MANUAL OF THE ADMINISTRATION
OF THE
MADRAS PRESIDENCY,
IN ILLUSTRATION OF THE
RECORDS OF GOVERNMENT & THE YEARLY ADMINISTRATION REPORTS

MANUAL OF THE ADMINISTRATION
OF THE
MADRAS PRESIDENCY,
IN ILLUSTRATION OF THE
RECORDS OF GOVERNMENT & THE YEARLY ADMINISTRATION REPORTS.

IN THREE VOLUMES

VOL. III—GLOSSARY,

Containing a Classification of terminology, a Gazetteer and Economic dictionary of the province, and other information, the whole arranged alphabetically and indexed.

GYAN

Published by

GYAN

Gyan Publishing House
5, Ansari Road
Daryaganj, New Delhi-110002
Phone: 011-47034999, 9811692060
E-mail: books@gyanbooks.com

Distribution Network
gyanbooks.com
India, USA, Canada, UK, Australia, France

ISBN : 978-81-212-4379-7 (PB)
First Published, 1893

2nd Impression 2020

Printed at: Gyan Press, Delhi.

MANUAL OF THE ADMINISTRATION

OF THE

MADRAS PRESIDENCY,

IN ILLUSTRATION OF THE

RECORDS OF GOVERNMENT & THE YEARLY ADMINISTRATION REPORTS.

IN THREE VOLUMES.

VOL. III.—GLOSSARY,

Containing a Classification of terminology, a Gazetteer and Economic dictionary of the province, and other information, the whole arranged alphabetically and indexed.

MADRAS:
PRINTED BY THE SUPERINTENDENT, GOVERNMENT PRESS.

1893.

NOTE.

1. A special note is necessary in introducing the third and concluding volume of the Manual.

2. *First object.*—The first object of the volume is to establish the necessary connection between the English and the vernacular languages in matters where this can be most suitably done by a publication made with Government resources. In considering that connection, it will be found that there are always three difficulties present; uncertain orthography, imperfect correlation between the languages, and multiplicity of synonyms even after correlation is established. It is the object of this volume to supply a definition in each of these cases of ambiguity; the definitions to be taken as standards whenever it is thought fit, or to the extent which is thought fit. In carrying out the process etymology has been added as a necessary attendant upon it.

3. Uncertain orthography arises chiefly in the form given to native words when they are employed in English writings. A statement of the past history and present condition of this question has been given at Volume I, pages 544–549. The words in question have been incorporated in Anglo-Indian usage during two centuries, in which period the peculiarities of the English language have made them assume very numerous shapes. Of late a movement has taken place, which is likely in the end to prove successful, in the direction of abandoning altogether the attempt to express such words on English principles, and instead of that of employing a method of strict transliteration from the exact letters of the original, combined with the use of the Continental and especially the Italian powers of the Roman alphabet, to which accents and other signs are applied. The latter is however in effect so far as writing is concerned a new language, and the country is in a state of transition from one style to the other. This therefore only adds to the number of forms at the present moment requiring to be treated by a glossary. The definition adopted in this case in the present volume is to place first as title the average Anglo-Indian form, and then next after it in brackets the average form on the purely transliterative or as it is in this book called Continental system. The average Anglo-Indian form means the form arrived at by applying Volume II, Appendix XXI. Though ignorance and fashion have introduced an extreme number of irregularities, yet it is a mistake to suppose that there is no system in the English style of orthography applied to native names. It is less regular than the Continental style, but in the usage of the best writers it displays an organic character and method quite its own. The selection of an average has therefore been the result of analysis and not arbitrary. The forms here selected for title may be said to be those which are now just beginning to go out of fashion, but which were exclusively in use in Southern India as late as twenty years ago. The average Continental form means the form arrived at by applying Volume II, Appendix XXIII. It rejects the diacritical marks shown in Volume II, Appendix XXIV, other than the acute accent. It is a form that may be used at any time without encumbering manuscript or embarrassing printers and is sufficient for all purpose of ordinary identification. In cases only where the Tamul character expresses Tamul words derived from the Sanscrit, for which purpose it is very defective, will the transliterations be found not suitable for practical requirements. The Continental forms where differing from the English forms re-appear as titles in the index at the end of the volume. By giving the two average forms cross-referenced in this manner it is believed that the difficulty of finding words has been reduced to a minimum. As regards the current text, or that portion of the matter not devoted to definition, it has been considered from the commencement of the work that a mixed or varying style of orthography was unsuitable to this publication. The choice was then between adopting either the English style throughout or the Continental style throughout; and this was found on experiment to be at the present date a choice between a slight archaism or decided pedantry. The former alternative was taken.

4. Imperfect correlation between the English and the vernacular languages appears chiefly in the process of ascertaining vernacular equivalents for English terms connected with the natural kingdom, and especially terms bearing on economical subjects. A vast amount of information has been acquired on this head in Southern India during the present century, but very little has been collated or put forward in a suitable, accurate, or accessible form. Nor has any attempt been made hitherto to analyze the native nomenclature in contraposition to European structural classification, yet such a process is very necessary if it is sought to go at all below the surface. The present volume aims at defining this subject on fixed principles of verification and with the greatest accuracy at present attainable; and the reader who will be at the trouble to set against one another the different parts of the work will find that the whole subject has been systematically elaborated. The results show that the natives of the country have a much more intimate acquaintance with structure in the natural kingdom than is generally supposed; and the establishment of the correlations will, it is believed, subserve many useful ends. There are 50,000 such correlations in the present volume.

5. Multiplicity of synonyms occurs in connection with the last-named subject, in the three branches into which that subject resolves itself; the Anglo-Indian terms (otherwise commercial), the scientific terms, and the vernacular terms. The number of aliases in these cases, and the great confusion and inconvenience thence arising are well known. It is not too much to say that the number of aliases in the scientific botanical system form one of the chief technical impediments to the compilation and diffusion of information regarding the economic uses of the vegetable kingdom. Thus to take the simplest example, in Drury's "Useful Plants," a modern and practical work, 50 per cent. of the botanical terms taken as title differ from the previous writer Roxburgh, and 10 per cent. are in turn altered by the later Flora of British India (Kew). When such a process is applied cumulatively to a number of economic writers the extent of the confusion which arises may well be conceived. The present volume has undertaken the function of collecting all the synonyms under each head, and selecting from them a standard, one for each head; and it is to be distinctly understood that no such term has been quoted in this volume without being exposed in an exhaustive manner to that process. In the case of Anglo-Indian (or commercial) terms, the one selected will be known by not being quoted as an alternative. In the case of scientific terms the same. In taking botanical names for standard in the vegetable economic system, the Flora of British India (Kew) has been nearly always followed where applicable; it is to be observed however that the object in this connection is not so much to get the best standard as to get any standard whatever to which variants can for the practical purpose mentioned be reduced. In the case of vernacular terms, the one selected in each language will be found with vernacular type next after title or sub-title. As a general principle it has been considered that one vernacular equivalent in each language, and that the most typical and generally applicable, is sufficient; as otherwise this work would have exceeded all limit. But in some cases vernacular alternatives are shown later in the text.

6. Etymologies of all the principal Anglo-Indian and vernacular terms will be found in the work. They may be said to be all new and form one of the chief parts of the labour of the undertaking. They number about 35,000. In the case of names of places, indigenous etymologies have been in the great majority of instances substituted for the Sanscrit corruptions usually received on the authority of stalapooraunams. The modern example of a Sanscrit corruption shown under the item Saint Thomas's Mount is an exact type of the process which has been going on for hundreds or rather probably for thousands of years. This matter contributes with others to show the fallacious nature of the old theory of Aryan invasion. Hindooism is indeed all absorbing, but it is only by great intellectual effort. Many place names so far from having the Sanscrit derivations usually assigned to them appear to belong to a period when the present Dravidian dialects had not yet branched off as such from the original Dravidian stock, or when they differed much less from each other than they do now. In matters other than place names also the general tendency of the volume will be found to be one of de-sanscritizing the etymology.

7. *Second object.*—The second object of this volume is in conjunction with the glossary titles to bring forward such general information on the different heads as either is available from indigenous and local sources alone, or has been compiled by former quasi-official labours and remains now almost inaccessible on the shelf; the work of reduction being in both cases such as none but a Government agency could in this country perform. Special attention may be drawn to the geographical items (about 5,000), which in conjunction with pages 47–169 of Volume II and various parts of Volume I form an approximate gazetteer to the province, as indicated in the Preface; and to the economic items (about 4,000), which form the only economic dictionary for the Presidency at present available. Information is however given on very many other subjects in which it appears desirable to illustrate European topics by ascertaining and exhibiting the native point of view; in this connection such heads as Astrology, Astronomy, Customs, Festivals, Literature, Natural history, Philosophy, Proper names, Religion, Weights and measures, &c., have been fully and systematically treated.

8. Books from which in certain cases free quotation has been made, and which therefore require to be specified, are:—in religion and philosophy, Ziegenbalg's Genealogie der Malabarischer Götter (1713); in economic flora, Roxburgh's Flora Indica (1832), Drury's works; in zoology Jerdon's, Day's, and Günther's works. All these authors except the one last mentioned have been South Indian writers.

9. The remark made in the Preface as to the admixture of original and compiled matter may be here repeated; with the proviso that there is much more original matter in this than there was in the two previous volumes. About one-twentieth of the descriptive matter mentioned in para. 7 is merely compiled; the remainder is matter either rewritten or original, and translations have been made of many native papers.

10. *Signs, &c.*—Round brackets ( ) indicate that the vernacular words contained therein are spelt on the new Continental system. Square brackets [ ] indicate current cross-references. The sign * indicates a form of spelling adopted by Government for official correspondence.

11. Throughout the bulk of the vernacular equivalents vernacular type has been given. A roman type to act as a substitute in one work for all the languages of Southern India would take the very inconvenient form shown in Volume II, Appendix XXIV. The typography has therefore been in the main polyglot in sixteen vernacular languages combined with the ordinary roman.

12. It will be found that there is a more sparse use of capital letters in the text than usual. This method has been indispensable for classifying matter, throwing catch-words into relief, and alphabetically arranging whole phrases, in columns so closely printed.

13. As the etymological and classificatory method employed often conflicts to a certain extent with the alphabetical, and also with a view to the different variations set out in paragraphs 3–5 above, it will be necessary when using the volume as a work of reference to constantly consult the index at the end (about 65,000 items). It is an integral part of the design. When either the commencement or the termination of a compound word falls quite naturally within the alphabetical arrangement of the main text, the reader is left to trace the word for himself; but in all other cases assistance is given through the index.

14. *Conclusion.*—It may be observed in summing up the contents of the present volume that its frequent use as a work of reference can scarcely fail to bring conviction as to the truth of the main thesis advanced in the first 188 pages of Volume I, a thesis however very imperfectly recognized at the date of the commencement of this publication; namely that the Dravidians or population of Southern India form one of the world's separate and very great nations, and that the exterior Aryan influence which has been brought to bear upon them has given only the thinnest veneer to their original characteristics and institutions.

15. Finally though no pains have been spared and every precaution has been taken, it will be impossible in a volume going into so many details but that some mistakes will eventually be found.

GLOSSARY.

A (अ - a, आ - á, *San.*; ا - alif, *Hind.*; அ - a, ஆ - á, *Tam.*). —**(1)** Short San. symbolic of Vishnoo, especially as the first letter of the three sounds in the sacred syllable om; also of Bramh. Long San. symbol of Shiva and Lutchmy. Hind. in arithmetic one; in almanacs and astronomical books, Sunday and Taurus. Short Tam. sign of the numeral 8. The long letter in all the Dravidian languages is the ordinary Dravidian vocative, followed constantly by long "o" if the reply is not immediate; thus (appá), then (appó). It is also the Dravidian direct interrogative, "o" being the interrogative of doubt. Among the lowest Tamulians "á" forms termination also of numerous expletive particles; and all these "á" sounds are nasally prolonged. Hence character for want of euphony given by Europeans on superficial acquaintance to Tamul, a mellifluous and resounding language.—**(2)** Sanscrit short is negative prefix.——*Achit* (अचित् - achit, San.). Not mind; that is to say matter. With the Shreeveishnavas chit or mind is the spirit of Vishnoo; this, achit or matter, and eeshwaran or supreme ruler, form the three predicates of the universe [shreeveishnava]. See Vol. I (89).——*Acsha tadiya* (అక్షతదియ - akshatadiya, Tel.). From (akshaya, san. undying + tritíya, san. third); observance gives permanency to actions then performed. Otherwise Balarama jayanty. Lunar holiday [pundigay, 3e]. 3rd tity of waxing moon of 2nd lunar month Veishaukham [mausam], between April 16th and May 16th. Anniversary of beginning of Tretayoog.——*Acshayam* (अक्षय - akshaya, San.). From (kshaya, san. destruction). Unfailing. The seventh day of a lunar month if it fall on a Sunday or Monday, the fourth if it fall on Wednesday, is called Acshaya or auspicious day; the reasons are astrological. Acshaya pautram, from (above + pátra, san. utensil), is a charitable allowance to Bramins from the gross produce.——*Adharmam* (अधर्म - adharma, San.). From (dharma, san. virtue). Vice, demerit; opposite of Dharmam. According to Jeinas it causes soul's continuance with the body.——*Adity* (अदिति - aditi, San.). From (diti, san. the mother of asuras). Not dity. One of the wives of Cashyapan, and the mother of the gods and sooras or divinities [asooran]; her offspring are called Audityans.——*Adweitam* (अद्वैत - advaita, San.). From (dvaita, san. duality). Non-duality or identity. Unity of God and all his emanations. Bramins and their followers are of three classes according to the distinctions made by a combination of creed and philosophy. The Smartas worship Shiva and prosecute the Adweitam development of vedantic philosophy; being followers of Shuncaracharry. The Madhwas worship Vishnoo and prosecute the Dweitam development; being followers of Madhwacharry. The Shreeveishnavas worship Vishnoo and prosecute the Vishishtaudweitam development; being followers of Ramaunoojacharry. Of the three philosophies the old or Adweitam is that which prevails most in Southern india. This system regards the supreme spirit and the human spirit as one; in a state of degradation through ignorance, but re-absorbed on obtaining true wisdom. The world is an illusion. All external objects are different forms of the one deity, besides whom there exists nothing else. As gold is one, though in various forms, as money, earrings and other ornaments; so the one sole existent deity is found in all the various forms that appear to exist around mankind. The body of man is a temporary prison. On its decease the soul flows into deity; as air in a closed earthen vessel, when such is broken, flows into the common atmosphere. The Adweitam denies the existence of moral evil. Many treatises in Tamul, Teloogoo and Canarese on Adweitam philosophy. See Darshanam for philosophy generally. See Vedauntam for the main body of philosophy which underlies the Adweitam. For the founder of Adweitam see Shuncaracharry. See also Vol. I (74), (76). Cf. Spinozism.——*Aghoran* (अघोर - aghóra, San.). From (ghóra, san. terrific). Euphemistic title of Shiva. A religious mendicant.——*Akhandam* (अखण्ड - akhanda, San.). Means undivided. Akhanda cauvery is the country of the broad undivided Cauvery. The W. portion of Trichinopoly district from Caroor to Tirpalatoray; the latter being place where Cauvery divides into two branches, Cauvery and Coleroon. Epithet also for lamps kept burning at Hindoo shrines.——*Akhilam* (अखिल - akhila, San.). From (khila, san. gap). Whole. Akhilandayya, from (anda, san. egg) is Shiva, the lord of the universe. Akhilaunda naicky is Parvaty. Hindoo 2nd or pers. name [peyar].——*Amaram* (अमर - amara, San.). From (mri, san. to die). Immortality. Amara cosham, from (kósha, san. vocabulary), otherwise Tricaundam meaning three parts, otherwise Naumalingaunooshausanam meaning name + gender + rules, is a Sanscrit vocabulary by Amaran found in all Indian languages. In verse. Synonymous words are collected into one or more verses and placed in fifteen chapters, which treat of as many subjects. Sixteenth contains homonymous terms arranged alphabetically, in the Indian manner, by final consonants. Seventeenth is a full catalogue of indeclinables, i.e., adverbs, prepositions, conjunctions, and interjections. Last chapter is on gender of nouns.——*Amareshwaran* (अमरेश्वर - amaréshvara, San.). From (mara, san. death + íshvara, san. lord). Either Vishnoo or Shiva.——*Amogham* (अमोघ - amógha, San.). From (muh, san. to err). Unerring. Amogha varshan, meaning one who showers benefits unerringly, was Jeina king of Toudeimundalam at end of 9th century of Christian era. The principal Jeina pooraunams were written in his reign by his spiritual preceptor Jainasainan acharry.——*Amoortam* (अमूर्त - amúrta, San.). From (múrta, san. shape). Artificial division of time as opposed to Moortam or practical division [caulam, 3]. It has no natural standard. Used in astrology. The following is a scale of Amoortam time:—100 trooty or atoms = 1 tatparam or speck, 30 tatparams = 1 nimisham or twinkling, 18 nimishams = 1 caushtay or bit, 30 caushtays = 1 calay or indian minute, 30 calays = 1 ghaticam or indian hour, 2 ghaticams = 1 cshanam or double hour, 30 cshanams = 1 day. Approximate actual value:—1 ghaticam = 24 English minutes 1 trooty being $\frac{1}{33750}$ of an English second.——*Amritam* (अमृत - amrita, San.). From (mrita, san. dead). Immortal. Ambrosia, the beverage of the gods, produced at the churning of the ocean; and cause of war between Sooras and Asooras. Hindoo 2nd or pers. name [peyar], as Amritam iyer, Amritammaul. Amritanaicken is common among non-bramins. Amrit mahaul is title of a cattle breeding establishment in Mysore. Amritam is plant title, as:—Anona squamosa, Citrus medica, var. limetta, Methonica superba, Phyllanthus emblica, Psidium guyava, Pyrus communis, Terminalia chebula, Tinospora cordifolia; see gloss. paragraphs.——*Anangan* (अनङ्ग - ananga, San.). From (anga, san. body). Incorporeal. Cauman, the Indian cupid.——*Ananta chatoordashy* (అనంతచతుర్దశి - anantachaturdashi, Tel.). From (ananta, san. vishnu, the infinite + chaturdashí, san. fourteenth day). Otherwise Ananta vratam and Anantapudmanaubha chatoordashy. Lunar festival [pundigay, 3a]. 14th tity of 6th lunar month Bhaudrapadam [mausam] first pácsham, between Sep. 1st and Sep. 30th, sacred to Vishnoo, the infinite or the lotus-navelled. The corresponding religious ceremony is observed by males only. At the break of day the Bramin family priest consecrates a vessel, by reciting certain formulas. He is then presented with cloths and money. Those who keep it take but one meal and tie a red silk string on the right arm. This festival, as well as that of Varalutchmy vratam in Shrauvanam [mausam] or August and of Kedaury vratam in Aushweejam [mausam] or October, is not obligatory; but having once kept it, the celebration always must be continued. Even the posterity of those who have observed it are subject to this law, till they get released from their tacit vow.——*Anantan* (अनन्त - ananta, San.). From (anta, san. end). The eternal deity, Vishnoo or Shiva. Also Audy sheshan [q.v.]. Ananta shayanan, from (shayana, san. bed), is he who has Sheshan the serpent for his couch, Vishnoo. Appears in comp.; Ananta narayanan, Ananta pudmanaubhan, Ananta sadaushivan, &c. Ananta teertan means the devotee of Vishnoo. Anantayya is common Hindoo 2nd or pers. name [anantapore, peyar]. Anantaraushy is an infinite quantity in mathematics. Anantam, alluding to spreading roots, is plant name common to:—Barleria prionitis, Cynodon dactylon, Hemidesmus indicus.——*Anaudy* (अनादि - anádi, San.). From (ádi, san. beginning). Immemorial. Anaudibeed is ground waste from time immemorial.——*Animisham* (अनिमिष - animisha, San.). From (nimisha, san. winking). One whose eyes do not wink; a god.——*Anyaunam* (अज्ञान - añána, San.). From (ñá, san. to know). Ignorance. In philosophy not merely a negative, but an active principle which, consisting of the three goonas, viz., Satwam, Rajas and Tamas, and preventing the soul from realizing its identity with Bramh, causes self to appear a distinct personality and matter to appear a reality. Hence equivalent to Pracrity or nature and termed a divine shacty, synonymous with Mauyay or illusion. Anyauny is a heathen in Christian publications.——*Anyauyam* (अन्याय - anyáya, San.). From (nyáya, san. rule). Injustice. Complaint of injustice. Plaint in a civil suit.——*Aparapacsham* (अपरपक्ष - aparapaksha, San.). Means latter + fortnight; dark fortnight. Lunar festival [pundigay, 3e]. The whole of waning moon of 6th lunar month Bhaudrapadam [mausam]; any 15 days between 1st Sep. and 15th Oct. Same as Bramha sauvitry in Bengal.——*Aranyam* (अरण्य - aranya, San.). From (ri, san.

to go). Place neither cultivated nor grazed. Forest. Suffix in place names; as Vedaranyam, meaning sacred writing + forest.
——*Aravam* (اروی - arví, Hind.; అరవము - aravamu, Tel.): From (rava, san. sound). Name for Tamul among Mussalmans, Teloogoo and Canarese, on account of its being destitute of aspirates. Not to be confounded with the Tamul word aravam, sound. The latter word means sound, whilst the former means being without sound. The people who are represented by Ptolemy as occupying the portion of the Coromandel coast near Nellore are called by him the *ἀρούαρνοι*, which may represent the Tamul fishermen. There is a large caste of Aravas or Tamul caupoos in the Teloogoo country.——*Arogyam* (आरोग्य - árógya, San.). From (róga, san. sickness). Health. Common Hindoo 2nd or pers. name among non-bramins. Also Arogyasawmy [peyar].——*Aroondhaty* (अरुन्धती - arundhatí, San.). From (rudh, san. to check); above suspicion. Star in the Great bear régarded as wife of Vasishtan, a pattern of chastity. Pointed out to bride at marriage ceremony. There is a Tamul proverb :—அம்மி மிதித்து அருந்ததி பார்த்ததுபோல— "like one standing on a grindstone and looking at Aroondhaty," meaning the same.
——*Asat* (असत् - asat, San.). From (sat, san. entity). Nonentity [sat].——*Atalam* (अतल - atala, San.). From (tala, san. bottom). Bottomless. Subterranean world. One of the 14 locams.——*Atchootan* (अच्युत - achyuta, San.). From (chyu, san. to fall). Means who cannot fall. Vishnoo. Hindoo 2nd or pers. name [peyar]. Atchoota deva royel was Rajah of Vijianugger of the Narsimha dynasty, next after Krishna deva. A.D. 1530-1542. His reign remarkable for grants to Bramins and temples. Conquered down to Tinnevelly, took away one of the Pandyan ruler's daughters and fixed a pillar of victory on the banks of the Tamrapurny. Fort of Kurnool built in his time. See Vol. I (153). Atchoota vijayaraghavan was the last of the Naick dynasty of Tanjore. Built forts at Arantaungy and Puttoocottah, Tripatore, and the Rajagopaulsawmy pagoda at Munnargoody. His refusal to give his daughter in marriage to the rajah of Madura, led to a war. Atchootan fought and was killed. Had previously made preparation for burning his women's apartments, which was done. Scene was the now unoccupied tower at the south-west corner of the Tanjore palace. See Vol. I (121); and II, 126.——*Avibhactam* (अविभक्त - avibhakta, San.). From (vibhaj, san. to divide). Undivided. Avibhacta cootoombam is the well known Indian undivided family. Roman law, and modern European law following it, look upon co-ownership as an exceptional and momentary condition of the rights of property. But here this order of ideas is reversed, and it may be said that separate proprietorship is always on its way to become proprietorship in common. As soon as a son is born, he acquires a vested interest in his father's substance, and on attaining years of discretion he is in certain contingencies permitted by the letter of the law to call for a partition of the family estate. As a fact however a division rarely takes place even at the death of the father, and the property constantly remains undivided for several generations though every member of every generation has legal right to an undivided share on it. The domain thus held in common is sometimes administered by an elected manager, but more generally it is managed by the eldest agnate, that is to say by the eldest representative of the eldest line of the stock. Such an assemblage of joint proprietors, a body of kindred holding a domain in common, is the simplest form of a village community in this country. There is no such thing as succession, properly so called, in an undivided family. The whole body of such a family, consisting of males and females, constitutes a sort of corporation; some of the members of which are coparceners, that is to say persons who on partition would be entitled to demand a share, while others are only entitled to maintenance. In Malabar and Canara, where partition is not allowed, the idea of heirship would never present itself to the mind of any member of the family. Each person is entitled to reside and be maintained in the family house, and to enjoy that amount of affluence and consideration which arises from his belonging to a family possessed of greater or less wealth. As he dies out his claims cease, and as others are born their claims arise. But the claims of each spring from the fact of their entrance into the family, not from their taking the place of any particular individual. Deaths may enlarge the beneficial interest of the survivors, by diminishing the number who have a claim upon the common fund, just as births may diminish their interests by increasing the number of claimants. But although the fact that one is the child of another, introduces the former into the family, it does not give him any definite share of the property, for the latter himself has none. Nor upon the death of the parent does the child succeed to anything, for the parent has left nothing behind to succeed to. Elsewhere also the position of an undivided family is the same, except that within certain limits each male member has a right to claim a partition if he likes. What happens when the family is broken up, can be seen under the head of Bhaugam or Partition. The detailed management of an undivided family is best illustrated again by what happens in the Malabar district. The senior male member in a Malabar family is by law the Carnaven, that is to say the natural guardian of every member within the family. He alone can sue and be sued as the representative of the family. In the absence of fraud or collusion, a decree against the Carnaven as such is binding upon the other members of the family, although they are not parties to the suit. The Carnaven for the time being has an almost absolute control over the distribution of the family income and the family expenditure. The Carnaven may delegate his powers of management, but he cannot, without the assent of those to whom the obligations are owing, that is to say the members of the family generally, assign his rights and privileges so as to be unable to resume them. His powers of management may however be limited by contract. The rights of the junior members of the Malabar family are the right of the males to succeed to the headship by seniority, and the right of the males and females to be supported in the family house. A separate maintenance will not be allotted to a junior member who voluntarily and without lawful excuse separates himself or herself from the family. They cannot call for an account, except as incident to a prayer for the removal of the manager for misconduct, nor claim any specific share of the income, nor even require that their maintenance or the fair outlay should be in proportion to the income. An absolute discretion in this respect is vested in the manager. Their position is analogous to what was the position of the members of a Roman family under the Patria potestas. The Carnavon is as much the guardian and representative for all purposes of property, of every member within the tarwaud, as the Roman father or grandfather. In South canara the custom is still more archaic, and there the senior female is the manager. Compare the headings Aliya santauna and Maroomakkatoyem, which explain the law of inheritance on the West coast. Certain reigning families in Malabar also preserve the custom of female management. The remarks just made apply for the most part to the headship of any joint Hindoo family. The law under which a Hindoo inherits his claims in the joint family can be seen under the two headings just named, and under that of Dauyam or inheritance.——**(3)** Sanscrit long is intensive particle.——*Achandraurcam* (ஆசந்திரார்க்கம் - ásandirárkkam, Tam.). From (chandra, san. moon + arka, san. sun). As long as the sun and moon endure.——*Ahy* (अहि - ahi, San.). From (han, san. destroy). Greek ἔχιδνα. Serpent.——*Amooctam* (आमुक्त - ámukta, San.). From (much, san. to set free). Liberated. Amoocta maulyada, from (málya, san. garland), otherwise Vishnoo chitteeyam, meaning story of Vishnoochittan or periyalwar, the Vishnoo devotee, is a poem by Alasauny peddanna, to show southern progress of Veishnava system. A story in this resembles Arabian nights [alaf leila]. A raucshasan having caught a dausy, purposed to kill and eat her. To this the dausy made up her mind; but begged permission first to relate some stories. She then narrated the Hindoo account of the origin of the world, and the whole of the Hindoo mythology. At last the raucshasan renounced his purpose [periyalwar].
——*Anandam* (आनन्द - ánanda, San.). From (nand, san. to gladden). Joy. The supreme spirit. Shiva; Hindoo 2nd or pers. name. Common among Madhwas [peyar]. Ananda rauz was Rajah of the Northern circars and 5th ancestor of the present Maharajah of Vizianagram. Ally of English, whom he assisted at battle of Condore against French in 1758. See Vol. I, 54.
——*Aradhyan* (आराध्य - árádhya, San.). From (rádh, san. to propitiate); fit to be propitiated. Sectarian title of Jangam or Lingayet bramins. They do not intermarry with any other classes of Bramins in the province to which they belong. They nevertheless act as gooroos or family instructors of the higher classes of natives. They adhere to caste; and though they believe in the unity of the deity as Mahadewan, symbolized by the lingam, they observe the Braminical initiation, and worship the sun by the repetition of the gayatry. By the Lingayets themselves they are considered only half converts to their system. Number in Presidency about 8,000.——*Arohanam* (आरोहण - áróhana, San.). From (ruh, san. to rise). Hoisting the flag when a festival begins [avarohanam]. In music the gradual raising of the pitch.——*Ayoodham* (आयुध - áyudha, San.). From (yudh, san. to attack). Weapon, tool. Ayoodhacutty is the Nayar's national weapon; connected in tradition with Parshooraman's battle-axe.——*Ayoodha poojay* (आयुधपूजा - áyudhapújá, San.). From (áyudha, san. weapon + pújá, san. worship). Lunar festival [pundigay, 6d]. The 9th day of the waxing moon of the 7th lunar month Aushweejam [mausam] between Sep. 23 and Oct. 24. The last day of Dusserah. On this day the Navarantry feast ends, and the people make offerings and supplications to the tools and implements which they use in the exercise of their various professions. The laborer brings his plough, hoe, or other instruments used in his work. These he piles together and offers a sacrifice, consisting of incense, flowers, fruits, rice, &c., after which he prostrates himself before them at full length; then returns them to their places. The mason offers the same adoration and sacrifice to his trowel, rule, &c. The carpenter does the same with the hatchet, adze, and plane. The barber, with his razors. The writing master makes an offering to the iron pencil or stylo with which he writes. In the same way the tailor to his needles, the weaver to his loom, and the butcher to his cleaver. The women bring together their baskets, their rice mill, the wooden cylinder with which they bruise the rice, and other household implements. The festival is concluded by erecting a roughly formed statue composed of flour paste. This represents

a shacty or female divinity. Being placed under a canopy, it is carried about through the streets and receives the homage of the inhabitants. The Ayoodha poojay is a feast so sacred that if a Hindoo is attacked on the day of its celebration, he will not take arms to defend himself. It is related that the general of the Soobah of the Deccan, who besieged Jinjee, chose this day for the assault, being persuaded the besieged would not defend themselves, and that he actually entered the place without meeting with the least resistance.

AB (अप् - ap, *San.*; آب - áb, *Hind.*). Water.——*Abdar* (آبدار - ábdár, Hind.). From (dár, pers. holder). A servant in charge of drinking water.——*Abdarkhana* (آبدار خانه - ábdár-khánah, Hind.). From (dár, pers. keeper + khánah, pers. house). Place where water is kept for drinking. From the fifth khun of the Moharram onwards many Mahomedans keep them in front of their houses, &c.——*Ab geena* (آبگینه - ábgínah, Hind.). Glass.——*Ab i dogh* (آب دوغ - ábidogh, Hind.). From (dogh, pers. curd). Butter milk.——*Ab i nishaut* (آب نشاط - ábinishát, Hind.). From (nishát, pers. pleasure). Nectar.——*Ab i noocra* (آب نقره - ábinukrah, Hind.). From (nukrah, pers. silver). Quicksilver.——*Abjajan* (अब्जज - abjaja, San.). Means lotus-born. Bramha.——*Abjam* (अब्ज - abja, San.). From (jan, san. to be born). Means water-born. Lotus; conch; moon.——*Abkur* (آبکار - ábkár, Hind.). From (kár, pers. doer). A distiller or seller of spirituous liquors.——*Abkarry* (آبکاری - ábkárí, Hind.). From (kár, pers. business). The revenue derived from taxes on the manufacture or sale of spirituous liquors. See Vol. I, 445.——*Ab o dauna* (آب و دانه - ábodánah, Hind.). From (dánah, pers. grain). Means of subsistence; destiny.——*Ab o hawah* (آب و هوا - ábohawá, Hind.). From (hawá, pers. air). Climate, considered here to depend greatly on the water.——*Abruck* (अभ्रक - abhraka, San.). See sep. title.——*Ab shola* (آب شوره - ábshorah, Hind.). From (shorah, pers. saltpetre). Water cooled by means of a solution of saltpetre; so sherbet.

ABAD (آباد - ábád, *Hind.*). From (búdan, pers. to live). Populous centre, city. Suffix in place names; as Dowlatabad, meaning fortune + city. Tippoo substituted fanciful Mahomedan names for native town-names. Khaulakabad for Chandagaul near Seringapatam, Salaamabad for Suttimungalam, Jafferabad for Goorramcondah. Cf. also his Feiz hissaur for Gooty, Khoorshadsooad for Dharwar. His Mint towns Nazarbar and Furruckbaub hissaur remain unrecognized. Cf. also Hyder's mint Farookhy near Calicut, and Hyder nugger for Bednore.——*Abadauny* (آبادانی - ábádání, Hind.). From (above + affix denoting multitude). Cultivation.

ABAH (عبا - abá, *Hind.*). From Arabic. A cloak worn very loose and open in front.

ABAUBIL (ابابيل - ababíl, *Ar.*, *Pers.* and *Dec.*; వానకోకిల - vánakókila, *Tel.*; മീവൽപക്ഷി - mívalpakshi, *Mal.*; தலையில்லாதகுருவி - talaiyilláthaguruvi, *Tam.*). Title from arabic. Ar. from (ibaul, ar. distinct); from segregating habit. Tel. from (vána, tel. rain + kókila, san. cuckoo); from appearance about rains. Mal. from (méval, mal. dwelling + pakshi, san. bird); from frequenting dwellings; cf. house-martin. Tam. from (talai, tam. head + illátha, tam. without + kuruvi, tam. small bird); from appearance. Arabic also (khuttáf). Tam. also (tagaivilánguruvi), meaning fatigue + without + bird. Swallows and swifts. Hirundinidæ, fissirostres, insessores, aves [pacshy, 4], of naturalists; bill short, broad base, depressed, compressed at tip, more or less curved, not notched; gape very wide; wings long, pointed; tarsi short; feet feeble; hind toe short; live on insects captured in the air, and for this purpose mouth wide, though bill small. Divided into:—Hirundininæ or swallows, and Cypselinæ or swifts; latter distinguished by having only ten tail feathers, wings being longer, narrower, smaller and differently formed bill, and by structure of feet, the fastest flying birds in the world.—"*a*" The Common indian swallow is Hirundo rustica, hirundininæ. Alias gutturalis, javanica, jewan, panayana; above glossy blue-black, chin, throat, and a narrow band on the forehead, deep ferruginous; beneath from the breast rufescent-white; length to end of outer tail feathers $7\frac{1}{2}$ inches; a cold-weather visitant, leaving towards end of March.—"*b*" The Common indian swift is Cypselus affinis, cypselinæ. Alias montanus, nipalensis. Above brown black, darkest on the back, and glossed with green; head brownish, paler on the forehead; body beneath brownish-black; tail short, nearly even, with the feathers not pointed; noisy bird; watchful at night; voice is a shivering scream.—"*c*" The Indian edible-nest swiftlet is Collacalia nidifica. Nest composed entirely of inspissated mucus from the large salivary glands.—"*d*" See also the two species given below.——*Musjid abaubil* (مسجد ابابيل - masjidababíl, Hind.). From breeding on old mosques. Title otherwise Red-rumped swallow. Hirundo daurica, hirundininæ. Alias alpestris, erythropygia, nipalensis. Above blue-black; beneath rufescent-white, with dusky streaks.——*Taurabaubil* (تار ابابيل - tárababíl, Hind.). From (tár, hind. palmyra, borassus flabelliformis, linn.). Hind. also (tálchatta), meaning palm sparrow. The Palm swift. Cypselus batassiensis, cypselinæ. Alias palmarum. Wholly glossy ashy-brown, darker on the wings and tail, and lighter and somewhat albescent beneath; wings about equal to the tail; length 5 or $5\frac{1}{4}$ inches; abounds wherever the palmyra and cocoanut palms are found; not remarkably speedy.

ABBAUS (عباس - abbás, *Hind.*). From (abasa, ar. to frown). The fierce. Name of the uncle of Mahomed and the founder of the family of Abbasides who ruled as caliphs from 749 to 1258 A.D. Mahomedan alam [ism]. Fem. is Abbausee.——*Abbaus ally* (عباس على - abbásalí, Hind.). Double alam.——*Abbaus ally khan* (عباس عليخان - abbásalíkhán, Hind.). Double alam + honorific title. Last of the jagheerdars of Oodayagherry in Nellore district. For treason against Government in collecting arms and ammunition, he was made a state prisoner and confined in the Chingleput fort, where he died in 1841. The present representative of the family is his grandson, Syed davood ally, drawing a monthly pension of Rs. 250.——*Abbausee bee* (عباسى بى - abbásíbí, Hind.). Alam with alaumat added.

ABBY (అబ్బి - abbi, *Tel.*). A lad. Term of address [ammy].——*Abboye* (అబ్బాయి - abbáyi, Tel.). Familiar form of Abby. Hindoo 2nd or pers. name [peyar].

ABD (عبد - abd, *Hind.*). From Arabic. Slave. Same as Arabic Ghoolaum, Bengallee Doss, and Tamul Adiyaun. In composition forms one of the commonest lacabs [q.v.]; being prefixed to any one of the ninety-nine attributes of God [allah]; or to the name of God himself, as Abdoollah. These names have now become so common as to be regarded as alams [q.v.]. All classes may take these names. In the following specimens note variations of the particle:—Abdool cawder, slave of the powerful; Abd oon nabee, slave of the prophet; Abdoor rabb, slave of the lord; Abd oos samad, slave of the eternal; Abd oosh shacoor, slave of the grateful. Abd again is sometimes prefixed in law documents to the signature of each witness, as a sign of humility [ism].——*Abd ool cawder* (عبدالقادر - abdulkádir, Hind.). From (kádir, ar. god, the powerful). Lacab used as alam. Full name, Sheikh abdool cawder jeelauny. Surnamed Ghouse ool azam, Peer peeraun, Peer e dastgheer. Mahomedan saint at Baghdad, where his tomb is still reverenced. Anniversary on 11th Rabee oos saunee [maheena]. Invoked here during epidemic, &c., when a large green flag is carried in his name.——*Abdoollah cootb shah* (عبدالله قطب شاه - abdulláhkutbsháh, Hind.). From (abdulláh, ar. slave of god + kutbsháh, ar. dynastic title). Fifth of Cootb shahy dynasty of Golcondah, from 1611 to 1672. Aurungzeeb while a prince invaded his dominions, at the instance of Abdoollah's minister, Meer joomla, whose son Abdoollah had imprisoned. Shivajee exacted large tribute in 1667. See Vol. I (149).——*Abdoollah khan* (عبدالله خان - abdulláhkhan, Hind.). Alam + pataun alaumat. Local ruler of Vellore under the last of the Beejapore sultans. Built a town called Abdoollahpooram about $2\frac{1}{2}$ miles from Vellore.——*Abdool nabee khan* (عبدالنبى خان - abdunnabíkhán, Hind.). From (abdunnabí, ar. slave of the prophet + khán, pers. pataun alaumat). Third of the Cuddapah nawaubs. Grandson of the founder of that line. Invaded and subdued Baramahaul in 1713. Consolidated Sidhout, Gundicote, Cumbum and Goorramcondah under his rule independent of the Nizam. Ceased to rule about 1732. See Vol. II, 75.——*Abd ool wahaub* (عبدالوهاب - abdulwahhláb, Hind.). Means slave of God, the bestower. Brother of Nawaub wallajah. Commandant and local Governor.

ABDAT (عبدت - abdat, *Hind.*). From Arabic. Female slave. Used like Abd, but not common. The proper form is Amat; this also rare [ism].——*Abdat ool cawder* (عبدةالقادر - abdatulkádir, Hind.). Woman's name. Slave of the powerful.

ABDHY (अब्धि - abdhi, *San.*). From (ap, san. water + dhá, san. to hold). Sea.——*Abdhicam* (अब्धिक - abdhika, San.). Lower or coast Keralam [adricam].

ABEER (أبير - abír, *Hind.*). From (abír, ar. ambergris), probably from perfume. A perfumed powder made up of sandalwood powder, zedoary, rose, musk, and camphor. Rubbed on face or body or sprinkled on clothes to scent them.

ABELMOOSHK (حب المشك - habbalmushk, *Ar.*). From (habb, ar. seed + mushk, ar. musk); from taste and odour. Same as Musk bendy or hibiscus abelmoschus; latter word was formerly a genus.

ABHAL (أبهل - abhal, *Ar.*; هوبير - húber, *Hind.*; ابهل - abhal, *Dec.*). Title from deccany. Ar. also (arar). Hind. also (úher). Greek ἀρκευθίς. Title otherwise Juniper. Giving False sandrach. Botanically Juniperus communis, linn., coniferæ [vricsham]. Diœcious bush; fleshy fruits, improperly called berries, which contain sugar, and are thus fermentable. A kind of Sandrach [q.v.], a whitish yellow, brittle, inflammable, resinous substance with an acrid aromatic taste exudes from cracks and incisions in stem. Berries medicinally stimulant, diuretic and carminative; nervine tonic in diseases of the brain and paralytic affections; substituted for british spiritus ætheris nitrosi; gives to pharm. juniperi fructus; preparations, oleum juniperi, spiritus junipori; officinal. Aromatic wood used for fumigating. No other species here. For real sandrach see Callitris quadrivalvis [sandrach].

ABHI (अभि - abhi, *San.*). Intensive prefix.——*Abhidharmam* (अभिधर्म - abhidharma, San.). From (dharma, san. virtue). Supreme truth. Jeina metaphysics.——*Abhidhaunam* (अभिधान - abhidhána, San.). From (dhá, san. to set). Vocabulary. Abhidauna chintaumany [chintaumany], a dictionary of synonyms by Homachundran.——*Abhigamanam* (अभिगमन - abhigamana, San.). From (gamana, san. going). Purification of temples.——*Abhijit* (अभिजित् - abhijit, San.). From (ji, san. to conquer). Victorious. Name of Vishnoo. Hence the name of the intercalary or fractional Nacshatram in Chaundra maunam [nacshatram]. See description of the almanac at Vol. I, 611. When astronomers have occasion for this, in dealing with the moveable lunar zodiac [mausam], they insert it between the 21st and 22nd Nacshatrams, in which case they take 3° 20′ from Oottarashaudham, and 1° 40′ from Shravanam; thus making it consist of 5°. The deity of Shravanam is Vishnoo, and it is the second month which give its name to intercalary periods [adhicam]; hence title. Abhijit is much used for astrological purposes. Abhijit, as a yogam star or leading star of a nacshatram [yogam], is the same as the European α Lyræ.——*Abhimaunam* (अभिमान - abhimána, San.). From (man, san. to think). The function of Ahancauram or self-conviction, or belief in self. Also means honor; whence Abhimauna pootran, an honorary son, by inferior kind of adoption not recognised by the law.——*Abhinayam* (अभिनय - abhinaya, San.). From (ní, san. to lead). Dancing. Chiefly that of the dancing girls of temples [devadausy]. The art of dancing is exhibited in six ways:— by movements of the eyes; by action of the features; by attitude of the breast; by position of the hands; by action of the feet; by calisthenic performances.——*Abhirauman* (அபிராமன் - abirâman, Tam.). Means very pleasing. Epithet of Shiva. Hindoo 2nd or pers. name. Feminine Abhiraumy; for Parvaty and Saraswaty, and Hindoo name [peyar].——*Abhishaicam* (अभिषेक - abhishéka, San.). From (sich, san. to sprinkle). Ablution. Pouring milk, &c., on the lingam. Inauguration of an idol, or of a rajah. Used by missionaries for baptism and ordination. Abhishaica maulay, from (málá, san. wreath), is a work in praise of Shiva, by Shiva pracausha desican of Conjeeveram, who lived in the seventeenth century; sacred book of Veerasheivas. Abhishaica shaunty, from (shánti, san. pacification), is a special ablution for pacifying the deity.——*Abhyantaram* (अभ्यन्तर - abhyantara, San.). From (antara, san. middle). Internal object. Opposite of Bauhyam, external object. Jeina term.

ABID (عابد - ábid, *Hind.*). From (abada, ar. to worship). Pious. A Mahomedan alam. Name of 4th imaum. Fem. Abida [ism].——*Abida bee* (عابدہ بی - ábidahbí, Hind.). Alam with alaumat added.——*Abid ally* (عابد علی - ábidalí, Hind.). Double alam.

ABOO (ابو - abú, *Hind.*). From Hebrew. Father. As prefix is a coonyat or genealogical surname. Cf. ab in Abraham. But such terms have come to mean here merely an alam. The coonyat is often used fancifully, by metaphors [ism].——*Abool abbaus* (ابوالعباس - abulabbás, Hind.). Father of the fierce, a man's name.——*Abool fazl* (ابوالفضل - abulfazl, Hind.). Father of excellence, a man's name.——*Abool hiyal* (ابوالحیل - abulhiyal, Hind.). Father of stratagems, for a fox.——*Aboo tooraub* (ابوتراب - abúturáb, Hind.). Father of dust, for a humble person.

ABRONY (चिवारि - chivári, *Conc.*; ಮಜ್ಜಿಗೆಸೊಪ್ಪುಗಿಡ - majjigesoppugida, *Can.*; అబ్రోణి - abróni, *Too.*; കൊട്ടക്ക - kottakka, *Mal.*; கடம்பு - kadambu, *Tam.*). Title from tooloo. Can. from (majjige can. buttermilk + soppu, can. leaf + gida, can. plant). Mal. from (kotta, mal. kernel + káya, mal. fruit). Can. also (abhrángugida). Tam. also (visálam). Title otherwise Butter milk-leaf plant, Panicled grewia. Botanically Grewia [dharmanam] microcos, linn., tiliaceæ [vricsham, 27]. Alias Arsis rugosa; Grewia affinis, ulmifolia; Microcos mala, paniculata, stauntoniana. Small shrub.

ABRUCK (अभ्रक - abhraka, *San.*; ابرک - abrak, *Hind.*; അഭ്രം - abhram, *Mal.*; அப்பிரகம் - appiragam, *Tam.*). Title from San. through Hind. San. from (ap, san. water + bhri, san. to bear); water-bearer; cloud. Trade name for Indian mica. Sometimes called talc, from the Arabic; not talc of European geologists [talc]. A hydrous silicate of magnesia. Splits into thin elastic plates. Indian mica is rarely found in large flakes, hence in little demand except for ornamenting small articles. Abruck navaneetam is mica made into an ointment; Abruck sindooram, red oxide of talc; Abruck paunshaunam, one of the thirty-two kinds of arsenic in its natural state. The following are varieties of Abruck.——*Gandhac abruck* (گندکی ابرک - gandakiabrak, Hind.; கெந்தகாப்பிரகம் - kendagáppiragam, Tam.). Yellow colored.——*Krishna abruck* (کالا ابرک - kálaabrak, Hind.; கிருட்டிணாப்பிரகம் - kiruttinâppiragam, Tam.). Black colored. Otherwise Vajraubhracam, meaning adamant mica. Dark gray. For ornamenting fans, pictures, &c. Calcined is given by Veidyans for fluxes.——*Manjal abruck* (پیلا ابرک - píláabrak, Hind.; மஞ்சளப்பிரகம் - mañjalappiragam, Tam.). Apple-green. Looks like yellow orpiment [hartául]. Granulated makes gold sand for sanding wet writing. For ornamenting, &c. Calcined is a pectoral medicine among Veidyans.——*Pon abruck* (سنہری ابرک - sunehríabrak, Hind.; பொன்னப்பிரகம் - ponnappiragam, Tam.). Gold colored.——*Racta abruck* (لال ابرک - lálabrak, Hind.; இரத்தாப்பிரகம் - irattáppiragam, Tam.). Red colored.——*Tain abruck* (தேனப்பிரகம் - ténappiragam, Tam.). Honey colored.——*Velly abruck* (سفید ابرک - safedabrak, Hind.; வெள்ளியப்பிரகம் - velliyappiragam, Tam.). Gray; the common kind. Granulated makes silver sand.

ABSINTH (दमन - damana, *San.*; सुरबंद - surabanda, *Mahr.*; افسنتین - afsantín, *Ar.*; برنجاسف - brinjásaf, *Pers.*; مستارو - mastáru, *Hind.*; ولایتی افسنتین - viláitíafsantín, *Dec.*; மாசிப்பத்திரி - másippattiri, *Tam.*). Title from arabic. San. from (dam, san. to subdue); from strong odour. Mahr. from (shúla, mahr. stomach-ache + banda, mahr. constraint); as curing colic. Dec. from (viláití, hind. foreign + afsantín, ar. worm wood). Tam. from (máchí, san. worm wood + patra, san. leaf). Greek ἀψίνθιον. Title otherwise Old woman, Santonin wood, Southern wood, Worm wood. Called worm wood as being vermifuge. Botanically Artemisia absinthium, linn., compositæ [vricsham, 74]. The product, or dried plants, brought chiefly from persia; contains a very bitter and azotized matter, insipid substance, resinous bitter green volatile oil, chlorophyle a trace, albumen, fecula, salts of potash, ligneous fibre and water; affords to medicine an extract, a tincture, tonic syrup, &c.; volatile oil is camphoraceous, of repulsive bitterness, used as a vermifuge; flower sometimes substituted for the hop in beer.——*Indian absinth* (नागदमनी - nágadamaní, San.; افسنتین ہندی - afsantínihindí, Ar.; برنجاسف کوهی - brinjásafikohí, Pers.; مجتری - majtarí, Hind.; مستارو - mastáru, Dec.; ಮಂಜಪತ್ರೆ - manjipatri, Can.; మాచిపత్రి - máchipatri, Tel.; തിരുനീറ്റിപ്പച്ച - tirunítippaçça, Mal.; වල්කොළොන්ද - valkolondu, Singh.; மாசிப்பத்திரி - másippattiri, Tam.). Title as of same genus. San. from (nága, san. serpent + dam, san. to subdue). Pers. from (brinjásaf, pers. worm wood + koh, pers. mountain). Can. from (máchí, san. worm wood + patra, san. leaf). Tel. similar. Mal. from (tiru, mal. holy + níru, mal. ashes + paçça, mal. foliage); from appearance of leaf. Tam. like teloogoo. San. also (grant'hiparní), meaning knot + leaf; (sharaparní), meaning arrow-leaved. Hind. also (gandmár); (nagdauna), from sanscrit. Tel. also (davanamu), meaning conquering. Mal. also (káttuchettippú), meaning forest + chrysanthemum indicum, linn.; from similarity of leaf. Title otherwise Arrow-leaf, Dona, Fellon herb, Fleabane, Indian worm wood, Mauchipatry, Mother-wort, Mug-wort, Southern wood, Wild shaumanty. Botanically Artemisia vulgaris, linn., compositæ [vricsham, 74]. Alias grata, indica, vulgaris. Suffruticose, erect; leaves white, tomentose below, pinnatifid, upper ones trifid, uppermost and branched ones undivided, and with the lobes oblong, obtuse, mucronate; capitules spicately panicled, oblong, panicle leafy and spreading, younger racemes nodding; outer scales of the younger pubescent involucre leafy, acute, of the inner ones scariose, obtuse; flowers small, greenish white; cultivated in gardens; leaves of slightly aromatic odour, bitterish taste. The dried plant used as a stimulant tonic in infusion; substituted for real absinth, but weaker.——*Madras absinth* (सुरपर्ण - suraparna, San.; مستارو - mastáru, Dec.; ಮಾಚಿಪತ್ರೆ - máchipatre, Can.; మాచిపత్రి - máchipatri, Tel.; നിലമ്പാല - nilampála, Mal.; වල්කොළොන්ද - valkōlondu, Singh.; மாசிப்பத்திரி - másippattiri, Tam.). Title from similarity of leaves. San. from (sura, san. divine + parna, san. leaf). Can. from (máchi, san. worm wood + patra, san. leaf). Tel. similar. Mal. from (nilam, mal. ground + pála, mal. milky plant). Tam. like teloogoo. Can. also (muttakárase), meaning pearl + solanum trilobatum, linn. Tel. also (mustarú). Tam. also (shinnappúkkottaikkarandai), meaning small + flower + sphæranthus indicus, linn. Title otherwise Madras worm wood, Mauchipatry. Botanically Grangea maderaspatana, poir., compositæ [vricsham, 74]. Alias Artemisia maderaspatana; Cotula maderaspatana; Grangea adansonii. Stems procumbent or diffuse, villous; leaves sinuately pinnatifid, lobes obtuse; peduncles terminal or leaf-opposed; heads of flowers subglobose, solitary, yellow; rice-fields; flowering in the cold season. The leaves veidyans consider stomachic, deobstruent and antispasmodic; prescribe in infusion and electuary, in cases of obstructed menses and hysteria; sometimes use in preparing antiseptic and anodyne fomentations. No other common species here.

ABWAB (ابواب - abwáb, *Hind.*). Plural of (báb, ar. door). Miscellaneous heads of taxation in addition to regular land assessment [baub].

ABYAZ (ابيض - abyaz, *Ar.*). White. Common in comp. Ex., where transl. is of 1st term:—Brassica alba (kardaliabyaz), brassica juncea; Jasminum sambac (vardiabyaz), rose. See gloss. paragraphs.

ACARAUTHY (अकारादि - akárádi, *San.*). From (akára, san. the first letter of the hindu alphabet + ádi, san. beginning). Dictionary [nigantoo].

ACASAULY (ಅಕಸಾಲಿ - akasáli, obl.; ಅಕಸಾಲಿಗ - akasáliga, pers. sing.; ಅಕಸಾಲೆರು - akasáléru, pers. pl., *Can.*). Caste, title. Canarese goldsmiths. First sub-division of the Punchaular or Cummaular. The corresponding terms are:—Hind. Badyo, Tel. Cumsauly, Tam. and Mal. Tattaun [jauty].

ACBAR (اكبر - akbar, *Hind.*). From (kabara, ar. great). Name of a son of Hoossain, whose death is celebrated at the Moharram ceremony. The historic emperor. Acbar nauma, from (námah, pers. history), is a still extant history of Acbar, by his minister Abool fazl. Acbarshahy was a silver rupee = 40 daums [q.v.]. Acbar is a common Mahomedan alam [ism].——*Acbar ally* (اكبر على - akbaralí, Hind.). Double alam.——*Acbar khan* (اكبر خان - akbarkhán, Hind.). Alam + alaumat.——*Acbar ood dowla* (اكبرالدولہ - akbaruddaulah, Hind.). Highest in the empire. Here it is a part of lacab.——*Acbar oon nissa begum* (اكبرالنسا بيگم - akbarunnisábegam, Hind.). Highest of ladies. Similar and alaumat suffixed.

ACBAUR (اخبار - akhbár, *Hind.*). Plural of (khabr, ar. news). Newspaper. Originally written intelligence of the proceedings of native courts circulated to other courts by appointed agents [khubber].

ACHAR (اچار - achár, *Pers.*). Through Port. Acid and salt relishes; pickles.

ACHARRY (आचारी - áchárí, *San.*). From (áchára, san. conduct). One who knows the rules of conduct [auchauram]. Among the Bramins a spiritual preceptor, who invests the student of three twice-born castes with sacred thread, and instructs him in law of sacrifices and mysteries of religion. Here it especially denotes among Bramins the head of a religious society or high priest of an important temple. Also suffixed to names of learned men, corresponding to Dr. in English. Specially assumed by Madhwa bramins. The word means in another sense a master of any craft. The title is taken by the five castes of Shoodra artisans, blacksmith, goldsmith, coppersmith, stonecutter and carpenter, in the Tamul and Teloogoo countries [cummaula, cumsala, punchaula]. The artisan castes have always maintained a struggle for a higher place in the social scale than that allotted to them by Braminical authority, and the ambiguity of this term may have something to do with their disputes [maryauday, mataum].

ACHEEN (اچين - áchín, *Pers.*; அச்சி - açci, *Tam.*). From (achih, malay. wood-leech). Portuguese Achem, or by adhesion of genitive preposition, Dachem. State and town at N.W. angle of Sumatra. There was once a notion that Sumatra was the Greek ταπροβάνη. There is a Tamul proverb:—அச்சியிலும் பிச்சைக்காரர் உண்டு; "there are beggars even in Atchy"; showing its reputation.

ACH ROOT (آچ - ách, *Hind.*). From (áchhuka, san. the tree). Same as Morinda.

ACRE (ஏகரா - égará, *Tam.*). The English land measure; sub-divisions here in 40ths goontas and 16ths of 40ths; or else in 16ths or annas, and 4ths of 16ths.

ACROOT (आक्षोट - ákshóta, *San.*; अक्रोड - akróda, *Mahr.*; جوز - jauz, *Ar.*; چار مغز - chármaghz, *Pers.*; اخروٹ - akhrot, *Dec.*; ಅಕ್ರೋಡು - akródu, *Can.*; అక్రోటు - akrótu, *Tel.*; அக்கரோட்டு - akkaróttu, *Tam.*). Title from deccany. San. from (aksh, san. to pervade), from spreading roots. Mahr. from sanscrit. Ar. from hebrew. Pers. from (chár, pers. four + maghz, pers. kernel); from partition of fruit. Dec., &c., from sanscrit. Pers. also (girdagán), meaning round fruit. Greek κάρυον βασιλικόν; Latin nux. Title otherwise Ban nut, French nut, Walnut, Welsh nut. Botanically Juglans regia, linn., combretaceæ [vricsham, 55]. Generic means Jovis glans. Flowers are in catkin; fruit a drupe; the pericarp contains tannic and gallic acid; all parts of plant possess a peculiar scent, tolerably pleasant, but causing headache to those who remain long in its shade in hot weather. Oil procured by heat is anthelmintic; edible portions are the two seed lobes crumpled up within the shell; twigs and leaves used for fodder; oil expressed from kernels used both for burning and culinary purposes; dyers obtain a blackish brown dye from it; wood from old tree is dark-colored and handsome. Several varieties, the best being the thin-shelled or Caughazee acroot. No other species here. For Belgaum walnut see Aleurites triloba [lumbang nut].

ACSHAM (अक्ष - aksha, *San.*). From (ash, san. to reach).—"*a*" Terrestrial latitude. Distance from equator, north or south, reckoned in degrees, minutes and seconds; the arc of the meridian intercepted between the equator and the place; all nations reckon latitude from the equator. Celestial latitude is Vicshaipam. Acsha bhaugam is a degree of terrestrial latitude. Acshacarnam is the hypothenuse [jyotisham].—"*b*" Eye. Common for seeds. Ex.:—Clitoria ternatea (gaváksha), cow's eye; Coix barbata (kókiláksha), cuckoo's eye; Elæocarpus ganitrus (rudráksha), roodran's eye; Thespesia populnea (kubéráksha), coobairan's eye. See gloss. paragraphs.

AD (ال - ad, *Ar.*). Al [q.v.] before d in Arabic single terms, as Ad deen meaning the religion.

ADAM (آدم - ádam, *Hind.*). From (adamah, heb. tawny). Mahomedan patriarchal alam [alam]. Compare:—Citrus medica, var. limetta, adam's apple; Musa paradisiaca, adam's fig; Tabernæmontana coronaria, adam's apple; Yucca aloifolia, adam's needle. See gloss. paragraphs.——*Adam's bridge* (சேது - shéthu, Tam.). Title from the Mahomedan tradition that Adam on his expulsion from paradise, crossed to Ceylon by this bridge. Tamul means artificial bund. Tam. also (tiruvanai), meaning holy + bund. Sanscrit name (nalasétu), meaning nalan, the monkey who constructed the causeway + bund. Also (rámasétu), meaning Rama + bund. Also (ádisétu), meaning first bridge. Isthmus; Madura dist., Ramnaud tal.; lat. 9° 5′; long. 79° 30′; from Madura E.S.E. 110 miles; from Ramnaud E.S.E. 48 miles. Narrow ridge of sand and rocks mostly dry, nearly closing the Gulf of Manaar on the north and north-east. Western extremity joins the eastern point of Rameshwaram island; eastern extremity joins the eastern point of Manaar island; with these two islands it almost connects Ceylon with the peninsula. Called the bridge of Rama by Bramins, as along it Rama aided by Hanooman with his host of monkeys marched when invading Ceylon. It really joined Ceylon to India until 1480, when a breach was made through rocks during a storm. A subsequent storm enlarged this and foot traffic then ceased. Length about 30 miles, breadth 1¼ miles, direction south-east to north-west. Partly above and partly below water; but when covered has now here above three or four feet of water [charitram].——*Adam's needle* (آدم كى سوئى - ádamkísuí, Hind.). Title from leaves. Botanically Yucca aloifolia, linn., liliaceæ [vricsham, 136]. Large plant; common, long, hard, flattened leaves, each tipped with a needle-like thorn; white flowers, hanging like bells. Yucca gloriosa, linn., or Spanish bayonet is distinguished from aloifolia by its leaves being much narrower and spikelike.

ADAMANCOTTAH (அதமங்கோட்டை - athamangóttai, *Tam.*). Means fort of Adaman, a local king. Tam. also (athátturáyangóttai), meaning Athautroyen, proper name + fort. Village, Salem dist., Dharmapoory tal.; pop. 1,694; acres 3,042; lat. 12° 05′; long. 78° 10′; from Dharmapoory S.W. 5 miles; from Salem N. 29 miles. Founded by Adaman rajah, son of Dharma rajah, who also founded Dharmapoory. The fort is now dismantled. Four veeraculls. Temple, apparently Jeina, near which stands an erect nude figure much like the great statue at Shravanabelgola in Mysore and Yenoor in South canara. There is an inscription on the plinth. Near this are some Braminical temples in ruins. Annual festival. West is a large tank seldom full. Large quantities of coarse cloth are manufactured in the surrounding villages. Cattle-fair largely attended.

ADAMBO (अर्जुन - arjuna, *San.*; جارل - járal, *Hind.*; ಮರುವಾಚಲ - maruváchala, *Can.*; അടമ്പു - atambu, *Mal.*; මුරුත - muruta, *Singh.*; கடலிப்பூ - kadalippú, *Tam.*). Title from mal. San. means white; from white timber. Mal. means close-grained. Tam. means sea flower. Can. also (maruva); (challa). Mal. also (katalpú). Title otherwise Jaural, Larger venteak, Oblong-leaved lagerstrœmia, Queen's flower, Sea flower. Giving one of the Indian bloodwoods. Botanically Lagerstrœmia [cadaly] flos-reginæ, retz., lythraceæ [vricsham, 58]. Alias Adambea glabra; Lagerstrœmia adambæ, reginæ. Cf. the Malay. Ornamental tree; very large; flower large, pale, rose-colored in the morning at sunset purplish, smelling like roses; petals 6, orbicular, waved, shortly unguiculate; leaves opposite, entire, oblong, glabrous; panicled terminal; calyx 6-cleft, longitudinally furrowed and plaited; capsule 3-6 valved, 3-6 celled; seeds numerous; cultivated in gardens on western coast. Flower religious; root, bark, leaves, and flowers, used medicinally; gives a gum-resin; timber reddish or sometimes nearly white, tough and very durable under water, though it soon decays under ground; much used for building and boats.——*Red adambo* (دوپاتى لتا - dopátílatá, Hind.; ಕೆಂಪುಬಂಗಡುಬಳ್ಳಿ - kempubangaduballi, Can.; అడుంబుబూరు - adumbubúru, Too.; చెవులపిల్లితీగ - chevulapillitíga, Tel.; ചുവന്നടമ്പു - chuvannatambu, Mal.; முசற்றாழை - musattazhai, Tam.). Title from colour of flowers. Hind. from (do, hind. two + páti, hind. side + latá, san. creeper); from two-lobed leaf. Can. from (kempu, can. red + bangadu, can. a plant so called + balli, can. creeper). Too. from (adumbu, too. the plant + búru, too. creeper). Tel. from (chevulapilli, tel. hare + tíga, tel. creeper). Mal. from (chuvanna, mal. red + atambu, mal. ipomæa biloba, forsk.). Tam. from (musal, tam. hare + tazhai, tam. leaf); hare-lipped leaf; from two-lobed leaf. Can. also (adumbaballi), meaning the plant + creeper. Tel. also (bálabanditíga), meaning young + binding + creeper. Tam. also (áttukkáladambu), meaning goat + foot + the plant; (adappangodi), meaning adambo creeper.

Title otherwise Adambo creeper, Goat's-foot convolvulus, Goat's foot creeper, Hare leaf, Rabbit weed, Sea-side potato. Botanically Ipomœa [calamby] biloba, forsk., convolvulaceæ [vricsham, 93]. Alias Convolvulus bauhiniaefolius, bilobatus, brasiliensis, carnosus, maritimus, pescapræ; Ipomæa bilobata, brasiliensis, comosa, crassifolia, halophila, maritima, orbicularis, pescapræ, rotundifolia. Perennial; creeping but never twining; leaves long petioled, roundish, deeply 2-lobed, smooth, fleshy, like bauhinia, and resembling impression of a goat's foot; peduncles axillary, solitary, 2-flowered; sepals oblong, acute; seeds covered with a brownish pubescence; flowers large, reddish purple; stems root at distant intervals; common on the sandy beach north and south of madras; sand-binder. Decoction used as fomentation in colic and rheumatism; goats, cows, and horses eat it, but the milk of the cows is tainted.——*White adambo* (വെള്ളടമ്പ് - vellatambu, Mal.). Title from colour of flowers. Title otherwise White goat's foot. Botanically Ipomæa [calamby] beladambœ, rœm. and sch., convolvulaceæ [vricsham, 93]. Specific name from Malayalam. Alias Convolvulus flagelliformis, fugosus; Ipomæa repens, rugosa. Frequent in moist soil about the banks of water-courses and under bunds of tanks; flowers usually pink, sometimes pure white.

ADANGAL (അടങ്ങൽ - atannal, *Mal.*; அடங்கல் - adangal, *Tam.*). From (adangu, tam. to be contained). The whole. An enclosure. Agreement for the performance of a work. Book containing accounts of whole village, the most important of the village accounts. See Vol. I, 112.

ADAUNY (ಅಡಾಣಿ - adáni, *Can.*). Compulsory labour. Adaunijana is an unpaid laborer.

ADAVOO (ಅಡವು - adavu, *Can.*). From (adu, tam. to be near, to support). Pledge. Simple non-usufructuary mortgage; in which the mortgagor retains the property, paying interest on the loan [otty, panayam]. Adavoocaur is the mortgagee. Adavoo chit is the mortgage deed.

ADAWLUT (عدالت - adálat, *Hind.*; అదాలతు - adálatu, *Tel.*). From (adl, ar. justice). A court of justice. The adawluts under the Mahomedan government were of four main classes:—"*a*" Nizaumat adawlut, the supreme court of criminal justice; the ruler's court.—"*b*" Diwanny adawlut, the civil court of the Diwaun.—"*c*" Fowjdarry adawlut, the magistrate's or police criminal court.—"*d*" Adawlut ool cauzy, the town court. See Vol. I, 267.——*Adawlut e badshahy* (عدالت بادشاهی - adálatibádsháhí, Hind.). From (bádsháh, ar. king). King's court. Same as Nizaumat.——*Adawlut e khafeefa* (عدالت خفیفه - adálatikhafífah, Hind.). From (khafífah, ar. small). Small cause court. A minor Diwanny court.——*Adawlut e maul* (عدالت مال - adálatimál, Hind.). From (mál, ar. revenue). Any Revenue court. Same as cutcherry.——*Adawlut e mautahat* (عدالت ماتحت - adálatimátahat, Hind.). From (máhtahat, ar. subordinate). Any subordinate court.——*Adawlut e mooctiar* (عدالت مختار - adálatimukhtár, Hind.). From (mukhtár, ar. independent). A court of competent jurisdiction.——*Adawlut e mooraufa e oolah* (عدالت مرافع اولی - adálatimuráfaiúlá, Hind.). From (muráfa, ar. suit + úlá, ar. first). A court of first instance.——*Adawlut e mooraufa e saunee* (عدالت مرافع ثانی - adálatimuráfaisání, Hind.). From (muráfa, ar. suit + sání, ar. second). A court of appeal.——*Adawlut ool cauzy* (عدالت القاضی - adálatulkází, Hind.). From (kází, ar. judge). Court of Cauzy, the chief judge of a town in civil causes and questions regarding Mahomedan religion. Under him again formerly the Mohtasib held a court for the adjudication of offences against morals; as drunkenness, gambling, &c.

ADDA (అడ్డ - adda, *Tel.*). From (arddha, san. half). A half measure of any sort. Thus:—"*a*" Canarese goldsmith's weight. 2 haugas = 1 adda; 2 addas = 1 hana [niray, 3c]. Approx. actual value:—1 adda = 3 grains. Same as Can. munjoty, Tel. doogoola, Tam. munjaudy.—"*b*" Canarese coin, 2 haugas = 1 adda; 2 addas = 1 caul or ¼ rupee [naunyam, 2c]. Approx. actual value:—1 adda = 2 annas. Same as Tel. baida. Compare Fanam.

ADDAM (అద్దము - addamu, *Tel.*). Looking-glass.——*Addapoo dosily* (అద్దపుడోసిలి - addapudósili, Tel.). Means looking-glass + handful. An allowance of grain made to the village barber.

ADDANKY (అద్దంకి - addanki,* *Tel.*). From (addakamu, tel. dyeing).—"*a*" Deputy tahsildarry, Nellore district. Pay Rupees 70.—"*b*" Town, Head-quarters of Deputy tahsildar and Sub-registrar; Nellore dist., Ongole tal.; pop. 7,480; acres 16,912; lat. 15° 49′; long. 80° 01′; from Madras N. 185 miles; from Naidoopett N. 129 miles; from Nellore N. 92 miles; from Ongole N.N.W. 21 miles; from the sea W. 28 miles. On Goondlacumma and on main road from Nellore to Hyderabad. Temple of Shinganacondah. Ruined fort in neighbourhood, built or restored 500 years ago by Haripaulan, son of Prataupa roodran. About 200 years ago the brother kings of the Mundapaty family of Ongole reigned in this part of the country. Being the centre of an extensive pulse-growing and cattle-breeding tract, has a large trade in gram. Connected by a good road with Santamauglore 28 miles distant in Kistna district, a station on the Bellary-Kistna railway. A road connects it with Darshy 18 miles distant.

ADEE (ಅಡಿ - adi, *Can.*; అడుగు - adugu, *Tel.*; അടി - ati, *Mal.*; அடி - adi, *Tam.*). The Dravidian foot [ady]. Varies from 9·4 inches English as in Madura to 11·32 as in N. arcot. Generally taken at 10·46. 12 angoolams = 1 adee; 3 adees = 1 guz [alavay, 1a]. Same as Hind. kuddum. Cf. jaun or span. 57,600 square feet = 1 cawny.

ADEENA (آدینه - ádínah, *Hind.*). From (ázín, pers. decoration). Friday [shumbah]. Mahomedan proper name, chiefly servant's [alam, ism].

ADHATODAY (वासक - vásaka, *San.*; अडुळसा - adulasá, *Mahr.*; اڈلسا - adalsá, *Hind.*; اڈرسا - adarsá, *Dec.*; ಆಡುಸೋಗೆ - ádusóge, *Can.*; ಏಡ್‌ಮುಟ್ಟಂದಿತಪ್ಪು - édmuttanditappu, *Too.*; అడ్డసరము - addusaramu, *Tel.*; ആടലോടകം - átalótakam, *Mal.*; අගලාතාර - agalátára, *Singh.*; ஆடாதோடை - ádáthódai, *Tam.*). Title from tamul. San. from (vása, san. perfume). Mahr., Hind., Dec., Tel., Mal. from (atarusha, san.). Can. from (ádu, can. goat + sógu, can. to touch). Too. from (éd, too. goat + muttu, too. touch + tappu, too. leaf). Tam. from (ádu, tam. sheep + todu, tam. to touch). San. also (atarusha), meaning disease + killing; also (vaidyamátá), meaning physician + mother, or physician's prime remedy; also (raktapittaghní), meaning plethora + killing; also (vájídanta), meaning horse + tooth, from flower. Title otherwise Malabar nut tree, Winter cherry. Botanically Adhatoda vasica, nees, acanthaceæ [vricsham, 101]. Alias Adhatoda pubescens, zeylonensium; Gendarussa adhatoda; Justicia adhatoda. Small shrub cultivated and in waste places, 8 to 10 feet high; flowers cold season, late; flower whitish, spotted, sulphur-colored at the throat, and at the limb with dark purple lines; all parts bitterish and aromatic; not browsed by any animals except goats, and even these crop only a few leaves; cf. the title and tamul. The whole dried plant is a well-known vegetable drug. Leaves expectorant, antispasmodic and antiperiodic; serviceable in coughs, asthma, chronic bronchitis, phthisis pulmonalis, and ague; used for british squill, senega, æther sulphuricus, and cinchona bark; flowers similar; preparations, infusion and electuary; root similar; fruit similar; fresh flowers bound over eyes for ophthalmia; the plant is mentioned but non-officinal in indian pharm. Leaves given as cattle medicine. A yellow dye obtained from leaf by boiling; when combined with indigo gives a greenish-blue. Wood white, soft; used for gunpowder charcoal and for brick-burning.

ADHELAH (ادهیلا - adhelá, *Hind.*). From (ádh, hind. half + dhelá, hind. half pice). Small coin. 4 damrees = 1 adhelah; 3 adhelahs = 1 anna [naunyam, 2e]. Approx. actual value:—1 adhelah = 4 pies. Sometimes equal to 1, 2 or 3 pies. Same as Can. dooddoo, Tel. dub, Mal. piesa, Tam. dooddoo. Compare Faloos.

ADHI (अधि - adhi, *San.*). Prefix meaning over.——*Adheenam.* (अधीन - adhína, San.). From (in, san. to go). Private.——*Adhicam* (अधिक - adhika, San.). Additional. Especially intercalary in astronomy, and in daily almanac prescribed by Bramins. See description of almanac at Vol. I, 611. Twelve lunations form a lunar year of about 354 solar days; so that the lunar falls behind the solar year of 365 solar days more than 11 solar days every lunar year. Hence intercalary months about every third year [mausam]. So often as the sun remains in the same sign of the zodiac during two Amavausyays [pundigay] or days of the moon's change, the month to which the last Amavausyay belongs is named twice over; it is first considered Adhicam or intercalary, and after being completed is reckoned over again, under its proper name. Distinguish from Abhijit or intercalated partial Nacshatram, used mainly in astrology. Adhicam is also prefixed to the name of a lunar day or tithy, to show that it is repeated on two consecutive days in the calendar [jyotisham]. Adhica vauram is a division of the crop in which a larger share is assigned to Bramins or other privileged persons.——*Adhicauram* (अधिकार - adhikára, San.). From (kri, san. to do). Authority, especially official. In Travancore, a division of a talook. Adhicaurapatrica, from (patriká, san. letter), is a power-of-attorney. Adhicaury is an officer. Deshaudhicaury, the head of a district or province; abbreviated here to Deshye. Graumadhicaury, the headman of a village. Cf. the Adigar of Ceylon.——*Adhipaty* (अधिपति - adhipati, San.). From (pati, san. master). Same as Adhicaury.——*Adhishtaunam* (अधिष्ठान - adhisht'hána, San.). From (st'há, san. to stand). Basement in architecture.——*Adhyacsharam* (अध्यक्षर - adhyakshara, San.). From (akshara, san. syllable). The mystic syllable Om [matam].——*Adhyaupanam* (अध्यापन - adhyápana, San.). From (ápana, san. teaching). Teaching of the vedas [matam].——*Adhyautmam* (अध्यात्म - adhyátma, San.). From (átmá, san. spirit). Overruling spirit.——*Adhyayanam* (अध्ययन - adhyayana, San.). From (ayana, san. going). Perusal of the vedas [matam].

ADIL (عادل - ádil, *Hind.*). From (adl, ar. justice). Just, equitable. Mahomedan alam [ism].

ADIRAMPUTNAM (அதிராம்பட்டணம் - athirámbattanam, *Tam.* adirámpatnam*). From (ativirarāma, san. the pándya king, so called + pattana, san. town). Village, Port. Tanjore dist., Puttoocottah tal.; pop. 10,748; acres 2,395; lat. 10° 21′; long. 79° 25′; from Gopaulputnam N.N.E. 2½ miles; from Madras S.S.W. 196 miles; from Moottoopett W.S.W. 8 miles; from Puttoocottah S.E. 7¾ miles; from Tanjore S.S.E. 35 miles. On Palk strait, 34 miles W. of Point calimere. The sharp angle of coast immediately above protects port from N.E. monsoon, while Ceylon on S.E. protects it from gales. On grand trunk road. Extensive traces of buildings, masonry works, &c., underground. A portion of town submerged. Old Shiva temple with inscriptions. Sea trade chiefly with Ceylon, whither rice in exchange for betel and timber. Fish sent inland as far as Trichinopoly. Large Government salt manufactory, salt-marsh between town and Point calimere being one of most extensive in Presidency. Gopaulputnam adjoins.

ADIVY (అడివి - adivi, *Tel.*). From (at, san. to wander). Forest. Prefix in plant-names [vricsham]. Suffix in place names, as Gopaulappadivy, meaning Gopaulan's forest.

ADJUTANT BIRD (बक - baka, *San.*). Title in jest from its strutting gait. San. from (vak, san. to go crookedly). Ciconidæ family, cultirostres, grallatores, aves [pacshy, 45], of naturalists. Storks. Bill very large and stout, lengthened, straight, or slightly ascending, and with lower mandible subrecurved, smooth, without a groove, less cleft than in herons [paddy-bird], nostrils, linear, near base of culmen; wings long, 2nd and 3rd, or 3rd and 4th quills longest; tail short; all anterior toes joined at base by membrane; claws blunt; of large size. Differ from herons in many points, readily distinguished by large size, bulky form, stouter and smoother bill, and by always having web between inner and middle toes, as well as the outer web. Their lower larynx has no proper muscles, and they consequently emit no sound except by striking the mandibles together; peculiar mechanism of the knee joint, by which they are enabled to rest on one leg without fatigue. Some are migratory and gregarious, others solitary; they breed on lofty trees or on house-tops, and lay two to four whitish eggs. The species best known to the natives are shown below.——*Beefsteak bird* (कांडेश्वर - kándéshvara, Mahr.; مانک جوڑ - mánikjor, Hind.; کالی - kálí, Dec.; శంఖ మెడకొంగ - shankumedakonga, Tel.). Title from flesh cooked as steak. Mahr. from (kánda, san. stick + íshvara, san. lord), from its long neck. Hind. from (mánik, hind. name of a saint + jor, hind. companion). Tel. from (shankha, san. conch + meda, tel. neck + konga, tel. crane); from white neck. Title otherwise White-necked stork. Ciconia leucocephala. Alias Ardea Cucocephala. Top of head black, whole neck white, rest of body black. Flesh cooked as steak. Mussalmans abstain from eating it.——*Common adjutant* (ہرگیلا - hargílá, Hind., Dec.; బకపక్షి - bakapakshi, Can.; పినుగులకొంగ - pínugulakonga, Tel.). Can. from (baka, san. crane + pakshi, san. bird). Tel. from (pínugu, tel. corpse + konga, tel. crane). Hind. also (dastah). Title otherwise Gigantic stork. Leptoptilos argala. Alias Ciconia marabou, nudifrons; Ardea dubia; Argala migratoria. A scavenger, attending slaughter-houses, and burning grounds; roosts on tops of houses. The Comercolly feathers are the under tail-coverts. Its head said to contain a Zahrmorah or poison killer stone.——*Laklak* (لقلق - laklak, Ar., Pers., Hind.; వడుమెకొంగ - vadumekonga, Tel.). Hind. means brightness. Hind. also (ujlí), meaning white; (hajilaglag); (dhak). Title otherwise White stork. Ciconia alba. Alias Ardea ciconia. Head, neck and all body pure white; legs red. The most gregarious of all storks.——*Small adjutant* (چنجرا - chinjara, Hind.; డొడల్కొంగ - dodalkonga, Tel.). Hind. also (madanchurí), meaning pleasing bird, ironical. Title otherwise Hair-crested stork. Leptoptilos javanica. Alias Argala immigratoria; Ciconia calva, capillata, cristata, nudifrons. Top of head entirely bald.

ADJUTANT'S HEDGE (సీమచిత్రమూలము - símachitramúlamu, *Tel.*). Title as being used in cantonments. Tel. from (síma, tel. foreign + chitramúla, san. plumbago zeylanica, linn.). Tel. also (kantapála), meaning thorn + milky plant. Title otherwise Foreign plumbago, Jew bush, Slipper plant. Botanically Pedilanthus tithymaloides, poir., euphorbiaceæ [vricsham, 118]. Road side weed, with cylindrical, succulent stems and dark-green, thick, fleshy leaves; bears small crimson unattractive flowers. No other species here.

ADONY (ادھونی - adhúní, *Hind.*; ఆదవాని - ádaváni, *Tel.* ádóni*). From (ádu, tel. to protect + ani, tel. border). Sanscrit name (yádavagiri), means Krishna of the Yaudava race + hill.——**(1)** Talook, Bellary district. Tahsildar's pay Rupees 200. Area 839 square miles; population 160,795; language Tel. and Can. N.E. talook of district. Bounded on the north by Toongabudra river, south by Aulore talook, east by Putticondah talook of Kurnool district, west by Toongabudra and Hagary rivers. The country is flat, though here and there are detached masses of rock. The country between Adony and Yemmiganore is also hilly. The highest hill in the talook is the Adony rock or rather cluster of rocks on which the fort is built. There are smaller hills at Cotecull, &c., but all are of volcanic origin and devoid of foliage. To the north of the town of Adony, the land gradually slopes away to the basin of the Toongabudra. The soil is chiefly red, though near Cosgy and in the south of the talook the black soil is abundant. For the non-agricultural classes weaving is the chief occupation. The Adony fabrics are thought highly of, and there is a demand for them even in the markets of other districts. Cotton carpets are made and sent to Bellary. Silk is obtained from Collegaul in the Coimbatore district and from South mysore; and silk and cotton cloths are exported in large quantities to Dharwar and the Hyderabad country. There is no great trade in grain, but a large trade in cotton and several steam presses. The Toongabudra channel is taken off from the Toongabudra river by the anicut at Toombiganore. The two most important tanks are at Chinna toombalam and Haulhervy. There are smaller ones at Adony, Chirtahully, and Isvy. Best camping grounds:—Canacaveed, Chinnatoombalam, Cosgy, Cowtaul, Halvy, Hatsahully, Mandavaram, Rampooram and Yemmiganore. Places of archæological interest:—Adony, Alsandigootty, Badinehully, Basaracode, Basarvully, Beichigherry, Cadabore, Cadimetla, Canacaveed, Capaty, Caumavaram, Chinnatoombalam, Chyangy, Coopgal, Coorvutty, Cosgy, Cottalchinta, Cowtaul, Dayyamdinney, Goorzaula, Gungavaram, Halvy, Hatsahully, Haulhervy, Hissaurmoorvany, Manchaula, Nandavaram, Nettecull, Nyaulacosgy, Parvatipooram, Peddacadabore, Peddatoombalam, Peekalbetta, Rampooram, Sultanpore, Tangardona, Vattoomoorvany, Yenoogabaula. Trig. stations in the talook:—Adony, Caumanagutt, Chyaugy, Halvy. The leading places, &c., in the talook are the following.——*Adony* (ఆదవాని - ádaváni, Tel.). See below.——*Akkachell* (అక్కచెల్లెలగుడ్డ - akkachellelagudda, Tel.). From (akka, tel. elder sister + chelle, tel. younger sister + gudda, can. hill). Hill; means the two sisters. A curious isolated rock not far from Cosgy.——*Balakilah* (بالا قلعه - bálákila, Hind.; బాలాకిలా - bálákilá, Tel.). From (bálá, hind. high + kila, hind. fort). Hill; this and Tauliboonda are the highest peaks of the range on which the citadel of Adony stands. Half-way up is a fine tank which is never dry, and on the summit grows a fig tree forming a landmark for 20 or 30 miles in every direction.——*Basaracode* (బసరకోడు - basarakódu, Tel.). From (basava, can. bull + kódu, can. hill top). Village; pop. 880; acres 1,717; lat. 15° 35′; long. 77° 25′; from Adony E.S.E. 7 miles; from Bellary N.E. 42 miles. Temple in a cave near Alasandigootty, hamlet of this place.——*Caumanagutt* (కామనగట్టు - kámanagattu, Tel.). From (kámanna, tel. proper name + gattu, tel. border). Trig. station; lat. 15° 48′ 38·30″; long. 77° 19′ 19·10″; height 2,101 feet; from Adony N. 13 miles; from Balsaladoddy W.S.W. 2¼ miles; from Bellary N.N.E. 52 miles.——*Chinna toombalam* (చిన్నతుంబళము - chinnatumbalamu, Tel.). From (chinna, tel. small + tumbalamu, tel. village called after tumbaláraya, a ruler). Village; pop. 2,279; acres 5,965; lat. 15° 48′; long. 77° 21′; height 1,220 feet; from Adony N. 11 miles; from Bellary N.N.E. 52 miles. Contains an important tank.——*Chyaugy* (చాగి - chyági, Tel.). From (chágamu, tel. liberality). Trig. station; lat. 15° 51′ 19·57″; long. 77° 05′ 30·65″; from Adony N.W. 22 miles; from Bellary N. 50 miles.——*Coopgal* (కుప్పిగల్లు - kuppigallu, Can.). From (kuppe, can. heap + kallu, can. stone). Village, Railway station; pop. 1,091; acres 1,722; lat. 15° 44′; long. 77° 17′; height 1,351 feet; from Adony N.N.W. 7 miles; from Bellary N.N.E. 46 miles. Coarse cumblies made.——*Cosgy* (కోశిగి - kóshigi, Tel.). From (kósha, san. treasury). The founder of the village is said to have found treasure. Sanscrit name (kóshapurí), means treasury + town. Village, Railway station; pop. 7,054; acres 3,807; lat. 15° 51′; long. 76° 17′; height 1,237 feet; from Adony N. 16 miles; from Bellary N.N.E. 53 miles. Built in an irregular manner. It is situated at the foot of a rock. According to tradition the town was founded by Soorappa naick, an officer of the Anagoondy rajah, who visited the place on a marauding expedition. On the rock are the ruins of some fortifications and temples. Near is the curious isolated rock known by the name of the sisters [akkachell].——*Cotecull* (కోటేకల్లు - kótékallu, Tel.). From (kóte, can. fort + kallu, can. stone). Village; pop. 1,921; acres 8,912; lat. 15° 41′; long 77° 26′; from Adony E.N.E. 8¼ miles; from Bellary N.E. 49 miles. Close to a hill of volcanic origin.——*Cowtaul* (కవుతాళం - kavutálam, Tel.). From (kavi, san. poet + tála, san. palm tree, borassus flabelliformis, linn.). Village; pop. 4,061; acres 9,209; lat. 15° 46′; long. 77° 11′; from Adony N.W. 14 miles; from Bellary N.N.E. 46 miles. The site of the village was originally a jungle of palm trees and was presented to a poet by the ruler of the country. The tomb of a fakeer, who died about 500 years ago, is shown in this village. His family still hold a neighbouring village as a jagheer. Weaving is carried on to a small extent.——*Goodicull* (గుడికల్లు - gudikallu, Tel.). From (gudi, tel. temple + kallu, can. stone). Village; pop. 3,617; acres 3,792; lat. 15° 45′; long. 77° 31′; from Adony E.N.E. 15 miles; from Bellary N.E. 57 miles. Close to Yemmiganore; weaving industry.——*Halvy* (హాల్వి - hálvi, Tel.). From (hálu, can. milk). Village; pop. 2,119; acres 5,798; lat. 15° 53′; long. 77° 10′;

from Adony N.N.W. 20 miles; from Bellary N.N.E. 53 miles. Contains a well said to have cost 5 lakhs of rupees. It was built by the Diwaun of Basaulut jung, and as he had been informed that he would live to see the well completed, he intentionally omitted to finish the parapet wall. Trig. station in lat. 15° 53′ 01·57″; long. 77° 09′ 35·65″; from Halvy village W.S.W. ¼ mile.——*Hatsahully* (హత్సహళ్లి - hattsahalli, Tel.). From (hattsa, can. green + halli, can. village). Village; pop. 1,734; acres 6,188; lat. 15° 47′; long. 77° 02′; from Adony W.N.W. 22 miles; from Bellary N. 45 miles. The confluence of the Hagary and Toongabudra is near Halcote, about 6 miles from Hatsahully.——*Haulhervy* (హాలహర్వి - hálaharvi, Tel.). From (hálu, can. waste land + haruvu, can. to spread). Village; pop. 1,720; acres 9,195; lat. 15° 50″; long. 77° 29′; from Adony N.E. 17 miles; from Bellary N.E. 59 miles. Contains an important tank.——*Hissaurmoorvany* (హిస్సారమురువణి - hissára-muruvani, Tel.). From (hisár, hind. fort + muruvu, tel. beauty + ani, tel. boundary). Village; pop. 2,356; acres 9,654; lat. 15° 46′; long. 77° 28″; from Adony N.E. 13 miles; from Bellary N.E. 55 miles. It contains numerous wells.——*Isvy* (ఇసివి - isivi, Tel.). Means skin disease. Tradition says that there was a pit near the village, the mud of which was used to cure the disease. Village; pop. 443; acres 5,491; lat. 15° 40′; long. 77° 17′; from Adony W.N.W. 2¾ miles; from Bellary N.N.E. 41 miles. Good brinjauls grown.——*Manchaula* (మంచాల - mantsála, Tel.). From (mantsamu, tel. raised platform + álaya, san. temple). Sanscrit name (mantrálaya), meaning holy prayer + temple. Village; pop. 1,082; acres 4,185; lat. 15° 57′; long. 77° 28′; from Adony N.N.E. 23 miles; from Bellary N.N.E. 65 miles. The Toongabudra had an anicut here, the remains of which still exist. A place of pilgrimage to Bramins, contains the tomb of a Bramin high priest.——*Maudhavaram* (మాధవరము - mádhavaramu, Tel.). From (mádhava, san. epithet of vishnu + pura, san. town). Village; pop. 1,808; acres 4,345; lat. 15° 56′; long. 77° 24′; height 1,078; from Adony N.N.E. 21 miles; from Bellary N.N.E. 62 miles. Irrigation under the Toongabudra channels.——*Nandavaram* (నందవరము - nandavaramu, Tel.). From (nanda, san. epithet of vishnu + pura, san. town). Village; pop. 3,251; acres 13,920; lat. 15° 51′; long. 77° 31′; from Adony N.E. 20 miles; from Bellary N.E. 62 miles.——*Naugaldinney* (నాగులదిన్నె - náguladinne, Tel.). From (nágu, tel. serpent + dinne, tel. mound). Village; pop. 3,223; acres 1,349; lat. 15° 55′; long. 77° 36′; from Adony N.E. 27 miles; from Bellary N.E. 69 miles. Was once a large and prosperous town, but has never recovered the effects of the great storm in 1851, when a great portion of the town was washed away. There are the remains of an old fort which was destroyed soon after the cession of the district. There are 200 looms in the village, but only very coarse cloths are made.——*Rampooram* (రాంపురము - rámpuramu, Tel.). From (ráma, san. incarnation of vishnu + pura, san. town). Village; pop. 1,683; acres 1,713; lat. 15° 57′; long. 77° 22′; from Adony N. 22 miles; from Bellary N.N.E. 62 miles. Has numerous cocoanut and betel gardens.——*Toongabudra* (తుంగభద్ర - tungabhadra, Tel.). See sep. title.——*Yemmiganore* (యెమ్మిగనూరు - yemmiganúru, Tel.). See sep. title.——**(2)** Town, Divisional and Talook head-quarters, Railway station; pop. 26,243; acres 4,939; lat. 15° 38′; long. 77° 19′; height 1,362 feet; from Bellary N.E. 41 miles; from Hospett E.N.E. 65 miles; from Hurpanhully E.N.E. 105 miles; from Madras N.W. 261 miles; from Tadpatry N.W. 69 miles. Trig. station in lat. 15° 38′ 52·79″; long. 77° 19′ 14·14″; height 2,000 feet; from Adony town N. 1½ miles; from Bellary N.E. 43 miles. The largest town but one in the district near the north-western frontier towards the territory of the Nizam. The fort of Adony, now in ruins, stands upon five rocky granite hills to the north-west of the town, two of the peaks being 800 feet high. Half way up is a fine tank of drinking water. Formerly the fort played a conspicuous part in the intestine wars of the Deccan. It secured the passage of the Toongabudra and its possession was therefore essential to an army, which, invading the Carnatic from the Deccan, wished to keep its retreat secure. Being fortified with eleven ramparts, one within another, it was considered impregnable. Traditionally founded in 1200 B.C. by Chunder sen in the reign of Bheemasainan of Beedar. It was taken by Krishna deva royer of Vijianugger early in the sixteenth century. Ramrauz, his successor, received it as a dowry with his wife, and appointed his brother Caunom rajah as governor. On the fall of the Vijianugger dynasty in 1565, it passed to the Mahomedan kings of the Adil shahy dynasty of Beejapore and Golcondah. They built the lower forts and the outer walls. The revenue of the district amounted then to 6 lakhs and 75,900 pagodas, and the military establishment consisted of 4,000 horse and 8,000 foot. Ferishta refers to it as "situate on the summit of a high hill "and containing many lakes and fountains of clear and sweet "water, with princely structures." In 1690 it was taken after a determined resistance by the generals of Aurungzeeb and included in the soobah of Beejapore. As the central authority of Delhi declined, Beejapore was merged in the territories of the Nizam, and the fortress and province of Adony became a family dependency of a younger branch of the house. In 1748 held by Moozuffer jung, and, on his death, in 1752, it descended, through the influence of M. Bussy, to his son. In 1757 it passed to Basaulut jung, the brother of the Soobahdar of the Deccan, who, making it his capital, attempted to establish an independent principality. Hyder ally twice attacked the fortress without success, and though in 1778 he defeated the Mahrattas under its walls, and in the following year laid waste the country round, it did not surrender. In 1782 Basaulut jung died, and Hyder ally soon afterwards. In 1786 Tippoo, by a siege of a month, took the fort and razed its battlements. After the peace, Adony was restored to the Nizam, and in 1799 was ceded to the English. Cloths of cotton and silk, the latter made from the Collegaul cocoons, and carpets, constitute its chief manufactures, and occupy more than a third of the total adult male population. Connected by rail with Madras and Bellary since 1870. Roads run to Gooty and Siroogooppa, while numerous country tracks converging on Adony act as feeders to the railway. Cholera used at one time to be frequently epidemic here, but, owing to recent municipal reforms in street-widening, cleansing, and sanitation, the health of the town has of late improved greatly. The tomb of Malik rahman khan, the first Mussalman governor, on the Taulibanda hill, is still an object of veneration. The Jumma musjid, built by his son, is the best specimen of Mahomedan architecture in this part of the country. The large square well close to the mosque was built by Vencannah punt, Diwaun to the former [charitram].

ADRAK (ادرك - adrak, *Hind.*). From (árdraka, san. ginger). Same as Ginger.

ADRY (अद्रि - adri, *San.*). From (ad, san. to protect). Mountain. Cf. Sheshaudry.——*Adricam* (अद्रिक - adrika, San.). Upper or mountain Keralam [abdhicam].

ADUL OIL (ஆதலையெண்ணெய் - áthalaiyenney, *Tam.*). Same as Rat aumanac [q.v.].

ADY (ಅಡಿ - adi, *Can.*; അടി - ati, *Mal.*; அடி - adi, *Tam.*). From (adu, tam. to approach); near the ground. Foot [adoo], bottom, source, beginning, vicinity, &c. Suffix in place names; as Coilady, meaning temple + vicinity. A title among lower classes. Originally a slave. Fifteen classes of slaves are recognized by ancient Hindoo law:—Anaucaulabhritan, taken as a slave in a time of famine; Auhitan, taken as a pledge; Autmavikrayee, one who sells himself; Bhactadausan, one who is a slave for his food; Creetan, one purchased; Critan, one who makes himself a slave for a definite term; Dauyaudoo-paugatan, inherited; Grihajautan, one born in the house of the owner by a female slave; Labdan, one acquired, as by gift; Panejitan, won in a wager; Pravrajyauvasitan, apostate, one who having entered religious order, forsakes it and thereby becomes a slave of the rajah; Rinadausan, one becoming a slave in payment of a debt; Tavauham, one who voluntarily makes himself a slave, saying, I am thine; Varavahritan, one who becomes a slave by marrying a female slave; Yooddhaprauptan, acquired in war.——*Adicherry* (அடிச்சேரி - adiççéri, Tam.). From (shéri, tam. village). Suburb.——*Adikole* அடிக்கோல் - adikkól, Tam.). From (kól, tam. rod). Measuring rod.——*Adima* (അടിമ - atima, Mal.). Bondage, slavery. Remains in Malabar as a kind of feudal dependency. Also the name of a land-grant. Most persons there under the rank of Nayar acknowledge a dependence upon some Tumbiraun or superior, being by that means Adiyauns. Persons of this description were not formerly allowed to possess land in Jenm right; and therefore, when a Jenmy made over land to a person in the condition of an Adiyaun, it went by the special name of Adima grant. This grant is almost the same at present day as the inam or maunyam of other districts. In it the land is made over in perpetuity to the grantee, either unconditionally as a mark of favor, or on condition of certain services being performed. But in either case a nominal fee of about two fanams a year is payable to the landlord to show that he still retains the proprietary title. Land bestowed as a mark of favor can never be resumed; but where it is granted as remuneration for certain services to be performed, like service inam, the non-performance of such services involving the necessity of having them discharged by others will give the landlord power to recover the land. The non-payment of the annual fee will form no ground for ousting the grantee, but it will be recoverable by action. The land will also revert if there are no heirs. Adima has been granted to Cheroomar and other low caste people to enable them to bury or burn their dead in spots where the latter were not liable to be disturbed. It has been largely granted in favor of village artisans, washermen, and others, who in return for the bulk of the rent of the land were bound to perform certain services. The hereditary property of native princes cannot be conferred on this tenure, the ruling prince having only the right of enjoyment during life, without power to alienate. For inam lands to higher castes, see Anoobhavam, Santaty bramhasom. Compare Coodima for ordinary tenancy. Also Chungautam, which however only applies to superior castes. For a succinct view of Malabar tenures, see Vol. II, 104, 105.——*Adimaday* (அடிமடை - adimadai, Tam.). From (madai, tam. channel). Head of a water channel.——*Aditchaul* (அடிச்சால் - adiççál, Tam.). From (shál, tam. furrow). The first furrow in ploughing.——*Adivauram* (அடிவாரம் - adivá-ram, Tam.). From (váram tam. slope). Foot of a hill.——

Adiyaul (அடியாள் - adiyál, Tam.). Means foot + fem. pers. termination. Female Pariah name. Masc. form adiyaun.——*Adiyaun* (അടിയാൻ - atiyán, Mal.). Literally slave. In Northern division of Malabar, term applies generally to Cheroomar, who were formerly real slaves. In South malabar it means a person, especially Teeyan, who without holding any land owns a dependence on some Tumbiraun or superior. This Tumbiraun being bound to protect the Adiyaun and redress his wrongs. The Teeyan acknowledging his dependent state by yearly presents, and being ready with personal services on the occasion of any private quarrel by his patron. This kind of dependency gives the patron no right of disposal of the person of his dependent as a slave, nor does it acquit the dependent individual of a superior obligation to the rajah or his representatives, the Deshavauly and Naudvauly, upon a public emergency. Individuals are often Adiyauns to the temple, which, by means of its representatives the Ooraular, is bound to protect them. Adiyaun also means a holder on Adima tenure. Also an Ambalavausy caste in Travancore [antaraulam].——*Adiyody* (അടിയോടി - atiyóti, Mal.). Means foot runner. Hindoo 3rd or caste name [peyar], especially among Nayars of Cadatnaud in North malabar.

ADYAR (அடையாறு - adaiyáru, *Tam.*). From (adai, tam. to silt up + áru, tam. river).—"*a*" River in Chingleput and Madras districts. Rises under Chembrambaukam tank, the surplus waters of which flow into it. After forming the southern boundary, it enters Madras district on the south-west, and flowing through it for 3 miles empties itself into the sea. On its banks are some of the largest and handsomest private residences of the city. The Buckingham canal crosses it at the south-western end of Madras district, with locks on either side of the river. Alwarpett and Mylapore are on the north bank. Its southern bank is the limit of Chingleput district. The river has no commercial value, but many natives in the neighbourhood make a living by fishing. It is crossed by three important bridges; one near the Mount, a second the Marmalong at Sydapett, and a third very long one near the sea called Elphinstone bridge erected in 1842.- "*b*" Zemindarry, Village; Chingleput dist., Sydapett tal.; pop. 1,830; acres 1,426; lat. of village 13° 01′; long. 80° 18′; from Sydapett E.S.E. 1¾ miles; from the sea W. 2½ miles. Includes Guindy and the Little mount. Peshcush Rs. 98.

AFEEM (افیم - afím, *Hind.*). Corruption of arabic (afyún). Greek ὄπιον. Opium [q. v.].

AFGHAUN (افغان - afghán, *Hind.*). Inhabitant of Afghanistaun. Pataun is here used instead.

AFOO (عفو - afú, *Hind.*). From (afá, ar. to efface). The eraser of sins. Attribute of God [allah].

AFSAR (افسر - afsar, *Hind.*). From Pers. crown. Component part of lacabs male and female [ism].——*Afsar oon nissa* (افسرالنسا - afsarunnisá, Hind.). Crown of women.

AFTAUB (آفتاب - áftáb, *Hind.*). Sun.——*Aftaubgeer* (آفتاب گیر - áftábgír, Hind.). From (gír, pers. catcher). A parasol. ——*Aftauby* (آفتابی - áftábí, Hind.). Acbar's gold coin, value Rs. 12 [naunyam, 2e].

AFZAL (افضل - afzal, *Hind.*). From (fadala, ar. to exceed). Excellent. Mahomedan slave-alam. Also part of lacab [ism]. ——*Afzal ood dowla* (افضل الدولہ - afzaluddaulah, Hind.). From (daulah, ar. empire). Eighth Nizam of Deccan and father of the present ruler. See Vol. I, 9.

AGAM (അകം - akam, *Mal.*; அகம் - agam, *Tam.*). Inside; mind; dwelling place; low land; grain. Prefix in place names, as Agattettara, meaning inside + village. Suffix in place names as Vaudikagam, meaning enclosure + inside.——*Agambadiyaur* (அகம்படியார் - agambadiyár, obl.; அகம்படியான் - agambadiyán, pers. sing.; அகம்படியார் - agambadiyár, pers. pl., Tam.). Corr. of Agamoodeiyaur. Caste-title. One of the principal elements in the agricultural population of the Marava country. These people are nearly connected with the Maravar by descent, and they also resemble them closely in appearance, habits and customs. The chiefs of the Maravar are accustomed to marry Agambadiyaur women; and of the children born of such marriages, the males must marry Agambadiyaur females and belong to their wives' caste, whilst the females must marry Maravar and belong to their husbands' caste. The honorific title of an Agambadiyaun is Sherveicáuran, or captain of a band. The Agambadiyaur are slightly less numerous than the Maravar; as they are somewhat inferior to them in estimation. Men of this caste are employed in large numbers by zemindars and others as retainers and domestic servants. They are also employed in temples. But the great body of them are poor and humble ryots. Number about 300,000; most in Madura and Tanjore [jauty].——*Agamodeiyaun* (அகமுடையான் - agamudaiyán, Tam.). From (udai, tam. owning). A land-holder. Among Tam. Bramins, respectful way to speak to a woman of her husband.——*Agapodwaul* (അകപ്പൊതുവാൾ - akappotuvál, obl.; അകപ്പൊതുവാൾ - akappotuvál, pers. sing.; അകപ്പൊതുവാൻമാർ - akappotuvánmár, pers. pl., Mal.). From (potuvál, mal. the caste). Caste-title. Temple servants in Malabar [jauty, podwaul].——*Agaporool* (அகப்பொருள் - agapporul, Tam.). From (porul, tam. subject matter). A treatise on the composition of amatory poems by Naurcavirajan, Jeina poet.——*Agappay* (அகப்பை - agappai, Tam.). A ladle of stick and half cocoanut shell. There is a Tamul proverb:—கண்ணாற் கண்டது பொய் அகப்பைக்குறி மெய்— "that which one has seen is false, the sign of agappay is true." The mark of the agappay on the grain-heap is taken as better evidence than what an eye-witness saw. Derisive of justice.——*Agattumaur* (അകത്തമ്മമാർ - akattammamár, Mal.). From (amma, mal. mother). Honorific form. A Braminy in Malabar [antarjanam]. Almost gosha. When compelled to travel, preceded by a Nayar woman who cries out to warn off male passengers [jauty, maryauday].——*Agavilay* (அகவிலை - agavilai, Tam.). From (vila, tam. price). The market price of grain.

AGAR AGAR (دریاکی پاچی - daryákípáchí, *Dec.*; اگراگر - agaragar, *Malay*; సముద్రపుపాచి - samudrapupáchi, *Tel.*; கடற்பாசி - kadarbási, *Tam.*). Title from malay meaning sea weed. Other vern. means sea + moss. Malay also (sajarkarang), meaning sea-weed. Title otherwise Ceylon moss, Edible sea-weed, Jaffna moss. Giving Lichen starch. Botanically the Gracilaria genus, algæ [vricsham, 163]. Rose-spored; distinguished by its cylindrical compressed or flat fronds. Alga zeylanica, Fucus amylaceus of chemists. The species best known to the natives is lichenoides or ceylon moss [q.v.]; grows on ceylon coast; a light purple or greenish sea-weed; in medicinal properties resembles carrageen or rock-moss, being emollient; in decoction constitutes a food for invalids and children; gives to pharm. decoctum gracilariæ; officinal, like iceland moss. Other common species are:—confervoides, spinosa.

AGARAM (அகரம் - agaram, *Tam.*). From (agára, san. house). Latin ager. Agricultural village, subsequently Bramin village. Suffix in place names; as Periyagaram, meaning large + agricultural village. Sometimes used by mistake for Agrahauram.

AGARIC (غاریقون - ghárikún, *Pers.*; اغاریقون - aghárikún, *Dec.*; காரிக்கூன், kárikkún, *Tam.*). An old sarmatian word and thence borrowed by the arabs. Title otherwise Garikoon, Hard amadou, Hard tinder, Male agaric, Moxa, Punk, Spunk, Touch-wood. Botanically Polyporus ignarius, fries., fungi [vricsham, 161]. Alias Boletus ignarius. A fungus growing on trees; powder a purgative. Anthelminticus is similar. The Soft amadou, female agaric, german tinder, vegetable tinder, surgeon's agaric, is fomentarius.

AGAROO (अगरु - agaru, *San.*). From (a, san. negative prefix + guru, san. heavy); from light wood.—"*a*" Botanically the Excæcaria genus, euphorbiaceæ [vricsham, 118]. Mostly woody shrubs, but some form small trees; leaves usually alternate, and either entire or with margin toothed; flowers produced in catkins; fruit three-celled. The species best known to the natives are:—Agallocha [tiger's milk], Sebifera [china tallow]. Other S. indian species indigenous or naturalized are:—baccata, cochin chinensis, indica, insignis, oppositifolia.—"*b*" Also used for Aquilaria agallocha [eaglewood].—"*c*" Agaroo gandham or eaglewood scent is Pterocarpus santalinus [red sanders].

AGASA (ಅಗಸ - agasa, obl.; ಅಗಸ - agasa, pers. sing.; ಅಗಸರು - agasaru, pers. pl., *Can.*). Caste-title; personal forms, Agasa, sing., Agasar, pl. Canarese washermen. The corresponding terms are:—Hind. Dhoby, Tel. Saucala, Mal. Veloottaidan, Tam. Vunnaun. They worship Oobbey, or the steam issuing from the boiling water in which the clothes are steeped. Animals are sacrificed to Oobbey, in order to preserve the clothes from burning. They follow no profession but that of washing, and in all public processions are bound without reward to carry a torch before the images and the chief officer of Government. Both men and women wash. Their proper beasts of burthen are asses. They confine their marriages to a few families which they know to be of pure descent. They marry a number of wives if they can afford it. They may eat meat and drink spirituous liquors. They rank in Canara with the Punchaulas [jauty].

AGASTYAN (अगस्त्य - agastya, *San.*; அகத்தியன் - agattiyan, *Tam.*). From (aga, san. mountain + as, san. to throw). Thrower of mountains, meaning pioneer over mountainous regions.—"*a*" One of the Sapta rishies who escaped in a vessel at Menoo's flood, all represented in sky in Ursa major. Agastyan is on apex of an obtuse triangle, and over it is a small star for his wife Anoosya. Is a chiranjeevy. Also called Atry, his wife Atreyee [matam].—"*b*" The better known historic Agastyan is a Maha moony. Also called Tamizhmoony, the Tamul sage. Sometimes ascribed to times of Coolashekharan, first Pandyan king. Answers to the North india vyausan. This Agastyan is in the sky the star Canopus. Also called Coombha yony, as born from a water jar. He was a Thibetan, and not bramin. Said to have been short of stature [irattaiyaur]. He came south as a missionary, and the Scaundapooraunam has account of his humbling the pride of the Vindhyas, causing them to lie at his feet. Hence his name Vindhyacootan, evidently amplification of Agastyan. Farther south occurred the incident of Vautaupy and Ilvalan [kaukar]. This is a well known legend of Odin in Scandinavia. Thence to promontory of Caunya comaury or Cape comorin, where he took up his residence on Agastyamullay or Mount pothigay [q.v.], near the present Courtallam. The highest peak is inaccessible, and popular belief for a hundred miles around considers him to reside there still. This Agastyan diffused worship of Shiva amongst Tamuls; and taught them medicine, chemistry, astronomy, and other sciences. His treatise on Tamul grammar contained 12,000 sootrams, but excepting fragments preserved in quotations by Tolgauppyan is not now extant. However most Tamul works ascribed to Agastyan are not his. He had a wife Lopamoodray, and a son by her Sagaran. He had twelve disciples to whom he taught the arts and sciences:—Adancottay asiriyan, Avinyaut nayar, Caukkaypaudinyan who wrote a standard grammar, Cazhauramban, Nuttattan, Panambauran who wrote the preface to Tolgauppyam, Shempootcheyan, Tolgauppyan who wrote the celebrated grammar, Tooralingan, Vauman, Veiyaubigan, and Vyepiyan. The Agastya nyaunam, or Agastyan's wisdom, otherwise Agastya paudal or Agastyan's chant, written in Shen tamul high dialect, teaches a pantheistic monotheism leaning to Sheivism. His Mooppath or thirty stanzas are like the wisdom of Solomon. In one of these he refutes notions about Shiva, Vishnoo, and Bramha; states that penance, bathing, and self-immolation are unne cessary for a passage to Keilausam; and instructs men to worship Parabrahm. Example from a hymn ascribed to Agastyan:—பரமானந்தம் பரமசுகதம் கேவலஞானமூர்த்திம் துவந்துவாதீதம் ககனசதிரிசம் தத்வம் அசியாதிலக்ஷியம் ஏகம் நித்யம் விமலமசலம்சர்வ்தாசாக்ஷிபூதம் பாவாதீதம் திரிகுணரகிதம் சற்குரும் தம்நமாமி.—"I salute the "great teacher, the bestower of divine happiness and supreme "bliss; the image of perfect wisdom; who is removed from all "opposite states; who is represented by the sky; who is "denoted by truth and other names; the one, eternal, stainless, "stable, and omniscient, the incomprehensible, who is without "the 3 goonams of satwam, rajas, and tamas."——*Agasteeshwaram* (അഗസ്തീശ്വരം - agastíshvaram, Mal.). From (íshvara, san. lord).—"*a*" Talook; Travancore state, Pudmanaubhapooram division; area 97 square miles; pop. 78,979. Sub-divided into six Pidaugas and contains 475 caras or villages. Bounded N. by Tovaula talook, E. by Tinnevelly district, S. by Indian ocean, W. by Yerraneel talook. Greatest length from N. to S. is 12 miles and greatest breadth from E. to W. is 10 miles. Except the Maroothamala, there are no hills. Soil generally loose, but sandy near coast. Good for paddy cultivation, and growing mangoes. Most people are ryots, but near Cottaur are traders. In Cottaur are silk-weavers, Shauliyas and Mahomedans, who make laced muslin cloths or country coarse cloths. Many Shaunaur. Palmyra jaggery exported through Colachel. Sources of water-supply are Palayaur, Poottanaur and Anantanaur. Anicuts across Palayaur. No water at all goes to sea. Tanks are Sooshindram, Porakye, Poottary and Tairoor.—"*b*" The village of same name is in lat. 8° 06'; long. 77° 33'; from Sooshindram S.E. $5\frac{1}{2}$ miles; from Trivandrum S.E. 46 miles; from the sea N. $1\frac{1}{4}$ miles.

AGATTY (അകത്തി - akatti, *Mal.*). Means remote. Island; Malabar dist.; pop. 1,183; sq. mile $1\frac{1}{4}$; lat. 10° 52'; long. 72° 28. One of the Laccadives, lying about 35 miles north-west of Cavarathy, most westerly of the Laccadive group. Lies north-east and south-west and has on its western side a fine lagoon. The coral shoal upon which it stands is between 6 and 7 miles in length and from $3\frac{1}{2}$ to 4 miles in breadth. Besides the main island, the reef also encloses the small uninhabited island of Caulipully, to south of Agatty proper and separated by a narrow and shallow channel. The main island is long and narrow, being nearly 5 miles in length, whilst its greatest breadth is under 1,000 yards. The southern portion consists of a strip, averaging for more than 2 miles of its length little over 100 yards in width. At about 5 miles north lie the uninhabited islands of Paraly, Tinnakara and Vangara, but these, though upon an extension of the Agatty coral shoal, are enclosed by a separate range of reefs and the channel between is deep. The island is divided into three cherries or sub-divisions, viz., Tekkancherry, Vadacancherry, and Yedacherry. The entire island is a Melacherry or low caste island. The people are exclusively Mahomedans. The language bears a closer resemblance to Tamul than that of the other northern islands. Fish is abundant. The soil is comparatively sterile. About two-thirds of the island are under cocoanut cultivation, the rest is waste; there are no large jungles. Lands claimed by Pundauram or circar are of small extent. Attempts have been made to form a tottam or artificial low land for cultivation of cereals, but the extent is trifling and the quality very poor. A plant called Ittlah grows in Bangara, from the root of which a sort of tapioca is obtained, used as diet for invalids. In June 1880, a British steamer, the Mahableshwar, was wrecked on the reefs of this group of islands.

AGATTY (اگتی - agti, *Dec.*; ಅಗಶಿ - agashi, *Can.*; అవిసె - avisi, *Tel.*; അകത്തി - agatti, *Mal.*; அகத்தி - agatti, *Tam.*). Corr. of (agasti, san.). Same as Sesban. Also applied to Linum, usitatissimum. Also 2nd term in:—Cadaba indica (káttagatti), wild agatty; Cassia alata (shímaiyagatti), foreign agatty; see gloss. paragraphs.——*Foreign agatty* (दद्रुघ्न - dadrughna, San.; दाद्मर्दन - dădmardana, Mahr.; दाद्दुपान - dáddupána, Conc.; داد مردن - dádmurdan, Hind.; ولایتی اگتی - viláitíagtí, Dec.; گلنگنگ - glenggang, Malay; ಸೀಮೆಅಗಸೆ - símeagase, Can.; సీమఅవిశ - símaavishi, Tel.; ശീമയകത്തി - shímayakatti, Mal.; අත්තෝර - attóra, Singh.; சீமையகத்தி - shímaiyagatti, Tam.). Title from being introduced from west indies. San. from (dadru, san. ringworm + han, san. to destroy). Hind. from (dád, hind. ringworm + murdan, pers. to kill). Dec. from (viláití, hind. foreign + agtí, hind. sesbania grandiflora, pers.). Can. from (síme, can. foreign). Tel., Mal. and Tam., similar. Singh. from (at, singh. elephant + tóra, singh. cassia tora, linn.). San. also (dvípágasti), meaning island + sesbania grandiflora, pers. Dec. also (dátkápattá), meaning ring-worm leaf. Tel. also (mettatámara), meaning dry ground + nelumbium speciosum, willd. Tam. also (vandugolli), meaning beetle + killer; as cure against poisonous bites of insects. Title otherwise Broad-leaved cassia, Ringworm shrub, Winged senna. Botanically Cassia [sooyarnacam] alata, linn., leguminosæ [vricsham, 48]. Alias Cassia bracteata, herpetica; Senna alata. Shrub, 8-12 feet; branches spreading, irregularly angled, glabrous; leaflets 8-14 pairs, obovate-oblong, very obtuse, mucronate, glabrous on both sides, or nearly so, the lowest pair close to the branch, and at a distance from the next pair; petiole triangular, without glands; racemes terminal; legumes long, enlarged on each side with a broad crenulated wing, about 5 inches long and $1\frac{1}{2}$ broad; large spike of yellow flowers; introduced from west indies, now quite run wild and met with in jungles. Juice of leaves, mixed with lime-juice, remedy for ring-worm; fresh leaves, sometimes simply bruised and rubbed upon eruption; held also to cure all poisonous bites, buboes, and other venereal affections, and to strengthen the body; a tincture of dried leaves operates as senna, and an extract from fresh leaves is substitute for extract of colocynth; in pharm. non-officinal.

AGAURY (اگاڑی - agárí, *Hind.*). From (ágá, hind. front). The tether for a horse's fore feet. Van of an army.

AGHAH (آغا - ághá, *Hind.*). From Turkish. Master; elder brother. Moghul alaumat [ism].——*Aghah baukir* (آغا باقر - ághábákar, Hind.). Alaumat prefixed to alam.

AGHIYAH (اگیا - agiyá, *Hind.*). Title from (ág, hind. fire); from mottled colour. Larks. Alaudinæ, fringillidæ [boosa priyam], conirostres, insessores, aves [pacshy, 27], of naturalists. The species best known to the natives are shown below. Other S. indian species are:—Alauda malabarica, crested malabar lark; Ammomanes phoenicura, rufous-tailed finch-lark; Otocoris penicillata, horned lark; Spizalauda deva, small crested lark; caged and is an excellent mocking bird.——*Bageyra* (بگیری - bagerí, Dec.). Title otherwise Indian ortolan, Short-toed lark, Social lark. Calandrella brachydactyla. Alias Alauda arenaria, callandrella, dulhunensis; Emberiza baghaira, olivacea. Upper parts pale rufescent sandy, streaked dusky; stripe over eye, whole under parts fulvous white, tinged earthy brown on breast, which is spotless in some, in a few slightly spotted; wings dusky brown, fulvous edgings, broader and deeper-colored on tertiaries, and tips of coverts with whitish edge to first developed primary; tail dusky, penultimate feather having outer web white-edged, outermost feather with outer web wholly white to near base, and also some of inner web; bill whitish horny, dusky on ridge of upper mandible; legs brownish darker at joints; irides dark brown; length $6\frac{1}{4}$ inches; rare in extreme south; appears in october and november in flocks, always retires to corn fields or grass for shelter during heat of day; seldom seen in afternoon or evening; towards end of March different flocks unite into vast troops, quite darkening air; great numbers are netted, taken by birdlime, or shot.——*Bharata pitta* (اگن - agin, Hind.; భరతపిట్ట - bharatapitta, Tel.). Hind. means fire. Tel. from (bharata, san. music master + pitta, tel. bird). Tel. also (agnipitta), meaning fire + bird. Title otherwise Singing bush-lark. Mirafra cantillans. Caged by natives for its song, imitates notes of other birds.——*Chandool* (چنڈول - chandúl, Dec.; చండోలిపిట్ట - chandólipitta, Tel.). Tel. also (dzuttupitta), meaning crest + bird. Title otherwise Pyramid-crested woodlark. Galerida cristata. Alias Alauda chendula, deva, galerita, gulgula; Galerida chendula.——*Charcharah* (چرچرا - charchará, Hind.; ఫ్లజిట్ట - flajitta, Tel.). Hind. means chattering. Tel. from (fla, tel. whistle + jitta, tel. bird). Hind. also (lípí). Title otherwise Madras bush lark. Mirafra affinis. Plumage above dusky brown with pale rufous edges to feathers. The redwinged bush-lark, called by natives forest lark or small lark, mirafra erythroptera, alias mirafra javanica, is similar, distinguished by its smaller size, and by the rufous colour extending over the whole of the primary quills; also by longer tail.——*Dabakchoory* (دبک چڑیا - dabakchiryá, Hind.; دبلی چڑی -.

dabakchurí, Dec.; పొట్టిపిచ్చుక - pottipittsuka, Tel.). Hind. from (dabak, hind. squat + chiryá, hind. sparrow). Tel. from (potti, tel. short + pittsuka, tel. sparrow). Hind. also (diyorá); (duri). Tel. also (paidipittsuka), meaning gold + sparrow. Title otherwise Black-bellied finch lark, Gold sparrow, Indian ortolan of some, Squat sparrow. Pyrrhulauda grisea. Alias Alauda gingica, crucigera. Male above pale brownish grey, wings and tail brown; deep brown or black band from base of bill through eyes, continued to occiput; common except on malabar coast; remarkable for sudden ascents and descents of its flight; young birds are plumaged like true larks; in the cold season sometimes collects in large flocks, and is then often shot for table as ortolan.——*Vaunambaudy* (भरद्वाज - bharadvája, San.; قبرة - kubbarah, Ar.; چکاوک - chakávak, Pers.; بھرت - bhurut, Hind.; ಟಿಟ್ಟಿಭ - tittibha, Can.; నేలపిచ్చుక - nélapittsuka, Tel.; വാനമ്പാടി - vánampáti, Mal.; வானம்பாடி - vánambádi, Tam.). Title from tamul. San. from (bharat, san. bearing + vája, san. food). Ar. from (kubbar, ar. to conceal). Tel. from (néla, tel. ground + pittsuka, tel. sparrow); from frequenting grass land. Tam. from (vánam, tám. sky + pádu, tam. to sing). Ar. also (hummarah). Tel. also (bharatapitta), meaning singer + bird. Title otherwise Indian sky-lark. Alauda gulgula. Alias Alauda arvensis, gangetica, gracilis, leiopus, malabarica. Above feathers dark brown, with fulvous margins; beneath fulvescent white, deeper on breast, spotted or streaked with dusky; ear-coverts spotted and tipped dusky; pale eye streak; erectile feathers of head moderately elongated; tail has outermost feather almost wholly fulvescent-white, and penultimate one has outer web, and sometimes the tip of inner web of same tint; bill horny brown, pale beneath; legs fleshy brown; irides dark brown; length 6½ inches; has much the plumage of the sky-lark of europe, but is smaller; under parts generally more rufescent; hill examples brighter than those in the plains; frequents grass land; rises into the air singing, but does not soar so high as the lavrock of england; no other species here of Alauda.

AGNY (अग्नि - agni, *San.*). From (ang, san. to go up). Latin ignis.—"*a*" God of fire in the Aryan system. The other two great deities being Indran god of the firmament, and Vayoo god of the wind. By orthodox Hindoos Agny is still invoked on many solemn occasions, as for instance at the nuptial ceremony. He is one of the eight Loca paulacans or guardians of the world, being regent of the S.E. As being useful to mankind he is called Veishwaunaran; as protector of the house, Grihapaty; as protector of the community, Vishpaty; as purifier, Pauvacan. His wife is Agneya, or Swauha. His vehicle is a ram. His heaven is Agny locam [matam].—"*b*" Also plant 1st term. Ex., where transl. is of 2nd term:— Ammannia baccifera (agnivéndramu), heat; Aquilaria agallocha (agnikáshtamu), wood; Cardiospermum halicacabum (agniballi), creeper, as shining in dark; Carthamus tinctorius (agnishikhá), flame, from flowers; Carum copticum (agnivardhana), increasing, as digestive; Crocus sativus (agnishikhá), flame, from flowers; Methonica superba (agnishikhá), flame, from flower; Plumbago zeylanica (agnimátá), mother, from raising blisters, and (agnishikhá), flame, from flowers; Premna integrifolia (agnimantha), churning, as producing fire by attrition; Semecarpus anacardium (agnimukhí), face, from corrosive properties; Vernonia anthelmintica (agnibíja), seed; digestive; Woodfordia floribunda (agnijvála), flame, from scarlet flowers. See gloss. paragraphs.——*Agnicoolam* (अग्निकुल - agnikula, San.). From (kula, san. race). The Aryan fire-race [rajpoot].——*Agnihotry* (अग्निहोतृ - agnihótri, San.). From (hu, san. to offer oblation). A Bramin priest who maintains a perpetual fire in his house. Rare now.——*Agnivendram* (शिलाभेद - shilábhéda, San.; داد ماری - dádmárí, Hind.; اگن بوتی - aginbútí, Dec.; అగ్నివేండ్రము - agnivéndramu, Tel.; കല്ലുർവഞ്ഞി - kallúrvaññi, Mal.; கல்லுருவி - kalluruvi, Tam.). San. from (shilá, san. stone + bhid, san. to break); useful in gravel. Hind. from (dád, hind. herpes + márí, hind. killing). Dec. from (agin, hind. fire + bútí, hind. plant); from use as blister. Tel. from (agni, san. fire + véndramu, tel. heat); similar. Mal. from (kallu, mal. stone + urukku, mal. to melt + vaññi, mal. any winding shrub). Tam. from (kal, tam. stone + uruvu, tam. to draw out); useful in gravel. Hind. also (banmarich), meaning forest chilly. Tam. also (nírmélneruppu), meaning water + upon + fire; cool to touch but causing blisters. Title otherwise Blistering ammannia, Culloorivy, Gravel plant, Water-fire. Botanically Ammannia baccifera, linn., lythraceæ [vriksham, 58]. Alias Ammannia vesicatoria. Herbaceous annual; erect; stem much branched, 4-sided; leaves sessile, opposite, lanceolate, attenuated, smaller nearer the flowers; calyx 4-cleft to the middle, lobes acute, accessory teeth very small; flowers very minute, aggregated in the axils of the leaves, almost sessile; tube of the calyx at first narrow and tightened round the ovary, in fruit cup-shaped; petals wanting; capsule longer than the calyx, 1-celled; flowers red; very minute; whole has strong smell like muriatic acid; leaves exceedingly acrid. Pounded leaves applied to herpetic eruptions; used in paste as a blister, but application much more painful than cantharides for which substituted; in pharm. non-officinal. Other species are:— cordata, floribunda, lanceolata, multiflora, octandra, pentandra, peploides, rotala, rotundifolia, salicifolia, tenuis.——*Agniyaur* (அக்கினியாறு - akkiniyáru, Tam.). From (áru, tam. river). Sanscrit name (aññánavimóchiní), means ignorance + emancipator. Written as Icunney aur in some maps. River; Trichinopoly dist., Poodoocottah territory. Rises in Coolatore irrigation tank; flows through Coolatore and Alangoody talooks to sea near Rajahmadam, after passing through Tanjore district. Near Peroongalore it is called Peroongalore river.

AGOOMBY (ಆಗುಂಬಿ - águmbi, *Can.*). Pass; South canara dist., Oodipy tal. Connects Mysore with Canara. The trunk road from Mangalore to the Nugger division of Mysore meets this pass, and much coffee and sandal-wood are conveyed through it to the coast, the pass being practicable for wheeled vehicles. The total length is about 5 miles, and the ascent is nowhere more than 1 in 18 feet.

AGOW (اگاؤ - agáu, *Hind.*). From (ágá, hind. front). An advance of money [tuccauvy]. Also collection of revenue before it is due.

AGRAM (अग्र - agra, *San.*). From (ang, san. to go); foremost. Greek ἀκρός. First. Amplitude of a celestial object; an arc measured on the horizon, contained between the east point and the centre of the object at its rising; and between the west point and the centre of the object at its setting. Or it may be taken as an angle at the zenith contained between the meridian of the place and the vertical circle passing through the object at rising or setting. Agra bhaugam is a degree of amplitude. Agrajyay is sine of the amplitude [jyotisham].——*Agra coty* (अग्रकोटि - agrakóti, San.). From (above + kóti, san. complement of an arc to 90). Azimuth of a celestial object; an angle at the zenith contained between the meridian of the place and a vertical circle passing through the object; it is measured by the arc of the horizon contained between the N. or S. points and the place where the circle of altitude meets the horizon [jyotisham].——*Agrahauram* (अग्रहार - agrahára, San.). From (hri, san. to offer). A village or part of one allotted to Bramins at a favorable assessment or free. The conditions on which these villages are held are explained by the words prefixed to them; see Sarwagrahauram, Bilmacta agrahauram, Cuttoobuddy agrahauram, &c. There are three main kinds as to rent paying:—"*a*" Sarwa maunyam, rent free;—"*b*" Jody, partially rent free;—"*c*" Trishwaicam where one-third part of the produce is given for rent. Agrahauram means also quarter of modern town inhabited by Bramins. See Vol. I, 112.——*Agrahayanam* (अग्रहायण - agraháyana, San.). From (háyana, san. year). A new name given to the solar month Margashiram [mausam] about December, when latter was made to commence the year many centuries before Christ [jyotisham].——*Agrapoojay* (अग्रपूजा - agrapújá, San.). From (pújá, san. worship). Fee paid to a Bramin priest in acknowledgment of his title for precedence.

AHAM (अहम् - aham, *San.*). Latin ego. Self.——*Ahancauram* (अहंकार - ahankára, San.). From (kára, san. making). Consciousness or egoism. Product of Mahat. In Vedauntam books it is called Chidabhausa swaroopam. In Saunkhyam it is the third of the eight elements of creation, viz., individualization. It is the operative principle of transmigration [matam, samsauram].

AHAS (अहस् - ahas, *San.*). From (a, san. negative prefix + há, san. to abandon); not abandoned by sun. Day.——*Aharganam* (अहर्गण - ahargana, San.). From (gana, san. collection). The number of days from a given minor epoch to the time for which a computation is made. Used in the calendars [punchaungam] for determining at what point of time a year or month begins. For the number of days expired since the epoch of the creation see Srishtyaudy dyooganam.—"*a*" The following table gives the figures for computing, for the beginning of any solar year [maunam], the solar Aharganam from the beginning of the Caliyoog, the mean solar sidereal year being $\frac{1577917500}{4320000}$ or 365d 15g 31v 15p [caulam] according to the Arya siddhauntam [maunam]:—

Years.	Time of corresponding periods.				Years.	Time of corresponding periods.		
	D.	G.	V.	P.		D.	G.	V.
1	365	15	31	15	100	36525	52	5
2	730	31	2	30	200	73051	44	10
3	1095	46	33	45	300	109577	36	15
4	1461	2	5	0	400	146103	28	20
5	1826	17	36	15	500	182629	20	25
6	2191	33	7	30	600	219155	12	30
7	2556	48	38	45	700	255681	4	35
8	2992	4	10	0	800	292206	56	40
9	3287	19	41	15	900	328732	48	45
10	3652	35	12	30	1000	365258	40	50
20	7305	10	25	0	2000	730517	21	40
30	10957	45	37	30	3000	1095776	2	30
40	14610	20	50	0	4000	1461034	43	20
50	18262	56	2	30	5000	1826293	24	10
60	21915	31	15	0	6000	2191552	5	0
70	25568	6	27	30	7000	2556810	45	50
80	29920	41	40	0	8000	2922069	26	40
90	32873	16	52	30	9000	3287328	7	30
100	36525	52	5	0	10000	3652586	48	20

—"*b*" The following table shows the figures for the solar months under Arya siddhauntam [maunam], so as to extend the operation to a date in the middle of the solar year :—

Solar months.	Signs.	Separately. D.	G.	V.	P.	Collectively ; end of each month. D.	G.	V.	P.
Chittray	♈	30	55	32	1	30	55	32	1
Veiyaushy	♉	31	24	12	1	62	19	44	2
Auny	♊	31	36	38	1	93	56	22	3
Audy	♋	31	28	12	2	125	24	34	5
Auvany	♌	31	2	10	1	156	26	44	6
Poorattaushy ...	♍	30	27	22	1	180	54	6	7
Arpisy	♎	29	54	7	1	216	48	13	8
Caugtigay	♏	29	30	24	2	246	18	37	10
Maurgaly	♐	29	20	53	1	275	39	30	11
Tye	♑	29	27	16	1	305	6	46	12
Maushy	♒	29	48	24	1	384	55	10	13
Pungoony	♓	30	20	21	2	365	15	31	15

—"*c*" The following table gives the figures for computing, for the beginning of any luni-solar year, the luni-solar Aharganam from the beginning of the Caliyoog, the mean lunation being $\frac{1577917828}{53433336}$ or 29d 31g 50v 6p 59s. 78 [caulam] according to the Soorya siddhauntam [maunam] :—

Years.	Time due to corresponding periods. D.	G.	V.	P.	S.	Years.	Time due to corresponding periods. D.	G.	V.	P.	S.
1	354	22	1	23	57,14	100	35436	42	10	55	14
2	708	44	2	47	54,28	200	70873	24	39	50	28
3	1063	6	4	11	51,42	300	106310	6	59	45	42
4	1417	28	5	35	48,56	400	141746	49	19	40	56
5	1771	50	6	59	45,70	500	177183	31	39	36	10
6	2126	12	8	23	42,84	600	212620	13	59	31	24
7	2480	34	9	47	39,98	700	248056	56	19	26	38
8	2834	56	11	11	37,12	800	283493	38	39	21	52
9	3189	18	12	35	34,26	900	318930	20	59	17	6
10	3543	40	13	59	31,40	1000	354367	3	19	12	20
20	7087	20	27	59	2,8	2000	708734	6	38	24	40
30	10631	0	41	58	34,2	3000	1063101	9	57	37	0
40	14174	40	55	58	5,6	4000	1417468	13	16	49	20
50	17718	21	9	57	37,0	5000	1771835	16	36	1	40
60	21262	1	23	57	8,4	6000	2126202	19	55	14	0
70	24805	41	37	56	39,8	7000	2480569	22	14	26	20
80	28349	21	51	56	11,2	8000	2834936	26	33	38	40
90	31893	2	5	55	42,6	9000	3189303	29	52	51	0
100	35436	42	10	55	14,0	10000	3543670	33	12	3	20

—"*d*" The following table shows tho figures for the lunar months, according to Soorya siddhauntam [maunam], so as to extend the operation to a date in the middle of the luni-solar year :—

Lunations.	Time due to the end of the respective mean lunar months. D.	G.	V.	P.	S.
1	29	31	50	6	59,78
2	59	3	40	13	59,56
3	88	35	30	20	59,34
4	118	7	20	27	59,12
5	147	39	10	34	58,90
6	177	11	0	41	58,68
7	206	42	50	48	58,46
8	236	14	40	55	58,24
9	265	46	31	2	58,01
10	295	18	21	9	57,80
11	324	50	11	16	57,56
12	354	22	1	23	57,36
13	383	53	51	30	57,14

If Arya siddhauntam elements were taken for this last, the mean lunation would bo $\frac{1577917500}{53433336}$ or 29d 31g 50v 5p·40s, 21, &c.—"*e*" The following example shows use and application of the above tables. Wanted the Solar aharganam for the beginning of the solar year 4924 of the Caliyoog, or 4923 complete, A.D. 1822, according to the Arya siddhauntam.

	Y.	D.	G.	V.	P.
By Table—"*a*" there is given for	4000 ...	1461034	43	20	0
	900 ...	328732	48	45	0
	20 ...	7305	10	25	0
	3 ...	1095	46	33	45
		1798168	29	3	45
Substract shodhyam ...		2	8	51	15
Aharganam, 1st Chittray ♈, which divide by		7)1798166(20	12	30	
Remainder		6			

which counted from Friday, gives Shoodha dinam Thursday. For a date in middle of year add the figures of table *b*. For dates of the luni-solar year, employ similarly tables c and *d* [jyotisham].——*Ahorautram* (अहोरात्र - ahórátra, San.). From (ahas, san. day + rátra, san. night). Day and night, natural day. 30 moohoortams = 1 ahorautram ; 7 ahorautrams = 1 vauram or week [caulam, 2]. Also called Pitry dinam [dinam].

AHKAUM (احکام - ahkám, *Hind.*). Pl. of (hukm, ar. order). Orders [hookum].

AHL (اهل - ahl, *Hind.*). Men.——*Ahl e calam* (اهل قلم - ahlikalam, Hind.). From (kalam, ar. pen). Clerks.——*Ahlecaur* (اهل کار - ahlikár, Hind.). From (kár, pers. business). Public servants.——*Ahl e hadees* (اهل حدیث - ahlihadís, Hind.). From (hadís, hind. tradition). Designation of Wahaubies.——*Ahl e shumsheer* (اهل شمشیر - ahlishamshír, Hind.). From (shamshír, pers. sword). Military officers.

AHMAK (احمق - ahmak, *Ar.*). From (hamaka, ar. to lack understanding). Fool or false. Plant 2nd term. Ex. :—Ficus glomerata (anjíreahmak), false european fig.

AHMAR (احمر - ahmar, *Ar.*). From (hamara, ar. to be red). Red. Plant 2nd term. Ex., where transl. is of 1st term :—Capsicum annuum (filfiliahmar), chilly ; Pterocarpus santalinus (sandaliahmar), sandal ; Rosa centifolia (vardulahmar), rose ; Trichosanthes palmata (hanzaliahmar), colocynth. See gloss. paragraphs.

AHMED (احمد - ahmad, *Hind.*). From (hamd, ar. praise). Most praised. Name of the prophet. Mahomedan alam. Fem. form is Ahmedy [ism].——*Ahmed ally* (احمد علی - ahmadalí, Hind.). Double alam.——*Ahmed bee* (احمد بی - ahmadbí, Hind.). Alam + female alaumat.——*Ahmed moohee ood deen* (احمدمحی الدین - ahmadmuhíuddín, Hind.). Alam + lacab.——*Ahmedy begum* (احمدی بیگم - ahmadíbegam, Hind.). Alam + alaumat.

AHOBALAM (అహోబలం - ahóbalam, *Tel.*). From (ahó, san. awe-inspiring particle of exclamation + bila, san. cave). Tel. also (diguvaahóbilam), meaning lower + place, so called. Sanscrit name (navanarasimha), meaning nine + Vishnoo, the man-lion god, nine incarnations being there represented by nine temples. Village ; Kurnool dist., Sirwail tal. ; pop. 108 ; acres 3,307 ; lat. 15° 08′ ; long. 78° 43′ ; from Chaugulmurry N.N.E. 13 miles ; from Kurnool S.E. 63 miles. Place of pilgrimage. Vishnoo temple to Narsimhan. The shrine consists of Digoova ahobalam temple at foot of hills ; Yegoova ahobalam temple, 4 miles higher up on Bhavanausy ; and a small pagoda at top of hills. These, with six other about the hill, form the Nava narsimhan, nine forms in which Vishnoo exhibited himself. Digoova ahobalam is a small ordinary shrine. At Pedda ahobalam the idol is kept in a rock-cut cave. Near it in a verandah is the Chentsoo bride of the sawmy. Upon one of the precipitous sides of a ravine is an iron pillar which barren women solicitous for children move round and adore. Built by Pratanpa roodran of Warangal in 13th century. Annual festival in March or April. Trig. station in lat. 15° 08′ 58·94″ ; long. 78° 47′ 00·61″ ; height 2,982 feet ; from Chagulmurry N.E. 16 miles ; from Pedda ahobalam E. 4½ miles.

AHTOOR (ஆற்றூர் - attúr, *Tam.* atúr *). From (áru, tam. river + úr, tam. village) ; on Vasishtanuddy. Sanscrit name (anantagiri), meaning infinite + mountain ; either from the many hills about the village or from Vishnoo the infinite.——**(1)** Talook, Salem district. Tahsildar's pay Rupees 200. Area 841 square miles. Length from east to west 29 miles, from north to south 34 miles. Language Tamul. In the south-east portion of the district between N. lat. 11° 19′ and 11° 52′ and E. long. 78° 19′ and 78° 53′. Bounded north by Cullacoorchy talook of South arcot, and Ootancaray talook of Salem district ; east by Cullacoorchy and Vriddhauchellam talooks, South arcot ; south by Perambalore talook, Trichinopoly ; and west by Salem and Namcull talooks. Hill bound on the north and south, and partially so on the west. On the north-west limit the Tennaunday mullay reaches eastward to the Cottapputty pass. East of this pass is a range which on the northern side takes the name of the Aryagownden naud and on the Ahtoor limits is termed the Chinna and Periya culroyens. The Collamullays enclose the talook to the south ; and, after a considerable drop towards the plain, the Putchamullays trend away to the south and east. The talook is divided by the Pytore mullay into two principal water-sheds, those of the Vasishtanuddy and Shwetanuddy. The soil alternates in stretches of red loam and black alluvium, its fertility being in many parts greatly reduced by the excessive quantity of lime contained. The higher hill ranges are syenite and gneiss, quartz occurring rarely. Talcose schist occurs in the north-east. Magnesian limestone and steatite are found. The magnetic iron beds are apparently inexhaustible. Trap dykes occur in many places, notably in the Pytore and Mullicaray hills and above Gungavully on a spur of the Putchamullays. South-east of Ahtoor in the Munjiny caradoo and Shevaroy hills may be seen long bands of a peculiar altered gneiss which, with trap dykes, form the backbone of the ridge. Auragalore is the only important weaving village. Strong country carts are made at Ahtoor, and iron is smelted there and at Condayampully, Mekkapilleiyore, Naugayamputty, Shendauraputty and Tammamputty. White stone pots are manufactured in Keeriputty, Mungalapooram and Naurakinar. Staple crops are varagoo on poonjah and paddy on nunjah lands. Other products are raggy, cholum, tinay, tovray, oolandoo, putchay-payar, shaumay, yelloo, avaray, cotton, sugar-cane, grain of all kinds, oilseeds, tobacco, chillies, coriander, saffron, mustard, ground-nut, vendayam, narypayar, tuttapayar, motchacottay, betel, cocoanuts, &c. Areca palms and palmyras abound along the river drainage lines. Exports are paddy, oil-seed, motchacottay, coriander, cotton, chillies, tobacco, indigo, betel-nut, saffron, jaggery, cadookye, capilapody, cocoanuts and tamarind. Garden produce is sent to South arcot from Varagore and villages north of Talavausal. The Trichinopoly markets are accessible from Tammamputty and from the south-east corner of the talook. Indigo is cultivated to some extent. Veeraganore exports plantains and East rajahpolliem cotton. Sugar is imported from Razipore and Salem, and salt from South arcot. Cloths are imported by Lubbays from Madras, and by others from Combaconam and other places. Cattle are scarce in comparison with other talooks of the district. Water is almost entirely raised by manual labour with picottahs. The water is said to be unwholesome for cattle. The anicuts on the Vasishtanuddy are: Bailore chinna anicut, Bailore periya anicut, Cottavaudy, Calyaumagherry, Abhinavam, Yaittapore, Chinnasamoodram, Yerrasamoodram, Peddanaickenpolliem, Appasamoodram, Ahtoor, Ammapolliem, Cauttcottay, Deviya coorchy and Talavausal. The anicuts on the Shwetanuddy are :—Condayampully, Shendauraputty, Gungavully periya anicut, Gungavully chinna anicut, Aneiyamputty, Poothore, Tittacherry, Veeraganore and Laddivaudy. Periya combay anicut, Mauvaur private anicut and Jangama samoodram agrahauram anicut are on the Periya combay, a tributary of the Shwetanuddy. On the Oonantaungal, another tributary of the Shwetanuddy are Oonantaungal, Moollcoorchy, and half a dozen other anicuts. The chief tanks are :—Yerrasamoodram near Peddanaickenpolliem, Chittairy near Auragalore, and Shendauraputty. A large tank called the Krishnapooram project is under construction. Camping grounds Ahtoor, Peddanaickenpolliem, Talavausal and Vaulapaudy. Zemindarry :—Sheccadiputty. Places of archæological interest :—Ahtoor, Alagaupooram, Auragalore, Bailore, Caliyamputty, Calpaganore, Cariya ramancoil, Cullanuttam, Moommoody, Munjany, Odiyattore, Periyairy, Ramanaickenpolliem, Tadavoor, Talavaputty, Tammamputty, Yetapoor. The leading places in the talook are the following:——*Ahtoor* (ஆற்றூர் - áttúr, Tam.). See below.——*Auragalore* (ஆறகளூர் - áragalúr, Tam.). From (áru, tam. six + agazh, tam. trench + úr, tam. village); from a fort with six trenches, which once existed. Village; pop. 2,214; acres 878; lat. 11° 34′; long. 78° 50′; from Ahtoor E. 13 miles; from Salem E. 44 miles. Old sculptured Shiva temple with inscriptions. Once in ten years the Keikkilar flock here for the Padeikkalam festival [pundigay]. Common cloths are largely manufactured. There is a marble idol of Booddha in the Shiva temple.——*Bodamullay* (போதமலை - póthamalai, Tam.). See sep. title.——*Collimullay* (கொல்லிமலை - kollimalai, Tam.). See sep. title.——*Culroyamullay* (கல்ராயன்மலை - kalráyanmalai, Tam.). See sep. title.——*Dookyampolliem* (துக்கியாம்பாளையம் - tukkiyámbálaiyam, Tam.). From (dukki, can. tillage + pálaiyam, tam. fortified village). Village; pop. 1,011; acres 1,925; lat. 11° 41′; long. 78° 27′; from Ahtoor W.N.W. 15 miles; from Salem E. 16 miles.——*Eeshwaramoortipolliem* (ஈச்வரமூர்த்திப்பாளையம் - ísuvaramúrttippálaiyam, Tam.). From (íshvara, san. the lord + múrti, san. image + pálaiyam, san. fortified village). Village; pop. 1,035; acres 2,067; lat. 11° 34′; long. 78° 26′; from Ahtoor W. 15 miles; from Salem E.S.E. 17 miles. There is a hill in the neighbourhood known as Eeshwaramully at the foot of which is a Shiva temple.——*Mungalapooram* (மங்கலப்புரம் - mangalappuram, Tam.). From (mangala, san. auspicious + pura, san. town). Village; pop. 1,714; acres 3,820; lat. 11° 34′; long. 78° 25′; from Ahtoor W. 16 miles; from Salem E.S.E. 16 miles. A fair is held every week on Saturdays.——*Munmullay* (மண்மலை - manmalai, Tam.). From (man, tam. earth + malai, tam. mountain). Hill; pop. 670; lat. 11° 26′; long. 78° 36′; from Ahtoor S.S.W. 11 miles; from Salem E.S.E. 31 miles. There is a cave here in which a gold image of Varadaraja permaul is secured. It is taken out on procession twice a year on the 18th of Audy [mausam] or 2nd august and on the last day of Poorataushy [mausam] or 15th october.——*Nadavaloor* (நடவலூர் - nadavalúr, Tam.). From (naduvu, tam. middle + úr, tam. village). Village; pop. 2,750; acres 4,508; lat. 11° 31′; long. 78° 43′; from Ahtoor S.E. 6½ miles; from Salem E.S.E. 35 miles.——*Olapaudy* (ஓலைப்பாடி - ólaippádi, Tam.). From (ólai, tam. palm leaf + pádi, tam. village). Village; pop. 600; acres 471; lat. 11° 38′; long. 78° 33′; from Ahtoor W.N.W. 7¾ miles; from Salem E. 23 miles. This and its neighbouring villages contain numerous palmyra trees.——*Oomayaupooram* (உமையாப்புரம் - umayáppuram, Tam.). From (umá, san. wife of shiva + pura, san. town). Sanscrit name (umápura), meaning Parvaty + town. A large tank said to have been constructed by Chenroya. A Shiva temple and a Vishnoo temple; pop. 977; acres 1,322; lat. 11° 38′; long. 78° 31′; from Ahtoor W.N.W. 9¾ miles; from Salem E. 21 miles. This is 3 miles south of Yetapoor and was given as Stree dhanam to Oomay, wife of Shiva, at Yetapoor by the then ruler Chenroya who built the temple at Yetapoor. Now a money grant is made to the temple and the village has become a circar village.——*Peddanaickenpolliem* (பெத்தநாயக்கன்பாளையம் - pettanáyakkanbálaiyam, Tam.). From (pettanáyakkan, tam. proper name + pálaiyam, tam. fortified village). Village; pop. 3,713; acres 3,350; lat. 11° 39′; long. 78° 33′; from Ahtoor W.N.W. 7¾ miles; from Salem E. 24 miles. Pedda naicken was the Poligar of this part of talook. He had three wives Chinnamma, Tirmullay ammaul, and Yerrammah, and built villages in his own name and in the names of his wives. To north of village, on northern bank of Vasishtanuddy, a mile and a half from it, is a small hill, containing a Vishnoo temple. This is a place of pilgrimage. Resorted to on Saturdays in the month of Poorataushy [mausam] or september. Large trade in palmyra jaggery, areca and cocoanuts with Tripatore, Salem, and Vaniyambaudy. A fair on Fridays.——*Putchamullay* (பச்சமலை - paççamalai, Tam.). See sep. title.——*Pytore mullay* (பைத்தூர்மலை - paittúrmalai, Tam.). See sep. title.——*Rajahpolliem* (இராசாப்பாளையம் - irásáppálaiyam, Tam.). From (rájá, san. king + pálaiyam, tam. fortified village). Village; pop. 1,969; acres 2,092; lat. 11° 26′; long. 78° 51′; from Ahtoor S.E. 18 miles; from Salem E.S.E. 46 miles. Noted for cotton.——*Shekkadiputty* (செக்கடிப்பட்டி - shekkadippatti, Tam.). From (shekku, tam. oil press + adi, tam. bottom + patti, tam. cattle fold). Zemindarry, Village; pop. 554; sq. miles 45; lat. of village 11° 43′; long. 78° 29′; from Ahtoor N.W. 14 miles; from Salem E.N.E. 19 miles. Peshcush Rs. 2,020.——*Shendauraputty* (செந்தாரப்பட்டி - shendárappatti, Tam.). From (shem, tam. red + tázhai, tam. fragrant screw-pine pandanus odoratissimus, linn. + patti, tam. cattle fold). Village; pop. 4,877; acres 3,044; lat. 11° 26′; long. 78° 34′; from Ahtoor S.S.W. 12 miles; from Salem E.S.E. 28 miles.——*Shwetanuddy* (சுவேதநதி - shuvéthanathi, Tam.). See sep. title.——*Tadavoor* (தடாவூர் - tadávúr, Tam.). From (tata, san. bank + úr, tam. village); on north bank of Shwetanuddy. Village; pop. 3,332; acres 4,576; lat. 11° 30′; long. 78° 45′; from Ahtoor S.E. 9¼ miles; from Salem E.S.E. 38 miles. Trishwaicam village. Ruined Shiva temple with inscriptions and copper-plate grant. Indigo factory.——*Talavausal* (தலைவாசல் - talaivásal, Tam.). See sep. title.——*Tammamputty* (தம்மம்பட்டி - tammambatti, Tam.). From (tamma, can. younger brother + patti, tam. cattle fold). Village; pop. 3,516; acres 3,204; lat. 11° 26′; long. 78° 32′; from Ahtoor S.W. 14 miles; from Salem S.E. 27 miles. On south bank of Shwetanuddy at foot of Collimullays. Shiva and Vishnoo temples. South east is Munmullay. Iron-smelting. London mission school. Car festival in Chittray [mausam] or april.——*Taundagowndenpolliem* (தாண்டக்கவுண்டன்பாளையம் - tándakkavundanbálaiyam, Tam.). From (tándakkavundan, tam. proper name + pálaiyam, tam. fortified village). Village; lat. 11° 33′; long. 78° 26′; from Ahtoor W.S.W. 15 miles; from Salem E.S.E. 17 miles. Situated near hill which contains pot stone quarries. Manufacture of stone pots.——*Vasishtanuddy* (வசிட்டாநதி - vasittánathi, Tam.). See sep. title.——*Vaulapaudy* (வாழப்பாடி - vázhappádi, Tam.). From (vázhai, tam. plantain tree, musa paradisiaca, linn. + pádi, tam. village). Town. On boundary between Salem and Ahtoor talooks. Formerly belonged to Salem talook. Indigo factory. Public bungalow. Part is held on Trishwaicam, and is called Agrahaura vaulapaudy; the other part for which no Trishwaicam is granted is Circar vaulapaudy.——*Veeraganore* (வீரகனூர் - víraganúr, Tam.). From (víragan, tam. brave man + úr, tam. village). Village; acres 4,174; lat. 11° 29′; long. 78° 47′; from Ahtoor S.E. 12 miles; from Salem E.S.E. 41 miles. North-east of Shwetanuddy. Brass vessels manufactured.——*Yetapoor* (ஏத்தாப்பூர் - éttáppúr, Tam.). From (yáta, can. picottah + pura, san. town). Sanscrit name (shrírámasamudra), meaning holy + Rama, the god + ocean; also (yátápura), meaning traveller + town. Village; pop. 3,386; acres 4,116; lat. 11° 40′; long. 78° 31′; from Ahtoor W.N.W. 10 miles; from Salem E. 21 miles. On north bank of Vasishtanuddy with topes of palms and nunjah fields on every side. Two temples of Shiva and Vishnoo. At Pootragownden polliem, one mile south of Yetapoor a fair on Tuesdays.——**(2)** Town, Talook head-quarters; Salem dist., Ahtoor tal.; pop. 9,295; acres 6,817; lat. 11° 36′; long. 78° 39′; from Madras S.W. 152 miles; from Namcull N.E. 39 miles; from Oossoor S.E. 94 miles; from Salem E. 30 miles; from Tripatore S. 62 miles; from Yercand E.S.E. 29 miles. On Vasishtanuddy, about three miles from foot of Periya culroyen. The eastern portion on south of river is Poothoopett, the western is Ahtoor proper. North of river is a large fort, the builder of which found an immense treasure of gold buried in seven iron pots, one of which is still in Vishnoo temple in fort. The fort is square, with batteries and bastions in the angles and sides. The highest point is the flagstaff battery in the centre of the south face. The glacis to the east is over-grown with trees. The south side is guarded by the river, which when in flood runs some 20 feet deep, and the other faces are protected by a ditch, which at the south-west angle is always full of water. The outer wall of the ditch is roughly, and the river bank strongly, revetted. The ramparts are of cut stone, well fitted without mortar. Inside are three large and one small bombproof chamber, the roofs of the larger magazines being accessible by hidden stairs. There are the remains of two houses, the larger of which was occupied by Company's officers. The lower part is in native, and the upper part in European, style. The smaller house was residence of Commanding officer. A large vaulted chamber, occasionally utilized as a Roman catholic chapel, formerly used as a cutcherry. On south face of ramparts is an old pleasure house, a roof on pillars with obtuse pointed arches. Near this is a water gate strongly defended, leading to river, and on west face is another leading into ditch. On south-west angle is another flagstaff battery. The fort gate is in centre of east face. The buildings inside fort, which contains temples of Shiva and Vishnoo and a shrine of Mooniyappan, the guardian of the fort, are called Cottay; those outside the fort and north of the river are Moollavaudy. Cart-building. Iron-smelting to a small extent. Much through traffic passes on the Cuddalore and Salem road. A spacious chuttram cost Rs. 25,000 by one Nutter sahib. Four indigo factories. London mission school.

AILANTO (महानिम्ब - mahánimba, *San.* and *Mahr.*; مهارکھ - mahárúkh, *Hind.*; مهانیم - maháním, *Dec.*; ಹೆಮ್ಮರ - hemmara, *Can.*; పెద్దమాను - peddamánu, *Tel.*; ମହାନିମ୍ବ - maháním, *Oor.*; പെരുമരം - perumaram, *Mal.*; பெருமரம் - perumaram, *Tam.*). Title from chinese, meaning tree of heaven. San. from (mahá, san. large + nimba, san. melia azadirachta, linn.); from similarity of leaf and bark. Hind. from (mahá, hind. large + rúkh, hind. tree). Dec. from sanscrit. Can. from (hedda, can. large + mara, can. tree). Tel. similar. Tam. from (perumai, tam. largeness + maram, tam. tree). San. also (pisháchavriksha), meaning demon + tree. Can. also (doddamanimara), meaning great + bead + tree. Tel. also (peyyápa), meaning large + melia azadirachta, linn. Tam. also (peruppi), meaning large + sterculia fœtida, linn. Title otherwise Large bastard poon, Large neem, Large yaipy, Tree of heaven, Tree of the gods. Botanically the Ailanthus genus, simarubeæ [vricsham, 33]. Lofty trees, with large alternate leaves and small flowers in terminal or axillary panicles. The species best known to the natives are Coromandel, Japanese, and Malabar. Cf. Water ailanto, another genus.——*Coromandel ailanto* (ارنا - arná, Hind.). Title from habitat. Hind. from (aranya, san. forest). Title otherwise Arnah. Botanically Ailanthus excelsa, roxb., simarubeæ [vricsham, 33]. Large tree; bark of trunk rough and scaly, gray within; leaves abruptly pinnated, tomentose when young, afterwards glabrous; leaflets ten to fourteen pair, coarsely toothed at the base; petals five, almost glabrous in the inside; filaments glabrous, shorter than the anthers; calyx five-cleft; samaræ linear-oblong, three to five, one-seeded; panicles terminal; flowers fascicled, green. Resembling the ash in general appearance; bare of leaf for several months, too brittle to stand much wind; much planted, growing rapidly from large cuttings; much attacked by white ants. Gum resembles moringa gum and consists of large rounded tears of a deep vinous red. Decoction of stem and root bark is tonic; substituted for british cinchona bark, calumba and gentian. Gives a dye. Wood soft, white, not durable.——*Japanese ailanto* (جپان ارنا - japánarná, Hind.). Title otherwise False varnish tree, Japan varnish tree. Botanically Ailanthus glandulosa, desf., simarubeæ [vricsham, 33]. Introduced; allied to malabarica.——*Malabar ailanto* (अतिसारहिता - atisárahitá, San.; गुग्गुलधूपवृक्ष - gugguladhúpavriksha, Mahr.; ಮಡ್ಡಿಧೂಪದಮರ - maddidhúpadamara, Can.; പൊന്നെല്യം - ponnalyam, Mal.; කුඹලු - kumbalu, Singh.; மட்டிப்பால்மரம் - mattippálmaram, Tam.). Title from habitat. San. from (atisára, san. dysentery + hita, san. useful); resin useful in dysentery. Mahr. from (guggula, mahr. the incense + dhúpa, san. incense + vriksha, san. tree). Can. from (maddi, can. muddy + dhúpa, san. incense + mara, can. tree). Mal. from (ponnu, mal. to float); from light wood. Tam. from (matti, tam. coarse + pál, tam. milk + maram, tam. tree). Singh. also (valbilin), meaning wild averrhoa bilimbi, linn. Title otherwise Walbiling, Wild blimbing [q. v.]. Giving Mutty paul. Botanically Ailanthus malabarica, dec., simarubeæ [vricsham, 33]. Alias Ailanthus pangelion. Pangelion, from malayalam. Tree, leaves abruptly pinnated; leaflets quite entire, ovate-lanceolate, unequal-sided, oblique at the base; panicles large, terminal; peduncles and calyx pubescent; petal glabrous, obovate, much longer than the calyx; samaræ oval, oblong, obtuse at both ends; flowers small, white; dense moist forests of western ghauts, to 3,000 feet, from s. canara to cape comorin; commonly painted, very ornamental; bark rough and very thick. Fragrant resinous balsam known as muttipaul exudes from trunk; this as commonly met is dark brown or grey plastic, opaque, agreeable in smell; contains much impurity; is very soft, having consistence of thick treacle, doubtless the reason why it is always mixed with fragments of earth which makes it more easy to handle; alcohol readily dissolves it; when burnt it gives out a fragrance. Muttipaul reduced to powder mixed with milk and strained is medicinally stimulant, astringent and expectorant; much given in dysentery; substituted for british gummi rubrum and benzoinum. Bark in decoction and tincture is tonic and stomachic; used in dyspeptic complaints; substituted for british calumba, quassia, and gummi rubrum. Both in pharm. non-officinal. Muttipaul is burnt in temples. Wood white, very soft and spongy.——*Water ailanto* (നീർപ്പൊന്നെല്യം - nírpponnalyam, Mal.). From (nír, mal. water + ponnalyam, mal. ailanthus malabarica, dec.). Botanically the Dolichandrone genus, bignoniaceæ [vricsham, 99]. Trees; flowers white; fruit, a flat capsule opening at margin. The species best known to the natives are:—arcuata [night paulay], crispa [flowering pauthiry], falcata [wody], rheedii [long-leaved wody].

AIR (ఏరు - éru, *Tel.*). River. Suffix in river names; as Pennair, meaning great + river. Also in place names; as Pulmanair, meaning Pullavan's tank. A thin pronunciation of Tamul aur [q.v.]; not the same as airy [q.v.], a sheet of water.

AIRY (ಏರಿ - éri, *Can.*; ഏരി - éri, *Mal.*; ஏரி - éri, *Tam.*). Tank. A large tank or natural reservoir for irrigation outside a principal village. Differ from Coolams which are generally artificial tanks, stone-built or otherwise, found in every village and town. Every hamlet has also its small pond called in Tamul coottay for drinking-water and cattle. Suffix in place names, especially in Tinnevelly; as Nangoonairy, meaning four + bends + tank; Ponnairy, meaning gold + tank. The same appears in the original of Cauvery.

AJAM (अज - aja, *San.*). From (aj, san. to go). Goat. Plant first term. Ex., where transl. is of second term:—Anisochilus carnosus (ajapáda), foot; Argyreia speciosa (ajántrí), bowels; Carum copticum (ajamóda), smell; Cuminum cyminum (ajájí), conquering; Gynandropsis pentaphylla (ajagandhi), smell; Odina wodier (ajashringí), horn; Zizyphus jujuba (ajapriya), liked. See gloss. paragraphs.——*Ajapye* (अजपायि - ajapáyi, San.; چپک - chipak, Hind.; دبک چڑی - dabakchurí, Dec.; ఆసకప్పిరగాడు - ásakappiragádu, Tel.; சீனட்டம் - shínattam, Tam.). San. from (aja, san. goat + pá, san. to drink). Hind. from note. Dec. from (dabakná, hind. to skulk + churí, hind. bird). Hind. also (andhíchurí), meaning blind bird. Tel. also (kappapitta), meaning frog bird. Goatsuckers or night-jars. The name Goatsucker from large size of mouth. Title otherwise Eye-jars, Fern-owls, Night hawks, Night-jars. Caprimulgidæ, fissirostres, insessores, aves [pacshy, 5], of naturalists [jantoo]. Closely related to Swifts, but with soft and dingy plumage of owls.—"*a*" The Jungle night-jar is Caprimulgus indicus. Alias Cinerascens, saturatior. Prevalent hue light ashy, with dusky pencillings and black streaks on the feathers of the middle of the head, back, &c., the lower parts rufescent ashy with dark bars and mottlings; its call is like "tew-yo-yo", frequently repeated.—"*b*" The Ice-bird is Caprimulgus asiaticus. Common Indian night-jar. Its note is like the sound of a stone scudding over ice.——*Ajauntry* (अजान्त्री - ajántrí, San.). From (aja, san. goat + antra, san. entrails) from creeping stems.—Silver-weed. Botanically the Argyreia genus, convolvulaceæ [vricsham, 93]. Scandent, rarely sub-erect, shrubs; leaves hairy; flowers showy, purple or rose, rarely white; fruit berry-like. The species best known to the natives are Malabarica [malabar creeper] and Speciosa [sea-shore paulay].——*Ajmood* (अजमोद - ajamóda, San.). From (aja, san. goat + móda, san. smell); goat-smelling, from seeds. Botanically the Carum genus, umbelliferæ [vricsham, 67]. Herbs, perennial or annual, with finely cut leaves and compound umbels; flowers white; fruit ovoid, ellipsoid or oblong curved. The species best known to the natives are:—Carui [caraway], copticum [ajwaun], roxburghianum [ajmood ajwaun]. Also applied in arabic to other genera, as Apium [karafs] and Hyoscyamus [persian ajwaun].

AJWAUN (यमानी - yamání, *San.*; ओंवा - ómvá, *Mahr.*; वोंवा - vómvá, *Conc.*; كمون ملوكى - kamúnimulúkí, *Ar.*; نانخواه - nánkháh, *Pers.*; اجوائن - ajwáin, *Hind.*; اجوان - ajwán, *Dec.*; ಓಮಗಿಡ - ómagida, *Can.*; వామము - vámamu, *Tel.*; ଜୁଆନି - juváni, *Oor.*; അയമോദകം - ayamódakam, *Mal.*; අසමෝදගම් - asamódagam, *Singh.*; ஓமம் - ómam, *Tam.*). Title from deccany. San. means pertaining to yavanas. Mahr. and conc. from sanscrit. Ar. from (kamún, ar. cumin, cuminum cyminum, linn. + mulúkí, ar. royal). Pers. from (nán, pers. bread + kháh, pers. demanding); appetiser. Hind. and dec. from sanscrit. Can. from (óma, can. the seed + gida, can. plant). Tel. from sanscrit. Mal. from (ajamódiká, san.), meaning goat smelling. Tam. from sanscrit. San. also (brahmadarbhá), meaning brahma, the creator + coosham grass, eragrostis cynosuroides, retz.; (yavániká), meaning introduced by yavanas; (agnivarddhana), meaning fire increasing; (dípyaka), meaning promoting digestion; (ugragandhá), meaning strong smelling. Ar. also (tálibulkabz), meaning enquirer of costiveness, from cure against costiveness. Pers. also (zányán). Can. also (ajámúlagida), meaning goat + root + plant. Tel. also (vámu). Tam. also (asamóthagam), meaning goat + smelling. Title otherwise Bengal jawauny, Brahma's coosham, Ethiopian cumin, Indian bishop's weed, Indian dill, Omam plant, Owa, Royal cumin, Sison, Sison cordial plant. Botanically Carum [ajmood] copticum, benth., umbelliferæ [vricsham, 67]. Alias Ammi copticum; Athamanta ajowan; Carum ajowan; Ligusticum ajowan; Ptychotis ajowan, coptica; Sison ajowan. Ajowan from hind. Annual; stem erect, dichotomous; calyx five-toothed; leaves few, cut into numerous linear or filiform segments, the uppermost simply pinnate; umbel seven to nine rayed; involucel few leaved; leaflets linear, entire; fruit strongly ribbed, covered with small blunt tubercles; flowers white; small, warm, aromatic seeds, resemble anise in virtues, with volatile oil. Seeds are medicinally stimulant, antispasmodic, of value in atonic dyspepsia and diarrhœa; the aqua known as Omam water or aqua ptychotis distilled from seeds is a valuable carminative, useful in disguising the taste of nauseous drugs and obviating their tendency to cause griping; the seeds yield also a crystalline essential oil, smelling like carbolic oil, substituted for british peppermint, caraway oil, and aniseed oil; all in pharm. officinal; seeds employed also in veterinary practice. Seeds form an ingredient of paun; used to give flavor and pungency to curries. Compare Sowa or dill, Anise, and Caraway.——*Ajmood ajwaun* (अजमोद - ajamóda, San.; अजमोदओंवा - ajamódaómvá, Mahr.; كرفس - karafs, Ar. and Pers.; اجمود - ájmúd, Hind.; اجموده اجوان کاجھار - ajmúdaajwánkájhár, Dec.; ಅಜಮೋದವೋಮ - ajamódavóma, Can.; అజమోదకము - ajamódaómamu, Tel.; அசமதாகம் - asamathágam, Tam.). Title as being from carum instead of hyoscyamus or sesseli [persian ajwaun]. San. from (aja, san. goat + móda, san. smell); from seeds. Mahr. from (ajamóda, san. the plant + ómvá, mahr. carum copticum, benth.). Hind. from sanscrit. Dec. from (ajamóda, san. the plant + yamání, san. carum copticum, benth.). Can. from (ajamóda, san. the plant + óma, can. carum copticum, benth.). Tel. similar. Tam. from sanscrit. Botanically Carum [ajmood] roxburghianum, benth., umbelliferæ [vricsham, 67]. Alias Apium involucratum; Pimpinella involucrata; Ptychotis roxburghiana. A distinctive s. indian species. Herbaceous; flowers small, white; cultivated; seeds nearly same as omum, but aroma inferior; carminative and stimulant; are a separate article in bazaar.——*Persian ajwaun* (पारसीकयमानि - párasíkayamáni, San.; खुरासानीओंवा - khurásáníóvá, Mahr.; بنج - banj, Ar.; بنگ - bang, Pers.; خراسانی اجواین کا پیڑ - khurásáníajváinkáper, Hind.; خراسانی اجوان کا جھاڑ - khurásáníajvánkájhár, Dec.; ادس پدس - adaspedás, Malay; ಕುರಾಸಾನಿ ಓಮ - kurásánióma, Can.; కురాసాని ఓమము - kurásániómamu, Tel.; குராசாணிஓமம் - kurásániyómam, Tam.). Title from original habitat. San. from (párasíka, san. persian + yamání, san. carum copticum, benth.). Mahr. means khorassan ajwaun. Ar. from (banja, ar. to stupify); from seed. Pers. from arabic. Hind. from (khurásání, hind. khorassan + ajváin, hind. carum copticum, benth. + per, hind. tree). Can., Tel. and Tam. similar. Tel. also (kurinjiómamu) by corruption. Greek ὑοσκύαμος μέλας, meaning black hog-bean. Title otherwise Henbane, Khorassan ajwaun, Kirmauny ajwaun. Botanically Hyoscyamus niger, linn., solanaceæ [vricsham, 94]. Alias Hyoscyamus agrestis, flavus. Common weed; stem viscous, branched; leaves oblong, sinuately toothed, or sinuate-pinnatifid, viscously pubescent, lower ones petioled, the rest half stem-clasping, sub-decurrent; flowers sub-sessile, erect, arranged on simple, unilateral, recurved, leafy, terminal spikes, the corolla minutely reticulated with purple veins on a pale rose-colored and yellowish ground, marked with a dark-purple throat; frequent in waste ground near houses; cultivated. Seeds are small, compressed, uniform, roundish, finely dotted, of a yellowish gray color, and have the odour of the plant and an oleaginous, bitter taste; called in latin faba porcina, faba suilla. Plant a powerful narcotic when its seeds are forming; its capsules, seeds, and leaves are used extensively in medicine and produce effects similar to opium; one of its powers is that of dilating the pupil in diseases of the eye when applied locally; gives to pharm. the dried leaves, hyoscyami folia, having alkaloid hyoscyamia, sedative, anodyne, and antispasmodic; preparations, tinctura hyoscyami, extractum hyoscyami; officinal; young leaves eaten by cattle. Another species Muticus, called in Hind. kohibhang or mountain hemp, is sometimes used for smoking. Natives give the same names to Sesseli indicum, w. & a., otherwise Indian meadow saxifrage; alias Cnidium diffusum; Ligusticum diffusum; flower small, white; seed used as medicine for cattle.

AKALKARAH (अकराकरभा - akarákarabhá, *San.*; अक्कलकरा - akkalakará, *Mahr.*; عاقرقرحا - áakarkarahá, *Ar.*; اکلکرا - akalkará, *Pers.*; اقلقرا - akalkará, *Hind.* and *Dec.*; ಅಕ್ಕಲಕಾರೆ - akkalákaré, *Can.*; అక్కలకర్ర - akkalakarra, *Tel.*; അക്കിക്കറുക - akkikkaruka, *Mal.*; அக்கராக்காரம் - akkarákkáram, *Tam.*). Title from hindostany. San. from (akará, san. branchless + karabhá, san. pellitory). Ar. also (audulkarah), meaning pellitory wood. Hind. also (akarkará). Greek πύρεθρον. Title otherwise Pellitory, Pellitory of Spain, Ring-flower. Botanically Anacyclus pyrethrum, dec., compositæ [vricsham, 74]. Alias anthemis pyrethrum. Plant with flower resembling a large daisy; root, when dry, is tough, fibrous, of the thickness of a quill, externally grey, internally white; pungency of root is not perceived till chewed for a few seconds, when it occasions at first a glowing heat in the mouth, soon followed by a pricking sensation in tongue and lips; gives to pharm. pyrethri radix, with acrid resinous principle pyrethrin; stimulant, locally applied; irritant and rubefacient sialagogue; used as masticatory and for relief of toothache; powder of root used in large quantities by Mahomedans to excite transpiration, being rubbed on skin. Root is an ingredient in snuffs. No other species here.

AKEEK (عقیق - akík, *Hind.*; சிலைமான்கல் - shilamángal, *Tam.*). Hind. from (akka, ar. to split). Tam. from (sulaiman, ar. solomon + kal, tam. stone). Hind. also (akíkiyamaní), meaning yemen cornelian. Agate, which word is from the river Achates in Sicily. A variegated form of silica, banded with different colors, or with opaque and translucent layer alternating. Commonly found lining cavities in basalt and other volcanic rocks. For the most part from Bombay, whither they are brought from Nimudra, a place situated on the left bank of the Nerbudda. Sometimes also found in the Northern circars. Those imported from Japan are much admired, being of a red color with white veins. The Tamul lapidaries often confound the Akeek proper with Akeek i bahree or Mocha stones. Agates are an aggregate fossil, consisting of chalcedony, cornelian, jasper, quartz, or flint, while the Mocha stone is a mere variety of chalcedony. See below.——*Akeek i bahree* (عقیق بحری - akíkibahri, Pers. and Hind.; యమునరాయి - yamunaráyi, Tel.). Pers. from (akík, ar. agate + bahr, ar. sea). Tel. from (yamuná, san. river jumna + ráyi, tel. stone). Mocha stone, being Saxon for moss-stone or moss agate and not Arabian. Variety of chalcedony found near Rajahmundry.——*Akeek i siyah* (गोमेद - góméda, San.; عقیق سیاہ - akíkisiyáh, Pers. and Hind.; ಗೋಮೇಧಿಕ - gómédhika, Can.; గోమేధికము - gómédhikamu, Tel.; ഗോമേദകം - gómédakam, Mal.; கோமேதகம் - kóméthagam, Tam.). San. from (gó, san. cow + méda, san. fat); from color. Hind. from (akík, ar. cornelian + siyáh, pers. black). Sardonyx. Brought from the Himalayas and the Indus.——*Akeek i soofeed* (शिवधातु - shivadhátu, San.; عقیق ابیض - akíkiabyaz, Ar.; عقیق سفید - akíkisufíd, Pers.; دودھیا عقیق - dúdhyáakík, Hind.; కురింజి - kurinji, Tel.; வைரமணி - vairamani, Tam.). San. means shiva's mineral, milk-white. Ar. from (akík, ar. cornelian + abyaz, ar. white). Pers. from (akík, ar. cornelian + sufíd, ar. white). Hind. from (dúdh, hind. milk + akík, ar. cornelian). Tel. corruption of (kuruvinda, san. the stone so called). Tam. from (vairam, tam. diamond + mani, san. gem). Chalcedony. Species of agate; milky white or pale yellow, often with an internal wavy structure.——*Akeek i soorkh* (عقیق سرخ - akíkisurkh, Pers. and Hind.; కరబొకు - karabóku, Tel.; அக்கிக்கல் - akkikkal, Tam.). Pers. from (akík, ar. agate + surkh, pers. red). Tel. from (kara, tel. hill + bóki, tel. pot); from want of lustre. Tam. from (akshi, san. eye + kal, tam. stone). Hind. also (akík i jigarí), meaning liver-colored cornelian. Cornelian. A sub-species of chalcedony, brought from Bombay, being usually found near Broach. Semi-pellucid, takes a high polish, opaque parts usually present the appearance of dots, eyes, veins, clouds, zones, or bands.

AKHTAR (اختر - akhtar, *Hind.*). From Persian. Star. Slave alam. Also component of lacabs.——*Akhtar e hind* (اخترهند - akhtarihind, Hind.). Star of India.

AKKA (అక్క - akka, *Tel.*; அக்காள் - akkál, *Tam.*). Elder sister. Term of friendly address among females towards elders. Also suffix in feminine proper names as Soobbakka, Ramakka. The Akkah coottattaur are the females attached to the Zenana of the late Maharajah of Tanjore and their descendants.

AKKASARY (عکسواری - akswárí, *Hind.*). From (aks, ar. shadow + wár, hind. suffix denoting possession). Neighbouring.

AL (ال - al, *Hind.*). The Arabic definite article. Before lunar letters, viz., the gutturals, palatals, and labials, it undergoes no change; as al khaulik, meaning the creator. But before a solar letter, viz., a lingual or a dental, it becomes an, ar, as, or ash, &c., according to the succeeding initial letter; as annabee, meaning the prophet, &c. When preceded by a syllable in composition, the vowel also itself is altered to oo; as Abdoollah, meaning slave of god, &c.——*Alabd* (العبد - alabd, Hind.). From (abd, ar. slave). Form of countersignature by a subordinate.——*Alcaudy* (القاضی - alkádi, Hind.). From (kazá, ar. mandate). Same as Cauzy.——*Algaroba* (خروب - kharrúb, Ar.). Same as Carob.——*Algoja* (الغوزہ - alghozah, Hind.). Flageolet [mookha veenay, saugeetam].——*Algowar* (അൾഗ്വാർ - algóvar, Mal.). Portuguese. Formerly the prison of the Inquisition at Goa.——*Alhagi* (الحاج - alháj, Ar.). Means the pilgrimage. Generic term; see Arabian manna.——*Alizarine* (العصارہ - alusárah, Hind.). From (usárah, ar. expressed juice). Commercial name of madder in the Levant. Product of Rubia peregrina, rubiaceæ [vricsham, 71]. Cf. munjeet.——*Alkali* (القلی - alkilí, *Ar.*). From (kaliy, ar. to calcine). Ashes, same as cauram. Southern india is particularly rich in alkaline and earthy minerals, one source of which is decaying granites [cauram, sarakk].

ALAF (الف - alaf, *Hind.*). From Arabic. A thousand.——*Alaf leila* (الف لیلہ - alaflailah, Hind.). From (lail, ar. night). Hindostany prose translation of the Arabian nights by Moonshee Abd ool careem of Lucknow, who lived about 1830. Text-book at Madras [amoocta maulyada, bribat katay, nummalwar].

ALAG (الگ - alag, *Hind.*). From (a, san. neg. + lagna, san. connected). Separate.——*Alaga poollary* (అలగాపుల్లరి - alagá-pullari, Tel.). From (pullari, tel. grass tax). Fine on stray cattle. See vol. I, 112.

ALAGAN (அழகன் - azhagan, *Tam.*). From (azhagu, tam. beauty). Vishnoo, the beautiful. Proper name among lower orders.——*Alagappa* (అలగప్ప - alagappa, Tel.). From (appa, tel. father). Hindoo 2nd or pers. name [peyar].——*Alagar hills* (அழகர்மலை - azhagarmalai, Tam.). From (malai, tam. hill). Tam. also (tenvéngadam), meaning south + tripatty. Sanscrit name (rishabhádri), meaning bull + mountain. Range of hills, Place of pilgrimage; Madura dist., Mailore tal.; lat. 10° 06′; long. 78° 17′; from Madura N.E. 15 miles; from Mailore N.W. 7¼ miles. About 12 miles in length; average height 1,000 feet. A great variety of geological formations found at the base. Sandstone predominates. On the south-east face at the foot of the hills stands the Cullar alagar covil, the ancient temple of the Cullar, with fortifications partly in ruins.——*Alagasingaran* (அளகசிங்கரன் - alagasingaran, Tam.). From singam, tam. lion). Epithet of Vishnoo. Hindoo 2nd or pers. name [peyar].

ALAH (علا - alá, *Hind.*). From Arabic. High. Component of lacabs [ism].——*Alah ood deen* (علاءالدين - aláuddín, Hind.). Glory of the faith.

ALAM (അളം - alam, *Mal.*; அளம் - alam, *Tam.*). From (al, tam. sharpness). Saltpan [ooppalam]. Salt marsh. So brackish and barren ground. Suffix in place names; as Cayaralam, meaning coir + marsh. Alavan is a salt maker.

ALAM (علم - alam, *Hind.*). From Arabic.——**(1)** Mahomedan personal name; the distinctive name of an individual in his family and amongst his familiar friends [ism]. Answers to Christian name of English, prénom of French, nomen of Latins, single name of Dravidian lower tribes, and second or deity name of Hindooized dravidians [peyar]. It has been described at vol. I (104), footnote. The following are further details. It is a word, usually single, meaning an attribute; but at the present day derived generally through precedents, such as:—"*a*" name and attributes of God,—"*b*" names of Mahomet, his family and his companions,—"*c*" names of patriarchs and prophets named in Koran,—"*d*" names of Imaums,—"*e*" names of tutelary saints. The following three cases are more original:—"*f*" heroic alams,—"*g*" alam from personal peculiarity, &c.,—"*h*" alams from planets, plants and flowers. Cases "*f*" to "*h*" apply chiefly to names of domestic servants and harem women. The following are the principal alams shown under all the above heads:—"*a*" Aleem, Allah, Allaum, Ally, Azam, Azeem, Azeez, Badee, Baseer, Bauky, Bauree, Bausit, Cabeer, Careem, Cawder, Cooddoos, Futtauh, Ghaffar, Ghafoor, Ghany, Hafeez, Hakeem, Haleem, Hameed, Haseeb, Haudy, Haukim, Hayaut, Hukk, Hye, Jaleel, Jubbaur, Kavee, Keiyoom, Khaulik, Lateef, Mabood, Majeed, Malik, Mateen, Momin, Moojeeb, Moosowir, Rabb, Raheem, Rahman, Rakeeb, Raoof, Rasheed, Ruzzauk, Salaam, Samad, Samy, Sattaur, Shacoor, Shaheed, Soobhaun, Towaub, Vakeel, Wadood, Wahaub, Wally, Wauhid, Wausya.—"*b*" Abbaus, Abid, Aboo bakr, Acbar, Ahmed, Aleema, Ally, Ameen, Ameena, Asad, Asghar, Athar, Ayeesha, Badr, Basheer, Baukir, Boorhaun, Caleem, Cassim, Coobrah, Coolsoom, Fareed, Faseeh, Fatimah, Ghaulib, Ghazanfar, Habeeb, Hafeez, Haleema, Hamza, Haneef, Hassan, Haumid, Haushim, Hoossain, Hyder, Imaum, Khadeejah, Mahdee, Mahmood, Mahomet, Mazhar, Misbah, Mooctiar, Moojtabah, Moonavar, Mooneer, Moortezah, Moostafah, Moozuffer, Nabee, Noor, Osman, Rasool, Rookia, Sajjaud, Sakeena, Shafee, Shubbeer, Shubber, Siddeek, Sufder, Tauhir, Teiyib, Tooraub, Yauseen, Zaheer, Zahra, Zeinab.—"*c*" Adam, Ayoob or job, Davood or david, Eesah or jesus, Haroun or aaron, Ibrahim or abraham, Idrees or enoch, Ishauk or isaac, Ismail, Khaleel a title of abraham, Khizr or elijah, Maryam or mary, Maseeh or messiah, Moosa or moses, Nooh or noah, Safee a title of adam, Saurah or sarah, Sicunder or alexander, Sooliman or solomon, Yacoob or jacob, Yahya or john, Yoonoos or jonas, Yoosoof or joseph, Zacriyah or zacharia, Zuleikhah who was potiphar's wife.—"*d*" Cauzim, Jaffer, Mahdee, Nakee, Razah, Saudic, Takee.—"*e*" Dastgheer, Fareed, Ghiyaus, Ghouse, Jeelauny, Madaur, Mahboob, Mansoor, Mohee ood deen, Nutter, Peer, Peeraun.—"*f*" Pahilwaun, Roostam.—"*g*" Dilaraum, Goolbadan, Goolrookh, Gowhar, Jamaul, Khoosh kadam, Mokhlis, Rowshan.—"*h*" Ajauyib or shoeflower, Chembeley or jasmine, Goolchaman or garden rose, Goolcheen or gardener, Goolkheir or persian hollyhock, Khoorsheed or sun, Mooshtary or jupiter, Nafarmaun or forget-me-not, Nargis or narcissus, Sanobar or fir, Shumshaud or cypress, Sosan or lily, Zohra or venus. Shiah alams differ from those of the Soonnees in that the alams of the first three caliphs, and of the saints mentioned above are not used; many of these express devotion to Ally and his direct lineage.——**(2)** Alam also means a military banner. Generally of copper brass, or steel. Compare standards of Greeks and Romans. A common form is the Punja or hand with five fingers extended. Alams carried at Moharram represent the ornaments affixed to the upper part of the colors of the Arab warriors. They are dedicated to different persons, and their processions take place on different nights and days as follows.——*Abbausee alam* (عباسی علم - abbásíalam, Hind.). To Abbaus, half brother of Hoossain.——*Alam e imaum cassim* (علم امام قاسم - alamiimámkásim, Hind.). To the martyr Cassim, paternal nephew of Hoossain. 7th day at noon.——*Baurah imaum* (بارة امام - bárahimám, Hind.). Means twelve saints. To Ally, and eleven descendants of Mahomet by his daughter Fatimah. 10th night.——*Hoossainy alam* (حسینی علم - husainíalam, Hind.). To Hoossain. 9th night.——*Hydary alum* (حیدری علم - haidaríalam, Hind.). To Mahomet's cousin and son-in-law, Ally. 10th night.——*Naul e moobaurak* (نعل مبارك - nalimubárik, Hind.). Means sacred horse shoe. To the shoe of Hoossain's war horse. 10th night.

ALAMORE (ఆలమూరు - álamúru, *Tel.*). From (álamu, tel. battle + úru, tel. village). Sanscrit name (sangrámanagara), meaning battle + town.—"*a*" Deputy tahsildarry, Godavery district, Pay Rs. 70.—"*b*" Village, Head-quarters of Deputy tahsildar; Godavery dist., Ramchendrapooram tal.; pop. 2,578; acres 2,573; lat. 16° 47′; long. 81° 55′; from Cocanada W.S.W. 26 miles; from Coonavaram S.E. 67 miles; from Ellore E. 51 miles; from Madras N.N.E. 270 miles; from Narsapore N.N.E. 27 miles; from Rajahmundry S.S.E. 17 miles; from Ramchendrapooram W.S.W. 10 miles. Near the Godavery.

ALAMPARVA (ஆலம்பறை - álambarai, *Tam.*). From (álam, tam. water + paravai, tam. expanse). Shrotriem village; Chingleput dist., Madrantacam tal.; pop. 411; acres 395; lat. 12° 17′; long. 80° 03′; from Chingleput S. 30 miles; from Madrantacam S.S.E. 18 miles; from Sydapett S.S.W. 53 miles; from the sea W. ¼ mile. Coast village near S. limit of district, midway between Pondicherry and Chingleput. The Mahomedan fort passed into hands of French in 1750 as a gift from Moozuffer jung, Soobahdar of the Deccan. In 1758 a severe naval engagement between the French and English squadrons was fought opposite this village. It was a French depôt and fort during the seige of Madras and was reduced by Sir Eyre Coote in 1760 on the collapse of the French power in that part of India. Formerly noted for excellent quality of drinking water and its cisterns, and for its oyster beds. The ruins of the fort still remain; it was square, of stone, and had towers at the angles.

ALANJY (अङ्कोल - ankóla, *San.*; अङ्कोळ - ankóla, *Mahr.*; اكول - akol, *Hind.*; اكولا - akolá, *Dec.*; ಅಂಕೋಲೆಮರ - ankólemara, *Can.*; ಅಂಕೋಲೆದಮರ - ankóledamara, *Too.*; ఊడుగ - údnga, *Tel.*; ଅଙ୍କୁଲ - ankúla, *Oor.*; അങ്കോലം - ankólam, *Mal.*; අංගොල - angóla, *Singh.*; அழிஞ்சில் - azhiñjil, *Tam.*). Title from tamul. San. from (ank, san. mark), marked by spines; from branchlets ending occasionally in spines. Mahr., &c., from sanscrit. Tam. from (azhi, tam. to destroy); antidote to poison. San. also (shódhana), meaning clearing, as removing poison. Can. also (guddadagónimara), meaning hill + sack tree, salvadora persica, linn.; (kallumávu), meaning stone + mangifera indica, linn. Tel. also (nallaankólamu), meaning black + alanjy. Oor. also (dolanku). Mal. also (chemmaram), meaning red-wood; (kárankólam), meaning black alanjy. Tam. also (karuppuazhiñjimaram), meaning black + alanjy. Title otherwise Ancola fruit plant, Hill sack tree, Nallancolam bark plant, Red-wood, Sage leaved alangium, Stone mango. Botanically Alangium lamarckii, thwaites, cornaceæ [vricsham, 69]. Generic from Tamul. Alias Alangium acuminatum, decapetalum, hexapetalum, karangolam, tomentosum. Karangolam is malayalum. Deciduous shrub; leaves alternate, narrow-oblong; petals six to ten; branches occasionally six pinescent; stamens twice the number of the petals; filaments hairy at the base; flowers solitary or aggregate in the axils of the leaves, whitish yellow, fragrant; drupe tomentose, one-seeded; flowers in april and may. Root-bark very bitter; is medicinally emetic, nauseant, alterative tonic and antipyretic; a remedy for bites of mad dogs and poisonous snakes; for british ipecacnanha, jamaica sarsaparilla, and pul. jacob. vera. Fruit edible, somewhat astringent; eaten by the poor. Sapwood light-yellow; heartwood brown, hard, close and even-grained; used for pestles, oil-mills, wooden cattle-bells, fuel, &c. No other common species here.

ALAR (அலர் - alar, *Tam.*). Flower.——*Alamail* (அலமேலு - alamélu, Tam.). From (mél, tam. over). Lutchmy on the lotus flower. The name of the goddess at Tripatty. A common female name at Madras [peyar].——*Alar magal* (அலர்மகள் - alarmagal, Tam.). From (magal, tam. daughter). Lutchmy, the lotus-born daughter.——*Alary* (அலரி - alari, Tam.). Sweet scented oleander, nerium odorum. Plant 2nd term. Ex., where transl. is of 1st term:—Homonoya riparia (káttalari), wild; Plumeria acutifolia (ízhattalari), ceylon; Polygonum barbatum (áttalari), river; Tabernæmontana dichotoma (káttalari), wild; Tamarix gallica (áttalari), river; Thevetia nereifolia (shímaiyalari), foreign. See gloss. paragraphs. Appears also as Araly.

ALAUMAT (علامت - alámat, *Hind.*). From (alam, ar. impression). Means a sign. Mahomedan tribal mark or surname.

Alaumat prefixed or suffixed to an Alam constitutes a sufficiently complete Mahomedan proper name [ism]. The following are the various alaumats :— Aghah, Bauno, Bee, Beg, Begum, Khan, Khanam, Khautoo, Khautoon, Mah, Meer, Mirzah, Nissa, Shareef, Sheikh, Syed. See each. See also vol. I (106), footnote, cl. 7 [ism].

ALAUWAH (الاوا - aláwá, *Hind.*). From (aláv, hind. fire in a pit). Circular pit dug in front of an ashoorkhana at Moharram. Fires are lit therein and by-standers fence across them with sticks or swords.

ALAVAY (அளவை - alavai, *Tam.*). From (ala, tam. to measure). Measure, whether linear, superficial, or cubic. See vol. II, 505.——(1) The following is an attempt to reduce to an average table and a standard value the linear measures of the Presidency taking them under five divisions according to nationality of the populations using, and adding Sanscrit.—"*a*" Average table of linear measures in Tamul districts :—8 yells or sesamum seeds = 1 nel or paddy seed, 8 nels = 1 viralcaday or finger-tip-breadth, 12 viralcadays = 1 jaun or span, 2 jauns = 1 moolam or cubit, 4 moolams = 1 maur or fathom, 2,000 maurs = 1 crosham, 4 croshams = 1 cautham or day's march. Extras :—12 ungoolams or English inches = 1 adee or English foot ; 2 viralcadays = 1 ungoolam or thumb-joint-length, 24 ungoolams = 1 gajam or yard ; 44 ungoolams or finger-tip-breadths = 1 tutchacole or artificer's yard ; $7\frac{1}{2}$ nauzhivazhies or Indian miles = 1 cautham. Approximate actual value :—1 moolam = 18 inches.—"*b*" Average table of linear measures in Teloogoo districts :—8 yavams or barley corns = 1 ungoolam or finger-tip-breadth, 12 ungoolams = 1 jena or span, 2 jenas = 1 moora or cubit, 4 mooras = 1 niloovoo or fathom, 2,000 niloovoos = 1 pargoo, 4 pargoos = 1 aumada or day's march. Approximate actual value :—1 moora = 18 inches.—"*c*" Average table of Canarese linear measures :—8 yaveys or barley corns = 1 ungoola or finger-tip-breadth, 12 ungoolas = 1 guenoo or span, 2 guenoos = 1 mola or cubit, 4 molas = 1 bauroo or fathom, 2,000 bauroos = 1 hardaury, 4 hardauries = 1 gauvada or day's march. Approximate actual value :—1 mola = 18 inches.—"*d*" Average table of linear measures of Malabar :—8 yen manies or sesamum seeds = 1 tora or dholl seed, 8 toras = 1 viral or finger-tip-breadth, 12 virals = 1 chaun or span, 2 chauns = 1 moolam or cubit, 4 moolams = 1 maur or fathom, 1,000 maurs = 1 nauzhiga or Indian mile, 4 nauzhigas = 1 cautham. Extra :—2 virals = 1 ungoolam or thumb-joint-length, 24 ungoolams = 1 kole or artificer's rod. Approximate actual value :—1 moolam = 18 inches.—"*e*" Average table of Mahomedan linear measures :—8 jows or barley corns = 1 ungool or finger-tip-breadth, 12 ungools = 1 bilisht or span, 2 bilishts = 1 haut or cubit, 2 hauts = 1 guz or yard, 2 guz = 1 baum or fathom, 2,000 baums = 1 coss. Extras :—4 ungools = 1 mootthy or fist ; 3 kadams or feet = 1 guz. Approximate actual value :—1 haut = 18 inches.—"*f*" Average table of Sanscrit linear measures :—8 yavams or barley corns = 1 ungoolam or finger-tip-breadth, 12 ungoolams = 1 vitasty or gocarnam or span, 2 vitasties = 1 hastam or cubit, 2 hastams = 1 gajam or yard, 2 gajams = 1 dandam or dhanoo or pole, 2,000 dandams = 1 crosham, 4 croshams = 1 yojanam or day's march. Extras :—10 ungoolams = 1 pradesham or thumb-forefinger span, $3\frac{1}{2}$ hastams = 1 yaumam or fathom ; 2 croshams = 1 gavyooty or cows' range ; 1,000 dandams = 1 crosham. Approximate actual value :—1 hastam = 18 inches.——(2) The following is an attempt to reduce to an average table and a standard value the superficial measures of the Presidency, taking them under five divisions according to nationality of the populations using, and adding Sanscrit.—"*a*" Average table of superficial measures in Tamul districts :—1 kole or rod square of 24 English feet = 1 coozhy = 576 square feet, $4\frac{1}{4}$ coozhies = 1 munny or ground, 24 munnies = 1 cawny or country acre, 5 cawnies = 1 vaily. Extras :—100 coozhies = 1 mah, 20 mahs = 1 vaily ; 256 coozhies = 1 chey ; 2 puddies = 1 bullah ; 8 puddies = 1 mercaul, 21 mercauls = 1 vithaicottay. Approximate actual value :—1 cawny = 57,600 square feet.—"*b*" Average table of superficial measures in Teloogoo districts :—1 kole or rod square of $52\frac{1}{2}$ English feet = 1 coonta = $2,756\frac{1}{4}$ square feet, 50 coontas = 1 gorroo, 8 gorroos = 1 cootchel. Extras :—50 coontas = 1 wet bharnam ; 100 coontas = 1 dry bharnam ; 20 nowts = 1 bharnam ; 600 coontas = 1 garce ; 20 coonchams = 1 pootty, 30 pootties = 1 veesam ; 16 parrahs = 1 veesam, 16 veesams = 1 catty. Approximate actual value :—1 gorroo = 3·16 acres.—"*c*" Average table of Canarese superficial measures :—4 bullahs = 1 coodoo or colagam, 20 coodoos = 1 khandaga. Extras :—1 moody = 1 acre. Approximate actual value :—1 dry khandaga = 64,000 square yards ; 1 wet khandaga = 10,000 square yards.—"*d*" Average table of superficial measures of Malabar :—10 yidangazhies = 1 parrah. Extras :—11 colagams or pothies = 6 acres. Approximate actual value :—1 parrah = $\frac{1}{8}$ of an acre.—"*e*" Average table of Mahomedan superficial measures :—60 guz or yards = 1 jareeb or chain, 1 jareeb square = 1 pucka beegah, 120 square beegahs = 1 chauver. Extras :—1 catcha beegah = 1,600 square yards. Approximate actual value :—1 guz = 33 inches, 1 pucka beegah = 3,025 square yards.—"*f*" Average table of Sanscrit superficial measures :—10 hastams or cubits = 1 vamsham or rod, 20 vamshams square = 1 nivartanam. Extras :—1 gocharmam or hide of land = 300 feet × 10 feet. Approximate actual value :—1 hastam = 18 inches.——(3) The following is an attempt to reduce to an average table and a standard value the grain measures of the Presidency, taking them under five divisions according to nationality of the populations using, and adding Sanscrit.—"*a*" Average table of grain measures in Tamul districts :—2 ollucks = 1 oyak, 4 oyaks = 1 puddy, 8 puddies = 1 mercaul, 5 mercauls = 1 parrah, 80 parrahs = 1 garce. Extras :—2 maunams = 1 puddy, 2 puddies = 1 bullah or vallam, 32 bullahs = 1 shalagay, 3 shalagays = 1 pothy, 8 pothies = 1 candy ; 40 bullahs = 1 cundaga ; 12 mercauls = 1 cullum ; 21 mercauls = 1 cottah. Approximate actual value :—1 garce = 194 c. ft., 768 c. inches.—"*b*" Average table of grain measures in Teloogoo districts :—4 giddas = 1 sola, 2 solas = 1 tavva, 2 tavvas = 1 maunica, 4 maunicas = 1 cooncham, 4 coonchams = 1 toom, 20 tooms = 1 pootty, $7\frac{1}{2}$ pootties = 1 garce. Extras :—2 tavvas = 1 adda ; 4 tooms = 1 nowt ; 4 pootties = 1 bharnam ; 4 chitties = 1 sola, 4 solas = 1 moonta ; 20 tooms = 1 pullepootty, $2\frac{1}{2}$ pullepootties = 1 malacapootty. Approximate actual value :—1 maunica = $157\frac{1}{2}$ c. inches.—"*c*" Average table of Canarese grain measures :—14 pucka seers = 1 kulsy, 3 kulsies = 1 moody, 42 moodies = 1 corjy. Extras :—4 seers = 1 solga, 4 solgas = 1 maunam, 4 maunams = 1 bullah, 4 bullahs = 1 colaga, 5 colagas = 1 punchacam, 4 punchacams = 1 candy or khandaga. Approximate actual value :—1 pucka seer = 70 c. inches.—"*d*" Average table of grain measures of Malabar :—2 ollucks = 1 oyak, 2 oyaks = 1 oory, 2 oories = 1 nauzhy, 4 nauzhies = 1 yidangazhy, 10 yidangazhies = 1 parrah. Approximate actual value :—1 yidangazhy = $113\frac{3}{4}$ c. inches.—"*e*" Average table of Mahomedan grain measures :—2 chittacks = 1 nowtauk, 2 nowtauks = 1 pow, 4 pows = 1 pucka seer. Approximate actual value :—1 pucka seer = 70 c. inches.—"*f*" Average table of Sanscrit grain measures :—12 mooshties or handfuls = 1 coodavam or anjaly or double palmful, 4 coodavams = 1 prastam, 4 prastams = 1 audhacam, 4 audhacams = 1 dronam, 16 dronams = 1 khaury. Extras :—20 dronams = 1 coombham. Approximate actual value :—1 audbacam = 448 c. inches.——(4) The following is an attempt to reduce to an average table and a standard value the liquid measures of the Presidency, taking them under five divisions according to nationality of the populations using, and adding Sanscrit.—"*a*" Average table of liquid measures in Tamul districts :—2 ollucks = 1 oyak, 4 oyaks = 1 puddy, 2 puddies = 1 mercaul, 4 mercauls = 1 paunay, $1\frac{1}{2}$ paunays = 1 audam, 2 audams = 1 cullum. Extras :—2 puddies = 1 chemboo ; 8 paunays = 1 pothy. Approximate actual value :—1 puddy = 113 c. inches ; $2\frac{1}{2}$ ollucks = 1 pint.—"*b*" Average table of liquid measures in Teloogoo districts :—4 giddas = 1 sola, 2 solas = 1 tavva, 2 tavvas = 1 maunica, 4 maunicas = 1 cooncham. Extras :—4 chitties = 1 sola, 4 solas = 1 moonta ; 2 tavvas = 1 adda, 4 addas = 1 cooncham. Approximate actual value :—1 maunica = $157\frac{1}{2}$ c. inches.—"*c*" Average table of Canarese liquid measures :—2 coodtays = 1 seer, 5 seers = 1 cootty, 4 cootties = 1 caulauda. Extras :—$1\frac{1}{4}$ coodtays = 1 siddy. Approximate actual value :—1 seer = 21 c. inches.—"*d*" Average table of liquid measures of Malabar :—2 ollucks = 1 oyak, 2 oyaks = 1 oory, 2 oories = 1 nauzhy, 4 nauzhies = 1 yidangazhy, $1\frac{1}{2}$ yidangazhies = 1 cootty, 16 cootties = 1 paudam. Extras :—3 yidangazhies = 1 chodana. Approximate actual value :—1 yidangazhy = $113\frac{3}{4}$ c. inches.—"*e*" Average table of Mahomedan liquid measures :—2 chittacks = 1 nowtauk, 2 nowtauks = 1 pow, 4 pows = 1 pucka seer. Extras :—5 chittacks = 1 cutcha seer. Approximate actual value :—1 pucka seer = 70 c. inches.—"*f*" Average table of Sanscrit liquid measures :—2 palams = 1 prasritam or palmful, 2 prasritams = 1 coodavam or anjaly or double palmful, 2 coodavams = 1 sharauvam or maunica, 2 sharauvams = 1 prastam, 4 prastams = 1 audhacam or pautram, 4 audhacams = 1 dronam. Approximate actual value :—1 audhacam = 448 c. inches.——(5) The heads of this glossary can be consulted for the different kinds of measure.

ALAVEE (علوی - alaví, *Hind.*). From (alí, ar. the caliph). Syeds descended from Ally by his other wives, but not by Fatimah daughter of the prophet.

ALBACA (اجاص - ijjás, *Ar.* ; آلو - álú, *Pers.* ; آلو بخارا - álú-bukhárá, *Hind.* and *Dec.* ; ఆల్పొగడా - álpogadá, *Tel.* ; ஆல்பொகடா - álbogadá, *Tam.*). Title from hindostany. Hind. from (álú, pers. plum, prunus + bukhárah, pers. bokhara town). Tel. and tam. from hindostany. Title otherwise Bokhara plum, Bollas, Bullas, Cabool prune, Wild damson. Botanically Prunus [auloo] communis, huds., var. insititia, rosaceæ [vricsham, 49]. Alias Prunus aloocha, bokhariensis. The prunes brought dried from cabool ; sub-acid, cold and moist ; digestive and aperient. Root astringent and gum may be used for gum arabic. For amygdalus or almond see Baudam ; for armeniaca or apricot see Mishmish.

ALCARA (هرکارہ - harkárah, *Hind.*). From (har, pers. every + kár, pers. business). French spelling for harcarra.

ALDEA (الضيع - addai, *Ar.*). Portuguese from Arabic. A hamlet. Fr. aldée is still used.

ALEEF (الف - alif, *Hind.*). First letter of Persian and Arabic alphabets.

ALEEM (علیم - alím, *Hind.*). From (ilm, ar. knowledge). Omniscient. Epithet of God, used as alam, or with Abd [ism]. Fem. is Aleema.——*Abd ool aleem* (عبدالعلیم - abdulalím, Hind.). Slave of the omniscient.——*Aleem khan* (علیم خان - alímkhán, Hind.). Alam + alaumat.

ALEEYAT (علیہ - alíyat, *Hind.*). From (ally, ar. caliph + female suffix). Female slave of Ally. Equivalent to Abd, and similarly used.

ALHAMD (الحمد - alhamd, *Hind.*). Praise.——*Alhamd oolillah* (الحمدالله - alhamdulilláh, Hind.). From (illáh, ar. to god). Praise be to god. Mahomedan ejaculation of thanksgiving.

ALIYA SANTAUNA (ಅಳಿಯಸಂತಾನ - aliyasantána, *Can.*). From (aliya, can. nephew + santána, san. succession). The law of inheritance by the female line among the Bunts, Nayars, &c., of Canara, being the equivalent of Maroomakkatoyem in Malabar further south [maroomakkatoyem]. The principle that the inheritance vests in the females in preference to the males is more consistently carried out in Canara, where even the management of property vests ordinarily in females, and not as in Malabar in the males. The following is an abstract translation of the original set of rules which make up the law. The law prescribes fourteen canons for the guidance of the three classes of people other than Bramins; these canons going by the names Jauty, Neety, Mauna, Maryauday, Hoottoo, Cattoo, Hindey, Moondey, Hetchoo, Cummy, Baly, Banna, Aly, and Ooly. Added to these fourteen canons are fourteen cuttaleys or commandments. The following are the fourteen canons in alphabetical order.——*Aly* (ಅಳಿ - ali, Can.). Death.—"*a*" That the eldest female, the eldest male children of the senior and junior maternal aunts shall stand entitled to aly ooly or succession to property on death. The eldest female is also the Yejmaun or manager answering to the Carnaven in Malabar.—"*b*" That the children of the elder and younger sisters shall not enter into a division of property.—"*c*" That the remaining members shall act in union.—"*d*" That if misunderstandings arise between the sisters, the elder sister shall provide the younger with a house and household articles, retaining herself the management of the property and the right to Oorisiry or participation and liability in respect of all that is either good or bad.—"*e*" That only the surviving heir, enjoyer of aly ooly, shall be entitled to Puttah putty honors.—"*f*" That on the death of such heir, the next surviving male member of the family shall succeed to the Puttah. ——*Baly* (ಬಳಿ - bali, Can.). Tribe. The Balies are sixteen in number, and they are enumerated.——*Banna niroobaly* (ಬಣ್ಣನಿರುಬಳಿ - bannanírubali, Can.). This refers to classes that have no places or marks of honor, but simply the color of a caste. They are three in number, viz.:—persons unfit to enter any of the higher classes; persons who have not established Balisauvirabramhas; persons who have no king for the country in which they live.——*Cattoo* (ಕಟ್ಟು - kattu, Can.). This precept contains the formal introduction of the Aliya santauna law, as shown in the following fixed rules:—"*a*" That the wife and children shall observe the Sootacam on the occasion of death, and shall participate in the effects of sin or virtue. Sootacam is impurity from child-birth, as Pautacam is impurity from death of relatives. They shall also share in the virtue accruing from gift and charity and in the fame or infamy arising from any deeds.—"*b*" That the Santaunam shall succeed to the property, and shall observe the Sootacam on the occasion of birth only, and not on that of death. Santaunam is literally offspring, and here applied to the successors of an Aliya santauna family or those who claim through them; in contradistinction to Cootoomba, applied to the wife and children.—"*c*" That no auspicious ceremony shall be celebrated through Bramins.—"*d*" That no Mahaulyam [pundigay, 6d] shall be performed for the deceased. This rule is not observed.—"*e*" That no Puncha gavyam [q.v.] shall be taken.—"*f*" That no Poonya homam [q.v.] shall be made with the use of the Darbhay on occasions of birth, as well as of death.—"*g*" That only the Nirmaulyam shall be taken on occasions of birth and of death in the names of those that brought forth the children in the former and in those of the death in the latter. Nirmaulyam is the remains of an offering presented to a deity, Shiva especially.—"*h*" That the Poojay and Abhishaica shaunty shall be performed besides the Samaraudhanay. Poojay is worship. Abhishaica shaunty is the anointing of the idol with milk, honey, sugar, ghee, curds, &c. Samaraudhanay is the feeding of Bramins on occasions of religious ceremonies.——*Cummy* (ಕಮ್ಮಿ - kammi, Can.). Inferiority. This rule contains the distinctions of respect which each caste observes towards the other.——*Hetchoo* (ಹೆಚ್ಚು - heççu, Can.). Superiority, similar.——*Hindey* (ಹಿಂದೆ - hinde, Can.). Behind [moondey].——*Hoottoo* (ಹುಟ್ಟು - huttu, Can.). This precept contains the abolition of the rival Makkala santauna law.——*Jauty* (ಜಾತಿ - játi, Can.). This precept enumerates the castes that are to follow the Aliya santauna law. They are:—Agasar, washermen; Audeycoragar, a hill-tribe; Carinyaurar, a class of pariahs; Coombaurar, potters; Cshowricar, barbers; Devadigar, menial servants who perform out-door services at temples; Haleypeiks, toddy-drawers, same as Billawar; Harischetties, merchants corresponding to comaties above the ghauts; Holeyar, pariahs; Jeinas; Malaicoodies, a hill-tribe; Malavar, a class of laborers; Mausaudicar, a class of bunts who eat flesh; Moondaular, a class of pariah; Nayar; Parivaurs, an inferior class of bunts; Punchaular, artizans; Shauliyar, weavers; Tooloovar. It will be observed that all are Shoodras and Pariahs.——*Maryauday* (ಮರ್ಯಾದೆ - maryáde, Can.). This contains the honor to be enjoyed from generation to generation "in the order of four, eight and sixteen." Those enjoying the highest dignities are meant by the four and those next to them the eight, and the last sixteen. They are:—Arasooputtah, title of kings; Pagady, fixed periodical tributes; Putty, occasional tributes, such as nuzzers, &c., as entered in certain lists or putties.——*Mauna* (ಮಾನ - mána, Can.). This contains the dignities to be enjoyed "in the order of four, eight and sixteen." They are:—Arasoo, privileges attached to kings; Ballaula, privileges attached to chiefs who rank next to kings; Heggadey, privileges attached to those who rank equally with Ballaulas; Keerty, honorary distinctions; Mauey, respect due to the social position of certain families; Nauma, title; Pirapp, line of descent; Stala, respect due to the holders of certain lands or premises.——*Moondey* (ಮುಂದೆ - munde, Can.). Before [hindey]. This gives different degrees of superiority consisting in the Puttah and Puttauvaly honors held by 4, 8 and 16 houses respectively. Puttah is an inscribed plate fastened on the forehead. It is here used to signify the dignity enjoyed by a person. Puttauvaly is the plural of Puttah. The sixteen houses refer to the 16 Balies.——*Neety* (ನೀತಿ - níti, Can.). This is the rule enacted for the guidance of the Jauty. Each of the classes shall behave itself in respect of its superiority or inferiority, and also in such a manner as the manners and customs peculiar to each class may direct.——*Ooly* (ಉಳಿ - uli, Can.). This enunciates succession by heirship to property. It provides:—"*a*" That excepting the wedding gift given to a married girl, the property that may be given to her by the husband of his own accord, however trifling it may be, even with the consent of the family, shall be taken away by the members of the family. The family here is Santauna not Cootoomba.—"*b*" That one shall assign to his children in gift movable or immovable property of his own acquisition, but not ancestral property.—"*c*" That on failure of heirs a girl of the same Baly that may be fostered shall be considered an adopted child. Adoption by a female having male issue is invalid.—"*d*" That no male shall be adopted.—"*e*" That no right shall be sold on the plea of absence of heirs, nor conferred on the wife and children on the same plea. The right refers to estates.—"*f*" That if a family become extinct without adoption, the heads of the country in the order of 4, 8 and 16 shall choose a girl and boy of the same Baly to stand as representatives of such extinct family.—"*g*" That these representatives alone shall succeed as heirs, but not the wife and children [maryauday].

ALKHAULAK (الخالق - alkhálak, *Hind.*). Means measured and cut. Over-coat; double breasted dress, made with long sleeves, and to fit to the form as low as the hips with skirts reaching down to the calf of the leg, tied across the chest on the left side.

ALLAH (الله - alláh, *Hind.*). From (al, ar. the + iláh, ar. god). Means worthy of adoration. Name of God as opposed to his ninety-nine attributes, which connected together in a certain order form the rosary of the Mahomedans, ending with Allah as the hundredth.——(1) The following are the attributes. They are divided into glorious and terrible. All are used with Abd [q.v.] to make common Mahomedan lacabs [q.v.], now used often in the sense of simple alams [q.v.].——*Adl* (عدل - adl, Hind.). From (adala, ar. to act uprightly). Just.——*Afoo* (عفو - afú, Hind.). From (afá, ar. to efface). Pardoner.——*Aleem* (علیم - alím, Hind.). From (alima, ar. to know). Omniscient.——*Ally* (علی - alí, Hind.). From (ala, ar. to become high). Exalted.——*Aukhir* (آخر - ákhir, Hind.). From (akkhara, ar. to put back). Last.——*Azeem* (عظیم - azím, Hind.). From (azima, ar. to become great). Great.——*Azeez* (عزیز - azíz, Hind.). From (azza, ar. to become strong). Who overcomes everything. Mighty.——*Badee* (بدیع - badí, Hind.). From (bida, ar. novel). Incomparable. Originator of creation not after the fashion of anything pre-existing.——*Barr* (بر - barr, Hind.). From (barra, ar. to be kind or righteous). Very benign. Righteous.——*Baseer* (بصیر - basír, Hind.). From (basira, ar. to see). All seeing. Seer.——*Bauky* (باقی - báki, Hind.). From (baká, ar. to endure). Eternal.——*Bauree* (باری - bárí, Hind.). Maker.——*Bausit* (باسط - básit, Hind.). From (basata, ar. to spread). Enlarger of means of subsistence, diffuser of souls in bodies. Spreader.——*Bautin* (باطن - bátin, Hind.). From (batn, ar. belly). Knower of secrets. Hidden.——*Bauyis* (باعث - báis, Hind.). From (baasa, ar. to revive). Quickener.——*Cabeer* (کبیر - kabír, Hind.). From (kibr, ar. great). Great.——*Careem* (کریم - karím, Hind.). From (karuma, ar. to be generous). Generous.——*Cawder* (قادر - kádir, Hind.). From (kadira, ar. to be strong). Powerful.——*Cooddoos* (قدوس - kuddús, Hind.). From (kadasa, ar. to sanctify). Holy.——*Futtauh* (فتاح - fattáh, Hind.). From (fataha, ar. to open). Opener of gates of sustenance. Accomplisher.——*Ghaffar* (غفار - ghaffár, Hind.). From (ghafara, ar. to cover). Forgiver.

——*Ghafoor* (غفور - ghafúr, Hind.). From (ghafara, ar. to cover). Forgiving.——*Ghany* (غنى - ghaní, Hind.). From (ghaná, ar. to be free from want). Independent.——*Hafeez* (حفيظ - hafíz, Hind.). From (hafiza, ar. to preserve). Guardian.——*Hakeem* (حكيم - hakím, Hind.). From (hakuma, ar. to know). Wise. ——*Haleem* (حليم - halím, Hind.). From (haluma, ar. to forbear). Clement.——*Humeed* (حميد - hamíd, Hind.). From (hamada, ar. to praise). Praised.——*Haseeb* (حسيب - hasíb, Hind.). From (hasaba, ar. to count). Reckoner.——*Haudy* (هادى - hádí, Hind.). From (hudá, ar. to guide). Guide.——*Haukim* (حاكم - hákim, Hind.). From (hakama, ar. to restrain). Ruler.——*Hukk* (حق - hakk, Hind.). From (hakka, ar. to become just). Really-existing; unchangeable in nature. Unchangeable.——*Hye* (حى - haí, Hind.). From (hai, ar. to live). Living.——*Jabbaur* (جبار - jabbár, Hind.). From (jabara, ar. to compel). Almighty supreme.——*Jaleel* (جليل - jalíl, Hind.). From (jalla, ar. glorious). Majestic.——*Jawmy* (جامع - jámi, Hind.). From (jamaa, ar. to collect). Collector.——*Kahhaur* (قهار - kahhár, Hind.). From (kahara, ar. to overcome by violence). Dominant.——*Kaubiz* (قابض - kábiz, Hind.). From (kabaza, ar. to grasp). Withholder of subsistence. Punisher of tyrants.——*Kavee* (قوى - kaví, Hind.). From (kuva, ar. to be strong). Strong.——*Keiyoom* (قيوم - kaíyúm, Hind.). From (kauma, ar. to stand up). Subsisting.——*Khabeer* (خبير - khabír, Hind.). From (khabara, ar. to have knowledge). Aware. ——*Khaufiz* (خافض - kháfiz, Hind.). From (khafaza, ar. to lower). Abaser.——*Khaulik* (خالق - khálik, Hind.). From (khalaka, ar. to create). Creator.——*Lateef* (لطيف - latíf, Hind.). From (latafa, ar. slender). Subtle.——*Majeed* (مجيد - majíd, Hind.). From (majada, ar. to glory). Glorious.——*Mateen* (متين - matín, Hind.). From (tanna, ar. to stay). Firm. ——*Maujid* (ماجد - májid, Hind.). From (majada, ar. to glorify). Glorious.——*Maulik* (مالك - málik, Hind.). From (milk, ar. property). King.——*Maulik ool moolk* (مالك الملك - málikulmulk, Hind.). From (málik, ar. lord + mulk, ar. kingdom). Lord of the world.——*Mauny* (مانع - máni, Hind.). From (manaa, ar. to forbid). Withholder.——*Moakhir* (موخر - muakhkhir, Hind.). From (akkhara, ar. to put back). Deferer. ——*Mohee* (محى - muhí, Hind.). From (hai, ar. to live). Restorer.——*Moheemin* (مهيمن - muhímin, Hind.). From (hamana, ar. to protect). Protector.——*Mohsee* (محصى - muhsí, Hind.). From (hasí, ar. to count). Comprehender.——*Moiz* (معز - muiz, Hind.). From (azza, ar. to become great). Honorer.——*Mokaddim* (مقدم - mukaddim, Hind.). From (kadama, ar. to go before). Bringer forward.——*Mokeet* (مقيت - mukít, Hind.). From (kava, ar. to become strong). Strengthener.——*Momeet* (مميت - mumít, Hind.). From (mata, ar. to die). Killer.——*Momin* (مومن - múmin, Hind.). From (amn, ar. safety). Giver of security.——*Moobdee* (مبدى - mubdí, Hind.). From (badá, ar to originate). Originator.——*Mooctadir* (مقتدر - muktadir, Hind.). From (kadr, ar. power). Prevailing. ——*Mooghny* (مغنى - mughní, Hind.). From (ghaná, ar. free from want). Enricher.——*Moojeeb* (مجيب - mujíb, Hind.). From (vajaba, ar. to approve). Approver.——*Mooksit* (مقسط - muksit, Hind.). From (kist, ar. equity). Equitable.——*Moontakim* (منتقم - muntakim, Hind.). From (nakama, ar. to chastise). Avenger.——*Moosowir* (مصور - musawwir, Hind.). From (saur, ar. to form). Fashioner.——*Mootakabbir* (متكبر - mutakabbir, Hind.). From (kibr, ar. great). Great.——*Mootally* (متعالى - mutaálí, Hind.). From (ulu, ar. high). Most sublime. ——*Mootee* (معطى - mutí, Hind.). From (atá, ar. to give). Giver.——*Moozil* (مذل - muzil, Hind.). From (zalla, ar. to demean). Destroyer.——*Moyeed* (معيد - muíd, Hind.). From (áda, ar. to return). Restorer.——*Naufy* (نافع - náfi, Hind.). From (nafa, ar. to be useful). Profiter.——*Noor* (نور - núr, Hind.). From (nára, ar. to shine). Light.——*Owval* (اول - awwal, Hind.). From (avila, ar. to precede). First.——*Raheem* (رحيم - rahím, Hind.). From (rahima, ar. to pity). Compassionate.——*Rahman* (رحمان - rahmán, Hind.). From (rahima, ar. to pity). Merciful.——*Rakeeb* (رقيب - rakíb, Hind.). From (rakaba, ar. to look). Guardian.——*Raoof* (رؤف - raúf, Hind.). From (ráfa, ar. to pity). Kind.——*Rasheed* (رشيد - rashíd, Hind.). From (rashada, ar. to guide aright). Director.——*Roufy* (رافع - ráfi, Hind.). From (rafa, ar. to elevate). Exalter. ——*Ruzzauk* (رزاق - razzák, Hind.). From (razaka, ar. to provide). Provider.——*Saboor* (صبور - sabúr, Hind.). From (sabara, ar. to endure). Patient.——*Salaam* (سلام - salám, Hind.). From (salama, ar. safe). Saviour.——*Samad* (صمد - samad, Hind.). From (samada, ar. to go to); from recourse being had to Him in exigencies. Eternal.——*Samee* (سميع - samí, Hind.). From (samia, ar. to hear). Hearer.——*Shaheed* (شهيد - shahíd, Hind.). From (shahada, ar. to bear witness). Knower.——*Shakoor* (شكور - shakúr, Hind.). From (shakara, ar. to thank). Grateful.——*Towaub* (تواب - tauwáb, Hind.). From (tába, ar. to repent). Acceptor of repentance.——*Vakeel* (وكيل - wakíl, Hind.). From (vakala, ar. to entrust). Advocate.——*Vaurs* (وارث - váris, Hind.). From (irs, ar. to inherit). Inheritor.——*Wadood* (ودود - wadúd, Hind.). From (wadda, ar. to love). Loving.——*Wahaub* (وهاب - wahháb, Hind.). From (wahaba, ar. to excel in liberality). Bestower.——*Walee* (ولى - walí, Hind.). From (valí, ar. to be near). Patron.——*Wally* (والى - wálí, Hind.). From (valí, ar. near). Governor.——*Wauhid* (واحد - wáhid, Hind.). From (ahad, ar. one). One. ——*Waujid* (واجد - wájid, Hind.). From (wajada, ar. to discover). Finder.——*Wausya* (واسع - wási, Hind.). From (wasa, ar. to extend). Comprehensive.——*Zar* (ضار - zárr, Hind.). From (zarra, ar. to harm). Distresser.——*Zauhir* (ظاهر - záhir, Hind.). From (zahara, ar. apparent). Evident.——*Zool jalaul o walikraum* (ذوالجلال والاكرام - zuljalálowalikrám, Hind.). From (zu, ar. master + jalál, ar. majesty + ikrám, ar. honor). Lord of Majesty and Liberality.——(2) *Allah hafiz* (الله حافظ - alláhháfiz, Hind.). From (háfiz, ar. guardian). God protect you. Expression used at parting.——*Allah ki coodrat* (الله کی قدرت - alláhkíkudrat, Hind.). The power of god.——*Allah o acbar* (الله اكبر - alláhuakbar, Hind.). From (akbar, ar. great). God is great. Common exclamation.

ALLEPPEY (ആലപ്പുഴ - álappuzha, *Mal.*). From (ála, mal. broad + puzha, mal. river). Greek *βάρις*. Town, Port, Judge's head-quarters; Travancore state, Quilon division, Ambalapoya tal.; pop. 22,768; lat. 9° 30′; long. 76° 23′; from Ambalapoya N.N.W. 8 miles; from Bombay S.S.E. 692 miles; from Cauttore S. 5 miles; from Cochin S. 33 miles; from Cottayam W.S.W. 14 miles; from Nagarcoil N.W. 115 miles; from Paravore S. 46 miles; from Poracaud N. 10 miles; from Quilon N.N.W. 44 miles; from Trivandrum N.N.W. 80 miles. Chief sea-port town of Travancore, seat of Commercial agent to Travancore government. On coast midway between Cochin and Quilon. The town lies on narrow strip of sea-coast between backwater and sea, and has a canal running from the former through it till within a few yards of the sea. Two good roads run along the banks of the canal from east to west, and the bazaars, merchants' godowns and places of business are situated on them. It communicates southward with Quilon and Trivandrum, northwards with Cochin, by canals parallel to coast and backwaters. Excellent anchorage always available, for although there is no protecting headland, a mud bank of about 1½ miles in length breaks the force of the roughest seas. This natural breakwater has shifted slightly within the last century. A similar deposit exists at Naracal. Light on the beach about one cable inland. Lat. 9° 30′ 0″; long. 76° 19′ 0″. White, revolving. 17 miles. Visible from all directions seaward. Masonry round white tower. To guide vessels to the smooth water anchorage during the south-west monsoon. Contains a very varied population, including even Arabs, Negroes, and Malays. Bartolomeo records that Alleppey was opened to foreign trade in 1762 and mentions the canal. In 1809 a detachment of European soldiers and Company's sepoys, who had halted here on their way up the coast, were massacred by the Nayars. Alleppey is the chief depôt of the Travancore government for the sale of forest produce, chiefly cardamoms. Is a place of considerable foreign trade. European merchants have settled here, and coir-matting and other industries are extensively carried on. Trade is chiefly in teak, cocoanuts, coir or cocoanut fibre, betel-nut, vegetable produce, coffee, ginger, fish, pepper, cardamoms, &c. The rajah has an establishment for building small craft.

ALLIGATOR (اليگيٹر - aligetar, *Hind.*). From Spanish lagarto. Anglo-indian for large lacertine amphibia of rivers.——*Alligator apple* (ولايتى پهل - viláitíphal, Hind.). Title from being eaten by alligators. Same as anona palustris.——*Alligator catfish* (ಮರವೆ - marave, Can.; మార్పు - márpu, Tel.; ମଗୁରା - magurá, Oor.). Oor. from (makara, san. alligator). Clarias magur, siluridæ [kizhautty], physostomi, teleostei, pisces [matsyam, 35], of naturalists [jantoo]. Specific name from oor. Alias Clarias batrachus, marpus, punctatus; Macropteronotus batrachus, magur; Silurus anguillaris, batrachus. Upper jaw the longer; head shagreened superiorly and covered with fine granules; two depressions on the head; dingy green or brownish superiorly, becoming lighter beneath; vertical fins usually with reddish margins; fresh and brackish waters of plains; lives long after removal from native element, being amphibious; attains foot and half in length; as food nourishing. No other common species here.——*Alligator pear* (ولايتى سيب - viláitíseb, Hind.). Title corruption of mexican, ahuacatl. Hind. means foreign pear. Title otherwise Avocado pear, Midshipman's butter, Subaltern's butter. Botanically Persea gratissima, gærtn., lauraceæ [vriesham, 111]. Alias Laurus persea. West indian bush. Fruit in outward appearance like a very large green pear; in centre is a stone about size of a walnut; the fleshy part of fruit around stone is of a bright yellow color, of the consistency of firm butter, flavor of a fresh walnut. Fruit gives an oil. Cf. Nanmuh.——*Alligator's nose* (भुइकुवाळे - bhuikuválé, Conc.; ನೀರುಗನಗಲು - níruganagalu, Can.; ನಿರುಗನ್ನ - nírugannéru, Tel.; മുതലമൂക്ക - mutalamúkku, Mal.; කිඹුල්වැන්න - kimbulvanna, Singh.; முதலைப்பூண்டு - muthalaippúndu, Tam.). Title from form of root. Conc. means ground pumpkin, cucurbita maxima, duch. Can. from (níru, can. water + ganagalu, can. nerium odorum, soland.). Tel. from (níru, tel. water + gannéru, tel. nerium odorum, soland). Mal. from (mutala, mal. alligator + múkku, mal. nose). Singh. from (kimbulá, singh. alligator + venna, singh. form). Tam. from (muthalai, tam. alligator + púndu, tam. plant); from form of root. Tam. also (áttalari), meaning river + nerium odorum, soland; (níralari), meaning water + nerium odorum, soland. Title otherwise Auttalary, Water gannair. Botanically Polygonum [water gannair] barbatum, willd., polygonaceæ [vricsham, 110]. Herb; stems several, erect, slender, smooth, 3–4 feet, joints slightly swelled; leaves lanceolar, smooth; racemes terminal, long, short peduncled; fascicles remote; flowers rose-colored, numerous; seeds triangular, dark and shining; flowering all year; common on banks of streams and water-courses. Leaves used in infusion in colic; seeds carminative. Another species is glabrum.

ALLIPOORAM (అల్లిపురము - allipuramu, *Tel.*). From (alli, tel. lily flower, nymphæa lotus, linn. + pura, san. town). Zemindarry, Village; Vizagapatam dist., Vizagapatam tal.; lat. of village 17° 43′; long. 83° 19′; from Vizagapatam N. 1½ miles; from the sea W. 2 miles. Suburb of Vizagapatam.

ALLOOR (అల్లూరు - allúru, *Tel.* allúr*). From (alláreddi, tel. proper name + úru, tel. village). Original name Panta alloor, meaning crops + alloor, in contradistinction to Aukoola alloor, meaning leaves + alloor in Ongole talook.—"*a*" Deputy tahsildarry, Nellore district. Pay Rs. 70.—"*b*" Village, Headquarters of Deputy tahsildar; Nellore dist., Nellore tal.; pop. 6,575; acres 20,918; lat. 14° 41′; long. 80° 06′; from Madras N. 110 miles; from Naidoopett N.N.E. 54 miles; from Nellore N.N.E. 17 miles; from Ongole S. 55 miles; from the sea W. 6 miles. Fine tank, improved by Sungam project. Large Shiva temple. Station of American baptist mission.

ALLY (علی - alí, *Hind.*). From (ala, ar. to become high). Eminent. Attribute of god [allah]. Name of son-in-law and companion of the prophet and the fourth caliph. The subsequent dispute as to the nature of his succession gave rise to the schism between the shiahs and soonnees [q.v.]. His titles are Asadoollah, Ghaulib, Hyder, Moortezah, Sufder, &c. Now common Mahomedan alam [ism].——*Ally ahmed* (علی احمد - alíahmad, Hind.). Double alam.——*Ally aubkhan* (علی خان - aliábkhán, Hind.). Alam + alaumat.——*Ally dost* (علی دوست - alídost, Hind.). Friend of Ally. Alam + term of devotion, like abd, mostly taken by Shiahs.——*Ally moosey razah* (علی موسی رضا - alímúserazá, Hind.). Triple alam.

ALMIRAH (الماری - almárá, *Hind.*; அலுமாரி - alumári, *Tam.*). From Gr. ἀρμαρὴ and Latin armorium, an armoury, through Portuguese almario; in old English ombry. Wardrobe, chest of drawers, sometimes book-case.——*Almauracoonair* (అల్మారాకోనేరు - almárákóneru, Tel.). From (kóneru, tel. pond). A square well into which steps descend.

ALOE (कुमारी - kumárí, *San.*; कोरफड - kórap'hada, *Mahr.*; लोलिसरु - lólisaru, *Conc.*; نبات الصبر - nabátussibr, *Ar.*; درخت صبر - darakhtisibr, *Pers.*; کماری - kumárí, *Hind.*; کنور - kanwar, *Dec.*; ಕತ್ತಾಳೆ - kattále, *Can.*; నాళిసర - nálisara, *Too.*; కలబంద - kalabanda, *Tel.*; കറ്റാഴ - kattázha, *Mal.*; කුමාරි - kumári, *Singh.*; கற்றாழை - kattázhai, *Tam.*). Title from syriac ('elwai). San. means maiden; plant with cool leaves. Mahr. from (kurá, mahr. eye + p'hada, mahr. pinnate leaf); from form of leaf. Conc. from (lóle, can. sticky + sara, can. string); from juice. Ar. from (nabát, ar. plant + sibr, ar. aloe). Pers. from (darakht, ar. tree + sibr, ar. aloe). Hind. from sanscrit. Can. from tamul. Too. from (lóle, can. sticky + sara, can. string). Tel. from (kaliyu, tel. to mix with + bandana, tel. mucilage); from slimy pulp. Mal. from tamul. Singh. from sanscrit. Tam. from (kal, tam. stone + tázhai, tam. screw-pine, pandanus odoratissimus, linn.); from hard blades of leaves. San. also (kantala), meaning thorn plant; (kanyá), meaning maiden. Ar. also (sabbárá). Dec. also (kalbandá). Greek ἀλόη. Title otherwise Demon leaf, Maiden plant, Stone screw-pine. Botanically the Aloe genus, liliaceæ [vricsham, 136]. Succulent plants, of liliaceous habit; stem short; leaves fleshy; flowers arranged in erect spikes or clusters; fruit membranous, consisting of three cells, each containing a great number of seeds. Leaves of several species furnish a bitter malodorous resinous juice, which when inspissated forms the drug aloes. The commercial kind of aloes are:—"*a*" Socotrine, Turkey, or Extract of spiked, from aloe socotrina, lamb.—"*b*" Genuine hepatic, Bombay, or East indian, from the same.—"*c*" Barbadoes, from aloe vulgaris, lam.—"*d*" Cape and Caballine, from several species.—"*e*" Mocha, from the socotrine species, being the refuse of the market.—"*f*" Indian so called, not East indian, from various indian species, especially aloe indica, royle, and aloe litoralis, koen.;—"*g*" Curacoa, from aloe vulgaris, lam. Socotrine aloes is reddish brown, its surface shining, structure transparent, fracture shelly, taste very bitter, the powder is of bright yellow color. Genuine hepatic aloes, produce of the same, differs in being opaque and olive-colored. Barbadoes aloes is in common usage termed hepatic, it is exported in gourds, ranges in color from dark-brown or black to red or liver-color, fracture dull or glossy, odour disagreeable, and increased by breathing upon the surface, powder dull olive-yellow. Cape aloes is deep brown, shining, of greenish tint and resinous fracture, edges transparent and ruby-colored, powder greenish-yellow, odour strong. Caballine aloes is now no longer found in commerce. Common bazaar aloes is black, brittle, of semi-vitreous fracture. Aloes are obtained by making transverse incisions through the leaves, and allowing the juice to drop out; this is evaporated to dryness by a gentle heat. In small doses, aloes used as a stomachic tonic; in larger doses purgative, and indirectly emmenagogue; locally applied, dissolved in glycerine, as a stimulant application in skin diseases; although aperient, yet unlike other cathartics the effect is not increased if given in large doses beyond a certain point; both aloe indica, royle, and aloe litoralis, koen., are in the pharmacopœia of india; common bazaar aloes is too impure for medical use. In veterinary practice:—purgative 3 to 5 drachms; alterative 1 drachm with 2 drachms of gentian every morning, until the bowels are acted upon; 1 drachm of ginger powder to each bolus. Various species of Agave, especially agave americana, l., are popularly called aloe; these are plants of mexico; botanically genus agave differs from genus aloe; from a chemical point of view also there is no analogy between the two [american aloe, bastard aloe]. A fourcroya also is called aloe [foreign aloe]. Again the word Aloes or Lign aloes, in latin Lignum aloes, is used in ancient writings to designate a substance totally distinct from the modern aloes, namely the resinous wood of Aquilaria agallocha, roxb., thymelæaceæ [eaglewood]. There is a Tamul proverb:—கற்றாழை நாற்றமும் பித்தளை வீச்சமும் போகாது—"The ill odour of the aloe and the bad smell emitted from brass will not leave them." There is another:—கற்றாழை சிறுத்தாலும் ஆனை அடி வைக்காது—"Though the aloe be small, the elephant will not tread upon it"; on account of its spikes. The species of aloe best known to the natives are shown below; all give aloes. Two agaves and a fourcroya also, as above said, come under this title; these give no aloes.——*American aloe* (कालकण्टल - kálakantala, San.; कंटल - kantala, Mahr.; راکس پتا - rákaspattá, Hind., Dec.; ಆನೆಕತ್ತಾಳೆ - ánekattále, Can.; ದಡ್ಡೊಳಿ - daddoli, Too.; రాకాసిమట్ట - rákáshimatta, Tel.; പനങ്കറ്റാഴ - panankattázha, Mal.; ஆனைக்கற்றாழை - ánaikkattázhai, Tam.). Title from native habitat. San. from (kála, san. black + kantala, san. aloe). Hind. from (rákas, hind. demon + pattá, hind. leaf); from large prickly leaf. Can. from (áne, can. elephant + kattále, can. aloe). Tel. from (rákási, tel. she devil + matta, tel. stem). Mal. from (pana, mal. palmyra, borassus flabelliformis, linn. + kattázha, mal. aloe). Tam. from (ánai, tam. elephant + kattázhai, tam. aloe). Hind. also (hathísingár), meaning elephant ornament; (barákanwar), meaning large aloe; (janglíkanwar), meaning wild aloe. Can. also (bhútále), meaning demon + aloe. Tel. also (kittanára), meaning canvas + fibre; (pítikalabanda), meaning dung + aloe. Mal. also (airóppakkaita), meaning european pandanus. Tam. also (alagai), meaning devil, wild aloe. Title otherwise Carata, Century plant, Demon aloe, Elephant aloe, Hill aloe, Palmyra aloe, Pitah fibre plant, Vegetable silk plant, Wild aloe. Botanically Agave americana, linn., amaryllidaceæ [vricsham, 145]. Alias Agave ramosa; Aloe americana. Thick, juicy, dull sea-green colored leaves, arranged in a rosette on a very short stalk; each leaf is 3–6 feet in length; margins are armed with strong, brown, curved spines and end by a straight spine; in this climate plant takes from five to seven years to attain full size, then a stalk shoots up in the centre at a rate of about 6 inches daily, and reaches a height of 20 or 30 feet; the upper half produces candelabra-like branches, which bear numerous yellowish green flowers; after flowering dies; originally a native of america, now common all over s. india; gives no aloes. Expressed juice of the leaves resolvent and alterative, especially in syphilis; leaves sometimes used as poultice; roots alterative and diuretic; substituted for british jamaica sarsaparilla; in pharm. non-officinal; not much used by natives. Much valued as hedge plant; chief importance arises from excellent fibres procured from leaves, called pitah thread. A variety variegata has leaves creamy white, striped with green. The only other species here is Vivipara [bastard aloe].——*Barbadoes aloe* (गृहकन्यका - grihakanyaká, San.; گھی کنور - ghíkanwar, Dec.; කොමාරිකා - kómárika, Singh.). Title from native habitat. San. from (griha, san. house + kanyá, san. aloe); garden vegetable. Dec. from (ghí, hind. ghee + kanwar, hind. aloe); from pulp of leaf. Singh. from (kumárí, san. aloe + ka, san. diminutive suffix). Title otherwise Yellow-flowered aloe. Botanically Aloe vulgaris, lam., liliaceæ [vricsham, 136]. Alias Aloe barbadensis, maculata, officinalis, perfoliata, vera, vulgaris. Stem short; leaves fleshy, stem-clasping, first spreading, then ascending, lanceolate, glaucous-green, flat, obovate, convex below, armed with distant reddish spines perpendicular to the margin; the parenchyma slightly colored brown, and very distinct from the tough leathery cuticle; spike cylindrical-ovate; flowers at first erect, then spreading, afterwards pendulous, yellow, with the three inner segments at the apex somewhat orange, not longer than the stamens. Yields aloes of a dark color and unpleasant odour; in quality inferior to socotrine [bombay aloe]. Pulp of leaf is emollient and cooling; applied in ophthalmia; it produces great cold and acts like ice.——*Bastard aloe* (بنس كيورا - banskeurá, Hind.; బలురక్కసి - balurakkasi, Tel.; மலைக்கற்றாழை - malaikkattázhai, Tam.). Title from low growth. Hind. from (bans, hind. bamboo, bambusa arundinacea, willd. + keurá, hind. pandanus odoratissimus, linn. f.). Tel. from (balupu, tel. plumpness + rakkasi, tel. she devil); from thick, recurved prickly leaves. Tam. from (malai, tam. hill + kattázhai, tam. aloe). Hind. also (ketgí), meaning pandanus odoratissimus, linn. in Hyderabad usage. Tel. also (brahmarákási), meaning bramin + she devil; (brahmarákshasi), meaning bramin + she devil; (samatta); (kittanára), meaning canvas + fibre; (píti-kalabanda), meaning dung + aloe. Tam. also (pirammarágási), meaning bramin + devil. Titles otherwise much the same as americana. Botanically Agave vivipara, linn., amaryllidaceæ [vricsham, 145]. Alias Fourcroya cantala. Stemless; leaves ovate oblong, acute, stiff, thick, recurved spreading, pale green, hoary, prickly at the edges; prickles collected, very small, orange brown; scape branched, bulbiferous of comparatively low growth. Same qualities as americana. Often used as hedge. The only other species here is Americana.——*Bombay aloe* (यवनकुमारी - yavanakumárí, San.; صبارة مقوطری - sabbárahi-sukkotrí, Ar.; درخت صبر سقوطری - darakhtisibrisukkotrí, Pers.; తురకకలబంద - turakakalabanda, Tel.; മക്കിക്കററാഴ - makkik-kattázha, Mal.; துலுக்கக்கற்றாழை - tulukkakkattázhai, Tam.). Title from place of import. San. from (yavana, san. ionia + kumárí, san. aloe); from place of growth. Ar. from (sabbárá, ar. aloe + sukkotrí, ar. socotrine). Pers. from (darakht, pers. tree + sibr, ar. aloe + sukkotrí, ar. socotrine). Tel. from (turaka, tel. turk + kalabanda, tel. aloe); from turkey. Mal. from (makki, mal. mecca, the place + kattázha, mal. aloe). Tam. from (tulukka, tam. turk + kattázhai, tam. aloe); from turkey. Pers. also (darakhtibolisiyáh), meaning black myrrh tree. Title otherwise Caballine aloe, Cape aloe, East indian aloe, Mocha aloe, Socotrine aloe, Spiked aloe, Turkey aloe, Yamauny aloe, Zanzibar aloe. Botanically Aloe socotrina, lamb., liliaceæ [vricsham, 136]. Alias Aloe perfoliata, var. succotrina, vera. Leaves minutely serrated, flowers scarlet at the base, pale in the middle, green at the point; native of socotra. Yields socotrine aloes; also the true hepatic superior aloes and mocha inferior aloes.——*Common indian aloe* (घृतकुमारी - ghritakumárí, San.; तांबडाबोळ - támbadábólá, Mahr.; گهیگوار - ghígavár, Hind.; گهی کنور - ghíkanwar, Dec.; చిన్నకలబంద - chinnakalabanda, Tel.; කොමාරිකා - kómáriká, Singh.; சோற்றுக்கற்றாழை - shóttukkattázhai, Tam.). San. from (ghrita, san. ghee + kumárí, san. daughter); from cooling ghee-like pulp. Mahr. from (támbada, mahr. copper + bóla, mahr. aloe). Hind. and Dec. from (ghí, hind. ghee + kanwar, hind. aloes). Tel. from (chinna, tel. small + kalabanda, tel. aloe). Singh. from (kumárí, san. aloe + ka, san. diminutive suffix). Tam. from (shóru, tam. pulp + kattázhai, tam. aloe). San. also (kadalaka), meaning small-leaved. Hind. also (ghiritkumárí), from sanscrit. Dec. also (kanwárpátha), meaning aloe plant. Tel. also (errakalabanda), meaning red + aloe. Singh. also (ratakomárika), meaning red aloe. Title otherwise Ghee aloe, Indian aloe. Botanically Aloe indica, royle, liliaceæ [vricsham, 136]. Alias Aloe perfoliata, rubescens. Common indigenous plant; leaves thorn-edged, thick, soft, pale-green, crossed with lines of spots; bears dull-red flowers; gives aloes. In native medicine fresh juice of leaves is cathartic and cooling. Pulp of leaves and seeds eaten in famine; leaves give fibre.——*Coromandel aloe* (چهوٹا راکس پٹا - chhotárákaspattá, Hind.; چهوٹا کنور - chhotákanwar, Dec.; ಶೀಮೆಕತ್ತಾಳೆ - shímekattále, Can.; చిన్నకలబంద - chinna-kalabanda, Tel.; ചെറുകററാഴ - cherukattázha, Mal.; சிறுகற்றாழை - shirugattázhai, Tam.). Title from habitat. Hind. from (chhotá, hind. little + rákaspattá, hind. aloe). Dec. from (chhotá, hind. little + kanwar, hind. aloe). Can. from (shíme, can. foreign + kattále, can. aloe). Tel. from (chinna, tel. small + kalabanda, tel. aloe). Mal. from tamul. Tam. from (shiru, tam. small + kattázhai, tam. aloe). Tel. also (chinnarákáshimatta), meaning small agave americana, linn.; (manchikattáli), meaning good + aloe. Title otherwise Sea-side aloe, Small indian aloe. Botanically Aloe litoralis, koen., liliaceæ [vricsham, 136]. A reddish-leaved species growing near east coast; gives aloes; ink prepared from juice.——*Foreign aloe* (சீமைக்கற்றாழை - shímaikkattázhai, Tam.). Title from being american. Tam. from (shímai, tam. foreign + kattázhai, tam. aloe). Tam. also (perundázhai), meaning big + screw-pine, pandanus odoratissimus, linn. f. Title otherwise Fetid aloe, Giant mexican lily, Great aloe. Botanically Fourcroya gigantea, vent., amaryllidaceæ [vricsham, 145]. Gives a fibre used in arts and manufactures; white, strong, fit for cordage or paper, 6–9 feet. No other species here.

ALOES (मुसंबरबोळ - musambarabóla, *Mahr.*; صبر - sibr, *Ar.*; بول سیاه - bolisiyáh, *Pers.*; مصبر - musabbar, *Hind.*; ایلوا - elwá, *Dec.*; ముషాంబరం - múshámbaram, *Tel.*; സന്നിനായകം - sanninâyakam, *Mal.*; කළුවෝල - kaluvóla, *Singh.*; கரியபோளம் - kariyabólam, *Tam.*). Title from syriac ('elwai). Pers. from (bol, pers. myrrh + siyáh, pers. black). Hind. from arabic. Mal. from (nanni, mal. convulsions + náyaka, san. lord). Singh. from (kalu, singh. black + vóla, singh. gum myrrh). Tam. from (karumai, tam. blackness + pólam, tam. myrrh). Ar. also (sibrisukkotrí), meaning socotra aloes. Tam. also (irattabólam), meaning red + myrrh. Title otherwise Cariyabolam, Moosambar. Resinous [raul] inspissated juice of the leaves of Aloe species [aloe]. American aloe plants give no aloes. Aloes wood is a misnomer for Eaglewood [q.v.], that being in turn from Tamul (agil).

ALSEE (अतसी - atasí, *San.*; अळशी - alasí, *Mahr.*; كتان - kattán, *Ar.*; زغیر - zaghír, *Pers.*; السی - alsí, *Hind.* and *Dec.*; ಅಗಸಿಗಿಡ - agasigida, *Can.*; అవిశి - avishi, *Tel.*; ଝୋଟୋ - jhottó, *Oor.*; ചെറുചണം - cheruchanam, *Mal.*; அளி - áli, *Tam.*). Title from hindostany. Hind. from sanscrit. Mal. from (cheru, mal. small + chanam, mal. indian flax, crotolaria juncea, linn.). Tam. from (ál, tam. to cultivate). San. also (umá), meaning weaving, as used in clothing. Hind. also (javas), from mahrattee; (musíná); (tisí), from sanscrit. Dec. also (ambárá). Can. also (alasigida); (atasigida); (háru). Tel. also (gógu); (madanagindzachettu), meaning pleasing + seed + plant; (nallaagisi), meaning black + alsee; (nallavishi), meaning black + alsee. Tam. also (alisi); (áliviraiççedi), meaning linseed plant; (shanal); (shirusanal), meaning small + crotolarea juncea, linn. Title otherwise Flax, Linseed plant, Small hemp. Botanically Linum usitatissimum, linn., lineæ [vricsham, 28]. Alias Linum arvense, mucronatum. Annual, erect, about 15 inches, glabrous slender stem; leaves alternate, lanceolate or linear, acute, entire; panicles corymbose; sepals ovate, acute or mucronate, with scarious or membranaceous margins; petals slightly crenated, three times larger than the calyx; stamens alternate with the petals, having their filaments united together near their basis; capsule roundish, pointed at the apex, five-celled, each cell divided into two partitions, containing a single seed; seeds oval, smooth, brown or white, mucilaginous outside, with oily and farinaceous kernels; flowers blue, bell-shaped. Tenacity of its cortical fibres places it at the head of textile plants; linen and cambric made from it. Has long been cultivated here for the seed and oil; there being no demand for flax till last few years, plant has after harvest usually been burnt, for if it stands it becomes poisonous for cattle; seldom covers whole fields; generally sown along side of fields bordering on roads and cattle-paths, as cattle will not eat it. The linseed-oil is obtained in two ways:—either cold drawn, when it is of a pale color; or by the application of heat at a temperature of not less than 200°, when it is of deeper yellow or brownish color, and is disagreeable in its odour. Linseed-meal is the oil-cake coarsely pulverised. Flax is prepared by steeping the plant, stripping off the bark, and beating so as to separate the fibres. Linseeds are medicinally demulcent, nutritive and emollient; much used in poultice which may be made either of the seed simply ground or of the pulverised cake; an infusion of the seeds called linseed tea is demulcent; linseed-oil is aperient, but seldom used as such, chief medicinal use in preparation of carron-oil, applied with cotton to burns and scalds, substituted for british olive oil; oil officinal in pharm.; the products are not much used by hindoos in medicine. Oil-cake given to cattle; unripe capsules eaten by natives; linseed-oil one of chief ingredients in oil varnishes and printer's ink; also used in soft soap; dried stalks of plant used as materials in building houses. Indian substitutes for flax are the following:—Ananas sativus, pine-apple fibre [ananas], susceptible of being split by carding and of being worked as flax; Calotropis gigantea, yercum fibre [yercum], employed in making cambrics, but the mode of picking it from the inner bark has always made it expensive, used for fishing lines, nets, bowstrings, gins for catching large game, and for the braminical cord worn over the right shoulder; Cryptostegia grandiflora, paulay fibre [paulay silk cotton], similar to yercum; Tylophora asthmatica, coorinjah fibre [indian ipecacuanha] containing strong white fibre. There are three forms of the linum plant, with white, red, or brown seeds; the white-seeded is best. No other species here.

ALTAMGHAH (التمغا - altamghá, *Hind.*). From (al, turk. red + tamghá, turk. a stamp). A royal grant under seal.

ALVANDAR (ஆளவந்தார் - álavandár, *Tam.*). From (ál, tam. to rule + vandán, tam. he who came). Hindoo 2nd or pers. name [peyar]. A Tamul poet. Wrote Tamul poetical version of Sanscrit Nyauna vausishtam; the standard work on Vedantism in South india. Is in 2,055 stanzas. Example:—அத்தமியாதசோதியருக்கநயனவிலாதாய் மெத்தியபிணியிலாதாய் மேவரும்பிறப்பிலாதா யெத்தலங்களினுமென்றுமியாவுமாயாவுஞ்செய்து முத்தியுமாகியோங்கு முதற்பரம்பொருளொன்றுண்டு. "There is a supreme "being; he is the sun who shines with unreflected light with- "out setting, he is infinite, he is free from infirmity, he is not "subject to birth, he is everywhere and at all times, he is all "and the creator of all, he is the final beatitude itself."

ALWAR (ஆழ்வார் - ázhvár, *Tam.*). From (ázh, tam. to be profound). Title of the 12 ancient devotees of Vishnoo, and generally a Veishnava title. Hindoo 2nd or pers. name [peyar]. The Alwars were born in various places and lived in different times. The Veishnavas on their arrival in Southern india had to dispossess the Sheivas, and the contest frequently took the form of public disputation, recorded examples of which were at Villipoottore in the Pandyan kingdom, at Warriore in the Chola kingdom, and at Shreepermatore in Tondeimundalam. The Veishnavas also occupied themselves in translating portions of the Vedas into Tamul poetry, now known as the Tirmozhy, Dravida prabandham, or Naulauyira prabandham; and the Alwar were the chief of these authors. A kind of deification has been assigned to them by viewing them as incarnations, of Vishnoo's arms, ornaments, or attendants. See vol. I (76). The 12 were as follows.——*Aundaul* (गोदा - gódá, San. ஆண்டாள் - ándál, Tam.). San. means born of the earth; counterpart of Seetay who was born of the furrow. Tam. means she who ruled. The daughter of Periyalwar, as born out of his Toolsy garden in Shreevillipoottore. Otherwise Shoodicodoot nautchy. She was a poetess and composed two poems Tirpauvay and Tirmozhy consisting of 173 stanzas in praise of Vishnoo, which now form part of Naulauyira prabandham.——*Bhootatt alwar* (भूतयोगी - bhútayógí, San.; பூதத்தாழ்வார் - púthattázhvár, Tam.). From (bhúta, san. devotee). Born in Mauvellipore. Contemporary with Poygay alwar. Considered incarnation of the mace borne in one hand by Vishnoo. He composed the second Tirvantaudy of 100 stanzas of Naulauyira prabandham.——*Coolashekhara alwar* (कुलशेखर - kulashékhara, San.; குலசேகராழ்வார் - kulaségarázhvár, Tam.). From (kula, san. family + shékhara, san. crest-jewel). Otherwise Coolashekhara permaul. A Chera king born in Colly city. He personates cowstoobham or the chest pendent of Krishna. A Cshatriya skilled in Tamul and Sanscrit; composed Permaul tirmozhy of 105 stanzas in Tamul, now a portion of Naulauyira prabandham, and Moocoondamaulay in Sanscrit.——*Mathooracavy alwar* (மதுரக்கவியாழ்வார் - mathurakkaviyázhvár, Tam.). Means sweet poet. Bramin in Pandyan kingdom in Tiroocolore, near Nangoonairy. Supposed to be incarnation of Veinateyan, composed Cunninoon shirtaumboo of 11 stanzas.——*Nummalwar* (நம்மாழ்வார் - nammázhvár, Tam.). Means our alwar. Otherwise Caurimauran, Shadagopan and Vacoolaubharanan. Born in Tirnagary on the Tamrapurny. A Vellaulan considered an incarnation of Senamoodelly one of the Vellaula saints; composed Tirvrittam of 100 stanzas, Tirvausiriya vrittam of 7 stanzas, Periya tirvantaudy of 87 stanzas, and Tirvye mozhy of 1,102 stanzas.——*Periyalwar* (विष्णुचित्त - vishnuchitta, San.; பெரியாழ்வார் - periyázhvár, Tam.). From (periya, tam. great). San. means Vishnoo + mind. Otherwise Garoodalwar. A bramin. Incarnation of the eagle vehicle of Vishnoo. Born in Shreevillipoottore. He lived in the time of Vallabhadeva pandyan of Madura, who gave him the title of Puttarpiraun or lord among the learned. He found a female child in a bush and devoted her to temple service. She is called in Tamul Aundaul or Shoodicodoot nauchiyaur and in Teloogoo Amoocta maulyada. He composed Tirpallaundoo of 12 stanzas and Tirmozhy of 461.——*Peyalwar* (भ्रान्तयोगी - bhrántayógí, San.; பேயாழ்வார் - péyázhvár, Tam.). From (péy, tam. wild). San. means mad sage; from his action and gesticulation. Born at Mylapore. Incarnation of Nandacam or Krishna's sword. Contemporary with Bhootatt alwar and Poygay alwar; composed the third Tirvantaudy of 100 stanzas.——*Poygay alwar* (कासारयोगी - kásárayógí, San.; பொய்கையாழ்வார் - poygaiyázhvár, Tam.). From (poygai, tam. pool). San. means pond sage. Incarnation of Paunchajanyam, the chunk of Vishnoo. Born at Conjeeveram. He began the Tirmozhy. Contemporary with Bhootatt alwar and Peyalwar, composed the first Tirvautaudy of 100 stanzas.——*Tirmangay alwar* (திருமங்கையாழ்வார் - tirumangaiyázhvár, Tam.). From (tiru, tam. sacred + mangai, tam. woman, meaning lakshmí); from his marriage with Coomoodavully, the lily handed woman, supposed to be a divine impersonation. Vishnoo's bow incarnate. Attached to the temple at Shreerungam. A Veydan or hunter, born in Tirvauly tirnagary near Shiyally. He obtained the title of Naurcavy permaul from the skill in composing the four kinds of poems Ausoo cavy or impromptu verse, Madhoora cavy or sublime verse in sweet style, Chitra cavy or varied verse, and Vistaura cavy or extended poem or epics like Bhauratam and Ramayanam. He constructed the temple at Shreerungam and caused the masons at last in lieu of receiving wages to be drowned in the Cauvery, since called Colladam or place of slaughter. Composed Periya tirmozhy of 1,814 stanzas, Tircooroom taundagam of 20 stanzas, Tirnedoom taundagam of 30 stanzas, and Tirvalookkootirkye, Periya tirmadal and Shiriya tirmadal of 227 stanzas.——*Tirmazhisay alwar* (भक्तिसारमुनि - bhaktisáramuni, San.; திருமழிசையாழ்வார் - tirumazhisaiyázhvár, Tam.). From (tirumazhisai, tam. place so called). San. means faith + excellence + sage. Born at Tirmazhisay, otherwise Maheesauram. Incarnation of Soodarshanam or the discus weapon. Composed Tiroochanda vrittam of 120 stanzas and Naunmookhan tirvantaudy of 96 stanzas.——*Tirpaunalwar* (திருப்பாணாழ்வார் - tiruppánázhvár, Tam.). From (tiru, tam. holy + pán, tam. song). Otherwise Paun permaul or music sage. Born in Warriore on the Cauvery. Incarnation of Shreevatsam or the curling mark of good fortune on Vishnoo's breast. A pariah. Composed Amalan audipiraun or Vishnoo the first god in 10 stanzas.——*Tondaradipody alwar* (भक्ताङ्घ्रिरेणुमुनि - bhaktánghrirénumuni, San.; தொண்டரடிப்பொடியாழ்வார் - tondaradippodiyázhvár, Tam.). Title from (tondan, tam. devotee + adi, tam. foot + podi, tam. dust); dust of the foot of devotees, a humble appellation. San. means same. Surnamed Viprauarrain or bramin Vishnoo, as bramin by birth and from his devotion to Vishnoo. Born in the Chola country. Incarnation of Vishnoo's garland veijayanty. Composed Tirmaulay of 45 stanzas and Tirpally yezhootchy in 10 stanzas [matam].

ALWYE (ആലുവാ൦ യ് - áluváy, *Mal.*). From (áru, mal. river + váya, mal. mouth).—"*a*" Village, Sanitarium; Travancore state, Cottayam division, Aulangaud tal.; lat. 10° 07; long. 76° 24′; from Aulangaud E. 4 miles; from Trivandrum N.N.W. 117 miles; from the sea E. 11 miles. On the Travancore-Cochin frontier. A sanitarium on the Periyaur, resorted to from Malabar. Annual fair. Considerable trade. Baskets, basket toys, and umbrellas of palmyra leaves manufactured.—"*b*" River; Travancore and Cochin states; Greek ψευδόστομος ποταμός. Named by the early Portuguese the Fiera d'Alva. A branch of the Periyaur, which it joins at Alwye town. Cochin derives drinking water from this.

AMA (अमा - amá, *San.*). With.——*Amavausyay* (अमावास्या - amávásyá, San.). From (above + vas, san. to dwell). Conjunction of sun and moon. Complement between end of fourteenth lunar tithy and exact conjunction of sun and moon in any month. Compare Arcaindoo sangamam which is instant of true conjunction. An infant born during period of Amavausyay holds life by uncertain tenure. The day so named is sometimes a day prior to actual new moon. It is however always the last day of the Krishna pacsham. A fast day for Bramins and orthodox Hindoos; lunar festival [pundigay, 3e]. There is a Tamul proverb—நித்தியம் கிடைக்குமா அமாவாசைச் சோறு?—"May new moon fare be expected daily?"; the household eat only once during day, but the food is superior and prepared with cooking utensils kept for sacred purposes. If a Bramin is present he offers oblations of sesamum grain and water to manes of dead, naming each in order as far back as the third generation [shrauddham]. The ancient Romans had the same ceremony at the Ides. Distinguish from Divasam or Tithy which is an anniversary on any date commemorative of parent, grand parent or great-grand parent. Compare the Mahaulya [pundigay, 6d] amavausyay and Mahaulya pacsham [pundigay, 6d], which come only once a year. The new moon days are specially kept by Tamuls in Audy or July, Auny or June and Tye [mausam] or January [jyotisham].

AMAH (ஆமா - ámá, *Tam.*). From Port. A wet nurse.

AMAL (عمل - amal, *Hind.*; அமல் - amal, *Tam.*). From (amala, ar. to transact). Transaction; administration. Business.——*Amaldar* (عملدار - amaldár, Hind.). From (dár, pers. holder). Factor. Native collector of revenue among Marhattas; retained now in Mysore and Hyderabad.——*Amaljaury* (عمل جاری - amaljárí, Hind.). From (jári, ar. execution). Execution, particularly of a decree.——*Ameel* (عامل - ámil, *Hind.*). Much the same as Amaldar; answers to a Deputy tahsildar in the British system.——*Amla* (عمله - amlah, Hind.). Plural of (ámil, ar. functionary). The clerical establishment of a court or office. Applied particularly to vernacular as distinguished from English department.

AMALAUPOORAM (అమలాపురం - amalápuram,* *Tel.*). From (amala, san. pure + pura, san. town).——**(1)** Talook, Godavery district. Tahsildar's pay Rs. 200. Area 506 square miles. Population 256,081 largely Braminical. Language Teloogoo. Central coast talook of district. Bounded north by Gowtamy branch of Godavery and Ramchendrapooram talook; south by sea; east by Coringa division and sea; and west by Vasishtam branch of Godavery and Narsapore and Tanookoo talooks. Flat and even land. Soil alluvial. There is no special industry. Cocoanut oil is manufactured. Trade is principally in cocoanuts, areca nuts, cocoanut oil, paddy, grains, oil seeds, cloths and cotton twist. The central part is noted for its cocoanut, areca nut and plantain plantations. These are exported by sea or by the navigable canals to Cocanada, Rajahmundry, Ellore, and other parts of the district. Irrigated by main canals from the anicut, the Lolla canal, Gunnavaram and Amalaupooram canals. These are navigable and supply water to the various branch irrigation channels. The branches of the Godavery known as the Vasishtam, Gowtamy, Old gowtamy, Veinateyam, and Cowshiky water the talook. In the bed of the Vasishta godavery are valuable islands formed by accumulated deposits of silt. Zemindarries:—Anautavaram, Buntoomilly, Craupa, Goottinadivy, Gopalpore, Keshanacoorroo, Maugaum, Moongondapollem, Nadavapully, Palivela, Potecoor, Shirasavilly sauvaram, Soorasauny yaunam, Vilasa, Zanoopully. Places of archæological interest:—Bendamoorlunka, Bodasacoorroo, Lutchmy polavaram, Moocteshwaram, Moommadivaram, Palivela,

Rauly. Principal Trig. stations :—Balsootippa, Candicooppa, Catacoorroo, Cherooklunka, Cottapollem beacon, Cottapully, Dantacoor, Deocootam, Depoolunka, Mogullamory, Pedalunka, Soollapully, Soorasauny yaunam beacon. The leading places, &c., in the talook are the following.——*Amalaupooram* (అమలాపురం - amalápuram, Tel.) ; see below.——*Ambaujipett* (అంబాజీపేట - ambájipéta, Tel.). From (ambáji, tel. proper name + péta, tel. suburb). Village ; lat. 16° 35′ ; long. 81° 59′ ; from Amalaupooram W. 4¼ miles ; from Cocanada S.W. 32 miles ; from the sea N. 12 miles. Hamlet of Mautsavaram. Large weekly market every Wednesday.——*Anautavaram* (అనాతవరము - anátavaramu, Tel.). From (ananta, san. vishnu + pura, san. town). Zemindarry, Village ; lat. of village 16° 36′ ; long. 82° 06′ ; from Amalaupooram N. E. 4 miles ; from Cocanada S.S.W. 26 miles ; from the sea N. 10 miles. Peshcush Rs. 1,755.——*Annampully* (అన్నంపల్లి - annampalli, Tel.). From (annamma, tel. proper name + palli, tel. village). Village ; lat. 16° 40′ ; long. 82° 11′ ; from Amalaupooram N.E. 12 miles ; from Cocanada S.S.W. 20 miles ; from the sea W. 12 miles. Site of a proposed lock.——*Balsootippa* (బలుసుతిప్ప - balusutippa, Tel.). From (balusu, tel. canthium parviflorum, lamk. + tippa, tel. mound). Trig. station ; lat. 16° 37′ 48·67″ ; long. 82° 18′ 25·13″ ; from Bramhasamvedyam N.N.E. 10 miles.——*Bendamoorlunka* (బెండమూర్లంక - bendamúrlanka, Tel.). See sep. title.——*Buntoomilly* (బంటుమిల్లి - bantumilli, Tel.). From (bantu, tel. servant + milli, tel. village). Zemindarry, Village ; acres 266 ; lat. of village 16° 35′ ; long. 82° 10′ ; from Amalaupooram E. 7½ miles ; from Cocanada S.S.W. 26 miles ; from the sea N. 6½ miles. Peshcush Rs. 200.——*Candicooppa* (కందికుప్ప - kandikuppa, Tel.). From (kandi, tel. pigeon pea, cajanus indicus, spr. + kuppa, tel. heap). Trig. station ; lat. 16° 35′ 31·00″ ; long. 82° 15′ 11·11″ ; from Pullamcoorroo E.S.E. 1 mile.——*Catacoorroo* (కటకుర్రు - katakurru, Tel.). From (kataka, san. hill slope + kurru, tel. hamlet). Trig. station ; lat. 16° 33′ 24·38″ ; long. 82° 12′ 21·33″ ; from Nadavapully S.S.W. 1¼ miles.——*Cherooklunka* (చెరుకులంక - cherukulanka, Tel.). From (cheruku, tel. sugar-cane, saccharum officinarum, linn. + lanka, tel. island).—"*a*" Trig. station ; lat. 16° 40′ 6·36″ ; long. 82° 18′ 18·84″ ; from Bramhasamvedyam N.N.E. 13 miles.—"*b*" Trig. station ; lat. 16° 40′ 14·99″ ; long. 82° 18′ 11·41″ ; from Bramhasamvedyam N.N.E. 13 miles.——*Cottapettah* (కొత్తపేట - kottapéta, Tel.). See sep. title.——*Cottapollem beacon* (కొత్తపాలెము - kottapálemu, Tel.). From (kotta, tel. new + pálemu, tel. fortified village). Trig. station ; lat. 16° 35′ 14·55″ ; long. 82° 19′ 14·73″ ; from Goottinadivy S.S.E. 6½ miles.——*Cottapully* (కొత్తపల్లి - kottapalli, Tel.). From (kotta, tel. new + palli, tel. village). Trig. station ; lat. 16° 32′ 37·26″ ; long. 82° 10′ 27·43″ ; from Cautrenicona S.W. 3 miles.——*Cowshiky* (కౌశిక - kaushika, Tel.). See sep. title.——*Craupa* (క్రాప - krápa, Tel.). Zemindarry, Village ; lat. of village 16° 38′ ; long. 82° 07′ ; from Amalaupooram N.E. 6 miles ; from Cocanada S.S.W. 24 miles ; from the sea N. 12 miles. Peshcush Rs. 2,362.——*Dantacoor* (దంతకూరు - dantakúru, Tel.). From (danta, san. ivory + úru, tel. village). Trig. station ; lat. 16° 34′ 50·28″ ; long. 82° 13′ 44·36″ ; from Geddanapully E.N.E. 1½ miles.——*Deocootam* (దేవకూటము - dévakútamu, Tel.). From (déva, san. god + kúta, san. peak). Trig. station ; lat. 16° 28′ 34·50″ ; long. 82° 3′ 45·64″ ; from Saumantacoorroo W. 2 miles.——*Depoolunka* (దేపులంక - dépulanka, Tel.). From (déva, san. god + lanka, tel. island). Trig. station ; lat. 16° 38′ 35·63″ ; long. 82° 15′ 33·84″ ; from Polavaram S.E. 1¼ miles.——*Godavery* (గోదావరి - gódávari, Tel.). See sep. title.——*Goottinadivy* (గుత్తినదివి - guttinadivi, Tel.). From (gutti, tel. cluster + adavi, tel. forest). Zemindarry, Village ; acres 34,822 ; lat. of village 16° 41′ ; long. 82° 17′ ; from Amalaupooram E.N.E. 17 miles ; from Cocanada S. 18 miles ; from the sea W. 6½ miles. Peshcush Rs. 651. Temple of Hanoomanta ; noted for dairy produce.——*Gopalpore* (గోపాలపురు - gópálapúru, Tel.). From (gopáludu, tel. proper name + úru, tel. village). Zemindarry, Village ; lat. of village 16° 42′ ; long. 81° 51′ ; from Amalaupooram N.W. 16 miles ; from Cocanada W.S.W. 33 miles ; from the sea N. 23 miles. Peshcush Rs. 18,439.——*Keshanacoorroo* (కేశనకుర్రు - késhanakurru, Tel. kesanakurru*). From (késhana, tel. proper name + kurru, tel. hamlet). Zemindarry, Village ; lat. of village 16° 38′ ; long. 82° 12′ ; from Amalaupooram E.N.E. 12 miles ; from Cocanada S.S.W. 22 miles ; from the sea W. 9 miles. Peshcush Rs. 11,381.——*Lolla* (లొల్ల - lolla, Tel.). Means ploughed ground leveller. Village ; acres 1,494 ; lat. 16° 49′ ; long. 81° 58′ ; from Amalaupooram N.W. 21 miles ; from Cocanada W.S.W. 30 miles ; from the sea W. 29 miles. Gives its name to a canal.——*Maugaum* (మాగాము - mágámu, Tel.). From (mahá, san. great + gráma, san. village). Zemindarry, Village ; lat. of village 16° 37′ ; long. 82° 06′ ; from Amalaupooram N.N.E. 4½ miles ; from Cocanada S.S.W. 25 miles ; from the sea N. 12 miles. Peshcush Rs. 1,745.——*Mautsavaram* (మాత్సవరము - mátsavaramu, Tel.). From (mátsa, tel. barren + pura, san. town). Town ; pop. 5,125 ; acres 2,331 ; lat. 16° 36′ ; long. 81° 59′ ; from Amalaupooram W.N.W. 5¼ miles ; from Cocanada S.W. 32 miles ; from the sea N. 12 miles.——*Mocaladibba* (మోకలదిబ్బ - mókaladibba, Tel.). From (móka, tel. grove + dibba, tel. mound). Village ; lat. 16° 38′ ; long. 82° 15′ ; from Amalaupooram E.N.E. 14 miles ; from Cocanada S. 22 miles ; from the sea W. 5¼ miles.——*Mogullamory* (మొగల్లమోరి - mogallamóri, Tel.). From (mogali, tel. fragrant screw-pine, pandanus odoratissimus, linn. + móru, tel. peak). Trig. station ; lat. 16° 27′ 40·96″ ; long. 82° 1′ 9·16″ ; from Bendamoorlunka N.N.E. 2 miles.——*Moocteshwaram* (ముక్తేశ్వరం - muktéshvaram, Tel.). From (mukta, san. blessed + íshvara, san. shiva, the lord). Village, Place of pilgrimage ; lat. 16° 39′ ; long. 82° 04′ ; from Amalaupooram N.N.E. 5½ miles ; from Cocanada S.S.W. 24 miles ; from the sea N. 14 miles. Ancient temple with Stala pooraunam. It faces Kotipully on the other side of the river.——*Moommadivaram* (ముమ్మిడివరము - mummidivaramu, Tel.). From (mummadi, tel. three shares + pura, san. town). Village ; acres 6,096 ; lat. 16° 38′ ; long. 82° 09′ ; from Amalaupooram N.E. 8 miles ; from Cocanada S.S.W. 22 miles ; from the sea N. 11 miles. Ancient Vishnoo temple. Sub-registrar's office. Abounds in gardens.——*Moongondapollem* (ముంగొండపాలెము - mungondapálemu, Tel.). From (munu, tel. front + konda, tel. hill + pálemu, tel. fortified village). Zemindarry, Village ; acres 578 ; lat. of village 16° 36′ ; long. 81° 57′ ; from Amalaupooram W.N.W. 6¼ miles ; from Cocanada S.W. 32 miles ; from the sea N. 14 miles. Peshcush Rs. 545.——*Mundapully* (మండపల్లి - mandapalli, Tel.). From (manda, san. saturn + palli, tel. village). Village ; pop. 420 ; lat. 16° 44′ ; long. 81° 54′ ; from Amalaupooram N.W. 14 miles ; from Cocanada W.S.W. 28 miles ; from the sea N. 24 miles. Cowshiky takes its origin here. Temple of Mandeshwaran whose idol is bathed in gingelly oil every Saturday.——*Nadavapully* (నడవపల్లి - nadavapalli, Tel.). From (nadava, tel. porch + palli, tel. village). Zemindarry, Village ; lat. of village 16° 36′ ; long. 82° 12′ ; from Amalaupooram E. 10 miles ; from Cocanada S.S.W. 24 miles ; from the sea W. 7 miles. Peshcush Rs. 3,092.——*Palivela* *(పలివెల - palivela, Tel.). Zemindarry, Village ; pop. 6,148 ; lat. 16° 42′ ; long. 81° 55′ 34″ ; from Amalaupooram N.W. 12 miles ; from Cocanada S.W. 29 miles ; from the sea N. 20 miles. Peshcush Rs. 18,894. Proprietary village on the Amalaupooram canal. Cottapettah is a hamlet. Temple with inscriptions.——*Pedalunka* (పెదలంక - pedalanka, Tel.). From (pedda, tel. large + lanka, tel. island). Trig. station ; lat. 6° 36′ 26·36″ ; long. 82° 13′ 9·43″ ; from Mooroomulla S.S.E. 4 miles.——*Pitchicalunka* (పిచ్చికలంక - piççikalanka, Tel.). See sep. title.——*Point godavery* (గోదావరిమోన - gódávarimona, Tel.). See sep. title.——*Potecoor* (పోతుకుర్రు - pótukurru, Tel.). From (pótu, tel. bull + kurru, tel. hamlet). Zemindarry, Village ; lat. of village 16° 37′ ; long. 82° 07′ ; from Amalaupooram N.E. 6 miles ; from Cocanada S.S.W. 24 miles ; from the sea N. 11 miles. Peshcush Rs. 910.——*Rauly* (రాళి - ráli, Tel.). From (ráyi, tel. stone). Village ; acres 4,255 ; lat. 16° 47′ ; long. 81° 50′ ; from Amalaupooram N.W. 20 miles ; from Cocanada W.S.W. 31 miles ; from the sea N. 28 miles. Ancient temple of Camandaleshwarasawmy with inscriptions. Temple of Keshava sawmy built by Chola king. Idol beautifully carved.——*Shirasavilly sauvaram* (శిరసవిల్లిసావరము - shirasavillisávaramu, Tel.). From (shiras, san. head + palli, tel. village + ságara, san. ocean). Zemindarry, Village. Peshcush Rs 300.——*Soollapully* (సుళ్ళపల్లి - sullapalli, Tel.). From (sudi, tel. whirlpool + palli, tel. village). Trig. station ; lat. 16° 29′ 57·77″ ; long. 82° 7′ 1·64″ ; from Gopavaram S. 2 miles.——*Soorasauny yaunum* (సూరసానియానము - súrasániyánámu, Tel.). From (súri, tel. the learned + sáni, tel. dancing girl + yánámu, tel. village of that name). Zemindarry, Village ; lat. of village 16° 29′ ; long. 82° 08′ ; from Amalaupooram S.S.E. 8 miles ; from Cocanada S.S.W. 32 miles ; from the sea N. 1¾ miles. Peshcush Rs. 529. The village was granted as an inam to a dancing girl named Soorasauny. Hence the name. Trig. station in lat. 16° 28′ 42·58″ ; long. 82° 8′ 18·72″ ; from Soollapully E.S.E. 3¼ miles.——*Teertaulamondy* (తీర్థాలమొండి - tírt'hálamondi, Tel.). From (tírt'ha, san. sacred water + mudi, tel. knot). Village ; lat. 16° 41′ ; long. 82° 22′ ; from Amalaupooram E.N.E. 22 miles ; from Cocanada S.S.E. 18 miles ; from the sea W. 1 mile. Near the embouchure of the Gowtamy branch of the Godavery. Temple of Bheiravasawmy. A place of pilgrimage.——*Vasishta godavery* (వసిష్ఠగోదావరి - vashisht'hagódávari, Tel.). See sep. title.——*Veinateyam* (వైనతేయము - vainatéyamu, Tel.). See sep. title.——*Vilasa* (విలస - vilasa, Tel.). Zemindarry, Village ; lat. of village 16° 37′ ; long. 82° 04′ ; from Amalaupooram N.N.E. 3½ miles ; from Cocanada S.S.W. 26 miles ; from the sea N. 12 miles. Peshcush Rs. 1,440.——*Zanoopully* (జనుపల్లి - dzanupalli, Tel.). From (dzanumu, tel. hemp, crotalaria juncea, linn. + palli, tel. village). Zemindarry, Village ; acres 411 ; lat. of village 16° 35′ ; long. 82° 03′ ; from Amalaupooram N. 1 mile ; from Cocanada S.S.W. 29 miles ; from the sea N. 10 miles. Peshcush Rs. 218.——**(2)** Town, Head-quarters of talook and District moonsif ; Godavery dist., Amalaupooram tal. ; pop. 9,254 ; acres 4,228 ; lat. 16° 34′ ; long. 82° 03′ ; from Cocanada S.S.W. 30 miles ; from Coonavaram S.E. 83 miles ; from Ellore E. 60 miles ; from Madras N.N.E. 260 miles ; from Narsapore E.N.E. 23 miles ; from Rajahmundry S.S.E. 33 miles ; from the sea N. 9½ miles. Noted for manufacture of cocoanut oil. The canal of this name is one of the three divisions of the central main canal, and is navigable as far as Amalaupooram, one mile above which the Bendamoorlunka canal is taken off.

AMANJY (அமிஞ்சி - amiñji, *Tam.*). Tam. from Hind. Compelled labor [amjy].

AMAR (अमर - amara, *San.*). From (a, san. not + mri, san. to die). Immortal.——*Amar sing* (امرسنگھ - amarsing, Hind.). From (above + simha, san. lion). The immortal lion. Proper name [peyar].

AMARAM (அமரம் - amaram, *Tam.*). From (amar, tam. war). The command of a thousand foot. A grant of revenue by a ruler on condition of military service.

AMAT (امت - amat, *Hind.*). From Arabic. Feminine of Abd, and similarly used [ism].——*Amat ool careem* (امت الکریم - amatulkarím, Hind.). Slave of the generous or of God.

AMAUN (امان - amán, *Hind.*). From (amana, ar. to be safe). Security. Part of lacab; as Amaun oon nissa, the peace of ladies.——*Amaunat* (امانت - amánat, Hind.). From (amn, ar. safety). Anything given in trust. Corruptly anaumat. Part of lacab; as Amaunat ally, given in trust to Ally. Amaunatgaud is a hawker.——*Amauny* (امانی - amáni, Hind.). From (amn, ar. safety). Anything held in trust, or under official management. The following is a Hindostany proverb:—امانی آبادانی اجارہ اجاڑ - "Government collection is prosperity, "farming is depopulation." Amauny reddy is a reddy having no mirassy right, appointed during temporary absence of mirassy holder. See vol. I, 112.

AMBAH (अम्बा - ambá, *San.*). From (amb, san. to go). Mother. Title of goddesses. Parvaty specially. Suffix in female proper names of the superior castes as Avayaumbah, Madhooraumbah. The Tamul Ammah is the title to more ordinary persons [ammah]. Distinguish Amman.——*Ambashuncaran* (அம்பாசங்கரன் - ambásangaran, Tam.). From (shankara, san. shiva, the pleasure maker). Hindoo 2nd or pers. name [peyar].——*Avayaumbah* (அவயாம்பா - avayámbá, Tam.). From (abhaya, san. fearless). Epithet of Doorga. Female name among Sheivites. Familiarly Avayam.

AMBALAM (അമ്പലം - ambalam, *Mal.*; அம்பலம் - ambalam, *Tam.*). From (ampu, mal. friendship + ála, mal. house). Drav. form of San. Sabhay. A public place of meeting in a village. Temple on W. coast. Suffix in place names; as Ayacaurambalam, meaning toll-gatherer + public place. Suffix in proper names among non-bramins, as Ponnambalam [peyar]. There is a Tamul proverb:—நுளையன் பேச்சு அம்பலமேறாது—"The words of a fisherman will not reach the assembly." Derisive of justice.——*Ambalacauran* (அம்பலக்காரன் - ambalakkáran, Tam.). From (káran, tam. door). Chairman of meeting. The head of a village, particularly of Shoodra village. A titular appellation of the Cullar tribes of the Tondiman's country. A caste numerous in Trichinopoly; less so in Tanjore, Salem, Coimbatore, and Madura; total for Presidency, about 156,000 [jauty].——*Ambalacottah* (അമ്പലക്കോട്ട - ambalakkótta, Mal.). From (above + kótta, mal. fort). Village; Cochin state, Moocoondapooram tal. Early seminary of Jesuits, who published here in 1577 first printed work in Malayalam.——*Ambalapady* (അമ്പലപ്പടി - ambalappati, Mal.). From (above + pati, mal. step). A certain step in a temple just outside sanctuary, on which only particular persons are entitled to sit. The right to this becomes a valuable dignity. The claim to it is derived from ancestry, but the dignity is saleable. It is however understood that it cannot be disposed of except to a person of the proper caste and necessary respectability. The Ooroyma is the office to which is attached the general superintendence of the affairs of a temple; a person who has attained the Ambalapady dignity in the village holds invariably also that of Ooroyma, that is to say he is the Ooraulan of the temple. But there are Ooraular who are not Ambalapadies. An Ambalapady is in a more secular sense the chairman of a public meeting [maryauday].——*Ambalapoya* (അമ്പലപ്പുഴ - ambalappuzha, Mal.). From (puzha, mal. river). Sanscrit name (ambarápagápura), meaning sky + river + town; town of the celestial ganges.—"*a*" Talook, Travancore state, Quilon division. Population 93,104. Sub-divided into 12 praverties and contains 72 caras or villages. Bounded N. by Shertala talook and Vembanaud lake, E. by Chungacherry and Tiroovalla talooks, S. by the Caurtigapully talook, and W. by the Indian ocean. Greatest length N. to S. is 15 miles and greatest breadth E. to W. is 10 miles. A great portion lies under water for part of year. Soil is alluvial and productive. Limited industry and trade in native cloths. The cultivation begins by draining and bunding the fields, and with the natural damp and one or two falling rains the paddy reaches maturity.—"*b*" Town, Tahsildar's and Moonsif's station; Travancore state, Quilon division, Ambalapoya tal.; pop. 7,243; lat. 9° 23′; long. 76° 25′; from Alleppey S.S.E. 8 miles; from Cottayam S.S.W. 17 miles; from Madras S.W. 370 miles; from Nagarcoil N.W. 108 miles; from Paravore S. 53 miles; from Quilon N.N.W. 36 miles; from Trivandrum N.N.W. 73 miles. On the coast. The country around consists of low-lying paddy lands. Connected by canal with Alleppey. Till 1754 capital of Ambalapoya, otherwise known as Chumbagacherry principality, which was added to the Travancore territories at the time of Martaunda vurma maharajah by his Dalavoy diwaun ramayyan. Famous in history as the scene of Fra Paolo Bartolomeo's protest against the compulsory attendance of Christians at Hindoo festivals. Pagoda of some importance. The interior apartment is covered with plates of copper and on top are three gilt spiral ornaments with a large gilt pillar in front of the gate. Great annual festival, held in April, attracts some local trade.——*Ambalavausy* (അമ്പലവാസി - ambalavási, obl.; അമ്പലവാസി - ambalavási, pers. sing.; അമ്പലവാസികൾ - ambalavásikal, pers. pl., Mal.). From (vas, san. to dwell). Caste-title. Temple servants in Malabar. Called Antaraulam in Travancore. A sort of Levite. Descendants of Numboory fathers and lower caste mothers; form intermediate class between the Numboories and the Nayar. Following Maroomakkatoyem. The following are different classes of them:—Chaukky, Gooroo, Mauraun, Mootad, Numbidy, Numby, Pooshpacan, Vauriyan. The lowest are the Mauraur. Numbers of all Ambalavausies about 18,000 in Malabar. See vol. II, 100 [jauty].

AMBASAMOODRAM (அம்பாசமுத்திரம் - ambásamuttiram, *Tam.* ambásamudram*). From (ambá, san. párvati, the mother + samudra, san. sea).——**(1)** Talook, Tinnevelly district. Tahsildar's pay Rs. 225. Area 481 square miles. Population 183,616. Language Tamul. W. of district. Bounded S.E. by Nangoonairy talook, E. by Tinnevelly talook, N. by Tencausy and Shuncaraneinarcoil talooks, and W. by the ghauts. The ghaut range is accessible by mountain paths from Cadayam, Alwarcoorchy, Paupanausam and Shingamputty. The southern portion is rocky and soil sandy, producing poor dry crops, shaumay and gram, and occasional palmyra topes. North of the Tamrapurny, except near the ghaut range, the high dry lands have the same character, the soil being derived partly from decayed gneiss, but largely from overlying quartz, and being of a red sandy character frequently impregnated with soda. At the foot of the ghauts and for five or six miles eastward red clays and loams of better quality are found. This portion is better wooded than the more eastern and southern portions. High quartz ridge forms the water-shed between the Tamrapurny and Chittaur. The whole of the Tamrapurny valley and portions of those of its affluents get the benefit of the south-west monsoon and obtain a first or caur crop; while the north-east monsoon commencing in October, supplies these lands again for a second crop. The villages of the river valley supply other parts of the talook with rice. Money-lending is pursued. Weaving has declined before the supply of piece-goods from Europe. Puttamaday mats, made of fine rushes found on the river banks and in tank beds, are in demand. Valuable timbers are derived from the forests. The talook contains the principal sources of the Tamrapurny, which rises on either side of Agastya mullay. From the north of this mountain flows the Serviaur which joins the Tamrapurny about four or five miles before it quits the mountain range at Paupanausam. Other tributaries of the Tamrapurny are to the north the Gatananuddy and the Ramanuddy draining considerable mountain areas and to the south the Manimoottaur and the Putchayaur. Shingamputty zemindarry in the south-west corner is well watered from the Manimoottaur. The Putchayaur fills a few tanks during the north-east monsoon. The irrigation system is very ancient. There are numerous anicuts across the Tamrapurny and its affluents. The Cunnadiyan is the finest anicut on the river. Zemindarries;—Oorcaud and Shingamputty. Places of archæological interest:—Alwarcoorchy, Ambasamoodram, Amboor, Auladiyore, Bramhadesam, Culladacoorchy, Paupanausam, Ravanasamoodram, Shermadevy, Shivasheilam, Tentribhoovanam, Tirpoodaymaroothore, Veeravanallore, Veirauvicoolam. The leading places, &c., in the talook are the following.——*Agastya mullay* (அகத்தியமலை - agattiyamalai, Tam.). See Pothigay.——*Alwar coorchy* (ஆழ்வார்க்குறிச்சி - ázhvárkkuriççi, Tam.). From (ázhván, tam. vaishnava devotee + kuriççi, tam. village). Village; pop. 4,829; acres 3,504; lat. 8° 48′; long. 77° 26′; from Ambasamoodram N.W. 7 miles; from Tinnevelly W. 21 miles. On left bank of Gatananuddy and on road to Tencaushy. Irrigated by Gatananuddy and Ramanuddy, affluents of Tamrapurny. Shiva and Vishnoo temples. Car festival in March.——*Ambasamoodram* (அம்பாசமுத்திரம் - ambásamuttiram, Tam.). See below.——*Aryanayagipooram* (அரியநாயகிப்புரம் - ariyanáyagippuram, Tam.). From (ariyanáyagi, tam. proper name + pura, san. town). Village; pop. 3,156; acres 6,531; lat. 8° 43′; long. 75° 35′; from Ambasamoodram E.N.E. 7 miles; from Tinnevelly W. 10 miles. On left bank of river Tamrapurny. Irrigated by Tamrapurny and Gatananuddy. Shiva temple. Car festival in March.——*Baunateertam* (வாணதீர்த்தம் - vánathírttam, Tam.). From (bána, san. asura so called + tírt'ha, san. place of sacred water). Waterfall; from Ambasamoodram W.S.W. 20 miles; from Tinnevelly W.S.W. 40 miles. On Tamrapurny [aroovy].——*Bramhadesam* (பிரம்மதேசம் - pirammathésam, Tam.). From (brahma, san. the god + désha, san. country). Greek *Βράχμη*. Village; pop. 3,279; acres 923; lat. 8° 44′; long. 77° 29′; from Ambasamoodram N. 2 miles; from Tinnevelly W. 17 miles. Ancient place referred to in ancient inscriptions. Formerly cusbah of talook of same name, Old and sacred temple, surrounded by a high granite wall, with two large gopoorams. A fine reservoir, surrounded by flight of steps and has a small spire in the centre. Annual car festival.——*Cadayam* (கடையம் - kadaiyam, Tam.). From (kadaiyan, tam. one of the kadai caste). Town; pop. 9,345; acres 7,138; lat. 8° 50′; long. 77° 24′; from Ambasamoodram N.N.W. 10 miles; from Tinnevelly W.N.W. 22 miles. On road to Courtallam from Ambasamoodram. Two Shiva and one Vishnoo temples. Among the Maravar habitations is a gigantic figure of potters' ware to whom offerings of poultry are made. Roman catholic church. Jaggery, coarse cloths, reed mats, and gunnies manufactured.——*Culladacoorchy* (கல்லடைக்குறிச்சி - kalladakkuriçci, Tam.). From (kal, tam. stone + adai, tam. to enclose + kuriççi, tam. village); from the masonry anicut, near the village. Town; pop. 13,602, including Terkk culladacoorchy, which practically is a part of the town; acres 6,122; lat. 8° 41′; long. 77° 30′; from Ambasamoodram S.S.E. 1½ miles; from Tinnevelly W. 16 miles. Wealthy trading and agricultural town on right bank of Tamrapurny and Cunnadiyan channel. Chiefly inhabited by Bramin landholders. Old stone column with inscription on high road near old fort.——*Culyauny teertam* (கலியாணிதீர்த்தம் - kaliyánith*í*rttam, Tam.). From (kalyání, san. párvatí, the auspicious deity + tírt'ha, san. a place of sacred water). Falls; lat. 8° 42′; long. 77° 25′; from Ambasamoodram W. 6 miles; from Tinnevelly W. 22 miles. Waterfall on Tamrapurny at Paupanausam [aroovy].——*Cunnadiyan* (கன்னடியன் - kannadiyan, Tam.). Means a Canarese man; after the constructor. Anicut; lat. 8° 41′; long. 77° 29′; from Ambasamoodram S.W. 1¾ miles; from Tinnevelly W. 18 miles. On Tamrapurny.——*Gatananuddy* (கடனாநதி - kadanánathi, Tam.). From (ghatana, san. junction + nadí, san. river). River; tributary of the Tamrapurny.——*Kodamailalagyan* (கோடமேலழகியன் - kódamélalagiyan, Tam.). From (kódam, tam. boundary + mél, tam. on + azhagu, tam. beauty). The beautiful village on the boundary. Ancient village; from Ambasamoodram W. 6 miles; from Tinnevelly W. 22 miles. Site of an anicut.——*Krishnaupooram* (கிருட்டிணப்புரம் - kiruttináppuram, Tam.). From (krishna, san. the god + pura, san. town). Village; pop. 3,585; lat. 8° 48′; long. 77° 25′; from Tinnevelly W.N.W. 22 miles. On left bank of Varattaur and on road to Courtallam. Shiva temple with fine sculptures. Chiefly inhabited by Lubbay weavers. Reed mats also made.——*Manimoottaur* (மணிமுத்தாறு - manimuttáru, Tam.). From (mani, tam. beauty + muttu, tam. pearl + áru, tam. river). River; Tributary of the Tamrapurny.——*Nathiyoony* (நதியுண்ணி - nathiyunni, Tam.). From (nadi, san. river + unni, tam. absorber). Ancient village; from Ambasamoodram W.N.W. 2½ miles; from Tinnevelly W. 19 miles. Site of an anicut.——*Oorcaud* (ஊர்க்காடு - úrkkádu, Tam. urkád*). From (úr, tam. village + kádu, tam. forest); tract with many villages. Zemindarry, Village, Head-quarters of a zemindar; pop. 3,182; acres 6,700; lat. 8° 43′; long. 77° 31′; from Ambasamoodram E.N.E. 1 mile; from Tinnevelly W. 15 miles. Peshcush Rs. 12,926.——*Paumbanaroovy* (பாம்பனருவி - pámbanaruvi, Tam.). From (pámbu, tam. snake + aruvi, tam. waterfall); from its appearance at a distance. Waterfall on Tamrapurny. Consists of two falls. This spot is a part of Vicramasingapooram [aroovy].——*Paupanausam* (பாவநாசம் - pávanásam, Tam.). See sep. title.——*Pottalpoothoor* (பொட்டற்புதூர் - pottarbuthúr, Tam.). From (pottal, tam. arid tract + puthu, tam. new + úr, tam. village). Village; pop. 1,734; acres 170; lat. 8° 48′; long. 77° 25′; from Ambasamoodram N.N.W. 8¼ miles; from Tinnevelly W.N.W. 22 miles. On left bank of Varattaur and on road to Courtallam. Given in endowment to a mosque. Four large tombs of Mahomedan priests. Market on Wednesdays. Mats and gunnies made, former by Lubbays.——*Puttamaday* (பத்தமடை - pattamadai, Tam.). From (pattai, tam. shrubbery + madai, tam. channel). Village; pop. 5,385; acres 2,115; lat. 8° 40′; long. 77° 38′; from Ambasamoodram E.S.E. 10 miles; from Tinnevelly W.S.W. 7¾ miles. On Cunnadiyan channel on road from Palamcottah to Paupanausam. Annual car festival and several minor festivals. Roman catholic chapel. Noted for fine reed mats.——*Ramanuddy* (இராமநதி - irámanathi, Tam.). From (ráma, san. the hero + nadi, san. river). River. Tributary of Gatananuddy.——*Serviaur* (சேர்வியாறு - shérviyáru, Tam.). From (shérvai, tam. junction + áru, tam. river). River. Tributary of the Tamrapurny.——*Shermadevy* (சேர்மாதேவி - shérmáthévi, Tam.). See sep. title.——*Shingamputty* (சிங்கம்பட்டி - shingambatti, Tam. singampati*). From (simha, san. lion + patti, tam. village). Zemindarry, Village; pop. of village 1,841; acres 5,003; lat. of village 8° 40′; long. 77° 28′; from Ambasamoodram S.S.W. 3½ miles; from Tinnevelly W.S.W. 17 miles. Peshcush Rs. 8,008.——*Tamrapurny* (தாம்பிரப்பருணி - támbirapparuni, Tam.). See sep. title.——*Tirpoodaymaroothore* (திருப்புடைமருதூர் - tiruppudaimaruthúr, Tam.). From (tiru, tam. holy + pudai, tam. place + marutham, tam. terminalia tomentosa, bedd. + úr, tam. village); from a tree, facing the western entrance of the pagoda, with a circumference of 25 feet. Village, Place of pilgrimage; pop. 1,619; acres 569; lat. 8° 44′; long. 77° 32′; from Ambasamoodram E.N.E. 3½ miles; from Tinnevelly W. 13 miles. At junction of Gatananuddy and Tamrapurny. Temple with unfinished gopooram on east face. South-east of temple is fine reservoir. Bathing takes place on Tye poosham [pundigay, 5a] about January. Car festivals in January. In neighbourhood of village is a stratum of white clay with which Sheiveites besmear themselves. The soil in neighbourhood is irrigated by Cunnadiyan channel.——*Veeravanallore* (வீரவநல்லூர் - víravanallúr, Tam.). From (víraván, tam. a brave man + nal, tam. good + úr, tam. village). Town; pop. 14,785; acres 2,500; lat. 8° 41′; long. 77° 34′; from Ambasamoodram E. 5¼ miles; from Tinnevelly W.S.W. 11 miles. On Palamcottah road. Population chiefly weavers. Old temple with inscriptions. Trade in colored cloths with Palghautcherry and Calicut. Weekly market on Sunday. Roman catholic chapel of St. James.——*Vicramasingapooram* (விக்கிரமசிங்கப்புரம் - vikkiramasingappuram, Tam.). From (vikrama, san. valour + simha, san. lion + pura, san. city). City of Vicrama simhan. Village, Place of pilgrimage; pop. 4,485; acres 5,654; lat. 8° 43′; long. 77° 25′; from Ambasamoodram W.N.W. 4¼ miles; from Tinnevelly W. 20 miles. On road to Paupanausam, and south of a range of low wooded hills. Pagoda with large gopooram over east gate.——(2) Town, Head-quarters of Tahsildar, District moonsif and Sub-registrar; Tinnevelly dist., Ambasamoodram tal.; pop. 9,944; acres 3,295; lat. 8° 43′; long. 77° 29′; from Madras S.S.W. 347 miles; from Palamcottah W. 20 miles; from Shermadevy W. 8 miles; from Shreevillipoottore S.S.W. 57 miles; from Tinnevelly W. 16 miles; from Tuticorin W. 48 miles. Temple, known as Agasteeshwaran coil, with ancient stone pillar. Car festivals twice a year. About one-third of population are Kcikkilar weavers. Cloths and muslins exported through this place to Travancore. Weekly market.

AMBATTAN (அம்பட்டன் - ambattan, *Tam.*). From (amba, san. near + st'há, san. to stand); he who stands near to cure. Originally offspring of a Veisya woman by a Bramin and whose profession is medicine. Caste-title. Tamul barbers. The corresponding terms are Hind. Hajaum; Can. Nayinda; Tel. Mungala; Mal. Vilakkatharavan. Many of them are doctors and surgeons as well, and their women are commonly employed as midwives. Barbers form about 1·2 per cent. of the Hindoo community. The village barber shaves the ryot, cuts his nails, trims his eyebrows and moustache, &c. He is often a musician. He is occasionally called upon to carry a torch before travellers at night [jauty].

AMBAUDY (അമ്പാടി - ampáti, *Mal.*). From (áyan, mal. cowherd + páti, mal. village). Mal. equivalent of sanscrit Gocoolam. Eldest female of the Zamorin's line, as coming originally from that family, worshipping Krishna. Ambaudy covilagam is her palace.

AMBAURY (عماری - amárí, *Pers.*; అంబారి - ambári, *Tel.*). From (amár, pers. inventor's name). A canopied seat. An open one is Howdah.

AMBER (عنبر - ambar, *Hind.*). From Arabic. Greek ἤλεκτρον; Latin Succinum. Fossilized resin of the black poplar. Generally stands in this country for ambergris; see below. For real amber see Karbah.——*Meenamber* (अम्बर - ambara, San.; عنبر - ambar, Ar.; شاه بوی - sháhbúi, Pers.; انبر - ambar, Hind. and Dec.; انبار - anbár, Malay; అంబరు - ambaru, Tel.; മീനമ്പർ - mínambar, Mal.; ම්‍ස්සම්බර - mussambara, Singh.; மீனம்பர் - mínambar, Tam.). San. from (am, san. quickly + vri, san. to surround). Tam. from (mín, tam. fish + ambar, hind. the perfume). Ambergris, meaning grey amber. Ambragrisea of chemists. A solid opaque, generally ash-colored, and brittle, fatty, inflammable substance, variegated like marble, very light, and has when heated a fragrant and singular odour. Is a concretion of the indigestible portions of the cuttle-fish, which form the food of the sperm whale. The nucleus of the mass is generally the horny beaks of these creatures, and the substance itself is found in the intestines of the sperm whale, or on the shores of the seas frequented by this species [hoot]. No other whale is known to be subject to these bezoars. Trading vessels find it floating on the Indian ocean, or adhering to rocks, chiefly among the Moluccas and other islands to the eastward, but also in the Maldives. Esteemed as perfumes, especially by the Mahomedans. Their physicians consider it also as an aphrodisiac. Substituted for British phosphorus. Used as a perfume, a drop or two of the essence mixed with lavender water.

AMBICAY (अम्बिका - ambiká, *San.*). From (amb, san. to go). One who is approached familiarly; mother. Parvaty. See vol. 1 (73). Ambica bhaugan from (bhága, san. portion) is one who has in his person a portion of Parvaty, Shiva. Ambica tanayan from (tanaya, san. son, the extender of the family) is Vigneshwaran, the son of Parvaty and Shiva; also Soobramanyan, their second son.

AMBOOR (అంబూరు - ambúru, *Tel.*; ஆமூர் - ámúr, *Tam.* ambúr*). From (ámai, tam. tortoise + úr, tam. village). Sanscrit name (kúrmapurí), means tortoise town; also (chamúru), means the yak. Greek ἀβούρ. Town; North arcot dist., Vellore tal.; pop. 10,586; acres 6,357; lat. 12° 47′; long. 78° 46′; from

Chittore S.W. 40 miles; from Vellore W.S.W. 30 miles. On south bank of Palaur, at foot of Cadapanuttam pass. Fertile soil. Topes. Railway station is within half a mile. Very ancient town and a Coorumbar stronghold. Lubbay traders settled forty years back. Trade with Mysore. Fort, on almost inaccessible Amboor droog, commands important pass into Carnatic. In 1749 Anwar ood deen, Nawaub of Arcot, was defeated by Moozuffer jung, under its walls. This was the first occasion in which European troops played a conspicuous part in Indian warfare. In 1768, it was gallantly defended by the 10th Regiment of Madras infantry. In 1781 it was captured by Hyder ally and restored by the Treaty of Mangalore. In the expeditions against Mysore in 1792 and 1799, it was occupied as a point of great importance on the line of communications. Fairs Friday.

AMBOOSIE (आम्रपेशी - ámrapéshí, *San.*; अंबोशी - ambóshí, *Mahr.*). Title from mahratta. San. from (ámra, san. mango + péshí, san. peel). Flesh or pulp of green mangoes, cut into oblong pieces and dried in sun; used in curries.

AMBOYNA (انبون - ambún, *Ar.*). Island in Molucca sea, belonging to Dutch.——*Amboyna wood* (شجر انبون - shajriambúnah, Hind.). Title from place of export. Also called Lingo wood, Kyaboca wood. Product of Pterospermum [mooch coondam] species, sterculiaceæ [vricsham, 26]. Fancy wood of various colors; obtained from the knotty excrescences or burrs of the trees; it is sawn in slabs 2 to 4 feet long and 3 to 8 inches thick; resembles the hue of the yew, is very hard and full of curls, the color being reddish-brown, varying to orange; ornamental and used for making small boxes, writing desks, and other fancy work; the wood is brought to singapore by traders, and thence goes to india and europe.

AMEEN (امین - amín, *Hind.*; அமீனா - amíná, *Tam.*). From (amn, ar. safety). A chief officer of Police or Revenue. A confidential agent; Lat. fide commissarius. A Principal sudder ameen was formerly a minor judge. A revenue ameen may be the manager for Government of an estate under attachment, a seller of distrained property, or merely a process server. Distinguish from Ameel [q.v.]. Mahomedan alam meaning faithful; as Syed ameen, alaumat + alam. Also used like Abd; as Ameen ood deen, faithful to religion. Feminine is Ameena, which was name of the prophet's mother [ism].

AMEER (امیر - amír, *Hind.*). From (amr, ar. command). Late Greek ἀμεραῖος. English admiral from (amíralbahr, ar. commander of the sea, dropping last word). A nobleman. The hereditary title of the ruler of Afghanistaun. The plural appears in English as Oomrah [q.v.]. Generally an alam; as Ameer beg, alam + alaumat. Also component part of lacabs; as Ameer ood dowla, prince of the kingdom [ism].——*Ameer ool oomrah* (امیرالامرا - amírulumará, Hind.). From (umará, ar. nobles). Noblest of nobles. Title of Commander-in-Chief.——*Ameer sing* (امیر سنگھ - amírsingh, Hind.). From (singh, mahr. honorific title). Rajah of Tanjore, who succeeded his brother Toolsajee, 1788. Deposed in 1798 for misgovernment. See vol. I, 50; II, 126.——*Ameerzauda* (امیر زادہ - amírzádah, Hind.). From (zádah, pers. born). Son of a prince. Cf. Mirzah.

AMINDIVY (അമിൻദിവി - amindivi, *Mal.*). Means ameen's island. Deputy tahsildarry in the five Laccadive islands which are attached to South canara district [laccadives]. Pay Rs. 70. The principal of the five islands, and the head-quarters of the Deputy tahsildar. A meteorological station.

AMINJICARAY (امجگرا - amjigirá, *Hind.*; அமிஞ்சிக்கரை - amiñjikkarai, *Tam.*). From (amiñji, tam. compulsory service + karai, tam. field). Zemindarry, Village; Chingleput dist., Chingleput tal.; pop. 292; acres 447; lat. of village 12° 33′; long. 80° 10′; from Chingleput S.E. 13 miles; from Sydapett S.S.W. 33 miles; from the sea W. 4¾ miles. Peshcush Rs. 91.

AMJY (امجی - amjí, *Hind.*; అంజి - amji, *Tel.*). Compelled labor. Tamul form is Amanjy.

AMLA (अम्ल - amla, *San.*). Sour.——*Amla shaucam* (अम्लशाक - amlasháka, San.). From (amla, san. sour + sháka, san. plant); from taste. Botanically the Antidesma genus, euphorbiaceæ [vricsham, 118]. Trees or shrubs; leaves alternate, simple, entire; flowers minute, and in spikes; fruit a small one-seeded drupe. The species best known to the natives are:—bunias [nolatauly], diandrum [carpenter's tamarind], ghæsembilla [gasambilla].——*Amlicah* (अम्लिका - amliká, San.). Sour. Plant name common to:—Oxalis corniculata, Phaseolus trilobus, Phyllanthus emblica, Tamarindus indica. See gloss. paragraphs.——*Aumlacam* (आमलक - ámalaka, San.). From (ámla, san. sour); from fruit.—"*a*" Botanically the Phyllanthus genus, euphorbiaceæ [vricsham, 118]. Trees or shrubs, often undershrubs; leaves small and arranged in opposite rows along smaller branches; flowers small, green, often with a yellow or purplish tinge and occur in clusters on edges of leaves; fruit is a small depressed or globular capsule; wood red. The species best known to the natives are:—distichus [brazil cherry], emblica [emblic myrobalan], maderaspatensis [lowly nelly], multiflorus [poolah], nirnri [neeroory], pendulus [white nelly], polyphyllus [forest nelly], reticulatus [netted nelly], urinaria [red neeroory]. Other S. indian species indigenous or naturalized are:—arboreus, asperus, baillonianus, canaranus, cyanospermus, fagifolius, fimbriatus, heyneanus, hohenhackeri, indicus, juniperinoides, lanceolarius, leschenaultii, littoralis, longipes, macraei, macrocalyx, malabaricus, miquelianus, neilgherrensis, nitidus, obliquus, peltandra, perrotetianus, rheedii, rotundifolius, simplex, stellatus, tomentosus, velutinus, wightianus, zeylanicus. —"*b*" Cf. also Flacourtia cataphracta (práchínámalaka), oriental phyllanthus.

AMMAH (அம்மா - ammá, *Tam.*). Dravidian corruption of (ambá, san.). Mother, mistress of the house. Title of respect to females. Affix to female proper names as Annammah, Rungammah [peyar]. This corresponds to Bye among the Mahrattas and Madhwas. In Tooloo the word strangely means father [appan]. Distinguish the Dravidian Amman.

AMMAN (ಅಮ್ಮ - amma, *Can.*; అమ్మ - amma, *Tel.*; അമ്മ - amma, *Mal.*; அம்மன் - amman, *Tam.*). Female of Ayen. The female deity among the Dravidians, always ruling demoniac influences or personages. For every village there is at any rate one temple dedicated to a goddess of this sort. For an analysis of the functions of these deities, see vol. 1 (78) and (81). The title has generally a prefix, as:—Ammannamman, Ancaulamman, Chinnamman, Cunnyamman, Mariyamman, Mootyaulamman, Mullamman, Naugauttamman, Osooramman, Padeivettamman, Periyamman, Polairamman, Ponniyamman, Shellamman, Taundoniyamman, Tooloocaunamman, Yellamman [q.v.]. The Mariyamman of the Tamuls is specially a deity of the small-pox, causing or protecting from that disease. There is a Tamul proverb:—வைசூரி வந்தவர்கள் அம்மா என்று கூப்பிடவேண்டும்—"Those who are attacked with small-pox "must call it the goddess." The representation of an Amman in the temples is generally a black stone or a piece of wood, and seldom an image. A poojarry, who is not a Bramin, is appointed for the daily worship. He anoints the symbol of the deity daily, and puts ashes on her head. For offering he breaks a cocoanut in front of the idol. This is the commonest offering. The villagers make frequent vows to the goddess, promising sacrifices if she fulfils desires, and occasionally they collect money by subscription and celebrate a feast. When any member of a family is seized by sickness, the poojarry is consulted, who announces to the worshipper the offering that must be presented. If cholera or other large epidemic breaks out, the village deity will rise into importance and the sacrificial rite will be more frequently performed. Sacrifice is specially made to the village goddess at sowing time and harvest; also for rain or fair weather. The Amman is brought out from time to time and carried around the village or town [matam].——*Amman coil* (அம்மன்கோயில் - ammangóyil, Tam.). From (above + kóyil, tam. temple). Temple of the village goddess.——*Ammannamma* (అమ్మన్నమ్మ - ammannamma, Tel.). Same as Amman.——*Ammany* (அம்மணி - ammani, Tam.). Familiar form of Amman. Name and title of address among Hindoo females. There is a Tamul proverb:—பொன்மணி அற்றவளை அம்மணி என்பானேன்? "Why should a woman, who has "no gold or ornament be called Ammany?" Pun on Ammany, which also means she who is bare [peyar].——*Ammapett* (அம்மாப்பேட்டை - ammáppéttai, Tam.). From (ammá, tam. village goddess + péttai, tam. suburb). Village; Salem dist., Salem tal.; pop. 7,003; lat. 11° 40′; long. 78° 14′; from Salem E.S.E. 1¼ miles. Suburb of Salem.——*Ammatchy* (അമ്മച്ചി - ammaççi, Mal.). Wife of a rajah on the west coast. Not a member of the royal household, and in nowise associated with the court. Cannot be seen in public with the rajah. Her issue occupy the same position as herself. The word is more commonly Cuttilamma in North malabar [maroomakkatoyem].——*Ammaul* (அம்மாள் - ammál, Tam.). Plural of Amman. Honorific title to females answering to Iyer among male Smartas [peyar]. Very often applied to goddesses.——*Ammavaur* (అమ్మవారు - ammaváru, Tel.). The same.——*Ammay* (அம்மை - ammai, Tam.). The same, especially as small-pox [veidyan].——*Ammayaur coondal* (அம்மையார்கூந்தல் - ammaiyárgúndal, Tam.). Tam. from (ammai, tam. matron + kúndal, tam. woman's hair); from intertwining habit. Title otherwise Virginian silk. Botanically Periploca sp., asclepiadeæ [vricsham, 88]. Plant is medicinally diuretic; gives fibre.——*Ammy* (అమ్మి - ammi, Tel.). A girl. Term of address to women [abby].——*Ammye* (అమ్మాయి - ammáyi, Tel.). Familiar form of Ammy. Term of address to young children of both sexes. Hindoo female proper name [peyar].

AMMAUN (அம்மான் - ammán, *Tam.*). Maternal uncle.——*Ammaun putcharisy* (चित्र - chitra, San.; کھیری - khirí, Hind.; ಅಚ್ಚೆಸೊಪ್ಪು - aççesoppu, Can.; నానబాల - nánabála, Tel.; දදකිරිය - dadakíriya, Singh.; அம்மான்பச்சரிசி - ammánbaççarisi, Tam.). Title from tamul. San. means variegated in color. Hind. from (kshírí, san. milk plant). Can. from (aççe, can. tattoo + soppu, can. leaf); from children marking their hands with milk of leaf stalks while playing. Tel. from (nánu, tel. to soak + pálu, tel. milk); from seeds tasting like raw rice. Singh. from (dada, singh. wild + kíriya, singh. milk plant). Tam. from (ammán, tam. maternal uncle + paççai, tam. green + arisi, tam. rice); uncle is jocose meaning false, and the seeds are something like raw rice. Botanically Euphorbia [milk hedge] indica, lam., euphorbiaceæ [vricsham, 118]. Alias Euphorbia decumbens, hypercifolia. Lightish colored bark; sweetish to the taste; the leaves smell like tea when carefully dried. Juice medicinally astringent and slightly narcotic, used in dysentery; bark purifies the blood; leaves and seeds, given in worm cases and bowel-affections of children. Leaves used as famine food. There are several allied species. Large ammaun putcharisy, otherwise pill-bearing spurge, is euphorbia pilulifera, l., alias hirta, a common weed. Red ammaun putcharisy is euphorbia rosea, retz. Small ammaun putcharisy, otherwise thyme-leaved spurge, is euphorbia thymifolia, burm., alias macrophylla; this is the commonest sort; branches pressing flat on the earth, colored, hairy; leaves opposite, obliquely ovate, serrate; flower axillary, crowded on short peduncles, small, greenish; calyx and corolla each of four semi-lateral parts.

AMMAYANAICKANORE (அம்மயநாயக்கனூர் - ammayanáyakkanúr, *Tam.* ammayanáyakanúr*). From (ammayanáyakkan, tam. proper name + úr, tam. village). Zemindarry, Village, Railway station; Madura dist., Dindigul tal.; pop. 3,820; square miles 97; lat. of village 10° 10′; long. 77° 57′; height 786 feet; from Dindigul S.S.W. 14 miles; from Madura N.W. 23 miles. Zemindarry was one of the five polliems which Hyder failed to resume, but it was afterwards sequestered by Tippoo sultan. On the British occupation, it was restored to its original status as a tributary polliem. Peshcush Rs. 13,668. On the route from Dindigul to Madura. Station for the Pulneys on the Negapatam line. Battle fought here in 1741 decided the fate of Dindigul, which thus fell into the hands of Chundah sahib.

AMOMUM (حماما - hamáma, *Ar.*). From (hamma, ar. to heat); from properties. The wild cardamom [q.v.] genus.

AMOOKRA (அமுக்குரா - amukkurá, *Tam.*). From (amungu, tam. to sink + kurá, tam. webera corymbosa, willd.); from size of plant. Same as Asgand [q.v.].

AMRAUTAM (आम्रात - ámráta, *San.*). From (ámra, san. mangifera indica, linn.). Hog-plum. Botanically the spondias genus, anacardiaceæ [vricsham, 45]. Deciduous glabrous trees, natives of tropical regions; leaves usually crowded at the tips of branches, alternate, odd-pinnate; flowers small; drupe fleshy; stone hard, thick. The species best known to the natives are:—dulcis [otaheite apple], mangifera [wild mango].

AMRAVATTY (அமராவதி - ámarávathi, *Tam.* amarávati*). From (ámra, san. mango tree, mangifera indica, linn. + vat, san. suffix of possession).—"*a*" Mythologically capital of Indran. The name has been applied by the Bramins to more than one town in Southern india [matam].—"*b*" Village, Place of pilgrimage; Kistna dist., Suttenapully tal.; pop. 2,252; acres 2,693; lat. 16° 34′; long. 80° 24′; from Crossoor E.N.E. 14 miles; from Masulipatam W.N.W. 58 miles. On south bank of Kistna. One of chief centres of ancient Vengy kingdom. The celebrated Booddhist stoopam, first discovered by Rajah Vencataudry naidoo's servants in A.D. 1796, stands south of village. Booddhist carvings were hidden under a large mound of earth called Deepauladinney, or mound of lanterns. The various subsequent excavations have laid bare a circular processional path, stone-flagged, with an inner and outer railing of carved marble. At the points of the compass were formerly four small chapels or perhaps entrances with pillars. In the centre must have been a dagoba, but of that there is now no trace. The pillars and slabs and cornices of the railings are covered with sculpture of an astonishing degree of excellence. The sculptures depict scenes in the life of Booddha and various Booddhist emblems and symbols. Inscriptions in the Goopta or Pali character are frequent. The central dagoba was commenced first with an enclosing rail. Subsequently the great outer rail was begun, the place having acquired celebrity. The sculptures of the inner rail were taken in hand, after which decay set in, and nothing further was done. These are the inferences from internal evidence. The central discs of the pillars alone have contained from 6,000 to 7,000 figures. If are added to these the continuous frieze above, and the sculptures above and below the discs on the pillars, there probably were not less than from 120 to 140 figures for each intercolumniation, say 12,000 to 14,000 in all. The inner rail probably contains even a greater number of figures than this, and they are so small as to resemble ivory carving. These figures and the other ornaments show the elaboration and finish of the Sawmy jewellery. Except the great frieze at Nakhon vat in Cambodia, there is not in any other part of the world a mass of sculpture equal in extent to what this must have been when complete. The subject of sculptures are very various:—animals, bulls, elephants, &c., well depicted; feasts, concerts of instruments; scenes from the life of Booddha, &c. This tope is identified with the Averashilah sangharaumam of Hwen thsang, and with the temple of the Diamond sand mentioned in the Tooth relic traditions. Close by the tope is a temple and a mosque for the construction of which many of the marbles from the tope were used. To the west is a mound called Coochy dibba, which probably contains remains. A number of rude stone burying-places, circles, dolmens, &c., are scattered about the neighbourhood especially near the hills, a few miles south-east of the village. In the village on the river bank is the handsome temple of Amareshwaran, built towards the close of last century by Rajah vencataudry naidoo. There was a much older temple here, which was repaired by Anoo vaima reddy of Condaveed in A.D. 1361. Near the temple are the remains of Vencataudry naidoo's palace. Half a mile to the west is the old fort of Dharanicottah on the river. This dates many centuries back, though the age is uncertain. The ancestors of the Reddies of Condaveed, who commenced to rule in A.D. 1328, lived here. On the rocks in the bed of the river opposite the Amareshwarasawmy temple are many rough sculptures and inscriptions. Leaden Andhra coins have been found here. For the country round Amravatty, see Cronnaud [charitram].—"*c*" River; Coimbatore and Trichinopoly districts. Has source in confluence of several jungle streams that run from the N.E. spur of Anamullay and Travancore hills bordering Oodamalpett talook. Flows into Anjanaud valley, whence it debouches into Coimbatore district near villages of Cullaupooram and Chuckragherry, and after flowing E.N.E. for about 140 miles through Oodamalpett, Dharaupooram and Caroor talooks, falls into the Cauvery in lat. 10° 58′ and long. 78° 14′, at Tirmookkoodal at the eastern extremity of Caroor talook on the Trichinopoly boundary. Crossed by seventeen anicuts. Being fed by the S.W. monsoon it flows with some regularity from June to end of August. It fails generally in September, and again increases in the N.E. monsoon till November. It then gradually falls until March, when it is practically dry save for spring channels. Very fully utilized for irrigation throughout its course, which is marked by an almost continuous though very narrow belt of wet land, except in the heart of the Dharaupooram talook. Navigation is possible only for the smallest description of boats. Chief places on its banks are Comauralingam, Dharaupooram and Caroor. Crossed by girder bridge of twenty-one arches at Caroor.

AMROOD (अमृतफल - amritap'hala, *San.*; شجر كمثرى - shajarikummasrá, *Ar.*; درخت امرود - darakhtiamrúd, *Pers.*; ناشپاتی - náshpátí, *Hind.* and *Dec.*). Title from persian. San. from (amrita, san. the undying, nectar + p'hala, san. fruit). Ar. from (shajar, ar. tree + kummasrá, ar. pear). Pers. from (darakht, ar. tree + amrúd, pers. pear). Hind. from (násh, pers. lamentation + pát, pers. leaves). Title otherwise Pear. Botanically Pyrus communis, linn., rosaceæ [vricsham, 49]. Small, thorny tree; thrives well on the neilgherries. Perry is fermented juice of pears. For malus or apple see Seb.

AMSH (अंश - amsh, *San.*). To divide.——*Amsham* (अंश - amsha, San.). A fraction. Part or portion, essence, principle. The soul is said to be an Amsham of the deity. Degree of latitude [acsham] or longitude [deshauntaram]. Third or fifth of scale treated as a dominant [sangeetam, swaram].——*Amshapatram* (അംശപത്രം - amshapatram, Mal.). From (patra, san. letter). Same as Pagoothy olay [q.v.].——*Amshom* (അംശം - amsham, Mal.). Another form of Amsham. Modern division of a talook in Malabar. Similar to the English parish. The headman is Adhicaury; the curnam is Menon. As the district has never been surveyed in detail, the areas of amshoms are not distinctly known. There is no such thing therein as a village, but a series of scattered homesteads and farms, where the owner of the land and his servants reside separate and apart, in single separate huts, or in scattered collections of huts. Subordinate to the amshom is the deshom or hamlet. For history of the amshom, see vol. I, 117 and II, 103. Amshom was formerly hobly, containing so many taras. See vol. I, 112.

AMUCK (اماک - amak, *Jav.*). Malay word from Java. Onslaught whether of many in battle, or of an individual.

AN (ان - an, *Ar.*). Al [q.v.] before n in Arabic single terms, as Annabee, meaning the prophet.

ANAMASAMOODRAM (అనమసముద్రము - anamasamudramu, *Tel.*). From (annamma, tel. proper name + samudra, san. ocean). Village; Nellore dist., Atmacore tal.; pop. 1,291; acres 6,307; lat. 14° 42′; long. 79° 43′; from Atmacore N.N.E. 6¼ miles; from Nellore N.W. 26 miles. Large tank. Fine and ancient mosque, with endowment of ten villages and scene of annual gathering of nine days to celebrate Oors of founder, Cauja rahmat ool lah. The trustee of mosque holds title of Peer zauda. Deserted temple north of village contains ten stone statues. The dyeing of white thread into red is carried on to a great extent.

ANAMOODY (ആനമുടി - ánamuti, *Mal.*; ஆனைமுடி - ánaimudi, *Tam.*). From (ánai, tam. elephant + mudi, tam. peak). Mountain, Plateau; Travancore state, Cottayam division, and Coimbatore dist., Pollachy tal. Highest point 8,837 feet, being the highest point in peninsular India. Situated in upper ranges of Anamullays averaging 7,000 feet above level of sea and with climate similar to Ootacamund. The plateau is uninhabited, except for occasional visits from ibex-hunters or the wild hill tribe of Poolayar. They sell honey to the people of the plains, which they obtain by swinging themselves by long chains of rattan rings over precipices. Between Anamoody and the next plateau lies an extensive grass plain watered by several streams.

ANAMULLAY (ஆனைமலை - ánaimalai,* *Tam.*). From (ánai, tam. elephant + malai, tam. mountain). Sanscrit name (gajashaila), meaning same.—"*a*" Village; Coimbatore dist., Pollachy tal.; pop. 6,343; acres 3,980; lat. 10° 35′; long. 76° 58′; from Coimbatore S. 29 miles; from Pollachy S.W. 7½ miles. On the Auliyaur, 8 miles from foot of hills. Timber centre for Anamullay hills. A good cart road connects it with Pollachy. Ruined Shiva temple destroyed by Tippoo sultan. Worship is kept up. Mahomedan musjid. Market for forest produce weekly. Chuckragherry droog fort on the summit of a small hill called Jeinacull droog.—"*b*" Range of mountains; Coimbatore dist., Pollachy tal. For description, see vol. II, 51.—"*c*" Hill; Madura dist., Madura tal. A remarkable rock, two miles in length and a quarter of a mile in breadth, supposed to represent the elephant sent to destroy the city of Madura by a Chola king. It is a solid block of gneiss; strata of felspar, mica, and quartz running horizontally through its mass, crossed by veins of a felspathic rock which pass through the entire vein. Porch and temple have been hewn out of the side.

ANANAS (अननास - ananása, *San.*; अननस - ananasa, *Mahr.*; अवनस - avanasa, *Conc.*; عين الناس - ainunnás, *Ar.* and *Pers.*; اننّاس - anannás, *Hind.*; انانس - anánas, *Dec.*; ಪರಂಗಿಹಲಸು - parangihalasu, *Can.*; ಪರಂಗಿಪೆಲಕಾಯಿ - parengipelakayi, *Too.*; అనాసచెట్టు - anásachettu, *Tel.*; കൈതച്ചക്ക - kaitaççakka, *Mal.*; അന്നക്കാ - annakká, *Singh.*; அன்னாசி - annási, *Tam.*). Title from Brazilian, through Arabic. Ar. from (ain, ar. eye + nás, ar. man), which is a corruption. Dec. is nearest the original. Can. from (parangi, can. foreign + halasu, can. jack, artocarpus integrifolia, willd.). Too. from (parangi, too. foreign + pelakayi, too. jack fruit). Tel. and Tam. are corruptions from analogy of Star anise [q.v.] or Illicium anisatum, linn. Mal. from (kaita, mal. screw-pine, pandanus odoratissimus, linn. + chakka, mal. jack fruit). Singh. from Tam. by perversion. Mal. also (kappaççakka), meaning ship + jack fruit. Tam. also (parangittázhai), meaning foreign + screw-pine; also (annattázhai), meaning pine-apple + screw-pine. Pine-apple shrub, so called because fruit resembles pine-cones; Brazilian nanas; Portuguese ananas; Mananazi of Zanzibar, m being a prefix; French Manasse. In Macassar called pandang, from its resemblance to Pandanus odoratissimus, linn., the screw-pine. Conversely the pandanus has been called wild ananas. Botanically Ananas sativus, schult., bromeliaceæ [vricsham]. Alias Ananassa sativa; Bromelia ananas. Perennial, 2-3 feet; flowers small, bluish; flowering in April-May; naturalised. Native of hot regions of Mexico and Panama. The Portuguese first introduced the seeds from the Moluccas into Bengal in Acbar's time. The plants are remarkable for their power of existing in the air without contact with the earth. Grows well in Southern india, though chiefly cultivated by Europeans. In Malabar coast, near Mahé, remarkably abundant. Fruit consists of a number of a pulpy ovaries cohering in a firm compact head, and terminated by a tuft of small leaves termed the crown. Large, greenish when young, and orange color when ripe. Fresh juice of the leaves powerful anthelmintic, that of the fruit antiscorbutic. Natives regard the fresh juice of the fruit as poisonous if hypodermically injected. The flavor of the fruit is heightened by cultivation, being somewhat acrid in its wild state. The natives say it is poisonous, perhaps on account of the eyes; consequently destroy it or give it away. A pleasant wine may be made with it. The plant itself forms hedges, and will grow with little care and in almost any soil. The fibre yielded by the leaves is nearly white, very soft, silky and pliant, and at the same time strong, durable, and susceptible of fine sub-division. It is as long in the staple as flax, and can be worked by the same machinery. It is proof against immersion in water. It forms most delicate fabrics as well as fishing lines, ropes, &c. The Ceylon pine-apple has the finest flavor. There is a striatifolia or stripe-leaved variety.

ANANDRAM (അനന്തരം - anantaram, *Mal.*). From (an, san. not + antaram, san. interval). Succeeding.——*Anandraven* (അനന്തരവൻ - anantaravan, Mal.). From (above + an, mal. personal suffix). Successor, heir to the Carnaven [q. v.]. All members of a tarwaud other than the Carnaven. Younger brothers, children and grandchildren in Makkatoyem; younger brothers and nephews in Maroomakkatoyem [maryauday].

ANANDRYE (അനന്തരായി - anantaráyi, *Mal.*). From (ananta, san. vishnu, the endless + rájá, san. king). Travancore ruler; gave name to a pagoda coin.

ANANTAPORE (అనంతపురము - anantapuramu, *Tel.* anantapúr*). From (anantá, san. name of a queen + pura, san. city). Sanscrit name (anantaságara), meaning Ananta's ocean, or boundless ocean, name applied to many large tanks. The later name is Handey anantapooram, meaning the eternal city of Handey hanoomappa naidoo; see below.——(1) Revenue district; situated inland; between 13° 40′ and 15° 14′ lat., and between 76° 55′ and 78° 11′ long.; bounded N. by Bellary district, E. by Kurnool and Cuddapah districts, S. and W. by Mysore; square miles 5,275; pop. 708,549; lang. Teloogoo and Canarese. Contains rivers Chitrauvaty and Pennair; no hills beyond 1,000 feet above the plain; sanitaria, none. The whole area of the district is represented by the following talooks as sub-areas:—Anantapore, Dharmavaram, Gooty, Hindoopore, Madaksira, Penoocondah, Tadpatry. For general administrative purposes the district is distributed between the following revenue and magisterial officers, who have their head-quarters at the places shown. The pay set opposite the subordinate officers gives the grade of the corresponding charge:—Collector, Anantapore; Head assistant collector, Penoocondah, in charge of Penoocondah, Hindoopore, Madaksira and Dharmavaram talooks; General deputy collector, Gooty, in charge of Gooty and Tadpatry talooks. Tahsildars; Anantapore, Rs. 175; Dharmavaram, Rs. 200; Gooty, Rs. 200; Hindoopore, Rs. 150; Madaksira, Rs. 150; Penoocondah, Rs. 150; Tadpatry, Rs. 200. Deputy tahsildars; Bookkapatam, Rs. 70, range situated in the east of Penoocondah talook; Calyaundroog, Rs. 100, range situated in the west of Dharmavaram talook; Ooravacondah, Rs. 70, range situated in the south-west of Gooty talook; Yaudiky, Rs. 70, range situated in the north-west of Tadpatry talook. Similarly judicial officers:—Judge, Bellary. District moonsifs; Gooty with jurisdiction extending over talooks of Adony of Bellary, Anantapore, Gooty and Tadpatry; Penoocondah with jurisdiction extending over talooks of Dharmavaram, Hindoopore, Madaksira, and Penoocondah. Similarly Public Works officers:—District engineer, Bellary; Sub-divisional officer, Anantapore. Contains Registration sub-districts; Anantapore, Bookkapatam, Calyaundroog, Dharmavaram, Gooty, Hindoopore, Madaksira, Ooravacondah, Penoocondah, Tadpatry. Contains Forest ranges; Anantapore, Hindoopore, Mootchoocottah, Penoocondah. Contains Municipality, Anantapore. Contains District board. Contains Talook boards; Anantapore embracing Anantapore talook; Gooty embracing Gooty and Tadpatry talooks; Hindoopore embracing Hindoopore and Madaksira talooks; Penoocondah embracing Penoocondah and Dharmavaram talooks. The following general references should be made to the preceding volumes:—general geography, I (1) to (29); general ethnology, I (29) to (109); general history, I (110) to (188); physical geography, II, 1; meteorology, II, 3; geology, II, 8; fauna, II, 21; flora, II, 26; mineralogy, II, 29. The following references in the preceding volumes will furnish details special to the district:—particulars about towns, II, 48; comparative population, II, 172; location of revenue officers, II, 378; registrars' and sub-registrars' stations, II, 420; rain-guage stations, II, 428; police divisions, II, 431; maps published, II, 436; survey topographical lists, II, 443; hospitals and dispensaries, II, 447; head-quarter stations of gazetted officers, II, 461; incidence of taxation, II, 463; weights and measures of the district, II, 505, Bellary. A special gazetteer account of the whole district is given at II, 52. For the detailed topography of the district, reference should be made to the talook notices in the present volume, viz.:—Anantapore, Dharmavaram, Gooty, Hindoopore, Madaksira, Penoocondah, Tadpatry.——(2) Talook, Anantapore district. Tahsildar's pay Rs. 175. The Gooty district moonsif exercises civil jurisdiction. Area 789 square miles. Population 97,315. Language Teloogoo. Centre of district. Bounded N. Gooty talook, E. Tadpatry tal. and Cadiry tal. of Cuddapah, S. Dharmavaram tal. and W. Royadroog tal. of Bellary. Highest point Chiyyaid droog, 1,200 feet above the level of the plain. The Pennair forms for some distance the northern boundary and separates it from the talook of Gooty. General appearance of the talook greatly undulating. The soil for the most part red and gravelly. In the north small tracts of black soil are found. Cholum and raggy are imported from Hindoopore and Madaksira and also jaggery and cocoanuts to a limited extent. Paddy and gram are sent to Kurnool and the Nizam's country and the western markets. Channels for irrigation are cut from the Pennair and Chitrauvaty. They are frequently silted up and have to be cleared again. At Bookkacherla there is an important irrigation project. The most important tanks in the talook are those at Agrahauram, Anantapore, Bramhanayaulair, Madigoobba, Marvapully, Raptaud and Singanamala. The Anantapore tank has for one of its feeders the Pundlair river, which crosses the trunk road at Raptaud. Camping grounds are at Anantapore, Garladinney, Maroor. Trig. stations are Devarcondah and Obooldevarcondah. The principal places, &c., in the talook are the following.——*Anantapore* (అనంతపురము - anantapuramu, Tel.). See below.——*Atmaccre* (ఆత్మకూరు - átmakúru, Tel.). From (yátamu, tel. water-lift + úru, tel. village). Village; pop. 1,882; lat. 14° 38′; long. 77° 24′; from Anantapore W. 16 miles. Known for cattle grazing.——*Bookkacherla* (బుక్కచెర్ల - bukkacharla, Tel.). From (bukka, tel. name of a king + cheruvu, tel. tank). Named after Bookkaroya of Vijianugger. Village; pop. 965; lat. 14° 35′; long. 77° 35′; from Anantapore S.S.W, 7¾ miles. There is an irrigation project here to consist of the construction of a great channel to take flood waters from the Pennair near Trimany and store them at Bookkacherla, whence they would flow to all lower tanks including Anantapore and Singanamala.——*Bookkaroya samoodram* (బుక్కరాయసముద్రము - bukkaráyasamudramu, Tel.). From (bhukkarája, san. name of a king + samudra, san. ocean). Named after the same village;

pop. 2,432; lat. 14° 42′; long. 77° 41′; from Anantapore N.E. 2 miles. Has four hamlets. An old fortified town. The great reservoir was constructed [anantapore] in SS. 1286 or A.D. 1364. A Teloogoo manuscript translated and published in English, under the title of "Wars of the Rajahs" relates the story of its construction and of the sacrifice of the girl, which accompanied the erection of the embankment. The principal ryots live in Anantapore.——*Bramhanayaulair* (బ్రాహ్మణయాలేరు - bráhmanayáléru, Tel.). From (bráhmana, tel. bramin caste + álu, tel. cockle shell + éru, tel. river); Bramin village on a river containing cockle shells. Village; pop. 486; lat. 14° 38′; long. 77° 33′; from Anantapore W.S.W. 7¾ miles. Contains an important tank.——*Chitrauvaty* (చిత్రావతి - chitrávati, Tel.). See sep. title.——*Chiyyaid* (చియ్యేడు - chiyyédu, Tel.). From (chiyya, tel. fat + vídu, tel. town). Village, Hill; pop. 1,037; lat. 14° 38′; long. 77° 47′; from Anantapore E.S.E. 9¼ miles. The highest point in Anantapore. At the summit are the remains of an old fort.——*Coodair* (కూడేరు - kúdéru, Tel.). From (kúdu, tel. junction + éru, tel. river). Village; pop. 1,403; lat. 14° 44′; long. 77° 28′; from Anantapore W.N.W. 12 miles. A detached hill here called Ramdroog, on which once stood a fort belonging to the chief of Oodirpicondah in Gooty talook. There is a small temple dedicated to Shiva as Sangameshwara sawmy; Sangam is the religious term for river junctions.——*Devarcondah* (దేవరకొండ - dévarakonda, Tel.). From (déva, san. god + konda, tel. hill). Hill; lat. 14° 40′; long. 77° 42′. Overlooks Anantapore. Chikkappa wodeyar's embankment to dam the Pundlair abuts on this hill. Trig. station in lat. 14° 40′ 32·10″; long. 77° 41′ 25·02″; height 1,840 feet; from Anantapore E. 3 miles.——*Garladinney* (గార్లదిన్నె - gárladinne, Tel.). From (gára, tel. cement + dinne, tel. mound). Village, Travellers' bungalow; pop. 1,122; lat. 14° 49′; long. 77° 38′; from Anantapore N. 10 miles. A camping station on Gooty-Bangalore road. Chuttram.——*Gumpamala* (గంపమల - gampamala, Tel.). From (gampa, tel. basket + mala, tel. hill); from its shape. Hill; lat. 14° 52′; long. 77° 43′; height 2,510 feet; from Anantapore N.N.E. 14 miles. At the base is the village of Singanamala.——*Madigoobba* (మడిగుబ్బ - madigubba, Tel.). Village; pop. 660; lat. 14° 38′; long. 77° 31′; from Anantapore W.S.W. 9¾ miles. Contains an important tank.——*Maroor* (మరూరు - marúru, Tel.). From (maruvu, tel. desert + úru, tel. village). Village, Travellers' bungalow; pop. 1,987; lat. 14° 30′; long. 77° 40′; from Anantapore S. 13 miles. A camping station on Gooty-Bangalore road. Chuttram.——*Nadimidoddy* (నడిమిదొడ్డి - nadimidoddi, Tel.). From (nadama, tel. middle + doddi, tel. enclosure). Village; pop. 1,199; lat. 14° 46′; long. 77° 50′; from Anantapore E.N.E. 14 miles. There was once a strong fort residence of a Baida poligar. Now in ruins. A descendant of family receives small pension.——*Oboolderurcondah* (ఓబుళదేవరకొండ - óbuladévarakonda, Tel.). From (óbuladévara, tel. proper name + konda, tel. hill). Trig. station; lat. 14° 34′ 19·57″; long. 77° 46′ 18·65″; height 2,325 feet; from Anantapore S.E. 11 miles; from Tadmurry W. 8½ miles.——*Padamatiyaulair* (పడమటియాలేరు - padamatiyáléru, Tel.). From (padamara, tel. west + álu, tel. cockle shell + éru, tel. river). Village; pop. 1,764; lat. 14° 40′; long. 77° 25′; from Anantapore W. 16¼ miles. Has a tank divided into three parts by hills. Inhabited mostly by native Roman catholics.——*Paulcherla* (పాలచర్ల - pálacharla, Tel.). From (pálu, tel. milk + cheruvu, tel. tank). Village; pop. 1,118; lat. 14° 30′; long. 77° 32′; from Anantapore S.W. 14 miles.——*Singanamala* (సింగనమల - singanamala, Tel.). From (singana, tel. proper name + mala, tel. hill). Village, Hill; pop. 2,881; lat. 14° 48′; long. 77° 46′; from Anantapore N.E. 11 miles. In ancient times the seat of a powerful chief. There are ruins of a large fort on the hill, and foundations of temples and of streets and houses are to be seen. The town is small. Built at the base of the Gumpamala hills. The only road to it passes over the apron of the calingula and under the bund of the tank; so that when the calingula is discharging, the village cannot be approached from the trunk road. The tank, which is one of the finest in the Anantapore district, was built by Shreerungarauz of Vijianugger.——*Tadmurry* (తాడిమర్రి - tádimarri, Tel.). From (tádi, tel. palmyra tree, borassus flabelliformis, linn. + marri, tel. banyan tree, ficus bengalensis, linn.). Village; pop. 1,748; lat. 14° 34′; long. 77° 54′; from Anantapore E.S.E. 19 miles. Among the hills on the east of the talook. There are traces of a strong fort built by a petty poligar named Sakey condauna naidoo, who possessed about ninety villages. He was deposed by Hyder when the latter overran the province. At one time Tadmurry was a large town and the cusbah of a talook, but in 1820 the villages were divided between the talooks of Anantapore, Tadpatry and Penoocondah. There was a Moonsif's court here till quite recently. The village presents a ruined appearance. The better class of merchants have long ago deserted it, but weaving is carried on on a small scale.——**(3)** Collector's head-quarters, Tahsildar's station, Divisional head-quarters, Municipality, and Talook board; Anantapore dist., Anantapore tal.; pop. 6,994; lat. 14° 41′; long. 77° 39′; from Bellary S.E. 56 miles; from Gooty S. 30 miles; from Madras N.W. 216 miles; from Penoocondah N. 40 miles. Built in A.D. 1364 by Chikkappa wodeyar, Diwaun to the Rajah of Vijianugger. Chikkappa raised an embankment against the river Pundlair near Devarcondah. At each end of the bund was a calingula, and close to each calingula he founded a village. The western was called after his wife Anantasangaram, and the eastern after his master Bookkaroya samoodram. Some time after his death the tank bund breached, and tradition says that to prevent similar disasters in future, Mosalamma, daughter-in-law of Basireddy of Bookkaroya samoodram, was offered as a sacrifice and built up in the breach. In 1569 Anantapore and the surrounding districts were bestowed on Handey banoomappa naidoo. This chief had assisted Rama rajah of Vijianugger to suppress an insurrection headed by a Golla named Salicatimma, and had even defeated the Sultan of Golcondah who was marching southwards to assist Timma. Hanoomappa naidoo settled at Bookkaroya samoodram in 1569 and died there in 1582. This poligar family held Anantapore for two centuries. In 1757 the town was besieged by the Mahrattas, who were bought off for a sum of Rs. 50,000. In 1775 Hyder ally, after taking Bellary and Gooty, demanded tribute from Anantapore. The tribute fixed was Rs. 45,000, and for sometime this was punctually paid. At length the tribute fell into arrears, and Hyder arrested the poligar and attached his property. From this time the family fell into obscurity. The two eldest sons were drafted into Hyder's army in which they lost their lives, and the third Shiddhappa naidoo was sent to Seringapatam. Crushed by these troubles the old poligar died in 1788. Soon after this Tippoo, who required all the available troops for active service and could spare none for distant garrisons, sent orders that all the males of the family were to be put to death. This order was at once carried out, and they were hanged on hooks just outside the town. The third son who had been at Seringapatam escaped and took refuge with the Rajah of Calastry. In 1799 he returned to Anantapore, but soon after submitted to the Nizam, who granted him the village of Sidrampore as personal property. On his death in 1801 the direct line became extinct, but some of the family were receiving pensions as lately as 1860. When the Kurnool and Bellary districts were ceded in 1800, Colonel Munro chose Anantapore for his residence, and for many years this was the head-quarters of the Ceded districts. In 1822 Mr. Campbell removed his office to Bellary on the ground that this was a more central place in the newly-constituted zillah of Bellary. In the following year however Mr. Robertson was directed to return to Anantapore. In 1830 the place became the head-quarters of the sub-division, and till 1869 a succession of Sub-collectors administered the five talooks of Anantapore, Dharmavaram, Penoocondah, Hindoopore and Madaksira. In 1869 a redistribution of divisions was made, and the Sub-collector was removed to Gooty. In 1882 the town became the head-quarters of the present Anantapore district [charitram].

ANANTASAUGARAM (అనంతసాగరము - anantaságaramu, *Tel.*). From (ananta, san. boundless + ságara, san. ocean). Village; Nellore dist., Atmacore tal.; pop. 3,220; acres 9,031; lat. 14° 34′; long. 79° 27′; from Atmacore W. 15 miles; from Nellore W.N.W. 39 miles. Two miles from north bank of Pennair. Considerable grain trade. Large tank fed by Kedamanair coming from Veligonda hills. Irrigates twelve villages and holds two years' supply. The bund between two rocky hills is revetted on both sides and at the top with large blocks of hornstone. On the bund 2 miles from the village stand a granite pillar 7 feet high, and an inscribed stone, commemorating the repair of the tank in A.D. 1521, in the reign of Krishna deva royel of Vijianugger, by Conda narsayya, who also made the tank at Calavoy, 4 miles away on the opposite side of the river.

ANASANDRA (బన్ని - banni, *Can.*; అనసండ్ర - anatsandra, *Tel.*; சீமைவெள்வேல் - shímaivelvél, *Tam.*). Title from teloogoo. Can. from (vahni, san. fire); from color of wood. Tel. from (ana, tel. corr. of vahni, san. fire + tsandra, tel. acacia sundra, dec.). Tam. from (shímai, tam. foreign + vel, tam. white + vél, tam. the tree, acacia sp.). Botanically Acacia [cantalam] ferruginea, dc., leguminosæ [vricsham, 48]. Alias Mimosa ferruginea. Tree, 20–25 feet, armed with conical stipulary thorns, occasionally unarmed; leaves bipinnated, glabrous; pinnæ three to six pair; leaflets ten to twenty pair, oblong-linear; spikes of flowers axillary, usually in pairs, many-flowered; corolla five-cleft; stamens slightly united at the base; legumes flat, lanceolate, rusty-colored two to six seeded; flowers small, pale yellow; found common; much resembles Acacia catechu, willd. [catechu] and Acacia sundra, dec. [sundra]. Gum similar to gum-arabic. Gives to pharm. anasandra bark, mentioned but non-officinal; dark rusty color. Anasandra bark steeped in jaggery water aids the distillation of arrack [q.v.]. A decoction with ginger and other ingredients is wash for the teeth. Wood reddish brown, streaked with a darker hue, heavy and durable, does not warp or crack, grain rather coarse and even; used in building and in the construction of carts, ploughs, &c.

ANAUR (दाडिम - dádima, *San.*; डाळिंब - dálimba, *Mahr.* and *Conc.*; شجر رمان - shajarirummán, *Ar.*; درخت انار - darakhtinár, *Pers.*; انار کا پیڑ - anárkáper, *Hind.*; انار کا جھاڑ - anárkájhár, *Dec.*; دالما - dálima, *Malay*; ದಾಳಿಂಬೆ - dálimbe, *Can.*; ದಾಳಿಂಬ - dálimba, *Too.*; దానిమ్మ - dánimma, *Tel.*; ଡାଳିମ୍ବ - dálimbó, *Oor.*; മാതളം - mátalam, *Mal.*; දෙළුම් - delum, *Singh.*; மாதளை - máthalai, *Tam.*). Title from hindostany. San. from (dal, san. to burst open); bursting when fully ripe. Mahr. and conc. from sanscrit. Ar. from (shajar, ar. tree + rummán, ar. pomegranate). Pers. from (darakht, ar. tree + nár, pers. pomegranate). Hind. from (anár, hind. pomegranate + per, hind. tree). Dec. from hindostany. Malay, &c., from sanscrit. Mal. from (mátulunga, san. citrus medica, linn.); perhaps from appearance. Tam. similar. San. also (karaka), meaning throwing out seeds; (bíjapúra), meaning filled with seeds. Hind. also (gulnár), for the male variety; (dárim). Can. also (hushidálimbé), meaning false + pomegranate. Tel. also (dálimba); (dálimma); (dádimachettu); (puvvudánimma), meaning flower + pomegranate; (pulladánimma), meaning sour + pomegranate; (tiyyadánimma), meaning sweet + pomegranate; (dálunimma). Mal. also (urumámpazham), from arabic, meaning pomegranate fruit; (tálimátalam), meaning creeping + anaur; (púmátalam), meaning flower anaur. Tam. also (púmáthalai), meaning flower pomegranate, for the male variety. Greek for rind σίδειον, for grains κόκκωνες. Latin, Punicum malum, Pomum granatum, Balaustium. Title otherwise Carthaginian apple, Dalimba, Goolnaur, Pomegranate. Botanically Punica granatum, linn., lythraceæ [vricsham, 58]. Large shrub, 15–20 feet; leaves opposite, oblong-lanceolate; foliage dark green like olive and myrtle; calyx five-cleft; petals five; peculiar fruit size of orange, composed of two whorls of carpels, one placed above the other, the lower consisting of three or four and the upper five to ten carpels; hard brown-yellowish rind, containing a reddish, seedy, juicy pulp; flowers nearly sessile, scarlet; all flowers produced at the extremities of the young branches formed the same year; longevity of tree remarkable; dried root bark occurs in quills or fragments of a greyish yellow color externally, and yellow internally, without odour but of an astringent, slightly bitter taste. Cultivated in red loam; often in backyards; ground prepared by digging pits 1 or 2 feet deep, filled with manure and watered; seed sown in south in auny or june or audy [mausam] or july; on coromandel in aushweejam or october and caurteecam [mausam] or november; sown in nursery; after one or two months transplanted; watered once a week, and pruned and manured occasionally; bears fruit after two or three years; gathered by hand; average price, one fruit for 6 pies. All parts of plant rich in tannic acid, and act medicinally astringents and anthelmintics; juice of ripe fruit contained in red succulent pulp, which covers seeds, slightly acid, extremely pleasant to taste, not unlike orange, very refreshing, well calculated to quench thirst in fevers, veidyans prescribe it combined with saffron when the habit is heated; bark of fruit and the flowers, useful astringents, commonly given by natives in decoction, combined with powdered cloves, in such bowel affections as are not accompanied with tenesmus; bark of root, administered by hakeems in diseases requiring astringents, and considered perfect specific in tape worm, then given in decoction; gives to pharm. root-bark, granati radicis cortex and the dried rind or pericarp, granati cortex, substituted for english male fern. Fruit universally eaten; keeps for a long time; bark formerly employed in dyeing leather, the yellow morocoo of tunis being still tinted with an extract; flower makes a red dye, especially with cotton cloths; stem gives gum; wood light yellow, with a small, darker colored, irregularly shaped heart-wood, compact and close-grained. Several varieties, those with yellow flowers being most rare. Sour and sweet varieties so called in the vernaculars. The male variety is called flowering in vernaculars. No other species here.——*Wild anaur* (कडवी - kadaví, Mahr.; بندارو - bandárú, Hind.; جنگلی انار کا جهاڑ - janglíanárkájhár, Dec.; బందార - bandára, Tel.; ବୋଡୋକ - bodoka, Oor.; വല്ലാരി - vallári, Mal.; விளாரி - vilári, Tam.). Mahr. from (katu, san. bitter). Dec. from (janglí, hind. wild + anár, hind. pomegranate, punica granatum, linn. + jhár, hind. tree); from similarity of leaves. Mal. from (vala, mal. net + ari, mal. grain); from netted wings surrounding seeds; cf. latin generic term. Tam. from malayalam. Tel. also (bárja). Tam. also (malaittanakku), meaning mountain + gyrocarpus jacquini, roxb.; (shivappumaram), meaning red + tree; (ilaimérgáymaram), meaning fruit-upon-leaf tree, probably from bullate floral leaf. Title otherwise Bastard cedar; sometimes wrongly called Wild bachnaug. Botanically Hymenodictyon excelsum, wall., rubiaceæ [vricsham, 71]. Alias Cinchona excelsa; Hymenodyction utile. Deciduous tree, 50 feet; smooth bark; leaves from oblong to roundish ovate, pubescent; stipules cordate; floral leaves oblong, colored, bullate; panicles terminal and axillary; anthers nearly sessile in tube of the corolla; calyx five-toothed; corolla infundibuliform, five-parted; capsule two-celled, many-seeded; seeds girded by a membranous reticulated border; flowers small, greenish; the lower pairs on two of the ramifications of the panicle are ornamented, each with a pair of colored floral leaves. Two inner coats of bark have qualities of cinchona, and when fresh in a stronger degree; in pharm. non-officinal, like cinchona. Leaves are cattle fodder. Inner bark used by tanners. Wood nearly color of mahogany and used for furniture. Another species is obovatum, less common.

ANAVINGA (भोगर - bhógara, *Mahr.*; چلا - chillá, *Hind.*; గురుగుడు - gurugudu, *Tel.*; ଗିରରି - girari, *Oor.*; ആനവണങ്ങി - ánavananni, *Mal.*; கடிச்சை - kadiççai, *Tam.*). Title from malayalam. Mal. from (ána, mal. elephant + vanannu, mal. to revere); from belief that elephants retire at the sight of it. Tel. also (kálamesara); (kámemosara); (chalakasavara); (pisiki); (gilugidu); (gidugudu). Title otherwise Caditchay, Caulamesara. Botanically Casearia tomentosa, roxb., samydaceæ [vricsham, 60]. Alias Anavinga lanceolata; Casearia canziala, elliptica, ovata. Small tree; leaves alternate, bifarious, ovate-oblong, serrulate, downy beneath, on short petioles; sepals five, villous; corolla none; peduncles short, axillary, one-flowered, surrounded at their base with villous involucres; flowers small, crowded into globular heads, pale green; jungles near coast; among bushes near pagoda wells. Very bitter in all parts; leaves used in medicated baths, and pulp of fruit is very diurotic; bark used as adulterant for kamela [q.v.] powder. Wood yellowish-white, moderately hard, rough, close-grained; used to make combs; does not warp. Other common species are:—Coriacea, very coriaceous and large leaves; Esculenta, large shrub, flowers greenish-yellow, in drying leaves turn very black on the upper side, has bitter purgative roots, leaves eaten; Glomerata, flowers small, greenish yellow; Graveolens; Rubescens, flowers greenish-yellow, western ghauts; Wynadensis, small graceful tree, flowers small, ghauts.

ANAY (ആന - ana, *Mal.*; அணை - anai, *Tam.*). From (an, tam. to approach). Artificial bank [anicut]. Causeway. Suffix in place names in southern districts; as Chittanay, meaning small + bund; Pairanay, meaning great + bund. Cf. Caray, natural bank. Cullanay is a stone dam, as opposed to earth only.

ANCANAM (అంకణము - ankanamu, *Tel.*; அங்கணம் - anganam, *Tam.*). From (ank, san. to go). Walking space. Superficial measure for house sites. The space enclosed by four pillars in a house. 32 square mooras or cubits = 1 ancanam; 607 ancanams = 1 acre [alavay, 2b]. Approximate actual value, 1 ancanam = 8 square yards. Generally a space 8 cubits long by 4 cubits broad. Compare Manay.

ANCAULAMMAN (అంకాళమ్మ - ankálamma, *Tel.*; அங்காளம்மன் - angálamman, *Tam.*). From (am, tam. beautiful + káli, tam. the goddess + amman, tam. mother). A special form of the Amman, somewhat Hindooized [matam] to represent Cauly or Bhadra cauly, Shiva's daughter-in-law. As a rule she is represented only by a stone or block of wood, but if specially depicted, her image has four arms and hands. Two of these she raises, holding in the right a weapon of wood and leather, encircled by a snake and in the left a noose, called Pausham, with which she draws the souls of dying people to herself. In one of the other two hands she holds the skull of Bramha, the fourth hand being empty. On her head she wears a crown. Behind her ears she has two flowers; and in them large earrings. Her hair is erect, and near her are two lamps. In the inner apartment of her pagodas stands her own representation or image, if any. In the outer one the following images may be found:—"*a*" Her husband Veerabhadran, the son of Shiva, having erect black hair, with a crown on his head, lion's teeth in the mouth, the mark of Shiva on his forehead, two white flowers behind his ears, and streams of fire issuing from his whole body. He has fourteen arms and hands, of which four are empty, and in the remaining ten he holds, respectively, a sword, a trident, a shield, a sort of drum, a bell, a flower, two arrows, and a large spear. He wears a long string of skulls, and has sometimes only four, sometimes sixteen, or more heads. According to the Pooraunams he should have 1,000 heads and 2,000 arms.—"*b*" Periya tumbiraun or the great lord, an image similar to that of Shiva, and meant to represent his son Veerabhadran as lord of the sacrifice of Dacshan.—"*c*" Troolan, a savage-hero.—"*d*" Ranaveeran, a demon hero, &c.—"*e*" Pauvaday vceran, a demon hero.—"*f*" Ooyirtoondilcauran, servants of Ancaulamman, whose business is to bring those who die by their own hands to her.—"*g*" Teecoothitt ammaul, a deified woman who leapt into the fire and made signs after her death.—"*h*" Cauttairy, a demoness, of whom the Tamulians are specially afraid. All these images, which are usually made of wood, are worshipped with offerings. The figures of clay within and without the enclosure of the pagodas are not worshipped. The representation or image of Ancaulamman herself, which stands in the inner apartment of the pagoda, is worshipped every Friday, or oftener. Besides these ordinary offerings, she obtains on occasion also a thank offering from devotees. Like the other goddesses, she enjoys a yearly movable festival, lasting seven or nine days, on which her image of metal is carried about every morning and evening; and the last and principal day is celebrated like the last day of Mariyamman's festival.——*Ancamma* (అంకమ్మ - ankamma, Tel.). Contr. from Ancaulamman.——*Aye ancaulammay* (ஆயியங்காளம்மை - áyiyangálammai, Tam.). From (áyi, tam. mother). Same as Ancaulamman.

ANCHATTY (அஞ்சட்டி - añjatti, *Tam.*). From (anche, can. the post + hatti, can. cattle-pen). Village; Salem dist., Oossoor tal.; pop. 536; acres 2,760; lat. 12° 21′; long. 77° 46′;

from Oossoor S.S.W. 27 miles; from Salem N.N.W. 57 miles. Near the Mysore frontier. Gallant defence in 1760 by Makhdoom ally, against superior forces of Khanda row.

ANCHEY (ಅಂಚೆ - anche, *Can.*). The post. Ancheyava is a postal runner. Anchey chauvady is the Post office. Anchey cheela is the leather wallet containing letters [anjel].——*Anchey meeda* (ಅಂಚೆಮಿಡ - anchemída, Can.). Means on relay. Phrase for sending sick persons from stage to stage escorted.

ANCOOSHAM (अंकुश - ankusha, *San.*). From (ank, san. to curve). Elephant goad. Ancoosha paushamaindy, from (pásha, san. cord + éndi, tam. holder), holder of an elephant goad and a cord, is Vigneshwaran, eldest son of Shiva.

ANDAMAN (انگمنین - angamanain, *Ar.*; திமைத்தீவு - timaittívu, *Tam.*). Ar. from (agamitae, malay name of the aborigines + ar. dual sign). Tam. from (tímai, tam. evil + tívu, tam. island). Islands in Bay of Bengal, inhabited by negrito race, partially occupied as convict settlement under the Government of India. Mentioned in a Tanjore temple inscription. Cf. Diospyros kurzii, andamanese marble wood; Pterocarpus indicus, andaman red-wood.

ANDAY (அண்டை - andai, *Tam.*). From (an, tam. to approach). Neighbourhood. Field-bund. Suffix in place names; as Kizhakkanday, meaning east + side.

ANDHRAM (आन्ध्र - ándhra, *San.*; ఆంధ్రము - ándhramu, *Tel.*). From (andhra, san. hunter). Sanscrit name for Teloogoo. The Teloogoo people were always divided into inland Andhras and maritime Calingas. The Andhras were better known than the Calingas to the early Aryans [q.v.]; hence the name. In pooranic times a dynasty of Andhra kings reigned in Northern india, probably Dravidian or some kindred race. The Andaræ are represented by Pliny, after Megasthenes, as a powerful people, and the Andre Indi have a place in the Peutinger Tables amongst the few Indian nations of which the author of those tables had heard. They were however placed by error north of the Ganges. Hwen thsang makes An-to-lo one of the southern kingdoms, and this has been held to mean Andhra. He gives the capital of the Andhra people as Ping-ki-lo, which may be Warangal. The connection between the Andhra dynasty and Southern india is stated in vol. I (132), foot-note. Andhram is one of the fifty-six countries of Tamul geography [bhaushay, charitram].——*Andhra deepacam* (आन्ध्रदीपक - ándhradípaka, San.). From (dípaka, san. lamp). Modern dictionary of Teloogoo, explained in Teloogoo, by Maumidy vencayya, merchant of Masulipatam in 1816. Only words used in poetry. Alphabetical in European method.——*Andhra dravida bhaushay* (आन्ध्रद्राविडभाषा - ándhradrávidabhásha, San.). Means Teloogoo-Tamul language. Comaurila bhatt's name for Dravidian languages, northern and southern.

ANDIPUTTY (ஆண்டிப்பட்டி - ándippatti, *Tam.*). From (ándi, tam. one of the caste + patti, tam. village). Village, Range of hills; Madura dist., Periyacoolam tal.; pop. 6,747; acres 8,975; lat. 10° 00′; long. 77° 40′; from Madura W.N.W. 34 miles; from Periyacoolam S.S.E. 9¾ miles. The range, 55 miles in length, runs from the Travancore chain and is known during the last 15 miles as the Naugamullay. Abounds in bison, deer, pig, cheetah, and at certain seasons elephants. The village is at the north-eastern spur of the range.

ANDRA (ఆంధ్ర - ándra, *Tel.*).—"*a*" Zemindarry; Vizagapatam dist., Gajapatinugger division; pop. 7,846. The ancestor of present proprietor obtained estate from Jeypore chief. On his descendants allying themselves with Vizianagram family, Andra passed under the patronage of that house. Assessed at the permanent settlement at Rs. 1,386.—"*b*" Village, Headquarters of zemindarry; Vizagapatam dist., Gajapatinugger division; pop. 899; lat. 18° 21′; long. 83° 15′; from Gajapatinugger W.N.W. 10 miles; from Vizagapatam N. 44 miles. A small village and is the residence of Andra zemindar.

ANDROTT (അന്ത്രോത്ത് - antrótt, *Mal.*). Island; Malabar dist.; pop. 2,999; square miles about 1¾; lat. 10° 48′; long. 73° 57′; from Calicut W. 139 miles. One of the Laccadives. Largest of the northern group of so called Cannanore islands attached to Malabar district. Lies east and west; has hardly any lagoon. Greatest length from south-east to the north-west is about 3½ miles; greatest breadth, about centre of island, is 1¼ miles. Coast line is scarcely at all indented, so that the island forms a regular oval figure. Surface is generally a level plain, elevated but a few feet above the sea, here and there varied by mounds formed mostly of heaped-up material excavated in forming tottam or arable land. Highest mound is probably not 40 feet above sea and average elevation not more than 7 or 8 feet. The island is divided into four sub-divisions or cherries:—Chemacherry, Keelcherry, Mecherry and Yedacherry. The first is on southern shore and separated from Yedacherry by the tottam or garden. Formerly these cherries were political and revenue sub-divisions, but now all matters are decided by the Ameen with the assistance of Carnaver, regardless of the cherry to which the latter belong. The Coral shoal upon which the island is situated is of considerable extent, but the coral crops up to surface only in immediate neighbourhood of land, reef being hardly anywhere above sixty yards from the beach; on the east the beach and reef are coincident. The people fall under three main classes:—Carnaver, sub-divided into Carnaver proper and Tanaca piranda coodiyauns; Maulim or pilots and sailors, sub-divided into Maulim proper and Oorcaur; Melacherry or tree-climbers. The first class of Carnaver is composed of the rich boat owners and Punchayetdars. The male members are distinguished by the title of Koya, a religious dignity. The island Carnaver, Ameen, and Cauzy, all belong to this class. The Tanaca piranda coodiyauns are less wealthy and cultivators. The second class or the Maulims are, as the name implies, sailors. They are generally Puttah coodiyauns, that is to say partly independent and partly dependent on the higher classes. The third class, Melacherries, are servants and toddy-drawers. These are generally Adima coodiyauns or serfs of the Carnavers, but they are at liberty to change their employers. The islanders in their customs and habits closely resemble the Moplahs of North malabar. All the people of the island profess Mahomedanism. Pundauram or crown lands comprise about one-fourth of the area and are scattered throughout the holdings of islanders, having been acquired by escheat or confiscation. The chief Pundauram possessions are East and West Valiya pundaurams. Chief produce is cocoanuts. Raggy, varagoo and millet, yams, sweet potatoes, bread-fruit trees, plantains, limes, areca palms, and betel vines are also grown to a limited extent. The only manufactures carried on are the manufacture of coir-yarn and of jaggery. Shark fins are cured for exportation in small quantities. The principal exports are coir-yarn, cocoanuts, jaggery and pindica a kind of sweetmeat, a little vinegar, lime pickle, and shark fins. Imports are rice, salt, areca nuts, betel, curry-stuffs, cooking utensils, both earthern and metal, implements of husbandry, clothes and occasionally cattle and ornaments. Teak, mango-wood and bamboos are also imported and used in repairing the wodams and small boats. As Andrott is the nearest island to the coast, many wodams from other islands call there for water, &c. The usual coast markets visited by islanders are Calicut, where they sell their goods, and Mangalore, where they usually purchase their supplies. Occasionally they call at Tellicherry and Cannanore.

ANDY (அந்தி - andi, *Tam.*). Means to meet. Evening, being the junction of day with night. Andivurnan, from (varna, san. color) is he who is red like the evening, Shiva.

ANGAH (انگا - angá, *Hind.*). From (anga, san. body). Otherwise Angy. Jacket. Worn in place of the Neemah [q.v.]; not so long, reaching only to the haunches. Is the body part of the angarkha, without the skirt and tails.——*Angarkha* (انگرکها - angarkhá, Hind.). From (rakhá, hind. preserver). Long coat. Same as the cabah [q.v.], without open flaps; breast and armpits covered.

ANGAM (अङ्ग - anga, *San.*). From (ang, san. to walk). Limb. For limbs of the Vedas, see Vedaungam.——*Angajan* (अङ्गज - angaja, San.). From (ja, san. be produced). Cauman, the Indian cupid.——*Anganyausam* (अङ्गन्यास - anganyása, San.). From (nyása, san. placing). The mental appropriation of various parts of the body to tutelary divinities, by touching the several parts and applying sacred ashes, accompanied with prayer. This is a very common form of prayer [matam].——*Anga pradacshinam* (அங்கப்பிரதட்சிணம் - angappirathadchinam, Tam.). From (pra, san. towards + dakshina, san. right side). Moving the body from the left towards the right side. Worship performed by rolling round a temple after a car, &c., in performance of a vow. See vol. I (83) [matam].

ANGAUDY (അങ്ങാടി - annáti, *Mal.*; அங்காடி - angádi, *Tam.*). From (ankam, mal. duel + átu, mal. to act). Place where duels are fought, hence a public square, bazaar. Suffix in place name; as Payyangaudy, meaning old + bazaar. Angaudy vaunibham is merchandise.

ANGAUM (هنگام - hangám, *Hind.*). Season.——*Angaumy* (هنگامی - hangámí, Hind.). Periodical. Angaumy sibbundy is a temporary establishment.

ANGAURACAN (अङ्गारक - angáraka, *San.*). From (angára, san. charcoal); from his fiery color. Planet Mars. Tam. Shevvye, means red-mouthed.

ANGOOR (द्राक्षा - drákshá, *San.*; द्राक्ष - dráksha, *Mahr.*; عنب - inab, *Ar.*; تاک - ták, *Pers.*; داکهلتا - dákhlatá, *Hind.*; انگورکی بیل - angúrkíbel, *Dec.*; انگر - anggur, *Malay*; ದ್ರಾಕ್ಷಿ - drákshi, *Can.*; ದ್ರಾಕ್ಷ - dráksha, *Too.*; ద్రాక్ష - dráksha, *Tel.*; മുന്തിരി - muntiri, *Mal.*; මිදි - midi, *Singh.*; திராட்சை - tirádchai, *Tam.*). Title from deccany. San. from (drá, san. to cause to run); as quenching thirst. Mahr. from sanscrit. Hind. from (dákh, hind. grape + latá, hind. creeper). Dec. from (angúr, pers. grape + bel, hind. creeper). Can., &c., from sanscrit. Singh. from sanscrit. San. also (mridvíká), meaning easily squeezed, soft fruited; (góstaní), meaning cow's udder; (svádví), meaning tasteful; (madhurasá), meaning honey + juice. Dec. also (habshíangúr), meaning abyssinian grape; (bokháraangúr), meaning bokhara grape. Singh. also (valmidi), meaning creeper + vine. Tam. also (kodimundiri), meaning creeper + anacardium occidentale, linn. Greek ἄμπελος οἰνοφόρος. Latin vitis sativa. Title otherwise Cow berry, Creeper cashew, Draucshay, Grape vine, Sweet berry, Vine. Botanically Vitis [draucshay] vinifera, linn., ampelideæ [vricsham, 42]. Stalks long; flowers greenish; fruit a berry, growing in bunches, and called grapes; native of the caspian; thrives between 32° and 50° of N. latitude; can be cultivated elsewhere. Raisins are dried grapes; currants are the dried uvæ of a small corinthian variety; juice of young fruit is verjuice, contains much tartaric and some citric and malic acid; must is the expressed juice of the ripe grape; must at a temperature between 60° and 80° Fahr. ferments, and this racked, sulphured, and fined, is wine; an ardent spirit is obtained by the distillation of a vinous liquid, which is brandy. Grapes can be successfully cultivated in s. india, and of a delicate flavor; french at pondicherry very successful; but owing to the heat by which vinous fermentation is rendered too quick wine cannot be made; periplus says that laodicean and italian wine was sent in small quantity to mouziris and nelkunda; wine is at the present day brought to india from persia; two sorts of shiraz wine, a red and a white [mooskiraut, sharaub]; small raisins called kismis, common in the bazaars, are brought from persia, made from the shiraz grape. For cultivation the grape vine is planted in pits from cuttings of old grape, and set 3 to 5 feet apart; watered once a week, pruned and trimmed once or twice a year; toddy and dried fish are applied as manure; bears after six years; average price, 5 lbs. per rupee; eaten by higher classes in hot weather.——*Country angoor* (रानद्राक्ष - ránadráksha, Mahr.; संबरबल्लि - sambaraballi, Conc.; انگور جنگلی - junglíangúr, Dec.; ಸಂಬಾರಬಳ್ಳಿ - sambáraballi, Can.; శంబారవల్లి - shembáravalli, Tel.; ചെമ്പരവള്ളി - chemparavalli, Mal.; சம்பாரவல்லி - shambáravalli, Tam.). Mahr. from (ráua, mahr. wild + drákshá, san. grape, vitis vinifera, linn.). Dec. from (janglí, hind. wild + angúr, hind. grape). Mal. from (chempara, mal. reddish + valli, mal. creeper); perhaps from red color of root. Tam. from malayalam. Conc. also (sávirasambára). Hind. also (panjerí). Title otherwise Indian grape vine, Indian wild vine, Red vine. Botanically Vitis [draucshay] indica, l., ampelideæ [vricsham, 42]. Alias Vitis rugosa. A wild, shrubby, climbing plant; fruit round, size of a large currant, fair eating.——*Dog angoor* (سگ انگور - sagangúr, Hind.). Title means like but inferior. Hind. from (sag, pers. dog + angúr, pers. grape). Title otherwise Banewort, Belladonna, Belladonna mandrake, Black cherry, Deadly nightshade, Dog grape, Dwale, Dway berry, Great morel, Naughtyman's cherry. Botanically Atropa belladonna, linn., solanaceæ [vricsham, 94]. Specific from its being used by Italian women to dilate pupils of eyes. Plant 3 feet high; thick, fleshy root, flowers large, very faint narcotic odour; berry large, roundish, at first green, when ripe of shining black color, containing many seeds, and violet-colored juice; every part poisonous; berries, when eaten, produce intoxication. Not indigenous. Gives to pharm. belladonnæ folia and belladonnæ radix; activity resides in alkaloid, atropia; powerfully sedative, anodyne, and antispasmodic, lactifuge, dilating the pupil, in overdoses powerfully poisonous; officinal. No other common species here.——*Jungle angoor* (బేడిసతివ్వ - bédisativva, Tel.; വലിയപർപ്പടകം - valiyaparppatakam, Mal.; காட்டுக்கொடி முந்திரிகை - káttukkodimundirigai, Tam.). Tel. from (bédisa, tel. a dye + tivva, tel. creeper). Mal. from (valiya, mal. large + parpatakam, mal. mollugo cerviana, ser.). Tam. from (kádu, tam. forest + kodimundirigai, tam. grape vine, vitis vinifera, linn.). Mal. also (chunnámbuvalli), meaning choonam creeper. Title otherwise Jungle grape vine, Large parpatacam. Botanically Vitis [draucshay] latifolia, r., ampelideæ [vricsham, 42]. Alias Vitis glabrata. Flowers small, reddish-brown; brown-colored seeds, about the size of those of coriandrum sativum, but pleasant, sub-aromatic and mucilaginous taste; medicinally cardiac and stomachic.

ANGREZ (انگریز - angrez, *Hind.*). The English.

ANGY (అంగి - angi, *Tel.*). From (angu, tel. beauty). Suffix in place names; as Relangy, meaning Cassia fistula, linn. [condray] + beauty.

ANICUT (அணைக்கட்டு - anaikkattu, *Tam.*). From (anai, tam. dam + kattu, tam. building). A dam, generally of masonry, to retain or divert running water for irrigational purposes [anay].

ANIL (चमरपुच्छ - chamarapuchha, *San.*; گلہری - gilehrí, *Hind.*; ಉಡತೆ - udate, *Can.*; ఉడుత - uduta, *Tel.*; അണ്ണാൻ - annán, *Mal.*; அணில் - anil, *Tam.*). San. from (chamara, san. chowry + puchha, san. tail). Can. and Tel. from (udugu, can. to grow lean). Terms co-extensive with the European genus Sciurus, sciuridæ [chamara pootcham], rodentia, mammalia [sastanam, 16], of naturalists [jantoo]. The species best known to the natives are malabaricus [malabar squirrel], palmarum, [anil pillay]. Other S. indian species are:—elphinstonei, layardi, macrourus, sublineatus, tristriatus. Pteromys is called Flying anil.——(1) *Anil pillay* (वृक्षशायिका - vrikshasháyiká, San.; گلہری - gilehri, Hind.; ಚಿಟ್ಟಿಳಿಲು - chittalilu, Can.; ఉడుత - uduta, Tel.; അണ്ണാക്കൊട്ടൻ - annákkottan, Mal.; அணிற்பிள்ளை - anirbillai, Tam.). San. from (vriksha, san. tree + sháyiká, san. sleeper). Can. from (chitti, can. small + alilu, can. squirrel). Tam. from (anil, tam. squirrel + pillai, tam. child, affix for small animals). Title otherwise Palm squirrel, Striped squirrel. Sciurus palmarum, sciuridæ, rodentia, mammalia [sastanam, 16], of naturalists. Alias pencillatus. Above dusky greenish gray with three yellowish white stripes along the whole length of the back, and two fainter lines on each side; beneath whitish; tail with the hairs variegated with red and black; ears rounded. Though termed palm squirrel only occasionally seen on palm trees. A legend states that when Hanooman was crossing the Saitoo, it was bridged over by all the animals. But a small gap remained which was filled by this squirrel. When Hanooman passed over, he placed his hand on the squirrel's back, and the marks of his five fingers have remained ever since. It is not unlike the chipmunk of America, Tamias striatus; but those are true ground squirrels having cheek-pouches and living in burrows.—"*a*" Allied is the Jungle striped squirrel, Sciurus tristriatus. Very similar to last, but generally darker, the face, forehead, back and haunches, more or less tinged with rusty-red, or reddish brown; the stripes small, narrower than in the common one, and not extending the whole length of the back; tail beneath distinctly rusty; sides darker than in palmarum. It differs in its voice, which is much less shrill.—"*b*" Another is the Travancore striped squirrel, Sciurus layardi. Much darker than the last, being of a dark dingy olive color with a tinge of ashy; middle of back, black with a short yellowish streak in the middle and a faint and shorter streak on each side; tail tipped black, rusty in the middle; lower parts somewhat ferruginous. Size of the last or a trifle larger.—"*c*" Lastly Neilgherry striped squirrel, Sciurus sublineatus. Of a dark grizzled olive color, tinged with tawny above and with three pale lines alternating with four dark ones on the back and croup, the outer dark lines narrower and somewhat less dark than the others; beneath lighter, more mixed with tawny; tail grizzled dusky olive and ferruginous. Fur remarkably dense, close and soft.—"*d*" Indian species of Sciurus akin to the above and not here found are:—Berdmorei or berdmore's ground-squirrel, Macclellandi or macclelland's ground-squirrel, Quinquestriatus or stripe-bellied squirrel, Tupaiodes or long-nosed squirrel.—"*e*" From these small squirrels are to be distinguished the large forest and strictly arboreal species [malabar squirrel].——(2) *Paravay anil* (اُڑن گلہری - urangilehrí, Hind.; ಹಾರುವಬೆಕ್ಕು - hárnvabekku, Can.; దుముకుడుత - dumukuduta, Tel.; പറയണ്ണിൽ - parayanil, Mal.; பறவையணில் - paravaiyanil, Tam.). Hind. from (uran, hind. flying + gilehrí, hind. squirrel). Can. from (háru, can. to leap + bekku, can. cat). Tel. from (dumuku, tel. to leap + uduta, tel. squirrel). Tam. from (paravai, tam. bird + anil, tam. squirrel). Title otherwise Flying squirrel, Oral. Pteromys petaurista, sciuridæ, rodentia, mammalia [sastanam, 16], of naturalists. Upper parts dusky-maroon black grizzled with white, the membrane and limbs above somewhat brighter and more rufous; the feet, the muzzle, and round the eyes, and terminal half of the tail, dark brown or black, the last sometimes with a little white towards the tip; under parts dingy brownish gray or nearly white. The male is distinguished by an irregular patch of rufous on the sides of the neck, which in the female is a sort of pale fawn. The female has six mammæ, two pectoral, and four ventral. Feet as in Sciurus palmarum or Striped squirrel. The skin of the flanks extended between the fore and hind feet, forming when expanded a wide parachute; tail rounded, hairy all round, as long as the body or longer. Found wherever there are extensive lofty forests. It lives chiefly on fruits of various kinds, also on bark, shoots, &c.; occasionally on beetles and the larvæ of insects. During the day it sleeps much, either sitting with its back bent into a circle, and its head thrust down to its belly, or lying on its back with the legs and parachute extended, a position it is fond of in sultry weather. During the night time it is incessantly moving. When wishing to pass from one tree to another at some distance, it does not descend to the ground, but leaping from the topmost branches sails through the air by means of the parachute, and reaches the lower part or trunk of the adjacent tree. These flights can be extended to ten yards or upwards, always in a diagonal and lowering direction. This genus is distinguished by its large round tail. The flying apparatus in the Flying squirrel is analogous to that of the Galæopithecus among Lemurs which however is not known in Southern india, and to that of the common flying fox among bats. Indian species of Pteromys not here found are:—Albiventer or white-bellied flying squirrel, Alboniger or black and white flying squirrel, Alborufus or red and white flying squirrel, Caniceps or grey-headed flying squirrel, Cineraceus or ashy flying squirrel, Fimbriatus or grey flying squirrel, Fuscocapillus or Small travancore flying squirrel, Magnificus or red-bellied flying squirrel, Melanopterus or black-flanked flying squirrel, Oral or brown flying squirrel, Pearsonii or hairy-footed flying squirrel, Spadiceus or red flying squirrel, Yunnanensis or yunnan flying squirrel. Belonging to a separate genus is the Small travancore flying squirrel, Sciuropterus fuscocapillus. This is distinguished by its small flat tail. In this the upper parts are a rufescent fulvous or dark-brownish isabelline hue, the hairs being fuscous with a fulvous tip; head darker and fuscous; lower parts rufous white, as are the cheeks and under lip; margin of the membrane rufo-fulvous; tail concolorous or nearly so with back above, with a whitish tip, and the lower surface blackish brown. Ears small, almost nude,

Tail bushy, the hair above one inch long at base, hardly distichous; moustaches long and black; fur long, porrect, very fine.

ANIL (النيل - annil, *Ar.*). Means the blue. Portuguese for indigo [indigo, neely]. Origin of term Aniline dye.

ANISE (शतपुष्पा - shatapushpá, *San.*; शोप - shópa, *Mahr.*; رازيانج - ráziyánaj, *Ar.*; باديان - bádiyán, *Pers.*; سونف - sonf, *Hind.* and *Dec.*; ادس منس - adasmanis, *Malay*; ದೊಡ್ಡಜೀರಿಗೆ - doddajírige, *Can.*; సోపు - sópu, *Tel.*; ପୋନ୍ନମୋୟିରି - ponnomoyiri, *Oor.*; പെരിഞ്ചീരകം - periñchírakam, *Mal.*; දේවදුරු - dévaduru, *Singh.*; சோம்பு - shómbu, *Tam.*). Title from (anísún, ar.). San. from (shata, san. hundred + pushpa, san. flower); from numerous flowers. Mahr. from hindostany. Malay from (adas, malay fennel + manis, malay sweet). Can. from (dodda, can. large + jírige, can. cuminum cyminum, linn.). Tel. from hindostany. Mal. from (peru, mal. large + jíraka, san. cumin seed); cf. sonf. Singh. from (déva, san. god + duru, singh. cuminum cyminum, linn.). Tam. from hindostany. San. also (misi), meaning maturing. Ar. also (shamár). Pers. also (válánibazarg), meaning large fennel. Malay also (jíramanis), meaning sweet cumin. Tel. also (peddajilakara), meaning large + cumin seed; (peddasadápa), meaning large + ruta graveolens, linn. Singh. also (mahaduru), meaning great cumin; (lokuduru), meaning great cumin; (simhalaasamódagam), meaning ceylon carum copticum, linn. Tam. also (peruñjíragam), meaning large + cumin seed. Greek ἄνισον. Seeds often confounded by the natives with sweet fennel seeds [sonf]. Title otherwise Ceylon ajwaun, Large cumin, Sweet cumin. Botanically Pimpinella anisum, linn., umbelliferæ [vricsham, 67]. Alias Anisum officinale, vulgare; Apium anisum; Sison anisum; Tragium anisum. Annual; small, white flowers; seed or rather small fruit, aniseed, is an imported article, chiefly from persia; aromatic, sweetish, warm-tasted; the smell is peculiarly inviting to rats; very common in bazaars; among the oldest of medicines and spices. Cultivated in red garden soil, dry; sown in small pits, tubers dug out after four months. Aniseed, or fructus anisi, is medicinally laxative, diuretic, carminative and stomachic; frequently used by the hakeems for children; substituted for british magnesia carbonas, and rhubarb. Essential oil obtained by distilling seeds with water; applied medicinally to both men and animals; in pharm., oleum anisi; from which essentia anisi; officinal. Seeds used in confectionery; from seeds is made the well-known cordial; essential oil used for scenting soaps and pomatums. Other species are candolleana, heyneana, leschenaultii. The dried capsules and seeds of the star-anise, Illicium anisatum, linn., as well as the leaves of the wood apple tree Feronia elephantum, corr., have both odour and properties of ordinary aniseed. Cf. also Sowa or dill, Ajwaun or indian dill, and Caraway.——*Star anise* (बादियान - bádiyána, Mahr.; نبات باديان خطائى - nabátibádiyánikhatái, Ar.; درخت باديان خطائى - darakhtibádiyánikhatái, Pers.; اناس پهل کا پير - anásphalkáper, Hind.; انس پهل کا جهاڑ - anasphalkájhár, Dec.; మరాటిమొగ్గ - marátimogga, Tel.; அன்னாசு - annásu, Tam.). Title from the capsules appearing in a starlike form, opening upwards + resemblance of flavor to real anise. Mahr. from arabic. Ar. from (nabát, ar. plant + bádiyán, ar. pimpinella anisum, linn. + khatái, ar. cathay), means chinese anise. Pers. from (darakht, pers. tree, &c.). Hind. from (anásphal, hind. star anise + per, hind. tree). Dec. from (jhár, hind. tree). Tel. from (maráti, tel. the country + mogga, tel. bud), indicating the capsule. Tam. from hindostany. Ar. also (ráziyánajikhatái), meaning chinese pimpinella anisum, linn. Hind. also (sonf), meaning equally fennel, anise. Tel. also (anásapuvvu), meaning anise + flower. Title otherwise Cathay anise, Chinese anise, Chinese fennel, Siberian cardamom, Yellow-flowered aniseed plant. Botanically Illicium anisatum, linn., magnoliaceæ [vricsham, 3]. Evergreen, smooth-leaved shrub, 20-25 feet; native of yanam and s.w. provinces of china. The capsules, fructus anisi stellati, or semen badiana of chemists, under name of chinese fennel now carried by inland trade from china to yarkund and thence to india; once brought into europe overland by way of russia and then called cardamomum siberiense; resemble stars, with six or eight points, pale-brown color, size of a rupee, and nearly a quarter of an inch thick; common in most bazaars and form part of mahratta buds [q.v.]; whole plant, especially fruit, has aromatic flavor of fennel or anise, sweetish and rather pungent; capsules abound in an essential oil; rather brown, lighter than water, with more difficulty congealed than true aniseed oil, but in other respects of the same properties. Powdered capsules are carminatives; officinal in pharm.; oil distilled from fruit is substitute for british oleum anisi. Fruit used in the fabrication of liqueurs; also as a condiment. No other species here.

ANJ (അഞ്ചു - añchu, *Mal.*). Five.——*Anjanaud* (അഞ്ചനാട് - añchanátu, Mal.). From (añchu, mal. five + nátu, mal. country). Tract of country; Travancore state, Cottayam division; square miles 231. Comprises a valley and hill range. Hills form a part of Pulneys and are divided into two ranges, higher having average elevation of 7,500 feet. Coffee, tea and cinchona plantations.——*Anjarcundy* (അഞ്ചരക്കണ്ടി - añcharakkanti, Mal.). From (añchara, mal. five-and-a-half + kanti, mal. piece of land). Mal. also (randattara), meaning two villages.—"*a*" River; Málabar dist., Chiracal tal. Rises in heavy forest land on western face of Wynaud ghaut slopes, and after a course of 40 miles divides into two branches forming island of Dharmapatam at its junction with sea. Navigable for boats at all seasons to Vengaud. The command of the traffic was formerly considered so important that Dharmapatam island, acquired by the company in 1734-35, was heavily fortified and garrisoned, and it was even proposed to give up the Tellicherry factory altogether and to build a new one on Dharmapatam island.—"*b*" Amshom; Malabar dist., Chiracal tal.; lat. 11° 52′; long. 75° 33′; from Calicut N.N.W. 46 miles; from Cannanore E. 10 miles; from the sea E. 11 miles. About 8 miles north of Tellicherry. It has no paid adhicaury or other village officers and is held by the family of Mr. Murdoch Brown on a lease of 99 years granted by the East india company on the 30th April 1817. It was formerly a small talook in North malabar lying between Cannanore and Dharmapatam island. In 1741, mortgaged by the Atchanmars or chiefs to the company for 60,000 silver fanams, equal to 12,000 rupees; debt increased to 80,000 fanams in 1749; ceded to the Chiefs of Tellicherry by Ravivurma, Regent of the Chiracal raj, 23rd March 1765; reduced by the Rajah of Chiracal and Cadatnaud under the requisition of Hyder ally, 1779; reoccupied by the Chief of Tellicherry, 1782; seized again by the Rajah of Chiracal, 1786; ceded to the company with the rest of Malabar under treaty with Tippoo, 18th March 1792. In 1797 the Company opened out at this place, then known as Randatarra, a plantation of about 1,000 acres for the cultivation of special products, such as coffee, pepper, cinnamon, nutmeg, cassia, cotton, sugar-cane, and sandal-wood plants, and appointed Mr. Murdoch Brown, who had originated the scheme, to be the overseer and manager. In 1803 the plantation was almost wholly destroyed by the Pychy rebels. In 1817 a lease for 99 years granted to Mr. Brown. The estate consists of five taras or deshoms of Anjarcundy, Camayatt, Maumba, Mooringairy, Paulairy, together with a strip of land on the opposite side of the Anjarcundy river in Cottayam talook, bounded by the dyke of ten feet in height constructed in 1800 for the defence of the plantation and containing about 40 acres of land.——*Anjengo** (അഞ്ചുതെങ്ങ് - añchutennu, *Mal.*). From (añchu, mal. five + tennu, mal. cocoanut tree).—"*a*" Sub-magistracy, pay Rs. 70. Malabar district, Cochin talook.—"*b*" Town; Travancore state, Trivandrum division, Cherankeel tal.; pop. 2,678; lat. 8° 40′; long. 76° 48′; from Alleppey S.S.E. 63 miles; from Attingal W.S.W. 4½ miles; from Bombay S.S.E. 750 miles; from Cannanore S.S.E. 240 miles; from Cape comorin N.W. 67 miles; from Calicut S.S.E. 185 miles; from Cochin S.S.E. 94 miles; from Caracoolam W.N.W. 16 miles; from Cottayam S.S.E. 65 miles; from Madras S.W. 390 miles; from Nagarcoil N.W. 56 miles; from Paravore S.S.E. 107 miles; from Quilon S.E. 19 miles; from Trivandrum N.W. 18 miles; from the sea E. ½ mile. A small seaport and fishing village on a narrow strip of land running north-west to south-east, about half way between Trivandrum and Quilon. It is in the possession of the British. Bounded north and south by Travancore state, east by Anjengo backwater, west by the Arabian sea. Surrounded on its land side by Cherankeel talook. Divided into two deshoms Cottadilly farm and Vaudikagam or Anjengo proper, including Poottara. Cottadilly is farmed to the Travancore government. The Subordinate magistrate at Anjengo is immediately subordinate to the Deputy collector of Cochin. In civil matters, Tungacherry is subject to Anjengo. The town formerly consisted of two rows of houses, traces of which still exist. Anchorage off Anjengo under 10 fathoms is foul rocky ground, outside of that depth the bottom is sand and shells. Ships cannot anchor under 10 or 11 fathoms; the prevalence of considerable surf on the coast, particularly southward, renders it unsafe for ships' boats to land and communication with the shore is carried on by means of country boats. In the monsoon landing is impracticable. There is uninterrupted inland water communication from Anjengo to Tiroor railway station, a distance of nearly 200 miles. Population consists of an indifferent breed between the lowest classes of Natives and Portuguese. The first political and commercial relations between Travancore and the East india company arose in 1673 when the Company established a factory at Anjengo. In 1684, the Company obtained permission from the Ranee of Attingal to occupy the site for purposes of trade; and in 1695 a factory with fortifications was erected. For a while Anjengo ranked as an important port. The Factor was Second in Council in Bombay; and under him were placed the ports of Colachel, Yeddowa and Vilinjam. Cottadilly was ceded to the English on 10th January 1731 as satisfaction for the murder of a Chief of Anjengo and his followers. During the wars of the Carnatic, Anjengo was useful as a depôt for military stores and as the point from which the first news of outward-bound ships reached Madras. In 1792, the town was reported to be in hopeless decline. In 1809, during the disturbances in Travancore, the roadstead was completely blockaded, and in the following year the post of Commercial resident was abolished and the station made subordinate to the Political resident at Trivandrum. It has now a forsaken appearance. The ruins of a fort and flagstaff are still to be seen on the coast. A British factory and some old monuments further bespeak its former affluence and present declension. The most ancient monument is dedicated to the memory of the wife of J. Braburn, Esq., Commodore of Anjengo. On a glass panel is inscribed the name of John Tollor, first British resident, 1777. The old tombs of former English officials and their families are interesting. The historian, Robert Orme, was born at Anjengo in 1728. He was the son of a physician attached to the Anjengo factory. Eliza Draper the object of Sterne's rhapsodies was the wife of a chief of Anjengo and lived at the station. There are two Roman catholic churches. The population mostly fish. One-third of Friday's haul goes to the church. Lemon-grass oil and coir yarn are manufactured at Anjengo. The coir yarn turned out in Anjengo is superior to that made elsewhere on the coast. Exports are coir, pepper, and bamboos.—"c" Lake; Travancore state; Trivandrum division, Cherankeel tal. Receives the Attingal or Vaumanapooram river and is formed chiefly by its waters, connected with the sea by a narrow bar. Its extreme length is 12 miles, extreme breadth $\frac{3}{4}$ of a mile. Its area is 8 square miles.——*Anjikeimal* (അഞ്ചിക്കൈമൾ - añchikkaimal, Mal.). From (añchu, mal. five + kaimal, mal. chief, title). Village; Cochin state, Canyanore tal. Suburb of Ernacolum. So called in memory of five chiefs who formerly shared the surrounding country. Large regularly built market. Considerable trade, chiefly in hands of Jews and Concanies.

ANJALY (अञ्जलि - añjali, *San.*). From (añj, san. to prepare). Double handful. Measure of capacity. 12 mooshties = 1 anjaly; 4 anjalies = 1 prastam [alavay, 3f]. Approximate actual value, 1 anjaly = 28 cubic inches. Same as Coodavam. Compare Mal. nauzhy, Tam. oyak.

ANJEER (उदुम्बर - udumbara, *San.*; شجر انجیر - shajarianjír, *Ar.* and *Pers.*; انجیر کا جهاڑ - anjírkájhár, *Hind.* and *Dec.*; انجیر - anjir, *Malay*; ಶೀಮೆಅತ್ತಿ - shímeatti, *Can.*; సీమఅత్తి - símaatti, *Tel.*; ശീമയത്തി - shímayatti, *Mal.*; රටඅත්තික්කා - rataattikká, *Singh.*; சீமையத்தி - shímaiyatti, *Tam.*). Title from malay. San. from (ud, san. prefix of superiority + ambara, san. sky); extending to heavens, from its tallness. Ar. from (shajar, ar. tree + anjír, ar. fig). Hind. from (anjír, ar. fig + jhár, hind. tree). Can., &c., from (shíme, can. foreign + atti, can. fig tree). Singh. from (rata, singh. foreign + atti, singh. fig tree, ficus glomerata, miq.). Tam. also (ténatti), meaning honey + fig tree. Hebrew teenah. Greek ἐρινεὸς or later συκῆ. The European fig tree. Botanically Ficus [atty] carica, linn., moraceæ [vricsham, 121]. A deciduous tree, 15 to 20 feet in height, with large rough leaves, forming a handsome mass of foliage. Imported and moderately successful. By incisions bark yields an acrid and caustic milk, containing a considerable quantity of India rubber. Uses of fruit are familiar.

ANJEL (അഞ്ചൽ - añchal, *Mal.*). A relay; so letter post, which is carried by relays [anchey].

ANJELY (ആഞ്ഞിലി - áññali, *Mal.*). Same as wild jack. Cf. Antiaris saccidora (arayáññali), half jack; Oroxylum indicum (payyáññali), soft jack.

ANJOOM (انجم - anjum, *Hind.*). Stars.——*Anjóoman* (انجمن - anjuman, Hind.). Galaxy of stars. Association.

ANKAM (അങ്കം - ankam, *Mal.*). Challenge. In Malabar, a duel, formerly frequent among the Nayar race. These combats arose from private feuds. A preparation and training for twelve years preceded the actual fight in order to qualify the combatants in the use of their weapons. They were not necessarily the principals in the quarrel, generally their champions. These undertook to defend the cause they had taken up till they were killed. Source of revenue to the local rajah, each combatant paying for the privilege of fighting [maryauday].

ANKAPULLY (అనకాపల్లె - anakápalle,* *Tel.*). From (anaka, san. small + palle, tel. village).——**(1)** Division; Vizagapatam district; area 310 square miles; population 135,147; language Teloogoo. Boundaries:—east, Vizagapatam talook; south, Sarwasiddhy talook; west, Golcondah and Sarwasiddhy talooks; north, Veeravilly and Srungavarapoocote talooks. Physical aspect, rugged in some parts and contain hills and scrub jungle on the northern side. Soil, red ferruginous, which is very fertile. Exports jaggery, paddy, gingelly and indigo. Imports iron, tin, copper, lead, pulses, oil seeds, wheat, piecegoods and yarn. Agriculture is the chief industry. River channels and tanks. River Shaurada irrigates mostly. Camping grounds:—Cassimcote and Sabbavaram. Place of archæological interest:—Maurtore. Principal trig. station:—Potecondah. The leading places in the division, &c., are the following.——*Ankapully* (అనకాపల్లె - anakápalle, Tel.). See below.——*Bharanicam* (భరణికము - bharanikamu, Tel.). From (bharani, san. the constellation + gráma, san. village). Proprietary estate, Village; pop. 899; lat. of village 17° 38′; long. 83° 06′; from Ankapully S.E. 5 miles; from Vizagapatam W.S.W. 16 miles; from the sea W. 12 miles. Peshcush Rs. 1,566.——*Cassimcote* (ఖాసింకోట - khásimkóta, Tel.). See sep. title.——*Eedoolpaucabonangy* (ఈదులపాకబోనంగి - ídulapákabónangi, Tel.). From (ídu, tel. wild date tree, phœnix sylvestris, roxb. + páka, tel. hamlet + bónangi, tel. place so called). Proprietary estate, Village; pop. 1,020. Peshcush Rs. 2,056.——*Gotivauda* (గొట్టివాడ - gotiváda, Tel.). From (gotti, tel. tree, spathium chinense, lour. + váda, tel. village). Village; pop. 895; lat. 17° 48′; long. 83° 10′; from Ankapully N.E. 11 miles; from Vizagapatam W.N.W. 13 miles; from the sea W. 18 miles.——*Maurtorè* (మారుటూరు - márutúru, Tel.). From (márata, tel. exchange + úru, tel. village). Village; pop. 1,351; lat. 17° 44′; long. 83° 04′; from Ankapully N. 3 miles; from Vizagapatam W. 18 miles; from the sea N. 16 miles. On two hills in the vicinity are rockcut shrines, mantapams, and images supposed to be Booddhist or Jeina.——*Moonagapauk* (మునగపాక - munagapáka, Tel.). From (munaga, tel. moringa pterygosperma, gærtn. + páka, tel. village). Proprietary estate, Town; pop. 5,785; lat. of town 17° 38′; long. 83° 02′; from Ankapully S.S.W. 4 miles; from Vizagapatam W.S.W. 20 miles; from the sea N. 11 miles. Estate originally comprised eight villages paying a peshcush of Rs. 24,636; now incorporated with Ankapully.——*Narsingapully* (నరసింగపల్లి - narasingapalli, Tel.). From (narasinga, tel. proper name + palli, tel. village). Village; pop. 332; lat. 17° 36′; long. 82° 55′; from Ankapully W.S.W. 11 miles; from Vizagapatam W.S.W. 28 miles; from the sea N. 12 miles.——*Potecondah* (పోటుకొండ - pótukonda, Tel.). From (pótu, tel. ox + konda, tel. hill). Trig. station; lat. 17° 48′ 11·48″; long. 83° 04′ 38·80″; height 1,952 feet; from Ankapully N. 8 miles; from Golcondah E.N.E. 38 miles.——*Rauvauda* (రావాడ - ráváda, Tel.). From (rávi, tel. poplar-leaved fig tree, ficus religiosa, linn. + váda, tel. village). Proprietary estate, Village; pop. 1,061; lat. of village 17° 35′; long. 83° 07′; from Ankapully S.E. $7\frac{1}{2}$ miles; from Vizagapatam W.S.W. 16 miles; from the sea N. $4\frac{1}{2}$ miles. Peshcush Rs. 3,751.——*Shaurada nuddy* (శారదానది - shárádánadi, Tel.). See sep. title.——**(2)** Deputy tahsildarry; Vizagapatam district; pay Rs. 100.——**(3)** Zemindarry; Vizagapatam dist., Ankapully division; pop. 135,147; square miles 310. Originally tributary to vizianagram rajahs. Passed entirely into the hands of the family by purchase at auction in 1802, subject to a peshcush to Government of Rs. 30,766 per annum. Resold by the rajah to Godey juggappa. Consists of sixteen villages and seventeen hamlets, and comprises some of the richest land in the district. Annual rent value, with five other attached estates, Rs. 1,76,090. Present peshcush Rs. 29,953.——**(4)** Town, Head-quarters of Deputy tahsildar; Vizagapatam dist., Ankapully division; pop. 17,010; lat. 17° 41′; long. 83° 03′; from Coraputt S.S.E. 79 miles; from Madras N.N.E. 362 miles; from Narsapatam E. 28 miles; from Parvatipore S.S.W. 79 miles; from Vizagapatam W. 18 miles; from Vizianagram S.W. 40 miles; from the sea N. 13 miles. On the Shaurada nuddy and the great trunk road. A rising municipal town of recent growth, and an agricultural centre, with an export trade in sugar and cotton. Most of surrounding country belongs to Rajah of Vizianagram. A political disturbance here was speedily quelled in 1832.

ANNA (آنه - ánah, *Hind.*; ಆಣೆ - ane, *Can.*; అణా - aná, *Tel.*; അണ - ana, *Mal.*; அணா - aná, *Tam.*). One-sixteenth; either of a rupee or of a measure of capacity or length. A half anna share is $\frac{1}{32}$; a quarter anna share is $\frac{1}{64}$. Sixteen annas denotes the whole. Four annas' interest denotes 300 per cent. per annum; for this is 25 per cent. per month, by which time interest is always here reckoned. No coin of this dimension is current. But there are copper pieces representing the half and quarter anna, and the pie, which is the twelfth part; and there are silver pieces of the value of two, four, and eight annas [nauuyam, 2e]. As superficial measure it is sometimes subdivided into 16 chittahs as in North arcot, or four quarters or $\frac{1}{64}$th parts as in South arcot [alavay, 2].

ANNAM (अन्न - anna, *San.*). From (ad, san. to eat). Food.——*Anna bhaidy* (कासीस - kásísa, San.; هيرا كشيش - hírákashísh, Hind.; அன்னபேதி - annabéthi, Tam.). Drav. all same. San. from (káshi, san. benares + ísha, san. lord); shiva, the lord of benares. Hind. from (hará, hind. green + kasís, hind. sulphus ferri). Tam. from (anna, san. food + bhédí, san. solvent). Sulphate of Iron. Otherwise Green copperas. The solution is called Green vitriol [toottam]. Ferri sulphas, ferri vitriolatum, sal martis, of chemists. When pure it is transparent, of a fine bright, though not very deep, grass green color, and of a nauseous astringent taste, accompanied with a kind of sweetness; wholly soluble in water; made by subjecting iron wire to the action of dilute sulphuric acid, and evaporating the solution to crystallisation. As a native drug, powerful chalybeate tonic, astringent, emmenagogue, antiperiodic and anthelmintic; in large doses poisonous. Locally applied, astringent and stimulant. Very ancient medicine [ospitry, voidyan]. Used also in dyeing, tanning, painting, &c.——*Anna daunam* (अन्नदान - annadána, San.). From (above + dána, san. gift). Charity of rice-giving.——*Annadaunaputty* (அன்னதானப்பட்டி - annathánappatti, Tam. annadánapati*). From (annathánan, tam. name of the founder + patti, tam. village). Zemindarry, Village; Salem dist., Salem tal.; pop. 187; acres 5,662; lat. of village 11° 39′ long. 78° 11′; from Salem W.S.W. 2 miles.

Principal village in Mittah of same name included within Salem municipality. Peshcush Rs. 3,790.——*Annam bhatt* (अन्नभट्ट - annambhatta, San.). From (above + bhatta, san. lord). A Madhya cavy. Logician born in Garikipaud, near Chintapully, about A.D. 1500. He studied at Condaveed. Wrote Tarca sangraham or compendium of the old system of logic of the Nyauyam school.——*Annapoornay* (अन्नपूर्णा - annapúrná, San.). From (above + púrna, san. filled). Otherwise Anna devatay, Aunay. δημήτηρ of Greeks; Ceres of Romans; Isis or orient deity of Egyptians. Probably connected with Anna perenna of the Romans. A beneficent form of the Hindoo Parvaty. Not a Tamulian deity. She is depicted as of a deep yellow color, standing or sitting on the lotus or water lily. She has two arms, and in one hand holds a spoon, in the other a dish. In her dress she is decorated like the other modern images of Parvaty. Annapoornay is a household goddess. Her festivals take place in the early part of the increase of the moon in the month Cheitram [mausam] or about april and those of the Roman goddess took place on the Ides of march. In the hymn addressed to her by the rishy Agastyan, she is personified as pitoo or material food. She is really the harvest deified [matam].

ANNAN (ಅಣ್ಣ - anna, *Can.*; అన్న - anna, *Tel.*; அண்ணன் - annan, *Tam.*). In Malayalam is archaic. From (annal, tam. greatness). Elder brother. Suffix of respect added to proper names, as Cooppannan, Ramannan. Common prefix in comp. of 2nd or pers. names [peyar]; see below. A term of familiar address in the vocative, especially common among the non-bramin castes.——*Annacharry* (அண்ணாச்சாரி - annáççári, Tam.). From (ásári, tam. colloquial for áchárya, san. preceptor). A Madhwa name. Hindoo 2nd or pers. name [peyar].——*Annacootty* (அண்ணாக்குட்டி - annákkutti, Tam.). From (kutti, tam. child). Hindoo 2nd or pers. name [peyar].——*Annaujee* (ಅಣ್ಣಾಜಿ - annáji, Can.). From (jí, hind. master). A Mahratta and Madhwa name. Hindoo 2nd or pers. name [peyar].——*Anny* (அண்ணி - anni, Tam.). Elder brother's wife. In vocative, term of familiar address towards females among non-bramin classes; corresponds to annah among males.

ANONA (ඇනෝනා - anóná, *Singh.*). From a hayti word. Custard-apple. Botanically the Anona genus, anonaceæ [vricsham, 4]. Trees or shrubs, natives of america; fruit globose, many-celled, fleshy and many-seeded. Cherimoyer, soft-fruited custard-apple tree, anona cherimolia, mill., is a peru plant. Alligator apple tree, giving cork wood, anona palustris is a fruit of west indies, eaten by alligators. The species best known to the natives are shown below.——*Common anona* (गण्डगात्र - gandagátra, San.; सीताफळी - sítáp'halí, Mahr.; अंदण - andana, Conc.; شجر شريفه - shajrisharífah, Ar.; درخت كاج - darakhtikáj, Pers.; شریفے کا پیڑ - sharífekáper, Hind.; سیتا پھل کا جھاڑ - sítáphalkájhár, Dec.; بواہنونا - buahnona, Malay; ದುರಂಜಿ - duranji, Can.; ಅಮೃತಕಾಯಿಮರ - amritakáyidamara, Too.; సీతాఫలముచెట్టు - sítáp'halamuchettu, Tel.; ആത്തച്ചക്ക - áttaççakka, Mal.; ඇනෝනා - anóná, Singh.; சீத்தா - shíttá, Tam.). San. from (ganda, san. pimple + gátra, san. body); from fruit. Mahr. from (sítá, san. the goddess + p'hala, san. fruit). Ar. from (shajr, ar. tree + sharífah, ar. noble). Pers. from (darakht, pers. tree + káj, pers. custard-apple). Hind. from (sharífah, ar. noble + per, hind. tree). Dec. means seeta's fruit tree. Malay from (buah, malay fruit + nona, malay anona). Too. from (amrita, san. nectar + káyi, too. fruit + mara, too. tree). Tel. means seeta's fruit tree. Mal. from (átta, mal. mexican name of anona + chakka, mal. artocarpus integrifolia, willd.); from appearance of fruit. Tam. from (sítá, san. the goddess); san. here also means furrow and the fruit is furrowed on rind. Hind. also (átá). Malay also (srikaya), meaning lutchmy + fruit. Can. also (amritamara), meaning nectar + tree. Mal. also (átta). Title otherwise Atah, Custard-apple, Custard jack, Nectar fruit, Pimple fruit, Seeta's fruit, Sugar apple, Sweet sop. Botanically Anona squamosa, linn., anonaceæ [vricsham, 4]. Shrub or small tree, 15–20 feet; leaves oblong, or oblong-lanceolate, glabrous, pellucid dotted, with heavy smell; calyx three-sepalled; petals six in a double row; exterior ones narrow lanceolate, three-cornered near the apex; inner ones scarcely any; peduncles axillary; flowers whitish green; flowering in march-april; domesticated everywhere. Fruit about size of an orange, full of black seeds, each of which is covered with a yellow edible pulp of delicate flavor. Originally from s. america. Ripe fruit medicinally a maturant when bruised and mixed with salt, applied to tumours; root drastic purgative. Fruit more delicate flavor than bullock's-heart; perfectly free from acid. Seeds contain acrid principle fatal to insects; dried unripe fruit, powdered and mixed with gram flour, used to destroy vermin in hair. Wood soft, close-grained.——*Netted anona* (लवली - lavalí, San.; रामफळी - rámap'halí, Mahr.; गोयिंचेअंदन - góyinchéandana, Conc.; لونا - launá, Hind.; رام پھل کا جھاڑ - rámphalkajhár, Dec.; نونا - nona, Malay; ರಾಮಫಲ - rámap'hala, Can.; రామాఫలముచెట్టు - rámáp'halamuchettu, Tel.; രാമച്ചീത്താമരം - rámaççíttámaram, Mal.; ආත්තා - áttá, Singh.; இராமசீத்தா - irámasíttá, Tam.). Title from appearance of fruit. San. from (lú, san. to cut); from sour fruit. Mahr. from (ráma, san. the hero + p'hala, san. fruit). Hind. from (laun, hind. salt). Dec. from (rám, hind. the hero + phal, hind. fruit + jhár, hind. tree). Singh. means grandmother, alluding to seetay; but is really a corruption from mexican (áta). Tam. from (ráma, san. the god + sítá, san. the goddess). San. also (rámasítá), meaning rama + seeta. Mal. also (parankiççakka), meaning portuguese + jack fruit, artocarpus integrifolia, willd. Tam. also (aninuná), meaning great + morinda, but really corrupted from anona; (manilaáttá), meaning manilla + custard-apple, anona squamosa, linn. Title otherwise Bullock's-heart, Foreign jack, Manilla custard-apple, Rama's fruit, West indian custard-apple. Botanically Anona reticulata, linn., anonaceæ [vricsham, 4]. Alias Rollinia sieberi. Flower largish, yellowish green, of a vinous smell; fruit like a bullock's-heart; pulp is yellowish white, containing seeds of an agreeable flavor; differs from custard-apple in having a perfectly smooth rind. Fruit eaten by natives, rarely by europeans; good fibre from bark of young twigs; dry unripe fruit yields black dye; fresh leaves give some indigo.——*Prickly anona* (نونا - nona, Malay; ಮುಳ್ಳುರಾಮಫಲ - mullurámap'hala, Can.; വിലാത്തിനൂണ - viláttinúná, Mal.; රටඇනෝනා - rataanóná, Singh.; புளிப்பலா - pulippalá, Tam.). Title from thorn-like points of fruit. Can. from (mullu, can. thorn + rámap'hala, can. anona reticulata, linn.). Mal. from (viláttí, mal. europe + núná, mal. morinda umbellata, linn.). Singh. from (rata, singh. foreign + anóná, singh. custard-apple, anona squamosa, linn.). Tam. from (puli, tam. acidity + palá, tam. jack tree, artocarpus integrifolia, willd.). Tam. also (mullusíttá), meaning thorn + custard-apple tree. Title otherwise Prickly custard-apple, Sour jack, Sour sop. Botanically Anona muricata, linn., anonaceæ [vricsham, 4]. Fruit resembles large Custard-apple [common anona] with soft thorn-like points to each pip; nutritious, but insipid. Wood inferior.

ANOO (अनु - anu, *San.*). Prefix, meaning after or with.——*Anoobhavam* (अनुभव - anubhava, San.; അനുഭവം - anubhavam, Mal.). From (bhú, san. to be). Enjoyment. Grant of hereditary land in Malabar, either rent free or at a pepper-corn rent, in reward of service. Also a present of betel or a cocoanut from the proprietor at the time of executing a deed of transfer of a garden or plantation to the person to whom the transfer is made as symbolical of the character of the land made over. See vol. I, 112.——*Anoobhavaumritam* (अनुभवामृत - anubhavámrita, San.). From (bhú, san. to be + amrita, san. nectar). A Veiraugya treatise. Exists only in Dravidian languages. It contains a treatise on the Oopanishad, a sort of exposition of pantheism; shows that the existence of a material world cannot be proved, and that all is Mauyam; and recommends retirement from domestic life and meditation with a view to the soul's purification and final beatitude.——*Anoobhogam* (अनुभोग - anubhóga, San.). From (bhuj, san. to eat). Same as Anoobhavam.——*Anooloma* (अनुलोम - anulóma, San.). From (lóman, san. hair). Means born in natural order. By Sanscrit theorists applied to those born of a higher-caste male and lower-caste female; as for instance a barber, who is supposed to be the offspring of a Bramin man and a Veisya woman. Opposed to Pratiloma [q.v.]. The six Anooloma castes are as follows. Three born of Bramins, by Cshatriya women and known as Moordhauvasicta, by Veisya women and known as Ambashta, by Shoodra women and known as Nishauda or Paurashava. Two born of Cshatriyas, by Veisya women and known as Mauhishya, by Shoodra women and known as Oogra. One born of Veisyas, by Shoodra women and known as Carana [jauty].——*Anoomaunam* (अनुमान - anumána, San.). From (má, san. to measure). Inference; one of the four processes, according to Nyauya philosophy, by which the mind arrives at true knowledge. The other three are pratyacsham or sense perception, oopamaunam or comparison, and shabdam or verbal testimony.——*Anooswauram* (अनुस्वार - anusvára, San.). From (svar, san. sound). The nasal sound marked by a dot above the line. Much use is made in the Dravidian languages, especially in Tamul and Teloogoo, of the nasals ṅ, ñ, ṇ, n, and m for the purpose of euphonising the harder consonants of each varga. This is called nunnation. All the nasals are regarded by native grammarians as modifications of the sound of m, the nature of each modification being determind by the manner in which m is affected by succeeding consonants. In Sanscrit the nasal consonants constitute the final characters of each of the five vargams. In Teloogoo and Canarese one and the same character, which is called anooswauram, is used to represent the whole of the nasal modification [bhaushay].

ANSAR (انصر - ansar, *Hind.*). From (nasara, ar. to succour). Victorious. Alam; as Ansar bee, alam + alaumat. Also component part of lacabs; as Ansar ood deen, victorious in religion [ism].

ANTAM (अन्त - anta, *San.*). End.——*Antacan* (अन्तक - antaka, San.). One who causes death. Epithet of Bharany, second lunar asterism, from Yaman the god of death who presides over it.——*Antaudy* (அந்தாதி - andáthi, Tam.). From (ádi, san. beginning). Tamul verse, the last word or syllable of a stanza in which is the first of the succeeding. Employed in various metres to assist the memory.——*Antyam* (अन्त्य - antya, San.). Last in mathematics. Pratamam, Madhyam, Antyam are first, mean, and last.——*Antya parny* (अन्त्यपर्णी - antyaparní, San.). From (parna, san. leaf); from terminal leaves. Botanically the Terminalia genus, combretaceæ [vricsham, 55]. Large trees of tropical regions; leaves mostly alternate, entire and clustered towards the points of branches; flowerspikes mostly slender, axillary; fruit ovoid, very various in size, smooth or angular or winged, one-seeded; wood moderately hard to very hard. The species best known to the natives are :—arjuna [white murdah], belerica [belleric myrobalan], catappa [catapang], chebula [chebulic myrobalan], citrina [harra], paniculata [flowering murdah], tomentosa, var. coriacea [leathery murdah], tomentosa, var. typica [black murdah]. Other s. indian species indigenous or naturalized are :—alata, bialata.

ANTAR (अन्तर् - antar, San.). Within.——*Antah caranam* (अन्तःकरण - antahkarana, San.). From (karana, san. organ). Mental powers embracing :—Booddhy or perception, Ahancauram or self-consciousness, Manas or volition, and Chittam or the reasoning faculty.——*Antah pooram* (अन्तःपुर - antahpura, San.). From (pura, san. place). Women's apartments.——*Antaram* (अन्तर - antara, San.). An intermediate space, a difference in computations.——*Antaraulam* (अन्तराल - antarála, San.). From (above + lí, san. to lie). Castes placed between the four original ones. Travancore name for Ambalavausy [q.v.]. Means intermediate castes between Bramins and shoodras. They officiate as temple servants. They mostly follow the nepotistic law [jauty].——*Antarjanam* (अन्तर्जन - antarjana, San.). From (jana, san. person). A Braminy in Malabar [agattamaur].——*Antarvedhy* (అంతర్వేది - antarvédi, Tel.). From (above + védi, san. sacrificial altar); vasishtan performed a yaugam here. Village, Port, Place of pilgrimage; Godavery dist., Narsapore tal.; pop. 6,494; acres 11,557; lat. 16° 20′; long. 81° 46′; from Bendamoorlunka W.S.W. 18 miles; from Cocanada S.W. 53 miles; from Madras N.N.E. 242 miles; from Narsapore S.S.E. 7½ miles. On Golcondah coast. The Vasishta branch of the Godavery falls into the sea at this place, and large vessels discharge and load near its mouth. Narsapore point lies to the east of the bar, and near it is a conspicuous obelisk, 75 feet high. Two ancient temples of Narsimhasawmy and Neelacunteshwaran. About 20,000 pilgrims resort to this place annually for the calyaunam of the idol in the first temple, which lasts for five days in January. Antarvedhy also forms the last of the seven sacred stations on the Godavery, at each of which devotees performing the ceremony of Sapta saugara yautray have to bathe. Trig. station in lat. 16° 21′ 51·53″; long. 81° 49′ 55·13″. Another in lat. 16° 20′ 47·08″; long. 81° 48′ 9·11″. Another in lat. 16° 19′ 46·57″; long. 81° 46′ 3·91″.——*Antaryaumy* (अन्तर्यामी - antaryámí, San.). From (above + yam, san. to check). The internal check, conscience.

ANT GRASS (அளத்துப்புல் - alattuppul, *Tam.*). Title from being found near ant-hills. Tam. from (alam, tam. saltpan + pul, tam. grass); maritime grass. Botanically Pommereulla cornucopiæ, linn. f., graminaceæ [vricsham, 156]. Small rare grass, growing under bushes on dry uncultivated ground; no other species here.

ANTISA (అంటిస - antisa, *Tel.*). Sticking. Plant name common to :—Achyranthes aspera, Cyathula prostrata, Sida cordifolia. See gloss. paragraphs.

ANWAR (انور - anwar, *Hind.*). From (núr, ar. light). The resplendent. Alam; as Anwar ally, double alam; Anwar khan, alam + alaumat. Also component part of lacabs; as Anwar ood deen, light of the faith [ism]. The ruler of the latter name was appointed by the Nizam as Nawaub of Ellore and Rajahmundry from 1725 to 1741; then Governor of Carnatic during the minority of the lawful Nawaub, Mahomed sayeed. On Mahomed sayeed's assassination he was confirmed as Nawaub in 1743, though a stranger to the preceding line. During the war between the English and the French in 1744, he continued to change sides. At the death of Nizam ool moolk, his patron, and the consequent contest for the Hyderabad throne, Chundah sahib joined one of the claimants and assisted by the French, marched against Anwar ood deen, who met him at Amboor and in an action fought there in 1749, was killed. His second son Mahomed ally or wallajah was confirmed by the British as Nawaub at Arcot. His descendants are the present Carnatic family. Anwar ood deen built Covelong. See vol. I (122), 44; and II, 252, 256 [charitram].

ANWAUR (انوار - anwár, *Hind.*); pl. of (núr, ar. light). Lights.——*Anwaur oos sooheily* (انوارالسهيلى - anwárussuhailí, Hind.). From (suhail, ar. the star canopus). A book of tales translated from the Arabic by the Persian poet Kashifee [nacshatram].

ANYAM (अन्य - anya, *San.*). Other.——*Anya coody* (அன்னியக்குடி - anniyakkudi, Tam.). From (kudi, tam. tenant). A cultivator who does not live in the village in which his land is [paracoody].——*Anyata* (ಅನ್ಯತ - anyata, Can.). A present made to junior relatives; in contradistinction to Oochita, a present made to non-relatives.

ANZEROOT (انزروت - anzarút, *Ar.*; گژاد - guzhád, *Pers.*; لائی - lái, *Hind.*). Ar. also (kohlifársí), meaning persian collyrium; (kohlikirmání), meaning kirman collyrium. Title otherwise Goojar, Persian collyrium, Sarcocolla. Product of Astragalus species, leguminosæ [vricsham, 48]. A gum exported from persia; made into an ointment and plaster, or into a medicated oil. For tragacanth of this genus see Kateerah.

APARAM (अपर - apara, *San.*). Other.——*Aparadinass* (అపరదినుసులు - aparadinusulu, Tel.). From (dinusu, tel. article). All grains other than the nine common grains [nava dhaunyam].

APARANJY (افرنجى - afranjí, *Ar.* and *Hind.*; ಅಪರಂಜಿ - aparanji, *Tel.*). From (afranj, ar. frank or european). Superior gold. The leaves are used in setting precious stones [pon raikk].

APHAINAM (अफेन - ap'héna, *San.*). From (ahi, san. serpent + p'héna, san. froth). Poppy. Botanically the Papaver genus, papaveraceæ [vricsham, 8]. Herbs with a milky juice; leaves lobed or toothed, and hairy; fruit capsular. The species best known are shown below.——*Corn poppy* (तांबडाखसखस - támbadákhasakhasa, Mahr.; نبات الخشخاش الاحمر - nabátulkhashkháshulahmar, Ar.; كوكنار سرخ - koknárisurkh, Pers.; لال پوست - lálpost, Hind.; لال خشخش کا جهاڑ - lálkhashkhashkájhár, Dec.; بنگه اپیون - bungapiun, Malay; ಕೆಂಪುಗಸಗಸೆ - kempugasagase, Can.; ಕಸಕಸ - kasakase, Too.; ఎర్రగసగసాలచెట్టు - erragasagasálachettu, Tel.; ചുവന്നകശകശ - chuvannakashakasha, Mal.; சிவப்புக்கசகசாச்செடி - shivappukkasagasáççedi, Tam.). Title from being found in corn fields. Mahr. from (támbadá, mahr. red + khashkhash, ar. poppy). Ar. from (nabát, ar. plant + khashkhásh, ar. poppy + ahmar, ar. red). Pers. from (koknár, pers. opium poppy + surkh, pers. red). Hind. from (lál, hind. red + post, hind. capsule). Dec. from (lál, hind. red + khashkhash, hind. poppy, papaver somniferum, linn. + jhár, hind. tree). Malay from (bung, malay flower + apiun, malay opium). Can. from (kempu, can. red + gasagase, can. poppy). Tel. from (erra, tel. red + gasagasálu, tel. poppy seed + chettu, tel. plant). Mal. from (chuvanna, mal. red + kashakasha, mal. poppy). Tam. from (shivappu, tam. red + kasagasá, tam. poppy + shedi, tam. plant). San. also (mudriká), meaning stamped with the seal, from capsules bearing impressions like seals. Mahr. also (jangalímudriká), meaning wild + the plant. Ar. also (khashkashimansúr), meaning scattered poppy, from its shedding petals quickly; (shakáik), from its extreme redness. Pers. also (lálá), from redness. Tel. also (errapóstakáyachettu), meaning red + poppy fruit + plant. Tam. also (shivappuppósdakkáyççedi), meaning red + poppy + plant. Title otherwise Blind-eyes, Canker, Canker-rose, Cockrose, Copper-rose, Cop-rose, Corn-flower, Corn rose, French poppy, Red poppy, Red-weed, Seal capsule. Botanically Papaver [aphainam] rhœas, linn., papaveraceæ [vricsham, 8]. Smaller plant than opium poppy and distinguished by much divided leaves and hairy flower stalks. Petals employed in pharmacy for sake of coloring matter; no active or narcotic principle in this species.——*Opium poppy* (अहिफेन - ahip'héna, San.; अफीण - ap'hína, Mahr.; कसकसे - kaskasé, Conc.; نبات الخشخاش - nabátulkhashkhásh, Ar.; كوكنار - koknár, Pers.; خشخاش کاپیڑ - khashkháshkáper, Hind.; خشخش کا جهاڑ - khashkhashkájhár, Dec.; بنگه مدت - bungmadat, Malay; ಗಸಗಸೆಗಿಡ - gasagasegida, Can.; ಕಸಕಸೆ - kasakase, Too.; గసగసాలచెట్టు - gasagasálachettu, Tel.; കറുപ്പ് - karuppa, Mal.; අබින් - abin, Singh.; கசகசாச்செடி - kasagasáççedi, Tam.). Title from yielding opium. San. from (ahi, san. serpent + p'héna, san. froth). Mahr. from sanscrit. Ar. from (nabát, ar. plant + khashkhásh, ar. poppy). Pers. from (kok, pers. cough + nár, pers. capsule). Hind. from (khashkhásh, ar. poppy + per, hind. tree). Malay from (bung, malay flower + madat, malay opium). Can. from (gasagase, can. poppy + gida, can. plant). Mal. from (karu, mal. black); from product. Tam. from (khashkhásh, ar. poppy + shedi, tam. plant). San. also (ap'héna), by corr. Mahr. also (khasakhasa), meaning poppy seed. Hind. also (afiyún). Malay also (apyun). Tel. also (nallamanduchettu), meaning opium + plant; (póstakáyachettu), meaning poppy fruit + plant. Tam. also (pósdakkáyççedi), meaning poppy plant. Greek μήκων, the product μηκώνιον. A Latin name for opium is Manus dei. Title otherwise Abiny, Balewort, Carnation flowered poppy, Cough capsule, Garden poppy, Joan silver-pin, Khaskas, Maw seed, Peony poppy, White poppy. Botanically Papaver [aphainam] somniferum, linn., papaveraceæ [vricsham, 8]. Alias Papaver album, indehiscens, nigrum, officinale, opiiferum.—"*a*" Herbaceous, annual, 2–3 feet; sepals two, deciduous; petals four; stem smooth, glaucous; leaves amplexicaul, repand, cut and toothed, teeth somewhat obtuse; capsules obovate or glabrous; peduncles drooping; seeds numerous, small, white; flower generally white, but to be found mixture of rose, lilac, or violet and white; naturalized by cultivation in india.—"*b*" All parts of the poppy abound in a narcotic milky juice, which is partially extracted, together with a quantity of mucilage, by decoction; seeds are not considered narcotic in europe, here in a slight degree; the mature capsules are called poppy-heads, devoid of odour, but of slightly bitter taste; milky inspissated juice of the plant is opium, derived by scratching immature capsules and not from foliage.—"*c*" Two kinds of opium are found in general commerce, the Turkey and East indian. The former is solid, compact, and transparent, somewhat brittle, of a dark-brown color. The latter has much less consistence, being sometimes not thicker than tar and always ductile; in color it is more dark, nauseous, but less bitter; it is cheaper, and not so strong as the turkey; it is often adulterated with oil of sesamum, cow-dung, the aqueous extract of the capsules, gum-arabic, tragacanth, aloes, and other articles. Good opium is not perfectly soluble in water, very inflammable and burns with a clear flame; its value consists in the quantity of the alkaloid morphine which it contains; this morphine is obtained in crystals from opium treated with alcohol and ammonia; the best opium contains from 8 to 9 per cent. of morphine. The seeds yield by expression a bland and very valuable oil, of a pale golden color, equal to that of the olive; by exposure to heat of sun in shallow vessels, it is rendered perfectly colorless.—"*d*" The use of the drug opium was transmitted by the arabs to the nations of the east, and in the first instance to the persians; there are no ancient chinese or sanscrit names for opium; the introduction of opium into india was connected with the spread of islamism, and may have been favored by the mahomedan prohibition of wine; barbosa, who visited calicut in 1511, mentions it among the more valuable drugs, imported from aden or cambay; the opium trade is one of the monopolies of government; great quantities are annually shipped to china; foreign opium is only admitted at a heavy duty.—"*e*" For cultivation the poppy plant requires a rich soil, plenty of manuring, and frequent irrigation; dew has the effect of facilitating the flow of juice, and, though increasing it in quantity, renders it of a darker color and more liquid than otherwise; a dry state of the atmosphere, accompanied by strong winds, is a favorable condition for elaborating the juice in the capsules; the practice in collecting it consists in making incisions into the capsules when the dew has evaporated, collecting the juice in pots, &c., and working it into masses or cakes. Opium is not made in southern india, except in very small quantities in mysore; chiefly imported from malwah.—"*f*" The pounded herb, dry capsule, seed, oil, and concrete juice of the immature capsule or opium are all medicinal. The heads or capsules possess anodyne properties; chiefly employed, boiled in water, as fomentations to inflamed or ulcerated surfaces; the syrup prepared from them with inspissated decoction used as an anodyne for children and to allay cough, &c. Veidyans prescribe seeds in diarrhœa. Oil from seeds also used as a demulcent medicine. The opium is in medicine primarily stimulant; secondarily narcotic, anodyne, and antispasmodic; and in overdoses a powerful poison; as an external application opium valuable in various rheumatic, neuralgic, &c., affections. The plant gives to pharm. the nearly ripe capsules, papaveris capsulæ, sedative and anodyne; preparations, decoctum papaveris, extractum papaveris, syrupus papaveris; also opium in numerous forms, hydrochlorate of morphia, one of the contained alkaloids; narcotine a contained neutral crystallizable body. The veidyans use opium freely in medicine; they give it to procure sleep, shorten cold fit of an intermittent fever in lockjaw, and to afford ease in certain stages of dysentery; they give it also externally, mixed with arrack, in conjunction with benzoin, bdellium, aloes, and ginger in rheumatic affections. The stimulant effects of opium are most apparent from small doses, which increase the energy of the mind and the frequency of the pulse; these effects are succeeded by languor and lassitude; in excessive doses it proves a violent and fatal poison; by habit, the effects of opium on the body are remarkably diminished; acetic acid is a perfect counter-poison for opium.—"*g*" The seed, the maw seed given to cage birds, has a sweet taste, used parched by the lower class of natives as a food, also much used by sweetmeat-makers. An intoxicating liquor is formed by macerating or infusing the poppy heads with water and sweetening with molasses; this is drunk by fakeers and others at festivals. Oil used for lamps and is prized by artists; also used as salad oil for cooking purposes; after the oil is extracted, the cake is sold as a food to the poorer classes. An account of the commercial treatment of opium will be found at vol. 1, 456.—"*h*" Varieties very numerous. The special quality called doodhy opium or milk opium coming from bengal is very soft, is dark in color, and contains a large quantity of milky juice; 1½ grains of this are equal to 1 of Malwah.

APPAN (ಅಪ್ಪ - appa, *Can.*; అప్ప - appa, *Tel.*; அப்பன் - appan, *Tam.*). Father. In Malayalam is archaic. In Tooloo means mother [ammah]. Suffix of respect added to proper names, as Ayyappan, Mooroogappan. Common prefix in comp. of 2nd or pers. names [peyar]; see below. In vocative a common mode of calling among non-bramins. The same to children among all castes.——*Apparow* (ಅಪ್ಪಾರಾವು - appárávu, Can.). From (rávu, can. king). A Mahratta name. Hindoo 2nd or pers. name [peyar].——*Appattoray* (அப்பாத்துரை - appátturai, Tam.). From (turai, tam. ruler). Hindoo 2nd or pers. name [peyar].——*Appaujee* (ಅಪ್ಪಾಜಿ - appáji, Can.). From (ji, hind. master). Marhatta name. Hindoo 2nd or pers. name [peyar].——*Appauroo* (அப்பாவு - appávu, Tam.). Familiar form of Appan. Common among non-bramins. Hindoo 2nd or pers. name [peyar].——*Appoo* (ಅಪ್ಪು - appu, Can.; அப்பு - appu, Tam.). Familiar form of Appan.——*Appoocootty* (அப்புக்குட்டி - appukkutti, Tam.). From (kutti, tam. child). Hindoo 2nd or pers. name [peyar].

APPAY (నాగదొండ - nágadonda, *Tel.*; அப்பை - appai, *Tam.*). Tel. from (nága, san. serpent + donda, tel. cephalandra indica, naud.); probably from color of fruit. Tam. means adhering. Tel. also (kunkumadonda), meaning red saffron powder + cephalandra indica, naud.; from color of fruit. Tam. also (appakkóvai), meaning appay plant + indian caper, cephalandra indica, naud. Title otherwise Appacovay, Beaked bryony, Saffron indian caper, Stinking indian caper. Botanically Rhynchocarpa fœtida, schrad., cucurbitaceæ [vricsham, 62]. Alias Æchmandra rostrata; Bryonia pilosa, rostrata. Climbing; stem slender, hairy or pubescent; tendrils simple; leaves on longish petioles, roundish cordate, sinuate, toothed, pubescent; male flowers usually two together, pedicelled, on a slender peduncle, longer than the petiole; calyx campanulate; female solitary, very shortly peduncled, in the same axils with the male, being ovate, rostrate, longitudinally striated, hairy, two to six seeded; seeds black, compressed, with thin margin. The root, small and of a light grey color, is sweet and mucilaginous to the taste; powder is medicinally demulcent; leaves eaten as greens. No other common species here.

AR (ار - ar, *Ar.*). Al [q.v.] before r in Arabic single terms, as ar-raheem, meaning the merciful.

ARA (അറ - ara, *Mal.*; அறை - arai, *Tam.*). From (aru, tam. to cut). Apartment. Suffix in place names; as Pulliyara, meaning sleep + room, so palace.

ARA (అర - ara, *Tel.*; അര - ara, *Mal.*). Half.——*Arapow* (అరపావు - arapávu, Tel.). From (pávu, tel. one-fourth).—"*a*" One-eighth of anything.—"*b*" Measure of weight. 2 arapows = 1 pow or ¼ seer [uiray, 2b]. Approximate actual value, 1 arapow = 472½ grs. Used in Bellary ⅛th of a seer of 21 tolahs. Compare Pollum.

ARAB (عرب - arab, *Hind.*). Mahomedans, originally natives of Arabia, and come to the southern districts by sea as sailors or merchants. Most numerous in S. arcot; less so in Tinnevelly, Tanjore and Malabar. Total for Presidency about 4,000. Araby is a turban worn by Arabs. In Anglo-Indian title means an Arab horse.——*Arabia* (عربستان - arabastán, Hind.). The country. Cf. Alhagi maurorum, arabian manna; Boswellia carterii, arabian olibanum; Cassia angustifolia, arabian senna plant; Coffea arabica, arabian coffee shrub; Costus speciosus, arabian costum; Jasminum sambac, arabian jasmine; Salicornia arabica, arabian gloss-wort; all naturalized.——*Arabian costum* (केमुक - kémuka, San.; पेवा - pévá, Mahr.; قسط - kust, Ar.; قسط شیرین - kustishírín, Pers.; کیو - keú, Hind.; ಪುಷ್ಕರ - pushkara, Can.; బొమ్మకచ్చిక - bommakaççika, Tel.; ചണ്ണക്കൂവ - channakkúva, Mal.; තෙබු - tebu, Singh.; கோட்டம் - kóttam, Tam.). Title from country whence brought. San. from (ka, san. head + am, san. to be sick). Ar. from (kushtha, san. the plant). Pers. from (kust, ar. costus + shírín, pers. sweet). Can. from (pushkara, san. nourishing). Mal. from (chanda, san. violent + kúva, mal. arrowroot, curcuma angustifolia, roxb.). Tam. from (kusht'ha, san. bad spotted); as useful in skin diseases. San. also (pushkara), meaning nourishing; (káshmíra), meaning produced in cashmere; (subandhu), meaning good friend; (padmapatra), meaning having leaves like nelumbium speciosum, willd.; (kusht'ha), meaning bad spotted. Hind. also (pachak). Mal. also (maruñchanna), meaning fragrant + the plant; (patimukam), corr. from (padmaka, san. the plant); (channa). Tam. also (kúgaimañjal), meaning arrowroot + turmeric, compare malayalam; (malaivasambu), meaning mountain + sweet flag, acorus calamus, linn. Title otherwise Elephant arrowroot, Mountain sweet flag, Showy costus, Sweet costus, Tsiana. Botanically Costus speciosus, smith, zingiberaceæ [vricsham, 144]. Generic name from (kusht'ha, san. the plant). Alias Amomum hirsutum; Banksia speciosa; Costus arabicus, vaginalis; Hellenia grandiflora; Tsiana speciosa. Tsiana from mal. Height 3–4 feet, dark green large lanceolate leaves, deep crimson bracteal heads, as large as a man's closed hand, pale lavender colored flowers, five inches across, its spirally twisted stem carries its leaves and flowers above the brushwood in jungles; frequenting moist, shady places. Infusion of pleasant-smelling, warm, knotty root prescribed by veidyans as stomachic and tonic; given in advanced stages of typhus fever. Rhizomes made into a preserve. Once thought to be the source of Costus, for which see Costum. No other species here.——*Arabian date* (تمر - tamar, Ar.). From (tamara, ar. to eat date). See Kharjooram.——*Arabian manna* (दुरालभा - durálabhá, San.; धमासा - dhamásá, Mahr.; شوك الجمل - shaukuljamal, Ar.; شترخار - shutrkhár, Pers.; جوانسا - javánsa, Hind.; جواسا - javásá, Dec.; గిరికర్ణిక - girikarnika, Tel.; കപ്പത്തുമ്പ - kappattumba, Mal.). Title from habitat. San. from (dur, san. prefix meaning difficulty + álabh, san. to touch); prickly bush. Mahr. from (dhanvayása, san. desert camel thorn). Ar. from (shauk, ar. thorn + jamal, ar. camel); being food of camel. Pers. from (shutr, pers. camel + khár, pers. thorn). Hind. from (yavása, san. camel thorn). Tel. from (girikarniká, san. mouse-eared camel thorn). Mal. from (kappal, mal. ship + tumba, mal. leucas indica, r. br.); foreign leucas. San. also (girikarniká), meaning mouse + eared; (yavása), meaning joining; (kaçchurá), meaning itchy plant, from causing itch. Pers. also (ushturkhár), meaning camel's thorn; (khárishutr), meaning camel's thorn. Title otherwise Camel thorn, Haj, Hebrew manna, Jawausah, Mouse ear, Ooshtarkhaur, Persian manna, Tooranjbeen. Botanically Alhagi maurorum, desv., leguminosæ [vricsham, 48]. Generic name from (alháj, ar. pilgrim). Alias Hedysarum alhagi. Low scrubby spiny bush; small simple leaves, flower smallish red; in hot season when smaller plants die, this sends forth leaves and flowers. During daytime in persia, &c., a sweet gummy substance exudes from the leaves and stems; this hardens and is collected; not found on the indian plant; occurs in small, round, unequal grains, the size of coriander seed, of yellowish white color, caking together and forming an opaque mass, in which are found portions of the thorns and fruits of the plant; is inodorous, flavor is sweetly saccharine, followed by slight acridity. As a medicine its effects correspond to those of ash manna, or fraxinus ornus; in pharm. non-officinal. Factitious manna, a compound of sugar or honey with scammony, is sometimes exposed for sale. No other species here [manna].

ARAGAUNY (అరగాణి - aragáni, *Tel.*). Catchment basin.

ARAM (அறம் - aram, *Tam.*). From (aru, tam. to decide); prescribed duty. Virtue. Mankind according to Tamulian authors were created for the purpose of enjoying one or other of four objects; Aram or virtue, Porool or wealth, Inbam or pleasure, and Veed or eternal happiness in another world. Aram itself has eight constituent parts:—viz., absence of scepticism; absence of covetousness; absence of disgust; absence of perplexity; absence of censoriousness; aiding the impoverished; elucidating the nature of charity; abundant love. Aram is elsewhere said to be of two kinds, viz., Illaram or domestic life, and Tooravaram or ascetic life; in the former, thirty-two acts of charity being prescribed. Arattay cauppone, from (káppón, tam. he who guards), is Ayenaur.——*Arantaungy* (அறந்தாங்கி - arandángi, Tam. arantángi*). From (aram, tam. charity + tángi, tam. support).—"*a*" Deputy tahsildarry, Tanjore district. Pay Rs. 70.—"*b*" Village, Head-quarters of Deputy tahsildar and Sub-magistrate and Sub-registrar; Tanjore dist., Puttoocottah tal.; pop. 2,708; acres 8,044; lat. 10° 10′; long. 79° 02′; from Combaconam S.S.W. 60 miles; from Madras S.S.W. 217 miles; from Mayavaram S.S.W. 78 miles; from Munnargoody S.W. 46 miles; from Negapatam W.S.W. 70 miles; from Puttoocottah S.W. 29 miles; from Tanjore S.W. 43 miles; from the sea W. 17 miles. Once noted for weaving industry. Ruined fort, formerly occupied by petty chieftain tributary to Rajah of Tanjore. Fair on Tuesdays. In early times of importance. Taken in fifteenth century from Cholas by the Saitoopaty general of the Pandyan ruler and annexed to dominions of latter. In seventeenth century belonged to Tanjore, and about 1646 was seized by Raghoonaut tevar. Restored by treaty, was again captured in 1698. Early in eighteenth century, the governorship of a son of the Kizhavan of Ramnaud. The fortress subsequently changed hands many times, the Tanjore rajah finally occupying it in 1749. Old Shiva temple with inscriptions.

ARAMANAY (ಅರಮನೆ - aramane, *Can.*; அரமனை - aramanai, *Tam.*). From (arasan, tam. king + manai, tam. house). Palace, court of justice, Government. Aramanay swaustyam from (svást'hya, san. competence) were estates kept by the old governments for supply of grain to troops. Cf. Havelly lands in Northern circars. See vol. I, 112.

ARAMBOLY (ആരുവാമൊഴി - áruvámozhi, *Mal.*). From (aru, tam. shiva + váy, tam. mouth + mozhi, tam. word). Village; Travancore state, Pudmanaubhapooram division, Tovaula tal.; lat. 8° 15′; long. 77° 34′; from Bhootapaundy E. 5 miles; from Trivandrum E.S.E. 41 miles; from the sea N. 13 miles. Pagoda of great sanctity. Chowky for collecting duties on dutiable exports and imports. The pass of same name leads to Tinnevelly from Travancore.

ARANASHT (ಅರನಷ್ಟ - aranashta, *Can.*). From (ara, can. royal + nashta, san. loss). Payment to ruling power. Analogous to existing license tax. See vol. I, 112.

ARANAY (ब्राह्मणी - bráhmaní, *San.*; سپلک - siplak, *Hind.*; ನಲಿಗಣ್ಣಿನಹಾವು - naliganninahávu, *Can.*; నలికండ్లపాము - nalikandlapámu, *Tel.*; അരണ - arana, *Mal.*; அரணை - aranai, *Tam.*). San. from (brahma, san. the god). Can. from (nali, can. agreeable + kannu, can. eye + hávu, can. snake). Tel. from (nali, tel. agreeable + kannu, tel. eye + pámu, tel. snake). Tam. from (aran, tam. beauty). The terms are co-extensive with the european family Lacertidæ, Sauria [godhicay], reptilia [sarpy, 7], of naturalists [jantoo]. This class of animals have a head covered with shields, which are symmetrically arranged; tongue slender, free, exsertile, terminating in a fork; scales on the back granular or rhombic, on the sides granular; on the belly larger, quadrangular or rounded, and arranged in cross bands; no longitudinal fold along the sides, but generally a fold across the throat; tail very long, rounded, with the scales arranged in rings, fragile; eyes diurnal, with eyelids; tympanum distinct; limbs four, well developed; do not attain to any considerable size; live generally on the ground and are not burrowing. The following are representative species in Southern india:—"*a*" Acanthodactylus nilgherrensis; Neilgherries; length ½ foot.—"*b*" Cabrita leschenaultii; alias Cabrita brunnea; Calosaura leschenaultii; Lacerta leschenaultii; brown, with two broad whitish bands on each side, length 5½ inches, head and trunk 2 inches; Coromandel coast, Salem and Coimbatore, especially near banks of Cauvery; frequents bushy ground, hedges of milk-hedge and clumps of prickly-pear. Its licking is considered poisonous, and there is a Tamul proverb:—அரணை கடித்தால் மரணம்—"if a streaked lizard bite, death ensues."

ARANGOTT (ആറന്നോട്ട - árannóttu, *Mal.*). From (áru, mal. river + annóttu, mal. the other side). A name for the local Vellattiry [q.v.] rajah who lived on the other side of the Ponnany river from Cranganore, the Chera viceroy or permaul's head-quarters.

ARASAN (அரசன் - arasan, *Tam.*). King.—"*a*" Frequent prefix in place names, as Arasanore, meaning king + village.—"*b*" Caste-title. The corresponding terms are:—Tel. raucha, Can. urs. A caste which claims Rajpoot origin. Relatives of the ruling family at Mysore are called by the Sanscrit term Rajpindey, but also by the vernacular Arasoo known in English as Urs. Arasapullies are one of the lower castes in Madura district living by cultivation and cooly work [jauty].

ARASILAUR (அரசிலையாறு - arasilaiyáru, *Tam.* arasillár*). From (arasu, tam. the peepul tree, ficus religiosa, linn. + ilai, tam. leaf + áru, tam. river). Sanscrit name (harinadí), meaning vishnoo river; from the tradition that it rose at the word of vishnoo. River; Tanjore dist., Combaconam tal. Affluent of the Cauvery.

ARAVAM (அரவம் - aravam, *Tam.*). From (arai, tam. to trail). Serpent.——*Aravacoorchy* (அரவக்குறிச்சி - aravakkuriççi, Tam. aravakurchi*). From (kuriççi, tam. village). Sanscrit name (vijayamangala), meaning victory + prosperity.—"*a*" Deputy tahsildarry, Coimbatore district. Pay Rs. 70.—"*b*" Village, Deputy tahsildar's and Sub-registrar's station; Coimbatore dist., Caroor tal.; pop. 4,514; acres 7,876; lat. 10° 46′; long. 77° 57′; from Caroor S.W. 17 miles; from Coimbatore E.S.E. 66 miles; from Erode S.S.E. 41 miles; from Madras S.W. 224 miles; from Ootacamund E.S.E. 90 miles; from Pollachy E. 61 miles; from Suttimungalam S.E. 68 miles. On road from Caroor to Dindigul. Fort built by a Mysore rajah. Occupied by British troops in 1768, 1783, and 1790. On the last occasion the fortifications were destroyed, and the site made over to the Poligar of Andiputty. Old Shiva temple highly sculptured. Branch station of the Roman catholic goa mission. Considerable trade carried on almost exclusively by Lubbays in hides, leather, cloth, &c. Market.——*Aravamoottoo* (அரவமுத்து - aravamuttu, Tam.). From (muttu, tam. pearl). Hindoo 2nd or pers. name. Common among non-bramins [peyar].

ARAY (அரை - arai, *Tam.*). From (aru, tam. to diminish). Waist, also half.——*Araymoody* (அரைமூடி - araimúdi, Tam.). From (múdu, tam. to cover). The fig-leaf shaped ornament worn with a string for decency by female children.——*Aray tookky* (அரைத்தூக்கி - araittúkki, Tam.). From (túkku, tam. to hang). Half-hanging; the pillory.

ARAYAN (അരയൻ - arayan, *Mal.*); a corruption of (arachan, mal. king). Caste-title. Fishermen on west coast [jauty].

ARCAN (अर्क - arka, *San.*). From (arch, san. to shine). Sun.——*Arcaindoo sangamam* (अर्केन्दुसङ्गम - arkéndusangama, San.). From (indu, san. moon + sangama, san. conjunction). The instant of true conjunction of the sun and moon; distinguished from Amavausyay [jyotisham].

ARCAUTY (ஆறுகாட்டி - árugátti, *Tam.*). From (áru, tam. way + kátti, tam. he who shows). A pilot.

ARCAUVATY (ಅರ್ಕಾವತಿ - arkávati, *Can.*; arkavati, *Mys. Gov.*). From (arka, san. copper + vat, san. suffix of possession). River. Rises to the west of Nundidroog in Bramhagherry just beyond the northern limits of Bangalore district, Mysore, through which it flows from north to south receiving the drainage of all the country between the central water-shed and western chain of hills. Tributary of the Cauvery, length about 120 miles.

ARCHACAN (अर्चक - archaka, *San.*). From (arch, san. to praise). Officiating priest in Vishnoo temple; as Gooroocal in Shiva temples and Poojarry in Shoodra temples dedicated to inferior deities [matam].

ARCONUM (அற்கோணம் - árgónam, *Tam.* arkónam*). From (áru, tam. six + kónam, tam. lane). Tam. also (arakkunam), meaning half + hill; still current among lower orders.—"*a*" Deputy tahsildarry, Wallajahpett talook, North arcot district. Pay Rs. 70.—"*b*" Village, Head-quarters of

Deputy tahsildar, Railway station ; North arcot dist., Wallajahpett tal. ; pop. 4,236 ; acres 1,493 ; lat. 13° 05′ ; long. 79° 43′ ; height 295 feet ; from Arnee N.E. 39 miles ; from Chittore E.S.E. 40 miles ; from Madras W. 42 miles ; from Ranipett E.N.E. 26 miles ; from Tripatty S.S.E. 42 miles ; from Vellore E.N.E. 38 miles ; from Wallajahpett E.N.E. 23 miles. Junction of North-west and South-west lines of Madras railway.

ARCOT * (ஆற்காடு - árgádu, *Tam.*). From (áru, tam. six + kádu, tam. forest) ; meaning Athonday's six fanes in Tondeimundalam jungle. Sanscrit name (shadáranya), meaning same. The ἀρκατοῦ βασίλειον σῶρα of Ptolemy. ἄρκατος is here represented not as a country, people, or city, but as the name of a prince. σῶρα is represented not as a nation, but as a city. The names given by the natives of the country to Ptolemy's informants appear to have been transposed.——**(1)** North arcot (ఉత్తరార్కాడు - uttaraárkádu, *Tel.* ; வடவார்க்காடு - vadavárgádu, *Tam.*). A district ; see sep. title.——**(2)** South arcot (దక్షిణార్కాడు - dakshinaárkádu, *Tel.* ; தென்னார்க்காடு - tennárgádu, *Tam.*). A district ; see sep. title.——**(3)** Talook, North arcot district. Tahsildar's pay Rs. 225. Area 432 square miles. Length from east to west 35 miles, breadth 12 miles. Population 176,878. Language Tamul. E of district. Bounded north by Wallajahpett talook, from which separated by Palaur ; east by Conjeeveram talook, Chingleput district ; south by Wandiwash talook and Arnee jagheer ; west by Vellore talook. Almost entirely undiversified plain. On west Vellore hills run into it for three or four miles, and in extreme east near Maumandore tank a few insignificant hills are found. All these elevations are bare and rocky without any jungle growth. Soil poor, being red and black clay mixed with large proportion of sand or gravel, and as there are no local jungles, the land does not get much manure. Beyond limestone, there are hardly any minerals, even building stone being scarce. Agriculture, weaving, and tanning are the only important industries. The last is with Lubbays, chiefly in Visauram. Tanned hides thence exported to Madras. Weavers are in forty villages, in which they have 1,700 looms. Chief weaving villages are Trivettore, Hasanampett, and Vencataroyenpett, producing ordinary country cloths. Large rivers are Palaur and Cheyaur. Latter only skirts talook. Palaur anicut feeds tanks of eighty villages, but that across Cheyaur does not benefit this talook. A few small streams rising in Vellore hills eventually fall into Cheyaur. Largest tank is Maumandore. Places of archæological interest :—Anamallore, Arapaukam, Arcot, Canyanore, Caranday, Coottiyam, Doosy, Keel minnal, Maumandore, Maungaud, Nauttairy, Panamagay, Peinginar, Pennagar, Peroongattore, Poonauvaty, Poongode, Puncha pandava mullay, Shirvanjiputt, Tandalam, Timiry, Tirpanamore, Tirparangaud, Trivettore, Vaulore, Velapaukam, Veliyanallore, Veliyattore, Veppore, Visauram, Voyapandal, Yeshayanore. Principal trig. stations :—Canyanore, Maumandore. The leading places in the talook are the following.——*Arcot* (ஆற்காடு - árgádu, Tam.). See below.——*Calaray* (கலவை - kalavai, Tam.). From (kaluva, tel. water lily, nymphæa). Village ; pop. 3,823 ; acres 1,153 ; lat. 12° 46′ ; long. 79° 28′ ; from Arcot S.S.E. 11 miles ; from Chittore S.E. 37 miles. Large tank.——*Canyanore* (கணியனூர் - kaniyanúr, Tam.). From (kaniyan, tam. member of the singer caste + úr, tam. village). Village ; pop. 1,378 ; acres 3,362 ; lat. 12° 48′ ; long. 79° 24′ ; from Arcot S.S.E. 7 miles ; from Chittore S.S.E. 33 miles. Inscription in forty lines north of village. Others on Vishnoo temple and on a rock in a tope. Trig. station in lat. 12° 47′ 09·13″ ; long. 79° 24′ 15·59″ ; height 643 feet ; from Arcot S.S.E. 8¾ miles ; from Mazbayore N. 1½ miles.——*Cheyaur* (செய்யாறு - sheyyáru, Tam.). See sep. title.——*Maumandore* (மாமண்டூர் - mámandúr, Tam.). See sep. title.——*Meileshwaram* (மைலேசுவரம் - mailésuvaram, Tam. maileshvaram*). From (mél, tam. west + íshvara, san. lord) ; so called to distinguish it from Keel visauram, one mile to the east. Sanscrit name (mayúréshvara), means peacock + lord, as if title was from (mayil, Tam.) peacock. Village ; pop. 3,644 ; lat. 12° 55′ ; long. 79° 19′ ; from Arcot W. 3¾ miles ; from Chittore S.S.E. 24 miles. Large lubbay village between Arcot and Vellore. Tumuli showing a double circle of large boulders. Circumference of largest, 140 yards, height 20 feet.——*Nauttairy* (நாட்டேரி - náttéri, Tam.). From (nádu, tam. country + éri, tam. tank). Village ; pop. 1,878 ; acres 4,780 ; lat. 12° 49′ ; long. 79° 32′ ; from Arcot E.S.E. 12 miles ; from Chittore S.E. 38 miles. Originally called Soorajadowlapooram. Granted to Bramins by Nawaub wallajah in Fusly 1195 in 128 shares.——*Palaur* (பாலாறு - páláru, Tam.). See sep. title.——*Poonauvaty* (புனாவதி - punávathi, Tam.). Sanscritized from (punal, tam. river + pathi, tam. village). Village ; lat. 12° 39′ ; long. 79° 36′ ; from Arcot S.E. 22 miles ; from Chittore S.E. 49 miles. On Cheyaur opposite Trivettore. Once large town, now deserted. Jeina remains.——*Poongode* (பூங்கோடு - púngódu, Tam.). From (pú, tam. flower + kódu, tam. multitude) ; flowery jungle. Sanscrit name (bháradvájáshrama), meaning bharadwaujan, the sage + hermitage. Village ; pop. 218 ; acres 229 ; lat. 12° 54′ ; long. 79° 24′ ; from Arcot E.S.E. 2 miles ; from Chittore S.E. 29 miles. Close to Palaur anicut. Temple of Bhauradwaujeshwaran, erected by a Chola king, one of temples of six forests [arcot].——*Poothoopaudy* (புதுப்பாடி - puthuppádi, Tam.). From (puthu, tam. new + pádi, tam. village). Village ; pop. 882 ; acres 1,340 ; lat. 12° 52′ ; long. 79° 25′ ; from Arcot S.E. 4 miles ; from Chittore S.E. 31 miles. Site of Palaur anicut.——*Puncha pandava mullay* (பஞ்சப்பாண்டவமலை - pañjappándavamalai, Tam.). See sep. title.——*Timiry* (திமிரி - timiri, Tam.). See sep. title.——*Trivettore* (திருவத்தூர் - tiruvattúr, Tam.). See sep. title.——*Visauram* (விசாரம் - visáram, Tam.). From (vishésha, san. remarkable + áru, tam. river) ; at the confluence of three streams. Tam. also (kízhvisáram), meaning east + visauram. Sanscrit name (válmíkyáshrama), meaning Vaulmeeky, the sage + hermitage. Village ; pop. 3,995 ; acres 2,016 ; lat. 12° 55′ ; long. 79° 19′ ; from Arcot W.N.W. 4½ miles ; from Chittore S.S.E. 24 miles. Tanning by Lubbays. Hides exported to Madras.——*Voyapandal* (வாழைப்பந்தல் - vázhappandal, Tam.). From (vázhai, tam. plantain tree, musa paradisiaca, linn. + pandal, tam. shed). Sanscrit name (kadalípura), means plantain town. Village ; pop. 2,297 ; acres 1,749 ; lat. 12° 38′ ; long. 79° 25′ ; from Arcot S. 19 miles ; from Chittore S.S.E. 45 miles.——**(4)** Town, Tahsildar's station ; North arcot dist., Arcot tal. ; pop. 10,928 ; acres 1,792 ; lat. 12° 54′ ; long. 79° 22′ ; height 580 feet ; from Arnee N.N.E. 16 miles ; from Chittore S.E. 27 miles ; from Madras W. 66 miles ; from Ranipett S.S.W. 1½ miles ; from Tripatty S. 51 miles ; from Vellore E. 14 miles. On right bank of Palaur, 5 miles from Arcot railway station. European station is Ranipett in Wallajahpett talook on left bank of Palaur, 3 miles from railway station, formerly a cantonment. Formerly known as old Arcot to distinguish it from Ranipett, which was then generally called Arcot. Athonday raised temples at Conjeeveram and five other places, and introduced cultivation. These were the six forests, meaning six fanes in the forest. The following is the legend connected with the later foundation of Arcot town. Nulla bomma naidoo and Timma naidoo, on a hunting excursion from Penoocondah, coming to the spot saw a hare chase a tiger and seize it by the throat. They considered this marvel to be auspicious and cut down the forest and built a stone-fort. Arcot is first mentioned in authentic history in the beginning of eighteenth century when it was chosen as seat of Mahomedan government of Carnatic instead of Jinjee. Davood khan improved the fort and laid out the town in eighteen streets with names after distinguished commanders. Some of these streets still exist. In 1712, in order to facilitate operations against Mysore, Saudat oollah khan, commander of the Delhi forces, transferred his headquarters to Arcot. In 1740 the Mahratta army of Hojy bhonslay overran the district. Dost ally was killed in battle and Arcot became the centre of operations. Sufder ally, who succeeded Dost ally, was murdered in 1742. His successor, Mahomed sayeed shared the same fate in 1744. During the next seven years Arcot changed hands as many times ; but after its capture and defence by Clive in 1751, an English garrison occupied the fort. In 1758 it surrendered to the French under Lally. Two efforts made in 1759 to regain possession failed. In 1760 Colonel Coote bombarded and captured the fort. For the next twenty years it remained in hands of Nawaub mahomed ally, the ally of the British. In 1780 it surrendered to Hyder ally who held it till 1783. Tippoo sultan succeeded to Hyder's conquests, and after destroying the fortifications abandoned it. Included in the cession of the Carnatic to the English in 1801. The Nawaubs of Carnatic actually resided here until the time of Mahomed ally, who removed to Madras and was followed by the wealthy Mahomedan families attending his court. Its large trade continued thereafter for some years, and much gold lace and chintz were manufactured and sold until Wallajahpett began to draw away its commerce. For many years now it has been a second-rate town, but its importance at one time may be judged of by the fact that it had 360 makauns or charitable institutions where fakeers were fed at the expense of the Nawaub and his nobles. The old fort of historical renown is now portion of the town, covered with houses and gardens. The thick masonry wall with which it was faced called the Shaharpanah or Defender of the city, had five gates, the chief of which was the Delhi gate, leading out upon the bed of the Palaur. This still stands. Tradition asserts that the chamber over the gate was a favorite resort of Clive. The tomb of Nawaub saudat oollah khan, between the palace and the fort, is a domed structure, about 50 feet in height, and built of green stone. The Jumma musjid was built by Zoolfacar khan and added to by both Saudat oollah khan and Anwar ood deen. A fakeer Tippoo owlia's tomb is regarded with veneration. Hyder selected this fakeer as his patron saint, and named his son after him. Beyond the exportation of rice to the west coast, there is no trade, and except manufacture of bangles, no special industry.

ARDHAM (अर्ध - ardha, *San.*). Half.——*Ardha bindoo* (अर्धबिन्दु - ardhabindu, San.). From (bindoo, san. dot). Semicircle in Teloogoo archaic writing. This was sounded as the last consonant in the French word façon, son. Occasionally the whole circle is used with the same purpose ; this still remains [anooswauram].——*Ardha naury* (अर्धनारी - ardhanárí, San.). From (nárí, san. female). A form of Shiva and Parvaty which on the right-hand half is Shiva and on the left-hand half is Parvaty. Symbol to indicate union of the active deity with passive matter ; whence creation. This form belongs more to Northern india. Not to be confounded with Hariharan [matam].——*Ardha swaram* (अर्धस्वर - ardhasvara, San.). From (swara, san. tone). A half tone in music.

ARDRAY (आर्द्रा - árdrá, *San.*). From (árdra, san. wet). The sixth lunar mansion.——*Ardrah darshanam* (आर्द्रादर्शन - árdrádarshana, San.). From (above + darshana, san. seeing); seeing the god Shiva at the full moon about Ardray. Otherwise Maurgaly tirmanjanam or Tirvauthiray. Luni-solar festival [pundigay, 5e]. Day of full moon in the ninth solar month Maurgaly [mausam], i.e., between December 14th and January 11th. Inasmuch as full moon is somewhere near the sixth constellation Ardray [nacshatram] on that occasion. Celebrated in pagodas of Shiva, particularly at Chidambaram to Sabhaupaty. It lasts for ten days.

ARECA (पूग - púga, *San.*; सुपारि - supári, *Mahr.*; شجرفوفل - shajrifaufal, *Ar.*; درخت پوپل - darakhtipúpal, *Pers.*; سپاری کا جہاڑ - supáríkájhár, *Dec.* and *Hind.*; پنانگ - pináng, *Malay*; ಅಡಿಕೆಮರ - adikemara, *Can.*; ಕಂಗು - kangu, *Too.*; పోకచెట్టు - pókachettu, *Tel.*; ଗୁଅ - guva, *Oor.*; കഴുങ്ങ് - kazhunnu, *Mal.*; පුවක් - puvak, *Singh.*; பாக்கு - pákku, *Tam.*). Title from (atakka, mal. betel-nut). San. from (pú, san. purify); clears mouth. Ar. from (shajr, ar. tree + faufal, ar. betel-nut). Pers. from (darakht, pers. tree + púpal, pers. betel-nut). Hind. from (supárí, hind. betel-nut + jhár, hind. tree). Can. from (atakka, mal. closed fruit). Tel. from (púga, san. areca palm + chettu, tel. tree). Oor. from (guaváka, san. filth-remover, areca palm). Mal. from (kramuka, san. areca palm). Tam. from sanscrit. San. also (guváka), meaning filth-remover; (kramuka), meaning attracting tree. Mahr. also (póp'hala), from arabic. Pers. also (shajarigirdchob), meaning round wood tree. Tel. also (vakkachettu), meaning betel-nut + tree; (kólapóka), meaning straight + areca palm. Mal. also (atakka), meaning closed fruit; (kavunnu); (kamuku). Tam. also (kamugu); (pákkuppanai), meaning areca nut + palmyra tree, borassus flabelliformis, linn. Title otherwise Betel-nut palm because its nut eaten with betel [q.v.] leaf, Betel palm, Cabbage tree, Catechu palm, Drunken date, Goovauk, Medicinal cabbage tree, Pauk tree, Penang palm, Soopaury. The nut is the Avellana indica of old writers; common name for the preparation of this in commerce being Kalipauk. Botanically Areca catechu linn., palmaceæ [vricsham, 149]. Generic name from (atakka, mal. nut). Alias Areca fanfel. Fanfel, compare arabic.—"*a*" Palm, 40–80 feet; spathe double; spadix much branched; male flowers numerous, above the female, sessile; calyx one-lobed, three-cornered, three-partite; petals three, oblong, smooth; stamens two-partite, inserted round the base of the style; female flowers one to three at the base of each ramification, sessile; calyx five-lobed, flowers small, white, fragrant, flowering in april, may. Is of remarkably erect growth with a slender, cylindrical, annulate stem, the inner part of which is generally hollow, and a tuft of feathering leaves at the extreme top; the nuts hang in bunches just below the leaves; native of cochin-china and malay islands and here cultivated; the most graceful of palms. The nuts vary greatly in size, and their quality depends solely on the amount of astringent matter they contain, a point which is judged by cutting them; if the medullary portion which intersects the astringent part be small, the nut is considered of good quality; but when the medullary portion is in large quantity, the nut is considered more mature, and not possessing so much astringency is esteemed less valuable. The ordinary nuts have a thin brown rind and in size are intermediate between walnuts and hazel-nuts; their general substance is of a faint oily grey color, thickly marked with curly streaks, of dark brown or black; they occur in the market sliced and in whole nuts, also boiled and raw, or split and dried hastily over a fire, or dried slowly in that manner. The nuts yield two astringent kinds of cutch [q.v.], respectively called in Tamul cuttacaumboo for chewing with betel-leaf and causcutty for medicine. Areca nut when in bulk as cargo, generates an excessive heat.—"*b*" Unlike the cocoanut palm the areca palm will thrive at high regions and at a distance from the sea. The best here grows in Travancore, Malabar, and the Nugger division of Mysore. In the Portuguese and Dutch period great quantities of areca nuts were exported. The palm is cultivated in sandy clay; best on sides of hills and margin of rivers and with moist climate; seed first sown in nursery in coombham or february and meenam [mausam] or march on w. coast; paddy husk is spread to prevent white ants; after transplanting, plants are daily watered for three or four years, soil being stirred very frequently; bears ten or twelve years after; nuts are gathered by climbing the trees; the cooly after gathering sways the tree till it touches the next and shifts to that without descending. The nuts are collected while the fruit is tender, and the husk or outer pod being removed, the kernel, a round fleshy mass remains, which is boiled in water; in the first boiling of the nut, when properly done, the water becomes red, thick, and starch-like, and this on removal of the kernel is evaporated into a substance like gambier or cutch; the boiled kernels being then removed, sliced, and dried, the red catechu-like substance is rubbed on them, and when dried again in the sun they become of a shining black color, and are ready for use; both nut in the pod and sliced nuts are exported; sometimes whole nuts are similarly treated.—"*c*" Dried nut is medicinally a nervine tonic and emmenagogue; the catch is powerful astringent and slight antiperiodic useful in gargle; both these in pharm. non-officinal; the dry expanded petioles serve as ready-made splints for fractures.—"*d*" The nut is one of the constituents of the famous masticatory, the betel-nut of the east; paun or the leaf of the piper betel, and shell-lime, are mixed with slices of the nut and chewed together; the lime gives a deep orange or red color to the coloring matter of the nut, and thus dyes the lips and tongue; this preparation strengthens the gums, sweetens the breath and improves digestion; the nut for this purpose is used in a young and tender state, or is prepared by boiling in water, sometimes combined with aromatics as camphor or cardamom; the effect of betel, when chewed, is due to the mutual reaction of the areca nut, betel leaf, lime, and saliva; the compound betel is much used for ceremonial purposes when any person of consideration visits another.—"*e*" A handsome bead is made by polishing the nut; a decoction of nut with cedrela toona, roxb., gives a red dye; the charcoal afforded by burning the nut in a close vessel is sold as a tooth-powder; the nut is also made into necklaces, rulers, tops of walking-sticks, and other small objects. With the tough, fibrous vegetable covering, or spatha, stretching over the blossom of the tree, the natives make vessels for holding water, arrack, &c.; it is also made into buckets, caps, dishes, and small umbrellas; the inside part readily separates from the other; it looks like fine, white china paper, and can be written on with ink.—"*f*" Wood used for furniture, trenails, bows, spear handles, and for scaffolding poles; very elastic; also used as the ridge-tree in building native houses; hard and peculiarly streaked, and so used in turnery for small ornamental work; can be split into laths.—"*g*" On the mountains of travancore and malabar grows the wild areca, seaforthia dicksonii, mars.; of this the poorer classes eat the nuts as a substitute for the common betel-nut, but no other part of the tree is employed for any useful purpose. There is a species areca alba from bourbon.—"*h*" There is a Tamul proverb:—செத்தவன் கையிலே வெற்றிலை பாக்குக் கொடுத்த சம்பந்தம்—"Like putting "betel and areca nut into the hand of the dead;" the giving of betel and nut being one of the marriage ceremonies. There is another:—ஊண்பாக்கு ஒழிய வீண்பாக்கு ஆகாது—"Betel is not good except after food." There is another:—வாழை வடக்கு ஈனும் வான் கமுகு தெற்கு ஈனும்—"Plantain trees put forth their bunches to the north, and "areca nut trees to the south." And another:—கை காய்த் தாற் கமுகு காய்க்கும்—"If the hand grow hard with water-"ing it, the areca palm will bear fruit;" because it needs careful watering. The Tamul poets compare this palm to an "arrow "shot from heaven."

ARFA (عرفہ - arafah, *Hind.*). From (arfát, ar. the hill); hill near Mecca. Hence ninth day of Buckreed, as hill then visited by pilgrims. Tenth of Buckreed is the festival. Eve of Shab e baraut also.

ARGELLIA (നാളികേരം - nálikéram, *Mal.*). An old erroneous transliteration for the cocoanut.

ARHAR (ارہر - arhar, *Hind.*). From (ádhakí, san. dholl). Same as Dholl.

ARHAT (अर्हत् - arhat, *San.*). From (arh, san. to deserve). Worthy. The name given by Jeinas to supreme being. His popular name is Jinan. Like deities of ordinary pantheon, has 1,008 sacred names [matam].

ARIANCOOPPAM (அரியங்குப்பம் - ariyanguppam, *Tam.*). From (ariyan, tam. sage, epithet of shiva or vishnu + kuppam, tam. hamlet). South arcot dist., lat. 11° 53′; long. 79° 51′; from Cuddalore N.N.E. 13 miles; from Pondicherry S.S.W. 3 miles; from Tindivanam S.S.E. 26 miles; from the sea W. 1¼ mile. In French territory. The fort and stream formed an important part of the outer defences of Pondicherry in the operations of 1746–60, between which dates they changed hands more than once. Captured by Admiral Boscawen in 1748.

ARIMOW (ارمو - arimau, *Malay*). Tiger. Compare:—Felis bengalensis (árimaukar), scandent plant tiger, because long and slender; Felis pardus (arimautálap), perfume box tiger, because spotted.

ARIYALORE (அரியலூர் - ariyalúr,* *Tam.*). From (ariyal, tam. toddy + úr, tam. village). Zemindarry, Town, Divisional head-quarters, District moonsif's station, General deputy collector's division; Trichinopoly dist., Oodayarpolliem tal.; pop. 6,730; lat. of town 11° 08′; long. 79° 8′; from Madras S.S.W. 156 miles; from Moosiry E.N.E. 44 miles; from Oodayarpolliem W.S.W. 15 miles; from Shreerungam N.E. 32 miles; from Trichinopoly N.E. 34 miles. History is exactly the same as for Oodayarpolliem. In 1871 twenty-seven villages were sold in satisfaction of debts incurred by the zemindar, and in 1873 the remaining thirty villages were sold. The estate is now held by a number of petty proprietors, who have no sunnud. The town is healthy. Connected by metalled roads with Perambalore and Keelpaloovore. Residence of the zemindar. His palace is almost in ruins. Two old Shiva and Vishnoo temples. Cattle and general market on Sunday.

ARJ (عرض - arz, *Hind.*). From Arabic; means breadth. Measurement of heap of grain round the bottom.

ARJOONAN (अर्जुन - arjuna, *San.*). From (arj, san. to be white). The friend of Krishnan and the principal Pandava hero in the war for the succession to the throne of Hastinapooram, detailed in the Mahabhaurat [q.v.]. To him Krishnan made the revelations contained in the episode called the Bhagavat geeta [q.v.]. According to a southern legend, Arjoonan took a pilgrimage from Telingana to Madura and Tinnevelly, and thence back to Dwarca. His penance, described in the poem Kirautarjooneeyam, is the subject of a large rock sculpture at Mauvellipore. He did penance in order to obtain the bow called Paushoopataustram, with which he afterwards overcame Dooryodhanan. See vol. I (72). The name Arjoonam is given to the tree White murdah [matam].

ARMEGAM (ஆறுமுகம் - árumugam, *Tam.*). From (árumugam, tam. proper name). Title otherwise Monapollem. Village, Port, Lighthouse; Nellore dist., Goodoor tal.; acres 238; lat. 13° 54′; long. 80° 15′; from Goodoor S.E. 29 miles; from Madras N. 55 miles; from Nellore S.S.E. 41 miles; from Poody N.N.W. 3 miles; from Toopily S.E. 10 miles. Named after a canoongo Armoogam moodelliar, by whose assistance the first English settlement on the Coromandel coast, consisting of a factory defended by twelve pieces of cannon, was established at this place in 1628. Light mainland, village of Monapollem. Lat. 13° 53′; long. 80° 15′. White; revolving. A flash every 20 seconds. 14 miles range. Visible from all directions seaward. Masonry column, white. Warns vessels off the Armegam shoal, 6 miles off shore. The shoal is about 10 miles long, the shallowest patch is $1\frac{3}{4}$ fathoms, and lies from $3\frac{1}{2}$ miles to $5\frac{1}{2}$ miles E. by N. of the lighthouse. The still water inside the shoal is called Blackwood's harbour [blackwood's harbour, doogarauzpatam].

ARMINY (ارمنی - armaní, *Hind.*). From (arman, ar. armenia). Armenian. Total for Presidency about 200. Cf. Carum carui (kamuniarmaní), armenian cumin, caraway; Prunus armeniaca (tuffáhiarmaní), armenian apple, mishmish.

ARMOOGAM (ஆறுமுகம் - árumugam, *Tam.*). From (áru, tam. six + mukha, san. face). Epithet of Soobramanyan. Hindoo 2nd or pers name [peyar]. Common among nonbramins. Name of a Canoongo near Poolicat, through whose influence the first English factory was formed on the Coromandel coast. See vol. II, 112 [armegam].

ARNAH (ارنا - arná, *Hind.*). From (aranya, san. forest). Same as Coromandel ailanto.

ARNAM (अरुण - aruna, *San.*). From (ri, san. to rise). Latin Aurora. Color of the sun-rise. Red [aroonan].——*Arnagiry* (அருணகிரி - arunagiri, Tam.). From (giri, san. hill). Trinomallee hill. Hindoo 2nd or pers. name [peyar].——*Arnauchellam* (அருணாசலம் - arunásalam, Tam.). From (achala, san. mountain). Trinomallee hill. Hindoo 2nd or pers. name [peyar].

ARNEE (ஆரணி - árani, *Tam.* árni*). From (áranam, tam. sacred writing). Title is feminine form and means cauly, the deity.——**(1)** Jagheer, North arcot. Area 180 square miles. Population 91,730. Language Tamul. Bounded north by Vellore talook; east by Arcot and Wandiwash talooks; south and west by Polore talook. Acquired early in seventeenth century by a Bramin Vadajee bhauscar punt, who accompanied Shahjee in his expedition into the Carnatic. With few interruptions held by his successors upon condition of paying an annual nuzzer of Rs. 10,000, and additional obligations of supporting members of the family, erecting no strong-hold in the country, retaining no military force, and imposing no unauthorised cesses. In 1761 the Nawaub dispossessed the jagheerdar. In 1762 the estate was restored. Again attached in 1771 and not given back till 1789, when Shreenivasa row was placed in possession by the Madras government. The present nuzzer amounts to a little more than Rs. 5,000, reductions on account of moturfa, &c., abandoned by the jagheerdar having been made in 1872. The estate is for the most part flat and open, without much jungle growth. There are three tracts of scrub, the largest in the south near the villages of Mooroogamungalam and Carappore; another on the north between Sirmeilore and Moollandram on the Arcot border; and the third on the west, by Castambaudy, where some 7,000 acres are covered with low trees fit for fuel. The few hills are of slight elevation. The highest are those near Sirmeilore, Poosimully cooppam, and Poottore. These are sparsely wooded and kept under strict conservancy. Besides these there are Devicapooram hill and Vunnaudroog. The soil is chiefly sandy mixed with red clay. There are scarcely any minerals. A little iron sand is found but not used. The principal manufacture is weaving. There are upwards of a thousand looms, distributed among fourteen villages, and producing some 200,000 women's cloths in a year, worth about Rs. 750,000. The best fabrics are woven in Arnee itself. Dyeing of piece-goods and mat-making are also carried on. Superior sort of pottery, glazed and unglazed, is also produced. The Cheyaur or Bauhoodah nuddy cuts off a small portion of the south-east of the jagheer, but the country is chiefly drained by the Seyaur or Camandala nuddy. There is also an extensive flood drain into which many of the tanks overflow and which never fails. The principal tanks are those of Caumacore, Paneiyore, Tirmullay samoodram, and Tutchore. Places of archæological interest:—Arnee, Calpoondy, Caumacore, Chaivore, Devicapooram, Laudambaudy, Maumandore, Moollandram, Moorcanandal, Poonalpaudy, Poondy, Poosimullaycooppam, Poottore, Shamboonarayananellore, Tutchore, Vadagacherry, Vedojeepooram. The leading places in the jagheer are the following.——*Arnee* (ஆரணி - árani, Tam.). See below.——*Cheyaur* (చెయ్యేరు - cheyyáru, Tel.). See sep. title.——*Colattore* (கொளத்தூர் - kolattúr, Tam.). From (kulam, tam. tank + úr, tam. village). Village; pop. 1,604; lat. 12° 44′; long. 79° 11′; from Arnee W.N.W. 10 miles; from Chittore S. 33 miles. Principal village of tributary Jagheer of that name.——*Coonnamungalam* (குன்னமங்கலம் - kunnamangalam, Tam. kunnamangalam*). From (kunram, tam. hill + mangala, san. prosperity). Village; pop. 2,500; lat. 12° 45′; long. 79° 12′; from Arnee W.N.W. 10 miles; from Chittore S. 32 miles. Large Mussalman mosque.——*Coonnatore* (குன்னத்தூர் - kunnattúr, Tam.). From (kunram, tam. hill + úr, tam. village). Village; pop. 1,555; lat. 12° 41′; long. 79° 16′; from Arnee W.N.W. $3\frac{1}{2}$ miles; from Chittore S.S.E. 37 miles. On road from Arnee to Vellore. Cavalry station in last century. In neighbourhood is European cemetery.——*Devicapooram* (தேவிகாப்புரம் - tévigáppuram, Tam.). See sep. title.——*Moollandram* (முள்ளண்டறம் - mullandaram, Tam.). From (mullai, tam. a jasmine, jasminum trichotomum, heyne + andaram, tam. temple). Village; pop. 2,307; lat. 12° 47′; long. 79° 18′; from Arnee N. $8\frac{1}{4}$ miles; from Chittore S.S.E. 32 miles. Two old temples.——*Poosimullay cooppam* (பூசிமலைக்குப்பம் - púshimalaikkuppam, Tam.). From (púshi, tam. to worship + malai, tam. mountain + kuppam, tam. village). Village; pop. 1,152; lat. 12° 47′; long. 79° 17′; from Arnee N.N.W. 8 miles; from Chittore S.S.E. 31 miles. Bungalow of Jagheerdar at foot of hill.——*Satyavijayanagaram* (சத்தியவிசயநகரம் - shattiyavijayanagaram, Tam.). See sep. title.——*Vinnamungalam* (விண்ணமங்கலம் - vinnamangalam, Tam.). From (vin, tam. sky + mangala, san. prosperity). Village; pop. 1,162; lat. 12° 35′; long. 79° 21′; from Arnee S.S.E. $6\frac{1}{4}$ miles; from Chittore S.S.E. 46 miles. Country locks are made here.——**(2)** Sub-magistracy, North arcot district. Pay Rs. 70.——**(3)** Town, Divisional head-quarters, Deputy tahsildar's station; North arcot dist., Arnee jagheer; pop. 11,469; lat. 12° 40′; long. 79° 19′; height 499 feet; from Chittore S.S.E. 40 miles; from Madras W.S.W. 74 miles; from Ranipett S.S.W. 18 miles; from Tripatty S. 67 miles; from Vellore 20 miles S.S.E. On the right bank of the Seyaur. Formerly a strong fortress, now much decayed. Once a station for European troops. The old fort, built by Ganapaty royel, brother of Krishna deva royel. Its site, including the glacis, does not belong to the Jagheerdar. In 1751 Arnee was stormed by Clive, when pursuing Rajah sahib; and under its walls, in 1782, Sir Eyre Coote defeated the troops of Lally and Hyder ally, capturing the fort with all the military stores lodged in it by the enemy. Here also the British army concentrated for the campaign of 1790. Noted for its muslins made of a mixture of silk and cotton and much worn by wealthy Bramin women. The celebrated Arnee muslins however are not made here but in Chingleput district not far from Maderpauk. Fair every Friday.——**(4)** Village; Chingleput dist., Ponnairy tal.; pop. 3,989; acres 1,865; lat. 13° 20′; long. 80° 09′; from Ponnairy W. $7\frac{1}{4}$ miles; from Sydapett N.N.W. 23 miles; from the sea W. 17 miles. Old Shiva temple with inscriptions.

ARNOOTTIMULLAY (அறுநூற்றிமலை - arunúttimalai, *Tam.*). From (aran, tam. shiva + úttu, tam. spring + malai, tam. mountain); as being the source of Vasishtanuddy passing by Bailore temple. Sanscrit name (arunódayagiri), meaning Aroonan, the dawn deity + rising + hill. Hill; Salem dist., Salem tal.; lat. 11° 47′; long. 78° 24′; from Salem N.E. 15 miles. Inhabited by hill-men.

AROOGAN (அருகன் - arugan, *Tam.*). From (arh, san. to deserve). Tamul of Arhat.

AROONAN (अरुण - aruna, *San.*). From (ri, san. to rise). Latin Aurora. The dawn. Mythologically the charioteer of the sun [matam].

AROOPATT MOOVER (அறுபத்துமூவர் - arubattumúvar, *Tam.*). From (aru, tam. six + pattu, tam. ten + mú, tam. three). The sixty-three gods. Popularly sixty-three Nauyanaur or Nauyanmaur. They were born in various places and lived in different times. In literature they are known as Tirtondar or holy servants; also Gooroomoorties or incarnations of the gooroo or Shiva in Augama philosophy; also Shivanadiyaur or servants of Shiva. These were the sixty-three champions of Shoiva faith against the heretical Jains. Their lives are given in the Tirtondar pooraunam, popularly Periyapooraunam, by Shekkilaun; otherwise Bhacta vilausam or life of devotees. The foremost are four viz.:—Appan, Maunica vauchacan, Sambandhan and Soondran. The following is the complete list:—Amarneety, Appan, Appoothy, Atibhactan, Calarchingan, Caleiyan, Calicauman, Calicumban, Caliyan, Canamboollan, Caricaul ammay, Caudavar cone, Cauriyan, Chandeshwaran, Cherma permaul, Cooleitchiray, Cooroomban, Coottoovan, Cotchongan cholan, Cotepooly, Cunnappan, Dandy, Eiyadigal, Eribhactan, Gananautan, Idangazhiyaun, Isainyauny, Iyarpageiyaun, Mangayarkk arasy, Maunacanjauran, Mauran, Meypporool nauyan, Mooneiyadoovaun, Moorkkan, Mooroogan, Moorty, Naminundy, Narsinga moonayan, Nedoomauran, Neelanakkan, Nesan, Poogazh cholan, Poogazh toonay, Pooshalan, Roodra pashoopaty, Sambandhan, Shacty, Shadeiyan, Shaukkiyan, Shertoonay, Shirappooly, Shirtondan, Shomausimauran, Soondran, Tillay vauzh andanar, Tircooripp tondan, Tirmoolan, Tirnaulay povaun, Tirnauvookk arasan, Tirneela cuntan, Tirneela cunta yauzhpaunan, Vauyilaun, Viraumindan, Yenaudy nauyan. See vol. I (78) [alwar, matam].

AROOVY (അരുവി - aruvi, *Mal.*; அருவி - aruvi, *Tam.*). From (aruvu, tam. to flow little by little). Mountain waterfall. Suffix in river names; as Tainaroovy, meaning honey + waterfall.—"*a*" The following are the best known falls in the Presidency:—Atripully, cochin state; Barapoley, near codyaul, coorg; Batlagoondoo, dist. Madura, tal. dindigul; Baunateertam, dist. tinnevelly, tal. ambasamoodram; Beypore river, near carcoor, dist. malabar, tal. yernaud; Bhawauny falls, attapaudy valley, dist. malabar, tal. yernaud; Burra chookky, dist. coimbatore, tal. collegaul; Capila teertam, dist. north arcot, tal. chundragherry; Catherine's fall, dist. neilgherry, tal. parangi-naud; Champacautavy teertam, dist. tinnevelly, tal. tencausy; Chinnaguddee, dist. cuddapah, tal. cuddapah; Chola river, near cholaudy pass, dist. malabar, tal. yernaud; Codavanaur falls, near manalore, dist. madura, tal. dindigul; Codayaur, near triparapp, travancore state; Colacumbey, dist. neilgherry; Courtallam, dist. tinnevelly, tal. tencausy; Culhutty, dist. neilgherry; Culyauny teertam, dist. tinnevelly, tal. ambasamoodram; Gersoppah, mysore state; Gollalair, dist. kurnool, tal. coilcoontla; Goondamallappa, dist. kurnool, tal. bunganapully; Gunganchookky, dist. coimbatore, tal. collegaul; Hariharateertam, dist. north arcot, tal. calastry; Hogeycull, dist. salem, tal. dharmapoory; Kartairy, dist. neilgherry; Keel talacoott, dist. madura, tal. pulney; Keilausacona, dist. north arcot, tal. carvetnugger; Lutchmanateertam, dist. coorg; Mail talacoott, dist. madura, tal. pulney; Matsyalunka, dist. cuddapah, tal. cuddapah; Nangaunjy falls, near cottavully, dist. madura, tal. pulney; Nellara, anamullays, dist. coimbatore, tal. pollachy; Neyyaur, travancore state; Nityapoojacona, dist. cuddapah, tal. sidhout; Palair, dist. kurnool, tal. coilcoontla; Paumbanaroovy, dist. tinnevelly, tal. ambasamoodram; Paupanausam, dist. tinnevelly, tal. ambasamoodram; Peddaguddee, dist. cuddapah, tal. cuddapah; Pembanmala cataract, travancore state; Penchalcondah, dist. nellore, tal. raupore; Poonampaura, cochin state; Poroondalaur, dist. madura, tal. pulney; Putchaur, dist. madura, tal. pulney; Pycarrah, dist. neilgherry; Saulunka, dist. cuddapah, tal. cuddapah; Shivasamoodram, cauvery falls, dist. coimbatore, tal. collegaul; Simhauchellam, dist. vizagapatam, tal. vizagapatam; Suddicootimadoogoo, dist. north arcot, tal. calastry; Tainaroovy, dist. tinnevelly, tal. tencausy; Talacona, dist. cuddapah, tal. voilpaud; Toombacadav, dist. coimbatore, tal. pollachy; Toomboor cona, dist. north arcot, tal. chundragherry; Toracadavaur, anamullays, dist. coimbatore, tal. pollachy; Vadavaroovy, dist. tinnevelly, tal. tencausy; Veigay falls, near guntamanaickanore, dist. madura, tal. madura.—"*b*" The following is the list reversed:—Arcot north, capilateertam, hariharteertam, keilausacona, suddicootimadoogoo, toomboorcona; Cochin, atripully, poonampaura; Coimbatore, burrachookky, gunganachookky, nellara in anamullays, shivasamoodram or cauvery falls, toombacadav, toracadavaur in anamullays; Coorg, barapoley, lutchmanateertam; Cuddapah, chinnaguddee, matsyalunka, nityapoojacona, peddaguddee, saulunka, talacona; Kurnool, gollalair, goondamallappa, palair; Madura, batlagoondoo, codavanaur, keeltalacoott, mail talacoott, nangaunjy, poroondalaur, putchaur, veigay falls near guntamanaickanore; Malabar, beypore river near carcoor, bhawauny falls attapaudy valley, chola river near cholaudy pass; Mysore, gersoppah; Neilgherries, catherine's fall, colacumbey, culhutty, kartairy, pycarrah; Nellore penchalcondah; Salem, hogeycull; Tinnevelly, baunateertam, champacautavyteertam, courtallam, culyaunyteertam, paumbanaroovy, paupanausam, tainaroovy, vadavaroovy; Travancore, codayaur near triparapp, neyyaur, pembanmala cataract; Vizagapatam, simhauchellam.—"*c*" Most of these can be seen under their respective heads.

ARRACK (आसव - ásava, *San.*; شراب - sharáb, *Hind.*; ಸಾರಾಯ - sáráya, *Can.*; సారాయి - sáráyi, *Tel.*; ചാരായം - chárâyam, *Mal.*; சாராயம் - sháráyam, *Tam.*). Title from (arak, ar. exudation). San. from (á, san. intensive prefix + sn, san. to distil). Hind. from (sharb, ar. to drink). Drav. from (sára, san. essence). Mal. also (rákku), corr. from Arabic. Tam. also (arakku), corr. from Arabic. Old form, Rack. Cf. Turkish rauky or spirit from grape-skins. Cf. French slang word riquiqui for brandy. Literally essence, spirit. Anglo-indian term, not native, for distilled spirits. Arracum spiritus tennior of chemists. The finest sort of arrack was formerly brought into Southern india from Batavia, where it was called kneip; this article was formerly a source of great revenue to the Dutch; it is distilled from malted rice. Another superior kind still comes from Colombo in Ceylon. This spirit is distilled from palm-juices, mostly cocoanut. Its average percentage of alcohol is 42. About 2·4 fluid ounces would contain one ounce of absolute alcohol by weight. What is called in Southern india, puttay arrack or pariah liquor or country liquor, and which is made in great abundance in every part of the country, is distilled from a fermented solution of jaggery, the coarse sugar obtained from the juice of the date, cocoanut, palmyra and other palms, or from the sugar-cane. In its preparation different barks such as Acacia leucophlæa, wild., Acacia ferruginea, dec., &c., are added to the hot sugar-solution, precipitating albuminous matters which would otherwise putrify and communicate a nauseous flavor; and also increasing by one-sixth the quantity of alcohol produced. Hence the name puttay. Sulphuric acid is sometimes used to assist fermentation. In an ordinary sample of this spirit, the percentage of alcohol by volume is found to be 45. 2·6 oz. contains one ounce weight of absolute alcohol. Rice-arrack is common in Ganjam and the north part of Vizagapatam. The rice is steamed and then spread to dry on mats; a root called Sondimund is then powdered and mixed with the steamed rice and the rice on cooling forms with the Sondimund a sort of cake or cakes which are placed in vats and water is pumped in and the mixture ferments for five or six days when it is 'wash' and ready for distillation. For native mode of distillation of arrack, see vol. I, 450. Arrack is sometimes made more exciting by the addition of opium, datura, or preparations from the hemp-plant. The presence of the first will be detected in the extract, previously if necessary bleached by resolution and filtration through animal charcoal, by adding a drop of ferric chloride, which will give a red color if opium is present. Extract containing datura will produce dilatation of the pupil if put into a cat's eye. Cannabis, the hemp-plant, may be detected by administering the extract to some small animal and comparing the effects with the symptoms of intoxication with bhang, ganjab, or other of those preparations. Arrack is used by Veidyans as an external application in burns, sprains, palsy, chronic rheumatism, &c. Also internally, when diluted, as a stimulant. The names of the varieties are as follows. The best is the cocoanut arrack, and the second best is the puttay. ——*Bassia arrack* (मधूकासव - madhúkásava, San.; موهےکی شراب - mohekísharáb, Hind.; ಇಪ್ಪೆಸಾರಾಯ - ippesáráya, Can.; ఇప్పసారాయి - ippasáráyi, Tel.; ഇരിപ്പച്ചാരായം - irippaççáráyam, Mal.; இலுப்பைச்சாராயம் - iluppaiççáráyam, Tam.). Distilled from fermented juice of flowers of Bassia longifolia, linn., sapotaceæ.——*Batavia arrack* (بتائی شراب - bataísharáb, Hind.; బత్తాయిసారాయి - battáyisáráyi, Tel.; വത്തായിച്ചാരായം - vattáyiççáráyam, Mal.; வத்தாவிச்சாராயம் - vattáviççáráyam, Tam.). Distilled from malted rice. No longer procured.——*Cocoanut arrack* (नारिकेलासव - nárikélásava, San.; ناریل کی شراب - nárelíkísharáb, Hind.; ತೆಂಗಿನಸಾರಾಯ - tenginasáráya, Can.; టెంకాయసారాయి - tenkáyasáráyi, Tel.; തെങ്ങിഞ്ചാരായം - tenniñcháráyam, Mal.; தென்னஞ்சாராயம் - tennañjáráyam, Tam.). Distilled from toddy of Cocos nucifera, linn., palmaceæ.——*Colombo arrack* (கொழும்புச்சாராயம் - kozhumbuççáráyam, Tam.). Arrack, mostly cocoanut arrack, brought from Ceylon.——*Date palm arrack* (खर्जूरासव - kharjúrásava, San.; سیندی کی شراب - sendíkísharáb, Hind.; ఈతసారాయి - ítasáráyi, Tel.; ഈന്തച്ചാരായം - íntaççáráyam, Mal.; ஈச்சஞ்சாராயம் - íççañjáráyam, Tam.). Distilled from toddy of Phœnix sylvestris, roxb., palmaceæ.——*Jaggery arrack* (गुडासव - gudásava, San.; گڑکی شراب - gurkísharáb, Hind.; ಬೆಲ್ಲಸಾರಾಯ - bellasáráya, Can.; బెల్లపుసారాయి - bellapusáráyi, Tel.; വെല്ലച്ചാരായം - vellaççáráyam, Mal.; வெல்லச்சாராயம் - vellaççáráyam, Tam.). Distilled from solution of jaggery from various palms, or from the sugar-cane.——*Palmyra arrack* (तालासव - tálásava, San.; تاڑی کی شراب - tárikísharáb, Hind.; ಪನೆಸಾರಾಯ - panésáráya, Can.; తాటిసారాయి - tátisáráyi, Tel.; പനഞ്ചാരായം - panañcháráyam, Mal.; பனஞ்சாராயம் - panañjáráyam, Tam.). Distilled from toddy of Borassus flabelliformis, linn., palmaceæ.——*Puttay arrack* (کیکرکی شراب - kíkarkísharáb, Hind.; ಪಟ್ಟೆಸಾರಾಯ - pattesáráya, Can.; పట్టసారాయి - pattasáráyi, Tel.; പട്ടച്ചാരായം - pattaççáráyam, Mal.; பட்டைச்சாராயம் - pattaiççáráyam, Tam.). Distilled from solution of jaggery from various palms or from sugar-cane, with bark of Acacia leucophlæa, willd., &c., added. The arrack usually sold. ——*Rice arrack* (तण्डुलासव - tandulásava, San.; چانول کی شراب - chánvalkísharáb, Hind.; ಅಕ್ಕಿಸಾರಾಯ - akkisáráya, Can.; బియ్యపుసారాయి - biyyapusáráyi, Tel.; അരിച്ചാരായം - ariççáráyam, Mal.; அரிசிச்சாராயம் - arisiççáráyam, Tam.). Distilled from malted grain of Oryza sativa, linn., graminaceæ.——*Sago palm arrack* (ماڑی کی شراب - maríkísharáb, Hind.; ಬೈನಿಸಾರಾಯ - bainisáráya, Can.; చిరుగుసారాయి - chirugusáráyi, Tel.; ഈരമ്പനച്ചാരായം - írumpanaççáráyam, Mal.; கூந்தற்பனைச்சாராயம் - kúndarbanaiççáráyam, Tam.). Distilled from toddy of Caryota urens, linn., palmaceæ.

ARROO (ఆర్రు - arru, *Tel.*). Means neck. Strip of land. Suffix in place names, especially in Northern circars; as Paumarroo, meaning snake + narrow land.

ARSATA (اڑسٹھ - arsath, *Hind.*; అడసట్ట - adasatta, *Tel.*). From (arsath, hind. sixty-eight); original being a monthly treasury account which contained sixty-eight columns. Valuation.

ARVENCAUD (அரவங்காடு - aravangádu, *Tam.*). From (aravam, tam. snake + kádu, tam. forest). Village, Valley; Neilgherry dist., Paranginand division; lat. 11° 22′; long. 76° 48′; from Coonoor W.N.W. 2⅓ miles; from Ootacamund E.S.E. 5½ miles. Valley separated from Kaity valley by a spur, on which is built the rest-house on the Ootacamund and Coonoor road. The drainage flows into Coonoor river. The old road to Ootacamund runs up the hollow; the present one being formed by a cutting along the northern side of the valley, a spur of Dodabetta. Village has a chuttram.

ARY (அரி - ari, *Tam.*). Ear of paddy. Arimerah is a deduction made from grain in the rick, and so in ear and stalk; in contradistinction to the usual merah from stock of threshed grain.——*Arittvaulcha* (അരിട്ടുവാഴ്ച - aríttuvázhcha, Mal.). From (above + itu, mal. to put + vázhcha, mal. reign). Coronation ceremony of a Malabar chieftain, from putting rice on his head [maryauday].

ARYAN* (आर्य - árya, *San.*). The original root means to plough; compare Latin arare, Greek ἀρόω, and English ear in the sense of till. In later Sanscrit, the root means noble; compare Greek ἄριστος, German ehre, and English erin. In Java it is still an honorary prefix. In Malabar means a sage. By European writers, Aryan as a language term is applied to the languages derived from the speech of the assumed primitive and homogeneous people whose earliest seats were somewhere in northern Europe or Asia, and who were the ancestors of the Indians, Persians, Celts, Greeks, Romans, Slavonians and Teutons. It is assumed that the ancestors of the Indic and Iranic nations went east and south, spreading over Cochin-China, Hindostan, Persia and Afghanistaun.——**(1)** The following is the list of the Aryan languages, the main heads being in small capital type, the sub-heads being in italic, and the languages usually classed as such being in ordinary type:—INDIC.—Sanscrit (extinct), Pracrit (extinct), Pali (extinct), Indian dialects, Gipsy dialects, &c.—IRANIC.—Zend (extinct), Cuneiform inscriptions (extinct), Parsee (extinct), Persian, &c.—CELTIC.—*Cymric*—Cornish (extinct), Welsh, Armorican.—*Gadhelic*—Gaelic, Erse, Manx, &c.—GRAECO-LATIN.—*Greek type*—Greek (extinct); sub-divided into Doric, Æolic, Attic and Ionic, Modern Greek, &c.—*Romance languages*—Latin (extinct), Portuguese, Spanish, Provençal and French, these being divided into Langue d'Oc and Langue d'Oil, Italian, Roumansch, Wallachian, &c.—SLAVONIC.—*Lettic*—Old Prussian (extinct), Lithuanian, Lettish.—*Eastern slavonic*—Ancient-Bulg. (extinct), Bulgarian. Russian.—*Western slavonic*—Polish, Bohemian.—TEUTONIC.—*High german*—Old and Middle high german (extinct), German.—*Low german*—Gothic (extinct), Anglo-Saxon (extinct), English, Old saxon (extinct), Old frisian (extinct), Old dutch (extinct), Platt-Deutsch, Frisian, Dutch.—*Scandinavian*—Old norse (extinct), Icelandic, Swedish, Danish, &c.——**(2)** The first main head or Indic is that which concerns this country. The Indo-Aryan language Sanscrit has been extinct for at least two thousand years, but it continues to be studied by the learned [sanscrit]. At the time when the Greek authors were producing their greatest works and when Rome had not as yet a literature, Sanscrit had already degenerated into various dialects. Among these were the Pracrit idioms, bearing somewhat the same relation to Sanscrit as Italian bears to Latin [hindostany, pracrit]; and ancient Pali, in which most of the sacred books of the Ceylonese boodhists were written, representing an intermediate stage between Sanscrit and Pracrit [pali]. The only authorities for Aryan history are the Ramayanam, the Mahabhaurat and Pooraunams. Each of these purports to be matter repeated by some person, stating what he heard from another. Thus the Bhagavat pooraunam is recited to king Paricshit by Shoocan, as he had heard it narrated to assembled sages by Sootan. According to these authorities, the country of the Indian aryans was called Bramhahvartam or Aryavartam, and was bounded by the rivers Saraswaty and Drishadwaty. The northern and southern limits were the Himalayan and Vindhya mountains. This country corresponded with the modern provinces of Lahore, Delhi, Agra, Oude and Allahabad. The country was at first divided between two principal families of the sun and the moon [vamsham]. Compare Grecian kings descended from Jupiter; and the Incas of Peru, the progeny of the sun. In the solar race came Rama [ramayanam], in the lunar came the personages of the Mahabhaurat [mahabhaurat]. The most adventurous emigrations took place through the lunar family. The Aryan dynasties, if they ever really ruled at all in India, which is doubtful, must have ended about the time of the Mahabhaurat. The year from which dates the Kalyoog, B.C. 3102, may mark the first entrance of Aryans in any numbers into India. After the occurrences told in the Mahabhaurat the most important principality of India became that of Magadham, and continued so for many centuries; capital Rajagriham. Chundragooptan, called by the Greeks Sandracottus, was the friend and ally of Seleucus Nicator, Alexander the Great's successor in Persia. Pautalipootram or Palibothra or Coosoomapooram, his capital, was situated near the confluence of the Sone and the Ganges, not far from the site of the modern Patna. The descendants of Chundragooptan were called Mowryae. At the beginning of the Christian era the principal kingdom in India was that of Avanty or Oujein, under Vicramadityan. He rendered important service to India by arresting the conquests of the Shancas, whence he is called the Shaucaury, or foe of the Shancas. The Samvat era dates from Vicramadityan, fifty-seven years B.C. The next prince of note is Salivahanan, king of Pratishtaunam in the Deccan. The Saca era counts from him, beginning seventy-eight years after Christ. These states, Magadham, Pautalipootram, Avanty and Pratishtaunam, are always spoken of as Aryan, and they are therefore here mentioned; but it is improbable that the rulers were Aryan, and it is certain that the populations were not. The present state of the case as regards Aryan influence in S. india can be seen at vol. I (32) [jauty].——**(3)** Title of the Malabar hill god Ayyappan. Prefix in place names thence derived.——**(4)** A paddy in Malabar, named after the Mahratta country. Has varieties:—black from color of ear growing; small; sand from growing near sea at cochin; golden, from appearance of ear.——**(5)** *Arya bhatta* (आर्यभट्ट - áryabhatta, San.). From (bhatta, san. learned man). Ardubrius of the Chronichon Paschale and Arjabahr of the Arabs. An early astronomer and mathematician of Northern india, born near Patna. Works well known here, and his figures of solar reckoning adopted in preference to those of Soorya siddhauntam [q.v.]. He affirmed the diurnal revolution of the earth on its axis, accounting for it by a current of aërial fluid, extending to a height of 114 miles above the earth's surface; and he calculated the earth's circumference to be 25,080 miles. He believed the moon and primary planets to be dark and only illumined by the sun; and he possessed the true theory of lunar and solar eclipses. His idea of the roundness of the earth is thus expressed:—"The terrestrial globe, a compound of earth, "water, fire and air, entirely round, encompassed by a girdle, "stands in the air, in the centre of the stellar sphere; like as a "ball formed by blossoms of anthocephalus cadamba is on every "side beset with flowerets, so is the earth-globe, with all crea-"tures, terrestrial and aquatic." And of the daily revolution he says:—"As a person in a vessel while moving forward, sees "an immovable object moving backwards; in the same manner "do the stars, however immovable, seem to move daily." Elsewhere of the same he says:—"The sphere of the stars is "stationary; and the earth, making revolution, produces the "daily rising and setting of stars and planets." He is also the earliest author that is known to have treated of algebra. In his Siddhauntam he deduced from observations the values of the mean motions of the sun, moon and planets, and of their apsides and nodes, and calculated eclipses. His chief work is the Arya bhatteeya sootram, which includes two other works, the Dashah geety sootram and the Aryaushta sootram. A later astronomer of the same name is called Laghoo arya bhatta or Arya bhatta the lesser [jyotisham].——*Aryacoott* (ஆரியக்கூத்து - áriyakkúttu, Tam.). From (áriyan, tam. juggler + kúttu, tam. dance). Dancing with pole and ropes.——*Aryam* (आर्य - árya, San.). Form of Nagry alphabet used on West coast. Cf. ἀριακή, Ptolemy's name for the Mahratta country.——*Aryanaud* (ആരിയനാട് - áriyanátu, *Mal.*). From (áriyan, mal. sage, epithet of ayyappan the village deity + nátu, mal. country). Meaning the country of Shaustauv. Pass, Village; Travancore state, Trivandrum division, Nedoovengaud tal.; lat. 8° 36′; long. 77° 08′; from Nedoovengaud E. 6¼ miles; from Trivandrum N.E. 13 miles; from the sea E. 17 miles.——*Aryancauv* (ആരിയങ്കാവ് - áriyankávu, *Mal.*). From (áriyan, mal. sage, epithet of ayyappan, the village deity + kávu, mal. sacred enclosure), meaning the grove of Shaustauv. Mal. also (áriyankóvil), meaning Ayyappan, the god + temple. Village; Travancore state, Quilon division, Shencottah tal.; lat. 8° 59′; long. 77° 11′; from Shencottah W. 7¼ miles; from Trivandrum N.N.E. 37 miles; from the sea E. 40 miles. On the main road from Quilon to Shencottah, in a circular valley about a mile from the head of the Aryancauv pass. Temple of Shaustauv, the forest deity. Chowky. Once a flourishing commercial town for the trade of Travancore with Tinnevelly. Now mostly in ruins. The pass to Tinnevelly district had been shut till recently, now re-opened.——*Aryavartam* (आर्यावर्त - áryávarta, San.). From (ávarta, san. thronged place). Dwelling-place of the Aryans. Also called Arya bhoomy. Menoo's name for the land extending from the eastern to the western sea and bounded on the north and south by the Himalaya and Vindhya mountains.

ARZ (عرض - arz, *Hind.*). Solicitation. Arzee is a petition. Arzeedar is a petitioner. Arzeedasht from (dásht, pers. which contained) is specially a written petition.

ARZAH (ارزه - arzah, *Ar.*). Cedar of Lebanon. Botanically Cedrus libani, barr., coniferæ [vricsham]. Timber resinous; fragrant odour, brown color, bitter taste, not subject to worms. For the Indian cedar see Deodar.

AS (اس-اص-اث-اش - as, *Ar.*). Al [q.v.] before s in Arabic single terms, as assamad meaning the eternal.

ASAD (اسد - asad, *Hind.*). From Arabic. Lion. Alam; as Asad beg, alam + alaumat. Also component part of lacab; as Asad ool lah, the lion of God [ashed, ism].

ASAF (آصف - ásaf, *Hind.*). From Arabic. Alam; as Asaf khan, alam + alaumat. Part of lacab; as Asaf ood dowlah, the distinguished minister of the state. Asaf was a title given by Tippoo to his principal civil officers.——*Asaf jah* (آصف جاه - ásafjáh, Hind.). Alam + alaumat. Founder of reigning family of Hyderabad. See vol. I (150), 9.

ASAFŒTIDA (हिंगु - hingu, *San.*; हिंगु - hingu, *Mahr.*; हिंगाझाड - hingájháda, *Conc.*; حلتيت - hiltít, *Ar.*; انگوزه - angozah, *Pers.*; هنگ - hing, *Hind.* and *Dec.*; ಇಂಗಿನಗಿಡ - inginagida, *Can.*; ಇಂಗು - ingu, *Too.*; ఇంగువచెట్టు - inguva-chettu, *Tel.*; കായം - káyam, *Mal.*; පෙරුංකායම් - perunkáyam, *Singh.*; பெருங்காயம் - perungáyam, *Tam.*). Title from (aza, pers. mastic + latin fetida). San. from (han, san. to kill); from overpowering other odours. Mal. from (káyu, mal. to be hot); from taste. Singh. from tamul. Tam. from (perumai, tam. greatness + káyam, tam. pungent drug). San. also (rámat'ha), meaning pertaining to ramata a people in the west of india; (bálhika), meaning produced in balkh. Pers. also (angushtikandah), meaning rotten finger, from appearance of root. Tam. also (urumbaram), from copper-like gum; (káyam), meaning pungency. Greek νάρθηξ. Title otherwise Devil's dung, Giant fennel, Rotten finger. Botanically Ferula [baulhicam] narthex, boiss., umbelliferæ [vricsham, 67]. Alias Ferula asafœtida; Narthex asafœtida. Product imported from afghanistaun, &c.; gum-resin having a nauseous bitter taste and fetid smell, obtained by incision from the thick fleshy root; occurs in irregular masses, partly composed of tears, of a dark pink, or if long kept of a dull yellow color; the fracture is vitreous, at first white, and passing to red by contact with the air, a property which distinguishes it from all other gum-resins; that which is moist and has a strong fetid garlic odour is chosen for medicinal use. Much resorted to by bramins as a remedy against flatulence and to counteract the effect of their cold vegetable food; veidyans use it in dyspepsia and amenorrhœa; substituted for british valeriate of quinine and zinc; often mixed with dirt, gravel and bits of rag; in pharm. officinal as powerful antispasmodic, stimulant, and anthelmintic; also in british. In veterinary practice:—in drachm doses with 2 of gentian or 1 of ginger daily, is beneficial for cold; in flatulency, 1 drachm to a pound of water and a drachm of ginger, drench. Used for seasoning curries and other food; an essential oil from root. Some asafœtida comes from other umbelliferous plants.

ASAL (اصل - asl, *Hind.*; அசல் - asal, *Tam.*). From Arabic. Original. Asal beriz is the original rent. Asal chit is the original or first copy of a bond. Asal jumma is the original revenue of a village, &c., without extra cesses; also the amount taken as the basis of a revenue settlement. Asal mokaddamah is an original suit in distinction to appeal suit. See vol. I, 112.

ASAY (அசை - asai, *Tam.*). Syllable.——*Asaipirittal* (அசைபிரித்தல் - asaibirittal, Tam.). Means syllable + division. Syllabation in grammar. The chief peculiarity of Dravidian, particularly Tamul, syllabation is its extreme simplicity and dislike of compound or concurrent consonants. No other combination of consonants is admitted than the duplication of mutes and the junction of the nasal and the mute. In Teloogoo, Canarese and Malayalam, the great majority of Dravidian words, and in Tamul all words without exception, including even Sanscrit derivates, are divided into syllables on the following plan. Double or treble consonants at the beginning of syllables, like 'str,' in 'strength,' are altogether inadmissible. At the beginning not only of the first syllables of every word, but also of every succeeding syllable, only one consonant is allowed. If in the middle of a word of several syllables, one syllable ends with a consonant and the succeeding one commences with another consonant, the concurrent consonants must be euphemically assimilated, or else a vowel must be inserted between them. At the conclusion of a word, double and treble consonants like 'gth' in 'strength' are as inadmissible as at the beginning; and every word must terminate in Teloogoo and Canarese in a vowel; in Tamul, either in a vowel or a semi-vowel, as 'l,' or 'r,' or in a single nasal, as 'n' or 'm.' This plan of syllabation is extremely unlike that of Sanscrit. Generally 'i' is the vowel which is used for the purpose of separating inadmissible consonants, as appears from the manner in which Sanscrit derivatives are Tamulised. Sometimes 'u' is employed instead of 'i.' Thus the Sanscrit preposition 'pra' is changed into 'pira' in the compound derivatives, which have been borrowed by the Tamul, whilst Krishna becomes (kiruttinan) ('tt,' instead of sh'), or even (kittinan). It may be observed that the Finnish, the Hungarian, and other languages of the same stock similarly allow of only one consonant at the beginning of a syllable. See vol. I (52); II, 205, 209.

ASGAND (अश्वगन्धा - ashvagandhá, *San.*; كاكنج هندى - káknajihindí, *Ar.*; كاكنۀ هندى - káknahihindí, *Pers.*; پنیر کا پیڑ - panírkáper, *Hind.*; ناٹ کی اسگند کا جھاڑ - nátkíasgandkájhár, *Dec.*; ಹಿರಿಮದ್ದಿನಗಿಡ - hirimaddinagida, *Can.*; పెన్నేరు - pennéru, *Tel.*; അമുക്കിരം - amukkiram, *Mal.*; அமுக்குரா - amukkurá, *Tam.*). Title from sanscrit through deccany. San. from (ashva, san. horse + gandha, san. smell); from roots having smell of horse. Ar. from (káknaj, ar. winter cherry, physalis + hindí, ar. indian). Pers. from arabic. Hind. from (panír, pers. cheese + per, hind. tree); seeds used to make cheese. Dec. from (nát, hind. country + asgand, hind. winter cherry + jhár, hind. tree). Can. from (hiri, can. large + maddu, can. medicine + gida, can. plant). Tam. from (amungu, tam. to sink + kurá, tam. webera corymbosa, willd.); from low size of plant. San. also (vájigandhá), meaning horse smelling. Hind. also (kákanj); (asgand). Can. also (sogadebéru); (angara); (amakíre). Tel. also (pillivéndramu), meaning cat + beat. Mal. also (pévetti), meaning devil + tree of useless timber. Greek στρύχνος ὑπνωτικός. Title otherwise Amookra, Burrwood, Cheese tree, Horse root, Winter cherry. Botanically Withania somnifera, dunal., solanaceæ [vricsham, 94]. Alias Physalis somnifera, flexuosa, sugunda, tomentosa. Perennial undershrub, 2–3 feet; stem two-forked, flexuous; leaves ovate, entire, in pairs, pubescent; calyx five-toothed, segments equal to the length of the tube; flowers axillary, crowded, nearly sessile; corolla campanulate, yellowish green; berry small, red, size of a pea, covered with a membranaceous, angular, inflated calyx; root resembles gentian root in external appearance. Fruit is medicinally diuretic, and root and leaves powerfully narcotic and alexipharmic; leaves moistened with warm castor-oil applied in cases of carbuncle. Seeds employed in coagulation of milk in making butter. Another species here is coagulans. Physalis alkekengi is the Winter cherry of Europe.

ASGHAR (اصغر - asghar, *Hind.*). From (saghara, ar. to lessen). Little. Name of a son of Hoossain, whose anniversary is celebrated at Moharram. Used as common alam [ism].

ASH (اش - ash, *Ar.*). Al [q.v.] before sh in Arabic single terms, as ash-shacoor, meaning the grateful.

ASHAMBOO (അശമ്പു - ashambu, *Mal.*). Means watershed. Plateau; Travancore state, Pudmanaubhapooram division, Tovaula talook. On the Mahendragherry hills. Extensive coffee estates. Europeans resort to it for health. Near is the famous water-fall Olakkarvy.

ASHAUM (احشام - ahshám, *Hind.*); pl. of (hashm, pers. state servant). Attendants. Irregular infantry with swords and matchlocks. Sometimes applied to garrison troops.

ASHOCAM (देवदारु - dévadáru, *San.*; دیودار - dendárí, *Hind.*; ಪುತ್ರಜೀವಿಮರ - putrajívimara, *Can.*; ಅಶೋಕ - ashóka, *Too.*; అశోకము - ashókamu, *Tel.*; ଦେବଦାରୁ - débadaru, *Oor.*; അശോകം - ashókam, *Mal.*; நெட்டிலிங்கு - nettilingu, *Tam.*). San. from (déva, san. divine + dáru, san. tree). Can. from (putra, san. son + jíva, san. life + mara, can. tree); supposed good for health of children. Mal. from (a, san. negative particle + shóka, san. grief); lovely. Tam. from (nettai, tam. tallness + alika, san. beauty); tall, beautiful evergreen. San. also (ashóka), meaning not causing sorrow. Hind. also (asok), from sanscrit. Tam. also (asógu). Title otherwise Asoca, Indian fir, Indian mast tree, Jambool deodar. Botanically Polyalthia [doodooga] longifolia, benth. & h. f., anonaceæ [vricsham, 4]. Alias Guatteria longifolia; Unona longifolia; Uvaria longifolia. Tree; long lance-shaped shining leaves, wavy at the edges; greenish star-like flowers; highly ornamental; planted in avenues. Timber whitish-yellow, light, very flexible, tolerably close and even-grained, used for making drum cylinders.——*Bengal ashocam* (अशोक - ashóka, San.; असोक - asóka, Mahr.; जस्सुन्दी - jassundí, Conc.; اسوک - asok, Hind.; ಅಶೋಕ - ashóka, Can.; అశోకము - ashókamu, Tel.; അശോകം - ashókam, Mal.; දියරතඹලා - diyaratambalá, Singh.; அசோகு - asógu, Tam.). Title from place where first found. San. from (a, san. negative particle + shóka, san. sorrow); sorrow dispeller; beautiful tree; seeta is supposed to have dispelled her sorrow under this tree when confined by ravanan. Mahr. from sanscrit. Hind. from sanscrit. Singh. from (diya, singh. water + ratambalá, singh. ixora coccinea, linn.); from affecting moisture. Tam. from sanscrit. San. also (vichitra), meaning many-colored; (vañjula), meaning worshipped; (kankéli), meaning water-sporting; (chháyá), meaning shady; (anganápriya), meaning dear to women; (krimikáraka), meaning worm producing. Title otherwise Water ixora, Wing-leaved ashocam. Botanically Saraca indica, linn., leguminosæ [vricsham, 48]. Alias Jonesia asoka, pinnata; Saraca arborescens. A tree of considerable size, bears compact clusters of flowers, varying in color from pale orange to scarlet; flowers during hot season; shade yielding ornamental tree; flower religious. Bark used in uterine affections; decoction in milk is generally prescribed. Wood light, reddish-brown, soft. No other common species here.

ASHOORA (آشوره - áshúrah, *Hind.*). From (ashr, ar. ten). The first ten days of the month of Moharram [q.v.]; see vol. I (96). Ashoorkhana from (khánah, pers. house) is house appointed for the ceremonies of Moharram.

ASHRAF (اشرف - ashraf, *Hind.*). From (sharafa, ar. to excel in glory). Most noble. Alam; as Ashraf ally, double alam. Also component part of lacab; as Ashraf oon nissa, noblest lady [ism].——*Ashrafee* (اشرفی - ashrafí, Hind.). A gold mohur. Not now legal tender in British territory. The full value is 16 rupees, but varies. Cf. Deenaur [naunyam, 2e].

ASHTAM (अष्ट - ashta, *San.*). Eight.——*Ashta bhauga maunyam* (अष्टभागमान्य - ashtabhágamánya, San.). From (bhága, san. division + mániyam, tam. estate). Estate paying only one-eighth of produce as revenue. See vol. I, 112.——*Ashta bhogam* (अष्टभोग - ashtabhóga, San.). From (bhóga, san. enjoyment). Enjoyment of the whole, or eight products of an estate. Or:—the land cultivated, Siddhy; produce of such land, Saudhyam; uncultivable or rocky land and its products, as minerals, &c., Paushaunam; property deposited on the land, Nicshaipam; treasure-trove, Nidhy; waters and their produce, Jalaumritam; actual privileges, Acshiny; prospective rights and privileges, Augaumy. See vol. I, 112.——*Ashtacam* (अष्टक - ashtaka, San.). Eighth. Specially eighth day of moon in certain months, when progenitors are worshipped [pundigay, 3e].——*Ashtadic* (अष्टदिक् - ashtadik, San.). From (dik, san. quarter). The usual eight cardinal points of the compass. For each of these there is an elephant [ashtadic gajam] and a divinity [ashtadic paulacan]. In astrology are added two others, viz., Vishoomboo, the ethereal regions, and Pautaulam, the abyss. The eight points are, especially in choosing spots for building houses, named after certain animals:—East, kite; South-east, cat; South, lion; South-west, dog; West, snake; North-west, rat; North, elephant; North-east, hare. The animals of the opposite points are natural foes to each other, the one being pursuer and the other the pursued [jyotisham, matam].——*Ashtadic gajam* (अष्टदिग्गज - ashtadiggaja, San.). From (gaja, san. elephant). Eight pairs of elephants, male and female, in the eight cardinal points of the heavens who support the earth. East, Eirauvatam and Apramay; South-east, Poondareecam and Capilay; South, Vaumanam and Pingalay; South-west, Coomoodam and Anoopamay; West, Anjanam and Taumracurny; North-west, Pooshpadantam and Soodanty; North, Saurwabhoomam and Anjanay; and North-east, Soopradeepam and Anjanauvaty. So eight poets in the court of Krishna deva royel of Vijianugger. They were Alasanny peddanna, Mookkoo timmana, Tenauly ramalingam, Pingaly sooranna, Bhattoomoorty, Ayyalrauz, Ramabhadran, and Cumsala veerabhadran [matam].——*Ashtadic paulacan* (अष्टदिक्पालक - ashtadikpálaka, San.). From (pálaka, san. protector). The deities who are regents of the eight points. Otherwise Dicpaty. According to the Tamulian geography borrowed from the Bramins, the earth consists of seven great insular continents and seven circumambient oceans, and beyond the seventh circumambient ocean, there is at each of the eight cardinal points a regent or protector of the earth. The images of these eight protectors of the earth are usually made of stone, or bricks and mortar; sometimes also of metal, at least that of Agny bhagavan. At the beginning of every festival of several days' duration, the Ashtadicpaulacas are placed at their respective sites within the enclosure of the pagoda, with ceremonies and muntrams; and when the festival is over, they are replaced in the temple with further ceremonies. They receive honor on other occasions also, and play an important part in the building of houses.—"*a*" Indran or Devendran, the king of the Devas, is regent of the east and protects the earth from giants and malignant spirits; he is inferior to none in power except Shiva, Vishnoo, and Bramha. He presides over the seasons and crops, and is worshipped at sowing and reaping. Sign a thunderbolt.—"*b*" Agny, the regent of the south-east, is the god of fire. He is represented as riding on a grey goat, flames of fire streaming round him. He has two faces, four hands or seven, and three legs, signifying the trident which fire forms. On his two heads he wears a crown, surrounded by fire, and in his hands he holds sacrificial implements and materials. The offerings to Agny consisting of ghee, plantains, cakes, &c., are accompanied with an incantation, that is repeated one hundred and eight times and are made particularly at marriages. Sign is smoke.—"*c*" Yaman, the regent of the south, is the god of death and king of hell, where he sits in judgment on departed souls. After death souls appear before him, and, when they have been confronted with Chitragooptan the recorder, by whom all actions are registered, the virtuous are conveyed to Swargam whilst the wicked are driven to the different regions of Naracam. Yaman is represented as quite black, with a crown on his head, and surrounded by fire. In his mouth he has a lion's teeth, and in his four hands he holds respectively a club, ropes, a trident, and a wine-jug. From the latter he gives wine to the dying to mitigate the bitterness of death. He also rides on a black buffalo. Of his many names the following may be mentioned:—Antacan, the destroyer; Chundan, the wrathful; Coott, the separator of soul and body; Dharman, the just; Maraly, the confounder; Nadoovan, the impartial; Naman, like Yama; Shaman, the just; Shengol cadavool, the god with the right sceptre; Tendisaykone, the king of the southern region. Sign is a lion.—"*d*" Nirrity, the regent of the south-west, is a giant of green color. He was elevated to the dignity by severe penance. On his head he wears a crown, and on his forehead Shiva's ashes; of his four hands one is empty, and in the other three he holds a banner with the sign of a fish, a ring, and a wine-jug. His vehicle is a crocodile. His sign is a dog.—"*e*" Varoonan, the regent of the west, is the god of the waters, clouds, and rain. He is represented with a green body, with two hands, of which one is empty and the other holds a sword. His head is adorned with a crown, his whole body with various ornaments, and his shoulders with garlands. His vehicle is a stag. His sign is a bull.—"*f*" Vayoo, the regent of the north-west, is the god of the wind. He is represented as having a grey color and four arms and hands, in which he holds a sword, a shield, a bow, and an arrow. Like the other gods, he wears a crown and various ornaments, and his vehicle is a Bhootam. His sign, an ass.—"*g*" Coobairan, the regent of the north, is the god of riches and the keeper of gold, silver, precious stones, pearls, and all the treasures in the earth, which he gives to those for whom they are destined by Eeshwaran. He has a deformed body of white color, with a crown on his head, and a club in one of his hands. His whole body is adorned with various ornaments, and his vehicle is a self-moving chariot. Coobairan is synonymous with a croesus in Tamul. Coobairan has various names, of which the following may be mentioned:—Alagaiyauly, ruler of Alacay, his capital; Dhanadan, he who gives riches; Dhanapaty, lord of riches; Haran tozhan, Haran's, i.e., Shiva's friend; Kinnara piraun, lord of the Kinnarans; Muntry, prime minister; Pingalan, the lord of the treasure; Pooroosha vauhanan, he whose vehicle is a man; Pooshpaca vimaunamoollavan, possessor of the self-moving chariot; Veishravanan, son of Vishravan. His sign is an elephant.—"*h*" Eeshaunan, the regent of the north-east, is a form of Eeshwaran. He is represented as having four arms and hands, of which one is empty, whilst he holds in the other three a small drum, a stag, and a sword. His head is adorned with a crown, and his whole body with the usual ornaments. Near him stands a bull, his vehicle. Being a form of Eeshwaran, he is regarded as the chief among the protectors of the earth, and he is believed to direct and control all. His sign is a crow [matam].——*Ashta lutchmy* (अष्टलक्ष्मी - ashtalakshmí, San.). Eight Lutchmies:—Dhanam or patroness of riches, Dhaunyam of grain, Dheiryam of courage, Showryam of heroism, Vidyay of science, Keerty of fame, Vijayam of victory, Rajyam of kingdom.——*Ashtamoody* (അഷ്ടമുടി - ashtamuti, Mal.). From (muti, mal. knot). Back-water; Travancore dist., Quilon division; Quilon tal. Adjacent to Quilon and connected with the sea by the Ivica bar. Fed by the Cullada river. The lake branches off into eight creeks, whence the name. Of sufficient depth for small vessels. Country crafts are constructed on the banks and launched into the sea through the opening in the bar. The banks rise abruptly and are of hard laterite soil. The area is 20 square miles with an average breadth of 2 miles. The extreme length is 10 miles and its extreme breadth 9 miles.——*Ashtamy* (अष्टमी - ashtamí, San.). Eighth day of any lunar fortnight. A lunar festival in some months [pundigay, 3e]. On this day in waning moon of fifth lunar month Shrauvanam [mausam] or august is celebrated the birth of Krishna under the name of Krishna janmaushtamy. This feast is known among the Smartas as Gocoolaushtamy and among the Veishnavas as Krishna jayanty or Shree jayanty. Also on West coast a luni-solar festival [pundigay, 5a]. This festival is celebrated in the bright fortnight in eighth solar month Vrishchicam [mausam], i.e., between November 15th and December 13th at Wycome in Travancore. On this day people afflicted with incurable disease come in crowds to see the god Shiva [maryauday].——*Ashtaucsharam* (अष्टाक्षर - ashtákshara, San.). From (akshara, san. character). A form of prayer. Omnamo narayanauya. The eight-lettered muntram prescribed to be uttered in daily prayer. Also used by exorcisers for the dispossession of demons. Four special muntrams are known, of which this is one. The other three are Punchaucsharam or the five-lettered muntram of Namashivauya, Shadaucsharam or the six-lettered muntram of Vishnaveynama, and Dwaudashaucsharam or the twelve-lettered muntram of Omnamo bhagavatey vausoodevauya. Beejaucsharam is the essential syllable with which the muntram of any deity opens. The sacred syllable om is sometimes called Yecaucsharam or one-lettered muntram [matam].——*Ashtaungam* (अष्टाङ्ग - ashtánga, San.). From (anga, san. member). Eight members of the body. A prostration in which worshippers touch the ground with the breast, forehead, hands, knees, insteps; then kiss the earth; half rise up and pass the left over the right forearm and vice versâ; then finally after again saluting the earth stand erect. See vol. I (89) [maryauday].——*Ashtauvadhauny* (अष्टावधानी - ashtávadhání, San.). From (avadhána, san. attention). One who undertakes to do any eight things at once; such as playing chess, composing stanzas with the omission of any given letter, reckoning correctly the grains of rice dropped on one's shoulders, &c.——*Ashta varnam* (अष्टवर्ण - ashtavarna, San.). From (varna, san. color). Eight distinguishing marks of the religion of Shiva.—"*a*" the Gooroo or spiritual teacher;—"*b*" the lingam or emblem of Shiva;—"*c*" the Jangama or Veerasheiva devotee;—"*d*" the vibhooty or sacred ashes;—"*e*" the roodraucsham or sacred bead;—"*f*" the tirmuntram or sacred charm;—"*g*" the paudodacam or water which has washed the feet of a spiritual teacher;—"*h*" the prasaudam or benediction of a spiritual teacher [matam].

ASHWAM (अश्व - ashva, *San.*). From (ash, san. to be able); strong and enduring animal. The genus Equus, equidæ, perissodactyla, ungulata, mammalia [sastanam, 21], of naturalists [jantoo]. The two species are asinus [gadhah], vulgaris [ghorah]. So plant first term. Ex., where transl. is of second term :—Glycosmis pentaphylla (ashvashákhóta), jack.; Ficus religiosa (ashvatt'ha), standing; Nerium odorum (ashvamáraka), killing; Shorea robusta (ashvakarna), ear; Withania somnifera (ashvagandhá), odour. See gloss. paragraphs.——*Ashwa medham* (अश्वमेध - ashvamédha, San.). From (médha, san. sacrifice). Horse sacrifice. Among the Aryans any one claiming to be a supreme ruler announced his intention of celebrating a horse sacrifice. A horse was selected and then turned loose to go where it pleased, only being followed by armed men. If another ruler contested the claim, he endeavoured to seize the horse. If the armed men came back unconquered and the horse with them, the claim was complete; the sacrifice was then conducted. He who offered a hundred such sacrifices was entitled to the throne of Indran [maryaday, matam].——*Ashwapaty* (अश्वपति - ashvapati, San.). From (pati, san. lord). Title borne by certain ancient rajahs.——*Ashwa rogam* (अश्वरोग - ashvaróga, San.). Horse-disease [bail, bursauty, chautahband, chuckrauval, dard-mondah, haddah, moongah, morghbyeza, motrah, pasoonah, porah, shembah].——*Ashwattam* (अश्वत्थ - ashvatt'ha, San.). From (st'há, san. to stand); tree in which resides the celestial fiery horse. Holy peepul tree. Supposed to be frequented by the gods as it is believed to be a transformation of Brihaspaty, the preceptor of the gods. It is reckoned an act of merit to plant and water it and worship and perform Pradacshinams round it. On Somavaura amavausyay days or every Monday on which the new moon falls, females go round this tree and worship it. Dry twigs of this tree are used to feed the sacred fires in households.——*Ashwiny* (अश्विनी - ashviní, San.). A name of Chauyay or shade, who took the form of a mare, and was approached by Sooryan in the form of a horse. On their nostrils touching she was impregnated with sun-beams, and became the mother of the Ashwiny comaurar or twins of the Hindoo zodiac, the physicians of the celestials, the Latin Castor and Pollux. The first of the twenty-seven nacshatrams [q. v.]. Its beginning follows immediately after the principal star in the last Nacshatram or Raivaty, nearly opposite to the very conspicuous star which indicates the fourteenth asterism, viz., Chitray. As a constellation it comprises three stars. As overlain by the fixed soli-sidereal zodiac, it is the first 13° 20′ of Maisham [jyotisham].

ASKA (అసికా - asiká, *Tel.* aska*). From (ashóka, san. king of that name).—"*a*" Deputy tahsildarry, Ganjam district. Pay Rs. 100.—"*b*" Proprietary estate; Ganjam district, Zemindarry tracts; population 7,928. Together with Coorlah and Devabhoomy contains a total population of 16,704. Square miles 14. Total quit-rent, Rs. 15,465-2-4, composed as follows :—Rs. 4,849 for Aska, Rs. 5,427 for Coorlah and Rs. 5,188 for Devabhoomy. The Aska estate originally formed a part of the Aska zemindarry; the latter was dismembered during the Moghul government of the Northern circars, 1560 to 1753, upon the death of Ram rowt row, the last zemindar, and divided amongst the neighbouring zemindars of Goomsoor, Dhauracote and Atagadah.—"*c*" Village, District moonsif's court, Registration office, Telegraph office, Deputy tahsildar's station, Ganjam dist.; pop. 3,909; lat. 19° 36′; long. 84° 42′; from Balligooda S.E. 63 miles; from Berhampore N.N.W. 23 miles; from Chetterpore N.W. 28 miles; from Chicacole N.N.E. 104 miles; from Madras N.N.E. 525 miles; from Russellcondah S. 23 miles. Traditionally founded by Asoca who gave it his own name. On the road from Berhampore to Russellcondah, immediately above the confluence of the Rooshcoolya and the Mahanuddy, and in a fertile tract of country chiefly planted with sugarcane. During the Goomsoor disturbances in 1835-36, temporarily occupied by troops. Temple with inscription said to have been executed by Asoca's own orders. Chief seat of the sugar trade in the district. Sugar works employ about 1,000 hands under English supervision. The Rooshcoolya is crossed here by a masonry bridge of nineteen span-arches.

ASMAUN (آسمان - ásmán, *Hind.*). From (ás, pers. millstone + mán, pers. suffix of similarity). Sky. There are seven among the Mahomedans:—First or Adam's residence composed of pure virgin silver; second or Enoch's and John the Baptist's, of gold; third or Joseph's, of pearls; fourth or Jesus', of pure white gold; fifth or Aaron's, of pure silver; sixth or Moses', of ruby and garnet; seventh, or Abraham's, of crystal [bheest].

ASOCA (अशोक - ashóka, *San.*). Means without sorrow. A ruler of the Mowrya dynasty of Magadham in N. india and grandson of its founder, Chundragooptan. He made Booddhism in place of Braminism the religion of the state. The king who set up the celebrated edict inscriptions is therein called Priyadarshy the beautiful, and Devanaumpriyan the beloved of the gods. Booddhist writings identify Priyadarshy with Asoca. The inscriptions above-named are of three distinct classes. Rock inscriptions, pillar inscriptions, and cave inscriptions. The five rock inscriptions hitherto known present five different texts of the same series of edicts which were published by Asoca in the tenth and twelfth years of his reign, or in 253 and 251 B.C. These five inscribed rocks have been found at far distant places, of which four are on the extreme eastern and western borders of India. Thus:—"*a*" At Shahbauzgurh, 40 miles to the east-north-east of Peshawar, and 25 miles to the north-west of Attock on the Indus.—"*b*" Near Khalsy on the west bank of the Jumna, just where it leaves the higher range of mountains to pass between the Doons, or valleys of Kyaurda and Dehra.—"*c*" At Girnar, near Joonaghur in Cuttywar, 40 miles to the north of Somnaut.—"*d*" At Dhowlee in Cuttack, 20 miles to the south of the town of Cuttack and the same distance to the north of the famous temple of Juggernaut.—"*e*" At Jowgada in the Ganjam district. This the only one in Madras presidency [jowgada]. There are no pillar or cave inscriptions in this presidency [charitram].

ASOO (असु - asu, *San.*). From (as, san. to be); life. A respiration.——*Asooran* (असुर - asura, San.). Demons and giants, who, like the Titans of the Greeks made war against the gods. See vol. I (73) to (78). Deityan is an older form than Asooran. Some say that a deluge intervening destroyed the deityans. In the oldest part of the Rig vedam the word Asooran is used for the supreme spirit, and is the same as the Ahoora of the Zoroastrians; but in the latter parts of the Rig vedam it signifies, as in the Pooranic mythology, a demon, and this change in its meaning probably grew out of the religious quarrel of Indian aryans with the Persians. Compare the change in meaning in the Greek δαίμων. According to the Vishnoo pooraunam, the origin of the Asoorans was as follows. Bramha being desirous of creating the four orders of beings, termed gods, demons, progenitors, and men, collected his mind into itself. Whilst thus concentrated, the quality of darkness pervaded his body; and then the demons called Asoorans were born, issuing from his thigh. The later beings of this class are Raucshasans. Asooradhroovam is the S. pole [matam].

ASRAH (آسرا - ásrá, *Hind.*). From Persian. Shelter, support. Asrahbhoomy is land having the support of water, land under irrigation.

ASSAMAD (الصمد - assamad, *Hind.*). From (samada, ar. to go to); from recourse being had to him in exigencies. The eternal [allah]. Mahomedan alam.

ASSES' EARS (ಕೊಣಜದಕಲ್ಲು - konajadakallu, *Can.*). From (konaja, can. name of a village + kallu, can. rock). Rocks; South canara dist., Mangalore tal.; lat. 13° 05′; long. 75° 05′; from Mangalore N.E. 21 miles; from Moodbidry N.E. 3 miles. Two perpendicular rocks on a small eminence. Form a well-known landmark.

ASTAM (अस्त - asta, *San.*). Means end or setting. Western ghauts. Astagiry, the same.

ASTAUNAH (آستانہ - ástánah, *Hind.*). From (ást'hána, san. place). Threshold; fakeers' residence. Astaunam in malayalam is audience-hall.

ASTRAM (अस्त्र - astra, *San.*). From (as, san. to throw). A missile weapon, as opposed to Shastram or arms.

ASWAD (اسود - aswad, *Ar.*). Black. Cf. Helleborus niger (kharbakiaswad), black hellebore; Justicia gendarussa (aslakiaswad), black vitex negundo. See gloss. paragraphs.

AT (الت - at, *Ar.*). Al [q.v.] before t in Arabic single terms, as at tauhir, meaning the pure.

ATAGADAH (అఠగడ - át'hagadá, *Tel.* átagadá*). From (áta, oor. eight + godo, oor. fort). Proprietary estate; Ganjam district, Zemindarry tracts; square miles 294; lat. of village 19° 36′; long. 84° 52′. The estate is perhaps the finest in the district. Contains 203 villages divided into three sub-divisions :—Colady mittah with sixty-eight villages; Bondacundy mittah with ninety-three villages; Bhidore mittah with 102 villages. Peshcush Rs. 59,927. Bounded :—north by Banpoor and Nyagar in Cuttack; south by the Rooshcoolya and Berhampore talook; east by Cullicote; west by Goomsoor. Country is mostly rich and fertile, being watered by three small rivers. In the centre it is mountainous, and south-east of Coracholly in Goomsoor are the Pundripada maliahs, an elevated tract covered with dense forest and abounding in game. The Bissoye of this tract was formerly a feudal dependent of the ancient Zemindars of Atagadah. The founder of the family was one Jagga doss, a hermit. The estate was sold by auction for arrears of tribute on the 15th July 1854. It was at first declared to have been bought by Government, but on appeal the Cullicote rajah was declared purchaser. The old sunnud was then cancelled. The transfer to the Cullicote rajah, in spite of his being a nephew of the last zemindar, caused dissatisfaction, and disturbances took place owing to oppressive management. In 1873 the feeling of discontent culminated in the zemindar's manager being waylaid and stabbed whilst on his way to Berhampore [cullicote].

ATAH (عطا - atá, *Hind.*). From (atú, ar. to give). Gift. Component part of lacabs [ism]. Atah ool lah, the gift of God. Compare Pers. buksh, in Khoodabuksh.

ATAR (अथर् - at'har, *San.*). Fire.——*Atarvan* (अथर्व - at'harva, San.). Aryan priest who has to do with fire and somam [veda]. The ancient sage of this name is represented as a Prajaupaty, Bramha's eldest son, as the first learner and earliest teacher of Bramha vidyay, and as the author of the Atarva veda. The Atarva veda, though so called, is not strictly a Veda like the Rig, Saumam and Yajoos, but a collection of formulas to avert consequences of mistakes in sacrifices [matam].

ATAUVANY (ಅಠವಣಿ - at'havani, *Can.*). Same as Attavanay. Register, cash book. Atauvany buntrote is a revenue peon.

ATCHAH (तिन्दुक - tinduka, *San.*; آبنوس - ábnús, *Hind.*; ಶೇಗುಮರ - shégumara, *Can.*; చేవమాను - chévamánu, *Tel.*; വീട്ടി - vítti, *Mal.*; ஆச்சா - áççá, *Tam.*). Any ebony tree. To be distinguished from Blackwood [q. v.]. Bauhinia racemosa, lam., Diospyros ebenum, koenig., and Diospyros melanoxylon, roxb., are well known Indian ebonies. They are all slow-growing trees, with dark-colored leaves. By age the interior of the wood becomes hard and black.

ATCHAN (അച്ചൻ - aççan, *Mal.*). From (ajja, prákrita of árya, san. noble). A father; used also as a title of respect [polliettatchan]; and in Malabar applied especially to the males of the royal family who have no office nor official rank in the state. Atchanmar is the honorific.——*Atchancoil* (അച്ചൻകോവിൽ - aççankóvil, Mal.). From (aççan, mal. lord, epithet of ayyappan, the village deity + kóvil, mal. temple).—" *a* " Village, Pass; Travancore district, Quilon division, Chenganore tal.; lat. 9° 5′; long. 77° 10′; from Chenganore E.S.E. 40 miles; from Trivandrum N.N.E. 43 miles; from the sea E. 41 miles. Village lies in an exceedingly wild part of the hills. Shrine sacred to Shauttan. Chowky. The pass, called on the British side Shencottah, connects Tinnevelly and Madura districts with Travancore; but, being more difficult for traffic than the Aryancauv road, is less used.—" *b* " River; Travancore district, Quilon division, Chenganore and Mauvelicara tals.; also known as Coolacudda river. Rises at the foot of the pass of the same name. Quitting the wild tract that borders its early course, the bed, generally sandy, interrupted however at intervals by rocks as it flows westwards, gradually widens to near three hundred yards, and the elevation of the banks diminishes and are bordered by cultivation. After a course of 70 miles north-west, it unites with the Pambah. Chief places on the river, Pundalam and Mauvelicara. It is navigable for 40 miles from its junction with the Pambah, boats ascending to Gonay for the greater part of the year.

ATCHOO (هتا - hattá, *Hind.*; అచ్చు - attsu, *Tel.*; அச்சு - aççu, *Tam.*). Tel. also (pana). A weaver's reed. A comb-like frame in a loom, through which the warp threads are passed, and by which the weft threads are pressed or battened together [nesavoo].

ATEES (अतिविषा - ativishá, *San.* and *Mahr.*; وجّ ترکی - vajjiturkí, *Pers.*; اتیس - atís, *Hind.*; وجّ ترکی - vajjiturkí, *Dec.*; అతివస - ativasa, *Tel.*; അതിവിടയം - ativitayam, *Mal.*; අතිවිඩයන් - atividayan, *Singh.*; அதிவிடையம் - athividaiyam, *Tam.*). Title from hindostany. San. from (ati, san. prefix meaning very + visha, san. poison); probably aryan name for a poisonous species misapplied to this non-poisonous indian species. Pers. from (vaj, pers. sweet-flag + turkí, pers. turkish). Hind. from sanscrit. Dec. from persian. Tel. from sanscrit by corruption, and is to some extent confounded with bachnaug or aconitum ferox, wall. Mal., Singh. and Tam. from sanscrit. Hind. also (atvíká), corr. from sanscrit. Cf. Aconitum ferox, wall. [bachnaug]; and see Jadwaur for non-poisonous aconites generally. Botanically Aconitum [bish] heterophyllum, wall., ranunculaceæ [vricsham, 1]. A plant of 1–3 feet high with a raceme of large flowers of a dull-yellow veined with purple, or altogether blue. Grows in the himalayas. The root, as met with in bazaars, occurs in small tubers, tapering towards a point, from one to one-and-a-half inches, or more in length, and from three-eighths to a quarter of an inch in thickness; grey externally, slightly wrinkled longitudinally, and marked here and there with rootlet scars, easily friable; internally white, farinaceous, inodorous, and of a pure bitter taste, devoid of acidity or astringency. The root is exceedingly bitter, mild antiperiodic, aphrodisiac and tonic, checking diarrhœa; may be administered internally with safety owing to comparative absence of poisonous properties; especially useful in convalescence after fever; is often adulterated with that of asparagopsis sarmentosa, kunth. [shatamooly]. Cf. also Methonica superba, lam. [wild bachnaug]. Used for British cinchona bark and phosphorus. Gives to pharm. aconiti heterophylli radix; tonic and antiperiodic; officinal. Alkaloid principle, atisine. Hydrochlorate of atisine is a white salt in very minute grains and has an intensely bitter taste.

ATHAR (اطہر - athar, *Hind.*). From (tahara, ar. to be clean). Pure. Mahomedan alam; as Athar hoossain, double alam [ism].

ATHONDAY (ஆதொண்டை - áthondai, *Tam.*). Means a creeper, Capparis horrida, linn. [thorny caper]. Name of illegitimate son of the Chola ruler Rajendra coolotoongan. Also called Tondaman chuckravurty. Conquered the Pallavas. Established the Tondeimundalam province. See vol. I (141).

ATI (अति - ati, *San.*). Intensive prefix. Common in many compounds. Ativeera rama pandiyan was a pandyan ruler of very ancient date, said to have been an author; the principal work attributed to him is the tamul neishadam; his real name was vallabha devan [charitram].——*Atimathooram* (यष्टिमधुका - yashtimadhuká, San.; ज्येष्टमध - jyésht'hamadha, Mahr.; سوس - sús, Ar.; مہک - mahak, Pers.; ملٹھی - mulatthí, Hind.; میٹھی لکڑی - míthílakrí, Dec.; اورت منس - uritmanis, Malay; ಅತಿಮಧುರ - atimadhura, Can.; అతిమధురము - atimadhuramu, Tel.; ഇരട്ടിമധുരം - irattimadhuram, Mal.; අතිමදුරං - atimaduram, Singh.; அதிமதுரம் - athimathuram, Tam.). Title from sweet roots. San. from (yashti, san. stick + madhu, san. sweet); from long sweet roots. Mahr. from sanscrit. Dec. from (míthí, hind. sweet + lakrí, hind. stick). Can. from (ati, san. prefix excessive + madhura, san. sweet). Tel. like canarese. Mal. from sanscrit. Singh. from tamul. Tam. like canarese. San. also (madhuyashtiká), meaning sweet stick; (madhuká), meaning sweet; (klítaka), meaning destroying impotency. Hind. also (jethímadh), from sanscrit. Singh. also (valmí), meaning honey creeper. Greek γλυκύῤῥιζη. Latin radix dulcis. Liquiritia, whence liquorice, is a corruption of glycyrrhiza. Title otherwise Honey creeper, Liquorice plant, Sweet root. Botanically Glycirrhiza glabra, linn., leguminosæ [vricsham, 48]. Alias Glycyrrhiza triphylla; Liquoritia officinalis. Malabar coast; but product most met with in bazaars is imported from Persia. Roots very long, about an inch thick, flexible fibrous, of a brown color; see description under abrus precatorius, linn., those roots being often substituted for these. By decoction and evaporation the roots yield the dry extract, called liquorice. Gives to pharm. glycyrrhizæ radix; officinal; has a power of covering the flavor of nauseous medicines; in high repute amongst veidyans chiefly in infusion, for coughs, consumptions, gonorrhœa, &c.; also considered mild laxative. Root gives a dye. No other species here.

ATMACORE (آتکور - átkúr, *Hind.*; ఆత్మకూరు - átmakúru, *Tel.* atmakúr *). From (yátamu, tel. water lift + úru, tel. village).——(1) Talook, Nellore district. Tahsildar's pay Rs. 175. Area 640 square miles. W. centre inland talook of district. Bounded:—North by Oodayagherry, west by E. ghauts, south by Raupore, east and north-east by Nellore and Cauvaly respectively. A portion of the talook formerly belonged to one Abbaus ally khan, Jagheerdar of Oodayagherry. For misconduct he was made a state prisoner and his lands were confiscated. The Veligondas occupy W. part of talook. The rest is generally flat, but there are isolated hills. Pennair divides talook into two unequal portions. The northern part is drained by Boggair which joins Pennair near Atmacore. Other streams are the Kedamanair and Beerapair. On the banks of the Pennair soil is clayey and fertile; elsewhere poor, especially in the north-east, where there is also great scarcity of water. Indigo largely grown on river banks and thread dyed in some villages. Numerous irrigation channels from Pennair. Water is also taken by lift from Boggair and other streams. There are several fine tanks, those of Anamasamoodram, Anantasaugaram, Atmacore, Calavoy and Mahimalore being specially noteworthy. Camping grounds:— Beylachirvella, Mahomedapooram, Shreecolan. Places of archæological interest:—Anamasamoodram, Anantasaugaram, Atmacore, Calavoy, Chejerla, Chirmana, Colagotla, Coollore, Cotiteertam, Gollapully, Mahimalore, Mungampulley, Nauvore, Nedoorpulley, Pautapaud, Pellcor, Permana, Poongode, Prabhagiriputnam, Shreecolan, Somashila, Vaushily, Veerlagoodipaud. Principal trig. stations:—Caraconda, Krishnamma, Raujally. The leading places, &c., in the talook are the following.——*Anamasamoodram* (అనమసముద్రము - anamasamudramu, Tel.). See sep. title.——*Anantasaugaram* (అనంతసాగరము - anantaságaramu, Tel.). See sep. title.——*Atmacore* (ఆత్మకూరు - átmakúru, Tel.). See below.——*Beerapair* (బీరపేరు - bírapéru, Tel.). See sep. title.——*Boggair* (బొగ్గేరు - boggéru, Tel.). See sep. title.——*Calavoy* (కలువాయ - kaluváya, Tel.). See sep. title.——*Caraconda* (కరకొండ - karakonda, Tel.). From (kara, tel. border + konda, tel. hill). Trig. station; lat. 14° 27′ 44·93″; long. 79° 22′ 01·76″; from Atmacore W.S.W. 23 miles; from Seetarampully W. 5 miles.——*Chejerla* (చేజర్ల - chéjarla, Tel.). See sep. title.——*Coollore* (కుల్లూరు - kullúru, Tel.). From (gulla, tel. shell + úru, tel. village). Village; pop. 2,837; acres 7,525; lat. 14° 30′; long. 79° 24′; from Atmacore W.S.W. 20 miles; from Nellore W. 41 miles. Coral and pearl merchants. On bank of Pennair and at foot of Veligondas. Old temple in ruins.——*Cotiteertam* (కోటితీర్థము - kótitírt'hamu, Tel.). From (kóti, san. contraction for kótíshvara, san. shiva, the hill lord + tírt'ha, san. place of sacred water). Village; pop. 1,621; acres 8,044; lat. 14° 34′; long. 79° 32′; from Atmacore W.S.W. 10 miles; from Nellore W.N.W. 34 miles. On right bank of Pennair. Lingam temple of Shiva as Coteshwarasawmy, repaired by Cota rauzooloo, a Cshatriya, and endowed with a Khandriga and inams in extent about acres 125. The chief festival, Calyaunam [pundigay, 6d] ootsavam, is celebrated in Maugham [mausam] or January. Bank of Pennair near the village is very strongly revetted. Irrigated by river channels from Pennair. Thread is dyed here.——*Devaroyapully* (దేవరాయపల్లె - dévaráyapalle,* Tel.). From (dévaráyadu, tel. proper name + palle, tel. village). Village; pop. 1,962; acres 6,549; lat. 14° 35′; long. 79° 29′; from Atmacore W. 12¾ miles; from Nellore W.N.W. 36 miles. Formerly head-quarters of Tahsildar. Wet lands irrigated by river channels as well as by Anantasaugaram tank. Pennair is encroaching and seems likely to wash the village away.——*Krishnamma* (కృష్ణమ్మ - krishnamma, Tel.). Means a proper name. Trig. station; lat. 14° 27′ 17·35″; long. 79° 47′ 46·28″; height 465 feet; from Anjagauripulley N. 2 miles; from Atmacore S.E. 14 miles.——*Mahimalore* (మహిమలూరు - mahimalúru, Tel.). See sep. title.——*Nadigadda* (నడిగడ్డ - nadigadda, Tel.). From (nadi, tel. middle + gadda, tel. mound). Village; pop. 877; clubbed with Maumoodore; acres 5,048; lat. 14° 35′; long. 79° 44′; from Atmacore E.S.E. 4⅘ miles; from Nellore W.N.W. 21 miles. Island in Pennair near mouth of Boggair.——*Pennair* (పెన్నేరు - pennéru, Tel.). See sep. title.——*Prabhagiriputnam* (ప్రభగిరిపట్నము - prabhagiripatnamu, Tel.). From (prabhákarudu, tel. proper name + pattana, san. town). Village; pop. 1,212; acres 9,609; lat. 14° 27′; long. 79° 47′; from Atmacore S.E. 14 miles; from Nellore W. 15 miles. Ancient fort and several pagodas restored by Pudma kesara, son of a ruler Varadarajah.——*Rajavole* (రాజవోలు - rájavólu, Tel.). From (rájá, san. king + prólu, tel. town). Village; pop. 1,241; acres 5,743; lat. 14° 43′; long. 79° 39′; from Atmacore N.N.W. 7¼ miles; from Nellore N.W. 31 miles. Irrigation under tank.——*Raujally* (రాజల్లి - rájalli, Tel.). From (rádzu, tel. king + palli, tel. village). Trig. station; lat. 14° 42′ 34·57″; long. 79° 39′ 16·43″; height 549 feet; from Atmacore N.N.W. 6½ miles; from Poongode N.W. 1⅓ miles.——*Somashila* (సోమశిల - sómashila, Tel.). See sep. title.——*Veligonda* (వెలిగొండ - veligonda, Tel.). See sep. title.——*Yerraconda* (ఎర్రగొండ - erragonda, Tel.). See sep. title.——**(2)** Village, Head-quarters of Tahsildar and Sub-registrar; Nellore dist., Atmacore tal.; pop. 3,760; acres 11,752; lat. 14° 37′; long. 79 40′; from Madras N.N.W. 112 miles; from Naidoopett N.N.W. 52 miles; from Nellore N.N.W. 26 miles; from Ongole S.S.W. 67 miles. 12 miles west of Sungam and 1 mile from north bank of Boggair. A low hill to west of village. Climate very hot in hot weather. One large tank fed by a channel from Boggair. The houses of Hindoos and Mahomedans are found side by side contrary to usual custom. Former residence of Oodayagherry jagheerdar. On tank-bund is an inscription stating that the tank was repaired by Conaity timmaratsayya of Vijianugger in A.D. 1549. Ruined temple to Alaganautasawmy. West on a hill is a stone statue, representing a Jeina teertancaran. Thread is dyed here.——**(3)** Deputy tahsildarry, Kurnool district. Pay Rs. 70.——**(4)** Village, Deputy tahsildar's station; Kurnool dist., Nundicotcore tal.; pop. 3,498; acres 10,916; lat. 15° 53′; long. 78° 38′; from Cumbum W.N.W. 40 miles; from Kurnool E. 36 miles; from Madras N.N.W. 218 miles; from Nundiaul N.N.E. 28 miles; from Nundicotcore E. 22 miles; from Pyaupaly N.E. 71 miles. On route from Kurnool to Guntoor. Former head-quarters of talook. Temples of Keshava sawmy and Siddeshwara sawmy. Large tank and tope for camping ground, both by Ambah naidoo a descendant of Poligar of Dornaul in beginning of eighteenth century. In January or February pilgrims halt on their way to Srisheilam.

ATOLL (അട്ടാലം - attálam, *Mal.*). Means sinking reef. Came to English through French atollon. A coral island consisting of a more or less perfect ring of coral rock surrounding a lagoon. The Maldive and Laccadive islands consist of atolls.

ATRY (अत्रि - atri, *San.*). From (ad, san. to eat). Devourer. In the epic Aryan period one of the ten Prajaupaties or lords of creation engendered by Menoo for the purpose of creating the universe. At a later period the mind-born son of Bramha and one of the seven rishies; otherwise the ancient Agastyan [matam].

ATTACK (अट्टक - attaka, *Mahr.*; اٹاک کا جہاڑ - atákkájhár, *Hind.*). Botanically Flacourtia [swaudoo cantacam] montana, grah., bixineæ [vricsham, 14]. Tree; fruit scarlet, size of a cherry; has agreeable acid taste.

ATTAP (اٹاپ - atáp, *Malay*). Title from javanese, meaning thatch. Title otherwise Java thatch. Botanically nipa fruticans, thunb., pandanaceæ [vricsham, 150]. Palm fronds used in thatching; fruit gives a dye. No other species here.

ATTAR (عطر - itr, *Hind.*; அத்தர் - attar, *Tam.*). From (itr, ar. perfume). Means essence. Title otherwise Otter, Otto. Attars are very strong oils, containing the essential oils of the plants and substances used in their preparation; a few drops are sufficient to produce an intensely strong perfume. These on ceremonial occasions, are offered to the guests on a piece of cotton, twisted at the end of a stick four or five inches long [paunsoopaury]. The best known attar is the essential oil extracted from the petals of roses. This is obtained by skimming off the essential oil from rose water which has been exposed to the air all night in large open vessels. It is said to take 200,000 roses to produce an ounce of attar of roses. Attar of roses is nearly colorless, solid below 80°, and liquefies at 84°. A compound of two oils, one liquid, the other solid and inodorous. Oleum rosæ of chemists. Adulteration effected by the addition of the volatile oil of the grass, Andropogon schœnanthus, linn., lemon or geranium oil. The following are two key-lists of the volatile and perfumed oils of s. india; further information must be traced in the glossary paragraphs through the small-type cross references at end of this volume; see also vricsham, 7, for the method of expressing the products, &c., of the plants in the dravidian languages:—"*a*" Acorus calamus, sweet flag; Andropogon iwaranousa, ibharancoosha; Andropogon martini, roussa grass; Andropogon muricatus, cuscus; Andropogon schœnanthus, lemon grass; Aquilaria agallocha, eagle wood; Artemisia vulgaris, indian absinth; Carum copticum, ajwaun; Cinnamomum camphora, camphor cinnamon; Cinnamomum tamala, cassia cinnamon; Cinnamomum zeylanicum, ceylon cinnamon; Citrus aurantium, orange; Citrus aurantium, var. bergamia, bergamot orange; Citrus medica, var. limonum, lemon; Citrus medica, var. medica proper, citron; Cuminum cyminum, cummin; Elettaria cardamomum, cardamom; Eugenia caryophyllata, clove; Excæcaria agallocha, blinding tree; Jasminum auriculatum, needle jasmine; Jasminum grandiflorum, common jasmine; Jasminum humile, yellow jasmine; Jasminum pubescens, musk jasmine; Jasminum sambac, arabian jasmine; Lawsonia alba, henna plant; Melaleuca leucadendron, var. minor, cajeput; Mesua ferrea, nauga champak; Michelia champaca, champak; Mimusops elengi, ilanjy; Myristica fragrans, common nutmeg; Myristica malabarica, malabar nutmeg; Nardostachys jatamansi, indian spikenard; Nicotiana tabacum, tobacco; Nigella sativa, sweet fennel; Pandanus odoratissimus, screw-pine; Pergularia minor, primrose creeper; Phœnix dactylifera, arabian date; Pimpinella anisum, anise seed; Piper cubeba, cubeb pepper; Piper nigrum, black pepper; Pogostemon patchouli, var. suavis, patchouli; Psidium guyava, var. pyriferum, white guava; Rosa centifolia, cabbage rose; Rosa damascena, damask rose; Santalum album, sandal; Saussurea lappa, costum; Styrax benzoin, benzoin.—"*b*" Absinth, artemisia; Ajwaun, carum; Aniseed, pimpinella; Benzoin, styrax; Blinding tree, excæcaria; Cajeput, melaleuca; Cardamom, elettaria; Champak, mesua, michelia; Cinnamon, cinnamomum; Citron, citrus; Clove, eugenia; Costum, saussurea; Cummin, cuminum; Cuscus, andropogon; Date, phœnix; Eagle wood, aquilaria; Fennel, nigella; Guava, psidium; Henna, lawsonia; Ibharancoosha, andropogon; Ilanjy, mimusops; Lemon, citrus; Lemon grass, andropogon; Nutmeg, myristica; Orange, citrus; Pepper, piper; Primrose creeper, pergularia; Rose, rosa; Roussa grass, andropogon; Sandal, santalum; Screw-pine, pandanus; Spikenard, nardostachys; Sweet flag, acorus; Tobacco, nicotiana.

ATTAVANAY (அட்டவணை - attavanai, *Tam.*). From (at'havana, mahr. remembrance). Cash book, ledger, register [atauvany].

ATTAY (जलौक - jalauka, *San.*; جونك - jonk, *Hind.*; ಜಿಗಣಿ - jigani, *Can.*; జలగ - jalaga, *Tel.*; അട്ട - atta, *Mal.*; அட்டை - attai, *Tam.*). Title from Tam. from (adu, tam. to adhere). San. from (jala, san. water + óka, san. dwelling). Can. from (jígí, can. adhesive). Tel. from sanscrit. Terms apply to family hirudinidæ, leeches of various genera. The officinal or green leech Sanguisuga medicinalis is of blackish green color, with six reddish brown, longitudinal streaks. The English, or speckled leech Sanguisuga medicinalis has six stripes spotted with black, the belly is greenish yellow, and spotted. The peculiar Madras leech is a bdella. Found in stagnant ponds and ditches, especially during the monsoon. It is larger than the European leech, and very voracious. Use by vaidyans and hakeems same as with Europeans; they wash the part always with soap and water previously. The large Horse-leech, is also common in stagnant pools, depressed body and dusky-colored back, belly yellowish green. The Ceylon leech, met with in the south, is a dangerous animal to foot travellers at certain seasons; seldom more than an inch long, broad behind, taper towards the forepart; color brown, or light-brown; substance nearly transparent; very active, powers of contraction and expansion are great; point so sharp that it makes its way through smallest openings, and attacks feet, legs and thighs. Twelve species of leech are enumerated in shastrams, six of which poisonous. The six that are fit for use are:—Capilah, or tawny leech; Pingalah, pale red tinge; Chunk mookhy, yellow and has a long sharp head; Mooshikah, dun; Poondareeca mookhy, brown color and with mouth like flower of nelumbo; and Shabarikah, which resembles leaf of lotus in color.——*Attapaudy* (അട്ടപ്പാടി - attapáti, Mal.). From (atta, mal. leech + páti, mal. village). Valley; Malabar district, Valavanaud talook. Site of the source of the Bhawauny.

ATTINGAL (ആറ്റുങ്ങൽ - áttunnal, *Mal.*). From (áru, mal. river + kal, mal. locative termination). Sanscrit name (stríbhága), meaning woman + portion; portion of the Travancore ranees. Village, Head-quarters of Tahsildar and Moonsif, Port; Travancore state, Trivandrum division, Cherankeel tal.; pop. 9,277; lat. 8° 42′; long. 76° 52′; from Anjengo N.E. 4¼ miles; from Alleppey S.S.E. 62 miles; from Cottayam S.S.E. 64 miles; from Madras S.W. 380 miles; from Nagarcoil N.W. 55 miles; from Paravore S.S.E. 106 miles; from Quilon S.E. 20 miles; from Trivandrum W.N.W. 18 miles; from the sea E. 5 miles. Ancient village on the Attingal or Vaumanapooram river, and on the main northern trunk road from Trivandrum. Constitutes, with seventeen surrounding villages, the hereditary domain of the Ranee or eldest princess of Travancore, who formerly possessed the sovereignty of the country, and with whom in the earliest periods of the English factory at Anjengo contracts were made. The country consisting of two adhicaurams or sub-divisions of the Cherankeel talook is still the private property of the Ranee. Through the Ranees, according to the custom of the Nayars, is still the line of succession to the throne. This district is administered by the princesses through their Cauryacauran or Manager. They reside here for a short time at least once a year, for change of air, river bathing and boating, and worship at their tutelar shrine. There is an ancient palace and pagoda here to which the Maharajah pays a state visit once a year in January for worshipping the family deity.

ATTIPAIR (അട്ടിപ്പേറ് - attippéru, *Mal.*). From (atti, mal. to come in contact + péru, mal. birth). Contraction for Neerattipair [q.v.].——*Alagya attippair* (അഴകിയഅട്ടിപ്പേറ് - azhakiyaattippéru, Mal.). From (azhakiya, mal. fair + attippéru, mal. title deeds of freehold property). Otherwise Peroomartam. A tenure approximating closely to Otty [q.v.], the mortgagee being in possession and enjoying the whole produce. There is a peculiarity however, that the sum advanced, which is always the full marketable value of the land for the time being, is not mentioned in the deed; and the landlord, in redeeming his property, does not repay the amount originally advanced, but the actual value of it in the market at the time of redemption. In other respects the same rules that apply to Otty mortgages are applicable to these also. Deeds of this kind are in use only at Palghaut and Temmalapooram. See vol. II, 104.——*Attippettola* (അട്ടിപ്പേട്ടോല - attippéttóla, Mal.). From (óla, mal. palm leaf). Title deeds of free-hold property.

ATTIRY (اتيري - attirí, *Mahl*). Means sea-shore. Male assembly. A division of a village in Maldives for the purposes of administration [varaungy].

ATTY (அத்தி - atti, *Tam.*). From (attu, tam. to attach); from the gum. Fig.—"*a*" Botanically the Ficus genus, moraceæ [vricsham, 121]. Trees or shrubs; natives of warm countries; have alternate rarely opposite entire or lobed leaves; the flowers are usually incomplete and unlike those of most fruit trees make no outward appearance, but are concealed within the fig on its internal surface. There is a Tamul proverb:— அத்தி பூத்ததுபோல் இருக்கிறது அவன்வந்தது; "his "coming is like the flowering of the fig-tree;" something that never happens. The fruit is turbinate, fleshy, soft and hollow within; consists of globose or angular achenes, with a dry thin rarely pulpy pericarp; under favorable circumstances a fruit or two is formed along the shoots at the base of almost every leaf. Several fig-trees throw out aërial roots from branches which grow into the ground and again throw out branches. The trees are large and of rapid growth. The timber is of little value, being light, open, and soft. Some yield useful caoutchouc; several yield fibres for cordage, for half stuff, for paper-making. The species best known to the natives are:—arnottiana [wild peepul], asperrima [bramha's banyan], bengalensis [banyan], benjamina [small tsiela], carica [anjeer], citrifolia [wild banyan], cunia [large bramha's banyan], excelsa [tall-fig], glomerata [cluster fig], heterophylla [red fig], infectoria [stone banyan], laccifera [nooga], oppositifolia [devil fig], racemosa [country fig], religiosa [peepul], repens [creeper fig], retusa [chinese banyan], scandens [stone fig], tomentosa [hill banyan], tsiela [tsiela], tuberculata [hill tsiela], vagans [hill peepul]. Other s. indian species indigenous or naturalized are:—acutiloba, angustifolia, guttata, macrocarpa, rumphii, wightiana. The so called figs proper are shown below.—"*b*" Also applied to some species of other genera. Cf. Gomphia angustifolia (chóratti), red atty; Nephelium longana (púvatti), flowering atty. See gloss. paragraphs.——*Cluster fig* (यज्ञो - डुम्बर - yañódumbara, San.; उंबर - umbara, Mahr.; درخت تين الاحمق - darakhtitínulahmak, Ar.; درخت ثمر پشه - darakhtisamarpashshah, Pers.; گولير کاجهاڑ - gulerkájhár, Dec.; ಅತ್ತಿ - atti, Can.; ಅತ್ತಿಮರ - artimara, Too.; మేడి - médi, Tel.; ଡିମ୍ବିରି - dimeri, Oor.; അത്തിയാൽ - attiyál, Mal.; අත්තික්කා - attikká, Singh.; அத்தி - atti, Tam.). Title from appearance of fruit in bunches. San. from (yaña, san. sacrifice + udumbara, san. fig tree) used in sacrifice. Mahr. from (udumbara, san. the plant); see below. Ar. from (darakht, ar. tree + tín, ar. ficus carica, linn. + ahmak, ar. false). Pers. from (darakht, ar. tree + samar, pers. fruit + pashshah, pers. gnat); fruit being insect-eaten. Mal. from (atti, mal. fig tree + ál, mal. banyan, ficus bengalensis, linn.). Tam. from (attu, tam. to attach); from its gum-giving property. San. also (udumbara), meaning extending to the sky; (yañavriksha), meaning sacrifice + tree, from being used in sacrifice; (haritáksha), meaning reddish green-eyed, from fruit; (jantup'hala), meaning insect + fruit, from fruits being full of insects. Ar. also (jammaiz). Pers. also (darakhtianjíriahmak), meaning false edible fig tree. Tel. also (bodda); (paidichettu), meaning gold + tree, from orange colored fruit. Singh. also (dimbul). Title otherwise Country fig, Guler, Gum fig, Insect fruit, Sacrificial fig, Wild fig. Botanically Ficus [atty] glomerata, miq., moraceæ [vricsham, 121]. Alias Covellia glomerata. Large tree; trunk crooked, bark of a rusty-greenish color, rough; leaves alternate, petioled, oblong or broad lanceolate, tapering equally to each end, entire, very slightly three-nerved, smooth on both sides; racemes compound or panicled, issuing immediately from the trunk or large branches; fruit pedicelled, nearly as large as the common fig, clothed with soft down, when ripe orange colored; common on banks of rivers. From the root exudes a fluid, caught in earthen pots, which veidyans consider as a calpam or powerful tonic; this is termed atty vair tunny; the bark astringent to ulcers and to remove poison of wounds made by a tiger or cat; the root used in dysentery, the milky juice given in piles and diarrhœa, and in combination with sesamum oil in cancer; fresh juice of ripe fruit used as adjunct to a metallic preparation given in diabetes and other urinary diseases; bark in combination with gingelly oil an external application in cancer. The fruit edible, but insipid, and is usually found full of insects; occasionally eaten raw and in curries by the poor. Gum is used as bird lime, and has a pleasant odour; tree gives fibre. Wood grey, soft, mottled on a longitudinal section; not durable, lasts well under water, consequently used for well-frames.——*Creeper fig* (بهوئی ڈومر - bhuídumar, Hind.; கொடியத்தி - kodiyatti, Tam.). Hind. from (bhuí, mahr. ground + udumbara, san. the fig tree, ficus glomerata, miq.). Tam. from (kodi, tam. creeper + atti, tam. fig tree). Botanically Ficus [atty] repens, roxb., moraceæ [vricsham, 121].——*Devil fig* (काकोदुम्बर - kákódumbara, San.; खरवत - kharavata, Mahr.; شجر تين بري - shajaritínibarrí, Ar.; درخت انجير دشتی - darakhtianjíridashtí, Pers.; جنگلی انجير کا پيڑ - janglíanjírkáper, Hind.; جنگلی گولير کا جهاڑ - jangligulerkájhár, Dec.; ಅಡವಿಅತ್ತಿ - adaviatti, Can.; కాకిమేడి - kákimédi, Tel.; പാറകം - párakam, Mal.; කොටදිඹුලා - kotadimbulá, Singh.; பேயத்தி - péyatti, Tam.). Title from growing wild. San. from (káka, san. crow + udumbara, san. ficus glomerata, miq.); as eaten by crows. Ar. from (shajr, ar. tree + tín, ar. ficus carica, linn. + barrí, ar. forest). Pers. from (darakht, pers. tree + anjír, pers. ficus carica, linn. + dashtí, pers. forest). Hind. from (janglí, hind. wild + anjír, pers. ficus carica, linn. + per, hind. tree). Dec. from (janglí, hind. wild + guler, hind. ficus glomerata, miq. + jhár, hind. tree). Can. from (adavi, can. wild + atti, can. fig tree). Tel. from (káki, tel. crow + médi, tel. fig tree). Mal. from (pára, mal. rock + akam, mal. inside). Singh. from (kota, singh. small + dimbul, singh. ficus glomerata, miq.). Tam. from (péy, tam. devil + atti, tam. ficus genus). Tel. also (bódamámidi), meaning bald mango; (verrimédi), meaning mad + fig tree; (verriatti), meaning mad + fig tree; (brahmamédi), meaning bramha, the god + fig tree; (bommamédi), by corr. Mal. also (péyatti), meaning devil's fig. Title otherwise Bramha's fig, Crow fig, Mad fig, Wild fig. Botanically Ficus [atty] oppositifolia, gasp., moraceæ [vricsham, 121]. Alias Covellia oppositifolia; Ficus hispida; Sycomorphe roxburghii. Small tree; young shoots scabrous, and covered with short hair, fistulous and interrupted at the insertion of the leaves; leaves opposite, round or oblong, slightly serrate, glandular in the axils of the veins beneath, shining above, downy beneath; fruit axillary and peduncled, racemose on the naked woody branches, round, about the size of a large nutmeg, covered with short white hair, with several equidistant ridges. Gives to pharm fruit, seeds and bark, non-officinal; fruit, seeds and bark emetic; bark antiperiodic and tonic. Fruit not often eaten; leaves lopped for cattle fodder; is from its being sown by birds, a great destroyer of houses and walls; soft fibre, fit for weaving. Wood soft, dirty grey, no heart-wood, no annual rings. The Ficus polycarpa, roxb., is a smaller species analogous; fruit size of pea.——*Red fig* (त्रायमाणा - tráyamáná, San.; బురోని - buróni, Tel.; വള്ളിത്തേരകം - vallittérakam, Mal.; වලහෙටු - valehetu, Singh.). Title from red leaves of a variety. San. from (trá, san. to protect); a curative. Mal. from (valli, mal. creeper + térakam, mal. ficus asperrima, roxb.). Singh. from (val, singh. forest + ehetu, singh. ficus tsiela, roxb.). Title otherwise Wild tsiela. Botanically Ficus [atty] heterophylla, linn., moraceæ [vricsham, 121]. Alias Ficus rubescens. Common in moist places. All rough and harsh; leaves alternate, short-petioled, stiff, membranaceous, roughish above and of a deep green, paler below, oblong-acute, acute at the base, serrated, entire or three-lobed, of all shapes; fruit axillary, solitary, rarely twin, between turbinate and globose, size of a large gooseberry. The juice of root internally administered in colic; the juice of leaves mixed with milk in dysentery; the bark of the root very bitter; pulverised and mixed with coriander seed is a remedy in affections of the chest.——*Stone fig* (கல்லிச்சி - kalliçhi, Tam.). Tam. from (kal, tam. stone + içhi, tam. ficus tsiela, roxb.); from hard leaf. Title otherwise Stone tsiela. Botanically Ficus [atty] scandens, roxb., moraceæ [vricsham, 121].——*Tall fig* (അത്തിമിറാൽ - attimirál, Mal.). Mal. from (atti, mal. ficus genus + ál, mal. ficus bengalensis, linn.). Botanically Ficus [atty] excelsa, vahl., moraceæ [vricsham, 121]. Tree; leaves alternate, bifarious, slightly scabrous beneath; fruit-receptacles axillary, solitary or paired, peduncled, somewhat turbinate, smooth, size of a cherry, yellow when ripe. Introduced from moluccas. The decoction of the root is powerful aperient.

AUCAUSHAM (आकाश - ákásha, *San.*). From (á, san. all round + kásh, san. to shine). Ethereal space; the inane of Lucretius; the fifth element of the Tamulians. Frequent in plant names, from roots floating or from being parasitic. Cf. Cassytha filiformis (ákáshavallí), air creeper; Corallocarpus epigæa (ákáshagadda), air tuber; Pistia stratiotes (ákáshatámara), floating water-lily. See gloss. paragraphs.——*Aucausha gamanam* (आकाशगमन - ákáshagamana, San.). From (gamana, san. going). Walking in the air; one of the sixty-four magical arts.——*Aucausha ramayya* (ఆకాశరామయ్య - ákásharámaya, Tel.). From (rámaya, tel. proper name). Means Rama in the sky. Signature often given to anonymous petitions.

AUCHAURAM (आचार - áchára, *San.*; اچار - áchár, *Hind.*). From (á, san. prefix meaning towards + char, san. to move). The rules of practice in caste and religion. Includes the division of a bramin's life into four periods, the conduct of a student in the house of his preceptor, investiture with the sacred cord, the five diurnal devotional acts, the domestic ceremonies of marriage, funeral rites, the various modes of gaining subsistence, the rules of diet, the laws concerning women, &c. The Vishnoo pooraunam contains a complete and systematic description of the Auchauram. Coolachauram is family usage. Deshachauram is custom of the country. Aucharanay is the same [maryauday, matam].

AUCHITAM (आचित - áchita, *San.*). From (áchi, san. to load with). Measure of weight. Generally a cart-load. More specifically 10 bhaurams = 1 auchitam [niray, 2f]. Approximate actual value, 1 auchitam = 1 ton, 16 cwts., 2 qts., 12 lbs.

AUD (अवि - avi, *San.*; بکرا - bakrá, *Hind.*; ಕುರಿ - kuri, *Can.*; గొర్రె - gorre, *Tel.*; ആട് - átu, *Mal.*; ஆடு - ádu, *Tam.*). Sheep and goat species, part of sub-family caprinæ, family bovidæ, order ruminantia, class mammalia [sastanam, 23], of naturalists [jantoo]. Cf. for plant terms:—Adhatoda vasica (ádusóge), what goats touch; Aristolochia bracteata (ádumuttadagida), what goats do not touch. Cf. for animal terms:—Cervulus muntjac (káttádu), forest goat; Tetraceros quadricornis (malaiyádu), mountain goat.——*Cooroombaud* (کربا - kurbá, Hind.; குறும்பாடு - kurumbádu, Tam.). Tam. from (kurumbu, tam. village in a desert tract). A short woolly sheep with crumpled horns [shemmariyaud].——*Pulleiyaud* (பள்ளையாடு - pallaiyádu, Tam.). Tam. from (pallai, tam. short and thick). An undersized goat; very prolific [vellaud].——*Shemmariyaud* (मेष - mésha, San.; لال بکرا - lálbakrá, Hind.; గొర్రె - gorre, Tel.; ചെമ്മരിയാട് - chemmariyátu, Mal.; செம்மறியாடு - shemmariyádu, Tam.). Hind. from (lál, hind. red + bakrá, hind. sheep). Tam. from (shem, tam. red + mari, tam. young one of sheep + ádu, tam. ovis). The ordinary sheep, browner than the goat, and hence so called; has some wool. The Shemmariyaud corresponds with Ovis aries, sub-family caprinæ, family bovidæ, order ruminantia, class mammalia [sastanam, 23], of naturalists [jantoo]. Horns in both sexes large, angular, heavily wrinkled, turned downwards almost into a circle, with their flat points directed forwards and outwards. No muffle; no beard; chaffron convex; large but immobile eye, pits in some, wanting in others; small feet-pits in all feet; inguinal glands distinct; two mammæ. The peculiar conformation of the mouth of the sheep, the lips being protected by hair, and the upper lip presenting a cleft, enables it to take bite much closer to the ground than cattle in general; and for this reason sheep can thrive on scanty pasture. Nellore district is famed for its large breed, the tallest in india; a good specimen stands across the withers thirty to thirty-six inches in height, and, when fattened, will weigh from 80 to 100 lb.; it has the usual form of twisted horns of moderate size, with a slight roman contour of the face; the prevailing color is white or a light brownish white with black points; the body is well covered with short fur or hair, with a light frill of hair frequently lining the throat and foreneck in the males; some have two long rounded pendulous lobules, from two to three inches in length, hanging side by side from the throat, which the natives term in tamul bells; the hair about the posterior part of the thighs, from the tail to hock, is longer and thicker than in most other parts; the tail is short; the ewes are hornless. The Madras sheep proper resembles a greyhound with tucked-up belly, having some coarseness of form; the feet light; limbs bony; sides flat; and tails short; it seldom exceeds twenty-two to twenty-eight inches in height; the horns are confined to the rams only, which, when the animal is well-grown, are generally of fair size, having the usual twist; these sheep have slight roman noses, and large ears in some instances and small pointed ones in others; they are covered with short, coarse hair, the prevailing color being red or brown, of which there are various shades, and many have the "bells" above mentioned depending from the throat; the ewes are an inch or two lower than the rams; they make fair nurses and milk well; a variety of this sheep is sometimes met with, in which the rams are hornless, the throat and foreneck lined with a thick shaggy coat of hair, extending like a frill from the throat to the breast, and often reaching to the knees. This Madras breed proper is found in the Chingleput, parts of the Kistna, Godavery, Ganjam, North arcot, South arcot, Salem, Trichinopoly, Tanjore, Madura and Tinnevelly districts. Neither the Madras, nor the Nellore breed furnishes wool or hair fit for textile purposes. Coimbatore district is famed for a breed of wool producing sheep; it is, on the whole, a small breed, the rams seldom exceeding twenty-six, and the ewes twenty-two inches in height; the rams carry large twisted horns, whilst the ewes are hornless the prevailing color is white with a black head; their carcases have a fair covering of wool, the staple being from four to five inches in length; the fleece of the best sheep seldom exceeds 3 lb. in weight; it is more frequently 1 or 2 lb.; these animals, though small, fatten well; their weight ranges from 50 to 60 lb., and very rarely 80 lb., live weight; this breed is generally imported into the malabar district from coimbatore. A woolly breed of sheep exist throughout Mysore and these are imported into South canara. The Mysore sheep are of three varieties, the Coorumba, Golla, and Yeediga; taking their names from the caste of people who keep them. Sheep are let in to land for manure; there is a Teloogoo proverb:—గొర్రె తిరిగిన నేల బంగారు—"It suffices if sheep merely walk over the land." There is a large mutton-eating population in Southern india, exclusive of Europeans. Agastya veidya einnoor speaks unfavorably of the mutton of the Cooroombaud as promoting too much bile. Kid, it says, is the lightest and safest of all kinds of animal food for the sick. Veidyans employ mutton suet in preparation of ointments; also administer it internally, with fruit of Azima tetracantha, lamk., nutmeg and cubebs, in hemoptysis, and in certain stages of phthisis pulmonalis. Sheep's tendon is used as a substitute for catgut for some purposes. Sheep's foot oil is used by tanners, shoe-makers, &c. Rams are sometimes kept for sport. The Tamul cooral has the following:—ஊக்க முடையா னொடுக்கம் பொருதகர் தாக்கற்குப் பேருந் தகைத்து—"The self-restraint of the energetic is like the "drawing back of a fighting ram in order to butt." Indian species of Ovis not here found are:—Blanfordii or blanford's wild sheep, Brookei or brooke's wild sheep, Cycloceros or punjaub wild sheep, Hodgsoni or argali or ovis ammon of thibet, Karelini or karelin's wild sheep, Nahura or burhel or blue wild sheep, Polii or marco polo's sheep, Vignei or vigne's wild sheep.——*Vellaud* (छाग - chhága, San.; چھيلا - chhela, Hind.; ಆಡು - ádu, Can.; మేక - méka, Tel.; വെള്ളാട് - vellátu, Mal.; வெள்ளாடு - velládu, Tam.). Tam. from (vel, tam. white + ádu, tam. ovis). The ordinary goat, a long legged animal, much commoner than the sheep. The Vellaud corresponds generally with Hircus ægagrus, alias Capra hircus, sub-family carprinæ, family bovidæ, order ruminantia, class mammalia [sastanam, 23], of naturalists. Domesticated from the Ibex. Characterized by having the horns sub-angular, recurved, compressed, seated on the crest of the forehead, and by their union, covering the top of the head. The males are generally bearded and emit a strong odour. There are several varieties, the chief of which are the long and short legged race. A large export trade in goat skins is now being established with America, and the demand is likely to increase. Goat's hair has been used for textile fabrics. The natives attach medicinal virtues to goat's milk which is abundant. The Mahomedans specially keep them for milking purposes. Flesh tough and tasteless, though much eaten by natives; veidyans consider it has virtues in incontinence of urine. Indian species of Capra not here found are:—Ægagrus or wild goat of asia minor, Megaceros or markhor, Sibirica or himalayan ibex.

AUDA (ఆడ - áda, *Tel.*). Female. Common for joining genera. Ex., where transl. is of second term:—Anisomeles ovata (ádabira), luffa acutangula; Cadaba indica (ádamorinika), mærua arenaria, var. glabra. See gloss. paragraphs.——*Audapaupa* (ఆడపాప - ádapápa, Tel.). From (above + pápa, tel. child). A community of Devadausies or pagoda dancers, maintained by the Shiva temple at Calastry [jauty].

AUDAK (आढक - ádhaka, *San.*; ಆಡಕ - ádaka, *Can.*). Mysore grain measure equal to 7 lbs. avoirdupois, or as a measure of capacity containing about 750 cubic inches. A minor mercaul [q.v.]. Distinguish from the small measures Oyak and Olluck [alavay, 3f].

AUDAM (ஆடம் - ádam, *Tam.*). Liquid measure, especially for oil; Tanjore and Trichinopoly. 20 seers = 1 audam; 6 audams = 1 pothy [alavay, 4a]. Approximate actual value, 1 andam = 1312½ cubic inches. Compare Paunay.

AUDAY (ஆடை - ádai, *Tam.*). Dress.——*Auday otty* (ஆடையொட்டி - ádaiyotti, Tam.). From (ádai, tam. dress + ottu, tam. to stick); from action of bristles. Title otherwise Round-leaved pupalia. Botanically Pupalia orbiculata, wight., amarantaceæ [vricsham, 106]. Alias Achyranthes orbiculata; Cyathula orbiculata. Sand-binder. An extensively spreading procumbent plant, the branches being often several feet long, round, pubescent, of a light brownish-green color; leaves when full grown coriaceous and nearly glabrous; spikes terminal, long, at first compact, but becoming interrupted as the plant increases in length; fascicles of flowers capitate, densely tomentose, bristles when full-grown not simple, but compound, or as it were pinnate, pale brown, attaching themselves to the clothes of passengers, cling to them with tenacity. Another species is atropurpurea. Cf. Indian burr.

AUDHOONICA (आधुनिक - ádhunika, *San.*). From (adhuná, san. now). Modern classics, as opposed to ancient [cavy].

AUDITYAN (आदित्य - áditya, *San.*). From (aditi, san. the mother of gods). Son of Adity. The sun. Auditya vauram Sunday. The twelve suns or the presiding deity of the sun for each month, beginning with Chittray [mausam] or April are :—Dhautry, Chuckran, Aryaman, Mitran, Varoonan, Amshooman, Hiranyan, Bhagavan, Diveshwaran, Pooshan, Savitry and Twashtry. They belong to a period before the time of the vedas, when the worship of the elements particularly of the sun, was first observed. Vishnoo is called chief of the Audityans. Auditya vurman was a common royal name among Cholas, Cadambas, Western chalookyas, Travancore line, &c. [matam].

AUDRY (अद्रि - adri, *San.*). From (a, san. not + drí, san. to split) ; not liable to be split. Vowel lengthened by composition. Hill. Suffix in place names ; as Totaudry, meaning praise + hill. Neelaudry is old name of Neilgherries.

AUDY (आदि - ádi, *San.*). First, ancient. Epithet of any of the Hindoo triad as well as of other deities. Common second name among non-bramins. Common also as prefix in second names, as :—Audayya from (ayya, tel. master) ; Audikeshava from (késhava, san. vishnu, the long-haired) ; Audinarrain from (náráyana, san. vishnu, the mover on the water) ; Audisheshoo from (shésha, san. serpent king) ; Audiyammah from (amma, tel. mother), female name ; Audiyappa from (appa, tel. father) [peyar].——*Audy rajah* (आदिराजा - ádirájá, San. ; ആഴിരാജാവു - ázhirájávu, Mal.). Title and San. from (ádi, san. first + rájá, san. king). Mal. from (ázhi, mal. the deep + rájá, san. king) ; the sea king ; this is the real meaning. Corruptly also Ally rajah. Honorific title of the chief male representative of the Cannanore Moplah family. Cannanore, originally included in the kingdom of the Colattiry or Chiracal rajahs, had become by the middle of sixteenth century chief seat of Moplahs and a Mahomedan state of some importance, almost independent of the Nayar king. Under the representative of this title the Portuguese were allowed to occupy a small fort in Cannanore where they had a church and college of Jesuits. A century later the Cannanore rajah's dominions reached 10 miles southward of Cannanore to the Tellicherry river, near which was his harbour of Dharmapatam. An Audy rajah in 1753 supported the English cause against the French. A treaty of offensive and defensive alliance between an Audy rajah and Thomas Hodges, Chief of Tellicherry, on behalf of the English East india company, was concluded in 1759. In 1766 an Audy rajah instigated Hyder ally to his successful invasion of Malabar, and was entrusted with the management of all the conquered states from Chiracal to Cochin, except Cochin, Coringote and Randatarra. On the capture of Cannanore by the British in 1784 the Beeby or female and real head of the house became tributary to the East india company. Cannanore was taken again in 1791, and has since remained in British hands. In the Cannanore family, as usual in Malabar, the succession goes in the female line. The last male ruler before the present was succeeded by his niece, whose husband died during the siege of Cannanore in 1790. She was succeeded by her daughter and grand-daughter. The latter died in October 1861, and the Madras government at first recognized her distant female relative to the exclusion of her son. But on further investigation of the case, Audy rajah's right to the succession was recognized [charitram].——*Audy sheshan* (आदिशेष - ádishésha, San.). From (above + shésha, san. remainder) ; as he is said to have existed prior to creation and to continue to exist after its destruction. Eternal matter, on which Vishnoo reposes during the night of Bramha, when the destructive power only is in operation. Represented as an immense snake forming by its many coils a bed on which Vishnoo sleeps ; and with its many heads erect, forked tongues projecting, forming a canopy over Vishnoo's head. Audy sheshan supports the eight elephants which support in turn the world. There is a popular tale of a dispute between him and Vayoo, regent of wind. The latter, in a trial of strength, blew against the thousand peaks of Mount meroo, and Audy sheshan covered each peak by one of his thousand heads. In the legend of Tripatty a special version of this tale is made. Vayoo made a feint, and ceased blowing. Audy sheshan lifted up one head to see where was Vayoo, when the latter suddenly returned and blew off the exposed peak, which was carried through the air and fell at Tripatty, a hill that now partakes of the sanctity of Mount meroo. Audy sheshan being mortified at the above, performed penance at Varauhagherry, and on the god appearing asked for conquest over Vayoo. In answer the god said, "Have "power to eat the wind." Hence by virtue of this permission snakes can live for a long time on air alone [matam].

AUDY (ஆடி - ádi, *Tam.*). Corruption of ashaudham, fourth lunar month. Fourth solar month [mausam].——*Audy amavausyay* (ஆடியமாவாசியை - ádiyamávásiyai, Tam.). Means fourth solar month + new moon day. Luni-solar festival [pundigay, 5a]. The new moon occurring in the fourth solar month Audy [mausam], i.e., between July 15th and August 14th. Observed only by Tamuls.——*Audy pathinett* (ஆடிப்பதினெட்டு - ádippathinettu, Tam.). Means fourth solar month + eighteen, number of day of month. Solar festival [pundigay, 2c]. Festival of Cauvery floods on eighteenth of fourth solar month Audy [mausam] about 2nd August among Tamuls. Popularly known as Pathinettaum perook, or flood of the eighteenth. Sometimes Audy perook, or July floods.——*Audy pooram* (ஆடிப்பூரம் - ádippúram, Tam.). Means fourth solar month + Poorva phalgoony, the eleventh lunar asterism. Luni-solar festival [pundigay, 5b]. On the day in the fourth solar month Audy [mausam], i.e., between July 15th and August 14th, when the moon is in the constellation, Pooram. Celebrated in pagodas of Shiva, in honor of Parvaty.——*Audy pundigay* (ஆடிப்பண்டிகை - ádippandigai, Tam.). Means fourth solar month + festival. Solar festival [pundigay, 2d]. Otherwise Dacshinauyana poonya caulam, or the auspicious time when the sun is supposed to enter on its southern course. On July 15th the first day of fourth solar month Audy [mausam]. A day of recreation on which Hindoos feast on boiled cocoanuts. Tarpanam also takes place [maryauday].

AUGAMAM (आगम - ágama, *San.*). From (ágam, san. to know). Otherwise (divyágama), meaning divine augamam. In law, a voucher. Twenty-eight sacred books, inculcating mystical worship of Shiva and Shacty, which with Sheiveites supersede most Pooraunams and Oopapooraunams. They recognize instead of the usual trinity, five great deities ; Bramha, Vishnoo, Roodran, Maheshwaran, and Sadaushivan. These are called the five Curtas. The Augamams are rare and little known. They are explained in Shivarchana chundricay, a treatise on Shiva worship by sage Vishweshwaran. All augamams are divided into four sections, namely, Nyaunapaudam or knowledge section, Yogapaudam or meditation section, Charyapaudam or section relating to practice of austerities, and Kriyapaudam or ceremonial section. Distinguish from Nigamam or vedic text. The Dacshinacharry shauctas follow the Nigamams ; the Vaumacharry shauctas follow the Augamams. Besides Sheiva augamams, there are two Veishnava augamams, Pauncharautram and Veikhaunasam. The following is the list of Sheiva augamams.——*Ajitam* (अजित - ajita, San.). From (a, san. negative prefix + ji, san. to conquer) ; invincible ; epithet of shiva, the supreme.——*Amshooman* (अंशुमान् - amshumán, San.). From (amshu, san. ray + mat, san. affix showing possession) ; the radiant.——*Analam* (अनल - anala, San.). Means fire.——*Bhedam* (भेद - bhéda, San.). From (bhid, san. to divide) ; difference.——*Bimbam* (बिम्ब - bimba, San.). Means reflected form, otherwise (mukhabimba), meaning face + reflection.——*Caumicam* (कामिक - kámika, San.). From (kam, san. to desire).——*Cauranam* (कारण - kárana, San.). Means cause ; as originant.——*Chintyam* (चिन्त्य - chintya, San.). From (chit, san. to know) ; object of meditation.——*Chundra nyaunum* (चन्द्रज्ञान - chandrañána, San.). From (chandra, san. moon + ñána, san. knowledge) ; knowledge of shiva.——*Deeptum* (दीप्त - dípta, San.). From (díp, san. to shine) ; luminous.——*Kiranam* (किरण - kirana, San.). From (krí, san. to scatter) ; means ray of light ; sun.——*Lalitam* (ललित - lalita, San.). Means love.——*Macootam* (मकुट - makuta, San.). Means crown.——*Nisvausam* (निश्वास - nishvása, San.). Means inspiration.——*Paurameshwaram* (पारमेश्वर - páraméshvara, San.). From (parama, san. supreme + íshvara, san. lord).——*Prodgeetam* (प्रोद्गीत - pródgíta, San.). From (pra, san. intensive prefix + udgíta, san. sung) ; perhaps from opening words.——*Rowravam* (रौरव - raurava, San.). From (ru, san. to kill) ; a place where the soul undergoes inordinate torture.——*Sahusram* (सहस्र - sahasra, San.). Means thousand ; perhaps in allusion to shiva with thousand heads, eyes, arms and feet.——*Santauna sarwottam* (सन्तानसर्वयुक्त - santánasarvayukta, San.). From (santána, san. succession + sarva, san. all + yukta, san. joined) ; he in whom is all succession.——*Siddham* (सिद्ध - siddha, San.). From (sidh, san. to accomplish), accomplished ; perfect ; epithet of shiva.——*Soocshmam* (सूक्ष्म - súkshma, San.). Means subtle.——*Sooprabhedhacam* (सुप्रभेदक - suprabhédaka, San.). From (su, san. intensive prefix + prabhédaka, san. separating).——*Swauyambhoovam* (स्वायम्भुव - sváyambhuva, San.). From (svayam, san. self + bhú, san. to be).——*Vautoolam* (वातुल - vátula, San.). From (váta, san. wind) ; crazy.——*Veeram* (वीर - víra, San.). Means heroism. Otherwise (víratantra), meaning heroic tantram.——*Vijayam* (विजय - vijaya, San.). Means victory.——*Vimalam* (विमल - vimala, San.). Means purity.——*Yogajam* (योगज - yógaja, San.). From (yóga, san. meditation + jan, san. to be born) ; fruits of meditation [matam].

AUHAN (अयस् - ayas, *San.* ; حديد - hadíd, *Ar.* ; آهن - áhan, *Pers.* ; لوہا - lohá, *Hind.* ; ಕಬ್ಬಿಣ - kabbina, *Can.* ; ఇనుము - inumu, *Tel.* ; ഇരിമ്പു - irimpu, *Mal.* ; இரும்பு - irumbu, *Tam.*). San. from (i, san. to go). Can. from (kappu, can. black + banna, can. color). Tel. from tamul. Tam. from (irul, tam. black + pon, tam. metal). Iron. Ferrum of chemists. Gray color and strong metallic lustre, susceptible of being heightened by polishing. Exceeds all metals in tenacity [dhautoo, loham]. For distribution see vol. II, 36. The native metal is scarce, most iron being found in form of oxide, in ochres, bog ores, and other friable earthy substances of brown, yellow, or red color [tavalay cull]. Iron obtained by smelting is not pure, but in the three following states, white crude iron, grey crude iron, and black cast iron, which last is commonly fused with white iron. Crude iron, especially grey, fused again in contact with air, unites, sparkles, loses weight, and becomes less brittle, and may be converted into bar iron by fusing it in charcoal and beating it. The purified or bar iron, is soft, ductile, flexible, and malleable. The same is converted into steel by being exposed to the action of heat, in contact with carbonaceous matter, which penetrates its substance; and by being tempered when red hot by immersion in water, by which it becomes harder, more elastic, and brittle. In the selection of ores the native manufacturer employs only those which are rich in metal, never mixing those of different qualities, and seldom using fluxes to suit particular ores. The clay iron stones and calcareous iron ores are neglected. The furnaces in which the ores are smelted are small and the walls are not thick. The only blast is that of the common native bellows made of cow skins inflated, and the metal does not flow freely enough to be separated from the scoriæ. The native process may be regarded as one for refining and not for smelting the ores. The silicious particles are got rid of, and the iron is agglutinated into a lump which descends to the bottom and is taken out in a state fit for working up. By this mode the subsequent heating and puddling which are required in the English process for cast iron are avoided. The process is economical for manufactures of a small kind. For s. indian steel see Wootz. Indian pharmacopœia articles are very numerous [ospitry]. For native medical uses see below, especially annabhaidy and iroomboo tooroo [veidyan]. Iron is not much valued here. There is a Tamul proverb :—எத்தனை புடம் இட்டாலும் இரும்பு பசும்பொன் ஆகாது "However much iron may be heated, "it will not become gold."——*Anna bhaidy* (அன்னபேதி - aunabéthi, Tam.). See sep. title. *Cauntam* (காந்தம் - kándam, Tam.). Magnetic oxide of iron. See sep. title.——*Cooshy* (कुशी - kushí, San.). Wrought iron.——*Iroomboo pody* (लोहचूर्ण - lóhachúrna, San.; لوهے کا بورا - lohekábúrá, Hind.; ಕಬ್ಬಿಣಾರಪೊಡಿ - kabbinarápodi, Can.; ఇనుమురాపొడి - inumurápodi, Tel.; ഇരിമ്പുപ്പൊടി - irimpuppoti, Mal.; இரும்புப்பொடி - irumbuppodi, Tam.). San. from (lóha, san. iron + chúrna, san. powder). Tel. from (rátsu, tel. to file + podi, tel. powder). Mal. and Tam. mean iron-powder. Iron filings. Ferri limatura of chemists. Not used as medicine by Hindoos. Used as tonic by Mahomedans, prescribed by them along with ginger and cumin seeds. In conjunction with vinegar, cadookye, and marootham bark, used for dyeing black; also with other ingredients, to give leather the same color.——*Iroomboo tooroo* (अयोमल - ayómala, San.; لوهیکا گو - lohekágú, Hind.; ಕಬ್ಬಿಣದತುಕ್ಕು - kabbinadatukku, Can.; ఇనుపతుప్పు - inupatuppu, Tel.; ഇരിമ്പുതുരുമ്പ് - irimputturuvu, Mal.; இரும்புத்துரு - irumbutturu, Tam.). San. from (ayas, san. iron + mala, san. refuse). Hind. from (lohá, hind. iron + gú, hind. impurity). Can. from (kabbina, can. iron + tukku, can. rust). Tel. from (inumu, tel. iron + tuppu, tel. rust). Rust of iron. Otherwise Impure red oxide of iron. Ferri peroxidum, Ferri rubigo of chemists. Native medicinal use, tonic, emmenagogue and anthelmintic. Substituted for British Tinctura ferri perchloride. Used by natives for nearly the same purposes in the arts, as iron filings. *Irooppoo kittam* (मण्डूर - mandúra, San.; ಕಬ್ಬಿಣದಕಿಟ್ಟ - kabbinadakitta, Can.; ఇనుపచిట్టెము - inupachittemu, Tel.; ഇരിമ്പുക്കിട്ടം - irimpukkittam, Mal.; இருப்புக்கிட்டம் - iruppukkittam, Tam.). Title from (irumbu, tam. iron + kitta, san. dirt). San. from (mand, san. to surround). Can. from (kabbina, can. iron + kitta, can. dross). Tel. from (inumu, tel. iron + chittemu, tel. dross). Scales of iron, oxidized iron.——*Swarnamaucshicam* (स्वर्णमाक्षिक - svarnamákshika, San.; ಕಲ್ಲಿದ್ದಲು - kalliddalu, Can.; స్వర్ణమాక్షికము - svarnamákshikamu, Tel.; பொன்னிமிளை - ponnimilai, Tam.). San. from (svarna, san. gold + mákshika, san. honey). Can. from (kallu, can. stone + iddalu, can. coal). Tam. from (pon, tam. gold + nimilai, tam. pyrite). Iron pyrites. Occurs dark yellow nodules with a golden lustre. As an alterative in tonic, generally used in combination with other medicines of its class, such as iron, talc, mercury, &c.——*Tandavaulam* (कान्तलौह - kántalauha, San.; తండువాళము - tanduválamu, Tel.; தண்டவாளம் - tandaválam, Tam.). Title from tamul. Tam. from (danda, san. stick + pálam, tam. bar of metal). San. from (kánta, san. beautiful + lauha, san. iron). Cast-iron.——*Taura maucshicam* (तारमाक्षिक - táramákshika, San.; ತಾರಮಾಕ್ಷಿಕ - táramákshika, Can.; తారమాక్షికము - táramákshikamu, Tel.; வெள்ளிநிமிளை - vellinimilai, Tam.). San. from (tára, san. radiating + mákshika, san. honey); on account of its likeness to honey. Tam. from (velli, tam. silver + nimilai, tam. pyrite). San. also (rúpyamákshika), meaning silver + pyrite. Tam. also (rajatanimilai), meaning silver + pyrite. Iron pyrites; variety with silvery radiated crystals. Same uses as Swarna maucshicam.

AUK (ఆకు - áku, *Tel.*). Leaf.—"*a*" Plant first term. Ex.:—Euphorbia cattimandoo (ákujemudu), leafy euphorbia.—"*b*" Plant second term. Ex., where transl. is of first term :—Cinnamomum iners (pattsáku), green; Launea pinnatifida (vádateduáku), rudder; Nicotiana tabacum (pogáku), smoke; Notonia grandiflora (kundéluchevviáku), hare's ear; Pistia stratiotes (níráku), water. See gloss. paragraphs.——*Aukroy* (कलिङ्ग - kalinga, San.; ఆకురాయి - ákuráyi, Tel.). Title from teloogoo. San. from (kali, san. strife + gam, san. to go); quarrelsome. Tel. from (ákuráyi, tel. file); from call like rasping of file. Cuckoo-shrikes or File-birds. Campephaginæ, laniadæ [pingalam], dentirostres, insessores, aves [pacshy, 19], of naturalists [jantoo].—"*a*" The black headed cuckoo-shrike is Volvocivora sykesii, called by natives small aukroy. Alias Campaphaga sykesii; Ceblepyris canus, fimbriatus. Head, neck and breast, deep black; whole upper plumage pale grey; tail black, outer feathers broadly tipped white; lower breast and abdomen pale grey, passing white on lower abdomen and lower tail-coverts; hunts in small parties, slowly examining the foliage; favorite food caterpillars and other soft insects; usually silent, but has harsh call.—"*b*" The grey cuckoo-shrike is Graucalus macei, called by natives large aukroy. Alias Graucalus nipalensis, papuensis. Whole upper plumage light plumbeous grey. Flesh eaten.

AUKHIR (آخر - ákhir, *Hind.*). Last, the end. Aukhiry chahaur shumba is the last Wednesday of Safar. So observances thereon [islam, shamba]. See vol. 1 (96).

AUL (آل - ál, *Hind.*). Same as Dyeing mulberry.

AUL (ಆಳ್ - álu, *Can.*; ആൾ - ál, *Mal.*; ஆள் - ál, *Tam.*). From (ál, tam. to rule). An individual. Aul amanjy is same as Amanjy. Aul cooly are wages of laborer. Aulotty from (óttu, tam. to drive) is an overseer. Aul pauttom is in Malabar hire of a laborer lent out to another person. Aul soonka was in Canara a tax once levied on cultivators who employed laborers, at so much per head of laborers. See vol. 1, 112.——*Aulcautty* (ஆள்காட்டி - álgátti, Tam.). Means man + pointer; from screeching on approach of man by night. Bird name common to :—Lobivanellus goensis, Ortygornis ponticeriana, Sarciophorus bilobus; see gloss. paragraphs.

AUL (ആൽ - ál, *Mal.*; ஆல் - ál, *Tam.*). From (álu, tam. to spread). Banyan tree, Ficus bengalensis, linn. Suffix in place names; as Otteiyaul, meaning Solitary banyan. Plant second term. Ex., where transl. is of first term :—Bombax malabaricum (mulláala), thorn; Ficus bengalensis (pérál), great; Ficus citrifolia (kátál), forest; Ficus infectoria (chuvannál), red; Ficus religiosa (arayál), king; Ficus retusa (biliála), white; Ficus tsiela (kuruvál), short; Stilpnophyllum elasticum (shímayál), foreign; Thespesia populnea (kallál), stone. See gloss. paragraphs.——*Aulamar cadavool* (ஆலமர்கடவுள் - álamargadavul, Tam.). From (above + amar, tam. to settle + kadavul, tam. god). Shiva, who teaches the four sons of Bramha seated with his face to the south under the shade of a banyan [matam].——*Aulambaudy* (ஆலம்பாடி - álambádi, Tam.). From (álam, tam. banyan tree, ficus bengalensis, linn. + pádi, tam. village). Village; Coimbatore dist., Collegaul tal.; lat. 12° 9′; long. 77° 47′; from Coimbatore N.N.E. 96 miles; from Collegaul E. 42 miles. On right bank of Cauvery. An important place in seventeenth century. Garrisoned by British troops in 1768, but relinquished on advance of Hyder's army. Ruined Shiva temple, well-sculptured and wrecked by Mahomedans. Old fort. In bed of Cauvery is the Smoking rock. Gives its name to a breed of cattle.——*Aulatore* (ആലത്തൂർ - álattúr, Mal. álatúr *). From (above + úr, mal. village).—"*a*" Deputy tahsildarry, Malabar district. Pay Rs. 70.—"*b*" Town, Head-quarters of Deputy tahsildar and Moonsif, Travellers' bungalow. Malabar dist., Palghaut tal.; pop. 3,517; lat. 10° 39′; long. 76° 35′; from Calicut S.E. 67 miles; from Cannanore S.E. 114 miles; from Madras W.S.W. 300 miles; from Malapooram S.E. 43 miles; from Manantoddy S.S.E. 86 miles; from Palghaut S.W. 12 miles; from Ponnany E.S.E. 43 miles; from Tellicherry S.E. 103 miles. In Cauttoocherry amshom on the road from Palghaut to Cochin frontier viâ Vadacancherry. Near lies Aulatore hill or Veloomala. The hill contains a large cave formerly inhabited and a ruined temple, a mosque and a Roman catholic church. Weekly market on Wednesdays. An important Hindoo temple called the Tripauvalore temple to Shiva lies in adjacent Vadakketara amshom. Navarautry ootsavam [pundigay, 6d] annually in September October, and fairs held during the period. Trig. station in lat. 10° 37′ 30·07″; long. 76° 34′ 26·80″; height 1,202 feet; from Chittalancherry N.W. 2 miles; from Palghaut S.W. 12 miles.——*Aulileimail pullicondone* (ஆலிலைமேற்பள்ளிகொண்டோன் - álileimérballigondón, Tam.). From (above + ilai, tam. leaf + mél, tam. on + palli, tam. bed + kondón, tam. one who has taken). Vishnoo.

AULAM (عالم - álam, *Ar.*). The universe. Lacab suffix originally peculiar to Syeds, now taken by any one; as Badr e aulam, meaning the full moon of the world.

AULAY (ആല - ála, *Mal.*; ஆலை - álai, *Tam.*). From (álu, tam. to resound). Sugar mill. Suffix in place names as Shotvaulay, meaning muddy ground + sugar mill. Also proper name in lower castes [peyar]. The native sugar mill is of wood with two uprights, one revolving round the other, and between the two the cane is pressed. Bullocks walk round and cause the mill to revolve. The cane is cut into pieces about two cubits long. These are inserted between the uprights, when the sap flows down, and the crushed cane comes out above. Each piece is crushed three times. A vat beneath the mill catches the juice. As soon as the vat is full, the juice is taken out in pots, poured into a vessel and boiled. When the juice has boiled for three or four hours, it becomes jaggery. It is then poured into a long wooden trough, and left to cool. When it has cooled, it is stirred with wooden trowels to cause it to harden. It is then made with the hand into balls and so sold [jaggery, sugar].——*Aulangaud* (ആലങ്ങാട് - álannátu, Mal.). From (above + kátu, mal. forest). So called owing to its productiveness in sugar. —"*a*" Talook, Travancore state, Cottayam division; area 208 square miles. Most northern talook of Travancore; pop. 66,753. Sub-divided into seven praverties and contains 103 caras or villages. Bounded N. and E. by the Cochin territory, S. by Todoopoya, Mooatpoya and Coonnatnaud talooks, W. and N.W. by Paravore talook. The greatest length, N. to S. is 10 miles; and greatest breadth, E. to W., is 25 miles. Soil productive. Cultivation and manufacture of sugar. The Alwye river irrigates.—"*b*" Village; Travancore state, Cottayam division, Aulangaud tal.; pop. 14,103; lat. 10° 07′; long. 76° 21′; from Alleppey N. 42 miles; from Cottayam N.N.W. 38 miles; from Madras S.W. 335 miles; from Nagarcoil N.N.W. 150 miles; from Paravore E.S.E. 5½ miles; from Quilon N.N.W. 85 miles; from Trivandrum N.N.W. 120 miles; from the sea E. 7¼ miles. Old town, once capital of the Aulangaud rajahs. In the Christian pettah are the remains of the largest Romo-Syrian church in the country.

AULIYAUR (ஆளியாறு - áliyáru, *Tam.*). From (áli, tam. embankment + áru, tam. river); from the high banks. River; Coimbatore district, Pollachy talook. Rises in Anamullays in Travancore territory, descends from hills in Navamullay in Cotore village and runs westwards. Receives its first tributary Ooppaur near Anamullay town, then takes a N.E. course, receives its main tributary the Palaur from Oodamalpett talook, a few miles below Anamullay town, and after keeping up that course for a distance it turns westwards, enters the frontiers of Cochin, passes by the talook of Chittoor of Cochin, then enters the frontier of Malabar, where known as Cunnaudy poya, passes by the talook of Palghaut, and empties itself into the Cullpauty, a few miles west of Palghaut. It is running throughout the year but is nowhere navigable. It is crossed by a bridge at Amarampolliem 4 miles from Pollachy on the Malabar road.

AULOO (आलु - álu, *San.*). From (ri, san. to move); moving, hence round. Yam.—"*a*" Botanically the Dioscorea genus, dioscoreaceæ [vricsham, 132]; extensive; herbaceous perennials or climbing plants, leaves generally entire, with strongly marked veins; flowers inconspicuous and hermaphrodite; tuberous roots used for food as substitutes for potatoes; some species poisonous. The dioscorea species best known to the natives are the yams shown below.—"*b*" Also applied to some other genera; cf. Gardenia latifolia (banpindálú), forest round yam; Ipomæa batatas (raktapindálu), red round yam; Manihot utilissima (pindálú), round yam; Pachyrhizus angulatus (shankhálú), conch yam; see gloss. paragraphs.——*Betel yam* (ఆరెటీగ - áretíga, Tel.; வெற்றிலைவள்ளி - vettilaivalli, Tam.). Title from being cultivated in betel gardens. Tel. from (áre, tel. bauhinia racemosa, lam. + tíga, tel. creeper). Tam. from (vettilai, tam. piper betel, linn. + valli, tam. dioscorea genus). Tel. also (áretéga), meaning bauhinia racemosa, lam. + root; (avatengatíga). Title otherwise Wild sesban yam. Botanically Dioscorea [auloo] oppositifolia, linn., dioscoreaceæ [vricsham, 132]. ——*Common yam* (رتالو - rotálú, Hind.; ಹೆಗ್ಗೆಣಸು - heggenasu, Can.; മുക്കിഴങ്ങ് - mukkizhannu, Mal.; රටකොඩොල් - ratakodól, Singh.; யாமிசுக்கிழங்கு - yámisukkizhangu, Tam.). Can. from (heççu, can. superior + genasu, can. dioscorea). Mal. from (mul, mal. thorn + kizhannu, mal. esculent root). Tam. means yam root. Mal. also (peruvallikkizhannu), meaning large + dioscorea + root. Title otherwise Cultivated yam. Botanically Dioscorea [auloo] sativa, linn., dioscoreaceæ [vricsham, 132]. Cooked is common article of food.——*Goa yam* (मध्वालु - madhválu, San.; कणगर - kanagara, Mahr.; कनंग - kananga, Conc.; ماؤ آلو - maúálú, Hind.; چھوٹا پنڈالو - chhotá-pindálú, Dec.; ಶೀಗೆಣಸು - shígenasu, Can.; ತೀಪೆಕೆರೆಂಗ್ - típekereng, Too.; గెనుసు - genusu, Tel.; ചക്കരക്കിഴങ്ങ് - chakkarakkizhannu, Mal.; කුකුළල - kukulala, Singh.; சிறுவள்ளி - shiruvalli, Tam.). Title from place of growth. San. from (madhu, san. sweet + álu, san. esculent root); as resembling sweet potato in appearance. Mahr. from (kana, mahr. grain + gara, mahr. pith). Conc. from mahratta. Hind. from (maú, mahr. soft + álu, san. esculent root). Dec. from (chhotá, hind. small + pindálu, san. dioscorea globosa, roxb.). Can. from (shí, can. sweet + genasu, can. dioscorea). Too. means sweet root. Mal. from (chakkara, mal. sugar + kizhannu, mal. esculent root). Singh. from (kukul, singh. cock + ala, singh. yam). Tam. from (shiru, tam. small + valli, tam. dioscorea genus). Tel. also (kummarabaddu), meaning potter + male organ. Mal. also (káttukizhannu), meaning wild root. Tam. also (káttukizhangu), meaning forest + esculent root. Title otherwise Goa potato, Kaawi yam. Botanically Dioscorea [auloo] aculeata, linn., dioscoreaceæ [vricsham, 132]. Alias Ubium aculeatum. Flowers small, whitish; tuber oval, very white; dug up in forests in cold season; common in curry.——*Humped yam* (पिण्डालु - pindálu, San.; چپریالو - chupriyálú, Hind.; గూనపెండలము - gúnapendalamu, Tel.; காய்வள்ளி - káyvalli, Tam.). Title from appearance of tuber. San. from (pinda, san. ball + álu, san. esculent root). Tel. from (gúni, tel. hump-backed + pendalamu, tel. dioscorea). Tam. from (káy, tam. fruit + valli, tam. dioscorea genus); from fruit. Tam. also (kaivalli), meaning hand + dioscorea genus. Botanically Dioscorea [auloo] globosa, roxb., dioscoreaceæ [vricsham, 132]. Round tubers internally white, and a six-sided twining stem bearing opposite or alternate, five to seven-nerved, long stalked leaves, expanding at the base; flowers small white; the female flowers few but fragrant, and in erect spikes; the male flowers abundant in pendulous tassels. A common species. Yields the best edible yam.——*Large yam* (दण्डालु - dandálu, San.; कोन - kóna, Conc.; خام آلو - khámálú, Hind.; اوبی - ubi, Malay; ಮುಡಿಗೆಣಸು - mudigenasu, Can.; ತೂನಕೆರೆಂಗ್ - túnakereng, Too.; నిలువుపెండలము - niluvupendalamu, Tel.; കാച്ചിൽ - káççil, Mal.; රොසකන්ද - rosakanda, Singh.; பெருவள்ளி - peruvalli, Tam.). Title from size of tuber. San. from (danda, san. stick + álu, san. esculent root). Hind. from (khám, pers. raw + álú, pers. potato). Can. from (mudi, can. knot + genasu, can. dioscorea). Too. from (túna, too. stake + kereng, too. root). Tel. from (nilutsu, tel. to stand + pendalamu, tel. dioscorea). Mal. from (káççu, mal. to warm). Tam. from (perumai, tam. greatness + valli, tam. dioscorea genus). Can. also (túnagenasu), meaning stake + dioscorea. Tel. also (gadimidondapendalamu). Mal. also (peruvallikkizhannu), meaning large + dioscorea + root; (kávattu), meaning fruit + seed. Tam. also (káççikkizhangu), from malayalam; (yámsgizhangu), meaning yam + esculent root. Title otherwise Pervully, Ubi yam, White yam, Wing-stalked yam. Botanically Dioscorea [auloo] alata, linn., dioscoreaceæ [vricsham, 132]. Alias Ubium alatum. Tuber oblong, white, stems four-angled, leaves deeply cordate. Favorite vegetable.——*Pondicherry yam* (रक्तालु - raktálu, San.; لال گرنیالو - lálguraniyálú, Hind.; దేశవాళిపెండలము - déshavális pendalamu, Tel.; புதுச்சேரிவள்ளி - puthuççérivalli, Tam.). Title from place of growth. San. from (rakta, san. red + álu, san. dioscorea); from reddish tubers. Tel. from (désha, san. country + váli, tel. common + pendalamu, tel. dioscorea). Tam. from (puthuççéri, tam. pondicherry + valli, tam. dioscorea). Tel. also (niluvupendalamu), meaning standing + dioscorea. Tam. also (pottukkarivalli), meaning spot + curry + dioscorea genus. Title otherwise Pondicherry sweet potato, Purple yam. Botanically Dioscorea [auloo] purpurea, roxb., dioscoreaceæ [vricsham, 132]. Tubers sometimes 3 feet long; a dull crimson red outside and of a glistening white within; flower small, whitish; cultivated; tuber has somewhat perfumed taste.——*Prickly yam* (कण्टकालु - kantakálu, San.; کانٹالو - kántálú, Hind.; اوندو - ondo, Malay; ముల్లుపెండలము - mullupendalamu, Tel.; നൂറങ്കിഴങ്ങ് - núrankizhannu, Mal.; කටුවල - katuvala, Singh.; நூறங்கிழங்கு - núrangizhangu, Tam.). Title from prickly stem. San. from (kantaka, san. thorn + álu, san. dioscorea). Hind. from sanscrit. Tel. from (mullu, tel. thorn + pendalamu, tel. dioscorea). Mal. from (núru, mal. starch + kizhannu, mal. root). Singh. means thorny yam. Tam. from malayalam. Tel. also (pandimukkudumpa), meaning pig + snout + root; (tsuntsugadda), meaning mouse + root. Mal. also (káttunúrankizhannu), meaning wild + starch + root. Tam. also (káttuvalli), meaning forest + dioscorea genus. Title otherwise Five-leaved yam, Mouse root, Pig-snout yam. Botanically Dioscorea [auloo] pentaphylla, willd., dioscoreaceæ [vricsham, 132]. Tubers oblong, large and white; stems herbaceous, twining, prickly; leaves digitate, downy; male flowers panicled, greenish white, fragrant; female flowers spiked. A common species. Tubers very acrid before preparation; male flowers eaten as greens.——*Roodrauck yam* (రుద్రాక్షపెండలము - rudrákshapendalamu, Tel.). Title from appearance of tuber. Tel. from (rudráksha, san. braminy bead + pendalamu, tel. dioscorea). Tel. also (káyapendalamu), meaning fruit + dioscorea. Botanically Dioscorea [auloo] crispata, r., dioscoreaceæ [vricsham, 132].——*Short yam* (ಕುಂಟಗೆಣಸು - kuntagenasu, Can.; చేదుబద్దుదుంప - chédubaddudumpa, Tel.). Title from small tuber. Can. from (kunta, can. short + genasu, can. dioscorea). Tel. from (chédu, tel. bitter + baddu, tel. male organ + dumpa, tel. root). Tel. also (sasibuddadumpa), meaning straight + rupture + root. Botanically Dioscorea [auloo] pulchella, roxb., dioscoreaceæ [vricsham, 132].——*Thorny yam* (कांटेकणग - kántékananga, Conc.; ಮುಳ್ಳುಗೆಣಸು - mullugenasu, Can.; ಮುಳ್ಳುಕೆರೆಂಗ್ - mullukereng, Too.; సుబ్బదుంప - subbadumpa, Tel.; മുള്ളൻകിഴങ്ങ് - mullankizhannu, Mal.; උයල - uyala, Singh.). Title from tubers armed with inoffensive prickles. Conc. from (kantaka, san. thorn + kananga, conc. dioscorea aculeata, linn.). Can. from (mullu, can. thorn + genasu, can. dioscorea). Too. from (mullu, too. thorn + kereng, too. root). Tel. from (subbu, tel. to come out + dumpa, tel. root). Mal. from (mullu, mal. thorn + kizhannu, mal. esculent root). Can. also (bilégenasu), meaning white + dioscorea. Botanically Dioscorea [auloo] tomentosa, hohenhacker, dioscoreaceæ [vricsham, 132].

AULOO (آلو - álú, *Pers.*). Cherry-tree. Botanically the Prunus genus, rosaceæ [vricsham, 49]. Trees and shrubs; margin of leaves rolled inwards; flowers in umbel-like clusters; fruit covered with mealy bloom; stone pointed at one or both ends and furrowed along edges; some spiny in wild state, but smooth when cultivated. The species best known to the natives are:—amygdalus [baudam], armeniaca [mishmish], cerasus [cherry], communis [albaca], domestica [auloochah], persica [shaft auloo].——*Auloo chah* (برقوق - burkúk, Ar.; آلو - álú, Pers.; آلوچہ - álúchah, Hind. and Dec.). Hind. from (álú, pers. prunus + chah, pers. diminutive suffix). Ar. also (jábizak). Title otherwise Common plum, Cultivated plum. Botanically Prunus [auloo] domestica, linn., rosaceæ [vricsham, 49]. Small, white flowers; waxy yellowish fruit; on neilgherries; gives to pharm. dried drupe, prunum, demulcent and laxative; official; the wood is not generally sound, but resembling a pear or cherry.——*Shaft auloo* (خوخ - khaukh, Ar.; شفتالو - shaftálú, Pers.; آڑو - arú, Hind.; شفتالو - shaftálú, Dec.). Pers. from (shafat, ar. the lip + álú, pers. prunus); from reddish color. Dec. from persian. Greek μηλέα περσική, Latin Persica. Title otherwise Peach. Botanically Prunus [auloo] persica, benth. and hook. f., rosaceæ [vricsham, 49]. Alias Amygdalus persica. With care grows and bears in mysore; leaves and kernels on distillation yield prussic acid; the nectarine is the variety lævis.

AULORE (ఆలూరు - álúru, *Tel.* alúr *). From (ávu, tel. cattle + úru, tel. village).——**(1)** Talook, Bellary district. Tahsildar's pay Rs. 175. Area 686 square miles. Population 88,088. Language Canarese and Teloogoo. E. talook of district. Bounded on the north by the Adony talook, E. Putticondah talook of Kurnool district and Gooty talook of Anantapore district, south by Gooty talook, and west by Bellary talook and the Hagary river. The surface is a uniform dead level, except for the low hills near Holagondy and the rocks near Ramandroog. The soil throughout is the best regar. Trees will not grow, for beneath the black soil there is a soft calcareous limestone, which renders the water in all the wells brackish. Almost every acre fit for cultivation has been taken up. The principal crops are cotton and cholum, and these are sent out to Bellary, the surrounding talooks, and Madras. Holagondy and Molagavelly are the centres of the trade, and many of the merchants here are very wealthy. Paddy and coarse cloths are imported. The Hagary river flows along the western boundary of the talook, but no channels are taken from it. The river changes its bed frequently, and on either bank for some distance the soil is deeply covered with drifted sand-heaps which prohibit cultivation. From the uniform dead level of the talook the storage of water is not easy, and there is no tank of any size. The largest is at Aulore cusbah; that at Arikera is second to it being about two miles from the cusbah, where a small gorge in the hills has been dammed up. Best camping grounds are:—Arikera, Aspry, Aulore, Ballore, Chintacoonta, Chippagherry, Gooliem, Harivaunam, Holagondy, Lingadahully, Molagavelly, and Virpapore. Places of archæological interest:—Aulore, Chippagherry, Coroocondah, Haulhervy, Nerniky, Rauvihaul, Sheedarhaul, Yellarty. Trig. stations in the talook:—Arkeribetta, Holagondy. The leading places, &c., in the talook are the following.——*Arikera* (అరికెర - arikera, Tel.). From (ari, can. stone + kere, can. tank). Village; pop. 1,397; acres 7,294; lat. 15° 24′; long. 77° 15′; from Aulore W.N.W. 2 miles; from Bellary N.E. 26 miles. Trig. station called Arkeribetta in lat. 15° 24′ 33·81″; long. 77° 13′ 48·48″; height 2,127 feet; from Arikera W.N.W. ¾ mile; from Aulore W.N.W. 2¾ miles; from Bellary N.E. 26 miles.——*Aspry* (అస్పరి - áspari, Tel.). Sanscrit name (ashvapurí), meaning horse + town. Village, Railway station; pop. 1,786; acres 9,907; lat. 15° 29′; long. 77° 26′; height 1,493 feet; from Aulore E.N.E. 12 miles; from Bellary N.E. 38 miles.——*Aulore* (ఆలూరు - álúru, Tel.). See below.——*Buntanáhaul* (బంటనహాళు - bantanahálu, Tel.). From (banta, can. servant + hálu, can. waste land). Village, Railway station; pop. 778; acres 3,010; lat. 15° 11′; long. 77° 21′; height 1,454 feet; from Aulore S.S.E. 16 miles; from Bellary E. 26 miles.——*Chikka hotore* (చిక్కహోతూరు - chikkahótúru, Tel.). From (chikka, can. small + hóta, can. he goat + úru, can. village). Village; pop. 2,379; acres 11,969; lat. 15° 27′; long. 77° 21′; from Aulore N.E. 6½ miles; from Bellary N.E. 33 miles.——*Chippagherry* (చిప్పగిరి - chippagiri, Tel.). Corruption of sanscrit; sanscrit name (shilpagiri), means fine art + mountain. Village; pop. 1,884; acres 13,683; lat. 15° 14′; long. 77° 22′; from Aulore S.S.E. 13 miles; from Bellary E.N.E. 28 miles. Formerly a larger place, but deserted on account of the want of water. On a rock in the centre of the town are the remains of some very fine temples. Inscriptions of the Vijianugger dynasty at the temple of Timmappasawmy.——*Gooliem* (గూళ్యము - gúlyamu, Tel.). From (gúle, can. desertion). Village; pop. 1,383; acres 3,007; lat. 15° 22′; long. 77° 07′; from Aulore W.S.W. 11 miles; from Bellary N.N.E. 17 miles. Formerly head-quarters of talook. During a storm in 1851 the Hagary river swept away the greater part of the houses. A small village has been built about a mile from the old site.——*Goommanore* (గుమ్మనూరు - gummanúru, Tel.). From (gumma, tel. grain receptacle + úru, tel. village). Village; pop. 598; acres 5,412; lat. 15° 10′; long. 77° 17′; from Aulore S. 16 miles; from Bellary E. 21 miles.——*Hagary* (హగరి - hagari, Tel.). See sep. title.——*Harivaunam* (హరివాణము - harivánamu, Tel.). From (hari, san. vishnu + bána, san. arrow). Village; pop. 2,108; acres 13,854; lat. 15° 38′; long. 77° 09′; from Aulore N.N.W. 19 miles; from Bellary N.N.E. 36 miles. Weaving is the chief trade.——*Haulhervy* (హాళహర్వి - hálaharvi, Tel.). From (hálu, can. waste land + haruvu, can. to spread). Village; pop. 1,825; acres 7,881; lat. 15° 20′; long. 77° 12′; from Aulore S.W. 6½ miles; from Bellary N.E. 21 miles. Inscriptions at temple of Anjaneyasawmy, Vijianagger dynasty.——*Hirey hotore* (ಹಿರೇಹೋತೂರು - hiréhótúru, Can.). From (hiré, can. big + hóta, can. he goat + úru, can. village). Village; pop. 1,805; acres 11,890; lat. 15° 27′; long. 77° 19′; from Aulore N.E. 5 miles; from Bellary N.E. 31 miles. On the Bellary-Kurnool road.——*Holagondy* (హొళగొంది - holagondi, Tel.). From (hole, can. water course + gondi, can. lane). Village; pop. 3,356; acres 11,953; lat. 15° 29′; long. 77° 06′; from Aulore W.N.W. 14 miles; from Bellary N.N.E. 25 miles. Situated among the hills in the north of the talook. To the west is a shady market-place with a temple. There are wealthy merchants here. Trig. station in lat. 15° 30′ 01·57″; long. 77° 04′ 49·65″; height 2,151 feet; from Aulore W.N.W. 15 miles; from Bellary N.N.E. 26 miles; from Holagondy village N.N.W. 1¼ miles.——*Molagavelly* (మొళగవల్లి - molagavalli, Tel.). From (mulaka, tel. solanum indicum, linn. + palli, tel. village). Village; pop. 3,216; acres 15,778; lat. 15° 21′; long. 77° 22′; from Aulore E.S.E. 7½ miles; from Bellary E.N.E. 31 miles. Centre of the cotton trade.——*Nuncherla* (నంచర్ల - nancharla, Tel.). From (nalla, can. good + cheruvu, tel. tank). Village, Railway station; pop. 1,014; acres 2,542; lat. 15° 14′; long. 77° 26′; height 1,553 feet; from Aulore S.E. 16 miles; from Bellary E.N.E. 32 miles.——*Ramandroog* (రామదుర్గము - rámadurgamu, Tel.). From (ráma, san. the god + durga, san. fort). Village, Hill; pop. 1,914; acres 9,387; lat. 15° 18′; long. 77° 17′; height 2,029 feet; from Aulore S. 7 miles; from Bellary E.N.E. 24 miles. Has a bold mass of rocks round it.——**(2)** Village, Talook head-quarters; pop. 2,766; acres 5,973; lat. 15° 24′; long. 77° 16′; height 1,493 feet; from Adony S.S.W. 17 miles; from Bellary N.E. 27 miles; from Hospett E. 58 miles; from Hurpanhully E.N.E. 94 miles; from Madras N.W. 258 miles; from Tadpatry W.N.W. 60 miles. On the Bellary-Adony trunk road. The head-quarters of the talook were transferred to Aulore from Gooliem in 1805. In the hills a few miles north-east are the ruins of an old city, with remains of temples, streets and houses. There is a travellers' bungalow.

AULY (سیپی - sípí, *Hind.*; ಚಿಪ್ಪುಮೀನು - chippumínu, *Can.*; గుల్లచేప - gullachépa, *Tel.*; മുരു - muru, *Mal.*; ஆளி - áli, *Tam.*). Tel. from (gulla, tel. shell + chépa, tel. fish). Oyster. Ostrea edulis of naturalists. South indian oysters small, but inferior to none in any part of the world. Coromandel coast oysters are best in months of May, June, July and August. Places where Coromandel coast oysters are found, of the best quality, are:—Alamparva, Ennore, Ramnaud, the best; Caricaul, Topotoray and Sadras, not quite so good; Fort St. David and Cuddalore, tolerably good. Malabar coast oysters are in season earlier than on Coromandel coast, and season ends in May. On Malabar coast best oysters procured at Calicut and Tellicherry. At the mouths of several rivers on west coast oyster-beds have been made by the natives. Best on west coast in the months of March, April and May. Variety called rock-oyster by English fishermen, occasionally met with in some parts of Coromandel coast; distinguished by being thin.

AUM (آم - ám, *Hind.*). From (ámra, san. mango). Mango. Cf. also Spondias mangifera (janglíám), jungle mango, and several similar.

AUMADA (ఆమడ - ámada, *Tel.*). Linear measure. 4 pargoos = 1 aumada [alavay, 1b]. Approximate actual value, 1 aumada = 10 miles. Compare San. yojanam, Hind. gow, Tam. cautham.

AUMANAC (एरण्ड - éranda, *San.*; एरंड - éranda, *Mahr.*; एरंडि - éradi, *Conc.*; شجرة الخروع - shajaratulkhirva, *Ar.*; درخت بید انجیر - darakhtibedanjír, *Pers.*; ارنڈی کا پیڑ - arandíkáper, *Hind.*; یرنڈی کا جھاڑ - yarandíkájhár, *Dec.*; جرك - jarak, *Malay*; ಹರಳು - haralu, *Can.*; alambuda, *Too.*; ఆముద - ámuda, *Tel.*; କଲ୍ଲୋ - kallo, *Oor.*; ആവണക്ക - ávanakku, *Mal.*; endaru, *Singh.*; ஆமணக்கு - ámanakku, *Tam.*). Title from tamul. Mahr. and conc. from sanscrit. Ar. from (shajar, ar. tree + khirva, ar. castor seed). Pers. from (darakht, pers. tree + bedanjír, pers. castor seed). Hind. and dec. from sanscrit. Tel. from (ámanda, san. castor-oil plant). Mal. from (ámanda, san. castor-oil plant). Singh. from sanscrit. Tam. like malayalam. San. also (ámanda), meaning a beautiful plant; (gandharvahasta), meaning gandharvan's hand, from serrate leaves; (pañchángula), meaning five fingered, from appearance of leaf. Can. also (audlagida), meaning castor-oil seed + plant; (karala). Tel. also (errámuda), meaning red + castor-oil plant. Mal. also (kotta), meaning seed; (pándiyávanakku), meaning paundy, the place + the plant. Tam. also (muttukkottaiççedi), meaning pearl + seed + plant; (kottaimuttuççedi), meaning seed + pearl + plant. Greek κρότων and κίκι; Latin ricinus. First Greek name and the Latin name derived from resemblance to a tick or dog louse. Second Greek name is from Egyptian. The name Palma christi, derived from its substitution by Christians on Palm sunday for true palm branches. Castor-oil is the Palmæ oleum of old pharmacologists. In Shakespeare's As you like it, Rosalind says, "Look "here, what I found on a palm tree," which means the Palma christi. Title otherwise Castor, Gandharva's hand, Jonah's gourd, Lamp-oil plant, Palma christi plant, Pearl-seed plant, Yerandam.—"*a*" Botanically Ricinus communis, linn., euphorbiaceæ [vricsham, 118]. Alias Ricinus vulgaris. Height 8-10 feet; root perennial; stem round, thick, jointed, channelled, glaucous, purplish-red color upwards; leaves alternate, large, deeply divided into seven segments, on long, tapering, purplish stalks; spikes glaucous, springing from the divisions of the branches; the males from the lower part of the spike, the females from the upper; capsules prickly; seeds oval, shining, black dotted with grey; flowering nearly all the year; cultivated; in hot countries it is a perennial, in cold an annual or biennial; found here wild, but generally cultivated.—"*b*" Two varieties, known respectively as fructibus minoribus; and fructibus majoribus; the former is a small distorted plant, as compared with latter. Distinguished in vernaculars as small and large. Oil made from seeds of small-seeded variety is viscid, nearly colorless or of pale-yellow color, and has a peculiar bland oily taste with a slight nauseous smell; this is called castor-oil. That from large seeded variety is much thicker, more or less of brown color, and has an acrid and very disagreeable nauseous taste and odour; this is called lamp-oil. But there is no difference between the oils of small and large seeds, if they are prepared in a proper manner, and by cold-drawn process.—"*c*" Skin of the seeds consists of three coverings; the active principle is found more or less throughout the entire seed; the oil is soluble in pure sulphuric ether and alcohol; combines easily with alkaline leys; being entirely soluble in highly rectified alcohol of specific gravity ·825, any adulteration of it with other fixed oils may be ascertained by dissolving a sample in eight times its weight of spirit; the fixed oil is not dissolved but floats on the surface; this however is not an infallible test.—"*d*" Cultivated in red sandy soil; dry ground prepared in south in chittray [mausam] or april; on coromandel in jyeshtam or june and ashaudham [mausam] or july, on w. coast in maidom or april and yedavam [mausam] or may, seed sown in south in auvany [mausam] or august and coromandel in shrauvanam [mausam] or august, on w. coast in maidom or april and yedavam or may; no nursery; seed sown in furrows; depends solely upon rain; grown usually as a field border, commonly on the border of cotton and sugar-cane fields; sometimes on isolated patches of a few square yards near dwelling houses; three to six months after sowing branches are cut and gathered; covered by leaves till rotten; then exposed to sun for two or three days and beaten with sticks and seeds separated; brought to market one month after; average price, 16 imperial seers for 1 rupee.—"*e*" The ordinary process of boiling seeds for oil is as follows:—The seeds are cleared of small stones and other substances, heated or toasted a little, and then beaten into a mass in stone mortars; this mass is boiled just like rice, when oil floats on the surface; the oil is then poured into another vessel and heated twice again; it is of a dark color; the mass precipitated at bottom of vessel at first boiling of seeds is made into bratties and used as fuel; this rough process is generally applied to the larger variety.—"*f*" The following is a Tamulian recipé for making an oil for domestic purposes. It will be observed that it is entirely the hot-drawn process:—Take five seers of the smaller castor-oil nuts, and soak them for one night in cold water; next morning strain this water off, throw it away, and put the nuts into a second quantity of fresh water, and boil them in it for two hours; after which strain the water off and throw it away as in the first instance; the nuts are then to be dried in the sun on a mat for three days, at the end of which time they are to be well-bruised in a mortar; add to the nuts thus bruised ten measures of water, and set them on the fire to boil, taking care to keep continually stirring the contents of the pot until all the oil appears at the top, when it is to be carefully strained off, and after being allowed to cool put into a bottle for use; the quantity of nuts mentioned in the above recipé ought to yield about one quart bottle full of oil; in place of the ten measures of plain water, the same quantity of cocoanut water may be used, being supposed to make the castor-oil of a paler and finer color,—"*g*" The following is the more scientific mode of making the oil:—The fresh seeds after having been sifted and cleaned from dust, stones, and all extraneous matters, are slightly crushed between two rollers, freed by hand from husks and colored grains, and enclosed in squares of clean gunny or canvas; the packets of seed then receive a slight pressure in an oblong mould which gives a uniform shape and density to them; the bricks as they are technically called are then placed alternately with plates of sheet iron in an ordinary screw press; on the application of a gradually increasing pressure, the oil exudes through the pores of the gunny and is received into clean tins. So far this is the cold-drawn process, giving the purest oil; the process however generally proceeds, and water in the proportion of a pint to a gallon of oil being added, the whole is boiled until the water has evaporated; the mucilage will then be found to have subsided and encrusted the bottom of the pan, whilst the albumen solidified by the heat has formed a thin layer between the oil and the water; great care must be taken to remove the pan from the fire the instant the whole of the water has evaporated, which may be known by the bubbles having ceased, for if allowed to remain longer, the oil which has hitherto been of the temperature of boiling water or 212°, suddenly rises to that of oil or nearly 600°, thereby heightening the color and communicating an empyreumatic taste and odour; the oil is then filtered through blanket, flannel or american drill, and put into cans for exportation; it is usually of a light straw color, sometimes approaching a greenish tinge; the cleansed seeds yield from forty-seven to fifty per cent. of oil.—"*h*" The oils made here are much stronger than those of France and Italy.—"*i*" Castor-oil is the well known laxative medicine; among hindoos used as remedy in cutaneous affections externally applied; bark of the root is a powerful purgative; fresh juice used as an emetic in poisoning by opium and other narcotics; plant gives to pharm. ricini semina, preparation oleum ricini, officinal, from the fructibus minoribus; lamp-oil, like castor-oil, is purgative.—"*j*" Castor-oil becomes readily rancid, then considered dangerous; but in that state it may be purified by calcined magnesia.—"*k*" Leaves are a favorite food of some silk-worms; castor-oil used for culinary purposes; seeds also put into curries.—"*l*" Lamp-oil employed for common and simple lamps, where viscidity and drying qualities no objection, and in horse medicine; seeds used by dyers to mix with colors and render them permanent. Castor-oil is used for burning in the better class of wicklamps and other domestic purposes; also used by natives for anointing the head; soap of good quality may be made from it; but cost and disagreeable smell preclude its general use.—"*m*" Wood white, soft, light, with large central pith.—"*n*" No other species here.——*Creeping aumanac* (കൊടിയാവണക്ക - kotiyávanakku, Mal.; புல்லாமணக்கு - pullámanakku, Tam.). Mal. from (koti, mal. creeper + ávanakku, mal. ricinus communis, linn.). Tam. from (pul, tam. small + ámanakku, tam. ricinus communis, linn.). Tam. also (kallámanakku), meaning stone + castor plant. Title otherwise Pillaumanac. Botanically Sebastiana chamælea, müller, euphorbiaceæ [vricsham, 118]. Alias Tragia chamælea. Perennial or herbaceous; flowers small, greenish; flowering in cold season. No other species here.——*Foreign aumanac* (பறங்கியாமணக்கு - parangiyámanakku, Tam.). Title from leaf. Same as Papaw.——*Rat aumanac* (निकुम्भ - nikumbha, San.; जंगलीएरण्ड - jangaliéranda, Mahr.; ತೊಟ್ಲಗಿಡ - totlagida, Can.; కాటిఆముద - kátiámuda, Tel.; ആതല - átala, Mal.; දෙඩ - deita, Singh.; எலியாமணக்கு - eliyámanakku, Tam.). Title from small size. San. from (ni, san. prefix of certainty + kumbha, san. pot); from oil-bearing seeds. Mahr. from (jangala, san. jungle + éranda, san. ricinus communis, linn.). Can. from (totte, can. shell + gida, can. plant); from shell of kernel. Tel. from (kádu, tel. forest + ámuda, tel. castor-oil plant). Tam. from (eli, tam. rat + ámanakku, tam. castor-oil plant); from small size. Tel. also (néláámuda), meaning ground + castor-oil + plant; (dundiga). Tam. also (áthalai); (érikkaraikkáttámanakku), meaning tank bund + jatropha curcas, linn. Title otherwise Adul oil plant, Lowly aumanac. Botanically Jatropha [nicoombham] glandulifera, roxb., euphorbiaceæ [vricsham, 118]. Alias Adenorhopium glaucum; Croton lobatum; Jatropha glauca. Small plant, one foot, erect, pubescent; leaves five to three cleft, serrated, smooth, glaucous, almost veinless; petioles sub-villose, longer than the leaves, with glandular hairs; petals of female flowers ovate, the length of the calyx; capsule muricated, as large as hazel nut; seed size of a pea; flowers small, greenish yellow; flowering all year; bunds of tanks. Gives to pharm. seeds and oil of seeds, non-officinal; oil stimulating, external application in chronic rheumatism and paralytic affections; much resembles castor-oil in appearance. Dried leaves dye cloth of a fine apple green color; seeds yield a clear limpid oil for burning; plant largely used for hedges.——*Small wild aumanac* (ವಿಲಾಯತಿಹರಲು - viláyatiharalu, Can.; காட்டுநேர்வாளம் - káttunérválam, Tam.). Can. from (viláyati, can. foreign + haralu, can. ricinus communis, linn.). Tam. from (kádu, tam. forest + nérválam, tam. croton tiglinm, linn.). Title otherwise Coral plant, French physic nut, Small physic nut, Tyle berry plant. Botanically Jatropha [nicoombham] multifida, linn., euphorbiaceæ [vricsham, 118]. Alias Adenorhopium multifidum. A very common, large, herbaceous shrub, ornamental, when kept down to a moderate size; large, much slit, vivid, bluish green leaves, above which rise bunches of small flowers somewhat resembling pieces of red coral. Seeds purgative and emetic; in pharm. non-officinal. Gives an oil.——*Wild aumanac* (काननेरण्ड - kánanéranda, San.; रानएरण्डी - ránaérandí, Mahr.; काडएराडे - kádaéradi, Conc.; دندنهری - dandinahrí, Ar.; دندبری - dandibarrí, Pers.; جنگلی ارنڈی - jangliarandí, Hind. and Dec.; ಕಾಡುಹರಳು - káduharalu, Can.; ಕಾಡಲಂಬುಡು - kádalambudu, Too.; అడవిఆముద - adaviámuda, Tel.; കാട്ടാവണക്ക - káttávanakku, Mal.; වලෙණ්ඩරු - valendaru, Singh.; காட்டாமணக்கு - káttámanakku, Tam.). San. from (kánana, san. forest + éranda, san. castor-oil plant, ricinus communis, linn.). Mahr. from (aranya, san. forest + éranda, san. castor-oil plant). Conc. from (kádu, can. forest + éranda, san. castor-oil plant). Ar. from (dand, ar. croton tiglium, linn. + nahr, ar. river). Pers. from (dand, ar. croton tiglium, linn. +

barr, ar. forest). Hind. from (janglí, ar. wild + arandí, hind. ricinus communis, linn.). Can. from (kádu, can. jungle + haralu, can. castor-oil plant). Too. from (kádu, too. jungle + alambudu, too. castor-oil plant). Tel. from (adavi, tel. forest + ámuda, tel. ricinus communis, linn.). Mal. from (kátu, mal. forest + ávanakku, mal. castor-oil plant). Singh. from (val, singh. wild + endaru, singh. castor-oil plant). Tam. from (kádu, tam. forest + ámanakku, tam. castor-oil plant). San. also (parvatéranda), meaning hill + castor-oil plant. Mahr. also (mogalíeranda), meaning moghul castor-oil plant; (jépálaérandí), meaning croton tiglium, linn. + castor-oil plant. Hind. also (safeddand), meaning white croton-oil plant; (pahárí arand), meaning mountain castor-oil plant. Can. also (turukaharalu), meaning turk + castor-oil plant; (ádaluharalu); (doddaharalu), meaning big + castor-oil plant; (maraharalu), meaning tree + castor-oil plant; (parangiharalu), meaning european + castor-oil plant; (dundiginagida); (bettadaharalu), meaning hill + castor-oil plant. Tel. also (kondaámuda), meaning hill + castor-oil plant. Singh. also (rataendaru), meaning foreign castor-oil plant. Tam. also (kadalámanakku), meaning sea + castor-oil plant. Title otherwise Moghul castor, Moochee wood plant, Physic nut, Purging-nut, Sea castor, Turkey castor. Botanically Jatropha [nicoomblam] curcas, linn., euphorbiaceæ [vricsham, 118]. Alias Castiglionia lobata; Curcas purgans; Ricinus americanus. Small tree or shrub; leaves scattered, broad-cordate, five-angled, smooth; panicles terminal, or from the exterior axils, cymose, many-flowered; male flowers at the extremities of the ramification on short articulated pedicels, the female ones in their divisions, with pedicels not articulated; calyx five-leaved; corolla five-petalled, campanulate, somewhat hairy; styles three, short; flowers small, green; ovary oblong, smooth; flowering nearly all year; planted near villages; fruit oval, size of a small nut, yellow or blackish; seeds size of a small bean, blackish. Viscid juice flowering from the plant gradually dries into a substance resembling shell-lac in color and consistence. Oil expressed from seed is of a pale color; it differs from castor and croton oil in its slight solubility in alcohol; but mixed with castor-oil its solubility is increased. Seeds used as a purgative by natives; their operation is stronger than castor and weaker than croton; and two or three may be taken for a dose; leaves warmed and rubbed with castor-oil are applied to inflammations when suppuration is wished for; juice is applied externally in hæmorrhoids; gum used like collodion to close wounds; quoted in pharm. non-officinal. Plant frequently used as a hedge-plant, as cattle will not touch the leaves; the juice is tenacious, and if blown forms large bubbles, owing to presence of caoutchouc; the oil has been imported to england as a substitute for linseed oil; oil used for burning in lamps; milky juice dyes linen black. Wood white, very soft, perishable. Baliospermum montanum [wild jamalgota] is also considered by the Tamulians a wild castor. Also croton tiglium [jamalgota].

AUMAY (تانبیل - támbel, *Hind.*; తాంబేలు - tábélu, *Tel.*; ஆமை - ámai, *Tam.*). Tam. from (ám, tam. water). Tortoise. Terms coextensive with families testudinidæ and emydidæ, chelonia, reptilia [sarpy, 1, 2], of naturalists [jantoo]. Of two sorts; Land or Testudinidæ, and Freshwater or Emididæ [coormam]. For Turtle see Cadalaumay. Land tortoises appear thus:—Shell very convex; toes distinct; feet club-shaped for walking; no web between the toes; shell with horny shield; caudal shields united into one. Freshwater tortoises appear thus:—Shell sometimes convex, generally more or less depressed; toes distinct, webbed; feet for walking and swimming; shell with horny shields; caudal shields separate. Only gradual transition from land proper to thoroughly aquatic. Development of webs indicates power of swimming. Kites carry to a height the small terrapen, and drop it so as to break the shell. Hindoo mythology represents the world as supported on the back of an elephant, itself sustained upon a round-backed tortoise. The following are the species of both kinds in s. india:—"*a*" Batagur elliotti, emididæ. The Batagur. Freshwater; large size. Kistna river. Posterior margin of shell strongly serrated; uniform brownish above, yellowish below. Feet during life dotted with brown.—"*b*" Emys trijuga, emididæ; alias Emys belangeri, sebæ, thermalis, Geoclemys seba. Common Terrapen or Ceylonese pond tortoise; freshwater. Has thorax and sternum solid, entirely bony, and united into an immovable carapace in the adult state. The upper shell more or less depressed. Feet with the toes broadly webbed. Claws strong, five anteriorly and four posteriorly. Rest on the water with the shell and the snout raised above its surface, suddenly disappearing at the approach of danger. Their pointed claws enable them to crawl easily over steep places; they are chiefly carnivorous. Food of the carnivorous, water-insects, frogs, small fishes, small aquatic birds and mammals; whilst they are persecuted by alligators and large fishes, and the young and eggs by numerous other animals. Not used as food by man, the flesh of most species having a very disagreeable smell, which is also perceptible when first taken out of the water in a net or by a hook baited with meat. There is a Tamul punning proverb:—ஊமை ஊரைக்கெடுக்கும் ஆமை கிணற்றைக் கெடுக்கும்—"The dumb man destroys a village, a tortoise destroys a "well." Easily kept in captivity, attain only a small size; all more or less ferocious. The head and feet can be completely retracted within the carapace. The terrapen is common in the peninsula: Full-grown at a length of from 7 to 8 inches.—"*c*" Pangshura tecta, emididæ. The Pangshure. Freshwater. Distinguished by its elevated back; shell brownish or blackish. The lower parts of the shell yellow with large blackish-brown spots. Habits like terrapen.—"*d*" Pangshura tentoria, emididæ; alias Batagur tentoria, Emys tectum, tentoria. The Dura. Similar to Pangshure, but shell more depressed. Upper shell uniform brown. On banks of the Kistna and tributaries.—"*e*" Testudo elegans, testudinidæ; alias actinodes, geometrica, stellata, megalopus. Land tortoise. The Starred tortoise. Has the head, feet, and tail completely retracted within the shell; entirely terrestrial being the worst swimmers of the whole class of reptiles, with the exception of the chameleon. Movements slow; food on vegetables; edible, of small size. Found in Coromandel coast, and the low jungles of the Carnatic; color and appearance blended with the rocky nature of the ground. Remain in concealment beneath shrubs or tufts of grass during the heat of the day. In rainy season in the greatest activity. ——*Cadal aumay* (कूर्म - kúrma, San.; رق - rakk, Ar.; باخه - bákhah, Pers.; کچھوا - kachhvá, Hind.; دریا کا تانبیل - daryá-kátámbel, Dec.; ಕಡಲಾಮೆ - kadaláme, Can.; సముద్రపుతాబేలు - samudraputábélu, Tel.; കടലാമ - kataláma, Mal.; கடலாமை - kadalámai, Tam.). Title from tamul. San. from (ku, san. prefix showing inferiority + úrmi, san. speed). Hind. from (kachhapa, san. tortoise). Dec. from (daryá, hind. sea + támbel, hind. tortoise). Rest mean sea tortoise. Turtle. Terms coextensive with families trionycidæ and chelonidæ, chelonia, reptilia [sarpy, 3, 4], of naturalists [jantoo]. Of two sorts:—Freshwater turtles or Trionycidæ and Marine turtles or Chelonidæ. Order chelonia [coormam]. For Tortoise see Aumay. The following is the description of the freshwater turtles:—Shell much depressed, covered with soft skin; feet for swimming; toes distinct, strongly webbed. The following is the description of the marine turtles:—Long, compressed, fin-shaped, non-retractile feet, toes being enclosed in a common skin, out of which one or two claws project; carapace broad and much depressed, so that when these animals are on shore and turned over on their back, they cannot regain their natural position; head large and globose, cannot be retracted within the shell; covered above with symmetrical horny shields, jaws armed with sharp horny sheaths. The shells of marine turtles are the tortoise-shell of commerce [zabl]. There is a Tamul proverb:—அவனை அவன் பேச்சிட்டுப் பேச்சு வாங்கி, ஆமைமல்லாத்திருப்போல் மல்லாத்திப்போட்டான்—"Having fished out his secrets by cunning he turned him upside "down as a turtle is turned." The following are the species of turtles of both kinds which are best known in Southern india:—"*a*" Caouana olivacea, gray. Indian loggerhead. Family Chelonidæ, marine. Alias Chelonia dussumieri, olivacea. Carnivorous, eating fishes, mollusca, and crustacea. Found on Coast of Malabar. Of no commercial value, flesh not esteemed and tortoise-shell of inferior quality.—"*b*" Caretta squamata. Hawk-bill turtle or Indian caret. Family Chelonidæ, marine. Alias Caretta imbricata; Eretmochelys squamata; Testudo squamata. Carnivorous, gives the best tortoise-shell. So named from its rather elongate and compressed, curved upper jaw, does not attain to the same size as the other turtles. Natives eat the flesh of green turtle.—"*c*" Chelonia virgata. Indian turtle, family Chelonidæ, marine. Herbivorous, feeding on algæ. In size equals the Atlantic turtle, which it rivals in flavor. The flesh is sometimes found to be poisonous.—"*d*" Dermatochelys coriacea. Family Chelonidæ, marine. Alias Sphargis coriacea, mercurialis. Testudo coriacea.—"*e*" Emyda vittata. Family Trionycidæ, freshwater. Has neck very long and flexible; head short, jaws covered with sharp horny sheaths, eyes small, slightly directed upwards, tail none; armed with strong claws, habits aquatic and carnivorous; does not attain a large size. When the water dries up buries itself deep in the mud. Characterized by black streaks and spots on the head and neck, whence the name.—"*f*" Halys elliotti. Tail short, not prehensile, terminates in a spine. Olive-green above; pearl-white beneath.—"*g*" Trionyx javanicus. Family Trionycidæ, freshwater. Alias Gymnopus cartilagineus, javanicus; Trionyx javanicus. The largest of the freshwater turtles, thoroughly aquatic and carnivorous.

AUMSAM (ஆமிசம் - ámisam, *Tam.*). From (amsha, san. share). Estimate. Especially of the yield of standing crop.

AUN (ஆண் - án, *Tam.*). From (ál, tam. to rule). A ruler, a male.——*Aundaul* (ஆண்டாளு - ándálu, Tam.). Literally she who ruled. Lutchmy. Hindoo female proper name [peyar]. Common among Veishnavas [alwar].——*Aunday* (ஆண்டை - ándai, Tam.). A master.——*Aundoo* (ആണ്ടു - ándu, Mal.; ஆண்டு - ándu, Tam.). Any dynastic year. Especially the year of the Collam era [q.v.].——*Aundy* (ಆಂಡಿ - ándi, Can.; ஆண்டி - ándi, Tam.). Sheiva mendicant. Some 70,000 in Presidency. Suffix in Tamul proper names of the inferior castes, as Pulney aundy [peyar].——*Aun vazhy* (ആൺവഴി - ánvazhi, Mal.). From (vazhi, mal. way). The male line in descent or Makkatoyem. Opposed to Penvazhy or Maroomakkatoyem.

AUNA (ఆన - ána, *Tel.*). Abbreviation for Anno Domini.

AUNA (آنہ - ánah, *Pers.*). Suffix meaning like; as Nuzrauna, meaning offering + like.

AUNAH (आना - áná, *San.*). Goldsmith's weight. 6 goonjams = 1 aunah; 2 aunahs = 1 mausham [niray, 3f]. Approximate actual value, 1 aunah = 11 grains.

AUNAY (ಆನೆ - áne, *Can.*; ആന - ána, *Mal.*; ஆனை - ánai, *Tam.*). From (éndu, tam. to support). Elephant. Aunesaul, from (shálá, san. hall) is an elephant stable. For Annacomban paddy see paddy. Aunacoova, from (kúva, mal. arrowroot) is Malabar arrowroot [elephant]. Common plant term, indicating size of plant or fruit, and often joining two genera. Ex., where transl. is of second term:—Adansonia digitata (ánaippuli), tamarindus indica, and (ánappuliyárai), oxalis corniculata; Adenanthera pavonina (ánaikkunrimani), abrus precatorius; Agave americana (ánaikkattázhai), aloe indica; Boucerosia umbellata (ánaikkallimulaiyán), boucerosia panciflora; Casearia tomentosa (ánavanaṁni), reverenced by; Curcuma aromatica (ánemañjal), curcuma longa, turmeric, and (ánakkúva), curcuma angustifolia, arrowroot; Elephantopus scaber (ánaççóvati), footmark, and (ánaiççeviyadi), ear + foot; Girardina heterophylla (ánaççoriyanam), tragia involucrata; Odina wodier (ánaikkárai), canthium parviflorum; Pedalium murex (áneneggilu), tribulus terrestris; Pothos scandens (ánapparuva), creeper; Scindapsus officinalis (ánaittippili), piper longum; Sida rhombifolia (ánaikkuruntótti), sida rhombifolia, var. retusa; Typha elephantina (ánaikkórai), cyperus. See gloss. paragraphs.

AUNY (ஆனி - áni, *Tam.*). From (háni, san. loss). Third solar month [mausam].——*Auny amavausyay* (ஆனியமாவாசியை - ániyamávásiyai, Tam.). Means third solar month + new moon day. Luni-solar festival [pundigay, 5a]. New moon festival of the third solar month Auny [mausam], i.e., between June 13th and July 14th. The floating festival at Trivellore falls on this date.——*Auny tirmanjanam* (ஆனித்திருமஞ்சனம் - ánittirumañjanam, Tam.). Means solar month + holy ablution. Luni-solar festival [pundigay, 6d]. The sacred bathing or anointing of the Lingam especially at Chidambaram which is always held when the moon stands in Pooshyam the eighth lunar mansion in third solar month Auny [mausam], i.e., between June 13th and July 14th. Occurs in June.

AUR (ആറ് - áru, *Mal.*; ஆறு - áru, *Tam.*). From (aru, tam. to cut). Natural current or river. Differs from Caulvyo and Vycaul, which are artificial channels. Suffix in river names; as Palaur, meaning milk + river. Not the same word as Airy [q.v.]. The corresponding teloogoo termination is Air.—"*a*" Into the Arabian sea no considerable rivers flow in this Presidency. Flowing towards the Bay of Bengal there are the Veigay through the district of Madura; the Cauvery with the towns of Tranquebar, Trichinopoly, and Tanjore; the Bhawauny; the Ponniaur dry in the hot season, with Cuddalore; the Palaur dry in the hot season, with Arcot and Vellore; the Pennair dry in the hot season, with Nellore; the Kistna with Masulipatam; the Toongabudra with Kurnool; the Hagary flowing through Bellary district; and the Godavery with Rajahmundry. The Rooshcoolya in the north-east falls into the Bay of Bengal near Ganjam; the Vamshadhaura falls into it at Calingapatam, and near it the Langoolya also from C. Provinces. Further south the deltas of the Godavery and Kistna water large districts. In the Carnatic, the Goondlacumma rises in the Eastern ghauts; the Pennair, Palaur, and Ponniaur rise in the east of Mysore and flow into the bay. The Cauvery at Trichinopoly divides into several branches, of which the Coleroon is the most important; it rises in the Western ghauts and flows south-east. The Veigay and Tamrapurny rise on the borders of Travancore and fall into Palk's strait and the Gulf of Manaar respectively.—"*b*" Common plant term from growing on river sides or in river beds, and sometimes joining two genera. Ex., where transl. is of second term:—Citrullus colocynthis (áttuttummatti), cucumis trigonus; Najas indica (áttuppási), moss; Polygonum barbatum (áttalari), nerium odorum; Tamarix gallica (áttuççavukku), casuarina equisetifolia; Trewia nudiflora (áttuppúvarasu), thespesia populnea. See gloss. paragraphs.——*Auttcaul* (ஆற்றுக்கால் - áttukkál, Tam.). From (kál, tam. channel). River channel.——*Autt pauchal* (ஆற்றுப்பாய்ச்சல் - áttuppáyççal, Tam.). From (páy, tam. to flow). River irrigation.——*Auttvary* (ആറ്റുവരി - áttuvari, Mal.). From (vari, mal. tax). Tax for irrigating from rivers.——*Auttvepp* (ആറ്റുവെപ്പ് - áttuveppu, Mal.). From (veppu, mal. deposit). A new land left by the receding of a river, so plantations thereon. Extended also to plantations by the sea [caravepp].

AUR (ആറു - áru, *Mal.*). Six.——*Aurnaulipaud* (ആറുനാഴിപ്പാട് - árunázhippátu, Mal.). From (above + názhi, mal. the measure + pátu, mal. chief, a title). Attendants on a rajah getting six nauzhies of paddy per diem [chungautam, maryauday].

AURAGVADHAM (आरग्वध - áragvadha, *San.*). From (araja, san. skin disease + vadh, san. to destroy). Curl brush bean. Botanically the Pithecolobium genus, leguminosæ [vriesham, 48]. Large shrubs or trees; leaves double pinnate; flowers white or yellowish; pods spirally twisted or very much curved; seeds surrounded by a thin pulp. The species best known to the natives are:—bigeminum [wild connay], dulce [corcapilly], saman [zamang tree]. Other species indigenous or naturalized are:—subcoriaceum, umbellatum.

AURAL (वाम - báma, *Mahr.*; جری - jirrí, *Ar.*; مارماهی - mármáhí, *Pers.*; کچیا مچھی - kachiyámachhí, *Hind.*; تمبو مچھی - tambúmacchí, *Dec.*; ಹಾವುಮೀನು - hávumínu, *Can.*; బొమ్మదాయ - bommadáya, *Tel.*; ବାମ - báma, *Oor.*; ആരൽ - áral, *Mal.*; තෙලියා - teliyá, *Singh.*; ஆரல் - áral, *Tam.*). Title from tamul. Ar. from (jirra, ar. to stretch); from length. Pers. from (már, pers. snake + máhí, pers. fish). Hind. from (kachiya, hind. sickle + machhí, hind. fish). Can. from (hávu, can. snake + mínu, can. fish). Mal. from tamul. Singh. from (tel, singh. oil); from being slippery. Tam. from (ár, tam. glistening). Ar. also (samakulhayát), meaning life-giving fish. Hind. also (bám). Tel. also (peddamaluguchépa), meaning large + eel + fish; (mundlachépa), meaning thorn + fish; (tirukachépa), meaning twist + fish. Tam. also (tirukkai), meaning to twist, from form. Title otherwise Lamprey, Sand eel, Spined eel. Rhynchobdella aculeata, rhynchobdellidæ, acanthopterygii, teleostei [matsyam, 24], of naturalists [jantoo]. Alias Macrognathus aculeatus; Mastacembelus pentophthalmos; Ophidium aculeatum; Rhynchobdella aral, ocellata, orientalis. Aral from tamul. Freshwater. Snout fleshy, elongated, with trilobed anterior extremity. Air-vessel extends from head to anus. Colors brownish or greenish, marbled superiorly, yellowish along abdomen; light band along body above lateral-line; from three to nine large black ocelli, having white or buff edge, along base of soft dorsal fin. Caudal with vertical brown bars, fins otherwise grayish. Pectoral sometimes yellow. Brackish waters within tidal influence, also throughout deltas of large rivers, absent from Malabar coast; attaining about 15 inches in length. Conceals itself in mud, and becomes drowned if placed in water so as to be unable to reach the surface, requiring to respire air directly. No other common species here.——*Rock aural* (ముడిబొమ్మదాయ - mudibommadáya, Tel.; கல்லாரல் - kalláral, Tam.). Title from adhering to stones and rocks. Tel. from (mudi, tel. old + bommadáya, tel. lamprey). Tam. from (kal, tam. stone + áral, tam. lamprey). Title otherwise Thorny-backed eel. Mastacembelus armatus, rhynchobdellidæ, acanthopterygii, teleostei [matsyam, 24], of naturalists. Alias Macrognathus armatus, caudatus, undulatus et hamiltonii; Mastacembelus marmoratus, ponticerianus. Freshwater. Snout trilobed at anterior extremity; usually rich brown, lighter on abdomen. In some blackish band goes through eye and is continued undulating along upper half of side; above this are sometimes black spots along base of soft dorsal fin, added to which there may be short black bands over back in situation of dorsal spines. Pectoral usually spotted, and dorsal and anal have usually bands or spots. Some are marbled all over the sides. A variety Marmoratus is by far the handsomest species, and found in Mysore and Bhawauny river. It is of a general purplish color, marbled all over with darker. Head has wide dark bands broken up into angular or irregularly shaped spots by narrow white lines. Pectoral with basal third purple, middle third with narrow yellow lines, and outer third yellow. A variety Ponticerianus, with rather pointed tail is common at Madras. The stone aural is found throughout fresh and brackish waters of plains and hills, attaining two feet or more in length. Good eating, especially when curried or fried. Another common species is Pancalus, much smaller.

AURANG (اورنگ - aurang, *Hind.*). From Persian. Factory, depôt for piece-goods. Company's term.

AURAUMAM (आराम - áráma, *San.*). From (á, san. intensive prefix + ram, san. to please). Garden, grove. Suffix in place names; as Draucsharaumam, meaning vine + grove.

AURAY (सुनिषण्णक - sunishannaka, *San.*; چپاتی کی بھاجی - chapátíkíbhájí, *Dec.*; మునుగుతామర - munugutámara, *Tel.*; ആരൽ - áral, *Mal.*; මහබුරුඩ - mahaburnda, *Singh.*; ஆரை - árai, *Tam.*). Title from tamul. San. from (su, san. well + nishanna, san. sunk down); from submerged habit. Dec. from (chár, hind. four + pát, hind. leaf + bhájí, hind. potherb); from leaflets. Tel. from (munugu, tel. to sink + támara, tel. nelumbium speciosum, willd.); submerged under water and leaf like lotus. Mal. from tamul. Tam. from (ár, tam. to eat); as being edible. San. also (chitradala), meaning having variegated leaves. Hind. also (godhi). Tel. also (mudugutámara), meaning shrinking + nelumbium speciosum, willd.; (chitlinta), meaning split-leaved; (árakúra). Botanically the Marsilea genus, marsileaceæ [vricsham]. Pseudoferns; with creeping rhizome and erect leaves consisting of a long stalk and two pairs of leaflets which are circinate when young, disposed in a cross, nerved somewhat after those of adiantum, and which at night fold up like the leaflets of many leguminosæ. The species best known to the natives are:—coromandeliana, quadrifolia.——*Sour auray* (अम्ललोणिका - amlalóniká, San.; चूका - chúká, Mahr.; तेलतुप्पि - télatuppi, Conc.; حمیض - hummaiz, Ar.; حماض سہ برگہ - hummáz i sihbargah, Pers.; انبوتی - ambotí, Hind.; انبوتی کی بھاجی - ambotíkíbhájí, Dec.; ಪುಲ್ಲಂಪುರಚಿ - pullampurachi, Can.; పుళియారలు - puliyáralu, Too.; పులిచింత - pulichinta,

Tel.; പുളിയാരൽ - puliyáral, Mal.; புளியாரை - puliyárai, Tam.). Title from taste of leaves. San. from (amla, san. sour + lóniká, san. sorrel plant). Mahr. from (chukriká, san. the plant). Ar. from (hamaza, ar. sour). Pers. from (hummáz, ar. sorrel + sih., pers. three + barg, pers. leaf). Hind. from (ambasht'há, san. the sorrel plant). Can. from (puli, can. acid + puniche, can. tamarindus indica, linn.). Too. from malayalam. Tel. from (puli, tel. sour + chinta, tel. tamarind tree). Mal. from (puli, mal. sour + áral, mal. marsilea). Tam. from (puli, tam. sour + árai, tam. marsilea). San. also (chángérí), meaning causing teeth to loose their soundness; (chukriká), meaning sour; (amliká), meaning sour; (ambasht'há), meaning acting like mother being medicinal plant; (dantashat'há), meaning tooth + rogue, as hurting teeth from sourness. Mahr. also (bhuísarapatí), meaning earth + creeping. Hind. also (sehpatí), meaning three-leafed; (amrul). Can. also (nírugóli), meaning water + coral jasmine, nyctanthes arbortristis, linn.; (hulihuniche), meaning acid + tamarind tree; (pullampunise); (hulichikkana). Tel. also (pullachinta), meaning sour + tamarind tree; (pullachanchali), meaning sour + digera arvensis, forsk. Tam. also (shusigam), meaning cleaner, as removing stains; (túsigam), meaning cleaner; (pulikkírai), meaning sour greens. Title otherwise Indian sorrel, Sour greens, Three-leaved sorrel, Tooth-rogue, Water coral jasmine, Yellow-wood sorrel. Botanically Oxalis corniculata, linn., geraniaceæ [vricsham, 31]. Alias Oxalis dillenii, monadelpha, prostrata, pusilla, repens, stricta; Oxys lutea. Creeping herb; stems decumbent, branched, radicating, leafy; stipules united to the base of the petioles; leaves palmately three-foliolate; leaflets obcordate, pubescent; peduncles two to five but mostly two-flowered, stamens monadelphous; sepals pubescent; petals emarginate; pistils as long as the longer stamens; capsule many-seeded, densely pubescent; flowers yellow; flowering nearly all year; a common weed on lawns and in gardens; the trefoil leaves, fold downwards at night; leaves are sour to taste, containing oxalic acid salts. Leaves, tender stalks and flowers used as cooling medicine, especially in dysentery; juice used externally to remove warts; fresh juice expressed from leaves relieves intoxication from datura. Used in chutney and curries, substitute for lime juice or tamarind; also eaten raw and cooked as a pot-herb, especially by mahomedans. Juice used to remove ink-spots. No other species here.

AURDRACAM (आर्द्रक - árdraka, *San.*). From (árdra, san. wet); moist root. Botanically the Zingiber genus, zingiberaceæ [vricsham, 141]. Generic name from sanscrit through arabic. Herbs, with creeping jointed woody root-stocks, from which are sent up every year stems surrounded by sheathing leaves arranged in two ranks; flowers are borne on cone shaped spikes, thrown up from the root-stock, and protected by bracts. The species best known to the natives are:—capitatum [jungle ginger], cassumunar [q.v.], officinale [ginger], zerumbet [false ginger]. Other S. indian species indigenous or naturalized are:—nimmonii, roseum, squarrosum.

AURSHAM (आर्ष - ársha, *San.*). From (rishi, san. vedic sage). Archæology. Natives understand by this what Europeans call pre-historic archæology. Antiquities here of that class range under the following heads, viz.:—"*a*" Sepulchral monuments, mounds and tumuli.—"*b*" Single stones, on which rude figures of warriors are represented, and flat stones, with rude sculptures representing combats, objects of worship, &c., with or without inscriptions; these are in the Canarese country called Veeracull, or heroic monuments.—"*c*" Shausanams or inscriptions in various characters cut in stone; these generally commemorate grants of land, &c.—"*d*" Vases, urns and lamps of clay and metal. Statues, whether those remarkable for their size and the uniformity of their sitting and standing attitudes, which belong to the Booddhist and Jeina worship, or the more varied personifications of the Braminical system.—"*e*" Sculptured excavations, as those of Mauvellipore, &c. Compare the notice on antiquities at vol. I, 526. Under the heading of each talook or similar geographical division in this volume will be found a complete list of the villages with antiquities contained in that talook or division. For pre-historic antiquities see:—Azhauram, Coday cull, Mady mottaur tauzhy, Mannauticull, Maundavar coozhy, Mausticull, Panndicoozhy, Paundoo cull, Raucshasagoondloo, Topicull, Vauly coody, Veeracull. For Jeina or Booddhist archæology see:—Basty, Baur, Betta, Cheityam, Dagoba, Sangharaumam, Tope, Vihauram. For general architecture see Staupatyam [charitram].

AUSAUMY (آسامی - ásámí, *Hind.*); pl. of (ism, ar. name). Individual. Ausaumiwar is individually. Ausaumiwar hisaub is an account showing name of each individual.

AUSAURY (ఆసారి - ásári, *Tel.*). Ganjam form of Acharry. Proceeding up the coast, the ch is softened.

AUSHRAMAM (आश्रम - áshrama, *San.*). From (á, san. intensive prefix + shram, san. to toil). A condition of life of which four should theoretically be passed through in succession by Hindoos of the three superior castes. These are as follows:—"*a*" That of the Brambacharry or practisor of vedam, who, from the time of his investment with the sacred cord, is required to tend the sacred fires and to follow his studies under, or in the presence of, his preceptor. A Bramhacharry, instead of passing on into the other Aushramams, may bind himself to remain a student for life, and such persons now constitute a numerous order.—"*b*" That of the Gribastan or householder, who, from his marriage, must strictly observe his religious duties, maintain the sacred fires, and liberally practise hospitality for the support of the other three orders.—"*c*" That of the Vaunaprastan or recluse, who, with or without his wife, retires to the desert feeding on leaves, roots and fruits, or on the hospitality of the second order, and continues to perform his daily rites.—"*d*" That of the sanyausy, for which see separate head [matam].

AUSHWINAM (आश्विन - áshvina, *San.*). From (ashviní, san. the first or horseheaded asterism); from full moon in the month occurring in or near that nacshatram. Seventh lunar month or about October.——*Aushwina shoeddham* (ఆశ్వినశుద్ధము - áshvinashuddhamu, Tel.; ஆசுவினசுத்தம் - ásuvinasuttam, Tam.). Means the seventh lunar month + bright fortnight. Otherwise Navaraatry. Lunar festival [pundigay, 3b]. The first tity of the seventh month Aushweejam [mausam] between September 15 and October 16, consecrated to the worship of the goddess Doorga. On this day Dusserah is begun.

AUSMAUN (ఆసుమాను - ásumánu, *Tel.*; ஆசுமனை - ásumanai, *Tam.*). From (ásu, tam. small thing, meaning the hollow bamboo answering to heck-box + manai, tam. board). Distinguish from Asmaun. A flat oblong board with rows of small upright pegs, each row having three or five. Round these pegs the thread is passed in the figure of 8, to be made into skeins [nesavoo].

AUSRYAPPAH (ஆசிரியப்பா - ásiriyappá, *Tam.*). From (ácbárya, san. teacher + pá, tam. verse); royal verse. Also called Agaval. A kind of versification in Tamul. The number of lines in each stanza is not defined, nor is there any settled rule for the number of feet requisite to each line. The Nunnool is in this metre.

AUSTRALIA (استريليا - ástreliyá, *Hind.*). The country. In addition to terms below see also:—Casuarina equisetifolia, australian swamp-oak; Dammara australis, australian dammer; Dentella repens, australian tooth-flower.——*Australian blackwood* (استريلياببول - ástreliyábabúl, Hind.). Title otherwise Tasmanian lightwood. Botanically Acacia [cantalam] melanoxylon, r. br., leguminosæ [vricsham, 48]. Introduced to Neilgherries, Pulneys, &c. They are now overgrown with this and Acacia dealbata, link. Wood hard and durable; heart-wood dark-brown and mottled soft, shining, even-grained; used chiefly for firewood.——*Australian gum tree* (شجر كافور - shajarikáfúr, Ar.; درخت كافور - darakhtikáfúr, Pers.; كافور كا پير - káfúrkáper, Hind.; كافور كا جهاڑ - kápúrkájhár, Dec.; ಕರ್ಪೂರಮರ - karpúramara, Can.; കർപ്പൂരമരം - karpúramara, Too.; కర్పూరపుచెట్టు - karpúrapuchettu, Tel.; கர்ப்பூரமரம் - karppúramaram, Tam.). Means camphor tree. Botanically the Encalyptus genus, myrtaceæ [vricsham, 56]. Mostly lofty trees, natives of australia and adjacent islands; leaves of a thick leathery texture, opposite in young plants but becoming alternate as the plants get older; flowers either solitary or in clusters; fruit closely enveloped in woody calyx; introduced into neilgherries where they thrive well. The red colored gum or kino is called botany bay kino; the best procured from corymbosa, rostrata, and citriodora; bitter, but has little smell. Kino useful in chronic bowel complaints, being mildly astringent; leaves yield essential oil, sometimes substitute for cajeput oil. Kino is applicable for tanning or dyeing; bark also is a powerful tanning substance; bark forms paper material. Wood strong and tenacious, durable; much used for firewood or charcoal; the rostrata, or yarrah of western australia, is particularly useful, resisting the white-ant and sea-worm or teredo navalis. The species best known is globulus or blue gum [q.v.]; other species on neilgherries are gummifera and robusta.

AUTCHY (ஆட்சி - ádchi, *Tam.*). From (ál, tam. to rule). Inheritance. Suffix in place names; as Maniyautchy, meaning grain + possession.——*Arasautchy* (அரசாட்சி - arasádchi, Tam.). From (arasu, tam. royalty). Royalty.——*Cawnyautchy* (காணியாட்சி - kániyádchi, Tam.). From (káni, tam. land). A domain obtained by inheritance.

AUTCHY (अक्षि - akshi, *San.*). Eye; suffix in female proper names as Canmautchy, meaning love + eye.

AUTMAM (आत्मा - átmá, *San.*). From (at, san. to move). The Supreme Being whether Bramha, Vishnoo, or Shiva. The living or individual soul. For transmigration see samsauram. The Hindoos believe that the soul or conscious life enters the body through the sagittal suture, lodges in the brain, and may contemplate through the same opening the divine perfections. Mind or the reasoning faculty is reckoned to be an organ of the body situated in the heart. The following verses are from the Tamul Bhagavat geeta, a rare work:—பீறிய போர்வையைப் பெயர்த்துப்பின்னரோர் வேறிய போர்வையை விரும்பு வாரொன ஆறிய வுடம்பினி னுதித்தவுண்மை தான் மாறி யோருடம்பினை மருவுமன்னனே—"As those who "throw away a tattered garment, desire another clothing, so "the reality or soul, O king, which appears in one mortal body "will enter into another body." உறுப்பான்மை மற்றதனுக் கொருநாளுமினமையாற செருப்பால் வெம்படைக் கலங்கள் சேதிக்க மாட்டாவா நெருப்பால் வெந்தழி யாது நீராலனைக்கொழுகாது மருத்தாலுஞ் சலியாது மற்றதன்றனியல்கேள்—"As the nature of the body at no "time appertains to the soul, the keenest weapons on battle "field cannot divide it. It cannot be burnt up and destroyed "by fire. The water cannot destroy it; nor can it be shaken "by the wind." எவ்வாப்பொருட்கும் பழையதனை யெங் குந்தானுயிருப்பதனை நில்லாத்தன்மை யில்லதனை நித்தியத்துவத்தை நிலைப் பேற்றை யல்லாப்புலனைகள் பதினாலுமறியா வறிவையறியாதே யில்லாப்பொருள் போலழியுமென விரங்குகின்றதென்கண்டோ—"Of all "beings it is the most ancient. It exists in all places. It is "unchangeable. It is eternal. It is immoveable. Besides "which it is the pure intelligence beyond the powers of the "fourteen caranams to conceive; what knowest thou then to "grieve as thou dost, as if the soul could be destroyed as other "perishable substances." மாயுமவராலுமுயிர் வாழுமவ ராலு மாயுமறி ஞோர்களழியாமை யறியாயோ நீயு மிவர் தாமுநிகழ் நானு நெறி தேரிலேயும் வகையா லுலகிலென்று முளமேகாண்—"Dost thou not know that "the wise neither grieve for the dead nor for the living. "Thyself, these princes, and I myself, when well considered "shall never cease to be."——*Autmanautma viraicam* (आत्मानात्मविवेक - átmánátmavivéka, San.). From (anátman, san. the not-soul + vivéka, san. discernment). Very succinct Tamul treatise on intellectual knowledge; from Sanscrit. Contains two divisions, on divine and human nature. In divinity there are three forms, actuated by one pervading mind. The three forms are Bramha, Vishnoo, Shiva, whose bodies are respectively red, blue, and white. In the pervading mind there are five properties or powers, analogous to five senses. They are one in council, diverse in operation; Bramha creating, Vishnoo preserving, Shiva destroying. There is only one supreme in the universe, the Trimoorty. In the human nature there is a compound of body and soul. In the soul there are five senses. In the body there are seven vital airs, which operate in various ways, by pulsation, &c. In the body there are nine apertures. The perfection of human nature consists in the restraint of the five senses, seven vital airs, and nine apertures; the mind being fixed in contemplating the supreme, who has five powers, and diversely operates by three forms, as creator, preserver, and destroyer.——*Paramautman* (परमात्मा - paramátmá, San.). The supreme soul-god [matam].

AUTTAUL (ஆத்தாள் - áttál, *Tam.*). From (agam, tam. house + ál, tam. pers. termination). House woman. Mother; epithet of Parvaty, mother of the world. Suffix in proper names among the lower castes, as Mauriyauttaul [peyar].

AUTTCAUL (ஆற்றுக்கால் - áttukkál, *Tam.*). From (áru, tam. river + kál, tam. channel). River; Madura district, Pulney talook. Rises in Aroongaunal hill, fertilises for three miles Peroompullam valley, then winds N.W. and west for three miles, and turning S.S.W. one mile and a half receives the Covanjy, the latter having run a course N. by E. six miles from its sources in the Permaul range. The river, now known as the Vardaputnam, winds N.W. three and a quarter miles to a dam constructed across it from which the channel runs north to Ayacoody. About two furlongs below the dam, a small branch is conveyed into a tank south of Ayacoody. The river now splits in two, unites again about a mile below, and half a mile further on is again dammed. The canal conveyed away on the right bank flows south of Pulney, and ultimately discharges itself into the large tank west of the temple. The river now assumes the name of the Varattaur, and running a devious course of four and a half miles N.W. by W. through an open tract discharges itself into the Palaur, one and a half mile W.S.W. of Pulney. Total length, 17 miles.

AUTTY (ஆத்தி - átti, *Tam.*). Plant of Mountain ebony or bauhinia class.——*Auttisoody* (ஆத்திசூடி - áttisúdi, *Tam.*). From (above + shúdu, tam. to wear); from the opening words. One of Avvay's aphoristic works taught in schools. Contains 108 aphorisms, each beginning with a different letter of the alphabet and its vowel combinations [avvay, condrayvendan]. Example, the opening:—ஆத்திசூடி யமர்ந்ததேவனை யேத்தி யேத்தித் தொழுவோமியாமே. நூல்.—அறஞ்செய விரும்பு. ஆறுவது சினம். இயல்வது கரவேல். ஈவது விலக்கேல். உடையது விளம்பேல். ஊக்கமது கைவி டேல். எண்ணெழுத்திகழேல். ஏற்பதிகழ்ச்சி. ஐயமிட் டுண். ஒப்புரவொழுகு. ஓதுவதொழியேல். ஔவியம் பேசேல். அஃகஞ்சுருக்கேல். கண்டொன்றுசொல் லேல். ஙப்போல்வளை. சனிநீராடு. ஞயம்படவுரை. இடம்படவீடிடேல் இணக்கமறிந்திணங்கு. தந்தை தாய்ப்பேண்—"Let us worship and praise continually the "god who is dear to that being who wears a garland made of "the flowers of the autty tree. Desire to do virtue. Anger "should be subdued. Do not conceal your means. Do not "prevent giving alms. Do not boast of your possessions. Do "not lose courage. Do not despise numbers and letters. Beg"ging is disgraceful. Give alms then eat. Conduct yourself "consistently. Cease not to learn. Do not speak enviously. "Make not grain scarce. Do not say one thing after seeing "another. Be united to your relatives like the letter ங, i.e. as "the letter ங is united to its kindred letters. Bathe on Satur"day. Speak so as to give pleasure. Do not build too large a "house. Be friendly on experiencing friendship. Protect your "father and mother." The style is not profound, but is extremely popular with the Tamulians [bhaushay].

AUTUNNY (اٹھنی - áthanni, *Hind.*). From (át'ha, mahr. eight + áná, mahr. sixteenth of a rupee). Eight anna silver piece, so called under Mahomedan government.

AUVANY (ஆவணி - ávani, *Tam.*). Corruption of Shrauvanam, the fifth lunar month. Fifth solar month [mausam].——*Auvany avittam* (ஆவணியவிட்டம் - ávaniyavittam, Tam.). Means fifth solar month + shravishtay, the twenty-third nacshatram. Luni-solar festival [pundigay, 5b]. Also called Oopaucarmam or Shrauvanam. On the day when the moon is in the nacshatram Shravishtay in the fifth solar month Auvany [mausam] between July 30th and August 27th. Festival peculiar to the three twice-born castes and is the annual renewal of their sacred order, a new thread being put on. One meal only is taken on this day.——*Auvany moolam* (ஆவணிமூலம் - ávanimúlam, Tam.). Means fifth solar month + nineteenth nacshatram. Luni-solar festival [pundigay, 5b]. On the day when the moon is in the constellation Moolam in the fifth solar month Auvany [mausam], i.e. between August 15th and September 14th; celebrated in temples of Shiva, in commemoration of miracles performed by him. Observed only by Tamuls [maryauday, matam].

AUVAURAY (ஆவாரை - ávárai, *Tam.*). Same as Tungaid.

AUVOODEIYAUR (ஆவுடையார் - ávudaiyár, *Tam.*). From (ávi, tam. life + udaiyán, tam. possessor). The lingam and yony combined. The emblem of Shiva among the ordinary Sheivites; but not among the Lingayets, who do not admit the Yony [matam].

AUVOOLAPULLY (ఆవులపల్లి - ávulapalli, *Tel.*). From (ávu, tel. cow + palli, tel. village). Range of hills; Cuddapah dist., Madanapully tal.; lat. 13° 28'; long. 78° 27'; from Cuddapah S.S.W. 75 miles; from Madanapully S.W. 8¾ miles. On the plateau above the ghauts. Highest peak, Auvoolapully droog, 3,850 feet, at the point of junction of Cuddapah and North arcot districts with Mysore.

AVA (अव - ava, *San.*). Prefix meaning down or diminution.——*Avacausham* (अवकाश - avakásha, San.). From (kásh, san. to shine). Interspace. A claim. Avacausha moory, from (muri, mal. note) is a deed of partition declaring the several rights and privileges of persons having a joint interest in property. Avacaushy is a rightful owner. See vol. I, 112.——*Avadhy* (अवधि - avadhi, San.). From (dhá, san. to place). Limit. Avadhy krayam is a conditional sale, to become absolute if the purchase-money be not repaid within a stipulated time.——*Avamauham* (अवमाह - avamáha, San.). From (avama, san. inferior + ahan, san. day). An expunged tity.——*Avanataumsham* (अवनतांश - avanatámsha, San.). From (avanata, san. bent down + amsha, san. degree). Altitude. Avanataumsha bhangam is a degree of altitude of any object above the horizon [jyotisham].——*Avarohanam* (अवरोहण - avaróhana, San.). From (ruh, san. to rise). Taking down a temple flag at close of festival [arohanam]. In music the gradual lowering of the pitch.——*Avasarpiny* (अवसर्पिणी - avasarpiní, San.). From (srip, san. to creep). A cycle of time among Jeinas. They divide each yoog into two cycles, Ootsarpiny or age of increase and Avasarpiny or age of decrease. Each cycle is again subdivided into six stages. That of the Ootsarpiny has:—Super bad, bad, bad good, good bad, good, and super-good times. Avasarpiny has the reverse series. Throughout Ootsarpiny men's ordinary age and stature increase, Avasarpiny the reverse. In the best stages there was no light of the sun or the moon, but day and night were formed by the reflection and non-reflection of the calpacam trees. Seem to refer to changes in globe due to precession. The present is the Avasarpiny cycle; the stage in which men now live is the fifth, bad time.——*Avastaunam* (अवस्थान - avast'hána, San.). From (above + st'hána, san. place). Division of the sun's total course southward or northward, viewed in relation to the nacshatrams. There are three:—Eirauvatam or northern, or northern declination; Jauradgavam or southern, or southern declination; and Veishwaunary or central, or a portion taken out of each. The European system does not recognize a Veishwaunary [jyotisham].——*Avastay* (अवस्था - avast'há, *San.*). From (st'há, san. to stand). Condition. The five kinds of Avastays are:—Activity, dream, deep sleep, abstraction of mind, insensibility. The Trimoorties, Bramha, Vishnoo and Shiva are three avastays of Bramh, in the different characters of creator, preserver and destroyer. The avastays are also sufferings and enjoyments from actions of former births. The saptauvastay, the seven stages of the soul from ignorance to knowledge of bramh and consequent felicity are :—anyaunam or ignorance, auvarnam or envelopement, vicshaipam or projection, parotcham or unperceived approximation to emancipation, aparotcham or union with deity, shocanivritty or relief from application and anandam or felicity [matam].——*Avatar* (अवतार - avatára, San.). From (tri, san. to cross). The descent of a deity upon earth and his incarnation as a man or animal. The story of the Ramayanam and Mahabhaurat turns wholly upon the doctrine of incarnations; all the chief dramatis personæ of the poems being impersonations of gods and demigods and celestial spirits. The most frequent references are to the ten avatars of Vishnoo, viz. :—"*a*" Matsyam, or fish avatar, under which form Vishnoo preserved Menoo the ancestor of the present human race during a universal deluge ; —"*b*" Coormam or tortoise avatar ; —"*c*" Varauham or boar avatar ;— "*d*" Narsimhan or man-lion avatar ; —"*e*" Vaumanan or dwarf avatar ;— "*f*" Bhaurgavan or Parshooraman ;— "*g*" Ramchendran or Codandaraman ; —"*h*" Krishna ; this is the most celebrated of Vishnoo's avatars, in which he is supposed to have been completely incarnate ; —"*i*" Booddha. The Bramins considered Booddha to have been a delusive incarnation of Vishnoo assumed by him to induce the Asooras to abandon the Vedas, by which they lost their supremacy ; —"*j*" Calky or white horse yet to come. An account of each will be found in this glossary. The following is a Sanscrit memoria technica for the ten greater Vishnoo avatars :—मत्स्य, कूर्म, वराह, नारसिंह, वामन, राम, राम, राम, कृष्ण कल्कि. Matsya, Coorma, Varauha, Naurasimha, Vaumana, Rama, Rama, Rama, Krishna and Calky. Here the three Ramas indicate Parshooraman, Ramchendran and Balaraman. The following are secondary avatars of Vishnoo :—Capilan ; Duttautreyan ; Dhanwantary, physician of the gods, who rose from the sea of milk when it was churned by the gods and asooras ; Haya greevan ; Mohiny or mauyay, a female form of vishnoo, said to have conversed with shiva, and thus to have produced ayenaur ; Nara narayanan ; Nauradan ; Sanacan ; Sanandanan ; Sanatcomauran ; Sanautanan ; Vrishabhayogy, the first of the twenty-four jeina saints ; Vyausan or veda vyausan ; Yaugapaty. Shiva even is said to have had some avatars. See vol. I (74) [matam].

AVADAVAT (रक्ताङ्ग - raktánga, *San.* ; منيا - muniyá, *Hind.* ; జీనువాయి - jínuváyi, *Tel.*). Title from ahmedabad whence imported into Europe. San. from (rakta, san. red + anga, san. body) ; from color of body. Hind. is properly the female only. Tel. from (jínu, tel. anchor + váyi, tel. mouth). Male birds are :—Hind. (lálmuniyá), meaning red + munia. Tel. (errajínuváyi), meaning red + munia. Hind. also (charchára), meaning talkative one ; (phiddari). Beng. also (sarmunia), meaning spotted munia. Title otherwise Loxia bird. Estreldinæ, fringillidæ, conirostres, insessores, aves [pacshy, 28], of naturalists [jantoo].—"*a*" The Black-headed munia so called in vernaculars is Munia malacca.—"*b*" The Spotted munia as called in Hindostany, or Crane munia as in Teloogoo, is Munia undulata ; alias Amadina punctularia, Lonchura nisoria, Munia lineoventer.—"*c*" The plain brown Munia is Munia malabarica. Alias Lonchura cheet, Loxia bicolor.—"*d*" The common Avadavat or Red waxbill is Estrelda amandava. Alias Amaduvade finch. Male in full summer plumage more or less crimson, darkest on throat, breast, supercilia, cheeks, and upper tail-coverts ; tail black, outer feathers more or less white tipped ; wings brown ; range of minute white feathers beneath eye, wing, flanks and sides of breast with numerous round white spots, and a few smaller specks on the back ; abdominal region infuscated ; lower tail-coverts black ; bill deep red, upper mandible black above ; irides crimson ; feet fleshy. Female olive-brown above with lores blackish, bounded by whitish semi-circle below eye ; few white specks occasionally on back ; rump and upper tail-coverts tinged crimson ; beneath paler brown, abdomen strongly tinged fulvous yellow ; lower tail-coverts dull white. After breeding males assume, by moulting, plumage similar to female. Large numbers taken and caged. Male has small pleasant voice ; also fights with spirit, for which purposes kept by natives.

AVALANCHEY (ಅವಲಾಂಚೆ - avalánche, *Can.*). From (auval, hind. first + anche, can. stage). From the post-house formerly located there.—"*a*" Halting-station, Valley ; Neilgherry district, Coondah division ; lat. 11° 18′ ; long. 76° 37′ ; from Ootacamund S.W. 10 miles. Old tappaul station. Now halting-station on Sisparra ghaut road, in valley of same name. Travellers' bungalow built of wood with zinc roof and in romantic situation. Also a chuttram. Near bungalow on eastern slopes of Coondahs are groups of cairns and burrows.—"*b*" River ; Neilgherry district, Coondah division. Rises on the Coondah range. Flows past village of same name from W. to E. ; winding amongst hills. Eventually flows into Bhawauny.

AVAN (அவன் - avan, *Tam.*). Person ; suffix in compounds at Caunavan, meaning forest + person.

AVANASHY (அவனாசி - avanási, *Tam.* Avanáshi*). From (agha, san. sin + náshi, san. destroyer). Ancient Tamul name (pukkoliyúr), meaning praise + to obtain + town ; also (tiruppukkoliyúr), meaning holy + pookkoliyore, the town so called. Sanscrit name (aghanáshi), meaning sin-destroyer.—"*a*" Deputy Tahsildarry, Coimbatore district. Pay Rs. 70.—"*b*" Village, Place of pilgrimage ; Coimbatore dist., Pulladam tal. ; pop. 1,321 ; acres 457 ; lat. 11° 12′ ; long. 77° 19′ ; from Coimbatore E.N.E. 25 miles ; from Erode W.S.W. 33 miles ; from Madras W.S.W. 240 miles ; from Ootacamund E.S.E. 40 miles ; from Pollachy N.N.E. 41 miles ; from Pulladam N. 14 miles ; from Suttimungalam S. 22 miles. On the trunk road, on an affluent of the Noyil, and 8 miles from Tirpore Railway station. Former head-quarters of talook, and previous to opening of Railway a posting stage on route to Neilgherries. Old Shiva temple. The Nundy is colossal. In the outer porch are two stone images of alligators, each vomitting forth a child. From a deep pit in the village the materials of a subterranean vault consisting of large slabs were removed. Dolmens in the neighbourhood. The bridge over the river is built in the old Hindoo style, as seen at Vijianugger, on stone pillars sunk in the bed with slabs resting on them. Weekly market, and large annual fair on the occasion of the car festival.

AVANIGADDA (అవనిగడ్డ - avanigadda, *Tel.*). From (avani, tel. earth + gaddu, tel. mound).—"*a*" Deputy tahsildarry, Kistna district. Pay Rs. 70.—"*b*" Village ; Kistna dist., Bunder tal. ; pop. 5,840 ; acres 6,020 ; lat. 16° 01′ ; long. 80° 58′ ; from Bezwada S.E. 39 miles ; from Guntoor E.S.E. 37 miles ; from Masulipatam W.S.W. 19 miles ; from Vinoocondah E. 78 miles ; from the sea W. 16 miles. Head-quarters of the talook sub-division. Vishnoo temple with five Chola inscriptions of the twelfth century. Weekly fair on Wednesdays.

AVARAY (ಅವರೆ - avare, *Can.* ; அவரை - avarai, *Tam.*). Dolichos lablab [country bean]. Also in comp. for other genera. Ex., where transl. is of first term :—Canavalia obtusifolia (kózhiyavarai), cock ; Cyamopsis psoralioides (chapparadavare), shed, (kottavarai), cluster, and (shíniyavarai), china ; Glycine javanica (kádavare), jungle ; Mucuna pruriens (púnaiyavarai), cat ; Phaseolus trilobus (shímaiyavarai), foreign ; Psophocarpus tetragonolobus (murukkavarai), curling ; Vigna catiang (válavarai), sword. See gloss. paragraphs.

AVERGAL (அவர்கள் - avargal, *Tam.*). Double plural of (avan, tam. he) ; honorific title used in reference to both sexes [avan, gauroo].

AVERJAH (آوارجا - awárijá, *Hind.* ; ಆವರ್ಜೆ - ávarji, *Can.*). From (áwárá, pers. scattered). Collection of detached notes. A rough day book.

AVISHY (అవిశి - avishi, *Tel.*). Sesbania grandiflora [west indian sesban]. Also in comp. for other genera. Ex., where transl. is of 1st term :—Bauhinia racemosa (adaviavishi), forest ; Cassia alata (símaavishi), foreign ; Linum usitatissimum (nalla-avishi), black. See gloss. paragraphs.

AVVAY (ಅವ್ವ - avva, *Can.* ; అవ్వ - avva, *Tel.* ; அவ்வை - avvai, *Tam.*). From (ambá, san. mother). Mother. Among Jeinas, a female ascetic. Honorifically Avvaiyaur, the celebrated Tamul poetess. Her real name not known. Her mother gave birth to her in a choultry near Warriore. Being exposed there, she was found and brought up by a Paunan or minstrel. She continued unmarried all her life. It is stated that by a panacea she prolonged her existence to 240 years, and then made the Mahaprastauna gamanam or great journey to the Imaus and died there. Her two books of moral aphorisms are called Auttisoody and Condray vendan. In both, the aphorisms are written in the order of the Tamul alphabet ; hence called the Golden alphabets of the Tamulians. Her other works are the Moothooray, Nalvazhy, Calvy oloocam, Asathy covay, Nunnool covay, Naunmany covay, Aroontamizh maulay, Darshanaputt, Nyauna cooral and Panthan antaudy. Of these the first eight are on ethics and religion, the ninth is on metaphysics, and the tenth is a panegyric on a wealthy merchant of the name of Panthan, who resided at Canveryputnam. There is also extant under her name a Nigantoo or dictionary in verse, containing the Tamul synonyms of the materia medica, but it is not in general use. The Hindoo system of moral philosophy involves four questions, viz., What is virtue, and how is it to be exercised ? What is wealth, and how is it to be acquired ? What is pleasure, and how is it to be enjoyed ? What is heavenly bliss, and how is it to be obtained ? Avvay compressed all the four questions and their answers within the compass of the following stanza :—
ஈதலறந் தீவினை விட்டீட்டல் பொருளெஞ்ஞான்றுங்,
காதலிருவர் கருத்தொக்க—ஆதரவு, பட்டதேயின்பம்
பரனை நினைந்திம் மூன்றும், விட்டதே பேரின்பவீடு.
"To give is virtue. That which is acquired without sin, is "wealth. The constant mutual affection of two, whose tastes "agree, is pleasure. To forsake these three, in the contemplation of the supreme being, is heavenly bliss." The following impromptu by her is well known :—நல்லார்களெல்லாரு நல்லாரேதன்மையால், வல்லாராற்கேடுபடாராயின்—நல்லறி, வாண்மக்கட் பற்பலர்க்கேயுண்டாகும் பெண்டிரும், மாண்புக்கெடுக்காவிடின்.—"All women would be "good by nature, if men did not spoil them ; and most men would "have a tolerable stock of sense, if the women did not make fools "of them." The subjoined stanza eulogizing the city of Conjeeveram is attributed to her :—வையகமெல்லாங் கழனியாய் வையகத்துட்—செய்யகமே நாற்றிசையின் றேயங்கள்—

செய்யகத்துள், வான்கரும்பேதொண்டை வளநாடு வான்கரும்பின், சாறே யந்நாட்டிற்றலையூர்கள் சாறட்ட, கட்டியேகச்சிப்புறமெல்லாம் கட்டியுட், டாணெற்றமான் சருக்கரைமாமணியே யாணெற்றுள் கச்சியகம்—"The "whole earth may be compared to an expanse of wet land; the "several countries of the earth, marked by their boundaries on "the four sides, are cultivated fields within it; Tondeivalanaud "is a lofty sugar-cane in one of these fields; the chief towns of "this country are the crude juice of this sugar-cane; Conjee-"veram and its vicinity are like a cake of unrefined sugar "obtained by boiling this juice; and a large concretion of "refined sugar in the midst of this cake represents the interior "of Canchy where the bull-borne deity resides." There is a Tamul proverb:—ஔவை சொல்லுக்கு அச்சம் இல்லை—"No fear about Avvay's sayings" [bhaushay].

AYACUT (ಆಯಕಟ್ಟು, - áyakattu, *Can.*; ആയക്കെട്ട - áyakkettu, *Mal.*; ஆயக்கட்டு - áyakkattu, *Tam.*). From (áyam, tam. extension + kattu, tam. to frame). Regulation, settlement. Measurement of lands, determining the boundaries of a village. Hence the whole land belonging to a village. The Nunjah ayacut is the wet land belonging to a village. The ayacut of a tank is the land irrigable by that tank. See vol. I, 112.

AYAH (ஆயாள் - áyál, *Tam.*). From Portuguese aio, tutor; aia, governess. A nurse for children, or a lady's maid.

AYAK (ആഴക്ക് - ázhakku, *Mal.*). From (ara, mal. half + uzhakku, mal. a measure). Mal. form of Olluck. A measure of capacity. 5 chavadoos = 1 ayak; 2 ayaks = 1 oyak [alavay, 3d]. Approximate actual value, 1 ayak = 3½ c. inches. Varies with the Yidangazhy.

AYAN (عين - aín, *Hind.*; ಐನ - aina, *Can.*; அயன் - ayan, *Tam.*). From Arabic. Actual. Also ordinary as distinguished from extra. Also used for circar lands as distinguished from inam or zemindarry. Also for the standard assessment of Government revenue. Also for amauny lands kept in hands of Government.

AYANAM (अयन - ayana, *San.*). From (ay, san. to go). A course. Sun's progress from one solstice to another. Oottarauyanam, or northward progress, from Tye [mausam] or january to end of Auny or june. Dacshinauyanam, or southward progress, from Audy [mausam] or july to end of Margaly or december. Two Ayanams compose a year [caulam]. The southward Ayanam is a night and the northward a day light of the gods. Twelve thousand divine years, each composed of such days constitute a maha yoog. In Oottarauyanam all Hindoos must devote themselves to study of Vedas; marriages and auspicious rites are performed; all acts done have a virtuous effect. In Dacshinauyanam everything done, though virtuous in itself, is unprofitable in effects; sin abounds. Ayanam is used loosely for solstitial and equinoctial points, when terms have contradictory appearance; see below. Also for the progress of sun through either southern or northern signs; perhaps original meaning. Distinguish from Avastaunam.——*Ayana caulam* (अयनकाल - ayanakála, San.). From (kála, san. time). The time from one equinox to the ensuing. Also the time of commencement of the tropical year or month; called in Tamul Ayana pirapp.——*Ayanaumsham* (अयनांश - ayanámsha, San.). From (amsha, san. degree). The arc between the sun's vernal equinoctial point, and the beginning of the fixed and artificial solar sidereal zodiac; being one of the most important elements in the whole of Hindoo astronomy, as it refers the sidereal to the tropical zodiac. For finding the Ayanaumsham at any particular time it need only be remembered that the fixed and movable solar zodiac are supposed to have been coincident at the expiration of the 3600th year of the Caly yoog; and that the equinoctial points are assumed by the Hindoos to have a retrograde motion of 54″ in a sidereal year. The Soorya siddhauntam says:—the Ayanaumsham moves eastward thirty times twenty in each Maha yoog. By that number or 600 multiply the Ahargaṇam, and divide the product by the number of seven days in a yoog, and of the quotient take the bhoojam or supplement to or excess over 180°, which multiply by 3, and divide the product by 10; the quotient is the Ayanaumsham [craunty pauta gaty, rishy]. At one time astronomers conceived the Ayanaumsham to librate in an arc of 27° of the ecliptic on each side of ♈, at another to revolve in an epicycle about the same point as a centre, at another to move round the platonic cycle in a period of 24,000 years.——*Dacshinauyanam* (दक्षिणायन - dakshináyana, San.). From (dakshina, san. south). Northern [ayanam] solstice.——*Maishauyanam* (मेषायन - mésháyana, San.). From (mésha, san. aries). Vernal equinox.——*Oottarauyanam* (उत्तरायण - uttaráyana, San.). From (uttara, san. north). Southern [ayanam] solstice.——*Toolauyanam* (तुलायन - tuláyana, San.). From (tula, san. libra). Autumnal equinox [jyotisham].

AYANDAH (آینده - áindah, *Hind.*). From (ámadan, pers. to come). Future.

AYAPPANAY (అయపని - ayapani, *Tel.*; அயப்பனை - ayappanai, *Tam.*). Tel. and Tam. naturalized terms, supposed erroneously to be from (ayam, tam, oleander shrub, nerium odorum, soland + panai, tam. palm). Botanically Eupatorium ayapana, vent., compositæ [vricsham, 74]. Specific term is S. american. A small shrub; branchlets reddish; leaves opposite, lanceolate; flowers yellow. The leaves have peculiar fragrant odour, and when first tasted slightly irritate tongue, but afterwards astringent quality is felt. When fresh bruised, applied to cleansing of foul ulcers; whole plant is aromatic, and good stimulant, tonic, and diaphoretic; a decoction of leaves makes good fomentation; quoted in pharm., but non-officinal. Agrimony hemp; otherwise Dutch agrimony, Hemp weed, Holy rope, Water agrimony, Water hemp; is from allied Eupatorium cannabinum, linn., a tall, erect plant with downy leaves and terminal crowded head of dull purple flowers, inhabiting damp, watery places. Another species is Polyanthum.

AYE (അഴി - azhi, *Mal.*). From (azhi, tam. to perish); place where the water is lost in the sea; river-mouth. Suffix in place names; as Maudye, meaning shallow + river-mouth.

AYE (ಆಯಿ - áyi, *Can.*; ஆயி - áyi, *Tam.*). Mother; suffix in female proper names among the lower castes as Mauriyaye the small-pox deity + mother. Chinnaye meaning little + mother, Ponnaye meaning gold + mother, and Shellaye meaning favorite + mother, are terms of familiar address towards young children of both sexes [peyar].

AYEEN (آئین - áín, *Hind.*). Statute. By secular authority, in distinction to those of the koran or sacred tradition.——*Ayeen e acbaree* (آئین اکبری - áíniakbarí, Hind.). From (akbarí, ar. belonging to akbar). A statistical and political account of the Moghul empire drawn up during Acbar's reign by his minister Abool fazl.

AYEESHA (عایشه - áíshah, *Hind.*). From (ásha, ar. live). Voluptuous. Name of daughter of Aboo bakr, and prophet's wife. Common female alam [ism].

AYEN (ஐயன் - aiyan, *Tam.*). From (ai, tam. lord + an, tam. pers. termination). Village deity. The male of Amman. Ayenaur is the honorific form and the one generally used. This is the only male deity among the Graumadevatays. When incorporated into the Hindoo system, he is also named Harihara pootran, or son of Shiva by Vishnoo as Mohiny. Represented in arts by human form in sitting posture, with red skin, crown on head, and pearls in his locks. On forehead he wears the mark of the Sheivas, made with sacred ashes of burnt cowdung. On his ears and neck he has pearls. On breast a sort of ribbon. His arms, hands, feet, &c., are covered with jewels and ornaments. In his right hand he holds a sceptre, as king among demons. Round body and left leg a belt, called Bauhoo puttay, which is also used by sages when they sit. On his shoulders are garlands. The upper part of his body is uncovered. Ayenaur's two wives, Pooranay and Poodcalay, are represented as having natural bodies of a yellow color, with crowns on their heads, holding flowers in their hands. Pooranay wears on her forehead the mark of Custoory, and Poodcalay that of Shiva made with sacred ashes. They sit to the right and left of Ayenaur. Pagodas of Ayenaur are very numerous, one in almost every village. They are small, and stand usually at some distance W. of village in a grove. At their entrance stand two door-keepers, called Moonnadiyaur or head-servants, who have crowns on their heads, thick sticks in their hands, and lions' teeth in their mouths. In the first room stand seven small figures of stone, called Saptamautahs, or seven matrons, who are under a curse. Their names are:—Baula shacty or young shacty; Bhagavaty or goddess; Bhoovana shacty or world-Shacty; Cauttairy or demoness; Mooyalcarashoory or the heroine of Shiva with the hare in his hand; Racta chamoondy or blood-Chamoondy; Tricarashoory or the three-handed demoness. These names differ from the Aryan saptamautahs. In same room are also two images of Vigneshwaran. All these are occasionally worshipped with offerings. In inner room is Ayenaur with his two wives, and round them stand seven figures of stone, representing virgins, which however are not worshipped. In front of the pagoda stands an altar of stone for living sacrifices; and by the side of it is frequently a vault with figures of wood, representing elephants, horses, birds, demons, &c., which are used at festivals as conveyances for Ayenaur and his wives. Close by the pagoda, on both sides of it, stand figures of clay, among which are Ayenaur's military commanders, called Palyacaurar. There are also horses on which he is supposed to ride about the fields, keeping off demons. These figures are presents to the god from people who call on him in sickness and recover, or from women who desire offspring. Ayenaur is worshipped daily, two or three times, with offerings and incense. For this a bramin is sometimes engaged. For the living sacrifices of pigs, goats, cocks, &c., with libations of strong drink, a Shoodra, usually a Pundauram or a Sheiva devotee, is engaged. After the harvest, is Ayenaur tirnaul, holy day of Ayenaur. It lasts seven or nine days, during which images of Ayenaur and wives are carried in the streets, morning and evening, on conveyances mentioned above. On last day, they are dragged on a car. At this festival, every inhabitant is bound to make an offering to the god according to his ability. There are no books regarding Ayenaur, but stories are related about him in the Sanscrit pooraunams, and forms of prayer have been made in his name. Of his various titles the following may be mentioned:—Arattay cauppone or the preserver of virtue; Aryan or priest; Ayyan or lord; Hariharan or Shiva-Vishnoo; Harihara pootrau son of Shiva-Vishnoo; Nullashevagan or the good warrior; Poodcalay manaulan or Poodcalay's husband; Pooncadal varnan or the sea colored; Poornaykizhavan or Pooranay's husband; Poorattavan or he who is by the side as watchman; Shauttan or teacher; Tirmoodishevagan or the warrior with the sacred crown; Vellaiyanneiyoorty or the rider on a white elephant; Yogy or ascetic, &c. There is a proverb:—ஐயனார் கோவில் செங்கல் அத்தனையும் தெய்வம்—"The bricks of Ayenaur's temple are so "many gods." Ayenaur's worship may be said to be chiefly south of the Palaur. Ayyappan, the hunting god of the Arayan tribe of the west coast and of the Coorgs, is the same deity. Tigers are there regarded as his dogs.——*Ayenaur tirnaul* (ஐயனார்த்திருநாள் - aiyyanárttirunál, Tam.). Holy day of Ayenaur [pundigay, 6 c]. Village movable festival celebrated for several days after the harvest in January [maryauday, matam].

AYICOTTAH (അഴിക്കോട്ട - azhikkótta, *Mal.*). From (azhi, mal. river mouth + kótta, mal. fort); on the Northern branch of the Periyaur. Town; Cochin state, Cranganore tal.; pop. 3,641; lat. 10° 10′; long. 76° 14′; from Ernacolum N.N.W. 15 miles; from Cranganore S.W. 2½ miles; from sea E. 1 mile. At N. extremity of southern Cranganore. According to tradition, St. Thomas landed here. In latter part of eighteenth century held by Dutch. During war with Tippoo sultan in 1790, garrisoned by Company. The mouth of the Chaulacoody and of one branch of the Alwye river is called Ayicottah. This is always navigable.

AYIVOO (അഴിവു - azhivu, *Mal.*). Expense.——*Ayishilavoo* (അഴിശിലവു - azhishilavu, Mal.). From (shilavu, mal. expense). The expense of preparing gardens allowed for in cases of Cooyicaunom [q. v.] lease. It bears the proportion of 20 per cent. to the valuation of trees settled when making the Cooyicaunom agreement. This expense being added to the value of the trees, the proprietor must if he redeems pay for both; or else the interest of the two sums, according to the usual rate of the place, is included in the Pramaunam or bond and deducted from the pauttom or Jenmy's rent. See vol. I, 112.——*Ayivoo cooyicaunom* (അഴിവുകുഴിക്കാണം - azhivukuzhikkánam, Mal.). From (kuzhi, mal. pit + kánam, mal. lease). By Malabar inversion for pit expense lease [cooyicaunom].

AYIYAM (അഴിയം - azhiyam, *Mal.*). Low land.——*Ayiyapaudam* (അഴിയപാടം - azhiyapátam, Mal.). From (pátam, mal. field). The lowest lying rice lands.

AYOOB (ایوب - aiyúb, *Hind.*). From Arabic. Job. Common alam [ism].

AYYAN (ಅಯ್ಯ - ayya, *Can.*; అయ్య - ayya, *Tel.*; അയ്യൻ - ayyan, *Mal.*; ஐயன் - aiyyan, *Tam.*). Father; master; elder brother. Tamul plural is Ayyar, always taken as title by Smarta bramins. Tamul honorific plural is Ayyangar, generally written Iyengar, always taken by Veishnavites. Cf. with these two the Mahratta row [q.v.]. Common suffix in 2nd or pers. names; as Ramayyan. This in Tamul must mean a Bramin; but not necessarily so in other languages. Ayenaur is the male village deity [ayen].——*Ayyaloo* (అయ్యలు - ayyalu, Tel.). Tel. plural of Ayyan. Hindoo 2nd or pers. name [peyar].——*Ayyam pidaury* (ஐயம்பிடாரி - aiyambidári, Tam.). From (ayyai, tam. mistress + pidári, tam. the village deity, so called). There is a Tamul proverb:—ஆட்டுக்கும் மாட்டுக்கும் இரண்டு கொம்பு, ஐயம்பிடாரிக்கு மூன்றுகொம்பு—"Sheep and "oxen have two horns, an Ayyam pidaury has three;" from the three horns sounded in her processions [pidaury].——*Ayyanavar* (ಅಯ್ಯನವರು - ayyanavaru, Can.). From (ayya, can. father). Lingayet priest.——*Ayyappa* (ಅಯ್ಯಪ್ಪ - ayyappa, Can.). From (appa, can. father). Hindoo 2nd or pers. name [peyar].——*Ayyasawmy* (அய்யாசாமி - ayyásámi, Tam.). From (svámi, san. lord). Hindoo 2nd or pers. name [peyar].——*Ayyatturay* (அய்யாத்துரை - ayyátturai, Tam.). From (turai, tam. ruler). Hindoo 2nd or pers. name [peyar].——*Ayyavayyan* (அய்யாவய்யன் - ayyávayyan, Tam.). Reduplication of Ayyan. Very common. Hindoo 2nd or pers. name [peyar].——*Ayyay* (ஐயை - aiyai, Tam.). Feminine of (ayyan). Bhadracauly or Shiva's inferior wife [jauty, matam].

AZ (اض - اظ - از - اذ - az, *Ar.*). Al [q.v.] before z in Arabic single terms, as az zikr, az zeinab, az zarb, az zohr.

AZADIRACHT (آزاد درخت - ázáddarakht, *Pers.*). From (ázád, pers. free + darakht, pers. tree). Same as Large neem.

AZAM (اعظم - azam, *Hind.*). From (azima, ar. to be great). Means highest. Alam; as Azam ally, double alám. Also component part of lacab; as Azam oon nissa, the highest woman. Literary designation of the last Nawaub of the Carnatic, Ghoolaum mahomed ghouse khan [ism].——*Azam jah bahaudur* (اعظم جاه بهادر - azamjáhbahádur, Hind.). From (jáh, pers. dignity + bahádur, pers. title). Last Nawaub of the Carnatic but one, Azeem jah being regent during Mahomed ghouse khan's minority. A.D. 1819–1825. See vol. I, 43.

AZAUN (اذان - azán, *Hind.*). From (izn, ar. permission). The summons to prayer proclaimed by the Mooazzin in mosques from the side of the building. The Mooazzin stands with his face towards Mecca with the points of his forefingers in his ears and recites the prescribed formula. The call is:—"God is "great; I bear witness there is no God but one God; I bear "witness that Mahomet is His prophet; come to pray; come to "salvation; God is great; there is no God but one." In the morning is added:—"prayer is better than sleep."

AZEEM (عظيم - azím, *Hind.*). From (azima, ar. to be great). Esteemed great. Epithet of god [allah]. Alam; as Azeem jah, alam + alaumat. Part of lacab; as Azeem ood dowlah, high in the realm.——*Azeem jah* (عظيم جاه - azímjáh, Hind.). From (jáh, pers. dignity). Regent of the last Nawaub of the Carnatic during his minority, which was 1819–1825, and after his death and the lapse of the line, the first Prince of Arcot, viz., 1867–1874. He received an annual allowance of three lakhs with a salute of fifteen guns. A new residence on the site of the old Royapettah police court was fitted up for him; but he did not leave his ancestral palace in Triplicane till his death in 1874. See vol. I, 45.——*Azeem ood dowla* (عظيم الدولہ - azímuddaulah, Hind.). From (daulah, ar. empire). Last Nawaub of the Carnatic but two. Nephew of the Nawaub who preceded him. The British placed him on the musnud in lieu of the son Hoossain ally. Delivered over the civil and military government of the Carnatic to the English by the Treaty of 1801. Died in 1819. See vol. I, 45.

AZEEZ (عزيز - azíz, *Hind.*). from (azza, ar. to be strong). Mighty. Attribute of God [allah]. Special title of ruler of Egypt. Feminine is Azeeza. Alam; as Azeez khan, alam + alaumat. Also component part of lacab; as Azeez ool moolk, dear to the state [ism].

AZHAGOO (அழகு - azhagu, *Tam.*). Beauty. The ten beauties to be courted by authors are according to Nunnool:—"*a*" brevity or conciseness; —"*b*" perspicuity or comprehensiveness; —"*c*" agreeableness; —"*d*" use of appropriate or reputable words; —"*e*" harmony or rhythm; —"*f*" profundity of thought; —"*g*" regularity of method; —"*h*" conformity with the opinions of the good and great so as not to puzzle the world; —"*i*" sterling worthiness of subject-matter; —"*j*" appropriate examples and illustrations.

AZHAURAM (ஆழாரம் - ázháram, *Tam.*). From (ázhi, tam. circle + aram, tam. cellar). Stone circle. The native cromlech. Similar to ancient stone circles of British. Both are circular and made of unhewn stones, and within each cinerary urns and bones are often found. The South indian circles however are comparatively small, rarely exceeding 8 or 10 feet in diameter, and the walls are complete all round and are built up with several stones, one over the other; while the British are much larger, the walls being composed of single stones, and avenues of stones generally connecting the circles together [phin].

AZMAYISH (آزمايش - ázmáish, *Hind.*). From (ázmúdan, pers. to try). Trial. Estimate of the crop, while standing made by subordinate revenue officer. Azmayish tareek is on probation.

B

B (ब - ba, *San.*; ب - be, *Hind.*). San. symbolic of Varoonan. Hind. numerically symbol for two; Monday as the second day of the week, and the constellation Gemini; also abbreviated for the seventh month Rajab.

BA (با - bá, *Hind.*). With.——*Bamojib* (بموجب - bamújib, Hind.). From (above + mújib, ar. reason). According to.——*Baushara* (باشرع - báshara, Hind.). From (above + shara, ar. law). Means according to the law. Classes of fakeers who observe koran; as distinguished from the beshara, without the law. Baushara marry and have fixed homes.

BABA (بابا - bábá, *Hind.*). From Turkish. A father. Term of affection to old persons and children; term of respect equivalent to Sir; head of an order of monks so called.——*Bababooden* (بابابڈن - bábábudan, Hind.; ಬಾಬಾಬುಡ್ಡನಗಿರಿ - bábábudnagiri, Can.; bababudan, Mys. Gov.). Can. also (chandradróna), meaning moon + valley. Range in the north of the Chicmagalore talook, Cuddore district, Mysore, between 13° 23′ and 13° 35′ N. lat.; 75° 37′ and 75° 51′ E. long. Derives its present name from a Mahomedan ascetic who planted there coffee seeds obtained at Mocha and introduced article to India. He lies buried in a cave in the hills.

BABOO (بابو - bábú, *Hind.*). From (vapra, san. father). Master. Hindoo title equivalent to Mr. or Esquire; not common here [peyar]. In Anglo-indian usage, a clerk who knows English, more particularly a Bengalee bramin. Forms also an alam; as Baboo khan, alam + alaumat [ism].

BABOOL (वर्वर - varvara, *San.* ; बाभूळ - bábhúla, *Mahr.* ; शामी - shamí, *Conc.* ; امغیلان - ummighílán, *Ar.* ; مغیلان - mughílán, *Pers.* ; ببول - babúl, *Hind.* ; کالی کیکر - kálíkikar, *Dec.* ; ಕರಿಜಾಲಿ - karijáli, *Can.* ; నల్లతుమ్మ - nallatumma, *Tel.* ; കരുവേലകം - karuvélakam, *Mal.* ; கருவேல் - karuvél, *Tam.*). Title from hindostany. San. from (vri, san. to cover); from thorny branches used as a dry fence. Mahr. from sanscrit. Conc. from (sham, san. to sacrifice); used in sacrifices as retaining heat. Ar. from (umm, ar. mother + ghílán, ar. devil); mother of devils, haunted by devils. Hind. from sanscrit. Dec. from (kálí, hind. black + kíkar, hind. acacia). Can. from (kari, can. black + jáli, can. acacia). Tel. from (nalla, tel. black + tumma, tel. acacia). Mal. from (karu, mal. black + vélakam, mal. acacia). Tam. from (karumai, tam. blackness + vél, tam. acacia). San. also (krishnakhadira), meaning black acacia catechu; (kálavarvara), meaning black babool; (yugaláksha), meaning pair + pivot, from thorns rising in pairs. Greek κόμμι; whence through the Latin, gum. Title otherwise Black acacia, Indian gum arabic tree, Shittim-tree of bible, Sunt-wood tree. Botanically Acacia [cantalam] arabica, willd., leguminosæ [vricsham, 48]. Alias Acacia nilotica, vera; Mimosa arâbica. Gum is Gummi arabicum, Gummi acaciæ of chemists. Tree, 30–40 feet, armed with stipulary thorns; leaves bipinnated; pinnæ about five pair; leaflets forty-five to twenty pair, glabrous; peduncles aggregated, axillary or forming a raceme by the abortion of the leaves; heads of flowers globose; stamens distinct; legumes stalked, thickish, contracted on both sutures between the seeds; flowers small, bright yellow, fragrant like violets; flowers may to october; of rapid growth, and thriving in black soil and barren wastes that would hardly produce any other tree; common everywhere except malabar coast; requires no water. Gum which exudes from bark is in form of irregular and broken tears, agglutinated in masses, each tear about half an inch in size and brown or red to light straw color; bark is in large thick pieces, coarsely fibrous, of a deep mahogany color, and astringent bitterish taste. Flower is religious. Tender leaves beaten into a pulp are given medicinally as an astringent; gum, when pure a substitute for real gum arabic, produce of acacia senegal, willd.; but dark and dirty tears are often mixed, and sometimes insoluble from containing bassorin; the bark in decoction is powerful astringent; fine powder of bark mixed with gingelly oil, external application in cancerous affections, used for british oak bark; mentioned in pharm. but non-officinal. Mixed with seeds of sesamum left after oil is expressed, gum is article of food with natives; seeds and pods of great value in hot season as food for flocks when grass is scarce. Bark is used for tanning, gives a buff tinge to the leather; pods yield a brown or black dye, with alum as a mordant; a substitute for more expensive dye-stuffs, and giving shades of drab; salts of iron deepen the black dye; decoction of bark or pods makes a soap; bark is added to arrack [q.v.] during manufacture to modify its quality; thin branches are tooth brushes, ends being beaten to make them soft; bark and seeds burnt and powdered are a tooth-powder; bark of slender twigs yields coarse fibre; young thorny twigs used for dry fences. The wood is small and often crooked, but very hard and tough, and makes ploughshares, naves of wheels, well curbs, sugar and oil presses, rice pounders, agricultural implements, tool handles, ship-building materials, &c., for which a bent wood is required; sapwood large, whitish; heart-wood pinkish white, turning reddish-brown on exposure, hard, mottled with dark streaks; it consists of darker and lighter colored bands of an equal width; very durable if well seasoned; also much used as firewood and to make charcoal. There is a Tamul proverb:—கருவேலமரத்திற்கு நிழலில்லை, கல்யாணத்துக்கு முறையில்லை—"The babool casts no shade, smiths observe no relation-" ship in marrying."——*Ashy babool* (वीरवृक्ष - víravriksha, San.; ورتولی - vartulí, Hind.; ಎಡತರಿ - edatari, Can.; వెలుతురు - velnturu, Tel.; අඳර - andara, Singh.; விடத்தேர் - vidattér, Tam.). Title from leaf like babool and of an ash gray color. San. from (víra, san. strong + vriksha, san. tree); from hard wood. Can. from (edatara, can. middling); of middling size as a shrubby tree. Tam. from (vidam, tam. inflammation + tér, tam. to remove); as cure in ophthalmia. Can. also (vadavinagida). Tam. also (vidattalai) by corruption; (mávilingai), meaning large + wood-apple tree, cratæva religiosa, forst., applied here from similar wood [nirvala, weaver's beam]. Title otherwise Sore eye plant. Botanically Dichrostachys cinerea, w. and a., leguminosæ [vricsham, 48]. Alias Acacia cinerea, dalea; Desmanthus cinereus; Mimosa cinerea. Shrub, 6–7 feet; thorns solitary; calyx five-toothed; pinnæ eight to ten pair; leaflets ciliated, thirteen to fifteen pair; petioles pubescent; spikes axillary, usually solitary, cylindric, drooping, rather shorter than the leaves; corolla five-cleft, petals scarcely cohering by their margins; flowers white or rose colored at the bottom, and yellow at top; legumes thick, curved; joints one-seeded. Leaves in form resembling babool, but of an ashy gray color; pink and yellow in flower, is caused by the change in color of the stamens as the flowers increase in age; flowers very showy; very common plant in dry arid soils in the plains and lower hills throughout presidency. The young shoots are bruised and applied in ophthalmia. Heart-wood red, extremely hard; wood too small to be of much use, makes tent pegs. No other common species here.——*Deccany babool* (دکھنی ببول - dakhanibabúl, Hind.). Same as Corcapilly.——*White babool* (سفید ببول - sufedbabúl, Hind.). From white bark. Velvail.

BABOON (میمون - maimún, *Ar.* and *Pers.*). Title from arabic through Italian. Ar. from (yumn, ar. auspiciousness). Equivalent to sub-family Cercopithecinæ, cercopithecidæ, quadrumana, mammalia [sastanam, 1], of naturalists [jantoo]. Otherwise dog-headed monkeys. See Bandar for the genera. See Lungoor for semnopithecinæ.

BABOONA (بابونج - bábúnaj, *Ar.* ; بابونه - bábúnah, *Pers.*, *Hind.* and *Dec.* ; ಶೀಮೆಶ್ಯಾಮಂತಿಗೆ - shímeshyámantige, *Can.* ; సీమశామంతి - símashámanti, *Tel.* ; ശീമജെവന്തി - shímajevanti, *Mal.* ; சீமைச்சாமந்தி - shímaiççámandi, *Tam.*). Pers. from (bábúnah, pers. village in asiatic turkey). Can. from (shíme, can. european + shyámantige, can. chrysanthemum indicum, linn.). Pers. also (babúnahigáu), meaning cow chamomile; (gâuchashm), meaning cows' eye. Greek παρθένιον. Title otherwise Camowyne, Chamomile, Cow eye chamomile, Europe shaumanty. Botanically Anthemis nobilis, linn., compositæ [vricsham, 74]. Brought to india from persia; cultivated in gardens of wealthy mahomedans. Flowers in infusion are simple bitter tonic; oil is stimulant and antispasmodic; gives to pharm. dried flower-heads, single or double, anthemidis flores, active principles, a volatile oil, and a bitter extractive; stimulant tonic and carminative; officinal.——*Country baboona* (சாமந்தி - shámandi, Tam.). Title otherwise Dog chamomile, German chamomile, Gowan, Horse chamomile, Wild chamomile. Botanically Matricaria chamomilla, linn., compositæ [vricsham, 74]. Substitute for European chamomile. No other species here.

BACANORE (വക്കനൂർ - vakkanúr, *Mal.*). Another name for Barcore.

BACHNAUG (वत्सनाभ - vatsanábha, *San.* ; बचनाग - bachanága, *Mahr.* ; بیش - bísh, *Ar.* ; بیشناگ - bíshnág, *Pers.* ; بچھناگ - bachhnág, *Hind.* and *Dec.* ; ವಸನಾಭಿ - vasanábhi, *Can.* ; ವತ್ಸನಾಬಿ - vatsanábi, *Too.* ; వసనాభి - vasanábhi, *Tel.* ; വത്സനാഭി - vatsanábhi, *Mal.* ; වත්සනාභ - vatsanábha, *Singh.* ; வசநாவி - vasanávi, *Tam.*). Title from hindostany. San. from (vatsa, san. calf + nábhi, san. destroyer); from poisonous properties. Ar. from (visha, san. poison). Pers. and hind. from sanscrit. Tel., &c., from sanscrit. San. also (visha), meaning poison; (nábhi), meaning destroyer. Hind. also (bis), meaning poison; (zahar), meaning poison; (singiyá), meaning horny; (singiyábis), meaning horny poison, from appearance of root; (teliyábis), meaning greased poison; (mitházahar), meaning sweet poison; (mahur), meaning sweet. Dec. also (bach). Tam. also (paççainávi), by corr.; (návi), corr. from (nábhi, san.). Title otherwise Butch, Indian aconite, Mahoor, Poison-root. Botanically Aconitum [bish] ferox, wall., ranunculaceæ [vricsham, 1]. Stem erect, 2–3 feet, slightly downy above; tubers 2–3 blackish, white inside; branches villous; leaves roundish-cordate, deeply five-parted; lobes pinnatifid, cuneate at the base, hairy on the brim beneath; racemes terminal, downy; flowers large, deep blue, hoary; helmet gibbous, semi-circular, slightly acuminated in front; cucullate petals slightly incurved. Grows in himalayas. Simple tuberous roots of an elongated conical form, like a carrot, 3 to 4 inches long and ¾ to 1¾ inches in greatest diameter; blackish brown; brittle, break with a resinous fracture, and readily reduced to a coarse powder; in this state destitute of smell, slightly bitter to the taste, the tongue being subsequently benumbed wherever touched on; somewhat resemble roots of sweet-scented flag [vashamboo]; sometimes steeped in cow's urine to preserve them from insects, and then unfit for use in medicine; found in every large bazaar. Roots much used medicinally as external application, being formed into a paste and spread upon the skin; internally, chiefly used in treatment of chronic intermittent fevers; used in large doses along with stimulants in snake-bite and scorpion sting; sedative, anodyne, and antiphlogistic; natives employ it in leprosy; for british aconitum napellus, linn.; gives to pharm. dried root, aconiti ferocis radix, active principle aconitia, officinal; much more potent than the aconite root of europe [wolf-strangler]. Used in hilly districts to poison arrows for wild beasts; has been used in warfare to poison wells and tanks. There are two well-known varieties:—The first is in Tamul vennauvy or white bachnaug being pale internally, in Hindostany meetah zahara or sweet poison. The other is in Tamul carnauvy or dark bachnaug being dark brown internally, in Hindostany singyah bish as looking like small horn of a deer or goat, also called in Hindostany teliyah bish from being generally greased to keep it from air. The root of Methonica superba, lam. [wild bachnaug] is common fraudulent substitute; no poison in it. For non-poisonous aconites see Atees and Jadwaur; for european aconite see Wolf-strangler.——*Wild bachnaug* (अग्निशिखा - agnishikhá, San.; कळलावी - kalalávi, Mahr.; वागानांक्त - vágánánkta, Conc.; کریاری - kariyárí, Hind.; ناٹ کا بچھناگ - nátkábachhnág, Dec.; ಕರಡಿಕನ್ನಿನಗಡ್ಡೆ - karadikanninagadde, Can.; ಬಲಿಪಪು - balipapú, Too.; అడవినాభి - adavinábhi, Tel.; മേത്തോന്നി - méttónni, Mal.; നിയാഗലാ - niyágalá,

Singh.; கார்த்திகை - kárttigai, Tam.). Title from use of root. San. from (agni, san. fire + shikhá, san. flame); from crimson flowers [bastard saffron, saffron, white chitramoolam]. Dec. from (nát, hind. country + bachnág, hind. aconite, aconitum ferox, wall.). Can. from (karadi, can. bear + kannu, can. eye + gadde, can. root). Tel. from (adavi, tel. forest + nábhi, san. aconite). Mal. from (mél, mal. excellent + tóuri, tam. red lily). Tam. from (kárttika, san. the month); november flower plant. San. also (lángalikí), meaning plough-like, from root; (hari-priyá), meaning dear to hary; (ahijihvá), meaning serpent's tongue; (uttamáraní), meaning superior fire; (amritá), meaning imperishable [chebulic myrobalan, emblic myrobalan, goolancha]; (garbhaghátiní), meaning causing abortion. Conc. also (shivashakti), meaning shiva + power. Can. also (shivashakti), meaning shiva + power; (shivaraktiballi), meaning shiva + red + creeper. Tel. also (pottidumpa), meaning short + root; (kalapagadda), meaning plough + root. Mal. also (kántal), meaning burning. Tam. also (akkiniççilam), meaning fire + water; (talaiççuruli), meaning head + to curl, from twisted petals; (kaunóvuppúndu), meainng eye disease + small plant; (návi), meaning aconite; (kalappaikkizhangu), meaning plough root; from the bend of the root suggesting the plough. Title otherwise Caurtigay plant, Country aconite, Flame flower, Hary's plant, Malabar glory lily, November flower plant, Plough root, Serpent's tongue, Superb lily. Botanically Methonica superba, lam., liliaceæ [vricsham, 136]. Generic name from malayalam. Alias Gloriosa superba. Slender climbing plant, with small narrow leaves and flowers of long, narrow, inverted, twisted petals, one half deep crimson and one half primrose color on first opening, but afterwards becoming altogether crimson; grows in dry jungles. The root is tuberous, cylindrical, bent at a right angle near one end, knotty at the angle, and occasionally much pointed at both ends; length from 3 to 5 inches; about size of a finger or thumb, sometimes larger when the plant grows in the sandy and wet soil; knot bears a mark of the stém on the upper surface, and gives an attachment to many thin rootlets by the lower; the root is covered with a thin, loose, and wrinkled epidermis, which is of brownish-grey or pale brown color, and the surface underneath the latter is brown or dark-brown if it is well dried root; this substance internally is of white color; its taste is bitter not acrid, and it is farinaceous in structure. The plant is religious. Veidyans apply the root in paste to the hands and feet of women in difficult parturition; mixed with honey it is given in gonorrhœa; it is not poisonous in twelve-grain doses, but on the contrary is alterative, tonic and antiperiodic; quoted in pharm., non-officinal; considered to possess nearly the same medicinal properties as the root of Aconitum ferox, wall., hence substituted for, or adulterated with, the true root. A salt is obtained from the root by repeated washing and grinding, throwing away the liquor, and washing the residuum carefully; the white powder thus obtained is bitter to the taste. No other common species here.

BACKDORE (باگ دور - bágdor, *Hind.*). Bridle-cord, rein.

BACKWATER (కయ్యి - kayyi, *Tel.*; காயல் - káyal, *Tam.*). Stretch of salt water close to the coast and separated from the sea by sand spits. Found on both coasts [cauyal].——*Back water tree* (నీటితుమికి - nítitumiki, Tel.). Tel. means water diospyros. Same as Gaub.

BADA (ಬಡ - bada, *Can.*). North.——*Badaga* (ಬಡಗ - badaga, Càn.). Literally northmen [vadooga]. Tribal-title; personal forms, Badaga, sing., Badagas, pl. Often called by the English Burghers.—"*a*" The most numerous, wealthy, and civilized of natives of Neilgherries. Speak an old Canarese dialect. Originally from North coimbatore and South mysore, then part of Congoo kingdom. Lingayet wodeyas are the most recent. They are almost all Sheiveites, while Mysore rajahs were converted to Veishnavite faith some centuries back.—"*b*" They are an active race, of moderate stature, with the usual Dravidian features, a prepossessing expression, and light complexion. They are accustomed to labor from their earliest youth; boys of from seven to ten years of age being employed to break stones upon the roads, whilst the women take an equal share with the men in working in the fields. This may in part account for their extreme thinness; they are generally a healthy, but they are not a robust race.—"*c*" The Badagas are Sheiva hindoos, but the worship is of a rude sort. The Shiva temple is in a conical form outside the village, with a nundy at entrance. Special deities are Hetteydeva, an old man, and Hiryadeva, who brought them to the mountains. There are other male and female gods. Like other tribes they worship at Rungasawmy peak, where Iroolas officiate as priests. Also at Hoolicull, where a Badaga officiates. A few Badagas are Lingayets. The principal temples are:—Hettey coil in Paranginaud; two dedicated to Mahalingasawmy at Tainaud in Paranginaud, and at Mailore in Merkoonaud; Jaday sawmy's temple at Nedooncoolam in Paranginaud; Hiriyasawmy temples, one at Kodanaud and one at Mailore. They are in perpetual fear of the Coorumbar on account of supposed sorcery. In the season for tilling the ground a Coorumban is sent for who sacrifices a lamb in the field, and afterwards holds the plough for a short distance. The annual ceremony to the Mahalingam is performed in the season for reaping. The temple is then thatched anew, the walls and floor are cleaned and repaired on a Sunday, and on the next day a Coorumban is sent for to reap a handful of the produce, which is hung in front of the temple, and some water, in which bark from a tree has been soaked, is poured on the idol. Plantains and flowers are then offered up, with prayers, to preserve the community from sickness. Afterwards should sickness occur no medicines are used.—"*d*" Badaga villages are not so picturesque as munds of Todahs. But their long rows of neatly-thatched or tiled houses stand in the midst of fields of coraly and shaumay and are surrounded by well-stocked farm yards, showing comfort and wealth. As the men work on coffee plantations, labor in their own fields is performed by women. A Badaga pays Rs. 150 or Rs. 200 for a wife. Badagas intermarry very closely. Betrothal is made by parents, but marriage only takes place when grown up. No polyandry, but divorce is easily obtained. Badagas both burn and bury their dead. The men wear the lungooty, and both sexes wear a large unbleached cloth, which is stiffened to render it water-tight and warm to an extent which makes it ungraceful. It is loosely wrapped round them; so loosely that as a Badaga man works in the fields, he is obliged to stop between every few strokes of his hoe to gather up his cloth and throw one end over his shoulder. They wear turbans of the same cloth with an end hanging behind. Their ornaments consist of brass, iron, or filigree silver earrings, necklaces, bracelets, and armlets; they also wear nose-rings. The men frequently carry a silver box for opium or any small treasure they may happen to possess, such as a charm, a title-deed, or paper. The women are tattooed in rows of dots about the chest and four marks thus ⁘ on the forehead. The women wrap the cloth round their bodies from below their arms to their knees and fasten it with a cord below their arms and around their hips; the arms and shoulders and their legs below the knees are bare. A scarf goes round the head, and is let fall behind. The women are of domestic habits, and affectionate mothers. The Badagas are a light-hearted race and fond of music. Their national melodies are quaint and original. They have many ballads of great length, which are sung to a monotonous kind of chant. They are the husbandmen of the hills, and are diligent in tilling the ground, from which they raise barley, the poppy, the amaranthus, and the grain which they furnish to the Todahs and consume themselves. They have buffaloes, oxen and goats in abundance, and live on their milk and ghee, and the grain above mentioned, which they grind into meal, and eat mixed with water, which forms a thick dough. They eat no animal food.—"*e*" Numbers about 250,000. They recognize eighteen subcastes. Of the seven highest each one has a history of its own. The first called the Wodeyar, a branch of the caste of the reigning family of Mysore, are aristocratic. They refuse to carry burdens and work for Europeans, and in consequence are poor. They possess only five villages. The Wodeyar will not eat with the other castes, and consider themselves as gooroos or priests. They wear the lingam. Second are the Congas. Their ancestors came from Sargore north-west of Goondloopett by the Guzzelhutty pass on the Coimbatore side of the hills. They wear the lingam. Adhicauries are divided into two sets, Lingadhicauries who wear lingam, and Maitadhicauries who come from village of Nellitoray. The Kanakar or accountants are the only class who read and write. They are also physicians and exorcists. Probably introduced by control of Tamul rulers, this officer being called Shanbogue in Mysore [conicopoly]. The Chittrey class came to the hills with the Wodeyar, in the train of the Rajah of Mailcottah, a ruined fort near head of Segore ghaut. The Belly or silver class are the most astute of Badagas. There is an out-caste tribe of this name in Mysore. Jackatalla close to Wellington is inhabited by these, whence Badaga proverb, "if "you are not wide-awake, do not go to Jackatalla." The Haurwar are a degenerate class of Bramins. They may be connected with the Harihara [q.v.] sect. They wear Braminical string and officiate at harvest festivals. Every second year they walk with bare feet over burning coals. The first settlers of this caste did not bring any women with them. These are the seven principal castes. The remaining are as follows:—Hatarar, Aneyar who live exclusively in todanaud, Marey, Custry who live at kaity and are also called gangalar, Doomas, Gonajar, Mannicar or gem caste. See vol. I (36); II, 106 [burgher, jauty].——*Badagara* * (വടകര - vatakara, Mal.). From (vata, mal. north + kara, mal. village). Town, Amshom, Port, Tahsildar's station, District moonsif's station, Custom house; Malabar dist., Cooroombranaud tal.; pop. 9,195; lat. 11° 36′; long. 75° 38′; from Bombay S.S.E. 530 miles; from Calicut N.N.W. 27 miles; from Cannanore S.E. 23 miles; from Cottacull N. 2 miles; from Madras W.S.W. 336 miles; from Malapooram N.W. 49 miles; from Manantoddy W.S.W. 31 miles; from Moottangal S. 3½ miles; from Palghaut W.N.W. 91 miles; from Ponnany N.N.W. 59 miles; from Tellicherry S.S.E. 12 miles. On the Malabar coast at the northern extremity of the Calicut backwater, and on the trunk road from Calicut to Cannanore. Population almost exclusively Moplahs. Fort belonged originally to the Chiracal rajahs, from whom it was wrested by the Cadatnaud family in 1564. It then passed into the possession of Tippoo, who made it the chief export customs station in his dominions. In 1790 taken from Tippoo by English and restored to Cadatnaud rajah, converted by him into Bramin feeding house, which was afterwards transferred to Parvantala temple in Badagara. Coasting steamers occasionally call. Chief exports are coffee and cocoanuts; imports, rice and salt.

BADAGY (ಬಡಗಿ - badagi, *Can.*). From (vardhaki, san. carpenter). Caste-title. Carpenters. The corresponding terms are:—Hind. badye; Tam. tutcha; Tel. vadla; Mal. acharry [jauty].

BADAK (بدک - badak, *Hind.*). Duck, anas or querquedula.

BADARY (बदरी - badarí, *San.*; زيزفون - zaizufún, *Ar.*). From (bad, san. to be firm). Jujube, lotus.—"*a*" Botanically the Zizyphus genus, rhamneæ [vricsham, 41]. Generic name from arabic. Trees or shrubs, often decumbent or sarmentose and frequently armed with sharp, straight or hooked prickles; leaves alternate, usually leathery; flowers fascicled, or in sessile or stalked cymes; fruit fleshy or dry, with a woody or bony stone; wood reddish, moderately hard or hard; no heart-wood. The species best known to the natives are:—glabrata [carook vauly], jujuba [bair], nummularia [forest bair], œnoplia [jackal bair], vulgaris [sinjid], xylopyrus [nutty bair]:—Other s. indian species indigenous or naturalized are:—horrida, rugosa, wynadensis.—"*b*" River. Rises in Bababooden hills and is chief tributary of Hemauvaty which it joins near Goroor, Arcalgode talook, Hassan district, Mysore.

BADEE (بديع - badí, *Hind.*). From (bida, ar. new). Epithet of God [allah]. Also part of lacab; as Badee ood deen, originator of religion.

BADR (بدر - badr, *Ar.*). Full moon. Part of mahomedan lacab; as Badr ood deen, full moon of the faith [ism].

BADSHAH (بادشاه - bádsháh, *Hind.*). Arabic form of the Persian padshah. Alaumat of Syeds and Masheiks; as Ameen badshah, alam + alaumat [ism].——*Badshahy* (بادشاهی - bádsháhí, Hind.). Royal; held under a royal grant.

BAEL (बिल्व - bilva, *San.*; बेल - béla, *Mahr.*; बेल्लाफल - béllápʼhala, *Conc.*; سفرجل هندی - safarjalihindí, *Ar.*; هل - shul, *Pers.*; بيل پهل کاپير - belphalkáper, *Hind.*; ಬೇಲ - béla, *Can.*; ಬೆಲ್ಲಪತ್ರೆ - bellapatre, *Too.*; మారేడు - márédu, *Tel.*; കൂവളം - kúvalam, *Mal.*; බෙලි - beli, *Singh.*; வில்லுவம் - villuvam, *Tam.*). Title from mahrattee. San. from (bil, san. to break); destroys diseases. Ar. from (safarjal, ar. quince + hindí, ar. indian). Hind. from (belphal, hind. bael fruit + per, hind. tree). Tel. from (máuu, tel. tree + rédu, tel. king). Mal. from (kúr, tam. sharpness + vilá, tam. wood-apple tree, feronia elephantum, corr.); from thorns. Tam. from sanscrit. San. also (shripʼhala), meaning holy + fruit; (mahákapittʼha), meaning large + feronia elephantum, corr.; (góharítakí), meaning cow + terminalia chebula, retz., from large size of fruit; (nílamalliká), meaning black jasminum sambac, ait.; (málúra), meaning happiness giving. Hind. also (síphal), meaning holy fruit; (sríphal), meaning holy fruit. Can. also (kumbalamara), by corruption from malayalam. Tel. also (shándilyamu). Mal. also (mávilávu), meaning large wood-apple tree. Tam. also (kúvilam), meaning sharpness + wood-apple tree, feronia elephantum, corr., from thorns. Title otherwise Bel, Bengal quince, Bilba, Cow gall, Dietetic bael, Golden apple, Holy fruit, Indian bael, Indian quince, Larger wood-apple, Mabura, Pumpkin tree, Stone apple, Thorny bengal quince, Thorny wood-apple. Botanically Ægle marmelos, corr., rutaceæ [vricsham, 32]. Alias Cratæva marmelos; Feronia pellucida. Large and erect tree, 20–30 feet, armed with sharp spines; leaves pinnate; leaflets oblong or broad-lanceolate, crenulated, unequal, middle one petiolate, lateral ones almost sessile; petals four to five, spreading; stamens distinct; style short, thick; flowers in panicles, axillary, on long pedicels, large, greenish white, fragrant; berry with a hard rind, smooth, many-celled, many-seeded; seeds covered with a transparent glutinous matter; bark ash-colored, branches few and irregular; flowers during hot season, and fruit ripens after the rains; very slow in growth; wild in forests of coromandel ghauts; ascends mountains to about 4,000 feet. From abundance and cheapness, wood-apple [q.v.] is substituted for bael fruit but they can be distinguished thus:—Bael-fruit is generally round, slightly obovate, often oblong; about size of an orange, and often as big as a pomegranate or larger; greenish yellow, smooth, slightly shining; rind very hard and woody; in centre of pulp, from five to eighteen cells, each of which contains one to twelve or more seeds and mucus; in small bael-fruits, the seeds are often absent in the cells; seeds are oblong, flat or compressed, woolly, and about size of a lime seed; mucus is thick, very tenacious, transparent, and terebinthinate in smell and taste; when fruit is quite ripe, pulp is brownish red with strong balsamic odour and taste; when very ripe or dry, pulp is very adherent to rind. Wood-apple is almost always round or spherical; generally about the size of an orange and sometimes as large as a pomegranate; dull white or greenish-white in color and not smooth; rind hard and woody, but more easily broken; no cells at all, and the seeds are embedded in the pulp; the seeds are small, round, and smooth; contains no mucus; in the same condition, the pulp is of reddish grey color, with a very sweet and agreeable taste and smell; in the same condition, the pulp and seeds are more or less loose from the rind. The bael tree gives a true gum occurring in tears of a yellowish color, like gum arabic, or in fragmentary tears resembling coarse brown sugar. Is sacred to shiva and leaves used in his worship, like toolsy to vishnoo; the triple leaf is also typical of the three gods of trimoorty; according to indian poets it sprang from the milk of shree, the goddess of abundance; is constantly alluded to as an emblem of increase and fertility in ancient sanscrit poems; is common about pagodas. Gives to pharm. the half-ripe fruit, belæ fructus, astringent, mild stimulant of intestinal mucus membrane; preparations, mistura belæ, extractum belæ, extractum belæ liquidum; officinal; also in british; specially used in chronic diarrhœa and dysentery; the half-ripe fruit is best suited for medicinal use, especially newly gathered; the root bark is on malabar coast a remedy in hypochondriasis, melancholia, and palpitation of the heart; the leaves in decoction are used in asthma. To make bael sherbet:—take two ounces of the strained soft gummy interior, from the ripe or half-ripe fruit, mix it with three or four ounces of water, sweeten it with sugar, add tamarind, and cool it artificially; a simple remedy for dyspepsia. The fruit is never eaten as dessert, though its pulp is sometimes made into a preserve with sugar; fruit is used as famine food. Mucus of seeds is used as an addition to mortar, especially for wells; rind yields a yellow dye, used with myrobalans in calico-printing. Wood yellowish white, hard, with a strong aromatic scent when fresh cut; no heart-wood, not durable, readily eaten by insects; of no great value; in godavery forests the native drum is made from it; in some parts used for the naves of wheels and sugar crushers. There is a wild variety, with far inferior fruit. No other common species here.——*Barber's bael* (नैबेल - naibéla, Mahr.). From fruit used for soap by barbers. Same as Wild lime.

BAFTA (بافته - báftah, *Hind.*). From (báftan, pers. to weave). Cotton articles loom-woven [sheelay].

BAGHAUVAT (بغاوت - baghávat, *Hind.*). From (baghá, ar. to exceed just bounds). Mutiny. Baghauvat e hind is the Indian mutiny.

BAGLAH (بگلا - baglá, *Hind.*). Means heron; term common to genera ardea, ardeola, ardetta, buphus, butorides, herodias.

BAHAH (بهاء - bahá, *Ar.*). From (bahu, ar. to be fair). Glory. Part of lacab; as Bahah ood deen, glory of the faith [ism].

BAHAR (باهر - báhar, *Hind.*). Outside.——*Baharjully* (బహర్జల్లి - baharjalli, Tel.). From (above + jala, san. water); from being outside the Colair. Distinguished from (bhítarjalli), meaning inside + water. Sanscrit name (gókarnapura), meaning cow + carnan, proper name + city. Zemindarry, Village; Godavery dist., Bheemavaram tal. A low and treeless flat tract of country to the east of the Colair. Contains several villages. This tract was formerly a wealthy city called Gocurnapooram. Since submerged. Again reclaimed. Peshcush Rs. 1,15,050.

BAHAUDUR (بهادر - bahádur, *Hind.*). From Turkish. A hero, warrior. A title of honor given to nobles under the Mahomedan government, and now to distinguished native officials. Heroic alam; as Bahaudur khan, alam + alaumat; or Bahaudur ally, double alam [ism].——*Bahaudry* (بهادری - bahâduri, Hind.). Short for Hyder's Bahaudry pagoda.——*Bahaudur shahy* (بهادر شاهی - bahádurshâhí, Hind.). Shah alam's gold coin, with his name and Hijra on the obverse, name of the mint city and the year of reign on the reverse. A pagoda or mohur.

BAHMAN (بهمن - bahman, *Hind.*). Bramin.——*Bahmany* (بهمنی - bahmaní, Hind.). Mahomedan dynasty from 1347 to 1527 A.D. Founded by Hassan khan otherwise Allah ood deen, an Afghaun, who adopted the title in compliment to his patron, a Bramin. Nothing can be added to what is said at vol. I (148) [charitram].

BAHOO (बहु - bahu, *San.*). From (bah, san. to increase). Much.——*Bahoolam* (बहुल - bahula, San.). From thick darkness. The darkening fortnight of the moon [jyotisham, pacsham].

BAHOOR (பாகூர் - págúr, *Tam.*). From (págu, tam. palmyra sugar + úr, tam. village). South arcot dist., Pondicherry territory; lat. 11° 48′; long. 79° 47′; from Cuddalore N.N.W. 6 miles; from Pondicherry S.S.W. 11 miles. Between Fort St. David and Pondicherry. Major Lawrence in August 1752 entirely routed the French army here.

BAHR (بحر - bahr, *Ar.*). Sea. Compare:—Delphinidæ (bintulbahr), daughters of the sea; Lodoicea seychellarum (nárjílibahrí), sea cocoanut.

BAICULL (ಬೇಕಲ್ - békal, *Can.*). From (bé, can. to burn + kallu, can. stone). Cota koulam of De varros. Town, subport; South canara dist., Cassergode tal.; pop. 5,090; lat. 12° 24′; long. 75° 05′; from Bangalore W.S.W. 177 miles; from Bombay S.S.E. 474 miles; from Cassergode S.S.E. 7½ miles; from Cautacutcherry N.N.W. 14 miles; from Madras W. 358 miles; from Mangalore S.S.E. 34 miles; from the sea E. ½ mile. Largest and best preserved fort in district, situated on headland running into sea with fine bay to south. May have been erected during the wars between Ikkairy and Chiracal rajahs. The fortifications bear traces of European science. Town is north of fort. The tract anciently under Cadamba dynasty. It subsequently became part of Vijianugger. On the destruction of the latter at Talicote, in 1565, it was seized by the rajah of Bednore and gave its name to a sub-division of that kingdom. It fell to Hyder ally in 1763, and on the overthrow of Tippoo in 1799, was incorporated with the dominions of the East india company. The present Cassergode talook was known as Baicull for more than half a century. Trig. station at Fort cavalier; lat. 12° 23′ 32·68″; long. 75° 04′ 31·08″; from Cassergode S.S.E. 7½ miles; from the sea E. ½ mile.

BAID (பேடு - pédu, *Tam.*). Village; suffix in place names, as Carimbaid, meaning black + village [paid].

BAIDA (ಬೇಡ - béda, *Can.*). Hunter.——*Baidagan* (ಬೇಡಗನು - bédaganu, Can.). Hunting god of the Todahs.

BAIDA (బేడ - béda, *Tel.*). See vol. 1, 615.—"*a*" A coin. 6 dubs = 1 baida; 2 baidas = 1 doogoola [naunyam, 2]. Approximate actual value, 1 baida = 2 annas. $\frac{1}{32}$ of kurruck pagoda. Same as Can. adda. Compare Silver fanam.—"*b*" Goldsmith's weight. 2 baidas = 1 doogoola [niray, 3]. Approximate actual value, 1 baida = 1¾ grains. $\frac{1}{32}$ of a pagoda weight. Same as Hind. goomchy, goonj; Tel. gooriginja; Tam. coondrimany.

BAIKREE (بيكرى - bekrí, *Hind.*). Same as Jungle sheep [q. v.].

BAIL (بيل - bel, *Hind.*). Meaning creeper; from the supposed resemblance of the inflamed vessels to a vegetable growth. Farcy in horses [ashwarogam].

BAIR (बदरी - badarí, *San.*; बोर - bóra, *Mahr.*; बोरिरूकु - bóriráku, *Conc.*; سدر - sidr, *Ar.*; كنار - kunár, *Pers.*; بيركا پيڑ - berkáper, *Hind.*; بيركا جهاڑ - berkájhár, *Dec.*; بدرا - bidara, *Malay*; ಯಲಚಿ - yalachi, *Can.*; ಬೊಗರಿ - bogari, *Too.*; రేగు - régu, *Tel.*; ലന്ത - lanta, *Mal.*; මසන් - masan, *Singh.*; இலந்தை - ilandai, *Tam.*). Title from hindostany. Mahr. from sanscrit. Ar. from (sidara, ar. to dazzle). Hind. from sanscrit. Malay from sanscrit. Mal. from tamul. San. also (kólí), meaning produced in colam; (karkandhu), meaning red + bearing, from red leaves and fruits; (bálóshta), meaning desired by children; (gudap'hala), meaning ball fruit; (madhurap'hala), meaning sweet fruit; (nripéshta), meaning liked by kings; (nripabadarí), meaning king's jujube; (p'halashaishira), meaning producing fruit in the dewy season; (prit'hukólí), meaning large jujube; (rájabadarí), meaning king's jujube; (rájavallabhá), meaning king's beloved; (rájakólí), meaning king's jujube; (sup'hala), meaning having good fruit; (svachha), meaning pure; (tanubíja), meaning having small seed; (ajapriya), meaning dear to goat; (vishama), meaning not smooth; (ubhayakantaka), meaning double-thorned; (dridhabíja), meaning hard seeded; (dviparní), meaning double-leaved. Hind. also (khikhrí); (kúl); (narikelikúl). Can. also (bogari); (yagachi); (jatimara); (yelanjimara). Mal. also (perintutali), meaning large scutia indica, brongn.; (malantutalí), meaning wild scutia. Singh. also (debara); (mahadebara). Tam. also (kullari); (véttiram). Title otherwise Blunt-leaved buckthorn, Chinese date tree, Common jujube, Egg plum, Indian cherry, Indian plum, Lotus of the lotophagi. Botanically Zizyphus [badary] jujuba, lamk., rhamneæ [vricsham, 41]. Generic name from arabic; specific name from same. Alias Rhamnus jujuba; Zizyphus mauritiana, sororia, trinervia. Small, stiff branched, hooked, thorny tree, 16 feet; stipulary prickles short, in pairs or solitary, often wanting, especially on the young branches; leaves elliptical or oblong, sometimes coarsely toothed at the apex, serrulated, acutish or obtuse or slightly cordate at the base, upper side glabrous, under side as well as young branches and petioles covered with dense tawny tomentum; cymes sessile or very shortly peduncled; ovary two-celled; styles two, united to the middle; drupe spherical, yellow when ripe; nut rugose, two-celled; flowers greenish yellow; wild and cultivated; very common. Fruit, the indian plum of most authors; perfectly round, of size of a very large cherry, smooth, shining, and of a tawny yellow color; has a peculiar perfume, rather acid in flavor, and not altogether unlike a siberian crab-apple; mahomet included it among the joys of paradise; the fruit of the cultivated tree is much larger than the wild. A kind of kino is produced from bark. Fruit mucilaginous, pectoral, and styptic; berries purify the blood and assist digestion; bark a remedy for diarrhœa; root used in decoction in fever and powdered to be applied to ulcers and old wounds; leaves form a plaster in strangury. Fruit often eaten, being sweet and mealy, also largely preserved in chutney; fruit of wild kind dried and powdered like the lotus of the lotophagi. Bark employed by tanners. Stem gives a gum. The wood is tough and tolerably strong. In gardens there is a variety with oblong fruit.——*Black bair* (చికిరేణి - chikiréni, Tel.). From dark bark and resemblance. Same as Dark sirissa.——*Female bair* (పెయ్యరేగు - peyyarégu, Tel.). Title from small size. Tel. also (peyyarodda). Botanically Grewia [dharmanam] orientalis, linn., tiliaceæ [vricsham, 27]. Shrubby; flowers small, white.——*Forest bair* (सम्ला - sámlá, San.; جهوٹا كروندا - jhútákarondá, Dec.; కానరేగు - kánarégu, Tel.; ବଇଞ୍ଚ - baincha, Oor.; കുരുമുള്ളി - kurumulli, Mal.; சொத்தைக்களா - shottaikkalá, Tam.). Title from habitat and resemblance. San. from (sa, san. with + amla, san. sour). Dec. from (jhútá, hind. false + karondá, hind. carissa carandas, linn.). Tel. from (kána, tel. forest + régu, tel. jujube tree, zizyphus jujuba, lamk.). Mal. from (kuru, mal. small + mulli, mal. thorny plant). Tam. from (shottai, tam. decayed + kalá, tam. the plant, carissa genus) [mauritius plum, tomi tomi]. Title otherwise Caunaraig, False carondah, Shottay calah, Strong iron-wood, Thorny iron-wood, Wild jujube. Botanically Flacourtia [swaudoocantacam] sepiaria, roxb., bixineæ [vricsham, 14]. Alias Sideroxylon spinosum. Shrub, 6 feet; thorns very numerous, patent, bearing both leaves and flowers; leaves obovate-oblong, older ones very rigid and coriaceous, serrate; peduncles axillary, solitary, one-flowered; flowers small green; berry very globular, size of a pea, succulent; seeds four to eight. An infusion of leaves and roots in snake-bites; bark fried in oil externally in rheumatism. Berries eatable; leaves thrashed out for cattle fodder; makes good fences from thorns. Wood only for fuel.——*Forest bair* (മലന്തുടലി - malantutali, Mal.; காட்டிலந்தை - káttilandai, Tam.). Mal. from (mala, mal. mountain + tutali, mal. thorny plant, scutia indica, brongn.). Tam. from (kádu, tam. forest + ilandai, tam. zizyphus jujuba, lamk.). Title otherwise Wild jujube. Botanically Zizyphus [badary] nummularia, w. & a., rhamneæ [vricsham, 41]. Alias Rhamnus nummularia; Zizyphus microphylla, rotundifolia. Shrub; flowers small, greenish-yellow. Fruit, small, round; cool and astringent. Plant gives a gum; used to make fences. Wood yellow, hard, compact.——*Jackal bair* (शृगालकोलि - shrigálakóli, San.; तोरण - tórana, Mahr.; कनेरीझाड - kanéríjháda, Conc.; سدربرى - sidribarrí, Ar.; كناربرى - kunáribarrí, Pers.; جنگلى بيرى - janglíberí, Hind.; ಸುರಿಮುಳ್ಳು - surimullu, Can.; ತೂರಿಮುಳ್ಳು - túrimullu, Too.; పరింగి - paringi, Tel.; ବରକୋଳି - barókóli, Oor.; തുടലിമുള്ള - tutalimullu, Mal.; එරමිණියා - eraminiyá, Singh.; நரியிலந்தை - nariyilandai, Tam.). Title from inferior fruit. San. from (shrigála, san. jackal + kóli, san. jujube, zizyphus jujuba, lamk.). Ar. from (sidr, ar. jujube + barr, ar. forest). Pers. from (kunár, pers. jujube + barr, ar. forest). Hind. from (janglí, hind. wild + berí, hind. jujube). Can. from (suri, can. knife + mullu, can. thorn). Mal. from (tutar, mal. chain + mul, mal. thorn). Tam. from (nari, tam. jackal + ilandai, tam. jujube). San. also (badara). Mahr. also (suran). Can. also (kanerigida). Title otherwise Jackal jujube, Oblique-leaved jujube. Botanically Zizyphus [badary] œnoplia, mill., rhamneæ [vricsham, 41]. Alias Rhamnus œnoplia; Zizyphus albens, napeca, scandens. Climbing, thorny shrub; flowers small greenish-yellow; common hedge plant; bark and root used medicinally; fruit eaten; the bark affords a kino; wood reddish, with the structure of a climber.——*Nutty bair* (गालयिझाड - gáláyijháda, Conc.; بيرى - berí, Hind.; ಕೊಡಚಿಗಿಡ - kodachigida, Can.; ಕೊಟ್ಟೆಮುಳ್ಳು - kottemullu, Too.; గొట్టి - gotti, Tel.; கொட்டையிலந்தை - kottaiyilandai, Tam.). Title from large nut of fruits. Tam. from (kottai, tam. seed + ilandai, tam. zizyphus jujuba, lamk.). Tam. also (káttilandai), meaning forest + zizyphus jujuba, lamk. Title otherwise Seed jujube. Botanically Zizyphus [badary] xylopyrus, willd., rhamneæ [vricsham, 41]. Alias Rhamnus xylopyrus; Zizyphus caracutta, elliptica, orbicularis, rotundifolia; caracutta from canarese. Tree; stipulary prickles solitary, or in pairs, or wanting; leaves alternate, broadly elliptical or orbicular, slightly cordate at the base, serrulated, under side pale, softly pubescent, finely reticulated, upper side pubescent when young; cymes short; ovary three-celled; styles three, united below; drupe size of cherry, turbinate, nut globose, hard, slightly rugose, three-celled; flowers greenish yellow. Kernels taste like filberts, eaten by natives; shoots and leaves eaten by cattle. Fruit used by shoemakers to blacken leather and to make blacking; bark imparts a black color. Wood is orange-colored, very hard and durable, and not heavy; used for torches.——*Small bair* (भूबदरी - bhúbadarí, San.; గద్దగోరు - gaddagóru, Tel.; തുടലി - tutali, Mal.). Title from size and resemblance. San. from (bhú, san. ground + badarí, san. the jujube tree, zizyphus jujuba, lamk.); from low shrubby habit. Tel. from (gadda, tel. kite + góru, tel. claw); from curved thorns like kite's claws. Mal. from (tutar, mal. chain); from chain-like thorns. San. also (súkshmabadarí), meaning small jujube; (laghubadarí), meaning short jujube; (badaravallí), meaning jujube creeper; from straggling habit; (bahup'hala), meaning many fruited. Title otherwise Jujube creeper, Kite's claw, Small jujube tree. Botanically Scutia indica, brong., rhamneæ [vricsham, 41]. Alias Ceanothus circumscissa, zeylanica; Celastrum zeylanica; Rhamnus circumcissus, myrtimus; Scutia rhediana. A small straggling shrub, bears small, greenish-yellow flowers; common.

BAJANTRY (بجنترى - bajantarí, *Hind.*). From (bájná, hind. to play upon an instrument). Village music; employed at ceremonies, before the god, to meet distinguished persons, &c. [sangeetam].

BAJRAH (कङ्गु - kangu, *San.*; बाजरी - bájarí, *Mahr.*; باجرا - bájrá, *Hind.* and *Dec.*; ಸಜ್ಜೆ - sajje, *Can.*; సజ్జ - saddza, *Tel.*; ଗଣ୍ଟିଆ - gautiya, *Oor.*; കമ്പം - kampam, *Mal.*; கம்பு - kambu, *Tam.*). Title from hindostany. San. from (ka. san. water + gam, san. to come out) [tinay]. Mahr. from hindostany. Tam. from (kanu, tam. joint); from jointed culms. Hind. also (lahrá).

Tel. also (gante). Title otherwise Bulrush millet, Couz-couz, Cumboo, Gero corn, Sadza, Spiked millet. Botanically Pennisetum spicatum, delile, graminaceæ [vricsham, 156]. Alias Alopecurus typhoides; Gramen panicum; Holcus spicatus; Panicum spicatum; Penicillaria spicata; Pennisetum cylindrica, typhoideum. Cereal or millet grass; culms erect, with roots from the lowermost joints or two, round, smooth, 3–6 feet, nearly as thick as the little finger; leaves alternate, sheathing, broad and long, mouths of the sheaths bearded; spikes terminal, cylindric, erect, 6–9 inches long; pedicels generally two-flowered, occasionally one to four flowered; flowers surrounded with many woolly, hispid, purple bristles or involucres; calyx two-flowered, one hermaphrodite, the other male, two-valved, exterior valvelet minute, interior one nearly as long as the corolla, retuse, both awnless; corolla of the hermaphrodite flower two-valved, of the male one-valved; stigma two-cleft, feathery; seeds ovoid, obtuse, rounded at the top, contracted at the base, of bluish-grey with a yellow point to their attachment, fixed on the long spike, very close, and thinning from the base to the summit. Grain contains about 10 per cent. of nitrogenous matter and 71 of starch. Except cholum this is the most cultivated grain in india; grown over the higher lands on the coast of coromandel; cultivated in black loam; dry ground prepared in south in auvany [mausam] or august, on coromandel in veishaukham or may and jyeshtam [mausam] or june, on w. coast in carcatacam [mausam] or july; ploughing and manuring; seed sown in south in poorataushy or september and arpisy [mausam] or october, on coromandel in ashaudham or july and shrauvanam [mausam] or august, on w. coast in carcatacam or july and chingom [mausam] or august; sown broadcast and ploughed in while under growth; again ploughed after twenty-five days; weeds cleared; if plants are dense some of them removed; watering crop; full grown crop has stalks green and ears brown; cut usually after three months, but on w. coast after six months; on w. coast the ears are plucked by the hand; ears brought to the threshing floor and trodden by bullocks and buffaloes; grain separated from chaff by winnowing in the wind; produce can be sold as soon as the grain is collected. As food used chiefly by lower classes, mostly in the cold weather; as flour and made into rotees or hand-bread, occasionally with buttermilk; with milk, &c., forms the staple food of many; considered heating, but is more nutritious than rice; green chopped stalks and leaves used as fodder for cattle. There are two well-marked varieties, one (bajrah) with greenish colored grain, and the other (bajri) with reddish grain. Other common species are:—alopecuros, hohenhackeri, holcoides.

BAKAUYAH (بقایا - bakáyá, *Hind.*). Plural of the Arabic (bakíyah). Old balances.

BAKHT (بخت - bakht, *Pers.*). Luck. In composition forms a lacab; as Bakhtauwar begum, fortunate lady [ism].

BAKK (بق - bakk, *Ar.*). Gnat.——*Bakk tree* (شجرة البق - shajaratulbakk, Ar.; پشہ غال - pashshaghál, Pers.). Ar. from (shajar, ar. tree + bakk, ar. gnat); from resort of gnats. Pers. from (pashshah, pers. gnat + ghál, pers. hive). Ar. also (dardár). Pers. also (sárakhdár), meaning gnat container; (pashshadár), meaning gnat holder. Hebrew becaim. Title otherwise Abete tree, Asp, Aspen, Aspen poplar, Gnat tree, Haps, Mulberry tree of scripture. Botanically Populus tremula, linn., alicaceæ [vricsham]. Long leaf-stalks cause the leaves to tremble with wind.

BALAGHAUT (بالا گہاٹ - bálághát, *Hind.*). From (bálá, pers. above + ghát, hind. hill). The country above any mountain passes. Highlands as opposed to lowlands; the latter being Talaghaut, or Payeen ghaut. The term was specially applied formerly to elevated country from Toongabudra and Kistna in N. to extremity of Mysore in the opposite direction; or between lat. 8° 10′ to 16°; long. 77° 20′ to 80° 10′. This district formed part of kingdom of Vijianugger. Conquered by Mahomedans, and upon fall of Moghul empire was split into various states. Hyder ally in turn conquered the country. On Tippoo's defeat by British, it was partitioned. The chief of Kurnool retained his ancient patrimony. Remainder was shared between Rajah of Mysore, British, and Nizam. In 1800 Nizam ceded his portion in commutation of subsidy. In 1841 Nawaub of Kurnool by misconduct incurred forfeiture. Excluding Mysore, the country has been divided into four administrative districts; Anantapore, Bellary, Cuddapah, and Kurnool. Term Balaghaut is still used locally for these four districts. In Salem district part of Oossoor and Krishnagherry talooks are called Balaghaut, being geographically a portion of Mysore plateau [charitram].

BALAH (बला - balá, *San.*). From (bala, san. strength); medicinal. Indian mallow. Botanically the Sida genus, malvaceæ [vricsham, 25]. Herbs or undershrubs, natives of tropical countries; leaves simple or lobed; fruit of five or more indehiscent carpels, each containing a single pendulous seed. Leaves of greater number employed for same purposes as marsh mallow, althæa officinalis, linn., and common mallow, malva sylvestris, linn., in europe; being soft, nearly inodorous, mucilaginous, and demulcent. The species best known to the natives are shown below. Compare also:—Canthium parviflorum (nágabalá), elephant tonic; Maranta dichotoma (bhadrabalá), auspicious tonic; Pæderia fœtida (rájabalá), king's tonic.——*Common balah* (बला - balá, San.; तुपकडी - tupakadí, Mahr.; तुप्कडी - tupkadí, Conc.; حلبۂ بری - hulbahibarrí, Ar.; شنبلید دشتی - shambalídidashtí, Pers.; جنگلی میتھی - janglímethí, Hind. and Dec.; ಕಲ್ಲಂಗಡಲೆಗಿಡ - kallangadalegida, Can.; ಕಡೀರು - kadíru, Too.; మయిలుమాణిక్యము - mayilumánikyamu, Tel.; കുറുന്തോട്ടി - kuruntótti, Mal.; කොටිකම්බලිල - kotikambalila, Singh.; மயிர்மாணிக்கம் - mayirmánikkam, Tam.). San. means strong. Ar. from (hulbah, ar. fenugreek trigonella fœnum-græcum, linn. + barr, ar. forest). Pers. from (shambalíd, pers. fenugreek + dasht, pers. forest). Hind. from (janglí, hind. wild + methí, hind. fenugreek). Can. from (kallu, can. stone + kadale, can. bengal gram, cicer arietinum, linn. + gida, can. plant). Tel. from tamul. Mal. from (kuru, mal. small + tuvatti, mal. the plant, abutilon indicum, g. don.); from size and resemblance. Tam. from (mayir, tam. hair + mánikya, san. ruby); valuable medicine for hair, leaves washing it black and soft. San. also (vátaghní), meaning rheumatism destroyer; (ahikhanda), meaning snake + fragment; (atibalá), meaning large + the plant; (mahábalá), meaning large + the plant. Hind. also (sufedbariyálá), meaning white sida. Can. also (bennegaragugida), meaning butter-melting plant. Tel. also (gúbatada), meaning owl + grewia tiliæfolia, vahl.; (muttavapulagamuchettu), meaning grandmother's pudding plant [lance-leaved balah, peramootty, shoondy, shrubby balah]. Mal. also (ánakkuruntótti), meaning elephant + the plant, the large variety; (vattúram), meaning round creeper. Tam. also (kurundótti). Title otherwise Large balah, Wild fenugreek. Botanically Sida [balah] rhombifolia, linn., malvaceæ [vricsham, 25]. Shrub; leaves rhomboid-lanceolate, serrated, under side hoary, with short tomentum; pedicels more than half the length of the leaf, jointed at the very base, axillary, solitary, usually collected into leafy corymbs at the extremity of the branches; carpels eight to eleven, slightly bicuspidate; flowers smallish, pale yellow. Bark yields very delicate, flaxy fibre. There is a variety retusa, common weed; roots used in diseases of cattle, and root boiled in oil used externally in rheumatism; leaves used for washing head. Another variety is rhomboidea; when seed is sown thick in a good soil, the plants grow tall and slender, without branches, and are fit for fibre; medicinal properties resemble those of other species; bark yields very delicate flaxy fibre. Another variety is scabrida.——*Dwarf balah* (గాయపాకు - gáyapáku, Tel.; බැවිල - bavila, Singh.; வேலிப்பாசி - vélippási, Tam.). Tel. from (gáyamu, tel. wound + áku, tel. leaf); being emollient. Tam. from (véli, tam. hedge + pási, tam. moss); diffuse hairy plant found on hedges. Tel. also (nélabenda), meaning ground + hibiscus esculentus, linn.; (nélatutti), meaning ground + abutilon indicum, g. don., from size and resemblance. Tam. also (pazhambási), meaning fruit moss. Title otherwise Hedge-moss, Wound-leaf. Botanically Sida [balah] humilis, willd., malvaceæ [vricsham, 25]. Alias Sida multicaulis, pilosa, radicans, unilocularis. During famine eaten as greens.——*Lance-leaved balah* (पट - pata, San.; तुपकडी - tupakadí, Mahr.; ವಿಷಕಡ್ಡಿ - vishakaddi, Can.; విషబొడ్డి - vishaboddi, Tel.; ചെറുപരുവ - cheruparuva, Mal.; සිරිවදිබලිල - sirivadibalila, Singh.; மலைதாங்கி - malaithángi, Tam.). San. from (pat, san. to split). Can. from (visha, can. poison + kaddi, can. small stick). Tel. from (visha, san. poison + boddi, tel. macaranga peltata, müll.). Mal. from (cheru, mal. small + paruva, mal. creeper, spathium chinense, lour.). Tam. from (malai, tam. mountain + tángu, tam. to support); found among hills and supposed to hold them up. Can. also (bhímanakaddi), meaning the hero bheeman + small stick. Tel. also (muttavapulagamuchettu), meaning great-grandmother pudding + plant [common balah, peramootty, shoondy, shrubby balah]; (sahadévichettu), meaning sahadevy, wife of sahadevan, the youngest of the five pandavas + plant, as sacred to her; (gáyapákuchettu), meaning wound + leaf + plant. Mal. also (malatánni), meaning hill supporter. Singh. also (hínanóda), meaning small + abutilon indicum, g. don. Tam. also (vattattiruppi), meaning circle + to turn; (ariválmanaippúndu), meaning knife + seat + plant, from lanceolate leaves; (ponmusuttai), meaning gold + the plant, ipomæa candicans, bot. mag. [indian parcira]; (káyappúndu), meaning wound + plant; (ariválmúkkan), meaning knife + nose, from lanceolate leaves. Title otherwise Horn bean-leaved sida, Sickle leaf, Wound plant. Botanically Sida [balah] carpinifolia, linn., malvaceæ [vricsham, 25]. Alias Sida acuta, lanceolata, scoparia, stauntoniana. Shrub, 4–6 feet; calyx five-cleft, without involucel; leaves narrow lanceolate, acuminated, slightly sprinkled with bristly hairs on the nerves beneath, coarsely simple serrated; pedicels axillary, solitary, not shorter than the petioles, jointed about the middle, sometimes arranged in a short, axillary, almost leafless branch; carpels five to nine, bi-rostrate; flowers yellow; flowering in august, december; common. Root resembles common liquorice, very bitter in taste. Medicinally an emollient and demulcent plant; the root is given in infusion with ginger in intermittent fevers, a valuable stomachic; the leaves made warm and moistened with gingelly-oil are employed to hasten suppuration; the juice of the leaves mixed with honey is given in dysentery and pains in the chest; gives to pharm. the root, non-officinal. Root strikes a blue color with salts of iron; good fibre from the stems.——*Mysore balah* (కుండివెలగ - kundivelaga, Tel.; அதிவாசர்

மனைப்பூண்டு - arivâlmanaippúndu, Tam.). Tel. from (kundu, tel. to subside + velaga, tel. wood-apple tree, feronia elephantum, corr.); small but like wood-apple tree. Tam. from (arivál, tam. knife + manai, tam. seat + púndu, tam. plant). Botanically Sida [balah] mysorensis, w. et a., malvaceæ [vricsham, 25]. Alias Sida glutinosa, urticæfolia. Erect undershrub.——*Prickly balah* (नागबला - nágabalá, San.; తెనల్లబెండ - ternallabenda, Tel.; அரிவாள்மனைப்பூண்டு - arivâlmanaippúndu, Tam.). Title from spines. San. from (nága, san. elephant + balá, san. the plant, sida rhombifolia, linn., var. retusa, linn.). Tel. from (tera, tel. plain + nalla, tel. black + benda, tel. hibiscus esculentus, linn.). Tam. from (arivál, tam. knife + manai, tam. seat + púndu, tam. plant). Tel. also (chinamuttama), meaning small + great-grandmother. Title otherwise Alder-leaved sida, Nauga balah. Botanically Sida [balah] spinosa, linn., malvaceæ [vricsham, 25]. Alias Sida alba, alnifolia. Shrub; flowers small, white; medicinal properties of the other species.——*Shrubby balah* (बला - balá, San.; चिकणा - chikaná, Mahr.; ಹೆತ್ತುತ್ತಿಗಿಡ - hettuttigida, Can.; తెల్లఅంటిస - tellaantisa, Tel.; കാട്ടൂരം - káttúram, Mal.; සිරිවැට - sirivatu, Singh.; நிலத்துத்தி - nilattutti, Tam.). San. means strong. Mahr. means strong. Can. from (hedda, can. large + tuttigida, can. mallow) [tootty]. Tel. from (tella, tel. white + antisa, tel. burr, achyranthes aspera, linn.). Mal. from (kátu, mal. forest + úram, mal. creeper). Tam. from (nilam, tam. ground + tutti, tam. mallow abutilon indicum, g. don.). San. also (suvarna), meaning good colored [coudray, nauga champak]. Tel. also (chiribenda), meaning small + hibiscus esculentus, linn.; (muttavapulagamuchettu), meaning great-grandmother + pudding + plant [common balah, lance-leaved balah, peramootty, shoondy]; (tellagorrachettu), meaning white + the plant so called. Tam. also (arivâlmanaippúndu), meaning knife + seat + plant. Title otherwise Ground mallow, Heart-leaved sida. Botanically Sida [balah] cordifolia, linn., malvaceæ [vricsham, 25]. Alias Sida herbacea, rotundifolia. Shrubby; flowers middle-sized, yellow; its mucilage, mixed with rice is given in dysentery and fevers, and its seeds in colic, tenesmus, and gonorrhœa; decoction of the root with ginger in intermittent fever; powder of the root-bark given with milk and sugar for frequent micturition and leucorrhœa.

BALAM (बल - bala, San.). From (bal, san. to support). Strength.——*Balabhadran* (बलभद्र - balabhadra, San.). Means strong and propitious one. Same as Balaraman.——*Baladevan* (बलदेव - baladéva, San.). Means the strong god. Same as Balaraman.——*Balarama jayanty* (బలరామజయంతి - balarámajayanti, Tel.). Means Balaraman, the god + day of rejoicing. Lunar holiday [pundigay, 6c], subject to intercalation. Same as Acsha tadiya.——*Balaraman* (बलराम - balaráma, San.). Means Rama, the strong. Son of Nundan and elder brother of Krishna. The patron of agriculture; the Yaudavas, to which tribe he belonged, being properly herdsmen and shepherds. When represented in arts he bears in one hand, as a staff, a country plough. When the Bramins had deposed Booddha from dignity of avatar of Vishnoo, they put Balaraman into his place as ninth avatar. He was married to one Raivaty. The Hercules of the Hindoos. Always represented as a white man [avatar, matam, vishnoo].——*Balcutcauram* (बलात्कार - balátkára, San.). From (above + kri, san. to do). Oppression.——*Balootah* (बलुता - balutá, Mahr.; بلوته - balútá, Hind.). From (balutem, mahr. allowance in kind assigned to village officers); one entitled to the fixed allowance. Corruptly Baloty. A collective name of the chief village public servants, such as the carpenter, blacksmith, potter, astrologer, &c. They are nominally twelve, and called Baurabalootah, but enumeration differs in different parts. The headman and accountant are sometimes included in the term and sometimes not.—"*a*" The Balootah are in Tamul villages termed Coody makkal and are:—Monigar, headman; Curnum, accountant; Neergunty, waterman; Taliyaur, watchman; Toty, village peon; Veidyan, doctor; Puttigaur, cattle-impounder; Vunnaun, washerman; Ambattan, barber; Tutchan, carpenter; Collan, blacksmith; Tattaun, goldsmith or shroff; Coosavan, potter; Tandalgaur, money-collector; Punchaungy, astrologer.—"*b*" In Teloogoo villages termed Graumachaukar and are:—Peddacaup, headman, moonsif; Curnum, accountant; Cummara, smith; Coommara, potter; Saucala, washerman; Mungaly, barber; Maudiga, leather-worker; Vettivaud, a sweeper; Talaury, watchman; Neergunty, water distributor; Shroff, money counter; Poorohit, priest.—"*c*" In Canarese villages termed Aya caurar, and are:—Gowda, headman; Shanbogue, accountant; Joshy, astrologer; Puttaury, corn measurer, or money-changer; Cummara, blacksmith; Badagy, carpenter; Coombaura, potter; Nauvithan, barber; Agasa, washerman; Barica, one who affixes the public seal to public papers; Talavaur, watchman; Neergunty, waterman.—"*d*" In Malabar villages termed Amshom oodyogastar and are:—Adhicaury, headman; Menon, accountant; Kolecar, peon.—"*e*" Distinguish the Balootah from the Punchaula or guild of artisans, whose members are only accidentally and individually village public servants. See vol. I, 112.——*Baly* (बलि - bali, San.). A religious offering, especially an animal sacrifice. A giant or Deitya king sent to Pautaulam by Vishnoo when the latter was incarnate as a dwarf [avatar]. Also called Baly chuckravurty, Mahabaly. Baly is the most popular legendary king in South india [mauvellipore]. His greatest feast falls on the full moon in the month of Caurtigay [mausam] or November. In Mysore popular songs are sung in his praise on the last day of the Navaurautry [pundigay, 6d]. He is worshipped in Malabar on the Wonaum [pundigay, 5c] festival. He does not die and is one of the seven Chiranjeevies. Vishnoo goes by the name of Balidhwamsy, for defeating him in the Vaumana avatar [matam].

BALANGHAS (കാവലം - kávalam, *Mal.*). Title from malayalam by inversion. Mal. from (káya, mal. fruit + valam, mal. manure). Title otherwise Edible sterculia. Botanically Sterculia [cauvalam] balanghas, linn., sterculiaceæ [vricsham, 26]. Alias Southwellia balanghas. Flowers small, flesh-colored; western coast forests, planted in gardens; seeds when roasted are like chestnuts; wood open grained and soft.

BALAPAM (بلفم - balfam, *Hind.*; ಬಳಪ - balapa, *Can.*; బలవు - balavu, *Too.*; బలపము - balapamu, *Tel.*; മാക്കല്ല് - mákkallu, *Mal.*; மாக்கல் - mákkal, *Tam.*). Tam. from (má, tam. flour + kal, tam. stone). Pot stone; a soft stone of a greyish blue color; easily worked, and is used for making small pots and dishes; with pencils of this school boys write upon books formed of cloth blackened and stiffened with gum [cadata]. There is a harder variety in Mysore called Shilaycull, as being used for making images [cull].

BALBIJ (بلبيج - balbíj, *Hind.*). Means strength, seed being aphrodisiac. Country mallow [tootty] seeds.

BALDAH (بلده - baldá, *Hind.*). Same as Belleric myrobalan.

BALIJE (బలిజె - balije, *Tel.*). According to some, from (bali, san. sacrifice + jan, san. to be born); from the tradition that the originator of the caste came out of the celebrated sacrifice made among five fires by Parvaty. Sometimes known as Gowry pootran or son of Gowry. Caste-title. Section of the old Cavaray tribe in Teloogoo district. Originally solely employed in making bangles, pearl or coral ornaments, and other female adornments; now the greater part engage in agriculture, and the caste ranks high. Contains many sub-divisions, usually after their ordinary occupations in times past. The worship is of Vishnoo combined with Gowry devy, their patron goddess. Widow remarriage is disallowed, but flesh-eating and drinking of spirits are permitted. The dead are buried. The caste affixes are Naidoo and Chetty, the latter being justly claimable only by those who are descended from the heads of the caste. About 780,000 in Presidency; most in Arcot north, Bellary, Canara, Cuddapah and Nellore. The following are the principal sub-divisions:—Gauzoola balije, from (gádzu, tel. glass bracelet); dealing in those articles. Linga balije, from (linga, san. symbol of shiva). Moonnooty goompoo, from (munnúru, tel. three hundred + gumpu, tel. crowd); a mixed caste, comprising the illegitimate descendants of Balijes and the male children of dancing girls. Moota cummaloo balije, from their earrings. Ooppoo balije, carry salt on donkeys in panniers. Pagadaula balije, deal in corals and pearls. Perika balije, from (perika, tel. a pack); same as ooppoo. Raulla balije, sell precious stones. Tota balije, carry on garden cultivation. Vauda balije, meaning boat balijes, are sailors. There is a teloogoo proverb:—బలిజె పుట్టుకపుట్టవలె బటావియా బుడ్డికొట్టవలె—"One must be born a balije to "crack a batavia bottle;" from drinking habits [jauty].

BALLA (బల్ల - balla, *Tel.*). Table.——*Ballacutt* (బల్లకట్టు - ballakattu, Tel.). From (above + kattu, tel. to fasten). Platform boat for taking carriages across ferries.

BALLABHY (वल्लभि - vallabhi, *San.*). Means master. A rajpoot dynasty in Goozerat from 319 to 658 A.D.; era called after them which dates from 319 A.D. See vol. I (117) [charitram].

BALLAR (بلر - ballar, *Hind.*). Plant name common to:—Dolichos lablab; Vigna catiang. See gloss. paragraphs.

BALLAULA (ಬಲ್ಲಾಳ - ballála, *Can.*). From (bali, can. path + álu, can. to rule); he who controls course of descent. Class title.—"*a*" Spiritual preceptors in canara, who exercise control over the sixteen balies or classes under the aliya santauna law; balagye or right-hand ballaulas come from chitpaudy, and yedagye or left-hand ballaulas come from nidambore; both in oodipy talook [maryanday].—"*b*" Also means a nobleman.—"*c*" So a dynasty designated hoysala from the founder sala having killed a tiger which became their family crest; known also as the yaudava dynasty of dwaura samoodram to distinguish it from another contemporaneous yaudava dynasty at devagiry; for brief description, see vol. I (140); and list vol. II, 250 [charitram].—"*d*" Also Jeina title.—"*e*" Hindoo third name [peyar].

BALLEY (బల్లె - balle, *Tel.*). Corruption of (palle, *Tel.*). Village; suffix in place names, as Nelaballey, ground + village.

BALLIGOODA (ಬಲ್ಲಿಗುಡಾ - balligudá, *Tel.* balliguda *). From (balli, oor. sand + gudá, oor. fort).—"*a*" Deputy tahsildarry; Ganjam district. Pay Rs. 250.—"*b*" Village, Maliah head-quarters of Special assistant agent and Assistant superintendent of police, Head-quarters of Sub-magistrate; Ganjam district, Chinna kimedy maliahs division; pop. 1,476; lat. 20° 11′; long. 83° 57′; from Berhampore N.W. 84 miles; from Chetterpore N.W. 91 miles; from Chicacole N. 131 miles; from Madras N.N.E. 540 miles; from Russellcondah W.N.W. 48 miles.

BALLIRUNGAM (ಬಿಳಿಗಿರಿರಂಗನಬೆಟ್ಟ - biligiriranganabetta, *Can.*; பிளிகிரிரங்கமலை - piligirirangamalai, *Tam.* biligirirangamalai *). From (bilu, can. white + giri, san. mountain + ranga, san. vishnu + malai, tam. mountain). Sanscrit name (shvétádri), meaning white + mountain. Title otherwise Biligherry rungam. Range of hills. Partly in Coimbatore district and partly in Mysore province. For description see vol. II, 61.

BALM (بلسان - balsán, *Hind.*). Means same as balsam, in the sense of aromatic resin.——*Balm of gilead* (اقويلا سمون رومي - akuvilásamúnirúmí, Ar.). From (akuvilásamún, ar. balsam + rúmí, ar. turkish). Title from place whence first brought. The Balm of scripture. Greek βάλσαμον. Title otherwise Balsam of gilead, Balsam of mecca, Opobalsam, Turkish balsam. Botanically Balsamodendron [balsam] opobalsamum, kunth., burseraceæ [vricsham, 35]. Alias Amyris gileadense; Protium gileadense. Distinct however from kiloovay [q.v.]. Tree of arabia, giving a gum-resin. When this first flows, it is yellowish, turbid; after standing some time, becomes clear and heavier, and changes to golden yellow, paler within; odour like anise; taste pungent and acrid; almost always adulterated with turpentine, olive oil or wax; soluble in alcohol. Originally brought from gilead in judea to egypt; mahomedans say it sprung from the blood of the slain in mahomet's conflict with the tribe of harb, and the prophet used the balm for the resuscitation of the dead. Obtained by cutting bark when juice is in strongest circulation, july, august, and september. As medicine scarcely known now in europe, but much used by hakeems as a stimulant. In turkey still used as a cosmetic. Opobalsamum of the ancients was the green liquor found in the kernel of the fruit; carpobalsamum is made by the expression of the ripe fruit; xylobalsamum, very inferior, is prepared by boiling the small twigs.——*Balm of mecca* (بلسان مكى - balasánimakkí, Hind.). Otherwise Opobalsam, the finest kind of Balm of gilead.

BALMATTA (ಬಲ್ಮಠ - balmat'ha, *Can.*). From (bal, can. great + mat'ha, san. convent). Portion of Attavar village, South canara dist., Mangalore tal.; situated in the town of Mangalore; from the sea 1½ mile. A hill formerly the site of the Collector's office, now occupied by the Basel german mission as their quarters.

BALSAM (بلسان - balsán, *Hind.*). Title from Hebrew baal samen, signifying royal oil. Botanically the Balsamodendron genus, burseraceæ [vricsham, 35]. Small, spiny, and balsamiferous trees; natives of arabia, deccan and south africa; foliage scanty; flowers small and green; fruits oval and drupe-like, with hard and thick nuts; give similarly named gum-resin. The species best known to the natives are:—berryi [kiloovay], kataf [african bdellium], mukul [mookul bdellium], myrrha [bole], opobalsamum [balm of gilead], roxburghii [indian bdellium]. In english applied to the Impatiens [gool mindie] genus. The Momordica genus is in english also called Balsam-apple or Balsam-pear [carolah]. See also Persian toolsy.

BALSAM (तैल - taila, *San.*; دهن البلسان - duhnulbalasán, *Ar.*; روغن بلسان - raughanibalasán, *Pers.*; بلسان كا تيل - balsánkátel, *Hind.* and *Dec.*; ತೈಲ - taila, *Can.*; తైలె - taile, *Too.*; తైలము - tailamu, *Tel.*; തൈലം - tailam, *Mal.*; தைலம் - tailam, *Tam.*). Title from hebrew; means royal oil. San. from (tila, san. sesamum seed, sesamum indicum, dec.). Ar. from (duhn, ar. oil + balasán, ar. balsam). Pers. from (raughan, pers. oil + balasán, ar. balsam). Hind. from (balsán, ar. balsam + tel, hind. oil). The product. Aromatic semi-solid exudations from trees [gond], a sub-division of resins [raul]. More solid than oleo-resins [teilam], but the dravidians do not distinguish these two. Hind. distinguishes, real balsams being from arabia. The best known so called balsam here is Gurjan balsam [q.v.], a dipterocarpus; but this is really an oleo-resin. True balsams are from balsamodendron and liquidamber trees. Balm is the same word, but generally confined to the arabian article or Balm of gilead.

BALY (बलि - bali, *San.*). San. means sacrifice. In Malay means to return; a land of quick return, from its unfailing irrigation throughout the year. Next island E. of Java, divided from it by a strait a mile and a half broad. Between S. lat. 6° 45′ and 8° 3′ 30″ and E. long. 114° 26′ and 115° 40′. The indigenous Balinese are same race as Malays and Javanese, but the island, like Cambodia, was reached by Indian aryans and is still under their influence. Balinese are divided into Bramins, Cshatriyas, Veisyas, and Shoodras; more strictly than Hindoos. The sacred language of Baly and Java is Kawy. See vol. I (113).

BAMBOO (بمبو - bambú, *Hind.*; ಬೊಂಬು - bombu, *Can.*). Onomatopæic from the crackling and explosions when they burn. Botanically the Bambusa genus, graminaceæ [vricsham, 156]. Tribe of gigantic grasses strong-rooted perennial plants with jointed hollow stems, rarely solid and varying greatly in size, terminating with branches furnished with grass-like leaves; do not survive seeding. The English bamboo-cane is a species of rattan. Bamboos are by natives distinguished as male and female, the latter embracing all the common species with hollow stems, the former title being applied to Bambusa stricta, roxb., which has a nearly solid core. Ctesias, B.C. 400, says that the Indian reeds were divided into male and female, the male having no ἐντερώνην. The species best known to the natives are shown below. With the bamboos are also classed by the natives:—dendrocalamus [bengal bamboo], crinum [poison bamboo], melocanna [berry bamboo], phragmites, and saccharum [naunal]. For the Bamboo fish see Talabone; so called from color and cylindrical form.——*Bengal bamboo* (پيا بانس - piyábáns, Hind.). Hind. from (piyá, hind. lover + báns, hind. bamboo), lover bamboo; from gracefulness. Hind. also (bishníbáns), meaning same. Botanically Dendrocalamus tulda, nees, graminaceæ [vricsham, 156]. Specific name from bengalee. Alias Bambusa tulda. Stems jointed, unarmed, smooth; leaves alternate, bifarious, sheathing, linear-lanceolate, broad, and sometimes cordate at the base; sheaths longer than the joints; panicles oblong, composed of numerous supra decompound ramifications, only appearing when the plant is destitute of leaves; spikelets lanceolate, sessile four to eight-flowered. No other species here.——*Berry bamboo* (വിഷമുള - vishamula, Mal.). Title from appearance of fruit. Mal. from (visha, san. poison + mula, san. bamboo, bambusa arundinacea, willd.), from quality of berries and other parts. Title otherwise Beesha, Berry-bearing bamboo, Rheede's bamboo. Botanically Melocanna rheedii, rupr., graminaceæ [vricsham, 156]. Alias Beesha rheedii. Beesha from malayalam meaning poison. Unarmed; leaves alternate, ovate-lanceolate, bifarious, smooth on both sides; sheaths villous bearded at the mouth; pericarp a large, fleshy, conical-curved and pointed fruit, with a single oval seed in each; the circumference near the base is 12–13 inches, the height from 50–70 feet, erect, and without the least flexure or inequality of surface, bare of branches, except near the extremity; common on travancore hills. Yields a tabasheer; is common for building; the natives make arrows and bows from the stems and pens from the younger shoots; the leaves are put on verandahs and roofs to keep away white-ants.——*Common bamboo* (वंश - vamsha, San.; वंस - bunsa, Mahr.; वासो - vásó, Conc.; قصب - kasab, Ar.; نى - naí, Pers.; بانس - báns, Hind.; بانسا - bánsá, Dec.; بلوح - buluh, Malay; ಬಿದ್ರು - bidru, Can.; ಬೆದ್ರು - bedru, Too.; వెదురు - veduru, Tel.; മുള - mula, Mal.; උණ - una, Singh.; மூங்கில் - múngil, Tam.). San. from (van, san. to sound); from crackling sound of cluster. Mahr. and conc. from sanscrit. Ar. from (kasaba, ar. to cut); from joints. Hind. and dec. from sanscrit. Can. from (biduvu, can. extension). Mal. means shoot; from appearance of plant, as it sprouts out of earth. San. also (téjana), meaning arrow, from being used for arrow shaft; (kíchaka), from rustling sound; (trinadhvaja), meaning chief among grass; (shataparvá), meaning having many knots; (yavap'hala), meaning having fruits like barley. Hind. also (magarbáns), meaning crocodile bamboo; (nalbáns), meaning tube bamboo. Malay also (mambu). Tel. also (bonguveduru), meaning hollow + bamboo; (pentiveduru), meaning female + bamboo, Tam. also (kuzháymúngil), meaning tube bamboo. Title otherwise Bamboo cane, Bans, Female bamboo, Hollow bamboo, King of grasses, Moongil, Thorn grass. Botanically Bambusa [bamboo] arundinacea, willd., graminaceæ [vricsham, 156]. Alias Arundo arborea, bambos; Bambusa orientalis; Nastus arundinaceus. A gigantic grass with a ligneous stem 70–90 feet, spinescent; grows in large compact clumps of thirty to hundred culms, all from one root. Stems erect, bending at the summit, jointed, hollow between the joints; branches alternate; thorns two or three, alternate on the joints; when double, a branchlet occupies the centre; when triple, the largest is strong, sharp, and somewhat recurved, occasionally wanting; leaves 4–8 inches long, sheathing, linear-lanceolate, upper sides and margins hispid, sheaths downy; when in flower, the tree is leafless and the extremities are covered with flowers like one large panicle composed of numerous verticillate spikes, each verticel composed of several oblong, jointed, sessile spikelets; calyx two to six-flowered, three-valved; flowers hermaphrodite and male; seeds size and appearance of oats; male flowers one to three above the hermaphrodite ones. The silicious concretion known as tabasheer is a bluish-white concrete light substance, a secretion from the joints of the reed in a state of disease, malformation, or fracture; consists of 90·50 per cent. of silica, a minute quantity of lime, and vegetable matter; refractive power is lower than that of any other body, whether solid or fluid; with certain oils, which it imbibes, it becomes as transparent as glass; absorbs water and becomes as white and opaque as if covered with white-lead; so far resembles silex as to form a kind of glass when fused with alkalies; is unaffected by fire and acids; sticks to the tongue. The bamboo is of rapid growth, and in four or five years is fit for many uses, but does not bear flower or fruit till it has reached a very considerable age, as for instance twenty-five, after which it perishes; large patches of jungle always flower together and at long irregular intervals; the jungle tribes regard these phenomena as the heralds of famine and sickness. Immense quantities of bamboos are floated down rivers of west coast. Tabasheer is medicinally a stimulant and aphrodisiac, in pharm. non-officinal; the root of the bamboo is diluent, the bark a specific in eruptions, and the leaves anthelmintic and emmenagogue. Seed eaten by the poorer classes like paddy; as it appears at the very season when drought occurs and other crops fail, it is of some advantage to the poor; it is a very unsafe aliment, being apt to produce diarrhœa and dysentery; rats are fond of it; young shoots are cut when tender, eaten like asparagus and used in chutneys; leaves and twigs form an important fodder, being largely consumed by elephants. The stem gives a fibre; the full-grown stems, while green, form convenient cases, which exhaling a perpetual moisture are capable of transporting fresh flowers, &c., for hundreds of miles; when ripe and hard they are converted into bows, arrows, and quivers, lance shafts, the masts of vessels, bed-posts, walking sticks, the poles of palanquins, the floors and supporters of rustic bridges, and a variety of similar purposes; in a growing state the spiny kinds are formed into stockades, which are impenetrable to any but regular infantry, aided by artillery; bruised and crushed in water, the leaves and stems form chinese paper, the finer qualities of which are only improved by a mixture of raw cotton and by more careful pounding; cut into lengths and the partitions knocked out, stems form durable water-pipes; slit into strips, they afford a durable material for weaving into mats, baskets, window-blinds, and even the sails of boats; a joint of bamboo answers the purpose of a bottle, and a section of it is a measure for liquids, &c., in bazaars; 21 bamboos of rice make 1 maund; as measure of length it is 14 yards; a piece of it is used as a blow-pipe and as a tube in a distilling apparatus; a small bit of it split at one end serves as tongs to take up burning charcoal, and a thin slip of it is sharp enough to be used as a knife in shelling betel-nuts, &c.; its surface is so hard that it answers the purpose of a whetstone, upon which the ryots sharpen their bill-hooks and sickles; from buoyancy it is used in numbers for floating heavier woods. The bamboo is next to the cocoanut palm the most useful and economical of all the vegetable products of the country; in no other plant is strength and lightness combined to such a degree. There is a Tamul saying:—ஆல்போற்றழைத்து, அறுகுபோல் வேரூன்றி மூங்கில்போற் சுற்ற முசியாமல் வாழ்ந்திருப்பீர்—"May you flourish as the banyan full of "boughs and foliage, spread like creeping stems of hurrially "grass, putting forth roots and prosper as the bamboo amid "unfailing kindred;" a congratulatory expression to a newly-married couple.——*Creeping bamboo* (लतावंश - latávamsha, San.). Title from habit and appearance. Same as Country rattan.——*Crow bamboo* (కాకివెదురు - kákiveduru, Tel.). Inferior bamboo. Same as Naunal.——*Dog bamboo* (ഞാങ്ങണ - ñánnana, Mal.). Inferior bamboo. Same as Naunal.——*Dwarf bamboo* (கடப்பைமரம் - kadappaimaram, Tam.). Title otherwise Chinese dwarf bamboo, Small bamboo. Botanically Bambusa [bamboo] nana, roxb., graminaceæ [vricsham, 156].——*Hog bamboo* (ಪಂಜಿಬೆದುರು - panjibeduru, Too.). From use in pig sticking. Same as Male bamboo.——*Mahableshwar bamboo* (कांटाबंस - kántábamsa, Mahr.). Mahr. from (kanta, san. thorn + vamsha, san. bamboo). Title otherwise Bamboo reed. Botanically Bambusa [bamboo] arundo, klein., graminaceæ [vricsham, 156]. Culms thorny; western ghauts.——*Male bamboo* (अखंडुवासो - akhanduvásó, Conc.; قصب - kasab, Ar.; نئی - naí, Pers.; بانس - báns, Hind.; بمبو - bambú, Dec.; ಗಂಡುಬಿದುರು - gandubiduru, Can.; ಪಂಜಿಬೆದುರು - panjibeduru, Too.; రాతివెదురు - rátiveduru, Tel.; അരിങ്കണ്ടം - arinkantam, Mal.; கல்மூங்கில் - kalmúngil, Tam.). Title from its strength and straightness. Conc. from (akhanda, san. not breaking + vamsha, san. bambusa arundinacea, willd.). Hind. from (vamsha, san.). Can. from (gandu, can. male + biduru, can. bamboo). Too. from (pañji, too. hog + beduru, too. bamboo); from use in pig sticking. Tel. from (ráyi, tel. stone + veduru, tel. bamboo). Mal. from (arim, mal. strong + kantam, mal. piece). Tam. from (kal, tam. stone + múngil, tam. bamboo). Hind. also (ghatbáns), meaning solid bamboo. Tel. also (sádhanapuveduru), meaning implement + bamboo; (gettiveduru), meaning solid + bamboo. Mal. also (karinkana), meaning black-knuckled. Title otherwise Dark bamboo, Hard bamboo, Hog bamboo, Stone bamboo. Botanically Bambusa [bamboo] stricta, roxb., graminaceæ [vricsham, 156]. Alias Bambusa verticillata; Dendrocalamus strictus; Nastus strictus. Small straight species; stems strong, elastic and nearly solid; thorns frequently wanting; inflorescence the same as in the common bamboo; verticels sessile, globular, numerous, entirely surrounding the branchlets; flowers hermaphrodite; corolla two-valved; extreme valves pubescent, sharply pointed; pistil woolly. Has often deciduous leaves; flowers frequently every year, does not die down after flowering; natives say it accomplishes the whole of its growth in two or three weeks during the rains; found in plains and lower hills. Leaves used sometimes as fodder. Natives use it for spears, shafts, and similar purposes.——*Poison bamboo* (विषमण्डल - vishamandala, San.; नागदवण - nágadavana, Mahr.; किरटिमारि - kiratimári, Conc.; سکھدرسن - sukhdarsan, Hind.; ناگن کے پتے کا جھاڑ - náginkepattekájhár, Dec.; ತೊಲ್ಡೊ - toldo, Can.; విషముంగలి - vishamungali, Tel.; പോളത്താളി - pólattáli, Mal.; තොලබො - tolabó, Singh.; விடமூங்கில் - vidamúngil, Tam.). Title from bamboo-like leaves and emetic bulbous root. San. from (visha, san. poison + mandala, san. ball). Mahr. means serpent subduer. Hind. from (sukha, san. pleasure + darshana, san. sight). Dec. from (nágin, hind. female serpent + pattá, dec. leaf + jhár, dec. tree). Tel. from tamul. Mal. from (póla, mal. bubble + táli, mal. creeper). Tam. from (visha, san. poison + múngil, tam. bamboo). Hind. also (barákanwar), meaning large aloe. Tel. also (késara) [ilanjy, kamela, nauga champak, saffron]; (lakshminárâyanachettu), meaning lutchmy + narayana + plant. Mal. also (vishamula), meaning poison bamboo. Tam. also (narivengáyam), meaning fox onion from being wild and having bulbous root like onion; (tudaivási), meaning to destroy + health, from nauseant root. Title otherwise Asiatic poison bulb, Asiatic squill, Bubble creeper, Fox onion, Kool-leaved african lily, Poison bulb crinum, Poison lily. Botanically Crinum asiaticum, linn., willd., amaryllidaceæ [vricsham, 145]. Alias Crinum defiscum, toxicarum. Stemless; leaves radical, linear, concave, 3–4 feet long, obtuse, pointed, margins smooth; umbels six to sixteen-flowered; flowers subsessile; roots bulbous, with a terminal fusiform portion, issuing from the crown, from which numerous fibrous roots proceed; flowers large, white, fragrant at night; corolla tube cylindrical, usually pale green, segments linear-lanceolate, margins broad, with a recurved process at the apex of each; plant indigenous; grows on the banks of streams and tanks. Succulent bitterish leaves bruised and mixed with castor-oil, form application for whitlows, &c.; juice for ear ache; root a substitute for the squill. The variety toxicarium gives to pharm. crini radix; nauseant and diaphoretic; officinal, like squill. Other common species are:—ornatum, pratense, revolutum, roxburghii. Compare genus Melocanna [berry bamboo].——*Striped bamboo* (कळक - kalaka, Mahr.; උණ - una, Singh.). Title from appearance of stem. Mahr. means stained. Botanically Bambusa [bamboo] vulgaris, schrad., graminaceæ [vricsham, 156]. Stems 20–50 feet, yellow or striped yellow and green.——*Thorny bamboo* (කටුඋණ - katuuna, Singh.). Singh. from (katu, singh. thorny + una, singh. bamboo). Botanically Bambusa [bamboo] spinosa, roxb., graminaceæ [vricsham, 156]. Alias Bambusa arundinacea. Mountains on north-east coast.

BAN (بن - ban, *Hind.*). Forest. Compare:—Glycosmis pentaphylla (bannímbu), forest lime; Jasminum angustifolium (banmallika), forest jasmine; Felis viverrina (banbirál), forest cat; Pterocles exustus (bantítar), forest partridge. See gloss. paragraphs.

BANAFSHAH (بنفسج - banafsaj, *Ar.*; بنفشه - banafshah, *Pers.*, *Hind.* and *Dec.*). Greek ἴον πορφυροῦν. The Violet. Botanically Viola odorata, linn., violaceæ [vricsham, 13]. The dry plant sold in the bazaar is a very small herb with thready branches; root small, fusiform, generally smooth, and from one to three lines in thickness; stem short, often divided and rough; leaves small, much shrivelled, but when moistened and spread they are elliptical or oblong; flowers retain their original color when new. As a drug whole plant is used, antipyretic and diaphoretic; preparations by compound and simple decoction. Viola tricolor is the pansy or heart's ease.

BANAJIGA (ಬಣಜಿಗ - banajiga, *Can.*). From (vanik, san. trader). The Canarese form of Bunniah [q.v.]. Common caste in Mysore; with various occupations. Many dancing girls are of this caste. The caste are permitted to eat meat and drink spirits. They are Shoodras, and do not, like the Bunniahs, claim to be Veisyas. Some are Veishnavas, and some Lingayets. Their gooroos are accordingly chief of the Shreeveishnava bramins or punchaungies of the Smarta bramins. The Linga banajigas are very strict in their observances, and abstain from flesh and spirits [jauty].

BANANA (بنان - bananá, *Malay*). W. indian variety of musa paradisiaca, plantain; sweeter.

BANDAH (بنده - bandah, *Pers.*). From (bandh, san. to bind). Slave. Part of lacab; as Bandah i ally, slave of Ally [ism].——*Bandaghee* (بندگی - bandagí, Hind.). From (bandh, san. to bind). Submission. Mahomedan term of salutation.——*Bandana* (بندهنا - bandhaná, Hind.). From (bandhana, san. tie). A yellow or red silk handkerchief [roomaul] with spots left white. The parts intended to remain undyed or white are tightly tied; hence the name. The spots are generally diamond shape. The term is often used for figured silk handkerchiefs of other descriptions. For figured cottons as opposed to figured silks, see Chintz [sheelay].

BANDAR (कपि - kapi, *San.*; वानर - vánara, *Mahr.*; قرد - kird, *Ar.*; بوزینه - búzínah, *Pers.*; بندر - bandar, *Hind.*; باندرا - bándrá, *Dec.*; کارا - kára, *Malay*; ಮಂಗ - manga, *Can.*; ಮಾಙ್ಙ - mançça, *Coorg*; ಮಂಗೆ - mange, *Too.*; కోతి - kóti, *Tel.*; ମାଙ୍କଡ଼ - mankodo, *Oor.*; കുരങ്ങൻ - kurannan, *Mal.*; රිලවා - rilavá, *Singh.*; குரங்கு - kurangu, *Tam.*). Title from hindostany. San. means brown. Mahr. from (vana, san. forest + nara, san. man). Ar. from (karida, ar. submissive); from docility. Pers. from (bú, ar. father + zannah, ar. suspicion); from vigilant habits. Hind. from (vana, san. forest + nara, san. man). Oor. from (markata, san. monkey). Mal. and Tam. from (kurai, tam. to clamour). Mahr. also (makadí), from (markata, san. monkey); also (kerda), from arabic. Can. also (kódaga). Mal. also (vellamanti), meaning white + monkey; also (moçça), meaning the munching one. Singh. also (vandurá), a generic name for the black monkey. Title otherwise Bonnet monkey. Macacus sinicus, cercopithecinæ [baboon], cercopitheoidæ, quadrumana, mammalia [sastanam, 1], of naturalists [jantoo]. Alias Cercocebus radiatus; Macacus radiatus; Simia sinica. Of generally dusky olive-brown color, paler and albescent on the belly, and somewhat ashy on the outer sides of the limbs; hairs on the crown of the head, radiated; tail, dusky brown above, whitish beneath. Found over all south, extending north to latitude 18°, where replaced by Bengal monkey, Macacus rhesus. It sometimes inhabits the jungles, and also lives in towns, carrying off fruit and grain from shops. It is the monkey most commonly found in menageries. For silenus species see Siyah bandar. Indian species not here found are:—Arctoides or brown stump-tailed monkey, Assamensis or hill monkey, Cynomolgus or crab-eating monkey, Leoninus or long-haired pig-tailed monkey, Nemestrinus or pig-tailed monkey, Pileatus or toque monkey, Rhesus or bengal monkey. There is a Tamul proverb:—இஞ்சிதின்ற குரங்குபோல்—"Like a "monkey that has eaten green ginger; i.e., suffering for one's "own folly." And another:—மர்க்கடநியாயத்தீர்ப்பு—"Monkey's judgment"; i.e., a corrupt judgment. The natives hold that the urine, discharged in a thick stream and which admits of being collected when dry, has property of curing rheumatic pains, applied with garlic. Chentsoos obtain a sale for even stones on which this monkey has made water. The hill people suffering from chronic fever sometimes drink its blood.——*Siyah bandar* (केसरिवानर - késarivánara, San.; سیاہ بندر - siyáhbandar, Pers. and Hind.; ಶಿಂಗಳೀಕ - shingalíka, Can.; ಕರಿಂಗೋಡೆ - karingóde, Coorg; కొండముచ్చు - kondamuttsu, Tel.; നീലൻ - nílan, Mal.; මහවඳුරා - mahavandurá, Singh.; கருங்குரங்கு - karungurangu, Tam.). Title from hindostany. San. from (késari, san. the maned lion + vánara, san. monkey). Pers. from (siyáh, pers. black + bandar, hind. monkey). Can. from (chinnala, mal. lion). Coorg from (kari, coorg, black + kóde, coorg, monkey). Tel. from (konda, tel. hill + muttsu, tel. thief). Mal. from (níla, san. black). Singh. from (mahá, san. great + vandurá, singh. black monkey). Tam. from (karumai, tam. blackness + kurangu, tam. monkey). Tel. also (gandangi), meaning great + body. Mal. also (chinnalakkurannu), meaning lion + monkey; (nílamanti), meaning black + monkey. Title otherwise Lion monkey, from form of tail. Macacus silenus, cercopithecinæ [baboon], cercopithecidæ, quadrumana, mammalia [sastanam, 1], of naturalists [jantoo]. Alias Inuus silenus Silenus veter; Simia ferox, silenus. Black, with a reddish-white hood or beard surrounding the face and neck; tail, with a tuft of hair at the tip. It is a native of the more elevated forests of the Western ghauts from latitude 14° to the extreme south, but most abundant in Cochin and Travancore. It frequents the most dense and unfrequented parts of the forests, at a considerable elevation. In its nature it is savage. In Ceylon there is the Semnopithecus ursinus or Wanderoo [q.v.]. There has been a certain amount of confusion between this animal and the lion monkey. They are both large monkeys, with great beards of light colored hair, but in no other respect do they resemble each other.

BANDHOO (बन्धु - bandhu, *San.*; بندھ - bandh, *Hind.*). From (bandh, san. to tie). Relation. The following are the terms for the different degrees of kindred in Sanscrit, Teloogoo, and Tamul, arranged for convenience under the English titles. They throw much light on Dravidian nomenclature.——*Aunt* (पितृष्वसा - pitrishvasá, San.; మేనత్త - ménatta, Tel.; அத்தை - attai, Tam.); father's sister. (मातृज्येष्ठष्वसा - mátrijyésht'hashvasá, San.; పెత్తల్లి - pettalli, Tel.; பெரியதாயார் - periyatháyár, Tam.); mother's elder sister. (मातृकनिष्ठष्वसा - mátrikanisht'hashvasá, San.; పినతల్లి - pinatalli, Tel.; சிறியதாயார் - shiriyatháyár, Tam.); mother's younger sister. (ज्येष्ठपितृव्यपत्नी - jyésht'hapitrivyapatní, San.; పెత్తల్లి - pettalli, Tel.; பெரியதாயார் - periyatháyár, Tam.); father's elder brother's wife. (कनिष्ठपितृव्यपत्नी - kanisht'hapitrivyapatní, San.; పినతల్లి - pinatalli, Tel.; சிறியதாயார் - shiriyatháyár, Tam.); father's younger brother's wife. (मातुलानी - mátulání, San.; మేనత్త - ménatta, Tel.; மாமி - mámi, Tam.); mother's brother's wife.——*Brother* (भ्राता - bhrátá, San.; సహోదరుడు - sahódarudu, Tel.; சகோதரன் - shagótharan, Tam.).——*Brother-in-law* (ज्येष्ठदेवर - jyésht'hadévara, San.; బావ - báva, Tel.; மச்சினன் - maççinan, Tam.); husband's elder brother. (कनिष्ठदेवर - kanisht'hadévara, San.; మరిది - maridi, Tel.; கொழுந்தன் - kozhundan, Tam.); husband's younger brother. (स्याल - syála, San.; బావమరిది - bávamaridi, Tel.; மச்சினன் - maççinan, Tam.); wife's brother. (ज्येष्ठभागिनीपति - jyésht'habhaginípati, San.; బావ - báva, Tel.; அத்திம்பேர் - attimbér, Tam.); elder sister's husband. (कनिष्ठभागिनीपति - kanisht'habhaginípati, San.; మరిది - maridi, Tel.; மாப்பிள்ளை - máppillai, Tam.); younger sister's husband. (षड्डक - shaddhaka, San.; షడ్డకుడు - shaddakudu, Tel.; சட்டகன் - shattagan, Tam.); wife's sister's husband.——*Cousin* (ज्येष्ठपितृव्यापत्य - jyésht'hapitrivyápatya, San.; పెత్తండ్రిబిడ్డలు - pettandribiddalu, Tel.; பெரியப்பன்மக்கள் - periyappanmakkal, Tam.); father's elder brother's children. (कनिष्ठपितृव्यापत्य - kanisht'hapitrivyápatya, San.; పినతండ్రిబిడ్డలు - pinatandribiddalu, Tel.; சிற்றப்பன்மக்கள் - shittappanmakkal, Tam.); father's younger brother's children. (पितृष्वस्रीय - pitrishvasríya, San.; మేనత్తబిడ్డలు - ménattabiddalu, Tel.; அத்தைமக்கள் - attaimakkal, Tam.); father's sister's children. (मातुलापत्य - mátulápatya, San.; మేనమామబిడ్డలు - ménamámabiddalu, Tel. மாமன்மக்கள் - mámanmakkal, Tam.); mother's brother's children. (ज्येष्ठमातृष्वस्रीय - jyésht'hamátrishvasríya, San.; పెత్తల్లిబిడ్డలు - pettallibiddalu, Tel.; பெரியதாயார்மக்கள் periyatháyármakkal, Tam.); mother's elder sister's children. (कनिष्ठमातृष्वस्रीय - kanisht'hamátrishvasríya, San.; పినతల్లిబిడ్డలు - pinatallibiddalu, Tel.; சிறியதாயார்மக்கள் - shiriyatháyármakkal, Tam.); mother's younger sister's children. (ज्ञाति - ñáti, San.; దాయాది - dáyádi, Tel.; தாயாதி - táyáthi, Tam.).——*Daughter* (दुहिता duhitá, San.; కూతురు - kúturu, Tel.; மகள் - magal, Tam.).——*Daughter-in-law* (स्नुषा - snushá, San.; కోడలు - kódalu, Tel.; மருமகள் - marumagal, Tam.).——*Elder* (ज्येष्ठ - jyésht'ha, San.; పెద్ద - pedda, Tel.; மூத்த - mútta, Tam.).——*Father* (पिता - pitá, San.; తండ్రి - tandri, Tel.; தகப்பன் - tagappan, Tam.).——*Father-in-law* (श्वशुर - shvashura, San.; మామగారు - mámagáru, Tel.; மாமனார் - mámanár, Tam.).——*Foster-brother* (धात्रीपुत्र - dhátríputra, San.; పెంపుడుసహోదరుడు - pempudusahódarudu, Tel.; வளர்ப்புச்சகோதரன் - valarppuççagótharan, Tam.).——*Foster-child* (पोष्यापत्य - póshyápatya, San.; పెంపుడుబిడ్డ - pempudubidda, Tel.; வளர்ப்புப்பிள்ளை - valarppuppillai, Tam.).——*Foster-father* (पोषकपिता - póshakapitá, San.; పెంపుడుతండ్రి - pempudutandri, Tel.; வளர்த்ததகப்பன் - valarttathagappan, Tam.).——*Foster-mother* (धात्री - dhátrí, San.; పెంపుడుతల్లి - pempudutalli, Tel.; வளர்த்ததாயார் - valarttatháyár, Tam.).——*Foster-sister* (धात्रेयी - dhátréyí, San.; పెంపుడుసహోదరి - pempudusahódari, Tel.; வளர்ப்புச்சகோதரி - valarppuççagóthari, Tam.).——*God-daughter* (धर्मदुहिता - dharmaduhitá, San.; దైవపుత్రి - daivaputri, Tel.; ஞானப்பெண் - ñánappen, Tam.).——*God-father* (धर्मपिता - dharmapitá, San.; దైవపితృ - daivapitri, Tel.; ஞானப்பிதா - ñánappithá, Tam.).——*God-mother* (धर्ममाता - dharmamátá, San.; దైవమాతృ - daivamátri, Tel.; ஞானத்தாயார் - ñánattáyár, Tam.).——*God-son* (धर्मपुत्र - dharmaputra, San.; దైవపుత్రుడు - daivaputrudu, Tel.; ஞானப்பிள்ளை - ñánappillai, Tam.).——*Grand-daughter* (पौत्री - pautrí, San.; మనమరాలు - manamarálu, Tel.; பேத்தி - pétti, Tam.); son's daughter. (दौहित्री - dauhitrí, San.; మనమరాలు - manamarálu, Tel.; பேத்தி - pétti, Tam.); daughter's daughter.——*Grand-father* (पितामह - pitámaha, San.; తాత - táta, Tel.; பாட்டன் - páttan, Tam.); paternal. (मातामह - mátámaha, San.; తాత - táta, Tel.; பாட்டன் - páttan, Tam.); maternal.——*Grand-mother* (पितामही - pitámahí, San.; అవ్వ - avva, Tel.; பாட்டி - pátti, Tam.); paternal. (मातामही - mátámahí, San.; అవ్వ - avva, Tel.; பாட்டி - pátti, Tam.); maternal.——*Grand-son* (पौत्र - pautra, San.; మనమడు - manamadu, Tel.; பேரன் - péran, Tam.); son's son. (दौहित्र - dauhitra, San.; మనమడు - manamadu, Tel.; பேரன் - péran, Tam.); daughter's son.——*Husband* (भर्ता - bhartá, San.; పెనిమిటి - penimiti, Tel.; புருடன் - purudan, Tam.).——*Mother* (माता - mátá, San.; తల్లి - talli, Tel.; தாயார் - táyár, Tam.).——*Mother-in-law* (श्वश्रू - shvashrú, San.; అత్తగారు - attagáru, Tel.; மாமியார் - mámiyár, Tam.).——*Nephew* (भ्रात्रीय - bhrátríya, San.; సహోదరునికొడుకు - sahódarunikoduku, Tel.; சகோதரன்மகன் - shagótharanmagan, Tam.); brother's son. (भागिनेय - bhágineya, San.; మేనల్లుడు - ménalludu Tel.; மருமகன் - marumagan, Tam.); sister's son.——*Niece* (भ्रात्रीया - bhrátríyá, San.; సహోదరునికూతురు - sahódarunikúturu, Tel.; சகோதரன்மகள் - shagótharanmagal, Tam.); brother's daughter. (भागिनेयी - bhágineyí, San.; మేనకోడలు - ménakódalu, Tel.; மருமகள் - marumagal, Tam.); sister's daughter.——*Parents* (पितरौ - pitarau, San.; తల్లిదండ్రులు - tallidandrulu, Tel.; தாய்தந்தைகள் - táytandaigal, Tam.).——*Sister* (भगिनी - bhaginí, San.; సహోదరి - sahódari, Tel.; சகோதரி - shagóthari, Tam.).——*Sister-in-law* (ज्येष्ठननान्दा - jyésht'hananándá, San.; వదినె - vadine, Tel.; பெரியநாத்தனார் - periyanáttanár, Tam.); husband's elder sister. (कनिष्ठननान्दा - kanisht'hananándá, San.; మరదలు - maradalu, Tel.; சிறியநாத்தனார் - shiriyanáttanár, Tam.); husband's younger sister. (स्याली -

syálí, San. ; వదినెమరదలు - vadinemaradalu, Tel. ; மச்சினி - maççini, Tam.) ; wife's sister. (प्रजावती - prajávatí, San. ; వదినె - vadine, Tel. ; அண்ணி - anni, Tam.); elder brother's wife. (कनिष्ठभ्रातृजाया - kanisht'habbhrátrijáyá, San. ; మరదలు - maradalu, Tel. ; தம்பிபெண்சாதி - tambibensáthi, Tam.) ; younger brother's wife. (याता - yátá, San. ; తోడికోడలు - tódikódalu, Tel. ; ஓரகத்தி - óragatti, Tam.) ; husband's brother's wife.——*Son* (पुत्र - putra, San. ; కొడుకు - koduku, Tel. ; மகன் - magan, Tam.).——*Son-in-law* (जामाता - jámátá, San. ; అల్లుడు - alludu, Tel. ; மருமகன் - marumagan, Tam.).——*Step-brother* (वैमात्रेय - vaimátróya, San. ; మారుసహోదరుడు - márusahódarudu, Tel. ; மாற்றாஞ்சகோதரன் - máttáñjagótharan, Tam.).——*Step-daughter* (सपत्नीदुहिता - sapatníduhitá, San. ; సవతికూతురు - savatikúturu, Tel. ; மறுதாரத்தின்மகள் - maruthárattinmagal, Tam.).——*Step-father* (మారుతండ్రి - márutandri, Tel. ; மாற்றாந்தகப்பன் - máttándagappan, Tam.).——*Step-mother* (सपत्नीमाता - sapatnímátá, San. ; సవతితల్లి - savatitalli, Tel. ; மாற்றாந்தாயார் - máttándáyár, Tam.).——*Step-sister* (वैमात्रेयी - vaimátréyí, San. ; మారుసహోదరి - márusahódari, Tel. ; மாற்றாஞ்சகோதரி - máttáñjagóthari, Tam.).——*Step-son* (सपत्नीपुत्र - sapatníputra, San. ; సవతికొడుకు - savatikoduku, Tel. ; மறுதாரத்தின்மகன் - márutharattinmagan, Tam.).——*Uncle* (मातुल - mátula, San. ; మేనమామ - ménamáma, Tel. ; மாமன் - mámau, Tam.) ; mother's brother. (ज्येष्ठपितृव्य - jyésht'hapitrivya, San. ; పెత్తండ్రి - pettandri, Tel. ; பெரியப்பன் - periyappan, Tam.) ; father's elder brother. (कनिष्ठपितृव्य - kanisht'hapitrivya, San. ; పినతండ్రి - pinatandri, Tel. ; சிற்றப்பன் - shittappan, Tam.) ; father's younger brother. (मातृज्येष्ठभगिनीपति - mátrijyésht'habhaginípati, San. ; పెత్తండ్రి - pettandri, Tel. ; பெரியப்பன் - periyappan, Tam.) ; mother's elder sister's husband. (मातृकनिष्ठभगिनीपति - mátrikanisht'habhaginípati, San. ; పినతండ్రి - pinatandri, Tel. ; சிற்றப்பன் - shittappan, Tam.) ; mother's younger sister's husband. (पितृभगिनीपति - pitribhaginípati, San. ; మేనమామ - ménamáma, Tel. ; அத்தைப்புருடன் - attaippurudan, Tam.) ; father's sister's husband. —*Wife* (भार्या - bháryá, San. ; పెండ్లాము - pendlámu, Tel. ; பெண்சாதி - pensáthi, Tam.).——*Younger* (कनिष्ठ - kanisht'ha, San. ; పిన్న - pinna, Tel. ; இளைய - ilaiya, Tam.).

BANDICOOT (इन्दूर - indúra, *San.* ; घूस - ghúsa, *Mahr.* ; خرموش - kharmúsh, *Pers.* ; گھونس - ghúns, *Hind.* ; گھوس - ghús, *Dec.* ; ಹೆಗ್ಗಣ - heggana, *Can.* ; ಪೆರ್ಗುಡೆ - pergude, *Too.* ; పందికొక్కు - pandikokku, *Tel.* ; ବୋଡ଼ୋମୁସା - bodomussa, *Oor.* ; പെരിച്ചാഴി - periççázhi, *Mal.* ; ඌරුමීයා - úrumíyá, *Singh.* ; பெருச்சாளி - peruççáli, *Tam.*). Title from teloogoo. Mahr. from hindostany. Pers. from (khar, pers. ass + músh, pers. mouse). Can. from (hedda, can. large + khanaka, san. rat). Tel. from (pandi, tel. pig + kokku, tel. bandicoot). Oor. means large rat. Mal. from tamul. Singh. from (úru, singh. large + míyá, singh. rat). Tam. from (perisu, tam. great + eli, tam. rat). Title otherwise Malabar rat, Pig rat. Mus [moosham] bandicota, muridæ, rodentia, mammalia [sastanam, 17], of naturalists [jantoo]. Generic name connected with (músha, san. rat) ; specific name from teloogoo. Alias Mus giganteus, malabaricus, nemorivagus. Dark dusky olive brown color above, with some black bristly hairs intermixed ; beneath lighter mixed with gray. The length of a large individual, head and body, has been known to be 15 inches. The incisors are dark olive green at the base, becoming yellow at the extremities. The molars have strong alveolar processes ; the anterior is divided into three portions by transverse ridges of enamel, the middle ones into two, and the posterior ones only partially so. They become quite tubercular when old. The tail is scaly with a few scattered, short, addressed, bristly hairs. The female has twelve teats. Found throughout S. india, and more prevalent than in north. In the fort at Madras it is exceedingly numerous, living during the day in drains, and entering houses at night. Does not occur in Neilgherries. Is eaten by lower classes of natives. Bones fragile, and easily killed. Its nests, when rifled, are found to contain rice stored up against dry season.

BANDICOY (வெண்டைக்காய் - veudaikkáy, *Tam.*). From (bhinda, san. hibiscus + káy, tam. fruit). Similar in all dravidian. Unripe fruit of hibiscus esculentus [common bendy].

BANDY (بنڈی - bandí, *Hind.* ; బండి - bandi, *Tel.* ; വണ്ടി - vanti, *Mal.* ; வண்டி - vandi, *Tam.*). A carriage or cart. Unknown in Bengal.——*Bandy pettah* (బండిమెట్ట - bandimetta, Tel. ; வண்டிப்பேட்டை - vandippéttai, Tam.). Tel. from (metta, tel. rising ground). From (above + péttai, tam. suburb). A cart-stand. ——*Bandy raipam* (బండిరేఫము - bandiréþ'hamu, Tel.). R. The letter ఱ ; still used in Teloogoo, obsolete at present day in Canarese.

BANEE (بنی - baní, *Hind.*). Bride. In composition makes a lacab ; as Banee bee, bride-like lady. Baney is the masculine ; as Baney miyaun, bridegroom + lord [ism].

BANGALORE (ಬೆಂಗಳೂರು - bengalúru, *Can.*). From (bengalu, can. a bean + úru, can. village).—"*a*" District in the south-east Mysore, sub-divided into the following talooks:—Annecull, Bangalore, Cancanhully, Closepett, Devanhully, Dodballapore, Hoscote, Maugady, Nelamungala.—"*b*" Talook near the centre, Bangalore district. Head-quarters at Bangalore. Contains the hoblies:—Agara, Bangalore, Begore, Halsore, Kengairy, Krishnarajpore, Vartore, Yelahunka, Yeswantapore. Principal places:—Bangalore, Baunasavaudy, Caucharkahully, Goonjore, Kampapore, Kengairy, Vartore, Yelahunka.—"*c*" Town in lat. 12° 59′ and long. 77° 38′. Seat of Government for Mysore and head-quarters of the Bangalore division of the Madras army. Consists of the pettah or old native town and the cantonment or Civil and Military station [hill-station, mysore].

BANGHY (بھنگی - bhangí, *Hind.*). From (vah, san. to bear). A yoke on which two articles are carried. The post mail that conveys parcels. So also the parcels themselves.

BANGLE (بنگڑی - bangrí, *Hind.*). A bracelet, generally of colored glass worn on the wrist by women. Also applied to any native ring-bracelet and anklet.

BANIJ (بنج - banij, *Hind.*). From (vanik, san. merchant). Trade, business. The Thug designation for victims.

BANKAH (वंक्रि - vaukri, *San.* ; بانکا - bánká, *Hind.*). From (vank, san. to be crooked). A bent trumpet like letter S, brass, of three pieces fixed into one another [sangeetam].

BANKSHAUL (بنگسال - bangsál, *Hind.*). From (vanik, san. trade + shálá, san. a house). Warehouse. Specially Government warehouse for salt, tobacco, &c.

BANOLAH (بنولا - banolá, *Hind.*). From (bángá, hind. cotton). Cotton seed [indian cotton].

BANS (بنس - báns, *Hind.*). Bamboo, bambusa arundinacea. Compare: Agave vivipara (banskeora), bamboo screw-pine. ——*Banslochan* (بنس لوچن - banslochan, Dec.). From (báns, hind. bamboo + lochan, hind. eye). Tabasheer.

BANTAM (வாந்தம் - vándam, *Tam.*). Town in Java. English first arrived there in 1602, following the Dutch. In the sequel the English were expelled by their rivals. See vol. I, 2. Madras was a dependency of the Bantam factory till 1653. Gives name to a small kind of fowl. Bantam work is gaudily varnished japan work.

BANYAN (न्यग्रोध - nyagródha, *San.* ; वड - vada, *Mahr.* ; بڑ - bar, *Hind.* ; بڑکا جھاڑ - barkájhár, *Dec.* ; برنگن - baringin, *Malay* ; ಆಲ - ála, *Can.* ; ಗೋಳಿದಮರ - gólidamara, *Too.* ; మఱ్ఱి - marri, *Tel.* ; ବୋରୁ - bóru, *Oor.* ; പേരാൽ - pérál, *Mal.* ; මහනුග - mahanuga, *Singh.* ; ஆல் - ál, *Tam.*). Title first bestowed on a tree of this species growing near gombroon or bunder abbas on persian gulf, under which the hindoo traders or banyans had built a small pagoda. San. from (nyak, san. turned downwards + ruh, san. to grow) ; from descending shoots. Mahr. from (vata, san. the tree). Hind. from the same. Can. from tamul. Mal. from (peru, mal. large + ál, mal. the banyan tree). Singh. from (mahá, san. great + nuga, singh. milky fig tree, ficus laccifera, roxb.). Tam. from (álu, tam. to spread) ; from spreading branches. San. also (vata), meaning circle, from its circumference ; (bahupád), meaning many-footed, from descending shoots ; (mánavriksha), meaning proud tree ; (skandhajanya), meaning produced from stem or cuttings ; (pátánga), meaning tree with descending branches ; (chiravriksha), meaning long-lived tree. Can. also (gólimara), from globular fruit. Tam. also (égavásam), meaning solitary tree ; (kánmaram), meaning forest tree. Title otherwise Arbor de rais, Bengal fig, Descending tree, Grove tree, Indian fig, Murry, Oval-leaved fig, Pagoda tree, Wad. Botanically Ficus [atty] bengalensis, linn., moraceæ [vriosham, 121]. Alias Ficus indica, vuta ; Urostigma bengaleuse. Vuta from sanscrit. Immense tree ; branches spreading very much ; lower ones rooting ; leaves alternate, ovate, bluntly acuminated, with parallel nerves, paler underneath, entire, downy when young, afterwards smooth ; fruit receptacles axillary, paired, sessile, as large as a middle-sized cherry, appearing and ripening in the hot season. Common everywhere ; it is remarkable for the singular property of letting a gummy kind of rootlet fall from its branches ; these form a natural support to the larger branches of the parent tree, forming a vast assemblage of pillar-like stems covering a considerable area round the original trunk ; as the banyan tree gets old, it breaks up into separate masses, the original trunk decaying and the props becoming separate trunks of the different portions ; if the seeds drop into the axils of the leaves of the palmyra tree, the roots grow downwards embracing the trunk in their descent, until they envelop every part except the top ; in old specimens the leaves and head of the palmyra emerge from the trunk of the banyan tree as if they grew from it ; these the hindoos regard with reverence and call holy marriages. Friar jordanus,

the quilon bishop of the fourteenth century, has the following:—
"there be also many other trees, and wonderful ones; among
"which is one which sendeth forth roots from high up, which
"gradually grow down to the ground and enter it, and then wax
"into trunks like the main trunk, forming as it were an arch;
"and by this kind of multiplication one tree will have at once
"as many as twenty or thirty trunks beside one another, and all
"connected together; 'tis marvellous! and truly this which
"I have seen with mine eyes, 'tis hard to utter with my tongue;
"the fruit of this tree is not useful, but poisonous and deadly."
The account of the banyan in paradise lost, b. ix, it may be noted, is an exact versification of pliny's description. The banyan is the hindoo emblem of immortality; in the end of time all nature will perish except one mystic banyan at the foot of which the deity will be enthroned. The seeds of the fruit are medicinally cooling and tonic; the white glutinous juice from the stems is applied in toothache and also to the soles of the feet when cracked and inflamed; the bark given in infusion is a tonic, used in diabetes; a balsam from bark is mixed with oil and applied to ulcerous affections of the ear and in deafness; a bath made from bark of root and stem is efficacious in leprosy, and mitigating pains in limbs; heated leaves are poultice to abscesses, &c. Fruit sometimes eaten by poorer natives. Rootlets from branches form substitute for tooth-brush, the ends being beaten so as to make them soft; birdlime is prepared from the tenacious milky juice; the leaves are sewn together and used as plates to eat; coarse rope made from the bark and from the aërial roots; paper from the bark. The wood is light coarse-grained and brittle of a light brown color, not strong nor durable but durable in water, used for well rings; the wood of the drop is stronger and tougher, and is used for yokes of bullock carts and other purposes. There is a Tamul proverb:—சிறு ருபத்தை உடைய பேரும் அருட்பொருளைச்செய்வார்: அது போல, சிறு விதை ஆகிய ஆலமரம் பெருநிழலைக் கொடுக்கும்—"Those who are of inferior stature may accomplish difficult things; the seed of the banyan is small, but the "tree affords a large shade."——*Bramha's banyan* (బొమ్మమఱ్ఱి - bommamarri, Tel.; തേരകം - térakam, Mal.; සීවනමද්දෙය - sívanamaddeya, Singh.). Title for distinction. Tel. from (bomma, tel. the god brahma + marri, tel. banyan, ficus bengalensis, linn.). Mal. altered from (peru, mal. large + akam, mal. inside); from large trunk. Tel. also (karása); (pindichettu), meaning flour + tree; (tellabarranki), meaning white + the tree, epicarpurus orientalis, blume; (karakarabuda), meaning rough. Title otherwise Carausa, Rough banyan. Botanically Ficus [atty] asperrima, roxb., moraceæ [vricsham, 121]. Tree or shrub; figs size of a gooseberry, yellow when ripe; common; leaves a substitute for sand-paper, similarly to epicarpurus orientalis [stunted jack].——*Chinese banyan* (क्षुद्र - kshudra, San.; नान्दुरकी - nándurakí, Mahr.; ಕಿರುಗೋಳಿಮರ - kirugólimara, Can.; ಶಿಡಿಗೋಳಿಮರ - shidigólimara, Too.; ఎఱ్ఱజువ్వి - erradzuvvi, Tel.; ഇത്തിയാൽ - ittiyál, Mal.; கல்லிச்சி - kalliççi, Tam.). San. means small. Can. from (kiru, can. small + gólimara, can. banyan tree). Tel. from (erra, tel. red + dzuvvi, tel. ficus tsiela, roxb.). Mal. from (itti, mal. parasitical plant + ál, mal. banyan tree). Tam. from (kal, tam. stone + iççi, tam. ficus tsiela, roxb.); from wood. Tel. also (billadzuvvi), meaning plate + ficus tsiela, roxb., from leaves; (emmóduga); (emmenta); (nandiréka); (hémanta). Title otherwise Oval-leaved fig, Shining-leaved fig, Willow fig. Botanically Ficus [atty] retusa, linn., moraceæ [vricsham, 121]. Alias Ficus benjamina, nitida. Large tree; figs globular; very common in subalpine tracts; fruit receptacles lateral, fascicled, globular, sessile, the size of a large pea, smooth. Bark of root, root itself, and leaves boiled in oil, form applications for wounds and bruises. A handsome avenue tree. Wood light-reddish-grey, close-grained, moderately hard, beautifully mottled; used for tables, door panels and other purposes.——*Foreign banyan* (ولايتی بڑ - viláitíbar, Dec.). From being introduced from eastern peninsula and spreading habit and descending aërial roots. Same as Indian caoutchouc.——*Hill banyan* (ಕಲ್ಲಾಲ - kallála, Can.; కొండమఱ్ఱి - kondamarri, Tel.; கல்லத்தி - kallatti, Tam.). Can. from (kallu, can. stone + ála, can. banyan tree). Tel. from (konda, tel. hill + marri, tel. banyan tree). Tam. from (kal, tam. stone + atti, tam. fig tree, ficus glomerata, miq.). Tel. also (pittamarri), meaning bird + banyan, from birds eating its fruit. Botanically Ficus [atty] tomentosa, roxb., moraceæ [vricsham, 121]. Alias Ficus mollis, pubescens; Urostigma tomentosum. Very large tree giving out root from its branches, like banyan; but fruit woolly the size of a large pea; common in subalpine tracts. Wood soft and light, and of little use even as fuel.——*Large bramha's banyan* (खरपत्र - kharapatra, San.; खर्वतेरूकु - kharvatérúku, Conc.; ಗರಗಸಮರ - garagasamara, Can.; ಪಾಜೇವು - pájévu, Too.; പൊരിന്തേരകം - porintérakam, Mal.; தரகதிமரம் - taragathimaram, Tam.). San. from (khara, san. rough + patra, san. leaf). Can. from (garagasa, can. a saw + mara, can. tree). Mal. from (peru, mal. large + térakam, mal. ficus asperrima, roxb.). Tam. a corruption from (téragattimaram, from mal.). Mal. also (tondittérakam), meaning thick-skinned + ficus asperrima, roxb.; (páróm), meaning hard as rock. Title otherwise Large carausa, Rough-leaf fig. Botanically Ficus [atty] cunia, buch., moraceæ [vricsham, 121]. Alias Ficus conglomerata. Middling-sized tree; fruit-receptacles turbinate, ribbed, pedicelled, size of a filbert, hairy, umbilicated, in pairs or threes on long procumbent, radical and cauline, compound, leafless branches, appearing all the year. Fruit administered in aphthous complaints, and boiled in milk in visceral obstruction. Rough leaves used for polishing furniture.——*Short banyan* (குறுவால் - kuruvál, Tam.). Same as Tsiela.——*Stone banyan* (प्लक्ष - plaksha, San.; पिंपरी - pimparí, Mahr.; پاکهل - pákhal, Hind.; ಕರಿಬಸರಿ - karibasari, Can.; కల్లుజువ్వి - kalludzuvvi, Tel.; ചക്കില - chakkila, Mal.; கல்லால் - kallál, Tam.). Title from hardness of wood. San. from (plush, san. to burn). Mahr. from (pippala, san. peepul tree, ficus religiosa, linn.). Hind. from sanscrit. Can. from (kari, can. charcoal + basari, can. the tree); makes charcoal. Tel. from (kallu, tel. stone + dzuvvi, tel. ficus tsiela, roxb.). Mal. from (chákku, mal. death + ila, mal. leaf); from deciduous habit. Tam. from (kal, tam. stone + ál, tam. banyan tree). San. also (parkati), meaning touching, growing in groups one touching another; (jati), meaning having roots. Hind. also (rámanjír), meaning rama's fig. Can. also (juvvimara), meaning swinging + tree; (basari). Mal. also (chuvannál), meaning red + banyan tree, from the bark. Tam. also (kurugu), meaning white, from grey wood; (kurugatti), meaning whiteness + fig tree. Title otherwise Chakkela, Waved-leaved fig, White fig. Botanically Ficus [atty] infectoria, roxb., moraceæ [vricsham, 121]. Alias Ficus venosa; Urostigma ægeirophyllum, ceylonense, infectorium, tjakela; tjakela from malayalam. Large tree; fruit size of a pea, roundish smooth, white when ripe; malabar, &c., up to 2,000 feet elevation; young shoots eaten in curries by natives; leaves make good elephant fodder; bark yields a fibre; galls used as mordant; wood grey, moderately hard not durable, makes charcoal.——*Wild banyan* (കാട്ടാൽ - káttál, Mal.; බූනුග - búnuga, Singh.). Mal. from (kátu, mal. forest + ál, mal. banyan tree). Singh. from (bú, singh. demon + nuga, singh. milky fig tree, ficus laccifera, roxb.). Title otherwise Demon fig. Botanically Ficus [atty] citrifolia, lam., moraceæ [vricsham, 121]. Decoction of bark is medicinal.

BANYAN (بنیا - banyá, *Hind.*). From (vanik, san. merchant). Cf. Bunniah. A Hindoo trader, especially of Goozerat. The term is not much used in this Presidency. In Bengal it is applied to the native man of business in the service of Europeans. In days of the early occupancy Bramins were thus called by corruption. Also an undershirt, originally of muslin such as Hindoo tradesmen wear; whence the name. Also the Banyan tree which see for its derivation [jauty].

BAOBAB (गोरखअम्ली - górakhaamlí, *Mahr.*; حوبب - bahubab, *Ar.*; گورك املی - gorakamlí, *Hind.*; هاتی ختیان - hátíkhatiyán, *Dec.*; ಬ್ರಹ್ಮಾಮ್ಲಿಕ - brahmámlika, *Can.*; పేరులేనిపెద్దమాను - péruléni peddamánu, *Tel.*; ஆனைப்புளி - ánaippuli, *Tam.*). Title from arabic. Mahr. from hindostany. Hind. from (gorakha, hind. proper name + amlí, hind. tamarindus indica, linn.); after the ascetic. Dec. from (hátí, hind. elephant + khatiyán, hind. silk cotton tree, eriodendron anfractuosum, dec.); from strong fibre. Can. from (brahma, san. god + ámla, san. tamarind tree); from general appearance. Tel. from (péru, tel. name + léni, tel. without + peddamánu, tel. great tree); nameless great tree. Tam. from (ánai, tam. elephant + puli, tam. tamarindus indica, linn.); rind like tamarind pod. Mahr. also (górakhachincha), from gorakhnaut or corakkan the sage, who taught under this tree. Ar. also (habhabú); (hujed). Hind. also (choramlí), meaning false tamarind; (bahmaníamlí), meaning bramin tamarind; (viláitíamlí), meaning foreign tamarind. Dec. also (barákhatiyán), meaning large silk-cotton tree. Can. also (magimávu), meaning great + mangifera indica, linn. Tam. also (papparappuli), meaning goozerat + tamarind tree; (púrimaram), meaning to grow stout + tree; (páppárappuli), meaning bramin + tamarind tree; (perukkamaram), meaning stout tree. Title otherwise Adansonia, African calabash, Bramin tamarind, Elephant silk-cotton, Elephant tamarind, Ethiopian sour gourd, Foreign tamarind, Gorakh's chinch, Gorakh's tamarind, Indian cork, Monkey-bread, Monster silk-cotton. Botanically Adansonia digitata, linn., malvaceæ [vricsham, 25]. Alias Adansonia baobab. Baobab from arabic. Tree of moderate height; trunk enormous, 30–40 feet in circumference; leaves digitate, quinate, glabrous, peticled; leaflets elliptical, slightly acuminated; petioles and peduncles pubescent; calyx five-partite, pubescent, silky inside; petals five, spreading, at length deflexed; flowers axillary, solitary on long pedicels; stamen tube adhering to the base of the petals; large, white, with purplish anthers. The fruit is large and oblong, varying in length and circumference from 8 or 9 to 15 inches; externally it bears a great resemblance to velvet, being soft and downy, and is of greenish-brown color; number of its cells varies from six to ten, but is generally eight; each cell is filled with a grey, sub-acid and farinaceous substance; black seeds, which are about half an inch in length and kidney-shaped, are embedded in the pulp; acidity of the fruit is due to tartaric acid and bitartrate of potassium. The bark is thick, light and covered with a thin greenish brown epidermis, which is rough from wrinkles, &c., but not scaly; pale-brown internally, odourless and tasteless; contains three per cent. of soluble and insoluble tannin, but no alkaloid or saponin. Bark is medicinally antiperiodic; acid farinaceous pulp surrounding seeds is astringent, refrigerant, and diuretic; used with buttermilk in dysentery; for british krameria, hæmatoxylum, quercus and acidum phosphoricum dilutum; both in pharm. non-officinal. Young leaves pounded used as a condiment; sherbet made from fruit; pulp eaten with sugar. Bark furnishes indestructible cordage and a coarse thread used for cloth and ropes; fruits are used as floats; all parts abound with thick mucilaginous juice. Timber pale colored, light, soft, useless. No other species here.

BAR (بر - bar, *Hind.*). Up, off.——*Barauward* (براورد - baráwurd, Hind.). From (above + áwurd, pers. brought). Estimate, muster roll.——*Bartarf* (برطرف - bartaraf, Hind.). From (above + taraf, ar. side). Dismissal.

BAR (பார் - pár, *Tam.*). Bank; suffix in Tinnevelly place names, as Shookkaunbar, meaning limestone + bank [par].

BARAMAHAUL (بارا محل - bárámahal, *Hind.*). From (bárá, hind. twelve + makal, hind. palace). The twelve provinces. A tract of country supposed to have included the modern talooks of Dharmapoory, Krishnagherry, Tripatore, Ootancaray in Salem district, and the Cungoondy zemindarry of North arcot; lat. 11° 47′ to 12° 47′; long. 77° 43′ to 79° 04′. Originally governed by the Anagoondy family. Passed in 1668 under the Mysore rule, then under the Nawaubs of Cuddapah, who were ousted by Hyder ally in 1759. Ceded to the English by Tippoo in 1792, when the name was soon after abandoned [charitram].

BARAUBAR (برابر - barábar, *Hind.*). From (bar, pers. bosom); chest to chest, or level. Regular, proper, opposite, exact.

BARBADOES (باربڈوس - bárbados, *Hind.*). Means island of pines. One of the British West indian islands. Plant first term. Ex.:—Adenanthera pavonina, barbadoes pride; Aloe vulgaris, barbadoes aloes; Cæsalpinia pulcherrima, barbadoes flower; Eugenia uniflora, barbadoes cherry; Gossypium barbadense, barbadoes cotton; Ipomæa quamoclit, barbadoes sweet william; Parkinsonia aculeata, barbadoes flower fence. See gloss. paragraphs.

BARBARA (बर्बर - barbara, *San.*). From (vri, san. to impede); stammerer. Same as Greek βάρβαρος. Any non-Aryan.

BARCAT (برکت - barakkat, *Ar.*). From (baraka, ar. to pray for one). Blessing. In lacab; Barcat oollah, blessing of God [ism].

BARCELORE PEAK (ಬಸರೂರುಶಿಖರ - basarúrushikhara, *Can.*). Sailors' corruption of Basroor [q.v.]. Distinguish from Barcore in Oodipy talook. Round mountain, about three and a quarter leagues inland, having Bednore mountains for its base.

BARCORE (ಬಾರ್ಕೂರು - bárkúru, *Can.*; വക്കനൂർ - vakkanúr, *Mal.*; barkúr *). Sanscrit name (dvádashakanyápura), meaning twelve + girl + town; from the twelve Jeina girls whom Bhootaulan married. Bacanore of Barbosa. Distinguish from Basroor or Barcelore in Coondapore talook. Village; South canara dist., Oodipy tal.; pop. 951; lat. 13° 28′; long. 74° 48′; from Coondapore S.S.E. 11 miles; from Mangalore N. 42 miles; from Oodipy N. 9½ miles; from the sea E. 4 miles. The port is Hangarcutta. On the Seetanuddy. Connected by road with Bednore and situated in a fertile well-watered country. The present town marks the site of a very ancient city, once the largest in Canara, and even in the sixteenth century of considerable importance. Barcore also gave its name to a former sub-division of Canara, comprising a portion of the western declivity of the ghauts; very hilly, and traversed by numerous mountain streams. This tract, formed part of the ancient Cadamba realm. As the capital of the Jeina kings of Tooloovam, the seat of Bhootaula pandya's government, and subsequently a stronghold of the Vijianugger rajahs who obtained possession of it in 1335, the ruined city possesses much interest. After the defeat of the Vijianugger power at Talicote in 1565, it passed into the hands of the Bednore rajah. In 1763, Hyder ally absorbed Bednore, and after the death of his son, Tippoo sultan, the country was incorporated in the British dominions. Traces of the great fort built by Harihara rajah about A.D. 1370 still exist, as also the tanks and part of the walls of Bhootaula pandya's palace. Ruins of Booddhist temples abound, and inscriptions dated A.D. 1383, 1390, 1430, 1522, and 1525, testify that in the fourteenth century Barcore was the seat of the viceregal government of the Royel of Vijianugger. Among the sculptures, one representing a procession of armed men, bearing a striking resemblance in equipments and general appearance to the Greek soldiery, and another of a centaur, deserve special mark. Tradition asserts that it was from here that the Aliya santauna law of inheritance was promulgated. The present town possesses some trade in brass and copper utensils.

BAREE (بڑی - barí, *Hind.*). Great. In composition makes a lacab; as Baree bee, great lady. Barey is the masculine; as Barey miyaun, great sir [ism].

BAREED (برید - baríd, *Ar.*). Post-horse. Title of Beedar rulers. A.D. 1498–1609. See vol. I (149).

BAREEJAH (بریجا - baríjá, *Hind.*). Same as Galbanum.

BARHAEE (بڑھئی - barhaí, *Hind.*). From (vardhaki, san. carpenter). A carpenter.

BARICA (బరిక - barika, *Tel.*). From (bari, tel. thief). Subdivision of Maula tribe. About 10,000.

BARK (برق - bark, *Hind.*). From (baraka, ar. to gleam). Lightning.——*Barkandauz* (برقنداز - barkandáz, Hind.). From (above + andáz, pers. who throws). Matchlock man.

BARK (பட்டை - pattai, *Tam.*). Technical term for chinchona bark [koinah]. Compare also the barks of:—Acacia farnesiana, piyvail; Acacia leucophlæa, velvail; Ailantus excelsa, peroomaram; Alangium lamarckii, nallancolam; Albizzia amara, woonja; Albizzia lebbek, sirissa; Bauhinia diphylla, yepy; Bauhinia variegata, ebony; Bruguiera gymnorhiza, mangrove; Calotropis gigantea, mudar; Cassia auriculata. tungaid; Cassia fistula, connay; Cinnamomum iners, cassia; Cinnamomum zeylanicum, cinnamon; Cissampelos pareira, pareira; Eugenia jambolana, nauval; Holarrhena antidysenterica, conessi; Melia azadirachta, margosa; Morinda citrifolia, morinda; Odina wodier, wodiya; Phyllanthus multiflorus, poolah; Punica granata, pomegranate root; Rhizophora mucronata, kunro; Salvadora persica, oogha; Samadera indica, niepa; Soymida febrifuga, rohan; Swertia chirata, chiretta; Terminalia tomentosa, marootham; Toddalia aculeata, lopez root. See gloss. paragraphs.——*Bark tree* (பட்டைமரம் - pattaimaram, Tam.). From use of bark as clothing. Same as Sack tree.

BARKHAST (برخواست - barkhást, *Hind.*). From (barkhástan, pers. to get up). The breaking up an assembly or court.

BAROO (برو - barú, *Hind.*). Wool of gomooty palm [q.v.].

BARR (ಬಾರು - báru, *Can.*). Troops, especially Mysore foot soldiers.——*Barcor* (ಬಾರೂರು - bárúru, Can.). From (báru, can. row + úru, can. village). Village; Salem dist., Krishnagherry tal.; pop. 1,228; acres 1,582; lat. 12° 18′; long. 78° 21′; from Krishnagherry S.S.E. 17 miles; from Salem N.N.E. 45 miles. Project work.

BARTEE (بڑتی - bartí, *Hind.*). From (bhritti, san. wages). Increase, especially of pay.

BARWAH (బారువ - báruva,* *Tel.*).—"*a*" Proprietary estate; Ganjam dist.; pop. 4,653; area 9 square miles. Sub-divided into Barwah and Pettah. Contains extensive plantations of cocoanut and palmyra trees. Quit-rent 3,900 rupees. The estate lies in the jurisdiction of the Sompett sub-magistrate.—"*b*" Town, Port, Sea-customs station; Ganjam dist., Sompett deputy tahsildar's range, Barwah estate tal.; pop. 3,921; lat. 18° 52′; long. 84° 38′; from Berhampore S.S.W. 32 miles; from Chetterpore S.W. 44 miles; from Madras N.E. 485 miles; from Poondy N.E. 17 miles; from Sonapore S.W. 20 miles. On the Orissa coast at the southernmost limit of the Ooriyah country. Identified with Ptolemy's ἀφητήριονεἰς τὴν χρυσῆν, the sailors taking Mahendragherry for their landmark. South-west there are large topes of cocoanut trees. North is a plain covered with sand drifts. Port is marked by two columns, black and white, 50 feet high, built on a site 15 feet above the sea, bearing north-west from the usual anchorage. Native passengers from Burmah land here and emigrants embark here for Burmah. Two old temples erected by Pandavas. Another old temple with seven images. Cocoanut oil is made in the neighbourhood.

BASAULUT (بسالت - basálat, *Ar.*). From (basala, ar. fierce). Ferocity.——*Basaulut jung* (بسالت جنگ - basálatjang, Hind.). Fierce in war. Descriptive + khitaub alaumat [ism]. Brother of tho Nizam salaubut jung and Nizam ally; and Jagheerdar of Guntoor. See vol. I (180) and 9.

BASAVA (ಬಸವ - basava, *Can.*). From (vrishabha, san. bull). Canarese name of Nundy, vehicle of Shiva. So Canarese proper name, and especially that of the founder of the Lingayet sect. This man was son of a sheiva bramin; while yet a boy, he refused to assume the sacred thread, because the initiatory rites required adoration of the sun; and in A.D. 1135 he fled from his home, accompanied by his sister, to calyaun, whose ruler bijjala was of the jeina religion; here he joined his maternal uncle, a bramin and the rajah's minister, who gave him employment and also gave him his daughter in marriage, and basava became prime minister on his uncle's death; the bulk of the people from north of calyaun to mysore adhered to him; but king bijjala opposed the movement, and was assassinated by two fanatics, on which the calyaun kingdom closed; basava disappeared at the shiva lingam temple, at the confluence of the kistna and maulprabha, but his sister's son, channa basava, extended the sect. For the sect, see Lingayet. See vol. I (70) to (94), and the following foot-notes:—history of rel. and phil. I (70), existing hindoo sects I (88), jeinas I (95) [matam].——*Basavy* (బసవి - basavi, Tel.). Devoted to the service of the nundy. The corresponding terms are:—Tel. bogam, Tam. devadausy. Prostitute caste [jauty].——*Baswant* (ಬಸ್ವಂತ - basvanta, Can.). From (above + ante, can. like). Pers. name among Lingayets and Mahrattas [peyar].

BASELLA (ಬಸಳೆ - basale, *Can.*). From (pasai, tam. stickiness); from leaf. Botanical genus. Vernacular also applied to Portulaca and Spinacea genera.

BASHAURAT (بشارت - bashárat, *Ar.*). Beauty. Prefixed to alam forms lacab; as Bashaurat ally, the beauty of Ally [ism].

BASHAW (باشا - báshá, *Hind.*). The old English form of Padshah, the Pers. form.

BASHEER (بشير - bashír, *Ar.*). From (bashara, ar. to rejoice). Comely. Prefixed to an alam forms a lacab; as Basheer ahmed, beauty of Ahmed the prophet [ism].

BASIREDDY (బసిరెడ్డి - basireddi, *Tel.*). From (basava, can. shiva's bull + reddi, tel. caste title). Otherwise Vasireddy. A family founded by one Vasireddy veerappa naidoo, who obtained the pergunnah of Nundigauma in Kistna district from the king of Golcondah in 1670. In 1794 the Zemindarry residence was changed from Chintapully on the Kistna to Amravatty. The present zemindars have pensions from Government [charitram].

BASROOR (ಬಸರೂರು - basarúru, *Can.*). From (basari, can. the waved leaved fig tree, ficus infectoria, miq. + úru, can. town). Sanscrit name (vasupura), meaning wealth + town; called after a king named Vasoo. Bracalor of Faria y Souza. Cf. Barcelore peak which is the hill. Village; South canara dist., Coondapore tal.; pop. 1,950; lat. 13° 37′; long. 74° 47′; from Coondapore E. 4 miles; from Mangalore N. 52 miles; from the sea E. 5 miles; from Shiroor S.S.E. 21 miles. Once of great celebrity, but now in ruins. Two miles inland from the present mouth of the Coondapore river. The walls and water gates still remain in good preservation.

BASSES (இராமப்பாதம் - irámappátham, *Tam.*). From (ráma, san. the god + páda, san. foot). Divided into great and little. Bassæ of Ptolemy's map of Taprobane. Rocks east of Ceylon. Believed to be remnants of a great island. Mahavanso states that early inhabitants of Ceylon were Yacshas, deported by Booddha to two beautiful islands, probably meaning the Basses before their submersion. See vol. I (4) [charitram].

BASTY (بستى - bastí, *Hind.*). From (vas, san. to dwell).—"*a*" A village. Basty daukkal from (above + dákhal, pers. entered) are lands included in village-sites. See vol. I, 112.—"*b*" A Jeina temple. Distinguish from Betta. A well-known group of basties is that at Shravanabelgola in Mysore. There are there two hills, Indragherry and Chundragherry. On the former stands a colossal Gomataroya [betta]. On a shoulder of the latter stand the basties, fifteen in number. All in Dravidian architecture [staupatyam], and are consequently built in gradually receding storeys, each of which is ornamented with small simulated cells. No instance occurs among them of the curvilinear shikharam or spire, universal with N. jeinas. Below the ghauts in Canara, Jeinism is the religion of the country, and nearly all temples belong to this sect, but the architecture is neither Dravidian style nor that of N. india, and belongs of Nepaul. One of the largest of Canara temples is Moodbidry. A basty is as to exterior much plainer than an ordinary Hindoo temple. The pillars look like logs of wood with the angles partially chamfered off, so as to make them octagons, and the sloping roofs of the verandahs show that the style itself cannot be far removed from a wooden original. In many places below the ghauts the temples are still wholly constructed in wood without any admixture of stone, and almost all the features of the Moodbidry temples may be found in wood at the present day. The feature however which presents the greatest resemblance to the northern styles is the reverse slope of the eaves above the verandah. The interiors of the Canara basties are in marked contrast with the plainness of the exteriors. Nothing can exceed the richness or the variety with which they are carved. No two pillars are alike. Their plans are those usual in Jeina temples; spacious, well-lighted porches, leading to a dark cell in which the image of one of the Teertancarans is placed. This is naked, as all the southern Jeinas belonged to the Digambaran sect [aursham, baur, cheityam, coil, goomta, jeina, laut, matam, maunasauram, staupatyam, tope, vihauram].

BATAGUR (سلحفات - sulahfát, *Ar.*; سنگ پشت - sangpusht, *Pers.*; کچھوا - kachhvá, *Hind.*; تانبل - támbel, *Dec.*; దాసరితాబేలు - dásaritábélu, *Tel.*; കാരാമ - kaáráma, *Mal.*; பறையாமை - paraiyámai, *Tam.*). Title from singhalese. Ar. from (surákh, pers. hole + pái, pers. foot); from hole in shell through which foot comes out. Pers. from (sang, pers. stone + pusht, pers. back). Tel. from (dásari, tel. vaishnava mendicant + tábélu, tel. tortoise); from the stripes resembling the broad forehead marks. Mal. from (kár, mal. black + áma, mal. tortoise). Tam. from (parai, tam. the caste + ámai, tam. tortoise); means black tortoise from the color of the pariah. Batagur elliotti, emydidæ [aumay], chelonia [coormam], reptilia [sarpy, 2], of naturalists [jantoo]. A freshwater tortoise of the Coromandel coast.

BATAIR (वर्त्तिका - vartiká, *San.*; بٹیر - bater, *Hind.*; ఎలిసె - elise, *Tel.*). Title from hindostany. San. from (vrit, san. to live); from going at large. True quails. Coturnicinæ, tetraonidæ [tittiram], rasores, aves [pacshy, 33], of naturalists [jantoo]. The species best known to the natives are shown below. Black quail [q.v.] is a separate family.——*Common quail* (लवा - lavá, Mahr.; بڑا بٹیر - barábater, Hind.; گھاگس - ghágas, Dec.; కోలంకిపిట్ట - kólankipitta, Tel.; കാട - káta, Mal.; பெரியகாடை - periyagádai, Tam.). Hind. from (bará, hind. large + bater, hind. quail). Tel. from (kóla, tel. arrow + anga, tel. stride + pitta, tel. bird); from swift running. Tam. from (periya, tam. large + kádai, tam. quail). Tel. also (gogireyelise); (gerijapitta); (púrédu), meaning flower + king. Title otherwise European quail, Large gray quail. Coturnix communis of naturalists. Alias Coturnix dactylisonans, indicus. Netted in great numbers, many are also caught in hair nooses. There is a Tamul proverb :—காடை இடம் ஆனால் நாட்டை ஆளலாம் —"If a quail crosses a man's path to the left, he will govern a "province."——*Rain quail* (بٹیر - bater, Hind. and Dec.; చిన్నయెలిసె - chinnayelise, Tel.; காடை - kádai, Tam.). Title from appearing about the rains. Tel. from (chinna, tel. small + yelise, tel. quail). Tam. from (kádu, tam, forest). Title otherwise Black-breasted quail. Coturnix coromandelica of naturalists. Alias Coturnix textilis. Do not rise at once.

BATAVIA (بتاوى - batáví, *Hind.*; வத்தாவி - vattávi, *Tam.*). Latin name for Holland. The native name is (sundkalapa) or sunda of the coco-palms [arrack]. The Sanscrit name is (jayakartá), meaning victory + maker. The latter appears colloquially as Jacatra. Town in Java. The capital of all the Dutch possessions in the Indies since its foundation in 1619. See vol. I, 2.——*Batavia lemon* (بتاوى ليمو - batávilímú, Hind.). From habitat. Pummelow.

BATTA (بهتا - bhattá, *Hind.*; బత్తా - battá, *Tel.*). From (bhát, hind. boiled rice). Subsistence. Daily allowance to servants in addition to regular pay, for travelling, temporary dearness of staple food-grain, &c. Also allowance paid by creditor for subsistence of a debtor in prison. Also allowance to witnesses summoned to court [pady].

BATTAH (بٹا - battá, *Hind.*; బత్తెము - battemu, *Tel.*). From (vat, san. to divide). Difference or rate of exchange. Not to be confounded with batta, subsistence money.——*Batwaudah* (بٹواره - batvárah, Hind.). From (vat, san. to divide). Disbursement [batta].——*Batye* (بٹائى - batái, Hind.). From (vat, san. to divide). Sharing, especially of crop. Revenue paid in kind to proprietor. See vol. I, 112.

BATTAN (بطن - batan, *Hind.*). Charadridæ family, pressirostres, grallatores, aves [pacshy, 38], of naturalists [jantoo]. Plovers. Nidificate on somewhat open ground, young are liable to be taken, and parent birds feign lameness to entice enemy away. Differ from Snipes and Sandpipers in shorter, stronger and harder bill, adapted for seizing insects and small shells off the surface of ground, and not for insertion into the soft mud. Divided into Charadrinæ, or true Plovers, containing Golden and Ringed-plovers; Vanellinæ, or Lapwing; Esacinæ or Stone plovers. The species best known to the natives are shown below.——*Chota battan* (چهوٹا بطن - chhotábatan, Hind.). Means small plover. Title otherwise Golden plover. Charadrius longipes, charadrinæ, of naturalists. Alias Charadrius pluvialis, virginicus, xanthocheilus, orientalis. Has a shrill whistling call, and flies very rapidly.——*Jungle hare* (كروان - karwán, Ar.; كروانك - karwának, Hind.; కన్యలేడి - kanyalédi, Tel.; கானமுசல் - kánámusal, Tam.). Title from peculiar motion. Tel. from (kána, tel. forest + lédi, tel. deer). Tam. from (kán, tam. jungle + musal, tam. hare). Title otherwise Bastard florican, Stone plover. Œdicnemus crepitans, esacinæ, of naturalists. Occurs in bushy wilds; when a flock is disturbed, they fly a short distance, and then squat close; long cry heard at night.——*Raiva* (زريا - zirriyá, Hind.; రేవ - réva, Tel.). Tel. means ford; from its haunt. Tel. also (bítuullangi), meaning timid lapwing. Title otherwise Indian ringed-plover. Ægialitis philippensis, charadrinæ, of naturalists. Alias Charadrius hiaticuloides.——*Titibham* (टिट्टिभ - tittibha, San.; ٹٹوری - titorí, Hind. and Dec.; యెనపచితవ - yenapachitava, Tel.; കുളക്കോഴി - kulakkózhi, Mal.; ஆள்காட்டி - álgátti, Tam.). San. from (tittí, san. the sound + bhá, san. to shine). Tel. from (yenumu, tel. buffalo + chitava, tel. bird so called). Mal. from (kulam, mal. tank + kózhi, mal. fowl). Tam. from (ál, tam. person + káttu, tam. to point); as enticing people away from its nest. Hind. also (titai); (tití). Tel. also (ullangipitta), meaning lapwing + bird. Title otherwise Red wattled lapwing, Sandpiper. Lobivanellus goensis, vanellinæ, of naturalists. Alias Charadrius atrogularis. Very numerous on sandy banks and shores of rivers; the strutting gait is supposed to indicate conceit; thence a story as defying the sea; said to sleep on its back with its legs upwards to prevent the sky from falling.

BAUB (باب - báb, *Ar.*). Door; section; head of accounts [abwab]. Baubat is an item.

BAUBER (بابر - bábar, *Pers.*). Lion. Mahomedan alam. Also part of lacab; as Bauber bakht, lion's luck [ism].

BAUD (باد - bád, *Hind.*). From Persian; means calamity. Remission on account of deficient produce. One-life grant by zemindars in favor of village artisans, &c. [inam]. See vol. I, 112.

BAUD (బాడు - bádu, *Tel.*). Waste; suffix in place names as Daggoobaud, meaning low + waste.

BAUDAM (बादाम - bádáma, *San.*; बादामी - badámí, *Mahr.*; شجرة لوز - shajaratullauz, *Ar.*; درخت بادام - darakhtibádám, *Pers.*; بادام کا جھاڑ - bádámkáper, *Hind.*; بادام کا جھاڑ - bádamkájhár, *Dec.*; بادم - bádam, *Malay*; ಬಾದಾಮಿ - bádámi, *Can.*; బాదంచెట్టు - bádamchettu, *Tel.*; ബദാം - bádám, *Mal.*; රට කොට්ටම්බා - ratakottambá, *Singh.*; வாதுமை - váthumai, *Tam.*). Title from persian. San. from persian. Ar. from (shajar, ar. tree + lauz, ar. almond). Pers. from (darakht, ar. tree + bádám, pers. almond). Hind. from (bádám, pers. almond + per, hind. tree). Mal. and tam. from persian. Singh. from (rata, singh. foreign + kottambá, singh. country almond, terminalia catappa, linn.). San. also (ingudí), meaning growing up, from tallness [catapang, fire-work plant]. Pers. also (bádamifársí), meaning persian almond. Malay also (lauzan). Tel. also (pársibádamchettu), meaning persian almond tree. Tam. also (pársiváthumai), meaning persian almond. Title otherwise Almond, Bitter almond, Hog tragacanth tree, Persian almond, Sweet almond. Botanically Prunus [auloo] amygdalus, baill., rosaceæ [vricsham, 40]. Alias Amygdalus communis. Tree of which produce is brought from the seaports of the persian gulf; the leaves are long and narrow, with an acute point and saw-like margin; fruit has kernel enclosed in shell or stone and surrounded by succulent covering like peach, apricot, plum, cherry; the kernel is the almond. Two varieties, sweet and bitter, distinguished by the taste of the kernel; bitter plant smaller than sweet; appearance of fruits correspond; taste, composition, and properties however totally different. Sweet almonds contain a fixed oil and emulsine; former is colorless, or very slightly yellow, with difficulty congealed, taste sweet, smell light, agreeable, and resembling that of the seeds; in properties and uses nearly identical with olive oil. Bitter almonds contain in addition a nitrogenous substance called amygdaline, which by combination with emulsine, produces a volatile oil and prussic acid; the oil of bitter almonds is extremely poisonous. Almond milk is made by almonds rubbed in a mortar with water, sugar, gum arabic. Sweet almonds are in native practice aphrodisiac, attenuant and detergent; used internally and externally; ingredient in many tonic and fattening mahomedan prescriptions; in pharm. as amygdalæ dulces. Bitter almonds are in pharm. amygdalæ amaræ; official only for the sake of expressed oil, oleum amygdalæ. The sweet almond is used for dessert, the part eaten being the two seed lobes. African almond tree is brabejum stellatum, proteaceæ. Java almond tree is canarium commune, burseraceæ. Compare also here:—Hydnocarpus venenata (janglíbádám), wild almond; Terminalia catappa (déshíbádám), country almond. See gloss. paragraphs.

BAUDARAUYANAN (बादरायण - bádaráyana, *San.*). From (badara, san. the place of pilgrimage + ayana, san. house); from place of retirement. Otherwise Vyausan or Veda vyausan. Founder of the Oottara mimaumsam or Vedauntam philosophy [matam, vedauntam]. See vol. I (74).

BAUDY (باڑی - bárí, *Hind.*; പാടി - páti, *Mal.*; பாடி - pádi, *Tam.*). Village in a jungle tract. Suffix in place names, as Vaniyambaudy, meaning oilmonger + village [paudy].

BAUGALOO (ಬಾಗಲು - bágalu, *Can.*). Door; suffix in place names, as Bheemanibaugaloo, meaning Bheeman's doorway or entrance.——*Baugalore* (ಬಾಗಲೂರು - bágalúru, Can. bágalúr *). From (above + úru, can. village); door of Balaghaut. Zemindarry, Village; Salem dist., Oossoor tal.; pop. 2,208; acres 37,840; lat. of village 12° 50′; long. 77° 55′; from Oossoor N.N.E. 7½ miles; from Salem N.N.W. 83 miles. Peshcush Rs. 14,483.

BAUGH (باگھ - bágh, *Hind.*). From (vyághra, san. tiger). A tiger [pooly]. Cf.:—Felis pardus (chítábágh), cheetah tiger; Felis tigris (pátáyatbágh), striped tiger; Felis viverrina (khufyahbágh), concealed tiger, of tiger like form; Hyæna striata (lakarbágh), stiff tiger. See gloss. paragraphs.

BAUGH (باغ - bágh, *Hind.*). Garden. Baugh o bahaur; from (bahár, pers. spring), is a well known Oordoo book of tales by Meer amman of Delhi, who lived about 1800.——*Baughayet* (باغات - bághát, Hind.). Plural of above. Garden lands watered usually by means of a well, and rendered fit for the growth of vegetables, fruit trees, superior crops of grain, chillies, tobacco, turmeric, &c.

BAUHAM (بام - bám, *Hind.*; பாகம் - págam, *Tam.*). From (báhu, san. arm). Means arm. Fathom. Linear measure. Distance between the finger tips of both arms when arms extended. 4 moolams or cubits = 1 bauham; 2,000 bauhams = 1 coss [alavay, 1]. Approximate actual value, 1 bauham = 6 feet. In Salem there are two bauhams, one 6 feet 4 inches, the other 8 feet. Same as San. dandam, Hind. baum, Can. bauroo, Tel. niloovoo, Tam. maur. Compare Poorsham. See vol. I, 609; II, 505, 517.——*Bauhoodah nuddy* (బాహుదనది - báhudánadi, Tel. báhudá *). From (báhu, san. hand + dá, san. to give + nadí, san. river); from a legend that a person regained his lost hand by bathing in the stream. River; Cuddapah dist., Madanapully, Voilpaud and Royachoty tals. Rises in Madanapully talook, and passing through western portion of Voilpaud, flows into Royachoty talook and joins with other streams in forming the Cheyair. Has water only during monsoon. A rocky stream with very rapid torrent.

BAUKIR (باقر - bákir, *Hind.*). From (bakara, ar. to rend). He who rends, so lion. Lacab of Mahomet's great-grandson. Mahomedan alam; as Baukir ally, double alam [ism].——*Baukiry* (باقری - bákirí, Hind.). From above. Tippoo's four-anna coin [naunyam].

BAUKY (باقی - bákí, *Hind.*). From (baká, ar. to remain). Balance; baukidar is a defaulter. Bauky also means the eternal, an epithet of God [allah]; is also an alam [ism].

BAULA (بالا - bálá, *Pers.*). Above.——*Baulakhana* (بالا خانہ - bálákhánah, Hind.). From (above + khánah, house). Origin of English balcony. Upper story.——*Baulbund* (بالا بند - bálâband, Hind.). From (above + band, pers. closed). Because a line runs along the top of the letters. Corruption by Marhattas to Baulbodh, which means instruction for youth. Devanagry character for Sanscrit. See vol. I (49) [bhaushay].

BAULAN (बाल - bála, *San.*). From (bal, san. to live). Youth. All the following are Hindoo 2nd or pers. names [peyar].——*Baulachendran* (బాలచంద్రుడు - bálachandrudu, Tel.). From (chandra, san. moon). Crescent moon till five or six days old [peyar].——*Baulagopaulan* (बालगोपाल - bálagópála, San.). From (above + gó, san. cow + pála, san. protector). Common epithet of Krishna in one of his manifestations as infant seated on a five-headed cobra, his right toe in his mouth, and his mother standing by with a peacock. Baulakrishnan is the same [matam].——*Baulajee* (ಬಾಲಾಜಿ - báláji, Can.). From (jí, hind. sir). Epithet of Vishnoo at Tripatty. Used by Beiraugies, common pers. name among Madhwas and Mahrattas [peyar, row].——*Baulakrishnan* (பாலக்கிருட்டிணன் - pálakkiruttinan, Tam.). Krishna in his youth [peyar].——*Baulasawmy* (బాలస్వామి - bálasvámi, Tel.). From (above + svámi, san. lord). Either Krishnan or Soobramanyan [peyar].——*Baulasoobbaroya* (ಬಾಲಸುಬ್ಬರಾಯ - bálasubbaráya, Can.). Young Soobramanyan, as the snake king [peyar].——*Baulasoobramanyan* (பாலசுப்பிரமணியன் - pálasuppiramaniyan, Tam.). Scandan in his youth [peyar].——*Baulasoondram* (பாலசுந்தரம் - pálasundaram, Tam.). Youthful beauty, applied to any god. Feminine Baulasoondry applied to a Shacty [peyar].——*Baulavendran* (బాలవేంద్రుడు - bálavéndrudu, Tel.). Young Indran [peyar].——*Baulyam* (बाल्य - bálya, San.). Minority. According to native usage, minority of a Hindoo extends, according to different authorities, to beginning or end of sixteenth year; and a Mahomedan is a minor till expiration of sixteenth year, unless symptoms of puberty appear earlier. British government has extended the period of minority for legal purposes to end of eighteenth year [maryauday].

BAULEY ROW (భాలేరావు - bhálérávu, *Tel.*). Means leader of spearmen. Family name of the zemindar of Moottiaulpaud [q v.], Nellore district.

BAULHICAM (बाल्हिक - bálhika, *San.*). Means coming from balkh. Giant fennel. Botanically the Ferula genus, umbelliferæ [vricsham, 67]. Natives of mediterranean and persian regions; stem tall-growing and pithy; leaves deeply divided; fruit compressed. The species best known are:—galbaniflua [galbanum], narthex [asafœtida], persica [sagapenum].

BAUN (بان - bán, *Pers.*). From (van, san. suffix of possession). Possessive particle added to nouns to indicate quality; as Mehrbaun, kindness + possessing.

BAUNAM (बाण - bána, *San.*). From (van, san. to sound). Fireworks. These are largely used at marriages and other festivities. Nitre [shorah], sulphur [gandhac], and the charcoal [kary] of calotropis gigantea [yercum], are taken according to certain proportions and pounded in earthern mortars; this powder is packed into bamboo tubes, horns of cattle, or earthern bottles, according to requirements; pounded steel filings are mixed for fire sprays, wheel rockets, &c.; to make bengal light nitre, sulphur and lime are pounded without charcoal; cups made of paper are filled with this powder and pasted at foot to small earthern saucers with paste made of tamarind seeds; the rockets are exactly like european, but not a borrowed manufacture.

BAUNDOO (ಬಾಂದು - bándu, *Can.*). Earthen embankment used as a demarcation mark. Baundinavar are officials of Revenue survey and Settlement department. See vol. I, 112.

BAUNO (بانو - báno, *Pers.*). Means a lady. Pataun female alaumat; as Azeez bauno, alam + alaumat. Also an alam; as Bauno bee, alam + alaumat [ism].

BAUP (باپ - báp, *Hind.*; బాబు - bábu, *Tel.*). From (vapra, san. father). A father. Term of endearment to young people. Hindoo 2nd or pers. name. Common to both sexes among Madhwas and Mahrattas. Baupanna, Baupayya and Baupamma, are common [peyar].

BAUPATLA (బాపట్ల - bápatla, * *Tel.*). From (bápana, tel. bramin + patla, tel. place). Sanscrit name (bhávapurí), meaning supreme being + town, called after Bhauva narrainsawmy, the god of the place.——**(1)** Talook, Kistna district. Tahsildar's pay Rs. 225. Area 679 square miles. Population 151,736. Language Teloogoo. Lies along the coast south of Guntoor and extends from near Nizampatam to Pedda ganjam salt factory. S.W. of district. Bounded on the north by Guntoor talook, east Repully talook, south Bay of Bengal, west Ongole talook of Nellore district, and Narsarowpett talook. Parallel to the coast and some miles inland runs a great sand ridge which shuts in the drainage flowing towards the sea and causes an enormous swamp with outlets to the sea at Chinna ganjam. The town of Baupatla itself is on this sand ridge and the old line of the Madras road is shown by avenues westwards along the ridge. The north-west portion is black cotton soil, flooded in wet weather by the local torrents which flow from the Condaveed hills and Narsarowpett, but dried up in the hot weather. Through this black soil runs the old line of the Guntoor-Madras road, with travellers' bungalows at Parchoor and Incolloo, a route practicable in dry weather and impassable after heavy rain. A large portion is deltaic alluvium and is under irrigation which makes the contrast the more striking between the expanse of rice fields under Kistna water and the barren villages a few miles to the north-west. Soil is sandy along coast, rest regar. Indigo and cotton manufacture. Agriculture is chief industry. Grain merchandise, also pulses and casuarina timber. The Commamore canal enters the north-east corner of the talook at Zaugarlamoody and leaves it at the south-west corner at Pedda ganjam, where it joins the Buckingham coast canal. Irrigation by Kistna anicut canals and springs. Camping grounds at Incolloo, Parchoor, Pedanandipaud. Places of archæological interest:—Annavaram, Appicatla, Baupatla, Caukmaunoo, Cauramchaid, Chebrole, Chinna ganjam, Collimerla, Collitippa, Commoor, Condapautore, Devarpully, Duggoopaud, Firangy dibba, Ganikepoody, Inagull, Incolloo, Keshavarapoopaud, Moonoopulley, Motoopully, Murripoody, Naugalla, Nundoor, Ooppootore, Partsore, Paulparroo, Pauvoolore, Pedda cheroocore, Ponnore, Poosapaud, Pooslore, Raitore, Santaravore, Swarna, Timirtipaud, Toorlapaud, Vangipooram, Vulloor, Yeedpoolapaud, Zaugarlamoody. Trig. stations:—Firangy-dibba, Juggayapollem, Paulparroo, Zaugarlamoody. The leading places, &c., in the talook are the following.——*Anoomilly* (అనుమిల్లి - anumilli, Tel.). From (anumu, tel. dolichos lablab, linn. + milli, tel. village). Village; pop. 4,049; acres 2,208; lat. 15° 47′; long. 80° 21′; from Baupatla S.W. 13 miles; from Masulipatam W.S.W. 60 miles; from the sea N. 4½ miles. Weaving cloths.——*Baupatla* (బాపట్ల - bápatla, Tel.). See below.——*Cauramchaid* (కారంచేడు - káramchédu, Tel.). From (káramu, tel. earth salt + jédu, tel. marsh). Village; pop. 2,779; acres 9,518; lat. 15° 53′; long. 80° 22′; from Baupatla W. 9¾ miles; from Masulipatam W.S.W. 58 miles. In a swamp. Old temple with inscription. Endowed choultry.——*Chebrole* (చేబ్రోలు - chébrólu, Tel.). From (che, tel. field + prólu, tel. town). Sanscrit name (chaturmukhapura), meaning four + face + city; from temple to bramha, the four-faced god. Village; pop. 3,647; acres 5,267; lat. 16° 12′; long. 80° 34′; from Baupatla N. 20 miles; from Masulipatam W. 42 miles; from the sea N. 23 miles. On edge of sandstone ridge overlooking Kistna delta, 1 mile from Commamore canal. Guntoor road enters talook in the neighbourhood. Ancient temple to Bramha, with four gates facing four points of compass. Gold and silver coins have been found. Inscriptions.——*Chercore* (చెరుకూరు - cherukúru, Tel.). From (cheruku, tel. sugar-cane, saccharum officinarum, linn. + úru, tel. village). Tel. also (peddacherukúru), meaning large sugar-cane village. Sanscrit name (ikshupurí), meaning sugar-cane + town. Village; pop. 2,472; acres 5,583; lat. 15° 59′; long. 80° 25′; from Baupatla N.W. 8½ miles; from Masulipatam W.S.W. 51 miles; from the sea N. 15 miles. Temple of Trivicramasawmy with inscriptions.——*Chinna ganjam* (చిన్నగంజాము - chinnagandzámu, Tel.). From (chinna, tel. small + gandzámu, tel. place so called). Sanscrit name (gandhapurí), meaning fragrance + town. Village, Salt factory; pop. 3,370; acres 10,978; lat. 15° 42′; long. 80° 17′; from Baupatla S.W. 21 miles; from Masulipatam W.S.W. 67 miles; from the sea W. 3 miles. Fragments of stone with Booddhist carvings and Pali inscriptions from a Booddhist tope of great antiquity lie about the Collitippa swamp adjoining.——*Chiraula* (చీరాల - chírála, Tel. chirala *). From (chíra, tel. cloth + ila, tel. place). Sanscrit name (kshírálaya), meaning milk + temple. Town; pop. 10,581; acres 5,864; lat. 15° 49′; long. 80° 23′; from Baupatla S.W. 10 miles; from Masulipatam W.S.W. 57 miles; from the sea N. 4 miles. Transferred from Nellore district in 1846. Large weaving population. Noted for cotton manufactures.——*Commamore* (కొమ్మమూరు - kommamúru, Tel.). See sep. title.——*Commoor* (కొమ్మూరు - kommúru, Tel.). From (komma, tel. branch + úru, tel. village). Sanscrit name (shringipura), meaning mountain + town. Village; pop. 2,651; acres 6,185; lat. 16° 04′; long. 80° 24′; from Baupatla N.N.W. 13 miles; from Masulipatam W. 53 miles. Inscriptions.——*Eepoorpollem* (ఈపూరుపాలెం - ípúrupálem, Tel.). See sep. title.——*Firangy dibba* (ఫిరంగిదిబ్బ - p'hirangidibba, Tel.). From (farangí, hind. european + dibba, tel. mound). Tel. also (p'hirangaladinne), meaning european + mound. Village; included in Pedda ganjam; near the line of the old Madras road. Portuguese here in 1240. Small fort at Cadavacodore in neighbourhood was a British outpost last century. Trig. station in lat. 15° 40′ 58·87″; long. 80° 15′ 10·75″; height 30 feet; from Baupatla S.W. 23 miles; from Pedda ganjam N.N.W. 2¾ miles; from the sea W. 3¾ miles.——*Incolloo* (ఇంకొల్లు - inkollu, Tel.). From (inku, tel. to dry + kollu, tel. pool). Village; pop. 3,132; acres 8,335; lat. 15° 50′; long. 80° 14′; from Baupatla W.S.W. 19 miles; from Masulipatam W.S.W. 67 miles; from the sea W. 19 miles. The old line of Madras road enters the district here. Several old temples and Naugacull considered Scythic. The figure wears a head-dress resembling a Phrygian cap. Travellers' bungalow. Endowed choultry.——*Juggayapollem* (జగ్గయపాలెము - jaggayapálemu, Tel.). From (jaggayya, tel. proper name + pálemu, tel. fortified village). Trig. station; lat. 15° 46′ 43·74″; long. 80° 25′ 20·13″; from Baupatla S.W. 11 miles. On the sea shore.——*Motoopully* (మోటుపల్లె - mótupalle, Tel.). From (mótu, tel. uneven + palle, tel. village). Sanscrit name (móhanapurí), meaning infatuating, epithet of shiva + town. Village, Port; pop. 893; acres 4,591; lat. 15° 44′; long. 80° 20′; from Baupatla S.W. 17 miles; from Masulipatam W.S.W. 66 miles. Fishing village about 30 miles from southern mouth of Kistna. Marco Polo stopped here about 1290 A.D. on his voyage up the coast, and describes the place. He mentions the trade in diamonds and fine cloths. Formerly used as a landing place for stores for French troops in Guntoor. Two old Chola temples with inscription.——*Narsayyapollem* (నరసాయపాలెము - narasáyapálemu, Tel.). From (narasáya, tel. proper name + pálemu, tel. fortified village). Village; pop. 1,784; acres 3,899; lat. 15° 57′; long. 80° 26′; from Baupatla N.W. 6 miles; from Masulipatam W.S.W. 51 miles; from the sea N. 11 miles. Lock on the canal. Manufacture of woollen blankets.——*Nayanipulley* (నాయనిపల్లె - náyanipalle, Tel.). From (náyadu, tel. surname + palle, tel. village). Village; pop. 2,259; acres 5,388; lat. 15° 47′; long. 80° 22′; from Baupatla S.W. 31 miles; from Masulipatam W.S.W. 60 miles; from the sea N. 2¼ miles. Two old temples.——*Nundoor* (నందూరు - nandúru, Tel.). From (nandí, san. sacred bull + úru, tel. village). Village; pop. 2,039; acres 2,935; lat. 16° 02′; long. 80° 33′; from Baupatla N.N.E. 8¼ miles; from Masulipatam W.S.W. 43 miles; from the sea N. 12 miles. Two inscriptions. Manufacture of woollen cumblies.——*Ooppootore* (ఉప్పుటూరు - upputúru, Tel.). From (uppu, tel. salt + úru, tel. village). Sanscrit name (lavanapurí), meaning salt + town. Village; pop. 2,036; acres 6,719; lat. 15° 57′; long. 80° 20′; from Baupatla W.N.W. 12 miles; from Masulipatam W.S.W. 58 miles; from the sea N. 18 miles. Ancient temples and inscriptions.——*Pandillapully* (పండిల్లపల్లె - pandillapalle, Tel.). From (pandili, tel. pandal + palle, tel. village). Village; pop. 3,123; acres 2,181; lat. 15° 46′; long. 80° 20′; from Baupatla S.W. 16 miles; from Masulipatam W.S.W. 63 miles; from the sea W. 5½ miles.——*Parchoor* (పర్చూరు - partsúru, Tel.). From (parutsu, tel. to level + úru, tel. village). Village; pop. 2,042; acres 6,486; lat. 15° 58′; long. 80° 19′; from Baupatla W.N.W. 13 miles; from Masulipatam W.S.W. 59 miles; from the sea N. 20 miles. A grant to the Bramins by Mookkanty pullava. Travellers' bungalow. Camping ground. Private endowed choultry.——*Paulparroo* (పాలపర్రు - pálaparru, Tel.). From (pála, tel. white + parra, tel. swamp). Village; pop. 1,623; acres 3,060; lat. 16° 04′; long. 80° 20′; from Baupatla N.W. 16 miles; from Masulipatam W. 57 miles; from the sea N. 26 miles. Trig. station in lat. 16° 03′ 17·33″; long. 80° 19′ 03·52″; height 53 feet; from Baupatla N.W. 16 miles; from Paulparroo S.W. 1 mile; from the sea N. 26 miles.——*Pauvoolore* (పావులూరు - pávulúru, Tel.). From (pávu, tel. one-fourth + úru, tel. village). Village; pop. 2,059; acres 4,098; lat. 15° 51′; long. 80° 12′; from Baupatla W. 20 miles; from Masulipatam W.S.W. 68 miles; from the sea W. 25 miles. Old temples with inscriptions and eight stone images of origin prior to the Bramínical religion.——*Pedda ganjam* (పెద్దగంజాము - peddagandzámu, Tel.). From (pedda, tel. great + gandzámu, tel. place so called). Sanscrit name (gandhapurí), meaning fragrance + town. Village; pop. 2,688; acres 13,623; lat. 15° 39′; long. 80° 16′; from Baupatla S.W. 24 miles; from Masulipatam W.S.W. 71 miles; from the sea W. 2 miles. Tidal lock connects Commamore canal with the Buckingham canal.——*Peraula* (పేరాల - pérála, Tel.). From (péru, tel. great + ráyi, tel. stone). Village; pop. 2,014; acres 2,813; lat. 15° 50′; long. 80° 24′; from Baupatla S.W. 8½ miles; from Masulipatam W.S.W. 57 miles; from the sea N. 4½ miles. Weaving industry.——*Ponnore* (పొన్నూరు - ponnúru, Tel.). See sep. title.——*Santaravore* (సంతరావూరు - santarávúru, Tel.). From (santa, tel. market + rávi, tel. the peepul tree, ficus religiosa, linn. + úru, tel. village). Village; pop. 1,933; acres 5,289; lat. 15° 49′; long. 80° 18′; from Baupatla W.S.W. 64 miles; from the sea N. 11 miles. Former Mahomedan outpost. Three ancient temples with inscriptions. Lock of the Buckingham canal.——*Swarna* (స్వర్ణ - svarna, Tel.). Means gold. Villages; pop. 2,251; acres 9,593; lat. 15° 51′; long. 80° 19′; from Baupatla W.S.W. 13 miles; from Masulipatam W.S.W. 60 miles; from the sea N. 12 miles. Until 1873 belonged to Vencatagherry rajah. On the Buckingham canal.

Three inscriptions. Manufacture of earthen bangles.——*Vangipooram* (వంగిపురము - vangipuramu, Tel.). From (vanga, tel. brinjaul, solanum melongena. linn. + pura, san. town). Sanscrit name (ahichhatrapura), meaning ahichatram, country so called + town. Village; pop. 1,967; acres 4,717; lat. 16° 08′; long. 80° 25′; from Baupatla N.N.W. 17 miles; from Masulipatam W. 51 miles; from the sea N. 25 miles. Inscriptions.——*Vulloor* (వల్లూరు - vallúrú, Tel. vallúr*). From (valle, tel. cloth + úru, tel. village). Village; pop. 2,576; acres 6,357; lat. 16° 07′; long. 80° 28′; from Baupatla N.N.W. 15 miles; from Masulipatam W. 49 miles; from the sea N. 22 miles. Inscriptions. ——*Zaugurlamoody* (జాగర్లమూడి - dzágarlamúdi, Tel.). From (dzágari, tel. watchman + púdi, tel. village). Village; pop. 2,328; acres 911; lat. 16° 14′; long. 80° 38′: from Baupatla N.N.E. 25 miles; from Masulipatam W. 36 miles; from the sea N. 26 miles. On the Commamore canal. Close to it is a lock with a bridge and under sluices to supply the Toongabudra. Old Shiva temple, with a large banyan tree close by said to be coeval with it, and several inscriptions.——**(2)** Town, Head-quarters of Tahsildar and District moonsif, Sub-engineers, and D.P.W. Sub-division officer; Kistna dist., Baupatla tal.; pop. 6,928; acres 8,300; lat. 15° 54′; long. 80° 30′; from Bezwada S.S.W. 43 miles; from Guntoor S. 27 miles; from Madras N. 193 miles; from Masulipatam W.S.W. 48 miles; from Vinoocondah E.S.E. 51 miles; from the sea N. 5½ miles. Carved figures of female furies, considered to be of Scythic origin. Old temple with sixteen inscriptions, most dating from time of Chola kings. Travellers' bungalow.

BAUR (باڑ - bár, *Hind.*). Rail in architecture. Important feature of Booddhist architecture. Generally they are found surrounding regular Booddhist topes [q.v.]; but they also enclose sacred trees [poonyoshadhy] temples [coil] and pillars [laut], and other miscellaneous objects [staupatyam].

BAURAH (بارا - bárá, *Hind.*). Twelve.——*Baurabaloty* (بارابلوهتی - bárábalúhtí, Hind.). The twelve village public servants [balootah].——*Bauradaree* (بارادری - bárádarí, Hind.). Literally having twelve doors. A summer house especially in a garden.——*Baurah fusly* (بارا فصلی - bárâfaslí, Hind.). From (above + faslí, hind. harvest year). Fusly 1212 or the year 1801, when Carnatic was finally ceded.——*Baurah wafaut* (باراوفات - báráwafát, Hind.). From (above + wafát, ar. death); prophet's death on the twelfth. A solemn festival on the 12th of Rabee ool owwal [maheena], on which date, A.H. 11, the prophet died. Sufficiently described at vol. I (96).—— *Baurakharee* (باراکهڑی - bárákharí, Hind.). From (above + khara, san. hard consonants). The song sung by gardeners when drawing water from their wells. Every line of it begins with a consonant. The following is a Hindostany proverb:— کڑکا سہے پالی کے بارا سہے مالی کے— "Pastorals suit the shepherd, "and the song of the well the gardener."

BAURAK (بارک - báruk, *Hind.*). From (baraka, ar. to propitiate). Blessing.——*Baurak allah* (بارک الله - bárakalláh, Hind.). From (above + alláh, ar. god). May God prosper you! Exclamation amongst Mahomedans.

BAURISH (بارش - bárish, *Hind.*). From (báridan, pers. to rain). Rain. Baurishputty is the rain fall account.

BAUROO (ಬಾರು - báru, *Can.*). See vol. I, 615; II, 505-520.— "*a*" Fathom [bauham]. 4 molas = 1 bauroo; 2,000 bauroos = 1 hardaury [alavay, 1].—"*b*" Bazaar weight. 20 maunds = 1 bauroo [niray, 2]. Approximate actual value, 1 bauroo = 500 lbs. In Bellary it is 518·4 lbs. Same as Hind. candy, Tam. bhauram.

BAUSIT (باسط - básit, *Hind.*). From (basata, ar. to spread). The provider. Epithet of God [allah]. Common alam, as Bausit khan, alam + alaumat [ism].

BAUZ (بعض - baaz, *Hind.*). Sundry. Bauzbaub, miscellaneous head in account. Bauz kharch, miscellaneous expenses.

BAWCHEE (वाकुची - vákuchí, *San.*; बावची - bávachí, *Mahr.*; باونچیاں - bávanchiyân, *Hind.*; باونچی - bávanchí, *Dec.*; ಬಾರುಂಚ - baruncha, *Can.*; కాలగింజచెట్టు - kálagindzachettu, *Tel.*; കാർക്കോൽ - kárkkól, *Mal.*; கார்ப்போகு - kárppógu, *Tam.*). Title from hindostany. San. from (váta, san. wind + kuch, san. to contract), destroying vauta rogam [malkangany, wild jeerah]. Mahr., &c., from sanscrit. Tel. from (kála, san. black + gindza, tel. seed + chettu, tel. plant); from dark brown seeds. Mal. from tamul. Tam. means dark flower plant. Tel. also (bhávanjichettu), from hindostany; (kárubhógichettu); (bapunga); (kórjashtamu). Mal. also (kárppókil). Tam. also (kárppuvá), meaning dark-flowered. Title otherwise Hazel-leaved psoralea. Botanically Psoralea corylifolia, L., leguminosæ [vricsham, 48]. Alias Trifolium. Herbaceous, erect, 2 feet; leaves simple, roundish-ovate, repand-toothed; racemes dense, spike-like, usually short, on long axillary solitary peduncles, pedicels much shorter than the calyx, about three together from each bractea; sepals five; legume the length of the calyx, one-seeded, indehiscent; flowers violaceous or pale flesh-colored; a common weed. The dark brown seed, size of large pin's head, oval-shaped, has aromatic unctuous taste, and certain degree of bitterness. Seed useful in skin diseases; also stomachic and deobstruent. Gives an oil. No other common species here.

BAZAAR (بازار - bázár, *Hind.*). From (bá, pers. food + zár, pers. place). A market-place. Any street composed chiefly of shops. Here and in Ceylon a single shop kept by a native. Bazaar nerruck is market rate; opposed to haut, occasional.

BAZAH (بزا - bazá, *Hind.*). Means ibis, geronticus papillosus. Platalea leucorodia (chamchábazá) is the spoon bill ibis; Threskiornis melanocephalus (sufedbazá) is the white ibis.

BDELLIUM (कौशिक - kaushika, *San.*; गुग्गुळ - guggula, *Mahr.*; مقل - mukl, *Ar.*; بوئے جهودان - búijahúdán, *Pers.*; گوگل - gúgal, *Hind.* and *Dec.*; ಗುಗ್ಗುಳ - guggula, *Can.*; గుగ్గుళ - guggula, *Too.*; గుగ్గిలము - guggilamu, *Tel.*; රත්දුම්මල - ratadummala, *Singh.*; மைசாட்சி - maisádchi, *Tam.*). Title from hebrew (bdólah). Pers. from (bú, pers. fragrance + jahúdán, pers. jews); used by them for fumigation. Hind. from sanscrit. Singh. from (rata, singh. country + dummala, singh. resin). Tam. from (mahisha, san. buffalo + akshi, san. eye); from color of drug. Tel. also (maisákshi). Singh. also (gugulu). Tam. also (kukkil). Title otherwise Foreign googal. A gum-resin [gond, googal]; akin to balm of gilead [q.v.] and myrrh [bole]; distinct from olibanum [q.v.]; is one of the many googals [q.v.]. Good bdellium is clean, bright, sticky, soft, sweet-smelling, yellowish, and bitter; mixed readily with water; is hot and dry; used in the same way as myrrh. The cheaper kinds of bdellium are used to give adhesiveness and polish to fine plaster on ceilings and pillars; these kinds are then dissolved, strained and mixed with molasses.——*African bdellium* (सैन्धवगुग्गुल - saindhavaguggula, San.; महिषबोल - mahishabóla, Mahr.; حبق هادی - habakihádí, Ar.; بهینسا بول - bhainsábol, Hind.). Title from place whence introduced. San. from (sindhu, san. sea + guggula, san. indian bdellium, balsamodendron roxburghii, arn.); as coming from barbary in africa from beyond sea. Mahr. from (mahisha, san. buffalo + vóla, san. myrrh, balsamodendron myrrha, nees.); given to increase its milk. Ar. from (habak, ar. basil + hádí, ar. a wild bull). Hind. from (bhains, hind. buffalo + bol, ar. myrrh); current in bombay for the gum-resin from barbary in africa. San. also (samudriyaguggula), meaning sea + googal, balsamodendron mukul, hook., as coming from beyond sea; (mahisháksha), meaning buffalo + eye, from appearance. Title otherwise Besabole, Foreign googal. Botanically Balsamodendron [balsam], kataf, kth., burseraceæ [vricsham, 35]. Alias Amyris kataf; Balsamea erythræa; Hemprichia erythræa. Gives a gum-resin, paler and more reddish than myrrh; much stronger, acrid taste, and a separate odour; is on a par with an indian googal.——*Indian bdellium* (कौशिक - kaushika, San.; गुग्गुळ - guggula, Mahr.; بهینسا گوگل - bhainságúgal, Hind.; بهیسا گوگل - bhaiságúgal, Dec.; ಗುಗ್ಗುಳ - guggula, Can.; గుగ్గిలపుచెట్టు - guggilapuchettu, Tel.; ගුගුළු - gugulu, Singh.; குக்குலு - kukkulu, Tam.). San. from (kósha, san. bark), exudation of bark [arabian jasmine]. Mahr. from (gud, san. to protect). Hind. from (bhainsá, hind. buffalo); given to increase its milk. Tam. from (gud, san. to preserve), as curative. San. also (guggulu); (aguru), meaning eagle-wood, from similar fragrance. Mahr. also (mahishabóla), meaning buffalo + myrrh. Tel. also (bódankichettu); (kondarégu), meaning hill + jujube tree, zizyphus jujuba, lamk.; (mahisákshi), meaning buffalo + eye, from color of drug. Singh. also (jatáyu). Tam. also (maisádchi), meaning buffalo-eyed; from color of drug. Title otherwise Buffalo googal, Buffalo myrrh, False myrrh, Roxburgh's googal. Botanically Balsamodendron [balsam] roxburghii, arn., burseraceæ [vricsham, 35]. Alias Amyris agallocha, commiphora; Balsamodendron agallocha. Small tree; trunk crooked, and clothed with many drooping crooked branches down to the ground; branchlets often ending in thorny points; calyx four-toothed; petals four; leaves alternate, petioled, oval or elliptic, serrulate, smooth on both sides; at the base or apex of the petiole on each side is generally a small leaflet giving the appearance of a ternate leaf; flowers on short peduncles, axillary, small, red, aggregate on the buds by the former year's leaves; berry drupaceous, red, smooth, size of a currant; nut two-celled, one-seeded; grows in scinde. Gives a fragrant gum resin; this is semi-pellucid and of a yellowish brown or dark-brown color according to its age, unctuous to the touch, but brittle; soon however softening betwixt the fingers; in appearance not unlike myrrh; of a bitterish taste and moderately strong smell; in burning it sputters owing to its moisture. Is collected in the cold season by making incisions in the tree and letting the resin fall on the ground. Medicinal properties, being same as myrrh [bole], are stimulant, expectorant and emmenagogue; internally as purifier of blood; substituted for british myrrh; in pharm. non-officinal. Is used by masons to mix with fine plaster.——*Mookul bdellium* (महिषगुग्गुल - mahishaguggula, San.; مقل - mukl, Ar.; بوئے جهودان - búijahúdán, Pers.; گوگل - gúgal, Dec.; රත්දුම්මල - ratadummala, Singh.). Title from syriac through arabic. San. from (mahisha, san. buffalo + guggula, san. indian bdellium, balsamodendron roxburghii, arn.); from bluish black color of drug. Ar. from syriac. Pers. from (bú, pers. scent + jahúdán, ar. jews); from being largely used by jews. Dec. from sanscrit. Singh. from (rata, singh. foreign + dummala, singh. resin); as coming from arabia. Ar. also (mukliarzak), meaning bdellium of a bluish tinge; (aflátan). Pers. also (raugbaniturb), meaning earth oil. Title otherwise Blue bdellium, Foreign googal, Jews' scent. Botanically Balsamodendron [balsam], mukul, hook., burseraceæ [vricsham, 35]. Specific name from syriac through arabic. Small thorny tree bearing trifoliate leaves; the outer bark peels off in thin flakes exposing the green under layer; gives one of the googals, but roxburghii much more common here [indian bdellium].

BE (بے - be, *Hind.*). From Persian. Without.——*Bebauk* (بے باق - bebák, Hind.). From (bák, ar. arrear). In full, of a receipt.——*Bebund* (بے بند - beband, Hind.). From (band, pers. bar). Insecure.——*Becharaugh* (بے چراغ - becharágh, Hind.). From (charágh, pers. lamp). Deserted, of a village.——*Begaury* (بیگاری - begárí, Hind.). From (kár, hind. work). Unpaid labor.——*Be insauf* (بے انصاف - beinsáf, Hind.). From (insáf, ar. justice). Injustice.——*Bejah* (بیجا - bejá, Hind.). From (já, pers. place). Inaccurate.——*Benaumy* (بینامی - benámí, Hind.). From (nám, pers. a name). Nameless. A sale or purchase made in the name of some one other than the actual vendor or purchaser. See vol. I, 112.——*Beshara* (بے شرع - beshara, Hind.). From (shara, ar. law). Without the law; of fakeers [baushara].——*Bewaurs* (بے وارث - bewáris, Hind.). From (wáris, ar. heir). Unclaimed.

BEAD TREE (अक्षद्रु - akshadru, *San.*; منکے کا جھاڑ - mankekájhár, *Dec.*). Title from use of seeds. San. from (asksha, san. bead + dru, san. tree). Dec. from (manká, hind. bead + jhár, hind. tree). Anglo-indian term for plants giving seeds used for ornament [munkah]; especially for Melia azedarach, linn. [neem]. Cf. also :—Abrus precatorius, coral bead; canna indica, indian bead.

BEARD-GRASS (वेणी - vẽní, *San.*). Title from hairy stalks. San. means braided hair. Botanically the Andropogon genus, graminaceæ [vricsham, 156]. The species best known to the natives are —aciculatus [keshinee], contortus [spear-grass], iwarancusa [ibharancoosha], martini [roussa grass], muricatus [cuscus], nardus [indian grass], pilosus [nutt grass], schœnanthus [lemon grass]. Other S. indian species indigenous or naturalized are :—bladhii, controversus, fascicularis, glaber, imberbis, pertusus, montanus, serratus, simillimus, scandens.

BEARER (மெய்க்காவலன் - meykkávalan, *Tam.*). From (mey, tam. body + kával, tam. guard). A man who carries a palankeen. So a body servant [boy].

BEAR HILL (ಡೇರ್‌ಬೆಟ್ಟ - dérbetta, *Can.*). From (dér, badaga contraction of dévaru, can. god + betta, can. mountain). Hill; Neilgherry district, Coondah division; lat. of trig. station 11° 15′ 47·29″; long. 76° 37′ 25·75″; height 8,304 feet; from Ootacamund S.W. 12 miles.

BED (بید - bed, *Hind.*). Means cane. Same as Indian willow.

BED (بید - bed, *Hind.*). Sense.——*Bedaur* (بیدار - bedár, Hind.). From (above + dár, pers. keeper). Vigilant. Mahomedan servant's alam. Also takhalloos [ism].

BEDAUNA (درخت سفرجل - darakhtisafarjal, *Ar.*; درخت بہی - darakhtibihí, *Pers.*; بہی کا پیڑ - bihíkáper, *Hind.*; بہی کا جھاڑ - bihíkájhár, *Dec.*; ಶೀಮೆದಾಳಿಂಬೆ - shímedálimbe, *Can.*; సీమదానిమ్మ - símadánimma, *Tel.*; சீமைமாதளை - shímaimáthalai, *Tam.*). Title from hindostany meaning quince seed. Ar. from (darakht, ar. tree + safarjal, ar. water fruit). Pers. from (darakht, ar. tree + bihí, pers. quince). Hind. from (bihí, pers. quince + per, hind. tree). Can. from (shíme, can. foreign + dálimbe, can. pomegranate, punica granatum, linn.). Tel. from (síma, tel. foreign + dánimma, tel. pomegranate, punica granatum, linn.). Tam. from (shímai, tam. foreign + máthalai, tam. pomegranate); from fruit and seed. Pers. also (darakhtitukhmiábí), meaning water-seed tree. Tam. also (péthaná). Greek κυδώνιον; Latin Malum cotoneum. The Greek from Cydonia, a city of Crete, whence the quince was first introduced. Title otherwise Apple of song of solomon, Cretan apple, Foreign pomegranate, Golden apple, Golden fruit of the hesperides, Melicoton, Quince, Water-fruit. Botanically Cydonia vulgaris, pers., rosaceæ [vricsham, 49]. Pyrus cydonia; Cydonia sumboshia. Little found in the bazaars here; brought to india from sea ports of persian gulf. Seeds inodorous, insipid, ovate, angled, reddish brown, coriaceous, contained within the cells of the pear which is yellowish; when long chewed, bitter. Bedauna seed is demulcent tonic, and restorative; highly valued by mahomedans all over the east; in pharm. non-officinal; contains prussic acid. Fruit astringent, edible with sugar in jelly and syrup; ripe fruit has a powerful odour, used to flavor preserves.

BEE (بی - bí, *Hind.*). Means lady. Syed and Sheikh female alaumat; as Careem bee, alam + alaumat [ism].——*Beeby* (بی بی - bibí, Hind.). From Persian. Lady. Lacab of females [ism]. Beeby fatimah, daughter of Mahomet, was wife of Ally. Among Sheikhs the title is commonly affixed to all women's names. The Beeby of Cannanore is the ruler of that neighbourhood, and exercises authority over three of the islands of the Laccadives, all of which formerly belonged to her ancestors. She is a Moplah mahomedan. The senior female member of the family always takes the title and position [bee, begum].——*Beejaun* (بی جان - bíján, Hind.). From (above + ján, hind. soul). Dear lady. Lacab of female; sometimes alam; as Beejaun bee, alam + alaumat [ism].

BEED (ಬೀಡು - bídu, *Can.*; బీడు - bídu, *Tel.*). Waste; suffix in place names, as Haleybeed, meaning old + waste. Poorantana beed from (purátana, san. old), is land long left fallow.

BEEDAR (بدر - bídar, *Hind.*). The city. Town, Nizam's dominions, Deccan; lat. 17° 53′; long. 77° 34′; from Hyderabad N.W. 75 miles. On right bank of Manjeerah. Capital under Bahmany kings, now much decayed. Noted for metal ware.——*Beedar earth* (بدری کھری - bidríkharí, Hind.). From (kharí, hind. chalk). Obtained at a hill near Beedar. Used for whitening soldiers' belts and helmets.

BEEGAH (بیگھا - bíghá, *Hind.*). From (vigraha, san. extension). Land measure. 20 bishwahs = 1 beegah; 120 beegahs = 1 chauver [alavay, 2]. Approximate actual value, 1 standard beegah = 3,025 square yards, but varies from one-third of an acre to one acre. See vol. I, 609.

BEEJAM (बीज - bíja, *San.*). From (vi, san. intensive prefix + jan, san. to produce). Seed. Also a mystic letter, the syllable which forms the essential part of the muntram of any deity [matam].——*Beeja ganitam* (बीजगणित - bíjaganita, San.). From (above + ganita, san. calculation). Calculation of seeds. Calculation of primary elements, algebra.——*Beejwary* (ಬೀಜವರಿ - bíjavari, Can.). From (above + wárí, hind. according to). Extent of land computed according to the quantity of seed required to be sown in it. See vol. I, 112.

BEER (بیر - bír, *Hind.*). Woman.——*Beerboty* (इन्द्रगोप - indragópa, San.; كاغنه - kághunah, Ar.; عروسك - arúsak, Pers.; بیربہوٹی - bírbahútí, Hind.; بیر بہوٹی - bírbahútí, Dec.; ಇಂದ್ರಗೋಪ - indragópa, Can.; ఆరుద్రపురుగు - árudrapurugu, Tel.; ഇന്ദ്രഗോപം - indragópam, Mal.; தம்பலப்பூச்சி - tambalappúççi, Tam.). Title from hindostany. San. from (indra, san. the sky god + gup, san. to protect); as nourished during rains. Pers. from (arús, pers. bride + pers. diminutive suffix). Hind. from (bír, hind. woman + bhú, san. earth + uthí, hind. grown). Tel. from (árdra, san. moist + purugu, tel. insect); from appearing in rainy season. Tam. from (tambalam, tam. red spittle + púççi, tam. insect); from crimson color. Tel. also (súryaputamupurugu), meaning sun + exposure + insect. Otherwise Lady fly, Scarlet moth. Mutella occidentalis, mutillidæ, hymenoptera; holometala, insecta [poochy], of naturalists [jantoo]. Alias Mutella antiguensis. Scarlet-velvet-colored insect, about the size of a large pea, but flat, commonly found in rainy weather on reddish sandy soil, near grass. Antennæ, eyes, legs, and under part of the body are black; sting long and filiform; abdomen marked with a black belt; it has no wings. Veidyans consider it efficacious in snake-bites, and tonic when dried and mixed with the root of Corallocarpus epigæa, hook. [caper]. Not to be confounded either with the foreign cochineal insect [kirmiz] or indigenous lac insect [jantoo, lac].

BEERA (బీర - bíra, *Tel.*). Elæodendron glaucum, pers., Olive-wood.——*Beerapair* (బీరేరు - bírapéru, Tel.). From (above + éru, tel. river). From color of waters which resemble scarlet fruit of plant. Sanscrit name (bhímanadí), meaning Bheeman's river. River; Nellore district, Atmacore and Nellore talooks. A small stream which carries off rain fall of north eastern portion of Atmacore talook and of small part of Cauvaly and Oodayagherry talooks, and falls into Pennair at Sungam just within limits of Nellore talook.

BEG (بیگ - beg, *Hind.*). From Turkish. Prince, lord. Moghul alaumat; as Ahmed beg, alam + alaumat [ism].——*Begum* (بیگم - begam, Hind.). Feminine of Beg. Princess. Moghul and Pataun female alaumat [ism]. Generally a title of rank, but among Syeds is commonly affixed to all women's names [bauno, bee, beeby, khanam, khautoon, nissa]. Many towns are hence named; as Begum bazaar, a suburb of Madras.

BEIDORE (ಬೈದೂರು - baidúru, *Can.*). From (baida, can. hunter + úru, can. town). Town, Port; South canara dist., Coondapore tal.; pop. 2,157; lat. 13° 52′; long. 74° 39′; from Coondapore N.N.W. 18 miles; from Mangalore N. 70 miles; from Shiroor S.S.E. 3 miles; from the sea E. 1 mile. Extreme north-western town of the Presidency at the terminus of the road crossing the ghauts into Mysore territory. Temple and sculptures. Formerly had a fort, and belonged to a Jeina ranee named Bheiradevy.

BEIRA (ಬೈರ - baira, *Can.*). From (bhéri, can. drum). Low caste proper name. Common among chucklers [peyar].

BEIRAM (بیرم - bairam, *Hind.*). From Turkish. Festival, same as Eed. Greater is Buckreed; lesser is Ramzaun [q.v.].

BEIRAUGY (बैरागी - bairágí, *San.*). From (vi, san. privative + rága, san. passion). A shoodra mendicant of the Veishnava sect. Profess physic; do not marry. For Sheiva see Yogy; for general see Sanyausy.

BEITAUL (بیتال - baitál, *Hind.*). Ghost.——*Beitaul pacheesy* (بیتال پچیسی - baitálpachísí, Hind.). From (above + pachísí, hind. twenty-five). Hindee edition of Vetaula puncha vimshaty [q.v.].

BEL (بیل - bel, *Hind.*). A hoe. Beldar is a laborer.——*Belha* (بیلہا - belhá, Hind.). Thug grave-digger.

BEL (بیل - bel, *Hind.*). Creeper.——*Bel bootah* (بیل بوٹا - belbútá, Hind.). From (above + bútá, hind. flower). Arabesque [staupatyam].

BELGAUM (బెలగాము - belagámu, *Tel.* belgám *). From (bila, san. cave + gráma, san. village). Village, Head-quarters of Senior assistant collector, District moonsif, Deputy tahsildar, and Assistant superintendent of Police, Sub-registrar's office, Hill jail; Vizagapatam dist., Parvatipore division; pop. 2,168; lat. 18° 46; long. 83° 28′; from Coraputt E. 45 miles; from Madras N.N.E. 440 miles; from Narsapatam N.N.E. 90 miles; from Parvatipore S. 1 mile; from Vizagapatam N. 72 miles; from Vizianagram N. 44 miles. For account of Belgaum zemindar, see Parvatipore. Police reserve located here to quell any disturbance in Central agency tracts.

BELLAMCONDAH (బెల్లంకొండ - bellamkonda, *Tel.*). From (bellamu, tel. jaggery + konda, tel. hill). Tel. also (bilamkonda), meaning cave + hill. Village, Hill; Kistna dist., Suttenapully tal.; pop. 1,503; lat. of trig. station 16° 30′ 19·16″; long. 80°03′ 32·15″; height 1,570 feet; from Crossoor W.S.W. 8¾ miles; from Masulipatam W.N.W. 79 miles. Hills crowned with the ruins of a fortress. The village stands at the foot of the hill, on the Guntoor-Nelgonda road. The fort constructed by the Condaveed reddies. After their power passed away in A.D. 1428 it passed under the Orissa rajahs. In 1531 Sultan coolee of Golcondah took the place. It again fell into the hands of the Carnatic kings, and was taken by the Mahomedans in 1578. At the close of the last century the English stationed a few sepoys at foot of hill in temporary mud huts. The works consist of a single stone wall connecting the principal elevated points of the hill, having tower bastions at the south-east and north-west angles, which terminate the principal front. The entrance is on this side, at about a third of its length from the latter bastion, and is gained by a winding pathway from the foot of the hill near the village. In shape it is somewhat of an equilateral triangle, enclosing an area of irregular elevation of about one-sixteenth of a square mile. The wall is in a ruinous state. The two bastions, that to the north-west 970, and to the south-east 1,090 feet above the plain, are the most perfect parts of the work, but even these from their overhanging position seem to threaten destruction to everything below them. The interior is overgrown with bushes and long grass which obstruct the passage to the eastern and western faces in many parts. There still remain some buildings of stone, the old magazine and godowns, the remains of a small mosque and a tomb of one of the Mussalman commanders, a small pond with good water, and a mound of earth thrown across part of the interior apparently intended as a passage to the northern part of the droog.

BELLARY * (بلہاری - balhárí, *Hind.*; బళ్లారి - ballári, *Tel.*). From (bala, san. name of a giant + hári, san. defeat); place where Bala the giant was killed. But probably there is some indigenous derivation.——(1) Revenue district; situated on the north-west corner of the Presidency, between 14° 29′ and 15° 58′ N. lat., and between 75° 42′ and 77° 41′ E. long.; bounded north by river Toongabudra, east by Kurnool and Anantapore districts, south and west by Mysore. Square miles 6,141. Population 900,126. Language Canarese and Teloogoo. Contains rivers Hagary and Toongabudra; mountains, Cumply and Sundoor; sanitarium, Ramandroog [hill-station]. The whole area of the district is represented by the following sub-areas:—Adony, Aulore, Bellary, Coodligy, Hoovinhadgully, Hospett, Hurpanhully, and Royadroog talooks, and Sundoor territory. For general administrative purposes the district is distributed between the following revenue and magisterial officers, who have their head-quarters at the places shown; which see separately. The pay set opposite the subordinate officers gives the grade of the corresponding charge:—Collector, Bellary. Head assistant collector, Hospett, in charge of Hospett, Hurpanhully, Hoovinhadgully and Coodligy talooks. Assistant collector or General duty deputy collector, Bellary, in charge of Bellary and Royadroog talooks. General duty deputy collector, Adony, in charge of Adony and Aulore talooks. Tahsildars at Adony, Rs. 200; Aulore, Rs. 175; Bellary, Rs. 225; Coodligy, Rs. 175; Hoovinhadgully, Rs. 150; Hospett, Rs. 175; Hurpanhully, Rs. 150; Royadroog, Rs. 175. Deputy tahsildars at Cumply, Rs. 70, range situated north-east of Hospett talook; Siroogooppa, Rs. 70, range situated in the northern extremity of the Bellary talook; and Yemmiganore, Rs. 70, range situated north-east of Adony talook. Sub-magistrate without revenue charge, Bellary, Rs. 100, jurisdiction extending over Bellary town. Similarly judicial officers:—Judge, Bellary. District moonsifs; Bellary, with jurisdiction extending over Bellary and Royadroog, and portion of Aulore talook; Narraindevarakery, with jurisdiction extending over Hospett, Hurpanhully, Hadgully, and Coodligy talooks. Contains Registration sub-districts; Adony, Aulore, Bellary, Coodligy, Cumply, Hoovinhadgully, Hospett, Hurpanhully, Siroogooppa, Royadroog and Yemmiganore. Contains forest ranges; Coodligy, Hospett, Royadroog, Sundoor. Contains municipalities; Adony, Bellary. Contains District board. Contains Talook boards; Bellary talook board embracing Bellary and Royadroog talooks; Hospett talook board embracing Hospett, Hadgully, Coodligy and Hurpanhully talooks; Adony talook board embracing Adony and Aulore talooks. The following general references should be made to the preceding volumes:—general geography, I (1) to (29); general ethnology, I (29) to (109); general history, I (110) to (188); physical geography, II, 1; meteorology, II, 3; geology, II, 8; fauna, II, 21; flora, II, 26; mineralogy, II, 29. The following references in the preceding volumes will furnish details special to the district:—latitudes and longitudes, II, 47; particulars about towns, II, 48; comparative population, II, 172; location of revenue officers, II, 380; registrars' and sub-registrars' stations, II, 420; rain-guage stations, II, 428; police divisions, II, 431; maps published, II, 436; survey topographical lists, II, 443; hospitals and dispensaries, II, 447; missionary stations, II, 455; head-quarter stations of gazetted officers, II, 461; incidence of taxation, II, 463; weights and measures of the district, II, 507; zemindarries, II, 294. A special gazetteer account of the whole district is given at II, 58. For the detailed topography of the district, reference should be made to the talook notices in the present volume, viz.:—Adony, Aulore, Bellary, Coodligy, Hoovinhadgully, Hospett, Hurpanhully, Royadroog, Sundoor.——(2) Talook, Bellary district. Tahsildar's pay Rs. 225. Area 962 square miles. Population 172,216. Language Canarese and Teloogoo. Centre of district. Situated between lat. 14° 57′ and 15° 44′ N. and long. 76° 41′ and 77° 13′ E. Bounded by Toongabudra river on the north, Aulore talook of Bellary and Gooty talook of Anantapore on the east, Hospett talook on the west, and Royadroog talook and Mysore on the south. Surface is mostly a level plain, sloping down from the Mincherry range to the Toongabudra and Hagary. About two-thirds are black cotton soil, and the remainder light brown soil changing in the vicinity of the hills into red gravel. In certain places the black soil is impregnated with saline matter which affects its fertility. The greater portion of the surplus grain of the talook finds its way to Bellary, but a considerable quantity of paddy is annually sent to the principal markets in the Doab. Dharwar supplies the greater portion of the wheat. A considerable supply of raggy is drawn from Mysore, especially in times of scarcity. Coarse country cloths and cumblies are chiefly woven in the talook, these being much used by the population. Large quantities of plantain leaves and fruits are brought weekly into Bellary from Camalaupooram in Hospett, Deshanore and Siroogooppa in Bellary talook. Copper and brass vessels at Hireyhaul, silk and cotton cheeras at Bellary, are the principal manufactures. Nuts and cocoanuts from the Mysore territory and rice from the Royadroog talook and the neighbouring districts are imported largely every week into the Bellary market. Jaggery is exported from Siroogooppa to the Nizam's territory. There are only five tanks, and these very insignificant. The Toongabudra and Hagary flow along the boundaries. In connection with the Hagary there are channels to the villages of Asoondy, Chauganore, Moka, Roopangoody, and Tolamaumidy. Larger channels are taken off from the Toongabudra by anicuts at Deshanore and Siroogooppa. The rainfall is very small. There are camping grounds at Courtney, Hireyhaul, Moka, Paramadevanhully. Places of archæological interest:—Bellary, Coorgode, Courtney, Hireyhaul, Kenchengode. Principal trig. stations:—Coorgode, Gooddadore, Kenchengode, Sooggaldevy. The leading places, &c., in the talook are the following.——*Bellary* (బళ్లారి - ballári, Tel.). See below.——*Brucepettah* (బ్రూసుపేట - brúsupéta, Tel.). See sep. title.——*Coorgode* (ಕುರುಗೋಡು - kurugódu, Can.). From (kuru, can. short + kódu, can. hill top); sanscrit name (nandikéshvara), meaning bull god + lord. Village; pop. 3,440; acres 11,092; lat. 15° 21′; long. 76° 53′; from Bellary N.N.W. 15 miles. Temple of Basaveshwara contains a representation of the bullock-god, 12 feet high, with small horns and facing the temple of Humpy. Several temples with inscriptions in old Canarese. Trig. station in lat. 15° 20′ 46·57″; long. 76° 51′ 57·65″; height 1,966 feet; from Bellary N.N.W. 15 miles; from Coorgode W. 1 mile.——*Copper mountain* (ತಾಂಬ್ರಬೆಟ್ಟ - támbrabetta, Can.). See sep. title.——*Courtney* (కుడతని - kudatani, Tel.). See sep. title.——*Cowl bazaar* (قول بازار - kaulbázár, Hind.). See sep. title.——*Deshanore* (దేశనూరు - déshanúru, Tel.). So called after Devarasayya who built the anicut. Village; pop. 2,169; acres 3,585; lat. 15° 39′; long. 76° 55′; from Bellary N. 35 miles. Anicut with channels on Toongabudra.——*Gooddadore* (ಗುಡ್ಡದೂರು - guddadúru, Can.). From (gudda, can. hill + úru, can. village). Trig. station; lat. 15° 18′ 48·57″; long. 77° 01′ 57·65″; height 1,674 feet; from Bellary N.N.E. 13 miles; from Gooddadore village W.N.W. ¼ mile.——*Hagary* (ಹಗರಿ - hagari, Can.). See sep. title.——*Hireyhaul* (ಹಿರೇಹಾಳು - hiréhálu, Can.). From (hiri, can. great + hálu, can. waste). Village; pop. 4,179; acres 8,299; lat. 15° 0′; long. 76° 53′; from Bellary S.W. 11 miles. On

Bangalore road, in plain at W. end of small pass. Formerly under Poligars of Royadroog. Taken by Moraury row, but shortly afterwards retaken after a siege of three months by Hyder ally. Remains of fort to be seen. Copper and brass vessels manufactured. Good camping ground and travellers' bungalow.——*Ibrahimpooram* (ఇబ్రాంపురము - ibbarámpuramu, Tel.). From (ibráhím, ar. proper name + pura, san. town). Village; acres 2,189; lat. 15° 05′; long. 77° 01′; from Bellary S.E. 5½ miles.——*Kenchengode* (ಕೆಂಚನಗುಡ್ಡ - kenchanagudda, Can.). From (kenchana, can. proper name + gudda, can. hill); after Kenchengowda, the founder. Village; pop. 1,202; acres 2,804; lat. 15° 37′; long. 76° 53′; from Bellary N. 33 miles. Remnants of large town on S. bank of Toongabudra. Near it is burial place of Pumpaupaty gowda, and ruins of stone fort, palace, and gardens erected by Kenchengowda, founder of the place. The latter contain a curious model of a labyrinth in stone. Several anicuts across river. Founder was a peasant who emigrated here during reign of Krishna deva royel of Vijiannugger, by whose permission he settled with the privileges of Nautgowdy. His descendants, Basava and Naugottama gowda, accompanied Ramranz of Vijianugger on an expedition against his brother at Adony, and were rewarded by privileges of Nowbut, Chanwar and Chaund. Kenchengode, Siroogooppa and its dependencies were conferred upon them for ever. Basava assumed title of rajah. He died after ruling fifty-two years, succeeded by his son Hampa gowda, in whose time Masood khan, Soobahdar of Adony, appropriated the revenue, leaving the Gowda the rights only of Nautgowdy, with an allowance. Trig. station in lat. 15° 35′ 40·57″; long. 76° 53′ 06·65″; from Bellary N. 31 miles; from Hirekal N.N.E. 1 mile.——*Mellorpettah* (మిల్లరుపేట - millarupéta, Tel.). See sep. title.——*Mincherry* (మించేరి - minchéri, Tel.). See sep. title.——*Moka* (మోక - móka, Tel.). So called after a princess who founded the city. Sanscrit ·me (mókshámbikápurí), meaning absolution + goddess [illegible]. Village; pop. 2,919; acres 6,263; lat. 15° 14′; long. 77° 06′; from Bellary N.E. 11 miles. Has a channel in connect[illegible] with the Hagary.——*Roopangoody* (ರೂಪನಗುಡಿ - rúpanagudi, [illegible]n.). From (rúpanna, can. a village deity + gudi, can. temp[illegible] Village; pop. 1,989; acres 5,619; lat. 15° 03′; long. 77° 0[illegible] from Bellary E.S.E. 12 miles. Has a channel in connection with the Hagary.——*Siroogooppa* (శిరుగుప్ప - shiruguppa, Tel.). See sep. title.——*Sooggaldevibetta* (ಸುಗ್ಗಲದೇವಿಬೆಟ್ಟ - sugaladévibetta, Can.). From (suggi, can. spring + dévi, can. goddess + betta, can. hill). Contains old copper mines. Trig. station in lat. 15° 04′ 34·57″; long. 76° 52′ 23·65″; height 3,285 feet; from Bellary S.W. 7¾ miles.——*Tekkalcote* (తెక్కలకోట - tekkalakóta, Tel.). From (tekkali, tel. robbery + kóta, tel. fort). Village; pop. 3,721; acres 10,621; lat. 15° 32′; long. 76° 55′; from Bellary N. 28 miles. Formerly capital of province given by Vijianugger ruler to first Nayar poligar of Bellary. Fell into hands of Mahomedans in sixteenth century, taken by Hyder when he overthrew the Balaghaut, and ceded by Nizam to British in 1800.——*Toongabudra* (తుంగభద్ర - tungabhadra, Tel.). See sep. title.——**(3)** Sub-magistracy, Bellary town. Pay Rs. 100. See on district above.——**(4)** Town, Cantonment, Head-quarters of Collector, Judge, Talook and Division, Deputy tahsildar's station, Railway station; Bellary dist., Bellary tal.; pop. 59,467; acres 15,882; lat. 15° 08′; long. 76° 58′; height 1,477 feet; from Adony S.W. 41 miles; from Hospett E.S.E. 38 miles; from Hurpanhully E.N.E. 67 miles; from Tadpatry W. 74 miles. On an arid plain stretching from the foot of a mass of granitic rock, and defended by two lines of fortifications. Very dry climate. A dependant of Krishna deva royel of Vijianugger built a fort here. His descendants held it even after Talicote, when Bellary passed to Beejapore. In 1650 Anoopa the Rajah of Bellary defeated the descendant of the Vijianugger rajahs, who had claimed tribute from him, and for a century the feud continued between the two families. On the district passing with its neighbours into the hands of the Nizam, Bellary was included in the estate of Adony which had been given to Basaulut jung, the Nizam's brother. In 1769 the poligar appealed to Hyder ally for help against Sufder jung and M. Bussy, who had been sent from Adony to collect tribute. Hyder defeated the Nizam's troops and seized the fort for himself. It was held by Tippoo sultan till 1792, when it fell by the partition treaty to the Nizam, who ceded it in 1800. The present fortifications were built by a staff of French engineers. Tradition is that after the new citadel had been completed, Hyder ally hanged them at the gate, as he found that the fort could be commanded by a higher rock. The summit constitutes the upper fort, unoccupied. The lower fort, containing the arsenal, guards the eastern base and is about half a mile in circumference. Southward of the rock and south-east of the lower fort stretches the native quarter, Cowl bazaar, Brucepettah, and Mellorpettah, to which the inhabitants were removed in 1816 from the fort. A large tank, nearly 3 miles in circumference. About half a mile south-west of the base of the rock are the regimental lines. The Church of St. Mary was erected in 1866 for soldiers. There are two churches of the London missionary society, one in Brucepettah and one in the Cowl bazaar. Of late years water has been scarce and old springs seem to be drying up. Chloride of soda and carbonate of lime appear largely in the soil. The opening of the railway has given an impetus to cotton traffic.

BELLIAPATAM (വളപട്ടണം - valapattanam, *Mal.*). From (valar, mal. to grow + pattana, san. town). Sanscrit name (vriddhipura), meaning growing town; also (vallabhapura), meaning town of vallabhan, the king; also (shivéshvara), meaning shiva + lord.—" *a* " Town; Malabar dist., Chiracal tal.; lat. 11° 56′; long. 75° 24′; from Bombay S.S.E. 486 miles; from Calicut N.N.W. 54 miles; from Poothiyangaudy N.N.W. 80 miles; from Cannanore N. 4¾ miles; from the sea E. 2½ miles. On left bank of river of same name, 4 miles from mouth and just below Mount delly. In 1735 the Company obtained permission from the Rajah of Chiracal to build a fort, named Madakara, near this place as a precaution against the transport of pepper and cardamoms by the river. Near Belliapatam Hyder ally, in his descent upon Malabar, gained a signal victory. He used a fleet to transport his horsemen across the river. Sacred temple in the south-east of the town. Port has a fair amount of coasting trade. Crafts of considerable size enter the river and take in the country produce brought to market by the Belliapatam and Taliparamba rivers, which here unite. Poon and teak spars are floated down the river and shipped here during the fine season.—" *b* " River; Malabar district, Chiracal talook. Otherwise Neytarpoya or ghee village river. Rises with the Lutchmanateertam and Paupnaushy in the Bramhagherry hills in the Kiggat naud sub-division of Coorg where called Barapoley, flows for several miles in almost a straight line and then westwards through Malabar district into the Arabian sea. Its upper course lies amid deep gorges and wild forest scenery, one of its tributaries falling over a perpendicular rock of great height, forming a cascade [aroovy] near Codyaul coffee estate. On the Coorg frontier it also forms a waterfall of 200 feet. At foot of the hills joins another large stream flowing from the range in north-east of Manattana. Immediately below junction, the united stream is spanned by Iritty bridge on high road from coast to Coorg and Mysore. From Iricore, where it is always navigable for large boats, it flows westward to Grovapoya. Here a third stream rising from the same sources joins it, the river widening considerably at the confluence. It then flows past and debouches into the sea 4 miles north-west of Belliapatam in lat. 11° 57′; long. 75° 21′. Numerous plantations of areca and cocoanut palms make the scenery of the lower stream picturesque. Total length, about 74 miles. Though its length is less than that of several other rivers in Malabar, it discharges more water into the sea than any of them.

BELLOO (വെളു - vellu, *Mal.*). From (velu, mal. white). Pariah proper name. Compare Biliya, Vellay [peyar].——*Belliky* (ಬೆಳ್ಳಿಕಿ - belliki, Can.). Village, Valley, Paranginaud division, Neilgherries; from Coonoor 22 miles; from Ootacamund 27 miles. Near the foot of the Coonoor ghaut, N. of the Kullaur. Two remarkable rock-cut caves with frescoes. The caves have several branch chambers. The roofs and façade bear rough paintings of men and animals. Near the second cave are the remains of a hypæthral circular temple with rude sculptures. Three rock inscriptions in the valley.——*Beltangady* (ಬೆಳ್ತಂಗಡಿ - beltangadi, Can.). From (belta, can. white + angadi, can. shop). Can. also (kuttiyár), meaning small river.—" *a* " Deputy tahsildarry, South canara district. Pay Rs. 70.—" *b* " Town in the village of Coottiyaur, Deputy tahsildar's station; South canara dist., Ooppinangady tal.; pop. 1,182; lat. 12° 59′; long. 75° 20′; from Coondapore S.E. 60 miles; from Madras W. 336 miles; from Mangalore E.N.E. 32 miles; from Oodipy S.E. 44 miles; from Poottore N.N.E. 17 miles; from Soobramanyam N.W. 31 miles. On the route from Mangalore to Chitaldroog. Formerly an ancient city. Jeina temple and fort of the Rajahs of the Bangara family.

BELOTE (بلوط - bálút, *Pers.*). Oak. Botanically the Quercus genus, cupuliferæ [vricsham]. Trees and shrubs; wood brown, very hard to extremely hard, heavy, generally with a distinct darker colored heart-wood; most indian species furnish wood which warps and splits in seasoning. The species best known to the natives are shown below. Compare in other genera:—Barringtonia acutangula, indian oak; Careya arboreya, patana oak; Casuarina equisetifolia, australian swamp oak; Schleichera trijuga, ceylon oak; Tectona grandis, indian oak. See gloss. paragraphs.——*British oak* (मायाफल - máyáp'hala, San.; ماجهل کا جهار - máphalkájhár, Dec.; மாசக்காய்ச்செடி - másakkáyçedi, Tam.). San. from (máyá, san. illusion + p'hala, san. fruit); false fruit, from galls. Tam. from (másakkáy, tam. gall-nut + shedi, tam. plant). Title otherwise Black oak, Common oak, Truffle oak. Botanically Quercus [belote] robur, linn., cupuliferæ [vricsham]. Native of europe; gives to pharm. the dried bark of the small branches and young stems, quercus cortex, non-officinal; active constituents are tannic and gallic acids; powerful astringent; acorns powdered with sugar and aromatics constitutes the racahout of the arabs.——*Cork oak* (بلوط - ballút, Ar.). Greek φελλός. Title otherwise Cork tree. Botanically Quercus [belote] suber, linn., cupuliferæ [vricsham]. Compare in other genera:—Hibiscus tiliaceus, cork wood; Millingtonia hortensis, cork tree; Mundulea suberosa, cork-leaved tephrosia. See gloss. paragraphs.——*Dyer's oak* (मायाफल - máyáp'hala, San.; माजूफल - májúp'hala, Mahr.; عفص - afas, Ar.; مازوپهل کا پیڑ - mázúphalkáper, Hind.; ماجهل کا جهار - máphalkájhár, Dec.; ಮಾಚಿಕಾಯಿ - máchikáyi, Can.; మాచికాయ - máchikáya, Tel.; മാച്ചിക്കായ - máchikkáya, Mal.; மாசக்காய் - másakkáy, Tam.).

Title from use of galls. San. from (máyá, san. illusion + p'hala, san. fruit); false fruit. Can. from (máchi, can. gall + káyi, can. fruit). Greek κηκίς. Title otherwise Aleppo gall oak, Gall oak, Nutgall oak. Botanically Quercus [belote] infectoria, oliver, cupuliferæ [vricsham]. Alias Quercus lusitanica, var. infectoria. A shrub 4-6 feet; when punctured by a cynips allows an astringent juice to exude, which becomes the gallnuts of commerce. Galls vary in size from half an inch to an inch in diameter; those that come out first are known in trade by terms, black, blue, or green galls; those afterwards gathered, inferior from being pierced, are called white galls. Galls are powerful vegetable astringents; antidote in poisoning by vegetable alkaloids; in pharm. astringent, tonic, antiperiodic, officinal; prescribed by veidyans. Galls also used for tanning and for making ink. Tamarisk galls found on the branches of tamarix articulata, vahl. are used here in the place of oak galls. ——*Holm oak* (بلوطالملك - ballútulmalik, Ar.; شاه بالوط - sháh-bálút, Pers.). Title from leaf like holly. Ar. from (ballút, ar. oak + malik, ar. king). Pers. from (sháh, pers. royal + bálút, pers. oak). Greek ἥμερις. Title otherwise Barbary oak, Evergreen oak, Holly-leaved oak, Holly oak, King's oak, Sweet acorn oak. Botanically Quercus [belote] ilex, linn., cupuliferæ [vricsham]. Native of spain; acorn eaten.

BENAKA (ಬೆನಕ - benaka, *Can.*). Corruption of Vinauyacan, the god. Generally appears as Benakappa.

BENCOOLEN (بانگ کولو - bángkaulu, *Malay*; బంకోలు - bankólu, *Tel.*). A settlement on W. coast of Sumatra, which pertained to English from 1685 to 1824, when given over to Holland. The English factory was from 1714 called Fort Marlborough.

BENDA (బెండ - benda, *Tel.*). Same as bendy [q.v.].——*Bendamoorlunka* (బెండమూర్లంక - bendamúrlanka, Tel.). From (above + úru, tel. village + lanka, tel. island). Otherwise Bundermalanka. Village, Port; Godavery dist., Amalaupooram tal.; lat. 16° 26'; long. 82° 01'; from Amalaupooram S.S.W. 9½ miles; from Antarvedhy E.N.E. 18 miles; from Cocanada S.S.W. 40 miles; from Madras N.N.E. 252 miles; from Yanam S.W. 26 miles. Small port on Golcondah coast, on the Vasishta veinateyam mouth of the Godavery. English factory established in 1751. Captured by Bussy together with Neelapully and Inzaram in 1757. Part of the territory ceded by Nizam's treaty with Colonel Forde, 14th May 1759. Grant confirmed by the Moghul's firmaun, 12th August 1765.

BENDY (भिण्ड - bhinda, *San.*; भेंडा - bhéndá, *Mahr.*; بھینڈی - bhendí, *Hind.*; ಬೆಂಡೆ - bende, *Can.*; బెండ - benda, *Tel.*; വെണ്ട - venda, *Mal.*; வெண்டை - vendai, *Tam.*). Rose-mallow. Botanically the Hibiscus genus, malvaceæ [vricsham, 25]. Herbs, shrubs, climbers or small trees; flowers large and showy, having five petals; fruits five-celled, with numerous seeds; mucilaginous properties; many eaten as pot-herbs; yield fibre. The species best known to the natives are shown below. Other s. indian species indigenous or naturalized are:—angulosus, canescens, lunarifolius, macrophyllus, micranthus, rugosus, solandra, trionum. For other genera, cf. where translation is of first term:—Abutilon indicum (adivibenda), forest; Pavonia odorata (chittibenda), small; Phyllanthus multiflorus (núgubenda), down; Sida cordifolia (chiribenda), small; Sida humilis (nélabenda), ground. See gloss. paragraphs. The Portia also is called Bendy tree, from similar flowers.——*China rose bendy* (जवा - javá, San.; जास्वंद - jásvanda, Mahr.; दसणेफूल - dasané-p'húla, Conc.; انغراه هندی - anghiráihindí, Ar. and Pers.; جاسون - jásún, Hind.; جاسوت - jásút, Dec.; ಕೆಂಪುಪುಂಡ್ರಿಕೆ - kempupundrike, Can.; ದಾಸನಪು - dásanapú, Too.; దాసాని - dásáni, Tel.; ചെമ്പരുത്തി - chemparutti, Mal.; සප්පත්තුමල - sappattu-mala, Singh.; சப்பாத்துச்செடி - shappáttuççedi, Tam.). Title from original habitat. San. from (jap, san. to mutter prayer); religious. Mahr. from (javásuma, san. shoe flower). Ar. from greek. Hind. and dec. from mahratta. Can. from (kempu, can. red + pundrike, can. nelumbium speciosum, willd.). Mal. from (chem, mal. red + parutti, mal. cotton, gossypium herbaceum, linn.); from likeness of flowers. Singh. from (sappattu, singh. shoe + mala, singh. flower). Tam. from (shappáttu, tam. shoe + shedi, tam. plant); from flowers used in blacking shoes [prickly pear]. San. also (japá), meaning useful in prayer and worship; (rudrapushpa), meaning roodran's flower; (ódhrapushpá), meaning orissa flower. Mahr. also (jásundí). Tel. also (dásána). Mal. also (aimparutti), meaning beauty + cotton. Tam. also (shembarattai), meaning red + the plant; (arattam), meaning blood; (shevvarattai), meaning red + the plant; (shivandavésai), meaning red harlot. Title otherwise Chinese shoe-plant, Jasoon, Javah, Ketmia, Orissa flower, Roodra's flower, Shoe-flower. Botanically Hibiscus [bendy] rosa-sinensis, linn., malvaceæ [vricsham, 25]. Alias Hibiscus javanicus; Malvaviscus rosa-sinensis. Shrub, 12–15 feet; stem arborescent, without prickles; leaves ovate, acuminated, coarsely toothed, and slightly cut towards the apex, entire at the base; pedicels axillary, as long as, or longer than, the leaves, jointed above their middle; involucel six to seven-leaved; calyx tubular, five-cleft; flowers large, single or double, crimson, yellow, or white, scentless; flowering all year; seeds unknown; cultivated in gardens. Flowers yield juice which turns rapidly to dark purple color, and is very mucilaginous. Flowers religious. Root triturated with oil used in menorrhagia; leaves emollient, resolvent and anodyne, prescribed in small-pox; flowers employed in fevers, syrup and infusion, the former preferable, substituted for british citric and tartaric acid; gives to pharm. expressed juice of the dark red petals, demulcent, non-officinal. Flowers make a pickle; flowers used to give red tinge to spirituous liquors; petals when rubbed on paper communicate a bluish purple tint, which forms substitute for litmus paper as chemical test; petals used for blackening and polishing shoes, whence one of the names; women employ them to color their hair and eye-brows black; bark contains fibre, clean, silky, fit for cordage. There are several varieties, with red, yellow, and flesh-colored flowers.——*Common bendy* (भिण्ड - bhinda, San.; भेंडा - bhéndá, Mahr.; भेण्ड - bhénda, Conc.; بامیه - bámiyah, Ar. and Pers.; رام ترائی - rámturái, Hind.; بھینڈی - bhendí, Dec.; ಬೆಂಡೆ - bende, Can.; ಬೆಂಡೆ - bende, Too.; బెండ - benda, Tel.; വെണ്ട - venda, Mal.; බණ්ඩක්කා - bandakká, Singh.; வெண்டை - vendai, Tam.). Hind. from (rám, hind. ráma + turái, hind. luffa acutangula, roxb.); from similar capsules. San. also (pátali), meaning red [edible paulay, jungle geranium, pauthiry, weaver's beam]; (gandhamúla), meaning fragrant + root. Hind. also (dhanrus). Title otherwise Bamiyah, Bandicoy plant, Common okro, Edible hibiscus, Esculent okro, Gobbo, Gombo, Nafey shrub, Okra, Okro, Vendy fibre plant, West indian ochro. Botanically Hibiscus [bendy] esculentus, linn., malvaceæ [vricsham, 25]. Alias Abelmoschus esculentus, longifolius; Hibiscus ficifolius, longifolius. Biennial shrub; 2-3 feet; stem herbaceous, hairy, without prickles; leaves on longish petioles, cordate, with three to five obtuse lobes, strongly toothed, scabrous on both sides, with short appressed rigid hairs; pedicels very short; involuc[illegible]aves ten, deciduous; capsule pyramidal, furrowed, elongate[illegible]minated; petals pale yellow, dark crimson at the base; common in all parts, handsome flowering; flowers all year. Fruit is [illegible] thin capsule, 4-6 or more inches long and about an inch in d[illegible]eter, with five to seven ridges corresponding to the valves; [illegible] cells, each of which latter contains a single row of round se[illegible]; it is covered with rough hairs and is green or purplish when fresh; it has a slightly sweet mucilaginous taste and a weak herbaceous odour; when grown in rich soil is considerably improved in quality. Whole plant, particularly capsules, replete with much mild mucilage; substituted for british pareira brava; gives to pharm. fresh immature capsules, hibisci capsulæ; valuable emollient and demulcent, diuretic; preparation, decoctum hibisci, officinal; dried fruit may be employed where not procurable in fresh state; fresh capsules bruised from a poultice; used in fact like marsh mallow, althæa officinalis [foreign tootty]. Young pods gathered green and pickled like capers; more mature pods cooked for table, agreeable flavor, slimy nature. Stem yields a fibre, exported to a slight extent as hemp, to which it bears resemblance. There are varieties of dwarf habit, free from the spine-like hairs.——*Cork wood bendy* (بولا - bolá, Hind.; ବଣିଆ - baniyá, Oor.; താളിപ്പരുത്തി - tálip-parutti, Mal.; බෙලිපත - belipatta, Singh.). Title from soft wood. Mal. from (táli, mal. a plant whose mucilaginous leaf or bark is used for cleaning head + parutti, mal. cotton, gossypium herbaceum, linn.). Title otherwise Cuba bast tree, Parootty. Botanically Hibiscus [bendy] tiliaceus, linn., malvaceæ [vricsham, 25]. Alias Hibiscus elatus, circinnatus, guineensis, similis; Paritium tiliaceum, tortuosum. Small tree; leaves crenulated, sometimes quite entire, roundish-cordate with a sudden acumination, seven to eleven-nerved, upper side glabrous, under hoary with pubescence; involucel ten-lobed, shorter than the calyx; capsule five-celled, five-valved; cells many-seeded; flowers large, sulphur with a blood-colored eye; flowering all year; west coast; tree abounds in mucilage. Bark used in medicine; rope cords and fine mats made from fibre of bark; timber soft and valueless. There is a variety called tortuosus.——*Hemp bendy* (नाली - náli, San.; अंबाडी - ambádí, Mahr.; انباڑی - ambárí, Hind.; انباڑا - ambárá, Dec.; ಹೊಲದಪುಂಡ್ರಿಕೆಗಿಡ - holada-pundrikegida, Can.; గోగు - gógu, Tel.; କନୁରିଆ - kanuriya, Oor.; കഞ്ചാവ് - kañchávu, Mal.; புளிச்சை - puliççai, Tam.). Title from yielding hemp. San. from (nála, san. tube). Mahr. from (ámrátaka, san. the plant). Hind. and dec. from mahrattee. Can. from (hola, can. dry land + pundrikegida, can. cannabis sativa, linn.). Mal. from (gañjika, san. cannabis sativa, linn.). Tam. from (puli, tam. sourness); from taste of young leaves [red hemp bendy]. San. also (bhangá), meaning breaking [kinnab]; (karnikára), meaning ear-ornament + to go, from flower serving as ear ornament [kaniyaur, tirauna]. Hind. also (pátsan), meaning sunn leaf; (rattiasan), meaning blood; (mastapát), meaning inebriating leaf. Can. also (pundi). Tel. also (gulugu); (pundikúra). Mal. also (káttuvellúram), meaning wild abutilon indicum, g. don. Tam. also (pulimañji), meaning acid + a winding shrub; (káççurai), meaning fruit + curling, from shape of fruit. Title otherwise Acid-leaved marool, Ambauree, Bastard jute, Bombay hemp, Brown hemp, Deccany hemp, Gogoo, Hemp-leaved hibiscus, Hemp mallow, Indian brown hemp, Poolitchay, Roselle hemp. Botanically Hibiscus [bendy] cannabinus, linn., malvaceæ [vricsham, 25]. Alias Hibiscus radiatus, vitifolius; Ketmia glandulosa. Small shrub; stem herbaceous, prickly; leaves palmately five-partite, glabrous, segments narrow lanceolated, acuminated, serrated; flowers almost sessile, axillary, solitary; leaves of the involucel about nine, subulate, prickly, with rigid bristles, shorter than the undivided portion of the calyx; calyx divided beyond the middle, segments slightly prickly, one-nerved; corolla spreading; fruit nearly globose, acuminated, very hairy; seeds few, glabrous; flowers pale sulphur, with a deep purple centre; carpels joined into a five-celled, five-valved capsule. Cultivated in red loam and black soil; cultivation, dry or wet; ground prepared on coromandel in caurteecam or november and margashiram [mausam] or december, ploughing the soil twice or thrice; seed sown in margashiram or december and pooshyam [mausam] or january; cut after three months; bundled and dried in the sun; at the threshing floor beaten with sticks and grain winnowed; brought to market after two months; average price 48 imperial seers for 1 rupee. Seeds an external application to pains and bruises. Young foliage of crop is acidulous, eaten as a vegetable; seeds roasted are eaten. Fibre, extracted by submerging the stalks in water for a number of days and pulling off the bark by hand; is soft, white and silky; used for gunny bags and cordage; stronger than, though not so good as, sunn; used in the manufacture of paper. Compare in other genera :—Cochlospermum gossypium (kondagógu), hill gogoo; Salvadora persica (varagógu), superior gogoo. See gloss. paragraphs.——*Hill bendy* (కొండబెండ - kondabenda, Tel.; மலைவெண்டை - malaivendai, Tam.). Tel. also (kondagógu), meaning hill + hibiscus cannabinus, linn. Botanically Hibiscus [bendy] collinus, roxb., malvaceæ [vricsham, 25]. Alias Hibiscus eriocarpus, simplex. Small tree, with spreading branches and three-lobed, heart-shaped, smooth leaves; large, full-expanding, pale rose-colored flowers, with dark puce-colored eye; flowering nearly all year. Gives fibre.——*Hill hemp bendy* (కొండగోగు - kondagógu, Tel.; නාපිරිත්ත - nápiritta, Singh.; மலைப்புளிச்சை - malaippuliççai, Tam.). Tel. from (konda, tel. hill + gógu, tel. deccany hemp plant, hibiscus cannabinus, linn.). Tam. from (malai, tam. mountain + puliççai, tam. hibiscus cannabinus, linn.). Botanically Hibiscus [bendy] furcatus, r., malvaceæ [vricsham, 25]. Alias Hibiscus aculeatus. Strong, white flaxy fibre, but being very prickly, is unfit for handling.——*Jasmine bendy* (सूर्यमणि - súryamani, San.; నిత్యమల్లె - nityamalle, Tel.). Title from flowers. San. from (súrya, san. sun + mani, san. jewel); from scarlet flowers. Tel. from (nitya, san. perennial + malle, tel. jasmine, jasminum sambac, ait.). San. also (pushparakta), meaning flower-red plant. Tel. also (adavinityamalle), meaning forest + the plant, jasminum sambac, ait.; (sallabudata), meaning cool + little one. Title otherwise Purple-flowered hibiscus. Botanically Hibiscus [bendy] hirtus, linn., malvaceæ [vricsham, 25]. Alias Hibiscus phœniceus, rosa-malabarica.——*Lotus bendy* (पद्मचारिणी - padmachárini, San.; सूर्यकांत - súryakánta, Conc.; گل عجائب - guliajáib, Pers., Hind. and Dec.; ಸೂರ್ಯಕಾಂತಿ - súryakánti, Can.; ചീനപ്പരുത്തി - chínapparutti, Mal.; செம்பரத்தை - shembarattai, Tam.). Title from flowers. San. from (padma, san. lotus, nelumbium speciosum, willd. + char, san. to act), lotus-like. Conc. from (súrya, san. sun + kánta, san. desire); which loves sun. Pers. from (gul, pers. flower + ajáib, pers. wonderful); from changing colors. Can. from (súrya, san. sun + kánti, san. desire). Mal. from (chína, mal. china + parutti, mal. cotton, gossypium herbaceum, linn.); a corruption. Tam. from (shem, tam. red + parattai, tam. hibiscus rosasinensis, linn.). San. also (st'hala-padma), meaning land lotus. Title otherwise Changeable rose, Chinese hibiscus. Botanically Hibiscus [bendy] mutabilis, linn., malvaceæ [vricsham, 25]. Alias Hibiscus sinensis; Ketmia mutabilis. Large bushy shrub, 8 feet high; large heart-shaped downy leaves; double flowers, somewhat like very large double roses, white on first opening in morning, then becoming cream-colored at night, finally of a deep rose tint next morning. Bark yields a strong fibre.——*Musk bendy* (लताकस्तुरिका - latákastúriká, San.; कस्तुरिभेण्ड - kastúribhénda, Mahr.; حب المشك - habbulmushk, Ar.; مشك دانہ - mushkdánah, Pers.; مشك بهيندى - mushkbhendí, Hind. and Dec.; ಕಾಡುಕಸ್ತೂರಿ - kádukastúri, Can.; కర్పూరబెండ - karpúrabenda, Tel.; കാട്ടുകസ്തൂരി - káttukastúri, Mal.; கத்தூரிவெண்டை - kattúrivendai, Tam.). Title from smell and taste. San. from (latá, san. creeper + kastúriká, san. musk). Mahr. from (kastúrí, san. musk + bhéndá, mahr. hibiscus esculentus, linn.). Ar. from (habb, ar. seed + mushk, ar. musk), from its odour and taste. Pers. from (mushk, ar. musk + dánah, pers. seed). Hind. from (mushk, ar. musk + bhendí, hind. hibiscus esculentus, linn.). Can. from (kádu, can. wild + kastúrí, san. musk). Tel. from (karpúra, san. camphor + benda, tel. hibiscus esculentus, linn.). Mal. from (kátu, mal. forest + kastúrí, san. musk). Tam. from (kastúrí, san. musk + vendai, tam. hibiscus esculentus, linn.). Dec. also (kálákastúrí), meaning black musk. Can. also (kádubende), meaning wild + hibiscus esculentus, linn. Tel. also (kastúribenda); (adavibenda). Mal. also (káttuparutti), meaning wild cotton. Tam. also (vettilaikkattúri), meaning betel-leaf, piper betel, linn. + musk; (káttupparutti), meaning forest + cotton plant, gossypium herbaceum, linn.; (pottagattutti), meaning box + abutilon indicum, g. don. from lobed leaf; (irattagattutti), meaning double-threaded cloth + inside + abutilon indicum, g. don.; (káttukkattúri), meaning forest + musk plant. Title otherwise Abel mooshk, Mooshkdanah, Musk-mallow, Musk okro, Musk plant, Target-leaved hibiscus, Wild bandicoy, Wild musk. Botanically Hibiscus [bendy] abelmoschus, linn., malvaceæ [vricsham, 25]. Specific name from Arabic meaning musk-seed. Alias Abelmoschus moschatus; Bamia abelmoschus; Hibiscus flavescens, moschatus. Stem herbaceous, hispid with spreading hairs, not prickly; leaves, and long petioles, hispid with rigid hairs, but otherwise glabrous, unequally and coarsely toothed, deeply five to seven lobes; lobes all spreading, oblong or lanceolate; pedicels harshly pubescent, axillary, about as long as the petioles; involucel-leaves six to ten, linear, hairy; capsule oblong, acuminated, hairy; petals sulphur-colored, dark crimson at the base; cultivated. Seeds of psoralea corylifolia, linn. [bawchee], are often sold for these, but the following descriptions will distinguish :—"*a*" seeds of hibiscus abelmoschus, linn., kidney shaped, slightly compressed, striated or marked with minute parallel elevated lines of the same color, and present a small but very distinct hilum in the concave border; brown in color, and about two lines in length; smell like that of the pure musk, though very faint, not being distinctly perceptible unless the seeds are put in the mouth and chewed or rubbed between the fingers; taste not bitter.—"*b*" seeds of psoralia corylifolia, linn., oval or oblong, and flat; brown or dark brown in color, and about two or two-and-a-half lines in length; smell aromatic, but musty or unctuous; taste slightly bitterish. The seeds of the present plant are medicinally cordial and stomachic; when bruised, given as an andidote to snake-bite; applied externally and internally; largely used in native perfumery and to scent medicated oils; in the days of hair powder they were exported to Europe for perfuming powder and pomatum. Mucilage used to clarify sugar; seeds sometimes employed for giving perfume to coffee; stem yields strong fibre; plant gives greenish-yellow oil.——*Red hemp bendy* (लालअंबाडी - lálaambádí, Mahr.; لال انبارى - lálambárí, Hind.; لال انبارا - lálambárá, Dec.; ಪುಂಡಿ - pundi, Can.; ಪುಂಡಿ - pundi, Too.; ఎర్రగోగు - erragógu, Tel.; പുളിച്ചീര - puliççíra, Mal.; புளிச்சை - puliççai, Tam.). Title from flowers. Mahr. from (lála, mahr. red + ambádí, mahr. hibiscus cannabinus, linn.). Hind. from (lál, hind. red + ambárí, hind. hibiscus cannabinus, linn.). Tel. from (erra, tel. red + gógu, tel. hemp plant, hibiscus cannabinus, linn.). Mal. from (puli, mal. sour + chíra, mal. greens). Tam. from (puli, tam. sourness) [hemp bendy]. Hind. also (patwa). Tel. also (símagógu), meaning foreign + hemp plant, hibiscus cannabinus, linn. Mal. also (puliççi), meaning sour. Tam. also (shivappukkáyççurai), meaning red + hibiscus cannabinus, linn.; (shímaikkáyççurai), meaning foreign + the plant; (shembuliççai), meaning red + hibiscus cannabinus, linn. Title otherwise Guinea sorrel, Indian sorrel, Red sorrel, Roselle, Thorny mallow. Botanically Hibiscus [bendy] sabdariffa, linn., malvaceæ [vricsham, 25]. Specific name from Turkish. Alias Hibiscus gossypifolius. Small bush; annual, glabrous, 1–3 feet; lower leaves undivided, upper palmately three to five-lobed, cuneate and entire at the base, lobes oblong lanceolate, acuminated, toothed; flowers axillary, solitary on very short pedicels; involucel segments about twelve; stems unarmed; capsule many-seeded; seeds smooth; flowers pale sulphur, with dark-brown eye; common in gardens. The so-called fruit is the calyx, which continues to enlarge after the other whorls of the flowers have fallen away. The seeds are reddish grey or reddish brown, odourless, and possess a feeble mucilaginous taste, about the size of, and bear some resemblance to, Kaladana seeds. The seeds are medicinally demulcent, diuretic and tonic, used in draught by bruising with water and straining through cloth; substituted for sweet nitre. The calyx and capsule, freed from the seeds, make tarts and jellies; leaves are used in salads; in the french west india islands, there is a cider from it, vin d'ozeille; contains a wholesome acid; the stem is cut when in flower and a fibre procured from the bark, rather fine and silky; gives an oil. Compare in other genera :—Dodonæa viscosa, jamaica switch sorrel; Oxalis corniculata, indian sorrel; Rumex vesicarius, country sorrel. See gloss. paragraphs.——*Spreading bendy* (పరుపుబెండ - parupubenda, Tel.; காட்டுவெண்டை - káttuvendai, Tam.). Tel. from (parutsu, tel. spread + benda, tel. hibiscus esculentus, linn.). Tam. from (kádu, tam. forest + vendai, tam. hibiscus esculentus, linn.). Tel. also (nélabenda), meaning ground + hibiscus esculentus, linn. Botanically Hibiscus [bendy] ficulneus, linn., malvaceæ [vricsham, 25]. Alias Abelmoschus ficulneus; Hibiscus prostratus, strictus; Lagunea aculeata. Shrub annual; flowers white, with a rose-colored eye; flowering nearly all year; seeds put in sweetmeats; valuable fibre; seeds yield oil.——*Syrian bendy* (اودا گڈهيل - údágudhel, Hind.). Hind. from (údá, hind. azure + gudhel, hind. hibiscus rosasinensis, linn.). Title otherwise Rose of sharon. Botanically Hibiscus [bendy] syriacus, linn., malvaceæ [vricsham, 25]. Bushy shrub, 4 feet high; leaves towards the base wedge-shaped, towards the apex three-lobed; large blue-lilac flowers with dark-purple eye; flowers give a dye.——*Thorny hemp bendy* (रानभेंडी - ránabhéndí, Mahr.; ముల్లుగోగు - mullugógu, Tel.; முள்புளிச்சை - mulbuliççai, Tam.). Title from prickly stems. Mahr. from (rána, mahr. wild + bhéndá, mahr. hibiscus esculentus, linn.). Tel. from (mullu, tel. thorn + gógu, tel. hemp plant, hibiscus cannabinus, linn.). Tam. from (mul, tam. thorn + puliççai, tam. hibiscus cannabinus, linn.). Tam. also (káttukkáyççurai), meaning forest + hibiscus cannabinus, linn. Botanically Hibiscus [bendy] surattensis, l., malvaceæ [vricsham, 25]. Shrub; a herbaceous plant with speckled prickly stems and yellow flowers; indigenous; bark gives fibre; leaves used as greens.——*Vine-leafed bendy* (भारद्वाजी - bháradvájí, San.; పిండి సొప్పు - pindisoppu, Can.; కారుపత్తి - kárupatti, Tel.; மணித்துத்தி - manittutti, Tam.). San. means relating to bharadwaujan. Tel. from (káru, tel. forest + patti, tel. cotton, gossypium herbaceum, linn.). Tam. from (mani, san. beauty + tutti, tam. abutilon indicum, g. don.). San. also (vanakárpása), meaning forest cotton. Tam. also (shiruthutti), meaning small + abutilon. Botanically Hibiscus [bendy] vitifolius, linn., malvaceæ [vricsham, 25]. Alias Hibiscus obtusifolia, truncatus. Shrub, biennial; leaves soft, toothed, angular; flowers large, sulphur with a dark-purple eye; flowering nearly all year. Leaves emollient. Fibre good color, strong, fit for cordage.

BENGAL (బంగాళ - bangála, *Tel.*). From (vanga, san. the country of east bengal). The province. Cf. :—Aleurites triloba, bengal walnut; Butea frondosa, bengal kino; Carissa carandas, bengal currant; Cicer arietinum, bengal gram; Crotalaria juncea, bengal hemp; Dendrocalamus tulda, bengal bamboo; Ficus bengalensis, bengal fig; Meriandra bengalensis, bengal sage; Panicum italicum, bengal grass; Rubia cordifolia, bengal madder; Wedelia calendulacea, bengal polymania; Zingiber cassumunar, bengal root. See gloss. paragraphs.——*Bay of bengal* (पूर्वाम्बुधि - púrvámbudhi, San.; బంగాళాఘాతము - bangálághátamu, Tel.; வங்காளக்குடாக்கடல் - vangálakkudákkadal, Tam.). San. means eastern ocean. Tel. from (bangála, tel. bengal + agádha, san. deep). Greek κόλπος γαγγητικός.

BENGUN (بینگن - baingan, *Hind.*). Bengalee form, and origin of latin melongena. Brinjaul.

BENJAMIN (لبان جاوى - lubánjáwai, *Ar.*). Title from (lubán, ar. frankincense + jáwaí, ar. of java). First syllable dropped. Same as Benzoin.

BENNIE OIL (تل - til, *Hind.*). Gingelly. Sierra leone title.

BEN OIL (بن - ban, *Hind.*). Same as Moringa or horse-radish oil.

BENT GRASS (दूर्वा - dúrvá, *San.*). Title from appearance of joints. San. from (dúrv, san. to hurt), from sharp grass blades. Hurrially grass.

BENZOIN (देवधूप - dévadhúpa, *San.*; شجر لبان - shajarilubán, *Ar.*; درخت حسن لبه - darakhtihasnlubah, *Pers.*; لوبان کا پیر - lobánkáper, *Hind.*; لوبانی عود کا جھاڑ - lobáníúdkájhár, *Dec.*; کومنجن - kominjan, *Malay*; ಸಾಂಬ್ರಾಣಿ - sámbráni, *Can.*; సాంబ్రాణిచెట్టు - sámbránichettu, *Tel.*; സാമ്പ്രാണി - sámbráni, *Mal.*; කළුවැල් - kaluval, *Singh.*; சாம்பிராணி - shámbiráni, *Tam.*). Title from (lubán, ar. frankincense + jáwaí, ar. java). San. from (déva, san. god + dhúpa, san. incense). Ar. from (shajar, ar. tree + lubán, ar. olibanum). Pers. from (darakht, pers. tree + hasnlubah, pers. olibanum). Hind. from (lubán, ar. olibanum + per, hind. tree) [indian olibanum]. Dec. from (lobáníúd, hind. olibanum frankincense + jhár, hind. tree). Tel. from (sámbráni, tel. incense + chettu, tel. tree). Singh. from (kalu, singh. agreeable + val, singh. creeper). Ar. also (bakhúr), meaning incense. Pers. also (hasílubán), meaning honey juice; (asaluljáwaí), meaning java honey. Tam. also (malákkásámbiráni), meaning malacca benzoin. Title otherwise Assa dulcis, Assa odorata, Gum benjamin, Gum benzoin, Java honey, Liquor cyrenaicus, Malacca benzoin. Botanically Styrax [dhoopam] benzoin, dryand, styraceæ [vricsham, 84]. The plant is a native of Java, Sumatra and Siam. Benzoin is the juice obtained by making incisions into the tree; this hardens on exposure to the air, that which flows first being the purest and most fragrant; it occurs in dry and hard grey masses, rather shining, brittle, formed of ovoid, whitish tears, like stripped almonds, and placed as it were in a cement of a greenish red porous mass; fracture resinous; odour sweet, peculiar, very agreeable, increased by friction; taste sweetish, sub-resinous, balsamic, irritating; powder yellowish grey, disposed to cake. Benzoic acid is obtained from the crude benzoin by sublimation, or boiling with an alkali; this acid, when pure, is colorless, and it fuses and sublimes at a moderate heat; if strongly heated it burns with a bright yellow flame. The resin is in medicine internally stimulant, expectorant; externally stimulant; the smoke given out acts as a disinfectant and drives away mosquitoes and flies; substituted for british balsams of peru and tolu; in pharm. officinal, benzoinum, contains volatile oil and a peculiar acid, benzoic acid; it is an ingredient in the old friar's balsam; the benzoic acid obtained from it enters into the composition of the paregoric elixir; is used in perfumery and burnt as incense.

BERBERRY (दारुहरिद्रा - dáruharidrá, *San.*; दारुहळद - dáruhalada, *Mahr.*; امبر باريس - ambarbárís, *Ar.*; پیل زهره - pílzahra, *Pers.*; دارهلد - dárhald, *Hind.*; മരമഞ്ഞൾ - maramaññal, *Mal.*; முள்ளுக்களா - mullukkalá, *Tam.*). Title from arabic. San. from (dáru, san. wood + haridrá, san. turmeric, curcuma longa, roxb.); from yellow dye of wood and root. Mahr. from sanscrit. Ar. from greek. Pers. from arabic. Hind. from sanscrit. Mal. means tree turmeric. Tam. from (mul, tam. thorn + kalá, tam. carissa); from black sour berries. San. also (dárví), meaning wooden [false calumba]. Ar. also (filzahraj), meaning elephant poison. Hind. also (chitra); (dárchob), meaning wood tree; (raswat), meaning hot juice. Greek for product is λύκιον ἰνδικὸν, the other λύκιον being from a buck thorn [rohitacam]. Title otherwise Chitrak, Chotra, Dyer's berberry, Indian berberry, Rasoot shrub, Thorny carissa, Tree turmeric, Wood turmeric, Yellow wood, Zarishk shrub. Botanically Berberis aristata, dec., berberideæ [vricsham, 6]. Alias Berberis angustifolia, chitria, tinctoria. Shrub, 6–10 feet; leaves simple, obovol, entire, or with distant, small, spiny teeth, glaucous, with the principal veins and nerves prominent beneath, but not above; racemes stalked, longer than the leaves; pedicels slender; petals six, distinctly biglandular; sepals five, spines deeply divided into three sharp rigid segments; flowers yellow. Berries shrivelled and much compressed; dark-brown or black in color; pleasantly acid in taste; about third of an inch long, and fifth broad; smooth, soft, and moist; pedunculate; contain dark brown pulp; generally contain no seeds, but sometimes one small, hard, and oblong seed in each. Native of himalayas. Wood whether from root or stem is called Darhald. The bark from wood, especially root, occurs in thin, brittle, slightly quilled or flat pieces; outer surface has a corky texture and a light-brown color; the inner surface is darker and a somewhat greenish yellow, and has a shining appearance, it is almost inodorous, but has a very bitter, somewhat mucilaginous taste. Watery extract called Rasoot or Rusot is prepared in hilly districts from sliced root, stem, and branches; it is dark brown like opium, bitter to taste, rich heavy smell; readily soluble in water, partly so in rectified spirit. Zarishk is a moist sticky mass of the dried fruits. Periplus enumerates λύκιον among commodities brought to barygaza; mentioned among indian drugs on which duty was levied at roman custom house of alexandria about A.D. 176–180; vases are preserved in collections of greek antiquities, made to contain λύκιον and bearing the name of the seller of the extract. Root bark in medicine diaphoretic, antiperiodic and tonic, of great value in intermittent and remittent fevers, and in general debility from whatever cause, substituted for british cinchona and its alkaloids; rasoot febrifuge and external remedy in eye-diseases, useful in all kinds of hæmorrhages and in diarrhœa, jaundice, &c., substituted for british argenti nitras; both in pharm. berberis cortex and extractum berberis, officinal. Medicinal preparations :—decoction, take of the wood in shavings or coarse powder six ounces, water two pints and a half, boil on a slow fire till the liquid is reduced to one pint; tincture, take of the wood in shavings or coarse powder six ounces, proof spirit one pint, macerate for seven days with occasional agitation, strain and add more proof spirit to make one pint; extract, take the shavings or coarse powder in any quantity, boil with water till the liquor becomes somewhat thick, strain and evaporate on a sand-bath to the consistence of an extract. Doses :—of the decoction, from two to six fluid ounces; of the tincture, from two to six fluid drachms; of the extract, from one to two drachms. Fruit eaten; also dried in sun like raisins; the zarishk is imported. Root and wood dark yellow and form yellow wood of persian authors; used for dyeing a yellow color; contains yellow coloring principle in a greater state of purity than common english berberry; wood used for fuel. Rasoot, &c., also from berberis asiatica, roxb.; bush with three to five-fold strong spinous shining leaves, spinous on the margin and abundant small pure yellow flowers. Also from berberis lycium, royle; shrub, 6–8 feet; spines trifid or simple; leaves oval, cuneated or elliptical, mucronate, smooth, under surface, glaucous, entire or spinulosely toothed; racemes short, many-flowered, corymbose, shorter than the leaves; pedicels elongated, one-flowered; berries purplish; flowers small, yellow. Other species are :—concinna, nepalensis.

BERHAMPORE * (బరంపురము - barampuramu, *Tel.*). From (brahma, san. the god + pura, san. town).——**(1)** Talook; Ganjam district. Tahsildar's pay Rs. 200. Area 496 square miles. Population 323,474. Language Teloogoo and Ooriya. E. coast of district. Bounded north by Cullicote, Atagadah, Biridy, Hoomma and Paulore zemindarries and Aska estate; east by the Bay of Bengal; south by Jalantra zemindarry; and west by Cheekaty, Chinna kimedy, Pedda kimedy, Shergadah and Dhauracote zemindarries. Consists of the old Mohiry zemindarry bought in on behalf of Government in 1844, and of the old Poobacondah and Ichapore khandams. On the east the country is an open plain, but to the west there are some small ranges of hills. The Kerandy or Mohiry hills traverse the talook in a north-westerly direction. The talook is on the whole fertile. Weaving of common fabrics for native wear and of fine cloths in silk and cotton is carried on. Irrigation works are the Hiradhaura channel from the Rooshcoolya and the Corautoly tampara fed by the Jayamungalam channel of the Godahaddoh. Camping grounds :—Berhampore, Chetterpore, Ganjam, Gopalpore and Ichapore. Places of archæological interest :—Ichapore, Jowgada, Lootchaupadah, Pooltah. Principal trig. stations :—Arjipollem beacon, Cavitey beacon, Ganjam, Gopalpore, Ichapore, Juggernautpore, Londabanso, Mattikhila, Maurcandy, Paulore, Relava, Sonapore, Torratarny. The leading places, &c., in the talook are the following.——*Arjipollem* (అర్జీపాలెము - arjipálemu, Tel.). From (arzí, hind. petition + pálemu, tel. fortified village).

Trig. station; lat. 19° 19′ 13·10″; long. 85° 01′ 21·40″; from Arjipollem N. ¾ mile; from Berhampore E. 12 miles; from the sea W. 1½ miles.——*Berhampore* (బరంపురము - barampuramu, Tel.). See below.——*Bodagherry* (బొడగిరి - bodagiri, Tel.). From (boda, oor. large + giri, san. hill). Trig. station, Peddakimedy zemindarry; lat. 19° 02′ 32·74″; long. 84° 37′ 35·12″; height 816 feet; from Borigy S.S.W. 2 miles; from Berhampore S.W. 22 miles; from Chetterpore S.W. 35 miles. Close to Nowgaum of either Jalantra or Sooradah zemindarry.——*Cavitey* (కవిటె - kavite, Tel.). Sanscrit name (udyánavana), meaning royal garden. Village; pop. 4,285; acres 3,232; lat. 19° 00″; long. 84° 45′; from Berhampore S.S.W. 21 miles; from Chetterpore S.W. 34 miles; from the sea W. 2 miles. The chief town of the coast. A great market for coir and other produce of cocoanut trees with which the area is thickly planted, and for plantains and garden produce. Has an extensive trade in coir-rope which is largely manufactured in this and neighbouring villages. Population consists chiefly of Teloogoo calingas. Trig. station in lat. 19° 02′ 00·31″; long. 84° 43′ 34·87″; height 282 feet; from Cavitey N.N.W. 2 miles; from Berhampore S.S.W. 20 miles; from the sea W. 3½ miles.——*Chetterpore* (ఛత్రపురము - chhatrapuramu, Tel.). See sep. title.——*Coojidibba* (కూజిదిబ్బ - kújidibba, Tel.). From (kúchi, tel. sharp-pointed + dibba, tel. mound). Trig. station, Biridy zemindarry; lat. 19° 28′ 04·77″; long. 85° 05′ 14·53″; height 1,117 feet; from Coojidibba E.N.E. 1 mile; from Berhampore N.E. 21 miles; from Chetterpore N.N.E. 7½ miles.——*Dandraushy* (ధనరాశి - dhanaráshi, Tel.). From (dhana, san. wealth + ráshi, san. heap). Trig. station, Mundasa zemindarry; lat. 19° 10′ 44·50″; long. 84° 46′ 49·07″; height 679 feet; from Haripooram N.E. 29 miles; from Berhampore S.S.W. 8½ miles; from Chetterpore S.W. 21 miles; from the sea W. 6½ miles. Somewhere about two miles south of Golantra.——*Dhobah dhobny* (ధోబాధోబుని - dhobádhobuni, Tel.). Trig. station, Peddakimedy zemindarry; lat. 19° 14′ 21·14″; long. 84° 23′ 24·48″; height 4,166 feet; from Berhampore W. 29 miles; from Chetterpore W.S.W. 44 miles.——*Ganjam* (గంజాము - gandzámu, Tel.). See sep. title.——*Gopalpore* (గోపాలపురము - gópálapuramu, Tel.). See sep. title.——*Ichapore* (ఇచ్ఛాపురము - içchápuramu, Tel.). See sep. title.——*Jowgada* (జౌగడ - dzaugada, Tel.). See sep. title.——*Juggernautpore* (జగన్నాథపురము - jagannát'hapuramu, Tel.). From (jagat, san. world + nát'ha, san. lord + pura, san. town). Trig. station; lat. 19° 18′ 59·08″; long. 84° 55′ 24·59″; height 194 feet; from Juggernautpore S.W. ¾ mile; from Berhampore E. 6½ miles; from the sea W. 7½ miles. On the Berhampore-Chetterpore road.——*Londabanso* (లొండాబాంసొ - londábánsó, Tel.). Trig. station; lat. 19° 23′ 36·21″; long. 84° 58′ 50·48″; height 573 feet; from Londabanso N.W. ¼ mile; from Berhampore N.E. 12 miles; from the sea N. 7½ miles.——*Mahendragherry* (మహేంద్రగిరి - mahéndragiri, Tel.). See sep. title.——*Mansoorcottah* (మనసూరుకోట - manusúrukóta, Tel.). See sep. title.——*Mattikhila* (మట్టిఖిలా - mattikhilá, Tel.). Trig. station; lat. 19° 19′ 21·00″; long. 84° 59′ 11·80″; height 255 feet; from Mattikhila W. 1½ miles; from Berhampore E. 11 miles; from the sea N. 2½ miles.——*Maula* (మాల - mála, Tel.). Means line. Trig. station, Mundasa zemindarry; lat. 18° 47′ 19·81″; long. 84° 33′ 17·02″; height 483 feet; from Berhampore S.S.W. 39 miles; from Chetterpore S.W. 51 miles; from the sea W. 2½ miles. One of the peaks of Mahendragherry.——*Maurcandy* (మార్కండి - márkandi, Tel.). Trig. station; lat. 19° 11′ 01·82″; long. 84° 52′ 25·82″; height 44 feet; from Maurcandy S.S.E. ½ mile; from Berhampore S.S.E. 8½ miles; from the sea W. ½ mile. Just south of the south end of Berhampore rampart.——*Mohiry* (మోహిరి - móhiri, Tel.). See sep. title.——*Muntridy* (మంత్రిడి - mantridi, Tel.). From (mantra, san. enchantment). Village; pop. 1,265; acres 749; lat. 19° 09′; long. 84° 49′; from Berhampore S. 8½ miles; from Chetterpore S.W. 19 miles; from the sea W. 4½ miles. Has a large tank irrigating 251 acres of this village besides others.——*Pandiyah* (పండియా - pandiyá, Tel.). Village; pop. 1,359; acres 521; lat. 19° 30′; long. 84° 53′; from Berhampore N.N.E. 14 miles; from Chetterpore N.W. 15 miles; from the sea N. 22 miles. Contains the lac fort [jowgada].——*Paulavalsa* (పాలవలస - pálavalasa, Tel.). From (pálu, tel. milk + valasa, tel. colony). Trig. station, Sompett division; lat. 18° 53′ 20·22″; long. 84° 35′ 19·78″; from Paulavalsa N. ¾ mile; from Barwah N.W. 3 miles; from Berhampore S.S.W. 32 miles; from Chetterpore S.W. 44 miles; from Sompett S.W. 3½ miles; from the sea W. 4 miles.——*Paulore* (పాలూరు - pálúru, Tel.). Trig. station; lat. 19° 26′ 49·97″; long. 85° 10′ 23·46″; height 579 feet; from Paulore E.S.E. ½ mile; from Berhampore E.N.E. 25 miles; from Chetterpore N.E. 10 miles; from the sea W. 1 mile.——*Poorshottapore* (పురుషోత్తపురము - purushóttapuramu, Tel.). See sep. title.——*Pudmye* (పట్మాయి - patmáyi, Tel.). Trig. station, Sompett division; lat. 18° 58′ 17·42″; long. 84° 39′ 49·22; from Berhampore S.S.W. 25 miles; from Chetterpore S.W. 37 miles; from Sompett N.E. 4 miles; from the sea W. 4½ miles.——*Rambha* (రంభ - rambha, Tel.). See sep. title.——*Raty beacon* (రతి - rati, Tel.). From (rati, san. the goddess + pura, san. town). Trig. station, Sompett division; lat. 18° 46′ 49·20″; long. 84° 34′ 11·80″. By position should be somewhere on coast just S.E. of Haripooram.——*Relava* (రలభా - ralabhá, Tel.). Trig. station; lat. 19° 15′ 27·10″; long. 84° 49′ 42·59″; height 301 feet; from Relava S.W. ¼ mile; from Berhampore S. 2½ miles; from the sea W. 9 miles. Just east of the Chicacole road beyond Holidiyabhadra.——*Rooshcoolya* (ఋషికుల్య - rishikulyá, Tel.). See sep. title.——*Ryegodo* (రైగొడొ - raigodo, Tel.). From (rai, hind. king + gudá, oor. fort). Trig. station, Peddakimedy zemindarry; lat. 19° 17′ 34·31″; long. 84° 41′ 42·51″; height 2,892 feet; from Toorboody S.E. 4 miles; from Berhampore W. 9 miles; from Chetterpore W.S.W. 23 miles.——*Sonapore* (సొన్నాపురము - sonnápuramu, Tel.). See sep. title.——*Soorlah* (సుర్లా - surlá, * Tel.). Village; pop. 1,520; acres 2,831; lat. 19° 06′; long. 84° 48′; from Berhampore S. 13 miles; from Chetterpore S.W. 24 miles; from the sea W. 1½ miles. Salt factory surrounded by extensive swamps.——*Torratarny* (తోరాతరణి - torátarani, Tel.). From (torá, oor. the local deity + tarani, oor. the local deity); after two goddesses Torratarny, to whom the hill is consecrated. Hill, Place of pilgrimage for Ooriyas. Trig. station in lat. 19° 29′ 20·66″; long. 84° 56′ 28·33″; height 708 feet; from Ryepore W. 1 mile; from Poorshottapore S. 2½ miles; from Berhampore N.N.E. 15 miles; from the sea W. 20 miles.——*Yalmel* (ఎల్మల్ - elmel, Tel.). From (ella, tel. boundary + mala, tel. hill). Trig. station, Sompett division; lat. 18° 50′ 38·32″; long. 84° 34′ 39·90″; from Berhampore S.S.W. 35 miles; from Chetterpore S.W. 47 miles; from Sompett S.S.W. 6½ miles; from the sea W. 3 miles.——**(2)** Sub-magistracy; Ganjam district. Pay Rs. 70.——**(3)** Town, Municipality, Head-quarters of Divisional officer, District engineer, Tahsildar, Sub-magistrate, District judge, District moonsif and Sub-registrar, Cantonment, Telegraph office; Ganjam dist., Berhampore tal.; pop. 25,653 including cantonment; acres 3,199; lat. 19° 18′; long. 84° 50′; from Balligooda S.E. 84 miles; from Chetterpore W.S.W. 15 miles; from Chicacole N.E. 94 miles; from Madras N.E. 518 miles; from Russellcondah S.S.E. 45 miles; from the sea W. 11 miles. On the great northern road. Built upon a rocky ledge, surrounded by an extensive cultivated plain, sloping towards the sea on the east and south, but on the west and north bounded by hills about 8 miles distant. The soil of the cantonment is dry and gravelly and in many places granite rocks protrude from the surface. In consequence of an epidemic of fever at Ganjam in 1815, the Collector's cutcherry and the military force was removed to Berhampore and located here till 1835. The town is a conglomeration of six revenue villages. The military lines are situated in a hollow in Baupore. The Madras bank has a branch. The chief industry is the weaving of tusser silk into gold embroidered turbans, dresses, and other articles of wearing apparel. Common native cotton cloths are also woven. Sugar and sugar-candy are manufactured largely. During the cold weather English vegetables are raised. Snipe, wild-fowls, and other game are plentiful during the season. The following are the travelling distances by road from Berhampore to different places:—

To	Viâ	Miles and Furlongs.
Aska	......	24 0
Balligooda ...	Calingyah	117 4
Bangalore ...	Chicacole, Toony, Bezwada, Nellore and Chittore.	773 6½
Bellary	Chicacole, Guntoor and Cumbum	681 ½
Bezwada ...	Chicacole, Vizianagram, Rajahmundry and Ellore.	373 ½
Bhandara ...	Kantilo, Sonapore and Ryepore	510 2
Bhandara ...	Khoordhah, Kantilo, Sonapore and Ryepore.	530 2½
Bhandara ...	Calingyah, Sonapore and Ryepore	461 7½
Boad	Coracholly and Kantilo	167 6½
Boad	Khoordhah and Kantilo	198 1
Calingyah ...	......	69 4
Cassimcote ...	Chicacole and Chittivalsa	179 6½
Chetterpore ...	......	14 3
Chicacole ...	Ichapore	99 ½
Chittore ...	Chicacole, Vizianagram, Bezwada and Nellore.	663 4
Cocanada ...	Chicacole and Samulcottah	262 7½
Cuddapah ..	Chicacole, Rajahmundry, Guntoor and Cumbum.	602 4
Cumbum ...	Chicacole, Rajahmundry and Guntoor ...	506 0
Cuttack ...	Ganjam and Khoordhah	116 5
Ellore	Chicacole and Rajahmundry	333 7½
Ganjam ...	......	19 0
Guntoor ...	Chicacole, Rajahmundry and Ellore ...	393 1
Jubbulpore ...	Russellcondah, Sonapore, Sumbulpore, Bilaspore and Mandla.	545 6½
Jubbulpore ...	Kantilo, Sonapore, Sumbulpore and Bilaspore.	614 3½
Jubbulpore ...	Kantilo, Ryepore and Mandla	591 8
Jubbulpore ...	Russellcondah, Sonapore, Ryepore and Mandla.	523 0
Kamptee ...	Calingyah, Dadpore, Kankar and Nagpore.	557 7½
Kamptee ...	Coradah, Dadpore and Kankar	539 3½
Kamptee ...	Kantilo, Sonapore, Arang and Ryepore ...	578 2½
Kamptee ...	Russellcondah, Sonapore, Arang and Ryepore.	509 7½
Kantilo ...	Coracholly	99 4½
Kantilo ...	Khoordhah	119 7
Khoordhah ...	Ganjam and Rambha	98 5
Madras	Chicacole, Rajahmundry, Guntoor and Nellore.	645 5
Masulipatam ...	Chicacole, Rajahmundry and Mogultoor ...	369 1½

To	Viâ	Miles and Furlongs.
Masulipatam ...	Chicacole, Rajahmundry and Ellore ...	378 6
Nagpore ...	Russellcondah, Sonapore, Arang and Ryepore.	499 7½
Nagpore ...	Kantilo, Sonapore, Arang and Ryepore ...	568 2½
Nellore	Chicacole, Rajahmundry and Guntoor ...	537 7
Ongole	Chicacole, Rajahmundry and Guntoor ...	461 4
Rajahmundry.	Ichapore, Chicacole and Toony	278 6½
Rambha ...	Ganjam	29 2
Russellcondah.	Aska	49 0
Ryepore ...	Khoordhah, Kantilo, Sonapore and Arang.	385 1
Ryepore ...	Kantilo, Sonapore and Arang	365 ½
Ryepore ...	Russellcondah, Sonapore and Arang ...	316 6
Samulcottah ...	Chicacole and Toony	254 7½
Secunderabad.	Chicacole, Toony and Bezwada	539 7
Sonapore ...	Birsola	17 0
Sonapore ..	Coracholly, Kantilo and Boad	194 6½
Sonapore ...	Khoordhah, Kantilo and Boad	215 1
Sonapore ..	Russellcondah and Calingyah	146 4
Sooradah ...	Aska	46 0
Sumbulpore ...	Khoordhah, Kantilo and Sonapore	268 7
Sumbulpore ...	Coracholly, Kantilo and Sonapore	248 4½
Sumbulpore ...	Aska, Calingyah, Comarcoll and Sonapore.	200 2
Toony	Chicacole and Cassimcote	217 3½
Vellore	Chicacole, Bezwada and Nellore ...	685 4
Vizagapatam ...	Chicacole and Chittivalsa	163 1½
Vizianagram ...	Chicacole and Chittivalsa	158 1½
Vizianagram ...	Chicacole and Palcondah	171 1½

BERIBERY (ബെരിബെരി - baribari, *Singh.*). Meaning weakness. Acute human disease presenting dropsical symptoms, paralytic numbness of the lower extremities, and oppressed breathing.

BERIZ (برز - beríj, *Hind.*). From (báriz, pers. head of an account). Same as Jumma. The aggregate of an account, especially of revenue assessment. Beriz zaubitah was a register under Mahomedan governments showing total assessment of each village.

BERLIAUR (ಬರಲಿಯಾರು - baraliyáru, *Can.*; barliyár *). From (baralu, can. dry + áru, tam. river). Village; Neilgherry district, Paranginaud division; pop. 2,184; lat. 11° 20′; long. 76° 53′; from Coonoor E. 4 miles; from Ootacamund E.S.E. 12 miles. One of the stages on the Coonoor ghaut, containing a chuttram and Government garden. Principal fruits produced are the mangosteen, nutmeg, clove, cocoa, and vanilla. Gives its name to a river. Coffee estate of same name S. of toll gate and village.

BESTA (బెస్త - besta, *Can.* and *Tel.*). From (bhriti, san. wages); hired laborer. Caste-title. The corresponding terms are:—Tam. shembadavan; Can. and Mal. moocwa. Fishermen and palankeen-bearers. They also cook in zemindars' families. Not numerous inland, but found there. They call themselves Soota coolam or cooking clan, and say they are the descendants of the rishy Soota maha moony. They are divided into Teloogoo bestaul and Parikithy bestaul, the difference being chiefly religious; the former get themselves branded on shoulders with Veishnavite emblems chunk and chuckram, but the latter do not. They employ Dausaries as the messengers of a death, and Saucalavaur as those of a birth or of the fact that a girl has reached womanhood. Their chief object of worship is Hanooman, a picture or figure of whom always in their houses. About 750,000; most in Bellary. The Boyies are very similar. There is a teloogoo proverb:—[illegible]—"The "youngest among Bramins, and the oldest among Bestas;" both are made drudges [jauty].

BETEL (വെററില - vettila, *Mal.*; வெற்றிலை - vettilai, *Tam.*). Title from malayalam through portuguese. The betel-vine. See betel pepper under pepper. Called also indian leaf; but not to be confounded with folium indicum of druggists, which is leaf of wild cassia or malabathrum.——*Betel and nut* (வெற்றிலைப் பாக்கு - vettilaippákku, Tam.). Small pieces of areca nut, spice, catechu [cutch, kath], and sometimes quicklime [choonam], rolled up in a leaf of the piper betel [paun], to be slowly masticated, answering the purpose of an aromatic, astringent and alkalescent condiment. This is much used for the relief of malaise; and is also commonly presented from one person to another in token of civility or affection; presentation is essential in ceremonial visiting and on marriage and other festive occasions [paunsoopaury].——*Betel leaf* (वीटिका - vítiká, San.; विडा - vidá, Mahr.; بیڑی - bírí, Hind.; بیڑا - bírá, Dec.; ಪಟ್ಟಿವೀಳ್ಯ - pattívílye, Can.; [illegible] - ákumadupu, Tel.; വെററിലമടിപ്പ - vettilamatippu, Mal.; வெற்றிலைச்சுருள் - vettilaiçurul, Tam.). Title from malayalam through portuguese. San. from (vi, san. prefix of intensity + it, san. to go). Mahr. from sanscrit. Hind. from sanscrit. Can. from (patti, can. wrapped + vílye, can. betel-leaf). Tel. from (áku, tel. leaf + madutsu, tel. to fold). Mal. from (vettila, mal. betel-leaf + matippu, mal. fold). Tam. from (vettilai, tam. betel-leaf + shurul, tam. roll). Tam. also (putti), meaning roll. The leaf of the betel-vine [pepper], especially when used to enclose the masticatory. Paun more generally used among anglo-indians in this sense. ——*Betel nut* (पूगीफल - púgíp'hala, San.; सुपारी - supárí, Mahr.; سپاری - supárí, Hind. and Dec.; پینڠ - pináng, Malay; ಅಡಿಕೆ - adike, Can.; వక్క - vakka, Tel.; അടക്ക - atakka, Mal.; පුවක්ගෙඩිය - puvakgediya, Singh.; கொட்டைப்பாக்கு - kottaippákku, Tam.). Title from use with leaf of the betel-vine. San. from (púga, san. areca palm + p'hala, san. fruit). Can. from malayalam. Mal. from (ata, mal. close + káya, mal. fruit), from covering. Singh. from (puvak, singh. areca palm + gediya, singh. fruit). Tam. from (kottai, tam. nut + pákku, tam. areca). Tel. also (pókavakka). Tam. also (pákku). Title otherwise Areca nut, Pauk, Penang nut. Nuces areca, Semen arecæ, of chemists. Nut of the Areca palm [q.v.].

BETTA (ಬೆಟ್ಟ - betta, *Can.*). Means a hill.—"*a*" A Jeina open courtyard on a hill containing a colossal image. Distinguish from Basty [q. v.]. As compared with the images, are not of a Teertacaran but of a Gomataroya so called, probably a corruption of Gowtama rajah [booddha]. Three of them are known. The largest is at Shravanabelgola in Mysore. The hill there called Indragherry is one mass of granite [caroom cull] about 400 feet in height, and probably had a mass or tor on its summit, either a part of the subjacent mass or lying on it. This the Jeinas undertook to fashion into a statue 70 feet 3 inches in height, and have acheived it with great success. Even in Egypt no statue surpasses it in height. The image at Caurcal in Canara which is next in size, being 41 feet 5 inches in height and which weighs about 80 tons, was evidently moved to the place where it now stands; its date is engraved upon it, A.D. 1432. The third at Yenoor in Canara is about 35 feet high; from the style of art in which it is executed it is probably the oldest of the three. All these three figures belong to the Digambaran sect of Jeinas, being entirely naked, and all possess the peculiarity of having twigs of the Bo-tree [peepul] of Shakya moony, the ficus religiosa, twisted round their arms and legs in a manner found nowhere else, and in having serpents at their feet [staupatyam].—"*b*" Makes proper names. Thus Bettada chauma rajah a Mysore rajah. Bettana, from (anna, tel. a brother), otherwise known as Tumby, was an illegitimate brother of Dalavoy saitoopaty of Ramnaud; vol. I (124).—"*c*" Suffix in place names, as Dodabetta, Devarbetta. Also prefix in ditto.——*Bettoo* (ಬೆಟ್ಟು - bettu, Can.). In Canara the third or worst kind of land for rice, situated on high ground, and imperfectly irrigated, yielding generally but one crop a year. See vol. I, 112.

BETTATNAUD (വെട്ടത്തനാട്ട - vettattanátu, *Mal.*). From (vettam, mal. heat + nátu, mal. country). Seat of ancient raj in Malabar district, Ponnany talook. This family became extinct and the estate escheated in 1793.——*Bettattpoothiyangaudy* (വെട്ടത്തുപുതിയങ്ങാടി - vettattuputiyannáti, Mal. vetatapudiyangádi *). From (vettattu, mal. a dynasty derived from chéramán's minister tólan, now extinct + putiya, mal. new + annáti, mal. bazaar).—"*a*" Deputy tahsildarry, Malabar district. Pay Rs. 70.—"*b*" Village, Deputy tahsildar's and Moonsif's station; Malabar dist., Ponnany tal.; pop. 6,353; lat. 10° 53′; long. 75° 58′; from Calicut S.S.E. 27 miles; from Cannanore S.S.E. 76 miles; from Madras W.S.W. 330 miles; from Malapooram S.W. 14 miles; from Manantoddy S. 62 miles; from Palghaut W.N.W. 49 miles; from Ponnany N. 6 miles; from Tellicherry S.S.E. 66 miles; from the sea E. 2¾ miles. Two miles east of the railway station. Sub-magistrate's and Judge's courts were built with the materials of the palace of the Bettatnaud rajahs, destroyed by Tippoo sultan in 1784. Has few Moplah mosques.

BEY (بے - be, *Hind.*). From Turkish. Same as Beg.

BEYPORE * (ബേപ്പൂർ - béppúr, *Mal.*). From (veppu, mal. deposit + úr, mal. village). Place formed by receding of sea. Sanscrit name (váyupura), meaning vayoo, the god + town.—"*a*" Town; Malabar dist., Yernaud tal.; pop. 3,672; lat. 11° 10′; long. 75° 50′; height 14 feet; from Bombay S.S.E. 560 miles; from Cadaloondy N.N.W. 4 miles; from Calicut S.S.E. 6 miles; from Molancadav S. 3 miles; from Munjery W.N.W. 22 miles; from the sea E. ¼ mile. Near mouth of river of same name. Formerly terminus of Madras railway, but station was abolished from 1st January 1888 on extension of line to Calicut. The terminus was on Chauliam island and incorrectly called Beypore. The port so called lies on north bank of river. The limits of port are:—north and south, the sea-shore within fifty yards of high-water mark spring-tides, from boundary pillars one-and-a-half miles north and south of the river's mouth; west, the anchorage between two lines running west from the boundary pillars to nine fathoms water; east, the banks of the river, backwater, creeks, and islands within fifty yards of high-water spring tides, and within a distance of one-and-a-half miles from the river's mouth. The anchorage for small vessels is inside the river, close to the north bank and immediately below a reef of laterite rock which projects far into the stream. The best anchorage in the roads for large vessels is in four-and-half to six fathoms and from two to three miles off shore. The bar admits craft of 300 tons to the river, and at low spring tides gives soundings of 12–14 feet. The Portuguese established a factory here, but it failed. Tippoo selected a spot 3 miles up the river as the site of the capital of Malabar and called it Ferokhee or Sultan putnam, but the plan came to nothing. Beypore was a regular port of call for steamers, before change of railway station. All the coffee of Ouchterlony valley, with much from East wynaud, comes here for export. Also teak floated down from forests. Rice and salt form staples of import trade. Iron ore, and wood in great abundance exist in vicinity. Five miles east is Chattaparamba or Field of Death, remarkable for its ancient stone circles and monuments. Beypore amshom was formerly known as Vadaparapnaud. In Beypore amshom there are four Covilagams called Manayatt, Nediyaul, Panangaud and Poothiya, belonging to the family of the Beypore branch of the Parapnaud family.—" *b* " River; Malabar district, Yernaud talook; also called Sharapoya or arrow river. Its two main branches rise respectively in the Coondahs and on lower ranges of S.E. Wynaud. The one, called the Gold river, passes over the ridge of ghauts in a long succession of rocky cataracts, lying a short distance south of the Carcoor pass, after draining an extensive tract of the Neilgherry. The other, called the Chola river, drains the Wynaud ghauts and falls from the crest of the Wynaud hills in a cataract [aroovy] close to a foot-path known as the Cholaudy pass. The two streams, after receiving many large feeders, unite in the midst of the Nelambore government teak plantations. After reaching the low country the river receives many affluents, the chief being the Carimpoya at its junction with which a massive timber bridge spans the joint stream, the Calakkampoya, the Carcoorpoya, and the Mappooram. Then flowing past Arriyacode, it joins the Codiyattore. It debouches into the sea at Beypore, being joined near its mouth by the Cadaloondy, with which it forms the island of Chauliam. Total length about 90 miles. Even in height of dry season boats of light draught can ascend as far as Maumbaud under the shadow of the Camel hump range. The sands are auriferous; lower classes make a small livelihood by washing sands after each annual flood.

BEZOAR (विषघ्न - vishaghna, *San.*; حجرالسم - hajarussamm, *Ar.*; پاد زهر - pádzahar, *Pers.*; زهر مهره - zahrmohrá, *Hind.*; پاؤ زهر - páuzahar, *Dec.*; گولیگا - goliga, *Malay*; ವಿಷಕಲ್ಲು - vishakallu, *Too.*; విషహారి - vishahári, *Tel.*; വിഷക്കല്ല് - vishakkal, *Mal.*; വിഷഗൽ - vishagal, *Singh.*; விடக்கல் - vidakkal, *Tam.*). Title from persian. San. from (visha, san. poison + han, san. to destroy). Ar. from (hajar, ar. stone + samm, ar. poison). Pers. from (pád, pers. antidote + zahar, pers. poison). Hind. from (zahar, pers. poison + mohrah, pers. shell). Dec. from persian. Drav. means poison + stone. Hind. also (kánízahrmohrá), meaning mineral bezoar. Malay also (mátika), meaning gem; (mántika). Tel. also (pámukallu), meaning snake + stone; (garudapattsa), meaning braminy kite + emerald. Tam. also (pámbukkal), meaning snake stone; (télgal), meaning scorpion stone. Two kinds according to European nomenclature; mineral and animal. The former a natural produce of india, persia, tartary, and other countries; chemically, silicate of magnesia and iron; no medicine so frequently resorted to by native practitioners, especially hakeems, in cholera; there are several varieties; that sought for in cholera is of pale green color, and easily ground with water on a stone; the paste is white and slightly odorous, the smell being often very feeble and somewhat like that of the prepared pipe clay; this is a variety of steatite or soap-stone. Animal bezoars are concretions named after the animal from which obtained, as fish-bezoar, goat-bezoar, snake-bezoar, &c.; the list of these has been much augmented since modern writers have extended that term to all the concretions in the body of animals; animal bezoar however is not considered as a variety of bezoar by native practitioners; it is called gorochanay [q. v.]; many snake-stones are mere animal bezoars. The following descriptions show the difference between the two classes of bezoar:—" *a* " Mineral bezoar; form not defined; it occurs in very irregular and angular pieces of various shape, like pieces of marble or any other stone; size unlimited, often as large as a fist, and sometimes much larger; surface generally rough, but smooth when covered with clay, which is the case sometimes; of various colors between white and green or yellowish-green, but generally pale green with one or two shades of yellow; structure amorphous.—" *b* " Animal bezoar or gorochanay; from defined and regular; oval, oblong, ovate, globular, or flat and circular; seldom of the size of an egg, but generally of various sizes below that; surface very smooth and glossy; color various, generally dark green, marbled, or bluish-brown; structure laminated and concentric.——*Bezoar nut* (గచ్చ - gattsa, Tel.). Title from pale green appearance of nut and kernel. Tel. from (gittsu, tel. to prick), from prickly legumes. Same as Bonduc.

BEZWADA (بجواڑا - bijwára, *Hind.*; బెజవాడ - bedzaváda, *Tel.* bezváda *). From (beddzamu, tel. deep gorge + váda, tel. village). Sanscrit name (vijayapura), meaning arjoonan, the victorious + town.——**(1)** Talook, Kistna district. Tahsildar's pay Rs. 150. Area 236 square miles. Population 85,736. Language Teloogoo. On left bank of Kistna. Centre of district. Bounded:—North by Vissanapett division and Noozveed zemindarry; south by the Kistna river; east by Noozveed zemindarry and west by Nundigauma talook and Nizam's dominions. Include the Condapully range to the north and on the south portion of the territory acquired by the Valloor zemindar. Partly hilly and partly plain. Regar soil predominates. Irrigation, by Kistna anicut and rain-fed tanks. Places of archæological interest:—Autcore, Bezwada, Chiggireddipaud, Condapully, Condore, Cowlore, Ganapavaram, Malacaupooram, Mogalrauzpooram, Potavaram, Todapully, Velgalair, Yanikepaud, Zakkampoody, Zoopoody. Trig. stations:—Bezwada, Yerragutt. The leading places, &c., in the talook are the following.——*Bezwada* (బెజవాడ - bedzaváda, Tel.). See below.——*Boodamair* (బుడమేరు - budaméru, Tel.). See sep. title.——*Condapully* (కొండపల్లె - kondapalle, Tel.). See sep. title.——*Cunkipaud* (కంకిపాడు - kankipádu, Tel.). From (kanki, tel. ear of corn + pádu, tel. village). Village; pop. 2,745; acres 2,496; lat. 16° 26′; long. 80° 48′; from Bezwada E.S.E. 12 miles; from Masulipatam N.W. 32 miles. Lock in the Masulipatam canal.——*Ibrampatam* (ఇబ్రహాముపట్టణము - ibrahámupattanamu, Tel.). See sep. title.——*Kistna* (కృష్ణ - krishna, Tel.). See sep. title.——*Valloor* (వల్లూరు - vallúru, Tel.). See sep. title.——*Yerragutt* (ఎఱ్ఱగట్టు - erragattu, Tel.). From (erra, tel. red + gattu, tel. hill). Trig. station; lat. 16° 40′ 29·79″; long. 80° 42′ 19·96″; height 1,273 feet; from Bezwada N.N.E. 12 miles; from Vellatore E.S.E. 1½ miles.——**(2)** Zemindarry; Kistna district, Bezwada talook. Zemindarry attached in 1830 and sold for arrears of revenue in 1846. The last holder, a widow, died a pensioner in 1853.——**(3)** Town, Municipality, Head-quarters of District moonsif, Head assistant collector, Talook, Superintending engineer, Executive engineer, Assistant engineer and Sub-registrar, Telegraph office, Railway station; Kistna dist., Bezwada tal.; pop. 20,741; acres 2,949; lat. 16° 31′; long. 80° 39′; from Guntoor N.N.E. 19 miles; from Madras N. 236 miles; from Masulipatam W.N.W. 42 miles; from Vinoocondah E.N.E. 66 miles. On Kistna, here crossed by ferry, and at junction of high roads from Madras to Calcutta and from Hyderabad to coast. Entrepôt for most canal traffic of Kistna delta and connected by canal with Ellore, Masulipatam, Cocanada and Rajahmundry. In ancient days religious centre of Vengy desham. About A.D. 605 captured by Chalookyas who came from Calyaun under Cobja vishnoovardhanan, and established the Eastern chalookya dynasty. Hwen thsang, Chinese pilgrim, resided in A.D. 639 at the Poorvashila booddhist monastery on a hill east of a town. In A.D. 1023 the Chola dynasty obtained possession of Vengy desham, and held the country till about A.D. 1228. Next held by Ganapaty dynasty of Warangal, who ruled till A.D. 1323, when they were in turn overthrown by Mussalmans. On the ruins of the Ganapaty kingdom rose a dynasty of local Reddy chiefs, who ruled at Condaveed till A.D. 1427, when they were subverted by Mussalmans of Golcondah cootb shahy dynasty. Between A.D. 1427 and A.D. 1515, under the sway of first a Gajapaty named Langoolya, then two of the early Vijianugger sovereigns, and then a succession of four Gajapaties, the last of whom was conquered by Krishnadeva royel in A.D. 1515. In 1565 Mussalmans regained possession of country after Talicote, and held it till British occupation, having their capital in hill fortress of Condapully. Numerous Booddhistic remains. Rock-cuttings on hill west of town, the Indraneeladry or Arjoonacondah of natives and Telegraph hill of English. Two marble statues of Booddha on west side of western hill. Of early Braminical period there are temples of Mulleshwaran, Arjoonan and Canaca doorga, with inscriptions, sculptured pillars, mantapams, and figures, besides rock-cuttings in the hills and small cave-temples. Traces of fort erected by East india company in 1760 and dismantled in 1820. For a description of the anicut, constructed here across the Kistna, see vol. I, 396. Trig. station in lat. 16° 31′ 15·47″; long. 80° 38′ 58·53″; height 703 feet; from Bezwada W. ½ mile. The following are the travelling distances by road from Bezwada to different places:—

To	Via	Miles and Furlongs.
Berhampore ...	Rajahmundry, Vizianagram, Chicacole and Ichapore.	373 0⅓
Chennore ...	Warangal	213 1
Chetterpore ...	Rajahmundry, Chicacole, Ichapore and Berhampore.	387 3⅓
Chicacole ...	Rajahmundry, Cassimcote, and Chittivalsa.	274 0
Chunda ...	Warangal, Chennore and Sirpore	315 2
Cocanada ...	Rajahmundry and Samulcottah	132 2
Cuddapah ...	Guntoor and Cumbum	229 3⅓
Cumbum ...	Guntoor	132 7⅓
Ellore	......	39 1
Ganjum ...	Rajahmundry, Chicacole, Ichapore and Berhampore.	392 0⅓
Guntoor ...	......	20 0⅓
Kamptee ...	Chennore, Chunda and Bowry	420 5
Madras ...	Guntoor, Ongole, Nellore and Wojelly ...	272 4⅓
Masulipatam ...	......	43 6⅓
Nagpore ...	Warangal, Chennore, Chunda and Warora.	410 5
Nellore ...	Guntoor, Ongole and Cauvaly	164 6½
Ongole	Guntoor	88 3⅓
Rajahmundry.	Ellore	94 2
Samulcottah ...	Ellore and Rajahmundry	124 2
Secunderabad.	Juggayapett, Sooryapett and Haitipamla.	166 6⅓
Sironchah ...	Chennore	228 0
Toony	Ellore and Rajahmundry	155 5
Vinoocondah ...	Guntoor	74 1⅓
Vizagapatam ...	Ellore, Rajahmundry and Cassimcote ...	217 2
Vizianagram ...	Ellore, Rajahmundry, Toony and Cassimcote.	240 5

BHACTAN (भक्त - bhakta, *San.*). From (bhaj, san. to worship). Devotee.——*Bhactavatsa* (భక్తవత్సలుడు - bhaktavatsudu, Tel.). From (above + vatsala, san. kind). Kind to adherents; epithet of Shiva or Vishnoo. Hindoo 2nd or pers. name. Common among non-bramin Veishnavites [peyar].——

Bhacty (भक्ति - bhakti, San.). Faith. Distinguished from Carmam [q.v.] or action, and Nyaunam [q.v.] or spiritual knowledge.

BHADRACHELLAM (భద్రాచలము - bhadráchalamu, *Tel.* bhadrachalam*). From (bhadra, san. lovely + achala, san. hill). Sanscrit name (rámatírt'ha), meaning rama, the hero + place of sacred waters; from rama having crossed the Godavery here on his way to Ceylon.——**(1)** Talook, Godavery district. Lying between lat. 17° 27′ and 17° 56′ and long. 80° 55′ and 81° 51′. Area with Rekapully, 911 square miles. Inhabitants, chiefly Koyas, a tribe of Gonds. Language Teloogoo. N.W. of district. Bounded N. by Cherla and Bustar, E. by Rekapully, S. and W. by the river Godavery. Ceded in 1860 by the Nizam, and thus formed part of Upper Godavery district, Central provinces. With Rekapully, transferred from the Central provinces to Madras in 1874; and the Rumpa country from the talook of Rajahmundry being added, together with parts of Yernagoodem and Peddapore talooks, the whole was formed into an Agency under the Godavery collector. The talook is flat, with the exception of a strip of land a few miles in breadth along the Godavery; it is covered with dense jungle with here and there a small village consisting of a few Koya huts. Soil good; black cotton soil on the bank of the river. In the interior sandy and rocky. Trade in timber and forest produce. No irrigation. Camping grounds:—Bhadrachellam, Doomagoodem, Lutchigoodem, Nellipauca, Nullamilly, Singavaram and Toomikicheroo. Zemindarry; Narrainpooram. Places of archæological interest:—Bhadrachellam, Devarpully, Doomagoodem, Lutchmanagootta, Nullapully, Purnashaula. Principal trig. station:—Singavaram. The leading places, &c., in the talook are the following.——*Bhadrachellam* (భద్రాచలము - bhadráchalamu, Tel.). See below. ——*Doomagoodem* (దుమ్ముగూడెము - dummagúdemu, Tel.). See sep. title.——*Godavery* (గోదావరి - gódávari, Tel.). See sep. title.——*Goondaula* (గుండాల - gundála, Tel.). From (gundamu, tel. a pit); from sacred springs of water in the Godavery. Zemindarry village; pop. 318; lat. of village 17° 39′; long. 80° 59′; from Bhadrachellam E.S.E. 3½ miles; from Cocanada W.N.W. 97 miles.——*Paupicondah* (పాపికొండ - pápikonda, Tel.). See sep. title.——*Purnashaula* (పర్ణశాల - parnashála, Tel.). From (parna, san. leaf + shálá, san. hut). Bower. Zemindarry village, Place of pilgrimage; pop. 270; lat. of village 17° 56′; long. 80° 56′; from Bhadrachellam N. 18 miles; from Cocanada N.W. 109 miles. On the Godavery. Celebrated shrine built over the spot whence Seeta was carried off by Ravanan. In a stream at the back of the temple is shown a foot-print made by Seeta. The villagers show peculiar formations of hills and rocks as relics of the death of Jatauyoo and the abduction of Seeta.——*Singavaram* (సింగవరము - singavaramu, Tel.). From (singamu, tel. lion + pura, san. town). Trig. station; lat. 17° 45′ 10·38″; long. 80° 58′ 36·22″; height 724 feet; from Bhadrachellam N.N.E. 6½ miles; from Singavaram S. 1½ miles.——**(2)** Zemindarry, Town, Talook head-quarters, Place of pilgrimage; Godavery dist., Bhadrachellam tal.; pop. 2,053; lat. of village 17° 40′; long. 80° 56′; from Cocanada W.N.W. 102 miles; from Coonavaram W.N.W. 25 miles; from Ellore N.N.W. 66 miles; from Madras N. 310 miles; from Narsapore N.N.W. 100 miles; from Rajahmundry N.W. 74 miles. Built on a knoll about 100 feet high, on the Godavery. Consist of one long narrow street. Celebrated temple of Rama. The temple is built on the top of a small hill, called Bhadrachellam and is surrounded by twenty-four lesser pagodas and surmounted by a lofty gopooram, which is out of all proportion to the edifice it surmounts. The space in the centre is paved. The building is approached by a flight of stone steps from the river. The temple is managed by the Nizam's officials. The Nizam contributes Rs. 13,000 annually towards the maintenance. Rama being said to have crossed the Godavery at this spot on his expedition to Ceylon, an annual festival is held in April. About a mile east of the village are dolmens. Diamonds are found in the neighbourhood. There is a hot spring in bed of Godavery. Peshcush of Zemindarry Rs. 16,709. The Ranee traces her descent from Annappa ashwa row, who received grant of the estate from Emperor of Delhi in 1324.

BHADRAM (भद्र - bhadra, *San.*). From (bhand, san. to be greeted with praise). Propitious.——*Bhadra* (ಭದ್ರ - bhadra, Can.). Means beautiful. River; Cuddore district, Mysore. Twin stream of the Toonga, which both united form the Toongabudra. Confluence with the Toonga at Coodaly in the Shimoga district, about 8 miles north-east of Shimoga.——*Bhadra cauly* (भद्रकाली - bhadrakálí, San.). From (above + kálí, san. the goddess of that name). S. indian usage for Cauly, περσεφόνη of Greeks; Proserpina of Romans; Isis of Egyptians. The Moloch of Indian mythology. The Caulica pooraunam details her ritual, &c. There is a temple to her at Cauly ghattam near Calcutta, whence latter name. She is here one of the forms in which the village goddess of the south has been assimilated into the Hindoo system. Differs but little from Doorga. Said to have been Shiva's wife, but to have become arrogant; in consequence of which she was banished to this world, where she is now one of the queens who rule over demons, and protect men from them. She is sometimes called the shacty or inferior wife of Veerabhadran, Shiva's third son. She is represented in a dancing attitude; for she danced once in emulation with Shiva. The latter is for this reason called Peyodaudy, the dancer with a devil, and represented in dancing attitude in the pagoda at Chidambaram, where at the annual great festival his dancing with Bhadra cauly is also acted. Bhadra cauly wears on her head a fiery crown, round which are serpents, and her whole body glows with fire. On her forehead she has Shiva's mark of sacred ashes, and in her mouth are two lion teeth. She has ten arms and hands; four of these are empty, and in the other six she holds respectively a rope, a parrot, a lance, a drum round which is a snake, a trident, and fire. An image of this description is found in her pagodas, together with Vigneshwaran, Veerabhadran and Aghoran. The last standing for Shiva is represented in a dancing attitude, having fourteen arms and hands, in which he holds various weapons. On his head he wears a crown; in his long erect locks are on one side Gungay and on the other the moon; on his forehead is the Sheiva sign made with sacred ashes; and on his feet are wooden slippers, in which he danced with Bhadra cauly; whilst garlands hang down from his shoulders. In the pagodas which have a sufficient income, Bhadra cauly is daily worshipped in the inner apartment, with offerings similar to those made to Shiva and Vishnoo, a Bramin usually officiating. The sacrifices made on the altars before the pagodas, consisting of swine, goats, cocks, strong drink, &c., are conducted by Shoodras or Pariahs. Bhadra cauly assists in the practice of black arts. Like the other Graumadevatays, Bhadra cauly enjoys an annual festival, which lasts seven or nine days. She has various names, and among them the following:—Alacay codiyaul or she on whose banner a devil is painted; Ayyay or mistress; Bheiravy or the shacty of bheiravan; Cauly or the black one; Chamoondy; Cungauly or she who wears skeletons; Devy or goddess; Madhoopaty or mistress of ardent spirits; Mauliny; Mautah or mother; Mautangy or the young woman; Moocunny or the three-eyed; Oolaviya manyay or walking deception; Shooly or she who wears a trident; Shoory or heroine-demoness; Vallanang or the malevolent goddess; Veery or heroine; Vetauly or demoness; Yauliyoorty or she who rides the lion; Yaumalay; Yendoly or the eight shouldered. The name frequently occurs in books, conjointly with coil, for a temple in which the female energy is worshipped. Very many Cauly coils are scattered over Southern india, and by traditional statement a human sacrifice was offered at the foundation of every one of them. The Tauntrica rites of the Atarvana vedam pertain to her worship. For Shiva's wife in her milder form see Parvaty. See vol. I (70) to (94), and the following foot-notes:—history of religion and philosophy I (70), conspectus of pantheon I (77), devil worship I (80), existing hindoo sects I (88) [matam].——*Bhadrachellam* (భద్రాచలము - bhadráchalamu, Tel.). The sacred place; see sep. title. Hindoo 2nd or pers. name [peyar].——*Bhadradeepam* (ഭദ്രദീപം - bhadradípam, Mal.; பத்திராத்திபம் - pattiraittíbam, Tam.). Means lamp of good fortune. Solar festival [pundigay, 6d] on the first day of fourth solar month Carcatacam [mausam] or 15th July and again on the first day of tenth solar month Macaram [mausam] or 12th January. Festival in Travancore. It is a kind of sun worship like the Pongal of the Tamuls, performed at the two ayanams or solstices of the year, calculated as occurring about 12th January and 15th July. The ceremony chiefly consists in the priests transferring, by means of muntrams or invocations, the spirit of the sun to sacred lamps. The Moorjapam, which is a special and extraordinary observance of the Bhadradeepam, is held every six years; this is supposed to compensate for any defect during the preceding six years. The Moorjapam is terminated by Laksha deepam [q.v.].——*Bhadray* (भद्रा - bhadrá, San.). Auspicious. Name of the second, seventh and twelfth days of any lunar fortnight, as auspicious days.

BHAEE (بھائی - bhái, *Hind.*). From (bhrátri, san. brother). Brother. Distinguish from Bye [q.v.].——*Bhaee paun lao* (بھائی پان لاؤ - bháipánláo, Hind.). Brother, bring Paun! A Thug signal.

BHAGAM (भग - bhaga, *San.*). From (bhaj, san. to enjoy). Fortune.——*Bhagavanta* (భగవంతుడు - bhagavantudu, Tel.). From (above + vat, san. suffix of possession). Epithet of the Supreme being. Hindoo 2nd or pers. name [peyar].——*Bhagavat* (भगवत् - bhagavat, San.). From (above + vat, san. affix showing possession). The fortunate one, the supreme being, especially Vishnoo. The monotheistic Cooral used it for the one supreme being. Thus:—"The essence of the supreme is defined by the "term bhagavat; the word bhagavat is the denomination of the "primeval and eternal god; the letter bh implies the cherisher "and supporter of the universe; by ga is understood the leader, "impeller, or creator; the dissyllable bhagam indicates the six "properties, viz., dominion, might, glory, splendour, wisdom and "dispassion" [matam].——*Bhagavat geeta* (भगवद्गीता - bhagavadgítá, San.). From (gítá, san. song). Also short, the Geetay. An episode of Mahabhaurat, in form of discourse between Avatar krishnan and his friend and pupil Arjoonan. After twelve years' wandering of Pandavas, the hostile armies met on plain of Cooroo cshetram. Arjoonan, seeing his relatives drawn up against him in battle array, was struck with compunction. Krishnan, who was acting as his charioteer, replied in a metaphysical discourse that as Arjoonan belonged to the military caste his duty was to fight. Renunciation of the world ought not to involve avoidance of action, or neglect of professional duties. The fight then went on and the Pandavas gained the victory. The Geetay is philosophically eclectic and claimed by all religious parties, and resembles Stoic philosophy of the Greeks. According to it, god is the soul of the world, its material cause as well as its efficient cause. The world is his body, formed by himself out of himself. Everything that exists is a portion of god, and every action that is performed is an action of god. Next to the doctrine concerning deity, the most distinguishing principle is the importance of quietism. To the wise man, pleasure and pain, gain and loss, victory and defeat, are the same. He is of the same mind to the good and to the bad. He is free from desire and aversion, hope and fear, unconcerned about the issue of his actions. The real author is unknown. It was at an early date placed in the Mahabhaurat. It is however, quite independent. Example from the Canarese version which is the best known—"ಯೆಲಾ ಕರ್ಮಗಳನ್ನು ಮನಸ್ಸಿನಿಂದ ಬಿಟ್ಟಂಥಾವನಾಗಿ ತಾನು ಮಾಡಿಸದೇ ವೊಂಭತ್ತು ಬಾಗಿಲುಗಳುಳ್ಳ ಈ ಶರೀರವೆಂಬ ಪಟ್ಟಣದಲ್ಲಿ ಜೀವನು ಇಂದ್ರಿಯಂಗಳನ್ನು ಸ್ವಾಧೀನಮಾಡಿಕೊಂಡು ಸುಖವಾಗಿ ಇರುವನು. ಸಮರ್ಥನಾದ ದೇವರು ಲೋಕಕ್ಕೆ ಕರ್ತೃತ್ವವನ್ನು ಕರ್ಮಗಳನ್ನು ಕರ್ಮದ ಫಲದಿಂದ ಕೂಡುವಿಕೆಯನ್ನು ವುಂಟುಮಾಡುವದಿಲ್ಲವು ಸ್ವಭಾವವಾಗಿಯೇ ಪ್ರವರ್ತಿಸುವದು. ಅರಸಾದ ದೇವರು ಪುಣ್ಯ ಪಾಪಗಳಿಂದ ಬರುವ ಸುಖದುಃಖಗಳನ್ನು ಹೊಂದುವದಿಲ್ಲ ಆದರೆ ಜ್ಞಾನವು ಅಜ್ಞಾನದಿಂದ ಮುಚ್ಚಲ್ಪಟ್ಟಿದೆ ಆದರಿಂದ ಈ ಜೀವಜಂತುಗಳು ತಪ್ಪಿನಡಿಯುತ್ತವೆ. ಯಾರಿಗೆ ಅಂಥಾ ಅಜ್ಞಾನವು ಜ್ಞಾನದಿಂದ ನಾಶವಾಗಿ ಹೋಗುವದೋ ಅವರಿಗೆ ಸೂರ್ಯನಹಾಗೆ ಆತ್ಮದಜ್ಞಾನವು ಆಮೇಲೆ ಪ್ರಕಾಶಿಸುವದು. ಆ ಭಗವಂತನಲ್ಲಿಯೇ ಬುದ್ಧಿಯು ಆತನಲ್ಲಿಯೇ ಚಿತ್ತವು ಆತನಲ್ಲಿಯೇ ಭಕ್ತಿಯು ನೆಲೆಗೊಂಡಿರುವವರು ಮತ್ತು ಆತನಲ್ಲಿ ನಂಬಿಕೆಯುಂಟಾದವರು ಜ್ಞಾನದಿಂದ ತೊಳೆಯಲ್ಪಟ್ಟ ಪಾಪಗಳುಳ್ಳವರಾಗಿ ಯೆಂದೆಂದಿಗೂ ತಿರುಗದ ಸ್ಥಳವನು ಶೇರುವರು—"As for the man who has his passions in subjection and who does not concern himself with worldly matters, "his soul sits at rest in the nine-gate city of its abode, neither "acting nor causing to act. The Almighty creates neither the "powers nor the deeds of mankind, nor the application of the "fruits of action; nature prevails. The Almighty receives "neither the vices nor the virtues of any one. Mankind are led "astray by their reason being obscured by ignorance but when "that ignorance of their souls is destroyed by the force of "reason, their wisdom shines forth again with the glory of the "sun, and causes the deity to appear. Those whose understanding are in him, whose souls are in him, whose confidence "is in him, and whose asylum is in him, are by wisdom purified "from all their offences, and go from whence they shall never "return." The following are the detailed contents of the eighteen chapters:—"*a*" The despondency of Arjoonan.—"*b*" On the nature of the soul and speculative doctrines; application to the Saunkhyam doctrine.—"*c*" Of works; devotion through action.—"*d*" Devotion through spiritual knowledge; of the forsaking of works.—"*e*" Of forsaking the fruits of works; devotion by means of the renunciation of actions.—"*f*" Of the exercise of soul; devotion by means of self-restraint.—"*g*" Of the principle of nature and the vital spirit; devotion through spiritual discernment.—"*h*" Of Pooroosham; devotion to the indivisible supreme spirit.—"*i*" Of the chief of secrets and prince of science; devotion by means of kingly knowledge and kingly mystery.—"*j*" Of the diversity of the divine nature; devotion to the divine virtues.—"*k*" Display of the divine nature in the form of the universe; the vision of the universal forms.—"*l*" On serving the deity in his visible and invisible forms; devotion through worship.—"*m*" Explanation of the terms cshetram and cshetranyan; devotion in connection with the cshetranyan.—"*n*" Of the three goonams or qualities; devotion in connection with the three qualities.—"*o*" Of Poorshottaman; devotion by the attainment to the highest person.—"*p*" Of good and evil destiny; devotion in regard to the lot of the Devas and of the Asoorans.—"*q*" Of faith divided into three species; devotion as regards the three kinds of faith.—"*r*" Of forsaking the fruits of action for obtaining eternal salvation; devotion as regards renunciation and emancipation. Distinguish from Bhagavat pooraunam [matam].——*Bhagavaty* (भगवती -bhagavatí, San.). ἀφροδίτη of Greeks, Venus of Romans, Isis of Egyptians. Lutchmy. Hindoo 2nd or pers. name. Applied to males and females [peyar]. Also a gold coin with the figure of the goddess Bhagavaty, called by Europeans pagoda.——*Bhageeraty* (பாகீரதி - págírathi, Tam.). From (bhagírath'a, san. a myth. king). Ganges, as daughter of Bhageeratan, patronymic. Hindoo 2nd or pers. name. Common to both sexes. Familiarly shortened into Baugy [peyar].——*Bhagwaun* (भगवान् - bhagaván, San.). From (above + vat, san. suffix of possession). The divine being [bhagavat].——*Bhaugavatam* (भागवत - bhágavata, San.). From (bhagavat, san, vishnu, the fortunate). Same as Bhagavat pooraunam. Also Shree bhaugavatam.——*Bhaugnugger* (بھاگ نگر - bhágnagar, Hind.). From (bhág, hind. fortunate + nagar, hind. city). Called after Bhaugmaty, the Hindoo mistress of one of the Golcondah nawaubs. Old name of Hyderabad in Deccan.——*Bhaugyam* (பாக்கியம் - pákkiyam, Tam.). Fortune. Hindoo 2nd or pers. name. Applied to males and females; also taken by native Christians [peyar].——*Bhaugyanautan* (பாக்கியநாதன் - pákkiyanáthan, Tam.). From (abave + nát'ha, san. master). Shiva, the master of the eight Bhaugyas or Siddhies. Hindoo 2nd or pers. name [peyar].

BHAICAM (भेक - bhéka, *San.*; مینڈک - mendak, *Hind.*; ಕಪ್ಪೆ - kappe, *Can.*; కప్ప - kappa, *Tel.*; തവള - tavala, *Mal.*; தவளை - tavalai, *Tam.*). San. from (bhi, san. to be timid). Hind. from (mandúka, san. frog). Tam. from (távu, tam. to leap). The frog and toad order of animals. Terms co-extensive with the European order Batrachia ecaudata, sub-class Batrachians. This sub-class is sometimes included under Reptiles [sarpy], but is here separated. Batrachians are distinguished from other divisions of vertebrate animals by passing through a metamorphosis; that is, after their embryonal life, undergoing changes which affect not only their external form but also their internal organs. Food consists of insects and worms, only the largest kinds feed on small vertebrates. The prey is swallowed entire. Moisture is necessary; they are found only in damp places or in the neighbourhood of water; when the hot season commences, those which are remote from water bury themselves deep enough in the ground to escape the dry atmosphere, falling into a state of lethargy identical with the winter-sleep of species inhabiting colder climates. Many are endowed with a powerful voice; skin sometimes smooth. Many live at some distance from water; all enter it at the season of propagation. The young ones or tadpoles have a thick ovate body without legs, terminating in a long, strong, compressed tail, which serves as an organ of locomotion in the water. They are true aquatic animals, having the same anatomical and physiological arrangement of the organs of circulation as fishes. Food consists chiefly of living or decaying vegetables, but also of decomposing animal substances. None are poisonous. The sub-class Batrachians has two orders here represented. The first order is that represented by the title, viz., of Batrachia ecaudata or Tail-less frogs, otherwise Batrachia salientia or Jumping frogs; in this order the body is broad and short, and in the perfectly developed state with four legs and without tail. The second order is that of burrowing Batrachians, Batrachia apoda or frogs without legs; in this order the body is long, cylindrical, without limbs, worm-like; a tail is absent or extremely short; skin is smooth and viscous, forming numerous annular folds; eyes are rudimentary, more or less hidden below the skin; constantly live below ground, burrowing like worms; food consists of mould and worms; these are not classed by natives among frogs, and go under the head of worm [keerah]. There is a Tamul proverb:—தவளை தாமரைக்குச் சமீபமாக இருந்தும் அதின் தேனை உண்ணாது; அதுபோல அறிவினர் கிட்ட இருந்தாலும் கற்றுக்கொள்ளார்கள்—"The frog "living near the lotus drinks not its honey, the illiterate though "they live near the learned remain ignorant."——(1) The following is a synopsis of the Batrachia ecaudata of Southern india, ranged down to species. The italics indicate the families, and the ordinary type indicates the species.——*Ranidæ.*—Rana hexadactyla [tank frog], cyanophlyctis, kuhlii, tigrina [bull frog], gracilis, verrucosa, rufescens, breviceps, dobsonii, beddomii, semipalmata, leptodactyla, diplosticta, phrynoderma, malabarica, curtipes, temporalis; Rhacophorus pleurostictus [tree frog], maculatus [choonam frog], malabaricus, beddomii, lateralis; Ixalus opisthorhodus, fuscus, silvaticus, saxicola, leucorhinus, femoralis, beddomii, pulcher, variabilis [tinkling frog], glandulosus, punctatus, chalazodes, flaviventris signatus; Nyctibatrachus pygmæus, major; Nannobatrachus beddomii.—*Engystomatidæ.*—Melanobatrachus indicus; Microhyla rubra, ornata; Callula obscura, olivacea, triangularis; Cacopus systoma, globulosus.—*Bufonidæ.*—Nectophryne tuberculosa; Bufo pulcher, hololius, beddomii, melanostictus [indian toad], microtympanum, parietalis.——(2) The following are the principal South indian species of the Ecaudata arranged alphabetically with a few particulars.—"*a*" Bufo melanostictus, bufonidæ [indian toad].—"*b*" Cacopus systoma, engystometidæ; color of the upper surface black or blackish brown with delicate primrose undulating marbling.—"*c*" Callula triangularis, engystomatidæ; a large triangular blackish spot occupying nearly the whole length of the backs.—"*d*" Ixalus glandulosus, ranidæ; a small tree frog, with very obtuse muzzle; green above, yellowish on the sides and limbs.—"*e*" Ixalus opisthorhodus, ranidæ; color of upper surface brown; under surface yellowish with mottlings; lower surface of hind limbs rose-colored; black band on each side of the head under each eye.—"*f*" Ixalus saxicola, ranidæ; dark olive green with dark marbling, and barred limbs.—"*g*" Ixalus signatus, ranidæ; a large x shaped marking on the back; generally greenish yellow on upper surface.—"*h*" Ixalus variabilis, ranidæ [tinkling frog]; color and marking subject to great variations; very difficult to capture.—"*i*" Microhyla rubra, engystomatidæ; found near rivers and sandy banks.—"*j*" Nectophryne tuberculosa, bufonidæ; skin of the upper parts tubercular.—"*k*" Rana breviceps, ranidæ; habit stout; head short; snout rounded; skin of upper parts smooth, greenish marbled with brown; with the aid of its shovel-like metatarsal tubercle it burrows in the ground.—"*l*" Rana curtipes, ranidæ; head and back bright buff above, sides deep maroon, legs dark purple with a few white spots, and abdomen white mottled.—"*m*" Ranacyanophlyctis, ranidæ; allied to hexadactyla, smaller.—"*n*" Rana diplosticta, ranidæ; pinkish olive colored, black spots on the sides; legs with dark cross-bars; abdomen light colored.—"*o*" Rana gracilis, ranidæ; allied to tigrina, but smaller size, greyish olive with large dark spots on the back and limbs; sometimes a triangular transverse spot between the eyes, with the point directed backwards; five broad short bands radiate from the orbit, forming two spots below the eye; uniform white below.—"*p*" Rana hexadactyla, ranidæ [tank frog].—"*q*" Rana rufescens, ranidæ; rufous color above whitish beneath; body rough and granulose; limbs barred; malabar coast.—"*r*" Rana tigrina, ranidæ [bull frog].—"*s*" Rana verrucosa, ranidæ; upper parts with prominent warts; malabar.—"*t*" Rhacophorus maculatus, ranidæ [choonam frog].—"*u*" Rhacophorus pleurostictus, ranidæ [tree frog]; variable in color.——**(3)** The following are the different batrachians distinguished by the natives.——*Bull frog* (वर्षाभू - varshábhú, San.; مینڈکا - mendká, Hind.; గోదురుకప్ప - góduru-kappa, Tel.; പേക്കൻ - pékkan, Mal.; மிடாத்தவளை - midát-tavalai, Tam.). San. from (varsha, san. rain + bhú, san. to be), produced in the rains. Tel. from (góda, tel. bull + kappa, tel. frog). Mal. from (bhéka, san. frog). Tam. from (midaru, tam. throat + tavalai, tam. frog). Rana tigrina, ranidæ, of naturalists. Alias Rana brama, cancrivora, crassa, latrans, mugiens, rugulosa, vittigera; Hoplobatrachus ceylanicus; Hydrostentor pantherinus; Pyxicephalus fodiens. Skin of the back with longitudinal folds; tympanum distinct, about two-thirds the size of the eye; lower jaw with two not very prominent apophyses in front; fourth toe one-third or one-half longer than the fifth; toes nearly entirely webbed, the web extending not quite to the tip of the fourth toe; a well-developed membranaceous fringe along the outer side of the fifth toe; a single small or large, blunt or shovel-shaped inner metatarsal tubercle. Color dark-brown above with large blackish spots. The males during the breeding season are pale greenish yellow with dark spots and a pale vertebral streak, and are smaller than the females which are greyish olive with dark spots. Its barking voice is familiar during the monsoon. This frog eats the smaller species.——*Choonam frog* (प्लव - plava, San.; اڑتی مینڈک - urtímendak, Hind.; ఉరుగుకప్ప - urugukappa, Tel.; ചൊറിത്തവള - choritta-vala, Mal.; சொறித்தவளை - shorittavalai, Tam.). San. from (plu, san. to fly). Hind. from (urtí, hind. flying + mendak, hind. frog). Tel. from (uruku, tel. to fly + kappa, tel. frog). Mal. from (chori, mal. scab + tavala, mal. frog). Tam. from (shori, tam. rough + tavalai, tam. frog). Otherwise Flying frog. Rhacophorus maculatus, ranidæ, of naturalists. Alias Burgeria maculata, Hyla leucomystax, maculata; Polypedates biscutiger, cruciger, leucomystax, maculatus, megacephalus, rugosus. Tympanum nearly as large as the eye; toes nearly entirely, fingers slightly webbed; discs of fingers and toes well-developed, about half the diameter of the tympanum; a single, small, inner metatarsal tubercle. Skin smooth above, strongly granular on the belly and under the thighs; a narrow fold above the tympanum. Coloration varies; the most constant markings are brownish cross-bars on the limbs, small, more or less distinct, round white or whitish spots on the hinder side of the thigh, and a more or less developed white streak on the upper lip. This species has the power of changing its colors; it is sometimes buff above, sometimes ashy-grey, chocolate-brown, tinged with rose or lilac, black spots being more or less visible. Frequently seen, adhering to vertical surface, walls and windows, by means of the discs on its fingers and toes.——*Indian toad* (स्थूलमण्डूक - st'húlamandúka, San.; دادر - dádur, Hind.; తలకప్ప - talakappa, Tel.; തേര - téra, Mal.; தேரை - térai, Tam.). San. from (st'húla, san. large + mandúka, san. frog). Hind. from (dardura, san. rain cloud). Tel. from (tala, tel. head + kappa, tel. frog). Bufo melanostictus, bufonidæ, of naturalists. Alias Bufo bengalensis, carinatus, dubia, gymnauchen, isos, scaber, spinipes; Phrynoidis melanostictus. Head with more or less elevated bony ridges; tympanum at least two-thirds the width of the eye; first finger generally extending beyond second; toes at least half-webbed; two moderate metatarsal tubercles. Upper surfaces with more or less prominent, generally spiny warts; parotoids very prominent, kidney-shaped or elliptic, more or less elongate. Color and markings yellowish or brownish above, the spines of the warts and the ridges of the head generally black; beneath immaculate or more or less spotted. Makes a chirping sound and sometimes a shrill whistle.——*Tank frog* (मण्डूक - mandúka, San.; مینڈکی - mendkí, Hind.; కప్ప - kappa, Tel.; തവള - tavala, Mal.; தவளை - tavalai. Tam.). Hind. is diminutive of (mendká). Tam. from (távu, tam, to leap). Otherwise common frog. Rana hexadactyla, ranidæ, of naturalists. Alias Dactylethra bengalensis; Rana cutipora, robusta. Skin smooth, with rows of pore round the neck, sides, and belly; toes and fingers pointed, the first finger extending a little beyond the second; toes webbed to the tips; fourth toe not very much longer than third and fifth; a membranaceous fringe along the margins of the first and fifth toes; metatarsus with a single small inner conical tubercle. Color generally bright grass-green, rapidly changing in spirit to chocolate brown, with a central green or yellow stripe, vertebral line, along the middle of the back, but the presence of this stripe is not constant. Very common in tanks and along the banks of rivers.——*Tinkling frog* (हरि - hari, San.; هری مینڈک - harímendak, Hind.; బొంతకప్ప - bontakappa, Tel.; പച്ചത്തവള - paççattavala, Mal.; பச்சைத்தவளை - paççaittavalai, Tam.). San. means green. Hind. from (harí, hind. green + mendak, hind. frog). Tel. from (bonta, tel. large + kappa, tel. frog). Tam. from (paççai, tam. green + tavalai, tam. frog). Ixalus variabilis, ranidæ, of naturalists. Tongue without a papilla; snout rounded; tympanum indistinct, about half the width of the eye; fingers very slightly, toes two-thirds webbed; discs moderate; a small inner metatarsal tubercle; skin smooth above, granular beneath; color and markings subject to great variations, the upper surface being bluish, greenish, brownish or blackish, uniform, or variously spotted or speckled with darker or lighter; Neilgherries; found in grass and among bushes; peculiar loud clear metallic tinkling call; natives say that it is a ventriloquist.——*Tree frog* (మంటికప్ప - mantikappa, Tel.; മരത്തവള - marattavala, Mal.; மணற்றவளை - manattavalai, Tam.). Tel. from (mannu, tel. mud + kappa, tel. frog). Mal. means tree + frog. Tam. from (manal, tam. sand + tavalai, tam. frog). Otherwise Green frog, Mud-frog. Rhacophorus pleurostictus, ranidæ, of naturalists. Alias Polypedates pleurostictus. Tympanum small, indistinct, not quite one-third the width of the eye, fingers very distinctly webbed at the base; discs well-developed; toes broadly webbed, the interdigital membrane extending to the discs of the third and fifth toes; metatarsus with a single tubercle; very variable in color; sometimes unspotted, at other times with gold spots or blackish spots; at times golden-yellow with brown spots; at other times brown with darker spots; banks of streams and in shrubs.——**(4)** For insects see poochy; for fishes see matsyam; for reptiles see sarpy; for birds see pacshy; for mammals see sastanam. A general conspectus of the fauna of s. india is given in vol. II, appendix IV.

BHAIDAM (भेद - bhéda, *San.*). From (bhid, san. to break); difference. In natural history a species. For category, see Padaurtam; for elementary substance, see Dravyam; for matter, see Bhootam; for organic and inorganic, see Indriyam and Anindriyam; for organic kingdom, see Ganam [jantoo, vricsham]; for organic class, see Vargam; for organic order, see Santaunam; for organic family, see Coolam; for organic genus, see Jauty; organic species is the present word. Oopa prefixed to either of the above means a sub-head. For inorganic minerals, see Dhautoo.

BHAM (भ - bha, *San.*). From (bhá, san. to shine). Star; planet.——*Bhaganam* (भगण - bhagana, San.). From (above + gana, san. group). Group of stars and planets. Revolution of planets in the zodiac or the period during which a planet moves from the first point of Ashwiny to the last point of Raivaty. It is shorter or longer as the orbit is small or large. Chundran or moon which has the smallest orbit takes twenty-seven days to complete a revolution; while Shany or Saturn which has the largest orbit takes thirty years for one revolution. Boodhan, Shoocran and Sooryan take one year; Angauracan, a year and a-half; Gooroo, twelve years. Any great circle in astronomy divided into twelve raushies or signs and sub-divided at each step sexagesimally into bhaugams, calays, vicalays, &c., i.e., degrees, minutes, seconds, &c. [jyotisham].——*Bhamundalam* (भमण्डल - bhamandala, San.). Means starry circle, as opposed to terrestrial globe. Also zodiac, solar or lunar; for the former cf. Raushy [jyotisham].——*Bhascaracharry* (भास्कराचार्य - bháskarácharya, San.). From (bháskara, san. sun, the light-maker, proper name + áchárya, san. preceptor). Last of the celebrated astronomers and mathematicians [siddhauntam]. Lived at Beedar. Author of Beeja ganitam on arithmetic, Leelauvaty on algebra, and Siddhaunta shiromany on astronomy. Knew principle of differential calculus.——*Bhascaran* (भास्कर - bháskara, San.). Light-giver; sun.——*Bhascara saptamy* (భాస్కరసప్తమి - bháskarasaptami, Tel.). Means sun + the seventh day of lunar fortnight. Same as Rata saptamy.——*Bhaunoo* (भानु - bhánu, San.). The sun. Hindoo 2nd or pers. name; applied to males and females. Bhaunmoorty, or sun-deity [moorty] is common [peyar].——*Bhaunoovidiya* (భానువిదియ - bhánuvidiya, Tel.). Means sun + the second day of the lunar fortnight. Lunar festival [pundigay, 3a], subject to intercalation. A feast held in the first lunar month Cheitram [mausam] between 15th March and 14th April in honor of sun.

BHANDAURA (ಭಂಡಾರ - bhandára, *Can.*). Treasury.——*Bhandaury* (ಭಂಡಾರಿ - bhandári, Can.). From above. Title among Bunts. Hindoo third name [peyar].

BHANG (भङ्गा - bhangá, *San.*; قنب - kinnab, *Ar.*; بنگ - bang, *Pers.*; بھنگ - bhang, *Hind.*; ಭಂಗಿ - bhangi, *Can.*; బంగి - bangi, *Tel.*; കഞ്ചാവില - kañchávila, *Mal.*; பங்கி - pangi, *Tam.*). San. from (bhanj, san. to break). Pers. and hind. from sanscrit. Mal. means ganjah leaf. Tam. from sanscrit. The dried leaves of the Cannabis sativa, linn. [kinnab]. Thence made drink of same name; plant with female flowers only used for this purpose; chiefly drunk by Mahomedans. The following is a recipe:—Take of hemp leaves, washed in water, one tolah or three drams, black pepper four annas' weight or forty-five grains, cloves, nutmeg and mace, of each one anna or eleven and one-fourth grains weight; triturate the leaves and other ingredients with one pow or eight ounces of water, milk, or the juice of water-melon seed, or cucumber seed, strain and drink the liquor. It is usually employed without the spices; the latter rendering it highly inebriating. Bhang is cheaper than ganjah [q.v.] and though less powerful is sold at such a low price that for one pice enough can be purchased to intoxicate a habituated person [mooskiraut, sharaub].——*Slow bhang* (بجر بهانگ - bajarbháng, Hind.). Tobacco.

BHANGRAH (केशराज - késharája, *San.*; माका - máká, *Mahr.*; काजलमावु - kájalamávu, *Conc.*; بهرنگراج - bharangráj, *Hind.*; بهنگرا - bhangrá, *Dec.*; ಕಾಡಿಗೆಗರುಗ - kádigegaruga, *Can.*; గుంటగలిజేరు - guntagalijéru, *Tel.*; କେସରଡା - kesardá, *Oor.*; കഞ്ഞുണ്ണി - kaññunni, *Mal.*; කීකිරිඳිය - kíkirindiya, *Singh.*; கரிசலாங்கண்ணி - karisalánganni, *Tam.*). Title from deccany. San. from (késha, san. lock of hair + ráj, san. to shine), from giving hair a glossy appearance. Conc. from (kájala, mahr. lamp-black); from dark stain of juice. Hind. and dec. from (bhringarája, san. the plant). Can. from (kádige, can. collyrium + garuga, can. the plant). Tel. from (gunta, tel. pond + galijéru, tel. trianthema decandra, linn.). Mal. from tamul. Tam. from (karisal, tam. blackness + á, tam. to become + kan, tam. eye), from blackening hair. San. also (bhringarája), meaning shining like bees; (suparna), meaning beautiful-leaved; (márkava), meaning useful in medicinal mixture. Hind. also (keshúriyá); (mochkand); (babri). Can. also (garuga); (ajágaragida), meaning not + wakeful + plant, hence causing sleep. Tel. also (guntakalagara), meaning pond + the plant; (galagara). Mal. also (kalaññiyam); (karishánkanni); (kayyenni); (kaiyántakara), meaning hand + cassia tora, linn. Tam. also (arubatham); (kaiyándagarai), meaning smallness + to become + the plant, cassia tora, linn.; (shárutbári); (kaigési); (kaivísi); (karippán), meaning that which is black, from dark juice; (shirugarisalánganni), meaning small + the plant. Title otherwise Bee plant, Eclipse plant. Botanically Eclipta alba, hassk., compositæ [vricsham, 74]. Alias Eclipta adpressa, dentata, erecta, parviflora, prostata; Micrelium asteroides; Rotula alba; Verbesina alba. Herbaceous; stem prostrate or erect; leaves lanceolate, serrate, somewhat waved; flowers nearly sessile, alternate in pairs; corolla white; in grassy, damp, or clayey soils. Whole plant alterative, tonic, cholagogue, purgative and diuretic; in paste with sesamum oil [gingelly] is local remedy in elephantiasis; substituted for british taraxacum in liver cases; root in pharm., but not officinal. No other common species here.——*Yellow bhangrah* (भृंगराज - bhringarája, San.; पिवळाभांगरा - pivalábhángará, Mahr.; پیلا بهنگرا - pílábhangrá, Hind. and Dec.; ಗರ್ಗರಿ - gargari, Can.; పసుపుగుంటగలిజేరు - pasupulaguntagalijéru, Tel.; പൊക്കയ്യണ്ണി - pókkayyanni, Mal.; பொற்றலைக் கையாந்தகரை - pottalaikkaiyándagarai, Tam.). Title from color of flowers. San. from (bhringa, san. beetle + ráj, san. to shine). Mahr. from (pivalá, mahr. yellow + bhángara, mahr. eclipta alba, hassk.). Hind. from (pílá, hind. yellow + bhangrá, hind. eclipta alba, hassk.). Tel. from (pasupu, tel. turmeric, curcuma longa, rox. + guntagalijéru, tel. eclipta alba, hassk.). Mal. from (pé, mal. devil + kayyanni, mal. the plant, eclipta alba, hassk.). Tam. from (pon, tam. gold + talai, tam. head + kaiyándagarai, tam. eclipta alba, hassk.). San. also (pítabhringi), meaning yellow eclipta alba, hassk. Mahr. also (pivalámaka), meaning yellow eclipta. Hind. also (bhánrá), meaning eclipta alba, hassk. Mal. also (ponnirakkayyanni), meaning golden colored eclipta alba, hassk. Tam. also (athigumbai), eclipta. Title otherwise Ceylon verbesina, Mary-gold verbesina. Botanically Wedelia calendulacea, less., compositæ [vricsham, 74]. Alias Jægreia calendulaceæ; Polymania benghalensis; Verbesina benghalensis, calendulacea; Wedelia benghalensis. Perennial, herbaceous, creeping; leaves opposite, broad-lanceolate, obtuse, entire; peduncles axillary; flowers bright yellow; has a slightly terebinthinaceous smell and camphoraceous taste. Leaves tonic, alterative; juice of leaves used as a snuff in cephalalgia. Leaves used in dyeing grey hair. There are other species:—biflora, urticæfolia.

BHARAM (भर - bhara, San.). From (bhri, san. to bear). Support.——*Bharany* (ഭരണി - bharani, Mal.). Means nourishing; name of the second lunar asterism. Also called Cock feast. Luni-solar festival [pundigay, 5c] held when the moon is in the constellation Bharany in twelfth solar month Meenam [mausam], i.e., between March 12th and April 11th. Popular feast in Malabar. Especially celebrated in Cranganore at the Bhagavaty temple. Cocks are slaughtered and sacrificed. All castes including low caste-people are free to go to the temple on this day. It corresponds to Holy festival in Bengal and Cauman pundigay in Tamul countries.——*Bharany deepam* (భరణిదీపం - bharanidípam, Tel.; பரணிதீபம் - paranithíbam, Tam.). Means the second nacshatram + lamp. Luni-solar festival [pundigay, 6d]. The day when the moon is in the asterism Bharany in the waxing moon of eighth solar month Caurtigay [mausam], i.e., between 15th November and 13th December. A feast of lights in honor of Vishnoo. This is just before Caurtigay deepam. No connection with Malabar bharany.——*Bharatan* (भरत - bharata, San.). From (bhri, san. to support). Aryan ruler, son of Dooshyantan by Shacoontalay. The legend of his birth forms the ground-work of Calidass's drama, Shacoontalay or the Lost ring. But there are several others of this name [bhauratam].——*Bharnam* (భరణము - bharanamu, Tel.). From (bhara, san. support).—"*a*" Measure of capacity in Ganjam. 4 poottics = 1 bharnam; 7½ bharnams = 1 garce [alavay, 3]. Approximate actual value, 1 bharnam = 18,200 cubic inches. Compare Colagam of Bellary.—"*b*" Superficial measure from seed measurement, in Ganjam. 20 nowts = 1 bharnam; 7½ bharnams = 1 garce [alavay, 2]. Approximate actual value, 1 bharnam = ½ acre. Wet bharnam is 50 coontas or 8,450 square feet, dry bharnam is 100 coontas or 16,900 square feet. See vol. I, 615; II, 510.

BHATT (भट्ट - bhatta, *San.*; بهٹ - bhat, *Hind.*). From (bhat, san. to nourish). Learned Bramin. Also simply a Hindoo third name. Common title of Mahratta bramins [poyar]. Also a caste-title, hereditary bards. Causby bhatt, from (káse, tel. working in stone) are stone masons.——*Bhattatiry* (ഭട്ടതിരി - bhattatri, Mal.). From (above + tiri, mal. holy, a title). The highest class of Kerala bramins, vulgarly known as Pattairy. Teachers of philosophy. A title of Vishishta bramins on W. coast.——*Bhattavritty* (भट्टवृत्ति - bhattavritti, San.). From (above + vrit, san. to live). An assignment of revenue or lands granted to Bramins at a low rent, or rent-free, for their subsistence; the lands in such case being mostly held in severalty [inam]. See vol. I, 112.

BHATTA (ಬತ್ತ - batta, *Can.*). From (bhakta, san. boiled rice). Rice before it is deprived of the chaff; paddy, which is probably derived from this word.

BHATTY (ಭಟ್ಟಿ - bhatti, *Can.*). A still. Bhattisoonka, from (sunka, can. tax) is still-head duty.

BHAUGAM (भाग - bhága, *San.*). From (bhaj, san. to divide).—"*a*" Partition. Condition of coparcenary among Hindoos [avibhactam] may be broken up under certain circumstances by partition of the joint property, each co-heir taking his appointed share. The effect of such division is to vest the divided share absolutely in each separate member and in his line after him. Sons may, at their will and irrespective of all circumstances, compel their father to divide with them the ancestral property. Sons who have demised being represented by their sons or grandsons, the latter also may force on such division. Should the father have become a devotee he is considered civilly dead, and the sons may proceed to division without him. His degradation from caste would operate according to Hindoo law in the same way, but the legislature have ruled that this circumstance shall not interfere with an individual's rights in property. The property of Nayar, that is to say Shoodra families on the West coast, who are subject to the Aliya santauna or Maroomakkatoyem laws of inheritance, is in the primitive condition and admits of no partition. The following descriptions of property, besides self-acquired property, are not subject to partition:—Lands endowed for religious purposes, and all things destined to religious uses. Regalities and ancient zemindarries which have vested in the eldest son. Land specially granted so as to maintain the rank and dignity of a family. Zemindarries held under grant from the ruling government and renewed to the eldest son. Self-acquired property created by a father while divided from his sons, should there be sons born after the division this vesting in the latter. Nuptial gifts received by a man with his wife, even although such come out of the joint property. Clothes and jewels habitually worn and which belong exclusively to the wearer. Dues attached to the office of a curnum, notwithstanding that the office itself may be ancestral. For inheritance see Dauyam [maryauday].—"*b*" Degree. In astronomy an arc equal to the one-three hundred and sixtieth part of the circumference of a circle, or one-thirtieth of a raushy. Fraction; numerator of a fraction. Bhauga anoobandham is an infinite series [jyotisham].—"*c*" Portion; suffix in place names, as Mettbhaugam, meaning rising ground + portion.——*Bhaujak* (भाजक - bhájaka, San.). From (bhaj, san. to divide). Divisor in arithmetic. Also called Haram.——*Bhaujyam* (भाज्य - bhájya, San.). From (bhaj, san. to divide). Dividend in arithmetic.

BHAUNCOTE (భానుకోట - bhánukóta, *Tel.*). From (bána, san. the asura + kóta, san. fort). Range of hills; Cuddapah dist., Poolivendla and Jummalmudoogoo tals.; lat. 14° 41′; long. 78° 16′; from Cuddapah W.N.W. 41 miles; from Poolivendla N. 18 miles. The village is sacred. Temple, to which pilgrimages are made in Caurtigay [mausam] or November. Ruins of a fort. The range separates Poolivendla from Jummalmudoogoo. It is altogether denuded.

BHAURAM (भार - bhára, *San.*; பாரம் - páram, *Tam.*). From (bhri, san to bear). A weight equal to 20 maunds [niray, 2]. Approximate actual value, 1 bhauram = 500 lbs. avoirdupois. Same as Can. bauroo, Hind. candy, Tel. pootty of Ganjam and Vizagapatam. See vol. I, 609; II, 506–520.

BHAURATAM (भारत - bhárata, *San.*). From (bharata, san. the king so called). Short term for Mahabhaurat. Bhaurata champoo, from (champu, san. work consisting of prose and verse) is the story in prose and verse by Ananta bhattan, modern, but favorite. Bhaurata tautparya nirnayam, from (tátparya, san. purport + nirnaya, san. settlement) is a verse summary by

Ananta teertan, with reference to his own doctrines. Bhaurata vilausam, from (vilása, san. play) is a modern drama by Ramachendra cavy royan of Madras.——*Bhaurata varsham* (भारतवर्ष - b'háratavarsha, San.). From (above + varsha, san. division). Northern india, as having been the kingdom of Bharatan, son of Rishabhan. It was divided into nine khandams; Casheroomat, Coomauricam, Gabhastimat, Gandharvam, Indra dweepam, Nauga dweepam, Sowmyam, Tamravurnam, Vauroonam. Cannot be satisfactorily identified. It did not include the peninsula south of the Vindhya range [aryavartam]. See vol. I (3) [charitram].

BHAURGAM (भार्ग - bhárga, *San.*; ತಗ್ಗಿಮರ - taggimara, *Can.*; భారంగి - bhárangi, *Tel.*). From (bharga, san. radiance); from curing efficacy. San. also (hañjiká), meaning killer, as an anthelmintic. Tel. also (brahmichettu), meaning bramha's tree, from ashy white bark; (chiritéku), meaning small + teak tree, tectona grandis, linn. Glory-tree. Botanically the Clerodendron genus, verbenaceæ [vricsham, 102]. Trees or shrubs sometimes rambling; leaves opposite, simple, occasionally lobed; cymes in axillary or terminal panicles, often leafy below; drupe globose, succulent; seeds oblong. The species best known to the natives are:—inerme [sangcooppy], infortunatum [saraswaty's leaf], phlomoides [tirootauly], serratum [knotted bhraungy], siphonanthus [bhraungy]. Other s. indian species indigenous or naturalized are:—Fragrans, flowers double, fragrant, leaves fœtid when bruised; Hastatum; Nutans, flowers white, drooping; Squamatum, flowers brilliant scarlet.

BHAUSH (भाष् - bhásh, *San.*). To speak.——*Bhaushay* (भाषा - bháshá, San.; மொழி - mozhi, Tam.). Language. Tamulians say that eighteen languages only have been granted by the deity:—Angam or that of bengal proper, Aroonam or that of agra, Calingam or telinga that of northern circars, Caumbojam or that of cambojam in north of india, Cheenam or chinese, Conganam or that of concan, Cosalam or that of oude, Cowshicam or that of cutch, Dravidam or tamul and its cognate languages, Magadham or that of maghada south of behar, Maraudam or mahratta, Papparam or goozeratty, Shauvagam or javanese, Shimhalam or singhalese, Sindhoo or sind, Shonacam or hindostany, Tooloovam or that of country between concan and canara, and Vangam or e. bengalee. See vol. I (38) to (61), and the following foot-notes:—dravidian conspectus I (38), morphological stages I (39), comp. with indo european I (40), comp. with turanian I (41), vocabulary I (41), history I (42), written characters I (46), existing languages in plains I (50), existing languages of hills I (51), tamul analysed, I, 52, tamul geographical names I (54), dravidian literature I (56); kolarian conspectus I (38), structure I (59), existing languages I (59); ooriyah particulars I (59); hindostany account I, 60; specimens of characters II, 177, statistics II, 183, anglo-indian spelling II, 185, new spelling II, 187-191, dravidian vocabulary II, 193, kolarian vocabulary II, 203, orthography of tamul II, 205, letter ழ II, 209, tamul topography II, 211-218.——*Bhaushicam* (பாஷிகம் - pásigam, Tam.). Means commentary on Vedas. Hindoo 2nd or pers. name. Common among Madhwas and Veishnavas. Teloogoo form is Bhaushyam [peyar].

BHAUVY (वापि - vápi, *San.*; ಭಾವಿ - bhávi, *Can.*; బావి - bávi, *Tel.*; வாவி - vávi, *Tam.*). Well with a flight of steps leading down to the water. Suffix in place names, as Cullbhauvy, meaning stone + well. There is a Canarese proverb:—ಮಾಡಿದ ಪಾಪಕ್ಕೆ ಮನವೇ ಸಾಕ್ಷಿ, ತೋಡಿದ ಭಾವಿಗೆ ಜಲವೇ ಸಾಕ್ಷಿ—"Conscience is "the witness of sins committed, and water is evidence of "the dug-up well."

BHAVAM (भव - bhava, *San.*). From (bhú, san. to be). Being. Bhavan is a name of Shiva. Bhavabooty was the dramatist at Court of Bhoja rajah of Oojjein, considered second only to Calidass. See also Bhawauny.——*Bhavanty* (భవంతి - bhavanti, Tel.). From (bhavana, san. house). A house built square with chamber in each corner; the middle being an area.——*Bhavanty roomaul* (భవంతిరుమాలు - bhavantirumálu, Tel.). From (above + rúmál, pers. handkerchief). Handkerchief with flower patterns in each corner.

BHAWAUNY (भवानी - bhavání, *San.* bhaváni *). A name of Parvaty as wife of Bhavan [bhavam].——**(1)** Ἥρα of Greeks, Juno of Romans, Isis of Egyptians. Hindoo 2nd or pers. name. Common to both sexes [peyer]. Similar is Bhawaunishuncar, Parvaty and Shiva combined [ardhanaury].——**(2)** Talook, Coimbatore district, Tahsildar's pay Rs. 150. Area 715 square miles. In N.E. corner of district, Population 119,869. Languages Tamul and Canarese. Bounded E. and N. by Cauvery; N.W. and W. by Burgoor hills; W. by Suttimungalam talook; S. by Erode talook. Cauverypooram pass, principal route from Mysore, formerly passed through talook. Burgoor ghaut route still takes some portion of foot and bullock traffic. Talook extremely hilly, and practically unexplored. Paulamullay and Burgoor hills are chief ranges, and Oorautchicottah hill is a striking feature from sharp conical shape. Climate feverish and hot in the plains, and the hills are not above fever range. The talook shares in both monsoons, but, except on and near the hills, general rainfall in S.W. monsoon is not so good in the interior as at Bhawauny town. The forests are on an imposing scale, and one object of Burgoor ghaut was opening up of hills for timber. Bison are common on hills, and this talook and Suttimungalam are the special home of the elephant. Rocks are gneissose, intersected by veins of quartz and in places covered by masses of once fluid limestone. Soils that are the product of these rocks are in general poor, much of the clay from the felspathic portion of the gneiss having been washed down to other districts; seven-eighths of the soils are red, above three-fourths being red sand or gravel. Pasture is abundant and cattle numerous and fairly good. The Burgoor breed partakes of Mysore characteristics and is well known. There is a moderate trade in forest produce, and Auvauray bark is largely collected and exported for tanning. Cotton carpets are well woven and dyed at Bhawauny, the Cauvery water being specially valuable in fixing. Other manufactures are gunny, common country cloths and wares. The drainage is to the Cauvery either direct or by the Bhawauny on the south. The Aupacoodal chain of tanks runs from the hills in the north to the Bhawauny on the south. Except one tank in Moogausipoothore, supplied by drainage water from the Attavanaipoothore channel, the whole irrigation is from rain-fed tanks, chiefly in the Aupacoodal series. The tanks receive no supply till N.E. monsoon. Yennamungalam is a large tank. There are several ruined tanks and old anicuts over jungle streams. There has been a project for extending Cauvery irrigation by the Nerinjipett anicut an ancient native structure which used to irrigate land on both sides of the Cauvery, but which breached in the eighteenth century. Places of archæological interest:—Andiyore, Aupacoodal, Bhawauny, Cauverypooram, Jambay, Paulamullay, Shaumpully. Principal trig. stations:—Bodamullay, Oorautchimullay, Paulamullay. The leading places, &c., in the talook are the following.——*Andiyore* (அந்தியூர் - andiyúr, Tam.). From (andi, tam. the place where three ways meet + úr, tam. village). Village; pop. 7,647; acres 7,507; lat. 11° 35′; long. 77° 38′; from Bhawauny N.W. 11½ miles; from Coimbatore N.E. 58 miles. Near foot of Burgoor ghaut. Bhawauny talook formerly took name from this village. Old fort. Shiva temple finely sculptured with inscriptions. Busy place with weekly market.——*Bhawauny* (பவானி - paváni, Tam.). See below.——*Bodamullay* (போதமலை - póthamalai, Tam.). From (bódha, san. wise man + malai, tam. mountain). Trig. station; lat. 11° 54′ 53·79″; long. 77° 35′ 48·32″; height 4,034 feet; from Bhawauny N.N.W. 33 miles; from Nadoocauvalchuttram W.S.W. 3½ miles.——*Burgoor* (பருக்கூர் - parukkúr, Tam.). See sep. title.——*Cauvery* (காவேரி - kávéri, Tam.). See sep. title.——*Cauverypooram* (காவேரிப்புரம் - kávérippuram, Tam.). See sep. title.——*Gowndapaudy* (கவுண்டப்பாடி - kavundappádi, Tam.). From (kavundan, tam. one of that caste + pádi, tam. village). Village; pop. 5,443; acres 5,433; lat. 11° 26′; long. 77° 36′; from Bhawauny W. 8½ miles; from Coimbatore N.E. 50 miles. Weekly market.——*Moyaur* (மொய்யாறு - moyyáru, Tam.). See sep. title.——*Mylambaudy* (மைலம்பாடி - mailambádi, Tam.). From (mayil, tam. peacock + pádi, tam. village). Village; pop. 2,986; acres 5,260; lat. 11° 31′; long. 77° 42′; from Bhawauny N.N.W. 5¾ miles; from Coimbatore N.E. 59 miles. Weekly market.——*Nerinjipett* (நெரிஞ்சிப்பேட்டை - neriñjippéttai, Tam.). From (nerińji, tam. tribulus terrestris, linn. + péttai, tam. suburb). Village; pop. 1,045; acres 1,756; lat. 11° 40′; long. 77° 48′; from Bhawauny N.N.E. 16 miles; from Coimbatore N.E. 70 miles. Site of stone anicut across Cauvery, proposed to reconstruct [paulamullay].——*Oorautchimullay* (ஊராச்சிமலை - úráççimalai, Tam.). From (úr, tam. village + ádchi, tam. possession + malai, tam. mountain). Means the hill owned by the village. Sanscrit name (védagiri), meaning sacred writing + hill. Village, Hill; pop. 485; acres 561; lat. 11° 29′; long. 77° 44′; from Bhawauny N.N.E. 2½ miles; from Coimbatore N.E. 60 miles. Temple on the hill. Trig. station; lat. 11° 28′ 33·80″; long. 77° 43′ 56·90″; height 1,437 feet; from Bhawauny N.N.E. 2½ miles; from Oorautchicottah village S.W. ½ mile.——*Paulamullay* (பாலமலை - pálamalai, Tam.). From (pálai, tam. ironwood tree, mimusops hexandra, roxb. + malai, tam. mountain). Trig. station; lat. 11° 41′ 30·39″; long. 77° 46′ 36·86″; height 4,924 feet; from Bhawauny N.N.E. 17 miles; from Nerinjipett N.N.W. 3 miles.——*Shaumpully* (சாம்பள்ளி - shámballi, Tam.). From (shámai, tam. millet, panicum miliare, lam. + palli, tam. village). Sanscrit name (sámbapura), meaning shiva + town. Village; pop. 2,698; acres 4,155; lat. 11° 50′; long. 77° 51′; from Bhawauny N.N.E. 28 miles; from Coimbatore N.E. 81 miles. Fort and old Shiva temple. Weekly market.——**(3)** Town, Talook head-quarters; Coimbatore dist., Bhawauny tal.; pop. 7,341; acres 5,038; lat. 11° 27′; long. 77° 43′; from Coimbatore E.N.E. 58 miles; from Erode N.N.W. 8 miles; from Madras W.S.W. 206 miles; from Ootacamund E. 65 miles; from Pollachy N.E. 71 miles; from Suttimungalam E. 30 miles. Also called Bhawauny coodal, being at junction of the Cauvery and Bhawauny. Chiefly inhabited by Bramins attached to temple. District head-quarters until 1805. Well-sculptured ancient Shiva temple of Sangameshwaran, bathing ghauts occupying extreme point of rock. Pilgrims in November. Ruined fort built by the poligar, who once held it under Madura. Both rivers crossed by fine masonry bridges. The bridge over Cauvery was completed in 1847, and immediately afterwards destroyed by freshes. It was rebuilt with twenty-six spans and again opened for traffic in 1851. Eight roads converge here, viz., the main roads to Salem, Coimbatore, Shunkerrydroog, and Suttimungalam; Hassanore ghaut and Burgoor ghaut roads; and the roads to Erode and Gowndapaudy. Good cotton cloths and carpets.——**(4)** River; Neilgherry, Coimbatore district, Bhawauny, Suttimungalam talooks. Perennial river. Rises in southern spurs of Coondahs about lat. 11° 15′; long. 76° 4′. First skirts S. base of Neilgherry hills, but diverges as it approaches Hoolicull droog, so that it is five miles from the base of the Coonoor ghaut at Mettapolliem, where it is 1,000 feet above sea. It receives Coondah and Coonoor rivers from S. and E. of Neilgherry, as well as from Malabar district. It enters low country in lat. 11° 9′; long. 76° 37′. At the Mailore or Shoondaputty ghaut it receives a considerable tributary and swells into a large stream. After a winding course eastward of 105 miles, during which it traverses Suttimungalam and Bhawauny talooks and receives several affluents, the Moyaur at Danaickencottah and the Noyil being the chief, it joins the Cauvery at Bhawauny town. It yields the channels, Arcancottah and Tadapully for Suttimungalam talook and Calingaroyan for Erode talook. The chief places on or near its banks are Mettapolliem, Danaickencottah, Suttimungalam, Gopichettipolliem, and Bhawauny. Fed principally by S.W. monsoon, and consequently receives its first freshes about the end of May; is at its highest from June to August, and thenceforward, with occasional floods in the north-east monsoon, gradually subsides throughout the hot weather. Fish abound but its waters are not considered wholesome by the natives. Its bed is granitic. The banks are finely wooded in places, and there are many islands in its course. At Mettapolliem it is crossed by a good masonry bridge.

BHEE (भी - bhí, *San.*). Fear.——*Bheeman* (भीम - bhíma, San.). Terrible. Ajax of Hindoos. Also called Bheemasainan or terrible warrior; also Vrikodaran signifying wolf-bellied, from his being a great eater. Second of the Pandava dynasty and its principal general. Killed Dooryodhanan, head of the Cooroos, in the war of Mahabhaurat. Vol. I (58), (79). Hindoo 2nd or pers. name, especially with Madhwas.——*Bheema rautry* (भीमरात्रि - bhímarátri, San.). Means Bheeman, the hero + night [pundigay, 6a]. The seventh night of the seventh month of the seventy-seventh year of a man's age, after which a person is exempt from all instituted observances, it being considered the end of his natural life.——*Bheemeshwaram* (भीमेश्वर - bhíméshvara, San.). From (above + íshvara, san. god). One of the twelve great lingams enumerated in the Kedaura calpam of the Nundy oopapooraunam. Worshipped at Draucsharaumam in the Godavery district. See vol. I (88).——*Bheeshanan* (भीषण - bhíshana, San.). Literally frightful, a form of Shiva.——*Bheeshman* (भीष्म - bhíshma, San.). A Cowrava chief and commander of Dooryodhanan's army on the first day of the combat, in Mahabhaurat.——*Bheeshma yecaudashy* (భీష్మ ఏకాదశి - bhíshmaékádashi, Tel.). From (bhíshma, san. terrible, the leader of the kurus + ékádashí, san. eleventh day). Lunar festival [pundigay, 3a] subject to intercalation. The eleventh day of waxing moon of eleventh lunar month Maugham [mausam] between 24th January and 23rd February. Fast day in honor of Bheeman. Ceremonies performed with til or sesamum.

BHEEMAVARAM (భీమవరము - bhímavaramu, *Tel.* bhímavaram*). From (bhíma, san. one of the five pándavas + pura, san. town). Sanscrit name (bhímapura), meaning same; (bhíméshvara), meaning shiva, the terrible + lord.——**(1)** Talook, Godavery district. Tahsildar's pay Rs. 175. Area 321 square miles. Population 121,994. Language Teloogoo. S. inland part of district. Bounded north by Tanookoo talook; south and east by Narsapore talook; west by Colair lake and Goodivauda talook of Kistna district. Whole surface is flat. Numerous channels intersect it in all directions. Soil is of five different kinds; permanently improved, regar pure, regar loamy, regar sandy, and alluvial. Principal products are white paddy, gingelly-oil seed, horse gram, and raggy. Woollen blankets manufactured in Chaunamilly, Cherkoomilly, Goomlore, Oondy and Yanikepully. Trade consists chiefly in paddy, taken in large quantities to Cocanada, Masulipatam, Narsapore and Rajahmundry for sale. Well supplied with means of irrigation. Principal canals are those of Aucveed, Chinnacaupooram, Gostanuddy and Oondy. Zemindarry:—Conitivauda. Places of archæological interest:—Ajjamore, Andalore, Ardhavaram, Aucveed, Bheemavaram, Chintaparroo, Commoochikkala, Coomoodavully, Cooppanapoody, Crovvidy, Dharmapooram, Doompagadapa agrahauram, Ganapavaram, Goomlore, Goonpoody, Keshavaram, Madivauda, Mogull, Nidamarroo, Nindracolan, Ooppooloor, Paulcodair, Paunuoova, Pedda caupavaram, Peddamiram, Pedda ramchandrapooram, Royacoodore, Veeravausaram, Vencataupooram, Yeloorpaud. The leading places, &c., in the talook are the following.——*Aucveed* (ఆకువీడు - ákuvídu, Tel.). From (áku, tel. leaf + vídu, tel. town). Village, canal; pop. 3,084; acres 2,785; lat. 16° 35′; long. 81° 25′; from Bheemavaram W.N.W. 10 miles; from Cocanada W.S.W. 62 miles; from Veeravausaram W.N.W. 17 miles. Two temples, 400 years old, and an older temple of a village goddess. In Bheemeshwara swamy temple are stone sculptures.——*Baharjully* (బహార్జల్లి - baharjalli, Tel.). See sep. title.——*Bheemavaram* (భీమవరము - bhímavaramu, Tel.). See below.——*Bondaudu* (బొండాడ - bondáda, Tel.). From (banda, tel. rock + váda, tel. village). Village; pop. 2,981; acres 6,085; lat. 16° 32′; long. 81° 30′; from Bheemavaram W. 4½ miles; from Cocanada W.S.W. 58 miles; from Veeravausaram W. 11 miles. Estate of this name was resumed in 1864 owing to arrears of revenue.——*Conitivauda* (కొణితివాడ - konitiváda, Tel.). From (kaniti, tel. elk + váda, tel. place). Zemindarry village; pop. 2,084; acres 1,767; lat. of village 16° 35′; long. 81° 42′; from Bheemavaram E.N.E. 10 miles; from Cocanada W.S.W. 45 miles; from Veeravausaram N.N.E. 5 miles. Peshcush Rs. 1,996.——*Crovvidy* (క్రొవ్విడి - krovvidi, Tel.). From (krotta, tel. new + vídu, tel. town). Zemindarry village; pop. 633; acres 1,336; lat. of village 16° 40′; long. 81° 29′; from Bheemavaram N.N.W. 10 miles; from Cocanada W.S.W. 56 miles; from Veeravausaram N.W. 14 miles. Mosque 300 years old, built by a Cootb shahy sovereign of Golcondah.——*Ganapavaram* (గణపవరము - ganapavaramu, Tel.). From (ganapati, tel. belly god + pura, san. town). Village; pop. 2,561; acres 1,529; lat. 16° 42′; long. 81° 30′; from Bheemavaram N.N.W. 11 miles; from Cocanada W.S.W. 54 miles; from Veeravausaram N.W. 15 miles. Temple with inscriptions dating from A.D. 1151 to 1273. A few mounds mark the site of the old fort. The temple is in charge of the zemindar of the Baharjully estate.——*Goonpoody* (గున్నపూడి - gunnpúdi, Tel.). From (gunna, tel. small + púdi, tel. village). Sanscrit name (pañcharámakshétra), meaning five + rama, the hero + sacred place. Town; pop. 1,891; acres 3,226; lat. 16° 33′; long. 81° 34′; from Bheemavaram E. ¼ mile; from Cocanada W.S.W. 54 miles; from Veeravausaram W. 6 miles. Identified with Puncha rama cshetram mentioned in the Bheema khandam of the Scandapooraunam. Old temples of Someshwarasawmy of considerable size.——*Gostanuddy* (గోస్తనది - góstanadi, Tel.). See sep. title.——*Oondy* (ఉండి - undi, Tel.). Village, canal; acres 4,731; lat. 16° 35′; long. 81° 30′; from Bheemavaram N.W. 5½ miles; from Cocanada W.S.W. 57 miles; from Veeravausaram W.N.W. 11 miles. The canal 18 miles long is navigable to Oondy; 5 miles below this being unnavigable.——*Ooppooloor* (ఉప్పులూరు - uppulúru, Tel.). From (uppu, tel. salt + úru, tel. village). Zemindarry village; pop. 786; acres 1,459; lat. of village 16° 38′; long. 81° 32′; from Bheemavaram N.N.W. 7½ miles; from Cocanada W.S.W. 53 miles; from Veeravausaram N.W. 11 miles. Vishnoo 400 years old. The idol is exclusively worshipped by Pariahs, an unusual feature.——*Veeravausaram* (వీరవాసరము - víravásaramu, Tel.). See sep. title.——**(2)** Town; Godavery dist., Bheemavaram tal.; pop. 2,364; acres 3,056; lat. 16° 32′; long. 81° 34′; from Cocanada W.S.W. 55 miles; from Coonavaram S.S.E. 74 miles; from Ellore E.S.E. 30 miles; from Madras N.N.E. 250 miles; from Narsapore W.N.W. 14 miles; from Rajahmundry S.S.W. 36 miles. On the Yenamadoorroo drain. Temple of Beemeshwarasawmy with inscription.——**(3)** Village, Place of pilgrimage; Godavery dist., Bheemavaram tal.; pop. 5,051; lat. 17° 03′; long. 82° 13′; from Cocanada N.N.W. 8 miles; from the sea W. 9 miles. Close to Samulcottah. Old town. Ancient and highly venerated temple, built of black granite and sculptured, erected by a Chalookya maharajah. His fort is about 20 yards from the temple. Numerous inscriptions. Annual car festival of Bheemeshwaran celebrated on Shivarautry [pundigay, 6a]. Aqueduct across the Yelair.

BHEEST (بهشت - bihisht, *Hind.*). Heaven. The Mahomedans, exclusive of the ninth which they do not term bheest, reckon eight heavens:—Daur ool jalaul or mansion of glory, composed of pearls; Daur oos salaam or mansion of rest, of ruby and garnet; Jannat ool mauwah or garden of mirrors, of yellow pewter; Jannat ool khoold or garden of eternity, of yellow coral; Jannat oon nayeem or garden of delights, of white diamond; Jannat ool firdows or garden of paradise, of red gold; Daur ool caraur or everlasting abode, of pure musk; Jannat ool adan or garden of eden, of red pearls. For hell see Dozak.——*Bheesty* (بهشتی - bihishtí, Hind.). Because he who gives water to the thirsty earns paradise. A water carrier, carrying leather bag on his back. Compare puckally who uses a double bag carried by buffalo or bullock.

BHEIRAVAN (भैरव - bhairava, *San.*; வயிரவன் - vayiravan, *Tam.*). From (bhíru, san. terrible). The Bheiravans are eight inferior forms or manifestations of Shiva, all of them of a terrible character:—Asitaungan, black-limbed; Caulan, black; Chundrachoodan, moon-crested; Crodhan, anger; Mahah, great; Rooroo, a dog; Samhauram, destruction; Tamrachoodan, red-crested. In these forms Shiva often rides upon a dog, for which reason he is called Shwashwan, or he whose horse is a dog. Bheiravy is Bhadra cauly, the wife of Shiva [matam].

BHEROONDAM (भेरुण्ड - bhérunda, *San.*). Falconidæ family, raptores, aves [pacshy, 2], of naturalists [jantoo]. Divided as follows:—"*a*" Falconinæ, True falcons [pattry].—"*b*" Accipitrinæ, hawks; comprises sparrow-hawks and goshawks; the eyes of all are yellow, in some with age becoming red; the goolaubchashm of indian falconers, the rose-eyed as opposed to the black-eyed falcons [shyainam].—"*c*" Aquilinæ, eagles; the largest of all falconidæ, inferior in courage to falcons and hawks, superior to kites and buzzards; divided into true eagles, kite eagles, hawk eagles, serpent eagles, and fishing eagles [cooralam].—"*d*" Buteoninæ, buzzards [shyainacam].—"*e*" Milvinæ, kites [chillam].

BHET (بھینٹ - bhet, *Hind.*). Interview ; the presentation of a gift made to a superior on the occasion of being presented to him.

BHILAWAUN (بھلاواں - bhilávân, *Hind.*). Means vesicant. Same as Marking-nut tree ; appears in trade as Bellaman.

BHISHAK (भिषक् - bhishak, *San.*). Means healer. Physician. ——*Bhishakpriyah* (भिषक्प्रिया - bhishakpriyá, San.). Physician's friend, from medical properties. Plant name common to :—Terminalia chebula ; Tinospora cordifolia. See gloss. paragraphs.

BHOGAM (भोग - bhóga, *San.*). From (bhuj, san. to enjoy). Enjoyment, use, produce. Teloogoo caste-title ; the corresponding terms are :—Tam. devadausy ; Can. basavy ; the males hold menial appointments about temples or provide music at ceremonies ; the females are the dancing girls and professional prostitutes [jauty]. Bhogamma is a female proper name [peyar]. Bhogan was an ancient Tamul sage and author ; said to be same as Fohi, who introduced Booddhism into China in latter part of first century of Christian era.——*Bhoga jausty* (భోగజాస్తి - bhógajásti, Tel.). From (above + jásti, tel. additional). Same as Fusl jausty, but less common. See vol. I, 112. ——*Bhoga nashty* (भोगनाष्टि - bhóganashti, San.). From (above + nashta, san. loss). Remission on double crop land, when there is no water for a second crop. See vol. I, 112.——*Bhogaul* (భోగాలు - bhógálu, Tel.). Indicating superiority. A paddy of the N. circars. There are several varieties named after Balaraman, Dasharatan, Seeta, &c. [paddy].——*Bhogyadar* (ಭೋಗ್ಯದಾರ - bhógyadára, Can.). From (above + dhri, san. to hold). A mortgagee.——*Bhogyaudy* (ಭೋಗ್ಯಾದಿ - bhógyádi, Can.). From (above + ádi, san. beginning). A form of mortgage in Canara. Land and its produce are separately mortgaged in that district. If the land itself is mortgaged for a sum of money, no interest is demanded, and as soon as the bargain is concluded the mortgagee is put in possession of the land. The mortgagor is sometimes permitted to reside upon the estate and allowed one or two moodas of land to cultivate, in the capacity of a tenant, but the mortgagee pays the circar rent and transacts the whole business of the estate as if he were the proper owner. The mortgage bonds always contain a clause that, as soon as the sum borrowed is repaid, the land is immediately to be returned to the mortgagor, the latter agreeing to pay the expenses of all improvements, to be adjusted by the friends of both parties. A certain portion of the produce of estates is frequently mortgaged for the discharge of interest on debts. In this case it is stipulated that, for the interest of the sum borrowed, a certain number of moodas of rice are to be paid annually, but that the person receiving the rice shall have no interference with the estate ; and that should the mortgagor fail in his payment, the land itself is to be made over to the mortgagee. The first of these mortgages is termed in Canarese Bhogyaudy or living mortgage, the other Toradavoo or dead mortgage. See vol. I, 112.——*Bhogy pundigay* (భోగిపండుగ - bhógipanduga, Tel. ; போகிப்பண்டிகை - pógippandigai, Tam.). Indran, the god of enjoyment + festival ; a feast at the beginning of the harvest. Solar festival [pundigay, 6a]. Immediately precedes Pongal and is generally looked upon as part of that feast. On 11th January the last day of ninth solar month Maurgaly [mausam]. No particular religious ceremonies. A period for relaxation. Presents are interchanged.

BHONSLAY (भोन्सला - bhónsalá, *Mahr.*). Family which claimed descent from the Rana of Oodayapore. To it Shivajee, founder of the Mahratta kingdom, belonged [charitram].

BHOO (भु - bhú, *San.*). Middle place. The Earth, ⊖ or ♁. Supposed by Hindoos to be centre of universe.——*Bhoobund* (భూబందు - búbandu, Tel.). From (above + bandha, san. tie). Boundary of estate.——*Bhoo carnam* (भूकर्ण - bhúkarna, San.). From (above + karna, san. ear). The radius of the equator [jyotisham].——*Bhoo champak* (भूचम्पक - bhúchampaka, San.). From (above + champaka, san. michelia champaca, linn.) ; from low habit and fragrant flowers. Botanically the Kœmpferia genus, zingiberaceæ [vricsham, 144]. Herbs of tropical east indies ; flowers appear before leaves from a very short stem and are highly ornamental ; roots tuberous. The species best known to the natives are :—galanga [indian galangal], rotunda [false zedoary]. Another is angustifolia.——*Bhoo chuckram* (भूचक्र - bhúchakra, San.). From (above + chakra, san. circle). The equator, equinoctial line. The ecliptic is craunty mundalam [jyotisham].——*Bhoogola shastram* (भूगोलशास्त्र - bhúgólashástra, San.). From (above + góla, san. sphere + shástra, san. science). Geography.—"*a*" Sanscrit Bhoogola shastram begins with celestial geography. There are in the first place the fourteen worlds divided into seven lower stalams or places, and seven upper locams or habitations. Thence eight elephants and eight serpents support the mountain Maha meroo and all the fourteen worlds. The eight elephants are :—Anjanam, Coomoodam, Eirauvautam, Poondareecam, Pooshpadantam, Saurwabhoomam, Soopradeepam, Vaumanam. The eight serpents are :—Anantan, Caurcotacan, Coolican, Dacshan, Mahapudman, Shankhan, Tacshacan, Vausooky. Of the eight serpents some make but one, called Sheshan or Audy sheshan, and said to have thousand heads. The names of the seven stalams are in descending order :—Atalam, Vitalam, Sootalam, Nitalam, Talautalam, Mahautalam, Pautaulam. Of these the last and lowest is hell, and is also called Yamalocam. The seven locams are in ascending order :—Bhoo locam, Bhoovar locam, Swar locam or Deva locam, Maha locam, Jana locam, Tapo locam, Satya locam. The first of these is the earth. The second is the space between the earth and the sun and the residence of the Siddhars and Moonies. The third or the space between the sun and the polar star is the residence of the 330,000,000 minor gods. The fourth is Vishnoo's residence. The fifth is the residence of rishies. The sixth that of Beiraugies or ascetics. The seventh, the Satya locam or true world, originally said to be Bramha's residence, whence called Bramha locam. In the more modern theologies however Sheivas hope to attain to Keilausam, Eeshwaran's paradise, and Veishnavas to attain to Veicoontam, Vishnoo's paradise. These fourteen worlds are each 50,000,000,000,000,000 leagues long and 25,000,000,000,000,000 leagues broad. Mount Maha meroo, which passes through all the fourteen worlds, is 1,600,000,000,000 leagues high and as many broad.—"*b*" The shastram next treats of mundane geography. On the mundane earth there are seven great islands or continents, otherwise dweepams, which are most of them named from the trees growing in them, as follows :—Coosham, Crowncham, Jamboo on which India is situated, Placsham, Pooshcaram, Shaucam, and Shaulmaly. The seven oceans on the earth with samoodram affixed are as follows :—Lavanam, salt ; Ney, ghee ; Nullatunneer, fresh water ; Paul, milk ; Sharcaray, sugar juice ; Tain, honey ; Tyre, curdled milk. The following is the disposition of the dweepams and samoodrams. The golden mountain, Maha meroo, is surrounded immediately by Jamboo dweepam, extending a hundred thousand leagues, around which flows the salt sea. Beyond this are Shauca dweepam and the sea of milk. Coosha dweepam is next, and the sea of Tyre or curdled milk. Next Crowncha dweepam and the sea of ghee. Next Shaulmaly dweepam and sea of sugar-cane juice. Next Placsha dweepam with the sea of honey. Next Pooshcara dweepam with the fresh water sea. Outside in a circular form around these is Chuckravaulagherry or wheel mountain, and to the east of that is Oodayagherry or sun-rising mountain. As to Jamboo dweepam, Oodayagherry. Astagiry, Himalaya, and Dacshinaurnavam or Saitoo are its boundaries. The former two mountains represent the Eastern and Western ghauts running along the coasts. Dacshinaurnavam is the southern ocean ; Saitoo is Rama's bridge. All that is known about Pooranic geography is shown at vol. I (1)—(5).—"*c*" More recently the geographical works indicate by fifty-six countries the whole known modern world. The countries according to the Chatoor acarauthy of Beschi, are Andhram, Angam, Aroonam, Avanty, Calingam, Caunada, Cannaudam, Caroosham, Cashmere, Caumbojam, Causham, Cheenam, Cholam, Collam, Concanam, Coodagam, Coolindam, Coontalam, Cooroo, Cooroogoo, Cosalam, Dravidam, Gaundhauram, Goorjaram, Ilautam, Kekayam, Keralam, Kirautam, Magadham, Malayalam, Maraudam, Matsyam, Maulavam, Nepaulam, Nishadham, Parparam, Paunchaulam, Paundyam, Podam, Poolindam, Pullavam, Shacam, Shaulavam, Shonacam, Shoorasenam, Sindhoo, Singhalam, Sowveeram, Tenganam, Tooloovam, Vangam, Vangaulam, Vidarbham, Wottiyam, Yavanam, Yoogandham. Of the countries here mentioned, Cashmere, Caumbojam, Nepaulam, Cannaudam are plain ; Calingam was an ancient kingdom near the godavery ; Dravidam is the southern tamul country ; Maulavam is probably malwah ; Maraudam the southern marava district ; Paundyam is the madura kingdom ; Keralam, the travancore and malayalam country ; Vangam is supposed to be the province of e. bengal ; Yavanam, arabia.—"*d*" Works on Bhoogola shastram in Tamul are rare. The Dravidians are essentially non-migratory. The pooraunams contain, in special sub-divisions, called Bhoovana cosham and Deshamaulay, geographical treatises, of which the first two chapters of the second book of the Vishnoo pooraunam deserve special notice. Gola deepam or globe lamp, a modern book, translated from the Sanscrit, treats of the geography of the pooraunams [charitram].——*Bhoojpattar* (भूर्ज - bhúrja, San. ; بھوج پتر - bhújpattar, Hind. and Dec. ; భుజపత్రి - bhujapatri, Tel.). San. from (bhúh, san. on the earth + jan, san. to be produced). Hind. from (bhúrja, san. the tree + patra, san. leaf). San. also (charmí), meaning leathery, from leather like leaves ; (mridutvak), meaning soft barked. Title otherwise Bhoj, Himalayan birch, Indian birch, Indian leather birch, Indian paper birch, Indian writing birch. Botanically Betula bhojpattra, wall., cupuliferæ [vricsham]. Specific name from hindostany. A birch of afghanistann, himalayas, thibet, japan, &c. ; products introduced ; the bark peels off in large sheets and is used for umbrellas, for writing upon, and for the flexible tubes of hookahs ; wood good, used for cups, commonly for turnery.——*Bhoomidevy* (भूमिदेवी - bhúmidéví, San.). From (above + déví, san. mistress). The goddess of the earth. A secondary wife of Vishnoo, as Gungay is of Shiva. Represented in arts as a woman with two arms and hands, holding in the one a lotus flower and letting the other hang down empty. Her color is yellow. On her head she wears a crown, whilst her black locks hang down as far as her feet. She wears jewels in her nose and red paste on her forehead, and is otherwise adorned like the other goddesses. She stands on a lotus flower in paintings, but there is no image of her in any pagoda. She is not worshipped and no offerings are made to her. See vol. I (79) [matam].——*Bhoomy* (भूमि - bhúmi, San.). Land. Of five kinds ; see Desham.——*Bhoo-*

nimbam (भूनिम्ब - bhúnimba, San.). From (above + nimba, san. melia azadirachta, linn.). Ground neem; from low size and bitter property. Botanically the Andrographis genus, acanthaceæ [vricsham, 101]. Annual herbs or very small shrubs, erect or procumbent. The species best known to the natives are:—echioides [coromandel chiretta], paniculata [french chiretta]. Other s. indian species indigenous or naturalized are:—affinis, lineata, lobelioides, macrobotrys, neesiana, serpyllifolia, viscosula, wightiana.——*Bhoonj* (భుంజ - bhunja, Tel.). From (bhúmi, san. earth + jan, san. to be born). Family designation of the Goomsoor zemindars, in Ganjam district. The zemindarry was annexed to British dominions in 1836, the chief having rebelled. The members of the family were removed to Vellore, with small pensions now all lapsed. The result of this annexation was suppression of meriah amongst Khonds. Vol. I, 49. ——*Bhoo puridhy* (भूपरिधि - bhúparidhi, San.). From (above + paridhi, san. that which surrounds). Same as Bhoo chuckram [jyotisham].——*Bhoopaty* (భూపతి - bhúpati, Tel.). From (above + pati, san. ruler). Any ruler.——*Bhoo stity* (भूस्थिति - bhúst'hiti, San.). From (above + st'há, san. to stand). Landed property.——*Bhootam* (भूत - bhúta, San.).—"*a*" Material element in philosophy. There are five, viz., earth, water, fire, air, and ether. Earth has smell or gandham; water, taste or rasam; air, touch or sparsham; fire, color or roopam; and pure ether, sound or shabdam. Besides these the elements have other qualities. Earth, which is the heaviest element, has the qualities of smell, sound, tangibility, visibility and taste; it enters largely into the formation of the body and of all solid and heavy substances. Water possesses sound, tangibility, visibility and taste; bestows the sense of coolness, fluidity, weight, and smoothness on bodies; and has the quality of happiness or satwagoonam, and of inertness or tamogoonam; and is transparent, producing light and weight; it forms the different fluids of the body. Air has sonorousness, tangibility and lightness; and from having the quality of action or rajogoonam in excess, has the moving powers and qualities of bodies. Fire possesses sound, tangibility and visibility, and gives taste; it produces the passions, bodily strength and valour. Ether or aucausham is separated from the others, and possesses the property of sound and form; it predominates in the organ of hearing, and fills up the porosities of living bodies as those of the bones, &c.; and possesses the quality of goodness or satwagoonam; this element is undistinguishable by the senses, and is only made known through the evidence of the understanding.—"*b*" Matter in the classification of natural history. As follows:—for category, see Padaurtam; for elementary substance, see Dravyam; for matter, see the present heading; for organic and inorganic, see Indriyam and Anindriyam; for organic kingdom, see Ganam [jantoo, vricsham]; for organic class, see Vargam; for organic order, see Santaunam; for organic family, see Coolam; for organic genus, see Jauty; for organic species, see Bhaidam. Oopa prefixed to either of the above means a sub-head. For inorganic minerals, see Dhautoo.—"*c*" A goblin. These are represented in the arts with small, thick bodies, of a red color, with pig tails round their heads, horrible faces, lion's teeth in their mouths, and various ornaments over their bodies. They were created for the purpose of being the servants of the gods and are content in doing the lowest services, which is not the case with the peygal. In this sense word is a constant prefix to plant names, generally when large.—"*d*" Also any living being.—"*e*" Bhoota chatoordashy, meaning spirits of the dead + fourteenth day is the same as deepauvaly. Bhoota nautan, meaning lord of demons is Shiva. Bhootaula pandya, meaning spirit-ruling pandyan, was a ruler in Canara who introduced the aliya santauna law. ——*Bhoovangherry* (புவனக்கிரி - puvanakkiri, Tam. bhuvanigiri *). From (bhuvana, san. world + giri, san. mountain).—"*a*" Deputy tahsildarry, Chidambaram talook, South arcot district. Pay Rs. 70.—"*b*" Deputy tahsildar's station; pop. 7,660; acres 1628; lat. 11° 27′; long. 79° 42′; from Chidambaram N.W. 4 miles; from Cuddalore S.S.W. 20 miles; from Madras S.S.W. 120 miles; from Tindivanam S. 54 miles; from Tricalore S.E. 47 miles; from Vriddhauchellam E. 23 miles; from the sea W. 10 miles. On route from Tranquebar to Vicravaundy. Five villages collected under this name. Formerly fort used as a grain depôt for Fort St. David. Weekly fair.——*Bhowman* (भौम - bhauma, San.). From (bhúmi, san. earth). Planet Mars [coojan, graham, mungalan].

BHOOJAM (भुज - bhuja, *San.*). From (bhuj, san. to bend). The whole arm from the shoulder to the tips of the fingers. Arm or side of a triangle or any mathematical figure, pratibhoojam being the opposite side. Also an arc, also the supplement of two or four right angles or the complement of three right angles. Tribhoojam is a triangle [jyotisham].——*Bhoojajyay* (भुजज्या - bhujajyá, San.). From (above + jyá, san. bow-string). Sine of the Bhoojam.——*Bhoojanga* (ಭುಜಂಗ - bhujanga, Can.). From (bhuja, san. zigzag + gam, san. to go); from crooked motion. Snake. Hindoo 2nd or pers. name. Common among Madhwas and Mahrattas [peyar].

BHRAUNGY (भार्गी - bhárgí, *San.*; भारंगी - bhárangí, *Mahr.*; بهارنگی - bahárangí, *Hind.*; ಭಾರಂಗಿ - bhárangi, *Can.*; భారంగి - bhárangi, *Tel.*; ஞரிவாளை - ñariválai, *Tam.*). Title from hindostany. San. from (bhrajj, san. to shine); from shining green leaves. Hind. from (bahár, hind. green + rang, hind. color); from leaf. Tam. from (nari, tam. fox + vélai, tam. gynandropsis pentaphylla, dec.). San. also (bráhmanayashtiká), meaning bramin + creeping plant; from shining whitish stems. Hind. also (arná). Tel. also (brahmi), meaning bramha's tree; from bright whitish stems and leaves; (hanjiká), meaning killer, anthelmintic; (chiritéku), meaning small + teak tree. Title otherwise Pipe flower, Tube flower. Botanically Clerodendron [bhaurgam] siphonanthus, r. brown, verbenaceæ [vricsham, 102]. Alias Siphonanthus indica. Small shrub, white tubular flowers three or four inches long, long strap like leaves.——*Knotted bhraungy* (बर्बर - varvara, San.; भारंग - bháranga, Mahr.; گنٹ بہارنگی - gantbahárangí, Hind.; گنڈ بہارنگی - gandbahárangí, Dec.; ಗಂಟುಭಾರಂಗಿ - gantubhárangi, Can.; గంటుభారంగి - gantubhárangi, Tel.; ചെറുതേക്ക - cherutékku, Mal.; කිණිහිරිය - kanhinda, Singh.; சிறுதேக்கு - shiruthékku, Tam.). Title from root. San. from (vri, san. to cover); curly and woolly [fragrant toolsy, vaily]. Hind. from (gant, hind. knob + bahárangí, hind. clerodendron); from root. Can. and tel. from hindostany. Mal. from (cheru, mal. small + tékku, mal. teak). Tam. from (shiru, tam. small + tékku, tam. teak, tectona grandis, linn.), from leaves. San. also (angáravallí), meaning fire + creeper; (dvidandi), meaning having two sticks; (bhárgí), meaning shining. Tel. also (bhramaramári), meaning beetle + killer. Mal. also (nápálu), meaning four + milk, four-sided milky plant; (kantabhárngí), meaning thorn + the shrub. Tam. also (kandubárangi), meaning knot + the plant [round leaved nelumbo]. Title otherwise Beetle-killer, Fire creeper. Botanically Clerodendron [bhaurgam] serratum, spreng., verbenaceæ [vricsham, 102]. Alias Clerodendron javanicum, macrophyllum, ternifolium; Volkameria farinosa, serrata. A large-leaved, coarse, unattractive shrub, better known than siphonanthus; young shoots four-sided; leaves opposite, 5–10 inches long, and broad in proportion, serrated; panicles terminal; flowers pale blue, with lower lip indigo-colored; nearly always in blossom; grows in dry jungles. Small, knobby, warm and slightly bitterish-tasted root is febrifuge and expectorant; remedy in febrile and catarrhal affections; quoted in pharm. but non-officinal. Infusion or decoction of leaves and tender stalks and roots are attenuant and diaphoretic; slightly bitter, and not unpleasant to taste. Leaves boiled with oil and butter are made into an ointment, useful in cephalalgia and ophthalmia. Seeds bruised and boiled in buttermilk are slightly aperient and administered in dropsy.

BHRIGOO (भृगु - bhrigu, San.). From (bhrajj, san. to shine). —"*a*" Planet Venus [graham, shoocran]. A male with the Hindoos.—"*b*" Son of Bramha. A rishy. Ancestor of Parshooraman. Vishnoo's breast bears the impression of his foot.

BHUNGHEE (بهنگی - bhangí, *Hind.*). A common sweeper.

BHURTY (بهرتی - bhartí, *Hind.*). From (bhri, san. to bear). Filling up; recruitment. A substitute. An accretion of land from alluvial deposit. In Canara Bhurty estates are those which are considered to pay the full amount of revenue that should be demanded from them under the Tarow [q.v.] system introduced in 1819. See vol. I, 112.

BHUTTOTE (بهٹوت - bhatot, *Hind.*). Among Thugs the strangler [banij].

BHYE (بائی - bái, *Hind.*). Same as Bhaee. Distinguish from bye.

BICHAUNAH (بچهانا - bichháná, *Hind.*). Bedding of any kind.

BICHOOR (بچهوا - bichhuá, *Hind.*). From (bichhú, hind. scorpion). Dagger with more than one blade.

BIDAUR (బిడారు - bidáru, *Tel.*). Caravan of Lumbaudies. Herd of loaded cattle.

BIDPAY (بید پای - bedpái, *Hind.*). From (védapriya, san. knowledge lover). Author of Punchatantram. Same as Pilpay.

BIJAUYA (బిజాయ - bijáya, *Tel.*). From (vijaya, san. success). Pass; Vizagapatam district, Royagada division. Leads from Parvatipore to Jeypore. The head of the pass rises to 3,000 feet above the sea, the average gradient being 1 in 20.

BIJJA (ಬಿಜ್ಜ - bijja, *Can.*). Learning.——*Bijjala* (ಬಿಜ್ಜಳ - bijjala, Can.). From (bijjavala, can. ganésha, the god). Also called Nissanka mulla and Tribhoovanamulla. A Jeina king of Calyaunapoora or Shilpagherry, in the Deccan, A.D. 1156—1168, who had Basava [q.v.] for his minister of State and was assassinated in the Lingayet insurrection. The history of revolution is contained in two works called Basava pooraunam and Bijjala charitram, the one text-book of Lingayets, the other of Jeinas. See vol. I (88) [charitram].

BIKH (بیخ - bíkh, *Pers.*). Same as Bish, and derived same.

BIKKY (ಬಿಕ್ಕಿ - bikki, *Can.*). Roodrauck; Hill emetic nut.

BIL (بال - bil, *Hind.*). From (ba, ar. with + al, ar. the). In, with, by, &c.——*Bilmacta* (بالمقطع - bilmakta, Hind.). From (above + makta, ar. agreement). According to agreement. In Northern circars a fixed quit-rent or revenue assessed at a rate below the usual standard. In the south land held at any fixed rate [inam]. See vol. I, 112.

BILAUTY (ولايتى - viláití, *Hind.*). From (viláyat, ar. foreign country). Foreign, exotic.

BILISHT (بلشت - bilisht, *Hind.*). Span. Linear measure, taken from the tip of the thumb to that of the little finger, both extended. 12 ungools = 1 bilisht ; 2 bilishts = 1 haut [alavay, 1]. Approximate actual value, 1 bilisht = 9 inches. Same as San. vitasty, Can. gueno, Tel. jena, Tam. jaun. See vol. I, 609 ; II, 505.

BILLA (بلا - billá, *Hind.*). A badge worn by peons.

BILLAWA (ಬಿಲ್ಲವ - billava, *Can.*). Altered form of Ilava. Canara tribe. Extract toddy from palm trees and collect forest produce. Devil worshippers.

BILY (ಬಿಳಿ - bilí, *Can.*). White.——*Bilicull* (ಬಿಳಿಕಲ್ಲು - bilikallu, *Can.*). From (bili, can. white + kallu, can. rock). Village, Hill ; Neilgherry dist., Todanaud division ; lat. 11° 29′ ; long. 76° 44′ ; from Ootacamund N. 5½ miles ; from Seegore S.S.E. 2½ miles. Five cairns have been opened here. They contained pottery, bronzes, iron implements, gold beads and earrings, &c. Contains a small natural tank. First stocked with fish from the plains about 1839. Enlarged in 1844. Coffee and fruit estates 107 acres.——*Biligiry* (ಬಿಳಿಗಿರಿ - biligiri, Can.). From (above + giri, san. hill). The sacred place in Mysore [ballirungam]. Hindoo 2nd or pers. name [peyar].——*Biliya* (ಬಿಳಿಯ - biliya, Can.). Means a white man. Hill-tribe proper name [belloo, peyar, vellay].

BIMLIPATAM * (بملى پٹن - bimlípatan, *Hind.* ; భీమునిపట్నము - bhímunipatnamu, *Tel.*). From (bhíma, san. the hero + pattana, san. town). Sanscrit name (bhímapattana), meaning same.——**(1)** Division ; Vizagapatam district ; area 218 square miles ; population 115,309 ; language Teloogoo. Centre coast of district. Boundaries :—east, Bay of Bengal ; south, Vizagapatam talook ; west, Srungavarapoocote and Ankapully talooks ; north, Vizianagram and Cheepoorpully talooks. The S.W. portion is studded with low hills, which are generally rocky ; the rest of the talook is flat and even, and is traversed by the Gostany. Soil, mostly red ferruginous series, and is suited for the growth of dry crops, i.e., gram, chillies, raggy and cumboo. The chief industry is agriculture. There is a large steam gunny factory and several indigo factories. Coarse cotton cloths, brass and copper vessels are also made. Salt is manufactured in two places. Commerce almost entirely seaborne. Oil-seeds, myrobalans, indigo, hides, skins, horns, are chief exports. The imports are piece goods, machinery, glass, hardware, wines and spirit, jute. Irrigation is mostly from tanks and from wells. The Gostany irrigates the lands along its course. Camping grounds, Chittivalsa and Sontyaum. Places of archæological interest :—Bhogaupooram, Bimlipatam, Bonye, Brihadauchellam, Daucmurry, Goodilova, Goodivauda, Potnore, Pudmanaubham, Rauvauda. Principal trig. stations :—Akkavaram, Amanaum, Anandapooram, Bimlipatam beacon, Chittivalsa, Cowlevauda beacon, Krishnapooram, Rajappa lowa. The leading places, &c., in the division are the following.——*Akkavaram* (అక్కవరము - akkivaramu, Tel.). From (akki, can. rice + pura, san. town). Trig. station ; lat. 18° 01′ 26·22″ ; long. 83° 30′ 36·09″ ; from Akkavaram N. ½ mile ; from Bimlipatam N. 9½ miles ; from the sea W. 7¼ miles.——*Amanaum* (అమనాం - amanám, Tel.). From (aman, hind. safety + gám, hind. village). Trig. station ; lat. 17° 56′ 51·22″ ; long. 83° 31′ 29·26″ ; height 838 feet ; from Bimlipatam N.N.E. 4 miles ; from Chittivalsa E.N.E. 3½ miles ; from the sea W. 2¾ miles.——*Anandapooram* (ఆనందపురము - ánandapuramu, Tel.). From (ánanda, san. proper name + pura, san. city). Built by Ananda rauz. Village ; pop. 2,286 ; lat. 17° 54′ ; long. 83° 25′ ; from Bimlipatam W.N.W. 5½ miles ; from Vizagapatam N.N.E. 15 miles ; from the sea W. 6 miles. Fair every Thursday. Trig. station in lat. 17° 53′ 50·92″ ; long. 83° 24′ 47·76″ ; from Anandapooram S. ½ mile ; from Bimlipatam W. 5½ miles ; from the sea W. 5½ miles.——*Bhogaupooram* (భోగాపురము - bhógápuramu, Tel.). From (bhóga, san. enjoyment + pura, san. a town). Village ; pop. 3,633 ; lat. 18° 02′ ; long. 83° 33′ ; from Bimlipatam N.N.E. 11 miles ; from Vizagapatam N.N.E. 28 miles ; from the sea W. 6 miles. Two inscriptions of Orissa dynasty dated A.D. 1175 and 1184, both recording grants in the reign of Anantavurma deva. An old fort, age not known.——*Bimlipatam* (భీమునిపట్నము - bhímunipatnamu, Tel.) ; see below.——*Chittivalsa* (చిట్టివలస - chittivalasa, Tel.). See sep. title.——*Conauda* (కోనాడ - kónáda, Tel.). See sep. title.——*Cowlevauda beacon* (కౌలువాడ - kauluváda, Tel.). From (kaul, hind. agreement + váda, tel. village). Trig. station ; lat. 17° 58′ ; long. 83° 34′ ; from Bimlipatam N.E. 6½ miles ; from Conauda S.W. 4½ miles ; from the sea W. 2 miles.——*Goodivauda* (గుడివాడ - gudiváda, Tel.). From (gudi, tel. temple + váda, tel. village). Village ; pop. 870 ; lat. 17° 56′ ; long. 83° 29′ ; from Bimlipatam N.N.W. 3½ miles ; from Vizagapatam N.N.E. 19 miles ; from the sea W. 5 miles. Two inscriptions of Anantavurma deva of the Orissa dynasty.——*Gostany* (గోస్తని - góstani, Tel.). See sep. title.——*Kistnapooram* (కృష్ణాపురము - krishnápuramu, Tel.). From (krishna, san. god + pura, san. town). Trig. station ; lat. 17° 59′ 35·3″ ; long. 83° 22′ 17·2″ ; from Bimlipatam N.W. 11 miles ; from Pudmanaubham N. ¼ mile ; from the sea W. 16 miles.——*Neelayyamma chuttram* (నీలయ్యమ్మసత్రము - nílayyammasatramu, Tel.). From (nílayyamma, tel. proper name + satramu, tel. choultry) ; called after the founder. A substantial choultry for natives ; from Bimlipatam N. 7 miles ; from Vizagapatam S. 28 miles.——*Potnore* (పొట్నూరు - potnúru, Tel.). From (pottu, tel. husk + úru, tel. village). Village ; pop. 2,276 ; lat. 18° 01′ ; long. 83° 22′ ; from Bimlipatam N.W. 12 miles ; from Vizagapatam N. 22 miles ; from the sea W. 17 miles. Ancient capital of the Maharajah of Vizianagram. Pillar of victory erected by Krishna deva roya. Two old forts. Deserted temple near a tank of large stones.——*Pudmanaubham* (పద్మనాభము - padmanábhamu, Tel.). Means vishnoo, the lotus-navelled deity. Sanscrit name (padmanábhapura), meaning vishnoo, the lotus-navelled deity + town. Village, Place of pilgrimage ; pop. 607 ; lat. 17° 59′ ; long. 83° 23′ ; from Bimlipatam N.W. 12 miles ; from Vizagapatam N. 20 miles ; from the sea W. 15 miles. Battle fought here between Vijiaram rauz II, great grandfather of the present Maharajah of Vizianagram, and the English on the 10th July 1794, in which the former was defeated and slain. On the top of a hill in the vicinity are two old sculptures of Vishnoo's chunk and chuckram, and an ancient temple. Worship has lately been revived and the place is held in much estimation. At the foot of the hill is another old temple declared to have been erected by Yoodishtiran.——*Rajappa lowa* (రాజప్పలోవ - rájappalóva, Tel.). From (rájappa, tel. proper name + lóva, tel. cave). Trig. station ; lat. 17° 57′ 14·86″ ; long. 83° 27′ 43·40″ ; from Bimlipatam N.N.W. 5 miles ; from the sea W. 7 miles.——*Santapilly* (శంతపల్లె - santapalle, Tel.). See sep. title.——*Sontyaum* (శొంఠ్యాము - sontyámu, Tel.). From (sonti, tel. dry ginger + gám, hind. village). Camping ground ; pop. 2,222 ; lat. 17° 52′ ; long. 83° 21′ ; from Bimlipatam W. 80 miles ; from Vizagapatam N. 11 miles ; from the sea W. 9 miles. Choultry and camping ground.——*Taullavalsa* (తాళ్లవలస - tállavalsa, Tel.). From (tádi, tel. palmyra tree, borassus flabelliformis, linn. + valasa, tel. colony). Village ; pop. 1,743 ; lat. 18° 02′ ; long. 83° 26′ ; from Bimlipatam N.N.W. 11 miles ; from Vizagapatam N.N.E. 24 miles ; from the sea W. 14 miles. Good choultry. On trunk roads from Ankapully and Vizagapatam to Vizianagaram.——*Vencatapore* (వెంకటాపురము - venkatapuramu, Tel.). From (vénkata, san. vishnu + pura, san. town). Village ; pop. 630 ; acres 112 ; lat. 17° 55′ ; long. 83° 23′ ; from Bimlipatam W.N.W. 6 miles ; from Vizagapatam N.N.E. 15 miles ; from the sea W. 6 miles. Chief place in Goodivauda talook of Vizianagram zemindarry.——**(2)** Deputy tahsildarry ; Vizagapatam district ; pay Rs. 70.——**(3)** Zemindarry ; Vizagapatam district, Bimlipatam division ; pop. 115,309 ; square miles 218.——**(4)** Town, Port, Deputy tahsildar's station ; Municipality ; Vizagapatam district, Bimlipatam division ; pop. 9,784 ; lat. 17° 53′ ; long. 83° 30′ ; from Calcutta S.W. 454 miles ; from Conauda S.W. 12 miles ; from Coraputt S.E. 57 miles ; from Madras N.N.E. 387 miles ; from Narsapatam E.N.E. 57 miles ; from Parvatipore S. 62 miles ; from Vizagapatam N.E. 18 miles ; from Vizianagram S. 16 miles. On Coromandel coast, on the Chittivalsa river. Though an open roadstead, the port is somewhat protected by the Oopada and Sugar-loaf headlands, and good anchorage in 6½ fathoms can be obtained half a mile off shore. The best anchorage in the roads is with the pagoda on Bimlipatam hill from W. to S. to W.S.W. ; Sugar-loaf hill from S.W. to S.W. by S. ; flagstaff, W. to W. by S. The river does not admit anything but masulah boats and these only during a portion of the year. During the remaining period the bar is silted up and boats load and unload on the beach. The coast between Bimlipatam and Vizagapatam is very bold, having 15 or 16 fathoms within 2 miles off shore. The Dutch east india company built a fort and factory here in the middle of the seventeenth century, about same time as the English company formed a settlement at Vizagapatam. In the war between England and the Batavian republic at close of eighteenth century, the Dutch lost all their possessions in India. The peace of Amiens, dated March 27, 1802, provided for their restoration, but this was precluded by the early renewal of the war. Actual restoration was made in 1819 to the king of Holland, agreeably to the convention of the allied powers in 1814. The Dutch then held their territory at Bimlipatam till the 1st of June 1825, when it was made over by a Dutch commissioner to the Collector, under the operation of the Treaty of March 1824 between His Britannic Majesty and the king of Holland. On the hill near the town is an old Vishnoo temple. In the town is a Shiva temple built by the Cholan. An inscription on the Garooda stambham of the Vishnoo temple records repairs. Tombstones of A.D. 1623 in the old burial-ground. Bimlipatam was for long celebrated for its cotton piece-goods. It is now the port of all the northern part of the district and has a good trade in seeds, hides, and indigo. Till 1846 Bimlipatam was a mere fishing village. About that time, Messrs. Arbuthnot and Company, having obtained the lease of the Palcondah estate, built a factory at Chittivalsa, for the manufacture of jaggery since converted into a gunny factory employing seven hundred hands and the exportation of oil-seeds. This trade is now shared by some half-dozen French and English houses and native firms. Imports are cotton-twist, piece-goods, machinery and liquor. Exports are sugar, indigo and oil-seeds. Principal buildings are the church, school-house, and clock tower. The Madras bank has a branch. Bimlipatam beacon trig. station is in lat. 17° 53′ 25·45″; long. 83° 29′ 12·36″; from Bimlipatam W.N.W. ¾ mile.——**(5)** River; Vizagapatam district, Bimlipatam and Srungavarapoocote divisions. **Also called Gostany or Chittivalsa river.**

BINGY (బింగి - bingi, *Tel.*). From (binga, can. fool). A caste of mendicant dramatists.

BINJ (बीज - bíja, *San.*; بینج - bínj, *Hind.*; ಬೀಜ - bíja, *Can.*; విత్తనము - vittanamu, *Tel.*; വിത്ത് - vittu, *Mal.*; விதை - virai, *Tam.*). Seed. The following are two key-lists in the briefest possible terms of the principal commercial seeds of s. india; further information must be traced in the glossary paragraphs through the small-type cross-references at end of this volume; see also vricsham, 7, for the method of expressing the products, &c., of plants in the dravidian languages.—"*a*" Bassia longifolia, common mohwah; Brassica juncea, indian mustard; Buchanania latifolia, chironjee; Cæsalpinia bonducella, bonduc; Cannabis sativa, indian hemp; Carthamus tinctorious, safflower; Carum carui, caraway; Carum copticum, ajwaun; Cassia auriculata, tungaid; Cassia tora, chakondah; Coriandrum sativum, coriander; Croton tiglium, purging croton; Cucumis trigonus, country cucumber; Cuminum cyminum, cummin; Daucus carota, carrot; Erythrina indica, common coral tree; Fœniculum vulgare, indian fennel; Gossypium arboreum, tree cotton; Hibiscus abelmoschus, musk bendy; Hordeum vulgare, barley; Hyoscyamus niger, henbane; Indigofera tinctoria, common indigo; Lepidium sativum, cress; Linum usitatissimum, flax; Momordica charantia, balsam apple; Pandanus odoratissimus, screw-pine; Panicum italicum, italian millet; Papaver somniferum, opium poppy; Pimpinella anisum, anise seed; Ricinus communis, castor oil; Sesamum indicum, gingelly; Trigonella fœnum-græcum, fenugreek.—"*b*" Ajwaun, carum; Anise seed, pimpinella; Balsam apple, momordica; Barley, hordeum; Bendy, hibiscus; Bonduc, cæsalpinia; Caraway, carum; Carrot, daucus; Castor oil, ricinus; Chakondah, cassia; Chironjee, buchanania; Coral tree, erythrina; Coriander, coriandrum; Cotton, gossypium; Cress, lepidium; Croton, croton; Cucumber, cucumis; Cummin, cuminum; Fennel, fœniculum; Fenugreek, trigonella; Flax, linum; Gingelly, sesamum; Hemp, cannabis; Henbane, hyoscyamus; Indigo, indigofera; Italian millet, panicum; Mohwah, bassia; Mustard, brassica; Poppy, papaver; Safflower, carthamus; Screw-pine, pandanus; Tungaid, cassia.

BINKY (ಬೆಂಕಿ - benki, *Can.*). Fire. Binky nawaub in old documents is for commandant of artillery.

BINNAM (భిన్నము - bhinnamu, *Tel.*). From (bhid, san. to break). Division of lands for land assignment. See vol. I, 112.

BINT (بنت - bint, *Ar.*). Daughter. Forms coonyat [q. v.]. Arabic, and not here adopted [ism].

BIRIDY (బిరిడి - biridi, *Tel.*; ବିରୋଲି - biroli, *Oor.* biridi *). Ancient zemindarry; Ganjam district; pop. 16,175; square miles 65. Contiguous to Callicote zemindarry, and impinging upon the southern extremity of the Chilka lake. Like the other zemindarry tracts lying contiguous to the Chilka lake, the estate owes its origin to Poorshottama gajapaty deo, king of Orissa, who granted the talook to Balaram soor, one of his sirdars, in 1489 A.D. The present zemindar is Shree vinauyaca soor maharta mardaraja bramharavaur roya. Peshcush Rs. 4,456. Contains Rambha [q.v.] and Coojidibba [q.v.] trig. stations.

BISFAYAJ (بسفایج - basfáij, *Ar.* and *Pers.*; کہنکلی - khanklí, *Hind.*; بسفایج - bisfáij, *Dec.*; വലിയപന്ന - valiyapanna, *Mal.*; வலியப்பன - valiyappana, *Tam.*). Pers. from (bass, pers. cat + páyah, pers. foot). Mal. from (valiya, mal. large + panna, mal. fern). Ar. also (azrásulkalb), meaning canine teeth; (sákibulhajr), meaning perforater of stone. Title otherwise Cat's foot. Botanically Polypodium species, polypodiaceæ. Leaves reduced to powder and taken with honey are emmenagogues and bring on abortions.

BISH (विष - visha, *San.*). From (vish, san. to pervade). Hindostany form. Poison. So especially the Aconitum genus, Ranunculaceæ [vricsham, 1]. Perennial, erect, rarely twining herbs; flowers irregular, racemed, blue purple white or yellow. The species best known to the natives are:—ferox [bachnaug], heterophyllum [atees], napellus [wolf-strangler]. For non-poisonous aconites, see Jadwaur. Compare in other genera:—Crinum asiaticum (vishamandala), poison ball; Heliotropium indicum (vishaghá), poison destroyer; Melocanna rheedii (vishamula), poison bamboo; Momordica charantia (vishakantaka), poison thorn; Pittosporum floribundum (vishári), poison destroyer; Strychnos nux vomica (vishatinduka), poison gaub. See gloss. paragraphs.

BISLEY (ಬಿಸಲೆ - bisale, *Can.*). From (bishi, can. heat + halu, can. forest). Village belonging to Mysore, Pass; South canara district, Mangalore talook. The pass was formerly of importance as connecting Mangalore with Seringapatam, but fell into disrepair and was for long practicable for pack-bullocks only. Recently opened as a fair weather road and continued to Ooppinangady. As being the shortest route to Soobramanya, where a great annual fair is held, the cattle-breeders on the other side use this route. The village stands at one end of the pass on the road from Bangalore to Mangalore.

BISM (بسم - bism, *Hind.*). From (ba, ar. in + ism, ar. name). In the name of.——*Bismillah* (بسم الله - bismilláh, Hind.). From (above + alláh, ar. god). In the name of God. Used by Mahomedans in the beginning of all actions or lessons and especially before eating. Ceremony observed when a child about four years four months old is set to read for the first time in a Maktab. Taken by fakeers as an alam; as Bismillah shah, alam + alaumat [ism].

BISSEE (బిసీ - biseí, *Tel.*). From (vishaya, san. a country). A province under the old Hindoo government of Orissa.——*Bissoye* (బిసోయి - bisóyi, Tel.). The chief of a Bissee. The family name of a race of hill chiefs in Northern circars [inam]. A Dora is a lower chief.

BISSEMCUTTACK (ବିଷମକଟକ - bishomokotóko, *Oor.*). From (vishama, san. rugged + kataka, san. hill side). Otherwise Bissemcote and Issemcote.——**(1)** Division; Vizagapatam district. Language chiefly Ooriya. Most northerly talook in district in country of the Deshye or outer Khonds. Boundaries:—north, Central provinces and Ganjam district; south, Royagada and Goonapore divisions; west, Calahundy; east, Ganjam district. Of the seven Khond mittahs proscribed by the officers of the Meriah agency in 1857 as addicted to human sacrifice. Consists of valleys and hills. Soil moderately fertile. Enjoys considerable trade through traffic between Central provinces and coast in grain, tobacco, saffron, mustard and gingelly seeds and unrefined sugar in exchange for iron, cloths, and salt. Irrigation by jungle streams. Contains 497 villages divided into eight sub-mittahs; Bhangoda, Canacalaudy, Cojiry, Cootragoda, Jagdalpore and Jigada, Ombadola, Sogata. The leading places in the division are the following.——*Bissemcuttack* (ବିଷମକଟକ - bishomokotóko, Oor.). See below.——*Cootragoda* (కుట్రగడ - kutragoda, Tel.). From (kutra, tel. intricate + gadá, oor. fort). Village; pop. 367; lat. 19° 37′; long. 83° 36′; from Bissemcuttack N.N.E. 7½ miles; from Narsapatam N.N.E. 150 miles; from Vizagapatam N. 132 miles. A mittah held under the Taut rajah by an Ooriya patro.——*Jagdalpore* (జగదల్పూరు - jagadalpúru, Tel.). From (jagadalli, tel. deity + pura, san. town). Village; lat. 19° 46′; long. 83° 35′; from Bissemcuttack N. 18 miles; from Narsapatam N.N.E. 154 miles; from Vizagapatam N. 142 miles. A mittah held under the Taut rajah by an Ooriya patro.——*Neemgherry* (నీంగిరి - nímgiri, Tel.). See sep. title.——*Ombadola* (ఒంబదోల - ombadóla, Tel.). Village; pop. 1,132; lat. 19° 49′; long. 83° 30′; from Bissemcuttack N. 22 miles; from Narsapatam N.N.E. 156 miles; from Vizagapatam N. 146 miles. A mittah held under the Taut rajah by an Ooriya patro.——**(2)** Deputy tahsildarry, Vizagapatam district, range situated to the extreme north of Vizagapatam. Pay Rs. 120.——**(3)** Village, Head-quarters of Taut rajah and Deputy tahsildar, Government hospital; Vizagapatam district, Bissemcuttack division; lat. 19° 30′; long. 83° 33′; from Coraputt N.E. 70 miles; from Madras N.N.E. 488 miles; from Narsapatam N.N.E. 138 miles; from Parvatipore N. 50 miles; from Vizagapatam N. 125 miles; from Vizianagram N. 96 miles. Population composed almost entirely of retainers and servants of the Taut rajah, a feudatory of Jeypore paying a tribute of Rs. 15,000 per annum and bound to render service with five hundred armed peiks or peons. The fort is called in Teloogoo Issemcote. Export trade in gram, tobacco, saffron, mustard, gingelly seeds and sugar. Imports are iron, cloth and salt.

BISWOOL (खदिर - khadira, *San.*; थेंबि - t'hémbi, *Mahr.*; بسول - bisúl, *Hind.*; కారుశీకాయ - kárushíkáya, *Tel.*; உசிலை - usilai, *Tam.*). Title from hindostany. San. from (khad, san. to be firm); from hard wood [catechu tree, shoondy, sundra]. Tel. from (káru, tel. wild + shíkáya, tel. acacia concinna, dec.). Tam. from (usi, tam. sharpness); from thorns [dark sirissa]. Tel. also (karrachika), meaning stain + soap-pod. Tam. also (shikkiri), meaning cleansing tree, from leaves used to cleanse hair; (udu), meaning arrow tree, from thorns. Title otherwise Fine-leaved acacia, Oosilay, Rusty mimosa. Botanically Acacia [cantalam] pennata, willd., leguminosæ [vricsham, 48]. Alias Acacia megaladena; Mimosa ferruginea, pennata. Large thorny climber and hedge plant; flowers small, yellow; flowering in rainy season. Wood porous, moderately hard.

BITLOBAN (कृष्णलवण - krishnalavana, *San.*; बिडलवण - bidalavana, *Mahr.*; ملح نفطی - milhiniftí, *Ar.*; نمک سیاہ - namakisiyáh, *Pers.*; کالا نمک - kálánamak, *Hind.*; پادرا نمک - pádránamak, *Dec.*; ಕರೇಉಪ್ಪು - karéuppu, *Can.*; కరియుప్పు - kariyuppu, *Too.*; నల్లఉప్పు - nallauppu, *Tel.*; കാരുപ്പ് - káruppu, *Mal.*; කළුලුණු - kaluluṇu, *Singh.*; கருப்புப்பு - karuppuppu, *Tam.*). Title from mahrattee. San. from (krishna, san. black + lavana, san. salt). Mahr. from (vit, san. excrement + lavana, san. salt). Ar. from (milh, ar. salt + nift, ar. bad smell). Pers. from (namak, pers. salt + siyáh, pers. black). Hind. from (kálá, hind. black + namak, pers. salt). Dec. from (pádrá, hind.

bad smell + namak, hind. salt). Drav. means black + salt. Singh. from (kala, singh. black + lunu, singh. salt). Hind. also (bidlon), from mahratta; (kálálon), meaning black salt; (pádálon), meaning bad smelling salt; (pádánamak), meaning bad smelling salt. Tel. also (gandhakauppu), meaning sulphur + salt. Black salt [ooppoo]; an impure chloride of sodium containing a little sulphuret of iron; the variety which has smell something like that of rotten eggs, see names above, is superior. Prepared by melting together for six or seven hours in an earthen pot an impure muriate of soda and emblic myrobalans, in proportion of fifty-six pounds of the muriate to twenty ounces of the dried myrobalans. On analysis 480 grains contained black oxide of iron 6 grains, sulphur 14 grains, muriate of lime 12 grains, muriate of soda 444 grains, loss 4 grains. Used as a tonic in dyspepsia and gout, as a deobstruent in obstruction of the spleen and mysenteric glands and as a stimulant in chronic rheumatism and palsy.

BITRAGOONTA (బిట్రగుంట - bitragunta, *Tel.*). From (bittara, tel. beautiful + gunta, tel. pond). Village; Nellore dist., Cauvaly tal.; pop. 2,046; acres 4,762; lat. 14° 49′; long. 80° 01′; from Cauvaly S.S.W. 7¼ miles; from Nellore N. 25 miles; from the sea W. 8 miles. Temple of Vishnoo on a hill close by, and annual festival. Many resort for marriages instead of Tripatty, the god being the same. South of the temple is a cave temple on a hill. There is a small tank at the foot of the hill called Sawmypooshcarny. Weaving industry. Trig. station in lat. 14° 47′ 57·58″; long. 80° 1′ 7·59″; height 153 feet; from Cadanootla W.N.W. 2 miles; from Cauvaly S. 8 miles; from the sea W. 8 miles.

BLACHANG (بالچان - bálachán, *Malay*). A caviare of strong odour prepared with spawns of shrimps and shrimps themselves in Straits settlements whence brought here.

BLACK (कृष्ण - krishna, *San.*). Enters into innumerable compounds.——*Black buck* (జింక - jinka, Tel.). Male jinka [q. v.].——*Black honey* (کالے مدھ کا پیڑ - kálemadhkáper, Hind.). Sweet juice taken from dark berries of phyllanthus [aumlacam] multiflorus [poolah]. Cf. white honey.——*Black oil tree* (مال کنگنی - málkangní, Hind.). Title from oil of seeds. Same as Malkangany.——*Black quail* (گولو - gullú, Dec.; పురిడి - puridi, Tel.; கருங்காடை - karungádai, *Tam.*). Title from black markings. Tel. means spirited one; properly the female. Tam. from (karumai, tam. blackness + kádai, tam. quail); properly the female. Male birds are:—Tel. (koladu), meaning spiritless one; Tam. (ángádai), meaning male quail. Title otherwise Black-breasted bustard quail. Turnix taigoor, turnicinæ, tinamidæ, rasores [pacshy, 34], of naturalists [jantoo]. Alias Turnix bengalensis, ocellatus, rufa. Distinct from Quail [batair]. Fighting qualities well known; kept for that purpose by Mussalmans.——*Black wood* (शिंशप - shimshapa, San.; شیشم - shísham, Hind.; ನೂಕೇಮರ - núkémara, Can.; నూకమాను - núkamánu, Tel.; കരിമരം - karimaram, Mal.; நூக்கமரம் - núkkamaram, Tam.). Title otherwise East indian rosewood. Anglo-indian name for what is in England termed rosewood, produced chiefly by several species of Dalbergia [malabar blackwood]. Carved furniture is chiefly of blackwood. Acacia melanoxylon, r. br., is called blackwood in Australia. To be distinguished from the ebonies [atchab, ebony, indian ebony, mountain ebony].——*Blackwood's harbour* (మోనపాలెమురేవు - monapálemurévu, Tel.). After Sir Henry Blackwood, admiral. Village, Port; Nellore district, Goodoor talook. A sheet of water north of Point poody between Armegam shoal and the mainland. Soundings from 4½ fathoms near shore to 6 or 7 fathoms contiguous to end of shoal. In the beginning of the century Colonel de Haviland drew attention to the anchorage at rear of Armegam shoal. The southern entrance between the shoal and the mainland is a mile broad of deep water caused by the set of the current past Poody spit. The northern entrance is three miles broad. The shoal itself is of great length. Sir Henry Blackwood, then Admiral on the station, had a complete chart of the whole harbour's soundings prepared. The boats in use here are lighter than those on other parts of coast. A railway might be constructed running down the spit and crossing the upper part of the Poolicat lake a little above Shreeharicote [armegam, doogarauzpatam].

BLATTY (വിലാത്തി - vilátti, *Mal.*; කිරිල්ල - kirilla, *Singh.*). Mal. means foreign. Botanically Sonneratia acida, linn. f., lythraceæ [vricsham, 58]. Small evergreen tree; leaves opposite, oval, oblong, quite entire, thick, veinless; branchlets drooping, four-angled, calyx campanulate; petals six, narrow lanceolate; fruit a berry, nearly globose, many-celled; seeds numerous, surrounded with a fleshy pulp, curved; flowers in threes or sometimes solitary, large purple; on banks of tidal backwaters; send out the curious, long, spindle-shaped excrescences four or five feet above the surface; acid bitter fruit. Natives eat the fruit mixed with other food; is cooling. Wood grey, soft, even-grained; substitute for cork. No other common species here. ——*River blatty* (लाङ्गली - lángalí, San.; ചെറുവള്ളൽ - cheruvallal, Mal.; දියකිරිල්ල - diyakirilla, Singh.; பொன்னாங்கண்ணிச்சக்களத்தி - ponnánganniççakkalatti, Tam.). Title from habitat. San. from (lángala, san. plough) [wild bachnaug]. Mal. from (cheru, mal. small + vallal, mal. creeper). Singh. from (diya, singh. water + kirilla, singh. sonneratia acida, linn. f.). Tam. from (ponnánganni, tam. alternanthera sessilis, r. br. + shakkalatti, tam. rival wife); similar and found together. San. also (kañchara), meaning water + moving. Title otherwise Counterfeit jaunaky, Water olive. Botanically Hydrolea zeylanica, vahl., hydrophyllaceæ [vricsham, 91]. Alias Nama zeylanica. Annual, herbaceous; stems erect, variously bent towards the extremities; leaves short, lanceolate, rather obtuse, marked below with numerous prominent parallel veins; racemes axillary, spreading, few-flowered, and with the pedicels and calyx pubescent; pedicels one-flowered, usually opposite to a small bracted leaf; flowers deep blue, with a white spot in the centre; calyx five-parted, divisions lanceolate, thickly covered with glandular hairs; corolla wheel-shaped, tube short, five-cleft, petals spreading, or even reflexed when fully open; flowers blue; borders of tanks and other wet places; flowering in cold season; leaves beaten into a pulp and applied as a poultice to ulcers. No other common species here.

BLIMBING (बिलंबी - bilambí, *Mahr.*; बिंबल - bimbala, *Conc.*; بلمبو کا پیڑ - bilambúkáper, *Hind.*; بلمبو کا جھاڑ - biambúkájhár, *Dec.*; بلمبنگ باسی - blimbingbási, *Malay*; ಬಿಲಿಂಬಿ - bilimbi, *Can.*; ಬಿಂಬುಲಿ - bimbuli, *Too.*; బిలిబిలి - bilibili, *Tel.*; വിലുംബി - vilumbi, *Mal.*; බිලිං - bilin, *Singh.*; கொச்சித்தமரத்தை - koççittamarattai, *Tam.*). Title from malay. Hind. from (bilambú, hind. the fruit + per, hind. tree). Tam. from (koççi, tam. cochin + tamarattai, tam. averrhoa carambola, linn.). Tel. also (pulusukáyachettu), meaning sour + fruit + tree. Mal. also (kariççakka), meaning black artocarpus integrifolia, willd. Tam. also (puliççakkáy), meaning sour fruit; (pulimá), meaning sour mango. Title otherwise Bilimby, Black jack, Cucumber tree, Sour fruit. Botanically Averrhoa [lavaly] bilimbi, linn., geraniaceæ [vricsham, 31]. Tree 15–20 feet; leaves slightly sensitive, alternate, unequally pinnated; leaflets oblong, lanceolate, acuminated, entire; calyx five-cleft, pubescent; petals five; flowers reddish purple, in racemes from the trunk; fruit oblong, obtuse-angled; seeds without aril. Fruit is borne on the tree hanging merely by slight thread-like footstalks, clusters of eight or ten, from the oldest branches, but principally from the trunk itself in size of a gherkin, with a smooth, thin, pale green, translucent rind, like that of the white grape; when ripe as soft as butter, somewhat of flavor of an unripe gooseberry; contains an abundant acid juice. Syrup from juice of fruit given as cooling drink in fevers. Fruit pickled or preserved with sugar.——*Sweet blimbing* (میٹھا کمرکھ - míthákamrakh, Hind.). From taste of fruit. Same as Coromandel gooseberry.

BLOODSUCKER (सरट - sarata, *San.*; حربا - hírbá, *Ar.*; آفتاب پرست - áftábparast, *Pers.*; گرگٹ - girgit, *Hind.*; گرگٹ - girgut, *Dec.*; ತೊಂಡೆ - tonde, *Can.*; తొండ - tonda, *Tel.*; ഓന്ത് - óntu, *Mal.*; ඌනා - úná, *Singh.*; ஓணான் - ónán, *Tam.*). Title because when excited changes in color, especially about the neck, from a yellow or grey to a dark red; as if sucking its own blood. San. from (sri, san. to move). Pers. from (áftáb, pers. sun + parast, pers. worshipper). Tam. from (óthu, tam. to pray); from motion of head up and down as if in act of prayer. The terms are nearly co-extensive with the family Agamidæ, sauria [godhicay], reptilia [sarpy, 10], of naturalists [jantoo] and to be distinguished from Chameleon [patchonty]. The bloodsuckers have a head covered with numerous, very small, flattish or convex shields; tongue thick, attached to the gullet along its whole base, not, or but slightly, notched in front; scales of the back, sides and belly imbricate, generally rhombic; tail long, tapering, not fragile; eye and eyelids well developed; pupil round; nostrils in a separate plate; teeth implanted on the edge of the bones of the jaws; generally a pair of canine teeth in front of each jaw; limbs well developed. They are land lizards, some living on trees or bushes, others inhabiting rocks or plains. They do not attain any considerable size. Mostly insectivorous, but many feed on vegetables. All are oviparous. The following are representative species in S. india:—"*a*" Bronchocela jubata; Alias Bronchocela gutturosa. Is called by natives green bloodsucker; insectivorous; more or less developed crest commences on the neck; tail exceedingly long; has some yellow spots on the neck.—"*b*" Calotes nemoricola. The whole genus Calotes is closely allied to Bronchocela; true tree lizards, some having tail rather compressed at the base, feed on insects, tender leaves and berries.—"*c*" Calotes ophiomachus. Alias Agama ophiomachus; Calotes viridis; Lacerta calotes. Is called by the natives the red bloodsucker. Dark green, with four or six narrow, vertical white bands on the body; are edged with brown in young specimens; head lighter-colored or red; tail with some white bands anteriorly, brown posteriorly, with darker rings; generally some white streaks or spots on the limbs; when alarmed at the sight of an enemy its head and part of its neck and the crest become of a blood-red color.—"*d*" Calotes rouxii. Is brownish, uniform or spotted with black.—"*e*" Calotes versicolor. Alias Agama tiedemanni, versicolor, vultuosa; Calotes rouxii, viridis. Is the bloodsucker proper. Coloration variable, sometimes uniform brownish or greyish-olive or yellowish; generally broad brown bands across the back, interrupted by a yellowish lateral band; black streaks radiate from eye and some are continued over the throat, running obliquely backwards;

belly frequently with greyish longitudinal stripes, along the median line being most distinct; young and half-grown specimens have dark, black-edged band across inter-orbital region; ground-color generally light brownish olive. This lizard can change to bright red, to black, and to a mixture of both. Change is sometimes confined to the head, at other times diffused over the whole body and tail. Common state is, with the tail and limbs black, head and neck yellow picked out with red, and the rest of the body red. These bright changeable colors are peculiar to the male during the breeding season, in the months of May and June. One of the most common lizards; found in hedges and trees.—"*f*" Charasia dorsalis. Alias Agama dorsalis. Is brownish yellow or dusk gray on the back; black band commences behind the eye and another behind the angle of the mouth; former continued on and spreads over the sides of the body; legs dotted with black; male sometimes of a brighter color, red or yellow on the back, black on the sides and on the belly. Rock lizard only found at some elevation above the sea.—"*g*" Dracones or dragons are tree lizards, jumping from branch to branch; they are supported in the air by their expanded parachutes, which are laid backwards at the sides of the animal while it is sitting or merely running; if the hind extremities of a dragon were cut off, it would lie helpless on the ground, but it would still move with great velocity if it were merely deprived of its wings. Most of the species have a short, low crest along the middle of the neck, more developed in the adult male than in the female and young; trunk rather slender, covered above and below with scales; tail long, slender, tapering to a point, not fragile; variegated colors. Draco dussumerii has the ground color of wings light; blackish violet reticulated lines occupy middle and outer half of wings, enclosing round light spots; only found in Malabar, Cochin, and Travancore.—"*h*" The genus Salea has the head tetrahedral, covered with small irregular shields; trunk slightly compressed, covered with scales; throat without pouch or fold; tail long, tapering, slightly compressed at the base, uniformly covered with scales; limbs well developed. Salea horsefieldii. Alias Mecolepis hirsutus, sulcatus, trispinosus; Salea jerdonii. Is generally a bright grass-green, marbled with brown, with red marks on the head and nape and with a few white scales on the sides; colors become darker at a low temperature; frequents bushes and hedges.—"*i*" The genus Sitana has only four toes behind. Head tetrahedral; snout of moderate length; body slightly compressed; tail longish, rounded, tapering; head covered with small, keeled scales; male provided with a very large, subtriangular appendage, which extends on to the belly; can be folded up like a fan, and in this state it is scarcely visible. Sitana minor is brownish, with series of rhomboidal dark spots along back, spot on the neck being the darkest; whitish line along each side of the back; gular appendage tri-colored, blue, black, and red; common in fields and low copses, avoiding wooded districts; the common prey of many raptatorial birds. Sitana ponticeriana is brown, with series of dark spots along the middle of back, spot on the neck being the darkest; whitish band along each side of the back; gular appendage tri-colored, blue, black and red.

BLOODWOOD (جارل - járal, *Hind.*; ಚಲ್ಲಾ - challá, *Can.*; അടമ്പു - atambu, *Mal.*; கடலிப்பூவாமரம் - kadalippúvámaram, *Tam.*). From red dye of wood. Indian bloodwood is lagerstrœmia flos-reginæ, retz. [adambo]. Jamaica bloodwood is gordonia hæmatoxylon, ternstrœmiaceæ. Norfolk island bloodwood is balogia lucida, euphorbiaceæ. Victoria bloodwood is eucalyptus corymbosa, myrtaceæ.

BLUE (नील - níla, *San.*). Common prefix.——*Blue gum* (கர்ப்பூரமரம் - karppúramaram, Tam.). Title from general color of foliage and from giving gum. Tam. from (karpura, san. camphor + maram, tam. tree); from smell and appearance of back of leaves. Title otherwise Fever gum. Botanically Eucalyptus [australian gum tree] globulus, labill., myrtaceæ [vricsham, 56]. Lofty tree; young shoots and foliage glaucous-white; leaves of the young trees opposite, sessile, and cordate, of the full-grown tree lanceolate or ovate-lanceolate, acuminate, falcate; veins rather conspicuous, oblique and anastomosing, the intra-marginal one at a distance from the edge; flowers large, axillary, solitary, or two to three together, closely sessile on the stem or on a peduncle not longer than thick; calyx tube broadly turbinate, thick, woody, and replete with oil-receptacles, more or less ribbed and rugose; border prominent; operculum thick, hard, and warty, depressed hemispherical; stamens infected in the bud, raised above the calyx by the thick edge of the disk; anthers ovate, with parallel cells; fruit semi-globular, the broad flat-topped disk projecting above the calyx, the capsule nearly level with it; valves flat. The best known here of the australian gums; from tasmania; introduced especially on neilgherries. The kino is inferior; the oil from leaves and young shoots is camphor-like, has been substituted for cajeput oil; wood strong, tough, and durable.——*Blue rock pigeon* (कपोत - kapóta, San.; पारवा - páravá, Mahr.; حمام - hamám, Ar.; کبوتر - kabútar, Pers., Hind. and Dec.; గుడిపావురాయి - gudipávuráyi, Tel.; അമ്പലപ്രാവു - ambalaprávu, Mal.; கோவிற்புறா - kóvirburá, Tam.). Title from ash-blue color. San. from (ka, san. wind + póta, san. young); from rapidity of motion. Ar. from (hamma, ar. hot); from its properties. Pers. from sanscrit. Tel. from (gudi, tel. temple + pávuráyi, tel. pigeon). Mal. from (ambalam, mal. temple + právu, mal. pigeon). Tam. from (kóvil, tam. temple + purá, tam. pigeon); from haunt. Hind. also (pureva). Tel. also (pávuramu); (pávuráyi). Mal. also (mátaprávu), meaning house + pigeon. Tam. also (malaippurá), meaning mountain + pigeon; (purá). Columba intermedia, columbinæ, columbidæ [capotam], gemitores [pacshy, 29], of naturalists [jantoo]. Alias Columba livia, œnas. Venerated by natives; if they build in the house it is a fortunate omen; very destructive to grain; the origin of most of the domestic pigeons of india; to be distinguished from the so-called rock pigeon [q.v.].

BO (بو - bú, *Hind.*). Fragrance.——*Bostaun* (بوستان - bústán, Hind.). From (above + sitán, pers. place). The work by the Persian poet and moralist Saady who lived 1184 to 1292 A.D.

BOA (ಬೋಆ - bóa, *Can.*). Todah temple on Neilgherries.

BOBBARCHY (باورچی - báwarchí, *Hind.*). Turkish. Cook.

BOBBERY (باپ رے - bápre, *Hind.*). From (báp, hind. father + re, hind. oh). Exclamation of surprise; so noise, quarrel; a bobbery pack is a pack of noisy mongrel dogs.

BOBBILY (بوبلی - búblí, *Hind.*; బొబ్బిలి - bobbili, *Tel.*). From (pedda, tel. great + puli, tel. tiger); called in honor of Sher mahomed khan.——(1) Division, Vizagapatam district; population 128,785; language Teloogoo. Boundaries:—north, Parvatipore division; east, Palcondah division; south, Cheepoorpully and Gajapatinugger divisions; west, Sanlore division. Consists of a plain with low line hills here and there. Black soil and red soil. Irrigation by tank and wells, and Vaigavaty and Swarnamookhy rivers. Camping grounds, Bobbily and Seetanagaram on the main road. Places of archæological interest:—Bobbily, Chitracote, Narrainpooram, Seetanagaram. Principal trig. station:—Rawal. The leading places, &c., in the division are the following.——*Bobbily* (బొబ్బిలి - bobbili, Tel.). See below.——*Chitracote* (చిత్రకోట - chitrakóta, Tel.). From (chitra, san. ornamental + kóta, san. fort); from site. Village; pop. 952; lat. 18° 37′; long. 83° 21′; from Bobbily N.W. 4¼ miles; from Vizagapatam N. 62 miles. Former capital of the Jeypore rajahs. Fort built by Vishwambhara deo maharajah, on a site well chosen for defensive purposes. A carved stone inside the gateway or Toorcavaudoo bears a hand, sun, moon, horse and two human figures. Close by is site of old city with stone walls and pillars of a temple still remaining.——*Langoolya* (లాంగుల్య - lángulya, Tel.). See sep. title.——*Narrainpooram* (నారాయణపురము - náráyanapuramu, Tel.). From (náráyana, san. vishnu, the mover on waters + pura, san. town). Village; pop. 2,767; lat. 18° 38′; long. 83° 36′; from Bobbily E.N.E. 13 miles; from Vizagapatam N.N.E. 66 miles. West are four old Shiva temples. On pillars and walls are inscriptions.——*Paultair* (పాల్తేరు - páltéru, Tel.). From (pálu, tel. milk + éru, tel. river). Village; pop. 3,464; lat. 18° 31′; long. 83° 27′; from Bobbily S.E. 4½ miles; from Vizagapatam N. 57 miles. Good earthenware.——*Peddapenky* (పెద్దపెంకి - peddapenki, Tel.). From (pedda, tel. large + penki, tel. a climbing shrub, gouania leptostachya, dec.). Village; pop. 3,026; lat. 18° 35′; long. 83° 33′; from Bobbily E. 9½ miles; from Vizagapatam N.N.E. 62 miles. Good gold and silver work. Girdles made.——*Rawal* (రావల్ - rával, Tel.). From (rávi, tel. poplar tree, ficus religiosa, linn.). Trig. station; lat. 18° 32′ 12·00″; long. 83° 35′ 39·31″; height 875 feet; from Bobbily E. 12 miles; from Vantaraum E. 1 mile.——*Seetanagaram* (సీతానగరము - sitánagaramu, Tel.). From (sítá, san. wife of ráma + nagara, san. town). Tel. also (peddabhógila), meaning large + village so called. Village; pop. 1,138; lat. 18° 39′; long. 83° 25′; from Bobbily N. 5¾ miles; from Vizagapatam N. 65 miles. Former head-quarters of a District moonsif. Old fort and inscriptions.——(2) Zemindarry; Vizagapatam district, Bobbily division; for an account of the zemindarry, *vide* vol. I, 60, foot-note.——(3) Deputy tahsildarry; Vizagapatam district. Pay Rs. 100.——(4) Town, Head-quarters of Zemindar and Deputy tahsildar, High school supported by the Rajah, Sub-registrar's office; Vizagapatam district, Bobbily division; pop. 14,468; lat. 18° 34′; long. 83° 24′; from Coraputt E.S.E. 44 miles; from Madras N.N.E. 422 miles; from Narsapatam N.E. 78 miles; from Parvatipore S.S.W. 15 miles; from Vizagapatam N. 60 miles; from Vizianagram N. 31 miles. Old mud fort, where a battle was fought between Runga row of Bobbily and Pedda vijiaram rauz of Vizianagram, assisted by the French in which the former was defeated and slain. In 1758 the fort was stormed by a force under Bussy. When all hope of maintaining it against the assailants had been abandoned by the garrison, the chiefs put to death their wives and children, and returned to die themselves on the walls. Peshcush Rs. 89,763. Bobbily runga row charitram is modern poem in three cantos on siege of Bobbily fort.

BODA (ବଡ଼ - boda, *Oor.*). Great.——*Bodagooda* (బొడగూడ - bodagudá, Tel.). From (above + gudá, oor. fort).—"*a*" Ancient zemindarry, Ganjam dist.; pop. 16,106; square miles 455.

Adjoins the old zemindarry of Sooradah, now incorporated in Goomsoor talook. Attached to the zemindarry by name are the contiguous Bodagooda maliahs which form a part of the charge of the Special assistant agent. One of the wildest parts of the district. For the most part hilly and overrun with jungle, amongst which there is some fine forest land. Streams watering the country are tributaries of large rivers. There are 153 villages and three mittahs or sub-divisions, viz., Coradahcona, Cotta and Jagary. The present zemindar is Shree kesora chendra sing. Peshcush Rs. 4,024.—" *b*" Village; Ganjam district, Zemindarry tracts; pop. unknown; lat. 19° 38′; long. 84° 27′; from Chetterpore W.N.W. 43 miles; from Russellcondah S.S.W. 24 miles.——*Boda kimedy* (బోడకిమిడి - bódakimedi, Tel.). Ooriya form of Pedda kimedy.

BODHAM (बोध - bódha, *San.*). From (budh, san. to know). Wisdom.——*Bodhagooroosawmy* (బోధగురుస్వామి - bódhagurusvámi, Tel.). Means wise preceptor. Epithet of Soobramanyan who was preceptor to his father Shiva. Hindoo 2nd or pers. name [peyar].——*Bodhamullay* (போதமலை - póthamalai, Tam.). From (bódha, san. wisdom + malai, tam. mountain). Hill; Salem dist., Salem tal.; lat. 11° 32′; long. 78° 16′; from Salem S.S.E. 8½ miles. A range of hills extending from Panamarattputty to a few miles from Singipooram in Ahtoor talook.——*Bodhan* (बोध - bódha, San.). Bramha, the teacher.——*Bodhisatwan* (बोधिसत्त्व - bódhisattva, San.). From (bódhi, san. perfect wisdom + sattva, san. essence). One who has the essence of perfect wisdom in him. Among Booddhists an ascetic who has arrived at the stage when there is only one more birth, before attaining the rank of a Booddha [matam].——*Bodhy* (बोधि - bódhi, San.). Wisdom tree. The bo-tree of the Booddhists. Peepul, Ficus religiosa, linn., under which Gowtaman attained Booddhahood, found in the precincts of every Booddhist temple [matam].

BODINAICKANORE (போடிநாயக்கனூர் - pódináyakkanúr, *Tam.* bodináyakanúr *). From (bódináyakudu, tel. proper name + úr, tam. village). Zemindarry, Village; Madura dist., Periyacoolam tal.; pop. 17,570; acres 19,698; lat. of village 10° 01′; long. 77° 24′; from Madura W. 52 miles; from Periyacoolam W.S.W. 15 miles. Peshcush Rs. 15,347. Estate was one of the original seventy-two Naicks' polliems of Madura, the family having emigrated from Gooty in 1336 A.D. Resumed by Hyder ally in 1776, and after an interval of semi-independence again reduced by Tippoo. Subsequently seized by Rajah of Travancore. In 1793 the Bodinaickanore chief recovered possession. In 1795 on the Company's officers proceeding to settlement of district, they were resisted by chief of Bodinaickanore, and the party was fired upon. It was one of the largest of the twenty-four polliems then settled, containing thirty villages and yielding about Rs. 70,000 per annum. The valley of this name lies between the Pulneys and the Travancore hills and is watered by the Tainy.

BOGGAIR (బొగ్గేరు - boggéru, *Tel.*). From (boggu, tel. charcoal + éru, tel. river). Sanscrit by corruption (bhrigunadí), meaning Bhrigoo, the sage + river. River; Nellore district, Atmacore and Oodayagherry talooks. Affluent of the Pennair. Rises among ghauts at Boggoo vencatapooram, drains country west and south of Oodayagherry droog, and flowing through Atmacore joins the Pennair a little above sungam, where the two rivers have overspread a considerable tract with alluvial deposits. The site of the source is called Boggootloo, where there is very thick bamboo forest. Runs during October, November, December. Not navigable. No bridges. One under contemplation at Boylachirvella, where at present is a small anicut by means of which water is taken to Atmacore tank. Atmacore talook to some extent and Oodayagherry talook almost entirely, depend upon the Boggair for irrigation.

BOHRAH (بوهرا - bohrá, *Hind.*). Through Goozeratty from (vyavahára, san. business). An offshoot of Shiahs, originally Bramin converts. They believe in seven imaums instead of twelve. The centre of this class is at Surat. But several families in Madras.

BOJAH (فقاع - fukká, *Ar.*; بوزا - bozá, *Pers.*; بوجا - bojá, *Hind.*). Fermented liquor obtained in Northern circars from raggy [q. v.], fermented with bark of margosa tree [neem] and further made intoxicating by addition of bachnaug [q. v.] or poison root. It somewhat resembles English country beer [mooskiraut, sharaub].

BOLAMPUTTY (பொலுவாம்பட்டி - póluvámbatti, *Tam.*). From (bólu, tel. hollow + patti, tam. cattle fold). Valley; Coimbatore district, Coimbatore talook; lat. 10° 58′; long. 76° 50′; from Coimbatore W. 11 miles. The valley of the Noyil.

BOLARUM (بولارم - bolárum, *Hind.*). Cantonment, 12 miles north of Hyderabad, and 5 miles north of Secunderabad.

BOLE (रसगन्ध - rasagandha, *San.*; बाळंतबोळ - bálantabóla, *Mahr.*; مر - murr, *Ar.*; بول - bol, *Pers.*, *Hind.* and *Dec.*; ಬೊಳ - bóla, *Can.*; బాలెంతబోళము - bálentabólamu, *Tel.*; ගන්ධරස - gandharasa, *Singh.*; வெள்ளைப்போளம் - vellaippólam, *Tam.*). Title from egyptian through persian. San. from (rasa, san. juice + gandha, san. fragrance). Mahr. from (bálanta, mahr. woman in child bed + vóla, san. gum-myrrh); useful in delivery. Ar. from (murara, ar. to be bitter); from taste. Singh. from sanscrit. Tam. from (vellai, tam. white + vóla, san. the gum); from whitish opaque markings on fracture. San. also (raktápaha), meaning blood destroyer. Hind. also (hírábol), meaning white bole. Singh. also (bólam). Tam. also (vázháttippólam), meaning woman in child bed + myrrh; (shivappólam), meaning white myrrh. Hebrew mor from its bitterness. Greek σμύρνα, and so Aeolic μύῤῥα and English myrrh. Title otherwise Bayee balsam, Myrrh, Woman's bole. Botanically Balsamodendron [balsam] myrrha, n. ab. e., burseraceæ [vricsham, 35]. A small tree with a whitish grey bark, rough abortive branches terminating in spines; found in arabia, likewise on the range of hills which on the african shore runs parallel to somauly coast; the source of true myrrh of european commerce. Myrrh is the gum-resin spontaneously deposited in the cortical layers; occurs in the form of tears of irregular shape and variable size; somewhat translucent, of a reddish yellow or reddish-brown color, has an agreeable aromatic odour, and a bitter acrid taste; is partly soluble in water, alcohol and ether; often adulterated with indian googals [q.v.]. The medicinal use is the same as of native googals; is in pharm., officinal, gummi resina myrrha of chemists. Used with olibanum [q.v.] as a constituent of incense, perfumes, and unguents. The googals are called False myrrh. With the στακτή or liquid myrrh of the ancients no drug of modern times has been indentified.——*Besabo'e* (महिषबोळ - mahishavóla. San.; بهينسابول - bhainsábol, Hind. and Dec.). Means Buffalo myrrh; like buffalo's eyes; also being given to increase its milk. Trade name in Bombay for the gum-resin from Africa. Same as African bdellium.——*Black bole* (بول سياه - bolisiyáh, *Pers.*). Aloes [cariya bolum].——*Hirabole* (هيرا بول - hírábol, Hind.). Means white myrrh. Another name for myrrh [bole].——*Woman's bole* (బాలెంతబోళము - bálentabólamu, Tel.). Title from being administered to women in child bed. Another name for myrrh.

BOLY (بولی - bolí, *Hind.*). Language.——*Khary boly* (کهری بولی - kharíbolí, Hind.). From (kharí, hind. plain + above). Common talk. Plain Hindee.

BOMBAY (मुंबई - mumbaí, *Mahr.*). From the local deity. The town so called. Cf.:—Aloe socotrina, bombay aloe; Cassia angustifolia, bombay senna; Crotalaria juncea, bombay hemp; Dalbergia latifolia, bombay blackwood; Hibiscus cannabinus, bombay hemp. See gloss. paragraphs.——*Bombay duck* (बोंबील - bómbíla, Mahr.). Trade name for dried and salted bummelo [q.v.], employed as relish with curries.

BOMMA (బొమ్మ - bomma, *Tel.*). From (brahma, san. the god). Cf. Ficus asperrima (bommamarri), bramha's banyan; Webera corymbosa (bommapápata), bramha's pavetta. See gloss. paragraphs.

BOMMA (బొమ్మ - bomma, *Tel.*). Puppet. Pariah proper name [peyar]. Bommalautas are a class of beggars who act plays in the streets.——*Bomrauz* (బొమరాజు - bommarádzu, Tel.). From (above + rádzu, tel. king). From comely appearance. Same as Carvetnugger [q.v.]. See vol. I, 58. A polliem. Formerly with Vencatagherry, Calastry, and Sydapore, constituted the district of Western polliems.——*Bomrauzpollem* (బొమరాజపాలెము - bomarádzupálemu, Tel.). From (bomarédzu, tel. proper name + pálemu, tel. camp). Village; North arcot dist., Carvetnugger zemindarry; lat. 13° 24′; long. 79° 40′; from Carvetnugger E. 11 miles; from Chittore E.N.E. 36 miles. Original village of the Bomrauz or Carvetnugger family; in ruins [western pollems].

BONDILY (బొందిలి - bondili, *Tel.*); so called from being settlers from Bundelcund. A caste with some Rajpoot ancestry. The Sheivites of this sect bury their dead, the Veishnavites burn them. Remarriage of widows is not permitted. Generally peons of zemindars. These or Bhatrauzool chiefly claim to be Cshatriyas [jauty].

BONDOO (బొందు - bondu, *Tel.*). Crop withered before ear.

BONDUC (पूतिकरञ्ज - pútikarañja, *San.*; गजगोटी - gajagótí, *Mahr.*; गजगो - gajagó, *Conc.*; شجر اكتمكت - shajariakitmakit, *Ar.*; درخت خاي ابليس - darakhtikháyahiiblís, *Pers.*; كتكليجى كا پهر - katkalíjekáper, *Hind.*; گجگے کا جہاڑ - gajgekáhár, *Dec.*; بوا گوری - buvágore, *Malay*; ಗಜ್ಜಿಗೆ - gajjige, *Can.*; ಗೆಜಿಗೆ - gejige, *Too.*; గచ్చ - gattsa, *Tel.*; കഴഞ്ചി - kazhañchi, *Mal.*; කුඹුරුවැල් - kumburuval, *Singh.*; கழற்சி - kazharchi, *Tam.*). Title from arabic meaning filbert; from resemblance; arabs also called areca nut bandak i hindee; according to some the filbert is bandak in arabic as coming from banadik or venice. San. from (púti, san. stinking + karañja, san. pongamia glabra, vent.); from kernels. Mahr. means wreath ball. Ar. from (shajar, ar. tree + akitmakit, ar. bonduc nut). Pers. from (darakht, pers. tree + kháyah, pers. testicle + iblís, pers. satan). Hind. from (karanja, san. pongamia glabra, vent. + per, hind. tree). Dec.

from (gajgá, hind. bonduc nut + jhár, hind. tree). Can. from (gâjje, can. foot-ball), seeds worn as ankle bells. Tel. from (gittsu, tel. to pinch) ; from prickly legumes. Singh. from (kumbura, singh. paddy-field + val, singh. creeper). Tam. from (kazhal, tam. foot) ; from seeds worn as ankle bells. San. also (kubérákshí), meaning coobairan, the god of wealth + eye [portia] ; (prakírya), meaning thrown, as in dice ; (kalimâraka), meaning caly + destroyer, from being used by pregnant women as a charm against abortion. Mahr. also (káutékaranja), meaning thorny pongamia glabra ; (ghánerákaranjal), meaning nauseous pongamia glabra ; (ságaragóti), meaning ocean + round pebble. Ar. also (bunduk), meaning a ball or filbert ; (hajarulukáb), meaning eagle-stone ; from resemblance of nut. Pers. also (bundukihindí), meaning indian filbert. Hind. also (katkaranj-káper), meaning bonduc nut tree ; (katakaranja), meaning country bunduc ; (ságargholá), meaning ocean pebble ; (karanjo). Can. also (sânnagejje), meaning small + spherical bells worn on ankles. Tel. also (nemaliadugu), meaning peacock + foot, from prickles ; (shukajambukamu), meaning parrot + eugenia jambolana, lam. Tam. also (kazhangu), meaning gaming, as used in games by boys as marbles ; (muzhal), from sounding pod ; (kazhargodi), meaning bonduc creeper ; (keççakkáyççedi), meaning bonduc seed plant. Title otherwise Akulmookt, Ankle-bell, Bezoar nut, Bonduc indorum, Caly's foe, Common nicker, Corunga nut, Eagle-stone creeper, Fever nut, Grey bonduc, Guilandina, Indian filbert, Molucca bean, Molucca nut, Nicker tree, Ocean pebble, Parrot jamboo, Peacock's foot, Stinking pongamia, Sumatra nicker, Thorny pongamia. Botanically Cæsalpinia [coobairaucshy] bonducella, flem., leguminosæ [vricsham, 48]. Specific name from (bunduk, ar.). Alias Guilandina bonducella ; Glycirrhiza aculeata. Common prickly climbing shrub ; leaves abruptly bipinnated, more or less pubescent, three to eight pair, with one to two small recurved prickles between them ; leaflets oval or ovate ; prickles solitary ; flowers yellow ; sepals five, nearly equal ; petals five, sessile ; flowers largish, sulphur-colored, spicately racemose ; legume ovate, two-valved, one to two-seeded, covered with straight prickles ; native of both indies. The seeds are nearly globular, $\frac{1}{2}$ to $\frac{3}{4}$ of an inch in diameter ; of a dull grey color, smooth, very hard ; the umbilicus is surrounded by a small, dark brown, semi-lunar, blotch opposite the microphyle ; the shell is very thick, and contains a white kernel, which consists of two cotyledons and a thick radicle having a very bitter taste ; the bark and wood of the root are hardly at all bitter ; a microscopic examination shows the presence in the cotyledons of mucilage, starch, oil, and albumen ; the cells of the testa are blackened by perchloride of iron, showing the presence of tannin. Bonduc nut was probably one of the eagle-stones of the ancients, the stones which they thought eagles brought from india [aloes, eaglewood]. Bitter kernels of nuts are medicinally tonic and antiperiodic, like quinine ; made into an ointment with castor oil, and applied externally in incipient hydrocele ; useful for dispersing swellings, restraining hæmorrhage, and keeping off infectious diseases ; given internally in leprosy ; anthelmintic ; fixed fat oil from them is useful in convulsions, palsy, &c. ; officinal in pharm. bonducellæ semina or guilandinæ semina ; preparation, pulvis bonducellæ compositus, powdered kernels mixed with black pepper ; substituted for british cinchona-bark, gentian and santonin. Oil used as a cosmetic ; necklaces of seeds strung upon red silk are worn by pregnant women ; plant well adapted for hedges ; seeds used by boys as marbles ; ashes used as mordant. The nearly allied cæsalpinia bonduc, roxb., is distinguished by its larger size, being much less hairy, no stipules, erect bracts, and yellow seeds in lieu of gray.——*Tall bonduc* (നെട്ടാവിൽ - nettávil, Mal.). Title from height and appearance. Same as Sack tree.

BONTA (బొంత - bonta, *Tel.*). Large. Frequent plant first term. So bonta cauky, large raven, graculus carbo.

BOOCHKAH (बुचका - buchaká, *Mahr.*). Entangled yarn or hair brought away in combing.

BOODAMAIR (బుడమేరు - budaméru, *Tel.*). From (budama, tel. cucumis trigonus, roxb. + éru, tel. river). River ; Kistna district, Bezwada, Goodivauda, Noozveed divisions. Two hill streams rising in Reddigoodem division, in the Vissanapett division, join together and go under this name. It flows 40 miles in the talook, first in a south-westerly direction and then turns south-east and falls into the lake of Collair, Goodivauda talook. Not navigable. Flows only in July, August and September.

BOODAURASINGHY (బుడారశింగి - budárashingi, *Tel.*). From (bidáramu, tel. caravan + shringa, san. peak). Ancient Zemindarry, Village ; Ganjam dist., Sompett tal. ; Deputy tahsildar's range ; pop. 4,278 ; square miles 43 ; lat. of village 18° 58′ ; long. 84° 29′ ; from Berhampore S.W. 32 miles ; from Chetterpore S.W. 46 miles. Small zemindarry extending along the foot of Mahendram mountain between Jalantra to the north, and Mundasa to the south. There is much bamboo jungle. The family traces back its descent to 1443. Its founder, Damodara nishanka, was a Shavara chieftain. The family has repeatedly intermarried with Mundasa, with whom it has also frequently been at feud. The present zemindar is Shree lutchmy narayana nishanka deo. Peshcush Rs. 525. Contains Mahendragherry trig. station.

BOODBOODIKEY (ಬುಡುಬುಡಿಕೆ - budubudike, *Can.*). From the sound of the rattle used by them. Class of religious mendicants in Mysore. Worship hanooman [q.v.]. Tell fortunes.

BOODDHA (बुद्ध - buddha, *San.*). From (budh, san. to know). Greek βούττα. Any sage.—"*a*" The teacher generally known as Booddha was the son of a ruler, Shooddhodanan, in Capilavast, capital of a country at foot of mountains of Nepaul. Personal name unknown. His mother's name was Mauyay, daughter of Sooprabooddhan. His wife was Yashodharay and he had a son Rahoolan and a cousin Anandan. His family name was Shakyan, and his clan name Gowtaman. Common titles given to him are :—Shakya moony, the sage of the shakya tribe ; Shakya prabhoo, the shakya lord ; Shakya simhan, the shakya lion ; Prabhoo gowtaman, the distinguished one of the gowtama family ; Bhagavat, the worshipful one ; Siddhaurtan, the one who has obtained perfection ; and Tataugatam, the one who has passed away. Very little is really known of his life. His death occurred according to some in 543, and according to others in 477 B.C. The Bramins at first raised Booddha to the dignity of the ninth avatar of Vishnoo, but when Booddhism had acquired strength, and persecuted the old Veishnava creed, they abandoned this position and substituted Balabhadran, nominal elder brother of Krishnan. There have been Booddhists in India who rejected this and worshipped an earlier Booddha, and Booddhists generally hold that one Booddha more, called Meitreyan, is yet to appear.—"*b*" The historic relations of Booddhism with S. india should be read in the foot-note on the history of the Hindoo religion, at vol. I (74). It no longer exists here as a separate creed. The following is however a summary of the doctrines, being as they are the foundation of the still remaining Jeinism. Strictly a Booddhist should never pray ; he should merely contemplate. The only god is what man himself can become. Carmam or act is to be got rid of as soon as possible, for action leads to continual existence, carried on through innumerable bodies till acts are adequately rewarded or punished ; and that all existence is an evil is a fundamental dogma of Booddhism. Hence the great end of the system is Nirvaunam, the being blown out or extinction ; this is similar to the nivritty or mocsham of the Bramins, and analogous to the ἀπολύτρωσις and ἐξανάστασις of the Bible. Booddhists regard men as divided into two classes :—first, those who are still attached to the world and worldly life ; secondly, those who by self-mortification are bent on being delivered from it. The first class are Oopausacans or laymen, the second are Shramanans or ascetics. Ten moral prohibitions are given :—Five are for all ; viz., kill not, steal not, commit not adultery, lie not, drink no strong drink. The other five are for the ascetics who have commenced the direct pursuit of nirvaunam ; viz., eat no food out of season, abstain from dances, theatres, songs, and music, use no ornaments or perfumes, abstain from luxurious beds, receive no gold nor silver. Besides these prohibitions and injunctions there are six transcendent perfections of conduct called Pauramitays which lead to the other shore of Nirvaunam and which are incumbent on all, viz., Daunam or charity or benevolence ; Sheelam or virtue or moral goodness ; Cshaunty or patience and forbearance ; Veeryam or fortitude ; Dhyaunam or meditation ; Pranyay or knowledge. Of these, that which especially characterizes Booddhism is the perfection of benevolence and sympathy displayed towards all living beings. Four others are sometimes added, viz., Oopauyam or expediency ; Balam or power ; Pranidhy or circumspection ; Nyaunam or knowledge of universal truth. The Bowddhans agree with the orthodox Hindoos in following three points :—in acknowledging braminical doctrine as foundation of their own, in admitting a trimoorty, in acknowledging transmigration [samsauram]. They differ in the following three points :—in not acknowledging the vedas as revealed, in not recognizing the division of caste, in considering the inferior gods as holy men.—"*c*" Four great Booddhist councils were held, which are often quoted in history, viz., by Ajauta shatroo, king of Magadham after Shakya moony's death ; by Caula ashocan, a century later ; by Asoca, 246 or 247 B.C. ; by Canishcan, king of Cashmere, 143 B.C. At the first council all the teachings and sayings of Shakya moony, who appears never to have written anything, were collected into three sets of books, called Tripitacam, or the three baskets or collections, which form the Booddhist sacred scriptures. These three collections are :—Sootra pitacam, collected by anandan, shakya moony's disciple, containing all the maxims and discourses of shakya moony and by no means brief like the braminical sootrams ; Vinaya pitacam containing books on morals and discipline ; Abhidharma pitacam, on metaphysics.—"*d*" The Booddhists are described in the following fragment of Cleitarchus :—"According "to the relation of cleitarchus, they place in opposition to the "bramins the pramanæ, a contentious and argumentative set of "men who deride the bramins as arrogant and ridiculous on "account of their studies in physiology and astronomy. They are "divided into the mountaineer, the naked, the citizen, and rural "sects."—"*e*" By the term Booddhist the Jeinas are generally intended among Tamuls. In one instance, in the standard history of Malabar, the name is applied to Mahomedans, showing that it was a strange one.—"*f*" See the whole of vol. I (70) to (94), and the following foot-notes ;—history of religion and philosophy I (70), jeinas I (95) [matam].——*Booddha's foot* (බුත්සරණ - butsarana, Singh.). Same as Indian shot.——*Booddhivantan*

(ಬುದ್ಧಿವಂತ - buddhivanta, Can.). Wise man; an elder in a village community.——*Booddhy* (बुद्धि - buddhi, San.). From (budh, san. to know). Greek σοφία. Wisdom; in Saunkhyam cosmogony, the first born from the Divine essence.——*Bowddham* (बौद्ध - bauddha, San.). Relating to Booddha.

BOODHAN (बुध - budha, *San.*; புதன் - puthan, *Tam.*). From (budh, san. to know). ποσειδῶν of Greeks, Neptune of Romans, Osiris of Egyptians. Wise. Name of the planet Mercury or its regent [graham]; ☿; sidereal period of revolution 87d 23h 16m; inclination of orbit [caesham] to ecliptic [craunty mundalam] about 7°. Tamulians deem it fortunate to be born when he is rising. In one of the zodiacs, he is seated on a carpet, holding in his hands a sceptre and a lotus; in another he is shown riding on an eagle; and elsewhere he is described as sitting in a car drawn by lions. The pooraunams give a brief legend that Chundran or the moon was placed in the house of Brihaspaty or Jupiter as his pupil, and that Taurah or the lunar path of twenty-seven asterisms, fell in love with Chundran, and seduced him while Brihaspaty was away at a sacrifice made by Indran or the firmament; and the result was the birth of Boodhan. Boodha vauram is Wednesday [vauram]. Must not be confounded with Booddha, the incarnation of Vishnoo [matam].

BOOGGA (بگا - buggá, *Hind.*; బుగ్గ - bugga, *Tel.*). From (bugabuga, tel. the sound of water as it comes out of the earth). Spring: suffix in place names, as Caushy boogga, meaning Benares + spring.——*Booggavunka* (బుగ్గవంక - buggavanka, Tel.). From (above + vanka, tel. channel). Otherwise Booggair River; Cuddapah district, Cuddapah talook. Rises in Palcondah hills and joins Pennair due north of Cuddapah. The springs on its banks produce the best supply of fresh water available in the latter town. Its water is taken off from anicuts to two large tanks and supplies several channels near the town.

BOOKHER OIL (بخور کا تیل - bukhúrkátel, *Hind.*). From (bukhúr, ar. incense + tel, hind. oil). Product of Liquidambar orientale [indian storax].

BOOKKA (బుక్క - bukka, *Tel.*). Means a person in Canarese. With his brother Hukka or Harihara, and assisted by the sage Vidyauranyan, whose name was given originally to the city, founded the Vijianugger dynasty. The two brothers belonged to the house of Warangal from which they immigrated on its capture by Mahomedans. Bookka ruled from 1350 to 1379 and was known also as Rajendra. Vol. I (148), (151) [charitram].——*Bookkapatam* (బుక్కపట్నము - bukkapatnamu, Tel. bukkapatnam). From (bhukka, san. the vijayanagar king + pattana, san. town).—"a" Deputy tahsildarry, Anantapore district. Pay Rs. 70.—"b" Village, Deputy tahsildar's station; Anantapore dist., Penoocondah tal.; pop. 4,063; acres 7,198; lat. 14° 12′; long. 77° 51′; from Anantapore S.S.E. 35 miles; from Bellary S.E. 88 miles; from Gooty S. 64 miles; from Madras W.N.W. 185 miles; from Penoocondah E.N.E. 16 miles. On right bank of Chitrauvaty. At E. end of tank, irrigating 3,483 acres, bund 3 miles long, erected four hundred years ago across Chitrauvaty, connecting two low ranges of hills. Besieged in 1740 by Poligar of Royadroog. Poligar of Bellary raised siege, and having been admitted as an ally within fortifications seized place. To the east are hills, well wooded.

BOOLAUK (بلاق - bulák, *Hind.*; புலாக்கு - pulákku, *Tam.*). From Turkish. Flat trinket set with pearls [moty] and precious stones [ratnam] appended to the septum of the nose.

BOOLBOOL (بلبل - bulbul, *Ar.*; هزار داستان - hazárdástán, *Pers.*; بلبل - bulbul, *Hind.* and *Dec.*; పికిలి - pikili, *Tel.*; இராப்பாடிக்குருவி - iráppádikkuruvi, *Tam.*). Title from arabic, which however means the nightingale and not this. Pers. from (hazár, pers. thousand + dástán, pers. note). Hind. from arabic. Tam. from (irá, tam. night + pádu, tam. to sing + kuruvi, tam. small bird). Brachypodidæ family, dentirostres, insessores, aves [pacshy, 22], of naturalists [jantoo]. Short legged thrushes. Sub-divided into:—Pycnonotinæ, true boolbools; Phyllornithinæ, green boolbools; Ireninæ, blue-birds; Oriolinæ, orioles. The species best known to the natives are shown below. See also the Mango bird.——*Green boolbool* (هریوا - harevá, Hind. and Dec.; వనభూషణము - vanabhúshanamu, Tel.). Title from color. Hind. from (hará, hind. green). Tel. from (vana, san. forest + bhúshana, san. ornament). Phyllornis jerdoni, phyllornithinæ, of naturalists. Alias Chloropsis cochinsinensis, cœsmarhynchos. Usual call is like the King crow, though softened. Good mocking bird.——*Hill boolbool* (پہاڑی بلبل - paháríbulbul, Hind. and Dec.; తురకపికిలి - turakapikili, Tel.; கொண்டலாத்தி - kondalátti, Tam.). Title from resort. Hind. from (pahár, hind. mountain + bulbul, ar. the bird so called). Tel. from (turaka, tel. mussalman + pikili, tel. bulbul). Tam. from (kondai, tam. crest). Title otherwise Red-whiskered boolbool. Otocompsa jocosa, pycnonotinæ, of naturalists. Alias Ixos monticolus, pyrrhotis; Lanius emeria. Chirruping notes.——*Madras boolbool* (بلبل - bulbul, Ar.; هزار داستان - hazárdástán, Pers.; بلبل - bulbul, Hind. and Dec.; పికిలి - pikili, Tel.; கொண்டலாத்தி - kondalátti, Tam.). Title from habitat. Pers. from (hazár, pers. thousand + dástán, pers. note). Tam. from (kondai, tam. crest). Pycnonotus hæmorhous, pycnonotinæ, of naturalists. Alias Hamatornis cafer, pseudocafer, pusillus; Ixos cafer. Note a harsh chirrup, like 'cheek by jowl,' by which name often called; can imitate the notes of other birds; commonly caged; sometimes kept for fighting, being held on the finger with a cord attached.——*Shoubiga boolbool* (شوبگا - shúbigá, Hind.; పచ్చపిట్ట - pattsapitta, Tel.; பச்சைப்புறா - paççaippurá, Tam.). Title from cry. Tel. from (pattsa, tel. green + pitta, tel. bird). Tam. from (paççai, tam. green + purá, tam. pigeon). Iora zeylonica, phyllornithinæ, of naturalists. Alias Iora melaceps, typhia. Flight causes a whirring sound; repeats word 'shoubhiga, shoubhiga,' before rain.——*Turmeric boolbool* (పొడపికిలి - podapikili, Tel.; மஞ்சள்குருவி - mañjalguruvi, Tam.). Title from color. Tel. from (podâ, tel. variegated color + pikili, tel. bulbul). Tam. from (mañjal, tam. turmeric + kuruvi, tam. small bird). Title otherwise White-browed bush boolbool. Ixos luteolus, pycnonotinæ, of naturalists. Loud, thrush-like warble.

BOOM (بوم - búm, *Hind.*). Means frequent crier. Bird name common to:—Atheno brama; Huhua nipalensis. See gloss. paragraphs.

BOON (بن - bun, *Hind.*). Coffee [q.v.] berry.

BOORAUK (براق - burák, *Hind.*). From (bark, ar. lightning); from swiftness. Animal sent from heaven through the angel Gabriel to convey the prophet from Jerusalem to heaven on occasion of his miraculous journey [leilatoolmirauj]. It had head and face of a man; ears long; forehead broad and shining like the moon; eyes black, like those of a deer, and brilliant as the stars; neck and breast of a swan; loins of a lion; tail and two wings of a peacock; stature of a soorahgye or yak, or of a mule; speed of lightning. Fac-similes made of wood, &c., are placed in ashoorkhanas [q.v.] during the Moharram [q.v.].

BOORCA (برقع - burka, *Hind.*). From Arabic. Sheet veil for women; thrown over the head, with a not-worked space opposite the eyes; voluminous enough to conceal almost the whole person; used by women who cannot afford to be carried [muckna].

BOORHAUN (برهان - burhán, *Hind.*). From (barhana, ar. to prove). Manifest evidence. Lacab of prophet. Alam; as Syed boorhaun, alaumat + alam. Also part of lacab; as Boorhaun ood deen, proof of the faith [ism].

BOOSAM (बुस - busa, *San.*). From (bus, san. to reject). Chaff, bran. Wheat bran is given in veterinary practice instead of gram, a day or two preparatory to physic.——*Boosa priyam* (बुसप्रिय - busapriya, San.). From (above + priya, san. lover). Chaffinch. Fringillidæ family, conirostres, insessores, aves [pacshy, 27], of naturalists [jantoo]. Finches. Divided into sub-families:—"a" Ploceinæ, weaver-birds [weaver bird].—"b" Estreldinæ; two forms in India, one the munias, with a thick tumid bill; the other the amadavads with a more slender, conic, and waxy red bill [avadavat].—"c" Passerinæ, sparrows [chiriyah].—"d" Emberizinæ, buntings.—"e" Fringillinæ; divided into grosbeaks, bull-finches, cross-bills, rose finches, true finches; only the rose finches are represented in S. india.—"f" Alaudinæ, larks; sub-divided into bush-larks, the true larks, and long-billed or desert larks; the latter are not represented in S. india [aghiyah].

BOOT (بت - but, *Hind.*). From (bhúta, san. spirit). Idol.——*Bootkhana* (بتخانہ - butkhánah, Hind.). From (above + khánah, pers. house). A temple. By some supposed to be the origin of pagoda [q.v.].

BOOTCHY (బుచ్చి - buççi, *Tel.*). Small.——*Bootchammah* (బుచ్చమ్మ - buççamma, Tel.). From (above + amma, tel. mother). Hindoo female proper name [peyar].——*Bootchireddipollem* (బుచ్చిరెడ్డిపాలెము - buççireddipálemu, Tel.). From (buççireddi, tel. proper name meaning small reddi + pálemu, tel. fortified village). Colloquially bootchy and polliem. Sanscrit name (rámakshétra), meaning rama, the god + sacred place; from tradition that rama visited place during exile. Village; Nellore district, Nellore tal.; pop. 4,317; acres 7,449; lat. 14° 33′; long. 79° 56′; from Nellore N.W. 9 miles; from the sea W. 20 miles. Near the Canigherry tank, the chief reservoir under the project of the Sungam anicut. Large Vishnoo temple built by Ramy reddy, resorted to in April for nine days. Fine cloths manufactured. Good gneiss building stone. Seat of Veishnava high priest called Addanky tautacharry. The Bootchireddipollem reddies are a well known family.

BORAH (بورا - borá, *Hind.*). Canvas sack for grain [gunny].

BORAX (بورک - búrak, *Hind.*). From (baraka, ar. to glisten) [bark]. Title is short for (búrakusságha), meaning polisher + gold or silversmith. Because it polishes silver [vengauram].

BORER (سرفہ - surfah, *Ar.*; ತೊಳೆತುಂಬಿ - toletumbe, *Can.*; తొలుచుతుమ్మెద - tolutsutummeda, *Tel.*; തുളവണ്ട് - tulavantu, *Mal.*; துளைவண்டு - tulaivandu, *Tam.*). Title from boring into coffee trees to deposit eggs. Ar. from (sarafa, ar. to eat wood). Can. from (tole, can. hole + tumbe, can. carpenter bee). Tel. from (tolutsu, tel. to bore + tummeda, tel. beetle). Tam. from (tulai, tam. to bore + vandu, tam. beetle). Anglo-indian name. Xylotrechus quadrupes, cerambycidæ, coleoptera, holometabola, insecta [poochy], of naturalists [jantoo]. The larva is called the borer, the white borer, or the worm. The insect is called the coffee-fly or borer beetle. In the latter stage the insect appears as a fly or winged beetle from six to nine lines in length, with a hard slimy coat, in color red and black, or yellow and black, in alternate transverse lines. It bores a passage into the stem of the coffee tree, generally a few inches above the ground. This passage, at first horizontal, afterwards takes an upward or spiral direction, and after a little a retreat is formed in which to deposit its larva. The tree soon begins to droop, and in a short time dies down to the point where the entry was effected.

BORIYAH (कट - kata, *San.*; بوریا - boriyá, *Hind.*; ಚಾಪೆ - chápe, *Can.*; చాప - tsápa, *Tel.*; പായ - páya, *Mal.*; பாய் - páy, *Tam.*). Mat. The following are two key-lists in the briefest possible terms of the articles used here for making mats; further information must be traced in the glossary paragraphs through the small-type cross-references at end of this volume; see also vricsham, 7, for the method of expressing the products, &c., of plants in the dravidian languages.—"*a*" Andropogon muricatus, cuscus, root; Borassus flabelliformis, palmyra, leaf in strips; Cocos nucifera, cocoanut, split leaf or cadjan; Corypha umbraculifera, talipot, leaf; Cyperus corymbosus, indian matting sedge, culms; Dendrocalamus tulda, bengal bamboo, bamboo chip; Hibiscus tiliaceus, corkwood bendy, fibre of bark; Maranta dichotoma, seetalpaty, split stem; Moringa pterygosperma, indian horse radish, fibre of bark; Pandanus odoratissimus, screw-pine, leaf; Phœnix farinifera, small date, leaf; Phœnix sylvestris, wild date, leaf; Phragmites roxburghii, large naunal, split stalk; Saccharum munja, moonj grass, leaf; Saccharum sara, moonshee grass, leaf; Saccharum spontaneum, naunal, culm; Typha angustifolia, small bulrush, leaf; Typha elephantina, bulrush, leaf.—"*b*" Bamboo, dendrocalamus; Bendy, hibiscus; Bulrush, typha; Cocoanut, cocos; Cuscus, andropogon; Date, phœnix; Horse radish, moringa; Moonj grass, saccharum; Moonshee grass, saccharum; Naunal, phragmites, saccharum; Palmyra, borassus; Screw-pine, pandanus; Sedge, cyperus; Seetalpaty, maranta; Talipot, corypha.

BORNEO (بورنيو - borneo, *Hind.*). The largest of the Oceanic islands. Cf.:—Dipterocarpus turbinatus, borneo tallow; Dryobalanops aromatica, borneo camphor; Metroxylon sagu, borneo sago.

BORREL (വിരൽ - viral, *Mal.*). Old term for Malabar inch.

BO TREE (බෝ - bó, *Singh.*). Knowledge tree. Plant name common to Ficus bengalensis, Ficus religiosa [bodhy].

BOTTELL (बतेला - batélá, *Mahr.*; ബൊത്തെല്ല - bottella, *Mal.*). From Portuguese batella. A boat used on the west coast. Single-masted, 30 to 85 tons.

BOY (بھوئی - bhoí, *Hind.*; బోయ - bóya, *Tel.*). Word is Dravidian; but cf. Bhaee.—"*a*" Caste-title; personal forms, Boy, sing., Boyies, pl. Called Beydar in Canarese. The same caste is found in Central india and Berar. The Madras boyies belong to Nellore and the Northern circars. Primarily fishermen; but employed in carrying letters and palankeens, and also as domestic servants; hence familiar call. The old native armies largely recruited from this caste, and some rose to power. The Poligars of Hurpanhully and Royadroog were boyies. Have several divisions, the chief of which are the Moolky boyies meaning arrow boyies, and the Paul boyies meaning milk boyies, who cannot intermarry. Their most peculiar custom relates to marriages, in which the bride besides having a golden talee tied to her neck has an iron ring fastened to her wrist with a black string and the bridegroom has the same. Widows may not remarry or wear black bangles, but they may wear silver bangles. The boyies bury their dead and use Maudigas as their messengers on such occasions. They mostly profess to be of the Veishnava sect. See vol. I (109); II, 231. Bestas are nearly the same [jauty].—"*b*" Also head of a Gond village.

BRAB (براب - bráb, *Hind.*). From Portuguese brava, wild. The palmyra [q.v.].

BRAHOOI (ब्रहुयि - brahúyi, *San.*). A tribe of mountaineers in khanship of Khelaut in Beloochistaun. Language has a Dravidian appearance, which may argue remote affinity [bhaushay].

BRAMH (ब्रह्म - bramha, *San.*; பிரமம் - piramam, *Tam.*). From (brih, san. to increase). Neuter gender. The supreme soul of the universe, self-existent, absolute, and eternal, from which all things emanate and to which all return. It receives no worship, but is the object of that abstract meditation which sages practise in order to obtain absorption into it. It is exactly the τὸ πλήρωμα, τὸ ἓν of the Greek philosophy. Cf. anima mundi. The following is a passage from a tamul shastram:—காலத்திரயத் திலும் ஆகாயம்போலும் ஒருபடித்தாயெங்கும் நிறைந்திருக்கின்ற நித்தியசுத்தாதி இலட்சணங்களுடனே கூடினவர் பிரமத்தின்பெயர்.—அந்தரியாமிமுதலான மூவகை அதிஷ்டானன்; ஒன்றான பிரமம், பரத்துவம், பரமான்மா, விசுத்தசித்து, தத்பதலட்சியார்த்தம், சருவாதிஷ்டானத்துரு. பிரமத்தின் சப்தாவஸ்தையின் இலக்கணம்; சைதன்னியம், சுயம்பிரகாசமா யிருக்கின்றபோது பிரமம்; மாயையுடனே கூடில் ஈசுரன்; அவித்தையிற் கூடில் சீவன்; அந்தக்கரணத்துடன் கூடில் பிரமாதா; இந்திரியங்களுடன் கூடில் பிரமாணம்; பரோட்சவிஷயத்துடன் கூடில் பிரமேயம்; பிரத்தியட்சவிஷயத்துடன் கூடில் பலம்—"He is "called bramh who combines the properties of the first cause, of "eternity and purity uniformly filling and pervading everywhere "like aucausham in all the three times past, present and future; "he is three vehicles of spirit called antaryaumy and he is "the one bramh, the supreme one, the paramautman, the pure "intelligence, the designated of the syllable tat and the sole vehi-"cle of whatever form, through which the state of bramh can be "realized. The characteristics of bramh in its revealed state:—"Cheitanyam is bramh when self-enlightened; Eeshwaran when "united to mauyay or illusion; Jeevan when joined to avidyay or "ignorance; Pramautah or the judge when connected with antah-"caranam or internal sense; Pramaunam or the measure or "standard when related to indriyam or sense; Prameyam or the "thing to be measured when united to an invisible object; Palam "or fruit when united to a visible object." The doctrine of Bramh is held only as a philosophical speculation, and has no influence on the exoteric religion of the country. There is a Tamul proverb:—பார்ப்பதற்கு அரிய பரப்பிரமம்—"It is impossible "to comprehend the supreme Bramh." The Veda is sometimes called Shabda bramh, spirit to be attained through the word, as opposed to Parabramh [q.v.] spirit to be attained through reflection. See vol. I (70) to (94), and the following footnotes:—history of religion and philosophy I (70), conspectus of pantheon I (77), existing hindoo sects I (88).——*Bramha* (ब्रह्मा - bramhá, San.; பிரமன் - piraman, Tam.). From (brih, san. to increase). Masculine gender. The son or creature of Bramh; sometimes styled Curta bramha, the creator Bramha. Ζεύς of Greeks, Saturn or Jupiter of Romans, Osiris of Egyptians.—"*a*" The first member of the Trimoorty. The supreme spirit manifested as the active creator of the universe. Probably the oldest of the Aryan non-elemental gods, and closely connected with the rise of the Bramins. The acceptance of three gods simultaneously in one, in the Trimoorty, is a late conception and not improbably developed in S. india. By a modern legend the four classes, Bramin, Cshatriya, Veisya, Shoodra, are symbolically stated to have proceeded from different parts of Bramha's body; the Bramin class from his head, and thence claiming pre-eminence.—"*b*" For Bramha as giving periods to the Braminical chronology, see Calpam and Caulam. In the pooraunams of the Veishnava class, it is stated that after the last great pralayam or destruction by a flood, the supreme being as Narayanan floated on the abyss of waters on a leaf of the banyan tree, which leaf has a symbolical meaning. From his navel the stalk of a lotus arose, in the flower of which Bramha was born as the creator. The Sheiva pooraunams ignore the above view. They state Vishwacarman to be the former of all things. Bramha is treated with contempt and obloquy. Thus Shiva cut off one of the heads of Bramha for his pride. Bramha suborned a ketaky flower to tell a lie with reference to the immensity of Shiva; and was sentenced by Shiva to be without temples and worshippers. Soobramanyan asked Bramha the meaning of the mystic syllable, om; and as Bramha could not tell it, Soobramanyan put Bramha in prison, and himself assumed the work of creation. These two last legends from the Scandapooraunam are repeated in many of the local legends of Sheiva temples in the Peninsula; in that of the Yecaumbareshwaran fane at Conjeeveram with great prominence.—"*c*" As creator Bramha's shacty is mauyay or matter; as the author of the vedams his shacty is Saraswaty. He is represented in the arts in S. india as having four heads and four faces. On each one he wears a crown; in his locks he has a string of pearls; on his forehead he has a spot of custoory. Two of his hands are empty, and the other two he raises, holding in the left a water-pot and in the right a rosary of Roodraucsham. The color of his body is tawny. He stands on a flower, and near him is his vehicle, the Annam or swan. There are no pagodas sacred to him; nor does his image stand in any other pagoda. Bramins occasionally chant a hymn in his honor, and mention his name at their offerings. No feast or fast is observed in his honor, but the term Bramhotsavam [q.v.] possibly retains traces of such in very ancient days.—"*d*" There are numerous stories related of Bramha in the Pooraunams, all more or less lewd. The following are some of his names:—Ajan or the unborn; Anantan or the endless; Anna voorty or the swan-rider; Bodhan or teacher; Gooravan or the old one; Hiranya garbhan or the gold-wombed; Malarone or the lotus-one; Marayavan or having vedam; Mauloondivandone or he who sprung from maul's or vishnoo's navel [pralayam]; Mediny padeittona or creator of the earth; Naul mookhan or the four-faced; Nyauny or the wise; Pitaumahan or grandfather; Swayambh or the self-existent; Varan or giver; Vauny kelvan or saraswaty's husband; Vaunore moothalvan or the first of the celestials; Vedan or author of hindoo vedas; Vidhy or fate, &c. Of the books specially written regarding him may be mentioned Bramhaustrapatalam so called from the miracle-working arrow which he grants to ascetics, and Bramhottara khandam or the last chapter of the Bramhapooraunam.—"*e*" The pre-ordinations of Bramha, regulated by the actions of former births, are written on men's skulls. Hence the two following proverbs:—எண்ணெய்போக முழுகினாலும் எழுத்துப்போகத் தேய்ப்பார் உண்டா—

"Although one bathe till the oil is washed out, can the writing "of Bramha be rubbed off?"—தலை எழுத்தைத் தலையைச் சிரைத்தால் போகுமா?—"Can you efface the writing on the "skull, by shaving the head?" See vol. I (70) to (94), and the following foot-notes:—history of religion and philosophy I (70), conspectus of pantheon I (77).——*Bramhacharry* (ब्रह्मचारी - brahmachárí, San.). From (above + áchári, san. observer), one who practises study and devotion. A young Bramin in a state of pupilage and not married.——*Bramhadand* (ब्रह्मदण्ड - brahmadanda, San.; फिरंगीधोतरा - p'hirangidhótará, Mahr.; شيال كانٹا - shiyálkánta, Hind.; بهرم ڈنڈی - bharamdandí, *Dec.*; ಅರಸಿನವುಮ್ಮೆತ್ತ - arasinavummetta, Can.; బ్రహ్మదండి - brahmadandi, Tel.; ବ୍ରହ୍ମଦଣ୍ଡି? ଓ କଣ୍ଟାକୁଷମ - kantákusham, Oor.; ബ്രഹ്മദണ്ഡി - brahmadanti, Mal.; பிரமதண்டு - piramathandu, Tam.). San. from (brahma, san. bramin + danda, san. staff); from white color of stem. Mahr. from (p'hirangí, mahr. frank + dhótará, mahr. datura fastuosa, linn.). Hind. means jackal thorn. Can. from (arasina, can. saffron, crocus sativus, linn. + ummetta, can. thorn apple, datura fastuosa, linn.). San. also (shrigálakantaka), meaning jackal thorn; (brahmí), meaning pertaining to a bramin; (brahmarákshasa), meaning bramin + demon. Hind. also (farangídhatúrá), meaning english or foreign datura; (píládhatúrá), meaning yellow datura. Can. also (balurakkisa), meaning great demon. Mal. also (ponnummattam), meaning gold + datura fastuosa, linn. Tam. also (kudiyóttippúndu), meaning family + expel + plant; (kurukku), meaning white plant. Title otherwise Bramin devil plant, Bramin's staff, Cardo santo, Coorook, Devil's fig, Fico del' inferno, Foreign datura, Gamboge thistle, Horned poppy, Infernal fig, Jackal thorn, Jamaica yellow thistle, Mexican poppy, Prickly argemone, Prickly poppy, Thistle oil plant, Yellow datura, Yellow thistle. Botanically Argemone mexicana, linn., papaveraceæ [vricsham, 8]. Alias Argemone mucronata, spinosa. Annual, herbaceous; variegated thistle-like leaves alternate, sessile, repand-sinuate, sharply toothed; sepals two to three; calyx prickly, glabrous; petals four to six; stem bristly; flowers solitary on erect peduncles; capsules prickly; seeds roundish, corrugated; flowers bright yellow. An introduction of not very remote date from south america and one of the most common weeds throughout south india; it springs up everywhere when the soil is left uncultivated. The seeds are small, round, hard, striated, dark brown and about the size of a small mustard-seed; they are full of oil, and if crushed on paper break with a noise and leave on it an oily stain; their kernel is white, minute and albuminous; the fixed oil yielded by these seeds on expression is quite tasteless with little or no smell, and its color is pale amber, or yellowish or reddish brown; the oil gives an orange red color with nitric acid; the root is small, fusiform, brown externally, pale-white internally and odourless with a slight bitterish taste; the stalks and leaves abound with a bitter yellow juice-like gamboge, which on drying forms a substance resembling opium. Medicinally; seeds are laxative, emetic, nauseant, expectorant and demulcent; oil a drastic purgative, nauseant and expectorant; root, an alterative tonic; seeds and oil have good effect in asthma; oil used externally in cutaneous diseases and muscular pains. Preparations:—as seeds abound in oil they cannot be reduced to fine powder, and the best way of using them is in emulsion, by bruising and rubbing with water and straining through cloth, resulting draught is whitish, quite tasteless, and is rendered palatable by adding sugar or honey; the oil may be taken floating in water, in emulsion with mucilage or with sugar; the root is used in decoction by boiling three ounces with one and a-half pint of water till reduced to one pint. Doses:—of the seeds, as a laxative and emetic from one drachm and a-half to two drachms and a-half, as a nauseant expectorant and demulcent and for asthma from forty grains to one drachm three or four times in the twenty-four hours; of the oil, as a purgative from twenty to thirty-five minims, as a nauseant and expectorant and for asthma from ten to fifteen minims three or four times in the twenty-four hours; of decoction, from two to three ounces, three times a day. The seeds substituted for squill, senega root, ammoniacum, balsamum tolutanum and ether; the oil for jalap, rhubarb, castor-oil and squill; the root for jamaica sarsaparilla. Seeds narcotic, especially when smoked with tobacco. Oil used in lamps and is cheap; also used by painters and for giving a shining appearance to wood; also employed in the process of dyeing red thread. There is a variety with white flowers. No other common species here.——*Bramhadauyam* (ब्रह्मदाय - brahmadáya, San.). From (above + dá, san. to give). Lands held by Bramins free of assessment [inam].——*Bramhagherry* (ബ്രഹ്മഗിരി - brahmagiri, Mal.). From (above + giri, san. hill). Can. name (marenádu), meaning shelter + country. Mountains; Malabar dist., Cottayam, Wynaud tals.; lat. of trig. station 11° 55′ 5·5″; long. 76° 02′ 09·8″; height 5,276; from Calicut N.N.E. 48 miles; from Cannanore E.N.E. 42 miles; from Madras W.S.W. 305 miles; from Malapooram N. 60 miles; from Manantoddy N. 9 miles; from Palghaut N.N.W. 90 miles; from Ponnany N.N.E. 77 miles; from Tellicherry E.N.E. 36 miles. On the edge of an elevated miniature plateau of grass and sholah land, the greater portion of which lies in Coorg. Forms the southern section of the chain of the Western ghauts, which constitutes a natural barrier for several miles between Coorg and Wynaud talooks. The sides are clothed with heavy forest, and in some places with coffee plantations. Among these hills are the sources of the principal tributaries of the Cauvery, the Lutchmana teertam, Paupnaushy, and Belliapatam which flows westwards; on the precipitous western face, the Barapoley and other cataracts leap down to the sea. Highest peak, Davasy betta, 5,276 feet.——*Bramhanacrauka* (బ్రాహ్మణక్రాక - bráhmanakráka, Tel.). From (bráhmana, san. bramin + kráka, tel. anger). Village; Nellore dist., Cauvaly tal.; pop. 3,213; acres 15,369; lat. 14° 50′; long. 79° 57′; from Cauvaly S.W. 8½ miles; from Nellore N.N.W. 27 miles; from the sea W. 13 miles. Up to A.D. 1790 gave its name to a talook. Large wet village being entirely flat. Two tanks. Two old temples. Trig. station in lat. 14° 49′ 37·44″; long. 79° 59′ 8·60″; height 38 feet; from Cauvaly S.S.W. 7¼ miles; from Jaldanky S.S.E. 4½ miles; from the sea W. 10 miles.——*Bramhanam* (ब्राह्मण - bráhmana, San.). From (brahma, san. sacred text). One of the two dual parts of each of the four old Vedams. Precept and illustration as against original dogma. Cf. the Talmud as against the Mosaic code, and the Hadees or Soonnat as against the Koran. However the Bramhanams are as much Shrooty or revelation as the Muntrams. In relation to caste Bramhanams are more important than the hymns. They are unsystematic prose compositions, intended to serve as ceremonial directories for the use of the priests, prescribing rules for the employment of the Muntrams at sacrifices, speculating as to the meaning and effect of certain verses and metres, and giving detailed explanations of the origin, import, and conduct of the sacrifices, with the occasional addition of controversial remarks and illustrations in the shape of legends. Each of the Samhitays or collections of Muntrams has its own one or more Bramhanams. Thus Rig vedam has the Eitareya bramhanam and the Cowsheetaky bramhanam. The two collections of the Yajoor vedam have the Teittireeya brámhanam and the Shatapata bramhanam. The Sauma vedam has eight Bramhanams, of which the best known are the Prowdham or Puncha vimsham, the Taundyam, and the Shadvimsham. The Atarva vedam has a Bramhanam, called Gopatam [matam].——*Bramha rautry* (ब्रह्मरात्रि - brahmarátri, San.). The night of Bramha, the calpam [q.v.] being his day light.——*Bramha samauj* (ब्रह्मसमाज - brahmasamája, San.). From (above + samája, san. assembly). A reform of Hindooism begun by Ram mohun roy in Bengal in 1830. A branch called Veda samauj was established in Madras in 1864. See vol. I (77) [matam].——*Bramha sampradayee* (ब्रह्मसम्प्रदायी - brahmasampradáyí, San.). From (above + sampradáyí, san. holder of any traditional doctrine). Another name for the Madhwacharry [q.v.] sect of Veishnavas. See vol. I (90).——*Bramhasom* (ബ്രഹ്മസ്വം - brahmasvam, Mal.). Means Bramins' property. Inam lands of Bramins. See vol. II, 105, 289.——*Bramha staupyam* (ब्रह्मस्थाप्य - brahmast'hápya, San.). From (above + st'hápya, san. established). Performance of the sacred thread ceremonial in favor of a Bramin. One of the seven meritorious acts.——*Bramhaudicam* (ब्रह्मादिक - brahmádika, San.). From (above + ádi, san. beginning). Incarnation of Bramha [avatar]. There is a very ancient tradition that there were nine such; and that they, as heads of families, became the progenitors of the human race. There is a frequent interchange of names between these, the seven great rishies, and the prajaupaties or patriarchs.——*Bramhaundam* (ब्रह्माण्ड - brahmánda, San.). From (above + anda, san. egg). The egg of the world, created by Bramha; also the visible sky, the shell of this egg. Also one of the eighteen pooraunams. Colloquially anything huge and collossal.——*Bramhotsavam* (బ్రహ్మోత్సవం - brahmótsavam, Tel.; பிரமோற்சவம் - piramórchavam, Tam.). From (brahma, san. sacred rite + utsava, san. festival); principal festival done with all pomp and ceremonies [pundigy, 6a]. Not now connected with Bramha the god. Annual festival at a pagoda in the early part of the year, lasting nine or ten days, in the bright fortnight of the month. It begins with hoisting a flag on a high pole in the first courtyard of the temple. After this, the morning and evening ceremonies are performed with more pomp and details than usual and the idol is taken in state through the principal streets both morning and evening, every day. Each day a separate vehicle is exhibited [tircalyaunam].——*Bramhya maunam* (ब्राह्म्यमान - bráhmyamána, San.). Reckoning of Bramha's time [calpam, maunam, yoog].

BRAMIN (ब्राह्मण - bráhmana, *San.*; برهمن - brahman, *Hind.*; بامن - báman, *Dec.*; ಬ್ರಾಹ್ಮಣನು - bráhmananu, *Can.*; బ్రాహ్మణుడు - bráhmanudu, *Tel.*; ബ്രാഹ്മണൻ - bráhmanan, *Mal.*; பிராமணன் - pirámanan, *Tam.*). From (brahma, san. religious devotion). The older English form is Brachman; which comes through the Greek and Latin authors. The caste is sufficiently described at vol. II, 225. For Bramin high priests see Acharry and Jiyyangar. For W. coast Bramins see Numboory. For the Gowda and Dravida distinction, see Dravida [jauty].——**(1)** *Braminy* (ब्राह्मणी - bráhmaní, San.). A Bramin woman.——*Braminy bead* (रुद्राक्ष - rudráksha, San.). San. means roodran's eye. Same as roodrauck.——*Braminy bull* (ककुद्मान् - kakudmán, San.; ಗೂಳಿಯೆತ್ತು - gúliyettu, Can.; ఆబోతు - ábótu, Tel.; കുട്ടൻ - kúttan, Mal.; இமிலெருது - imileruthu, Tam.). San. from (kakud, san. hump of a bull +

mat, san. suffix of possession). Tel. from (ávu, tel. cow + pótu, tel. mate). Tam. from (imil, tam. hump + eruthu, tam. ox). The humped Indian ox.——*Braminy butter* (நெய் - ney, Tam.). An old name for ghee.——*Braminy duck* (بهمنی بدک - bahmaní-badak, Dec.). Casarca rutila, from marks on forehead resembling caste-mark.——*Braminy kite* (بهمنی چیل - bahmaníchíl, Dec.; బాపనచిలువ - bápanachiluva, Tel.). Haliastur indicus, from being sacred.——*Braminy kite creeper* (கருடக்கொடி - karudakkodi, Tam.). From being cure against snake-bites. Same as Isharmool.——*Braminy myna* (بهمنی مینا - bahmaní-mainá, Hind.; பாப்பாத்திமைனா - páppáttimainá, Tam.). Temenuchus pagodarum, from bright yellow legs as if by turmeric which bramin females use in daily bathing.——(2) *Ardha bramin* (അർദ്ധബ്രാഹ്മണ - arddhabráhmana, Mal.). From (ardha, san. half + above). Half bramins. The fishermen appointed by Parshooraman to officiate as Bramins to the people, and subsequently superseded by a colony of pure Bramins. The former were evidently an indigenous and native priesthood.——*Arya bramin* (ആര്യബ്രാഹ്മണ - áryabráhmana, Mal.). The Bramins brought by Parshooraman to the West coast from Ahichatram, in the north of India, in Aryabhoomy to replace the Ardha bramins.——*Odra bramin* (ఓఢ్రబ్రాహ్మడు - ódhrabráhmadu, Tel.). Orissa bramin.——*Vishwa bramin* (விசுவப்பிராமணன் - visuvappirámanan, Tam.). From Vishwacarman, the divine architect. Epithet taken by artisans as his alleged descendants.

BRAN PLANT (బుడ్డచెట్టు - buddachettu, *Tel.*; தவுட்டை - tavuttai, *Tam.*). Title from appearance of fruit. Tel. from (budda, tel. bubble + chettu, tel. tree). Tam. from (tavidu, tam. bran). Tel. also (jibilikechettu). Title otherwise Soft-leaved grewia. Botanically Grewia [dharmanam] hirsuta, vahl., tiliaceæ [vricsham, 27]. Alias Grewia helicterifolia, pilosa. Shrub; flowers small, white, becoming yellow; fruit hairy.——*Dog bran-plant* (కుక్కబుడ్డ - kukkabudda, Tel.). Title from being wild. Tel. from (kukka, tel. dog + budda, tel. grewia hirsuta, vahl.). Tel. also (medakava); (nalli). Botanically Grewia [dharmanam] pilosa, lam., tiliaceæ [vricsham, 27]. Alias Grewia carpinifolia, commutata, flavescens. Shrub; flowers small, whitish. Wood yellowish-white, hard, divided into triangular wedges proceeding from the centre towards the four corners and sides.

BRATAYOODA (برتيودا - bratayúdá, *Malay*). From (bhárata, san. the work + yuddha, san. war). Javanese bhauratam.

BRATTY (اپلی - aplí, *Hind.*; పిడక pidaka, *Tel.*; விராட்டி - virátti, *Tam.*). Title from tamul. Tel. from (pidutsa, tel. a lump). Tam. from (varattu, tam. to dry up). A round flat dry cake, prepared with cowdung and husks of grain, or small pieces of dry grass or straw; used as fuel and burns like a scented turf.

BRAZIL (برزیل - brazil, *Hind.*). Title from portugnese braza, meaning live coal, from color of wood found in the country. A good many S. indian naturalized plants have this name, from origin.——*Brazil cherry* (लवणी - lavaní, San.; रायआंवळी - ráyaámvalí, Mahr.; राजावाळो - rájáváló, Conc.; هرپهاریوڑی - harpháreurí, Hind.; هرفالیوڑی - harfáleurí, Dec.; ಕಿರುನೆಲ್ಲಿ - kirunelli, Can.; ಕರನೆಲ್ಲಿ - karinelli, Too.; రాచఉసిరిక - rátsausirike, Tel.; നെല്ലിപ്പുളി - neliippuli, Mal.; அருநெல்லி - arunelli, Tam.). San. from (lavana, san. salt). Mahr. from (ráya, mahr. king + ámvalí, mahr. phyllanthus emblica, linn.). Hind. from (hariparvari, san. the tree). Can. from (kiru, can. small + nelli, can. phyllanthus emblica, linn.). Tel. from (rátsa, tel. kingly + usirike, tel. phyllanthus emblica, linn.). Mal. from (nelli, mal. phyllanthus emblica, linn. + puli, mal. sour). Tam. from (aru, tam. minuteness + nelli, tam. phyllanthus emblica, linn.). Hind. also (núrí), meaning bright fruit. Mal. also (arinelli), meaning small nelly. Title otherwise Country gooseberry, Country star gooseberry, Hill gooseberry, Long-leaved phyllanthus, Otaheite gooseberry, Small nelly. Botanically Phyllanthus [aumlacam] distichus, müll., euphorbiaceæ [vricsham, 118]. Alias Averrhoa acida; Cicca disticha; Frinkia ramiflora; Phyllanthus longifolius. Small tree; calyx four-parted; leaves pinnated, 1–2 feet long, often flower-bearing; leaflets numerous, alternate, stalked, nearly orbicular, 1–3 inches long; petioles round, smooth, sometimes ending in a short raceme of male flowers; racemes numerous, terminal, axillary, and from the old buds on the naked branches; flowers numerous, small, reddish, in globular heads; drupe three to four-lobed, grooved, white, size of gooseberry; hard stone in centre; acid in taste; flowering in hot season; much cultivated in gardens; has spread itself all over the neilgherry, pulney and shevaroy mountains. Root is an active purgative and seeds also are cathartic. Fruit is eaten raw, pickled and preserved. Wood inferior. Cf. Indian winter cherry.——*Brazil wood* (بقم - bakm, Ar.). Same as Sappan.

BREAD-FRUIT (ചക്ക - chakka, *Mal.*). Title from fruit cooked looking like bread and being used as food. Mal. corruption of (chakra, san. round). Same as Common jack fruit.

BRIDE FISH (عارس مچھی - árasmaçchí, *Hind.*; செங்கரை - shengárai, *Tam.*). Title from gay colors. Hind. from (áras, hind. bride + maçchí, hind. fish). Tam. from (shem, tam. red + kárai, tam. equula genus). Lutjanus [taumbam] marginatus, percidæ [panayairy], acanthopterygii, teleostei, pisces [matsyam, 1], of naturalists [jantoo]. Alias Diacope axillaris, marginata, xanthopus; Genyoroge marginata; Mesoprion gaimardi, marginatus. Scales in oblique rows above lateral-line horizontal, below lateral-line extend to hind edge of eye. Colors purplish-yellow above lateral-line, and golden below it; no lateral blotch; colors of back continued to lower third of dorsal fin and cease at dark grey longitudinal band which has a lighter one above it, edged superiorly black and margined with white; caudal dark purplish red having white edge; pectoral, ventral and anal flesh-colored having yellowish tint. On the Malabar coast specimens are frequently taken that have a black lateral-blotch; also on the Coromandel coast some have lateral-mark faintly developed, but it is more commonly absent. Sea, attaining at least 16 inches in length.

BRIHASPATY (बृहस्पति - bríhaspati, *San.*). From (brih, san. prayer + pati, san. lord).—"*a*" Son of Angiran, and gooroo to the devatays; represented in the arts as a yellow man, seated on a water-lily; he is regent of the planet jupiter; considered to be of benevolent influence; hence brihaspaty vauram or thursday. In vedas identical with Agny, as almost the same epithets are applied. The saying is:—if a person be born under this planet, he will be endowed with an amiable disposition, possess palaces, gardens and lands, and be rich in money and corn; he will possess much religious merit, and have all his wishes gratified; bramins however will not be so fortunate as those of other castes, for brihaspaty being a bramin does not wish to exalt those of his own caste.—"*b*" Name stands also for the planet itself in common usage, ♃; sidereal period of revolution 4332d 14h 2m, or rather under twelve terrestrial years; inclination of orbit 1° 19′.—"*c*" Brihaspaty maunam, from (above + mána, san. measure) is the year for this earth according to Jupiter reckoning; founded on the period during which he describes one sign or a twelfth part of his orbit. This period is not identical with the common solar year though near it. See below under vatsaram.—"*d*" Twelve approximate years is one full revolution of Jupiter. This is a terrestrial very familiar Dravidian period. Compare mahamagham feast. The following is a Hindostany proverb:—باره برس پیچھے کوڑے کے بھی دن پھرتے ھیں—"after twelve years, even a dunghill "begins to prosper;" the theory being that the fortune of everything changes each twelve years.—"*e*" Five revolutions again of Jupiter make up the cycle of sixty years called in Tamul Vyauzhachuckram. The names of the five vatsarams or periods or revolutions are as follows:—Samvatsaram meaning dwelling together presided over by agny; Parivatsaram meaning full year by arcan; Idvatsaram by chundran; Anoovatsaram meaning after year, by bramha; Oottara vatsaram meaning latter year, by shiva. The name of each individual year of the Vatsaram, that is to say of each Brihaspaty maunam year, sometimes called Jupiter months, is determined from the Nacshatram in which Brihaspaty rises and sets heliacally; and they follow in the order of the lunar months. They are as follows:—Caurteecam, Agrahayanam, Pooshyam, Maugham, Phaulgoonam, Cheitram, Veishaukham, Jyeshtam, Ashaudham, Shrauvanam, Bhaudrapadam, Aushweejam. On the W. coast, the zodiacal names are applied to these Jupiter months, but the word Vyauzham meaning jupiter is always appended; ex. Meena vyauzham. Caurteecam is placed the first in the cycle of 12. It may therefore be inferred that there was a time when the Hindoo solar year, as well as the Brihaspaty cycle of 12, began with the sun's entrance in or near the Nacshatram kritticay.—"*f*" The whole cycle of 60 terrestrial years is explained in vol. I, 612, para. 17 of foot-note, and a list of the years in the order of their appearance is given at appendix XXXVI of vol. II. The following is the list in alphabetical order, showing the meaning of the names. ——*Acshayam* (अक्षय - akshaya, San.). From (a, san. prefix of negation + kshaya, san. ruin). Otherwise Cshayam. 60th.——*Anandam* (आनन्द - ánanda, San.). Means happiness. 48th.——*Angeerasam* (आङ्गिरस - ángirasa, San.). From (angiras, san. the sage). 6th.——*Bhavam* (भव - bhava, San.). From (bhú, san. to be). 8th.——*Caulayoocty* (कालयुक्ति - kálayukti, San.). From (kála, san. time + yukti, san. junction). 52nd.——*Chittrabaun* (चित्रभानु - chitrabhánu, San.). From (chitra, san. variegated + bhánu, san. beauty). 16th.——*Crodhanam* (क्रोधन - kródhana, San.). From (krudh, san. to become angry). 59th.——*Crodhy* (क्रोधी - kródhí, San.). From (krudh, san. to become angry). 38th.——*Dhautoo* (धातु - dhátu, San.). From (dhá, san. to support). 10th.——*Doondoobhy* (दुन्दुभि - dundubhi, San.). Means a kettle drum so called from its sound. 56th.——*Doonmookhy* (दुर्मुख - durmukha, San.). From (dur, san. bad + mukha, san. face). 30th.——*Doormaty* (दुर्मति - durmati, San.). From (dur, san. bad + mati, san. mind). 55th.——*Eeshwaram* (ईश्वर - íshvara, San.). From (ísh, san. to protect). 11th.——*Hevilamby* (हेमलम्ब - hémalamba, San.). From (héma, san. gold + lamb, san. to hang). 31st.——*Jayam* (जय - jaya, San.). From (ji, san. to conquer). 28th.——*Keelakam* (कीलक - kílaka, San.). From (kíl, san. to bind). Nail. 42nd.——*Kharam* (खर - khara, San.). Means hard. 25th.——*Manmatum* (मन्मथ - manmat'ha, San.).

From (mana, san. mind + mat'h, san. to excite). 29th.——*Nalam* (अनल - anala, San.). From (nal, san. to shine). 50th. ——*Nandanam* (नन्दन - nandana, San.). From (nand, san. to gladden). 26th.——*Paraubhavam* (पराभव - parábhava, San.). Means defeat. 40th.——*Paridhaury* (परिधावी - paridhávi, San.). From (pari, san. all round + dháv, san. to run). 46th.——*Paurtivam* (पार्थिव - párt'hiva, San.). From (prit'hiví, san. earth). 19th.——*Pingalam* (पिङ्गल - pingala, San.). Means tawny color. 51st.——*Plavam* (प्रव - plava, San.). From (plu, san. to swim). Superior. 35th.——*Plavangam* (प्लवङ्ग - plavanga, San.). From (plava, san. boat + gam, san. to go). 41st.——*Prabhavam* (प्रभव - prabhava, San.). From (pra, san. intensive prefix + bhú, san. to become). First.——*Prajotputty* (प्रजापति - prajápati, San.). From (prajá, san. people + utpatti, san. origin). Fifth.——*Prumadeecham* (प्रमादी - pramádí, San.). From (pra, san. intensive prefix + mad, san. to rejoice). 47th.——*Prumaudy* (प्रमाथी - pramát'hí, San.). From (pra, san. intensive prefix + mat'h, san. to excite). 13th.——*Pramodootam* (प्रमोद - pramóda, San.). From (pramóda, san. bliss). 4th.——*Ractaucshy* (रक्ताक्षि - raktákshi, San.). From (rakta, san. blood + akshi, san. eye). 58th. ——*Raucshasam* (राक्षस - rákshasa, San.). From (rakshas, san. hurt). 49th.——*Roodrotcaury* (रुधिरोद्गारी - rudhiródgárí, San.). From (rudhira, san. blood + udgri, san. to vomit). Otherwise Oodgaury. 57th.——*Rowdry* (रौद्र - raudra, San.). From (rudra, san. shiva). Terrible. 54th.——*Sadhauranam* (साधारण - sádhárana, San.). Means ordinary. 44th.——*Sarwadhaury* (सर्वधारी - sarvadhárí, San.). From (sarva, san. all + dhri, san. to hold). 22nd.——*Sarwajit* (सर्वजित् - sarvajit, San.). From (sarva, san. all + ji, san. to conquer). 21st.——*Shaurvary* (शार्वरी - shárvarí, San.). From (sharvara, san. darkness). 34th.——*Shobhacrit* (शोभकृत् - shóbhakrit, San.). From (shóbha, san. beauty + kri, san. to do). 37th.——*Shoobhacrit* (शुभकृत् - shubhakrit, San.). From (shubha, san. happiness + kri, san. to do). 36th.——*Shooclam* (शुक्ल - shukla, San.). Bright. The third year of the Tamul Jovian cycle.——*Shreemookham* (श्रीमुख - shrímukha, San.). From (shrí, san. prosperity + mukha, san. face). 7th.——*Siddhaurty* (सिद्धार्थी - siddhárt'hí, San.). From (siddha, san. accomplished + art'ha, san. object). 53rd.——*Soobhaun* (सुभानु - subhánu, San.). From (su, san. well + bhá, san. to shine). 17th. ——*Sowmyam* (सौम्य - saumya, San.). From (sóma, san. moon). 43rd.——*Tauranam* (तारण - tárana, San.). From (tar, san. to cross). Raft. 18th.——*Vegoo dhaunyam* (बहुधान्य - babudhánya, San.). From (bahu, san. copious + dhánya, san. crop). 12th. ——*Vibhavam* (विभव - vibhava, San.). From (vi, san. intensive prefix + bhú, san. to be). 2nd.——*Vicaury* (विकारी - vikárí, San.). From (vikára, san. change). The 33rd.——*Vicramum* (विक्रम - vikrama, San.). From (vi, san. intensive prefix + kram, san. to step). 14th.——*Vicrit* (विकृति - vikriti, San.). From (vi, san. mean + kriti, san. work). 24th.——*Vijayam* (विजय - vijaya, San.). Means success. 27th.——*Vilamby* (विलम्बी - vilambí, San.). From (vilamba, san. tardiness). 32nd. ——*Virodhicrit* (विरोधकृत् - viródhakrit, San.). From (viródha, san. opposition + kri, san. to do). Otherwise Rodhacrit. 45th. ——*Virodhy* (विरोधी - viródhí, San.). From (viruddh, san. to oppose). 23rd.——*Vishoo* (वृष - vrisha, San.). From (vrish, san. to rain). 15th.——*Vishwauvasoo* (विश्वावसु - vishvávasu, San.). From (vishva, san. all + vasu, san. wealth). 39th.——*Vyayam* (व्यय - vyaya, San.). Means expense. 20th.——*Yoovam* (युवा - yuvá, San.). Means youth. 9th [jyotisham].

BRIHAT (बृहत् - brihat, *San.*). Great.——*Brihadambah* (बृहदम्बा - brihadambá, San.). From (above + ambá, san. mother). Parvaty. A shacty as worshipped at Poodoocottah, after which the tondiman takes his family title Shree brihadambah doss. ——*Brihad jautacam* (बृहज्जातक - brihajjátaka, San.). From (above + játaka, san. nativity). Astrological work by Varauha mihiran. So called to distinguish from Laghoo jautacam or small book on astrology by the same author. Consists of twenty-five chapters on horoscopy [jyotisham].——*Brihat katay* (बृहत्कथा - brihatkat'há, San.). From (above + kat'há, san. story). Sanscrit book known to Europeans through Arabic translation into the Alaf leila or 1,001 nights.——*Brihat samhitay* (बृहत्संहिता - brihatsamhitá, San.). From (above + samhitá, san. composition). Astrological work by varauha mihiran; consists of three parts, tantram, horah, and shaukhay; first teaches to find by calculation the position of planets, second the lucky and unlucky indications, third the prognostics relating to various matters; the last part is extant and is generally known by above title, consists of 100 chapters and 4,000 couplets. The astronomical work by the author is known as Puncha siddhaunticay [jyotisham].

BRINDONES (भिरंड - bhiranda, *Mahr.*). Title is a portuguese corruption from mahrattee. Same as Mate mangosteen.

BRINJARRY (بنجارہ - banjárah, *Hind.*; బంజారి - banjári, *Tel.*). From (vanik, san. a trader). Perhaps confounded with Persian (biranj), rice. Title otherwise Banjaura. Traders who travel over the country with pack-bullocks, carrying grain, salt, &c., from market to market; some are hindoos and some mussalmans; first came to deccan with moghul camp as commissariat carriers; speak mahrattee; numbers inconsiderable; the soogaulies and lumbaudies are probably divisions of the same tribe. See vol. I (61), (69), 195 [janty].

BRINJAUL (वार्त्ताकी - vártákí, *San.*; वांगी - vángi, *Mahr.*; वायिंगण - váyingana, *Conc.*; شجر بادنجان - shajaribázinján, *Ar.*; درخت بادنجان - darakhtibádinján, *Pers.*; ڈورلے کا پیڑ - dorlekáper, *Hind.*; بینگن کا جھاڑ - baingankájhár, *Dec.*; ترونگ - tirong, *Malay*; ಬದನೆ - badane, *Can.*; ಬದನೆ - badane, *Too.*; వంగ - vanga, *Tel.*; ବାଂଗିନୋ - bángino, *Oor.*; വഴുതിന - vazhutina, *Mal.*; වම්බටු - vambatu, *Singh.*; கத்தரி - kattari, *Tam.*). Title from persian through portuguese bringella. San. from (vártam, san. health); health-producing. Ar. from (shajar, ar. tree + bázinján, ar. brinjaul). Pers. from (darakht, pers. tree + bádinján, pers. egg plant fruit). Hind. from (dorlá, hind. egg plant fruit + per, hind. tree). Dec. from (baingan, dec brinjaul + jhár, dec tree). Can. corruption from malayalam. Mal. from (vazhu, mal. sliding + tala, mal. head), from the slippery sides of the fruits. San. also (hingulí), meaning growing, healthy; (bhantákí), meaning maintaining the fire of digestion; (pítap'hala), meaning yellow fruit; (kulí), meaning hand, from leaves; (mahatí), meaning large; (simhí), meaning injuring; (dushpradharshiní), meaning not to be touched; (dírghavártákí), meaning long + the plant. Can. also (káchigida). Tel. also (nidupuvanga), meaning long + brinjaul; (mulaka); (chirivanga), meaning small + brinjaul; (mettavanga), meaning dry land + brinjaul; (níruvanga), meaning water + brinjaul. Mal. also (nílavazhutina), meaning blue brinjaul. Tam. also (vazhuthalai); (níttakkattari), meaning long brinjaul; (mullukkattari), meaning thorn + brinjaul; (kárkkattari), meaning black brinjaul. Greek *στρύχνος*. Title otherwise Aubergine, Bengun, Egg-plant, Jew's-apple, Mad-apple, Malum insanum, Rage-apple, Wangee. Botanically Solanum [cooly] melongena, linn., solanaceæ [vricsham, 94]. Specific name from arabic. Alias Melongena tereta; Solanum esculentum, incanum, longum, undatum, zeylanicum. Perennial; stem herbaceous, woody at the base, clothed with star-shaped hairs; ovate, serrated leaves; flowering peduncles reflexed; fertile peduncle solitary, sterile one racemose; calyx campanulate; corolla angular, purple flowers; bears large, smooth, shining fruits or berries which are of the shape and size of a small hen's egg; the latter are either ovate, oblong, violet or white; or globular, violet; or more or less globular, white, or white striped on a violet ground. Garden produce; in cultivation requires good soil and abundance of water; cultivated in red or black earth; ground prepared in south in auvany or august and maushy [mausam] or february, on coromandel in shrauvanam or august and bhaudrapadam or september, on w. coast in yedavam or may; ground ploughed and manured; seed sown in south in poorataushy or september and pungoony or march, on coromandel in shrauvanam or august and bhaudrapadam or september, on w. coast after 10th maidom or april transplantation being made by the 1st of yedavam or may; sown in nursery in all cases; seedlings are transplanted a foot apart when about six inches high; while under growth ground is weeded and watered twice a week; the fruit when full ripe becomes yellow; the brinjauls are gathered six weeks after transplantation when tender; those for seeds next year are left; average price in south 480 pollums or 66 lbs. per rupee; on coromandel 1 viss per 1 anna; on w. coast six hundred fruits for a rupee. Seeds are medicinally stimulant, leaves narcotic. Fruit is eatable after undergoing a process by which bitter acrid matter is removed:—"*a*" made into curries, either with potatoes, or shrimps, or both;—"*b*" roasted under hot ashes and mashed and seasoned with salt, onions, chillies and lime-juice or mustard oil;—"*c*" cut into slices and fried in oil;—"*d*" when young and tender pickled with mustard oil, chillies, salt, &c. For culinary purposes, one of the best vegetables in india. Many varieties distinguished by the shape and color of the fruit, which ranges from white through yellow and red. For a wild brinjaul see Elephant shoonday.——*Creeper brinjaul* (वेलवाङ्गी - vélavángí, Mahr.). From habit and fruit. Tomato [europe brinjaul].——*Europe brinjaul* (वेलवांगी - vélavángí, Mahr.; ولایتی بینگن - viláitibaingan, Dec.; تماتی - tamátí, Malay; ಗೊಂದಹಣ್ಣುಗಿಡ - gondahannugida, Can.; సీమవంగ - símavanga, Tel.; പേത്തക്കാളി - péttakkáli, Mal.; මහාරටතාමැටි - maháratatámatti, Singh.; சீமைத்தக்காளி - shímaittakkáli, Tam.). Title from habitat, having come from s. america. Mahr. from (valli, san. creeper + vángí, mahr. egg plant, solanum melongena, linn.); from trailing habit and fruit like brinjaul. Dec. from (viláití, hind. foreign + baíngan, hind. solanum melongena, linn.). Can. from (góndu, can. gum + hannu, can. fruit + gida, can. plant); from appearance of pulp. Tel. from (síma, tel. european + vanga, tel. egg plant, solanum melongena, linn.). Mal. from (pé, mal. demon + takkáli, mal. the plant, physalis). Singh. from (mahá, san. great + rata, singh. foreign + támatti, singh. the plant, from tomato). Tam.

from (shímai, tam. foreign + takkáli, tam. the plant, physalis). Hind. also (gurbaigan), meaning jaggery brinjaul, from taste. Can. also (chapparadabadanegida), meaning pandal + brinjaul plant, solanum melongena, linn.; (kadagólu), means churning stick. Tel. also (símatakkáli), meaning foreign + the plant, physalis; (karpúravanga), meaning camphor + brinjaul, solanum melongena, linn. Tam. also (erumaittakkáli), meaning buffalo + the plant, physalis; (shímaimanattakkáli), meaning foreign + the plant, solanum nigrum, linn. Greek λυκοπέρσιον. Title otherwise Amorous apple, Buffalo wintercherry, Creeper brinjaul, Devil wintercherry, Golden apple, Love-apple, Sweet brinjaul, Tomato, Wolf peach. Botanically Lycopersicum esculentum, miller, solanaceæ [vricsham, 94]. Alias Amatula rubra; Lycopersicum solanum; Solanum lycopersicum, pomum amoris. Trailing plant introduced from south america, chiefly cultivated for europeans; flower small, cream-colored; large, red, or sometimes yellow, fruit; this eaten as salad and in sauce; two varieties, the large imported kind is size of an orange nearly, the small about size of a plum raised from country seeds. No other common species here.——*Pandaul brinjaul* (పందిటివంకాయ - panditivankáya, Tel.). Title from growing over pandauls and bearing fruit like brinjaul. Same as Moon flower.——*Prickly brinjaul* (कण्टकारिका - kantakáriká, San.; डोरली - dórəlí, Mahr.; चिंचर्टि - chincharti, Conc.; حدق بری - hadakibarrí, Ar.; بادنجان بری - bádanjánibarrí, Pers.; جنگلی بینگن - janglíbaingan, Hind.; ڈورلا - dorlá, Dec.; ನೆಲಗುಳ್ಳ - nelagulla, Can.; ಗುಳ್ಳ - gulla, Too.; నేలములక - nélamulaka, Tel.; കണ്ടകാരിച്ചുണ്ട - kantakáriççunta, Mal.; කටුවැල්බටු - katuvalbatu, Singh.; கண்டங்கத்தரி - kandangattari, Tam.). San. from (kantaka, san. thorn + ri, san. to go). Ar. from (hadak, ar. wild brinjaul + barr, ar. forest). Pers. from (bádanján, pers. brinjaul, solanum melongena, linn. + barr, ar. forest). Hind. from (janglí, hind. wild + baingan, hind. brinjaul). Can. from (nela, can. ground + gulla, can. the shrub, solanum ferox, linn.). Tel. from (néla, tel. ground + mulaka, tel. solanum ferox, linn.). Mal. from (kantakári, san. the plant + chunta, mal. solanum verbascifolium, linn.). Singh. from (katu, singh. thorny + valbatu, singh. solanum). Tam. from (kantaka, san. thorn + kattari, tam. solanum melongena, linn.). San. also (nidigdhiká), meaning destroying completely; (vyághrí), meaning tiger-like, from thorns; (chitrap'halá), meaning having variously colored fruits; (kshudrá), meaning small; (kshudrakantaká), meaning having small thorns; (kshudrap'halá), meaning having small fruits; (ráshtriká), meaning produced in country; (dhávaní), meaning running; (dushpradharshiní), meaning not to be touched; (dusparshá), meaning not to be touched [caunjory, indian nightshade]; (brihatí), meaning growing; (bahukantaká), meaning having many thorns; (bahup'halá), meaning having many fruits; (kshétrajá), meaning produced in field; (kshuriká), meaning cutting; (kapatéshvarí), meaning goddess of deceit; (pítatandulá), meaning yellow rice, from seeds; (putraprada), meaning son giving; (sarpatanu), meaning serpent's body. Hind. also (katái); (rengní). Can. also (rámagulla). Tel. also (vákudu), meaning growing by the side of streams [carondah]; (nélamulláku), meaning ground + thorn + leaf; (pinnamulaka), meaning small + solanum ferox, linn.; (tellanélamulaka), meaning white + the plant; (tellavákudu), meaning white + the plant. Mal. also (kantankattiri), meaning thorny solanum melongena, linn. Title otherwise Jacquin's nightshade, Yellow-berried nightshade. Botanically Solanum [cooly] xanthocarpum, schrad. & wendl., solanaceæ [vricsham, 94]. Alias solanum diffusum, jacquini, virginianum. Procumbent, diffuse, prickly; leaves sinuately pinnatifid, prickly on both surfaces, with naked margins; racemes simple, which as well as the calyx are prickly; corolla bluish purple; if plant strongly armed, fruit smaller; if plant less armed, fruit larger; has small, bitterish and sub-acid fruit. The dried plant expectorant and diuretic; the mouth fumigated with smoke of burning seeds to relieve toothache; decoction of root given with long pepper and honey in cough and cattarrh, and with rock salt and asafœtida in spasmodic cough; gives to pharm. stems, flowers and fruit, non-officinal. The fruit used in curries.——*Sweet brinjaul* (گر بینگن - gurbaingan, Hind.). From taste. Same as tomato [europe brinjaul].

BRITASTAUN (व्रतस्थान - vratast'hána, *San.*). From (vrata, san. religious duty + st'hána, san. place). Mentioned in the Bramhaunda pooraunam as the place of religious duty. Is supposed by some to be the island of Great britain. It is also called Shwetadweepam or the White island. Swarna dweepam or the Golden island is conjectured to be Ireland. The British islands are sometimes identified with the Chundra dweepam of pooraunams; likewise with Tricalasham, or the island with three peaks, viz., Rajatacootam, Ayacootam, and Swarnacootam. If the original Aryan stock had a more northerly origin than is generally supposed, there is nothing very improbable in these identifications.

BROOM GRASS (جہاڑو - jhárú, *Hind.* and *Dec.*; ಹಂಚಿಹುಲ್ಲು - hanchihullu, *Can.*; చీపురుగడ్డి - chípurugaddi, *Tel.*; துடைப்பப்புல் - tudaippappul, *Tam.*). Title from use by sweepers. Hind. from (jhárná, hind. to sweep). Tel. from (chípuru, tel. broom + gaddi, tel. grass). Tam. from (tudaippam, tam. broom + pul, tam. grass). Tel. also (puchikagaddi). Title otherwise Jhauroo, Sweeper grass. Botanically Aristida setacea, retz., graminaceæ [vricsham, 156]. Alias Chætaria setacea. Grass found on dry, barren soil. Cattle will scarcely eat it. Stalks are tied into bundles and used as brooms by sweepers; serves for tooth-picks; used for making tatties. No other common species here.

BRUCEPETTAH (బ్రూసుపేట - brúsupéta, *Tel.*). Town; pop. 27,473. Suburb of Bellary. Commenced in 1815 by Mr. Bruce, the judge, to shelter a number of people who were ejected from the fort.

BUCKAUL (بقال - bakkál, *Hind.*). From (bakala, ar. herb); seller of greens. Hence shop-keeper generally [bunniah].

BUCKINGHAM CANAL (உப்புவாய்க்கால் - uppuváykkál, *Tam.*). Title from the Duke of Buckingham, Governor of Madras. Tam. from (uppu, tam. salt + váykkál, tam. canal). Otherwise called the East coast canal. In the early part of this century, two canals, known as Cochrane's canal and the South coast canal, existed. The former led from the Cooum northwards as far as Doogarauzpatam, and the latter from Paupanchauvady in Chingleput district southwards to the mouth of the Palaur, near Sadras. Passengers and light cargoes of firewood, fish, &c., were carried by these canals. Cochrane's canal has been from time to time extended north so as to reach Pedda ganjam in Kistna district, where through the local Commamore canal it joins with the Kistna delta high level canals. The S. coast canal has similarly been extended south to Mercaunam in S. arcot district. During the administration of the Duke of Buckingham as Governor of Madras, these canals were connected by a fresh excavation, five miles in length, running through the heart of Madras from the mouth of the Cooum to Adyar river. This was one of the famine relief works of 1877-78. The whole canal, including the new central excavation, is sometimes called the Buckingham canal; otherwise only the northern section. Through communication now existing between the Godavery delta, the Kistna delta, and the Buckingham canal system, passengers can go by canal from Mercaunam to Cocanada, distance 462 miles. The bottom breadth of the canal is 30 feet and the depth varies from 2½ to 3½ feet; but in the Poolicat lake there is from 5 to 6 feet of water. All boats sail when the wind suits, otherwise they are towed or poled; the crew consist of two to three men. Passenger boats ordinarily accomplish 25 miles per diem, but with extra trackers and moving day and night 50 miles could be attained. Boats ply both by day and night, but in very dark nights navigation is tedious and difficult in the Poolicat lake. There is no stream beyond that which is due to ebb and flow of tide, except at a point 7 miles north of Doogarauzpatam, where the canal runs for a mile through the stream of the Swarnamookhy river, which when in floods flows from two to three miles per hour; this velocity only lasts for a few days in each year during October and November. Navigation is seldom entirely interrupted, but it is difficult during high floods in October and November, and at low tides afterwards until the silt deposited in the canal by freshes is removed. In May and June, when the water is low, the transit of heavily laden cargo boats may be impeded at times. Cargoes carried to the south consist principally of grains, condiments, salt, fish, firewood, choonam shells and charcoal; while those taken northwards are chiefly cocoanuts, coir, palmyra rafters, fish, salt, jaggery and young plantain trees. See vol. I, 405. The following is the itinerary from the Palaur to Santaravore on the Commamore canal:—

Name of stage.	Distance.		Remarks.
	M.	F.	
Palaur river ...	...	...	
Sadras ...	4	0	Large town; P.W.D. bungalow; camping ground good in town 1 mile from canal; supplies plentiful; water good and abundant; good camping ground also on bank of canal; good road hence to Chingleput 19½ miles distant.
Tirporore ...	14	0	
Covelong ...	7	0	A large village; good bungalow; ground dry and good near village and canal; good topes; water plentiful and good; hence to Chingleput distant 20 miles, a good road.
Adyar river ...	16	0	
Madras	3	0	
Ennore	10	0	
Poolicat ...	15	0	Camping ground 1 mile north of Poolicat on south bank of lake; ground dry and good in large and shady topes; water plentiful and good. Travellers' bungalows.
Tettoopett ...	10	4	A small village on sandy ridge between canal and sea; a large chuttram, good topes, and good water.
Cusbah ...	9	0	A large village; camp just north of it, in good topes; ground high and sandy; good water here, but only in two or three wells.
Royadorvoo ...	12	0	Small village; good topes; good water.
Pambaly ...	8	0	Small village; ground low and swampy; no shade; water scarce and not good.
Doogarauzpatam.	4	0	Small town; chuttram and travellers' bungalow; post office a good camping ground 3 miles short of this, 1 mile from Pambaly.
Siddhavaram ...	11	0	Large village; good topes and water.

Name of stage.	Distance. M.	Distance. F.	Remarks.
Kistnapatam ...	12	0	Large village; 2 miles from canal; good water 1 mile distant; camping ground low, and swampy; a good place to camp is at Miday, 3 miles further south in the Kistnapatam back-water. A good road to Nellore distant 17 miles. Collector's Conamoola bungalow 4 miles to E.
Codoor	11	0	Large village; good topes and water. A good road to Nellore distant 14½ miles.
Corattore and Meipaud.	9	0	Large village, 1 mile from canal; camping ground confined, but dry, among paddy fields on bank of canal; water from river channels good and plentiful; better ground with shade 1½ miles north.
Pennair river ...	4	0	River three branches with connecting canal 2½ miles; boats sailed or poled across.
Rama teertam.	7	0	Small village; good water and topes.
Iskapully ...	8	0	Small village, 1 mile from canal; camp on dry sandy plain between canal and sea; no shade, and water not good; better ground 1 mile further north and ½ mile west of canal. A good road to Nellore distant 22½ miles.
Chippilair river	5	4	Shallow river, easily crossed.
Toommalapenta	6	0	Large village; good tope; good camping ground; water good.
Ramapatam ...	10	4	Small town; good bazaars; camp on dry sandy ground on bank of canal; good topes, water good and plentiful; a good road to Tettoo, 3 miles distant.
Chaukicherla ...	4	0	Large village.
Alagaunipollem	3	0	Small village.
Munnair river.	4	0	Shallow river, 210 yards wide.
Oondlapollem...	2	0	Large village; road to Shingaroyacondah 4 miles distant.
Paucala ...	3	0	Large village.
Palair river ...	2	4	Shallow river, 150 yards wide.
Mooshy river ...	1	0	Deep river, 175 yards wide.
Maunore	3	4	Large village.
Eetamookkala.	1	4	Large village.
Cottapatam ...	4	4	Small town 1½ miles from canal; large bazaar; camp on east bank of canal; ground dry and extensive; water good and plentiful ½ mile distant; no shade near camping ground; road to Ongole distant 10 miles 5 furlongs.
Goondlacumma river.	8	2	Deep river, 150 yards wide.
Canoopurty ...	3	4	Large village.
Pedda ganjam.	4	4	Small village; good water.
Firangy dibba.	2	2	Desolate place; Dutch factory here 200 years ago.
Santaravore ...	8	0	Hence to Vaitpollem distant 3¼ miles, a fair weather track.

BUCKOOL (बकुल - bakula, *San.*). From (vak, san. to go crookedly). Same as Mimusops elengi [ilanjy]. Cf. Elengi.

BUCKREED (بكرعيد - bakríd, Hind.). Hind. from (bakrá, hind. sheep + íd, ar. festival); from sacrifice of sheep, &c., commemorating sacrifice of Ismael by Ibraham. Festival [eed] on ninth and tenth of Zool hijja [maheena]. Otherwise Eed ooz zoohah, festival of forenoon; Eed i coorbaun, festival of sacrifices; Eed i cabeer, great feast; Baree eed, great feast, &c. In Turkey Coorbaun beiram, feast of sacrifices. Sufficiently described at vol. I (97).

BUCKUM (بقم - bakm, *Hind.*). Same as Cæsalpinia or Sappan.

BUD (بد - bad, *Hind.*). Bad.——*Budmash* (بدمعاش - badmaásh, Hind.). From (above + maásh, pers. livelihood). A vagabond.——*Budzaut* (بدذات - badzát, Hind.). From (above + zát, ar. race). A blackguard; term of abuse.

BUDGEROOK (ಬಜಾರರೊಕ್ಕ - bajárarokkha, *Can.*). From (bajára, can. bazaar + rokkha, can. money). The Portuguese Basaruco. A coin struck at Cochin, lead and tin, cast in a mould, about 4 to 1 peisa, 60 to a Cochin fanam, 48 to Anjengo fanam. Same as damree, pie [naunyam, 2]. See vol. I, 609.

BUDGEROW (بجرا - bajrá, *Hind.*). Term for vessels which trade from Cutch, Goozerat, and the Malabar coast, to the Gulf of Persia, the coast of Arabia and the Red sea. Also used for large canal boats on East coast; these have a cabin and a mast and are either sailed or rowed or dragged by track-rope; round-bottomed, and without keel.

BUDL (بدل - badl, *Hind.*). Substitute.——*Budly* (بدلى - badlí, Hind.). A substitute, a person or thing taken in representation or exchange of some other person or thing.

BUDWAIL (బద్వేలు - badvélu, *Tel.* badvél*). From (batta, tel. cloth + prólu, tel. town).——**(1)** Talook, Cuddapah district. Tahsildar's pay Rs. 150. Area 755 square miles. Population 92,152. Language Teloogoo. N.E. of district. Bounded on the north by Cumbum talook of the Kurnool district, east by Oodayagherry talook of the Nellore district, south by Sidhout talook and west by Proddootore and Cuddapah talooks. Hilly. Covered with forests in some places. Its distinguishing feature is a want of water. Soils, red, black and sowdoo. Amongst the hills there are many old lead mines now no longer worked, and there is a considerable amount of undeveloped mineral wealth. Iron stone is common. Chief product is indigo. The only product exported is indigo, and the quantity is calculated at 4,000 maunds annually. The only river is the Saglair, which is not utilized. The tanks at Budwail and Pormaumilla are, however, amongst the finest in the district. Camping grounds, Budwail and Pormaumilla. Places of archæological interest:—Budwail, Chennamambapooram, Cutteragundla, Jangamrauzpully, Palgoorallpully, Pormaumilla, Shuncavaram, Siddhavaram, Sullagirigela, Varicoonta. The principal trig. station:—Lunkamala. The leading places, &c., in the talook are the following.——*Budwail* (బద్వేలు - badvélu, Tel.). See below.——*Calasapaud* (కలశపాడు - kalasapádu, Tel.). From (kalasha, san. pot + pádu, tel. village). Village; pop. 1,679; acres 3,002; lat. 15° 07′; long. 78° 59′; from Budwail N.N.W. 26 miles; from Cuddapah N. 44 miles. Head-quarters of S.P.G. mission.——*Cavalacoontla* (కవులకుంట్ల - kavulakuntla, Tel.). From (kavi, san. poet + kunta, tel. pond). Village; pop. 2,994; acres 20,297; lat. 15° 03′; long. 79° 04′; from Budwail N. 21 miles; from Cuddapah N.N.E. 41 miles.——*Cherlapully* (చెర్లోపల్లి - cherlópalli, Tel.). From (cheruvu, tel. tank + palli, tel. village). Village; pop. 3,657; acres 8,934; lat. 15° 00′; long. 79° 05′; from Budwail N. 18 miles; from Cuddapah N.E. 38 miles.——*Cundimulloyapully* (కందిమల్లాయపల్లి - kandimalláyapalli, Tel.). From (kandimalláya, tel. proper name + palli, tel. village). Village, Place of pilgrimage; pop. 1,590 of Somireddipully of which it is a hamlet; lat. 14° 49′; long. 78° 55′; from Budwail W.N.W. 13 miles; from Cuddapah N. 23 miles.——*Cutteragundla* (కత్తెరగండ్ల - katteragandla, Tel.). From (kattera, tel. marble stone + gandala, can. cave). Village; pop. 3,984; acres 12,345; lat. 15° 01′; long. 79° 00′; from Budwail N.N.W. 19 miles; from Cuddapah N.N.E. 37 miles. Vijianugger inscriptions dated A.D. 1526, 1530 and 1547, three in a Vishnoo, and one in a Shiva temple.——*Dornaul* (డోరనాల - dóranála, Tel.). See sep. title.——*Jangamrauzpully* (జంగమరాజుపల్లి - jangamarádzupalli, Tel.). See sep. title.——*Lunkamala* (లంకమల - lankamala, Tel.). See sep. title.——*Lutchmipollem* (లక్ష్మిపాలెము - lakshmipálemu, Tel.). From (lakshmí, san. the goddess + pálemu, tel. fortified village). Sanscrit name (anantarájapura), meaning vishnoo, the king of anantan the serpent + town. Village; lat. 14° 47′; long. 79° 07; from Budwail N. 2 miles; from Cuddapah N.E. 26 miles. Vishnoo temple.——*Matsyalunka* (మత్స్యలంక - matsyalanka, Tel.). From (matsya, san. fish + lanka, tel. island). Tank; from Budwail S.W. 6 miles; from Cuddapah N. 38 miles. Natural pool in the Lunkamalas, held sacred.——*Moonnelly* (మున్నెల్లి - munnelli, Tel.). From (munu, tel. early + nelli, tel. emblic myrobalan, phyllanthus emblica, linn.). Village; pop. 2,765; acres 9,304; lat. 14° 55′; long. 79° 00′; from Budwail N.N.W. 14 miles; from Cuddapah N.N.E. 31 miles.——*Narsapore* (నరసాపురము - narasápuramu, Tel.). From (narasayya, tel. proper name + pura, san. town). Village; pop. 1,524; acres 2,003; lat. 15° 03′; long. 78° 59′; from Budwail N.N.W. 23 miles; from Cuddapah N.N.E. 40 miles. Former residence of a poligar.——*Nullamullay* (నల్లమల - nallamala, Tel.). See sep. title.——*Palgooraullapully* (పలుగురాళ్లపల్లి - palugurállapalli, Tel.). From (paluguráyi, tel. flat stone, generally applied to white marble + palli, tel. village). Village; pop. 2,628; acres 12,467; lat. 14° 52′; long. 78° 59′; from Budwail N.W. 12 miles; from Cuddapah N.N.E. 28 miles.——*Pormaumilla* (పోరుమామిళ్ల - pórumámilla,* Tel.). From (póru, tel. battle + mámidi, tel. mango tree, mangifera indica, linn.). Sanscrit name (gópínandapattana), meaning the cowherd nundan, foster father of krishnan + town. Village; pop. 3,099; acres 2,326; lat. 15° 00′; long. 79° 02′; from Budwail N.N.W. 18 miles; from Cuddapah N.N.E. 38 miles. Once the residence of a poligar, the ruins of whose fort are to the north.——*Saglair* (సగిలేరు - sagiléru, Tel.). See sep. title.——*Shuncavaram* (శంఖవరము - shankhavaramu, Tel.). From (shankha, san. chunk shell + pura, san. town). Village; pop. 3,532; acres 126,632; lat. 15° 03′; long. 79° 02′; from Budwail N.N.W. 22 miles; from Cuddapah N.N.E. 40 miles. South are the remains of a small fort. Two old temples one of Vishnoo and the other of Shiva. The former is ruined and contains fine sculpture on the outer wall. An old Teloogoo inscription of Vijianugger in front of the temple.——*Somireddipully* (సోమిరెడ్డిపల్లి - sómireddipalli, Tel.). From (sómireddi, tel. proper name + palli, tel. village). Village; pop. 1,720; acres 12,078; lat. 14° 50′; long. 78° 57′; from Budwail W.N.W. 12 miles; from Cuddapah N.N.E. 25 miles.——*Veligonda* (వెలిగొండ - veligonda, Tel.). See sep. title.——*Yeddadoogoo canama* (ఎడ్డదుగుకనమ - eddadugukanama, Tel.). See sep. title.——**(2)** Town, Talook head-quarters; Cuddapah dist., Budwail tal.; pop. 5,443 excluding hamlets; acres 1,555; lat. 14° 45′; long. 79° 06′; from Cuddapah N.E. 24 miles; from Madanapully N.N.E. 90 miles; from Madras N.W. 139 miles; from Sidhout N.N.E. 20 miles. In the Cumbum valley east of the Nullamullays. Formerly under a poligar tributary to Vijianugger, from whom it was annexed by Necnam khan of Cuddapah. Two old temples. An important centre of trade. Large tank. The hamlet of Lutchmipollem has ancient temple of Prasanna vencateshwarasawmy.

BUFFALO (کھلگا - khulgá, *Hind.*). Title from portuguese. Old english forms are buffle and buff. Originally applied to the common indian ox; then the domestic buffalo was called the water-buffalo.——*Buffalo lime* (جاروک کرباؤ - járukkarbau, Malay). Same as Sour lime.——*Buffalo reed* (எருவை - eruvai, Tam.). From being eaten by buffaloes. Same as Naunal.

BUGGALAH (بگلہ - bagalah, *Hind.*). From portuguese through mahrattee. Coasting vessel. Same as Budgerow.

BUGGLECONDAH (బొగ్గులకొండ - boggulakonda, *Tel.*). From (boggu, tel. charcoal + konda, tel. hill); from color of rocks. Hill; Kistna dist., Narsarowpett tal. Steep basaltic hill rising about 1,200 feet above the plain near Vinoocondah. Frequent earthquakes. No crater observed. There are three peaks, central one highest.

BUKSH (بخش - bakhsh, *Pers.*). From (bakshídan, pers. to give). Gift. Sheikh alaumat; as Ilauhee buksh, alam + alaumat. Bukshish is a gift. Bukshy is a paymaster; under the moghul system frequently one with the commander-in-chief; in mysore a superior magistrate.

BULLAH (ಬಳ್ಳ - balla, *Can.*; வள்ளம் - vallam, *Tam.*). See vol. I, 615; II, 508, 509, 518.—"*a*" Measure of capacity. 2 puddies = 1 bullah; 40 bullahs = 1 cundaga [alavay, 3]. Approximate actual value, 1 bullah = 245 cubic inches. In Bellary equal to 4 maunams of 16 seers of 84 tolahs. In Coimbatore, equal to 2 pucka puddies of 144 tolahs. In Salem equal to 48 double handfuls or 2 seers; of which there are two, one of 150 tolahs and the other of 86. In Trichinopoly equal to 2 puddies of 116 tolahs. In South arcot equal to 590 tolahs when heaped. Compare Mercaul of Tanjore, Moonta of Nellore, and Cooncham of Ganjam.—"*b*" Superficial measure in dry land. 4 small puddies = 1 bullah [alavay, 2]. Approximate actual value, 1 bullah = 3·82 acres. In Salem, there are two bullahs, 96 and 64 fathoms square respectively, fathom being 6 feet 4½ inches. This gives 8·6 acres and 3·82 acres respectively. Compare Gorroo of Nellore and Kurnool.

BULLY (బల్లి - balli, *Tel.*). Lizard.——*Bullipully canama* (బల్లిపల్లెకనమ - ballipallekanama, Tel.). From (above + palli, tel. village + kanama, tel. pass). Ghaut; Cuddapah district, Poollampett talook; from Cuddapah S.E. 63 miles; from Poollampett S.S.E. 28 miles. Between the Veligonda and Sheshachellam hills leading from Cuddapah to North arcot district.

BUMMELO (बोंबील - bómbila, *Mahr.*; కుక్క_ముట్టె - kukkamutte, *Tel.*). Title from mahrattee. Tel. from (kukka, tel. dog + mutte, tel. clupea longiceps). Tel. also (kukkasavára), meaning dog + ophiopehalus striatus; from snake-like form and pursuing other fishes for prey. Title otherwise Bombay duck, Dog herring. Harpodon nehereus, scopelidæ, physostomi, teleostei [matsyam, 36], of naturalists [jantoo]. Specific name from bengalee. Alias Harpodon microps; Laurida microps; Osmerus nehereus; Salmo microps; Sauridichthys ophiodon; Saurus nehereus, ophiodon; Triurus microcephalus. Body compressed, snout, short and obtuse; lower jaw longer; colors, head, back, and sides semi-transparent like gelatine, light-greyish, with minute star-like black or brownish dots; anterior part of abdomen pale, silvery-bluish; rest greyish-white; cheeks and opercles pale silvery-bluish, dotted like body; fins transparent, colored like body, but more closely dotted, as to appear greyish and black at their extremities, in some specimens the fins are black; iris golden; highly esteemed as food, whether fresh or salted; in latter form employed as relish with curries; seas and estuaries; most common at bombay decreasing down malabar coast; not common at madras but augments up coromandel coast. No other common species here.——*False bummelo* (चोरबोंबील - chórabómbila, Mahr.; బడిముట్టె - badimutte, Tel.; അരണ - araṇa, Mal.; உழுவை - uluvai, Tam.). Title from being similar but inferior. Mahr. means false bummelo. Tel. from (badi, tel. small + mutte, tel. clupea longiceps). Mal. means green house lizard. Tam. from (ulu, tam. to be worm-eaten); from appearance of spots as if worm-eaten).—"*a*" The above is Saurida tumbil, scopelidæ, physostomi, teleostei [matsyam, 36], of naturalists [jantoo]. Specific name from (támba, mahr. sky red); from its reflections. Alias Aulopus elongatus; Laurida tombel; Osmerus tumbil; Salmo tumbil; Saurida argyrophanes, tombil, undosquamis; Saurus argyrophanes, badimottah, tumbil, undosquamis. Badimottah from teloogoo. Eyes with broad adipose lids; cleft of mouth extending to behind the orbit; scales over body and head, with some on base of caudal fin; brownish-gray along back, becoming white beneath, whole having yellow reflections; in some dorsal and upper half of caudal fins are barred in spots; in others there are no spots, middle of pectoral and ventral are sometimes almost black; sea; as food rather dry and insipid; 8 inches. No other common species here.—"*b*" Title otherwise Flat head, Crocodile fish, is applied to genus Platycephalus, cottidæ, acanthopterygii, teleostei, pisces [matsyam, 22], of naturalists. Head broad; iris possesses two semi-circular flaps which can be brought together under the stimulus of light; wounds from the spines occasion violent irritation; natives call these two-mouthed fish.

BUND (बन्ध - bandha, *San.*; بندھ - bandh, *Hind.*; బందు - bandu, *Tel.*). From (bandh, san. to tie). An agreement. Confinement. The wall of earth, mostly artificial, that supports the lower end of a tank. Also masonry bank built across a stream so as to retain water above it. Also an embankment to preserve a roadway across plains inundated in the rainy season. Also suffix denoting agent; as Dufterbund, dufter + tyer.——*Bandikhana* (بندیخانہ - bandíkhánah, Hind.). From (above + khánah, pers. house). Jail.——*Bandiwaun* (بندیوان - bandíwán, Hind.). Prisoner.——*Bund e charaunah* (بند چرانا - bandicharáṇa, Hind.). From (above + charáná, hind. pasture). Poundage on cattle straying into grain fields.——*Bundobust* (بندوبست - bandóbast, Hind.). From (bastan, pers. to tie). Literally tying and binding, both words being derived from the same persian verb. Sometimes inverted as Bustobund. Settlement of revenue to be paid to Government, or to a zemindar. Arrangement, of any undertaking, great or small. See vol. I, 112.

BUNDA (بندہ - bandah, *Hind.*). From (bastan, pers. to bind). Servant.——*Bunda nawauz* (بندہ نواز - bandahnaváz, Hind.). From (above + naváz, pers. liberator). Otherwise Ghesoo darauz or the long-ringletted. A great walee. His shrine is at Goolburga. His sandal [q.v.] there is on 16th of 11th month zoolcada [maheena] and his oors [q.v.] on 18th.

BUNDER (بندر - bandar, *Hind.*). From Persian. Any seaport. Bunder boat is a harbour boat. Shah bunder from (sháh, pers. king), is a harbour-master.——(1) Talook, Kistna district. Tahsildar's pay Rs. 175. Area 514 square miles. Population 159,575. Extends from the Kistna embouchure including the Island of Divy, past Masulipatam along the coast of the north. Bounded :—north by Goodivanda talook and Bheemaveram talook of the Godavery district, east and south by the Bay of Bengal, west by the Kistna, Sullapully zemindarry and Goodivanda talook. Irregular in shape, flat throughout the division. Probably reclaimed from the sea by the Kistna. Interspersed with Kistna canals, one of which is navigable. The coast is lined with mangrove [q.v.] forest yielding abundant supply of firewood. Soil is swampy and sandy in the sea coast, rest regar [q.v.]. Agricultural industry, grain and oil-seeds exported. Cotton piece-goods imported by the sea. Irrigation by Kistna anicut canals and rain-fed tanks. A considerable extent is uncultivated because of the injury done to the soil by the inundation of 1st November 1864. Camping grounds—Goodoor and Masulipatam. Places of archæological interest :—Avanigadda, Goodoor, Masulipatam, Pedana, Talagadadivy. Trig. station :—Cara, Caucarlamoody, Chilacalpoody, Chinnapondrauca, Cottapoody, Jimjair, Krittivenn temple, Lutchmeepooram, Masulipatam church, Narrainpooram, Peddagollapolliem beacon, Peddaputnam, Poteypully, Rajah's house city station, Sandala, Saupalamondy. The leading places, &c., in the talook are the following.——*Avanigadda* (అవనిగడ్డ - avanigadda, Tel.). See sep. title.——*Bunder* (بندر - bandar, Hind.). See below.——*Buntoomilly* (బంటుమిల్లి - bantumilli, Tel.). From (bantu, tel. hero + milli, tel. village). Village, formerly a salt factory; pop. 671; acres 967; lat. 16° 23′; long. 81° 18′; from Masulipatam N.N.E. 17 miles; from the sea N. 6½ miles.——*Cara* (కర - kara, Tel.). Means a bank. Trig. station; lat. 16° 11′ 1·94″; long. 81° 13′ 10·50″.——*Caucarlamoody* (కాకర్లమూడి - kákarlamúdi, Tel.). From (kákara, tel. momordica charantia, linn. + púdi, tel. village). Trig. station; lat. 16° 15′ 32·75″; long. 81° 14′ 29·19″.——*Chilacalpoody* (చిలకలపూడి - chilakalapúdi, Tel.). From (chilaka, tel. parrot + púdi, tel. village). Trig. station; lat. 16° 11′ 22·24″; long. 81° 12′ 19·55″.——*Chinna pondrauca* (చిన్నపాండ్రాక - chinnapándráka, Tel.). From (chinna, tel. small + pándráka, tel. place so called). Trig. station; lat. 16° 20′ 55·52″; long. 81° 20′ 57·67″.——*Codoor* (కోడూరు - kódúru, Tel.). From (kódę, tel. bull + úru, tel. village). Village; pop. 3,643; acres 22,024; lat. 6° 01′; long. 81° 05′; from Bezwada S.E. 44 miles; from Guntoor E.S.E. 43 miles; from Madras N.N.E. 202 miles; from Masulipatam S.S.W. 15 miles; from Vinoocondah E. 85 miles; from the sea N. 7¼ miles. Large village.——*Cottapoody* (కొత్తపూడి - kóttapúdi, Tel.). From (kotta, tel. new + púdi, tel. village). Trig. station; lat. 16° 13′ 58·02″; long. 81° 13′ 36·81″.——*Devarcote* (దేవరకోట - dévarakóta, Tel. devarakót*). From (dévara, tel. king + kóta, tel. fort). Zemindarry, Village. Peshcush Rs. 81,397.——*Divy* (దివి - diví, Tel.). See sep. title.——*Gilacaladindy* (గిలకలదిండి - gilakaladindi, Tel.). From (gilaka, tel. the sunn plant, crotolaria juncea, linn. + dindi, tel. stumps). Village; pop. 1,159. Fishing village.——*Goodoor* (గూడూరు - gúdúru, Tel.). See sep. title.——*Hamsal divy* (హంసలదీవి - hamsaladívi, Tel.). From (hamsa, san. swan + dívi, tel. island). Sanscrit name (hamsadvípa), meaning same. Village; pop. 940; acres 32,055; lat. 16° 05′; long. 81° 11′; from Masulipatam S. 7 miles. Site of point Divy light-house.——*Jimjair* (జింజేరు - jimjéru, Tel.). From (jimjiri, tel. chain). Trig. station; lat. 16° 17′ 7·19″; long. 81° 16′ 25·71″.——*Kistna* (కృష్ణ - krishna, Tel.). See sep. title.——*Krittivenn temple* (కృత్తివెన్నుదేవునిగుడి - krittivennudévunigudi, Tel.). From (krittivennu, tel. place so called

+ déva, san. god + gudi, tel. temple). Trig. station; lat. 16° 22′ 5·25″; long. 81° 25′ 1·19″.——*Lutchmeepooram* (లక్ష్మీపురము - lakshmípuramu, Tel.). From (lakshmí, san. the goddess + pura, san. town). Trig. station; lat. 16° 23′ 31·99″; long. 81° 29′ 12·53″. ——*Masulipatam* (మచిలీపట్టణము - machilipattanamu, Tel.). See sep. title.——*Mopidevy* (మోపిదేవి - mópidévi, Tel.). From (mópi, tel. widow + dévi, san. queen). Zemindarry, Village, Place of pilgrimage; pop. 2,246; acres 367; lat. of village 16° 04′; long. 80° 58′; from Masulipatam W.S.W. 16 miles; from the sea W. 16 miles. A place of pilgrimage.——*Narrainpooram* (నారాయణపురము - náráyanapuramu, Tel.). From (náráyana, san. vishnu, mover on waters + pura, san. town). Trig. station; lat. 16° 19′ 54·16″; long. 81° 18′ 28·60″.——*Ooppootair* (ఉప్పుతేరు - upputéru, Tel.). See sep. title.——*Pedana* (పెడన - pedana, Tel.). From (pedali, tel. a kind of tree, randia malabarica, lamk. + vana, san. forest). Village; pop. 4,740; acres 3,153; lat. 16° 16′; long. 81° 11′; from Masulipatam N. 7½ miles. Temple of Agasteeshwara sawmy with inscriptions.——*Pedda gollapollem beacon* (పెద్దగొల్లపాలెము - peddagollapálemu, Tel.). From (pedda, tel. large + gollapálemu, tel. the village). Trig. station; lat. 16° 21′ 5·72″; long. 81° 28′ 50·53″.——*Peddaputnam* (పెదపట్నము - pedapatnamu, Tel.). From (pedda, tel. large + pattana, san. town). Trig. station; lat. 16° 18′ 10·25″; long. 81° 20′ 49·27″.——*Poteypully* (పోతేపల్లి - pótépalli, Tel.). From (pótu, tel. ox + palli, tel. village). Trig. station; lat. 16° 12′ 34·21″; long. 81° 12′ 53·81″.——*Rajah's house city station* (రాజావారియిల్లు సిటీస్టేషను - rájáváriyillusitístéshan, Tel.). Trig. station; lat. 16° 10′ 41·24″; long. 81° 10′ 32·23″.——*Sandala* (సందల - tsandala, Tel.). Trig. station; lat. 16° 24′ 12·75″; long. 81° 27′ 20·84″.——*Saupalamondy* (చాపలమొండి - tsápalamondi, Tel.). From (tsápa, tel. mat + mondi, tel. bare spot). Trig. station; lat. 15° 43′ 37·18″; long. 80° 52′ 22·76″.——*Talagadadivy* (తలగడదీవి - talagadadívi, Tel.). From (talagada, tel. pillow + díví, tel. island), from shape. Village; pop. 2,115; acres 15,544; lat. 15° 55′; long. 80° 59′; from Masulipatam S.W. 23 miles; from the sea W. 5½ miles. Temple of Doorgaumba in the hamlet of Ganapeshwaram with inscriptions.——(2) Sub-Magistracy, Kistna district, pay Rs. 70.——(3) French lodge; Kistna district, Bunder tal.; pop. 100. Of the extensive French territory, of which the city of Masulipatam was formerly the capital, there only remains to France, at present in the city, one lodge. This lodge is at present unoccupied. The chief of the factory of Yanam places there a native overseer with an assistant. The village of Francepett, about 2 miles north-west of Masulipatam and two pieces of land, of which one is situated about one mile from the same city, depend on the lodge.——(4) Another name for Masulipatam; also called Mutchlee bunder, or fish-harbour.

BUNGALOW (بنگلہ - banglah, *Hind.*). Bengal fashioned house; that is built with pent roof and of one floor. Term now extended to any house that stands apart in its own grounds. Public bungalows are houses for travellers built by Government on the public roads. Distinguish from Buggalah.

BUNGANAPULLY (بینگن پلی - bainganpallí, *Hind.*; బంగనపల్లె - banganapalle,* *Tel.*). From (benaka, can. corruption of vináyaka, san. the god of wisdom + palle, tel. village).——(1) Native state, Kurnool district. Western portion hilly. Round sudder station, topes; otherwise territory flat and bare. The hills are composed of clay, slate and altered sandstones. The Rampore pass road runs through for 30 miles E. to W. Thermometer from 50° at night in December to 105° at noon in May. November, December, and January are cool, dry months. February, March, April, and May increasingly hot. S.W. monsoon during June, July, August, and September and N.E. in October. Average annual rainfall 30 inches. Fever endemic but not severe. Soils black cotton in south and red gravel elsewhere. Lime at Palcore and among hills. Population; Caupoos, Boyies or Beydar, Weavers, Maulas, Maudigas. Nawaub's family is Shiah. For further particulars, see vol. I, 41, 42 and vol. II, 62. The leading places, &c., in the state are as follows.——*Bunganapully* (బంగనపల్లె - banganapalle, Tel.). See below.——*Camalapoory* (కమలాపురి - kamalapuri, Tel.). From (kamala, san. lotus, nymphæa lotus, linn. + purí, san. town). Sanscrit name (kamandaléshvarapura), meaning shiva, the water-jar lord + town. Village; pop. 537; lat. 15° 12′; long. 78° 18′; from Bunganapully S. 7½ miles; from Kurnool S.S.E. 45 miles. All snakes here said to be harmless, and persons bitten are brought here for cure with earth and water from temple of Camandaleshwaran.——*Chenchely mullay* (చెంచెలిమల - chenchelimala, Tel.). See sep. title.——*Nandavaram* (నందవరము - nandavaramu, Tel.). From (nandana, san. proper name + pura, san. town). Called after Nandanan, the ruler. Sanscrit name (nandinípura), meaning doorga, the rejoicer + town; also (nandanapura), meaning shiva, the rejoicer + town. Village; pop. 1,209; lat. 15° 22′; long. 78° 20′; from Bunganapully N.E. 5 miles; from Kurnool S.S.E. 35 miles. Temple of Chowdeshwary in which pedigrees of five hundred families of Nandavareeky bramins who emigrated here in days of Nandana chuckravurty, tenth century A.D. are preserved.——*Pasoopoola* (పసుపుల - pasupula, Tel.). From (pasupu, tel. turmeric, curcuma longa, roxb. + ila, tel. ground). A village; pop. 606; lat. 15° 20′; long. 78° 04; from Bunganapully W. 14 miles; from Kurnool S. 34 miles. Old military camping ground on Rampore pass road. Goondamallappa waterfall [aroovy], 2 miles to west in Yerramalas, 80 feet high and throughout the year.——*Yauganty* (యాగంటి - yáganti, Tel.). From (yága, san. sacrifice + gandi, tel. pass). A place of pilgrimage; lat. 15° 20′; long. 78° 14′; from Bunganapully W.N.W. 3 miles; from Kurnool S.S.E. 36 miles. Temple to Shiva. In narrow valley surrounded by hills on three sides. Festival on Mahashivarautry [pundigay, 6a]. Perennial thermal spring irrigates betel [q.v.] and plantain [q.v.] gardens. Two caves on hill scarp N. of temple.——*Yerramala* (ఎర్రమల - erramala, Tel.). See sep. title.——*Zoorrair* (జూర్రేరు - dzurréru, Tel.). See sep. title.——(2) Village; Kurnool dist., Bunganapully state; pop. 3,330; lat. 15° 19′; long. 78° 17′; from Cumbum W.S.W. 61 miles; from Kurnool S.S.E. 38 miles; from Madras N.W. 210 miles; from Nundiaul S.W. 21 miles; from Pyaupaly E.N.E. 33 miles. On route from Bellary to Guntoor in a plain near the entrance to a broad defile formed by two parallel ranges of low hills branching to N.E. and S.E. Divided by the Zoorrair, into two parts, which are again sub-divided into Condapettah and Santapett on the right bank, and Cangarauzpett and Cusbah pettah on the left. Fort, on left bank, of lime stone with mud. The walls enclose Nawaub's zenana and his residence. In the pettah, N. of fort, are strong stone houses. Diamond mines near a low range of hills half mile from town. The matrix of the gems is a sandstone breccia lying under compact sandstone, of which the hills in the neighbourhood are composed. This breccia is composed of a mixture of colored jasper, quartz, and hornstone, cemented by a silicious paste. It passes into a pudding-stone of rounded pebbles of the above materials, cemented by an argillo-calcareous earth of a loose friable texture, in which the diamonds are found. This is also the case with the diamond alluvium found at the base of the hills washed by the pennair, near Chennore and Condapettah in Cuddapah. The process of mining is simply digging out the graves, breaking up the larger pieces of the breccia, washing and sifting the fragments, and spreading them out on the ground. The diamonds are easily detected by the practised eye of the native. No diamonds [vajram] of greater value than 300 or 400 rupees have been discovered here for many years.

BUNGAUR (سنہری سانپ - sunehrísámp, *Dec.*; ಚಟ್ಟೆಕಂದ್ಮೂಡೆ - chattekandmude, *Can.*; బంగారుపాము - bangárupámu, *Tel.*; மஞ்சட்சாரை - manjadchárai, *Tam.*). Dec. from (sunehrí, hind. golden + sámp, hind. snake). Tel. from (bangáru, tel. gold + pámu, tel. snake). Tam. from (manjal, tam. turmeric + shárai, tam. striped or rat snake). Title otherwise Banded bungaur, Rock-snake. Bungarus fasciatus, elapidæ [naug], ophidii colubriformes venenosi, ophidia [sarpam], reptilia [sarpy, 27], of naturalists [jantoo]. Alias Bungarus annularis; Pseudoboa fasciata. It varies in size from four to six or eight feet. Body with alternate broad black and yellowish rings, extending across the belly; there are from twenty-five to thirty-three of these black rings round the trunk; the first is the broadest and produced into a triangular process, the point of which rests on the vertical shield. Head black anteriorly and on the sides separated from the triangular process by a yellow V-like mark. Lower parts and throat uniform yellow. The hexagonal vertebral shield, and hard, blunt and almost bony end of tail, are very strongly marked. These are diurnal terrestrial snakes, but like others they generally prefer the shade to the sunshine. They are found in the open country, in grass and low jungle, and in fields. They live in holes in the ground, sometimes down among the roots of trees at a considerable depth. They are not frequently seen in inhabited places, though they at times find their way into huts and houses. Their bite is very dangerous, but does not cause many deaths, probably because it is not so much in the way of being met with as the cobra [q.v.] or krait [q.v.]. Its fangs are relatively to those of the cobra very small, and its bite in dogs causes death much slower than the cobra's bite. It is less valued by snake-charmers than the cobra, as it does not erect its head, nor is it amenable to tuition. The bungaur is not aggressive and tries to escape when discovered, but if attacked it retaliates fiercely. It lies coiled in curves, and when disturbed jerks itself out like a spring, but without extending its whole length of body. See Krait, which is Bungarus cæruleus.——*Sea bungaur* (கடற்பாம்பு - kadarbámbu, Tam.). Not unlike Bungaur fasciatus [bungaur], from the black and yellow-ringed markings. The Platurus genus of naturalists [jantoo]. One of the genera of Hydrophidæ or sea-snakes [chittal, tuttapaumb]. Are poisonous snakes inhabiting the sea, but transitional between land and sea forms. Has several characters like land snakes. Tail not prehensile. Ventral shields like those of land snakes. Body sub-cylindrical and not compressed. The eye is small. Tail longer and thicker in males than in females. Poison fang short.—"*a*" Platurus fischeri. Has trunk surrounded by thirty-six black rings; black band crosses the occiput; upper part of the snout yellow; upper labials black; 30 inches long.—"*b*" Platurus scutatus. Alias Coluber laticaudatus; Hydrophis colubrinus; Hydrus colubrinus; Laticauda scutata; Platurus fasciatus. Has crown of the head black; first and second black mark of the head and neck are joined below by a black longitudinal band, commencing from the chin; snout and side of the head yellow; with a black band running through the eye. The number and width of the black cross bands do not constitute specific characters in these snakes. Length of the tail varies with the sex. A common species. 5 feet long.

BUNJAR (بنجر - banjar, *Hind.*). From (bandhyá, san. barren). Land before cultivated, but now lying waste or fallow.

BUNNIAH (بنیا - baniyá, *Hind.*). A Hindoo trader [banyan].

BUNT (ಬಂಟ - banta, *Can.*). Means servant. Tooloo agricultural caste. Many have migrated into Coorg. They correspond to the Tamul vellaular and Malayalam nayar and form the main Shoodra population of the northern portion of Canara. In Malabar and south of Canara as far as Cassergode, they are called Nayars and their language is Malayalam. From Cassergode to Bramhahwar they are termed Bunts and speak Tooloo. To the north of Bramhahwar they are called Naudavar and speak Canarese [jauty].——*Buntrote* (ಬಂಟ್ರೋತು - bantrótu, Tel.). From (above + rautu, tel. horseman). A peon, originally mounted. ——*Buntwaul* (ಬಂಟ್ವಾಳ - bantvála, Can. bantvál *).—"*a*" Deputy tahsildarry, South canara district. Pay Rs. 70.—"*b*" Town, Deputy tahsildar's station; South canara dist., Mangalore tal.; pop. 3,551; lat. 12° 53'; long. 75° 05'; from Bangalore W. 172 miles; from Bombay S.S.E. 442 miles; from Coondapore S.S.E. 56 miles; from Madras W. 335 miles; from Mangalore E. 14 miles; from Oodipy S.S.E. 37 miles; from Poottoor N.W. 14 miles; from the sea E. 15 miles; from Soobramanyam W.N.W. 41 miles. On N. bank of Netrauvaty, so far navigable by boats. During war with Tippoo sultan town was partially destroyed by rajah of Coorg, who carried off half the inhabitants as prisoners. Formerly of importance as head-quarters of talook of same name. The talook was dismembered in 1852 and merged in present Mangalore talook. Possesses considerable traffic, being an entrepôt for the produce of Mysore on its way to the coast and vice versâ. Has a wealthy temple of Vencatramanan owned by Concany bramins, in which a car festival is celebrated annually in the month of March.

BURGHER (බර්ගර් - burgar, *Singh.*). From Dutch, meaning citizen. Ceylon term, but some Burghers are to be found in this Presidency. The Dutch admitted people of mixed descent to a kind of citizenship, and such people were distinguished by this name from pure natives. The word now used in same sense as half-caste, and Eurasian in India. The Badagas of the Neilgherries are sometimes called Burghers by confusion with the above [jauty].

BURGOOR (ಬರ್ಗೂರು - bargúru, *Can.* bargúr *). From (baragu, can. millet, panicum miliaceum, linn. + úru, can. village). Village, Hill range, Ghaut; Coimbatore dist., Bhawauny tal.; pop. 4,059; lat. of village 11° 48'; long. 77° 35'; from Bhawauny N.N.W. 26 miles; from Coimbatore N.E. 68 miles. The range lies between Bhawauny and Collegaul talooks, and is connected on the north and west with the Collegaul hills. It is a long narrow plateau watered by the river of the same name, ending in the Burgoor pass leading into Mysore. 30 miles in length. About 3,000 feet in height, with peaks rising to above 4,000 feet. Contains twenty-eight villages. The climate is dry, but water is got freely by digging wells. The hills are not much affected by either monsoon and are healthy. Inhabitants are chiefly Canarese lingayets. Their deity is Mautheshwaran, whose temple is on a hill of that name in Collegaúl; they have also the usual village gods. The sholagar are a servile tribe. The Burgoor cattle are well known. Small game, deer, panthers, tigers and bison are to be met with. The ghaut, along which passes the road from Erode to Collegaul, is passable by carts, the gradient being one in sixteen. Burgoor village is five miles further on and at the north edge of the plateau in a depression in the hills. Connected with the railway at Erode by a good road about 45 miles in length.

BURRAH (بڑا - bará, *Hind.*). Great. Common in composition. Burrah fusly sometimes corruptly for Baurah fusly [q.v.].

BURSAUT (برسات - barsát, *Hind.*). From (varsha, san. rain). The rainy season.——*Bursauty* (برساتی - barsátí, Hind.). Horse disease peculiar to India. Appears in rainy season, in form of chancre-like sores on skin, face, tongue, lips and fetlock joints. A horse [ghorah] which has, or has had, bursauty is unsound [ashwarogam].

BURTY (బర్తి - barti, *Tel.*). Corruption of (parti, *Tel.*). Uncultivated land; suffix in place names, as Penooburty, meaning large + uncultivated land.

BUS (بس - bas, *Hind.*). Anglo-indian exclamation. Enough.

BUSSORAH (بصره - basrah, *Hind.*). From (basarah, ar. whitish stone); as situated on such ground. Town at head of the Persian gulf.——*Bussorah gum* (صمغ بصره - simaghibasrah, Hind.). Same as Hog gum [q.v.].

BUTCH (بچ - bach, *Dec.*). From (vatsa, san. calf); from use as animal poison. Short for Bachnaug. Also with another derivation stands for sweet flag.

BUTTER (வெண்ணெய் - venney, *Tam.*). Tam. means white ghee. Prefix.——*Butter fish* (پفته - paftah, Hind.). Title from mucous secretion of body. The genus Callichrous, siluridæ [kizhautty], physostomi, teleostei, pisces [matsyam, 35], of naturalists [jantoo]. Length not exceeding one foot; lower jaw projects beyond the upper; eye behind and partly below, the cleft of the mouth; good for food. The species best known to the natives are:—bimaculatus [two-spotted shark], malabaricus [malabar shark].——*Butter tree* (मधुवृक्ष - madhuvriksha, San.). San. from (madhu, san. butter or honey + vriksha, san. tree). Anglo-indian name given to several trees whose fruits or bark yield a solid oily or fatty substance. Examples are:—Bassia butyracea [butter mohwah]; Garcinia indica, cokum butter; Garcinia morella, gamboge butter; Myristica fragrans, nutmeg butter; Persea gratissima, midshipman's butter; Theobroma cacao, cocoa butter. See gloss. paragraphs.

BUTTY (బట్టి - batti, *Tel.*). From hindostany [bhatty]. A still; suffix in places names, as Antarbutty, inside + still.

BYE (بائی - bái, *Hind.*; బాయి - báyi, *Tel.*). From (bái, mahr. woman). Term of respectful address towards a mother or an elderly female. Suffix in feminine proper names among Madhwa and Mahratta women, as Rama bye, Roocma bye. Compare ammah among Tamuls and Teloogoos [peyar]. In northern India the term means a dancing-girl. Distinguish from bhaee, bhye.

BYEBARANG (विडङ्ग - vidanga, *San.*; बावडंग - bávadanga, *Mahr.*; برنج کابلی - biranjikábulí, *Ar.* and *Pers.*; باوبرنگ - báubarang, *Hind.*; بائی برنگ - báíbarang, *Dec.*; ವಾಯುವಿಳಂಗ - váyuvilanga, *Can.*; వాయువిడంగము - váyuvilangamu, *Tel.*; ବାୟିବିଡଙ୍ଗ - báyibidanga, *Oor.*; വായ്വിളങ്ങം - váyvilankam, *Mal.*; වලංගසාල් - valangasál, *Singh.*; வாயுவிளங்கம் - váyuvilangam, *Tam.*). Title from deccany. San. from (vid, san. to break), as vermifuge. Ar. from (biranj, ar. rice + kábulí, ar. cabul). Hind. from (báu, hind. flatulence + biranj, pers. seed). Can. from (váyu, san. wind + vidanga, san. the plant). Oor. from (váyu, san. wind + vidanga, san. the plant). Mal. from (váya, mal. mouth + vilakku, mal. to clean). Tam. from (váy, tam. mouth + vilangu, tam. to clear). San. also (chitratandula), meaning variegated rice; (krimighna), meaning worm-killer. Tam. also (vellal). Title otherwise Cabool rice, Wind berry, Worm-killer. Botanically Embelia ribes, burm., myrsineæ [vricsham, 81]. Generic name from singhalese. Alias Embelia glandulifera, ribesioides. Large climbing shrub; tender shoots and peduncles hoary; leaves alternate, oblong, entire, glabrous; panicles terminal, hoary; calyx and corolla five-parted; stamens inserted in the middle of the petals; flowers numerous, very small, greenish yellow; tube of calyx concave; berries succulent; grows in dry jungles. The berries as occurring are something like black-pepper; very smooth; almost always have a thin peduncle or stalk attached to them, and possess a very slight pungent taste; with regard to color, there are two varieties, grey or reddish-grey and dull brown. Medicinally berries are carminative, stomachic, and anthelmintic; enter into composition of applications for ringworm and other skin diseases; are also aperient; they are used largely in the adulteration of black-pepper [q.v.]. No other common species here.

BYGHONEY (ಬೈಗಣಿ - baigani, *Can.*). Coffee [q.v.] and cinchona [koinah] estates, Paranginaud, Neilgherries. From Kotagherry S.E. 4 miles. 192 acres.

BYLE (بیل - bail, *Hind.*). From (bala, san. strength). Bullock.

BYLE (ಬೈಲು - bailu, *Can.*; బైలు - bailu, *Tel.*). From (veli, tam. outside). A plain; an open field, especially for rice [vayal].

BYNEE PALM (ಬೈನಿ - baini, *Can.*). Bastard sago [q.v.].

C (क - ka, *San.*; க - ka, *Tam.*). The who or the unknown; any chief god. Tam. sign for the numeral one.——*Catapayaudy* (कटपयादि - katapayádi, San.). From (ka + ta + pa + ya, the san. letters + ádi, san. beginning). System of algebra [beeja ganitam] where consonants, not vowels, represent figures.

CAABA (کعبه - kabah, *Hind.*). From (kaab, ar. a cube). Any square building. Whence especially the temple at Mecca, the object of the haj [q.v.]. This contains the black stone touched or kissed by pilgrims; probably originally a lingam [q.v.]. Said to have been built by Abraham and Ismail. Since made by Mahomet the kibla for his followers all over the world.

CABAH (قبا - kabá, *Hind.*). From (kab, ar. a piece of cloth sewed inside a shirt near the opening at the neck). A long gown with flaps in the skirt; the skirt and breast open, and sometimes slit in the armpits [chapkan, sheelay].

CABBAGE WOOD (کھتیان - khatiyán, *Dec.*). From softness. Wood of eriodendron anfractuosum [silk cotton].

CABEER (کبیر - kabír, *Hind.*). From (kibr, ar. great). Great. An attribute of God [allah]. Mahomedan alam, as Cabeer ally, double alam [ism].

CABOB (كباب - kabáb, *Hind.*). From Arabic root meaning to heat. Small piece of meat roasted on a skewer and seasoned with salt, pepper, asafœtida and garlic. Also origin of term cubobs [cubeb pepper].——*Cabob cheeny* (كباب چینی - kabáb-chíní, Hind.): From (above + chiní, hind. china); introduced into commerce by chinese from the eastern islands, its native habitat. Term for Cubebs [cubeb peper] in bengal, Pimento [china pepper] in madras.

CABOOL (قبول - kabúl, *Hind.*). From (kabala, ar. to accept). Consent.——*Caboolyat* (قبولیت - kabúliyat, Hind.). A counter-agreement.

CABOOL (کابل - kábul, *Hind.*). Capital of Afghanistan.——*Cabool country bean* (باقلۂ کابلی - báklahikábulí, Pers.; سیم - sem, Hind. and Dec.). Pers. from (báklah, ar. bean, dolichos + above). Title otherwise Broad bean, Tare, Vetch. Botanically Vicia faba, linn., leguminosæ [vricsham, 48]. Alias Faba vulgaris. Annual herb; farinaceous edible seeds; can be grown at bangalore.——*Cabool rice* (برنج کابلی - biranjíkábulí, Ar.). Same as Byebarang.

CABZA (قبضہ - kabza, *Hind.*). From (kabaza, ar. to grasp). A dagger; dagger mark used instead of signature.

CACSHAM (कक्ष - kaksha, *San.*). From (kash, san. to rub). Orbit. The path described by a planet [graham] or comet [dhoomkait] round the sun [sooryan]; more or less in the form of an ellipse, with the sun in one of the foci not in the centre [caindram]. No native terms for ellipse and focus. That point in the planet's orbit which is furthest from the sun is the aphelion [mandotcham]; the point nearest the sun is the perihelion [chalotcham]. The points in the orbit of a planet which intersect the ecliptic [craunty mundalam] are the nodes [pautam]. See Jyotisham.

CADA (കട - kata, *Mal.*; கட - kada, *Tam.*). To cross, go.——*Cadatnaud* (കടത്തനാട് - katattanátu, Mal.). From (katattu, mal. transport + nátu, mal. country). Sanscrit name (ghatótkachapura), meaning giant of that name + town. Cottanara of Pliny, κοττοναρικὴ of the periplus, which calls it the district where the best pepper was produced. Town; Malabar district, Cooroombranaud talook. Gave its name to one of the ancient chieftainships into which Malabar district was formerly divided; stretching from the sea-coast up the western declivity of the Western ghauts. The first Cadatnaud rajah was a Nayar of eminence, who about 1564 wrested this tract from the Rajah of Chiracal. The invasion of Tippoo interrupted the line. On the expulsion of the latter in 1792, the Nayar rajah was restored and his family have held the estate ever since. The rajah resides at Coottipooram.——*Cadav* (കടവ് - katavu, Mal.). Ford; suffix in place names as Molancadav, meaning bamboo ford.——*Cadavool* (கடவுள் - kadavul, Tam.). From (kada, tam. to surpass). The deity, especially Shiva.——*Caday* (കട - kata, Mal.; கடை - kadai, Tam.). From (kada, tam. to go) [cadav]. Gate. Also last. Also place, shop. Suffix in place names as Poothoocaday, meaning new market.——*Cadaycaul* (கடைக்கால் - kadaikkál, Tam.). From (kadai, tam. last + kál, tam. channel). The most distant channel or portions of a field.——*Cadaycaur* (கடைக்காரன் - kadaikkáran, Tam.). From (kadai, tam. shop + káran, tam. agent). A shopkeeper.——*Cadaycoolam* (ಕಡೇಕುಲ - kadékula, Can.). From (above + kula, san. family). The lowest of the castes, Pariah.——*Cadaygaul* (ಕಡೇಕಾಲ - kadékála, Can.). From (kadai, tam. last + kála, san. time). The later cultivating season, under N.E. monsoon [hingaur, parvam, peira].——*Cadaypoke* (கடைப்போக்கு - kadaipókku, Tam.). From (kadai, tam. gate + pó, tam. to go). The flood-gate of a tank [poramboke].

CADA (கடா - kadá, *Tam.*). Buffalo.——*Cadauvady* (கடாவடி - kadávadí, Tam.). From (above + adi, tam. to beat). A second threshing of corn performed by buffaloes.

CADAGAM (கடகம் - kadagam, *Tam.*). From (kat, san. to surround). Fortification; suffix in place names [catacam].

CADAL (കടൽ - katal, *Mal.*; கடல் - kadal, *Tam.*). Sea.—"*a*" Suffix in place names as Shircadal, meaning small sea.—"*b*" Sea-colored or maritime or foreign as having come from over sea. Plant first term, often joining two genera. Ex., where transl. is of second term:—Jatropha curcas (kadalámanakku), ricinus communis; Lodoicea seychellarum (kadattengu), cocos nucifera; Lumnitzera racemosa (katakkantal), kandelia rheédhii; Morinda citrifolia (katappilávu), artocarpus integrifolia. See gloss. paragraphs.——*Cadalay* (கடலை - kadalai, Tam.). Foreign as having been introduced from abroad. Same as Bengal gram.——*Cadaloondy* (കടലുണ്ടി - katalunti, Mal.). From (above + untu, mal. to push); from rapidity of river current. τύνδις in the Periplus.—"*a*" Village, Port; Malabar dist., Yernaud tal.; lat. 11° 7'; long. 75° 52'; from Beypore S.S.E. 4 miles; from Bombay S.S.E. 565 miles; from Calicut S.S.E. 10 miles; from Munjery W. 20 miles; from Parpauangaudy N.N.W. 5 miles. Small port at mouth of river of same name; native vessels occasionally come for country produce.—"*b*." River; Malabar dist., Yernaud tal.; about lat. 10°. 59' N.; long. 76° 17' E. Rises in southern slopes of Coondah mountains, meanders westerly with many serpentine windings, and after flowing via Tiroorangaudy, empties into sea at Cadaloondy. One branch joins the Beypore river opposite to place of that name and forms island of Chaulyam. The river is known by different names in different parts of its course; at Malapooram it is called Noorandy and Anakkayam, at Tiroorangaudy, it is Tiroorangaudy, &c. The bed is exceedingly narrow and rocky with high banks fringed with wood and groves of areca and other palms at intervals. Teak and other timber, also rafts of bamboos, are floated down to the coast to the depôts at Beypore and Cullye near Calicut.——*Cadaly* (கடலி - kadali, Tam.). From color of flowers. Crape myrtle, Indian lilac. Botanically the Lagerstrœmia genus, lythraceæ [vricsham, 58]. Large trees or shrubs, with opposite entire leaves and terminal panicles of purplish or white flowers; fruits contain winged seeds; ornamental. The species best known to the natives are:—flos-reginæ [adambo], indica [china mindie], lanceolata [venteak], parviflora [chennangy].

CADAMBA (कदम्ब - kadamba, *San.*). Plants of Adina, Anthocephalus, and Stephegyne genera; especially the second. See below. Line ruling in W. of Mysore and in Canara from at least commencement of Christian era. Shortly after that reduced by Chalookyas. The founder of the family was Mayoora vurman. Capital Banavausy is mentioned by Ptolemy. Banner was a monkey, and signet a lion [charitram]. See vol. I (136); II, 251. Cadamban is Soobramanyan, son of Shiva, the tree being sacred to him.——*Blue cadamba* (நீலக்கடம்பு - nílakkadambu, Tam.). Same as Lowly nelly.——*Common cadamba* (कदम्ब - kadamba, San.; कळंब - kalamba, Mahr.; کدم - kadam, Hind. and Dec.; ಕಡಹ - kadaha, Can.; కదిమి - kadimi, Tel.; କଦମ୍ବ - kadambo, Oor.; കടമ്പ - katamba, Mal.; කොළොං - kolom, Singh.; கடம்பு - kadambu, Tam.). Title from sanscrit. San. from (kad, san. to kill); from curing virtue. Mahr., &c., from sanscrit. San. also (priyaka), meaning agreeable; (kádambarí), meaning liquor distilled from its flower; (nadíja), meaning river born; (dévavriksha), meaning divine tree; (dásavriksha), meaning serving + tree, useful in worship. Can. also (kadavá). Tel. also (kadapachettu); (mogulukadimi), meaning male + the tree; (nripálakadambamu), meaning king + the tree; (rudrákshakadamba), meaning shiva + eye + the tree. Singh. also (halamba). Tam. also (vellaikkadambu), meaning white + the tree, from color of wood. Botanically Anthocephalus cadamba, miq., rubiaceæ [vricsham, 71]. Specific name from sanscrit. Alias Cephalanthus orientalis; Nauclea cadamba, citrifolia, orientalis; Sarcocephalus cadamba. Large tree with a perfectly straight erect trunk, spreading branches, and thick foliage; leaves opposite, between bifarious and decussate, oval, smooth, entire; petioles smooth; peduncles terminal, solitary; heads of flowers globose; calyx five-partite; capsules four-sided, four-celled; seeds numerous, not winged; flowers small, orange-colored, fragrant. Bark used medicinally as febrifuge and tonic. Fruit eaten; foliage as fodder for cattle. Planted for shade. Wood white, with a yellowish tinge, soft, even-grained. No other common species here.——*Sea cadamba* (சமுத்திரக்கடம்பு - shamuttirakkadambu, Tam.). From resemblance and being on sea-coast. Same as Common indian oak.——*Water cadamba* (کدم - kadam, Hind.; ಹೆದುಮರ - hedumara, Can.; నీరుకదిమి - nírukadimi, Tel.; നീർക്കടമ്പ - nírkkatamba, Mal.; நீர்க்கடம்பு - nírkkadambu, Tam.). Title from habitat. Can. from mahratta, meaning yellow wood tree. Tel. from (níru, tel. water + kadimi, tel. anthocephalus cadamba, miq.). Tam. from (nír, tam. water). Mal. also (káttuchakka), meaning wild jack, artocarpus integrifolia, willd. Tam. also (pattakkadambu), meaning stripe + cadamba tree. Title otherwise Female cadamba, Wild jack. Botanically Stephegyne parvifolia, korth., rubiaceæ [vricsham, 71]. Alias Cephalanthus pilulifer; Nauclea orientalis, parvifolia. Tree 30–40 feet, glabrous except in the axils of the nerves on the under side of the leaves; branches brachiate; leaves opposite, ovate or oval, bluntish; general peduncles opposite, terminal, bearing a pair of small deciduous leaves, partial ones scarcely so long as the globose head of flowers; limb of calyx very short, and almost truncated; lobes of corolla spreading; capsule containing two cocci splitting at the inner angle; flowers small, yellow; malabar, mysore. Wood close-grained and of light chestnut-color, if exposed to wet it soon rots; used for packing cases, flooring, &c.——*Yellow cadamba* (धाराकदम्ब - dhárákadamba, San.; हेदू - hédú, Mahr.; ھلدو - haldáu, Hind.; ಎತ್ತೇಗು - ettégu, Can.; పసుపుకదిమి - pasupukadimi, Tel.; ହୋଲଣ୍ଡ - holonda, Oor.; മഞ്ഞക്കടമ്പ - maññakkatamba, Mal.; කොළොං - kolom, Singh.; மஞ்சக்கடம்பு - mañjakkadambu, Tam.). Title from wood. San. from (dhárá, san. turmeric); from color of wood. Mahr. from (héma, san. gold + dru, san. tree); from yellow wood. Hind. means turmeric wood. Can. from (ede, can. middling size + tégu, can. tectona grandis, linn. f.). Tel. from (pasupu, tel. yellow). Mal. from (mañña, san. yellow). Tam. from (mañjal, tam. saffron). Can. also (hedde), by corruption from mahratta; (pettégu), meaning brittle + teak; (arasanatégu), meaning saffron + teak. Tel. also (dádugu); (bandáru), meaning saffron [golla's plate, wild anaur]; (bettaganapa), meaning strength + great. Title otherwise

Model wood, Saffron teak, Saffron wood, Turmeric wood, Yellow wood. Botanically Adina cordifolia, hook. f., rubiaceæ [vricsham, 71]. Alias Nauclea cordifolia. Tree 40–50 feet; leaves opposite, decussate, cordate, roundish, pubescent on the upper side, tomentose on the under; general peduncles axillary, one to three together, partial one shorter than the general, rather longer than the globose head of flowers; calyx five-partite, segments clavate; corolla pubescent, lobes spreading; capsule two-celled; seeds six, winged at the extremities; flowers small, yellow, flowering in rainy season. Growing abundantly in mountainous parts of Coromandel coast. Wood yellow, moderately hard, even-grained; no heart-wood, no annual rings. Seasons well, takes a good polish, and is durable, but somewhat liable to warp and crack, it does not stand wet. Resembles box, but is lighter. No other common species here.

CADATA (ಕಡತ - kadata, *Can.*). A cloth covered with a composition of charcoal [adoopp kary] and gum [gond], used instead of a slate [cull palagay] for writing on with chalk or steatite [balapam]. Leaves of such folded together are used as account books in Canara. Writing is effaced with wet sponge or cloth.

CADEEM (قديم - kadím, *Hind.*). From (kidama, ar. to go before). Ancient. Hereditary cultivator as distinguished from poyacarries or strangers [oolcoody].

CADIAPATAM (കടിയപട്ടണം - katiyapattanam, *Mal.*). From (katiya, mal. large + pattana, san. town). Village, Port; Travancore state, Pudmanaubhapooram division, Yerraneel tal.; pop. 11,249; lat. 8° 8′; long. 77° 21′; from Bombay S.S.E. 790 miles; from Cochin S.S.E. 143 miles; from Colachel S.E. 4½ miles; from Quilon S.E. 70 miles; from Shaunaurgoody W. 17 miles; from Trivandrum S.E. 33 miles; from Yerraneel S. 5 miles. 17 miles N.W. of Cape comorin. Unsafe anchorage between the shore and two rocky islets. At the adjoining village of Moottam, a bay affords some shelter from N.W. winds. There is a lighthouse here.

CADIRY (కదిరి - kadiri,* *Tel.*). From (khadira, san. acacia catechu, willd.); tree under which a local idol of narsimhan [q.v.] was found.——**(1)** Talook, Cuddapah district. Tahsildar's pay Rs. 175. Area 1,158 square miles. Population 134,715. Language Teloogoo. Most western and largest talook in Cuddapah district. Irregular in shape. Extreme length 45 miles, extreme breadth 35 miles. Bounded north by Poolivendla talook, from which it is separated by a rocky range of hills; west by Hindoopore and Penoocondah talooks of Anantapore district; south by Madanapully talook; east by Royachoty talook. Very rocky and barren, and cut up by detached rocky hills perfectly destitute of vegetation. It is hot, though from 1,500 to 2,000 feet above the sea, and has the reputation of being unhealthy. Soil very poor, chiefly coarse red sand mixed with disintegrated granite [caroom cull] or soda [munn cauram]. Regar [q.v.] or black soil is met with in patches here and there. Towards Anantapore and Poolivendla frontiers extensive jungles, but wood small and ordinary. The hills are unproductive. Ordinary jungle products of lac [q.v.], honey [shahad], bees [tainee], wax [mom], and dyeing roots collected by jungle tribes. Iron-stone found and roughly smelted. Limestone [choonam] procurable, and granite for building purposes. Chief products, beyond the local requirements of rice [paddy] and sadza [bajrah], are horse-gram, cholum [q.v.], sugar-cane [q.v.], and cotton [q.v.]; scarcely any indigo is cultivated. A good deal of jaggery [q.v.] is produced, and there is a considerable trade in this article by importation from Madanapully talook; it is then exported to the northern talooks of the district and elsewhere. Formerly silk used to be manufactured, and much care was devoted to the cultivation of mulberry trees, which were grown under wells from cuttings. Rivers are the Maddoolair, and the Paupughny. The latter passes through the south and south-western portions. But they are of little advantage for irrigation. The five largest tanks are those of Cadiry, Moottiaulcheroo, Puntoolacheroo, Putnam, and Wonkamuddy. The principal channels are the Cadiry, Codavandlapully caulwa, and the Tippamuddy caulwa. In addition to Government wells there are 7,980 private wells. Upon these the ryots chiefly depend for their water-supply during the hot months. The wells are constructed at great cost and with considerable labor. They are often from 30–40 feet in depth, and four pairs of bullocks are frequently used during the day for drawing the water. Places of archæological interest:—Cadiry, Doragull, Putnam. Principal trig. stations:—Eeshwaramala, Ingalore, Palcondah, Peipaud droog. The leading places, &c., in the talook are the following.——*Cadiry* (కదిరి - kadiri, Tel.). See below.——*Chitrauvaty* (చిత్రావతి - chitrávati, Tel.). See sep. title.——*Coccunty* (కొక్కంటి - kokkanti, Tel.). From (kokku, tel. rat + kannu, tel. eye); after a person of that name. Village; pop. 2,817; acres 17,379; lat. 13° 56′; long. 78° 19′; from Cadiry S.E. 14 miles; from Cuddapah S.W. 52 miles. Seat of an old poligar family.——*Coorly* (కుర్లి - kurli, Tel.). From (kuri, can. sheep). Village; pop. 1,783; acres 13,328; lat. 14° 17′; long. 78° 15′; from Cadiry N.N.E. 12 miles; from Cuddapah W.S.W. 44 miles.——*Eeshwaramala* (ఈశ్వరమల - íshvaramala, Tel.). From (íshvara, san. shiva, the lord + mala, tel. hill). Trig. station; lat. 14° 01′ 56·05″; long. 78° 22′ 39·44″; height 3,161 feet; from Cadiry E.S.E. 13 miles; from Chaumalgondy S. 2 miles; from Cuddapah S.W. 45 miles.——*Ingalore* (ఇంగలూరు - inagalúru, Tel.). From (ingalamu, tel. charcoal + úru, tel. village). Village, Trig. station; pop. 1,401; acres 8,489; lat. 14° 02′ 25·08″; long. 78° 06′ 54·91″; height 2,900 feet; from Cadiry S.W. 7½ miles; from Devarcondah S.S.W. 15 miles; from Cuddapah W.S.W. 59 miles.——*Moottiaulcheroo* (ముత్యాలచెరువు - mutyálacheruvu, Tel.). From (mutyamu, tel. pearl + cheruvu, tel. tank). Village; pop. 1,002; acres 8,476; lat. 14° 06′; long. 78° 08′; from Cadiry W. 4½ miles; from Cuddapah W.S.W. 55 miles. The tank is never empty.——*Palcondah* (పాలకొండ - pálakonda, Tel.). See sep. title.——*Paupughny* (పాపఘ్ని - pápaghni, Tel.). See sep. title.——*Peipaud droog* (పైపాడుదుర్గము - paipádudurgamu, Tel.). From (pai, tel. upper + pádu, tel. village + durga, san. fort). Trig. station; lat. 14° 19′ 58·41″; long. 78° 12′ 52·16″; height 2,289 feet; from Putnam N.E. 8½ miles; from Cadiry N. 15¾ miles; from Cuddapah W.S.W. 44 miles.——*Putnam* (పట్నము - patnamu, Tel.). Means town. Village; pop. 2,061; acres 10,274; lat. 14° 14′; long. 78° 09′; from Cadiry N.N.W. 9¼ miles; from Cuddapah W.S.W. 51 miles. Tank. Five miles north on the hills is a fine old fort.——*Talpoola* (తలుపుల - talupula, Tel.). From (talupu, tel. door). Village; pop. 2,761; acres 11,989; lat. 14° 14′; long. 78° 18′; from Cadiry N.E. 11½ miles; from Cuddapah W.S.W. 41 miles. Seat of an old jagheerdar's family.——*Tanacull* (తనకల్లు - tanakallu, Tel.). From (tanuku, tel. to burn + kallu, tel. stone). Village; pop. 3,236; acres 11,052; lat. 13° 55′; long. 78° 15′; from Cadiry S. 13 miles; from Cuddapah S.W. 57 miles.——*Toommala* (తుమ్మల - tummala, Tel.). From (tumma, tel. babúl tree, acacia arabica, willd.). Village; pop. 1,823; acres 13,244; lat. 13° 56′; long. 78° 07′; from Cadiry S.S.W. 13¼ miles; from Cuddapah S.W. 62 miles. Ruins of a fort. During last century held as military fief of Gooramcondah by a Mussalman general.——**(2)** Town, Talook head-quarters, Place of pilgrimage; Cuddapah dist., Cadiry tal.; pop. 6,059; acres 13,301; lat. 14° 06′; long. 78° 12′; from Cuddapah W.S.W. 51 miles; from Madanapully N.N.W. 45 miles; from Madras W.N.W. 160 miles; from Sidhout W.S.W. 60 miles. Parwarish khan obtained this as a jagheer [q.v.]. It was resumed by the Mahrattas in 1756; and restored in 1764 by Meer sahib who resumed it again in 1773. In 1799 Alam khan took possession of Cadiry. Cumr ood deen fixed his peshcush [q.v.] at 8,050 Canteroy pagodas [q.v.]. Refusing to pay the peshcush due, he was attacked but escaped, and the jagheer was again resumed. The family is now extinct. Large number of ancient tombs and mosques south of town. Pagoda festival in February and March. People come from Bellary and Mysore. Two days after car procession pariahs are allowed to enter temple after bathing in the Maddoolair [ooppooloor].

CADJAN (جولی - jaulí, *Hind.*; كجنگ - kajang, *Malay*; తాటాకు - tátáku, *Tel.*; ഓല - óla, *Mal.*; ஓலை - ólai, *Tam.*). Malay means a dressed nipah palm leaf. Tel. from (tádi, tel. palmyra + áku, tel. leaf). Dried leaves of cocoanut, talipot, and palmyra palms [taur]. Used as a thatch, which resists rain better than tiles, but roofs made of them should be relaid before commencement of rainy season. The cadjans of talipot and palmyra palms are written on with an iron style for accounts, &c. [olay]. The letters are sometimes blackened with ink [mashy]. Distinguish from catjang.——*Cadjan snake* (پتےکا سانپ - pattekásámp, Hind.; వానపాము - vánapámu, Tel.; ஓலைப் பாம்பு - ólaippámbu, Tam.). Title from color. Hind. from (pattá, hind. leaf + sámp, hind. snake). Tel. from (vána, tel. rain + pámu, tel. snake). Tam. from (ólai, tam. cadjan + pámbu, tam. snake), from color. Title otherwise Chameleon snake. Tropidonotus stolatus, colubridæ [paumb], ophidii colubriformes, ophidia [sarpam], reptilia [sarpy, 17], of naturalists [jantoo].

CADOO (கடு - kadu, *Tam.*). Strength.——*Cadookkay* (கடுக்கை - kadukkai, Tam.). From (kadumai, tam. strength); medicinal. The tree Cassia fistula, linn. [condray]. Cadookaiyan is Shiva, the tree being sacred to him.——*Cadookye* (கடுக்காய் - kadukkáy, Tam.). Means sharp fruit. Chebulic myrobalan.

CAFFRE (كافر - káfir, *Hind.*). From (kufr, ar. unbelief). An infidel or non-Mahomedan.——*Caffree* (كافری - káfirí, Hind.). Huge, from association. Plant first term. Ex.:—Capsicum grossum (káppirimilagáy), large chilly.

CAHATA (කහට - kahata, *Singh.*). Means bitter; astringent; from bark. Same as Coomby.

CAHILAH (كاهلا - káhilá, *Hind.*). From (káhil, ar. indolent). Ill-health; especially fever [jwaram].

CAINDRAM (केन्द्र - kéndra, *San.*). From Greek κέντρον. Centre of a circle. The argument of an equation. Caindraubhimookham or towards centre is centripetal and caindra paraunmookham or away from centre is centrifugal. Caindra chyooty is deviation from centre or eccentricity.——*Dwiteeya caindram* (द्वितीयकेन्द्र - dvitíyakéndra, San.). From (dvitíya, san. second). The supplement to a whole circle of mean anomaly [mandam]; being the distance of the higher apsis [mandotcham] from a planet in any point of its orbit [cacsham].——*Manda caindram* (मन्दकेन्द्र - mandakéndra, San.). From (manda, san. anomaly),

Argument of anomaly.——*Patana caindram* (पतनकेन्द्र - patana-kéndra, San.). From (patana, san. latitude). Argument of the latitude.——*Ravy caindram* (रविकेन्द्र - ravikēndra, San.). Means sun + argument. Argument of the equation for the sun's place. ——*Shashy caindram* (शशिकेन्द्र - shashikéndra, San.). Means moon + argument. Situation of the moon in the rising sign, also in the fourth, seventh or tenth from it. Moon's anomaly. ——*Sheeghra caindram* (शीघ्रकेन्द्र - shíghrakéndra, San.). From (shíghra, san. parallax). The commutation; being the distance of the sun from a superior planet; or the distance of an inferior planet from the sun [jyotisham].

CAJAUNAH (خزانه - khazánah, *Hind.*). From (khazana, ar. to lay up). A treasury [bhandaura]. Cajaunchy, treasurer.

CAJEPUT (کائی پتی - káipattí, *Hind.*; کائی بوتی - káibútí, *Dec.*; کیو پتہی - kayuputih, *Malay*; கையாப்புடை - kaiyáppudai, *Tam.*). From (kayu, malay, wood + putih, malay, white). Title otherwise White australian tea tree, White wood tree. Botanically Melaleuca leucadendron, l., myrtaceæ [vricsham, 56]. Moderate-sized tree; dark, evergreen, willow-like foliage; ash-grey withered-looking bark in layers, like thin paper; small whitish flowers; native of indian archipelago. Oil distilled from leaves is clear and limpid, of a light green color, very volatile, diffusing a powerful odour, having a warm aromatic taste, something resembling that of camphor [q.v.], followed by a sense of coolness. Favorite native medicine both externally and internally; gives to pharm. cajuputi oleum, diffusible stimulant, antispasmodic and diaphoretic, externally applied, rubefacient. Oil dissolves caoutchouc or indian rubber, by which means a good varnish [rangh] may be made.

CAJJALY (कज्जलि - kajjali, *San.*). From (kajjala, san. lamp-black); called after the color. Otherwise Æthiop's mineral. Black sulphide of mercury [krishna paspam, rasam], prepared by rubbing together equal parts of sulphur [gandhac] and mercury [rasam] till globules disappear [caujal].

CAL (कल् - kal, *San.*). To count, do, incite, sound, go.——*Calacuntam* (कलकण्ठ - kalakant'ha, San.). From (kala, san. low voice + kant'ha, san. throat). Sylviadæ family, dentirostres, insessores, aves [pacshy, 23], of naturalists [jantoo]. Warblers. Divided into the following sub-families:—"*a*" Saxicolinæ, Stone-chats, Wheat-ears and Robins [shyaumay].—"*b*" Ruticillinæ, Red-starts [neelcunty, tirtira].—"*c*" Calamoherpinæ, Grass warblers [cumpajitta].—"*d*" Drymoicinæ, Wren warblers [indian tailor bird].—"*e*" Phylloscopinæ, Tree-warblers.—"*f*" Sylviinæ, Grey-warblers.—"*g*" Motacillinæ, Wagtails and Pipits [pilkya]. ——*Calay* (कला - kalá, San.; కళ - kala, Tel.). From (kal, san. to count).—"*a*" Measure of space. An arc of one minute of a degree. 60 vicalays = 1 calay or minute; 60 calays = 1 bhaugam or degree.—"*b*" Measure of time. 30 caushtays = 1 calay; 30 calays = 1 moohoortam [caulam, 2]; approximate actual value, 1 calay = 1 English minute and 36 English seconds; this is in natural and popular solar reckoning. Also $\frac{1}{60}$th of a lunar day or about 24 minutes.—"*c*" Also a phase of the moon, or digit of her diameter. The orb of the moon is divided into sixteen of these, but as one is considered constant, and the other fifteen revolve round it like a garland of flowers on a string, each revolving calay corresponds to a tity or lunar day [tity].—"*d*" Maha calay is conjunction [amavausyay] or opposition [powrnimay] of the sun and moon [jyotisham]. Vicalay, from (vi, san. prefix of division) is either an arc [bhoojam, chaupam] of one second of space, or an Indian minute in the sexagesimal division of the sowram day [caulam, 6].——*Caligherry* (کلگیری - kalgírí, Hind.; కలిగిరి - kaligiri, Tel.). From (kali, tel. buttle + giri, san. hill). Village; Nellore dist., Cauvaly tal.; pop. 1,995; acres 6,112; lat. 14° 50'; long. 79° 44'; from Cauvaly W.S.W. 21½ miles; from Nellore N.W. 33 miles; from the sea W. 28 miles. Small village but formerly head-quarters of a District moonsif and Talook tahsildar. Large tank, the bund of which is on the south-west side instead of on the east as is generally the case in Nellore district. To be distinguished from Canigherry and again from Canigherry reservoir [q. v.]. Soil fertile. Moosaufer khana [q. v.].——*Calingam* (कलिङ्ग - kalinga, San.). From (kali, san. strife). Latin regio calingarum.—"*a*" One of the fifty-six countries of Tamul geography [bhoogolashastram]. Was one of the five out-lying kingdoms of ancient Pooranic india; on the northern part of east coast, with its capital about half way down the coast. Mentioned by Mahabhaurat, Megasthenes, Pliny, Booddhist legends, Hwen thsang, &c. All that is known of this kingdom is fully stated in volume I (13) and (130)—(132) [charitram]. Calinganagaram was modern Rajahmundry. Modern Calingas are a quasi Braminical agricultural class in Vizagapatam; branch of Gowda [q.v.] bramins; have almost abandoned Braminical achauram [q.v.]; support themselves by agricultural operations; speak Ooriya. Calingaroya or kings of Calingam are a division of the Tamul cullar [q.v.]. Kintaly calingas are Calingas from Coontalam or the Canarese uplands. Calingam is also plant name common to Dillenia indica and Holarrhena antidysenterica; see gloss. paragraphs.——*Calingapatam* * (కళింగపట్నము - kalingapatnamu, Tel.). From (kalinga, san. the country + pattana, san. town). Greek δανδάγυλα. Town, Port, Light-house; Ganjam dist., Chicacole tal.; pop. 4,844; acres 1,626; lat. 18° 21'; long. 84° 09'; from Bapanapaud S.W. 22 miles; from Chetterpore S.S.W. 91 miles; from Chicacole E.N.E. 15 miles; from Madras N.E. 437 miles; from Maufooz bunder E.N.E. 14 miles viâ Chicacole. Presumed to be an ancient capital of the kingdom of Calingam. On the Orissa coast [q.v.], at the mouth of the Vamshadhaura, and at the southern extremity of Ganjam district. Light on the point in lat. 18° 19' 0", long. 84° 07' 30"; white; fixed; 8 miles range; visible from all directions seaward; obelisk of cut stone, column white, capital dark blue; to warn vessels off a small reef. The reef extends from the shore half a mile seawards. In passing vessels ought not to approach nearer than 8 fathoms. Best anchorage is in 6½ to 7 fathoms. Town is situated between S. bank of river and the point. The only port [toray] with any shelter and which is not a perfectly open roadstead between Coringa 150 miles south, and Dhaumrah in Orissa 250 miles north. Greatest depth of water over the bar is 14 feet 6 inches, and for 220 yards there is a depth of 12 feet. Rising in importance as a harbour [toray] and a regular port of call for steamers. Communication between the shore and shipping is rarely interrupted. During the monsoons [q.v.] a large number of native vessels lie up in the river. Connected by roads with Chicacole and the interior. Country around is barren. Five stone images in a shed in a field worshipped by Sheiveites, reputed of great age. Considerable mosque [q.v.] called the Durgah [q.v.] of Syed mahomed madany owlia, who was martyred here. The villages of Hoosompolavalsa, Jalloovalsa, Mooppidy, Narayanavalsa and Raullapaud, were granted by the Nawaub [q. v.] for the support of the durgah. Syed ishauk madany, another celebrated Mussalman warrior of the same period, is also buried here. A mound near the present town was plainly the site of the ancient city and small gold coins are sometimes found. Salt factory. Exports are rice, seeds, hides [chamrah], &c.——*Calingaroyan* (கலிங்கராயன் - kalingaráyan, Tam.). Means Calinga king. Village; Hamlet attached to Maitt nausoovanpolliem village; Coimbatore dist., Erode tal.; lat. 11° 26'; long. 77° 43'; from Coimbatore E.N.E. 58 miles; from Erode N.N.W. 8 miles. Gives name to channel fed by Bhawanny, across which there is an anicut [q.v.] close to the town of that name and running adjacent to the South indian railway and the Cauvery throughout the whole length of Erode talook. It used to run on into Caroor across the Noyil by an aqueduct and into the Amravatty near Caroor. Traces of this are still to be met. For a large part of the year there is a considerable surplus into the Noyil, benefiting the Poogalore channel. The left bank is artificial up to the tail, the other natural. The total length of the channel is 60 miles and the total fall about 122 feet, giving an average fall of 2 feet per mile. Crossed by forty-two natural drainages which are sources of danger, owing to suddenness of floods and quantity of sand brought down. The left bank is planted with palmyras [q.v.]. On the right bank the land is generally used for gardens irrigated by baling.——*Calingyah* (కళింగియా - kalingiyá, Tel.). From (kalinga, san. the kingdom so called). Hill, Ghaut; Ganjam dist., Goomsoor tal., Maliahs division; lat. 20° 04'; long. 84° 20'. The ghaut [q.v.] is the only good road from Goomsoor into the Maliahs [q.v.]. The ascent is five miles long; gradient severe for heavy loaded cart [bandy].——*Calky* (कल्कि - kalki, San.). From (kalka, san. sin). The great white horse of Vishnoo's coming incarnation, which will stamp with its right foreleg as the sign of the end of all things [avatar]. Its appearance closes the Kalyoog [q.v.]. Compare Revelations, chapter 19, v. 11—31. The divinity will then begin a new exercise in creating other worlds and other creatures. The Vishnoo pooraunam predicates as follows:—"Towards the end "of the Kaly [q.v.] age there will be reigning over the earth "kings of a churlish spirit and a violent temper, and ever "addicted to falsehood and wickedness. They will inflict death "on women, children, and cows; they will seize upon the "property of their subjects. They will be of limited power, "and will for the most part rapidly rise and fall; their lives will "be short, their desires insatiable, and they will display but "little piety. The people of the various countries intermingling "with them will follow their example, and the barbarians being "powerful in the patronage of the princes, whilst purer tribes "are neglected, the people will perish. Wealth and piety will "decrease day by day, until the world be wholly depraved. "Then property alone will confer rank; wealth will be the only "source of devotion; passion will be the sole bond of union "between the sexes; falsehood will be the only means of "success in litigation; and women will be objects merely of "sensual gratification. The earth will be venerated but for its "mineral treasures; the Braminical thread will constitute a "Bramin; external types will be the only distinctions of the "several orders of life; dishonesty, will be the universal means "of subsistence; weakness will be the cause of dependence; "menace and presumption will be substituted for learning; "liberality will be devotion; simple ablution will be purifica-"tion; mutual assent will be marriage; fine clothes will be "dignity; and water afar off will be esteemed a holy spring "[teertam]. Amidst all castes he who is the strongest will "reign over a principality thus vitiated by many faults. The "people, unable to bear the heavy burdens imposed upon them "by their avaricious sovereigns will take refuge amongst the "valleys of the mountains, and will be glad to feed upon wild "honey [shahad], herbs, roots, fruits, flowers, and leaves; their "only covering will be the bark of trees, and they will be "exposed to the cold and wind and sun and rain. No man's "life will exceed three and twenty years. Thus in the Kaly age "shall decay constantly proceed until the human race ap-"proaches its annihilation. Then when the practices taught by "the Vedams [q.v.] and the institutes of law shall nearly have "ceased, and the close of the Kaly age shall be nigh, a portion "of that divine being who exists of his own spiritual nature in "the character of Bramha [q.v.], and who is the beginning and "the end, and who comprehends all things, shall descend upon "the earth. He will be born in the family of Vishnoo yashas, "an eminent Bramin of Shambhalam village, as Calky, and be "endowed with the eight super-human faculties. By his irresis-"tible might he will destroy all the Mlechas [q.v.] and thieves, "and all whose minds are devoted to iniquity. He will then "re-establish righteousness [dharmam] upon earth; and the "minds of those who live at the end of the Kaly age will be "awakened and will be as pellucid as crystal. The men who "are thus changed by virtue of that peculiar time shall be as "the seeds of human beings, and shall give birth to a race "who shall follow the laws of the Kritam [q.v.], age, or age of "purity. As it is said; when the sun and moon, and the lunar "asterism [nacshatram] Tishyam and the planet Jupiter [brihas-"paty] are in one mansion, the Kritam age shall return [calpam, "matam]."——*Caly* (कलि - kali, San.). Evil [kalyoog].——*Calyam* (कल्य - kalya, San.). From (kal, san. to do). Accomplished, sound, healthy, auspicious.——*Calyaun* (कल्याण - kalyána, San.). Means beautiful, propitious. Common ancient geographical name. One town still known by that name 33 miles N.E. of Bombay. Another was capital of Chalookyas of Deccan in the ninth to twelfth centuries; this is in the Nizam's district of Nuldroog, about 40 miles E.N.E. of the fortress called by that name. A third was a port of Canara between Mangalore and Coondapore, in lat. 13° 24′, on the same river as Barcore; see Calyaunapooram. See vol. I (138) [charitram].——*Calyaunam* (कल्याण - kalyána, San.). Marriage. For ceremonies see vol. I (108), and II, 235. Calyaunacoory, from (kuri, mal. lottery), is a marriage entertainment, and so other entertainment to which the guests invited are expected to subscribe according to their means [maryanday]. Calyauna mantapam, from (mandapa, san. hall), is the hall of temple in which the idol is placed when its marriage is yearly celebrated [coil, pagoda]. Calyaunam is also Hindoo 2nd or pers. name. Calyaunaraman similarly the auspicious Raman; Calyaunasoondram, the auspicious Shiva, &c. Feminine Calyauny [peyar]. Calyaunam, from use on festive occasions, is also plant first term often joining two genera. Ex., where transl. is of second term:—Cucumis melo, var. utilissimus (kaliyánappúsani), cucurbita maxima; Erythrina indica (kaliyánamurukkam), butea frondosa. See gloss. paragraphs.——*Calyaunapooram* (ಕಲ್ಯಾಣಪುರ - kalyánapura, Can.). From (kalyána, san. auspicious + pura, san. town). Sanscrit also (shilpagiri), meaning architecture + hill. καλλιένα of Cosmas.—"*a*" Village; South canara dist., Oodipy tal.; pop. 5,582; lat. 13° 24′; long. 74° 46′; from Mangalore N. 38 miles; from Oodipy N. 4½ miles; from the sea E. 3 miles. Former capital of the Calachoorya king Bijjala. First place in which the Portuguese built a church in South canara. There is now a large colony of Native christians.—"*b*" Village; Tinnevelly district. Ancient town once near Korkay; same as Manapaday veed.——*Calyaundroog* (కల్యాణదుర్గము - kalyánadurgamu, Tel. kalyándrúg*). From (kalyána, san. felicity + durga, san. fort).—"*a*" Deputy tahsildarry, Anantapore district, situated in the west of Dharmavaram talook. Pay Rs. 100.—"*b*" Village, Deputy tahsildar's station, Fort; Anantapore dist., Dharmavaram tal.; pop. 4,205; lat. 14° 33′; long. 77° 09′; from Anantapore W.S.W. 35½ miles; from Bellary S.S.E. 42¾ miles; from Dharmavaram W.N.W. 42¾ miles; from Gooty S.W. 53¼ miles; from Madras W.N.W. 235 miles; from Penoocondah N.W. 46¼ miles. Six miles west of the route from Madras to Bellary. Has diminished in importance. Fortified hill close to town. District moonsif's court formerly.——*Caly's foe* (कलिमारक - kalimáraka, San.). From (kali, san. evil + máraka, san. destroyer). Title as being a charm against abortion. Same as Bonduc.——*Tricalingam* (త్రికళింగము - trikalingamu, Tel.). From (tri, san. three). Ancient name for the total of the three separate communities into which the Calingas were divided. See vol. I (130). Compare the three great Tamul countries of the south, Paundyam, Cholam, Cheram. Pliny says, "Insula "in Gange est magnæ magnitudinis gentem continens unam, "Modgalingam nomine." This is pure Teloogoo for three Calingams (múdukalingam). Tricalingam is the name of a ruined city between Dharanicottah and Amravatty [q.v.], containing the ruins of a very fine dagoba [q.v.].

CALABASH (قرع يابس - karaiyábis, *Ar.*). Title through the Portuguese calabaça, from the Arabic (karah) a gourd, and (aibasah) dry. The dry rind of a gourd used as a bottle or float. They are of two kinds the long and the round, the long make lutes and the round make sounding drums for the Sitaur [q.v.] and Veenay [q.v.].

CALACHOORYA (कलत्सूरि - kalatsúri, *San.*). Title otherwise Calabhoorya. Dynasty from Bundelcund that moved south and ruled in Calyaunnapooram in Deccan [q.v.]. Reduced by Chalookyas, but again subverted the latter. Their restoration was for but a short time, and their territories were absorbed by the Hoysala ballaulas [q.v.] and the Yaudavas [q.v.] as those dynasties became powerful. See vol. I (138) [charitram].

CALAM (قلم - kalam, *Hind.*). From (kalama, san. reed). Cf. Latin calamus. A pen, or a reed used as one. Especially pen with which God pre-recorded the actions of men. It was the first thing created; and it wrote down the quantity of every individual thing to be created and all that was, and all that will be to all eternity.——*Calama* (കഴമ - kazhama, Mal.). From sanscrit. A superior Malabar paddy growing in deep water. Growth six months. Varieties black and white, from color of ear growing [paddy].——*Calam caury* (قلم کاری - kalamkárí, Hind.). From (above + kárí, hind. workmanship). Hand-painted, as opposed to stamped.

CALAM (കളം - kalam, *Mal.*; களம் - kalam, *Tam.*). Threshing floor; suffix in place names, as Nadoovacalam, meaning middle + threshing floor.——*Cala cooripp* (களக்குறிப்பு - kalakkurippu, Tam.). From (above + kurippu, tam. memorandum). Account of the grain on the threshing floor.——*Calamathy* (களமதி - kalamathi, Tam.). From (above + mathi, tam. to estimate). Estimate of the grain on the threshing floor.——*Calanaday* (களநடை - kalanadai, Tam.). From (above + nadai, tam. custom). The allowance given to village servants [merah]. See vol. I, 112.——*Cala pitchay* (களப்பிச்சை - kalappiççai, Tam.). From (above + piççai, tam. alms). Grain from the threshing floor given in charity.——*Calappady* (களப்படி - kalappadi, Tam.). From (above + padi, tam. allowance). Grain from threshing floor given to laborers or village public servants [merah]. See vol. I, 112.——*Calattmode* (களத்துமேடு - kalattumédu, Tam.). From (above + médu, tam. high ground). The raised ground of the threshing floor.——*Calavausam* (களவாசம் - kalavásam, Tam.). From (above + vási, tam. portion). Same as calappady.

CALAM (கலம் - kalam, *Tam.*). Otherwise written Cullum. Hollow vessel. Measure of capacity [alavay, 3]. Varies in each district with the mercaul. 1 mercaul = 1 cooroony; 2 cooroonies = 1 pathakk; 2 pathakks = 1 toony; 3 toonies = 1 calam. In South arcot there are two calams, goondoo and royajee. Compare Cottah. See vol. I, 609; II, 506, 507, 509, 515, 518 and 519.

CALAM (களம் - kalam, *Tam.*). Black.——*Calah* (களா - kalá, Tam.). Any black fruited tree. Large calah is Carondah. Shottay calah, from (shottai, tam. insect-eaten) is forest bair.——*Calamara* (కలమర - kalamara, Tel.). Corruption of (kálámadwán, hind. black chrysophrys). Same as Black rock cod.——*Calaminder wood* (කළුමැදිරිය - kalumediriya, Singh.; காலேமிந்தாரம் - kálémindaram, Tam.). Singh. means black tree. Title otherwise Coromandel wood by corruption. Botanically Diospyros [indian ebony] hirsuta, linn. f., ebenaceæ [vricsham, 83]. Tree of great size, from ceylon [q.v.]; wood has a dingy ground sometimes running into white streaks; used in cabinet work, like zebra and rosewood. Quæsita has the same name.——*Calar* (களர் - kalar, Tam.). From black color of soil. Soil impregnated with alkali [munn, ooppoo].——*Calarvah* (களர்வா - kalarvá, Tam.). From (kalari, tam. jungle); wild desert tree. Large tooth-brush tree.——*Caloo* (කළු - kalu, Singh.). Black. Ex.:—Cassia absus (kalukollu), black dolichos biflorus; Justicia gendarussa (kaluveraniya), black shrub.

CALAMBAC (كلمبك - kálámbak, *Malay*). Eagle wood.

CALAMINA (كلمينا - kalmína, *Hind.*). Mediæval Latin name for Mylapore. May be corruption of Coromandel.

CALANDAR (قلندر - kalandar, *Ar.*). A religious mendicant [baushara, beshara, fakeer].

CALANJY (கழஞ்சு - kazhañju, *Tam.*). From (kazhagu, tam. game); from use by boys like marbles.—"*a*" Seed of Cæsalpinia bonducella, flem. [bonduc]; smooth, grey, hard, nearly spherical. Otherwise Molucca bean [coondrimany, munjaudy].—"*b*" So a goldsmith's weight. 20 munjaudies = 1 calanjy; 12 calanjies = 1 pollum [niray, 3]. Approximate actual value, 1 calanjy = 82 grains, which is above natural weight of seed. In Tinnevelly, $\frac{1}{12}$th of a pollum of 5¼ tolahs. In Tanjore ⅜th of a tolah or 72 grains. The base of the outer wall of the great temples at Tanjore, Conjeeveram and other places is covered with inscriptions, recording gifts of land, cows, money for lamps, meat offerings and other pious purposes; the same generally specified in calanjies of gold. See vol. I, 609; II, 518.

CALASSY (خلاصی - khalásí, *Hind.*). From (khalas, ar. freed); as non-combatant. A lascar, tent-pitcher, native sailor, artillery man.

CALASTRY (కాళహస్తి - kálahasti,* *Tel.*; காளாத்தி - kálátti, *Tam.*). From (kála, san. serpent + hasti, san. elephant); from tradition that a serpent [cobra] and an elephant [q.v.] worshipped shiva here. Tel. also (pottappinádu), means country of pottapy naick. Sanscrit name (dakshinakailása), meaning southern paradise; also (shrípura), means city of lutchmy; or else spider town, from tradition that a spider [shilandy poochy] worshipped shiva here; also (nárâyanavana), meaning vishnoo, the mover on the waters + forest.——**(1)** Zemindarry, North arcot. Area 874 square miles. Population 70,566. Language Teloogoo. Only portion lies in N. arcot, the rest being in Nellore. The N. arcot portion lies at extreme N.E. corner of district. Bounded on W. by Chundragherry talook and Carvetnugger zemindarry, N. and N.E. by Nellore, S.E. by Trivellore talook of Chingleput, and S. by Carvetnugger and Chingleput district. Its outline is very irregular. Suttivaid division of Chingleput divides it into two portions. The Zemindar divides his estate into the talooks of Calastry, Cutchinaud, and Pamoor, which are again sub-divided into several maugaunams [q.v.]. For Government administrative purposes, the N. arcot portion is divided into two divisions, Calastry on the north-west and Maderpauk on the south-east, each in charge of a Deputy tahsildar. The Pamoor talook has its villages scattered in five revenue talooks in Nellore district:—in Atmacore, 7; in Cauvaly, 24; in Oodayagherry, 81; in Cundoocore, 7; in Canigherry, 71; total, 190. The peshcush [q.v.] of Calastry is Rs. 1,73,812, paid in North arcot on the whole estate. A further account will be found at vol. I, 58. Places of archæological interest:—Akkoorty, Amarambaud, Calastry, Cullivaid droog, Cunnaly, Cunnambaukam, Cutchore, Goodimallam, Ingavaurpollem, Maderpauk, Moderimbaid, Nambaukam, Oorandore, Penoobauca, Pillacore, Pulloor, Santapett, Singamala, Sooratipully, Tondamanaud, Tripoorauntacapooram, Veeraraghavapooram, Vellauttcottay, Yerpett. Principal trig. stations:—Pillamode, Yerpett. The leading places in the zemindarry are the following.——*Calastry* (కాళహస్తి - kálahasti, Tel.). See below.——*Caushy boogga* (కాశిబుగ్గ - káshibugga, Tel.). From (káshí, san. benares + bugga, tel. spring). River; Perennial stream which issues near Yerpett. Believed to flow underground from Benares.——*Cutchore* (కచ్చూరు - kaççúru, Tel.). From (kaççi, tel. weaver + úru, tel. village). Village; pop. 439; lat. 13° 18′; long. 79° 56′; from Calastry S.S.E. 34½ miles; from Chittore E. 54 miles; from Maderpauk S.W. 13 miles. Twelve miles north of Trivellore railway station. Old Jeina basty [q.v.] with grantam [q.v.] inscriptions. Mud fort in ruins.——*Maderpauk* (மாதர்ப்பாக்கம் - mátharppákkam, Tam.). See sep. title.——*Pennaloorpett* (పెన్నలూరుపేట - pennalúrupéta, Tel.). From (penna, tel. river pennéru + úru, tel. village + péta, tel. suburb). Village; pop. 569; lat. 13° 41′; long. 79° 53′; from Calastry E.S.E. 10¾ miles; from Chittore N.E. 61 miles; from Maderpauk N.W. 20 miles. Chiefly agricultural. Mud fort in ruins. Station of Zemindar's tahsildar.——*Pillamode* (పిల్లమోడు - pillamódu, Tel.). From (pilla, tel. small + módu, tam. hill). Trig. station; lat. 13° 51′ 22·84″; long. 79° 45′ 23·26″; height 499 feet; from Calastry N. 7¼ miles; from Pillamode S.S.W. ⅜ mile.——*Swarnamookky* (స్వర్ణముఖి - svarnamukhi, Tel.). See sep. title.——*Tainimullay* (தேனேமலை - ténémalai, Tam.). See sep. title.——*Tondamanaud* (தொண்டமாநாடு - tondamánádu, Tam.). See sep. title.——*Tripoorauntacapooram* (త్రిపురాంతకపురము - tripurántakapuramu, Tel.). From (tripurántaka, san. shiva, the destroyer of the giant tripura + pura, san. town). Village; pop. 1,027; lat. 13° 27′; long. 79° 54′; from Calastry S.S.E. 22½ miles; from Chittore E.N.E. 54 miles; from Maderpauk W. 9½ miles. Ruined hill fort.——*Vencatagherry droog* (వెంకటగిరిదుర్గము - venkatagiridurgamu, Tel.). Title means Vencatagherry fort. Trig. station; lat. 13° 58′ 28·77″; long. 79° 30′ 34·69″; height 3,080 feet; from Calastry N.W. 22 miles; from Chittore N.N.E. 59 miles.——*Yerpett* (ఏర్పేట - yérpéta, Tel.). From (éru, tel. river + péta, tel. suburb); from source of the Caushy boogga. Village, C.N.S. Railway station; pop. 500; lat. 13° 41′; long. 79° 38′; from Calastry W.S.W. 8¼ miles; from Chittore N.E. 47 miles. At the junction of the Vencatagherry and Naidoopett roads. Favorite halting place. At the foot of a hill west of the village is a small temple of Oottaleshwaran. Here the Caushy boogga issues. Trig. station in lat. 13° 42′ 59·75″; long. 79° 36′ 28·01″; height 2,235 feet; from Calastry W. 9¼ miles; from Yerpett N.W. 2¼ miles.——**(2)** Deputy tahsildarry, Calastry zemindarry, North arcot. Pay Rs. 100.——**(3)** Town, Zemindar's and Deputy tahsildar's head-quarters, Place of pilgrimage; North arcot dist., Calastry zemindarry; pop. 11,754; lat. 13° 45′; long. 79° 45′; height 368 feet; from Arnee N.N.E. 80 miles; from Chittore N.E. 55 miles; from Madras N.W. 61 miles; from Ranipett N.N.E. 62 miles; from Tripatty E.N.E. 21 miles; from Vellore N.N.E. 69 miles. On the right bank of the Swarnamookhy, at the extremity of the Nagary hills. These hills are considered so holy in the neighbourhood that it is not permitted to quarry stone or gravel from them. A large proportion of the residents are in the employ of the Zemindar. In the Shiva temple Shiva manifests himself in the form of a mysterious and imperceptible current of air. Hence the lingam [q.v.] is called Vayoo lingam. The sacred lamp over the idol however always sways. Europeans are not allowed to enter. South-east of the temple is a rock-cut mantapam [q.v.], the Manicarnica ghaut, with sculptures. The Shivarautry [pundigay, 6a] festival takes place during ten days in Maushy [mausam] or February. Chief days from fifth to eighth. Trade in grain, bangles [gauzoo], glass-beads and other articles. Cloth is woven.

CALAUBAT (کلابتون - kalábatún, *Hind.*). From (kal, hind. instrument + bátná, hind. to twist); plate drawn. Gold thread. The following is the method of making it. A piece of silver [velly] about the length and thickness of a man's forefinger is gilded at least three times heavily with the purest gold, all alloy being previously carefully discharged from the silver. This piece of gilt-silver is beaten out to the size of a stout wire, and is then drawn through successive holes in a steel plate until the wire is as fine as a hair. The gilding is not disturbed by this process, and the wire finally appears as if of fine gold [pon]. It is then flattened in a skilful manner on a highly polished steel anvil, with a steel hammer, also polished. The metal wire is then wound upon silk thread, as follows. The silk [puttoo] is very slightly twisted, and is rolled upon a winder. The end is then passed over a polished steel hook fixed to a beam in the ceiling of the workshop; and to it is suspended a spindle [cathir] with a long thin bamboo shank, slightly weighted to keep it steady, which nearly touches the floor. The workman gives the shank of the spindle a sharp turn upon his thigh, which sets it spinning with great rapidity. The gold wire, which has been wound on a reel as it passes behind the maker, is then applied to the bottom of the silk thread near the spindle, and twists itself upwards, being guided by the workman as high as he can conveniently reach, or nearly his own height, upon the thread. The spindle is then stopped. The thread now covered with wire is wound upon the spindle and fastened in a notch of the shank, when the silk thread is drawn down and the spindle is again set spinning with the same result as before. Certain lengths of the gold thread are made into skeins, and so sold or used by weavers. Indian brocades, whether gold or silver, never tarnish. This is the result of the absolute purity of the metals [loham] employed [nesavoo].

CALAVOY (కలువాయ - kaluváya, *Tel.*). From (kaluva, tel. water-lily, nymphæa stellata, willd. + páya, tel. stream). Village; Nellore dist., Atmacore tal.; pop. 3,518; acres 7,804; lat. 14° 31′; long. 79° 27′; from Atmacore W.S.W. 16¾ miles; from Nellore W. 38 miles. Two miles from south bank of Pennair. Soil very fertile. Many betel [q.v.] leaf gardens. Indigo [q.v.], saffron [country saffron] and ginger [q.v.] extensively cultivated. Large tank, with goddess Mullammah. Temple of Shiva under the designation of Chennakeshwarasawmy, repaired about 200 years ago by Cota polireddy. Daily worship maintained, and a Navaunicam [pundigay, 6d] held at irregular intervals, when villagers raise subscriptions. Has an inam of acres 19·24. Mosque [q.v.] with an inam of acres 100·82.

CALAVYE (கலவாய் - kalaváy, *Tam.*). Means black-lipped. The genus Serranus, percidæ [panayairy], acanthopterygii, teleostei, pisces [matsyam, 1], of naturalists [jantoo]. The species best known to the natives are shown below.——*Red perch* (சிகப்புக்கலவாய் - shigappukkalaváy, Tam.). Title from dull lake color. Tam. from (shivappu, tam. redness). Serranus [calavye] sonnerati, percidæ [panayairy], acanthopterygii, teleostei [matsyam, 1], of naturalists. Alias Epinephelus nigripinnis; Perca rubra; Serranus erythræus, pachycentron, pachycentrum. Scales on head, body; badly marked line, much similar to lateral-line, along scales near bases of dorsal and anal fins; dull lake, head and body to below first half of spinous dorsal fin covered with net-work of blue lines enclosing spots from one-sixth diameter of eye to spaces larger than it. Indistinct spots over whole body. Fins of darker color than body, especially at edges, caudal with dull blue or white spots. Sea; common at Madras, attains at least 3 feet.——*Sore-headed perch* (పాముమీను - pámumínu, Tel.; കറുപ്പ് - karúppu, Mal.; வடுத்தலைக்கலவாய் - vaduttalaikkalaváy, Tam.). Title from appearance. Tel. from (pámu, tel. snake + mínu, tel. fish). Mal. from (karuppu, mal. black). Tam. from (vadu, tam. mole + talai, tam. head). Tel. also (pillipunni), meaning cat + small; (sakalátubonta), meaning broad cloth + mullus genus, from yellow color. Serranus [calavye] lanceolatus, percidæ [panayairy], acanthopterygii, teleostei [matsyam, 1], of naturalists. Alias Epinephelus lanceolatus; Holocentrus lanceolatus; Perca suggalathoo bontoo; Serranus horridus. Suggalathoo bontoo from teloogoo. Scales usually with raised circular lines upon them, especially in forepart of body, about fifteen rows between sixth dorsal spine and lateral-line. Colors vary with age, very young being of fine citron or sulphur ground-color, having irregular vertical bands and markings, which become more distinct as the age advances. About to a foot or over 18 inches in length, ground-color continues bright yellow, with five vertical, blackish-blue bands, first from orbit over opercle: second from nape to opercle joins first band in its posterior margin, and coalesces with third behind or above pectoral fin; third proceeding from bases of seven dorsal spines, passes downwards to abdomen; fourth passes from fifth to last dorsal ray, and descends to base of anal fin; last surrounds free portion of tail. Fins yellow with black spots or blotches, forming confluent bars at bases, which on pectoral are disposed in undulating arched bands. In adult black bands disappear, ground-color becomes greyish-brown, whole being reticulated with greyish-black lines. Fins retain most of their original yellow color but amount of black decreases. Sea to Malay archipelago, attaining a large size. About 51 inches long.——*Spotted perch* (புள்ளிக்கலவாய் - pullikkalaváy, Tam.). Title from spots on fins. Tam. from (pulli, tam. spot).

Serranus [calavye] hexagonatus, percidæ [panayairy], acanthopterygii, teleostei [matsyam, 1], of naturalists. Alias Epinephelus hexagonatus, merra; Holocentrus hexagonatus, merra; Perca hexagonata; Serranus confertus, merra et faveatus, nigriceps. Reddish brown with light reticulation; body, pectoral, soft dorsal, and caudal fins covered with hexagonal, or rounded markings. In some the dark blotches become more confluent, light reticulations being indistinct. Sea; over 8 inches in length. ——*Striped perch* (రాతిబొంత - rátibonta, Tel.; வரிக்கலவாய் - varikkalaváy, Tam.). Title from stripes. Tel. from (ráyi, tel. stone + bonta, tel. mullus genus); from brown color. Tam. from (vari, tam. stripe). Serranus [calavye] boenack, percidæ [panayairy], acanthopterygii, teleostei [matsyam, 1], of naturalists. Alias Bodianus boenack; Epinephelus boenach, formosus; Perca rahtee bontoo; Sciæna formosa; Serranus boenach, formosus. Rahtee bontoo from teloogoo. Scales covering forehead and preorbital. Colors when alive brilliant, but fading after death. Generally yellowish-brown, snout pale blue, lips and throat spotted with deeper blue, about five fillets of the same color diverge from orbit and cross opercles and branchial membranes. Blue and tortuous horizontal lines pass from head towards tail below lateral-line, above it are about eight more directed backwards, upwards, and continued to dorsal fin; these blue lines are likewise continued on to the other fins, except occasionally on the ventrals, which become nearly black at their extremities. Some blue spots exist anterior to base of ventral fin of male, also occasionally on jaws. Sea.——*Yellow perch* (කහලවෑය - kahalaveyá, Singh.; மஞ்சக்கலவாய் - mañjakkalaváy, Tam.). Title from color of fins. Tam. from (mañjal, tam. country saffron). Serranus [calavye] flava-cæruleus, percidæ [panayairy], acanthopterygii, teleostei [matsyam, 1], of naturalists. Alias Bodianus macrocephalus; Cynichthys flavo-purpuratus; Epinephelus flavo-cæruleus; Holocentrus flavo-cæruleus, gymnosus; Perca flava-purpurea; Serranus borbonicus. Scales thickly covering snout, pre- and sub- orbitals, and posterior half of the maxilla; about eighteen rows between lateral-line and sixth dorsal spine; those on chest and abdomen very small, about sixty-five rows between lateral-line and median line of abdomen. Head and body deep purplish blue; free portion of tail and all fins gamboge [q.v.] yellow; yellow on snout, maxilla, chest, and opercular spines; indistinct darkish band along base of spinous and first third of rayed portion of dorsal fin; ventral and caudal with fine black tips. Sea; nearly $10\frac{1}{2}$ inches in length.

CALAY (கலை - kalai, *Tam.*). To break up, disperse, mix.——*Calagary* (కలగరి - kalagari, Tel.). From (kaliyu, tel. to mix + ari, tel. suffix of agency). Water let into the field immediately after sowing, in order to make the seed sprout.——*Calappay* (हल - hala, San.; هل - hal, Hind.; ಹಲ - hala, Can.; నాగలి - nágali, Tel.; കരി - kari, Mal.; கலப்பை - kalappai, Tam.). San. from (hal, san. to plough). Tam. from (kalai, tam. to break up). A plough without the yoke [yair]. There are two main varieties, the wet and the dry plough; the former is a light implement. The instrument consists of a simple stick, with a natural crook at the end, and with a handle fastened to it. This plough does not turn up the soil [munn], for there is nothing to answer the purpose of a coulter or mould-board. According as the angle formed by the head with the share [caur] is acute or obtuse, the plough is known by different names. The latter is usually preferred. The plough is drawn by a pair of bullocks or buffaloes [q.v.] in a yoke which are guided by the ploughman himself with a goad. The light plough with three shares is used as a harrow also [gorroo]. To convert this into a drill, the zaddigam [q.v.] or drill head, with three bamboo [q.v.] tubes fitted into it, can also be affixed.——*Calathy* (கலதி - kalathi, Tam.). From (kalathai, tam. confusion). Moodevy, the goddess of ruin [kettay]. This is a Dravidian conception.

CALEEM (كليم - kalím, *Ar.*). From (kaláma, ar. to say). Eloquent speaker. Part of lacab, as Caleem ool lah, speaker with God, lacab of Moses [moosa]. Now an ordinary alam [ism].

CALF'S GRASS (वत्सप्रिय - vatsapriya, *San.*; كانشورا - kánshurá, *Hind.*; ಕನ್ನೆಸೊಪ್ಪು - kannesoppu, *Can.*; వెన్నవెదురు - vennaveduru, *Tel.*; දියමනේරිය - diyamanériya, *Singh.*; கானாவாழை - kánávazhai, *Tam.*). Title from leaves used to feed calves. San. from (vatsa, san. calf + priya, san. dear). Can. from (kanna, can. beloved + soppu, can. leaf). Tel. means butter bamboo. Tam. from (kánam, tam. forest + vázhai, tam. plantain, musa paradisica, linn.). San. also (lángalí), meaning sticky, from leaf [cocoanut, wild bachnaug]; (jalapippalí), meaning water + long pepper, piper longum, linn.; (kañchata), meaning to shine, from glossy leaves. Hind. also (kána). Tel. also (vennamudda), meaning butter + lump, from leaf; (nírukasuvu), meaning water + grass; (vennadévikúra); (ganjigadda), meaning gruel + root. Tam. also (kanrukkuttippul), meaning calf + grass; (kánángirai), meaning forest + vegetable; (kózhikkánángirai), meaning fowl + forest + vegetable; (kánángózhai), by corruption. Title otherwise Blue spiderwort. Botanically Commelyna communis, linn., commelynaceæ [vricsham, 139]. Root fibrous, stems branched; creeping, branchlets marked with a line of hairs, leaves sessile, ovate-lanceolate, acuminate, rounded at the base, margin waved, spathes opposite the leaves, rounded cordate, acute, folded, smooth, with roughish margins, peduncles in the spathe two, the longer one one-flowered, the shorter three-flowered; flowers bright blue; flowering in rains. Weed on banks of water-courses; sending suckers into the ground; improperly called a grass. Leaves used by natives for feeding young calves, when they wish to wean them from their milk; also as human food mixed with other greens [keeray]. Other common species are:—Benghalensis or common spiderwort; flowers bright blue; common everywhere; flowering in rains; leaves eaten as greens during famine [cshaumam]; seeds eaten plain or prepared by heating when they swell. Obliqua; the root useful in vertigo, fevers, and bilious affections, and as an antidote to snake-bites. Polyspatha; flowers light blue; mountains near coimbatore at 3,000 feet.

CALICO (कार्पास - kárpása, *San.*; کپڑا - kaprá, *Hind.*; ಶಲ್ಲ - shallá, *Can.* and *Tel.*; വെള്ളശ്ശീല - vellashshíla, *Mal.*; காரிக்கம் - kárikkam, *Tam.*). For title see below. San. from (karpása, san. cotton tree, gossypium herbaceum, linn.). Mal. from (vella, mal. white + shíla, mal. cloth). Tam. from (kári, tam. blackness), as generally applied to unbleached calico. White plain cotton cloth, originally manufactured at Calicut, whence the title through the French calicot. Calico manufacture is one of the oldest known institutions of this country. Most so-called calico however now comes from England. Sold as bleached and unbleached. For colored calico, see Chintz.

CALICUT* (കോഴിക്കോട് - kózhikkótu, *Mal.*; கள்ளிக்கோட்டை - kallikkóttai, *Tam.*). Title from arabic corruption. Mal. from (kózhi, mal. cock + kótu, mal. fort); the land within range of cock-crow is said to have been given to the zamorin [q.v.]. Tam. means milk-hedge, euphorbia genus + fort. Sanscrit name (kukkutapura), meaning cock + town; also (gópakútapurí), meaning shepherd + crowd + town; from the zamorin, the head of the yeraudies or shepherds. Calicut has given its name to Calico cloth, through the Portuguese.——(1) Talook, Malabar district. Tahsildar's pay Rs. 175. Area 339 square miles. Occupies a central position in the district. Situated in lat. 11° 10′ and 11° 32′ and long. 75° 47′ and 76° 11′. Form is an irregular quadrilateral. Length 30 miles, breadth from 7 to 17 miles. Central coast of district. Bounded north and north-east by Cooroombranaud and Wynaud talooks; east by Wynaud and Yernaud talooks; south by Yernaud talook; west by Arabian sea. Comprises forty-one amshoms [q.v.]. In 1866 six amshoms were transferred from Cooroombranaud. Consists mostly of low hills covered with jungle. The higher grounds are usually laid out in terraces for the cultivation of dry grains [q.v.]. The banks of the rivers are thickly wooded; some infested with alligators. There being but little surf small-craft can ply. The ports [toray] are however nearly all shut during the south-west monsoon [q.v.]. Similarly the passes. The Ootoomullays, separating this talook from Wynaud and Yernaud, contain large quantities of teak [q.v.], timber and bamboos [q.v.], which are floated down the rivers to Calicut and Beypore during the rains. Soil about the seaboard is brown or white sand; in interior red with gravel approaching in certain parts to a mixture of red and brown. In Caurannore amshom, there is a dam known as the Moolyaurnada, which is constructed for the protection of cultivation. The Conolly canal passes through the amshoms of Casaba, Cottooly, Cutcherry, Yedacaud, Caurannore, Makkada and Yelattore, and connects the Cullye with the Yelattore river. Principal rivers are the Yelattore and a stream which rises in the Vauvoomala or Camel hump [q.v.] mountains, flows in the direction of Tirvambaudy and Coottiyaudy, and joins the Beypore river east of Paloor. A third river rising in the ghauts [q.v.], in the vicinity of Tamracherry, joins the Beypore river 12 miles from the sea. Small tanks and large wells are numerous, particularly in the town of Calicut; cultivation is, however, almost entirely dependent upon the rains. Places of archæological interest:—Annacherry, Beypore, Calicut, Canniparamba, Chevayore, Codoly, Covoor, Iringallore, Kilacote, Padinyauttmoory, Poottore, Talacoolattore, Tirvangaud, Valayanaud, Varacull, Yedacaud, Yelattore. Principal trig. station:—Poccoonn. The leading places, &c., in the talook are the following.——*Calicut* (കോഴിക്കോട് - kózhikkótu, Mal.). See below.——*Canniparamba* (കണ്ണിപറമ്പ - kanniparamba, Mal.). From (kanni, mal. salt pan + parampa, mal. high ground). Village; pop. 3,666; lat. 11° 16′; long. 75° 59′; from Calicut E. 11 miles; from Chevayore E.S.E. 8 miles; from the sea E. 11 miles. Temple dedicated to Shiva, Vishnoo, Ganapaty, Ayyappan and Dacshina moorty, 132 feet square. On the rocky pinnacle of a hill is a pit from which holy water gushes out daily in the morning in Yedavam [mausam] or May-june for 20 minutes, when it again becomes dry. The water also begins to flow on the occasion of Shivarautry [pundigay, 6a] festival in Coombham [mausam] or February-March.——*Chervannore* (ചെറുവണ്ണൂർ - cheruvannúr, Mal.). From (cheruman, mal. member of the tribe + úr, mal. village). Village; pop. 3,514; lat. 11° 11′; long. 75° 55′; from Calicut S.S.E. 5 miles; from Chevayore S.W. $6\frac{1}{4}$ miles; from the sea E. 2 miles. Temple to Shiva, Soobramanyan, Ayyappan, Ganapaty, and Dacshina moorty; roof is copper-plated. Festival annually for forty-one days called Mundala vilakk in December and January. The Malabar spinning and weaving company, limited, set up mills in this village in 1888, and in August of that year commenced spinning cotton [q.v.]. The shareholders are exclusively natives.——*Chevayore* (ചേവായൂർ - chévâyúr, Mal. chevayur*). From (chéva, mal. military service + úr, mal. village); nayar village held on military tenure. Village, Tahsildar's station; pop. 6,761; lat. 11° 17'; long. 75° 51'; from Calicut N.E. 3¾ miles; from Cannanore S.E. 49 miles; from Madras W.S.W. 320 miles; from Malapooram N.W. 24 miles; from Manantoddy S.S.W. 39 miles; from Palghaut W.N.W. 65 miles; from Ponnany N.N.W. 34 miles; from Tellicherry S.S.E. 39 miles; from the sea E. 3½ miles. Sepulchral rock-cut cave with erect pillar in middle of main chamber.——*Covoor* (കോവൂർ - kóvúr, Mal.). From (kó, mal. king + úr, mal. village). Village; pop. 4,953; lat. 11° 16'; long. 75° 53'; from Calicut E. 4 miles; from Chevayore S.E. 2 miles; from the sea E. 4½ miles. Rock-cut cave.——*Mammally* (മമ്മളി - mammalli, Mal.). From (man, mal. earth + palli, mal. village). Village. In Chervannore amshom, about 7 miles from Calicut, coffee-curing establishment under European management.——*Molancadav* (മൊളാങ്കടവു - molankatavu, Mal.). From (mula, mal. bamboo, bambusa arundinacea, willd. + katavu, mal. ford). Village, Port; lat. 11° 14'; long. 75° 49'; from Beypore N. 4¾ miles; from Bombay S.S.E. 550 miles; from Calicut S.E. 7¼ miles; from Chevayore S. 4 miles. At mouth of Cullye.——*Padinyauttmoory* (പടിഞ്ഞാറ്റുമുറി - patiññâttumuri, Mal.). From (patiññâru, mal. west + muri, mal. village). Village; pop. 4,910; lat. 11° 19'; long. 75° 51'; from Calicut N.N.E. 5¼ miles; from Chevayore N. 2 miles; from the sea E. 4 miles. Rock-cut caves from which a quantity of pottery was unearthed.——*Poccoonn* (പൊക്കുന്നു - pokkunnu, Mal.). From (pokkam, mal. height + kunnu, mal. hill). Hill, Trig. station; lat. 11° 14' 27·20"; long. 75° 51' 50·49"; height 279 feet; from Calicut E.S.E. 3 miles; from Chevayore S.S.E. 2¾ miles; from the sea E. 3½ miles.——*Poothiyangaudy* (പുതിയങ്ങാടി - putiyannâti, Mal.). Means new bazaar. Village, Port; lat. 11° 18'; long. 75° 47'; from Bombay S.S.E. 540 miles; from Calicut N.N.W. 4 miles; from Chevayore W.N.W. 4 miles; from Yelattore S.S.E. 3 miles. Small port of call for country craft taking in cocoanuts [q.v.] and other produce. Many Moplahs here. Residence of Moplah tangal [q.v.] of pure Arab extraction. Eight mosques [q.v.]. Jumma musjid [q.v.] 72 by 30 feet. Annual festival.——*Poothoopaudy* (പുതുപ്പാടി - putuppâti, Mal.). From (putu, mal. new + pâti, mal. village). Village; lat. 11° 29'; long. 76° 2'; from Calicut N.E. 21 miles; from Cannanore S.E. 49 miles; from Chevayore N.E. 18 miles; from the sea E. 25 miles. Four miles from foot of Tamracherry ghaut. Hotel used as resting place by travellers between Calicut and Wynaud.——*Talacoolattore* (തലക്കുളത്തൂർ - talakkulattúr, Mal.). From (tala, mal. head + kulam, mal. tank + úr, mal. village). Village; pop. 4,156; lat. 11° 22'; long. 75° 48'; from Calicut N. 8 miles; from Chevayore N.N.W. 6¼ miles; from the sea E. 2 miles. Old temple.——*Tamracherry* (താമരശ്ശേരി - támarashshéri, Mal.). See sep. title.——*Valayanaud* (വളയനാട് - valayanátu, Mal.). From (valaya, san. bracelet + nátu, mal. country). Village; lat. 11° 14'; long. 75° 51'; from Calicut S.E. 2 miles; from Chevayore S. 3 miles; from the sea E. 2 miles. Ancient temple; roof of the shrine is copper-plated; 192 feet long by 144 feet broad. Elaborate sculptures on the gopooram [q.v.]; temple belongs to the Zamorin; annual festival lasting for eight days is celebrated in Macaram [mausam] or January-february, when the image of Bhagavaty [q.v.] is taken in procession on an elephant's back with great pomp.——*Yelattore* (എലത്തൂർ - elattúr, Mal.). See sep. title.——(2) Deputy tahsildarry, Malabar district. Pay Rs. 70.——(3) Town, Head-quarters of Collector, District and Sub-judge, Moonsif, and Deputy tahsildar, Lighthouse. Malabar dist., Calicut tal.; pop. 66,078; lat. 11° 15'; long. 75° 49'; from Bangalore S.W. 168 miles; from Beypore N. 6 miles; from Bombay S.S.E. 553 miles; from Cannanore S.E. 50 miles; from Cochin N.W. 93 miles; from Madras W.S.W. 330 miles; from Mangalore S.E. 130 miles; from Manantoddy S.S.W. 40 miles; from Malapooram N.W. 24 miles; from Molancadav N. 1¼ miles; from Palghaut W.N.W. 67 miles; from Ponnany N.N.W. 33 miles; from Poothiyangaudy S.S.E. 4 miles; from Tellicherry S.S.E. 39 miles; from Yelattore S.S.E. 7 miles. In extensive palm groves. One of largest ports in presidency. Limits of port are:—north, boundary pillar north of the new custom house [chowky]; south, boundary pillar south of the custom house; the sea-shore between them to within fifty yards of high-water mark spring-tides; east, the harbour or backwater [cauyal], and the Cullye river as far as the junction of Conolly's canal with all creeks and channels leading thereto, and so much of the shores thereof, whether of the main land or the islands, as are within fifty yards of high-water spring-tides; west, the space enclosed by two lines running due west from the boundary pillars to nine fathoms water. Light on the sandy beach; lat. 11° 15' 05"; long. 75° 45' 35"; white; fixed, 14 miles range; visible from all directions seaward white column; to guide vessels to the anchorage clear of the reef, which lies about one mile S. 30° W. from the light. A small red light is exhibited from head of pier as guide for small coasting craft when entering port. The best anchorage for large vessels is marked by a buoy, and is with lighthouse E. to E. by N. in five to six fathoms, and from two to three miles off shore. A soft mud bank which from time to time forms off the lighthouse stills the surf in ordinary sea-breezes. The entrance from anchorages, particularly from southward is cumbered by Coote reef, so called from one of the Company's vessels having grounded on it. See vol. II, 148. There is a modern legend of the ruins of a town built by the Portuguese lying under the water. An iron screw-pile pier extends out to 12 feet of water. According to native tradition, Chermaun, having divided Malabar among the ancestors of the present chieftains, had nothing remaining to bestow on Tamoory [zamorin], the ancestor of the chief whom the Portuguese found in possession. He accordingly gave Tamoory his sword, with all the territory in which a cock crowing at a small temple could be heard. His successors extended their dominions south and east with the aid of the Moplahs. They are no longer independent, but are stipendiaries of the crown. In 1498, Vasco de Gama arrived at Calicut, but was inhospitably received by the Zamorin. In 1501, Pedralvarez Cabral established a factory, which was immediately afterwards destroyed by the Moplahs, and the whole colony massacred. Cabral bombarded the town; and in the following year De Gama destroyed all the shipping in the roadstead, and laid nearly all the houses in ruins. In 1510, Albuquerque again attacked Calicut, burnt the Zamorin's palace, and wrecked the town; but the natives drove him back to Cochin with great loss. In 1513 the Zamorin made peace with the Portuguese, who erected a factory, the origin of the present establishment. English factory established by permission of the Zamorin of Calicut in 1616; establishment expelled by the Dutch in 1664; agency re-established in 1668; port ravaged by Captain Kidd in 1695; captured by Hyder ally in 1766, when the Zamorin set fire to his palace and with his family died in the flames; grant of factor and all existing privileges confirmed and ratified by Hyder ally on his conquest of Malabar, 23rd February 1766; further ratification by Hyder ally by treaty, dated 8th August 1770; British dispossessed by Hyder ally, 1779; reduced by Major Abingdon, 1782; factory and privileges restored according to treaty with Tippoo, 1784; taken by Tippoo in 1789, who treated the inhabitants with great cruelty; the city was almost entirely demolished and most of the materials taken to Nullore where they were utilized in building the fort of Furruckabad [q.v.]. In 1790, the Mysore force was totally defeated in the neighbourhood of Calicut. Tippoo's general was made prisoner with 900 of his men, and 1,500 more laid down their arms at Furruckabad. Under the treaty dated 18th March 1792 which deprived Tippoo of half his dominions, Calicut fell to the share of the East india company, and was formally incorporated with the British dominions. After this event the scattered survivors of the population returned and rebuilt their dwelling. Since the cession to the British, Calicut has steadily advanced in trade and population; and with the exception of fanatical Moplah outbreaks, the peace has been undisturbed. Owing to the Moplah outrages, a detachment of European infantry was stationed here in 1849. It was removed to the outpost at Malapooram in 1851, but again brought back on the assassination of the Collector, Mr. Conolly, in 1855. The French settlement dates from 1722, since which year it has been three times in British possession. In 1817, it was finally restored with Mahé to the French, who still hold a few houses and the land adjoining. The Danish government established a factory in 1752. It was partially destroyed in 1784, and soon after incorporated in the British settlement. An unsuccessful attempt was made in 1792 to re-establish the claims of Denmark. The present town of Calicut dates from the thirteenth century. The barracks stand north of the town, as also the old Portuguese quarter with a Roman catholic church built by the Zamorin and presented to Portugal in A.D. 1525, and a convent. The southern portion contains the timber depôt, Cullye, and the Moplah quarter; above which lie the sea customs and salt offices, the lighthouse and mercantile houses, facing the sea. Round the Maunanchira tank, a fine reservoir of fresh water, are grouped the chief public offices and many important buildings. The suburbs consist of detached villages joining Calicut to Beypore, and surrounded with groves of palm, mango [q.v.] and jack [q.v.] trees. The French loge consists of 6 acres on the sea-shore, about half a mile north of Calicut lighthouse and adjoins the old District jail; apparently obtained by the French from the Zamorin. Beyond the fact that the landed property and houses are untaxed, there is nothing to distinguish the loge from the rest of Calicut. When the Zamorin's influence was supreme on the Malabar coast [q.v.], Calicut was a place of great trade; though Cochin, its rival, under Portuguese and Dutch influence, has, with its greater natural facilities, always had an advantage. Imports are now chiefly grain, salt [ooppoo], and piece-goods; exports, produce of the cocoanut [q.v.], coffee [q.v.], pepper [q.v.], timber, ginger [q.v.], &c. In May 1842 a Basel mission was established here. In 1855 a carpenter's workshop and a weaving establishment with six looms were opened. In 1868 a mercantile mission shop was opened. In 1874 the mission started tile works. There are seven important Hindoo temples in the town. They are Aricodicauv, Beiraugy matam, Bilauticoolam, Cokkolicode, Talee, Tirvannore, and Varacull. Talee temple is in the heart of the town close to the Zamorin's old palace dedicated principally to Shiva, though Vishnoo, Bhagavaty, Ganapaty and Ayyappan are also worshipped. The Tirvannore temple is very ancient; has a newly-erected gateway in style precisely similar to the basties at Moodbidry in South canara erected by

Jeinas. There are no less than forty mosques in the town. The most important are the two Jumma musjid, Shekkindepully and Palayapully. Large kotiyehs [q.v.] and puttimars [q.v.] are built on the beach $1\frac{1}{2}$ miles south of the lighthouse by the entrance of the Cullye river or creek, where the shore is smooth, being partially protected by the Coote reef. There is a club for Europeans on the beach, which was started on the 8th February 1864. The following are the travelling distances by road from Calicut to different places :—

To	Via	Miles and Furlongs.	
Alleppey	Taunore, Chowghaut and Cochin ...	130	5
Angaudipooram...	Arriyacode and Munjery	52	1
Angaudipooram...	Condotty and Munjery	42	6
Angaudipooram...	Condotty and Malapooram	43	4
Arriyacode ...	......	27	4
Bangalore ...	Manantoddy and Seringapatam	222	0
Bangalore ...	The Tamracherry ghaut and Seringapatam.	213	0
Bangalore ...	The Carcoor ghaut and Mysore	225	6
Bellary ...	The Tamracherry ghaut, Manantoddy and Seringapatam.	374	7
Cannanore ...	Badagara and Tellicherry	59	1
Cassergode ...	Badagara, Tellicherry and Cannanore ...	116	2
Chowghaut ...	Taunore and Ponnany	47	7
Cochin ...	Taunore, Chowghaut and Cottaparamba.	97	6
Coimbatore ...	Malapooram and Palghaut	115	3
Culpetta ...	Tamracherry	44	3
Dindigul ...	Malapooram and Palghaut	187	3
Goodalore ...	Arriyacode, Nelambore and the Carcoor ghaut.	70	1
Goondloopett ...	Arriyacode, Nelambore, the Carcoor ghaut and Goodalore.	100	3
Goondloopett ...	The Tamracherry ghaut, Culpetta and Perambaudy.	87	5
Madras	Bangalore and Ranipett	418	$7\frac{1}{2}$
Madras	Palghaut, Coimbatore, Salem, Vellore and Ranipett.	422	4
Madura	Malapooram, Palghaut and Dindigul ...	227	$4\frac{1}{2}$
Mahé	Badagara	39	4
Malapooram ...	Condotty	31	4
Manantoddy ...	The Tamracherry ghaut and Culpetta ...	63	1
Mangalore ...	Badagara, Tellicherry, Cannanore and Cassergode.	145	2
Mangalore ...	Cannanore and Paulore	182	1
Munjery	Condotty	30	1
Mysore	The Tamracherry ghaut, Culpetta and Manantoddy.	133	1
Mysore	The Tamracherry ghaut and Goondloopett.	124	1
Mysore	Carcoor ghaut and Goondloopett	136	7
Negapatam ...	Malapooram, Palghaut, Coimbatore, Trichinopoly and Tanjore.	337	4
Nelambore ...	Arriyacode	43	5
Ootacamund ...	Arriyacode, Sholacull and the Sisparra ghaut.	99	7
Palamcottah ...	Palghaut, Dindigul and Madura	323	$2\frac{1}{2}$
Palghaut ...	Arriyacode, Munjery and Angaudipooram.	93	1
Palghaut ...	Taunore and Trittaula	86	6
Palghaut ...	Condotty, Munjerry and Angaudipooram.	83	6
Palghaut ...	Malapooram and Angaudipooram ...	84	4
Palghaut ...	Mannar and Malapooram	86	4
Ponnany	Taunore	33	6
Quilon	Taunore, Chowghaut and Cochin	185	7
Salem	Palghaut, Coimbatore and Erode	214	0
Salem	Malapooram, Palghaut, Coimbatore and Bhawauny.	215	7
Seringapatam ...	The Tamracherry ghaut, Culpetta, Manantoddy and Mysore.	142	5
Seringapatam ...	The Tamracherry ghaut and Goondloopett.	133	5
Seringapatam ...	Carcoor ghaut and Goondloopett	146	3
Sholacull	Arriyacode and Vandoor	54	1
Sisparra	Arriyacode, Sholacull and Sisparra ghaut.	65	5
Tamracherry ...	......	19	0
Tanjore	Malapooram, Palghaut and Trichinopoly.	281	4
Taunore	......	19	6
Tellicherry ...	Badagara	45	1
Trichinopoly ...	Malapooram, Palghaut, Oodamalpett and Caroor.	246	6
Trichinopoly ...	Malapooram, Palghaut and Coimbatore...	244	2
Trittaula ...	Beypore and Taunore	49	6

CALIDASS (कालिदास - kálidása, *San.*). From (kálí, san. the deity + dása, san. servant). The well-known poet and dramatic author, anterior to Christian era, at court of Vicramadityan [q.v.] rajah of Oojjein [navaratnam]. His chief poems are Comaura sambhavam and Maigha dootam [maha cauvyam]. Besides these, he wrote Saitoo cauvyam, building of Rama's bridge [adam's bridge]; and three plays, Shacoontalay [q.v.], Vicramorrvashy, and Maulavicaugnimitram. Shacoontalay, in seven acts, is the most celebrated. There was a later Calidass at Canouj.

CALIMERE POINT (கள்ளிமேடு - kallimédu, *Tam.*). From (kalli, tam. milk hedge plant, euphorbia tirucalli, linn. + médu, tam. mound). Tám. also (kódikkarai), meaning cape + shore. Greek καλλιγικόν, Latin calingon. Village, Port, Promontory; Tanjore dist., Tritrapoondy tal.; acres 2,544; lat. 10° 17′; long. 79° 52′; from Madras S. 194 miles; from Moottoopett S.E. 23 miles; from Tanjore S.E. 57 miles; from Tritrapoondy S.E. 21 miles; from Vedaranyam S.E. 6 miles. Most southerly point on Coromandel coast [q.v.]. Ought not to be approached within $5\frac{1}{2}$ or 6 fathoms. Two pagodas [q.v.] near each other are about a mile from the shore and $5\frac{1}{2}$ miles N.N.W. of S. extremity of point. Trig. station in lat. 10° 17′ 33·26″; long. 79° 54′ 40·51″; from Tritrapoondy S.E. 23 miles; from Coditaray E.N.E. $3\frac{1}{2}$ miles; from Codiyacaul E. 3 miles; on the sea shore.

CALINGULA (கலிங்கல் - kalingal, *Tam.*). From (kazhi, tam. to discharge + kal, tam. stone). A water-way constructed in the bunds of tanks to permit the escape of surplus water, so as to prevent the bund [q.v.] bursting; usually set with upright stones to admit of partial bunding up.

CALIPH (خليفه - khalifah, *Hind.*). From (khalafa, ar. to succeed). Mahomedan rulers, successors of the prophet.——*Caliphate* (خلافت - khiláfat, Hind.). The office of caliph, the head of Islam, according to the Soonnees. The Shiahs do not recognize the caliphate, but substitute the office of imaum [q.v.].

CALPAM (कल्प - kalpa, *San.*). From (klip, san. to arrange). ——(1) Medical treatment. Any preparation made to strengthen the body.——(2) The first Vedaungam [smrity, vedaungam]. A ceremonial directory or rubric set out in the form of short aphoristic sootrams [q.v.] or rules, called Shrowtam, because serving as guides for the application of the Muntram and Bramhanam portion of Shrooty to the conduct of sacrificial rites. There are Shrowta sootrams for each of the five Sambitays of the Veda. Thus, for the Rig vedam there are the Aushwalauyanam, Saunkhyauyanam, and Shownacam shrowta sootrams; for the Sauma vedam, the Mashacam, Lautyauyanam, and Draubyauyanam; for the Teittireeyam or Black yajoor vedam, the Aupastambam, Bowdhauyanam, Satyaushaudham, Hiranyacaishy, Maunavam, Bhauradwaujam, Vaudhoonam, Veikhaunasam, Lowgaucshy, Meitram, Katam, and Varauham; for the Vaujsaneyin, or White yajoor vedam there is only the Cautyauyanam; for the Atarva vedam only the Cooshicam [matam]. ——(3) In Hindoo natural philosophy the bright half of Bramha's day [caulam, 2], or one thousand Mahayoogs [q.v.].—"*a*" A date is assigned to the creation calculated backwards to the time when all the planetary bodies [graham], with nodes [pautam] and apsides [mandotcham], must have been found in conjunction in the first degree of Maisham [q.v.] or Aries. In like manner calculation is made forward until a similar conjunction of planetary bodies and movable points in the heavens will occur. And both these periods added together make up 4,320,000,000 or 4,320 millions of solar sidereal years; corresponding to one thousand great ages [mahayoog], or one calpam. At the close of the bright day of Bramha a collapse of the universe takes place, which lasts through a night of Bramha, equal in duration to his day, during which period the three worlds are converted into one great ocean, when the lotus-born god, expanded by his deglutition of the universe, and contemplated by the yogies and gods in Jana locam, sleeps on the serpent sheshan. At the end of that night he awakes and creates anew. See Caulam.—"*b*" Within the period of a calpam or bright day of Bramha, fourteen Menoos reign, and a Manwantaram, or period of Menoo, is consequently the fourteenth part of a Calpam. In the present Calpam six Menoos, of whom Swauyambhoovan was the first, have already passed away, the present Menoo being Veivaswatan. In each Manwantaram seven rishies [q.v.], certain deities, an Indran, a Menoo, and the kings, his sons, are created and perish. A thousand of the systems of four yoogs [q.v.], as has been above explained, occur coincidently with these fourteen Manwantarams, and consequently about seventy-one systems of four yoogs elapse during each Manwantaram, and measure the lives of the Menoo and the deities of the period.—"*c*" According to another division a calpam is the sum of fourteen Manwantarams, with a Sundhyay, or twilight of 1,728,000 solar years.—"*d*" The Manwantaram, or reign of each Menoo, and the four lesser ages, Satyam, Tretay, Dwauparam and Kaly are not astronomical, but a sub-division after the greater astronomical periods had been adjusted.—"*e*" Calpam is often shortly used for the destruction of the world.——(4) *Calpacam* (कल्पक - kalpaka, San.). One of the five miraculous trees of Indran's devalocam or paradise yielding whatever is desired. Appears to be analogous to the tree of life in the garden of Eden. There is a Tamul proverb :—கற்பகத்தின் காக்கை சார்ந்த காகமும் அமுதம் உண்ணும்—"Even a crow that "lives in the calpacam tree feeds on ambrosia" [amritam]. Calpa droomam, from (druma, san. tree), is the same.——*Calpadinam* (कल्पदिन - kalpadina, San.). From (above + dina, san. day). The day on which the Calpam began, or its anniversary. ——*Calpastaunam* (कल्पस्थान - kalpast'hána, San.). From (above + st'hána, san. abode); chapter on pharmacy. Standard treatise on pharmacy. Treats in its introduction of the different countries which produce vegetable drugs [desham, munn].

CALPENY (കല്പേനി - kalpéni, *Mal.*). Means stone-quarry. Island; Malabar dist.; pop. 1,236; from Calicut W.S.W. 166 miles. One of the Laccadives. About 44 miles due south from Andrott in lat. 10° 7′ N. and long. 73° 38′ E. Coral shoal upon which it stands is about 8 miles in length and $3\frac{1}{2}$ to 4 in width. Besides the main island, which alone is inhabited, there are two small rocky islands to the south-west separated from the mainland and each other by narrow channels and a long narrow island called Cheriyam, about $1\frac{1}{2}$ miles north of the main island. These four islands together form a figure resembling a bottle with an elongated neck running north by east to south by west. The extreme length from the north point of Cheriyam to the south point of Calpeny is about 7 miles, and the greatest width about three-quarters of a mile. On the east the reef forms the shore line of Calpeny and Cheriyam, and on the south lies a short distance from the beach. On the west it trends outward so as to enclose a magnificent lagoon [cauyal] of still water over 7 miles in length and from 2 to 2½ miles broad as its widest point. The channels between the various islands are at low water very shallow, and the islanders can easily pass on foot from one to another. It was from these shoals particularly that between the main islands and Cheriyam, that cowries [q.v.] were formerly gathered. The main island is about 3 miles long. Only the southern portion is inhabited, as only here good drinkable water is procurable. All uncultivated portions are covered with a dense jungle of screw-pine [q.v.], &c. This island contains a considerable plot of low arable land adapted to the cultivation of a few coarse grains. In physique the inhabitants are inferior to those of the other islands. Nearly all the work is done by the women. The Carnaver class claim to have derived their descent from the Numboory bramins of Malabar, and their houses are generally distinguished by the word illam [q.v.]. The island is divided into four sub-divisions or cherries, viz., Keelcherry, Mecherry, Tekkancherry, Vadacancherry. In the arable ground the same coarse grains are cultivated as in Andrott. In sea products, Calpeny is peculiarly rich. The turtle [cadal aumay], killed for oil but not for eating, is very common. Coir-yarn is the chief manufacture, generally of an inferior quality. The people are exclusively Mahomedans. A large English steamship, "the Amelia," was wrecked upon the reef in April 1880.

CALUMBA (کلمبہ - kalambah, *Pers.*; کلمبے کا پیڑ - kalambekáper, *Hind.*; کلمبےکاجہاڑ - kalambekájhár, *Dec.*; కలంబావేరు - kalambávéru, *Tel.*; கொழும்புவேர் - kozhumbuvér, *Tam.*). Title as having first reached england from columbo. Hind. from (kalamba, hind. colombo + per, hind. tree). Tel. and tamul mean columbo root. Hind. also (chobchíní), meaning china root. Giving China root, Columbo root. Botanically Cocculus [vansanavully] palmatus, dec., menispermaceæ [vricsham, 5]. Alias Cocculus colombo; Jateorhiza columba, miersii, palmata; Menispermum columba, palmatum. Shrub; flower small, green; native of mozambique, introduced. Root met with in slices of one to two inches diameter, half an inch thick, much wrinkled, greyish externally, bright yellow within; the taste is bitter, smell heavy, powder of a greenish grey color, and very apt to attract moisture from the air; very subject to decay and becomes perforated by small worms. Gives to pharm. calumbæ radix; contains a bitter crystallizable principle, calumbin, and a bitter neutral principle, berberina; valuable tonic and stomachic.——*False calumba* (दार्वी - dárví, San.; दारुहळद - dáruhalada, Mahr.; جہاڑکی ہلدی - jhárkíhaldí, Dec.; ಮರದರಸಿನ - maradarasina, Can.; ಮರಮಂಜಳ - maramanjal, Too.; మానుపసుపు - mánupasupu, Tel.; മരമഞ്ഞൾ - maramaññal, Mal.; වෙනිවැල් - venival, Singh.; மரமஞ்சள் - maramañjal, Tam.). Title as substitute for calumba. San. from (dáru, san. wood) [berberry]. Mahr. from (dáru, san. tree + halada, mahr. turmeric). Dec. from (jhár, hind. tree + haldí, hind. turmeric, curcuma longa, roxb.); from color of root used as dye. Can. from (mara, can. tree + arasina, can. turmeric). Tel. from (mánu, tel. wood + pasupu, tel. turmeric). Mal. from (maram, mal. wood + maññal, mal. turmeric). Tam. from (maram, tam. tree + mañjal, tam. turmeric); from ligneous yellow stem. San. also (dáruharidrá), meaning wood turmeric; (pítadru), meaning yellow tree, from dye. Dec. also (haldíkájhár), meaning turmeric tree [country saffron]. Can. also (doddamaradarasina), meaning large + tree turmeric. Title otherwise Maramanjal, Tree turmeric, Yellow tree. Botanically Coscinium fenestratum, colebr., menispermaceæ [vricsham, 5]. Alias Coscinium wallichianum; Menispermum fenestratum. Climbing plant with thick ligneous stem and branches; leaves alternate, petioled, cordate, entire, five to seven-nerved, smooth and shining above, very hoary below, acuminate or obtuse, three to nine inches long, two to six broad; petioles downy, shorter than the leaves; flowers in small globular heads, numerous, sub-sessile, villous, of an obscure green; female umbels several from the same bud, rising from the branches, on thick downy peduncles; the latter longer and thicker in fruit; calyx six-leaved; three exterior sepals oval, downy outside; three interior ones longer; petals six, filaments very downy; style recurved; berries round, villous, size of a large filbert; seed one; flowers greenish; indigenous in malabar forests. Round, yellow colored, bitterish root, about one inch in circumference. Cylindrical woody stems, diameter 1 to 4 inches, covered with a pale corky bark. Wood and bark tonic and stomachic; useful in debility and atonic dyspepsia; substituted for british columba, gentian, and cinchona [koinah] bark; gives to pharm. non-officinal, stems, like calumba root. Wood yields a yellow dye [shauyam]. Wood itself is of a bright greenish yellow color, and open porous structure, having no concentric rings, but conspicuous medullary rays; taste purely bitter; sometimes confounded with darhald [q.v.], the stem of the berberry [q.v.]; the wood is much less hard than that of the berberry, and of a lighter color.

CALYE (قلعی - kalaí, *Ar.*). From (kala, ar. mine); where produced. Tin. As verb, to line brass [pittalay] or copper [taumram] vessels with a coating of tin [tagaram].

CAM (क - ka, *San.*). Water.——*Calamby* (कलम्बी - kalambí, San.). From (ka, san. water + lamb, san. to hang). Aquatic bindweed. Title otherwise American bindweed, Morning glory. Botanically the Ipomæa genus, convolvulaceæ [vricsham, 93]. Twining prostrate creepers, or rarely low and erect shrubs; leaves, entire, lobed or divided; flowers large and showy; many yield purgative roots, others edible. Genus very scattered in vernacular terminology. The species best known to natives are:—angustifolia [seeta's knot], aquatica [tooty coora], batatas [sweet potato], beladamboe [white adambo], biloba [red adambo], bonanox [moon flower], coccinea [caushy ratnam], cymosa [laldana], digitata [giant sweet potato], hederacea [kaladana], muricata [false kaladana], pentaphylla [hill giant sweet potato], pestigridis [tiger's foot], quamoclit [indian pink], reniformis [rat's ear], sepiaria [luldanah], turpethum [turbith]. Other s. indian species indigenous or naturalized are:—Bracteata, in tamul called mortar flower from shape; Campanulata, stem straight, large bell-shaped flowers pale rose at the mouth deepening to dark crimson at the bottom; Chryseides, stem twisted; Dasysperma, one to three-flowered, flowers deep cream-colored tinged with yellow and with a lilac purple eye; Dissecta, coromandel coast [q.v], called in tamul hare's gourd; Eriocarpa, flower small, rose-colored, plant eaten in times of famine; Obscura, flower largish, white, with cream-colored plica, and a dark purple eye; Palmata, flowers very large, white, lilac purple; Purpurea or morning glory, profusion of flowers every shade of color from white through blue and crimson to dark purple; Rumicifolia; Staphylina, flowers very numerous; Tridentata; Uniflora; Vitifolia; Wightii.——*Calasham* (कलश - kalasha, San.; کلس - kalas, Hind.). San. from (ka, san. water + lá, san. to take). Pot. A rounded pinnacle or ball on the top of a temple [coil, shikharam]. Calashapoojay is placing a water-jar in a chamber as type of Doorga [q.v.].——*Calauyam* (कलाय - kaláya, San.; वाटाणे - vátáné, Mahr.; बट्टणे - battané, Conc.; مٹر - matar, Hind.; بٹانی کا جہاڑ - batánekájhár, Dec.; ಬಟಾಣಿ - batáni, Can.; کچنگ - kachang, Malay; ಬಟಾಣಿ - batáni, Too.; పటాణి - pat'háni, Tel.; പട്ടാണിപ്പയറു - pattánippayaru, Mal.; රටගොරාද්‍ය - ratagoradya, Singh.; பட்டாணி - pattáni, Tam.). San. from (ka, san. wind + lá, san. to take), causing vayoo [bengal gram]. Mahr. from hindostany. Mal. from (pattáni, mal. patán + payar, mal. pulse); favorite pulse among patauns. San. also (satínaka), meaning troubling; (harénu), meaning destroying; (khandika), meaning eaten. Ar. also (himmas) [bengal gram]. Hind. also (golmatar), meaning round pea. Can. also (badagida). Tel. also (pattáni); (gundushanagalu), meaning round + bengal gram, cicer arietinum, linn. Tam. also (vellaippattáni), meaning white + pisum sativum, linn. Greek ἐρέβινθος. Title otherwise Common pea, Dantzic pea, Garden pea, Puttauny. Botanically Pisum sativum, linn., leguminosæ [vricsham, 48]. Alias Pisum exhorticatum, quadratum, humile, umbellatum. Annual tendril climber; leaves having three pairs of entire glaucous leaflets and large leafy stipules; large flowers white or variegated with red; indigenous in central india; here only cultivated; grows well at bangalore. Not much cultivated except for European tables. There is a Hindostany proverb:—ایک چنے کے دو دال—"Two halves of a pea;" or two chips of the same block. Many varieties. More valuable and prolific than P. arvense, linn.——*Camalam* (कमल - kamala, San.). From (ka, san. water + al, san. to adorn). Lotus, nelumbium speciosum, willd. [nelumbo].——*Camala moodray* (కమలముద్ర - kamalamudra, Tel.). Means camalam or lotus stamp. Otherwise Camala mauda. Ancient gold coin of a cup-like form; stamped on one side with the lotus flower, whence name, and with the chunk [q.v.]. Generally half pagoda [mauda].——*Camalaupooram* (కమలాపురము - kamalápuramu, Tel. kamalápuram *). Means camalam or lotus town.—"*a*" Deputy tahsildarry, Cuddapah district. Pay Rs. 70.—"*b*" Village, Deputy tahsildar's station, Railway station; Cuddapah dist., Cuddapah tal.; pop. 5,082; acres 4,408; lat. 14° 36′; long. 78° 43′; height 462 feet; from Cuddapah N.W. 13¼ miles; from Madanapully N. 72 miles; from Madras N.W. 152 miles; from Sidhout W.N.W. 22 miles. At the junction of Paupughny and Pennair. Once residence of a poligar [q.v.]. Family now extinct. Two old temples. Two Government plantations near the town on the Paupughny. Trade in rice.—"*c*" Town; Bellary dist., Hospett tal.; pop. 5,314; acres 23,494; lat. 15° 18′; long. 76° 31′; from Bellary W.N.W. 31½ miles; from Hospott E.N.E. 7 miles. Suburb of Vijianugger. Built beneath the embankment of a large tank, supplied by the Toongabudra. Until 1820 the residence of the last surviving representative of the Vijianugger dynasty. There are many ruined buildings, one converted into a bungalow [q.v.]. Chiefly remarkable for its iron foundries; the large iron [auhan] pans required for boiling down the juice of the sugar-cane [q.v.], largely grown in the neighbourhood, being made here.——*Camalay* (கமலை - kamalai, Tam.). From (ka, san. water + al, san. to adorn). The lotus, a name of lutchmy [q.v.]. Hindoo 2nd or pers. name of females and males. Similarly Camaleshan; from Vishnoo, husband of Lutchmy the lotus-goddess [peyar].——*Capotam* (कपोत - kapóta, San.). From (ka, san. wind + póta, san. young one); from rapid motion. Columbidæ family, gemitores, aves [pacshy, 29], of naturalists [jantoo]. Pigeons and Doves, ordinarily so called, which feed chiefly on grains, often on shoots and buds of plants, and a few partially on fruit [pazham]. Differ from green pigeons [haritaulam] by more terrestrial habits, more dull and sombre colors, various shades of dark-blue, red-brown, and grey predominating, often adorned with a beautiful iridescence or play of colors on neck, and in many with marked neck spot. Divided according to general tone of coloring and habits into :—" *a* " Palumbinæ, Wood-pigeons or cushats. Feet fitted for perching; tail somewhat long and rounded. More frugivorous and bud-eating than ordinary Pigeons and Doves, only twelve tail-feathers, denizens of woods and forests, feed partly on trees and partly on the ground [sholah pigeon].—" *b* " Columbinæ, Rock-pigeons. Feet fitted for walking; tarsus longer and less feathered; find their food mostly on the ground. Comprise the blue Rock-pigeons and the so-called Stock-pigeons and their allies, from some species of which the domestic Pigeons have sprung [blue-rock pigeon].—" *c* " Turturinæ, bonap., Doves. Feet fitted for walking on ground, tail somewhat lengthened, rounded or graduated, pale tips to outer feathers; of delicate make, with small heads; neck usually without the iridescent play of the Columbinæ, but frequently adorned with neck spots as in the Palumbinæ, or with rings; colors usually pale, compared with pigeons. Mostly feed on the ground on grain, pulse, and other small seeds, not in general gregarious, though large numbers may be seen feeding together. Chiefly frequent open and cultivated country, a few preferring highly wooded or forest districts; many are very familiar, feeding close to houses and stables. Breed on low trees, or shrubs, constructing the usual slight platform nest; they breed at all seasons of the year [tootroo].——*Caunjicam* (काञ्जिक - káñjika, San.). From (ka, san. water + añj, san. to shine); water by distinction. Rice vinegar [caudy].

CAMAUL (كمال - kamál, *Ar.*). From (kamala, ar. to complete). Perfection. Prefixed to an alam forms a lacab, as Camaul ahmed, perfection of Ahmed the prophet [ism].

CAMBATTIGA (కంబట్టిగ - kambattiga, *Tel.*). Corruption from (kembattakki, can. red paddy rice). A Bellary paddy.

CAMBAUKUM (காம்பாக்கம் - kámbákkam, *Tam.*). From (kámbu, tam. bamboo, bambusa arundinacea, willd. + pákkam, tam. village). Village; Chingleput dist., Trivellore tal.; pop. 742; acres 15,874; lat. 13° 35′; long. 79° 58′; from Suttivaid N.N.W. 10 miles; from Sydapett N.W. 44 miles; from Trivellore N.N.W. 30½ miles. Near Calastry zemindarry. Cambaukum droog is a trig. station in lat. 13° 34′ 29·90″; long. 79° 54′ 13·72″; height 2,548 feet; from Sydapett N.W. 44 miles; from Trivellore N.N.W. 30 miles. Principal peak in the Naugalaupooram and Suttivaid ranges. Remains of a fine hill fort with palaces and other buildings. On the hill is a tableland half square mile in area, which it was at one time proposed to convert into a sanitarium for troops. The forest in the vicinity promises to be of great value. This plateau is the only approach the district possesses to a hill climate, but the range is decidedly feverish in the hot months, until cleansed by the first falls of the south-west monsoon [q.v.].

CAMBAY (खंभात - khambhát, Mahr.; கம்பை - kambai, Tam.). Title from mahratta. Mahr. corruption from (stambhatírtha, san. sacred pillar pool); from a pool sacred to shiva under the form of pillar god. Town in Goozerat, at the head of the gulf of same name.——*Cambay pebble* (گجراتی کنکر - gujrátíkankar, Hind.; గుజరాతిరాయి - gudzarátiráyi, Tel.; கம்பைக்கல் - kambaikkal, Tam.). Title from cambay, town of goozerat. Hind. from (kankar, hind. pebble). Brought from Goozerat and resembles in color a mixture of milk and water. It changes color when held in different positions [ratnam].

CAMBODIA (कम्बोज - kambója, *San.*). From (kambu, san. neck + ójas, san. strength). One of the non-Aryan tribes of the north-west famous for their horses. When the Aryan travellers or colonists proceeded to the country which is the modern French cochin china, they took this name with them. The Cambodia ruins of extraordinary vastness and architectural elaboration are numerous. The country is known to the modern natives under the name of Champah [baly]. Gamboge [q.v.] is derived from this word. The country also exports eaglewood [q.v.]. Its chief produce is rice. Abrus precatorius is Cambojy in sanscrit. And compare :—Phyllanthus multiflorus (krishnakámbóji), black fruited abrus; Securinega leucopyrus (shvétakámbóji), white fruited abrus.

CAMEES (قمیص - kamís, *Hind.*). From the portuguese camisa through arabic. A short coat, shirt [coortee, sheelay].

CAMEL (اونٹ - únt, *Hind.*). Rather common prefix [ottagam].——*Camel hump* (വാവ്വൽമല - vávúlmala, Mal.). Title from appearance. Mal. from (vával, mal. large bat + mala, mal. hill). Peak, Malabar dist., Wynaud tal. Trig. station; lat. 11° 25′ 34·05″; long. 76° 10′ 23·03″; height 7,677 feet; from Calicut E.N.E. 26 miles; from Manantoddy S.S.E. 26 miles; from Munjery N. 22 miles. The highest peak in Wynaud, and a conspicuous landmark from all points on the coast and from sea. Covered to the summit with virgin forest.——*Camel thistle* (ऊंटकटारी - úntakatárí, Mahr.; اونٹ کٹارا - úntkatárá, Hind.; ಬ್ರಹ್ಮದಂಡ - brahmadanda, Can.; వేమదొండ - vémadonda, Tel.). Title from food of camels. Mahr. from (únta, mahr. camel + katára, mahr. dagger); from dagger-like bristles of plant. Hind. from (únt, hind. camel + katárá, hind. the plant). Can. from (brahma, san. deity + danda, san. stick); from white stem [bramhadand]. Tel. from (vému, tel. margosa tree, melia azadirachta, linn. + donda, tel. cephalandra indica, naud.). Hind. also (katárá), meaning plant with dagger-like bristles. Title otherwise Globe thistle, Vaimdonda. Botanically Echinops echinatus, dec., compositæ [vricsham, 74]. Erect, much branched; leaves pinnatifid, pubescent and viscid above, hoary-tomentose beneath; divisions ovate-lanceolate, waved, smooth; heads of flowers terminal, solitary, globose, spinous, florets pale lilac, tube slender, division linear-acute, revolute; pappus short, brush-like, ovary very hairy; flowering february and march; camels eat it; no other common species here.——*Camel thorn* (اشترخار - ushturkhár, Pers.). Title from being camel's food. Arabian manna.

CAMPHOR (कर्पूर - karpúra, *San.*; कापूर - kápúra, *Mahr.*; كافور - káfúr, *Ar.*, *Pers.* and *Hind.*; کاپور - kápúr, *Dec.*; کپور - kapur, *Malay*; ಕರ್ಪೂರ - karpúra, *Can.* and *Too.*; కర్పూరము - karpúramu, *Tel.*; കർപ്പൂരം - karppúram, *Mal.*; කපුරු - kapuru, *Singh.*; கற்பூரம் - karppúram, *Tam.*). From sanscrit through arabic. Greek καφουρά. Camphora of chemists. Product of Cinnamomum camphora, nees. and eberm. [camphor cinnamon], and Cinnamomum zeylanicum, breyn. [ceylon cinnamon]; chiefly the former. Is a vegetable principle arising from the separation by sublimation of the concrete volatile oil contained in wood of the trees; it is not a gum resin [gond, googal]. Impure camphor of the shops is concrete, grey, granular, moist, full of heterogeneous particles; refined camphor is in flat cakes, white, semi-transparent, having a crystalline appearance; in either case has a fragrant odour, and a hot taste; inflammable and so volatile as to exhale when left exposed in a warm air; odour very penetrating, taste hot and bitter like peppermint; weight sensibly decreases by keeping, owing to evaporation; insoluble in water, burns without residue or blackening, though it emits dense smoke. The bazaar dealers moisten it to increase its weight, and fresh cakes often contain about one-fourth their weight of fluid. The article here sold comes, like the one imported into europe, from formosa and japan. Camphor is prepared by boiling chips of the wood in a retort; the wood is cut into billets and boiled in water in iron pots covered with earthenware heads filled with straw; the camphor volatilises and concretes on the straw; it is afterwards purified by sublimation and made into cakes. In medicine camphor is primarily a diffusable stimulant and diaphoretic; secondarily a sedative, anodyne, and antispasmodic; and in large doses an acro-narcotic poison; as external application used in the form of liniment for rheumatism, sprains, &c.; camphor water or julep is a vehicle for other medicines; spirits of camphor are prepared by dissolving one drachm of camphor in one ounce and one drachm of rectified spirits of wine. Gives to pharm. preparations :—aqua camphoræ, spiritus camphoræ, tinctura camphoræ cum opio, linimentum camphoræ, linimentum camphoræ compositum; officinal. In veterinary practice used in fever and for destroying worms in cancer. Camphor is constantly burnt in ceremonies; placed among clothes as insectifuge. The above is the ordinary or China camphor. Borneo or Sumatra or green camphor comes from Dryobalanops aromatica, gærtn.; natives consider this more highly medicinal than the ordinary. Sumatra camphor is often called Barus camphor from town of that name and this has the highest reputation. Camphor may also be procured from thyme, marjoram, ginger, sage, &c. The so called Mercury camphor is rascapoor [q.v.], an impure sub-chloride of mercury. Vemana has a verse :—ఉప్పు కప్పురంబు నొక్కపోలికనుండు; చూడచూడ రుచుల జాడ వేరు; పురుషులందు పుణ్యపురుషులు వేరయా, వి— " Salt and camphor are of one semblance, but if you examine " and try the flavors, their tastes are diverse; thus do the excellent differ from other men."——*Camphor creeper* (कर्पूरवल्ली - karpúravallí, San.). From smell. Same as Country lavender or Country borage.——*Camphor grass* (கற்பூரப்புல் - karppúrappul, Tam.). From fragrance. Same as Lemon grass [q.v.].——*Camphor leaf* (कर्पूरपत्त्र - karpúrapattra, San.). From flavor. Same as Indian sage.——*Camphor root* (عروق الكافور - urúkulkáfúr, Ar.). From (urúk, ar. roots + káfúr, ar. camphor). Same as Long zedoary.——*Camphor tomato* (కర్పూరవంగ - karpúravanga, Tel.). From flavor. Same as Europe brinjaul or tomato.——*Camphor tree* (கற்பூரமரம் - karppúramaram, Tam.). From smell and appearance of back of leaves. Same as Blue gum.——*Camphor turmeric* (کپور هلدی - kapúrhaldí, Hind.). From smell. Same as Long zedoary.

CANACAM (కనకము - kanakamu, *Tel.*). Means gold. Hindoo 2nd or pers. name of females and males [bungaur, ponnoo, tungam]. Similar is Canacaratnam meaning gold gem; Canacasabhaupaty from shiva, lord of the golden hall at chidambaram; Canacasabbhay from the sacred hall itself. Ponnambalam is the same among non-bramins [peyar].

CANAM (कण - kana, *San.*). From (kan, san. to grow small). Atom.——*Canaudan* (कणाद - kanáda, San.). From (above + ada, san. eater); from his abstemious habit. Author of the ancient Veishaishicam philosophy, or physical branch extension of Nyauyam [q.v.]. He is also called Ooloocan, meaning owl, probably in derision. See vol. I (74).——*Canishtam* (कनिष्ठ - kanisht'ha, San.). Literally least. x in the algebraic form $ax^2 + b = y^2$. ——*Canwa* (कण्व - kanva, San.). One of the very ancient rishies. Recently the earliest writer on Teloogoo grammar; at court of one Andhra roya on banks of Godavery. Ancient royal dynasty in the modern Behar; see vol. I (117), (132) [charitram].

CANAMA (కనుమ - kanama, *Tel.*). From (kanu, tel. to see). Ravine or hill pass [ghaut]. A breach in the bank of a tank, whether accidental or artificial. Suffix in place names, as Raupore canama [canavye, cundy].

CANARA (ಕನ್ನಡ - kannada, *Can.*). From (karnáta, san. from karu, tam. black + nádu, tam. country). Anglo-indian name for part of west coast which lies below ghauts from Mount delly northward to Goa territory. Comprises two British districts N. and S. canara, the latter in this Presidency. Term unknown to the natives in this sense. The name meaning black country, from black cotton soil [regar] prevailing there, was a corruption of Carnautacam [carnatic]. Throughout sixteenth century applied to country above ghauts, sometimes even to the whole kingdom of Narsingam or Vijianugger. Gradually, and owing to local application at Goa, where the natives were from the first known to the Portuguese as Canarija, the name became appropriated to the low country on the coast between Goa and Malabar, which was subject to the kingdom in question; much in the same way that Carnatic came at a later date to be misapplied on other side of peninsula. The tract is bounded on the north by Goa; east by Mysore and Coorg; south by Coorg and Malabar; west by the Arabian sea. It lies between lat. 12° 11′ to 15° 30′; long. 74° 9′ to 75° 44′, and has an area of 7,720 square miles. The Jeinas, who have nearly vanished from many other parts of India, are here still numerous. The early history is obscure. Soon after middle of last century it fell into hands of Hyder ally; and on fall of his son Tippoo in 1799 it passed to the East india company [charitram].——*Canarese* (ಕನ್ನಡ - kannada, *Can.*). From (kár, tam. black + nádu, tam. country). English name for the Carnauta or as it was later called Cannada language; the language of the Carnatic [q.v.]. The term Carnautam was once a generic term, including both the Teloogoo and Canarese people and their languages. Then the Teloogoo people branched off. There are in the Presidency about 1,300,000 persons who talk Canarese; most in Canara, Coimbatore, and Salem. See vol. I (50) [bhaushay].

CANAVAN (கணவன் - kanavan, *Tam.*). From (kan, tam. eye). Master. Vishnoo.

CANAVUTTAM (கணவட்டம் - kanavattam, *Tam.*). From (kshana, san. moment + vattam, tam. circle); fast-going. The royal Paundy horse emblem. See vol. I (119).

CANAVYE (கணவாய் - kanaváy, *Tam.*). A gap or dip in a mountain range, by which travellers can pass at the lowest level from one side to the other. For principal passes see Ghaut [canama].

CANCHOOLYA (கஞ்சுளிய - kañjuliya, *Tam.*). From (kanjuli, tam. jacket). A class of votaries of Angauly. See vol. I (87).

CANDAHAR (गान्धार - gándhára, *San.*; قندهار - kandahár, *Hind.*). The town of afghanistaun; was an ancient province.——*Candahar tree* (गन्धारी - gandhárí, San.; قندهاری - kandahárí, *Hind.*). Same as Cashmere tree.

CANDEL (கண்டல் - kandal, *Tam.*). The tree, kandelia rheedii, w. &. a. Its juice is astringent and used to dye sailcloths, boat-ropes, fishing-nets to preserve them from decay. Poo candel is variety bearing fragrant flowers; pey candel is a wild one.——*Candel bark* (കണ്ടൽതോലി - kantaltoli, Mal.; கண்டற்பட்டை - kandarbattai, Tam.). Mal. from (kantal, mal. the tree, kandelia rheedii, w. and a. + toli, mal. bark). Title otherwise Mangrove bark. Used for tanning [chamrah]. The barks known in S. india as Mangrove bark are from following trees:—Avicennia officinalis, Bruguiera gymnorhiza, Ceriops candolleana, Ceriops roxburghiana, Kandelia rheedii, Rhizophora mucronata. See gloss. paragraphs.

CANDY (खण्डशर्करा - khandasharkará, *San.*; قند - kand, *Ar.*; مصری - misrí, *Hind.*; ಕಲ್ಲುಸಕ್ಕರೆ - kalkanda, *Can.*; కలకండ - kalakanda, *Tel.*; കൽക്കണ്ടു - kalkantu, *Mal.*; கற்கண்டு - kargandu, *Tam.*). Title from arabic. San. from (khanda, san. piece + sharkará, san. sugar); sugar in pieces. Ar. from (khanda, san. piece). Hind. means sugar of egypt, misr, through which country it was imported into turkey. Drav. means stone + piece. Crystal, especially of cane sugar [q.v.].

CANDY (खंडी - khandí, *San.*; ఖండి - khandí, *Tel.*; കണ്ടി - kanti, *Mal.*; கண்டி - kandi, *Tam.*). From (khand, san. to divide). The Portuguese wrote it candil. See vol. I, 609; II, 506, 519.—"*a*" Bazaar weight. 20 maunds = 1 candy [niray, 2]. Approximate actual value, 1 candy = 500 lbs. avoirdupois. Not commonly used by natives. Used by Europeans and Mahomedans, for measure called by natives bhauram. Corresponds broadly with the Arabian bahaur. Varies with the weight of one maund. Is also different for different materials. Same as Tel. pootty in Ganjam and Vizagapatam, Tam. bhauram.—"*b*" Measure of capacity. 20 colagams = 1 candy [alavay, 3]. Bellary and Mysore. In Coimbatore a candy is 24 shalagays. In some Teloogoo districts candy is used for pootty. Same as cundaga.—"*c*" Cubic measure. Approximate actual value, 1 candy = 12½ cubic feet. Used in Malabar in measuring wood. It is a cube measuring a kole or 28¾ inches to the side. The cubical contents of a block of wood is obtained there by multiplying half the circumference of the block reduced to koles, by its length.—"*d*" Superficial measure. 120 beegahs = 1 candy [alavay, 2]. Approximate actual value, 1 candy = 75 acres. Same as Hind. chauver.

CANDY (కంది - kandi, *Tel.*). From (kandi, tel. to redden). Formerly common Anglo-indian for dholl.

CANGOTE (കണ്ണവം - kannavam, *Mal.*). Inflected form from (kan, mal. eye + akam, mal. abode); beautiful abode. Village; Malabar dist., Cottayam tal.; from Calicut N.W. 41 miles; from Tellicherry N.E. 13 miles. Large hilly tract, formerly a military post. Small redoubt on a hill in ruins. Good bungalow for travellers and substantial stone-bridge thrown over small river by pioneers in 1822-23. Celebrated pagoda, known as Toticalam, about one mile north-north-west of Cangote. There are three rock-cut caves in Toticalam, paved with bricks. Mosque in the amshom known as Cangote mosque. The rich jenmy known as Cangote numbiyaur joined rebellious Pychy rajah of Cottayam and disturbed the peace of the talook for a series of years. He eventually fell into the hands of the authorities and was hanged on the hill near the bungalow, his estate being declared escheated in 1805. Cangote escheat is of large extent and lies in Cangote and Manattana amshoms. The forests are peopled by Cooritchiyar.

CANIGHERRY (కనిగిరి - kanigiri,* *Tel.*). From (khani, san. mine of precious stones + giri, san. mountain). Tel. also (kanakagirivijayamártándadurgamu), meaning gold + hill + vijayamartaundan, meaning the prosperous sun, the local name of shiva + hill fort. Sanscrit name (kanakagiri), means gold + mountain.——**(1)** Talook, Nellore district. Tahsildar's pay Rs. 150. Area 1,014 square miles. N. central inland part of district. Lat. 15° 1′ to 15° 35′ N.; long. 79° 07′ to 79° 44′ E. Separated on E. from Cundoocore talook by the Choondy hills; from Cumbum talook of Kurnool district on W. by the Veligondas [q.v.]; Zemindarry talook of Podily, belonging to Vencatagherry, skirts the northern boundary; south bordered by Oodayagherry talook. Portion belongs to the Vencatagherry and Calastry zemindarries respectively, and the villages thereof are interspersed throughout all parts of the talook. In eighteenth century Hyder ally invaded Nizam's dominions, and took possession of the talook, destroying town and fort of Canigherry. On defeat of Tippoo it reverted to Nizam, who afterwards gave it to the English with the Ceded districts [q.v.]. It was first attached to Cuddapah district, then transferred to Kurnool, and finally made part of Nellore district. The most barren talook in the district, though palmyra trees are abundant in N.W. corner. Intersected by two streams, the Munnair and the Palair. Rock hills abound. Soil, red loam. Coarse cloths, such as doopty [q.v.] sheets and female white cloths manufactured to a large extent. These, ghee and lamp oil seeds, are exported to Nellore, Naidoopett and Calastry, &c., by road. Most of the paddy [q.v.] consumed in the talook is imported from the villages of Cauvaly, Cundoocore and Nellore talooks. Cloths, iron [auham] and sundry articles, &c., are received from Madras viâ Buckingham canal to Oollipollem and thence by road and bandy tracts to different principal villages. Jaggery [q.v.], cloths, and tamarind [q.v.] from Vellore, pulses [dholl] from Ongole, chillies [q.v.] and tobacco [pogauk] from Guntoor, are also largely imported. Petty merchants buy brass vessels manufactured at Meilavaram and Wonipenta and sell in the northern talooks from village to village. There are nine tanks. Nundanavanam the largest, below the Veligonda range. In almost all the villages there is garden cultivation with the aid of private wells. Camping grounds:—Canigherry, Gogoolpully, Hajipooram, Mogullore, Pamoor, Pedda alvalapaud, Pedda irlapaud, Vaimlapaud. Principal trig. stations:—Lingamgoonta, Pitcherlacondah, Tellanullamala. The leading places, &c., in the talook are the following.——*Canigherry* (కనిగిరి - kanigiri, Tel.). See below.——*Cattakindy pulley* (కట్టకిందిపల్లె - kattakindipalle, Tel.). From (katta, tel. bund + kinda, tel. under + palle, tel. village). Village, Head-quarters of the Tahsildar of Maurella talook of Vencatagherry zemindarry; pop. 1,722; lat. 15° 25′; long. 79° 18; from Canigherry W. 16 miles; from Nellore N.W. 81 miles. An ancient temple to Shiva as Eeshwarasawmy. Annual festival about March. Fine tank. ——*Gogoolpully* (గోగులపల్లి - gógulapalli, Tel.). See sep. title. ——*Inimerla* (ఇనిమెర్ల - inimerla, Tel.). From (inumu, tel. iron + maru, tel. barren land). Village; pop. 1,632; acres 10,511; lat. 15° 07′; long. 79° 30′; from Canigherry S. 20½ miles; from Nellore N.W. 57 miles. Consists of two portions, old and new. On banks of Munnair. Two tanks.——*Irlapaud* (ఇర్లపాడు - irlapádu, Tel.). From (irri, tel. deer + pádu, tel. village). Village; pop. 4,407; acres 15,486; lat. 15° 12′; long. 79° 38′; from Canigherry S.S.E. 15 miles; from Nellore N.N.W. 57 miles. Good tank. Produces tobacco which is sent to Nellore and Bootchireddipollem, &c., station of Revenue inspector. Fine betel leaf gardens.——*Lingamgoonta* (లింగంగుంట - lingamgunta, Tel.). From (lingamma, tel. proper name + gunta, tel. pond); after a concubine of the royel of Vijianugger. Village; pop. 1,536; acres 5,837; lat. 15° 31′; long 79° 22′; from Canigherry N.W. 14¾ miles; from Nellore N.W. 86 miles. Choultry on the ghauts. Trig. station in lat. 15° 33′ 14·93″; long. 79° 19′ 43·76″; height 1,648 feet; from Canigherry N.W. 18 miles; from Vaimlapaud W.N.W. 4 miles.——*Maurella* (మారెళ్ళ - marélla, Tel.). See sep. title.——*Mogullore* (మొగల్లూరు - mogallúru, Tel. mógallúr *). From (mogili, tel. screw-pine, pandanus odoratissimus, linn. + úru, tel. village). Sanscrit name (kétakipattana), means screw-pine + city; still used by banyans. Village; pop. 1,841; lat. 15° 20′; long. 79° 27′; from Canigherry S.W. 8 miles; from Nellore N.W. 72 miles; Vencatagherry zemindarry. Head-quarter station of Tahsildar of Canigherry till 1879 and formerly the Deputy tahsildar's centre of Gogoolpully division.——*Munnair* (మన్నేరు - mannéru, Tel.). See sep. title.——*Nundanavanam* (నందనవనము - nandanavanamu, Tel.). From (nandana, san. pleasure + vana, san. garden). Village; pop. 1,775; acres 7,912; lat. 15° 28′; long. 79° 19′; from Canigherry W.N.W. 15¾ miles; from Nellore N.W. 84 miles. Betel and sugar-cane gardens, fine tank.——*Palair* (పాలేరు - páléru, Tel.). See sep. title.——*Pamoor* (పామూరు - pámúru, Tel.). See sep. title.——*Pedda alvalapaud* (పెద్దఅలవలపాడు - peddalavalapádu, Tel.). Means town of abilities. Distinguished from chinna alvalapaud. Village; pop. 2,380; acres 13,160; lat. 15° 20′; long. 79° 40′; from Canigherry S.E. 9½ miles; from Nellore N.N.W. 64 miles. On the Palair and is on the Cumbum and Oollipollem road. Temple of Bagadigunga. Annual festival.——*Pitcherlacondah* (పిచ్చర్లకొండ - picherlakonda, Tel.). From (pina, tel. small + cheruvu, tel. tank + konda, tel. hill). Trig. station in lat. 15° 12′ 01·52″; long. 79° 33′ 34·23″; height 1,283 feet; from Canigherry S. 14 miles; from Irlapaud W. 5 miles.——*Tellanullamala* (తెల్లనల్లమల - tellanallamala, Tel.). From (tella, tel. white + nalla, tel. black + mala, tel. hill). Trig. station in lat. 15° 13′ 45·93″; long. 79° 09′ 20·76″; height 2,733 feet; from Canigherry W.S.W. 29 miles; from Tangootore N.E. 3½ miles.——*Veeraramapooram* (వీరరామాపురము - vírarámápuramu, Tel.). From (vírarárma, san. pándya king of that name + pura, san. town). Village; pop. 521; acres 1,439; lat. 15° 26′; long. 79° 19′; from Canigherry W. 15½ miles; from Nellore N.W. 82 miles. Shiva temple. Agrahauram [q.v.] granted to a Smarta priest called Shuncaracharry [q.v.].——*Veligonda* (వెలిగొండ - veligonda, Tel.). See sep. title.——**(2)** Village, Head-quarters of Tahsildar, Sub-registrar and District moonsif; pop. 3,710; acres 8,209; lat. 15° 24′; long. 79° 33′; from Madras N.N.W. 164 miles; from Naidoopett N.N.W. 104 miles; from Nellore N.N.W. 72 miles; from Ongole W.S.W. 36 miles. Connected by road with Cundoocore, Podily and Cumbum. A road partially constructed to Pamoor. Consists of Newpettah and Pautore. Spinning instruments and country razors manufactured. Hill said to contain treasure. At western edge of hill are ruins of Andavaroyadoo's temple. To east of hill at the foot is a ruined temple to Singariroyadoo. On adjoining hill, once fortified, is a table-land about a square mile in area where a town once stood and was occupied in the tenth century by Caucateeya prataupa roodran of Warangal. His son built the town and fortified the hill. Subsequently seized by the Golcondah mussalmans. Ancient temple to Shiva, as Martaundeshwarasawmy. Annual festival about March. Mahomedans have a festival about December.——**(3)** Canigherry reservoir, from (kanivádu, tel. person so called + giri, san. hill). Called after the digger, and a hill near it; has no connection with the above. Artificial reservoir in Nellore talook. From Nellore N.W. 12 miles. See vol. I, 402. The old tank which preceded the present was miraculously formed by a sage living in the jungle near Moonoolapoody.

CANNADA (ಕನ್ನಡ - kannada, *Can.*). Later name for the Canarese language [bhaushay].——*Cannaudam* (கன்னடம் - kannádam, Tam.). Tamul for the Canarese country [bhoogolashastram].

CANNANORE * (കണ്ണൂര് - kannúr, *Mal.*). From (kannu, mal. eye + úr, mal. village); beautiful village. Sanscrit name (vélápuri), meaning sea-shore + town.—"*a*" Deputy tahsildarry. Malabar district. Pay Rs. 100.—"*b*" Town, Port, a Native regiment and European detachment are stationed here, Cantonment, Municipality, Head-quarters of talook, Deputy tahsildar and District moonsif, Lighthouse. Malabar dist., Chiracal tal.; pop. 27,418; lat. 11° 52′; long. 75° 25′; from Belliapatam S. 4¾ miles; from Bombay S.S.E. 508 miles; from Calicut N.N.W. 50 miles; from Chiracal S. 3½ miles; from Madras W.S.W. 345 miles; from Malapooram N.W. 72 miles; from Manantoddy W. 42 miles; from Palghaut N.W. 113 miles; from Ponnany N.N.W. 82 miles; from Tellicherry N.W. 11 miles. Populous sea-port of great antiquity. On north of a small bay, open to south, but sheltered on west by a bluff headland running north and south and surmounted by a fort and other buildings which render it easily distinguishable at sea. The port limits are:—north boundary pillar one mile north of the fort; south, boundary pillar two miles south of the fort; east, sea-shore between them to within fifty yards of high-water mark, spring tides; west, space enclosed by two lines running due west from the boundary pillars to nine fathoms water. Light on the fort rampart near the beach; lat. 11° 51′ 10″; long. 75° 21′ 45″; red; fixed, 6 to 8 miles range; visible from all directions seaward. Small masonry tower of a light yellow color. The best anchorage for large vessels in the roads is with the flagstaff N.E. by N. to N.E. by E. in from 5½ to 6 fathoms and about 2½ miles off shore. Small coasting craft find shelter in the bay under guns of fort. According to the legend of the partition of his dominions by Cherma permaul, Cannanore was included in the kingdom of the Colattiry or Chiracal rajahs, to whom it belonged till the invasion of Malabar by Hyder ally. In 1501 Cabral landed here, and being well received planted a colony. In 1505 later Vasco da Gama erected a factory. Fort St. Angelo on the promontory north of the bay, commanding the native town and south-east of the cantonment was built by the Portuguese. In 1656 the Dutch effected a settlement, for the protection of which they built the present fort, which they occupied till 1766, when it fell into the hands of Mysore troops. In 1784 Cannanore was captured by the British, and the reigning princess became tributary to the East india company. It was on the conclusion of the treaty of Mangalore given back to the Moplah family. In 1791 having become the property of Tippoo, it was besieged and taken by the British. Since that date it has remained in British hands. The descendant of the old Cannanore moplah sultans, Ally rajah, resides in the east of the bay. Within the Moplah quarter stands the fishing village of Tye, with a Roman catholic chapel, once a Portuguese factory. Modern trade is principally in pepper, grain, timber, and cocoanuts; vast quantities of the last are exported northwards. Anglican, German, and Roman catholic missions are established here, with schools attached. Cotton fabrics are manufactured chiefly by the mercantile branch of the German mission. A bazaar known as Tekky bazaar, is used by the native troops. About three miles north of the fort is the Central jail at Oodayancoonn. The Cannanore town was once the residence of the Chiracal rajah and contained a village known as Caunattore with 390 Numboory houses, almost all of which have now become extinct. The following are the distances from Cannanore to different places:—

To	Via	Miles and Furlongs.	
Alleppy	Calicut, Taunore, Chowghaut, Cottaparamba and Cochin.	189	6
Badagara ...	......	28	0
Bangalore ...	Periya ghaut and Seringapatam	216	0
Bangalore ...	Perambaudy and Seringapatam	197	7
Bellary	Perambaudy and Seringapatam	350	6
Bellary	Periya ghaut and Seringapatam	368	7
Calicut	Tellicherry	59	1
Cangote	......	30	4
Chowghaut ...	Tellicherry, Calicut and Taunore... ...	107	0
Cochin	Tellicherry, Calicut, Taunore, Chowghaut, and Cottaparamba.	156	7
Coimbatore ...	Calicut and Palghaut	174	4
Cuddapah ...	Perambaudy, Seringapatam and Bangalore.	354	3
Dharwar	Perambaudy, Seringapatam and Harihar.	397	1¼
Dindigul	Calicut, Malapooram, and Palghaut ...	246	4
French Rocks ...	Perambaudy and Seringapatam	125	0
French Rocks ...	Periya ghaut, Manantoddy and Mysore...	143	1
Goodalore ...	The Periya ghaut and Manantoddy ...	111	1
Goodalore ...	Coottooparamba, the Coottiyaudy ghaut and Manantoddy.	109	7
Harihar	Perambaudy and Seringapatam	305	0
Honore	Mangalore	190	3¼
Hoonsoor ...	Cangote and the Perambaudy ghaut ...	87	5
Kurnool	Perambaudy, Seringapatam, Bangalore and Gooty.	420	7
Kurnool	Seringapatam and Bellary	442	6
Madras	Seringapatam, Bangalore and Colaur ...	403	6½
Madras	Perambaudy, Seringapatam, Bangalore and Vellore.	411	7
Madura	Calicut, Malapooram, Palghaut and Dindigul.	286	5½
Mahé	Tellicherry	18	3
Malapooram ...	Calicut	90	5
Manantoddy ...	Coottooparamba and the Coottiyaudy ghaut.	57	7¾
Manantoddy ...	Cangote and the Periya ghaut	59	1
Mangalore ...	Poolore and Pauney mangalore	123	0
Mangalore ...	Cassergode	86	1
Mercara	Cangote, the Perambaudy ghaut and Veera rajendrapett.	71	3
Mysore	Periya ghaut and Manantoddy	127	1
Mysore	Perambaudy ghaut and Yelwaul ...	115	4
Mysore	Coottiyaudy ghaut and Manantoddy ...	125	7½
Negapatam ...	Calicut, Palghaut, Trichinopoly and Tanjore.	396	9
Nellore	Perambaudy, Seringapatam, Bangalore and Chittore.	434	6
Ongole	Perambaudy, Seringapatam, Bangalore, Chittore and Nellore.	511	1
Ootacamund ...	The Periya ghaut, Manantoddy and the Goodalore ghaut.	141	1
Ootacamund ...	The Coottiyaudy ghaut, Manantoddy and Goodalore.	139	7½
Palamcottah ...	Calicut, Palghaut, Dindigul and Madura	382	3½
Palghaut	Calicut and Malapooram	143	5
Paumben ...	Calicut, Palghaut, Dindigul, Madura and Ramnaud.	384	4½
Ponnany	Tellicherry, Calicut and Taunore ...	92	7

To	Via	Miles and Furlongs.	
Poonamallee ...	Perambaudy, Seringapatam, Bangalore and Ranipett.	392	2½
Quilon	Calicut, Taunore, Chowghaut, Coottooparamba, and Cochin.	345	0
Ramnaud ...	Calicut, Palghaut, Dindigul and Madura.	347	4¾
Sadaushivagarh (Carwar).	Mangalore	249	7¾
Salem	Calicut, Palghaut and Coimbatore ...	273	1
Secunderabad ...	Perambaudy, Seringapatam, Bangalore and Kurnool.	557	6
Seringapatam ...	The Perambaudy ghaut and Hoonsoor ...	118	4
Seringapatam ...	The Periya ghaut, Manantoddy and Mysore.	136	5
Seringapatam ...	Coottiyaudy ghaut and Manantoddy ...	135	3¾
Tanjore	Calicut, Palghaut and Trichinopoly ...	340	5
Tellicherry ...	......	14	0
Trichinopoly ...	Calicut, Palghaut, Coimbatore and Caroor.	303	3
Veera Rajendrapett.	Cangote and the Perambaudy ghaut ...	51	5
Vellore	Perambaudy, Seringapatam, Bangalore and Krishnagherry.	328	4
Yelwaul	Cangote and the Perambaudy ghaut ...	107	1

CANNAUD (కన్నాడు - kannádu, *Tel.*). From (kanama, tel. defile + nádu, tel. country). Ancient name for hilly portion of Kurnool district, distinguishing from Renaud, black cotton land of adjoining Coondair valley.

CANNING SEAT (கானிங்சீட்டு - káningsíttu, *Tam.*). After Lady Canning. A prominent point on Dolphin's Nose road, with views over Coimbatore plains. Neilgherry district. Parangi-naud division; lat. 11° 22′; long. 76° 53′; from Coonoor E.N.E. 3 miles.

CANOO (కను - kanu, *Tel.*). Prominent.——*Canoogonda* (కనుగొండ - kanugonda, Tel.). From (above + konda, tel. hill). Hill; Cuddapah dist., Madanapully tal. Two sculptured gatekeepers or Dwaura paulacans [q.v.] of temple on the hill. Trig. station in lat. 13° 46′ 59·05″; long. 78° 20′ 28·44″; from Peddapolliem N. 1¼ miles.

CANOON (قانون - kánún, *Ar.*). From Greek κανών. A rule, canon.——*Canoongo* (قانونگو - kánúngo, Hind.). From (above + go, pers. who speaks). An expounder of the laws, but applied especially to village accountant [curnum]. See vol. I, 112.——*Canoon i fittib* (قانون في الطب - kánúnifittib, Hind.). From (above + fí, ar. in + tibb, ar. medicine). Arabic work known in Europe as Canons of Avicenna. Author was Aboo ally ool hoossein ben abd oollah ibn e seenah; born in Bokhara, A.D. 980, and died at Hamadaun in Persia, A.D. 1036. Treats of medicine and diseases in general, simple and compound medicine, their qualities and virtues, also of anatomy; consists of five books.

CANOOPURTY (కనుపర్తి - kanuparti, * *Tel.*). From (kanaka, san. gold + parti, tel. village). Sanscrit name (kanakapuri), meaning gold + city. Village, Salt factory; Nellore dist., Ongole tal.; pop. 3,838; acres 10,643; lat. 15° 35′; long. 80° 15′; from Madras N. 169 miles; from Motoopully S.S.W. 10½ miles; from Nellore N. 78½ miles; from Ongole E.N.E. 12½ miles; from Paudarty N.N.E. 8½ miles. Close to Buckingham canal. Founded by a Rajah, one Oodauyana. Said to have been destroyed by an inundation of the sea, and ninety-nine temples entirely buried. In many places the bull and lingam [q.v.] are carved on the rocks, and there is an immense stone shausanam [q.v.] with an inscription. Half hidden in the sand are several sculptured nundies and lingams. Shiva temple of Yeleshwara-sawmy of great antiquity and rebuilt one hundred and twenty years ago. Villagers say that opposite to this temple there lies buried in the sand a very large bell-metal chariot at the site of a still older temple.

CANTAM (कण्ट - kanta, *San.*). From (kant, san. to go). Thorn.——*Cantacam* (कण्टक - kantaka, San.). Prickle.—"*a*" Plant first term. Ex., where transl. is of second term:—Artocarpus integrifolia (kantakap'hala), fruit; Azima tetracantha (kantangúr), vitis vinifera; Dioscorea pentaphylla (kantakálú), esculent root; Lasia lourierii (kantakachóramu), curcuma zedoaria.—"*b*" Plant second term. Ex., where transl. is of first term:—Achyranthes aspera (kándakantaka), stem; Argemone mexicana (shrigálakantaka), jackal; Euphorbia tirucalli (trikantaka), three; Hygrophila spinosa (ékakantaka), one; Momordica charantia (vishakantakí), poison; Solanum ferox (sitakanta), white; Trapa bispinosa (jalakantaka), water; Tribulus terrestris (svádukantaka), sweet; Zyzyphus jujuba (ubhayakantaka), double; Zyzyphus napeca (bahukantaká), many. See gloss. paragraphs.——*Cantalam* (कण्टल - kantala, San.). From prickly branches. Botanically the Acacia genus, leguminosæ [vricsham, 48]. Prickly shrubs or trees, erect or climbing; leaves bipinnate, with minute leaflets; flowers small, and collected in large numbers in globular heads, or in long spikes; pod ligulate or oblong, not jointed, usually compressed and dry. The species best known to the natives are:—arabica [babool], catechu [q.v.], concinna [soap pod wattle], farnesiana [piyvail], ferruginia [anasandra], intsia [corindah], latronum [vellay mool vail], leucophlæa [velvail], melanoxylon [australian black wood], pennata [biswool], planifrons [ooday vail], suma [white sundra], sundra [q.v.], tomentosa [coday vail]. For the allied Mimosa genus see Shoondy.

CANTEROY (ಕಂಠೀರವ - kant'hírava, *Can.*). From (kant'ha, san. throat + rava, san. noise); lion-voiced. Canteroy narsa rajah, a Mysore ruler, about 1638, made the first recorded gold coinage. His gold fanam [q.v.] became standard denomination of the currency in mysore; this bore the image of the narsimha avatar, and varied in weight from six to eight grains. The canteroy pagoda went 6 to 5 star pagodas; equal to 10 gold fanams, say = Rs. 2-14-8. The following were local varieties of the canteroy pagoda:—Cuddapah, 1,200 to 100 star pagodas; Seringapatam, 1,203¾ to 100; Coimbatore, 1,191¼ to 100; Salem, 1,181½ to 100. There was a later Canteroy rajah in A.D. 1704–14, also called Mookarasoo or the dumb king [charitram].

CANY (കണി - kani, *Mal.*). From (kan, mal. eye). Sight.——*Caniyaun* (കണിയാൻ - kaniyán, Mal.). From (above + án, mal. personal suffix). Tribe of astrologers and umbrella-makers in Malabar. Said to descend from a numboory and teeya woman; hence a polluting caste, members of which cannot approach a bramin within 24 feet. Follow makkatoyem [q.v.] law. Marriage and death ceremonies however seem to have a maroomakkatoyem [q.v.] origin. Numbers about 13,000 [jauty].——*Canyanore* (കണയന്നൂർ - kanayannúr, Mal.). From (kaniyán, mal. astrologer + úr, mal. village).—"*a*" Talook, Cochin state; pop. 88,847. Principal places:—Canyanore, Channera, Chittoor, Ernacolum, Neendacara, Nettoor, Tripoontora, Vellaurapully.—"*b*" Village; Cochin state, Canyanore tal.; lat. 9° 55′; long. 76° 27′; from Chittoor S.S.W. 60 miles; from Cochin E.S.E. 12 miles; from Ernacolum E.S.E. 10 miles; from Trichore S.S.E. 43 miles; from Tripoontora E.S.E. 4½ miles; from Madras S.W. 340 miles; from the sea E. 10 miles.

CANYAY (कन्या - kanyá, *San.*). From (kana, san. little). The solar sign Virgo ♍ [mausam, rausby]. A maid of nine or ten.——*Canya comaury* (कन्याकुमारी - kanyákumárí, San.). From (above + kumárí, san. daughter). Sanscrit form of Comorin [q.v.].——*Canya shoolcam* (कन्याशुल्क - kanyáshulka, San.). From (above + shulka, san. price). Money given to the parents of the bride by the bridegroom [maryauday].——*Caunyacoobja* (कान्यकुब्ज - kányakubja, San.). From (above + kubja, san. crooked); from canouj, the country of the hunch-backed girl. Bramins from Canouj, found in Madras town [jauty]. Speak hindee. Tall, athletic, but coarser in features than other bramins. Eat flesh; in other respects very strict in ceremonial observances, many enlist as sepoys.

CAPAULAM (कपाल - kapála, *San.*). From (ka, san. head + pál, san. to protect). Skull. Capauly is Shiva as wearing a garland of skulls.——*Caupaulica* (காபாலிக - kábáliga, Tam.). Caste-title. Followers of Bheiravau, a form of Shiva bearing a skull [jauty].

CAPE (كيپ - kep, *Hind.*). Prefix to articles from Cape Verde island or Cape of Good hope, chiefly latter.——*Cape aloes* (كيپ كا صبر - kepkásibr, Hind.). Same as Bombay aloes.——*Cape gooseberry* (مكاؤ - makáo, Hind.). Same as Indian winter cherry.——*Cape jasmine* (गन्धराज - gandharája, San.; گل چاندنی - gulichándní, Pers. and Hind.). San. from (gandha, san. fragrance + ráj, san. shining); from glossy foliage and fragrant flowers. Pers. from (gul, pers. rose + chándní, hind. moon-light). Title otherwise Wax-flower. Botanically Gardenia [gandharajah] florida, linn., rubiaceæ [vricsham, 71]. Glossy foliage, leaves obovate; large, cream-white, fragrant flowers having appearance of a small camellia.——*Cape merchant* (కొపుదారుడు - kópudárudu, Tel.). From (kópu, tel. mercantile house + dár, pers. holder). Old Anglo-indian by false analogy for Copedaur, a warehouse-keeper.——*Cape weed* (كيپ كي پاچي - kepkípáchi, Hind.). A dye lichen, the Roccella tinctoria [cull pausy], from Cape Verde islands.

CAPEMARRY (కేపుమారి - képumári, *Tel.*; கெப்புமாரி - képpumári, *Tam.*). From (képu, tel. offspring + mári, tam. one who barters). Kidnapper; rogue; term of abuse. Wandering pickpockets; especially N. arcot [cuttiry].

CAPER (كبر - kabar, *Ar.*). Title from arabic. Botanically the Capparis genus, capparideæ [vricsham, 11]. Trees or shrubs, erect, decumbent or climbing, unarmed or with stipulary thorns; leaves simple; flowers white or colored, often showy; fruit fleshy; seeds many imbedded in pulp. The species best known to the natives are shown below. Other S. indian species indigenous or naturalized are:—Divaricata; as shrub very narrow linear leaf, never flowers; as tree, leaves much broader; red flowers; wood for fuel. Diversifolia; flowers largish, purple rose-color. Erythrocarpus, giving fruit. Floribunda; flowers white. Grandiflora; low, thorny shrub, large handsome flowers. Heyneana; flowers white or pale-lilac. Moonii; large white or rosy flowers, resembling a tassel, from the abundant stamens. Pedunculosa; near point calimere in tanjore. Roxburghii; flowers large, white, slightly tinged with yellow; hedges and forests. Sepiaria; straggling, thorny shrub; flowers very showy; febrifuge; an excellent hedge plant; wood white, hard. Term also includes plants of Corallocarpus, Cephalandra, and Zehneria genera.——*Braminy kite caper* (कदम्ब - kadamba, San.; اذان الفيل - ázánulfíl, Ar.; لفا - lufá, Pers.; اكاس كدّه - ákásgaddah, Hind.; ركس كدّا - rakkasgaddá, Dec.; ಆಕಾಶಗರುಡ ಗಡ್ಡೆ - ákáshagarudagadde, Can.; ఆకాశగరుడ - ákáshagaruda, Tel.; കൊല്ലംകോവ - kollankóva, Mal.; ගොපලංගා - gopalangá, Singh.; கொல்லங்கோவை - kollangóvai, Tam.). Title as antidote to snake-bite, because the kite kills snakes. San. from (kad, san. to kill); from curing virtue [cadamba]. Ar. from (ázán, ar. ear + fíl, ar. elephant). Hind. from (ákás, hind. air + gaddah, hind. tuberous root). Dec. from (rakkas, hind. demon + gaddá, hind. root). Can. from (ákásha, san. sky + garuda, san. braminy kite + gadde, can. root). Tel. from (ákásha, san. sky + garuda, san. braminy kite); from roots living in air, without water, and antidote to snake-bite. Tam. from (kol, tam. to kill + kóvai, tam. cephalandra indica, naud.). Hind. also (kadam), from sanscrit; (rákasgaddah), meaning demon root; (garajphal), meaning thunder-fruit. Tel. also (ákáshagadda), meaning sky + root; (nágadonda), meaning snake + cephalandra indica, naud.; (murudonda), meaning beauty + cephalandra indica, naud. Tam. also (karudan), meaning braminy kite, as antidote to snake-bite. Cf. crow creeper. Title otherwise Air-living bryony, Demon root, Elephant ear, Naugadonda, Sky root, Snake caper. Botanically Corallocarpus epigæa; hook., cucurbitaceæ [vricsham, 62]. Alias Æchmandra epigæa; Bryonia epigæa, glabra. Climbing shrub; stem glabrous, often very flexuose at the joints; tendrils simple; leaves somewhat fleshy on longish petioles, cordate, usually three-lobed, densely covered on both sides with short bristly hairs; lobes rounded, the lateral ones the broadest, and slightly two-lobed, all remotely and slightly toothed; male flowers shortly racemose at the apex of a long thickish peduncle; calyx campanulate; females short peduncled, solitary, in the same or different axils from the males; flowers yellow; berry ovate, rostrate, glabrous, few-seeded; seeds white, compressed. Root lives in the air without water; root in shape like english garden turnip, more pointed at top; bitterish, mucilaginous, sub-acid taste; when dried, resembles calumba [q.v.] root. Root chiefly used as external application, with cummin seed [jeerah], onions [piyauz], and castor-oil, forming liniment for chronic rheumatism and contracted joints; also internally, anthelmintic and deobstruent, alterative and gently aperient; veidyans prescribe it internally in latter stages of dysentery and old venereal complaints; usually administered in powder, of a very pale color; an antidote for snake poison in mysore.——*Ceylon caper* (वाघंटी - vághantí, Mahr.; ತೊಟ್ಲಗಿಡ - totlagida, Can.; చిట్టిగార - chittigára, Tel.; துரத்திமரம் - turattimaram, Tam.). Mahr. means tiger-like; from curved thorns. Can. from (totlu, can. the vegetable + gida, can. plant) [rat aumanac]. Tel. from (chitti, tel. small + gára, tel. balanites roxburghii, planch.). Tam. from (turatti, tam. iron crook + maram, tam. tree); from crooked thorns. Tel. also (palleke); (pálaki). Tam. also (áthondai), meaning untouchable, from thorns [thorny caper]. Title otherwise Wagantee. Botanically Capparis [caper] zeylanica, linn., capparideæ [vricsham, 11]. Alias Capparis acuminata, brevispina, rheedii, rotundifolia, wallichiana, wightiana. Scrambling shrub; stem armed with yellow thorns in pairs at the leaves; flowers largish, the two upper petals tinged yellow; common on dry rocky ground; flowering end of cold season. Fruit, size of small pear. Green fruit used in pickles.——*Common caper* (करीर - karíra, San.; नेपती - népatí, Mahr.; كريركا پر - karerkáper, Hind.; كريل كا جهاڑ - karelkájhár, Dec.). San. from (krí, san. to hurt); a prickly plant. Dec. from sanscrit. Botanically Capparis [caper] aphylla, roth., capparideæ [vricsham, 11]. Alias Capparis sodada; Sodada decidua. Dense branching shrub; stipules thorny, nearly straight; leaves, on the young shoots only, linear-subulate, mucronate; flowers corymbose; corymbs nearly sessile, from the axils of the stipules; fruit globular, pointed. Top shoots and young leaves, made into a powder, used as a blister in native medicine. Fruit eaten. Common for fuel, burning with strong flame even when green; wood also durable, from its bitter qualities.——*Indian caper* (बिम्बिका - bimbiká, San.; तोंडली - tóndalí, Mahr.; तेंडे - téndlé, Conc.; كبر هند - kabarihind, Ar.; كبر هندى - kabarihindí, Pers.; كندورى كى بيل - kandúríkíbel, Hind. and Dec.; ತೊಂಡೆ - tonde, Can.; ಮನೋಲಿ - manóli, Too.; దొండ - donda, Tel.; കോവ - kóva, Mal.; කොවක්කා - kóvakká, Singh.; கோவை - kóvai, Tam.). San. from (bimba, san. ball); from oblong or conical berries. Mahr. from (tundikérí, san. the plant). Ar. from (kabar, ar. capparis spinosa, linn. + hind, ar. indian). Hind. from (kandúrí, hind. the fruit + bel, hind. creeper). Can. from (tonde, can. bloodsucker + balli, can. creeper); like teloogoo. Tel. from (tundikérí, san. cephalandra indica, naud.). Tam. from (kó, tam. to string as flowers). San. also (jívaka), meaning living, medicinal; (píluparní), meaning having leaves like careya arborea, roxb.; (kadalá), meaning small-leaved; (tundikérí), meaning resembling lips; (raktap'halá), meaning red fruit. Hind. also (talkhiyah), meaning bitter plant; (dandápandúkíbel), from teloogoo meaning fruit + tree; (bhimb), from sanscrit. Can. also (kondeballi), meaning shelter + creeper. Tel. also (kákidonda), meaning crow + plant so called [bitter snake-gourd]; (binká); (tiyyadonda), meaning sweet + the plant; (káyadonda), meaning fruit + the plant [rama's caper]. Mal. also (tonti), by corruption from canarese. Tam. also (nallukóvai), meaning good + the plant; (periyakkóvai), meaning large + the plant; (vimbam), meaning small ball. Title otherwise Covay, Indian coccinia, Jeevacam, Large-flowered bryony, Red bitter melon, Scarlet-fruited gourd, Telkacha. Giving Covay fruit. Botanically Cephalandra indica, naud., cucurbitaceæ [vricsham, 62]. Alias Bryonia grandis, moimoi; Coccinia indica; Cucurbita dioica; Momordica covel, monodelpha. Climbing shrub; diœcious white flowers; oblong bright scarlet edible fruit two inches in length; flowering throughout year; common in hedges. Juice of leaves applied to bites of all animals. Ripe fruit eaten raw; while green used in curries. Compare in other genera:—Clitoria ternatea (karudathondai), braminy kite caper; Bauhinia malabarica (pulladonda), sour caper; Echinops echinatus (vémadonda), neem caper; Rhynchocarpa fœtida (kunkumadonda), saffron caper; Trichosanthes palmata (kákidonda), crow caper; Zehneria umbellata (tiyyadonda), sweet caper. See gloss. paragraphs.——*Rayhola caper* (कवुंतेल - kavuntél, Mahr.; وگهوتى - vaghutti, Malay; రేగుట్టి - régutti, Tel.; வெள்ளைத்துரத்திமரம் - vellaitturattimaram, Tam.). Title corruption from teloogoo. Tel. from (rédu, tel. king + gutti, tel. cluster); from flower cluster; compare specific racemifera. Tam. from (vellai, tam. white + turatti, tam. iron crook + maram, tam. tree); properly applies to a curved thorny variety; wood is white. Tel. also (dudippi) [coomby]; (guli); (gullemu). Botanically Capparis [caper] grandis, linn. f., capparideæ [vricsham, 11]. Alias Capparis bisperma, maxima, obovata, racemifera. Shrub, or small tree, covered all over with greyish pubescence; stipules very short, and wart-like, wanting on the younger branches; leaves roundish-ovate, glabrous above, pubescent beneath; corymbs terminal, almost umbelliform, many-flowered; ovary and berry globose, the latter two-seeded; flowering in may; trunk thick; wood hard, heavy, and durable, much used.——*Rama's caper* (घोयंट - ghóyanta, Conc.; ಶೀದೊಂಡೆ - shídonde, Can.; ಶೀಪೆಮನೋಲಿ - shípemanóli, Too.; నేతిదొండ - nétidonda, Tel.; കരിവിവള്ളി - karivivalli, Mal.; இராமக்கோவை - irámakkóvai, Tam.). Title from dark color of plant. Can. from (shí, can. sweet + tondeballi, can. indian caper, cephalandra indica, naud.). Too. from (shípe, too. sweet + manóli, too. indian caper). Tel. from (neyyi, tel. ghee + donda, tel. indian caper). Mal. from (karivi, mal. waste land + valli, mal. creeper). Tam. from (ráma, san. proper name + kóvai, tam. indian caper). Tel. also (tiyyadonda), meaning sweet + the plant; (pótudonda), meaning male + the plant. Tam. also (kárkkóvai), meaning black + the plant. Title otherwise Rama covay. Botanically Zehneria umbellata, thw., cucurbitaceæ [vricsham, 62]. Alias Bryonia amplexicaulis, rheedii, sinuosa, theodonta, umbellata; Karivia amplexicaulis, umbellata; Momordica umbellata. Theodonta from teloogoo. Karivia from malayalam. Diœcious; root tuberous; stems glabrous; tendrils simple; leaves very short-petioled, cordate, or sagittate, hirsute at the base, from oblong and entire or roundish and angled to more or less deeply three to five-lobed or sometimes palmately five-partite, sinuate and sharply toothed, scabrous above, smoothish beneath, somewhat coriaceous; male flowers umbelled or shortly racemose at the apex of a long slender peduncle; pedicels with a small narrow-oblong bracteole about their middle; calyx campanulate; females on a different plant, solitary, short-peduncled; berry about the size of a pigeon's egg, oblong, slightly angled; seeds orbicular, surrounded with a warted zone; flowers small yellowish; common in hedges; flowering nearly all year; the ripe and unripe fruit, as well as the boiled roots, are eaten. No other common species here.——*Thorny caper* (हुङ्कार - hunkára, San.; गोविंदी - gövindí, Mahr.; اردندا - ardandá, Dec.; ఆదొండ - ádonda, Tel.; ଓସର୍ଵ - oserva, Oor.; වල්ලඟිරිය - vallangiriya, Singh.; ஆதொண்டை - áthondai, Tam.). San. means roaring. Mahr. from (góvinda, san. cow-protector, krishna); the fruit is said to cry out govinda in the mouth of the eater. Hind. from (árá, hind. cross + dandá, hind. bar); from plant being impenetrable. Tel. from tamul. Tam. from (á, tam. negative particle + todu, tam. to touch); from prickles. San. also (krakara), meaning producing the sound kra. Hind. also (ultákántá), meaning reversed thorn. Tel. also (doddichettu), meaning cattle pen + tree; (árudonda); by corruption from hindostany. Tam. also (káttotti), meaning fruit + hook. Title otherwise Cattle-pen plant. Botanically Capparis [caper] horrida, linn. f., capparideæ [vricsham, 11]. Alias Capparis quadriflora, terniflora, zeylanica. Extensively straggling thorny shrub; young leaves and shoots have a rich, chestnut colored tinge; large, white, tassel-formed flowers. Leaves applied medicinally as a counter-irritant; root-bark is sedative, stomachic and antihidrotic in decoction; substituted the leaves for dill [sowa] fruit; the root-bark for bismuthi subnitras and acid. hydrocyanic. dil. Fruit made into pickle. Hedge plant, being quite impenetrable. Wood yellowish-white, moderately hard; faint, wavy, concentric line of soft tissue.

CAPILEY (घटीयन्त्र - ghatíyantra, *San.*; موٹھ - moth, *Hind.*; ಕಪಿಲೆ - kapile, *Can.*; కపిలె - kapile, *Tel.*; കവല - kavala, *Mal.*;

கவலையேற்றம் - kavalaiyéttam, *Tam.*). San. from (ghata, san. pot + yantra, san. machine). Tam. from (kavalai, tam. earthern bucket + éttam, tam. picottah). A pulley sheave. It projects over the side of a well, and the water is raised in a large leathern bucket [yaittachaul], by a pair of bullocks that walk down a declivity. Generally the bullocks back up again without being detached. Where two pairs are available, they are detached, and walk round while the other pair draw down [mhote, picottah].

CAPOOK (کپوک - kapuk, *Malay*). Same as Silk-cotton tree.

CAPPER HILL (கேப்பர்மலை - kápparmalai, *Tam.*). From captain capper, who acquired the hill in 1796. Original name (vandippálaiyam), meaning cart + fortified village. Mountain; South arcot district, Cuddalore talook. A low plateau of laterite [q.v.]. In 1796 Captain Capper enclosed a piece of land on the hill and built a house there; no longer standing. In 1805 he transferred the property to Captain Fraser to whom a grant was given for it by Government. The property on reverting to Government was sold by auction to weavers. District jail now on the hill.

CAPPIAUR (കപ്പിയാർ - kappiyár, *Mal.*). From syriac. Sexton among Malabar syrian christians.

CAPSY (ಕೆಪಸಿ - kepasi, *Can.*). Botanically Debregeasia longifolia, wedd., urticaceæ [vricsham, 119]. Alias Conocephalus niveus; Debregeasia velutina; Missiessaya velutina; Morocarpus longifolius; Urtica longifolia. Small erect weak tree; fruit capitate yellow; common in western jungles to 7,000 feet; fishing lines made of bark; heart-wood reddish-brown, hard; sapwood white. No other common species here.

CAPY (कपि - kapi, *San.*). Brown.——*Capilan* (कपिल - kapila, San.). Founder of the Saunkhyam philosophy [darshanam, saunkhyam]. See vol. I (74). Perhaps nickname like Canaudan [q.v.]. Author of two works; viz., original Saunkhya sootrams, sometimes called Saunkhya pravachanam, comprising 526 aphorisms in six books; and a short work called Tatwa samausam or Compendium of principles [matam]. One of the forty-nine Madura professors [madura college].

CAR (کار - kár, *Pers.*). Work [caur].——*Caravan* (کاروان - kárwán, Hind.). From (above + ván, pers. suffix of possession). A string of travellers with beasts of burden [taundah].——*Caravansary* (کاروان سرائی - kárwánsarái, Hind.). From (above + sarái, pers. building). An inn.——*Carbaur* (کاروبار - károbár, Hind.). From (above + bár, pers. load). Business, affairs. Carbaury is a manager.——*Carcoon* (کارکن - kárkun, Hind.). From (above + kun, pers. doer). An inferior revenue officer in charge of a taraf, or division of a talook, corresponding to modern Revenue inspector. See vol. I, 112.

CAR (கரு - karu, *Tam.*). Black [calam, caulam, caur].——*Caraid* (కరేడు - karédu, Tel.). From (kari, tel. black + vídu, tel. town). Sanscrit by corruption (kharapurí), meaning kharan, the raucshasan + town. Village, Port; Nellore dist., Cundoocore tal.; pop. 3,574; acres 12,550; lat. 15° 11′; long. 80° 06′; from Cundoocore E. 10¾ miles; from Nellore N. 51 miles. Hardly any trade by sea now. Noted for betel gardens. Ancient temples of Caulahasteeshwara sawmy, Keshava sawmy, Veerabhadra sawmy. In braminical tradition Kharan brother-in-law of Ravanan was killed by Rama here. Noted for dyeing [shauyam] cloths. Large tank. Festival of Shiva in February.——*Carangooly* (கருங்குழி - karunguzhi, Tel. karunguli*). From (karumai, tam. blackness + kuzhi, tam. pit). Town; Chingleput dist., Madrantacam tal.; pop. 3,887; acres 1,205; lat. 12° 32′; long. 79° 57; from Madrantacam N.N.E. 2¼ miles; from Sydapett S.W. 39 miles; from the sea W. 18 miles. At the forty-eighth mile stone on the great southern trunk road from Madras. Former cusbah of talook of same name, which included roughly speaking eastern half of Madrantacam talook. On banks of channel in an old mango tope stands travellers' bungalow. Was head-quarters of collectorate until 1825, when removed to Conjeeveram. The fort was occupied during Anglo-french wars of the Carnatic [q.v.], being regarded as an outpost of Chingleput. These two places, with Wandiwash and Ootramallore, formed a quadrilateral on the line of attack between Madras and Pondicherry. As early as 1755 it was a point of dispute. In 1757 it was evacuated by English in the face of advancing French troops. The following year the English attempted to recover it by surprise, but were repulsed with loss; a failure which was repeated in 1759. A few months later Colonel Coote, after a few days' bombardment, captured the fort. This was the first decisive action in the successful campaign of 1759-60, which led to the victory of Wandiwash. During Hyder's invasion of the district in 1780, Carangooly, with other forts in the Carnatic, fell into his hands. On the 19th January 1781 it was captured by the English and thereafter remained in the undisturbed possession of the British. Its ramparts for some time formed a quarry for stones. The fortifications were destroyed in 1782. A Mahomedan mosque inside the fort is built of the materials of a Hindoo temple and contains a Chola inscription. On the hill behind the house are remains of two rude stone redoubts connected by a way protected by a stone wall. These are clearly native works. Trig. station in lat. 12° 32′ 09·05″; long. 79° 55′ 57·44″; height 412 feet; from Madrantacam N.N.E. 2 miles; from the sea W. 17 miles.——*Caratchy* (करकटल - karakatla, Mahr.; కరేపు - karipe, Tel.; എഴുത്തുകോര - ezhuttamkóra, Mal.; கரச்சி - karaççi, Tam.). Title from tamul. Tel. from (kari, tel. black). Mal. from (ezhuttam, mal. painted + kórá, mal. polynemus indicus). Tam. from (karumai, tam. blackness). Pristipoma [caripey] maculatum, percidæ [panayairy], acanthopterygii, teleostei [matsyam, 1], of naturalists [jantoo]. Alias Anthias maculatus; Lutjanus maculatus; Perca caripe; Pristipoma caripa. Caripe, caripa from teloogoo. Scales in oblique rows above lateral-line and horizontal below; greyish, becoming white beneath, and having purplish tinge about head; blackish band over snout; second from occiput touches posterior edge of orbit, and descends over opercles; vertical black band, about eight scales wide, passes over nape and terminates about three scales below lateral-line; posterior to this are six black blotches, three or four above, and two or three below lateral-line, not forming bands, but placed like squares on chess board. Spinous dorsal with large black mark between fourth and seventh or even eighth spines; soft dorsal with dark band along centre, both dorsals with edges stained black, as is also the caudal. Sea; 16 inches.——*Caricaulan* (கரிக்காலன் - karikkálan, Tam.). Means black-legged. Chola king, who invaded Ceylon. See vol. I (126) [charitram].——*Caricauttah* (கரிக்காத்தாள் - karikkáttál, Tam.). From (above + ká, tam. to protect). Epithet of cauly, the black deity. A name of the village goddess [ancaulamman].——*Carimaraly* (கரிமரலி - karimarali, Tam.). From (above + marali, tam. yama). Black death. Hindoo 2nd or pers. name [peyar].——*Carimbadam* (കരിമ്പടം - karimpatam, Mal.). From (above + pata, san. cloth). A cumbly.——*Caripey* (కరేపు - karipe, Tel.). The genus Pristipoma, percidæ [panayairy], acanthopterygii, teleostei, pisces [matsyam, 1], of naturalists [jantoo]. Moderate as food; air-bladder gives isinglass. The species best known to the natives are:— furcatum [pyckeely], hasta [caukkan], maculatum [caratchy].——*Carippauly* (കരിപ്പാലി - karippáli, Mal.). From (above + pál, mal. milk); juicy rice with black husk. A Malabar paddy. There are the usual dark and white varieties, from color of ear growing. Also a hill variety [paddy].——*Carisal* (கரிசல் - karisal, Tam.). Blackness. Carisal caud is cotton soil [regar].——*Cariya* (கரிய - kariya, Tam.). Black. Prefix in place names, as in Cariyamungalam, meaning the prosperous village with dark soil.——*Cariya bolam* (கரியபோளம் - kariyabólam, Tam.). Black aloes [aloes].——*Cariyan* (கரியன் - kariyan, Tam.). Means black man. Pariah proper name. Carooppan is the same; and Carooppy is female [peyar].——*Cariyavan* (கரியவன் - kariyavan, Tam.). Vishnoo, the black.——*Carnatic* (कर्णाटक - karnátaka, San.; کرناٹک - karnátik, Hind.; ಕರ್ಣಾಟಕ - karnátaka, Can.; కర్ణాటక - karnátaka, Tel.; கர்நாடகம் - karnádagam, Tam.). From (kár, tam. black + nádu, tam. country). In allusion to the black regady [regar] soil. The term is found in Varauha mihiran. There are other black countries in this sense; tracts of black soil being found scattered throughout the valley of the Kistna, and occupying the lower plains and flats of Coimbatore, Salem, Madura, Tanjore, Ramnaud and Tinnevelly.—" *a* " The Carnatic proper may be defined as bounded:—to the south by the plateau of Mysore; to the east by a line passing through Nundidroog, Penoocondah, Adony, Ryechore, and Goolburga to Beedar, its most northern point; to the north by an irregular line passing from Beedar by Calyaun, Sholapore, Punderpoor, and Kolhapore to Gheriah, or Viziadroog, on the sea. The whole tract is comprised between latitude 12° and 18°, and longitude 73½° and 77½°, forming an area of about 115,000 square miles and containing at present from ten to twelve millions of inhabitants. The most ancient history is almost unknown. The country was probably divided between princes of the Chera and Cadamba families. The Chalookya family of Calyaun, the Yaudava princes of Chundragherry, and the Ganapaty princes of Warangal had probably small portions. About the tenth century the country fell into the hands of the Cholas. About the middle of the eleventh century the family of the Ballaula appears to have arisen. The Vijianugger dynasty, which came into power about 1336 and survived till 1565, conquered the whole of the Peninsula south of the Toongabudra river. They were completely overthrown by the Mahomedans in 1565, and retired first to Penoocondah, and then to Chundragherry, one branch of the family settling at Anagoondy.—" *b* " The Nawaubs of Arcot, were known as Nawaubs of the Carnautaca payeen ghaut, or that adjunct to the Carnatic proper which lay below ghauts. But the English in error dropped the distinctive term Payeen ghaut [q.v.] and applied the unmeaning term Carnatic to the whole country below the ghauts on the eastern side of the Peninsula. By just the same error the term Canara [q.v.] was extended to the country below the Western ghauts. The English carnatic was divided into Southern, Central and Northern. The first is the country S. of Coleroon; comprising Poodoocottah, Tinnevelly, Madura, part of Trichinopoly, and Tanjore. Central carnatic is the country between Coleroon and Pennair comprising the larger portion of Trichinopoly, the whole of North and South arcot, Chingleput and a section of Nellore. Northern carnatic was limited by the Pennair on one extremity, and Guntoor on the other, including within it the remainder of Nellore. The English carnatic extended from lat. 8° 10′ to lat. 16°, and from the sea on the east to long. 77° 20′ on the west. See vol. I (176).—"c" In 1801 the title of Nawaub of the Carnatic became nominal, the British Government obtaining all actual power. The last Nawaub dying in 1855 without heirs, the titular dignity expired. See vol. I, 43 [charitram].——*Carnautacam* (कर्णाटक - karnátaka, San.). Otherwise Carnautam. Old name for the Canarese people; the inhabitants of the proper Carnatic.——*Carnautaca rajakkal* (கருணாடகராசாக்கள் - karunádagarásákkal, Tam.). From (karnátaka, san. the country + rájá, san. king). Modern work. A Savistaura charitram, or general history being original history of peninsula, and the only one of its kind. Author Narayanan of the Ananta kone or poligar race of Jinjee. Composed while Lord W. Bentinck was Governor of Madras. It embraces period from commencement of Kalyoog corresponding with installation of Parichit, son of Abhimanyan and grandson of Arjoonan, down to Kalyoog 4908, being Acshayam year of the Hindoo cycle; era of Vicramadityan 1864, Shalivahana saca 1729, A.D. 1807-8. The first caundam, on primeval matters. The Bramhaundam, or mundane egg; the greater and lesser periods; periodical deluge; Avatars of Vishnoo; birth of Krishnan, about 100 years before end of Dwaupar yoog, and his building Dwarca, on sea coast, and reigning there. Second caundam deals with royal line of Hastinapooram. Accounts of Pandavas, and other persons, similar to Mahabhaurat. A long lapse of time given to the descendants; Vicramadityan conquered and ended that race. Kalyoog 3700 is fixed as commencement of Hijra. Hindoo kings ruled 591 years after that period. Rise of Mahomedan ascendancy. Third caundam. Account of Vilauyet or original country of the Mahomedans. Rise of Mahomed. Invasion of Delhi from Persia. Extension of irruption into Deccan. Plunder of Carnautacam country, extending to Seringapatam. Ramaunoojan was then at Seringapatam. Another invasion in the year of the Hijra 622. Fourth caundam on Delhi affairs. Fifth caundam gives account of Timur, Acbar, Jehaungeer. Aurungzeeb sent Zoolfacar khan to conquer the Carnatic; fought with the Mahrattas, took Jinjee. Davood shah made Killadar of Jinjee. Sixth caundam concerning Mahrattas, and Tooloovam country, and upper Carnautaca desham. A shepherd of the Coorumba tribe discovered treasure, raised troops, and laid the foundation of Anagoondy, and afterwards of Vijianugger. He was named Pravada deva royel. Seventh caundam on the Hassan dynasty of the Deccan kingdom. Eighth caundam concerning lower Carnautacam country. Ascendancy gained by the Sheivas. Notice of Tamul poets; Cumban, Poogazhendy, Ottacoottan. Cumban composed his poetical version of the Ramayanam in Shal. Sac. 807. Notice of some Chola kings. Veishnava teacher Ramaunoojan flourished Shal. Sac. 939. Tribhoovana chuckravurty became Soondra paundy tevar, Fusly 460. Veera paundya cholan was his son. Ramaunoojan lived in his time. Notice of first inroad made by Mahomedans into Carnatic. Many details concerning Ramaunoojan. Caricara cholan flourished 570 Fusly. Villipoottooran, a poet in the Congoo desham, translated Mahabhaurat into Tamul verse, at promised reward of five gold hoons [q.v.] each stanza on his task being finished, king gave him only five fanams [q.v.] each stanza. Origin of Jinjee. A treasure was discovered by one Ananta kone, a shepherd, who raised troops therewith; and getting aid from other chiefs, established himself as a rajah, Jinjee being his capital; this was Fusly 600. He cut a canal for irrigation near Trinomallee, which in the course of time having become filled up, was restored by Nawaub wallajah, Fusly 1184. Ananta kone gave to his tribe the name of Shamanar. He was succeeded by Krishna kone, Fusly 650 and Conairy kone, Fusly 680 both of them built sacred edifices. His son was Govinda kone Fusly 700. Pulliya kone, Fusly 720, made roads, choultries, &c. The dynasty now gave way before a Coorumba tribe named Vadooga yiday or north country shepherds. The first king of this tribe was Gopy lingan, Fusly 740. He built a brick fort at Shendamungalam. He formed some tanks, and left others unfinished. In his time, his feudatories built several forts with bricks in different places, as Aspore, Pelagooppore, Cooppamgolore, &c. He formed channels to bring down streams for irrigation from mountain-springs; among which the one named Gopy lingan shoonay remains to this day. He ruled with great equity. Afterwards, Fusly 800, Narsinga wodeyar became viceroy. The Maha royer of Anagoondy, Vijianugger, and Penoocondah sent an army against the aforesaid Gopy lingan, and having conquered the country he delivered it over to Narsinga wodeyar, to be held sending tribute to the royer. About this time the rajah of Wandiwash named Bhoopaty roya wodeyar ruled according to an inscription dated in Shal. Sac. 1341. Veera vijaya royer was also a ruler over that district. Vellaula royer ruled Fusly 750. He made additions to the shrine at Trinomallee. He paid tribute to the royer. After he fell the country being divided among petty chiefs. The royer sent an army into the Carnatic, which consisted of 100,000 men under command of Veiyyappa naick, Toopauky krishnappa naick, Vijaya raghavanaickar, and Vencatappa naickar. In Fusly 870, Veiyyappa naick came and collected tribute extensively. He encamped near Vellore. The chief at Chittore, and other chiefs of the Tondaimundalam, had an interview with him. He fixed their rate of tribute. Mention is made among others of Bomma reddy of Calastry. The royer's general afterwards went to Jinjee. The chiefs of the Chola mundalam had an interview with him, and their tribute was also settled. Veiyyappa naick continued at Jinjee with his army. He gave it in charge to the subordinate generals to go and levy tribute on the Paundyam, Cholam and Cheram kingdoms. In Tanjore, Trichinopoly, Madura and Tirnagary, the kings respectfully answered to the demand. Thus the eastern Carnautacam, as distinguished from Mysore, &c., became subject to the royer. He derived three crores of rupees from this country, and in consequence he divided the whole into three parts, under three viceroys. Krishnappa naick at Jinjee governed the country from Nellore to Coleroon, Vijayaraghavan at Tanjore governed the fertile country washed by the Cauvery river, and to Vencatappa naickar was assigned the country south of the latter. Notices follow of the proceedings of these viceroys. A Mahomedan coalition was formed against the royer. The principal viceroy of the latter was recalled, with his troops; and Toopauky naick thenceforward assumed independency at Jinjee. His successors with their dates and proceedings are mentioned. The last of them Appa naickar is described as weak and vicious to an extreme. He came to the throne, Fusly 1030, and in his time a Mahomedan confederacy, the formation of which is ascribed to the treachery of Bomma rajah of Chingleput, brought a deluge of Mahomedan troops into the lower Carnatic. The siege of Jinjee, and its capture, after great resistance are described with considerable force and spirit, and at much length, as the author is writing about his native place. The proceedings of Vijayaraghavan at Tanjore are also alluded to; he purchased peace. Trimal naickar of Madura by the assistance of the Cullar routed and repelled the Mahomedans, who returned discomfited to Jinjee. Irruption of the Mahrattas into the country, seizure of Tanjore, tribute imposed by them on other places. Proceedings of Shivajee in the lower Carnatic. Arrival of the English at Chennaputnam. Notice of other Europeans. From this time forwards, there is a minute and generally correct detail of the proceedings of the English and French in connexion with the Nawaub on the one part, and Chundah sahib, &c., on the other part. The French capture of Jinjee is circumstantially stated. The whole of the connected and subsequent transactions are interwoven with details as to motives on the part of native princes, little known to English historians. Hyder ally and Tippoo's proceedings are fully described, and the narrative closes practically with final capture of Seringapatam and its celebration at Madras [charitram].——*Carnautam* (कर्णाट - karnáta, San.). From (karu, tam. black + nádu, tam. country). The Carnatic.——*Carnautighur* (கருநாடகக்கிரி - karunádagakkiri, Tam.). From (karnátaka, san. the country so called + giri, san. hill). Hill; North arcot district, Polore talook. Strong hill fort, on a spur of the Jawaudies which terminates in a huge rock on which citadel is built. Improved by Mahrattas. Citadel separated from the rest of fort by narrow neck of rock 50 yards broad. A few ruined buildings. Trig. station in lat. 12° 34′ 45·28″; long. 79° 07′ 03·62″; height 3,124 feet; from Polore N.W. 5¾ miles; from Pottaray W.N.W. 2¾ miles.——*Caroo* (काल - kálá, San.; كالا - kála, Hind.; ಕರಿ - kari, Can.; నల్ల - nalla, Tel.; കറു - karu, Mal.; கரி - kari, Tam.). Black. In the different languages plant first term joining two genera. Ex., where transl. is of second term:—Albizzia amara (nallarégu), zizyphus jujuba; Albizzia odoratissima (karintakara), cassia tora; Andrographis paniculata (karivému), melia azadirachta; Anisomeles malabarica (karintumba), leucas indica; Aristida depressa (nallaputiki), grewia salvifolia; Averrhoa bilimbi (kariçcakka), artocarpus integrifolia; Cajanus indicus (kariuddugida), phaseolus mungo, var. radiatus; Cassia absus (karinkollu), dolichos biflorus; Cassia pumila (nallajiluga), æschynomene aspera; Clerodendron inerme (nalla-uppi), capparis sepiaria; Clitoria ternatea (kálízír), cuminum cyminum; Curculigo orchioides (kálímúslí), asparagopsis sarmentosa; Curculigo orchioides (nallatádi), borassus flabelliformis; Dalbergia latifolia (karumduvarai), diospyros embryopteris; Eugenia jambolana (kálájám), psidium guyava; Garuga pinnata (karuvémbu), melia azadirachta; Guizotia abyssynica (kálítil), sesamum indicum; Hymenodictyon excelsum (kálábachnág), aconitum ferox; Indigofera echinata (karuneruñjil), tribulus terrestris; Ipomæa obscura (nallakokkita), argyreia speciosa; Justicia gendarussa (kálíshambálí), vitex negundo; Justicia gendarussa (karinekki), vitex negundo; Linum usitatissimum (nallaagisi), sesbania grandiflora; Maba buxifolia (nallamaddi), terminalia arjuna; Manisuris granularis (nallaponuku), gyrocarpus jacquini; Miliusa velutina (nalladuddugu), polyalthia cerasoides; Monochoria vaginalis (karinkuvalayam), nymphæa; Ormocarpum sennoides (nallakáshana), bauhinia acuminata; Ougenia dalbergioides (kálápalasa), butea frondosa; Picrorhiza kurrooa (kálíkutkí), helleborus niger; Pongamia glabra (karunduvarai), cajanus indicus; Pterocarpus marsupium (karintakara), cassia tora; Rhynchosia cyanosperma (nallagurigindza), abrus precatorius; Shorea robusta (nallamaddi), terminalia arjuna; Shorea talura (karimarutu), terminalia; Sonchus arvensis (nallatapeta), asystasia coromandeliana; Vernonia anthelmintica (kálájíre), cuminum cyminum; Zanthoxylum rhetsa (karimurikku), erythrina indica. See gloss. paragraphs.——*Caroomaun* (கருமான் - karumán, Tam.). From (karumai, tam. blackness). Same as Collan. Can. cummara, Tel. cummary. Blacksmith or ironsmith, who makes and repairs all ironwork for the village [jauty].——*Caroongauly* (கருங்காலி - karungáli, Tam.). From (káli, tam. the deity). Black cauly or Doorga.——*Carooppan* (கறுப்பன் - karuppan, Tam.). Otherwise (pathinettámbadik-karuppan), meaning eighteen steps + carooppan, the deity; as worshipped when cauvery rises eighteen steps on river ghaut. A ferocious village deity.——*Carootawauv* (കറുത്തവാവ് - karuttavávu, Mal.). From (karutta, mal. dark + vávu, mal. moon's change). New moon [amavausyay].——*Caroo vaimboo* (கருவேம்பு - karuvémbu, Tam.). From (above + vémbu, tam. margosa tree, melia azadirachta, linn.); from leaf darker than margosa. Botanically the Murraya genus, rutaceæ [vricsbam, 32]. Trees or shrubs without spines, having pinnate leaves, and terminal many flowered cymose inflorescence; the fruit is succulent. The species best known to the natives are:—exotica [foreign conjy], kœnigii [curry-leaf tree].——*Carvanore* (കരുവന്നൂർ - karuvannúr, Mal.). From (karuván, mal. a blacksmith + úr, mal. village). River; Cochin state, between Trichore and Moocoondapooram talook. Rises in Combalcherry hill, the British-Cochin boundary, and passes between 10° 10′ and 10° 25′ through Moocoondapooram and Trichore, and falls into the Cranganore backwater. Total length about 50 miles. Does not run during February, March and April, the hot months. Navigable for ordinary boats up to Poothoocand. Crossed by two bridges; the Carvanore bridge ten miles south of Trichore, and Manaly bridge six miles south-east of Trichore.——*Cary* (കരി - kari, Mal.; கரி - kari, Tam.). Black. Prefix in place names, as Carimpoya, meaning the dark-colored river.

CARACAL (वनबिडाल - vanabidála, *San.*; سیاہ گوش - siyáhgosh, *Pers.* and *Hind.*; ಶಿವಂಗಿ - shivangi, *Can.*; శివంగి - shivangi, *Tel.*; ചിവിഞ്ഞി - chivinni, *Mal.*; சிவிங்கி - shivingi, *Tam.*). Title from turkish, meaning black-eared; distinguish from kerkal, the leopard. San. from (vana, san. wild + bidála, san. cat). Pers. from (siyáh, pers. black + gosh, pers. ear). Title otherwise Indian lynx, Siyahgosh. Felis [marjauram] caracal, felidæ [deeptaucsham], digitigrada, carnivora, mammalia [sastanam, 9], of naturalists [jantoo]. General color unspotted vinous brown or bright fulvous brown; paler beneath, almost white in many; tail concolorous with the body, tapering, with the tip black; lower parts with some obscure spots, at times distinct, on the belly, flanks and inside of limbs; ears black externally, white within, a long dark ear-tuft; a black spot where the moustaches grow, and another above the eye, also a line down each side of the nose. The Caracal has the long limbs, ears, skull and dentition of a true lynx, but the cheeks are not whiskered, as is the case with the lynx. The Caracal is easily tamed, and is trained to catch birds, hares, etc.

CARAFT (قرابہ - karábah, *Hind.*). From (karabah, ar. water-bag), stitched on one side. Jar [carboy].

CARAM (कर - kara, *San.*). Hand.——*Caraulam* (कराल - karála, San.). Terrible. Carauly is Parvaty.——*Cary* (करी - karí, *San.*). From (kara, san. hand); having a trunk. Elephant [q.v.].——*Caryvauhanan* (करिवाहन - kariváhana, San.). From above + váhana, san. vehicle). Indran who has the elephant for his vehicle.

CARAMBAY (கரம்பை - karambai, *Tam.*). Sterile ground, suffix in place names. Anaudy carambay is immemorial waste.——*Carambacoody* (கரம்பக்குடி - karambakkudi, Tam.). From (above + kudi, tam. village). Village, Head-quarters of Deputy tahsildar; Trichinopoly dist., Poodoocottah state; pop. 2,842; lat. 10° 27′; long. 79° 11′; from Poodoocottah E.N.E. 23 miles; from Trichinopoly S.E. 40 miles. On road to Puttoocottah. Two extensive gardens belonging to the State. The ancestral home of Tondiman rulers. Temple to Carooppan. Fair on Wednesday. Mats, coarse cloths, and bell-metal [cunts] vessels manufactured. Once an important place.

CARAMBOLA (करंबेळ - karambéla, *Mahr.*). Corruption of (karmaranga, san. food appetizer, the fruit). Same as Coromandel gooseberry [q.v.].

CARANAM (करण - karana, *San.*). From (kri, san. to do).—"*a*" Bond [pramaunam]. Specifically in Malabar the title-deed by which land is transferred or acquired under the Jenm system of land tenure. The six kinds of Caranams culminating in acquired Jenm are according to old book authorities:—Cooyicaunom, Caunom, Otty, Otticoompooram, Coodimaneer or neermoothal or jenmpanayam, and Neerattipair or full jenm. The first is a sort of cowle [q.v.] for reclaiming waste land and contains slight proprietorship. The second is a lease. The third Otty, is really mortgage. The fourth and fifth are cases where the mortgagor has less and less rights. The sixth is complete transfer of jenm. According to some authorities, between Otty and Otticoompooram there is another Keividotty. By a peculiar Malabar inversion the deeds are called Caranam-attipair, not Attipair caranam; and so on. For a sketch of the modern aspects of the whole question of land transferred, see vol. II, 104. The transactions are there viewed from the point of view of the tenant as merely in succession Veroompanttom or plain lease, Caunom or quasi-mortgage, Otty or real mortgage, and Neerattipair or sale of jenm.—"*b*" The proper form of Curnum [q.v.].—"*c*" An astrological element importing the time during which the moon's motion from the sun amounts to 6°, and being half of an astrological Tity [caulam, 4]. The moon's synodical revolution is divided into eleven Caranams, seven of which are ordinary and movable, called Charam; and four extraordinary and fixed, called Stiram. The following are the caranams:—Bavam, Baulavam, Cowlavam, Teitilam, Garam, Vanikk, Bhadram, Shacoony, Chatooshpadam, Naugavam, Kimstooghnam. The last four are the fixed. The first caranam begins when the moon is 6° from the sun; and the seven movable ones being eight times repeated in successive order, include 342°. The moon's synodical orbit [cacsham] being considered as divided into 360°, there remains 18° which she wants to complete her revolution [bhaganam]; and these are allotted to the eighth, ninth and tenth caranams; but the first six degrees [bhaugam] after the conjunction belong to the eleventh or last. Punchaungams [q.v.] give ending of each caranam [jyotisham].——*Caranappiya* (കരണപ്പിഴ - karanappizha, Mal.). From (above + pizha, mal. fine). A fine for having executed documents on an unstamped or insufficiently stamped leaf or paper.

CARAT (قیراط - kírát, *Hind.*). From arabic through greek. A bean of the κερατεία, carob tree, Ceratonia siliqua, l. For gold, the twenty-fourth part of any alloy. For diamonds [vajram] a fixed weight of $3\frac{1}{6}$ troy grains, divided into 4 carat grains and further sub-divisions. Cf. Retty.

CARAUR (قرار - karár, *Hind.*; కరారు - kararu, *Tel.*; கரார் - karár, *Tam.*). From (karra, ar. to settle). An agreement. Caraur nauma is an agreement deed [oodambadikay].

CARAWAY (सुषवी - sushaví, *San.*; विलायतीजिरे - viláyatíjiré, *Mahr.*; كروية - karwiyah, *Ar.*; زیرهٔ ارمنی - zírahiarmaní, *Pers.*; ولایتی زیرہ کا پیڑ - viláitízírahkáper, *Hind.*; ولایتی زیرہ کا جہاڑ - viláitízírahkájhár, *Dec.*; ಸೋಪುಗಿಡ - sópugida, *Can.*; సీమసోపు - símasópu, *Tel.*; රටදුරු - rataduru, *Singh.*; சீமைச்சோம்பு - shímaiççómbu, *Tam.*). Title directly from arabic, indirectly from the country caria. San. from (su, san. well + su, san. to beget); curative [black jeerah, carolah]. Mahr. from hindostany. Pers. from (zírah, pers. cumin seed, cuminum cyminum, linn. + armaní, pers. armenian). Hind. from (viláití, hind. foreign + zírah, pers. cumin seed + per, hind. tree). Can. from (sópu, can. caraway seed + gida, can. plant). Tel. from (síma, tel. foreign + sópu, tel. anise seed). Singh. from (rata, singh. foreign + duru, singh. cuminum cyminum, linn.). Tam. from (shímai, tam. foreign + shómbu, tam. anise seed, pimpinella anisum, linn.). Ar. also (kamúniarmaní), meaning armenian cumin; (kamúnirúmí), meaning turkish cumin. Pers. also (zírahirúmí), meaning turkish cumin; (zírahisiyáh), meaning black cumin. Tel. also (kékuvittulachettu), meaning cake seed plant. Tam. also (kékkuvirai), meaning cake seed, from use [tootty]. Greek κάρος, Latin careum, from Caria the country of the plant. Title otherwise Andalusian caraway, Armenian cumin, Black cumin, Cake seed, Foreign anise, Foreign cumin, Mountain cumin, Persian caraway, Roman cumin, Turkish cumin. Botanically Carum [ajmood] carui, linn., umbelliferæ [vricsham, 67]. Specific name from arabic. An erect plant not unlike a carrot [gaujar]; flowers small, whitish; not cultivated here, and introduced at a not very early date. Gives to pharm. dried fruit, carui fructus, active principle, a volatile oil; preparations, oleum carui, aqua carui; officinal; stomachic and carminative; an ingredient in many prescriptions. Seed is used parched and powdered to flavor curries, or raw and entire to put into cakes; also in flavoring drinks. The oil is used for scenting soap [sauboon]. For cumin see Jeerah.

CARAWILLA (کوریالا - kauriyálá, *Hind.*; سنپولادارسانپ - sampoládársámp, *Dec.*; ರಕ್ತಕನ್ನಾಡೆ - raktakannáde, *Can.*; කරවලා - karavalá, *Singh.*). Title and hindostany from singhalese. Dec. from (sampolá, hind. zigzag + sámp, hind. snake). Can. from (rakta, can. blood + kannu, can. eye + ádu, can. to play). Hypnale nepa, crotalidæ [pit piper], ophidii viperiformes, ophidia [sarpam], reptilia [sarpy, 29], of naturalists [jantoo]. The genus Hypnale has only this species. Alias Coluber nepa; Cophias hypnale; Hypnale carawala; Trigonocephalus hypnale, zara. Found in Malabar, on the Anamullays and in Ceylon. The largest size is 19 inches, the tail accounting for two and a half inches. Head broad, triangular; snout covered with numerous small shields above, the crown of the head being normally shielded. Body of moderate length, with keeled scales in seventeen rows. Tail rather short, not prehensile, terminating in a short cervical scale. Brown or grey, or reddish olive, with a double dorsal series of brown or black spots; the spots of both sides sometimes confluent into cross-bands. Sides and belly finely marbled and dotted with brown or black. Upper lip brown or black, well marked by a darker line running from behind the eye to the angle of the mouth; a more or less distinct white or whitish temporal streak above the dark line, sometimes continued along the side of the neck, with an interrupted brown band above and below it. Chin and throat blackish and brownish variegated with yellow or grey. Sometimes specimens occur of a more uniform coloration; the dorsal spots on each side of the throat are the most constant markings, as described. The carawilla is much dreaded, although its bite is but exceptionally fatal to man, and in such cases death does not occur before the lapse of some days.

CARAY (కర - kara, *Tel.*; கரை - karai, *Tam.*). From (karai, tam. to be dissolved). The natural shore of a sea, river, tank, &c. [cara]. Several portions of the Tinnevelly coast are called Caraychoott, the coast circuit; whilst a caste of fishermen farther north are called Caraiyaur, coast people. The last portion of two names of places mentioned by Ptolemy represents the Tamul, viz., καλαικαρίας and περιγκαρεῖ. If the latter word had been written περυγκαρεῖ, it would have been perfectly accurate Tamul, letter for letter, for great shore. In the Cauvery channels the riparian villages are divided into Carays for the supply of labor to maintain Coramboos [q.v.]. In the Balaghaut [q.v.] talooks of Salem district a Caray is a curnum's and moonsif's charge. Also merely a portion of land, especially a share in a Mirassy [q.v.]. So freehold or private property. See vol. I, 112. Also suffix in place names, especially in southern districts. As Ootancaray, meaning water spring + bank; Tencaray, meaning south + bank [garay]. Compare Anay, artificial bank.——*Aroothy caray* (அறுதிக்கரை - aruthikkarai, Tam.). From (aruthi, tam. decisive + above). Permanent shareholders in a village. Cf. mirassidar and pasuncaray.——*Cara* (കര - kara, Mal.; కర - kara, Tel.). Bank. Malabar houses are generally built round a tract of paddy land, and according to their bearings, are named Vadakkara, northern bank; Tekkara, southern bank, and so forth. Hence cara comes to mean hamlet, parish. The caras have no separate boundaries and no distinct names, but are comprehended in the deshom [q.v.]. They formerly contained husbandmen subordinate to the Deshavaūly in military matters, and to the Tarwaud carnaven in civil matters. See vol. I, 112.——*Caraicauran* (கரைக்காரன் - karaikkáran, Tam.). From (above + káran, tam. possessor). Officer in charge of a caray: same as Caraidar, but with a Tamul instead of a Hindostany termination.——*Caraicutt* (கரைக்கட்டு - karaikkattu, Tam.). From (above + kattu, tam. protection). A buttress for strengthening a bank [bund].——*Caraidar* (கரைதாரன் - karaitháran, Tam.). From (above + dár, hind. agent). Monigar.——*Caraiyaulan* (கரையாளன் - karaiyálan, Tam.). Means landlord. Tribal title of Yidayar [peyar].——*Caraiyaur* (கரையான் - karaiyán, pers. sing.; கரையார் - karaiyár, pers. pl., Tam.). Caste-title. The καρέοι of Ptolemy. Division of the Shembadavar or fishermen. Numbers about 7,000.——*Caramana* (കരമന - karamana, Mal.). From (above + mana, mal. house). Meaning houses on the bank. Sanscrit name (kharávása), meaning kharan's abode. River; Travancore state, Trivandrum division, Nedoovengaud, Neittincara and Trivandrum talooks. Rises in the north-western slopes of Agastya cootam. After a winding irregular course, westerly at its rise, then southerly and lastly south-westerly it discharges itself into the sea at a small headland, termed Covalam, three miles from Poondora. It receives the Kiliyaur about three miles from the sea. Length, 41 miles. Confined by high and steep banks for the greater part of its course. Bed is rocky and narrow. Navigable for boats for about ten miles inland. During the rains rafts are floated down upon it from a great distance. Trivandrum and a large Bramin village are situated on its bank. Crossed by a strong stone bridge at the village from whence it takes its name. The Caramana bramin village is in lat. 8° 27′; long. 77° 01′; from Trivandrum S.E. 2¼ miles; from the sea E. 3 miles.——*Caravepp* (കരവെപ്പു - karaveppu, Mal.). From (above + veppu, mal. planting). Plantation on elevated ground, in contradistinction to Auttvepp [q.v.] on low ground.——*Caraypottanaur* (கரைப்பொட்டானாறு - karaippottánáru, Tam.). From (karai, tam. boundary + podu, tam. to form + áru, tam. river). River that marked the boundary between Chera, Chola and Paundya kingdoms. River; Trichinopoly district, Moosiry talook. Flows through Cautpoottore mittah and several villages in extreme W. of talook, falling into Cauvery at Sheelapillapoottore, 12 miles W. of Moosiry. An embankment carries the boundary from the river southwards [carvauttaur].

CARBOY (قرابه - karábah, *Hind.*). Leather water jar [caraft].

CARCAM (कर्क - karka, *San.*). From (krí, san. to injure). A crab [raushy].——*Carcasham* (కర్కశము - karkashamu, Tel.). Literally rough. A dispute. Carcashabhoomy is a field, the boundary, &c., of which is in dispute or under litigation.——*Carcatacam* (कर्कटक - karkataka, San.). Fourth solar month [mausam] when the sun is in cancer the fourth sign [raushy].——*Carcata shringy* (कर्कटशृङ्गी - karkatashringí, San.). Crab or scorpion + horn. From appearance of galls. Plant name common to Pistacia integerrima, Rhus succedanea, Terminalia chebula; see gloss. paragraphs.

CARCAUROO (कर्कारु - karkáru, *San.*). Means white. Title otherwise Gourd, Pumpkin, Squash. Botanically the Cucurbita genus, cucurbitaceæ [vricsham, 62]. Large climbing herbs, hispid or hairy; leaves stalked, cordate, ovate, five-angular or lobed; flowers solitary, yellow, very large; fruit fleshy, indehiscent, often large; seeds ovoid or oblong, compressed, margined or not. The species best known to the natives are shown below. For melons and cucumbers see Oorvauroo; for water-melons see Indravully; for white pumpkin see Wax gourd. See also:—Adansonia digitata, ethiopian sour gourd; Benincasa cerifera, wax gourd; Cephalandra indica, scarlet fruited gourd; Citrullus colocynthis, bitter gourd; Lagenaria vulgaris, bottle gourd; Luffa ægyptiaca, washing gourd; Trichosanthes anguina, club gourd. See gloss. paragraphs.——*Common pumpkin* (कूष्माण्ड - kúshmánda, San.; कोहळा - kóhala, Mahr.; مجدبه - majdabah, Ar. and Pers.; کدیما - kudímah, Hind.; پیٹھہ - pethah, Dec.; ಬೂದಿಕುಂಬಳಬಳ್ಳಿ - búdikumbalaballi, Can.; బూడిదగుమ్మడి - búdidegummadi, Tel.; കുമ്പളം - kumbalam, Mal.; கலியாணப்பூசணி - kaliyánappúsani, Tam.). San. from (ku, san. diminutive prefix + úshma, san. heat + anda, san. ball); from cooling seeds. Mahr. from sanscrit. Ar. from (jaduba, ar. land affected with drought). Can. from (búdi, can. ash + kumbalaballi, can. pumpkin plant, cucurbita maxima, duch.). Tel. from (búdide, tel. ashes + gummadi, tel. pumpkin). Tam. from (kalyána, san. auspicious + púsani, tam. pumpkin, cucurbita maxima, duch.); used in feasts. Hind. also (kumrá), meaning gourd; (kondhá), meaning ash-colored; (sufedkaddú), meaning white gourd; (kondhákumrá), meaning ash-colored gourd. Dec. also (kaddú), meaning gourd. Tel. also (pendligummadi), meaning marriage pumpkin; (pottigummadi), meaning short pumpkin. Tam. also (púsani). Greek σίκυς. Title otherwise Festive pumpkin, Summer squash, Turban pumpkin, White gourd, White pumpkin. This or common pumpkin is the melon of old english horticulturists, the true melon being their musk melon. Sometimes confounded with the great pumpkin. Botanically Cucurbita [carcauroo] pepo, dec., cucurbitaceæ [vricsham, 62]. Cultivated near huts, often spreading over roof. Seeds anthelmintic; in pharm. non-officinal. Fruit eaten as a vegetable. Seeds give fixed drying oil.——*Great pumpkin* (कूष्माण्ड - kúshmánda, San.; दुद्दिणि - duddini, Conc.; میٹھا کدو - míthákaddú, Hind. and Dec.; ಕುಂಬಳಬಳ್ಳಿ - kumbalaballi, Can.; తీపెకుంబుడ - típekumbuda, Too.; గుమ్మడి - gummadi, Tel.; ବୋଇତାଳୁ - boitalu, Oor.; മത്തൻ - mattan, Mal.; කොමඩු කායි - kumbalakáyi, Singh.; பூசணி - púsani, Tam.). San. from (ku, san. prefix of diminution + úshma, san. heat + anda, san. ball); from cooling seeds. Hind. from (míthá, hind. sweet + kaddú, hind. gourd). Can. from (kumbala, can. the plant + balli, can. creeper). Tel. from sanscrit. Mal. from (mad, san. to be intoxicated). Tam. from (pú, tam. flower + shanai, tam. to grow luxuriantly). San. also (punyalatá), meaning beautiful creeper; (dadhip'hala), meaning curd fruit, from acid taste [wood-apple]. Hind. also (lálkumrá), meaning red gourd; (safaríkumrá), meaning journey gourd; (kaddú), meaning gourd. Can. also (chinikáyiballi); (bésinikáyeballi). Tel. also (tiyyagummadi), meaning sweet + the plant; (erragummadi), meaning red + the plant; (karbúdzudósa), meaning melon, cucumis melo, linn. + cucumber, cucumis sativus, linn. Mal. also (chakkarakkumbalam), meaning sweet + cucurbita pepo, dec.; (chakkaraççora), meaning sweet + lagenaria vulgaris, ser. Tam. also (parangikkáy), meaning portuguese + fruit; (sharkkaraippúsani), meaning sugar + pumpkin; (arasánikkáy), meaning king fruit; (animulai), meaning beauty + breast; (shímaippúsani), meaning foreign + pooshany plant. Title otherwise Common gourd, Portuguese fruit, Red gourd, Spanish gourd, Squash gourd, Sweet gourd, Sweet pumpkin, Winter squash. Botanically Cucurbita [carcauroo] maxima, duchesne, cucurbitaceæ [vricsham, 62]. Flower very large, yellow; brownish red, globular shaped, bluntly ribbed gourd of great size; largest known fruit. Cultivated in any soil rich in vegetable deposit; dry cultivation; ground prepared in hot weather by hand-hoeing two or three times; dry leaves burnt on the spot and dried cowdung also applied; the soil invariably well manured; seed sown a month later, being pressed into ground with the finger about an inch deep at equal distances; the seedlings are watered every day for about three months; the soil is also stirred once or twice; weeding is carefully attended to; when the plants begin to creep, pandauls [q.v.] are raised and the plants creep over them; by poor people twigs of trees are placed; the fruit is generally gathered when full ripe, about five months after sowing, and brought to market immediately; average price one anna for a fruit. Seeds anthelmintic; mixed with sugar or honey; substituted for british kousso and male-fern; in pharm. non-officinal. The dried pulp eaten with rice; when boiled, tastes somewhat like a young carrot [gaujar]; the leaves make good greens. An oil from the seeds.——*True musk melon* (سفری کمرا - safaríkumrá, Hind.). Title from odour. Hind. means journey gourd. Title otherwise Cocoanut squash, Elector's-cap gourd, Jerusalem artichoke gourd, Lima squash, Marrow squash, Melon pumpkin, Musk pumpkin, Red gourd, Scallop squash, Squash, Squash gourd, Turk's cap gourd. Botanically Cucurbita [carcauroo] moschata, duchesne, cucurbitaceæ [vricsham, 62]. Alias Cucurbita melopepo, maxima. Leaves five-palmate and often marked with whitish blotches; petiole hairy but not prickly; fruiting peduncled, angular and furrowed; calyx segments of the female flower large foliaceous. Fruits of two forms; one smooth and somewhat oblong in shape, the other fluted and flattened spheroidal. Very extensively cultivated. Yellow flesh of fruit cooked and eaten. A mild, bland, pale-colored oil, from seeds.

——*Vegetable marrow* (ஷீமைப்பூசணி - shímaippúsani, Tam.). Title from softness. Tam. from (shímai, tam. foreign + púsani, tam. pumpkin, cucurbita maxima, duch.). Title otherwise Egg-shaped gourd. Botanically Cucurbita [carcauroo] ovifera, linn., cucurbitaceæ [vricsham, 62]. Introduced; of easy culture in good rich soil.

CARDAMOM (एला - élá, *San.*; एल - éla, *Mahr.*; आल - ála, *Conc.*; قاقلة صغار - kákilahisighár, *Ar.*; قاقلة خرد - kákilahi-khurd, *Pers.*; الايچى - iláichí, *Hind.*; الاچى - iláchí, *Dec.*; پور - puvar, *Malay*; ಏಲಕ್ಕಿಗಿಡ - élakkigida, *Can.*; ಏಲಕಿ - élaki, *Too.*; ఏలకి - élaki, *Tel.*; ഏലം - élam, *Mal.*; ඇන්සාල් - ensál, *Singh.*; ஏலம் - élam, *Tam.*). Title from (chhard, san. to vomit + hamámá, ar. amomum genus); reckoned an anti-emetic. San. from (il, san. to send down); correcting foul-breath and removing nausea. Mahr. and conc. from sanscrit. Ar. from (kákilah, ar. cardamom + sighár, ar. small). Pers. from (kákilah, ar. cardamom + khurd, ar. small). Hind. and dec. from sanscrit. Can. means cardamom rice plant. Too., &c., from sanscrit. San. also (drávidí), meaning produced in south india; (gandha-kuti), meaning fragrant flower-bud; (upakuñchiká), meaning small; (bahulá), meaning giving many fruits; (chandrabálá), meaning child of camphor, from smell; (nishkuti), meaning departing from the bud; (prit'hvíká), meaning large; (chhardi-kághna), meaning vomiting + destroyer; (chhardikáripu), meaning vomiting + enemy. Ar. also (shushmír); (khairbavá); (helbavá), meaning aromatic cardamom. Pers. also (hel). Hind. also (chhotíiláichí), meaning lesser cardamom; (gújratíiláichí), meaning goozerat cardamom. Dec. also (chhotíiláchí), meaning small cardamom. Malay also (kapulaga). Can. also (yálakki-gida). Tel. also (sannaélaki), meaning small + cardamom. Mal. also (élattari), meaning cardamom seed. Tam. also (shit-télam), meaning small cardamom; (irávadi); (iláñji). Greek καρδάμωμον. Title otherwise Cluster cardamom, Lesser cardamom, Long malabar cardamom, Officinal cardamom, Round cardamom, Small cardamom, True cardamom, White cardamom. Botanically Elettaria cardamomum, maton., zingiberaceæ [vricsham, 144]. Generic name from (élattari, mal. cardamom seed). Alias Alpinia cardamomum; Amomum cardamomum, ensal, racemosum, repens; Zingiber ensal. Ensal from singhalese. Native of india; stem perennial, reed-like, erect, jointed, 6–9 feet, enveloped in the sheaths of the leaves; leaves lanceolate, acuminate, sub-sessile, entire, 1–2 feet long; sheaths slightly villous; scapes several, flexuose, jointed, branched, 1–2 feet long; flowers alternate, short-stalked, solitary at each point of the racemes; calyx funnel-shaped, three-toothed, finely striated; corolla tube as long as the calyx; limb double; exterior portion of three oblong, concave, nearly equal divisions; inner lip obovate, longer than the exterior divisions, curled at the margins; apex three-lobed, marked in the centre with purple-violet stripes; capsule oval, somewhat three-sided, three-celled, three-valved; seeds numerous, angular; flowers pale-greenish white. Produces fruit for several years; grows abundantly, both wild and under cultivation, in the moist shady mountain forests of north canara, coorg and wynaud at elevation of 2,500 to 5,000, above sea; is truly wild in canara, and the anamullay, cochin and travancore forests; there is a small cardamom island in the laccadive group, west of malabar, inhabited by moplahs. The seeds as occurring are small, almost black, nearly triangular, with an aromatic taste, and a camphoraceous smell; semina cardamomi minoris, fructus cardamomi of chemists; a volatile oil is procured from the seeds by aqueous distillation, which has a strong aromatic taste, soluble in alcohol; it loses its odour and taste by being kept too long. The plant grows as a spontaneous seedling in woods of high land, cultivation being merely clearing of ground from trees; previous to commencement of rains cultivators ascend mountain sides, and seek a spot where cardamom plants are growing; here they make small clearings, in which the admission of light occasions the plant to develop in abundance; about two years after the first clearing the plants begin to flower, and five months later ripen some fruits, but a full crop is not got till at least a year after; the plants continue productive six or seven years. On the lower range of the pulney hills, near dindigul, at an elevation of about 5,000 feet above the sea, the cardamom plant is actually cultivated in the shade; the natives burn down the underwood, and clear away the small trees of the dense sholahs, which are damp all the year round; the cardamoms are then sown, and when a few inches high are planted out, either singly or in twos, under the shade of the large trees; they take five years before they bear fruit. In harvesting, the clusters of cardamom are plucked by hand; the stem being pruned to permit fresh stems to shoot; the capsules are separated and strewn on ground and dried in sun; that part of the stalk which adheres to the capsules is removed by heating the capsules over a fire in a pit; 100 pollums [q.v.] of capsules dried are sold at $7\frac{1}{2}$ rupees. Plant gives to pharm. dried capsules, cardamomum, stimulant, carminative; preparation, tinctura cardamomi composita; also in british pharm. Used in veterinary practice in cordial preparations. Capsules are used by natives in flavoring sweetmeats and certain cooked dishes; also as a spice; sometimes chewed in betel-leaf [paun]. In commerce there are three varieties of cardamoms, the short, long-longs, and short-longs:—Short are more coarsely ribbed and of a brown color, and are called the malabar cardamoms or wynaud cardamoms, reckoned the best of the three; long-longs are more finely ribbed, and of a paler color, seeds are white and shrivelled; short-longs merely differ from the latter in being shorter or less pointed. It is usual to mix the several kinds together when ready for exportation. Large cardamoms distinct from these are furnished by species of Amomum. No other species here.——*Cardamom hills* (ഏലമല - élamala, Mal.). From (élam, mal. elettaria cardamomum, maton. + mala, mal. mountain). Range of hills. Travancore state, Cottayam division, Todoopoya, Mooatpoya, Meenachel, and Chungacherry talooks. Detached from W. ghauts. Divided roughly into Margary alam and Coonny alam groups, both very sparsely populated and unhealthy. Coonny alam, though lower lies within influence of the sea-breeze and enjoys rather better climate than Margary alam. The chief produce is cardamoms, which brings in a large revenue. They thrive best at 3,000 feet. A few small coffee-estates on southern slopes.——*Ethiopian cardamom* (قاقلۂزنگی - kákilahizangí, Pers.). Same as Wild cardamom.——*Galangal cardamom* (خلنجن قاقل - khulanjankákilah, Ar.); from flavor. Same as Greater galangal.——*Greater cardamom* (بڑی الاچی کا پیڑ - baríiláchíkáper, Hind.). From size of capsules. Same as Wild cardamom.——*Punneer cardamom* (پنیر کا پیڑ - panírkáper, Hind.); from seeds used in making cheese. Same as Country asgand.——*Raven cardamom* (قاقلۂ غراب - kákilahighuráb, Pers.). From being wild. Same as Wild cardamom.——*Siberian cardamom* (نبات بادیان خطائی - nabátibádiyánahikhatáí, Ar.). Title from being once imported into europe through russia from china. Arabic means chinese anise plant. Same as Star anise. ——*Wild cardamom* (स्थूलैला - st'húlailá, San.; थोरावेळा - t'horávélá, Mahr.; قاقلۂکبار - kákilahikibár, Ar.; قاقلۂ کلان - kákilahikalán, Pers.; بڑی الایچی کا پیڑ - báríiláichíkáper, Hind.; بڑی الاچی کا جہاڑ - baríiláchíkájhár, Dec.; ದೊಡ್ಡಯಾಲಕ್ಕಿಗಿಡ - doddayálakkigida, Conc.; అడవిఏలకి - adaviélaki, Tel.; പേരേലം - pérélam, Mal.; காட்டேலம் - káttélam, Tam.). San. from (st'húla, san. large + élá, san. cardamom, elettaria cardamomum, maton.). Mahr. means large + cardamom. Ar. from (kákilah, ar. cardamom + kibár, ar. great). Pers. from (kákilah, pers. cardamom + kalán, pers. great). Hind. from (barí, hind. large + iláíchi, hind. cardamom + per, hind. tree). Can. from (dodda, can. large + yálakki, can. cardamom seed + gida, can. plant). Tel. from (adavi, tel. wild + élaki, tel. cardamom). Mal. from (peru, mal. large + élam, mal. cardamom). Tam. from (kádu, tam. forest + élá, san. cardamom). San. also (brihadupakuñchiká), meaning large + cardamom. Mahr. also (mót'hávélá), meaning large cardamom. Ar. also (hílizakr), meaning large cardamom; (kákilahizanjí), meaning ethiopian cardamom. Pers. also (kákilahighuráb), meaning crow cardamom; (kákilahizakr), meaning large cardamom. Dec. also (iláchídánah), referring to seed; (jangliiláchí), meaning wild cardamom; (haidarábádíiláchí), meaning hyderabad cardamom. Tel. also (peddaélaki), meaning large + cardamom. Tam. also (periyayélam), meaning large cardamom. Title otherwise Ethiopian cardamom, Greater cardamom, Jungle cardamom, Raven cardamom. Botanically Amomum subulatum, roxb., zingiberaceæ [vricsham, 144]. Capsules larger and inferior to real cardamom. The following is a description of capsules:—ovate or bluntly triangular, with a tuft of fibres at its smaller end, which is often destroyed in course of time; generally 1 inch in length and $1\frac{1}{2}$ inches in circumference; ribbed; coriaceous; and reddish brown color. And the following of the seeds:—small; almost round or bluntly angular; brown; and feebly aromatic in taste and smell, the latter not being distinct until they are bruised or chewed. Medicinally same as real cardamoms. The following are other Amomum cardamoms:—Moringa [q.v.] cardamom is amomum aromaticum, roxb.; flower middle-sized, pale-yellow, the tip tinged with red down the middle; capsule ovate, size of a nutmeg, similar to true cardamoms; native of chittagong. Java cardamom is amomum maximum, roxb.; introduced from malay islands; pungent taste but not so grateful as real cardamom. Grains of paradise are amomum melegueta, roscoe; otherwise malaguetta pepper; native of guinea; capsule oblong, somewhat triangular, beaked, of dark reddish-brown color, hairy, powerfully aromatic; the seeds are of bright golden brown color, excessively hot, acrid and aromatic; used in cattle medicines; used to give false strength to beer and other liquors.

CARICAUL (காரைக்கால் - káraikkál, *Tam.*). From (kárai, tam. thorny webera, canthium parviflorum, lamk. + kál, tam. channel). Greek κορέλη. French territory and town; Tanjore dist.; pop. 92,516; square miles 60; town, lat. 10° 55′ N.; long. 79° 52′ E.; from Combaconam E. 31 miles; from Madras S.S.W. 152 miles; from Mayavaram S.E. 16 miles; from Munnargoody N.E. 31 miles; from Nagore N. 8 miles; from Negapatam N. 12 miles; from Tanjore E.N.E. 47 miles; from Tranquebar S.S.W. $7\frac{1}{2}$ miles. On the Coromandel coast, about $1\frac{1}{2}$ miles from the mouth of the Arasilaur. Central coast part of district. Light at the mouth of the river; lat. 10° 55′ 0″; long. 79° 50′ 35″; white; fixed; 9 miles; visible from all directions seaward; flagstaff; as a guide to the anchorage. The territory is bounded north, south, and west by Tanjore district; and east by Bay of Bengal. Eighty-one other villages ceded to them on 21st December 1749 by Rajah of Tanjore. French seized town in 1736, and constructed a fort, which was taken by the English on April 5, 1760, restored in 1765, again taken in 1778, and finally restored by treaty in 1814 on condition that no fortifications should be erected therein. By terms of treaty, no military are to be retained but such as required for police. Caricaul formed the base of Lally's operations against Tanjore. The town carries on a brisk trade with Ceylon, Europe, and the French colonies, exporting rice and importing chiefly European articles and timber. An administrateur, subordinate to Pondicherry, is in charge of settlement. There are also a colonial inspector, a commandant of troops, a judge and other officers. On the subject of inland customs a convention exists with the Madras government, and all salt consumed in French territory is by treaty purchased from the English. Revenue about 400,000 francs; expenditure about 277,000 francs. The soil is watered by six small rivers, branches of Cauvery. These periodically overflow their banks, fertilizing the country. Fourteen principal canals and their branches afford irrigation. The territory contains 108 villages. The following are besides Caricaul the principal villages, giving their names each to a sub-district.——*Cotcherry* (கோட்டுச்சேரி - kóttuççéri, Tam.). From (kódu, tam. boundary + shéri, tam. village); pop. 10,646.——*Nedoongaud* (நெடுங்காடு - nedungádu, Tam.). Means long forest; French, Nedouncadou; pop. 5,931; lat. 10° 58′; long. 79° 49′; from Caricaul N.W. 5 miles; from Tanjore E. 44 miles; from the sea W. 5½ miles.——*Nullazhandore* (நல்லழுந்தூர் - nallazhandúr, Tam.). From (nal, tam. good + azhundu, tam. ridge in a betel garden + úr, tam. village); pop. 7,724; lat. 10° 57′; long. 79° 47′; from Caricaul N.W. 6½ miles; from Tanjore E. 42 miles; from the sea W. 7¼ miles.——*Prauvidayanaur* (பிராவிடையனாறு - pirávidaiyanáru, Tam.). See sep. title.——*Tirmullay rajanputnam* (திருமலைராசன் பட்டணம் - tirumalairásanbattanam, Tam.). Means trimal naicks' town. French, Grande aldée; lat. 10° 53′; long. 79° 52′; from Caricaul S. 3¼ miles; from Tanjore E. 46 miles. Is a port.——*Tirnoolaur* (திருநூலார் - tirunúlár, Tam.). From (tiru, tam. holy + núl, tam. writing + áru, tam. river). French, Tirnoular; pop. 9,186; lat. 10° 55′; long. 79° 50′; from Caricaul W. 3 miles; from Tanjore E.N.E. 44 miles; from the sea W. 4½ miles.

CARM (كرم - karm, *Ar.*). From (karama, ar. to be generous). Gift. Prefixed to an alam forms a lacab; as Carm ally, gift of Ally [ism].——*Careem* (كريم - karím, Hind.). From (karama, ar. to be generous). Clement. An attribute of God [allah]. Common alam; as Careem beg, alam + alaumat. Also part of lacab; as Careem ood deen, generous in faith [ism].

CARMAM (कर्म - karma, *San.*). From (kri, san. to do). Action. Any act of piety; as sacrifice, marriage-ceremony, funeral obsequies. Fate as the consequence of acts. Action. Also action in a previous birth, good or evil, entailed on the soul and resulting in the enjoyments and sufferings of the present or a future state [samsauram]. Also religious action such as sacrifice, ablution, and especially as originating in the hope of future recompense and as opposed to speculative religion or spiritual knowledge; such rites are expounded in the augamams; they are thus one of the three means of salvation:—viz:, carmam, works; bhacty, faith; and nyaunam or spiritual knowledge. Also simply periodical religious rites according to the rules of the shastrams; obligation imposed by peculiarities of tribe or occupation. In Booddhism, it is especially prominent and is the supreme controlling power of the universe, the instrumental cause of birth and death. It is by destroying this cause and getting rid of its operations by following a prescribed course of discipline, that men can ensure freedom of action, good or bad, and attain nirvaunam [q.v.] or liberation from existence [matam].——*Carma caundam* (कर्मकाण्ड - karmakánda, San.). From (above + kánda, san. section). Act; section. Exoteric portion of vedic writing [nyauna caundam].——*Carmauntaram* (कर्मान्तर - karmántara, San.). From (above + antara, san. interval). Funeral ceremonies after burial [shavacaud] or cremation [shoodcaud]. Full details at vols. I (108); II, 237.

CARNAM (कर्ण - karna, *San.*). From (kri, san. to do); useful. Literally ear. Surd, hypothenuse, diagonal, true distance of a planet [graham] from earth.——*Carnan* (कर्ण - karna, San.). Supposed to be born of Coonty's ear. One of the Pandavas. There is a Tamul proverb:—கார்த்திகைக்கு மேல் மழையும் இல்லை, கர்ணனுக்கு மேல் கொடையும் இல்லை—"No rain "better than november, no liberality superior to that of carnan" [mahabhaurat, mausam].

CARNAVEN (കാരണവൻ - káranavan, *Mal.*). Means the originator. Managing head of a family or tarwaud [q.v.] in Malabar. Where the Makkatoyem [q.v.] law of descent of property is observed, he is the father, elder brother, &c. Where Maroomakkatoyem [q.v.] is observed, which is the usual case, he is the maternal uncle or eldest brother. As an exception to the general rule, in some few Shoodra families a custom exists by which the management is vested in the senior female in preference to the senior male member of the family [aliyasantauna]. The Carnaven is the natural guardian of every member within the family. He alone can sue and be sued as the representative of the family. In the absence of fraud or collusion, a decree against the Carnaven as such is binding upon the other members of the family, although they are not parties to the suit. The Carnaven for the time being has an almost absolute control over the distribution of the family income and the family expenditure. He may delegate his powers of management, but he cannot, without the assent of the members of the family generally, assign his rights and privileges so as to be unable to resume them. His powers of management may however be limited by contract. Alienations by a Carnaven, whether in the form of gifts, sales or mortgages, are invalid unless made with the assent, express or implied, of the junior members. The whole of the tarwaud property is liable for a tarwaud debt properly incurred by the Carnaven [maryauday].——*Carnavaty* (കാരണവത്തി - káranavatti, Mal.). Female Carnaven.——*Carnavenpaud* (കാരണപ്പാട് - káranavappátu, Mal.). From (above + pátu, mal. rank, a title). Rank of a Carnaven.

CAROB (خروب - kharrúb, *Ar.*; كشاء شامى - kisáishámí, *Pers.*; خرنوب - kharnúb, *Hind.*). Ar. from (kharaba, ar. devastated); desert plant. Pers. from (kisá, ar. cassia fistula, linn. + shám, ar. syria); from resemblance of fruits. Title otherwise Algaroba [manilla tamarind], Bread tree, Kharnoob, Locust bean, Locust tree, St. john's bean, St. john's bread, Syrian cassia. Called St. John's bread from the idea that the pod constituted the honey on which John the Baptist fed in the desert. The shells of the carob are supposed to have been the husks which the prodigal son desired to eat. Greek κερατωνία, Latin ceraunia, Spanish algaroba. Pods called keratia, from resemblance to a curved horn. Botanically Ceratonia siliqua, linn., leguminosæ [vricsham, 48]. Pod, 6 to 8 inches in length, an inch in breadth, flattened on the sides; seeds of a reddish brown immersed in a sweetish pulp; native of mediterranean coast; imported. The seed is the original of the jeweller's carat [q.v.]. Seeds used in coughs attended with much expectoration; had formerly a place in british materia medica; husk of pod antacrid, purgative, pectoral, and astringent. Saccharine matter in which seeds are imbedded is nutritious, forms an important constituent in patent cattle foods. Wood hard, heavy, excellent as fuel, and valued for cabinet-work.

CAROLAH (सुषवी - sushaví, *San.*; कारली - kárali, *Mahr.*; कारांत - kárati, *Conc.*; قثاءالبرى - kisáulbarrí, *Ar.*; سيما هنك - símáhang, *Pers.*; کرولا - karolá, *Hind.*; کريلا - karelá, *Dec.*; ಹಾಗಲ - hágala, *Can.*; ಕಂಚಾಲ - kanchála, *Too.*; కాకర - kákara, *Tel.*; କରେଣ - karena, *Oor.*; കൈപ്പ - kaippa, *Mal.*; කාරවල්ලි - káravalli, *Singh.*; பாகல் - págal, *Tam.*). Title from sanscrit through hindostany. San. from (su, san. prefix meaning well + su, san. to bring forth); from medicinal virtues [black jeerah, caraway]. Mahr. from (káravélla, san. the plant). Conc. from mahratta. Ar. from (kisá, ar. cucumber, cucumis sativus, linn. + barr, ar. forest). Pers. from (sím, pers. silver + áhang, pers. cucumber). Hind. from (káravélla, san. the plant). Dec. from hindostany [bitter luffa]. Mal. means bitter. Singh. from (káravélla, san. the plant). Tam. from (pávu, tam. to spread). San. also (káravélla), meaning grown with effort [vailay]; (káravallí), from (káravélla); (krimighna), meaning insect killer; (vishakantaki), meaning with poisonous thorn as an antidote to poison; (dírghakáravélla), meaning long-fruited variety; (hrasvakáravélla), meaning short-fruited variety. Hind. also (bárákarelá), meaning large momordica; (lambákarelá), meaning long momordica. Can. also (úrubágala), meaning village + the plant. Tel. also (peddachétiánuga), meaning large + bitter + lagenaria vulgaris, ser.; (peddakákara), meaning large + the plant; (kurilla); (uchi); (pottikákara), meaning short + the plant; (tellakákara), meaning white + the plant; (úrakákara), meaning village + the plant; (mettakákara), meaning dry land + the plant; (kásara). Mal. also (pával), meaning spreading plant; (pántippával), meaning paundy, the place + the plant; (metippával), meaning treading + the plant; (rájavalli), meaning king's creeper. Tam. also (shinnappágal), meaning small + the plant; (kombuppágal), meaning horn + the plant, from shape of fruit; (mithippágal), meaning to tread down + the plant, ground creeper; (nilappágal), meaning ground + the plant; (kalakkodi); (panrippudal), meaning pig + the plant, from fruit short and thick; (malappirkku), meaning hill + luffa acutangula, roxb.; (égaravalli); (káravalli); (athalai). Title otherwise Balsam apple, Balsam pear, Hairy momordica, Paugal, Pauvakkah, Pig gourd, Small snake-gourd, Spiked bitter cucumber. Botanically Momordica charantia, linn., cucurbitaceæ [vricsham, 62]. Alias Momordica humilis, muricata. Climbing; stems more or less hairy; leaves palmately five-lobed, sinuate, toothed, when young more or less villous on the under side, particularly on the nerves; peduncles slender, with a reniform bracteole, male ones with the bracteole about the middle, female with it near the base; fruit oblong or ovate, more or less tubercled or muricated; seeds with a thick notched margin and red aril; flowers middle-sized, pale yellow; commonly cultivated. The whole plant mixed with cinnamon [q.v.], long pepper [q.v.], rice [q.v.], and marotty [q.v.] oil given in cutaneous diseases; juice of leaves mixed with warm water is anthelmintic. Green gourd is bitter, but wholesome, and used in curries, &c. There are two varieties; one having fruit larger and more oblong, the other with fruit smaller, more ovate, muricated and tubercled; the smaller is best. Other common species are:—Cochin-chinensis; fruit about 4 inches in diameter, ovate, pointed, bright red, covered with conical pointed tubercles. Cymbalaria; root tuberous; flower, small, white; rare species; grows on banks of water-courses. Dioica, see below [prickly carolah].——*Buffalo carolah* (എരിമപ്പാവൽ - erimappával, Mal.; இருப்பவல் - iruppaval, Tam.). Title from being wild and inferior. Mal. from (erima, mal. buffalo + pával, mal. momordica charantia, linn.) [prickly carolah]. Title otherwise Indian cudweed, Indian everlasting. Botanically Gnaphalium indicum, linn., compositæ [vricsham, 74]. Alias Gnaphalium multicaule, pluricaula, polycaulon, strictum. Stems herbaceous, many, diffuse, tomentose; leaves obovate oblong or oblong-linear, mucronate, more or less tomentose, lower ones attenuated at the base, upper ones sessile; capitula aggregated into an interrupted simple or branched spike; involucral scales linear, obtuse, scariose, straw-colored or reddish; flowers very small, yellow; flowering in february and march; root has little sensible taste or smell; root alterative, prescribed in decoction [kwautam] in cachexia, scrofula and syphilis. Other common species are:—hypoleucum, luteo-album, pulvinatum.——*Prickly carolah* (फागिल - p'hágila, Conc.; دھارکرولا - dhárkarolá, Hind.; ಮಾಡಹಾಗಲ - mádahágala, Can.; ಕಾಡಕಂಚಾಲ - kádakanchála, Too.; ఆగాకర - ágákara, Tel.; വെമ്പാവൽ - vempával, Mal.; තුම්බකරවිල - tumbakaravila, Singh.; பழுப்பாகல் - pazhuppágal, Tam.). Title from exterior of fruit. Hind. from (dhár, hind. stripe + karolá, hind. momordica charantia, linn.). Can. from (made, can. strong + hágala, can. the plant). Too. from (kádu, too. wild + kanchála, too. the plant). Tel. from (áda, tel. female + kákara, tel. the plant, momordica charantia, linn.). Mal. from (ven, mal. white + pával, mal. the plant, momordica charantia, linn.). Singh. from (tumba, singh. long + káravalli, singh. the plant). Tam. from (pazhu, tam. to become yellowish + págal, tam. the plant). Can. also (madehágala), meaning strong + the plant. Tel. also (pótuágákara), meaning male + the plant; (pótukákara), meaning male + the plant, momordica charantia, linn.; (púágákara), meaning flower + the plant; (adavikákara), meaning jungle + the plant; (adavipótukákara), meaning forest + the plant; (kárkótakamu). Mal. also (erimappával), meaning buffalo + the plant [buffalo carolah]. Tam. also (kátuppágal), meaning forest + the plant. Title otherwise Bristly balsam apple, Buffalo carolah, Male carolah. Botanically Momordica dioica, roxb., cucurbitaceæ [vricsham, 62]. Alias Momordica hispida, missionis, tuberosa. Climbing, diœcious; root tuberous; stems glabrous; leaves long-petioled, cordate at the base, from entire to three to four-lobed, toothed, upper side slightly scabrous, under smooth or nearly so; peduncles slender, with entire bracteoles, male with the bracteole close to the flower, and concealing the lower part, female one small near the base; fruit ovate, muricated; seeds oval, surrounded with a large red aril; flowers large yellow. Mixed with cocoanut [q.v.], pepper [q.v.], and red sandal [q.v.], applied in the form of liniment, relieves head-ache; mucilaginous-tasted root is used in piles; tender green fruit and tuberous roots of the female plant are eaten. There are several varieties, differing chiefly in leaves.

CARONDAH (करमर्दक - karamardaka, *San.*; करवंद - karavanda, *Mahr.*; कारांजे - káránjé, *Conc.*; کروندے کا پیر - karondekáper, *Hind.*; کروندے کا جہاڑ - karondekájhár, *Dec.*; ಹಿರಿಕಳವಿ - hirikalavi, *Can.*; ಕಂಡೇಪುಳಿ - kamrdépuli, *Too.*; ఓక - óka, *Tel.*; କେରେଣ୍ଡୋ - kerendo, *Oor.*; കരണ്ട - karanta, *Mal.*; මහකරඹ - mahakaramba, *Singh.*; பெருங்களா - perungalá, *Tam.*). Title from hindostany. San. from (kara, san. hand + mard, san. to crush). Mahr. from sanscrit. Conc. from sanscrit. Hind. from (karamardaka, san. the tree + per, hind. tree). Can. from (hiri, can. big + kalavi, can. the tree). Mal. from (kri, san. to do). Singh. from (maha, singh. large + karamba, singh. carissa). Tam. from (perumai, tam. greatness + kalá, tam. carissa sp.). San. also (krishnapákap'hala), meaning black + ripe + fruit; (krishnap'hala), meaning black fruit; (avigna), meaning not trembling; (karámlaka), meaning hand + sour; (sushéna), meaning having beautiful clusters. Hind. also (barákarondá), meaning large carissa. Can. also (korindagida); (karavadi); (kareki); (heggerjige). Tel. also (peddakalivi), meaning large + carissa spinarum, a. dec.; (vákudu) [prickly brinjaul]; (kalive); (vákalivi); (váka). Mal. also (kalávu). Tam. also (kalá), meaning black, from ripe berry. Title otherwise Bengal currant bush, Black-fruit, Calah, Caranda, Corindah, Jasmine-flowered carissa, Large calah, Large carondah, Thorny carissa. Botanically Carissa carandas, linn., apocynaceæ [vricsham, 87], Carandas from (karanda, san.). Alias Capparis carandas; Carissa congesta, jasminonerium; Echites spinosa. Small gnarled tree; leaves opposite, ovate, mucronate, nearly sessile, shining; calyx five-toothed; corymbs terminal and axillary, many-flowered; spines always in pairs at the divisions of the branches, and at every other pair of leaves, strong and sharp, two-forked; flowers pure white; flowering in hot season; berry black; when ripe, in shape, size, and color bears a strong resemblance to a damson; bears within it a number of small seeds; common. Unripe fruit medicinally astringent; ripe fruit cooling, acid, and useful in bilious complaints; root bitter stomachic. Fruit great value for making preserves; in its unripe state used for tarts and puddings; has when cooked much of the flavor of the green gooseberry; natives eat it raw; it has to be thrown into salted water shortly before being eaten whereby the taste is improved; wine is also made in a small quantity at Goa for local consumption. Shrub makes strong fences from sharp thorns; milky juice exudes from wounded part of fruit, very adhesive; fruit used as mordant [sauram]. Wood hard, smooth, close-grained; used for turning and combs, and to make dry fences; the wood of a very old tree turns quite black and acquires a strong fragrance. There is a Tamul proverb:—அன்றைக்குத் தின்கிற பலாக் காயிலே இன்றைக்குத் தின்கிற களாக்காய் பெரிது— "The calah fruit of to-day is better than the jack fruit of the "future." Other common species are:—Macrophylla, much larger flowers than any of the other species, and its thorns are always recurved; fruit superior to carandas. Paucinervia, flowers white with a slight dash of rose. Spinarum, flowers white, a smaller bush than carandas.——*False carondah* (جہاٹا کروندا - jhátákarondá, Dec.). From fruit similar but inferior. Same as Forest bair.——*Hill carondah* (ಅಂಡುವನ - anduvana, Can.; மலைக்களா - malaikkalá, Tam.). Title otherwise Bleaberry, Whortleberry. Botanically Vaccinium genus, vacciniaceæ [vricsham, 77]. Low-growing heath-like shrubs met with generally in mountainous districts or moist healthy places; leaves alternate, generally evergreen; flowers solitary or clustered; fruit is a globular four or five-celled berry with many seeds in each compartment; found on neilgherries. The species best known to the natives are:—Leschenaultii; otherwise carbolic acid plant, farkle berry; tree; flowers red; grows on mountains; the fruit, about as large as currants, is eaten, an agreeable acid; wood rose-colored, with red heart, wavy grained, good for cabinet work; there is variety rotundifolia. Neilgherrense, shrubby; flowers whitish or rose-colored; fruit green, little red.——*Thorny carondah* (முள்ளுக்களா - mullukkalá, Tam.). From spines and black sour berries. Same as Berberry.

CAROOK (கருக்கு - karukku, *Tam.*). Jagged.——*Carook vauly* (वातदल - vátadala, San.; ಚಿಟಿಪಾಲ - chitipála, Can.; కాకుపాల - kákupála, Tel.; கருக்குவாளி - karukkuváli, Tam.). Title from tamul. San. from (váta, san. rheumatism + dala, san. leaf). Can. from (chiti, can. small + pále, can. alstonia scholaris, r. br.). Tel. from (káki, tel. crow + pála, can. milky tree). Tam. from (karukku, tam. jagged edge + vál, tam. sword), from serrate leaf. Tam. also (kadikkai); (karukkattámaram); (karukkuvánimaram); (karukkuváççi), meaning jagged-edged adze tree. Title otherwise Jagged jujube, Three-nerved zizyphus. Botanically Zizyphus [badary] glabrata, heyn., rhamneæ [vricsham, 41]. Alias Zizyphus trinervia. Tree, 20 feet, unarmed; leaves alternate, ovate-oblong, obtuse, crenate-serrated-glabrous, three-nerved; cymes axillary, scarcely longer than the petioles, few-flowered; drupe turbinate, yellow, with a soft gelatinous pulp; calyx five-cleft; petals obovate, unguiculate; styles two, nearly distinct; ovary two-celled; nut hard and thick, rugose, obovate, flattened, one to two-celled; flowers small, greenish yellow. Leaves have little sensible taste or smell, but decoction [kwautam] given to purify blood. Bark affords kino-like gum [gond] by exudation and decoction. Timber, light brownish, hard and close-grained.

CAROOR (கரூர் - karúr,* *Tam.*). From (karu, tam. black + úr, tam. village); from the dark grey gneiss quarried about three miles to the south-west. Greek κάρουρα βασίλειον κηροβόθρου, Caroor the capital of the cherapaty. Tam. also (kadáram), meaning brown; also (kázhagam), meaning blackness; also (vañji), meaning the creeper, tinospora cordifolia, miers. Sanscrit name (garbhapurí), meaning interior + town.——(1) Talook, Coimbatore district. Tahsildar's pay Rs. 175. Area 612 square miles. Population 201,044. Language Tamul. S.E. of district. Bounded N. by Erode talook, from which it is separated by Noyil; W. by Dharaupooram talook; S. by Dindigul talook of Madura and Coolitalay talook of Trichinopoly districts; E. by the Cauvery and Coolitalay talook of Trichinopoly. As the border talook between Trichinopoly and former Mysore territory, was once the scene of incessant military movements. Is open undulating plain with no hills and only a few insignificant rocky extrusions. The bulk is poor uplands with fertile bottoms and good wet lands along the borders of the river. The climate is very hot from March to June, after which time it is tempered by the south-west winds. Soils are of the usual gneissose and quartzose character, with beds of nodular or agglomerated limestone [choonam]. Towards the south the surface is little but hard kankar [q.v.] which however produces fair crops. White quartz crops up in many places, especially on road from Poogalore to Caroor. Dark grey gneiss of superior quality is quarried about three miles S.W. of Caroor. Soils are either red or grey, the former being ferruginous and the latter calcareous; there is no black soil; 7 per cent. of the dry land is classed as red loam and 93 per cent. as red sand; in wet lands about 98 per cent. is red loam and 2 per cent. red sand. The soil of the dry lands is generally inferior, but a regular and abundant rainfall, gives good crops. Pastures are fairly abundant, the usual grass being the indigenous coray [q.v.]. Hides [chamrah] are imported and exported, and there is trade in cloth, grain and money at Aravacoorchy, Caroor and Pullaputty. A considerable trade in grain and oil-seeds finds an outlet by Caroor railway station. Tanning [chamrah] used to be well represented at Caroor; it is still carried on at Pullaputty. Brass [pittalay] is made in Caroor. Products are almost entirely rural, save brass ware, leather and common cloths. Rivers are the Amravatty, Cauvery and Noyil. The Cauvery is not embanked in this talook below Vaungal, and, as the surface of the country is little above its ordinary full level, floods cause considerable damage by the sand which they deposit on the wet lands fed by the Neroor channel. This river feeds three good channels. The banks of the Amravatty are low, and the lands bordering the river are irrigated by anicuts and coramboos [q.v.] of sand and brushwood in the bed of the river. Nine channels are supplied by the Amravatty. The banks of the Noyil are high and steep, and its floods are very intermittent. It is useless for irrigation except by the Poogalore channel. The only considerable jungle streams are the Codavanaur and Nangaunjy, which, running from the south, fall into the Amravatty above Caroor town. There are two considerable rain-fed tanks, Ooppidamungalam and Velliyanay. There is much baling from channels. Zemindarry, Andiputty. Places of archæological interest :—Aravacoorchy, Caroor, Chinna dharaupooram, Inninganore, Modacore, Moonnore, Naugampully, Neroor, Paramatty, Pavitram, Poogalore, Poongambaudy, Pullapolliem, Somore, Tandony, Tennilay, Vaungal, Venjamam goodalore, Vettaimungalam. Principal trig. station :—Rungamullay. The leading places, &c., in the talook are the following. ——*Amravatty* (ஆமராவதி - ámarávathi, Tam.). See sep. title. ——*Aravacoorchy* (அரவக்குறிச்சி - aravakkuriççi, Tam.). See sep. title.——*Aundauncoil* (ஆண்டாங்கோவில் - ándángóvil, Tam.). From (ándán, tam. lord + kóvil, tam. temple). Sanscrit name (sundararangapura), meaning beauty + vishnoo + town. Village; pop. 3,391; acres 5,270; lat. 10° 57′; long. 78° 05′; from Caroor W. 3¼ miles; from Coimbatore E. 73 miles. On Amravatty. Remains of old temple 2 furlongs W. of village.——*Calingaroyan* (கலிங்கராயன் - kalingaráyan, Tam.). See sep. title.——*Caroor* (கரூர் - karúr, Tam.). See below.——*Cauvery* (காவேரி - kávéri, Tam.). See sep. title.——*Chinna dharaupooram* (சின்னதாராப்புரம் - shinnathárappuram, Tam.). Means small dharaupooram. Sanscrit name (kíchakapura), meaning hollow bamboo, bambusa arundinacea, willd. + town. Village; pop. 1,885; acres 1,851; lat. 10° 51′; long. 77° 54′; from Caroor W.S.W. 17¼ miles; from Coimbatore E.S.E. 61 miles. On Amravatty. Old Shiva temple. Part of bastions of old mud fort still standing.——*Neroor* (நெரூர் - nerúr, Tam.). From (nirai, tam. fulness + úr, tam. village). Village; pop. 6,104; acres 5,663; lat. 11° 00′; long. 78° 11′; from Caroor E.N.E. 5½ miles; from Coimbatore E. 80 miles. Two old Shiva and Vishnoo temples.——*Noyil* (நொய்யல் - noyyal, Tam.). See sep. title.——*Ooppidamungalam* (உப்பிடமங்கலம் - uppidamangalam, Tam.). From (uppu, tam. salt + idam, tam. place + mangala, san. prosperity). Village; pop. 5,184; acres 8,716; lat. 10° 54′; long. 78° 12′; from Caroor S.E. 6 miles; from Coimbatore E.S.E. 80 miles. Wesleyan mission station. Large market.——*Paramatty* (பரமத்தி - paramatti, Tam.). From (param, tam. best + atti, tam. ficus racemosa, linn.). Sanscrit name (paraméshtʼhipura), meaning supreme god + town. Village; pop. 1,434; acres 3,307; lat. 10° 57′; long. 77° 58′; from Caroor W. 11 miles; from Coimbatore E. 66 miles. Market. An old Soobramanya sawmy temple.——*Pavitram* (பவித்திரம் - pavittiram, Tam.). Means holy. Village; pop. 4,423; acres 7,078; lat. 10° 58′; long. 78° 02′; from Caroor W. 6½ miles; from Coimbatore E. 69 miles. An old temple.——*Poogalore* (பொகலூர் - pogalúr, Tam., púgalur*). From (pugazh, tam. fame + úr, tam. village). Village, Railway station; pop. 4,757; acres 6,454; lat. 11° 03′; long. 78° 02′; height 504 feet; from Caroor N.N.W. 9½ miles; from Coimbatore E. 71 miles. Ancient and well-sculptured Shiva temple on a small hill close to the Cauvery. The channel of this name has its head near Oonjalore and irrigates a few acres in Erode talook. It crosses the Noyil by an anicut just above its junction with the Cauvery.——*Pooliyore* (புலியூர் - puliyúr, Tam.). From (puli, tam. tiger + úr, tam. village); from shiva who is said to be clad in tiger's skin. Sanscrit name (vyághrapurí), meaning tiger + town. Village; pop. 2,762; acres 2,960; lat. 10° 57′; long. 78° 11′; from Caroor E. 4 miles; from Coimbatore E. 80 miles. An old Shiva temple.——*Pullaputty* (பள்ளப்பட்டி - pallappatti, Tam.). From (pallan, tam. member of the peasant caste + patti, tam. cattle fold). Village; pop. 7,653; acres 4,919; lat. 10° 43′; long. 77° 56′; from Caroor S.W. 21 miles; from Coimbatore E.S.E. 66 miles. Inhabited by Lubbays. Formerly included in Aravacoorchy. Market.——*Rungamullay* (இரங்கமலை - irangamalai, Tam.). From (ranga, san. vishnu + malai, tam. mountain). Hill; a temple on the hill. Trig. station; lat. 10° 38′ 50·93″; long. 77° 57′ 31·80″; height 3,099 feet; from Caroor S.S.W. 24 miles; from Periya manjavaly W.S.W. 3 miles.——*Shendamungalam* (சேந்தமங்கலம் - shéndamangalam, Tam.). From (shéndan, tam. skanda, the red god + mangala, san. prosperity). Sanscrit name (skandamangala), meaning same. Village; pop. 5,174; acres 14,392; lat. 10° 40′; long. 77° 54′; from Caroor S.W. 25 miles; from Coimbatore E.S.E. 66 miles.——*Tennilay* (தென்னிலை - tennilai, Tam.). From (ten, tam. south + nilai, tam. site). Village; pop. 9,546; acres 22,302; lat. 10° 56′; long. 77° 53′; from Caroor W. 16 miles; from Coimbatore E.S.E. 59 miles. On road from Trichinopoly to Coimbatore. Distributed through sixty-seven hamlets and divided into four sections. Market.——*Velliyanay* (வெள்ளியணை - velliyanai, Tam.). From (velli, tam. white + anai, tam. artificial bank). Sanscrit name (rajatagiri), meaning silver mountain or keilausam. Village; pop. 5,762; acres 11,180; lat. 10° 51′; long. 78° 10′; from Caroor S.S.E. 7½ miles; from Coimbatore E.S.E. 78 miles. An old temple. Market.——*Venjamam goodalore* (வெஞ்சமாங்கூடலூர் - veñjamángúdalúr, Tam.). From (veñjamam, tam. hot battle + kúdalúr, tam. village so called). Village; pop. 4,461; acres 11,392; lat. 10° 49′; long. 78° 03′; from Caroor S.S.W. 12 miles; from Coimbatore E.S.E. 71 miles. Old Shiva temple.——**(2)** Town, Talook head-quarters, District moonsif's and Sub-registrar's station, Railway station; Coimbatore dist., Caroor tal.; pop. 10,750; acres 2,489; lat. 10° 58′; long. 78° 07′; height 391 feet; from Calicut E. 154 miles; from Coimbatore E. 76 miles; from Erode S.E. 35 miles; from Madras S.W. 210 miles; from Mangalore S.E. 253 miles; from Ootacamund E.S.E. 96 miles; from Pollachy E.N.E. 76 miles; from Suttimungalam S.E. 68 miles. On rising ground on the left or north bank of the Amravatty and near its confluence with the Cauvery. Of great antiquity and at or near the Scandapooram of the old Congoo country. Ancient capital of the Cherans or Keralans. The κηρόβοθρος of Ptolemy was the Cherapaty or lord of Cheram. Is also one of the seven sacred stalams or Shivaulyams of Congoo country. During the struggles between the rival dynasties of Chera, Chola, and Paundya, the town changed hands more than once. After the absorption of the Chera by the Chola dynasty it was still of importance and was provided with a good stone fort. With the rise of the Naicks, it fell to the kingdom of Madura; but was frequently attacked and occupied by the Mysore armies, until towards the end of seventeenth century it was finally annexed to the latter kingdom, and became its most important frontier post. In 1736, Chundah sahib besieged it unsuccessfully. In 1760, it was captured by the English after a short siege, and held by a British garrison till 1768, when it was retaken by Hyder ally, to whom its possession was confirmed by Treaty in 1769. In 1783, Colonel Lang held the fort for a few months. It was a third time captured in 1790 by General Meadows, and again restored in 1792. At the close of the second Mysore war, in 1799, it was finally ceded to the English, and was abandoned as military station in 1801. A monument to British who fell in the siege of 1790 is on the south bank of the river. Old Shiva temple of Pashoopateeshwaran built by a Cholan king. The lingam [q.v.] is 5 feet high. Old Vishnoo temple. In 1806 Roman coins were found. The fort is now demolished. Considerable trade. The Jesuit mission was established in 1639. The Wesleyan mission have also station. Sub-collector's head-quarters formerly. Cf. alloor [cranganore].

CARPANG (کرپان - karpán, *Hind.*; കരപ്പൻ - karappan, *Mal.*; கரப்பான் - karappán, *Tam.*). From (karai, tam. to be emaciated). Eruption on children, unaccompanied with fever [veidyan]. Common, from age of three or four months, to three years. Spreads over every part of body. Clusters of from three to five, or more, light-colored papulæ, each size of a mustard seed; and terminates in large loose, yellowish or brown scabs. Carpang plant; from cure against carpang, is same as Lowly corandy.——*Cadoovaun carpang* (கடுவான்கரப்பான் - kaduvángarappán, Tam.). From (kadu, tam. to give throbbing pain). Not common, between knees and ankles.——*Cheng carpang* (செங்கரப்பான் - shengarappán, Tam.). From (shem, tam. red). Red gum, Strophulus intertinctus, hardly a disease. ——*Colly carpang* (கொள்ளிக்கரப்பான் - kollikkarappán, Tam.). From (kolli, tam. fire brand). Between two and four years. Red spots, size of a six-pence, consisting of innumerable small papulæ. It terminates in a brownish itchy scab.——*Cooshta carpang* (குட்டக்கரப்பான் - kuttakkarappán, Tam.). A white scabby scraf spreading over whole surface of body.——*Munday carpang* (மண்டைக்கரப்பான் - mandaikkarappán, Tam.). From (mandai, tam. skull). Crusta lactea, or milk cap. On forehead and scalp.

CARPAUSY (कर्पासी - karpásí, *San.*). From (kri, san. to do); as being useful. Cf. Latin carbasus. Title otherwise Cotton [q.v.]. Botanically the Gossypium genus, malvaceæ [vricsham, 25]. Herbs or perennial shrubs, indigenous to asia and america; leaves grow upon stalks and are generally heart-shaped, and most commonly three or five-lobed, with the lobes sharp or rounded; flowers large and showy; fruit, three or five-celled capsule; seeds clothed with cotton wool. The species best known to the natives are :—arboreum [tree cotton], barbadense [american cotton], barbadense, var. acuminatum [peruvian-cotton], herbaceum [indian cotton]. Cf. the Bombax and Eriodendron genera.

CARPET SNAKE (चित्रमण्डल - chitramandala, *San.*; कुण्डली - kundalí, *Mahr.*; افعی - afaí, *Ar.*; لپیٹا سانپ - lapetásámp, *Hind.*; సురటపాము - suratapámu, *Tel.*; ചുരുട്ടപ്പാമ്പ - churuttappámbu, *Mal.*; சுருட்டை - shuruttai, *Tam.*). Title from pattern of back. San. from (chitra, san. variegated + mandala, san. circle). Mahr. from (kundala, san. coil). Ar. from (faá, ar. malignant). Hind. from (lapetá, hind. coiling + sámp, hind. snake). Drav. means coil. Hind. also (sabzíkásámp), meaning grass snake; (churímársámp), meaning fowl-killing snake; (angulsámp), meaning inch snake, from small size; (gaddhámárúsámp), meaning donkey killing snake; (marúrísámp), meaning twisting snake. Title otherwise Asp. Echis carinata, viperidæ [viriyan], ophidii viperiformes, ophidia [sarpam], reptilia [sarpy, 30], of naturalists [jantoo]. Alias Pseudoboa carinata. A small viper [viriyan], one of the true vipers. Brown or brownish grey, with a series of sub-quadrangular or ovate whitish spots, edged with blackish brown; a sub-semicircular whitish band on each side of each of the dorsal spots, enclosing a round, dark-brown, lateral spot. A pair of oblong brown, black-edged spots on the crown of the head convergent anteriorly; a brown spot below and an oblique broad streak behind the eye. Belly whitish, with more or less numerous round brown specks. The carpet-viper is fierce and aggressive. It is always on the defensive, ready to attack; it throws itself into a double coil, the folds of which are in perpetual motion, and as they rub against each other, they make a loud rustling sound very like hissing. This sound is produced by the three or four outer rows of carinated scales above-mentioned, which are very prominent, and point downwards at a different angle to the rest; their friction against each other causing the sound. This viper does not really hiss. Its fangs are very long and mobile like those of the Daboia [chain viper, penjera]. Its eye has a peculiarly vicious appearance. It is very active and can dart a considerable distance a foot or more, to strike its prey; it is the most active and aggressive of all poisonous snakes. Kills, if at all, by slow poisoning followed by gangrene or mortification. The following different kinds are distinguished in Tamul and Teloogoo.——*Blood carpet snake* (నెత్తురుసురత - netturusurata, Tel.; இரத்தச்சுருட்டை - irattaççuruttai, Tam.). The bite of which causes vomiting of blood.——*Lizard-tail carpet snake* (బల్లితోకసురత - ballitókasurata, Tel.; அரணைவாற்சுருட்டை - aranaivárchuruttai, Tam.). With a tail like green lizard.——*Long carpet snake* (పొడుగుసురత - podugusurata, Tel.; நெடுஞ்சுருட்டை - nedunjuruttai, Tam.). The largest.——*Red carpet snake* (ఎర్రసురత - errasurata, Tel.; செஞ்சுருட்டை - shenjuruttai, Tam.). The yellow kind.——*Short carpet snake* (పొట్టిసురత - pottisurata, Tel.; குறுஞ்சுருட்டை - kurunjuruttai, Tam.). The smallest.——*Swelling carpet snake* (వాపుసురత - vápusurata, Tel.; ஊதுசுருட்டை - úthusuruttai, Tam.). The bite causes swelling.

CARPOOR (कर्पूर - karpúra, *San.*). Same as Capoor and Camphor.——*Carpoora teilam* (कर्पूरतैल - karpúrataila, San.; کافور کا تیلم - káfúrkátailam, Dec.). Names mean oil of camphor on account of the smell. Oil of turpentine, obtained by distillation from that article. For the turpentine, oleo-resin itself see Ganda firoza.——*Carpoor maram* (కర్పూరమాను - karpúramánu, Tel.; கர்ப்பூரமரம் - karppúramaram, Tam.). Title from appearance and smell of leaf. Same as Blue gum [q.v.]; and generally applied to the whole eucalyptus genus [australian gum tree].

CARSHAM (कर्ष - karsha, *San.*). From (krish, san. to obtain). Measure of weight. 16 maushams = 1 carsham; 4 carshams = 1 palam [niray, 2, 3]. Approximate actual value, 1 carsham = 13 drs., 9 grs. Compare pollum. See vol. I, 609.

CARVETNUGGER (కార్వేటినగరము - kárvétinagaramu, *Tel.* kárvetnagar*). From (kárvédu, tel. local ruler + nagara, san. city). Tel. also (bommarádzupálemu), bomrauz [q.v.] being the family name.——**(1)** Zemindarry, North arcot district. Population 275,830. Language Teloogoo. N. centre of district. Bounded on the north by Chundragherry talook and Calastry zemindarry; on the east by Calastry zemindarry and Chingleput district; on the south by Wallajah talook; on the west by Chittore talook. Divided by the zemindar for revenue purposes into Narrainavaram, Pulliputt, and Trittany talooks. For criminal administration Government divide it into Narrainavaram and Trittany divisions. The Peshcush [q.v.] of Carvetnugger is Rs. 1,73,912 paid in three instalments. An historical and statistical account will be found in foot-note on page 58, vol. I. Places of archæological interest:—Arangoolam, Aroombaukam, Carimbaid, Carvetnugger, Cauverypooram, Chevarambaukam, Chinnammapett, Colattore, Coopaid, Cutchore, Damodara maharajpooram, Daumarpaukam, Eechambaudy, Kembarapollem, Makharauz droog, Maumandore, Melapoondy, Moodipully, Nagary, Naickenpollem, Narrainavaram, Naugapoody, Nediyam, Nindra, Payanore, Permanellore, Pulliputt, Santaunavengopaulpooram, Tirvaulangaud, Trittany, Velancherry, Vellauttcottay, Yogimullavaram. Principal trig. stations:—Alligore, Pinnauk, Poollore, Nagary nose. The leading places in the zemindarry are the following.——*Alligore* (அல்லிக்கூரு - allikkúru, Tam.). From (alli, tam. water-lily, nymphæa lotus, linn. + úru, tam. village). Trig. station; lat. 13° 16′ 14·90″; long. 79° 45′ 53·08″; from Carvetnugger E.S.E. 21 miles; from Trittany N.E. 9 miles; from Vijayapooram E. 2 miles.——*Arangoolam* (அரங்குளம் - árangulam, Tam.). From (arugan, tam. jain god + kulam, tam. tank). Village; lat. 13° 14′; long. 79° 43′; from Carvetnugger S.E. 20 miles; from Chittore E. 39 miles. Arangoolam naud was part of Chundragherry cottam, in the ancient Tondaimundalam. Jeina temple.——*Arnanuddy* (అరుణానది - arunánadi, Tel.). From (aruna, san. red + nadí, san. river). Sanscrit name (araninadí), meaning tree, ficus religiosa, linn. + river. River. Local name for Narrainavaram river. Takes its source in Sadaushiva condah hills, runs east into the Chingleput district. Flows August to December.——*Bomrauzpollem* (బొమ్మరాజుపాలెము - bomarádzupálemu, Tel.). See sep. title.——*Carvetnugger* (కార్వేటినగరము - kárvétinagaramu, Tel.). See below.——*Cooshastaly* (కుశస్థలి - kushast'hali, Tel.). See sep. title.——*Makharauz droog* (మఖరాజుదుర్గము - makharádzudurgamu, Tel.). From (makharádzu, tel. proper name + durga, san. fort). Hill; lat. 13° 23′; long. 79° 32′; from Carvetnugger E.S.E. 3¾ miles; from Chittore E.N.E. 30 miles; from Narrainavaram W.S.W. 6¾ miles; from Poottore S.W. 5 miles. Old hill fort by Makharauz, the first of the present Carvetnugger zemindars, for his Zenana [q.v.] in war.——*Nagary* (నగరి - nagari, Tel.). See sep. title.——*Narrainavaram* (నారాయణవరము - náráyanavaramu, Tel.). See sep. title.——*Pinnauk* (பிண்ணாக்கு - pinnákku, Tam.). Means oil-cake. Trig. station; lat. 13° 09′ 59·90″; long. 79° 38′ 19·08″; height 725 feet; from Carvetnugger S.S.E. 20 miles; from Trittany W.S.W. 1½ miles.——*Poollore* (పుల్లూరు - pullúru, Tel.). From (pulla, tel. reed + úru, tel. village). Trig. station; lat. 13° 13′ 57·70″; long. 79° 23′ 38·28″; height 1,914 feet; from Poollore E.S.E. 1½ miles; from Narrainavaram S.W. 20 miles; from Poottore S.W. 19 miles.——*Poottore* (புத்தூர் - puttúr, Tam.). See sep. title.——*Pulliputt* (பள்ளிப்பட்டு - palippattu, Tam.). From (palli, tam. rice-working caste + pattu, tam. village). Sanscrit name (shayanapuri), meaning town of rest; village where god slept. Village, Head-quarters of Zemindar's revenue talook; pop. 1,139; lat. 13° 20′; long. 79° 29′; from Carvetnugger S. 5½ miles; from Chittore E.N.E. 25 miles; from Trittany N.W. 16 miles. Military station under Mahomedan, had a mint. Fair Saturday. Rough cloths woven.——*Royalcheroo* (రాయల్చెరువు - ráyalcheruvu, Tel.). From (ráyalu, tel. the ruler + cheruvu, tel. tank); called after krishna deva royel. Village; pop. 383; lat. 13° 30′; long. 79° 26′; from Carvetnugger N.N.W. 7¼ miles; from Chittore N.E. 28 miles; from Narrainavaram W.N.W. 14 miles; from Poottore W.N.W. 12 miles. Once important, on road from Tripatty to Conjeeveram, but pilgrims now go by rail. Said that one of Krishna deva royel's daughters was buried in bund to prevent escape of water [anantapore]. Large choultry endowed by Zemindar.——*Tirvaulangaud* (திருவாலங்காடு - tiruválangádu, Tam.). From (tiru, tam. sacred + álam, tam. banyan tree, ficus bengalensis, linn. + kádu, tam. forest). Sanscrit name (vatáranya), means forest of banyan trees. Village, Place of pilgrimage; pop. 1,855; lat. 13° 08′; long. 79° 49′; from Carvetnugger S.E. 29¼ miles; from Chittore E. 46 miles; from Trittany E. 12 miles. Ancient temple to Shiva as Devarsinga permaun, with goddess Bramaraulacaumbicay. Of the sixty-four in which Shiva has danced, this first. Bramhotsavam [pundigay, 6a], in March-April. Ardray [pundigay, 5c] festival in December. Also a temple to Cauly [q.v.]. Three miles N. of Chinnammapett railway station.——*Trittany* (திருத்தணி - tiruttani, Tam.). See sep. title.——*Veligaram* (வெளிகரம் - veligaram, Tam.). See sep. title.——**(2)** Town, Head-quarters of zemindarry; North arcot district, Carvetnugger zemindarry, Narrainavaram division; pop. 6,046; lat. 13° 25′; long. 79° 29′; from Arnee N.N.E. 53 miles; from Chittore E.N.E. 28 miles; from Madras W.N.W. 60 miles; from Ranipett N.N.E. 35 miles; from Tripatty S. 15 miles; from Vellore N.N.E. 41 miles. Named after Carvetrauz, son of Bomrauz [q.v.], the founder of Bomrauzpollem, a village close to Carvetnugger. On high ground, but being surrounded by hill and jungle is feverish. Formerly strongly fortified. Zemindar's palace is modern. About 3 miles S.E. is Makharauz droog. It had two temples, one Shiva and one Vishnoo. The idol of the latter was moved to the new settlement. Carvetrauz being warned in a dream not to disturb the other, it is still worshipped in the deserted village. Fair Tuesday. Noted for oranges [q.v.].

CASAUREE (त्रिपुटी - triputí, *San.*; लांख - lánkha, *Mahr.*; کھساری - khisárí, *Hind.*). Title from hindostany. San. from (tri, san. three + puta, san. pod); triangular wedge-shaped pod. Hind. also (matar), meaning pea, pisum sativum, linn. [calauyam]. Greek λάθυρος; Latin cicercula. Title otherwise Chickling vetch, Everlasting pea, Vetch. Botanically Lathyrus sativus, linn., leguminosæ [vricsham, 48]. A pulse; flower large, blue; gives to pharm. seeds, non-officinal; affords wholesome green fodder; seeds eatable. The sweet pea is Lathyrus odoratus, with pink and white blossoms.

CASH (ಕಾಸು - kásu, *Can.*; காசு - kásu, *Tam.*). From (karsha, san. the coin); through Portuguese caixa. Coin or money in general. Thus pon cash, gold coin; velly cash, silver coin; shemboo or red cash, copper coin.—"*a*" Again in the old Madras currency, a small indeterminate copper coin, of which ten were equal to one doody [q.v.], being then less than half a pie. In Travancore sixteen cash at present date go to the chuckram [q.v.], and each is thus less than half a pie. The East india company issued copper pieces made at Birmingham at the end of last century in the form of one, five, ten, and twenty cash pieces, the last weighing 180 grains.—"*b*" The following varieties of old cash do not include the various kinds named after places where found; where not otherwise mentioned the impression is in accordance with the name:—Ashwapaty; lord of the horse, impression of horse. Aunay; elephant cash, cheran or congoo dynasty. Batavia; struck by dutch government of java and by the e. i. c. Bhootaky basavanna; from (bhútaki, can. demon + basava, can. bull); impression of bull on one side and of a demon on other. Bowddhan; struck by rulers professing booddhism, with impression of a booddha. Calyauna basavanna; struck by bijjala roya of calyaun; impression of bull, lingam, moon and sun. Camala moodray; lotus stamp. Chattrapaty; from (chhatrapaṭi, can. umbrella-lord). Chuckram; from (chakra, san. disc). Deva roya; struck by deva royel, of vijianugger; on one side figure of an ox, on other his name. Gajapaty; struck by prataparoodran of cuttack; impression of elephant. Ganapaty; struck by ganapaty deva of warangal. Garooda; from (garuda, san. the sacred kite). Goonta; from (gunta, tel. depressed). Hanooman; from the monkey god. Harihara roya; struck by that king of vijianugger; on one side impression of a bull, on other his name in nagry [baulbund, devanagry]. Jinka moodray; from the antelope. Matsya moodray struck by paundyan kings; impression of a fish. Mayoora vurman; struck by mayoora vurman king of banavausy, with impression of peacock. Motoopully; from place so called; struck by mookkanty maharauz. Nacshatra moodray; star stamp. Neelacunta; impression of a bull on one side, on the other the royal name neelacunta in nagry. Prataupa deva roya; struck by that king of vijianugger; impression of bull on one side, and his name in canarese on the other. Ramnaud; struck by saitoopaty of ramnaud; on one side his name in tamul, on the other a ceylonese dagger. Sarpa moodray; snake stamp. Shaunaur; the venetian ducat or sequin, the large numbers of which on the malabar coast testify to the once extensive commerce with italy by way of red sea; so called from figure of doge standing in front of st. mark's cross, mistaken for toddy drawer preparing to climb palmyra tree; have still a limited circulation. Shunkha; conch. Simha moodray; lion. Vencatapaty; struck by vencatapaty roy, rajah of chundragherry; impression of vencateshwaran, on other side his name. Vishnoovardhanan; struck by vishnoo vardhana ballaula, king of dwaura samoodram, with figure of ramaunoojan. Vrishchica moodray; scorpion.—"*c*" The present scale may be considered to be as follows:—2 cash = 1 dooggauny [naunyam, 2 a.c.d.]; approximate actual value, 1 cash = 1 pie. In Tamul countries, it is generally used for a pie; in Teloogoo districts a cash is generally $\frac{1}{4}$th of a dooggauny or otherwise $\frac{1}{10}$th of a dooggauny [damree, daum, roowa]. See vol. I, 609.

CASHAM (కశము - kashamu, *Tel.*; கசம் - kasam, *Tam.*). From (kasi, tam. to ooze out). Spring [oott].——*Casacaul* (கசக்கால் - kasakkál, Tam.). From (above + kál, tam. channel). Lands irrigated by well springs [caulvye, channel].

CASHEEDA (کشیدہ - kashídah, *Hind.*). From (kashídan, pers. to draw); as drawn or worked by the needle. Mixed texture of cotton and silk [puttoo] embroidered with the needle; used for caps [topee], &c. Working it forms leisure occupation of majority of Mahomedan females.

CASHEESHA (കശീശ - kashísha, *Mal.*). From Syriac. Presbyter among Malabar syrian christians.

CASHEW (शोफहर - shóp'hahara, *San.*; काजू - kájú, *Mahr.*; काज्जु - kájju, *Conc.*; بلادر فرنگ - baládurifarang, *Ar.*; بادام فرنگی - bádámifarangí, *Pers.*; کاجو کا پیڑ - kájúkáper, *Hind.*; کاجو کا جھاڑ - kájúkájhár, *Dec.*; جمبو مونت - jambumonat, *Malay*; ತುರಕಗೇರು - turakagéru, *Can.*; ಗೋಂಕುದಮರ - gónkudamara, *Too.*; ముంతమామిడి - muntamámidi, *Tel.*; കശുമാവ് - kashumávu, *Mal.*; කජු - kaju, *Singh.*; முந்திரி - mundiri, *Tam.*). Title through french acajou, from brazilian acajaiba; distinguish from catechu. San. from (shóp'ha, san. morbid swelling + hri, san. to take away). Mahr. from european term. Ar. from (baládur, ar. semecarpus anacardium, linn. f. + farang, ar. european); as a variety. Pers. from (bádám, pers. prunus amygdalus, baill. + farangí, pers. european). Hind. from (kájú, hind. cashew-nut + per, hind. tree). Can. from (turuka, can. turkish + géru, can. marking-nut plant). Too. from (góku, too. cashew fruit + mara, too. tree). Tel. from (munta, tel. pot + mámidi, tel. mangifera indica, linn.); from jug-like fruit. Mal. from (caju, port. cashew tree + mávu, mal. mangifera indica, linn.). Tam. from (muga, tam. to smell + tirigai, tam. the cashew plant). Hind. also (hijlíbádam). Malay also (jambuirung). Can. also (kempugéru), meaning red + semecarpus anacardium, linn. f. Tel. also (jídimámidi), meaning corrosive sap, marking nut + mango tree. Mal. also (pórtukimávu), meaning portuguese mango tree; (parankimávu), meaning foreign mango tree; (kappalchérmaram), meaning foreign + semecarpus anacardium, linn. f.; (pátirimávu), meaning christian mango tree; (kappalmávu), meaning-ship + mango tree. Tam. also (uttamabalam), meaning superior + fruit; (shigidimá), meaning gum + mango; (sháram), meaning juice; (tirigai), meaning twist, from appearance; (kottaimundirigai), meaning nut + cashew tree, to distinguish from (kodimundiri), meaning creeper + cashew tree [angoor]. Title otherwise Bean of Malacca, Cardole oil tree, Cashew-apple, Cashew-nut, Christians' mango, Foreign almond, Foreign marking-nut, Hijlee baudam, Kajo, Portuguese mango, Pot mango, Promotion nut tree, Ship mango, Turkish marking-nut. Botanically Anacardium occidentale, linn., anacardiaceæ [vricsham, 45]. Alias Acajouba occidentalis; Cassuvium pomiferum. Small tree, native of west indies; trunk short, thick, and very crooked, bark considerably rough; leaves oval, alternate, with roundish or emarginate apex; calyx five-cleft nearly to the base; petals five, linear-lanceolate, pale, yellow with pink stripes; stamens usually nine, with one longer than the others; style solitary; panicles terminal, with male and hermaphrodite flowers mixed together; flowers greenish red; fruit or cashew-nut a kidney-shaped ash-brown nut, one inch, sessile on the apex of a yellow or crimson-colored torus, called cashew-apple; flowering twice a year; in coast forests near the sea; resembles the walnut, and its leaves have a similar scent. The kernel of the nut is enclosed in a coriaceous covering consisting of two layers, between which is a thick black oil known as cardole oil; this oil is acrid to an extraordinary degree, whilst the kernels, which are roasted and eaten, are quite bland. The nuts yield also by expression a very sweet-tasted edible oil, much superior to european olive oil, but not so cheap as ground-nut [q.v.] oil; as the nuts are generally roasted and eaten, this oil is seldom obtained. The gum [gond] from trunk occurs in stalactiform masses, and varies in color from reddish to pale yellow; when placed in water it swells and forms a jelly-like mass and a portion of it dissolves; this solution is rendered turbid by oxalate of ammonium, and gives a copious white precipitate with alcohol; it is not precipitated by borax [vengauram] or sulphate of iron [annabhaidy]; the gum is obnoxious to insects. Cardole oil is medicinally powerful rubefacient and vesicant, used as an anæsthetic in leprosy [cooshtam], and as a blister in warts, corns and ulcers; the bark is given internally in infusion; apple is succulent and possesses a peculiar cooling quality; the juice of the apple is of use in diarrhœa and diabetes; whole plant gives to pharm. gum, cardole oil, cashew-nut oil, and cashew spirit. The dried kernels are eaten as dessert like almonds [baudam] after being toasted; in this state they are palatable when eaten with salt, but indigestible; they impart a flavor to madeira wine; mixed with cocoa they make a good chocolate; the juice of the apple expressed and fermented yields a pleasant wine, and distilled a spirit is drawn from it. Bark used in tanning [chamrah]; cardole oil applied to prevent attack of white-ants; gum is a good varnish [rangh] and a fair substitute for gum-arabic [q.v.], collected while the sap is rising, small in quantity. Wood red, moderately hard, close-grained; makes good charcoal [adoopp-kary]. A variety grows in travancore, whose nuts have no oil. No other common species here.——*Country cashew* (රටකජු - ratakaju, Singh.). From likeness of taste. Same as Ground-nut.

CASHMERE (काश्मीर - káshmíra, *San.*; کشمیر - kashmír, *Hind.*). From (kashyapa, san. the sage + míra, san. mountain side).—"*a*" The valley province of W. himalayas. Colonized by sage Cashyapan [q.v.] about B.C. 3000. Various Hindoo dynasties ruled over the country until annexed to Moghul dominions in 1586 A.D. Wrested from Mahomedans by Runjeet singh in 1819. Granted to Rajah goolaub singh by the British on the conclusion of Panjaub war in 1846 A.D. and his descendants now rule over it.—"*b*" Woollen fabric once solely manufactured there [shawl].—"*c*" Prefix in plant names from place of growth.——*Cashmere flower* (काश्मीरजन्मा - káshmírajanmá, San.). Same as saffron.——*Cashmere nut* (کشمیری پستہ - kashmírípistah, Ar.). Same as Mishmish.——*Cashmere tea* (چاء کشمیری - cháikashmírí, Pers.). Same as Lemon grass.——*Cashmere tree* (काश्मरी - káshmarí, San.; शिवणी - shivaní, Mahr.; جگنی چکر - juganíchukar, Hind.; ಕಾಶ್ಮೀರಮರ - káshmírimara, Can.; గుముడుటేకు - gumudutéku, Tel.; ଗୁମ୍ବାରି - gumbári, Oor.; കുമിഴ് - kumizh, Mal.; දෙමට - demata, Singh.; குமிழ் kumizh, Tam.). Title from habitat. San. from (kash, san. to destroy); from destroying bile. Tel. from (gumudu, tel. cluster, gmelina asiatica, linn. + téku, tel. teak, tectona grandis, linn. f.). Mal. and tam. means globular, probably from use in ornamental knob work. San. also (gambhárí), meaning difficult to be conveyed and heavy; (gandhárí), meaning produced in candahar; (gándháryá), meaning pertaining to candahar; (vidárí), meaning rending asunder [giant sweet potato, shoonday]; (sarvatóbhadrá), meaning auspicious on all sides; (shríparní) meaning holy-leaved. Hind. also (gumar). Can. also (gumbari). Tel. also (peddagumudutéku), meaning large + the tree; (kasmiryamu), from sanscrit; (gumudu), meaning clustering; (chittungudu); (belligummudu); (peddagumudu), meaning large + the tree, gmelina asiatica, linn.; (teggummudu), meaning teak + gmelina asiatica, linn. Mal. also (kumbil). Tam. also (perungumizh), meaning large + the tree. Title otherwise Candahar tree, Cashmere timber tree, Cooml, Cooml teak, Gambhauree, Gandharee, Heart-leaved gmelina, Large goomidy. Botanically

Gmelina arborea, linn., verbenaceæ [vricsham, 102]. Alias Cumbul rheedii; Gmelina rheedii. Cumbul from mal. Arboreous, unarmed; short thick trunk; branchlets and the young leaves covered with a greyish powdery tomentum; leaves long-petioled, cordate or somewhat produced and acute at the base, acuminate, the adult ones glabrous above, greyish tomentose beneath, with two to four glands at the base; panicles tomentose, axillary, and terminal; raceme-like cymules decussate, trichotomous, few-flowered; bracts lanceolate, deciduous; the acutely dentate calyx eglandulose; flowers large, sulphur-colored, slightly tinged with red outside the tube; flowering in the hot season; grows rapidly and the seeds may be planted in beds. Root is bitter, tonic, stomachic and laxative, given in cough, rheumatism, fever and indigestion, and is anthelmintic. Fruit eaten by khonds and other wild hill tribes. Leaves used as fodder, deer are fond of them; shade is good; ashes used as mordant [cauram]. Wood yellowish, greyish or reddish-white with a glossy lustre, close and even-grained, soft, light and strong, durable, does not warp or crack; annual rings marked either by a white line or by more numerous pores in the spring wood; wood easily worked, readily takes paint or varnish [rangh]; very durable under water; highly esteemed for planking, furniture, domestic utensils, door panels, carriages and palankeens, well-work, boats, toys, packing cases, and all ornamental work; not readily attacked by insects. The Small cashmere tree, otherwise Lowly cooml, Oval-leaved gmelina, Rais madre de deos, Small goomidy, is Gmelina asiatica, linn., alias Gmelina lobata, parviflora, Premna parvifolia; thorny shrub; leaves opposite, petioled, ovate, tomentose underneath, with frequently a sharp short lobe on each side; spines axillary, opposite, horizontal, pubescent at the tip, the length of the petioles; flowers from the end of the tender twigs on peduncles; fruit a berried drupe size of a jujube [bair], black, smooth; flowers large, bright sulphur; drooping; flowering all the year; leaves have quality of thickening water, and rendering it mucilaginous when agitated in it, so becoming useful drink in gonorrhœa, &c., requiring demulcents; quoted in pharm., but non-officinal; wood only used as fuel.

CASHOON (کشون - kashún, *Hind.*). A battalion [pataulam]. Turkish word introduced by Tippoo sultan.

CASHYAPAN (कश्यप - kashyapa, *San.*). According to the Mahabhaurat, the Ramayanam and the Pooraunams, he was the son of Mareechy, the son of Bramha; and he was the father of Vivaswat, the father of Menoo. He married thirteen of the daughters of Dacshan and two of Veishwaunaran and became the father of the gods, demons, men, beasts, and reptiles [adity]. He is therefore called a Prajaupaty. He is also according to some, one of the seven great Rishies. The word resembles the mythological and astronomical κασσιόπεια [caushyapy]. It without doubt represents some very ancient race who inhabited the Central asiatic chain, in which traces of the name are so plentifully found, as in the Kob i kas or Caucasus, the Caspian, and Cashmere [q.v.]. Of the forty-nine gotrams of Bramins cashyapa is one [matam].

CASONDY (कासमर्द - kásamarda, *San.*; होडुतैकिलो - hódutaikiló, *Conc.*; کسوندی - kasondí, *Hind.*; بڑی کسونڈی - barikasondí, *Dec.*; ದೊಡ್ಡತಗಚೆ - doddatagache, *Can.*; ಆನೆತಜಂಕ್ - ánetajank, *Too.*; కసింద - kasinda, *Tel.*; നാറ്റന്തകര - náttantakara, *Mal.*; පනිතෝර - panitóra, *Singh.*; நாற்றந்தகரை - náttandagarai, *Tam.*). Title from hindostany. San. from (kása, san. cough + mard, san. to crush). Dec. from (barí, hind. large + kasondí, hind. the plant). Can. from (dodda, can. big + tagache, can. cassia tora, linn.). Tel. from (kasi, tel. itching); as cure. Singh. from (pani, singh. sweet + tóra, singh. cassia tora, linn.). Tam. from (náttam, tam. fetidness + tagarai, tam. plant, cassia tora, linn.); from leaves. Hind. also (gajarság), meaning elephant greens. Can. also (kóltagache), meaning stick + cassia tora, linn. Tel. also (kasivinda), meaning itching. Mal. also (ponnáviram), meaning gold + cassia auriculata, linn., from yellow flowers; (péyáviram), meaning wild + cassia auriculata, linn. Singh. also (petitora); slender tora. Tam. also (péyávirai), meaning wild + cassia auriculata, linn.; (ponnávirai), meaning gold + cassia auriculata, linn. Title otherwise Casandy, Fetid cassia, Negro coffee, Occidental cassia, Round-podded cassia, Rubbish cassia, Stinking weed, Wild cassia. Botanically Cassia [soovarnacam] occidentalis, linn., leguminosæ [vricsham, 48]. Alias Cassia fœtida, planisiliqua, sophera; Senna occidentalis. Annual; erect, branches glabrous; leaflets three to five pairs, without glands between them, ovate-lanceolate, very acute, glabrous on both sides; petiole with a large sessile gland near its tumid base; flowers longish-pedicelled, upper ones forming a terminal raceme, lower ones three to five together, on a very short axillary peduncle; legumes long when ripe, when dried surrounded with a tumid border nearly cylindrical; flowers yellow; common, particularly among rubbish; leaves when bruised exhale disagreeable odour; very nearly allied to cassia sophera, linn. [stinking casondy]. Seeds used under the name of fedegozo seeds on the zambesi as a substitute for coffee [q.v.]. The leaves purgative; in pharm., but non-officinal.——*Baskee casondy* (باس کی کسوندی - báskíkasondí, Hind.). Means stinking casondy [q.v.].——*Hill casondy* (కొండకసింద - kondakasinda, Tel.). Same as Toddaly.——*Stinking casondy* (कासमर्द - kásamarda, San.; रानटांकळा - ránatánkalá, Mahr.; باس کی کسوندی - báskíkasondí, Hind.; سڑی کسونڈی - sarikasondí, Dec.; ಕಾಸಮರ್ದವು - kásamardavu, Can.; పైడితంగేడు - paiditangédu, Tel.; പൊന്നാന്തകര - ponnántakara, Mal.; උරුතෝර - úrutóra, Singh.; பொன்னாவிரை - ponnávirai, Tam.). Title from disagreeable smell of plant. San. from (kása, san. cough + mard, san. to crush). Mahr. from (rána, mahr. wild + tánkalá, mahr. cassia tora, linn.). Hind. from (bás, hind. stink + kasondí, hind. cassia occidentalis, linn.). Dec. from (sarí, hind. fœtid + kasondí, hind. cassia occidentalis, linn.). Tel. from (paidi, tel. gold + tangédu, tel. cassia auriculata, linn.). Mal. from (pon, mal. gold + takara, mal. cassia tora, linn.). Singh. from (úru, singh. large + tóra, singh. cassia tora, linn.). Tam. from (pon, tam. gold + ávirai, tam. cassia auriculata, linn.). San. also (svarnamayahari), meaning gold + cassia auriculata, linn.; (talapóta), probably corruption from (stalapadma, san. cassia angustifolia). Dec. also (janglítáklah), meaning wild cassia tora, linn.; (kasoya); (kasota); (kasmardah). Tel. also (tagara); (nútikasinda), meaning well + cassia occidentalis, linn.; (kondakasinda), meaning hill cassia occidentalis [toddaly]. Tam. also (periyatagarai), meaning large + cassia tora, linn.; (péràvirai), meaning large + cassia auriculata, linn. Title otherwise Baskee casondy, Casoudy, Fetid cassia, Golden tungaid, Large tagaray, Round-podded cassia. Botanically Cassia [soovarnacam] sophera, linn., leguminosæ [vricsham, 48]. Alias Cassia chinensis, coromandeliana, esculenta, indica, purpurea, sopheroides, torosa, torulosa; Chamæfistula coromandelina, sophera, torosa; Senna esculenta, purpurea, sophera. Annual; erect, branched, glabrous; leaflets six to twelve pairs, lanceolate or oblong-lanceolate, acute, with a single gland near the base of the petiole; racemes terminal or axillary, few-flowered; upper petal retuse; legumes long, linear, turgid, almost cylindrical, but when dry flatten; when immature and dried, compressed, glabrous, many-seeded; suture keeled; seeds horizontal with cellular partitions; flowers middle-sized, yellow; flowering nearly all year; smell of plant heavy and disagreeable. Bark, leaves, and seeds are cathartic; juice of leaves with lime-juice is specific in ringworm [dadroo], made into a plaster and combined with sandal-wood; leaves quoted in pharm., but non-officinal. Leaves eaten in curries.

CASSA (अंजन - añjana, *Mahr.*; गंडपटकलि - gandapatakali, *Conc.*; کاشان - káshán, *Dec.*; ಅಲಮರು - alamaru, *Can.*; ಅಲಿಮರು - alimaru, *Too.*; అల్లిచెట్టు - allichettu, *Tel.*; കാശാവു - káshávu, *Mal.*; දොඩන්කහ - dodankaha, *Singh.*; காசா - kásá, *Tam.*). Title from tamul. Mahr. means collyrium [champak, yaipy]. Dec. from tamul. Tel. from (allu, tel. to spread + chettu, tel. tree). Singh. from (dodam, singh. orange + kaha, singh. turmeric, curcuma longa, roxb.); from dye. Tam. from (káy, tam. to shine). Can. also (ganduképala), meaning male + ixora coccinea, linn. Too. also (ollekodi), meaning water-snake + sprout. Mal. also (káyávu), by corruption; (kaláyam); (netunchetti), meaning tall + ixora coccinea, linn. Singh. also (valíkaha), meaning sand + turmeric. Tam. also (káyámbúççedi); (shirugásá), meaning small + the plant; (vaççi); (púvai), meaning beautiful; (alli), meaning dark plant, from blue flowers; (káyá), meaning shining tree; (perungásá), meaning large + the tree. Title otherwise Iron-wood tree. Botanically Memecylon edule, roxb., melastomaceæ [vricsham, 57]. Alias Memecylon cordatum, edule, ramiflorum, sessile, tinctorium, umbellatum. Shrub, arborescent, 10–12 feet; calyx with a hemispherical or subglobose tube; petals four; branches terete; leaves shortly petioled, ovate or oblong, one-nerved; peduncles axillary, and below the leaves on the elder branches bearing a more or less compound corymb of pedicellate flowers; stamens shortish; style about the length of the stamens; fruit globose, crowned with the four-toothed limb of the calyx; fruit one to two-seeded; flowers bluish purple; flowering in beginning of hot season. Leaves in infusion are medicinally anti-inflammatory. Astringent pulpy berries, when ripe, eaten by natives. Leaves are used by mat-makers in conjunction with myrobalan [q.v.] and vattangy cuttay or sappan [q.v.] wood in imparting a deep red tinge to the mats [boriyah]; they are also used in preparing shempunjy or red cotton [red cotton wool]; as an auxiliary with chayroot [q.v.] give a yellow dye [shauyam]. Wood strong, durable, very hard, and close-grained; substitute for boxwood. Other species are:—amabile, amplexicaule, angustifolium, gracile, heyneanum, procerum, terminale.

CASSERGODE (ಕಾಸರಗೋಡು - kásaragódu, *Can.*; കാഞ്ഞിരോട് - káññirótu, *Mal.*; kásaragód*). From (kásara, can. wild buffalo + kódu, can. peak). Mal. from (kááñiram, mal. strychnos nux vomica, linn. + kótu, mal. place).——(1) Talook, South canara district. Tahsildar's pay Rs. 200. S. coast of district. Boundaries; north, part of Mangalore talook and the river Netrauvaty; south, Cavvye river; east, Coppinangady talook and part of Coorg; west, the Arabian sea. Comprises low undulating hills intersected with rivers. Soil sandy on the coast and laterite [q.v.] elsewhere. The chief industry is agriculture. Rice, pepper [q.v.], cardamoms [q.v.] and areca-nuts [q.v.] are exported. The imports consist of cotton-goods, hardware and articles of European manufacture. Cultivation depends mainly upon rains, which are plentiful. Later crops are raised partly by supplies of water drawn from streams, natural pools, private tanks and wells. Camping grounds on the coast road; Baicull, Cassergode, Cautacutcherry, Coombla, Hosdroog, Manjeshwar. On the road from Mangalore to Mercara, Cauv, Pauneymangalore. Places of archæological interest:—Adoor, Anantapooram, Baicull, Bangramanjeshwar, Cassergode, Cauv, Chundragherry, Hosdroog, Muddore, Poodoor, Shiry, Tenka coombla, Vittal. Principal trig. stations:—Baicull, Bullamaley, Coondoodakamaley, Moochil. The leading places, &c., in the talook are the following.——*Adoor* (ಅಡೂರು - adúru, Can.). From (adi, can. bottom + úru, can. village). Village; pop. 2,252; lat. 12° 34′; long. 75° 14′; from Cassergode E.N.E. 15 miles; from Mangalore S.E. 32 miles; from the sea E. 16 miles. Shiva temple once in ruins, but now repaired. Temple of Ganesh with inscription.——*Ajanore* (ಅಜಾನೂರು - ajánúru, Can.). From (aja, san. the unborn brahma + úru, can. village). Village; pop. 6,971; lat. 12° 20′; long. 75° 7′; from Cassergode S.S.E. 13 miles; from Mangalore S.S.E. 40 miles; from the sea E. 1 mile. On coast road half way between Mangalore and Cannanore.——*Alaratnaud* (അലവട്ടനാട് - alavattunátu, Mal.). From (alavu, mal. measure + atta, mal. devoid + nátu, mal. country). A subdivision of the talook, comprising nine villages.——*Baicull* (ಬೇಕಲ - békal, Can.). See sep. title.——*Baudore* (ಬಾಡೂರು - bádúru, Can.). From (bádu, can. fence + úru, can. village). Village; pop. 1,330; lat. 12° 39′; long. 75° 04′; from Cassergode N. 11 miles; from Mangalore S.E. 19 miles; from the sea E. 7½ miles.——*Bauyaur* (ಬಾಯಾರು - báyáru, Can.). Village; pop. 2,854; lat. 12° 41′; long. 75° 04′; from Cassergode N. 13 miles; from Mangalore S.E. 16 miles; from the sea E. 8 miles.——*Bullamaley* (ಬಲ್ಲಮಲೆ - ballamale, Can.). Trig. station; lat. 12° 48′ 34·54″; long. 75° 07′ 46·07″; height 818 feet; from Cassergode N.N.E. 22 miles; from the sea E. 16 miles.——*Cassergode* (ಕಾಸರಗೋಡು - kásaragódu, Can.). See below.——*Charvuttore* (ചാർവത്തൂർ - charvvattúr, Mal.). From (charuvu, mal. slope + úr, mal. village). Village; pop. 4,615; lat. 12° 13′; long. 75° 12′; from Cassergode S.S.E. 22 miles; from Mangalore S.S.E. 49 miles; from the sea E. 3½ miles.——*Chundragherry* (ಚಂದ್ರಗಿರಿ - chandragiri, Can.). See sep. title.——*Colnaud* (ಕೊಲನಾಡು - kolanádu, Can.). From (kole, can. murder + nádu, can. country). Village; pop. 2,653; lat. 12° 46′; long. 75° 05′; from Cassergode N. 19 miles; from Mangalore E.S.E. 15 miles; from the sea E. 12 miles.——*Coombla* (ಕುಂಬಳೆ - kumbale, Can.). See sep. title.——*Coondoodakamaley* (ಕುಂದುದ್ದಕಮಲೆ - kunduddakamale, Can.). Trig. station; lat. 12° 23′ 28·29″; long. 75° 16′ 19·81″; height 1,896 feet; from Bailore E. 2½ miles; from Cassergode E.S.E. 17 miles; from the sea E. 13 miles.——*Hosdroog* (ಹೊಸದುರ್ಗ - hosadurga, Can.). See sep. title.——*Madakye* (ಮಡಕ್ಕಯಿ - madakkayi, Can.). From (mada, can. shrine of a demon + kaya, can. swamp). Village; pop. 4,225; lat. 12° 20′; long. 75° 10′; from Cassergode S.E. 15 miles; from Mangalore S.S.E. 42 miles; from the sea E. 4 miles.——*Manjeshwar* (ಮಂಜೇಶ್ವರ - manjéshvara, Can.). See sep. title.——*Moochil* (ಮುಚ್ಚಿಲು - muççilu, Can.). Trig. station; lat. 12° 37′ 04·64″; long. 75°·21′ 54·10″; height 1,215 feet; from Cassergode E.N.E. 24 miles; from the sea E. 27 miles.——*Mooliyaur* (ಮುಳಿಯಾರು - muliyáru, Can.). From (muli, can. thatch grass + áru, can. plough). Village; pop. 3,717; lat. 12° 31′; long. 75° 09′; from Cassergode E. 8½ miles; from Mangalore S.E. 31 miles; from the sea E. 10 miles.——*Neeleshwar* (ನೀಲೇಶ್ವರ - niléshvara, Can.). See sep. title.——*Oodiyauvar* (ಉದಿಯಾವರ - udiyávara, Can.). From (udaya, san. rising + pura, san. town). Village; pop. 2,054; lat. 12° 44′; long. 74° 56′; from Bombay S.S.E. 440 miles; from Cassergode N.N.W. 18½ miles; from Caup S.S.E. 35 miles; from Mangalore S.S.E. 9½ miles; from Oodipy S.S.E. 42 miles. Moplah village.——*Payashwany* (ಪಯಸ್ವಿನಿ - payasvini, Can.). See sep. title.——*Perdaul* (ಪೆರ್ಡಾಲ - perdála, Can.). From (peru, can. to obtain + dálu, can. shield). Village; pop. 4,617; lat. 12° 36′; long. 75° 06′; from Cassergode N.N.E. 8½ miles; from Mangalore S.E. 23 miles; from the sea E. 8½ miles.——*Pullacorcode* (ಪಳ್ಳಕೊರ್ಕೋಡು - pallakorkódu, Can.). From (palla, can. pit + kora, can. short + kódu, can. hill top). Village; pop. 4,932; lat. 12° 29′; long. 75° 01′; from Cassergode W. 1 mile; from Mangalore S.S.E. 27 miles; from the sea E. ½ mile.——*Vittal* (ವಿಟ್ಲ - vitla, Can.). From (vitt'hal, san. vishnu). Village; pop. 2,834; lat. 12° 45′; long. 75° 08′; from Cassergode N.N.E. 19½ miles; from Mangalore E.S.E. 19 miles; from the sea E. 15 miles. Formerly owned by petty Jeina rajah or Heggadey [q.v.]. The family receives a pension. Temple of Punchaliugeshwaran of great antiquity.——**(2)** Town, Port, Talook head-quarters; South canara dist., Cassergode tal.; pop. 5,943; lat. 12° 30′; long. 75° 02′; from Baicull N.N.W. 7 miles; from Bombay S.S.E. 460 miles; from Coombla S.S.E. 2½ miles; from Coondapore S.S.E. 80 miles; from Madras W. 360 miles; from Mangalore S.E. 27 miles; from Oodipy S.S.E. 60 miles; from Poottore S.W. 22 miles; from Soobramanyam W.S.W. 42 miles. Kangercoté of the Tohfatool moojauhideen. On the Chundragherry river, on route from Mangalore to Cannanore. The town is in rear of a backwater [cauyal]. Connected by road with Coorg and Mysore. When the country along the coast was divided by Mayoora vurman into sixty-four sections under different Bramin governors, this was one of the four centres. A fort, built by Shivappa naick when he subjected the petty rajahs of Tooloovam, is now in total ruins.

CASSIA (كاشا - kassá, *Hind.*). From syriac; means peeled. Ancient term for Cassia bark otherwise Cassia lignea [cassia cinnamon], used medicinally like cinnamon bark. Cassia buds are the dried flower-buds of the same tree, used for flavoring like cloves. Cassia oil is distilled from leaves and bark of the same tree, used also for flavoring. The term has been applied by botanists to a genus [soovarnacam] including great variety of different plants; similar origin, but changed meaning.

CASSIBOR (धान्याक - dhányáka, *San.*; धणा - dhaná, *Mahr.*; कोतंबरि - kótambari, *Conc.*; كزبرة - kuzbarah, *Ar.*; كشنيزسبز - kushnízisabz, *Pers.*; كوتهمير - kothmír, *Hind.* and *Dec.*; كاتومبر - kátumbar, *Malay*; ಕೊತ್ತುಂಬರಿ - kottumbari, *Can.*; ಕೊತ್ತಂಬರಿ - kottambari, *Too.*; ధనియాలు - daniyálu, *Tel.*; ଧନିଆ - dhoniya, *Oor.*; കൊത്തമ്പാല - kottampála, *Mal.*; කොත්තමල්ලි - kottamalli, *Singh.*; கொத்தமல்லி - kottamalli, *Tam.*). Title from arabic, corrupted. San. from (dhánya, san. grain). Arabic from syriac. Pers. from (kushníz, pers. coriander + sabz, pers. green). Hind. from persian. Can. from (kustumburu, san. coriander). Tel. from sanscrit. Tam. from (kustumburu, san. coriander). San. also (kustumbarí), meaning small coriander; (hridyagandha), meaning of agreeable smell. Arabic also (nabátijuljulán). Tel. also (kottamalli). Mal. also (kottamalli). Singh. also (dhaníya). Tam. also (uttambari); (tanigam). Greek κορίαννον, κόριον, κορίανδρον, from κόρις bug, on account of smell of growing plant and unripe fruit. Title otherwise Coriander, Cottamully, Dhanyah. Botanically Coriandrum sativum, linn., umbelliferæ [vricsham, 67]. Annual plant; flowers small, white; the fruit is coriander seed. Cultivated in soils of a saline nature; ground prepared in south in auvany or august or poorataushy or september; on coromandel [q.v.] in ashaudham or july or shrauvanam or august and aushweejam [mausam] or october; prepared by ploughing and manuring; seed sown in cartigay or november broadcast; while under growth weeds cleared; full grown crop, one foot high; cut or pulled up after three months; the plants are heaped for three days; afterwards put in the sun and seeds separated; brought to market ten days afterwards; average price thirty-five imperial seers for one rupee. Dried fruit and volatile oil used as an aromatic stimulant in colic; gives to pharm. ripe fruit dried, coriandri fructus, properties similar to those of carum carui; officinal. In veterinary practice the young plants are used when horses are overpurged from physic; giving five or six handfuls. Eaten as a vegetable; seeds universally used as a condiment [chutney], form one of the ingredients in curry [q.v.]; also used in confectionery and for flavoring spirits; favorite condiment on account of its flavor and warm taste. Volatile oil gained from fruit by distillation in water. No other species here.

CASSIM (قاسم - kásim, *Ar.*). From (kasama, ar. to divide). A divider. Name of the prophet. Alam; as Cassim bee, alam + alaumat [ism].——*Cassimcote* (ఖాసింకోట - khásimkóta, Tel. kasimkót). From (kásim, ar. name of the founder + kóta, san. fort). Proprietary estate, Town, Head-quarters of the proprietrix; Vizagapatam district, Ankapully division; pop. 7,672; lat. of town 17° 40′; long. 83° 01′; from Ankapully W.S.W. 3½ miles; from Vizagapatam W. 21 miles; from the sea N. 13 miles. Under Mussalman rule, a fowjdarry [q.v.] of Chicacole circar [q.v.]. After the Northern circars [q.v.] came into British hands in 1768, it remained head-quarters of a division. When in 1802 Chicacole circar was transferred to Ganjam, Cassimcote remained attached to Vizagapatam. It was here that Colonel Forde's troops made their rendezvous with those of Vizianagram, previous to battle of Condore and taking of Masulipatam in 1758-59. Peshcush Rs. 13,901.

CASSUMUNAR (वनार्द्रक - vanárdraka, *San.*; كسومونر - kasumunar, *Hind.*; కారల్లము - kárallamu, *Tel.*). Title from bengalee. San. from (vana, san. forest + árdraka, san. ginger, zingiber officinale, roscoe). Tel. from (káru, tel. wild + allamu, tel. ginger). Hind. also (bumadabemada); (banada), by corruption from sanscrit. Tel. also (kúrapasupu), meaning curry + turmeric, curcuma longa, rox.; (kárupasupu), meaning wild + turmeric. Title otherwise Bengal root, Curry turmeric, Downy-leaved ginger, Wild turmeric. Botanically Zingiber [aurdracam] cassumunar, roxb., zingiberaceæ [vricsham, 144]. Root tuberous; stems erect, round, 3–5 feet; leaves bifarious, linear-lanceolate; scapes radical, 6–12 inches long; spikes oblong, strobiliform, closely imbricated with numerous obovate acuminate villous bracts; flowers large, pale sulphur; flowering in july and august. A plant, with strong camphoraceous smell; rhizome much larger than that of common ginger [q.v.], tastes hot and bitterish.

CATACAM (కటకము - katakamu, *Tel.*). From (kat, san. to surround). Fortification; suffix in place names [cadagam].

CATAMARAN (கட்டுமரம் - kattumaram, *Tam.*). From (kattu, tam. to bind + maram, tam. wood). Raft consisting of three logs of very light buoyant wood, such as the Erythrina indica [common coral tree]. Erroneously said to be made of the cocoanut [q.v.] tree, a wood which sinks at once in water.

The length is from 20–25 feet, and breadth 2½–3½ feet. The logs are secured together by three spreaders and cross-lashings through small holes; the centre log being much the largest, with a curved surface at the fore end, which trends and finishes upwards to a point. The side logs are similar in form, but smaller, having their sides straight, and fitted to the centre log. The catamaran is generally navigated by two men, sometimes by one only. Catamarans are used mostly for deep-sea fishing. They also convey letters to and from the shore; the man who takes it has leaf of the areca [q.v.] tree tied round his waist, in which he encloses it.

CATAPANG (इंगुदी - ingudí, *San.*; बदामिरूकु - badámirúku, *Conc.*; درخت بادام هندی - darakhtibádámihindi, *Pers.*; هندی بادام کا پیڑ - hindíbádámkáper, *Hind.*; جنگلی بادام کا جهاڑ - janglíbádamkájhár, *Dec.*; کتپانگ - katapáng, *Malay*; ನಾಟುಬಾದಾಮಿ - nátubádámi, *Can.*; ಬಾದಾಮು - bádámu, *Too.*; నాటుబాదముచెట్టు - nátubádamuchettu, *Tel.*; അടമരം - atamaram, *Mal.*; කොට්ටඹා - kottambá, *Singh.*; நாட்டுவாதுமை - náttuváthumai, *Tam.*). Title from malay. San. from (ing, san. to grow up) [baudam, firework plant]. Pers. from (darakht, pers. tree + bádám, pers. almond, prunus amygdalus, baill. + hindí, pers. country). Hind. from (hindí, hind. country + bádám, hind. almond + per, hind. tree). Dec. from (janglí, hind. wild + bádam, hind. almond + jhár, hind. tree). Can. from (nátu, can. country + bádámi, can. the tree). Tel. similar. Mal. from (ata, mal. close + maram, mal. tree). Tam. from (nádu, tam. country + váthumai, tam. almond tree). San. also (déshabádáma), meaning country almond; (tailap'hala), meaning oil-fruited. Can. also (bádámi); (olágramara), meaning indigenous + tree; (úrubádámi), meaning country + tree; (tari). Tel. also (bádamuchettu); (tápasataruvu), meaning sage + tree. Mal. also (náttubádám), meaning country almond; (kottakkuru), meaning kernel nut. Tam. also (amandimaram), perhaps from english almond; (váthumai) [baudam, katcerah]. Title otherwise Bengalee baudam, Broad-leaved terminalia, Country almond, Indian almond, Jungle almond, Malabar almond, Malay almond. Botanically Terminalia [antya parny] catappa, linn., combretaceæ [vricsham, 55]. Specific name from malay. Alias Adamaram; Bucida buceras; Juglans catappa; Terminalia intermedia, moluccana, myrobalana, subcordata. Adamaram from malayalam. Tree, 50 feet; leaves about the extremities of the branchlets, short-petioled, obovate, cuneate or slightly cordate at the base, a little repand, with a large gland beneath on either side the midrib near the base; racemes axillary, solitary, simple shorter than the leaves; drupe compressed, oval, with elevated margins, convex on both sides; flowers small, dull white, with a hairy glandular disk at the bottom of the calyx; found in gardens, &c.; is in flower and fruit throughout the year; bears fruit three times a year on the malabar coast; a malayan species, cultivated in india. Drupe contains one kernel which has a fine filbert-like flavor, with a crispness like that of a fresh walnut, resembles a small fold of white paper; the kernel yields upwards of fifty per cent. of a pure bland oil, very similar to almond oil, for which it may be used as a substitute; this kept for a time deposits a large quantity of stearine; the color is a deep straw. Bark astringent; kernels and oil are in pharm. non-officinal. Kernels are eaten; oil expressed from seeds is like almond oil cake used to feed pigs; tusser [q.v.] silkworms feed on the leaves. Makes a good avenue [shaulay] tree; bark and leaves yield a black pigment [rangh], to dye teeth and make indian ink [mashy]; gives a gum [gond]. Wood red with lighter-colored sapwood, hard; levers of picottahs [q.v.] are made of it; texture is very like that of mango [q.v.].

CATAURY (کتاری - katárí, *Hind.*). From (katár, hind. dagger). Pointings in embroidery [zardozy].

CATECHU (खदिर - khadira, *San.*; खैर - khaira, *Mahr.*; खैरु - khairu, *Conc.*; کهیر ببول - khairbabúl, *Hind.*; کتهے کی کیکر - katthekíkíkar, *Dec.*; ಕಗ್ಗಲಿಮರ - kaggalimara, *Can.*; ಕಾಚು - káchu, *Too.*; పొడలమాను - podalamánu, *Tel.*; ଖଇରୁ - khoiru, *Oor.*; ഖദിരം - khadiram, *Mal.*; කිහිරි - kihiri, *Singh.*; ஓதலை - óthalai, *Tam.*). Title from teloogoo and canarese for the product [cutch]. San. from (khad, san. to be firm), strong timber. Mahr. from sanscrit. Hind. from (sanscrit + babúl, hind. acacia arabica, willd.). Dec. from (katthá, hind. cutch + kíkar, hind. acacia sp.). Can. from (kaggallu, can. to be firm + mara, can. tree). Tel. from (poda, tel. variegation + mánu, tel. tree). Oor. and singh. from sanscrit. Tam. from (ótham, tam. moisture + ali, tam. to preserve), as thriving on dry soil. San. also (jívamangalyá), meaning life + auspicious, from cutch being good for health; (arunaki), meaning red, from color of cutch. Can. also (taremara), meaning to tear, of thorns + tree. Tel. also (nallatsandra), meaning black + acacia sundra, dec.; (kátsuchettu), meaning cutch tree. Greek ἀχάνθη. Title otherwise Black catechu, Cutch acacia, Kath acacia, Medicinal acacia, Wodalee gum tree. Botanically Acacia [cantalam] catechu, willd., leguminosæ [vricsham, 48]. Alias Acacia polyacantha, sundra, wallichiana; Mimosa catechu, catechuoides, sundra. Sundra, from (tsandra, tel. acacia sundra, dec.). Gregarious, thorny, deciduous tree, 30–40 feet; dark brown bark; branches armed with stipulary thorns, occasionally unarmed; foliage delicate; leaves bipinnated; pinnæ ten to thirty pair; leaflets numerous, ranged like teeth of small comb; young shoots, petioles, and peduncles more or less pubescent; petioles sometimes armed below with a row of prickles; spikes axillary one to four together, shorter than the leaves; corolla five-cleft; petals united; stamens distinct; legumes thin, flat, glabrous, four to eight-seeded; flowers small, white, or pale yellow, flowering nearly all year; chiefly found in malabar; closely allied to acacia sundra, dec., and suma, kurz. [sundra, white sundra]. The watery extract is black cutch [cutch]; a concentrated and solidified product of a decoction from the chips of the brown heart-wood; an astringent juice, soluble in water; not to be confounded with gambier [q.v.]; not a gum [gond] or resin [raul], any more than indigo [q.v.]. Ordinary black cutch occurs as dry, brown externally, reddish or pale within, fracture brilliant, or dull according to the kind; in flat, round, cylindrical, or irregular pieces, inodorous, of extremely astringent taste, followed by an agreeably sweet flavor; often adulterated with starch and clay; that used for medicinal purposes is clean, dark, and easily fractured. The tree also yields direct a pale yellow gum, often occurring in tears one inch in diameter, generally less than half an inch in size; it is sweet to the taste and soluble in water; it forms a strong mucilage. For making the cutch, chips of the heart-wood are boiled in earthen pots, and the clear liquor is strained off; when the residuum is of sufficient consistence, it is poured into clay moulds; a finer form generally called kath [q.v.] which is the hindostany for cutch, is made by putting twigs in the decoction, on which the substance then crystallizes. A mixture of cutch and myrrh [q.v.], called kathbol, is given to women after confinement as a tonic and to promote the secretion of milk; in general medicine a powerful astringent; also antiperiodic and antiscorbutic; for british kino, pale catechu, oakgalls and logwood; gives to pharm. catechu nigrum; active principles, peculiar form of tannin, mimotannic acid and catechin; powerful astringent tonic; preparations, infusum catechu, tinctura catechu, pulvis catechu compositus; officinal. The purer kath is used as an ingredient in the prepared paun [q.v.] or betel-leaf. Cutch contains a greater proportion of tannin than other astringent substances, and 1 lb. of this is equal to 7 or 8 lb. of oak-bark for tanning [chamrah]; it is now largely exported to europe and america for its tannin; it is also used in dyeing [shauyam], a solution of cutch being by the action of lime [choonam] or of alum [padicauram] changed into a dull red color. Timber dark colored; hard and heavy; close-grained and durable, works smoothly and stands a good polish, though somewhat brittle, much valued where strength is required, used for ploughs [calappay], pestles, &c., in house-building and the construction of carts; not attacked by white-ants [q.v.]; the wood is however inferior to the other species of the genus.

CATHAY (خطا - khatá, *Ar.*). From (khitan, the dynasty which ruled over the country). Northern china [cheen]. Name by which for nearly thousand years the whole of China has been known to nations of Inner asia and to those whose acquaintance with it was got by that channel [charitram]. Frequent plant title in introduced plants.

CATHERINE FALL (கோட்டக்கிரியருவி - kóttakkiriyaruvi, *Tam.*). Means kotagherry water-fall. Water-fall, Neilgherry district, Paranginaud division; lat. 11° 23′; long. 76° 54′; from Coonoor N.E. 5 miles; from Ootacamund E.S.E. 11 miles. In a stream south of Kotagherry. Height 250 feet [aroovy].

CATJANG (کچنگ - kachang, *Malay*). Distinguish from Cadjan. Pulse [dholl].

CATTANAR (കത്തനാർ - kattanár, *Mal.*). From (kartá, san. lord). Priest of Malabar syrian christians.

CATTAY (கட்டை - kattai, *Tam.*). From (kattu, tam. to become confined). Anything dwarfish.——*Cataboma* (కట్టబొమ్మ - kattabomma, Tel.). Means short Bomma. In Anglo-indian the Cat. Poligar of Punchaulamcoorchy, near the present town of Ottapidauram in Tinnevelly district. Tried and hanged in 1799 for rebellious conduct against Government. Vol. I (122) [charitram].

CATTY (ಕಟ್ಟಿ - katti, *Can.*; కట్టి - katti, *Tel.*). A measure of grain, now obsolete; 3,200 rupees' weight. A land measure; 32 coontas = 1 catty [alavay, 2b]. In Godavery there are three superficial catties in which the coonta measures 80, 84 and 96 feet square respectively, thus giving 12·8 acres, 14·11 acres and 18·4 acres respectively. In Kistna the superficial catty is 17 acres. In Vizagapatam it is 16 veesams or 19·478 acres. Compare Cootchel.

CAU (கா - ká, *Tam.*). To guard; also grove.——*Caupaud* (കാപ്പാട് - káppátu, Mal.). From (kával, mal. guard + pátu, mal. place). Mal. also (káppáttannáti), meaning caupaud, the place + bazaar. Village, Port; Malabar dist., Cooroombranaud tal.; lat. 11° 23′; long. 75° 46′; from Badagara S.S.E. 18 miles; from Bombay S.S.E. 540 miles; from Calicut N.N.W. 9½ miles; from Quilandy S.S.E. 4¼ miles; from Yelattore N.N.W. 2¼ miles. Place where Vasco da Gama's expedition first dropped anchor.——*Caupoo* (కాపు - kápu, Tel.). From (káyu, tel. to watch).

A cultivator [inam]. So a caste-title, the great cultivating body of the Teloogoo districts. Numbers about a million. Arava caupoo, from (aravamu, tel. tamul), are tamul by origin and speech. Cantsara caupoo, from (kantsara, tel. brazier), are braziers. Conda caupoo, from (konda, tel. hill), are in the elevated land of the eastern ghauts [q.v.]; speak khond; style themselves conda dorloo, but have no proprietary right in the land they cultivate. Conidey caupoo, from (konidi, tel. half handfull), a class of half-cultivators. Dausla caupoo, from (dása, san. slave). Desoory caupoo, from (désúru, tel. place so called). Gauzoola caupoo, from (gádzu, tel. glass bracelet). Morasoo caupoo, from (morasu, tel. rude). Motauty caupoo, from (mátádu, tel. an inferior revenue servant); a class whose duty is to look after the crops. Munney caupoo, from (manne, tel. chieftain). Panta caupoo, from (panta, tel. crop); regular husbandmen. Pauknauty caupoo, from (pákanádu, tel. country so called). Pedacunty caupoo, from (peda, tel. wrong + kannu, tel. eye + kápu, tel. the caste); wrong side or left side; a class of caupoos whose females do not wear the talee [q.v.] or a bodice to cover their breasts. Tota caupoo, from (tóta, tel. garden); division of vellaula. Velama caupoo, from (velama, tel. noble). Velnauty caupoo, from (velnádu, tel. country so called) [jauty].——*Cauttaun* (காத்தான் - káttán, Tam.). The protector. Foster son of Cauly [q.v.]. Otherwise Cauttavaroyen. Proper name among lower orders. Cauttaun and Cauttye are the English jack and jill. Compare Veeran [peyar].——*Cauttye* (காத்தாயி - káttáyi, Tam.). From (above + áyi, tam. mother). Cauly, the protector [ancaulamman]. Female proper name among the lower orders [peyar].——*Cauv* (കാവ് - kávu, Mal.). From (kákku, mal. to guard). A grove consecrated to the village deity. Prefix in place names, as Cauvachery, meaning grove + village. Suffix in place names as Aryancauv, meaning Ayyappan's grove.——*Cauvady* (కావడి - kávadi, Tel.). From (kávu, tam. to carry on the shoulder + tadi, tam. pole). Pole for carrying burthens, resting on the shoulder, and having a rope at each extremity by which the articles to be conveyed are slung. The Banghy of Northern india. Sometimes written Cowry. Cauvadicaur is a cauvady carrier, commonly accompanying a palankeen.——*Cauval* (കാവൽ - kával, Mal.; காவல் - kával, Tam.). Guard. Prefix in place names as in Cauvalpaud, meaning the guarding village. Similarly suffix, as Tirnellicauval, meaning the guardian of the holy nelly tree.——*Cauvalcutt* (காவற்கட்டு - kávargattu, Tam.). From (above + kattu, tam. bundle). A bundle of paddy sheaves given to watchmen.——*Cauvalgar* (కావలికాడు - kávalikádu, Tel.; காவற்காரன் - kávargáran, Tam.). Title from tamul. Tel. from (above + kádu, tel. man). Tam. from (above + káran, tam. doer). Village watchman, who acts as a messenger and guide for travellers [inam]——*Cauval merah* (కావలిమేర - kávaliméra, Tel.; காவல்மேரை - kávalmérai, Tam.). From (above + méra, tel. share). Share of grain given to the watchmen of village from threshing floor [calam].——*Cauval mooray* (காவல் முறை - kávalmurai, Tam.). From (above + murai, tam. turn). Turn for watching.——*Cauval nigoody* (காவல்நிகுதி - kávalniguthi, Tam.). From (above + niyati, san. obligation). Fees paid by cauvalgars for the enjoyment of their privileges.——*Cauval vazhak* (காவல்வழக்கு - kávalvazhakku, Tam.). From (above + vazhakku, tam. custom). Customary fees paid to a watchman.——*Cauvaly* (కావలి - kávali, Tel.). A tax on ploughs once levied owing to turbulence of inhabitants, and the proceeds employed in augmenting the police force. Also the right to levy black-mail enjoyed by poligars and main cauvalgars. See vol. I, 112. For place of this name, see sep. title.——*Cauvery* (காவேரி - kávéri, Tam.). From (ká, tam. grove + éri, tam. tank); from its original source in a garden tank. Tam. also (shittiraiççilamban), meaning april + mountain fresh; as it rises in chittray [mausam] or april from the mountain floods; also (ponni), meaning gold possessor. Sanscrit name (dakshinagangá), means south + ganges; also (ardhagangá), meaning half ganges; also (kákanadí), meaning crow + river, from black color of sand. The earliest mention is that of Ptolemy. Greek χάβηρος; καμάρα of the Periplus. River; Salem, Trichinopoly, Tanjore districts. Rises in the mountains of Coorg at Taley cauvery, 50 miles from Mangalore in lat. 12° 25′; long. 75° 34′. Flows first easterly for 33 miles and then turns north-east for 8 miles, at which point it touches Mysore and for 20 miles forms its boundary towards Coorg, still flowing north-easterly. In Coorg it is joined by the Cacabey, Cadanore, Chikkaholey, Cummaholey, Moottaureymootta, and Swarnauvaty. Flows through Mysore, generally south-easterly for 95 miles, to Talacaud; from whence, its course being first north-easterly and subsequently easterly, it forms the boundary between Mysore and Coimbatore district for 40 miles, when it finally leaves the former territory. At Seringapatam it entirely encircles the fortress and island. At Sosiley it receives its first great auxiliary stream, the Cubbany, which flowing past Nanjangode, brings into its course the alluvium of Wynaud. Farther on the Muddore falls into it, and now greatly enlarged in its limits it occupies a bed of nearly a mile broad, varying from 15–20 feet deep, before it reaches the western point of Shivasamoodram. The passage of the river before Shivasamoodram and residence upon the island of that name were formerly difficult, but the jagheerdar of the island erected two stone bridges over the two branches of the river. After passing under the bridges the northern branch of the river winds along the southern side of a mountain until it reaches the high land forming the island on the eastern side. Here it begins to descend with considerable rapidity till it arrives at the head of the cataract Gunganchookky, so called in consequence of a rajah of the island whose name was Gungan having about 700 years ago leapt his horse down at this place at the command of the divinity of the island, in order to cleanse himself from a pollution he had unknowingly received. Part of the site of the ancient Hindoo city of Gungan pauray may still be traced here. A little above the cataract, this branch of the river encircles a smaller island. The fall on the southern branch of the river is called Barchookky, and is about two miles from Gunganchookky. After leaving Shivasamoodram, the Cauvery gradually descends until it receives the Bhawauny at the village of the same name. About Bhawauny there are numerous islands. At Caroor the Amravatty, and a little higher the Noyil fall into the Cauvery. All these streams, now united into one bed, wind in a serpentine course. After forming the boundary between Coimbatore and Salem districts for a considerable distance, the river enters Trichinopoly districts. Passing the rock of Trichinopoly, it divides at the island of Shreerungam into two channels, which enclose between them the delta of Tanjore. This delta is 70 miles in length from the apex to the sea and has a base of 80 miles. After Shreerungam, the river is divided into two branches; of which the northern is called the Coleroon and falls into the sea at Devicottah, while the other breaks up into many small streams reaching the sea at Negapatam and Tranquebar. On the seaward face of the delta are the open roadsteads of Negapatam and Caricaul. Large as is the supply of water in the Cauvery it is nearly exhausted before it reaches the sea at Cauveryputnam. The course of the Cauvery is over an extensive and generally barren surface of granitic rocks, with scarcely any woods or jungle on its banks. It consequently brings down no vegetable alluvium, but a rich clay, rendering the plains of Tanjore the most fertile portion of the South of India. During the inundation, the river is navigable through the low country for craft. Those in use are circular baskets from 9–14 feet in diameter, covered with buffalo leather. In these cotton [q.v.], sandal-wood, saltpetre [shorah], and other wares are brought down the river, and as the violence of the current precludes their upward navigation, they are taken to pieces, the basket-work abandoned, and the leather taken back on men's heads. Seringapatam, Trichinopoly, Tanjore, Combaconam and Mayavaram are on its banks. For a description of the irrigation works, see vol. I, 399, &c. Total length, about 475 miles; estimated area of drainage basin, 28,000 square miles. The area of delta is 2,760 square miles, and irrigation system supplies about 835,208 acres, yielding a revenue of Rs. 35,30,336. The whole of the course of the Cauvery is to the natives holy ground. Even the Ganges is said to resort under-ground once in the year to the source of the Cauvery to purge itself from the pollution contracted from the crowd of sinners who have bathed in its waters. At its source at Taley cauvery, and at Bhaugamundalam, where it receives its first tributary, are ancient temples largely frequented by pilgrims in October and November. There is a Tamul proverb:—புல்லும் பூமியும் கல்லும் காவேரியும் உள்ளமட்டும்—"As long as vegetation, earth, "rocks and the Cauvery exist" [shausanam].——*Cauvery falls* (காவேரியருவி - kávériyaruvi, Tam.). Shivasamoodram, Barchookky and Gunganchookky in Coimbatore; Hogeycull in Salem. Former generally meant [aroovy].——*Cauverypauk* (காவேரிப்பாக்கம் - kávérippákkam, Tam. kávéripák*). From (kávéri, tam. the river + pákkam, tam. village). Village; North arcot dist., Wallajahpett tal.; pop. 6,259; acres 2,914; lat. 12° 54′; long. 79° 30′; height 389 feet; from Chittore S.E. 33 miles; from Wallajahpett E. 6¾ miles. Flourishing agricultural village midway between Arcot and Conjeeveram, south of large tank to which it gives name. Formerly a small fort near tank bund. Clive gained victory over French here in 1752. Captured by French in 1757. Tank largest in district, having bund four miles long north to south. Has much silted up. Fed by channel from Palaur, and in its surplus weir are head waters of Corteliaur, which supplies Madras with drinking-water. Waterfowl abundant. On bund a bungalow.——*Cauverypooram* (காவேரிப்புரம் - kávérippuram, Tam.). Means cauvery town. Village, Pass; Coimbatore dist., Bhawauny tal.; pop. 6,725; acres 37,909; lat. 11° 54′; long. 77° 48′; from Bhawauny N. 32¾ miles; from Coimbatore N.N.E. 82 miles. On right bank of Cauvery. Fort stands at mouth of one of passes from Mysore. Fort and pass were points of strategic importance throughout Mysore wars, the pass 30 miles in length being much used for convoys in the final struggle. Outpost of Trimal naick of Madura against the inroads of the Curtar [q.v.] of Mysore. In 1768, captured by Colonel Wood; 1769 retaken by Hyder ally. The pass has been almost abandoned in favor of the route viâ Suttimungalam and Hassanore. Old well-sculptured Shiva temple in the village with many inscriptions. Also a ruined fort. Large number of resident Canarese bramins. Weekly market.——*Cauveryputnam* (காவேரிப்பட்டணம் - kávérippattanam, Tam.). Means Cauvery town.—"*a*" Sanscrit name (cháritrapura), meaning historic fame + town. Greek χάβηρος ἐμποριόν. Village, Place of pilgrimage; Tanjore dist., Shiyally tal.; pop.

2,846; lat. 11° 09′; long. 79° 53′; from Neythavausal S. 1½ miles; from Shiyally S.E. 9 miles; from Tanjore E.N.E. 53 miles. Resorted to by the Hindoos for bathing. Fattan of Rasheedood deen. Compare putnam for Madras now-a-days. Ancient seaport with extensive commerce, gold dust being a part of the commodities. Ceased to be of importance in fifteenth century, partly owing to silting up of Cauvery. Nothing now remains but a few sandy mounds with fragments of brick strewed over them, and traces of temples. Trig. station in lat. 11° 7′ 53·37″; long. 79° 54′ 6·08″; from Shiyally S.E. 11 miles; from Cauveryputnam S.E. 1½ miles; from Mailayore E.S.E. 3 miles; from Neythavausal S.S.E. 2¾ miles; from the sea W. ⅛ mile.—" *b* " Town; Salem dist., Krishnagherry tal.; pop. 4,457; acres 206; lat. 12° 25′; long. 78° 15′; from Krishnagherry S. 8 miles; from Salem N. 53 miles. On right bank of Ponniaur. The fort which commands the pass of Palcode was taken by the English in 1767, and almost immediately recaptured by Hyder ally, who strengthened the works, and used them as a support in the following campaign, until his withdrawal above the ghauts [q.v.], when Colonel Wood again captured the place. In 1790 Cauveryputnam was Colonel Maxwell's head-quarters before advancing against Tippoo. Trade in oil, oil-seed and grain is considerable; while the cloths woven here supply the demand of the greater part of the talook. Large weekly fair for cattle.

CAUCATEEYA (काकतीय - kákatíya, *San.*). Dynasty of Warangal. Otherwise called Ganapaty. See vol. I (132), (142) [charitram].

CAUD (కాడు - kádu, *Tel.*; காடு - kádu, *Tam.*). From (kadu, tam. hard). Uncultivated jungle tract. Suffix in place names, as Yercaud, meaning tank + forest. Compare Coody, Naud, Oor.——(1) *Caudaurambam* (காடாரம்பம் - kádárambam, Tam.). From (above + árambha, san. beginning). Upland where dry grain is raised.——*Caudcaul* (காடுகாள் - kádugál, Tam.). From (above + ká, tam. to protect). Mauriyamman.——*Cauttairy* (காட்டேரி - káttéri, Tam.). From (above + éru, tam. to pervade). Same as caudcaul.——*Cautvauram* (കാട്ടുവാരം - káttuváram, Mal.). From (above + váram, tam. share). A tax on lands bordering on waste in lieu of any assessment on tracts that may be cultivated within the waste. See vol. I, 112.——(2) *Beed caud* (బీడుకాడు - bídukádu, Tel.). From (bídu, tel. waste + above). Uncultivated land.——*Cautcaud* (ಕಾಟುಕಾಡು - kátukádu, Can.). Jungle cultivation in which the plots are changed every year. Same as Coomry and Ponacaud on W. coast.——*Shavacaud* (சவக்காடு - shavakkádu, Tam.). From (shava, san. corpse + above). Burial ground. Vedantists, lingayets, the five artisan castes, beiraugies, sanyausies, the gooroos of sects and all the races and tribes not admitted into hindooism, bury their dead. As life becomes extinct, the body is made to assume the attitude to be preserved in the procession and in the grave. It is borne to the grave in a car, on the shoulders of relatives or friends. On reaching the burial place, the priest recites prayers, and the body is seated on a ledge with its face looking northwards; salt and ashes of cow-dung are placed on the head [maryauday].——*Shoodcaud* (சுடுகாடு - shudugádu, Tam.). From (shudu, tam. to burn + above). Burning-ground. Those not mentioned under Shavacaud burn their dead. When it appears that one of those classes is about to die, a space is prepared with earth mingled with cow-dung, and strewed with sacred Darbhay [q.v.] grass, and over it a clean cloth is spread, on which the dying man is placed. Next, the chief priest or Poorohit performs a Praunyaschittam [q.v.] or general expiation, by the efficacy of which he is delivered from all his sins. After this the ten gifts or Dasha daunam [q.v.] are prepared. These consist of cows, lands, millet-seed, gold, butter, clothes, grain of various kinds, sugar, silver, and salt, and are offered to bramins on the day of the funeral. The more valuable of these are distributed by the rich only. After the last breath those who are present weep for a reasonable time, and then the chief mourner performs ceremonies, till in due time the body is placed on a litter and carried to the place where it is to be burnt, the chief mourner walking foremost with fire in a vessel, and others following. Having arrived at the place, the party dig a trench of inconsiderable depth over which the funeral pile is erected. The corpse being placed on it, the chief mourner makes the sacrifice called Homam [q.v.] and other ceremonies, after which he sets fire to the pile and retires with the company, while the four bearers should remain with the corpse till it is consumed [carmauntaram, maryauday, matam].——*Vettcaud* (வெட்டுக்காடு - vettukkádu, Tam.). From (vettu, tam. to cut + above). Land cleared of jungle and brought under cultivation.

CAUDY (अम्ल - amla, *San.*; خل - khall, *Ar.*; سرکہ - sirkah, *Pers.* and *Hind.*; ಕಾಡಿ - kádi, *Can.*; కాడి - kádi, *Tel.*; കാടി - káti, *Mal.*; காடி - kádi, *Tam.*). San. from (am, san. to make sick). Ar. from (khalla, ar. to become spoiled), from the sweet flavor spoiling by fermentation. Drav. root means burning or biting. Vinegar [sharb]. Acetum of chemists. An impure acetic acid [tezaub] made by the acetous fermentation of sweet fruits [pazham], rice [q.v.], toddy [q.v.], sugar [q.v.], honey [shahad], &c.; each kind of vinegar is named after the substance from which it is produced. Imported english distilled or white wine vinegar is preferred medicinally; the best native kind is that prepared from the toddy of the palmyra [q.v.] tree, colored with burnt paddy [q.v.]. For making this the alcoholic liquid is placed in earthen jars half imbedded in the soil and left until the acetification has been accomplished. Natives use it in medicine externally as a repellent, and in composing certain discutient fomentations; also mix it with gingelly [q.v.] oil to make cooling embrocation for head in cephalalgia; some veidyans [q.v.] and hakeems [q.v.] render it stronger by distillation; used internally it is not only refrigerant, but, especially when taken in warm gruel, powerful diaphoretic; bengal gram vinegar is a common menstruum for medical purposes. The following are vinegars most commonly found in the bazaar.——*Barley vinegar* (सौवीर - sauvíra, San.). San. from (su, san. good + víra, san. spirituous liquor). From husked grains of barley [jow] boiled and steeped in water.——*Bengal gram vinegar* (चणकाम्ल - chanakámla, San.; خل الحمص - khallulhams, Ar.; سرکہ نخود - sirkahinakhúd, Pers.; بوٹ کا سرکہ - bútkásirkah, Hind.; கடலைப்புளிப்பு - kadalaippulippu, Tam.). Acid drops of water on the leaves of cicer arietinum, linn., or bengal gram [q.v.].——*Date vinegar* (खर्जूराम्ल - kharjúrámla, San.; سیندھی کا سرکہ - sendhíkásirkah, Hind.; ಖರ್ಜೂರಕಾಡಿ - kharjúrakádi, Can.; ఈతకాడి - ítakádi, Tel.; ഈന്തിങ്കാടി - íntinkáti, Mal.; ஈச்சங்காடி - íççangádi, Tam.). From toddy of phœnix sylvestris, roxb., the date palm [wild date].——*Grain vinegar* (धान्याम्ल - dhányámla, San.; அரிசிக்காடி - arisikkádi, Tam.). Tam. from (arisi, tam. rice + above). From acetous fermentation of powdered paddy [q.v.]. Also called Caunjicam.——*Grape vinegar* (द्राक्षाम्ल - drákshámla, San.; انگوری سرکہ - angúrísirkah, Hind.; ದ್ರಾಕ್ಷಿಕಾಡಿ - drákshíkádi, Can.; ద్రాక్షకాడి - drákshakádi, Tel.; മുന്തിരിങ്ങക്കാടി - muntirinnakkáti, Mal.; திராட்சக்காடி - tirádchakkádi, Tam.). From fruit of vitis vinifera, linn., the grape vine [angoor].——*Husk vinegar* (तुषाम्ल - tushámla, San.). From husks of fried oolundoo [black gram] and barley [jow], boiled together for acetous fermentation.——*Palmyra vinegar* (तालाम्ल - talámla, San.; تاڑی کا سرکہ - tárikásirkah, Hind.; ಪನೇಕಾಡಿ - panékádi, Can.; తాటికాడి - tátikádi, Tel.; പനങ്കാടി - panankáti, Mal.; பனங்காடி - panangádi, Tam.). Otherwise Culloo caudy or Toddy vinegar. From toddy of borassus flabelliformis, linn., the palmyra [q.v.].——*Rice vinegar* (आरनाल - áranála, San.; கஞ்சிக்காடி - kañjikkádi, Tam.). San. from (ára, san. brass + nála, san. odour). Tam. from (kanji, tam. gruel from the smell + above). From fermentation of boiled rice.——*Six-month vinegar* (ஆறுமாதக்காடி - árumáthakkádi, Tam.). Water in which rice has been washed and various ingredients mixed, kept six months; used medicinally for jaundice, incipient dropsy, &c.

CAUFIR (کافر - káfir, *Hind.*). From (kufr, ar. infidelity). One who denies, an infidel [caffre]. Abusive epithet by Mahomedans to all non-Mahomedans. Of these there are five classes:—those who do not believe in the great first cause; those who do not believe in the unity of God; those who do not believe in revelation; idolators; deniers of the mission of Mahomet.

CAUFOOR (کافور - káfúr, *Hind.*). From arabic, means camphor [q.v.]. Otherwise known as Malik caufoor. A slave taken during the conquest of Goozerat by Allah ood deen's general. Subsequently rose to highest offices. He was the first Mahomedan general who invaded the Deccan [q.v.], against which he made four expeditions. The first in 1306, and the last in 1312 was against the Yaudavas of Devagherry. In 1309 he reduced the Ganapaty of Warangal; led a successful expedition against the Yaudavas of Dwaura samoodram in 1310. Murdered in 1316 being suspected of his master's assassination. Vol. I (120) [charitram].

CAUGAZ (کاغذ - kághaz, *Hind.*). From Persian. Paper; document. Acbaur caugaz is a newspaper.

CAUJA (خواجہ - khwájah, *Hind.*). A title like gentleman, squire. Title of persons eminent for sanctity or learning. Denomination of Syeds out of respect. Title of Dervishes. Alaumat of one whose father is a Moghul and mother a Seidaunee; as Cauja fareed, alaumat + alam; Cauja nimat ool lah, title + lacab [ism].

CAUJAL (कज्जल - kajjala, *San.*; کاجل - kájal, *Hind.*; ارانگ پرا - arángpara, *Malay*; ಕಾಡಿಗೆ - kádige, *Can.*; ಕಾಡಿಗೆ - kádige, *Too.*; కాటుక - kátuka, *Tel.*; മഷി - mashi, *Mal.*; மை - mai, *Tam.*). San. from (kad, san. prefix showing defectiveness + jvala, san. flame). Malay from (aráng, malay, charcoal + para, malay, portion); from similarity. Tel. from (káru, tel. black). Tam. means blackness. Lamp-black. The carbon or smoke formed by burning vegetable substances in confined air. It constitutes the basis of lithographic and printing inks [mashy], and also of an oil paint [rangh]. Usually obtained by fixing a copper pan over the flame arising from burning gingelly [q.v.] oil, in which pan the lamp-black is collected [cajjuly].

CAUKKAY (काक - káká, *San.*; కాకి - káki, *Tel.*; காக்கை - kákkai, *Tam.*). From (kai, san. to caw). Crow [caurvam]. Plant first term, often joining two genera, from color or inferiority.

Ex., where transl. is of second term :—Abrus precatorius (kákachiñchá), tamarindus indica ; Gmelina arborea (kákódúmbarí), ficus glomerata ; Saccharum spontaneum (kákiveduru), bambusa arundinacea ; Strychnos nux vomica (kákatinduka), diospyros embryopteris ; Toddalia aculeata (kákkattutali), scutia indica ; Trichosanthes palmata (kákidonda), cephalandra indica ; see gloss. paragraphs. Constantly also within the same genus.——*Caukkan* (காக்கன் - kákkan, Tam.). Title from being dark like crow. Tam. also (korukkai). Pristipoma [caripey] hasta, percidæ [panayairy], acanthopterygii, teleostei [matsyam, 1], of naturalists [jantoo]. Alias Coius gudgutia ; Lutjanus hasta ; Mesoprion gutgutia ; Polotus nitidus ; Pristipoma chrysobalion, commersonii, kaakan. Kaakan from tamul. Four or five interrupted lines of grey along sides, three or four being above lateral line ; sometimes they coalesce and form bands. Two or three rows of spots along dorsal fin, and in adult single row of dull blotches at base of the fin. Sea ; $1\frac{1}{2}$ feet.——*Caukkay pon* (कांस्यपत्र - kámsyapatra, San. ; سون پیتل - sunpítal, Dec. ; ಕಾಗಿಬಂಗಾರ - kágibangára, Can. ; ಅಬರಕು - abaraku, Too. ; కాకిబంగారు - kákibangáru, Tel. ; കാക്കപ്പൊൻ - kákkappon, Mal. ; காக்காய்ப்பொன் - kákkáyppon, Tam.). San. from (kámsya, san. brass + patra, san. leaf). Dec. from (sun, hind. gold + pítal, hind. brass). Can. from (kági, can. crow + bangára, can. gold). Tel. similar. Tam. from (kákkai, tam. crow + pon, tam. gold) ; inferior gold. Tam. also (kañjattagadu), meaning white copper or brass + leaf. Mica or glittering earth [abruck]. Also tinsel of brass leaf glittering like gold.——*Caukoola canama* (కాకులకనము - kákulakanama, Tel.). From (káki, tel. crow + kanama, tel. ravine). Pass ; Kurnool dist., Marcapore tal. ; lat. 16° 15′ ; long. 79° 37′ ; from Kurnool E.N.E. 102 miles ; from Marcapore N.N.E. 40 miles. Crosses N.E. extension of the Nullamullays, on high road between Cumbum and Pulnaud talook of Kistna district.——*Jala caukkay* (जलकाक - jalakáka, San. ; پنکوا - pankavvá, Hind.). From (jala, san. water + káka, san. crow) ; from habitat. Hind. from (páni, hind. water + kavvá, hind. crow). Graculidæ family, piscatores, natatores, aves [pacshy, 58], of naturalists [jantoo]. Cormorants. The species best known to the natives are shown below.—"*a*" Large cormorant, called in vernaculars, large crow, water crow, black heron. Graculus carbo. Alias Carbo cormoranus. Rare towards south.—"*b*" Small cormorant not distinguished by separate vernacular. Graculus javanicus. Alias Carbo melanognathus ; Phalacrocorax niger ; Picus pygmæus. Common.—"*c*" Snake cormorant ; title from long neck ; called (bánuá) in deccany. Plotus melanogaster, plotinæ, graculidæ. Float low on the water, often with nothing, but the head and neck visible, and swim and dive with rapidity.——*Samoodra caukkay* (समुद्रकाक - samudrakáka, San. ; تیہاری - tehári, Hind. ; సముద్రపుకాకి - samudrapukáki, Tel.). San. from (samudra, san. sea + káka, san. crow) ; from habitat and appearance. Hind. also (gangachíl), meaning ganges kite ; (machhalouka), meaning fish snatcher. Tel. also (rámadásu), meaning rama's devotee. Laridæ family, vagatores, natatores, aves [pacshy, 53], of naturalists [jantoo]. S. indian sub-families :—Larinæ or gulls, Sterninæ or terns. The species best known are :—Little diving petrel, pelicanoides urinatrix. Great black-headed gull ; kroikocephalus ichthyætus, seen on sea coast at madras, voice deep like that of the raven. Brown-headed gull, xema brunnicephala, frequently follows ships for miles to pick up garbage. Laughing gull, xema ridibunda, note is a hoarse cackle. Largest tern, sylochelidon caspius. Gull-billed tern, gelochelidon anglicus. Small marsh tern, hydrochelidon indica. Large river tern, seena aurantia. European tern, sterna nirundo. Black-bellied tern, sterna javanica. Little tern, sternula minuta. Large sea tern, thalasseus cristatus. Smaller sea tern, thalasseus bengalensis. Indian skimmer, rhynchops albicollis.

CAUL (కాలు - kálu, *Tel.* ; കാൽ - kál, *Mal.* ; கால் - kál, *Tam.*). The leg, foot. In Malabar, any tree that serves as a standard of the pepper vine or betel-vine. Figuratively a reach of water, like English arm of sea. So a channel [q.v.]. Suffix in place names as Tencaul, meaning southern channel. Also stands for road and land. Also one-fourth.——*Caucauvery* (காக்காவேரி - kákkávéri, Tam.). From (kál, tam. quarter + kávéri, tam. the cauvery) ; small Cauvery. On account of the stream which brought down high freshes and contained a perpetual supply like the Cauvery river. Zemindarry, Village ; Salem dist., Salem tal. ; pop. 1,844 ; area 1,830 acres ; lat. of village 11° 27′ ; long. 78° 16′ ; from Salem S.E. 16 miles. Chief village in Mittah of same name. Peshcush Rs. 2,641.——*Caulauda* (ಕಾಲಾಡ - káláda, Can.). From (above + áda, can. the liquid measure of 20 seers of 70 cubic inches each). Liquid measure. 4 cootties = 1 caulauda ; $2\frac{1}{2}$ caulaudas = 1 maund [alavay, 4c]. Approximate actual value, 1 caulauda = 385 cubic inches. S. canara for oil. Compare Marcam or Mercaul of Kistna, Colagam of Coimbatore.——*Caul shetty* (கார்சட்டை - kárchattai, Tam.). From (above + shattai, tam. dress). Trousers.——*Caulvye* (ಕಾಲಿವೆ - kálive, Can. ; కాలవ - kálava, Tel. ; கால்வாய் - kálváy, Tam.). From (above + váy, tam. place). A channel [q.v.], generally of irrigation.——*Caulvyecomaury* (کوماری - komárí, Hind. ; கால்வாய்க்கோமாரி - kálváykkómári, Tam.). From (above + váy, tam. mouth + gó, san. cow + mári, san. contagious disease). Foot and mouth disease of cattle [pashoorogam]. Not largely destructive of life in Southern india ; the mortality rarely exceeding 3 per cent. here though it rises to 50 in Europe. Sheep [shemmariyaud], goats [vellaud], pigs [soor] and poultry are liable and it has been conveyed by means of the milk [paul] of affected cows [pashoo] to the human subject. The absence of purging and the affection of the feet distinguish this disease from rinderpest [vishajooram], but both maladies may co-exist in the same animal.——*Caulwa* (కాలవ - kálava, Tel.). Means channel.—"*a*" Deputy tahsildarry, Kurnool district. Pay Rs. 70.—"*b*" Village, Head-quarters of Deputy tahsildar, a Sub-registrar and an hospital are situated here. The head-quarters of the Deputy tahsildar have been temporarily moved to Baitamcheroo after the advent of the railway. Kurnool dist., Nundiaul tal. ; pop. 2,284 ; acres 6,519 ; lat. 15° 37′ ; long. 78° 14′ ; from Cumbum W. 60 miles ; from Kurnool S.E. 17 miles ; from Madras N.W. 223 miles ; from Nundiaul W.N.W. $20\frac{3}{4}$ miles ; from Pyaupaly N.E. 41 miles. On the bank of a spring channel, the town being built on the bed of red purple shales. Two large ruined temples. Extensive wet cultivation under the spring channel [q.v.]. Three miles distant is Boogga tepid spring, a halting place on Kurnool-Nundiaul road. On Shivarautry [pandigay, 6a] a car festival at this Boogga [q.v.].——*Coott caul* (میخ - mekh, Hind. ; குத்துக்கால் - kuttukkál, Tam.). Hind. means a nail. Tam. from (kuttu, tam. to plant + kál, tam. post). Upright posts in a loom [nesavoo, tarry].

CAULAM (काल - kála, *San.* ; کال - kál, *Hind.* ; காலம் - kálam, *Tam.*). From (kal, san. to go). Time in general or any particular time or season. Death, destiny. Blackness [calam, car, caur]. Also one of the Dravyams [q.v.] of the Veishaishicam philosophy [matam].——(1) For Dravidian time generally see vol. I, 609. Average table of ditto :—60 cunnimays or twinkles otherwise nodies or finger-snaps = 1 vinaudy or indian minute, 60 vinaudies = 1 nauzhigay or indian hour, colloqnially nauzhy, $7\frac{1}{2}$ nauzhigays = 1 jaumam or watch, 2 jaumams = 1 nairam or half day light, 2 nairams = 1 pagal or day light, 1 irauppagal or night and day = 1 naul or natural day, 7 nauls = 1 kizhamay or week, 4 kizhamays = 1 tingal or month, 12 tingals = 1 aundoo or year. But notice that Vinaudy and Nauzhigay are borrowed from sanscrit, no native terms for minute and hour having survived. The Cunnimay is ·4 english seconds, the Vinaudy is 24 english seconds, the Nauzhigay is 24 english minutes.——(2) The following is the most ancient and still best known table of time from the sanscrit. It runs from the excessively minute to the almost infinitely great. The day is the sauvanam or natural and civil day from sunrise to sunrise, and the table is popular and not scientific, as will be seen from the fact that 360 sunrises make up here the year. 15 nimishams or eye winks = 1 caushtay, 30 caushtays = 1 calay, 30 calays = 1 moohoortam, 30 moohoortams = 1 dinam or day, or sunrise, 30 dinams = 1 mausam or month, 2 mausams = 1 ritoo or season, 3 ritoos = 1 ayanam or half-year, 2 ayanams = 1 varsham or year of men, 360 varshams = 1 devavarsham, or year of gods, 12,000 devavarshams = 1 mahayoog or great age, 1,000 mahayoogs = 1 calpam or bramha's day time, 2 calpams = 1 bramha's day, 30 bramha's days = 1 bramha's month, 12 bramha's months = 1 bramha's year, 100 bramha's years = 1 mahapralayam or bramha's flood. Taking the dinam as 24 english hours, the Nimisham here is ·213 english seconds, the Caushtay is 3·2 english seconds, the Calay is 1 english minute and 36 english seconds, the Moohoortam is 48 english minutes. The following is a tabular view of the longer periods of the same, dividing also the 12,000 devavarshams between the four yoogs [q.v.] :—

Kritam,	4,800	years of the gods	× 360=	1,728,000	years of mortals.
Tretay,	3,600	do. do.	× 360=	1,296,000	do.
Dwauparam,	2,400	do. do.	× 360=	864,000	do.
Kaly,	1,200	do. do.	× 360=	432,000	do.
				4,320,000	Maha yoog.
				1,000	
				4,320,000,000	Day of Bramha.
				2	
				8,640,000,000	Day and night of Bramha.
				360	
				3,110,400,000,000	Year of Bramha.
				100	
				311,040,000,000,000	Age of Bramha, 3 billions and odd of years.

The world is now, A.D. 1892, in the 4,993rd year of the iron age ; 51 years of Bramha have elapsed ; 49 of Bramha's years are yet to come, when all matter will become spirit, and all be absorbed into the essence of Bramha ; after a million of ages Bramha will rise from his stupor and will again diversify himself. See vol. I, 609. The following is the authentic account of such time in the Vishnoo poorraunam :—"Time is a form of "Vishnoo ; hear how it is applied to measure the duration of "Bramha, and of all other sentient beings. Fifteen twinklings "of the eye make a Caushtay ; thirty Caushtays, one Calay ; and "thirty Calays, one Moohoortam ; thirty Moohoortams constitute a day and night of mortals ; thirty such days make a "month, divided into two half months ; six months form an Ayanam ; two Ayanams compose a year. The southern Ayanam "is a night, and the northern a day, of the gods. Twelve "thousand divine years, each composed of three hundred and "sixty such days, constitute the period of the four yoogs or "ages. They are thus distributed:—the Kritam age, has four "thousand divine years; the Tretay, three thousand; the Dwau- "param, two thousand; and the Kaly age, one thousand; so "those acquainted with antiquity have declared. The period "that precedes a yoog is called a Sundhyay, and it is of as many "hundred years as there are thousands in the yoog; and the "period that follows a yoog, termed the Sundhyaumsham, is of "similar duration. The interval between the Sundhyay and "the Sundhyaumsham is the yoog, denominated Kritam, Tretay, "&c. The Kritam, Tretay, Dwauparam and Kaly, constitute a "great age, or aggregate of four ages; a thousand such aggre- "gates are a day of Bramha, and fourteen Menoos reign within "that term. Hear the division of time which they measure. "Seven rishies, certain secondary divinities, Indran, Menoo, and "the kings, his sons, are created and perish at one period; and "the interval, called a Manwantaram, is equal to seventy-one "times the number of years contained in the four yoogs, with "some additional years: this is the duration of the Menoo, the "attendant divinities, and the rest, which is equal to 852,000 "divine years, or to 306,720,000 years of mortals, independent "of the additional period. Fourteen times this period consti- "tutes a Bramha day. At the end of this day a dissolution of "the universe occurs, when all the three worlds, earth, and the "regions of space, are consumed with fire. The dwellers of "Maha locam or region inhabited by the saints who survive "the world distressed by the heat, repair then to Jana locam "or region of holy men after their disease. When the three "worlds are but one mighty ocean, Bramha, who is one with "Narayana, satiate with the demolition of the universe, sleeps "upon his serpent-bed; contemplated, the lotus born, by the "ascetic inhabitants of the Jana locam; for a night of equal "duration with his day; at the close of which he creates anew. "Of such days and nights is a year of Bramha composed; and a "hundred such years constitute his whole life. One Paraur- "dham, or half his existence, has expired, terminating with the "Maha calpam called Pudmam. The Calpam or day of Bramha "termed Vaurauham is the first of the second period of Bramha's "existence."——(3) There is a division of time also into Moortam or sensible time and Amoortam or artificial time.— "*a*" The following is a specimen of Moortam time:—10 goor-vaucsharams or long syllables = 1 asoo or respiration, 6 asoos = 1 vinaudy or indian minute, &c. So also the table from eye-winks in head "2" above, or in head "6" below.—"*b*" The following is a specimen of Amoortam time:—100 trooties or atoms = 1 tatparam or speck, 30 tatparams = 1 nimisham or twinkling, 18 nimishams = 1 caushtay or bit, 30 caushtays = 1 calay or indian minute, 30 calays = 1 ghaticam or indian hour. With the calay as before, this makes the atom $\frac{1}{33750}$ of a second. It is called artificial time however because the scale goes down below limits of senses, and there is really no exact equivalence with anything else.——(4) The following is the scale of scientific lunar time:—60 soorams = 1 param or indian second, 60 params = 1 vighaticay or indian minute, 60 vighaticays = 1 ghaticay or indian hour, 30 ghaticays = 1 caranam or half lunar day, 2 caranams = 1 tity or lunar day, 15 tities = 1 pacsham or lunar fortnight, 2 pacshams = 1 chaundra mausam or lunar month or lunation, 12 chaundra mausams = 1 chaundra samvat-saram or maunam or lunar year. A mean tity or lunar day is the time during which the moon moves through 12° of her synodical orbit [cacsham] supposed to be divided into 360°; its duration is therefore 59g. 3v. 58p. hindoo sidereal or star time, or 23h. 37′ $27\frac{1}{5}''$ european time.——(5)—"*a*" The following is the scale of scientific fixed star or nacshatram [q.v.] time. This is the scale used by S. indian astronomers who compute in solar time, in dividing the nacshatram day or time of the equinoctial points [ayanam] rising twice. It is purely sexagesimal. The nacshatram days are considered equal throughout the year. 60 soorams = 1 param or indian second, 60 params = 1 vighaticay or indian minute, 60 vighaticays = 1 ghaticay or indian hour, 60 ghaticays = 1 dinam or day. Approximate actual value:—1 vighaticay or Indian minute = 24 english seconds.—"*b*" The following two tables convert the European sexagesimal scale of hours, minutes, seconds and sixtieths of seconds, into the above named Hindoo sexagesimal scale of dinams, ghaticays, vighaticays, params, soorams; and vice versâ:—

First table. European hours, minutes and seconds into Hindoo time.

European time.	Hindoo time.	European time.	Hindoo time.
1	2	3	4
H. M. S. S.‴	G. V. P. S.	H. M. S. S.‴	D. G. V. P. S.
1	2 30	10	0 25
2	5 0	20	0 50
3	7 30	30	1 15
4	10 0	40	1 40
5	12 30	50	2 5
6	15 0	60	2 30
7	17 30		
8	20 0		
9	22 30		
10	25 0		

Second table. Hindoo ghaticays, vighaticays and params into European time.

Hindoo time.	European time.	Hindoo time.	European time.
5	6	7	8
G. V. P.	H. M. S. S.‴	G. V. P.	H. M. S. S.‴
1	0 24	10	4 0
2	0 48	20	8 0
3	1 12	30	12 0
4	1 36	40	16 0
5	2 0	50	20 0
6	2 24	60	24 0
7	2 48		
8	3 12		
9	3 36		
10	4 0		

The first, second, &c., term in the left-hand column indicated by letters is equated to the first, second, &c., term indicated by letters respectively of the right-hand column, in each case. The figures read below them show the correct equivalence. The following are two examples of application:—

EXAMPLE I.

To convert 15h. 21m. 35s. into Hindoo time.

	G.	V.	P.	S.
First table. 10h. =	25			
5h. =	12	30		
20m. =		50		
1m. =		2	30	
30s. =		1	15	
5s. =			12	30
Answer ...	38	23	57	30

EXAMPLE II.

To convert 56g. 37v. 23p. into European time.

	H.	M.	S.	S.‴
Second table. 50g. =	20			
6g. =	2	24		
30v. =		12		
7v. =		2	48	
20p. =			8	
3p. =			1	12
Answer ...	22	38	57	12

——(6) An astronomical Sowram day is the time taken by the sun in describing one degree [bhaugam] of the ecliptic [craunty mundalam], and consequently longer or shorter as the sun is in apogee or perigee. The following is the scale used in the Sowram time thence resulting:—3,600 nimishams or winks = 1 alipalam, 60 alipalams = 1 caushtacalay or indian second or vipalam, 10 caushtacalays = 1 prauna calay, 6 prauna calays = 1 vicalay or indian minute or palam, 60 vicalays = 1 dandam or indian hour, 60 dandams = 1 dinam or day. Approximate actual value:—1 vicalay or indian minute = 24 english seconds. Observe that here the sexagesimal order is interrupted after the vicalays, which are only sub-divided into 6 prauna calays for the purpose of procuring a numerical division of time equal to the number of minutes of a degree contained in the circumference of a circle, being 21,600. It may be converted into degrees, &c., or space divisions, by the following table:—

Terms for time.		Terms for longitude [sauyanam]. Used also for dividing circle in many other astronomical operations.	
European term.	Sanscrit ditto.	European scientific symbols.	Hindoo scientific terms.
Year	Samvatsaram.	360°	12 Raushies or Signs.
Month	Mausam ...	30°	1 Raushy or 30 Bhaugams.
Day	Dinam ...	1°	1 Bhaugam.
Indian hour ...	Dandam ...	1′	Calay.
Indian minute.	Vicalay ...	1″	Vicalay.
	Prauna calay.	10‴	1 Prauna calay.
Indian second ...	Caushtacalay.	1‴	Caushtacalay.

——(7) The following table shows the current names in the different languages of the practical divisions of time when the day is divided sexagesimally :—

Language.	60 =	60 =	60 =	7 =	2 =	2 =	6 =	2 =	
English ...	Indian second.	Indian minute.	Indian hour.	Day ...	Week ...	Fortnight ...	Month ...	Half-year ...	Year.
Sanscrit ...	Parum ...	Vinaudy ...	Naudy ...	Dinam ...	Vauram ...	Pacsham ...	Mausam...	Ayanam ...	Samvatsaram.
Mahratta ...	.....	.....	Ghady ...	Dinam ...	.....	Pacsham ...	Mausam...	Ayanam ...	Samvatsaram.
Arabic ...	Sauniya ...	Dakeekah ...	Saut ...	Yowm ...	Oosboo ...	Oosbooaun ...	Shahar ...	.....	Sanut.
Persian ...	Sauniya ...	Lahza ...	Saut ...	Roz ...	Haftah ...	.....	Mauh ...	Shosh mauhee.	Saul.
Hindostany.	.....	Pal ...	Ghurry ...	Din ...	Haftah ...	Pandarwaura.	Maheena..	Cheh mauhee.	Baras.
Deccany ...	.....	Pal ...	Ghantah ...	Din ...	Haftah ...	Pandarwaura.	Maheena...	Cheh mauhee.	Baras.
Malay ...	.....	Saut ...	Jam ...	Yum ...	Jaumad ...	.....	Chandra...	.....	Saunn.
Canarese ...	.....	Vighaligey...	Ghaligey ...	Dinam ...	Vauram ...	Pacsham ...	Tingal ...	Ayanam ...	Varsham.
Tooloo ...	.....	Vighaligey...	Ghaligey ...	Dinam ...	Vauram ...	Pacsham ...	Tingal ...	Ayanam ...	Varsham.
Teloogoo ...	Nimisham.	Vighadiya ...	Ghadiya ...	Dinum ...	Vaurum ...	Pacsham ...	Mausam...	Ayanam ...	Samvatsaram.
Malayalam.	Mautray...	Vinaudicay.	Nauzhiga ...	Divusum...	Autchavuttam.	Pacsham ...	Mausam...	Ayanam ...	Collam.
Singhalese...	.....	Vinaudiya...	Naudy ...	Divusum...	.....	Pacsham ...	Mausam...	Ayanam ...	Varsham.
Tamul ...	Cunnimy.	Vinaudy ...	Nauzhigay...	Naul ...	Vauram ...	Pacsham ...	Mausam ..	Ayanam ...	Varsham.

——(8) For the special features of time among those of Jeina faith see Avasarpiny.——(9) Caulam also means weather. The following are Tamul proverbs on that head. Cf. Caurtey and Mausam :—தூரமண்டலம் சேரமழை, சேரமண்டலம் தூரமழை—"a distant halo round the moon betokens speedy "rainfall ; but a halo close around her shows the rain is very "distant." காலைசெம்மானம் கங்கமழை, அந்தி செம்மானம் அழுதாலும் மழையில்லை—"red sky in the morn-"ing means speedy rain, red sky in the evening means none "though you cry for it." அகல்வட்டம் பகல்மழை—"a "large halo, a rainy day." அந்தி ஈசல் பூத்தால், அடைமழை யதிகரிக்கும்—"if white-ants take wing in the even-"ing, it prognosticates excessive rain." அந்திமழை யழுதாலும் விடாது—"the evening rain will not cease even if one "should weep." எறும்புமுட்டைகொண்டு திட்டையேறின் மழைபெய்யும்—"if ants carry their eggs to a higher "place, it will rain." காய்ந்தவானம்பெய்ந்தால் விடாது—"rain after drought will not soon cease." காலைச்செல் பூத்தால் அடுத்தமழையடங்கும்—"should winged white-ants "come out in the morning the heavy rain will cease." தட்டான் தாழப்பறந்தால் தப்பாமல் மழைவரும்—"if a "butterfly flies low, it is sure to rain." பனிப்பெய்தால் மழையில்லை, பழம் இருந்தால் பூஇல்லை—"when there is dew "there is no rain, when fruit is ripe there is no blossom." புற்றிலே ஈசல் புறப்பட்டாலும், மண்ணிலேகறையான் கூடினாலும் மழை வரவேவரும்—"when winged white-"ants issue out of a hole, and white-ants swarm, it will certainly "rain." மின்னுக்கெல்லாம்பின்னேமழை—"lightning is "always followed by rain." வடக்கே கறுத்தால் மழைவரும் ; "darkening in the north betokens rain" [caur, jyotisham].——(10) *Caulah* (کالا - kálá, Hind.). Black. Caulah pauny is black water ; the sea, with special reference to transportation.——*Caulak* (कालक - kálaka, San.). Literally black. Unknown quantity in algebra [neelak]. Known quantity is roopam.——*Caulamookham* (कालमुख - kálamukha, San.). From (above + mukha, san. face). A Sheiva sect. One of the six divisions of orthodox Sheivism.——*Caulan* (काल - kála, San.). Shiva.——*Caula rautry* (कालरात्रि - kálarátri, San.). From (above + rátri, san. night). The last night of a calpam.——*Caulaugny* (कालाग्नि - kálágni, San.). From (above + agni, san. fire); fire at end of time. The final fire destined to burn up the world.——*Caulaun* (सर्पच्छत्र - sarpachhatra, San. ; कळंबें - kalambém, Mahr. ; فطر - futr, Ar. ; کلاه دیو - kuláhideu, Pers. ; قدرتی - kudratí, Hind. ; کتے کی چھتری - kuttekíchhatrí, Dec. ; పుట్టకొక్కు - puttakokku, Tel. ; നായ്കുട - náykuta, Mal. ; காளான் - kálán, Tam.). Title from tamul. San. from (sarpa, san. serpent + chhatra, san. umbrella) ; from growing about snake hills. Ar. from (fatara, ar. to split) ; from its splitting the earth in coming up. Pers. from (kuláh, pers. cap + deu, pers. demon). Hind. means self-produced. Dec. from (kuttá, hind. dog + chhatrí, hind. umbrella). Tel. from (putta, tel. ant hill + kokku, tel. bandicoot). Mal. from (náya, mal. dog + kuta, mal. umbrella) ; from being wild. Tam. from (kálam, tam. poison) ; some species being poisonous. San. also (chhatraka), meaning small umbrella ; from figure of plant ; (chhatra), meaning same. Ar. also (ushshulghuráb), meaning raven's nest. Pers. also (samárúgh) ; (chatrimár), meaning snake's umbrella. Can. also (anabe). Mal. also (kún). Tel. also (puttagodugu), meaning ant hill + umbrella ; (kukkagodugu), meaning dog + umbrella. Title otherwise Demon cap, Dog umbrella, Mushroom, Raven's nest, Snake umbrella. Botanically the order fungi [vricsham, 161]. Plants without green color or any distinction as to stem and leaf ; some are poisonous ; the safest being the mushroom, agaricus campestris. The principal edible genera here are :—Agaricus, Clavaria, Coprinus, Fistulina, Hydnum. Not much used by natives. The following are the characters of wholesome fungi :—"*a*" Found growing in fields or in open grassy places in forests.—"*b*" Scattered, each rising direct from the ground ; never collected into clumps nor found growing upon trees.—"*c*" The stem breaks easily when touched ; it springs from the centre of the pileus ; the cap is thick relatively to the gills.—"*d*" They should not be acid in flavor nor smell.—"*e*" Have bright rosy or pink gills and show no yellow stain when bruised. ——*Caulauvadhy* (कालावधि - kálávadhi, San.). From (above + avadhi, san. limit). Season for cultivation [vellaumay].——*Cauley* (کالے - kále, Hind.). Black ; name from personal peculiarity ; as Cauley khan, alam + alaumat [ism].——*Caulingy* (కాళింగనది - kálinganadi, Tel.). From (kálinga, san. the snake on hood of which krishna danced + nadí, san. river). River ; N. arcot and Nellore district. Rises in North arcot district and, flowing through that district, enters Polore division of Nellore and, running south-east by the villages of Munnaurpolore and Sooloorpett, falls into Poolicat lake. Bridge over it at Sooloorpett. Freshes come down in October to January. Total course is about 50 miles.——*Cauliyore naud* (காழியூர்நாடு - kázhiyúrnádu, Tam.). From (káli, tam. the goddess + úr, tam. village + nádu, tam. country). Part of Cauliyore cottam in the ancient Tondaimundalam. In the present Arcot talook, North arcot district [arnee].——*Cauly* (कालि - káli, San. ; کالی - kálí, Hind. ; காளி - káli, Tam.). The wife of Shiva ; same as Devy or Doorga. More usually Bhadra cauly [q.v.] Caulyauttaul, from (áttál, tam. mother) and Cauly amman, from (amman, tam. goddess) are other forms.

CAUM (کام - kám, *Hind.*). Work.——*Caumdaury* (کامداری - kámdárí, Hind.). From (above + dárí, pers. holding). Agency [carbaur].

CAUMAM (காமம் - kámam, *Tam.*). From (gráma, san. village). Village.——*Caumacoottam* (காமக்கோட்டம் - kámakkóttam, Tam.). From (above + kóttam, tam. village). Town or cottam where the Coorumba tribes once flourished. Caumacotatty is the goddess Parvaty.

CAUMAM (काम - káma, *San.*). From (kam, san. to wish). Desire. Plant first term, from pleasing appearance and taste. Ex. :—Cycas circinalis (kámamaram), meaning love tree ; Ipomæa quamoclit (kámalatá), meaning love creeper ; Mangifera indica (kámap'hala), meaning love fruit ; Ocimum basilicum (kámakastúri), meaning love musk ; see gloss. paragraphs. ——*Cauma baunam* (कामबाण - kámabána, San.). From (above + bána, san. arrow). The arrow of love. Cauman's five arrows are :—"*a*" The ally or small lotus or nymphæa [indian water-lily] alba which causes confusion or distraction of mind, and terminates in the privation of every power, excepting that of thinking and speech ;—"*b*" the champak [q.v.], or some say mango [q.v.], which causes sensual desire, and terminates in hot breathing and weeping ;—"*c*" the asbocam [q.v.] tree which causes possession, and terminates in lassitude, grief, and aversion to food ;—"*d*" the jasmine [q.v.] which causes great heat, and terminates in intoxication of sensual desire ;—"*e*" the neelam or blue flower, which causes intention, or eagerness of mind, and terminates in death [matam].——*Caumadhain* (कामधेनु - kámadhénu, San.). From (above + dhénu, san. cow). The heavenly cow which yields all desires, as an earthly cow gives milk. Called also Soorabhy. Produced at the churning of the ocean by Vishnoo [coormam, matam].——*Cauman* (काम - káma, San.). Latin cupido, Greek ἔρως. The god of love. This name is frequently used in the north, but Moroogan and Manmatan [q.v.] are more common southern usage [matam].——*Cauman pundigay* (காமன்பண்டிகை - kámanbandigai, Tam.). Cauman's festival. Otherwise Hootaushana powrnimay or fire the oblation-eater + full moon; from cauman's burning on that day. In Bengal and Mysore called Holy. Lunar festival [pundigay, 6a], subject to intercalation. The fifteenth tity or full moon of the twelfth lunar month Phaulgoonam [mausam] between 26th February and 27th March. Festival on near approach of vernal equinox [maishauyanam]. Also to commemorate the destruction of Cauman by Shiva [manmatan]. All classes of Hindoos sport on this day in honor of Govindan, who is carried about in a palankeen. Cf. the Latin saturnalia. The classes of society are confounded whilst it lasts. At the close of the festival a pile is lighted, on which a cake is placed. In Travancore cocks are offered by Nayars, who kill them before the door of the temple of Cauly or Bhagavaty [bharany, maryauday].——*Caumaroopam* (कामरूप - kámarúpa, San.). From (above + rúpa, san. form). Having the power to change the form at will. Also name of ancient country, now part of Assam.——*Cauma shastram* (कामशास्त्र - kámashástra, San.). From (above + shástra, san. science). Science of love. Treated by natives physically and classed under Veidya shastram.——*Caumautchy* (कामाक्षी - kámákshí, San.; காமாட்சி - kámádchi, Tam.). From (above + akshi, san. eye). Parvaty as having fascinating eyes. Hindoo 2nd or pers. name common to both sexes. Familiarly Caumoo [peyar].——*Caumayya* (కామయ్య - kámayya, Tel.). From cauman, god of love. Hindoo 2nd or pers. name [peyar].

CAUMAUTY (ಕಾಮಾಟಿ - kámáti, *Can.*; காமாட்டி - kámátti, *Tam.*). From (karmat'ha, san. skilled in work).* A bricklayer [inam]. Used as term of abuse [moottaul].

CAUN (कानन - kánana, *San.*; కాన - kána, *Tel.*; கானம் - kánam, *Tam.*). Jungle. Plant first term, often joining two genera. Ex., where transl. is of second term:—Flacourtia ramontchi (kánarégu), zizyphus jujuba; Guizotia abyssinica (kánel), sesamum indicum; Jatropha curcas (kánaneranda), ricinus communis; Ormocarpum sennoides (kánanashigru), moringa pterygosperma; Plumeria alba (kánanakaravíra), nerium odorum; Spondias mangifera (kánanámra), mangifera indica; Vernonia anthelmintica (kánanajíraka), cuminum cyminum. See gloss. paragraphs.——*Caunaraig* (కానరేగు - kánrégu, Tel.). Same as Forest bair [q.v.].

CAUN (காண் - kán, *Tam.*). To see; to worship.——*Caunicay* (காணிக்கை - kánikkai, Tam.). Present to a deity or preceptor [maryauday, wolfa].

CAUNARY (كانرى - kánarí, *Malay*). Botanically the Canarium genus, burseraceæ [vricsham, 35]. Balsamiferous trees with compound leaves; flowers panicled; fruit a triangular drupe of one seed. The species best known to the natives are:—commune [elemi], strictum [black dammer].

CAUNCHY (पिण्डार - pindára, *San.*; پنڈالو - pindálú, *Hind.* and *Dec.*; ಕಾಟ್ಕುಂಬಳ - kátkumbala, *Can.*; ମୋଣ୍ଡା - momda, *Oor.*; കാഞ്ഞി - káñchi, *Mal.*; ஆற்றுப்பூவரசு - áttuppúvarasu, *Tam.*). Title from malayalam. San. from (pinda, san. ball + ri, san. to go). Hind. from sanscrit. Can. from (kádu, can. wild + kumbil, mal. cashmere tree, gmelina arborea, linn.); from similarity of leaves. Tam. from (áru, tam. river + púvarasu, tam. portia tree, thespesia populnea, corr.). Can. also (kanchimara). Tam. also (káñji) [indian elm, jow]. Title otherwise Pindauloo, Pindaura, River portia. Botanically Trewia nudiflora, linn., euphorbiaceæ [vricsham, 118]. Alias Rottlera hoperiana, indica; Tetragastis osssea; Trewia macrophylla, macrostachys. Large tree; stipules linear-subulate, very caducous; leaves broad ovate, acute or acuminate, cordate or obtuse or subcuneate at the base, entire, five-nerved, membranaceous, biglandular at the base, young ones villous or pubescent on both sides and below, especially in the lower part, sprinkled with gold shining, very small, waxy glands, but soon altogether destitute of them; racemes axillary, males often exceeding the leaves, flower-bearing almost the whole length, females few-flowered; bracts very small; male calyx globose; segments of the female calyx long-acuminate, here and there cohering in pairs; anthers emarginate at the base and apex; ovary pale tawny, silky; fruit four to three coccous, sub-globose, smooth, pendulous; seeds smooth; in sandy places near the shore; flowering in february and march; small, whitish, greenish flowers. Wood white, soft, not durable. No other common species here.

CAUNDAL (காந்தல் - kándal, *Tam.*). Means burning, from burning ground. Neilgherry district, Todanaud division; lat. 11° 24'; long. 76° 43'; from Ootacamund N.W. 1¼ miles. Suburb of Ootacamund.——*Caundy* (காந்தி - kándi, Tam.). From (kándu, tam. to be sun burnt). Female proper name among the lower orders [peyar].

CAUNDAM (काण्ड - kánda, *San.*). A portion of a book; specially in epics and vedas. Distinguish from khandam.

CAUNG (காங்கு - kángu, *Tam.*). From (kán, tam. forest); from habitat. Botanically the Hopea genus, dipterocarpeæ [vricsham, 24]. Large, glabrous or hoary tomentose, resinous trees; heart-wood yellowish brown, hard, smooth, even-grained, seasons well. The species best known to the natives are shown below. Other s. indian species indigenous or naturalized are:—dichotoma, glabra, malabarica, odorata.——*Common caung* (காங்கு - kángu, Tam.). Botanically Hopea [caung] wightiana, wall., dipterocarpeæ [vricsham, 24]. Large tree; young branches and petioles densely pubescent; leaves ovate-oblong, rounded at the base and attenuated towards the apex into a very obtuse point, glabrous except on the rib above; panicles axillary, generally three together, shorter than, or as long as, the leaves; flowers pink, secund, bracteolate at the base of their very short pedicels; calyx glabrous; corolla hairy on the outside; stamens fifteen, alternately single and double; anthers terminated by a long bristle; fruit and calycine wings glabrous, bright crimson; very common in western forest; an echinate excrescence, much like young fruit of a spanish chestnut, is produced in the axils of the leaves, probably the formation of some insect in the bud of the panicle; large tracts are met with never apparently flowering, but abundantly covered with the abortive fruit-like excrescence; timber very valuable.——*Water caung* (ಕಿರಲ್ಬೋಗಿ - kiralbógi, Can.; ഇരിമ്പകം - irimpakam, Mal.; நீர்க்காங்கு - nírkkángu, Tam.). Title from habitat. Mal. from (irimpu, mal. iron + akam, mal. inside); from strong wood. Tam. from (nír, tam. water + kángu, tam. hopea genus). Can. also (tirpu). Botanically Hopea [caung] parviflora, bedd., dipterocarpeæ [vricsham, 24]. Large handsome tree, petioles, panicles, and calyx hairy; leaves short-petioled, glabrous, ovate to oblong, furnished with glands in the axils of the veins beneath; flowers secund, sub-sessile, numerous, very minute, fragrant; stamens fifteen, alternately single and in pairs; stigma three-cleft; common in both moist and dry forests; excrescences as in common caung; produces a gum [gond]; wood brown, hard, and close-grained, valued in south canara for building temples.

CAUNJIRAY (காஞ்சிரை - káñjirai, *Tam.*). From (káy, tam. fruit + shira, tam. to destroy). Same as Poison nut.

CAUNJORY (वृश्चिकाली - vrishchikálí, *San.*; खाजकुल्लि - khájrakulli, *Conc.*; کانچکوری - kánchkurí, *Hind.*; ದೂಲಗೊಂಡಿ - dúlagondi, *Can.*; దూలగొండి - dúlagondi, *Tel.*; ചൊറിഞ്ഞണം - choriññanam, *Mal.*; වල්කහම්බිලියා - valkahambiliyá, *Singh.*; காஞ்சொறி - káñjori, *Tam.*). Title from tamul. San. from (vrishchika, san. scorpion + álí, san. friend); from similar burning sensation. Conc. from (khájara, mahr. stinging + kuirí, mahr. cowhage, mucuna pruriens, dc.). Hind. means cowhage, mucuna pruriens, dc. [common cowitch]. Tel. from (dúla, tel. itching + gondi, tel. wretch). Mal. from (chori, mal. itch). Singh. from (val, singh. creeper + kahambiliyá, singh. nettle, urtica). Tam. from (káy, tam. to be hot + shori, tam. to itch), as causing itching and burning sensation. San. also (dusparshá), meaning not to be touched [indian nightshade, prickly brinjaul]; (durálabhá), meaning not to be touched [arabian manna]; (samudrántá), meaning extending to the sea; (kachhurá), meaning itchy; (vrishchikapatri), meaning scorpion + leaf; from causing burning sensation on contact. Can. also (turachi) [common cowitch]. Tel. also (peddadúlagondi), meaning large + the plant; (télumanichettu), meaning scorpion + gem + plant. Mal. also (kotittúva), meaning creeper + nettle. Tam. also (erumaikkáñjori), meaning buffalo + the plant; (púnaikkáñjori), meaning cat + the plant; (vellaikkáñjori), meaning white + the plant; (shendotti), meaning good defence; (kannísi). Title otherwise Calycine tragia, Scorpion leaf, White caunjory. Botanically Tragia involucrata, muller, euphorbiaceæ [vricsham, 118]. Annual, twining; leaves oblong-lanceolate, acute, sharply serrated, alternate; closely covered with stinging hair; female bracts five-leaved, pinnated; flowers axillary in small clusters, several together on the same foot-stalk, upper ones male, under ones female; flowers small, greenish; flowering nearly all year; the hair sting like nettle; small root with no sensible taste nor smell. The root medicinally an alterative; the root in decoction [kwautam] internally against suppression of urine; the juice mixed with cow's milk and sugar given as a drink in fevers and itch; fruit made into paste applied to boils to hasten suppuration.——*Small caunjory* (कासघ्नी - kásaghní, San.; खाजकुल्लि - khájrakulli, Conc.; کاچکوری - káchkurí, Hind.; کانچکوری کا جہاڑ - kánchkuríkájhár, Dec.; ಕಿರುತುರಚಿ - kiruturachi, Can.; చిన్నదూలగొండి - chinnadúlagondi, Tel.; சிறுகாஞ்சொறி - shirugáñjori, Tam.). Title from size. San. from (kása, san. cough + han, san. to kill). Conc. means stinging cowhage. Hind. means cowhage, mucuna pruriens, dc. Can. from (kiru, can. small + turachi, can. tragia involucrata, müller). Tel. from (chinna, tel. small + dúlagondi, tel. tragia involucrata, müller). Tam. from (shiru, tam. small + káñjori, tam. tragia involucrata, müller). San. also (grahíni), meaning seizing; (virúpa), meaning shapeless. Can. also (sannaturachi), meaning small + tragia involucrata, müller. Tel. also (révatidúlagoudi), meaning regar soil + tragia involucrata, müller. Tam. also (karuppukkáñjori), meaning black + tragia involucrata, müller; (púnaikkáñjori), meaning cat + tragia involucrata, müller. Title otherwise Black caunjory, Hemp-leaved tragia. Botanically Tragia cannabina, l., euphorbiaceæ [vricsham, 118]. Annual; stem twining, hispid; leaves hairy, stinging, three-parted, lanceolate, petioled; peduncles lateral, solitary, one-flowered, the length of the leaves; flowers small, yellowish; hair stings like that of common nettle; root has, in dried state, but little taste or smell; in more succulent condition rather pleasant odour. Root is medicinally diaphoretic and alterative.

CAUNOM (കാണം - kánam, *Mal.*). From (kánuka, mal. to see). That which is seen; so deposit; so the tangible lump sum advance, bearing interest, on receiving which a west coast jenmy gives a lease of his land when desirous of raising money, which he cannot do by Veroompauttom [q.v.]. So by the elliptical technical language of Malabar that form of lease, or that tenure, itself. Caunom is the most ordinary form of lease-hold in Malabar. The origin was that the tenant was required to give a year's rent or pauttom in advance to the proprietor, either as a necessary security for payment or as a bonus for the profit he was allowed to enjoy [cuttacaunom, moonpauttom], and this turned to a permanent advance bearing interest. Looking to the fact of this advance, caunom is half a lease and half a mortgage. The following are the details. The landlord leases an estate to a tenant, giving him possession, but taking from him a sum of money or store of grain as deposit, and agreeing to pay him a small interest on this. At the end of the specified term, almost invariably twelve years, and always so where a fee has been paid, the landlord can demand repossession on payment of the amount taken in deposit and of compensation for any improvements that may have been made. During the tenancy, the tenant pays the whole profits to the landlord, after deducting the expenses of cultivation, the Government dues, and interest on the principal lent. The whole surplus is supposed to be paid over to the landlord, but the terms vary according to special agreement. The tenant cannot be ousted till the expiry of the term, except for injury to the estate. The tenant may obtain an extension of the term on payment of a renewal fine, theoretically supposed to be one-fifth of the sum originally lent. Should the landlord himself desire to raise a further sum of money on the land, and the tenant be unwilling to advance it, the landlord may assign the property to a third party, who will be entitled to possession on paying off the sum originally advanced by the first tenant. The latter however in his turn has the option of advancing the required sum and remaining in possession if he pleases [caunom poorangcadom]. To sum up, the rights of the landlord are to redeem at the end of the term on payment of what is due, to receive payment of the rent fixed as it falls due, or to deduct it from the refund of caunom if it is in arrears at the time of redemption, and to create what is called a mailcaunom or higher mortgage. The rights of the tenant are to assign his term, and to claim compensation for unexhausted improvements at the time of redemption. The caunom deed is the second of the six Pramaunams or Caranams or deeds of transfer of property recognized in the Malabar Sanscrit shastrams as culminating in acquired jenm [caranam]. It follows their Cooyicaunom or pitting lease, and precedes Otty or real mortgage. In North malabar the caunom sum is larger than in South malabar. For a conspectus of Malabar tenures see vol. II, 104; caunom is given there as coming next above Veroompauttom in the interests of tenant; for a stage higher see Otty. ——(1) *Caunacaur* (കാണക്കാരൻ - kánakkáran, Mal.). From (above + káran, mal. holder). The lessee or mortgagee.—— *Cauna coyoovan* (കാണക്കൊഴുവൻ - kánakkozhuvan, Mal.). From (above + kozhuvan, mal. tenant). Lessee or mortgagee [coyoovan].——*Cauna jenma maryauda arinyaver* (കാണജന്മമര്യാദയറിയുന്നവർ - kánajanmamaryádayariyunnavar, Mal.). From (above + janmam, mal. birthright + maryáda, mal. custom + ari, mal. to know). Assessors by whom the value of an estate is determined and the proportion of the caunacaur and jenmy adjusted.——*Cauna palisha* (കാണപ്പലിശ - kánappalisha, Mal.). From (above + palisha, mal. interest). Interest on caunom deposited by lessee or mortgagee.——*Cauna pauttom* (കാണപ്പാട്ടം - kánappáttam, Mal.). From (above + páttam, mal. rent). The yearly rent payable by a Caunacaur. It does not usually exceed one-third of the net produce. It is opposed to Veroompauttom, the rent of a simple lease, where no deposit has been made and which is generally at least two-thirds.—— *Caunatoga* (കാണത്തുക - kánattuka, Mal.). From (above + tuka, mal. amount). Amount of deposit in caunom.——*Caunavacausham* (കാണാവകാശം - kánávakásham, Mal.). From (above + avakásha, san. claim). A Caunacaur's claim.——*Caunom poorangcadom* (കാണമ്പുറങ്കടം - kánampurankatam, Mal.). From (above + puram, mal. outside + katam, mal. debt). An expedient of Jenmies for raising more money on land already made over to a tenant on caunom, from the same tenant. It is a separate transaction. It sometimes takes place at the time of arranging the caunom, in which case it is referred to in the caunom deed. At other times it is effected after the lessee has come into possession; in that case the fact of the caunom or lease is alluded to in this deed, and the landlord engages to pay off both the caunom and the new loan together. The loan of Poorangcadom gives the Caunacaur an additional lien upon the property.——(2) *Cootticaunom* (കുറ്റിക്കാണം - kuttikkánam, Mal.). From (kutti, mal. stump + above). Stump mortgage. In this a landlord assigns on caunom a tract of forest land, receiving a stipulated fee for every tree felled by the mortgagee. ——*Cooyicaunom* (കുഴിക്കാണം - kuzhikkánam, Mal.). From (kuzhi, mal. pit + above). A special pitting lease antecedent to caunom. Lease by which land is let for improving. The tenant under this pays no real caunom and ordinarily no rent to the jenmy, and at the end of his term receives compensation [chamayam] for all trees planted, houses and walls built, &c., but only for such improvements as are of a permanent nature. If there happen to be any trees on the land at the time of leasing, the tenant pays rent for them. The tenant can be ousted for neglecting to improve the property according to agreement. He on his side cannot give up the property before the fixed time, but he can transfer his estate or any lesser one. Where no express period has been stipulated this lease is considered to run for twelve years. Cf. Cuttacaunom for another lease prior to Caunom and Coodiyiroopp for house-lease.—— *Cuttacaunom* (കട്ടക്കാണം - kattakkánam, Mal.). From (katta, mal. lump + above). Ground-breaking lease. Another name for Moonpauttom or step between Veroompauttom and Caunom, or tenure of a simple lessee who deposits in his Jenmy's hands a single year's rent as security for due fulfilment of his lease contract, and for payment of rent. Cuttacaunom does not carry with it a right to hold for twelve years; the security is returned without interest at the end of the lease. The cultivator pays the full established pauttom besides. This differs from the payments under Caunom, Otty, and the higher tenures in that no interest is claimable on it.——*Nauticaunom* (നാട്ടിക്കാണം - nátikkánam, Mal.). From (nátu, mal. to inspect + above). A sum after inspection. A sum in compensation to himself deducted by a proprietor from the tenant's deposit or loan in Caunom and Otty for the depreciation of the estate by neglect. ——*Pautta caunom* (പാട്ടക്കാണം - páttakkánam, Mal.). From (páttam, mal. rent + above). Rent.——*Tooshicaunom* (തൂശിക്കാണം - túshikkánam, Mal.). From (túshi, mal. iron style + above). Fee paid to the writer who draws a transfer deed.—— *Vettoocaunom* (വെട്ടുകാണം - vettukánam, Mal.). From (vettu, mal. to dig + above). Form of caunom where compensation [chamayam] is payable to an outgoing tenant for having cleared and levelled land, in other words for tillages.

CAUNOOGA (ಕಾನಗ - kánaga, *Can.*; కానుగ - kánuga, *Tel.*; പുന്നു - punnu, *Mal.*; புங்கு - pungu, *Tam.*). Title from canarese. Can. from (kánu, can. hard). Tel. from (kánu, tel. hard) [karanj]. Mal. from tamul. Tam. from (punmai, tam. inferiority); inferior wood [karanj, malabar poon]. Tel. also (peddasápara), meaning large + symplocos racemosa, rox.; (errapattséri), meaning red + dalbergia paniculata, roxb. Botanically Dalbergia [yooga pattricay] lanceolaria, linn., leguminosæ [vricsham, 48]. Alias Dalbergia arborea, frondosa. Tree, 30 feet; bark smooth; leaves pinnate; leaflets about five pairs, alternate, cuneate oval, emarginate, when very young silky; panicles axillary, pubescent; flowers secund, racemose along the alternate branches of the panicles, small, bluish white; calyx hairy; alæ as long as the vexillum, about twice as long as the keel; corolla papilionaceous; ovary very slightly pubescent; legume lanceolate, one to four-seeded or less; handsome and quick-growing; mountains of south of peninsula; taller and straighter than sissoo [q.v.]. The bark in infusion is given in dyspepsia, and the leaves rubbed over the body in leprosy [cooshtam] and cutaneous diseases; a fixed fat oil procured from the seeds used in rheumatic affections; milk which exudes from the roots applied to ulcers. Wood white, moderately hard; not durable; no heart-wood; may be used for building purposes.——*Creeper caunooga* (తీగకానుగ - tígakánuga, Tel.; പന്നിവള്ളി - pannivalli, Mal.; கொடிப்புங்கு - kodippungu, Tam.). Title from habit and resemblance. Tel. from (tíga, tel. creeper + kánuga, tel. dalbergia lanceolaria, linn.). Mal. from (panni, mal. hog + valli, mal. creeper). Tam. from (kodi, tam. creeper + pungu, tam. dalbergia lanceolaria, linn.). Tel. also (mottasirli); (surli); (chiratalabódi). Mal. also (muyalvalli), meaning hare + creeper. Title otherwise Hog creeper. Botanically Derris scandens, benth., leguminosæ [vricsham, 48]. Alias Brachypterum scandens; Dalbergia scandens. Twining shrub; leaflets opposite, oblong-lanceolate, obtuse at the apex; petioles channelled; calyx with two small bracteoles at its base, truncated, with a short tooth opposite the keel; vexillum callous at the base of the limb; wings ciliated at the base; legume almost sessile, linear-lanceolate, two to three-seeded; racemes axillary, longer than the leaves; pedicels fascicled, slender; flowers numerous, white or pale-rose, fragrant; flowering in august. There are other species:—canarensis, heyneana, ovalifolia, robusta, uliginosa.

CAUNTAM (कान्त - kánta, *San.*; लोहकान्त - lóhakánta, *Mahr.*; مقناطيس - maknátís, *Ar.*; آهن ربا - áhanrubá, *Pers.*; چمك پتهر - chamakpatthar, *Hind.*; بتو برنى - batubrani, *Malay*; సూదంటురాయి - súdanturáyi, *Tel.*; അയസ്കാന്തം - ayaskántam, *Mal.*; කාන්තගල - kántagala, *Singh.*; காந்தம் - kándam, *Tam.*). San. from (kam, san. to long for). Mahr. from (lóha, san. iron + kánta, san. magnet). Ar. from greek. Pers. from (áhan, pers. iron + rubá, pers. attractor). Hind. from (chamak, hind. flash + patthar, hind. stone). Malay from (batu, malay, stone + brani, malay, bold). Tel. from (súdi, tel. needle + antu, tel. to stick + ráyi, tel. stone). Mal. from (ayas, san. iron + kánta, san. attracting). Singh. from (kánta, san. loadstone + gala, singh. stone). Tam. from sanscrit. Ar. also (hajrulmighnátís), meaning magnet stone. Pers. also (sangichamak), meaning stone + flash. Malay also (basibrani), meaning bold iron. Loadstone. Otherwise Magnet. Forri oxidum magneticum of chemists. A combination of the protoxide and peroxide of iron. Chief use is in making the mariner's compass; but veidyans consider to possess tonic and deobstruent qualities, and prescribe powder in conjunction with aromatics and sulphur [gandhac], in consumption and dropsy. Arakk cauntam, from (arakku, tam.) lac, is a red kind. Cull cauntam is magnetic iron stone, used medicinally in anæmia and gastritis; according to their shape magnets are called oorlay or round, tagatt or flat, &c. Caunta munn is magnesite, see vol. II, 38, wherein is found carbonate of magnesia; magnesia or oxide of magnesium, obtained from the latter by applying heat; and sulphate of magnesia or epsom's salts. Caunta shatroo, from (shatru, san. enemy), are things which counteract the magnetic power; as blue-vitriol [mayil toottam], salammoniac [nowshandar] and saltpetre [shorah].——*Cauntan* (कान्त - kánta, San.). Lover. Suffix in proper names as Lutchmicauntan [peyar].——*Caunty* (कान्ति - kánti, San.). Brightness, love. Plant second term. Ex.:—Hibiscus mutabilis (súryakánti), lover of the sun; flower opens when sun is up and like it in color and form. Ipomæa bonanox, var. grandiflora (chandrakánti), lover of the moon; flower opens when moon is up and white in color.

CAUR (كار - kár, *Hind.*). Work [car].——*Cauram* (कार - kára, San.). From (kri, san. to do). Doing. Abstract agency. Suffix in compounds; as Balautcauram, meaning by force + doing, violence. Distinguish from cauram, alkali.——*Cauran* (കാരൻ - káran, Mal.; காரன் - káran, Tam.). Doer. Personal agency suffix in compounds; as Carmacauran, meaning work + doer, artisan.——*Cauranam* (कारण - kárana, San.). From (kri, san. to do). Cause. According to Sheiva philosophy it is threefold, viz.:—"*a*" moothal cauranam, material or proximate cause, the clay from which pot is made, the primitive Mauyay out of which the universe is produced;—"*b*" toonay cauranam, auxiliary or instrumental cause as the wheel of the potter, the Shacty or energy of shiva;—"*c*" nimitta cauranam, the efficient cause or agent as the potter, Shiva in the production of the world [matam].——*Caurchoby* (كارچوبى - kárchobí, Hind.). From (above + chob, pers. stick); from the frame of wooden laths on which the embroidery is done. Solid embroidery in gold thread [calaubat], employed for cushions of state, elephant trappings, &c. [zardozy].——*Caurgah* (كارگاه - kárgáh, Hind.). From (above + gáh, pers. place). Manufactory.——*Caurinda* (كارنده - kárindah, Hind.). From (above + suffix denoting agent). Servant, revenue clerk.——*Caurjy* (కార్జి - kárji, Tel.). From (above + jí, hind. honorific address). Head of a village [inam].——*Caury* (कारी - kárí, San.). From (kri, san. to do). A doer. Suffix of agency in compounds; as adhicaury, meaning over + doer.

CAUR (ಕಾರು - káru, *Can.*; కారు - káru, *Tel.*; கார் - kár, *Tam.*). Means dark [calam, car, caulam] or wild. Prefix in place names as in Caurcoody, meaning village with dark soil.—"*a*" The wet season of the year corresponding to either of the monsoon [q.v.] periods. The S.W. monsoon is sometimes called Moongaur [q.v.], and the N.E. Hingaur [q.v.]. In Tamul countries Caur is generally restricted to S.W., and then equivalent to Poonausa [q.v.] of N. districts. Natives consider that there is a second burst of the S.W. in August and September; this is sometimes called Caur specially.—"*b*" The term indicates also the paddy [q.v.] of the corresponding season. The following are different kinds of Caur paddy:—Aroovaul caur means sickle, from sickle-shaped grain; Auny caur is from the month of sowing; Chittray caur from month of reaping; Coolla caur means short stalk; Eroomay caur means buffalo, being coarse; Mottay caur means blunt, from shape of grain; Mutta caur means palm stem, from color of grain; Oonday caur means ball, from roundish rice; Peroom caur means large size; Pody shandicaur means small and stubborn grain which cannot be easily husked off; Pooldy caur means raised on dry ground; Pooncaur means flower, being soft and superior; Shem caur means red, from color of grain; Tella caur means white, from color of ear growing. Compare Pishaunam.—"*c*" Cauriyan means the black man. Pariah proper name. Caury is feminine [peyar].—"*d*" Plant first term, often joining two genera, meaning wild. Ex., where transl. is of second term:—Atylosia scarabæoides (káruulava), dolichos biflorus; Bridelia retusa, var. roxburghiana (káratti), ficus glomerata; Carallia integerrima (káralli), memecylon; Caralluma adscendens (kárallamu), zingiber officinale; Dysophylla cruciata (kárutumma), leucas indica; Gardenia latifolia (káringuva), ferula narthex; Hibiscus vitifolius (kárupatti), gossypium herbaceum; Laggera aurita (kárupogáku), nicotiana tabacum; Phaseolus adenanthus (káralatsanda), vigna catiang; Rhynchosa viscosa (kárukandi), cajanus indicus; Sterculia colorata (káruboppáyi), carica papaya; Zingiber cassumanar (kárupasupu), curcuma longa. See gloss. paragraphs.—"*e*" Plant first term, meaning black. Ex.:—Aleurites triloba (kárankólam), black alangium lamarckii; Aristolochia bracteata (kárirattam), black blood, from flowers; Indigofera echinata (kárnegilu), black tribulus terrestris; Jatropha curcas (kárnoççi), black vitex; Zehneria umbellata (kárkkóvai), black cephalandra indica. See gloss. paragraphs.——*Caurallam* (मकरसिंग - makarasinga, Mahr.; కారల్లము - kárallamu, Tel.; கள்ளிமுளையான் - kallimulaiyán, Tam.). Title from teloogoo. Mahr. means monkey horn. Tel. from (káru, tel. forest + allamu, tel. ginger, zingiber officinale, roscoe). Tam. from (kalli, tam. euphorbia tirucalli, linn. + mulai, tam. sprout); from fleshy leafless stems. Tel. also (tavatichettu), meaning bran + plant. Tam. also (ezhumán); (ezhumánbuli). Title otherwise Bran plant, Monkey's horn, Spurge sprout, Wild ginger. Botanically Caralluma genus, asclepiadeæ [vricsham, 88]. Generic from teloogoo. Fleshy, erect, nearly leafless herbs, with very thick stem and branches which are almost cylindrical or angular; leaves minute and dropping off; flowers solitary or in pairs at the upper nodes; follicles long and slender with hairy seeds. The species best known to the natives are:—Adscendens, curious looking fleshy plant with angular stems; flowers often nodding; used in pickles and chutney [q.v.]; young tetragonal stems used as famine food. Attenuata, dry plains at foot of neilgherries. Edulis. Fimbriata, flowers yellowish above, transversely purple-streaked, underneath yellow.——*Cauraumany* (காராமணி - kárámani, Tam.). From (kár, tam. black + á, tam. cow + mani, tam. grain). From dark grain and serving as fodder. Cow gram.——*Caurcal* (ಕಾರ್ಕಲ - kárkala, Can.). From (kare, can. black + kallu, can. stone); black stone found here in abundance.—"*a*" Deputy tahsildarry, South canara district. Pay Rs. 70.—"*b*" Village, Port, Deputy tahsildar's station; South canara dist., Oodipy tal.; pop. 4,115; lat. 13° 13′; long. 75° 02′; from Coondapore S.E. 35 miles; from Madras W. 355 miles; from Mangalore N.E. 26 miles; from Oodipy E.S.E. 18 miles; from Poottore N.N.W. 34 miles; from Soobramanyam N.W. 56 miles; from the sea E. 16 miles. On one of the main lines from Mysore to Mangalore. Once a populous Jeina town. Jeina statue and group of temples. The image called Goomta [gomataroya] is made of one piece of granite [caroomcull], the extreme dimensions of which above ground are 41 feet 5 inches in height, 10½ feet in breadth, and 10 feet in thickness and there are probably 3 feet more under ground. It was erected, according to an inscription on it in A.D. 1432. Only three of these great monolithic Jeina statues are known to exist, the others being at Shravanabelgola in Mysore and Yenoor in this district. This one represents Bauhoobalin, son of Vrishabhanautan, the first of the Teertancarans, and was erected by Veera paundyan. The principal basty [q.v.] is an elaborately sculptured building whose forms very closely follow those of wooden originals, as do most of the structures of the Western coasts. This is especially noticeable on the roof. The pillars of the mantapam and the base of the handsome monolithic pillar in front are well sculptured. The designs of some of the figure sculptures are purely Veishnava; for instance Vishnoo on the Garoodan, the boy Krishnan with the serpent, &c. The scroll work and the devices on some of the square pillar bases are admirably designed; amongst others an intricately twisted rope ornament and a geometrical pattern strongly recalling to mind that in constant use on Japanese pottery, of which the matrix is the swasticam [q.v.]. On one of the pillar shafts is a band like the plaits of a woman's hair. Near the village are the ruins of the palace of Bheirava arsoo wodeyar, the most powerful of the Jeina rajahs of Tooloovam, who was overthrown by Shivappa naick of Ikkairy. A high monolithic Dhwaja stambham [q.v.], a kind of obelisk, a Hindoo temple [coil] containing a figure of Ananta shayanan, and a Jeina impaling stone, are the other curiosities of this village. There are several inscriptions all in Canarese in the Ananta pudmanaubhan temple, dating from A.D. 1334 to 1592. There is a small lake here. The village is the centre of a considerable rice trade [betta].

CAUR (కారు - káru, *Tel.*). To flow.——*Caurem* (కారేము - káremu, Tel.). Hollowed trunk of a palm tree shaped like a canoe and balancing like a see-saw, to draw up water [picottah].——*Caurempoody* (కారెంపూడి - kárempúdi, Tel.). From (káremu, tel. hollow trunk of a palm tree used to conduct water + púdi, tel. village). Village, Head-quarters of District moonsif; Kistna dist., Pulnaud tal.; pop. 1,941; acres 4,265; lat. 16° 26′; long. 72° 46′; from Dauchepully S. 11¼ miles; from Masulipatam W.N.W. 94 miles. Scene of the cock-fights mentioned in the ballads of the Pulnaud heroes. This sport still survives. Several cromlechs have been opened in this neighbourhood. Temple of Sooreshwarasawmy. Two storied mantapams [q.v.]. Fourteen inscriptions, one of the reign of Coolotoonga chola A.D. 1154, others of the reign of the Regent Roodramma.

CAUR (കാർ - kár, *Mal.*; காறு - káru, *Tam.*). Ploughshare [calappay].——*Cauraulan* (കാരാളൻ - kárálan, Mal.). From (above + álu, mal. to own). Worker. The agent or deputy for the Ooraulan, or founder in the management of the lands of Malabar temples; the enjoyer of the Cauroyma tenure given therefor.——*Cauroyma* (കാരായ്മ - káráyma, Mal.). The office of Cauraulan or temple land bailiff in Malabar [ooroyma]. So the tenure by which these hold certain temple lands. For conspectus of Malabar tenures, see vol. II, 104.——*Cauroymacaur* (കാരായ്മക്കാരൻ - káráyamakkáran, Mal.). Same as Cauraulan.

CAURAM (क्षार - kshára, *San.*; كهار - khár, *Hind.*; காரம் - káram, *Tam.*). San. from (kshar, san. to flow); a corrosive substance. Hind. and Drav. from sanscrit. Distinguish from cauram, suffix [caur]. Any alkali; substance changing the colors of the vegetable blues to green, and yellows to brown; neutralising acids [tezaub] and forming with them salts; has a peculiar hot, bitter, and caustic taste. Alkaline ashes [sujjeekhaur] are obtained by natives in the ruder parts of the country by burning plants. So more specifically a body, which having a two-fold attraction for organic fibres and coloring particles serves as a bond of union between them and thus gives fixity to coloring substances, constituting them dyes [shanyam]; the tamulians have a large assortment of these; their chief mineral mordants are alum [padicauram], and the salts of iron; alkalies derived from the ashes of many plants are used as mordants, when mineral are absent.——**(1)** The following are two keylists in the briefest possible terms of the principal vegetable mordants of s. india for which vernacular names are known; further information must be traced in the glossary paragraphs through the small type cross-references at end of this volume; see also vricsham, 7, for the method of expressing the products, &c., of plants in the dravidian languages:—"*a*" Abrus precatorius, indian liquorice, ashes; Acacia intsia, corindah, bark and leaves; Achyranthes aspera, indian burr, ashes; Adhatoda vasica, malabar nut, ashes; Alstonia scholaris, dita, ashes; Amarantus spinosus, thorny spinach, ashes; Averrhoa carambola, coromandel gooseberry, fruit; Bambusa arundinacea, common bamboo, ashes; Bassia latifolia, wild mohwah, bark; Bauhinia purpurea, purple mountain ebony, bark; Bauhinia variegata, variegated mountain ebony, bark; Cæsalpinia bonducella, bonduc, ashes; Calotropis gigantea, mudar, ashes; Carissa carandas, carondah, fruit; Cassia fistula, indian laburnum, ashes; Cedrus deodara, deodar, ashes; Erythrina indica, common coral tree, ashes; Euphorbia nereifolia, leafy milk hedge, ashes; Euphorbia tirucalli, round milk hedge, ashes; Ficus infectoria, stone banyan, galls; Gmelina arborea, cashmere tree, ashes; Holarrhena antidysenterica, tellicherry bark, ashes; Indigofera tinctoria, indigo, ashes; Luffa ægyptiaca, oil-giving luffa, ashes; Mangifera indica, mango, dry unripe fruit; Musa paradisiaca, plantain, ashes; Nerium odorum, oleander ashes; Pennisetum spicatum, spiked millet, ashes; Pistacia integerrima, zebra wood tree, galls; Pistacia vera, pistachio nut tree, galls; Pongamia glabra, indian beech, bark; Quercus infectoria, dyer's oak, galls; Salicornia brachiata, glosswort, ashes; Salvadora oleoides, large tooth-brush tree, galls; Shorea robusta, common saul, ashes; Suæda indica, indian saltwort, ashes; Suæda nudiflora, sea side indian saltwort, ashes; Symplocos racemosa, californian cinchona, ashes; Tamarindus indica, tamarind, fruit; Tamarix dioica, cypress tamarisk, galls; Tamarix gallica, indian tamarisk, galls; Vitex negundo, notchy, ashes.—"*b*" Bamboo, bambusa; Banyan, ficus; Beech, pongamia; Bonduc, cæsalpinia; Burr, achyranthes; Carondah, carissa; Cashmere tree, gmelina; Cinchona, symplocos; Coral tree, erythrina; Corindah, acacia; Deodar, cedrus; Dita, alstonia; Glosswort, salicornia; Gooseberry, averrhoa; Indigo, indigofera; Kino, butea; Laburnum, cassia; Leadwort, plumbago; Liquorice, abrus; Malabar nut, adhatoda; Mango, mangifera; Milk hedge, euphorbia; Millet, pennisetum; Mohwah, bassia; Mountain ebony, bauhinia; Mudar, calotropis; Notchy, vitex; Oak, quercus; Oleander, nerium; Pistachio nut, pistacia; Plantain, musa; Saltwort, suæda; Saul, shorea; Spinach, amarantus; Tamarind, tamarindus; Tamarisk, tamarix; Tellicherry bark, holarrhena; Tooth-brush tree, salvadora; Zebra-wood tree, pistacia.——**(2)** The different kinds of ordinary mineral cauram are shown in the sub-paragraphs below.——*Appalacauram* (پاپڑ كهار - páparkhár, Hind.; پپڑ كهار - papparkhár, Dec.; అప్పలాకారము - appalákáramu, Tel.; പപ്പടക്കാരം - pappatakkáram, Mal.; அப்பளாக்காரம் - appalákkáram, Tam.). Title from (appalam, tam. thin cake). Hind. from (pápar, hind. thin cake). A sub-carbonate of soda [sowdoo] from a particular kind of pooneer [q.v.] containing saltness or acidity mixed with much sharpness. It produces a burning sensation on the tongue and is used chiefly in the manufacture of the thin wafer-like biscuits called poppadams [q.v.].——*Caudy cauram* (काडिखार - kádikhára, Mahr.; كاڑى كهار - kárikhár, Hind.; ಕಾಡಿಕಾರ - kádikára, Can.; కాడికారము - kádikáramu, Tel.; കാടിക്കാരം - kátikkáram, Mal.; காடிக்காரம் - kádikkáram, Tam.). Hind. from (kárí, hind. stick), from appearance, stick caustic. Nitrate of silver, argenti nitras of chemists, but the bazaar article is impure; occasionally prepared by hakeems [q.v.]; in large doses an irritant poison; in medicinal doses astringent, sedative and antispasmodic; taken internally darkens the skin; the strongest and most manageable caustic known.——*Munn cauram* (மண் காரம் - mangáram, Tam.). From (man, tam. earth + above). General term for soda. A crude carbonate of soda is here obtained in two ways; as an efflorescence on the soil, from the ashes of certain saltworts or plants containing sodium. The former is Sujjee matty, or sowdoo [q.v.]; the latter is Sujjee khaur [q.v.], the barilla of commerce.——*Oovar munn cauram* (చవిటిమన్నుప్పు - tsavitimannuppu, Tel.; உவர்மண்காரம் - uvarmangáram, Tam.). Tel. from (tsavitimannu, tel. fuller's earth + uppu, tel. salt). Tam. from (uvar, tam. salt + man, tam. earth + kshára, san. alkali). An impure carbonate of soda made from dhoby's earth, otherwise Oovar munn, otherwise Soonnapoo sowdoo.——*Padicauram* (स्फटिकारि - sp'hatikári, San.; पटिकार - patikára, Mahr.; زاج - záj, Ar.; زاك - zák, Pers.; پهٹكرى - phitkarí, Hind.; پهٹكرى - phatakrí, Dec.; توس - tawas, Malay; ಪಟಿಕಾರ - patikára, Can.; ಪಟಿಕಾರ - patikára, Too.; పటికారము - patikáramu, Tel.; ചീനിക്കാരം - chínikkáram, Mal.; ചീനാക്കാരം - chínakkáram, Singh.; படிக்காரம் - padikkáram, Tam.). San. from (sp'hatika, san. crystal + ari, san. foe); crystal-rival in lustre. Mal. from (chini, mal. chinese + káram, mal. alkali). Tam. from sanscrit. Mahr. also (turatí), from the acid astringent taste. Ar. also (shib); (zájiabyaz), meaning white vitriol. Pers. also (zákisufíd), meaning white vitriol; (zákibillaur), meaning crystal vitriol. Tam. also (shínakkáram), meaning china + alkali. Alum. Alumen of chemists. Double salt composed of sulphate of potash and sulphate of alumina; found native in small quantities, but has long been produced artificially from different ores; brittle, inodorous, crystallises in transparent octahedrons; has an acid, sweetish, astringent taste; the common impure alum contains potash [jharkanamak]. Veidyans employ it as astringent, styptic and antiseptic [ospitry, veidyan]; pharm. preparation is alumen exsiccatum. In veterinary practice; equal parts of alum and calomel are used in cancer of the feet; three drachms each of alum and catechu [q.v.] are used for soft doing, when not arising from diseased liver; four drachms of alum in a bottle of water are used for sore mouth. Used for clarifying muddy water; it dissolves in five parts of water at 60°, and the solution reddens blues; the dyers [shauyam] use it for fixing and giving brilliancy to colors in chintz and other paintings, particularly purple and deep red; chucklers employ it in preparing soft white leather. Goldsmiths use it to brighten gold ornaments.——*Poongauram* (सर्ज्जिकाक्षार - sarjjikákshára, San.; सज्जाखार - sajjákhára, Mahr.; ملح القلى - milhulkilí, Ar.; شخار - shikhár, Pers.; سجى - sajjí, Hind.; سجى كهار - sajjíkhár, Dec.; ಸೂಜಾಕಾರ - sújákára, Can.; చవిటికారము - tsavitikáramu, Tel.; ചാരം - cháram, Mal.; பூநீறுக்காரம் - púnírukkáram, Tam.). San. from (sarja, san. impure carbonate of soda + kshára, san. alkali). Ar. from (milh, ar. salt + kilí, ar. alkali). Hind. from sanscrit. Can. from sanscrit. Tel. from (tsaudu, tel. fuller's earth + kshára, san. alkali). Mal. from (kshára, san. alkali). Tam. from (pú, tam. flower + níru, tam. ashes + kshára, san. alkali). San. also (sarjiká). Hind. also (chínákálon), meaning white salt; (sajjílon), meaning sujjee salt. Dec. also (chaurkánamak), meaning fuller's salt. Tel. also (tsavitimannuppu), meaning fuller's earth + salt. Tam. also (valaiyaluppu), meaning glass bracelet + salt. Nitre of the Bible. A carbonate of soda mixed with various impurities, popularly called soda [munn cauram]; obtained from pooneer [q.v.] or from dhoby's earth [q.v.]; compare sujjeekhaur from vegetables. Poongauram is found in the bazaar, in regular whitish cakes about third part of an inch thick; has smell like new-burnt quicklime. When purified employed by veidyans as antacid and alterative; substituted for british carbonate and bicarbonate of soda; in water poured over lemon juice, sweetened with sugar, forms a pleasant effervescing draught. It is used in preparing the lac [q.v.] dye in the process of glass-making [ounnaudy] and soap-making [sauboon]; it is also used in dyeing cloth and leather, and by painters; it is one of the ingredients employed in preparing red cotton [potee] and likewise in the process of dyeing [shauyam] leather red.——*Vengauram* (टङ्कण - tankana, San. and Mahr.; بورق - búrak, Ar.; تنكار - tangár, Pers.; تنكال - tinkál, Hind.; سهاگا - sohágá, Dec.; پيجار - pijár, Malay; ಬಿಳಿಗಾರ - biligára, Can.; వెలిగారము - veligáramu, Tel.; പൊങ്കാരം - ponkáram, Mal.; വെംഗാരം - vengáram, Singh.; வெங்காரம் - vengáram, Tam.). San. from (tank, san. to bind); from astringency. Ar. from (baraka, ar. to glisten). Pers. from sanscrit. Hind. from sanscrit. Can. from (bili, can. white + kára, can. alkali). Tel. from (vella, tel. white + kshára, san. alkali). Mal. from (pon, mal. gold + káram, mal. alkali); used to melt gold. Tam. from (ven, tam. white + kshára, san. alkali). San. also (tagara). Ar. also (milhussághah), meaning goldsmith's salt. Malay also (patteri). Mal. also (vellakkáram), meaning white alkali. Singh. also (puskara); (lansipuskara), meaning dutch borax. Borax. Sodæ subboras, Sodæ biboras of chemists. Imported from north-west. Sold in transparent, colorless, crystalline masses or pieces of various sizes, inodorous, with a cool saltish styptic taste; after exposure to air becomes covered with a whitish efflorescence. Medicinally astringent lotion in hot eruptions on body; also gargle; criminally used to procure abortion; pharm. preparations are mel boracis, glycerinum boracis; with veidyans, refrigerant, diuretic, emmenagogue, parturifacient and lithontriptic; locally applied, stimulant; never used alone. Used as flux for metals [loham] by goldsmiths and tinmen; with it veishnavites prepare the red tirchoornam [q.v.] for their forehead marks.

CAURAY (नागबला - nágabalá, *San.*; कायिलि - káyili, *Conc.*; ಕಾಕೆಗಿಡ - kákegida, *Can.*; ಕಕ್ಕೆಂಡಲ್ - kakkendel, *Too.*; బలుసు - balusu, *Tel.*; കണ്ടകാരം - kantankára, *Mal.*; කර - kara, *Singh.*; காரை - kárai, *Tam.*). Title from tamul. San. from (nága, san. elephant + bala, san. strength). Can. from (káke, can. hot + gida, can. plant). Tel. from (bala, san. strength). Mal. from (kantaka, san. thorn + kára, mal. thorny plant). Tam. from (kár, tam. blackness). San. also (gángéruki), meaning water + casting. Can. also (kirani); (káre); (kákigida), meaning hot plant. Mal. also (cherukára), meaning small thorny plant. Tam. also (shengárai), meaning red canthium; (mathukkárai), honey + the plant [common emetic nut]. Title otherwise Honey cauray, Thorny webera. Botanically Canthium parviflorum, lam., rubiaceæ [vricsham, 71]. Alias Gardenia micrantha; Plectronia parviflora; Webera tetrandra. Canthium from Malabar name. Small shrub, usually with opposite horizontal thorns a little above the axils, sometimes unarmed; leaves opposite, ovate, often fascicled on the young shoots; racemes short, axillary, few-flowered on each side; drupe obovate, slightly emarginate, compressed, furrowed on each side; corolla with short tube, segments woolly inside or sometimes glabrous; nut two-celled; seeds solitary; flowers small, yellow. Scraggy, thorny shrub, found in waste lands, with small fruit about the size of a pea. Bark and young shoots used in dysentery. Fruit eaten; leaves in curries, leaves used as famine food. A hedge plant. Wood very hard. Other common species are:—angustifolium, didymum [black cauray], and neilgherrense.——*Black cauray* (उरसुल - ursul, Mahr.; ಎದ್ದರಾಣಿಕೆಮರ - eddaránikemara, Can.; నల్లబలుసు - nallabalusu, Tel.; ତୋଲନ - tolan, Oor.; පොරවමාර - poravamárá, Singh.; நக்கேணி - nakkéni, Tam.). Title from wood. Tel. from (nalla, tel. black + balusu, tel. canthium parviflorum, lam.). Singh. from (porava, singh. hatchet + mára, singh. tree). Tam. from teloogoo. Can. also (abalu). Tel. also (nakkena); (níralli), meaning water + nymphæa lotus, linn.; (nallarégu), meaning black + zizyphus jujuba, lam. Singh. also (galkaranda), meaning stone + pongamia glabra, vent. Title otherwise Black jujube, Hatchet tree, Stone pongamia. Botanically Canthium didymum, roxb., rubiaceæ [vricsham, 71]. Alias Canthium cymosum; Cupia cymosa; Gardenia parviflora; Plectronia didyma; Psydrax dicoccos; Rondeletia cymosa; Webera cymosa. Unarmed shrub; leaves oval, more or less acuminated, glabrous, coriaceous; upper side shining, under with glandular hollows in the axils of the nerves; cymes axillary, peduncled, much shorter than the leaves; calyx-limb with five often inconspicuous teeth; corolla-tube hairy inside; stigma much exserted, mitre-shaped, slightly two-lobed at the apex, drupe when ripe compressed and somewhat didymous, obovate, wrinkled and tubercled, marked with a furrow on each side; flowers white, very fragrant; interior mountains of the coromandel coast; hard wood.——*Elephant cauray* (ஆனைக்காரை - ánaikkárai, Tam.); from size. Same as Wodier.——*Manilla cauray* (മണിലക്കാര - manilakkára, Mal.). Same as Edible paulay.——*Sweet cauray* (மதுக்காரை - mathukkárai, Tam.). From taste of seeds. Common emetic nut.

CAURAY (ಗಾರೆ - gáre, *Can.*; ಗಚ್ಚಿ - gaççi, *Too.*; గార - gára, *Tel.*; കുമ്മായം - kummáyam, *Mal.*; காரை - kárai, *Tam.*). Mal. from (kummu, tam. to beat in a mortar). Tam. from (karai, tam. to dissolve). Mortar or plaster covering walls. Mutty-cauray is a coarse, and Sannacauray is a fine, kind.

CAURTEY (కార్తె - kárte, *Tel.*). From (krittiká, san. the constellation, so called); not connected with caur [q.v.], darkness. Primarily the period of the sun's stay in the nacshatram Kritticay, which was once the first of the twenty-seven nacshatrams [q.v.], some 2,500 years ago. Thence extended to other nacshatrams which follow. Now the period in which the sun lies in any nacshatram. Each Caurtey is divided into four quarters [jyotisham].—"*a*" The caurteys enable ryots roughly to forecast season and pursue cultivation on some system. Caurteys fifth to seventeenth include whole period when rains are due. Kritticay, third, early may, hottest part of year, is of evil influence being ruled by fire; no native builds a house in this caurtey; with first rain if any in this, ploughing is begun; these are the showers in advance of s.w. monsoon, arising from cyclonic disturbance by change of monsoons. Rohiny, fourth, end of may, is cooler and there are sometimes showers here also; if enough rain has fallen here or in june dry crops are put down after a heavy shower; commonest are raggy, cumboo, varagoo, gingelly, cotton. Mrigashiram fifth caurtey begins early in june;—మృగశిర చిందిస్తే ముసలిఎద్దు రంకె వేయును—"if there "be drizzle in mrigashiram, it will make even an old bull "bellow;" that is, for joy; if no rain falls a drought is expected for following five caurteys, till middle of august; with first showers in this caurtey, the more general sowing of paddy, cumboo, raggy, &c., is begun. Ardray, sixth, end of june; if there should be thunder in this without rain, it presages drought for next sixty days; but if it rains then it is held to continue for next six caurteys, till end of september;—అరుద్ర ఉరిమిస్తే అరువై రోజులవరకు, అరుద్రలో వరుషం వస్తే, ఆరుకార్తెలు కురుసును—"if there "be thunder in ardray, the rain will fail for sixty days; but if it "rain then, it will continue for the next six caurteys;" this caurtey is inauspicious for either sowing or transplanting. Poonarvas, seventh, early july, a second sowing of paddy is tried in this if first had failed; also various pulses and grams. Pooshyam, eighth, latter half of july; in this cumboo and other dry crops are transplanted. Aushlaisham, ninth, early august; in this slight showers are usual;—ఆశ్లేషవాన అరికాలు తేమ—"rain "in aushlaisham just suffices to wet the sole of the foot;" transplanting of paddy is begun. Magham, tenth, latter half of august; in this transplantation is continued; if there should be lightning and thunder in this caurtey it is taken as a certain sign of an on-coming good season;—మఘపురిమితే మదురుమీద కఱ్ఱ అయినా పండును—"if magham thunders even the dry stalk on the "wall-coping will yield fruit;" on the other hand if there should be no thundery rain during tenth and eleventh caurteys, natives hold it as an indication of coming famine. Poobbam, eleventh, early september; in this the ryots do not sow but transplantation is continued;—పుబ్బలో చల్లుటకంటె దిబ్బలో చేసేది మేలు—"it is "better to throw the seed into the rubbish heap than to sow it "in poobbam;" if it should rain well now, it is expected to continue;—పుబ్బ రేగినా బూతు రేగినా నిలవదు—"if it rains hard in "poobbam, or if a foul tongue wags, either will be unceasing." Oottaram, twelfth, middle of september; in this if there should be rain and thunder it is certain to continue; in fact the end of this s.w. and beginning of n.e. monsoons will unite;—ఉత్తర ఉరిమి కురిసినా పాము తెరిమి కరచినా తిరగదు—"if there be rain with thunder "in oottaram it will not cease, if a snake pursues and bites it "will not be without effect." If there has been no rain before and there should be no rain either in magham or in poobbam or oottaram that is till end of september it is an unmistakeable indication of coming drought and famine;—మఘపుబ్బలు వరుసైతే మహాక్షామము; ఉత్తర చూచి ఎత్తర గంప—"failure of rain in magham "and poobbam, forebodes a famine; but wait till oottaram, and "if it does not rain even then, it is best to emigrate with your "basket." In oottaram caurtey the peira or second dry crop cultivation is begun; and latest sown paddy is transplanted;—ఉత్తరలో చల్లితే ఊబుడనిచే దావికి లేదు—"crop sown in oottaram gives a "meagre yield." Hastam, thirteenth, early october; in this the n.e. monsoon sets in;—హస్తమే అతివాన కాలము అది తెలిసి గొర్లు బోయలారా, బండమీద దొడ్డు వేయండి—"that hastam is the season of heavy rain "is foreseen by the sheep which ask the herdsmen to fold them "on the rocks;" similarly in chitta and swauty, fourteenth and fifteenth;—చిత్త చిత్తగించి స్వాతి దయచేసి విశాఖ విసిరికొట్టకుంటె వీసానికి పుట్టెడు పండును—"if chitta be kind and swauty show favor "and vishaukham does not blow a hurricane, one veesam of land "will yield a pootty of grain;" swauty or october rains are the heaviest of all;—స్వాతివానకు సముద్రాలు నిండును—"rain in swauty "fills the sea;" in chitta and swauty no new crops are sown as they are liable to be destroyed by insects. Vishaukham, sixteenth, or early november; in this rain is considered healthy;—విశాఖ కురిస్తే విషములన్నీ పోవును—"rain in vishaukham takes away "poison;" the first sown paddy crops are then reaped as also the grams; garden crops are also raised and second crop raggy is sown. Anooraudhay, seventeenth, latter half of november; with this the rain is supposed to terminate; rain during this caurtey sets the ryot's mind at ease, as having sufficient for the season;—అనూరాధ కురిస్తే మనోరోగాలు పోవును—"rain in anooraudham drives away mental anxiety." Though rain is not generally expected after caurtigay, december, it is possible it may fall during jyeshtam and moolam, the next two caurteys or till end of december; but such rains are not desired as injurious and likely to cause blight in flowering pulses;—మూలలు మూసిన కురుసును, జేష్ఠవాన కురుసును, మూలవాన ముంచకత్తెరదు—"rain in "jyeshtay and moolam are injurious; rain in moolam will not "fail to ruin the farmer." After this the rains cease and night dews are heavy and bring the grain to maturity; in tye, or january-february is celebrated tye pongal feast with first fruits of harvest season. For tamul seasons see Mansam and Caur. For general proverbs on weather see Caulam.—"*b*" The following table shows the twenty-seven Caurteys of the year, their duration, and the corresponding solar months and seasons:—

Number.	Caurteys or nacshatrams of the Lunar Zodiac dwelt in by the Sun.	Date of Sun's entrance into each caurtey.	No. of days in each.	Corresponding Solar Months [mausam].	Corresponding Signs of Solar Zodiac [raushy].	Date of Sun's entrance into each sign.	Sanscrit Seasons [ritoo].	Tamul Seasons [ritoo].	Teloogoo Seasons [ritoo].	Malayalam Seasons [ritoo].
	1	2	3	4	5	6	7	8	9	10
1	Ashwiny	11th April	14							
2	Bharany	25th April	14	Chittray ...	Maisham, Aries ...	12th April ...				
3	Kritticay	9th May	14							
4	Rohiny	23rd May	14	Veiyaushy ...	Vrishabham, Taurus.	13th May	Vasantam, spring.	Yila venil, mild heat.		
5	Mrigashiram	6th June	14							
6	Ardray	20th June	14	Auny ...	Mitoonam, Gemini ...	13th June ...			Yendacaur, hot season.	
7	Poonarvas	4th July	14				Greeshmam, scorching season.	Moothir venil, extreme heat.		
8	Pooshyam	18th July	14	Audy ...	Carcatacam, Cancer.	15th July ...				
9	Aushlaisham	1st August ...	14							
10	Magham	15th August ...	14							Varsham, rainy season.
11	Poobham	29th August ...	14	Auvany ...	Simham, Leo	15th August ...	Varsham, rainy season.	Caur, gloomy.		
12	Qottaram	11th September ...	13							
13	Hastam	25th September ...	14	Pooratanshy.	Canyay, Virgo ...	15th September...				
14	Chitta	9th October ...	13						Vaunacaur, rainy season.	
15	Swanty	22nd October ...	15	Arpisy ...	Toolaum, Libra ...	16th October ...				
16	Vishaukham	4th November ...	14				Sharat, light rains.	Coothir, cold.		
17	Anooraudhay	18th November ...	13	Caurtigay ...	Vrishchicam, Scorpio.	15th November...				
18	Jyeshtay	1st December ...	13							
19	Moolam	14th December ...	13							
20	Poorvashaudham ...	26th December ...	13	Maurgaly ...	Dhanoos, Saggittarius.	14th December ...				
21	Oottarashaudham ...	9th January ...	13				Hemantam, dews and fogs.	Moon pany, evening dew.		
22	Shravanam	22nd January ...	13	Tye ...	Macaram, Capricorn.	12th January ...				
23	Dhanishtay	4th February ...	13						Muntsoocaur, dewy season.	Venil, hot season.
24	Shatabhishay	17th February ...	13	Maushy ...	Coombham, Aquarius.	12th February ...				
25	Poorva Bhaudram ...	2nd March ...	14				Shishiram, cold.	Pin pany, morning dew.		
26	Oottara Bhaudram ...	16th March	13	Pungoony ...	Meenam, Pisces ...	12th March ...				
27	Raivaty	29th March	13							

CAURTIGAY (కార్తికము - kártikamu, *Tel.*; கார்த்திகை - kárttigai, *Tam.*). From (krittiká, san. the third lunar asterism). Otherwise Tircartigay, Caurtigay vilakk, Caurtigay deepam. Luni-solar festival [pundigay, 5c]. The day in the eighth solar month Caurtigay [mausam] when the moon enters the third Nacshatram, i.e., between November 15th and December 13th. A holy day sacred to the Pleiades and their foster son Scandan [soobramanyan]. Very similar to Deepauvaly and specially observed by Tamuls. A relic of sun-worship [bharany deepam, pongal]. On the evening of this day lamp lights are placed along the pial, at the door and other parts of the house, in the cowstall, at the well, &c. Also kept in honor of Shiva, who destroyed on that day Tripoorausooran [tripooran]. The Sheivites consider the whole month more sacred than others and many abstain from animal food during the month, who at other times use it, and keep it as a season of fast. The mondays in this month are regarded as fast days, called Caurtigay somavauram. Caurtigay is kept with particular state at Trinomallee, whither pilgrims flock. During three days a great lamp is lighted on the mountain top. The lamp, which is in a large stone cauldron, is fed with butter or ghee [q.v.] and camphor [q.v.] which the people send from all parts; the match is composed of pieces of linen of several cubits length. The Bramins collect the remains of this lamp, which they present to the worshippers, who every day mark their forehead with it. It is in imitation of this sacred lamp that the worshippers of Shiva make in their houses a large cake of rice flour, kneaded with water. They make a hole in the middle which they fill with butter or ghee, and light a small match; they then worship the fire, and fast the whole day, and after six o'clock at night they eat the cake [maryauday].——*Caurtigay plant* (கார்த்திகை - kárttigai, Tam.). From the month caurtigay or november, the time of flowering. Wild bachnaug.——*Caurtigay pourrnimay* (கார்த்திகைப்பௌர்ணிமை - kárttigaippaurnimai, Tam.). Full moon of caurtigay or november when vanabhojanam [q.v.] is celebrated.——*Caurtikeyan* (कार्त्तिकेय - kárttikéya, San.). From (krittiká, san. the pleiades). N. indian name of Soobramanyan.

CAURVAM (कारव - kárava, *San.*). From (ká, san. bad + rava, san. sound). Corvidæ family, conirostres, insessores, aves [pacshy, 25], of naturalists [jantoo]. Divided into the following sub-families:—corvinæ, garrulinæ, dendrocittinæ, fregilinæ, and streperinæ. Corvinæ are the crows and magpies. The species best known to the natives are shown below.——*Beggar's crow* (عقعق - akak, Ar.; کلاغ ابلق - kulághiablak, Pers.; ٹکا چور - takkáchor, Hind.; لٹورا - latorá, Dec.; గోకరాయి - gókaráyi, Tel.). Title from belief that its call forebodes approach of guests to the house. Ar. from its call. Pers. from (kulágh, pers. crow + ablak, ar. piebald). Hind. from (takká, hind. money + chor, hind. thief). Tel. from (góku, tel. to scratch + ráyi, tel. stone), from sound. Ar. also (shajají). Hind. alsc (handícbacha), meaning pan scraper, imitative of its cry; (mahalat), meaning large shrike; (kotri). Tel. also (kondakátigádu), meaning hill + forester. Dendrocitta rufa, dendrocittinæ, corvidæ. Alias Pica rufiventris, vagabunda. Whole head, neck and breast sooty brown, or blackish, deepest on forehead, chin and throat, passing into dusky cinereous; scapulars, back, and upper tail-coverts dark ferruginous; wing coverts and outer web of secondaries light grey, almost whitish in some; rest of quills black; tail ashy-grey, feathers all broadly tipped with black, least so on centre feathers; beneath from breast ferruginous or fulvous; bill black; irides blood-red; legs dark slaty; length 16 inches; common in well-wooded districts; occasional about towns; flies from tree to tree with a slow undulating flight; natives consider it of shrike genus [pingalam]; usual harsh cry of the magpie; also clear whistling, somewhat metallic call; also a feeble indistinct note at the pairing season, which the male utters, and the female responds to in a sort of chuckle. The long-tailed magpie is dendrocitta leucogastra, malabar coast; has a loud call.——*Carrion crow* (غراب - ghuráb, Ar.; کلاغ سیاه - kulághisiyáh, Pers.; ڈھال کوا - dhálkavvá, Hind.; دھیڑی کوا - dherikavvá, Dec.; ಸುಬ್ಬುಕಾಗೆ - subbukáge, Can.; మాలకాకి - málakáki, Tel.; അന്തങ്കാക്ക - antankákka, Mal.; அண்டங்காக்கை - andangákkai, Tam.). Title from food. Ar. from (gharaba, ar. remote), from far-sightedness. Pers. from (kulágh, pers. crow + siyáh, pers. black). Hind. from (dhál, hind. shield + kavvá, hind. crow). Dec. from (dherí, hind. pariah + kavvá, hind. crow); from black color. Can. from (subbu, can. name of a serpent + káge, can. crow). Tel. from (mála, tel. the caste + káki, tel. crow). Tam. from (andu, tam. to approach + káka, san. crow); familiar crow. Ar. also (ghurábulbain), meaning raven of separation; (abka); (hátim), meaning unlucky. Hind. also (dhár). Tel. also (bontakáki), meaning large + crow. Beng. also (dadkag). Title otherwise Indian corby, Indian raven, Karrial. Corvus culminatus, corvinæ, corvidæ. Alias Corvus corax, enca, macrorhynchos, orientalis. Above glossy black, dull black beneath; tail slightly rounded; wings reach nearly to end of the tail; bill straight at base and high, culmen raised, curving strongly towards tip; bill and legs black irides dark brown; length 21 inches; wing $13\frac{1}{2}$; tail $7\frac{3}{4}$; almost as familiar as the common crow; voice hoarser and shorter than european crow.——*Common crow* (काक - káka, San.; زاغ - zágh, Ar.; کلاغ - kulágh, Pers.; کوا - kavvá, Hind. and Dec.; ಕಾಗೆ - káge, Can.; కాకి - káki, Tel.; കാക്ക - kákka, Mal.; காக்கை - kákkai, Tam.). San. from (kai, san. to caw). Hind., &c., from (káka, san. crow). San. also (váyasa), meaning the long-lived. Hind. also (desíkavvá), meaning country crow; (patikavvá), (kág). Tel. also (manchikáki), meaning good crow; euphemistic. Tam. also (nallakkákkai), meaning good crow. Corvus splendens, corvinæ, corvidæ. Alias Corvus dauricus, monedula, impudicus. Forehead, sinciput, and lores, glossy black; occiput, nape, hind neck, and sides of neck, purplish ashy; back, wings and tail black with rich purple and steel-blue reflections; chin, throat and sides of neck, in part black with steel reflections; breast ashy tinged dark; middle of abdomen dull black slightly tinged steel-blue; length varies from 15 to above 18 inches; bill and legs black; irides deep brown; found in vast numbers in every town and village; crow's nest almost exclusively selected by cuckoo to deposit her eggs in. The common crow is the vehicle of Shany [q.v.]. The sight of a single crow is inauspicious, two not so. The cawing of a crow is to be estimated by the following formula:—measure the length of the shadow by the foot and add 12 to the number of feet ascertained; then divide by 7 and the remainder will determine the import of the note; one good luck, 2 gain, 3 rain, 4 conflict, 5 feasting, 6 victory; if on dividing by 7 there is no remainder the note means death. Natives attribute to crows five peculiarities:—going forth very early of a morning; never being seen to pair; eating together; bathing before going to their nest; warningtheir companions of apparent danger. There is a Tamul proverb:—காகம் இல்லாத ஊர் பாவி இல்லாத ஊர்—"A village without a crow "is a village without a sinner;" the two are rare. The Tamul Cooral has the following:—காக்கை கரவா கரைந்துண்ணு மாக்கமு மன்னநீ ரார்க்கே யுள—"The crows do not "conceal their prey, but will call out for others while they eat "it; wealth will be with those who show a similar disposition."

CAUSH (काश् - kásh, *San.*). To shine.——*Casie chetty* (காசிச்செட்டி - kásiççetti, Tam.). From (káshí, san. benares, proper name + shetti, tam. member of the caste). A modern Singhalese author of a book called Tamul Plutarch.——*Caushta calay* (काष्ठाकला - kásht'hákalá, San.). From (kásht'ha, san. stick; a measure of length or time + kalá, san. part). Measure of time. Time taken up by one respiration. 10 caushta calays = 1 prauna calay; 6 prauna calays = 1 vicalay or palam [caulam, 6]. Approximate actual value, 1 caushta calay = ·4 second. $\frac{1}{36000}$th of dandam [caulam, 6]. Same as San. vipalam [caulam, 6] or param [caulam, 4, 5].——*Caushtay* (काष्ठा - kásht'há, San.). Measure of time. 15 nimishams or winkings = 1 caushtay; 30 caushtays = 1 calay [caulam, 2]. Approximate actual value, 1 caushtay = 3·2 English seconds. Also $\frac{1}{30}$th of a calay [q.v.] of 48 seconds or 1·6 seconds.——*Caushy* (काशी - káshí, San.).—"*a*" Benares, the sacred city. The first of six sacred places. The other five are Ayodhyay, ancient oudh; Mathooray or muttra; Mauyay or gaya; Canjy or conjeeveram; and Avanticay or oojjein. The Sheiva system had its earliest stronghold in Caushy. Pilgrimages from the south are still made thither on special occasions. Tencaushy, or South benares, is Madura. The Caushy of Sanscrit theoretical geography lies in 27° 35′ of latitude N. and 4° 37′ E. from Lunka. Hindoo 2nd or pers. name; common to both sexes. Similarly Caushinautan meaning Shiva, lord of Benares; and Caushy vishwa lingam, meaning the universe lingam of Benares [peyár]. Caushiyautray, from (yátrá, san. journey) is a pilgrimage to Benares [charitram].—"*b*" Plant first term. Compare:—Impatiens balsamia (kásittumbai), benares leucas indica; Ipomœa coccinea (káshiratnamu), benares gem; Lagenaria vulgaris (káship'hal), benares fruit; Solánum pubescens (kásiuste), benares solanum verbascifolium. See gloss. paragraphs.——*Caushy ratnam* (కాశీరత్నము - káshiratnamu, Tel.). Tel. from (káshí, san. benares + ratna, san. precious stone). Title otherwise Crimson quamoclit, Scarlet creeper, Scarlet-flowered bind-weed, Star glory. Botanically Ipomæa [calamby] coccinea, linn., convolvulaceæ [vricsham, 93]. Alias Convolvulus phœniceus; Ipomæa phœnicea; Quamoclit phœniceum. Creeper; leaves cordately subreniform, angularly toothed at the margin and sometimes three-lobed, lobes acute, dentato-sinuate at the margin, glabrous on both sides; peduncles many-flowered, loosely spiked; sepals equal, awned; flowers large, bright scarlet; common, flowering in cold season.

CAUSHT (كاشت - kásht, *Hind.*). From (káshtan, pers. to sow). Cultivation.

CAUT (காடு - kádu, *Tam.*). Oblique form of caud, forest. Prefix in place names, as in Cautpaudy, meaning forest + village.

CAUTCHY (காட்சி - kádchi, *Tam.*). From (kán, tam. to see). Appearance, so perception. Of perception seven species are recognised in the augamam logic of the south, viz.:—"*a*" Ayya cautchy, doubt perception or indistinct apprehension.—"*b*" Tirip cautchy, change perception or mistaking one thing for another.—"*c*" Vicalpa cautchy, difference perception or discrimination, to distinguish things one from another especially in the five particulars of name, kind, quality, action and substance.—"*d*" Porivauyil cautchy, sense perception or perception through the senses with the aid of the mental faculties.—"*e*" Mana cautchy, mind perception or ideas formed in the mind of things perceived by the senses.—"*f*" Anoobhava cautchy, experience perception or perception by actual experience or exercise of the affections towards objects perceived.—"*g*" Yoga cautchy, meditation perception or spiritual perception by abstract devotion of knowledge of events past, present or future. Each of the above division has two sub divisions; one pooram, relating to external or secular affairs and the other again, relating to religious or spiritual affairs [matam].

CAUTHAM (കാതം - kátam, *Mal.*; காதம் - kátham, *Tam.*). From (kádam, ar. a step). League. Linear measure. 7½ nauzhivazhies = 1 cautham [alavay, 1 a, d]. Actual value varies from 5 to 10 miles. In Malabar between 5 and 6 miles. Compare San. yojanam, Pers. farsang, Hind. gow, Can. gauvada, Tel. aumada. See vol. I, 609; II, 505.

CAUVALAM (കാവളം - kávalam, *Mal.*). From (káya, mal. fruit + valam, mal. manure). Title otherwise Stink tree. Botanically the Sterculia genus, sterculiaceæ [vricsham, 26]. Trees or shrubs, native of tropical regions; leaves simple, palmately lobed or digitate; flowers in drooping panicles; fruits consist of five or fewer more or less woody pieces called follicles, each containing several albuminous seeds. The species best known to the natives are:—balanghas [q.v.], colorata [wild papaw], fœtida [bastard poon], guttata [piymaram], urens [false kateerah], villosa [odul tree]. Other s. indian species indigenous or naturalized are:—alata, populifolia.

CAUVALY (కావలి - kávali, * *Tel.*). Means guard.——(1) Talook, Nellore district. Tahsildar's pay Rs. 175. Area 548 square miles; lat. 14° 40′ to 15° 04′ N.; long. 79° 38′ to 80° 09′ E. Centre coast part of district. Bounded:—north by Cundoocore talook; west by Oodayagherry talook; south by Atmacore and Nellore talooks; east by the sea. The talook is generally flat but there are a few isolated hills. The north-west is drained by the Appoolair and its tributaries. A smaller stream of the same name falls into the sea near Zoovvaldinney. Along the coast the climate is healthy and good water abundant. The west is dry and rocky. To the west and north-west are extensive low jungles, in parts very dense. Soil is poor. Large beds of laterite [q.v.] are frequently met with. Indigo [q.v.] and rice [q.v.] are the principal agricultural products. On the uplands there is a large area cultivated with dry crops. Along the coast are many palmyra [q.v.] and casuarina [chowkmaram] plantations both private and circar. Tanks are numerous except in the west and north-west, but their supply is uncertain being derived from local drainage. There are no ports proper in the talook; but Chennayapollem, Toommalapenta, and Zoovvaldinney are used by native craft. Since the construction of the Buckingham canal [q.v.], the sea-borne trade has fallen off. Weaving is carried on to a considerable extent, and there is an extensive trade in cattle with Cuddapah and Bellary. Camping grounds:—Bitragoonta, Bramhanacrauka, Cadanootla, Caligherry, Cauvaly, Jakkepully goodoor, Maddoorpaud, Moosnore, Roodracote, Taullapollem, Toommalapenta, Zoovvaldinney. Places of archæological interest:—Anneymadoogoo, Bitragoonta, Bramhanacrauka, Cauvaly, Chentsoo gaunipollem, Chinnacrauka, Chintalapollem, Gattoopulley, Jaldanky, Moosnore, Timmasamoodram, Toommalapenta. Principal trig. stations:—Akkapollem, Allimadoogoo, Annagauripollem, Bitragoonta, Bramhanacrauka, Cauvaly, Colladinney, Cottapully, Gavaravaram, Jadagegoola, Jaldanky, Keshavaram, Moongamore, Ootoorpullepollem beacon, Shiddancondore, Siripooram, Somavarapaud, Vaudapollem, Zoovvaldinney. The leading places, &c., in the talook are the following.——*Akkapollem* (అక్కపాలెము - akkapálemu, Tel.). From (akka, tel. elder sister + pálemu, tel. fortified village). Trig. station in lat. 14° 52′ 30·36″; long. 80° 01′ 4·97″; from Boodamgoonta E.S.E. 2½ miles; from Cauvaly S.S.W. 3½ miles; from the sea W. 7 miles.——*Allimadoogoo* (అల్లిమడుగు - allimadugu, Tel.). From (alli, tel. water-lily, nymphæa lotus, linn. + madugu, tel. pool). Trig. station in lat. 14° 47′ 9·30″; long. 80° 4′ 17·65″; from Cauvaly S.S.E. 11 miles; from Moongamore S.S.E. 3 miles; from the sea W. 3¾ miles.——*Annagauripollem* (అన్నగారిపాలెము - annagáripálemu, Tel.). From (anna, tel. elder brother + gáru, tel. term of respect + pálemu, tel. fortified village). Trig. station in lat. 14° 49′ 15·28″; long. 80° 6′ 25·53″; from Cauvaly S.E. 7 miles; from Zoovvaldinney N. 2½ miles; from the sea W. 1¼ miles.——*Bitragoonta* (బిట్రగుంట - bitragunta, Tel.). See sep. title.——*Bramhanacrauka* (బ్రాహ్మణక్రాక - bráhmanakráka, Tel.). See sep. title.——*Caligherry* (కలిగిరి - kaligiri, Tel.). See sep. title.——*Cauvaly* (కావలి - kávali, Tel.). See below.——*Chennayapollem* (చెన్నయపాలెము - chennayapálemu, Tel.). From (chennaya, tel. proper name + pálemu, tel. fortified village). Village, Port for native craft; pop. 1,032; acres 3,192; lat. 14° 59′; long. 80° 06′; from Cauvaly N.N.E. 6 miles; from Madras N. 129 miles; from Toommalapenta N. 6 miles; from Nellore N.N.E. 37 miles; from Ramapatam S. 4 miles. Export used to be sea-fish. The Buckingham canál runs through. Covered densely with palmyra trees.——*Chinna annalore yepinaupy* (చినఅన్నలూరుయేపినాపి - chinaannalúruyépinápi, Tel.). Two villages clubbed. Village; pop. 4,675; acres 23,122; lat. 14° 55′; long. 79° 44′; from Cauvaly W. 21 miles; from Nellore N.N.W. 36½ miles; from the sea W. 26 miles. Coarse cloths manufactured.——*Chippilair* (చిప్పిలేరు - chippiléru, Tel.). From (chippa, tel. shell + éru, tel. river). Village; pop. 2,114. Close to Zoovvaldinney.——*Colladinney* (కోళ్లదిన్నె - kólladinne, Tel.). From (kódi, tel. fowl + dinne, tel. mound). Trig. station in lat. 14° 48′ 58·28″; long. 80° 5′ 17·71″; from Cauvaly S.S.E. 7¾ miles; from Moongamore E.N.E. 2¼ miles; from the sea W. 2½ miles.——*Cottapully* (కొత్తపల్లి - kottapalli, Tel.). From (kotta, tel. new + palli, tel. village). Trig. station in lat. 14° 55′ 43·67″; long. 79° 58′ 1·39″; from Boodamgoonta N.N.W. 3¾ miles; from Cauvaly W.N.W. 5 miles; from the sea W. 10 miles.——*Gavaravaram* (గవరవరము - gavaravaramu, Tel.). From (gavara, tel. a class of merchants + pura, san. town). Trig. station; lat. 14° 49′ 48·01″; long. 80° 1′ 12·45″; from Bitragoonta N.E. 1¾ miles; from Cauvaly S. 6 miles; from the sea W. 7½ miles.——*Jadagegoola* (జడగోగుల - jadagógula, Tel.). From (jadagógu, tel. matted hair hemp plant, hibiscus cannabinus, linn.). Trig. station; lat. 14° 48′ 2·13″; long. 80° 5′ 15·27″; from Cauvaly S.S.E. 8½ miles; from Moongamore E.S.E. 1½ miles; from the sea W. 3¼ miles.——*Jaldanky* (జల్దంకి - dzaldanki, Tel.). See sep. title.——*Keshavaram* (కేశవరము - késhavaramu, Tel.). From (késhava, san. vishnu, the god with the hair + pura, san. town). Sanscrit name (késhavapura), meaning vishnoo's city. Village; pop. 1,404; acres 7,548; lat. 14° 55′; long. 79° 52′; from Cauvaly W. 12 miles; from Nellore N.N.W. 34 miles; from the sea W. 17 miles. Water scarce. Trig. station in lat. 14° 54′ 41·65″; long. 79° 51′ 40·34″; height 208 feet; from Cauvaly W. 12 miles; from Timma samoodram E.N.E. 2¼ miles; from the sea W. 17 miles.——*Maddoorpaud* (మద్దూరుపాడు - maddúrupádu, Tel.). From (maddi, tel. terminalia arjuna, bedd. + úru, tel. village + pádu, tel. village). Trig. station; lat. 14° 57′ 38·08″; long. 80° 1′ 42·27″; from Cundoocore S.S.E. 19 miles; from Roodracote S.S.W. 1½ miles; from the sea W. 5¼ miles.——*Moongamore* (ముంగమూరు - mungamúru, Tel.). See sep. title.——*Munnair* (మన్నేరు - mannéru, Tel.). See sep. title.——*Ootoorpullepollem beacon* (ఊటూరుపల్లెపాలెందీపస్తంభము - útúrupallepálemdípastambhamu, Tel.). From (úta, tel. spring + úru, tel. village + palle, tel. village + pálemu, tel. fortified village). Trig. station; lat. 14° 50′ 34·92″; long. 80° 7′ 44·61″; from Cauvaly S.E. 7½ miles; from Chennayapollem S. 10 miles; from the sea W. ¼ mile.——*Shiddancondore* (శిద్దనకొండూరు - shiddanakondúru, Tel.). From (shiddana, tel. proper name + konda, tel. hill + úru, tel. village). Village; pop. 964; acres 2,970; lat. 14° 48′; long. 79° 50′; from Cauvaly W.S.W. 15¼ miles; from Nellore N.N.W. 27 miles; from the sea W. 21 miles. A ruined temple of Siddheshwara sawmy on the hill close by. Trade in bulls and sheep. Coarse cloths woven and taken to Madras. Trig. station in lat. 14° 47′ 39·93″; long. 79° 48′ 56·76″; height 331 feet; from Cauvaly W.S.W. 17 miles; from Vaimlapaud W.S.W. 4 miles; from the sea W. 21 miles.——*Siripooram* (సిరిపురము - siripuramu, Tel.). From (siri, tel. wealth + pura, san. town). Trig. station; lat. 14° 56′ 47·07″; long. 79° 59′ 31·24″; from Cauvaly N.W. 4 miles; from the sea W. 7½ miles.——*Somavarapaud* (సోమవరప్పాడు - sómavarappádu, Tel.). From (sómavaramu, tel. place so called + pádu, tel. village). Trig. station; lat. 14° 47′ 9·41″; long. 79° 53′ 55·12″; from Cauvaly S.W. 13 miles; from Krishtapaud S.W. 1 mile; from the sea W. 16 miles.——*Toommalapenta* (తుమ్మలపెంట - tummalapenta, Tel.). See sep. title.——*Vaudapollem* (వాడపాలెము - vádapálemu, Tel.). From (váda, tel. village + pálemu, tel. fortified village). Trig. station; lat. 14° 48′ 53·24″; long. 80° 7′ 29·86″; from Cauvaly S.S.E. 10 miles; from Zoovvaldinney E.N.E. 1 mile; from the sea W. ¼ mile.——*Zoovvaldinney* (జువ్వలదిన్నె - dzuvvaladinne, Tel.). See sep. title.——**(2)** Town, Head-quarters of District moonsif and Sub-registrar; Nellore dist., Cauvaly tal.; pop. 5,611; acres 11,087; lat. 14° 55′; long. 80° 03′; from Madras N.N.W. 127 miles; from Naidoopett N.N.E. 70 miles; from Nellore N. 33 miles; from Ongole S. 42 miles; from the sea W. 5¾ miles. On Great northern road. Travellers' bungalow, large tank, choultry and hospital. Remains of an ancient temple to Veerabhadran [q.v.], son of Shiva, and ruins of a Covilammashacty pagoda. Trig. station in lat. 14° 55′ 13·20″; long. 80° 0′ 32·92″; from Cauvaly W.N.W. 2 miles; from Maddoorppaud S.W. 3½ miles; from the sea W. 6¼ miles.

CAUVY (गैरिक - gairika, *San.*; गेरु - géru, *Mahr.*; طين مغر - tínimaghar, *Ar.*; گل سرخ - gilisurkh, *Pers.*; گیرو - gerú, *Hind.*; ಕಾವಿಕಲ್ಲು - kávikallu, *Can.*; ಕಾವೆಕಲ್ಲು - kávekallu, *Too.*; కావి - kávi, *Tel.*; കാവി - kávi, *Mal.*; සිවංගුරු - sivanguru, *Singh.*; காவி - kávi, *Tam.*). San. from (giri, san. mountain). Mahr. from hindostany. Ar. from (tín, ar. earth + maghar, ar. red). Pers. from (gil, pers. earth + surkh, pers. red). Hind. from sanscrit. Can. from (kávi, can. red + kallu, can. stone). Tam. from (ká, tam. to preserve). Ar. also (maghra), meaning red substance; (tínulahmar), meaning red earth; (tínifársí), meaning persian earth. Ochre or Reddle. Cauvycull is red chalk. The following are the different kinds of Cauvy.——*Gopy cauvy* (گوپی - gopí, Hind.; గోపికావి - gópikávi, Tel.; கோபிக்காவி - kóbikkávi, Tam.). From (gópí, san. milk-maid + kávi, tam. ochre). A faint yellow ochre.——*Pooraun cauvy* (पीतगैरिक - pítagairika, San.; طين الاصفر - tínulasfar, Ar.; گل زرد - gilizard, Pers.; پیلا گیرو - pilágerú, Hind.; ಹಳದಿಕಾವಿ - haladikávi, Can.; ಮಂಜಳಕಾವೆ - manjalkáve, Too.; పసుపుకావి - pasupukávi, Tel.; பூரான்காவிக்கல் - púrángávikkal, Tam.). San. from (píta, san. yellow + gairika, san. ochre). Ar. from (tín, ar. earth + asfar, ar. yellow). Pers. from (gil, pers. earth + zard, pers yellow). Hind. from (pilá, hind. yellow + gerú, hind. ochre). Can. from (haladi, can. yellow + kávi, can. ochre). Too. from (manjal, too. yellow + káve, too. red stone). Tel. from (pasupu, tel. yellow + kávi, tel. ochre). Tam. from (púrán, tam. centipede + kávi, tam. ochre + kal, tam. stone); from color of common centipede. San. also (suvarnagairika), meaning gold ochre. Common yellow ochre. Used by moochees [q.v.] as yellow paint [rangh]. In conjunction with vinegar [caudy], used in dyeing [shauyam] a buff color.——*Sheemay cauvy* (طين ارمنی - tíniarmaní, Ar.; گل ارمنی - giliarmaní, Pers.; گل ارمنی - giliarmaní, Hind.; پھول گیرو - phúlgerú, Dec.; సీమకావి - símakávi, Tel.; കാവിക്കല്ലു - kávikkallu, Mal.; சீமைக்காவிக்கல் - shímaikkávikkal, Tam.). Ar. from (tín, ar. earth + armaní, ar. armenian). Pers. from (gil, pers. earth + armaní, pers. armenian). Hind. from persian. Dec. from (phúl, hind. flower + gerú, hind. ochre); from fragrance. Tel. from (síma, tel. foreign + kávi, tel. ochre). Mal. from (kávi, mal. ochre + kallu, mal. stone). Tam. from (shímai, tam. foreign + kávi, tam. ochre + kal, tam. stone). Ar. also (hajariarmaní), meaning armenian stone. Hind. also (kábulímattí), meaning cabul earth. Tam. also (kargávi), meaning stone + ochre. Armenian bole [ghil arminy].——*Shivappoo cauvy* (रक्तोपल - raktópala, San.; रक्तधातु - raktadhátu, Mahr.; طين الاحمر - tínulahmar, Ar.; گل سرخ - gilisurkh, Pers.; لال گیرو - lálgerú, Hind.; ಚಂದ್ರಗಾವಿ - chandragávi, Can.; ಚಂದ್ರಕಾವಿ - chandrakávi, Too.; ఎర్రకావి - errakávi, Tel.; சிவப்புக்காவிக்கல் - shivappukkávikkal, Tam.). San. from (rakta, san. red + upala, san. stone). Mahr. from (rakta, san. red + dhátu, san. mineral). Ar. from (tín, ar. earth + ahmar, ar. red). Pers. from (gil, pers. earth + surkh, pers. red). Hind. from (lál, hind. red + gerú, hind. ochre). Can. from (chandra, can. moon + kávi, can. ochre); from color of rising moon. Tel. from (erra, tel. red + kávi, tel. ochre). Tam. from (shivappu, tam. red + kávi, tam. ochre + kal, tam. stone). Tam. also (pungávi), meaning flower + ochre; (kargávi), meaning stone + ochre. Red ochre. Contains much oxide of iron. Used by moochees as a red paint and by dyers in dyeing a nankeen color [shauyam]. The native form of Ghil arminy.

CAUY (காயு - káyu, *Tam.*). To be hot.——*Causcutty* (காசுக்கட்டி - kásukkatti, Tam.). From (káyçu, tam. to boil + katti, tam. lump). Balls formed of a compound of superior catechu [q.v.] with different spices.——*Cautchal* (காய்ச்சல் - káyççal, Tam.). Tam. from (káyu, tam. to be hot). Fever [jwaram, veidyan].——*Cauyal* (காயல் - káyal, Tam.). Means lagoon or backwater, liable to dry up. Now called Old cauyal. Village; Tinnevelly dist., Tencaray tal.; pop. 1,004; acres 5,478; lat. 8° 40′; long. 78° 09′; from Madras S.S.W. 329 miles; from Poonnacauyal N.N.W. 3¼ miles; from Shreeveicoontam E. 14 miles; from Tinnevelly E. 29 miles; from Tuticorin S.S.W. 9¼ miles; from the sea W. 2 miles. Once a famous port near the extreme south of India, at the mouth of the Tamrapurny in the Gulf of Manaar, now long abandoned. Two or three miles higher up the river lies the site of Korkay, each port in succession having been destroyed by the retirement of the sea. Tuticorin may be considered the successor of those ancient marts. Marco Polo landed here and describes it as belonging to Ashar, the eldest of five brothers, who reigned in the Malabar and Tinnevelly regions. Abd oor ruzzauk names it as a place situated opposite the island of Sérendib, otherwise called Ceylon. Nicholas Conti calls it Cahila, the site of a pearl-fishery. Vasco da Gama, writing the word Caell, notices that with a Caufir or Christian people it had a Mahomedan king. It is still inhabited partly by Mahomedans and partly by Roman catholics. For two or three miles north of the present village of Cauyal, and a mile and a half inland as far as Mauramungalam, the whole plain is covered with broken tiles, remnant of Arabian and other pottery and China porcelain [kaolin]. There are several Jeina statues. Two old Shiva and Vishnoo temples. Modern trade chiefly in pearls [moty] and precious stones [ratnam]; paddy [q.v.], rice [q.v.] and cocoanuts [q.v.] from Ceylon; timber and betel-nuts [q.v.] from Travancore; and palmyra jaggery [q.v.], &c.——*Cauyalputnam* (காயற்பட்டணம் - káyarbattanam, Tam. káyalpatnam *). From (káyal, tam. lagoon + pattana, san. town). Village, Port; Tinnevelly dist., Tencaray tal.; pop. 11,465; acres 8,162; lat. 8° 34′; long. 78° 10′; from Madras S.S.W. 340 miles; from Old cauyal S.S.E. 8 miles; from Poonnacauyal S. 5 miles; from Shreeveicoontam E.S.E. 15 miles; from Tinnevelly E.S.E. 33 miles; from Veerapaundyanputnam N. 3 miles; from the sea W. ½ mile. North of the Tamrapurny and on the western shore of the Gulf of Manaar.——*Cauyam* (காயம் - káyam, Tam.). Pungency. Plant second term. Ex., where transl. is of first term:—Allium cepa (vengáyam), white; Cuminum cyminum (attuvákkáyam), red; Ferula narthex (perungáyam), large. See gloss. paragraphs.——*Cauyancollam* (കായങ്കുളം - káyankulam, Mal.). From (káyal, tam. lagoon + kóvilakam, mal. palace). Title otherwise Cully quilon, meaning stony + the town so called [collam].—"*a*" Town, Port, Travancore state, Quilon division, Caurtigapully tal.; lat. 9° 10′; long. 76° 33′; from Alleppey S.S.E. 23 miles; from Bombay S.S.E. 710 miles; from Poracaud S.S.E. 14 miles; from Trivandrum N.N.W. 57 miles; from Aripaud S. 7½ miles. Formerly a Dutch commercial town, and now a place of considerable inland and foreign trade. About 3 miles to the interior of the backwater of the same name between Alleppey and Quilon. Abreast the town is an opening into the Arabian sea, which only admits small coasters; but there is water communication by the backwater with Cochin on the north and Quilon on the south. Also connected with Madura by a road leading through the ghauts at the Atchancoil pass. Another road connects it with the one from Quilon to Shencottah, and by means of these two roads the town carries on an extensive trade with several important places in Madura and Tinnevelly districts. Formerly capital of the independent state of Quilon. In 829 A.D. the Syrian church was founded here. Captured by the Dutch in 1661. In 1745, the rajah submitted to Travancore; and fifteen years later, the state was finally absorbed by its more powerful neighbour. Some irregular fortifications are seen to the north.—"*b*" Backwater; Travancore state, Quilon division, Caurtigapully talook. One of the links of the chain of water communication between Trivandrum and Cochin. Extreme length 19 miles, extreme breadth 2 miles, average breadth one mile and a quarter. Area of the lake is 23 miles. Separated from the sea by a narrow strip of coast line. Along the banks extensive coir [q.v.] manufacture is carried on by hand labor.——*Palaya cauyal* (பழயகாயல் - pazhaiyagáyal, Tam.). From (pazhaiya, tam. old + káyal, tam. town, so called). Same as Cauyal.——*Poonnacauyal* (புன்னக்காயல் - punnak-káyal, Tam.). From (punai, tam. newness + káyal, tam. the town). New cauyal as distinguished from cauyal or old cauyal. Village, hamlet of Shendamungalam village; Tinnevelly dist., Tencaray tal.; lat. 8° 38′; long. 78° 10′; from Cauyal S.E. 2¾ miles; from Cauyalputnam N. 5 miles; from Madras S.S.W. 330 miles; from Shreeveicoontam E.S.E. 15 miles; from Tinnevelly E.S.E. 31 miles. With roadstead, on the north-west coast of the Gulf of Manaar, South of Tuticorin. The approach from the south is dangerous, in consequence of an extensive reef stretching in that direction; but a ship having safely made its way past that danger may anchor securely in 7 or 8 fathoms, with bottom soft mud, and 2 miles from the beach. In 1551, two hospitals and a seminary founded by Portuguese. In 1552, fort taken by the Vijianugger troops, Countinho, the Portuguese captain of the fishery, being defeated. In 1553, the fort retaken by a fleet from Calicut. In 1556, there was a garrison of fifty men only. Shortly after 1563, when Cæsar Frederic visited the coast, the fishers for pearls [moty] still continued to pay for permission to the representative of the King of Portugal; the Madura Naicks had therefore not yet succeeded in gaining supreme power. In 1570, great famine on the fishery coast. Father Henriquez established famine relief houses, in some of which fifty persons were fed daily. Don Sebastian limits to the Christian fishermen the tithes on pearls. Dutch factory demolished in 1782. See vol. II, 156.

CAUYAM (काय - káya, *San.*). From (chi, san. to construct). The body.——*Cauyasiddhy* (कायसिद्धि - káyasiddhi, San.). From (above + siddhi, san. perfection). Corporeal perfection attained by religious austerities. Especially attainment of the eight superhuman powers known as ashta siddhies.——*Cauyast* (कायस्थ - káyast'ha, San.; کایتھ - káyath, Hind.). From (above + st'há, san. to stand). Otherwise Cauyet. Supreme spirit. Accountant caste in Bengal and N.W. india. A few members here. See vol. II, 229.

CAUYAM (قایم - káyim, *Hind.*). From (kauma, ar. to stand). Permanent.——*Cauyam goottadar* (قایم گتہ دار - káyimguttahdár, Hind.; ಕಾಯಂಗುತ್ತೇದಾರ - káyamguttédára, Can.). From (above + guttedár, hind. renter). Holder of land on a fixed assessment. ——*Cauyamgueny* (ಕಾಯಂಗೇಣಿ - káyamgéni, Can.). From (above + géni, can. lease). A permanent rent, or lease; same as Moolgueny.——*Cauyam jummabundy* (قایم جمعبندی - káyim-jamabandí, Hind.). From (above + jamabandi, pers. settlement). A permanent settlement. See vol. I, 112.

CAUZIM (کاظم - kázim, *Ar.*). From (kazama, ar. to restrain anger). One who restrains his anger. Name of seventh Imaum. Mahomedan alam; as Cauzim ally, double alam [ism]. Cauzimy was the one-anna piece of Tippoo sultan [naunyam].

CAUZY (قاضی - kázi, *Hind.*; కాజి - káji, *Tel.*). From (kazá, ar. a mandate). With the article before the Arabic form, thus Alcaudy, it became the Spanish alcalde. Under the Mahomedan empire, a civil and criminal judge. Under British rule he became an adviser to the courts on points of Mahomedan law. Duties now confined to the preparation and attestation of deeds of conveyance and other legal instruments, and the general superintendence and legalization of the ceremonies of marriage [shaudy], funerals [janauza], and other domestic occurrences among the Mahomedans. Alam, as Cauzy khan, alam + alaumat [ism].——*Cauzy ool kozzat* (قاضی القضاة - káziulkuzzát, Hind.). From (above + kuzzát, ar. judges). The chief cauzy.

CAVALLIUM (కవిలె - kavile, *Tel.*). Generic term. Same as False kateerah.

CAVAR (கவர் - kavar, *Tam.*). To seize, to rob.——*Cavara* (കവര - kavara, Mal.). Caste-title. Basket-makers of Malabar. They speak a corrupt Tooloo [jauty].——*Cavarathy* (കവരത്തി - kavaratti, Mal.). From (kavaru, mal. plunder + tívu, mal. island). Island; Malabar dist., pop. 2,021; from Calicut S.W. 220 miles. One of the Laccadives. In lat. 10° 32′ N. and long. 72° 40′ E. About 74 miles N.W. from Calpeny and 38 S.E. from Agatty. Coral [moongah] shoal least extensive of any. Length from north-east to south-west about 3½ miles; greatest breadth about three-quarters of a mile. Island is situated just within the reef on the east; on the west there is a lagoon [cauyal] which at its widest part is about half a mile broad. At southern end there was formerly a separate island, but it is now connected with the main island by a narrow strip of land about 50 yards wide. The islets attached are Pitty and Sooheliparra. The former, a mere sand bank on a coral limestone foundation, lies about 15 miles north-west of Cavarathy and is frequently visited for fishing purposes. The coral shoal of Sooheliparra lies about 40 miles south-west of Cavarathy. It is composed of Valiyakara or large shore at the northern extremity of lagoon, and of Cheriyakara or little shore at the southern extremity. These two islets, formerly common property of Cavarathy islanders, were confiscated by the Pundauram [q.v.] or circar. Valiyakara is completely overrun with jungle, throughout which scattered cocoanut [q.v.] trees occur; Cheriyakara lies east and west and has extreme length of three-quarters of a mile. Breadth at widest point does not exceed quarter of a mile. Area is 81¼ acres. It contains no jungle. Covered with coarse long grass and a kind of small shrub. The inhabited portion of Cavarathy is divided into four cherries, viz., Melacherry or Mecherry on the north-west coast; Tekkeycherry on the east coast; Poragacherry to the south; Pullicherry on the south-west shore; Poragacherry is separated from Mecherry and Pullicherry by a small valley apparently excavated formerly for grain cultivation. The body of the island is the common property of the people. Over a part however the Pundauram asserts exclusive claims. The soil of Cavarathy is poor. Beans, plantains [q.v.] and brinjauls [q.v.], areca [q.v.] palms, tamarind [q.v.] trees, and betel [q.v.] vines are grown to a small extent. People depend almost entirely upon their cocoanut cultivation. Manufactures consists mainly of coir [q.v.] yarn. Inhabitants are exclusively Mahomedans.

CAVVYE (കവ്വായി - kavváyi, *Mal.* kavváyi *). From (kai, mal. canal + váya, mal. mouth). Village, Port, River: Malabar dist., Chiracal tal.; lat. 12° 6′; long. 75° 14′; from Bombay S.S.E. 485 miles; from Calicut N.N.W. 69 miles; from Cannanore N.W. 20 miles; from Mangalore S.S.E. 56 miles; from Yetticoolam N. 5¾ miles; from the sea E. 2¼ miles. Northern frontier town of Malabar. At mouth of a backwater of same name near Mount delly. The ancient town and port of Neeleshwar were about 12 miles up this backwater. The surrounding country is a sandy plain. Inhabitants are Moplahs. The English established a factory in 1750, and about that time French built a fort on south side of river. This fort and another of native construction are now in ruins. Dolmen [coday cull] and four menhirs.

CAVY (कवि - kavi, *San.*). From (ku, san. sound). Poet in Telinga country. There were three Audycavies or original cavies, founders of Teloogoo literature; Nannayya bhatt, Tiecana somayaujy, and Yerrah pragada. The Audy cavies were followed by others nearly equal to them called Madhya cavies, or middle cavies; for instance:—Adidam sooranna, Amareshwaran, Anantamautyan, Bammera potaranz, Bhattoomoorty, Bhauscaran, Caucamauny moorty, Ketana, Mookkoo timmana, Mullanna, Peddauna, Pingaly sooranna, Pooshpagiry timmana, Ramau, Ramabhadran, Runganautan, Shreenautan, Tautam bhatt, Telaganauryan, Tenauly ramalingam, Veerabhadran, Vennelacunty soorayya and Zakkanna. Antya cavies, or last cavies, are quite modern. Caviraja sawmy is a literary title [peyar]. Cavy royan is a general term for a great poet [inam].

CAWDER (قادر - kádir, *Hind.*). From (kadara, ar. to be strong). Powerful. An attribute of God [allah]. A common Mahomedan alam; as Cawder ally, double alam; Cawder beg, alam + alaumat [ism].——*Cawder wally* (قادر ولی - kádirwalí, Hind.). From (above + walí, ar. saint). Mahomedan saint, with shrine at Nagore near Negapatam; the Mahomedan inhabitants of which are chiefly Lubbays [q.v.] of Shafayee sect. His sandal [q.v.] is ninth of sixth month Jamaudy ool aukhir [maheena], and his oors [q.v.] on tenth. Mussalman ship-captains and sailors frequently make vows to Cawder wally [meeraun sahib].

CAWNY (ಕಾಣಿ - káni, *Can.*; కాణి - káni, *Tel.*; காணி - káni, *Tam.*). From (kán, tam. to see); that which is known and recognised. Landed property, land.—"*a*" A land measure. 100 coozhies = 1 cawny [alavay, 2 a]. Approximate actual value, 1 cawny = 57,600 square feet or 1·322 acres; for purposes of cultivation a cawny is divided into 100 coozhies, and for house building purposes into 24 munnies [q.v.] or grounds of 60 by 40 feet each; in parts of madura and trichinopoly cawny is equal to 100 coozhies of 21 square feet or 44,100 square feet or 1·01 acres; sometimes cawny is equal to 57,600 square native adees, in which case it is less than an acre. See vol. I, 609; II, 506, 507, 509.—"*b*" In numbers, an 80th fractional part, or in Telinga usage one 64th.—"*c*" Cawnyautchy, from (ádchi, tam. possession), is a term given by Vellaular to communal rights of villagers, lands, offices, fees, held in free and hereditary property; when the lands fell into the hands of bramins, it was called swaustyam [q.v.]; when the same property was possessed by mahomedans or christians, it was called mirass [q.v.], which is the term now usually employed; pasancarny [q.v.] in tamul and Sarwadauyam mean the same thing; see vol. I, 112.—"*d*" Cawny cauran is a hereditary proprietor of land. Hill tribe living towards the south of travancore; same as those in the north called malaiyarasar [q.v.]; sometimes spoken of as vailanmaur or spearmen; live together in small clans, each hamlet under a headman; in south speak tamul and further north malayalam; somewhat superior in several respects and not regarded with abhorrence felt towards the poolayar [jauty]. See vol. I (111).

CAZHOO (கழு - kazhu, *Tam.*). Vulture [gidh].——*Cazhoo-goomullay* (கழுகுமலை - kazhugumalai, Tam.). From (kazhugu, tam. vulture + malai, tam. mountain). Sanscrit name (gridhráchala), meaning vulture + mountain. Town, Hill, Place of pilgrimage; Tinnevelly dist., Shuncaraneinarcoil tal.; pop. 4,228; acres 23,445; lat. 9° 08′; long. 77° 45′; from Ottapidauram N.W. 27 miles; from Tinnevelly N. 28 miles; from the sea W. 49 miles. Large isolated rock in Yettiyaupoorau zemindarry, with rock-cut temple and Jeina sculptures and inscriptions. The temple, to Soobramanyan, is a fine monolithic work, much in the style of Seven pagodas [q.v.], with porticos round. On the rock-face are inscriptions in archaic characters, with numbers of Jeina figures of saints. One side of the hill was occupied by Jeinas; the other by the Sheivas, who carved the small temple out of the solid rock, almost a counterpart of a portion of the Keilausam at Ellora. The Jeina inscriptions are written in Vattezhoot [q.v.]. Each is in a different form, but all in the same alphabet; the sculptors apparently having diversified the work by varying the exact shape of the letters on each inscription. In the same rock is a cave-temple dedicated to Ganesh, known as the Pillaiyaur coil, with a space round the shrine for the pradacshinam or circumambulation ceremony. Annual festival in January, February and March, at which time a large cattle-fair also takes place.

CAZHOOTHAY (கழுதை - kazhuthai, *Tam.*). Ass, sign of Vayoo regent of north-west [ashtadicpaulacan].

CEDED DISTRICTS (صوبجات مرفضہ - súbajátimuaffizah, *Hind.*). Territory south of Toongabudra ceded to company by Nizam in 1800 after defeat and death of Tippoo sultan. Embraced present districts of Anantapore, Bellary, Cuddapah, and Kurnool, with the Pulnaud. See vol. I (25) and the description of the separate districts in vol. II. For the history of the cession, see vol. I (186).

CEYLON (सिंहल - simhala, *San.*; سرانديب - sarandíb, *Hind.*; ಸಿಂಹಳ - simhala, *Can.*; సింహళము - simhalamu, *Tel.*; ഈഴം - ízham, *Mal.*; இலங்கை - ilangai, *Tam.*). Ancient Tam. (ஈழம் - ízham). Title (sílan) is Malay or very ancient Dravidian, meaning cocoanut. Ancient Tamul means same as title. Compare the Ilavar of Malabar. Simhala is the name by which it was called by the later Booddhistic writers, being a Sanscrit corruption of the original, and meaning lion's abode. Hence the modern term Singhalese. Singhala dweepam or Singhala island appears in the Greek of Cosmas as σιελεδίβα. The Greeks thought this the largest island in the world. From Singhala dweepam comes the Arabic Serendib. A descriptive name for Ceylon in some pooraunams is Ratna dweepam, or island of gems. The Sanscrit Lunka again meaning beautiful was the old mythological name of Ceylon in the old literature of Booddhism and Braminism. This name was unknown to the Greeks and Romans. Lunka was in early Sanscrit legend the capital town of the kings of the race of Poclastyau known as Yacshans, and remarkable as the capital of Ravanan the abductor of Seeta, with whom Rama fought. The Ramayanam [q.v.] was written long before Ceylon was known to the Bramins; but, on their migrating south, their poets discovered in the then visible rocky chain across the gulf of Manaar the bridge built by Rama, with Hanooman, Soogreevan and their monkies represented by the Dravidian inhabitants. Thenceforward Lunka was held to be the island of Ceylon. The city of Ravanan itself was supposed to the south of Trincomalee and to have been swallowed up by the sea. In this sense Ceylon has always been considered the land of wonders. The following is a Hindostany proverb :—لنکا میں سے جونکلے سو باون گزکا— "All who come from Lunka are 52 yards high." The Greek ταπροβάνη represents the Sanscrit (támraparni), meaning copper-leaved. பொருணை is the Tinnevelly river, meaning toddy river, but with copper-colored sand; and hence the Sanscrit by corruption. For history and account of the island, see vol. I, page 32.——**(1)** The following are places in the island which have been mentioned in connection with the history of this Presidency, with the Tamul identifications attached.——*Adam's bridge* (சேது - shéthu, Tam.). Tam. from (si, san. to bind). Lat. 9° 10′; long. 79° 40′. The Tamul Veishnavite name is Tirvanay or holy bund. A reef of sunken rocks connecting the north of Ceylon with the mainland of this Presidency 30 feet wide with 3 or 4 feet of water above it at high tide.——*Adam's peak* (சிவனடிப்பாதம் - shivanadippátham, Tam.). See Dharmarajacull.——*Allaipitty* (அல்லைப்பிட்டி - allaippitti, Tam.). From (allai, tam. the creeper + pitti, tam. basket). Lat. 9° 40′; long. 79° 55′. Small island off Jaffna in the north.——*Amsterdam island* (காரைத்தீவு - káraittívu, Tam.). Tam. from (kárai, tam. a shrub, canthium parviflorum, lam. + tívu, tam. island). Lat. 9° 51′; long. 80° 1′. Island on the north coast of Ceylon.——*Anooraudhapoora* (அநுராதப்புரம் - anuráthappuram, Tam.). From (anurádha, san. prosperous; name of a prince + pura, san. city). Lat. 8° 25′; long. 80° 20′. Principal town in North central province of Ceylon; situated 68 miles north-east of Putlam and 92 miles north of Candy. On the Aripo river; the ancient capital till the eighth century. Among the ruins are many colossal dagobas, stoopams, temples and tanks, and the sacred Bo tree or peepul tree said to have been brought from Gya in Behar about 240 B.C., an object of pilgrimage for the Booddhists. The great tanks in the neighbourhood have recently been restored.——*Aripo* (அரிப்பு - arippu, Tam.). Means sifting. Lat. 8° 50′; long. 79° 55′. Town in Northern province; situated on the western coast in Condatchy bay, 141 miles north of Colombo. Centre of pearl fishery. Also river in north-west, falling into the sea by several mouths, in lat. 8° 50′; long. 79° 55′.——*Basses* (இராமப்பாதம் - irámappátham, Tam.). See sep. title.——*Batticaloa* (மட்டக்களப்பு - mattakkalappu, Tam.). From (mattam, tam. smallness + kalappu, tam. a shallow at sea). Lat. 7° 44′ 30″; long. 81° 40′ 30″. Port in district of same name. Eastern province, 68 miles S. of Trincomalee. It is situated on a small island. Also river in Eastern ceylon, falling into the sea in lat. 7° 44′ 30″; long. 81° 40′ 30″.——*Belligaum* (வலிக்காமம் - valikkámam, Tam.). From singhalese meaning sand village. Lat. 5° 59′ 30″; long. 30° 40′. Village in Southern ceylon; situated on a small bay, nearly midway between Galle and Madura. Fishing port.——*Bentotte* (வேந்தோட்டை - véndóttai, Tam.). From singhalese meaning demon's port. Lat. 6° 20′; long. 79° 59′. Village in Galle district, Southern province; situated about midway between Galle and Colombo, at the mouth of a river of the same name.——*Calanigunga* (கழனிக்கங்கை - kazhanikkangai, Tam.). From singhalese meaning beautiful river. River in Western ceylon, rising near Adam's peak, and falling into the sea 3 miles north of Colombo in lat. 7° 59′; long. 79° 50′.——*Calpentyn* (கற்பிட்டி - karbitti, Tam.). From (kal, tam. stone + pitti, tam. a basket). Lat. 8° 12′; long. 79° 41′. Town in North-western ceylon; situated on the west side of the Gulf of Calpentyn, 92 miles north of Colombo.——*Caltura* (கழுத்துறை - kazhutturai, Tam.). From singhalese meaning dark water ferry. Lat. 6° 42′; long. 79° 54′. Town in the district of same name, Western province; situated 26 miles south of Colombo, at the mouth of the Caloogunga. Climate salubrious.——*Candy* (கண்டி - kandi, Tam.). Lat. 7° 24′; long. 80° 43′; height 1,680. Capital of Candy district, Candy division, Central province. It is 74½ miles distant by rail from Colombo and 113 miles from Trincomalee. The town lies in a valley formed by the surrounding hills.——*Chilaw* (சலாபம் - shalábam, Tam.). Tam. means diving. Lat. 7° 34′; long. 79° 47′. A place on the west coast, North-western province, an old seat of the pearl-fishery. The name was commonly applied by the Portuguese to the whole aggregation of shoals or Baixos de Chilao in the Gulf of manaar between Ceylon and the coast of Madura and Tinnevelly. Fifty-three miles north of Colombo.——*Colombo* (கொழும்பு - kozhumbu, Tam.). From singhalese meaning harbour. Lat. 6° 57′; long. 79° 50′. Capital of Colombo district, Western province. Situated 74½ miles from Candy, with which it is connected by railway. Port of call for steamers.——*Coothiramullay* (குதிரமலை - kuthiramalai, Tam.). From (kuthirai, tam. a horse + malai, tam. mountain). Lat. 8° 32′; long. 79° 50′. North-western Ceylon.——*Dharmarajacull* (தருமராசக்கல் - tarumarásakkal, Tam.). Meaning Dharmarajan's or Booddha's rock. Steep rock near Adam's peak, ascended by 127 steps cut horizontally on the face. See sep. title.——*Dondra* (தேவன்றுறை - tévanrurai, Tam.). From (tévan, tam. title of marava rulers + turai, tam. port). Lat. 5° 55′; long. 80° 35′ 30″. Village situated near Madura on a promontory of the same name; the most southerly point in the island.——*Galle* (காலி - káli, Tam.). In singhalese means rock. Lat. 5°; long. 80° 10′. Sea-port in Galle district, Southern province. Port of call for steamers.——*Gungaroyen* (கங்கைராயன் - kangairáyan, Tam.). From (gangá, san. the ganges + rájá, san. king). River in Northern ceylon, falling into the sea in lat. 9° 26′; long. 80° 20′.——*Haarlem* (நயினாத்தீவு - nayináttívu, Tam.). Tam. from (nayinár, tam. a lord + tívu, tam. corruption of dvípa, san. island). Lat. 9° 41′; long. 79° 54′. Island on the south-west of Jaffna.——*Irrantivo* (இரணத்தீவு - iranattívu, Tam.) From (iranam, tam. brackish ground + tívu, tam. corruption of dvípa, san. island). Island in the Gulf of manaar.——*Jaffna* (யாழ்ப்பாணம் - yázhppánam, Tam.). From (yázh, the lute + pánan, a lute player); called after a blind minstrel of that name from the Chola country, who by permission of the Singhalese king obtained possession of Jaffna, then uninhabited and introduced there a colony of the Tamul people. Ancient Tamul name is (erumaimullaittívu), from the shrub so called + island. Lat. 9° 47′; long. 80° 9′. γαλίβα of Ptolemy. Otherwise Jaffnapatam. A very ancient Tamul settlement. Capital in district of same name of Northern province. Situated about 220 miles north of Colombo and about 250 miles south of Madras. Old Dutch station.——*Lunka* (இலங்கை - ilangai, Tam.). Means beautiful. River in Eastern ceylon, falling into the sea in lat. 7° 14′; long. 81° 46′.——*Madura* (மாத்துறை - mátturai, Tam.). From singhalese meaning great port. A different word from the Madura of the mainland. Lat. 6° 56′ 30″; long. 80° 33′. Village in district of same name, Southern province; situated 26 miles south-east of Galle at the mouth of the Neelgunga. Also island on south coast.——*Maha voya* (மகாவோயை - magávóyai, Tam.). From singhalese meaning large stream. River in Eastern ceylon, flowing into the sea in lat. 7° 30′; long. 79° 31′.——*Mahawaligunga* (மகாவலிகங்கை - magávalikkangai, Tam.). From singhalese meaning great sand river. Largest river in Ceylon, flows N.E. for 200 miles, falling into the sea on the east coast into the Bay of Trincomalee in lat. 8° 17′; long. 81° 25′.——*Manaar* (மன்னார் - mannár, Tam.). See sep.

title.——*Mantotte* (மாதோட்டம் - máthóttam, Tam.). From (má, tam. the mango tree + tóttam, tam. garden). Lat 8° 54′; long. 79° 54′. Village in Mantotte district, North-western Ceylon, on the road from Colombo to Jaffna, 13 miles from Aripo. Also sub-division of Manaar district, North-western Ceylon.——*Nallore* (நல்லூர் - nallúr, Tam.). From (nal, tam. good + úr, tam. village). Lat. 9° 49′; long. 80° 8′. Village in Jaffna district, Northern province, situated 2 miles north of Jaffna.——*Newara ellia* (நுவரெலி - nuvareli, Tam.). From singhalese, meaning city plain. Lat. 7°; long. 8° 45′; height 6,200. Village and Sanitarium. In Walapane district, Central province, Ceylon; situated 47 miles south-east of Candy.——*Palk bay* (பாக்குக்குடாக்கடல் - pákkukkudákkadal, Tam.). Between lat. 9°; long 79° and lat. 10° 20′; long. 80° 5′. Bay between the north part of Ceylon and this continent.——*Palmyra point* (பள்ளிமுனை - pallimunai, Tam.). Tam. from (palli, tam. the caste of cultivators + munai, tam. point). Lat. 9° 51′; long. 80° 12′. Extreme north-east point.——*Peradeniya* (பேராதனை - pérâthanai, Tam.). From singhalese meaning guava swamp. Lat. 7° 8′; long. 80° 42′. Station on Candy and Colombo railway; situated 71 miles from Colombo. Botanic garden.——*Pigeon island* (குருவிமுனை - kuruvimunai, Tam.). Tam. from (kuruvi, tam. a small bird + munai, tam. point). Lat. 8° 43′; long. 81° 12′. Also called Elizabeth island. Island in Trincomalee bay.——*Point pedro* (பருத்தித்துறை - paruttitturai, Tam.). Tam. from (parutti, tam. cotton + turai, tam. port). Lat. 9° 50′; long. 80° 35′. Town in Northern province; situated on the east coast, 21 miles from Jaffna.——*Pollannarrua* (பொள்ளனருவை - pollanaruvai, Tam.). Lat. 8°; long. 81°. Ancient city now in ruins. For 450 years the capital of the Singhalese kings.——*Rotterdam* (அனலைத்தீவு - analattívu, Tam.). Tam. from (anala, san. fire + tívu, tam. corruption of dvípa, san. island). Lat. 9° 38′; long. 79° 45′. Island in North ceylon.——*Tamana newara* (தம்மனநுவரை - tammananuvarai, Tam.). From (tammana, tam. proper name + nuvarai, tam. corruption of nagara, san. city). Lat. 8° 4′; long. 80°. The most ancient town in the island, situated about 6 miles east of Putlam, North-western Ceylon.——*Trincomalee* (திருக்கோணமலை - tirukkónámalai, Tam.). From (tiri, tam. three + kónam, tam. corner + malai, tam. mountain). Lat. 8° 31′; long. 81° 23′. Principal station, in district of same name, in Eastern province; situated 113 miles north-east of Candy and 137 miles south-east of Jaffna. It has a strong fort and one of the finest harbours in the world. British naval station, but the trade is inconsiderable. To the south-west of Trincomalee are the remains of the great artificial tank of Candelay and others, from which this part of the island was formerly irrigated.——**(2)** Plant first term, as in :—Cinnamomum zeylanicum, ceylon cinnamon; Diospyros ebenum, ceylon ebony; Elæodendron glaucum, ceylon tea; Garcinia morella, ceylon gamboge; Gracilaria confervoides, ceylon moss; Gymnema lactiferum, var. lactiferum proper, ceylon cow-plant; Litsæa zeylanica, ceylon litsæa; Memecylon edule, ceylon memecylon; Pancratium zeylanicum, ceylon pancratium; Pavonia zeylanica, ceylon pavonia; Plumbago zeylanica, ceylon leadwort; Sanseviera roxburghiana, ceylon sanseviera; Schleichera trijuga, ceylon oak; Trichodesma zeylanicum, ceylon borage. See gloss. paragraphs.——**(3)** *Ceylon oak* (कोशिंब - kóshimba, Mahr.; మయిరోంగ - mayirótanga, Tel.; ରସ - rasam, Oor.; പൂവം - púvam, Mal.; කෝන් - kón, Singh.; பூமரம் - púmaram, Tam.). Mal. from (pú, mal. flower + akam, mal. inside); from fine timber. Tam. from (pú, tam. flower + maram, tam. tree). Can. also (sagade); (akota); (sagarimara); (kunghas). Tel. also (posuku). Oor. also (kolakusumu); (ghuntiakusumu). Tam. also (kumbáthiri), meaning hill + trumpet flower tree, stereospermum chelonoides, dec.; (koñji) [conjy]; (púvatti), meaning flower + fig tree, ficus. Title otherwise Flowering fig, Gum-lac tree, Honey tree, Lac tree [taloora saul]. Botanically Schleichera trijuga, willd., sapindaceæ [vricsham, 43]. Alias Melicocca pubescens, trijuga; Schleichera pubescens; Scytalia trijuga; Stadmannia trijuga. Deciduous tree, 50 feet; leaves abruptly pinnate; leaflets opposite, about three pairs, oblong or broadly lanceolate, quite entire, nearly glabrous; calyx five-cleft; petals none; racemes axillary or below the leaves round the base of the young shoots, solitary, simple or compound; drupe globose, pointed, with a dry pericarp; seeds one to two, rarely three, covered with a pulpy aril; flowers small, greenish; confined to dry forests; flowers early in hot season. Fruit sometimes quite smooth, though often armed with prickles, caused by some insect; pulpy aril is agreeable acid. Bark is astringent; powdered and rubbed up with oil, used in itch. Fruit eaten. Oil expressed from the seed used for burning; quantity of lac [q.v.] produced on the young branches; gives a yellowish resin [raul]. Produces a red, strong, hard and heavy wood, which is used to make pestles, spokes for bandy wheels and other purposes, where much strength in small space is required, and as crushes for sugar; rice and oil mills, screw rollers for sugar mills, cotton presses and ploughs, &c. No other common species here.——*Ceylon plum* (विकङ्कत - vikankata, San.; वेहळी - véhalí, Mahr.; పెద్దకానరేగు - peddakánarégu, Tel.; ବାଉଚ - bávich, Oor.). San. from (vi, san. intensive prefix + kank, san. to go), spreading. Tel. from (pedda, tel. large + kánarégu, tel. flacourtia ramontchi, l'her). Tel. also (nakkanérédu), meaning fox + rose apple tree, eugenia jambos, linn. Title otherwise Esculent flacourtia, Fox rose-apple, Wild jujube. Botanically Flacourtia [swandoocantacam] ramontchi. l'herit, var. sapida, bixineæ [vricsham, 14]. Alias Flacourtia sapida. Small tree or shrub; thorns scattered, naked; leaves serrated, elliptical, obtuse, older ones membranaceous; male flowers, stamens closely arranged on the dilated torus; female, stigmas five to seven, radiating, linear, furrowed above; peduncles axillary, many-flowered; flowers small, greenish. Fruit size of plum and of sharp sweetish taste. Almost the same as the typical Ramontchi [mauritius plum]. After child-birth among natives, seeds are ground to powder with turmeric [country saffron] and rubbed over body to prevent rheumatic pains from exposure to damp winds; native inoculators for small-pox use the thorns for breaking the pustules on the ninth or tenth day; the fruit and leaves are eaten. Wood red, hard, close and even-grained; splits, but does not warp, and is durable.

CHABOOTRAH (چبوترہ - chabútrá, *Hind.*). From (chatvara, san. quadrangular court). Raised mound used for assemblies.

CHAD (چڑھ - char, *Hind.*). Rising.——*Chadsaul* (چڑھ سال - charsál, Hind.). From (above + sál, hind. year). Year in which a maximum amount of revenue is derived.

CHAID (జేడు - jédu, *Tel.*). From (chedu, tel. to spoil). Muddy ground; suffix in place names, especially in the northern districts, as Cauramchaid, meaning the alkaline swamp.

CHAIGO (ചേക - chéka, obl.; ചേകോൻ - chékón, pers. sing.; ചേകോർ - chékór, pers. pl., *Mal.*). From (chéka, mal. service). Another name for Ilava or toddy-drawer caste in Malabar.

CHAINOO (చేను - chénu, *Tel.*). Field; suffix in place names as Goodiselchainoo, meaning the field with the huts [chey].——*Chainy* (ചേനി - chéni, Mal.). Village. Suffix in place name, as in Pullachainy [jainy].

CHAIN VIPER (سنکلدار سانپ - sankaldársámp, *Hind.*; ರಕ್ತಮಸಲೆ - raktamasale, *Can.*; కట్లపురుగు - katlapurugu, *Tel.*; ചേനത്തണ്ടൻ - chénattantan, *Mal.*; තිත්පොලඟා - titpolangá, *Singh.*; கண்ணாடிவிரியன் - kannádiviriyan, *Tam.*). Title from the series of rings on back. Hind. from (sankal, hind. chain + dár, pers. having + sámp, hind. snake). Can. from (rakta, san. blood + masalu, can. to boil); from its poisonous bite. Tel. from (kattu, tel. stripe + purugu, tel. worm). Mal. from (chénattandu, mal. arum stem + an, mal. personal suffix); from similarity. Singh. from (tit, singh. spotted + polangá, singh. viper). Tam. from (kannádi, tam. looking glass + viriyan, tam. viper). Hind. also (chamaktásámp), meaning shining snake; (baingankekhetkásámp), meaning brinjaul field snake; (gobarkásámp), meaning dung snake; (khúnísámp), meaning bloody snake; (átishbársámp), meaning fire-emitting snake; (shaffáfsámp), meaning bright snake. Tel. also (penjera), meaning big + snake [penjera]. Mal. also (vellikkattan), meaning silver + band. Title otherwise Necklace snake, Russell's viper. Also Cobra monil and Cobra manilla from the Portuguese, meaning beaded cobra; but it is a viper, not colubriform. Also Tic polonga in Ceylon. Daboia elegans, viperidæ [viriyan], ophidii viperiformes, ophidia [sarpam], reptilia [sarpy, 30], of naturalists [jantoo]. There is only this species of the genus Daboia. Alias Coluber russellii; Daboia pulchella, russellii; Vipera daboia, elegans. One of the true vipers [viriyan]. Greyish brown or light chocolate color with three series of large black, white-edged rings, those of the middle series ovate, those of the outer circular; sometimes very small, black, white-edged ocelli are scattered between the rings. A yellow line on each side of the upper surface of the head, the two lines convergent on the snout. Rostral and labial shields yellow, with brown margins; a sub-triangular brown, black-edged spot below the eye. Belly uniform yellowish, or marbled with brownish; generally more or less numerous, semi-circular brown spots on the hinder margins of the ventral shields. It is not as venomous as the cobra [q.v.]. The blood usually remains fluid after death from the poison of the chain viper, the human subject being excepted; whereas after cobra poisoning it generally coagulates firmly on being removed from the heart and great vessels. The Chain viper is nocturnal in its habits; in confinement it is sluggish and does not readily strike, unless roused and irritated, when it bites with great force and determination. When disturbed, it hisses fiercely, and when it strikes, does so with great vigour. Its long, movable fangs are very prominent objects and with them it is capable of inflicting a very deep as well as poisoned wound. The markings on its body are very beautiful and justify the synonym, Vipera elegans; compare tamul above. It lives on small animals, such as rats [ely], mice [shoondely], and frogs [bhaicam]. It will go into water. It is, however, terrestrial in its habits. Its loud hissing when disturbed is calculated to warn those who come within its dangerous proximity. Though so deadly, it has not the reputation of causing many deaths; but this may be owing to the fact that it is less known. The adult varies in length from three to four feet or so. It prevails in the plains as well as in the hills [penjera].

CHAKKAN (ചക്കൻ - chakkan, *Mal.*). From (chekkan, mal. lad). Pariah proper name [chikka, peyar]. Dist. from chokkan.

CHAKKELA (ചക്കില - chakkila, *Mal.*). Means death + leaf; from deciduous character. Same as Stone banyan.

CHAKONDAH (चक्रमर्दक - chakramardaka, *San.*; टांकळा - tánkalá, *Mahr.*; तैकिलो - taikiló, *Conc.*; سنجسبویه - sanjisabúyah, *Ar.*; سنگسبویه - sangisaboyah, *Pers.*; چکوندا - chakondá, *Hind.*; تروٹا - tarotá, *Dec.*; ಗುಂಡುತಗಚೆ - gundutagache, *Can.*; ತಜಂಕ್ - tajank, *Too.*; తంటెపుచెట్టు - tantepuchettu, *Tel.*; തകര - takara, *Mal.*; තෝර - tóra, *Singh.*; தகரை - tagarai, *Tam.*). Title from hindostany. San. from (chakra, san. ring + mard, san. to crush); from curing ringworm. Can. from (gundu, can. round + tagache, can. the plant). Mal. from tamul. Tam. from (tagar, tam. destroy); useful remedy. San. also (prabhunát'ha), meaning lord of lords, medicinal. Ar. also (kulkul); (ainussárátín), meaning crab's eyes; referring to seeds. Pers. also (kulkul). Hind. also (chakonr); (panwár). Can. also (tagache) [dyeing mulberry]; (tagarchi); (tagarasi). Tel. also (tagarisha). Singh. also (pani-tóra), meaning sweet cassia. Title otherwise Fœtid cassia, Oval-leaved cassia, Ringworm plant, Tagaray. Botanically Cassia [soovarnacam] tora, linn., leguminosæ [vricsham, 48]. Tora from singhalese. Alias Cassia fœtida, gallinaria, inodora, obtusifolia, tagera, toroides, tula; Senna tora, toroides. Tagera from malayalam. Annual, with spreading branches; leaflets three pairs, with a gland between the one to two lower pairs, but without any between the uppermost, cuneate-obovate, obtuse, glabrous or pubescent on the under side; small yellow flowers on long pedicels, upper ones forming a short terminal raceme, lower ones one to two together on a short axillary peduncle; upper petals obcordate; legumes very long, sharp-pointed, four-sided, many-seeded, each suture two-grooved; seeds liver-colored and slightly compressed. Leaflets all fold up closely at night; the whole plant has a fetid smell; the leaves when full grown are mucilaginous, and have a nauseous taste, but when young they are mild. Formed into a paste with lime-juice, fresh leaves cure ringworm [dadroo]; administered in infusion they act as a mild cathartic; substituted for british santonin [absinth] and alexandrian senna; quoted in pharm. non-officinal; leaves fried in castor-oil are applied to foul ulcers; on west coast make a warm poultice to hasten suppuration of boils; seeds ground and mixed with butter-milk allay irritation in itch, a warm remedy in gout, sciatica, and pains in the joints. Seeds a substitute for coffee [q.v.] when roasted and ground. The leaves are used to adulterate senna [q.v.]; are known by their wedge-shaped and ciliated margins. Seeds in combination with Wrightia tinctoria, br. [paula indigo], are used in preparing a blue dye [shauyam]; generally fixed with lime water.——*Large chakondah* (பெரிய தகரை - periyatagarai, Tam.). Tam. from (periya, tam. large + tagarai, tam. cassia tora, linn.). Title otherwise West indian bead tree. Botanically leucæna glauca, benth., leguminosæ [vricsham, 48]. Introduced tree common in gardens; chucklers collect the seeds and string them as fancy ornaments in bags, baskets, necklaces, &c. No other species here.——*Lowly chakondah* (ನೆಲತಗಚೆ - nelatagache, Can.; నల్లజీలుగ - nallajíluga, Tel.). Title from being prostrate. Can. from (nela, can. earth + tagache, can. cassia tora, linn.). Tel. from (nalla, tel. black + jíluga, tel. æschynomene aspera, linn.). Title otherwise Black solah, Lowly senna. Botanically Cassia [soovarnacam] pumila, lam., leguminosæ [vricsham, 48]. Alias Senna prostrata. Suffruticose, procumbent; branches slightly hairy; leaflets twelve to thirty pair, with an erect slender stalked peltate gland close to the lowest pair, linear-oblong, unequal-sided, mucronate, more or less hairy or pubescent; rachis not margined; stamens five, nearly equal; flowers supra-axillary, one to three together, yellow; legumes flat, linear, six to seven-seeded, slightly pubescent, constructed between the seeds; stipules lanceolate-subulate; flowering in the rainy season. Cattle eat it.——*Needle chakondah* (ஊசித்தகரை - úsittagarai, Tam.). Title from shape of pod. Tam. from (úsi, tam. needle + tagarai, tam. cassia tora, linn.). Botanically Phaseolus [moodgam] semi-erectus, linn., leguminosæ [vricsham, 48]. Alias Phaseolus psoraloides. Erect shrub; young shoots and racemes pubescent, leaflets lanceolate, acute, silky-pubescent underneath; stipules sessile, erect, striated, persistent; racemes much longer than the leaves, with flowering part elongated; peduncle very long and stout; calyx five-toothed; keel circinate; legumes pendulous, nearly straight, long-linear, many-seeded, pubescent, seeds slightly truncated at both ends.

CHAKSOO (چاکسو - cháksú, *Hind.*). From (chakshu, san. eye); useful in eye-disease. Same as Black horse gram.

CHAL (चल - chala, *San.*). From (chal, san. to move). Moving.——*Chala carnam* (चलकर्ण - chalakarna, San.). From (above + karna, san. ear). The true distance of a planet [graham] from the earth, in contradistinction to its mean distance; or the radius of the Cacsham [q.v.], or deferent [carnam].——*Chalawany* (چلونی - chaláuní, Hind.; சிலாமணி - shilámani, Tam.). From (chalná, hind. to go). Current [jaury, rupee].——*Chalgueny* (ಚಾಲಗೇಣಿ - chálagéui, Can.). From (above + géni, can. rent). Tenancy-at-will, or occupation on paying rent for a short or indefinite term. See vol. I, 112.——*Chalookya* (चालुक्य - chálukya, San.). San. from (chaluka, san. water-pot). Alleged tradition of first king having been born out of spray of water-pot. As a dynasty may have been Agnicoolam rajpoots. As a race were Dravidians of the Deccan [q.v.]. See vol. I (138); II, 250 [charitram].

CHALGOZAH (چلغوزہ - chalghozah, *Hind.*). From (chil, pers. pinus genus + ghozah, pers. walnut). The seeds are the κόκκαλοι of hippocrates and πιτυΐδες of dioscorides; the tree is the πίτυς of ancient greeks and πεύκη κωνοφορὸς of theophrastus. Title otherwise Italian stone pine. Botanically Pinus [devadauram] pinea, linn., coniferæ [vricsham]. The nuts [cottay] are of an oily, mild and agreeable taste.

CHALLY (ചിള്ളി - chilli, *Mal.*; சல்லி - shalli, *Tam.*). Mal. means trifling. Tam. from (chhallí, san. rind, from chhí, san. to cut). Small copper coin, a fractional part of a larger coin. There is a Tamul proverb:—அனாச்சல்லியை வைத்து எருக்கு இலையைக் கடந்ததுபோல—"As one leaped over a yercum "[q.v.] leaf under which he had concealed a half chally;" foolishly showing what might have remained concealed [reis].

CHALTAH (भव्य - bhavya, *San.*; मोटाकरमल - mótákaramala, *Mahr.*; چالتا - chaltá, *Hind.*; ಬೆಟ್ಟಕಣಿಗಿಲ - bettakanigila, *Can.*; కలింగ - kalinga, *Tel.*; ରାଇ - rai, *Oor.*; ചലിത - chalita, *Mal.*; හොඬපර - hondapara, *Singh.*; உவா - uvá, *Tam.*). Title from hindostany. San. from (bhú, san. to exist), means handsome. Mahr. from (mótá, mahr. large + karamala, mahr. dilleuia pentagyna, roxb.). Hind. means moving, as medicinal. Can. from (betta, can. hill + kanigila, can. nerium odorum, sol.); from flowers. Tel. compare tellicherry bark. Mal. from hindostany. Tam. means pleasing tree. San. also (ravya), meaning hill tree. Can. also (kádkanigila), meaning wild + nerium odorum, sol. Tel. also (peddakalinga), meaning large variety; (uvva). Tam. also (ugâ), meaning pleasing. Title otherwise Large flowered dillenia, Oogah, Oovah, Sand-paper tree, Wild gannair. Botanically Dillenia indica, linn., dilleniaceæ [vricsham, 2]. Alias Dillenia elliptica, speciosa. Tree, 40 feet; leaves oblong, serrated, glabrous, appearing with the flowers; sepals and petals five; peduncles solitary, terminal, one-flowered; stamens all equal in length; styles and carpels about eighty; seeds hairy; carpels joined into a spurious, many-celled, many-seeded berry, crowned by the radiant stigmas; flowers large, showy, with white petals and yellow anthers. Ornamental tree of spreading habit, with bright green leaves having conspicuous lateral nerves ending in a tooth at the margin, and fragrant flowers, 9 inches in diameter, followed by fruit enclosed in five thickened persistent sepals forming a ball the size of the fist; fruit as they hang resemble enormous green apples; found in dense forests at no great elevation in malabar, northern circars [q.v.], orissa, godavery forests; much cultivated, particularly by natives about temples. Bark and leaves are medicinally astringent; ripe fruit similarly laxative. The fleshy accrescent calyces which surround the fruit are eaten; tasted raw these have the exact flavor of a very sour unripe apple [seb], and when cooked with sugar resemble apple similarly; contain much fibre; commonly mixed in curry [q.v.], especially prawn; acid juice sweetened with sugar forms cooling drink. Leaves, which are hard and rough, used for polishing furniture and tinware [bramha's banyan]. Wood tough, used to make gun-stocks and for boats, very durable under water.——*Small chaltah* (करमळ - karamala, Mahr.; ಕಾಡುಗಣಿಗಿಲ - káduganigila, Can.; ಮಲೆಗೇರು - malegéru, Coorg; చిన్నకలింగ - chinnakalinga, Tel.; ରାଇ - rái, Oor.; நாய்த்தேக்கு - náyttékku, Tam.). Mahr. is applied also to coromandel gooseberry [q.v.]. Can. from (kádu, can. wild + kanigila, can. nerium odorum, sol.); from odour. Coorg from (male, can. hill + géru, can. the marking nut tree, semecarpus anacardium, linn.). Tel. from (chinna, tel. small + kalinga, tel. dillenia indica, linn.). Tam. from (náy, tam. dog + tékku, tam. teak, tectona grandis, linn. f.); from inferiority. Can. also (kóltégu), meaning tall teak; (machil). Tel. also (ravudana). Tam. also (pinnai), meaning handsome tree, generally calophyllum inophyllum, linn. [common poon]. Title otherwise Dog teak, Hairy dillenia. Botanically Dillenia pentagyna, roxb., dilleniaceæ [vricsham, 2]. Alias Colbertia coromandeliana; Dillenia augusta, pilosa; Wormia coromandeliana. Tree, 20 feet; leaves broadly lanceolate, sharply toothed or serrated, appearing after the flowers; peduncles from the axils of the scars of the former year's leaves, several together, one-flowered; inner row of stamens longer than the others; styles five; flowers gold-colored, fragrant; seeds immersed in a gelatinous pulp; carpels joined into a ribbed baccate fruit. Flowers, buds, and fruit when green eaten by the natives. Wood close-grained, strong, tough, fibrous and durable even under ground, reddish brown, ornamental wavy surface on one side, easily worked, subject to warp and crack; used in house and ship-building, and adapted for cabinet purposes; as it splits easily, is much used for firewood.

CHAMARAM (चमर - chamara, *San.*). Tail of yak [chowry].——*Chamara pootcham* (चमरपुच्छ - chamarapuchha, San.). From (puchha, san. tail); from bushy tail. Family sciuridæ, rodentia, mammalia [sastanam, 16], of naturalists [jantoo]. Three well marked groups in Southern india, distinguished by size, coloration and habits. First, large squirrels [malabar squirrel]. Secondly, striped squirrels, which, from best known species Sciurus palmarum, have been named Palmists; of small size, and affect the ground [anil pillay]. Thirdly, flying squirrels; divided into two smaller groups, one of large size, and with the tail round and hairy throughout, Pteromys [paravay anil], the other of smaller size with the tail flat, and the hairs distichous, Sciuropterus. The squirrels of medium size with grizzled fur are confined to the south-east Himalayas, and the provinces north-east of Bengal; they are not here represented.

CHAMAUR (چمار - chamár, *Hind.*; ಚಂಬಾರ - chambára, *Can.*). From (charma, san. skin). Leather dresser, chuckler [inam].

CHAMAYAM (ചമയം - chamayam, *Mal.*). From (chamayuka, mal. to get ready). Generically compensation for improving land. Used specifically of compensation to tenant for his building fixtures [coodiyiroopp] as opposed to compensation for plantings [cooyicaunom] and tillages [vettoocaunom]. See vol. I, 112; II, 104.

CHAMBALEE (चंबेलीअत्तर - chambéliattara, *Mahr.*). From (chambélí, mahr. jasminum grandiflorum, linn. + attara, mahr. essential oil). Essential oil of jasmine [attar].

CHAMGADAL (जतुका - jatuká, *San.*; चामचिराई - chámachiráí, *Mahr.*; خفاش - khaffásh, *Ar.* and *Pers.*; چمگادر - chamgádar, *Hind.*; چمگدل - chamgadal, *Dec.*; ದೊಡ್ಡಬಾವಲೆಹಕ್ಕಿ - doddabávaléhakki, *Can.*; పెద్దగబ్బిలము - peddagabbilamu, *Tel.*; ବାଦରା - bádará, *Oor.*; குருட்டுவவ்வால் - kuruttuvavvál, *Tam.*). Title from deccany. San. from (jatu, san. lac); lac-brown. Mahr. means leather-winged. Ar. from (khafisha, ar. small eye). Hind. from (charma, san. leather + gídar, hind. jackal); i.e., leather or winged fox. Can. from (dodda, can. large + bávale, can. bat + hakki, can. bird). Tel. from (pedda, tel. large + gabbilamu, tel. bat). Oor. from (vátuli, san. flying fox). Tam. from (kurudu, tam. blindness + vavvál, tam. bat). Family Noctilionidæ, cherioptera, mammalia [sastanam, 5], of naturalists [jantoo]. Nectule bats or Great bats. These have no facial membrane; head, short and obtuse; lips, large; wings, long; tail usually free at the tip.—"*a*" The first of the family is the Long-armed bat, Taphozous longimanus. Alias Taphozous brevicaudus, cantori, fulvidus; Vespertilis longimanus. Ears oval, with many distinct folds, naked except at the base; tragus, securiform; fur, thick, close, fuscous black or dark fuscous brown above; beneath paler, except on the throat, the hairs being conspicuously tipped with gray; the upper hairs all white at their base; face nude; it and the membranes, dark brownish black. Young individuals are fulvescent and become gradually blacker with age. Very common about large towns. It frequents dark out-houses, cellars, stabling, old temples.—"*b*" Next is the Black-bearded bat. Taphozous melanopogon. Alias Taphozous philippinensis. Ears, moderate, oval, with the outer margin extending under the eyes, dilated into a large rounded lobe; the tragus, leaf-shaped; the head, muzzle, and chin covered with short hairs. Above brown or reddish brown; beneath brownish white, with a long black collar or beard round the throat of the male, surrounded by a light brown band. Many males, however, it is stated, want this collar. The females are brownish mouse gray above, lighter beneath. Has been found in Canara.—"*c*" Next is the White-bellied bat, Taphozous saccolaimus. Alias Taphozous crassus, pulcher. Muzzle, angular, naked, very acute; nostrils, small, close; ears, distant, shorter than the head, large inner margin recurved, outer ditto, dilated, reaching to the commissure of the mouth; tragus, wide, securiform; fur, short, smooth, blackish on the head, chestnut-brown on the back; beneath dirty white or black-brown above with white pencillings; pure white below.—"*d*" Last is the Wrinkled-lipped bat, Nyctinomus plicatus. Ears large; tail thick; above smoky or snuff-brown; paler and somewhat ashy beneath. Frequents ruins, dark buildings, and occasionally, the hollows of trees. Attracts attention by a hissing noise.—"*e*" Indian species of this family not here found are:—Nyctinomus tragatus, Taphozous kachhensis, Taphozous theobaldi.—"*f*" For vespertilion bats, see Vavvaul; for vampires see Kaffaush.

CHAMOONDY (चामुण्डा - chámundá, *San.*). From (chandamunda, san. two asuras killed by kálí). Village goddess, especially in Coorg. Like Bhadra cauly [q.v.]. Represented somewhat like Pidaury [q.v.]. However she does not sit, but stands on the buffalo-head of the giant Mahishan [q.v.], whom she slew with the two weapons of Vishnoo called Chunk [q.v.] and Chuckram [q.v.], held in two of her four hands [dusserah]. In Chamoondy's pagodas, which are not numerous, stand the following images:—Chamoondy, both of stone and of metal; Ooyirtoondilcauran [ancaulamman]; Veerabhadran [q.v.], usually of wood; Vigneshwaran [q.v.]; Yevalcaura pey, a demon who serves-her as messenger [matam]. See vol. I (78).

CHAMPAK (चम्पक - champaka, *San.*; पिवलाचांपा - pivaláchámpá, *Mahr.*; चांप्या - chámpyá, *Conc.*; چمپے کا پیڑ - champekáper, *Hind.*; چمپے کا جھاڑ - champekájhár, *Dec.*; چمپکا - champaka, *Malay*; ಸಂಪಿಗೆ - sampige, *Can.*; ಸಂಪಯಿ - sampayi, *Too.*; సంపంగి - sampangi, *Tel.*; ଚାଂପା - chámpá, *Oor.*; ചെമ്പകം - chempakam, *Mal.*; සපු - sapu, *Singh.*; சண்பகம் - shanbagam, *Tam.*). Title from champah, a province of cambodia, where the tree grows. San. from (champ, san. to move) [pagoda tree]. Mahr. from (pivalá, mahr. yellow + champaka, san. the tree). San. also (kusuma), meaning flower [bastard saffron]; (dípapushpa), meaning lamp-flower; (vanamáliká), meaning garland of wood; (sukumára), meaning beautiful; (chámpéya), meaning produced in champah; (hémánga), meaning golden limbed; (hémapushpaka), meaning golden flowered; (añjana), meaning collyrium [cassa, yaipy]; (gandhap'halí), meaning fragrant fruit. Tel. also (gangarávi), meaning large + the tree, ficus religiosa, linn. [portia]; (kánchanamu), meaning gold [purple mountain ebony, toddaly, white mountain ebony]. Tam. also (shambangi), commonly creeper champak; (vandunámalarmaram), meaning flower-tree untouched by beetles, from strong scent [common vengay]; cf. foreign agatty. Title otherwise Anjanam, Beetle's foe, Golden-flowered champak, Indian magnolia, Sampaugy. Botanically Michelia champaca, linn., magnoliaceæ [vricsham, 3]. Specific name from sanscrit. Alias Michelia rheedii, suaveolens. Tree, 30–40 feet; petals numerous, disposed in several rows; leaves alternate, entire, lanceolate, acuminated, glabrous; flowers on short peduncles, axillary; spathe of one leaf; carpels two-valved; seed several; flowers large, lemon colored, fragrant. Large shady tree; a kind of magnolia; much resembling mango [q.v.] in habit and shape of leaves, with foliage of a dull green hue and flowers like an unfolded tulip produced in great numbers, followed by straw colored fruits, which open and permit the seeds to hang out by long funicular cords; wild in western forests; common, cultivated about temples. The fresh bark is covered externally by a light brown epidermis, which can be easily removed by friction; beneath this, it is of a reddish brown color mottled with longitudinal green stripes, and pale yellow scars of irregular form; the inner surface is yellowish and fibrous, taste feebly bitter, with a faint aroma; it contains tannic and gallic acids; bark collected on hills of w. coast. Flowers offered in temples, especially to vishnoo; flowers rubbed on the body at marriages, &c.; is one of those with which the five arrows of cauman [cauma baunam] are tipped; its aromatic scent is so strong that bees [tainee] never light upon it. Bark of the root red, bitter, and very acid; when pulverised emmenagogue; quoted in pharm., non-officinal; flowers beaten up with oil applied to fetid discharges from the nostrils; all parts are powerfully stimulant. Preparations:—flowers, infusion and tincture, flowers in coarse powder two ounces and a half to one pint of boiling water or rectified spirit; bark, decoction, boiling two ounces and a half in two pints of water till reduced to one pint. Substituted:—the flowers for spirit. ammon. arom., tinct. moschi, tinct. cardamomi comp., and tinct. cascarillæ; the bark for cinchona [koinah] and its alkaloids. Fruit edible. Flowers used to ornament the hair; bark yields sampaugy oil; the seeds destroy vermin; when boiled, flower yields a yellow dye [shauyam], communicating an agreeable perfume to the fabric dyed; the flowers give a volatile oil, which somewhat resembles ilang [ilang ilang] for which it is used as an adulterant. Wood soft, seasons and polishes well; sap-wood white; heart-wood light olive-brown.——**(1)** *Champakacherry* (ചെമ്പകശ്ശേരി - chempakashshéri, Mal.). From (above + shéri, mal. village). A principality including Collam and Ambalapoya.——*Champakallee* (چنپا کلی - champákallí, Hind.). From (above + kallí, hind. bud). An ornament formed of rays representing the unblown flower of Michelia champaca, linn., worn loosely round the neck and reaching half way down the bosom [zewar].——**(2)** *Creeper champak* (تونکی - tonki, Malay; సీతామనోహరము - sítámanóharamu, Tel.; கொடிசம்பங்கி - kodisambangi, Tam.). Title from habit and similar fragrance of flowers. Tel. from (sítá, san. rámá's wife + manas, san. mind + hri, san. captivate); seeta's delight. Tam. from (kodi, tam. creeper + champaka, san. michelia champaca, linn.). Tel. also (álapála). Tam. also (tongippú), meaning to hang + flower from drooping flowers. Title otherwise Cowslip creeper, Primrose creeper, Seeta's heart joy, West coast creeper. Botanically Pergularia minor, andr., asclepiadeæ [vricsham, 88]. Alias Asclepias odoratissima; Cynanchum odoratissimum; Pergularia odoratissima. Extensive climber, with heart-shaped, pointed leaves of a dull green color, bears bunches of flowers resembling those of the cowslip, but of a dead, heavy, greenish yellow, scenting the air when in blossom during the hot months with much fragrance; thick cylindrical seed-pods, six inches long. Another species is Pallida.——*Forest champak* (ವನಸಂಪಿಗೆ - vanasampige, Can.). From habitat and sulphur colored flowers. Same as Wild mountain ebony.——*Golden champak* (कनकचम्प - kanakachampa, San.). From yellow fragrant flowers. Same as Shilandy.——*Lowly champak* (भूमिचम्पक - bhúmichampaka, San.). From low size and fragrant flowers. Same as False zedoary.——*Nauga champak* (नागकेसर - nágakésara, San.; नागचांपा - nágachámpá, Mahr.; नागचांपे - nágachámpé, Conc.; ناگیسر - nágesar, Hind. and Dec.; ನಾಗಸಂಪಿಗೆ - nágasampige, Can.; ನಾಗಸಂಪೈ - nágasampai, Too.; నాగకేసరము - nágakésaramu, Tel.; ନାଗେଶ୍ୱର - nágésvoro, Oor.; വെളുത്തചെമ്പകം - velutta-chempakam, Mal. ; නාගහ - nágaha, Singh. ; சிறுநாகம் - shirunágam, Tam.). Title from resort of serpents and odour of flowers. San. from (nága, san. serpent + késara, san. filament). Mahr. from (nága, san. serpent + champaka, san. the tree). Hind. from sanscrit. Can. from (nága, san. serpent + sampige, can. michelia champaca, linn.). Too. from (nága, san. serpent + sampai, too. champaka). Mal. from (velutta, mal. white + chempakam, mal. the tree michelia champaca, linn.). Singh. from (na, singh. serpent + gaha, singh. tree). Tam. from (shiru, tam. small + nágam, tam. the plant). San. also (késara), meaning filament of flower [ilanjy, kamela, poison bamboo, saffron]; (nágapushpá), meaning serpent + flower; (nága), meaning serpent; (suvarna), meaning of good color [common condray, shrubby balah]; (kiñjalka), meaning filament of flower; (pannagakésara), meaning serpent + filament. Mahr. also (t'hórachámpá), meaning large champak. Tel. also (gajapushpamu), meaning elephant + flower; (nágachampakamu), meaning serpent + the tree; (chíkatimánu), meaning darkness + tree [yellow mangosteen]. Tam. also (pálai), meaning having milk [dita, edible paulay, eve's apple, ground paulay, monkey face paulay, nakchiknee silk cotton, pauchonty, paula indigo, paulay silk cotton, tellicherry bark]; (nángal); (malainángal), meaning mountain + the plant; (nírnángal), meaning water + the plant; (irulmaram), meaning dark tree. Title otherwise Iron-wood champak, Iron-wood tree [cassa, chowkmaram, dark vail, deccany deodar, foreign ilanjy, yellow condray], Nahor oil plant, Nagaisar, Serpent champak, White champak. Botanically Mesua ferrea, linn., guttiferæ [vricsham, 22]. Alias Calophyllum nagassar, - nagassaricum; Mesua coromandelina, roxburghii, speciosa. Nagassar from sanscrit. Tree, 40 feet; straight stem, sepals four, unequal; petals four, alternate with the sepals; leaves oblong-lanceolate, acuminated, glaucous beneath, upper side shining, midrib and margins colored; flowers stalked, axillary, large, white, fragrant; fruit about the size of a small apple, one-celled, one to four-seeded. Cultivated about temples, very showy; bears flowers in february in great profusion; fruit reddish and wrinkled when ripe; rind like that of chestnut, in size, shape, and taste; the bark, wood, and roots are bitter and sweet-scented; at the bottom of the tender fruits, tenacious and glutinous oleo-resin [raul] exudes with a sharp aromatic smell. Religious; blossoms extremely fragrant; one of cauman's arrows [cauma baunam]. Kernels yield by expression a fixed oil useful in itch; the oleo-resin possesses all the properties of canada balsam. Fruit eaten. Oil used for burning; flowers dried are mixed with other aromatics, such as white sandal-wood, and used for perfuming ointment; attar [q.v.] prepared from flowers; flower buds are used for dyeing [shauyam] silk; tree affords an excellent shade. Heart-wood dark red, extremely hard, very durable. No other common species here.——*Neilgherry champak* (पिवळाचांपा - pivaláchámpá, Mahr.; پیلا چمپا - píláchampá, Dec.; වල්සපු - valsapu, Singh.; நீலகிரிசண்பகம் - nílagirisanbagam, Tam.). Mahr. from hindostany. Hind. from (pílá, hind. yellow + champá, hind. michelia champaca, linn.). Singh. from (val, singh. wild + sapu, singh. champak). Botanically Michelia nilagirica, zenker., magnoliaceæ [vricsham, 3]. Alias Michelia pulneyensis. Leaves elliptic, glabrous, acuminated; stipules and spathes silky; petals eight, in two rows; stamens shorter than the column of fructification; carpels one-seeded, warty; ovaries numerous, one-ovuled; flowers white, sometimes with a tinge of yellow; flowering during the rains. Magnolia-like tree; common on higher ranges of western hills; wood strong, close, fine-grained, very hygrometrical; used for building purposes, beams and rafters.——*Sultan champak* (سلطان چمپا - sultánchampá, Hind.). Title from flower. Same as Common poon.——*Wild champak* (جنگلی چمپا - janglichampá, Hind.). Same as Pagoda tree.

CHAMRAH (चर्म - charma, *San.*; جلد - jild, *Ar.*; چرم - chirm, *Pers.*; چمڑا - chamrá, *Hind.*; ಚರ್ಮ - charma, *Can.*; తోలు - tólu, *Tel.*; തോൽ - tól, *Mal.*; தோல் - tól, *Tam.*). Title from hindostany. San. from (char, san. to move), as protecting motion. Pers., hind. and can. from sanscrit. Mal. and tam. from (toli, tam. to strip off). Skin or hide. In English commercial language skins are of those animals such as calves, deer, goats, lambs, &c., which, when prepared, are used in the lighter works of book-binding, the manufacture of gloves, parchment, &c.; while hides are of the ox, horse, &c., which, when prepared are used in the manufacture of shoes, harness, &c.; the tamulians do not make this distinction. The manufacture of leather in this Presidency is considerable and the quality of the article good, considering the low rank of the artisans, called chucklers. Leather-working has been successfully practised by European tanners at Pondicherry. Hoonsoor in Mysore, Guntoor, Bangalore and Madras, the leather there made being scarcely inferior to that made in Europe. The following is the native method of working. First the skins, whether of sheep, goats, cows or buffaloes, are steeped in water in a pit with choonam [q.v.] at say two tooms [q.v.] for every hundred skins; this is within an hour after the skins are brought to the tannery; they are kept thus steeped for four days, by which time the hair on the skins will fall away; they are then taken out, and the choonam and other matter which may adhere is scraped off with a knife; after this they are well washed with water. Secondly, tungaid [q.v.] bark, at ten maunds for every hundred sheep and goat skins and for every ten cow and buffalo skins is thrown into water in a wooden trough and well soaked, so that the sap may come out and mix with the water; into this decoction the skins are thrown, after they have been scraped and washed as above said; they are left in the trough for eight days, being stirred up and down every day; on the ninth day, the tungaid bark is taken out, but nothing else which may be at the bottom of the trough; after this five maunds of new tungaid bark are thrown in, and the skins are left to soak in the juice for another eight days, turning them every day as before; this is sufficient for sheep and goat skins; but if they be skins of cows and buffaloes, new tungaid bark must be thrown in the same manner three times; that is to say, the skins must soak in the decoction for twenty-four days; afterwards they are taken out, the watery matter is wrung out, and the skins are well scraped. Thirdly, ink-nuts or chebulic myrobalans [q.v.] are well pounded, and the powder thrown into a wooden trough; into this trough hot water is poured; the decoction is left to cool; and subsequently the skins which have been steeped in the tungaid bark juice and scraped, are thrown into the decoction; there they remain one whole night; early morning next day, they are turned and left again the whole of a day and night; on the third day morning, they are taken out, wrung and smoothed with a knife. Fourthly, the skins are piled one above another, on a table; and oil at one maund for hundred sheep and goat skins or twenty cow and buffalo skins, is poured over them; after this they are dried on ropes in the shade so that the oil may soak into the skins. Fifthly, each of the skins is taken from the rope, and well rubbed over with a flat stone or a flat piece of wood; they are then dried again until they are completely dry; after this, every four skins are rolled together and thrashed upon a stone; then each of them is firmly drawn over the edge of an upright iron rail, until it becomes soft; after this, the inside of each skin is well rubbed over with a red hot brick. The expense of preparing skins in this way is some twenty rupees for every hundred sheep and goat skins and two hundred and fifty rupees for every hundred cow and buffalo skins. Skins and hides are principally from the goat, sheep [aud], buffalo [khoolgah], and bullock [maud]; also from the spotted deer [cheetal], hog deer [cheetal], dromedary [ottagam], barking deer [jungle sheep], elephant [q.v.], horse [ghorah]; bison [gowr], ravine deer [q.v.], ibex [saddle back], nilghye [q.v.], samber [q.v.], pig [soor], wild boar. Mineral articles employed in the process of tanning are alum, iron filings, quick lime, rust of iron, sulphate of iron [annabhaidy]. The following are two key-lists in the briefest possible terms of the principal vegetable tanning materials of s. india for which vernacular names are known; further information must be traced in the glossary paragraphs through the small-type cross references at end of this volume; see also vricsham, 7, for the method of expressing the products, &c., of plants in the dravidian languages.—"*a*" Acacia arabica, babool, bark and pods; Acacia catechu, catechu, bark and cutch; Albizzia lebbek, common sirissa, bark; Albizzia procera, hill sirissa, bark; Anacardium occidentale, cashew, bark; Anogeissus acuminata, pauchimaun, leaf; Avicennia officinalis, ooppata mangrove, bark; Barringtonia acutangula, small indian oak, bark; Bridelia retusa, var. genuina, thorny vengay, bark; Bruguiera gymnorhiza, candel mangrove, bark; Buchanania latifolia, chironjee, bark; Cæsalpinia coriaria, divy-divy, pods; Careya arborea, hindostany slow match, bark; Cassia auriculata, tungaid, bark; Cassia fistula, indian laburnum, bark; Garuga pinnata, garooga, bark; Kandelia rheedii, candel mangrove, bark; Loranthus longiflorus, gooloom, bark and bruised wood; Odina wodier, wodier, bark; Prosopis spicigera, shamee, bark; Punica granatum, pomegranate, root-bark and fruit rind; Rhizophora mucronata, white candel mangrove, bark; Shorea robusta, common saul, bark; Terminalia belerica, belleric myrobalan, dried fruit; Terminalia chebula, chebulic myrobalan, dried fruit and galls; Terminalia citrina, citrine myrobalan, dried fruit; Uncaria gambier, gambier, cutch; Zizyphus jujuba, bair, bark.—"*b*" Babool, acacia; Bair, zizyphus; Cashew, anacardium; Catechu, acacia; Chironjee, buchanania; Divy-divy, cæsalpinia; Gambier, uncaria; Garooga, garuga; Gooloom, loranthus; Laburnum, cassia; Mangrove, avicennia, bruguiera, kandelia, rhizophora; Myrobalan, terminalia; Oak, barringtonia; Pauchimaun, anogeissus; Pomegranate, punica; Saul, shorea; Shamee, prosopis; Sirissa, albizzia; Slow match tree, careya; Tungaid, cassia; Vengay, bridelia; Wodier, odina.

CHAND (चन्द् - chand, *San.*). To please, gladden.——*Chandanam* (चन्दन - chandana, San.). Red-wood. The inner wood of any plant which is red or reddish black.——*Chandas* (छन्दस् - chhandas, San.). From (chhad, san. to please). Metre.——*Chandoo* (چندو - chandú, Hind.). Intoxicating substance made of babool [q.v.] leaves and opium [aphainam] boiled, distilled, and prepared in chinese fashion [madak, mookhadiraut].——*Chaund** (چاند - chánd, Pers.). From (chandra, san. moon). Moon. Alam. In composition makes a lacab; as Chaund bee, moon-like lady [ism]. Plant second term from white flowers, as in:—Gardenia florida (gulichándní), moon rose; Rauwolfia serpentina (chhotáchánd), young moon. See gloss. paragraphs.

CHANDWAH (चांद - chánda, *Mahr.*; چندوا - chandwá, *Hind.*). From (chandra, san. moon); from silvery transparent color.

The genus Ambassis, percidæ [panayairy], acanthopterygii, teleostei, pisces [matsyam, 1], of naturalists [jantoo]. Small bony fishes; body deep and compressed, more or less transparent; eaten by the poorer classes, easily dried without salt. The species best known to the natives are shown below.——*Red chandwah* (लालचान्द - lálachánda, Mahr.; لال چندوا - lálchandwá, Hind.). Hind. from (lál, hind. red). Mahr. also (rangachánda), meaning painted ambassis. Ambassis [chandwah] ranga, percidæ [panayairy], acanthopterygii, teleostei [matsyam, 1], of naturalists. Specific name from mahratta. Alias Ambassis alta, barlovi, lala; Chanda lala, ranga. Olive, having dark mark composed of spots on shoulder, being remains of band present in the young; margins of vertical fins usually dark; young is of bright yellow or orange color, with four or five dark vertical bands formed of fine black dots; first dorsal nearly black, second and anal as well as occasionally the ventral have deep black edges; yellow spots sometimes present, subject to great variations in accordance with age; freshwater; few inches.——*Striped chandwah* (गाडेचिरि - gáudéchiri, Mahr.; ఆకురాతి - ákuráti, Tel.; କର୍ତ୍ତକନା - kartkana, Oor.). Mahr. from (gávadí, mahr. cow + chirí, mahr. fine stripe); from color and stripes. Tel. from (ákuráyi, tel. file); from oblong figure and markings on skin granulated like a file. Mahr. also (náma), meaning white striped; (p'húla), meaning flowery, from white spots on fish; (bágóda), meaning tiger-like, either from spots or from teeth curving forwards; (chándanáma), striped ambassis; (bágódanáma), meaning tiger-spotted and striped. Title otherwise Aukrauty. Ambassis [chandwah] nama, percidæ [panayairy], acanthopterygii, teleostei [matsyam, 1], of naturalists. Specific name from mahratta. Alias Ambassis bogoda, oblonga, phula; Bogoda nama; Chanda nama, phula et bogoda; bogoda from mahratta; phula from mahratta; bogoda nama from mahratta; chanda nama from mahratta. Lower jaw much longer than upper. Scales minute, scarcely visible on head; in young specimens captured from stagnant water, mucus often causes scales to be overlooked. Lateral-line always indistinct. Colors yellowish-olive covered over with minute black dots which on shoulder are collected into oblong patch, having longest diameter vertical; summit of head and top of eyes black. Fins orange, upper half of first dorsal deep black; dark upper edge to second dorsal; caudal dark with light outer margin; anal with black mark over bases of spines. Shows considerable local variations. Throughout freshwaters; three or four inches.——*White chandwah* (سفید چندوا - sufedchandwá, Hind.). Hind. from (sufed, hind. white). Ambassis [chandwah] gymnocephalus, percidæ [panayairy], acanthopterygii, teleostei [matsyam, 1], of naturalists. Alias Ambassis dussumieri, vachelli; Chanda dussumieri; Lutjanus gymnocephalus; Priopis argyrozona. Chanda from mahratta. Lower jaw the longer. Scales two rows on suborbital ring of bones, the lower of which is much the deeper. Lateral line interrupted from eighth to twelfth scale, in some cases entirely. Colors silvery with bright longitudinal lateral band, brown spots on upper third of body in front half; blackish between second and third dorsal spines, black edge to caudal. Variation in length of second and third dorsal spines, sometimes one, sometimes the other being longer. Sea; four inches; captured in backwaters.

CHANGAUDA (ചങ്ങാടം - channátam, *Mal.*). From (sam, san. together + ghat, san. to unite). σάγγαρα of the Periplus. Canoe formed out of single tree [jungar]. See vol. I (44).

CHANNEL (கால் - kál, *Tam.*). Common irrigation term [caulvye].——*River channel* (ఏటికాలవ - étikálava, Tel.; ஆற்றுக்கால் - áttukkál, Tam.). Channel for irrigation issuing from a river as distinguished from a spring or tank.——*Spring channel* (جهرے کا نالا - jharekánálá, Hind.; ಊಟೆಕಾಲಿವೆ - útekálive, Can.; ఊటకాలవ - útakálava, Tel.; ஊற்றுக்கால் - úttukkál, Tam.). Channel for irrigation issuing from a spring instead of from a river or tank.——*Supply channel* (వరవకాలవ - varavakálava, Tel.; குளக்கால் - kulakkál, Tam.). Tel. from (vattsu, tel. to arrive + kálava, tel. channel). Tam. from (kulam, tam. tank + kál, tam. channel). Channel from any source or sources which feeds a tank.

CHAP (چپ - chap, *Pers.*). Left.——*Chapraus* (چپراس - chaprás, Hind.). From (above + rást, pers. right). The brass plate which a messenger wears on his shoulder belt, as a badge of office. On the chapraus is engraved the name of the office to which the messenger belongs [billa, chooprassy].

CHAPKAN (چپکن - chapkan, *Hind.*). From (chipakná, hind. to adhere); from its close fit. A long gown with flaps in the skirt and the skirt open and breast covered; sometimes having slits in the armpits [cabah, sheelay].

CHAR (चर् - char, *San.*). To move, act, practise.——*Characun* (चरक - charaka, San.). A medical writer in Vedic times, and the author of Characa samhitay, one of the standard Hindoo medical works. He received materials from Agnivesan, and he from Atreyan. This book was translated into Arabic before the eighth century.——*Charaucharum* (चराचर - charáchara, San.). From (chara, san. movable + achara, san. immovable). The world, the aggregate of all things.——*Charitram* (चरित - charita, San.). History. Of the eighteen pooraunams, four only contain dynastic lists, representing all the indigenous history possessed by Hindoos; these are Matsyam, Vishnoo, Bhaugavatam and Vayoo [carnautaca rajakkal, congoodesha rajakkal]. See vol. I (110)—(188), and the following foot-notes:—Sans. legends I (114), dynasties of n. india I (116), ceylon I (117), paundy kingdom I (119)—(124), chola I (125)—(125), chera I (126)—(127), kerala I (128), pullava I (129), vengy I (132), andhra I (132), calinga I (132), knowledge of anc. foreigners I (133), hoysala ballaula I (140), yadava of devagherry I (140), tondaimundalam I (141), mahomedan imp. dynasties I (143), mahomedan sub-kingdoms I (146), condaveed I (150), nellore I (150), gajapaty I (151), vijianugger I (151), hurpanhully I (154), growth of english I (155)—(160), madras in seventeenth century I (163), mahrattas I (166), e.i. company I (166)—(171), const. hist. of brit. government I (172), first siege of madras I (174), second siege I (178), northern circars I (179), british acquisitions I (188), native rulers II, 250, annals II, 257, governors II, 268, acquisitions II, 272, fort st. george II, 279, attached native states II, 285.——*Charmaudy* (ಚಾರ್ಮಾಡಿ - chármádi, Can.). From (charama, san. west + adri, san. mountain).—"*a*" Village; South canara district, Ooppinangady talook; pop. 700; lat. 23° 03′; long. 75° 28′; from Mangalore E.N.E. 42 miles; from Poottore N.E. 26 miles.—"*b*" Pass; South canara district, Ooppinangady talook also known as the Boon ghaut or Coffee ghaut, and as the Codicull ghaut. Opened in 1864, and now one of the main lines for wheeled traffic, specially for coffee [q.v.] transport, between Mangalore and Mysore.——*Charry* (चारि - chári, San.). From (char, san. to practise). An observer. Suffix in compounds as Bramhacharry, meaning religious devotion + observer, religious student.——*Chauram* (चार - chára, San.). From (char, san. to move). Motion. Especially the daily aspect or position of the planets [graham]. Chaura caundam, from (above + kánda, san. stick, measure) is ascensional difference. Chaurajyay, from (above + jyá, san. bow-string; sine) is the sine of the ascensional difference.——*Chaurvaucan* (चार्वाक - chárváka, San.). From (cháru, san. elegant + váka, san. speaking). The Pyrrho and Epicurus of India. Founder of the materialistic school of philosophy [sarwa darshana sangraham]. The Chaurvaucans are sometimes called Locauyatans. They reject all the Pramaunams [q.v.], except Pratyacsham, perception by the senses; they admit only four Tatwams [q.v.], viz., earth, air, fire, and water, and from these cheitanyam [q.v.] or intelligence is produced; they affirm that the soul is not different from the body, and that all the phenomena of the world are spontaneously produced without even the help of Adrishtam or the unseen. They deny the existence of god or any divine being or first cause; the earth, the visible sky, the expanse of either, the sun, the moon, are self-produced; there is no distinction between moral good and evil, and no state of rewards or punishments after death [samsauram]; hence there is no need to entertain any dread, or reverence, of any superior, or inspecting being. The divisions into which the Chaurvaucan class was formerly distinguished were eleven:—Sowtrauntican, Yogachauran, Veibhaushican, Nirgranta vandy of the Shamanan, Ashwacan, Bhattacharry, Prabhacaran, Mayauvaty, Parausharyan, Nishwausangy, Puncharautry. See vol. I (70) to (94); and the following foot-notes:—history of rel. and phil., I (70), existing hindoo sects I (88) [matam].

CHAR (چار - chár, *Hind.*). Four [chow, chatoor].——*Charkhauny* (چارخانی - chárkhání, Hind.). From (above + khánah, hind. square). Chequered muslin [doriyah, sheelay].——*Charpoy* (چارپائی - chárpái, Hind.). From (above + pái, pers. a foot). A bedstead being plain frame of wood set on four short legs; cords or broad tapes [navaur] are stretched along and across the frame to form the bed. Precisely the same are found in the old sculptures, and they are the same as those of the ancient Egyptians. It is correctly described in the following quotation from Ibn batuta:—"The bedsteads in India are very light. A "single man can carry one, and every traveller should have his "own bed, which his slave carries about on his head. The bed "consists of four conical legs, on which four staves are laid; "between these they plait a sort of ribbon of silk or cotton. "When you lie on it you need nothing else to render the bed "sufficiently elastic [cot, cuttil]."——*Char yauree* (چار یاری - cháryárí, Hind.). From (above + yár, pers. companion). Followers of the four companions, the Soonnees [q.v.].

CHAR (چاء - chá, *Dec.*). From chinese. Same as Tea.

CHARAS (چرس - charas, *Hind.*). The exudation of the flowers of hemp [kinnab] collected in the early morning and prepared for use as an intoxicating drug [mooskiraut].

CHARAUNAH (چرانا - charáná, *Hind.*). Means grazing. So fines on cattle trespassing on corn fields [condy].

CHARCOAL TREE (کوئلے کا جہاڑ - kolsekájhár, *Dec.*). Title from making good charcoal [adooppkary] for gunpowder. Same as Indian nettle.

CHAR PALM (சாற்றுப்பனை - sháttuppanai, *Tam.*). Title means toddy palm. Same as Palmyra.

CHARVANAM (चर्वण - charvana, *San.*). Title from (charv, san. to masticate). Masticatory. Tobacco [pogauk] and many other vegetable substances are extensively used as masticatories by S. indian natives. They stimulate salivary glands, which adapt themselves to increased demand. The following are two key-lists of the principal masticatories of s. india for which vernacular names are known; further information must be traced in the glossary paragraphs through the small-type cross-references at end of this volume; see also vricsham, 7, for the method of expressing the products, &c., of plants in the dravidian languages:—"*a*" Acacia catechu, catechu, cutch; Alpinia officinarum, lesser galangal. root; Areca catechu. areca, nut; Caryota urens, bastard sago palm, fruit; Cinnamomum zeylanicum, ceylon cinnamon, bark; Cocos nucifera, cocoanut, dry nut; Elettaria cardamomum, cardamom, capsule; Eugenia caryophyllata, clove tree, flower buds; Myristica fragrans, common nutmeg, nutmeg and mace; Nicotiana tabacum, tobacco, leaf; Piper betel, betel pepper, leaf; Piper cubeba, cubeb pepper, berry; Strychnos nux-vomica, poison-nut, nut; Zingiber officinale, ginger, rhizome.—"*b*" Cardamom, elettaria; Catechu, acacia; Cinnamon, cinnamomum; Clove, eugenia; Cocoanut, cocos; Galangal, alpinia; Ginger, zingiber; Nutmeg, myristica; Pepper, piper; Poison nut, strychnos; Sago palm, caryota; Tobacco, nicotiana.

CHATOOR (चतुर - chatur, *San.*). Latin quatuor. Four.——*Chatoor acarauthy* (चतुरकारादि - chaturakárádi, San.). From (akárádi, san. dictionary). Dictionary of Tamul explained in Tamul, by Beschi [veeramamoony]. Consists of four distinct dictionaries. The first, Peyar, shows the several meanings of every word. The second, Porool, shows the several words bearing the same meaning. The third, Togay, shows the subordinate species of the technical and general terms of science and literature. The fourth, Today, is a rhyming dictionary. The last is the only one which is entirely arranged in alphabetical order, the words in the others being collected into general classes and resembling therefore vocabularies rather than dictionaries [acarauthy, nigantoo].——*Chatooram* (ചതുരം - chaturam, Mal.). Quadrangular. Plant first term often joining two genera as in:—Averrhoa carambola (chaturappuli), quadrangular tamarindus indica.——*Chatoordashy* (चतुर्दशी - chaturdashí, San.). From (above + dasha, san. ten). The fourteenth day in a lunar fortnight. Lunar festival [pundigay, 3e] held on the fourteenth tity [q.v.] of either of fortnight of any month [anantachatoordashy, bhootachatoordashy, naracachatoordashy].——*Chatoor mookhan* (चतुर्मुख - chaturmukha, San.). From (mukha, san. face). The four-faced Bramha [matam, naul mookhan].——*Chatoorta palam* (चतुर्थफल - chaturt'hap'hala, San.). From (above + p'hala, san. result). The second inequality or equation of a planet [graham], answering to the annual parallax [sheeghram] of a superior planet and the elongation of an inferior one.——*Chatoorty* (चतुर्थी - chaturt'hí, San.). The fourth day in a lunar fortnight. Is sacred to Vigneshwaran. Lunar festival [pundigay, 3e] held on the fourth tity of either fortnight of any month [pillaiyaur chatoorty, vinauyaca chatoorty].——*Chatoor varnam* (चतुर्वर्ण - chaturvarna, San.). From (varna, san. color). The four castes of Hindoos [jauty].——*Chatoor yoog* (चतुर्युग - chaturyuga, San.). From (yuga, san. period of time). Same as mahayoog [caulam].——*Chatoosunga* (ಚತುಸ್ಸಂಗ - chatussanga, Can.). From (above + sanga, san. assemblage). The four old Aryan castes, Bramha, Cshatriya, Veisya and Shoodra.——*Chatrangam* (चतुरङ्ग - chaturanga, San.). From (above + anga, san. member). Chess. The Tamul cooral has the following:—அரங்கின்றி வட்டாடி யற்றே நிரம்பிய நூலின்றிக் கோட்டி கொளல்—"To speak in an assembly "without fulness of knowledge, is like playing at chess on a "board without squares" [chowsar, pacheesy, shatranj].

CHATTAM (చట్టము - tsattamu, *Tel.*; ചട്ടം - chattam, *Mal.*; சட்டம் - shattam, *Tam.*). Means a frame. Tabular account. A regulation.——*Chattagar* (چٹےکار - chattekár, Hind.; சட்டைக்காரன் - shattaikkáran, Tam.). Tam. from (shattai, tam. dress + káran, tam. possessor). One who wears European dress; an East indian.——*Chattay* (ಚಟ್ಟೆ - chatte, Can.; చట్ట - tsatta, Tel.; சட்டை - shattai, Tam.). Dress.——*Chatty* (भाण्ड - bhánda, San.; هانڈی - handí, Hind.; هنڈی - handí, Dec.; بالنگا - bálanga, Malay; ಚಟ್ಟಿಗೆ - chattige, Can.; ಚಟ್ಟಿ - chatti, Too.; చట్టి - tsatti, Tel.; ചട്ടി - chatti, Mal.; சட்டி - shatti, Tam.). Title from tamul. Tam. from (shattam, tam. mould). Malay also (priyuk). Tel. also (kunda). Tam. also (pánai). Earthen pot, spheroidal in shape. There are three distinct branches of earthenware manufacture which though similar in their manipulation are different in their results; the red porous earthernware used for chatties and cooking vessels, the black used for similar purposes, and the fine white which resembles some of the biscuit earthenware of Europe. The red porous earthenware differs very materially in quality according to the locality from which the clay [calimunu] is selected; some is made of a common coarse earthy loam [pasalay munn] which has very little tenacity, and yields a brittle kind of pottery neither susceptible of much finish nor of being glazed; most of the pottery of southern india is of this description, the vessels which are mostly of round form are thrown thick in the neck and upper parts or sides; they are cut off the wheel and left open in the bottom with vertical sides, they are then allowed to harden a little in the necks and as soon as they will bear to be handled the sides are thinned out by beating with a flat mallet upon a rounded stone or very hard round piece of wood held inside the vessel which is turned about and beaten till it is closed; this makes a thin light vessel but at a great sacrifice of time, from eighteen to twenty of these is a good day's work. Black earthenware is a mere variety of the red and in most instances it is the same kind of pottery blackened by the simple process of damping or checking the fire when it is beginning to decline, and thus throwing a great deal of smoke amongst the wares when the heat is not sufficiently intense to burn it off; a better, and stronger kind of black earthenware is manufactured at bangalore from a fine dense clay that contains both manganese [q.v.] and iron [auhan]; this approaches the black stoneware of egypt and is strong and sonorous when struck. White earthenware differs from the others in being conducted with more care and cleanliness, some attention being paid to the sifting of the materials and to the ornamenting and finishing of the articles; the material selected is a decaying white granite resembling the cornish stone of england or the grauen of germany; this is carefully washed and decanted to free it from sand or impurities, it is then allowed to subside, the water is poured off and the soft clay is collected on a clean cloth and laid on a heap of white wood ashes to dry; a small percentage of alkali [cauram] is thus absorbed through the cloth and is incorporated through the mass by kneading; this clay or decayed white granite is the true kaolin [q.v.] or porcelain earth of china and europe; it is abundant in southern india and occurs in beds of enormous extent and of every variety of color; it possesses the valuable qualities of combining with a large percentage of silica, felspar, baryta or other stony bodies and of resisting the most intense heats, but in southern india it is employed alone and produces a soft brittle porous ware which is not susceptible of being well glazed; the reason is that the kaolins require flint [teetatty cull], felspar [mauvayira cull], or stone to open them, and exposure to a long continued and steady heat before they are thoroughly burnt in the biscuit state; they also require a hard frit or porcelain glaze, which cannot be prepared without expensive machinery, the firing also involves a great consumption of fuel as the heat must be kept up steadily for forty or sixty hours.

CHATTRAM (छत्त्र - chhattra, *San.*). From (chhad, san. to cover). Umbrella or parasol [coday]. The umbrella is highest of insignia of regality. A vermilion umbrella everywhere in the east signifies imperial authority [maryanday]. Also name for the order fungi [caulaun].——*Chattrapaty* (छत्रपति - chhattrapati, San.). From (above + pati, san. lord). Title conferred on rulers, being higher than rajah or maharajah [q.v.].

CHAUGAL (چھاگل - chhágal, *Hind.*). A leathern bottle with spout to it, used for carrying water on journey [carboy].

CHAUGULMURRY (చాగలమర్రి - chágalamarri, *Tel.*). From (chágamu, tel. liberality + marri, tel. banyan, ficus bengalensis, linn.). Village, Head-quarters of Tahsildars; Kurnool district; Sirwail talook; pop. 3,115; acres 3,699; lat. 14° 58′; long. 78° 38′; from Cumbum S.W. 54 miles; from Kurnool S.S.E. 69 miles; from Madras N.W. 168 miles; from Nundiaul S.S.E. 36 miles; from Pyaupaly E.S.E. 60 miles. Built upon beds of calcareous limestone [choonam cull] and shale. About five miles north is Moottiaulpaud. Near is Shiva temple with tepid spring, resorted to at Shivarautry [pundigay, 6a].

CHAUKYAUN (ചാക്യാൻ - chákyán, *Mal.*). From (shakya, san. buddhist ascetic). Caste-title. Half bramins in Malabar [ambalavausy]. They sing and play before the temple gods, or before Bramins. The women are called Nangiyaur [jauty].

CHAULA (ചാല - chála, *Mal.*). From (shálá, san. hall). A hut of the lower castes or of artizans.——*Chaulacoody* (ചാലക്കുടി - chálakkuti, Mal.). From (chála, mal. road + kuti, mal. house); being village in form of street, which on w. coast is not usual. River; Cochin state, Moocoondapooram tal.; lat. between 10° 10′ and 10° 25′; long. between 76° 10′ and 76° 45′. Chief river of Cochin state. Rises in the Anamullays in Coimbatore district, where it is known as the Cholayaur, and flows directly west into the sea at Paliport, being known by various names along its route. Total length about 80 miles.

CHAULMOOGRA (برنج موگرا - biranjmograá, *Pers.*; چال موگرا - chálmográ, *Hind.* and *Dec.*). Pers. from (biranj, pers. rice grain + mográ, pers. jasminum sambac, ait.); with reference to seeds. Hind. from (cháwal, hind. rice grain + mográ, hind. jasminum sambac, ait.). Title otherwise Fragrant marotty, Rice grain jasmine. Botanically Gynocardia odorata, r. br., bixineæ [vricsham, 14]. Alias Hydnocarpus odoratus. Large tree, attaining size of an oak or sycamore; entire, glossy, alternate leaves; large yellow sweet-scented flowers, about 1½ inches across, growing in clusters on the old wood; the fruit is large and globular, about the size of a shaddock [pummelow], and contains numerous seeds immersed in pulp. The seeds, 1 to 1¼ inches long and about half as much in diameter, are of irregular ovoid form, and more or less angular or flattened by mutual pressure; they weigh on an average about thirty-five grains each; the testa is very thin, about $\frac{1}{25}$ of an inch, brittle, smooth, dull-grey; the copious oily albumen encloses a pair of large, plane, leafy, heart-shaped cotyledons with a stout radicle. The oil expressed from kernel of seeds is reddish brown and slightly viscid with a peculiar and nauseous smell and taste; it bears the greatest resemblance to croton [jamalgota] oil in its appearance and smell; during the rainy and cold seasons, a portion of it congeals and is thrown down at the bottom of the bottle in the form of a grey or yellowish-white crystalline fat; this fat is liquified by heat. The active principle of the oil is gynocardic acid; it is useful in all the forms of leprosy [cooshtam], tubercular, anæsthetic and mixed, but the first-named variety is the one most benefited; the internal use should always be assisted by its external application to the affected parts in combination with margosa [noom] oil, oil of pongamia glabra [karanj], &c. Preparation:—the oil taken floating on water or milk, the seeds in the form of pill or coarse powder. Doses:—of the oil, from five to fifteen minims or drops; of the seeds, from five to fifteen grains or more. Gives to pharm. chaulmoogra seeds, gynocardiæ semina, alterative tonic, in large doses emetic; and chaulmoogra ointment, unguentum gynocardiæ; officinal. In s. india, chaulmoogra is rarely obtainable, and marotty [q.v.] oil is a substitute.

CHAULYAM (ചാലിയം - cháliyam, *Mal.*). From (cháliyan, mal. a weaver). Island; Malabar dist., Yernaud tal.; lat. 11° 09′; long. 75° 51′; from Calicut S.S.E. 7 miles; from Munjery W.N.W. 21 miles; from the sea E. ½ mile. Rocky islet southward of entrance to Beypore river and connected with the mainland by a groyne. Contains old masonry foundations for formidable fortress for protection of entrance to Beypore river. Perhaps by Tippoo [furruckabad]. Site of abandoned Beypore railway station. Portuguese had factory here.——*Chaulyan* (ചാലിയൻ - cháliyan, Mal.). From (jála, san. woven texture). Weavers of Malabar [jauty].

CHAUMA (ಚಾಮ - cháma, *Can.*). Black. Common name of Mysore rajahs, as Chauma rajendra wodeyar.

CHAUN (ചാൺ - cháu, *Mal.*). Span. Linear measure. 12 virals = 1 chaun; 2 chauns = 1 moolam [alavay, 1 d]. Approximate actual value, 1 chaun = 9 inches. Same as San. gocurnam, vitasty; Hind. bilisht; Can. gueuoo; Tel. jena; Tam. jaun. Compare San. pradesham, Tam. adee, wottay.

CHAUPA (حصير - hasír, *Hind.*; చాప - tsápa, *Tel.*; பாய் - páy, *Tam.*). Hind. from (hasira, ar. to contract). Tel. from (tsápu, tel. to extend). Tam. from (pávu, tam. to spread). Mat; made of bamboo [q.v.], caldera bush [screw-pine], palmyra [q.v.] leaves, rattan [q.v.], &c. [boriyah]. Also sail of boat.

CHAUPAH (چهاپا - chhápá, *Hind.*; ചാപ്പ - cháppa, *Mal.*). A seal [moodray], stamp, punched coin [naunyam]. Chaupah kayitham, from (kákitamu, tel. paper) is stamped paper. Chaupah khana, from (khánah, pers. house) is a printing office.

CHAUTAH (چهاتا - chhátá, *Hind.*). Chest.——*Chautahband* (چهاتا بند - chhátáband, Hind.). From (above + band, pers. bound). Chest influenzá in horses [ashwarogam].

CHAUVADY (چاوڑی - cháurí, *Hind.*; ಚಾವಡಿ - chávadi, *Can.*; చావడి - tsávadi, *Tel.*; ചാവടി - chávati, *Mal.*; சாவடி - shávadi, *Tam.*). From (chau, mahr. four + váta, san. road); place where four roads meet. Appears in Anglo-indian as choultry [q.v.]. A hall, used by travellers as a resting-place, and also intended for the transaction of a public business. A building of this kind formed the earliest court-house. In the old Madras archives there is frequent mention of the Justices of the Choultry. The Moonsif of every village still holds court in the village choultry. Pillared hall attached to a temple [coil, pagoda] in front of the vimaunam [q.v.], but this is more properly called Mantapam [q.v.]. Distinguish from chuttram [q.v.]. Constantly used as suffix for place names [chowky, moosaufer khana].

CHAUVER (چاور - chávar, *Hind.*). From (cháhúra, mahr. the measure). Superficial measure. 120 beegahs = 1 chauver [alavay, 2 e]. Approximate actual value, 1 chauver = 75 acres. Varies with beegah. Same as candy applied to land.

CHAUYAY (छाया - chháyá, *San.*). From (chhad, san. to cover). Shadow, the consort of Sooryan.——*Chauyah sootan* (छायासुत - chháyásuta, San.). From (above + suta, san. son). Born from darkness. One of the names of Saturn [shany].——*Madhyama chauyay* (मध्यमछाया - madhyamachháyá, San.). From (madhyama, san. middle + above). The midday shadow of a gnomon [shunk].——*Sama mundala chauyay* (सममण्डलछाया - samamandalachháyá, San.). From (sama, san. equal + mandala, san. disc + above). The midday shadow of a gnomon when the sun is east or west of it.——*Vishoova chauyay* (विषुवछाया - vishuvachháyá, San.). From (vishu, san. equinox + above). The shadow of a gnomon when the sun is in the equinoctial points [ayanam, jyotisham].

CHAYROOT (چرول - chirval, *Hind.*; چرول کا جهاڑ - chirvalká-jhar, *Dec.*; ಚಾಯಬೇರು - cháyabéru, *Can.*; చిరివేరు - chiriveru, *Tel.*; ସୁରବୁଳି - surbuli, *Oor.*; ചായവേർ - cháyavér, *Mal.*; සායමුල් - sayamul, *Singh.*; சாயவேர் - sháyavér, *Tam.*). Title from malayalam. Can. from (cháya, can. color + béru, can. root). Tel. from (chiru, tel. small + véru, tel. root). Mal. from (cháyam, mal. color + vér, mal. root). Hind. also (chirvalkílakrí), meaning chirwal wood. Tam. also (imbúral), meaning iron-taint plant; (irámésuvaramvér), meaning rameshwaram root, from place of growth; (shiruvér), meaning small + root. Title othewise Chiroovair, Chirwal, Dye root, Indian madder, Rameshwaram root, Shauyavair. Botanically Oldenlandia [field parpatam] umbellata, linn., rubiaceæ [vricsham, 71]. Alias Hedyotis hispida, indica, umbellata; Oldenlandia hispida, puberula. Small plant, suffruticose, erect or diffuse, slightly scabrous; calyx four-parted; corolla rotate, four-cleft; leaves opposite or verticillate, linear, paler on the under side, margins recurved; stipules ciliated with bristles; peduncles alternate, axillary, bearing a short raceme; partial peduncles one to three-flowered; capsule globose with a wide dehiscence; flowers white. Weedy annual or biennial; growing spontaneously in sandy soil near the sea and extensively cultivated on coromandel coast; small, narrow, pale-green leaves. Cultivated roots orange-colored, very slender and from one to two feet, but wild are shorter and yield more coloring matter; the coloring matter resides entirely in the bark of the root, the inner portion being white and useless; roots of two years' growth are preferred when procurable; chayroot rapidly deteriorates by being kept in any dark place. Cultivated in sandy soil on sea coast; ground prepared on coromandel in pooshyam or january, maugham or february, and phaulgoonam [mausam] or march, land being first dug with momatties [q.v.] and then ploughed up four times and levelled; grounds afterwards watered regularly; seed sown in phaulgoonam or march and cheitram or april; seeds of one-fourth maunica [q.v.] mixed with sand of 16 maunicas are sown direct on the land; watered daily twice for nine days through sieve of palmyra [q.v.] fibre, so that the seeds may not be disturbed; on the tenth day when seeds sprout water mixed with dung is sprinkled on the crop by hand; from the eleventh day pure water is sprinkled forenoon and afternoon; thenceforward watered more rarely; after three months cattle dung mixed with sand is sprinkled; after six months the crop is rooted up; brought to market after one month; average price, 9 imperial seers for 1 rupee. The leaves are expectorant; dried and powdered are mixed with flour and made into cakes, and given in asthmatic complaints and consumption. Roots yield a blue dye, which by different mordants [cauram] is changed from pale to a very deep red, and with which turbans and handkerchiefs are dyed; the basis of the dye is alizarine; chayroot holds the same place amongst indian dye stuffs as madder does in europe; for producing the brilliant and fast red dye for which madras handkerchiefs were once famous, it is used along with the morinda [dyeing mulberry], and with alum [padicauram] as a mordant; when employed with ventilago [pappily] it gives the chocolate color formerly so much prized in the bandana [q.v.] or poolicat handkerchief; with iron [auban] it gives a black, and with safflower [bastard saffron], lime [choonam] juice and soda [munn cauram] an unstable red color [shauyam]. The following is a detailed account of the mode of dyeing yarn with chayroot:—The yarn, being washed and untwisted that it may not become entangled, and being so separated that every part may be equally penetrated by the coloring matter, is divided into bundles of thirty or forty threads, through each of which at the middle and extremities a cotton thread is loosely sewed, but so as to allow of every thread being exposed to the sun's rays when hung up, and the threads spread out on a bamboo. The yarn is washed and cleansed in cold water, aided by half an hour's manipulation; it is then kept in water in covered vessels till it acquires a putrid smell, which takes place in from twenty-four to thirty-six hours, and during this period it is occasionally pressed and worked for a quarter of an hour together; it is then washed as clean as possible, beaten on a stone or earthen pot, and hung up to dry. While this process is going on, a lye or mordant [cauram] is prepared of the ashes of the plantain [q.v.] or other tree in cold water; it is an object to have the lye of sufficient strength, which is determined by adding to a small quantity about half as much gingelly [q.v.] oil and giving to it a gentle motion; should it turn immediately white, having no visible globules of oil swimming on the surface, it is good; the quantity required of clean lye being poured off and strained, sheep dung, in the proportion of three ounces to a pint of lye, is dissolved in one-half of it; and this solution is again strained; the other half of the lye is mixed with half its bulk of gingelly oil and half as much tsiky or saponaceous water procured during and retained from former process, being, in fact, a solution of soap in water; the two liquors are then mixed together, and if things are favorable a milky scum arises; the proportions required for say half a pound of yarn would be, gingelly oil half a pint by two pints, tsiky a quarter of a pint, sheep dung two or three ounces. The yarn having been soaked in this mordant is dried in the sun for some hours; it is then again soaked and dried as before; the same night it is treated with an additional portion of mordant, is put into covered vessels, and allowed to remain till morning; if any mordant remain the same process is again repeated; the yarn is at night moistened with the lye first prepared, diluted with one-third of its bulk of water, and put into covered vessels; the yarn in drying, should have the position constantly changed, to prevent the lye from accumulating in the lower part; next day the yarn is spread out to dry; then it is taken in at night, and treated with lye; this alternate soaking or thorough moistening with lye at night and exposure during the day are continued without intermission till the yarn appears saturated with lye, or in fact till the oil is converted into soap [sauboon]; this, if the lye is sufficiently strong, may occupy five days; this is ascertained by washing a few inches from off the bundle in water holding some astringent in solution; a whitish scum will arise, and it is from the feeling of this scum when worked between the hands, and the appearance of it afterwards, that the state is determined; the workman being satisfied of the completion of this process, the yarn is again moistened for one day, morning and evening, with much diluted lye or plain water; the yarn may be immediately washed, but the process is much improved by retaining it for some weeks, to allow the animalizing matter to get fixed; the yarn is then washed in a tank till nothing of the mordant seemingly remains, but the smell and a certain softness to the touch; occasionally the whole process is again repeated. The yarn being thus thoroughly impregnated with the mordant, a cold infusion of cassa [q.v.] leaves in water is made, and after some hours the yarn is put into it and handled in such a manner as to expose every thread to its action; it is allowed to remain therein all night; the quantity of leaf used in the infusion is so great that it resembles a paste; next morning the water is wrung out from the yarn, the adhering leaves are shaken off, and fresh leaves with an equal quantity of chayroot substituted; for half a pound of yarn a handful of each is sufficient; after two hours the yarn is laid in the liquor; the same process is repeated on the third day; by this time the yarn usually changes to a reddish-yellow color, with occasional red spots. A liquor in which to soak the yarn is now prepared of a handful of chayroot in water; on the fourth day the yarn will appear in the evening of a light red color; it is treated in the same manner as on preceding days, and a similar liquor to the last-named is prepared for soaking it in at night. On the fifth day the yarn is washed in a tank, and afterwards dried in the sun; as usual, for soaking it in at night, a liquor is prepared of pounded cassa leaves, mixed with gingelly oil sufficient to form a dry paste, of which about half an ounce is mixed in the usual portion of water; after standing two hours, a handful of chayroot is added, and the yarn immediately immersed for the night. The mode of proceeding on the sixth day is similar, but the liquor for the night is prepared wholly of chayroot. On the seventh day the yarn is again washed, dried, etc.; on this and the next day it is immersed in a liquor composed of equal parts of cassa leaves and chayroot in water. The yarn is now boiled in a liquor composed of that strained from it at the last night's process, with the addition of chayroot, a handful for half a pound of yarn, and sufficient water to give room to agitate the yarn freely; the pot containing the liquor is placed on the fire, which is kept up briskly till it begins to boil; it is then kept simmering till a rose-colored froth rises and covers the surface, when the fire is withdrawn, and the pot with its contents allowed to cool gradually; during the boiling the contents of the pot are stirred quickly, so as to expose the yarn as little as possible to the action of the air. When cold, the yarn is taken out and washed in a tank, beaten as usual, and dried in the sun; its color should be a bright and lively red; if it fail, it is occasionally brightened by steeping once more in a liquor composed with cassa leaves and chayroot, the former being mixed first with a little gingelly oil; a temporary brilliancy is further given by putting it in a cold infusion of sappan [q.v.] wood. See also Shauyam for dyeing with other dyes.——*Counterfeit chayroot* (இம்பூறற்சக்களத்தி - imbúrar-chakkalatti, Tam.). Title from inferiority. Tam. from (imbúral, tam. oldenlandia umbellata, linn. + shakkalatti, tam. rival wife); meaning counterfeit chayroot. Botanically Oldenlandia [field parpatam] dichotoma, kœn., rubiaceæ [vricsham, 71]. Alias Hedyotis affinis, dichotoma, diffusa, linifolia; Oldenlandia affinis, capillaris, linifolia, pusilla. Annual, erect or decumbent with erect branches; branches slightly four-angled, scabrous on the angles; leaves linear, attenuated at both ends, flaccid; stipules usually with two to three bristles, sometimes without any; flowers on long and capillary pedicels, rarely axillary and solitary, sometimes two to three from the apex of a slender elongated peduncle, usually several, arranged in very lax peduncled axillary or terminal naked racemes; corolla infundibuliform; capsule nearly globose, with a not very prominent ridge on the apex; flowers white; flowering in rainy season.——*Wild chayroot* (क्षेत्रपर्पटी - kshétraparpatí, San.; کھیت پاپر - khetpápar, Hind.; వెర్రినేలవేము - verrinélavému, Tel.; වල්පත්පාඩගම් - valpatpádagam, Singh.). San. from (kshétra, san. field + parpata, san. mollugo genus). Cf. mollugo stricta [wild tirye]. Tel. from (verri, tel. mad + nélavému, tel. andrographis paniculata, nees.). Singh. from (val, singh. jungle + patpádagam, singh. mollugo cerviana, sering.). Botanically Oldenlandia [field parpatam] corymbosa, linn., rubiaceæ [vricsham, 71]. Alias Hedyotis biflora, burmanniana, intermedia; Oldenlandia biflora, herbacea, ramosa. Annual, diffuse, glabrous or scabrous; leaves linear or linear-lanceolate, tapering at both ends; peduncles solitary, axillary, alternate, shorter than the leaves, one to three-flowered; corolla shortly-tubular; calyx-segments in fruit somewhat subulate, distant, with the sinus wide; capsule glabrous, roundish-ovate, gibbous at the base, narrower towards the crown; flowers small, white; flowering in rainy season. Whole plant used medicinally in decoction, alterative.

• CHEBEERA (اطريلال - atrílál, *Hind.*; ಸೀಬಿಗಿಡ - síbigida, *Can.*; చేబీర - chébíra, *Tel.*; കാരക്കാഞ്ഞിരം - kárakkáññiram, *Mal.*; මහනෙලු - mahanelu, *Singh.*; காரக்கானிராம் - kárakkánirám, *Tam.*). Title from teloogoo. Tel. from (chédu, tel. bitter + bíra, tel. luffa acutangula, rox.). Mal. from (kár, mal. black + káññiram, mal. strychnos nux-vomica, linn.). Singh. from (maha, singh. great + nelu, singh. strobilanthes sp.). Tam. from malayalam. Title otherwise Bitter luffa. Botanically Peristrophe bicalyculata, nees, acanthaceæ [vricsham, 101]. Alias Dianthera bicalyculata, malabarica; Justicia bicalyculata, ligulata, malabarica. Stem hexagonal, bough and hairy; leaves ovate-acuminate, glabrous or puberulous, peduncles axillary, bitrifid, their branches dichotomous; flowers solitary, pale-rose; common involucre of one leaf linear, double the length of the flower-head; calyx small, membranaceous; corolla pubescent, nearly half an inch long; flowering in cold season. Whole plant, macerated in an infusion of rice, a remedy in poisonous snake-bites; has properties of fumitory and is used in its stead, but has not its bitterness. Other common species are:—lanceolaria, montana, undulata. Cf. French chiretta.

CHECKBUNDY (چك بندى - chakbandí, *Hind.*). From (chak, hind. division of land + bandí, hind. limit). Defining of boundaries of detached piece of land [inam].

CHEE (چهی - chhí, *Hind.*). Fie.——*Cheechee* (چهی چهی - chhíchhí, Hind.). A disparaging term applied to half-castes.

CHEEKATY (చీకటి - chíkati, • *Tel.*). From (chitkiti, oor. a wild hog). Ancient zemindarry, Village; Ganjam dist., pop. of village 3,396; square miles 118; lat. of village 19° 12′; long. 84° 40′; from Berhampore S.W. 13 miles; from Chetterpore W.S.W. 27 miles. South-east of Pedda kimedy. In general open and well cultivated. Watered by the Bauhoodah. Said to have been granted by a king of Cuttack to Kashauno, a Sirdar, who conquered the country from the aboriginal wild tribes, and built a fort in A.D. 881. The number of villages is 129 and the country is divided into the six mittahs of Bodopolonko, Cotilingy, Jayantipooram, Krishnapooram, Patrapooram and Talatampara. The last named mittah is entirely separated from the rest of the estate and is the most fertile. The present zemindar is Shree vishwambhara rajendra deo. Peshcush Rs. 33,904. The Rajah possesses a substantially-built house at Cheekaty.

CHEEMA (చీమ - chíma, *Tel.*). Ant [choomtee].——*Cheemacoorty* (చీమకుర్తి - chímakurti, Tel.). From (chíma, tel. ant + gutti, tel. collection). Tel. also (chímakutika), meaning ant + hut. Village, Hill; Nellore dist., Ongole tal.; pop. 3,407; acres 14,282; lat. 15° 35′; long. 79° 55′; from Nellore N. 78½ miles; from Ongole W.N.W. 13 miles; from the sea W. 24 miles. On trunk road from Ongole to Cumbum. The deity is Sautchy ramalingasawmy, that at Ramateertam at foot of hill is Mocsharamalingasawmy. The ascent to the hill is exceedingly difficult, otherwise it could be made a good hot weather resort. Trig. station in lat. 15° 37′ 12·36″; long. 79° 52′ 04·69″; height 2,093 feet; from Ongole W.N.W. 17 miles; from the sea W. 23 miles.

CHEEN (चीन - chína, *San.*; چين - chín, *Hind.*; சீனம் - shínam, *Tam.*). China [bhoogolashastram, cathay, china].

CHEEPOORPULLY (చీపురుపల్లె - chípurupalle, • *Tel.*). From (chípuru, tel. broom + palle, tel. village). Tel. also (kótachípurupalle), meaning fort + the place.——(1) Division, Vizagapatam district; area 547 square miles; population 138,896; language Teloogoo. N. coast of district. Boundaries:—north, Palcondah talook; east, Chicacole talook of Ganjam and Bay of Bengal; south, Bay of Bengal and Bimlipatam division; west, Vizianagram and Gajapatinugger talooks and Bobbily division. Dry barren tract excepting a few localities. Intersected by hillocks in several places. Soil is of the red ferruginous series and sandy, with nodulous kankar [q.v.] underlying. Tobacco [pogauk] and chillies [chilly] are largely exported. Fine cloths of native thread are woven and exported to various places. Camping ground at Ranastalam. Places of archæological interest:—Cheepoorpully, Cotapollem, Dooppalvalsa, Gadabavalsa, Gargoobilly, Goozerattipett, Sher mahomed pooram. Principal trig. stations:—Cotcherla beacon, Pindy, Ramchendrapooram beacon, Rauvipulley, Tamauda, Yerramunty. The leading places, &c., in the division are the following.——*Bontalacodoor* (బొంతలకోడూరు - bontalakódúru, Tel.). From (bonta, tel. quilt + kódúru, tel. place so called). Important village; pop. 2,109; lat. 18° 28′; long. 83° 26′; from Cheepoorpully N.W. 16 miles; from Vizagapatam N. 52 miles; from the sea N. 46 miles. Residence of Puttsauley proprietors of Ganjam. Trade in tobacco and chillies. Manufacture of fine cloths with native thread.——*Cheepoorpully* (చీపురుపల్లె - chípurupalle, Tel.). See below.——*Cooppily* (కుప్పిలి - kuppili, Tel.). From (kuppa, tel. heap + palli, tel. village). Proprietary estate, Village, Salt station; pop. 2,696; lat. of village 18° 10′; long. 83° 51′; from Cheepoorpully S.E. 18 miles; from Vizagapatam N.E. 47 miles; from the sea N. 1 mile. Consists of sixteen Jiroyaty [q.v.]

villages with some advantage for irrigation. Peshcush Rs. 8,429.——*Cotcherla beacon* (కొచ్చర్ల - koççarla, Tel.). From (kóta, tel. fort + cherla, tel. village). Trig. station; lat. 18° 09′ 00·90″; long. 83° 49′ 34·42″; from Cheepoorpully S.E. 18 miles; from Cooppily S.W. 2½ miles; from the sea N. 1 mile.——*Dooppalvalsa* (దుప్పలవలస - duppalavalasa, Tel.). From (duppi, tel. spotted deer + valasa, tel. colony). Village; pop. 415; lat. 18° 09′; long. 83° 47′; from Cheepoorpully S.E. 15 miles; from Vizagapatam N.E. 42 miles; from the sea N. 2 miles. Close to Chicacole, on the Vizagapatam side of the river. Old mosques, pillar, called Boorralcote, fifteen feet high, said to have been built by Mussalmans with the skulls of fallen enemies [chicacole].——*Kintaly* (కింతలి - kintali, Tel.). From (kindu, tel. low + talamu, tel. ground). Proprietary estate, Village; pop. 1,783; lat. of village 18° 20′; long. 83° 54′; from Cheepoorpully E. 19 miles; from Vizagapatam N.E. 56 miles; from the sea N. 10 miles. Cloth manufactures. The estate is fertile and contains 11 villages in all. Peshcush Rs. 7,349.——*Pindy* (పిండి - pindi, Tel.). Means flour. Trig. station; lat. 18° 19′ 41·97″; long. 83° 47′ 39·87″; from Cheepoorpully E. 12 miles; from Pondore S. 1 mile; from the sea N. 13 miles.——*Pondore* (పొందూరు - pondúru, Tel.). From (ponnu, tel. gold + úru, tel. village). Pop. 4,682; lat. 18° 21′; long. 83° 48′; from Cheepoorpully E. 12 miles; from Vizagapatam N.E. 53 miles; from the sea N. 15 miles. Manufacture of cloths.——*Ramchendrapooram beacon* (రామచంద్రపురము - rámachandrapuramu, Tel.). From (rámachandrudu, tel. proper name + pura, san. town). Trig. station; lat. 18° 07′ 18·44″; long. 83° 44′ 44·01″; from Cheepoorpully S.E. 15 miles; from the sea N. 2 miles.——*Ranastalam* (రణస్థలము - ranast'halamu, Tel.). From (rana, san. battle + st'hala, san. a place). Village; pop. 1,771; lat. 18° 12′; long. 83° 45′; from Cheepoorpully S.E. 12 miles; from Vizagapatam N.E. 43 miles; from the sea N. 6 miles. Camping station. Choultry [q.v.] and rest-house. Head-quarter of Cotapollem tannah [q.v.].——*Rauvipulley* (రావిపల్లె - rávipalle, Tel.). From (rávi, tel. peepul tree, ficus religiosa, linn. + palle, tel. village). Trig. station; lat. 18° 15′ 03·36″; long. 83° 51′ 11·18″; from Cheepoorpully E. 17 miles; from the sea N. 7 miles.——*Sher mahomedpooram* (شیر محمد پور - shermuhammadpúr, Hind.; షేరుమహమ్మదుపురము - shérumahammadupuramu, Tel.). Proprietary estate, Village; pop. 2,492; lat. 18° 17′; long. 83° 53′; from Cheepoorpully E. 17 miles; from Vizagapatam N.E. 54 miles; from the sea N. 9 miles. So named by Runga row, its founder, in honor of the designation Sher of his patron Sher mahomed khan, Fowjdar [q.v.] of Chicacole. Ruins of a palace and old mosques. The estate consists of 27 villages and has some fine tanks. Is in close proximity to Chicacole. Peshcush Rs. 19,325.——*Tamauda* (తామాడ - támáda, Tel.). From (támara, tel. lotus, nelumbium speciosum, willd. + váda, tel. village). Trig. station; lat. 18° 11′ 00·00″; long. 83° 48′ 00·00″.——*Yerramunty* (ఎర్రమంటి - yarramanti, Tel.). From (erra, tel. red + mannu, tel. soil). Trig. station; lat. 18° 16′ 15·98″; long. 83° 55′ 19·22″; from Cheepoorpully E. 20 miles; from the sea N. 6 miles.——**(2)** Deputy tahsildarry, Vizagapatam district. Pay Rs. 70.——**(3)** Town, Deputy tahsildar's station; Vizagapatam dist., Cheepoorpully division; pop. 2,658; lat. 18° 18′; long. 83° 37′; from Coraputt E.S.E. 66 miles; from Madras N.E. 417 miles; from Narsapatam N.E. 77 miles; from Parvatipore S.S.E. 33 miles; from Vizagapatam N.N.E 45 miles; from Vizianagram N.E. 19 miles; from the sea N. 20 miles. Also called Cotacheepoorpully from the fact of its having once contained a fort built by a family named Mandapautivaur. Fort south of the village. Is the head-quarter of the Ameen of the Coomaraum tannah.

CHEER (सरल - sarala, *San.*; صنوبرالهند - sanobarulhind, *Ar.*; صنوبر هندی - sanobarihindí, *Pers.*; سرل - saral, *Hind.*; چیرکا جھاڑ - chírkájhár, *Dec.*; దేవదారు - dévadáru, *Tel.*; ചരലം - charalam, *Mal.*; හාවා - hává, *Singh.*; சுருள்தேவதாரி - shuruldévathári, *Tam.*). Title from deccany. San. means straight. Ar. from (sanobar, ar. deodar, cedrus deodara, loud. + hind, ar. indian). Pers. from arabic [deodar]. Hind. from sanscrit. Tel. from (déva, san. god + dáru, san. wood) [deccany deodar, deodar, large neeroory]. Mal. from sanscrit. Tam. from (sarala, san. the tree + déva, san. deity + dáru, san. pine). San. also (shrívása), meaning lutchmy + abode. Tam. also (shímaithévathári), meaning foreign + erythroxylon monogynum, roxb. Title otherwise Emodi pine, English deodar, Ganda firoza tree, Long-leaved pine, Sharal. Botanically Pinus [devadauram] longifolia, roxb., coniferæ [vricsham]. N. indian tree. Exudes, or yields to incisions, a very fine turpentine called Ganda firoza [q.v.]; tar [keel] is also obtained from it. Ganda firoza used internally as a stomachic, and externally as a plaster applied to abscesses for suppuration. Wood like deodar [q.v.], employed for making torches; a substitute for english deal.

CHEERA (ചീര - chíra, *Mal.*). From (jíra, san. cuminum cyminum, linn.); grain resembling seeds of cumin [jeerah]. A Malabar paddy. Congan cheera means the Congoo country whence introduced; Cottampaula cheera means seeds of coriandrum sativum, linn., from fragrancy; Custoory cheera means musk, from smell [paddy].

CHEETAH (चित्रक - chitraka, *San.*; चित्ता - chittá, *Mahr.*; نمر - namir, *Ar.*; یوز - yúz, *Pers.*; چیتا - chítá, *Hind.*; ಚಿರತೆ - chirate, *Can.*; ಕಿರುಬ - kiruba, *Coorg*; ಚಿರ್ತೆ - chirte, *Too.*; చిరుతపులి - chirutapuli, *Tel.*; କୋରଡପୋତ୍ରିଆ - koradapottria, *Oor.*; ചെമ്പുലി - chempuli, *Mal.*; චිත්‍රක - chitraka, *Singh.*; சிறுத்தைப்புலி - shiruttaippuli, *Tam.*). Title from hindostany. San. from (chitra, san. variegated). Mahr. from sanscrit. Ar. from (namara, ar. spotted). Pers. from (úzídan, pers. to seek); as used in hunting. Hind. from sanscrit. Can. from (chiru, can. small). Coorg from (kiru, can. small). Tel. from (chiruta, tel. small + puli, tel. tiger). Mal. from (chem, mal. red + puli, mal. tiger). Tam. from (shiruttai, tam. cheetah + puli, tam. tiger). San. also (chitravyághra), meaning spotted tiger. Pers. also (yúzpalang), meaning cheetah tiger. Hind. also (lakarbágh), means tree-tiger. Can. also (sivangi). Called also the Hunting leopard because trained to hunt the antelope. Cynaelurus jubatus, felidæ [deeptaucsham] digitigrada, carnivora, mammalia [sastanam, 9], of naturalists [jantoo]. Alias Felis jubata, guttata, venatica; Gueparda guttata. This animal was the Leopardus of the ancients, who considered, with the Arabs of the present day in Northern africa, that it was a breed between the lion and the pard; arguing from the mane or tuft of hair on the neck. To this species the English have applied the Indian name cheetah, which however is a name really for all spotted cats; cheetah-baugh being spotted tiger, cheetal the spotted deer, &c. A tall, slim animal, with body much drawn in at the flanks like a greyhound; purely cat-like head with short round ears; long tail, much compressed at the end; in color a bright rufous fawn, more or less deep, sometimes a bright nankeen, dotted with numerous small black spots which are single, and not in rosettes, as in the pards; a black streak from the corner of the eye down the face; ears black at base externally, the rest whitish; the tail spotted, but having three or four black rings at the tip, and the extreme tip is always white; the hair of the belly is lengthened with a shaggy fringe-like appearance; the fur generally is coarse; the nozzle is black, whereas in the tiger it is pink, and in a pard dusky pink; the pupils of the eye contract circularly. The cheetah is in much request as a necessary appanage to regal state among native rulers. For this purpose the adult animal is always caught, it being considered that a young leopard would never turn out well for the purposes of the chase. Antelope [jinka], gazelle [q.v.], and nilghye [q.v.] are its chief food in the wild state. On a hunting party, the cheetah is carried on a cart, hooded; and when the game is raised the hood is taken off. The cheetah then leaps down, sometimes on the opposite side to its prey, and pursues the antelope. If the latter are near the cart, the cheetah springs forward with amazing velocity, perhaps exceeding that which any other quadruped possesses. This great velocity is not unlike the sudden spring by which the tiger seizes its prey, but it is often continued for three or four hundred yards. If within this distance the cheetah does not seize its prey, he stops; but apparently more from anger or disappointment than from fatigue for his attitude is fierce; and he has been known immediately afterwards to pursue with equal rapidity another antelope that happened to be passing. If the game is at too great a distance when the cheetah's eyes are uncovered, he in general gallops after it until it approaches so near that he can seize it by a rapid spring. This gallop is as quick as the course of well-mounted horsemen. Sometimes, but rarely, the cheetah endeavours to approach the game by stealth, and goes round a hill or rock until he can come upon it by surprise. An oil obtained from the cheetah's intestines is used in cases of rheumatic affections like tiger fat. The bones and hair are reduced to powder and mixed with gingelly [q.v.] oil, blue stone [mayil toottam] or bichloride of mercury [rascapoor], and used as an application in cases of syphilitic complaints. The flesh, boiled in milk, has virtues in epilepsy [honiga, pooly].

CHEETAL (पृषत - prishata, *San.*; چیتل - chítal, *Hind.*; ماجنگن توتول - mánjangantutul, *Malay*; ಸಾರಗ - sáraga, *Can.*; దుప్పి - duppi, *Tel.*; ଝ୍ୟାଥୋ - jhyátho, *Oor.*; പുള്ളിമാൻ - pullimán, *Mal.*; புள்ளிமான் - pullimán, *Tam.*). Title from hindostany. San. from (prish, san. to sprinkle); sprinkled with white spots. Hind. from (chitra, san. spotted). Malay from (mánjangan, malay, deer, cervus rusa + tutul, malay, spotted). Can. from (sáranga, san. spotted). Tam. from (pulli, tam. spot + mán, tam. deer). Hind. also (chitra), from sanscrit meaning variegated; also (chitri). Can. also (hulle), meaning spotted one. Title otherwise Gangetic stag, Spotted deer. Axis maculatus, cervidæ [mrigam], ruminantia, mammalia [sastanam, 24], of naturalists [jantoo]. Alias Cervus axis, nudipalpebra; axis major et medius. General color yellow or rufous fawn with numerous white spots, and a dark dorsal streak from the nape to the tail; head brownish and the muzzle dark; chin, throat and neck in front white; lower parts and thighs internally, whitish; ears brown externally, white within; tail longish, white beneath. The basal tine is directed forwards, and in old individuals has often one or two points near the base. Length, about 4½ to nearly 5 feet; height at shoulder 36 to 38 inches. Found along the Western and Eastern ghauts [q.v.], Northern circars [q.v.],

&c. Incinerated antler gives Hartshorn [sing]. Not here found is Axis porcinus or hog deer.

CHEHOOR (چهور - chehur, *Hind.*). Large mountain ebony.

CHEITRAM (चैत्र - chaitra, *San.*). The first solar month [mausam].——*Cheitrotsavam* (சைத்திரோற்சவம் - shaittirórchavam, Tam.). From (above + utsava, san. feast). Otherwise Chittray tirvizhah. Solar festival [pundigay, 2d], held in the first solar month Chittray [mausam], i.e., between 12th April and 12th May. Feast at Madura.

CHEITYAM (चैत्य - chaitya, *San.*). From (chitá, san. funeral pyre). Originally meant some funeral monument. Rock-cut assembly halls of the Booddhists found on the west coast. These halls correspond in every respect with the churches of the Christian religion. Their plans, the position of the altar or relic casket, the aisles, and other peculiarities are the same in both, and their uses are identical, in so far as the ritual forms of the one religion resemble those of the other. The monuments which are in S. india called topes [q.v.] or stoopams are called cheityams in Nepaul. Distinguish from Vihauram [q.v.].

CHELAH (چیلہ - chelá, *Hind.*). From (chéta, san. servant). Disciple. Especially Hindoo-converted to Mahomedanism.

CHELAMA (చెలమ - chelama, *Tel.*). Freshwater pond scooped out of sand on sea-shore and in dry river beds [casham, oott].

CHELICA (చెలిక - chelika, *Tel.*). Fallow field; suffix in place names as Chintalchelica, meaning the fallow with the tamarind trees.

CHELINGO (ചലാന്തി - chalanti, *Mal.*; சலங்கு - shalangu, *Tam.*). From arab. (shalandi). W. coast sailing vessel.

CHELLAM (अचल - achala, *San.*). From (a, san. negative prefix + chal, san. to move); a mountain. Anglo-indian suffix in mountain and place names as Vriddhauchellam, meaning ancient + mountain.——*Chelamayya* (చలమయ్య - chalamayya, Tel.). From (achala, san. mountain + ayya, tel. master). Hindoo 2nd or pers. name. Similar are Chelamanna, Chelapaty, &c. [peyar].

CHELLAN (چلان - chalán, *Hind.*). From (chal, san. to go). Literally, going. A pass or way-bill for persons or goods [rawauna]. Hence chellan paper or coarse country paper [caugaz].

CHELLOO (చెల్లు - chellu, *Tel.*). From (chellu, tel. to pass as money). Payment.——*Chelloo bauky* (ಸಲ್ಲುಬಾಕಿ - sallubáki, Can.; చెల్లుబాకి - chellubáki, Tel.). From (báki, ar. balance). Annual statement of demand, collection and balance of revenue in a village [dowle vasool bauky, jumma vasool bauky]. See vol. I, 112.

CHEM (చెం - chem, *Tel.*; ചെം - chem, *Mal.*; செம் - shem, *Tam.*). Red. Beautiful. Prefix in place names as Chemmalacherry, meaning village of the red mountain [shen].——*Chemboo* (செம்பு - shembu, Tam.). Means a metal-pot. Liquid measure. 3¼ seers = 1 chemboo; 4 chemboos = 1 paunay [alavay, 4 a]. Approximate actual value, 1 chemboo = 216 cubic inches. Trichinopoly wholesale for ghee. Compare cooncham of Ganjam, mercaul of Tanjore, bullah of Trichinopoly. Chemboo krishnan is Krishnan in one of his manifestations, as a child carrying a pot.——*Chembrambaukam* (செம்பரம்பாக்கம் - shembarambákkam, Tam.). From (above + parambu, tam. hill + pákkam, tam. village). Zemindarry, Village; Chingleput dist., Sydapett tal.; pop. 910; acres 1,182; lat. 13° 02′; long. 80° 07′; from Madras W. 16 miles; from Sydapett W. 11 miles; from the sea W. 15 miles. In S.W. of talook. Has immense tank, which derives supply from anicut thrown across Cooum at Corattore through new Bungaur channel. Like the Red hills tank, an old work extended and improved. 20 miles in circuit. See vol. I, 403. There is a Tamul proverb:—செம்பரம் பாக்கத்தான் பெயர் பெற்றான் மாங்காட்டான் நீர் பெற்றான்—"Those "at Chembrambaukam get the name, those at Maungaud get the "water;" meaning that the tank does not benefit the former village.——*Chempay* (ചെമ്പ - chempa, Mal.). Same as Common sesban.——*Chenat nayar* (ചെനാട്ട് നായർ - chenáttunáyar, Mal.); called after a person of that name. Government forest; Malabar district, Palghaut talook. Escheated in early years of century to Government. Contains Yelivaul or Rat's tail hill well known to ibex [saddle back] hunters and two forest rest-houses, one at Carimala and one at Dhony.——*Chenchely mullay* (చెంచెలిమల - chenchelimala, Tel.). From (chennu, tel. beautiful + cheli, tel. damsel + mala, tel. hill). Village, Hill; Kurnool dist., Bunganapully native state; pop. 1,895; lat. 15° 09′; long. 78° 21′; from Bunganapully S.S.E. 12 miles; from Kurnool S.S.E. 50 miles. Formerly a separate estate, but in 1814 added to Bunganapully.——*Chengalroya* (చెంగల్రాయుడు - chengalráyadu, Tel.). From (above + kaluva, tel. lily + ráyadu, tel. king). Vishnoo, lord of the red lily or lotus [nelumbo]. Also Soobramanyan. Hindoo 2nd or pers. name [peyar].——*Chengam* (செங்கம் - shengam, Tam.). From (above + kamam, tam. field).—"*a*" Deputy tahsildarry, South arcot district. Pay Rs. 70.—"*b*" Town, Deputy tahsildar's station, Pass; South arcot dist., Trinomallee tal.; pop. 2,231; acres 2,210; lat. 12° 19′; long. 78° 50′; from Chidambaram N.W. 87 miles; from Cuddalore W.N.W. 76 miles; from Madras S.W. 116 miles; from Tindivanam W. 57 miles; from Tricalore N.W. 37 miles; from Trinomallee W.N.W. 19¾ miles; from Vriddhauchellam N.W. 64 miles. Two old Shiva and Vishnoo temples and old temple of Cauly; inscriptions of Chola and Vijianugger. The pass connects Salem and South arcot. It lies between lat. 12° 21′ and 12° 23′ 45″ N.; long. 78° 50′ and 78° 52′ 35″ E. As the direct route to the Baramahaul [q.v.] from the Carnatic [q.v.], it has been the scene of several important events. In 1760, Makhdoomally entered the Carnatic by this pass; and here, in 1767, Hyder ally, pursuing the British in their retreat on Trinomalee, received a severe defeat. In 1791 Tippoo led his forces, the last army that invaded the British carnatic, by the same route.——*Chengammah* (చెంగమ్మ - chengamma, Tel.; செங்கம்மா - shengammá, Tam.). From (above + amma, tel. mother); epithet of lutchmy, the beautiful. Familiarly Chennoo. Hindoo 2nd or pers. name [peyar].——*Chenna basaya* (ಚೆನ್ನಬಸವ - chennabasava, Can.). From (chenna, can. beautiful + basava, can. proper name). The nephew of the elder basava [q.v.]. He succeeded as head of the new sect of Lingayets [q.v.], on the death of his uncle. The harana basagy ascribed to him is a philosophical statement of the new phase of the Sheiva creed. The Chenna basava pooraunam is also ascribed to him. In this the Bramins are derided. It was evidently written after the overthrow of the Jeinas.——*Chennacooppam* (చెన్నకుప్పము - chennakuppamu, Tel.). From (chennappa, tel. proper name + kuppam, tam. hamlet). Original name of Madras [chennaputnam].——*Chennakeshavan* (చెన్నకేశవుడు - chennakéshavudu, Tel.). From (above + késhavudu, tel. vishnu). Hindoo 2nd or pers. name [peyar].——*Chennungy* (नाना - náná, Mahr.; ಚನ್ನಂಗಿಮರ - channangimara, Can.; చెన్నంగి - chennangi, Tel.; ସଲୋର - salora, Oor.; கச்சக்கட்டைமரம் - kaççakkattaimaram, Tam.). Title from teloogoo. Can. from (channa, can red + angi, can. body + mara, can. tree); from the wood. Tel. from (chennu, tel. beauty + anga, san. body). Tam. from (kaççal, tam. tender + kattai, tam. wood + maram, tam. tree). Tel. also (chinángi). Title otherwise Loose strife. Botanically Lagerstrœmia [cadaly] parviflora, roxb., lythraceæ [vricsham, 58]. Tree; branches quadrangular; leaves opposite, entire, from oblong or oval and obtuse to ováte and acute, pale beneath; peduncles axillary, three to six-flowered; calyx six-cleft, even; petals six, flattish, shortly unguiculate; the six outer stamens longer than the rest; capsule oblong, two to four-celled; flowers small, white, fragrant, very numerous. Gives a sweet gum-resin [googal]; bark used in dyeing [shauyam] skins [chamrah] black. Wood very hard, grey or greyish-brown, often with a reddish tinge, darker colored near the centre; hard, tough, elastic, seasons well, works freely, and is fairly durable; used for ploughs and other agricultural implements, for construction, for buggy shafts and axe handles; it gives a very good charcoal [kary]. There are two varieties, one with under sides of the leaves downy and the other the same glabrous.——*Chennaputnam* (چیناپٹن - chínápatan, Hind.; చెన్నపట్టణము - chennapattanamu, Tel.; சென்னப்பட்டணம் - shennappattanam, Tam.). From (shennappa, tam. proper name + pattana, san. town). Name for the enlarged Chennacooppam. Name for Madras universally now used by natives. Also called Putnam or the city by eminence [charitram].——*Chennaur* (சென்னாறு - shennáru, Tam.). From (above + áru, tam. river). Sanscrit name (sanatkumáranadí), meaning sanatcomauran son of bramha + river. River; Salem dist., Dharmapoory, Oossoor tals. Works of importance are Sungambasavan anicut and channel, supplying tank of same name near Mauraundahully and the Mullapooram anicut further down.——*Chennay* (சென்னை - shennai, Tam.). Short name for Chennaputnam.——*Chennore* (చెన్నూరు - chennúru, Tel.). From (chennu, tel. fine + úru, tel. village); after chennakeshwarasawmy, the local deity. Village; Nellore dist., Goodoor tal.; pop. 3,958; acres 8,132; lat. 14° 09′; long. 79° 50′; from Goodoor W. 3¾ miles; from Nellore S.S.W. 24 miles; from the sea W. 22 miles. Vishnoo temple to Chennakeshwarasawmy, by Chola kings.——*Chetput* (சேத்துப்பட்டு - shéttuppattu, Tam.). From (shéttu, tam. red + pattu, tam. village). Title otherwise Chittapett. Village; North arcot dist., Polore tal.; pop. 2,321; acres 1,384; lat. 12° 28′; long. 79° 23′; height 1,450 feet; from Chittore S.S.E. 55 miles; from Polore E.S.E. 15½ miles. Once head-quarters of talook in South arcot. The fort now in ruins was, next to Jinjee, the most important in this part of the Carnatic [q.v.]. Held by the Mahrattas till 1690, when it was occupied by Delhi troops. After the accession of the Carnatic nawaubs, entrusted to a killadar [q.v.] appointed by the Soobahdar of the Deccan [q.v.]. Shah nawauz khan, Nauzir jung's diwaun, fled here after the battle of Jinjee in 1750. It was again seized by the Mahrattas, but in October 1757 taken by the French. After the battle of Wandiwash in 1760, taken by Coote. In 1782 a drawn battle was fought under its walls between Hyder and the British. In 1783 by the treaty with the Mahrattas, the place was given up in exchange for Cumbum. As first constructed, the fort measured

540 yards by 430, and was defended by fourteen towers. Manufacture of native shoes. Weekly fair. Old Shiva temple with Tamul inscriptions.

CHEMOODOO (చెముడు - chemudu, *Tel.*). Means milk-hedge, euphorbia tirucalli, linn. Village, Head-quarters of zemindar; Vizagapatam dist., Saulore division; pop. 1,746; lat. 18° 38′; long. 83° 16′; from Saulore N. 8¾ miles; from Vizagapatam N. 64 miles. Ruined fort. The zemindarry was a dependency of Jeypore, and fell under Vizianagram with the rest of the hill zemindarries in the time of Poosapauty seetaram rauz. The family belong to the Condarauz caste, and their ancient title is Ranasimham. Peshcush Rs. 4,655.

CHENGAN (ചെങ്കൻ - chenkan, *Mal.*). From (shankha, san. conch). Fisherman.——*Chenganaud* (ചെന്നനാട - chennanátu, Mal.). From (above + nátu, mal. country). The old principality of Quilon.——*Chenganore* (ചെന്നന്നൂർ - chennannúr, Mal.). From (above + úr, mal. village).—"*a*" Talook, Quilon division; pop 81,301. Chenganore talook is sub-divided into seven praverties and contains 133 caras or villages. It is bounded N. by Tiroovalla talook, E. and S. by Coonnatore and Mauvelicara talooks and W. by Caurtigapully talook. Its greatest length N. to S. 12 miles and its greatest breadth from E. to W. is 20 miles. Its area is 160 square miles. Towards east a picturesque forest and towards west gravelly; soil is productive.—"*b*" Town, Tahsildar's station; Travancore state, Quilon division, Chenganore tal.; pop. 9,230; lat. 9° 17′; long. 76° 36′; from Alleppey S.E. 20 miles; from Cottayam S. 21 miles; from Madras S.W. 360 miles; from Nagarcoil N.N.W. 94 miles; from Paravore S.S.E. 62 miles; from Quilon N. 27 miles; from Trivandrum N.N.W. 61 miles; from the sea E. 10 miles. Has a large pagoda [q.v.] to Bhagavaty [q.v.]; has every January a festival lasting for a month.

CHENNA (چینا - chíná, *Hind.*). From san. Same as Varagoo.

CHENTSOO (చెంచు - chentsu, *Tel.*). Assumed as from (chañch, san. to go), from wandering habit; but probably a dravidian word. Wild tribe, found in Nellore, Kurnool, Cuddapah and Kistna.—"*a*" Chentsoo language, like Yanaudy, is merely a corrupt Teloogoo. A Chentsoo vocabulary is given in the second volume.—"*b*" The features of this tribe are small and animated; cheek bones higher and more prominent than generality; nose flatter and nostrils more expanded; eyes are black and piercing; in stature they are short; the hair very long and rolled up at back or near the crown like that of a woman; is shaggy and crimped; in person they are usually slightly made, but well formed, except about the knee which is large, and the leg; the color of skin is slightly darker than usual. The men go nearly nude. The women dress in style of wandering female coravars [q.v.], wear copper ornaments and rosaries of Goorivenda ginjas [indian liquorice], and smear faces with oil of Buchanania latifolia [chironjee] and Pongamia glabra [karanj]. Formerly the chentsoo men used to wear on their heads caps made of leaves of trees; the elders still carry a spear, a hatchet, or a matchlock; the juniors a bamboo [q.v.] bow and an arrow of reeds, tipped with iron; sometimes poison is applied to the ends of the arrows; they are not now good marksmen, but serve as beaters.—"*c*" Chentsoos worship Ahobalam narsimha sawmy, and present honey [shahad], saurapappoo [chironjee], &c., on festivals at Ahobalam temple. They also worship Vencateshwaran, Veerabhadran, and Gandoolaveeran, to whom they make rice-offerings. They add a lamp sacrifice when they worship Goorappa, Ancaulamman, Yidamma, Potrauz, Sooncoolamma, Mauriyamman, Mullammah, &c. No forehead marks as a rule.—"*d*" When at home they live in small communities called goodems [q.v.]. They frequent chiefly the tract of jungle covering the westernmost range of the eastern ghaut line, between the pennair river and the kistna, and known locally as the nullamullays [q.v.] and the lunkamullays [q.v.]; also the palcondah hills to west of the nellore district, and specially the nundicanama pass, on the road between cumbum and gooty, where they serve as watchmen and guides. They inhabit clearings in the forest; they live in beehive-shaped huts like the nicobarian tribes, of wicker-work, with walls about three feet high, and a conical straw roof, with a screen for a door; they look on weaving and other manufacturing arts with contempt. Each goodem has a headman, who decides all disputes, assisted by elders of neighbouring goodem; he is not known by any particular titles, but is entitled to precedence on all occasions of marriage or other ceremonies, and to a portion of the flesh of the animals killed by any member of the goodem; in former times he used to dispose of murder cases also; the murderer, on proof of guilt, being put to death with the same weapons with which the murder was committed. They eat cholum [q.v.], and raggy [q.v.]; also a species of wild tubers called chentsoo gaddah, and the flesh of all animals killed in the chase excepting tiger [pooly], cheetah [q.v.] and wolf [konye]; in last case they do not boil the meat, but heat it over the fire; the flesh of the lungoor [q.v.] or condamoottsoo is much relished [malayarasa]; in the hot months a species of lizard is eaten. They have no distinction of caste such as prevents their eating and drinking together; they practise polygamy, but the western chentsoos do not intermarry with the eastern chentsoos, nor with those on the northern side of the kistna; the chentsoos do not marry with the teloogoos on the plains. Chentsoo widows, like the wandering lumbaudies [q.v.], generally marry the brother of their former husband; if there is no brother, they are allowed to marry others. Cremation is not practised by chentsoos. They look upon the jungle minor produce, such as honey, gall-nut [mauchicoy], and the like, as their exclusive property; they also claim the privilege of collecting a small fee from the pilgrims to srisheilam on occasions of festivals, in return for which they undertake to act as their guide without molestation; some chentsoos are employed by villagers on plains to watch fields during harvest; their chief occupation is collection of jungle produce and the chase.—"*e*" Numbers about 5,000. They are divided into five tribes or gotrams. Bonta chentsoo, from (bonta, tel. quilt), are a sub-division, who live in patch-work tents [jauty].

CHEPAUVANY (چھپاونی - chhapáuní, *Hind.*). From (chhapáná, hind. to hide). Concealment of cultivation of lands in order to defraud the revenue. May be by ryot or curnum, or both. See vol. I, 112.

CHEQUIN (ചക്കിൻ - chakkin, *Mal.*). From portuguese. Cochin silver coin; 10 equal to 3 Sicca rupees [chick].

CHER (ചേറു - chéru, *Mal.*). Soil [sher, shey].——*Cher laubham* (ചേർലാഭം - chérlábham, Mal.). From (above + lábha, san. gain). Cultivator's share of profit.——*Chermakkal* (ചെറുമക്കൾ - cherumakkal, Mal.). From (above + makkal, mal sons). Slaves in general.——*Cherman* (ചെറുമൻ - cheruman, pers. sing.; ചെറുമർ - cherumar, pers. pl., Mal.). From (above + an, mal. personal suffix). Caste-title. Lower class in Malabar connected with rice cultivation. Aborigines of the country when it passed under the rule of the Nayar. See vol. II, 99. Very black, and hair often woolly, small in stature. They are lower in the social scale than the Teeyar. In trade or barter they in native usage lay down their goods, retire to a prescribed distance, and leave the payment to be adjusted by the man of higher rank. The Cheroomar are of two sections, one of which, the Iraya cheroomar, are of slightly higher social standing than the Poolayar [jauty].

CHER (ചെറു - cheru, *Mal.*). Small [chit]. Prefix in place names as Chercoonn, meaning small hill.——*Cheriya* (ചെറിയ - cheriya, Mal.). Small. Plant first term, often joining two genera, as in:—Antidesma ghæsembilla (cheriyakottam), small costus speciosus; Celosia argentia (cheriyatakkamaniyan). small sphæranthus indicus. See gloss. paragraphs.——*Cheriya coonyoottacaur* (ചെറിയകുഞ്ഞൂട്ടക്കാർ - cheriyakuññúttakkár, Mal.). From (cheriya, mal. small + kuññúttan, mal. young boy + kár, mal. personal suffix). Temple boys in Travancore.——*Cher jenmam* (ചെറുജന്മം - cherujanmam, Mal.). From (above + janmam, mal. birthright). Inferior rights; applied to the fees receivable by the carpenter and smith in Malabar. See vol. I, 112.——*Cheroo* (ചെറു - cheru, Mal.). Small. Plant first term, often joining two genera, as in following, where transl. is of second term:—Ærua lanata (cherupúla), bombax malabaricum; Aganosma caryophyllata (cherupával), momordica charantia; Clerodendron serratum (cherutékku), tectona grandis; Cyathula prostrata (cherukataláti), achyranthes aspera; Limnanthemum cristatum (cheruchittámbal), nymphæa stellata; Limonia acidissima (cherukáttunárakam), atalantia monophylla; Linum usitatissimum (cheruchanam), crotolaria juncea. See gloss. paragraphs.——*Cherpalcherry* (ചെർപ്പുള്ളശ്ശേരി - cherppullashshéri, Mal. cherpalcheri *). From (above + pilla, mal. child + shéri, mal. village); after the god ayyappan.—"*a*" Deputy tahsildarry, Malabar district. Pay Rs. 70.—"*b*" Village, Deputy tahsildar's station, Sub-registrar's office, Travellers' bungalow; Malabar dist., Valavanaud tal.; pop. 4,877; lat. 10° 53′; long. 76° 22′; from Calicut S.E. 44 miles; from Cannanore S.E. 92 miles; from Madras S.W. 305 miles; from Malapooram S.E. 20 miles; from Manantoddy S.S.E. 65 miles; from Palghaut W.N.W. 24 miles; from Perindalman S.E. 7¾ miles; from Ponnany E.N.E. 27 miles; from Tellicherry S.E. 81 miles. Annexed to Mysore in 1766. From 1792 to 1800 station of the Southern superintendent under Bombay, and in 1860 head-quarters of old Nedoonganaud talook. Temple called Ayyappan cauv. Festival for ten days in February-March. Weekly market on wednesdays.

CHERAM (சேரம் - shéram, *Tam.*). Tam. means toddy. The country so called. Nothing can be added to what has been stated at vol. I (126) to (128) [charitram].——*Cherambaudy* (ചേരമ്പാടി - chérampáti, Mal.). From (shéran, tam. the ruler + páti, tam. village); village of cherma permaul. Village, Public bungalow; Neilgherry dist., Wynaud S.E. division; lat. 11° 31′; long. 76° 19′; from Goodalore W. 15 miles; from Ootacamund W.N.W. 30 miles. Chief market of Cherangode. Coffee [q.v.], cinchona [koinah], and blue gum [q.v.] estates, from Devaulah N.W. 7¼ miles, 326 acres.——*Cheran* (சேரன் - shéran, Tam.). Chera ruler. The title was specially applied to the rajahs of Travancore, Coorg, and Malayalam country proper;

see vol. II, 250.——*Cherangode* (ചേരങ്കോട് - chérankótu, Mal.). From (chéran, mal. the king + kótu, mal. fort); site of one of cherma permaul's forts. Amshom; Neilgherry dist., Wynaud S.E. division; pop. 2,440; lat. 11° 32′; long. 76° 21′; from Goodalore W.N.W. 12½ miles; from Ootacamund W.N.W. 28 miles. In 827 A.D., the Permaul became a convert to Islam, and having partitioned his kingdom, started for Arabia, dying in 832 A.D. at Zaphar [cherma permaul]. Kerala veera vurman, better known as the rebel Pychy rajah, had a fort in this tract during early years of present century. The temple of Cherval-lore is of great antiquity. Cherambaudy is chief market.——*Cherapaty* (சேரப்பதி - sherappathi, Tam.). From (above + pati, san. ruler). Same as Cheran. κηροβόθρος of Ptolemy, and κηπροβότρος of Periplus, where the π is an error [charitram].——*Cherma permaul* (ചേരമാൻ പെരുമാൾ - chéramán-perumál, Mal.). From (above + mahá, san. great + perumál, mal. chief). The viceroy from Cheram country, who administered the Malayalam country. Especially one of the ninth century who afterwards established himself as an independent ruler. He founded the town of Calicut, and all the royal races of Malabar claim descent from him. Towards the close of his reign, he became a convert to Mahomedan faith, divided his kingdom among his relatives and dependants and sailed for Mecca which he reached about A.D. 827. He died at Zaphar in Arabia in A.D. 832, and his tomb is still seen there [charitram, collam]. See vol. I (129); II, 68, 103, 134.——*Chermaun* (ചേരമാൻ - chéramán, Mal.). From (above + mahán, san. great man). Any king of Cheram country.——*Chernaud* (ചേരനാട് - chéranátu, Mal.). From (above + nátu, mal. country). The Cheram or Salem country. Called by the Canarese and so in Sanscrit the Keralam country. Also an old talook of Malabar now included in Yernaud.

CHEROO (చెరువు - cheruvu, *Tel.*). From (chéru, tel. to collect). An artificial lake, called tank. Common suffix in place names; as Baitamcheroo, meaning cane + tank [cherla, chira].——*Cherankeel* (ചിറയിങ്കീഴ് - chirayinkízh, Mal.). From (chira, mal. tank + kízh, mal. below).—"*a*" Talook, Travancore state, Trivandrum division; pop. 87,072. Its greatest length N. to S. is 14 miles and greatest breadth E. to W. is 8 miles. It is subdivided into eleven praverties and contains eighty-eight caras or villages. The talook is bounded N. by Quilon and Cottauracara talooks, E. by Nedoovengaud talook, S. by Trivandrum talook and W. by the Indian ocean. Partly hilly and partly interspersed with backwaters and lagoons [canyal]; soil laterite [q.v.] or clay and sand. The chief industries are fishing, coir rope-making and burning of shells and converting the same into quick lime [choonam]. Cocoanut [q.v.] and cocoanut-oil are the chief articles of export. Rivers are chief sources of irrigation. Camping ground at Warkully.—"*b*" Village, Tahsildar's station; Travancore state, Trivandrum division, Cherankeel tal.; pop. 10,388; lat. 8° 40′; long. 76° 49′; from Attingal S.W. 3½ miles; from Trivandrum N.W. 17 miles; from the sea E. 1½ miles. Extensive and regular town with pagoda [q.v.] and palace.——*Cherla* (చర్ల - cherla, Tel.). Plural locative form. Tank. Suffix in place names as Chitticherla, meaning small + tank [cheroo].——*Cheroo maunyam* (చెరువుమాన్యము - cheruvumányamu, Tel.). From (above + mányamu, tel. inam). Tank-inam; granted to a person who has dug a tank at his own expense, for keeping its banks in repair and to reimburse him gradually for his first outlay [dasbandam].

CHEROOT (چُٹّا - chuttá, *Hind.*; ಹೊಗೆಬತ್ತಿ - hogébatti, *Can.*; చుట్ట - tsutta, *Tel.*; ചുരുട്ട് - churuttu, *Mal.*; சுருட்டு - shuruttu, *Tam.*). Title from tamul. Hind. from teloogoo. Mal. and tam. mean a roll. Dried leaves of tobacco plant [pogauk], formed into small rolls for smoking, both ends being open. The three main sorts are Trichinopoly, Lunka [q.v.] and Manilla, the last imported. European manufacturers make up the tobacco in cigar shape, and call them by fancy names; they are then not properly cheroots [mookhadiraut].

CHERRY (ചേരി - chéri, *Mal.*; சேரி - shéri, *Tam.*). From (shér, tam. to gather). A group of houses occupied by the same caste among the lower classes. Suffix in place names; as Pondicherry, meaning new village [chainy, coodiyiroopp, jainy].——*Parcherry* (பறைச்சேரி - paraiççéri, Tam.). Pariah quarter.

CHERRY (چواری - chuárí, *Hind.*). Named from Keresoun, a town of Pontus. Botanically Prunus [auloo] cerasus, linn., rosaceæ [vricsham, 49]. Not here cultivated. Compare:—Atropa belladonna, black cherry; Malphigia glabra, barbadoes cherry; Phyllanthus distichus, brazil cherry; Physalis angulata, winter cherry; Withania somnifera, winter cherry; Zizyphus jujuba, indian cherry. See gloss. paragraphs.

CHETTERPORE (ఛత్రపురము - chhatrapuramu, *Tel.* chatrapur *). From (chhatra, san. umbrella + pura, san. town). Sanscrit name (sattrapura), meaning choultry + town. Town, Head-quarters of Collector; Ganjam dist., Berhampore tal.; pop. 3,135; acres 880; lat. 19° 21′; long. 85° 03′; from Balligooda E.S.E. 91 miles; from Berhampore E.N.E. 14 miles; from Chicacole N.E. 103 miles; from Madras N.E. 525 miles; from Russellcondah S.S.E. 47 miles; from the sea W. 2½ miles. Once site of East india company's stud farm. On high road between Berhampore and Cuttack, 28 miles from frontier of Bengal. Situation picturesque. The town overlooks the sea about 60 feet above sea-level. Healthy but relaxing. In 1831 the Collector first took up his residence here. The Maliah reserve force of constables is located at Chetterpore. The onslow institution founded by Mr. Onslow, a former Collector, for the education of natives, is supported by the rent of the Collector's house and other property. Provisions for Europeans have usually to be brought from Berhampore. The following are the travelling distances by road from Chetterpore to different places:—

To	Viâ	Miles and Furlongs.	
Aska	Ganjam and Poorshottapore	47	3
Aska	Berhampore	38	3
Berhampore ...	......	14	3
Bezwada ...	Berhampore, Mansoorcottah, Chicacole, Toony and Ellore.	387	3
Chicacole ...	Mansoorcottah, Berhampore and Ichapore.	113	2½
Cuddapah ...	Chicacole, Bezwada, Guntoor and Cumbum.	616	7
Cuttack ...	Manickaputnam and Juggernaut or Pooree.	119	2
Cuttack ...	Rambha and Khoordhah	102	2
Ellore	Chicacole and Toony	348	2½
Ganjam ...	......	4	5
Guntoor ...	Berhampore, Chicacole, Toony and Ellore.	407	4
Juggernaut or Pooree.	Manickaputnam	63	5
Khoordhah ...	Rambha	84	2
Madras ...	Chicacole, Rajahmundry, Ellore, Guntoor and Nellore.	660	0
Manickaputnam.	......	43	4
Nellore ...	Chicacole, Rajahmundry, Bezwada, and Guntoor.	552	2
Ongole	Chicacole, Rajahmundry and Guntoor ...	475	7
Rajahmundry.	Chicacole and Toony	293	1½
Rambha ...	......	14	7
Russellcondah.	Berhampore and Aska	62	8
Russellcondah.	Ganjam and Poorshottapore	37	5
Sonapore ...	Aska, Russellcondah and Coormingyah ...	160	7
Sonapore ...	Khoordhah, Kantilo and Boad	200	6
Toony	Chicacole and Cassimcote	233	6½
Vizagapatam ...	Chicacole and Chittivalsa	177	4½
Vizagapatam ...	Chicacole and Chittivalsa	172	0½

CHETTY (శెట్టి - setti, *Tel.*; செட்டி - shetti, *Tam.*). From (shettu, tam. trade). Not the same as the Bombay sait [q.v.]. See vol. I (66); II, 227 [jauty].—"*a*" Primarily a member of any trading caste in Southern india, answering to the Banyans [q.v.] of Western and Northern india. It is applied in this sense, without reference to caste or race, to the Parsee engaged in the trade, the Mahomedan bohrah [q.v.], the Teloogoo comaty [q.v.], the Tamul vellaulan [q.v.], the Silk-weaver, and the Cavaray [q.v.]. Amongst the Teloogoo races the title is given to the Gauzoola balije [q.v.] or bangle-makers, the Vauniyar or oil-pressers, the Ilay vauniya or cloth-merchants, and the Comaties or grocers and general dealers. In the Tamul country it is given to the Nautcottays or general merchants, and to the Coosavar or potters. The Tooloo race take Chetty as a title.—"*b*" The word also represents a caste proper. Number in presidency about 260,000; mostly in Coimbatore, Madura, Malabar and Tanjore. Some of the Chetty families abstain from animal food and otherwise follow the pure Vellaula customs, and very probably are of the true Vellaula caste. Men of ordinary pully or vunniya castes, however, as they rise in the world, assume the title of chetty or pillay, according as they pursue trade or agriculture; and the classes of chetties and pillays thus newly formed have now become so numerous that it is difficult to distinguish the true castes from them. There are Tamul proverbs:—ஆதாயமில்லாத செட்டி ஆற்றைக்கட்டி இறைப்பானா?—"Will a Chetty dam up a river and drain out "its waters for nothing?" கெட்டாலும் செட்டி செட்டியே கிழிந்தாலும் பட்டு பட்டே—"Though reduced in circum-"stances a Chetty is a Chetty; silk is silk though never so "torn." செட்டிக்கு வேளாண்மை சென்மப் பகை—"The "chetty has a natural aversion to agriculture." செத்தால் தெரியும் செட்டியார் வாழ்வு—"The wealth of the Chetty "will be known after death."—"*c*" Also a mere Hindoo third name. Chettiar is honorific plural [peyar].——*Berichetty* (బేరిసెట్టి - bérisetti, Tel.). From (béramu, tel. trade). Claim to be the only representative of a true Veisya stock belonging to the left-hand castes [yidangay]. They are distinct from ordinary Comaties or Chetties. Some worship Shiva and some Vishnoo, and a few are Lingavant who do not marry into families with a different worship. All the divisions wear the sacred thread. None tolerate widow remarriage. Unlike Comaties, the daughters are sometimes married after puberty. About 20,000.——*Chetty grass* (ചെട്ടിപ്പുല്ല് - chettippullu, Mal.). Probably from being introduced into malabar by chetties or tamul shoodras. Same as raggy.——*Nautcottay chetty* (நாட்டுக்கோட்டைச்செட்டி - náttukkóttaiççetti, Tam.). Corruption of Nauttarasancottay, small village near Shivagunga. A trading class of the Vunniya or Pully caste of the Tinnevelly and other southern districts. They are found all over the coast and seaport towns in the peninsula and the islands of the Indian ocean. All speak Tamul and follow Hindooism; are large spice merchants, and have the marked African protruding lips and nose sharply cut at the forehead. They are keen, active traders. However wealthy they may be, they usually live in the most penurious manner. They seclude their wives [jauty]. They claim to be a good caste, and assert that they emigrated to Madura thousands of years ago from a town called Cauvery-putnam in consequence of persecution. But the other Chetties will not admit the truth of their story, and allege that they are the descendants of a Mahomedan man and a Culla woman.——*Vellaun chetty* (வெள்ளாஞ்செட்டி - velláñjetti, obl., Tam.). From (vellán, tam. a member of the vellála caste). A trading Vellaulan. About 40,000.

CHETWYE (ചേറ്റുവായ - chéttaváya, *Mal.*). From (chettu, mal. to cut + vazhi, mal. way).—"*a*" Village; Malabar dist., Ponnany tal.; lat. 10° 32′; long. 76° 05′; from Bombay S.S.E. 608 miles; from Cochin N.N.W. 41 miles; from Calicut S.S.E. 52 miles; from Madras S.W. 340 miles; from Ponnany S.S.E. 19 miles; from Trichore W. 12 miles. A strip of land on sea-coast insulated by estuaries of the Chetwye and Cranganore. Sometimes called Manapooram, meaning sandy-side from nature of the soil. Has travellers' bungalow. Extends nearly 27 miles from south-east to north-west, with a breadth varying from 2 to 4 miles. Forms part of the township of Vaudanpully and adjoins the territory of Cochin. In 1715 permission granted by the Zamorin to the English to build a warehouse. In 1717, wrested from the Zamorin by the Dutch, who built a fort and made it the capital of their province of Pauppinivuttam. Taken by the Portuguese from the Dutch. In 1776 Hyder ally overran the district and captured the fort. In 1790 it was taken by Colonel Hartly, and passed into British possession on the conclusion of peace in 1792. It was leased to the Cochin rajah for Rs. 40,000 per annum until 1805, in which year it came under the direct administration of the East india company.—"*b*" River; Malabar dist., Ponnany tal.; lat. 10° 31′ N.; long. 76° 6′ E. The mouth and about 6 miles of course lie in British territory, and for about 2 miles more it forms boundary between British territory and Cochin native state. At end of this 8 miles the river widens out into a lake, partly natural and partly artificial.

CHEY (చే - ché, *Tel.*; செய் - shey, *Tam.*). From (shey, tam. to do). Cultivated ground; field [chainoo]. So measure of a corn field; very variable, from 1 to 2 acres [alavay, 2 a]. In tel. also means hand, from same root.——*Chejerla* (చేజెర్ల - chejerla, Tel.). From (above + cherla, tel. village). Sanscrit name (kapótéshvara), meaning dove + lord.—"*a*" Village; Kistna dist., Narsarowpett tal.; pop. 1,140; acres 2,329; lat. 16° 19′; long. 79° 53′; from Masulipatam W. 84 miles; from Narsarowpett W.N.W. 14½ miles. The legend told in the Mahabhaurat of the king who sacrificed his own flesh to redeem the life of a dove hunted by a hawk is transferred to this place. Three caves in the rock, probably ancient. Many remains of shrines. Ten inscriptions. A large baobab [q.v.] tree here considered indigenous. Between temple and west tank are heaps of debris from smelting of iron ore. Industry now extinct. Marble stone [shalavay cull] quarried.—"*b*" Village; Nellore dist., Atmacore tal.; pop. 2,665; acres 7,808; lat. 14° 31′; long. 79° 37′; from Atmacore S. 7 miles; from Nellore W. 28 miles. Ancient temple of Vishnoo as Chennakeshavan. Has an inam of acres 31·96. Temple to Shiva as Neelacuntan, with inam of acres 25·82. In some villages near this, viz., Canoopoorpulley shrotriem, Gollapully, Padair, and Timmayyapollem shrotriem, diamonds [vajram] were formerly found. The remains of the old works are still visible.——*Cheyair* (చెయ్యేరు - cheyyéru, Tel. cheyér *). From (above + éru, tel. river). Sanscrit corruption, for tel. (cheyyi), hand (báhudánadí), meaning hand-giving + river; from the legend of a person who regained his lost hand by bathing in the stream. River; Cuddapah dist., Madanapully, Voilpaud, Royachoty, Poollampett and Sidhout tals. Tributary of the Pennair. Formed by several streams rising in the south and south-west extremities of the sub-division of Cuddapah district, the principal of which are the Punchanuddy and the Bauhoodah nuddy. The several tributaries combine in Royachoty talook near Royavaram. The river then flows through the Palcondah hills, dividing the latter from the Sheshachellam range, receiving during this part of its course the combined waters of the Manndavair and the Chittair which drains the north-east portion of Royachoty talook. After winding through the valley which once formed the petty kingdom of Chitwail it flows into the Pennair near the boundary of Sidhout and Poollampett talooks. It finds an exit through the Soonkesala pass in the Eastern ghauts [q.v.]. Two miles from Culcada is a branch of this stream. Its water is extensively used for irrigation by means of channels. Crossed by a railway bridge at Nundalore. The original bridge was partly swept away by flood in October 1870 and 1874; on the former occasion many of the passengers in a train were drowned. The present bridge was completed in May 1879. The river is dry for six months in the year. It is not navigable.——*Cheyaur* (செய்யாறு - sheyyáru, Tam. cheyár *). From (above + áru, tam. river). Sanscrit corruption (báhudánadí), meaning hand-giving river; see cheyair. Sanscrit also (skandanadí), meaning Soobramanyan's river; from a legend that the river arose from his peacock's pecking at the mountain. River; North arcot and Chingleput districts. Rises in the Jawaudy range near Chengam in lat. 12° 30′ N.; long. 78° 50′ E. First flows southward into S. arcot. After passing through Polore talook and Arnee jaghire it forms boundary between Wandiwash and Arcot talooks. Tributaries in N. arcot are the Camandala nuddy or Padavaid, Mricanda nuddy, Bheemanuddy, and Munjalaur, all rising in the Jawaudy hills. Enters Chingleput district 10 or 12 miles west of Ootramallore, flowing past Trivettore and watering many rich villages in that division by channels taken off it. Among others it fills the tank of Ootramallore village, with a revenue of Rs. 25,000 dependent on it. It joins the Palaur in Chingleput district in lat. 12° 45′; long. 79° 55′.——*Cheypota* (చెయిపోత - cheyipóta, Tel.). From (cheyyi, tel. hand + póyu, tel. to pour). Irrigation by hand from pools.

CHICACOLE * (శ్రీకాకుళము - shríkákulamu, *Tel.*). From (shikhá, san. head + kula, san. house), as being capital of calingam. Sanscrit name (shikhápura), meaning extremity + town. Mahomedan name (mahfuzbandar), from the port, named after máufooz khan. Also called (gulshanábád), meaning happy rose garden.——(1) Talook; Ganjam district. Tahsildar's pay Rs. 175. Area 461 square miles. Population 194,367. Language Teloogoo. S. coast of district. Bounded north by Parlakimedy and Tekkaly estates, east by Bay of Bengal and south, and west by Vizagapatam district. Consists of the Havelly [q.v.] or Home lands of the old Chicacole circar. Formerly part of the territory of the Gajapaty rajahs of Orissa, but shortly after their overthrow in 1568, came together with the rest of the Circars [q.v.] under the Cootb shahy rule, and their governors resided in the town. Hindoo influence finally succumbed in 1724 only when Asaf jah, Viceroy of the Deccan [q.v.] and first Nizam ool moolk, took actual possession, collected the revenue, and appointed a civil and military establishment. With the rest of the Northern circars [q.v.] it was assigned by the Nizam to the French in 1753. Ceded with the rest of the Northern circars by the Nizam to the British in 1759. Actual possession was taken in 1766. Under Mahomedan rule, divided into the three divisions of Cassimcote, Chicacole and Ichapore. The first two, on British occupation became parts of Vizagapatam district, the demesne lands or Chicacole havelly being leased to the Rajah of Vizianagram till 1787, when they came under direct administration. In 1802 transferred to Ganjam. The country rises gradually from the sea towards the northern boundary. There are a few hills and Vamshadhaura flows through it. The talook is not very fertile. Soil, regar [q.v.], sand, and black clay. Weaving, lacquered ware are the industries. Exports, rice [q.v.], gingelly [q.v.] and pulses [dholl]. Irrigation works are the Wadauda and Doosy channels of the Langoolya and the Bheiry, Nayira, Poorshottapore, Nagaricatacam, Joolmoor, Polauky, Malagaum, Loocoolaum and Gariboola channels of the Vamshadhaura. Camping grounds, Chicacole, Cotabommauly and Narsannapett. Places of archæological interest:—Arsavully, Balaga, Bheiry, Booravully, Calingapatam, Chicacole, Corlaum, Cullepully, Dirghausy, Gaura, Goozerauttipett, Ippily, Joolmoor, Oorgam, Peddapaud, Polauky, Poorshottapore, Raugole, Ronanky, Santa bommauly, Shreecoormam, Silagaum, Singoopooram, Vamarvully. Principal trig. stations:—Bendy, Boddapaud, Caukarpully, Jogipaud beacon, Lakkavaram, Linganlavalsa, Maudigapooram, Moony, Peddacondah, Pokalpett beacon, Raullapaud, Saulihoondaum, Tirwaula. The leading places, &c., in the talook are the following.——*Arsavully* (అరసవల్లి - arasavalli, Tel.). From (arasa, can. king + palli, tel. village). Sanscrit name (harshavalli), meaning gladdening earth; happy spot. Village; pop. 346; acres 1,294; lat. 18° 17′; long. 83° 58′; from Chetterpore S.W. 101 miles; from Chicacole E. 1 mile; from the sea N. 5½ miles. Ancient temple with old inscriptions; said to have been founded by Indran himself; rich endowments.——*Bendy* (బెండి - bendi, Tel.). Trig. station; lat. 18° 42′ 16·75″; long. 84° 22′ 17·88″; from Bendy W. 1¼ miles; from Tekkaly E.S.E. 4¼ miles; from Chicacole N.E. 43 miles; from the sea W. 4¾ miles.——*Bharanigaum* (భరణిగామము - bharanigámu, Tel.). From (bharaní, san. 2nd lunar asterism + gráma, san. village). Proprietary estate, Village; pop. 36. Peshcush Rs. 82.——*Boddapaud* (బొడ్డపాడు - boddapádu, Tel.). From (bóda, oor. large + pádu, tel. village). Trig. station; Lat. 18° 29′ 05·35″; long. 84° 10′ 58·29″; from Sariya boddapaud N. ¾ mile; from Cotabommauly S.W. 2¾ miles; from Chicacole N.E. 21 miles; from the sea W. 9½ miles.——*Boddaum* (బొడ్డాం - boddám, Tel.). From (bóda, oor. large + gám, oor. village). Proprietary estate, Village; pop. 329; acres 776; lat. of village 18° 26′ 15″; long. 84° 13′ 12″; from Chetterpore S.W. 82 miles; from Chicacole N.E. 20 miles; from the sea W. 2½ miles. Peshcush Rs. 89.——*Calingapatam* (కళింగపట్నము - kalingapatnamu, Tel.). See sep. title.——*Caukarpully* (కాకరపల్లి - kákarapalli, Tel.). From (kankara, tel. gravel + palli, tel. village). Trig. station; lat. 18° 30′ 33·23″; long. 84° 15′ 50·00″; from Cotabommauly E. 3¼ miles; from Chicacole N.E. 26 miles; from the sea W. 6 miles. Somewhere close to Cotabommauly.——*Chicacole* (శ్రీకాకుళము - shríkákulamu, Tel.). See below.——*Chinnamallipooram* చిన్నమల్లిపురము - chinnamallipuramu, Tel.). Trig. station, Parlakimedy zemindarry; lat. 18° 40′ 30·46″; long. 84° 06′ 14·88″; height 1,616 feet; from Chinnamallipooram N.W. 1¼ miles; from Chicacole N.N.E. 29 miles; from Chetterpore S.W. 78

miles.——*Chinnatoongaum* (చిన్నతుంగాం - chinnatungám, Tel.). From (chinna, tel. small + tunga, san. hill). Zemindarry, Village; pop. 416; acres 428; lat. of village 18° 32′; long. 84° 16′; from Chetterpore S.W. 74 miles; from Chicacole N.E. 28 miles; from the sea W. 6 miles. Peshcush Rs. 424.——*Corlaum* (కొర్లాం - korlám, Tel.). From (kóra, tel. steep + lámu, tel. hollow in a hill). Village; pop. 1,370; acres 1,229; lat. 18° 18′; long. 84° 7′; from Chetterpore S.W. 93 miles; from Chicacole E. 11 miles; from the sea N. 1¾ miles. Temple built three-hundred years ago over one male and two female images.——*Danta* (దంత - danta, Tel.). Means ivory. Zemindarry, Village; pop. 3,420; acres 5,738; lat. of village 18° 33′ 05″; long. 84° 10′ 12″; from Balligooda S.S.E. 111 miles; from Berhampore S.W. 66 miles; from Chetterpore S.W. 78 miles; from Chicacole N.E. 23 miles; from Madras N.E. 450 miles; from Russellcondah S.S.W. 98 miles; from the sea W. 14 miles. Peshcush Rs. 2,309.——*Deodangar* (దియోడంగర్ - diyódangar, Tel.). From (dévatá, san. god + nagara, san. city). Trig. station, Parlakimedy zemindarry; lat. 18° 54′ 35·18″; long. 84° 06′ 03·52″; height 4,535 feet; from Moonshingy E. 3¼ miles; from Chicacole N.N.E. 44 miles; from Chetterpore W.S.W. 68 miles.——*Gottipully* (గొట్టిపల్లి - gottipalli, Tel.). From (gutta, tel. rock + palli, tel. village). Zemindarry, Village; pop. 5,348; acres 2,571; lat. of village 18° 38′; long. 83° 57′; from Chetterpore W.S.W. 84 miles; from Chicacole N. 94 miles; from the sea N. 30 miles. Peshcush Rs. 2,034.——*Jogipaud beacon* (జోగిపాడు - dzógipádu, Tel.). From (yógí, san. sage + pádu, tel. village). Trig. station; lat. 18° 27′ 00·00″; long. 84° 16′ 00·00.″——*Joolmoor* (జుల్మూరు - dzulmúru, Tel.). From (zulm, hind. oppression + úru, tel. village). Village; pop. 3,480; acres 3,569; lat. 18° 30′; long. 84° 05′; from Chetterpore S.W. 84 miles; from Chicacole N.N.E. 17¾ miles; from the sea W. 17 miles. Formerly chief town of a sub-division. Old mud fort, traditionally a residence of the Orissa rajahs. Most of the population are Ooriya bramins.——*Lakkavaram* (లక్కవరము - lakkavaramu, Tel.). From (lóka, san. world + pura, san. town). Trig. station; lat. 18° 31′ 41·76″; long. 84° 18′ 30·15″; from Aucausha lakkavaram W. 1 mile; from Gopalpore S.E. 2 miles; from Chicacole N.E. 29 miles; from the sea W. 4½ miles, where road bungalow near Nowpada.——*Langoolya* (లాంగుల్య - lángulya, Tel.). See sep. title.——*Lingaulavalsa* (లింగాలవలస - lingálavalasa, Tel.). From (linga, san. emblem of shiva + valasa, tel. colony). Trig. station; lat. 18° 18′ 18·79″; long. 84° 00′ 56·02″; from Chicacole E.N.E. 5 miles; from the sea N. 5 miles.——*Malagaum* (మలగాము - malagámu, Tel.). From (mala, tel. hill + gráma, san. village). Sanscrit name (malagráma), meaning same. Proprietary estate, Village; pop. 737; lat. of village 18° 28′; long. 84° 17′; from Chetterpore S.W. 81 miles; from Chicacole N.E. 24 miles; from the sea W. ½ mile. Peshcush Rs. 570.——*Maudigapooram* (మాదిగపురము - mádigapuramu, Tel.). From (mádiga, tel. the caste + pura, san. town). Trig. station; lat. 18° 41′ 36·68″; long. 84° 23′ 40·12″; from Chicacole N.E. 41 miles; from the sea W. 7½ miles.——*Moonagavalsa* (మునగవలస - munagavalasa, Tel.). See sep. title.——*Moony* (ముని - muni, Tel.). Means a sage. Trig. station; lat. 18° 38′ 53·78″; long. 84° 23′ 14·65″; from Chicacole N.E. 38 miles; from the sea W. 6 miles.——*Moorkhy* (మూర్ఖి - murkhi, Tel.). Trig. station, Tarlah zemindarry; lat. 18° 46′ 42·74″; long. 84° 28′ 55·45″; from Chicacole N.E. 49 miles; from Chetterpore S.W. 54 miles; from the sea W. 6½ miles.——*Nagaricatacam* (నగరికటకము - nagarikatakamu, Tel.). From (nagarí, san. small town + kataka, san. hill side). Village; pop. 1,550; acres 841; lat. 18° 34′; long. 84° 01′; from Chetterpore S.W. 86 miles; from Chicacole N.N.E. 20 miles; from the sea W. 26 miles.——*Narsannapett* (నరసన్నపేట - narasannapéta, Tel.). See sep. title.——*Peddacondah* (పెద్దకొండ - peddakonda, Tel.). From (pedda, tel. large + konda, tel. hill). Trig. station; lat. 18° 25′ 45·60″; long. 84° 09′ 02·50″; from Raulla godiyavalsa N.N.W. 1½ miles; from Chicacole N.E. 17 miles; from the sea W. 7 miles.——*Peddatoongaum* (పెద్దతుంగాం - peddatungám, Tel.). From (pedda, tel. large + tunga, san. hill). Zemindarry, Village; pop. 433; acres 382; lat. of village 18° 33′; long. 84° 15′; from Chetterpore S.W. 75 miles; from Chicacole N.E. 27 miles; from the sea W. 10 miles.——*Pokalpett beacon* (పుక్కెల్లపేట - pukkellapéta, Tel.). From (póka, tel. areca palm, areca catechu, linn. + péta, tel. suburb). Trig. station; lat. 18° 13′ 03·08″; long. 83° 59′ 03·66″; from Chicacole S.S.E. 5½ miles; from the sea W. 1 mile. Staff No. 1 on the mouth of Chicacole river in coast series chart No. 6.——*Poorshottapore* (పురుషోత్తపురము - purushóttapuramu, Tel.). From (purushóttama, san. vishnu, the best of men + pura, san. town). Village; pop. 2,718; acres 3,724; lat. 18° 28′; long. 84° 00′; from Chetterpore S.W. 92 miles; from Chicacole N.N.E. 13 miles; from the sea N. 17 miles. On right bank of Vamshadhaura. Large mud fort about a mile square, contains Shiva lingams and a female rock-cut figure. Two miles south is a hill called hill of the Pandavas.——*Raullapaud* (రాళ్లపాడు - rállapádu, Tel.). From (ráyi, tel. stone + pádu, tel. village). Trig. station; lat. 18° 23′ 12·83″; long. 84° 06′ 39·10″; from Chicacole E.N.E. 13 miles; from the sea W. 7 miles.——*Saulihoondaum* (సాలెహుండాం - sálehundám, Tel.). From (sále, tel. a weaver + hundám, tel. an estate). Village, Hill; pop. 2,150; acres 2,114; lat. 18° 20′; long. 84° 06′; from Chetterpore S.W. 93 miles; from Chicacole E.N.E. 10 miles; from the sea N. 4½ miles. The hill, a conspicuous land-mark at sea, has a temple and the remains of a substantial stone causeway leading to it. Trig. station in lat. 18° 20′ 05·31″; long. 84° 04′ 18·52″; height 413 feet; from Chicacole 9 miles E.N.E; from the sea 5¼ miles N.——*Shreecoormam* (శ్రీకూర్మము - shríkúrmamu, Tel.). See sep. title.——*Talasamoodram* (తలసముద్రము - talasamudramu, Tel.). From (tala, tel. head + samudra, san. ocean). Zemindarry, Village; pop. 862; acres 1,156; lat. of village 18° 21′; long. 84° 07′; from Chetterpore S.W. 90 miles; from Chicacole E.N.E. 12 miles; from the sea W. 4¼ miles. Peshcush Rs. 2,383.——*Tilaury* (తిలారి - tilári, Tel.). Means oilman. Zemindarry, Village; pop. 6,832; acres 1,143; lat. of village 18° 29′; long. 84° 08′; from Chetterpore S.W. 83 miles; from Chicacole N.E. 18 miles; from the sea W. 11 miles. Peshcush Rs. 3,654.——*Tirwaula* (తిరివాల - tiriväla, Tel.). Trig. station; lat. 18° 29′ 28·44″; long. 84° 13′ 53·40″; from Chicacole N.E. 24 miles; from the sea W. 6¼ miles.——*Vamarvully* (వమరవల్లి - vamaravalli, Tel.). From (vamramu, tel. white-ant + palli, tel. village). Village; pop. 3,093; acres 3,044; lat. 18° 19′; long. 84° 08′; from Chetterpore S.W. 91 miles; from Chicacole E.N.E. 13 miles; from the sea W. 2 miles. Salt station. Thatched shed built over fifty small images. Annual festival largely attended.——*Vamshadhaura* (వంశధార - vamshadhára, Tel.). See sep. title.——*Wadauda* (వాడాడ - vádáda, Tel.). From (váda, tel. boat + váda, tel. village). Village; pop. 1,621; acres 2,467; lat. 18° 16′; long. 83° 59′; from Chetterpore S.W. 103 miles; from Chicacole S.E. 3½ miles; from the sea N. 3 miles.——(2) Town, Municipality, Divisional, Talook and District moonsif's head-quarters; Ganjam dist., Chicacole tal.; pop. 18,241; lat. 18° 17′; long. 83° 57′; from Balligooda S. 131 miles; from Berhampore S.W. 90 miles; from Chetterpore S.W. 103 miles; from Madras N.E. 425 miles; from Russellcondah S.S.W. 123 miles; from the sea N. 7 miles. Formerly called Maufooz bunder from a small port so called at mouth of river, Maufooz khan being son of Anwar ood deen afterwards Nawaub of Arcot. On north bank of Langoolya. The great northern trunk road passes through town. Climate salubrious. Probably earliest capital of the Calingam kingdom. Inhabitants are mentioned by Pliny. Capital transferred to Calingapatam. In modern times once a military cantonment and still an important recruiting station. In 1815 head-quarters of the district. Head-quarters of the District court until its transfer to Berhampore in 1864. Mosque built in 1641 by Sher mahomed khan, first Mussulman fowjdar [q.v.] has a large enclosed garden and burial ground. Four miles north on the Berhampore road are two cairns. Close to one of the ways to the Langoolya is a rock with sculptured lingams. South-west, across the river, is an octagon pillar, said to have been built of the skulls of men killed in battle by Mahomedans [dooppalavalsa]. Temple of Kota anjaneyasawmy, of modern construction, built over an image of Hanooman now dismantled. Town celebrated for fine muslins [q.v.], but industry has declined. The following are the travelling distances by road from Chicacole to different places:—

To	Viâ	Miles and Furlongs.	
Aska	Ichapore and Berhampore	123	0½
Aska	Ichapore and Digoopoody	124	1½
Bangalore ...	Rajahmundry, Bezwada, Ongole, Nellore and Chittore.	674	5½
Bellary	Guntoor and Cumbum	582	0½
Berhampore ...	Ichapore	99	0½
Bezwada... ...	Toony, Rajahmundry and Ellore ...	274	0
Bissemcote ...	Goonapore	103	7
Cassimcote ..	Chittivalsa	80	6
Chetterpore ...	Ichapore and Berhampore	113	3½
Chittore ...	Rajahmundry, Bezwada, Ongole and Nellore.	564	3½
Cocanada ...	Toony and Samulcottah	163	7
Cuddapah ...	Rajahmundry, Guntoor and Cumbum. ...	503	2½
Cumbum ...	Rajahmundry, Bezwada and Guntoor ...	406	7½
Cuttack ...	Ichapore, Berhampore, Ganjam and Khoordhah.	215	5½
Ellore	Toony and Rajahmundry	234	7
Ganjam... ...	Ichapore, Berhampore and Chetterpore ...	118	0
Guntoor ...	Toony, Rajahmundry and Bezwada ...	294	0½
Joonaghur ...	Battily, Bissemcote and Mookoly ...	174	1
Kamptee ...	Palcondah, Nowrungapore, Kankar, Sangarhy and Nagpore.	486	4
Kamptee ...	Bissemcote, Mookoly, Joonaghur, Kankar and Weiragarh.	515	2¼
Kamptee ...	Battily, Bissemcote, Mookoly, Joonaghur and Ryepore.	523	7¼
Kamptee ...	Nowrungapore, Dhamtery and Ryepore ...	514	3½
Kankar ...	Palcondah and Nowrungapore	268	1
Kankar ...	Battily, Bissemcote, Mookoly and Joonaghur.	294	0¾
Khariar... ...	Battily and Joonaghur	211	7¾
Kimedy ...	Savarcote	40	5
Madras ...	Toony, Rajahmundry, Bezwada, Guntoor and Nellore.	546	4½
Masulipatam ...	Toony, Rajahmundry and Ellore ...	279	5½
Masulipatam ...	Rajahmundry and Mogultoor	270	1
Nagpore ...	Palcondah, Kankar and Sangarhy ...	476	4
Nagpore ...	Bissemcote, Mookoly, Joonaghur, Kankar, and Weiragarh.	505	2¼
Narrainpooram	Palcondah	77	6

To	Viâ	Miles and Furlongs.
Nellore	Toony, Rajahmundry, Bezwada and Guntoor.	438 6½
Nowrungapore.	Palcondah	142 6
Ongole	Toony, Rajahmundry, Bezwada and Guntoor.	362 3½
Palcondah ...	......	25 0
Parvatipore ...	Palcondah	53 6
Rajahmundry...	Toony	179 6
Russellcondah .	Ichapore and Berhampore	147 0½
Ryepore ...	Bissemcote, Mookoly, Joonaghur and Khariar.	330 5¾
Ryepore ...	Nowrungapore and Dhamtery	321 2
Ryepore ...	Nowrungapore and Kankar	341 1
Samulcottah ...	Chittivalasa, Cassimcote, Toony and Juggampett.	155 7
Sangarhy ...	Palcondah and Kankar	408 7
Secunderabad...	Toony, Rajahmundry and Bezwada ...	440 6½
Sonapore ...	Birsola	93 1½
Sonapore ...	Bissemcote, Mookoly and Madnapor ...	232 2
Sumbulpore ...	Berhampore, Khoordah and Sonapore ...	367 7½
Toony	Chittivalasa and Cassimcote	118 3
Vizagapatam ...	Chittivalasa	64 1
Vizianagram ..	Chittivalasa	59 1
Vizianagram ...	Palcondah	72 1
Weiragarh ...	Battily, Bissemcote, Mookoly and Joonaghur.	408 2¼

CHICK (چق - chik, *Hind.*). From Turkish. Screen-blind made of finely-split bamboo [q.v.], loosely fastened together in parallel lines by perpendicular strings, and often painted. It is hung or framed in doorways or windows, both in houses and in tents [tatty]. Also on the West coast short for chickeen, a sum of four rupees; the Venetian zecchino, cecchino, or sequin [chequin]. See vol. I, 609.

CHICKEN MUTTY (چکنی مٹی - chiknímattí, *Hind.*). From (chikná, hind. unctuous + mattí, hind. earth). Potter's clay [calimunn].

CHICKLEDAR (صيقل گر - saikalgar, *Hind.*; చికిలిదారుడు - chikilidárudu, *Tel.*). From (saikal, ar. polish + agent suffix). Polisher of arms [inam], armourer.

CHICKRAINY (చికిరేణి - chíkiréni, *Tel.*). Same as Dark sirissa.

CHICKRASSY (چکرسی - chukrásí, *Hind.*; چٹگام - chatgám, *Dec.*; ದುಲ್ಮರ - dulmara, *Can.*; చిట్టిగాంగుచెట్టు - chittigángu-chettu, *Tel.*; അകിൽ - akil, *Mal.*; හුලන්හික්ගස් - hulanhikgas, *Singh.*; மதகரிவேம்பு - mathagarivémbu, *Tam.*). Tel. means chittagong wood tree. Tam. from (mathagiri, tam. place, so called + vémbu, tam. neem tree, melia azadirachta, linn.) [javanese cedar]. Tel. also (máganimánu), meaning mahogany tree. Tam. also (agil) [eagle-wood, tiger's milk]. Title otherwise Bastard cedar [large neem, soymida], Jamaica cedar, Chittagong wood [toon], Indian mahogany. Botanically Chickrassia tabularis, ad. juss., meliaceæ [vricsham, 36]. Chickrassia from hindostany. Alias Chickrassia nimmonii, velutina; Swietenia chickrassia. Tree of large size, often 8–10 feet in girth with a thick straight trunk 60 or 80 feet to first bough, rust colored deeply cracked bark; calyx short, five-toothed; petals five-erect; leaves abruptly pinnated; leaflets five to eight pair, nearly opposite, obliquely ovate-oblong, unequal-sided, obtusely acuminated, quite entire, more or less conspicuous, hairy in the axils of the nerves beneath; panicles terminal, erect; capsule ovoid, three-celled, three-valved, dehiscent, septifragal; stamen-tube sub-cylindrical, rather shorter than the petals, striated, with ten short antheriferous teeth; seeds numerous, expanding downwards into a wing, and imbricated in a double series across the cells; flowers large, greenish white; found sparingly in most hill forests. Bark powerfully astringent, though not bitter. Flower yields red and yellow dyes [shauyam]; stem gives a transparent, amber-colored gum [gond]. Wood light color, well veined and close in the grain, much used for furniture; cedar-like smell; one of the woods known to europeans as bastard cedar; also one of the chittagong woods; its timber used in the interior of the palace of one of the candyan kings is known to have lasted many hundreds of years; much esteemed by cabinet-makers; as furniture it is light, cheap, and durable; but warps to the hot land-wind [q.v.]. No other common species here.

CHIDAMBARAM (سلمبرم - silambaram, *Hind.*; சிதம்பரம் - shithambaram, *Tam.*). From (chit, san. wisdom + ambara, san. atmosphere), Old Tamul name (tillaivanam), meaning tree excæcaria agallocha, willd. + forest; also (tillai); also (shévaiyúr), meaning worship + town; also (puliyúr), meaning tiger town, as the residence of a rishy with a tiger's leg [wycome]; also (manru), meaning hall. Sanscrit name (chitrakúta), meaning beauty + hall; also (pundaríkapura), meaning white lotus, nelumbium speciosum, willd. + town.——**(1)** Talook, South arcot district. Tahsildar's pay Rs. 250. Area 402 square miles. Population 282,275. Language Tamul. S.E. of district. Boundaries:—North, Cuddalore and Vriddhachellam talooks; east, Bay of Bengal and the Coleroon; south, the Coleroon; west, Oodayarpolliem talook, Trichinopoly district. Flat for the most part. Soil, regar [q.v.] for the most part, sandy in the north-eastern part in about thirty-five villages. Manufacture of female cloths of both coarse and fine description. Irrigation:—Pelandoray and Shauttatope anicuts across the Vellaur; Keeranore anicut across the Manimooctah nuddy; Vadavaur and Rajah vycaul channels from the Coleroon; Khan sahib's canal. Places of archæological interest:—Chidambaram, Porto Novo, Shivapoory, Shreemooshnam. Principal Trig. stations:—Ayyampett, Coleroon beacon, Cootchore, Podaiyore, Porto novo. The leading places, &c., in the talook are the following.——*Ayyampett* (அய்யம்பேட்டை - ayyambéttai, Tam.). From (ayyan, tam. the god ayyanár + péttai, tam. suburb). Trig. station; lat. 11° 21′ 49·83″; long. 79° 27′ 09·52″; height 224 feet; from Chidambaram W.S.W. 20 miles; from Polliemcottah W. 4 miles; from the sea W. 27 miles.——*Bhoovangherry* (புவனக்கிரி - puvanakkiri, Tam.). See sep. title.——*Chidambaram* (சிதம்பரம் - shithambaram, Tam.). See below.——*Coleroon* (கொள்ளடம் - kolladam, Tam.). See sep. title.——*Coodalayauttore* (கூடலையாற்றூர் - kúdalaiyáttúr, Tam.). From (kúdal, tam. junction + áru, tam. river + úr, tam. village). Village; pop. 560; acres 855; lat. 11° 25′; long. 79° 31′; from Chidambaram W. 15 miles; from Cuddalore S.W. 29 miles; from the sea W. 22 miles. At the confluence of the Vellaur and the Manimooctah nuddy. Important Shiva temple.——*Cootchore* (குச்சூர் - kuççúr, Tam.). From (kuççu, tam. hut + úr, tam. village). Trig. station; lat. 11° 13′ 12·40″; long. 79° 35′ 18·46″; height 25 feet; from Chidambaram S.W. 15 miles; from Conavausal N.N.E. ¾ mile; from the sea W. 22 miles.——*Khan sahib's canal* (கான்சாயப்புவாய்க்கால் - kánsáyappuváykkál, Tam.). See sep. title.——*Killay* (கிள்ளை - killai, Tam.). Means a black species of parrot. Village; pop. 3,105; acres 3,810; lat. 11° 27′; long. 79° 49′; from Chidambaram E.N.E. 6¾ miles; from Cuddalore S. 19 miles. On the coast. Annual festival called Maushimagham [pundigay, 5b].——*Mannargoody* (மன்னார்குடி - mannárgudi, Tam.). See sep. title.——*Paravanaur* (பரவனாறு - paravanáru, Tam.). See sep. title.——*Podaiyore* (பொடையூர் - podaiyúr, Tam.). From (pudai, tam. side + úr, tam. village). Trig. station; lat. 11° 21′ 26·64″; long. 79° 33′ 29·18″; height 42 feet; from Chidambaram W.S.W. 12 miles; from Cholattiram S.E. ¾ mile; from the sea W. 21 miles.——*Polliemcottah* (பாளையங்கோட்டை - pálaiyangóttai, Tam.). From (pálaiyam, tam. fortified village + kóttai, tam. fort). Village; pop. 5,726; acres 6,919; lat. 11° 22′; long. 79° 31′; from Chidambaram W.S.W. 15 miles; from Cuddalore S.W. 30 miles; from the sea W. 20 miles. Former possession of a Mahomedan family who held it as a jagheer [q.v.] from the Nawaubs of the Carnatic [q.v.]. Some members of this family still survive and hold inam lands in Polliemcottah and surrounding villages. Besieged by the French in 1754 and relieved by the English. Old fort.——*Porto novo* (பரங்கிப்பேட்டை - parangippéttai, Tam.). See sep. title.——*Rajah vycaul* (இராசாவாய்க்கால் - irásáváykkál, Tam.). From (rájá, san. king + váykkál, tam. channel). Otherwise North rajah vycaul to distinguish from South rajah vycaul of Tanjore. Channel; from Chidambaram S. 3 miles; from Cuddalore S. 30 miles; from the sea W. 11 miles. Large irrigation channel which takes off from the Coleroon and irrigates 19,000 acres.——*Shauttatope* (சாத்தத்தோப்பு - sháttatóppu, Tam.). From (sháttan, tam. epithet of ayyanár + tóppu, tam. grove). Village; pop. 701; lat. 11° 28′; long. 79° 35′; from Chidambaram W.N.W. 11 miles; from Cuddalore S.W. 23 miles; from the sea W. 16 miles. Site of an anicut on the Vellaur.——*Shreemooshnam* (ஸ்ரீமுட்டணம் - shirímuttanam, Tam.). See sep. title.——*Vadavaur* (வடவாறு - vadaváru, Tam. vadavár *). From (vada, tam. north + áru, tam. river). Channel; from Chidambaram S.W. 17 miles; from Cuddalore S.W. 38 miles; from the sea W. 24 miles. A channel branching from the Coleroon, irrigating 10,000 acres and feeding Veeraunam tank.——*Veeraunam* (வீராணம் - viránam, Tam.). See sep. title.——*Vellaur* (வெள்ளாறு - velláru, Tam.). See sep. title.——

(2) Town, Municipality, Talook head-quarters, S.I. railway station; pop. 18,640; acres 1,105; lat. 11° 24′; long. 79° 44′; height 16 feet; from Cuddalore S.S.W. 21 miles; from Madras S.S.W. 120 miles; from Tindivanam S. 57 miles; from Tranquebar N.N.W. 26 miles; from Tricalore S.E. 51 miles; from Vriddhachellam E.S.E. 26 miles; from the sea W. 8 miles. In an alluvial plain on the route from Tranquebar to Arcot, half way between the Coleroon and the Vellaur. In 1749 the ill-fated expedition under Captain Cope against Devicottah halted at Chidambaram on its retreat to Fort St. David. In 1750 the armies of Moraury row and Moozuffer jung met here. In 1753 the French took the neighbouring fort of Bhoovangherry and occupied the Chidambarám pagoda on its being evacuated by the English garrison. In the same year the French and Mahratta forces met at Chidambaram before marching to Trichinopoly. In 1759 an attempt to capture the pagoda by the English failed; the garrison however surrendered in 1760. Hyder improved the defences and placed a garrison in the pagoda [q.v.] to maintain his line of communication with Pondicherry. In 1781, Sir Eyre Coote attacked the pagoda but was driven off. This attack was probably made on the west entrance. The Shiva pagoda covers an area of 39 acres in the centre of the town. Known as the Sabhanaicker coil. It contains the Aucausha lingam or air-lingam, also known as the Chidambara rahasyam, one of the five lingams [q.v.] of the elements found in Southern india. It was probably built by a Chola mundalam ruler. There are five halls known as Canacasabhay, Chit sabhay, Deva sabhay, Nritya sabhay and Rajah sabhay. There are also a Vishnoo coil and a Pillaiyaur coil, the latter containing an idol of Ganesh, the largest in India. In the centre is the shrine of Parvaty, a beautiful building containing a golden canopy with superb fringes of bullion. The mantapam [q.v.] has more than 1,100 carved pillars, each a solid block. The lights from the gopooram [q.v.], 122 feet high, can be seen at sea 10 miles distant. The greater part of the temple is of granite [caroom cull], and the whole of the stone must have been carried 40 miles and across the Vellaur river. The stone-work was mutilated by Hyder ally. The tank is called Shiva gungay or Hemapooshcarny. There is a black granular deposit at the bottom, the composition of which is curious. It does not adhere to the hand like mud. This is said to be owing to the quantity of oil, honey [shahad] and ghee [q.v.] which flowing into the tank from the temple daily when the idol is washed and anointed has in the course of years been carried to the bottom and affected the deposit. After two or three days' exposure to the sun thin deposit cakes into a stiff clay. The pagoda is the property of the class of Deecshita bramins. The Hindoos of Ceylon and the Nautcottay merchants of Madura contribute largely to its support. A French author mentions the existence of a remarkable stone chain in the pagoda, each link of which was 3 feet long, and its entire length 548 feet. No trace of this remains. The Ardrah darshanam [pundigay, 5e], held in December or January, lasts for ten days and is attended by from 60,000 to 70,000 persons. Weaving of silk and cotton cloths is carried on. A remarkable feature in the town is the large number of chuttrams; there are sixty-nine in all. The Caushimutt, the largest, is capable of holding eight hundred or nine hundred persons. There is a Tamul proverb :—சிதம்பரத்திலே பிறந்த பிள்ளைக்குத் திருவெம்பாவை கற்றுக் கொடுக்கவேண்டுமோ ?—"Is it necessary to teach holy "verses to a child born and brought up at Chidambaram ?" And another—பொன்னம்பலத்துக்கும் புவனகிரிப் பட்டணத்துக்கும் என்றைக்கும் உண்டான இழவு—"The "golden hall of Chidambaram and the town Bhoovangherry are "always in trouble, having been so often attacked."

CHIKAN (چکن - chikan, *Hind.*). Net-work.——*Chikan dozeé* (چکن‌دوزی - chikandozí, Hind.). From (above + dozí, pers. sewing); forming meshes by sewing. Cotton embroidery on muslin [q.v.]. Includes figured or flowered work; also net-work formed by breaking down the texture of the cloth with the needle, and converting it into open meshes.

CHIKAT POOLDY (சிகத்துப்புழுதி - shigattuppuzhuthi, *Tam.*). From (sheykál, tam. field + puzhuthi, tam. fine mould). Wet lands which have been ploughed but not sown.

CHIKKA (ಚಿಕ್ಕ - chikka, *Can.*). Small. Common name of Mysore rajahs, as Chikka deva, Chikka rajah. Prefix in place names, as Chikmagalore, meaning small + daughter + village.

CHIKSAH (چکسا - chiksá, *Hind.*). A perfumed powder made up of a great variety of ingredients the principal being sandal [q.v.], zedoary [q.v.], benzoin [q.v.], camphor [q.v.], &c., used by Mahomedan females.

CHIKTY (چکتی - chiktí, *Hind.*; அடையொட்டி - ádaiyotti, *Tam.*). Hind. from (chikat, hind. gummy). Tam. from (ádai, tam. dress + ottu, tam. to stick), from sticky fruit. Title otherwise Paroquet burr, West indian burweed. Botanically Triumfetta annua, linn., tiliaceæ [vricsham, 27]. Annual; leaves ovate, toothed, smooth above, somewhat hairy on the nerves beneath; peduncles axillary, three-flowered; flowers small, yellow. Fruit size of large pea [calauyam]. Other common species are :—Neglecta, flowers yellow. Pilosa, flowers yellow; fruit small, size of cherry. Rhomboidea, flowers yellow; fruit about size of a vetch seed; eaten as pot-herb in times of scarcity; coarse, strong bark. Rotundifolia, flowers small, yellow.

CHILBINJ (چل‌بینج - chilbínj, *Dec.*). Same as Clearing-nut.

CHILKA * (చిలక - chilaka, *Tel.*). Means a parrot. Lake, Canal; Ganjam dist.; Biridy, Paulore and Cullicote zemindarries; lat. 19° 28′ to 19° 56′ N.; long. 85° 08′ to 85° 38′ E.—"*a*" The lake is an extensive marine lagoon [cauyal] on the north-western side of the Bay of Bengal, forming the northern boundary of the Northern circars and dividing Ganjam from Pooree district in Bengal. Bounded east and south by a low sandy ridge in places little more than 200 yards wide, which separates it from the Bay of Bengal; and north-west by the mountains which extend from the Mahanuddy to the Godavery. Northward it loses itself in endless shallows, sedgy banks, and islands just above the surface, formed from the silt which the rivers bring down. It communicates with the sea by a single narrow mouth, cut through the sandy ridge, in lat. 19° 42′; long. 85° 40′. It is pear shaped; 44 miles in length from north-east to south-west; the northern half has a mean breadth of about 20 miles, while the southern half tapers into an irregularly curved point, barely averaging 5 miles wide. Area, 344 square miles in the dry weather, increasing to about 450 during the rainy season. Average depth, from 3 to 5 feet, scarcely anywhere exceeding 6 feet. The bed is a very few feet below the high-water level of the sea, although in some parts it is slightly below low-water mark. The distant inner portion of the lake keeps about 2 feet higher than the exterior ocean at all stages of the tide. It receives a branch of the Mahanuddy. The narrow tidal stream, which rushes through the neck connecting the lake with the sea, suffices to keep the water distinctly salt during the dry months from December to June. But as soon as the rains have set in, and the rivers come pouring down upon its northern extremity, the sea-water is gradually driven out, and the Chilka passes through various stages of brackishness until it becomes a fresh-water lake. The Chilka is the result of a breach of the sea over a flat sandy shore, whose elevation is above the level of the country within. Poolicat lake is of similar formation. Old documents show that a century ago the neck of land was only from half a mile to a mile broad in places where it is now two miles. On the other hand, the opening in the bar, which was a mile wide in 1780 and had to be crossed in large boats, was described forty years later as choked up. Shortly before 1825, an artificial mouth had to be cut; and although this also rapidly began to silt up, it remained as late as 1837 more than three times its present breadth. The villagers allege that it still grows narrower year by year; and the difficulty in maintaining an outlet forms one of the chief obstacles to utilizing the lake as an escapement for the floods that desolate the delta. The scenery is varied, and in parts picturesque. In the south and west it is dotted with a number of small rocky islands. Proceeding northwards, the lake expands into a majestic sheet of water. Half-way across is Nalbanah, or the reed forest, an island about 5 miles in circumference, scarcely anywhere rising more than a few inches above water level. It is altogether uninhabited, but is regularly visited by thatchers from the mainland, who cut the reeds and high grasses with which it is completely covered. On the eastern side lie the islands of Parikad, with new silt formations behind, and now partially joined to the narrow ridge of land which separates the Chilka from the sea. At some places they emerge almost imperceptibly from the water; at others they spread out into well-raised rice-fields. Their northern extremity slopes gracefully down to the lake like an English park, dotted with fine trees, and backed by masses of foliage. Water-fowl of all kinds are abundant. Salt-making is largely carried on in Parikaud. Beyond the northern end of Parikaud, the lake gradually shallows until it becomes solid ground. At this point the Pooree rivers empty themselves into the lake, and silting is going on steadily. The northern shores of the Chilka comprise the pergunnahs of Sirye and Chowbiskud, and these tracts have to bear the greatest suffering in times of general inundation in Pooree. Until Ganjam was deserted on account of its unhealthiness, the Chilka lake was during the hot months a frequent resort of Europeans from this Presidency. At the southern extremity of the lake stands the village of Rambha, having an extensive trade in grain with Orissa, for which it gives salt in exchange.—"*b*" The Chilka canal, connecting the southern extremity of the lake with the Rooshcoolya river, is 7 miles in length, and navigable throughout the year. Large quantities of grain and salt are carried along it. The present canal terminates at Ganjam.

CHILLA (چله - chhillah, *Hind.*). From (chehl, pers. forty). Any period of forty days; as a forty days' fast, forty days after child-birth, &c.; called mundalam by hindoos.

CHILLAM (चिल्ल - chilla, *San.*). From (chill, san. to sport). Milvinæ, falconidæ [bheroondam], raptores, aves [pacshy, 2], of naturalists [jantoo]. Kites. Bill short and weak, waved nostrils at base; wings long and pointed; tarsi short and strong; toes broad and well-padded beneath. The species best known to the natives are shown below.——*Braminy kite* (क्षेमङ्करी - kshémankarí, San.; رو مبارك - rúmubárak, Pers.; گرڑپکھ - gararpakh, Hind.; بہمنی چیل - bahmaníchíl, Dec.; ಗರುಡ - garuda, Can.; గరుత్మంతుడు - garutmantudu, Tel.; ഗരുഡൻ - garudan, Mal.; கருடன் - karudan, Tam.). Title from its sacred character. San. from (kshéma, san. happiness + kri, san. to do); as a bird of good omen. Pers. from (rú, pers. face + mubárak, ar. auspicious). Hind. from (garuda, san. the kite + pakshi, san. bird). Dec. from (bahmaní, hind. bramin + chíl, hind. kite). Can. from (garut, san. wing + dí, san. to fly); from being much on the wing. Tel. from (garut, san. wing + vat, san. having). Mal. and tam. like canarese. San. also (shankarachilla), meaning shiva's kite, of bengal. Hind. also (dhobíchíl), meaning washerman's kite; (chúhámár), meaning rat-killer. Tel. also (garudálváru), meaning braminy kite + ruler [garoodan]; (shemberrid), from (shembarundu, tam.), meaning red kite; (pisgenda), from ghond. Title otherwise Maroon-backed kite, Rufous kite. Haliastur indus, alias Haliaetus ponticerianus; Milvus ponticerianus, rotundicaudus. Adult, head, neck and body below, as far as the middle of the abdomen, white, rest of the plumage rich chestnut rufous. Length 21 inches. Young bird pale brown, feathers of head, neck, and lower parts lighter streaked, upper feathers spotted, with fulvous or whitish wings, reach somewhat beyond the end of the tail. Abundant on sea coasts, and in the vicinity of wet cultivation; rare in dry plains. Usual food is carrion. Much on the wing. Usually selects a palm tree to build in. Has a peculiar squeal; but is not so noisy a bird as the pariah-kite [q.v.]. Natives regard it as the vauhan [q.v.] of Vishnoo. At the cry of Hary! Hary! the birds assemble, and animal food is tossed to them. The birds are expert fishers. There is a Tamul proverb:—வெண்டலைக் கருடன் வந்திடமானுல் எவர் கைப்பொருளும் தன் பொருள் ஆகும்—"When a Braminy kite crosses one from "right to left he may become possessed of the wealth of all." Friar Jordanus, the Quilon Bishop of the fourteenth century, has the following:—"There is also in this India a certain bird, big "like a kite, having a white head and belly, but all red above, "which boldly snatches fish out of the hands of fishermen and "other people, and indeed these birds go on just like dogs."——*Honey kite* (माधव - mádhava, San.; شهديلا - shahdílá, Hind.; ಜೇನುಅಲವೆ - jénualave, Can.; తేనెగద్ద - ténegadda, Tel.; தேன்பருந்து - ténbarundu, Tam.). Title from feeding on honey. San. from (madhu, san. honey). Hind. from (shahad, hind. honey). Can. from (jénu, can. honey). Tel. from (téne, tel. honey + gadda, tel. kite). Tam. from (tén, tam. honey + parundu, tam. kite). Tel. also (jutalu), of yerkalas. Title otherwise Crested honey buzzard. Pernis cristata, alias Pernis bharatensis, elliotti, maculosa. Found in forest. Feeding by preference on honey [shahad], and the young of bees [tainee] and wasps. Thickly feathered in defence against the stings.——*Pariah kite* (घार - ghára, Mahr.; حداة - hidát, Ar.; غليواز - ghilíwáz, Pers.; چيل - chil, Hind. and Dec.; ಹದ್ದು - haddu, Can.; మాలగద్ద - málagadda, Tel.; பறைப்பருந்து - paraipparundu, Tam.). Title from color. Mahr. from (gridhra, san. kite). Pers. from (ghiliu, pers. to fly high). Hind. from the cry. Tel. from (mála, tel. the caste + gadda, tel. kite). Tam. from (parai, tam. the caste + parundu, tam. kite). Ar. also (abulkhattáf), meaning father of swallows; (abussalti), meaning father of sharpness in seizing. Pers. also (zughan). Tam. also (karumbarundu), meaning dark kite. Milvus govinda, alias Haliaetus lineatus; Milvus ater, cheele, indicus. Adult, head and neck pale brown, or rufous or reddish, upper plumage brown; male 23 to 24 inches. Young bird brown, numerously spotted with whitish, or streaked on the head, neck, and lower parts, and the other feathers edged and tipped pale. Closely related to Milvus ater of Europe. Very common. Pick up garbage of all kinds. Vast numbers in large towns. Collect in numbers without any apparent object, especially towards evening. May often be seen seated on the entablatures of buildings, with their breast to the wall, and wings spread out, as represented in Egyptian monuments. Cry is a prolonged tremulous squeal.

CHILLARAY (چلره - chilrah, *Hind.*). Miscellaneous.——*Chillar cash* (சில்லறைக்காசு - shillaraikkásu, Tam.). From (above + kásu, tam. coin). Madura coin, 1,320 to 1 star pagoda.

CHILLIMILLY (چلميرى - chalmerí, *Hind.*). Brazil cherry.

CHILLUM (چلم - chilam, *Hind.*). The part of the hookah [q.v.], which contains the tobacco [pogauk], charcoal balls [adoopp kary] and fire.

CHILLY (मरिच - maricha, *San.*; مرچ - mirch, *Hind.*). Title from mexican, whence came through indian archipelago. San. from (mri, san. to kill); from pungency. Late greek κάψικον. Title otherwise Capsicum, Garden ginger, Guinea pepper, Pod pepper. Botanically the Capsicum genus, solanaceæ [vricsham, 94]. Annual or perennial herbs, glabrous or nearly so; leaves entire or with margins wavy; fruit variable in form and size, many-seeded; fruits and seeds possess hot pungent properties; for ordinary culinary purposes only two kinds are required, the annuum or common country kind, and the minimum or very small sort called bird's-eye; cayenne pepper or guinea pepper or red pepper, is powder of the ripe dried pods of one or other species, or sometimes several mixed; before pulverizing the pods are called chillies. The species best known to the natives are shown below.——*Bird's eye chilly* (मरीच - marícha, San.; فلفل احمر - filfiliahmar, Ar.; پلپل سرخ - pilpilisurkh, Pers.; لال مرچ - lálmirch, Hind.; لال مرچى - lálmirchí, Dec.; چبئى روت - chabairawit, Malay; ಪರಂಗಿಮೆಣಸಿನಗಿಡ - parangimenasinagida, Can.; సూదిమిరప - súdimirapa, Tel.; കപ്പൽമുളക - kappalmulaku, Mal.; මිරිස් - miris, Singh.; ஊசிமிளகாய் - úsimilagáy, Tam.). Title from smallness of pod. San. from (mri, san. to kill); from pungency. Ar. from (filfil, ar. chilly + ahmar, ar. red). Pers. from (pilpil, pers. chilly + surkh, pers. red). Hind. from (lál, hind. red + marícha, san. chilly). Can. from (parangi, can. european + menasu, can. pepper, piper nigrum, linn. + gida, can. plant). Tel. from (súdi, tel. needle + miriyamu, tel. pepper). Mal. from (kappal, mal. ship + mulaku, mal. pepper, piper nigrum, linn.). Singh. from sanscrit. Tam. from (úsi, tam. needle + milagáy, tam. chilly); from shape of fruit. Hind. also (gáchmirch). Mal. also (kántári), meaning heat producing, from extreme pungency. Tam. also (shímaippaççaimilagáy), meaning foreign + green + pepper + fruit. Title otherwise Bird pepper, Needle chilly, Small-podded capsicum. Botanically Capsicum [chilly] minimum, roxb., solanaceæ [vricsham, 94]. Alias Capsicum, baccatum, fastigiatum. Very fiery; used chiefly for making chilly vinegar [candy].——*Caffree chilly* (كافرى مرچ كا پيڑ - káfrímirchkáper, Hind.; كافرى مرچى كا جهاڑ - káfrímirchíkájhár, Dec.; ഉപ്പേരിമുളക - uppérimulaku, Mal.; காப்பிரிமிளகாய் - káppirimilagáy, Tam.). Hind. from (káfrí, hind. large + mirch, hind. chilly, capsicum annuum, linn. + per, hind. tree). Mal. from (uppéri, mal. curry + mulaku, mal. capsicum). Tam. from (káfri, hind. large + milagáy, tam. chilly). Tam. also (kudamilagáy), meaning pot chilly; from shape of fruit. Title otherwise Bell-pepper from bell-shaped fruit, Giant capsicum. Botanically Capsicum [chilly] grossum, willd., solanaceæ [vricsham, 94]. A very large species with mild fruit, size of small apple, skin fleshy and tender. Cultivated chiefly for europeans; who either use them in stews, or have them opened, stuffed with certain spices, and pickled in vinegar. There is a variety of this, Cerasiformis, giving Cherry pepper.——*Common chilly* (मरीच - marícha, San.; मिरशेंग - mirashénga, Mahr.; मिरसांग - mirasánga, Conc.; فلفل احمر - filfiliahmar, Ar.; پلپل سرخ - pilpilisurkh, Pers.; مرچ كا پيڑ - mirchkáper, Hind.; مرچى كا جهاڑ - mirchíkájhár, Dec.; ಮೆನಸಿನಕಾಯಿ - menasinakáyi, Can.; ಪರೆಂಗಿಮುಞ್ಚಿ - parengimunchi, Too.; మిరప - mirapa, Tel.; ଲଙ୍କାମରିଚ - laukámáucho, Oor.; കപ്പൽമുളക - kappalmulaku, Mal.; මිරිස් - miris, Singh.; மிளகாய் - milagáy, Tam.). San. from (mri, san. to kill); from pungent taste, properly pepper. Mahr. from (mirachí, mahr. chilly + shénga, mahr. pod). Ar. from (filfil, ar. chilly + ahmar, ar. red). Pers. from (pilpil, pers. chilly + surkh, pers. red). Hind. from sanscrit. Can. from (menasu, can. pepper + káyi, can. fruit). Too. from (parengi, too. european + munchi, too. pepper). Tel. from (miriyamu, tel. pepper). Mal. from (kappal, mal. ship + mulaku, mal. pepper, piper nigrum, linn.). Singh. from sanscrit. Tam. from (milagu, tam. pepper, piper nigrum, linn. + káy, tam. pod). Hind. also (gáchmirch). Dec. also (lálmirchíkájhár), meaning red + chilly + plant. Can. also (p'harengimenasinakáye), meaning european pepper fruit; (kempumenasu), meaning red pepper. Tel. also (miriyapukáya), meaning pepper + fruit; (mirchi). Mal. also (parankimulaku), meaning foreign pepper; (mulaku), meaning pepper; (valiyakappalmulaku), meaning large foreign pepper. Singh. also (ratamiris), meaning foreign chilly. Title otherwise Curry pepper, Europe pepper, Guinea pepper, Large foreign pepper, Large-podded capsicum, Laul mirch, Pod-pepper, Red-pepper, Spanish pepper. Botanically Capsicum [chilly] annuum, linn., solanaceæ [vricsham, 94]. Alias Capsicum angulosum, cordiforme, longum, milleri, olivæforme, sphæricum, tetragonum. Annual of dark green color, introduced from south america. 1–2 feet, stem herbaceous; calyx five-toothed; corolla five-cleft; leaves solitary, scattered, entire; peduncles extra-axillary, one-flowered; fruit oblong, pendulous or erect, red, yellow, or variegated; flowers white. The pods are taper, scarlet or yellow-colored, and filled with a pulp which contains many small, flat, kidney-shaped seeds. The acridity of pod depends on an alkaloid capsicine; it differs from the other kinds of pepper [q.v.] in being pungent without being aromatic; the ash should not exceed six per cent., and the pepper should give up twenty-five per cent. of its weight to alcohol and 9 or 10 to ether. Cultivated in black loam dry or wet, chiefly in cold season; ground prepared in south in audy [mausum] or july, on coromandel in shrauvanam or august and bhaudrapadam or september, ploughing four or five times; seed of a year old sown in south in arpisy or october; on coromandel in shrauvanam or august and bhaudrapadam or september; seeds sown in nursery in both cases; while under growth weeds are cleared and water given every four or five days; full grown crop shows chillies red, flowers white, leaves green, 2 feet high; chillies gathered when ripe three months after transplantation by the hand; chillies then dried on mats in sun and stored; produce brought to market in one month; dried chilly is sold in south by weight at the rate of about 1¼ rupee per toolaum [q.v.] of 14⅖ lbs.; on coromandel 1 viss [q.v.] per three or four annas. Dried ripe fruit is in medicine substituted for british peppermint oil and the mustard flour imported from europe; gives to pharm. capsicum fruit the ripe fruit dried, capsici fructus, activity residing in a resinous principle, capsicine; acrid stimulant, locally applied, rubefacient; preparation tinctura capsici; officinal. In veterinary practice, take a handful of cayenne pepper, make into paste with an ounce of black pepper, and apply to mange parts, wash after four hours and repeat after a week. Chillies are a principal ingredient in all curries, promoting digestion; by pouring hot vinegar upon pods, chilly vinegar is prepared. There are numerous varieties. There is a Tamul proverb:—ஆனைக்குத் தறடும் அன்னத்துக்கு மிளகாயும் வேண்டும்—"An elephant requires a goad, and "boiled rice a chilly."——*Nepaul chilly* (नैपालमरीच - naipálamarícha, San.). Botanically Capsicum [chilly] nepalense, owen, solanaceæ [vricsham, 94].——*Shrubby chilly* (बृहन्मरीच - brihanmarícha, San.; मिरची - mirachí, Mahr.; فلفل احمر - filfiliahmar, Ar.; پلپل سرخ - pilpilisurkh, Pers.; مرچ - mirch, Hind.; مرچى - mirchí, Dec.; چبئى سابرنگ - chabaisábrang, Malay; ಮೆಣಸು - menasu, Can.; మిరప - mirapa, Tel.; മുളക - mulaku, Mal.; ගස්මිරිස් - gasamiris, Singh.; மிளகாய் - milagáy, Tam.). San. from (brihat, san. large + marícha, san. pepper). Mahr. from (maricha, san. pepper). Ar. from (filfil, ar. chilly + ahmar, ar. red). Pers. from (pilpil, pers. chilly + surkh, pers. red). Hind. from sanscrit. Tel. from (miriyamu, tel. pepper). Mal. from tamul. Singh. from (gasa, singh. tree + miris, singh. chilly). Tam. from (milagu, tam. pepper, piper nigrum, linn. + káy, tam. pod). Title otherwise Goat pepper, Golcondah chilly,

Spur pepper. Botanically Capsicum [chilly] frutescens, linn., solanaceæ [vricsham, 94]. A common large species; qualities the same as annuum. Two varieties, red and yellow.

CHILWAH (چلوا - chilwá, *Hind.*). From sanscrit. Otherwise White carp. The genus Chela, cyprininæ, cyprinidæ, physostomi, teleostei, pisces [matsyam, 39], of naturalists [jantoo]. Bright silvery fishes, long in the body, with small heads and upturned mouths, the dorsal fin being placed very far back. They keep mostly at the surface of the water, feeding on insects. Good eating. The species best known to the natives are :—argentea, bacaila, clupeoides, gora, phulo, untrahi.

CHINA (چینی - chíní, *Pers.*). Chinese [cheen]. So often anything foreign.——*China anise* (نبات بادیان خطائی - nabátibádiyánikhátái, Ar.). Same as Star anise.——*China castor* (درخت بید انجیر خطائی - darakhtibedanjirikhatái, Pers.). Same as Jamalgota.——*China corn* (کنگنی - kanguí, Hind.). Same as Tinay.——*China cotton* (ചീനപ്പരുത്തി - chínapparutti, Mal.). Same as Lotus beudy.——*China date* (خرماہ چین - khurmahichín, Hind.). Same as Bair.——*China date plum* (چین کا گاب - chínkágáb, Hind.). Same as Chinese gaub.——*China dolichos* (چین کی کلتھی - chínkíkulthí, Hind.). Same as Cow gram.——*China dwarf bamboo* (چینی بمبو - chíníbambú, Hind.). Same as Dwarf bamboo.——*China fennel* (نبات بادیان خطائی - nabátibádiyánikhatái, Ar.). Same as Star anise.——*China fever plant* (گندھالی - gandhálí, Hind.). Hind. means fetid bough. Same as Gandhalee.——*China flower* (گل چینی - gulchíní, Hind.). Same as Shaumanty.——*China fruit creeper* (ಚೀನಿಕಾಯಿಬಳ್ಳಿ - chínikáyiballi, Can.). Same as Great pumpkin.——*China grass* (اتنگن - utangan, Hind.; انجورا - anjúrá, Dec.). Title otherwise Grass-cloth plant, Nettle, Ramee grass, Rhea. Botanically Urtica nivea, linn., urticaceæ [vricsham, 119]. Alias Bœhmeria nivea. Perennial, herbaceous; leaves large, alternate, of equal shape, broadly ovate or elliptic-rounded, acuminate, cordate at the base, or more often shortly cuneate near the petiole, more seldom alternate or truncated at the base, crenate-serrate, snowy-tomentose beneath, scabrous above; stipules free; glomerules loosely cymose-panicled; fructiferous perigonium elliptic or oblong-compressed, hairy; easy of cultivation and of luxuriant and rapid vegetation. Fibres of bark used for textile fabrics. The common nettle is dioica. The malabar nettle, devil's nettle, fever nettle is crenulata; common in western coast moist forests; with natives the sting brings on fever.——*China honey suckle* (विलायतीचमेली - viláyatíchamélí, Mahr.). Same as Rangoon creeper.——*China lablab* (சீனியவரை - shíniyavarai, Tam.). Same as Guar.——*China laurel* (നൂലിത്താലി - núlitáli, Mal.). Same as Nolatauly.——*China olive* (چین کا زیتون - chínkázaitún, Hind.). Same as Elemi.——*China pepper* (चीनिमिर्संग - chínimirsánga, Conc.; سیتل چینی - sítalchíní, Hind.; کباب چینی - kabábchíní, Dec.; ಗಂಡಮೆಣಸು - gandamenasu, Can.; മലയാളമുഞ്ചി - malayálamunchi, Too.; ചീനമുളക - chínamulaku, Mal.). Conc. means chinese pepper. Hind. from (sítal, hind. cool + chíní, hind. chinese pepper). Dec. means chinese cubebs [cubeb pepper]; from resemblance. Can. from (ganda, can. male + menasu, can. pepper, piper nigrum, linn.). Too. from (malayála, too. malabar + munchi, too. pepper). Mal. from (chína, mal. chinese + mulaku, mal. pepper). Mal. also (kappalmulaku), meaning foreign pepper. Title otherwise Allspice, Bayberry, Cabobcheeny of madras, Indian allspice, Jamaica allspice, Jamaica pepper, Pimento, Stal cherry of bengal, Wild cinnamon, Wild clove. Botanically Pimenta acris, wight, myrtaceæ [vricsham, 56]. Alias Caryophyllus racemosus; Eugenia acris; Myrcia acris, pimentoides; Myrtus acris, aromatica, caryophyllata. Tree; 20–30 feet; young branches acutely four-angled; leaves opposite, elliptic-oval, obtuse, very glabrous, upper side reticulated with elevated veins; peduncles compressed, axillary and terminal, trichotomous, corymbose, rather longer than the leaves; calyx limb five-partite, segments roundish; berry globose, one to four-seeded; flowers small, white; introduced from west indies. Berries have an aromatic odour, resembling a mixture of cinnamon, cloves and nutmegs; bark astringent and aromatic. Gives to pharm. dried unripe berries, pimenta. properties similar to clove; officinal. Leaves and berries used in cooking; berries yield oil of pimento by distillation. Timber is hard, red and heavy. No other common species here.——*China root* (چوب چینی - chobchíní, Hind.). See sep. title.——*China shoe plant* (جاسوت چینی - jásútichíní, Hind.). Same as China rose bendy.——*China smilax* (چوب چینی - chobchíní, Hind.). Same as Common china root.——*China sugar-cane* (چین کا گنا - chínkáganná, Hind.). Same as Sweet cholum.——*China tallow* (तोयपिप्पली - tóyapippalí, San.; پپلیانگ - pippalíyáng, Hind.). San. from (tóya, san. water + pippalí, san. long pepper, piper longum, linn.); from capsules like pepper. Title otherwise Poplar-leaved croton, Water long-pepper. Botanically Excæcaria [agaroo] sebifera, muell. arg., euphorbiaceæ [vricsham, 118]. Alias Carumbium sebiferum; Sapium sebiferum. Tree; leaves long-petioled, rhombovate, entire, sharply accuminate at the apex, sub-membranaceous; racemes spiciform, terminal, at length far exceeding the leaves; bracts very broadly ovate, acute, many-flowered, many times shorter than the aggregated pedicles; male calyx two to three-cleft, female three-partite, one to two of the segments often cleft, and the calyx then becomes irregularly and spuriously five-partite; stamens most frequently two; styles connate below into a column, above recurved, spreading; capsules largish, globose ellipsoid, sub-acute, thinly fleshy, long, black; seeds furnished under the skin with a thick, white, tallowy bed, forming a spurious aril; native of china. The vegetable tallow is obtained from kernels by expression; by boiling it becomes as hard as bees' wax [mom]. Vaidyans prepare with dry and fresh plant and mustard-seed, oil a decoction, used as liniment in fever. In candles the tallow gives a bright, clear, inodorous flame, without smoke, has to be cased in wax to make it firm; from shell and stone or seed, oil is extracted, used for lamps; leaves are valuable as dye [shauyam]. Timber is white and close-grained and well-fitted for printing-blocks.——*China tree* (ಚೀನಾಚೆಟ್ಟು - chínáchettu, Tel.). Same as China mindie.——*China tuber* (ചീനക്കിഴങ്ങ് - chínikkizhannu, Mal.). Same as Sweet potato.——*China water-lily* (چین کا نیلوفر - chínkánílofar, Hind.). Same as Nelumbo.——*China wood* (دال چینی - dálchíní, Hind.). Same as Country cinnamon.——*China yam* (ചീനക്കിഴങ്ങ് - shínikizhannu, Mal.). Same as Sweet potato.

CHINA ROOT (चीनी - chíní, *Mahr.*). From (chína, san. the country). An esteemed medicine in China. Title otherwise Chob cheeny [calumba], Nunnaury [indian sarsaparilla], Rough bindweed. Botanically the Smilax genus, smilaceæ [vricsham, 131]. Climbing shrubs, natives of the warmer temperate and tropical regions; root stocks tuberous or fibrous; stem usually prickly; leaves stalked, net-veined; flowers in globular heads, sessile or stalked in the axils of leaves; fruit pulpy, one to three-seeded. The species best known to the natives are shown below. Other S. indian species indigenous or naturalized are:—hohenhackeri, macrophylla, macula, zeylanica. Calumba [q.v.] is called by the natives China root.——*Common china root* (چوب چینی - chobchíní, Pers., Hind. and Dec.; పరంగిచెక్క - parangichekka, Tel.; චීනඅල - chínaalla, Singh.; பறங்கிச்சக்கைச்செடி - parangiççakkaiççedi, Tam.). Pers. from (chob, pers. stick + chíní, pers. china). Tel. from (parangi, tel. european + chakka, tel. wood). Tel. also (gálichekka). Tam. also (parangippattaiççedi), meaning foreign bark plant. Title otherwise Foreign wood. Botanically Smilax [china root] china, linn., smilaceæ [vricsham, 131]. Woody climber; gives a large, tuberous, knotty root of a dark reddish, brown color on the outside, and reddish white within; brought from china; resembles sarsaparilla. A preparation obtained by a prolonged boiling of the root in water; tonic, used in rheumatism and syphilitic complaints.——*Indian china root* (ہندی چوب چینی - hindíchobchíní, Hind. and Dec.). Botanically Smilax [china root] lanceæfolia, roxb., smilaceæ [vricsham, 131]. Indigenous. Gives to pharm. roots, non-officinal; like jamaica sarsaparilla.——*Large china root* (بڑی چوب چینی - baríchobchíní, Hind. and Dec.). Botanically Smilax [china root] glabra, roxb., smilaceæ [vricsham, 131]. The commonest of the indigenous species. Scandent; stem and branches unarmed, terete, smooth; leaves lanceolate, acuminate, rotund at the base, three-nerved, nerves smooth, glaucous beneath; umbels axillary, simple sessile, solitary; calycine segments broad, obcordate; anthers sessile; roots tuberous. Gives to pharm. roots, non-officinal; like jamaica sarsaparilla.——*Oval-leaved china root* (جنگلی عشبہ - janglíushbah, Hind.; కొండతామర - kondatámara, Tel.; കല്ത്താമര - kaltámara, Mal.; மலைத்தாமரை - malaittámarai, Tam.). Hind. from (janglí, hind. wild + ushbah, ar. sarsaparilla, smilax officinalis, linn.). Tel. from (konda, tel. hill + támara, tel. lotus, nelumbium speciosum, willd.). Mal. from (kal, mal. stone + támara, mal. lotus, nelumbium speciosum, willd.). Tam. from (malai, tam. mountain + támarai, tam. lotus, nelumbium speciosum, willd.). Tel. also (kistapatámara); (kondaguravatíga); (kondadantena), meaning hill + the tree, clitoria ternatea, linn.; (sitapachettu). Mal. also (kariviláuti). Title otherwise Hill lotus, Wild sarsaparilla. Botanically Smilax [china root] ovalifolia, roxb., smilaceæ [vricsham, 131]. Indigenous. Stems climbing, cylindric, larger parts armed with sharp, incurved prickles; tendrils paired, simple; leaves alternate, short-petioled, oval, five to seven-nerved, smooth, entire; petioles short-winged, channelled; umbels axillary, compound; umbellets globular; flowers greenish; berries red, smooth, succulent, two to three-seeded; common in jungles in malabar and travancore; flowering in the hot season. Root like saraparsilla.——*Sarsaparilla china root* (शारिबा - sháribá, San.; عشبۂ مغربی - ushbahimaghrabí, Ar.; عشبۂ مغربی - ushbahimaghrabí, Pers.; سالسا - sálsá, Hind.; عشبہ - ushbah, Dec.; సీమసుగంధపాల - símasugandhapála, Tel.; നറുനീണ്ടി - narunínti, Mal.; சீமைநன்னாரி - shímainannári, Tam.). San. from (shrí, san. to destroy). Ar. from (ushbah, ar. sarsaparilla + maghrabí, ar. western); from its virtues being first known in andalusia in spain. Dec. from (ashaba, ar. fresh). Tel. from (síma, tel. foreign + sugandhapála, tel. sarsaparilla, hemidesmus indicus, r. br.). Mal. from (naru, mal. fragrance + nílu, mal. to spread). Tam. from (shímai, tam. foreign + nannári, tam. hemidesmus indicus, r. br.). Ar. also (ushbatunnár), meaning fiery sarsaparilla. Tel. also (sarasavéru); from juicy root. Tam. also (shárasam); from juice. Title otherwise Foreign núnnaury, Jamaica sarsaparilla. Botanically Smilax [china root] officinalis, humb. & bonpl., smilaceæ [vricsham, 131]. Native of central america; roots several feet in length, about the thickness of a quill, with joints at short distances; the root bark, in which the virtue resides, is white, grey, or reddish; brought from abroad. An alterative tonic, useful in syphilitic and chronic rheumatic affections; gives to pharm. the dried root, sarsæ radix; acrid bitter resin [raul], a trace of volatile oil, and a crystalisable principle, smilacine; officinal.

CHINGLEPUT* (چنگلپیٹ - changalpet, *Hind.*; செங்கற்பட்டு - shengarbattu, *Tam.*). From (shengazhunír, tam. flower plant, nymphæa odorata, willd. + pattu, tam. village). Sanscrit name (kuvalayapura), meaning water-lily, nymphæa genus + town.——(1) Revenue district; situated on the Coromandel coast; between 12° 14′ and 13° 45′ N. lat., and between 79° 37′ and 80° 23′ E. long.; bounded N. by Nellore district, E. by Bay of Bengal, S. by South arcot district, W. by North arcot district; square miles 2,842; pop. 981,381; lang. Tamul and Teloogoo. Contains rivers Adyar, Cheyaur, Cooum, Corteliaur, Nagary, Narrainavaram, Palaur; ports Covelong, Ennore, Poolicat; mountains Cambaukum and Naugalpore range; sanitaria Ennore, Poonamallee military invalid cantonment. The whole area of the district is represented by the following sub-areas:—Chingleput talook, Conjeeveram talook, Madrantacam talook, Ponnairy talook, Sydapett talook, Trivellore talook. For general administrative purposes the district is distributed between the following revenue and magisterial officers, who have their head-quarters at the places shown. The pay set opposite the subordinate officers gives the grade of the corresponding charge:—Collector, Sydapett; Sub-collector, Chingleput, in charge of Chingleput, Conjeeveram and Madrantacam talooks; General deputy collector, Sydapett, in charge of Sydapett and Ponnairy talooks. General charge deputy collector at Sydapett, in charge of Trivellore talook. Tahsildars—Chingleput, Rs. 175; Conjeeveram, Rs. 200; Madrantacam, Rs. 225; Ponnairy, Rs. 150; Sydapett, Rs. 175; Trivellore, Rs. 175. Deputy tahsildars—Conjeeveram, Rs. 100, range situated in the south of Conjeeveram talook; Ootramallore, Rs. 70, range situated in the north-west of Madrantacam talook; Poonamallee, Rs. 70, range situated in the north of Sydapett talook; Shreepermatore, Rs. 70, range situated in the north of Conjeeveram talook; Suttivaid, Rs. 70, range situated in the north of Trivellore talook. Similarly judicial officers:—Judge, Chingleput; District moonsifs, Chingleput with jurisdiction extending over Chingleput, Madrantacam, and a portion of Conjeeveram talooks, Poonamallee with jurisdiction extending over Sydapett and Ponnairy talooks, Trivellore with jurisdiction extending over Trivellore and a portion of Conjeeveram talooks. Similarly Public works officers:—District engineer, St. Thomas' mount; Sub-divisional officer, Chingleput. Contains Registration sub-districts:—Chingleput, Conjeeveram, Madrantacam, Ootramallore, Ponnairy, Poonamallee, Shreepermatore, Suttivaid, Sydapett, Tirporore, Trivellore, and Wallajahbad. Contains Forest ranges:—Trivellore, Chingleput, Sydapett. Contains Municipality, Conjeeveram. Contains District board; and Talook boards, Chingleput embracing Chingleput, Madrantacam and Conjeeveram talooks, Trivellore embracing Trivellore talook, and Sydapett embracing Sydapett and Ponnairy. The following general references should be made to the preceding volumes:—general geography, I (1) to (29); general ethnology, (29) to (109); general history, (110) to (188); physical geography, II, 1; meteorology, II, 3; geology, II, 8; fauna, II, 21; flora, II, 26; mineralogy, II, 29. The following references in the preceding volumes will furnish details special to the district:—latitudes and longitudes, II, 47; particulars about towns, II, 48; coast survey, II. 161; lighthouses, II, 169; comparative population, II 172; location of revenue offices, II, 381; revenue settlement of the district, II, 407; registrars' and sub-registrars' stations, II, 420; ports, II, 423; salt factories, II, 426; rain-gauge stations, II, 428; police divisions, II, 431; maps published, II, 436; survey topographical lists, II, 443; hospitals and dispensaries, II, 447; head-quarter stations of gazetted officers, II, 461; incidence of taxation, II, 463; weights and measures of the district, II, 509; zemindarries, II, 294; special public works, I, 403. A special gazetteer account of the whole district is given at II, 65. For the detailed topography of the district, reference should be made to the talook notices in the present volume, viz.:—Chingleput, Conjeeveram, Madrantacam, Ponnairy, Sydapett, Trivellore.——(2) Talook, Chingleput district. Tahsildar's pay Rs. 175. Area 436 square miles Population 137,291. Languages Tamul, Teloogoo. S. centre of the district. Bounded south and south-east by the Palaur; east by the Bay of Bengal; north by Sydapett talook; and west by Conjeeveram talook. The East coast canal [q.v.] runs for about 26 miles along the eastern border and the South indian railway traverses the western side for about 21 miles. The country is rocky and poor, being covered with low hills and extensive scrub jungles. The soil is mostly red ferruginous loam in the interior and sandy towards the west. The talook produces no manufactures of any consequence. The only river irrigation is from the Palaur, either by spring channels bringing the water directly to the fields, or flood channels which fill tanks when the river is in fresh. The bulk of the irrigation is precarious, being derived from rain-fed tanks with small catchment basins. Camping grounds, Chingleput and Goodoovaucherry. Petty zemindarries:—Aminjicaray, Ammanampaukam, Arambaukam, Attavuttam, Basavasamoodram, Bommarajapooram, Carmaurapaukam, Condacauricooppam, Coodiperambaukam, Coonnatore, Coonnavaukam, Iroombilicherry, Itchancauranay, Mercaundayoottangooly, Nadoovacaray, Narasancooppam, Neroombore, Panancautcherry, Pandore, Paukkam, Periyacauttpaukam, Peroombaid, Poondandalam, Shooracooppam, Shooraudimungalam, Tepanamputt, Vayalore, Vengapaukam, Vittalaupooram. Places of archæological interest:—Chingleput, Covelong, Goodoovancherry, Munnivaukam, Sadras, Saulvancooppam, Seven Pagodas, Shingapermaulcoil, Tircalicoondram, Tircatchore, Tirporore, Tirvadanday, Tirvadishoolam, Vembaukam, Vullam. Principal Trig. stations:—Manamay coonnattore, Poothoopaukam, Tircalicoondram, Tirmany. The leading places in the talook are the following.——*Adyar* (அடையாறு - adaiyáru, Tam.). See sep. title.——*Aminjicaray* (அமிஞ்சிக்கரை - amiñjikkarai, Tam.). See sep. title.——*Arambaukam* (ஆரம்பாக்கம் - árambákkam, Tam.). From (áram, tam. garden + pákkam, tam. village). Zemindarry, Village; pop. 336; acres 983; lat. of village 12° 34′; long. 80° 12′; from Chingleput S.E. 14 miles; from Sydapett S. 32 miles; from the sea W. 2¼ miles. Peshcush Rs. 2,192.——*Chingleput* (செங்கற்பட்டு - shengarbattu, Tam.). See below.——*Covelong* (கோவளம் - kóvalam, Tam.). See sep. title.——*East coast canal* (கிழக்கரைவாய்க்கால் - kizhkkaraiváykkál, Tam.). See sep. title.——*Goodoovancherry* (கூடுவாஞ்சேரி - kúduváñjéri, Tam.). See sep. title.——*Goondore* (குண்டூர் - kundúr, Tam.). From (gundu, tel. rock + úr, tam. village). Village; pop. 2,714; lat. 12° 42′; long. 80° 02′; from Sydapett S.S.W. 28 miles; from the sea W. 16 miles. Part of Chingleput town.——*Manamay coonnattore* (மணமைக்குன்னத்தூர் - manamaikkunnattúr, Tam.). From (manal, tam. sand + mai, tam. blackness + kunram, tam. hill + úr, tam. village). Trig. station; lat. 12° 34′ 24·25″; long. 80° 12′ 18·77″; height 76 feet; from Chingleput S.S.E. 14 miles; from Nulloor E. 2 miles; from the sea W. 2½ miles.——*Neroombore* (நெரும்பூர் - nerumbúr, Tam.). From (narumai, tam. fragrance + úr, tam. village). Zemindarry, Village; pop. 1,022; acres 1,930; lat. of village 12° 31′; long. 80° 07′; from Chingleput E. 13 miles; from Sydapett S. 36 miles; from the sea W. 6¼ miles. Peshcush Rs. 1,246.——*Palaur* (பாலாறு - pálaru Tam.). See sep. title.——*Pandore* (பாண்டூர் - pándúr, Tam.). From (pándi, tam. pándya kingdom + úr, tam. village). Zemindarry, Village; pop. 767; acres 1,419; lat. of village 12° 32′; long. 80° 05′; from Chingleput S.S.E. 12 miles; from Sydapett S. 35 miles; from the sea W. 8¾ miles. Peshcush Rs. 1,024.——*Paulore* (பாலூர் - pálúr,* Tam.). From (pál, tam. milk + úr, tam. village). Village, Railway station; pop. 3,523; acres 5,715; lat. 12° 46′; long. 79° 58′; height 287 feet; from Chingleput W. 6¾ miles; from Sydapett S.W. 27 miles; from the sea W. 23 miles.——*Ponvilainda calattore* (பொன்விளைந்தகளத்தூர் - ponvilaindugalattúr, Tam.). From (pon, tam. gold + vilai, tam. to grow + kalattúr, tam. village, so called). Village; pop. 2,017; acres 2,986; lat. 12° 37′; long. 80° 02′; from Chingleput S. 5½ miles; from Sydapett S.S.W. 32 miles; from the sea W. 15 miles. Same as Calattore railway station.——*Poothoopaukam* (புதுப்பாக்கம் - puthuppákkam, Tam.). From (puthu, tam. new + pákkam, tam. village). Trig. station; lat. 12° 48′ 30·37″; long. 80° 13′ 58·41″; height 153 feet; from Chingleput E.N.E. 15 miles; from Teiyore N. 2¼ miles; from the sea W. 5¼ miles.——*Sadras* (சதுரங்கப்பட்டணம் - shathurangappattanam, Tam.). See sep. title.——*Saulvancooppam* (சாளுவன்குப்பம் - sháluvanguppam, Tam.). See sep. title.——*Seven pagodas* (மாவலிப்புரம் - mávalippuram, Tam.). See sep. title.——*Shingapermaulcoil* (சிங்கப்பெருமாள்கோவில் - shingapperumálgóvil, Tam. singaperumálkoil *). From (shingam, tam. lion + perumál, tam. vishnu, the great god + kóvil, tam. temple). Village, Railway station; pop. 430; acres 175; lat. 12° 46′; long. 80° 03′; height 140 feet; from Chingleput N. 5 miles; from Sydapett S.W. 23 miles; from the sea W. 16 miles. Old Vishnoo temple with inscriptions.——*Tircalicoondram* (திருக்கழிக்குன்றம் - tirukkazhikkunram, Tam.). See sep. title.——*Tirmany* (திருமணி - tirumani, Tam.). From (tiru, tam. sacred + mani, san. gem). Trig. station; lat. 12° 39′ 04·47″; long. 80° 01′ 18·25″; height 768 feet; from Chingleput S. 2¼ miles; from Manapaukam N.N.E. 3 miles; from the sea W. 15 miles.——*Tirporore* (திருப்போரூர் - tirupporúr, Tam.). See sep. title.——*Tirvadishoolam* (திருவடிசூலம் - tiruvadisúlam, Tam.). From (tiru, tam. holy + adi, tam. foot + shúla, san. trident). The real name is (tiruvidaiççuram), meaning holy + shepherd + jungle. Village; pop. 342; acres 1,623; lat. 12° 42′; long. 80° 05′; from Chingleput E. 3¾ miles; from Sydapett S. 26 miles; from the sea W. 13 miles. Amongst the hills east of Chingleput. Small temple of local repute. A fort, probably one of the last Coorumbar-strongholds, built in the time of Athonday chuckravurty, and renewed at a later period and strengthened by two chiefs, who defied the power of Vijianugger. The story of their final overthrow, brought about by treachery, is remembered in the neighbourhood.——*Vandalore*

(வண்டலூர் - vandalúr,* Tam.). From (vandal, tam. silt + úr, tam. village). Village, Railway station; pop. 541; acres 1,377; lat. 12° 53′; long. 80° 06′; height 111 feet; from Chingleput N.N.E. 15½ miles; from Madras S.W. 19 miles; from Sydapett S.W. 13 miles; from the sea W. 12 miles. On the great southern trunk road. Site of an entrenched camp during the Carnatic wars. A substantial upstair house erected by General Joseph Smith in 1765. Inscription of Vijianugger dynasty on base of temple.——*Vedachellam* (वेदाचल - védáchala, San.). From (véda, san. the sacred writings + achala, san. mountain). Village, Hill; lat. 12° 37′; long. 80° 06′; from Chingleput S.E. 8 miles; from Sydapett S.S.W. 30 miles; from the sea W. 9 miles. Hill on which stands temple of Tircalicoondram.——*Vembaukam* (வெண்பாக்கம் - venbákkam, Tam.). From (ven, tam. white + pákkam, tam. village). Village; pop. 407; acres 855; lat. 12° 46′; long. 80° 00′; from Chingleput N.N.W. 5 miles; from Sydapett S.W. 25 miles; from the sea W. 20 miles. Between village and Shingapermaulcoil railway station are sepulchral stone circles [azhauram].——**(3)** Town, Divisional, Talook, and Judge's head-quarters, Railway station; pop. 3,466; acres 233; lat. 12° 42′; long. 80° 01′; height 128 feet; from Arcot E. 45 miles; from Bangalore E. 162 miles; from Conjeeveram E.S.E. 23 miles; from Cuddalore N. 65 miles; from Madras S.W. 34 miles; from St. Thomas' mount S. 26 miles; from Sydapett S.W. 28 miles; from Tanjore N. 145 miles; from the sea W. 17 miles. At the junction of the Chingleput-arconum branch with the main line of the S.I. railway. The climate, except during hot winds, is cool, and place healthy. Surrounded by hills, 500 feet in height, and these with the large tank and several lesser sheets of water lend to the scenery, especially after rains, an appearance of picturesque beauty seldom met with on the plains. The large tank is two miles long by one broad, and is formed by bunding up surplus water of country ten miles to northward. The supply is far in excess of what is required for irrigation, and it is consequently full during hot weather. The clay of town is best in district for bricks [shengal] and there are many kilns [shoolay]. The town consists of the villages of Chingleput, Goondore and Nuttam, all reckoned separate for revenue. The fort was erected at the end of sixteenth century, when Vijianugger rajahs held their court alternately here and at Chundragherry. About 1644 it passed into hands of Golcondah chiefs, by whom it was surrendered to Nawaubs of Arcot. By latter it was surrendered in 1751 to Chundah sahib. In 1752 Clive bombarded it and compelled French garrison to surrender. After reduction of Fort St. David, Madras government, apprehensive of an attack on Madras, called in all the garrisons and stores from outlying forts; and Chingleput was abandoned in 1758. On advance of French from south it was again garrisoned. Lally finding it impregnable left it in his rear and passed on to Madras. During siege that followed the garrison of Chingleput rendered invaluable assistance by securing country north of Palaur, and by harassing rear of investing enemy. In 1780 British force, after destruction of General Baillie's column, found refuge here, and during the wars with Mysore this fortress was once taken by the enemy, re-occupied by the British, and twice unsuccessfully besieged. The fort is of Hindoo origin. Roman catholic and Free church missions here. A detachment, consisting generally of two companies of native infantry, were formerly stationed. A cave a mile east has been made into a Lingam [q.v.] temple. Formerly a Booddhist hermit's cell. Three miles from the town, close to the southern trunk road, are cairns. Between the town and the Palaur causeway are sepulchral circles [azhauram]; also near the suburb of Nuttam. On Trichinopoly road is a large mound surrounded by megalithic graves [raucshasagoondloo]. The following are the travelling distances by road from Chingleput to different places:—

To	Viâ	Miles and Furlongs.	
Bangalore ...	Vellore, Amboor and Oossoor	193	6
Bellary	Ranipett, Pulmanair, Madanapully and Anantapore.	304	0
Berhampore ...	Madras, Nellore, Bezwada, Rajahmundry and Chicacole.	680	4
Bezwada ...	Madras, Nellore, Ongole and Guntoor.	307	3½
Chicacole ...	Madras and Rajahmundry	581	3½
Chittore ...	Ranipett	80	4½
Conjeeveram ...	Wallajahbad	20	4
Cuddalore ...	Caroongooly and Pondicherry	79	1
Cuddapah ...	Madras, Nagary and Kircambaudy ...	201	3
Cuddapah ...	Ranipett, Chittore and Royachoty ...	181	7½
Ellore	Madras, Nellore, Ongole and Bezwada.	346	4½
Ganjam	Madras, Nellore, Bezwada, Vizianagram, Chicacole and Berhampore.	699	4
Guntoor	Poonamallee, Nellore and Ongole ...	287	8
Madras	Goodoovancherry, Pallavaram and Saint Thomas' mount.	34	7
Masulipatam ...	Madras, Nellore, Ongole and Baupatla.	314	2
Mayavaram ...	Pondicherry, Cuddalore, Chidambaram and Shiyally.	130	3
Negapatam ...	Pondicherry, Cuddalore, Chidambaram, Shiyally and Tranquebar.	159	5
Nellore	Madras and Sooloorpett	142	5
Ongole	Madras and Nellore	219	0
Ooloondoorpett ...	Villoopooram	88	5
Pallavaram ...	Goodoovancherry	22	7
Pondicherry ...	Caroongooly and Kilyanore	67	2

To	Viâ	Miles and Furlongs.	
Rajahmundry ...	Poonamallee, Nellore, Ongole and Bezwada.	401	5½
Ranipett	Conjeeveram	50	3
Sadras	......	19	4
Saint Thomas' mount.	Goodoovancherry and Pallavaram ...	26	3
Salem	Ooloondoorpett	171	6
Samulcottah ...	Madras, Nellore, Ongole and Rajahmundry.	431	5½
Shiyally	Pondicherry, Cuddalore and Chidambaram.	117	2
Tanjore	Vicravaundy, Panrooty and Combaconam.	161	3
Tanjore	Pondicherry, Cuddalore and Combaconam.	175	7
Tindivanam ...	Caroongooly	41	1
Tranquebar ...	Pondicherry, Cuddalore, Chidambaram and Shiyally.	137	3
Trichinopoly ...	Volcondapooram	165	4
Vellore	Ranipett	64	1
Villoopooram ...	Caroongooly, Tindivanam and Vicravaundy.	65	3
Vizagapatam ...	Madras, Nellore, Ongole, Bezwada and Cassimcote.	524	5½
Vizianagram ...	Madras, Nellore, Ongole, Bezwada and Soobaraum.	548	0½
Volcondapooram.	Caroongooly, Villoopooram and Ooloondoorpett.	125	1½

CHINNA (చిన్న - chinna, *Tel.*; ஷின்ன - shinna, *Tam.*). Small. Common prefix in place names. Chinnamma is a name of the village goddess. Chinnasawmy, from (svámí, san. master), hindoo 2nd or pers. name; and so many others, as chinnadoray, chinnayyan [peyar], &c. Chinnaye is term of endearment to children of either sex [peyar]. Plant first term often joining two genera as in:—Aloe littoralis (chinnarákásbimatta), small agave americana; walsura ternatea (chinnavalasa), small guizotia abyssinica. See gloss. paragraphs.——*Chinna cash* (ஷின்னக் காசு - shinnakkásu, Tam.). Small cash. Money. 5 chinna cash = 1 cash or pie [naunyam, 2 a]. Same as cash in Teloogoo districts.——*Chinna hagary* (చిన్నహగరి - chinnahagari, Tel.). From (above + hagari, tel. river so called). Can. also (janagahalla), meaning janaga, proper name + river. River; Bellary dist., Royadroog tal.; rises in Mysore in lat. 14° 15′; long. 76° 22′; about 4 miles south-west of Chitaldroog. Flows north-easterly through Mysore and Bellary, and falls into the Hagary in lat. 14° 56′; long. 77° 05′.——*Chinna kimedy* (చిన్నకిమిడి - chinnakimedi, Tel. chinnakimedi *). From (above + kimedi, tel. the place). Sanscrit name (pratápagiri), meaning king so called + hill. Ancient zemindary, Village; Ganjam dist., Zemindarry tracts; pop. 35,954; square miles 2,130; lat. of village 19° 29′; long. 84° 37′; from Chetterpore W.N.W. 29 miles; from Russellcondah S. 31 miles. Formerly a part of the adjacent zemindarry of Peddakimedy, and along with that estate originally belonged to Parlakimedy. In 1607 the Parlakimedy rajah gave his younger son, Ananga bheema deo kesary, that portion of his estate called Ananga bheema deo kimedy, subsequently sub-divided into Vijianugger or Pedda kimedy and Prataupagherry or Chinna kimedy. In 1768, the united estate was in the hands of Bheema deo, the most turbulent zemindar in the district. At his death in 1776, one of his sons, Mony deo, kept Vijianugger or Pedda kimedy, and the other, Juggannauta deo, succeeded to Prataupagherry or Chinna kimedy. Owing to feuds and disturbances between the two families, the Privy council decided in 1876 that the estate was to be made over to the adopted son of the late zemindar's widow, herself a sister of the neighbouring zemindar of Pedda kimedy. Peshcush Rs. 20,826. Annual income Rs. 63,621. Sub-divided into the five Mittahs of Goodaury, Khaury, Prataupagherry, Siddheshwaram, and Votyausy. Number of villages, 159. There are besides nineteen agrahaurams [q.v.]. The Godahaddoh flows through the zemindarry, and joins the Rooshcoolya near Injily. The zemindar's fort is situated at Poodamary, and there the zemindars used to live. The extensive Chinna kimedy maliahs, 11,975 square miles, which were formerly attached to this zemindarry, have been resumed by Government.——*Chinnam* (చిన్నము - chinnamu, Tel.). Goldsmith's weight. 4 gooriginjas = 1 chinnam, 9 chinnams = 1 pagoda weight [niray, 3b]. Approximate actual value, 1 chinnam = 6 grains. Same as Can. hana, Tam. and Mal. pana tookkam. Compare Tel. chowlam.——*Chinnapanam* (ஷின்னப்பணம் - shinnappanam, Tam.). Small fanam. Money. 3¾ doodies = 1 chinnapanam; 2 chinnapanams = 1 panam [naunyam, 2a]. Approximate actual value, 1 chinnapanam = 1 anna 3 pies. Tamul districts. Compare Can. hauga.——*Chinnapuddy* (ஷின்னப்படி - shinnappadi, Tam.). Half of puddy [alavay, 3a]. Compare Ardhaseer, Maunam.——*Chinny* (چینی کا جہاڑ - chíní kájhár, Hind.; ಚಿನ್ನಿ - chinni, Can.; చిన్ని - chinni, Tel.; ஷின்னி - shinni, Tam.). Hind. by corruption from tamul. Title otherwise Birch-leaved acalypha. Botanically Acalypha [maumsicay] fruticosa, forsk., euphorbiaceæ [vricsham, 118]. Alias Acalypha amentacea, betulina, spiciflorus. Shrub, pubescent, with sessile, waxy, golden-yellowish glands; leaves rhomb-ovate, acute at both ends, serrated, beneath covered and shining with golden glands; spikes unisexual, very shortly peduncled, or androgynous and males; males commonly shorter than the leaves, erect, hoary; androgynous ones increased at the base by one to four female bracts; female spikes lax-flowered, five to eight bracteate; female bracts one-flowered, exceeding the capsule; male calyx externally pubescent; ovary densely hairy; capsules hoary tomentose; seeds smooth; flowers greenish. Leaves have pleasant and aromatic taste and odour. Leaves prescribed by veidyans as a stomachic in dyspeptic affections and cholera; attenuant and alterative.

CHINTA (చింత - chinta, *Tel.*). Tamarind [q.v.].——*Chintala* (చింతల - chintala, Tel.). Locative plural form. Suffix in place names; as Renta chintala, meaning two + tamarind trees.——*Chintalapoody* (చింతలపూడి - chintalapúdi, Tel.). From (above + púdi, tel. village).—"*a*" Deputy tahsildarry, Godavery district. Pay Rs. 70.—"*b*" Village, Deputy tahsildar's station, Sub-registrar's office; Godavery dist., Ellore tal.; pop. 713; acres 6,201; lat. 17° 03′ 25″; long. 81° 02′ 04″; from Cocanada W. 81 miles; from Coonavaram S.S.W. 39 miles; from Ellore N.N.W. 25¼ miles; from Madras N.N.E. 272 miles; from Narsapore N.W. 62 miles; from Rajahmundry W. 50 miles. Formerly constituted the zemindarry of Zoopullivaur, resumed by Government. Ruined fort of the late zemindars. A temple of Shiva named Vaigilingasawmy and rebuilt by one Poornananda yogy, in the year 1705 Shalivahanan [q.v.].

CHINTAUMANY (चिन्तामणि - chintámani, *San.*). From (chintá, san. thought + mani, san. jewel). The gem which gives all desires. Common pers. or second name among Jeina bramins [peyar]. Title of treatises as Ganita chintaumany, astrological; Tarca chintaumany, logical; Vivaica chintaumany, religious; &c.——**(1)** The great Tamul Jeina poem is Jeevaca chintaumany, Jeevacan being the hero. One of the five Tamul classics. Otherwise Jinamata nool, meaning jeina + doctrine + treatise. The design of this work is to represent the Jeina system in an attractive form. It is founded on a similar story in Maha pooraunam, a Sanscrit Jeina work. Author's name Tirtevar, lived in Mylapore some eight hundred years ago. The following stanzas may be taken as a specimen of the style:—இலங்கலாழியினுன் களிற்றீட்டம்போற் கலங்குதெண்டிரைமேய்ந்துகணமழை பொலங்கொள்கொன்றையினுன் சடைபோன்மின்னி விலங்கல்சேர்ந்து விண்ணேணியிட்டார்த்தவே—"Like a herd of elephants belonging to some "resplendent emperor, the gregarious clouds, having grazed on "the clear waves of the troublous ocean, darting lightnings, "resembling the beautiful golden flowers of the Condray [q.v.] "on the dark hair of Shiva, having reached the mountains and "climbed the sky, wide opening bellowed aloud."—அஞ்சனகோலினாற்ற நாகமோராருயிர்குன்றிற் குஞ்சர மலறிவீழக் கூர்நுதியெயிற்றிற்கொல்லும் பஞ்சியின் மெலவிதேனும் பகைசிறிதென்னவேண்டா மஞ்சித்தற்காக்கல்வேண்டுமெரும் பொருளாகவொன்றான்—"A snake "that cannot sustain the blow of a bodkin, with its sharp pointed "tooth will kill an elephant like a mountain with a waterfall, "and cause it to fall roaring to the ground; think not a foe "small, though more unsubstantial than cotton, but fear and "guard yourselves against him. Such was his hard doctrine." The Chintaumany contains 3,145 stanzas or verses, and is divided into thirteen sections, called Ilambacam, as follows.—"*a*" *Naumagal ilambam* (நாமகளிலம்பம் - námagalilambam, Tam.). From (námagal, tam. sarasvatí, the tongue daughter + lamba, san. section). First book 408 verses, begins with invocations to deity, to Aroogan [q.v.], to virtue, and to the assembly of the wise; aim and analysis of whole work. Then book commences. Five parts:—Description of country Hemaungadam. Description of city Rajamaupooram. Description of king's palace. History of Satchandan the king and Vijayay his queen, father and mother of Jeevacan. The king leading a sensual life, neglected his kingdom; a plot formed by his minister, who assassinated him and usurped the throne. Jeevacan's birth in burning-ground of a wild forest, his rescue by a rich merchant, who educated him, &c. His mother had fled from country and was leading life of a devotee.—"*b*" *Govindaiyaur ilambam* (கோவிந்தையாரிலம்பம் - kóvindiyárilambam, Tam.). From (góvindá, san. cow finder, female proper name). Second book, 84 verses, early exploits of Jeevacan. Pashoocauvalan gave his daughter Govindaiyaur to Jeevacan.—"*c*" *Gaundharva tattaiyaur ilambam* (காந்தருவத்தத்தையாரிலம்பம் - kándaruvattattaiyárilambam, Tam.). From (gandharva, san. celestial singer + tattai, tam. parrot). Third book, 358 verses, story of Tattaiyaur, female player on veenay [q.v.]. Jeevacan entered lists with other competitors, excelled in his performance, and married her.—"*d*" *Goonamaulaiyaur ilambam* (குணமாலையாரிலம்பம் - kunamálaiyárilambam, Tam.). From (guna, san. merit + málá, san. garland). Fourth book, 315 verses, story of two young women Goonamaulay and Sooramunjary, who contended for superiority with regard to scented powders which they possessed. Jeevacan decided in favor of Goonamaulay, and she married him. Also account of a man who was metamorphosed into a dog and by Jeevacan was remetamorphosed into a man.—"*e*" *Pudmaiyaur ilambam* (பதுமையாரிலம்பம் - pathumaiyárilambam, Tam.). From (padmá, san. lakshmí, the lotus deity). Fifth book, 246 verses, travels of Jeevacan in distant lands, where he met with Pudmay, a daughter of the king of Pullavam. When she was gathering flowers, she was bitten by a snake, but was healed by Jeevacan, who married her.—"*f*" *Cshemachariyaur ilambam* (சேமசரியாரிலம்பம் - shémasariyárilambam, Tam.). From (kshéma, san. the country of prosperity, so called + char, san. to move). Sixth book, 145 verses, visit of Jeevacan to Cshemadesham, where he performed prodigies and married Cshemasoondary, daughter of a king.—"*g*" *Canacamaulaiyaur ilambam* (கனகமாலையாரிலம்பம் - kanagamálaiyárilambam, Tam.). From (kanaka, san. gold + málá, san. garland). Seventh book, 332 verses, Jeevacan's journey to Sooshaina desham, where he shot at a mark and gained king's daughter.—"*h*" *Vimalaiyaur ilambam* (விமலையாரிலம்பம் - vimalaiyárilambam, Tam.). From (vi, san. suffix of privation + mala, san. stain). Eighth book, 107 verses, journey of Jeevacan to Nunnaud, where he met his mother in Dandacauranyam [q.v.]. He returned to his own city, and connected himself with a merchant, whose daughter, Vimalay, he married.—"*i*" *Sooramunjariyaur ilambam* (சுரமஞ்சரியாரிலம்பம் - shuramañjariyárilambam, Tam.). From (sura, san. god + mañjarí, san. flower cluster). Ninth book, 108 verses, Jeevacan's marriage with Sooramunjary, mentioned in Goonamaulaiyaur ilambam.—"*j*" *Manamagal ilambam* (மணமகளிலம்பம் - manamagalilambam, Tam.). From (manamagal, tam. the bride, the marriage daughter). Tenth book, 224 verses, Jeevacan shot at a target and married daughter of his maternal uncle, king of Videham. The assassin of Jeevacan's father tried to put him to death. Jeevacan met him, slew him, and ascended the throne of his ancestors.—"*k*" *Poomagal ilambam* (பூமகளிலம்பம் - púmagalilambam, Tam.). From (púmagal, tam. lakshmí, the flower daughter). Eleventh book, 251 verses, conquest of Hemaungadam, his father's dominions, from the hands of the usurper.—"*l*" *Ilakkanaiyaur ilambam* (இலக்கணையாரிலம்பம் - ilakkanaiyárilambam, Tam.). From (lakshana, san. lucky mark). Twelfth book, 249 verses, nuptials of Jeevacan and Ilakkanay, his maternal uncle's daughter.—"*m*" *Moocty ilambam* (முத்தியிலம்பம் - muttiyilambam, Tam.). From (mukti, san. renunciation). Thirteenth book, 318 verses, religious acts of Jeevacan and his wives, the partition of his dominions among his sons, and the renunciation of all secular pursuits and objects by himself and his female associates.——**(2)** *Chintaumany veidyan* (चिन्तामणिवैद्य - chintámanivaidya, San.). From (above + vaidya, san. physician). Tamul physicians who follow Agastyan; in opposition to Malayalam who style themselves Ashtaunga hridaya veidyans and follow Bhappatan, Characan and Sooshrootan [veidyan].

CHINTOO (చింతు - chintu, *Tel.*). Botanically the Gymnosporia genus, celastrineæ [vricsham, 40]. Erect shrubs, often thorny; leaves alternate; flowers small in cymes or racemes. The species best known to the natives are shown below. Other s. indian species indigenous or naturalized are:—ovata, rothiana, wallichiana.——*Large chintoo* (कांगुणी - kángunuí, Mahr.; مالکنگنی - málkangní, Hind. and Dec.; ತಂದ್ರಸಿಗಿಡ - tandrasigida, Can.; పెద్దచింతు - peddachintu, Tel.; வாலுளுவை - váluluvai, Tam.). Hind. means celastrus paniculata, willd. [malkangany]. Tel. from (pedda, tel. large + chintu, tel. the tree, gymnosporia). Tam. from (val, tam. strength + ul, tam. to exist); medicinal. Tel. also (dantichettu); (gajachinui), meaning elephant + gymnosporia; (gettsangi); (bhávunji) [bawchee]. Title otherwise Spindle tree [malkangany], Thorny staff tree. Botanically Gymnosporia [chintoo] montana, roxb., celastrineæ [vricsham, 40]. Alias Catha montana; Celastrus crenata, montana, senegalensis. Small tree; flowers small; greenish-white; ovary and capsule occasionally only two-celled, and young branches sometimes pointed with a thorn. Deep scarlet-colored oil from seeds by expression; used for medicinal purposes. Leaves used for fodder. Wood pinkish white, soft but close-grained, no heart-wood, no annual rings, durable.——*Small chintoo* (చిన్నిచెట్టు - chinnichettu, Tel.; கட்டாஞ்சி - kattáñji, Tam.). Tel. from (chinna, tel. small + chettu, tel. tree). Tam. from (kattum, tam. wild). Botanically Gymnosporia [chintoo] emarginata, roth., celastrineæ [vricsham, 40]. Alias Celastrus emarginata. Shrub, thorny, flower small, whitish yellow; makes good fences and fuel; wood white, hard.

CHINTZ (चित्रकार्पास - chitrakárpása, *San.*; छीट - chhíta, *Mahr.*; چھینٹ - chhint, *Hind.*; ಚೀಟಿಗುದ್ದೆ - chítigudde, *Can.*; చీటిగుడ్డ - chítigudda, *Tel.*; ചീട്ടി - chítti, *Mal.*; சீட்டி - shítti, *Tam.*). Title from hindostany which is from (chitra, san. spotted); plural form has become singular. San. from (chitra, san. variegated + kárpása, san. cotton cloth). Can. from (chíti, can. print + gudde, can. cloth). Tel. from (chitra, san. variegated + gudda, tel. cloth). Mal. and tam. are short forms. Properly cotton stuffs printed in colors with white spots; same as Bandana [q.v.] for silk [puttoo]. Generally however cotton stuffs with patterns of different colors impressed upon a white or light-colored ground. The best known sites of present manufacture are Arnee, Masulipatam, and Sydapett. Those of Masulipatam are of various hues and each piece is two cubits in breadth and twelve in length. These are used for under garments by native women. They have enjoyed a world-wide celebrity ever since the days of Arrian, and probably of the Mahabhaurat. They are prized for the freshness and permanency of their dyes [shauyam], the colors being brighter after washing than before. There is still a great demand for them in Burmah, the Straits, and Persian gulf, but European goods have begun to destroy this immemorial industry of India. Nearly all the Masulipatam chintzes are copied from Persian designs of sprigs of flowers, and of the knop and flower and tree of life pattern. The chintzes of Arnee and Sydapett are eight by two cubits, and are used for pillow covers and other purposes as well as for under garments of native women. At Combaconum spotted chintzes are still printed for the Straits, and are there called Shaurangs [q.v.]. Very bold printing is done at Wallajahpett in North arcot for sale to Mussalmans at Hyderabad and Bangalore. At Madura large quantities of the stained cloths for which it is celebrated are manufactured. They are coarse and printed in only two colors, red and black, with mythological subjects taken from the Ramayanam and Mahabhaurat. They are made chiefly for the service of the temples, and are rare to get, except by favor of the priests. Sometimes they are worked up in yellow by hand-painting [calam caury]. At Poolicat peculiar chintzes have been made till recently. The practical industry of chintz manufacture may be divided into two branches:—the first including handkerchiefs [roomaul] and turbans [puggry], cloths for males and females, or dhoties [q.v.] and sauries [q.v.], bed-covers [palampores], canopies, and prayer cloths, all with the exception of the last being for strictly domestic use; the second including cloths of special manufacture, nearly always hand-painted, used as canopies over the images of Hindoo gods and at marriage or other ceremonies. Masulipatam in the Kistna district, Palcole and Gollapoilem near Cocanada in the Godavery district, Nagore and Combaconam in the Tanjore district, and Paramacoody and Paumben in the Madura district, are the chief places where the former kinds are made; and for the other variety Calastry, Salem, Palcoie, and Masulipatam are noted. The fine deep red of chintzes is obtained from the roots of the small plant Oldenlandia umbellata, linn., rubiaceæ, growing wild in sandy soils which are occasionally overflowed by the sea [chayroot]. The blue is from indigo [q.v.]. The yellow is from the leaf galls of Terminalia chebula, retz., combretaceæ [chebulic myrobalan]. Green is obtained by the addition of yellow to the indigo blue. The plain cloth is first soaked in a preparation of milk and gall-nut [mauchicoy]. When the cloth is dry the black outline of the pattern, if the pattern has one, is stamped by the block; or in the case of hand-painted cloths drawn with a rude brush or pencil of bamboo [q.v.] which is kept supplied with ink, a preparation of iron [auhan] and alum [padicauram], by pressure of the palm of the hand on a coil of thread soaked in the liquid and twisted round the middle of the instrument. The red color is applied next by block or hand. To bring out the color the cloth must then be boiled repeatedly, the red becoming deeper and deeper. If blue is also required the process is in every case performed by hand without the aid of blocks. The portions of the patterns which are required to remain red are covered with wax applied with an iron instrument divided at the end similarly to a draughtsman's inking pen, the wax melted by a slow fire being held in a bag or pouch formed generally of human hair through which the iron shaft passes. The cloth may then be dipped in the indigo dye as the parts covered by the wax will retain their original color uninjured. In some cases, such as in the sacred cloths of Calastry, the blue is applied with the same brush as the black outline and the waxing process is thus avoided, but the color is not so permanent. The yellow is also applied by the same method. The hand-painting process is precisely similar to the other only that the work is done without the aid of blocks. On account of the tedious process of repeated boilings which the red color needs, two months are required for the preparation of each cloth. **For plain cotton, see Punj.**

CHIPKALEE (मुसली - musalí, *San.*; पाल - pála, *Mahr.*; سام ابرص - sámmiabras, *Ar.*; چلپاسه - chalpásah, *Pers.*; چھپکلی - chhipkalí, *Hind.*; سپلک - siplak, *Dec.*; چچک - chichak, *Malay*; ಹಲ್ಲಿ - halli, *Can.*; బల్లి - balli, *Tel.*; പല്ലി - palli, *Mal.*; පල්ලි - palli, *Singh.*; பல்லி - palli, *Tam.*). San. from (mus, san. to destroy). Mahr. from (palli, san. lizard). Ar. from (sámm, ar. poisonous + abras, ar. leprosy); from use of electuary in leprous affections. Hind. from (chip, hind. the noise + palli, san. lizard). Dec. from hindostany. Malay from the noise. Tel. also (gauli). Title otherwise Gecko, House lizard, Wall lizard. Gecko is from the cry. The terms are co-extensive with family Geckotidæ, sauria [godhicay], reptilia [sarpy, 9], of naturalists [jantoo]. The chipkalee has a head broad and depressed with large eyes; body of moderate breadth; tail thick at the base, tapering, generally somewhat deformed, easily breaks off and easily renewed; limbs stout, of moderate length, with at least four toes well developed. Frequenting houses, rocks, and trees; generally able to run up and along the surface of a wall or of any other perpendicular object; carnivorous, destroying insects [poochy], moths [patingah], and even the younger and weaker members of their own species; have even been seen devouring their own tail; of fierce habits, fighting between themselves. The chirp of the chipkalee is never disregarded since it may bear a message of great consequence to the family or individual. A small book called the shastram of the lizard contains information regarding its chirping. On hearing it the facts to be observed are the point of the compass [ashta dic], the hour of the day [caulam, dinam], &c. These being known, recourse is made to formula, and it is ascertained whether the omen is auspicious or not. There is a Tamul proverb:—ஊருக்கெல்லாம் சாஸ்திரம் சொல்லுகிறபல்லி கூழ்ப்பானையில் விழுந்தாற்போல— "As if a lizard, the oracle of the whole village, should fall into "a pot of gruel;" spoken of a person injuring his own reputation. The following is a Hindostany proverb:—جتنا سانپ لنبا اتنی هی گوه چوڑی—"The lizard is as wide as the snake is "long;" that is to say, "six of one and half a dozen of the "other." Bruised body made into electuary, in conjunction with aromatics; used by veidyans in leprous affections [cooshtam]; hence arabic name. The following are the representative species in Southern india:—"*a*" Eublepharis hardwickii. Ground lizard unable to climb walls. Pale reddish white, two very broad bands across the trunk; three or four rings round the tail, deep brown or black, brown portions being edged with black, broader than the ground color; limbs reddish olive, with black dots on elbows, and knees.—"*b*" Gecko guttatus. Alias Gecko reevesii; Lacerta annulatus, gecko, guttatus, teres, verus; Platydactylus guttatus. Above ash-colored, with numerous round pale-orange spots; one of the most common.—"*c*" Gymnodactylus deccanensis. Reddish olive, with narrow white, black-edged cross-bands; first semi-circular, from one eye across the nape to the other eye; trunk with three and tail with five or six bands; similar band across the forearm and across the lower hind leg.—"*d*" Gymnodactylus indicus. Alias Goniodactylus indicus. Brownish or greenish, irregularly marbled with darker along the vertebral line; conceals itself under stones in daytime.—"*e*" Gymnodactylus littoralis. Brown, with a series of paler marks along the back and tail; a black spot on the nape; Malabar.—"*f*" Gymnodactylus malabaricus. Dark brown above, marbled with black spots, and a white spot on the nape; Malabar.—"*g*" Gymnodactylus mysoriensis. Greyish brown, with light stripe down the centre of back, and series of dark-brown marks on head, back and sides; legs and feet banded; two and a half inches long; the young has the tail flesh-colored.—"*h*" Hemidactylus leschenaultii. Olive-colored, marbled with grey.—"*i*" Hemidactylus maculatus. Alias Hemidactylus pieresii; Nubilia argentii. Brownish olive above, irregularly spotted or banded with brown; brown band runs from the first upper labial through the eye to above the ear; common.—"*j*" Hemidactylus punctatus. Scales of abdomen dotted, brown above; limbs and tail reddish, with dark bands; pale-yellow streak from muzzle to tail, bordered beneath by a dark line; another dark line from nostrils to behind the eye.—"*k*" Hemidactylus sykesii. Brownish olive above, with cross series of rounded brown spots, sometimes confluent into bands; two brown streaks behind the eye and one before it.—"*l*" Hemidactylus triedrus. Alias Gecko triedrus. Brownish olive.

CHIPPY (कोमलशरीरी - kómalasharírí, *San.*; گھونگے - ghunge, *Hind.*; ಚಿಪ್ಪುಹುಳ - chippuhula, *Can.*; చిప్పపురుగు - chippa-purugu, *Tel.*; ചിപ്പി - chippi, *Mal.*; சிப்பி - shippi, *Tam.*). Title from (shipi, san. light). San. from (kómala, san. soft + sharíra, san. body). Hind. from (kambuka, san. shell). Can. and tel. mean shell + worm. Mollusc. One of the primary sub-kingdoms of animals [jantoo], comprising cuttle-fish and ordinary univalve and bivalve shells, or Cephalopoda, Gasteropoda, Pteropoda, and Lamellibranchiata. Shell fish are largely used by natives for food when available. On the coast purely marine species are not common or easily procured, but in lagoons [cauyal] bivalves are abundant and often collected as food. The commonest edible shell fish are the Cockle, cordium edule [mutty], the Oyster, ostrea edulis [auly], and the Snail, helix pomatia [nuttay]. Other common molluscs are the Chunk [q.v.], turbinella rapa, and the Pearl oyster [sadaf], meleagrina margaritifera [moty].——*Chippautchy* (ಚಿಪ್ಪಾಚಿ - chippáchi, Can.). From (akshi, san. eye). Hill-tribe female proper name [peyar].

CHIRA (ചിറ - chira, *Mal.*). A tank [cherla, cheroo].

CHIRACAL (ചിറക്കൽ - chirakkal, *Mal.* chirakal *). From (chira, mal. tank + kal, mal. suffix of place); from the palace near the tank.——**(1)** Talook, Malabar district. Tahsildar's pay Rs. 175. Area 648 square miles; most northerly coast talook of the district. Bounded north by Cassergode talook of South canara; east by Coorg; south by Cottayam talook; west by the Arabian sea. Formerly comprised the talooks of Cavvye and Chiracal. The terraced character of the laterite [q.v.] formation is conspicuous, more particularly in that portion lying north of the Belliapatam river. These terraces are as a rule unproductive, but where they break off in abrupt cliffs the soil is extensively cultivated with cocoanut [q.v.], jack [q.v.] and pepper [q.v.]. The flats between the laterite terraces are thickly peopled; along the coast, the beach, except at Mount delly and to the south of Cannanore, is low and sandy; the outlying spurs of the ghauts are covered with scrub jungle and the ghauts themselves are in great part also covered with scrub, the heavy forest having disappeared. Laterite is met with in abundance. Coarse cotton cloths are made at places in the interior by rude appliances. At Cannanore is a weaving establishment under the

German mission. In the Central jail, Cannanore, carpentry and other works are carried on. Cooniyimungalam is noted for its brass [pittalay] works, chiefly lamps. Neither dams nor irrigation canals are to be met with. Sultan's canal, between the river of Payyangaudy and a branch of another which runs north, joins the Cavvye immediately to south of the town of that name. It is three miles in length, cut through low paddy [q.v.] ground. It was executed at the expense of the Beeby of Cannanore with the object of having a safe inland navigation from Neeleshwar in South canara to Caccaud. It is now shallow and impassable at low tide. Places of archæological interest:—Ayicode, Cadalye, Cadambairy, Calarivaudacull, Calliaud, Cannanore, Caunyarangaud, Cavvye, Cayaralam, Cayivellore, Chercoonn, Chertalam, Choolaly, Chova, Cooniyimungalam, Coormattore, Coottiyairy, Coottiyauttore, Coottore, Cunnaupooram, Keelara, Madool, Malaputtam, Maniyore, Maudye, Molappilaugaud, Mount delly, Oorpilatchicauv, Payyannore, Payyavore, Polaudy, Taliparamba, Trichambaram, Vaudeshwaram, Vellore, Yedacaud, Yelayavore, Yelome, Yeraumala. Principal trig. station:—Delly. The leading places, &c., in the talook are the following. ——*Anjarcundy* (അഞ്ചരക്കണ്ടി - añcharakkanti, Mal.) See sep. title.——*Belliapatam* (വളപട്ടണം - valapattanam, Mal.). See sep. title.——*Calliaud* (കല്ലിയാട് - kalliyátu, Mal.). From (kallu, mal. stone + átu, mal. country). Sub-village; lat. 12° 1′; long. 75° 38′; from Calicut N.N.W. 53 miles; from Cannanore N.E. 18 miles; from the sea E. 23 miles. On the route from Cannanore to Seringapatam. Five rock caves.——*Cannanore* (കണ്ണൂർ - kannúr, Mal.). See sep. title.——*Caraur sheema* (കരാർശീമ - karárshíma, Mal.). Means agreement territory. Mal. also (karárinakkam), meaning agreement + union; name by which known among natives. Tract of land about 2,364 acres in extent in Cannanore town belonging to the Moplah rajah of Cannanore, Ally rajah [audy rajah]; and held by his family under an agreement entered into with the British government. The rajah exercises no sovereign or judicial powers but in respect of this tract is merely an Inamdar. His palace is situated in the old town of Cannanore and is known as the Aracull palace. A lamp is kept burning day and night in one of the rooms in the palace, the belief being that if extinguished the prosperity of the house would be destroyed. The peshcush [q.v.] payable on Caraur sheema and the Laccadive islands is Rs. 15,000 per annum. An abatement of Rs. 5,250, was allowed in 1822 as compensation for the loss of the Amindivy islands attached to South canara district.——*Cavvye* (കവ്വായി - kavváyi, Mal.). See sep. title.——*Chiracal* (ചിറക്കൽ - chirakkal, Mal.). See below.——*Coonyimungalam* (കുഞ്ഞിമംഗലം - kuññimannalam, Mal.). From (kuññi, mal. child + mangala, san. prosperity); from Shaustav temple. Amshom; pop. 9,759; lat. 12° 05′; long. 75° 17′; from Calicut N.N.W. 66 miles; from Cannanore N.N.W. 17 miles; from the sea E. 4 miles. Ramantaly narayancunnore temple. Image of Shaustauv [q.v.]. Old temple on the western slope of Mount delly and close to the sea. Contains Vattezhoot [q.v.] inscriptions. Noted for manufacture of brass utensils, chiefly native lamps.——*Delly* (ഏഴിമല - ézhimala, Mal.). See sep. title.——*Iricore* (ഇരിക്കൂർ - irukkúr, Mal.). See sep. title.——*Madakara* (മടക്കര - matakkara, Mal.). See sep. title.——*Maudye* (മാടായി - mátáyi, Mal.). See sep. title.——*Payyannore* (പയ്യന്നൂർ - payyannúr, Mal.). See sep. title.——*Ponacaud* (പൊനക്കാട് - ponakkátu, Mal.). From (punam, mal. high ground + kátu, mal. forest). Village; lat. 12° 02′; long. 75° 26′; from Calicut N.N.W. 58 miles; from Cannanore N.N.E. 12 miles; from the sea E. 14 miles. A small sub-village north of Taliparamba where in ancient times stood the palace of Colattiry rajah's wife.——*Punniyore* (പന്നിയൂർ - panniyúr, Mal.). See sep. title.——*Randatarra* (രണ്ടുതറ - rantattara, Mal.). See sep. title.——*Shreecundapooram* (ശ്രീകണ്ഠപുരം - shríkandapuram, Mal.). From (shrí, san. holy + kanda, mal. skanda, the god + pura, san city). Town; lat. 12° 3′ N.; long. 75° 33′ E.; from Calicut N.N.W. 57 miles; from Cannanore N.E. 16 miles; from the sea E. 22 miles. On the right bank of the principal tributary of the Belliapatam. Inhabited almost exclusively by Moplahs [q.v.] who settled here under the protection of a Choolaly chief, a feudatory of the Colattiry [q.v.] rajahs. Mosque, founded by Malik ibn e deenaur in the ninth century A.D.——*Sultan's canal* (സുൽത്താൻതോട് - sultántótu, Mal.). See sep. title.——*Taliparamba* (തളിപ്പറമ്പ - talipparamba, Mal.). See sep. title.——*Vyetalmala* (വയിത്തൽമല - vayitalmala, Mal.). See sep. title.——*Yetticolam* (എട്ടിക്കുളം - ettikkulam, Mal.). From (etti, mal. strychnos nux vomica, linn. + kulam, mal. tank). Village, Port; lat. 12° 1′; long. 75° 15′; from Bombay S.S.E. 490 miles; from Calicut N.N.W. 64 miles; from Cannanore N.N.W. 15 miles; from Cavvye S. 6 miles; from Maudye W. 4 miles; from Poothiyangandy N.N.W. 60 miles. Picturesquely situated in a bay just under Mount delly promontory, commanded by the old Mount delly redoubt. Inhabited by Moplah merchants, who supply Cannanore and Tellicherry with firewood.——(2) Village, amshom; Malabar dist., Chiracal tal.; pop. 10,390; lat. 11° 55′; long. 75° 24′; from Calicut N.N.W. 52 miles; from Cannanore N.N.W. 4 miles; from the sea E. 3 miles. Former head-quarters of the talook. The rajah of Chiracal, formerly a powerful chief, belonged to the Colattiry family. The country was in 1789 devastated by Tippoo sultan, and the rajah induced one of his followers to shoot him through the head. It was from one of these rajahs that the British first obtained a permanent footing at Tellicherry. Descendants of this line still live in the neighbourhood.

CHIRAM (चिर - chira, *San.*). Long.——*Chiranjeevy* (चिरञ्जीवी - chirañjívi, San.). From (above + jív, san. to live). Endowed with a long life. Seven immortal sages who will be produced in successive manwantarams [q.v.]:—Ashwattauman, Baly, Hanooman, Kripan, Parshooraman, Vibheeshanan, Vyausan. When Hindoos bathe in oil seven drops of oil are scattered on the ground in a row for the seven chiranjeevies and joined together by running the finger over them; after which the oiled finger is applied to the head, this being thought to promote longevity.

CHIRAUG (چراغ - chirágh, *Pers.*). Lamp [deepam]. Prefixed to alam makes a lacab; as Chiraug ally, lamp of Ally. Mostly taken by Shiahs [ism]. Cf. Becharaug.——*Chiraughaun* (چراغان - chírághán, Hind.); plural of chiraug. A common ceremony observed by lower order of mussulmans on the sixteenth night of zilkada [maheena] in honor of Bundanawauz [q.v.] when lamps made of silver or paste are lighted with ghee [q.v.] and fautihas [q.v.] offered.——*Chiraughy* (چراغی - chirághí, Hind.). An allowance for keeping lamps constantly burning at the tomb [durgah] of a Mahomedan saint [walee], or for illuminating a mosque [musjid].

CHIRETTA (कैरात - kairáta, *San.*). From (kiráta, san. mountaineer). Title otherwise Chirayta, Creyat, Country gentian, Kariyat, King of bitters. Chiefly the Swertia genus, gentianaceæ [vricsham, 90]; annual or perennial herbs; leaves generally opposite; flowers blue lurid or whitish, sometimes with yellow glands; fruit one-celled, two-valved; seeds membraneous, winged; the species best known to the natives are shown below; other s. indian species indigenous or naturalized are angustifolia, pulchella. See however also the genera:—andrographis [bhoonimbam, french chiretta, coromandel chiretta], enicostema [small chiretta], erythræa [roxburgh's chiretta], and exacum [country chiretta, purple chiretta].——*Blue-flowered chiretta* (اودے پھول کا چرایتہ - údahphúlkácharáitah, Hind.; శిలాజిత - shilájitu, Tel.). Tel. from (shilá, san. stone + ji, san. to conquer); found on stony ground [shilajit]. Tel. also (salárasa), meaning stone + juice. Title otherwise Elegant ophelia. Botanically Swertia [chiretta] affinis, clarke, gentianaceæ [vricsham, 90]. Alias Ophelia elegans. Shrub, erect, ramous above, obsoletely four-sided; leaves sessile, narrow, ovate-lanceolate, tapering to a slender point, three-nerved, lateral nerves close to the margin; branches ascending, slender, bearing at each point lateral few-flowered cymes, forming together a large, many-flowered, leafy panicle; calyx lobes narrow-lanceolate, acute, about two-thirds the length of the corolla; lobes of the corolla obovate-cuspidate; foveæ bound with longish coarse hairs; flowers pale blue. Stems medicinally resemble himalayan chiretta.——*Coromandel chiretta* (چرایتہ - charáitah, Hind. and Dec.; గొర్రెచీమిడి - gorrechímidi, Tel.; മലകുലുക്കി - malakulukki, Mal.; கோபுரந்தாங்கி - kóburandángi, Tam.). Tel. from (gorre, tel. sheep + chímidi, tel. mucus). Mal. from (mala, mal. mountain + kulukku, mal. to shake); found on mountains; cf. lance-leaved balah. Tam. from (gópura, san. tower + tángu, tam. to support); found on towers. Tel. also (tsalavapurikáda), meaning cool + stem. Mal. also (píttumba), meaning dirt + leucas indica, r. br. Botanically Andrographis [bhoonimbam] echioides, nees., acanthaceæ [vricsham, 101]. Alias Justicia ciliaris, echioides. Herbaceous, hairy; leaves oblong, sub-sessile somewhat crenated; racemes rigid, reflexed; capsules four-seeded; flowers whitish with dark purple spots; flowering nearly all the year. For paniculata see French chiretta.——*French chiretta* (भुनिम्ब - bhúnimba, San.; चिराईत - chiráíta, Mahr.; किरातु - kirátu, Conc.; قصب الذريرة - kasabuzzarírah, Ar.; نی نهاوندی - naiinihávandí, Pers.; چرایتہ - charáitah, Hind. and Dec.; ನೆಲಬೇವು - nelabeva, Can.; ಕಿರ್ಯಾತ್ - kiryát, Too.; నేలవేము - nélavému, Tel.; നിലവേപ്പ് - nilavéppu, Mal.; බිංකොහොඹ - binkohomba, Singh.; நிலவேம்பு - nilavémbu, Tam.). Title as introduced from isle of france. San. from (bhú, san. earth + nimba, san. margosa, melia azadirachta, linn.); from being a bitter shrub. Mahr. from (kiráta, san. mountaineer). Ar. from (kasab, ar. reed or plant + zaríráh, ar. worm-wood, artemisia); cf. absinth. Pers. from (nai, pers. reed + nihávand, pers. name of place). Hind. from (kiráta, san. mountaineer). Can. from (nela, can. ground + bévu, can. margosa tree). Too. from (kirata, san. mountaineer). Tel. from (néla, tel. ground + vému, tel. margosa). Mal. from (nilam, mal. earth + véppu, mal. margosa). Singh. from (bin, singh. ground + kohomba, singh. margosa). Tam. from (nilam, tam. ground + vémbu, tam. margosa tree). San. also (kunimba), meaning earth margosa; (mahátikta), meaning great + bitter; (anáryatikta), meaning non-aryan margosa; to distinguish from real margosa tree called (áryatikta). Ar. also (kasabbuvá), meaning odorous reed. Hind. also (mahátitah), meaning very bitter; (kiryát), from san. meaning non-aryan. Can. also (úrakiriyátu), meaning village + chiretta. Tel. also (karivému), meaning black + margosa. Mal. also (karakkáññiram), meaning blackness + strychnos nux vomica, linn. Singh. also (húbinkohomba), meaning small + the plant. Tam. also (kiriyáttu); (vérkkiriyáttu). Title otherwise Ground neem, King of bitters, Non-aryan bitter. Botanically Andrographis [bhoonimbam] paniculata, nees, acanthaceæ [vricsham, 101]. Alias Justicia paniculata. Annual, 1–2 feet; stem quadrangular, pointed, smooth, leaves opposite, on short petioles, lanceolate, entire; calyx deeply five-cleft; corolla bilabiate, lips linear, reflected, upper one three-toothed, lower one two-toothed; flowers remote, alternate, on long petioles, downy, rose-colored or white, streaked with purple; capsules erect, somewhat cylindrical; seeds three to four in each. Dried stem sold in bazaars with the root attached; occurs in pieces of about a foot or more in length, quadrangular, of a lightish-brown color, and persistent bitter taste. Has properties similar to those of chiretta; the bitter is due to a non-basic principle, there being no alkaloid; medicinally forms basis of french and portuguese bitter tincture known on malabar coast as drogue amére; gives to pharm. dried stalks and root, andrographis caules et radix, bitter tonic and stomachic, very analogous to quassia or gentian in its action; officinal. For echioides see Coromandel chiretta.——*Himalayan chiretta* (कैरात - kairáta, San.; चिराईत - chiráíta, Mahr.; जिरत्ते - jiratté, Conc.; قصب الزريرة - kasabuzzarírah, Ar. and Pers.; چرايته کا پير - charáitahkáper, Hind.; چرايته کا جهار - charáitahkájhár, Dec.; ಕಿರಿಯಾತು - kiriyátu, Can.; ಕಿರಿಯಾತು - kiriyátu, Too.; నేలవేము - nélavému, Tel.; നിലവേപ്പു - nilavéppu, Mal.; கிராயத்து - kiráyathu, Tam.). San. from (kiráta, san. a mountainous tribe, the country they inhabit). Ar. from (kasab, ar. reed + zarírah, ar. chiretta). Tel. from (néla, tel. ground + vému, tel. margosa). Mal. from (nilam, mal. ground + véppu, mal. margosa), from low size and bitterness. San. also (bhúnimba), meaning ground margosa; (haima), meaning pertaining to gold; (suvarnabhúmijá), meaning produced in gold earth; (kirátiká); (kirátatikta), meaning bitter tree of mountaineers; (naipála), meaning coming from nepaul; (anáryatiktá), meaning bitter plant of the non-aryans. Hind. also (kiriyat). Can. also (chiryáta); (nelabévu), meaning ground + margosa. Tel. also (shilásattu), meaning stone + essence, growing among hills; (shilárasamu), meaning stone + juice [indian storax, shilajit]. Mal. also (kiriyáttu). Tam. also (nilavémbu), meaning ground + margosa. Title otherwise Ground margosa, Nepaul chiretta, Worm-seed plant. Botanically Swertia [chiretta] chirata, ham., gentianaceæ [vricsham, 90]. Specific name from hindostany. Alias Agathotes chirayta; Gentiana chirayta; Ophelia chirata. A slender branching annual, 2–3 feet high; small stalks of light-grey color; from northern india. Stems single, round, jointed; branches decussated, occasionally angular at the extremities; leaves opposite, amplexicaul, lanceolate, very acute, entire, three to five-nerved; flowers numerous, stalked, the whole upper part of the plant forming an oblong decussated panicle; calyx four-cleft; petals spreading, four-parted, divisions equal to those of the calyx; capsules one-celled, two-valved, slightly opening at the apex; seeds numerous; flowers yellow. All parts extremely bitter, identical with gentian; the dried plant is the form generally presented; stems about three feet long, of the thickness of a goose quill. Valuable as a tonic and febrifuge; long been used in hindoo medicine; parts used, the dried stalks with pieces of the root adhering to them; a decoction [kwautam] of these or an infusion of them in hot water; the root is the bitterest part; officinal in pharm.; the flowers even share the intense bitterness of the whole drug.——*Mahableshwar chiretta* (مها بليشوار کا چرايته - mahábleshwárkácharáitah, Hind.). Title from original habitat. Botanically Swertia [chiretta] decussata, nimmo, gentianaceæ [vricsham, 90]. Stem quadrangular, four-winged, ascending, densely leafy; leaves round, ovate, stem-clasping, five-nerved, mucronulate, glabrous, decussate; cymes many-flowered; calyx divisions lanceolate-acuminate; corolla white, four-divided, segments ovate-elliptic, their rounded pits surrounded by long fringes; filaments united at the very base. ——*Oodah chiretta* (اودا چرايته - údácharáitah, Hind.). Same as Purple chiretta.——*Purple chiretta* (بڑا چرايته - barácharáitah, Hind.; اودا چرايته - údácharáitah, Dec.). Title from color of flowers. Hind. from (bará, hind. large + charáitah, hind. chiretta, swertia chirata, ham.). Dec. from (údá, hind. purple + charáitah, hind. chiretta). Hind. also (habshícharáitah), meaning large chiretta. Title otherwise Country gentian. Botanically Exacum bicolor, roxb., gentianaceæ [vricsham, 90]. Alias Exacum grandiflorum. Small plant, 1–2 feet; stem and branches tetragonal; leaves sessile, sub-acute, ovate, three to five-nerved, margins smooth; calyx four-cleft; flowers axillary, solitary, on short pedicels; corolla white, having the segments tipped with blue; found on margins of rivers; valuable febrifuge; just like gentian; in pharm. but non-officinal. Other species are:—cochin-chinensis, courtallense, pedunculatum, insignis, perottetii, tetragonum, wightianum.——*Roxburgh's chiretta* (چرايته - charáitah, Hind.; ಕಾಡುಕೆಂಪುಜೀರಿಗೆಗಿಡ - kádukempujírigegida, Can.). Can. from (kádu, can. jungle + kempu, can. red + jírige, can. cuminum cyminum, linn. + gida, can. plant); from similar seeds. Title otherwise Wild cumin [wild jeerah]. Botanically Erythræa roxburghii, g. don., gentianaceæ [vricsham, 90]. Alias Chironia centaurioides. Herbaceous; stem erect; lowermost leaves rosulate, obovate oblong, obtuse; cymes one to two dichotomous, spreading; flowers lateral, ebracteate, star-like, pink; wild plant, common in cultivated fields after rains; whole plant powerfully bitter, in pharm. but non-officinal. No other species here.——*Small chiretta* (چهوٹا چرايته - chhotácharáitah, Hind.; نائی کا جهار - náíkájhár, Dec.; చెవుకుర్తిచెట్టు - chevukurtichettu, Tel.; வெள்ளறுகு - vellarugu, Tam.). Hind. from (chhotá, hind. small + charáitah, hind. chiretta), from bitterness. Tam. from (vel, tam. white + arugu, tam. the grass, cynodon dactylon, pers.). Tel. also (golimidi); (nélagulimidi), meaning ground + the plant; (nélagurugudu), meaning ground + casearia tomentosa, roxb.; (nélaguli), meaning ground + capparis grandis, linn. f.; (vallari). Title otherwise White doob grass. Botanically Enicostema littorale, bl., gentianaceæ [vricsham, 90]. Alias Adenema hyssopifolia, hyssopifolium; Cicendia hyssopifolia; Exacum hyssopifolium; Gentiana verticillaris, verticillata; Hippion hyssopifolium; Slevotia orientalis, verticillata. Annual, herbaceous; stem quadrangular, angles slightly winged, leaves opposite, decussate, linear-lanceolate, tapering at the base, embracing the stem with the short petioles, three-nerved, paler below; calyx five-cleft; segments margined, reflexed at the point, permanent, closely embracing the base of the mature capsule; corolla tubular, five-cleft; segment spreading, oblique at the base, remaining attached to the capsule till the latter bursts; flowers six to eight together in axillary whorls, sessile, white; capsule two-valved, one-celled; seeds numerous, small, round, small white. Whole plant medicinal; tonic, stomachic, and laxative; useful in dyspepsia and general debility; substituted for british gentian, on account of bitterness; in pharm., but non-officinal. No other common species here.

CHIRIYAH (चट - chata, *San.*; عصفور - usfúr, *Ar.*; کنجشک - kunjashk, *Pers.*; چڑيا - chiriyá, *Hind.*; چڑی - churí, *Dec.*; ಗುಬ್ಬಿ - gubbi, *Can.*; ఊరపిచ్చుక - úrapittsuka, *Tel.*; കുരികിൽ - kurikil, *Mal.*; அடைக்கலாங்குருவி - adaikkalánguruvi, *Tam.*). Title from hindostany. Ar. from (asa, ar. rebel + farra, ar. fly); from legend that it flew off when summoned by adam to be named. Tel. from (úru, tel. village + pittsuka, tel. sparrow). Mal. from (kuru, mal. small + kili, mal. bird). Tam. from (adaikkalam, tam. shelter + kuruvi, tam. small bird); from resorting to houses for protection. Hind. also (khánchurí), meaning house sparrow, cf. house martin; (gauriya), meaning yellowish white. Can. also (gubichi). Mal. also (atakkáppakshi), meaning shelter + bird. Tam. also (úrkkuruvi), meaning village + bird. Sparrows. Passerinæ, fringilidæ [boosapriyam], conirostres, insessores, aves [pacshy, 27], of naturalists [jantoo].—"*a*" The Indian house sparrow is Passer indicus. Alias Passer domesticus. Differs very little from that of Europe. Builds in thatched roofs, under the eaves of houses. Note like the European.—"*b*" Yellow-necked sparrow, or hill sparrow, or sugar-cane sparrow, according to the natives is Passer flavicollis; common in thin forest jungle. Lives in small parties.

CHIRONJEE (प्रियाल - priyála, *San.*; पियाल - piyála, *Mahr.*; پيال کا پير - piyálkáper, *Hind.*; چرونجی کا جهار - chironjíkájhár, *Dec.*; ಮೊರವೆ - morave, *Can.*; చార - tsára, *Tel.*; ଚର - chara, *Oor.*; മുരൾ - mural, *Mal.*; காட்டுமா - káttumá, *Tam.*). Title from deccany. San. from (priya, san. dear). Can. from (morave, can. resounding + mara, can. tree). Mal. from (mura, san. fragrant plant). Tam. from (kádu, tam. forest + má, tam. mango, mangifera indica, linn.) [wild mango]. San. also (chára), meaning moving, as medicinal; (tápasapriya), meaning dear to hermits; (rájádana), meaning eaten by kings [monkey-face paulay]. Mahr. also (chárólí), from sanscrit. Tel. also (chinamorali), meaning small + the tree; (chárumámidi), meaning juice + mango tree. Mal. also (kálamaram). Tam. also (aimá); (tumbí). Title otherwise Charolee oil plant, Cuddapah almond, Hermit's tree, Jungle mango, Moræda. Botanically Buchanania latifolia, roxb., anacardiaceæ [vricsham, 45]. Alias Chirongia sapida; Spondias elliptica. Chirongia from deccany. Tree, 30 feet; leaves alternate, entire, broadly oval or obovate, obtuse; calyx small, obtusely five-cleft; petals five, sessile recurved; branches of the panicles hirsute, terminal, and axillary, with the flowers crowded, assuming the appearance of a corymb at the tops of the branches; flowers small, greenish white; flowers in december and january, ripens fruit in may. The fruit is a sub-globose, slightly compressed drupe, half inch in diameter, of a deep purple color; stone hard, two-valved; kernels laterally compressed like a vetch seed, brown, mottled with darker brown, rather more than ¼ inch in length, and rather less than ¼ inch in breadth; slight pressure separates the oily cotyledons, which have a very agreeable nutty flavor. Habitat, mountains on the coromandel and malabar coasts; cuddapah, belgaum and mysore forests. Gives gum [gond] resembling bussorah gum [hog gum]; brittle, pale, horn-colored, tinged with brown, tasteless, soluble in water, except a small insoluble portion of bussorine; a good clear and very adhesive mucilage and can be substituted for gum-arabic [q.v.]. Oil extracted from seeds, pale straw color; also a black varnish [rangh], similar to semecarpus anacardium [marking nut]. Gum administered in diarrhœa; oil from kernels of fruit used as substitute for almond oil. Kernels used in confectionery as substitute for almonds [baudam]; mixed with milk are eaten by higher classes to promote fatness. Bark used by tanners [chamrah]. Wood greyish-brown, moderately hard with a small dark-colored heart-wood; seasons well and is fairly durable if kept dry. Other common species are :—angustifolia, lanceolata.

CHIRY (ചിരി - chiri, *Mal.*). Small [cher, chinna, chit, chota, coor, shir].——*Chiriyan* (ചിരിയൻ - chiriyan, Mal.). From (cheriya, mal. young). Pariah proper name [peyar].——*Chiry mat* (ఛిరిచాప - chiritsápa, Tel.). From (above + tsápa, tel. mat). Fine mat [boriyah] of bulrushes [coray].

CHISHT (چشت - chisht, *Pers.*). A Persian town.——*Chishtiya* (چشتیہ - chishtiyah, Hind.). A class of singing fakeers [q.v.] founded by Cauja bunda nawauz chishty, alias the long ringletted [bunda nawauz].

CHIT (चित् - chit, *San.*). From (chit, san. to perceive). Intelligence. Chit is four kinds, viz., jeevan, eeshwarau, jagat and paramautman. It has four oopaudhies or states of being :—chit or intelligence when in entire abstraction; antaryaumy when united to mauyay or illusion; hiranyagarbham when joined with mauyay soocshma shareeram or subtle body of mauyay; and viraut poorooshan or male energy when dwelling in mauyay stoola shareeram or gross body of mauyay [achit, matam].——*Cheitanyam* (चैतन्य - chaitanya, San.). Intelligence. ——*Cheitanyan* (चैतन्य - chaitanya, San.). A reformer. Gave his name to a Veishnava sect in Bengal and Orissa. See vol. I (77), (85) [matam].——*Chidambaram* (चिदम्बर - chidambara, San.). From (above + ambara, san. robe). Spirit-robed [jeina]. Hindoo 2nd or pers. name. Similarly Chidambarasawmy [peyar]. Cf. Digambara. For talook of this name see sep. title.——*Chitram* (चित्र - chitra, San.). From (chit, san. to perceive). Variegated, spotted. Chitracaury is a small caste of teloogoo painters, about 1,000. Chitravadhay, from (vadha, san. killing) is torture. Chitravully, from (valli, san. creeper) is parvaty.——*Chitramoolam* (चित्रक - chitraka, San.; चित्रमूल - chitramúla, Mahr.; चित्रमूल - chitramúla, Conc.; شيطرج - shítraj, Ar.; شيتره - shítarah, Pers.; چترا - chitrá, Hind.; چتر مولم - chitarmulam, Dec.; ಚಿತ್ರಮೂಲ - chitramúla, Can.; ಚಿತ್ರಮೂಲ - chitramúla, Too.; చిత్రమూలము - chitramúlamu, Tel.; കൊടുവേലി- kotuvéli, Mal.; නෙතුල් - netul, Singh.; சித்திரமூலம் - shittiramúlam, Tam.). San. from (chitra, san. variegated). Mahr. from (chitra, san. variegated + múla, san. root). Mal. from (kotu, mal. cruel + vér, mal. root); from blistering root. San. also (chitravallí), meaning variegated creeper; (dípiká), meaning shining; (dáruna), meaning cruel; (vahni), meaning fire, from its raising blister [shamee]; (agnishikhá), meaning flame of fire [saffron, wild bachnaug]; (agnimátá), meaning mother of fire. Hind. also (chítrak), meaning variegated; (chitá), meaning variegated; (chitarmul), meaning variegated root. Tam. also (kodivéli), corrupted from (kodivéri), meaning pungent rooted; (athiganári), meaning having strong smell; (shittiragam), meaning variegated; (akkini), meaning fire, from blistering root. Blister root, Chitrak, Leadwort. Botanically the Plumbago genus, plumbagineæ [vricsham, 79]. Herbaceous plants or shrubs.—"*a*" Officinal leadwort, otherwise Fire plant, Rosy-flowered leadwort, is Plumbago rosea, linn. Alias Plumbago coccinea; Thela coccinea. Small erect shrub; perennial, stems jointed, smooth, flexuous; branches nearly bifarious; leaves alternate, ovate, waved, smooth, entire; petioles short, stem-clasping, channelled; raceme axillary and terminal, smooth; flowers moderate sized, pale, pinkish-scarlet flowers in cold season. Bruised root, in natural state, acrid and stimulating, tempered with bland oil used as external application in rheumatic and paralytic affections; also prescribed internally in small doses for same complaints; gives to pharm. non-officinal, root-bark, like mezereon bark; for raising a blister, fresh bark of root is taken and rubbed into a paste with water and rice flour.— "*b*" Ceylon leadwort, otherwise White-flowered leadwort is Plumbago zeylanica, linn. Alias Plumbago flaccida, sarmentosa. Small slender shrub; perennial, stems jointed, smooth, flexuous; branches nearly bifarious; leaves alterative, ovate, waved, smooth, entire; racemes axillary and terminal, covered with much glutinous hair; outer bract much larger than the lateral ones, glutinous; flowers pure white, clammy to touch; flowering nearly all year; grows in hedges and waste places. Medicinal properties same as rosea, but milder.—"*c*" Blue-flowered leadwort, otherwise Cape leadwort is Plumbago capensis, thunb. A small prostrate growing shrub, bears in the hot and rainy seasons a profusion of pale, azure blue flowers of the same size and form of rosea.—"*d*" Pedilanthus tithymaloides (símachitramúlam), is foreign plumbago. Pupalia atropurpurea (valiyakotuvéli), is large plumbago. See gloss. paragraphs.—— *Chitravaty* (చిత్రావతి - chitrávati, * Tel.). From (chitra, san. varied color + vat, san. suffix of possession). River, Anantapore district, Hindoopore, Penoocondah, Dharmavaram, Anantapore and Tadpatry talooks. Rises in Mysore and enters Anantapore district near Codicondah. Is dammed near Bookkapatam by an immense bund which joins two hills. In this way the large tank is formed. About 20 miles lower down it is again dammed and forms the Dharmavaram tank. A little lower it is joined by the Maudair river and winding through the hills joins the Pennair near Gundicote in lat. 14° 48′; long. 78° 16′; near Gandlore near the Gundicote gorge. A high flood in 1851 submerged the village of Sowtapully. Crossed by a railway bridge near Condaupooram station.——*Chittajan* (चित्तज - chittaja, San.). From (above + jan, san. to be born). Cauman, as produced in the mind [manmatan].——*Chittrah* (चित्रा - chitrá, San.). The fourteenth lunar mansion [nacshatram]. See chitta.——*Chittray* (சித்திரை - shittirai, Tam.). First tam. solar month [mausam] or april. One born in that month. Pariah proper name [peyar]. Chittray shilamban or April floods is cauvery [q.v.].——*Chittray pournamy* (చిత్రాపౌర్ణమి - chitrápaurnami, Tel.; சித்திராப்பௌர்ணமி - shittirâppaurnimi, Tam.). Means the first solar month + full moon day. Otherwise Chittray poornay, Chittray conjee; the latter from distribution of conjee [q.v.] in honor of chitragooptan. Luni-solar festival [pundigay, 5a]. The fifteenth tity [q.v.] or full moon day in first solar month Chittray [mausam], i.e., between 12th April and 12th May. Celebrated by offerings of boiled rice, milk and jaggery [q.v.] in honor of Chitragooptan, the secretary of Yaman, who records the vices and virtues of mankind. On this occasion Hindoos eat but one meal [maryauday].

CHIT (چٹّی - chítí, *Hind.*). A letter, document. The Tamulians use the word for a ticket, or for a playing card.—— *Chittah* (چٹھا - chitthá, Hind.). From (chíthi, hind. memorandum). A rough note book or account book for land or cash. See vol. I, 112.

CHIT (చిరు - chiru, *Tel.*; ചിറു - chiru, *Mal.*; சிறு - shiru, *Tam.*). Small [cher, chinna, chiry, chota, coor, shir]. Prefix in place names, as Chittore, meaning small + village.——*Chitikey* (ಚಿಟಿಕೆ - chitike, Can.). Means snap of the fingers [nody]. Castanets. Small shells of ivory [dant] or hard wood which dancers rattle in their hands [sangeetam].——*Chittack* (چھٹاک - chhaták, Hind.; చటాకు - chatáku, Tel.; சிற்றாழாக்கு - shittázhákku, Tam.). Tam. from (shiru, tam. small + ázhákku, tam. one-eighth of a measure). Small olluck, or half olluck.—"*a*" Bazaar weight. 5 tolahs = 1 chittack; 2 chittacks = 1 nowtauk [niray, 2e]. Approximate actual value, 1 chittack = 2 oz. and 25 grs. Ganjam and Vizagapatam. Compare Pollum of Tinnevelly.—"*b*" Measure of capacity. 2 chittacks = 1 nowtauk [alavay, 3c]. Approximate actual value, 1 chittack = $4\frac{3}{8}$ cubic inches. $\frac{1}{16}$th of a pucka seer. Compare Tel. gidda, Mal. oyak. See vol. I, 609; II, 514.——*Chittal* (دریا کا سانپ - daryákásámp, Hind.; చిట్టులి - chittuli, Tel.; കടൽപാമ്പ് - katalpámbu, Mal.; கடற்பாம்பு - kadarbámbu, Tam.). Title from teloogoo. Hind. means sea-snake. Tel. from (chiru, tel. small + uli, tel. hissing). Mal. from (katal, mal. sea + pámbu, mal. snake). Tam. similar. Genus formerly called Chittulia. The terms are co-extensive with the genus Hydrophis, hydrophidæ [tuttapaumb], ophidii colubriformes venenosi, ophidia [sarpam], reptilia [sarpy, 28], of naturalists [jantoo]. This genus furnishes the greater proportion of sea-snakes found on these coasts. They present considerable variety of form and coloration. They are all poisonous and entirely pelagic. The following are the species under Hydrophis :—"*a*" Chloris. Sometimes called Soodarshanam, from (su, san. good + darshana, san. sight). Alias Gracilis obscura. Trunk greenish-olive above, yellowish on the side and below; blackish bands across the back, much narrower and fainter on the sides, and extend round the belly; head and anterior part of the belly entirely black. Young specimens have the markings of a deep black; the coasts of Madras; 40 inches long, tail 3 inches.—"*b*" Cærulescens. Alias Hydrophis hybrida; Hydrus cærulescens. Yellowish, with from thirty-seven to forty-six rhombic blackish spots on the back.—"*c*" Curta. Alias Hydrophis propinquus; Hydrus curtus; Lapemis curtus. Black bands across the back; yellowish ground-color between them, yellowish streak on the temple; tail black, with only two yellow transverse spots at its root.—"*d*" Cyanocincta. The Chittal proper. Alias Hydrophis striata, subannulata, sublævis; Hydrus striatus. Greenish olive on the back, yellowish on the sides and belly; trunk with from fifty to seventy-five black cross-bands. In young and half-grown specimens they surround the body entirely and are sometimes joined by a black band running along the whole line of the ventral shields. Head greenish olive above and yellowish on the sides; in the young black, variegated with yellow, yellow color sometimes forming a frontal and temporal band. One of the commonest sea-snakes; length of more than 6 feet. Old males have a remarkably thick and rounded tail.—"*e*" Diadema. Head blackish above, with yellow band over each superciliary and the temple; lower jaw and belly yellowish; tail with from seven to nine blackish cross bars.—"*f*" Ellioti, Alias Aturia ornata. Broad blackish-olive bands across the back, separated by very narrow whitish transverse stripes. Head uniform greenish olive. Lower parts and sides whitish; tail with narrow yellowish cross bands. Distinguished from ornata by a shorter head, stouter body, and by the coloration.—"*g*" Fasciata. Alias Anguis mamillaris; Hydrus fasciatus. Trunk with deep-black rings; lower parts from the chin to the extremity of the tail being deep black; head uniform black, with two or three yellowish dots behind the eye; tail black, with three short yellowish bars across its basal half.—"*h*" Gracilis. Alias Hydrophis microcephala, obscurus; Hydrus gracilis; Microcephalophis gracilis; Thalassophis microcephala. Neck very slender; anterior part of the body surrounded by blackish rings; hinder half of the body is greenish-olive above and whitish below.—"*i*" Jerdonii. Alias Kerilia jerdonii. Trunk with black cross bands, broadest on back.—"*j*" Lapemoides. Alias Aturia lapemoides. Black rings round the body; ventral shields blackish; head black above, with yellow band on each side; lower parts of the head greyish. Tail black, with white ring round its base.—"*k*" Lindsayi. Alias Aturia lindsayi; Hydrophis gracilis. Neck very slender; trunk greenish olive above, yellowish on the side and below; broad blackish bands across the back; those on the neck form complete rings; the middle and posterior extend only to the middle of the side. The whole head and anterior part of the belly are black. Similar to chloris. Shorter neck.- "*l*" Longiceps. Alias Chitulia fasciata. Broad blackish-olive cross bands, rounded and narrower on the sides than on the back; sides and all the lower parts uniform whitish; head uniform greenish olive above, superciliary edged whitish; tail with eleven blackish vertical bars.—"*m*" Major. Alias Hydrophis mentalis; Pelamis shavii. Belly covered with scales; back of the trunk with thirty-one large rhombic black spots.—"*n*" Melanosoma. Black rings of the body so broad that the yellowish ground-color only appears in narrow vertical, stripes on the side; head nearly uniform blackish.—"*o*" Ornata. Alias Aturia ornata; Chitulia inornata; Hydrophis lævis, schlegelii; Thalassophis schlegelii. Blackish olive above and whitish below.—"*p*" Robusta. Alias Hydrophis nigrocincta. Narrow, black rings, extending round the belly, sometimes interrupted on the side and dilated on the back; head without markings; throat and belly whitish. Six feet long.—"*q*" Spiralis. Alias Hydrophis melanurus; Hydrus spiralis. Black rings round trunk; series of round black spots alternating with the black rings along the vertebral line; head black above, with horse shoe-shaped yellow mark; lower half of the upper lip, the chin and throat yellowish; belly black along its anterior half; posterior part of the tail black.—"*r*" Stricticollis. Body with blackish rings; head yellow above, with irregular blackish confluent spots; whitish below; tail with eleven blackish vertical bars.—"*s*" Subcincta. Trunk with broad dark cross bands, about as broad as the interspaces, not extending downwards to the middle of the side; a series of small, roundish, blackish spots along the lower part of the sides.—"*t*" Viperina. Alias Disteira præscutata; Hydrophis doliata; Thalassophis viperina. Back with rhombic black spots; head without markings.——*Chittaur* (சிற்றாறு - shittáru, Tam. chittár*). From (above + áru, tam. river). Sanscrit name (chitránadí), meaning beautiful + river. River; Tinnevelly district, Tencaushy and Tinnevelly talooks. With its branches drains an extent of mountains not much less than the basin of the Tamraparny, though sources do not extend so far into heart of mountains. The Chittaur is crossed by many anicuts [courtallam].——*Chittivalsa* (చిట్టివలస - chittivalasa, Tel.). From (above + valasa, tel. colony).—"*a*" Village; Vizagapatam dist., Bimlipatam division; pop. 1,891; lat. 17° 56′; long. 83° 28′; from Bimlipatam N.N.W. 4 miles; from Vizagapatam N. 19 miles; from the sea N. 6½ miles. On river of same name lying on road from Bimlipatam to Vizianagram and Chicacole. Large jute [q.v.] factory belonging to Messrs. Arbuthnot and Co. Sugar [q.v.] formerly manufactured; now only gunnies [q.v.] made. The Chittivalsa river is bridged here. Trig. station in lat. 17° 55′ 55·00″; long. 83° 28′ 37·06″; from Bimlipatam N.N.W. 3 miles; from Chittivalsa S.E. 1¼ miles. From the sea N. 5 miles.—"*b*" River; Vizagapatam dist., Bimlipatam division. Otherwise called Gostany and Bimlipatam river. Rises in lat. 18° 19′ N.; long. 82° 58′ E., at the summit of the Gaulicondah hill, and after a south-easterly course of 58 miles during which it passes Gopaulpully and Jaumy, flows into the sea at Bimlipatam.——*Chittoor* (ചിറ്റൂർ - chittúr, Mal.). From (above + úr, mal. village).—"*a*" Talook, Cochin state; pop. 67,702. An isolated portion of the State surrounded by Malabar and Coimbatore districts. The Aunamala flows for fifteen miles through the talook; known as Auliyaur in Coimbatore, and Cunnaudy in Palghaut. Most of the talook is overrun with forests. Principal places:—Chittoor, Colinjappaura, Moolattara, Nemmaura, Nullapully, Tattamungalam, Vallangy.—"*b*" Town; Cochin state, Chittoor tal.; pop. 10,400; lat. 10° 42′; long. 76° 47′; from Ernacolum N.N.E. 59½ miles; from Cochin N.E. 60 miles; from Trichore E.N.E. 37 miles; from Tripoontora N.N.E. 60 miles; from Madras S.W. 285 miles; from the sea E. 52 miles. Contains one of the Rajah's palaces and many native official establishments.——*Chitty* (చిట్టి - chitti, Tel.). Small.—"*a*" Plant first term often joining two genera as in:—Capparis zeylanica (chittigára), small balanites roxburghii; Pavonia odorata (chittibenda), small hibiscus esculentus. See gloss. paragraphs.—"*b*" A small vessel. Measure of capacity. 4 chitties = 1 sola [alavay, 4b]. Approximate actual value, 1 chitty = 15⅓ cubic inches, or 18 tolahs. Nellore. Compare Sola of Ganjam, Olluck of Madras, Oory of Malabar.——*Chitty paumb* (پانی کا سانپ - páníkásámp, Hind.; చిట్టిపాము - chittipámu, Tel.). Hind. from (páni, hind. water + sámp, hind. snake). Tel. from (chiru, tel. small + pámu, tel. snake). Between a rain snake and freshwater snake. Atretium schistosum, colubridæ [paumb], ophidii colubriformes, ophidia [sarpam], reptilia [sarpy, 17], of naturalists [jantoo].——*Chitwail* (చిట్వేలు - chittivélu, Tel. chitvél*). From (above + prólu, tel. town).—"*a*" Deputy tahsildarry, Cuddapah district. Pay Rs. 70.—"*b*" Village, Deputy tahsildar's station; Cuddapah dist., Poollampett tal.; pop. 3,066; acres 3,919; lat. 14° 10′; long. 79° 22′; from Cuddapah S.E. 40 miles; from Madanapully N.E. 70 miles; from Madras N.W. 98 miles; from Poollampett E.N.E. 8¾ miles; from Sidhout S.E. 32 miles. Head-quarters of the former petty principality of the Matly rajahs. The poligar was one of the chief Hindoo lieutenants of the Vijianugger kings west of the ghauts [q.v.]. He was wealthy, his dominions being situated in the rich Cheyair and Pennair valleys, which now form a portion of Poollampett talook. Munro found the poligar encumbered with debt, and the only mode of realizing the revenue was in dispossessing him. The two brothers, the heads of the family, were allowed 10 per cent. of the net revenue, represented by a pension of Rs. 1,723, which has lately ceased.

CHITTAGONG (چٹگام - chatgám, *Hind.*). From (chatur, san. four + gráma, san. village). District along North-east of Bay of Bengal. Exports large quantity of rice [q.v.]. Chittagong wood is same as Toon, Chickrassy.

CHITTORE (చిత్తూరు - chittúru, *Tel.* chittoor*). From (chiru, tel. small + úru, tel. village).——(1) Talook, North arcot district. Population 200,249. Language Teloogoo. Tahsildar's pay Rs. 175. Area 793 square miles. Centre of district. Bounded north by Chundragherry; east by Carvetnugger and part of Wallajah; south by Goodiyattam; and west by Pulmanair and Poonganore. Length from north to south, about 30 miles, and breadth about 25 miles. Includes polliems of Bungaur, Goodipaud, Naraganty and Toomba. The talook a plain, broken by an infinite number of naked rocky hills, which rise abruptly and are difficult of access, being covered with enormous granite [caroom cull] boulders. The plain of the north, out of which these hills rise, is fairly level; but in the south there is a fall of some 500 feet to the level of the Palaur. The trees are small, though large enough for agricultural implements, and afford an ample supply of firewood. Soil is good, being generally a red clay mixed with sand and fertilized by the vegetable matter and rocky detritus carried down from the hills. These are covered with a scanty scrub jungle, affording abundance of leaf manure, and with coarse grasses upon which many cattle graze. The mineral products are iron [auban], lime [choonam] and building stone, and a soft sort of soap stone called Balapam [q.v.], found near Narsingaroyanipett and formed into cups and kitchen utensils, in Calijaveed, Gungaudharanellore, and Mooccanapully. The iron was once largely utilized and smelted in the villages of Eechinairy, Pootramuddy, Veerishettipully, but the industry has greatly declined. Weaving [nesavoo] is carried on in a few villages. In Græmespett and Santapett, suburbs of Chittore, the fabrics are of a superior quality; but elsewhere only the common cloths are woven. The formation of the country is such as naturally to produce an immense number of jungle streams, which eventually form four principal rivers, called Aragonda, Chittore, Eiraula and Vencatagherry. These generally flow eastwards into the Poyney, which passing southwards forms the boundary between Chittore and Wallajah talooks. All have sandy beds which only contain water during the rainy season, and are at times impassable torrents. The number of dasbandam [q.v.] tanks is very great, and most of them are in bad repair. As the valleys are small no reservoir is of any great size. Places of archæological interest:—Adenapully, Ammavaurpulley, Aragonda, Artala, Baulecooppam, Bommasamoodram, Calavagoonta, Cattamanchy, Cawnipaukam, Chittore, Eiraula, Gerigelapulley, Govindareddipulley, Irvauram, Krishnapooram, Mahadevamungalam, Mahimundalam, Mailpaudy, Mogily, Nargull, Pardaraumy, Paulauntope, Poolicull, Pootalputt, Taulambaid, Vailcore, Vauvilitote, Vencatagherry, Veppancherry, Vullimullay, Yaudamurry. Principal Trig. stations:—Bodimala, Mogily, Moorcambutt. The leading places, &c., in the talook are the following.——*Aragonda* (అరగొండ - aragonda, Tel.). From (ara, tel. half + konda, tel. hill); small hill. Village; pop. 1,959; acres 2,991; lat. 13° 17′; long. 79° 00′; from Chittore W.N.W. 10 miles. In a fertile valley. Formerly depôt for merchandise passing to and from Ceded districts. Trade in grain, jaggery [q.v.], tamarind [q.v.] and cumblies [q.v.]. Also river.——*Bodimala* (బోడిమల - bódimala, Tel.). From (bódi, tel. bare + mala, tel. hill). Trig. station; lat. 13° 12′ 38·90″; long. 79° 06′ 36·08″; from Chittore W.S.W. 2 miles; from Tenabunda W.S.W. 1 mile.——*Bungaur* (బంగారు - bangáru, Tel. bangáru*). Called after a person of that name. Village; acres 160 square miles; lat. 13° 12′; long. 78° 57′; Polliem. Peshcush Rs. 11,647.——*Cattamanchy* (కట్టమంచి - kattamanchi, Tel.). From (katta, tel. tank-bund + manchi, tel. goodness). Village; pop. 1,278; acres 1,923; lat. 13° 14′; long. 79° 09′; from Chittore N.E. 1½ miles. Suburb of Chittore.——*Chittore* (చిత్తూరు - chittúru, Tel.). See below.——*Goodipaud* (గుడిపాడు - gudipádu, Tel.). From (gudi, tel. temple + pádu, tel. village). Zemindarry; pop. 461; square miles 33·18; lat. 13° 06′; long. 79° 09′; from Chittore S.S.E. 9 miles. Peshcush Rs. 2,852.——*Mahimundalam* (మహిమండలము - mahimandalamu, Tel.). From (mahí, san. earth +

mandala, san. globe). Village; pop. 3,110; acres 3,598; lat. 13° 04′; long. 79° 16′; from Chittore S.E. 14 miles. Three miles west of Vullimullay. At the foot of Mahimundala droog. Impregnable upon all sides except east, which is protected by barriers of loose stones, in addition to walls of fort. Old fortifications improved by Mahrattas and Mahomedans.——*Mailpaudy* (மேல்பாடி - mérbádi, Tam.). From (mél, tam. upper + pádi, tam. village). Village; pop. 2,245; acres 2,635; lat. 13° 04′; long. 79° 19′; from Chittore S.E. 17 miles. On E. of talook. Ancient Jeina temple now to Shiva.——*Mogily* (మొగిలి - mogili, Tel.). From (mogulu, tel. cloud). Sanscrit name (méghapuri), means town of clouds. Village pass; pop. 181; lat. 13° 11′; long. 78° 53′; from Chittore W. 18 miles. Sacred place. Formerly settlement of Linga balije [q.v.] or Canarese merchants, who traded between plains and plateau in pepper [q.v.], &c. Expelled by poligars. A subterranean passage leads from hills here to naicknairy ghaut [q.v.]. Trig. station in lat. 13° 09′ 56·32″; long. 78° 52′ 09·30″; height 2,461 feet; from Chittore W.S.W. 19 miles; from Mogily S. 1½ miles.——*Moorcambutt* (మురకంబట్టు - murakambattu, Tel.). From (murukku, tam. indian coral tree, erythrina indica, lamk. + pattu, tam. village). Trig. station; lat. 13° 15′ 39·36″; long. 79° 07′ 40·46″; height 1,786 feet; from Chittore N.N.W. 3¼ miles.——*Naraganty* (నారగంటి - náraganti, Tel. naragunti*). From (nára, san. water + kallu, tel. stone). Zemindarry; square miles 41·66. Peshcush Rs. 6,510.——*Nargull* (నారగల్లు - náragallu, Tel.). From (nára, san. water + kallu, tel. rock); as being near the Poyney. Sanscrit name (náradagiri), means nauradan's hill. Village; pop. 873; lat. 13° 08′; long. 79° 15′; from Chittore S.E. 9½ miles. On R. bank of Poyney. Original seat of Naraganty poligar. Fort is in ruins. Adjacent village of Narsingaroyanipett has taken its place. Hyder ally died in the neighbourhood and a rough masonry platform still marks the spot.——*Peilaudy* (పైలాడి - pailádi, Tel.). From (peyya, tel. cow + vádi, tam. village). Village.——*Pootalputt* (పూతలపట్టు - pútalapattu, Tel.). From (púta, tel. flower + pattu, tel. village). Village; pop. 2,337; acres 3,431; lat. 13° 20′; long. 79° 9′; from Chittore N. 9½ miles. On Cuddapah road, at confluence of Eiraula and Poyney. Temple built by a Chola king. The bones of deceased persons are brought from all parts and deposited here.——*Poyney* (పొయిని - póyini, Tel.). See sep. title.——*Santapett* (సంతపేట - santapéta, Tel.). From (santa, tel. market + péta, tel. suburb). Hind. name (dilerábád), meaning dilair, the brave, proper name + city. Village; pop. 1,688; lat. 13° 14′; long. 79° 08′; from Chittore N.N.E. ½ mile. Suburb of Chittore.——*Toomba* (తుంబ - tumba, Tel.). From (tumbi, tel. bottle gourd plant, lagenaria vulgaris, ser.). Polliem; pop. 354; acres 25,277; lat. 13° 16′; long. 78° 53; from Chittore W. 17 miles. Peshcush Rs. 1,783. Polliem on W. of Chittore, eight villages.——*Vullimullay* (வள்ளிமலை - vallimalai, Tam.). From (valli, tam. consort of skanda + malai, tam. mountain). Village, Hill; pop. 839; acres 602; lat. 13° 05′; long. 79° 19′; from Chittore S.E. 15 miles. 1½ miles N.N.W. of Mailpaudy. Former site of Jeina worship. Shiva temple on hill, founded by a Chola king. Within a large natural cave. The adjoining village, Cotanuttam, was a large Coorumba settlement.——**(2)** Town, Head-quarters of Collector, District judge, Assistant collector, District superintendent of Police, Civil surgeon; North arcot dist., Chittore tal.; pop. 9,965; acres 1,516; lat. 13° 13′; long. 79° 08′; from Arnee N.N.W. 40 miles; from Madras W. 81 miles; from Ranipett N.W. 26 miles; from Tripatty S.W. 37 miles; from Vellore N. 21 miles. On S. bank of Poyney in a valley 80 miles from the sea and within influence of north-east monsoon [q.v.], but sea breeze is not regular. The climate is salubrious. Formerly private estate of Arcot family, and in 1781 occupied by the British troops under Sir Eyre Coote. Military station until 1874. The soil particularly suitable for mango [q.v.] topes. Large quantities exported. Upon the opposite bank of the river is suburb Santapett, and a mile to W. Græmespett. Cattamanchy is suburb on N. On the east is Vailcore, a large city in time of Janamejayan maharajah. The following are the travelling distances by road from Chittore to different places:—

To	Viâ	Miles and Furlongs.	
Anantapore ...	Pulmanair and Cadiry	163	2½
Arnee ...	Vellore	45	4
Bangalore ...	Vencatagherry, the Mogily pass, Pulmanair and Colaur.	110	2
Bellary ...	Colaur, Paul Samoodram and Anantapore.	267	1
Bellary ...	Pulmanair and Cadiry	228	4½
Berhampore ...	Nellore, Ongole, Bezwada, Rajahmundry and Vizianagram.	663	4
Calastry ...	Chundragherry and Tripatty	67	6
Chingleput ...	Ranipett and Wallajahbad	80	4½
Colaur ...	Vencatagherry, the Mogily pass and Pulmanair.	68	4
Cuddalore ...	Vellore and Trinomallee	137	6
Cuddalore ...	Vellore, Arnee, Jinjee and Villoopooram ...	129	2
Cuddalore ...	Ranipett, Wandiwash, Tindivanam and Pondicherry.	125	1½
Cuddapah ...	Daumalcheroo ghaut, Peelair and Royachoty.	101	3
Gooty ...	Royachoty and Tadpatry	191	6
Gooty ...	Pulmanair, Cadiry and Anantapore ...	195	6½

To	Viâ	Miles and Furlongs.	
Madras ...	Ranipett, Shreepermatore and Poonamallee.	100	6½
Masulipatam ...	Tripatty and Nellore	297	2
Nellore ...	Chundragherry, Kircambaudy, Calastry and Wojelly.	125	5
Peelair ...	Daumalcheroo	35	½
Pondicherry ...	Ranipett, Wandiwash and Tindivanam ...	113	2½
Poonamallee ...	Ranipett and Shreepermatore	83	2½
Poongarore ...	The Mogily pass and Pulmanair	44	5½
Pulmanair ...	Vencatagherry and the Mogily pass ...	26	0
Ranipett ...	Shercaud	30	1½
Royachoty ...	Daumalcheroo ghaut and Peelair	60	0
Tripatty ...	Chundragherry	44	8
Vellore ...	Narharipett	22	0
Wallajahbad ...	Arcot	66	4½

CHOB (چوب - chob, *Pers.*). A stick, mace. Chobdar is a mace-bearer. Attendant of Indian nobles, and in former days of Anglo-Indian officials of rank. They are still a part of the state of the Viceroy, Governors, and Judges of High courts; these chobdars carry a staff overlaid with silver.——*Chob cheeny* (چوب چینی - chobchíní, Hind.). Same as China root [china].

CHOCAPAUD (చొక్కపాడు - tsokapádu, *Tel.*). From (tsokkamu, tel. faultless + pádu, tel. village). Mittah, Village; Ganjam dist., Goomsoor maliahs tal.; pop. 7,377; lat. of town of same name 20° 17′; long. 84° 31′; from Chetterpore N.N.W. 72 miles; from Russellcondah N.N.W. 26 miles.

CHODA (چوڑا - choda, *Hind.*). North indian form of chola [q.v.].——*Chodavaram* (చోడవరము - chódavaramu, Tel. chódavaram*). From (above + pura, san. town). Village, Head-quarters of Deputy tahsildar, Viravilly division. District moonsif; Vizagapatam dist., Veeravilly division; pop. 5,474; lat. 17° 50′; long. 82° 59′; from Coraputt S.E. 68 miles; from Madras N.E. 368 miles; from Narsapatam N.E. 23 miles; from Parvatipore S.S.W. 72 miles; from Vizagapatam N.W. 26 miles; from Vizianagram S.W. 37 miles. Temple of Keshava sawmy with six inscriptions dating from A.D. 1391; also another temple of Gowreshwarasawmy of great antiquity.

CHODANA (ചോതന - chótana, *Mal.*). From (shódhana, san. examination). A liquid measure [alavay, 4d]. Approximate actual value, 1 chodana = 370 or 560 cubic inches. Cocoanut-oil measure on coast south of Calicut. See vol. I, 309; II, 516.

CHOGA (چوغہ - choghah, *Hind.*). From turkish. A long sleeved garment like a dressing gown. Generally of soft woollen material [pushm] and embroidered on the back, sleeves, and shoulders [sheelay].

CHOKKAM (ಚೊಕ್ಕ - chokka, *Can.*; சொக்கம் - shokkam, *Tam.*). From (chóksha, san. clean). Pure.——*Chokkalingam* (சொக்கலிங்கம் - shokkalingam, Tam.). From (above + linga, san. emblem of shiva). Epithet of shiva [chokkanautan]. Non-bramin Hindoo 2nd or pers. name. Chokkan and Chokkoo are contractions; feminine Chokky [peyar]. A Chokkalingam, otherwise known as Chokkanautan, was ninth Naick ruler of Madura, 1660 to 1682. Married the famous Mungammaul [q.v.]. Dethroned and imprisoned by his ministers in 1677. Vol. I (121) [charitram].——*Chokkanautan* (சொக்கநாதன் - shokkanáthan, Tam.). From (above + nát'ha, san. lord). Shiva. Especially at the Madura temple. His shacty is Meenautchy.——*Chokkatoo* (ಚೊಕ್ಕಟು - chokkatu, Can.). From (chokkata, can. pure). A breed of buffalo [khoolgah] found in the country bordering Kistna river.

CHOKKYE (చొక్కాయి - tsokkáyi, *Tel.*). Tel. from (tsottsu, tel. to enter + káya, san. body). Coat, especially a short one [sheelay].

CHOKRA (چھوکرا - chhokrá, *Hind.*). A boy, especially one about a household or a regiment.

CHOLAM (சோழம் - shózham, *Tam.*). Name appears also as Shozhagam and Shozhiyam. Means south. Greek terms in which the name occurs are σῶραι νόμαδες—ἀρκάτου βασίλειον σῶρα—ὀρθουρὰ βασίλειον σώρναγος—παραλία σωρητῶν or σωριγῶν—παραλία σωριγγῶν. In Pliny, Sora; in Asoca's inscriptions Chora; in Hwen Thsang Choliya. Nothing can be added to what has been said at vol. I (122) to (125) [charitram].——*Cholagan* (சோழகன் - shózhagan, Tam.). Chola king.——*Cholan* (சோளன் - shólan, Tam.). The Chola king. Prefix in place names, as in Cholapooram, meaning the Chola king's town.——*Cholavaram** (சோழவரம் - shózhavaram, Tam.). From (shózhan, tam. the king + pura, san. city). Village; Chingleput dist., Ponnairy tal.; pop. 2,252; acres 1,479; lat. 13° 14′; long. 80° 14′; from Ponnairy S.S.W. 7 miles; from Sydapett N. 15 miles; from the sea W. 11 miles. On high road from Ponnairy to Madras. Old Shiva temple with inscriptions. Largest tank in talook. Receives water turned from Corteliaur for purpose of feeding Red hills tank, which it supplies by means of a regulating sluice at south end of its bund. The tank irrigates acres 2,838, revenue Rs. 11,154.——*Choliya* (چولیا - choliyá,

Hind.). Amongst the Malays, any native of S. india [kling]. So the Mahomedans in Malabar, who are of Arab descent like Lubbays [q.v.], but chiefly Shiahs [q.v.].

CHOLEE (چولی - cholí, *Hind.*). A bodice which extends low enough to cover the breast. It has tight sleeves, which reach half way or less down from the shoulder to the elbow, and a narrow border of embroidery [casheeda], or silk [puttoo], &c., of a different color sewed on round all its edges. It is put on as a spencer, and the two ends tied together in front. Never longer, as that would approximate too much to the Hindoo manner of having it entirely down to the elbows. Hindoos avoid shorter cholees for a contrary reason [cunchaly, sheelay].

CHOLERA HORN (தாரை - tárai, *Tam.*). Corruption of Collery horn, meaning horn used by Cullar. A long brass horn, often used at funerals and festivals.

CHOLUM (यवनाल - yavanála, *San.*; जवारी - javárí, *Mahr.*; जोळु - jólu, *Conc.*; ذرت - zurat, *Ar.*; جاورس هندی - jávarsi-hindí, *Pers.*; جواری - javárí, *Hind.*; جاری - járí, *Dec.*; ಜೋಳ - jóla, *Can.*; ಜೋಳ - jóla, *Too.*; జొన్న - dzonna, *Tel.*; జొన్న - jonna, *Oor.*; ചോളം - chólam, *Mal.*; சோளம் - shólam, *Tam.*). Title from tamul. San. from (yavana, san. ionians, any foreigner + nála, san. hollow stalk); introduced from africa [mecca cholum]. Ar. means whiteness. Pers. from (jávars, pers. millet + hindí, pers. indian). Hind. from sanscrit. San. also (júrna), meaning injurious, from difficulty in digestion; (raktajúrna), meaning red + great millet. Hind. also (jaundrí); (kurbí), meaning the stalk. Can. also (bilíjóla), meaning white + millet; (kágejóla), meaning crow + millet. Tel. also (telladzonna), meaning white + great millet; (bontadzonna), meaning large + great millet; (giddadzonna), meaning short + great millet; (pattsadzonna), meaning yellow + great millet; (kondadzonna), meaning hill + great millet; (rámuditalambrálu), meaning rama, the hero + rice poured over the head of the bride and the bridegroom during marriage. Mal. also (chavalam). Tam. also (shonnal), from teloogoo; (mappuççólam), meaning indigestion + the millet; (shivappuççólam), meaning red + the plant; (shenjólam), meaning red + the plant; (muttuççólam), meaning the large kind, resembling pearls; (vellaiççólam), meaning white + the plant. The stalk was the reed of St. Mathew, and its spikelets the hyssop of St. John. Title otherwise Dhourra, Great millet, Guinea corn, Indian millet, Jawaury, Jonua, Soft grass. Botanically Sorghum vulgare, pers., graminaceæ [vricsham, 156]. Alias Andropogon sorghum; Holcus bicolor, dona, durra, rubens, sorghum; Sorghum bicolor, nigrum. An annual, cane-like, corn-grass, 8–10 feet; culms erect; panicles contracted, dense, hermaphrodite; calyxes hairy; corolla three-valved, awned; similar to indian corn [mecca cholum], but not so strong in growth, producing a dense head of spikelets, bearing numerous small corn-grains, thrice the size of mustard seed [rayaun]; the heads of some kinds are so heavy that three or four stems have to be tied together near the top for mutual support; the grains enclosed in, but free from the hard shining outer glumes; very hard; little different from maize [mecca cholum] in chemical composition; contain about 9 per cent. of nitrogenous matter and 70 of starch. Cultivated in black loam; cultivation, dry; ground prepared in south in punggoony [mausam] or march or chittray or april, on coromandel in jyeshtam or june and ashaudham or july, on w. coast in maidom or april and yedavam or may; ploughing the ground several times, folding sheep three or four nights and otherwise manuring; seed sown in south at the end of veiyaushy or may or at the beginning of auny or june, on coromandel in caurteecam or november and margashiram or december, on w. coast in maidom or april and yedavam or may; no nursery; crop is dependent on rain; cut after four or five months; brought to threshing floor [calam] and trodden by cattle; grain is separated from chaff by winnowing fans; brought to market at once if wanted; average price eighteen imperial seers for 1 rupee. In places where the arid soil and scorching influences of the sun are uncongenial to the production of other grain, this millet can be most successfully cultivated; the best season is when the rain is light and not too frequent; a year of heavy rain is invariably a bad cholum season; under suitable irrigation several crops may be secured during the year; red gram and green gram [q.v.] are often sown with it. Forms the principal article of food among agricultural classes on tablelands, as rice [paddy] does of those of the lower country; the meal is made into cakes; or the grains are parched and eaten with salt, or made into a paste and mixed with chillies [q.v.], goor [q.v.], &c.; occupying the same place to many natives that oats do in scotland; when crushed makes also a good auxillary food for cattle [maud], horses [ghorah], swine [soor], poultry, and sheep [aud]; dry stalks and leaves are chopped to form the ordinary cattle fodder of the country for some months of the season; also a forage for horses when gram [q.v.] is not obtainable. An intoxicating drink called pachwye [q.v.], is made from this grain in ganjam. Three varieties, black, white and yellow cholum. There is a Teloogoo proverb:—తెల్లపూలు పండులుపండితే, తెల్ల జొన్నలుపండును, బలుసపండ్లుపండితే పచ్చజొన్నలుపండును—"If fruits "from plants bearing white flowers are plentiful, the white "jonna grows well; if the balsoo or canthium parviflorum "[canray] fruits well, the yellow cholum grows well." There is a Tamul proverb:—சோம்பேறிக்குச் சோளம் வெள்ளாண்மை—"Cholum is the crop for a lazy man." Requires little care. Cf. Soppa.——*Cholum bird* (گلابی مینا - gulábimainá, Hind. and Dec.; పరిగెపిట్ట - parigepitta, Tel.; ചോലപ്പക്ഷി - chólappakshi, Mal.; சூறைக்குருவி - shúraikkuruvi, Tam.). Title from plundering cholum fields. Hind. from (guláb, hind. rose colored + mainá, hind. starling); from color of plumage. Tel. from (parige, tel. ortolan + pitta, tel. bird). Mal. from (chólam, mal. great millet, sorghum vulgare, pers. + pakshi, mal. bird); from feeding on great millet. Tam. from (shúrai, tam. plunder + kuruvi, tam. small bird). Hind. also (tilyer). Tel. also (palisa). Title otherwise Rose-colored starling, Rosy myna. Pastor roseus sturninæ, sturnidæ [myna], conirostres, insessores, aves [pacshy, 26], of naturalists [jantoo]. Alias Turdus suratensis. Whole head with crest, neck and breast fine glossy black with purple reflections; wings and tail black with green gloss; rest of plumage pale salmon or light rose color. Usually makes appearance about November, associating in vast flocks, and committing great devastations on the cholum fields.——*Mecca cholum* (यवनाल - yavanála, San.; मकाना - makáná, Mahr.; जोळु - jólu, Conc.; خندروس - khandarús, Ar.; گندم مکہ - gandumimakkah, Pers.; مکہ جوار - makkahjavár, Hind.; مکہ جاری - makkahjárí, Dec.; جگنگ - jagung, Malay; ಮೆಕ್ಕೆಜೋಳ - mekkejóla, Can.; ಜೋಳ - jóla, Too.; మొక్కజొన్న - mokkadzonna, Tel.; మొక్క - mokka, Oor.; മക്കച്ചോളം - makkaççólam, Mal.; மக்காச்சோளம் - makkáççólam, Tam.). Title from mecca, place in arabia, which means west generally. San. from (yavana, san. ionian; any foreigner + nála, san. reed). Mahr. from (maká, mahr. maize + dáná, mahr. grain). Ar. from greek. Pers. from (gandum, pers. wheat, triticum vulgare, linn. + makkah, ar. mecca). Hind. from (makkah, ar. mecca + javár, hind. sorghum vulgare, pers.). Dec. from (makkah, ar. mecca + járí, hind. sorghum vulgare, pers.). Can. from (mekka, can. a country + jóla, can. great millet, sorghum vulgare, pers.). Tel. from (mokka, tel. stump + dzonna, tel. great millet); from the ear growing on the side of the stalk and not on the top as in other cereals [dhaunyam]; but confusion here with title meaning. Tam. from (makká, tam. mecca + shólam, tam. great millet). Ar. also (khálávan); (zurratulmakkah), meaning mecca cholum; (hintahirúmí), meaning turkey wheat. Pers. also (khoshahimakkí), meaning mecca corn-head. Hind. also (makkahbhuttah), meaning mecca corn-head; (bhutta), meaning corn ear or head; (makai); (barájavár), meaning large cholum. Can. also (hidijóla), meaning handful + great millet; (doddajóla), meaning large + great millet. Tel. also (mosanam); (munukadzonna). Mal. also (pontiççólam), meaning rising cholum. Tam. also (tulukkaççólam), meaning turk + great millet. Title otherwise Guinea wheat, Indian corn, Maize, Makka cholum, Makkye, Turkey wheat. Botanically Zea mays, linn., graminaceæ [vricsham, 156]. Alias Mays americana, vulgaris, zea; Zea alba, altissima, americana, minor, praecox, vulgaris. A large species of great millet, or cane-like grass, 4–5 feet high; erect, simple; culm tapering, smooth; leaves broad, flat, membranaceous, sheaths slightly compressed; ligula short, membranaceous; silky-ciliated, two-keeled; male raceme terminal, peduncled, simple or generally furnished below with single or many spreading branches; spikelets twin, one short, one longer pedicelled; female spikes axillary, solitary, sessile; sheaths four to five, spathiform; stigmas numerous, exserted; spikelets numerous, sessile, in many rows, rows approximated by pairs; male spikelets oblong, two-flowered, each flower with two paleæ, male sessile; glumes two, externally pubescent, upper one shorter; paleæ two, nearly equal; stamens three; filaments subulate; anthers linear, four-sulcate, two-celled, two-lobed; ovary oblique, sessile, roundish-ovate, externally convex, smooth, glabrous. Bears a dense head of closely packed grains, enclosed in a sheath called the cob; the grains are rounded, crustaceous at the surface, smooth, naked, shining, of gilded, white, or purplish shades; inodorous, insipid; flour slightly yellowish. Native of south america; not much cultivated in southern india, except as a garden crop. The green cobs are gathered and cooked like peas [calauyam] or asparagus; plant has also been employed in the manufacture of sugar [q.v.]; when the grain is ripened, it is usually dried before a fire, and ground into a meal called hominy for making porridge; very nutritious and contains 6 to 7 per cent. of a yellowish fat; stalks are cattle fodder. Yields a fibrous material capable of being spun and woven like flax [alsee]. No other species here.——*Sweet cholum* (देवधान्य - dévadhánya, San.; शाळू - shálú, Mahr.; دخن - dukhn, Ar.; دیو دھان - deudhán, Hind.; ولایتی جاری - viláitíjárí, Dec.; ಇಂಪಿಗಿಡ - impigida, Can.; ಅರಿಜೋಳ - arijóla, Too.; తెల్లజొన్న - telladzonna, Tel.; അരിച്ചോളം - ariççólam, Mal.; இறுங்கு - irungu, Tam.). Title from taste. San. from (déva, san. god + dhánya, san. grain); excellent grain, from sweetness. Hind, from sanscrit. Dec. from (viláití, hind. foreign + járí, hind. great millet, sorghum vulgare, pers.). Can. from (impu, can. sweet + gida, can. plant). Tel. from (tella, tel. white + dzonna, tel. great millet). Mal. from (ari, mal. rice + chólam, mal. great millet). Tam. from (irugu, tam. to grow luxuriantly). Hind. also (sádádeudhán), meaning ordinary broom corn. Title otherwise American broom corn, Chinese sugar-cane, Coffee corn,

God's grain, Imphee cane, Kaffir corn, Sorgho, Sugar millet, Sweet reed, Taam of egypt. Botanically Sorghum saccharatum, pers., graminaceæ [vricsham, 156]. Alias Andropogon saccharatum, saccharatus; Holcus dochna, saccharatus. Annual millet; erect; panicles verticillate, rays nodding; calyx hairy; spikelets sessile, entirely or interruptedly villous, shining, at length glabrate; pedicels scarcely equalling their own floret. Stalks thick and full of a sugary medulla. It can be cut down two or three times a year, and will sprout again. As a forage plant unsurpassed; it makes a fifth to a fourth of its bulk in good syrup; affords a sugar [q.v.] and a liquor like cider.——*Wild cholum* (गनेरे - ganéré, Conc.; ಕಾಡುಜೋಳ - kádujóla, Can.; ನಾತಪೂ - nátapú, Too.; അരിപ്പൂ - arippú, Mal.). Title from appearance of seeds. Can. from (kádu, can. wild + jóla, can. sorghum vulgare, pers.). Too. from means fragrant flower. Mal. from (ari, mal. small + pú, mal. flower). Can. also (nátahú), meaning fragrant flower. Mal. also (konnimmullu), meaning concany thorn, as being foreign and the stems hairy. Title otherwise Lantana, Wild sage. Botanically Lantana indica, roxb., verbenaceæ [vricsham, 102]. Alias Lantana alba, dubia. Shrubby, erect, straight; branches twiggy, four-sided, strigose and hairy; leaves opposite, short petioled, elliptic or rounded-ovate or subcordate, acuminate at the ends, coarsely serrate-crenate, much wrinkled, scabrous above, hoary and villous beneath; peduncles axillary, spreading, thickend upwards; heads of flowers hemispherical, light-purple; throat yellow, scentless; fruit dark-violet, of the size of a pea; most parts of the country; flowering all the year; there are several varieties with white, orange, and pale violet flowers. Used for hedges.

CHOMA (ಚೋಮ - chóma, *Can.*). From (sóma, san. moon); being born on monday. Pariah proper name [peyar, soman].

CHONAUCHALAN (शोणाचल - shonáchala, San.). From (shóna, san. red + achala, san. mountain). Trinomalee in S. arcot. There is a Tamul proverb:—சும்மா கிடைக்குமா சோணாசலன் பாதம் ?—"Can one approach the feet of Cho-"nauchalan without effort?"

CHONTEE (چونٹی - chontí, *Hind.*). From (chúdá, san. hair tuft on the head). False hair braided together, having a large golden knob or cup above and several smaller ones below. This is plaited with the natural hair of the head. Silk [puttoo] and cotton [q.v.] thread are also used to tie the hair [zewar]. This is one of the marriage [shandy] presents of bridegroom to bride.

CHOOCRA (ಚುಕ್ರ - chukra, *Can.*). From (shukra, san. venus); born on friday. Pariah proper name [peyar, shoocran].

CHOODAY (चूडा - chúdá, *San.*). From (chud, san. to conceal). Same as Coodoomy.——*Choodaumany* (चूडामणि - chúdámani, San.). From (above + mani, san. jewel). Poetical lexicon on plan of Sanscrit Amara cosham [q.v.] by Mundala poorooshan, Jeina ascetic, lived in time of Rajah krishnaroya of Vijianugger, in beginning of sixteenth century. A vocabulary consisting of 989 stanzas, in 12 chapters. One of the three classical Tamul dictionaries [nigantoo], the other two being Divaucaram [q.v.] and Pingalanday. The subjects are as follows:—names of gods, names of men, beasts, plants, places, synonyms, artificial objects, abstract nouns, verbal nouns, words relating to sound, &c., explanations of words, explanation of numbers like the sixty-four sciences, &c. There are numerous editions. A superior edition, with a number of additional stanzas by Vedagiry moodelliar, has been printed at Jaffna.

CHOOGAL (چگل - chugal, *Hind.*). Acbar's thirty rupee gold coin.

CHOOK (چک - chuk, *Hind.*; కోయలు - koyalu, *Tel.*; ഉമരി - umari, *Mal.*; உமரி - umari, *Tam.*). Tam. from (uvar, tam. saltishness); common on salt grounds and from taste; cf. indian saltwort. Tel. also (barillakóyalu), from yielding barilla; (koyyapippali), meaning stick + long pepper, piper longum, linn. Tam. also (káttumari), meaning forest + the plant; (shittumari), meaning small + the plant; (pavazhappúndu), meaning coral plant, from appearance. Title otherwise Coral plant [small wild aumanac], Crab-grass, English sea-grape, Frog-grass, Glosswort, Grasswort, Marsh samphire, Saltwort. Botanically Salicornia brachiata, roxb., salsolaceæ [vricsham, 108]. Perennial; stems erect; branches numerous, decussate; joints clubbed; spikes cylindrical; flowers greenish, conspicuous, three-fold, opposite; flowering in cold season; grows plentifully on low wet ground, overflowed by spring tides. One of the numerous sources of the alkali [q.v.] sujjeekhaur [q.v.], or barilla, or saltwort soda [munn cauram]; used in medicine, in pharm., non-officinal. During famine plant eaten as greens. Ashes used as mordant [cauram]. Other common species are:—arabica, herbacea.

CHOOL (ചൂൽ - chúl, *Mal.*). Broom stick; term of abuse.

CHOOLLY (ചുള്ളി - chulli, *Mal.*). From (shul, tam. small). Any thorny plant. Plant second term, as in:—Acanthus illicifolius (payinnáchulli), green thorn; Barleria buxifolia (karinculli), black thorn; Hygrophila spinosa (vayalchulli), field thorn. See gloss. paragraphs.

CHOOMTEE (पिपीलिका - pipílika, *San.*; نمل - naml, *Ar.*; مور - mor, *Pers.*; چیونٹی - chiúntí, *Hind.*; چمٹی - chumtí, *Dec.*; سامت - sámut, *Malay*; ಇರುವೆ - irive, *Can.*; ಪಿಜಿನು - pijinu, *Too.*; చీమ - chíma, *Tel.*; ഉറുമ്പ - irumpu, *Mal.*; පිපීලිකා - pipílaka, *Singh.*; எறும்பு - erumbu, *Tam.*). Title from hindostany. San. from (pid, san. to pinch), a reduplicated form. Ar. from (namala, ar. to bite). Hind. and dec. from (kíta, san. insect). Can. from (iri, can. to pierce). Mal. from (úru, mal. to crawl). Tam. from (eri, tam. to pierce). Terms synonymous with the family formicidæ, hymenoptera, holometabola, insecta [poochy], of naturalists [jantoo]. Ants. Distinguished by the wingless state of the abortive females, length of basal joint of antennæ in females and neuters and by the first and second joints of the abdomen being knotted. Neuters smaller than males. Males smaller than females. Females and neuters furnished with stings in many species. In his third book Herodotus makes the statement that there are in India ants as large as foxes [lomree], which keep golden treasures in their holes. The legend, whatever is it may mean, does not pertain here. There is a Tamul proverb:—எறும்பின் கண் அதன் அளவுக்குப்பெரிது, ஆனையின் கண் அதன் அளவுக்குச்சிறிது—"The eyes of an "ant are large for its size, the eyes of an elephant are small for "its size." There is another:—எறும்பு ஊரக் கல்குழியும்—"By the continual creeping of ants a stone will become hollow." The following are the principal kinds distinguished. Observe that the white-ant [q.v.] is not an ant.——*Black ant* (کالی چیونٹی - kálíchiúntí, Hind.; کالی چمٹی - kálichumtí, Dec.; ಕಟ್ಟಿರುವೆ - kattirive, Can.; కట్టెచీమ - kattechíma, Tel.; കട്ടിറുമ്പ - kattirumpu, Mal.; கட்டெறும்பு - katterumbu, Tam.). Hind. from (kálí, hind. black + chiúntí, hind. ant). Tel. from (katte, tel. stick + chíma, tel. ant), from the hard body. Mal. from (katta, mal. stout + irumpu, mal. ant). Tam. from (kattai, tam. stick + erumbu, tam. ant). Formica compressa, formicidæ, hymenoptera, holometabola, insecta [poochy], of naturalists. Found everywhere except on the western coast. Lives in numerous societies in the ground. Food chiefly sugar [q.v.].——*Jumping ant* (پرکی چمٹی - parkíchumtí, Dec.; ರೆಕ್ಕೆಇರುವೆ - rekkeirive, Can.; ರೆಂಕೆದಪಿಜಿನ್ - renkedapijin, Too.; రెక్కచీమ - rekkachíma, Tel.; പുളിയിറുമ്പ - puliyirumpu, Mal.; இறகெறும்பு - iragerumbu, Tam.). Dec. from (par, hind. wing + chumtí, dec. ant). Can. from (rekke, can. wing + irive, can. ant). Mal. from (puli, mal. tamarindus indica, linn. + irumpu, mal. ant). Tam. from (iragu, tam. wing + erumbu, tam. ant). Drepanognathus saltator, formicidæ, hymenoptera, holometabola, insecta [poochy], of naturalists. Alias Harpegnathus saltator. Found in Malabar. Makes surprising jumps when disturbed. Bites severely. Nest underground. Feeds on insects.——*Red ant* (لال چیونٹی - lálchiúntí, Hind.; لال چمٹی - lálchumtí, Dec.; ಕೆಂಪಿರುವೆ - kempirive, Can.; ಕೆಂಪಿಜಿನ್ - képijin, Too.; కొరవిచీమ - koravichíma, Tel.; ചോനൻ - chónan, Mal.; දිමියා - dimiyá, Singh.; முசிறு - musiru, Tam.). Title from color. Hind. from (lál, hind. red + chiúntí, hind. ant). Can. from (kempu, can. red + irive, can. ant). Tel. from (koravi, tel. fire brand + chíma, tel. ant); from burning on biting. Mal. means red one. Formica smaragdina, formicidæ, hymenoptera, holometabola, insecta [poochy], of naturalists. Female pale, shining green. Found in Malabar, but rare in the Carnatic [q.v.]. Forms a nest of living leaves, which it draws together without detaching from the branch, and unites with a fine white web; bites severely; lives chiefly on vegetable secretions. Forms a temporary web round the flowers or fruit of the Eugenia malaccensis [malaca jaumoon], Artabotrys odoratissimus [madmaunty], &c., for the purpose of feeding undisturbed.——*Small red ant* (چھوٹی لال چمٹی - chhotílálchumtí, Dec.; ಚಿಕ್ಕಿರುವೆ - chikkirive, Can.; ಮರ್ಲಪಿಜಿನ್ - marlapijin, Too.; ఎర్రచీమ - errachíma, Tel.; പാമ്പിറുമ്പ - pámbirumpu, Mal.; சிற்றெறும்பு - shitterumbu, Tam.). Dec. from (chhotí, hind. small + lál, hind. red + chumtí, dec. ant). Can. from (chikka, can. small + irive, can. ant). Too. from (marla, too. to madden + pijin, too. ant). Tel. from (erra, tel. red + chíma, tel. ant). Mal. from (pámbu, mal. snake + irumpu, mal. ant). Tam. from (shiru, tam. small + erumbu, tam. ant). Formica timida, formicidæ, hymenoptera, holometabola, insecta [poochy], of naturalists. All the body covered with long scattered hairs. Found on Malabar coast; lives chiefly on vegetable secretions. Has nest underground.

CHOONAM (चूर्ण - chúrna, *San.*; चुन्ना - chunná, *Mahr.*; كلس - kils, *Ar.*; آهک - áhak, *Pers.*; چونہ - chúnah, *Hind.*; چنہ - chunnah, *Dec.*; کاپور - kapur, *Malay*; ಸುಣ್ಣ - sunna, *Can.*; ಸುಣ್ಣ - sunna, *Too.*; సున్నము - sunnamu, *Tel.*; നൂറ - núru, *Mal.*; හුනු - hunu, *Singh.*; சுண்ணாம்பு - shunnámbu, *Tam.*). Title from sanscrit through hindostany. San. from (chúrn, san. to powder). Pers. from (áh, pers. vapour). Mal. from (nurunnu, mal. to be pulverized). Lime, whether slaked or unslaked, but the former is generally meant. Calx of chemists. Slaked lime or quicklime is limestone mixed with wood, coal [nilakary], or charcoal [adoopp kary], and exposed to a strong heat; the carbonic acid is expelled, and a substance results white, of a pale gray tint, opaque, inodorous, and its taste acrid and alkaline; when water is poured upon this it heats, crackles, swells, and a bulky white powder is obtained. Choonam is prepared in the interior from a gravelly sort of limestone dug out of quarries, and then called cull choonam; and along the coast from shells washed out of salt-water marshes, and then called kilinjal choonam; the following is the mode of preparing the former; the pebbles or gravel stones are first beat with wooden pestles to separate the aluminous clay which adheres to them; after they are thus cleaned, they are sorted, as of a white or brown quality; in some places the stone is burnt, by simply laying alternate layers of stone and charcoal on the ground, in the proportion of two parts of charcoal to one of stone, and thus allowed to burn out; the stone, after being burnt, is slaked by laying small quantities in heaps and throwing water on them, and as soon as the heat begins, the whole is mixed up together and stirred about till it is reduced to a dry powder; the lime is now considered fit for the use of the builder. Kilinjal choonam is manufactured much in the same way, excepting that it is again cleansed by the manufacturer in a dry state, by strewing it down against the wind, as corn is winnowed to separate the chaff; the burning also is differently performed; the charcoal is mixed up with the shells, and burnt in large open kilns [collvye], with a grated bottom and longitudinal flue, communicating with four or more lateral openings. Cull choonam forms a coarse sandy powder, and kilinjal choonam a very fine impalpable one. From these two substances all the mortar for building throughout Southern india is prepared. They are mixed with clean sharp river sand in various proportions, according to the use for which they are intended. For brick-work one part and a half to three of sand [manal] is mixed, with one or two of the fine slaked lime; for the coarse undercoat plastering from one to two of sand with two of lime; and for the last and fine upper coating two to three of sand with as many of lime. When the mortar [cauray] is prepared for the brick-work in rough plastering it is beat up with pure water in long stone troughs, with wooden pestles about a yard and a half long and shod with iron hoops. The following is a Hindostany proverb:—کوٹو تو چونا نہیں خاک سے دونا—"Well-beaten it is "plaster; unbeaten it is worse than dust." Choonam intended for fine plastering and ornamental works is ground by women on an oblong granite [caroom cull] stone and a cylindrical upper stone about four inches in diameter; the mixture is sometimes ground two, three and four times, to bring it to the required fineness and purity. In all the operations of choonam work jaggery [q.v.] water, that is to say, a solution of molasses or coarse sugar [q.v.], is invariably added by the builders; intimate union of the coarse particles of the lime with the sharp sand is effected by the saccharine acid in the molasses. Lime water [choonam tunny] is a useful antacid. Lime liniment is composed of equal parts of lime water and a bland oil. Lime is used internally in enlargements of spleen; externally as a caustic. Pharm. preparations of quicklime are:—Calcis hydras, properties caustic and escharotic, internally administered a corrosive poison, masticatory [charvanam]; liquor calcis, antacid, alterative, astringent; liquor calcis saccharatus; linimentum calcis. Calx chlorata is the well known deodoriser. Calcis phosphas is alterative, antacid. The finest choonam from oyster shells [chippy choonam] is chewed with betel-leaf [betel]. There is a Tamul proverb:—சுண்ணாம்பில் இருக்கிற சுருட்சம்—"The essence of paun [q.v.] is in the choonam." Slaked choonam in conjunction with butter milk [paul] is sometimes used in preparing a stringy mixture, employed by painters to give adhesion to colors [rangh].——(1) *Choonam cauray* (ಸುಣ್ಣದಗಾರೆ - sunnadagáre, Can.; சுண்ணாம்புக்காரை - shunnámbukkárai, Tam.). Tam. from (above + kárai, tam. mortar). Flooring with plaster alone, not with brick [shengal] or stone [cull].——*Choonam cull* (चूर्णखण्ड - chúrnakhanda, San.; چونے کا پتھر - chúnekáphattar, Hind.; ಸುಣ್ಣದಕಲ್ಲು - sunnadakallu, Can.; సున్నపురాయి - sunnapuráyi, Tel.; കുമ്മായക്കൽ - kummáyakkal, Mal.; சுண்ணாம்புக்கல் - shunnámbukkal, Tam.). San. from (chúrna, san. choonam + khanda, san. fragment). Hind. from (chúná, hind. choonam + patthar, hind. stone). Tel. from (sunnamu, tel. lime + ráyi, tel. stone). Mal. from (kummáyam, mal. lime + kal, mal. stone). San. also (karkara), meaning nodular stone. Tam. also (shukkángal), meaning fragment stone; very common. Limestone. Indurated carbonate of lime. See vol. II, 39. Lime is an oxide of metal calcium. It is known as quicklime before being slaked with water; the expression quicklime is in allusion to its corrosive property. It is literally calcic oxide or carbonate of lime deprived of its carbonic acid. On being slaked it is converted into calcic hydrate, which on being mixed with sand [manal] forms mortar or cement [cauray]. The quality or richness of a limestone is generally perceptible to the eye, but when this is not the case it may be detected by the violence of the effervescence produced on the application of sulphuric or muriatic acid [gandhac ka tezaub, namak ka tezaub], or by heating a fragment before the blow-pipe so as to convert it into quicklime. Chalk [sheemay choonam] is a soft amorphous carbonate of lime, which can be converted into quicklime by calcination and used for all the purposes of ordinary limestone; it is composed of forty-four parts of carbonic acid and fifty-six parts of lime; pure chalk dissolves readily in dilute muriatic acid, and gives no precipitate with the addition of ammonia water. Marble [shalavay cull] is limestone capable of receiving a polish. The two uni-colored conditions are white marble and black marble; but streaked and parti-colored marbles are frequent. The coloring is derived from accidental minerals, or from metallic oxides producing the coloring and veining, and from the presence of imbedded shells [chippy], corals [moongah], and other organisms.——*Choonam tunny* (चूर्णजल - chúrnajala, San.; چونے کا پانی - chúnekápání, Hind.; ಸುಣ್ಣದನೀರು - sunnadaníru, Can.; సున్నపునీళ్లు - sunnapuníllu, Tel.; சுண்ணாம்புத்தண்ணீர் - shunnámbuttannír, Tam.). Employed in bleaching and washing linen, in paper-making, in certain dyeing [shauyam] processes, and also in dressing leather [chamrah]. Veidyans prepare it as Europeans do; adding to ½ lb. of quicklime 12 pints of boiling soft water; they prescribe it mixed with gingelly [q.v.] oil of sesamum seeds, and sugar [q.v.], in obstinate cases of gonorrhœa.——(2) *Chippy choonam* (சிப்பிச்சுண்ணாம்பு - shippiççunnámbu, Tam.). Lime made from oyster [auly] shells.——*Chunk choonam* (சங்குச்சுண்ணாம்பு - shanguççunnámbu, Tam.). From conch shells.——*Cull choonam* (கற்சுண்ணாம்பு - karchunnámbu, Tam.). From common limestone.——*Kilinjal choonam* (கிளிஞ்சிற்சுண்ணாம்பு - kiliñjirchunnámbu, Tam.). From sea-shells.——*Moottoo choonam* (முத்துச்சுண்ணாம்பு - muttuççunnámbu, Tam.). Lime of pearls [moty], said to be luxury of kings with their betel [q.v.] leaf.——*Nuttay choonam* (நத்தைச்சுண்ணாம்பு - nattaiççunnámbu, Tam.). From snail [nuttay] shells.——*Sheemay choonam* (पाण्डुमृत् - pándumrit, San.; विलायतीचुण्णा - viláyatíchunná, Mahr.; طین ابیض - tíniabyaz, Ar.; گل سفید - gilisufed, Pers.; کھری مٹی - kharímattí, Hind.; ولایتی چنہ - viláitíchunnah, Dec.; کپور نگرس - kapuringgris, Malay; ಶೀಮೆಸುಣ್ಣ - shímesunna, Can.; ಶೀಮೆಸುಣ್ಣ - shímesunna, Too.; సీమసున్నము - símasunnamu, Tel.; ശീമനൂറു - shímanúru, Mal.; රටහුනු - ratahunu, Singh.; சீமைச்சுண்ணாம்பு - shímaiççunnámbu, Tam.). San. from (pándu, san. white + mrit, san. clay). Mahr. from (viláyatí, mahr. foreign + chunná, mahr. lime-stone). Ar. from (tín, ar. earth + abyaz, ar. white). Pers. from (gil, pers. earth + sufed, pers. white). Hind. from (kharí, hind. chalk + mattí, hind. earth). Dec. from (viláití, hind. european + chunnah, hind. choonam). Malay from (kapur, malay, lime + inggris, malay, english). Can. from (shíme, can. europe + sunna, can. lime). Too. from (shíme, too. england + sunna, can. chalk). Tel. from (síma, tel. foreign + sunnamu, tel. lime). Mal. from (shíma, mal. europe + núru, mal. lime). Singh. from (rata, singh. foreign + hunu, singh. choonam). Tam. from (shímai, tam. foreign + shunnámbu, tam. lime). San. also (dvípasudhá), meaning island lime. Hind. also (kharí). Chalk. Otherwise carbonate of lime. Carbonas calcis, Creta of chemists. A soft limestone. Contains much carbonic acid. Imported, native chalk being too hard for use. Opaque, of a white-gray color. Geological chalk formations occur at Ootatoor near Trichinopoly; and these extend towards Vriddhauchellam, Cuddalore and Pondicherry, where the chalk occurs tinged of various colors, of red, purple, grey and black. Red chalk is plentiful in Travancore; black chalk occurs near Vullam in Tanjore. Creta præparata or prepared chalk is medicinally antacid, astringent and absorbent; finely-powdered chalk, sprinkled over ulcers, excoriations, &c., acts by absorbing discharges. Used in polishing metals [loham], and glass [cunnaudy], and in painting [rangh] and whitewashing.

CHOONDY (చుండి - tsundi, *Tel.* chundi *). From (tsundu, tel. dung-fly). Zemindarry, Village; Nellore district, Cundoocore talook; pop. 3,670; lat. of village 15° 10′; long. 79° 44′; from Cundoocore W.S.W. 14 miles; from Nellore N.N.W. 53 miles; from the sea W. 25½ miles. Peshcush Rs. 21,219. The zemindarry is separated from Canigherry talook by a range of hills running north and south for about 15 miles of considerable elevation and the slopes covered with dense jungle. Consists of forty-four villages and forty-four hamlets in Cundoocore talook; extent 124¾ miles. Sunnud [q.v.] confirmed in 1842. Ruined fort west of the village. North of the tank on a hill is a ruined temple built by the ancestors of the present zemindar. Old fort near Pauta choondy, built by Reddy chiefs. Some other old temples built by same. Festival of Janardanasawmy in March. Festival of Ramalingasawmy in February. Large tank. Betel [q.v.] gardens. A fine garden founded by present zemindar. Trig. station in lat. 15° 11′ 05·93″; long. 79° 43′ 58·76″; height 834 feet; from Cundoocore W.S.W. 14 miles; from Timmareddipollem N.N.W. 6 miles; from the sea W. 26 miles.

CHOONGAM (ചുങ്കം - chunkam, *Mal.*). From (shulka, san. duty). Duty, tax. Choonga chauvady is toll-gate or custom-house [chowky].

CHOONTAL (ചൂണ്ടൽ - chúntal, *Mal.*). From (chúntu, mal. to fish). Fish-hook.——*Choonta palm* (ചൂണ്ടപ്പന - chúntappana, Mal.). From (above + pana, mal. palm), from use made of the branches. Same as Bastard sago palm.

CHOOP (چپ - chup, *Hind.*). Be silent!

CHOOPATTY (چپاتی - chapátí, *Hind.*). A thin flat unleavened cake of bread generally of coarse wheaten meal, baked upon a griddle or slightly baked or toasted over an open fire. The usual form of native bread [hopper, rotee].

CHOOPRASSY (چپراسی - chaprásí, *Hind.*). From (chap, pers. left + rást, ar. right). A servant wearing a chapraus [q.v.] or badge. Bengal term. In Madras, Peon from Portuguese.

CHOORNAM (चूर्ण - chúrna, *San.*; சுண்ணம் - shunnam, *Tam.*). From (chúrn, san. to powder). Carbonate. A salt, formed by the union of carbonic acid with base as the carbonate of lime, of copper, &c. For different carbonates see several heads under Cauram.

CHOORWEY (چُروے - churwe, *Hind.*). Paddy [q.v.] well soaked in water, and dried in the sun; then toasted in an earthen pot till one or two grains begin to burst, after which pounded in a wooden mortar and winnowed.

CHOOVANNA (ചുവന്ന - chuvanna, *Mal.*). Red. Compare in plants:—Aloe indica (chuvannakattázha), red aloe; Ficus infectoria (chuvannál), red banyan. See gloss. paragraphs.

CHORA (चोर - chóra, *San.*). Pali for Chola [cholam].

CHORNAULY (ചുരണാലി - churanáli, *Mal.*). From (svarna, san. gold + áryan, mal. the paddy so called). Gold colored paddy [q.v.]. Cautt chornauly means jungle variety; Cheriya chornauly means small; Mala chornauly means hill; Valiya chornauly means large; Veloottа chornauly means white.

CHORY (چوری - chorí, *Hind.*). From (chur, san. to steal). Theft. Chorimaul is stolen property. Chorinam is land enjoyed free of rent unauthorizedly.——*Choram* (चोर - chóra, San.). Means theft, corresponding to english bastard or false [cullan]. Plant first term often joining two genera, as in:—Adansonia digitata (chóramli), false tamarindus; Atalantia monophylla (chornimbuve), false citrus. See gloss. paragraphs.

CHOTA (چھوٹا - chhotá, *Hind.*). Small [cher, chinna, chiry, chit, coor, shir]. Plant first term often joining two genera, as in, where transl. is of second term:—Aloe littoralis (chhotárákaspattá), agave americana; Alpinia officinarum (chhotákulanjan), galangal; Canavalia ensiformis (chhotísem), dolichos lablab; Enicostema littorale (chhotácharáitah), swertia chirata; Trichodesma indicum (chhotákhurfá), portulaca oleracea; Xanthium strumarium (chhotágokhrú), tribulus terrestris. See gloss. paragraphs.——*Chota hazree* (چھوٹا حاضری - chhotaházirí, Hind.). From (above + házirí, ar. attendance). Small breakfast; refreshment taken by Europeans in the early morning before or after the morning exercise.——*Chotee* (چھوٹی - chhotí, Hind.). Little, feminine. In composition makes a lacab; as Chotee begum, little lady [ism].——*Chotey* (چھوٹے - chhote, Hind.). Little, masculine. In composition makes a lacab; as Chotey sahib, little lord [ism].

CHOTY (చోటు - tsótu, *Tel.*). Place; suffix in place names as Royachoty, meaning the king's place.

CHOULTRY (چاؤری - cháurí, *Hind.*). Anglo-indian form of Chauvady [q.v.].

CHOVOOR (ചൊവ്വൂർ - chóvúr, *Mal.*). From (shiva, san. the deity + úr, mal. village). Sanscrit name (shukapura), meaning bird + village. Ancient village, Malabar district, Ponnany talook, 6 miles E. of Ponnany. Close to modern Yedappaul. One of the sixty-four graumams of Keralam [keraloputty]. This was the second or seceding colony of Namboory bramins, adopting Sheivite religion. Cf. Punniyore in Chiracal talook.

CHOW (چو - chau, *Hind.*). Four [char, chatoor, naul].——*Chowanny* (چوانی - chauanní, Hind.). Four-anna piece.——*Chowdry* (چودهری - chaudhrí, Hind.; చౌదరి - chaudari, Tel.). Means holder of four. The headman of a trade [inam]. Title of a class of Mahomedans.——*Chowgaun* (چوگان - chaugán, Hind.). From persian. Four corners, viz., the meidaun; so Polo or horse-golf.——*Chowk* (چوک - chauk, Hind.). From (chatushka, san. quadrangle). A square, market.——*Chowkam* (చౌకము - tsaukamu, Tel.; சவுக்கம் - shavukkam, Tam.). From (chatushka, san. consisting of four). A square. The box containing the lingam [q.v.] of lingayets.——*Chowkidar* (چوکیدار - chaukídár, Hind.). From (above + dár, pers. keeper). A watchman.——*Chowky* (چوکی - chaukí, Hind.). Station of police or of customs, originally placed where four ways meet [chauvady].——*Chowlam* (ಚೌಲ - chaula, Can.; చవలము - tsavalamu, Tel.).—"*a*" Money. 2 doogoolams = 1 chowlam; 4 chowlams = 1 mauda [naunyam, 2b]. Approximate actual value, 1 chowlam = ½ rupee. Nellore and Kistna. ⅛th of a kurruck pagoda. No coin current. Same as Hind. neem tunkah.—"*b*" Goldsmith's weight. 2 doogoolam = 1 chowlam; 4 chowlams = 1 mauda [niray, 3b]. Approximate actual value, 1 chowlam = 6¾ grains. ⅛th of a pagoda weight. Compare Can. bana, Tel. chinnam, Mal. and Tam. pana tookkam. See vol. I, 609.——*Chowrausy* (چوراسی - chaurásí, Hind.). From (chatur, san. four + ashíti, san. eighty). Eighty-four. Multiple of number of months [mausam] by number of days in week [vauram]; multiple of signs of zodiac [raushy] by number of planets [graham]; multiple of terrestrial years making up Jupiter's year [brihaspaty] by the days of a quarter lunation [chaundra mausam] by which the moon passes through seven nacshatrams [q.v.]. Enters into the whole scheme of the Hindoo, Booddhist, and Jeina religions, cosmogonies, rituals, and legendary tales. There are eighty-four forests, eighty-four bazaars, eighty-four places of pilgrimage, eighty-four gooroos of the sect of Ramaunoojan. An ankle ring or an elephant's howdah [q.v.] is called Chowrausy from that number of bells upon it. The Shwetaumbarans have eighty-four siddhauntams [q.v.]. There are eighty-four points of difference between the Digambarans and Shwetaumbarans, regarded as of importance. Asoca raised 84,000 columns throughout India. In the opinion of Booddhists the life of man reached at one period 84,000 years. Compare the number 360, the days comprised in the year, adopted by most eastern nations; founded on the natural lunar year before the exact period of a lunation [chaundra mausam] was fully understood. The 360 parts into which the circle was divided by the Hindoos, as well as the Greeks, are evidently dependent on the number of the days of the early year. 360 is 6 times 60 or the years of the Jovian cycle [brihaspaty chuckram]. The respirations of a healthy man are said by the Jogies to be 360 in the course of a ghurry [q.v.]. Rama's auxiliaries, in his attack on Lunka, were 360,000 monkeys. Compare again 1,008 or 12 × 84. Shiva has, like Krishnan, 1,008 names.——*Chowsar* (چوسر - chausar, Hind.). From (above + sár, hind. dice). Otherwise Takhta i nard, meaning chess board. Cloth chess played with dice four or six-sided, and thrown by the hand and not from boxes, and full lengthways [chatrangam, pacheesy].——*Chowsingha* (रोहिष - róhisha, San.; भेकर - bhékara, Mahr.; چوسنگا - chausinghá, Hind.; جنگلی بکرا - janglíbakrá, Dec.; ಕೊಂಡಕುರಿ - kondakuri, Can.; కొండగొర్రె - kondagorre, Tel.; କୁତ୍ର - kutra, Oor.; വരിമാൻ - varimán, Mal., மலையாடு - malaiyádu, *Tam.*). Title from hindostany. San. from (róhita, san. red). Hind. from (chau, hind. four + singh, hind. horn). Dec. from (janglí, hind. wild + bakrá, hind. sheep). Can. from (konda, tel. hill + kuri, can. sheep). Tel. from (konda, tel. hill + gorre, tel. sheep). Mal. from (vari, mal. stripe + mán, mal. deer). Tam. from (malai, tam. mountain + ádu, tam. sheep). Tel. also (adavigorre), meaning forest + sheep. Title otherwise Four-horned antelope. Tetraceros quadricornis, antelopinæ, bovidæ, ruminantia, mammalia [sastanam, 23], of naturalists [jantoo]. Color a uniform brownish bay above, beneath lighter, and whitish inside the limbs and in the middle of the belly; forelegs dark, also the muzzle and edge of the ears, which are white within, with long hairs; fetlocks dark within, with more or less distinct whitish rings. Length from 40 to 42 inches; height at shoulder 2 feet to 26 inches; at the croup a little higher. Anterior horns up to 1½ inches; posterior horns 4 to 5. The anterior horns [sing] in the South of India generally have rarely more than a knob or corneous tip, which often falls off, leaving a black callous skin. Abounds in the hills of the Eastern ghauts [q.v.] from near Madras northwards.——*Chowt* (چوتھ - chauth, Hind.; சவுத்து - shavuttu, Tam.). From (chaut'ha, mahr. from chaturt'hi, san. fourth). One-fourth part. The tribute; equal ¼th, of actual Government collections, formerly levied by the Mahrattas from provincial governors as compensation for leaving their districts unplundered. See vol. I, 112.——*Chowtah* (چوتھا - chauthá, Hind.). A canvas covered palankeen used in the army.——*Chowty* (چوتھی - chauthí, Hind.). Same as Chatoorty. A Mahomedan ceremony observed fourth day after marriage when the wedding bracelets are untied from the wrists of the bride and bridegroom [shaudy].

CHOW (చవు - tsavu, *Tel.*). From (chava, mahr. taste); examination or test. A weight equal to 5⅔ grains, by which pearls [moty] are valued.

CHOWGHAUT (ചാവക്കാട് - chávakkátu, *Mal.* chávakád *). From (chávu, mal. death + kátu, mal. forest).—"*a*" Deputy tahsildarry, Malabar district. Pay Rs. 70.—"*b*" Town, Deputy tahsildar's and Munsif's station, Port; Malabar district, Ponnany talook; pop. 6,077; lat. 10° 35′; long. 76° 05′; from Bombay S.S.E. 605 miles; from Calicut S.S.E. 48 miles; from Cannanore S.S.E. 98 miles; from Chetwye N. 3½ miles; from Madras S.W. 334 miles; from Malapooram S. 32 miles; from Manantoddy S. 82 miles; from Palghaut W.S.W. 42 miles; from Ponnany S.S.E. 16 miles; from Tellicherry S.S.E. 87 miles; from Trichore W.N.W. 12 miles; from Velliangode S.S.E. 12 miles. Half way between Cochin and Calicut at north end of backwater, with small ports of Attacooy and Coorcooy subordinate to it. The port is not at Chowghaut itself, which is inland but at Chetwye. Head-quarters of Chowghaut talook till 1860, when latter was amalgamated with Cootnaud and Bettatnaud into present Ponnany talook. Inhabitants chiefly Christians and Moplahs. Trade in salt-fish and cocoanuts [q.v.].

CHOWK (چوک - chauk, *Hind.*). Whip [coradah].——*Chowk maram* (सर्पूहल - sarpúhala, Mahr.; चब्किरूकु - chabkirúku, Conc.; جنگلی سرو - janglísaro, Hind. and Dec.; اراو - aráu, Malay; ಕೇಸರಿಕೆಮರ - késarikemara, Can.; ಚಬುಕುಮರ - chabukumara, Too.; చవుకుమాను - tsavukumánu, Tel.; ചവുക്ക - chavókku, Mal.;

കസാഗഹ - kasagaha, Singh.; சவுக்கு - shavukku, Tam.). Title from tamul. Hind. from (janglí, hind. wild + saro, pers. cypress, cupressus sempervirens, linn.). Can. from (késha, san. hair + mara, can. tree). Tel. from (tsavuku, tel. whip + mánu, tel. tree). Singh. from (kasa, singh. whip + gaha, singh. tree). Tam. from persian, meaning whip; from slender cord-like branches. Hind. also (janglíjháú), meaning wild tamarisk. Mal. also (chólamaram), meaning shade tree; (káttáti), meaning wind + shaking. Tam. also (shivamaram), meaning red tree; from reddish wood.—"*a*" Terms for the whole genus casuarina, casuarinaceæ [vricsham, 127]. Leafless trees, with slender cord-like, generally pendulous branches, which are striated with sheathing joints, having much resemblance to the genus equisetum or horse-tails; flowers inconspicuous; male flowers in spikes or catkins; female flowers in compact heads, becoming a woody cone about an inch in length, with many cells, each containing a small winged nut-fruit.—"*b*" Terms apply particularly to Casuarina equisetifolia, forst. Alias Casuarina litoralis, litorea, muricata. Title otherwise Australian fir, Australian swamp oak, Beef wood, Casuarina, Casuarina pine, Forest oak, He-oak, Horse-tail casuarina, Iron-wood tree [cassa, dark vail, deccany deodar, foreign ilanjy, nauga champak, yellow condray], Shade tree, She-oak, Swamp oak, Tinian pine, Whip tree, Wild cypress, Wild tamarisk, Wind-whirl. Tree, 60 feet high; trunk straight, as in firs and pines; bark smooth, brown; branches scattered; leaves verticelled, slightly furrowed, jointed, joints ending in a cup, in which the next joint sits; stipules annular; male aments cylindric, terminating the leaves; scales six to eight in a verticel, united at the base, pointed and woolly; flowers, as many as divisions in the verticel; corolla two opposite, boat-shaped, ciliate scales; filaments single; anthers two-lobed; female flowers on a different tree; aments oval, short, peduncled; scales six to eight in a verticel, with a single flower between each; corolla none; germs oblong; style dividing into two long, recurved, garnet-colored portions; stigmas simple; strobiles oval, size of a nutmeg, armed with the sharp points of the two-valved capsule; seeds small, with a large, wedge-shaped, membranaceous wing; flowering in hot season. Indigenous on the coast of chittagong and the burmese provinces and southward as far as queensland; introduced here beginning of century; has a considerable superficial resemblance to a larch or other finally-feathered conifer, making an acceptable variety in the plains, where real pines will not grow; it flourishes in a low sandy soil and is always the first that springs up from land relinquished by the sea. Grows freely, ripening its seed in great abundance; it grows in ten years to the height of about 30 feet, generally very straight, and where the main shoot is broken or lopped off, throws out secondary shoots readily which are usually erect; it requires to have water at the roots, at least 10 feet from the surface of the ground. Cut down to 6 feet, and kept clipt, forms a dense bush hardly to be recognised. Bark slightly astringent, employed in infusion as tonic; quoted in pharm. but non-officinal. Favorite avenue [shaulay] tree, especially in narrow roads, and if kept stunted as above-mentioned forms good hedge; largely planted for fuel [lukdy]; great changes have been made along the east coast by planting dry tracts of drifting sand with it; bark gives brown dye [shauyam] called extract of casuarina; stem gives a resin [raul]. Wood of equisetifolia is very hard, reddish in color, and in density and appearance somewhat resembles trincomalee [trincomalee tree]; is well adapted for posts, and bears submersion in water; much grown for firewood, but is well adapted for rafters and building purposes; the timber, according to weight, is without exception the strongest wood known for bearing cross strains.—"*c*" The species stricta, quadrivalvis, paludosa and leptoclada have also been introduced on the neilgherries from australia.

CHOWLAH (چولا - chaulá, *Hind.*). Same as Cow gram.

CHOWRY (चामर - chámara, *San.*; چونری - chaunrí, *Hind.*; சவரி - shavari, *Tam.*). From (chamara, san. yak). A fly-waver. Next in dignity to the umbrella. May be made either of strips of sandal-wood, or of ivory [dant]; but the most esteemed are those made of the tail of the Himalayan yak set in a handle, whence title [chamaram, maryauday].

CHUCKLER (சக்கிலி - shakkili, obl.; சக்கிலியன் - shakkiliyan, pers. sing.; சக்கிலியர் - shakkiliyar, pers. pl., *Tam.*). Caste-title. The corresponding terms are:—Hind. chamaur; Can. and Tel. maudiga; Mal. tolcollan. Occupation is leather working, in which they had a monopoly until the Mahomedans and Lubbays disturbed it. Whether they or the pariahs are the lowest is subject of dispute. Chucklers will not take food or water from pariahs, nor latter from former. Chucklers, like pariahs, are outside the Hindoo caste system. They are not allowed to enter the portico of a pagoda [q.v.]. Chucklers dwell outside the village walls, are as above said tanners, workers in raw hides and in leather [chamrah], shoe and harness makers; also messengers, scavengers, and executioners. They make the leather bags for drawing water and any other leather article for villagers of their own village gratis. They are never horse-keepers. Very few read or write. The race as a rule are of a dark black hue, short in stature, and of very slender frame; lower limbs particularly slight, and calf and foot delicate. They still eat creatures that most races regard as unclean. In villages, where they perform the lowest menial offices, they are paid by portions of the crops and some small privileges. Though low in caste, their women are held to be of the Pudminy [q.v.] kind, that is to say of peculiar beauty of face and form, and very virtuous. In Madura the men are left-hand and the women right-hand [jauty, yidangay].

CHUCKRAM (चक्र - chakra, *San.*). From (kram, san. to move). A wheel or circle. The sharp quoit or discus, an ancient Hindoo missile weapon, whirled from forefinger; so especially the miraculous weapon of either Vishnoo or Shiva. An ancient silver coin once generally current in the s. of India, being the same to the gold pagoda that the anna is since to the silver rupee. It had under it again the copper cash [q.v.], which was its sixteenth. There was once a Tanjore silver chuckram, 22½ to 1 star pagoda [q.v.]. A very small silver chuckram still remains in Travancore. This is in size the split half of a pea. It weighs grains 5$\frac{7}{10}$, and 28½ go to 1 rupee. The present Travancore circulation consists of this coin in whole and half pieces; and the copper cash in four forms, single, double, quadruple and octuple or eight cash. The last is equal to the half silver chuckram. Chuckrams being small and globose, are exceedingly difficult to count or handle; they are measured or counted by means of a chuckram board, a small square wooden plate with a given number of holes, the exact size and depth of a chuckram; a small handful of coins is thrown on the board, which is then shaken gently from side to side, so as to cause a single chuckram to fall into each cavity, and the surplus if any is swept off with the hand. See vol. I, 609; II, 292. Chuckram means a cycle of years. Also a wheel used to drain water from fields on the west coast. Also Hindoo 2nd or pers. name; common to both sexes [peyar].—(1) *Chuckerbutty* (ചക്രവർത്തി - chakravatti, Mal.). Bengal form of Chuckravurty [peyar].—*Chuckrabala* (चक्रबल - chakrabala, San.). From (above + bala, san. power). Multiplication of the square. The principle on which algebraic problems of the form $ax^2 + b = y^2$ are solved.—*Chuckrapauny* (சக்கரப்பாணி - shakkarappáni, Tam.). From (above + páni, san. hand). Epithet of Vishnoo, the discus-handed deity. Hindoo 2nd or pers. name [peyar].—*Chuckraunkam* (चक्राङ्क - chakránka, San.). From (above + anka, san. figure caused by branding). Mark of the discus of Vishnoo, stamped with a hot iron on the persons of his worshippers [matam].—*Chuckrauvaul* (چکراول - chakrával, Hind.). From (above + ávali, san. row). Ring-bone in horses [ashwarogam].—*Chuckravurty* (चक्रवर्त्ती - chakravartí, San.). From (above + vartí, san. turning). He whose chariot wheels roll; a king. Veishnava second name. In Bengal Chuckerbutty [peyar]. Title assumed by many small rajahs.—*Chuckroon* (ചക്രം - chukram, Mal.). Anjengo coin, 27 to 1 rupee.—*Chuckry* (چکری - chakrí, Hind.). Mangalore coin, 16 to 1 pagoda [q.v.].—(2) *Brihaspaty chuckram* (बृहस्पतिचक्र - brihaspatichakra, San.). The jovian cycle of sixty years [brihaspaty].—*Cauly chuckram* (காளிச்சக்கரம் - kálіççakkaram, Tam.). A gold coin having a figure of the goddess, formerly current in the south.—*Nacshatra chuckram* (नक्षत्रचक्र - nakshatrachakra, San.). From (nakshatra, san. star + above). The sphere of the fixed stars [bhamundalam].—*Prauk chuckram* (प्राक्चक्र - prákchakra, San.). From (prák, san. prior + above). An epicycle on which the degrees of precessional variation [ayanaumsham] are counted.—*Raushy chuckram* (राशिचक्र - ráshichakra, San.). From (ráshi, san. sign of the zodiac + above). The zodiac [raushy].—*Shooly chuckram* (சுழிச்சக்கரம் - shuzhiççakkaram, Tam.). From (shuzhi, tam. a circle + above). Madura coin, 276 to 100 star pagodas.—*Veerabhadra chuckram* (ವೀರಭದ್ರಚಕ್ರ - vírabhadrachakra, Can.). From (vírabhadra, can. the son of shiva, especially worshipped in the mahratta country + above). Hindoo gold coin struck by the princes of Bednore [ikkairy].

CHUDDER (چادر - chádar, *Pers.* and *Hind.*; چدر - chaddar, *Dec.*). A large piece of cloth or sheet, of one and a half or two breadths, thrown over the head, so as to cover the whole body. Men sleep rolled up in it [sheelay]. Term is applied to the cloths spread over Mahomedan tombs. Also to woollen shawls [q.v.] manufactured at Rampore in the Punjaub.

CHULLAH (چهلا - chhallá, *Hind.*). Toe ring made of gold or silver, very thin [zewar].

CHUNDA (ചന്ത - chanta, *Mal.*). From (sam, san. together + dhá, san. to hold). Association. Market [santa, shandy].—*Chundavila* (ചന്തവില - chantavila, Mal.). From (above + vila, mal. price). Market price.

CHUNDAH (چندا - chandá, *Hind.*). Moon-like [chand, chundran]. In composition forms a lacab; as Chundah miyaun, moon-like lord [ism].—*Chundah sahib* (چنداصاحب - chandá-sáhib, Hind.). Son-in-law of Dost ally [q.v.], the second of the Carnatic [q.v.] nawaubs of the first hereditary line. Rival of Wallajah [q.v.] for the Arcot throne. Put an end to the Naick government of Madura by seizing on Trichinopoly and Madura. Subsequently defeated by the Mahrattas and confined at Sattaura for eight years, when he was released by Dupleix, who espousing his cause marched to Trichinopoly against Mahomed ally. Defeated there, Chundah sahib surrendered himself to a Tanjore general, by whom he was assassinated. See vol. 1 (177) and 44 [charitram].

CHUNDAN (चण्ड - chanda, San.). From (chanda, san. wrathful). Yaman, the god of death. Also Shiva. Also an asooran killed by cauly; hence Chundy is parvaty [chamoondy]. ——*Chundaula* (चण्डाल - chandála, San.; چنڈال - chandál, Hind.). As supposed to be savage and cruel. Sanscrit term for outcaste, especially one sprung from union of Shoodra man and Bramin woman [janty].

CHUNDRAGHERRY (చంద్రగిరి - chandragiri,* *Tel.*). From (chandra, san. moon + giri, san. mountain); from tradition that the moon worshipped shiva here.——**(1)** Talook, North arcot district. Tahsildar's pay Rs. 150. Area 548 square miles. Average length 35 miles, average breadth 16 miles. Population 100,194. Language Teloogoo. N. of district adjoining Cuddapah frontier. Bounded north by talooks of Pollampett and Voilpaud of that district, west by Poonganore zemindarry, south by Chittore talook and Carvetnugger zemindarry, and east by portions of that estate and of Calastry. Chundragherrycottam was a division of Toudaimundalam. Includes the polliems of Cullore and Poolicherla. Constituted in 1849, out of the two old talooks of Pennamurry and Tripatty. In the amalgamation the Toombapollem and some neighbouring Government villages were transferred from Pennamurry to Chittore. Hilly and picturesque. The Eastern ghauts [q.v.] run through the north and the Carvetnuggur hills occupy most of the south. The Tirmullay range, upon which the sacred temple of Tripatty stands, are the most considerable hills. This range, upwards of 2,000 feet high, forms portion of the Eastern ghaut line, and is about 100 square miles in extent. The chief valleys are those of Daumalcheroo, Maumandore, Naugapootla, and Tripatty. The forests are the most extensive and valuable in the district. The best are along the eastern slopes of the Tripatty hills, being the southern continuation of the Baulapully jungles of Cuddapah. Soil [munn] chiefly consists of black and red clays mixed with sand, of which the red soil is considered the more fertile. Limestone [choonam cull] is found and iron sand [manal] is gathered and smelted. The two principal rivers are the Daumalcheroo and Swarnamookhy. The latter is the more important and is held in reverence by the people. Remarkable tank at Rungampett. Contains two divisions, Chundragherry and Tripatty, in charge respectively of a Tahsildar and Deputy tahsildar; the latter being subordinate to the Tahsildar in revenue but not in magisterial matters. Places of archæological interest:—Auttore, Chennayyagoonta, Chettipulley, Chigoorvauda, Chundragherry, Comaurpulley, Daumalcheroo, Dauminaid, Dharmarajapooram khandriga, Kircambaudy, Moondlapoody, Mullauvaram, Mungalam, Mungaupooram, Nullappa reddigauripulley, Peroor, Pillapollem, Raghavapooram, Tirchanore, Tripatty lower, Tripatty upper. Principal trig. stations:—Peddadroog, Tellaraullapett. The leading places, &c., in the talook are the following.——*Bheemanuddy* (భీమనది - bhímanadi, Tel.). From (bhíma, san. one of the five pándavas + nadí, san. river). River. Rises near Mungalapenta in Poolicherla polliem, and unites with the Swarnamookhy near Narsingapooram. Some white decomposed shale near spring of the river is regarded as ashes resulting from sacrifice by Bheeman. ——*Calyaunanuddy* (కళ్యాణనది - kalyánanadi, Tel.). From (kalyána, san. prosperity + nadí, san. river). River. Affluent of the Swarnamookhy. Comes down the Shanmala valley, north of Chundragherry, and is rarely quite dry.——*Chiratanore* (చిరతానూరు - chiratánúru, Tel.). From (chirata, tel. panther + úru, tel. village). Sanscrit name (shríshukapurí), means holy city of shoocabramha, the sage. Tamul name (alamélumangáppuram), means town of lutchmy, the woman on the flower; also (tiruççánúr), meaning same as sanscrit. Village, Place of pilgrimage; pop. 1,786; acres 1,966; lat. 13° 37′; long. 79° 30′; from Chittore N.E. 37 miles; from Chundragherry E. 9 miles. Pond called Pudmasaras with floating festival in April-May. Annual Brambotsavam [pundigay, 6a] also in October-November. Under management of Mahant [q.v.] of Tripatty. The goddess said to be wife of Shree vencatesha sawmy, deity of Upper tripatty. Pilgrims now invariably visit the goddess after they perform their vows at Upper tripatty. Thread marriages and marriages avowed to be performed at Upper tripatty are now performed in the temple of the goddess.——*Chundragherry* (చంద్రగిరి - chandragiri, Tel.). See below.——*Cullore* (కల్లూరు - kallúru, Tel.). See sep. title.——*Daumalcheroo* (దామల్‌చెరువు - dámalcheruvu, Tel.). See sep. title.——*Gauzoolamundem* (గాజులమండెం - gádzulamandem, Tel.). From (gádzu, tel. glass bracelet + mandem, tel. factory). Village; pop. 2,387; acres 4,492; lat. 13° 36′; long. 79° 33′; from Chittore N.E. 39 miles; from Chundragherry E. 13¼ miles. Manufacture of glass beads.——*Kircambaudy* (கரக்கம்பாடி - karakkambádi, Tam.). From (karukkan, tam. the name of the founder of the village + pádi, tam. village). Village; pop. 2,147; acres 20,004; lat. 13° 40′; long. 79° 33′; height 275 feet; from Chittore N.E. 42 miles; from Chundragherry E.N.E. 15 miles. Poligar of this place fell in 1759 and village was sacked and burnt by English.——*Krishnapoorampolliem* (కృష్ణాపురంపాళెము - krishnápurampálemu, Tel.). From (krishnápura, san. city of krishna + pálemu, tel. fortified village). Zemindarry; pop. 1,433; square miles 15·68 or 10,032 acres; lat. 13° 41′; long. 79° 36′; from Chittore N.E. 45 miles; from Chundragherry E.N.E. 17 miles. Polliem resumed about 1848. ——*Maumandore* (మామండూరు - mámandúru, Tel.; மாமண்டூர் - mámandúr, Tam. mámandúr*) From (má, san. lakshmí, the goddess + vindu, tam. vishnu + úr, tam. village). Village; pop. 658; acres 5,462; lat. 13° 45′; long. 79° 30′; height 569 feet; from Chittore N.N.E. 44 miles; from Chundragherry N.E. 14¾ miles. Industry in stones for rubbing sandal-wood into powder out of a sandstone [manal cull] called Gandhapoosaunarye, quarried by Woddar near Tripatty and Maumandore. Every pilgrim carries away one of these stones.——*Pedda droog* (పెదదుర్గము - pedadurgamu, Tel.). From (pedda, tel. large + durga, san. fort). Trig. station; lat. 13° 33′ 03·90″; long. 79° 23′ 37·08″.——*Permaulpully* (పెరుమాళ్ళపల్లె - perumállapalle, Tel.). From (perumál, tam. vishnu, the great god + palle, tel. village). Village; pop. 2,105; lat. 13° 31′; long. 79° 05′; from Chittore N.N.W. 20 miles; from Chundragherry W.S.W. 20 miles. Copper [taumram] images made.——*Poodiputla* (పుదిపట్ల - pudipatla, Tel.). From (puthu, tam. new + patla, tel. place). Village; pop. 2,040; acres 5,348; lat. 13° 36′; long. 79° 25′; from Chittore N.E. 33 miles; from Chundragherry E.N.E. 3¼ miles.——*Poolicherla* (పులిచెర్ల - pulicherla,* Tel.). From (puli, tel. tiger + cherla, tel. village). Village, Polliem; pop. 2,473; acres 36,005; lat. 13° 35′; long. 79° 05′; from Chittore N. 26 miles; from Chundragherry W. 18 miles. Peshcush Rs. 5,585. *Poyney* (పోయిని - póyini, Tel.). See sep. title.——*Renigoonta* (రేణిగుంట - rénigunta, Tel.). See sep. title.——*Swarnamookhy* (స్వర్ణముఖి - svarnamukhi, Tel.). See sep. title.——*Tellaraullapett* (తెల్లరాళ్లపేట - tellarállapéta, Tel.). From (tella, tel. white + ráyi, tel. stone + péta, tel. suburb). Trig. station; lat. 13° 43′ 25·90″; long. 79° 20′ 54·08″; height 3,739 feet; from Chundragherry N. 10 miles; from Tirmaley N.W. 4 miles.——*Tirmaley* (திருமலை - tirumalai, Tam.). See sep. title.——*Toomboor cona* (తుంబురుకోన - tumburukóna, Tel.). From (tumburu, san. diospyros embryopteris, pers. + kóna, tel. ravine). Sanscrit name (tumburutírt'ha), meaning toombooroo, the sage so called + place of sacred waters. Valley, Waterfall; from Tripatty N. 5 miles. Rishies lived here. There is a cave having communication with Tripatty temple. Now infested with wild beasts [aroovy].——*Tripatty* (తిరుపతి - tirupati, Tel.). See sep. title.——*Vencatachellam* (வெங்கடாசலம் - vengadásalam, Tel.). See sep. title.——**(2)** Town, Tahsidar's station; North arcot dist., Chundragherry tal.; pop. 4,790; acres 8,060; lat. 13° 35′; long. 79° 22′; from Arnee N. 63 miles; from Chittore N.N.E. 29 miles; from Madras W.N.W. 74 miles; from Ranipett N. 45 miles; from Tripatty W. 7 miles; from Vellore N.N.E. 48 miles. On right bank of Swarnamookhy, east of hills on which stands the fort. The old town has disappeared. Many deserted temples, old tanks, and fine carved mantapams. Fort was originally built in A.D. 1000 by a Yaudava rajah, Immady narsimhan. Ten rajahs of that dynasty reigned till the Vijianugger dynasty, of whom Krishna deva roya reduced the place. In A.D. 1592, Vencatapaty of the Vijianugger dynasty retired here from Penoocondah, which had been the Vijianugger capital since 1564. In A.D. 1639 Shreerungaroyer of Vijianugger signed in the palace the treaty by which the site of the Presidency town was made over to the English [madras]. The fort fell in 1646 into the power of the Golcondah chief, from whom it was wrested a century later by the Nawaub of Arcot. In 1758, it was held by nawaub Abd ool wahaub khan, who assumed the protection of the sacred town of Tripatty. In 1782, it was captured by Hyder ally and remained subject to Mysore until the treaty of Seringapatam in 1792. The hill fort must have been impregnable by storm. The style is similar to that of Vellore fort. A lower fort encloses two mahauls. Two miles south is a ruined temple called Jangamvaurygoody below the Addacondah hill.——**(3)** Village, Hill, River; South canara district, Cassergode talook; pop. 1,410; lat. 12° 28′; long. 75° 03′; from Cassergode S.S.E. 2¼ miles; from Mangalore S.S.E. 29 miles; from the sea E. 1½ miles. Large ruined square fort on a hill, south of river of same name. Built by Shivappa naick, first ruler of the Ikkairy line [payashwany].

CHUNDRAM (ചന്ത്രം - chantram, *Mal.*). Treasury.——*Chundracaur* (ചന്ത്രക്കാരൻ - chantrakkáran, Mal.). From (above + káran, mal. doer). Inferior officer under Praverticauran [q.v.].

CHUNDRAN (चन्द्र - chandra, *San.*). From (chand, san. to shine). The moon [chand, chundah]. He is generally a male, riding on a car drawn by an antelope [jinka]; he presides over Somavauram, Monday [vauram]. Is also occasionally represented as female. According to one version, when the moon is in opposition to the sun, it is the god Chundran; but when in conjunction with it, the goddess Chundry. The moon was worshipped as male and female, by the Egyptians. Cf. Latin lunus and luna [matam]. Used as Hindoo 2nd or pers. name in composition. Chundranautan is the moon-lord. Chundrashekharan is Shiva, the moon-crowned. Chunder sen is moon-like chief. Ramchendran is moon-like Rama [peyar]. Plant first term, from white color or flowering at moon rise, as in:—Elettaria cardamomum (chandrabálá), daughter of the moon; Ipomæa bonanox, var. grandiflora (chandrakánti), fond of the moon; Mirabilis jalapa (chandramalle), moon jasmine; Solanum ferox (chandrapushpá), moon flower. See gloss. paragraphs. Chundra maunam [q.v.] is the system of calculating the years, months, &c. Chundra punchaungam is the lunar calendar. Chundra samvatsaram is the lunar year. The Hindoo astrologers say:—if a person be born under the planet Soman, he will have many friends, will possess elephants, horses, and palankeens, be honorable and powerful, will live upon excellent food, and will rest on superb couches [jyotisham].——*Chaundram* (चान्द्र - chándra, San.). Lunar.——*Chundrachoodan* (चन्द्रचूड - chandrachúda, San.). From (above + chúda, san. head). Moon-crested. Shiva.——*Chundragooptan* (चन्द्रगुप्त - chandragupta, San.). From (above + gupta, san. protected). Greek σανδρακόττος. The discovery of the identity gave the first date to early Indian history. Diodorus distorts the name into Xandrames, and Curtius into Agrammes. King of Magadha and founder of the Mowrya dynasty, 325 B.C. to 188 B.C. Drove the Greeks out of India. Formed an alliance with Seleucus, whose daughter he married and received a Greek ambassador named Megasthenes at his court, whose writings comprise nearly all that is known of ancient India. Died 301 B.C. [charitram].——*Chundramowleeshwaran* (चन्द्रमौलीश्वर - chandramaulíshvara, San.). From (above + mauli, san. head + íshvara, san. ruler). Shiva at Tripatty.——*Chundra shekharan* (चन्द्रशेखर - chandrashékhara, San.). From (above + shikhara, san. head). Shiva. There was a Paundy king of Madura of this name about 1558. Driven out by rajah of Tanjore who was in turn conquered by a Vijianugger general; latter seized the country and threw off his master's allegiance; his own son Viswanautha naick defeated him and founded the Naick dynasty of Madura. Vol. I (124), (154) [charitram].——*Chundravamsham* (चन्द्रवंश - chandravamsha, San.). From (above + vamsha, san. lineage). The race of the moon. The name of an Aryan [q.v.] tribe supposed to have entered India about the twelfth century B.C., and to have superseded the more peaceable solar race [soorya vamsham] which had entered seven or eight hundred years before. The lunar race ruled in Benares, Magadham, and near the modern Delhi; it had two chief branches, one called Yadoo, in which Krishnan was born, and the other Pooroo, to which the Pandavas, the heroes of the Mahabhaurat [q.v.], belonged. Yadoo has eight branches, of which the Jhareja and Bhatty in Cutch and Jessulmeer are the most powerful. See vol. I (115) [charitram].——*Chundricay* (चन्द्रिका - chandriká, San.). Moon-light. Plant name common to:—Lepidium sativum; Rauwolfia serpentina. See gloss. paragraphs.

CHUNDRAS (چندرس - chandras, *Hind.*). Corruption of pers. (sandrús). Same as Sandrach [dammer].

CHUNGAUTAM (ചങ്ങാതം - channátam, *Mal.*). From (sanghâta, san. union). Companionship. Money paid for convoy. This name was given originally to certain responsible guides in the Nayar country who escorted travellers from one inhabited place to another, guaranteeing their security with their own lives, like the Bhatts of Goozerat. So when a person wished to place himself under the special protection of a man of consequence, as a Deshavauly, Naudvauly, or Rajah he paid from 4 to 64 fanams annually for Chungautam, making sometimes an assignment on particular lands for the payment. The patron sometimes furnished a peon for ordinary times. There were four classes of officers about the rajah, whose posts were not hereditary but within his gift; viz., Moonnaulipaud, attendants with a daily allowance of three nauzhies [q.v.] of paddy [q.v.], youthful attendants; Aurnaulipaud [q.v.], attendants with double the above allowance; Pundaurapaud, treasury officials; and the present Chungautipaud. The temples often subjected themselves to Chungautam money to rajahs to ensure the benefit of their power.——*Chungauticoory* (ചങ്ങാതിക്കുറി - channátikkuri, Mal.). From (above + kuri, mal. lottery). Mutual benefit society on west coast. Might always be composed indiscriminately of Nayars, Teeyar, Moplahs, &c. Is at the present day merely a loan club.

CHUNK (शङ्ख - shankha, *San.*; سنکھ - sankh, *Hind.*). From (sham, san. to soothe); from sound when held to ear. Title otherwise Conch shell. Turbinella rapa of naturalists [chippy]. A large convolute shell, five inches long by three broad, regarded with religious veneration. Large quantities are obtained from the muddy bottom of the sea off the south coast, like the pearl oyster [sadaf], by means of divers. The fishery is a monopoly, the property of Government. Unlike the pearl oyster the chunk is always found, and the fishing has been regularly leased out by Government to the highest bidder. The fishery is chiefly worked at Keelakaray in the Ramnaud territory, and Tuticorin in the Tinnevelly district. The chunks lie at the bottom in from 2 to 5 fathoms of water. The divers carry a bag round their necks, and dive and grope over the bottom; 20 chunks are a good haul for one plunge. The fishing season is from October to March. The chunks are sawn into narrow rings or bracelets, armlets, beads, and are worn as ornaments [nagay] for the arms, legs, fingers, &c., by Hindoo women. Many of them are also buried with the bodies of opulent and distinguished persons. Those which, from being taken with the living mollusc [chippy], are called green chunks, are most in demand. The white chunk, which is the dead shell thrown upon the beach by strong tides, having lost its gloss and consistency, is not much considered. The value of the green chunk depends upon its size. The Jangam [q.v.] religious mendicants and those of the Veeramootty sect, blow them as horns, a hole being bored through the base. When blown they give a loud, sharp, and piercing sound. They are also used in Hindoo worship to call the attention of the gods to their worshippers. In ancient times, the Indian warriors had the chunk for their sole trumpet. Krishnan's chunk was called Paunchajanyam, and Vishnoo's Darendram. The pictures and figures of Vishnoo always represent him with a chunk shell in one hand and a discus or Chuckram [q.v.] in the other. A chunk shell is the national emblem of Travancore. It was also one of the insignia of royalty of the Chalookya dynasty when ruling at Calyaun in the upper Carnatic [q.v.]. Chunks used to be sent to Bengal where they were cut into cowries for coin [naunyam]. They are also used as lamps in temples [coil]. The conch shell, used for pouring water on the gods, is a smaller one, the Mazza rapa of naturalists. There is a Tamul proverb:—சங்கிலே வார்த்தால் தீர்த்தம், சட்டியிலே வார்த்தால் தண்ணீர்—"If poured into a conch water becomes sacred, if "into a chatty it is what it is;" meaning that things depend on circumstances. The abnormal Valamboory chunk, with its spiral opening to the right, is of exceptional value, and has been sometimes priced at a lakh of rupees. The Jalanchalam is poetical name for some super-eminent form of chunk, not identified. The following is from the Chintaumany:—கலம்புரியகலல்குற்று யார்தவ்வையர் சிலம்புரிதிருர்தடிபரவச்செல்பவள்வலம் புரிசஙகு சலம்வளைஇயதொத்தனள் குலம்புரித் திணைய தோர்கொடியினீர்மையால்—"She, vijayay, who bore the "slender frame of a tender creeper, who was distinguished by "high birth and noble virtues, whose easy graceful steps while "moving with sounding anklets claimed the homage of all her "elders and matrons from a noble race of modest virtue, was like "the jalanchalam conch amongst the valamboory conches." The following are different kinds of chunk.——*Jalanchalam* (சலஞ்சலம் - shalañjalam, Tam.). A chunk of super-eminent qualities, said to be found surrounded by one thousand ordinary valamboory chunks; see above.——*Mool chunk* (முட்சங்கு - mudchangu, Tam.). From (mul, tam. thorn). With thorn-like points.——*Putty* (பட்டி - patti, Tam.). Short chunk.——*Shool chunk* (சூற்சங்கு - shúrchangu, Tam.). From (shúl, tam. impregnation). Containing pearls [moty].——*Tauzham chunk* (தாழஞ்சங்கு - tázhañjangu, Tam.). From (tázhi, tam. pan). With a wide mouth.——*Valamboory* (வலம்புரி - valamburi Tam.). From (valam, tam. right + puri, tam. spiral). Otherwise Nundyauvarttam or Nundyauvuttam, or shell of happy convolutions. A chunk turning to the right; see above. Both short and long.——*Yidamboory* (இடம்புரி - idamburi, Tam.). From (idam, tam. left + puri, tam. spiral). The ordinary chunk opening to left.

CHUPPER (چھپرا - chhaprá, *Hind.*; ಚಪ್ಪರ - chappara, *Can.*). From (chhad, san. to cover). A temporary thatched structure, as for living in the jungle, for the celebration of a marriage, giving water to travellers, a screen addition to an ordinary building, &c. Thatching materials used are:—naunal [q.v.], palmyra [q.v.] leaves, straw of the common grains, and the spice grass Andropogon schœnanthus [lemon grass]. Cocoanut [q.v.] leaves are made into a kind of coarse matting, called tennam keet [q.v.], used for thatch [cottye, pandaul]. Plant first term from growing over sheds, as in:—Cyamopsis psoralioides (chapparadavare), chupper bean; Lycopersicum esculentum (chapparadabadanegida), chupper brinjaul. See gloss. paragraphs.

CHURRUCK (چرخ - charkh, *Pers.*). From (chakra, san. wheel). Wheel.——*Churruck poojah* (چرخ پوجا - charkhpújá, Hind.). From (pújá, hind. worship). Penitential ceremony formerly observed by the lower orders on the day the sun enters maisham [mausam, raushy], for expiation of sins. They were suspended, by an iron hook passed through the skin of the back, to one end of a lever, which was raised on the top of a high pole and whirled round by means of a rope fixed to the other end. Those who could afford it had it done by deputy [shirry].

CHUTNEY (तेमन - témana, *San.*; چٹنی - chatní, *Hind.*; ಉಪ್ಪಿನಕಾಯಿ - uppinakáyi, *Can.*; ఊరుగాయ - vúrugáya, *Tel.*; ഉപ്പിലിട്ടതു - uppilittatu, *Mal.*; ஊறுகாய் - úrugáy, *Tam.*). San. from (tim, san. to be wet). Tel. from (úru, tel. to soak + káya, tel. unripe fruit). Mal. from (uppu, mal. salt + idu, mal. to put). Tam. from (úru, tam. to soak + káy, tam. unripe fruit). Condiment, half sauce, half pickle [curry]. The better classes amongst the natives, more especially Mahomedans, use these. The following is a list of principal articles under botanical names:—Averrhoa bilimbi, blimbing, fruit; Averrhoa carambola, coromandel gooseberry, fruit; Bambusa arundinacea, common bamboo, stems; Capsicum minimum, bird's eye chilly, fruit; Carissa carandas, carondah, fruit; Citrus aurantium, orange, fruit; Citrus aurantium, var. bergamia, bergamot orange, fruit; Mangifera indica, mango, fruit; Phyllanthus emblica, emblic myrobalan, fruit; Zizyphus jujuba, bair, fruit.

CHUTTRAM (सत्त्र - sattra, *San.*; چھتر - chhattar, *Hind.*; சத்திரம் - shattiram, *Tam.*). From (sattra, san. abode). A house where pilgrims and travelling members of the higher castes are entertained and fed gratuitously for a day or two. Chuttrams much resemble the ancient hostelries of Europe. They are charitable foundations for the lodging and entertainment of a certain number of guests for a specified time; one day, three days, and sometimes longer. Some are founded merely for the relief of Bramins; others, for all classes of the natives; and some in former days even for the accommodation and entertainment of Europeans. Chuttrams are mostly terraced, and built of quarry stones [cull], or brick [shengal] and choonam [q.v.]. The smaller ones are single square rooms, open towards the street, where the roof is supported by large square pillars. In the walls are excavations for lamps, which are lighted in the night; but they have no windows. Every large chuttram has a pond or tank near it, partly to serve for the daily ablutions of the Hindoos and partly to allay thirst. Distinguish from chauvady or choultry, which is merely an open assembly hall. Common suffix in place names. Compare moosaufer khana.

CHY (چی - chí, *Pers.*). Suffix denoting agent; as Cajaunchy, treasurer.

CINNAMON (کنامون - kinamon, *Ar.*). From hebrew. Botanically the Cinnamomum genus, lauraceæ [vricsham, 111]. Evergreen trees or shrubs; leaves opposite or alternate; flowers small, in axillary and sub-terminal panicles; the fruit berry-like, one-seeded, in a cup-like calyx. The species best known to the natives are shown below. Other s. indian species indigenous or naturalized are:—Cecidodaphne; tree; malabar. Glanduliferum; giving nepaul camphor wood, nepaul sassafras; in pharm. non-officinal. Perottetii; tree; flowers brown; neilgherries. Sulphuratum; common in wynaud, coorg, western slopes of neilgherries, etc. Compare malabathrum. Also condray for cassia.——**(1)** *Cinnamon stone* (गोमेदक - gómédaka, San.; یاقوت زرد - yákútizard, Hind.; గోమేధికము - gómédhikamu, Tel.; கோமேதகம் - kóméthagam, Tam.). Title from color. San. from (gó, san. cow + méda, san. fat); of the color of cow's fat. Hind. from (yákút, ar. garnet + zard, pers. yellow). Tel. and tam. from sanscrit. Yellowish-brown stone, a species of garnet [tamrah] found in Ceylon, &c. Has the same names as sardonyx [akeekisiyah, ratnam].——**(2)** *Camphor cinnamon* (कर्पूर - karpúra, San.; कापूर - kápúra, Mahr.; شجرکافور - shajari-káfúr, Ar.; درخت کافور - darakhtikáfúr, Pers.; کافورکا پیڑ - káfúr-káper, Hind.; کاپورکا جھاڑ - kápúrkájhár, Dec.; کپور - kapur, Malay; ಕರ್ಪೂರ - karpúra, Can.; కర్పూరపుచెట్టు - karpúrapuchettu, Tel.; കർപ്പൂരം - karppúram, Mal.; කපුරු - kapuru, Singh.; கர்ப்பூரம் - karppúram, Tam.). Title as the source of ordinary camphor. San. from (krip, san. splendour). Ar. from (shajar, ar. tree + káfúr, ar. camphor). Pers. from (darakht, pers. tree + káfúr, ar. camphor). Tam. also (shúdan), meaning hot thing. Title otherwise Camphor laurel, Camphor tree, China camphor, Common camphor, Dutch camphor, Formosa camphor, Japan camphor, Officinal camphor. Botanically Cinnamomum [cinnamon] camphora, nees et eber, lauraceæ [vricsham, 111]. Alias Camphora officinarum; Laurus camphora, camphorifera. Trunk lofty; flowers small, pale, greenish yellow; fruit a drupe, the size of a pea. Wood white, damasked with reddish waves, of aromatic odour; made into boxes, preservative against insects. The chief source of camphor in this country; see that head. — *Cassia cinnamon* (तेजपत्र - téjapatra, San.; दालचिनी - dálachiní, Mahr.; زرنب - zarnab, Ar. and Pers.; تالیس - tálís, Hind.; برمی کا جھاڑ - barmíkájhár, Dec.; మొద్దులవంగపట్టచెట్టు - moddulavanga-pattachettu, Tel.; ഇലവങ്ങം - ilavannam, Mal.; பெரியலவங்கப்பட்டை - periyalavangappattai, Tam.). Title from (quása, hebrew, to peel off) and flavor. San. from (téja, san. pungent + patra, san. leaf). Mahr. from (dáru, san. wood + chiníya, mahr. chinese). Tel. from (moddu, tel. thick + lavangapattachettu, tel. cinnamomum zeylanicum, breyn.). Mal. from (lavanga, san. clove, eugenia caryophyllata, willd.). Tam. from (periya, tam. big + lavangapattai, tam. plant, cinnamom zeylanicum. breyn.). San. also (tamálapatra), meaning leaves of the tree [malabathrum]; (tamála) [ceylon gamboge, karanj, yellow mangosteen]; (tvacha), meaning bark. Hind. also (sadrus); (taj); (dálchíní), meaning cinnamomum zeylanicum, breyn.; (motídálchíní), meaning thick cinnamomum zeylanicum, breyn. Tel. also (nagacheraloo); (tálishapatri) [indian plum, taulisham]; (lavangachettu) [lavangam]. Mal. also (karuva), meaning black. Tam. also (shirunágappú), meaning the tree, mesua ferrea, linn. [nauga champak] + flower; (tálisappattiri) [taulisham]; (ilavangappattai), meaning cloves + bark, properly cinnamomum zeylanicum, breyn. Greek *κασσία*. Title otherwise Cassia bark tree, Cassia bud tree, Cassia lignea tree. Botanically Cinnamomum [cinnamon] tamala, nees, lauraceæ [vricsham, 111]. Specific name from sanscrit. Alias Cinnamomum albiflorum, nitidum; Laurus cassia. Moderate-sized evergreen tree fifty to sixty feet, on malabar coast. Immature flowers, flores cassiæ, gathered and dried, called cassia buds; of a dark brown color; the flavor resembles cinnamon [ceylon cinnamon]. The bark resembles that of ceylon cinnamon in appearance, smell and taste, but may be readily distinguished by being thicker in substance and more pungent; this is cassia lignea, cortex cassiæ, cortex casseæ ligniæ, of chemists; it is stripped from the twigs by running a knife along the branch. The leaves and bark are also distilled and furnish cassia oil. Medicinal uses of this bark same as ceylon cinnamon; used especially in veterinary practice in cordial preparations. The buds are used like cloves [lavangam]; the oil for flavoring [cassia].——*Ceylon cinnamon* (त्वच - tvacha, San.; दालचिनी - dálachiní, Mahr.; दालचिनी - dálchiní, Conc.; دارصینی - dársíní, Ar.; دارچینی - dárchíní, Pers.; دارچینی کا پیڑ - dárchíníkáper, Hind.; دال چینی کا جھاڑ - dálchíníkájhár, Dec.; کولتمنس - kulitmanis, Malay; ಲವಂಗಪಟ್ಟೆಮರ - lavangapattemara, Can.; ඉජන් - ijin, Too.; లవంగపట్టచెట్టు - lavangapattachettu, Tel.; ഇലവങ്ങം - ilavannam, Mal.; කුරුඳු - kurundu, Singh.; இலவங்கப்பட்டை - ilavangappattai, Tam.). Title from habitat. San. from (tvak, san. bark). Mahr. from (dáru, san. wood + chiníya, mahr. chinese). Conc. from mahratta. Ar. from (dár, ar. wood + síní, ar. chinese). Pers. from arabic. Hind. from persian. Dec. from hindostany. Can. from (lavanga, san. cloves + patte, can. bark + mara, can. tree). Tel. from (lavanga, san. clove tree + patta, tel. bark + chettu, tel. tree). Mal. from (lavanga, san. clove tree, eugenia caryophyllata, willd.). Tam. from (lavanga, san. clove tree + pattai, tam. bark); from similar flavor and property. San. also (gudatvacha), meaning sugar bark, refers to the bark of the tree; (tápiñchha), meaning heat + sheltering; (vasana), meaning bark; (dárusitá), meaning wood + white, is cinnamon in sticks. Conc. also (tikké). Ar. also (kirfabisailániyah), meaning ceylon bark. Pers. also (salíkhahisailániyah), meaning ceylon cassia. Hind. also (kalamidárchíní), meaning cinnamon in quills; (taj), meaning cassia lignea. Can. also (dálchinimara); (lavangachakkemara), meaning the tree. Tel. also (sannalavangapattachettu), meaning thin + the tree. Mal. also (karuva), meaning black; (varanam); (cheriyayilavannam), meaning small cinnamon. Tam. also (shannalavangappattai), meaning small + cinnamon; (karuvá). Hebrew kinamon, Greek *κιννάμωμον*, Latin xylocinnamum; the modern cinnamon however is a different product from that of the greeks and romans, which was not a bark, nor rolled up into pipes, but consisted of the tender shoot of the same plant; the ancient article was of much higher value. Title otherwise Common cinnamon, Sweet bark, True cinnamon. Botanically Cinnamomum [cinnamon] zeylanicum, breyn., lauraceæ [vricsham, 111]. Alias Cinnamomum cassia, verum; Laurus cassia, cinnamomum, malabathrum, nitida; Persea cinnamoma. Small evergreen tree, with willow-like branches and alternate, oblong, elliptical, smooth, entire leaves, with longitudinal veins running from the base to the apex; flowers inconspicuous, with unpleasant smell; fruit a small berry; native of ceylon. The inner aromatic bark is cinnamon; requires to be distinguished from country cinnamon [q.v.] which is very inferior; real cinnamon occurs in small closely rolled quills, containing several smaller quills within them of a light yellowish-brown color, fragrant odour, and warm sweet aromatic taste; country cinnamon is a much larger and thicker bark, generally curved, but seldom completely quilled, the taste less sweet, with some degree of astringency, and the smell less fragrant. Cassia lignea [cassia cinnamon] is also frequently substituted in commerce for cinnamon; by the ancients these two were never carefully distinguished. Four kinds of real cinnamon are distinguished:—Ceylon, Tellicherry, Malabar, and Java. Ceylon cinnamon is the most esteemed; Tellicherry or bombay cinnamon is grown at tellicherry; Malabar or madras cinnamon is of inferior quality, it is grown on the coromandel coast; Java cinnamon is from a separate species, javanicum. The culture of cinnamon was begun in ceylon about 1770 under the dutch. The shrubs grow in clusters and are decorticated when the shoots are from 1 to 3 inches in diameter; cinnamon is prepared by making longitudinal incisions in the bark which separates from the branches, and rolls up in the form of a pipe about the size of the finger; scraped and dried is of a brown color, and the cinnamon of commerce; the best cinnamon is procured from branches three years old; oil of cinnamon is obtained from the bark by distillation after it has been macerated in sea-water, and a fatty matter is procured from the fruit by boiling. Cinnamon is largely combined with other medicines as a condiment, and is indicated in all cases characterised by feebleness; gives to pharm. inner bark of shoots from the truncated stocks, cinnamomi cortex, virtues reside principally in a volatile oil, oleum cinnamomi, in addition to which it contains tannin and a peculiar acid, cinnamic acid, aromatic, stimulant, and carminative; it is closely allied in medical properties and uses to cloves [lavangam]. Cinnamon is used in curry [q.v.] and enters into the preparation known as paun [q.v.]. Three oils obtained:—oil of cinnamon is prepared from chips; oil of cinnamon leaf is procured by macerating the leaves; cinnamon camphor obtained by distillation from the roots. Ceylonese distinguish honey cinnamon, serpent cinnamon, fragrant cinnamon, astringent cinnamon; these do not constitute separate species.——*Country cinnamon* (तिलक - tilaka, San.; रानदालचिनी - ránadálachiní, Mahr.; टिक्कि - tikki, Conc.; جنگلی دارچینی - janglídárchíní, Hind.; جنگلی دال چینی - janglídálchíní, Dec.;

ಅಡವಿಲವಂಗ - adavilavanga, Can.; ಇಜಿನ್ಮರ - ijinmara, Too.; అడవిలవంగపట్టచెట్టు - adavilavangapattachettu, Tel.; കാട്ടുകറുവ - káttukaruva, Mal.; காட்டுக்கருவா - káttukkaruvá, Tam.). Title from being indigenous. San. means mark on the forehead [peacock gingelly, tirootauly]. Mahr. from (rána, mahr. forest + dálachíní, mahr. cinnamomum tamala, nees.). Hind. from (janglí, hind. wild + dárchíní, pers. cinnamon, cinnamomum zeylanicum, breyn.). Dec. from hindostany. Can. from (adavi, can. jungle + lavanga, san. cinnamon tree). Tel. from (adavi, tel. forest + lavangapattachettu, tel. tree, cinnamomum zeylanicum, breyn.). Mal. and tam. from (kádu, tam. forest + karuvá, tam. cinnamon tree, cinnamomum tamala, nees.). San. also (tamálapatra), meaning cinnamomum tamala, nees. + leaf. Hind. also (dálchíní), meaning cinnamon; (sadrus); (tálispatar); (tálispatrí); (barhmi); (tajpát); (putruj). Can. also (kádudalchíni), meaning jungle + cinnamon; (dálchínimara); (kádulavanga), meaning jungle + cinnamon. Tel. also (ákupatrikamu); (tálishapatri); (paççákuchettu), meaning green + leaf + tree. Mal. also (ilavannam). Tam. also (shembilá), meaning red + jack tree, artocarpus integrifolia, willd.; (pulippilá), meaning sour + jack tree, artocarpus integrifolia, willd.; (tálisappattiri) [indian plum, taulisham]; (ilavangam) [lavangam]. Title otherwise Wild cinnamon tree. Botanically cinnamomum [cinnamon] iners, reinw., lauraceæ [vricsham, 111]. Alias Cinnamomum eucalyptoides, malabathrum, nitidum, rauwolffii; Laurus iners, malabathrum. Small tree; leaves coriaceous, oval or oblong, nearly equally attenuated at both ends, usually three-nerved, almost veinless, lateral nerves nearly reaching the apex, shining and glabrous above, glaucous beneath; aromatic when bruised; panicles equalling or exceeding the leaves, slender, peduncled, lax, branchlets three-flowered, and with the flowers equalling the pedicel; lobes of the calyx falling off at the middle. Inner bark substituted in the bazaars for cassia lignea [cassia cinnamon]; is however, a much larger and thicker bark; generally curved, but seldom completely quilled; and its smell and taste are quite different from those of cassia [q.v.]. The dried buds partake of the carminative properties of cinnamon and cassia; the seeds bruised and mixed with honey [shahad] or sugar [q.v.] given in dysentery and coughs, and combined with other ingredients in fevers; inner bark quoted in pharm. like cinnamon, but non-officinal. Bark a condiment in curries.——*Martaban cinnamon* (کیو گدیس - kayogadis, Malay). Title from place of growth. Botanically Cinnamomum [cinnamon] parthenoxylon, meissn., lauraceæ [vricsham, 111]. Fruit yields an oil used in rheumatic affections; infusion of root substitute for sassafras.——*Wild cinnamon* (காட்டுக்கருவா - káttukkaruvá, Tam.). From similar flavor of berries. Same as China pepper.

CIRCAR (سرکار - sarkár, *Hind.*). From (sar, pers. head + kár, pers. business). Government. Chief authority. Also a small province. In the Mahomedan land revenue system each soobah [q.v.] was divided into a certain number of circars, each circar into pergunnahs or mahauls. See vol. I, 112. Prefix in place names, showing that the village was once Amauny as opposed to lease [sar].——**(1)** *Circar avacausham* (സർക്കാരവകാശം - sarkáravakásham, Mal.). From (above + avakásha, san. claim). Government dues [mail vauram].——*Circar cauryastan* (സർക്കാർകാര്യസ്ഥൻ - sarkárkáryast'han, Mal.). From (above + káryast'ha, san. agent). A public servant.——*Circar gueny wurg* (ಸರಕಾರಗೇಣಿವರ್ಗ - sarakáragénivarga, Can.). From (above + géni, can. rent + varga, san. class). Estates lapsed to Government.——*Circar moothal* (സർക്കാർമുതൽ - sarkármutal, Mal.). From (above + mutal, mal. money). Public money.——**(2)** *Northern circars* (سرکارات شمالی - sarkárátishimálí, Hind.). The expression "the Circars" was first used by the French in the time of Bussy for the Nizam's governments of the country from a little south of the Kistna to Orissa. The Circars of Chicacole now Vizagapatam district, Rajahmundry and Ellore now in Godavery district, and Condapully now in Kistna district, were the subject of a grant from the Great moghul obtained by Clive in 1765, confirmed by treaty with the Nizam in 1766. Guntoor now also included in Kistna district devolved eventually by the same treaty, but did not come permanently under British rule till 1803. These were then called by the English the Northern circars. The tract lay about between lat. 15° 40′ to 20° 17′; long. 79° 12′ to 85° 20′. Its sea-coast commenced at Motoopully in Bauputla, Kistna district in lat. 15° 43′; long. 80° 19′, and held a direction north-east for 450 miles to the vicinity of Ganjam in lat. 19° 35′; long. 85° 20′. Its greatest width was towards the south-west, where it extended about 100 miles in breadth inland, but in one part, towards the north-eastern extremity, the breadth was not more than 18 miles. The tract contained the important towns of Ganjam, Chicacole, Vizianagram, Vizagapatam, Coringa, Masulipatam, Ellore, and Nizampatam. In the early part of the Christian era, the Kesary [q.v.] or lion kings of Orissa held sway there, followed by the Gajapaty [q.v.] or elephant dynasty in the north and Narapaty [q.v.] in the south, then by the Bahmany [q.v.], the Cootb shahy [q.v.], and the Asaf jahy. A sketch history of the Northern circars from the year 1471 onwards will be found at vol. I (179) [andhram, calingam].

CIRCASSIA (سرکاشیه - sarkáshiya, *Hind.*). The country.——*Circassian bean* (سرکاشیه کی پھلی - sarkáshiyakíphallí, Hind.). Bean of False red sanders.

CLEARING NUT (कतक - kataka, *San.*; निर्मळा - nirmalá, *Mahr.*; चिलबीयि - chilabíyi, *Conc.*; نرملی - nirmalí, *Hind.*; چل بینج کا جھاڑ - chilbínjkájhár, *Dec.*; ಚಿಲ್ಲಿ - chilli, *Can.*; చిల్లచెట్టు - chillachettu, *Tel.*; କୋତକ - kotaka, *Oor.*; തേറ്റാമരം - téttámaram, *Mal.*; ඉංගිනි - ingini, *Singh.*; தேற்றா - téttá, *Tam.*). Title from its power of clearing muddy water. Mahr. from (nir, san. negative particle + mala, san. dirt). Oor. from sanscrit. Tam. from (téttu, tam. to clear up). San. also (payahprasádí), (ambuprasádí), (tóyaprasádana), all meaning water-clearing; (guchhap'hala), meaning cluster fruited; (ruchya), meaning palatable; (tiktap'halá), meaning bitter fruited; (tiktamarícha), meaning bitter piper nigrum, linn.; (khataka); (kata). Can. also (chali); (chittu). Tel. also (indupuchettu); (induga). Tam. also (akkólam). Title otherwise Water-filter nut. Botanically Strychnos [mooshty] potatorum, linn., loganiaceæ [vricsham, 89]. Alias Caniram tetankotta; strychnos tetankotta. Tetankotta, from (téttánkotta), malayalam clearing nut. Small tree; calyx five-parted; corolla funnel-shaped; leaves opposite, from ovate to oval, glabrous, pointed; bark deeply cracked; corymbs from the tops of the old shoots round the base of the new ones, bearing in ternary order many small, greenish-yellow, fragrant flowers; berry shining black when ripe, one-seeded, size of cherry [auloo]; tree common in mountainous districts, larger than nux-vomica [poison nut], flowers during hot season; the one seed is the clearing nut. Property of clearing water depends upon the albumen and casein which seeds contain; seeds sliced and digested in water yield a thick mucilaginous liquid, which, when boiled, yields a coagulum or albumen, and by subsequent addition of acetic acid [sirkey ka tezaub], it furnishes a further coagulum or casein. Flower religious; one of the flowers with which the arrows of the cauman are tipped [cauma baunam]. Seeds pulverized and mixed with honey [shahad] are applied to boils to hasten suppuration, and with milk given in sore eyes; seeds are remedy in diabetes and gonorrhœa; sometimes applied over the abdomen in the form of paste to relieve colic; mucus or thin pulp round seeds, and the pericarp or testa of fruit are emetic; substituted for british ipecacuanha; seeds are in pharm. non-officinal. Ripe pulp of fruit eaten; seeds used by distillers to render spirit more intoxicating. Ripe seeds are dried and sold in the bazaars to clear muddy water and render it potable; one of the seeds is rubbed very hard for a minute or two round the inside of an earthen vessel, into which the water is poured and left to settle; in a short time the impurities subside and leave the water perfectly limpid and tasteless. Wood white when fresh cut, turning yellowish-grey on exposure, hard, close-grained, seasons well.

CLEFT GRASS (கமரிப்புல் - kamarippul, *Tam.*). Tam. from (kamar, tam. crevice + pul, tam. grass). Title otherwise Indian fescue, Malabar meadow grass. Botanically Festuca indica, retz., graminaceæ [vricsham, 156]. Alias Digitaria malabarica; Poa malabarica. Culm in moist places erect, in dry procumbent, azure green; panicle contracted, erect, half the part at the same time flowering and spreading, then contracted and the other part flowering; spikelets compressed, somewhat six-flowered, sub-aristate; malabar; coromandel [q.v.] mountains.

CLOSEPETT (ಕುಲೀಸ್‌ಪೇಟೆ - kulíspéte, *Can.*; closepet, *Mys. Gov.*).—"*a*" Talook in the south-west, Bangalore district, Mysore, head-quarters at Closepett. Contains the hoblies:—Beirmungala, Chennaputna, Closepett, Coongull, Honganore, Maukaly, Moodigerey, Mullore, Virpautchipore. Principal places:—Cagalipore, Chennaputna, Closepett, Coodacull, Coodlore, Honganore, Jakkairy, Jaulavangala, Mullore, Melnaickenhully, Mungalvaurapett, Sogaula, Soogganhully.—"*b*" Town; lat. 12° 43′; long. 77° 19′; from Bangalore S.W. 27 miles. On the Bangalore-Seringapatam road. Named after Sir Barry Close, Resident; called Hospett, in Hindostany navapett, meaning new town, also Ramagherry. The horse-breeding establishment of the Sillahdars, since removed to Coongal in Toomcore district, was formerly here.

CLUB GRASS (नल - nala, *San.*; అల్లికి - alliki, *Tel.*; அலிகை - aligai, *Tam.*). Title from shape of culms. Tel. from (allu, tel. to spread). San. also (kastéru), meaning resting in water. Tel. also (gittigadda); (billappa); (boddutunga), meaning round + cyperus rotundus, linn.; (gundatunga), meaning round + cyperus rotundus, linn. Title otherwise Bull-rush, Club-rush, Round toonga. Botanically the Scirpus genus, cyperaceæ [vricsham, 155]. Grasses; inflorescense in solitary spikes or several together, clustered and forming heads; glumes imbricated on every side, none of the scales empty; style jointed at the base and deciduous; flowers furnished with bristles beneath the ovary. The species best known to the natives are:—Grossus; culm triquetrous, leafy at the base; in stagnant waters. Juncoides; culms cæspitose, sheathed. Kyssor; specific from sanscrit; culms 5-6 feet, triangular, hispid; western coast. Maritimus, glaucous club-rush, salt-marsh club-rush, sea-side club-rush, spurt-grass: creeping; culms triquetrous. Mucronatus. Subulatus; culm round, three-cornered at the apex, sheathed, leafless; in sandy localities.

CLUSTER GRASS (குஞ்சப்புல் - kuñjappul, *Tam.*). Title from habit. Same as Wild raggy.

CO (കോൻ - kón, *Mal.*; கோ - kó, *Tam.*). King.——*Coil* (కోవెల - kóvela, Tel.; കോയിൽ - kóyil, Mal.; கோவில் - kóvil, Tam.). From (above + il, tam. abode). In Malabar it has its original meaning, a palace [covilagam]. So a temple [covil, cshetram]. A Dravidian temple consists architecturally of four main parts :—the vimaunam [q.v.], or actual temple, which is square in plan and surmounted by a pyramidal roof; the mantapam [q.v.], or porch; the gopooram [q.v.], or gateway towers; and the chauvady [q.v.], or pillared hall. The gopooram is much higher than the temple proper. The following are the other parts :—Calyauna mautapam, Dhwaja stambham [q.v.], Dwaura mantapam, Mandiram, Moola staunam [q.v.], Praucauram [q.v.], Rath [q.v.]. The parts according to religious treatises are Mayan, the body; Sarpaugra mantapam, the head; Ardha mantapam, the neck; Maha mantapam, the chest; Darshana mantapam, the abdomen; Moolastaunam, the holy place; Yauga shaulay, the place of offerings; Madapully, the kitchen. Another division is into the Garbhagriham or womb of the house, the Antaranlam or ante-temple, and the Ardhamantapam or front portico [matam]. Coil is common suffix in place names, as Atchancoil. Or prefix, as in Coilputty.——*Coilputt* (கோயிற்பற்று - kóyirbattu, Tam.). From (kóyil, tam. temple + pattu, tam. connexion). Lands, &c., belonging to a temple [devadauyam].——*Coilputty* (கோவிற்பட்டி - kóvirbatti, Tam. koilpati *). From (kóvil, tam. temple + patti, tam. village).—"*a*" Zemindarry; Tinnevelly dist., Shauttore tal. Peshcush Rs. 3,230. Annual revenue Rs. 10,580.—"*b*" Village, Railway station; Tinnevelly dist., Shauttore tal.; pop. 2,740; acres 2,238; lat. 9° 10′; long. 77° 55′; height 287 feet; from Shauttore S.S.W. 12½ miles; from Tinnevelly N.N.E. 33 miles. Ancient rent-free village on the Madura-Palamcottah road. Famous temple. Perennial spring known as Agastya teertam. About a mile south-west is a remarkable rock with a cavern. Weekly fair on Monday. Trig. station in lat. 9° 09′ 42·93″; long. 77° 54′ 01·80″; height 534 feet; from Paundavarmungalam N.N.W. 1¾ miles; from Shauttore S.S.W. 13 miles.——*Coil tumbooraun* (കോയിത്തമ്പുരാൻ - kóyittampurán, Mal.). From (kóyil, mal. palace + tampurán, mal. lord). A class of quasi-noble Nayars, regarded as Cshatriyas; and from their ranks are chosen the consorts of the princesses. The men give cloth to Shoodra females, while the women are united to Numboory bramins [jauty].——*Colachel* (കൊല്ലംചൽ - kolláççal, Mal.). From (kollam, mal. palace + kal, mal. suffix of place). Greek κωλίας. Village, Port; Travancore state, Pudmanaubhapooram division, Yerraneel tal.; pop. 18,699; lat. 8° 10′; long. 77° 19′; from Yerraneel S.W. 4½ miles; from Bombay S.S.E. 790 miles; from Cadiapatam N.W. 4½ miles; Tengyeputnam S.S.E. 7½ miles; from Trivandrum S.E. 29 miles. In a diminutive bay. Of increasing importance for coasting steamers. Land is rather high and bold. Landing place sheltered by a reef. Cherma permaul took ship here to Mecca [randatarra]. Ancient seaport. Danes once had a factory and commercial resident. Referred to by Bartolomeo as safe harbour well known to ancients. Trade with coast and Ceylon. S. Travancore coffee [q.v.] prepared and exported. Salt [ooppoo] manufactured.——*Collam* (കൊല്ലം - kollam, Mal.). From (kóvilakam, mal. palace). Distinguish from Covalam [covelong]. Title otherwise Northern collam. Mal. also (pantaláyinikollam), meaning port collam. Village, Port; Malabar dist., Cooroombranaud tal.; lat. 11° 27′; long. 75° 43′; from Badagara S.E. 11¾ miles; from Bombay S.S.E. 540 miles; from Calicut N. 15 miles; from Cuddalore E. 3¾ miles; from Quilandy N. 1½ miles. The Pandarany of Portuguese writers, Plandrina of Frier Odoric, Fandreeah of Rowlandson's Tohfat ool moojauhideen, and Fandabraina of Ibn batuta. The place where the Malayalam era was started in the north, as distinguished from that of Southern collam or Quilon. Bhagavaty temple. Mosque of antiquity. Formerly favorite starting and landing place for Mahomedan pilgrims to and from Mecca. On a rock on the sea-shore is a deeply cut foot-print chiselled out of a natural hollow, 3¼ long by 10 to 12 feet broad, said to be print of Adam's foot [condaveed], as he landed from across the ocean; his next step took him to Adam's peak [dharmarajacull] in Ceylon. For the collam era see Saca. There are three other collams :—"*a*" Southern collam; otherwise Quilon, in Travancore state; till recently head-quarters of Government of that state [quilon].—"*b*" Cauyan collam, otherwise Cully quilon, in Travancore [cauyancollam].—"*c*" Tirvanjy collam in Cochin, the ancient seat of Chera government on West coast [tirvanjicoolam].——*Coloo* (కొలువు - koluvu, Tel.; கொலு - kolu, Tam.). From (kolutsu, tel. to worship). Sitting of a king or idol in state.——*Coloopoo* (కొలుపు - kolupu, Tel.). Festival of village deity [grauma devatay].——*Conaud* (கோநாடு - kónádu, Tam.). From (above + nádu, tam. country). Former name of a talook, which with Laulgoody was amalgamated in 1861 into present Trichinopoly talook.——*Conaun* (கோனான் - kónán, Tam.). From (kón, tam. king). A shepherd proper name; common among the lower orders [peyar]. Title of the Yiday caste.——*Cone* (കോൻ - kón, Mal.; கோன் - kón, Tam.). King [carnautaoa rajakkal, kone]. Prefix in place names, as Congaud, meaning royal forest.——*Covil* (കോവിൽ - kóvil, Mal.). From (above + illam, mal. house). Palace, temple [coil].——*Covilagam* (കോവിലകം - kóvilakam, Mal.). From (above + akam, mal. inside). Apartments of a rajah's palace. So a branch of a royal tarwand [q.v.]. It answers to Tauvery among the subjects. The Zamorin rajah of Calicut's tarwaud [q.v.] has three Covilagams :—Eastern or kizhakk, Western or padinyaur, New or poothiya. The eldest female in these three is the head of the tarwaud. She enjoys certain of the common lands attached to the Ambaudy covilagam or chief palace so called, and is regarded as the holder of a staunam or dignity. Next after her follow in succession the five eldest males of the tarwand, who stand in the order of their respective ages, and who are known respectively as:—Zamorin [q.v.], Yeralpaud, Moonalpaud, Yeddatralpaud, Nedootralpaud. To each of them a certain portion of the tarwaud property is allotted to enable him to maintain his staunam or dignity, and he is called a Coorvaulcha [q.v.] or Joint ruler. As soon as a member of the royal tarwand attains to a staunam of dignity, he theoretically loses his place in the Covilagam of his origin; but practically now when there are no political powers to be exercised, he is allowed to manage the common property of his branch.

COAST (கரை - karai, *Tam.*). In books of the eighteenth century means the Coromandel coast specifically. παραλία, the shore, was applied in a similar specific way, in Ptolemy to the coast near Cape comorin. The Madras Army was not long back called the Coast army. See however also the other terms below. ——*Coromandel coast* (சோழமண்டலக்கரை - shózhamandalakkarai, Tam.). Sailor's term. The Coromandel coast is the παραλία σωρητῶν or ϛωριγῶν of Ptolemy, and also the district τῆς ἰδίως λεγουμένης παραλίας τωριγγῶν or σωριγγῶν, in which the mouth of the κάβηρος, or Cauvery, was situated. Begins at Calimere point, 130 miles north-east of Adam's bridge and in lat. 10° 16′, long. 79° 55′, and holds a direction due north across the estuaries of the Cauvery, which either inclose or traverse a delta, having a base of 82 miles towards the sea. The coast continues to hold a northerly direction in lat. 15° 27′, where the river Goondlacumma is considered to bound it to the northward, and retains the same character of slight elevation and general sandy formation with shallow water along shore. Throughout this distance there is no shelter for large ships, except at Madras. During the closing months of the year, when the coast is exposed to the north-east monsoon [caur], it is nearly deserted. At all times a heavy sea rolls on shore from the vast expanse of the Bay of Bengal, and causes a surf, which precludes communication from the ships lying at anchor with the land by European built boats. The coast throughout is, with little exception, low and sandy, and the sea shallow near the shore, with sounding gradually increasing with the distance from land. The surf wave breaks from 3 feet in fine weather to 12 or 14 feet high in gales; it breaks at 300 feet from shore in calm and at 450 to 1,000 feet in stormy weather. Poolicat shoal, 14 miles north of Madras city, and Covelong reef, 25 miles south, are points of danger on the coast. Commencing with the north-east wind, a current of variable velocity sets in from the north in a direction parallel with the shore. This generally increases in strength in the course of the day and decreases during the night, and is moreover influenced by the strength of the wind. It appears to reach its maximum velocity about the 1st of November, when in conjunction with the tide it amounts to three miles per hour; and from this time decreases until the 10th of December, when it amounts to a small fraction of a mile per hour only. The current is always stronger in the afternoon than in the morning. The geological appearances in several places along the coast of Coromandel render it probable that the whole coast was heaved up at some remote period. That extensive estuaries must have indented the coast previous to that period is shown by the fossil remains, both pelagic and terrestrial, many miles removed from the present shore. The revenue districts along the Coromandel coast are Madura, Tanjore, South arcot, Chingleput, and Nellore. See vol. II, 158.——*Golcondah coast* (గోలుకొండరేవు - gólukondarévu, Tel.). Sailor's term. Begins from the Goondlacumma river in lat. 15° 27′; namely at Pedda devanampaud, Ongole talook, extending thence to the southern point of the district of Vizagapatam, in lat. 17° 15′, where begins the Orissa coast. In the south-western part, the Golcondah coast contains the estuaries of the branches of the river Kistna, and those more numerous of the river Godavery; and in that part is so low, that when prolonged and violent gales from the north-east are simultaneous with great land floods, the coast is extensively inundated and great devastation takes place. The most important maritime places on the Golcondah coast are Motoopully, Masulipatam and Coringa, Narsapore, Point godavery, and Wattauda. The hills on the Golcondah coast are connected in some places with the Eastern ghauts [q.v.], and as this range approaches the south-west, its distance from the shore gradually increases, leaving space for the plain comprised in Northern circars [q.v.] and Carnatic [q.v.]. See vol. II, 164. ——*Malabar coast* (ಮಲಯಾಳತೀರ - malayálatíra, Can.; മലയാംകര - malayámkara, Mal.). Sailor's term. Begins at Mount delly and stretches generally south-east as far as Cape comorin, a distance of 325 miles. Is the coast south of the Concan [q.v.]. With little exception, low, and either muddy or sandy, having numerous shallow inlets extending a considerable distance into the land, and called by Anglo-indian backwaters [cauyal]. This coast was a fixed starting point in ancient oriental geography. According to Friar Jordanus, Bishop of Quilon, Lesser india embraced Sindh and the coast as far as some point immediately north of Malabar. Greater india extended from Malabar indefinitely to the eastward and included Champah or Cambodia [q.v.]. India Tertia was the east of Africa. Other writers changed the names, but with similar divisions [india]. See vol. II, 147.——*Orissa coast* (ఓఢ్రరేవు - ódhrarévu, Tel.). Sailor's term; at S. point of Vizagapatam district, in lat. 17° 15′; and extends north beyond this Presidency.——*West coast* (மேற்கரை - mérgarai, Tam.). General Anglo-indian term. Meant in earliest writings the west coast of Sumatra. Now always means W. coast of this peninsula from Travancore to Canara. The climate is warm, but equable, temperature being seldom lower than 68° or higher than 88°; the mean temperature 78°. March, April and May constitute the hot season, the south-west monsoon [caur] setting in about the beginning of June. The most remarkable feature of this country is the great range of the Western ghauts, for a description of which see under ghaut. For coast see vol. II, 147. For separate accounts of Travancore, Cochin, Malabar, and South canara, see vol. II, appendix XII.

COBBARY (கொப்பரை - kopparai, *Tam.*). The white kernel of the cocoanut [cocoanut, coppray].

COBJA (कुब्ज - kubja, *San.*). From (ku, san. prefix implying want + ubj, san. to make straight). Hunch-backed [coon]. Cobja vishnoovardhanan dethroned the sovereign of Vengy and established the Eastern chalookya [q.v.] dynasty, which, fixing its capital at Rajahmundry, extended its conquests to the borders of Orissa and ruled for four centuries. Vol. I (132) [charitram].

COBRA (नाग - nága, *San.* and *Mahr.*; ناگ سانپ - nágsámp, *Hind.*; ನಾಗೆರಹಾವು - nágerahávu, *Can.*; మంచిపాము - manchipámu, *Tel.*; വിഷത്താൻ - vishattán, *Mal.*; නයා - nayá, *Singh.*; நல்லப்பாம்பு - nallappámbu, *Tam.*). Title from portuguese. San. from (nagna, san. naked). Tel. from (manchi, tel. good + pámu, tel. snake); euphemistic to avert snake's anger. Mal. from (visha, san. poison + attán, mal. honorific suffix). Singh. from sanscrit. Tam. from (nalla, tam. good + pámbu, tam. snake). Tel. also (manchinágamu), meaning good + cobra; (nágupámu), meaning cobra + snake. Tam. also (nágappámbu), meaning cobra + snake. Title otherwise Cobra de capello, Binocellate cobra, Spectacled cobra. Cobra de capello is in Portuguese snake of the small hood, from the appearance of a hood which it produces by the expanded skin about the neck. Friar Jordanus, the Quilon Bishop of the fourteenth century, has the following:—"There be also venomous animals, such "as many serpents, big beyond bounds, and of divers colors, "black [black cobra], red [red cobra], white, and green [whip "snake], and parti-colored; two-headed [domoonh], also three-"headed and five-headed. Admirable marvels!" The last might be suggested by the appearance of a cobra with dilated hood and spectacles. Naga tripudians, elapidæ [naug], ophidii colubriformes venenosi, ophidia [sarpam], reptilia [sarpy, 27], of naturalists [jantoo]; erroneously spelt Naja by early writers. Alias Coluber naja; Naja atra, kaouthia, larvata, lutescens. There is only this one species. Body and tail of moderate length; belly flat; head rather high and short, not very distinct from neck, which is very dilatable, the anterior ribs being elongate. The shields of the head normal, but the loreal is absent. Nostrils wide, lateral between two shields; eye of moderate size, with round pupil. One præthree, sometimes two or four post oculars. Six upper labials, the third and fourth entering the orbit; the third forms the lower half of the anterior margin of the orbit. Scales smooth, much imbricate, in numerous series round the hood. Anal entire. Sub-caudals two-rowed. The fang is grooved, with foramen at its extremity; one or two small ordinary teeth at a short distance behind it. The neck is marked between the tenth and seventeenth transverse series of scales with a white, black-edged ⊃ or ⋙ enclosing at either extremity a black ocellus. This pattern is entirely on the steel-brown skin, and is only seen when the cervical disk is expanded; then the scales are distant from one another like grains of linseed [alsee] symmetrically arranged in rows; at other times the scales are imbricate and conceal the pattern. The general color varies from light olive, or even buff, to dark-brown; this color is entirely on the scales, the interstitial skin being white, occasionally with dark cross-bands. A common variety has numerous narrow light cross-bars, generally in pairs. Under parts ash or dark mottled; anteriorly a lateral black spot corresponding to the position of the ocellus on the neck; two or three series of ventrals between the fifteenth and thirtieth are very dark, nearly black. The colors are variable in shade, and they mark caste according to the Tamulians. As a rule the cobras found on the coast are much lighter than those of inland districts. They seldom exceed 3 or 4 feet in length, and are about an inch and a quarter thick with a small head. Cobras never attack without distending the hood. They raise the anterior third of the body from the ground, slide slowly along on the posterior two-thirds, and with the hood dilated remain on the alert, darting the head forward to the attack when anything hostile approaches. This attitude is very striking, and few objects are more calculated to inspire awe than a large cobra, when with his hood erect, hissing loudly, and his eyes glaring, he prepares to strike. Nevertheless they are not aggressive; unless interfered with or irritated, they crawl along the ground with the neck undilated, looking not unlike innocent snakes; but the moment they are disturbed they assume the menacing attitude. The cobra is a nocturnal snake; that is to say it is most active in the night; but it is often seen moving about in the day. It is oviparous; the eggs, from eighteen to twenty-five in number, are obovate and about the size of those of a pigeon [capotam]; the shell is white, but tough and leathery. The cobras feed on small animals, bird's eggs, frogs [bhaicam], fish, or insects; they rob hen-roosts and swallow the eggs whole; they prefer taking their food at dusk or in the night. They drink water, but they will live for months in captivity without touching food or water. They go into water readily and swim well, but are essentially terrestrial snakes. They can climb and occasionally ascend trees in search of food. Cobras are not unfrequently found in the roofs of huts, holes in walls, fowl houses, old ruins, under logs of wood, in cellars, old brick kilns [collvye], and old masonry of stone, brickwork or mud. Their chief enemies are the jungle-fowl [q.v.], which destroy the young brood, and the herpestes or ichneumons [mongoose], which will attack and master the largest cobra. The cobras are the favorites of the snake-charmers, who make them assume a dancing motion opposite a pipe [jeenboorra, magady] which is played before them. These snake-catchers render them harmless by extracting the fangs when they are young, or when they are caught. A piece of stout cloth is put before the cobra on which it bites; the cloth is then suddenly drawn back, tearing out the fangs with it. The snake-charmers say that their charms and musics make the poison ineffective; but these are quickly reproduced, unless with the fang all the reserve fangs and germs are removed, in which case the snake is harmless for life. The cobra poison, when thoroughly inoculated by a fresh and vigorous snake is quickly fatal. Paralysis of the nerve-centres takes place, and death occurs with great rapidity sometimes in a few minutes, especially when the fangs, having penetrated a vein, inoculate the poison immediately into the venous circulation. None of the reputed antidotes [snake-stone] will cure the bite of the cobra if the snake is full-grown and if its poison fang is full and be not interfered with by clothing. The most probable remedy in all cases of snake-bite is the injection of ammonia. The Tamul Cooral has the following:—உடம்பாடிலாதவர் வாழ்க்கை குடங்கருட்பாம்போ டுடனுறைந்தற்று—"Living with "those who do not agree with one is like dwelling with a cobra "in the same hut." There is a Tamul proverb:—கடிக்கிறநாகம் கலந்து உறவாகுமா—"Will the biting cobra mix in "friendly intercourse?" The following different kinds are recognized among the Dravidians. All are deadly, except Hill cobra and Male cobra, which are not real cobras.——*Black cobra* (నల్లనాగు - nallanágu, Tel.; കൃഷ്ണസർപ്പം - krishnasarppam, Mal.; கருநாகம் - karunágam, Tam.). Same as pariah.——*Black-hooded cobra* (నల్లతాచుపాము - nallatátsupámu, Tel.). Black on the hood unusually deep.——*Bramin cobra* (బాపననాగు - bápananágu, Tel.; பாப்பாரநாகம் - pápparanágam, Tam.). Same as red.——*Chetty cobra* (శెట్టినాగు - shettinágu, Tel.; செட்டிநாகம் - shettinágam, Tam.). Otherwise Merchant cobra, so called from its habit of looking about on all sides when lifting up its head.——*Crab cobra* (ఎండ్రినాగు - endrinágu, Tel.; நண்டுதின்னிநாகம் - nanduthinninágam, Tam.). Alleged to live upon crabs [nundoo].——*Flower cobra* (పూనాగు - púnágu, Tel.; பூநாகம் - púnágam, Tam.). The smallest kind found amongst flowers; extremely venomous.——*Foliage cobra* (ఆకునాగు - ákunágu, Tel.; தழைநாகம் - tazhainágam, Tam.). Found among leaves.——*Hill cobra* (కొండనాగు - koudanágu, Tel.). See sep. title.——*Jasmine cobra* (మల్లెనాగు - mallenágu, Tel.). From frequenting those flowers.——*Male cobra* (சாரை - shárai, Tam.). See Rat-snake.——*Mogily cobra* (باڑی کا سانپ - bárikásámp, Hind.; మొగిలినాగు - mogilinágu, Tel.). Frequents the Caldera bush [screw-pine].——*Pariah cobra* (మాలనాగు - málanágu, Tel.; பறைநாகம் - parainágam, Tam.). Same as black.——*Red cobra* (ఎర్రనాగు - erranágu, Tel.; செந்நாகம் - shennágam, Tam.). Same as bramin.——*Shell cobra* (శంఖునాగు - shankhunágu, Tel.). Plain hood without any mark.——*Wheat cobra* (గోధుమనాగు - gódhumanágu, Tel.; கோதுமைநாகம் - kóthumainágam, Tam.). A cobra with a short, thin body.

COCA (کوکا - koka, *Hind.*). Title from mexican. Title otherwise South american coca bush, South american spadic bush. Botanically Erythroxylon coca, lam., lineæ [vricsham, 28]. Distinguish both from cocoa and cocoanut. Shrub of upright, bushy habit with alternate entire ovate leaves about $1\frac{1}{2}$ inches in length and small, greenish-white flowers; from south america; leaves dried and mixed with burnt lime form a masticatory [charvanam]; leaves can be infused as tea [q.v.]; immediate effect with american natives said to be a gentle excitement, with sensation of high enjoyment; its use lessens desire for food, and enables the consumer to undergo an enormous amount of fatigue from an increased nervous energy; has evidently some analogies to betel-nut [q.v.]; has not equal effects with europeans as far as observed. For the only indigenous species of this tree see Deccany deodar.

COCANADA (కాకినాడ - kákináda, *Tel.*). From (káki, tel. crow + nádu, tel. country); perhaps from the dark clay soil. ——**(1)** Division, Deputy tahsildarry, Godavery district. Pay Rs. 100. Area 126 square miles, containing sixty-one towns and villages. Population 120,907. Language Teloogoo. E. coast of district. Boundaries:—N. Pittapore division; S. Yanam and Ramchendrapooram talook; E. sea; W. Ramchendrapooram talook. Extends all along the coast. Soil of a regar [q.v.] clay [çalimunn] and generally fertile. Paddy [q.v.], jaggery [q.v.], hides [chamrah], castor [aumanac], and gingelly [q.v.] seeds, largely exported. Cigars are manufactured. Irrigation by canals. Yelair irrigates about twenty villages. A few villages by Godavery floods. Places of archæological interest:—Bheemavaram, Inzaram, Juggannautapooram, Neelapully, Sarpavaram. Principal trig. stations:—Gorrepoody, Manjair, Mullavarammol, Polecore, Raipore, Rameshwaram, Timmapooram, Vaucalpoody lighthouse. The leading places, &c., in the division are the following.——*Atchootapooratrayam* (అచ్యుతాపురత్రయం - açcutápuratrayam, Tel.). From (açcutápura, tel. town so-called + traya, san. triad); being composed of atchootapooram, bootchampett and rameshwaram. Sanscrit name (ráméshvara), meaning rama, the lord, from the temple of rama now existing. Zemindarry, Village; pop. 1,793; lat. of village 16° 57′; long. 82° 13′; from Cocanada W. 3 miles; from the sea W. 5¼ miles. ——*Bheemavaram* (భీమవరం - bhímavaramu, Tel.). See sep. title.——*Cocanada* (కాకినాడ - kákináda, Tel.). See below.—— *Coringa* (కోరంగి - kórangi, Tel.). See sep. title.——*Goorcozaunapully* (గురుజానపల్లి - gurudzánapalli, Tel.). From (guruja, tel. diamond + palli, tel. village). Zemindarry village; pop. 1,447; lat. of village 16° 54′; long. 82° 15′; from Cocanada S. 3½ miles; from the sea W. 1½ miles. Peshcush Rs. 1,251. Salt factory.—— *Gorrepoody* (గొర్రెపూడి - gorrepúdi, Tel.). From (gorre, tel. sheep + púdi, tel. village). Trig. station; lat. 16° 51′ 44·26″; long. 82° 14′ 24·24″; from Cocanada S.S.W. 6 miles; from Congodo E. 1¼ miles; from the sea W. 3½ miles.——*Hope island* (కోరంగిదీవి - kórangidívi, Tel.). See sep. title.——*Inzaram* (ఇంజరము - indzaramu, Tel.). See sep. title.——*Juggannautapooram* (జగన్నాథపురము - jagannát'hapuramu, Tel.). From (jagannát'hudu, tel. proper name + pura, san. town). Government village; pop. included in Cocanada; lat. of village 16° 56′; long. 82° 16′; from Cocanada S. 1 mile; from the sea W. 1 mile. Formerly Dutch. Salt factory.——*Manjair* (మంజేరు - manjéru, Tel.). From (manju, san. beautiful + éru, tel. river). Trig. station; lat. 16° 49′ 21·25″; long. 82° 14′ 25·37″; from Cocanada S.S.W. 9 miles; from the sea W. 5 miles; from Seela N.E. 1½ miles.—— *Mullavaram* (మల్లవరము - mallavaramu, Tel.). From (mallaya, tel. proper name + pura, san. town). Trig. station; lat. 16° 43′; long. 82° 18′; from Cocanada S. 16 miles; from the sea W. 4½ miles; from Tallaraiv S.E. 5 miles.——*Neelapully* (నీలపల్లి - nílapalli, Tel.). See sep. title.——*Pengoodoor* (పెనుగుదురు - penuguduru, Tel.). From (penu, tel. large + kuduru, tel. halting place). Zemindarry village, Salt factory; pop. 1,493; lat. of village 16° 54′; long. 82° 14′; from Cocanada S.W. 4 miles; from the sea W. 2½ miles.——*Polecore* (పోలేకుర్రు - pólékurru, Tel.). From (póli, tel. proper name + kurru, tel. hamlet). Trig. station; lat. 16° 46′ 00·00″; long. 82° 16′ 00·00″; from Cocanada S. 11 miles; from the sea W. 4 miles; from Tallaraiv S. 1 mile. ——*Raipore* (రేపూరు - répúru, Tel.). From (rédu, tel. king + pura, san. town). Trig. station; lat. 16° 56′ 54·21″; long. 82° 13′ 58·69″; from Cocanada W. 3½ miles; from Covoor N.E. ¾ mile; from the sea W. 4½ miles.——*Ramanayyapett* (రమణయ్యపేట -ramanayyapéta, Tel.). From (ramanayya, tel. proper name + péta, tel. suburb). Zemindarry village; pop. 1,451; acres 904; lat. of village 16° 59′; long. 82° 17′; from Cocanada N. 3 miles; from the sea W. 2 miles.——*Rameshwaram* (రామేశ్వరము - ráméshvaramu, Tel.). From (ráma, san. the god + íshvara, san. lord). Trig. station; lat. 16° 58′ 48·75″; long. 82° 14′ 32·24″; from Cocanada N.N.W. 3 miles; from Maudhavaputnam S. ¾ mile; from the sea W. 3½ miles.——*Samulcottah* (సామర్లకోట - tsámarlakóta, Tel.). See sep. title.——*Sarpavaram* (సర్పవరము - sarpavaramu, Tel.). From (sarpa, san. snake + pura, town). Village, Place of pilgrimage; pop. 1,374; lat. 17° 00′; long. 82° 16′; from Cocanada N. 4½ miles; from the sea W. 3½ miles. Ancient Vishnoo temple founded by a Rishy, with fourteen inscriptions. North is a small lake called Naurudagoondam. A large pagoda [q.v.].——*Tallaraiv* (తల్లరేవు - tállarévu, Tel.). From (tádi, tel. palmyra, borassus flabelliformis, linn. + révu, tel. harbour). Zemindarry village; lat. of village 16° 47′; long. 82° 16′; from Cocanada S. 12 miles. Ships repaired.——*Timmapooram* (తిమ్మాపురం - timmápuramu, Tel.). From (timmayya, tel. proper name + pura, san. town). Zemindarry village; pop. 1,160; lat. of village 17° 02′; long. 82° 19′; from Cocanada N.N.E. 6 miles; from the sea W. 3 miles. Trig. station; lat. 17° 02′ 06·27″; long. 82° 17′ 11·79″; from Cocanada N.E. 6 miles; from the sea W. 4 miles; from Panasapaud N.E. 2 miles.——*Vaucalpoody* (వాకలపూడి - vákalapúdi, Tel.). From (váka, tel. stream + púdi, tel. village). Zemindarry, Village, Lighthouse; pop. 891; lat. of village 17° 00′; long. 82° 19′; from Cocanada N.N.E. 5 miles; from the sea W. 1 mile. Lighthouse is a Trig. station; lat. 17° 00′ 49·87″; long. 82° 19′ 30·78″; from Cocanada N.N.E. 3 miles; from the sea W. ½ mile; from Tammavaram S. 1½ miles. Light 500 yards from the shore. White; flashing. A flash every 20 seconds. 14 miles range. Visible from all directions seaward. White column. To lead clear of the shoals to the northward of the Point godavery.——*Yanam* (యానాము - yánámu, Tel.). See sep. title.——*Yelair* (ఏలేరు - élérn, Tel.). See sep. title.——**(2)** Sub-magistracy, Godavery district. Pay Rs. 70. ——**(3)** Town, Port, Municipality, Collector's Divisional and Deputy tahsildar's head-quarters, Sub-judge's Court, Telegraph office, District registrar's office, Marine office; Godavery dist., Cocanada division; pop. 40,553; lat. 16° 56′; long. 82° 16′; from Coonavaram E.S.E. 76 miles; from Coringa N. 10 miles; from Ellore E.N.E. 76 miles; from Madras N.N.E. 288 miles; from Narsapore N.E. 50 miles; from Ooppauda S.S.W. 12 miles; from Rajahmundry E.S.E. 31 miles. On Golcondah coast [q.v.], at the northern extremity of the Godavery delta. Connected by canal with Samulcottah and the Godavery at Dowlaishweram. Includes the old town of Juggannautapooram formerly a Dutch settlement which is connected with Cocanada proper by an iron girder bridge across the salt creek, completed in 1865. For lighthouses see Vaucalpoody and Hope island. In 1802 a dock was constructed to receive ships of the Royal navy not drawing more than 14 feet of water. A great impetus was given to trade of place during American civil war, when large quantities of cotton were shipped. The shipping has increased and communication is kept up with Calcutta, Madras and Rangoon. Many mercantile houses have been established and a branch of the Bank of Madras opened. Chief exports are cotton [q.v.], gingelly-oil [q.v.] seed, cheroots [q.v.], sugar [q.v.] and rice [q.v.]. Imports are iron [anhan], copper [taumram], gunny [q.v.] bags, and various liquors. The following are the travelling distances by road from Cocanada to different places:—

To	Viâ	Miles and Furlongs.	
Berhampore ...	Samulcottah and Chicacole	262	7½
Bezwada	Rajahmundry and Samulcottah ...	132	2
Chicacole... ...	Toony and Samulcottah	163	7
Chunda	Rajahmundry, Mungaputnam and Chennore.	359	3
Cuddapah ...	Rajahmundry, Guntoor and Cumbum...	361	5½
Cumbum	Rajahmundry and Guntoor	275	1½
Cuttack	Chicacole, Toony and Samulcottah ...	379	4½
Ellore	Rajahmundry and Bezwada	93	1
Guntoor	Rajahmundry and Bezwada	152	2½
Madras	Masulipatam and Nellore	379	1
Madras	Rajahmundry, Bezwada and Nellore...	404	6½
Masulipatam ...	Mogultoor	99	0
Masulipatam ...	Rajahmundry and Mogultoor	128	3
Nellore	Masulipatam and Ongole	271	3.
Nellore	Rajahmundry, Ellore and Ongole ...	297	0½
Ongole	Mogultoor and Masulipatam	195	0
Ongole	Rajahmundry and Ellore...	220	5½
Raghavapooram.	Rajahmundry and Lakkavaram ...	104	5
Rajahmundry ...	Samulcottah	38	0
Securderabad ...	Rajahmundry, Bezwada and Sooryapett	299	0½
Sironchah ...	Rajahmundry and Dammapett ...	272	1
Vizagapatam ...	Samulcottah, Toony and Cassimcote ...	107	1
Vizianagram ...	Samulcottah, Toony and Soobaraum ...	130	4

COCHIN* (കൊച്ചി - koççi, *Mal.*). The final "n" is from the Portuguese. Cf. coleroon, comorin. Vern. means small place. Sanscrit name (bálápurí), means city of maidens; also (góshrínagarí), means cow + wealth + town. Also called Cheriya anantapooram as opposed to Periya anantapooram or Trivandrum. Local name for the province is Mautacshmah, meaning palace + country; also Mautabhoo, meaning same; also Perimpadapp, meaning great + creation, the great centre of population.——**(1)** Native state; situated on the west of the Presidency; between 9° 48′ and 10° 50′ N. lat., and between 76° 5′ and 76° 58′ E. long.; bounded N. by Malabar district, E. by Malabar and Coimbatore districts, S. by Travancore state, W. by Malabar district and the sea; pop. 600,278; lang. Malayalam. Contains rivers Alwye, Carvanore, Chaulacoody, Ponnany, Tattamungalam; ports Maulipooram, Naracal. The whole area of the state is represented by the following subareas:—Canyanore, Chittoor, Cochin, Cranganore, Moocoondapooram, Talapully and Trichore talooks. The following general references should be made to the preceding volumes:—general geography, I (1) to (29); general ethnology, I (29) to (109); general history, I (110) to (188); physical geography, II, 1; meteorology, II, 3; geology, II, 8; fauna, II, 21; flora, II, 26; mineralogy, II, 29. The following references in the preceding volumes will furnish details special to the district:—particulars about towns, II, 48; coast survey, II, 150; lighthouses, II, 168; ports, II, 423; missionary stations, II, 455. A special gazetteer account of the whole state is given at II, 68. Places of archæological interest:—Caccaud, Cochin, Cranganore, Nidoombara tully, Pauraul, Poonilaurava, Putticaud, Tircore, Tirvillamala, Trichore. The leading places, &c., in the State are the following.——*Ambalacottah* (അമ്പലക്കോട്ട - ambalakkótta, Mal.).

See sep. title.——*Anjikeimal* (അഞ്ചിക്കൈമൾ - añchikkaimal, Mal.). See sep. title.——*Annamanada* (അന്നമനട - annamanata, Mal.). From (annamman, mal. the food goddess, so called + nata, mal. entrance). Village; lat. 10° 14′; long. 76° 22′; from Irinyaulacode S.E. 12 miles; from Ernacolum N.N.E. 18 miles; from Trivandrum N.N.W. 128 miles; from the sea E. 12 miles. Capital of a small tract called Adoor graumam.——*Aunamala* (ആനമല - ánamala, Mal.). From (ána, mal. elephant + mala, mal. mountain). River. Rises in the mountains of Coimbatore, where called Auliyaur [q.v.], and flows 15 miles through forest taking different names. Stone-bridge near Tattamungalam. Joins with Ponnany river west of Parly railway station.——*Ayicottah* (അഴിക്കോട്ട - azhikkótta, Mal.). See sep. title.——*Caccaud* (കക്കാട് - kakkátu, Mal.). From (kal, mal. rock + kátu, mal. jungle). Village; pop. 216; lat. 10° 39′; long. 76° 06′; from Ernacolum N.W. 47 miles; from Trichore N.W. 13 miles; from Vadacancherry W. 12 miles; from the sea E. 6 miles. Rock-cut cave with pillars.——*Canyanore* (കണയന്നൂർ - kanayannúr, Mal.). See sep. title.——*Carvanore* (കരുവന്നൂർ - karuvannúr, Mal.). See sep. title.——*Chaulacoody* (ചാലക്കുടി - chálakkuti, Mal.). See sep. title.——*Chennamungalam* (ചേന്നമംഗലം - chénnamangalam, Mal.). From (shéndan, tam. skanda, the god + mangala, san. prosperity). Village; lat. 10° 10′; long. 76° 16′; from Cochin N. 14 miles; from Ernacolum N.N.W. 14 miles; from the sea E. 4 miles. The residence of Polliott atchan, a rich jenmy [q.v.]. Family once hereditary ministers of rajah of Cochin.——*Cheranore* (ചേരാനൂർ - chéranúr, Mal.). From (chéran, mal. chéra king + úr, mal. village). River. Rises in Vallangy hills and runs for 4 miles in rocky channel. It is then joined by others. Passes 20 miles through Trichore district and joins Carvanore river.——*Chittoor* (ചിറ്റൂർ - chittúr, Mal.). See sep. title.——*Cochin* (കൊച്ചി - koççi, Mal.). See below.——*Codacherry* (കോടശ്ശേരി - kótashshéri, Mal.). See sep. title.——*Colinjappaura* (കോഴിഞ്ചാമ്പാറ - kozhiñchánpára, Mal.). From (kozhi, mal. wither + pára, mal. rock). Village; pop. 4,314; lat. 10° 44′; long. 76° 53′; from Chittoor E.N.E. 6 miles; from Trichore E.N.E. 45 miles; from Ernacolum N.E. 65 miles; from the sea E. 60 miles. On the road to Pollachy. Fair held on Wednesdays.——*Coonnancoolam* (കുന്നംകുളം - kunnankulam, Mal.). From (kunnam, mal. hill + kulam, mal. tank). Town; pop. 4,004; lat. 10° 39′; long. 76° 6′; from Ernacolum N.N.W. 48 miles; from Trichore N.W. 13 miles; from Vadacancherry W. 13 miles; from the sea E. 6 miles. Large Christian town, with Syrian and Church missionary society establishments. One Malayalam bimonthly paper is published here.——*Cranganore* (കൊടുങ്ങല്ലൂർ - kotunnallúr, Mal.). See sep. title.——*Cullvetty bazaar* (കൽവെട്ടിബജാർ - kalvettibajár, Mal.). See sep. title.——*Ernacolum* (എറണാകുളം - eranákulam, Mal.). See sep. title.——*Irinyaulacode* (ഇരിഞ്ഞാലക്കോട - iriññálakkóta, Mal.). From (iru, mal. two + chála, mal. palace + kótu, mal. place). Village talook head-quarters; pop. 884; lat. 10° 21′; long. 76° 16′; from Chittore S.W. 43 miles; from Cochin N. 27 miles; from Ernacolum N. 26 miles; from Trichore S. 12 miles; from Tripoontora N.N.W. 29 miles; from Madras W.S.W. 330 miles; from the sea E. 6 miles. Has a large temple whose annual festival is in April-May. Weekly fair on Wednesdays.——*Keicherry* (കൈച്ചേരി - kaiççéri, Mal.). From (kai, mal. hand + chéri, mal. village). River. Rises at foot of hills and after 27 miles through Talapully district enters Trichore lake. During monsoon [q.v.] waters are made to irrigate lands by dams.——*Mattancherry* (മട്ടാഞ്ചേരി - mattáñchéri, Mal.). See sep. title.——*Maulipooram* (മാലിപ്പുറം - málippuram, Mal.). See sep. title.——*Moocoondapooram* (മുകുന്ദപുരം - mukundapuram, Mal.). See sep. title.——*Moolattara* (മൂലത്തറ - múlattara, Mal.). From (múla, mal. corner + tara, mal. village). Village. Anicut here on the Aunamala river. It irrigates a large tract of territory.——*Naracal* (ഞാറക്കൽ - ñárakkal, Mal.). See sep. title.——*Neliampathy* (നെല്ല്യാമ്പതി - nelyámpati, Mal.). See sep. title.——*Nemmaura* (നെന്മാറ - nemmára, Mal.). From (nal, mal. good + mári, mal. rain). Village; pop. 4,601; lat. 10° 35′; long. 76° 38′; from Chittoor W.S.W. 14 miles; from Trichore E. 26 miles; from Ernacolum N.N.E. 46 miles; from the sea E. 40 miles. At foot of Neliampathy hills. Has a pagoda. Is the head-quarters of a Sub-magistrate.——*Nidoombara tully* (നിടുമ്പരതളി - nitumbaratalli, Mal.). From (netumpura, mal. barracks, the long house + tali, mal. temple). Village; lat. 10° 45′; long. 76° 18′; from Ernacolum N. 50 miles; from Trichore N. 14 miles; from the sea E. 21 miles. Temple with inscriptions.——*Nullapully* (നല്ലേപ്പിള്ളി - nalléppalli, Mal.). From (nalla, mal. good + palli, mal. village). Village; pop. 4,306; lat. 10° 44′; long. 76° 50′; from Chittoor N.E. 3¾ miles; from Ernacolum N.E. 62 miles; from the sea E. 56 miles. Consists mostly of Bramins.——*Olloor* (ഒല്ലൂർ - ollúr, Mal.). From (ul, mal. interior + úr, mal. village). Village; lat. 10° 29′; long. 76° 17′; from Trichore S.S.E. 3½ miles; from the sea E. 13 miles. Syrian population and church.——*Oorgam* (ഊരകം - úrakam, Mal.). From (úr, mal. village + akam, mal. inside). Town; pop. 1,109; lat. 10° 26′; long. 76° 16′; from Ernacolum N.N.W. 30 miles; from Trichore S. 7 miles; from the sea E. 9 miles. Large temple and a palace. Festival in temple, March-April.——*Otchantora* (ഓച്ചന്തുറ - óççantura, Mal.). From (óççan, mal. a drum beater + tura, mal. harbour). Village; pop. 2,280; lat. 10° 01′; long. 76° 17′; from Ernacolum N.W. 3 miles; from Cochin N. 3½ miles; from the sea E. ¼ mile.——*Paliport* (പള്ളിപ്പുറം - pallippuram, Mal.). See sep. title.——*Pazhayanore* (പഴയന്നൂർ - pazhayannúr, Mal.). See sep. title.——*Periyaur* (പെരിയാറ് - periyáru, Mal.). See sep. title.——*Poonyicara* (പൂഞ്ഞിക്കര - púññikkara, Mal.). See sep. title.——*Putticaud* (പട്ടിക്കാട് - pattikkátu, Mal.). From (patti, mal. cattle fold + kátu, mal. jungle). Village; lat. 10° 33′; long. 76° 22′; from Ernacolum N.N.E. 40 miles; from Trichore N.E. 8 miles; from the sea E. 20 miles. Formerly remarkable for the robberies committed on travellers. Now a celebrated place amongst sportsmen. Several dolmens [coday cull]. In the forests in the vicinity are several deserted temples, solidly built of granite [caroom cull].——*Shoranore* (ചെറുവണ്ണൂർ - cheruvannúr, Mal.). See sep. title.——*Talapully* (തലപ്പിള്ളി - talappalli, Mal.). See sep. title.——*Tattamungalam* (തത്തമംഗലം - tattamannalam, Mal.). See sep. title.——*Tircore* (തൃക്കൂർ - trikkúr, Mal.). From (tirukku, mal. border + úr, mal. village). Village; lat. 10° 28′; long. 76° 19′; from Ernacolum N. 32 miles; from Irinyaulacode N.E. 8 miles; from the sea E. 14 miles. Temple in a cave.——*Tirvanjicoolam* (തിരുവഞ്ചിക്കുളം - tiruvañchikkulam, Mal.). See sep. title.——*Tirvillamala* (തിരുവില്വാമല - tiruvillámala, Mal.). From (tiru, mal. holy + villán, mal. bowman + mala, mal. hill); hill of rama, the bowman. Sanscrit name (bilvádri), means bael [q.v.] tree, ægle marmelos, corr. + mountain. Village; lat. 10° 44′; long. 76° 28′; from Ernacolum N. 52 miles; from Trichore N.E. 20 miles; from Vadacancherry N.E. 13 miles; from the sea E. 33 miles. Temple and rock-cut caves.——*Trichore* (തൃശ്ശിവപ്പേരൂർ - trishshivappérúr, Mal.). See sep. title.——*Tripoontora* (തൃപ്പൂണിത്തറ - trippúnittara, Mal.). See sep. title.——*Vadacancherry* (വടക്കാഞ്ചേരി - vatakkáñchéri, Mal.). From (vatakku, mal. north + chéri, mal. village). Talook head-quarters; lat. 10° 40′; long. 76° 17′; from Chittore W.S.W. 34 miles; from Cochin N. 47 miles; from Ernacolum N. 47 miles; from Trichore N.N.E. 9½ miles; from Tripoontora N.N.W. 49 miles; from Madras S.W. 318 miles; from the sea E. 19 miles. On road to Trichore. Moonsif's court. Syrian christians.——*Vellaurapully* (വെള്ളാരപ്പിള്ളി - vellárappalli, Mal.). From (vella, mal. white + áru, mal. river + palli, mal. village). Village; lat. 10° 8′; long. 76° 28′; from Canyanore N. 14 miles; from Cochin N.E. 17 miles; from Ernacolum N.E. 15 miles; from the sea E. 17 miles. An isolated portion of the State surrounded by Travancore territory, on northern bank of Periyaur. Sanitarium and watering place. The Rajah has a country residence.——*Vypeen* (വൈപ്പി - vaippi, Mal.). See sep. title.——*Yenamacull* (ഏനാമാക്കൽ - énámákkal, Mal.). From (énam, mal. ready + má, mal. large + kal, mal. stone). Village.——**(2)** Talook, Cochin state; pop. 89,758. Principal places:—Andicadav, Ayicull, Cheralye, Cochin, Maulipooram, Naracal, Neirambalam, Otchantora, Palloorty, Poonyicara, Yedacotchy, Yedavancaud and Yelangoonnapoya.——**(3)** British talook, Malabar district. Surrounded by Native state of Cochin, but under Malabar Collector [malabar]. Southernmost talook of the district. Area 1½ square miles, including seventeen detached plots known as paumoms or farms situated in lat. 9° 58′ 7″ N. and long. 76° 17′ E. Bounded north by the Native state of Cochin and backwater, south by the Cochin state, east by the river and the Cochin state, and west by the sea. Comprises three amshoms. Anjengo, Cochin and Tungacherry. Open seaboard. Form irregular being intersected here and there by the Cochin and Travancore states. Surface level. The Cochin inner harbour lies to the north of the town. About a mile in length is British territory, the rest belonging to the Native cochin state. There is an uninterrupted water communication from Cochin to Anjengo and thence to Trivandrum on the south and to Tiroor, a Railway station in Ponnany talook on the north. Soil alluvial and sandy; congenial to cocoanut palm, which is the chief product. Paddy [q.v.] is the only grain grown, and that to but a small extent. Staple produce is the cocoanut [q.v.]. Chief exports include the produce of Cochin and Travancore states and consist of cocoanut oil, coir [q.v.], fibre, coffee [q.v.], pepper [q.v.] and ginger [q.v.]. The chief imports are food grains, piece-goods, liquors and spices. Manufactures are cocoanut oil, coir-matting, casks, coir-yarn and lemon-grass [q.v.] oil. There are two small dams in the south of the town constructed for the purpose of protecting paddy cultivation from salt-water. Extensive protective works were at one time carried out at Cruz milagre about two miles to the north of the Cochin river-mouth to prevent the river from forcing for itself a new outlet. Small tanks are numerous, but the cultivation is entirely dependant upon south-west monsoon [q.v.]. There is a good camping ground in the heart of the town facing the Police station. The leading places, &c., in the talook are the following.—— *Anjengo* (അഞ്ചുതെങ്ങ് - añchutennu, Mal.). See sep. title.—— *Cochin* (കൊച്ചി - koççi, Mal.). See below.——*Tungacherry* (തങ്കശ്ശേരി - tankashshéri, Mal.). See sep. title.——**(4)** British town, Port, Head-quarters of Deputy collector, Sheristadar magistrate, Civil surgeon, Port office, Assistant superintendent of sea customs, Adhicaury, Telegraph office; Malabar dist., Cochin tal.; pop. 15,698; lat. 9° 58′ 04″; long. 76° 17′ 07·51″; from Bangalore S.W. 224 miles; from Bombay S.E. 648 miles; from Calicut S.E. 95 miles; from Cannanore S.E. 145 miles; from Chittoor S.W. 60 miles; from Cottayam N.N.W. 30 miles; from Ernacolum S. 3 miles; from Madras S.W. 345 miles; from Maulipooram S. 2½ miles; from Mangalore S.E. 220 miles; from Trichore S. 41 miles; from Tripoontora W. 6½ miles. On S. bank of principal entrance to Travancore estuary. Formerly on bank of a river, but in A.D. 1341 changes took place in backwater and whether from cyclone winds, or earthquake, or other causes Vypeen island was formed; a circumstance commemorated by an era of its own, known as Poothooveppoo or New deposit [vypeen]. The town is now fronted to N. by this island. The town extends for a mile along the Travancore estuary and then joins Mattancherry and the Jews settlement. It is half a mile in width. The numerous quaint old Dutch buildings give it a picturesque appearance. The chief native quarters are Cullvetty bazaar and Amravatty, the latter inhabited by Chetties and goldsmiths. The water-supply is bad and drinking water is brought by boats from Alwye, 20 miles distant. Light on a small mound, which formed a bastion of the old fort to the south of the harbour. Lat. 9° 57′ 47″; long. 76° 13′ 45″. White; fixed, 15 miles range. Visible from all directions seaward. White laterite [q.v.] column. Adjoining the lighthouse are the European residences facing the sea. Of late years, the sea had threatened to encroach, but stone groins were thrown out at right angles to river bank, and the foreshore has been reclaimed. Though it has the greatest depth of water of any Madras harbour, port is closed during Cochin S.W. monsoon [caur]. The best anchorage in the roads is from 5½ to 6½ fathoms soft ground, 2 to 2½ miles off shore. The stream of tide is strong and its times of change irregular, influenced by the evaporation from, or the fall of rain upon, the immense area of backwater [cauyal], of which Cochin river-mouth is the outlet. At the anchorage abreast the bar, the ebb sets west-north-west, but the tendency is to the north-west; racing over the sand-banks on the northern side of river entrance it always produces heavy breakers there, which a ship's boats should avoid. The bar at the river's mouth is a narrow strip of land having 13 feet on it at low water, but the rise and fall being only 3 feet at spring tides, only vessels drawing less than 14½ feet are taken in. The bar is marked by two buoys. The best channel does not always remain at the same spot. There is at times a surf on the bar occasioned by the strong ebb running out against the sea breezes when there is any swell outside. The river inside is deep seven to nine fathoms. Under the old wall of the fort, the depth of water is about twenty or thirty feet. Cochin is the only port south of Bombay where large ships can be built. In 1820 and 1821 three frigates for the royal navy were built. Smaller vessels for the Indian navy have also been built, and many ships from 500 to 1,000 tons burthen for the merchant service. The principal material is teak, procured from Western ghauts, but frequently so much injured in the passage down the torrents, as to be unfit for the construction of any but small craft of from 50 to 250 tons burthen. Repairs to sailing vessels are still executed. Cochin was one of the first spots in India visited by Europeans. Tradition asserts that St. Thomas labored in this region in 52 A.D., leaving behind him the colony of Christians called Nasrauny moplahs; and that in the first year of Christian era Jews settled on the site of their present colony. The latter afterwards established their head-quarters at Cranganore where they remained until driven back in the sixteenth century by the Zamorin's moplahs. From copper plates still extant, it is put beyond doubt that the Syrian christian and Jewish churches were firmly established in Cochin by the eighth century. In 1500, Cochin was visited by Cabral, after his attack on Calicut. He met with a friendly reception from the rajah, who is described as a reluctant vassal of the Zamorin. Cabral returned to Portugal with a cargo of pepper, and was followed by Inande nova castelho. In 1502, Vasco da Gama, on his second voyage, established a factory here. In 1503, Albuquerque arrived just in time to succour the Cochin rajah, who was besieged by the Zamorin in the island of Vypeen. He built the Cochin fort called Manuel cottah, the first European fort in India in 1507. The fort was enlarged in 1525 by Menezes. Albuquerque returned to Portugal, leaving Cochin guarded by only a few hundred men under Duarte pacheco. The Zamorin invaded the country but was compelled to retreat to Calicut. In 1505, Francisco Almeyda arrived as the first Portuguese viceroy of India. He was succeeded in 1510 by Albuquerque. On Christmas day 1524, Da Gama was buried here, according to Correa, in the principal chapel of the Franciscan monastery, now used as the Protestant church. His body was in 1538 removed to Portugal. In 1530, St. Francis Xavier preached in these parts and made many converts. In 1557, the church of Santa cruz was consecrated as the cathedral of a bishop. In 1577, the Society of Jesus published at Cochin the first book printed in India. In 1585 Cochin was visited by Ralph Fitch. In 1616 the English, under Keeling, engaged to assist the Zamorin in attacking Cochin, on the understanding that a English factory was to be established there. These relations were however broken off, and the factory was built some years later with the consent of the Portuguese. In 1663, the town and fort were captured from the Portuguese by the Dutch, and the English retired to Ponnany. The Dutch greatly improved the place and its trade, building substantial houses after the European fashion and erecting quays, &c. In 1776 the state was subjugated by Hyder. In 1778, Adrien Van Moens completely altered the fort, providing it with new ditches and building seven strong bastions. In 1795, on the conquest of Holland by the French, it was besieged and captured by Major Petrie. In 1796 a Dutch superintendent of Police, Justice of the Peace and Attorney-General in criminal cases, a criminal and civil court and a court of appeal were constituted at Cochin. The college for the guardianship of orphans and minors, a Dutch institution answering to the Court of Wards, a separate orphan house, an hospital for lepers at Paliport, and a matrimonial college were also continued. In 1800, Cochin was placed under the Malabar commissioners; in 1801, the Cochin commission was abolished and it was placed under the principal Collector of Malabar. The establishment was afterwards reduced to that of a Principal sudder ameen and Joint magistrate and of a Tahsildar-magistrate. In 1806 the English blew up the cathedral, destroying at the same time some of the quays, the best houses in the place, and the fort. This drove away the wealthier Dutch families. In 1814 finally ceded to the British by treaty at the time when the other Dutch indian settlements, captured the same year, were restored to Holland. British duties abolished in 1836. British resident appointed 1839. The Dutch church passed into the hands of the English. The Jews here are of two kinds; the fair Jews, of more recent arrival and settlement in the country; and the black Jews, who reside apart in a village outside the town [cranganore, ernacolum]. The latter have a synagogue. The Protestant church, formerly the principal chapel of the Franciscan monastery and probably dedicated to St. Anthony, which escaped the general destruction in 1806, is a plain massive building, with a nave 142 feet long by fifty-one broad. Its exact age is unknown; but from inscriptions on the floor it certainly existed before 1546, and is therefore the oldest European church in India, except perhaps the Calicut church. It contains some curious epitaphs. One tombstone is sometimes pointed out as that of Vasco da Gama, because it has the word 'Vasco' on it, the rest of the name being obliterated, but the coat of arms above is not that of Da Gama. The façade of the church was surmounted by an ornamented bronze cross and a weathercock 6 feet high which could be perceived some 10 miles off at sea. In 1865 these were pulled down. There are altogether nine Christian churches in the town; two Protestant, six Roman catholic and one Syrian. There are two temples; Amman coil dedicated to Bhagavaty, and Janardana devasom in Amravatty. Nearly all traces of the old fort have disappeared. The building now occupied as court house and talook cutcherry was formerly the Roman catholic convent. The Custom-house is situated on the boundary limits of British and Native cochin. The parade ground occupies the heart of the town beyond the Protestant church. Cochin is known for gold [pon] and silver [velly] work and wood and ivory [dant] carving. Two weekly English newspapers are published in addition to a Malayalam paper. There is a Tamul proverb:— கொச்சிக்குப் போனவன் செய்தியைப்பார், தன்குருவை விற்றவன் செய்தியைப்பார்—"See the result of his having "gone to Cochin, and of one who betrayed his Gooroo;" meaning that Tinnevelly tamul should stay at home. The following are the travelling distances by road from Cochin to different places:—

To	Viâ	Miles	Furlongs
Alleppey	......	32	6
Badagara ...	Cottaparamba, Chowghaut, Taunore and Calicut.	128	7
Calicut	Cottaparamba, Chowghaut and Taunore.	97	7
Cannanore ...	Cottaparamba, Chowghaut, Taunore, Calicut and Tellicherry.	156	7
Chowghaut ...	Cottaparamba	49	7
Coimbatore ...	Palghaut	116	7
Dindigul ...	Palghaut and Pulney	188	7
Madras	Palghaut, Coimbatore and Salem ...	429	1
Madura	Palghaut, Pulney and Dindigul ...	229	0½
Mané	Cottaparamba, Chowghaut, Taunore and Calicut.	137	2
Mangalore ...	Cottaparamba, Chowghaut, Calicut, Cannanore and Cassergode.	243	0
Ootacamund ...	Palghaut, Coimbatore and the Coonoor Ghaut.	171	7¾
Palghaut ...	Cottaparamba, Trichore and the Coodranghaut.	86	0

To	Via	Miles and Furlongs.	
Ponnany	Cottaparamba and Chowghaut	64	0
Quilon	Alleppey and Cauyancollam	88	0
Salem	Palghaut, Coimbatore, Avanashy and Bhawauny.	216.	3
Taunore	Cottaparamba, Chowghaut and Ponnany.	78	0
Tellicherry ...	Cottaparamba, Chowghaut, Taunore and Calicut.	142	7
Trichinopoly ...	Palghaut, Coimbatore and Pulladam ...	245	6
Trichinopoly ...	Palghaut and Dharaupooram	248	2
Trichore ...	Cottaparamba	43	7
Trittaula	Trichore	111	3
Trivandrum ...	Quilon	130	0

——(5) Native town ; Cochin state, Cochin tal. ; lat. 9° 58′ 7″ ; long. 76° 17′ ; from Chittoor S.W. 61 miles ; from Ernacolum W. 2 miles ; from Madras S.W. 347 miles ; from Trichore S. 38 miles ; from Tripoontora W. 7 miles. Also called Cochin bunder. Consists of four conjoined villages, on the Travancore estuary, half a mile south of the British town of Cochin, in the midst of the populous tract lying between the backwater and the sea. Connected by canals with Trichore for 45 miles. Former capital of the State ; and near it tradition places the gold reefs said to have been once worked. Gives its name to the form of elephantiasis known as Cochin leg [cullvetty, mattancherry].——(6) River ; Cochin state. Rather the tidal opening of a large system of backwaters [cauyal] in which numerous rivers from ghauts [q.v.] lose themselves. The backwaters extend north into Cochin territory and south into Travancore and afford a means of conveying the produce of this extensive tract. The rush of water across the bar is so great as to maintain a depth on it of about twelve feet, which enables ships of considerable size to come into harbour and load in smooth water.——(7) *Cochin leg* (हस्तिपद - hastipada, San. ; فیل پا - fílpá, Pers. ; هاتھی کا پاؤں - háthíkápáun, Hind. ; ಆನೆಕಾಲು - ánékálu, Can. ; ఏనుగకాలు - énugakálu, Tel. ; മന്ത - mantu, Mal. ; ஆனைக்கால் - ánaikkál, Tam.). San. from (hasti, san. elephant + pada, san. leg). Pers. from (fíl, ar. elephant + pá, pers. leg). Hind. from (háthí, hind. elephant + páun, hind. leg). Tel. from (énuga, tel. elephant + kálu, tel. leg). Mal. from (manda, san. slow) ; from the gait. Tam. from (yánai, tam. elephant + kál, tam. leg). Tam. also (perungál), meaning large + leg. Title because first observed in Malabar. Lepra tuberculosa seu nodosa. Called Elephantiasis, but this was not the Greek. &c. ; see Cooshtam. Otherwise Barbadoes leg. The appearance is familiar. Begins with fever [jwaram] and pain in the leg, extending as high up as the thigh. These gradually subside, but leave a thickening of the cuticle, which continues to increase in size and in duration with every attack of fever [veidyan].

COCHRANE CANAL (கொக்கரேன்வாய்க்கால் - kokkarénváykkál, *Tam.*). Called after Cochrane, a contractor. Canal ; Chingleput dist., Ponnairy and Sydapett tals. Now part of Buckingham canal [q.v.]. Ran north from Black town through the Poolicat lake as far as Doogarauzpatam.

COCK UP (फितादा - p'hitáda, *Mahr.* ; کروا - korvá, *Hind.* ; ಕುಳಂಜಿ - kulanji, *Can.* ; పండుచేప - panduchépa, *Tel.* ; ଦୁରୁଆ - durruá, *Oor.* ; നരിമീൻ - narimín, *Mal.* ; கொடுவாய் - koduváy, *Tam.*). Title from erect sharp spines of dorsal fin. Hind. from tamul. Can. from (kuli, can. pit + añji, can. be alarmed) ; used when small. Tel. from (pandu, tel. old + chépa, tel. fish). Mal. from (nari, mal. tiger + mín, mal. fish). Tam. from (kodumai, tam. frightfulness + váy, tam. mouth). Can. also (madávu), applied only to a large nayar fish, cf. english jack and pike. Tel. also (panduminu), meaning old fish. Mal. also (nadimín), meaning river fish. Tam. also (panrimín), meaning hog + fish. Title otherwise Indian perch, Nayar fish. Lates calcarifer, percidæ [panayairy], acanthopterygii, teleostei [matsyam, 1], of naturalists [jantoo]. Alias Coius vacti ; Holocentrus calcarifer, heptadactylus ; Lates nobilis ; Perca calcar, pandoomenoo ; Plectropoma calcarifer. Shoulder bone serrated ; air vessel thin, but furnishes a good isinglass [meen vajram] ; grey, with dash of green along back, and silvery on abdomen ; during monsoon it has a tinge of purple ; immature are usually darker than adults ; seas, backwaters, and mouths of tidal rivers, up which last it often ascends long distances to prey upon weaker neighbours ; excellent eating when from the vicinity of large rivers ; salts well, and from it some of the best Tamarind-fish [q.v.] is prepared. No other common species here.

COCOA (کوکو کا جہاز - kokokájhár, *Dec.*). Title corrupted from cacauat mexican ; to be distinguished from coca [q.v.] and cocoanut [q.v.]. Title otherwise Cacao, Chocolate tree. Botanically Theobroma cacao, linn., sterculiaceæ [vricsham, 26]. Habitat central america ; cultivated in ceylon. The cocoa fruit or capsule is oval, from 2½ to 4 inches long and about the same in circumference, yellow and five-celled, each cell containing generally from eight to ten seeds ; the seed is ovoid or oval, black and covered with a membranous and succulent aril ; the alkaloid of cocoa is theobromine, identical in its effects on the system with theine [tea] or caffeine [coffee]. The roasted and broken seeds are sometimes exported from ceylon and sold by native merchants at madras. Prepared cocoas are made by powdering the roasted seeds and removing a portion of the concrete oil by heat, and in the cheaper kinds sugar and farinaceous substances are added ; chocolate consists of the kernels of the seeds, which are first roasted, then deprived of their shells, and lastly reduced by grinding between heated stones into a paste, mixed with sugar and spices and pressed into cakes.

COCOANUT (नारिकेल - nárikéla, *San.* ; नारली - náralí, *Mahr.* ; नार्ल - nárla, *Conc.* ; شجرةالنارجيل - shajaratunnárjíl, *Ar.* ; درخت نارگیل - darakhtinárgíl, *Pers.* ; ناریل کا پیڑ - nárelkáper, *Hind.* ; ناریل کا جہاز - nárelkájhár, *Dec.* ; کالپا - kálapa, *Malay* ; ತೆಂಗಿನಗಿಡ - tenginagida, *Can.* ; ತಾರೆ - táre, *Too.* ; టెంకాయచెట్టు - tenkáyachettu, *Tel.* ; ନଡ଼ିଆ - nodiya, *Oor.* ; തെങ്ങ - tennu, *Mal.* ; පොල්ගහ - polgaha, *Singh.* ; தென்னை - tennai, *Tam.*). Title from a spanish word macoco applied to a monkey's or other grotesque face ; no connection with cocoa or coca. San. from (nála, san. tube + ka, san. water + ír, san. to throw) ; from water springing up when the top of a tender cocoanut is cut ; the sanscrit has originated the persian (nargíl), which appears in cosmas indicopleustes as ἀργέλλιον ; in the periplus it is said that ναύπλιος was exported in small quantity from the marts of azania, for ΝαΓΠλιος there has been suggested ΝαΡΓΙλιος from this sanscrit word. Mahr., &c., from sanscrit. Ar. from (shajar, ar. tree + nárikéla, san. cocoanut). Pers. from (darakht, pers. tree + nárikéla, san. cocoanut). Can. from (tenka, can. south + gida, can. plant). Singh. from (pol, singh. cocoanut + gaha, singh. plant). Tam. from (ten, tam. south) ; as coming from ceylon. San. also (trinarájá), meaning grass king [bamboo] ; (dirghavriksha), meaning tall tree ; (sadáp'hala), meaning always fruiting [neeroory] ; (rasáyanataru), meaning juice + abode + tree ; (lángalí), meaning resembling plough, ploughshare-like spathe [wild bachnaug]. Ar. also (shajarijauzulhind), meaning indian nut tree. Pers. also (darakhtibádinj), meaning cocoanut tree. Malay also (kálambar). Tel. also (kobbarikáyachettu), meaning dried cocoanut + tree ; (errabondálakobbarichettu), meaning red + spathe + cocoanut tree ; (guddzunárikadamu), meaning juice + cocoanut tree. Tam. also (tengu), meaning south tree ; (édagam), meaning leaf tree, applied to both palmyra and cocoanut ; (tázhai), meaning shady tree ; (kéli), applied specially to red variety. Title otherwise Argell, Cocoanut palm, Coker nut, Coquer nut, Indian nut, King of grasses [bamboo], Naurail, Naurikelam, Southern tree. To be distinguished as above said from Theobroma cacao of tropical america, which gives the cocoa bean ; and from Erythroxylon coca of peru which gives coca leaves. It has been assumed in these pages that it gave its name to Paundy, Chera and Congoo countries, and the Porny or Tamrapurny river through its product toddy ; see those heads. Botanically Cocos nucifera, linn., palmaceæ [vricsham, 149]. Alias Palma cocos.—"*a*" Spathe axillary, cylindric, oblong, terete, bursting longitudinally ; spadix erect, or nearly so, winding ; male flowers numerous, approximate, sessile, above the female ; calyx three-sepalled ; leaflets minute, broadly cordate, fleshy ; petals three ; female flowers usually one, occasionally wanting, near the base of each ramification of the spadix ; corolla six-petalled. Tall cylindrical tree rising to a height of from 30 to 100 feet with a diameter of about 1½ feet at the bottom and one foot at the top ; the tree is surmounted by numerous wavy leaves and their foot-stalks are often called branches ; the leaves are about 15 feet long ; a number of narrow and long leaflets are ranged along the two sides ; amidst these leaves hang the fruits. Specially abundant in ceylon, sumatra, java, the eastern archipelago, malabar and coromandel ; along the western side of the bay of bengal it is found as high as calcutta ; it will not grow in egypt ; the native accounts say that the cocoanut was brought from ceylon to india.—"*b*" The cocoanut requires a tropical sun, a saline atmosphere, sandy porous soil, and abundance of fresh water ; it is thus in a great measure a littoral plant, attaining earliest maturity, greatest size, and greatest fruitfulness close to the sea, although growing also and yielding fruit at a distance from it ; in the former position, should the soil be loose and friable, though of the most meagre description, such as sea sand and shells, it grows luxuriantly without the aids of cultivation, manure, or the proximity of inhabited houses ; when planted beyond 1 or 200 feet from the seashore, it neither grows well nor affords fruit, unless on rich soil, or in the proximity of dwellings ; it is self-propagating ; its keel-shaped nut, protected from the salt water by its tough and thick though light covering sails on the ocean to barren spots, where it germinates and causes even the smallest islets to become covered with clumps of the palm. When artificially cultivated, ground prepared four or five months before planting. Soils suitable for a cocoanut plantation are as follows, particularly observing that stony grounds, or those overlying rocky foundations, are to be avoided :—soils mixed with sand, either dark colored or river-washed [manal] ; sand mixed with clay, ferruginous earth, or black mould [pasalay munn] ; clayey soils where the under-strata consist of sand [calimunn] ; sand and clay, even when mixed with gravel and pebbles [adaimunn] ; seashore banks of backwaters, rivers, tanks, and paddy-fields ; alluvium of rivers and backwaters, provided a yard and a half of land is to be generally seen above water-level [vandal munn] ; marshy land even in brackish soils, but not where salt is formed in crystals by evaporation [calar munn]; all level lands exposed to the sea-breeze where the soil is good, as the valleys between hills, tanks, and ditches which have been filled up; lastly, even the floors of ruined houses well worked up, and any places much frequented by cattle and human beings on account of the ashes and salts of ammonia from the urine, &c., deposited day by day in the soil. Ripe nuts carefully collected should alone be employed as seed, and for this purpose they are usually gathered from february to may; seed from very young or very old trees is avoided; after having been kept for a month to six weeks they are planted; this may take place in january to april, or again in august, provided the rains are not heavy; the seed-beds are dug 2 feet deep and the nuts planted 1 foot apart; the nuts are laid on their sides, leaving 2 inches of their surface exposed; ashes, or ashes and salt, are freely placed in the trenches, these acting both as a manure and as a preventative against insects; the seed-bed thus prepared is kept moist, but not soaked; the germinated seeds are transplanted when they are in their second to their sixth or even twelfth month; in damp localities the transplanting is done in the hot season, otherwise during the rains; the seedlings are now put out in the plantation, pits 12 yards apart having been prepared for them; in rich soils the pits may be small, but in poor soils 1 to 2 yards wide and 2 to 3 feet deep; in cold clay soils these pits are filled with sand; in marshy land, walls are constructed around them; ashes are often freely mixed with the prepared soil to be put into the pits, as this prevents attacks of beetles destructive to trees; cultivation of turmeric [country saffron], arrowroot, [malabar arrowroot], &c., in the pits along with the cocoanuts is beneficial; the soil round the seedlings is also often kept damp by a bed of leaves, particularly such as will not encourage, but rather check, the approach of ants into the prepared soil; if the soil be naturally poor, salt, ashes, paddy-straw, fish manure, goats dung, and dry manures are added during the first year. By the end of the first year the normal leaves will begin to form and at this stage the soil around the plants is dressed and ashes added; every succeeding year the ground is opened out and manured about the commencement of the rains, the soil being replaced and levelled about the close of the rains; by the fourth year the stem begins to appear and has about twelve leaves, it is distinctly visible by the fifth year, when the tree has about twenty-four leaves; the spathes commence to be formed by the sixth year, and plant is then 1 to 2 feet above the ground, but in exceptionally favorable climates and soils it may be three or four times that height; the first few spathes do not form flowers or fruits, but presently they begin to do so, and in three or four more years the tree is in full bearing; about six months after flowering the fruits set, and by the end of the year they are fully ripe; as a rule a cocoanut throws out a spathe and a leaf every month; each flowering spike yields from ten to twenty-five nuts; the produce of a tree in full health and properly tended may be from fifty to one hundred and even two hundred nuts a year, the yield depending greatly, on the suitability of the climate and soil for cocoanut cultivation; a safe average would be one hundred nuts a year to each tree in full bearing; in good situations, the fruit is gathered four or five times in the course of the year; fruit-bearing power is improved by taking toddy [q.v.] during first two years of its productiveness only. The tree continues bearing from seventy to eighty years; it is in its highest vigour from twenty-five to thirty years of age, but will attain the age of a hundred years. Cocoanut trees have great enemies in the shape of two beetles; one of these is a large curculio, rhynchophorus sach, called the red beetle, nearly as large as the english stag-beetle; the other is the oryctes rhinoceros, so called from its projecting horn; the red beetle is so called from the red mark on the upper part of its breast; its attacks are on the nut, but those of the rhinoceros beetle are on the terminal bud of the palm stem; when so injured the bud dies, and the crown of the leaves falling off, leave the cocoanut tree a mere bare stem; the same result occurs to other palms, the palmyra, the areca, in which the top bud, or cabbage [q.v.], as it is called, is destroyed. Cocoanut palms may be easily transplanted, and indeed often with advantage; some of the fibrous roots should be cut away, and manure, together with a little salt, placed in the pit in which it is intended to plant the tree.—"*c*" There is scarcely a part of the plant which cannot be applied to some use; the chief are the oil from the nuts, the nuts themselves, the fibres, the leaves, the stem, and the toddy; see below; the natives say that its uses are as numerous as the days of the year. Friar jordanus, the quilon bishop of the fourteenth century, has the following:—"first of these is a "certain tree called nargil, which tree every month in the year "sends out a beautiful frond like a date palm tree, which frond "or branch produces very large fruit, as a big as a man's head; "there often grow on one such stem thirty of those fruits as "big as I have said; and both flowers and fruits are produced "at the same time, beginning with the first month and going "up gradually to the twelfth, so that there are flowers and "fruit in eleven stages of growth to be seen together; a wonder! "and a thing which cannot be well understood without being "witnessed; from these branches and fruits is drawn a very "sweet water; the kernel at first is very tender and pleasant to "eat, afterwards it waxeth harder, and a milk is drawn from "it as good as milk of almonds, and when the kernel waxeth "harder still, an oil is made from it of great medicinal virtue; "and if any one careth not to have fruit, when the fruit-bearing "stem is one or two months old, he maketh a cut in it, and "bindeth a pot to this incision, and so the sap, which would "have been converted into fruit, drops in, and it is white like "milk and sweet like must, and maketh drunk like wine, so "that the natives do drink it for wine, and those who wish not "to drink it so, boil it down to one-third of its bulk, and then it "becometh thick like honey, and 'tis sweet and fit for making "preserves like honey, and the honeycomb; one branch gives "one potful in the day and one in the night on the average "throughout the year, thus five or six pots may be found hung "upon the same tree at once; with the leaves of this tree they "cover their houses during the rainy seasons; the fruit is that "which we called nuts of india; and from the rind of that fruit "is made the twine with which they stich their boats together "in those parts; there is another tree of a different species, "which like that gives all the year round a white liquor pleasant "to drink, which tree is called tari; there is also another "called belluri, giving a liquor of the same kind, but bitter." Ludovico di varthema says:—"ten useful things are derived "from this tree; the first utility is wood to burn; nuts to eat; "ropes for maritime navigation; thin stuffs, which, when they "are dyed, appear to be made of silk; charcoal in the greatest "perfection; wine; water; oil; and sugar; and with its leaves "which fall, that is, when a branch falls, they cover the houses; "and these ward off water for half a year."—"*d*" Several distinct varieties:—king cocoanut, very handsome, of a golden orange color, never attaining to more than fifteen or twenty feet high; dwarf cocoanut, about fifteen feet; bramin cocoanut producing large handsome nuts, deep golden color, esteemed for milk they contain, considered inferior as regards quality of kernel; and others [taur].——**(1)** The principal products of the cocoanut palm are for convenience shown separately below.——*Arrack* (سیندھی کی دارو - sendhíkídárú, Hind.; റാക്ക് - rákku, Mal.; தென்னங்கள்ளுச்சாராயம் - tennangalluççáráyam, Tam.). This distilled from cocoanut toddy after it has undergone fermentation and becomes sour [sharaub]. See sep. title.——*Branch* (മട്ടൽ - mattal, Mal.; தென்னமட்டை - tennamattai, Tam.). The thin branches form a substitute for tooth-brush, the ends being beaten so as to make them soft.——*Cabbage* (ناریل کا کرد - nárelkákrud, Hind.; കുമ്പ് - kúmpu, Mal.; தென்னங்குருத்து - tennanguruttu, Tam.). The terminal bud at summit of tree. A tender vegetable when cooked; but cannot be obtained without destroying the tree.——*Cotton* (ناریل کی روئی - nárelkíruí, Hind.; టెంకాయచెట్టుపత్తి - tenkáyachettupatti, Tel.; അടിച്ചാര - atiççára, Mal.; தென்னம்பஞ்சு - tennambañju, Tam.). This is a soft, downy, light brown-colored substance, found on the outside of the lower part of the compound leaves of the cocoanut tree, where they spring from the stem and are partially covered with what is called punnauday [q.v.], or coarse vegetable matting [q.v.] of the tree. The cocoanut cotton is used for stopping blood in cases of wounds, bruises, leech-bites, &c.——*Fibre* (ناریل کا نار - nárelkánár, Hind.; ചെകരിനാർ - chekarinár, Mal.; தேங்காய்நார் - téngáynár, Tam.). The fibres covering the nut are when separated known as coir [q.v.]. The coir is separated from the shell by forcing the nut upon the point of an iron spike or sharp piece of hard wood, fixed firmly in the ground. In this manner the husks of 1,000 nuts can be separated from the shells by one man daily. These husks are subsequently thrown into salt or fresh water to soak, or buried in sand within the influence of sea-water for six or twelve months. The fibres are then separated from the cellular and other matter by beating with heavy mallets, and in some places by rubbing between the hands also. The various steps of this process differ in some particulars in different places. The coir from the Laccadives is the best. Though its quality varies according to the kind of nut from which it is taken, yet a great deal depends on the mode of its preparation. Good coir is known by its clear yellow color, the filaments being fine and even. The coir is manufactured into cordage of various sizes. It is well known to be one of the best materials for cables on account of its lightness, elasticity, and strength. It is also very durable and little affected by salt water. Numerous instances have been related of ships furnished with cables of this material, riding out a storm in security, while stronger made though less elastic ropes of other vessels have snapped in two, and when even chain cables have given way. Ropes made of it are used over the greater part of the country for almost all purposes. It is much used for stuffing mattresses, cushions, and saddles. The planks of the masulah [q.v.] boats are stitched together by thin ropes of this material. The loose fibre answers well as oakum, not being liable to rot. Of late years, it has been manufactured in England into a great many articles, such as brushes, brooms, matting, door-mats and netting for sheep folds, stair-carpets, table-mats, fancy baskets, and even bonnets and hats. For fibre generally, see Naur.——*Flower* (ناریل کا پھول - nárelkáphúl, Hind.; പൂക്കുല - púkkula, Mal.; தென்னம்பூ - tennambú, Tam.). The flowers contain a powerfully astringent property which is used medicinally. It is from the flower and spathes, before the flower has expanded, that the toddy or palm-wine is obtained.——

Gum (தென்னம்பிசின் - tennambisin, Tam.). Procured in very small quantities and not put to any use.——*Husk* (ناریل کا پوست - nárelkápost, Hind.; ചൊരി - chokari, Mal.; கதம்பை - kathambai, Tam.). Tam. also (téngaymattai), meaning cocoanut + fruit + fibrous husk; (urimattai), meaning stripped + husk. The nuts are enclosed in a thick fibrous husk from which the coir of commerce is obtained by maceration and beating. The husk itself is employed as a scrubbing or polishing brush.——*Jaggery* (ناریل کا گڑ - nárelkágur, Hind.; బెల్లం - bellam, Tel.; ചക്കര - chakkara, Mal.; தென்னம்வெல்லம் - tennamvellam, Tam.). This is yielded abundantly by cocoanut toddy. The sugar is obtained from the pure sweet toddy, drawn morning and evening, by simple evaporation over a slow fire. After being boiled for some time, the liquid becomes like honey [shahad]. By further boiling a coarse looking brown sugar [q.v.] is obtained, which is formed into cakes of various shapes and sizes. These are afterwards dried in smoke, and to preserve them from humidity they are further tied up in dried plantain [q.v.] leaves, each piece by itself. Particular care is taken that the vessels into which the toddy is collected for the above purpose are quite clean, so that it should be pure and free from acidity. It is considered a very valuable addition to choonam [q.v.] in building.——*Kernel* (ناریل کا مغز - nárelkámaghz, Hind.; തേങ്ങ - ténna, Mal.; தேங்காய் - téngáy, Tam.). In its young and green state, the cocoanut contains a clear albuminous fluid, with a sweetish taste and a slight degree of astringency; see Water. But as the nut advances to its full maturity, the fluid disappears, and the hollow is filled by the almond-like dried albumen, which is the germinating organ. This pulp or kernel, when young, can be easily removed by a spoon. It is used grated in curries, or its milk is expressed from it. The white and solid albumen is often cut into ornaments of flowers and fruits, meant to represent the garlands given to visitors of distinction. They are worn by Tamul women at particular festivals. When cut in pieces and dried in the sun, the kernel is called coppray [q.v.], which forms an extensive article of commerce. From the coppray cocoanut oil is expressed; see Oil. The refuse oil-cake, ponnauk [q.v.], forms an excellent manure. Reduced to powder, kernel is used as a tooth powder, and also as antiseptic and disinfectant. Used also as masticatory [charvanam].——*Leaf* (ناریل کا پتا - nárelkápattá, Hind.; തെങ്ങോല - tennóla, Mal.; தென்னோலை - tennólai, Tam.). The full-grown leaves which are pinnate are from 18–20 feet long. These, when split through the middle, are woven into mats [boriyah, chaupa] called cadjans [q.v.], and are employed for thatching bungalows. This thatching is preferred to straw, as lighter, more durable, and not attracting rats and reptiles. Cadjan roofs resist rain better than tiles, if the thatching is put on just before the monsoons. These mats are also used as screens and for sleeping upon. The leaves split into thin strips are used for writing on with a style. The leaves of the palmyra [q.v.] and talipot [q.v.] palms are however preferred for that purpose. The dried, old leaves, are used as torches. The large petioles, midribs of the compound leaves, serve as paddles for canoes or small rafts; yokes, fishing-rods, palings, stakes, wattling, brushes, combs, &c. The finer midribs of the leaflets form strong brooms for the garden or for the decks of ships, lasting longer than those formed of the culms of the common broom-grass [q.v.]. Aristida setacea, retz. The alkaline ash [sujjee khaur] obtained by burning worn-out cadjans is used for washing cloths [dhoby's earth].——*Marine soap* (ناریل کا بیسن - nárelkábesan, Hind.; தேங்காயெண்ணெய்ச்சப்பு - téngáyenneyççappu, Tam.). Soap made with cocoanut-oil, useful for washing linen in salt water. The component parts are soda [sowdoo], cocoanut, lard, and water [sauboon].——*Matting* (پنارا - panára, Hind.; കോച്ചാട - kóççáta, Mal.; தென்னம்பன்னாடை - tennambannádai, Tam.). This is a web-like tissue, formed of strong fibres, holding a position similar to ochrea of the rhubarb tribe, or the pericladium of umbelliferous plants. It does not look unlike coarse, brown cloth, and is somewhat stiff. It is stripped off in large pieces by the shaunaur, who make it serve as a strainer for the toddy; the latter usually contains some impurities as well as insects, these being attracted to it by its sweetness. In some places it is woven into a coarse article of apparel used by fishermen. This punnauday or mattula is nothing more than the so-called cocoanut cotton in its maturity.——*Milk* (ناریل کا دودھ - nárelkádúdh, Hind.; തേങ്ങാപ്പാൽ - ténnáppál, Mal.; தேங்காய்ப்பால் - téngáyppál, Tam.). The milk extracted by pressure from fresh kernel is used in curries and confectionery. When well boiled with rice [q.v.] and some of the kernel, the dish is known as cocoanut conjee [q.v.], and is given to the poor on particular occasions by native christians. The milk is oil in a transition state, or oil in a natural emulsion with vegetable albumen and water. After the hair has been cleansed by soap [sauboon], or other detergent material, this milk is poured on the head and rubbed well into the hair, some smearing even the body with it; it is then washed off by water. This application leaves the hair soft and silky. The milk has been employed in debility, incipient phthisis, and cachexia. In large doses it proves aperient, and in some cases actively purgative. It is one of the best recipes for freckles.——*Nut* (ناریل - nárel, Hind.; തേങ്ങ - ténna, Mal.; தேங்காய் - téngáy, Tam.). The nut, when perfect, is about the size of a child's head, and is covered with a quantity of rough fibre, which, when separated and cleaned, is termed coir [q.v.]. Underneath the fibrous covering is the shell, and in it is contained the kernel and a milky fluid. The shell is very hard and susceptible of a fine polish. On festive occasions, old and well-seasoned nuts are fixed on stakes by the roadside or gates to serve as torches, for which they are well-fitted by the oil within and the fibrous husk without. The ripe nut is sometimes sawn through transversely, the kernel and shell removed, the two halves of the fibrous husk answering as above said as scrubbing crushes for floors and certain articles of furniture. Cocoanuts are hourly broken and offered to the native deities.——*Oil* (नारिकेलतैल - nárikélataila, San.; ناریل کا تیل - nárelkátel, Hind.; کھوپریکا تیل - khoprekátel, Dec.; ತೆಂಗಿನಾಯನ್ನೆ - tenginávanne, Can.; టెంకాయనూనె - tenkáyanúne, Tel.; വെളിച്ചെണ്ണ - veliççenna, Mal.; தேங்காயெண்ணெய் - téngáyenney, Tam.). The freshly-prepared oil is nearly as fluid as water, of a pale-yellowish color, and almost inodorous but after a few days it acquires a peculiar rancid odour and taste; many attempts have been made to divest the oil of this smell, which renders it inapplicable for the perfumers' use, but only with partial success; the oil is solid at low temperatures; the best oil is exported from cochin and the neighbouring ports on the malabar coast. The oil is ordinarily obtained by expression from the dried kernel, chiefly by mill pressure. When the oil is required for edible purposes, the kernel of the fresh nut is taken, rasped and mixed with boiling water; this yields by pressure a milky fluid, which, on being boiled until all the water has evaporated, produces a clear edible oil; only just sufficient water to moisten the pulp is added, as a larger proportion prolongs the operation and deteriorates the product. Each tree is calculated to yield at least two and half gallons of oil per annum. Oil is much used for liniments and other external applications; employed as a local application in baldness and in loss of hair after fevers and debilitating diseases; used internally as a substitute for cod-liver oil, but in such cases it is not the commercial oil, but the oleine obtained by pressure, retined by being treated with alkalies [cauram] and then repeatedly washed with distilled water; its prolonged use internally is apt to disturb the digestive organs and induce diarrhœa. The oil is used for culinary purposes, especially in travancore [yennay]. In the more northern and eastern districts, it is chiefly employed for burning in lamps; it is used largely in england in the manufacture of candles and soap [sauboon]; for the candle maker the stearine is separated from the oleine, the former product being used for candles, for which it is most applicable on account of the high temperature required to fuse it; the oleine is then made over to the soap-boiler for conversion into soap; soap made from cocoanut oil is lighter than water, and consequently floats in that medium, whilst from its being the only soap which will dissolve freely in salt water it is usually called marine soap; in southern india the oil is made into soap by boiling with a proper proportion of dhobies' earth [q.v.], salt [ooppoo], saltpetre [shorah], quicklime [choonam] and water.——*Oil cake* (کھل - khal, Hind.; തേങ്ങാപ്പിണ്ണാക്ക - ténnáppinnákku, Mal.; தேங்காய்ப்புண்ணாக்கு - téngáyppunnákku, Tam.). The refuse or oil-cake after extracting the oil from the kernel; it is considered an excellent food for fattening pigs and poultry; the best manure to young cocoanut trees.——*Porcupine wood* (ناریل کا کھیر - nárelkákhair, Hind.; തെങ്ങിന്തായ്മരം - tennintáymaram, Mal.; தென்னஞ்சேகு - tennañjégu, Tam.). The porcupine wood of commerce is the produce of two palms, the palmyra and the cocoanut, chiefly however of the latter. The wood is either cut longitudinally or transversely. The pieces of speckled wood are very small.——*Root* (ناریل کی جڑ - nárelkíjar, Hind.; തെങ്ങിൻവേർ - tenninvér, Mal.; தென்னம்வேர் - tennanvér, Tam.). The long fibrous roots are made use of as tooth-brushes. They contain an astringent principle. They are used also as brushes for painting with, and are sometimes chewed instead of the areca-nut [q.v.] with the leaf of the betel [q.v.]. A decoction [kwautam] of these roots with ginger [q.v.] and jaggery [q.v.] is considered highly efficacious in remittent and intermittent fevers. This decoction is also employed, mixed with the fresh oil, as a gargle in certain cases of sore mouth and throat.——*Sago* (തെങ്ങിനൂറു - tenninnúru, Mal.; மாவு - mávu, Tam.). A farinaceous substance contained in the stem, a substitute for real sago [q.v.].——*Shell* (نارڑی - nárutí, Hind.; ناریل کا چپا - nárelkáchuppá, Dec.; టెంకాయచిప్ప - tenkáyachippa, Tel.; ചിരട്ട - chiratta, Mal.; கொட்டாங்கச்சி - kottángaççi, Tam.). Tam. also (téngayódu), meaning cocoanut shell. Within the fibrous husk of the nut is the shell, which is very brittle, though its structure somewhat fibrous. Cut in various ways it is formed into cups and drinking vessels, into pictures, funnels and lamps. It is susceptible of a high polish and admits of being turned in an agreeable manner. Those shells which are tolerably circular are used for the bodies of cups and vases, the feet and covers being made of wood and ivory [dant]. Common buttons are also made of the cocoanut shell and are considered better than those of horn, as they do not, like that material, absorb the

50

moisture, which causes horn [sing] buttons to swell and burst. The shell forms a valuable charcoal [adooppkary]. Yields also, when burnt, a black paint [rangh], which, in fine powder and mixed with choonam [q.v.], is used for coloring walls of houses. ——*Spathe* (ناریل کا پالا - nárelkápálá, Hind.; കൊതുമ്പു - kotumpu, Mal.; பாளை - pálai, Tam.). The tough fibrous covering of the blossom. Cocoanut trees of vigorous growth send forth nine, ten, and even twelve clusters of buds every year, but those on which little care has been bestowed and which are consequently feeble, produce only four or five spathes. The old, tough spathe is converted by the Shaunaur into a coffer or light box, which serves to hold the knives and apparatus which he carries with him up the tree. It is also used for making sheathes for daggers and other knives. The natives soak it in water and prepare from it a kind of coarse, short cordage, with which they tie the thatch on their houses, &c.——*Stem* (ناریل کی پیڑ - nárelkíper, Hind.; തെങ്ങിന്തടി - tennintati, Mal.; தென்னமரம் - tennamaram, Tam.). The stem during the period of most abundant bearing, considered to be between ten and thirty-five years' growth, is so soft and spongy at its centre that it is merely used for fences, water-pipes, &c.; but when old, and has ceased to bear fruit, it goes under the name of porcupine wood [q.v.], which, in Ceylon, is converted into chairs, ladies' work boxes, drums, rafters, small boats, spear-handles, and a variety of fancy articles. The living stem is said to possess such elasticity as to cause a cannon ball to rebound and be reflected from it.——*Tenneerk* (ഈർക്കൽ - írkkal, Mal.; தென்னீர்க்கு - tennírkku, Tam.). The woody ridge which runs along the back of the cocoanut leaf. With it natives make baskets for catching fish and brooms; they also use bundles of it as torches.——*Toddy* (ناریلی - nárelí, Hind.; ناریل کی سیندی - nárelkísendí, Dec.; టెంకాయకల్లు - tenkáyakallu, Tel.; തെങ്ങിൻകള്ള - tenninkallu, Mal.; தென்னங்கள்ளு - tennangallu, Tam.). This is obtained from the unexpanded spadix. This spadix, which is compound, is closely enveloped in a dense, tough spathe, which becomes quite ligneous when old. To procure the toddy, the spadix is bound firmly round with the young leaves, or strips of fibre from the under surface of the petiole. This is to prevent the spathe from opening. It is now struck all over with a small piece of wood or the handle of the toddy-knife. This operation of brushing is repeated morning and evening regularly for four, five, or six days. After this, an earthen vessel is tied on to the spadix, two or three inches of the latter having been previously cut off by a sharp knife. The toddy does not begin to exude until the second day and sometimes later. The fluid is then collected morning and evening, the extremity of the spadix being cut a little every day. This cutting is necessary, as the toddy, which is viscid, would otherwise concrete on the wound, and prevent further flow. Fruit is never looked for in the spadix which has been subjected to such treatment [shaunaun]. When taken early in the morning toddy has a pure sweet taste. It is slightly stimulant and gently aperient. Fermenting toddy is used by bakers as yeast, the bread made with it being remarkably light. Toddy is artificially brought to the vinous and acetous fermentations, and in the former state an alcoholic spirit is distilled from it which forms one of the arracks of commerce. One hundred gallons of toddy produce, by distillation, twenty-five gallons of arrack [q.v.]. Eight gallons of sweet toddy, boiled over a slow fire, yield two gallons of a luscious syrup, from which, by further boiling, a coarse brown sugar [q.v.] is produced, known in commerce as jaggery [q.v.]. Good vinegar [caudy] is made from cocoanut toddy, particularly at Mahé.——*Vinegar* (سرکا - sirká, Hind.; കാടി - káti, Mal.; தென்னங்காடி - tennangádi, Tam.). This is the liquid left after toddy has passed through the vinous and acetous fermentations. The acetous fermentation is hastened by the husks of paddy [q.v.]. Used extensively in the making of pickles [caudy].——*Water* (ناریل کا پانی - nárelkápání, Hind.; یلنیر کاپانی - elnírkápání, Dec.; ഇളനീർ - ilanír, Mal.; இளநீர் - ilanír, Tam.). Liquor amnii. This is a liquor contained within the kernel of the cocoanut while it is yet growing, and is refreshing and extremely pleasant to the taste, particularly in hot weather. It may be drunk to almost any quantity without injury, and is considered by the native doctors as a purifier of the blood. As the kernel approaches to maturity the liquor is diminished in quantity, becoming somewhat more sharp and a little aperient in its best state. It has the appearance of water with a small admixture of milk in it. It is used by bricklayers in preparing a fine whitewash. It is also employed in making the best and purest kind of castor [aumanac] oil, a certain portion of it being mixed with the water in which the seeds are boiled.——*Young leaf* (ناریل کا کابا - nárelkágábá, Hind.; കുരുത്തോല - kuruttóla, Mal.; குருத்தோலை - kuruttólai, Tam.). The unexpanded leaves are used in making ornaments for decorating houses, arches, and places of worship on festive occasions [coondal]. These ornaments are in the forms of birds, crowns, flowers, &c. Mats of fine quality are made in the Laccadives from leaves just before they unfold, cut out of the heart of the tree; involving the loss of the bunch of fruit which accompanies. The leaves of the chowk or unproductive trees are chiefly employed. These mats are used by W. coast islanders for the sails of their smaller boats.——**(2)** *Double cocoanut* (جہازی ناریل - jaházínárel, Hind.). Title from size and appearance. Hind. means ship cocoanut as coming from sea. Same as Sea-cocoanut.——*Maldive cocoanut* (مالدیپ کا ناریل - máldíbkánárel, Hind.). Same as Sea-cocoanut.——*Sea-cocoanut* (अब्धिनारिकेल - abdhinárikéla, San.; نارجیل بحری - nárjílibahrí, Ar.; نارگیل بحری - nárgílibahrí, Pers.; دریا کا ناریل - daryákánáriyal, Hind.; دریا کا ناریل - daryákánárel, Dec.; సముద్రపుటెంకాయ - samudraputenkáya, Tel.; കടൽതെങ്ങ - katalteuna, Mal.; මූදුපොල් - múdupol, Singh.; கடற்றெங்கு - kadattengu, Tam.). Title from being often found floating in sea. San. from (abdhi, san. sea + nárikéla, san. cocoanut, cocos nucifera, linn.). Ar. from (nárjíl, ar. cocoanut + bahr, ar. sea). Hind. from (daryá, hind. sea + náriyal, hind. cocoanut). Tel. from (samudra, san. sea + tenkáya, tel. cocoanut, cocos nucifera, linn.). Singh. from (múdu, singh. sea + pol, singh. cocoanut). Tam. from (kadal, tam. sea + tengu, tam. cocoanut tree). Hind. also (jaházínárel), meaning ship + cocoanut. Dec. also (zahrínárel), meaning poison cocoanut; inner husk reckoned an antidote more efficacious than bezoar stone. Mal. also (akráritennu). Title otherwise Coco de mer, Double cocoanut, Jahauzinaurel, Maldive cocoanut, Zahrinaurel. Botanically Lodoicea seychellarum, labill., palmaceæ [vricsham, 149]. Alias Cocos maldivica. Very tall tree confined to the seychelles islands; fruit resembles two cocoanuts fastened together; it is convex on one side, and almost flat on the other, oblong, and somewhat pointed at both ends; shell dark-colored and contains kernel, not unlike that of ordinary cocoanut, but drier and more insipid; old belief was that fruit was produced on a palm [taur] growing below sea; fruit formerly in repute as a universal antidote, now only an object of curiosity; shells are made into drinking cups and scallops, used by devotees. No other common species here.

CODA (കോട - kóta, *Mal.*; கோடு - kóda, *Tam.*). Crooked, west, border [code].——*Codacherry* (കോടശ്ശേരി - kótashshéri, Mal.). From (kóta, mal. west + chéri, mal. village). Mountain; Cochin state, Moocoondapooram tal.; lat. 10° 21′ to 10° 22′; long. 76° 23′ to 76° 28′; from Ernacolum N.N.E. 26 miles; from Irinyaulacode E. 10 miles; from the sea E. 16 miles. Mountainous tract, extending along the Chaulacoody river, containing timber. Feverish, inhabited by a few jungle people, 2,000 feet in elevation. Elephants [q.v.] and bison [gowr] abound.——*Codaga* (ಕೊಡಗ - kodaga, Can.). From (kuda, tam. west). The Coorg language or tribe [bhaushay, jauty].——*Codambaukam* (கோடம்பாக்கம் - kódambákkam, Tam. kódambákam *). From (kódam, tam. border + pákkam, tam. village). Village, Railway station; Chingleput dist., Sydapett tal.; pop. 2,206; acres 1,471; lat. 13° 03′; long. 80° 16′; height 28 feet; from Sydapett N. 1¾ miles; from the sea W. 4½ miles.——*Codavanaur* (கொடவனாறு - kodavanáru, Tam.). From (kudavu, tam. crookedness + áru, tam. river). River; Madura dist., Dindigul tal. Rises in the Bhootamullay hills. After fertilizing the tableland of Patchalore is joined four miles from its source by the Kullaur, from the Valrangatty hill. Thence it flows S.E. 3½ miles; E. by N. 2 miles, through a narrow wooded valley; is joined by the Collooparay stream running s. from the tableland of Periyaur; then flows in a winding course easterly, obstructed by rocks, and precipitates itself down the mountains to the N.E. of Manalore; thence skirting the hills a short distance through a deep forest, it enters the plains, and joined by a large rivulet from the Audalore hill four miles W. of Auttore, winds past the above place. Subsequently joins the Cauvery. To its junction with the Kullaur, it is known as the Oomaiyaur. In the rainy season it is very deep and rapid. Principal tributary is the Vagatchay [aroovy].——*Coday* (கோடை - kódai, Tam.). From (kodumai, tam. severity). Hot season. For seasons generally see canlam, caur, and caurtey.——*Codoo* (കൊടു - kotu, Mal.; கோடு - kódu, Tam.). Bent.——*Codoon* (கொடும் - kodum, Tam.). Rough; applied to Tamul, as opposed to the Shen.——*Codoonga cutty* (കൊടുങ്ങക്കത്തി - kotunnakkatti, Mal.). From (kodu, mal. bent + katti, mal. knife). The knife worn for defence by the Nayars of Malabar, fastened to a hook attached to a leathern girdle at the back of the body.——*Codvaul* (கொடுவாள் - koduvál, Tam.). From (kodu, tam. bent + vál, tam. a saw). Sickle [arivaul].——*Codyartanaur* (கொடியர்த்தனாறு - kodiyarttanáru, Tam.). From (kodiya, tam. cruel + arattan, tam. mars, the red planet + áru, tam. river). River; Madura district, Pulney talook. Tributary of the Tenaur. Rises in the Pulneys and flowing westerly receives, about four miles from its source, a large stream from the Cowdamully range on the right. Leaving the hills, and after a tortuous course of 25 miles during which it receives numerous large mountain streams it is joined at Mungaputty by the Cheggataur, after which it is known as the Tenaur.

CODACHAUDRY (ಕೊಡಚಾದ್ರಿ - kodachádri, *Can.*). From (kutacha, san. the tree, holarrhena antidysenterica, wallich + adri, san. hill). Mountain; South canara dist., Coondapore tal.; trig. station lat. 13° 51′ 24·48″ N.; long. 74° 54′ 32·56 E.; height 4,411 feet; from Coondapore N.E. 19 miles; from Mangalore N. 68 miles; from the sea E. 17 miles. Peak of the Western ghauts [q.v.], forming boundary between Shimoga district of Mysore state, and Coondapore talook. A well-known landmark. On the Mysore side it rises 2,000 feet from the plateau. Towards the west it falls precipitously to the plain of Canara for 4,000 feet, and affords a view as far as the sea. Half-way up is a temple to Hully deva. It used to be known to mariners as False barcelore peak [barcelore].

CODAY (கொடை - kodai, *Tam.*). From (kodu, tam. to give). Charity. Prefix in place names, as in Codavausal, meaning charity + gateway.——*Codavausal* (குடவாசல் - kudavásal, Tam.). From (above + vásal, tam. entrance); charity place. Otherwise Codavoyil.—"*a*" Deputy tahsildarry, Tanjore district. Pay Rs. 70.—"*b*" Town, Deputy tahsildar's station; Tanjore dist., Nunnilam tal.; pop. 7,785; acres 1,706; lat. 10° 52′; long. 79° 31′; from Combaconam S.E. 9½ miles; from Madras S.S.W. 160 miles; from Mayavaram S.S.W. 20 miles; from Munnargoody N. 14 miles; from Negapatam W.N.W. 25 miles; from Nunnilam W. 8½ miles; from Tanjore E.N.E. 24 miles. Two old temples, Shiva and Vishnoo. Former cusbah [q.v.] of talook now merged in Nunnilam talook.

CODAY (குடை - kudai, *Tam.*). Umbrella. Made of screw-pine [q.v.], palmyra [q.v.], talipot [q.v.], areca [q.v.], &c. Plant first term, from form of leaves or use. Ex., where transl. is of second term:—Acacia tomentosa (kudaivél), acacia; Chloris barbata (kudaippul), grass; Corypha umbraculifera (kudaippanai), borassus flabelliformis. See gloss. paragraphs.——*Codapanay* (குடைப்பனை - kudaippanai, Tam.). Means umbrella palm; from use made of leaves. Same as Talipot.——*Coday cull* (ಕೊಡೆಕಲ್ಲು - kodekallu, Can.; குடைக்கல் - kudaikkal, Tam.). Vernacular means umbrella + stone. Ortholithic stone with a wide cross slab. The European dolmen [aursham, paundoo cull].

CODAYAUR (കോതയാർ - kótayár, *Mal.*). From (gódá, san. water-giving + áru, mal. river). River; Travancore state, Pudmanaubhapooram division, Cullcoolam and Vilvancode talooks. Rises in the Moolautchy mountains. Its course is at first south-westerly through a wild and wooded tract. It flows into the Tamrapurny, 14 miles from its mouth. Length, 20 miles. Its banks are precipitous and bed rocky. During the latter part of its course, the stream becomes more tranquil and for a short distance rafts may be floated upon it. Several waterfalls are formed by it during its course, two of which are upwards of 40 feet in height. One of the waterfalls is near Tirparapp, near which stands a very ancient Shiva temple. There was a project to divert the water of this river southwards, so as to irrigate Cullcoolam and Yerraneel talooks, but the scheme was subsequently given up [aroovy].

CODE (कोटि - kóti, *San.*; ಕೋಡು - kódu, *Can.*; കോട്ട - kótu, *Mal.*; கோடு - kódu, *Tam.*). From (kut, san. to curve). Summit of a hill. Suffix in place names as Palcode, meaning milk + summit; Pullicode, meaning caste so called + summit [coda, gode].——*Codicondah* (కొడికొండ - kodikonda, Tel.). From (kodi, tel. peak + konda, tel. hill). Village; Anantapore dist., Hindoopore tal.; pop. 1,198; lat. 13° 50′; long. 77° 49′; from Anantapore S. 58 miles; from Hindoopore E. 19¼ miles. Formerly a flourishing head-quarter town. The ruins of the jail, talook cutcherry [q.v.], court, and judge's bungalow can still be seen. The small rock is fortified and has a needle-like projection on the summit forming a conspicuous landmark; whence the name. Is on right bank of Chitrauvaty.

CODY (ಬಳ್ಳಿ - balli, *Can.*; കൊടി - koti, *Mal.*; கொடி - kodi, *Tam.*). Flag, creeper.——**(1)** Plant first term often joining two genera. Ex., where transl. is of second term. Barleria prionitis (kodippasalai), basella; Cæsalpinia coriaria (kodivélam), acacia; Citrus medica, var. medica proper (kodimáthalai), punica granatum; Derris scandens (kodippungu), dalbergia lanceolaria; Ipomæa hederacea (kodikákkattán), clitoria ternatea; Pergularia minor (kodisambaugi), michelia champaca; Sarcostemma brevistigma (kodikkalli), euphorbia tirucalli; Vitis vinifera (kodimundiri), anacardium occidentale. See gloss. paragraphs.——**(2)** Plant second term. Ex., where transl. is of first term:—Aristolochia indica (garudakkodi), braminy kite; Artabotrys odoratissimus (manóranjanballi), mind + to please; Barleria prionitis (vettilaikkodi), piper betel; Cardiospermum halicacabum (agniballi), fire; Cocculus villosus (káttukkodi), wild; Convolvulus sp. (gauriballi), the goddess; Dæmia extensa (ugurusuttuballi), whitlow; Hemidesmus indicus (párgodi), milk; Heptapleurum venulosum (pisukkodi), unctuous; Memecylon amplexicaule (ollekodi), good; Methonica superba (shivaraktiballi), shiva red; Mucuna pruriens (náyisonaguballi), dog + writhing; Piper betel (ilaikkodi), leaf; Pothos scandens (adikebíluballi), areca nut + hedge; Pterolobium indicum (bádabakkaballi), fence + lean; Rubia cordifolia (shávalgodi), cock; Sarcostemma brevistigma (sómaballi), moon; Smilax pseudochina (káttukkodi), wild; Trichosanthes cucumerina (kádáduballi), jungle + sheep; Vitis indica (sambáraballi), spicery; Vitis quadrangularis (sanduballi), joint. See gloss. paragraphs.——**(3)** *Codicaul* (கொடிக்கால் - kodikkál, Tam.). From (above + kál, tam. post). A betel-vine garden.——*Codicaul vellaulan* (கொடிக்கால்வெள்ளாளன் - kodikkálvellálan, Tam.). A class of Vellaular who cultivate betel [janty].——*Codishaunty* (കൊടിശാന്തി - kotishánti, Mal.). From (koti, mal. flag + shánti, mal. priest). The highest priest in a temple.

COFFEE (बुंद - búnda, *Mahr.*; شجرة القهوة - shajaratulkahwah, *Ar.*; درخت قهوه - darakhtikahwah, *Pers.*; بن کا جهاڑ - bunkájhár, *Hind.* and *Dec.*; کوپی - kopi, *Malay*; ಕಾಪಿಗಿಡ - kápigida, *Can.*; ಕಾಪಿಗಿಡ - kápigida, *Too.*; కాపిచెట్టు - kápichettu, *Tel.*; കാപ്പി - káppi, *Mal.*; කෝපි - kópi, *Singh.*; காப்பிச்செடி - káppiççedi, *Tam.*). Title from arabic through malay. Ar. from (shajar, ar. tree + kahwah, ar. coffee). Pers. from (darakht, pers. tree, &c.). Hind. from (bun, ar. coffee berry + jhár, hind. tree). Can., &c., from arabic. Hind. also (bunkafí), meaning coffee seed. Malay also (káváh). Can. also (bondagida); (búnugida), meaning coffee plant. Mal. also (bunnu). Title otherwise Arabian coffee. Botanically Coffea arabica, linn., rubiaceæ [vricsham, 71]. Alias Coffea laurifolia, vulgaris. Large erect bush, quite smooth in every part; leaves oblong-lanceolate, acuminate, shining on the upper side, wavy, deep green above, paler below; stipules subulate, undivided; peduncles axillary, short, clustered; corolla white, tubular, sweet-scented, with a spreading five-cleft limb; anthers protruded; berries oval, deep purple, succulent, two-seeded. Native of africa of the region between the 10th and 15th degrees of north latitude, but thrives anywhere in a suitable soil and locality within the tropics; it was in use in persia a.d. 875, and avicenna fully describes it circa a.d. 1000; introduced here, and now very common in a cultivated state on the west side of the presidency, and run wild in some forests. The young fruit, which is red on ripening, is about the size of a small cherry, each containing two seeds, closely united; these, on being separated, constitute the coffee berries of commerce, and on being ground and roasted, the coffee powder of european shops. The value of commercial coffee depends upon the texture and form of the berry, the color and flavor; coffee powder contains in the raw state, about 0·75 per cent. of caffeine, reduced to 0·25 in the process of roasting, 10 to 13 per cent. of fat, 13 of nitrogenous substances, and between 6 and 7 of salts, potassium, magnesium and calcium in combination with phosphoric acid and chlorine. The plant was brought across the red sea from abyssinia and cultivated on the mountains of arabia as late as about the year 1450, less than half a century before the discovery of america and the passage to india by the cape; its product was introduced into europe at venice about 1615, at marseilles 1641, london 1652, and paris 1657; the plant was introduced into southern india more than two centuries ago by a mahomedan pilgrim, bababooden [q.v.]; this man, on his return from a pilgrimage to mecca, brought a few berries with him, and taking up his abode on the hills in western mysore, which still bear his name, planted them near his hut; from the trees thus raised by the fakeer bababooden, most of those cultivated in native gardens in mysore and coorg have been derived; for a long time the culture was entirely in the hands of natives, but about fifty years ago it began to attract the attention of europeans; since that time the industry has been taken up by european capitalists. The elevation at which the plant can be most profitably cultivated in southern india varies from 2,000 to 4,000 feet above sea-level, and the average annual rainfall of the coffee zone is from 80 to 100 inches; but the greater portion of this occurs during the south-west monsoon, so that in most districts there is a long dry season; the chief coffee districts here are mysore, coorg, wynaud, the neilgherries, and travancore, all sections of the western ghaut [q.v.] range, but there are also numerous estates on other isolated hill ranges, such as the shevaroys, anamullays, &c. For cultivation ground prepared in south from caurtigay or november to auny or june, on w. coast from macaram or january to maidom or april; the jungle is felled and burnt and pits 18 inches cube made 5–6 feet apart; seed sown in south in tye or january, on w. coast in toolaum [mausam] or october and vrishchicam or november; in nursery beds the seed being laid 2 or 3 inches apart; after transplanting to pits land is kept free of weed; failure in first planting is supplied; the plants when they have attained the height of 2–3 feet are topped to promote lateral growth; when the tree is bearing pruning is required every year to remove old wood; full grown crop shows bunches of red berries at each joint that is about 4 inches apart along the primaries; the trees begin to bear during the third year; ripe berries are picked by hand; they are then passed through a pulper to remove the pulp; the seeds are then washed and dried; the seeds are sent to market about four weeks after being picked. The crops have suffered much of late years from a disease called the coffee blight, which is caused by a fungus, hemileia vastatrix, spreading over the leaves, whose functions it completely destroys, resulting in a failure of the coffee crops; no cure has as yet been discovered. Medicinally the effect of the coffee alkaloid is to stimulate the nervous system; it increases the action of the heart, kidneys and skin, its diaphoretic property aiding its generally stimulating effects in rendering its use desirable in hot climates and hot weather [char, sharb]; it has the power of removing drowsiness and of retarding the access of sleep for some hours, and is prescribed in various derangements of the viscera and in nervous headaches; a strong decoction of coffee is capable of arresting diarrhœa; it is given to disguise the taste of nauseous medicines, particularly quinine [koinab], senna [q.v.], and epsom salts [bhaidy ooppoo]; a strong decoction allays the severity of a paroxysm of spasmodic asthma; in poisoning by opium [aphainam] or other narcotic poisons, a strong infusion without milk or sugar is an effectual stimulant; it is also advantageously given in the depression after drunkenness. The decoction of coffee berries is used as an ordinary drink like tea [q.v.] all over the world. Wood white, moderately hard, close-grained; pores very fine and extremely fine; medullary rays fine, numerous. Cultivated species other than the arabica are Wightiana, w. & a., in arid places from coorg to travancore, fruit much broader than long, with a deep furrow; and Travancorensis, w. and a., occurring in travancore, fruit broader than long. Liberian coffee is coffea liberica, hiern., natives of west tropical africa, taller and stronger than arabica, yielding a larger leaf and berry.

COILCOONTLA (కోయిలకుంట్ల - kóyilakuntla, *Tel.* koilkuntla *). From (koyila, tel. temple + kunta, tel. pond).——**(1)** Talook; Kurnool district. Tahsildar's pay Rs. 225. Area 572 square miles. Population 86,544. Language Teloogoo. S. of district. Bounded N. by Nundiaul talook, E. by Sirwail talook, S. by Jummalmudoogoo talook of Cuddapah district, and Tadpatry talook of Anantapore district and W. by Putticondah talook. Bunganapully jagheer is at W. end. The western and southern portions are hilly and gravelly, the hills being flat-topped as at Ooppalapaud and Aulvacondah. The eastern half of the talook and the plains about the Coondair are of black cotton soil [regar]. The chief products are white cholum [q.v.], cotton [q.v.], indigo [q.v.], bengal gram [q.v.], and wheat [geung]. Indigo manufacture is the principal industry, cotton and indigo the chief exports. Fine limestone [choonam cull] is procured in the Coondair. Rivers are the Coondair, and its tributaries, Palair, Gollalair, and Zoorrair. Owk timma rauz tank and Timmanayanipett tank are reservoirs formed by damming-up main drainage channels of a watershed at the points of their emergence from a hill gorge. Places of archæological interest:—Aulvacondah, Calgotla, Coilcoontla, Colimigoondla, Condaupoobram, Cumpamulla, Dornipaud, Goolladoorty, Goondoopaupaula, Govindinney, Injaid, Moodigode, Mookmulla, Nandavaram, Nitchenametla, Owk, Persomala, Sowdardinney, Toommalpenta, Vullampaud. Principal trig. station:—Ramavaram. The leading places, &c., in the talook are the following.——*Aulvacondah* (ఆలవకొండ - álavakonda, Tel.). From (áluvu, tel. sweet potato, ipomæa batatas, lam. + konda, tel. hill). Village; pop. 1,677; acres 8,722; lat. 15° 08′; long. 78° 17′; from Coilcoontla S.W. 8 miles; from Kurnool S.S.E. 49 miles. Veerabhadran temple.——*Bodamanore* (బోదమ్మనూరు - bódammanúru, Tel.). From (bódamma, tel. proper name + úru, tel. village). Village; pop. 1,286; acres 3,802; lat. 15° 04′; long. 78° 27′; from Coilcoontla S.S.E. 13 miles; from Kurnool S.S.E. 57 miles. Formerly held by Poligars of Hanoomatgoondam family. After division in seventeenth century, they held this village and under Aurungzeeb obtained four additional. Latter resumed in 1729 by Nawab of Cuddapah. In 1778, Hyder expelled Poligar, Yerra timma reddy, who soon after died leaving no heirs. His widow, Bootchammah, was restored by the Nizam's officers in 1792; but she was deprived of the village in 1796, and received some small inams in land for her maintenance. Her adopted son was held to have no right to the inheritance. ——*Coilcoontla* (కోయిలకుంట్ల - kóyilakuntla, Tel.). See below. ——*Colimigoondla* (కొలిమిగుండ్ల - kolimigundla, Tel.). From (kolimi, tel. furnace + gundu, tel. rock). Village; pop. 871; acres 2,604; lat. 15° 05′; long. 78° 09′; from Coilcoontla S.W. 18 miles; from Kurnool S. 52 miles. Several temples. Five by Chola kings. Four deserted. Annual festival in Narsimhasawmy temple on 14th Veishaukham [mausam] or may.——*Coondair* (కుందేరు - kundéru, Tel.). See sep. title.——*Dornipaud* (దోర్నిపాడు - dórnipádu, Tel.). From (tórana, san. gate + pádu, tel. village). Village; pop. 1,810; acres 7,839; lat. 15° 12′; long. 78° 30′; from Coilcoontla S.E. 9 miles; from Kurnool S.S.E. 50 miles. Inscription.——*Gollalair* (గొల్లేరు - golláléru, Tel.). From (golla, tel. a shepherd + éru, tel. river). River. A rivulet rises on Ooppalapaud plateau to E. of Booragala; a masonry dam sends water to Owk tank. The surplus joins Palair 3 miles E. of Owk [aroovy].——*Goolladoorty* (గుల్లదుర్తి - gulladurti, Tel.). From (gudi, tel. temple + durti, tel. village). Village; pop. 1,701; acres 5,453; lat. 15° 10′; long. 78° 24′; from Coilcoontla S. 5 miles; from Kurnool S.S.E. 50 miles. Residence of branch of Nossam poligar family of Narsimha reddy.——*Nelabilam* (నేలబిలం - nélabilamu, Tel.). From (néla, tel. ground + bila, san. cave). A place of pilgrimage; from Coilcoontla south-west 20 miles. Subterranean cavern 170 feet deep. A perennial spring flows into bowels of the earth. A built staircase to bottom. ¼ mile E. of Bandarlapulley.——*Nossam* (నోసం - nósam, Tel.). See sep. title.——*Ooppalapaud* (ఉప్పలపాడు - uppalapádu, Tel.). See sep. title.——*Owk* (ఔక - auka, Tel.). See sep. title.——*Palair* (పాలేరు - páléru, Tel.). See sep. title.——*Ramavaram* (రామవరము - rámavaramu, Tel.). From (ráma, san. the god + pura, san. town). Village; pop. 532; acres 2,471; lat. 15° 17′; long. 78° 10′; from Coilcoontla W.N.W. 13 miles; from Kurnool S.S.E. 38 miles. Trig. station in lat. 15° 17′; 32·94″; long. 78° 09′ 07·61″; height 1,714 feet; from Coilcoontla W.N.W. 15 miles; from Ramavaram N.W. 1½ miles.——*Sangaputnam* (సంగపట్నము - sangapatnamu, Tel.). See sep. title.——*Sowdardinney* (సవుదరదిన్నె - savudaradinne, Tel.). From (sódarudu, tel. brother + dinne, tel. mound). Village; pop. 921; acres 2,672; lat. 15° 14′; long. 78° 21′; from Coilcoontla W. 1 mile; from Kurnool S.S.E. 44 miles. Temple of Janardanasawmy. ——*Timmanayanipett* (తిమ్మనాయనిపేట - timmánáyanipéta, Tel.). From (timmánáyadu, tel. proper name + péta, tel. suburb). Village; pop. 1,458; acres 512; lat. 15° 01′; long. 78° 12′; from Coilcoontla south-west 18 miles; from Kurnool S.S.E. 56 miles. Very large tank. Weekly market on Fridays.——*Yerragoody* (ఎర్రగుడి - erragudi, Tel.). From (erra, tel. red + gudi, tel. temple). Village; pop. 730; acres 4,055; lat. 14° 59′; long. 78° 16′; from Coilcoontla south-west 18 miles; from Kurnool S.S.E. 59 miles. Best tobacco [pogauk] grown in the Presidency. ——*Yerramala* (ఎఱ్ఱమల - erramala, Tel.). See sep. title.——*Zoorrair* (జుఱ్ఱేరు - dzurréru, Tel.). See sep. title.——**(2)** Town, Talook head-quarters; Kurnool dist., Coilcoontla tal.; pop. 3,962; acres 5,172; lat. 15° 14′; long. 78° 22′; from Cumbum W.S.W. 57 miles; from Kurnool S.S.E. 44 miles; from Madras N.W. 198 miles; from Nundiaul S.S.W. 21 miles; from Pyaupaly E. 38 miles. Old fortified town. In eighteenth century given in jagheer to relatives of Cuddapah nawaub. Subsequently captured by the Nawab of Bunganapully and recaptured by Sarfrauz khan, brother of the Cuddapah nawaub. Again beseiged about 1760 A.D., the Poligar having rebelled against the Cuddapah nawaub. Weekly market on Fridays. Grand annual festival in Rungaswamy temple on 14th Veishaukham [mausam] or may.

COIMBATORE * (கோயமுத்தூர் - kóyamuttúr, *Tam.*). From (kóni, tam. the local goddess so called + muttu, tam. pearl + úr, tam. village).——**(1)** Revenue district; situated inland; between 10° 14′ and 12° 19′ N. lat., and between 76° 35′ and 78° 14′ E. long.; bounded N. by Mysore state, E. by Salem and Trichinopoly districts, S. by Madura and Travancore state, W. by the Neilgherries, Malabar district and Cochin state; square miles 7,860; pop. 2,004,839; lang. Tamul and Canarese. Contains rivers Amravatty, Bhawauny, Cauvery, Noyil; mountains Anamullays, Biligherry Rungam hills; sanitaria none. The whole area of the district is represented by the following sub-areas:—Bhawauny talook, Caroor talook, Coimbatore talook, Collegaul talook, Dharaupooram talook, Erode talook, Oodamalpett talook, Pollachy talook, Pulladam talook, and Suttimungalam talook. For general administrative purposes the district is distributed between the following revenue and magisterial officers who have their head-quarters at the places shown. The pay set opposite the subordinate officers gives the grade of the corresponding charge:—Collector, Coimbatore. Sub-collector, Erode, in charge of Erode, Dharaupooram, Caroor and Bhawauny talooks. Head assistant collector, Pollachy, in charge of Pollachy, Oodamalpett and Pulladam. General deputy collector, Suttimungalam, in charge of Suttimungalam and Collegaul. Tahsildars:—Bhawauny, Rs. 150; Caroor, Rs. 175; Coimbatore, Rs. 200; Collegaul—this Tahsildar is also the District moonsif of Collegaul and his consolidated pay is Rs. 250; Dharaupooram, Rs. 200; Erode, Rs. 225; Oodamalpett, Rs. 175; Pollachy, Rs. 175; Pulladam, Rs. 225; and Suttimungalam, Rs. 200. Deputy tahsildars:—Aravacoorchy, Rs. 70, range situated in the south of Caroor talook; Avanashy, Rs. 70, range situated in the north of the Pulladam talook; Caungyam, Rs. 70, range situated in the north of Dharaupooram talook; Coimbatore, Rs. 70, range situated in the south-east of the Coimbatore talook; Mettapolliem, Rs. 70, range situated in the north of the Coimbatore talook; Peroondoray, Rs. 70, range situated in the south-west of the Erode talook; Taulavaudy, Rs. 70, range situated in the north-west of the Suttimungalam talook. Similarly judicial officers:—Judge, Coimbatore; District moonsiffs, Coimbatore with jurisdiction extending over Coimbatore talook and that portion of Pulladam talook lying to the south of the Noyil river, Erode with jurisdiction extending over Erode, Bhawauny, Suttimungalam and that portion of the Pulladam talook to the north of Noyil river, Oodamalpett with jurisdiction extending over Oodamalpett, Pollachy, and part of Dharaupooram talook, Caroor with jurisdiction extending over Caroor and part of Dharaupooram talook, Collegaul with jurisdiction extending over Collegaul talook. Similarly Public works officers:—District engineer, Coimbatore. Contains Registration sub-districts:—Aravacoorchy, Avanashy, Bhawauny, Caroor, Caungyam, Codoomoody, Coimbatore, Collegaul, Dharaupooram, Erode, Ganapaty, Goodalore, Gopichettipolliem, Mettapolliem, Oodamalpett, Peroondoray, Pollachy, Pulladam, Shoolore, Suttimungalam, Taulavaudy. Contains Forest ranges:—Bhawauny, Bolamputty, Collegaul, Jadagam, Mettapolliem, Oodamalpett, Pollachy, Ponautchy, Pulladam, Sholacaray, Suttimungalam, Toonacadav. Contains Municipalities Caroor, Coimbatore, Erode. Contains District board and Talook boards, Coimbatore talook board embracing Coimbatore talook, Suttimungalam talook board embracing Suttimungalam talook, Collegaul talook board embracing Collegaul talook, Erode talook board embracing Erode, Bhawauny, Caroor and Dharaupooram talooks, Pollachy talook board embracing Pollachy, Oodamalpett and Pulladam talooks. The following general references should be made to the preceding volumes:—general geography, I (1) to (29); general ethnology, I (29) to (109); general history, I (110) to (188);

physical geography, II, 1; meteorology, II, 3; geology, II, 8; fauna, II, 21; flora, II, 26; mineralogy, II, 29. The following references in the preceding volumes will furnish details special to the district:—latitudes and longitudes, II, 47; particulars about towns, II, 48; comparative population, II, 172; location of revenue officers, II, 381; revenue settlement of the district, II, 408; registrars' and sub-registrars' stations, II, 420; rain-guage stations, II, 428; police divisions, II, 431; maps published, II, 436; survey topographical lists, II, 443; hospitals and dispensaries, II, 447; head-quarter stations of gazetted officers, II, 461; incidence of taxation, II, 463; weights and measures of the district, II, 509; zemindarries, II, 296. A special gazetteer account of the whole district is given at II, 71. For the detailed topography of the district, reference should be made to the talook notices in the present volume, viz.:—Bhawauny, Caroor, Coimbatore, Collegaul, Dharaupooram, Erode, Oodamalpett, Pollachy, Pulladam, Suttimungalam.——**(2)** Talook, Coimbatore district. Tahsildar's pay Rs. 200. Area 804 square miles. Unsurveyed tracts are 56 square miles in addition. Population 260,811. Languages, Tamul and Canarese. Includes lower slopes of Neilgherries. Situated in W. of district, at foot of Neilgherries which bound it on W. and N.; the Palghaut gap is close to S.W. extremity; Malabar and Cochin bound it on W. and S.; Pollachy and Pulladam talooks bound it on S. and E. and Suttimungalam on N.E. A large open plateau of considerable elevation sloping away from foot of Neilgherries to the south-east. Lambton peak within 6 miles of Coimbatore town. To W. Velliyangherry hills, within 15 miles of Coimbatore town form a defence against S.W. monsoon [q.v.]. Further to S.W. is Palghaut gap, through which in the monsoon rush masses of vapour. On the other side of the narrow gap rise abruptly the spurs of the Anamullays known as the Cootchimullay range, while the peaks of the Anamullays bound the landscape in the south. Traversed by the Bhawauny in the north and the Noyil in the south. The talook itself is no way picturesque. Forests were considerable, but denudation has taken place in Bolamputty valley. Climate pleasant. Elevation is in itself considerable, but chief salubrity is due to S.W. monsoon, through Palghaut gap from end of May. Rainfall is scanty. Soils are derived from the disintegration of the gneiss rocks, interpenetrated with lime [choonam], and in parts enriched by the organic vegetable soils [munn] from the hills. Kankar [q.v.] is abundant, and crystalline limestone [choonam cull] is found. Rock is very near the surface everywhere, and trees are stunted and poor. There are some tracts of black cotton soil [regar] and red loam. On dry black soil two crops are usually raised; cholum [q.v.] in the south-west and cotton [q.v.] in the north-east monsoon. In garden lands the speciality is wheat [geung], largely grown from October to February. Wet cultivation is excellent; giving crops of paddy [q.v.], sugar-cane [q.v.], betel [q.v.], cocoanuts [q.v.], plantains [q.v.], &c. Sugar-boiling is carried on. Paper-making has died out. Tanning [chamrah] is well represented. Weaving is represented by the commonest manufactures. Silk [puttoo] has been attempted, but was a failure commercially, and the worms are liable to suffer from the heat in the summer. Chief exports are wheat, chillies [q.v.], tobacco [pogauk], jaggery [q.v.], and cotton; the first to the Neilgherries, the next three to the West coast, and the last to Bombay. The Noyil and its tributaries supply water by anicuts to channels and tanks. The Kullaur has no anicuts, but earth dams supply two channels. There are besides eleven rain-fed tanks and five jungle streams. Camping grounds:—Coimbatore, Pothanore and Mathoocaray. Proprietary estates:—Caroonjaumy gowndenpolliem, Meilairipolliem, Naickampolliem, Nauchipolliem, Paulatooray, Tumbagowndenpolliem, Vellimullayputnam, all held by one person paying Rs. 1,182 peshcush. Places of archæological interest:—Annoor, Bolamputty, Cauramaday, Circarshaumacoolam, Coimbatore, Covilpolliem, Cullmaday, Mettapolliem, Moottconampolliem, Panapolliem, Peroor, Vellalore. Principal trig. stations:—Attimullay, Coimbatore. The following are the leading places, &c., in the talook.——*Agrahaura vellalore* (அக்கிரகாரவெள்ளலூர் - akkiragáravellalúr, Tam.). From (akkiragáram, tam. bramin village + vellam, tam. flood + úr, tam. village). Village; pop. 5,259; acres 3,992; lat. 10° 59′; long. 77° 04′; from Coimbatore S.E. 5 miles. Also called Circar agrahaura vellalore. On Noyil near Pothanore. Wet lands are of high value. ——*Annoor* (அன்னூர் - annúr, Tam.). From (anu, tam. smallness + úr, tam. village). Village; pop. 2,112; acres 3,194; lat. 11° 14′; long. 77° 09′; from Coimbatore N. 19 miles. On road to Suttimungalam. Ancient Shiva temple with inscriptions. Once fortified. Veeraculls [q.v.]. Weekly market.——*Attimullay* (அத்திமலை - attimalai, Tam.). From (atti, tam. fig tree, ficus racemosa, linn. + malai, tam. mountain). Trig. station; lat. 10° 55′ 10·48″; long. 76° 56′ 50·33″; height 2,562 feet; from Coimbatore S.S.W. 6½ miles; from Yettimaday N. 2¼ miles.——*Bolamputty* (போளுவாம்பட்டி - póluvámbatti, Tam.). See sep. title.——*Cauramaday* (காரமடை - kára-madai, Tam. karaimadai *). From (kárai, tam. canthium parviflorum, lamk. + madai, tam. sluice). Village, Railway station; pop. 6,208; acres 2,992; lat. 11° 14′; long. 77° 00′; height 1,207 feet; from Coimbatore N. 16½ miles. Old Vishnoo temple. Large circles of rough boulders. Annual car festival and cattle fair.——*Chettippolliem* (செட்டிப்பாளையம் - shettippálaiyam, Tam.). From (shetti, tam. one of that caste + pálaiyam, tam. fortified village). Village; pop. 3,173; acres 5,920; lat. 10° 55′; long. 77° 05′; from Coimbatore S.E. 7½ miles. On route to Dindigul.——*Coimbatore* (கோயமுத்தூர் - kóyamuttúr, Tam.). See below.——*Coordoomullay* (குறடுமலை - kuradu-malai, Tam.). From (kuradu, tam. hook + malai, tam. mountain). Sanscrit name (agastyagiri), meaning agastyan's hill. Hill; lat. 11° 07′; long. 76° 56′; height 5,033 feet; from Coimbatore N.W. 9 miles.——*Goodalore* (கூடலூர் - kúdalúr, Tam. gúdalúr *). From (kúdal, tam. junction + úr, tam. village). Village, Railway station; pop. 2,299; acres 4,669; lat. 11° 09′; long. 76° 59′; height 1,430 feet; from Coimbatore N. 10½ miles.——*Kullaur* (கல்லாறு - kalláru, Tam.). See sep. title.——*Maroothamullay* (மருதமலை - maruthamalai, Tam.). From (marutham, tam. terminalia tomentosa, bedd. + malai, tam. mountain). Hill, Place of pilgrimage; from Coimbatore N.W. 11 miles.——*Mathoocaray* (மதுக்கரை - mathukkarai, Tam. madukarai *). From (madhu, san. honey + karai, tam. border). Village, Railway station; pop. 2,030; acres 7,001; lat. 10° 54′; long. 76° 59′; height 1,117 feet; from Coimbatore S. 6½ miles. Weekly market.——*Meilairipolliem* (மைலேரிப்பாளையம் - mailérippálaiyam, Tam.). From (mayiléri, tam. skanda, the peacock rider + pálaiyam, tam. fortified village). Shrotriem village; pop. 1,716; acres 2,038; lat. 10° 52′; long. 77° 04′; from Coimbatore S.S.E. 9¾ miles. A salubrious climate.——*Mettupolliem* (மேட்டுப்பாளையம் - méttuppálaiyam, Tam.). See sep. title.——*Noyil* (நொய்யல் - noyyal, Tam.). See sep. title.——*Peroor* (பேரூர் - perúr, Tam.). See sep. title.——*Poothoor* (புதூர் - puthúr, Tam.). From (puthu, tam. new + úr, tam. village). Village; pop. 2,004; acres 2,122; lat. 10° 52′; long. 76° 57′; from Coimbatore S.W. 10 miles.——*Pothanore* (போத்தனூர் - póttanúr, Tam.). See sep. title.——*Shinganallore* (சிங்காநல்லூர் - shingánallúr, Tam. singánallúr *). From (shingamma, tam. proper name + nal, tam. good + úr, tam. village); originally a bramin inam granted by shingammaul. Sanscrit name (simhapurí), meaning lion + town. Village, Railway station; pop. 8,719; acres 6,100; lat. 11° 00′; long. 77° 06′; height 1,242 feet; from Coimbatore E. 5¼ miles. Once entirely inam now ryotwarry. Town and fort destroyed by Mahrattas. Recovered under British rule. Now a busy place. ——*Shirmoogay* (சிறுமுகை - shirumugai, Tam.). From (shiru, tam. small + mugai, tam. crowd). Village; pop. 1,318; acres 964; lat. 11° 20′; long. 77° 03′; from Coimbatore N. 23 miles.——*Toodiyalore* (துடியலூர் - tudiyalúr, * Tam.). From (tudi, tam. dance of the seven virgin goddesses + úr, tam. village). Village, Railway station; pop. 1,254; acres 1,483; lat. 11° 05′; long. 76° 59′; height 1,470 feet; from Coimbatore N. 5¾ miles. Large market place.——*Tumbagowndenpolliem* (தம்பக்கவுண்டம்பாளையம் - tambakkavundambálaiyam, Tam.). Means Tumba gownden's fortified village. Zemindarry, Village; pop. 583; acres 701; lat. of village 10° 52′; long. 77° 01′; from Coimbatore S. 9 miles. Shrotriem [q.v.] village. ——*Vellalore* (வெள்ளலூர் - vellalúr, Tam.). See sep. title. ——*Velliyangherry* (வெள்ளியங்கிரி - velliyangiri, * Tam.). From (velli, tam. silver + giri, san. mountain); after keilausam, the silver mountain of shiva. Hill; lat. 11° 00′; long. 76° 44′; from Coimbatore W. 18 miles. A Punchalingam [q.v.] and place of pilgrimage.——**(3)** Deputy tahsildarry, Coimbatore district. Pay Rs. 70.——**(4)** Town, Collector's, Judge's and Talook head-quarters, Railway station; Coimbatore dist., Coimbatore tal.; pop. 46,383; acres 2,308; lat. 11° 00′; long. 77° 00′; height 1,342 feet; from Bangalore S. 140 miles; from Bombay S.E. 600 miles; from Calicut E. 80 miles; from Erode W.S.W. 56 miles; from Madras S.W. 268 miles; from Mangalore S.E. 196 miles; from Ootacamund S.S.E. 32 miles; from Pollachy N. 25 miles; from Seringapatam S. 100 miles; from Suttimungalam S.S.W. 40 miles. Near left bank of the Noyil, in a dry and well-cultivated tract, on declivity and near base of Neilgherries and on the N. of Palghaut gap. Better suited for the residence of Europeans than most towns of the Presidency, having wide streets, good natural drainage, an abundant water-supply, and a cool temperature. An abundant supply of brackish water is available, but on the south side is a tank 3 miles in length. The European quarter is eastward of the town and detached from it. In the time of Hyder the town contained 4,000 houses; but it suffered in Mysore wars. From its position, commanding the approach to Palghaut on the west, and to the Guzzelhutty pass on the north, it was formerly of strategical importance. Originally belonging to the Cheran dominions it fell to the Madura naicks, by whom it was considered one of their chief strongholds, and afterwards to Mysore. Little is known of it till the time of the Mysore conquests. Both Hyder and Tippoo made it their head-quarters several times. It then had a fort. In 1768, the British took it, and again lost it, and in 1783 it was again taken and retaken. In 1790 the Company's forces a third time occupied it, but Tippoo, after a siege of five months, compelled the garrison to surrender. In 1792 provisionally, and in 1799 finally, the town was ceded to the British, and from that time it ceased to be a military station. It became district head-quarters on amalgamation of two divisions in 1805. A palace built by Tippoo sultan, is utilized as a cutcherry [q.v.]. It is a terraced massive building with open quadrangles. The large musjid [q.v.] was also erected by Tippoo. The town is the centre of a considerable trade. It contains a handsome English church. The jail is noted for its plan and management. Three missions are stationed here, viz., the Roman catholic french mission, headed by a Bishop, whose cathedral is a marked object in entering the town by rail; the London mission, whose premises are near the Collector's office; and the Lutheran mission. Trig. station in the Central Jail, Coimbatore tal.; lat. 11° 00′ 38·60″; long. 77° 00′ 39·53″; height 1,441 feet. The following are the travelling distances by road from Coimbatore to different places:—

To	Viâ	Miles and Furlongs.	
Avanashy ...	......	26	2
Bangalore ...	Annoor, Hassanore and Seringapatam.	213	3
Bangalore ...	Guzzelhutty and Seringapatam ...	199	1
Bangalore ...	Collegaul and Shivasamoodram ...	203	5
Bellary	Hassanore and Seringapatam	366	2
Bhawauny ...	Avanashy	63	5
Calicut	Palghaut and Malapooram	115	3
Cannanore ...	Palghaut, Malapooram, Calicut and Tellicherry.	174	4
Caroor	Pulladam and Caungyam	79	3
Caungyam ...	Pulladam	41	6
Cochin	Palghaut	116	7
Collegaul	Hassanore ghaut	114	6
Cuddalore ...	Salem and Ooloondoorpett	220	4
Dencanicottah ...	......	34	7
Dharaupooram ...	Pulladam	50	3
Dindigul	Pulladam and Dharaupooram	106	7
Erode	Avanashy	61	0
Guzzelhutty ...	Dencanicottah	44	0
Harihar	Hassanore, Seringapatam and Shimoga.	320	4
Hassanore ...	Suttimungalam	61	7
Kotagherry ...	Mettapolliem and the Shirmoogay ghaut.	43	5½
Madras	Avanashy, Erode, Salem, Tripatore, Vellore and Poonamallee.	312	2
Madras	Avanashy, Bhawauny, Omalore, Vellore and Poonamallee.	308	0
Madras	Avanashy, Bhawauny, Salem, Tripatore, Vellore and Poonamallee.	310	0
Madura	Dindigul	147	0½
Mettapolliem ...	......	22	6
Mysore	Annoor and Hassanore	124	4
Negapatam ...	Trichinopoly and Tanjore	222	1
Omalore	Avanashy and Bhawauny	109	5
Ootacamund ...	Mettapolliem and the Coonoor ghaut ...	55	0¾
Ootacamund ...	Kotagherry	58	3½
Palamcottah ...	Dindigul and Tirmungalam	242	6½
Palghaut ...	Walayaur	30	7½
Paumben ...	Dindigul, Madura and Ramnaud ...	244	7½
Pulladam ...	......	22	0
Quilon	Palghaut and Cochin	205	0
Ramnaud ...	Dindigul and Madura	218	4½
Salem	Avanashy and Erode	98	5
Salem	Avanashy and Bhawauny	100	4
Seringapatam ...	Guzzelhutty pass	120	4
Seringapatam ...	Annoor, Hassanore and Mysore ...	134	0
Shivasamoodram.	Hassanore and Collegaul	124	6
Suttimungalam.	Annoor	41	3
Tanjore	Pulladam and Trichinopoly	166	1
Tellicherry ...	Palghaut, Malapooram and Calicut ...	160	4
Trichinopoly ...	Pulladam, Caungyam, Caroor and Laulapett.	128	7
Vellore	Avanashy, Erode, Salem, Vaniyambaudy and Pullicondah.	223	6
Vellore	Avanashy, Bhawauny, Omalore and Vaniyambaudy.	227	7
Vellore	Avanashy, Bhawauny, Salem, Vaniyambaudy and Pullicondah.	225	7

COIR (கயிறு - kayiru, *Tam.*). Cocoanut fibre [q.v.].

COKAM (कोक - kóka, *San.*). Imitative term. Cuculidæ family, scansores, insessores, aves [pacshy, 15], of naturalists [jantoo]. Cuckoos. Comprise here:—Cuculinæ or true or parasitic cuckoos; all of which deposit their eggs in the nests of other birds [koel]. Phœnicophainæ, or malkohas, who live on insects, and make their own nests [crow pheasant, jungle parrot].

COKUM-BUTTER (كوكم كا تيل - kúkamkátel, *Hind.*). Product of mate mangosteen [q.v.] plant.

COL (கோல் - kol, *Tam.*). Metal [loham].——*Collan* (கொல்லன் - kollan, Tam.). Ironsmith. The corresponding terms are:—Hind. lohaur; Can. cummaura; Tel. cummara; Mal. collan. The Indian smith sits at the forge, and rises to his feet only when he uses a two-handed hammer. Hence the Tamul proverb:—இளகின இரும்பைக்கண்டால் கொல்லன் குண்டியைத் தூக்கி அடிப்பான்—"When the smith perceives that "the iron is soft, he will raise himself to the stroke" [jauty].——*Collangode* (കൊല്ലങ്കോട് - kollankótu, Mal. kolangód *). From (kollan, mal. a blacksmith + kótu, mal. place).—"*a*" Town; Malabar dist., Palghaut tal.; pop. 2,558; lat. 10° 37′; long. 76° 44′; from Calicut E.S.E. 74 miles; from Palghaut S. 10 miles. In Padinyaurattara amshom. Travellers' bungalow built on site of a ruined fort. Formerly seat of petty chieftain, Vengoonauttil numbidy. Family still reside. Cautchancoorchy temple, to Vishnoo. The mantapam [q.v.] and the surrounding wall of Shreecovil or shrine, are painted with incarnations [avatar] of Vishnoo. As a preliminary to yaugam by any Numboory bramin the sacrificer must come first to this temple and receive from the Vengoonauttil numbidy, the moon-plant or Sarcostemma brevistigma, w. & a. [somam], the blackwood or Acacia catechu, willd. [catechu], and the skin of a black antelope [jinka].—"*b*" River; Malabar district, Palghaut talook. Locally called Gayatry nuddy; rises in Collangode bluff or Malaya mountains being N.W. extremities of Anamullays. Joins Ponnany river near Wottapollem station.——*Collat cauran* (கொல்லற்றுக்காரன் - kollattukkáran, Tam.). From (kollaru, tam. trowel + kára, san. door). The Teloogoo is beldar. Bricklayer caste [jauty].

COL (கொல் - kol, *Tam.*). To kill.——*Coleroon* (கொள்ளடம் - kolladam, Tam.). Portuguese corruption; cf. cochin, comorin. Tam. from (kol, tam. to kill + idam, tam. place); place of slaughter from tradition that the workmen were drowned when the temple was built at Shreerungam [tirmangay alwar]. River. The Cauvery divides into two branches at Shreerungam. One is called the Cauvery proper, and the other branching to the left the Coleroon, this having been an artificial diversion. In full flood the Coleroon is now in places nearly a mile wide, whilst the original stream of the Cauvery disappears before reaching the sea. The absence of notice of the Coleroon in Ptolemy's tables is an indication of its modern origin. The Coleroon leaves the main channel at the upper end of Shreerungam, about 10 miles west of Trichinopoly, in lat. 10° 53′ N. and long. 78° 39′ E. After a north-easterly course of about 94 miles, it falls into the Bay of Bengal at Atchaulpooram, 3½ miles from Porto novo, in lat. 11° 26′ N. and long. 79° 52′ E. For the greater part of its length the Coleroon forms the boundary between Trichinopoly and South arcot districts on the left and Tanjore on the right bank. As compared with the Cauvery proper, its course is more direct and its fall more rapid, and consequently it naturally tends to carry off the larger volume of water. To counteract this tendency and maintain the proper water-supply of the Tanjore delta, the great anicut was constructed in 1856 across the channel of the Coleroon by Sir Arthur Cotton. In the same year a second dam, known as the lower anicut was thrown across the Coleroon, 70 miles below Shreerungam, in order to regulate the irrigation of South arcot. This dam consists of a hollow bar of masonry, 8 feet high and as many broad, the interior being filled with sand rammed down. The total length is 1,901 feet and in the rear is an apron of masonry. The lower anicut also feeds the great Veeraunam tank by the Vadavaur channel and by several canals irrigates Tanjore district. In South arcot, the main channels from the Coleroon are the Khan sahib, the Iron company's, the Rajahvycaul, the Bhootangoody, and the Caraugooly canals. The Coleroon is affected by the tide for 5 or 6 miles from its mouth. Boat traffic is considerable. See vol. I, 400. Coleroon beacon is a trig. station, Chidambaram talook; lat. 11° 26′ 31·62″; long. 79° 51′ 18·44″; from Chidambaram E.N.E. 8¾ miles; from Taundavaroya cholaganpettah N.E. 2½ miles; on the seashore.——*Colley* (ಕೊಲೆ - kole, Can.). Killing.——*Colleycull* (ಕೊಲೆಕಲ್ಲು - kolekallu, Can.). Tomb stone in honor of warriors killed in battle [aursham, veeracull].——*Collimullay* (கொல்லிமலை - kollimalai, Tam.). From (kolli, tam. killer + malai, tam. mountain), meaning haunt of wild beasts. Tam. also (valliyam), meaning shepherd village. Sanscrit name (chaturagiri), meaning square mountain, from the conformation. Range of hills; Salem district, Ahtoor and Namcull talooks; lat. 11° 11′ to 11° 30′; long. 78° 19′ to 78° 32′; height 4,663 feet; from Ahtoor S.W. 15 miles; from Salem S.E. 16 miles. For description see vol. II, 84.——*Colliverpan* (கொல்லிவெற்பன் - kolliverban, Tam.). From (kolli, tam. hill, so called + verban, tam. hill-ruler). See vol. I (427). Any ruler of the Cheram country [charitram].——*Colly* (கொல்லி - kolli, Tam.). Mountain in Salem, the modern Collimullays. See vol. I (127); II, 84 [charitram].

COL (கொள் - kol, *Tam.*). Buy.——*Colagam* (ಕೊಳಗ - kolaga, Can.; கொளகம் - kolagam, Tam.). From (above + agam, tam. inside); hollow vessel used in buying.—"*a*" Measure of capacity. 4 bullahs = 1 colagam; 20 colagams = 1 cundaga [alavay, 3c]. About = 3 bushels or 10 cubic feet and 1,500 cubic inches. Used in Bellary. Colagam of Mysore is 560 cubic inches, same as Coodoo and Pothy. Compare Bharnam.—"*b*" Superficial measure [alavay, 2c, d]. Approximate actual value, 1 colagam = $\frac{1}{16}$ acre. Land required to sow one colagam of paddy. See vol. I, 609; II, 508, 516.

COLA (ಕೋಲ - kóla, *Can.*). Jujube [bair].——*Colacumbey* (ಕೋಲಕಂಬೆ - kolakambe, Can.). From (above + kambe, can. a low hill). Village, Hill, River; Neilgherry district, Merkoonaud division; lat. 11° 17′; long. 76° 47′; height 5,601; from Coonoor S.W. 6 miles; from Ootacamund S.S.E. 9 miles. Coffee [q.v.] tract. Waterfall highest on Neilgherries, N. of hill has an unbroken fall of 400 feet. There are cromlechs [azhauram] and sculptured slabs [aroovy].

COLAH (கோலா - kólá, *Tam.*). From (kól, tam. stick); from long slender body and pointed head. Garfish, Garpike. The genus Belone, scombresocidæ, physostomi, teleostei, pisces [matsyam, 37], of naturalists [jantoo]. Bones green; indifferent as food. The species best known to the natives are Green pike, Stork pike. Cf. also Bottle-nosed pike, flying pike, which the natives connect.——*Bottle-nosed pike* (வட்டமூக்குக்கோலா - vattamúkkukkólá, Tam.). Tam. from (vattam, tam. circular form + múkku, tam. nose + kólá, tam. flying fish, exocætus pœcilopterus). Anacanthus barbatus, sclerodermidæ, plectognathi, teleostei [matsyam, 44], of naturalists. Alias Alatarius barbatus; Aluterus barbatus; Balistes barbatus; Pogonognathus barbatus; Psilocephalus barbatus. Body strongly compressed. Dull brown or gray, fins yellow, the caudal with about six vertical or angular dark bands not so wide as the ground-color. Sea. 10 inches. No other common species here.——*Flying pike* (பறவைக்கோலா - paravaikkólá, Tam.). Title from poising in air by long pectoral fins. Tam. from (paravai, tam. bird + kólá, tam. flying fish, exocætus pœcilopterus). Exocætus pœcilopterus, scombresocidæ, acanthopterygii, teleostei [matsyam; 37], of naturalists. Bluish along back, becoming silvery on sides and beneath. Pectoral with many rounded and oval spots, sometimes transversely arranged in bands, in others irregularly placed. Two had black spots up on the dorsal fin; ventral white or with spots. Sea. No other common species here.——*Green pike* (వాలకద్దెర - válakaddera, Tel.; വാളക്കതിരാൻ - válákkatirán, Mal.; பசுங்கோலா - pasungólá, Tam.). Title from green back. Tel. from (válu, tel. long + kaddera, tel. stork pike, belone strongylurus). Mal. from (vál, mal. sword + katirán, mal. the fish, gobius giuris). Tam. from (pasumai, tam. greenness + kólá, tam. flying fish, exocætus poecilopterus). Belone [colah] annulata, scombresocidæ, physostomi teleostei [matsyam, 37]. Alias Belone cylindrica, gigantea, indica, melanurus; Mastacembelus annulatus, choram. Upper surface of head and back green, with steel-blue reflections minutely dotted with black, fading into silvery-white on abdomen. Side of upper jaw of a dark olive, of the lower silvery. Black line passes from upper third of angle of mouth along base of teeth. Cheeks and opercles silvery. Membranes of dorsal caudal, and pectoral fins of light greenish-gray, minutely dotted with black, especially at margins. Anal and ventral anteriorly white, dotted with black. Iris silvery, margin of orbit black. Seas and estuaries. 2 feet. Food of indifferent quality, used by natives.——*Stork pike* (तोलटोला - tóla, Mahr.; بگلہ مچھی - baglahmaççhí, Hind.; వడ్లముక్కు - vadlamukku, Tel.; കോപ്ല - kópla, Mal.; கொக்குமீன் - kokkumín, Tam.). Title from stork-like neck. Hind. from (baglah, hind. paddy bird, ardeola leucoptera + maççhí, hind. fish); from long nose. Tel. from (vadlu, tel. paddy + múkku, tel. snout), from form of the snout. Tam. from (kokku, tam. stork + mín, tam. fish). Tel. also (kaddera). Mal. also (kokku), meaning long beak. Tam. also (úsikkazhutti), meaning needle-necked fish. Title otherwise Long-nosed fish. Belone [colah] strongylurus, scombresocidæ, physostomi, teleostei [matsyam, 37], of naturalists. Alias Belone caudimaculata, strongylura; Esox; Mastacembelus strongylurus. Free portion of tail compressed, much deeper than wide and without any distinct lateral keel; summit of head and back yellowish-green, with minute brown dots, fading into silvery on sides, and white on abdomen; cheeks and opercles silvery; deep blue longitudinal band, bordered beneath by another broader one of silver, passes along posterior half of sides; dorsal with orange along upper edge, it and sometimes anal bright yellow, rays dotted with brown; pectoral and ventral diaphanous, the latter occasionally with a black spot at the base; caudal yellowish or greenish, minutely dotted with black, having round bluish-black spot in centre near root; iris silvery; upper surface of eye bluish-black; seas and coasts; 2 feet.

COLAM (കുളം - kulam, *Mal.*; குளம் - kulam, *Tam.*). From (kuli, mal. to bathe). A bathing pond. Prefix in place names as Colattore, meaning village with the tank [coolam].——*Colair* (కొల్లేరు - kolléru, Tel.). From (kollu, tel. pond + éru, tel. river). Lake; Godavery and Kistna dists., Goodivauda tal.; 158 square miles; lat. 16° 31′ to 16° 47′; long. 81° 08′ to 81° 25′; from Goodivauda N.N.E. 10 miles; from Masulipatam N. 25 miles. A stretch of fresh water, half lake, half swamp, sometimes covering more than 100 square miles in the monsoon. It is of oval shape. In the dry weather it is about 25 miles in length and 10 in breadth. The Boodamair, Ooppootair, Tammilair, and Veyyair, feed it. The last is a tidal river and is its only outlet. At no time is it very deep. Abounds in waterfowl, and fairly stocked with fish. Contains numerous fertile islets many of which are inhabited and cultivated. Many smaller ones are submerged during floods. Cultivators obtain no proprietary rights in their lands, but hold them on annual leases. There are in the lake forty-four villages, which have been nominally reduced to twenty-seven. In 1860 there was considerable cultivation in the lake by means of mechanical contrivances. In 1869 the lake was brought under anicut [q.v.] irrigation, and the Ooppootair was left open as a tidal outlet between the sea and the lake. The Colair has been caused by the land-making activity of the Godavery and Kistna rivers, acting together with the monsoon [q.v.], which blows up an intervening beach or bank of sand between any low-lying unfilled tract and the sea. The lake is thus the natural depression between the Godavery and Kistna alluvial deltas. At the present time its dimensions are gradually being reduced by reclamation and embankments. Two copper plates of the early Pullava dynasty were found in the lake, and legend connects the place with Langoolya gajapaty, king of Orissa from 1237 to 1282. The general of an opposing force, wishing to capture the Gajapaty fort of Colleticote, is said to have cut the Ooppootair channel leading the lake waters into the sea, and to ensure success he sacrificed his daughter [anantapore, royalcheroo], whence the breach is called Perantaul canama to this day. The principal route across the lake is from Ellore to Keicalore.——*Colleticote* (కొల్లేటికోట - kollétikóta, Tel.). From (kolléru, tel. lake so called + kóta, tel. fort). Island; Kistna dist., Goodivauda tal.; pop. 513; acres 956; lat. 16° 38′; long. 81° 20′; from Goodivauda N.E. 24½ miles; from Masulipatam N.N.E. 32 miles. Old fort on an island in Colair lake said to have been built by Langoolya gajapaty, and the site of a battle. Figure of a female deity on a mound.——*Collore* (ಕೊಲ್ಲೂರು - kollúru, Can.; కొల్లూరు - kollúru, Tel.). From (kolanu, can. pond + úru, can. town). Can. also (múkámbi), meaning doorga, the dumb goddess; from tradition that she gave speech to a dumb cottayam king. Sanscrit name (kólápura), meaning jujube tree, zizyphus jujuba, lam. + town.—"*a*" Part of Valasheemey village, Place of pilgrimage; South canara dist., Coondapore tal.; lat. 13° 52′; long. 74° 52′; from Coondapore N.E. 18 miles; from Mangalore N. 69 miles; from the sea E. 14 miles. In a valley at the foot of the Western ghauts. Important temple to Moocaumbicay. Noted car festival.—"*b*" Ghaut; South canara dist., Coondapore tal.; lat. 13° 52′ to 13° 53′ 20″ N.; long. 74° 53′ to 74° 54′ E. Pass in Western ghauts, connecting Mysore with Canara.—"*c*" Village; pop. 371; acres 906; lat. 16° 42′; long. 80° 04′; from Crossoor N.W. 14 miles; from Masulipatam W.N.W. 81 miles. Once held by the Noozveed zemindar and afterwards by Vasireddy vencataudry naidoo. Temples with inscriptions. Old diamond [vajram] mines not worked now, whence came the Kohinoor. The mines were visited by Tavernier in the reign of Aurungzeeb, and by Marco polo and by Nicolo conti.

COLAM (കോലം - kólam, *Mal.*). Distinguish from Cholam; connected with Collam. Beauty.—"*a*" A floor ornament commonly formed at the entrance of a native house. The ornaments are renewed every morning. They contain various devices. In some a temple car is drawn, in others trees, birds, flowers, &c. They are connected with the prevalent ideas regarding the evil-eye. There is a Tamul proverb:—எல்லாரும் தடுக்கின்கீழ் நுழைந்தால் அவன் கோலத்தின்கீழ் நுழைவான்—"If all can hide themselves under a small mat, "he can conceal himself under the colam;" he is so cunning.—"*b*" North malabar. The country subject to the Colattiry rajah extending originally from the Tooracherry river to Chundragherry, later from Tellicherry to Neeleshwar in Canara [charitram, chiracal, keralam].——*Colastry* (കോലത്തിരി - kólattiri, Mal.). Portuguese form of Colattiry or Colatnaud. Distinguish from Calastry [q.v.] of the E. coast.——*Colaswaroopam* (കോലസ്വരൂപം - kólasvarúpam, Mal.). From (above + svarúpa, san. dynasty). The Colattiry rajah.——*Colatnaud* (കോലത്തുനാട് - kólattunátu, Mal.). From (above + nátu, mal. country). Same as Colam or North malabar.——*Colattiry* (കോലത്തിരി - kólattiri, Mal.). From (above + tiri, mal. holy, title). The dynasty of Colam, Colastry, Colatnaud, or North malabar [vellattiry]. Collattiries were the agents of the Permauls who had their head-quarters at Tirvanjicoolam in Cochin. Their jurisdiction extended over lands around Collam as the title signifies. On the departure of the last of Permauls to Mecca, they became independent. They are now respectively the Chiracal rajahs in Malabar and the Travancore rulers [charitram].

COLANDAY (குழந்தை - kuzhandai, *Tam.*). From (kuzhavu, tam. young). Child; also term of address to children of both sexes. Colandasawmy, the son-god, Soobramanyan, is Hindoo 2nd or pers. name, common among non-bramins [peyar].

COLE (ಕೋಲು - kólu, *Can.*; കോൽ - kól, *Mal.*; கோல் - kól, *Tam.*). Stick [kole]. Straight or tall. Plant first term, as:—Cassia occidentalis (kóltagasigida), straight cassia. Dillenia pentagyna (kóltégamara), straight teak. See gloss. paragraphs.——*Colauttam* (கோலாட்டம் - kóláttam, Tam.). From (above + áttam, tam. dance). Generally a game or exercise with two painted and ornamented sticks held one in each hand; in which boys or girls move round in a circle singing in chorus and keep time by dancing and beating their sticks against each other. Jaday colauttam or pinnal colauttam is a special kind of the same exercise in which dancing girls or school boys, by moving in different directions, plait into one rope separate strings held in one hand, while they keep time by beating their sticks against those of their comrades.——*Coiy* (കോലി - kóli, Mal.). From (kól, mal. stick); from size of grain, long and slender. A Malabar paddy [q.v.].

COLLAY (கொல்லை - kollai, *Tam.*). Dry field; especially backyard, or small garden at back of village houses. Suffix in place names, as Pinnacollay, meaning the field with the pinnay tree. Also high ground not capable of artificial irrigation. Plant first term. Ex., where transl. is of second term:—Phaseolus trilobatus (kollaippayaru), phaseolus mungo; Strigia euphrasioides (kollaippalli), lizard. See gloss. paragraphs.

COLLEGAUL (கொள்ளேகாலம் - kollégálam, *Tam.* kollegál *). Sanscrit name (kóhalagálava), meaning cohalan, the sage + gaulavan the sage; from their residence in the place.——

(1) Talook, Coimbatore district. Tahsildar's pay Rs. 150. Area 1,076 square miles. Population 88,533. Language Canarese. N. of district. Bounded N. and W. by Mysore. S. by Suttimungalam and Bhawauny talooks, E. by Bhawauny talook and Salem district, N. and N.E. by Cauvery. Forms part of mysore plateau, and is separated from Coimbatore district proper on the south and east by chains of mountains pierced here and there by passes, of which the chief are Guzzelhutty and Hassanore ghauts on S., Nadoocauvalcauverypooram on E. and Burgoor ghaut [q.v.] on S.E. General elevation from 2,500 to 3,000 feet with peaks and ranges from 4,000 to 5,000 feet. Forest on the south and east are vast and almost untrodden except by wild tribes. The sandalwood [sandal] under process of reservation. Talook is ill-provided with roads. Two main lines run up from the low country, one by Taulavaudy through Mysore territory and the other by Andiyore and Burgoor in Bhawauny talook. The latter road is out of order. Soil generally good. Of the assessed area, 77 per cent. is in the black and red loam series, 23 per cent. being red sand. At the Mautheshwaramullay festivals on Deepauvaly [pundigay, 6d], Shivarautry [pundigay, 6a], and Yoogaudy [pundigay, 6d], there are large cattle fairs. Kowthully, Ponautchy and Shengady, are notable for cattle of the pure Aulambaudy breed [maud]. Garden cultivation is little practised. Wheat [geung] is grown on dry land from July to October, and sugar-cane [q.v.] is a dry land as well as a wet crop. Raggy [q.v.] is also grown on dry land. Mulberry trees are grown to a considerable extent for feeding silkworms [puttoo]. There are few industries other than those of agriculture, cattle breeding, and weaving. There are about 2,000 looms [tarry] in the talook. Silk rearing and weaving are carried on to some extent, and the gold-laced cloths and handkerchiefs of Collegaul are good and well-known; Aulhully, Congarhully, Hindvaudy, and Shinganallore are chief breeding places, and Collegaul is the chief seat of manufacture. The sources of irrigation are the Cauvery, Goondal and Honnal. There are four masonry dams across the Goondal feeding the Polliem, Doddarunganautanhulla, Paupanacaulvye and Danakeray caulvye channels. Oottampully and Terampully are watered by a tank supplemented by the surplus water of a tank in Agra in Mysore province supplied by the Honnal. The Cauvery irrigates about 31 acres of wet land in the village of Danakeray, through which a channel from an anicut across the river, situated within the limits of the village, runs to two jagheer [q.v.] villages in the talook. Irrigation wells are hardly known. Camping grounds, Basavanuttam, near Bylore, Gergagundy, Hanoor and Moordigooddey. The only Jagheerdarry is :—Moollore and Ooginyam, Suttegaul. Rs. 2,236 peshcush. Places of archæological interest :—Aulambaudy, Bastipooram, Collegaul, Martahully, Nulloor, Oojipooram, Shengapaudy, Shinganallore, Shivasamoodram, Suttegaul. Principal trig. stations :—Bandahully droog, Ponautchybett. The leading places, &c., in the talook are the following. ——*Aulambaudy* (ஆலம்பாடி - álambádi, Tam.). See sep. title.——*Ballirungam* (பிளிகிரிரங்கமலை - piligirirangamalai, Tam.). See sep. title.——*Bandhully* (ಬಂಡಹಳ್ಳಿ - bandahalli, Can.). From (banda, can. rock + halli, can. hamlet). Sanscrit name (páshánapurí), meaning rock + town. Village; pop. 1,882; acres 17,454; lat. 12° 10′; long. 77° 23′; from Coimbatore N.N.E. 84 miles; from Collegaul E. 16½ miles. There was a fort on top of hill called Vicramadoorgam. Garrisoned in time of Hyder and Tippoo. The descendants of soldiers are still living. Trig. station; lat. 12° 12′ 13·00″; long. 77° 22′ 42·14″; height 4,276 feet; from Bandhully N.N.W. 3 miles; from Collegaul E.N.E. 15 miles.——*Burgoor* (பருக்கூர் - parukkúr, Tam.). See sep. title.——*Bylore* (ಬೈಲೂರು - bailúru, Can.). From (bailu, can. open plain + úru, can. village). Village, forest tract; pop. 365; lat. 11° 49′; long. 77° 17′; from Coimbatore N.N.E. 59 miles; from Collegaul S.S.E. 25 miles. Sandal-wood plantations.——*Cauvery* (காவேரி - kávéri, Tam.). See sep. title.——*Collegaul* (கொள்ளேகாலம் - kollégálam, Tam.). See below.——*Congarhully* (ಕೊಂಗರುಹಳ್ಳಿ - kongaruhalli, Can.). From (kongaru, can. the people of the konga country + halli, can. (hamlet). Village; pop. 1,620; acres 763; lat. 12° 08′; long. 77° 16′; from Coimbatore N.N.E. 80 miles; from Collegaul E.S.E. 8 miles.——*Coondore* (குண்டூர் - kundúr, Tam.). From (kunru, tam. hill + úr, tam. village). Village; pop. 1,687; acres 937; lat. 12° 08′; long. 77° 04′; from Coimbatore N. 78 miles; from Collegaul W.S.W. 5½ miles. Temple on hill to Prabhalingasawmy.——*Goondal* (குண்டல் - kundal, Tam.). From (gundu, can. round stone). Sanscrit name (bhárgavanadí), meaning bhaurgavan, the sage + river. River. Rises in Biligherry rungam hills in Mysore territory, about 20 miles south of Collegaul and empties itself into the Cauvery at Sharagore, 3 miles north of the cusbah. Feeds a series of tanks in the talook.——*Haurvanpooram* (ஆருவன்புரம் - áruvanburam, Tam.). From (hárnva, can. bramin + pura, san. town). Village; pop. 1,414; acres 637; lat. 12° 09′; long. 77° 12′; from Coimbatore N. 81 miles; from Collegaul E. 3 miles. Rich paddy [q.v.] fields.——*Kowthully* (ಕವಾಡಹಳ್ಳಿ - kavádahalli, Can.; கவுதள்ளி - kavuthalli, Tam.). From (kaváda, can. bullock's burden + halli, can. hamlet). Village; lat. 12°.4′; long. 77° 29′; from Coimbatore N.N.E. 81 miles; from Collegaul E.S.E. 23 miles. Europeans are acquiring lands for gold prospecting.——*Madhooranhully* (ಮಧುವನಹಳ್ಳಿ - maduvanahalli, Can.). From (madhu, san. honey + vana, san. forest + halli, can. hamlet). Sanscrit name (madhuvanapurí), meaning honey + forest + town. Village; pop. 2,607; acres 1,439; lat. 12° 09′ 14″; long. 77° 11′ 22″; from Coimbatore N. 81 miles; from Collegaul E. 2¾ miles. Mulberry cultivated. Silkworms reared.——*Mautheshwarumullay* (மாதேசுவரமலை - máthésuvaramalai, Tam. máthesvaramalai *). Means mountain of the great lord or shiva. Sanscrit name (mahádéváshvaragiri), meaning great + god + lord + mountain. Village, Hill, Place of pilgrimage; pop. 1,499; lat. 12° 02′; long. 77° 35′; from Coimbatore N.N.E. 82 miles; from Collegaul E.S.E. 30 miles. Cattle-breeding. Resorted to during Deepauvaly [pundigay, 6d] and on new-moon days, especially in Tye [mausam] or january-february. Large annual cattle [maud] fair in November attracts from Mysore, Salem, &c.——*Moodicoondam* (முடிக்குண்டம் - mudikkundam, Tam.). From (mudi, tam. top + kunram, tam. mountain). Village; pop. 2,065; acres 3,254; lat. 12° 08′; long. 77° 08′; from Coimbatore N. 79 miles; from Collegaul S.W. 1½ miles. A mart for sale of spices from low country.——*Moollore* (முள்ளூர் - mullúr, Tam.). From (mullu, tam. thorn + úr, tam. village). Shrotriem village; pop. 1,858; acres 1,797; lat. 12° 10′; long. 77° 06′; from Coimbatore N. 80 miles; from Collegaul W.N.W. 3 miles. On banks of the Cauvery. Rich soil.——*Ponautchipoly* (பொன்னச்சிப்பொளி - ponnáççippoli, Tam.). From (ponnáççi, tam. proper name + poli, tam. field-bund). Village; lat. 12° 09′; long. 77° 41′; from Coimbatore N.N.E. 88 miles; from Collegaul E. 33 miles. Bounded on one side by mountain range abounding with magnificent forests.——*Ponautchy bett* (ಪೊನ್ನಾಚ್ಚಿಬೆಟ್ಟ - ponnáççibetta, Can.). Trig. station; lat. 12° 08′ 19·67″; long. 77° 41′ 12·04″; height 4,970 feet; from Collegaul E. 36 miles; from Ponautchy E.N.E. 3½ miles.——*Seetaur* (சித்தாறு - shíttáru, Tam.). From (shíttá, tam. custard-apple tree, anona reticulata, linn. + áru, tam. river). River. Tributary of Cauvery.——*Shivasamoodram* (சிவசமுத்திரம் - shivasamuttiram, Tam.). See sep. title.——*Sutteyaul* (சத்தேகாலம் - sattégálam, Tam.). See sep. title.——**(2)** Town, Talook head-quarters; Coimbatore dist., Collegaul tal.; pop. 9,946; acres 2,813; lat. 12° 09′; long. 77° 09′; from Coimbatore N. 81 miles; from Erode N.W. 70 miles; from Madras W.S.W. 223 miles; from Ootacamund N.N.E. 58 miles; from Pollachy N. 102 miles; from Suttimungalam N. 46 miles. On the Cauvery and at the extreme north-west of the talook. Old Shiva temple well sculptured and containing inscriptions. Ruined fort.

COLLERY (கள்ளர் - kallar, *Tam.*). From (kal, tam. to steal). Corrupted form of Cullar [cholera-horn].——*Collery stick* (கள்ளர்தடி - kallardadi, Tam.). From (above + tadi, tam. stick). Throwing stick or bomerang used by the Cullar.

COLLVYE (ಕಾಳವೆ - kálave, *Can.*; காளவாய் - kálaváy, *Tam.*). From (kála, san. black + váy, tam. mouth); black-mouthed. A kiln [shoolay]. Distinguish from Caulvye.

COLLY (ಕೊಳ್ಳಿ - kolli, *Can.*; కొల్లి - kolli, *Tel.*). A stream.

COLLY (கொள்ளி - kolli, *Tam.*). Means fire-brand. Pariah female proper name [peyar].

COMALAM (कोमल - kómala, *San.*). Grace.——*Comala vully* (कोमलवल्ली - kómalavallí, San.). From (above + vallí, san. creeper); graceful creeper. Mauriyamman.

COMARAN (கொமரன் - komaran, *Tam.*). Youth. The son god Soobramanyan [comauran, coomauran]. Non-bramin Hindoo 2nd or pers. name [peyar].——*Comararole* (కొమరవోలు - komaravólu, Tel.). From (komaru, tel. beautiful + prólu, tel. town). Lake; Vizagapatam dist., Golcondah tal.; acres 2,542; lat. 17° 43′; long. 82° 44′; from Narsapatam N.E. 6½ miles; from Vizagapatam W. 38 miles. One of main sources of irrigation in district.

COMATY (కోమటి - kómati, *Tel.*). From (gó, san. eye + mushti, san. fist); from their vigilant habit. Trading caste in northern districts. Girls are married in childhood; widows not remarried. In many localities a comaty must marry his uncle's daughter if any, whether liked or not. Polygamy is allowed. There is a teloogoo proverb :—ధనియాలజాతి—"Coriander seed "caste;" treating a comaty roughly is the only way of dealing with him, as rubbing the coriander [cassibor] seed before sowing, is the only way of making it sprout. And another—కోడికిసుఖంలేదు, కోమటికి విశ్వాసంలేదు—"A fowl has no happiness "and a comaty has no faith." And another—కోమటికొట్టితే కొట్టుకొట్టి—"A comaty is a coward, if you hit him he runs away." And another—కోమటి సాక్ష్యము—"Comaty's evidence;" meaning shuffling evidence. There are two sub-divisions, smarta and veishnava comaties, who form separate classes and neither eat together nor intermarry. The males assume affix of Chetty. Number some 375,000, mostly in Godavery, Kistna and Nellore. There is a class called gowra comaty, from (gavara, tel. merchant), number about 9,000 [jauty].

COMAURAN (कुमार - kumára, *San.*). From (ku, san. grief + már, san. to kill); gladdener. A young man, son [comaran, coomaran]. Comauragooroo, the son-preceptor Soobramanyan who taught his father Shiva [gooroonautan], is non-bramin Hindoo 2nd or pers. name. Comaurasawmy the same, very common [peyar].——*Comauradhaury* (ಕುಮಾರಧಾರಿ - kumáradhári, Can.). From (above + dhárá, san. stream); called after soobramanyan. River; South canara district, Ooppinangady talook. Rises in lat. 12° 37′ N., and long. 75° 45′ E., in the Bisley ghaut on the boundary between Coorg and Hassan district of Mysore, below the Soobramanyam range of the Western ghauts. Flows westwards towards the Malabar coast. Near Ooppinangady it joins the Netrauvaty and the combined stream, under the latter name, flows into the sea near Mangalore. In the lower part of its course it is much used for navigation; small boats can proceed even above Ooppinangady.——*Comaurila bhatt* (कुमारिलभट्ट - kumárilabhatta, San.). From (above + bhatta, san. lord, title). A Bramin of Berar, in the eighth century. He excited an opposition to the Booddhists and Jeinas, which has been exaggerated by tradition into an extermination of Booddhists from the Himalayas to Cape comorin. His doctrine was a revival of the old Adweitam [q.v.] philosophy. He travelled into Southern india and had for disciple Shuncaracharry [q.v.]. See vol. I (75), (76).——*Comaury* (कुमारी - kumárí, San.). A young girl; goddess Doorga as a maiden [comorin, cunny].

COMBACONAM (کمکرن - kumkaran, *Hind.*; கும்பகோணம் - kumbagónam, *Tam.* kumbakónam*). From (kumbha, san. water pot + kóna, san. lane). Old Tamul (kudandai), meaning pot + place; used by Veishnavas.——(1) Talook, Tanjore district. Tahsildar's pay Rs. 250; area 342 square miles; pop. 377,658; language Tamul chiefly. N.W. of district. Bounded north by the Coleroon, which separates it from Trichinopoly and South arcot districts; south by Tanjore and Munnargoody talooks; east by Nunnilam and Mayavaram talooks; and west by the Coleroon, which separates it from Trichinopoly district. The talook is a plain tract consisting chiefly of paddy [q.v.] fields, gardens, &c. Soil is clayey, alluvial in part. Industry chiefly agricultural, but also brass [pittalay] vessels and weaving. The Cauvery and its branches give irrigation. Places of archæological interest:—Ammangoody, Anacoody, Aundauncoil, Audootoray permaul coil, Aurore, Caditchambaudy, Carooppore, Combaconam, Coorchy, Cottore, Cutchicutt, Devaroyapett, Koelasharcay, Mahadaunapooram, Mailayore, Manalore, Manjamully, Nauchiyaurcoil, Nullore, Nundivanam, Paupanausam, Pauparajapooram, Pundanallore, Putteeshwaram, Runganautapooram, Saucottah, Sawmymullay, Shenganore, Shivapooram, Shivaulyam, Shreenivasanullore, Soondrapermaulcoil, Sooryan coil, Tircaray cauvore, Tirchiray, Tirmungalacoody, Tirnaugeswaram, Tirnirayore, Tirpanandaul, Tirpatoray, Tirpirambiam, Tirvadamaroothore, Tirvalanjooly, Tirvoypaud, Tirvulliyangoody, Tookkautchy, Tribhoovanam, Tundantottam, Tyaugasamoodram, Vailacoody, Valangimaun, Veeramangoody, Villiyavarambal. Principal trig. stations:—Aulangoody, Combaconum college, Poottaharam, Tirpanandaulmantapam, Veeramungalam. The leading places, &c., in the talook are following.——*Arasilaur* (அரசிலையாறு - arasilaiyáru, Tam.). See sep. title.——*Audootoray* (ஆடுதுறை - áduthurai, Tam. áduturai*). From (ádu, tam. sheep + turai, tam. ford). Village, Railway station; pop. 104; lat. 10° 55′; long. 79° 15; from Combaconam W.S.W. 12 miles; from Tanjore N.N.E. 10 miles. Old Shiva temple.——*Aulangoody* (ஆலங்குடி - álangudi, Tam.). From (ál, tam. banyan tree, ficus bengalensis, linn. + kudi, tam. village). Trig. station; lat. 10° 49′ 55·23″; long. 79° 26′ 43·04″; height 73 feet; from Combaconam S.S.E. 9 miles; from Tillayaul nellore S.S.E. 9½ miles.——*Capistalam* (கபித்தலம் - kabittalam, Tam.). From (kapi, san. monkey + st'hala, san. place). Abode of Hanooman. Sanscrit name (kapist'hala), meaning same. Village; pop. 2,894; acres 1,255; lat. 10° 57′; long. 79° 18′; from Combaconam W. 7½ miles; from Tanjore N.E. 15 miles. On the Cauvery.——*Cauvery* (காவேரி - kávéri, Tam.). See sep. title.——*Coleroon* (கொள்ளடம் - kolladam, Tam.). See sep. title.——*Combaconam* (கும்பகோணம் - kumbagónam, Tam.). See below.——*Haridwauramungalam* (அரித்துவாரமங்கலம் - arittuváramangalam, Tam.). From (hari, san. vishnu + dvára, san. door + mangala, san. prosperity). Vishnoo is said to have entered the earth here to visit shiva's feet. Village; pop. 1,869; acres 1,796; lat. 10° 50′; long. 79° 24′; from Combaconam S. 8¾ miles; from Tanjore E.N.E. 15 miles. A Shiva temple.——*Mahadaunapooram* (மகாதானபுரம் - magáthánappuram, Tam.). From (mahá, san. great + dána, san. gift + pura, san. town). Place of great charity. Village; pop. 5,265; acres 957; lat. 11° 00′; long. 79° 30′; from Combaconam E. 6 miles; from Tanjore N.E. 25 miles. Inscription near the river.——*Narasingapett* (நாரசிங்கன்பேட்டை - nárasinganbéttai, Tam. narasingampet*). From (narasimha, san. vishnu, the man lion god + péttai, tam. village); from narsingan, the ruler of the place. Village, Railway station; pop. 2,018; acres 932; lat. 10° 02′; long. 79° 33′; height 65 feet; from Combaconam E.N.E. 10¾ miles.——*Nauchiyaurcoil* (நாச்சியார்க்கோவில் - nácçiyárkkóvil, Tam.). From (náççi, tam. honorable woman; epithet of a goddess + kóvil, tam. temple). Village; pop. 3,348; acres 752; lat. 10° 55′; long. 79° 29′; from Combaconam E.S.E. 5¾ miles; from Tanjore E.N.E. 23 miles. Old Vishnoo temple, highly sculptured and containing inscriptions.——*Paupanausam* (பாவநாசம் - pávanásam, Tam. pápanásam*). From (pápa, san. sin + násha, san. destruction). Village, Railway station; pop. 1,688; acres 1,062; lat. 10° 55′; long. 79° 18′; height 104 feet; from Combaconam W.S.W. 8 miles; from Tanjore N.E. 13 miles. Old Shiva temple with inscriptions.——*Poottaharam* (புத்தகரம் - puttagaram, Tam.). From (puthu, tam. new + agaram, tam. village). Trig. station; lat. 10° 56′ 30·27″; long. 79° 31′ 30·05″; height 47 feet; from Combaconam E.S.E. 7½ miles; from Tondaman tottam E. 2 miles.——*Pundanallore* (பந்தனல்லூர் - pandanallúr, Tam.). From (pandam, tam. torch + nal, tam. good + úr, tam. village). Sanscrit name (kandukapura), meaning ball + town. Village; pop. 1,136; acres 784; lat. 11° 08′; long. 79° 33′; from Combaconam N.E. 15½ miles; from Tanjore N.E. 35 miles. Old Shiva temple with inscriptions in old Tamul. Ruined fort with two Shiva and Vishnoo temples, also in ruins.——*Putteeshwaram* (பட்டீச்சுவரம் - pattísuvaram, Tam.). From (patti, tam. offspring of kámadhénu the wishing cow + íshvara, san. lord); shiva as worshipped by patty. Village; pop. 1,851; acres 1,345; lat. 10° 55′; long. 79° 23′; from Combaconam S.W. 3½ miles; from Tanjore E.N.E. 17 miles. Inscription of Chola dynasty in the temple of Sabhaupaty. Parts of the temple are well sculptured. Cloth weaving.——*Sawmymullay* (சுவாமிமலை - shuvámimalai, Tam.). From (svámí, san. deity + malai, tam. hill). Sanscrit name (skandagiri), meaning soobramanyan + hill. It is supposed to be one of the three summits of Keilausam [q.v.]. Village, Sub-Registrar's office, Hill; pop. 3,828; acres 648; lat. 10° 57′; long. 79° 22′; from Combaconam W. 3 miles; from Tanjore N.E. 18 miles. Old Shiva temple with inscriptions on the hill. In the hamlet of Vyausamungalam is another old Shiva temple. Centre of weaving industry.——*Soondrapermaulcoil* (சுந்தரப்பெருமாள்கோவில் - shundarapperumálgóvil, Tam. sundaraperumálkoil*). From (sundara, san. beautiful + perumál, tam. vishnu, the great lord + kóvil, tam. temple). Village, Railway station; pop. 2,689; lat. 10° 56′; long. 79° 22′; height 97 feet; from Combaconam W.S.W. 4½ miles; from Tanjore N.E. 15 miles. Old Vishnoo temple, built by a Chola king. Centre of weaving industry.——*Tircaraycauvore* (திருக்கராக்காவூர் - tirukkaraikkávúr, Tam.). From (tiru, tam. holy + karai, tam. field + ká, tam. grove + úr, tam. village). Sanscrit name (garbharakshakapura), meaning interior + protection + town; also (mádhavívana), meaning the spring flower creeper, hiptage madablota, gærtn. + forest. Village; pop. 1,096; acres 868; lat. 10° 52′; long. 79° 20′; from Combaconam S.W. 9 miles; from Tanjore E.N.E. 11 miles. Old Shiva temple with Chola inscriptions.——*Tirmungalacoody* (திருமங்கலக்குடி - tirumangalakkudi, Tam.). From (tiru, tam. sacred + mangalá, san. párvatí, the auspicious deity + kudi, tam. village). Sanscrit name (mangaléshvara), meaning parvaty + shiva. Village; pop. 2,508; acres 1,091; lat. 11° 02′; long. 79° 31′; from Combaconam N.E. 8½ miles; from Tanjore N.E. 28 miles. Old Shiva temple with inscriptions in Grantam [q.v.].——*Tirnaugeswaram* (திருநாகேசுவரம் - tirunágésuvaram, Tam.). From (tiru, tam. sacred + nága, san. serpent + íshvara, san. lord). The residence of Audy sheshan, the chief of serpents. Town; pop. 5,041; acres 521; lat. 10° 58′; long. 79° 28′; from Combaconam E. 3¼ miles; from Tanjore E.N.E. 23 miles. Old Shiva temple. Notable Vishnoo temple near, called Oopily appan covil. Weaving centre.——*Tirpanandaul* (திருப்பனந்தாள் - tiruppanandál, Tam.). From (tiru, tam. holy + panai, tam. palmyra tree, borassus flabelliformis, linn. + talam, tam. place). Village; pop. 795; acres 1,803; lat. 11° 06′; long. 79° 30′; from Combaconam N.N.E. 11 miles; from Tanjore N.E. 30 miles. Richly endowed Shoodra mutt, contains an old and valuable library of cadjan-leaf Tamul volumes. Trig. station at Mantapam in lat. 11° 05′ 30·43″; long. 79° 29′ 43·07″; height 80 feet; from Combaconam N.N.E. 10 miles; from Veeracunn N.E. 1¾ miles.——*Tirpirambiam* (திருப்பிரம்பியம் - tiruppirambiyam, Tam.). From (tiru, tam. sacred + pirambu, tam. cane + ayam, tam. place). Sanscrit name (pralayámbápura), meaning flood + goddess + town. Village; pop. 1,707; acres 1,441; lat. 11° 00′; long. 79° 23′; from Combaconam N.W. 4½ miles; from Tanjore N.E. 20 miles. Old Shiva temple with inscriptions.——*Tirvadamaroothore* (திருவிடைமருதூர் - tiruvidaimaruthúr, Tam.). See sep. title.——*Tirvalanjooly* (திருவலஞ்சுழி - tiruvalañjuzhi, Tam.). From (tiru, tam. sacred + valam, tam. right hand side + shuzhi, tam. whirlpool). From a whirlpool in the cauvery there. Said to be connected with the fact that shiva has a hole on the right side of his head. Village; pop. 1,101; acres 1,516; lat. 10° 56′; long. 79° 22′; from Combaconam W.S.W. 3½ miles; from Tanjore N.E. 17 miles. Old Shiva temple with inscriptions and fine gopooram. The sculptures of Jeina.——*Valangimaun* (வலங்கிமான் - valangimán, Tam.). From (valangai, tam. right hand + mán, tam. deer). Cf. Shiva. Town, Sub-registrar's office; pop. 7,244; acres 3,234; lat. 10° 53′; long. 79° 26′; from Combaconam S.S.E. 4¾ miles; from Tanjore E.N.E. 18 miles. Old Shiva temple with inscriptions.——*Veeramungalam* (வீரமங்கலம் - víramangalam, Tam.). From (víra, san. hero + mangala, san.

prosperity). Trig. station; lat. 10° 52′ 20·74″; long. 79° 21′ 00·36″; height 92 feet.——*Veppatore* (வெப்பத்தூர் - véppattúr, Tam.). From (vémbu, tam. neem tree, melia azadirachta, linn. + úr, tam. village). Town; area 3,354; pop. 5,788; lat. 11° 01′; long. 79° 29′; from Combaconam N.E. 5¼ miles; from Tanjore N.E. 25 miles.——*Vinaickunteroo* (விநாயக்கன்தெரு - vináyakkanderu, Tam.). See sep. title.——(2) Deputy tahsildarry, Tanjore district. Pay Rs. 100.——(3) Town, Municipality, Railway station, Head-quarters of Sub-collector, Sub-judge, and District moonsifs of Combaconam and Valangimaun; Tanjore dist., Combaconam tal.; pop. 54,307; acres 1,257; lat. 10° 57′; long. 79° 25′; height 85 feet; from Madras S.S.W. 157 miles; from Mayavaram W. 20 miles; from Munnargoody W. 20 miles; from Negapatam W.N.W. 34 miles; from Tanjore N.E. 20 miles. Large and populous town in a low level tract between two considerable branches of the Cauvery, over which is a handsome bridge. Extends about 2 miles in length from north to south and 1 mile in breadth from east to west. Though only with a slight elevation above the sea, it is remarkably healthy. One of the most ancient towns in the Presidency. It is the centre of the Braminical religion and literature, and was once the capital of the Chola kingdom. Combaconam was the seat of the Zillah court of the district from its first establishment in 1806 until 1863, when it was removed to Tanjore. Also from 1860 to 1863 head-quarters of the Sub-collector. A branch mutt of Shuncaracharry [q.v.], founder of the Adweitam [q.v.] philosophy, is presided over by a chief gooroo of Smarta [q.v.] bramins. There are sixteen temples, twelve dedicated to Shiva and four to Vishnoo. Two of the temples are important; the larger dedicated to Vishnoo and the smaller to Shiva. The Vishnoo temple has a great gopooram [q.v.], of twelve storeys and 147 feet high, richly ornamented with figures, the ceiling being especially well painted. Near this is a small porch and two processional cars of carved wood of elaborate design, one of great size. The Shiva temple called Coombheshwaran pagoda is approached by a corridor 330 feet long and 15 feet wide. The principal gopooram is 128 feet high, and leads to a court 83 feet by 55 feet. The Ramasawmy temple has only one gopooram leading into the enclosure. The car of the Shaurngapauny temple is the one of the largest in Southern india. Besides the usual annual festivals, the Maha magham [pundigay, 5c], occurring once in twelve years and celebrated in February, draws an immense concourse from all parts of the country. Brick remains of the palace of the Chola are also found in the neighbourhood. Situated in the most fertile and most thickly populated part of the delta, Combaconam has always been a great centre of trade and manufactures; the latter consisting chiefly of silk [puttoo] and cotton [q.v.] cloths and metal [loham] ware. From the Government provincial college at this town come many of the best educated natives of the south. Trig. station at Combaconam college; lat. 10° 58′ 10·75″; long. 79° 25′ 29·38″; height 124 feet.

COMBOO (கொம்பு - kombu, *Tam.*). A branch [comma]. A common musical horn.——*Combairy mookkan* (చెట్టురుకుపాము - chetturukupámu, Tel.; കൊമ്പേറിമൂർഖൻ - kompérimúrkhan, Mal.; கொம்பேறிமூக்கன் - kombérimúkkan, Tam.). Tel. from (chettu, tel. tree + uruku, tel. to spring + pámu, tel. snake). Mal. from (kompu, mal. branch + éru, mal. to ascend + múrkhan, mal. poisonous snake). Tam. means branch-ascending and long-nosed by corruption. A tree-snake, not poisonous. Dendrophis picta, dendrophidæ [tree-snake], ophidii colubriformes, ophidia [sarpam], reptilia [sarpy, 20], of naturalists [jantoo]. Alias Ahætulla bellii, boii; Coluber decorus, pictus, russell; Leptophis maniar, pictus. Obtuse snout. Bronze brown above, sometimes with yellow vertebral on front part of trunk; yellow band along each side, along the outer series of scales, and has a black or blackish edge either below or above and below, upper black margin being continuation of black band which commences behind the eye. Lower parts white or yellow. One of the most common species. Variations occur in the coloration. Food consists of lizards [chipkalee], and frogs [bhaicam]. When old ferocious and bites readily; length 4 feet.——*Comban* (گینڈا - gendá, Hind.; കൊമ്പൻ - kompan, Mal.). Tusker or male elephant [q.v.]. Here applied to rhinoceros.

COMB TREE (کنگوی کا جھاڑ - kangoíkájhár, *Hind.*). From shape of leaf. Same as Tootty.

COMERCOLLY (کمارکھالی - kumárkhálí, *Hind.*). Title from a town in lower Bengal. Otherwise Marabou [q.v.] feathers. The fine ash or slate colored feathers so called are the under tail-coverts of adjutant [q.v.] birds.

COMMA (కొమ్మ - komma, *Tel.*). Branch [comboo].——*Commamore* (కొమ్మమూరు - kommamúru, Tel.). From (above + úru, tel. village). Depopulated village, canal; Kistna district, Baupatla talook. Canal, begun as an irrigation channel in 1858–59, was continued in 1877 to meet the Buckingham canal [q.v.]. The head of the canal is at the twelfth mile from Seetanagram, and continues in a south-westerly direction to Pedda ganjam, where connected with Buckingham canal by a tidal lock. At Chebrole bridge, 10 miles from Guntoor, a considerable traffic quits the canal for Guntoor. Three other locks exist at Collimera, Nullamada and Santaravore.——*Commy* (కొమ్మి - kommi, Tel.). Same as Tirauna.

COMORIN (കന്യാകുമാരി - kanyákumári, *Mal.*; குமரி - kumari, *Tam.*). Title is Portuguese corruption from tamul. Cf. cochin, coleroon. Mal. from (kanyá, san. youthful + kumárí, san. virgin). Tam. means a virgin. The κομαρία ἄκρον καὶ πόλις of Ptolemy. Compare Cambojam or Khmer. The Periplus says:—"After this there is another place called κομάρ, where there is a "βριάριον, for which read φρούριον, and a harbour, where also "people come to bathe and purify themselves, . . . for it is "related that a goddess was once accustomed to bathe there "monthly." This monthly bathing in honor of Doorga is still continued. Through encroachments of sea, the harbour has disappeared; but a freshwater well remains in the centre of a rock, some way out at sea. In the Sanscrit legend the virgin goddess was daughter of a shepherdess, born at same date as Krishnan; Krishnan's father was instructed in a dream to remove Krishnan to the house of the shepherdess and to take in return the child born there for fear of Krishnan being killed by Cumsan, Krishnan's maternal uncle. The goddess is otherwise the incarnation of Mauyay [q.v.] or illusion. Or sometimes taken as Doorga [q.v.]. Or again there is a legend that a virgin leapt into the sea. Coomary is regarded by Pooraunic writers as the name of a river, one of the seven great sacred rivers [gungay] of India. Coomary sherpan denotes lord of the Coomary sea-coast. The term Comorin is in some writings used for the whole of the southern portion of the peninsula. Village, Cape, Place of pilgrimage, Sanitarium, Travancore state, Puduanaubhapooram division, Agasteeshwaram talook; lat. 8° 5′; long. 77° 36′; from Sooshindram S.E. 8 miles; from Bombay S.S.E. 810 miles; from Madras S.S.W. 390 miles; from Manacoody E. 4½ miles; from Trivandrum S.E. 49 miles. The cape is extreme southern point of peninsula. Formed of a circular low sandy point, not discernible above 3½ or 4 leagues. Within two or three cables' length of the south-east portion lies a sloping rocky islet, high above water, with other rocks about it, on which the sea breaks. There are several groups of rocks appearing above water. Westward of this islet the shore is sandy and barren, but eastward it abounds with trees. The land is safe to approach within about two miles, the depth in some places increasing towards shore. Eastward of the rocky islet and about three miles from it is a fort. To north-east the coast is little frequented for 166 miles; as navigation northwards into Bay of Bengal is obstructed by Adam's bridge. Inland, the cape rises in a gradual slope to the base of the ghauts [q.v.], the nearest of which at 4 miles north-west is an isolated, very sharp conical hill, 1,403 feet high, often mistaken for the cape itself. A small white, square pagoda crowns the extremity of the cape. A residency on the coast a little distance from the pagoda [q.v.] is resorted to by Europeans for health. Pilgrims come to worship the goddess and to bathe in the holy waters of the sea, this being one of the five renowned bathing places. There is a Bramin village near the pagoda and habitations of shaunaur and fishermen a little away from it. Sand of different colors is found. The legend of this is that Shiva at Sooshindram wanted to marry the goddess, but the marriage negotiations were broken off and the rice and other grains prepared for the ceremony were converted into sand [manal]. The country around is sandy and consists of palmyras [q.v.].

COMPOUND (کمپونگ - kampung, *Malay*). Means village. Applied by Europeans to the enclosure in which a house stands.

COMPRADORE (خرچ بردار - kharchbardár, *Hind.*). Portuguese from comprar, to purchase. Hind. from (kharch, hind. expenditure + bardár, pers. carrier). A house steward. Cf. curts.

CONA (ಕೋಣ - kóne, *Can.*; కోన - kóna, *Tel.*). From (kóna, san. corner). Recess; valley. Ravine; suffix in place names, especially in the Ceded districts [q.v.], as Punchalingaulacona, meaning ravine of the five lingams.——*Conair* (ಕೋಣೆರಿ - kónéri, Can.; కోనేరు - kóneru, Tel.). From (above + éri, can. tank). A square tank with steps.——*Conamoogam* (கோணமுகம் - kónámugam, Tam.). From (mukha, san. face). A delta. The principal deltas in S. india are those of the Godavery, the Kistna, the Pennair, and the Cauvery. Vol. I, 391.——*Conamoola* (కోనమూల - kónamúla, Tel.). From (múla, tel. corner). Site of Collector's bungalow at Krishnapatam, Nellore district.——*Conaseema* (కోనసీమ - kónasíma, Tel.). From (kóna, tel. valley + síma, tel. tract). The Godavery delta.——*Conauda* (కోనాడ - kónáda, Tel.). From (above + nádu, tel. country). Greek name παρθαλις. Village, Promontory, Port; Vizagapatam dist., Bimlipatam division; pop. 4,128; lat. 18° 1′; long. 83° 37′; from Bimlipatam N. 12 miles; from Madras N.E. 400 miles; from Santapilly S.W. 6½ miles; from Vizagapatam N.E. 30 miles. The point is 2½ miles south of the village. The anchorage for native vessels is in about 5½ fathoms. British vessels seldom visit the port. The Champauvaty falls into the sea here. Salt factory.

CONCAN (कोंकण - kónkana, *San.*; کوکن - kokan, *Hind.*; கொங்கணம் - konganam, *Tam.*). In ancient geography signified a kingdom south of Goa. Evidently allied to the Congoo country inland. Now a narrow strip of land, bounded on the east by the Western ghauts from Bombay to Goa. One of Hwen Thsang's nine divisions of s. india; capital Kong-kienna-pu-lo, or Concanapooram. This was the ancient kingdom of the

Cadambas, which for a time rivalled that of the Chalookyas [charitram].——*Concanasta* (कोंकणस्थ - kónkanast'ha, San.). Bramins distinct from concanies. Immigrants from Goa and Bombay canarese districts. Smartas. Are among dravida bramins.——*Concany* (कोंकणी - kónkaní, Mahr.). Pertaining to concan; used of persons or things. Concany bramins are puncha gowdas [q.v.] and are saraswats; included among gowdas; they are by religion rigvedies and madhwas. By occupation they are chiefly traders. Found throughout west coast, especially in Travancore and Cochin. Their family god is at Tripatty.——*Concany resin* (कोंकणधूप - kónkanadhúpa, San.). Same as White dammer.——*Sapta concanam* (सप्तकोंकण - saptakónkana, San.). The seven Concans of Sanscrit geography. See vol. I (128).

CONCH (शंख - shankha, *San.*). Title from greek κόγχη, which is from sanscrit. San. from (sham, san. to grow calm); from soothing sound when held to ear. Same as chunk [q.v.].——*Conch flower* (शङ्खपुष्पी - shankhapushpí, San.). Title from white color. Same as Keshinee and Crow-creeper.——*Conch yam* (शङ्खालु - shankhálu, San.). Title from color of root. Same as Wayaka.

CONDAH (కొండ - konda, *Tel.*). From (kunru, tam. rock). Hill; suffix in place names, as Penoocondah, meaning great hill.——*Conda dora* (కొండదొర - kondadora, Tel.). From (dora, tel. chieftain). Tribe in the mountains of Goomsoor.——*Condakirla auva* (కొండకిర్లఆవ - kondakirlaáva, Tel.). From (kondakara, tel. hill side + áva, tel. lake). Lake; Vizagapatam dist., Sarwasiddhy tal.; lat. 17° 36′; long. 83° 02′; from Vizagapatam S.W. 20 miles; from Yellamanchily N.E. 9 miles; from the sea N. 8¾ miles. One of main sources of irrigation in district. Fed by hill streams and supply-channels from the Shaurada nuddy.——*Condanaroos* (صحرائی سانپ - sahráisámp, Hind.; కొండనరుసు - kondanarusu, Tel.). From (above + arusu, tam. king). Desert snake. Term co-extensive with the family Psammophidæ, ophidii colubriformes, ophidia [sarpam], reptilia [sarpy, 19], of naturalists [jantoo]. The family approaches in some respects the Dryophidæ, or whip snakes [q.v.]. The only species known here is Psammophis condanarus. Alias Coluber condanarus; Psammophis indicus, tæniata. Back brown, with black edge along each side; brown, black-edged band along second outer series of scales, separated from back by a brownish-grey band, and from the belly by a yellow one; belly yellow, with black line along each side; head uniform light brown above; yellow, black-edged streak from rostral shield along canthus rostralis above the orbit to the neck; a second along the upper half of the labial shields.——*Condapully* (కొండపల్లె - kondapalle, Tel.). From (above + palle, tel. village); called after condadoo a shepherd. Hind. name (mustafánagar), meaning the chosen + city. Village, Hill, Bungalow; Kistna dist., Bezwada tal.; pop. 4,758; acres 8,295; lat. 16° 37′; long. 80° 35′; from Bezwada N.N.W. 8½ miles; from Masulipatam N.W. 50 miles. Picturesquely situated. Now unimportant, but formerly of some strength, giving its name to the province called Moostafahnugger by Mahomedans. Built about A.D. 1360 by Anoovaima reddy of Condaveed and called Condapully after the shepherd Condadoo, who showed the site to the Reddy king. From the Reddy dynasty it passed to the Rajah of Orissa, and from them it was taken in 1471 by Mahomed shah II of Goolburga. The garrison revolted about 1476 and in 1477 the place stood a siege of six months, at the close of which the young king with his own hands killed the Bramins officiating at a Hindoo temple in the fort. In 1481 the encampment at the foot of Condapully was the scene of the tragic fate of the aged minister Cauja mahomed gawaun. Taken about 1515 by Krishna deva roya and restored to the Orissa rajahs when the Kistna was made the boundary between their territory and that of Vijianugger. Taken about 1521 by Sultan coolee cootb shah of Golcondah. For the next fifty years it remained the out-post of the Mahomedan power. In 1557 Bezwada and Ibrampatam, both in the neighbourhood of Condapully were attacked by the Commandant of Condaveed. It was a favorite residence of Ibrahim shah, king of Golcondah, 1530–1580, and during the reign of his great grandson, Sultan abdoollah, 1661–1669, the Bala hissar was built of Burmese teak [q.v.]. In July 1687 the fortress was treacherously surrendered to Aurungzeeb. On the 10th March 1766 General Calliaud took it by assault from Nizam ally. A small detachment of Company's troops was stationed at the foot of the hill until January 1859, when the station was abandoned. The only remaining barrack room is now utilized as a travellers' bungalow. Manufacture of small figures and toys from a very light wood growing on the hills.——*Condaveed* (కొండవీడు - kondavídu, Tel.). From (above + vídu, tel. town). Sanscrit name (kundinapura), meaning basin + city. Hind. name (murtazánagar), meaning moortezah khan, the general + town. Hill range village; Kistna dist., Narsarowpett tal.; pop. 2,129; acres 3,314; lat. 16° 15′; long. 80° 17′; from Guntoor S.W. 13 miles; from Narsarowpett E. 13½ miles. There are two forts on the hill and one below; the last attributed to Krishna deva royel. The fortifications are much overgrown with jungle, but in good preservation. The greater part of the works are on the western side of the mountain, the principal summits of the ridge of the pettah being connected by a wall extending nearly 1½ miles to the south. From the southern extremity a line almost at right angles passes over one of the highest peaks at half a mile from which it descends about the same distance and forms a junction with the southern face of the fort in the plain. A second line projects from the above-mentioned peak in a north-westerly direction. From the northern front of the lower fort a line of works extends up the mountain in an easterly direction until it joins the central ridge. There are also some detached works within the cultivated parts as well as a line on the high ridge immediately east of the central one. The lower fort was a strong enclosure at the foot of the hill, 5 furlongs in length by 2½ in breadth, facing W.N.W. The walls are built of stone, with a parapet and loop-holes, well defended by bastions in the main line and cavaliers at the angles. That at the N.W. angle is the most perfect. The houses remaining in the fort are in ruins and chiefly occupied by Mussalman families. There are two small bungalows constructed in recent years by European officials. For history of the Condaveed reddies see vol. I (150). The Mahomedans, who captured Condaveed in 1565 on the overthrow of the Vijianugger dynasty, changed the name to Moortezahnugger after Moortezah khan, a distinguished General of Mahomed coolee cootb shah. The fortress remained under Mussalman rule until 1752, when it was given by the Nizam to the French. In 1757 Bussy only succeeded in capturing the place by starving out the garrison. This was the last instance of hostilities at Condaveed. The Fowjdar of Condaveed subsequently removed his residence to Guntoor, leaving in the fort a Killadar with a small force. The place was finally made over to the English in September 1788. On the highest peak of the hills, three miles east of the village, is a small mantapam [q.v.] built over an impression of Vishnoo's foot, called by Mussalmans Adam's foot [adam's peak, collam, dharmarajacull]. East of the town is a large ruined sculptured Vishnoo temple with an inscription, dated 1564, built in the time of the Reddy sovereigns. Inside the building known as the Treasury is a small temple with sculptured figures. Fifty yards west of this is an inscription dated A.D. 1525. Shiva temple of Ramalingam, north of the village, has an inscription dated A.D. 1666 recording its erection, and a finely sculptured figure of Veerabhadran. At Condaveed Mahomedans extract essences and fragrant oils [attar] from various flowers which are sent to Hyderabad for sale. They also manufacture a strong rough brown paper. The range of hills of this name occupies the north-east corner of the talook and overlooks the town of Guntoor. It forms a connected chain running by north-east and south-west for 9½ miles, besides some unconnected heights to the north-east which extend it two and three miles further. Colonel Lambton placed a Trigonometrical station upon the highest peak, rather to the southward of the middle of the range. The outline of the ridge is uneven, having many projecting conical peaks and at a mile north of the station it is very low. To the south-west of the station it forms a box or tableland which connects the main ridge with a parallel or collateral ridge, about four miles long, terminating on the south by a conical peak called Sunna condah. The village of Condaveed lies at the western foot of the central ridge. Trig. station in lat. 16° 15′ 16·92″; long. 80° 19′ 48·04″; height 1,664 feet.——*Condayya* (ಕೊಂಡಯ್ಯ - kondayya, Can.). From (above + ayya, tel. master). Hindoo 2nd or pers. name [peyar].——*Condla* (కొండ్ల - kondla, Tel.). From (konda, tel. hill). Locative plural form. Suffix in place names as Goolcondla, meaning the bird's hill.

CONDAY (கொண்டை - kondai, *Tam.*). Top knot, in men or women [coodoomy].——*Condaicutty* (கொண்டைக்கட்டி - kondaikkatti, Tam.). From (above + kattu, tam. to tie); from wearing hair done up into a knot on top of the head. A class of Vellaular [jauty]. Number about 1,800.

CONDRAY (கொன்றை - konrai, *Tam.*). Plants of cassia [q.v.] genus, especially cassia fistula, linn. Includes also a Pithecolobium. Note that there are four species of cassia in the market:—Cassia lignea or bark [cassia cinnamon], Cassia fistula [common condray], Cassia buds [cassia cinnamon], and Cassia senna [senna].——*Common condray* (आरग्वध - áragvadha, San.; भावई - bhávaí, Mahr.; कक्काई - kakkáí, Conc.; خیار شنبر - khiyárshambar, Ar.; خیار چنبر - khiyárchambar, Pers.; کرمالہ - girmálah, Hind.; املتاس - amaltás, Dec.; ಕಕ್ಕೆ - kakke, Can.; ಕೊಂಡೆ - konde, Too.; రేల - réla, Tel.; ସୁନାରି - sunari, Oor.; കൊന്ന - konna, Mal.; ඇහැල - ahala, Singh.; கொன்றை - konrai, Tam.). San. from (áraja, san. a red variety of cutaneous disease + vadh, san. to kill); as a curative [wild condray]. Ar. from persian. Pers. from (khiyár, pers. cucumber, cucumis sativus, linn. + chambar, pers. necklace); from structure of pod. Can. from (kakku, can. to scratch) [wild condray]. Mal. from (kón, mal. king); perhaps from flowers worn as garland by kings. Tam. like malayalam. San. also (suvarnaka), meaning having golden color [nanga champak, shrubby balah]; (rájavriksha), meaning king + tree; (rájataru), meaning king + tree. Ar. also (kathalulhind), meaning indian cucumber. Can. also (kondemara); (araginamara); (árévatamara); (takkemara). Tel. also (kólaponna), meaning straight + calophyllum inophyllum, linn. Mal. also (svarnáviram), meaning gold + cassia auriculata, linn., from yellow flowers. Tam. also (sharakkonrai), meaning wreath

+ the plant. Greek γλυκοκάλαμον, κασσία μέλαινα. Bark in Greek σῦριγξ, in Latin fistula. Title otherwise Amaltas, Black cassia, Common cassia, Connay, Gold flower tree, Indian laburnum, King's tree, Pudding-pipe tree, Purging cassia, Shara condray. Botanically Cassia [soovarnacam] fistula, linn., leguminosæ [vricsham, 48]. Alias Bactyrilobium fistula; Cassia fistula, rhombifolia; Cathartocarpus fistula. Tree, middling size, with usually smooth bark; dense dark-green foliage; leaflets about five pairs, broadly ovate, obtuse or retuse, glabrous; petioles without glands; racemes terminal, long, lax, drooping; flowers on long pedicels; legumes cylindric, pendulous, glabrous, smooth, dark brown, nearly 2 feet in length; cells numerous, each containing one smooth, oval, shining seed, immersed in black pulp; pendulous racemes of flowers bright yellow, fragrant; like laburnum; flowering from may to september; common in dry forests. Mucilaginous pulp surrounding the seeds is medicinally laxative, consisting chiefly of sugar [q.v.] and gum, entering into composition of confection of senna; flowers are given in decoction in stomachic affections; roots are a febrifuge; bark and leaves rubbed up and mixed with oil are applied to pustules; root is a strong purgative; leaves parched are eaten for medicinal purposes; gives to pharm. cassiæ pulpa, officinal, also in british. Pulp of pods used as famine food. Bark used by tanners; the proportion of astringent extract being much smaller than in auriculata, and tends to thicken the leather [chamrah];' bark used along with terminalia; ashes used as mordant [cauram]; an astringent gum [gond] exudes. Wood strong, elastic and durable, close and straight-grained, dark brown color often finely mottled, and works well; used in ship-building and for bows and axles, and is also suited for furniture.——*Peacock condray* (மயிற்கொன்றை - mayirkkonrai, Tam.). Title from flower. Same as Gold mohur tree, and as Foreign tungaid.——*Red condray* (ఉరిమిడి - urimidi, Tel.; රතුවා - ratuvá, Singh.; சிவப்புக்கொன்றை - shivappukkonrai, Tam.). Title from rose-colored flower. Singh. from (ratu, singh. red); from pink flowers. Tam. from (shivappu, tam. redness + konrai, tam. cassia fistula, linn.). Tel. also (usikimánu). Tam. also (varikkonrai), meaning stripe condray; (karungonrai), meaning black condray, from dark fruit. Title otherwise Horse cassia, Roxburgh's cassia. Botanically Cassia [soovarnacam] marginata, roxb., leguminosæ [vricsham, 48]. Alias Cassia emarginata, roxburghii; Cathartocarpus marginatus, roxburghii. Small tree with dull light brown bark and wide-spreading branches; small leaflet foliage; racemes of small rose-colored flowers, something like weeping ash; the fruit is cylindric, 8--12 inches long, as thick as a man's little finger, of a dark brown color and having transverse partitions. Planted in gardens for ornamental purposes. Wood close-grained, hard and durable, works smoothly and stands a good polish, when fresh deep rose colored, eventually turns reddish brown.——*Tree condray* (కొండతంటెపుచెట్టు - kondatantepuchettu, Tel; വലിയതകര - valiyatakara, Mal.; වල්ඇහැළ - valahala, Singh.; வெள்ளைத்தகரை - vellaittagarai, Tam.). Title from size. Tel. from (konda, tel. hill + tantepuchettu, tel. cassia tora, linn.). Mal. from (valiya, mal. large + takara, mal. cassia tora, linn.). Singh. from (val, singh. jungle + ahala, singh. cassia fistula, linn.). Tam. from (vellai, tam. white + tagarai, tam. cassia tora, linn.). Tam. also (mañjakkonrai), meaning yellow + condray tree; (kunduppúkkonrai), meaning globe flower condray. Title otherwise Sulphur-flowered cassia, Surat condray, Tree senna, Wild condray. Botanically Cassia [soovarnacam] glauca, lam., leguminosæ [vricsham, 48]. Alias Cassia arborescens, enneaphylla, planisiliqua, sulphurea, surattensis; Senna arborescens. Tree, with numerous branches spreading in every direction, young ones irregularly angled; leaflets four to six pair, with an erect gland between each of the two to three lower pair, oval, broadest at or below the middle, the upper ones the largest, under side glaucous and slightly pubescent; stipules linear-subulate, falcate; racemes axillary, corymbiform, long-peduncled, erect, crowded near the ends of the branches, about half the length of the leaves; petals all nearly equal; anthers all fertile, equally long, the two lower on rather longer filaments than the others; legumes drooping, linear, straight, thin, the margin a little tumid; flowers large, sulphur, long-pedicelled; the pedicels subtended by an ovate caducous bract; flowering nearly all year. Cultivated in gardens. Bark and leaves prescribed in diabetes and gonorrhœa.——*Wild condray* (आरग्वध - áragvadha, San.; کچلورا - kachlorá, Hind.; ಕಾಡಕೊಂದೆ - kádakonde, Can.; ಕಕ್ಕೆಮರ - kakkemara, Too.; കാട്ടുകൊന്ന - káttukonna, Mal.). Title from resemblance. San. from (araja, san. skin-disease + vadh, san. to kill) [common condray]. Can. from (kádu, can. wild + konde, can. cassia fistula, linn.). Too. from (kakke, too. cassia fistula, linn. + mara, too. tree) [common condray]. Mal. from (kátu, mal. forest + konna, mal. cassia fistula, linn.). Title otherwise Venezuela soap bark tree, Wight's inga. Botanically Pithecolobium [auragvadham] bigeminum, benth., leguminosæ [vricsham, 48]. Alias Inga bigemina, wightiana; Mimosa bigemina, lucida. Tree unarmed; leaves conjugately or bipinnated; pinnæ one to two pair, with a gland between each pair; leaflets two to three pair, ovate-lanceolate, accuminated, shining, with a gland between each pair; racemes panicled, terminal, many-flowered; flowers in small globose heads, white; legumes spirally twisted; flowering in hot season. Decoction of leaves, medicine for leprosy [cooshtam] and stimulant for growth of hair; hard and tough wood.——*Yellow condray* (ಸೀಮೆತಂಗೆಡಿ - símetangedi, Can.; కొండతంగేడు - kondatangédu, Tel.; മഞ്ഞക്കൊന്ന - maññakkonna, Mal.; වා - vá, Singh.; மஞ்சள்கொன்றை - manjalgonrai, Tam.). Title from color of flowers. Can. from (síme, can. foreign + tangedi, can. cassia auriculata, linn.). Tel. from (konda, tel. hill + tangédu, tel. cassia auriculata, linn.). Mal. from tamul. Tam. from (mañjal, tam. yellow + konrai, tam. cassia fistula, linn.). Tel. also (kurumbi), meaning clustering. Singh. also (aramaná). Tam. also (karungonrai), meaning black, condray from heart-wood; (malaiyávirai), meaning hill + cassia auriculata, linn.; (shímaiyávirai), meaning foreign + cassia auriculata, linn. Title otherwise Foreign tungaid, Hill tungaid, Iron-wood [cassa, chowkmaram, dark vail, deccany deodar, foreign ilanjy, nauga champak], Manjal condray, Sumatra senna. Botanically Cassia [soovarnacam] siamea, lamk., leguminosæ [vricsham, 48]. Alias Cassia florida, sumatrana; Senna sumatrana. Small tree, every branch terminating in a large panicle of deep yellow blossoms; in flower nearly all year; common wild in jungles; also planted and ornamental. Sap-wood whitish, rather large; heart-wood dark-brown, nearly black, very hard; very durable; good fuel for locomotives.

CONDY (கொண்டி - kondi, *Tam.*). Stray cattle.——*Condy otty* (கொண்டியோட்டி - kondiyótti, Tam.). From (above + ótti, tam. driver). A class employed on the Cauvery channels, whose duty is that of keeping stray cattle off the channel and river-banks and off the fields.

CONGA (కొంగ - konga, *Tel.*; கொக்கு - kokku, *Tam.*). Any crane, stork or heron [adjutant bird, deerghachauchoocam, paddy bird]. Compare, where transl. is of first term :—Anastomus oscitans (gullakonga), shell; Ardeola leucoptera (guddikonga), blind; Ardetta cinnamomea (dósikonga), sinner; Buphus coromandus (svátikonga), rainy season; Butorides javanica (dósikonga), sinner; Ciconia leucocephala (shankumedakonga), conch + neck; Herodias alba (málakonga), pariah; Herodias garzetta (nallamukkukonga), black + bill; Leptoptilos argala (pínugulakonga), corpse; Phœnicopterus roseus (púgonga), flower; Platalea leucorodia (gantemukkukonga), spoon + bill; Tantalus leucocephalus (errakálikonga), red + leg. See gloss. paragraphs. The Tamul Cooral has the following :—கொக்கொக்க கூம்புங்பருவத்து மற்றதன் குத்தொக்க சீர்த்த விடத்து—"At the time when "one should use self-control, let him restrain himself like a "heron; and let him, like it, strike when there is a favorable "opportunity." There is a Tamul proverb :—கடல்வற்றிக் கருவாடு தின்னலாமென்று உடல் வற்றிச் செத்ததாம் கொக்கு—"It is said that the stork died while waiting for the "ocean to dry, in the hope of getting a supply of dried fish."

CONGOO (கொங்கு - congu, *Tam.*). Means toddy. The country so called; otherwise Poozhy or country of dry fields. Ancient Hindoo kingdom comprising the modern Salem and Coimbatore districts. Existed from the commencement of the Christian era down to the end of the ninth century, when it was overthrown by the Chola kings of Tanjore and annexed to their dominions. To the east were the Chola and Paundyan kingdoms; and on the west, the Keralam. Two dynasties Ratta and Gunga are said to have ruled the country. The capital of the first was Scandapooram somewhere near Guzzelhutty pass, removed to Talacaud near Collegaul in Coimbatore district, in the third century. Jeinism and subsequently Sheivism was the prevailing religion of the kings, who seem to have had considerable intercourse with the west from the discovery of numerous coins of the Roman emperors. This kingdom was subsequent to Cheram. See vol. 1 (13), (129) [charitram]. There is a Tamul proverb :—கொங்கிலே குறுணி விற்கிறது இங்கு என்னத்திற்கு—"Why remain here when grain sells cheap in the "Congoo country;" showing its fertility.——*Caungyum* (காங்கயம் - kángayam, Tam. kángyam *). From (kongu, tam. country so named + ayam, tam. ground).—"*a*" Deputy tahsildarry, Coimbatore district. Pay Rs. 70.—"*b*" Village, Deputy tahsildar's station; Coimbatore dist., Dharaupooram tal.; pop. 6,956; acres 13,847; lat. 11° 00′; long. 77° 36′; from Coimbatore E. 40 miles; from Dharaupooram N. 18½ miles; from Erode S.S.W. 26 miles; from Madras S.W. 230 miles; from Ootacamund E.S.E. 63 miles; from Pollachy N.E. 45 miles; from Suttimungalam S.S.E. 39 miles. Trace of ancient kingdom of Congoo [q.v.] remains in this name. Elevated on dry gravelly soil. Former head-quarters of district, and till 1874 of Sub-collector. Once famous for breed of cattle [maud]. Still noted for ponies. Busy market town. A mile S. is large Shiva temple.——*Conganan* (கொங்கணன் - konganan, Tam.). Very ancient Tamul philosopher and physician, native of Coimbatore country. Instructed by the Aryan missionary Agastyan on Pothigay [q.v.]; probably one of his first converts. Wrote against polytheism, Conganar nyaunam; and two treatises on medicine, Cadaycaundam and Goona vaugadam. Example from Nyaunam:—கடவுளொன்றுவனுண்டே வேதமொன்றே காரணசற் குருதீட்சைதானுமொன்றே—யடைவுடனே யவனருளும் பதவியொன்றே யம்புவியின் மனுப்பிறவியானதொன்றே—நடைவழியும் பலமனுவோர்க் கொன்

ஹேயல்லால் நால்வேதமறுசமய நடைக்கைவேறுய்த்— திடமுடையதேவர்பலருண்டென் போர்கடீய்நரகுக்குள் ளாவர் திண்ணந்தானே—"There is but one God, there is "but one Veda, there is but one way of initiation by the good "spiritual guide, there is but one kind of bliss which he grants, "and there is but one genus amongst mankind upon the earth. "They who hold the contrary by asserting that there are four "Vedas and six sects and many gods, will surely enter the fiery "hell" [concan].——*Congoo desha rajakkal* (கொங்குதேசராசாக்கள் - konguthésarásákkal, Tam.). From (above + désha, san. country + rájá, san. king). A book describing the series of the Congoo or Chera rulers, from Veera roya chuckravurty to rajah Mulladevan: It contains distinct chapters on the Chola, Hoysala, and Vijianugger kingdoms, these rulers having been successively conquerors of the Congoo country.

CONICOPOLY (கணக்கப்பிள்ளை - kanakkappillai, *Tam.*). From (kanakku, tam. account + pillai, tam. title of the pillai caste). Caste-title. The corresponding teloogoo term is curnum. A village accountant. Now mostly used at Madras for a shipping clerk. See vol. I, 112.

CONIMERE (கூனிமேடு - kúnimédu, *Tam.*). From (kúni, tam. humped + médu, tam. mound). South arcot dist., Tindivanam tal.; pop. 1,933; acres 4,675; lat. 12° 05′; long. 79° 56′; from Cuddalore N.N.E. 27 miles; from Pondicherry N.N.E. 11 miles; from Tindivanam S.E. $19\frac{1}{4}$ miles; from the sea W. $\frac{1}{2}$ mile. Factory established by East india company in 1682; firmaun [q.v.] for fortified settlement and liberty of trade obtained from Ramrauz on a present of 800 pagodas, 1688; withdrawn on the purchase of Fort St. David, 1698; ceded with the rest of the soobah of Arcot by treaty with Azeem ool dowla, 31st July 1801. The factory stood on a sand-hill about 500 or 600 yards from the sea and covered an area of about 400 feet square. The foundations are still in existence.

CONJEE (काञ्चिक - káñjika, *San.*; کانجی - kánjí, *Hind.*; గంజి - ganji, *Tel.*; கஞ்சி - kañji, *Tam.*). Means boilings in tamul. Starch. So the water in which rice or other starchy grains has been boiled. The article being used as invalid diet, the word is applied to such slops generally. There is a Tamul proverb:— துழாவிக் காய்ச்சாதது கஞ்சியும் அல்ல, வினவிக்கட்டாதது கலியாணமும் அல்ல—"Conjee requires continued "stirring while boiling, and marriage requires careful consider-"ation before being entered on." Conjee is used in making paper and as a paste, also by weavers in preparing thread for the loom [nesavoo]; also by dyers [shauyam], bleachers, and washermen [dhoby]; sometimes by bricklayers, mixed with whitewash to increase adhesion. Distinguish from conjy.

CONJEEVERAM* (کنچی - kanchí, *Hind.*; காஞ்சீபுரம் - káñjíppuram, *Tam.*). From (káñchí, san. abrus precatorius, linn. + pura, san. city). Sanscrit name (káñchípura), meaning shining city; also (mókshapurí), meaning emancipation + city; also (satyavratakshétra), the menoo, so called + sacred place, from the plain on which the town is built. Tamul name (kaççi); also (tirukkaççi); also (perumálkóvil), meaning vishnoo, the great god + temple, the last in use among the veishnavas. Kien-chi-pu-lo of Hwen thsang. Indigenous name is Cutchy, from which the Sanscrit is corrupted; meaning the heart-leaved moon-seed plant, tinospora cordifolia, miers [goolancha].——**(1)** Talook, Chingleput district. Tahsildar's pay Rs. 200. Area 514 square miles. Population 176,123. Languages Tamul, Teloogoo. W. of district. Bounded north by Trivellore talook, east by Sydapett and Chingleput talooks; and south and west by North arcot district. The general appearance is monotonous, there being only low conical hills on the north-east. The general level rises gradually, from the Palaur towards the north and west. There is an entire absence of wood, and scrub jungle is to be found in very small quantities. Along the northern bank of the river palmyra [q.v.], cocoanut [q.v.] and tamarind [q.v.] trees have been planted. The soil is generally inferior, being either stony or mixed with lime [choonam], gravel, soda [sowdoo] and laterite [q.v.]. Crops are those general in Sydapett and Chingleput, with the addition of indigo [q.v.]. The weaving [nesavoo] industry has been reduced by the competition of Manchester goods. Country cloths of all kinds are still manufactured. There is a considerable trade in manufactured brass [pittalay] and other metals [loham], as well as jewellery. There are also a good many indigo vats and godowns scattered over the talook, but this industry seems to be languishing. Coarse paper-making on a small scale is also carried on. The chief sources of irrigation are the Palaur and Corteliaur. The Palaur irrigation is by means of the usual flood and spring channels [q.v.] on both banks of the river in the south of the talook and by the Cumbacaul channel. Camping grounds:— Balchetty chuttram, Royajee chuttram and Shreepermatore. Petty zemindarries:—Agaram, Baulanallore, Bheemantaungal, Bheemapooram, Cariyamungalam, Cattagaram, Caundavellore, Cauranayputt, Cauranaytaungal, Chittore, Chowkantaungal, Conoor, Cotore, Jamoonamputt, Keevalore, Moothoocore, Nemmaily, Ooloondey, Periyantaungal, Shattiray, Shelayanore, Soomitrambaid, Tandalam, Tattanore, Todoocaud, Vallacottah, Vayalore, Veipore, Vullam, Yerayore. Places of archæological interest:—Aurpaukam, Conjeeveram, Cooram, Madooramungalam, Manimungalam, Mookkayalore, Muttavaid, Orattoor, Peroondore, Poollalore, Shreepermatore, Tennairy, Tirpacooly, Tripattycoondram, Vadakkapett, Yelayanaurvainore. Principal Trig. station, Malayaputt. The leading places, &c., in the talook are the following.——*Baulanallore* (பாலநல்லூர் - pálanallúr, Tam.). From (bála, san. proper name + nal, tam. good + úr, tam. village). Zemindarry, Village; pop. 556; acres 1,053; lat. of village 12° 55′; long. 79° 58′; from Conjeeveram N.E. 15 miles; from Sydapett S.W. 22 miles. Peshcush Rs. 455. Many Christians.——*Caundavellore* (காந்தவேலூர் - kándavélúr, Tam.). From (kánta, san. beautiful + vélúr, tam. town, so called). Zemindarry, Village; pop. 474; acres 2,200; lat. of village 12° 55′; long. 79° 55′; from Conjeeveram N.E. 12 miles; from Sydapett W. 25 miles. Peshcush Rs. 595. Noted for quarry stones.——*Cauranayputt* (காரணப்பட்டு - káranappattu, Tam.). From (kár, tam. black + anai, tam. bund + pattu, tam. village). Zemindarry, Village; acres 197; lat. of village 12° 54′; long. 79° 59′; from Conjeeveram N.E. 15 miles; from Sydapett S.W. 22 miles. Peshcush Rs. 60. Formerly country residence of Collector of Chingleput.——*Cauranaytaungal* (காரணைத்தாங்கல் - káranaittángal, Tam.). From (kár, tam. black + anai, tam. bund + tángal, tam. pond). Zemindarry, Village; pop. 270; acres 436; lat. of village 13° 00′; long. 80° 02′; from Conjeeveram N.E. 20 miles; from Sydapett W. 17 miles. Peshcush Rs. 148.——*Chengalroyan chuttram* (செங்கல்ராயன்சத்திரம் - shengalráyansattiram, Tam. chengalráyanchattram*). From (shengalráyan, tam. proper name + sattra, san. choultry). Tam. also (uvvéri), meaning penance + tank. Village, Railway station; pop. 405; lat. 12° 56′; long. 79° 45′; from Conjeeveram, N. 6 miles; from Sydapett W. 36 miles. Poor pilgrims obtain provisions in this village on tickets.——*Cheyaur* (செய்யாறு - sheyyáru, Tam.). See sep. title.——*Conjeeveram* (காஞ்சீபுரம் - káñjíppuram, Tam.). See below.——*Cotore* (கோட்டூர் - kóttúr, Tam.). From (kóttam, tam. agricultural tract + úr, village). Zemindarry, Village; pop. 1,369; acres 1,806; lat. of village 13° 00′; long. 79° 52′; from Conjeeveram N.E. 12 miles; from Sydapett W. 28 miles. Peshcush Rs. 1,509.——*Cumbacaul* (கம்பக்கால் - kambakkál, Tam.). From (kambai, tam. river so called + kál, tam. channel). Channel. Taken off the Palaur at the same anicut which supplies Cauverypauk tank in the North arcot district, about 25 miles west of Conjeeveram. Flows along a ridge which runs on the western and northern sides of the talook, and fills chains of tanks, sometimes two, three, and four deep on each side of its course. The total irrigation thus supplied supports a revenue of about Rs. 44,000. It is a native work, improved about thirty years ago, and there is a project restoring the entire native scheme, which included a branch running south-east across the Conjeeveram and Chingleput talooks, and which was designed to irrigate lands up to within a few miles of the coast near Tirporore.——*Daumal* (தாமல் - támal, Tam.). From (támarai, tam. lotus, nelumbium speciosum, willd.). Village; pop. 2,356; acres 4,591; lat. 12° 53′; long. 79° 39′; from Conjeeveram W.N.W. $8\frac{1}{4}$ miles; from Sydapett W. 43 miles. Westernmost village of the district. Large Shiva temple. Large tank.——*Keelcherry* (கீழ்ச்சேரி - kízhççéri, Tam.). From (kízh, tam. east + shéri, tam. village). Village; pop. 1,355; acres 649; lat. 13° 02′; long. 79° 54′; from Conjeeveram N.E. 16 miles; from Sydapett W. 25 miles. Inhabited by Roman catholic descendants of immigrants who came from Guntoor during famine of 1787 under Father Manente.——*Malayaputt* (மலையப்பட்டு - malaiyappattu, Tam.). From (malai, tam. mountain + pattu, tam. village). Trig. station; lat. 12° 54′ 51·70″; long. 80° 03′ 19·65″; height 468 feet; from Colatore N. 21 miles; from Conjeeveram E.N.E. 21 miles.——*Manimungalam* (மணிமங்கலம் - manimangalam, Tam.). From (mani, tam. beauty + mangala, san. prosperity). Village; pop. 1,767; acres 2,725; lat. 12° 55′; long. 80° 06′; from Conjeeveram N.E. 23 miles; from Sydapett S.W. 14 miles. One of the 16 pergunnahs of the old jagheer [q.v.] of Chingleput. A temple with apsidal gopooram [q.v.], Permaul coil and erect stone in front of it. Rajagopaul permaul temple.——*Mappaid* (மப்பேடு - mappédu, Tam.). From (má, tam. great + pédu, tam. village). Village, Government; pop. 2,101; acres 3,881; lat. 13° 02′; long. 79° 55′; from Conjeeveram N.E. 17 miles; from Sydapett W. 24 miles. ——*Maugaral* (மாகரல் - mágaral, Tam.). From (má, tam. great + kazhal, tam. the bonduc creeper, cæsalpinia bonducella, flem.). Sanscrit name (mahákarapura), meaning mahacaran, the long-armed giant + town. Village, Government; pop. 1,488; acres 2,686; lat. 12° 43′; long. 79° 49′; from Conjeeveram S.S.E. 9 miles; from Sydapett W.S.W. 37 miles.——*Mosarwaukum* (முசரவாக்கம் - musaravákkam, Tam.). From (musiru, tam. large red ant + vákkam, tam. village). Village; pop. 2,099; acres 3,104; lat. 12° 52′; long. 79° 40′; from Conjeeveram W. 6 miles; from Sydapett W. 42 miles. Rich agricultural village on the great western trunk road. Site of an entrenched camp occupied by Hyder.——*Palaur* (பாலாறு - páláru, Tam.). See sep. title.——*Paranthoor* (பறந்தூர் - paranthúr, Tam.). From (parundu, tam. a kite + úr, tam. village). Sanscrit name (gridhrapura), meaning vulture + town. Village, Government;

pop. 1,471 ; acres 3,274 ; lat. 12° 57′ ; long. 79° 48′ ; from Conjeeveram N.N.E. 7½ miles ; from Sydapett W. 33 miles.——*Perambaukam* (பேரம்பாக்கம் - pérambákkam, Tam.). From (peru, tam. great + pákkam, tam. village). Village ; pop. 1,415 ; acres 1,359; lat. 13° 02′ ; long. 79° 52′ ; from Conjeeveram N.N.E. 15½ miles ; from Sydapett W. 27 miles.——*Poollalore* (புள்ளலூர் - pullalúr, Tam.). See sep. title.——*Shreepermatore* (சிரீப்பெரும்பூதூர் - shirípperumbúthúr, Tam.). See sep. title.——*Tirpacooly* (திருப்பக்குழி - tiruppakkuzhi, Tam.). From (tiru, tam. holy + pul, tam. a bird + kuzhi, tam. pit). Sanscrit name (jatáyutírt'ha), meaning jatauyoo, the sacred kite + place of sacred waters ; also (gridhrasaras), meaning vulture + tank. Village, Government ; pop. 1,582 ; acres 1,439 ; lat. 12° 53′ ; long. 79° 41′; from Conjeeveram W.N.W. 5¾ miles ; from Sydapett W.S.W. 41 miles. Temple to Jatauyoo.——*Wallajahbad* (والاجاهباد - wálájáhbád, Hind.). See sep. title.——**(2)** Deputy tahsildarry, Chingleput district. Pay Rs. 100.——**(3)** Town, Municipality, Talook, special town magistrate, Sub-registrar's head-quarters, Place of pilgrimage, Railway station ; Chingleput dist., Conjeeveram tal. ; pop. 42,548 ; acres 2,276 ; lat. 12° 50′ ; long. 79° 46′ ; height 274 feet ; from Arcot E. 27 miles ; from Bangalore E. 140 miles ; from Chingleput W.N.W. 20 miles ; from Cuddalore N. 75 miles ; from Madras W.S.W. 45 miles ; from St. Thomas' mount W. 37 miles ; from Sydapett W. 38 miles. One of the seven holy cities of India, called the Benares of the south. Second in antiquity to Surat. On the railway between Arconum and Chingleput, in a valley on route from Madras to Arcot. The town is five or six miles long ; the streets are mostly broad, and planted on both sides with cocoanut and bastard cedar trees ; many gardens and topes, under the shade of which weavers have their looms [nesavoo, tarry]. The Vaigavaty on the west contributes to fertility of valley. An inscription of Poolikeshy of the Chalookyan dynasty is to the effect that he conquered the Chola king and burned Conjeeveram. The date of this ruler is about 489 A.D. In fourteenth century became the capital of Tondaimuudalam. After the fall of the Vijianugger family in 1644 was subject to Golcondah princes, and afterwards, passing under Mahomedan rule, became part of Arcot dominions. Captured by Clive from French in 1751 ; in same year, taken by Razah sahib ; recaptured by Clive in 1752 ; in 1757, the French beaten off in an attack upon the pagoda set fire to the town ; in 1758 British garrison was temporarily withdrawn on account of the expected advance of the French upon Madras, but was soon sent back with reinforcements ; retaken from the French in 1759 and plundered by Hyder ally in 1780. Conjeeveram succeeded Carangooly as Collector's head-quarters in 1825 and remained so till 1830, the Collector's records and treasury remaining there for thirty years longer. There are three divisions in the place connected with religion ; namely, Jeina canjy, Shiva canjy, and Vishnoo canjy. As to Jeina canjy there are a few houses on the west side of the river where there is a temple, containing a representation of Booddha. Hwen thsang speaks of it as the capital of Dravida ruled by the Chola dynasty, and a great Booddhist centre. About the eighth century began a Jeina epoch, and traces of this religion still exist in the neighbourhood. There is a local legend of a dispute between Booddhists and Jeinas, and the latter being crushed in oil-mills [gaunam]. According to popular belief there are ten thousand lingams [q.v.] here. They may be seen set up at every turn. The largest and oldest temple of Conjeeveram is to Shiva, and the object of worship there is the earth-lingam [puncha lingam]. This is the head-quarters of the Adweitam [q.v.] doctrine. The enclosure possesses some large gopoorams, several mantapams and a hall of 1,000 pillars. The great tower erected over the grand entrance is the highest building of the kind in India. There are two handsome porches in front of the great gopooram built by Krishna deva roya of Vijianugger. Between the vimaunam [q.v.] and the great gopooram [q.v.] is a very old stone building covered with inscriptions. The building was often made into a fort during the wars of the Carnatic. Hyder ally has left the mark of his cannon shot on the large doors of the eastern gate as well as on the tower and gateway itself. A smaller temple dedicated to Vishnoo under the name of Varadaraja sawmy is the richest and most important religious institution in Conjeeveram. It is the centre of the Vishishtaudweitam [q.v.] school of ethics. It has two enclosures, the inner one being closed to Europeans and unbelievers. The first gopooram is severe in outline and is not plastered over with figures of Hindoo mythology. It has a number of inscriptions. The third important temple is to Caumautchy, wife of Shiva, and is devoted to worship of material good and pleasure. Besides these there are Gajendra varada in Ashtabhooja agrahauram, Jwarahareeshwaran in good preservation and wonderfully rich in sculpture, Oolacalanda permaul, Keilausa nautan, apparently coeval with the shore temple at the Seven pagodas [q.v.] which it strongly resembles and older than any temple yet found in Conjeeveram, Anaicapatangauvoodaiyaur or Anaicapatangeshwaran, Veicoonta perumal, Matangeshwaran very old, Moocteshwaran, Cutcheshwaran or Cutchaleshwaran parts very old, Eirauvateshwaran and Tripoorauntaceshwaran, Pandava perumal with old vimaunam, Tricaleshwaran, and Lutchmaneshwaran. There is a large mosque marking burial place of a fakeer from Beejapore. The tanks of the town are highly sacred. The finest is Sarwa teertam on outskirts of town to south of Shiva temple. Its sides are studded with small pagodas. The great annual festival in May is attended by 50,000 pilgrims. Trade consists almost solely of grain, for which Conjeeveram is the emporium of a large extent of surrounding country both in Chingleput and North arcot ; and cloth manufactured by the large weaver community. Two quarters of the town, Sheikhpett and Pillay polliem, are almost exclusively inhabited by weavers. The products of the looms consist chiefly of cotton handkerchiefs and native cloths for men and women. There is also a little silk-weaving. The cotton thread used is entirely English. The artificers of the town are clever workers in brass [pittalay] and copper [taumram]. They also turn out native jewellery of the usual kinds. The Scottish free church has a mission, and there is also a High school maintained by Patchiappa's charities. There is a Tamul proverb :—காஞ்சிபுரத்திற்குப் போனால் கால் ஆட்டி உண்ணலாம்—"If you go to Conjeeveram you may eat without "labor ;" meaning that there are so many choultries there.

CONJY (अश्वशाखोट - ashvashákhóta, *San.* ; بن نيمبو - bannímbú, *Hind.* ; గోలుగు - golugu, *Tel.* ; கொஞ்சி - koñji, *Tam.*). Title from tamul. To be distinguished from conjee. San. from (ashva, san. horse + shákhóta, san. epicarpurus orientalis, blume). Hind. from (ban, hind. forest + nímbú, hind. citrus medica, linn., var. limonum, brandis). Hind. also (gurgití), meaning blood sucker's root, from its fondness for it. Tel. also (gonjichettu) ; (kondagolugu), meaning hill-conjy. Tam. also (káttukkoñji), meaning wild conjy. Title otherwise Blood sucker root, Wild lemon. Botanically Glycosmis pentaphylla, correa, rutaceæ [vricsham, 32]. Alias Glycosmis arborea, chylocarpa ; Limonia arborea, pentaphylla. Erect, unarmed shrub ; leaflets three to five, oblong, entire or toothed ; panicles contracted ; petals broadly oval ; filaments broader towards the apex and suddenly contracted below the anther ; flowers small, white. Very common ; smooth, roundish, red fruit, about the size of a cherry ; wood bruised with water a specific in snake-bite ; fruit edible.——*Foreign conjy* (कुंटी - kuntí, Mahr. ; ಅಂಗಾರಕಗಿಡ - angárakagida, Can. ; నాగగోలుగు - nágagolugu, Tel. ; சீமைக் கொஞ்சி - shímaikkoñji, Tam.). Can. from (angáraka, san. fire + gida, can. plant) ; perhaps from red berries. Tel. from (nága, san. snake + golugu, tel. glycosmis pentaphylla, corr.). Tam. from (shímai, tam. foreign + koñji, tam. glycosmis pentaphylla, corr.). Title otherwise Andaman satin-wood, China box, Honey bush, Nauga conjy. Botanically Murraya [caroovaimboo] exotica, linn., rutaceæ [vricsham, 32]. A large handsome bushy shrub, with shining dark green foliage of pinnate leaves, leaflets six or eight, an inch or two long, alternate, obovate, rigid, and quite smooth ; bears several times during the hot and rainy seasons, in great profusion, corymbs of not large white flowers, fragrant during day ; bears in cold season numerous small red berries, not unlike holly ; shrub resembles a box tree. Religious plant. Planted for ornament. Wood light-yellow, close-grained, very hard, apt to crack ; resembles boxwood.——*Nauga conjy* (నాగగోలుగు - nágagolugu, Tel.). Same as Foreign conjy.

CONKY (కొంకి - kónki, *Tel.* ; முருவல்செடி - muruvalsedi, *Tam.*). Tam. from (muruval, tam. laugh + shedi, tam. plant), from bright leaves. Tel. also (embúdichettu) ; (kankiputri). Tam. also (kárindu), meaning black mimosa ; (ilaççaikkettayilaiççedi), meaning bashfulness + destitute + plant. Title otherwise Bashful tree, Laughing plant, Lettuce tree, Shameless plant, Strumpet plant, West indian cock's-spur. Botanically Pisonia alba, spanoghe, nyctagineæ [vricsham, 105]. Alias Pisonia morindifolia. Ramous shrub, six or seven feet high ; dense foliage of large, lanceolate, pale lettuce-green leaves ; leaves keep green if in shade and become a pale yellow color if fully exposed to the sun. Another species is aculeata ; tall woody climber ; flowers small, greenish-white ; flowering in march and april ; common ; bark and leaves a counter-irritant for swellings and rheumatic pains.

COO (कु - ku, *San.*). Prefix implying depreciation or low situation or deficiency. Earth, sin. As a verb means to sound indistinctly.——*Codandam* (कोदण्ड - kódanda, San.). From (ku, san. bent + danda, san. stick). A bow, especially the bow of Rama, which none but him can wield. Hindoo 2nd or pers. name. Common to both sexes. Appears as Codandaraman [peyar].——*Coobairan* (कुबेर - kubéra, San.). From (above + béra, san. body) ; of deformed body. πλοῦτος of Greeks. God of wealth, and regent of north. Originally the chief of evil spirits, afterwards the god of riches. Compare the legends of northern nations. He lives in a palace Alacay, and is borne in an aerial car Pooshpacam [q.v.]. His shacty [q.v.] is coobairy. See vol. I (78) [ashtadicpaulacan, matam].——*Coobairaucsham* (कुबेराक्ष - kubéráksha, San.). Coobairan + eye. Plant name common to :—Thespesia populnea; Cæsalpinia bonducella; Stereospermum suaveolens. See gloss. paragraphs.——*Coobairaucshy* (कुबेराक्षी - kubérákshí, San.). From (kubéra, san. the god + akshi, san. eye) ; from flower like coobairan's eyes. Botanically the Cæsalpinia genus, leguminosæ [vricsham, 48]. Robust erect trees, shrubs or woody prickly climbers; leaves large, abruptly bi-pinnate ; flowers showy, yellow, in copious axillary racemes; pod oblong or strap-shaped, thin and flat, or thick and sub-turgid, smooth but in sub-genus guilandina armed all over with wiry spines. The species best known to the natives are:—bonducella [bonduc], coriaria [divy divy], pulcherrima [gold mohur tree], sappan [q.v.], sepiaria [mysore thorn]. Other s. indian species indigenous or naturalized are:—digyna, mimosoides, nuga.——*Coogay* (கூகை - kúgai, Tam.). Dwarfed demons [cooly]. They form part of Shiva's ganam [q.v.]. Also name for a large hooting owl [oolóocam].——*Cooja* (كوزه - kúzah, Hind.). An earthen bottle for water [goglet].——*Coojan* (कुज - kuja, San.). From (ku, san. earth + jan, san. to be born). Cf. bhowman. Planet Mars, ♂. Sidereal period of revolution [bhaganam] is 686d 23h 31m. Inclination to the ecliptic [craunty mundalam] is 1° 51′ [jyotisham].——*Coomadwaty* (ಕುಮುದ್ವತಿ - kumadvati, Can.). Can. also (kundáru), meaning jasmine river. Cf. Coondair. Tributary of the N. pinauking or Pennair; Colaur and Toomcore districts, Mysore, length about 30 miles; joins the Pennair near Hindoopore, Anantapore district. Also name for coondair [q.v.].——*Coomaran* (குமரன் - kumaran, Tam.). From (ku, san. grief + mri, san. to die); gladdener. The same as Comauran. Name of Soobramanyan.——*Coomary* (குமரி - kumari, Tam.). Means virgin [cunny]. Comorin.——*Coomary sherpan* (குமரிச்சேர்ப்பன் - kumariççérppan, Tam.). From (shérppu, tam. coast). A title of the Paundy kings.——*Coombharan* (कुम्भर - kumbhara, San.). From (above + bhara, san. supporting). Shiva, the earth supporter.——*Coomeroo* (कुमेरु - kuméru, San.). From (above + méru, san. the mountain); evil meroo [q.v.], because abode of the demons. The southern hemisphere [golam], or south pole [asoora dhroovam], a region where Yaman presides over the Asoorans and Deityans [soomeroo].——*Coomry* (ಕುಮರಿ - kumari, Can.). From (kumbari, mahr. hill slope of poor soil). A kind of dry cultivation [vellaumay] carried on in forests by hill tribes during the rainy season. The trees standing upon the spot selected are felled and burnt; after which the ground is cultivated with rice [paddy], raggy [q.v.], &c., and sometimes with cotton [q.v.] and tobacco [pogauk]. The same space is not cleared again for cultivation for eight or ten years. Jhoom of bengal, Ponam of malabar, Ponacaud of salem [cautcaud, coomaky]. See vol. I, 112.——*Coonby* (کنبی - kumbí, Hind.; ಕುಣ್ಬಿ - kunbi, Can.). The chief agricultural caste of the Deccan [q.v.] and concan [concan, jauty].——*Cooncoomam* (कुंकुम - kumkuma, San.). From (ku, san. to sound); from sound of dry petals. Same as Saffron.——*Coondam* (कुन्द - kunda, San.). From (ku, san. earth + dó, san. to cut); breaks through the earth in sprouting. Jasmine.——*Coondapore* (ಕುಂದಾಪುರ - kundápura, Can.). See sep. title.——*Coondarpy* (కుంద్పి - kundarpi, Tel.). From (kundamu, tel. the jasmine flower, jasminum pubescens, willd.). Village; Anantapore dist., Dharmavaram tal.; pop. 2,255; lat. 14° 17′; long. 77° 04′; from Anantapore S.W. 47 miles; from Dharmavaram W. 47½ miles. Poligar fort built on hill. An inscription relates that a Mussalman ruler received from Conaity naidoo the villages of Penoocondah, &c., and gave him, in return, part of the country of Coondarpy. Five very old temples in the town. Trig. station here in lat. 14° 18′ 02·77″; long. 77° 04′ 31·64″; height 2,996 feet; from Anantapore S.W. 46 miles; from Coondarpy village N. ½ mile; from Dharmavaram W. 47½ miles. ——*Coopah* (कूप - kúpa, San.). Bottle [cooppy].——*Coopam* (കൂപം - kúpam, Mal.). From (above + ápa, san. water). Hollow. Cooparajyam, the second part of the Malabar coast. See vol. I (127) [charitram]. Extends from Payashwany to Poothooputnam on the Cotta river. Corresponds to ancient Colatnaud and to modern N. malabar. Other divisions are Keralam proper, Mooshicam, Tooloovam [cooum].——*Coopaty* (कुपति - kupati, San.). From (above + puti, san. master). A form of Shiva, the lord of the earth.——*Cooppy* (குப்பி - kuppi, Tam.). From (kúpí, san. bottle). Bottle [coopah].——*Cooralam* (कुरल - kurala, San.). See sep. title.——*Coorava* (കുരവ - kurava, Mal.). From (above + rava, san. sound); harsh sound. A shrill ululation produced by vibration of tongue between lips and teeth. By women at marriages, devil-dancing, &c.——*Coormam* (कूर्म - kúrma, San.). See sep. title.——*Coosava* (குசவ - kusava, obl.; குசவன் - kusavan, pers. sing.; குசவர் - kusavar, pers. pl., Tam.). From (ku, san. earth). Potmakers or brick [shengal] and tile [wóde] burners. The corresponding terms are:—Hind. coomhaur; Tel. coommara; Can. coombaura; Mal. coosava. The coosavan is the potter of a village, and generally furnishes each house or family once with a set of earthenware gratis; the servants of the circar [q.v.], civil and military, when travelling on duty are supplied by him with pots [chatty], as they are by the toty [q.v.] with straw and firewood; when they depart, the pots, unless they have been used by persons of an inferior caste, are taken back. These people are in some parts held in repute as sorcerers; they worship the kiln [shoolay], and generally call themselves sheivites. The men dig the clay [calimunn]; then women carry it to the place where the wheel is fixed, where it is softened and tempered and put on the earthen wheel by the men; the wheel is horizontal and is generally spun round by a woman, the man moulding and shaping it with his hands, while the simple impetus serves for the formation of the vessel; a batch of pots is put in the kiln once in a couple of months or so; fuel being laid in the bottom, the pots are arranged over it, and the kiln is covered with earth to exclude the air and to keep in the vapour; while the pottery is in the furnace, worship is paid to a demon called choolay maudan [q.v.]; on the third day the ware is taken out. The women and girls carry large loads of pottery on their heads, secured with ropes, to the markets for sale. Numbers about 300,000 [balootah, jauty].——*Coosham* (कुश - kusha, San.). From (above + shí, san. to strew); strewn on ground to sit upon.—"*a*" Sacrificial grass, which, on occasion of offerings made to the gods, is placed upon the ground as a seat for them, having its tips towards the east; also used at offerings to ancestors. Otherwise Darbhay [q.v.].—"*b*" The name of the fourth of the great insular continents or Dweepam [q.v.].—"*c*" Vishnoo had three sons; Cooshan, Lavan, and Manmatan [q.v.]. Cooshan was the first born to him in his incarnation [avatar] as Rama by his wife Seetay.—"*d*" Botanically the Eragrostis genus, graminaceæ [vricsham, 156]. Love grass. Hardy, handsome grasses distinguished by having inflorescence in compound or decompound panicles; glumes four to ten-flowered; seeds loose, two-horned, not furrowed. The species best known to the natives are:—bifaria [squirrel ginger], ciliaris [wild cumboo], ciliata [wild coraly], cynosuroides [darbhay], plumosa [shaumay grass]. Other s. indian species indigenous or naturalized are:—atropurpurea, cretacea, kœnigii, mangalorica, nigra, nutans, parviglumis, procera, punctata, stenophylla, tenella, viscosa.——*Cooshastaly* (కుశస్థలి - kushast'hali, Tel.). From (kusha, san. sacred grass + st'hali, san. wild tract). River; North arcot dist., Carvetnugger zemindarry, Narrainavaram division and Chingleput dist., Trivellore tal. Local name of Nagary. Rises near Pautagoonta. Runs east, between August and December. Crossed by railway bridge N. of Nagary railway station. Flows also through Chingleput and joins Corteliaur [q.v.].——*Cooshauvaty* (ಕುಶಾವತಿ - kusháwati, Can.; kushavati, Mys. Gov.). River. Two streams of this name, one a tributary of the Paupughny, the other of the Chitrauvaty. Colaur district, Mysore.——*Cooshtam* (कुष्ठ - kusht'ha, San.). See sep. title.——*Cooum* (کهاری - khári, Hind.; கூவம் - kúvam, Tam.). Title from (kúpa, san. a well). Hind. means brackish. Tamul because river issues from a well [coopam]. The name is mentioned in the Tamul devauram [q.v.] as the more common name of a sacred place of Shiva called Tirvitcolam. River in Chingleput and Madras district; lat. 13° 02′ to 13° 4′; long. 79° 50′ to 80° 20′. Rises at a village near Shreepermatore in Conjeeveram talook, Chingleput district, about 30 miles distant from Madras. Joined by the old Bungaur channel. Irrigates Cadambatore, Tinnanore and other villages in neighbourhood of railway, and from an anicut [q.v.] thrown across it at Corattore sends down a supply to Chembrambaukam tank through new Bungaur channel. It then irrigates Ayanambaukam, Vauyalanullore, and other villages of Sydapett talook, and flowing through the town of Madras, falls into the sea at the Marine villa in lat. 13° 4′ N.; long. 80° 20′ E. Within Madras town limits it expands and is to a great extent stagnant, having seldom volume enough to force its bar and receiving much of the sewage of the neighbourhood. About a mile from its mouth it divaricates, forming two nearly equal branches; the left or more northern, close to the point of parting, receiving a water course running from the north. After this accession the left branch flows by the southern rampart of Black town [q.v.] and subsequently by the south-west face of the fort. The right branch takes a direction first south, subsequently south-east, and both joining about 300 yards from the sea inclose what is called the island [q.v.]. Commercially the river is of little importance, except that the branches that encircle the island are the connecting link between the northern and southern sections of the Buckingham canal [q.v.]. The river is crossed by seven fine bridges in the Madras talook, viz., the Napier, the Wallajah, the Periamett, the Harris, the College, the Commander-in-Chief's and the Chintaudripett.——*Coova* (കൂവ - kúva, Mal.). From (kúvu, mal. to cry + kai, mal. stem); from hollow stems through which children blow bubbles. W. coast arrowroot. The different kinds in Malábar are:—Aunacoova, costus speciosus, sm.; Nyetticoova, curcuma angustifolia, roxb.; Malancoova, kœmpferia rotunda, willd., and Manyalcoova, curcuma longa, roxb.——*Coovid* (കൂവിട - kúvita, Mal.). From (kúvu, mal. to cry aloud + ita, mal. place). The distance at which a loud call is heard. A measure of distance = 6,666 yards. Compare coss, croe and crosham. Distinguish from covid.——*Cooy cooy* (കൂയികൂയി - kúyikúyi, Mal.). From the sound. Portuguese cucuya. A cry of warning.——*Cosalam* (कोसल - kósala, San.). From (ku, san. the earth + sal, san. to attain prominence). Two countries of this name. N. cosalam was an extensive kingdom including Ayodhyay, S. cosalam was the modern Berar province. One of Hwen thsang's nine southern kingdoms was Kiao sa-lo, perhaps the latter. See vol. I (117) [charitram].

COO (కు - ku, *Tel.*). The name of the Khonds [q.v.] among themselves. Compare Coyi similarly for the Gonds [q.v.].

COODA (கூட - kuda, *Tam.*). From (kodu, tam. steep), referring to the steep ghaut [q.v.] which formed the W. line of

Tamul-speaking country; hence West [coda]. Cf. Congoo, Coorg.——*Coodagam* (குடகம் - kudagam, Tam.). Coorg [bhoogolashastram].

COODAH (குடா - kudá, *Tam.*). From (kudai, tam. to scoop). Gulf. Owing to the continuous shore, the only gulf of Southern India is Manaar [q.v.], separated from Palk's strait by the islands of Rameshwaram and Manaar and several rocks between them, called Adam's bridge [q.v.].

COODAL (கூடல் - kúdal, *Tam.*). From (kúdu, tam. to join). Junction. Grove, especially a thick grove of palmyra [q.v.] trees. Compare Cauv. Suffix in place names, as Bhawauny coodal, meaning the place where the bhawauny joins the cauvery. Ancient name for town of Madura.

COODAPA (కుడప - kudapa, *Tel.*). From (kudiyu, tel. to sink as in mud). Wet ploughing [paddy]. Opposite of gaddavary.

COODLIGY (ಕೂಡ್ಲಿಗಿ - kúdligi, *Can.*; కూడ్లిగి - kúdligi,* *Tel.*). From (kúdu, tel. junction).——(1) Talook, Bellary district. Tahsildar's pay Rs. 175. Area 863 square miles. Population 94,296. Language Canarese. S. of district. Bounded N. by Hurpanhully and Hospett talooks and Sundoor state, E. by Molacaulmooroo talook of the Mysore territory, S. by Cancooppa talook of the same territory, and W. by Hurpanhully and Hoovinhadgully talooks. On the N.E. the Comaurasawmy range is prolonged to the neighbourhood of Goodicottah. There are low hills all round the cusbah [q.v.] also. The highest point is Jarimaley. Three-quarters of the talook are waste. The red and mixed soils largely predominate; they are very poor and in consequence lightly assessed. Cholum [q.v.], tamarind [q.v.], chillies [q.v.], cocoanuts [q.v.], lamp-oil [q.v.] seeds and gram [q.v.], are sent to the Bellary markets, and jaggery [q.v.], to Moondrigy in Dharwar. A small quantity of rice [q.v.] is imported for the wealthier classes, chiefly from the Mysore districts. Good woollen cumblies [q.v.], are woven at Nimbalgherry. The Chinna hagary river, to be distinguished from the Hagary in the Bellary talook, flows through the west of the talook. Its water is not utilized in any way for irrigation. The principal sources of irrigation are the tanks of Choranore, Coodligy, Cottore, Hanshy, and Oojany. Camping grounds :—Choranore, Coodligy, Cottore, Goodicottah, Hoolikerey, and Nimbalgherry. Places of archæological interest :—Ambaly, Baivore, Bennicull, Cottore, Devalaupooram, Goodicottah, Hailya, Hoolicoontey, Oojany, Sangameshwaram, Shiranaickenhully, Sovainahully, Veerandroog. Principal Trig. station :—Jarimaley. The leading places, &c., in the talook are the following.——*Chinna hagary* (చిన్నహగరి - chinnahagari, Tel.). See sep. title.——*Choranore* (ಚೋರನೂರು - chóranúru, Can.). From (chóra, san. robber + úru, can. village). Village; pop. 1,584; acres 9,802; lat. 14° 55′; long. 76° 35′; from Bellary W.S.W. 30 miles; from Coodligy E. 10 miles. Large tank.——*Cottore* (కొట్టూరు - kottúru, Tel.). From (kotta, tel. new + úru, tel. village). Village; pop. 6,136; acres 8,707; lat. 14° 49′; long. 76° 16′; from Bellary W.S.W. 51¼ miles; from Coodligy W.S.W. 12 miles. Founded by a hermit, Basappa. Formerly Moonsif's court. A large tank. A place of pilgrimage for Lingayets. Cotton [q.v.] and silk [puttoo] weaving. Chief market place.——*Goodicottah* (గుడికోట - gudikóta, Tel.). From (gudi, tel. temple + kóta, tel. fort). Village; pop. 1,418; acres 14,192; lat. 14° 49′; long. 76° 40′; from Bellary S.W. 28 miles; from Coodligy E.S.E. 17¼ miles. Once the seat of a powerful poligar [q.v.]. Ruins of a fort and palace and fragments of sculpture.——*Hailya* (ಹೇಳ್ಯ - hélya, Can.). Village; acres 5,013; lat. 14° 51′; long. 76° 16′; from Bellary W.S.W. 49 miles; from Coodligy W.S.W. 11 miles. Inscription of a local dynasty near a mantapam [q.v.].——*Hanshy* (హనిశి - hanishi, Can.). From (panasa, tel. jack tree, artocarpus integrifolia, willd.). Village; pop. 1,345; acres 4,019; lat. 14° 57′; long. 76° 21′; from Bellary W.S.W. 43 miles; from Coodligy W.N.W. 5¾ miles. Contains a large tank.——*Jarimaley* (ಜರಿಮಲೆ - jarimale, Can.). See sep. title.——*Nimbalgherry* (నింబళగిరి - nimbalagiri, Tel.). From (nimba, san. margosa tree, melia azadirachta, linn. + giri, san. hill). Village; pop. 1,160; acres 8,161; lat. 14° 42′; long. 76° 24′; from Bellary S.W. 47 miles; from Coodligy S. 14½ miles. Cumblies woven.——*Oojany* (ఉజని - ujani, Tel.). From (ut, san. intensive prefix + jaya, san. victory). Sanscrit name (ujjayaní). Village; pop. 2,999; acres 11,249; lat. 14° 43′; long. 76° 20′; from Bellary S.W. 51 miles; from Coodligy S.S.W. 14½ miles. Important tank. A place of pilgrimage. Seat of Lingayet [q.v.] chief Cooroo. Well built temple dedicated to Mowla siddheshwaran.——*Veerandroog* (ವೀರನದುರ್ಗ - víranadurga, Can.). From (víra, san. a hero + durga, san. fort). Sanscrit name (víradurga). Hill; lat. 14° 51′; long. 76° 26′; from Bellary W.S.W. 41 miles; from Coodligy S. 3¾ miles. Has a strong fort which Tippoo sultan unsuccessfully attacked.——(2) Village, Talook head-quarters; Bellary dist., Coodligy tal.; pop. 3,343; acres 5,494; lat. 14° 54′; long. 76° 26′; from Adony S.W. 78½ miles; from Bellary S.W. 39 miles; from Hospett S. 23 miles; from Hurpanhully E.N.E. 29 miles; from Madras W.N.W. 291 miles; from Tadpatry W.S.W. 108 miles.

COODOO (ಕೊಡು - kudu, *Can.*). Means small [coor].—"*a*" Measure of capacity. 4 bullahs = 1 coodoo, 20 coodoos = 1 cundaga [alavay, 3 c]. [Approximate actual value, 1 coodoo = 560 cubic inches. Mysore. Same as Colagam. Compare Mercaul of Tinnevelly.—"*b*" Superficial measure. Same table [alavay, 2 c]. Approximate actual value, 1 coodoo = 3,200 square yards of dry land or 500 square yards of wet land. Land requiring a coodoo of seed.——*Coodoomy* (குடுமி - kudumi, Tam.). From (kudu, tam. narrow or small); to distinguish from conday which is the whole tuft of hair made into a knot at the top; this latter is generally met with in the aborigines. A tuft of hair left on the head, usually about a foot long knotted at the end. Used by Hindooized Tamulians and regarded as a sign of respectability. There is a Tamul proverb :—அரைத்து மீந்தது அம்மி சிரைத்து மீந்தது குடுமி—"After grinding "the stone remains; after shaving the head, the coodoomy "remains." In the Tamul poem, Shiva vaucyam, the coodoomy is opposed, along with other Hindoo practices, thus: "The four "vedams, the sacrificial coosham [q.v.] grass, the coodoomy, the "ascetic's staff which Bramins carry; when born, were the "Bramin's cord [poonool] and the coodoomy born with you?" When the Bramins were brought by Parshooraman to the west coast their coodoomy was removed from the back to the front of the head to prevent their returning to their former home and people [conday, keraloputty, maryauday].——*Coodtay* (ಕುಡ್ತೆ - kudte, Can.); means narrow-mouthed vessel. Liquid measure, 2 coodtays = 1 cutcha seer [alavay, 4 c]. Approximate actual value, 1 coodtay = 10¾ cubic inches. S. canara, for oil. Compare Gidda of Kistna and Vizagapatam.

COODRAT (قدرت - kudrat, *Ar.*). From (kadara, ar. to be strong). Power. Part of lacab; as Coodrat haleem, power of God [ism].

COODY (കുടി - kuti, *Mal.*; குடி - kudi, *Tam.*). Agricultural village, habitation. Suffix in place names, especially in Tanjore and Madura [goody]. Compare Caud, wild tract. Also an inhabitant.——*Coodicauval* (കുടിക്കാവൽ - kutikkával, Mal.). From (above + kával, mal. guard). Village watch system.——*Coodima* (കുടിമ - kutima, Mal.). General term for tenancy in Malabar, other than Adima [q.v.]. Occupation of an estate for a season, either under lease or mortgage [panayam] tenure. See vol. II, 105.——*Coodimaneer* (കുടിമനീർ - kutimanír, Mal.). From (above + nír, mal. water). The last stage before actual transfer of Jenm, in the W. coast system of mortgage or land-transfer. See Cannam and Otty.——*Coodippaka* (കുടിപ്പക - kutippaka, Mal.). From (above + paka, mal. enmity). Resentment by the whole family of a wrong done to a member.——*Coodisay* (குடிசை - kudisai, Tam.). Hut. Suffix in place names.——*Coodivauram* (குடிவாரம் - kudivàram, Tam.). From (above in sense of inhabitant + vára, san. share). The share of the produce from land or salt pans [ooppalam] assigned to the cultivator [mail vauram]. See vol. I, 112. Cf. Coy laubham on west coast.——*Coodiyaun* (குடியான் - kudiyán, Tam.). An inhabitant, especially one who has caste. Often short as Coody.——*Coodiyiroopp* (കുടിയിരിപ്പ - kutiyirippa, Mal.; குடியிருப்பு - kudiyiruppu, Tam.). From (above + iruppu, tam. abode). Inhabitant's residence. Quarter occupied by people of some one tribe or caste; thus Chetty coodiyiroopp, the chetties' quarter. Compare agrahauram and cherry. Specification in a deed of conveyance of permission to a tenant to reside on a rented or mortgaged estate, in which case he is entitled to remuneration for any buildings he may have erected when his tenancy ends. In Malabar, also two fanams paid by tenant for land taken up for houses.——*Coody ayacut* (குடி ஆயக்கட்டு - kudiáyakkattu, Tam.). From (áyakkattu, tam. total extent of land). The total of inhabitants of a village.——*Coody makkal* (குடிமக்கள் - kudimakkal, Tam.). From (above + makkal, tam. men). Village public servants [balootah].——*Coody maraumut* (குடிமராமத்து - kudimarámattu, Tam.). From (marammat, ar. repairs). Contribution of labor for petty repairs to irrigation work, which the ryots are bound to give by immemorial custom. There is a law now for enforcing it or collecting its value; not often applied. See vol. I, 112. Much the same as amjy [q.v.].——*Coody oodambadicay* (குடியுடம்படிக்கை - kudiyudambadikkai, Tam.). From (udanbadikkai, tam. contract). Same as puttah.——*Coody pillay* (குடிப்பிள்ளை - kudippillai, Tam.). From (pillai, tam. title of respect). A division of the Pariahs [q.v.]; generally barbers.——*Coody taram* (குடித்தாரம் - kudittaram, Tam.). From (taram, tam. rate). Assessment according to individuals [ryotwarry], as opposed to lump village settlement [mottafeisal]. See vol. I, 112.

COOKOORAM (कुकुर - kukura, *San.*). From (kuk, san. to seize). Family Canidæ, digitigrada, carnivora, mammalia [sastanam, 12], of naturalists [jantoo]. Dog. Fore feet with five toes, the thumb raised; hind feet usually with four. Head more or less conical, and pointed in front, the jaws being produced; legs of nearly equal length. The tongue smooth. In domestic dogs there is often a fifth claw on the hind feet, but only connected by skin, and called the dew-claw. The skull partakes of the characteristics of both cat [poonay] and bear [richam]. The bark is peculiar to the domesticated dog [nye] and may have arisen in imitation of the tones of the human voice. The wild dog only whines, howls and growls. It is probable that the domestic dog has descended from different species of wolf and jackal. The wild dog is called dhole. The pariah dog [pye] is merely a mongrel, run wild and half-starved. The poligar [q.v.] dog is an immense creature peculiar to the south [combay]. The dog is mentioned by the Hebrew scriptures always in terms of aversion; the Hindoos have not the same feeling, but Mahomedans treat it as unclean. • The family contains the fox [lomree], jackal [q.v.], wild dog [dhole] and wolf [konye].

COOLAM (कुल - kula, *San.*). From (kul, san. to accumulate). A family. Cf. Gotram, the tribe. In natural history a family. For category, see Padaurtam; for elementary substance, see Dravyam; for matter, see Bhootam; for organic and inorganic, see Indriyam and Anindriyam; for organic kingdom, see Ganam [jantoo, vricsham]; for organic class, see Vargam; for organic order, see Santaunam; for organic family, see the present head; for organic genus, see Jauty; for organic species, see Bhaidam. Oopa prefixed to either of the above means a sub-head. For inorganic minerals, see Dhautoo.——*Coola bhrashta* (कुलभ्रष्ट - kulabhrashta, San.). From (bhrashta, san. fallen). A class of outcaste Bramins. Very few.——*Coolacurny* (کلکرنی - kulkarní, Hind.; ಕುಲಕರ್ಣಿ - kulakarni, Can.). From (above + karni, can. accountant). Village accountant [shanbogue]. See vol. I, 112. ——*Coola devatay* (कुलदेवता - kuladévatá, San.). From (above + dévatá, san. god). Household god. No house is supposed to be without its tutelary divinity, but the notion attached to this character is far from precise [matam].——*Coola parvatam* (कुलपर्वत - kulaparvata, San.). From (above + parvata, san. mountain); chief mountain. A system of seven chains of mountains in S. india according to Tamul geography:—Mahendram, Malayam, Sahyam, Shooctimat, Ricsham, Vindhyam, and Pauripautram. Mahendram is the eastern ghauts [q.v.]. Malayam, the hills of malabar proper, the south part of the western ghauts [q.v.]; sahyam, the northern parts of the western ghauts; shooctimat is doubtful; ricsham, the mountains of góndwana; vindhyam is here applied to the eastern division of the vindhyam mountains; pauripautram, or pauriyautram as it is frequently written, applies to the northern and western portions of the same range. Ptolemy has seven ranges, but his names are not in accord [bhoogolashastram, charitram]. See vol. I (4).——*Coolashekharan* (कुलशेखर - kulashékhara, San.). From (above + shékhara, san. crown). Title of the Paundy and Travancore kings [charitram].——*Coolashekharaputnam* (குலசேகரப்பட்டணம் - kulaségarappattanam, Tam. kulasekharapatnam *). From (kulashékhara, san. pándya king, the family head + pattana, san. town).—"*a*" Deputy tahsildarry, Tinnevelly district. Pay Rs. 100.—"*b*" Town, Port, Deputy tahsildar's station; Tinnevelly dist., Tencaray tal.; pop. 15,924; acres 2,928; lat. 8° 24′; long. 78° 06′; from Madras S.S.W. 346 miles; from Ootangoody N.E. 22 miles; from Palamcottah S.E. 31 miles; from Shermadevy E.S.E. 39 miles; from Shreevillipoottore S.S.E. 81 miles; from Shreeveicoontam S.S.E. 20 miles; from Tinnevelly S.E. 33 miles; from Trichendore S.W. 8 miles; from Tuticorin S.S.W. 29 miles. On Gulf of Manaar, adjoining Manápaud point and more than 30 miles east-north-east of Cape comorin. The anchorage, although not good, is used by native craft. One of the trade centres of the district.——*Coolauchauram* (कुलाचार - kuláchára, San.). From (above + áchára, san. usage). Family usage [maryauday].——*Coolotoongan* (कुलोत्तुङ्ग - kulóttunga, San.). From (above + uttunga, san. lofty). Otherwise known as Rajendra, 1064—1113. One of the greatest of the Chola rulers. In A.D. 1064 conquered the whole of the Paundyan kingdom and for a time annexed it. Crushed the Pullavas of Conjeeveram [charitram].——*Cooly* (कुलि - kuli, San.). Means cluster, from fruits. Nightshade. Botanically the Solanum genus, solanaceæ [vricsham, 94]. Shrubs, herbs or small trees, spinous or unarmed, natives of hotter parts; leaves alternate or sub-opposite in equal pairs, entire lobed or pinnatifid; inflorescence terminal at first, but in the course of growth bending downwards to give place to a shoot; fruit a berry containing many seeds. The species best known to the natives are:—Ferox [elephant shoonday], indicum [indian nightshade], melongena [brinjaul], nigrum [indian hounds' berry], pubescens [rameshwaram shoonday], torvum [hill shoonday], trilobatum [prickly shoonday], tuberosum [potato], verbascifolium [shoonday], xanthocarpum [prickly brinjaul]. Other s. indian species indigenous or naturalized are:—Biflorum; Bigeminatum; Denticulatum; Dulcamara, otherwise bitter sweet, fellon wood, fellonwort, foxgrape, woody nightshade; shrubby twining plant, with scarlet, oval, bitter and juicy berries; gives to pharm. the dried young branches; alterative, diuretic, diaphoretic; officinal; berries poisonous; Giganteum; Gracilipes; thorny under-shrub, small; fruit collected by hakeems [q.v.] to be applied to otitis; eaten by natives; Wightii.

COOLAM (കുളം - kulam, *Mal.*; குளம் - kulam, *Tam.*). From (kuli, mal. to bathe). Tank, piece of water formed by damming up a valley or hollow between hills. Suffix in place names, especially in Madura and Tinnevelly [colam].——*Coolacaul hills* (குளக்கால்மலை - kulakkálmalai, Tam.). From (above + kál, tam. a channel + malai, tam. hill). Range of hills; Tinnevelly dist., Nangoonairy tal. and Travancore state. Accessible by steep paths from village of same name. To south the range breaks into several semi-detached mountains, some forested to the summit as that called Mahendragherry, others bare or covered with short grass. At southernmost part of higher ranges, Cape comorin, locally known as the Nose presents a mass of solid gneiss rock with a precipitous face turned towards the north of many hundred feet clear fall. It is conspicuous on fine days as far as Tinnevelly, 35 miles distant. There are several small coffee-estates in the more sheltered valleys of the higher elevations on the Tinnevelly side, and almost the whole of the western Travancore slopes of this range have been denuded of forest to make way for coffee [q.v.] between the elevations of 1,500 and 3,500 feet. A well-frequented bridlepath leads over into these estates from Tircooroongoody, and different points of the Tinnevelly side of the range are accessible by two other well-known paths starting from the same point. Another good path ascends the mountains from Panagoody, eight miles further south.

COOLEE (قلی - kulí, *Hind.*). From turkish. Slave. Distinguish from Cooly.

COOLITALAY (குழித்தலை - kuzhittalai, *Tam.* kulitalai *). From (kuzhi, tam. hollow land + talai, tam. field) [cooy, coozhy]. ——(1) Talook, Trichinopoly district. Tahsildar's pay Rs. 150. Largest in district. Area 901 square miles. Greatest length from N. to S. 44 miles, greatest breadth from E. to W. 23 miles. Population 243,700. Language Tamul. S.W. of district. Lies south of Cauvery, which forms its N. boundary and separates it from Moosiry talook. Bounded E. by Trichinopoly talook and Poodoocottah state, and S. by Madura district and Poodoocottah state, W. by Caroor talook of Coimbatore and Dindigul talook of Madura district. The S. portion of talook, consisting of zemindarry of Maroongapoory and thirty-two Government villages, comprised the old Manapaurey talook, and was transferred from Madura to Trichinopoly in 1856. The northern and central portions are flat, while the west and south-west are hilly in parts and present a somewhat varied aspect. The wildest part of the talook, and, indeed, of the whole district, is the Cadavore zemindarry in the extreme S.W. Along the border of the Cauvery the prevalent soil is alluvial regar [q.v.], while in the southern parts of the talook it consists chiefly of red loam [shevvalmunn] and red sand interspersed with regar in the lowlying tracts. In the portion of the talook irrigated by the Cauvery the soil is very fertile, as it is enriched by river deposit. In the centre and south the soil is very poor and is impregnated with soda [munn cauram] and saltpetre [shorah]. The principal manufactures are cloth, coir [q.v.] ropes, and grass mats [boriyah]. Steel [wootz] is manufactured at Vencatanaickenputty. Glass bangles [gauzoo] at Valanaud in the Maroongapoory zemindarry. The principal sources of irrigation are the Amravatty, Cauvery and Maumoondy. The principal channels from the Cauvery are:—Cuttalay vycaul, Krishnaroyapooram naut vycaul, Mahadaunapooram vycaul, Mardoor naut vycaul and Nangapooram vycaul. There are 307 tanks. The two largest are Maravanore and Shivalore, both in Manapauray division, supplied from the Maumoondy. Camping grounds:—Covilputty and Toovarancoorchy on the Madura road; Cullputty and Veiramputty on the Dindigul road; Laulapett, Manapauray, Manavausy, and Poodoocottah on the Caroor road. Places of archæological interest:—Cadambar coil, Mahadaunapooram, Manapauray, Periyaputty, Ratnagherry, Shivauyam, Shoondakyepauray, Tircambiliyaur, Tirmookkoodal, Togamullay, Vettoovauttalay. The leading places, &c., in the talook are the following.——*Cadavore* (கடவூர் - kadavúr,* Tam.). From (kadavu, tam. gyrocarpus jacquini, roxb. + úr, tam. village). Tam. also (pillaimuzhungi), meaning child + devourer. Zemindarry, Village; pop. 3,830; area 154 square miles; lat. of village 10° 36′; long. 78° 15′; from Coolitalay S.S.W. 28½ miles; from Trichinopoly W.S.W. 37 miles. Zemindarry was formerly included in Madura district, and transferred to Trichinopoly in 1856. Zemindar is of Teloogoo extraction and of Tottiya naick caste. His family came from Gooty. The village is in south of zemindarry, and being in a horse-shoe shaped valley with only one outlet, situation is picturesque. Hills on Madura side rise to 2,000 feet. Present peshcush Rs. 13,410.——*Carooppore* (கருப்பூர் - karuppúr, Tam.). From (karuppu, tam. blackness + úr, tam. village). Village; pop. 1,863; acres 5,192; lat. 10° 30′; long. 78° 24′; from Coolitalay S.S.W. 30½ miles; from Trichinopoly S.W. 33 miles. ——*Cauvery* (காவேரி - kávéri, Tam.). See sep. title.——*Coolitalay* (குழித்தலை - kuzhittalai, Tam.). See below.——*Cuttalay* (கட்டளை - kattalai, * Tam.). From (kattu, tam. plenty + talai, tam. field). Village, Railway station; pop. 2,110; acres 2,696; lat. 10° 57′; long. 78° 14′; height 346 feet; from Coolitalay W. 16 miles; from Moosiry W. 18 miles; from Trichinopoly W. 36 miles.——*Keel pagoothy* (கீழ்ப்பகுதி - kízhappaguthi Tam.). From (kízh, tam. east + paguthi, tam. portion). Town; pop. 4,019. In Cadavore zemindarry.——*Krishnaroyapooram* (கிருட்டிணராயபுரம் - kiruttinaráyapuram, Tam.). Means krishnaroya's town. Village; pop. 3,346; acres 4,777; from Coolitalay W. 11 miles; from Trichinopoly W. 30 miles.——*Laulapett* (லாலாப்பேட்டை - iláláppéttai, Tam. lálápet *). Means laulah's village. Village, Railway station; pop. 992; lat. 10° 57′; long. 78° 23′; height 317 feet; from Coolitalay W. 5½ miles; from Moosiry W. 7 miles; from

Trichinopoly W.N.W. 26 miles.——*Mahadaunapooram* (மகாதானப்புரம் - magáthánappuram, Tam.). From (mahá, san. great + dána, san. gift + pura, san. town); the great gift to bramins by krishnaroya wodeyar of mysore. Tam. also (pazhaya-sengadam), meaning old + red + jungle. Town; pop. 6,682; acres 8,462; lat. 10° 57′; long. 78° 22′; from Coolitalay W. 8½ miles; from Trichinopoly W.N.W. 28½ miles. On R. bank of Cauvery. Large Shiva temple, remains of an extensive ruined camp near the town, and a well-constructed stone bathing-place assigned to a Chola king.——*Manapauray* (மணப்பாறை - manappárai, Tam.). See sep. title.——*Marcongapoory* (மருங்காப்புரி - marungáppuri, Tam. marungápuri *). From (maru, tam. fragrance + ká, tam. garden + purí, san. town). Zemindarry, Village; pop. 1,163; 177 sq. miles; lat. of village 10° 26′; long. 78° 28′; from Coolitalay S. 34 miles; from Trichinopoly S.W. 32½ miles. Zemindarry. Was formerly attached to Madura district, and transferred to Trichinopoly district in 1856. No sunnud [q.v.] has been given to the zemindar [q.v.], so his estate is still an unsettled polliem [q.v.]. The zemindar is of Teloogoo extraction and of the Tottiya naick caste. His family is supposed to have come from Gooty. The town is small but picturesquely situated among low hills, and contains an interesting ruined palace belonging to the Zemindar. Zemindarry now under Court of Wards. Peshcush Rs. 20,586.——*Maumoondiyaur* (மாமுண்டியார் - mámundiyár, Tam.). See sep. title.——*Nangavaram* (நங்கவரம் - nangavaram, Tam.). From (nangai, tam. woman + varam, tam. town). Sanscrit name (ádimúla-samudra), meaning first + principal + tank; name derived from an extensive tank, the bed of which has since been converted into wet fields. Village; pop. 4,592; acres 7,935; lat. 10° 52′; long. 78° 36′; from Coolitalay E.S.E. 9 miles; from Trichinopoly W.N.W. 11 miles. Large wet village.——*Poroondalore* (பொருந்தலூர் - porundalúr, Tam.). From (porundal, tam. success + úr, tam. village). Village; pop. 2,154; acres 3,045; lat. 10° 41′; long. 78° 30′; from Coolitalay S. 17½ miles; from Trichinopoly W.S.W. 20½ miles.——*Ratnagherry* (இரத்தினகிரி - irattinagiri, Tam.). See sep. title.——*Reddiyaputty* (இரெட்டியபட்டி - irettiyappatti, Tam.). From (reddi, tel. reddy caste + patti, tam. village). Town; pop. 2,595; acres 2,057; lat. 10° 33′; long. 78° 24′; from Coolitalay S.S.W. 27½ miles; from Trichinopoly S.W. 31 miles. A ruined fort of the Zemindar of Comauravaudy is situated to N. of Yelangacoorchy, hamlet of this village. Yelangacoorchy itself is a Mahomedan village where a weekly market is held.——*Shivalore* (சிவலூர் - shivalúr, Tam.). From (shival, tam. partridge + úr, tam. village). Town; pop. 3,870; acres 5,137; lat. 10° 38′; long. 78° 29′; from Coolitalay S. 21 miles; from Trichinopoly W.S.W. 23 miles. Large tank.——*Shivauyam* (சிவாயம் - shiváyam, Tam.). From (shiva, san. the god + ayam, tam. ground). Sanscrit name (shiválaya), meaning shiva temple. Village; pop. 3,010; acres 9,029; lat. 10° 52′; long. 78° 28′; from Coolitalay S. 5 miles; from Trichinopoly W. 20 miles. Old Shiva temple, and place of pilgrimage. Rock-cut cave [ratnagherry].——*Shoondakyepauray* (சுண்டைக்காய்ப்பாறை - shundaikkáyppárai, Tam.). From (shundai, tam. solanum pubescens, willd. + káy, tam. fruit + párai, tam. rock). Sculpture on a rock, and rock-cut cave.——*Togamullay* (தோகைமலை - tógaimalai, Tam.). From (tógai, tam. peacock + malai, tam. hill); hill resembling peacock. Resorted to as a place of pilgrimage; pop. 2,828; acres 3,360; lat. 10° 44′; long. 78° 29′; from Coolitalay S. 14½ miles; from Trichinopoly W.S.W. 20 miles.——*Veiga nallore* (வைகநல்லூர் - vaiganallúr, Tam.). From (vaigai, tam. river so called + nal, tam. good + úr, tam. village). Town; pop. 3,369; acres 4,109; lat. 10° 57′; long. 78° 29′; from Coolitalay N.W. ½ mile; from Trichinopoly W.N.W. 20½ miles. Attached to Coolitalay.——*Veiyyamputty* (வையம்பட்டி - vaiyyambatti, Tam. vaiyampati *). From (vaiyyam, tam. bullock cart + patti, tam. village). Village, Railway station; pop. 1,544; acres 3,214; lat. 10° 34′; long. 78° 24′; height 712 feet; from Coolitalay S.S.W. 26½ miles; from Trichinopoly S.W. 30½ miles. Weekly market on Saturday.——*Vetticootty* (வெட்டிக்குட்டி - vettikkutti, Tam.). From (vetti, tam. way + kattu, tam. dam); embankment village. Village; lat. 10° 58′; long. 78° 20′; from Coolitalay W. 10¾ miles; from Trichinopoly W.N.W. 30½ miles. Gave its name to a former talook [manapauray]. A hamlet of Shittalavye, the population of which is 1,959.——**(2)** Village, Head-quarters of Talook, District moonsif and Sub-registrar, Railway station, Head assistant collector's division; Trichinopoly dist., Coolitalay tal.; pop. 1,451; acres 577; lat. 10° 56′; long. 78° 29′; height 293 feet; from Ariyalore W.S.W. 45½ miles; from Madras S.W. 191 miles; from Madura N.N.E. 72 miles; from Moosiry S.W. 1¾ miles; from Shreerungam W.N.W. 18½ miles; from Trichinopoly W.N.W. 21 miles. On south bank of Cauvery. Itself only small village, but centre of three or four other villages which almost adjoin and together form a small town. The greater part of the land round the village is highly cultivated, and there are numerous clumps of cocoanut [q.v.], &c.

COOLITORA (കുഴിത്തുറ - kuzhittura, *Mal.*). From (kuzhi, mal. deep + tura, mal. ford) [cooy, coozhy]. Town, Tahsildar's station. Travancore state, Pudmanaubhapooram division, Vilvancode tal.; lat. 8° 19′; long. 77° 15′; from Alleppey S.E. 99 miles; from Cottayam S.S.E. 97 miles; from Madras S.S.W. 385 miles; from Nagarcoil W.N.W. 18 miles; from Paravore S.S.E. 141 miles; from Quilon S.E. 56 miles; from Trivandrum E.S.E. 21 miles; from the sea N. 7½ miles. Large Nayar town. Rock-cut temple sculptures and inscriptions. The Tamrapurny is also called after this village. Crossed by a large bridge.

COOLLAUDA (కుల్లాడ - kulláda, Tel.). From (kulála, san. potter + váda, tel. street). Village; Ganjam dist., Goomsoor tal.; pop. 1,975; acres 567; lat. 19° 59′; long. 84° 41′; from Chetterpore N.N.W. 48 miles; from Russellcondah N.E. 3¾ miles. Former stronghold of the Goomsoor rajahs. Had once 5,000 houses and a strong mud fort, the ruins of which are still visible. Scene of a battle between zemindar Dhananjaya bhoonj and the English. Fort captured by the latter in May 1815. Curious overhanging sacred rock in neighbourhood called Baughdevy, or the tiger goddess. An oath taken at this rock is binding in any transaction. On the hill are two large stones fastened with iron pins. Also a temple and old palace overgrown with jungle.

COOLSOOM (كلثوم - kulsúm, *Ar.*). Plump. Name of the grand-daughter of the prophet [mahomed] and the sister of Hoossain [q.v.]. Common female alam; as Coolsoom bee, alam + alaumat [ism].

COOLTEE (كلتهى - kulthí, *Hind.*). From (kulatthá, san. dolichos biflorus, linn.). Same as Madras horsegram.——*China cooltee* (چين كى كلتهى - chínkíkulthí, Hind.). Tam. means chinese bean. Same as Guar.

COOLY (ಕೂಲಿ - kúli, *Can.*; కూలి - kúli, *Tel.*; கூலி - kúli, *Tam.*). Hire. Also hired laborer. Distinguish from Coolee.——*Coolitchaicam* (കൂലിച്ചേകം - kúliççékam, Mal.). From (above + chékam, mal. service). The service under Coolitcham.——*Coolitcham* (കൂലിച്ചം - kúliççam, Mal.). In Malabar a tenure by which land is granted rent-free or on a low rent to Nayars on condition of armed service. See vol. I, 112.——*Cooliyaul* (ಕೂಲಿಯಾಳು - kúliyálu, Can.; கூலியாள் - kúliyál, Tam.). From (above + ál, tam. laborer). A laborer; generally short as cooly.

COOMAK (كمك - kumak, *Hind.*). From persian. Help.——*Coomaky* (ಕುಮಕಿ - kumaki, Can.). That which aids. In Canara a defined portion of forest, from which the proprietor of the village or estate has the privilege of supplying himself with wood for house-building, &c., with leaves and twigs for manure, fodder, &c. [cautcaud, coomry]. See vol. I, 112.

COOMBHAM (कुम्भ - kumbha, *San.*). From (kumb, san. to cover). Pot, water-jar. Sign Aquarius [raushy]. Measure of capacity. 20 dronâms = 1 coombham [alavay, 3 f]; approximate actual value, 1 coombham = 2 cubic feet, 1,280 cubic inches; obsolete.——*Coombaura* (كمهار - kumhár, Hind.; ಕುಂಬಾರ - kumbára, Can.). From (kumbha, san. pot + kri, san. to make). The corresponding terms are :—Tam. coosava; Tel. coommara; Mal. coosava. Canarese potters and indigo-dyers [jauty].——*Coombhacam* (कुम्भक - kumbhaka, San.). From (kumb, san. to cover). Power of suspending respiration to secure attention to divine and superhuman things [yogam].——*Coombhauraty* (कुम्भारति - kumbhárati, San.). From (above + áram, san. to leave). Sacred light waved before an idol.——*Coombha yony* (कुंभयोनि - kumbhayóni, San.). Means born in water-jar. Agastyan [jyotisham, nacshatram].——*Coomby* (पीलु - pílu, San.; कुंभ - kumbha, Mahr.; कुंबियो - kumbiyó, Conc.; كهمبى - khumbí, Hind.; كمبى - kumbí, Dec.; ಗುಡ್ಡದಪ್ಪೆ - guddadaippé, Can.; దద్దల - daddal, Too.; బుదదనేడి - budadanédi, Tel.; പീലു - pílu, Mal.; කබට - kabata, Singh.; ஆவிமா - ávimá, Tam.). Title from deccany. San. from (pil, san. to check) [toothbrush tree]. Hind. from (kumbhi, san. the tree). Can. from (gudda, can. hill + ippé, can. bassia longifolia, linn.). Mal. from sanscrit. Singh. means astringent; from bark. Tam. from (ávam, tam. saffron, crocus sativus, linn. + má, tam. mangifera indica, linn.); from color of wood. San. also (kumbhí), meaning jug-fruit; from apple-like fruits. Can. also (doddáladamara); (gongumara). Tel. also (budadarvi); (budadarmi); (budadarini); (dudippi) [raghota caper]; (arayachettu). Mal. also (ukamaram), meaning strength + tree. Title otherwise Cahata, Carey's tree, Hill mohwah, Hindostany slow match, Myrtle bloom. Botanically Careya arborea, roxb., myrtaceæ [vricshám, 56]. Large tree; leaves oval, serrulate, dentate; flowers several, large, greenish white; berry ovate, crowned with the segments of the calyx, four-celled, many-seeded; calyx four-parted; petals four. Tree flowers in april, generally when destitute of leaves; fruit about size of an apple [seb], and has peculiar and unpleasant smell. Bark astringent; flowers are given as a tonic in sherbet [q.v.] after child-birth. Bark is made into a coarse cordage and used by match-lockmen as slow match for guns; also used for tanning [ehamrah]. Gum [gond] forms with water a tolerably thick mucilage of a dark-brown color. Sap-wood whitish, large; heart-wood dull red, sometimes claret-colored, very dark in old trees, even-grained, beautifully mottled. Timber is tough, strong, and durable, close and even-grained, inferior to teak [q.v.] in its direct cohesive strength, admits of a fine polish, red colored, resembling mahogany; used for posts of houses and cart framing, and for the edging of wells, is well adapted for furniture and cabinet purposes, favorite wood in some parts for charcoal [adoopp kary]. Other common species are:—herbacea, sphærica.——*Coommara* (ಕುಮ್ಮರ - kummara, Tel.). From (kumbha, san. pot + kára, san. maker). Tel. potters and indigo dyers. The corresponding terms are:—Tam. coosava; Can. coombaura; Mal. coosava [jauty].

COOMBLA (ಕುಂಬಳೆ - kumbale, *Can.*). Village, Port; South canara district, Cassergode talook; pop. 2,620; lat. 12° 36′; long. 74° 59′; from Bombay S.S.E. 444 miles; from Cassergode N.N.W. 8¾ miles; from Madras W. 360 miles; from Mangalore S. 19 miles; from Manjeshwar S.S.E. 7½ miles. On a bold peninsula in a lagoon [cauyal], separated from the sea by a sand-spit and communicating with it by a narrow channel, on which the village of Canipooram is situated. Town once considerable, now decayed. Formerly joined by a bridge to Canipooram. The rajah of Coombla, whose ancestors ruled the southern part of Tooloovam [q.v.] and who is now a Government pensioner, resides at a small distance. There is a fort built by the Ikkairy [q.v.] rajahs.

COOML (குமிழ் - kumizh, *Tam.*). Means a ball; from use of wood in ornamental knobwork. Same as Cashmere tree.——*Lowly cooml* (நிலக்குமிழ் - nilakkumizh, Tam.). Same as Small cashmere tree.

COON (கூன் - kún, *Tam.*). From (kúnu, tam. to curve). Hunchback [cobja].——*Coon paundyan* (கூன்பாண்டியன் - kúnbándiyan, Tam.). The last but one of the old line of Paundyan kings, so deformed [charitram, soondra paundy tevar].

COONCH (कुञ्च - kuñch, *San.*). To be small. Cf. Cotchoo.——*Cooncham* (కుంచము - kuntsamu, Tel.). A measure of grain, about eight handfuls.—"*a*" Measure of capacity. 4 maunicas = 1 cooncham; 4 coonchams = 1 toom [alavay, 3 b]. Varies from 227½ to 980 cubic inches. Compare Cooroony and mercaul. Sometimes = chittah, or $\frac{1}{16}$th of pucka seer or 4⅜ cubic inches.—"*b*". Superficial measure. Land taking cooncham of seed, 20 coonchams = 1 pootty [alavay, 2 b]. Variable. See vol. I, 609; II, 511, 512, 513, 519.——*Coonjam* (குஞ்சம் - kuñjam, Tam.). Dwarfishness [cotchoo].——*Coonjan* (குஞ்சன் - kuñjan, Tam.). A dwarf [cotchan]. Familiarly Coonjy, Coonjoo for either sex. Hindoo 2nd or pers. name [peyar].

COONDAIR (కుందేరు - kundéru, *Tel.*). From (kundu, tel. to sink + éru, tel. river). From its low bed. Sanscrit name (kumudvatí), meaning water-lily, nymphæa lotus, linn. + possessor [coomadwaty]. River; Kurnool and Cuddapah districts. Rises on the western side of the Yerramala at the site of an ancient tank called Cocndoocheroo. Takes a northerly course for a short distance, winds round the Vandootla plateau into the Coondair valley, to which it gives its name, and flows in a southern direction with great rapidity and falls into the Pennair near Camalaupooram. It is not fordable in the rainy season for a few days. It is not at all navigable and runs for about seven months in the year. A bridge was built over it in 1864 at the place where it crosses the Kurnool-Cumbum high road.

COONDAM (कुण्ड - kunda, *San.*). From (kut, san. to burn); used in cooking. Pot [chatty].——*Coondan* (कुण्ड - kunda, San.). From (kut, san. to burn); as destroying reputation. The child of a woman by another man while her husband is living. Golacan is distinct, being the bastard child of a widow [jauty].——*Coondodaran* (कुण्डोदर - kundódara, San.). From (above + udara, san. belly). Attendant on Shiva. See vol. I (78) [matam].

COONDAPORE (ಕುಂದಾಪುರ - kundápura, *Can.* coondapoor *). From (kunda, san. jasminum pubescens, willd., epithet of vishnu + pura, san. town). Sanscrit name (kundapura), meaning same [coo].——**(1)** Talook, South canara district. Tahsildar's pay Rs. 150. Area 512 square miles. N. coast of district. Boundaries:—On the north, North canara under Bombay presidency; south, Oodipy talook; east, Mysore territory; west, Arabian sea. Coondapore and some other ports on sea-shore were in early part of sixteenth century seized by Portuguese, and the more inland tract was included within the Vijianugger raj until its overthrow in 1565. Subsequently this territory became part of state of Bednore, and Coondapore was one of the principal ports of the rajah; on the overthrow of the latter by Hyder ally in 1763 it became incorporated with his dominions, and when Tippoo in 1799 fell beneath the attack of the British it became part of the British district of North canara. On the partition of that district in 1860 it was temporarily attached to Bombay. The talook comprises a narrow and rugged tract of land between Western ghauts [q.v.] and sea, and is traversed by seven rivers, some of which are navigable. The ghaut [q.v.] slopes and the spurs running into the tract are clothed with dense forest. Soil generally fertile. Agriculture is the chief industrial pursuit of the people, the principal vegetable products being rice [q.v.], cocoanuts [q.v.] and areca-nuts [q.v.]. There are two sea-ports in the talook, one of which Coondapore gungolly has considerable trade, the chief articles of export being rice, paddy [q.v.], cocoanuts and salted fish, while the imports consist mostly of salt [ooppoo], dry grains [q.v.], oils [yennay] and cotton piece-goods. The cultivation is almost entirely dependant upon rains, of which the average fall is 150 inches. Places of archæological interest:—Beidore, Coondapore, Huttiyangady, Ooppoonda. Principal trig. stations:—Coondabhagavatygoodda, Goonjanagoodda. The leading places, &c., in the talook are the following.——*Barcelore peak* (ಬಸರೂರುಶಿಖರ - basarúrushikhara, Can.). See sep. title.——*Basroor* (ಬಸರೂರು - basarúru, Can.). See sep. title.——*Beidore* (ಬೈದೂರು - baidúru, Can.). See sep. title.——*Codachaudry* (ಕೊಡಚಾದ್ರಿ - kodachádri, Can.). See sep. title.——*Cody* (ಕೋಡಿ - kódi, Can.). Means outlet. Village; pop. 2,170; lat. 13° 29′; long. 74° 44′; from Coondapore S. 11 miles; from Mangalore N.N.W. 42 miles; from the sea E. ¼ mile. On peninsula between Coondapore backwater and sea. Has a brackish water lake with large fish.——*Collore* (ಕೊಲ್ಲೂರು - kollúru, Can.). See sep. title.——*Coonda bhagavatygoodda* (ಕುಂಡಭಗವತಿಗುಡ್ಡ - kundabhagavatigudda, Can.). From (kunda, san. pit + bhagavati, san. goddess + gudda, can. hill). Trig. station; lat. 13° 42′ 09·68″; long. 74° 46′ 33·08″.——*Coondapore* (ಕುಂದಾಪುರ - kundápura, Can.). See below.——*Goonjanagoodda* (ಗುಂಜನಗುಡ್ಡ - gunjanagudda, Can.). From (gunja, san. abrus precatorius, linn. + gudda, can. hill). Trig. station; lat. 13° 47′ 13·68″; long. 74° 41′ 01·08″; height 116 feet; from Naugore S.E. 1¾ miles; from Coondapore N.N.W. 11 miles; from the sea E. 1¼ miles.——*Gungavully* (ಗಂಗವಳ್ಳಿ - gangavalli, Can.). See sep. title.——*Gungolly* (ಗಂಗೊಳ್ಳಿ - gangóli, Can.). From (gangá, san. the ganges + ávali, san. range). Village, Port; pop. 1,142; lat. 13° 38′; long. 74° 43′; from Coondapore N.N.W. 1½ miles; from Mangalore N.N.W. 54 miles. Port of Coondapore. On the north bank near mouth of Coondapore river. Tippoo had a dock [dhony].here.——*Gurgat* (ಗರಗತ - garagata, Can.). River. Coondapore river. One of the five streams which forms Gungavully river.——*Harnaud* (ಹಾರ್ನಾಡು - hárnádu, Can.). From (háruva, can. bramin + nádu, can. country). A Maugauny or sub-division of Coondapore talook comprising 15 villages; pop 6,258.——*Hosangady* (ಹೊಸಂಗಡಿ - hosangadi, Can.). See sep. title.——*Hyderghur* (حيدر گڑھ - haidargarh, Hind.). See sep. title.——*Kirmooneshwar* (ಕಿರಿಮುನೇಶ್ವರ - kirimunéshvara, Can.). From (kirimuni, can. the name of the sage who founded the temple + íshvara, san. shiva). Halting place in village of Naugore; lat. 13° 46′; long. 74° 40′; from Coondapore N.N.W. 10 miles; from Mangalore N.N.W. 63 miles; from the sea E. ½ mile. The large Agrahauram [q.v.] was destroyed about 1790 A.D. by a band of Mahrattas under Baula row.——*Naickancuttey* (ನಾಯಿಕನಕಟ್ಟೆ - náyikanakatte, Can.). From (náyaka, can. proper name + katte, can. bund). Sub-port; pop. 966, is population of village in which situated; lat. 13° 49′; long. 74° 40′; from Beidoor S.S.E. 4 miles; from Bombay S.S.E. 360 miles; from Coondapore N.N.W. 13 miles; from Mangalore N.N.W. 66 miles; from the sea E. ¾ mile. On the north of a creek about twelve miles below Hog island, and at the foot of the Collore ghauts leading to Mysore.——*Ooppoonda* (ಉಪ್ಪುಂದ - uppunda, Can.). Village; pop. 2,638; lat. 13° 50′; long. 74° 47′; from Coondapore N.N.W. 15 miles; from Mangalore N.N.W. 69 miles; from the sea E. 1 mile.——*Shiroor* (ಶಿರೂರು - shirúru, Can.). See sep. title.——*Shuncara narayanam* (ಶಂಕರನಾರಾಯಣ - shankaranaráyana, Can.). From (shankara, san. happiness-giving shiva + náráyana, san. vishnu, the water-dweller). Village; lat. 13° 36′; long. 74° 54′; from Coondapore E.S.E. 12 miles; from Mangalore N. 51 miles; from the sea E. 12 miles. Large temple of Shuncaranarayanan. Car festival.——*Vadairhobly* (ವಡೇರಹೋಬಳಿ - vaderahóbali, Can.). From (odeya, can. lord + hóbali, can. division of a district). Village; pop. 1,726; lat. 13° 37′; long. 74° 44′; from Coondapore S. 1¼ miles; from Mangalore N.N.W. 52 miles; from the sea E. 1 mile.——**(2)** Town, Divisional and talook head-quarters; South canara district, Coondapore talook; pop. 3,617; lat. 13° 38′; long. 74° 44′; from Bangalore N.W. 198 miles; from Barcore N.N.W. 12 miles; from Bombay S. 376 miles; from Madras W. 380 miles; from Mangalore N. 53 miles; from Naickancuttey S.S.E. 13 miles; from Oodipy N.N.W. 20 miles; from Poottore N.N.W. 70 miles; from Soobramanyam N.W. 90 miles; from the sea E. 1½ miles. Light on the north side of the entrance to the river; red fixed; 3 miles range; flagstaff; guide to vessels making the port; exhibited from 1st October to 31st May. Town is on south of an estuary receiving five fresh-water rivers. The surrounding country is remarkably beautiful. The fort, probably built by Rajahs of Bednore and improved by Portuguese, still exists somewhat inland from village, and a strong, well-built redoubt on sea-face built by Hyder commands entrance to river. The town is healthy, but its trade is languishing. Rice is produced in the neighbourhood.

COONDOOR (كندر - kundur, *Ar.*). From (kundu, san. incense). Same as True olibanum.

COONGILYAM (குங்கிலியம் - kungiliyam, *Tam.*). From (guggila, san. dammer). Male frankincense, Saumbrauny [q.v.] being the female. Compare, where transl. is of first term:—Boswellia serrata, var. glabra (vellaikkungiliyam), white; Canarium strictum (karuppukkungiliyam), black; Pistacia lentiscus (púnaikkangungiliyam), cat's eye, from yellowish brown color; Vateria indica (vellaikkungiliyam), white. See gloss. paragraphs.

COOÑJARAM (कुञ्जर - kuñjara, *San.*). From (kuñja, san. tusk + rá, san. to give). Elephant [aunay, gájam].——*Coonjaramoodaiyone* (குஞ்சரமுடையோன் - kuñjaramudaiyón, Tam.). From (above + udai, tam. possession + ón, tam. personal termination). Vigneshwaran, the elephant-owner [gaja mookhan].

COONN (കുന്ന് - kunnu, *Mal.*; குன்று - kunru, *Tam.*). From (kunnu, tam. to decrease) [coor]. Hill. Suffix in place names as Candamcoonn, meaning hill with the field. Prefix in place names, as Coonnamungalam, meaning prosperous hilly village. ——*Connemowe* (കുന്നുമാവു - kunnumávu, Mal.). From (above + mávu, mal. mango tree, mangifera indica, linn.). Village; Travancore state, Cottayam division; Paravore talook. Chief seat of Roman catholic bishop.——*Coondah* (ಕುಂದ - kunda, Can.; குந்தா - kundá, Tam. kundahs *). From (kunru, tam. hill).—— "*a*" Division, Neilgherries. Area 101 square miles. Bounded north by Toudanaud, south by the Malabar district, east by Merkoonaud, west by the Malabar district. The division was considered part of Mysore territory till fall of Seringapatam in 1799 when it was annexed to Malabár. In 1863 it was transferred to Coimbatore. The division is much exposed to action of S.W. monsoon [caur]. The valleys are covered with evergreen sholahs [q.v.] and are very fertile; but the greater portion of the tract is composed of rocky ridges and sterile grassy hills. The Bhawany river intersects the division and the Coondah river skirts the northern boundary. Camping grounds at Avalanchey, Banghy tappaul and Sisparra. Places of archæological interest:—Avalanchey, Mailcoondah, Yenicullmund.—"*b*" Mountain range; Neilgherry dist., Coondah div.; pop. 1,411; between lat. 11° 11′ and 11°·20′; long. 76° 29′ and 76° 45′; from Ootacamund S.S.W. 7½ miles. A lofty ridge forming western wall of Neilgherry plateau. Summits are rocky and precipitous and in many parts rise almost perpendicularly several thousand feet from Nelambore country beneath. From extreme S.W. angle of district the range runs in a S. direction, rapidly decreasing in height, until it reaches Coimbatore gap, to S. of which rise Anamullay hills. The sides, covered at places with grass, slope down to the valley of the Coondah river, which separates this range from the rest of the tableland. The three highest points are Avalanchey peak, 8,502 feet; Bear hill, 8,353 feet; and Macoorty, 8,402 feet. The ground is broken and tea-planting is less developed than in rest of district. The Bhawauny rises in this range. The best large game shooting on the Neilgherries is here.—"*c*" River; Neilgherry dist., Coondah div. Called also Bigooly. Rises on E. face of Coondah range. Drains S.E. slopes of Dodabetta and S.E. slopes of Coondah range. Joins the Bhawauny.——*Coondram* (குன்றம் - kunram, Tam.). From (kunru, tam. to decrease). Hill; suffix in place names as Tircalicoondram [coonnam, goonam].——*Coondrimany* (குன்றிமணி - kunrimani, Tam.). From (kunri, tam. plant, abrus precatorius, linn. + mani, tam. seed). Seed of the plant Abrus precatorius, linn., used as goldsmith's weight. 4 nels or paddy grains = 1 coondrimany; 2 coondrimanies = 1 munjaudy [niray, 3 a]. Approximate actual value, 1 coondrimany = 1⅗ grains. Same as San. goonjam, Hind. goomchy or retty, Can. hauga, Tel. gooriginja, Mal. coonnycooroo. See vol. I, 609.——*Coondry* (குன்றி - kunri, Tam.). From (kunru, tam. to decrease); from small size. Same as Indian liquorice.——*Coonnam* (குன்றம் - kunram, Tam.). Hill; suffix in place names as Neycoonnam, meaning ghee + hill [coondram, goonam].——*Coonnoova* (குன்னுவ - kunnuva, obl.; குன்னுவன் - kunnuvan, pers. sing.; குன்னுவர் - kunnuvar, pers. pl., Tam.). From (kunru, tam. hillock). The predominant caste found on the Pulneys. They are Vellaular from the Coimbatore district. There are Eastern coonnoovar and Western coonnoovar. Amongst the Western coonnoovar the following custom prevails. When an estate is likely to descend to a female on default of male issue, she is forbidden to marry an adult, but goes through the ceremony of marriage with some young male child, or in some cases with a portion of her father's dwelling-house, on the understanding that she shall be at liberty to consort with any man of her caste to whom she may take a fancy, and her issue so begotten inherits the property which is thus retained in the woman's family. Cf. Maroomakkatoyem. The women wear a profusion of silver [velly] or brass [pittalay] or iron [auhan] bangles on their arms and legs; and rings through the dividing cartilage of the nose; and tie their cloths in peculiar manner, knotting it over the breast and fastening it with a bandage round the waist. The Coonnoovar profess Sheivism, but they worship a mountain god Vaulappan meaning deity of the sword [jauty].——*Coonoor* * (ಕುನ್ನೂರು - kunnúru, Can.). From (kunna, san. small + úru, can. village).—"*a*" Deputy tahsildarry, Neilgherry district. Pay Rs. 100.—"*b*" Town, Municipality, Sanitarium, Deputy tahsildar's station; Neilgherry district, Paranginaud division; pop. 6,049; lat. 11° 20′; long. 76° 50′; height 5,954 feet; from Coimbatore N.N.W. 28 miles; from Devaulah E.S.E. 29 miles; from Kotagherry S.S.W. 7½ miles; from Madras W.S.W. 264 miles; from Ootacamund S.E. 8½ miles; from Pundalore E.S.E. 33 miles. For description, see vol. II, pp. 73–74 [hill-station].—"*c*" Ghaut; Neilgherry district, Paranginaud division. Projected some years after the construction of the Kotagherry ghaut. Completed in 1833. Starting from Mettapolliem, it runs six miles due west to Kullaur along the level, crossing in its course the Bhawauny and Kullaur streams. From Kullaur the ascent begins. The old road follows N. side of the gorges of Kartairy and Coonoor rivers, the distance from foot to Coonoor bridge at head of pass being nearly nine miles. The average gradient is about one in twelve, but towards the top the gradient is as steep as one in five, and in some places it is reversed. The new ghaut, completed in 1871, begins the ascent at Kullaur, and is 16 miles long. Its gradient is 1 in 18½ feet. It has thirty-two timber bridges, of spans varying from 12 to 70 feet. Its width is about 18 feet. It follows N. side of gorge for about 13 miles, crossing and recrossing the old ghaut at nine points. It then passes to W. side of gorge of Coonoor river, and meets old ghaut at bridge at the head of ghaut [q.v.]. There are twelve zigzags.—"*d*" River; Neilgherry district, Paranginaud division. Formed of three streams terminating in a wedge-like promontory at a point where the united waters break over the stony lip of the ghaut and rush down the gorge under the name of Coonoor river until it empties itself into the Kartairy river.

COONTA (కుంట - kunta, *Tel.*). From (kunda, san. a pit). Same as goonta [q.v.]. Small tank. Compare cottam.—"*b*" Square superficial measure. 32 coontas = 1 catty [alavay, 2b]. Very variable. 12 to 36 feet to the side. Generally considered a square rod [cshetra ganitam]. In Kistna $\frac{1}{40}$th of a cootchel. Compare Tel. goonta and Tam. coozhy. See vol. I, 609; II, 510, 511.——*Coontla* (కుంట్ల - kuntla, Tel.); plural locative form. Small tank. Suffix in place names; as Coilcoontla, meaning the tanks with the temple [goontla].

COONTAM (कुन्त - kunta, *San.*). Lance.——*Coontalam* (कुन्तल - kuntala, San.). From (above + lá, san. to take). Having the shape of spear-point. Ancient name for upland Canarese country [carnatic]; or the Deccan [q.v.] in the English sense. Here the Andhras, Chalookyas, Yaudavas, and other dynasties ruled till the Mahomedan conquest. Then the name fell into disuse, and was re-placed by Andhram, Carnataucam, and Maharashtram, derived from languages spoken by inhabitants [charitram].——*Coonty* (कुन्ती - kunti, San.). Otherwise Coontidevy. The mother of the Pandoos [mahabhairat].

COONYAT (كنيت - kunyat, *Hind.*). From (koun, ar. to be). Surname of relationship; as when a person or a thing is described as the father [aboo], son [ibn], mother [oom], or daughter [bint], of some other person or object. Employed very often also fancifully, as the father of the universe, &c. Coonyats from aboo are now often used as ordinary proper names [ism]. See vol. I (105), cl. (3).

COOPPA (కుప్ప - kuppa, *Tel.*; குப்பை - kuppai, *Tam.*). Tel. from (kádu, tel. to bring together). Tam. from (kuvi, tam. to heap up). Mound, heap, stack of grain [coolam]. Forms Hindoo 2nd or pers. names, as Cooppammah, Cooppan, Cooppoonautan, Cooppoosawmy. Feminine Cooppy. Cooppoo, common to both sexes [peyar].——*Cooppacaud* (குப்பக்காடு - kuppakkádu, Tam.). From (above + kádu, tam. suffix denoting abundance). Country town in contradistinction to principal town. ——*Cooppacutt* (కుప్పకట్టు - kuppakattu, Tel.). From (above + kattu, tel. a rule). Allowance of grain from the general heap given to village servants [calappady]. See vol. I, 112.——*Cooppam* (కుప్పము - kuppamu, Tel.; குப்பம் - kuppam, Tam.).—"*a*" A village of small houses and huts inhabited by people of the lower castes, such as fishermen, &c. This name extends along the coast between Poolicat and Point calimere and inland from Cuddalore as far as the Eastern ghauts [q.v.]. The group of pointed roofs is the chief feature. Suffix in place names as Munjacooppam, meaning saffron + village [cooray, goodem].—"*b*" Village, Deputy tahsildar's station, Railway station, Sub-registrar's station; North arcot dist., Cungoondy zemindarry; pop. 3,405; lat. 12° 45′; long. 78° 23′; height 2,237 feet; from Arnee W. 64 miles; from Chittore W.S.W. 60 miles; from Cungoondy W. 6 miles; from Madras W. 131 miles; from Ranipett W. 67 miles; from Tripatty S.W. 94 miles; from Vellore W. 55 miles. Largest place in zemindarry. Large weekly market.——*Cooppamainy* (हरितमञ्जरि - haritamañjari, San.; खोकि - khókli, Mahr.; कुंकिमफल - kumkmip'hala, Conc.; کپی کا جہاڑ - kuppíká-jhár, Dec.; ಕುಪ್ಪಿಗಿಡ - kuppigida, Can.; బంగారకాయి - bangárakáyi, Too.; కుప్పంటి - kuppanti, Tel.; ଇନ୍ଦ୍ରମରିଷ - indramaris, Oor.; കുപ്പമേനി - kuppaméni, Mal.; කුප්පමේනියා - kuppaméniyá, Singh.; குப்பைமேனி - kuppaiméni, Tam.). Title from tamul. San. from (harita, san. green + mañjari, san. cluster of blossoms); from greenish flowers. Dec. from tamul. Can. from (kuppe, can. rubbish heap + gida, can. plant). Too. from (bangára, too. gold + káyi, can. unripe fruit). Tel. from (kuppa, tel. dunghill + antu, tel. to adhere). Oor. from (indra, san. thunderer, the god + márisha, san. amarantus blitum, var. oleraceus, linn.); appears after rains. Tam. from (kuppai, tam. rubbish heap + méni, tam. beauty); dung-hill beauty; compare acalypha, meaning plant of no beauty. Tel. also (murukonda), meaning beauty + hill; (puppanti), by corruption; (murupindi), meaning beauty + flour; (kuppichettu), meaning dung hill + plant [anise]; (pindi). Tam. also (kuppaivéni), meaning rubbish heap + beauty; (tiruméni), meaning sacred + beauty; (kadukkan), meaning that which is severe; (púnaivanangi), meaning cat-worshipped plant, from attraction of root to cats; cf. catmint; (oduvadakki), meaning boil + controller [tirye]. Title otherwise Cat plant, Indian acalypha, Rubbish plant, Three-seeded mercury. Botanically Acalypha [maumsicay] indica, linn., euphorbiaceæ [vricsham, 118]. Alias Acalypha spicata. Small annual common weed, widely distributed; 1–2 feet; leaves ovate-cordate, serrated, on long petioles; spikes axillary, as long as the leaves, male flowers uppermost, enclosed in a cup-shaped involucre opening on the inner side, striated, serrated; stamens eight to sixteen, styles three; capsules tricoccous, three-celled, one-seeded; flowers small, greenish; flowers all year. The root bruised in hot water is cathartic; leaves emetic, nauseant and expectorant, efficacious in catarrhal and bronchial affections of children, for british vinum ipecacuanhæ and senega.——*Cooppa manjal* (കുപ്പമഞ്ഞൾ - kuppamaññal, Mal.). Means rubbish heap + turmeric; from inferiority. Same as Monkey country saffron.——*Cooppay* (குப்பை - kuppai, Tam.). Heap [coolam]; suffix in place names; as Neycooppay, meaning ghee + heap.

COOR (കൂറ് - kúru, *Mal.*). Share [coroo].——*Coorvaulcha* (കൂർവാഴ്ച - kúrvázhcha, Mal.). From (above + vázhuka, mal. to reign). The step or throne which the rajahs of Malabar ascend. Answers to puttam [q.v.] in Tamul. The share of Government entrusted to a subordinate prince of the ruling family in Malabar. See vol. II, 144.

COOR (కురు - kuru, *Tel.*; കുറു - kuru, *Mal.*; குறு - kuru, *Tam.*). Small, narrow, short, defective [coodoo, cora]. Cf. Coonn.——*Coondal* (கூந்தல் - kúndal, Tam.). From (kúr, tam. to be sharp pointed); anything long and flowing. Woman's hair. Also applied to the white tender cocoanut [q.v.] leaves, split and hung up as an ornament in making up toranams [q.v.] or festoons on occasions of festivals in temples and houses. Cf.:—Porana racemosa (turóbathaikkúndal), drowpady's hair.——*Coondal palm* (கூந்தற்பனை - kúndarbanai, Tam.). From numerous long and thin spadices. Same as Talipot.——*Coora* (కూర - kúra, Tel.). Pot herb [keeray]. Compare, where transl. is of first term:—Allmania nodiflora (pendlipeddakúra), marriage + large; Amarantus campestris (chirrikúra), small; Amarantus gangeticus (tótakúra), garden; Amarantus viridus (chilakalakúra), parrot; Corchorus acutangulus (gánugapindikúra), oil-cake; Ipomæa reniformis (elukachevikúra), rat + ear; portulaca oleracea (pappukúra), dholl. See gloss. paragraphs.——*Cooral* (குறள் - kural, Tam.). See sep. title.——*Cooraly* (குறளி - kurali, Tam.). From (kuru, tam. to grow short). Dwarf. There is a Tamul proverb:—கொடுத்ததைக் கொடுக்கும் குறளிப் பிசாசு—"The dwarf demon returns only that which had been given to "it." Jugglery is attributed to power of a dwarf demon, which, retaining the materials entrusted to it, gives them one by one to the juggler as he wants them [cooly, cootty shauttan, matam].——*Cooray* (கூரை - kúrai, Tam.). Means pointed. Thatch-roof. Suffix in place names; as Ilooppacooray, meaning tree, bassia longifolia, linn. + thatch-roof [cooppam, goodem].——*Coorcha* (కొరచ - koracha, Tel.). From being short of stature. A tribe almost peculiar to Ceded districts [q.v.]. Speak mixture of Teloogoo and Tamul. Compare Cooritchiya. Naturally bamboo color, but tanned darker by the sun; faces oval with prominent bones and something of a tartar appearance; figures of both sexes very ungainly; the men average 5 feet 3 inches, the women 4 feet 9 inches; men wear hair tied in a large knot [conday] on one side of top of head as seen in sculptured figures on old stone monuments; women wear strings of small red and white glass beads and shells round the neck and falling over the bosom, also as seen in old bas-reliefs. The males do poojah [q.v.] at no temple nor do they reverence Bramins. Coorchar live in portable huts of mats, interwoven from long grass, spread over a bamboo [q.v.] frame; men marry about eighteen with girls who have attained maturity, girls go to husband's house two months after marriage; when they die married people are burned, unmarried are buried naked. They carry salt [ooppoo] and grain from one market to another by droves of cattle [maud] and asses [gadah], and also make bamboo mats [boriyah] and baskets [tokrah]. They carry with them the framework of their hut [coodisay], and while one part of the tribe proceeds with the baggage animals, the others settle for a time and employ themselves in making mats and baskets and in begging and stealing. They often commit burglaries and dacoities [dacoity, jauty].——*Coorchaid* (కురుచేడు - kuruchédu, Tel.). From (above + chédu, tel. swamp). Village, Bellary-kistna state railway station; Nellore dist., Darshy division; pop. 2,421; lat. 15° 54′; long. 79° 37′; from Darshy N.W. 11½ miles; from Nellore N.N.W. 103 miles; from Ongole N.W. 41 miles. Seat of much trade. East is a temple of Caulahasteeshwaran built by Chola kings. Also an old stone fort. Vishnoo temple built or restored 150 years ago by zemindar of Vencatagherry. Yearly marriage [calyaunam] festivals are celebrated for nine days in Maugham [mausam] or February. Inside the fort is the Ameen's cutcherry [q.v.].——*Coorchy* (കുറിച്ചി - kuriççi, Mal.; குறிச்சி - kuriççi, Tam.). From (kurumai, tam. littleness). Village in coorinjy or brush-wood tract [cooroomporay]. Suffix in place names, especially in Arcot south, Tinnevelly and Trichinopoly; as Cullacoorchy, meaning thief + village. Prefix in place names; as Coorchimala, meaning hill country + mountain.——*Coorinjah* (குறிஞ்சா - kuriñjá, Tam.). From (kurumai, tam. shortness); as growing on hilly inferior soil. Same as Indian ipecacuanha.——*Coorinjy* (குறிஞ்சி - kuriñji, Tam.). From (kurumai, tam. littleness).—"*a*" Hilly tract covered with underwood [desham].—"*b*" Same as Common vengay.—"*c*" Red coorinjy is Gluta travancorica, bedd., anacardiaceæ [vricsham, 45]. Large tree; leaves crowded about the apex of the branches, alternate, entire, elliptic, attenuated at both ends, glabrous, petioles very short, ciliated, panicles terminal, and from the upper axils, crowded, canescent, shortly pubescent; calyx irregularly and slightly five-toothed, splitting irregularly and caducous; bracts ovate, cymbiform; petals five, imbricate; fruit depressed, transversely oblong, with a rough brownish rind. Valuable timber tree, very straight stem; wood reddish, fine grained, takes a good polish, and is well adapted for furniture.——*Cooritchiya* (കുറിച്ചിയർ - kuriççiya, Mal.). From (kuriççi, tam. hill-village). A primitive Malabar tribe. Compare Coorcha. See vol. II, 99.——*Coorivey* (ಕುರಿವೆ - kurive, Can.). From (kuru, tam. narrow + vây, tam. mouth). A fish-trap basket made like mouse-trap, with narrowing entrance and springy bamboo [q.v.] spikes projecting inwards so as to prevent return.——*Coorlah* (కుర్లా - kurlá, Tel. kurla *). Zemindarry, Ganjam dist.; pop. 4,189: sq. miles 5; quit-rent, Rs. 5,427; lat. 19° 27′ 26″; long. 84° 44′ 17″; from Chetterpore W.N.W. 21 miles; from Russellcondah S.S.E. 32 miles.——*Cooroo* (കുറു - kuru, Mal.; குறு - kuru, Tam.). Small, short. Compare:—Andropogon muricatus (kuruvéru), small root; Flacourtia sepiaria (kurumulli), small thorn. See gloss. paragraphs.——*Cooroocum* (குறுக்கம் - kurukkam, Tam.). Means shortness. A land measure [alavay, 2]. Very variable, from ¾ acre to 7 acres.——*Cooroomullay* (குருமலை kurumalai, Tam.). From (kurumai, tam. small + malai, tam. mountain). Sanscrit name (kurangagiri), meaning antelope + hill. Village, Hill; Tinnevelly dist., Ottapidauram tal.; pop. 1,790; 75 sq. miles; lat. 9° 04′; long. 77° 54′; from Ottapidauram N.W. 15½ miles; from Tinnevelly N.N.E. 27 miles; from the sea W. 33 miles. The hill is conserved by the Zemindar. Good game; antelopes [jinka], buck and deer. Wild cows [gowr] also plentiful.——*Cooroony* (కురుని - kuruni, Tel.; குறுணி - kuruni, Tam.). From (kurumai, tam. shortness).—"*a*" Measure of capacity. 2 cooroonies = 1 pathakk [alavay, 3 a]. See calam. Same as mercaul. Its mark is ஞ. Compare cooncham.—"*b*" Superficial measure. 8 puddies = 1 cooroony; 21 cooroonies = 1 vithaicottay [alavay, 2 a]. Approximate actual value, 1 cooroony = 3,362 square feet. Same as mercaul. Compare Tel. cooncham, Mal. parrah. See vol. I, 609.——*Cooroopaum* (కురుపాము - kurupámu, Tel. kurupám*). From (kuru, tel. small + pámu, tel. snake). Zemindarry, Village; Vizagapatam dist., Parvatipore division; pop. 2,281; lat. of village 18° 51′; long. 83° 36′; from Parvatipore E.N.E. 10 miles; from Vizagapatam N.N.E. 82 miles. The zemindarry, with the exception of Goomahoondah which was added by Gopinauta deo of Parlakimedy about middle of eighteenth century, was granted to Sanyausy dora by Vishwambhara deo of Jeypore. Shivarama rauz of Cooroopaum joined in the rebellion against the Poosapauties, which broke out about period of establishment of first Chief in Council; and he attacked the company's troops on their advance into Jeypore in 1774. He and all his family subsequently arrested but set at liberty shortly before death of Vijayaram rauz in 1794 with a small pension for maintenance. The zemindarry was restored to the old family in 1796, and the permanent settlement of 1802 was made with Shivaraman's son, Chinna sanyausy rauz. Old fort in the village. Present peshcush Rs. 14,370.——*Cooroovay* (குறுவை - kuruvai, Tam.). From (kurumai, tam. shortness). Inferior reddish paddy; shortest crop. Tanjore and Tinnevelly. Aroovathaun cooroovay means sixty days' crop; Caroom cooroovay means black; Cull cooroovay means stone, from hard grains; Matta cooroovay means coarse; Mye cooroovay means jet-black; Shem cooroovay means red [paddy].——*Cooroovy* (குருவி - kuruvi, Tam.). Any small bird [pitta].——*Coorpoo* (കുറുപ്പ് - kuruppu, Mal.). From (kurumpu, mal. fight); chief, a military title among nayars. Hindoo third name [coorumba, peyar].——*Coorumba* (குறும்ப - kurumba, Tam.). See sep. title.——*Coorvitchy* (குருவிச்சி - kuruviççi, Tam.). See sep. title.——*Coory* (കുറി - kuri, Mal.). See sep. title.——*Cootchoo* (तन्तुकाष्ठ - tantukásht'ha, San.; కుంచె - kunche, Tel.; കുഞ്ചം - kuñcham, Mal.; குச்சு - kuççu, Tam.). Title from tamul. San. means thread + stick. Tam. also (pávátti), meaning warp + slackener. Weaver's long brush, with which the warp [pauv] threads when laid out between trestles [muttay coothiray] are separated from one another, and starched to stiffen them [nesavoo].——*Coottam* (குற்றம் - kuttam, Tam.). See sep. title.

COORAL (குறள் - kural, *Tam.*). From (kurumai, tam. shortness) [coor].——**(1)** A metre of two lines; the first tetrameter, the second trimeter. This metre is species of the well known Venbah [q.v.]; one of two metres in which most Tamul classics are composed, the other being Vroottam [q.v.]. Instead of making first foot of first verse rhyme with that of second verse, which is rule, the poet often makes it rhyme with last foot of first verse.——**(2)** The chief Dravidian classic, author Tirvulloovan [q.v.]. The work has three parts, treating of virtue, wealth, and pleasure; the three chief objects of human existence, or the three poorooshaurtams [q.v.]. These three parts contain 133 chapters of ten distichs each, resembling the Sanscrit sootrams [q.v.]. The poem invokes, not Ganesh or Saraswaty [q.v.], but 'the everlasting god.' The chapter then following is in praise of rain [mazhay]; after which are discussed virtue and moral excellence. Then follow songs on the duties of husbands, wives, and children, again on love, hospitality, gratitude, patience, back-biting, benevolence, &c. The third part is erotic; though possibly with a secondary meaning. There is no trace in the Cooral of the mysticism of the modern Pooraunic system; of Bhacty [q.v.], or exclusive enthusiastic faith in any one deity of the Hindoo pantheon; of exclusive attachment to any of the sects into which Hindooism has been divided since the era of Shuncaran [q.v.]; or even of acquaintance with the existence of any such sects. Beschi [veeramaumoony] translated the Cooral into Latin. The best commentary is by the Bramin Parimelazhagan. The Cooral is the real Tamul Dravidian ethical work as distinguished from such Hindooized works as Devauram [q.v.], Tirvauchacam [q.v.], &c. The following stanzas are specimens of the style:—பீலிபெய் சாகாடு மச்சிறுமப்பண் டஞ் சாலமிகுத்துப் பெயின்—"The axletree of a bandy "loaded only with peacocks' feathers will break if it be greatly "overloaded."—சிறைநலனுஞ் சீரு மிலனெனினு மாந்த ருறைநிலத்தொ டொட்ட லரிது—"It is a hazardous thing "to attack men in their own country, although they may neither "have power nor a good fortress [cottay]."—பெருமைக்கு மேனைச் சிறுமைக்குந் தத்தங் கருமமே கட்டளைக்கல்—"A man's deeds are the touch-stone of his greatness and "littleness."—அன்பறிவு தேற்ற மவாவின்மை யிந்நான் கு நன்குடையான் கட்டே தெளிவு—"Let the choice by a "king fall upon him who largely possesses these four things, "love, knowledge, a clear mind, and freedom from covetousness."—குடிமடிந்து குற்றம் பெருகு மடிமடிந்து மாண்ட வுஞற்றி லவர்க்கு—"Procrastination, forgetfulness, idleness, and sleep; these four things form the ship "which is desired by those who are destined to destruction."—செயற்கை யறிந்தக் கடைத்து முலகத் தியற்கை யறிந்து செய்ல்—"Though you are acquainted with the theoretical "methods of performing an act, understand the ways of the "world and act accordingly."—சொல்லுதல் யார்க்கு மெளிய வரியவாஞ் சொல்லிய வண்ணஞ் செயல்—"To "say how an act is to be performed is indeed easy for any one, "but far difficult it is to do according to what has been said."—பொருள்கருவி காலம் வினையிடனோ டைந்து மிருடீர வெண்ணிச் செயல்—"Do an act after a due consideration "of the following five, viz., money, means, time, execution, and place."—உளரெனினு மில்லாரோ டொப்பர் களனஞ்சிக் கற்ற செலச்சொல்லாதார்—"Those who through fear of "the assembly are unable to set forth their learning in an "interesting manner, though alive, are yet like the dead."—இளைதாக முண்மரங் கொல்க களையுநர் கைகொல்லுங் காழ்த்த விடத்து—"A thorny tree should be felled while "young, for when it is grown it will destroy the hand of the "feller."—இருநோக் கிவளுண்க ணுள்ள தொருநோக்கு நோய்நோக்கொன் றந்நோய் மருந்து—"There are two "looks in the dyed eyes of this fair one; one causes pain, and "the other is the cure thereof."—மதியு மடந்தை முகனு மறியா பதியிற் கலங்கிய மீன்—"The stars have become "confused in their places, not being able to distinguish between "the moon and the maid's countenance."—இன்னா தினனில் லூர் வாழ்த லதனினு மின்னா தினியார்ப் பிரிவு—"Painful is it to live in friendless town, but far more painful "is it to part from one's lover."——(3) The later members of Madura college [q.v.] all made what are called impromptus in praise of Cooral. The following are examples, being an exact specimen of the Tamul panegyric style.—"*a*" Accauracany nutchman's stanza:—கலைநிரம்பிக் காண்டற் கினிதாகிக் கண்ணி னிலைநிரம்பு நீர்மைத்தெனினு நெறிலவிலா வானூர் மதியந் தனக்குண்டோ வள்ளுவர்முப்பானு னயத்தின் பயன்—"The moon full of calay or illumination "pleases the external eye, in like manner as the Cooral full "of calay or knowledge pleases the intellectual eye. But "nevertheless she cannot be compared to Valloovar's production; for she is neither spotless, nor does she retain her "form and splendour unchanged like it." Full of calay [q.v.] means full moon.—"*b*" Calattorekizhaun's stanza:—ஒருவரி ருகுறளே முப்பாலின் னோதுந் தருமமுத நான்குஞ்சாலு மருமறைகளைந்துஞ் சமயநூலாறு நம்வள்ளுவனர் புந்திமொழிந்த பொருள்—"He who studies the two-"lined verses in the three divisions of Vulloovar's cooral will "obtain the four things; virtue, wealth, pleasure and eternal "happiness. For they contain the substance of the five "Vedams and the six systems of the sects." The five Vedams include Bhauratam, and the six systems [darshanam] are Saunkhyam, Yogam, Nyauyam, Veishaishicam, Poorva mimaumsam and Oottaramimaumsam.—"*c*" Capilan's stanza:—தினை யளவுபோதாச் சிறுபுன்னீர்நீண்ட பனையளவுகாட்டும் படித்தான் மனையளகு வள்ளைக்குறங்கும் வளநாடவள் ளுவனார் வெள்ளைக்குறட்பாவிரி—"O king of the fertile "country where the birds reared in houses are lulled by the "women's songs! Vulloovar's cooral is short in words but "extensive in sense, even as in a drop of water on the blade of "the Tinay [q.v.] grass may be seen reflected the image of the "palm-tree."—"*d*" Marootwan damodaran's stanza contains at the same time a recipe for headache:—சிந்நீர்க்கண்டந் தெறிசுக்குத்தேனளாய் மோந்தபின்யார்க்குந் தலைக் குத்தில் காந்தி மலைக்குத்தமால்யானை வள்ளுவர்முப் பாலாற் தலைக்குத்துத்தீர்வுசாத்தற்கு—"O king, who re-"sembles the huge elephant [q.v.] which thrust its tusk at the "mountain. All are relieved of their headache by smelling of "the Seendil salt, and sliced dry-ginger mixed with honey "[shahad]; but Shauttau was relieved of his own headache by "hearing the three parts of the Cooral recited." Seendil salt is produced from stalk of tinospora cordifolia [goolancha].—"*e*" Mathooray paulausriyan's stanza:—வெள்ளிவியாழம் விளங் கிரவிவெண்டிங்கள் பொள்ளெனநீக்கும் புறவிருளைத் தெள்ளிய வள்ளுவரின் குறள்வெண்பா வகிலத்தோ ருள்ளிருணீக்குமொளி—"The planets [graham] Venus "[shoocran], Jupiter [brihaspaty], Sun [sooryan] and Moon "[chundran] can swiftly dispel the darkness from the face of "the earth; but the Cooral of the learned Vulloovar can more "swiftly dispel the darkness from the hearts of men."—"*f*" Nappaulattan's stanza:—அறந்த கனியான்ற பொருட்டிரி யின்பு சிறந்தநெய்செஞ்சொற்றீத்தண்டு குறும்பா வள்ளுவனா ரேற்றினா ரைவைத்து வாழ்வார்களுள்ளிரு ணீக்கும் விளக்கு—"Vulloovar has lit a lamp for dispelling "darkness from the hearts of those who live in the world; "having virtue for its bowl, wealth for its wick, pleasure "for its oil, the fire of expression for its flame, and the "short stanza for its stand."—"*g*" Paranan's stanza:—மாலுங் குறளாய் வளர்ந்திரண்டு மாணடியான் ஞாலமுழுது நயந்தளந்தான் வாலறிவின் வள்ளுவருந் தங்குறள் வெண்பாவடியால்வையத்தா ருள்ளுவவெல்லாமளந்தா ரோர்ந்து—"Maul [q.v.] in his cooral or dwarfish incarnation "[avatar] measured the whole earth with his two expanded feet; "but Vulloovar has measured the thoughts of all mankind with "his verse of two short feet."—"*h*" Sheettalay shauttanaur's stanza:—மும்மலையு முன்னாடு முந்நதியு மூப்பதியு மும் முரசுமுத்தமிழு முக்கொடியு மும்மாவுந் தாமுடைய மன்னர் தடமுடிமேற் ரூரன்றே பாமுறைதேர் வள்ளு வர்முப்பால்—"The three parts composed by Vulloovar are "each a garland on the crowns of the three kings, Cheran, Cholan "and Paundyan; who are respectively possessed of the three "mountains Colly [q.v.], Nery [q.v.], and Pothiyamullay [pothigay]; the three countries Cheram [q.v.], Cholam [q.v.], and "Paundyam [q.v.]; the three rivers Porny [q.v.], Cauvery "[q.v.], and Veigay [q.v.]; the three cities Caroor [q.v.], "Warriore [q.v.], and Madura [q.v.]; the three kinds of drums "Mungala moorass, Vetti moorass, and Coday moorass; the three "dialects of Tamul colloquial, poetical, and dramatic; the three "banners Vittcody, Poolicody, and Meenacody; and the three "horses Canavuttam [q.v.], Paudalam [q.v.], and Coram [q.v.]." The names of each triad are here inserted [bhausahay].

COORALAM (कुरल - kurala, *San.*). From (ku, san. to sound) [coo]. Eagles. Aquilinæ, falconidæ [bheroondam], raptores, aves [pacshy, 2], of naturalists [jantoo]. Bill straight at base, and then greatly arched at tip, edges waved; nostrils in front of cere; tail long and large; tarsi long, inner toe and claw strongest. The species best known to the natives are shown below.——*Cauly cheel* (کالی چیل - kálíchíl, Hind.; నల్లగద్ద - nallagadda, Tel.; கரும்பருந்து - karumbarundu, Tam.). All mean black kite. Title otherwise Spotted eagle. Aquila nævia. Alias Aquila melanaetus, clanga, vittata. Adult, richly empurpled brown on scapulars. Paddy [q.v.] fields or tanks. Has a clanging cry, like the sound, 'jeb, jeb, jeb.'——*Gilherimar* (گلہری مار - gilehrímár, Hind.; ಅಲೆಗದ್ದೆ - alegadde, Can.; ఉడతగద్ద - udatagadda, Tel.; புன்செய்ப்பருந்து - punseypparundu, Tam.). Hind. from (gilehrí, hind. squirrel + már, pers. killer). Can. from (ale, can. to roam + gadda, tel. kite). Tel. from (udata, tel. squirrel + gadda, tel. kite). Tam. from (punsey, tam. dry land + parundu, tam. kite). Hind. also (bághátíjammash), meaning garden eagle. Title otherwise Dwarf eagle. Aquila pennata. Alias Aquila minuta; Butaquila strophiata; Spizaetus milvoides. Head and neck pale orange brown, some of the feathers lengthened, entirely brown, forming a rudimentary crest. Crows [caurvam] pursue it.——*Gootimar* (گوٹیمار - gútímár, Hind.). Hind. from (gútí, hind. cocoon + már, hind. destroyer); from feeding on cocoons. Hind. also (jayadhá), meaning slender necked; (pahárítísá), meaning mountain buzzard. Title otherwise Long-legged eagle. Aquila hastata. Alias Limnaetus unicolor; Spizaetus punctatus. Adult, above glossy hair brown, most feathers tipped with white; throat and breast unspotted brown; breast, abdomen, pale fawn or yellowish white, closely barred with brown.——*Jammash*

(جمش - jammash, Dec.; బూరగ - búraga, Tel.). Dec. means bird of chase. Tel. from (bóru, tel. large + váyi, tel. mouth). Title otherwise Imperial eagle. Aquila imperialis. Alias Aquila bifasciata, chrysaetos, heliaca, mogilnik, nipalensis. Adult fine rich glossy dark brown, head and hind neck orange buff. Rare. ——*Kohassa* (کوهسا - kohsá, Hind.; ఆల - ála, Tel.; ஆளா - álá, Tam.). Hind. from (koh, pers. mountain + sá, pers. like). Tam. from (álam, tam. water); as water-bird. Title otherwise Grey-backed sea eagle. Haliætus leucogaster. Alias Blagrus leucogaster; Falco blagrus, dimidiatus, maritimus; Icthyactus cultrungis. Adult, head, neck and entire underparts pure white. Wings reach beyond the end of the tail, which is wedge-shaped. On coast, and larger rivers. Lives on sea snakes. Preys on the osprey [machrangah]. Natives say that when breeding it makes a ladder of fresh boughs with leaves to place the fish on, to keep them fresh.——*Machrangah* (مچھرنگا - machhrangá, Hind.; కొర్రమీనుగద్ద - korramínugadda, Tel.; விராலடிப்பான் - virá-ladippán, Tam.). Hind. from (maççhí, hind. fish + ranga, san. sport); fish-loving. Tel. from (korramínu, tel. ophiocephalus striatus + gadda, tel. kite). Tam. from (virál, tam. ophiocephalus striatus + adi, tam. to kill). Hind. also (maççhariya), meaning fish killer. Tel. also (hugguli), of Yerkalas. Title otherwise Osprey, Fish hawk. Pandion haliætus. Alias Pandion fluvialis, indicus. Head and nape white, feathers of the forehead and crown with dark brown stripes, upper plumage rich; hair brown; quills blackish; tail pale brown, with dark bars, whitish on the inner web; on coast, large rivers and tanks. Plunges from great height into the water.——*Mhorangy* (मोराङ्गीघार - mórángí-ghára, Mahr.; مهرنگی - muhrangí, Hind.; కుందేటిసాళ్వ - kundéti-sálva, Tel.; இராசாளி - irásáli, Tam.). Mahr. from (móra, mahr. peacock + anga, mahr. body + ghára, mahr. kite); from reddish body with white spots. Hind. from (muhr, hind. peacock + anga, mahr. body). Tel. from (kundélu, tel. hare + sálvamu, tel. hawk). Tam. from (rájá, san. king + áli, tam. tawny eagle). Nisaetus bonelli. Alias Aquila intermedia; Nisaetus grandis, niveus. Adult, above dark hair brown, with white about head and back of neck; beneath white. Hilly districts. Much on the wing. Preys on game.——*Sabcheer* (سبچیر - sabchír, Hind.; గుమ్మ - gumma, Can.; నల్లపాములగద్ద - nallapá-mulagadda, Tel.). Hind. means crested hawk. Tel. from (nalla, tel. black + pámugadda, tel. serpent eagle). Hind. also (tilaíbáj), meaning spotted hawk. Tel. also (bottagenda), from ghond. Title otherwise Crested serpent eagle. Spilornis cheela. Specific from (chilla, san. bengal kite). Alias Buteo bacha, melanotis; Circaetus nipalensis, undulatus; Falco albidus; Hæmatornis undulatus. Adult, head black, feathers white on their basal portion, and for nearly two-thirds their length, showing a conspicuous full black and white crest; jungly countries.——*Saumpmar* (سانپ مار - sámpmár, Hind.; ಮಲ್ಪತರ್ - malpatar, Can.; పాములగద్ద - pámulagadda, Tel.; பாம்புப்பருந்து - pámbup-parundu, Tam.). Hind. from (sámp, hind. serpent + már, pers. killer). Tel. from (pámu, tel. snake + gadda, tel. kite). Tam. from (pámbu, tam. serpent + parundu, tam. kite). Title otherwise Common serpent eagle. Circaetus gallicus. Alias Circaetus brachydactylus. Adult, brown above and on the head, lower parts white, feathers all marked with broad stripes or spots. Head is large, full and puffy, plaintive scream. Usually solitary; chief food snakes [paumb] and lizards [chipkalee].——*Shahbauz* (شاه باز - sháhbáz, Pers. and Dec.; ಜುಟ್ಟುಭೈರಿ - juttubhairi, Can.; జుట్టుభేరి - dzuttubhéri, Tel.; குடுமிப்பருந்து - kudumipparundu, Tam.). Pers. from (sháh, pers. king + báz, ar. hawk). Can. from (juttu, can. crest + bhairi, can. falcon). Tam. from (kudumi, tam. hair-knot on the head + parundu, tam. kite); from long crest. Tam. also (kudumiyán), meaning the crested one. Title otherwise Crested hawk eagle. Limnaetus cristatellus. Alias Falco cirrhatus, lathami. Adult, deep black, tipped with white; head and neck fulvescent brown, upper plumage glossy hair brown; beneath the foreneck and breast pure white. Has a long crest.——*Wokhaub* (मोरघार - móraghára, Mahr.; عقاب - ukáb, Ar.; آل - álah, Pers.; عقاب - ukáb, Hind. and Dec.; సాళ్వము - sálvamu, Tel.; ஆளி - áli, Tam.). Title from deccany. Mahr. from (móra, mahr. peacock + ghára, mahr. vulture). Ar. from (akaba, ar. to pursue). Hind. from arabic. Tam. from (ál, tam. to rule). Ar. also (nasr). Title otherwise Tawny eagle. Aquila fulvescens. Alias Aquila punctata, fusca, nævioides, vindiana. Adult, tawny brown, head and throat dusky or almost black. Unknown in Malabar. Rare in Carnatic [q.v.]. Subsists by robbing other birds of prey. Shrill scream.

COORAUK (خوراک - khurák, *Hind.*). From (khurdan, pers. to eat) [coord]. Batta [q.v.] given by villagers to peons [q.v.] sent to collect Government dues.

COORBAUN (قربان - kurbán, *Ar.*; കുര്ബാന് - kurubán, *Mal.*). From (karaba, ar. to draw near); one who draws near to god. Sacrifice. Prefixed to an alam forms a lacab; as Coorbaun hoossain, the oblation of Hoossain. Mostly taken by Shiahs [ism]. The mass among Malabar syrian christians.

COORCHY (کرسی - kursí, *Hind.*). A seat. Base of a column. ——*Coorchy nauma* (کرسینامه - kursínámah, Hind.). From (above + námah, pers. list). List of those who sat on the throne, pedigree [vamsham].

COORD (خرد - khurd, *Hind.*). From (khurdan, pers. to eat) [coorauk]. Ate, the verb.——*Coordboord* (خردبرد - khurdburd, Hind.). From (above + burd, pers. took away). Embezzlement of public money.

COORG (क्रोडदेश - króḍadésha, *San.*; کُرگ - korak, *Hind.*; ಕೊಡಗು - kodagu, *Can.*; కొడుగు - kodugu, *Tel.*; കുടക - kutaku, *Mal.*; குடகு - kudagu, *Tam.*). Title through hindostany. San. from (króda, san. hog + désha, san. country); from tradition that inhabitants had nails on hands and feet like a boar [soor]. San. also means hollow country or country of heights and hollows. San. also (brahmakshétra), meaning bramha, the god + holy place, site of bramha's penance; also (matsyakshétra), meaning fish + holy place, from tradition that vishnoo became incarnate in the fish [matsyam] in a tank here. Drav. from (kuda, tam. west) [coda, cooda]. Province under the Government of India, but occupied entirely by a Dravidian race. Lies between north latitude 11° 56′ and 12° 50′, and between east longitude 75° 25′ and 76° 14′. The following are the principal rivers:—Cauvery, Lutchmana teertam, Swarnauvaty. The following are the principal hills:—Benganaud, Bramhagherry, Cotey betta, Iggootappa coond, Maulamby mullay, Pooshpagherry, Somamullay, Tadyandamole. The following are the large towns:—Codlipett, Colepett, Fraserpett, Mercara, Shanivaursantey, Somavaurpett, Veerarajendrapett. The province is divided into the following talooks:—Kiggatnaud, Mercara, Nunjarajputna, Padinaulknaud, Yedenaulknaud, Yelsauvirasheemey. Each of these except part of Nunjarajputna and Yelsauvirasheemey talooks is divided into nauds, these being again sub-divided into graumams, and the graumams being composed of vargams or detached farms after the manner of the west coast. In the two talooks just named there are hoblies as in Mysore, these containing collections of regular villages. For further particulars regarding Coorg see vol. I, 25. The following are the principal places, &c., with vernacular identifications and etymologies.——*Ammattinaud* (ಅಂಮತ್ತಿನಾಡು - ammattinádu, Can.; ammattinad, Coorg Gov.). From (ambata, can. the wild mango, spondias mangifera, willd.). Naud in Yedenaulknaud talook. ——*Anjigairinaud* (ಅಂಜಿಗೇರಿನಾಡು - anjigérinádu, Can.; anjigerinad, Coorg Gov.). From (añjiga, can. fear + giri, san. mountain). Naud in Kiggatnaud talook.——*Armairy* (ಅರ್ಮೇರಿ - arméri, Can.; armeri, Coorg Gov.). From (arame, can. very small + éri, can. tank-bund). Village in Yedenaulknaud talook.—— *Barapoley* (ಬರಪೊಳೆ - barapole, Can.). From (bara, can. empty + pole, can. river). River in Kiggatnaud [belliapatam].——*Benganaud mullay* (ಬೆಂಗನಾಡಮಲೆ - bénganádamale, Can.). From (bége, can. wild fire + nádu, can. country). An offshoot from the Western ghauts, running in an easterly direction towards Mercara. The Benganaud and the Noorokal range make up with the Western ghauts the watershed of the upper basin of the Cauvery, a valley which between Mercara and Naulknaud is 15 miles broad.——*Bettayetnaud* (ಬೆಟ್ಟಯೆತ್ನಾಡು - bettayetnádu, Can.; bettyetnad, Coorg Gov.). From (betta, can. hill + yettu, can. bullock). Naud in Kiggatnaud talook. ——*Bhaugamundala* (ಭಾಗಮಂಡಲ - bhágamandala, Can.; bhagamandala, Coorg Gov.). From (bhágya, san. wealth + mandala, san. region). Village in Padinaulknaud talook, near the source of the Cauvery. Head-quarters of Tauvnaud.—— *Bilhauda hobly* (ಬಿಳಹಾದಹೋಬಳಿ - bilahádahóbali, Can.; bilahahobli, Coorg Gov.). From (bila, san. cave + hádi, can. road). Hobly in Yelsauvirasheemey talook.——*Bolloor* (ಬೊಳ್ಳೂರು - bollúru, Can.; bollur, Coorg Gov.). From (bólu, can. hollow + úru, can. village.). Village in Kiggatnaud talook.——*Boyikerey* (ಬೋಯಿಕೆರೆ - bóyikere, Can.; boyikere, Coorg Gov.). From (bóyi, can. fowler + kere, can. tank). Village in mercara talook.——*Bramhagherry* (ಬ್ರಹ್ಮಗಿರಿ - brahmagiri, Can.; brahmagiri, Coorg Gov.). From (brahma, san. the god + giri, san. hill). Name borne by two hills, one at the source of the Cauvery, the other at the source of the Lutchmana teertam. The latter known in Mysore as Davasy betta.——*Cadanga mullay* (ಕಡಂಗಮಲೆ - kadangamale, Can.). From (kadangu, can. trench); from the defensive war-trenches of the Coorgs. Mountain lying west of Coorg.——*Cadyetnaud* (ಕಡಿಯೆತ್ತುನಾಡು - kadiyettunádu, Can.; kadyetnad, Coorg Gov.). From (kade, can. end + yettu, can. bullock). Naud in Padinaulknaud talook.——*Caggodloonaud* (ಕಗ್ಗೋಡ್ಲುನಾಡು - kaggódlunádu, Can. kaggodlunad, Coorg Gov.). From (kallu, can. stone + gódalu, can. a stall for cattle). Naud in Mercara talook.——*Chennayyancottah* (ಚೆನ್ನಯ್ಯನಕೋಟೆ - chennayyanakóte, Can.). From (chennayya, can. proper name + kóte, can. fort). Principal place in Yedenaulknaud talook.——*Codantora* (ಕೊಡಂತೊರೆ- kodantora, Can.). From (kódu, can. hill top + tore, can. a river). Pass.——*Comauradhaury* (ಕುಮಾರಧಾರಿ - kumáradhári, Can.). From (kumára, san. god of war + dhárá, san. stream). River rises in the west of Nunjarajputna talook and flows westwards into South canara.——*Coóndada betta* (ಕುಂದದಬೆಟ್ಟ - kundadabetta, Can.). From (kundu, coorg, height); otherwise Hattore hill. Mountain.——*Cooshal nugger* (ಕುಶಾಲನಗರ - kushálanagara, Can.). From (khushhál, hind. joyous + nagara, san. town). Fort. Otherwise called Fraserpett.——*Cotey betta* (ಕೋಟೆಬೆಟ್ಟ - kótebetta, Can.; kotebetta, Coorg Gov.). From (kóte, can. fort). Mountain in Nunjarajputna talook.——*Cottore* (ಕೊಟ್ಟೂರು -

kottúru, Can.; kottur, Coorg Gov.). From (kotta, can. uppermost + úru, can. village). Village in Padinaulknaud talook. ——*Culla holey* (ಕಲ್ಲಹೊಳೆ - kallahole, Can.). From (kallu, can. stone + hole, can. river). River joining the Barapoley at about the Coorg frontier where the combined streams enter Malabar and debouch near Chiracal into the sea.——*Davasy betta* (ದವಸಿ ಬೆಟ್ಟ - davasibetta, Can.). From (davasa, can. corn). Mountain. The source of Lutchmana teertam.——*Fraserpett* (ಫ್ರೇಜರ್‌ಪೇಟೆ - p'hréjarpéte, Can.). See sep. title.——*Gadinaud* (ಗಡಿನಾಡು - gadinádu, Can.; gadinad, Coorg Gov.). From (gadi, can. boundary). Naud in Nunjarajputna talook.——*Gowdhully* (ಗೌಡ ಹಳ್ಳಿ - gaudahalli, Can.; gaudhalli, Coorg Gov.). From (gauda, can. village headman + halli, can. village). Village in Yelsauvirasheemey talook.——*Hanoomanbetta* (ಹನುಮಾನ್‌ಬೆಟ್ಟ - hanumánbetta, Can.). From (hanúmán, san. monkey god). Mountain lying to the west of Coorg. ——*Hatgatnaud* (ಹತ್ತುಗಟ್ಟುನಾಡು - hattugattunádu, Can.; hatgatnad, Coorg Gov.). From (hattu, can. ten + gattu, can. pass + nádu, can. country). Naud in Kiggatnaud talook.——*Haulairy* (ಹಾಲೇರಿ - háléri, Can.). From (hálu, can. milk + éri, can. tank). Estate of the Coorg rajahs. Also a village.——*Hauringy* (ಹಾರಂಗಿ - háringi, Can.). Can. also (hattihole), meaning cattle-fold + river; (svarnávatí), meaning gold possessor. River. Separates the Mercara and Nunjarajputna talooks, and flows into the Cauvery.——*Hebbauley* (ಹೆಬ್ಬಾಳೆ - hebbále, Can.). From (hedda, can. big + bálé, can. plantain). One of the principal places in Nunjarajputna talook.——*Hoodikery cauntamorenaud* (ಹುದಿಕೇರಿಕಾಂತಮೂರುನಾಡು - hudikérikántamúrunádu, Can.; hudikerikantmurnad, Coorg Gov.). From (hudi, can. dam + kéri, can. street + kánta, san. pleasing + múru, can. three + nádu, can. country). Naud in Mercara talook.——*Horamaley* (ಹೊರಮಲೆ - horamale, Can.). From (hora, can. outside + male, can. hill). Mountain.——*Horoor noorokkalnaud* (ಹೊರೂರುನೂರೊಕ್ಕಲ್‌ನಾಡು - horúrunúrokkalnádu, Can.; horurnurokkalnad, Coorg Gov.). From (hora, can. outside + úru, can. country + núru, can. hundred + okkala, can. family + nádu, can. country). Naud in Mercara talook.——*Hutty holey* (ಹಟ್ಟಿಹೊಳೆ - hattihole, Can.). From (hatti, can. cattle-fold + hole, can. river). River, otherwise Hauringy.——*Iggootappa coond* (ಇಗ್ಗುತಪ್ಪಕುಂಡು - iggutappakundu, Can.; iggutappakundu, Coorg Gov.). From (iggu, can. malayalam god + appa, can. father + kundu, coorg, height). Hill in Padinaulknaud talook. Near the Pauditora pass.——*Jambore* (ಜಂಬೂರು - jambúru, Can.; jambur, Coorg Gov.). From (jambu, san. rose-apple tree, eugenia jambos, linn. + úru, can. village). Village in Nunjarajputna talook.——*Jomamullay* (ಜೋಮಮಲೆ - jómamale, Can.). From (jóma, coorg, ox). Mountain. In Padinaulknaud talook; overlooks the Codantora pass.——*Kiggatnaud* (ಕಿಗ್ಗಟ್ಟುನಾಡು - kiggattunádu, Can.; kiggatnad, Coorg Gov.). From (kiri, coorg low + gattu, can. pass). Talook. In the south. Head-quarters at Hoodikery. Contains the following nauds:—Anjigairy, Bettayet, Hatgat, Moodgairy, Tauvalgairy. Principal place:—Baudaga.——*Lutchmana teertam* (ಲಕ್ಷ್ಮಣತೀರ್ಥ - lakshmanatírt'ha, Can.; lakshmantirtha, Coorg Gov.). From (lakshmana, san. brother of ráma + tírt'ha, san. holy water). Can. also (doddahole), meaning great + river. River, rises in Kiggatnaud talook. Called Doddaholey, chief river of South coorg, tributary of the Cauvery [aroovy].——*Mahadevapett* (ಮಹಾದೇವಿಪೇಟೆ - mahádévipéte, Can.). From (mahá, san. great + dévi, san. goddess + péte, can. suburb); called after mahadevamma, the principal queen of dodda veera rajendra. Native portion of Mercara town.——*Mercara* (ಮಡಿಕೇರಿ - madikéri, Can.). See sep. title.——*Naulknaud* (ನಾಲ್ಕುನಾಡು - nálkunádu, Can.; nalknad, Coorg Gov.). From (nálku, can. four + nádu, can. village). Village in Padinaulknaud talook near the foot of Tadyandamole. The site of the principal country palace of the Coorg rajahs. ——*Naupocloo* (ನಾಪೊಕ್ಲು - nápoklu, Can.; napoklu, Coorg Gov.). Village. In north lat. 12° 19′; east long. 75° 43′, near the right bank of the Cauvery, or 9½ miles south-west of Mercara. Head-quarters of Padinaulknaud talook.——*Nidtad hobly* (ನಿಡ್ತಡಹೋಬಳಿ - nidtadahóbali, Can.; nidtahobli, Coorg Gov.). From (nitta, can. long). Hobly in Yelsauvirasheemey talook.——*Noojicull* (ನೂಜಿಕಲ್ಲು - nújikallu, Can.). River. In the north of Padinaulknaud talook, drains the Sampaujy valley.——*Nunjarajputna* (ನಂಜರಾಜಪಟ್ಣ - nanjarájapatna, Can.; nanjarajpatna, Coorg Gov.). From (nanjarája, can. proper name + pattana, san. town).—"*a*" Talook to the north of Coorg proper. Head-quarters at Fraserpett. Contains the following nauds or hoblies:—Gadinaud, Mootnaud, Nunjarajputna hobly, Ramasawmy canavey hobly, Yedavanaud. Principal places:—Hebbauley, Moolsogey, Sirangala, Somavaurpett, Tarinore, &c.—"*b*" Hobly in Nunjarajputna talook.——*Padinaulknaud* (ಪಡಿನಾಲ್ಕುನಾಡು - padinálkunádu, Can.; padinalknad, Coorg Gov.). From (hadinálku, can. fourteen + nádu, can. country).—"*a*" Talook in the west. Head-quarters at Naupocloo. Contains the following nauds:—Benga, Cadyet, Cooyyangairy, Padinaulk, Tauv. Principal places:—Bhaugamundala, Colkerey, Coombla, Naupocloo, Nelabey, Yavacapaudy.—"*b*" Naud in Padinaulknaud talook.——*Pauditora* (ಪಾಡಿತೊರ - páditora, Can.). From (pádi, coorg, name of a village + tora, can. pass). Pass, two miles to the north-east of Tadyandamole. ——*Permauley mullay* (ಪೆರುಮಾಳೆಮಲೆ - perumálemale, Can.). From (perumál, can. vishnu, the great). Mountain lying west of Coorg.——*Pooshpagherry* (ಪುಷ್ಪಗಿರಿ - pushpagiri, Can.; pushpagiri, Coorg Gov.). From (pushpa, san. flower + giri, san. hill). Can. also (subrahmanyagiri), meaning soobramanyan, the god + hill. Hill in the north-west between Coorg and South canara. Called also Soobramanyam. 5,626 feet.——*Shanivaursantey* (ಶನಿವಾರಸಂತೆ - shanivárasante, Can.; shanivarsante, Coorg Gov.). From (sanivára, can saturday + sante, can. market). Can. also (hemmage), meaning great + loom. Town. In north lat. 12° 44′; east long. 75° 56′, 23 miles north of Mercara. Head-quarters of Yelsauvirasheemey talook.——*Siddheshwar* (ಸಿದ್ಧೇಶ್ವರ - shiddéshvara, Can.). From (siddha, san. sage + íshvara, san. god). Hill on the eastern frontier in Yedenaulknaud talook.——*Sirangala* (ಸಿರಂಗಲ - sirangala, Can.). One of the principal places in the Nunjarajputna talook.——*Somavaurpett* (ಸೋಮವಾರಪೇಟೆ - sómavárapéte, Can.; somvarpet, Coorg Gov.). From (sómavára, can. monday + péte, can. suburb). Can. also (nagarúru), meaning fortified town + village. Town in north lat. 12° 36′; east long. 75° 54′, in Nunjarajputna talook, on the main road, N.E. 14 miles of Mercara.——*Swarnauvaty* (ಸುವರ್ಣಾವತೀ - suvarnávatí, can.; suvarnavati, Coorg Gov.). From (suvarna, san. gold + vat, san. suffix of possession). River, a tributary of the Cauvery.——*Tadyandamole* (ತಡಿಯಂಡಮೋಳ್ - tadiyandamól, Can.; tadiandamol, Coorg Gov.). From (tadi, coorg, broad + ande, can. place + mólu, coorg, hill). Highest mountain in Coorg, 5,729 feet in the south-west of Padinaulknaud talook.——*Taley cauvery* (ತಲೆಕಾವೇರಿ - talekávéri, Can.). From (tale, can. head + kávéri, can. the river). Mountain. Source of the Cauvery.——*Tarinore* (ತರನೂರು - tarinúru, Can.). From (tari, can. rice land + úru, can. village). One of the principal places in Nunjarajputna talook. ——*Tauvalgairy moornaud* (ತಾವಳಗೇರಿ ಮೂರುನಾಡು - távalagérimúrunádu, Can.; tavalgerimurnad, Coorg Gov.). From (távale, can. convalescence + giri, san. mountain + múru, can. three + nádu, can. country). Naud in Kiggatnaud talook.——*Tauvnaud* (ತಾವುನಾಡು - távunádu, Can.; tavunad, Coorg Gov.). From (távu, can. refuge). Naud in Padinaulknaud talook.——*Titimaty* (ತಿತಿಮತಿ - titimatí, Can.; titimati, Coorg Gov.). From (tati, can. good season + mati, can. wish). Village in Kiggatnaud talook. ——*Veera rajendrapett* (ವೀರರಾಜೇಂದ್ರಪೇಟೆ - víraréjéndrapéte, Can.). See sep. title.——*Yavacapaudy* (ಯವಕಪಾಡಿ - yavakapádi, Can.). From (yavaka, san. barley, hordeum vulgare, linn. + pádi, can. village). One of the principal places in Padinaulknaud talook.——*Yedavanaud* (ಯೆಡವನಾಡು - yedavanádu, Can.; yedavanad, Coorg Gov.). From (yeda, can. left side). Naud in Nunjarajputna talook.——*Yedenaulknaud* (ಯೆಡೆನಾಲ್ಕುನಾಡು - yedenálkunádu, Can.; yedenalknad, Coorg Gov.). From (yede, can. middle + nálku, can. four + nádu, can. country).—"*a*" Talook south of the Cauvery. Head-quarters at Veera rajendrapett. Contains the following nauds:—Ammatty, Beppoo, Yedenaulk. Principal places:—Ammatty, Aramarey, Caurmaud, Chennayancottah, Cooclore, Ketmalore.—"*b*" Naud in Yedenaulknaud talook.——*Yelsauvirasheemey* (ಯೆಳುಸಾವಿರಶೀಮೆ - yélusávirashíme, Can.; yelusavirshime, Coorg Gov.). Can. also (itterigashíme), meaning two + tax + country; from the district having once paid taxes to two parties the Coorg and the Mysore kings. The Seven thousand country, having reference to its revenue value. The most northern talook of Coorg. Head-quarters at Shanivaursantey. Contains the following hoblies:—Bilhauda, Codly, Nidtad. Principal places:—Doddacodly or Codlipett.

COORK (قرق - kurk, *Hind.*). Enclosure. To travel in coork is to travel with private menials separate from camp [derah].

COORMAM (कूर्म - kúrma, *San.*). From (ku, san. prefix of littleness + úrmi, san. speed); slow in motion [coo].——**(1)** The Chelonian or Tortoise order of reptiles [sarpy]. Reptiles with the bones of the thorax united into a carapace. The synopsis will be found under Sarpy. The following are brief notes on the families.—"*a*" *Testudinidæ* (स्थलकूर्मीयकुल - st'halakúrmíyakula, San.). From (st'halakúrma, san. land-tortoise). Land tortoises. Toes distinct; feet for walking, without web between the toes; shell very convex with horny shields; caudal shields united into one [aumay].—"*b*" *Emididæ* (जलकूर्मीयकुल - jalakúrmíyakula, San.). From (jala, san. water + kúrma, san. tortoise). Fresh-water tortoises. Toes distinct; feet for walking and swimming, with a web between the toes; shell more depressed with horny shield; caudal shields separate [aumay].—"*c*" *Trionycidæ* (त्रिणखकूर्मीयकुल - trinakhakúrmíyakula, San.). From (tri, san. three + nakha, san. claw + kúrma, san. tortoise). Fresh-water turtles. Toes distinct; feet for swimming, strongly webbed; shell covered with soft skin [cadal. aumay.]—"*d*" *Chelonidæ* (समुद्रकूर्मीयकुल - samudrakúrmíyakula, San.). From (samudra, san. sea + kúrma, san. tortoise). Marine turtles. Feet without distinct toes, fin-shaped [cadal. aumay].——**(2)** For insects see poochy, for fishes see matsyam, for batrachians see bhaicam, for birds see pacshy, for mammals see sastanam. A general conspectus of the fauna [jautoo] of s. india is given in vol. II, appendix IV.——**(3)** The second incarnation [avatar] of Vishnoo. Concerning this the Vishnoo poorannam gives the following:—"The moony "Doorvausan, a portion of Shiva, cursed Indran the king of the "gods for having disrespectfully treated a garland of celestial "flowers which he had given him; in consequence of which “thenceforward the three worlds and Indran lost their vigour; all vegetable products, plants and herbs withered and died; and all beings became devoid of steadiness, &c. Then, the three regions being thus-wholly divested of prosperity and deprived of energy, the Daunavans and sons of Dity; the enemies of the gods, who were incapable of steadiness, and agitated by ambition, put forth their strength against the gods. They engaged in war with the feeble and unfortunate divinities; and Indran and the rest being overcome in fight, fled for refuge to Bramha, who being unable to help them sent them to Vishnoo; and he, after having been duly praised by the gods, smiled upon the prostrate divinities and thus spake. With renovated energy, oh gods, I will restore your strength. Do you act as I enjoin. Let all the gods, associated with the Asoorans, cast all sorts of medicinal herbs into the sea of milk; and then taking the mountain Mandaram [q.v.] for the churning stick, the serpent Vausooky for the rope, churn the ocean together for ambrosia; depending upon my aid. To secure the assistance of the Deityans, you must be at peace with them, and engage to give them an equal portion of the fruit of your associated toil; promising them that by drinking the amritam [q.v.] that shall be produced from the agitated ocean they shall become mighty and immortal; whilst I will take care that the enemies of the gods shall not partake of the precious draught, but that they shall share in the labour alone. Being thus instructed by the god of gods, the divinities entered into alliance with the demons; and they jointly undertook the acquirement of the beverage of immortality. They collected various kinds of medicinal herbs, and cast them into the sea of milk, the waters of which were radiant as the thin and shining clouds of autumn. They then took the mountain Mandaram for the staff and the serpent Vausooky for the cord, and they commenced to churn the ocean for the amritam. The assembled gods were stationed by Vishnoo at the tail of the serpent; the Deityans and Daunavans at its head and neck. Scorched by the flames emitted from his inflated hood, the demons were shorn of their glory; whilst the clouds driven towards his tail by the breath of his mouth, refreshed the gods with reviving showers. In the midst of the milky sea, Vishnoo himself, in the form of a tortoise, served as a pivot for the mountain as it was whirled around. The holder of the mace and discus was also present in other forms [mauyan] amongst the gods and demons, and assisted to drag the monarch of the serpent race, and in another vast body he sat upon the summit of the mountain. With one portion of his energy, unseen by gods or demons, he sustained the serpent king; and with another, he infused vigour into the gods.” From the ocean, thus churned, arose Dhanwantary, the physician of the gods, bearing in his hand the cups of Amritam, Lutchmy the spouse of Vishnoo, celestial nymphs, &c. A popular notion is widely diffused among a great variety of people that the world, composed of flat earth and vaulted firmament, with organic beings enclosed between and suspended in the midst of the waters, is exactly figured by a turtle or tortoise [aumay], composed of arched upper shell resting upon the lower plate, with the living animal between, floating in the sea. The triple arrangement is indicated by the three classes of Roman divinities, Dii cœlestes terrestres et inferni. The Coormam avatar [q.v.] is held in these pages to indicate the discovery of the use of the grape-vine [angoor, matam].

COOROOK (குருக்கு - kurukku, *Tam.*). Same as Bramhadand.

COOROOM (قروم - kurúm, *Hind.*). The metal chromium [loham]. See vol. II, 36.

COOROOMBRANAUD (കുറുമ്പ്രനാട്ട് - kurumbranátu, *Mal.* kurumbranád *). From (kurumban, mal. hill-tribe so called + nátu, mal. country); country of the coorumbar [q.v.] who migrated into wynaud after the nayars came in. Talook, Malabar district. Tahsildar's pay Rs. 200. Area 538 square miles. Centre coast of district. Bounded north by Cottayam talook, east by Wynaud talook; south by Calicut talook, west by the Arabian sea. Soil of interior is generally red, much impregnated with laterite [q.v.]; gradually assumes a rich loam in parts cultivated with paddy [q.v.]; towards the coast it is brown loose earth. Comprises the old talooks of Cadatnaud and Cooroombranaud. About one-half under cultivation. Six amshoms [calicut] were transferred to Calicut talook. Rivers are Coottiyaudy, Mahé and Nadoovannore. Ferries are numerous. Dam at Paulayaud for the exclusion of salt water from the paddy cultivation lying above the dam; also a dam at Cauttampully in Panangaud amshom [q.v.]. Ayyanicada is an old one between Oollairy and Aricoolam amshoms. Places of archæological interest:—Badagara, Caurayaud, Chembra, Chervannore, Collam, Coottipooram, Cowntara, Eindalacondah, Iringannore, Keelariyore, Meppayore, Moottangal, Panangaud, Ponmairy, Tirvangore, Vaulicherrycottah, Viyyore, Yedacherry, Yeraumala. Coorumbranaud was until late years a principality under its own chiefs, the last of whom became extinct in A.D. 1779 [charitram]. Principal trig. stations:—Nadoovauram, Poracaud. The leading places, &c., in the talook are the following.——*Agalapoya* (അകലാപ്പുഴ - akaláppuzha, Mal.). From (akala, mal. broad + puzha, mal. river). River. A broad backwater 16 miles long joining the Nadoovannore river at its mouth. Connected with the Coottiyaudy river by the Payoly canal one mile in length. ——*Badagara* (വടകര - vatakara, Mal.). See sep. title.——*Cadatnaud* (കടത്തനാട്ട് - katattanátu, Mal.). See sep. title.——*Caupaud* (കാപ്പാട്ട് - káppátu, Mal.). See sep. title.——*Chombaula* (ചോമ്പാൽ - chombál, Mal.). From (chempu, mal. copper + ála, mal. workshop). Village, Port; lat. 11° 41′; long. 75° 36′; from Badagara N. 5¾ miles; from Bombay S.S.E. 515 miles; from Calicut N.N.W. 33 miles; from Mahé S.E. 2¾ miles; from Moottangal N.W. 3¼ miles. On the open coast. Basel evangelical mission started here in 1849; orphanage transferred from Cannanore in 1872; weaving establishment since 1883. The mission has out-stations at Badagara and Moorat.——*Collam* (കൊല്ലം - kollam, Mal.). See sep. title.——*Coottipooram* (കുറ്റിപ്പുറം - kuttippuram, Mal.). From (kutti, mal. boundary + puram, mal. beyond). Amshom; pop. 7,076; lat. 11° 41′; long. 75° 43′; from Badagara N.E. 8½ miles; from Calicut N.N.W. 30 miles; from the sea E. 9 miles. Ten miles north-east of Badagara, fortified palace of Cadatnaud porlattiry valiya rajah or senior rajah of Porlattiry dynasty at Cadatnaud.——*Coottiyaudy* (കുറ്റിയാടി - kuttiyáti, Mal.). See sep. title.——*Cotta* (കോട്ട - kótta, Mal.). See sep. title.——*Cottacull* (കോട്ടക്കൽ - kóttakkal, Mal.). From (kótta, mal. fort + kal, mal. suffix of place). Village, Port; pop. 5,252; lat. 11° 34′; long. 75° 39′; from Badagara S.S.E. 2½ miles; from Bombay S.S.E. 525 miles; from Calicut N.N.W. 24 miles; from Tricody N.N.W. 4¾ miles. At the mouth of the Cotta. Former resort of pirates, who captured all vessels not carrying the pass of the Cadatnaud rajah.——*Keelariyore* (കീഴരിയൂർ - kízhariyúr, Mal.). From (kízhu, mal. low + ariyúr, mal. small village). Amshom, Village; pop. 5,571; lat. 11° 29′; long. 75° 47′; from Calicut N.N.W. 17 miles; from Badagara S.E. 12 miles; from the sea E. 7½ miles. 15 miles south-east of Badagara; two rock-cut caves. ——*Keelore* (കീഴൂർ - kízhúr, Mal.). From (kízhu, mal. low + úr, mal. village). Village; lat. 11° 32′; long. 75° 40′; from Badagara S.S.E. 5¾ miles; from Calicut N.N.W. 21 miles; from the sea E. 2 miles. Large annual cattle fair and festival in December.——*Mahé* (മയ്യഴി - mayyazhi, Mal.). See sep. title. ——*Mailady* (മേലടി - mélati, Mal.). From (mél, mal. above + ati, mal. foot). Amshom, Village; pop. 9,526; lat. 11° 31′; long. 75° 39′; from Calicut N.N.W. 21 miles; from Badagara S.S.E. 6 miles; from the sea E. 1¼ miles. Ten miles from Quilandy. Shiva temple roofed with copper [taumram]. Festival and cattle [maud] market in Vrishchicam [mausam] or November-December.——*Moottangal* (മുട്ടുങ്കൽ - muttunkal, Mal.). From (muttu, mal. hindrance + kal, mal. rock); a nest of pirates. Amshom, Village, Port; pop. 5,075; lat. 11° 38′; long. 75° 37′; from Badagara N. 2¾ miles; from Bombay S.S.E. 520 miles; from Calicut N.N.W. 29 miles; from Chombaula S.S.E. 3¼ miles. Formerly haunt of pirates. Old temple with inscriptions.——*Nadaupooram* (നാദാപുരം - nádápuram, Mal.). See sep. title.——*Nadoovannore* (നടുവണ്ണൂർ - natuvannúr, Mal.). From (natu, mal. middle + van, mal. large + úr, mal. village). Village; pop. 2,605; lat. 11° 29′; long. 75° 49′; from Badagara S.E. 15 miles; from Calicut N. 16 miles; from the sea E. 11 miles. Head-quarters of old Cooroombranaud talook. Travellers' bungalow; market every Saturday.——*Nadoovauram* (നടുവാരം - natuváram, Mal.). From (natu, mal. centre + váram, mal. declivity). Trig. station; lat. 11° 44′ 12·62″; long. 75° 49′ 35·30″; height 4,557 feet; from Badagara N.E. 17 miles; from Coottiyaudy N.N.E. 6 miles; from the sea E. 18 miles.——*Pandacull* (പന്തക്കൽ - pantakkal, Mal.). From (pantal, mal. corr. from bandar, hind. harbour + kal, mal. suffix of place). Village. A detached French settlement belonging to Mahé.——*Payoly* (പയ്യോളി - payyóli, Mal. payóli *). From (payya, mal. the nád so called + oli, mal. beauty). Village, Canal; lat. 11° 31′; long. 75° 42′; from Badagara S.E. 7¼ miles; from Calicut N.N.W. 20 miles; from Quilandy N. 6 miles; from the sea E. 3½ miles. Travellers' bungalow on an eminence overlooking the river; weekly market on Monday. Lock on the canal, which connects Agalapoya backwater with Coottiyaudy river.——*Pooramala* (പുറമല - puramala, Mal.). From (puram, mal. outer + mala, mal. hill). Village, Hill; lat. 11° 04′; long. 76° 31′; from Badagara S.E. 69 miles; from Calicut E.S.E. 48 miles; from the sea E. 24 miles.——*Poracaud* (പുറക്കാട്ട് - purakkátu, Mal.). From (puram, mal. outside + kátu, mal. forest). Trig. station; lat. 11° 28′ 33·07″; long. 75° 41′ 27·37″; height 260 feet; from Badagara S.S.E. 9¼ miles; from Keelariyore W.S.W. 5½ miles; from sea E. 1½ miles. ——*Pynaud* (പയ്യനാട്ട് - payyanátu, Mal.). From (payya, mal. flat + nátu, mal. country). Petty principality, Village. Part of the ancient kingdom of Collam annexed by the Zamorin [q.v.]. ——*Quilandy* (കൊയിലാണ്ടി - koyilánti, Mal.). See sep. title. ——*Sacrifice rock* (വെള്ളിയാങ്കല്ല് - velliyánkallu, Mal.). See sep. title.——*Tooracherry* (തുറശ്ശേരി - turashshéri, Mal.). From (tura, mal. ford + shéri, mal. village). Village. Ford of the Poothooputnam river near Keelore. Boundary of different marriage customs, &c.——*Tricody* (തൃക്കോടി - trikkoti, Mal.). From (tri, mal. fortune + koti, mal. flag). Village, Port; lat. 11° 30′; long.

75° 40′; from Badagara S.S.E. 7 miles; from Bombay S.S.E. 530 miles; from Calicut N.N.W. 21 miles; from Cottacull S.S.E. 4¾ miles; from Cuddalore N. 2¼ miles.——*Yedacara* (എടക്കര - etakkara, Mal.). From (etam, mal. palace + kara, mal. village). Amshom; Town; pop. 5,908; lat. 11° 23′; long. 75° 49′; from Badagara S.E. 19 miles; from Calicut N. 10 miles; from Cannanore S.E. 42 miles; from Quilandy S.E. 6¾ miles; from the sea E. 4 miles. On the north of backwater. Population consist of Moplahs.——*Yedacherry* (എടച്ചേരി - etaççéri, Mal.). From (eta, mal. middle + chéri, mal. village). Lat. 11° 40′; long. 75° 40′; from Badagara N.E. 6 miles; from Calicut N.N.W. 30 miles; from the sea E. 5¾ miles. Five miles from Badagara. Ganapaty temple. Cadatnaud rajah maintains Bramin feeding-house.

COORTAH (کرتا - kurtá, Dec.). Loose shirt or under gown worn both by Hindoos and Mahomedans; reaching down to the ankles and put on by being thrown over the head. Instead of always having the slit or opening in the centre of the front, it has it not unfrequently on one side of the chest. It has no strings, but a button at its upper end [sheelay].——*Coortee* (کرتی - kurti, Hind.). Jacket reaching nearly to the waist and sometimes lower; has very short sleeves; worn by Mahomedan women [cunchaly, sheelay].

COORUMBA (കുറുമ്പ - kurumba, *Mal.*; குறும்ப - kurumba, *Tam.*). From (kuru, tam. short); from small stature [coor, cora]. Very ancient Dravidian shepherd tribe. Their language a rude Tamul.—"*a*" For Coorumba bhoomy see below. As a dominant race they had numerous petty principalities over the whole peninsula. Numerous sites attributed to them and still called Coorumbar cottam [q.v.] are to be met. The ruins of Coorumbar forts even are still visible, being heaps of mould. The power of the Coorumbar survived longest in the North carnatic [q.v.], particularly in the hills.—"*b*" The modern Coorumbar have lost all traces of their ancient civilization, and retain no recollection of their history. At the present day they are scattered through the districts of Malabar, Coimbatore, Cuddapah, Bellary, Tanjore, Trichinopoly, the Neilgherries, Mysore and Poodoocottah state. The most compact body occupy the slopes of the Neilgherries. The Coorumbar of North arcot district, who are the next best known, are foreigners from Mysore, the remnants probably of those who after peopling the country surrounding Conjeeveram, were ousted by the Cholas; they speak old Canarese; they tend only sheep and goats [aud], and weave the long wool of the former, called in the plains Coorumbaud.—"*c*" The members of this tribe, especially as shown on Neilgherries, are small in stature, have a spare form of body, with peculiar wedge-shaped face and obtuse facial angle, cheeks hollow, with prominent molars or cheek bones; slightly pointed chin; eyes moderately large and frequently blood-shot. Color of irides dark-brown; the nose has deep indentation at the root about 1¾ inches in depth, which is general, and when contrasted with the profile or line with the ridge of the nose and os frontis, it gives them a very peculiar expression of feature. The hair is long and black and is grown matted and straggling, somewhat wavy, and is sometimes tied into a knot [conday], with a piece of cord on the crown or back of the head, while the ends are allowed to be free and floating. They have scarcely any moustache or whiskers and a straggling scanty beard; occasionally one is met with full moustache, whiskers and beard. The women have much the same physiognomy as the men, somewhat softened in expression. The men seldom have any covering except the lungooty [q.v.]; some of the women have only a waist cloth, and others wear a square cloth which reaches from under the arms to the knee. Occasionally, when they can afford it, both men and women adopt the ordinary dress of natives. The women too, are fond of ornaments, and wear necklaces and nose rings, earrings, and bracelets of glass [gauzoo] and iron.—"*d*" The Coorumbar of the plains worship Shiva. Those on Neilgherries worship Cooribhattroyan or lord of sheep and the wife of Shiva under the name of Musny. Also a rough round stone under the name of Hiryadeva, setting it up either in a cave or in a circle of stones; to this they make poojah [q.v.], and offer cooked rice at the sowing time. They are dreaded as sorcerers.—"*e*" Hill Coorumbar are still shepherds by caste and occupation. Their villages are called mottas. These consist generally of only four or five huts made of mud and wattle with thatched roofs. The front of a house is sometimes whitewashed and ornamented with rude drawings of men and animals in red earth [cauvy] or charcoal [adoopp kary]. They store their grain in large oval baskets and for bottles they use gourds. They clear a patch round about the village and sow the ground with raggy [q.v.], tinay [q.v.] or keeray [maurisham]. They dig up roots [gaddah] for food and collect jungle produce; honey [shahad], resin [raul], gallnuts [mauchicoy], &c., which they barter with low country traders, and they are clever in catching game in nets. Hill Coorumbar occasionally take work on coffee [q.v.] plantations, and some earn a livelihood by officiating as priests to the Badagas. They are also employed as musicians at weddings feasts and funerals of the other tribes, where they play on clarionets [naugaswaram], drums [paray], tambourines, &c. They make baskets [tokrah] of rattan [q.v.] and milk vessels out of a joint of bamboo [q.v.], as well as nets. Their women do not labor in the fields, but confine themselves to the limited work of their households, fetching water, cooking, &c. Coorumbar profess some caste scruples, and will not eat with any tribe but the Badagas. They will accept uncooked food from Todahs though not from Kotar. They bury their dead [shavacaud]. They have no marriage ceremony; but occasionally, when two have been living together for some time, they will enter into an agreement, in the presence of friends, to remain united for life; and in a family where a succession of such unions has taken place, they will, once in two or three generations, perform a ceremony, and hold a festival in celebration of them. This is done by pouring pots of water over one another, the pairs seating themselves together for this purpose, the ablution commencing with the seniors. They then put on new cloths, and end the day in feasting.—"*f*" Coorumbar of the plains wear coarse woollens and occasionally engage in cultivation [vellanmay]. These, like the Pariahs, enjoy some privileges which seem to have come down to them from a time when they were occupants of the land who had to be propitiated by immigrant tribes. In some parts of Mysore a Coorumban is required to turn the first furrow for the farmer in spring. On the Neilgherry plateau the Todah, who exacts a tribute in token of superiority from all the other cultivating classes, himself presents an offering of the first fruits to the hill Coorumbar.—"*g*" The following stories are told of the Coorumbar and the new settling Moodelliars and Vellaular. The Coorumbar constructed low wicket gates to their gardens, so that the new comers must be forced to bow on entering. But the Moodelliars and Vellaular instead of entering head foremost put their feet in first, and thus treated the Coorumbar with contempt. It was the custom of the Coorumbar, that, if one of their people died, the whole family should have the head shaved. One of the seniors of the tribe of Coorumbar died, and by custom the whole tribe at one time sat down to have their heads shaved. At the instigation of the Moodelliars and Vellaulars a barber charged his associates each to kill his man, which they did by cutting his throat as he was shaved. The women, thus suddenly widowed, had a great pile of fire kindled, into which they leaped and died.—"*h*" Numbers about 120,000 for whole Presidency. See vol. I. (141); II, 54, 66, 109 [jauty].——*Cooroóba* (ಕುರುಬ - kuruba, Can.). Canarese form of Coorumba. The aboriginal cultivators of South canara. Also found in the Balaghaut [q.v.]. They worship Junjappa, a box supposed to contain the garments worn by Krishnan. The Haley cooroóba do not weave blankets [cumbly]; the Handey cooroóba section, who take service in towns, is regarded as the highest of the race; the Maisa cooroóba are the lowest in rank. Betta cooroóba or hill cooroóbas are met with chiefly in forests along south-western boundary of Mysore and among hills at foot of Neilgherries; they earn a livelihood by felling timber, at which they are very expert; they are a diminutive race, the men being about 5 feet 2 inches in height, but they are very active and capable of enduring great fatigue [jauty].——*Cooroom poray* (குறும்பொறை - kurumborai, Tam.). From (kurum, tam. short + porai, tam. hill). A village in a hilly country [coorchy]. ——*Coorumba bhoomy* (குறும்பபூமி - kurumbappúmi, Tam.). Formerly the country down the sea-coast from Pennair to Palaur, and across peninsula from Coromandel [q.v.] to Malabar coast [q.v.]. The Coorumba bhoomy of the east coast Coorumbas had twenty-four forts between the Pennair and Palaur and extending inland a considerable distance. This country was taken possession of by Athonday, the illegitimate son of ruler called Coolotoonga cholan and the conquered country went henceforth by the name of Tondaimundalam. See vol. I (141).——*Coorumbaud* (குறும்பாடு - kurumbádu, Tam.). Means coorumban's sheep. A particular kind of sheep [aud].——*Coorumbiyattiry* (കുറുമ്പിയാതിരി - kurumpiyátiri, Mal.). From (kurumpora, mal. the hilly district of kurumbranád to the east of calicut + tiri, mal. holy, title). Title of the Calicut zamorin's family [charitram]. ——*Coorumboo* (குறும்பு - kurumbu, Tam.). From (kuru, tam. short); deficient in fertility. Village of arid tract [paulay].—— *Coorumbranaud* (കുറുമ്പ്രനാട് - kurumbranátu, Mal.). Means coorumba + country. Hilly district to north-east of Calicut. See sep. title.

COORVITCHY (குருவிச்சி - kuruviççi, *Tam.*). From (kuru, tam. small + iççi, tam. ficus tsiela, roxb.); from size and resemblance [coor]. Botanically the Ehretia genus, boragineæ [vricsham, 92]. Tropical trees or shrubs with paniculate or corymbose flowers, usually white; fruit is a berry-like drupe with two or four stones each containing a single seed. The species best known to the natives are shown below.——*Prickly coorvitchy* (ಕೊಡ್ಲಿಮುರ್ಕಮರ - kódlimurkamára, Can.; బొక్కడి - bokkadi, Tel.). Title from acutely serrate leaves. Can. from (kodli, can. hatchet + murku, can. break + mara, can. tree). Tel. also (pótubokada), meaning male + the plant; (donkaburra); (bokkudu) [indian pennywort]. Botanically Ehretia [coorvitchy] acuminata, br., boragineæ [vricsham, 92]. Alias Ehretia serrata. Tree; leaves alternate, oblong, and broad lanceolate, acutely serrate, smooth; calyx five-cleft; corolla five-parted; panicles terminal, and from the exterior axils; flowers small, greenish-white, fragrant, numerous, aggregate in somewhat remote subsessile fascicles; drupes round, pulpy, red when ripe; found in some gardens; an introduction from northern bengal.——*Rough coorvitchy* (پالے کا جہاڑ - pálekájhár, Hind. and Dec.; ಎನ್ನೆಬುಡಿಗೆಗಿಡ - ennebudigegida, Can.; బాపనబూరి - bápanabúri, Tel.; ලින්තඹල - líntambala, Singh.; குருவிச்சி - kuruviççi, Tam.). Title from roughness of leaves. Hind. from (pálá, hind. nutriment + jhár, hind. tree). Can. from (enne, can. oil + budige, can. small earthen vessel + gida, can. plant). Tel. from (bápana, tel. bramin + búri, tel. wheaten cake). Singh. from (hín, singh. small + tambala, singh. colocasia antiquorum, schott.). Tel. also (pittapisinika), meaning bird + maba buxifolia, pers.; (telladzuvvi), meaning white + ficus tsiela, roxb. Tam. also (kuruviççai). Title otherwise Box-leaved coorvitchy. Botanically Ehretia [coorvitchy] buxifolia, roxb., boragineæ [vricsham, 92]. Alias Cordia retusa. Large ramous shrub or very small tree; leaves alternate, fascicled, sessile, reflexed, cuneiform, very scabrous, shining; peduncles axillary, two to six-flowered; pedicles very short; flowers small, white; calyx five-parted, segments lanceolate; corolla campanulate, five to six-cleft; berry succulent, red, quadrilocular; nuts two; common in dry barren places. Root has sweetish warm taste in fresh state; root is medicinally an alterative, especially for venereal affections; considered antidote to vegetable poisons; in pharm. but non-officinal, like elm bark; fruit eaten by lower classes.——*Smooth coorvitchy* (दत्रंग - datranga, Mahr.; دترنگا - datrangá, Hind.; ಕಪ್ಪುರ - kappura, Can.; ఆడబుక్కుడు - ádabukkudu, Tel.; ମୋସୋନିଆ - mosoniya, Oor.). Title from leaves. Mahr. from (danta, san. ivory + ranga, san. color); from greyish white wood. Hind. from mahratta. Tel. from (áda, tel. female + bukkudu, tel. the plant ehretia). Tel. also (peddapuliméra), meaning large + the tree, so called; (páladantamu), meaning white + ivory; (shiragadamu). Title otherwise Paula dantam. Botanically Ehretia [coorvitchy] lævis, roxb., boragineæ [vricsham, 92]. Alias Ehretia punctata; Beurreria lævis. Tree; leaves short-petioled, ovate or oval, quite entire, pubescent below at the axils of the nerves, otherwise glabrous; corymbs lateral or sub-axillary, dichotomous, many-spiked; pedicels slightly hairy; calyx deeply five-cleft; corolla subrotate; stamens exserted; flowers small, white; flowering from october to february. Has a bilocular four-seeded berry, which eaten; also inner bark in times of much scarcity; wood greyish-white, hard, tough, durable.

COORY (കുറി - kuri, *Mal.*). From (kuru, mal. small) [coor, cora]. Mark. Lottery. Short for Chungauticoory.——*Cooricalyaunam* (കുറിക്കല്യാണം - kurikkalyánam, Mal.). From (above + kalyánam, mal. marriage). An entertainment given under Chungauticoory.——*Coorimooppan* (കുറിമൂപ്പൻ - kurimúppan, Mal.). From (above + múppan, mal. head). The president of the Chungauticoory.——*Cooripp* (കുറിപ്പ് - kurippu, Mal.). A memorandum [chit].

COOSAM (कञ्चुक - kañchuka, *San.*; سانپ کی جالی - sámpkíjálí, *Hind.*; ಕುಪ್ಪಸ - kuppasa, *Can.*; కూసము - kúsamu, *Tel.*; പാമ്പിഞ്ചട്ട - pámbiñchatta, *Mal.*; பாம்புச்சட்டை - pámbuççattai, *Tam.*). San. from (kañch, san. to bind). Hind. from (sámp, hind. snake + jálí, hind. integument). Tel. contraction for (kuppasamu, tel. a long jacket). Mal. and tam. means snake + jacket. Snake skin. Kept with valuable cloths to prevent damage. Used in medicine [cobra].

COOSAMBAH (कुसुम्भ - kusumbha, *San.*). From (kus, san. to embrace); from flowers yielding a fast red dye. Same as Bastard saffron.

COOSHKY (خشکی - khushkí, *Hind.*). From (khushk, pers. dry). Unirrigated land [metta, poonjah].

COOSHTAM (कुष्ठ - kusht'ha, *San.*; جزام - juzám, *Ar.*; کوڑ - kor, *Hind.*; ಕುಷ್ಠ - kushtha, *Can.*; కుష్ఠము - kusht'hamu, *Tel.*; കുഷ്ഠം - kusht'ham, *Mal.*; குட்டம் - kuttam, *Tam.*). From (ku, san. bad + st'ha, san. spot) [coo]. Greek ἐλεφαντίασις. Skin disease, especially Leprosy or lepra arabum. The mild form of leprosy appears at first in faint spots, of a brownish red tint, little elevated above level of sound skin and attaining size of the palm of the hand; commonly permanent and unchanged for many years, other symptoms then supervening; but usually they increase in size, become more raised and acquire a deeper tint. They blend with neighbouring patches, so that large surfaces of trunk or limbs become involved, and then their originally circular form is less evident. After a time the patches are extremely tender to touch, and an itching sensation and slight scabbiness attends them. Then they lose their feeling, especially in the centre which becomes depressed, and thus an annular aspect is acquired, the interior portion being pale, harsh, and dry and the hairs upon it blanched; enlargement of patches takes place, chiefly by additions at circumference of pre-existing spots. The contagion of true leprosy is sluggish; liable to be endemic on sea coast or estuaries, with those who live much on putrid fish and intermarry closely. The following are considered useful in leprosy:—chaulmoogra oil [q.v.], madaur root [yercum], vallauray [indian pennywort], cashew-nut oil [cashew], gurjan oil [q.v.], wood oil [q.v.], arsenic [paushaunam], and corrosive sublimate [shavveeram]. In Bhavishya oottara pooraunam, eight varieties of cooshtam are mentioned, viz.:—blisters on feet; deformity of generative organs; cutaneous fissures; elephantiasis; ulcers; coppery blotches, lepra maculosa; black leprosy or lepra græcorum of the highest degree of scabbedness, a universal canker of the whole body; and white leprosy or lepra mosaica. The following are varieties of cooshtam recognized at present day.——*Alausaca cooshtam* (अलसककुष्ठ - alásakakusht'ha, San.). Mild form in which tubercles are large, of a red color and very itchy.——*Capaula cooshtam* (कपालकुष्ठ - kapálakusht'ha, San.). Means potsherd. Black and purplish patches resembling broken pieces of a black earthen vessel.——*Caroom cooshtam* (கருங்குட்டம் - karunguttam, Tam.). Black leprosy.——*Caucanaca cooshtam* (काकनककुष्ठ - kákanakakusht'ha, San.). From (kákanantiká, san. the plant, abrus precatorius, linn.). Red and black spots.——*Charma dala cooshtam* (चर्मदलकुष्ठ - charmadalakusht'ha, San.). From (charma, san. skin + dala, san. petal). Mild form, red spots.——*Dadroo cooshtam* (दद्रुकुष्ठ - dadrukusht'ha, San.). From (dadru, san. herpes). Patches are elevated, black, round, and spreading.——*Dadroomundala cooshtam* (दद्रुमण्डलकुष्ठ - dadrumandalakusht'ha, San.). From (dadru, san. herpes + mandala, san. round). Patches are of a slightly dark reddish color, itchy, spreading and elevated into tubercles.——*Gaja charma cooshtam* (गजचर्मकुष्ठ - gajacharmakusht'ha, San.). From (gaja, san. elephant + charma, san. skin). Ichthyasis simplex.——*Kilausa cooshtam* (किलासकुष्ठ - kilásakusht'ha, San.). From (kila, san. to become white). Resembling white leprosy; the skin becomes spotted without producing ulcers.——*Kitima cooshtam* (किटिमकुष्ठ - kitimakusht'ha, San.). Patches of a dark yellow color, like the cicatrices of healed ulcers.——*Neer cooshtam* (நீர்க்குட்டம் - nírkkuttam, Tam.). Water leprosy; with discharge of matter.——*Owdoombara cooshtam* (औदुम्बरकुष्ठ - audumbarakusht'ha, San.). From (udumbara, san. fig, ficus glomerata, miq.). Livid blotches resembling the ripe fig [anjeer].——*Paumay cooshtam* (पामाकुष्ठ - pámákusht'ha, San.; சொறிசிரங்கு - shorisirangu, Tam.). San. from (pámá, san. itches). Tam. from (shori, tam. to scratch + shirangu, tam. scab). Herpes, scab.——*Peroom vyaudhy cooshtam* (பெருவியாதிக்குட்டம் - peruviyáthikkuttam, Tam.). From (peru, tam. great + vyádhi, san. disease). Causing the dropping off of the fingers, toes, &c.——*Poondareeca cooshtam* (पुण्डरीककुष्ठ - pundaríkakusht'ha, San.). Means white lotus, nelumbium speciosum, willd. Patches are pale red in the centre, with dark dull red edges, and resemble the petals of the lotus [nelumbo], when exposed to the sun.——*Ricsha jihva cooshtam* (ऋक्षजिह्वकुष्ठ - rikshajihvakusht'ha, San.). From (riksha, san. bear + jihvá, san. tongue). Patches are shaped like the tongue of a bear [ricsham]; hard and red round their edges, dark in the centre.——*Sidhma cooshtam* (सिध्मकुष्ठ - sidhmakusht'ha, San.). From (sidhma, san. a blotch). Small, white, coppery or red spots, which spread over large surfaces accompanied with a thin mealy dust; lepra vulgaris.——*Veipaudicay cooshtam* (वैपादिकाकुष्ठ - vaipádikákusht'ha, San.). From (vipadá, san. misfortune). Sores form in hands and feet, about the nails, accompanied with small tubercles of a red color.——*Vellay cooshtam* (வெள்ளைக்குட்டம் - vellaikkuttam, Tam.). White leprosy. White albaras of the Arabians, and λεύκη of the Greeks.——*Vispota cooshtam* (विस्फोटकुष्ठ - visp'hótakusht'ha, San.). Means boil. Eruptions are of a dark yellow or red color, and the skin is dry and thin.——*Yeca cooshtam* (एककुष्ठ - ékakusht'ha, San.). From (éka, san. singular). There is no perspiration, and the patches are very large and of a dark brown color, and oblong, like the scales of a fish and rough like an elephant's skin. Ichthyasis.

COOSINY (కుశిని - kushini, *Tel.*; குசினி - kusini, *Tam.*). From french cuisine. A cook room. Coosinicauran is a cook.

COOSOOR (قصور - kusúr, *Hind.*). From (kasr, ar. defect). Deficiency.

COOST (قسط - kust, *Ar.*). Ar. from sanscrit. Same as Costum.

COOT (കൂട്ടം - kúttam, *Mal.*). From (kúdu, tam. to assemble). Assemblage. In Malabar a collection of houses, containing five-hundred or six-hundred persons whose members form a voluntary assembly. The coot formerly answered many purposes:—Nadoocoot, for arbitration; Nayautcoot, for hunting; Yogacoot, for meditation; Nizhalcoot, under shade of a tree to discuss tara [q.v.] affairs; Padacoot, for war. See vol. II, 104. In the Laccadive islands there are periodical coots for killing the rats which infest the coconut [q.v.] trees [maryauday].——*Coottaula* (കൂട്ടാല - kúttála, Mal.). From (above + ála, mal. shed). Naudvauly's house in Malabar.——*Coottauly* (கூட்டாளி - kúttáli, Tam.). From (áli, tam. possessor). Partner in business.

COOT (कुट् - kut, *San.*). To divide.——*Cootaury* (कुठारी - kut'hárí, San.). An elephant goad [ancoosham].——*Coottacam* (कुट्टक - kuttaka, San.). Algebra [beejaganitam, catapayaudy].

COOTAM (कूट - kúta, *San.*; కూటం - kútam, *Tel.*; കൂടം - kútam, *Mal.*; கூடம் - kúdam, *Tam.*). Peak. Suffix in hill names; as Agastyacootam, meaning agastyan + peak; Tricootam, meaning three + peak.

COOTB (قطب - kutb, *Hind.*). From (kataba, ar. to draw together). A pivot, axis. The pole star [al roocoabah], according to which the Kibla [q.v.] is constructed in Mahomedan mosques [musjid]. The highest title of Mahomedan saints. Part of lacab; as Cootb ood deen, the pole star of the faith [ism]. ——*Cootb shahy* (قطب شاهی - kutbsháhí, Hind.). From (above + sháh, pers. royal title). Branch of Bahmany dynasty, which after the dismemberment in 1489 A.D., established itself at Golcondah. Founded by Cootb ool moolk, tarafdar [q.v.] of Telingana [q.v.], who assumed the royal title in 1512. It lasted till 1687, when Golcondah was taken by the Moghul emperor Aurungzeeb [charitram]. See vol. I (149); II, 252.

COOTCHEL (కుచ్చెల - kuççela, *Tel.*). From (kuççe, tel. heap). A heap of cut corn. A land-measure in the Northern circars [q.v.] yielding such a heap = 8 gorroos or 1,000 coontas [alavay, 2b]. Approximate actual value, 1 cootchel = 25 acres.

COOTHIRAY (குதிரை - kuthirai, *Tam.*). From (kuthi, tam. to jump). Horse [ghorah].——*Coothiraymookh* (ಕುದುರೆಮುಖ - kuduremukha, Can.). From (kudure, can. horse + mukha, san. face); from its appearance at sea. Called Somsha parvat near Somsha in Mysore. Hill, South canara dist., Ooppinangady tal. Peak of Western ghauts [q.v.] on boundary between Cadoor district of Mysore and South canara. Conspicuous landmark to sailors. Can be ascended from west by a bridlepath. Bungalows. Trig. station in lat. 13° 07′ 42·85″; long. 75° 18′ 23·85″; height 6,215 feet; from Poottore N.N.E. 26 miles [hill-station]. ——*Muttay coothiray* (மட்டைக்குதிரை - mattaikkuthirai, Tam.). From (mattai, tam. palm-stem + kuthirai, tam. horse). Trestle for preparing the warp [pauv] in weaving [cootchoo, nesavoo].

COOTKEE (कटुका - katuká, *San.*; خربق هند - kharbakihind, *Ar.*; خربق هندی - kharbakihindí, *Pers.*; کٹکی - kutkí, *Hind.*). Title from hindostany. San. from (katu, san. pungent). Ar. from (kharbak, ar. hellebore + hind. ar. indian). San. also (róhiní), meaning red plant. Hind. also (pakhánbed), meaning gentian root. Title otherwise Bitter root. Botanically Picrorhiza kurrooa, benth., scrophularineæ [vriesham, 95]. Perennial; flowers sessile, deep blue, in dense spikes; fleshy-rooted plant allied to speedwell; imported. Root intensely bitter tonic and antiperiodic; substituted for british gentian, calumba [q.v.] and cinchona [koinah] bark; in pharm. non-officinal. No other common species here.——*Black cootkee* (कटुरोहिणी - katuróhiní, San.; कुटकी - kutakí, Mahr.; कडुकरोहिणी - katukaróhiní, Conc.; خربق اسود - kharbakiaswad, Ar.; خربق سیاه - kharbakisiyáh, Pers.; کٹکی - kutkí, Hind.; کالی کٹکی - kálíkutkí, Dec.; ಕಟುಕರೋಹಿಣಿ - katukaróhini, Can.; కటుకరోహిణి - katukaróhini, Tel.; കടുകരോഹിണി - katukurohani, Mal.; කළුරණ - kalúrana, Singh.; கடுகுரோகணி - kadugurógani, Tam.). Title from color of root. San. from (katu, san. pungent + ruh, san. to grow). Mahr. from (katukí, san. the plant). Ar. from (kharbak, ar. hellebore + aswad, ar. black). Pers. from (kharbak, ar. hellebore + siyáh, pers. black). Hind. from (katukí, san. the plant) [shaumay]. Dec. from (kálí, hind. black + kutkí, hind. hellebore). Can., &c., from sanscrit. San. also (krishnabhédá), meaning black + sort; (liptángí), meaning having the body anointed; (matsyapittá), meaning fish + bile; (shakuládaní), meaning eaten by fishes. Mal. also (katukirámani), by corruption. Tam. also (kadurógini). Title otherwise Bear's-foot, Black hellebore, Christiana, Christmas rose, Christ's wort, Fish bile, Giant christmas rose, Large-flowered hellebore, Nepaul hellebore. Botanically Helleborus niger, linn., ranunculaceæ [vriesham, 1]. Alias Helleborus altifolius, grandiflorus. Herbaceous plant, native of nepaul; large white rose-like flowers and a black root, with nauseous acrid taste; roots as occurring are in pieces four to six inches long, black all through their substance, externally of a greyish color, with numerous joints; used by farriers [naulbund] as purge for horses [ghorah], cautiously among hakeems [q.v.] as drastic cathartic in mania. The english stinking hellebore is helleborus fœtidus, willd. White hellebore or veratrum album is a different plant.

COOTOOMBAM (कुटुम्ब - kutumba, *San.*). From (kuti, san. house). Household. Family, or wife and children. Avibhacta cootoombam is the hindoo undivided family [avibhactam].

COOTT (കൂത്തു - kúttu, *Mal.*). Dance.——*Coottooparamba* (കൂത്തുപറമ്പ - kúttuparamba, Mal. kúttaparamba *). From (above + paramba, mal. high ground).—"*a*" Deputy tahsildarry, Malabar district. Pay Rs. 70.—"*b*" Town, Deputy tahsildar's station; Malabar dist., Cottayam tal.; lat. 11° 50′; long. 75° 36′; from Calicut N.N.W. 42 miles; from Cannanore E.S.E. 14 miles; from Cottayam E. 1 mile; from Madras W.S.W. 330 miles; from Malapooram N.N.W. 62 miles; from Manantoddy W. 29 miles; from Palghaut N.W. 102 miles; from Ponnany N.N.W. 75 miles; from Tellicherry N.E. 7¼ miles; from the sea E. 10 miles. Public bungalow [q.v.]; old fort in ruins; large meidaun [q.v.] on high road to Periya pass.

COOTTAM (குற்றம் - kuttam, *Tam.*). From (kurai, tam. to be imperfect) [coor, cora]. Fault. The ten faults or improprieties to be avoided by every writer are according to the Nunnool:—paucity of words; prolixity; tautology; contradiction; the use of inappropriate words; ambiguity; too great simplicity; irrelevancy; unequalness; unmeaningness. For beauties of composition see heading Azhagoo.——*Coottavauly* (குற்றவாளி - kuttaváli, Tam.). From (áli, tam. possessor). A criminal.

COOTTAM (குட்டம் - kuttam, *Tam.*). Literally depth. Also means small, young [cootty]. Tank; suffix in place names as Aunaicoottam, meaning elephant + tank.——*Coottaudan* (കുട്ടാടൻ - kuttátan, Mal.). From (kuttanátu, mal. the low land near ambalappuzha). A Malabar paddy. Black and white varieties as usual [paddy].——*Coottiyaudy* (കുററിയാടി - kuttiyáti, Mal. kuttiyádi *). From (kutti, mal. small + átu, mal. country). Village, Pass. River; Malabar dist., Cooroombranaud tal.; pop. 4,893; lat. 11° 39′; long. 75° 48′; from Badagara E.N.E. 12 miles; from Calicut N. 27 miles; from the sea E. 13 miles. Once a strong military post. Jumma musjid [q.v.]. The pass leads from head of the navigable waters of Cotta river into N. wynaud. At first made for military purposes in connection with Pychy rajah's rebellion. Only practicable for foot-passengers and beasts of burden. Coottiyaudy river is navigable from Badagara up to 30 miles. Large quantities of timber are floated to Yelattore and Badagara.——*Cootty* (കുട്ടി - kutti, Mal.; குட்டி - kutti, Tam.). Small [coottam].—"*a*" Term of familiar address to boys and girls in family. Also suffix in Tamul proper names as Annacootty, meaning elder brother + little one. Pariah proper name [peyar]. A term applied by Numboories to their east coast Puttar servants [boy].—"*b*" Plant first term. Ex., joining two genera, where translation is of second term:— Epicarpurus orientalis (kuttippilá), artocarpus integrifolia; Limonia acidissima (kuttivilá), feronia elephantum; Sponia wightii (kuttippilá), artocarpus integrifolia. See gloss. paragraphs.—"*c*" Means stump of wood; vessel made by scooping it out. Liquid measure [alavay, 4 c, d]. For oil. Varies from 105 to 175 cubic inches. Same as toony.—"*d*" Also stake to mark limit, hence boundary, and prefix in place names as Coottipeoram, meaning boundary + town. Coottinell is an allowance in grain made by proprietors for keeping up the fences and enclosure of an estate.——*Cootty shauttan* (குட்டிச்சாத்தான் - kuttiççáttán, Tam.). From (above + shástá, san. punisher). A goblin invoked in juggling tricks. See vol. I (81) [cooly, cooraly, matam].

COOVAH (کوا - kuá, *Hind.*). Subterranean passage in fort.

COOY (കുഴി - kuzhi, *Mal.*; குழி - kuzhi, *Tam.*). A square measure [coozhy], considerable variety in different places. Also a pit, especially in which a cocoanut [q.v.] tree is planted; whence in Malayalam planting trees. See vol. I, 609; II, 518. ——*Cooyicaunom* (കുഴിക്കാണം - kuzhikkánam, Mal.). See sep. title.——*Cooyicoor* (കുഴിക്കൂറു - kuzhikkúru, Mal.). From (above + kúr, mal. share). The profit to which the tenant is entitled under Cooyicaunom [chamayam].——*Cooyivett* (குழிவெட்டு - kuzhivettu, Tam.). From (above + vettu, tam. to dig). Earth work, digging at so much per pit.——*Cooyivila* (കുഴിവില - kuzhivila, Mal.). From (above + vila, mal. price). Value of the planted trees.

COOZHAY (குழை - kúzhai, *Tam.*). Short [coor].——*Coozay paumb* (گیدها سانپ - gídhásámp, Hind.; குழைப்பாம்பு - kúzhaippámbu, Tam.). Hind. from (gídhá, hind. dwarf + sámp, hind. snake). Tam. from (kúzhai, tam. short + pámbu, tam. snake). Hind. also (chhotásámp), meaning little snake. Terms co-extensive with the family Calamaridæ, ophidii colubriformes, ophidia [sarpam], reptilia [sarpy, 15], of naturalists [jantoo]. The Dwarf snakes or Calamaridæ are very small; always found on the ground, beneath stones, fallen trees, or turf; their food chiefly of insects and worms; they themselves fall an easy prey to other snakes, especially to the Bungaur [q.v.] and hill cobra [q.v.]; they never bite. The following are the South indian species:—"*a*" Aspidura copii. Scales in seventeen rows; brownish above, minutely dotted with black; series of pairs of black spots runs along the back; twenty-six pairs of spots on the trunk; belly white, marbled with black.—"*b*" Calamaria leucocephala. Black above; head, neck, the two outer series of scales, and the lower parts white.—"*c*" Geophis microcephalus. Alias Rhabdosoma microcephalum. Scales in thirteen series; brown; back with three more or less distinct series of small dark spots; blackish band with whitish edges along each side of the body, more distinct towards and on the tail than anteriorly; oblique yellowish streak behind angle of the mouth; belly nearly uniform brownish black, only margin of scutes remaining whitish.—"*d*" Macrocalmus lateralis. Brown; dark-brown band, enclosing a regular series of whitish dots, runs along the side, bordering the belly; back with two series of indistinct brownish-black spots; irregular series of very small black dots along each side of the belly, which is whitish; blackish subcaudal band.——*Coozhay vaulan* (குழைவாலன் - kúzhaiválan, Tam.). Tam. from (above + vál, tam. tail). The term may be considered co-extensive with the family Uropeltidæ, ophidii colubriformes, ophidia [sarpam], reptilia [sarpy, 14], of naturalists [jantoo]. Have short tail; bear some resemblance to the Typhlopidæ [domoonh]; live under ground; conical head, generally very stout neck, rigid body, short, strong, and posteriorly shielded tail, adapted for burrowing; head always narrower than the neck, which is generally slightly swollen and the thickest part of the trunk; nasal large; eye very small; do not attain to a considerable size; they are by no means scarce, but escape observation from their peculiar mode of life; in order to collect them it is necessary to dig for them to a depth of 4 feet; they are viviparous; live on insects and worms. The following are the South indian species:—"*a*" Melanophidium wynaudense. Alias Plectrurus wynaudensis. Black; posterior two-thirds of belly irregularly black and white.—"*b*" Plectrurus guntheri. Purple above, each scale with a lighter margin; belly yellow, color rising up on the sides in triangular markings, which are alternate with similar markings of black, purple spots sometimes joining those of the other side by narrow stripes crossing the belly.—"*c*" Plectrurus perrotetii. Uniform brownish or blackish.—"*d*" Rhinophis pulneyensis. Alias Plectrurus pulneyensis. Brownish-black; yellow bard from the labials runs along each side of the front part of the body; spots sometimes extend across the belly; yellow band along each side of the tail.—"*e*" Rhinophis sanguineus. Alias Rhinophis microlepis. Uniform black above; belly with the three outer series of scales scarlet, many of the scales and ventral shields having a black spot; caudal shield black, with yellow median streak and with red outer margin; large black spot on lower side of the extremity of the tail.—"*f*" Silybura beddomii. Brown; each scale on the sides with a pair of whitish dots; each ventral shield with a small whitish spot; yellowish line along the side of the neck; vent and tip of the tail yellow.—"*g*" Silybura bicatenata. Black above and below, each scale on the back with a yellowish margin; yellow band along each side of the body; lower parts entirely black.—"*h*" Silybura brevis. Brown above; lower part of sides and the belly yellowish, densely marbled with brown; sides of throat yellowish, immaculate; lower part of the tail black, with broad white band on each side.—"*i*" Silybura elliotti. Alias Colobarus ceylanicus; Siluboura ceylanica, nilgherriensis; Uropeltis ceylanicus. Blackish brown above and below; narrow yellowish streak runs from the angle of the mouth along each side of the neck; sometimes irregular small yellowish spots along the sides and on the back; lower part of the tail completely encircled by a yellow band.—"*j*" Silybura macrolepis. Black; broad, irregular, yellowish band along each side of the front part of trunk; traces of a similar narrow band are visible along the sides of the body; yellow band along each side of the lower part of the tail.—"*k*" Silybura ocellata. Ground color of male yellowish olive, darker towards head and tail; female dull brownish; young dark purplish brown; all with series of yellow, black-edged ocelli; series of irregular, transverse, yellow, black-edged spots along each side of the belly; belly brownish.—"*l*" Silybura shorttii. Black; numerous irregularly disposed scales are white; irregular white band from angle of mouth along each side of the front part of trunk; yellowish band along each side of tail.

COOZHY (കുഴി - kuzhi, *Mal.*; குழி - kuzhi, *Tam.*). Pit [cooy]. Superficial measure. 100 coozhies = 1 cawny [alavay, 2 a]. Approximate actual value, 1 coozhy = 576 square feet; but very variable. Compare Tel. goonta, Tam. gooly. See vol. I, 609; II, 506, 507, 509.——*Coolitalay* (குழித்தலை - kuzhittalai, Tam.). See sep. title.——*Coolitora* (കുഴിത്തുറ - kuzhittura, Mal.). See sep. title.——*Maundavar coozhy* (மாண்டவர்க் குழி - mándavarkkuzhi, Tam.). From (mándavar, tam. dead men + above). Ancient kistvaens. They contain earthen jars, with fragments of human bones in earth [aursham, mady moottaur tauzhy, paundicoozhy].

COPAL (चन्द्रस - chandrasa, *Mahr.*; سندروس - sandrús, *Ar.*; چندرس - chandras, *Hind.*). Title is mexican term for gum resins generally [googal]. Natives connect it with Gopaulan or Krishnan. Mahr. from (chandra, san. moon + rasa, san. juice); being a white gum [gond]. Used in America specially for gum-resin of Hymenæa gum trees. Indian copal is piney dammer [q.v.]. American copal occurs in yellow flat fragments while Indian copal is in round colorless masses. American copal, imported from south america through bussorah, is employed by bandy-makers for preparing a varnish; resembles amber so much that jewellers make it into necklaces, &c., passed off as amber [karbah]. Australian or New zealand copal is Dammara australis.

COPE (కొప్పు - kópu, *Tel.*). Mercantile house [aurang, bankshaul].——*Copedaur* (కొప్పుదారుడు - kópudárudu, Tel.). From (above + dár, pers. suffix of possession). A warehouse-keeper. A contractor for long-cloths [cape merchant].

COPPER MOUNTAIN (ತಾಂಬ್ರಬೆಟ್ಟ - támbrabetta, *Can.*). Can. also (jóladaráshi), meaning heap of cholum [q.v.], from shape. Sanscrit name (támrakúta), meaning copper peak. Hill; Bellary dist., Bellary tal.; lat. 15° 03′ 45″; long. 76° 55′ 45″; from Bellary S.S.W. 6¾ miles. Highest point of Mincherry range, which is four miles south of Bellary. So called because Hyder ally worked the ore here.

COPPRAY (کھوپرا - khoprá, *Hind.*; کھوپرےکی بٹی - khoprekíbattí, *Dec.*; ಕೊಬ್ಬರಿ - kobbari, *Can.*; కొబ్బెర - kobbera, *Tel.*; കൊപ്പര - koppara, *Mal.*; கொப்பரை - kopparai, *Tam.*). Dry kernel of cocoanut [cobbary].

CORA (ಕೊರ - kora, *Can.*; కొర - kóra, *Tel.*). Small [coor]. Defective. Narrow, sharp, rude.——*Coraga* (ಕೊರಗ - koraga, Can.). Means a low set of people. A prædial tribe found in South canara. Their traditions there are that an abyssinian brought an army from anantapore, of which they formed a part; the army was at first victorious, but afterwards being defeated the coragar were driven into the forests. They are physically strong, with a forehead of moderate size, and black skin. In former times they were slaves. There are three clans; the Andey coraga, Vastra coraga, and Sappoo coraga [jauty]. Under Hindoo rule, the Andey coragar were considered so unclean that they were not permitted to spit on the ground, but had a pot suspended from the neck into which they expectorated. The Vastra coraga clan wear the shrouds taken from the dead. The Sappoo have leaves as a covering. The tribe follow makkala santauna.——*Coraly* (ಕೊರಲಿ - kórali, Can.). See sep. title.——*Coramboo* (குரம்பு - kurambu, Tam.). From (kuru, tam. small + varambu, tam. ridge). A dam of sand, brushwood, loose stones, &c., running out from the bank of a river, sloping diagonally for a long distance upstream, to turn the river water into a channel [q.v.] for irrigation; the fall being made less than that of the river the water is delivered higher than it could be direct from the river. Also simply bund [q.v.] in rice-field [anay].——*Coraputt* (కొరాపట్టి - kórápatti, Tel.). From (kórá, tel. rude + patti, tel. village).—"*a*" Division; Vizagapatam district; language Ooriya. Boundaries:—E. Calahundy and Royagada and Parvatipore divisions; S. Pottinghy division; W. Padair and Mulkangherry divisions; N. Jeypore and Nowrungapore divisions.—"*b*" Deputy tahsildarry, Vizagapatam district, pay Rs. 200.—"*c*" Village, Head-quarters of Special assistant agent, Superintendent and Assistant superintendent of Police and Deputy tahsildar; Vizagapatam dist., Jeypore zemindarry, Coraputt magisterial division; pop. 163; lat. 18° 48′; long. 82° 46′; from Jeypore S.E. 11 miles; from Madras N.N.E. 422 miles; from Narsapatam N. 78 miles; from Parvatipore W. 46 miles; from Vizagapatam N.N.W. 85 miles; from Vizianagram N.W. 65 miles. A healthy, well-laid town on an open rolling plateau. Head-quarters of Agency police reserve. Granted to Government free of charge for this purpose by the late Maharajah.——*Corava* (குறவன் - kuravan, Tam.). The corresponding terms are:—Tel. and Can. yerkala, Mal. corava. Wandering tribe closely connected with the Coorumbar [q.v.]. They are darker than most natives in complexion. They worship a goddess called Polairamma. They march with tents [derah], hawking goods and telling fortunes; deal largely in salt [ooppoo], which they carry from the salt-pans [ooppalam] on the coast into the interior, returning with grain; some make boxes and baskets of bamboo [q.v.] twigs, and palmyra [q.v.] leaves; others breed pigs [soor] and donkeys [gadhah]; others collect honey [shahad] and other jungle produce; those that reside in madras town sell leaves called carepauk [curry-leaf tree] used as a curry [q.v.] stuff. Polygamy is common; and if a man owe money to his neighbour, he pledges his wife or daughter to his creditor, who may either live with them or transfer them to another person; on the release of the debtor, he reclaims his wife and any children that may have been born in the interval. The Coravar bury their dead [shavacaud]. There is a Tamul proverb:—குரங்குப் பிணமும் குறப் பிணமும் கண்டவர் இல்லை—"No one ever saw the dead "body of a monkey, or the corpse of a Coravan." There is a tamul proverb:—குறத்தி பிள்ளை பெற்றால் குறவன் காயம் தின்பான்—"If the wife of a Coravan is brought to "bed, her husband takes the prescribed stimulant;" this is in jest, but in fact the wife makes her husband taste the medicine lest her rivals should poison her. Also a Malayalam proverb:—കുരങ്ങു ചത്ത കുറവൻ—"A Coravan whose monkey is dead;" meaning one who has lost his livelihood, rearing up monkeys and exhibiting them to public being one of their occupations. Numbers about 60,000. The following are some principal subdivisions:—Bajantry corava, from (bajantri, hind. musician); also called jangama corava; bellary and canara, residing in small tents or in grass huts outside the walls; they will not labor; the men are musicians, and with their women make grass screens or tatties [q.v.]; at harvest times they beg and pilfer from the reapers; the women tattoo the arms and foreheads of the hindoo women; they marry when the bride and bridegroom are about eighteen years of age; polygamy is allowed, and they live virtuously, never prostituting their children; they keep in their houses idols of the figure of hanooman [q.v.], and mark their foreheads with the marks of the veishnava sect. Cashby corava, from (kasbi, hind. prostitute); also agaurypaulwauley, sitters at the door of their tents; differ in appearance from bajantry coravar, resemble in figure and countenance the teloogoo people; found throughout deccan [q.v.]; are basket-makers and sell brooms; but their chief subsistence is from their young women, one of whom from their earliest infancy they devote to the gods; the goddess to whose service their lives are dedicated is maddalamma, also hoolijeeva, near bellary, and chetwye, a divinity made by sprinkling red lead [sendoor] on the tarwar tree, the cassia auriculata [tungaid]; the devoted women sometimes bear children, who are admitted into the caste; the colors seen amongst them vary from the fairness of the bramins to that of the darkest of the shoodra races; no one can read or write; they abstain only from cow's flesh and pork; the women dress with the cholee [q.v.] or bodice and saury [q.v.]; they are rarely permitted to reside inside towns, or only then at some ruined spot remote from respectable people; they bury their dead, and place the deceased's usual food at the head of the grave, auguring most favorably if it be eaten by a crow and next if by a cow, if rejected by crow and cow they deem the deceased to have lived a depraved life and fine the surviving relatives. Caukka corava, from (kákka, mal. crow); in travancore; they eat crows. Patra corava, from the dancing girls having bells on their feet and ankles [jauty].——*Coray* (கோரை - kórai, Tam). See sep. title.——*Corcapilly* (دکھنی ببول - dakhaníbabúl, Hind.; کورکا پلی - korkápalí, Dec.; ಸೀಮೆಹುಣಿಸೆ - símehunise, Can.; ಚಕ್ಕುಲಿಮರ - chakkulimara, Too.; సీమచింత - símachinta, Tel.; കുക്കമ്പുളി - kúrkkampuli, Mal.; கொறுக்காய்ப்புளி - korukkáyppuli, Tam.). Title from tamul. Hind. from (dakhaní, hind. deccan + babúl, hind. acacia arabica, willd.). Dec. from tamul. Can. from (síme, can. foreign + hunise, can. tamarindus indica, linn.). Tel. from (síma, tel. foreign + chinta, tel. tamarindus indica, linn.). Mal. from (kúrkka, mal. sharp + puli, mal. sour, tamarindus indica, linn.). Tam. from (kurukku, tam. to shrink + káy, tam. fruit + puli, tam. tamarind tree); from fruit. Can. also (chaklimara). Tel. also (símachinduga), meaning foreign + albizzia odoratissima, benth. Title otherwise Foreign tamarind, Manilla tamarind, Sappan fruit tree, Sweet babool, Sweet-fruited inga. Botanically Pithecolobium [auragvadham] dulce, benth., leguminosæ [vricsham, 48]. Alias Inga dulcis; Mimosa dulcis. Tree, 30 feet; extreme branches pendulous, armed with short straight thorns; leaves bigeminate; leaflets oblong, very unequal-sided; petiole shorter than the leaflets; pinnæ and leaflets each one pair; flowers capitate, heads shortly peduncled, racemose, the racemes panicled; legumes irregularly turgid, much twisted; seeds glabrous, smooth, half imbedded in a firm whitish edible pulp; flowers small, yellowish-greenish; flowering in january and february; cultivated and common; in general appearance resembles the english hawthorn. The spaniards introduced the tree to the e. indies from mexico. Pulp of fruit eatable. Good hedge plant; coppices well; oil from flattened black seeds, of the consistence of castor [aumanac] oil, light-colored. Wood hard, coarse grained and brittle, of a reddish brown color, when sawn emits an unpleasant odour. Used for country carts, packing boxes, and the pannelling of doors.——*Corindah* (चिलारी - chilárí, Mahr.; కొరింద - kórinda, Tel.; ഇഞ്ച - iñcha, Mal.; வெள்ளிண்டு - vellindu, Tam.). Title from teloogoo. Tel. means thorny mimosa. Mal. from (chínna, mal. cleaning pod); (ínna), by corruption whence the word being joined with soap pod wattle [q.v.]. Tam. from (vellai, tam. white + indu, tam. mimosa species); from wood. Mal. also (attu), meaning bruised; soft bark used for washing body after bruising. Title otherwise Angular-stalked acacia. Botanically Acacia [cantalim] intsia, willd., leguminosæ [vricsham, 48]. Specific name from malayalam. Alias Acacia cæsia; Mimosa intsia. A procumbent or climbing shrub; branches angled, armed with recurved prickles; pinnæ five to eight pair, leaflets about nine pair, linear-oblong; petioles armed with recurved prickles on the under side, with a large convex gland near the base, and a small one between each of the one to three last pairs of pinnæ; panicles large, terminal; peduncles three to four together, heads of flowers globose; legumes broadly-linear, flat and thin; flowering in rainy season. Large thorny climbing shrub, hedge plant. Bark used in dyeing [shauyam] with morinda [dyeing mulberry], or lac [q.v.], giving brightness; fresh leaves also. Wood white, soft, porous. The hill variety is cæsia, otherwise gray acacia.——*Cority* (కొరితి - koriti, Tel.). Tel. from (kóra, tel. sharp); from spines. Tel. also (sálichettu), (alasále), (gortichettu), (gortidonka). Botanically Plecospermum spinosum, trecul., urticaceæ [vricsham, 119]. Alias Batis spinosa. Small straggling tree or sub-scandent shrub; common. Used for hedges. Wood greyish-white, with a small bright orange-yellow heart-wood, which is very hard; in the heart-wood the pores are filled with a yellow resinous substance; wood used to give a yellow dye [shauyam] with californian cinchona [lodh] and turmeric [country saffron]. No other common species here.——*Corote* (കോരോട്ട് - kórótt, Mal.). Adjectival form from (kóra, mal. cyperus juncifolius, rottl.). Village; Malabar dist., Wynaud tal.; lat. 11° 45′; long. 75° 56′; from Calicut N.N.E. 34 miles; from Manantoddy W.S.W. 8½ miles. In Tondarnaud amshom, place of considerable trade, chiefly in hands of Moplahs; travellers' bungalow; two temples Tondarcottah and Bhagavaty cauv; two mosques Corottangaudipully and Corottpoothiyapully.——*Corra* (కొఱ్ఱ - korra, Tel.). Means small grain. Same as Tinay.——*Corteliaur* (கொற்றலையாறு - korttalaiyáru, Tam. kortalayár *). From (kórai, tam. cyperus genus + talai, tam. place + áru, tam. river). Cf. Coray. Sanscrit name (kushast'halí), meaning coosham grass, eragrostis cynosuroides, retz. + land [cooshastaly]; also (vriddhakshíranadí), meaning old + milk + river. River; N. Arcot dist., Wallajah tal. and Chingleput dist., Ponnairy and Trivellore tals. Rises in surplus from calingula [q.v.] of Cauverypauk tank in North arcot. Swelled by accretions from tanks of Wallajah talook, and by the Mahendranuddy and Tappoor, it flows through the Trivellore and Ponnairy talooks. At Keshavaram it is crossed by an anicut [q.v.] which throws water down the old Bungaur channel. It then runs in a north-easterly direction to Puttrapermatore, near which it is joined by the Trittany and Nagary [cooshastaly]. At Velliyore tambrapaukam it is again tapped by an anicut for the supply of Cholavaram and Red hills tanks, and again by Seemaupooram anicut it fills large tanks of Minjoor, Vulloor, &c. It then falls into Ennore backwater about 12 miles north of Madras. Chief source of Madras [q.v.] water supply. See vol. II, 92. It is said that at one time the bed of the present Corteliaur was occupied by the Palaur. It was the delay caused by a sudden fresh in the Corteliaur that led to the destruction of General Baillie's column by Hyder ally in 1780 [poollalore].

CORADAH (کولڈا - koldá, *Hind.*; కొరడా - koradá, *Tel.*; കൊരടാ - koratá, *Mal.*).—"*a*" A long whip [chowk] of cotton [q.v.] rope, about an inch and-a-half in diameter at the thick end, where it is grasped, and tapering to a point at the other extremity; about 9 feet long. Formerly in use under Mahomedan governments.—"*b*" Mittah, Village; Ganjam dist.; 34 sq. miles; lat. of village 19° 56′; long. 84° 20′; from Balligooda S.E. 29 miles; from Chetterpore W.N.W. 60 miles.

CORAH (کورا - korá, *Hind.*). Means brown. Unbleached cotton cloth. Undyed silk [puttoo].

CORAKKAN (கோரக்கன் - kórakkan, *Tam.*). From (gó, san. cow + raksh, san. to protect); cowherd. One of the nine siddhar [q.v.], who acquired supernatural powers by intense austerities. Versed in poetry, medicine, and chemistry. Ganjah is called Corakkar mooly or Corakkan's drug. Compare Gorakha chincha or Gorakha's tamarind [baobab].

CORAL TREE (मन्दार - mandára, *San.*). From (mand, san. to be beautiful) [white mountain ebony]. Title from flowers. Botanically the Erythrina genus, leguminosæ [vricsham, 48]. Tropical trees and tuberous herbs, with clusters of very large, long flowers, which are usually of the brightest red; frequently stems are defended by stiff prickles; leaves are trifoliate, with long stalks; pods mostly long, narrow and round with red seeds used for necklaces. The species best known to the natives are shown below. The term includes also plants from genera bombax, breynia, zanthoxylum.——*Black coral tree* (കരിമുരിക്ക - karimurikku, Mal.). From glossy black seeds. Same as Rhotsa.——*Common coral tree* (पारिजात - paríjáta, San.; मन्दार - mandára, Mahr.; पंगिरो - pangiró, Conc.; پانگرا - pángrá, Hind. and Dec.; دودڤ - dudap, Malay; ಕೆಂಪುವಾರ್ಜಿಪ್ಪೆಮರ - kempuvárjippemara, Can.; ಪೊಂಗರೆಮರ - pongaremara, Too.; బార్జము - bárjamu, Tel.; ଚଲୋଧୋନ - chalodhona, Oor.; മുരിക്ക - murikku, Mal.; එරබදු - erabadu, Singh.; முருக்கம் - murukkam, Tam.). San. from (párí, san. ocean + jan, san. to be produced) [coormam, coral jasmine]. Mahr. from (mand, san. to be beautiful). Can. from (kempu, can. red + várjippemara, can. the tree). Tel. from sanscrit. Tam. from (murugu, tam. beauty). San. also (madaja), meaning produced from intoxication; (palitamandára), meaning grey + the plant. Hind. also (farad); (paltmandar), from sanscrit; (panjírá). Can. also (páriváladamara); (hongara); (pongara); (hálivánamara). Tel. also (bádidamu); (bádamu); (bádisechettu), meaning adze + tree; (bádchamu); (mahámeda); (muççikarra), meaning mootchy's wood. Mal. also (mullumurikku), meaning thorn + the tree; (karimurikku), meaning black + the tree; (kalyánamurikku), meaning auspicious + the tree; from beauty of flowers. Tam. also (kalyánamurukkam); (muççimaram), meaning mootchy tree, useful to mootchies in toy work; (shavusayam). Title otherwise Bastard teak [palaus], Moorkkam wood tree, Mootchy wood tree, Red bean. Botanically Erythrina [coral tree] indica, lamk., leguminosæ [vricsham, 48]. Alias Erythrina corallodendron, cuneata, orientalis. Tree, 10-30 feet, armed with prickles; petioles and leaves unarmed; leaves pinnately trifoliolate; leaflets glabrous, entire, the terminal ones broadly cordate; racemes terminal, horizontal; calyx spathaceous; contracted and five-toothed at the apex; corolla papilionaceous; vexillum about three times shorter than the calyx, and four times longer than the alæ; petals of keel distinct; stamens monadelphous, with the sheath entire at the base, thence diadelphous with the tube split; legumes six to eight-seeded; flowers scarlet. A stiff-looking tree; bears in march at the ends of its stems handsome clusters of the large, brilliant, flowers, being quite destitute of leaves at the time; has a dark-brown gum [gond]. The fresh bark has a smooth grey suber, and bears small fissured corky lenticels arranged in perpendicular rows; on rubbing off the thin suber a green surface is exposed; the outer portion of the bark is granular and brittle, the inner consists of numerous layers of liber cells interlaced so as to form an open network; the bark has a disagreeable flavor, but is not bitter. The flowers have no scent; there is a tamul proverb:—பொற் பூவின் வாசனையும் முருக்கம் பூவின் வாசனையும்சரி—"The smell of a flower "made of gold and that of the moorkkam flower are alike, both "beautiful but odourless;" there is another:—வித்தை அற்றவன் அழகு வாசனை இல்லா முருக்கம்பூப்போல—"The "beauty of the unlettered is like the inodorous moorkkam "flower." The trifoliate leaf is taken to be symbolical of the trinity [trimoorty]; the centre leaflet representing Vishnoo, its right bramha, its left Shiva. Bark used medicinally, being antibilious, febrifuge, anthelmintic and useful as a collyrium in ophthalmia; leaves applied externally to disperse venereal buboes, and to relieve pain on the joints. Young tender leaves eaten in curries; flowers much eaten by squirrels [anil], and crows [caurvam] and other birds feed on the insects which resort to the tree. Tree used in malabar for support of the betel [q.v.] vines; from being armed with numerous prickles, it serves as hedge-plant; dried flowers on being boiled yield a red dye [shauvam]; bark yields a fibre; ashes used as mordant [cauram]. Wood called mootchy wood is light and soft, does not warp or split; varnished toys from northern circars [q.v.] are made of this wood [condapully]; also for cowry [q.v.] boxes, and sword sheaths; also for rafts, and is hollowed out into canoes [munjy]. ——*Cotton coral tree* (ഉന്നമുരിക്ക - unnamurikku, Mal.). From red flowers and cottony fibres of pods. Same as Red cotton tree. ——*Devil coral tree* (पारिभद्र - páribhadra, San.; යකෙරබදු - yakerabadu, Singh.). Title from prickles. San. from (párí, san. ocean + bhadra, san. happy); beautiful tree from the ocean [coormam]. Singh. from (yak, singh. devil + erabadu, singh. the coral tree, erythrina indica, lamk.). Botanically Erythrina [coral tree] ovalifolia, roxb., leguminosæ [vricsham, 48]. Tree, armed with prickles; leaflets oval; petioles armed; vexillum obcordate; racemes terminal, horizontal; flowers very large, scarlet, variegated with orange, sulphur and dark purple. Found in cuttack.——*Poolah coral tree* (अरुणी - aruní, San.; سرسرونی - sursaruní, Hind.; ಗಂಡುಪಚ್ಚೆರಿ - gandupaççeri, Can.; పగడపుచెట్టు - pagadapuchettu, Tel.; പവിഴപ്പൂല - pavizhappúlá, Mal.; பவழப்பூலா - pavazhappúlá, Tam.). San. from (aruna, san. red); from berries. Can. from (gandu, can. male + paççeri, can. the tree, so called). Tel. from (pagadamu, tel. coral + chettu, tel. tree). Tam. from (pravála, san. coral + púlá, tam. the plant, phyllanthus multiflorus, willd.); from berries. Can. also (kádu-nugge), meaning wild moringa pterygosperma, gærtn.; (kempu-huligida), meaning red + tiger + plant. Tel. also (errapuru-gudu), meaning red + tree, phyllanthus multiflorus, willd. Tam. also (shigappuppúlá), meaning red + the plant. Title otherwise Poolah shrub, Red poolah, Wild moringa. Botanically Breynia rhamnoides, müller, var. genuina, euphorbiaceæ [vricsham, 118]. Alias Melanthesa rhamnoides; Phyllanthus rhamnoides, vitisidæa; Rhamnus vitisidæa. Shrub; leaves oval, rounded at the apex, acute at the base, glabrous; peduncles axillary, the inferior ones paired, male, upper ones solitary, female, about the length of the petiole; fruit embraced by the short calyx; berries globose, bright red, mealy when ripe; flowers small, greenish; flowering nearly all the year; native of coromandel coast [q.v.]. Dried leaves smoked like tobacco [pogauk] for swollen tonsils; leaves are used in discussing tumors, especially carbuncles, applied warm with castor-oil; bark of root mixed with long pepper [q.v.] and ginger [q.v.] drunk as a tonic. Cattle eat leaves. Employed for ornamental hedges. Wood white and durable, employed by hill tribes for various economical purposes. No other common species here.——*Thorny coral tree* (ಕಿಚಿಗೆ - kichige, Can.; ముల్లుమోదుగ - mullumóduga, Tel.; முள்முருக்கம் - mulmurukkam, Tam.). Tel. from (mullu, tel. thorn + móduga, tel. butea frondosa, roxb.). Tam. from (mul, tam. thorn + murukkam, tam. erythrina indica, lamk.). Botanically Erythrina [coral tree] stricta, roxb., leguminosæ [vricsham, 48]. Tree armed with white prickles; petioles rarely prickly; leaves unarmed, terminal; leaflet reniform-cordate, pointed; calyx spathaceous, entire, acute, short; vexillum about ten times longer than the calyx and twice the length of the keel; keel much longer than the wings, its petals uniting; stamens monadelphous, with the sheath entire at the base, diadelphous upwards; racemes terminal, horizontal; legume two to three-seeded; flowers large, dark purple scarlet; western ghauts; flowering in march.——*White coral tree* (मन्दार - mandára, San.; पांगार - pángára, Conc.; پانگرا - pángrá, Hind.; ముల్లుమోదుగ - mullumóduga, Tel.; வெள்ளைக்கலியாணமுருக்கம் - vellaikkaliyánamurukkam, Tam.). Title from flowers. San. from (mand, san. to be beautiful). Tel. from (mullu, tel. thorn + móduga, tel. butea frondosa, roxb.). Tam. from (vellai, tam. white + kaliyánamurukkam, tam. coral tree, erythrina indica, lamk.). Hind. also (dauldhak), meaning white, butea frondosa, roxb. Tel. also (munimóduga), meaning demon + butea frondosa, roxb.; from prickles. Botanically Erythrina [coral tree] suberosa, roxb., leguminosæ [vricsham, 48]. Tree, with corky deeply-cracked bark; branches unarmed, except at the insertion of the petioles; stipules lanceolate; petioles pubescent, prickly; leaves unarmed; leaflets tomentose below, terminal one rhomboid and acuminated, occasionally reniform and rounded; calyx tubular, two-lipped; vexillum much longer than the calyx and more than twice the length of the keel; keel cordate, many times longer than the small wings, its petals united; stamens monadelphous; racemes axillary, sometimes terminal, spreading; legume two to three-seeded; flowers large, whitish rose scarlet; circars [q.v.]; flowering in march and april.

CORALY (ಕೊರಲೆ - korali, *Can.*). Means small [cora] grain. Same as White tinay.——*Wild coraly* (ಕಾಡುನವಣೆಹುಲ್ಲು - kádunavanehullu, Can.). Can. from (kádu, can. wild + navane, can. panicum italicum, linn. + hullu, can. grass). Can. also (kádukambuhullu), meaning wild + pennisetum spicatum, delile + grass; from emarginate hairs. Botanically Eragrostis [cooshan] ciliata, nees, graminaceæ [vricsham, 156]. Alias Poa ciliaris. Culms erect, rigid, smooth, 1–2 feet; leaves pubescent at the mouth of the sheaths; panicle columnar, 2–4 inches, hairy at the insertion of the branches; spikelets six to twelve-flowered, outer valve three-nerved, cuspidate, margins ciliated; seed obovate-globose, smooth, dark-colored; dry barren ground. Cattle eat it.

CORAM (கோரம் - kóram, *Tam.*). From (ghóra, san. terrible). Horse. Cf. vol. I (125).

CORANDY (குறண்டி - kurandi, *Tam.*). From (kurandu, tam. to be crumpled or coiled); from slender branches spreading and taking root. Botanically the Lepidagathis genus, acanthaceæ [vricsham, 101]. Generic character similar to barleria [nail dye], but habit of plant is different; native of elevated, dry, barren ground, all over coromandel [q.v.]; flowers, rainy and cold season; capsules burst as in barleria. The species best known to the natives are shown below. Another species is scariosa.——*Lowly corandy* (भुईतेरडा - bhuítéradá, Mahr.; ಗಂಟುಕಾಲುಗಡ್ಡೆ - gantukálugadde, Can.; கீழ்க்குறண்டி - kízhkkurandi, Tam.). Mahr. from (bhúmi, san. ground + téradá, mahr. impatiens balsamina, linn.). Can. from (gantu, can. knot + kálu, can. black + gadde, can. root). Tam. from (kízh, tam. low + kurandi, tam. lepidagathis genus). Tam. also (karappánbúndu), carpang + shrub; as useful in carpang [q.v.]. Title otherwise Carpang plant. Botanically Lepidagathis [corandy] cristata, willd., acanthaceæ [vricsham, 101]. Stem suffruticose, diffuse, and with the linear lanceolate leaves, glabrous; spikes capitate-congested, conglomerated near the root, on the branches axillary, woolly; bracteas and bracteoles conformable, oblong, mucronate; calyx four-parted, segments mucronately aristate, the inferior one bifid; flowers small, rose-colored; flowering in the cold season. ——*Milk corandy* (பாக்குறண்டி - pákkurandi, Tam.). Tam. from (pál, tam. milk + kurandi, tam. the thorny shrub, lepidagathis). Botanically Lepidagathis [corandy] pungens, nees, acanthaceæ [vricsham, 101]. Stem shrubby, very ramous; leaves spinously dentate; spikes binate or ternate, capitately congested, axillary, villous; dorsal bracteæ ovate, and like the fertile ones and bracteoles oblong-lanceolate, rigid, spinous at the apex; calyx four-parted, segments mucronate, spinulose, the inferior one bifid at the apex.

CORAY (मुस्ता - mustá, *San.*; తుంగ - tunga, *Tel.*; കോര - kóra, *Mal.*; கோரை - kórai, *Tam.*). Title from tamul. San. from (mus, san. to destroy); medicinal. Tam. from (kuru, tam. small). Sedges and bulrushes. Botanically the Cyperus genus, cyperaceæ [vricsham, 155]. Stem triangular, leafy at the base; spikelets in two rows, imbricated, in clusters or heads, with a leaf-like involucre under them; glumes several in each spikelet, with one flower in each; seed without bristles; roots of several species tuberous, edible, aromatic. The species best known to the natives are shown below. Other s. indian species indigenous or naturalized are:—Arenarius, stem long. Aristatus, triquetrous culm. Articulatus, culm terete. Atroferrugineous, culm, slender, erect, smooth. Castaneus, culms triangular. Cephalotes, creeping; culm triangular. Dehiscens, culm one-leaved at the base, triquetrous above. Difformis, culm triquetrous. Distans, culm triangular, glabrous. Haspan, culm triquetrous at base, sometimes sheathed and leafless, or leafy. Mucronatus, creeping; culms terete. Nilagiricus, root ascending, fibrous; culm, smooth, thin. Niveus, culm slender, triangular. Oryzeticola, culm lofty. Pennatus, greenish-glaucous; culm trigonal, leafy at the base. Petræus, root cæspitiferous; culms very low. Polystachyus, culm triangular, leafy at the base. Procerulus, smooth. Pumilus, culm leafy at the base. Punctatus, culms triangular. Pusillus, culm terete. Racemosus, firm and tall culm. Retzii, culm triquetrous, smooth, leafy at the base. Seminudus, leafless. Squarrosus, leaves linear. Tenuiflorus, root creeping; culm triquetrous, leafy below. Tenuispica, root cæspitiferous; culms erect. Tortuosus, smooth triangular culm. Tuberosus, root tuberous; culm triangular, leafy at the base. Verticillatus, culm leafy. Vulgaris, culms triangular. Wightii, culm flaccid; root fibrous.——**(1)** *Common sedge* (मुस्तक - mustaka, San.; मोथा - mót'há, Mahr.; भद्रमुष्टि - bhadramushti, Conc.; صاب - sáb, Ar.; موتھا - mothá, Hind.; کورے کا جھاڑ - korekájhár, Dec.; ಭದ್ರಹುಲ್ಲು - bhadrahullu, Can.; తారిపంటి - táripanti, Too.; తుంగ - tunga, Tel.; മുത്തങ്ങ - muttanna, Mal.; කලාඳුරු - kalánduru, Singh.; கோரை - kórai, Tam.). San. from (mus, san. to destroy). Mahr. from sanscrit. Hind. from sanscrit. Can. from (bhadra, san. prosperous + hullu, can. gross). Mal. from sanscrit. San. also (dhanakúta), meaning wealth + heap; (bhadramustaka), meaning excellent + the grass, strictly cyperus pertenuis, roxb.; (gundrá), meaning protecting; (kaivartikamustá), meaning fisherman + the grass. Hind. also (baránágarmothá), meaning large, cyperus pertenuis, roxb. Can. also (koranárigadde); (gókinaguddi); (abdahullu), meaning sea grass. Tel. also (bhadratungamuste); (bhadramuste); (tungamuste); (parivellamu); (púrigaddi), meaning thatch grass; (bhadratunga), meaning prosperous + the plant; (skákhatunga), meaning branch + the plant. Mal. also (karimuttanna), meaning the black + the grass; (pottappullu), meaning worthless grass.

Tam. also (shilandiyarisi), meaning spider + rice; (ambutham), meaning water + to give; (shadámáñji), meaning bushy hair + pulp of fruit [jatamansy]. Title otherwise Indian papyrus, Small sedge, Spider sedge, Toonga. Giving Coray [nalam, straight sedge] root, Shilandy flour. Botanically Cyperus [coray] rotundus, linn., cyperaceæ [vricsham, 155]. Alias Cyperus bicolor, bulbosus, hexastachyus, hydra, litoralis, procerus, var. benghalensis, jemenicus, tetrastachyus. Culms 2–4 inches high, semiterete, three-cornered; root bulbous, tunicate, with bulbiferous fibres; spikelets linear-lanceolate, acuminate, ten to sixteen-flowered, alternate in the apex of the culm, lower two double; scales ovate-lanceolate, acuminate; style trifid; seed oblong, three-cornered, involucre with alternate leaflet; two lower ones longer than the spikes; leaves filiform, all radical, far sheathing. In sandy situations on coromandel coast [q.v.] becomes a troublesome weed in the gardens; tuber has an agreeable fragrance and an aromatic balsamic bitter taste; natives use it at festivals, powdering it up and sprinkling powder on the images. Tubers are used medicinally as stimulant, diaphoretic, stomachic and tonic; veidyans recommend decoction in fevers, and where there is a tendency to dropsy, in quantity of half a cupful twice daily; quoted in pharm. but non-officinal. Cattle eat the greens; pigs eat the tubers; the latter can be used as flour in times of scarcity, and eaten roasted or boiled having then the taste of potatoes [q.v.]. Tubers used by perfumers on account of fragrance, giving an essential oil. With the grass mat manufacturers make the common floor mats called Coray poy, staining them like those made of the caldera bush [screw-pine].——*Creeping grass sedge* (ഊർപ്പുൽ - úrppul, Mal.; ஊர்ப்புல் - úrppul, Tam.). Tam. from (úr, tam. to creep + pul, tam. grass). Botanically Cyperus [coray] pangorei, rottb., cyperaceæ [vricsham, 155]. Alias Papyrus pangorei. Next to Rotundus, the most important species. Root, perennial; culms 3–6 feet, naked, obsoletely three-sided, smooth; leaves consisting of two or three sheaths embracing the base of the culms; umbels decompound; umbellets subsessile; involucre about four-leaved, one or two longer than the umbel; spikelets alternate, many-flowered; seeds elliptically triangular; common in ditches and borders of tanks. Mats common at calcutta are made from this grass; when green, they are split into three or four pieces, which on drying contract sufficiently to bring the margins in contact or to overlap each other; in this state they are woven.——*Demon sedge* (రక్కిసతుంగ - rakkisatunga, Tel.). Tel. from (rakkisa, tel. she devil + tunga, tel. cyperus rotundus, linn.); from being the largest species on coromandel coast. Botanically Cyperus [coray] roxburghii, an. ab. e., cyperaceæ [vricsham, 155]. Alias Cyperus elatus. Umbel decompound and supra-decompound; contracted; rays elongated, compressed and trigonal, fascicled and umbelled from many fastigiate cylindric sub-sessile spikes; spikelets imbricated, linear, ebracteolate twelve to sixteen-flowered; scales closely imbricated, embracing, roundish-ovate, obtuse with a small mucro; caryopsis oblong, three-cornered, acute at both ends, smooth; leaflets of the many-leaved involucre twin, outer ones largest and with the radical leaves broad; involucels narrow, shorter than the umbellet; culm triquetrous, angles rough above, sides concave.——*Fisherman's sedge* (कैवर्त्तमुस्तक - kaivartimustaka, San.; പാറപ്പുല്ല - párappullu, Mal.). Title from being found on sea shore. San. from (kaivarta, san. fisherman + mustaka, san. cyperus rotundus, linn.). Mal. from (pára, san. shore + pul, mal. grass). Title otherwise Lofty cyperus. Botanically Cyperus [coray] venustus, r. br., cyperaceæ [vricsham, 155]. Culm triquetrous, leafy at the base, glabrous; leaves three-nerved, flat, scabrous at the margin; umbel compound, many-rayed, rays somewhat digitately branched at the apex; involucre five-leaved, very long; spikes spicately arranged in long branches, patent, narrow linear, compressed, ten to sixteen-flowered; scales keeled and boat-shaped, ovate, mucronate, lineolate; style exserted; achenium oblong, slightly arched, externally convex-angular, very finely dotted, a half shorter than the scale.——*Flood sedge* (پٹی - patí, Hind.; జలతుంగ - jalatunga, Tel.; പൊട്ടപ്പുല്ല - pottappullu, Mal.). Title from binding banks from floods. Tel. from (jala, san. water + tunga, tel. cyperus rotundus, linn.). Mal. from (potta, mal. worthless + pul, mal. grass). Mal. also (íra), meaning moist. Botanically Cyperus [coray], puncticulatus, vahl., cyperaceæ [vricsham, 155]. Alias Cyperus bacha, inundatus, procerus. Tall; culm triangular, glabrous; leaves stiff, keeled flat, somewhat scabrous on the margin and keel; umbel decompound, somewhat eight-rayed, large, diffuse; rays bracteately three to five-cleft, branches many-spiked; spikes spicately arranged, much spreading, broadly linear, twenty to twenty-six flowered; involucre three-leaved, very long; scales roundish-elliptic, shortly mucronate, keeled; stamens two; achenium obliquely sub-cordate, compressed at the sides, dotted and slightly scabrous, bright chestnut, shorter by half than the scale. Helps to bind banks from rapidity of water in streams.——*Indian matting sedge* (గొడ్డుతుంగ - goddutunga, Tel.; කලැහි - kalehi, Singh.). Tel. from (goddu, tel. beast + tunga, tel. cyperus rotundus, linn.). Botanically Cyperus [coray] corymbosus, rottb., cyperaceæ [vricsham, 155]. Alias Cyperus, tegetus. Culm triangular, leafless, sheathing at the base, glabrous; umbel compound, corymbiform, somewhat seven-rayed, longer rays brachiately branched; involucre somewhat four-leaved, twice exceeding the umbel; leaflets flat, scabrous at the margin; spikes four to twelve, spicately fascicled, patent, linear, compressed, twelve to thirty-two flowered; scales oblong, rounded emarginate at the apex, keeled and boat-shaped, five-nerved, rusty, keel green; achenium oblong, triquetrous, nearly three times shorter than the scale; wings of the rhacheola slowly becoming rusty and loosening. Floor mats [boriyah] are largely made of this.——*Large sedge* (పెద్దశాక - peddasháka, Tel.). Tel. from (pedda, tel. large + sháka, tel. cyperus rotundus, linn.). Botanically Cyperus [coray] umbellatus, burm., cyperaceæ [vricsham, 155]. Root fibrous; culms erect, 4–6 feet, smooth, bluntly angled, leafy at the base; leaves long, one equalling the culm; involucre three to six-leaved, leaflets unequal, the largest 2–3 feet; umbel decompound, with many unequal rays; spiklets numerous, spiked, alternate, three to four-flowered; seed elliptic, triangular.——*Straight sedge* (नागरमुस्तक - nágaramustaka, San.; नागरमोथा - nágaramót'há, Mahr.; سعد - sud, Ar.; مشک زمین - mushkizamín, Pers.; ناگرموتها - nágarmothá, Hind.; ناگرموتہ - nágarmotah, Dec.; ಕೊನ್ನಾರಿಗಡ್ಡೆ - konnárigadde, Can.; కోలతుంగ - kólatunga, Tel.; കോര - kóra, Mal.; கோரை - kórai, Tam.). San. from (nagara, san. town + mustá, san. cyperus rotundus, linn.); from being found near calcutta. Pers. from (mushk, pers. musk + zamín, pers. land). Hind. and dec. from sanscrit. Can. from (kora, can. short + nára, can. smell + gadde, can. root). Tel. from (kóla, tel. straight + tunga, tel. cyperus rotundus, linn.). Mahr. also (laválá). Can. also (kommarigadde). Tam. also (muttakkásu). Title otherwise Calcutta sedge. Botanically Cyperus [coray] pertenuis, roxb., cyperaceæ [vricsham, 155]. Alias Mariscus cyperus. Culm 3–4 feet, trigonal above; leaves few, radical, shorter than the culm; umbel compound and decompound; involucre nearly equalling the umbel; spikelets lanceolate, many-flowered; caryopsis three-cornered. Root is cordial, stomachic, and desiccant; also regarded as diaphoretic and diuretic; quoted in pharm. but non-officinal; root also aromatic and used for perfuming the hair.——*Striped sedge* (ಬಿಳಿಜಂಬುಹುಲ್ಲು - bilijambuhullu, Can.; വരപ്പുല്ല - varappullu, Mal.). Can. from (bili, can. white + jambu, can. reed for thatch + hullu, can. grass). Mal. from (vara, mal. stripe + pul, mal. grass). Title otherwise Fox-tail cyperus. Botanically Cyperus [coray] alopecuroides, rottb., cyperaceæ [vricsham, 155]. Culms triangular, glabrous; leaves flat, scabrous on the margin; umbel decompound, about nine-rayed, rays very unequal, umbellets three to seven-rayed, partial rays densely covered with spikes on every side, forming elongated cylindrical compound spikes; involucre three to five-leaved, longer than the umbel, partial about eighteen-flowered; scales broad-elliptic, mucronate, obsoletely seven-nerved; western coast.——*Tail sedge* (ದಬ್ಬೆಜಂಬುಹುಲ್ಲು - dabbejambuhullu, Can.; ഈര - íra, Mal.; වල්හිරි - valhíri, Singh.). Title from thin stalks. Can. from (dabbe, can. thin slip + jambu, can. sedge or reed + hullu, can. grass). Mal. means moist. Botanically Cyperus [coray] iria, linn., cyperaceæ [vricsham, 155]. Iria from malayalam. Culm triquetrous, glabrous; leaves flat, flaccid, rough on the margins; umbel six to eight-rayed; involucre very long, three to four-leaved; rays very unequal, branched and fascicled at the apex; spikes linear-compressed, eight to twenty-flowered, flowers distant; scales rounded, obovate-emarginate, very shortly mucronate, five-nerved; achenium elliptic, triangular, mucronate, as long as the scale. Yields fibre.——*Thorny sedge* (മുള്ളൻപുല്ല - mullanpullu, Mal.). Mal. from (mullu, mal. thorn + pul, mal. grass). Botanically Cyperus [coray] pygmæus, rottb., cyperaceæ [vricsham, 155]. Alias Cyperus diffusus. Culms cæspitose, triangular, glabrous, leafy at the base; leaves longer than the culm, keeled and flat, scabrous at the margin; heads of flowers solitary, ovate-globose, glomerate, sometimes in threes or fours; involucre four to seven-leaved, very long; spikes lanceolate, ten to sixteen to twenty-four flowered; scales oblong, acutely mucronate, convex and keeled, three-nerved; achenium oblong, terminated by the persistent style, convex and obtusely angled externally, brownish, one-third shorter than the scale.——*Water sedge* (జలతుంగ - jalatunga, Tel.). Tel. from (jala, san. water + tunga, tel. cyperus rotundus, linn.). Botanically Cyperus [coray] procerus, vahl., cyperaceæ [vricsham, 155]. Alias Cyperus tenuiflorus. Culm triquetrous, leafy at the base; leaves longer than the culm, keeled, spongy and thickish; umbel compound, many-rayed, rays brachiately branched above, flexuose; spikes spicately arranged, distichous, much spreading, linear, compressed, many-flowered; involucre three-leaved, leaflets scabrous on the margin and keel, one very long; scales ovate, elliptic, rounded at the apex, nine-nerved, keeled and navicular, pale-chestnut; achenium obovate, triangular; a half shorter than the scale.——*Wet land sedge* (ವುಸುಮಾನಿಹುಲ್ಲು - vusumánihullu, Can.; చలితుంగ - tsalitunga, Tel.). Can. from (ose, can. charmed + hullu, can. grass). Tel. from (tsali, tel. cold + tunga, tel. cyperus rotundus, linn.); from growing in moist soil. Botanically Cyperus [coray] compressus, linn., cyperaceæ [vricsham, 155]. Leaves glabrous, flat, longer than the triangular culm, younger ones serrulated on the margin; umbel one to six-rayed, rays three to six-spiked at the top, very unequal, one almost undeveloped; involucre three to six-leaved, very long; spikes lanceolate and linear, compressed, twenty-four to thirty-six flowered; scales keeled, acute and mucronate, many-nerved, green; achenium obovate, triquetrous, one-third the length of the scale.——(2) *Coraiyaur* (கோரையாறு - kóraiyáru, Tam.). From (kórai, tam. reed, cyperus + áru, tam. river). River; Tanjore dist., Munnargoody and Tritrapoondy tals. Branch of Vennaur. Source 2 miles N.W. of Needamungalam; course S.E. running from June to December; navigable below Mootoopett; crossed by three bridges.

CORINGA (కోరంగి - kórangi, *Tel.*). Means small cardamoms. Sanscrit corruption (kurangam), meaning a stag, after the golden stag in ramayanam. Kalingou of Pliny. Allosygne of others.—"*a*" Town, Port, Sea custom superintendent's station; Godavery dist., Cocanada division; pop. 4,517; lat. 16° 48′; long. 82° 16′; from Cocanada S. 9¼ miles; from Coonavaram E.S.E. 82 miles; from Ellore E.N.E. 74 miles; from Inzaram N.N.E. 6¾ miles; from Madras N.N.E. 283 miles; from Narsapore E.N.E. 43 miles; from Rajahmundry E.S.E. 33 miles. South of the estuary of the Coringa river. At the entrance is a bar with 12 or 14 feet of water at spring tides. Within the bar the depth is from 2½ to 4 fathoms. The lighthouse on the mainland, 4¾ miles from Cocanada, warns vessels off the Godavery shoals; white; fixed. 14 miles range; visible from all directions seaward; masonry tower, horizontal alternate bands of black and white. Trig. station; lat. 16° 49′ 09·93″; long. 82° 23′ 07·84″. Early Dutch settlement, and once the greatest seaport and shipbuilding centre on the coast, but owing to the extension of the delta seaward now of little commercial importance. Being situated on a low site near the coast it has frequently been subjected to inundations by the sea and to the effects of hurricanes and storms. The rising of the sea in May 1787 was so high that vessels were drifted as far inland as Rajahmundry. In 1802 there was a dock [dhony] for the repair of ships of the Royal navy. Still frequented by native craft and ship-building yards are at work in the hamlet of Tullaraiv. Considerable business with Rangoon and Moulmein is still carried on by small vessels.—"*b*" River; Godavery dist., Cocanada division. The branch of the Godavery opening into Coringa bay.

CORJY (ಕೊರ್ಜಿ - kórji, *Can.*; ఖోర్జం - khórjam, *Tel.*). Otherwise written Corge.—"*a*" Measure of capacity. 42 moodies = 1 corjy [alavay, 3 c]. Approximate actual value, 1 corjy = 1,764 pucka seers or 44 Indian maunds, or 70 cubic feet, 520 cubic inches. Compare Garce.—"*b*" Madras town cloth measure. A bale. 20 tauns or pieces = 1 corjy [alavay, 1 c].

COROMANDEL (சோழமண்டலம் - shózhamandalam, *Tam.*). From (shózham, tam. the kingdom + mandala, san. region). Land of the cholas. The name occurs on the temple inscription of Tanjore and in an inscription of A.D. 1101 at a temple to Varauhasawmy near Seven pagodas [q.v.], and is still quite current. Cf. Eelamundalam or ceylon, Chera mundalam, Tondaimundalam, &c. The Portuguese first gave the name to the east coast, and since then common with sailors. In San Bartolomeo it appears as Ciola mandala [coast].——*Coromandel ebony* (آبنوس دکھنی - ábnúsidakhaní, Hind.). See sep. title.——*Coromandel gooseberry* (कर्मरङ्ग - karmaranga, San.; कमरख - kamarakha, Mahr.; कंबल - kamrbala, Conc.; کھمرک - khamrak, Hind. and Dec.; بلمبنگ منس - blimbingmanis, Malay; ದಾರೆಹುಳಿ - dárehuli, Can.; దారెపులి - dárepuli, Too.; తమరతము - tamaratamu, Tel.; ചതുരപ്പുളി - chaturappuli, Mal.; தமரத்தை - tamarattai, Tam.). Title from habitat and flavor of fruit. San. from (karma, san. work + ranga, san. desire), making food palatable. Hind. and dec. from sanscrit. Malay from (blimbing, malay, averrhoa bilimbi, linn. + manis, malay, sweet). Can. from (dáre, can. edge + huli, can. tamarind); from angular fruit. Mal. from (chatura, san. square + puli, mal. tamarindus indica, linn.); from angular fruit. Tam. from (tamaram, tam. lac); from yellowish fruit. Mahr. also (karambala). Hind. also (míthákamaranga), sweet carambola. Tel. also (karamonga). Tam. also (shagadam). Title otherwise Caramba, Carambola, Carambola apple, Country gooseberry, Curmrung, Sweet blimbing. Botanically Averrhoa [lavaly] carambola, linn., geraniaceæ [vricsham, 31]. Specific name from sanscrit. Tree, 15–20 feet; leaves slightly sensitive, alternate, unequally pinnated; leaflets ovate, acuminated, two to five pair on small petioles; calyx glabrous; stamens five; flowers disposed in short racemes arising from smaller branches on the trunk; corolla five-petalled, campanulate; petals yellowish purple; fruit acutely five-angled, with a smooth yellowish rind; seeds with aril. Fruit rather larger than hen's egg; previous to becoming quite ripe possesses a flavor somewhat between that of sorrel and a green gooseberry; when perfectly ripe, semi-transparent and of a fine rich amber, contains a large quantity of quadroxalate of potash, has a strong and agreeable scent as nearly as possible like that of quince [bedauna], as well as a peculiar flavor. Leaves, root, and fruit used as cooling medicine. Fruit eaten, preserved and pickled; leaves are a good substitute for sorrel [sour auray]. Unripe fruit astringent and used as a mordant [cauram]; juice used in removing iron moulds from linen; leaves are good fodder. Wood light red, hard, close-grained. There is a small variety having fruit smaller by about half; when ripe of a deep-green color and not nearly so handsome a fruit, without the acidity of the ordinary kind, but also entirely without its fine flavor. No other common species here.——*Coromandel red wood* (ناتکا چندن - nátkáchandan, Hind.). Same as Soymida.

COROMANDEL (கருமணல் - karumanal, *Tam.*). Title Dutch or Anglo-indian corruption by analogy with the real Coromandel; for which see above. Tam. from (karu, tam. black + manal, tam. sand). Town; Chingleput dist., Ponnairy tal.; pop. 4,639; acres 9,513; lat. 13° 27′; long. 80° 21′; from Ponnairy N.E. 11 miles; from Sydapett N. 30 miles. Lies opposite Poolicat. One of oldest Dutch settlements on East coast, and mentioned as early as 1499 by Italian travellers. Some half-deserted European bungalows still remain. The inhabitants at present are fishermen. There is also a thriving ship-building [dhony] yard for native craft.

COROO (కోరు - kóru, *Tel.*). Share [coor]. Coroo graumam is a Ryotwar [q.v.] or Government village, as one in which the circar [q.v.] shares; as opposed to inam [q.v.], shrotriem [q.v.], and zemindarry [q.v.] villages. Sangoroo, from (sagamu, tel. half) is a half share.

CORROO (కుర్రు - kurru, *Tel.*). From (kúru, tel. to collect). Small hamlet. Suffix in place names, as Keshana corroo meaning keshanna's hamlet.

CORUNDUM (कुरुविन्द - kuruvinda, *San.*; کرنڈ - kurand, *Hind.*; కురివిందము - kurivindamu, *Tel.*; കുരുവിന്ദം - kuruvindam, *Mal.*; குருந்தம் - kurundam, *Tam.*). Title from hindostany. Also called Adamantine spar. A sort of sapphire [neelam], as including the grey and darker-colored opaque crystallized specimens. Greenish color. Pure alumina, crystallizing in the hexagonal system. Sapphire and ruby [laul] are forms of corundum, and emery is a granular variety, mixed with magnetite or hæmatite. This stone is, with the exception of the diamond [vajram], the hardest substance known [coorvinda cull, ratnam]. See vol. II, 38.

CORUNGA (கழங்குக்காய் - kazhangukkáy, *Tam.*). Tam. from (kazhagu, tam. game + káy, tam. fruit); from use of nut as marbles by boys. Same as Bonduc nut.

COSHAM (कोश - kósha, *San.*). From (kush, san. to embrace). A registry of village lands, a dictionary [acaranthy, nigantoo]. Also sheath of a plant [vricsham], seed-vessel, cocoon [peelah]. Also one of the five sheaths [puncha cosham] to the soul [autmam] in philosophy [vedauntam].

COSS (क्रोश - krósha, *San.*). From (krush, san. to cry out). Indian league. 2,000 baums = 1 coss; 4 coss = 1 gow [alavay, 1 e]. Approximate actual value, 1 coss = 2¼ miles. Cutcha coss is half of pucka. In Mysore the Sultanny coss is about 4 miles. Same as San. crosham, Hind. croe, Can. hardaury, Tel. pargoo. See vol. I, 609; II, 505.

COSTUM (कुष्ठ - kusht'ha, *San.*; قسط - kust, *Ar.*; کوست - kost, *Pers.*; کوٹ - kút, *Hind.*; پچک - pachak, *Dec.*; గోష్టము - góshtamu, *Tel.*; கோட்டம் - kóttam, *Tam.*). Title from sanscrit. San. from (ku, san. bad + st'ha, san. spot). Ar., &c., from sanscrit. San. also (kósht'ha); (káshmíra), meaning cashmere plant [arabian costum]. Hind. also (kustitalkh), meaning bitter costus. Tel. also (changalikóshtamu). Greek κόστος. There was κόστος ἀραβικός, white, best of all; κόστος ἰνδικός, dark; and κόστος συριακός, pale yellow. Title otherwise Costus [eagle wood], Coost. Botanically Saussurea lappa, clarke, compositæ [vricsham, 74]. Alias Aplotaxis lappa; Aucklandia costus. The root is imported; has a pungent, aromatic taste, with odour resembling orris root, which natives call by same name. Has been used in hindoo medicine from earliest ages. Is narcotic when smoked and aromatic and stimulant internally. Is a valuable perfume and is a preservative to woollen cloths; exported to china, where reduced to powder and burnt in temples. Two varieties of this root are recognised according to their taste as sweet and bitter. Another species is Candicans. The present genus is distinct from Arabian costum [q.v.].

COT (கட்டில் - kattil, *Tam.*). From (kattu, tam. to bind). A bedstead [cuttil]. It is universal as a sea-term; used in the south; answers to north indian charpoy [q.v.].

COTAUR (కొట్టారు - kot'háru, *Tel.*; கொட்டாய் - kottáy, *Tam.*). From (kódu, tam. to bend); from slope. A pent-house for cattle [cottye, pandaul]. A depôt for the sale of salt [ooppoo].

COTCHOO (കൊച്ചു - koççu, *Mal.*). Small [coonch, coonjam].——*Cotchan* (കൊച്ചൻ - koççan, Mal.). Lad [coonjan].——*Cotchilitty* (दद्रुमारि - dadrumári, San.; കൊച്ചിളച്ചിപ്പുല്ല് - koççilaççippullu, Mal.; கொச்சிலித்திப்புல் - koççilittippul, Tam.). Title from malayalam. San. from (dadru, san. ringworm + mári, san. killer). Mal. from (koççu, mal. small + ila, mal. tender + pullu, mal. grass). Tam. from malayalam. Title otherwise Dauby dooby, Ringworm killer [chakoudah]. Botanically Xyris indica, linn., xyridaceæ [vricsham, 140]. Annual, 1 foot; leaves radical, ensiform, on one edge slit into a sheath for the scape, pointed, smooth; head globular; scales roundish; scape naked, round, striated, the length of the leaves, each supporting a round, flower-bearing head; calyx three-leaved; petals three, unguiculate, with oval crenate borders, just rising above the scales; flowers bright yellow. Considered of great medicinal virtue on the malabar coast [q.v.]; juice of leaves mixed with vinegar [caudy] applied externally in itch; leaves and root boiled in oil applied in leprosy [cooshtam]. Gives fibre. There are other species:—anceps, lappacea, nilagiriensis, oryzetorum, pauciflora, walkeri.

COTE (कोट - kóta, *San.*; کوٹ - kot, *Hind.*; కోట - kóta, *Tel.*). From (kut, san. to curve). Fort. Suffix in place names; as Dhauracote, meaning stream + fort; Srungavarpoocote, meaning peak + town + fort [kota].——*Cotappa condah* (కోటప్పకొండ - kótappakonda, Tel.). From (kótappa, tel. shiva + konda, tel. hill). Hill of Coteshwaran, a name of Shiva. Sanscrit name (kotéshvaragiri), meaning shiva, hill-lord + mountain. Mountain, Place of pilgrimage; Kistna dist., Narsarowpett tal. The shrine upon the hill is modern. It is 600 feet above the plain, and is approached by a winding flight of stone steps. Festival at new moon [amavausyay] in February, attended by about 60,000 persons, at which there is considerable trade in timber. Trig. station in lat. 16° 09′ 09·73″; long. 80° 04′ 47·49″; height 1,588 feet; from Narsarowpett S. 6 miles.——*Cotepaud* (కోటపాడు - kótapádu, Tel.). From (above + pádu, tel. village). Village, Head-quarters of Jeypore maharajah's ameen [q.v.]; Vizagapatam dist., Jeypore division; pop. 3,257; lat. 19° 09′; long. 82° 22′; from Jeypore N.W. 27 miles; from Vizagapatam N.W. 116 miles. Formerly head-quarters of a Deputy tahsildar. Eighteen old mud forts. Small temple on an island in a lake, temple on the edge of the lake, a stone image of a goddess, and a Mahomedan tomb. The lake is semi-circular in shape and is a mile long and about two furlongs broad. Dug in the name of Damayanty, wife of Nalan, after whom it is called Damayanty saras. The town is the centre of a vast tract of wet paddy [q.v.] cultivation.——*Cotiote* (കോട്ടയത്ത് - kóttayatt, Mal.). Adjectival form of Cottayam.——*Cotta* (കോട്ട - kótta, Mal.). Means fort. River; Malabar dist., Cooroombranaud tal.; lat. 11° 34′ N.; long. 75° 39′ E. From a fort commanding entrance to the sea. Formerly haunt of pirates. Drains heavy mass of virgin forest on W. slopes of Wynaud ghauts, and for its length discharges more than usual quantity of water. Navigable at all seasons for boats for 20 miles to Coottiyaudy. Length about 46 miles. The water communication on this river is linked on the north with Badagara by the Badagara canal, and on the south by the Payoly canal, with the extensive natural backwater [cauyal] communication of the Agalapoya river.——*Cottah* (कोट - kóta, San.; کوٹا - kotá, Hind.; కోట - kóta, Tel.; കോട്ട - kótta, Mal.). Fort. Suffix in place names; as Poodoocottah, meaning new + fort [cottay, kota].——*Cottaur* (കോട്ടാർ - kóttár, Mal.). From (kótta, mal. fort + áru, mal. river). Greek κοττιάρα μητρόπολις. Town, Head-quarters of Sub-magistrate and District moonsif; Travancore state, Pudmanaubhapooram division, Agasteeshwaram tal.; pop. 19,968; lat. 8° 10′ N.; long. 77° 29′ E.; from Sooshindram N.W. 2 miles; from Alleppey S.E. 116 miles; from Cottayam S.S.E. 115 miles; from Madras S.S.W. 387 miles; from Nagarcoil S. 1¼ miles; from Paravore S.S.E. 157 miles; from Quilon S.E. 75 miles; from Trivandrum E.S.E. 39 miles; from the sea N. 5¾ miles. Large Bramin village known as Vaudeshwaram with old Shiva temple. Mentioned by Ptolemy as in the country of the ἄϊοι; also mentioned, as παραλία in the Periplus, identical in part with South travancore. Cottora of Pliny and Cottara of the Peutinger tables; not to be confounded with Cottonara [cadatnaud]. The greatest commercial town in South travancore. Ancient pagoda [q.v.] with inscription of Paraucrama paundyan. St. Francis Xavier's church in heart of town where is a festival every year. Weaving colony. Situated on main road to Tinnevelly through Aramboly pass [ghaut].——*Cottauram* (കൊട്ടാരം - kottáram, Mal.). From (above + agára, san. house). Palace; branch of a covilagam [q.v.] of a rajah's family in Malabar.——*Cottay* (कोट - kóta, San.; கோட்டை - kóttai, Tam.). Fort. Suffix in place names as Armoogamcottay, meaning proper name + fort [cote, cottah, kota]. The Tamul Cooral has the following:—இருபுனலும் வாய்ந்த மலையும் வருபுனலும் வல்லரணு நாட்டிற் குறுப்பு—"The constituents of a kingdom are the two waters "[mazhay, neer], from above and below, well situated hills and "an indestructible fort [kila]."——*Cottayam* (കോട്ടയം - kóttayam, Mal.). See sep. title.——*Cottay peak* (கோட்டை - kóttai, Tam.). Means fort. Mountain; Madura and Tinnevelly dists., Travancore state, Periyacoolam tal.; Trig. station; lat. 9° 31′ 14·30″; long. 77° 26′ 41·40″; height 6,617 feet; from Madura S.W. 56 miles; from Periyacoolam S.S.W. 42 miles. Peak of Western ghauts [q.v.] at junction of Madura and Tinnevelly boundaries.——*Cotwaul* (کوتوال - kotwál, Hind.). From (above + wál, hind. lord). Chief officer of police. Under native governments the cotwaul exercised magisterial power [inam, killadar]. Cotwaul chauvady was the cotwaul's court.

COTT (கொத்து - kottu, *Tam.*). Cluster. Suffix in place names as Vadacott, meaning north cluster. Also prefix in plant names as Cottavaray, meaning cluster bean [guar]. Cottvaunam is freckled or mackerel sky.

COTTA (కొత్త - kotta, *Tel.*). New.——*Cottapatam* (కొత్తపట్నము - kottapatnamu, Tel. kottapatam *). From (above + pattana, san. town). Port, Head-quarters of Superintendent of Customs and Sub-magistrate and Sub-registrar; Nellore dist., Ongole tal.; pop. 5,653; acres 16,603; lat. 15° 27′; long. 80° 12′; from Eetamookkala N.E. 6¼ miles; from Madras N. 159½ miles; from Nellore N. 60¼ miles; from Ongole E.S.E. 8¾ miles; from Paudarty S.S.W. 1¾ miles. Originally built as addition to village of Alloor. Northernmost and largest port in the district. Carries on an extensive trade by sea in grain, oil-seeds [yennay], and other produce of the Cumbum and Doopaud tracts. The sea-borne trade is however to a large extent diverted to the Buckingham canal [q.v.] which is 1½ miles from the town. Population chiefly Comaties. Salt [ooppoo] manufactory.——*Cottapettah* (కొత్తపేట - kottapéta, Tel.). From (above + péta, tel. suburb).—"*a*" Deputy tahsildarry, Godavery district, Pay Rs. 70.—"*b*" Village, Deputy tahsildar's station; Godavery dist., Amalaupooram tal.; lat. 16° 43′; long. 81° 56′; from Amalaupooram N.W. 12 miles; from Cocanada S.W. 28 miles; from Coonavarum S.S.E. 71 miles; from Ellore E. 51 miles; from Madras N.N.E. 267 miles; from Narsapore N.E. 20 miles; from Rajahmundry S.S.E. 21 miles; from the sea N. 22 miles. Hamlet of Palivela.

COTTAH (கோட்டை - kóttai, *Tam.*).—"*a*" Measure of capacity. 21 mercauls = 1 cottah [alavay, 3 a]. Approximate actual value, 1 cottah = 7 cubic feet. Tinnevelly. Varies with mercaul. Compare Calam.—"*b*" Superficial measure. 21 mercauls = 1 cottah [alavay, 2 a]. Approximate actual value, 1 cottah = 1·62 acres. Same as dhaunyacottay and vithaicottay. Compare Tel. garce or veesam of Vizagapatam, Tam. cawny. See vol. I, 609; II, 519.

COTTAM (కొట్టము - kottamu, *Tel.*; கோட்டம் - kóttam, *Tam.*). From (kódu, tam. to bend). A cow-house. Division of country in early Dravidian history. Applied to a Coorumba fort in Coorumba bhoomy [q.v.] in ancient tondaimundalam province. See vol. I (141). Suffix in place names as Manavore cottam.——*Cottacaraiyaur* (கொட்டக்கரையாறு - kottakkaraiyáru, Tam.). From (kottam, tam. cow-stall + karai, tam. bank + áru, tam. river). River; Madura dist., Ramnaud zemindarry. Wide and rapid stream formed by junction of two rivulets that enter district on west near Cokkarney. Flows into Rajasingamungalam lake, the superfluous waters of which are conveyed by a channel [q.v.] issuing from a large calingula [q.v.] on the northern bank. This channel runs in an east-south-easterly course five miles, crosses the high road by Armoogam cottah, and flows south-east nearly two miles; thence it pursues an east-south-east course towards Cunnanyendal, runs south-east from that village about a mile, separates into two branches on the west of the high road, and communicates with the sea by two mouths about a mile distant from each other.——*Cottagam* (கோட்டகம் - kóttagam, Tam.). Tank. Suffix in place names; as Pannaycauran cottagam, meaning husbandman's tank.

COTTAMULLY (கொத்தமல்லி - kottamalli, *Tam.*). Corruption from (kustumburu, san. the plant). Same as Cassibor.

COTTAUN (आकाशवल्ली - ákáshavallí, *San.*; आकाशवेल - ákáshavéla, *Mahr.*; کتان کا پیر - katánkáper, *Hind.*; کتان کا جہار - katánkájhár, *Dec.*; رمبوت پوتری - rambutputri, *Malay*; ಬೆಳುಬಳ್ಳಿ - béluballi, *Can.*; పాచితీగ - páchitíga, *Tel.*; ആകാശവള്ളി - ákáshavalli, *Mal.*; கொத்தான் - kottán, *Tam.*). Title from tamul. San. from (ákásha, san. sky + valli, san. creeper); from parasitic growth. Malay from (rambut, malay, hair + putri, malay, princess). Can. from (bélu, can. a kind of insect + balli, can. creeper). Tel. from (páchi, tel. moss + tíga, tel. creeper). Tam. from (kottam, tam victory); from curing virtues. Mahr. also (amaravéla), meaning sky + creeper. Hind. also (ákásbel), meaning sky-creeper. Tel. also (antaravalli), meaning growing in mid air + creeper; (núlutíga), meaning thread + creeper; (sítammapógunúlu), meaning seetay, the goddess + mother + yarn; cf. Seeta's knot. Tam. also (erumaikkottán), meaning buffalo + the plant; (indiravalli), meaning indran + creeper, air creeper; (nandai), meaning to dissolve; medicinal. Title otherwise Air plant, Air-creeper, Leafless creeper, Princess's hair, Moss creeper, Seeta's yarn, Thread creeper. Botanically Cassytha filiformis, linn., lauraceæ [vricsham, 111]. Alias Caladium cochin-chinense; Cassytha aphylla; Volutella aphylla. Parasitic leafless thread-like plant found twisting round branches of trees; spikes lateral, ascending; calyx three-leaved; segments very small, round; petals three, larger than the calyx; flowers small, white, rather remote; bracteas three-fold, embracing the fructification; fruit a drupe with a one-seeded nut, round. The juice mixed with sugar [q.v.] is applied to inflamed eyes; whole plant pulverised and mixed with dry ginger [q.v.] and butter is used in the cleaning of inveterate ulcers. Plant put as a seasoning into butter-milk [mor], especially by bramins in south. Juice mixed with gingelly [q.v.] oil is employed in strengthening roots of hair. For moodacottaun or palsy curer see Oolinja.

COTTAY (बीज - bíja, *San.*; گٹھلی - guthlí, *Hind.*; ಬೀಜ - bíja, *Can.*; విత్తు - vittu, *Tel.*; അണ്ടി - anti, *Mal.*; கொட்டை -

kottai, *Tam.*). Nut, kernel, or large seed [pazham]; one of the Dravidian terms for plant products added to the word root [vricsham].——**(1)** The following are two key-lists of the edible nuts of s. india; further information must be traced in the glossary paragraphs through the small-type cross-references at end of this volume; see also vricsham, 7, for the method of expressing the products, &c., of plants in the dravidian languges.—"*a*" Aleurites triloba, lumbang nut; Anacardium occidentale, cashew; Arachis hypogæa, ground nut; Artocarpus incisa, ratadel; Artocarpus integrifolia, bread-fruit; Avicennia officinalis, ooppata mangrove; Bauhinia racemosa, small-flowered mountain ebony; Buchanania latifolia, chironjee; Cocos nucifera, cocoanut; Coffea arabica, coffee; Euryale ferox, makhanah; Juglans regia, walnut; Nelumbium speciosum, sacred lotus; Nymphæa lotus, red indian water-lily; Nymphæa stellata, blue indian water-lily; Pistacia vera, pistachio nut; Prunus amygdalus, almond; Semecarpus anacardium, marking-nut tree; Sterculia fœtida, bastard poon; Sterculia urens, false tragacanth; Terminalia belerica, belleric myrobalan; Terminalia catappa, country almond; Terminalia chebula, chebulic myrobalan; Trapa bispinosa, water caltrops.—"*b*" Almond, prunus; Bread-fruit, artocarpus; Caltrops, trapa; Cashew, anacardium; Chironjee, buchanania; Cocoanut, cocos; Coffee, coffea; Country almond, terminalia; False tragacanth, sterculia; Ground nut, arachis; Lotus, nelumbium; Lumbang nut, aleurites; Makhanah, euryale; Mangrove, avicennia; Marking nut, semecarpus; Mountain ebony, bauhinia; Myrobalan, terminalia; Pistachio nut, pistacia; Poon, sterculia; Ratadel, artocarpus; Walnut, juglans; Water-lily, nymphæa.——**(2)** Compare also the following non-edible nuts:—Adhatoda vasica, malabar nut; Areca catechu, betel nut; Cæsalpinia bonduc, bezoar nut; Cæsalpinia bonducella, corunga nut; Calophyllum wightianum, keena nut; Carum bulbocastanum, great earth nut; Corypha umbraculifera, talipot nut; Entada scandens, lady-nut; Jatropha curcas, physic nut; Moringa pterygosperma, bennut; Randia dumetorum, emetic nut; Sapindus trifoliatus, soap nut; Strychnos nux vomica, vomit-nut; Strychnos patatorum, water filter nut; Terminalia citrina, gall nut.——**(3)** For oil nuts and seeds see Yennay.

COTTAYAM (കോട്ടയം - kóttayam, *Mal.*). From (kótta, mal. fort + akam, mal. within) [cote].——**(1)** The northern division of Travancore, divided into eleven talooks. Has more than a third of population of whole state, some 900,000.——**(2)** Talook; Travancore state, Cottayam division; pop. 64,958. Greatest length, N. to S. 10 miles. Greatest breadth, E. to W. 20 miles. Sub-divided into seven pravertics and containing eighty-one caras or villages. Bounded N. by Yaittoomanore and Meenachel talooks, E. by Chungacherry and Meenachel talooks, S. by Chungacherry and Ambalapoya talooks, and W. by Vembanaud lake and Shertala talook. In some places hilly, in others low with paddy-fields. Soil is productive. The principal industries are coppray [q.v.], coir [q.v.], pepper [q.v.], dry ginger [q.v.], and molasses [jaggery]. Irrigated by Meenachel river.——**(3)** Town, Head-quarters of Division and Tahsildar; Travancore state, Cottayam division, Cottayam talook; pop. 14,607; lat. 9° 36′; long. 76° 33′; from Alleppey E.N.E. 14 miles; from Bombay S.S.E. 680 miles; from Cochin S.E. 31 miles; from Madras S.W. 350 miles; from Nagarcoil N.W. 113 miles; from Paravore S.S.E. 43 miles; from Quilon N. 47 miles; from Trivandrum N.N.W. 80 miles; from the sea E. 14 miles. On Meenachel river in the middle of fine scenery, about eight miles to the interior of the eastern bank of the Vembanaud backwater [cayal], along which it extends for some distance. It crowns the bank of a large navigable stream and is on the main road to Peermaid. Former head-quarters of the Cottayam rajahs. Almost wholly inhabited by Syrian christians, who form a thriving community. Head-quarters of the Church mission society since 1816. Cross with Pahlava [q.v.] inscription in the old church, tablet with Pahlava inscriptions, and Syrian copper plates. Manufacture of molasses. Lately become of importance, as all trade from Madura country by Peermaid pass over ghauts [q.v.] is carried here, and thence by boats through backwaters to Alleppey. There are celebrated native physicians here.——**(4)** Talook, Malabar district, Tahsildar's pay Rs. 175. Area 462 square miles. Comprises the old talooks of Cottayam and Tellicherry. North centre coast of district. Bounded north by Chiracal, east by Coorg and Wynaud, south by Wynaud and Cooroombranaud, and west by the sea. The country, 8 miles in a parallel with the coast, is composed of open ridges between the cultivated valleys. A few eminences are wooded. There is very little flat land beyond a belt along the coast about Tellicherry and cultivated valleys. Whole eastern portion is one dense wood with a few cultivated spots to the foot of the ghauts [q.v.]. In island of Dharmapatam only flat ground is that under wet cultivation and marsh, rest is undulating ground falling in cliffs towards the sea. Opposite is a rocky island, called Grove island. About half a mile west of Tellicherry is a ridge of rocks which affords shelter for craft. Cangote forest belongs to Government. The soil in some parts towards the coast is brown and sandy; on the rising grounds in interior it is rich and gravelly; the cultivated valleys a brown loam; towards mountains and in forests rich and black; productions are rice [paddy] of different kinds, cocoanut [q.v], betel [q.v.], areca-nut [q.v.], cardamom [q.v.], pepper [q.v.] in great quantities and dry grains [q.v.] of sorts. Cottayam is celebrated for its pepper crops. Iron [auhau] is found but not worked. Cloths of inferior sorts are made. In Nittore, suburb of Tellicherry, weaving is carried on by Basel mission. Arrack [q.v.], jaggery [q.v.], oil [yennay] from coppray [q.v.] and other nuts are manufactured. Copper [taumram] vessels are manufactured at Tellicherry and at Mattanore in Pychy amshom. Eighty square miles under cultivation. Places of archæological interest:—Cannavam, Cathirore, Coottooparamba, Cottayam, Cullye, Dharmapatam, Keelore, Manattana, Meilanjenm, Nittore, Paunore, Peringalam, Pinaroy, Poottore, Shivapooram, Tellicherry, Tirvangaud, Tricaniyore and Triprangottore. Principal trig. station:—Dharmapatam. The leading places, &c., in the talook are the following.——*Bramhagherry* (ബ്രഹ്മഗിരി - brahmagiri, Mal.). See sep. title.——*Candamcoonn* (കണ്ടംകുന്ന് - kantamkunnu, Mal.). From (kantam, mal. field + kunnu, mal. hill). Village; pop. 10,641; lat. 11° 52′; long. 75° 38′; from Tellicherry N.E. 10 miles; from Calicut N.N.W. 44 miles; from the sea E. 16 miles.——*Cangote* (കണ്ണവം - kannavam, Mal.). See sep. title.——*Cathirore* (കതിരൂർ - katirúr, Mal.). From (katir, mal. spike of corn + úr, mal. village). Amshom, Village; pop. 9,933; lat. 11° 47′ N.; long. 75° 35′ E.; from Calicut N.N.W. 40 miles; from Tellicherry N.E. 4 miles; from the sea E. 4¾ miles. Head-quarters of the British troops during the Cotiote rebellion, 1796–1805. Two rock-cut caves. Formerly seat of Tahsildar and subsequently of District moonsif.——*Chauvacherry* (ചാവശ്ശേരി - chávashshéri, Mal. chávacheri *). From (chával, mal. cock + shéri, mal. village). Amshom, Village; pop. 4,150; lat. 11° 57′; long. 75° 39′; from Calicut N.N.W. 49 miles; from Tellicherry N.E. 16 miles; from the sea E. 20 miles. Moplah bazaar [q.v.] and palace to the north. Culloor temple and Paulote mosque [musjid].——*Codoly* (കൊടുവള്ളി - kotuvalli, Mal.). From (kotu, mal. steep + valli, mal. village); from a fort of that name at the mouth of the river. Otherwise Tellicherry river. River. Rises on the western slopes of the Wynaud ghaut.——*Coottooparamba* (കൂത്തുപറമ്പ - kóttuparamba, Mal.). See sep. title.——*Cotiote* (കോട്ടയത്ത് - kóttayatt, Mal.). See sep. title.——*Cottayam* (കോട്ടയം - kóttayam, Mal.). See below.——*Cottiyore* (കൊട്ടിയൂർ - kottiyúr, Mal.). From (kóttam, mal. temple + úr, mal. village). Village, Place of pilgrimage; lat. 11° 52′; long. 75° 54′; from Calicut N. 42 miles; from Tellicherry E.N.E. 26 miles; from the sea E. 34 miles. Annual festival in April-May. Shiva temple called Trichercoonn. On road from Manattana to Wynaud.——*Cullye* (കല്ലായി - kalláyi, Mal.). From (kal, mal. stone + azhi, mal. river mouth). Mal. also (karinnóttukalláyi), meaning cullye of caringode, to distinguish it from calicut cullye. Amshom, Village, Port; pop. 6,666; lat. 11° 43′; long. 75° 34′; from Bombay S.S.E. 510 miles; from Calicut N.N.W. 34 miles; from Mahé N.W. ¾ mile; from Talye S.E. 2¼ miles; from Tellicherry S.E. 4 miles. Inside the bar of the Mahé river, which can be entered by small sized country craft. Contains two caves cut out of laterite [q.v.]. Also Parimatam temple and Cullye mosque. There is little coasting trade. A land customs station of the French settlement frontier.——*Dharmapatam* (ധർമ്മടം - dharmmatam, Mal.). See sep. title.——*Iritty* (ഇരിട്ടി - iritti *, Mal.). Meaning dark from the shade of trees. River. Rises in Perambaudy ghaut in Coorg. Is crossed by a large iron girder bridge.——*Irvenaud* (ഇരുവൈനാട് - iruvainátu, Mal.). From (iru, mal. two + vazhi, mal. line + nátu, mal. country); this tract of land was formerly governed by the numbiyaur, but belonged to the colattiry rajahs and hence the name. Village.——*Manattana* (മണത്തണ - manattana, Mal.). From (mana, mal. nambúri house + tanal, mal. shade). Amshom; pop. 4,190; lat. 11° 55′; long. 75° 48′; from Calicut N. 45 miles; from Tellicherry E.N.E. 21 miles; from the sea E. 28 miles. Twenty-eight miles from Tellicherry and 8 from Cangote; once a military post. Redoubt on the summit of a low hill.——*Meilanjenm* (മൈലാഞ്ജന്മം - mailánjanmam, Mal.). From (mailán, mal. a family of that name in malabar + janmam, mal. a freehold). Amshom, Village; pop. 3,154; lat. 11° 44′; long. 75° 34′; from Calicut N.N.W. 37 miles; from Cottayam S.S.W. 5¾ miles; from Tellicherry E. 2½ miles; from the sea E. 1⅓ miles. Two rock-cut sepulchral caves. Part is included in the Tellicherry municipality.——*Meroompoya* (മെരുമ്പായി - merúmpáyi, Mal.). From (meruvam, mal. game + páyu, mal. to run). Name in the first part of its course. Otherwise Anjarcundy and Dharmapatam, lower down, called after those villages. River. Rises in Periya ghaut and after a course of 40 miles divides into two branches forming the island of Dharmapatam near Tellicherry.——*Paunore* (പാനൂർ - pánúr, Mal.). From (pána, mal. water pot + úr, mal. village). Amshom, Village; pop. 9,374; lat. 11° 46′; long. 75° 38′; from Calicut N.N.W. 37 miles; from Tellicherry E. 6½ miles; from the sea E. 7 miles. Seven miles from Tellicherry, formerly seat of District moonsif; populous Moplah village; ruins of an old fort. Sub-registrar's station.——*Periya peak* (പേരിയശിഖരം - périyashikharam, Mal.). From (periya, mal. great + shikhara, san. peak). Mountain. Pass leading into Cottayam talook; wheeled traffic.——*Pychy* (പഴശ്ശി - pazhashshi.

Mal.). See sep. title.——*Smuggler's pass* (ഗുഢച്ചുരം - gúdhachuram, Mal.). See sep. title.——*Talye* (തലായി - taláyi, Mal.). From (tala, mal. head + azhi, mal. river mouth). Village, Port; from Tellicherry S.E. 1½ miles. Small port on the open coast.——*Tellicherry* (തലശ്ശേരി - talashshéri, Mal.). See sep. title.——*Yelara* (ഏഴറ - ézhara, Mal.). From (ézhu, mal. seven + ara, mal. store room). Village, Port; also called Agaram. At the mouth of a small stream, the bar of which cannot be crossed even by small craft. The English factors at Tellicherry had a warehouse here for collecting pepper [q.v.].——(5) Town; Malabar dist., Cottayam tal.; pop. 7,227; lat. 11° 49′; long. 75° 35′; from Calicut N.N.W. 42 miles; from Cannanore E. 12 miles; from Tellicherry N.E. 6¾ miles; from the sea 8½ miles. Contains palaces of Cottayam rajahs; temple known as Trikyecoonn. The rebel Pychy rajah belonged to one of the branches of the Cottayam family. There are three mosques, called Chervancherry musjid, Cotiote jumma musjid, Moothiyanga jumma musjid [q.v.].

COTTON (قطن - kutn, *Ar.*). Wool or down surrounding seeds of various plants.——*American cotton* (قطن امریقہ - kutniamríkah, Hind.; சீமைப்பருத்தி - shímaipparutti, Tam.). Tam. means foreign + cotton. Title otherwise Barbadoes cotton, Bourbon cotton, Egyptian cotton, Foreign cotton, Georgian cotton, Long-stapled cotton, Mexican cotton, New orleans cotton, Sea island cotton, West indian cotton. Botanically Gossypium [carpausy] barbadense, linn., malvaceæ [vricsham, 25]. Alias Gossypium javanicum, nigrum, racemosum. A glabrous annual, stem erect, much branched; leaves, rotund ovate, sub-cordate, less than one-third cut into three to five lobes, or only angled, the upper ones entire; lobes ovate to lanceolate, oblong, acute, sinus almost rounded; inflorescence solitary flowered, extra axillary; bracteoles broadly ovate, cordate, not united together, at the base deeply laciniated; flowers yellow, often almost white, rarely fully expanding; capsule ovate-conic, acute, three to four locular, six to nine-seeded; seeds black, glabrous below the floss. Long fine easily separable cotton; fruits the whole year; uses precisely the same as herbaceum.——*Bengal cotton* (قطن بنگالہ - kutnibangálah, Hind.). Botanically Gossypium [carpausy] neglectum, tod., malvaceæ [vricsham, 25]. A large bush, chiefly grown as a field crop, and sometimes seen not more than 18 inches high; leaves, three, five, seven-lobed, but extra tooth in sinus less distinct and lobes more linear and simply acute, rarely bristle-tipped; densely coated with long spreading hairs, and, if hybridised with herbaceum, var. wightianum [indian cotton], having stellate hairs as well; stipules broad, linear; infloresence on short lateral branches, two to four-flowered; flowers yellow with purple centre or yellow with purple tinge; bracteoles very large with greatly elongate lateral ears but in shape above ovate acute, toothed; ovary pointed, boll of cotton sometimes elongating from the capsule so as to resemble a kidney-cotton; seed with green velvet below the floss. Constituting to a large extent the so-called Bengals of commerce. For hybrids of this species, see the remarks under Indian cotton. May itself be only a hybrid between arboreum [tree cotton] and herbaceum [indian cotton]. Another sub-arboreous species is Peruvian cotton [q.v.].——*Flowering cotton* (பூப்பருத்தி - púpparutti, Tam.). From similar flowers. Same as Portia.——*French cotton* (قطن فرانسیس - kutnifránsís, Hind.). Cotton in fruit of Calotropis gigantea [yercum].——*Golden silk cotton* (درخت کتیرهٔ هندی - darakhtikatírahihindí, Pers.; پیلی کپاس - pílíkapás, Hind.; پیلی کپاس کا جھاڑ - pílíkapáskájhár, Dec.; ಅರಸಿನಬೂರಗ - arasinabúraga, Can.; కొండగోగు - kondagógu, Tel.; କୋଣ୍ଟୋପଳାସ - kontópalás, Oor.; ശീമപ്പഞ്ഞിമരം - shímappaññimaram, Mal.; ඇලඉඹුල් - elaimbul, Singh.; கோங்கு - kóngu, Tam.). Title from color of flowers. Pers. from (darakht, pers. tree + katírah, pers. tragacanth + hindí, pers. indian), from use of gum as substitute. Hind. from (pílí, hind. yellow + kapás, hind. gossypium herbaceum, linn.), from flowers. Can. from (arasina, can. turmeric + búraga, can. bombax malabaricum, dec.). Tel. from (konda, tel. hill + gógu, tel. hibiscus cannabinus, linn.). Mal. from (shíma, mal. foreign + paññi, mal. cotton + maram, mal. tree). Singh. from (ela, singh. white + imbul, singh. eriodendron anfractuosum, dec.). Tam. means large tree [red-cotton tree]. Hind. also (katírá), meaning tragacanth [false kateerah, kateerah]; (hindíkatíra), meaning indian tragacanth. Tel. also (kong). Tam. also (kóngilavu), meaning the tree + the silk cotton, bombax malabaricum, dec.; (tanakku) [odul tree, tanakk]. Title otherwise False tragacanth tree, Hill hemp, Kateerah gum tree [velvail], Leaf-bellows tree, Yellow-flowered cotton. Botanically Cochlospermum gossypium, d.c., bixineæ [vricsham, 14]. Alias Bombax gossypium. Tree, 50 feet; leaves palmately five-lobed, lobes acuminated, quite entire, upper-side becoming glabrous; under tomentose; sepals five, oval-oblong, unequal, at length reflexed, the two exterior ones smaller; petals five emarginate, unequal-sided; capsules shortly obovate; seeds numerous, somewhat reniform; flowers large, yellow, panicled; peduncles somewhat joined at the base. Flowers appear in february or march when destitute of leaves; flowers are followed by a five-lobed capsular fruit, as large as a goose egg, which separates into two layers, showing a whitish membranous endocarp and numerous seeds the size of a small pea [calauyam] enclosed in long cottony fibres. Clear white gummy substance exudes from every part of the tree if broken, called gum kateerah [q.v.]; this is one of the country or false tragacanths; it is generally in large vermicular pieces, transversely fissured, and showing a tendency to split up into flat scales sometimes in large flat pieces like tragacanth; when moistened it swells up into a bulky transparent jelly, which may be diffused in a large quantity of water, but is only very sparingly soluble; its solution in water is neutral; the portion insoluble in water yields with alkalies [cauram] a thick mucilage of a pinkish color, which is not precipitated by acids [tezaub]; it has three varieties, white, red and black; black the worst; the red or intermediate employed for medicinal purposes. Gum kateerah is used as a demulcent in coughs. Cotton from seeds used for stuffing pillows, &c.; gum [gond] used in shoe-making; seeds give an oil. Wood extremely soft, grey; no heart-wood. Gum-kateerah comes also from Eriodendron anfractuosum, dec. [silk cotton], and Sterculia urens, roxb. [false kateerah]. No other common species here.——*Hedge cotton* (युग्मफला - yugmap'halá, San.; اترن کی بیل - utrankíbel, Hind.; جٹپ - jutup, Dec.; ಉಗುರುಸುತ್ತುಬಳ್ಳಿ - uguru-suttuballi, Can.; దుష్టుపుచెట్టు - dushtupuchettu, Tel.; ଉତ୍ତୁରୁରି - uttururi, Oor.; വേലിപ്പരുത്തി - vélipparutti, Mal.; මඩහංගු - madahangu, Singh.; வேலிப்பருத்தி - vélipparutti, Tam.). Title from being a hedge-plant bearing fruit with cottony fibres inside. San. from (yugma, san. couple + p'hala, san. fruit); fruits appear in pairs. Hind. from (utran, hind. the plant + bel, hind. creeper). Dec. means matted, from bristly pods. Can. from (uguru, can. finger nail + suttu, can. round + balli, can. creeper); useful in whitlow. Tel. from (dushtu, tel. corruption from dzuttu, tel. hair-tuft + chettu, tel. plant); bearing bristly pods [kakrasinghy]. Mal. from (véli, mal. hedge + parutti, mal. cotton, gossypium herbaceum, linn.). Tam. similar. San. also (yugap'halá), meaning double-fruited. Hind. also (sagowání); (jutak), meaning hair-knot. Can. also (juttuveballi), meaning hair-knot + creeper; (hálkoratiga). Tel. also (jittupuchettu), meaning hair-knot + plant, distinguished from Seeta's knot; (guruticlettu). Tam. also (uttámaní), meaning best + odour; ironical as it is with a fœtid scent; (uttamathâli), meaning best + convolvulus genus; (açcánimúli), meaning linch pin + plant; (kudagaram). Title otherwise Dog's bane, Hair-knot plant, Linch pin plant, Ootran, Whitlow plant. Botanically Dæmia extensa, r. br., asclepiadeæ [vricsham, 88]. Generic from arabic. Alias Asclepias echinata; Cynanchum cordifolium, extensum. Twining, shrubby; leaves roundish-cordate, acuminated, acute, auricled at the base, downy, glaucous beneath; stamineous corona double; outer one ten-parted, inner one five-leaved; peduncles and pedicles elongated, filiform; margins of corolla ciliated; flowers in umbels, pale green, purplish inside; follicles ramentaceous; has a fœtid scent; common weed of coromandel coast [q.v.]. The whole plant has emetic and expectorant virtues, much used in diseases of children; decoction of leaves anthelmintic; juice of fresh leaves in asthma; juice of leaves mixed with choonam [q.v.] in rheumatism; leaves quoted in pharm. but non-officinal. Very fine strong fibre [naur], like flax twine [alsee].——*Indian cotton* (कर्पासी - karpásí, San.; कापूस - kápúsa, Mahr.; काप्पुसु - káppusu, Conc.; قطن - kutn, Ar.; پنبہ - pambah, Pers.; کپاس - kapás, Hind. and Dec.; کپس - kapas, Malay; ಹತ್ತಿ - hatti, Can.; ಪರ್ತಿ - parti, Too.; పత్తి - patti, Tel.; କପା - koppa, Oor.; പരുത്തി - parutti, Mal.; කපු - kapu, Singh.; பருத்தி - parutti, Tam.). San. from (kri, san. to do); as being useful. Mal. from tamul. Singh. from sanscrit. Tam. from (pari, tam. to preserve); as being useful. San. also (mághani), meaning produced in maugham [mausam] or february; (anagniká), meaning cultivated; (tundikéri), meaning useful in face diseases [indian caper]. Mahr. also (dévakápúsa), meaning god + gossypium. Ar. also (kurfus), from sanscrit. Tam. also (uppambarutti), meaning to swell + cotton; (tálipparutti), meaning the creeper so called + cotton; (venbarutti), meaning white cotton; (uttiri); (panju). Title otherwise Common cotton, Country cotton, Herbaceous cotton, Indian lint, Native cotton, Short-stapled cotton, Thread cotton. Botanically Gossypium [carpausy] herbaceum, linn., malvaceæ [vricsham, 25]. Alias Gossypium indicum.—"*a*" The following is botanically the typical herbaceum:—perennial and bushy in the warmer areas, annual where killed by winter; stems erect, sparsely hairy, branches spreading, the bush sub-pyramidal; leaves pale green, thick, leathery, and larger and broader than in the variety wightianum, see below, half segmented into three to five, often seven lobes; lobes ovate-rotund, constricted below, the middle one acuminate, all shortly bristle-tipped; upper surface reticulate, pubescent, with longer hairs on the veins and felted below when young with bifid or trifid not stellate hairs, margins ciliate; stipules linear lanceolate, those nearer the peduncles shorter and broader; flowers longer than the bracteoles, petals obovate, unequally cuneate, yellow, with a large purple patch, slightly united together below; peduncles about half the length of the petioles; bracteoles ovate sub-obtuse, cordate, incisodentate, the entire portion sub-rotund, united to each other below, in texture thinner and more numerously veined than in indian cotton; capsule ovate-rotund four to five-celled, cells six to seven-seeded, seeds ovate, beaked at the hilum; under-velvet or fuzz as it is often called short, firmly adhering, whitish-grey; wool fairly long and white. The following is its variety wightianum, which is the chief form here practically found :—stems erect, somewhat hairy, branches spreading and ascending; leaves when young densely matted, with short, thick, stellate hairs, which fall off in patches leaving a few scattered all over both surfaces; ovate-rotund, almost obsoletely cordate, three to five, rarely seven-lobed, lobes ovate, oblong, acute, constricted at the base into the rounded sinus which in the young leaves rises up as a fold; stipules on the peduncles almost ovate, the others linear-lanceolate acuminate; flowers yellow with a deep purple patch at the base, becoming reddish on the outside on passing maturity; bracteoles small, slightly united at the base, ovate cordate, acute, shortly toothed; peduncles erect in flower, recurved in fruit, one-fourth the length of the petioles; capsule small, ovate acute, four-celled, with eight seeds in each cell; seeds small, ovate, sub-rotund, velvet very short and firmly adhering, wool white or whitish-red. There are an indefinite number of hybrids ranging to the typical herbaceum on the one side and to the sub-arboreous neglectum [bengal cotton] on the other side. The plant varies in height, seldom exceeding 2 or 3 feet; flowers succeeded by a capsule, which when ripe bursts open, presenting a mass of white filaments, and these after separation from the seed which is size of a small pea [calauyam], form the vegetable wool or cotton of commerce. The seeds are round, dark-brown and about the size of black pepper [q.v.]; if examined soon after the removal of the cotton, they are clothed with greyish down; their kernel is greenish, albuminous and slightly sweet in taste. The seeds contain a large proportion of oil [yennay], but the remains of the fibre [naur] adhere with such tenacity to the seed that it absorbs the whole of the oil expressed, from which it cannot be separated without much difficulty; the varieties of cotton with loose seeds, such as peruvian cotton [q.v.] have not this objection. Root has little taste or smell.—"*b*" *σινδόνες*, muslins [q.v.]; *ὀθόνια*, plain cottons; *περιζώματα*, sashes; *ζῶνα σκιωταί*, sashes striped with different colors; *πορφύραι*, purple cloth; and *σινδόνες μολόχινια*, muslins of the color of mallows, were exported in arrian's time from southern india to all the ports on the arabian and east african coasts; cotton was first imported into england from india in 1783.—"*c*" From the point of view of commercial growths so called there are four kinds of indian cotton in this presidency, viz., Tinnevelly, Westerns, Cocanadas, and Salems. Tinnevelly growth comes from tinnevelly district and southern portion of madura; Westerns come from bellary, anantapore and portions of kurnool and cuddapah; Cocanadas come from the kistna district. Salem growth comes from salem and coimbatore districts. Tinnevelly growth is the most valuable of these, it has a strong though not particularly long staple and a very pure white color, it is in demand among spinners in europe for mixing with american cotton [q.v.]. Westerns have been sub-divided into westerns proper and northerns, the latter being the chief cotton of cuddapah and kurnool; the staple of western proper is rough, but fairly long and strong and of a good white, but, owing to imperfections in cleaning, always contains broken leaf; that of northerns is silkier, and has a slightly reddish tinge. Cocanadas have a staple fairly long, strong, and silky; it takes dyes more readily than other growths. Salem growth is inferior, and is used in adulterating tinnevelly growth.—"*d*" For cultivation purposes, there are two forms of indigenous cotton usually grown, depending on south-west and north-east monsoons [q.v.] respectively. In northern circars [q.v.] known merely as poonausa [q.v.] pratty and peira [q.v.] pratty, or early and late cotton. They are in teloogoo generally white and red, and in tamul ookkam meaning swelling and naudam meaning country. Late cotton is grown on irrigated lands in the ganjam district; in all other districts, the crop is grown on dry or unirrigated lands and is often sown with dry grains [q.v.]. The white or ookkam kind is sown in black cotton soil [carisal, regar]; it lasts from six to twelve months; the tinnevelly and western growths are mainly from this variety. The red or naudam variety is grown generally on red or gravelly soils [sevval munn] and lasts from three to four or five years; salem growth is mostly from this variety; the inferior cottons of the presidency belong to naudam. Besides these, small quantities of various quite exotic cottons are grown in certain localities; but such are not herbaceum. In cultivation the shrub requires little care; cultivation dry as above said and depends solely on rainfall; ground prepared in south in chittray or april or else veiyaushy or may, on coromandel in ashaudham or july; ploughing and manuring; seed sown in south in arpisy or october, on coromandel in shrauvanam [mausam] or august; mostly sown with either varagoo [q.v.], dholl [common dholl] or raggy [q.v.] in separate drills, every sixth being cotton; the grain crop is first harvested, and the cotton then alone occupies the field; the cotton seed is specially prepared before being sown by being rubbed in cow-dung [shauny] and then well dried in the sun, and it requires to be sown at once afterwards; sown broadcast; the seedlings appear between the third and seventh day; when they are three weeks old, the plantation is hand-weeded, which process is repeated two or three times during growth of plant; frequently when the seedlings are but a fortnight old, a plough is run through the field to loosen the earth as well as to facilitate the removal of weeds; the plant generally begins to flower about the fourth, and to ripen its fruit at about the sixth month of its growth, but in some rare instances, this does not take place until the eighth month. The cotton crop is remarkably liable to the attacks of numerous insects, especially aphides and larvæ of moths [patingah], and to one or more fungous parasites; rats [ely], squirrels [anil], mice [shoondely], and other larger animals are destructive. As the pods ripen and burst, the cotton is picked at intervals of three or four days; the crop continues to be gathered for a period of two months. The produce thus collected is next freed from seed; this operation is conducted by means of a charka [rautnam]; the cotton, as brought in from the field, is freed, to a certain extent, of its capsules, stalks, leaves, &c., and then submitted to the charka; in most districts the cotton is previously spread out on a common charpoy [q.v.] or country cot [q.v.] and beaten with switches, when a portion of the minute particles of earthy or other extraneous matter still adhering falls through; this beating or thrashing is also intended to loosen the wool from the seed, in order to facilitate the operation of ginning; the operation of ginning is generally performed by females, who hold the seed in the left hand to feed the cylinders, and with the right simultaneously turn the charka; a woman, by manual labor alone can clean only about four pounds of cotton, whereas with the charka she can free from about twenty-five to thirty pounds in a day of ten hours. The following is the native method of packing:—to a strong perpendicular wooden post, a cross piece like the balance of a scale is suspended, the post being partly buried in the ground; to the cross piece, a bag of cumbly [q.v.] or gunny [q.v.] is attached intended as a covering to the bale; from five to six maunds [q.v.] of cotton are now thrown in and compressed by men, who jump into the gunny and stamp down the cotton with their feet; from six to ten men are sometimes thus employed, while others are engaged in bringing the sides of the covering together, and securing them by sewing; in some places the gunny bags are hung by three ropes from the roof of the house, a fourth also attached to the roof hangs free in the centre, to which the men stamping the cotton hold on; these bales vary in size and shape according to the mode by which they are to be conveyed to the nearest market for export, which may be by either pack bullocks or carts. The great proportion of the cotton produced in the ceded districts [q.v.] and kurnool is sent to madras for export; some also sent to bombay; the cotton produced in godavery, kistna, and nellore is sent to cocanada and to madras; the produce of southern districts is exported from tuticorin.—"*e*" The chief use made of cotton in medicine is as a local application to burns, in which it proves serviceable chiefly by excluding the air and maintaining an equable temperature; it has also been applied, on this principle, to erysipelatous and inflamed surfaces; substituted for british lint and tow. Decoction of cotton root is however demulcent; native practitioners prescribe this in cases of strangury and gravel; dose, half a tea-cupful or more twice daily. Oil also medicinally a demulcent. The gum [gond] which exudes from the stem is diuretic. The young leaves and shoots are prescribed for children in dysentry, colic, and hysterics. Seeds increase the secretion of milk, also said to be antidote to snake-poison. Gives to pharm., officinal, collodion, collodium; preparation of gun cotton with ether and rectified spirit, used as application to wounds, ulcers, skin diseases, &c.—"*f*" Cotton seed cake is a valuable food for cattle and also an excellent manure. Oil is used for burning in lamps. Gun cotton is a preparation of cotton which is steeped in sulphuric [gandhac tezaub] and nitric acid [shorey ka tezaub], washed in water several times, and then dried in a water bath, leaves no ash when exploded by heat.—"*g*" Cotton generally is used for the same purposes as hemp [kinnab], flax [alsee], hair and wool [pushm] are in England. The woven texture forms the clothing of the whole population, besides being used in a thousand different ways for carpets [shatranjee], tents [derah], screens [purdah], pillows, curtains, ropes, nets, red cotton wool, &c.—"*h*" There are a great many varieties of cotton goods in the market, whose value depends on the length, strength, and fineness as well as softness of the material, the chief distinction being between the long and short stapled. The kinds of cotton cloths, proceeding from coarse to fine are:—dungry, calico, madapollem, muslin; see each head. For figured cottons see Chintz [banolah, chintz, poonjam, potee, tauga]. In the godavery district excellent cloths are still made at ooppauda, near cocanada, and in the villages about neelapully and narsapore; tent cloth of superior quality is also manufactured in the villages near rajahmundry; in nellore fine shirtings are made at covoor, and pocket handkerchiefs [roomaul], and, when ordered, muslins suitable for ladies' dresses; exceedingly fine muslins are made at yaipalgoonta in the oodayagherry talook, and strong tent cloths at cundoocore; fine cloths are made in the talooks of goodoor, raupore, nellore and cauvaly; handkerchiefs are specially woven at valaparla in the ongole talook, and curtain cloths at gundavaram, toorimerla and nidimooshily in the nellore talook; dyeing [shauyam] is done at several places in the cundoocore, ongole and nellore talooks; the betilla is a certain kind of white east indian chintz made at masulipatam, and known under the name of organdi [q.v.]; cotton carpets [shatranjee] of large size for houses and tents and of a smaller size for the native troops are made at adony, whence they are exported in large quantities to all parts of southern india; colored stuffs are not, as in europe, printed by means of wooden blocks, but painted with a brush made of coir [q.v.], which approaches near to horse-hair, becomes very elastic, and can be formed into any shape the painter chooses; the colors employed are indigo [q.v.], indigofera tinctoria, linn.; curcuma or indian saffron [country saffron], a plant which dyes yellow, and gum-lac [q.v.], together with some flowers, roots, and fruits which are used to dye red. ——*Jungle cotton* (वनभेंडा - vanabhéndá, Mahr.; جنگلی کپاس - janglíkapás, Hind. and Dec.; పిల్లమంకెన - piliyamankena, Tel.; ഊരൻ - úran, Mal.; ஒட்டுத்துத்தி - óttuttutti, Tam.). Title from fine fibre. Mahr. from (vana, san. wild + bhénda, mahr. hibiscus esculentus, linn.). Hind. from (janglí, hind. wild + kapás, hind. gossypium herbaceum, linn.). Tel. from (pilla, tel. small + mankena, tel. pentapetes phœnicea, linn.). Mal. from (úru, mal. to creep). Tam. from (ódu, tam. shell + tutti, tam. abutilon indicum, g. don.). Hind. also (banakrá), meaning forest calotropis gigantea, r. br., from fibre. Tam. also (óttatti), meaning shell fig. Title otherwise Angular-leaved urena, Shell tootty. Botanically Urena lobata, linn., malvaceæ [vricsham, 25]. Generic name from malayalam. Herbaceous; leaves roundish, with three or more short obtuse lobes, more or less velvety, five to seven-nerved, with one to three glands on the nerves; segments of involucel five, oblong-lanceolate, equal to the expanded calyx; carpels densely pubescent, echinate; flowers middle-sized, rose-colored; flowering in august to october; common in waste places during the rain. Abounds in strong fibres, substitute for flax [alsee]. There is a variety scabriuscula. Other common species are:—repanda, sinuata.——*Nakchiknee silk cotton* (मधुमालति - madhumálati, San.; ناک چھکنی - nakchhikní, Hind. and Dec.; పాలకూర - pálakúra, Tel.; വട്ടക്കാക്കക്കൊടി - vattakkákkakkoti, Mal.; කිරිඅඟුණ - kirianguna, Singh.; பாலை - palai, Tam.). Title from hindostany; and fibre passes for cotton. San. from (madhu, san. sweet + málati, san. the plant, jasminum grandiflorum, linn.). Hind. from (nák, hind. nose + chhikní, hind. sneezing); from use in colds and eye diseases to cause sneezing. Tel. from (pála, tel. white + kúra, tel. pot-herb). Mal. from (vatta, mal. round + kákkakkoti, mal. the creeper, echites macrophylla, r. h.). Singh. from (kiri, singh. white + anguna, singh. hoya genus). Tam. from (pál, tam. milk) [dita, edible paulay, eve's apple, ground paulay, monkey face paulay, nauga champak, pauchonty, paula indigo, paulay silk cotton, tellicherry bark]. San. also (dugdhiká), meaning milk plant. Tel. also (dúdipála), meaning cotton + the plant [needle paulay]. Tam. also (kodippálai), meaning milk creeper; (kurinjákkírai), meaning creeper so called, gymnema sylvestre, r. br. + vegetable; from expectorant character. Title otherwise Twining swallow-wort. Botanically Dregea volubilis, benth., asclepiadeæ [vricsham, 88]. Alias Apocynum tiliæfolium; Asclepias volubilis; Hoya viridiflora. Twining; leaves ovate or cordate, acuminate, membranaceous, glabrous on both sides; corolla glabrous, segments ovate, acutish; leaflets of the staminal crown flat above, oboval, very obtuse, inner angle short, obtuse; follicles divaricate, thick, obtuse, rusty farinaceous; flowers smallish, green, inodorous; flowering march till may. Rambling membranaceous-leaved plant with insignificant, green, inodorous flowers; native of malabar. Leaves are applied to boils and abscesses; leaves quoted, non-officinal, in pharm.; roots and tender stalks are emetic and expectorant. Gives good fibre [naur] whence name. No other common species here.——*Paulay silk cotton* (പാല - pála, Mal.; கருடப்பாலை - karudappálai, Tam.). Title from milky juice and fibre. Mal. from (pál, mal. milk). Tam. from (garuda, san. braminy kite + pálai, tam. milky plant); from antidote to poison. Cf. Dita. Tam. also (pálai), meaning milk plant [dita, edible paulay, eve's apple, ground paulay, monkey face paulay, nakchiknee silk cotton, nauga champak, pauchonty, paula indigo, tellicherry bark]. Title otherwise Braminy kite paulay, India-rubber paulay. Botanically Cryptostegia grandiflora, r. br., asclepiadeæ [vricsham, 88]. Alias Nerium grandiflorum. Shrub; leaves opposite, elliptic, bluntly acuminated, shining above, minutely reticulated with brown beneath; calyx five-parted, segments lanceolate with undulated margins; corolla funnel-shaped, tube furnished with five enclosed narrow bipartite scales inside, covering the anthers, being opposite them; stamens enclosed; stigmas globosely conical; corymbs trichotomous, terminal; flowers large, reddish purple; follicles divaricate, acutely triquetrous. Large, over-spreading, and extensively-growing, scandent plant, throwing out twig-like stems of great length, bearing in pairs oblong, pointed, smooth, deep-green leaves, from three to four inches long; large, bell-shaped, bright rich-purple flowers; flowering all year. Yields a fine strong fibre resembling flax [alsee], which may be spun into the finest yarn; the milky juice gives a moderate caoutchouc [pauchonty], for rubbing out pencil-marks. No other common species here.——*Peruvian cotton* (పైడిపత్తి - paidipatti, Tel.). Tel. from (paidi, tel. gold + patti, tel. cotton plant); from color of flowers. Title otherwise Brazil cotton, Chain seed cotton, Kidney cotton, Maranham cotton, Pernambuco cotton. Botanically Gossypium [carpausy] barbadense, linn., var. acuminatum, roxb., malvaceæ [vricsham, 25]. Sub-arboreous; leaves, three to five-lobed, lobes divergent, ovate, acute, the middle one slightly the longest; flowers large, bracteoles broadly ovate, deeply cordate and glandular at the base; capsule ovate, acuminate, cells eight to ten-seeded, black glabrous except the long white wool. The seeds adhere together in a very peculiar manner; the cotton is easily and completely separable, milk-white, and of a long staple, but it is harsh and woolly to the touch. Gives fibre; seeds being easily separable from cotton give an oil by expression.——*Red-cotton tree* (शाल्मली - shálmalí, San.; सावरी - sávarí, Mahr. and Conc.; رگت سینبل - ragatsembal, Hind.; کانٹوں کا کھتیان - kántonkákhatiyán, Dec.; ಕೆಂಪುಬೂರಗ - kempubúraga, Can.; ಮುಳ್ಳಾಲ - mullála, Too.; బూరుగు - búrugu, Tel.; ଶିମୁଳି - simuri, Oor.; പൂള - púla, Mal.; කටුඉඹුල් - katuimbul, Singh.; முள்ளிலவு - mullilavu, Tam.). Title from reddish hue of the cotton when new. San. from (shál, san. to shine); beautiful when in flowers without leaves [silk-cotton tree]. Mahr. and conc. from sanscrit. Hind. from (rakta, san. blood + sembal, hind. silk cotton). Dec. from (kántá, hind. thorn + khatiyán, hind. eriodendron aufractuosum, dec.). Can. from (kempu, can. red + búraga, can. silk-cotton tree). Too. from (mullu, too. thorn + ála, too. silk-cotton tree). Tel. from (bura, tel. large). Oor. from sanscrit. Singh. from (katu, singh. thorny + imbul, singh. eriodendron anfractuosum, dec.). Tam. from (mul, tam. thorn + ilavu, tam. silk-cotton tree). San. also (púraní), meaning filling up, as used in stuffing pillows; (kukkutavandaka), meaning cock + praiser, from red flowers; (raktapushpá), meaning red + flowered [galangal]; (mócha), meaning liberating; (kantakidruma), meaning thorny tree; (st'hiráyu), meaning long-lived, cf. Silk cotton; (yamadruma), meaning tree of infernal regions, because it makes a great show of flowers but produces no fruit to eat. Mahr. also (kántésámvarí), meaning thorny silk-cotton tree. Hind. also (kántísemal), meaning thorny silk cotton. Dec. also (kántonkásemal), meaning thorny silk cotton; (lálkhatiyán), meaning red silk cotton. Can. also (mullubúraga), meaning thorny silk cotton; (mullelavu), meaning thorn + silk-cotton tree. Tel. also (mundlabúrugu), meaning thorn + the tree; (kondabúrugu), meaning hill + the tree; (pinnabúrugu), meaning small + the tree. Oor. also (bouro). Mal. also (mullilavu), meaning thorny silk-cotton tree; (unnamurikku), meaning cotton + erythrina indica, lamk. Tam. also (kóngu), meaning large tree [golden silk cotton]. Title otherwise Cock's comb silk cotton, Cotton coral tree, Kapok fibre tree, Malabar semul, Mocharas gum tree, Poola, Red semul, Red silk cotton, Seven-leaved silk cotton, Shaulmaly, Thorny silk cotton, Yama's silk cotton. Botanically Bombax malabaricum, dc., malvaceæ [vricsham, 25]. Alias Bombax ceiba, heptaphylla; Salmalia malabarica. Salmalia from sanscrit.—"*a*" Gigantic tree; trunk straight, often 80 or 100 feet to the first bough, of great girth, generally furnished with very large buttresses; armed with thorns on the bark; leaves divided into finger-like portions rising from one point; large red flowers appearing while the tree is without leaves in the hot season, followed by large pods containing white hairs resembling cotton, but wanting in the property of spinning into a thread [nool].—"*b*" The seeds are about the size of black pepper [q.v.], brown, smooth and roundish, with a very small and short but distinct ridge on one side of the hilum. The young fruits form part of mahratta buds [q.v.]. The bark of the stem or trunk varies much in appearance according to the age and size of the plant from which it is taken; that from the trunk of a well grown up tree after it begins to blossom is externally brown, rough, scaly and often covered with some short and blunt prickles, and internally reddish-brown, it is quite odourless and possesses no particular taste; the root bark is covered with a thin and ash-colored epidermis, and is deep or reddish-grey internally, it is also devoid of taste and smell; the extract of bark is dark in color and slightly saltish in taste, and odourless; the resemblance it bears to the mocharas, for which see below, is so great that if it is made to dry in any of the forms of the latter, it will pass for it, but it does not keep dry, its deliquescence and saline taste depending upon the large quantity of salt it contains. The root is long, fleshy, and whitish, brittle; this is not as sometimes said in error the soofaid moosly [q.v.], but the semul moosly [q.v.]. No gum [gond] is produced from stem on making incisions however deep, but a very small quantity is exuded spontaneously from time to time. This or mocharas [q.v.] has at least three varieties in the bazaar [q.v.]. The first variety occurs in very irregular, nodular, smooth, opaque, light or pale-brown pieces with internal cavities; the cavities are generally small and numerous, but sometimes few and large; in the latter case, the pieces often assume the appearance of a shell. The second is a mere sub-variety of the first and the only difference between them is that the pieces in the former are very hard, heavy, dark-brown and cannot be reduced to powder without great difficulty; they are sometimes so smooth that they shine, and possess but few cavities. The third and most common variety consists of very irregular, angular and hard fragments or pieces of various size and of a dark or dirty brown color. The drug in all its varieties is odourless and possesses an astringent and demulcent taste; when placed in water it swells up to a considerable size, and some tannin enters into solution, the insoluble portion resembles tragacanth [katecrah]. As regards the production of mocharas, if the plant is not very large, the exudation is only very small and occasional; the matter exuded is for some days at the beginning yellowish red or of flesh color, and then assumes a brownish hue; after some months it gradually acquires the form described above in the first variety; the second variety is produced in the same way if the plant is much larger and older; when the tree is very large and older than sixty or seventy years, the exudation of the resin [raul] occurs every year soon after the rainy season; a large quantity of thick, brown and viscid fluid flows spontaneously from a natural crack, fissure, or wound in the bark of the stem or large branch and collects on the ground; when dry, this forms the most common and abundant kind of mocharas in the bazaar, described above as the third variety; mocharas is the product of diseased action in the cells of the bark; whilst the third variety is the cheapest and most common, the first is the most efficacious as a drug. A dark brown but clear oil is obtained by expression from the seeds.—"*c*" Parts medicinally used are the gum, seeds, dry young fruit, tap-root of the young plant, bark, cotton; the young fruit is more common and abundant than the gum. In physiological actions:—the gum is astringent and demulcent; the seeds nutrient and demulcent; the young fruit stimulant-diuretic, tonic, aphrodisiac, expectorant, and exercises beneficial influence over membrane of genito-urinary organs; the tap-root [semul moosly] is demulcent, tonic, slightly diuretic, and aphrodisiac; the bark is demulcent, diuretic, tonic, and slightly astringent; the cotton is employed externally for its mechanical properties of softness and elasticity in padding splints and covering burned and inflamed surfaces, &c. Preparations:—of the gum are simple and compound powder, compound powder being mocharas, bengal-kino [q.v.], opium [aphainam] and dry pulp of emetic-nut [q.v.]; of the seeds, emulsion; of the dry young fruits, simple powder, prepared after removing stalks; of the tap-root, simple powder, by pulverizing dry slices of the tap-root; of the bark, decoction and extract. Doses:—of the simple powder of the gum, from twenty to forty grains; of the compound powder of the gum from sixteen to thirty-two grains; of the seeds, from two to three drachms; of the powder of the fruit, from thirty grains to one drachm; of the powder of the tap-root, from forty to eighty grains; of the decoction, from one to two fluid ounces; of the extract, from seven to fifteen grains. Substituted:—the gum for kino, rhatany and log-wood; the seeds for tragacanth, sweet-almonds [baudam] and copaiba; the young fruit, tap-root and bark, for pareira brava [indian pareira], broom tops, phosphorus, cantharides, calumba [q.v.], gentian [chiretta] and spiritus ætheris nitrosi. The mocharas is in pharm., but not officinal.—"*d*" Leaves and twigs lopped for fodder; flower buds eaten as pot-herb. The cotton which surrounds the seeds is sometimes used for stuffing cushions and quilted bed covers [rizye], being very light and soft; useless for textile purposes. Wood white when fresh cut, turning dark on exposure; very soft, perishable; no heart-wood; no annual rings; not durable, except under water when it lasts tolerably well; used for planking, packing-cases and tea boxes, toys, scabbards, fishing-floats, water conduits, and the lining of wells; makes a poor fuel; used for avenue planting [shaulay].—"*e*" A white flowering variety of tree much rarer than the red. No other common species of the genus here. Compare in other genera:—Cochlospermum gossypinum (arasinabúraga), yellow red-cotton tree; Eriodendron anfractuosum (bilibúraga), white red-cotton tree.——*Red-cotton wool* (پوتی - potí, Hind.; ಕೆಂಪುಹತ್ತಿ - kempuhatti, Can.; ఎఱ్ఱప్రత్తి - errapratti, Tel.; செம்பஞ்சு - shembañju, Tam.). Title otherwise Shempunjy, Potee. Round red cake of cotton. An inferior kind of this is the cotton impregnated with red coloring matter of prickly pear [q.v]; better kind is made by impregnating the cotton with the coral jasmine [q.v.] flower, nyctanthes arbor-tristis; the best of all is from bastard saffron [q.v.] or safflower, carthamus tinctorius. When this article is soaked in water, the latter becomes red ink [mashy].——*Silk cotton* (शाल्मली - shálmalí, San.; पाण्ढरसांवरी - pándharasámvarí, Mahr.; سفید سینبل - sufedsembal, Hind.; کتیان - khatiyán, Dec.; کپوک - kapuk, Malay; ಬಿಳಿಬೂರಗ - bilibúraga, Can.; ಆಲ - ála, Too.; బూరగ - búraga, Tel.; മുള്ളില്ലാപ്പൂള - mullilláppúla, Mal.; ඉඹුල් - imbul, Singh.; இலவம் - ilavam, Tam.). Title from silky wool of fruit. San. from (shál, san. to shine) [red-cotton tree]. Mahr. from (pándhara, mahr. white + sámvarí, mahr. red-cotton tree, bombax malabaricum, dec.); from white flowers. Hind. from (sufed, hind. white + sembal, hind. bombax malabaricum, dec.). Dec. means cotton. Can. from (bili, can. white + búraga, can. red-cotton tree). Mal. from (mullu, mal. thorn + illá, mal. not having + púla, mal. red-cotton tree). San. also (móchá), meaning setting free gum; (chiráyu), meaning long living, Cf. Red-cotton tree; (shvétashálmalí), meaning white silk cotton, from the flowers. Hind. also (túláper), meaning silk-cotton tree. Mal. also (paññimaram), meaning cotton tree; (púla), red-cotton tree. Singh. also (púraná), meaning filling, perhaps from cotton used to stuff bed. Title otherwise Cabbage wood, Capook, Ceiba cotton, God tree, Ilavam, Kapok floss, Khatian, Stuffing cotton, White cotton, White semul, White silk cotton, White tree cotton. Botanically Eriodendron anfractuosum, dc., malvaceæ [vricsham, 25]. Alias Bombax pentandrum; Ceiba pentandra; Eriodendron orientale; Gossampinus rumphii. Large deciduous tree, 50–60 feet; trunk prickly at the base; branches growing out horizontally from the stem, three from one point; leaflets five to eight, quite entire, or serrulated towards the point, lanceolate, mucronate, glaucous beneath; petals five, united at the base, filaments jointed at the base, each bearing two to three versatile anfractuose anthers; style crowned with a five to six-cleft stigma; capsule five-celled five-valved; cells many-seeded; seeds smooth, black, embedded in very fine silky cotton; flowers white, springing from the branches. Common, planted about villages and temples; leaves fall during the cold season; grows rapidly and is very ornamental; has a black and opaque pseudo-gum called Khatian [q.v.] gond, which is like that of the moringa [q.v.]. Very young fruits, demulcent and astringent in medicine; part of mahratta buds [q.v.]; a solution of the gum is given in conjunction with spices in bowel-complaints; bark is astringent, used to suppress vomiting. The large stems are hollowed out to form canoes; the cotton obtained from the pods is only of use for stuffing pillows and cushions; the texture is too loose to admit of its being spun and used in fabrication of cloth; as it easily catches fire it is put in tinder boxes and employed in the preparation of fire works [baunam]; an oil is extracted from the seeds of a dark-brown color; in s. canara fibre extracted suitable for paper. A soft almost worthless wood, used for toys, floats, and such purposes. Compare common coral tree. There is a Tamul proverb:—இலவு காத்த கிளி ஆனேன்—"I am "like the parrot that waited for the silk-cotton pod"; spoken of one disappointed; a parrot on seeing a green pod on a silk-cotton tree believed it would ripen into fruit, when it burst and the cotton was blown away.——*Thorny silk cotton* (முள்ளிலவு - mullilavu, Tam.). From prickles. Same as Red-cotton tree.——*Tree cotton* (देवकापूस - dévakápúsa, Mahr.; دیو کپاس - deukapás, Hind.). Mahr. and hind. from (déva, san. god + kárpása, san. gossypium); from being grown about temples and hermitages. Botanically Gossypium [carpausy] arboreum, linn., malvaceæ [vricsham, 25]. Arborescent, cultivated in gardens only or near temples; not a regular field crop; leaves, five to seven-lobed with an extra tooth in the left side sinus or both sides of the central lobe; thick, leathery, sub-glabrous or with short, abortively stellate hairs on the leaves and longer hairs on the petioles and young stems; lobes bristle-tipped; petiole long, rigid; stipules falcate; inflorescence axillary, generally one-flowered; peduncle about three-fourths the length of the petiole, but jointed above the middle, bearing a small leaf and two stipules at the joint; flowers small, purple, a little less than twice the length of the bracteoles; bracteoles medium-sized, base with round ears, apex ovate, acute toothed or sub-entire; ovary rounded; seeds with greyish black velvet underneath the floss. Its cotton is used only for making turbans [puggry]. Oil for burning in lamps. For sub-arboreous species see Bengal cotton and Peruvian cotton.——*Yama's silk cotton* (यमद्रुम - yamadruma, San.). Same as Red-cotton tree.——*Yellow cotton* (پیلی کپاس - pílikapás, Hind.). From yellow flowers. Same as Golden silk cotton.

COTTYE (கொட்டாய் - kottáy, *Tam.*). From (kódu, tam. to bend); from slope. Shed [cotaur, pandaul].——*Cottye ootsavam* (கொட்டாயுற்சவம் - kottáyurchavam, Tam.). Means shed + feast. Tabernacle feast held at various pagodas [pundigay, 6d]. Special celebration at Shreerungam, in a large and decorated pandaul erected for the occasion. This ends in Mooccoty yecaudashy [q.v].

COTY (कोटि - kóti, *San.*). From (kut, san. to bend). Point. End of a bow. Edge, border. The complement of an arc to 90°. Compare Bhoojam. Also one of the sides of a right-angled triangle [trikonam]. Crore [q.v.], as an extreme number. Suffix in proper names as Dhanacoty, he who has a crore of wealth. Prefix in proper names; as Cotilingam, crore of lingams. Also by itself Pariah proper name of both sexes [peyar].——*Cotijyay* (कोटिज्या - kótijyá, San.). From (above + jyá, san. bow-string, sine). The cosine of an angle in a right-angled triangle.——*Cotipully* (కోటిపల్లి - kótipalli, Tel.). From (kóti, tel. border + palli, tel. a village). Tel. also (gókavaram-raghudévapuramu), to distinguish from rajahmundry raghoodevapooram. Sanscrit name (kótip'hali), meaning crore + good fruits; from high sanctity.—"*a*" Deputy tahsildarry, Godavery district. Pay Rs. 100.—"*b*" Village, Deputy tahsildar's station, Place of pilgrimage; Godavery district, Ramchendrapooram talook; pop. 2,509; lat. 16° 41′; long. 82° 04′; from Cocanada S.W. 22 miles; from Coonavaram S.E. 78 miles; from Ellore E. 60 miles; from Madras N.N.E. 268 miles; from Narsapore N.E. 28 miles; from Rajahmundry S.E. 28 miles; from Ramchendrapooram S. 9¾ miles. Considered sacred. On left bank of Gowtamy-godavery. Belongs to Maharajah of Vizianagram. Only portion of district which belongs to him, with the exception of a few yards of land at Rajahmundry on which there is a small Beiraugy's shed. Numerous ancient temples. Every twelfth year the feast of Pooshcaram [pundigay, 6d]. Great festival at Shivarautry [pundigay, 6a].——*Shooddha coty* (शुद्धकोटि - shuddhakóti, San.). From (shuddha, san. pure + above). The sine of an angle in a right-angled triangle.

COUNTRY (देश - désha, *San.*; ناٹ - nát, *Hind.*; ನಾಡು - nádu, *Can.*; నాడు - nádu, *Tel.*; നാട് - nátu, *Mal.*; நாடு - nádu, *Tam.*). Indigenous as opposed to Sheemay or foreign [seema], implying that the Indian article resembles the European article named. Especially plant first term; see below; these are the commonest, but a great many more might be added.——*Country aconite* (ناٹ کا بچھناگ - nátkábachhnág, Dec.). Same as Wild bachnaug.——*Country almond* (நாட்டுவாதம்கொட்டை - náttuváthamkottai, Tam.). Fruit of the Catapang tree.——*Country bean* (शिम्बिक - shimbika, San.; वाल - vála, Mahr.;

بلر - ballar, Hind. and Dec.; ಅವರೆ - avare, Can.; ಅಬರೆ - abare, Too.; అనుము - anumu, Tel.; ବାଇଲୋ - báilo, Oor.; മൊച്ച - moçça, Mal.; மொச்சை - moççai, Tam.). San. from (sham, san. to pacify). Can. from tamul. Tam. from (moççu, tam. sheep-smell); from smell of seeds. San. also (sitashimbika), meaning white bean; (shvétashimbika), meaning white bean. Mahr. also (pávatá). Hind. also (chhotásem), meaning small dolichos lablab, linn.; (semkíphallí), meaning the dolichos pod; (lobia), meaning vigna catiang, endl. Can. also (holadavare), meaning field + bean, dry crop; (chilávari); (tammegida). Tel. also (tellachikkudu), meaning white + the plant; (chikkudu); (adavichikkudu), meaning forest + the plant; (anapuchikkudu), meaning bean + the plant; (káruchikkudu), meaning forest + the plant. Mal. also (vellavara), meaning white bean. Tam. also (avarai), meaning generally garden variety; (vellavarai), meaning white + the plant; (káttumoççai), meaning forest + the plant; (karuppumoççai), meaning black + the plant; (vellai-moççai), meaning white + the plant. Title otherwise Ballar [cow gram], Black-seeded bean, Egyptian kidney-bean, Hyacinth bean, Japan lablab, Lablab, Purple hyacinth bean, White hyacinth bean. Botanically Dolichos [shimby] lablab, linn., leguminosæ [vricsham, 48]. Specific name from arabic. Alias Dolichos albus, benghalensis, cultratus, cuspidatus, ensiformis, ignosus, mungo, purpureus, racemosus, spicatus, tetraspermus; Ensiformis sinensis; Lablab bengalensis, cultratus, leucocarpus, lignosus, microcarpus, nankinicus, niger, perennans, purpureus, vulgaris; Phaseolus tetraspermus. Wide-twining perennial or in cultivation annual herb; leaves pinnately trifoliolate; leaflets entire; racemes axillary, elongated; pedicles short; corolla papilionaceous; calyx bibracteolate, campanulate, tubular four-cleft; legume broadly scimitar-shaped, gibbous below the apex, and ending abruptly in a straight or recurved cuspidate point; seeds longitudinally oval, of various colors; flowers red, purple, or white; the stems attain a length of 16–20 feet; the recurved flat oblong pod is $1\frac{1}{2}$ to 2 inches long by $\frac{1}{2}$ to $\frac{3}{4}$ inch broad; two to four-seeded; the seed is a sort of round bean; the whole plant has in field cultivation a very disagreeable smell. Cultivated dry in any good soil; ground prepared in summer months, after rain, a selected spot being hand-hoed, weeds removed; dried leaves are burnt on the spot and ashes mixed with soil; seed sown a month or so later, either by hand or broadcast; under growth weeds are cleared and ground watered every few days; ashes and cow-dung applied as manure; pandauls [q.v.] raised for support of the plants; plant attains a height of over a foot, when the leaves become yellow and fall off; the pods however are generally gathered when young, those for seeds only being left to become full ripe; the pods can be plucked three months after sowing; the pods are dried in the sun for three days after which they are beaten or trodden and the seeds collected; the seeds are afterwards sifted and dried; average price fifteen imperial seers one rupee. When young and tender, seeds are good substitutes for french beans [lobyah]; being cheap are much eaten by poorer classes; they are not palatable, but rec-koned wholesome; cattle are fed with the seed; haulms are given as fodder; cultivated about the doors of the natives, form arbours. Several varieties differing in color of seeds and forms of legumes. Compare also:—Arachis hypogæa. underground bean; Cæsalpinia bonduc, molucca bean; Canavalia ensiformis, sword bean; Ceratonia siliqua, locust bean, st. john's bean; Dolichos biflorus, two-flowered bean; Entada scandens, match-box bean; Erythrina indica, red bean; Glycine javanica, japanese bean; Glycine soja, soy bean; Mucuna monosperma, negro-bean; Mucuna pruriens, horse-eye bean; Nelumbium speciosum, egyptian bean; Phaseolus grahamianus, graham's bean; Phaseo-lus lunatus, country haricot bean; Phaseolus vulgaris, haricot bean; Prosopis glandulosa, texas mesquit-bean; Prosopis pubes-cens, screw bean; Psophocarpus tetragonolobus, goa bean; Pyrus aucuparia, quick bean; Semecarpus anacardium, malacca kidney bean; Strychnos ignatii, st. ignatius bean; Vigna catiang, runner bean. See gloss. paragraphs.——*Country borage* (पाषाणभेदी - páshánabhédí, San.; पत्थरचूर - patt'harchúr, Mahr.; కర్పూరవల్లి - karpúravalli, Tel.). Title from resemblance, as to hairy leaves. San. from (páshána, san. stone + bhid, san. to break); useful in gravel. Mahr. from (prastara, san. stone + chúrn, san. to powder); useful in gravel. Tel. from (karpúra, san. camphor + vallí, san. creeper); from smell of leaves and flowers. Botanically Coleus aromaticus, benth., labiatæ [vric-sham, 103]. Alias Coleus amboynicus, crassifolius; Plectranthus amboynensis, aromaticus. Shrub, 2–3 feet; branches tomen-tosely pubescent, or hispid; leaves petiolate, broad, ovate, crenated, rounded at the base, or cuneate, very thick, hispid on both surfaces, or clothed with white villi, very fragrant, floral leaves hardly equal in length to the calyx; racemes simple; whorls twenty to thirty-flowered or more; calyx tomentose; tube of corolla about twice as long as the calyx, defracted at the middle; throat dilated; lower lip a little dilated, boat-shaped; flowers smallish, pale blue, very aromatic. Low growing wide-spreading herb; stem fruticose at the base; solid succulent leaves; native of the moluccas; common in gardens, but rarely flowers. Expressed juice, powerful carminative, given for colic of children. Leaves eaten and mixed with articles of food. The species barbatus is cultivated in gardens for the roots, which are pickled. Osmirrhizon is used by hindoo females to scent their hair. Other species are:—malabaricus, parviflorus.

——*Country chiretta* (بڑا چرائتہ - barácharáitah, Hind.). Same as Purple chiretta.——*Country cotton* (कार्पासी - kárpásí, San.). Same as Indian cotton.——*Country french beans* (کھرسنبل - kharsanbal, Hind.). Same as Country lobyah.——*Country gall nut* (కరక - karaka, Tel.). Tel. from (kara, tel. stain); fruit stains finger black and used in making ink [mashy]. Same as Chebulic myrobalan.——*Country gooseberry* (அருநெல்லி - arunelli, Tam.). Tam. from (aru, tam. minuteness + nelli, tam. emblic myrobalan); from small size. Same as Brazil cherry.——*Country horse-radish* (முருங்கை - murungai, Tam.). Same as Moringa.——*Country ipecacuanha* (جنگلی پکوان - janglípikván, Hind.). Same as Indian ipecacuanha.——*Country lavender* (उत्पलभेद - utpalabhéda, San.; कपूर्लि - kapúrli, Mahr.; साविर सम्बार - sávirasambára, Conc.; پنجیری کا پیڑ - panjeríkáper, Hind.; پنجیری کا جہاڑ - panjeríkájhár, Dec.; ದೊಡ್ಡಪತ್ರೆಬಳ್ಳಿ - doddapatreballi, Can.; ಸಂಬಾರಬಳ್ಳಿ - sambáraballi, Too.; కర్పూరవల్లి - karpúravalli, Tel.; കാട്ടുകൂർക്ക - káttukúrkka, Mal.; ගල්කප්පරවල්ලිය - galkapparavalliya, Singh.; கர்ப்பூரவள்ளி - karppúravalli, Tam.). Title from similarity to borago officinalis which has hairy leaves. San. from (utpala, san. fleshless + bhid, san. to break), probably cures emaciation. Hind. from (panjerí, hind. caudle + per, hind. tree). Can. from (dodda, can. large + patri, san. leaf + balli, can. creeper). Too. from (sambára, too. spicery + balli, too. creeper). Tel. from (karpúra, tel. camphor + valli, san. creeper) [country borage]. Mal. from (kátu, mal. forest + kúrkka, mal. the plant). Singh. from (gal, singh. stone + karppúravalli, tam. the plant), common among rocks. Tam. from (karpúra, san. camphor + valli, san. creeper); from smell. San. also (ajapáda), meaning sheep + foot; (induparní), meaning moon + leaf, from white round leaf; (karpúravallí), meaning camphor + creeper; (váluká), meaning sand plant. Ar. also (vardiafrásiún). Hind. also (sitákápanjerí), meaning seeta's caudle. Dec. also (ajwánkápattá), meaning carum copticum, benth. + leaf. Can. also (patriballi), meaning leaf-creeper; (kuruvéluballi), meaning fragrant grass creeper. Tel. also (karavéru), meaning the plant + root; (ómamuákuchettu), meaning carum copticum, benth. + leaf + plant, from similarity; (rógachettu), meaning disease + plant; (pindibanda), meaning flour + rock; as being able to powder rock. Mal. also (karppúra-valli); (chómara); (kúrkka); (patukúrkka), meaning rough + the plant. Title otherwise Ajwaun-leaf creeper, Camphor creeper, Caudle plant, Moon-leaf creeper, Seeta's caudle, Thick-leaved lavender. Botanically Anisochilus carnosus, wall., labiatæ [vricsham, 103]. Alias Anisochilus crassus; Lavandula carnosa; Plectranthus carnosus, crassifolius, dubius, strobiliferus. Herbaceous pot plant; stem erect, tetragonal; leaves petiolate, ovate-roundish, crenated, cordate at the base, thick, fleshy, tomentosely villous on both surfaces; spikes on long peduncles; calyx with upper lip, with ciliated edges, lower lip truncate, quite entire; corolla bilabiate, upper lip bluntly three to four-cleft, lower lip entire; flowers lilac. Plant yields a volatile oil. Fresh juice from leaves mixed with sugar [q.v.] and gingelly [q.v.] oil, is a cooling liniment for the head; leaves and stems in infusion are a mild expectorant. Other species are:—dysophylloides, eriocephalus, scaber, sericeus, suffruticosus.——*Country liquorice* (گمچی - gumchí, Dec.). Same as Indian liquorice.——*Country mallow* (துத்தி - tutti, Tam.). Same as Tootty.——*Country radish* (मूलक - múlaka, San.; मुळा - mulá, Mahr.; मूलंगि - múlangi, Conc.; فجل - fujl, Ar.; ترب - turb, Pers.; مولی - múlí, Hind.; ملی - mullí, Dec.; لوباک - lobak, Malay; ಮುಲ್ಲಂಗಿ - mullangi, Can.; ಮುಲ್ಲೆಂಗಿ - mullengi, Too.; ముల్లంగి - mullangi, Tel.; കനകപ്പാല - kanakap-pála, Mal.; முள்ளங்கி - mullangi, Tam.). San. from (múla, san. root), from officinal part. Ar. from (fajala, ar. thick). Pers. means earth. Hind. from sanscrit. Can. from (mullu, can. thorn). Mal. from (kanaka, san. gold + pála, mal. milk-plant). Tam. from (mul, tam. thorn), thorn-like. San. also (vrittatrina), meaning round grass. Can. also (múlangi); (mugabíja). Tam. also (rádismulangi), meaning radish root; (shivappumullangi), meaning red + radish. Greek ῥαφανὶς ἀγρία; Latin raphanus. Title otherwise Charlock, Indian radish. Botanically Raphanus sativus, linn., cruciferæ [vric-sham, 10]. Alias Raphanus radicula, rotundus, oblonga, according to shape.—"*a*" Annual herb of the cabbage [kobee, sarshapam] family; unknown wild; bears purplish flowers; root grows to an enormous size, sometimes as large as a man's leg, rising partly above ground like a stem; it is pale red or white colored without the pleasant pungency of the english plant but mild and tender. The seeds are roundish, reddish-grey or reddish-brown, vary in diameter from a half to one line, odourless and mucilaginous in taste. The root and seeds yield with water a milky distillate, from which a small quantity of oil may be obtained by rectification; it is colorless, heavier than water, and has the taste but not the smell of radishes; the oil contains sulphur [gandhac]; it forms a white precipitate with corrosive sublimate [shavveeram], and yellow with bichloride of platinum [goorootwam]; it dissolves with tolerable facility in water. Seeds diuretic, laxative and lithon-triptic; roots used for urinary and syphilitic diseases. Leaves are a vegetable; young pods used for pickling, a substitute for capers [q.v.]; root eaten cooked or raw; oil from seeds used in cooking. Several varieties.—"*b*" Wild country radish so called in vernaculars, otherwise wall radish, wild endive, wild radish, wild tobacco, is laggera aurita, schultz-bip., compositæ [vricsham, 74]; alias blumea aurita, conyza aurita; annual herbaceous or somewhat shrubby plant, flower small, yellow; smells strongly of turpentine [carpoora teilam], found particularly along the walls in old buildings and in graveyards. There is another species of laggera called pterodonta.—"*c*" Compare also:—Daucus carota (kempúmullangi), red country radish; and (pattsamullangi), yellow country radish; Sonchus oleraceus (káttumullangi), forest country radish. See gloss. paragraphs. ——*Country sarsaparilla* (ناتكا عشبہ - nátkáushbah, Dec.). Same as Indian sarsaparilla.——*Country sorrel* (चुक्र - chukra, San.; حماض - hummáz, Ar.; ترشہ - turshah, Pers.; چوکا - chúká, Hind.; چکہ - chukkah, Dec.; ಸುಕ್ಕೆಸೊಪ್ಪು - sukkesoppu, Can.; చుక్కకూర - tsukkakúra, Tel.; සුරි - suri, Singh.; சுக்கங்கீரை - shukkangírai, Tam.). San. means sourness. Ar. from (hamz, ar. acid). Pers. from (tursh, pers. acid). Hind. from sanscrit. Can. from (sukki, can. insipid + soppu, can. greens). Tel. from (chukra, san. the plant + kúra, tel. pot-herb). Tam. from (shukkam, tam. species of bryonia + kírai, tam. vegetable). San. also (amlavétasa), meaning sour, calamus rotang, linn.; (chukriká), meaning sour [sour auray]; (shatavédhí), meaning piercing a hundred, from curing hundred diseases. Ar. also (habakikhúrásání), meaning khorassan mint. Dec. also (chukkekíbhájí), meaning country sorrel greens. Tel. also (pullaprabba), meaning sour rattan. Singh. also (katutampalá). Title otherwise Bladder-dock, Bladder sorrel, Mint of khorassan. Botanically Rumex vesicarius, linn., polygonaceæ [vricsham, 110]. Stem low, branched; leaves somewhat fleshy, petioled, ovate or deltoid, obtuse or acutish, usually cuneate-attenuate from a cordate or sub-hastate base, uppermost ones narrower; racemes simple or panicled, leafless; fascicles two to five-flowered, remote; pedicels one-flowered or generally bearing two flowers at the top, connate at the back; valves very large, entire, very unequal, calliferous or almost naked; grows in fields during rains; medicinally cooling and aperient, and to certain extent diuretic; eaten raw and as pot-herb [keeray]. Other common species are:—dentatus, nepalensis, wallichii.——*Country walnut* (నాటుక్రోతు - nátuakrótu, Tel.). Lumbang nut.

COURTALLAM (குற்றாலம் - kuttálam, * *Tam.*). Title from sanscrit. Sanscrit name (triktúáchala), meaning three + peak + mountain; also (trikúta), meaning three + peak; also (drutikshétra), meaning drooty, the sage + sacred place; also (kuddála), meaning mountain ebony, bauhinia variegata, linn., from the name of the tree in the shiva temple. Village, Sanitarium. Place of pilgrimage; Tinnevelly dist., Tencaushy tal.; pop. 1,095; acres 1,324; lat. 8° 56′; long. 77° 19′; from Tencaushy W.S.W. 3½ miles; from Tinnevelly W.N.W. 32 miles. On the Chittaur. Although only 700 feet above sea-level, Courtallam receives the south-west monsoon [caur] through an opening in the ghauts [q.v.] and possesses the climate and flora [vricsham] of a much higher elevation. The valley allows an easy communication between the Carnatic [q.v.] and Malabar. There are several bungalows and good roads in all directions. Very sacred temple with some good sculpture and a number of inscriptions. The lingam [q.v.] is to Coottaulanauta sawmy. Mantapams [q.v.] and choultries [q.v.] for visitors. Festival in August when Hindoos come to bathe. Celebrated three waterfalls. The lowest is Vadavaroovy, the northern fall. It consists of two falls, the united height of which is about 180 feet. The upper pool of this fall is called Pongoo maucadal, the boiling great sea, the depth of which is 38 feet. The second fall is Champakautavy teertam, the sacred bathing place of the Champak [q.v.] forest. The third is Tainaroovy, the honey fall. The highest fall is 2,000 feet above the sea. The average temperature of the water is 72° to 75° and invalids derive great benefit from bathing in it. The bathing place is under a shelving rock, affording a natural shower-bath. The spices cultivated at Courtallam were introduced in 1800 [aroovy, hill-station].

COURTNEY (కుడతని - kudatani, *Tel.*). From (kúdu, can. junction + ani, tel. border). Sanscrit name (kumárapura), meaning town of the son-god, who destroyed a giant. Village, Railway station; Bellary dist., Bellary tal.; pop. 4,866; acres 19,356; lat. 15° 13′; long. 76° 48′; height 1,577 feet; from Bellary W.N.W. 11 miles. A large decayed village of considerable antiquity. Contains a good tank and the remains of a strong fort. There is a curious hill composed of scoriæ about three miles beyond this place, close to the Antapore pass, on the right of the road, about fifty feet high and four hundred feet in circumference. The summit is rounded and the surface partially covered with patches of dry grass, from which crop out masses of tufaceous scoriæ. It sounds hollow when trodden on. Either volcanic or remains of an ancient furnace. The local tradition is that the mound is composed of the ashes of an enormous raucshasan whose funeral pile it was. Still another account makes it to be the ashes of a funeral pile raised over the corpses of soldiers killed in battle. Courtney was formerly an important Jeina stronghold, but one of the principal basties [q.v.] is now occupied by Sheiva images, while another has been converted into a mosque [musjid], and a third forms the mutt [q.v.] of a Jangam priest. The large image of one of the Teertancarans [q.v.] is seen cast outside the western gate, with its feet buried in the soil. According to tradition, a Chola king built a number of temples here and dug wells. Numerous inscriptions on stone in the Haleycannada character, headed by representations of the lingam [q.v.], the sun and the moon, and mutilated sculptures are seen scattered about the ruins of the old fort. Travellers' bungalow.

COVELONG (كولم - kollam, *Hind.*; கோவளம் - kóvalam, *Tam.*). Means a headland. Sanscrit name (nityakalyánapura), meaning daily marriage city. According to Bramins the native goddess is Comalammah. Also called Saudat bunder, or auspicious port, so called by Anwaroodeen [q.v.] the first nawaub of Arcot who built a fort there in 1745. Village, Port, Canal; Chingleput dist., Chingleput tal.; pop. 2,044; acres 486; lat. 12° 47′; long. 80° 18′; from Arcot E. 62 miles; from Chingleput E.N.E. 19¾ miles; from Cuddalore N.E. 80 miles; from Madras S. 20 miles; from Sadras N.N.E. 20 miles; from Sydapett S.S.E. 17 miles. On the Coromandel coast [q.v.]. One of the earliest European settlements and formerly of strategical importance. The approach from the south and south-east is dangerous in consequence of a rocky shoal projecting upwards of a mile into the sea in that direction. In ancient times it was a town of a cautham [q.v.] or 10 miles, including Covelong, Tiravadam and Mauvellipore. See Seven pagodas. Going to ruin, it became a wilderness. Mahomedan accounts state that it was a shahar [q.v.] or great town, with many suburban adjuncts. They say a dead body of a holy person came ashore here enclosed in a chest with a writing that the body should be given a tomb [durgah], which was done. A mosque [musjid] was built in days of Nawaub Saudat oollah khan over tomb. Covelong was a Dutch settlement, and the Imperial east india company of Ostend built a fort, which has disappeared. The ruins now in existence belong to the Saudat bunder fort. Occupied in 1750 by the French by stratagem. In 1752 French garrison surrendered to Clive. The fortifications were then blown up. Covelong possesses a Roman catholic church, alms-house [lungarkhana], and orphanage founded and supported by grants from the DeMonte family, formerly rich merchants of Madras. The salt pans [ooppalam] to the west of the village are large, and there is some export trade in this article. Excellent oysters [auly] are found here.

COVID (കൊവിടം - kovitam, *Mal.*). From covado, portuguese word for cubit. Cloth measure 15, 27, or 36 inches. Distinguish from Coovid.

COVOOR (కోవూరు - kóvúru, *Tel.*). From (kóyarádzu, tel. proper name + úru, tel. village). Village; Nellore dist., Nellore tal.; pop. 5,893; acres 5,546; lat. 14° 30′; long. 80° 02′; from Nellore N. 3¼ miles; from the sea W. 13½ miles. One Coya rauz while on pilgrimage to Benares encamped at this place, and afterwards built the village. Two temples of Codandá ramasawmy and Mullicarjoonasawmy, with annual festivals. An agricultural centre on the northern bank of the Pennair on the Nellore trunk road. Noted for manufacture of white handkerchiefs [roomaul] and turbans [puggry]. Good laterite [q.v.] stone is quarried.

COWITCH (कन्दुरा - kandurá, *San.*; كواچھ - kaváchh, *Hind.*; దురదగొండి - duradagondi, *Tel.*). Title from hindostany. San. means pungent, itching. Hind. from (kapikachhu, san. the plant). Tel. from (durada, tel. itching + gondi, tel. wretch). San. also (katóla). Tel. also (suruticheţtu). Cf. Pappily. Botanically the Mucuna genus, leguminosæ [vricsham, 48]. Well known in tropical countries from the character of seed-pods which are thickly covered with stinging hairs easily detached and causing irritation if they fall on body; all are twiners or tall climbers, with trifoliate leaves and long stalked often pendulous racemes of large purple white or yellow flowers, rising singly or in clusters from gland-like swellings; the pods are thick and leathery. The species best known to the natives are shown below. With natives also includes a Tragia.——*Buffalo cowitch* (గేదెదూలగొండి - gédedúlagondi, Tel.). Tel. from (géde, tel. buffalo + dúlagondi, tel. mucuna pruriens, dc.). Tel. also (tillakáda). Botanically Mucuna [cowitch] atropurpurea, dc., leguminosæ [vricsham, 48]. Alias Carpopogon atropurpurea. Perennial; leaflets ovate, acuminated; racemes drooping, long-peduncled, sometimes compound; pedicels long, slender, compressed; calyx-segments broadly-ovate, obtuse; legume oblong-oval, deeply furrowed along the sutures, obliquely plaited, two or sometimes one-seeded, copiously covered with brown stinging hairs; seed oval, more convex on the one side, and there furnished its whole length with the linear hilum; flowers large, dark-purple; flowering in february and march.——*Common cowitch* (आत्मगुप्ता - átmaguptá, San.; कुहिली - kuhilí, Mahr.; खवल्यावालि - khavalyáváli, Conc.; كواچھ - kaváchh, Hind.; کاچکوری - káchkurí, Dec.; ಕಾಡವರೆ - kádavare, Can.; ನಾಯಿಸೊಣಗುಬಳ್ಳಿ - náyisonaguballi, Too.; దూలగొండి - dúlagondi, Tel.; କଇଞ୍ଚ - kaincho, Oor.; നായ്ക്കുരണ - náykkúruna, Mal.; ආචාරියපලු - áchâriyápalu, Singh.; பூனைக்காலி - púnaikkáli, Tam.). San. from (átman, san. self + gup, san. to protect); having hidden properties. Hind. from (kapikachhu, san. the plant). Can. from (kádu, can. wild + avare, can. bean, dolichos lablab, linn.). Too. from (náyi, too. dog + sonagu, too. writhing + balli, too. creeper). Tel. from (dúla, tel. itching + gondi, tel.

wretch). Oor. from (kapikachhu, san. the plant). Mal. from (náya, mal. dog + kuruna, mal. the plant, jasminum pubescens, wild.). Singh. from (áchāriyá, singh. blacksmith + palu, singh. joint). Tam. from (púnai, tam. cat + kál, tam. foot); from grey hairs. San. also (kapikachhu), meaning monkey's itch; (markatí), meaning relating to monkey [indian burr]; (právrisháyaní), meaning growing in rainy season; (vánarí), meaning pertaining to monkey, from tawny hair on pod. Mahr. also (kavachakuirí), meaning armour + cowhage. Hind. also (kivánchh); (goncha). Dec. also (kánchkurí) [caunjory]. Can. also (turachi) [caunjory]; (náyisonaguballi), meaning dog + writhing + creeper. Tel. also (pilliadugu), meaning cat + foot; (tótadúlagondi), meaning garden + the plant. Mal. also (chorivalli), meaning itch creeper. Tam. also (púnaiyavarai), meaning cat + the plant, dolichos; (púnaippidukkan), meaning cat's testicles; from hairy pods. Title otherwise Cat bean, Cowhage, Donkey's eye, Flea plant, Horse-eye bean, Monkey's itch. Botanically Mucuna [cowitch] pruriens, dc., leguminosæ [vricsham, 48]. Alias Carpopogon pruriens; Dolichos pruriens; Mucuna prurita, utilis; Stizolobium pruriens. Annual, twining; branches pubescent or slightly hairy; leaves pinnately trifoliolate; leaflets ovate, upper side glabrous, under sprinkled with adpressed silvery hairs; racemes shorter than the leaves, drooping; pedicels shorter than the calyx; calyx cleft to the middle, white with adpressed hairs, segments broad-lanceolate; corolla papilionaceous; vexillum cordate, incumbent on the alæ, alæ oblong-linear, sometimes slightly cohering, keel straight below, slightly falcate in the upper part, terminated by an acute beak; legume slightly curved like an S; densely clothed with rigid stinging hairs, six-seeded; flowers large, dark purple, papilionaceous; common lofty climbing herb; flowering in the cold season. Root in infusion is given in cholera [vaunty bhaidy]; syrup thickened with the hairs till it is of the consistence of honey [shahad], is anthelmintic; the leaves are applied to ulcers, and the beans are aphrodisiac; a vinous infusion of the pods is remedy for dropsy; the seed absorbs the poison of scorpions; gives to pharm. hairs of pod, mucuna, mechanical anthelmintic, officinal. Pod eaten like any other bean [shimby].——*Elephant cowitch* (ఏనుగదూలగొండి - énugadúlagondi, Tel.; കാകവള്ളി - kákavalli, Mal.). Title from size. Tel. from (énuga, tel. elephant + dúlagondi, tel. mucuna pruriens, dec.). [negro-bean cowitch]. Mal. from (kákka, mal. crow + valli, mal. creeper). Tel. also (peddadúlagondi), meaning large + the plant, mucuna pruriens, dc. Botanically Mucuna [cowitch] gigantea, dc., leguminosæ [vricsham, 48]. Alias Carpopogon giganteum; Dolichos giganteus; Stizolobium giganteum. Climbing, perennial; leaflets ovate, acute adult ones glabrous; flowers almost umbellate, at the apex of long pendulous peduncles; pedicels long, slender; three lower segments of the calyx short, tooth-like, the other very short; legumes linear-oblong, deeply furrowed along the sutures, not plaited, armed with stiff, stinging hairs, three to six-seeded; seeds oval; flowers large, sulphur-colored. Bark, pulverised and mixed with dried ginger [q.v.] and other ingredients, rubbed over parts affected by rheumatism.——*Negro-bean cowitch* (मोतीकुहिली - mótíkuhilí, Mahr.; ಆನೆಪೆಬಳ್ಳಿ - anipeballi, Can.; ఏనుగదూలగొండి - énugadúlagondi, Tel.; பெரியதெள்ளுக்காய்ச்செடி - periyathellukkáyççedi, Tam.). Mahr. from (mótí, mahr. pearl + kuhilí, mahr. cowhage plant, mucuna pruriens, dec.). Can. from (anipe, can. negro bean + balli, can. creeper). Tel. from (énuga, tel. elephant + dúlagondi, tel. the plant, mucuna pruriens, dec.) [elephant cowitch]. Tam. from (periya, tam. big + tellu, tam. flea + káy, tam. fruit + shedi, tam. plant); highly irritating pods. Mahr. also (songarvi). Botanically Mucuna [cowitch] monosperma, dec., leguminosæ [vricsham, 48]. Alias Carpopogon monospermum; Mucuna anguina. Perennial; leaflets ovate, pubescent when young; racemes short, somewhat corymbiform, short-peduncled, drooping; pedicels long; lowest calyx-segments long-pointed, the others very short; legumes semi-oval, deeply furrowed along the sutures, obliquely plaited, one-seeded, covered with stinging hairs; seed kidney-shaped; flowers large, dark-purple; flowering in cold season. Pod eaten.——*Small cowitch* (చిన్నదూలగొండి - chinnadúlagondi, Tel.). Same as Small caunjory.

COWKAB (كوكب - kaukab, *Hind.*). Star [nacshatram].——*Cowkab i bakht* (كوكب بخت - kaukabibakht, Hind.). Means star of prosperity. Jehaungeer's large silver coin. Weight 50 tolahs.——*Cowkab i saad* (كوكب سعد - kaukabisaad, Hind.). Means auspicious star. Jehaungeer's small silver coin. Weight 5 tolahs.——*Cowkab i tauly* (كوكب طالع - kaukabitáli, Hind.). Means star of fortune. Jehaungeer's maximum silver coin. Weight 100 tolahs [naunyam].

COWLE (قول - kaul, *Hind.*). From (kála, ar. to say). A promise on the part of a superior. Especially a document granted to holder of land, specifying special terms of tenure. The special agreement is generally to pay a small but increasing rent for land for a certain number of years when it becomes liable to the same rent as other cultivated lands; sometimes to hold land for a term, subject to not touching trees thereon. See vol. I, 112.——*Cowl beera* (قول بيرا - kaulbírah, Hind.). From (above + biráh, hind. betel). Betel of contract. Mahomedan ceremony of giving betel [q.v.] to the nearest male relative of a girl at the time of betrothment, to obtain his consent.——*Cowle bazaar* (కౌలుబజారు - kaulubadzáru, Tel.). From (above + bázár, pers. market). Village; pop. 25,987, including cantonment. Suburb of Bellary containing the finest military market in Southern india.——*Couledar* (قولدار - kauldár, Hind.). From (above + dár, pers. holder). A ryot [q.v.] holding lands on cowle. See vol. I, 112.

COWM (قوم - kaum, *Hind.*). Mahomedan sect. There are four principal called after their respective founders.——*Hambalee* (حنبلی - hambalí, Hind.). Hambalites, from founder Ibne hambal, chiefly found at Baghdad, in Arabia.——*Hanafee* (حنفی - hanafí, Hind.). Hanifites, from founder Aboo haneefa, found in Turkey and Usbec tartary; also all over India; comprising persons from four tribes Syed [q.v.], Sheikh [q.v.], Moghul [q.v.], and Pataun [q.v.].——*Malakee* (مالکی - málikí, Hind.). Malekites, from founder Malik bin ins, most prevalent in Barbary and other parts of Africa.——*Shahfayee* (شافعی - sháfaí, Hind.). Shafeites, from founder Aboo abdoollah shahfayee; frequent in Southern india; comprising the Navayats [q.v.] and Lubbays [q.v.].

COWNDINYAN (कौण्डिन्य - kaundinya, *San.*). A divine sage and originator of a gotram [q.v.].——*Cowndinyanuddy* (కౌండిన్యనది - kaundinyanadi, Tel.). From (above + nadí, san. river). Otherwise Goodiyattam river. River; North arcot dist., Goodiyattam, Poonganore, Pulmanair tals. Receives in Goodiyattam talook the surplus of the Dundapully tank, fed by a Mysore river and several other streams and falls into the Palaur.

COWRAVA (कौरव - kaurava, *San.*). From (kuru, san. ruler so named). The descendants of Cooroo [mahabhaurat]. An inferior race in the Peninsula are known as Cooroos; and Teloogoo pariahs are by some called Cowrava jauty. There has been some confusion between the Hindoo and Dravidian terms.

COWRY (کوڑی - kaurí, *Hind.*; గవ్వ - gavva, *Tel.*; கவடி - kavadi, *Tam.*). From (kaparda, san. shell used as a coin). Tam. also (palagarai). A small shell, the Cypræa moneta of naturalists. Small, white, or yellow kinds found on the shores of the Laccadive and Maldive islands, &c. The commoner kinds still pass current as coin in payment of fractional parts of a pice in the Ceded districts [q.v.]. There is a Hindostany proverb:—غریب کو کوڑی اشرفی هی—"A cowry is a gold mohur [q.v.] to a pauper." A currency table is as follows:—26 cowry = 1 damrée; 1 damree = 3 daums; 25 daums = 1 pice. But the pieces are mostly imaginary. With cowries the women of the lower orders form bracelets and other ornaments. Also sewed like buttons on their dress by Brinjarry women. The title-word is also another form of Cauvady [q.v.], by corruption.

COWSHIKY (కౌశిక - kaushika, *Tel.*). From (kaushika, san. sage of that name). River; Godavery dist., Amalaupooram tal. Branches off from the Gowtamy near Mundapully and falls into the sea near Bendamoorlunka after flowing through Amalaupooram, Gangalcoorroo, Indoopully, &c. Not navigable. Dry during part of year.

COY (కాయ - káya, *Tel.*; കായ - káya, *Mal.*; காய் - káy, *Tam.*). Unripe fruit [pazham]. Plant second term. Ex., where transl. is of first term:—Acacia concinna (shínikkáya), cleaning; Anamirta cocculus (pollakkáya), blister; Averrhoa bilimbi (puliççakkáy), sour; Benincasa cerifera (parangikkáy), portuguese; Capsicum annuum (milagáy), pepper; Cucumis melo, var. momordica (peddakáya), large; Cucurbita maxima (arasánikkáy), king; Grewia microcos (kottakka), kernel; Lagenaria vulgaris (gubbakáya), round. See gloss. paragraphs.——*Coy dhaunyam* (காய்த்தானியம் - káyttániyam, Tam.). From (above + dhánya, san. grain). Pulses, all sorts of seeds contained in pods or legumes [dholl]. Distinguished from cathir dhaunyam or ear grain or cereal [dhaunyam].

COY (കൊഴു - kozhu, *Mal.*). Ploughshare [caur].——*Coy laubham* (കൊഴുലാഭം - kozhulábham, Mal.). From (above + lábha, san. profit). A tenant's profit after deducting, expenses of cultivation and proprietor's share. Cf. Coodivauram.——*Coyoovan* (കൊഴുവൻ - kozhuvan, Mal.). From (above + an, mal. suffix, having). A tenant.——*Coy panayam* (കൊഴുപണയം - kozhupanayam, Mal.). From (above + panayam, mal. mortgage). Another name for Caripanayam, usufructuary mortgage [panayam].——*Coy punnam* (കൊഴുപണം - kozhupanam, Mal.). From (above + panam, mal. money). Two fanams given by tenant to proprietor in exchange for a piece of iron, typifying the ploughshare, concurrently with a deed by which he engages to improve the produce of the estate that he temporarily occupies.

COYI (కోయి - kóyi, *Tel.*). The name of the Gonds among themselves. Compare Coo similarly for the Khonds.

COZHY (கோழி - kózhi, *Tam.*). Means cock. Another name of Warriore; and Cozhy vendan is a chola king as ruler of Warriore. Gives its name to coins [naunyam], figure of cock stamped. For the gallinaceous fowl see Moorghy and Jungle fowl.

CRAB OIL PLANT (परुष - parusha, *San.*; کرپا - karapa, *Malay*; කඩොල් - kadol, *Singh.*; கண்டலெங்காய் - kandalangáy, *Tam.*). Title corruption from malay. San. means knotted. Tam. from (kandal, tam. rhizophora + káy, tam. fruit); from resemblance of fruits. Title otherwise Indian wooden pomegranate. Botanically Carapa moluccensis, lam., meliaceæ [vricsham, 36]. Alias Carapa obovata; Xylocarpus granatum. Generic from malay. Tree; leaves abruptly pinnated, leaflets two-pair, elliptical, obtuse, entire; calyx four-cleft; petals four, reflexed; stamen tube eight-cleft at the apex, the segments two-parted; style short, with a broad concave stigma; fruit spherical, six to twelve-seeded, the pericarp splitting into four valves; seeds angled, with a spongy integument; flowers small, yellowish; native of malabar, common. Fat expressed from seeds. Gives a clear, brown, brittle resin [raul]. Oil used as hair-oil and for burning purposes. Wood white, turning red on exposure, hard; used for house-posts, handles of tools, wheel spokes, boats; stands brackish water better than saul [q.v.].

CRAMAM (क्रम - krama, *San.*). From (kram, san. to move). Motion. Order, regularity. Crama vazhakk or dauvah [q.v.] is regular suit. In astronomy declination [craunty].——*Cramajyay* (क्रमज्या - kramajyá, San.). From (above + jyá, san. sine). The sine of a planet's declination. Paramaupama cramajyay, from (paramápama, san. the greatest declination) is the sine of planet's greatest declination [crauntijyay, jyotisham].

CRANGANORE (കൊടുങ്ങല്ലൂർ - kotunnallúr, *Mal.*). From (kóta, mal. west + kóvil, mal. palace + úr, mal. village) [coda, cooda]; western capital of the cheras, probably distinguishing it from caroor their eastern capital. Mal. also (allúr), meaning dark village, formed perhaps by analogy after caroor, the eastern capital of the cheras; also (kurumbálaya), meaning coorumba deity + temple. Sanscrit name (mahádévapura), means city of shiva the great god; also (kótilingapurí), means crore + phallic emblem of shiva + town; also (shríkótarapurí), means prosperity + cave + town. Greek μούζιρις; from mooyiricode which is the old name of krishnamcottah, just opposite to cranganore. Muziris primum emporium Indiae of Pliny.—"*a*" Talook, Cochin state; pop. 20,950. Boundaries:—north Moocoondapooram talook, east Moocoondapooram talook and Travancore territory, south Ayicottah river, west the sea. The talook forms the territory of the Cranganore chief. The line of the Rajahs is still extant. They found their claim to this territory as having been granted to their family by Cherma permaul, the chief of whose guard was their ancestor. The affairs are managed by Cochin. Principal places:—Ayicottah and Cranganore.—"*b*" Town, Talook head-quarters, Port; Cochin state, Cranganore tal.; pop. 10,011; lat. 10° 12′; long. 76° 15′; from Bangalore S.W. 211 miles; from Bombay S.E. 648 miles; from Calicut S.S.E. 75 miles; from Cannanore S.S.E. 126 miles; from Chittoor S.W. 50 miles; from Cochin N. 16 miles; from Ernacolum N.N.W. 16 miles; from Madras S.W. 341 miles; from Mangalore S.E. 207 miles; from Paliport N.N.E. 5 miles; from Trichore S. 22 miles; from Tripoontora N.N.W. 20 miles. Pliny says:—"To those bound for India, it is most convenient to depart "from Okelis. They sail thence with the wind Hipyalus in forty "days to the first emporium of India, Muziris, which is not a "desirable place to arrive at on account of pirates infesting the "neighbourhood, who hold a place called Nitrias, while it is not "well supplied with merchandize. Besides, the station for ships "is at a great distance from the shore, and cargoes have both to "be landed and to be shipped by means of small boats. There "reigned there when I wrote this Caelobothras [keralapootran]. "Another port belonging to the nation is more convenient, "Neacyndon, which is called Becare [cullada]. There reigned "Pandion [paundyan] in an inland town far distant from the "emporium called Modura [madura]. The region however from "which they convey pepper to becare in boats formed from "single logs is Cottonara [cadatnaud]." The Periplus says:—"To the kingdom under the sway of Keprobotras [keralapoot-"ran] Tundis [cadaloondy] is subject, a village of great note "situate near the sea. Mouziris, which pertains to the same "realm, is a city at the height of prosperity, frequented as it is "by ships from Ariake and Greek ships from Egypt. It lies near "a river at a distance from Tundis of five hundred stadia, whether "this is measured from river to river or by the length of the "sea voyage, and it is twenty stadia distant from the mouth "of its own river. The distance of Nelkunda [cullada] from "Mouziris is also nearly five hundred stadia, whether measured "from river to river or by the sea voyage, but it belongs to a "different kingdom, that of Pandion. It likewise is situate near "a river and at about a distance from the sea of one hundred and "twenty stadia." Ariake is the Mahratta country [maharashtram]. Cranganore is situated on the Alwye river, which has a bar at the entrance, with 5 or 6 feet of water; inside there are 14 or 16. Till 1314, when Vypeen harbour was formed, Cranganore was the only opening in the backwater [cauyal] and outlet for the Periyaur and it must at that time have been the best harbour on the coast. The traditions of Jews, Christians, Bramins, and of the Keraloputty, agree in making Cranganore the residence of the Permauls and of the first resort of western shipping. It was the seat of government of Cherma permaul, A.D. 341, and the earliest settlement of Jew and Christian immigrants. Jews now there claim to have been residents since A.D. 378. The section of Jews known as White jews, claim a peculiar connection with Cranganore. According to their account, their ancestors escaped from Jerusalem at the time of its final destruction, and the descendants of the fugitives made their way to the west coast of India, where, in the year of the world 4250 or 490 of the Christian era, the local ruler granted them a settlement at Cranganore, where they were joined by others of their nation, and in which place they remained about a thousand years; but, as one of their number stated, "discord arising "among ourselves, one of our chiefs called to his assistance an "Indian king, who came upon us with a great army, destroyed "our houses, palaces and strongholds, dispossessed us of Cranga-"nore, killed part of us, and carried part into captivity." The present Jewish synagogue is two centuries old. Christians have been here during the whole of the Christian era. Cranganore is prominent in all narratives earlier than the sixteenth century, especially in connexion with the Malabar christians, and it was the site of one of the seven churches founded by St. Thomas and the first place at which he labored, about A.D. 52. The names of the seven churches were Cauyal, Collam, Cottacauyal, Cranganore, Gokkamungalam, Niraunam, Paulore. In all of these except Cauyal and Cranganore, churches still exist. A colony of Syrian christians then settled here in A.D. 345, and their establishment continued to prosper until they invoked the aid of the Portuguese in 1502. The latter forced the greater part of them to acknowledge the authority of the Papal see which is exercised by the Bishop of Cranganore and Vicar-general of Malabar. Cranganore was already in decay when the Portuguese arrived. They eventually established themselves with a strong fort in 1523, which they enlarged in 1565 and which the Dutch took from them in 1662. The Dutch purchased the site from the Cranganore rajah, lost it to Tippoo in 1776, recaptured it in 1778, but sold it again in 1789 to Tippoo. The fort was dismantled by Tippoo's troops in 1790, and there is now hardly a trace of it left. The place was ceded to the British at the general pacification which closed the war provoked by the Sultan's attack on Travancore. The present town consists of two villages, Mettala and Lakmaleshwaram. In the latter are the ruins of old pagodas [q.v.]. Amongst others is that of Bhagavaty, where the feast of Bharany [pundigay, 5c] is held in March. The remains of the ancient watch-tower, and the palace of the titular rajah of Cranganore, are of interest. A Portuguese tomb, dated A.D. 1551, was lately discovered here. Shuncaracharry [shuncaran], the Sheiva reformer, was born near here.—"*c*" Backwater; Cochin state, Cranganore tal.; lat. between 10° 12′ and 10° 15′; long. 76° 15′ and 76° 17′; from Cranganore E. 1 mile. Is the estuary of the Carvanore river.

CRAUCA (క్రాక - kráka, *Tel.*). From (kragu, tel. to become hot). Heat. Suffix in place names; as Bramhanacrauka, hot place inhabited by bramins. Generally near a rock or hill.

CRAUNTY (क्रान्ति - kránti, *San.*). From (kram, san. to go). Astronomical declination [cramam]. The declination of a celestial body is its distance from the equinoctial [naudy mundalam]; if the body is on the north side of the equinoctial, it has north declination; but if on the south side, south declination. Or, it is the arc of a celestial meridian, or circle of declination, contained between the object and the equinoctial. The equinoctial being merely the projection of the terrestrial equator [niracsham], declination corresponds with terrestrial latitude [acsham]. Parallels of declination are small circles parallel with the equinoctial.——*Crauntam* (क्रान्त - kránta, San.). From (kram, san. to go). Conjunction [sangamam]. The Crauntam of any planet [graham] is when it is in conjunction with the moon [chundran], as the time of new moon [amavausyay] is the sun's own Crauntam. Mars [coojan]. Saturn [shany], Rahoo ☊ [q.v.] and Kait ☋ [q.v.], have a bad influence in Crauntam, and mark unlucky days. The other planets have also their Crauntam, but being innoxious they are not noticed in the Punchaungam [q.v.].——*Crauntijyay* (क्रान्तिज्या - krántijyá, San.). From (above + jyá, san. sine). The sine of the declination [cramajyay].——*Craunty bhaugam* (क्रान्तिभाग - krántibhága, San.). From (above + bhága, san. part). The declination of a point of the ecliptic.——*Craunty coty* (क्रान्तिकोटि - krántikóti, San.). From (above + kóti, san. complement). Co-declination.——*Craunty mundalam* (क्रान्तिमण्डल - krántimandala, San.). From (above + mandala, san. great circle). The ecliptic. That is to say the great circle representing the sun's apparent but the earth's real path of annual revolution [bhaganam] in the heavens. The plane of the earth's orbit [cacsham] is inclined to the plane of the equator [naudy mundalam] at an angle, called the obliquity of the ecliptic, of 23° 27½′. The ecliptic is divided into twelve equal parts, of 30 degrees each, called signs [raushy]; a belt in the heavens extending 8 degrees on each side of the ecliptic is the solar zodiac [raushy chuckram]. The point of the ecliptic where the sun crosses from the south to the north side of the equator is the first point of Aries; and where it crosses from the north to the south side, the first point of Libra. These are also the equinoctial points [craunty pautam], occurring about 21st of March and 23rd of September, when days and nights are of equal length throughout the world. The real constellations [nacshatram] have to be distinguished from the artificial signs of the zodiac or ecliptic, for, owing to a slow motion of the equinoctial points produced by the attraction of the sun, moon, and planets, upon the spheroidal figure of the earth, the longitude [sauyanam] of the fixed stars is increased at the present rate of about 50·1 seconds annually, the equinox having a retrograde motion from east to west to that amount. This is precession of equinoxes [ayanaumsham], and a complete revolution occupies 25,868 years. About 2,000 years ago the position of the vernal equinox [maishauyanam] coincided with the constellation Aries [maisham], but on account of precession this point is now in the actual constellation Pisces [meenam]. It is still customary to call the point of the spring equinox the first point of Aries. The autumnal equinox [toolauyanam] is similarly the first point of Libra [toolaum]. Cf. mausam (1), b. The obliquity of the ecliptic is considered by Hindoos to be constantly 24°; it is somewhat surprising that those who were able to discover though imperfectly the precessional variation, for they make it 54 seconds, should not have suspected the diminution of the obliquity.——*Craunty pautagaty* (क्रान्तिपातगति krántipátagati, San.). From (above + páta, san. falling + gati, san. going). Literally the motion of the nodes of the ecliptic; precessional variation.——*Craunty pautam* (क्रान्तिपात - krántipáta, San.). From (above + páta, san. falling). The nodes of the ecliptic, or the equinoctial points [jyotisham].

CREYAT (کریات - kiryát, *Dec.*). Title corruption from (kiráta, san. mountaineer), as growing on hills. Same as Chiretta.

CROE (کروہ - kroh, *Hind.*). From (krósha, san. the distance). Same as coss.

CRONNAUD (క్రొన్నాడు - kronnádu, *Tel.*). From (krotta, tel. new + nádu, tel. country). Old name of Amravatty country.

CRORE (کرور - karor, *Hind.*). From (kóti, san. the number) [coty]. 100 lakhs [q.v.] of anything or 10 millions. In Persia, the crore is only five lakhs, 500,000. Crory was a collector of revenue with Mahomedans.

CROREMUND (ಕ್ರೂರಮಂಡು - krúrmandu, *Can.*). From (kurumai, tam. littleness + úr, tam. village + mande, can. fold). Village, Neilgherry dist., Todanaud division; lat. 11° 24′; long. 76° 38′; from Ootacamund W. 7½ miles. On the Pycarrah river. Bungalow, built in January 1862, is in ruins.

CROSHAM (क्रोश - krósha, *San.*). From (krush, can. to cry). Distance at which a cry may be heard [coovid]. Indian league. 2,000 dandams = 1 crosham; 4 croshams = 1 yojanam [alavay, 1 f]. Approximate actual value, 1 crosham = 2¼ miles. Same as Hind. coss, croe, Can. hardaury, Tel. pargoo.

CROW (کوا - kavvá, *Hind.*). Prefix [caurvam].——*Crow creeper* (अपराजिता - aparájitá, San.; शंखपुष्पी - shankhapushpí, Mahr.; शंखपुष्पि - shankapushpi, Conc.; نبات بيخ حيات - nabátibíkhihayát, Ar.; درخت بيخ حيات - darakhtibíkhihayát, Pers.; کوا تھینتی - kavváthenthí, Hind.; گھٹی کی جڑ کا جھاڑ - ghuttíkíjarkájhár, Dec.; ಶಂಖಪುಷ್ಪ - shankhapushpa, Can.; ಶಂಕ - shanka, Too.; డింటెన - dintena, Tel.; ശംഖപുഷ്പം - shankhapushpam, Mal.; කටරොළු - katarolu, Singh.; காக்கணம் - kákkanam, Tam.). Title from dark flowers. San. from (a, san. negative prefix + paráji, san. to be defeated). Mahr. from (shankha, san. conch + pushpa, san. flower). Ar. from (nabát, ar. tree + bíkh, ar. root + hayát, ar. life). Pers. from (darakht, pers. tree + bíkh, ar. root + hayát, ar. life). Hind. from (kavvá, hind. crow + thenthí, hind. ball). Dec. from (ghutti, hind. purgative + jar, hind. root + jhár, hind. tree). Can. from (shankha, san. conch + pushpa, san. flower). Mal. from (shankha, san. conch + pushpa, san. flower), from shape of flowers. Tam. from (kákkai, tam. crow + anangu, tam. beauty); from crow dark flowers. San. also (gavákshí), meaning cow's eye; (rómavallí), meaning hair creeper; (vrishapádí), meaning bull-footed; (khadiraká), meaning firm; (aparájiká), meaning unconquered; (nílagirikarní), meaning blue + mouse ear; (girikarní), meaning mouse ear. Mahr. also (gókarni), meaning cow's ear. Ar. also (mázariúnihind), meaning indian daphne mezereum, linn.; from its diuretic and purgative properties. Hind. also (aprájita), meaning unconquered; (visnukrantí); (khágin), meaning female corby; (sufedaparájitá), meaning white variety. Dec. also (phíkekíjarkájhár), meaning insipid root tree. Tel. also (nalladintena), meaning black + the plant; (telladintena), meaning white + the plant. Mal. also (shankunkuppi), meaning conch + bottle; (kákkanámkodi); (áral). Singh. also (nilkatarolu), meaning blue + crow creeper; (sudukatarolu), meaning white + crow creeper. Tam. also (kákkattán), meaning crow [kaladana]; (karuvilai), meaning blackness + to grow; (karisanni); (káválai), meaning fruit + gynandropsis pentaphylla, dec.; (karudakkóvai), meaning braminy kite + cephalandra indica, naud., cf. Braminy kite caper; (karudathondai), meaning braminy kite + indian caper; (vellaikkákkattán), meaning white + the plant. Title otherwise Blue mouse ear, Braminy kite caper, Bull's foot, Conch flower, Cow's ear, Cow's eye, Crow's beak, Hair creeper, Indian daphne, Life root tree, Mouse ear, Mussel-shell creeper, Wing-leaved clitoria. Botanically Clitoria ternatea, linn., leguminosæ [vricsham, 48]. Alias Clitorea spectabilis; Lathyrus spectabilis; Ternatea vulgaris. Climbing herbaceous plant; calyx five-cleft; leaves unequally pinnated; leaflets two to three pairs, oval or ovate; stem pubescent, peduncles short, axillary, solitary, one-flowered; bracteoles large, roundish; flowers resupinate; legumes slightly pubescent, one-celled, many-seeded; flowers white or blue; flowering all year; common in woods of malabar. The fresh root is white, fleshy, often one inch or more in diameter, but pieces the size of a quill are preferred, it has an acrid taste; the root bark is soft, thick and fibrous and easily separated; the central portion of the root is composed of very large pitted vessels easily visible to the naked eye. The seeds are rather more than two-eighths of an inch long and resemble vetch seeds; they are mottled green and black; the testa is hard and contains two cotyledons made up of relongated thin-walled cells full of large starch granules; they have an acrid, bitter taste. Flower sacred to doorga [q.v.]. Seeds cathartic; the powder of the roasted seeds in drachm doses is a good purgative, substituted for british rhubarb and jalap [q.v.]; root demulcent, diuretic, and laxative; the fresh root or root-bark, in doses from one to two drachms, in infusion, relieves the irritation of the bladder and urethra and acts at the same time as a diuretic and laxative; the root is given in substance ground into powder in cases of croup, it sickens and sometimes produces vomiting, the dose is half a pagoda [q.v.] weight for a child of two or three years old; gives to pharm. seed and root-bark, non-officinal. A blue-dye is procured from corollas, but not permanent. There are three or four varieties:—one with flowers deep indigo blue; one azure blue; one pure white; one with double flowers. No other common species here.——*Crow pheasant* (चकोर - chakóra, San.; تذرج - tazraj, Ar.; تدرو - tadrau, Pers.; مہوکھا - mahokhá, Hind.; ಕಳ್ಳಿಕಾಗಿ - kallikági, Can.; జెముడుకాకి - jemudukáki, Tel.; ചെമ്പോത്ത - chempóttu, Mal.; கள்ளிக்காக்கை - kallikkákkai, Tam.). Title from appearance. San. from (chak, san. to be satisfied). Can. from (kalli, can. milk-hedge + kági, can. crow). Tel. from (jemudu, tel. euphorbia tirucalli, l. + káki, tel. crów). Mal. from (chem, mal. red + póttu, tam. indian cuckoo). Tam. from (kalli, tam. euphorbia tirucalli, l. + kákkai, tam. crow). Tam. also (shembugam). Title otherwise Coucal. Centropus rufipennis centropodinæ. cuculidæ [cokam], scansores, insessores [pacshy, 15], of naturalists [jantoo]. Alias Centropus bubutus, castanopterus, philippensis, pyrrhopterus. Whole head, neck, lower back, upper tail-coverts, and all under-parts richly empurpled black; tail glossed with green; upper part, back and wings bright deep rufous bay; legs black; very common; call is a 'whoot,' repeated slowly; when alighting on a tree, it raises its tail over its back. Lesser indian coucal is Centropus viridis; rare.

CROWNCHAM (क्रौञ्च - krauñcha, *San.*). From (kruñch, san. to move crookedly); from peculiar motion. Heron [paddy bird] or curlew [deergha chanchoocam].——*Crownchateev* (கிரௌஞ்சத்தீவு - kirauñjattívu, Tam.). From (above + tívu, tam. island). Sanscrit name (krauñchadvípa), meaning the same. Island; Tinnevelly dist., Ottapidauram tal.; lat. 8° 46′; long. 78° 14′; from Ottapidauram S.E. 16 miles; from Tinnevelly E. 35 miles. Has on it remains of a fort and other buildings. Is within the harbour of Tuticorin near the Devil's point.

CSHANAM (क्षण - kshana, *San.*). Means a glance. Twinkling of the eye. Measure of time. 2 ghaticams or indian hours = 1 cshanam or double hour, 30 cshanams = 1 dinam or day. Approximate actual value, 1 cshanam or double hour = 48 English minutes. Same as moohoortam [caulam, 2]. Same term appears also in other values.

CSHATRAM (क्षत्र - kshatra, *San.*). From (kshi, san. to govern). Dominion.——*Cshatriya* (क्षत्रिय - kshatriya, San.). The χατριαῖοι of Ptolemy, who located them towards Rajpootana. The second or military and regal caste of the Aryans [q.v.], represented in modern times in a way by Rajpoots [q.v.]. Said to have been produced from the breast or arms of Bramha. Their duty was to protect the earth, the cattle, and Bramins. Kings, governors, and all intrusted with civil and military affairs in general belonged to the Cshatriya caste. Parshooraman vowed that he would extirpate the whole Cshatriya race, and thrice seven times, says the Vishnoo poorauuam, he cleared the earth of them; a legend which intimates probably a violent and protracted struggle between the Bramins and Cshatriyas for domination in India. Some northern zemindars call themselves Cshatriyas. Bhatrauz, Bondily, Condarauz, Rauz, are classes who claim a Cshatriya origin [jauty].

CSHAYAM (क्षय - kshaya, *San.*). From (kshi, san. to wane). Waning.——*Cshaya samvatsaram* (क्षयसंवत्सर - kshayasamvatsara, San.). From (above + samvatsara, san. year). A luni-solar year with two intercalary months and one expunged month [mausam].——*Cshaya tity* (क्षयतिथि - kshayatit'hi, San.). From (above + tit'hi, san. day). An expunged lunar day [tity].

CSHEERAM (क्षीर - kshíra, *San.*). From (ghas, san. to eat). Milk [paul, sheer].——*Csheericay* (क्षीरिका - kshíriká, San.). Means milky tree. Monkey-face plants. Botanically the Mimusops genus, sapotaceæ [vricsham, 82]. Large milky juiced trees with thick entire smoothed leaves and clusters of small white often sweet-smelling flowers thought to resemble face of monkey; the fruits are globose or ellipsoid with one or two hard smooth seeds marked with a small egg-shaped scar; several species yield hard, durable and very heavy timber. The species best known to the natives are:—elengi [ilanjy], hexandra [monkey-face paulay], kauki [edible paulay], roxburghiana [jointed paulay].

CSHETRAM (क्षेत्र - kshétra, *San.*). From (kshi, san. to dwell). Soil; field; superficies; plane figure in geometry; place; body [shareeram]; sacred place [teertam]; in malayalam temple. ——*Cshetra ganitam* (क्षेत्रगणित - kshétraganita, San.). From (above + ganita, san. calculation). Geometry. Sixth book of a well-known Ganitam or mathematics. It treats of superficial measurements or land measuring, of the terms used in the science of measures, of the mode of measuring, of casting up accounts, and of allowances to be made in measuring, &c.—"*a*" The fundamental measure is the inch [ungoolam]. Twelve of these inches are one jaun [q.v.] or span. Sixty-four jauns are one gada or bamboo. Four gadas by which is understood one square bamboo is a coonta [q.v.]. The following is a table showing the sub-divisions of the coonta expressed as mere aliquot parts:—

1 Coonta, or say 4,000 country square feet, is equal to
- 2 Ara coontas.
- 4 Pautica.
- 8 Paraca coontas.
- 16 Veesam coontas.
- 32 Ara veesam coontas.
- 64 Cawny veesam coontas.
- 128 Ara cawny coontas.
- 256 Para cawny coontas.

To find the number of coontas in a square, add the number of bamboos of two opposite sides, multiply the amount by that of the two other opposite sides likewise added together, and divide the product by four; the quotient will be the number of coontas which the square contains; or take half the amount of two of the opposite sides, and multiply it by half the amount of the two others, the product will be the number of coontas. The following is a table for finding out the area of a piece of ground below the size of a coonta:—

Length of the field.	Breadth.	Area.
$\frac{1}{4}$ bamboo or 32 feet	$\frac{1}{4}$ bamboo or 32 feet is	1 pautica coonta or $\frac{1}{4}$ coonta.
$\frac{1}{4}$ Do. 32 ,,	$\frac{1}{8}$ Do. 16 ,,	1 paraca coonta or $\frac{1}{8}$ coonta.
$\frac{1}{4}$ Do. 32 ,,	$\frac{1}{8}$ Do. 8 ,,	1 veesam $\frac{1}{16}$ coonta.
$\frac{1}{4}$ Do. 32 ,,	$\frac{3}{16}$ Do. 12 ,,	1 Do. ara coonta or $\frac{3}{32}$.
$\frac{1}{4}$ Do. 32 ,,	$\frac{1}{16}$ Do. 4 ,,	1 ara veesam $\frac{1}{32}$.
$\frac{1}{4}$ Do. 16 ,,	$\frac{1}{4}$ Do. 16 ,,	1 veesam $\frac{1}{16}$.
$\frac{1}{4}$ Do. 16 ,,	$\frac{1}{16}$ Do. 4 ,,	1 cawny $\frac{1}{64}$.
$\frac{1}{4}$ Do. 16 ,,	$\frac{1}{64}$ Do. 1 ,,	1 para cawny $\frac{1}{256}$.
$\frac{3}{4}$ Do. 48 ,,	$\frac{3}{4}$ Do. 48 ,,	9 veesam coontas $\frac{9}{16}$.
$\frac{3}{4}$ Do. 48 ,,	$\frac{3}{16}$ Do. 12 ,,	2 veesam coontas and 1 cawny coonta or $\frac{9}{64}$.
$\frac{3}{4}$ Do. 48 ,,	$\frac{1}{8}$ Do. 8 ,,	1 veesam coonta and 2 cawny coontas or $\frac{6}{64}$.
$\frac{3}{4}$ Do. 48 ,,	$\frac{1}{16}$ Do. 4 ,,	3 cawny coontas or $\frac{3}{64}$.
$\frac{3}{4}$ Do. 48 ,,	$\frac{3}{64}$ Do. 3 ,,	2 cawny coontas and 1 para cawny coonta or $\frac{9}{256}$.
$\frac{3}{4}$ Do. 48 ,,	$\frac{1}{32}$ Do. 2 ,,	6 para cawny coontas or $\frac{6}{256}$.
$\frac{3}{4}$ Do. 48 ,,	$\frac{1}{64}$ Do. 1 ,,	3 para cawny coontas or $\frac{3}{256}$.
$\frac{3}{4}$ Do. 48 ,,	$\frac{1}{128}$ Do. $\frac{1}{2}$,,	$1\frac{1}{2}$ Do. $\frac{3}{512}$.
$\frac{3}{16}$ Do. 12 ,,	$\frac{3}{16}$ Do. 12 ,,	9 Do. $\frac{9}{256}$.
$\frac{1}{8}$ Do. 8 ,,	$\frac{1}{8}$ Do. 8 ,,	1 cawny coonta or $\frac{1}{64}$.
$\frac{1}{16}$ Do. 4 ,,	$\frac{1}{16}$ Do. 4 ,,	1 para cawny coonta or $\frac{1}{256}$.
$\frac{1}{64}$ Do. 1 ,,	$\frac{1}{64}$ Do. 1 ,,	1 gocara cawny coonta or $\frac{1}{4096}$.

Dwisamam is a quadrilateral figure where two sides are of equal and two others of different lengths; for this multiply the longest of the four sides by either of the adjoining sides, do the same with the two remaining sides; add the products; half this sum is the area required. Vishamam is a quadrilateral, all the sides of which are of different lengths; for this add the two smallest sides, and multiply half their amount by the longest, the product is the area. Samam is an equilateral parallelogram; for this take half the length of two opposite sides, and multiply it by half the amount of the other sides; the product will be the area required. Ayatam is an oblong rectangle; calculate this as for samam. Trisamam is a quadrilateral, three sides of which are of equal lengths; calculate this as for samam and the next, mookonam. Mookonam is a triangle, of which there are three different kinds; in this multiply the base by half the perpendicular height or the perpendicular height by half the base, the product is the area. Valayaucrity is the circle [chuckram, mundalam]; in this multiply the diameter by three, the product will be the circumference [paridhy]; multiply half the circumference by the radius, the product is the area; or multiply the circumference by the diameter, deduct a fourth part of the product, the remainder is the area. Maddalaucrity and damaroocaucrity are drum-shaped figures, like drums with convex and concave sides respectively; for these double the diameter going through the middle, add to it the diameter of the two extremities, divide the amount by four, multiply the quotient by the diameter of the length, the product gives the area. Ardha chandricay is the crescent moon; for this add the chord [chaupam] to the greatest width of crescent, multiply the amount by the same width, half the product is the area. Chunk [q.v.] is the conch figure; for this deduct half the amount of the short diameter from the long diameter, square the remainder; do the same with half of the short diameter, and add the two products together; multiply the amount by three; divide this product by four; the quotient is the area. Locoony [q.v.] is a piece of ground in the middle of a field, and for some reason to be deducted from the whole; if these be quadrilaterals, measure them according to the rules already given, and deduct them from the field in which they are comprised; the same rule applies to the velicoony or piece of ground lying on one or more sides, and to be deducted.—"*b*" The following is a common table in teloogoo country for beeja pramaunam or seed measure showing the amount ordinarily taken by one pootty [q.v.] or $7\frac{1}{2}$ acres of land, and the produce thence ordinarily arising:—

Name of crop.	Quantity of seed.	Produce.
Sugar-cane	19 Candies.	1000 Mds. of sugar.
Common chilly	4 Coonchams.	30 Candies.
Telinga potato	7 Candies.	70 ,,
Country saffron	9 ,,	90 ,,
Sweet potato	9 ,,	80 ,,
Paddy	60 Coonchams.	30 ,,
Cholum	3 ,,	25 ,,
Raggy	5 ,,	20 ,,
Gingelly	5 ,,	15 ,,
Indian cotton	12 ,,	30 ,,
Shaumay	5 ,,	15 ,,
Bajrah	5 ,,	20 ,,
Green gram, black	12 ,,	10 ,,
Black gram	10 ,,	10 ,,
Green gram	12 ,,	6 ,,
Country bean	10 ,,	5 ,,
Aumanac	10 ,,	8 ,,
Bengal gram	10 ,,	6 ,,
Madras horse gram	12 ,,	8 ,,
Guar	10 ,,	5 ,,

—"*c*" The following are the number of plants generally found on one pootty or $7\frac{1}{2}$ acres of land:—tobacco [pogauk], 1,200; cocoanut [q.v.], 400; mango [q.v.], 200 [ganitam, shastram].

CSHITY (क्षिति - kshiti, *San.*). From (kshi, san. to dwell). Earth [bhoomy].——*Cshitijam* (क्षितिज - kshitija, San.; افق - ufak, Hind.). From (above + jan, san. to be born). Horizon. The sensible horizon is a plane conceived to touch the earth at the point where the observer is situated, and meeting the celestial sphere [golam] in a circle; but when the observer is elevated above the earth's surface, the limit of his view is the visible or apparent horizon; and the angle between the visible and sensible horizons is the dip. A great circle of the sphere passing through the centre of the earth, and parallel with the sensible horizon, is the rational horizon. To the horizon circle, which is the only apparent one, almost all the celestial motions are referred; it is the common termination of day and night; and it marks out the times of the rising and setting of the sun and stars [jyotisham].

CUBBALDROOG (ಕಬ್ಬಾಳದುರ್ಗ - kabbáladurga, *Can.*). Hill-fort in Malvully talook, Mysore district. Formerly used as a penal settlement under Hindoo and Mussalman dynasties on account of its pestilential climate; now uninhabited.

CUBBANY (ಕಬ್ಬನಿ - kabbani, *Can.*; കബ്ബനി - kabbani, *Mal.*) From sanscrit. Sanscrit name (kapiní), meaning ape river; also (kapilá), meaning reddish brown river. River. Tributary of Cauvery. Rises in W. ghauts [q.v.] and flowing easterly through Mysore district falls into Cauvery near Narsapore. The confluence is of great sanctity. Two tributaries feed it from south, the Noogoor and Goondal. It is perennial, averaging from 150 to 200 yards in width. It and tributaries drain nearly whole of N. and S. wynaud, but beds being rocky and shallow no traffic beyond floating timber.

CUDDALORE (گولور - gúlúr, *Hind.*; கூடலூர் - kúdalúr, *Tam.*). From (kúdal, tam. junction + úr, tam. village); junction of the paravanaur and the guddilam. Also called Tegnapatam. Mahomedan name (islámábád), meaning safety + city. The European fort is Fort St. David.——(1) Talook, South arcot district. Tahsildar's pay Rs. 225; area 448 square miles; pop. 337,303. Language Tamul. E. coast of district. Boundaries:—north, French territory and Villoopooram talook; east, Bay of Bengal; south, Chidambaram talook; west, Vriddhauchellam and Tricalore talooks. Physical aspect generally flat. There are sandy ridges on the sea coast and high lands of laterite [q.v.] formation from Capper hill westward. Soils, black clay, black loamy, black sandy, red loamy, red sandy, and arenaceous loamy and arenaceous sandy [munn]. Weaving [nesavoo], indigo [q.v.] and ground-nut [q.v.] trade are principal industries. Irrigation by Ponniaur, Guddilam, river channels, and Permaul tank. Camping ground, Vadacott on the Madras-Combaconam trunk road. Includes the mittahs of Alaginuttam, Chennappanaickenpolliem, and Nadooveeraputt. Places of archæological interest:—Cuddalore, Fort St. David, Manantavilandapoottoor, Panrooty, Teertanagary, Tircanteshwaram,

Tirmauncooly, Tirpapooliyore, Tirvendipooram, Trivetty, Tyaugavully, Vengadampett, Yeydanore. Principal Trig. stations :—Guddenguddy, Keelmaumputt, Morandicooppam, Ramapooram, Tirmauncooly, Vengadampett, Vullum. The leading places, &c., in the talook are the following.——*Alaginuttam* (அழகிநத்தம் - azhaginattam, Tam.). From (azhagi, tam. handsome woman, epithet of a village goddess + nattam, tam. village). Mittah ; pop. 423 ; acres 1,285 ; lat. 11° 48′ ; long. 79° 44′ ; from Cuddalore N.W. 7 miles ; from the sea W. 7 miles. Peshcush Rs. 2,103.——*Capper hill* (கேப்பார்மலை - képparmalai, Tam.). See sep. title.——*Chennappa naicken polliem* (சென்னப்பநாயக்கன்பாளையம் - shennappanáyakkanbálaiyam, Tam.). From (shennappanáyakkan, tam. proper name + pálaiyam, tam. fortified village). Mittah ; acres 4,568 ; lat. 11° 44′ ; long. 79° 40′; from Cuddalore W. 9¾ miles ; from the sea W. 11 miles. Weaving industry and cloth manufacture. Peshcush Rs. 3,991.——*Coodicaud* (குடிக்காடு - kudikkádu, Tam.). From (kudi, tam. inhabitant + kádu, tam. forest). Village ; acres 1,547 ; lat. 11° 41′ ; long. 79° 48′ ; from Cuddalore S.S.W. 2½ miles ; from the sea W. 1 mile. Salt factory.——*Coorinjipaudy* (குறிஞ்சிப்பாடி - kuriñjippádi, Tam. kurinjipádi *). From (kuriñji, tam. coorinjah tree, tylophora asthmatica, w. & a. + pádi, tam. village). Town ; pop. 4,597 ; acres 1,733 ; lat. 11° 33′ ; long. 79° 38′ ; from Cuddalore S.W. 16 miles ; from the sea W. 12 miles. Weaving industry and weekly market.——*Cuddalore* (கூடலூர் - kúdalúr, Tam.). See below.——*Fort. St. David* (தேவனாம்பட்டணம் - tévanámbattanam, Tam.). See sep. title.——*Guddenguddy* (கட்டங்குடி - kattangudı, Tam.). From (gadda, can. bank + kudi, tam. village). Trig. station ; lat. 11° 40′ 07·35″ ; long. 79° 44′ 14·45″ ; from Cuddalore S.W. 6¼ miles ; from Ramapooram S. 1½ miles ; from the sea W. 5 miles.——*Guddilam* (கடிலம் - kadilam, Tam.). See sep. title.——*Keelmaumputt* (கீழ்மாம்பட்டு - kízhmámbattu, Tam.). From (kízh, tam. east + mámbattu, tam. the village). Trig. station ; lat. 11° 42′ 23·23″ ; long. 79° 38′ 7·82″ ; height 290 feet ; from Cuddalore W. 12 miles ; from Poothoopolliem W. 12 miles ; from the sea W. 13 miles.——*Malattaur* (மலட்டாறு - malattáru, Tam.). See sep. title.——*Morandicooppam* (மொழாண்டிக்குப்பம் - mózhándikkuppam, Tam.). From (mózhándi, tam. proper name + kuppam, tam. village). Trig. station ; lat. 11° 40′ 16·15″ ; long. 79° 37′ 22·74″ ; height 335 feet ; from Cuddalore W.S.W. 13 miles ; from Alagappasamoodram S. ½ mile ; from the sea W. 13 miles.——*Munjacooppam* (மஞ்சக்குப்பம் - mañjakkuppam, Tam.). See sep. title.——*Nadooveeraputt* (நடுவீரப்பட்டு - naduvírappattu, Tam.). From (nadu, tam. middle + víran, tam. proper name + pattu, tam. village). Mittah [q.v.] village ; pop. 4,878 ; lat. 11° 43′ ; long. 79° 40′ ; from Cuddalore W. 10¼ miles ; from the sea W. 11 miles. Includes Chennappanaickenpolliem, one of old farms granted to Company in 1762 as jagheer [q.v.] by the Nawaub of Carnatic [q.v.].——*Nellicooppam* (நெல்லிக்குப்பம் - nellikkuppam, Tam. nellikuppam*). From (nelli, tam. emblic myrobalan tree, phyllanthus emblica, linn. + kuppam, tam. village). Railway station, Mussalman place of pilgrimage ; pop. 1,112 ; acres 370 ; lat. 11° 46′ ; long. 79° 43′ ; height 48 feet ; from Cuddalore W.N.W. 7½ miles ; from the sea W. 8 miles. Has a European sugar [q.v.] factory and a distillery of country arrack [q.v.].——*Panrooty* (பண்ருட்டி - panrotti, Tam.). See sep. title.——*Paravanaur* (பரவனாறு - paravanáru, Tam.). See sep. title.——*Parvatipooram* (பார்வதிப்புரம் - párvathippuram, Tam.). From (párvatí, san. the mountain deity so called + pura, san. town). Sanscrit name (uttarañánachidambara), meaning future + wisdom + the town so called. Place of pilgrimage ; pop. 1,021 ; acres 2,505 ; lat. 11° 33″ ; long. 79° 35″ ; from Cuddalore S.W. 20 miles ; from the sea W. 15 miles.——*Ponniaur* (பெண்ணையாறு - pennaiyáru, Tam.). See sep. title.——*Poothoopolliem* (புதுப்பாளையம் - puthuppálaiyam, Tam.). From (puthu, tam. new + pálaiyam, tam. fortified village). Lat. 11° 45 ; long. 79° 48′ ; from Cuddalore N.N.W. 2½ miles ; from the sea W. 1¾ miles. Suburb of Cuddalore.——*Ramapooram* (இராமாப்புரம் - irámáppuram, Tam.). From (ráma, san. proper name + pura, san. town). Trig. station ; lat. 11° 42′ 47·50″ ; long. 79° 45′ 24·74″; height 183 feet ; from Cuddalore W. 3¾ miles ; from Ramapooram N.E. 2 miles ; from the sea W. 4¾ miles.——*Random shot* (குண்டுக்கிராமம் - kundukkirámam, Tam.). See sep. title.——*Singarcoil* (சிங்கர்க்கோவில் - shingarkkóvil, Tam.). From (shingam, tam. the lion + kóvil, tam. temple) ; temple of vishnoo, the lion-man god. Place of pilgrimage ; pop. 824 ; acres 353 ; lat. 11° 52″ ; long. 79° 50″ ; from Cuddalore N. 10 miles ; from the sea W. 2¼ miles.——*Toortanagary* (தீர்த்தனகரி - tírttanagari, Tam.). From (tírt'ha, san. place of sacred waters + nagarí, san. city). Village, Place of pilgrimage ; pop. 1,392 ; acres 1,504 ; lat. 11° 34′ ; long. 79° 43′ ; from Cuddalore S.S.W. 12 miles ; from the sea W. 5½ miles. Old Shiva temple with inscriptions.——*Tirmauncooly* (திருமாணிக்குழி - tirumánikkuzhi, Tam.). From (tiru, tam. holy + máni, tam. phallic emblem + kuzhi, tam. pit). Tam. also (mânikkuzhi), meaning same. Village ; pop. 1,302 ; acres 1,048 ; lat. 11° 44′ ; long. 79° 44′ ; from Cuddalore W.N.W. 6½ miles ; from the sea W. 7 miles. Hamlet of Tirvendipooram. Very ancient Shiva temple elaborately sculptured with inscriptions. Trig. station ; lat. 11° 44′ 7·76″ ; long. 79° 43′ 56·34″ ; height 192 feet ; from Cuddalore W.N.W. 5½ miles ; from Tirmauncooly E. ½ mile ; from the sea W. 6½ miles.——*Tirpapooliyore* (திருப்பாப்புலியூர் - tiruppáppuliyúr, Tam.). From (tiru, tam. holy + páthiri, tam. the trumpet-flower tree, stereospermum chelonoides, dec. + puli, tam. tiger + úr, tam. village). There is still an old pauthiry [q.v.] tree known as stala vricsham in the shiva temple. Tam. also (páthirippuliyúr), meaning same ; also (tiruppáppúr), by corruption ; also (páthirikkuppam), meaning same ; distinguished from (kuppam), short for munjacooppam. Sanscrit name (pátalapura), meaning trumpet-flower tree + town. Village, Place of pilgrimage and Railway station ; acres 1,308 ; lat. 11° 45′ ; long. 79° 47′ ; height 19 feet ; from Cuddalore N.W. 3 miles ; from the sea W. 3 miles.——*Tirvendipooram* (திருவேந்திப்புரம் - tiruvéndippuram, Tam. tiruvendipuram *). From (tiru, tam. sacred + véndan, tam. king + pura, san. town). Sanscrit name (ahíndrapura), means serpent + king + town. Village, Place of pilgrimage ; pop. 2,784 ; acres 1,499 ; lat. 11° 45′ ; long. 79° 45′ ; from Cuddalore W.N.W. 4½ miles ; from the sea W. 5½ miles. One of the villages of the old Tirvendipooram farm granted 1750 by Nawaub Mahomed ally as jagheer [q.v.] to Company. Firmaun [q.v.], from Moghul confirming the grant by way of inam [q.v.], 12th August 1765. Old Vishnoo temple with inscriptions.——*Trivetty* (திருவதி - tiruvathi, Tam.). See sep. title.——*Tyaugavully* (தியாகவல்லி - tiyágavalli, Tam.). From (tiyágan, tam. shiva, the giver + valli, tam. shepherd village). Village, Place of pilgrimage ; pop. 1,392 ; acres 3,610 ; lat. 11° 37′ ; long. 79° 47′ ; from Cuddalore S.S.W. 6¾ miles ; from the sea W. 1½ miles. Ancient Shiva temple buried in sand.——*Veerapermanullore* (வீரப்பெருமாநல்லூர் - vírapperumánallúr, Tam.). From (virapperumán, tam. proper name + nalla, tam. good + úr, tam. village). Village ; pop. 3,641 ; acres 2,249 ; lat. 11° 47′ ; long. 79° 29′ ; from Cuddalore W.N.W. 23 miles ; from the sea W. 24 miles.——*Vellaur* (வெள்ளாறு - velláru, Tam.). See sep. title.——*Veloodaiyanputt* (வேலுடையான்பட்டு - véludaiyánbattu, Tam.). From (vél, tam. spear + udaiyán, tam. possessor + pattu, tam. village). Soobramanyan's village. Place of pilgrimage ; pop. 1,495 ; acres 2,822 ; lat. 11° 36′; long. 79° 34′ ; from Cuddalore W.S.W. 19 miles ; from the sea W. 17 miles.——*Vengadampett* (வெங்கடாம்பேட்டை - vengadámbéttai, Tam.). From (vengadan, tam. name + péttai, tam. suburb). Trig. station ; lat. 11° 36′ 55·01″ ; long. 79° 38′ 37·18″ ; height 218 feet ; from Cuddalore S.W. 14 miles ; from Vaigacollay S.S.E. 1¾ miles ; from the sea W. 10 miles.——*Vullam* (வல்லம் - vallam, Tam.). From (val, tam. hillock). Trig. station ; lat. 11° 39′ 22·58″ ; long. 79° 33′ 40·60″ ; height 317 feet ; from Cuddalore W.S.W. 17 miles ; from Nadoocooppam S.S.E. 1¼ miles ; from the sea W. 18 miles.——**(2)** Town, Head-quarters of district and talook, Railway station ; South arcot dist., Cuddalore tal. ; pop. 47,355 ; acres 2,827 ; lat. 11° 43′ ; long. 79° 49′ ; height 19 feet ; from Chidambaram N.N.E. 23 miles ; from Madras S.S.W. 99 miles ; from Pondicherry S.S.W. 16 miles ; from Porto novo N. 16 miles ; from Tindivanam S.S.E. 36 miles ; from Tricalore E.S.E. 41 miles ; from Vriddhauchellam E.N.E. 33 miles. On the backwater connecting the Guddilam and Paravanaur, close to sea. The municipality embraces the Old town or Cuddalore proper, Fort St. David, Bandipolliem, Devanamputnam, Munjacooppam, Poothoopolliem, Tirpapooliyore, and nine smaller villages. The residences and offices of the Collector and Judge are in Munjacooppam, which with Fort St. David constitutes European quarter. The river mouths having silted up, only native craft can come up to the town ; but good anchorage in 6 to 8 fathoms can be obtained in the roads 1½ miles from shore. Light on cross-trees of flagstaff ; lat. 11° 43′ 0″ ; long. 79° 46′ 15″ ; red, fixed, 5 miles ; visible from all directions seaward ; a guide to the anchorage. In 1682, the Company opened negotiations with the Khan of Jinjee to settle here. The first building was erected in 1683, and in the following year a formal lease was obtained for the site of the present port and the old fortress. During the next ten years trade increased so rapidly that the Company erected Fort St. David and rebuilt their warehouses. In 1702 the whole of the fortifications were rebuilt. On the fall of Madras in 1746, the British administration withdrew to Cuddalore, which was soon afterwards twice unsuccessfully besieged by the French under Dupleix. In the same year Commodore Barnet, commanding the English squadron, died at Cuddalore. In 1749 the Jesuits were expelled from the settlement as spies in the French service. In 1752 the head-quarters of the Presidency were removed from here to Madras. In 1755, Lord Clive was in command at Cuddalore. In 1758 the French occupied the town and stormed and destroyed the fort. In 1760, after the battle of Wandiwash, it was retaken by a British detachment. In 1782 it again fell into the hands of the French and their ally Tippoo sultan, by whom the fortifications were sufficiently renewed to enable it to withstand in the following year a siege and several assaults. During the siege a drawn battle was fought in the roadstead between the French and English fleets. On the 1st February 1785 Cuddalore was formally restored to the British under the treaty of Versailles, and in 1801 included in the cession of the Carnatic [q.v.]. A street in Cuddalore is called after Clive. At Munjacooppam is the old garden house built in 1738 where the Governors and Deputy governors of Fort St. David formerly had their residence; now occupied by the Collector. Cuddalore carries on a large inland trade with Madras in indigo, oils and sugar, which are manufactured locally; and it exports by sea great quantities of grain. Laterite [q.v.] for making roads is quarried in the neighbourhood. The following are the travelling distances by road from Cuddalore to different places:—

To	Viâ	Miles and Furlongs.	
Arnee	Villoopooram, Jinjee and Chetput ...	83	6
Bangalore	Trinomallee and Oossoor	188	7
Bellary	Ranipett, Chittore, Pooriganore and Cadiry.	352	2
Caricaul	Chidambaram, Shiyally and Tranquebar.	67	6
Chidambaram ...	Poothoochuttram	25	4
Chingleput	Pondicherry and Tindivanam ...	79	1
Chittore	Pondicherry, Tindivanam, Wandiwash and Ranipett.	125	1½
Chittore	Villoopooram, Jinjee, Arnee and Vellore.	129	2
Chittore	Trinomallee and Vellore	137	6
Coimbatore	Salem, Bhawauny and Avanashy ...	220	4
Combaconam ...	Chidambaram, Shiyally and Mayavaram.	73	2
Cuddapah	Ranipett and Chittore	226	4½
Cuddapah	Pondicherry, Chingleput and Madras.	280	4
Dindigul	Trichinopoly	172	3
Jinjee	Villoopooram	52	1
Madras	Pondicherry, Tindivanam and Chingleput.	114	0
Madura	Combaconam, Tanjore and Tripatore.	199	0
Madura	Trichinopoly	192	3½
Mayavaram ...	Chidambaram and Shiyally	51	2
Negapatam ...	Chidambaram, Shiyally, Tranquebar and Caricaul.	80	4
Nellore	Pondicherry, Chingleput and Madras.	221	6
Oossoor	Trinomallee and Royacottah ...	156	0
Palamcottah ..	Combaconam, Tanjore and Madura.	294	6
Palamcottah ...	Negapatam and Ramnaud	316	5
Point calimere ...	Chidambaram, Shiyally, Tranquebar and Negapatam.	118	1
Point calimere ...	Mayavaram and Tritrapoondy ...	119	5
Pondicherry ...	......	11	7
Ramnaud	Negapatam and Tondy	222	4
Ranipett	Wandiwash	95	0
St. Thomas' mount.	Pondicherry, Chingleput and Pullavaram.	105	4
Salem	Vriddhauchellam and Talavausal ...	119	1
Salem	Ooloondoorpett and Talavausal ...	120	0
Shiyally	Chidambaram	38	1
Talavausal ...	Vriddhauchellam	77	6
Talavausal ...	Ooloondoorpett	77	5
Tanjore	Chidambaram and Combaconam ...	96	6
Tindivanam ...	Pondicherry	38	0
Tranquebar... ...	Chidambaram and Shiyally	58	2
Trichinopoly ...	Vriddhauchellam and Volcondapooram.	111	3½
Trichinopoly ...	Chidambaram, Shiyally, Combaconam and the Anicut.	125	6
Trinomallee ...	Manaloorpett	64	5
Vellore	Pondicherry, Wandiwash and Ranipett.	112	3
Vellore	Villoopooram, Jinjee and Arnee ...	107	2
Vellore	Manaloorpett and Trinomallee ...	115	6
Villoopooram ...	......	29	5
Vriddhauchellam ...	......	38	0
Wandiwash... ...	Pondicherry and Tindivanam ...	56	4

CUDDAPAH* (కడప - kadapa, *Tel.*). Means threshold. Sanscrit name (kripánagara), meaning cripay, proper name + town. Hind. name (neknámábád), meaning necnamkhan + town. Greek καρίγη.——**(1)** Revenue district; situated inland; between 13° 26′ and 15° 14′ N. lat., and between 77° 54′ and 79° 31′ E. long.; bounded N. by Kurnool district, E. by Nellore district, S. by North arcot district and Mysore state, W. by Mysore state and Anantapore district; square miles 8,722; pop. 1,272,072; language Teloogoo. Contains rivers Cheyair, Chitrauvaty, Coondair, Paupughny, Pennair, and Saglair. Mountains, Eastern ghauts [q.v.], Palcondah hills and Sheshachellam hills. The whole area of the district is represented by the following sub-areas:—Budwail talook, Cadiry talook, Cuddapah talook, Jummalmudoogoo talook, Madanapully talook, Poolivendla talook, Poollampett talook, Proddootore talook, Royachoty talook, Sidhout talook, and Voilpaud talook. For general administrative purposes the district is distributed between the following revenue and magisterial officers, who have their head-quarters at the places shown. The pay set opposite the subordinate officers gives the grade of the corresponding charge:—Collector, Cuddapah; Sub-collector, Madanapully, in charge of Cadiry, Madanapully, Royachoty and Voilpaud talooks; Head assistant collector, Cuddapah, in charge of Proddootore, Jummalmudoogoo and Poolivendla talooks; General deputy collector, Sidhout, in charge of Budwail, Sidhout and Poollampett talooks; General charge deputy collector, Cuddapah, in charge of Cuddapah talook. Tahsildars, Budwail, Rs. 150; Cadiry, Rs. 175; Cuddapah, Rs. 225; Jummalmudoogoo, Rs. 200; Madanapully, Rs. 175; Poolivendla, Rs. 175; Poollampett, Rs. 200; Proddootore, Rs. 175; Royachoty, Rs. 175; Sidhout, Rs. 150 and Voilpaud, Rs. 175. Deputy tahsildars, Camalaupooram, Rs. 70, range situated in the north and west of Cuddapah talook; Chitwail, Rs. 70, range situated in the east of the Poollampett talook; and Peelair, Rs. 70, range situated in the east of the Voilpaud talook. Sub-magistrate, Cuddapah, Rs. 100, jurisdiction extending over Cuddapah town. Similarly judicial officers:—Judge, Cuddapah; District moonsifs, Cuddapah with jurisdiction extending over the whole of Cuddapah talook and 58 villages of Poolivendla talook and 62 villages of Royachoty talook; Proddootore with jurisdiction extending Proddootore, Jummalmudoogoo, Budwail and the remaining half of Poolivendla; Nundalore with jurisdiction extending Sidhout and Poollampet talooks; Madanapully with jurisdiction extending Madanapully, Cadiry, Voilpaud talooks and the remaining half of Royachoty talooks. Similarly Public works officers:—Executive engineer, Cuddapah, Budwail, Sidhout, and Jummalmudoogoo. Contains Registration subdistricts, Budwail, Cadiry, Chitwail, Cuddapah, Jummalmudoogoo, Madanapully, Peelair, Poolivendla, Poollampett, Proddootore, Royachoty, Sidhout, Voilpaud. Contains Forest ranges, Budwail, Cadiry, Codoor, Cuddapah, Madanapully, Proddootore, Rajampett, Royachoty, Sidhout, Voilpaud. Contains one Municipality, Cuddapah. Contains District board; and Talook boards, Proddootore embracing Proddootore and Jummalmudoogoo, talooks, Poolivendla embracing Poolivendla talook, Sidhout embracing Sidhout and Budwail talooks, Poollampett embracing Poollampett talook, Cuddapah embracing Cuddapah talook, Cadiry embracing Royachoty and Cadiry talooks, Madanapully embracing Madanapully and Voilpaud talooks. The following general references should be made to the preceding volumes:—general geography, I (1) to (29); general ethnology, I (29) to (109); general history, I (110) to (188); physical geography, II, 1; meteorology, II, 3; geology, II, 8; fauna, II, 21; flora, II, 26; mineralogy, II, 29. The following references in the preceding volumes will furnish details special to the district:—latitudes and longitudes, II, 47; particulars about towns, II, 48; comparative population, II, 172; location of revenue officers, II, 382; revenue settlement of the district, II, 409; registrar's and sub-registrar's stations, II, 420; rain-guage stations, II, 428; police divisions, II, 431; maps published, II, 436; survey topographical lists, II, 443; hospitals and dispensaries, II, 447; missionary stations, II, 455; head-quarter stations of gazetted officers, II, 461; incidence of taxation, II, 463; weights and measures of the district, II, 510. A special gazetteer account of the whole district is given at II, 74. For the detailed topography of the district, reference should be made to the talook notices in the present volume, viz.:—Budwail, Cadiry, Cuddapah, Jummalmudoogoo, Madanapully, Poolivendla, Poollampett, Proddootore, Royachoty, Sidhout, Voilpaud.——**(2)** Talook, Cuddapah district. Tahsildar's pay Rs. 225. Area 764 square miles. Population 137,520. Language Teloogoo. Centre of district. Lies along either bank of Pennair. Bounded south and east by Palcondahs, north partly by Lunkamalas and partly by artificial boundaries from Proddootore and Budwail talooks, west by artificial limits alone from Poolivendla talook. Includes the old division of Jummalmudoogoo and Proddootore talooks, Chennore and Camalaupooram. The Cuddapah valley is a basin completely shut in by hills on three sides, the Lunkamala and Sheshachellam ranges spreading from the eastern confines of the talook along its northern and south-eastern boundaries respectively. These hill ranges are both covered with large timber. The talook lies beyond the limit of the black cotton soil [regar] which overspreads the western talooks of the district. The prevailing soil is alluvial, overlying to no great depth beds of argillaceous slates [cullpalagay]. The soil is not generally good, and is often rendered worthless by profusion of saltpetre [shorah], common salt [ooppoo], and soda [sowdoo], which all occur in efflorescence. The well-known diamond [vajram] sandstone is a feature of interest. This formation is the diamond-yielding quartzites, or altered sandstones [manal cull]. These beds occur very generally in the Ceded districts [q.v.], and at Bunganapully in Kurnool district and are systematically mined for diamonds. The Cuddapah mines however are only shallow pits, dug in the débris and gravel at the foot of the hill range above Canoopurty and Chennore. The local beds of kankar [q.v.] are of extreme usefulness. Rice [paddy] and indigo [q.v.] are alternately grown under tanks. Cuddapah indigo has obtained a reputation as the best in S. india, and commands in the home markets about eight annas per pound more than Madras indigo. It is extracted from the plant steeped when green. Cholum [q.v.] is the staple dry grain [q.v.], and cotton [q.v.] is also widely grown. Cuddapah melons [common melon] deserve notice; they are cultivated in the river beds in March and April. The bulk of indigo and cotton is purchased by resident merchants and brokers; but some also is sent to Madras. Grain is but little exported; supplies, especially of wheat [geung], &c., are drawn largely from the sub-division of the district. Most of the large towns are engaged wholly in trade of agricultural produce, especially indigo. Chief industry is weaving of coarse cloths. The Pennair traverses the talook from west to east, and receives within its limits the Coondair from the north near Camalaupooram, the Paupughny from the south below the same town, and the Boggair with several confluents due north of Cuddapah town. Irrigation consists of river channels [q.v.], spring channels, Cuddapah-kurnool irrigation canal, tanks and wells. Places of archæological interest:—Animela, Booggalpulley, Camalaupooram, Chennore, Chintacommadinney, Chintalaputtore, Cocatam, Codoor, Commaddy, Coppole, Cuddapah, Hanoomangootty, Indoocore,

Nundimundalam, Ooppalore, Ooratore, Ootcore, Pandillapully, Pauchikelapaud, Paulgherry, Pedda cheppully, Peddanapaud, Pooshpagherry, Potladoorty, Pydicaulwa, Sadipiraula, Sambatore, Sankatipulley, Shiddhareddy bhaucarapett, Shivaulapulley, Talpanore, Tappotla, Vedoorore, Veldoorty, Vulloor, Yellatore, Yerragoodipaud. The leading places, &c., in the talook are the following.——*Accauyapully* (అక్కాయపల్లి - akkáyapalli, Tel.). From (akkayya, tel. proper name + palli, tel. village). Village; pop. 1,040; acres 278; lat. 14° 29′; long. 78° 52′; from Cuddapah south ½ a mile.——*Animela* (అనిమెల - animela, Tel.). From (ani, tel. battle + ila, tel. ground). Village; pop. 2,845; acres 9,453; lat. 14° 28′; long. 78° 33′; from Cuddapah W. 20¾ miles. Temple of Sangameshwaran on high ground at the junction of the Mogamoorair and the Paupughny. Never completed. Four other old temples.——*Booggawunka* (బుగ్గవంక - buggavanka, Tel.). See sep. title.——*Camalaupocram* (కమలాపురము - kamalápuramu, Tel.). See sep. title.——*Cauzypett* (قاضی پیٹھ - kázípeth, Hind.; కాజీపేట - kájípéta, Tel. kázipet *). From (kází, ar. proper name + péta, tel. suburb). Village; pop. 1,833; lat. 14° 39′; long. 78° 49′; from Cuddapah N.N.W. 12 miles.——*Chennore* (చెన్నూరు - chennúru, Tel.). From (chennu, tel. beautiful + úru, tel. village). Village; pop. 4,279; acres 4,448; lat. 14° 34′; long. 78° 51′; from Cuddapah N. 5¾ miles. On Pennair, on route from Cuddapah to Hyderabad. Ferry station. Old temples. Large stretch of wet cultivation under Kurnool-cuddapah canal. Noted for melons.——*Chintacommadinney* (చింతకొమ్మదిన్నె - chintakommadinne, Tel.). From (chinta, tel. tamarind tree, tamarindus indica, linn. + komma, tel. branch + dinne, tel. mound). Village; pop. 3,084; acres 14,977; lat. 14° 26′; long. 78° 50′; from Cuddapah S.W. 4¼ miles. In the hamlet of Cottapettah a grand festival of goddess Gungammah.——*Commaddy* (కొమ్మద్ది - kommaddi, Tel.). From (komma, tel. branch + maddi, tel. terminalia arjuna, bedd.). Village; pop. 2,027; acres 8,599; lat. 14° 33′; long. 78° 29′; from Cuddapah W. 26 miles. Old stone fort.——*Coondair* (కుందేరు - kundéru, Tel.). See sep. title.——*Cotlore* (కొట్లూరు - kotlúru, Tel.). From (kottu, tel. store house + úru, tel. village). Village; pop. 2,148; acres 6,725; lat. 14° 37′; long. 78° 47′; from Cuddapah N.N.W. 10 miles.——*Cuddapah* (కడప - kadapa, Tel.). See below.——*Krishnapooram* (కృష్ణాపురము - krishnápuramu, Tel.). From (krishna, san. the god + pura, san. town). Village, Railway station, Canal terminus; pop. 231; acres 158; lat. 14° 29′; long. 78° 49′; height 435 feet; from Cuddapah W.N.W. 2¾ miles.——*Lunkamala* (లంకమల - lankamala, Tel.). See sep. title.——*Naugapootla* (నాగపుట్ల - nágaputtala, Tel.). From (nága, san. snake + putta, tel. ant hill). Ghaut [q.v.]. In the Palcondah hills [palcondah].——*Ooppalore* (ఉప్పలూరు - uppulúru, Tel.). From (uppalamu, tel. salt marsh + úru, tel. village). Village; pop. 1,777; acres 9,379; lat. 14° 36′; long. 78° 26′; from Cuddapah W.N.W. 30 miles. Former residence of a poligar [q.v.]. Three temples.——*Palcondah* (పాలకొండ - pálakonda, Tel.). See sep. title.——*Paulgherry* (పాలగిరి - pálagiri, Tel.). From (pálu, tel. milk + giri, san. mountain). Village; pop. 4,567; acres 13,916; lat. 14° 28′; long. 78° 29′; from Cuddapah W. 25 miles. Two old temples. Vijianugger inscriptions.——*Paupughny* (పాపఘ్ని - pápaghni, Tel.). See sep. title.——*Pauta cuddapah* (పాతకడప - pátakadapa, Tel.). From (páta, tel. old + kadapa, tel. the town). Village; pop. 1,969; acres 1,826; lat. 14° 30′; long. 78° 52′; from Cuddapah N.E. 1½ miles. Large agricultural suburb of Cuddapah.——*Pedda cheppully* (పెద్దచెప్పల్లి - peddacheppalli, Tel.). From (pedda, tel. large + chennu, tel. beautiful + palli, tel. village). Village; pop. 2,068; acres 2,135; lat. 14° 33′; long. 78° 40′; from Cuddapah W.N.W. 13½ miles. Near the Paupughny. Vishnoo temple. Watered by spring channels [q.v.].——*Pennair* (పెన్నేరు - pennéru, Tel.). See sep. title.——*Pooshpagherry* (పుష్పగిరి - pushpagiri, Tel.). From (pushpa, san. flower + giri, san. mountain). Village, Hill; lat. 14° 36′; long. 78° 48′; height 756 feet; from Cuddapah N.N.W. 8¾ miles. Hamlet of Cotlore. On the Pennair about two miles from the anicut newly constructed by the Irrigation and Canal company. Of great sanctity. Pagoda [q.v.] on a hill. Festival towards the end of April lasting eight days. Pilgrims bathe in the river and walk round the hill, six or seven miles in circumference.——*Puttoor* (పత్తూరు - pattúru, Tel.). From (patti, tel. cotton + úru, tel. village). Village; pop. 2,773; acres 15,109; lat. 14° 39′; long. 78° 49′; from Cuddapah N.N.W. 11½ miles. Old temple of Indranautasawmy. Two other temples. Chola kings built six shrines and a mantapam [q.v.] south of the temple of Gadaudhara sawmy.——*Soorya comauroola canama* (సూర్యకుమారులకనమ - súryakumárulakanama, Tel.). From (súrya, san. the sun + kumára, san. son + kanama, tel. pass); from a local ruler. Ghaut [q.v.] in the Palcondah hills.——*Vulloor* (వల్లూరు - vallúru, Tel.). From (val, tam. hillock + úru, tel. village). Village; pop. 3,189; acres 3,631; lat. 14° 34′; long. 78° 46′; from Cuddapah N.W. 9¼ miles. On the Bellary road. Large number of mosques [musjid] and temples and old fort. Noted for paddy [q.v.].——*Wonootlacona* (వానూతలకోన - vónútalakóna, Tel.). From (vána, tel. rain + núyi, tel. spring + kóna, tel. ravine). Village, Place of pilgrimage; lat. 14° 26′; long. 78° 40′; from Cuddapah W.S.W. 13½ miles. Remarkable on account of its spring and the temple dedicated to Narsimhasawmy in the hamlet of Chinna dausaripully.——*Yerragoodipaud* (ఎఱ్ఱగుడిపాడు - erragudipádu, Tel.). From (erra, tel. red + gudi, tel. temple + pádu, tel. village). Village; pop. 1,171; acres 3,223; lat. 14° 37′; long. 78° 39′; from Cuddapah W.N.W. 17 miles. Vijianugger inscription.——*Yerragoontla* (ఎఱ్ఱగుంట్ల - erraguntla, Tel.). From (erra, tel. red + gunta, tel. pond). Village, Railway station; pop. 1,362; acres 3,379; lat. 14° 38′; long. 78° 35′; height 547 feet; from Cuddapah N.W. 22 miles. Station for Proddootore. Former residence of a poligar. Good lime-stone [choonam cull] quarry.——**(3)** Deputy tahsildarry, Cuddapah district. Pay Rs. 100.——**(4)** Town, Municipality, Collector's, Judge's, Divisional and talook head-quarters, Railway station; Cuddapah dist., Cuddapah tal.; pop. 17,379; acres 1,075; lat. 14° 29′; long. 78° 52′; height 454 feet; from Madanapully N.N.E. 68 miles; from Madras N.W. 137 miles; from Sidhout W. 10 miles. On north bank of Boggair in the Pennair valley, six miles south of latter river. Being enclosed on three sides by bare sandstone hills, it is one of the hottest towns in the district, the mean temperature in the shade from March to July being 79° F. The native town is unhealthily situated and squalidly built. Place of importance under Vijianugger its immediate rulers being the chiefs of Chitwail. Fort improved towards the close of the sixteenth century by Necnam khan who accompanied Meer joomla, vizier [q.v.] of the Mahomedan king of Golcondah, in his expedition into the Balaghaut [q.v.] and Carnatic [q.v.]. Necnam khan was left in charge of the Chennore talook, and annexed the lands and fortresses of Budwail, Cumbum, Gundicote, Jummalmudoogoo and Sidhout, which were under poligars tributary to the Vijianugger rajahs. He built the present city on the site of the encampment of Meer joomla's army. It was at first called Necnamabad, but subsequently took that of the ancient Hindoo village adjoining, viz., Karipah coil. Compare vernacular at head. The town was taken by Mahomed coolee cootb shah of Golcondah in A.D. 1589, who broke the idol of the great temple and sacked the city. Afterwards ruled by Afghaun nobles under the Adil shahy and Cootb shahy [q.v.] sovereigns of Beejapore and Golcondah. It was not till the beginning of the eighteenth century, when the Nawaub of Cuddapah had absorbed the whole of the Balaghaut except Gooty, and had extended his conquests to the Baramahaul [q.v.] that Cuddapah appeared as the capital of a separate kingdom. In 1817 made the head-quarters of the district and in 1821 a military cantonment. The cantonment was abolished in 1868. Four mosques [musjid] about 300 years old. Parts of the Nawaub's palace have been utilized as a treasury and jail. Two large tanks near the town. Large temple of Vencateshwarasawmy, the Tripatty deity, in the suburb. Hindoos from the country north of Cuddapah make a point of visiting the Devoony cuddapah temples or Vencateshwaran's lower temples, before proceeding to the Tripatty temple or Vencateshwaran's upper temple. The railway was opened in 1868. Trade consists chiefly in the export of indigo and cotton. Principal industry is weaving of coarse cloth. The following are the travelling distances by road from Cuddapah to different places :—

To	Viâ	Miles	Furlongs
Bangalore ...	Goolcheroo ghaut, Royachoty, Madanapully and Hoscote.	156	4
Bellary ...	Yaumavaram and Gooty	152	1
Berhampore ...	Guntoor, Rajahmundry, Chicacole and Ichapore.	602	4
Bezwada ...	Cumbum and Guntoor	229	3½
Budwail ...	Vattimadoogoo	35	0
Budwail ...	Sidhout	31	5
Cannanore ...	Royachoty, Bangalore, Seringapatam and Perambaudy.	355	3
Chagulmurry ...	Doovvoor	38	2
Chetterpore ...	Cumbum, Bezwada and Chicacole ...	616	7
Chicacole	Guntoor, Ellore and Rajahmundry ...	503	2½
Chingleput ...	Chittore, Ranipett and Wallajahbad ...	181	7½
Chittore	Goolcheroo ghaut, Royachoty, Peelair and Daumalcheroo ghaut.	101	3
Cocanada	Cumbum, Guntoor and Rajahmundry.	361	5½
Cuddalore ...	Chittore and Ranipett	266	4¼
Cumbum	Budwail	96	4
Cuttack	Guntoor, Ellore, Chicacole and Berhampore.	719	1
Daumalcheroo ...	Royachoty, Peelair and Daumalcheroo pass.	80	6
Dharwar	Gooty, Bellary and Humpasaugar ...	302	4
Ellore	Cumbum, Guntoor and Bezwada ...	156	6¼
French Rocks ...	Royachoty, Madanapully, Bangalore and Chennaputna.	233	5
Goorramcondah.	Goolcheroo ghaut and Royachoty ...	56	2
Gooty	Yaumavaram	97	7
Guntoor	Cumbum and Vinoocondah	209	3
Hyderabad residency.	Nundiaul, Kurnool and Jedcherla ...	254	1
Kamptee ...	Kurnool, Secunderabad and Nirmal ...	576	5
Kircambaudy ...	......	82	2
Kurnool ...	Doovvoor and Nundiaul	123	0
Madanapully ...	Royachoty	75	5
Madras	Nundalore, Kircambaudy, Nagary and Poonamallee.	166	4
Madras	Royachoty, Chittore, Arcot and Shreepermatore.	202	1½

To		Viâ	Miles and Furlongs.	
Mangalore	...	Royachoty, Bangalore, Chenroyputna and Manjarabad.	377	4
Mangalore	...	Royachoty, Bangalore, Seringapatam and Mercara.	399	0
Masulipatam	...	Cumbum, Guntoor and Bezwada ...	161	4
Masulipatam	...	Cumbum and Guntoor	145	5½
Mercara ...	...	Royachoty, Bangalore, and Seringapatam.	313	2
Nagary ...	...	Nundalore and Kircambaudy	107	7
Nellore ...	...	Budwail, the Dornaul pass and Ooppalapaud.	107	7
Nellore ...	...	Sidhout and Budwail	104	4
Nundiaul	...	Chagulmurry...	78	0
Ongole ...	...	Budwail and Cumbum	165	1½
Ootacamund	...	Royachoty, Poonganore, Bangalore, Seringapatam and Seegore.	328	7
Peelair ...	...	Goolcheroo pass and Royachoty	66	2½
Pondicherry	...	Chittore and Ranipett	214	5½
Poonamallee	...	Nundalore, Kircambaudy and Nagary.	152	0
Poonamallee	...	Royachoty, Chittore, Arcot and Shreepermatore.	189	5½
Pooongancre	...	Goolcheroo ghaut, Royachoty and Goorramcondah.	89	5
Rajahmundry	...	Guntoor and Ellore	323	5½
Ranipett ...	...	Royachoty and Chittore	131	4½
Royachoty	...	Goolcheroo ghaut	32	3
Secunderabad	...	Nundiaul, Kurnool and Jedcherla ...	258	7
Seringapatam	...	Royachoty, Bangalore and Maddore ...	235	7
Tadpatry	...	Yaumavaram	65	2
Vellore ...	...	Royachoty, Peelair, Daumalcheroo Pass and Chittore.	123	3
Vizagapatam	...	Guntoor, Ellore, Rajahmundry and Cassimcote.	446	5½
Vizianagaram	...	Guntoor, Ellore, Rajahmundry and Soobaraum.	470	0½

CUFNEE (كفنى - kafní, *Hind.*). From (kafan, ar. a shroud). Hind. also (alfá). Cloth about fifteen feet long, and a yard wide; in the centre of its breadth a slit is made through which the head is passed, where a collar is sewed on; one-third of the cloth hangs behind reaching down to the calf of the leg, and two-thirds before; the superfluous quantity in front is tucked up by means of the cummerbund [q.v.], which at the same time forms a sort of bag to receive the contributions of the charitable [sheelay].——*Cufnee choory* (كفنى چڑيا - kafníchiryá, Hind.; كفنى چڑى - kafníchuri, Dec.; ಕೊಗ್ಗರನೆಹಕ್ಕಿ - koggaranehakki, Can.). Title from deccany. Hind. from (kafní, hind. fakeers' coat + churí, hind. bird); from sitting posture as if dressed in a fakeer's coat. Can. from (koggara, can. stooping + hakki, can. bird). Trogonidæ family, fissirostres, insessores, aves [pacshy, 6], of naturalists [jantoo]. The species best known is Harpactes fasciatus, alias Trogon malabaricus. Note like the mewing of a cat [poonay].

CULL (शिला - shilá, *San.*; शील - shíla, *Mahr.*; حجر - hajar, *Ar.*; سنگ - sang, *Pers.*; پتهر - patthar, *Hind.*; پهتر - phattar, *Dec.*; بتو - batu, *Malay*; ಕಲ್ಲು - kallu, *Can.*; ಕಲ್ಲು - kallu, *Too.*; రాయి - ráyi, *Tel.*; കല്ല് - kallu, *Mal.*; ගල - gala, *Singh.*; கல் - kal, *Tam.*). San. from (shi, san. to sharpen). Mahr. from sanscrit. Ar. from (hajara, ar. to resist). Hind. from (prastara, san. flat surface). Stone.——(1) The stones now in general use for building and for decorative and domestic purposes are granite [caroom cull], marble [shalavay cull], basalt [caroom palingoo cull], hornblende [shalavay cull], augite, laterite [q.v.], sandstone [manal cull], and steatite [sowcaura cull]. The modes of quarrying are various, by fire, wedges, and gunpowder. Stratified rocks generally split in the direction of the strata; so that the surface of separation show only the surfaces of the seam. But in the laminæ of the Balaghaut [q.v.] gneiss the case is different; on the surfaces of the laminæ are seen the strata, and their seams along the surface of the split, and therefore its direction is at an angle with that of the seams themselves. The natives have availed themselves of the peculiarity this gneiss has of splitting in a direction opposite to that of the strata, to obtain laminæ of any thickness. On the convex surface of the gneiss they light a fire, the intensity of which is proportionate to the thickness of the slab to be obtained; and after having kept it up for a certain length of time they extinguish it, and pour cold water on the heated surface of the rock. This sudden refrigeration producing an instantaneous contraction of the heated portion of the rock, extending as deep as the heat had penetrated, it is detached at that depth from the parent rock, and the laminæ are easily removed, and cut in as many pieces as required. The curvature of these laminæ being the segment of a very large circle, in the small dimensions they are generally cut they appear nearly straight, and are used for all architectural purposes, as columns, door-posts, steps, &c. Another and very different method is used to split granite, porphyry [dhoomra cull], green stone [putchay cull], or other unstratified rocks. This consists in making several square perforations, little more than an inch deep, with a hammer and a steel punch, in the rock, in a line and in the direction it is to be split. This done, the workmen put wedges in the holes, and strike on them with force, until the granite breaks. Blasting by gunpowder is much more modern than either of the above. The size of some of the stones in the ancient temples is very remarkable. The gateway of Shreerungam near Trichinopoly is built of single blocks of granite, each upwards of 40 feet in length; and at Humpy there are stones weighing from 20 to 30 tons, which have been raised to the height of at least 15 or 20 feet. The principles employed were probably the inclined plane, the lever, and manual labor. The word cull is a suffix in place names, as Namcull, meaning mark + rock; Goontacull, meaning quarry + stone; Varacull, meaning stripe + rock. Also prefix in place names, as in Cullore, meaning stone + village.——(2) The following general classification of lithology is adopted in this work:—*Igneous rocks.*—Granitic group or Granite, syenite, &c.; Trappean group or Trap, green stone, &c.; Volcanic group or Basalt, lava, &c.—*Aqueous rocks.*—Sand group or Sand stone, conglomerate, &c.; Clay group or Clay, shale, &c. Lime group or Limestone, &c.—*Metamorphic rocks.*—Sub-crystalline family—Arenaceous group or Quartzite, &c.; Argillaceous group or Clayslate, &c.; Calcareous group or Altered limestone, &c.; Crystalline family—Quartzose group or Quartz rock, gneiss, &c.; Argillaceous group or Schists, &c.; Calcareous group or Crystalline limestone, &c.——(3) Igneous rocks are such as are believed to have undergone fusion. For purposes of this work, these are divided into granitic, trappean, and volcanic.—*Granitic group.*—This group embraces those irregularly crystallized rocks which consist of some proportion of the minerals, quartz, felspar, mica, and hornblende. First, granite [caroom cull], which typically is a ternary compound of quartz, felspar, and mica. Second, syenite; also a ternary rock of quartz, felspar, and hornblende. And lastly, varieties of these, in which one or other of the constituent minerals is replaced by others allied to them, such as epidote, tourmaline [q.v.], talc, or chlorite. There is not however always this ternary aggregation of the minerals. One or other may be absent when the rock becomes a binary form, as binary granite, &c. While the crystalline arrangement of the different minerals may be such that a descriptive term is necessary to distinguish the rock, as in the case of graphic granite when the minerals are arranged after the manner of a written character, or porphyritic syenite, &c., when one or more constituents are scattered in crystals or crystalline masses at intervals throughout a more uniform mass or paste of the other minerals. The granitic rocks are also distinguished as being rich in silica or quartz, both free and in combination.—*Trappean group.*—This includes those rocks which come under the general term Trap [padicutt cull]. The traps are generally compact granular crystalline aggregates of the minerals felspar and hornblende, and according to the preponderance of one mineral over the other, may be divided into felspathic traps, i.e., felsites or felstones and hornblendic traps, i.e., green stone, diorite, &c.; while there are intermediate varieties according to the arrangement of the minerals, or the introduction of some other constituent, or allied mineral. With some developments of trap are often found associated a set of rocks which must have been the mechanical accompaniments of the igneous action at the time, or the ejected dust and ashes, &c.; and these come under the general term Trappean ash. The term trappean is adopted to include such rocks as are intermediate between those of the granitic and volcanic groups.—*Volcanic group.*—The Lavas and their accompanying Volcanic ash come under this head; as do all the other igneous rocks which are made up of augite and felspar. With the preponderance of either of these are the two divisions of Trachytes and Dolerite respectively; and there are intermediate varieties.——(4) Aqueous rocks are deposited by water, in contradistinction to igneous rocks, the formation of which has been due to heat. For purposes of this work, these are divided into clay, lime, and sand—*Clay group.*—This includes the Clays and Shales, or those rocks which show a plastic tendency, and which contain alumina in their constitution, thus possessing a soapy feel to the touch.—*Lime group.*—This includes such rocks as are made up of lime, or mainly of that mineral. The terms sandstone and conglomerate are applied when the rock is made up of finely comminated particles, or pebbles, &c., of limestone; so that the names Calcareous sand stone, and Limestone conglomerate or Conglomeratic limestone are met with. Limestones have been formed mechanically, chemically, or organically; but always in water as a general rule, and they are therefore aqueous rocks.—*Sand group.*—This includes such rocks as are made up of siliceous sand; either extremely coarse with large pebbles and gravel, when there is a conglomerate or pudding stone; or containing angular fragments of rock, forming what is called a breccia; or altogether made up of coarse or large-grained and angular sand, when the rock is termed a grit; or consisting of ordinary sand, fine or coarse, when there is a sand stone [manal cull].——(5) Metamorphic rocks are those which have undergone a change of structure and become crystalline. The term is especially applied to sedimentary formations, which, through the agency of heat or chemical action, have acquired crystalline structure. For purposes of this work, they are divided into the sub-crystalline family, arenaceous, argillaceous, and calcareous, and the crystalline family, quartzose and argillaceous.—*Sub-crystalline family. Arenaceous group.*—This includes such rocks as have belonged to the sand group of the aqueous division; but which have since been metamorphosed and now go by the general name quartzite.—*Argillaceous group.*—This includes such rocks as are supposed to have belonged to the clayey group of the aqueous division; and which come under the general term Slate [cull palagay].—*Calcareous group.*—This includes such rocks as have been ordinary limestone ; and which may come under the general term Sub-crystalline Limestone, or Altered limestone in contradistinction to the true crystalline limestone of the crystalline family of metamorphic rocks.—*Crystalline family. Quartzose group.*—This includes such rocks as are mainly made up of the mineral quartz and which appear to have been originally Sand stones, or, at any rate, members of that group ; as also rocks which are of a more variable constitution, though still showing the original siliceous elements, these last coming under the general term Gneiss.—*Argillaceous group.*—This includes such metamorphic rocks as are supposed to have been originally Clays, or Clay-slates, with their varieties and which come under the general term Schist.——**(6)** Common compound.—"*a*" Plant first term often joining two genera. Sometimes from habitat on rocky ground, sometimes from hardness of fruit, wood, &c., though this often happens from former. Ex., where transl. is of second term :—Alangium lamarckii (kallumávu), mangifera indica ; Bauhinia tomentosa (kallattimara), ficus glomerata ; Canna indica (kalvázhai), musa paradisiaca ; Sebastiana chamælea (kallámanakku), ricinus communis ; Smilax ovalifolia (kaltámara), nelumbium speciosum ; Solanum verbascifolium (kallatti), ficus glomerata ; Thespesia populnea (kallál), ficus bengalensis. See gloss. paragraphs.—"*b*" Fish first term, generally from living in rocky river beds. Ex., where transl. is of second term :—Discognathus lamta (karguravai), ophiocephalus genus ; Eleotris butis (kallára), polynemus indicus ; Homaloptera brucei (kargendai), barbus genus ; Mastacembelus armatus (kalláral), rhynchobdella aculeata ; Minous monodactylus (karbiláççai), ostracion genus. See gloss. paragraphs.—"*c*" Mammal first term. From habitat. Ex., where transl. is of second term :—Leggada platythrix (kallelaka), mus genus.——**(7)** The following are terms with Cull prefixed.——*Cullada* (കല്ലട - kallata, Mal.). From (above + ata, mal. block). Mal. also (kannétti), meaning eye + beauty. Greek νελκύνδα ; the point being βακάρη.—"*a*" Village ; Travancore state, Quilon division, Quilon and Coonnatore tals. ; lat. 9° 02′ ; long. 76° 44′ ; from Coonnatore S. 2½ miles ; from Quilon N.E. 10 miles ; from Trivandrum N.N.W. 41 miles ; from the sea E. 11 miles. The Cannetty of the Keraleputty. It is divided into Eastern cullada or Kizhakk cullada, and Western cullada or Padinyaur cullada ; the former is in Coonnatore talook and has a population of 6,622, and the latter is in Quilon talook and has a population of 4,498. Nelkunda is mentioned by various authors under varying forms of the name. It is Melkunda in Ptolemy, who places it in the country of the Aii. In the Peutingerian table it is Nincylda, and in the Geographer of Ravenna, Nilcinna. At the mouth of the river on which it stands was its shipping port βακάρη now represented by Markary lat. 12° N. The Periplus mentions exports and imports only at the two ports of Baragaza and Nelcynda. Fine muslins and ordinary cottons are the principal commodities of the first ; tortoise-shell [zabl], precious stones [ratnam], silk [puttoo], and pepper [q.v.] of the second ; the pepper was brought from Cottonara [cadatnaud].—"*b*" River ; Travancore state, Quilon division, Putnapooram, Coonnatore and Quilon tals. Formed principally by union of five large streams issuing from ghauts [q.v.], but swelled by numerous others as it proceeds westward. Its branches as they pass through the more hilly parts descend by a succession of cataracts, of which Meenmooty is the most remarkable. The banks till it reaches Cullada village rise boldly from its stream, which flows over a sandy bed, whose varying breadth in some places expands to nearly three hundred yards. The course is generally north-west and it terminates in the Ashtamoody estuary near Quilon by several mouths. Length, 70 miles. Putnapooram, Mahanuddy, and Coonnatore are towns on its bank. Not much used for cultivation. Navigable for about 25 miles from the coast, but difficult. During rains, boats can ascend to Putnapooram. The large tributary streams that flow into the Cullada transport the timber cut on their banks.——*Cullanay* (கல்லணை - kallanai, Tam.). From (above + anai, tam. bund). Another name for Rama's bridge [adam's bridge].——*Cullcary* (جھوٹا کوئلہ - jhútá-koelá, Hind. ; ارانگ تنا - arángtanah, Malay ; సీమబొగ్గు - símaboggu, Tel. ; കൽക്കരി - kalkari, Mal. ; கற்கரி - kargari, Tam.). Title from tamul. Hind. from (jhútá, hind. false + koelá, hind. coal). Malay from (aráng, malay, charcoal + tanah, malay, earth). Tel. from (síma, tel. foreign + boggu, tel. charcoal). Mal. from tamul, Tam. from (kal, tam. stone + kari, tam. charcoal). Anthracite. Otherwise Blind coal, Glance coal. An aqueous rock. Coal [nilakary] deprived of most of its volatile ingredients, and consisting almost wholly of carbon [kary], with a shining surface, burning without flame. See vol. II, 32.——*Cullcootaca* (ಕಲ್ಲುಕುಟುಕ - kallukutuka, Can.). From (kuttu, can. to strike). Stone-cutters in Canara. Speak mahratta and canarese. They assert that they are descendants of vishwa carman ; belong to the punchaulas [q.v.]. Dark, middle-sized and strong [cull tutcha].——*Cullhutty* (ಕಲ್ಹಟ್ಟಿ - kalhatti, * Can.). From (above + hatti, can. village). Village ; Neilgherry dist., Todanaud division ; lat. 11° 29′ ; long. 76° 42′ ; from Ootacamund N.N.W. 5½ miles. On the Seegore ghaut, three miles below its head. Halting place. The bungalow commands a fine view of the waterfall. Oranges [q.v.], apples [seb], peaches [shaft auloo], and pears [amrood] thrive. Near Cullhutty was an ancient fort called Mullaycotey or hill fort said to have been possessed by the Wodeya of Oommatore, a feudatory to the empire of Vijianugger but who on the decline of that kingdom became independent. The Oommatore chief was in 1613 subdued by the Mysore ruler, Rajah wodeyar, and his dominions then became part of Mysore kingdom. There are still living near Mullaycotey beydar or huntsmen, whose ancestors were in the service of the Oommatore chief as tax-gatherers. The falls at Cullhutty, 170 feet high, are picturesque. Also a river, a continuation of the stream running out of the Ootacamund lake ; before it reaches Seegore it is joined by another small stream from Marlemund. Also a Coffee [q.v.] estate, Todanaud, Neilgherries, just below the Travellers' bungalow ; 110 acres. Another just below the waterfalls ; 64 acres. Fruit estate, north of the Cullhutty stream and close to the waterfalls ; 6 acres. Cullhutty mullay is an estate, Moonanaud amshom, S.E. wynaud from Pundalore N. 1 mile ; 175 acres [aroovy].——*Cullicote* (కల్లికోట - kallikóta, Tel. kallikót *). From (above + kóta, tel. fort). Ancient zemindarry, Village ; Ganjam dist., Ganjam tal., Deputy tahsildars' range ; pop. 62,066 ; square miles 213 ; lat. 19° 28′ N. to 19° 49′ N. ; long. 84° 57′ to 85° 14′ E. ; lat. of village 19° 36′ ; long. 85° 08′ ; from Chetterpore N.N.E. 18 miles ; from Russellcondah E.S.E. 38 miles. On the northern boundary of the Presidency, adjoining Banpur country in Orissa. The family founded by one Rama boya. Poorshottama gajapaty deo, King of Orissa, confirmed him as zemindar of the talook in A.D. 1374. At a later period the zemindar kept Mahrattas out of the district and obtained title of Mardaraja deo. Occupied by British troops in 1769, and again from 1771 to 1775. The adjoining talook of Atagadah was bought in 1854 and now forms part of estate. Soil very fertile. Stretching along western shore of Chilka lake, possesses great natural advantages. The zemindar's residence is 15 miles from Rambha, in a basin surrounded and almost touched by adjacent hills. Peshcush Rs. 18,975. Revenue Rs. 19,000.——*Cullnaur* (शंखपलिता - shankhapalitá, Mahr. ; حجر کتان - hajarikatán, Ar. ; پنبهٔ کوهی - pambahikohí, Pers. ; پتھر کا نار - pattharkánár, Hind. ; ಕಲ್ನಾರು - kaláru, Can. ; ಕಲ್ನಾರು - kalnáru, Too. ; రాతినార - rátinára, Tel. ; கல்நார் - kalnár, Tam.). Title from tamul. Ar. from (hajar, ar. stone + katán, ar. flax). Pers. from (pambah, pers. cotton + koh, pers. mountain). Hind. from (patthar, hind. stone + nár, hind. fibre). Can. from (kallu, can. stone + náru, can. fibre). Tel. from (ráyi, tel. stone + nára, tel. fibre). Tam. from (kal, tam. stone + nár, tam. fibre). Asbestos. Otherwise Amianthus, Earth flax, Mountain flax. An igneous rock. Magnesian fossil found in Mysore, &c. ; its texture is delicately fibrous, its color flaxen, and its fibres flexible. The ligniform asbestos in external appearance resembles wood, its fibres are somewhat rigid, and its color is a dusky brown. Has the quality of resisting fire ; the silky filaments, when mixed with oil, may be woven into a fire-proof cloth.——*Cullore* (కల్లూరు - kallúru, Tel.). From (above + úru, tel. village).—"*a*" Village, Polliem ; North arcot dist., Chundragherry tal. ; pop. 265 ; acres 23,028 ; lat. 13° 33′ ; long. 79° 02′ ; from Chittore N.N.W. 24 miles ; from Chundragherry W. 22 miles. Peshcush Rs. 4,060. Site of the source of the Daumalcheroo.—"*b*" Pass ; North arcot dist., Chundragherry tal. In Eastern ghauts [q.v.], leading from lowland talooks to those above ghauts [q.v.]. It runs along the Daumalcheroo valley and through the Cullore polliem to the Cuddapah district. Along it passes the trunk road between Madras and Cuddapah.——*Cull palagay* (ಕಲ್ಲಿನಹಲಿಗೆ - kallinahalige, Can. ; రాతిపలక - rátipalaka, Tel. ; കല്പലക - kalpalaka, Mal. ; கற்பலகை - karbalagai, Tam.). Means stone + slab. Slate. A fissile non-crystalline argillaceous rock, the planes of separation in which are not due to bedding, but to cleavage. The term is popularly applied to hardened shales, which are bedded, not cleaved ; and to schists, which are crystalline.——*Cullpauty* (കല്പാത്തി - kalpátti, Mal.). From (above + pátti, mal. trough) ; from rocky bed of the river.—"*a*" Village ; Malabar dist., Palghaut tal. ; lat. 10° 47′ ; long. 76° 41′ ; from Calicut E.S.E. 66 miles ; from Palghaut N. 2 miles. The most important of the nineteen separate settlements or Graumams of the Bramin community called Puttar who belong to this talook. Forms part of Palghaut municipality.—"*b*" River ; Malabar dist., Palghaut tal. The most important of the rivers intersecting the talook. Locally called Nelanuddy. Takes its source at Chentaumaracoolam in hills north of Walayaur. Unites with Cunnaudy river near Parly railway station, and with Colangode river a little further on.——*Cull poo* (రాతిపువ్వు - rátipuvvu, Tel. ; கற்பூ - karbú, Tam.). Means flower stone. Any fossil or organic remains, animal or vegetable, imbedded in rocks.——*Cullroyamullay* (கல்ராயன்மலை - kalráyanmalai, * Tam.). From (kalráyan, tam. name of a local poligar + malai, tam. mountain). Range of hills ; S. arcot, Salem dists., Ahtoor tal. ; pop. 6,038 ; lat. 11° 38 to 12° 04′ N. ; long. 78° 32′ to 78° 52′ E. ; from Ahtoor N. 4 miles ; from Salem E. 21 miles. The principal part of the group is in Ahtoor talook. East of the Tennaunday mullays and separated from them by the Cottapputty pass. Inhabited principally by Malayaulies. The range has no general name among the natives, but every principal division bears a different appellation. The extreme southern and south-west part is known as the Periya or Great cullroyen ; this is the loftiest part of the range. The low western part is known as Chinna or Little cullroyen. The north-east end has the name Coorumbagownda mullay. The hills are divided into the five poliputs of Aryagownden, Chinna cullroyen, Coorumbagownden, Jadaygownden, and Periya cullroyen. These again are sub-divided into nauds. Periya cullroyen jagheer contains Keelnaud, about 20 square miles, in which are the Codicullaur, Sholaiyaur, Varattaur, Vellapaurayaur, and Vellaur rivers; the principal peaks are Aviyaraumanmullay, Chinna tripattymullay and Deetchagirymullay. Aryagownden jagheer contains the Sholaiyaur and Vellapaurayaur rivers and Vadakmullay and Yairimullay peaks. Chinna cullroyen jagheer contains the Periyaur and Vellaur rivers and the Condacullmullay, Deetchagirymullay, and Tencullmullay peaks. Periya cullroyen jagheer contains the Oppooraur river and the Aviyaraumanmullay peak. The hills were formerly held by petty native chiefs, who recklessly denuded the slopes. Cary raman pagoda on the Periya cullroyens is held in high esteem by the Malayanlies, and strangers are required to uncover their feet on approaching it.——*Culltutcha* (கற்சச்சன் - kattaççan, Tam.). From (taççan, tam. artisan). Tamul stone cutters [cullcootaca].——*Cull vetty bazaar* (കൽവെട്ടിബജാർ - kalvettibajár, Mal.). From (kalvetti, mal. stone cutter + bázár, hind. bazaar). Village; Cochin state, Cochin tal.; lat. 9° 57′; long. 76° 17′; from Ernacolum S.W. 3 miles; from the sea E. ½ mile. Chief native quarter of Cochin, mostly Moplahs. Narrowly escaped destruction by fire on New year's day 1876, and again on 4th January 1889. The canal of this name is about six miles long. Starting from Cullvetty it joins the river at Cullancherry. Owing to silting, through navigation is possible only during monsoons.——*Cull wodda* (ಕಲ್ಲೊಡ್ಡ - kallodda, Can.). From (odda, can. the caste). Stonemason woddas [q.v.].——**(8)** The following are the different kinds of Cull.——*Caroom cull* (నల్లరాయి - nallaráyi, Tel.; കരിങ്കല്ല് - karinkallu, Mal.; கருங்கல் - karungal, Tam.). Vernacular means black stone. The only general term for granitic rocks, though these are often light-colored and variegated. Granite, the first of the igneous rocks rich in silica composed of felspar quartz, and mica. The felspar almost always orthoclase; a second felspar, usually oligoclase, being frequently present also. In some forms of granite the mica absent; then it becomes aplite or pegmatite. Granite is one of the most common rocks in S. india, and is met with both in strata and unstratified. The best granite quarries are at Bangalore, Sadras, Cuddapah, Vizagapatam and Bellary. The prices vary in different localities, according to the cost of labor and the hardness of the stone. There is a variety of green stone [putchay cull] resembling the white stone of Scotland which is much used for building and ornamental purposes in Madras; it occurs in many parts here and is known as fire stone or grey granite. It is hard and durable, but more expensive than true granite from the greater labor of quarrying and cutting the blocks. Ornamental granites of bright colors occur in several localities. Those of Salem, Chittore and Seringapatam are flesh-colored, red, green, yellow and grey. Those of Arcot and Goodoovancherry are pure white. The Bellary and Bangalore syenites are red, grey, and white with the colors blended in about equal proportions. Some of the pale-grey granites and pegmatites or binary granites of Southern india contain a large proportion of felspar which leads to their decay. The carvings at Conjeeveram, Sadras and Chidambaram have lost their sharpness from this cause; while, on the other hand, those at Tadpatry, Vontimittah, Hirey toombal, and other places in the Ceded districts [q.v.], are nearly as sharp as when first executed. In a few temples and Mahomedan tombs, the most richly cut pillars and ornaments are hewn out of basalt, augite, or basaltic hornblende. The best specimens of this kind of carving are at Vellore, Seerah, Tinnevelly, Humpy, Adony and Anagherry. The carvings have often a polished surface resembling black marble, or hornblende [shalavay cull], but they are so hard as to strike fire with steel. Many of the temples of Southern india are constructed of granite. Its preservation, and the sharpness of its carvings testify to its great durability; and the age of these buildings is constantly under-estimated. In addition to the general use of this material for building and religious sculptures, the natives occasionally make domestic articles of it, such as round millstones, pestles and mortars, door-posts, lintels, &c. For gneiss which passes by insensible gradations into granite, natives have no separate term.——*Caroom palingoo cull* (கரும்பளிங்குக்கல் - karumbalingukkal, Tam.). From (karum, tam. black + palingu, tam. crystal + kal, tam. rock). Tam. also (mégavarnakkal), meaning cloud + color + stone. Basalt, a volcanic rock. Composed of augite and labradorite, often with olivine in disseminated grains. The term is chiefly applied to the hard, black, crystalline form of dolerite, and especially to that variety of the rock which exhibits prismatic structure.——*Caureeya cull* (నల్లసీసము - nallasísamu, Tel.; காரீயக்கல் - káríyakkal, Tam.). Means black lead stone. Graphite. A form of carbon [kary], occurring pure or mixed with more or less iron oxide, in crystalline rocks. See vol. II, 32.——*Cavvy cull* (కావిరాయి - káviráyi, Tel.; காவிக்கல் - kávikkal, Tam.). Means red ochre stone. Red chalk. A mineral dye. The essential ingredient is peroxide of iron [auhan], whether as an anhydrous red hæmatite or the hydrated brown and yellow limonites [cauvy, sheemay choonam].——*Choonam cull* (சுண்ணாம்புக்கல் - shunnámbukkal, Tam.). Limestone [kankar, shookkaun cull].——*Coolancull* (سنگریزه - sangrezah, Pers. and Hind.; పలుకురాయి - palukuráyi, Tel.; கூழாங்கல் - kúzhángal, Tam.). Title and Tam. from (góla, san. sphere + kal, tam. stone). Hind. from (sang, pers. stone + rezah, pers. fragment). Tel. from (paluku, tel. piece + ráyi, tel. stone). Shingle. Loose pebbles, especially those on the sea-shore.——*Coorvindacull* (కురువిందరాయి - kuruvindaráyi, Tel.; குருவிந்தக்கல் - kuruvindakkal, Tam.). From (kuruvinda, san. emery). Grey flint. An aqueous rock. A grey, heavy, and nearly pure silicious fossil usually found in nodules, particularly in Salem district. It is collected and pounded by stone-cutters, who with it in conjunction with seed lac [q.v.] and by means of heat, prepare an aggregate, hard grindstone, with which they cut into regular shapes many valuable stones, less hard than the grey flint itself, such as copals, cornelians, jaspers, agates, &c. Other stones of a harder nature, such as the diamond, ruby, emerald and sapphire can only be cut by the diamond [corundum, ratnam].——*Dhoomra cull* (தூமிரக்கல் - túmirakkal, Tam.). From (dhúmra, san. dark red). Porphyry. An igneous rock composed of a compact finely crystalline mass, in which large crystals of felspar are imbedded. A porphyritic granite, syenite, green stone, &c., is a rock in which the felspar is in large distinct crystals.——*Manal cull* (ಉಸುವುಕಲ್ಲು - usuvukallu, Can.; ఇసుకరాయి - isukaráyi, Tel.; மணற்கல் - manargal, Tam.). Sand stone, a rock composed of sand cemented together. An aqueous rock. Near Tadda and Podily in Nellore there are beds of white sand stone of superior working quality, and a valuable building material. At Shreepermatore and at Vriddhauchellam there are immense beds of another kind, used by natives for rice mills and grindstones. At Sadras there is one of the finest quarries in the Presidency; the grindstones made from which are equal to those imported from England. At Panuambauray in Tinnevelly district there is a sort of bath stone valuable for building. The Godavery anicut [q.v.] is built of a sharp grained sand stone of a bluish color and variable in hardness and durability; exposure hardens the surface of this stone probably from the lime [choonam] which it contains. The Kistna anicut is built of a coarser description of sand stone blended with gneiss and containing grey quartz and garnets of a light pinkish color, but not valuable. This rock occurs in large inclined strata lying loosely upon each other, it is easily quarried, and is a handsome building material, but being very brittle, it is not susceptible of a finely chiseled surface. The specific gravity of this stone is 157 lb. per cubic foot.——*Mauvayira cull* (மாவயிரக்கல் - mávayirakkal, Tam.). From (má, tam. flour + vayiram, tam hardness). Felspar. A group of minerals, one or the other species being a principal constituent of almost all igneous rocks. Orthoclase, albite, oligoclase, and labradorite are felspars; all consist of double silicates of alumina and one or more alkalies [cauram] or alkaline earths [sowdoo], and crystallize in the oblique or anorthic system.——*Ooray cull* (कष - kasha, San.; محک - mihakk, Ar.; معیار - miyár, Pers.; کسوٹی - kasotí, Hind.; بتوجی - batuuji, Malay; ಒರೆಗಲ್ಲು - oregallu, Can.; ಒರೆಕಲ್ಲು - orekallu, Too.; ఒరగల్లు - oragallu, Tel.; ഉരക്കല്ല് - urakkallu, Mal.; உரைகல் - uraigal, Tam.). San. from (kash, san. to rub). Ar. from (hakka, ar. to rub). Pers. from (ár, ar. to measure). Hind. from sanscrit. Malay from (batu, malay, stone + uji, malay, to assay). Tel. from (orayu, tel. to rub + kallu, tel. stone). Tam. from (urai, tam. to rub + kal, tam. stone). Touch stone. Lat. lapis lydius. A silicious fossil black, smooth, and somewhat glossy. Introduced into S. india from the more northern and western tracts of India. Used by gold and silversmiths for ascertaining the purity and exact color of metals [loham]; the stone is first well rubbed with the metal to be tried, it is then pressed against a dark-colored wax [mom], and on this it leaves a small portion of the metal from which the whole is judged.——*Padicutt cull* (మెట్టునాప - mettunápa, Tel.; படிக்கட்டுக்கல் - padikkattukkal, Tam.). Means step stone. The German trap, which also means stair; a name originally applied to tabular green stone and basaltic rocks, from their frequently occurring in hills with step-like terraces on the sides; subsequently used for all igneous rocks not distinctly granitic.——*Palingoo cull* (स्फटिक - sp'hatika, San.; بلور - billaur, Hind.; స్ఫటికపురాయి - sp'hatikapuráyi, Tel.; பளிங்குக்கல் - palingukkal, Tam.). San. from (sp'hat, san. to split). Crystal. A mineral [dhautoo] or salt [ooppoo] having regular polyhedral structure. All crystalline forms known are divided into six systems:—the cubical or isometric; the pyramidal, dimetric, or tetragonal; the prismatic, trimetric, or orthorhombic; the hexagonal or rhombohedral; the moneclinic or oblique; and the triclinic or anorthic [vencull].——*Parookkay cull* (గులకరాయి - gulakaráyi, Tel.; பருக்கைக்கல் - parukkaikkal, Tam.). Gravel. Loose pebbles, with or without sand.——*Paroomanal cull* (பருமணற்கல் - parumanargal, Tam.). From (paru, tam. big + manal, tam. sand + kal, tam. stone). Grit. A sand stone in which the grains of quartz are angular.——*Putchay cull* (ಪಚ್ಚೆಕಲ್ಲು - paççekallu, Can.; పచ్చరాయి - pattsaráyi, Tel.; பச்சைக்கல் - paççaikkal, Tam.). Green stone. A general name for igneous rocks, composed principally of felspar and hornblende. Certain plutonic rocks containing augite are also called green stones.——*Sarpaunga cull* (పాముకన్నెరాయి - pámuvanneráyi, Tel.; சருப்பாங்கக்கல் - sharuppángakkal, Tam.). The mottled appearance of rock resembling serpent's skin [coosam]. Serpentine. A mineral, usually of a greenish color, consisting of hydrous silicate of magnesia. Or a rock composed of the mineral in a more or less pure state. See vol. II, 39.——*Shalavay cull* (مرمر - marmar, Hind.; తలవరాయి - tsalavaráyi, Tel.; சலவைக்கல் - shalavaikkal, Tam.). Dravidian means cold stone. Any stone which when polished feels specially cold to the touch; generally applied to marble, that is to say to the finer and more crystalline forms of limestone [choonam cull] capable of being polished. Black marble and black and white marble exist in the Ceded districts [q.v.]; a greenish kind veined with black exists in the Bababooden [q.v.] mountains in the Western ghauts [q.v.]; and a grey and dirty white sort, variegated with black and coarse grained on the surface exists in the Tinnevelly district. At present the manufacture in the article is insignificant and confined to small miscellaneous articles for domestic use. The term is also applied to hornblende, a silicate of various bases, usually lime [choonam], magnesia or iron [auhan], or combinations of these with each other, part of the silica being often replaced by alumina; the crystallization is oblique; hornblende is an important constituent of many igneous rocks, such as syenite, diorite, &c.; hornblende is formed into images [shilay] and ornaments for public buildings.——*Shaunay cull* (शाण - shána, San.; سلی کا پتھر - sillíkápatthar, Hind.; సానరాయి - sánaráyi, Tel.; ചാണ - chána, Mal.; சாணைக்கல் - shánaikkal, Tam.). Hone, whetstone [tripatty cull].——*Shemboo tee cull* (செம்புத்தீக்கல் - shembuttíkkal, Tam.). From (shembu, tam. copper + tí, tam. fire + kal, tam. stone). Copper pyrites. Sulphide of copper [taumram] and iron [auhan], containing, when pure, 34·6 per cent. of copper, crystallizing in the pyramidal or tetragonal system.——*Shencull* (செங்கல் - shengal, Tam.). Means red stone. Brick. See Shengal.——*Shory cull* (బొంతరాయి - bontaráyi, Tel.; சொறிக்கல் - shorikkal, Tam.). Tel. from (bonda, tel. fissure + ráyi, tel. stone) [vettoocull]. Tam. from (shori, tam. rough + kal, tam. stone). Laterite [q.v.].——*Sookkaun cull* (సున్నపురాయి - sunnapuráyi, Tel.; சுக்கான்கல் - shukkángal, Tam.). Limestone [choonam cull, kankar].——*Sowcaura cull* (سنگ جراحت - sangijaráhat, Hind.; బలపపురాయి - balapapuráyi, Tel.; சவுக்காரக்கல் - shavukkárakkal, Tam.). Pers. from (sang, pers. stone + jaráhat, pers. wound). Tel. from (balapamu, tel. pot stone + ráyi, tel. stone). Tam. means soap + stone. Tam. also (mákkal), meaning flour + stone [balapam]. Soap stone. Otherwise steatite. A metamorphic rock. Has a soft and greasy feel; is of a yellowish white or greenish gray color; sometimes spotted or veined; with little lustre or transparency; is composed of silica, magnesia, alumina, oxide of iron, and water in various proportions; is soft enough to be easily cut, but is tough and hardens by exposure; is used for carving small models of buildings, making boxes, trays, or other ornaments. At Kurnool and Salem and near Mysore there are very fine white soap stones, and near Chittore there is a valuable description, similar to the Cornish serpentine, procurable in large blocks and suitable for many statuary and other similar decorative purposes; there is a quarry of good pot stone at the Nagary hills. When oiled this stone resembles in a great degree black marble [shalavay cull]. In its laminated form this is Abruck [q.v.]. See vol. II, 39.——*Tavalay cull* (தவளைக்கல் - tavalaikkal, Tam.). From (tavalai, tam. frog). Iron stone. Any ore of iron [auhan].——*Teecull* (అగ్నిశిల - agnishila, Tel.; தீக்கல் - tíkkal, Tam.). Means fire stone. Pyrites. Several sulphides of metals [loham] are thus termed; iron pyrites, copper pyrites, &c. Used alone generally signifies iron pyrites [auhan].——*Teetatty cull* (अग्निप्रस्तर - agniprastara, San.; حجرالنار - hajarunnár, Ar.; آتش زنہ - átishzanah, Pers.; چقماق - chakmák, Hind.; بتوافي - batuapi, Malay; ಚಕಮುಕಿಕಲ್ಲು - chakamukikallu, Can.; ಚಕಮುಕಿಕಲ್ಲು - chakamukikallu, Too.; చకిముకిరాయి - chakimukiráyi, Tel.; தீத்தட்டிக்கல் - títtattikkal, Tam.). San. from (agni, san. fire + prastara, san. stone). Ar. from (hajar, ar. stone + nár, ar. fire). Pers. from (átish, pers. fire + zanah, pers. emitter). Hind. from turkish. Malay from (batu, malay, stone + api, malay, fire). Can. from hindostany. Tel. from (chakimuki, tel. the noise produced by striking flint against steel + ráyi, tel. stone). Tam. from (tí, tam. fire + tattu, tam. to strike + kal, tam. stone). Flint. An aqueous rock. Siliceous concretion, usually translucent and tolerably homogeneous, occurring in chalk [sheemay choonam] or limestone [choonam cull]. See vol. II, 40.——*Tripatty cull* (తిరుపతిరాయి - tirupatiráyi, Tel.; திருப்பதிக்கல் - tiruppathikkal, Tam.). An inferior species of novaculite, or hone stone, of a dark green color. Occasionally to be met with, particularly near Tripatty. Used by barbers for sharpening razors [shaunay cull].——*Ven cull* (తెల్లరాయి - tellaráyi, Tel.; வெண்கல் - vengal, Tam.). Means white stone. Tam. also (palingukkal), meaning crystal + stone [palingoo cull]. White translucent quartz. Pure silica, crystallizing in the hexagonal system. Found in large, cracked, shapeless masses. In the state of powder, rubbed over fine choonam [q.v.] work to give it lustre and durability. A species called fat quartz is employed in Mysore in making glass [cunnaudy].——*Vettoo cull* (బొంతరాయి - bontaráyi, Tel.; வெட்டுக்கல் - vettukkal, Tam.). Title and Tam. from (vettu, tam. to cut + kal, tam. stone). Tel. from (bonda, tel. hole + ráyi, tel. stone) [shory cull]. Laterite. [q.v.].——**(9)** For precious stones see Ratnam; for archæological remains see Aursham.

CULLACOORCHY (கள்ளக்குறிச்சி - kallakkuriççi, *Tam.* kallakurchi *). From (kallan, tam. thief + kuriççi, tam. village) [cullan].——**(1)** Talook, South arcot district; Tahsildar's pay Rs. 175; lat. 11° 33′ to 12° 05′ N.; long. 78° 40′ to 79° 15′; area 868 square miles; pop. 240,181. Language Tamul. S.W. of district. Bounded:—north, Trinomallee talook; east, Tricalore talook; south, Vriddhauchellam talook and Ahtoor talook of Salem district; west, Ootancaray and Ahtoor talooks of Salem district. Physical aspect is rocky intercepted by jungle streams. Soil sandy and clayey. Agriculture, weaving and petty trade in sundry articles and wood. Irrigation by tanks, anicuts [q.v.], wells and channels [q.v.]. Places of archæological interest:—Bramhacoondam, Rishivandyam, Rowta nullore, Shuncaraupooram, Tirvarungam, Tyaugadroog, Varanjaram. The leading places, &c., in the talook are the following.——*Aryagownden* (அரியக்கவுண்டன்மலை - ariyakkavundanmalai, Tam.). After a person of that name. Zemindarry, Hills; pop. 892; lat. 11° 53′; long. 78° 43′; from Cuddalore W. 74 miles; from Cullacoorchy N.W. 22 miles. Zemindarry is inhabited exclusively by Malayaulies. Considerable trade in wood carried on with the plains.——*Bramhacoondam* (பிரம்மக்குண்டம் - pirammakkundam, Tam.). From (brahma, san. the god + kunda, san. sacrificial pit of fire). Pop. 1,346; acres 573; lat. 11° 59′; long. 78° 58′; from Cuddalore W.N.W. 60 miles; from Cullacoorchy N.N.W. 17 miles. White vibhooty [q.v.] found here is said to be the ashes of the sacred fire made by Bramha.——*Chinna salem* * (சின்னச்சேலம் - shinnaççélam, Tam.). From (shinna, tam. small + shélam, tam. town of that name). Tam. also (shélam). Village; pop. 6,091; acres 4,984; lat. 11° 38′; long. 78° 55′; from Cuddalore W.S.W. 60 miles; from Cullacoorchy S.W. 9 miles; from Salem E. 50 miles. On the route from Salem to Cuddalore. Coarse strong cloths extensively manufactured.——*Chittalore* (சித்தலூர் - shittalúr, Tam.). From (shittal, tam. cloth + úr, tam. village). Pop. 2,172; acres 3,211; lat. 11° 41′; long. 79° 07′; from Cuddalore W. 46 miles; from Cullacoorchy E.S.E. 8¾ miles. Annual festival on the birthday of Ancaulamman [q.v.]. Mahomedan sacred place with mosque [musjid] containing the tomb of Shah abbans barauny, a Syed fakeer [q.v.]. At the Buckreed [q.v.] a number of fakeers assemble.——*Congaroya polliem* (கொங்கராயப்பாளையம் - kongaráyappálaiyam, Tam.). From (kongu, tam. the country + rájá, san. king + pálaiyam, tam. fortified village). Pop. 3,007; acres 3,524; lat. 11° 39′; long. 79° 08′; from Cuddalore W.S.W. 45 miles; from Cullacoorchy S.E. 10 miles. North are dolmens [coday cull] formed of granite [caroom cull], one or two of which are large enough to give shelter to 200 people.——*Coorumbagownden* (குரும்பக்கவுண்டன்மலை - kurumbakkavundanmalai, Tam.). After a person of that name. Zemindarry, Hills; pop. 2,503; lat. 11° 53′; long. 78° 53′; from Cuddalore W. 63 miles; from Cullacoorchy N.W. 13 miles. Zemindarry inhabited by Malayaulies and hill-men. Wood trade with the plains is extensively carried on. The hills lie between 11° 51′ and 12° 1′ N. lat. and 68° 42′ and 78° 55′ E. long.——*Cullacoorchy* (கள்ளக்குறிச்சி - kallakkuriççi, Tam.). See below.——*Cullroyen* (கல்ராயன் - kalráyan, Tam.). See Cullroyamullay.——*Gomookhanuddy* (கோமுகநதி - kómuganathi, Tam.). See sep. title.——*Jadaygownden* (சடையக்கவுண்டன்மலை - shadaiyakkavundanmalai, Tam.). After a person of that name. Zemindary, Hills; pop. 3,082; lat. 11° 45′; long. 78° 51′; from Cuddalore W. 65 miles; from Cullacoorchy W. 12 miles. Zemindarry inhabited by Malayaulies. Trade in wood with the plains.——*Manimooctah* (மணிமுத்தா - manimuttá, Tam.). See sep. title.——*Mayoór nuddy* (மயூரநதி - mayúranathi, Tam.). From (mayúra, san. peacock + nadí, san. river). Sanscrit name (mayúra), means peacock [mayil]. River. Tributary of the Manimooctah. At the confluence is an old and famous Shiva temple.——*Moosamanaur* (மூசமனாறு - musamanáru, Tam.). From (mu, tam. three + shaman, tam. equal + áru, tam. river). River. Large jungle stream. Rises in the Cullroyens and falls into the Ponniár. Irrigates a few villages in Cullacoorchy talook.——*Paukambaudy* (பாக்கம்பாடி - pákkambádi, Tam.). From (pákkam, tam. agricultural district + pádi, tam. village). Pop. 944; acres 2,248; lat. 11° 33′; long. 78° 52′; from Cuddalore W.S.W. 64 miles; from Cullacoorchy S.S.W. 15 miles. Palmyra [q.v.] jaggery [q.v.] manufactured.——*Ponniaur* (பெண்ணையாறு - pennaiyáru, Tam.). See sep. title.——*Rishivandyam* (இருசிவந்தியம் - irusivandiyam, Tam.). From (rishi, san. sage + vandya, san. fit to be worshipped). Pop. 2,124; acres 2,903; lat. 11° 49′; long. 79° 08′; from Cuddalore W.N.W. 45 miles; from Cullacoorchy E.N.E. 10½ miles. Old and large Shiva temple.——*Shuncaraupooram* (சங்கராபுரம் - shangaráppuram, Tam.). From (shankara, san. shiva, the pleasure giver + pura, san. town). Pop. 1,453; acres 629; lat. 11° 53′; long. 78° 57′; from Cuddalore W.N.W. 58 miles; from Cullacoorchy N.N.W. 11 miles. Cattle-breeding centre. Old Shiva temple.

——*Torsalore* (தொறசலூர் - torasalúr, Tam.). From (toru, tam. cattle herd + shál, tam. abundance + úr, tam. village). Village; pop. 1,070; acres 2,730; lat. 11° 46′; long. 79° 07′; from Cuddalore W. 47 miles; from Cullacoorchy E.N.E. 7 miles. Slippers manufactured.——*Tyaugadroog* (தியாகத்துருக்கம் - tiyágatturukkam, Tam.). See sep. title.——**(2)** Town, Headquarters of talook; South arcot dist., Cullacoorchy tal.; pop. 3,816; acres 1,980; lat. 11° 44′; long. 79° 00′; from Chidambaram W.N.W. 54 miles; from Cuddalore W. 54 miles; from Madras S.W. 128 miles; from Tindivanam S.W. 57 miles; from Tricalore S.S.W. 22 miles; from Vriddhauchellam N.W. 30 miles. Remains of a small fort, the site of which is now held on puttah [q.v.].

CULLAN (ಕಳ್ಳ - kalla, *Can.*; కల్లుడు - kalludu, *Tel.*; கள்ளன் - kallan, *Tam.*). From (kal, tam. to steal). Means a thief. Hill tribe or Pariah proper name. Feminine Cully [peyar]. Also a tribe now chiefly inhabiting part of country east of Madura, and found scattered throughout Tinnevelly, Salem, Tanjore, Chinglepur and Coimbatore districts. Called Collery in the old English writers. In ancient times inhabited whole country from Trichinopoly to Cape comorin. In recent history these people sided with the Mahomedans and the British against the French. Their hereditary chieftain is the Rajah or Tondiman of Poodoocottah. The tradition among them is that they and the Maravar of Ramnaud are from the same stock. Like the Maravar they take Tevar [q.v.] as tribal title. A common title also is Ambalacaurar [q.v.] or palace servants. Nominally of the Sheiva sect, they are mostly devil-worshippers. They usually bury their dead [shavacaud]. They have a first and second marriage like the Maravar. Divorce and remarriage of widows are allowed. Marriage of near relatives is usual. The Western cullar of Madura are polyandrists. It constantly happens there that a woman is the wife of either ten, eight, six, or two husbands, who are held to be fathers jointly and severally of any children that may be born of her. Many Cullar practise circumcision. The tribal weapon is the boomerang [collery stick]. The tribe is sub-divided into numerous minor communities distinguished by family titles such as the following:—Calacooday, Caudavaroya, Caulingaroya, Malavaroya, Mauthooraur, Menautroya, Panniconda, Ponnapoonda, Pullavaroya, Raujauly, Shervaicauran, Shirnautroya, Sholaga, Sholangateva, Tanjiroya, Tengonda, Tondiman, Vaundaiyan, Vunniya. There is a Tamul proverb:—கதிர் நூல் குறைந்தாலும் கள்ளச்சி கழுத்து நூல் குறையாது—"Though the thread on the spindle diminishes, that on the neck "of a Culla woman does not;" because she is never without a husband. And another:—வெள்ளாளன் மரபே மரபு கள்ளர் திருட்டே திருட்டு—"Of all ranks that of the "Vellaulan is foremost, of thefts that of the Cullan is notorious." Number about 400,000. As plant first term cullan means false or imitative. Ex.:—Kœmpferia rotunda (kallakúve), false curcuma angustifolia; Sida rhombifolia, var. retusa (kallangadalegida), false cicer arietinum. See gloss. paragraphs.——*Culla cammattam* (കള്ളക്കമ്മട്ടം - kallakkammattam, Mal.). From (above + kammattam, mal. coinage). Counter-feit coin [naunyam].——*Cullacoorchy* (கள்ளக்குறிச்சி - kallakkuriçci, Tam.). See sep. title.——*Cullasarakk* (கள்ளச்சரக்கு - kallaçcarakku, Tam.). From (above + sharakku, tam. goods). Smuggled goods [sarakk].

CULLAUDAN (கல்லாடன் - kalládan, *Tam.*). From (kal, tam. to learn + ádu, tam. to play). One of the forty-eight professors of the Madura college [q.v.]. He composed a treatise on grammar [lacshanam] and rhetoric called Cullaudam. It is exceedingly difficult. There is a Tamul proverb:—கல்லாடம் படித்தவனோடு மல் ஆடாதே—"Do not contend with him "who has studied cullaudam."

CULLY (கள்ளி - kalli, *Tam.*). Same as Milk hedge, euphorbia sp. Also plant second term in other genera. Ex., where transl. is of first term:—Bryophyllum calycinum (viranakkalli), ulcer; Kalanchoe laciniata (malaikkalli), hill; Opuntia dillenii (mullukalli), thorn; Plumeria acutifolia (perungalli), large; Sarcostemma intermedium (kodikkalli), creeper; Soymida febrifuga (shurakkalli), fever. See gloss. paragraphs.

CUM (کم - kam, *Hind.*). From persian. Deficient. Low.——*Cum bakht* (کم بخت - kambakht, Hind.). From (above + bakht, ar. fortune). Unfortunate.——*Cumbaury* (ಕಂಬಾರಿ - kambári, Tel.). From (above + bhára, san. burden). A sub-renter.——*Cumbhurty* (کم بہرتی - kambharti, Hind.; ಕಂಭರ್ತಿ - kambharti, Can.; కంభర్తి - kambharti, Tel.). From (above + bharti, hind. full assessment). Land whose assessment is fixed below the full or bhurty [q.v.] standard of assessment [inam]. See vol. I, 112.——*Cummishara* (کم شرح - kamsharah, Hind.). From (above + sharah, ar. rate). Reduction to a lower grade.——*Cummy* (کمی - kamí, Hind.). From persian. Deficiency, decrease.——*Cumzarf* (کم ظرف - kamzarf, Hind.). From (above + zarf, ar. vessel or capacity). Base; a term of abuse.——*Cumzaut* (کم ذات - kamzát, Hind.). From (above + zát, pers. race). Low-born; a term of abuse.

CUM (கம் - kam, *Tam.*). Labour.——*Cumbala* (கம்பள - kambala, obl.; கம்பளத்தான் - kamalattán, pers. sing.; கம்பளத்தார் - kambalattár, pers. pl. **Tam.**). From (kambalam, tam. agricultural country). Otherwise Tottiya. An agricultural caste, sub-division of the vadoogar, descendants of a tribe from north of vijianugger; occupied western parts of madura kingdom beginning of sixteenth century; these enlisted largely in military service under naick rulers, but under british government they settled down to agricultural life. In dress, they love bright-colored handkerchiefs [roomaul], which they wear round their heads; the women wear several rows of red glass beads round their necks and a profusion of metal and earthenware bangles [gauzoo] round their arms. They are veishnavites; both men and women are specially addicted to magic and are regarded with awe; they cure snake-bites by incantations. They are uncommonly industrious and energetic and are great proficients in the art of reclaiming waste-lands. Numbers about 27,000 [jauty].——*Cumban* (கம்பன் - kamban, Tam.). From cumba, naud the country of his birth. Author of Tamul ramayanam [q.v.]. Posthumous son of a ruler of Cumba naud, who was assassinated. Born in poverty at Tirvilandore. Brought up by one Siddayyan of Vennainullore. Later on Rajendra chola invited him to Warriore. The Ramayanam being in Sanscrit, Cumban, Ottacoottan, and other court poets, undertook to imitate it in Tamul. Cumban's was best. Varagoona paundyan of Madura then invited him. There he composed Saraswaty antaudy [q.v.] in thirty stanzas in praise of Saraswaty [q.v.] Cumban's ramayanam consists of 12,016 stanzas, arranged in five books. Other works are Cauncby pooraunam, Cauncby pillay tamul, Chola cooravanjy, Shilay yezhoopatt and Yair yezhoopatt. His son Ambicaupaty, carrying on an intrigue with the king's daughter, was impaled alive, and he died after having lingered on the stake for a couple of days, repeating incessantly the subjoined verse:—எரியுதெரியுதென்னுள்ளீரலைப்பற்றி யெரியுதவியுதில்லை யென்செய்வேன் பொறியரவ நஞ்சிலேதோய்ந்த நளினவிழிப்பெண்ணணங்குநெஞ்சிலேயிட்டநெருப்பு—"What can I do? The fire which the "divine damsel with venomed eyes has kindled in my heart "burns within me, it burns without extinguishing." Cumban effected his escape into the Paundyan country, whence he sent to the king the following stanza:—வில்லம்பு சொல்லம்பு மேதினியிலிரண்டுண்டு வில்லம்பு சொல்லம்பை வெல்லாது வில்லம்பு பட்டுதெதெ வென்மார்பிற் பார்வேந்தேயுன்கிளையைச் சுட்டுதடா வென்வாயிற்சொல்—"There are two kinds of arrows on earth, of which one is shot "out from the bow, and the other from the mouth. O king! "thine arrow from the bow has hit my breast, but mine, the "word of my mouth, has burnt up thy race." After his flight he was reduced to poverty. He died aged sixty at Nattarasancottay in Ramnaud, and was buried there in a sitting posture. His grave forms an object of pilgrimage. The earth thence is given to stupid children.——*Cumma* (కమ్మ - kamma, Tel.). Sub-tribe of the Balijes, now often agricultural. Besides Vishnoo the Cummavaur worship Gungay. Numbers about 800,000; mostly in North arcot, Kistna, and Nellore.——*Cummara* (కమ్మర - kammara, Tel.). Ironsmith. The corresponding terms are:—Can. cummaura, Mal. peringollan, Tam. colla. Distinguish from Cummaulan.——*Cummattam* (கம்மத்தம் - kammattam, Tam.). From (kammam, tam. labor). A grant of a village for a wife's private expenses, generally for betel [q.v.]. Also land which a zemindar [q.v.] or inamdar keeps in his own hands, cultivating by laborers. See vol. I, 112.——*Cummaulan* (கம்மாளன் - kammálan, Tam.). From (kam, tam. smithery + ál, tam. to rule). The Sanscrit is Punchaula [q.v.].—"*a*" The five-fold guild of Tamul artisans. Distinguish from Balootah or set of village public servants; also from Cummara and Cumsaula. See vol. I (67) for the five classes composing the Cummaular or Punchaular in different languages. They take the title of Acharry, teacher, priest; also of Puttan, a corruption of Bhattan; also in the south, of Vishwa bramin.—"*b*" In religion they like the weaver classes are divided into three sects, viz., Sheiva, Veishnava and Lingayet; but those professing the Veishnava faith are comparatively very few. The self-called Vishwa bramins are mostly Sheiva sect, worshipping also Caumautchy amman, Cauly, and village gods. All Cummaular wear threads, and in large towns where they are congregated in communities, have their own priests to officiate at marriages and funerals [carmauntaram, shavacaud]. Cummaular are quiet and respectable men, but they have an aversion to Bramins, and have their own gooroo or family priest and their own books. They have as an idol a figure like a sitting Booddha. Some say they are the descendants of Booddhists, partially converted under persecution to an ostensible Braminism.—"*c*" They form the chief of the left-hand castes [yidangay]. Most bury their dead in a sitting posture; to obtain which, as death comes on, they raise the upper part of the body against a wall, to which by a peg or nail they secure the head. The veishnava artisans burn their dead. The malayalam artisans practise polyandry, with one wife to three or four brothers.—"*d*" The following is a legend about the Cummaular. In the town of Manda anciently the Cummaular lived closely united together; and were employed by all ranks of men, as there were no artificers besides them. They feared and respected no king, which offended certain kings, who combined against them, taking with them all kinds of arms. But as the fort in which the Cummaular lived was entirely constructed of loadstone [cauntam], this attracted and drew the weapons away from the hands of the assailants. The kings then promised a great reward to any who should burn down their fort. No one dared to do this. At length the courtezans [devadausy] of a temple engaged to effect it and took the pledge of betel [q.v.] and areca [q.v.], engaging thereby to do so. The kings greatly rejoicing, built a fort opposite, filled with such kind of courtezans, who by their singing attracted the people from the fort. One of these at length succeeded in extracting from a young man the secret, that if the fort were surrounded with varagoo [q.v.] straw set on fire, it might be destroyed. The king accordingly had this done; and in the burning down of the fort, many of the Cummaular lost their lives; some took to ships belonging to them, and escaped by sea. In consequence there were no artificers in that country. Those taken in the act of endeavouring to escape were beheaded. One woman of the tribe, being pregnant, took refuge in the house of a Chetty, and escaped, passing for his daughter. From a want of artificers, who made implements for weavers, husbandmen and the like, manufactures and agriculture ceased, and great discontent arose in the country. The king being of clever wit, resorted to a device to discover if any of the tribe remained to remedy the evils complained of. This was to send a piece of coral [moongah], having a fine tortuous aperture running through it, and a piece of thread to all parts of the country, with promise of great reward to any one who should succeed in passing the thread through the coral. None could accomplish it. At length the child that had been born in the Chetty's house undertook to do it; and, to effect it, he placed the coral over the mouth of an ant-hole, and having steeped the thread in sugar, placed it at some little distance. The ants [choomtee] took the thread and drew it through the coral. The king seeing the difficulty overcome, gave great presents, and sent much work to be done, which the child under the counsel and guidance of its mother performed. The king sent for the Chetty and demanded an account of this young man, which the Chetty detailed. The king had him plentifully supplied with the means of making ploughshares [caur], and having him married to the daughter of a Chetty, gave him grants of land for his maintenance. He had five sons, who followed the five different branches of work of the Cummaular tribe. The king gave them the title of Punchaular; down to the present day there is an intimate relation between these five branches, and they intermarry with each other; while as descendants of the Chetty tribe, they wear the poonool [q.v.] or caste-thread of that tribe. Those of the Cummaular that escaped by sea are said to have gone to China [q.v.].

CUMBLY (कम्बल - kambala, *San.*; کمل - kammal, *Hind.*; ಕಂಬಳಿ - kambali, *Can.*; కంబళి - kambali, *Tel.*; കമ്പിളി - kampili, *Mal.*; கம்பளி - kambali, *Tam.*). San. from (ka, san. body + val, san. to cover). A coarse woollen blanket. Cumblies are woven in almost every district of the wool [pushm] of the country. The wool is spun by hand; the yarn is sized with the juice of the common squill; the woof is beaten with a hand batten [atchoo] in the way that sailors adopt in forming mats for protecting riggings, no reed being used. A finer description of cumbly, of which the sepoy [q.v.] cloaks were formerly made, is manufactured in Bellary district. Mysore cumblies are of superior quality, in black and white colors. Most cumblies are made in pieces of two or three feet broad and five or six or more long and most are coarse, of a dark or black color. The better kind are larger and finer, and striped or spotted black and white [nesavoo].

CUMBOO (கம்பு - kambu, *Tam.*). From (kanu, tam. joint); from jointed culms. Any culmed stalk. Generally means Bajrah.——*Cumboo grass* (கம்பம்புல் - kambambul, Tam.). Title from resemblance. Tam. from (kambu, tam. pennisetum spicatum, delile + pul, tam. grass). Title otherwise Stalk grass. Botanically Panicum [priyangoo] grossarum, linn., graminaceæ [vricsham, 156]. Spike compound; common ones, six to twelve, secund-flowered, alternate; spikelets solitary, ovate, glabrous, sub-sessile; neuter floret two-valved; caryopsis oblong, transversely wrinkled; culm creeping; leaves ovate-lanceolate, softly pubescent.——*Mady cumboo* (మడుపుకర్ర - madupukarra, Tel.; மடிக்கம்பு - madikkambu, Tam.). Tel. from (madutsu, tel. to fold + karra, tel. stick). Tam. from (madi, tam. to fold + kambu, tam. stick). Warp-beam [nesavoo].

CUMBUM* (کہم - khamam, *Hind.*; కంభము - kambhamu, *Tel.*). From (kambhadu, tel. proper name).——**(1)** Talook, Kurnool district. Tahsildar's pay Rs. 150. Area 1,056 square miles. Population 117,602. Language Teloogoo. Average breadth, 25 miles; length, 85. E. of district. Bounded N. by Marcapore talook, W. by Nullamullays, E. by Veligondas, S. by Budwail talook of Cuddapah district. Nearly half area covered with hills and jungles, offshoots of Nullamullays. Several gorges were closed by native rulers, and reservoirs formed. Chief is Cumbum tank. A few miles south of Cumbum, the valley is crossed by crest of water-shed between Goondlacumma and Saglair. Nundicanama ghaut [q.v.] and Muntraula canama pass lead across the Nullamullays. Red and loamy soils prevail. About 1,500 acres of black soil near Giddalore in the south. Principal products are paddy [q.v.], yellow cholum [q.v.], arika [khoda millet], corra [tinay], sadza [bajrah], dholl [q.v.], wheat [geung], bengal-gram, horse-gram [q.v.] and castor-oil seeds [aumanac]. Cotton [q.v.] and indigo [q.v.] formerly cultivated. Garlic [lussoon] in Toorimilla valley. Principal rivers are Goondlacumma, Saglair, and Zampalair, which rise in Nullamullays. Cumbum tank, largest in district, covers more than 4 sq. miles. Others are Caucarla and Comaravole. The Yenoomoolair in S. is utilized by channels built by Zemindar runga reddy about A.D. 1750. Places of archæological interest:—Allinagaram, Anoomoonapully, Ardaveed, Aucveed, Basineypully, Baudinauyanipully, Bogole, Bolloopully, Comaravole, Commanore, Cottacote, Cumbum, Daddavauda, Dwaurcacherla, Giddalore, Goodimittah, Jallivaury poollalcheroo, Krishnamshettipully, Mallaupooram, Mocshagoondam, Moondlapaud, Narsimhoonipully, Nemilygondam, Nullagoontla, Ooyyaulavauda, Piticauyagoondla, Podillacondapully, Potavaram, Raucherla, Rauzoopollem, Reddicherla, Rowtampully, Salcalaveed, Sarwireddipully, Sooravarapully, Tauticherla, Toorimilla, Yadavully, Yerrabollem, Yidamacull. Principal Trig. stations:—Bheiranicondah, Cuttoolacondah. The leading places, &c., in the talook are the following.——*Aucveed* (ఆకువీడు - ákuvídu, Tel.). From (áku, tel. leaf + vídu, tel. town). Village; pop. 3,155; acres 9,598; lat. 15° 34′; long. 78° 59′; from Cumbum W. 11 miles; from Kurnool E.S.E. 62 miles. Ancient weapons discovered in the valley.——*Basineypully* (బసినేపల్లి - basinépalli, Tel.). From (basava, can. bull + palli, tel. village). Village; pop. 1,959; acres 4,408; lat. 15° 27′; long. 79° 11′; from Cumbum S. 10 miles; from Kurnool E.S.E. 77 miles. E. are two dolmens [coday cull]. S. deserted Veerabhadrau [q.v.] temple. On hill deserted temple of Lutchmy [q.v.]. A third deserted temple of Obleshwarasawmy near which are inscriptions.——*Bestavaurpettah* (బేస్తవారపుపేట - béstavárapupéta, Tel.). From (béstavâramu, tel. thursday + péta, tel. suburb); from its market on Thursdays. Village; pop. 1,633; acres 549; lat. 15° 33′; long. 79° 09′; from Cumbum S. 2 miles; from Kurnool E.S.E. 72 miles. Comaties carry on trade with coast districts.——*Bheiranicondah* (భైరవునికొండ - bhayiravunikonda, Tel.). From (bhairáva, san. shiva, the fearful + konda, tel. hill). Trig. station; lat. 15° 37′ 41·94″; long. 79° 02′ 16·61″; height 3,048 feet; from Bogole W.N.W. 3½ miles; from Cumbum W.N.W. 8 miles.——*Cottucote* (కొత్తకోట - kottakóta, Tel.). From (kotta, tel. new + kóta, tel. fort). Village; pop. 826; acres 3,555; lat. 15° 19′; long. 78° 54′; from Cumbum S.W. 25 miles; from Kurnool S.E. 63 miles. Fort by Chenchalamma runga reddy ancestor of Nossam poligars. Battle fought in 1779. The place also figured during the last conflict with Hyder. Mosque [musjid] in E. of village [moondlapaud].——*Cumbum* (కంభము - kambhamu, Tel.). See below.——*Cuttoolacondah* (కత్తులకొండ - kattulakonda, Tel.). From (katti, tel. sword + konda, tel. hill). Hill. Trig. station in lat. 15° 47′ 19·94″; long. 78° 52′ 17·61″; height 2,848 feet; from Boyalpully N.W. 9 miles; from Cumbum N.W. 23 miles.——*Daddavauda* (దద్దవాడ - daddaváda, Tel.). From (daddamu, tel. temple + váda, tel. village). Village; pop. 2,136; acres 4,968; lat. 15° 23′; long. 79° 03′; from Cumbum S.S.W. 16 miles; from Kurnool E.S.E. 70 miles. Inscriptions of Warrangal dynasty.——*Giddalore* (గిద్దలూరు - giddalúru, Tel.). From (gidda, tel. cow + úru, tel. village). Village B.K.S. railway station; pop. 2,631; acres 5,367; lat. 15° 23′; long. 78° 58′; from Cumbum S.W. 19 miles; from Kurnool E.S.E. 66 miles. On Saglair at E. flank of Nullamullays between Cumbum and the Nundicanama pass. Temple of Pautaula naugeshwarasawmy in a cave, and Vishnoo temple on hill, both ancient. Ruined fort defending the approach to Cumbum. Three inscriptions at Pautaula naugeshwarasawmy.——*Goondlacumma* (గుండ్లకమ్మ - gundlakamma, Tel.). See sep. title.——*Jallivaury poollalcheroo* (జల్లివారిపుల్లలచెరువు - dzallivári-pullalacheruvu, Tel.). From (dzallivâru, tel. a family so called + pullalacheruvu, tel. reed tank so called). Village; pop. 1,603; acres 3,014; lat. 15° 32′; long. 78° 59′; from Cumbum W.S.W. 12 miles; from Kurnool E.S.E. 62 miles. Former seat of Poligar [q.v.]. Remains of ancient fort. In neighbourhood is the water-fall of Nemilygondam, where Goondlacumma issuing from plateau of Goondlabramheshwar makes sudden descent into plains. At the foot is large pool. Litigation settled on its banks by swearing over its waters. One who perjures himself after bathing would be immediately stung by wild bees [taince] to death. Temple to Rungasawmy.——*Krishnamshettipully* (కృష్ణంశెట్టిపల్లి - krishnamshettipalli, Tel.). From (krishnamshetti, tel. proper name + palli, tel. village). Village; pop. 1,895; acres 3,550; lat. 15° 22′; long. 78° 55′; from Cumbum S.W. 21 miles; from Kurnool E.S.E. 63 miles. At E. entrance of Nundicanama pass. Temple of Bheemeshwara sawmy. A mile west is inscription.——*Mocshagoondam* (మోక్షగుండము - mókshagundamu, Tel.). From (móksha, san. salvation + gundamu, tel. a pit). Sanscrit name (muktéshvara), meaning absolution + lord. Shrotriem village; pop. 1,365; acres 12,749; lat. 15° 27′; long. 79° 07′; from Cumbum S.S.W. 8¾ miles; from Kurnool E.S.E. 72 miles. On road to Cumbum. Seat of native astrologers who calculate the punchaungams [q.v.]. E. is Shiva temple on hill called Moocteshwaram, where Shivarautry [pundigay, 6a] is held.——*Moondlapaud* (ముండ్లపాడు - mundlapádu, Tel.). See sep. title.——*Nullamullay* (నల్లమల - nallamala, Tel.). See sep. title.——*Nundicanama* (నందికనమ - nandikanama, Tel.).

See sep. title.——*Ooyyaulavauda* (ఉయ్యాలవాడ - uyyálaváda, Tel.). From (uyyála, tel. a swing + váda, tel. village). Place of hanging. Village; pop. 2,465; acres 5,861; lat. 15°. 13′; long. 78° 56′; from Cumbum S.S.W. 29 miles; from Kurnool S.E. 70 miles. In 1847 a disturbance was caused by Narsimha reddy, pensioned poligar [q.v.] of this place and grandson of Jayaram reddy the last powerful zemindar [q.v.] of Nossam. He unsuccessfully attacked Coilcoontla treasury and sheltered himself in hill forts of Yerramalas and Nullamullays. At Giddalore he gave battle to Lieutenant Watson and killed the Tahsildar of Cumbum. He then escaped into the Nullamullays, and was subsequently captured near Persomala in Coilcoontla talook and hanged. His head was kept hung in the fort on the gibbet till 1877. Inscription dated A.D. 1385 of Vijianugger dynasty.——*Poollalcheroo* (పుల్లలచెరువు - pullalacheruvu, Tel.). From (pulla, tel. reed + cheruvu, tel. tank). Tel. also (mádanapullalacheruvu), meaning maudana; proper name + village, so called. Village; pop. 1,552; acres 3,852; lat. 15° 30′; long. 78° 58′; from Cumbum W.S.W. 14 miles; from Kurnool E.S.E. 62 miles. Poligar of this place descended from Baupa naidoo mentioned under Baswapore. In 1779 he was expelled by Hyder and fled to the Carnatic [q.v.]. He again took possession of his district in 1791 and received sixteen additional villages from the Nizam's officers. On the transfer of the district to the Company, these sixteen villages were resumed and the peshcush [q.v.] of the old ones raised. As the Poligar refused to come to terms with Munro, he was expelled. The family has since been pensioned.——*Rauvipaud* (రావిపాడు - rávipádu, Tel.). From (rávi, tel. peepul tree, ficus religiosa, linn. + pádu, tel. village). Village; pop. 2,587; acres 2,564; lat. 15° 35′; long. 79° 12′; from Cumbum E. 3 miles; from Kurnool E.S.E. 75 miles. On the Goondlacumma. Sanitarium from Cumbum. Vishnoo temple.——*Saglair* (సగిలేరు - sagiléru, Tel.). See sep. title.——*Toorimilla* (తురిమిళ్ల - turimilla, Tel.). From (turu, can. cow + milli, tel. hamlet). Village; pop. 2,726; acres 4,998; lat. 15° 31′; long. 79° 02′; from Cumbum W.S.W. 9 miles; from Kurnool E.S.E. 65 miles. On Goondlacumma. Two miles distant is Sharabheshwarasawmy temple with inscription. Hermitage of the rishy Jamadagny. Visited at Shivarautry [pundigay, 6a]. Old temple between this and Aucveed, called Paupa vimochanam, with inscriptions.——*Veligonda* (వెలిగొండ - veligonda, Tel.). See sep. title.——*Yenoomoolair* (ఎనుములేరు - enumuléru, Tel.). From (enumu, tel. buffalo + éru, tel. river). River. Tributary of Goondlacumma.——*Zampalair* (జంపలేరు - dzampaléru, Tel.). From (dzammu, tel. bulrush, typha elephantina, roxb. + éru, tel. river). River. Tributary of Goondlacumma.——(2) Town, Head-quarters of Tahsildars, Revenue divisional officer, D.P.W. sub-divisional officer, B.K.S. railway station; Kurnool district, Cumbum talook; pop. 5,914; acres 2,903; lat. 15° 35′; long. 79° 09′; from Kurnool E.S.E. 72 miles; from Madras N.N.W. 188 miles; from Nundial E.N.E. 42 miles; from Pyanpaly E.N.E 93 miles. Country around formerly part of Vijianugger kingdom and of that of Andhra kings of Warangal. Cumbum was capital of a sub-division of Balaghaut in the south of Cuddapah, governed by a Naick poligar, tributary to Vijianugger, from whom it was taken by Necnam khan of Cuddapah and subsequently by Hyder. A company of invalid sepoys [q.v.] was stationed here till 1859, when it was removed and a detachment of sowars [q.v.] or mounted police maintained till 1866. The town, though surrounded by wet cultivation, was not unhealthy till 1866, when a malarious form of fever appeared and decimated the population. Large tank, W. of town, by bund 57 feet high across the Goondlacumma between two hills, has a circumference of 13 miles and an area of four square miles. Repaired by Varada rajamma, a wife of Krishna deva royel. The fort was dismantled some years ago. In the town is mosque [musjid] built of remains of a temple. Chief market place resorted to by traders from Guntoor and Pulnaud, who import chillies [q.v.], tobacco [pogauk], saffron [country saffron], salt [namak, ooppoo], &c. The following are the travelling distances by road from Cumbum to different places:—

To	Viâ	Miles and Furlongs.	
Bellary	Nundicanama ghaut and Gooty ...	170	0¼
Bezwada	Guntoor	132	7¼
Bunganapully ...	Nundicanama ghaut	72	1½
Canigherry ...	Hanoomantapaud	32	4
Chicacole	Guntoor, Bezwada and Rajahmundry...	406	7½
Cocañada	Bezwada and Rajahmundry	275	1½
Cuddapah ...	Budwail	96	4
Ellore	Vinoocondah and Bezwada	172	0¼
Gooty	Nundicanama ghaut	120	6¼
Guntoor	Vinoocondah	112	7
Guntoor	Vemlapaud ghaut and Ongole	137	0½
Hyderabad ...	Doopaud and Devarcondah	179	4½
Kurnool	Nundicanama ghaut and Nundiaul ...	101	3¼
Madras	Cuddapah	263	0
Madras	Nellore	225	6
Masulipatam ...	Vinoocondah and Guntoor	160	7½
Masulipatam ...	Ongole and Baupatla	163	7½
Nellore	Canigherry and Caligherry	118	0
Nellore	Canigherry and Shingaroyacondah ...	128	4
Ongole	Podily	68	5
Secunderabad ...	Devarcondah	184	2¼
Secunderabad ...	Kurnool and Janampettah	236	2¼

CUMMER (كمر - kamar, *Hind.*). Loins.——*Cummerbund* (كمربند - kamarband, Hind.). From (above + band, pers. band). Waist-band or sash. Chiefly used by the Mahomedans; the manner in which the dhoty [q.v.] is worn by the Hindoos rendering it less necessary in their case. Hindoos however use it in full dress. Ornamentation is confined to the ends, into which colored threads, and occasionally gold, are introduced [sheelay]. Habitually worn in an ornamental form by domestic servants, peons [q.v.], and irregular troops.——*Cummer cooshye* (كمركشائی - kamarkushái, Hind.). From (above + kushádan, pers. to loosen). Loosening the girdle. Fees once exacted by guards for allowing a prisoner [keidy] the liberty of undressing.——*Cummerputty* (كمرپٹی - kamarpattí, Hind.). From (above + pattí, hind. band). A simple flat ring about an inch and a half broad, which encircles the waist, and curved at the ends where they are hooked [zewar].

CUMPA (కంప - kampa, *Tel.*). Dried brambles; bush.——*Cumpacottah* (కంపకోట - kampakóta, Tel.). From (above + kóta, tel. fort). A hedge of dry thorns round a village as a defence, a sort of abattis.——*Cumpajitta* (కంపజిట్ట - kampajitta, Tel.). From (kampa, tel. bush + jitta, tel. bird). Grass-warblers, or Reed-warblers. Calamoherpinæ, sylviadæ [calacuntam], dentirostres, insessores, aves [pacshy, 23], of naturalists [jantoo]. The species best known to the natives are shown below.—"*a*" Large cumpajitta is Acrocephalus brunnescens. Alias Acrocephalus arundinaceus; Malacocircus abnormis. A winter visitant. Clings strongly to stalks of grain. Harsh clucking kind of note.—"*b*" Red cumpajitta otherwise Paddy field warbler is Acrocephalus agricolus. Paddy [q.v.] fields in cold weather. Migratory going north to breed.—"*c*" Small cumpajitta called podnah in hindostany, also tiktiky, is Acrocephalus dumetorum. Alias Acrocephalus montanus; Salicaria arundinacea; Sylvia montana. Note a sharp titick titick, resembling sound made by a flint and steel.

CUMPLY (ಕಂಪಲಿ - kampali, Can. kampli *). From (kampiliráya, can. proper name).—"*a*" Deputy tahsildarry, Bellary district. Pay Rs. 70.—"*b*" Town, Deputy tahsildar's station; Bellary dist., Hospett tal.; pop. 10,529; acres 5,839; lat. 15° 25′; long. 76° 39′; from Adony W.S.W. 48 miles; from Bellary N.W. 27¾ miles; from Hospett N.E. 17¾ miles; from Hurpanhully N.E. 59½ miles; from Madras W.N.W. 292 miles; from Tadpatry W.N.W. 99 miles. On the Toongabudra, 7 miles, from an important anicut [q.v.]. Old fort in ruinous state but densely populated. Its position is strong with river in front, and wet cultivated ground intersected by aqueducts in rear. Built by one of the Naicks of Bellary feudatory to Vijianugger, and was besieged by Hanoomappa naick of Bellary without success, after he had defeated the Vijianugger rajah in the plain of Cumply. Industries are weaving, especially of silk [puttoo] cloths; and the manufacture of wooden colored toys. Market once a week.—"*c*" Range of hills; Bellary district, Hospett talook.

CUMQUOT (قمقوت - kumkot, *Hind.*). Title from (kinkú, chinese, golden orange). Title otherwise Golden orange. Botanically Citrus [jambeeram] japonica, rutaceæ [vricsham, 32]. Small tree, native of Japan and China. Fruit resembles a diminutive orange [q.v.] about the size of a litchy [q.v.]. Preserve is made from it by Chinese.

CUMR (قمر - kamr, *Ar.*). Moon. The Mahomedan astrology call it the celestial messenger and fix its orbit [cacsham] in the first heaven. One born under the influence of this planet [graham] is supposed to be a gambler, a liar, subject to diseases, &c. Part of lacab; as Cumr oon nissa, moon of ladies; Cumr ood dowla, moon of the empire [ism].——*Cumr ood deen* (قمرالدين - kamruddín, Hind.). From (above + dín, ar. religion). The first Soobahdar [q.v.] of the Deccan [q.v.]. See vol. I, 9.

CUMSAM (कंस - kamsa, *San.*). Bell metal [cunts].——*Cumsaula* (కంసాల - kamsála, obl.; కంసాలి - kamsáli, pers. sing.; కంసాలులు - kamsálulu, pers. pl., Tel.). Teloogoo goldsmith caste or guild. Distinguish from Cummaulan. The corresponding terms are:—Can. acasauly, Tam. and Mal. tattaur [jauty].

CUNCAULAN (கங்காளன் - kungálan, *Tam.*). From (kankála, san. skeleton). Shiva, the wearer of bones. Cuncauly is Bhadracauly as wife of Cuncaulan.

CUNCHA (కంచ - kancha, *Tel.*). A hedge. Hence a government pasture farm, as enclosed [maita].——*Cunchacacherla* (కంచకచెర్ల - kanchakacherla, Tel.). From (above + cherla, tel. village). Greek κοντακόσσυλα. Village; Kistna dist., Nundigauma tal.; pop. 1,547; acres 7,290; lat. 16° 41′; long. 80° 26′; from Masulipatam N.W. 60 miles; from Nundigauma S.E. 9½ miles. Close to diamond [vajram] mines of Partiaul.

CUNDAM (खण्ड - khanda, *San.*; കണ്ടം - kantam, *Mal.*; கண்டம் - kandam, *Tam.*). From (khand, san. to divide). Portion. Suffix in place names; as Eivailicundam, meaning five + hedge + portion.——*Cundaga* (ಖಂಡುಗ - khandaga, Can.). From (khanda, san. portion). A measure = 4 punchacams [q.v.].—"*a*" Bazaar weight. 10 toolaums = 1 cundaga [niray, 2 c]. Approximate actual value, 1 cundaga = 205 lbs., 11 oz., and 7 drs. Compare Tel. cuntlam, Tam. pothy.—" ƀ " Measure of capacity. 40 bullahs = 1 cundaga [alavay, 3a, c]. Approximate actual value, 1 cundaga = 5 cubic feet and 1,510 cubic inches. In Bellary there is a very much larger wholesale cundaga of 5,376 pucka seers or 211 cubic feet, and 1,712 cubic inches. Compare Cullum of N. arcot, S. arcot and Chingleput. See vol. I, 609; II, 508, 509.——*Cundigay* (கண்டிகை - kandigai, Tam.). Field-division. Suffix in place names.——*Cundy* (గండి - gandi, Tel.; കണ്ടി - kanti, Mal.). Pass; suffix in place names; as Bondacundy, meaning stocks + pass [gundy]. A piece of ground. Suffix in place names as Anjarcundy, meaning five + half + ground.

CUNDAN (கந்தன் - kandan, *Tam.*). Tam. form of Scandan; the god of war. Non-bramin second name. Cundasawmy is very common [peyar].——*Cundoocore* (కందుకూరు - kandukúru, Tel.). See sep. title.

CUNDANORE (కందనూరు - kandanúru, *Tel.*). From (kandena, tel. grease + úru, tel. village). Because carts conveying stone to Alampore temple were formerly greased here. Ancient form of the name of Kurnool.

CUNDAUYAM (కందాయము - kandáyamu, *Tel.*). Fixed portion of tax payable at a certain time So rent paid in money as distinguished from rent paid in kind. See vol. I, 112.

CUNDOO (കണ്ടു - kantu, *Mal.*; கண்டு - kandu, *Tam.*). From (kan, mal. to see). Seen.——*Cundezhoott* (കണ്ടെഴുത്തു - kantezhuttu, Mal.). From (above + ezhuttu, mal. writing). Record of actual produce.——*Cundookrishy* (കണ്ടുകൃഷി - kantukrishi, Mal.). From (above + krishi, san. tillage). The home farm of a ruling power [havelly]. See vol. II, 289.——*Cundoomoothal* (கண்டுமுதல் - kandumuthal, Tam.). From (above + muthal, tam. stock). Actual produce.

CUNDOOCORE (కందుకూరు - kandukúru, *Tel.* kandukúr *). From (kandudu, tel. skanda, the god + úru, tel. village) [cundan]. Sanscrit name (skandapurí), meaning the god scandan + town. —(1) Talook, Nellore district. Tahsildar's pay Rs. 175. Area 787 square miles. N. centre coast part of district. Boundaries :—N. Ongole talook, Podily division; E. Bay of Bengal; S. Cauvaly talook; W. Canigherry talook. Lat. 14° 57′ to 15° 30′ N.; long. 79° 40′ to 80° 09′; E. Choondy zemindarry in west is separated from talook by a range of hills running north and south for about 15 miles; of considerable elevation and slopes covered with dense jungle. Every village has a handsome tope.[q.v.]. Laterite [q.v.] abundant and largely used for building purposes. Consists of extensive plains devoted to dry crop cultivation on a superior soil. The tract lying between the lower reach of the Moosy and Palair river in the centre is of superior regady [regar]. In the villages along the coast line the soil resembles that of the coast villages of Ongole talook, and is sandy. In the north-west and extreme west it is stony and sterile. Noted for good sheeting cloths; also for dyed cloths. In Paricondapaud boxes, toys, chairs, &c., are made. Manufacture of good indigo [q.v.]. Earthen bangles [gauzoo] manufactured in some villages. Great charities performed by Cotamma, a Caupoo widow at Oolavapulley. Intersected by the Munnair, Palair and Yelicair. The principal tanks are Caraid, Mautsavaram and Mopaud. Camping grounds :—Bitragoonta, Cundoocore, Goodlore, Mautsavaram, Oolavapulley, Ramapatam, Wogore. Places of archæological interest :—Anantasaugaram, Choondy, Condamoottsoopollem, Cundoocore, Goondlapollem, Jillellamoody, Lingasamoodram, Maulecondah, Mautsavaram, Ramapatam, Shaunampoody, Shingaroyacondah. Principal trig. stations :—Cancherla, Choondy, Daritippa, Goorayagoonta, Jendaltippa, Lutchmeepooram, Netvauripollem, Paujerla peddatippa, Poolipaud, Ramapatam beacon, Tettoo, Yeloorpaud. The leading places, &c., in the talook are the following.——*Bingini-pully* (బింగినిపల్లి - binginipalli, Tel.). From (binga, can. gold color + palli, tel. village); from vishnoo, the gold-colored god. Village; pop. 1,933; acres 3,147; lat. 15° 13′; long. 80° 07′; from Cundoocore E. 11 miles; from Nellore N. 53 miles. Till recently a large salt export station. Temples of Ramalingasawmy and Chennakeshavasawmy. Tank.——*Buddepoody* (బద్దెపూడి - baddepúdi, Tel.). From (baddamu, tel. boundary + púdi, tel. village). Village; pop. 1,091; acres 3,850; lat. 15° 08′; long. 79° 58′; from Cundoocore S.S.E. 6½ miles; from Nellore N. 46¼ miles; from the sea W. 9 miles. 5 miles east of the route from Nellore to Guntoor. Formerly gave its name to a talook and also to a range of the Public works department. Two temples of Shiva and Vishnoo. Fair trade in indigo.——*Caraid* (కరేడు - karédu, Tel.). See sep. title.——*Caumeypully* (కామేపల్లి - kámépalli, Tel.). From (kámayya, tel. proper name + palli, tel. village). Village; pop. 1,741; acres 4,028; lat. 15° 21′; long. 79° 52′; from Cundoocore N.N.W. 10½ miles; from Nellore N. 62 miles; from the sea W. 19 miles. In Choondy zemindarry. Residence of Appa cavy, a famous Teloogoo scholar and poet, 500 years ago. Temple of Vengopaulsawmy. Betel [q.v.] gardens. Tank.——*Chelamchaila* (చలంచేలు - chalamchéla, Tel.). From (chalama, tel. spring + chénu, tel. field). Village; pop. 1,179; acres 12,839; lat. 14° 59′; long. 79° 59′; from Cundoocore S. 16¼ miles; from Nellore N. 36 miles; from the sea W. 7½ miles. A dense jungle. Tank. Large stone image of Nundy [q.v.] held in high veneration specially in cases of difficult delivery. Temples of Keshava sawmy and Shuncarasawmy.——*Choondy* (చుండి - tsundi, Tel.). See sep. title.——*Cuncherla* (కంచెర్ల - kancherla, Tel.). From (kanche, tel. hedge + cherla, tel. village). Trig. station in lat. 15° 05′ 33·77″; long. 79° 43′ 49·47″; height 571 feet; from Cundoocore W.S.W. 16 miles; from Timmareddipollem W. 3 miles; from the sea W. 24 miles.——*Cundoocore* (కందుకూరు - kandukúru, Tel.). See below.——*Daritippa* (దరితిప్ప - daritippa, Tel.). From (dari, tel. border + tippa, tel. mound). Trig. station in lat. 15° 00′ 36·47″; long. 79° 57′ 40·10″; from Cundoocore S. 14 miles; from Pippallavauripollem N.W. 3½ miles; from the sea W. 9 miles.——*Dauva goodore* (దావగూడూరు - dávagúdúru, Tel.). From (dáva, vulg. for dóva, tel. way + gúdúru, tel. place so called). Village; pop. 838; acres 2,133; lat. 15° 19′; long. 79° 59′; from Cundoocore N.N.E. 7¾ miles; from Nellore N. 59½ miles; from the sea W. 10½ miles. Temple of Chennakeshavasawmy. Formerly gave its name to a talook.——*Goodlore* (గుడ్లూరు - gudlúru, Tel.). From (guddu, tel. egg + úru, tel. village). Village; pop. 2,039; acres 10,813; lat. 15° 04′; long. 79° 57′; from Cundoocore S. 10½ miles; from Nellore N. 43 miles; from the sea W. 10 miles. Good trading town. Ruined fort formerly held by a Poligar [q.v.]. An old temple of Chennakeshavasawmy. In the tank called Lingamgoonta there are the remains of an old palace built by a former rajah for his concubine.——*Goorayagoonta* (గురయగుంట - gurayagunta, Tel.). From (guravayya, tel. proper name + gunta, tel. pond). Trig. station; lat. 15° 2′ 4·43″; long. 80° 0′ 52·72″; from Chennayapollem W.N.W. 6¼ miles; from Cundoocore S.S.E. 13 miles; from the sea W. 5¼ miles.——*Ilavara* (ఇలవర - ilavara, Tel.). From (iluvaramu, tel a hut). Sanscrit by corruption (ilvalapurí), meaning ilvalan, the giant + town. Village; pop. 1,591; acres 4,276; lat. 15° 22′; long. 79° 52′; from Cundoocore N.N.W. 11½ miles; from Nellore N. 64 miles; from the sea W. 19 miles. Temple of Lutchmy narrainsawmy.——*Jendaltippa* (జెండలతిప్ప - jendalatippa, Tel.). From (jéndra, tel. a caste + tippa, tel. mound). Trig. station; lat. 15° 5′ 11·59″; long. 80° 2′ 55·71″; from Cundoocore S.E. 11 miles; from Ramapatam N.W. 3¾ miles; from the sea W. 3 miles.——*Lingasamoodram* (లింగసముద్రము - lingasamudramu, Tel.). From (lingamma, tel. proper name + samudra, san. ocean). Tel. also (tsundilingasamudramu), meaning choondy, the place + lingasamoodram, the place, as distinguished from lingasamoodram in cauvaly. Village; pop. 4,316; lat. 15° 06′; long. 79° 46′; from Cundoocore S.W. 14 miles; from Nellore N.N.W. 47½ miles; from the sea W. 21½ miles. Coral [moongah] and pearl [moty] merchants.——*Lutchmeepooram* (లక్ష్మీపురము - lakshmípuramu, Tel.). From (lakshmí, san. the goddess + pura, san. town). Trig. station; lat. 15° 0′ 4·15″; long. 80° 0′ 46·82″; from Cundoocore S.S.E. 15 miles; from Siripooram N. 4 miles; from the sea W. 5¾ miles.——*Maulecondah* (మాలెకొండ - málekonda, Tel.). From (mále, tel. dwelling + konda, tel. hill). Sanscrit name (mályádri), meaning garland + mountain. Village, Hill, Place of pilgrimage; lat. 15° 11′; long. 79° 41′; from Cundoocore W.S.W. 17 miles; from Nellore N.N.W. 55 miles; from the sea W. 28 miles. 3¾ miles W.N.W. of Choondy. Ancient temple dedicated to Vishnoo, as Lutchmy narsimhasawmy. Visited every Saturday, and persons who have vows to perform, feed the visitors. Hill considered a place of great sanctity. Formerly surrounded by dense jungle. Mantapam [q.v.] supported by fourteen pillars constructed by Mullayya reddy and a stone tank at the foot of the hill. Another temple in Lutchmakkapett dedicated to Lutchmy. Inam [q.v.] was granted in the time of Atchoota deva roya.——*Mautsavaram* (మాచవరము - mátsavaramu, Tel.). From (mátsamma, tel. proper name meaning great lakshmí + pura, san. town). Sanscrit name (mahálakshmípura), meaning great + lutchmy the goddess + town. Village; pop. 1,883; acres 4,129; lat. 15° 08′; long. 79° 56′; from Cundoocore S. 6 miles; from Nellore N. 47 miles; from the sea W. 11 miles. Large tank. Trade in cattle. On a small hill 1 mile north of village there was a temple demolished by a Mahomedan invasion. Old temple of Mullicarjoonan. Stone statues.——*Mooshy* (ముశి - mushi, Tel.). See sep. title.——*Moottiaulpaud* (ముత్యాలపాడు - mutyálapádu, Tel.). See sep. title.——*Munnair* (మన్నేరు - mannéru, Tel.). See sep. title.——*Netvauripollem* (నేతివారిపాలెము - nétivárípálemu, Tel.). From (nétiváru, tel. family name; ghee family + pálemu, tel. fortified village). Trig. station; lat. 15° 22′ 44·22″; long. 79° 51′ 06·23″; height 190 feet; from Cundoocore N.N.W. 13 miles; from Ilavara W. 1½ miles; from the sea W. 20 miles.——*Nundanavanam* (నందనవనము - nandanavanamu, Tel.). From (nandana, san. pleasing + vana, san. grove). Village; pop. 1,156; acres 3,173; lat. 15° 18′; long. 80° 02′; from Cundoocore N.E. 8 miles; from Nellore N. 58½ miles; from the sea W. 7½ miles. Temple of Vencateshwarasawmy.——*Ooppalpaud* (ఉప్పలపాడు - uppalapádu, Tel.). From (uppalamu, tel. salt marsh + pádu, tel. village). Village; pop. 2,058; acres 2,923; lat. 15° 10′; long. 79° 48′; from Cundoocore W.S.W. 10 miles; from Nellore N.N.W. 51 miles; from the sea W. 21 miles. Noted for its breed of cattle [maud].——*Palair*

(పాలేరు - pálóru, Tel.). See sep. title.——*Palcore* (పలుకూరు - palukúru, Tel.). From (paluku, tel. echo + úru, tel. village). Village; pop. 2,371; acres 7,377; lat. 15° 16′; long. 79° 59′; from Cundoocore N.E. 4¼ miles; from Nellore N. 56 miles; from the sea W. 9 miles. Five old temples. One large tank.——*Pamoor* (పామూరు - pámúrú, Tel.). See sep. title.——*Paucala* (పాకల - pákala, Tel.). See sep. title.——*Panjerla peddatippa* (పాజెర్లపెద్దతిప్ప - pájerlapeddatippa, Tel.). From (pájerla, tel. place so called, meaning snake village + pedda, tel. large + tippa, tel. mound). Trig. station; lat. 15° 3′ 57·30″; long. 80° 0′ 39·89″; from Cundoocore S.S.E. 11 miles; from Rotoolore N.E. 2 miles; from the sea W. 5½ miles.——*Poolipaud* (పులిపాడు - pulipádu, Tel.). From (puli, tel. tiger + pádu, tel. village). Trig. station; lat. 15° 14′ 22·63″; long. 80° 01′ 04·04″; height 126 feet; from Cundoocore E.N.E. 5½ miles; from Palcoorpett S.E. 2¾ miles; from the sea W. 7 miles.——*Ramapatam* (రామయ్యపట్నము - rámayyapatnamu, Tel.). See sep. title.——*Raurore* (రావూరు - rávúru, Tel.). From (rádzu, tel. a class of people + úru, tel. village). Village; pop. 1,759; acres 3,997; lat. 15° 01′; long. 80° 04′; from Cundoocore S.S.E. 15½ miles; from Nellore N. 39¼ miles; from the sea W. 1¾ miles. Large tank. Bhatrauzool or flattering beggars live here.——*Sangameshwaram* (సంగమేశ్వరము - sangaméshvaramu, Tel.). From (sangama, san. confluence + íshvara, san. lord); from shiva's temple at the junction of the palair and the makkair. Hill and temple; lat. 15° 21′ 10″; long. 79° 46′ 13″; from Cundoocore N.W. 15 miles; from Nellore N.N.W. 63¾ miles; from the sea W. 25½ miles. Temple of Sangameshwara sawmy with an annual festival in February.——*Shingaroyacondah* (శింగరాయకొండ - shingaráyakonda, Tel.). See sep. title.——*Tettoo* (తెట్టు - tettu, Tel.). Means stone fence. Trig. station; lat. 15° 2′ 43·26″; long. 80° 3′ 4·89″; from Cundoocore S.E. 13 miles; from Ramapatam W.N.W. 2½ miles; from the sea W. 3 miles.——*Vennore venkannapollem* (వెన్నూరువెంకనపాలెము - vennúruvenkanapálemu, Tel.). From (vennúruvenkanna, tel. proper name + pálemu, tel. fortified village). Village; pop. 2,131; acres 912; lat. 15° 23′; long. 79° 58′; from Cundoocore N. 11 miles; from Nellore N. 63½ miles; from the sea W. 13 miles. Noted for breed of cattle. Tank. Temple of Gopaulsawmy, festival held in April.——*Yelicair* (ఏలికేరు - elikéru, Tel.). See sep. title.——*Yeloorpaud* (ఏలూరుపాడు - élúrupádu, Tel.). From (élu, tel. to reign + úru, tel. village + pádu, tel. waste); from high site. Trig. station; lat. 15° 0′ 55·00″; long. 80° 2′ 25·07″; from Chennayapollem W.N.W. 4 miles; from Cundoocore S.S.E. 15 miles; from the sea W. 3½ miles.——**(2)** Town, Head-quarters of Tahsildar and Sub-registrar; Nellore district, Cundoocore talook; pop. 7,577; acres 17,773; lat. 15° 13′; long. 79° 57′; from Madras N. 146 miles; from Naidoopett N. 88½ miles; from Nellore N. 53 miles; from Ongole S.S.W. 23 miles; from the sea W. 12 miles. Large and flourishing commercial town. Remains of an old fort constructed during the fowjdarry [q.v.] of Malik aslam khan. Remains of another fort wholly under cultivation, west of the village, built during reign of Krishna deva royel. Very old temples of Someshwaran and Janardanan. Five old mosques [musjid], all with inams. In a pond there is a seven-headed tomb, for seven warriors slain in a battle at Allinugger, alias Gundavaram, Nellore talook, whose headless corpses dropped here from the backs of their horses [ghorah] flying from the battle field. This is supported by an inam [q.v.] and yeomiah [q.v.]. There is also a Durgah [q.v.] in honor of the saint Shah jehaungeer. Festival of Ancamma celebrated once in three years about July. Noted for breed of cattle.

CUNGOONDY (కంగుంది - kangundi,* *Tel.*). From (kanama, tel. valley + gondi, tel. corner) [canama].——**(1)** Zemindarry, North arcot. Area 346 square miles. Length from N.W. to S.E. about 25 miles; breadth about 18 miles. Population 54,052; Language, Teloogoo. S.W. of district. Bounded north-west by Mysore; north-east by Pulmanair; and south and south-east by Salem. The estate long with present Zemindar's family, probably a creation of Vijianugger dynasty, whose princes settled in neighbourhood. Hyder ally threw one of the poligars into jail at Seringapatam; and Tippoo placed a garrison in the town of Cungoondy. The Company seized the fort in 1792, but restored it in 1794. It formed portion of the Krishnagherry division of the Baramahaul [q.v.]. In 1816 it was attached for arrears and settled. Peshoush [q.v.] was about Rs. 23,000. The greater part of zemindarry lies above ghauts [q.v.]. The soil is poor gravelly loam, which gets more fertile in the north-east parts near Pulmanair talook. Lime [choonam], building stones [cull], and iron [auhan] are the only known mineral [dhautoo] products. The gold region of Colaur is just to the west of Cungoondy. The Cooroobas [q.v.] breed sheep and weave cumblies [q.v.]. Others raise Mysore bullocks [maud], and Cungoondy used once to furnish animals for use in the artillery. The Palaur passes through the estate from north-west to south-east in a rocky bed of no great breadth. It frequently comes down in flood, when owing to the great fall its course is very impetuous and it is for the time impassable. The sources of irrigation are chiefly tanks. Wells are infrequent, and spring channels [q.v.] unknown. The zemindar divides his country into three talooks:—the Byle seema or open country of the north-west; the Chettoo seema or wooded country of the middle; and the Canama kinda seema below the ghauts on the south-east. Places of archæological interest:—Cungoondy, Toommishy. The leading places, &c., in the zemindarry are the following.——*Cooppam* (కుప్పము - kuppamu, Tel.). See sep. title.——*Cungoondy* (కంగుంది - kangundi, Tel.). See below.——*Palaur* (பாலாறு - páláru, Tam.). See sep. title.——*Ramanaickanpett* (రామనాయకంపేట - rámánáyakampéta, Tel.). From (rámanáyakudu, tel. proper name + péta, tel. suburb). Village; pop. 1,244; lat. 12° 40′; long. 78° 35′; from Chittore S.W. 53 miles; from Cungoondy S.E. 10¼ miles.——**(2)** Sub-magistracy, North arcot district. Pay Rs. 100.——**(3)** Village, Hill; North arcot dist., Cungoondy tal., Zemindarry; pop. 652; lat. 12° 46′; long. 78° 29′; from Arnee W. 57 miles; from Chittore S.W. 54 miles; from Madras W. 127 miles; from Ranipett W. 61 miles; from Tripatty S.W. 89 miles; from Vellore W. 48 miles. At the foot of a precipitous hill, fortified and formerly of great strength but now dilapidated. Once chief place in the zemindarry but lately almost depopulated. Zemindar's palace. The droog is in lat. 12° 46′; long. 78° 29′; from Cungoondy S. ½ mile, ascended by flight of steps in bad order; half way up is a cave filled with the bones and horns of cattle.

CUNJOOMULLAY (கஞ்சமலை - kañjumalai, *Tam.*). From (kánchana, san. gold + malai, tam. mountain); so called on account of gold washings made here. Sanscrit name (káñchanagiri), meaning same. Hill; Salem district. Salem talook; A hog backed and detached hill, otherwise known as the shark's fin, famous for its stores of magnetic iron [cauntam]. The Porto novo iron [auhan] company obtained its ores here. Trig. station in lat. 11° 36′ 58·63″; long. 78° 06′ 04·47″; height 3,238 feet; from Salem W.S.W. 7¼ miles.

CUNN (கண் - kan, *Tam.*). Eye. In vocative is term of endearment.——*Cungaunam* (கண்காணம் - kangánam, Tam.). From (above + kán, tam. to see). A watch over fields and produce on behalf of Government.——*Cungauny* (கண்காணி - kangáni, Tam.). An inspector of crops. The village grain measurer; in some places his place is supplied by the Toty. Often used of one who takes native laborers to the coffee [q.v.] estates of Ceylon [inam].——*Cunnan* (കണ്ണൻ - kannan, Mal.; கண்ணன் - kannan, Tam.). The fair-eyed one. Vishnoo. Familiarly Cunnoo. Non-bramin, Hindoo 2nd or pers. name. Feminine Cunny [peyar].——*Cunnaudy* (दर्पण - darpana, San.; آئینه - áínah, Pers. and Hind.; كاچ - kacha, Malay; ಕನ್ನಡಿ - kannadi, Can.; ಕನ್ನಡಿ - kannadi, Too.; అద్దము - addamu, Tel.; കണ്ണാടി - kannáti, Mal.; கண்ணாடி - kannádi, Tam.). San. from (drip, san. to light). Pers. from (áhan, pers. iron; from being used in its manufacture). Malay from (kacha, san. brilliancy, from kach, san. to shine). Tel. from (abda, san. glass). Tam. from (kan, tam. eye + ádi, tam. mirror). Glass ὕαλος ἀργή, glass of a coarse kind was exported from Egypt to the west coast according to the Periplus; but glass of an inferior quality is made in several parts of Southern india. The manufacture is confined entirely to small phials and women's bracelets [gauzoo]. On the Mysore plateau the frit employed for making glass is composed of one part of fat quartz [veu cull] and six parts of a kind of coarse soda [munn cauram]. To give glass a green tinge, to the frit are added a further quantity of prepared soda, an iron ore, a red oxide of iron, and a proportion of calcined copper [taumram]; all which materials being mixed and put into the crucible and properly disposed in the furnace, the fire is kept up for nine days and nine nights. To give glass a red tinge, to the frit are added an additional proportion of prepared soda and a quantity of a certain red ore; after which the whole are fused together for fifteen days and fifteen nights. To make blue glass, to the frit are added a further proportion of soda, calcined copper, a quantity of powdered iron ore and a blue substance which may be smalts. To give glass a yellow color, it is enamelled with the melted calces of lead [eeyam], tin [tagaram] and zinc [tootnaug]. In the Poodoocottah country, where glass rings are made of a superior quality to those of mysore, the frit is prepared by adding to fine river sand [manal] a very strong solution of the alkaline earth oovar munn [q.v.] which contains much soda [munn cauram]; this mixture is formed into lumps, which are dried and then fused for many hours together; in order to make glass a certain quantity of poongauram [q.v.] is added to the powdered frit, and the whole fused together for many hours. Bhoota cunnaudy, from (bhúta, san. demon), meaning anything great and superhuman, is a microscope. Doora drishty cunnaudy, from (dúra, san. distance + drishti, san. sight) is a telescope. Mookha cunnaudy, from (mukha, san. face) is a looking glass. Mookkoo cunnaudy, from (múkku, tam. nose) are spectacles. Nilay cunnaudy, from (nilai, tam. fixed) is a mirror. Soorya caunta cunnaudy, from (súrya, san. sun + kánta, san. that which loves) is a burning glass.——*Cunnimay* (கண்ணிமை - kannimai, Tam.). From (above + imai, tam. to twinkle). Wink. Dravidian measure of time. 60 cunnimays = 1 vinaudy [caulam, 1]. Approximate actual value, 1 cunnimay = ·4 english second. Same as nimisham, caushta calay, and vipalam [caulam, 6].——*Cunnoor* (கண்ணூறு - kannúru, Tam.). From (above + úru, tam. touch, evil). Evil-eye. There is a Tamul proverb:—கல்

எறிக்குத் தப்பினாலும் கண் எறிக்குத் தப்பக் கூடாது—"Though one may escape the cast of a stone, he cannot escape "the glance of an evil-eye." To avert this as regards fruits [pazham], &c., in a garden, it is common to put up some object of attraction as a water-pot white-washed, inverted on a stump, and dotted with black spots, &c. In some enclosures grotesque images are seen.

CUNNAUN (கன்னான் - kannán, *Tam.*). From (kan, tam. brass-work). The corresponding terms are:—Tel. cantsara, Can. bogaura, Mal. mooshaury. Cummaulan or artisan caste; work in mixed metals [loham], such as brass [pittalay], &c.

CUNNY (கன்னி - kanni, *Tam.*). Maiden. Cunniyammaul is Parvaty [comaury, comorin, coomary].

CUNTLAM (కంట్లము - kantlamu, *Tel.*). A bullock load. Bazaar weight [niray, 2b]. Approximate actual value, 1 cuntlam = 200 lbs. In Cuddapah a wholesale weight of cotton [q.v.]; 60 maunds or 13 cwts. 44 lbs. of raw cotton or 15 or 3 cwts. 39 lbs. of cleaned. Compare Cundaga, Pothy.

CUNTS (कांस्य - kámsya, *San.*; پچرس - pachras, *Hind.* and *Dec.*; کڠسا - gangsa, *Malay*; ಕಂಚು - kanchu, *Can.*; ಕಂಚಿ - kanchi, *Too.*; కంచు - kantsu, *Tel.*; ഓട് - ótu, *Mal.*; வெண்கலம் - vengalám, *Tam.*). Title from teloogoo [cumsam]. San. from (kam, san. to love). Hind. from (pánch, hind. five + rasa, san. mineral); mixture of several metals, strictly a metallic alloy of copper, brass, tin, lead and iron. Malay, &c., from sanscrit. Mal. from (oti, mal. to break), brittle. Tam. from (ven, tam. white + kalam, tam. vessel). Mixed metal [loham], bell-metal, queen's metal; any amalgam of zinc [tootnaug] and copper [taumram].

CUPPAL (കപ്പൽ - kappal, *Mal.*; கப்பல் - kappal, *Tam.*). Ship [dhony] or foreign [q.v.]; corresponding to sheemay [q.v.]. Plant first term. Ex., joining two genera, where transl. is of second term:—Alhagi maurorum (kappattumba), leucas indica; Anacardium occidentale (kappalmávu), mangifera indica; Ananas sativus (kappaççakka), artocarpus integrifolia; Capsicum annuum (kappalmulaku), piper nigrum; Ipomæa batatas (kappalkizhannu), root; Pimenta acris (kappalmulaku), piper nigrum. See gloss. paragraphs.

CUPPATRAULA (కప్పట్రాళ్ల - kappatrálla, *Tel.*). From (kappu, tel. roof + rayi, tel. stone). Village; Kurnool district, Putticondah talook; pop. 1,999; acres 9,613; lat. 15° 35′; long. 77° 40′; from Kurnool W.S.W. 33 miles; from Putticondah N.E. 16½ miles. Former seat of a powerful poligar [q.v.]. Family now pensioned. Hill fort. Amethystine quartz in the hills. Annual festival at hill temple from 15th to 23rd Maugham [mausam] or February.

CURCAS (کرکس - karkas, *Hind.*). Same as Wild aumanac.

CURNUM (కరణము - karanamu, *Tel.*). From (karaṇa, san. doing); hence clever. Village accountant [inam]. San. grauma caranam or cauyast; Tam. conicopoly; Can. shanbogue; Mal. menon; Hind. patwarry; Ar. canoongo. In the Tamul country usually a Shoodra, and takes the title of Pillay; in the Teloogoo country usually a Bramin. A village clerk who keeps the accounts [kanak] of cultivation [vellaumay], and registers everything connected with it, and whose duties are remunerated either by a grant of land or certain small shares [merah] or perquisites from the crops of the village, or by a money allowance from Government. In the early days of the East india company this class were their brokers, agents, and interpreters [doobash]. There is a Tamul proverb:—இடைக்கணக்கன் செத்தான், இனிப் பிழைப்பான் நாட்டான்—"the curnum middleman "is dead, henceforth the peasant may prosper." And another:—எழுத்துக்குப் பாங்மாறின கணக்கனும் உடுக்கைக்குப் பாங்மாறினதாசியும் வருத்தம் அடைவார்—"the curnum "who neglects his accounts, and the dancing girl [dausy] who is "careless about her dress, will come to trouble." And another:—கணக்குக்குஞ்சையும் காக்கைக்குஞ்சையும் கண்டஇடத்திலே கண்ணைக்குத்து—"bore through the eyes of a "young curnum and a young crow [caurvam] wherever you find "them;" both bad. See vol. I (67); II, 229.——*Curneecam* (కరణీకము - karaníkamu, Tel.). The office of curnum.——*Curnum putty* (కరణపట్టి - karanampatti, Tel.). From (patti, tel. list). Tax levied on village curnums in certain zemindarries in proportion to the merah [q.v.] enjoyed by each.——*List curnum* (లిస్టుకరణము - lístukaranamu, Tel.). Whose name is recorded as employed by Government. See vol. I, 112.

CURRA (కఱ్ఱ - karra, *Tel.*). Stain from juice, or stick from straight slender stem. Plant first term. Ex., where transl. is of second term:—Acacia pennata (karrachíka), acacia concinna; Cyperus dilutus (karratunga), cyperus rotundus; Desmodium pulchellum (karraantinta), desmodium diffusum; Manihot utilissima (karrapendalamu), dioscorea; Rhynchosia velutina (karraulava), dolichos biflorus. See gloss. paragraphs.

CURRY (व्यञ्जन - vyañjana, *San.*; سالنا - sálná, *Hind.*; ಕಡಿ - kadi, *Can.*; కూర - kúra, *Tel.*; കൂട്ടാൻ - kúttan, *Mal.*; கறி - kari, *Tam.*). Title from tamul. Tam. from (kari, tam. to eat by biting). San. from (vyañj, san. to anoint). Tel. from (kúdu, tel. to mix). Mal. from (kúttu, mal. to mix). A bit, a morsel, a chip, &c. A dish made originally of sour milk [paul], with salt [ooppoo], pepper [q.v.], turmeric [country saffron], and other spices, and eaten with rice [q.v.] or pulse [dholl]. As now prepared for Anglo-indians, meat or vegetables [keeray] are used instead of the sour milk [chutney, poppadam, vadagam]. Made up curry powder [masaulay] is composed of many substances, turmeric being the principal ingredient; coriander [cassiber] seeds and black pepper are the ingredients next in importance, while small quantities of cayenne pepper [q.v.], cardamoms [q.v.], cumin [jeerah] and fenugreek [maitee] are also indispensable; ginger [q.v.], cloves [lavangam] and allspice [china pepper] are sometimes added. The following are two key-lists of the condimentary curry ingredients of S. india; further information must be traced in the glossary paragraphs through the small-type cross references at end of this volume; see also vricsham, 7, for the method of expressing the products, &c., of plant in the dravidian languages.—"*a*" Allium cepa, onion, bulb; Allium sativum, garlic, bulb; Andropogon schœnanthus, lemon grass, leaf; Apium graveolens, celery, root and petioles; Bassia longifolia, common mohwah, oil; Borassus flabelliformis, palmyra, jaggery, nut and toddy; Brassica campestris, sub-species campestris, colza, leaf, oil and seed; Brassica campestris, subspecies napus, rape, leaf, oil and seed; Capsicum annuum, common chilly, fruit; Capsicum frutescens, shrubby chilly, fruit; Capsicum grossum, caffrie chilly, fruit; Capsicum minimum, bird's-eye chilly, fruit; Capsicum nepalense, nepaul chilly, fruit; Carum carui, caraway, seed; Carum copticum, ajwaun, seed; Carum roxburghianum, ajmood ajwaun, seed; Caryota urens, bastard sago palm, toddy and jaggery; Cassytha filiformis, air plant, leaf; Cinnamomum iners, country cinnamon, bark and leaf; Cinnamomum tamala, cassia cinnamon, bark, leaf and bud; Cinnamomum zeylanicum, ceylon cinnamon, bark and leaf; Citrus aurantium, var. bergamia, bergamot orange, rind; Cocos nucifera, cocoanut, toddy, vinegar, jaggery, oil and cocoanut water; Coriandrum sativum, coriander, seed and green plant; Crocus sativus, saffron, stigmas; Cucumis sativus, common cucumber, oil of seed and young fruit; Cuminum cyminum, cummin, seed; Curcuma longa, turmeric, tuber; Elettaria cardamomum, cardamom, capsule; Eriodendron anfractuosum, silk-cotton tree, young fruit; Eugenia caryophyllata, clove tree, flower bud; Ferula narthex, asafœtida, gum; Fœniculum vulgare, indian fennel, leaf and seed; Garcinia cambogia, malabar gamboge, fruit; Garuga pinnata, garooga, fruit; Illicium anisatum, star anise, fruit; Lepidium sativum, cress, seed and green plant; Loranthus longiflorus, gooloom, bark; Mangifera indica, mango, kernels and dried fruit; Mentha piperita, peppermint, leaf; Mentha pulegium, pennyroyal; Mentha sativa, indian peppermint, leaf; Mentha viridis, spearmint, leaf; Moringa pterygosperma, indian horse radish, leaf, flower, pod and root; Murraya kœnigii, curry-leaf tree, leaf; Myristica fragrans, common nutmeg, nutmeg and mace; Myristica malabarica, malabar nutmeg, fruit; Nigella sativa, small fennel, seed; Ocimum basilicum, sweet basil, leaf or whole plant; Origanum marjorana, marjoram, leaf; Papaver somniferum, opium poppy, seed; Peucedanum graveolens, dill, seed; Phœnix sylvestris, wild date, toddy; Phyllanthus distichus, brazil cherry, fruit; Phyllanthus emblica, emblic myrobalan, fruit; Pimenta acris, pimento, leaf and berry; Pimpinella anisum, anise, seed; Piper betel, betel pepper, leaf; Piper chaba, chaab pepper, fruit; Piper cubeba, cubeb pepper, dried berry; Piper longum, long pepper, berry; Piper nigrum, black pepper, dried berry; Pteroselinum sativum, parsley, leaf; Saccharum officinarum, sugar-cane, jaggery and sugar; Sesamum indicum, gingelly, oil; Spondias mangifera, hog plum, fruit and leaf; Tamarindus indica, tamarind, fruit and leaf; Terminalia catappa, country almond, oil; Thymus vulgaris, thyme, leaf; Trigonella fœnum-græcum, fenugreek, green plant and seed; Vitex trifolia, water notchy, fruit; Zanthoxylum alatum, tejbul, fruit; Zanthoxylum rhetsa, rhetsa, fruit; Zingiber officinale, ginger, rhizome.—"*b*" Air plant, cassytha; Ajwaun, carum; Aniseed, pimpinella; Asafœtida, ferula; Basil, ocimum; Brazil cherry, phyllanthus; Caraway, carum; Cardamom, elettaria; Celery, apium; Chilly, capsicum; Cinnamon, cinnamomum; Clove tree, eugenia; Cocoanut, cocos; Colza, brassica; Coriander, coriandrum; Country almond, terminalia; Cress, lepidium; Cucumber, cucumis; Cummin, cuminum; Curry-leaf tree, murraya; Date, phœnix; Dill, peucedanum; Fennel, fœniculum, nigella; Fenugreek, trigonella; Gamboge, garcinia; Garlic, allium; Garooga, garuga; Gingelly, sesamum; Ginger, zingiber; Gooloom, loranthus; Hog plum, spondias; Horse radish, moringa; Lemon grass, andropogon; Mango, mangifera; Marjoram, origanum; Mohwah, bassia; Myrobalan, phyllanthus; Notchy, vitex; Nutmeg, myristica; Onion, allium; Orange, citrus; Palmyra, borassus; Parsley, pteroselinum; Pennyroyal, mentha; Pepper, piper; Peppermint, mentha; Pimento, pimenta; Poppy, papaver; Rape, brassica; Rhetsa, zanthoxylum; Saffron, crocus; Sago palm, caryota; Silk-cotton tree, eriodendron; Spearmint, mentha; Star anise, illicium; Sugar-cane, saccharum; Tamarind, tamarindus; Tejbul, zanthoxylum; Thyme, thymus; Turmeric, curcuma.——*Curry-leaf tree*

(सुरभिनिम्ब - surabhinimba, San.; कहिनिम्ब - karhinimba, Mahr.; करबेवु - karabévu, Conc.; کریاپات - kariyápát, Hind.; کرے پاك - karepák, Dec.; ಕರಿಬೇವು - karibévu, Can.; ಬೇಸೊಪ್ಪು - bésoppu, Too.; కరివేప - karivépa, Tel.; ବାସଙ୍ଗ - básang, Oor.; കറുവേപ്പ - karuvéppu, Mal.; කරපිංචා - karapiñcha, Singh.; கருவேம்பு - karuvémbu, Tam.). Title as used in curries, but really a corruption of tamul. San. from (surabhi, san. fragrant + nimba, san. neem tree, melia azadirachta, linn.). Hind. from (kariyá, hind. black + pát, leaf), from color of leaf. Dec. from hindostany by corruption. Can. from (kari, can. black + bévu, can. the neem tree). Too. from (bé, too. to cook + soppu, too. leaf). Tel. from (kari, tel. black + vépa, tel. the neem tree). Tam. from (karumai, tam. blackness + vémbu, tam. margosa tree, melia azadirachta, linn.). San. also (krishnanimba), meaning black neem; (krishnapatra), meaning black leaved; (kaidarya), meaning juice + praised [maroothani]; (kálasháka), meaning black vegetable. Mahr. also (jhirang); (jiraní); (karépáka). Hind. also (bursanga); (harri); (katním); (simboli); (kareaphal); (kariphalli). Dec. also (karnívím), meaning bitter neem. Tel. also (karépákuchettu); (karimpákuchettu). Title otherwise Black neem, Carepauk tree, Citron wort, Fragrant neem, Kikuel oil tree [tooth-brush tree], Simbolee oil tree. Botanically Murraya [caroovajmboo] kœnigii, spr., rutaceæ [vricsham, 32]. Alias Bergera kœnigii; Nimboo meloides. Nimbo, from (nimba, san. margosa). Small tree with pinnate leaves; leaflets alternate, ovate, acuminate, pubescent, somewhat serrated; panicles corymbiform, terminal; calyx five-cleft; petals five, spreading; berry one-celled, one-seeded; flowers small, white; common in jungles and much cultivated in native gardens; whole plant has peculiar odour; flowers in hot season. The roots spread widely and send up numerous suckers; they have a thick soft bark, the parenchyme of which is loaded with oil globules and has an agreeable odour and taste like fresh ginger [q.v.]; the leaves yield to distillation a small quantity of volatile oil resembling that obtained from bael [q.v.] leaves. Root medicinally laxative; bark and roots stimulant and used externally in eruptions, and in infusion to check vomitings in cholera [vaunty bhaidy]; tender leaves boiled in milk [paul], bruised, and applied as a poultice, to bites of poisonous animals; fresh leaves eaten raw in dysentery; infusion of toasted leaves stops vomiting; substituted for british peppermint [poodeenah] oil; leaves generally stomachic and tonic; leaves, bark and root quoted in pharm., non-officinal. Leaves used for seasoning curries, and mixed in curry pastes; retain their flavor when dry. Pulp of fruit gives a white juice, which blackens the skin like walnuts [acroot]; a yellow, clear, and transparent oil is procured from seeds, known as simbolee oil. Wood greyish-white, hard, durable. No other common species here.

CURTA (కర్త - karta, Tel.; കർത്താവ - karttáv, Mal.; கர்த்தா - karttá, Tam.). From (kri, san. to do). An agent, husband, proprietor, heir, managing member of a family. Also one of the five supreme deities in augamam [q.v.] philosophy.——*Curtaukkal* (கர்த்தாக்கள் - karttákkal, Tam.). Plural form. Title of the Naick rulers at Madura.

CURTS (خرچ - kharch, *Hind.*). Plural (ikhráját). From (kharaja, ar. to issue forth). Expense of any kind; a cess levied on cultivators to provide for expenses; debit side of an account. Curtsdar, debtor; Curtskhah, creditor. Compare Compradore.

CUSBAH (قصبه - kasbah, *Hind.*). From (kasab, ar. a tract). Market town, principal village.

CUSCUS (वीरण - vírana, *San.*; वाळा - válá, *Mahr.*; भाणावलो - bhánávaló, *Conc.*; اسیر - usír, *Ar.*; خس - khas, *Pers.* and *Hind.*; بالا - bálá, *Dec.*; اکرونگی - akarwangi, *Malay*; ಲಾವಂಚ - lávancha, *Can.*; ಮುಡ್ಯಾಲ - mudyala, *Too.*; వట్టివేరు - vattivéru, *Tel.*; രാമച്ചം - rámaççam, *Mal.*; සවැන්දරා - savandará, *Singh.*; வெட்டிவேர் - vettivér, *Tam.*). Title from persian. San. from (víra, san strong); from scent [false ginger]. Malay from (akar, malay, scandent plant + wangi, malay, fragrant). Tel. from tamul. Mal. from (lámajjaka, san. the grass) [lemon grass]. Tam. from (vettu, tam. to cut + vér, tam. root); in tanjore and south always connected with cooroovair or coleus osmirrhizon. San. also (ushíra), meaning root in demand; (bahumúla), meaning many roots; (ranapriya), meaning battle + liking; (víratara), meaning very strong; (lámajjaka), meaning destroying sap. Ar. also (izkhar). Pers. also (bíkhiwálá), meaning great root. Hind. also (khaskhas); (usir). Can. also (mudivala), meaning to adorn + tail; (báladahullu), meaning tail + grass; (kasuvuhullu); (nesehullu), meaning to jump + grass; (kádukaridappasajjehullu), meaning wild + black + thick + bed + grass. Tel. also (avuruganddi); (nallavattivéru), meaning black + cuscus + root, properly coleus osmirrhizon; (tellavattivéru), meaning white + cuscus + root; (vidavalivéru); (vákila); (kasavu), meaning grass. Mal. also (vettivér), meaning cut root. Singh. also (savandana); (savanna). Tam. also (vilámiççamvér), from sanscrit; (vizhalvér), meaning excellent + root; (viranam), meaning heroic. Title otherwise Khas-khas, Vettivair. Botanically Andropogon [beard grass] muricatus, retz., graminaceæ [vricsham, 156]. Alias Agrostis verticillata; Anatherium muricatum; Andropogon aromaticus, festucoides, squarrosus; Phalaris zizainia, zizanoides; Rhaphis muricata; Vetiveria odorata. Vetiveria from tamul. Root perennial, fibrous; culms numerous, smooth, slightly compressed at the base, 4–6 feet; leaves bifarious near the base, narrow, erect; florets in pairs, awnless, male and hermaphrodite, the former pedicelled, latter sessile. Tufted grass, consists of many long, spongy, brown fibres, common on coast; abundantly in rich moist ground; the lowest part of the culms, with or without a portion of its roots, is cut; contains a resin [raul], and some volatile oil which is difficult to extract. Infusion of root is gentle stimulant, and makes drink in fevers; reduced to powder, roots given for bile in bilious affections; and, mixed with milk, externally as cooling applications to skin irritations; in pharm. non-officinal. Cattle will not eat the grass, except when quite young. Roots have fragrant odour, especially when moistened; used for manufacture of screens or blinds [tatty], being interwoven with wicker work which, applied to doors and windows during hot weather and moistened, give out fragrant odour and cool the apartment; the culm is used for thatching.——*Black cuscus* (ಕರಿಲಾವಂಚ - karilávancha, Can.). Title from color of root. Same as Ibharancoosha.

CUSH (کش - kash, *Pers.*). From (kashídan, pers. to draw). Suffix in compounds; as Peshcush, first + drawn, first charge.

CUSTOMER (ஆயக்காரன் - áyakkáran, *Tam.*). Tam. from (áya, san. revenue + káran, tam. possessor). In old books the native official who exacted customs duties [sayer].

CUSTOORY (कस्तूरि - kastúri, *San.*; مشك - mishk, *Hind.*). San. from (ka, san. head + stu, san. to praise). San. also (mriganábhi), meaning deer + navel; (nábhi), meaning navel; (mushka), meaning scrotum.—"*a*" Title otherwise Musk. Moschus of chemists. The inspissated and dried secretion from the preputial follicles of moschus moschiferus, which animal however is not represented in s. india; in its recent state, it has the consistence of an electuary of a reddish brown color; but by being kept, it becomes dry and crumbly; odour powerful and peculiar, bitterish heavy taste; when of rather light-brown color, and granulated, it is impure; if dark, homogeneous and divided in many parts by a thin cuticle, it is of good quality; musk is adulterated either by dried blood or asphaltum [shilajit]; factitious musk may be made by digesting together rectified oil of amber, one part with nitric acid [shorey katezaub], four parts, to be afterwards well washed in water; smell similar to that of musk or ambergris [meenamber], and may be substituted for them as medicine. Medicinally stimulant and antispasmodic; used in the low stages of febrile diseases as a stimulant and in various nervous affections as an antispasmodic; in veterinary practice a scruple with two drachms of gentian [chiretta] given daily to horses [ghorah] suffering from rheumatism or cold. The chief Indian musk-scented animal is the so-called musk rat [q.v.] in reality a shrew, but its odorous secretion is not utilized. Compare also Civet and Musk rat.—"*b*" Proper name common to both sexes. Custoorirungan means vishnoo with musk mark on forehead [peyar].—"*c*" Plant first term. From fragrance. Ex.:—Acacia farnesiana (kastúritumma), musk babool; Hibiscus abelmoschus (kastúribenda), musk bendy; Jasminum pubescens (kastúrimallige), musk jasmine; Triphasia trifoliata (kattúriyelumiççai), musk lime. See gloss. paragraphs.

CUTCH (कात - káta, *Mahr.*; کات - kát, *Hind.*; کتھا - katthá, *Dec.*; کچو - kachu, *Malay*; ಕಾಚು - káchu, *Can.*; ಕಾಚು - káchu, *Too.*; కాచు - kátsu, *Tel.*; കാത്ത - káttu, *Mal.*; காசுக்கட்டி - kásukkatti, *Tam.*). Title from malay. Mahr. from (kvát'ha, san. decoction); extract by boiling. Hind. from (kvát'ha, san. extract). Can., &c., from (kásu, can. to boil). Mal. from hindostany. Tam. from (káyççu, tam. to boil + katti, tam. lump); inspissated lump by boiling. Mal. also (káshikkatti). Tam. also (kattakkámbu), from (gátahgambir, malay, gambier gum); (kásu). Also called Black catechu, Pegu catechu. Catechu nigrum of chemists. Formerly called Terra japonica, or Terra catechu; as believed to be mineral. Now only Pale cutch or gambier [q.v.] retains this name. Product of Acacia catechu, willd., leguminosæ [catechu] and other plants. Four principal kinds are found in the Madras market. First, the dark colored Catechu nigrum, from Acacia catechu; second, Catechu pallidum, imported from Singapore, the product of Uncaria gambier, roxb. [gambior]; third, a dark catechu from Areca catechu, linn. [areca]; fourth, white catechu, grey or pale brown externally and white internally, also known as Hyderabad catechu. There is cutch also from Acacia suma [white sundra] and sundra [sundra].

CUTCHA (کچا - kaççá, *Hind.*). Crude; in contradistinction to pucka, complete. When there are different measures or weights of same name, the smaller is cutcha. So also green, unripe. Also current, not closed. A cutcha-built house is one built with unburnt bricks [shengal], and clay [calimunn] for mortar [cauray].——*Cutcha seer* (کچا سیر - kaççáser, Hind.). From (above + ser, hind. seer). Small seer. Bazaar weight. 8 pollums = 1 cutcha seer; 5 cutcha seers = 1 viss [niray, 2 c, e]. Approximate actual value, 1 cutcha seer = 9$\frac{7}{8}$ oz. Used in every district except Malabar and Tinnevelly. In Kurnool it is equal to 8$\frac{1}{4}$ oz. In Bellary it is 8 oz. and 10$\frac{1}{2}$ drams. See vol. I, 609; II, 506, 507, 509.

CUTCHAM (கச்சம் - kaççam, *Tam.*). Tortoise [aumay, coormam].——*Cutchaleshwaran* (கச்சாலேசுவரன் - kaççálesuvaran, Tam.). From (kaççálai, tam. the tortoise shrine in conjeeveram + íshvara, san. lord). Epithet of Shiva. Hindoo 2nd or pers. name. Familiarly Cutchay, Cutchoo, Cutchauloo. The short forms are applied to females also. Cutchan is the tortoise catcher or eater, Pariah proper name [peyar].

CUTCHERRY (کچهری - kachehrí, *Hind.*). From (kutsita, san. bad + hri, san. to take); from dealing with petty criminal cases. A revenue or police office; or its establishment. Cutcherrycull or stone of office is name given to some old stone monuments [aursham].

CUTCHY (கச்சி - kaççi, *Tam.*). Means the heart-leaved moonseed plant, tinospora cordifolia, miers [goolancha]. Native name of Conjeeveram. Changed by Bramins into Canjy.——*Cutchinaud* (கச்சிநாடு - kaççinádu, Tam.). Same as Cunchinaud. One of the two ancient talooks into which Calastry zemindarry was divided; the other being Calastry.

CUTT (కట్టు - kattu, *Tel.*; കെട്ട് - kattu, *Mal.*; கட்டு - kattu, *Tam.*). Dam. Suffix in place names as Pullicutt, meaning village + dam. As a verb means to bind, construct or pay.——*Cuddauyam* (కడాయము - kaddáyamu, Tel.). From (kattu, tel. to bind). Compulsory work.——*Cutla* (కట్ల - katla, Tel.). Locative plural form. Suffix in place names; as Motacutla, meaning rude + embankment.——*Cutla paumb* (کٹان کا سانپ - kattánká-sámp, Hind.; కట్లపాము - katlapámu, Tel.; കെട്ടുവരിയൻ - kattu-variyan, Mal.; கட்டுவிரியன் - kattuviriyan, Tam.). Hind. from (kattu, tel. ring + sámp, hind. snake). Tel. from (kattu, tel. band + pámu, tel. snake). Mal. and Tam. from (kattu, tam. band + viriyan, tam. a viper). Snake with rings. Odontomus nympha, colubridæ [paumb], ophidii colubriformes, ophidia [sarpam], reptilia [sarpy, 17], of naturalists [jantoo].——*Cutlay* (కట్లె - katle, Can.; கட்டளை - kattalai, Tam.). From (kattu, tam. to bind). Rule. Measure. Goldsmith's weight. 24 cutlay pagodas = 1 pollum [niray, 3 a]. Approximate actual value, 1 cutlay pagoda = 56 grains. Compare Hind. miscal, Tel. kurruck-varahah, Tam. varauhan.——*Cutnam* (కట్నము - katnamu, Tel.). From (kattu, tel. to pay). Present made to superiors; present by relations to each other at the time of a marriage [bhet, nuzzer, wolfa].——*Cuttachootta* (కట్టచుట్ట - kattatsutta, Tel.). From (kattu, tel. band + tsutta, tel. coil). Terms co-extensive with the family Oligodontidæ, ophidii colubriformes, ophidia [sarpam], reptilia [sarpy, 16], of naturalists [jantoo]. The Oligodonts have the head nearly always with symmetrical arrow-shaped markings. The following are the known species in Southern india:—"*a*" Oligodon affinis. Small. Scales in seventeen rows; body brownish grey; back crossed by about thirty-eight short black streaks; belly white, with sub-quadrangular black spots, both colors being distributed in nearly equal; Anamullay hills.—"*b*" Oligodon brevicauda. Scales in fifteen rows; body greyish violet; a band runs along the vertebral line; ground-color of the belly the same as of the upper parts, with black quadrangular spots; sub-caudals whitish; Anamullay mountains.—"*c*" Oligodon elliotti. Scales in fifteen rows; Madras.—"*d*" Oligodon fasciatus. Scales in fifteen rows; body brownish olive; trunk with about twenty-seven broadish, brown, black-edged cross-bands, each slightly interrupted by a narrow yellow vertebral line; belly whitish, with small brown spots, more numerous on the sides than in the middle.—"*e*" Oligodon modestus. Scales in fifteen rows; brown spot below eye; body uniform greyish brown; belly white, with quadrangular black spots.—"*f*" Oligodon spilonotus. Scales in fifteen rows; head with symmetrical brown, black-edged markings; back with eight-shaped brown, black-edged transverse spots; distant from one another; lower parts uniform white.—"*g*" Oligodon spinipunctatus. Scales in seventeen rows.—"*h*" Oligodon subgriseus. Scales in fifteen rows. Back with numerous cross streaks, formed by the black edges of some of the scales, and interrupted by three more or less distinct, narrow whitish lines, one of which runs along the vertebral line; belly uniform white; southern parts of peninsula.—"*i*" Oligodon sub-punctatus. Body greyish, dorsal series of round black spots edged with white; belly whitish; coast of Malabar.—"*j*" Simotes bicatenatus. Of fierce habits, but harmless; has scales in nineteen rows; light brownish, with three rather indistinct dark longitudinal bands, one along the back; belly yellowish; sub-caudals nearly uniform yellowish.—"*k*" Simotes binotatus. Alias Xenodon dubium. Scales in seventeen rows; head with three angular white, black-edged cross bands; back with a series of pairs of square, brownish-grey, black-edged; lower parts uniform white; Coast of Malabar.—"*l*" Simotes russellii. Alias Coluber arnensis, monticolus, russellii; Coronella russellii. Scales in seventeen rows; brownish olive, with the bands on the head very distinct; body with well-defined black, white-edged cross bands; belly uniform white.—"*m*" Simotes trilineatus. Scales in seventeen rows; body reddish brown above and below, with three longitudinal bands; one runs along the vertebral line and is yellowish; the others are white, bordering the sides of the belly.—"*n*" Simotes venustus. Alias Xenodon venustum. Scales in seventeen rows; ground-color greyish or reddish brown, with three series of rounded black, yellow-edged spots; belly white, with quadrangular black spots, both colors being distributed in equal proportions.——*Cuttil* (കട്ടിൽ - kattil, Mal.). From (kattu, mal. to bind). Bedstead [cot]. Cuttil staunom, from (st'hána, mal. place) is property given by a Nayar to his wife and children [maroomakkatoyem].——*Cuttingia* (కట్టింగ్య - kattingyá, Tel.). Village, Mittah, Ghaut; Ganjam dist., Bodagooda tal., Maliah division; pop. 550; lat. 19° 41′; long. 84° 14′; from Balligooda S.S.E. 38 miles; from Chetterpore W.N.W. 56 miles. West of Bodagooda. Small mittah [q.v.] paying a quite-rent of 50 rupees. The mittahdar was formerly a feudal dependent of the Bodagooda rajahs. In consequence of a contest in 1807 between the Cuttingia sirdar [q.v.] assisted by the Chief of Sooradah, and the Godapore and Bodagooda zemindars assisted by the Shergadah people, a sunnud [q.v.] was granted to Cuttingia. Fort of the Taut [q.v.] rajah of Cuttingia. Ghaut from Sooradah viâ Meercote to Bammoonigaum, the most direct route to centre of Chinna kimedy maliahs.——*Cuttiwaukum* (கத்திவாக்கம் - kattivákkam, Tam.). From (kattu, tam. dam + pákkam, tam. village); from being near the mouth of the corteliaur. Village; Chingleput dist., Sydapett tal.; pop. 4,359; acres 1,177; lat. 13° 13′; long. 80° 23′; from Madras N. 12 miles; from Poolicat S. 14 miles; from Sydapett N.N.E. 15¾ miles; from the sea W. ¼ mile. Commonly known as Ennore, though that village is at the north bank of the backwater. A fishing village on a backwater into which falls the Corteliaur, and through which runs the Buckingham canal [q.v.] connecting with Madras. Being once a favorite resort of Europeans from Madras it has several European bungalows, but the place is chiefly notable for the extensive salt-pans in its neighbourhood. In 1769 Hyder encamped near this.——*Cuttoo* (కట్టు - kattu, Can.; కట్టు - kattu, Tel.; கட்டு - kattu, Tam.). From (kattu, tam. to bind). A rule, tie, band.——*Cuttoobuddy* (కట్టుబడి - kattubadi, Tel.). From (above + badi, tel. suffix meaning state). A favorable quit-rent [jody] on lands given to public servants, especially in zemindarries [inam].——*Cuttoobuddy buntrote* (కట్టుబడి బంట్రోతు - kattubadibantrótu, Tel.). From (kattubadi, tel. the tenure, so called + bantrótu, tel. peon). Peons who are paid for their services by grants of land subject to quit-rent only [inam]. They are divided into Grauma cuttoobuddy and Jangicuttoobuddy. The former are strictly village servants, and are required to perform service throughout the year. The latter are only called out for service on emergent occasions. See vol. I, 112.——*Cuttoo goottagay* (கட்டுக்குத்தகை - kattukkuttagai, Tam.). From (above + kuttagai, tam. lease). Joint renting.——*Cuttoo togay* (கட்டுத்தொகை - kattuttogai, Tam.). From (above + togai, tam. total). Grand total.——*Cuttooviriyan* (కట్టెడ - katteda, Tel.; கட்டுவிரியன் - kattuviriyan, Tam.). Band viper. Name applied to all small banded snakes [viriyan].

CUTTACAUMBOO (கத்தக்காம்பு - kattakkámbu, *Tam.*). Means gatah gambier [q.v.], from malay. Areca [q.v.] nut cutch [q.v.] chewed with betel-leaf [paun].

CUTTALAY (धामा - dhámá, *Mahr.*; కచ్చెలి - kaççeli, *Tel.*; கத்தலை - kattalai, *Tam.*). The genus Sciæna, sciænidæ, acanthopterygii, teleostei, pisces [matsyam, 12], of naturalists [jantoo]. The species best known to the natives are shown below.——*Black cuttalay* (నల్లకచ్చెలి - nallakaççeli, Tel.; ବୋଟାହଲ - botahl, Oor.; கருங்கத்தலை - karungattalai, Tam.). Tel. from (nalla, tel. black). Tam. from (karumai, tam. blackness). Sciæna [cuttalay] coitor, sciænidæ, acanthopterygii, teleostei [matsyam, 12], of naturalists. Alias Bola coitor; Corvina coitor, nalla-katchelee; Johnius coitor; nalla-katchelee from teloogoo. Snout scarcely overhanging jaws but prominent and swollen superiorly, upper jaw somewhat longer; scales cycloid on snout and below eyes, elsewhere ctenoid; lateral-line makes a gradual curve, and above commencement of anal becomes straight, its tubes give off a single branch on either side; colors silvery shot with gold and purple, upper half of first dorsal blackish; soft dorsal, caudal, and anal dark externally, whilst last fin has darkish basal band; larger rivers, descending to sea at seasons; attains a foot.——*Gray cuttalay* (سفید کتالی - sufedkattále; Hind.; வெள்ளைக்கத்தலை - vellaikkattalai, Tam.). Tam. from (vellai, tam. white). Sciæna [cuttalay] albida, sciænidæ, acanthopterygii, teleostei [matsyam, 12], of naturalists. Alias Bola coibor; Corvina albida, neilli. Jaws equal in front, or upper slightly longer, cleft of mouth slightly oblique; three pores across front of snout; free edge of skin of snout with five orifices and slight lateral lobe; bluntish knob below symphysis of lower jaw behind base of which is large open pore; short barbel between central pore and anterior lateral one, and very minute one at posterior pore; scales cycloid on head, elsewhere ctenoid, fine ones covering bases of soft and anal, and in adult whole of caudal fin; those anterior to base of first dorsal fin are much smaller than those posteriorly; lateral-line becomes straight opposite the anal fin; colors silvery, with light streak along each row of scales, first dorsal in young with black inter-spinous membrane, but only having black outer edge in adult; second dorsal stained gray at upper third; dark bluish mark on opercles, most distinct in young; ventral, anal, and caudal yellowish; sea; common, but not in esteem for table; 3 feet.——*Rusty cuttalay* (துருக்கத்தலை - turukkattalai, Tam.). Tam. from (turu, tam. rust). Sciæna [cuttalay] belengeri, sciænidæ, acanthopterygii, teleostei [matsyam, 12], of naturalists. Alias Corvina belengeri, lobata; Johnius belengeri; Sparus. Snout rounded, overhanging upper jaw which is in advance of lower; cleft of mouth almost horizontal; snout with three open pores across base; free edge of skin has one central and a second opening on either side dividing it into four lobes; five rather small open pores on lower jaw; scales form a thick covering for the base of the soft dorsal fin; lateral-line curves to opposite end of anal where it becomes straight, at first indistinct; tubes with one or two branches; colors dark-gray, dorsals, anal, and caudal almost black; dark blotch on opercle; some specimens much lighter; sea; common on western coast.——*Striped cuttalay* (చారికల్లకచ్చెలి - tsárikallakaççeli, Tel.; കത്തല - kattala, Mal.; வரிக்கத்தலை - varikkattalai, Tam.). Title from broad black stripes. Tel. from (tsára, tel. stripe + kalla, tel. false). Mal. from (kal, mal. stone + tala, mal. head). Tam. from (vari, tam. stripe). Tam. also (kuruvai), meaning short fish; (kurungattalai), meaning small sciæna genus. Sciæna [cuttalay] maculata, sciænidæ, acanthopterygii, teleostei [matsyam, 12], of naturalists. Alias Corvina maculata; Johnius maculatus; Perca sarikullah. Sarikullah from teloogoo. Upper jaw overlapping lower, and being itself overhung by the snout; transverse row of four pores across snout, free edge of skin with five orifices and a lateral lobe; central pore below mandibular symphysis; scales ctenoid, except on cheeks; lateral-line curves to below middle of soft dorsal when it proceeds straight, tubes have usually a single branch on either side; colors silvery-gray, abdomen whitish, cheeks tinged golden; five broad black bands, sometimes interrupted, extend over back, first from nape passes backwards and downwards, and shortly after crossing lateral-line abruptly terminates; second commencing opposite from fifth to seventh dorsal spines passes backwards and downwards, terminating opposite middle of ventral fin; third arising opposite second and third dorsal rays or between two dorsal fins passes downwards parallel to second band; fourth commences below centre of second dorsal and descends to lateral-line; fifth taking same course is below last few dorsal rays; occasionally there is a sixth over free portion of tail; upper two-thirds of first dorsal stained black, becoming more indistinct with age; caudal slightly tinged black, other fins yellowish; sea; a foot in length; not good eating. ——*White cuttalay* (తెల్లకచ్చెలి - tellakaççeli, Tel.; வெள்ளைக் கத்தலை - vellaikkattalai, Tam.). Tel. from (tella, tel. white). Tam. from (vellai, tam. white). Sciæna [cuttalay] miles, sciænidæ, acanthopterygii, teleostei [matsyam, 12], of naturalists. Alias Corvina celebica, dorsalis, miles, sampitensis, soldado, wolfii; Holocentrus miles; Johnius celebicus, miles; Labrus tella katchelee; Pseudosciæna miles; Tella katchelee from teloogoo. Cleft of mouth moderately oblique; snout not overhanging jaws which are of about equal length anteriorly, or the upper slightly longer; scales cycloid on head and chest, ctenoid on remainder of body; lateral-line becomes straight above hind edge of anal, its tubes arborescent posteriorly; colors grayish darkened with green along back, becoming white on sides and abdomen, sometimes a small brown spot in front of each dorsal ray; outer edges of fins in some specimens dark, except ventral which is white; sea; 2 feet.

CUTTY (కత్తి - katti, *Tel.*; கத்தி - katti, *Tam.*). From (krit, san. to cut). Knife. Cutticauran is a toddy-drawer. Cutti-chatty are toddy drawer's knives and pots. Cunnamcutty is a burgler's tool.——*Cuttimandoo* (కత్తిమందు - kattimandu, Tel.; கத்திமருந்து - kattimandu, Tam.). Tel. from (above + mandu, tel. medicine); from serving as a cement to fix knives into handles. Title otherwise Caoutchouc plant, Cement plant, Knife-mending plant. Botanically Euphorbia [milk hedge] cattimandoo, w. ell., euphorbiaceæ [vricsham, 118]. Specific name from teloogoo. Shrub or small tree; stem erect, five-sided, with prominent repand angles; stipulary thorns paired, short, subulate; leaves sessile, succulent, deciduous, obovate, subcuneate, cuspidate, glabrous; peduncles crowded, three-flowered, middle one usually sterile, and lateral one fertile, flowering after the fall of the leaf. Abounds in milky sap, of nature of gutta-percha [q.v.], which after being boiled and formed into cakes or cylinders, becomes resinous or brittle. Fresh milk employed as outward application in rheumatism. Hardened milk employed as cement for fixing knives into handles and other similar purposes, which is effected by heating it; articles may easily be moulded by the hand from it [pauchonty].——*Cuttipanam* (കത്തിപ്പണം - kattippanam, Mal.). From (above + panam, mal. money). Tax on toddy-drawing.——*Cuttiry* (కత్తెరదొంగ - katteradonga, Tel.). Tel. from (kattera, tel. scissors + donga, tel. thief). Pick-pocket.

D (ड - ḍa, द - da, *San.*; ڈ - ḍál, د - dál, *Hind.*). The cerebral. San. epithet of shiva. Hind. in arithmetic 4; the fourth day of the week [vauram], Wednesday; the planet [graham] Mercury [boodhan]; the sign [raushy] Leo [asad, simham].

DABBILY (డబ్బిలి - dabbili, *Tel.*). Knave; term of abuse.

DABKY (دبکی - dabkí, *Hind.*; పురిడిపిట్ట - puridipitta, *Tel.*; ଗୁଣ୍ଡ୍ରୁ - gundru, *Oor.*). Hind. means squatter. Tel. from (puridi, tel. quail + pitta, tel. bird). Tel. also (chinnadábapitta), meaning small + quarrel + bird; (telladábapitta), meaning white + quarrel + bird. Title otherwise Button quail. Turnix sykesii, turnicinæ, tinamidæ, rasores [pacshy, 34], of naturalists [jantoo]. Alias Turnix variabilis, dussumierii. Most diminutive game-bird of S. india. Flushed with great difficulty. Low plaintive moan of a single note.

DACOIT (ڈکیت - dakait, *Hind.*; தீவட்டிக்கள்ளன் - tívattikkallan, *Tam.*). From (dákná, hind. to shout); because dacoits call out at the entrance of the village they are about to plunder, to terrify villagers. Tam. from (tívatti, tam. torch + kallan, tam. robber). A member of a gang of dacoity robbers. By law, to constitute dacoity, there must be five or more in the gang committing the crime [deevatticollay].

DACSH (दक्ष् - daksh, *San.*). To be able.——*Dacshan* (दक्ष - daksha, San.). Very ancient mythological personage. An avatar [q.v.] of Bramha [q.v.]. His head was cut off by Veerabhadran [q.v.], and on the intercession of the gods was replaced by that of a he-goat. He had many daughters of whom twenty-seven became the wives of the moon [chundran], forming the lunar asterisms [nacshatram], and others the wives of Cashyapan [q.v.], becoming by him the mothers of gods, demons, men and animals [adity, matam]. See vol. I (71).——*Dacshinacharry* (दक्षिणाचारी - dakshináchárí, San.). From (dakshina, san. right-hand + áchára, san. conduct). Division of the Shauctas [q.v.], followers of the right-hand or purer ritual. The left-hand are Vaumacharries. See vol. I (87).——*Dacshina dhroovam* (दक्षिणध्रुव - dakshinadhruva, San.). South pole or dhroovam [q.v.].——*Dacshina golam* (दक्षिणगोल - dakshinagóla, San.). Southern sphere. Dacshina golaurdham is southern hemisphere [golam].——*Dacshina gungay* (दक्षिणगङ्गा - dakshinagangá, San.). From (dakshina, san. south + gangá, san. the ganges). Ganges [gungay] of the south, especially Cauvery.——*Dacshinam* (दक्षिण - dakshina, San.).—"*a*" Right side, as distinguished from left. Compare dexter and δεξιός.—"*b*" South. δαχιναβάδης of Periplus. The Aryans coming from the west applied term to country on their right hand. In like manner country before them became poorvam or east, and the inhabitants poorvyas or easterns; another word for east (práchi) supplied the Greeks with name πρασία for people of Gangetic valley. Thus dacshinam came to mean Southern india. Compare the Anglo-indian word Deccan [q.v.].—"*c*" Prefix in place names as Dacshina caushy, meaning southern benares.——*Dacshina mandotcham* (दक्षिणमन्दोच्च - dakshinamandóçça, San.). Southern apsis [mandotcham]. Perihelion.——*Dacshina moorty* (दक्षिणामूर्ति - dakshinámúrti, San.). From (dakshina, san. south + múrti, san. image). Agastyan [q.v.], as dwelling in Pothigay [q.v.] in the south. Shiva facing south in his malevolent aspect [aulamarcadavool]. Hindoo 2nd or pers. name [peyar].——*Dacshinaupata janmauna* (दाक्षिणापथजन्मान - dakshinápat'hajanmána, San.). From (dakshina, san. south + pat'ha, san. road + janma, san. birth). South indian aborigines, dravidians.——*Dacshinaurnavam* (दक्षिणार्णव - dakshinárnava, San.). From (dakshina, san. south + arnava, san. sea). The southern ocean, meaning ocean round Ceylon [q.v.].——*Dacshinauyanam* (दक्षिणायन - dakshináyana, San.). Southward progress. Northern solstice [ayanam].——*Dacshinauyana poonyacaulam* (தட்சணாயனப் புண்ணியக்காலம் - tadchanáyanappunniyakkálam, Tam.). Means northern solstice [ayanam] + auspicious time. Same as Audy pundigay.——*Dacshinay* (दक्षिणा - dakshiná, San.; ദക്ഷിണ - dakshina, Mal.). Means right. A gift made to Bramins.

DAEMIA (دیمیہ - dímia, *Ar.*). Hedge cotton [q.v.] shrub.

DAF (دف - daf, *Hind.*; డప్పు - dappu, *Tel.*). A large flat drum or tambour without cymbals [paray, sangeetam, tappattay].

DAFA (دفعہ - dafa, *Hind.*). From (dafa, ar. to impel); coming of a party of men to a place at once. Section. Turn. A band of policemen usually twelve [duffedar, taundah].

DAGAH (دغا - daghá, *Hind.*). From persian. Fraud.——*Dagahjauda* (دغا جھارا - daghájhárá, Hind.). From (jhárá, hind. search). Account of lands clandestinely sown.——*Daghah bauz* (دغاباز - daghábáz, Hind.; దగాబాజి - dagábáji, Tel.). From (báz, pers. player). A sharper [pashapa].

DAGLAH (ڈگلہ - daglah, *Hind.*). From (dhágá, hind. thread + ghálná, hind. to put in). A quilted jacket with long loose sleeves and open cuffs [sheelay].

DAGOBA (देहगोप - déhagópa, *San.*). From (déha, san. body + gup, san. to hide). Word came through the singhalese. A conical erection surmounting relics inside. Booddhist topes. Common in Ceylon. Corresponds to a relic monument which is still erected in Thibet over the body or the ashes of the Llamas. The dagoba is a later development of the sepulchral tumulus of the earlier races [aursham, paundicoozhy, tope].

DAHR (دهر - dahr, *Hind.*). From (dahra, ar. to befal). World, nature, eternity.——*Dahree* (دهری - dahrí, Hind.). Those who believe in eternity of matter and deny the existence of a creator, materialists.

DAKOREE (वरटा - varatá, *San.*; زنبور - zumbúr, *Ar.* and *Pers.*; ڈکوری - dakorí, *Dec.*; تابون - tábuwan, *Malay*; ಕಣಜದಹುಳ - kanajadahula, *Can.*; ಕೊಂಡೊಲು - kúndolu, *Too.*; కందిరీగ - kandiríga, *Tel.*; കടന്നൽ - katunnal, *Mal.*; குளவி - kulavi, *Tam.*). Title from deccany. San. from (vri, san. to encircle); as wheeling round [varatam]. Ar. from (zumbar, ar. to walk proudly). Dec. from (dák, hind. sting). Can. from (kanaja, can. granary + hula, can. insect). Tel. from (kandu, tel. to blister + íga, tel. fly). Mal. from (katu, mal. fierce). Tam. from (kozhuthu, tam. to hollow out). Wasp. Co-extensive with family sphegidæ, hymenoptera, holometabola, insecta [poochy], of naturalists [jantoo]. Distinguished by its metallic lustre. Introduces its eggs into the body of the pupa of some other insect, which it thrusts into key holes and other apertures of houses, and encloses the whole with moistened earth. The young parasite, after undergoing its transformations, gnaws its way into light, and emerges a four-winged fly. The Ampulex compressa, which drags about cockroaches [jhingoor] into which it has implanted its eggs, belongs to this family.

DALADAY (දළදා - daladá, *Singh.*). From (dala, singh. tooth + dá, singh. relic). The left canine tooth of Booddha, the most highly venerated relic among the Booddhists, now at Candy in Ceylon [dagoba].

DALAM (दल - dala, *San.*). From (dal, san. to be divided) [dholl]. Army.——*Dalavoy* (தளவாய் - talaváy, Tam.). From (above + vah, san. to lead). A military commander, or minister of state, title still borne by ministers of Mysore and Travancore. Answers to the Mussalman diwaun [q.v.].——*Dalavoy saitoopaty* (தளவாய்சேதுபதி - talaváysethuppathi, Tam.). Commander + title. Otherwise Sadeiyakka tevar, the third Saitoopaty [q.v.] of Ramnaud; 1635–1645. Deposed by his younger brother Tumby [bettana] on his attempting to proclaim his adopted son Raghoonaut tevar as his successor. Restored in 1640. Murdered by Tumby five years after restoration. See vol. I (124) [charitram].

DALAY (തല - tala, *Mal.*; தலை - talai, *Tam.*). From (st'hala, san. place) [talam]. Place. Suffix in place names; as Aulandalay, meaning place of the banyan [q.v.] tree [talay].

DALLAUL (دلال - dallál, *Hind.*). From (dalla, ar. to point out). A broker [doobash].

DALOYET (ڈھلیت - dhalait, *Hind.*). From (dhál, hind. shield). An armed attendant. Superior class of peons [q.v.] attached to the person of a chief European officer [duffedar].

DAM (दम् - dam, *San.*). To subdue.——*Damam* (दम - dama, San.). The power by which the organs [indriyam] and faculties are kept in subjection [yogam].——*Damayanty* (दमयन्ती - damayantí, San.). From fascinating men. The heroine of Neishadam [q.v.].——*Dammoo* (దమ్ము - dammu, Tel.). From (dama, san. mud). Moisture. Suffix in place names; as Varidammoo, meaning paddy + moisture.——*Damodaran* (दामोदर - dámódara, San.). From (dáma, san. cord + udara, san. belly). Krishnan tethered as a child by a cord round his belly. Nonbramin Hindoo 2nd or pers. name [peyar].——*Damodaraputnam* (தாமோதரப்பட்டணம் - támótharappattanam, Tam.). From (dámódara, san. krishna, proper name + pattana, san. city). Village, Port; Madura dist., Ramnaud zemindarry; lat. 9° 47′; long. 79° 07′; from Madras S.S.W. 240 miles; from Madura E.S.E. 63 miles; from Paushiputnam S.S.W. 1½ miles; from Ramnaud N.N.E. 32 miles; from Tondy N.E. 4½ miles. On Palk's straits [jalasand].

DAMAROO (डमरु - damaru, *San.*). From (dam, san. imitative + ri, san. to give). A kettle drum [paray, sangeetam]. Damarcam, similar, is the drum of Shiva [dindimam]. Damaroocaucrity is a drum-shaped figure in geometry [cshetra ganitam].

DAMASHOY (داماساہی - dámásáhí, *Hind.*). From (dámásáh, hind. merchant's name); who dying insolvent distributed all his property in just proportion among his creditors [curtskhah]. Proportionate distribution.

DAMBAM (डम्भ - dámbha, *San.*). From (dambh, san. to cheat). Hypocrisy, vain show. Dambacharry vilausam, from (vilásam, san. play), is a Tamul drama by Vishwanautan; plot from real life, to ridicule the life of a fop.

DAMMA (دمہ - dammah, *Hind.*). From (dam, pers. breath). Asthma in horses [ashwarogam, ghorah].

DAMMER (यक्षधूप - yakshadhúpa, *San.*; डामर - dámara, *Mahr.*; ڈامر - dámar, *Hind.*; دمر - damar, *Malay*; ಗುಗ್ಗುಳ - guggula, *Can.*; ರಾಳ - rála, *Too.*; గుగ్గిలము - guggilamu, *Tel.*; ചെഞ്ചല്യം - cheñchalyam, *Mal.*; දුම්මල - dummala, *Singh.*; குங்கிலியம் - kungiliyam, *Tam.*). Title from malay, where it means generically resin [raul]. San. from (yaksha, san. the demi-god + dhúpa, san. incense). Mahr. from hindostany. Hind. from malay. Can. from (gud, san. to preserve); useful in nervous diseases [googal]. Too. from (ri, san. to go). Mal. from (chem, mal. red + cháyilyam, mal. vermillion) [shangarf]. A hard, dark-colored, brittle, resinous substance [gond, raul], which exudes from trees of Dammara genus in the Eastern islands and New zealand, whence imported here. Used when melted for spreading over packages, as substitute for pitch [keel, zift]. Indigenous dammers are from other trees; see below.——*Amboyna dammer* (ابنون کا ڈامر - ambúnahkádámar, Hind.). Dammer proper from amboyna [q.v.]; see above.——*Australian dammer* (استریلیہ کا ڈامر - ástreliyákádámar, Hind.). Dammer proper from new zealand; see above.——*Black dammer* (राळधूप - ráladhúpa, Mahr.; کالا ڈامر - káládámar, Hind. and Dec.; ಮಂದಧೂಪ - mandadhúpa, Can.; నల్లరోజనము - nallarójanamu, Tel.; തെള്ളി - telli, Mal.; கருப்புக்குங்கிலியம் - karuppukkungiliyam, Tam.). Title from shining black resin; in contrast to the white dammer tree, vateria indica, linn., which is in these pages called piney dammer [q.v.]; in the north however the article which goes by the name of black dammer is the product of shorea robusta, gærtn. [common saul]; see saul dammer. Mahr. from (rála, mahr. the resin + dhúpa, san. incense). Hind. from (kálá, hind. black + dámar, hind. resin). Can. from (manda, san. slow + dhúpa, san. incense). Tel. from (nalla, tel. black + rójanamu, tel. probably corruption of english rosin). Mal. from (teli, mal. to sift); sifted resin, from its transparency. Tam. also (karuppudámar), meaning black dammer. Resin of Canarium [caunary] strictum, roxb., burseraceæ [vricsham, 35]. Large tree; young parts densely clothed with rusty-colored pubescence; leaflets nine to fifteen, stalked, ovate or ovate-lanceolate, acuminated, at length serrulate-ciliate, hairy; abundant in all the moist ghaut [q.v.] forests on west coast to 4,000–4,500 feet, never seen in dry forests; brilliant crimson foliage; flowers early in the year. Resin [raul] from incisions in trunk is transparent and of a deep brownish yellow or amber color, when held between the eye and the light, but when adhering to the tree has a bright shining black appearance; is a true copaline resin [copal]; is found in large stalactitic masses; insoluble in cold, but partially soluble in boiling alcohol with the addition of camphor [q.v.]; when powdered readily soluble in oil of turpentine [ganda firoza]; emits a more resinous smell and burns with more smoke than white or piney dammer. Quoted in pharm. but non-officinal; a substitute for burgundy pitch in making plasters. Used for many small purposes, as in the manufacture of bottling-wax [mom]; its solution in turpentine forms a tolerable varnish [rangh]; when submitted to destructive distillation it yields about 78 per cent. of oil, resembling that obtained from common colophony; a considerable article of trade with some hill tribes.——*Burmah dammer* (برمی کا ڈامر - barmekádamar, Hind.). Another name for Poonyet [q.v.].——*Cowdee dammer* (کوڑی ڈامر - kaurídámar, Hind.). Same as Australian dammer.——*Dhoona dammer* (धुनाडामर - dhúnádámara, Mahr.). Means sounding dammer, from sound of incense smoke. Same as Saul dammer.——*Dhoop dammer* (धूपडामर - dhúpadámara, Mahr.). Means incense dammer, from use Same as White dammer in either of its applications.——*East indian dammer* (ولایتی ڈامر - viláitídámar, Hind.) Dammer proper from molucca, borneo, java, sumatra, &c.; see above.——*Green dammer* (ہرا ڈامر - harádámar, Hind.). Same as Tambaga dammer.——*Indian dammer* (ناتک کا ڈامر - nátkádámar, Hind.). Term applied to either Black, Piney, or Saul dammers.——*Piney dammer* (कुन्दुर - kundura, San.; चन्द्रस - chandrasa, Mahr.; سندروس - sandrús, Ar.; چندروس - chandrús, Hind.; چندرس - chandras, Dec.; ಬಿಳಿಗುಗ್ಗಿಳ - biliguggila, Can.; ಲೋಭಾನ - lóbhána, Too.; తెల్లగుగ్గిలము - tellaguggilamu, Tel.; വെള്ളക്കുന്തുരുക്കം - vellakkunturukkam, Mal.; குந்துருக்கம் - kundurukkam, Tam.). Title piney, from (payan, mal. gum-yielding tree, vateria indica, linn.). San. from (kundu, san. gum olibanum) [coondoor]. Mahr. from arabic. Can. from (bili, can. white + guggila, can. dammer). Too. from (labana, ar. juice). Tel. from (tella, tel. white + guggilamu, tel. dammer). Mal. from (vella, mal. white + kunduruka, san. gum olibanum). Tam. from (kunduruka, san. gum olibanum). San. also (dhúpa), meaning incense [dhoop dammer]. Mal. also (pantam), meaning tied, probably from use as torch light [deevatty]. Title otherwise Gum animi, Indian copal, Piney tallow, White dammer. Resin of Vateria indica, linn., dipterocarpeæ [vricsham, 24]. Native of Ceylon and Malabar. Known to ancients, but wrongly included by them under the mineral σανδαράκη or realgar [manoshilay]. On wounding the bark of tree a white pellucid fragrant acrid and bitter honey-like resin [raul] exudes, which in the sun becomes yellow and brittle, and looks like amber; insoluble in water; when powdered dissolves in turpentine [gandafiroza]; half-petrified is superior to that obtained from living trees. This dammer is found in bazaar [q.v.] in two forms:—First, large compact and very hard lumps of all shapes, varying externally from bright orange to dull yellow, and internally from light green to light yellow, green predominating; has a shining vitreous fracture, and greatly resembles amber [karbah]; more soluble in alcohol and burns with less smoke, and gives out more fragrant smell, than black dammer [q.v.]. Second small or large masses of a cellular structure, of a shining appearance, and a balsamic odour; greatly inferior to the first sort.——*Poonyet dammer* (پونیت ڈامر - punyatdámar, Hind.). Same as Burmah dammer.——*Raul dammer* (राळडामर - ráladámara, Mahr.). Same as Saul dammer.——*Rock dammer* (ಕಲ್ಲುಗುಗ್ಗಿಲ - kalguggila, Can.; ಕಲ್ಲುರಾಳ - kalluráLa, Too.; ഉറപ്പിന്പശ - urappinpasha, Mal.; உரப்புப்பிசின் - urappuppisin, Tam.). Title from being found in rock-like masses. Can. from (kallu, can. stone + guggila, can. dammer). Too. from (kallu, too. stone + rála, too. dammer). Mal. from (urappu, mal. the tree + pasha, mal. gum). Tam. from (urappu, tam. hardness; applied to the tree, hopea odorata, roxb. + pisin, tam. gum). Resin of Hopea odorata, roxb. [caung].——*Saul dammer* (राल - rála, San.; राळ - rála, Mahr.; قنقهر - kankahar, Ar.; لعل معبری - lalimabarí, Pers.; رال - rál, Hind. and Dec.; دمر بتو - damarbatu, Malay; കുങ്കില്യം - kunkilyam, Mal.; குங்கிலியம் - kungiliyam, Tam.). Title from being obtained from saul [q.v.] tree. San. from (ri, san. to go); applied to resins [raul] which disappear on combustion. Pers. from (lal, pers. resin + mabar, ar. coromandel coast). Malay from (damar, malay, dammer + batu, malay, stone). Mal. from tamul. Tam. from (gud, san. to preserve); useful in nervous diseases [googal]. San. also (ashvakarnaniryása), meaning the tree, shorea robusta, gærtn. + gum; (sálavéshta), meaning shorea robusta, gærtn. + exudation; (sálaniryása), meaning shorea resin; (sarjaniryása), meaning shorea resin. Mahr. also (dhúna), meaning sounding resin, from sound of incense smoke [dhoona dammer]. Resin of Shorea robusta, gærtn. [common saul].——*Tambaga dammer* (തമ്പകഡാമർ - tampakadámar, Mal.). Resin of tambaga saul.——*White dammer* (سفید ڈامر - sufeddámar, Hind.; اجلا ڈامر - ujládámar, Dec.; வெள்ளைக்குங்கிலியம் - vellaikkungiliyam, Tam.). Hind. from (sufed, hind. white + dámar, hind. dammer). Dec. from (ujlá, hind. white + dámar, hind. dammer). Tam. from (vellai, tam. white + kungiliyam, tam. dammer). Term applied either to Dammer proper or to Piney dammer.——*Yellow dammer* (कोङ्कणधूप - kónkanadhúpa, San.; पांढरीविशेष - pándharívishésha, Mahr.; विशेषधूपु - vishéshadhúpu, Conc.; کندر - kundur, Ar., Pers. and Hind.; فرنگی عود کا جھاڑ - farangíúdkájhár, Dec.; دمر - damar, Malay; ಗುಗ್ಗುಳ - guggula, Can.; గుగ్గిలము - gúggilamu, Tel.; മഞ്ഞക്കുങ്കില്യം - maññakkunkilyam, Mal.; குந்துருக்கம் - kundurukkam, Tam.). San. from (kónkana, san. the country so called + dhúpa, san. smoke). Mahr. from (pándhara, san. white + vishésha, mahr. frankincense). Conc. from (vishésha, san. special + dhúpa, san. incense). Pers. from arabic. Dec. from (farangí, hind. foreign + úd, ar. frankincense + jhár, hind. tree). Can. and tel. from (guggula, san. dammer). Mal. from (mañña, mal. yellow + kunkilyam, mal. dammer). Tam. from (kunduruka, san. olibanum) [indian olibanum, piney dammer]. San. also (yakshadhúpa), meaning demi-god + incense; (kundu) [coondoor]. Dec. also (farangíkundur), meaning foreign incense. Can. also (sámbráni), meaning frankincense [saumbrauny]. Tel. also (andugu), meaning burning + tree; (p'harangisámbráni), meaning european + incense; (tellaguggilamu), meaning white + dammer. Mal. also (parankisámpráni). Tam. also (vellaikkungiliyam), meaning white + dammer. Title otherwise Concany resin, Country resin, Doopada [piney tree], Googal, Indian resin, White frankincense. Resin of Boswellia [olibanum] serrata, var. glabra, roxb., burseraceæ [vricsham, 35]. Alias Boswellia balsamifera, glabra; Canarium balsamiferum; Chloroxylon dupada. Dupada, from (dhúpadá, san. incense giving). Tall erect tree covered with greenish ash-colored bark; leaves alternate, unequally pinnate, at the extremities of the branchlets; leaflets six to ten pairs, opposite, broadly lanceolate, obtuse, serrated, glabrous; flowers numerous, on short pedicels, small, white; calyx small, five-toothed; petals five; capsule three-angled, three-celled, three-valved; seeds solitary, surrounded by a membranaceous wing; racemes simple, terminal, fascicled, shorter than the leaves. The fragrant gum resin is same as that of indian olibanum [q.v.] but dries quicker. With wood oil [q.v.], this gum resin [googal] makes a useful coarse varnish [rangh] for doors, windows, &c.; also as a pitch [keel] in dock-yards and by farriers [naulbund] for certain plasters; melted with gingelly [q.v.] oil, is used for covering corks in bottles to preserve them from white-ants [q.v.]; khonds [q.v.] and ooriyas [q.v.] make the leaves into eating plates, and roll up tobacco [pogauk] in them as a cheroot [q.v.]. Wood is heavy, hard and durable.

DANDAM (दण्ड - danda, *San.*). From (dand, san. to punish). A stick; a pole, as a measure of length [kole]; a column of troops [pataulam], army [dalam]; an uninterrupted series; oar of a boat; pole of a banner [dhwajam] or tent [derah].—"*a*" A linear measure, equivalent to fathom. 4 hastams = 1 dandam; 2,000 dandams = 1 crosham [alavay, 1 f.] Approximate actual value, 1 dandam = 6 feet. Same as Hind. baum, Can. bauroo, Tel. niloovoo, Mal. and Tam. maur.—"*b*" Measure of time. 60 vicalays or indian minutes = 1 dandam or indian hour; 60 dandams = 1 dinam or day [caulam, 6]. Approximate actual value, 1 dandam = 24 english minutes. Same as San. ghaticam [caulam, 4, 5], Tam. nauzhy, nauzhigay [caulam, 1].——*Dandacam* (दण्डक - dandaka, San.). From (danda, san. an uninterrupted series). Ancient forest lying between Godavery and Nerbudda. Rama and Seetay's adventures transferred here. Dandacauranyam is the same [charitram].——*Dandaca naud* (தண்டகநாடு - tandaganádu, Tam.). Part of Yeyil cottam in the ancient Tondaimundalam. In the present Conjeeveram talook, Chingleput district.——*Dandapauny* (தண்டபாணி - tandabáni, Tam.). From (danda, san. stick + páni, san. hand). Shiva or Vishnoo with staff in hand. Familiarly Dandoo. Hindoo 2nd or pers. name [peyar].——*Dandla* (దండ్ల - dandla, Tel.). From (dandu, tel. army). Locative pl. Suffix in place names; as Velidandla, meaning outer army.——*Dandoo* (தண்டு - tandu, Tam.). Means staff. Familiar contraction of Dandapauny or Shiva, the staff-handed god; also Soobramanyan. Hindoo 2nd or pers. name [peyar]. Also means army. Moon dandoo is vanguard and pin dandoo is the rear. There is a Tamul proverb:—தண்டிலே போனால் இரண்டிலே ஒன்று—"If you go into the army, one "of the two" is certain; life or death.——*Dandy* (दण्डी - dandí, San.; ڈنڈی - dandí, Hind.).—"*a*" Any one who bears a staff. Especially religious mendicants, of the order founded by Shuncaracharry [shuncaran]; these are divided into ten classes, each of which is distinguished by a peculiar name, as Teertam a sacred water, Aushramam an order, Giry a hill, which is added to the proper name of the individual as Poorshottamagiry; they are hence known collectively as the Dashnamy [q.v.], or tennamed gosains [gosain, matam].—"*b*" Also a rower, a boatman.—"*c*" Also a hammock-shaped conveyance for travellers, slung on a pole with straps for the feet and back, and carried by two bearers, suited for hill travelling.—"*d*" Also one of the sixty-three devotees [aroopatt moover] of shiva, who is said to have been born blind and afterwards to have received sight.

DANT (दन्त - danta, *San.*). From (dá, san. to cut). Tooth So ivory. Physiological characteristics of this are that transverse sections of the dentine substance show lines of different colours or striata proceeding in the arc of a circle and forming by their decussations minute curvilinear lozenge-shaped spaces. South indian ivory when first cut looks whiter than african, but is more apt eventually to become yellow [elephant]. Vegetable ivory is name given to osseous albumen in the nut of a dwarf south american palm, the phytelephas macrocarpa; these nuts called corossos are used by turners in imitation of elephant ivory. Dant is also frequent plant second term. Ex., where transl. is of first term:—Adhatoda vasica (vájídanta), horse; Argemone mexicana (brahmadanti), bramin; Baliospermum montanum (nágadanti), serpent; Ehretia lævis (páladantamu), white; Heliotropium indicum (nágadanti), serpent; Musa paradisiaca (guchhadantika), cluster of flowers. See gloss. paragraphs.——*Danta shatham* (दन्तशठ - dantashat'ha, San.). Tooth + rogue; from being bad for teeth from acidity. Plant name common to:—Diospyros embryopteris; Feronia elephantum; Oxalis corniculata. See gloss. paragraphs.——*Paula dantam* (పాలదంతము - páladantamu, Tel.). Meaning white + ivory, from wood. Same as Smooth coorvitchy.

DAR (دار - dár, *Pers*). From (dáshtan, pers. to keep). Suffix of possessor or agent; as Jagheerdar, jagheer + owner.

DAR (در - dar, *Hind.*). In.——*Darobast* (دروبست - darobast, Hind.). From persian. All, whole, altogether [hama].——*Darwauja* (دروازه - darvázah, Hind.). From (váz, pers. open). A gateway [dwauram].——*Darwillah* (درینولا - darínwilá, Hind.). From (above + ín, pers. this + wilá, ar. time). In this connection; phrase used in official papers to connect the substance of the paper with the salutation with which it usually opens.——*Daryaft* (دریافت - daryáft, Hind.). From (above + yáft, pers. finding). Investigation [taniky].

DARBHAY (दर्भ - darbha, *San.*; दर्भ्यां - darbhyá, *Conc.*; داب - dáb, *Hind.*; کشا - kushá, *Dec.*; ದರ್ಭೆ - darbhe, *Can.*; ದರ್ಭೆ - darbhe, *Too.*; దర్భ - darbha, *Tel.*; ആറ്റുദർഭ - áttudarbha, *Mal.*; කුසතණ - kusatana, *Singh.*; தருப்பை - taruppai, *Tam.*). Title from sanscrit. San. from (drí, san. to tear); from leaf margins acutely serrate. Conc. from sanscrit. Mal. from (áru, mal. river + darbha, san. the grass). Singh. from (kusha, san. the grass + trina, san. grass). San. also (kusha), meaning earth-strewn, from being strewn on ground and sat upon during devotion or sacrifice; (pavitra), meaning purifier; (kut'ha), meaning adhering to finger. Hind. also (kúthá). Can. also (kushadarbha), meaning sacrificial grass. Tel. also (áshvaláyanadarbha), meaning the sage + the plant; (kushadarbha). Tam. also (nákkaruttánbul), meaning tongue + to cut + grass; alluding to legend that serpents greedily licked the amritam that had fallen upon darbhay and had their tongues forked. Title otherwise Coosha grass, Cutting grass, Daub, Meadow grass, Sacrificial grass, Thatch grass [naunal], Tongue grass [haleem]. Distinguish from Doob or Doorvay, which is Cynodon dactylon, pers. [hurrially]. Botanically Eragrostis [coosham] cynosuroides, retz., graminaceæ [vricsham, 156]. Alias Briza bipinnata; Imperata arundinaceæ; Poa cynosuroides. Root creeping;

culm stout, reed-like, clothed at the base with withered sheaths; leaves rigid, flat, or the younger root ones convolute, elongated, nearly a foot long; raceme compound, close, elongated, branches scattered, dense, racemose; spikelets sessile, secund, distichous, nine to fifty-flowered; florets lanceolate, ovate, shining. Coarse grass, common in dry ground; culms straight round and smooth, one to three feet in height; leaves long and numerous, with sharp points, and margins acutely sawed downwards; its long roots keep it fresh throughout the year. Especially holy, and in demand in votive offerings and religious ceremonies [coosham]; it is then strewed upon the altar, or held by bramins in their hands whilst repeating the ritual; it is also placed on the ground with its tips to the east, as a seat for the idols; in the shrauddham [q.v.], the funeral cake [pindam] is placed on darbhay grass, and before offering it, water in which white flowers and sandal [q.v.] paste are immersed is poured on the cake; a dying hindoo, when no hopes of his surviving remain, should be laid on a bed of darbhay in the open air, with other ceremonies [shoodcaud]. The following is from the 4th vedam:—"thee, o darbhay, the learned proclaim a divinity not "subject to age or death; thee they call the armour of indran, "the preserver of regions, the destroyer of enemies; a gem "that gives increase to the field; at the time when the ocean "resounded, the clouds murmured, and lightnings flashed, then "was darbhay produced, pure as a drop of fine gold." Has medicinally diuretic and stimulant properties; produces an excellent rope fibre. The intellect of a clever man is said to be sharp as the point of a darbhay leaf.——*Bramha's darbhay* (ब्रह्मदर्भा - brahmadarbhá, San.). Same as Ajwaun.——*Wild darbhay* (ಕಾಡುದಬ್ಬೆಹುಲ್ಲು - kádudabbehullu, Can.). Can. from (kádu, can. wild + dabbehullu, can. split grass, eragrostis cynosuroides, retz.). Title otherwise Barn-yard grass, Cock's shin grass. Botanically Panicum [priyangoo] crus galli, linn., graminaceæ [vricsham, 156]. Alias Echinachloa crus corvi, crus galli; Oplismenus crus galli; Panicum crus corvi. Culms filiform, creeping at the base, above nearly erect; leaves soft, downy; spikes compound, alternate, secund; flowers imbricated in two rows; glumes and outer paleæ of the neuter floret hispid, awned or mucronate. Found on pasture lands, middle-sized, delicate, and rare; will not make hay, but cattle eat it.

DARD (درد - dard, *Pers.*). Pain.——*Dard mondah* (درد مونڈھا - dardmondhá, Hind.). Means shoulder-pain. Bad shoulder in horses [ashwarogam, ghorah].

DAROGHAH (داروغہ - dárúghah, *Hind.*). A Mongol word. A superintendent of any department, as salt, stamps, &c.

DARSHAM (दर्श - darsha, *San.*). From (drish, san. to see). Sight. New moon [amavausyay].——*Darshanam* (दर्शन - darshana, San.). From (drish, san. to see). Demonstration. And so system of philosophy. The six recognised systems or Shad darshanam are:—Nyauyam of gowtaman, Veishaishicam of canaudan, Saunkhyam of capilan, Yogam of patanjaly, Poorva mimaumsam of jeiminy, Oottara mimaumsam or Vedauntam of veda vyausan. All these ascribed to celebrated rishies had once adherents; now only vedauntam remains in s. india, where considered the orthodox sheiva philosophy. In the hands of Shuncaracharry [shuncaran] vedauntam became Adweitam [q.v.] pursued by Sheiva smartas, in the hands of Madhwacharry [q.v.] it became Dweitam [q.v.] pursued by Veishnava madhwas, in the hands of Ramaunoojacharry [q.v.] it became Vishishtaudweitam [q.v.] pursued by Veishnava shree veishnavas. A detailed account of the seven main propositions of early Braminical philosophy, of the six concrete philosophies which grew out of them, and of the three developments of Vedauntam, has already been given in the foot-note on the History of Hindoo religion at vol. I (74). Darshanam with lay Hindoos generally means simply performance of religious duties, visiting temples, seeing or reverencing idols, &c. Sarwa darshana sangraham [q.v.] is name of a treatise on the fifteen systems of philosophy, by Maudhavacharry [matam]. Darshanam is also a short term for Ardrah darshanam [q.v.].

DARSHY (దరిశి - darishi, *Tel.* darsi *). From (dari, tel. border) [darty].——(1) Zemindarry, Deputy tahsildar's division, Nellore, Pay Rs. 100. Area 616 square miles N.W. inland, part of district. Bounded:—north by Vinoocondah talook of Kistna district; east by Ongole talook; south by Podily division; west by Marcapore talook of Kurnool district. A flat tract of black cotton land [regar], diversified by abrupt steep bare rocky hills of gneiss. These hills spring from the dead level of the plain and rise steeply to a height of several hundred feet. They are few in number in the eastern part of the division but numerous in the west. There are patches of jungle in places but the general character of the country is bare. Soil is regar clay diversified in places by red loam and red sand. Coarse cloths and cumblies [q.v.] are to some extent manufactured. Lands are generally irrigated by tanks and wells. There are no river anicuts [q.v.] or other important irrigation works. Best camping grounds:—Indlacheroo and Potlapaud. Bellary-Kistna railway passes through north of division; there are stations at Coorchaid and Donacondah. Places of archæological interest:—Bhoomavaram, Bodanampaud, Boddicoorapaud, Chendalore, Coorchaid, Cotapully, Cotcherlacote, Cullore, Darshy, Donacondah, Gungavaram, Maurella, Moollamore, Naidoopollem, Polavaram, Poleypully, Potacamore, Potlapaud, Rajampulley, Salivendra Saumantapoody, Shivarampooram, Somavarapaud, Taullore Toommidelapaud, Tummalore. Principal trig. stations are:—Chendalore, Pidacaltippa. The leading places, &c., in the division are the following.——*Chendalore* (చందలూరు - chendalúru, Tel.). From (chandrappa, tel. proper name + úru, tel. village). Village; pop. 2,565; acres 8,227; lat. 15° 48′; long. 79° 38′; from Darshy W.N.W. 5¾ miles; from Nellore N.N.W. 96 miles; from Ongole N.W. 36 miles. A commercial place. Unboiled saltpetre [shorah] or sowdoo [q.v.] is made here; average 20 candies [q.v.] a year. This village with its tank was founded or restored by Bollapulley chundrappa naidoo during the reign of Chola kings. East are the two temples of Shiva as Chenna mulleshwarasawmy and Vishnoo as Chennakeshwarasawmy. Yearly marriage [calyaunam] festival, and occasional processions of the idols on special days. Trig. station in lat. 15° 47′ 13·10″; long. 79° 40′ 00·63″; height 1,377 feet; from Basireddipollem E. 2½ miles; from Darshy W.N.W. 4 miles.——*Coorchaid* (కురుచేడు - kuruchédu, Tel.). See sep. title.——*Cotapully* (కోటపల్లి - kótapalli, Tel.). From (kóta, tel. fort + palli, tel. village). Village; lat. 15° 49′; long. 79° 32′; from Darshy W. 14 miles; from Nellore N.N.W. 160 miles; from Ongole W. 43 miles. Inscriptions near a ruined temple.——*Cotcherlacote* (కొచ్చర్లకోట - koççarlakóta, Tel.). From (kotta, tel. new + cheruvu, tel. tank + kóta, tel. fort). Village; pop. 1,536; lat. 15° 50′; long. 79° 23′; from Darshy W. 23 miles; from Nellore N.N.W. 104 miles; from Ongole W.N.W. 51½ miles. Old fort founded by Gajapaty maharajah, son of Mullicarjoona ganapaty, who afterwards retired to Calingam [q.v.], from which place his son Mookkanty ruled. Captured by Prataupa roodran of Warangal and remained in the possession of these rulers for 24 years subsequently falling under the Vijianugger rulers. Three inscriptions dated A.D. 1310, 1533 and 1135. Sowdoo [q.v.] manufactured here, average 80 candies a year. East and west are the temples of Shiva as Ramalingasawmy and Vishnoo as Varadarajasawmy. Yearly festival performed for the latter nine days [navaunicam]. The Goondlacumma runs on the west of the village and turns towards the north.——*Darshy* (దరిశి - darishi, Tel.). See below.——*Goondlacumma* (గుండ్లకమ్మ - gundlakamma, Tel.). See sep. title.——*Mooshy* (ముశి - mushi, Tel.). See sep. title.——*Pidacaltippa* (పిడకలతిప్ప - pidakalatippa, Tel.). From (pidaka, tel. cowdung cake + tippa, tel. mound). Trig. station in lat. 15° 49′ 45·16″; long. 79° 45′ 51·50″; height 484 feet; from Darshy N.N.E. 5 miles; from Toommachintala E. 4 miles.——*Poleypully* (పోలేపల్లి - pólépalli, Tel.). From (póli, tel. proper name + palli, tel. village). Village; lat. 15° 53′; long. 79° 28′; from Darshy N.N.W. 18 miles; from Nellore N.N.W. 104¾ miles; from Ongole W.N.W. 48¼ miles. Copper-plate inscription of A.D. 1536.——*Potacamore* (పోతకమూరు - potakamúru, Tel.). From (potakamu, tel. necklace jewel + úru, tel. village); from its beautiful situation. Village; pop. 3,611; lat. 15° 44′; long. 79° 49′; from Darshy E.S.E. 6½ miles; from Nellore N. 89½ miles; from Ongole N.W. 24 miles. A commerical place. Fort and trench, now in ruins, on the west. A large tank on the north. The Dornaul vaug [q.v.] on the south. Vishnoo temple. Inside the fort is the Ameen's cutcherry [q.v.]. Marriage festival of Chennakeshwarasawmy and Mulleeshwarasawmy, celebrated in Jyeshtam [mausam] or june, lasts nine days.——*Taullore* (తాళ్లూరు - tállúru, Tel.). From (tádi, tel. palmyra tree, borassus flabelliformis, linn. + úru, tel. village). Village; lat. 15° 44′; long. 79° 56′; from Darshy E. 14 miles; from Nellore N. 88¾ miles; from Ongole N.W. 19 miles. Inscription of A.D. 1579.——(2) Town, Head-quarters of Deputy tahsildar and Ex-officio Sub-registrar, Hospital; Nellore dist., Darshy division; pop. 2,526; lat. 15° 46′; long. 79° 43′; from Madras N.N.W. 188 miles; from Naidoopett N. 126½ miles; from Nellore N.W. 93 miles; from Ongole N.W. 30 miles. Connected by roads with Podily and Addanky. The water supply is very bad and gives guinea worm [naudy vranam].

DARTY (దరి - darti, *Tel.*). Corruption of (dari, tel.). Border, or nearness. Cf. Darshy. Suffix in place names; as Paudarty, meaning confines of the jungle.

DARYAH (دریا - daryá, *Hind.*). Sea [samoodram]. Plant first term. Ex.:—Gracilaria lichenoides (daryákákañjál), sea weed; Lodoicea seychellarum (daryákánárel), sea cocoanut. See gloss. paragraphs.——*Daryah bahaudurghur* (دریا بہادر گڑھ - daryábahádurgarh, Hind.). From (above + bahádur, pers. haidar so called + garh, hind. fort). Island; South canara dist., Oodipy tal.; pop. nil; lat. 13° 20′; long. 74° 43′; from Mangalore N.N.W. 34 miles; from Oodipy W. 4 miles. About half a mile from the mainland. Small coasters find shelter under its lee from north-westerly gales. Ruins of fortifications by Hyder ally and Tippoo.

DAS (दश - dasha, *San.*; دس - das, *Hind.*). Latin decem. Ten.——*Dasbandam* (దశబంధము - dashabandhamu, Tel.). From (above + bundh, san. to bind). Abatement of one-tenth of the revenue on account of compensation for some public work, as the construction of a tank, &c. [inam]. See vol. I, 112.——

Dasha daunam (दशादान - dashadána, San.). From (above + dána, san. gift). Ten gifts to Bramins made in the last extremity as a pass-port to the other world. Or occasionally when a daughter is given in marriage [maryauday].——*Dashagreevan* (दशग्रीव - dashagríva, San.). From (above + gríva, san. neck). The ten-necked Ravanan [q.v.]; his ten necks were probably provinces.——*Dasham* (दश - dasha, San.). Ten.——*Dasha moolam* (दशमूल - dashamúla, San.). From (above + múla, san. root). Medicine. Compound decoction [kwautam] prepared from the roots of ten plants:—Ægle marmelos, corr. [bael]; Desmodium gangeticum, dec. [shaulicay]; Gmelina arborea, linn. [cashmere tree]; Oroxylum indicum, vent. [pajanely]; Premna integrifolia, linn. [moonnay]; Solanum indicum, linn. [indian nightshade]; Solanum xanthocarpum, sch. and wendl. [prickly brinjaul]; Stereospermum suaveolens, dec. [pauthiry]; Tribulus terrestris, linn. [nerinjy]; Uraria lagopoides, dec. [orila].——*Dashamy* (दशमी - dashamí, San.). Tenth day of a lunar fortnight [pacsham]. Lunar festival [pundigay, 3e] occurring twice in every lunar month [vijaya dashamy].——*Dashnamy* (दशनामी - dashanámí, San.). Ten-named; from the ten chief branches into which the sect is divided. See Gosain, Dandy.

DAS (दस् - das, *San.*). To destroy.——*Dasyoo* (दस्यु - dasyu, San.). In the vedas, evil beings, enemies of the gods and men [dausan]. Used for men and not for demons in the Eitareya bramhanam, in Menoo, and in the Mahabhaurat. Applied later to the dark Dravidians, &c., met by the Aryans. More general terms are the very ancient Deityan [q.v.], the less ancient Asooran [q.v.], and the comparatively recent Raucshasan [q.v.].——*Dausan* (दास - dása, San.). From (dás, san. to hurt) [dasyoo]. Demon, barbarian, slave. In Anglo-indian, Doss. A servant. Often used in composition to form a name; as Bhagwan dausan, the slave of God; compare the use of the Mussalman Ghoolaum. Common name among lower orders; familiarly Dausoo. Dausappan is another form [peyar]. Also a general name applied in the vedas to evil beings or demons [deityan], hostile to the human race and to indran; it is opposed there to aryan [q.v.].——*Dausarapada* (ದಾಸರಪದ - dásarapada, Can.). From (above + pada, san. verse). Sacred moral songs generally in Canarese by Poorandara dausan, Canacadausan and others, and recited by devotees of Vishnoo. The following is specimen of the Canacadausan:—ಅಡವಿಯೊಳಗಾಡುವ ಮೃಗಜಾತಿ ಪಕ್ಷಿಗೆ ಯಡಿಗಳಿಗೆ ಯಾಹಾರವನು ಯಿತ್ತವರು ದಾರೋ—ಪಡದ ಜನನಿಯು ದೆರವಿ ಸ್ವಾಮಿ ಹೊಣೆಕಾರನಾಗಿ ಬಿಡದೆ ರಕ್ಷಿಪನಿದಕೆ ಸಂದೇಹ ಬೇಡಾ—"Who daily feeds the beasts of "forests? Doubt not therefore that God will protect and bring "us up, just as the mother who begot us would."——*Dausary* (ದಾಸರಿ - dásari, Tel.). Dravidian form of Dausan. Vishnoo mendicant. Wear an upright white line on the forehead, and sound a conch [chunk] shell and a small gong [q.v.] or bell. The caste, like Sautaunies, is reinforced by idle members of lower Shoodra classes, who, being branded by the gooroos of Tripatty and other shrines, become thereby Dausaries. They wander about singing hymns to an accompaniment upon a stringed instrument or upon a drum called tappoo. Some Shoodra castes engage them to chant in front of the corpse at funerals, and many, accompanying bands of pilgrims travelling to Tripatty, stimulate religious excitement by singing sacred songs. A few called Yeroodandy take young bulls that have been devoted to a sawmy [q.v.] and teach them to perform tricks. Some Dausaries exhibit the Panda sairvay [q.v.] performance, which consists in being possessed by the spirit of a deity and beating themselves on the body with a flaming torch [pandam]. They wear as a distinction a garland of toolsy [q.v.] seeds. Every Dausary is a Tengalay [q.v.]. They have six divisions, called Balije, Janapa, Pully, Vulloova, Gungeddoola, and Golla dausaries, which neither eat together nor intermarry. Beyond prohibiting widow remarriage they have no social restrictions. Numbers about 85,000 [jauty].——*Dausary pitta* (దాసరిపిట్ట - dásaripitta, Tel.). Means mendicant + bird; striped bird. Bird name common to:—Leucocerca albofrontata; Pomatorhinus horsfieldii. See gloss. paragraphs.——*Dausy* (தாசி - tási, Tam.). The feminine of dausan. A woman dedicated to a temple. Properly Devadausy; which see. Numbers about 50,000.

DASHT (دشت - dasht, *Pers.*). Forest. Plant second term. Ex.:—Andropogon martini (gaznahidashtí), forest nettle; Sida rhombifolia, var. retusa (shambalídidashtí), forest fenugreek. See gloss. paragraphs.

DAST (دست - dast, *Hind.*). Hand.——*Daskat* (دستخط - dastkhat, Hind.). From (above + khat, pers. writing). Handwriting, signature [keiyoppam].——*Dastah* (دستہ - dastah, Hind.). A quire of paper.——*Dastak* (دستک - dastak, Hind.). Noise produced by the clapping of hands. A summons, passport.——*Dastauna* (دستانہ - dastánah, Hind.). From (ánah, pers. suffix of resemblance). Gloves of leather [chamrah], cloth, &c. [sheelay].——*Dastaur* (دستار - dastár, Hind.). Turban [puggry].——*Dastavaiz* (دستاویز - dastáviz, Hind.). From (above + áviz, pers. hanging). Document.——*Dastgheer* (دستگیر - dastgír, Hind.). From (above + gír, pers. holder). Protector. Title of the highest of Mahomedan saints [abdool cawder]. His other titles are Azam, Cawder, Ghouse, Jeelauny, Mahboob. Mohee ood deen; see each of those heads. Common alam; as Dastgheer beg, alam + alaumat [ism].

DATURA (धत्तूर - dhattúra, *San.*; تاتورہ - tátúrah, *Pers.*; دھتورہ - dhatúrah, *Hind.*; دھتورا - dhatúrá, *Dec.*; ಉಮ್ಮತ್ತ - ummatta, *Can.*; ఉమ్మెత్త - ummetta, *Tel.*; ഉമ്മത്ത - ummatta, *Mal.*; අත්තන - attana, *Singh.*; ஊமத்தை - úmattai, *Tam.*). Title from sanscrit through hindostany. San. from (dhús, san. to embellish + túri, san. thorn-apple). Hind. and dec. from sanscrit. Tel. from (unmattá, san. the insane plant). Tam. from (unmad, san. to madden); from virtue of plant. Tam. also (ilagam) from shining flowers. Title otherwise Thorn-apple. Botanically the Datura genus, solanaceæ [vricsham, 94]. Annual, soft-wooded, single-stemmed shrubs; natives of india; narcotic and poisonous; flowers large and white; fruit, a capsule of numerous seeds, about size of a walnut [acroot]. The species best known are shown below. The term also includes an Argemone and a Xanthium.——*Burdock datura* (अरिष्ट - arishta, San.; शंकेश्वर - shankéshvara, Mahr.; حسك صغير - hasakisaghír, Ar.; خسك خرد - khasakikhurd, Pers.; چھوٹا گوکھرو - chhotágokhrú, Hind. and Dec.; తలనొప్పిచెట్టు - talanoppichettu, Tel.; மருளூமத்தை - marulúmattai, Tam.). Title from resemblance. San. means perfect [neem, soap-nut tree]. Ar. from (hasak, ar. caltrops, tribulus terrestris, linn. + saghír, ar. small), from small bristly germs. Pers. from (khasak, pers. caltrops, tribulus terrestris, linn. + khurd, pers. small). Hind. from (chhotá, hind. small + gokhrú, hind. tribulus terrestris, linn.). Tel. from (tala, tel. head + noppi, tel. ache + chettu, tel. plant). Tam from (marul, tam. bewilderment + úmattai, tam. datura). Tel. also (verritalanoppichettu), meaning mad + headache + plant; (párshvapuchettu), meaning side + plant, as being cure for headache on one side; (marulamátangi), meaning intoxication + she-devil; (marulatíga), meaning intoxication + creeper, from the idea that the traveller treading upon the plant becomes intoxicated and loses his way. Greek ξάνθιον. Title otherwise Burdock, Burrweed, Confusion creeper, Ditchbur, Headache plant, Indian xanthium, Lesser burdock, Louse-burr, Small burdock. Botanically Xanthium strumarium, linn., compositæ [vricsham, 74]. Alias Xanthium indicum, orientale. Involucre fruit-bearing; oval, pubescent between the prickles and at the base of the beaks; beaks hooked at the apex; flowers small, white; common on the road-sides in most parts of the country, flowering in february and march; rank weed-like plant. Whole plant diaphoretic and sedative in decoction [kwautam]; oil used in medicine and burned. No other species here.——*Downy datura* (धुस्तूर - dhustúra, San.; مائل - másil, Ar.; سادہ دھتورا - sádahdhatúrá, Hind.; తెల్లఉమ్మెత్త - tellaummetta, Tel.; ഉമ്മത്ത - ummatta, Mal.; வெள்ளையூமத்தை - vellaiyúmattai, Tam.). Title from appearance. San. from (dhús, san. to embellish + túri, san. thorn-apple). Hind. from (sádah, hind. white + dhattúra, san. thorn-apple). Tel. from (tella, tel. white + ummetta, tel. thorn-apple, datura). Mal. from (unmad, san. to be mad). Tam. from (vellai, tam. white + úmattai, tam. thorn-apple plant); from flowers. Botanically Datura metel, linn., solanaceæ [vricsham, 94]. Specific name from arabic. Grows wild everywhere; properties similar to other species.——*Europe datura* (சீமையூமத்தை - shímaiyúmattai, Tam.). Title otherwise Apple of Peru, Common thorn-apple, Devil's-trumpet, Dewtry, Jamestown weed, Stink-weed, Stramonium. Botanically Datura stramonium, linn., solanaceæ [vricsham, 94]. Not found here. There is however a variety Tatula, so called from the Persian, with purple flowers.——*Foreign datura* (فرنگی دھتورا - farangídhatúrá, Hind.). From being introduced from america and from having bristly fruits like datura. Same as Bramhadand.——*Purple datura* (कृष्णधत्तूर - krishnadhattúra, San.; कालोदुतुरो - kálóduturó, Conc.; مائل اسود - másiliaswad, Ar.; مائل سیاہ - másilisiyáh, Pers.; اودہ دھتورا - údahdhatúrá, Hind.; کالا دھتورا - káládhatúrá, Dec.; کاچو بنگ - káchubung, Malay; ಕರಿಉಮ್ಮತ್ತೆ - kariummatte, Can.; ಕರಿಉಂಬೆ - kariumbe, Too.; నల్లఉమ్మెత్త - nallaummetta, Tel.; കരിയുമ്മത്ത - kariyummatta, Mal.; කළුඅත්තන - kaluattana, Singh.; கருவூமத்தை - karuvúmattai, Tam.). Title from color of flowers. San. from (krishna, san. black + dhattúra, san. thorn-apple). Conc. from (kála, san. black). Ar. from (másil, ar. datura plant + aswad, ar. black). Pers. from (siyáh, pers. black). Hind. from (údah, hind. purple). Dec. from (kálá, hind. black). Can. from (kari, can. black + ummatte, can. datura). Too. from (kari, can. black + umbe, too. datura). Tel. from (nalla, tel. black + ummetta, tel. thorn-apple). Mal. from (kari, mal. black + ummatta, mal. thorn-apple). Singh. from (kalu, singh. black + attana, singh. thorn-apple). Tam. from (karumai, tam. blackness + úmattai, tam. thorn-apple). San. also (kálahémika), meaning black thorn-apple; (maháshat'ha), meaning great + wicked; (krishnónmattá), meaning black thorn-apple; (rájadhúrta), meaning king + cheat; (kanaka), meaning gold; (rájadhattúra), meaning king thorn-apple; (bhrántá), meaning maddening; (krishnapushpá), meaning black blossomed; (shiva), meaning auspicious [chebulic myrobalan]; (krúradhúrta), meaning cruel cheat; (sachiva), meaning companion, from usefulness; (krúradhattúra), meaning cruel thorn-apple; (snigdhá), meaning cooling; (vishuráti), meaning poison + enemy. Ar. also (másimiaswad), meaning black datura. Pers. also (tátúrahisiyáh), meaning black datura. Hind. also (láldhatúrá), meaning red datura; (gharbhúlí), meaning house-forgetting. Malay also (rotikubung). Mal. also (nílaummatta), meaning black thorn-apple. Tam. also (úthávúmattai), meaning violet + thorn-apple plant; (ponnúmattai), meaning gold + thorn-apple plant. Greek στρύχνος μανικὸς. Title otherwise Asiatic dátura, Foolish plant, Indian datura, Indian hose in hose, Indian thorn-apple, Insane plant, King rogue, Mad plant, Oblivion plant, Purple thorn-apple. Botanically Datura fastuosa, linn., solanaceæ [vricsham, 94]. Alias Datura hummata; Stramonium fastuosum. Hummata, from (ummatta, mal. datura genus). Annual, 2–3 feet; leaves ovate, acuminated, repandly toothed, unequal at the base, and as well as the stem smooth; stamens enclosed; fruit prickly: calyx five-lobed. Leaves are of a heavy odour, and mawkish, faintly bitter, nauseous taste; fruit, a capsule, size of a walnut [acroot], containing seeds; seeds are brownish or black, flattened, kidney-shaped, without odour except when bruised, and have a bitter weakish taste, poisonous; large blossoms, white tinged with purple, resemble in form three or four large extinguishers projecting one slightly out of the other; sweet-scented at night; flowers all year; grows wild on waste lands; very common; the best known thorn-apple. Seeds were used by priests of delphi and other ancient oracles to produce prophecies; flower is here sacred to mahadevan [q.v.], and whole plant regarded with awe. All parts medicinal; fresh leaves bruised used in poultices for sedative action; leaves in oil rubbed on body in itch or rheumatism; in asthma dried leaves may be smoked like tobacco [pogauk]; seeds used in tincture as anodyne and antispasmodic, very dangerous if incautiously used; powdered root used by hakeems [q.v.] in epilepsy; in very small doses a few seeds with root of anacylus pyrethrum [akalkarah] and cloves [lavangam] are chewed as an aphrodisiac; an alkaloid, daturina, from the seeds, is now substituted for belladonna, in ophthalmic practice; leaves and seeds quoted in pharm. but not officinal. Seeds used to render liquor more intoxicating, being burned upon charcoal [adoopp kary] with vessels inverted to catch the smoke; seeds also used in powder for same purpose, being more powerful thus; put into food to intoxicate persons it is designed to rob, frequently with sweetmeats [halwah], curries [q.v.], &c.; also sometimes used by ganjah-smokers mixed with ganjah [q.v.].——*White datura* (उन्मत्ता - unmattá, San.; धोतरा - dhótará, Mahr.; दुतुरो - duturó, Conc.; ماثل ابيض - másiliabyaz, Ar.; ماثل سپيد - másilisupíd, Pers.; سادہ دھتورا - sádahdhatúrá, Hind.; اجلا دھتورا - ujládhatúrá, Dec.; ಬಿಳಿಉಮ್ಮತ್ತೆ - biliummatte, Can.; ಉಂಬೆ - umbe, Too.; తెల్లఉమ్మెత్త - tellaummetta, Tel.; ഉമ്മത്ത - ummatta, Mal.; සුදුඅත්තන - suduattana, Singh.; வெள்ளையூமத்தை - vellaiyúmattai, Tam.). Title from color of flowers. San. from (unmad, san. to be mad). Mahr. and conc. from (dhattúra, san. the white thorn-apple). Ar. from (másil, ar. datura plant + abyaz, ar. white). Pers. from (másil, ar. datura plant + supíd, pers. white). Hind. from (sádah, hind. white + dhattúra, san. thorn-apple). Dec. from (ujlá, hind. white + dhattúra, san. thorn-apple). Can. from (bili, can. white + ummatte, the plant). Tel. from (tella, tel. white + ummetta, tel. datura). Singh. means white datura. Mal. from (unmatta, san. insane). Tam. from (vellai, tam. white + úmattai, tam. thorn-apple) [downy datura]. San. also (mátula), meaning unequalled, from being the most powerful narcotic; (kanaka), meaning gold; (dhúrta), meaning wicked; (kanakapushpá), meaning golden blossomed; (kanakakantakap'hala), meaning golden thorn-apple; (shivapriyá), meaning dear to shiva; (shyámá), meaning dark-colored [tinay]; (kanakónmattá), meaning golden thorn-apple; (kitava), meaning cheat; (madana), meaning maddening [common emetic nut]; (móhana), meaning depriving of consciousness; (unmóhin), meaning confounding; (shaivashékhara), meaning shiva's crest jewel; (shat'ha), meaning a rogue. Ar. also (másimiabyaz), meaning white datura. Pers. also (tátúrahisupíd), meaning white datura. Hind. also (sufeddhatúrá), meaning white datura. Botanically Datura fastuosa, linn., var. alba, solanaceæ [vricsham, 94]. Alias Datura alba, metel, stramonium. Shrub; leaves ovate-acuminate, repand-dentate, unequal at the base, smooth; stem herbaceous; capsules nodding, covered with prickles; flowers very large, white; flowering all year. A strong narcotic though not so virulently poisonous as the simple fastuosa. ——*Yellow datura* (پیلا دھتورا - piládhatúrá, Hind.). From yellow flowers and fruits similar to datura. Same as Bramhadand.

DAU (दा - dá, *San.*). To give.——*Dadny* (دادنی - dádní, Hind.). From (dádan, pers. to give). Money advanced to contractors, &c.——*Daunam* (दान - dána, San.). Gift. Suffix in place names; as Devadannam, meaning god's gift.——*Dauyam* (दाय - dáya, San.). Gift, inheritance. Native writers treat inheritance as an aspect of partition [bhaugam]; the reason being that the normal state of property is that of being joint property, and the amount of interest which each member has in the property is only the share which he would be entitled to in the event of a partition. Remembering this limitation the following description of Hindoo inheritance is applicable. All legitimate sons, living in a state of union with their father at the time of his death, succeed equally to his property, real and personal, ancestral and acquired. In former times, the right of primogeniture prevailed to a certain extent. The right of representation is also admitted as far as the great grandson; and the grandson and great-grandson, the father of the one and the father and grandfather of the other being dead, will take equal shares with their uncle and grand-uncle respectively. Indeed the term pootran or son has been held to signify, in its strict acceptation, a grandson and great-grandson. An adopted son is a substitute for a son of the body, where none such exists, and is entitled to the same rights and privileges. In default of sons, the grandsons inherit, in which case they take per stirpes, the sons however numerous of one son, taking no more than the sons however few of another son. In default of sons and grandsons, the great-grandsons inherit; in which case they also take per stirpes, the sons, however numerous, of one grandson taking no more than the sons, however few, of another grandson. They will take the shares to which their respective fathers would have been entitled had they survived. In default of sons, grandsons, and great-grandsons in the male line, the inheritance descends lineally no farther, and the widow inherits according to the law as current in Bengal, whether her late husband was separated, or was living as a member of an undivided family [avibhacta cootoombam]; but, according to other schools, the widow succeeds to the inheritance in the former case only, an undivided brother being held to be the next heir. If there be more than one widow, their rights are equal. Inheritance taken as an actual process can only apply to property which was held in absolute severalty by its last male owner. Further, a person so inheriting becomes the point of departure for a new coparcenary, so that the property soon falls again under the laws of partition. Inheritance under a will [wasyat] is a novelty among the Tamulians. However wills are recognized by the courts with the restriction that the testators cannot bequeath property which they were incompetent to alienate during their lifetime. The principle of property devolving to a man's male child or children is on the West coast called Makkatoyem, as opposed to Maroomakkatoyem in Malabar and Aliya santauna in Canara, or the principle of property passing to the children, male or female, of the sister; see those headings. For Mahomedan inheritance see Vaurs [maryauday].——*Dutt* (दत्त - datta, San.). See sep. title.

DAUB (ڈاب - dáb, *Hind.*). A list [dufter, zaubitah]. Physician's recipe. A sword belt.

DAUB (داب - dáb, *Hind.*). From (darbha, san. the grass). Same as darbhay. Distinguish from Doob.

DAUBY DOOBY (दद्रुमारी - dadrumárí, *San.*). Title from bengalee. San. means ringworm killer; from virtue. Same as Cotchilitty.

DAUCHEPULLY (డాచేపల్లె - dáchépalle, Tel. dáchepalie*). From (tátsu, tel. snake + palle, tel. village). Village, Tahsildar's station; Kistna dist., Pulnaud tal.; pop. 2,823; acres 8,299; lat. 16° 36′; long. 79° 47′; from Bezwada W. 58 miles; from Guntoor W.N.W. 52 miles; from Madras N. 242 miles; from Masulipatam W.N.W. 96 miles; from Vinoocondah N. 37 miles. Old fort built by Condaveed reddies. The Naugilair flows past town, and is unfordable for some hours after rain. Temple called Naickraul's goody. Oldest inscription is in the Naugeshwarasawmy temple, A.D. 1213. There are remains of old forts in the neighbourhood, chiefly at Oblapully near Gaumalpaud, where are also some small temples with carved stones and inscriptions dated A.D. 1222, 1290 and 1459.

DAUD (داد - dád, *Hind.*). From (dadru, san. herpes); as curing herpes. Plant first term. Ex.:—Ammannia baccifera (dádmárí), itch killer.

DAUDAH (دادا - dádá, *Hind.*). Grandfather. Lacab. Sometimes taken by fakeers, as Daudah shah, alam + alaumat [ism].

DAUKKAL (داخل - dákhal, *Hind.*). From (dakhl, ar. entrance). Registration, entry.——*Dauklah* (داخله - dákhilah, Hind.). A receipt for payment.

DAUM (دام - dám, *Hind.*). From (dramma, san. drachma). $\frac{1}{30}$ seer [q.v.]. A Mahomedan copper coin equivalent to about $\frac{1}{8}$ penny; now obsolete. In the reign of Acbar, 40 daums were reckoned to a rupee; in that of Alumgheer, $46\frac{1}{3}$; at later periods, 80 and 90. Much the same as peisa. To "care a dam" meant originally nothing but this and was not slang language [damree, dirhem].——*Damree* (دمڑی - damrí, Hind.; దమ్మిడి - dammidi, Tel.). From (dramma, san.). Greek δράχμη. Copper coin. 12 damrees = 1 anna [nannyam, 2 e]. Approximate actual value, 1 damree = 1 pie. Same as Hind. pie, Tel. roowa, Tam. cash. Used for any very small copper coin [daum, dirhem]. See vol. I, 609.

DAUMALCHEROO (దామల్ చెరువు - dámalcheruvu, *Tel.*). From (támara, tel. lotus, nelumbium speciosum, willd. + cheruvu, tel. tank).—"*a*" Village; North arcot dist., Chundragherry tal.; lat. 13° 28′ N.; long. 79° 5′ E.; from Chittore N. 19 miles; from Chundragherry W.S.W. 20 miles. In S.E. of talook and at entrance of valley leading to Cullore ghaut. Large tank. Considerable trade.—"*b*" Pass. By this Shivajee made his first descent upon the Carnatic [q.v.] in 1676. Here in 1740, Dost ally, the Nawaub [q.v.], was killed in battle with the

Mahrattas. During Hyder's invasion of Carnatic in 1780-81, it formed the main route for supplies of his troops. An earthen embankment crosses the road and continues over the hills on either side. It extends to Tripatty on one side and to Yelagherry in Salem on the other, and was built by Chola kings to mark their boundary.—"c" River; North arcot dist., Chundragherry tal. Rises in Cullore polliem, flows down ghaut [q.v.], and passes for a short distance along the west of Chundragherry talook into Chittore talook, where it is known as the Poyney.

DAUN (دان - dán, *Pers.*). From (dánistan, pers. to know). Suffix denoting knowledge; as Kadr daun, merit + knower.——*Daunish* (دانش - dánish, Hind.). Wisdom.——*Daunishmund* (دانشمند - dánishmand, Hind.). From (above + mand, pers. possessive particle). The wise. Mahomedan servant's name [ism].

DAUR (दारु - dáru, *San.*; دار - dár, *Hind.*). From (drí, san. to split). Tree [droomam].—"a" Plant first term, often joining two genera. Ex., where transl. is of second term:—Berberis aristata (dáruharidrá), curcuma longa; Rubia cordifolia (dárhald), curcuma longa.—"b" Compare also where transl. is of first term:—Cedrus deodara (dévadáru), divine [deodar]; Cordia myxa (bhúkampadáruka), earthquake; Morinda umbellata (pítadáru), yellow. See gloss. paragraphs.——*Darhald* (دارهلد - dárhald, Hind.). Means wood turmeric, from yellow root and wood. Berberry wood, whether from stem or root.

DAUR (دار - dár, *Hind.*). House.——*Daur ool caraur* (دارالقرار - dárulkarár, Hind.). From (above + karár, ar. everlasting). Third Mahomedan heaven of pure musk [custoory].——*Daur ool jalaul* (دارالجلال - dáruljalál, Hind.). From (above + jalál, ar. majesty). First Mahomedan heaven of pearls [moty].——*Daur oos salaam* (دارالسلام - dárussalám, Hind.). From (above + salám, ar. peace). Second Mahomedan heaven of ruby [laul] and garnet [tamrah].

DAUVAH (دعوى - davá, *Hind.*). From (daú, ar. to claim). A claim, law-suit [firyaud].

DAVOOD (داؤد - dáúd, *Hind.*). From hebrew, beloved. David. Common alam; as Davood ally, double alam; Davood bee, alam + alaumat [ism]. Compare:—Chrysanthemum coronarium (gulidáúdí), david's flower.——*Davood khan* (داؤد خان - dáúdkhán, Hind.). Alam + pataun suffix. General of Zoolfacar khan and Nawaub [q.v.] of Carnatic [q.v.] in 1701. See vol. I (170).

DAWAULY (دوالى - duálí, *Hind.*). From (duál, pers. a leather strap). String round loins, to which lungooty [q.v.] is attached [tusma]. Cf. Cummerbund.

DAWK (ڈاک - dák, *Hind.*). Relays of men or cattle for the conveyance of letters, post, palankeens, &c., along a road [anchey meeda]. Thence the mail or letter-post [anchey]. To travel dawk is to travel with relays of bearers. A dawk bungalow [q.v.] is a travellers' rest-house [moosaufer khana] at the end of a stage [majil]. Dawk gharry is a stage carriage [tappaul].

DAYEE (धात्री - dhátrí, *San.*; داى - dái, *Hind.*; దాది - dádi, *Tel.*; தாதி - táthi, *Tam.*). San. from (dhé, san. to suck). Midwife. Wet nurse [amah, ayah].

DECAMALLEE (डिकामाली - dikámálí, *Mahr.*; خون خام - khúnikhám, *Pers.*; ڈکاملی - dikámalí, *Hind.*; ಡಿಕ್ಕಾಮಲ್ಲಿಮರ - dikkámallimara, *Can.*; ಡಿಕ್ಕಾಮಲ್ಲಿ - dikkámalli, *Too.*; చిన్నకారింగువ - chinnakáringuva, *Tel.*; കൊലലാകഡ - kolalákada, *Singh.*; கும்பைமரம் - kumbaimaram, *Tam.*). Title from hindostany. Pers. from (khún, pers. blood + khám, pers. raw). Hind. from mahratta, meaning juicy. Tel. from (chinna, tel. small + káru, tel. wild + inguva, tel. asafœtida, ferula narthex, boiss.). Can. also (bikkegida), meaning flesh + plant. Tel. also (tellamanga), meaning white + randia dumetorum, lamk.; (káringuva), meaning wild + asafœtida, from similar gum-resin [hill emetic nut]; (chiribikki), meaning small + gardenia latifolia, ait.; (chittamatta), meaning small stem; (garaga) [bair]; (tellakáringuva), meaning white + wild + asafœtida, ferula narthex, boiss. Tam. also (kambippisin), meaning wiry gum, being always mixed with twigs, applies to product; (kambalippisinmaram), meaning woollen cloth + gum + tree. Title otherwise Cumby resin tree, Gum yielding gardenia, White emetic nut. Botanically Gardenia [gandharajah] lucida, roxb., rubiaceæ [vricsham, 71]. Alias Gardenia resinifera. Small tree, unarmed, with resinous buds; leaves short-petioled, oblong or oval or obovate, obtuse or bluntly pointed, glabrous, bright shining olive-green, with simple parallel nerves and prominent veins; limb of calyx with five divisions, sprinkled on the inside with stoutish bristles; corolla hypocrateriform; tube long, striated; limb five-partite, divisions as long as, or a little shorter than, the tube; berry drupaceous, even, oblong, crowned with the calyx; nut very hard, thick, and long, with two parietal receptacles; flowers somewhat terminal, solitary shortly pedicelled, large, three or more inches across, pure white, fragrant; flowering in march and april; found throughout presidency, particularly in dry jungles in elevated parts of the country. A yellow gum-resin [googal] from buds and wounds in bark occurs in the form of very hard earthy-looking masses of a dull olive-green color; the odour is peculiar and offensive; though something like myrrh [q.v.]; it is never found pure, being always mixed with twigs and other impurities; like gum elemi [q.v.]. Gum-resin is antispasmodic and insecticide; possesses nearly similar virtues to myrrh; more active as external application; employed, dissolved in spirits, for cleaning ulcers. Gardenia gummifera, linn. f., alias gardenia arborea is a small tree or large shrub, found in similar localities to gardenia lucida, roxb.; flowers somewhat terminal, solitary, shortly pedicelled, large, pure white, fragrant; flowering in march and april; wood yellowish-white, hard, close-grained; might serve as a substitute for boxwood; the total want of pubescence, structure of the stipules, length of the calyx, and sharpness of its divisions, distinguish lucida from gummifera.

DECCAN (दक्षिण - dakshina, *San.*; دکهن - dakhan, *Hind.*; దక్కనము - dakkanamu, *Tel.*; தக்கணம் - takkanam, *Tam.*). Means south [dacshinam]. Properly India south of the Vindhya range, the Peninsula of the British. Taken in this sense, it comprehends the valley of the Nerbudda, the narrow tract of lowland forming a belt round the coast of the peninsula, and the vast expanse of triangular tableland, which, resting on each side upon the Eastern and Western ghauts [q.v.], is supported at its base by the Sub-Vindhyan range, termed the Sautpoora mountains. The Deccan was formerly an island, the Vindhya range being its northern shore, and the sea flowing over Hindostan to the foot of the Himalayas. The Deccan in the terminology of the English signifies only the elevated tract situated between the Nerbudda and Kistna rivers. Deccan has been often applied also politically to specific states, e.g., by the Portuguese in sixteenth century to Mahomedan kingdom of Beejapore, and in more recent times by English to state of Hyderabad.——*Deccany* (دکهنى - dakhaní, Hind.). Literally, southern. Hindostany as spoken in S. india. Though also written in the Persian character, this variety of Oordoo [q.v.] retains a much larger proportion of Indian, as opposed to Persian words, and is altogether more archaic in its grammatical forms than the language of the north. A certain proportion of its peculiarities must be ascribed to its separate development, as the tongue of Mahomedan colonies severed for some centuries from their original country. See vol. I (60) [bhaushay].——*Deccany grass* (ساوان - sáván, Hind.). Title from place of growth. Same as Shaumay.——*Deccany hemp* (انبارا - ambárá, Hind). Title as distinguished from bengal hemp [sunn]. Same as Hemp bendy.

DEECSH (दीक्ष् - díksh, *San.*). To prepare for sacrifice [yaugyam].——*Deecshitan* (ದೀಕ್ಷಿತ - díkshita, Can.). One who is initiated for making sacrifice. Title of Bramin priests, especially temple priests, at Chidambaram. Hindoo third name [peyar].

DEEN (دين - dín, *Hind.*). From (dána, ar. to submit) [dyaunat]. The faith. The practical part of Islam, consisting of recital of the kalima [q.v.], prayer [namauz] and ablution, and fasting [roza], which are incumbent upon all Mussalmans; and alms [zakaut] and haj [q.v.], which are enjoined upon those who can afford them [islam]. The cry of excited Mahomedans, is Deen, Deen! Part of lacab; as Faseeh ood deen, polished in religion [ism].——*Deenah* (دينا - díná, Hind.). Faithful. Mahomedan servant's name [ism].

DEENAM (दीन - dína, *San.*). Poor.——*Deenadayaul* (தீனதயாளு - tínathayálu, Tam.). From (above + dayálu, san. merciful). One who is compassionate towards the poor. Epithet of any deity. Hindoo 2nd or pers. name [peyar].

DEENAUR (دينار - dínár, *Hind.*). From latin denarius through arabic. An old gold coin equivalent to modern 2¼ rupees, formerly used by Mahomedans. The term is now used for any gold coin [dirhem, naunyam].

DEEP (दीप् - díp, *San.*). To shine.——*Deepam* (दीप - dípa, San.). Lamp. So a festival [pundigay, 6d] with illuminations [bhadra deepam, caurtigay deepam, laksha deepam, vishnoo deepam].——*Deepauvaly* (దీపావళి - dípávali, Tel.; தீபாவளி - tíbávali, Tam.). From (dípa, san. lamp + ávalí, san. row). Lunar festival [pundigay, 6d], subject to intercalation. Kept on the fourteenth lunar day [tity] of the waning moon in seventh lunar month Aushweejam [mausam] between 15th October and 14th November. In Bengal it is Cauly poojah. Compare Holy or Cauman pundigay in early spring. The following is a Hindostany proverb:—آدھ گاؤں دوالی آدھ گاؤں پھاگ—"One half the "village plays Deepauvaly, and the other half Holy;" half the village is at feud with the other half. In Malabar Deepauvaly is regarded as the new moon [amavausyay] in Toolaum [mausam] or October. The chief observance is an oil bath early in the morning, which is considered equivalent to bathing in the Ganges. Fireworks [baunam] and crackers are also used in large quantities and guns are fired. New clothes are put on. This feast is a relic of fire-worship [bhoota chatoordashy, maryauday, naraca chatoordashy, yama tarpanam].——*Deepdandam* (दीपदण्ड - dípadanda, San.). From (dípa, san. lamp + danda, san. stick). Lamp-bearing pillar.——*Deepdaun* (ديپدان - dípdán, Hind.). From (dípa, san. lamp + dána, san. giving). Offering of a lamp to an idol.——*Deeptaucsham* (दीप्ताक्ष - díptáksha, San.).

From (above + aksha, san. eye); from glittering eyes. Cat family. Felidæ, digitigrada, carnivora, mammalia [sastanam, 9], of naturalists [jantoo]. The animals of the cat family have the smallest number of molars, and hence their jaws are short and strong; the head is rounded, and the limbs powerful. Their teeth are particularly cutting. All are essentially carnivorous, and they are the type of the tribe and order. Their footfall is noiseless, from the thick pads with which the under surface of their feet is furnished. To preserve their claws sharp, they are habitually kept withdrawn between the toes, by the action of an elastic ligament which acts on the last joint of each toe, bending it upwards. When the animal is about to strike, the flex or tendons pull down this last phalanx and the claw is thus exerted. Their fur is usually dense and short. Their limbs are of moderate length and very powerful, and they can take astonishing bounds. Their vision is adapted for night as well as for day, and all are nocturnal in habits, or nearly so. Their sense of hearing is very acute, and their long whiskers are delicate organs of touch. The tongue is furnished with rough papillæ, directed backwards and somewhat recurved. The clavicle is rudimentary, and imbedded among the muscles. They usually take their prey by suddenly springing on it from a concealed spot, and if they fail in seizing it rarely pursue. They are generally solitary, but occasionally hunt in families. The cat tribe comprises the following animals:—Cheetah [q.v.], Domestic cat [poonay], Fishing tiger cat [meencolly poonay], Jungle cat [q.v.], Leopard or smaller pard [kerkal], Leopard cat [shivingy poonay], Indian lynx [caracal], Panther or larger pard [honiga], Rusty spotted cat [poolly poonay], Tiger [pooly]. The lion [simham] belongs to this tribe, but no longer exists in Southern india.

DEERGHA CHANCHOOCAM (दीर्घचंचुक - dírghachañchuka, San.). From (dírgha, san. long + chañchu, san. bill). Ibises. Tantalidæ family, cultirostres, grallatores, aves [pacshy, 47], of naturalists [jantoo]. Divided into the following sub-families:—Tantalinæ, bill very large, thick, rounded, smooth; legs long. Plataleinæ, bill very broad, flat, and depressed. Anastomatinæ, bill very thick, stout, coarse, gaping in the middle. Ibisinæ, bill long, thin, curved; differ from previous by long, slender, curved, and channelled beaks, and are called curlews here; breeding on trees, feeding their young till full grown. The species best known to the natives are shown below.——*Black ibis* (کالا بزا - kálábazá, Hind.; నల్లకంకణము - nallakankanamu, Tel.; கருநாரை - karunárai, Tam.). Title from color of head. Hind. from (kálá, hind. black + bazá, hind. ibis). Tel. from (nalla, tel. black + kankanamu, tel. kind of bustard). Tam. from (karumai, tam. blackness + nárai, tam. heron). Title otherwise Black curlew, King curlew, Warty-headed ibis. Geronticus papillosus, ibisinæ.——*Glossy ibis* (کیوری - kewari, Hind.; తాటికంకణము - tátikankanamu, Tel.). Title from plumage. Tel. from (tádu, tel. palmyra, borassus flabelliformis, linn. + kankanamu, tel. kind of bustard). Falcinellus igneus, ibisinæ. Alias Falcinellus bengalensis. Flies in flocks, rapidly in form of wedge.——*Pelican ibis* (ڈوک - dok, Hind.; ఎర్రకాలికొంగ - errakálikonga, Tel.; കരിനാര - karinára, Mal.; செங்கானாரை - shengánárai, Tam.). Title from appearance. Tel. from (erra, tel. red + kálu, tel. leg + konga, tel. crane). Mal. from (kari, mal. black + nára, mal. heron). Tam. from (shem, tam. red + kál, tam. leg + nárai, tam. heron). Tantalus leucocephalus, tantalinæ. Alias Tantalus gangeticus. Plumage white; quills and tail richly glossed green black; legs fleshy red. Stalks about shallows with bill in the water, partially held open.——*Shell ibis* (शंखबक - shankhabaka, San.; گونگلا - gonglá, Hind.; గుల్లకొంగ - gullakonga, Tel.; വെള്ളനാര - vellanára, Mal.; நத்தைக்குத்திநாரை - nattaikkuttinárai, Tam.). Title from feeding on molluscs. San. from (shankha, san. conch shell + baka, san. heron). Tel. from (gulla, tel. shell + konga, tel. crane). Mal. from (vella, mal. white + nára, mal. heron). Tam. from (nattai, tam. snail + kuttu, tam. to pick + nárai, tam. heron). Anastomus oscitans, anastomatinæ. Alias Anastomus albus, typus. Lives chiefly on molluscs [chippy].——*Spoon-bill ibis* (چمچا بزا - chamchábazá, Hind.; గంటెముక్కుకొంగ - gantemukkukonga, Tel.). Title from shape of bill. Hind. from (chamchá, hind. spoon + bazá, hind. ibis). Tel. from (gante, tel. spoon + mukku, tel. bill + konga, tel. crane). Platalea leucorodia, plataleinæ. Frequently in company with white ibis.——*White ibis* (سفید بزا - sufedbazá, Hind.; ಕಂಕ - kanka, Can.). Title from color of hind parts. Hind. from (sufed, hind. white + bazá, hind. ibis). Threskiornis melanocephalus, ibisinæ. Alias Ibis macei, bengala, religiosa, stricticollis. Head and neck nude, black; rest white.

DEER'S FOOT (هرن پادی - haranpádí, Hind.). Title from form of leaf. Hind. from (harina, san. deer + páda, san. foot). Title otherwise Corn bindweed. Botanically Convolvulus [tauly] arvensis, l., convolvulaceæ [vricsham, 93]. Stem slender, prostrate or twining, striated, angled; leaves narrow-sagittate, sub-auricled; sepals ovate-obtuse; capsule smooth; peduncles one to two-flowered, with two small bracts; flowers rose-colored, fragrant; common in the black soil [regar] of the deccan [q.v.].

DEH (ده - deh, *Hind.*). A village [graumam].——*Dehaut* (دیہات - dehát, Hind.). From arabic. Plural of deh. An entire village held as inam [inam].——*Dehjhaurah* (دہجھارا - dehjhárá, Hind.). From (above + jhárá, hind. examination). An account showing the number of houses, shops, cattle, population, looms, ploughs, &c., of which a town or village consists.——*Dehwaur* (دہوار - dehwár, Hind.). From (above + wár, pers. according to). Village by village.

DELLY (ഏഴിമല - ézhimala, *Mal.*). Means rat-hill; because infested by rats. Sanscrit name (saptashaila), meaning seven hills. Otherwise Yaimullay. Portuguese travellers styled the hill Monte d'Eli; hence the corruption into Delly, &c.—"*a*" Mountain, Malabar district, Chiracal talook. A detached hill forming prominent landmark visible 27 miles at sea. There are creeks on either side, the junction of which make it an island. Once a noted place for sea-pirates. The first Indian land seen by Vasco da Gama [cannanore]. A project set on foot for the construction of a harbour [toray] was abandoned on account of expense. The shore is bold and safe to approach, there being 7 and 8 fathoms at 1 and 2 miles' distance, 20 and 22 fathoms at 2 or 2½ leagues' distance; and at 15 leagues' distance abreast the mount soundings are lost. This is the narrowest part of the channel between the main and Laccadive islands, the distance being 27 leagues between Yeliculpainy bank and Mount delly. Abreast of this headland there is frequently a drain of current to the southward, with a short confused swell, the effect of brisk north-westers, which greatly prevail here. Modern fort built on a bluff projecting into the sea by the Portuguese, from whom it was taken by the Dutch. Acquired by the French by purchase from the Chiracal rajah on 24th February 1754. Surrendered to English according to terms of capitulation of Mahé, dated 10th February 1761. Taken by Sirdar khan, Tippoo's general, 1779. Restored to English by treaty of Mangalore, dated 11th March 1784. Much large game, samber [q.v.], panthers [honiga], &c.—"*b*" River; Malabar dist., Chiracal tal. Rises in ghaut [q.v.] mountains; lat. 12° 15′; long. 75° 22′, and loses itself in a number of creeks to east and north-east of the mount. One or more of these join the Neeleshwar and the chief stream flows south and enters sea in angle of the bay formed immediately to south of mount itself. The sluggish water is favorable to crocodiles [mugger]. Total length 30 miles.—"*c*" Trig. station; Malabar dist., Chiracal tal.; lat. 12° 01′ 37·04″; long. 75° 14′ 40·51″; height 720 feet; from Cannanore N.W. 16 miles; from Maudye W. 4½ miles; from the sea E. 1 mile.

DENCANICOTTAH (ಡೆಂಕನಿಕೋಟೆ - denkanikóta,* *Can.*). From (denkani a corruption of dakshina, san. southern + kóta, san. fort) [dacshinam, deccan].—"*a*" Deputy tahsildarry, Salem district. Pay Rs. 70.—"*b*" Town, Deputy tahsildar's station, Hills; Salem dist., Oossoor tal.; pop. 4,355; acres 2,772; lat. 12° 32′; long. 77° 50′; from Madras W.S.W. 170 miles; from Namcull N.N.W. 94 miles; from Oossoor S. 14¾ miles; from Salem N.N.W. 65 miles; from Tripatore W. 53 miles; from Yercaud N.N.W. 59 miles. To the west of Dencanicottah proper, which is on a hill, is the fort and fort pettah, also on an eminence; a valley with a tank lying between. The fort commands the approaches from Kelamungalam, Tully and Oossoor. A large portion has been dismantled. Dencanicottah proper is well laid out. Besides the town proper, and the fort pettah, there is the Tair [q.v.] or Car pettah about half mile south-east round the tank and temple of Bettroya sawmy and mostly occupied by votaries of the temple. The place is feverish. There is a large colony of Iyengar bramins in the old pettah [q.v.], and there are also many Mussalmans and Chetties. Trade in dry grains [q.v.], especially raggy [q.v.]; silk-worms [puttoo] were formerly bred. Rough pottery [chatty] is produced to a great extent. The Lumbaudies have their home in the Dencanicottah jungles. The Iroolar also frequent these jungles. Sandal-wood [q.v.] and atchah [q.v.] wood abound in the hills. The hills contain the finest forest in the district. Formerly gave its name to a talook [q.v.]. Ceded to the British in 1792. The camping grounds are Shoolagherry, Oossoor, Oodenapully.

DENGUE (ڈینگ - deng, *Hind.*; ಕೀಲಮ್ಮ - kílamma, *Can.*; కీళ్ళమ్మవారు - kíllammavárn, *Tel.*; முடக்குமாரி - mudakkumári, *Tam.*). Title from the spanish. Hind. from spanish. Can. from (kílu, can. joint + amma, can. goddess of small-pox). Tel. from (kílu, tel. joint + ammaváru, tel. goddess). Tam. from (mudakku, tam. to bend + mári, tam. epidemic). Hind. also (joronkábukhár), meaning joint + fever. Fugitive and erratic epidemic rheumatism, with fever [jwaram]. West indian term, but lately used here.

DEODAR (देवदारु - dévadáru, *San.*; देवदार - dévadára, *Mahr.*; صنوبر هند - sanobarihind, *Ar.*; صنوبر هندی - sanobarihindí, *Pers.*; دیودار - deudár, *Hind.*; دیودارو - deudárú, *Dec.*; ದೇವದಾರಿ - dévadári, *Can.*; దేవదారి - dévadári, *Tel.*; ദേവതാരം - dévatáram, *Mal.*; දේවදාර - dévadára, *Singh.*; தேவதாரி - tévathári, *Tam.*). Title from sanscrit through hindostany [deo, deva]. San. from (déva, san. god + dáru, san. tree) [cheer, deccany deodar, large neeroory]. Ar. from (sanobar, ar. fir, abies excelsa, dec. + hind, ar. indian). Pers. from arabic. Hind., &c., from sanscrit. San. also (suradru), meaning divine tree. Ar. also (shajaratideudár), meaning deodar tree. Pers. also (darakhtideudár), meaning deodar tree. Hind. also (kilankáper), meaning kilan tree; (nashtar), meaning lancet. Can. also (gundugururagi). Title otherwise Deodar cedar, Deodar pine, Devadauram, Fountain tree, Himalayan cedar, Indian cedar, Indian sanobar, Lancet tree, Sacred indian fir, Sooradauroo. Botanically Cedrus deodara, loud., coniferæ [vricsham]. Alias Abies deodara; Pinus deodara. Specific name from sanscrit, through hindostany. The great cedar of the Himalayas. Large tree, coma pyramidal, large, branches verticillate, lower ones somewhat hanging down, upper ones spreading, all pendulous at the apex; leaves spreading or pendulous at the top of the shortened branchlets, somewhat thirty-fasciculately collected, shortish, straight, stiffish, somewhat quadrangular, sides slightly compressed, green, bluntishly mucronate at the apex; male aments solitary, erect, oblong, acute; antheriferous bracts stalked, ovate above, rounded and denticulate at the apex; cones solitary, erect on a short branchlet or on a two-cleft branchlet twin, oval or oval-oblong, very obtuse, not umbilicate; scales numerous, imbricated, somewhat woody; bracts small, much shorter than the scale; nuts obovate, narrowed at the base, shorter than the obovate-triangular wing. Yields a coarse fluid kind of turpentine [ganda firoza], called kelonkatel, used as a stimulant to foul ulcers and skin diseases, and in leprosy [cooshtam]; quoted in pharm. but non-officinal. Ashes used as mordant [cauram]. Wood durable. For the Cedar of lebanon see Arzah. Compare also:—Acrocarpus fraxinifolius, pink cedar; Bischoffia javanica, var. genuina, red cedar; Cedrela toona, east indian cedar, moulmein cedar, singapore cedar, white cedar; Cedrus atlantica, african cedar, silver cedar; Chickrassia tabularis, bastard cedar, jamaica cedar; Erythroxylon monogynum, red cedar; Guazuma tomentosa, bastard cedar; Melia azedarach, bastard cedar, white cedar; Soymida febrifuga, bastard cedar, red cedar. See gloss. paragraphs.——*Deccany deodar* (देवदारु - dévadáru, San.; देवदारु - dévadáru, Conc.; دیودار - deudár, Hind.; دیوداروُ - deudárú, Dec.; ದೇವದಾರು - dévadáru, Can.; ದೇವದಾರು - dévadáru, Too.; దేవదారు - dévadáru, Tel.; ദേവദാരു - dévadáru, Mal.; දේවදාර - dévadára, Singh.; தேவதாரம் - tévatháram, Tam.). San. from (déva, san. god + dáru, san. tree); a medical fragrant tree [cheer, deodar, large neeroory]. Hind., &c., from sanscrit. San. also (amarabhúruha), meaning god + tree. Hind. also (nátkádeudár), meaning country cedar. Can. also (adavigóranti), meaning jungle + lawsonia alba, lamk.; (kuruvakamara), meaning lawsonia alba, lamk. Tel. also (adavigóranta), meaning forest + nail-dye plant, lawsonia alba, lam. Tam. also (shemmanatti), meaning red + that which has smell, from flesh-colored fragrant wood; (shembuliççai), meaning red + sour, from red wood and sour leaves; (káttuççandanam), meaning forest + santalum album, linn. Title otherwise Bastard sandal, Indian sethia, Iron-wood [cassa, chowkmaram, dark vail, foreign ilanjy, nauga champak, yellow condray], Jungle nail dye, Malabar cedar, Red-wood, Shemmanatty wood. Botanically Erythroxylon monogynum, roxb., lineæ [vricsham, 28]. Alias Erythroxylon indicum, sideroxyloides; Sethia indica. Small tree; petals five; leaves alternate, obovate or oblong, obtuse, cuneate at the base, feather-nerved, reticulated with veins, under side pale; pedicels axillary, one to three, about twice as long as the petiole, one-flowered; calyx five-lobed; styles combined nearly to the apex, longer than the stamens; drupes oblong, triangular, three-celled, two of the cells small, abortive, and without seeds; flowers small, greenish; flowering nearly all year; native of malabar; grows in dry jungles. Young leaves and tender shoots medicinally refrigerant; bruised and mixed with gingelly [q.v.] oil are applied as liniment to head; bark occasionally administered in infusion as tonic; substituted for anthemis, cascarilla and pot. acet.; leaves possibly contain some principle like erythroxylon coca, lam. [coca]; wood in powder used for sandal-wood [q.v.]; in famine time leaves eaten by starving poor. Empyreumatic oil or wood-tar of a reddish brown color is procured from the wood, used for preserving wood employed in construction of native boats [munjy]; timber flesh colored and excellent, of small size, known as bastard sandal, being used as substitute for sandal-wood.——*English deodar* (சீமைதேவதாரி - shímaithévathári, Tam.). Same as Cheer.——*Jambool deodar* (جمبول دیودار - jambuldeudár, Hind.). Same as Ashocam.——*Neeroory deodar* (देवदारु - dévadáru, San.). Title from similar appearance. Same as Large neeroory.

DERAH (ڈیرا - derá, *Hind.*; గుడారము - gudáramu, *Tel.*; തമ്പു - tambu, *Mal.*; கூடாரம் - kúdáram, *Tam.*). Tent. Their use has long been known to some of the wandering tribes; of a sort more like the old Roman tent than the Arab shamyauna [q.v.]. The following are different parts of tents, or kinds of tents as known to Europeans.——*Bechoba* (بے چوبہ - bechobah, Hind.). From (be, hind. without + chob, hind. pole). A tent without a pole. The peaked roof is made by a folding frame, on the umbrella principle.——*Canaut* (قنات - kanát, Hind.). The vertical side wall of a tent. Generally separate and attached all round as soon as the roof is pitched.——*Chick* (چق - chik, Hind.). From turkish. A hanging screen made of split bamboos [q.v.], fastened together in parallel lines by perpendicular strings, and sometimes painted [tatty].——*Dochoba* (دو چوبہ - dochobah, Hind.). From (do, hind. two + chob, pers. pole). Double-poled tent of oblong shape.——*Dosootee* (دو سوتی - dosútí, Hind.). From (do, hind. two + sút, pers. thread). A native made drill cloth, the threads of which are double; used for the outer covering of tents.——*Durbar ka derah* (دربار کا ڈیرا - darbárkáderá, Hind.). Tent used on durbar [q.v.] occasions.——*Durree* (دری - darí, Hind.). Carpet of country-made cotton [q.v.] cloth resembling drill, but colored [shatranjee].——*Fly* (سقف - sakf, Hind.). From (sakafa, ar. to cover in). The roof of a tent, sometimes single, sometimes double.——*Fowj ka derah* (فوج کا ڈیرا - faujkáderá, Hind.). Army, tent.——*Gadah* (گاڑا - gárá, Hind.). Coarse thick cloth.——*Hatrah* (ہتھوڑا - hatorá, Hind.). From (háth, hind. hand + torná, hind. to break). Mallet.——*Kharwah* (کھاروا - khárwá, Hind.). A coarse red cotton cloth.——*Khaum* (کھام - khám, Hind.). Tent-pole.——*Khootee* (کھوٹی - khútí, Hind.). Peg.——*Maij ka derah* (میز کا ڈیرا - mezkáderá, Hind.). From (mez, hind. table). Mess tent.——*Nowcar ka derah* (نوکر کا ڈیرا - naukarkáderá, Hind.). Servant's tent.——*Pakwaun ka derah* (پکوان کا ڈیرا - pakwáukáderá, Hind.). Cooking-tent.——*Paul* (پال - pál, Hind.). From (pá, san. to protect). A small tent with two light poles, a ridge bar, and steep sloping sides; the walls, if any, are very short, often not more than 6 inches high. Sometimes a second ridge above carries a second roof over the first; this makes a common shooting tent.——*Purdah* (پردہ - pardah, Hind.). A curtain.——*Pyekhana ka derah* (پائیخانہ کا ڈیرا - páikhánahkáderá, Hind.). Necessary tent.——*Rowty* (راوتی - ráutí, Hind.). A tent on the principle of the Paul but much higher and with canauts which have doors in them. Sometimes used to mean thereby the ordinary Paul.——*Saleetah* (شلیتا - shalítá, Hind.). Canvas sack [gunny] for packing different parts of the tent.——*Saumaun ka derah* (سامان کا ڈیرا - sámánkáderá, Hind.). Baggage tent.——*Shamyauna* (شامیانہ - shámiyánah, Hind.). From (sháh, pers. royal + miyánah, pers. centre). An awning or flat-roofed tent used by civil officers to hold their office or by natives for their zenanas [q.v.]. In the former case there are often no walls, it being pitched in front of the ordinary pyramidal tent.——*Shikar ka derah* (شکار کا ڈیرا - shikárkáderá, Hind.). Hill tent.——*Soorauk* (سوراخ - súrákh, Hind.). Eyelet.——*Sowar paul* (سوار کا ڈیرا - sawárkáderá, Hind.). Tent for a mounted soldier.——*Sywaun* (سائبان - sáibán, Hind.). From (sáyah, pers. shade + bán, pers. keeper). Side prolongations of the fly of a tent.——*Tabaila ka derah* (طبیلے کا ڈیرا - tabelekáderá, Hind.). Stable tent.——*Yek choba* (ایک چوبہ - ekchobah, Hind.). From (ek, hind. one + chob, pers. staff). Single-poled tent, the ordinary square tent.

DERVISH (درویش - darvísh, *Hind.*). From (dar, pers. door + áviz, pers. hanger on). Foreign term for a Mahomedan religious mendicant. There are several orders of Dervishes; the chief in S. india are Cawdiriya, Chishtiya, Madauriya, Nakshbundiya, Rafayee. Term fakeer [q.v.] generally substituted [calandar].

DESHAM (देश - désha, *San.*; دیس - des, *Hind.*). From (dish, san. to point). Point of the compass [dic, disay]. Country. Suffix in place names; as Bramhadesham. The following particulars are given by the Calpastaunam [q.v.] incidentally to medical matters; but see also the five-fold division below. All countries are situated either high, low or middle.—"*a*" The first, Jangala desham, is a high mountainous country, in which shrubs are thorny and trees very large. Salt water found by digging deep. The air clear and serene, and horizon [cshitijam] appears at an immense distance. The natives usually thin and fond of home. Adversity affects them, and the few disorders they are subject to are chiefly nervous [vautam].—"*b*" The second is Anoopa desham, or low country. A luxuriant appearance proceeding from general verdure and abundance of tanks, which are covered with Nautsoo or Utricularia stellaris, linn. Numberless fish. The whole is encompassed by high mountains, Trees large, and the plain is studded with palmyras [q.v.] and date trees [kharjooram]. The inhabitants are subject to catarrhal and hæmorrhoidal disorders, to obstructions in the abdomen, and to swollen legs. They are in general indolent, large, and have a soft flesh. The phlegm disorders [sheetam] prevail. The plants growing in such countries yield plentiful juices, but mostly sweet.—"*c*" The third country, Sandhauranam, approaches according to its position either the one or the other. And is either Jangala saudhauranam or Anoopa saudhauranam. The best medicines may be procured in this kind of country, provided attention is paid to the weather [caulam] and the season of the year.——**(1)** *Desha caval* (தேசக்காவல் - tésakkával, Tam.). From (above + kával, tam. guarding). System of guarding a tract of country against marauders. Desha cauvalgar was the equivalent of a poligar [q.v.].——*Deshacoyma* (ദേശക്കോയ്മ - déshakkóyma, Mal.). From (above + kóyma, mal. authority). Same as Deshavanly.——*Desha hasheel* (దేశహాశీలు - déshahásbilu, Tel.). From (above + háshilu, mahr. duty). Inland duty.——*Deshast* (ದೇಶಸ್ಥ - déshast'ha, Can.). From (above + st'há, san. to stay). Class of bramins originally from the Mahratta country. Speak Mahratta. Divided into Smartas [q.v.], and Madhwas [janty].——*Deshaudhicaury* (ദേശാധികാരി - déshádhikári, Mal.). From (above + adhikári, san. headman). The headman of a Deshom.——*Deshauntaram* (देशान्तर déshántara, San.). From (above + antara, san. space). Foreign country. The distance of any two meridians [raikhay] on the surface of the earth [bhoomy], or longitude; the governments of different nations fix one meridian and reckon the others; as half round the globe [golam] is 180 degrees, the greatest longitude a place can have is 180 E. or W. For celestial longitude see Dhroovacam and Sauyanam.——*Deshavauly* (ദേശവാഴി - déshavázhi, Mal.). From (above + vázhu, mal. to reign). Military chief of a Deshom [q.v.]. The number of Nayars or fighting men attached to a Deshavauly was from twenty-five to hundred; if it exceeded the latter number, he ranked as a Naudvauly [q.v.].——*Deshcoolacurny* (దేశకులకర్ణి - déshakulakarni, Tel.). From (above + kulakarni, can. accountant). Formerly a district accountant, compiling from village accountants [curnum].——*Deshmoukh* (దేశముఖ్యుడు - desamukhyudu, Tel.). From (above + mukhya, san. chief). Same as Deshpandya.——*Deshom* (ദേശം - désham, Mal.). From (dish, san. to point out). In Malabar a hamlet, a sub-division of an amshom [q.v.], which is again a sub-division of a talook [q.v.]. See vol. II, 103. Stands also for the proprietary possession of a village and the rank derived from it.——*Deshpandya* (దేశపాండ్య - déshapándyá, Tel.). From mahratta. A revenue head of a district under the old Governments [inam].——*Deshyam* (देश्य - déshya, San.). Primitive Teloogoo words, such as (gurram) a horse, (kannu) an eye, (illu) a house, and so forth; which like corresponding English words are considered primeval and not to be traced to any root. A sub-division of this class is Anya deshyam, or local. Thus the words (polati), (toyyali), (melata), and many other words for woman; (rautu) a soldier, (reddi) a farmer, (gidda) a bullock, (muduca) old, (bittari) beauty, (bittali) naked, and many more; some of which are supposed to be Tamul and others Cannadam.——*Deshye* (దేశాయి - désháyi, Tel.). From (désha, san. country + adhi, san. over). Same as Deshpandya.——(2) The following are the five kinds of country according to the Dravidians, with their characteristics.——*Coorinjy* (குறிஞ்சி - kuriñji, Tam.). From (kurumai, tam. shortness); hilly tract. The chief of the tracts are styled porooppan [q.v.], verpan [q.v.], and shilamban [q.v.]; the peculiar deity is scandan [q.v.]; the employments of its people are sowing mountain paddy [q.v.], watching millet [q.v.], collecting honey [shahad], digging of roots [gaddah], &c.; its water is mountain streams; its melody is coorinjy punn; its drum [paray] is tondagam; its birds are parrots [totah] and peacocks [mayil]; its flowers are known as november-flower [wild bachnaug], &c.; its trees are vengay [common vengay], coorinjy maram, sandal [q.v.] tree, teak [q.v.], aquila [eagle-wood], ashocam [q.v.], poon [q.v.]; its inhabitants are coravar, caunavar, coorattiyar; its lute is coorinjy yauzhtiram; the food of its inhabitants are bamboo rice [moongil arisy], mountain rice [eivana nel], tinay [q.v.], bulbous roots, honey, &c.; its villages are known by the name of shiroocoody [q.v.]; its beasts are tiger [pooly], bear [ricsham] elephant [q.v.], lion [simham], &c.——*Marootham* (மருதம் - marutham, Tam.). Agricultural tract. The chiefs of the district are styled ooran [q.v.] and kizhavan [q.v.]; the peculiar deity is indran [q.v.]; its inhabitants are the ploughmen and the labourers, their employments being ploughing, sowing, reaping, celebrating festivals, &c.; its water is rivers and canals; its birds are the heron [paddy bird], swans [hamsam], indian nightingale, ducks [badak], &c.; its beasts, cattle [maud], &c.; the food of the inhabitants is shumbah [q.v.] rice [q.v.], &c.; its plants are the ape face-flower plant [ilanjy], the lotus [nelumbo], the water-lily [q.v.], &c.; its trees are the marootham [murdah], terminalia, the caunchy [q.v.] and the vanjy [goolancha]; the villages are called peroor [q.v.] and moothore [q.v.].——*Moollay* (முல்லை - mullai, Tam.). Woodland or sylvan tract. The chiefs are styled cooroomporay [q.v.] naudan and tondral [q.v]; its peculiar deity is krishnan [q.v.]; the inhabitants are cowherds and shepherds, their occupations being feeding cows, grappling with bulls, dancing hand in hand, &c.; their food is shaumay [q.v.], varagoo [q.v.], and pulses [dholl]; its waters are jungle streams; its birds are jungle fowls [q.v.], &c., and the beasts are the stag and the hares [mosal]; the plants are the november-flower, or jasminum trichotomum, heyne, the vanamullicah, jasminum angustifolium, vahl., &c. [jasmine]; the trees are chiefly cassia [condray] and memecylon edulo, roxb. [cassa]; and its villages are styled paudy [q.v.].——*Neydal* (நெய்தல் - neydal, Tam.). From (ney, tam. to be unctuous); from nature of earth. Maritime tract. The chiefs are styled shairpan [q.v.] and poolamban [q.v.]; the ruling deity is varoonan [q.v.]; its inhabitants are fishermen and salt makers, &c.; their occupations being fishing and salt-making, &c.; their food is fishes, lobsters, &c.; its water is sea water or salt water; the birds are water-crow [caukkay], &c.; the beasts are the soorah [q.v.] fish, squalus carcharias; the plants are pandanus odoratissimus, linn. [screwpine], and aumbal, nymphæa alba, linn. [indian water-lily], &c.; the trees are the silk-cotton tree [q.v.], &c.; and its villages are styled pattinam and paukam [q.v.].——*Paulay* (பாலை - pálai, Tam.). From (pál, tam. whiteness, bleakness). Arid or desert tract. The rulers of the desert tract are styled caulay; its peculiar deity is doorga [q.v.]; its inhabitants are the veyda [q.v.] caste, their occupations being mostly plundering; the food is plunder on which they mainly subsist; its water is well-water; the birds are the dove [capotam], kite [chillam], and eagle [cooralam]. The plants are poolah [q.v.], paulay [q.v.] and cuily [q.v.]; the beasts are wild dogs [dhole]; the trees are the coorah, webera corymbosa, willd., l. [tirauna], and the marah or white cadamboo, Barringtonia racemosa, blume [common indian oak], and the villages of the arid tracts are styled cooruniboo [q.v.].

DEVA (देव - déva, *San.*). From (div, san. to shine) [deo, dinam]. Greek θέος, Latin deus.—"*a*" A secondary god in the Aryan mythology. Mortals possessed of some merit reside in the form of devas in the Devalocam, but when their merit [carmam] is exhausted they must again be born on earth as men or animals, or go to a place of suffering in hell [naracam] for the expiation of previous demerit [samsauram]. The devas are divided into four classes, or vagays, or ganams, with a vasoo [q.v.] or chief for each crore [q.v.] of devas therein. Thus there are:—first Dwaudashaudityan, the twelve audityans [q.v.], literally suns, their class numbering with them 120,000,000; secondly Yecaudasharoodran, the eleven roodrans [q.v.], their class comprising in all 110,000,000; thirdly Ashta vasoos, the eight vasoos, their class including themselves containing 80,000,000; fourthly Ashwinies [q.v.] who are the two physicians of the gods and chiefs of a class containing 20,000,000. There are thus 33 crores, or 330 millions of devas; the 33 crores of gods is a common expression. The term Shiva ganam is frequently used of a single celestial of Shiva's paradise [keilausam], especially with reference to one sent down on earth to bear a human or other form; and either as a punishment for a crime or to accomplish some purpose. The plaster figures outside the gopoorams [q.v.] of temples [coil] and the rows of figures bending on one knee to Shiva in the sculptures at the seven pagodas [q.v.] are devas of this class. Of the devas few only are known by names, but here and there paintings exhibiting various stories concerning them are found in the houses of the opulent. See vol. I (73), (78).—"*b*" The Tamuls always use the term Devan monotheistically. The following are from the Vausishtam [alvandar]:—தீவினையெல்லா மறுத்து மங்கல மெல்லாமுதவுந் தேவபூசை, யாவதெனக்கேட்டலுமே யருள்செய்வான் றெய்வந்தானியாதென்றேதிற், கேவலமே வரிபல்ல வரனல்ல பூதவுடற்கிடைத்ததல்ல மோவுமன மன்றடியு முடிவுமில்லாச் செயப்படாவுணர்வே தேவம்.—"When Vasishtan [q.v.] asked Shiva, what is "the divine worship which will remove all misery and produce "all happiness? Shiva graciously declared; to teach you what "the deity is, know that that which alone is, that which is not "Vishnoo, nor Shiva, nor anybody formed of the five elements "[bhootam], nor the ceasing mind; but that which is the self-"existing uncreated wisdom without beginning and without end, "that is the deity."—தேகமுதற் பிரிவுகளாய்ச் சிறியனவாம் பொருள்களிலத் தெய்வமுண்டோ, பாகமறப் பணதியற வடிமுடிவற்றுள வுணர்வே பரம போத, மாகவிஞ லதுதெய்வ மருச்சித்தற் குரித்தாகு மறிவிலாத, மூகருக்கு வடிவுமுதலருச்சனையே யியல்பென்று மொழியுமன்றே.—"Is this deity in the multifarious bodies "[shareeram] of insignificant objects? No. That which is "infinite wisdom, immeasurable, inoperative, without beginning "and without end; that is the deity, which is worthy of worship. "But to the ignorant, the worship of images and forms is "natural." Avvay, the Tamul poetess says:—தெய்வமொருவனேயென்று வுணரவல்லார்க்கு, அருவினைகளைந்து மறும்.—"They who are able to understand that there is one "only God, will lose their deep rooted five sinful actions" [matam].—"*c*" Plant first term denoting excellence. Ex., joining two genera, where transl. is of second term:—Canna indica (dévakéli), musa paradisiaca; Pimpinella anisum (dévaduru), cuminum cyminum; Plumeria acutifolia (dévaganagalu), nerium odorum; Randia uliginosa (dévatámalle), jasminum sambac. See gloss. paragraphs. There are many others where the genus is the same.——*Deo* (ديو - deu, Hind.; ଦିଓ - divó, Oor.). From (déva, san. god). A divinity [deva]. Ooriya title.——*Deodar* (ديودار - deudár, Hind.). See sep. title.——*Deva bramin* (దేవబ్రాహ్మణుడు - dévabráhmanudu, Tel.). Title of certain of the carpenters' caste in contradistinction to the Go-bramins or cow bramins. Cf. Vishwa bramin.——*Deva darshanam* (देवदर्शन - dévadarshana, San.). From (above + darshana, san. seeing). Visiting an idol. Particularly such a visit paid by the bride and bridegroom, with their friends, at a particular period after their marriage [maryauday].——*Devadattan* (தேவதத்தன் - tévathattan, Tam.). From (above + dá, san. to give); god-given. Name of the conch shell of Arjoonan. Often used in grammatical examples and then equivalent to any one or a certain person [peyar].——*Devadauram* (देवदारु - dévadáru, San.). From (above + dáru, san. tree); from fragrant resin of the genus. Fir, Pine-tree. Botanically the Pinus genus, coniferæ [vricsham]. Trees, generally confined to the northern hemisphere; leaves evergreen and sharp-pointed; wood generally very resinous, not homogeneous, consisting of alternate layers of soft and spongy spring wood and of hard and darker colored autumn wood; indian species have a distinct heart-wood. For the resinous products see Keel, Carpoora teilam, and Ganda firoza. The species best known to the natives are:—longifolia [cheer], pinea [chalgozah]. The anglo-indian term Deodar [q.v.] is for cedrus deodara and erythroxylon monogynum, conifers. The natives give the name to some other plants also.——*Devadausan* (தேவதாசன் - tévathásan, Tam.). From (above + dása, san. slave). Slave of the deity. Proper name [peyar].——*Devadausy* (தேவதாசி - tévathási, Tam.). From (above + dási, san. slave).—"*a*" The dancing girls of Swargam [q.v.], the world of the gods. The most celebrated among them are Menakay, Oorvashy, Rambhay, and Tilottamay.—"*b*" The official name of the girls who are devoted to dancing in the Shiva and Vishnoo temples. Cf. the ἱερόδουλοι of Corinth. Every temple, according to its size, entertains a set of them to the number of eight, twelve, or more; they perform their religious duties at the temple to which they belong twice a day, morning and evening; they are also obliged to assist at all public religious ceremonies; at private entertainments they come for payment [nautch]. They are reared to this life from their infancy; they are taken from any caste, and are not unfrequently of respectable birth; the life to which the daughter is destined brings no disgrace on the family; until recently in the native population these women were the only females who were allowed to learn to read. The dancing girl caste have special laws for adoption [dutt] and inheritance [dauyam]; a dancing girl can adopt a daughter, with the permission of the authorities of the pagoda [q.v.] to which she belongs; the property descends in the female line first, and then to males as in other castes; in the failure of issue, the property goes to the pagoda to which she belongs as a rule, it is seldom that these women have children of their own. In some places there exists two kinds of dancing girls, the dancing women differing from the pagoda dancers; these are distinguished as dausy and devadausy. Dancing girls, when performing, are accompanied by two men singers, who while singing also play the cymbals [jaulry]; one or more old women join in the song, and clap their hands during the performance; these are generally dancing girls who have given up the profession from age or other causes; the accompaniment is usually from a drone [tootty] and clarionet [naugaswaram]; their songs comprise praises in honor of the several idols. Nautches are given at marriage ceremonies and feasts, and on other public occasions; among zemindars are of almost daily occurrence; dancing girls frequently receive valuable presents in money, shawls, gold bangles or rings, which are bestowed on them during performance. Devadausies are without exception prostitutes; they receive a fixed allowance out of the temple endowment [devadauyam]; some are the concubines of one of the priests or of some native of consideration, while others are common women, as are all who do not serve in the temple; they are not allowed to marry. Their male children usually call themselves moodellies [q.v.] and pillays [q.v.], if in good circumstances; and have no difficulty in acquiring a proper position in society; the female children are generally brought up to the trade of the mothers; it is customary with a few castes to present their superfluous daughters to the pagodas with a view to their being brought up as dausies [bhogam, jauty].——*Devadauyam* (தேவதாயம் - tévatháyam, Tam.). From (above + dáya, san. a gift). Lands or allowances for the support of a devastaunam [devasom, inam].——*Devadiga* (ದೇವಡಿಗ - dévadiga, Can.). From (above + adiga, can. slave). Menial servant who performs out-door services at temples. Numbers about 20,000 [jauty].——*Devagherry* (దేవగిరి - dévagiri, Tel.). From (above + giri, san. mountain). Hill; Vizagapatam district, Jeypore zemindarry, Royagada magisterial division. Circular hill without much jungle. Five deep pools of pure water on top. Also cave containing lingams [q.v.] and a garden with plaintain [q.v.] trees. Largely resorted to on Shivarautry [pundigay, 6a]. Situated near Calyaunasingapooram.——*Devaky* (देवकी - dévakí, San.). The mother of Krishnan. Devaky meindan, from (maindan, tam. son) is Vishnoo.——*Devamany* (देवमणि - dévamani, San.). From (above + mani, san. jewel). Shiva.——*Devamboo* (தேவாம்பு - tévámbu, Tam.). From (above + ambu, san. water). Water of the gods; the Ganges. Hindoo 2nd or pers. name. Also common with baptized Native christians [peyar].——*Devanagry* (देवनागरी - dévanágarí, San.). From (above + nagara, san. a city). Character in which Sanscrit is usually written [baulbund, nagry].——*Devanaickam* (தேவநாயகம் - tévanáyagam, Tam.). From (above + náyaka, san. lord). Epithet of any superior deity, especially of indran. Feminine Devanaicky. Hindoo 2nd or pers. name. Common among non-bramins. Also among Native christians [peyar].——*Devanna* (ದೇವಣ್ಣ - dévanna, Can.). From (above + anna, can. elder brother). Hindoo 2nd or pers. name [peyar].——*Devarbetta* (ದೇವರಬೆಟ್ಟ - dévarabetta, Can.). From (above + betta, can. hill). Hill; Neilgherry district, Todanaud division, Trig. station; lat. 11° 23′ 22·18″; long. 76° 34′ 11·07″; height 8,371 feet; from Ootacamund W. 12 miles; from Macoorty peak N.N.E. 1½ miles.——*Deva roya* (దేవరాయ - dévaráya, Tel.). From (above + rájá, san. king). Rajah of Vijianugger of the Harihar dynasty A.D. 1406–1412. Distinguish from Krishnadeva roya [q.v.].——*Devarsinga permaun* (தேவர்சிங்கப்பெருமாள் - tévarsingapperumán, Tam.). From (above + simha, san. lion + perumán, tam. lord). Shiva who is a lion of the gods.——*Devasahauyam* (தேவசகாயம் - tévasagáyam, Tam.). From (above + saháya, san. companion). Hindoo 2nd or pers. name. Common among non-bramins. Also among Native christians [peyar].——*Devashikhaumany* (தேவசிகாமணி - tévasigámani, Tam.). From (above + shikhá, san. the crest + mani, san. gem). Hindoo 2nd or pers. name. Common among non-Bramins. Also among Native christians [peyar].——*Devasholah* (ದೇವರಶೋಲೆ - dévarashóle, Can.). From (above + shóle, can. a plantation). Village, Hill; Neilgherry district, Merkoonaud division; lat. 11° 19′; long. 76° 43′; height 7,417 feet; from Coonoor W.S.W. 9 miles; from Ootacamund S. 6½ miles. The hill is one of the principal eminence on the Neilgherries, half way between Mailcoondah and Dodabetta. Connected with Ootacamund by a driving road. Formerly clothed with thick forest of which a large portion has been cleared and planted. The cinchona [koinah] estate here on E. face of the hill has 1,000 acres. Devasholah bett is another name for Snowdon.——*Devasom* (ദേവസ്വം - dévasvam, Mal.). See sep. title.——*Devastaunam* (देवस्थान - dávast'hána, San.). From (above + t'hána, san. place). A temple; also land or allowances for the support of a temple [devadauyam, devasom, inam].——*Devatay* (देवता - dévatá, San.). Benign spirits governed by Indran. Properly the inhabitants of the North pole [soomeroo]; for the devatays are said to have sunshine when the deityans [q.v.] have darkness and vice versâ. The evil spirits are pishauch.——*Devaujee* (దేవాజీ - déváji, Tel.). From (above + aji, tel. master). Madhwa second name. Familiarly Devoo [peyar].——*Devaulah* (ദേവാല - déválа, Mal. dévála*). From (above + álaya, san. abode). Sanscrit name (déválaya), meaning same. Village, Head-quarters of Head assistant collector up to March 1889 when they were transferred to Pundalore. Public bungalow; Neilgherry district, Wynaud S.E. division; lat. 11° 29′; long. 76° 26′; from Coimbatore N.W. 53 miles; from Coonoor W.N.W. 29 miles; from Goodalore W.S.W. 8 miles; from Madras W.S.W. 290 miles; from Ootacamund W.N.W. 21 miles. Four miles from head of Carcoor ghaut [q.v.] on high road to Vythery. Weekly market. Was of considerable importance during early period of gold mining speculations. Most houses now empty. Three miles west on the W. slopes of mountains are a large number of ancient mining shafts, 70 or 80 feet deep, and sometimes so close together that it is dangerous to walk through the jungle. Old forest trees are to be seen growing out of them.——*Devaunga* (ದೇವಾಂಗ - dévánga, Can.; దేవాంగ - dévánga, obl. Tel.). From (above + anga, san. body), from a tradition of divine origin. Otherwise Jendravar. Weavers. The Devaungas are divided into Canarese and Teloogoo. The canarese wear the lingam [q.v.]; the hereditary chiefs are called yejmaun, these take cognizance of all caste offences; the whole of the class can intermarry; they are allowed a plurality of wives whom they purchase from their parents; the wives are not shut up, nor are they divorced, except for adultery; they eat no animal food nor use any intoxicating substance, except as a medicine; they bury the dead [shavacaud]. The teloogoo devaungas are divided into two sects, veishnava and sheiva, but both sects intermarry, the wife always adopting the religion of the husband; the widows were formerly expected to bury themselves alive with their husbands' bodies, this caste are allowed to eat animal food; but not to drink spirituous liquors; they offer sacrifices to the shacties [q.v.]. Numbers about 140,000; chiefly in Coimbatore, Godavery, Salem and Vizagapatam [jauty].——*Devauram* (देवार्ह - dévárha, San.; தேவாரம் - téváram, Tam.). From (above + arh, san. to adore). Collection of songs in tamul extolling the 1,008 Sheiva pagodas [q.v.], of which songs 574 are extant. Later than Tirvauchacam [q.v.]; composed chiefly by Nyauna sambandhan [q.v.], a native of Shiyally, near Chidambaram, with his disciples Soondran [q.v.] and Appan [q.v.]; these three held the most distinguished place amongst the sixty-three [aroopatt moover] devotees of Shiva. The Tirvauchacam and Devauram together are called Tamul vedam [tirvye mozhy]; opposed to jeinism [bhaushay, cooral].——*Devautidevan* (देवातिदेव - dévátidéva, San.). From (above + ati, san. intensive + above). God of gods. Epithet of Vishnoo and of Shakya moony.——*Devayaunay* (தெய்வயானை - teyvayánai, Tam.). Tam. by corruption from (daiva, san. divine + yánai, tam. elephant); supposed to be brought up by eirauvatam [q.v.], the divine elephant [q.v.]. Wife of Soobramanyan.——*Devendran* (देवेन्द्र - dévéndra, San.). From (above + indra, san. lord). Otherwise Indran [q.v.]. ζεύς of Greeks; Jupiter tonans of Romans; Osiris of Egyptians. The chief of the secondary gods. In the vedas the ruler over the deities of the atmosphere, not of heaven. He afterwards came to be considered the lord of all the gods and retained that place until the notion of the trimoorty [q.v.] came into being. Strabo describes the Hindoos as worshippers of Jupiter pluvius, meaning Indran. He was later also regent of the east quarter [ashtadicpaulacan]. His weapon is the vajram [q.v.] or thunderbolt. His paradise is Swargam [q.v.], which is modelled according to the court of a Hindoo king. To it great numbers of people limit their aspirations, higher degrees being promised to ascetics. He is represented in S. india with four arms and hands. With two of these he holds a lance; in the third he holds the Vajrauyoodham, or thunderbolt, the fourth is empty. The Vajrauyoodham, which makes persons invincible, he gives to those who practise austerities in his honor. On his head he wears a crown; in his hairlocks, pearls [moty] and precious stones [ratnam]; and on his ears, neck, breast, arms, and feet, ornaments of various descriptions. From his shoulders garlands hang down, and his seat is an exalted throne [simhausanam]. His whole body is full of eyes, said to be owing to the curse of the Rishy gowtaman, but meaning originally the stars of the firmament. He has the following among other names :— Ayiran cunnan or the thousand-eyed; Cary vauhanan or he that has the elephant as his vehicle; Maigha vauhanan or he who has the clouds as his vehicle; Pauca shausanan or conqueror of the giant Paucan; Poorhootan or the much invoked; Poorohitan or priest; Shoonauseeran or the leader of the celestial hosts; Vajrapauny or holder of the thunder-bolt; Vaunore comaun or king of the celestials; Vailvikvendan, or lord of sacrifice; Vinmoozhoothauly or ruler of the whole sky [matam].——*Devicapooram* (தேவிகாப்புரம் - tévigáppuram, Tam.). From (déviká, san. goddess + pura, san. town); called after parvaty. Jagheer village; North arcot dist., Arnee jagheer; pop. 2,334; lat. 12° 30′; long. 79° 18′; height 801 feet; from Arnee S.S.W. 12 miles; from Chittore S.S.E. 50 miles. Noteworthy for its temples. Most important, dedicated to Brihadambah, is in town. That of her spouse, Canacagireeshwaran, crowns the adjacent hill. The former was built by Chola rajah tondiman chuckravurty, who began his mission of temple building here. Second in importance only to Trinomallee. The goddess is one of the four brought into existence by Bramha.——*Devicottah* (தீவுக்கோட்டை - tívukkóttai, Tam.). From (tívu, tam. island + kóttai, tam. fort). Sanscrit name (dévíkóta), meaning doorga, the goddess + fort; also (bánapura), meaning baunan, the asooran + town; also (shónitapura), meaning baunan, the red asooran + town; also (ushávana), meaning ooshay, the daughter of baunan + garden; also (kótivarsha), meaning edge + country; also (kóttavipura), meaning town of doorga or town of the mother of baunan. Village, Tanjore dist., Shiyally tal.; pop. 8,451; lat. 11° 22′; long. 79° 51′; from Madras S. 122 miles; from Shiyally N.N.E. 10 miles; from Tanjore N.E. 60 miles; from Tranquebar N. 24 miles. On small island at mouth of Coleroon. The entrance of the river is difficult and dangerous of access from the Coleroon shoal, which stretches 4 or 5 miles to the south-east. Taken by the English, 1749. Ceded in 1749, with thirty-one surrounding villages, to the English by Rajah Prataup sing, on condition of his receiving military aid whenever required. Fortress abandoned by the English garrison in 1758 on the fall of Fort St. David to Lally and the approach of a large French force. Evacuated by the French in 1760 after Coote's victory at Wandiwash, and regarrisoned by the English. Included in the old Cuddalore district about 1787. Ruined fort said to have been built by a Chola rajah; formerly a mile in circumference with walls 18 feet high.——*Deviputnam* (தேவிப்பட்டணம் - tévippattanam, Tam.). From (déví, san. goddess + pattana, san. city). Sanscrit name (navapáshána), meaning nine stones representing the navagraham or nine planets [graham]. The stones are near the sea. Town, Port, Place of pilgrimage; Madura dist., Ramnaud zemindarry; pop. 3,905; lat. 9° 28′; long. 78° 56′; from Madras S.S.W. 264 miles; from Madura E.S.E. 59 miles; from Moodiapatam N. 3¼ miles; from Ramnaud N.N.E. 8¾ miles; from Tirpaulancoody S. 5¼ miles. Connected with Madura and Ramnaud by a road. One of the most holy bathing-places in S. india. Old Amman temple south of town, and large musjid [q.v.]. Also Shiva and Vishnoo temples. Formerly from this place to Tirpoollauny existed the Poorauranyam forest.——*Devy* (देवी - déví, San.; தேவி - tévi, Tam.). Feminine of deva.—"*a*" The goddess Parvaty. Specially in the war of amazons and devas against the asoorans. The episode in the Marcandeya poorannam, known as Sapta shaty as containing seven hundred shlocams, or Devy mahautmyam [q.v.], narrates the wars of Devy with Shoombhan, Nishoombhan, Mahishausooran, and their hosts of asoorans. Devy is also a name used by the shactibhactans in their mysteries; the same as the Latin Bona dea.—"*b*" Title to deities and Madhwa females especially. Hindoo third name [peyar].—"*c*" Phrase used for the small-pox [ammay].—"*d*" Moodevy is elder goddess or elder sister of lutchmy [q.v.] and is the goddess of misfortune; see sep. title. ——*Dewal* (देवालय - déválaya, San.; ديول - deval, Hind.; దేవళము - dévalamu, Tel.). From (déva, san. god + álaya, san. house). Hindoo temple in which an idol is placed [coil, pagoda].

DEVASOM (देवस्व - dévasva, *San.*; ദേവസ്വം - dévasvam, *Mal.*). From (déva, san. god + sva, san. wealth) [deo, deva]. ——(1) Territorial property attached to a temple [devadauyam, devastanam].——(2) The following are the principal Devasoms in North malabar, with the talook indicated.——*Cadalye* (കടലായി - katalâyi, Mal.), Chiracal.——*Calarivaudacull* (കളരിവാതുക്കൽ - kalarivátukkal, Mal.), Chiracal.——*Caunkole* (കാങ്കോൽ - kánkól, Mal.), Chiracal.——*Caunyarangaud* (കാഞ്ഞിരങ്ങാട് - kaññirannátu, Mal.), Chiracal.——*Chaulyle* (ചാലയിൽ - chálayil, Mal.), Chiracal.——*Chercoonn* (ചെറുകുന്ന - cherukunnu, Mal.), Chiracal.——*Collat vishaurical* (കൊല്ലത്ത് വിഷാരിക്കൽ - kollattvisháríkkal, Mal.), Cooroombranaud.——*Cottiyore* (കൊട്ടിയൂർ - kottiyúr, Mal.), Cottayam.——*Maudye cauv* (മാടായിക്കാവു - mátáyikávu, Mal.), Chiracal.——*Oorpilatchicauv* (ഊർപ്പിഴച്ചിക്കാവു - úrppizhaççikkávu, Mal.), Chiracal.——*Payyannore* (പയ്യന്നൂർ - payyanúr, Mal.), Chiracal.——*Payyavore* (പയ്യാവൂർ - payyávúr, Mal.), Chiracal.——*Perlacherry* (പെരളശ്ശേരി - peralashshéri, Mal.), Chiracal.——*Ramantaly* (രാമന്തളി - rámantali, Mal.), Chiracal.——*Taliparamba* (തളിപ്പറമ്പ - talipparamba, Mal.), Chiracal.——*Tirvangaud* (തിരുവങ്ങാട് - tiruvannátu, Mal.), Cottayam.——*Trichambaram* (തൃച്ചംബരം - triççambaram, Mal.), Chiracal.——*Vayattore* (വയത്തൂർ - vayattúr, Mal.), Chiracal.——*Yedacaud* (എടക്കാട് - etakkátu, Mal.), Chiracal.——(3) The following are similarly the principal Devasoms in South malabar.——*Caricaud* (കരിക്കാട് - karikkátu, Mal.), Yernaud. *Cautchancoorchy* (കാച്ചാങ്കുറിശ്ശി - káççánkurishshi, Mal.), Palghaut.——*Chamravattam* (ചമ്രവട്ടം - chamravattam, Mal.), Ponnany.——*Cherpalcherry cauv* (ചെർപ്പുളശ്ശേരിക്കാവ് - cherppullashshérikkávu, Mal.), Valavanaud.——*Codicoonnat* (കൊടിക്കുന്നത്ത് - kotikkunnattu, Mal.), Ponnany.——*Culleycoolangaru yaimore bhagavaty* (കല്ലേക്കുളങ്ങര ഏമൂർ ഭഗവതി - kallékkulanaraémúrbhagavati, Mal.), Palghaut.——*Gooroovayore* (ഗുരുവായൂർ - guruváyúr, Mal.), Ponnany.——*Irinyaulacode ccodal maunicam* (ഇരിഞ്ഞാലക്കുടക്കൂടൽ മാണിക്കം - irinnálakkutakútalmánikkam, Mal.), Moocoondapooram.——*Munjairy coonnat* (മഞ്ചേരിക്കുന്നത്ത് - mañchérikunnattu, Mal.), Yernaud.——*Niroomgythacottah* (നിറുമ്കൈതക്കോട്ട - nirumkaitakkótta, Mal.), Yernaud.——*Panavanna* (പനവന്ന - panavanna, Mal.), Valavanaud.——*Paracaut cauv* (പരക്കാട്ട് കാവ് - parakkáttukávu, Mal.), Palghaut.——*Permanna* (പെരുമണ്ണ - perumanna, Mal.), Calicut. ——*Polore* (പോലൂർ - polúr, Mal.), Calicut.——*Poottoore* (പുത്തൂർ - puttúr, Mal.), Calicut.——*Pullavore* (പല്ലാവൂർ - pallávúr, Mal.), Palghaut.——*Pundalore* (പന്തല്ലൂർ - pantalúr, Mal.), Yernaud. ——*Rampooram* (രാമപുരം - rámapuram, Mal.), Valavanaud.——*Shreevalyanaud cauv* (ശ്രീവളയനാട്ട് കാവു - shrívalayanáttukávu, Mal.), Calicut.——*Talee* (തളി - tali, Mal.), Calicut.——*Tirmandhauncoonn* (തിരുമാന്ധാംകുന്ന - tirumándhánkunnu, Mal.), Valavanaud.——*Tirnavoya* (തിരുനാവായി - tirunáváyi, Mal.), Ponnany.——*Tirvaipru* (തിരുവേഗപുരം - tiruvégapuram, Mal.), Valavanaud.——*Tirvannore* (തിരുവണ്ണൂർ - tirvannúr, Mal.), Calicut.——*Tirvaulattore* (തിരുവാലത്തൂർ - tiruválattúr, Mal.), Palghaut.——*Tirvillamala* (തിരുവില്ലാമല - tiruvillámala, Mal.), Talapully.——*Tricalungottore* (തൃക്കലങ്ങോട്ടൂർ - trikkalannóttúr, Mal.), Yernaud.——*Tricalayore* (തൃക്കളയൂർ - trikkalayúr, Mal.), Yernaud.——*Tricandiyore* (തൃക്കണ്ടിയൂർ - trikkantiyúr, Mal.), Ponnany.——*Tripauvalore* (തൃപ്പാവലൂർ - trippávalúr, Mal.), Palghaut.——*Triprangode* (തൃപ്രങ്ങോട - triprannótu, Mal.), Ponnany. ——*Tripriaur* (തൃപ്രയാർ - tripráyár, Mal.), Ponnany.——*Trishiva peroor vadaknautan* (തൃശ്ശിവപ്പേരൂർവടക്കുന്നാഥൻ - trishshivappérúrvatakkunát'han, Mal.), Trichore.——*Trittaula* (തൃത്താല - trittála, Mal.), Ponnany.

DEVAUNGA (वनमानुष - vanamánusha, *San.*; شرمندی بلی - sharmindíbillí, *Hind.*; ಅಡವಿಮನುಷ್ಯ - adavimanushya, *Can.*; ಚೆಂಗೆಕುಳಿ - chíngekuli, *Coorg*; దేవాంగిపిల్లి - dévángipilli, *Tel.*; തേവാങ്കം - tévánkam, *Mal.*; උනහපුලුවා - unahapuluvá, *Singh.*; தேய்வாங்கு - téyvángu, *Tam.*). Title from tamul; distinguish from devaunga, weaver, under deva. San. from (vana, san. wild + mánusha, san. man). Hind. from (sharmindí, hind. bashful + billí, hind. cat). Can. from (adavi, can. forest + manushya, san. man). Tam., &c., from (téyvu, tam. emaciation + anga, san. body). Can. also (bálegappe), meaning plantain frog; (nidugappe), meaning long frog. Title otherwise Lemur or slender loris. Loris gracilis, lemuridæ, quadrumana, mammalia [sastanam, 2], of naturalists [jantoo]. Alias Stenops gracilis. The light-colored variety of the loris in Ceylon has a spot on its forehead, somewhat resembling the naumam [q.v.] worn by Veishnavites, and so called the Naumadham. Lemurs are also natives of Madagascar. They have given their name to Lemuria, the submerged continent which once lay between Madagascar and South india. From the slowness of its movements the Lemur is also called the Indian sloth. Found in most forests but difficult to observe owing to small size and nocturnal habits. Lives almost entirely in trees. The fur is soft, dense, and woolly. The nostrils, unlike those of either group of monkeys [bandar], have a curved opening, and the tail is never prehensile. The extremities of the lemur differ remarkably from those of the monkeys in having a long, sharp, curved claw on the first finger of the hinder pair, and generally in the broad, flat character of the nails of the other fingers. The form of the face is somewhat fox-like in the prolongation of the muzzle and affords a physiognomical character which will be readily recognised. It is not common on the Malabar coast. Its eyes are a remedy for certain diseases of the eyes among the Tamul doctors; also used as love potions. A thin person is called a Devaunga. The lemur occurs also in Ceylon. There is a link between the lemurs and the bats [vavvaul] in the Galæopithecus or flying lemur. The limbs of these animals are connected with a membrane as in the flying squirrels [paravayanil] and flying foxes [q.v.]. They have not however been found in India. The Nycticebus tardigradus or slow-paced lemur is also not found here.

DEVIL'S GOAD (भूतांकुश - bhútánkusha, *San.*; गणसूर - ganasúra, *Mahr.*; భూతాలభైరి - bhútálabhairi, *Tel.*). Title from being powerful remedy. San. from (bhúta, san. devil + ankusha, san. iron goad). Tel. from (bhúta, san. devil + bhairi, hind. hawk). Botanically Croton [ghantabeejam] oblongifolius, roxb., euphorbiaceæ [vricsham, 118]. Tree; younger branches with the young leaves and inflorescences covered sparingly with yellowish scales; stipules stiff, subulate; leaves more or less elliptic or ovate or obovate, toothed or entire, acute at both ends, below at the base biglandulose; racemes abounding in flowers; bracts one to three-flowered; segments of the female calyx triangular-lanceolate, of the male pale at the margin and densely scurfy; stamens ten to twelve; filaments woolly near the base; styles once deeply bipartite; capsules sub-globose, covered with scurfy scales; flowers small, green; flowering in march; anamullays and malabar near coast. The root is twisted, often somewhat flattened, bark thickish, externally light-brown and scaly, internally yellowish, mottled with brown, substance compact and resinous, odour highly aromatic, taste peppery and camphoraceous. Seeds purgative; gives to pharm. non-officinal oil of seeds, like croton [jamalgota] oil. Wood whitish to yellow, close-grained, moderately hard; liable to crack in seasoning.

DHADAY (ಧಡೆ - dhade, *Can.*; ధడియము - dhadiyamu, *Tel.*). Bazaar weight. 2 viss = 1 dhaday; 4 dhadays = 1 maund [niray, 2c]. Approximate actual value, 1 dhaday = 6 lbs. 4 oz. avoirdupois. Same as Hind. dhurrah. Vol. I, 609; II, 506, 510, 516.

DHAN (धन् - dhan, *San.*). To move.——*Dhanak* (دهنك - dhanak, Hind.). From (dhanushka, san. a small bow). Narrow ribbon with five to seven strands of gold [pon] in the web; used for bodices [cholee].——*Dhanoor mausam* (धनुर्मास - dhanurmása, San.). Ninth solar month, i.e., between 14th December and 11th January when the sun is in sagittarius [dhanoos]. Hence the offerings to idols and the feastings in that month. Solar observance [pundigay, 2]. This is otherwise called Shoonyamausam or empty month, as no marriages and other good actions should then be performed. Hindoos rise very early in the morning, bathe in cold water and worship the idol with offerings of pongal and fruits, before sunrise. The same course is pursued in temples every day of the month. The last day of the month is Bhogy pundigay, the first of the next month being the grand Pongal [q.v.] feast [maryauday].——*Dhanoos* (धनु - dhanu, San.). A bow; sagittarius, the ninth zodiacal sign [rausby].——*Dhanwantary* (धन्वन्तरि - dhanvantari, San.). From (dhanvan, san. bow + tar, san. move); moving in a curve; epithet of the sun. The physician of the gods holding ambrosia [amritam, coormam] in his hands. Sanscrit treatises on medicine bear his name, Tamul treatises that of Agastyan.

DHAR (धर - dhara, *San.*). From (dhri, san. to bear) [dhau]. Support; restraint.——*Dharan* (धर - dhara, San.). Bearer or supporter. Suffix in proper names as Gungaudharan or Shiva, supporter of the ganges [peyar].——*Dharanicottah* (ధరణికోట - dharanikóta, Tel.). From (dharaní, san. earth + kóta, san. fort). Tel. also (dípáladinne), meaning lamp + mound. Sanscrit name (dhanakataka), meaning wealth + fort. Greek πιτύνδρα. Village; Kistna dist., Suttenapully tal.; pop. 1.489; acres 6,374; lat. 16° 35'; long. 80° 23'. The well-known old fort 1 mile west of the Booddhist tope [q.v.] at Amravatty on the Kistna. In the fort are two old temples with inscriptions and other remains. The fort was built in time of Jeinas by a king name Mookkanteshwaran, a name appearing variously as Mookkanty rajah and Mookkanty pullava [amravatty]. Has a ferry.——*Dharany* (धरणी - dharaní, San.). Earth [bhoomy].——*Dharaupooram* (தாராபுரம் - tárappuram, Tam.). See sep. title.——*Dharmacurta* (धर्मकर्ता - dharmakartá, San.; ధర్మకర్త - dharmakarta, Tel.). From (dharma, san. charity + kartá, san. doer). The chief manager or trustee of a pagoda [q.v.].——*Dharmadausan* (தருமதாசன் - tarumathásan, Tam.). From (dharman, san. duty + dása, san. servant). Slave of duty. Hindoo 2nd or pers. name. Common among non-bramins [peyar].——*Dharmalingam* (தருமலிங்கம் - tarumalingam, Tam.). From (dharma, san. proper name + linga, san. emblem of shiva). Shiva as worshipped by dharman or dharmarajan. Hindoo 2nd or pers. name. Common among non-bramins [peyar].——*Dharmam* (धर्म - dharma, San.). From (dhri, san. to hold) [dhauray]; that which is to be held fast. Ordinance; charity; religious merit [aram]; justice. One of the four objects of existence; the other three being:—artam, wealth; caumam, pleasure; mocsham, absolution. Generally includes faith [bhacty] and works [carmam].——*Dharman* (தருமன் - taruman, Tam.). God of death; Yoodhishtiran, the mythological hero. Hindoo 2nd or pers. name; also suffix in proper names. Feminine Dharmy [peyar].——*Dharmapatam* (ധർമ്മടം - dharmmatam, Mal.). From (dharma, san. charity + pattana, san. town).—"*a*" Amshom, Port, Island; Malabar dist., Cottayam tal.; pop. 6,411; acres 3,840; lat. 11° 46'; long. 75° 30' from Bombay S.S.E. 504 miles; from Calicut N.N.W. 41 miles; from Tellicherry N.W. 2¼ miles. Dehfattan of Ibn batuta, Darmaftan of the Tohfat ool moojauhideen, Tormapatani of Varthema. An island. Amshom [q.v.] lying in river of same name, immediately north of Tellicherry. The Anjarcundy river splits into two branches as it approaches the sea, and the land lying between them and the sea forms the island. Formerly belonged to the kingdom of Colattiry but ceded to the English in 1734. Taken by the Rajah of Chiracal in 1788 but retaken in 1789. Old redoubt and an old rock-cut cave. One of the earliest Arabic mosques [musjid], now entirely demolished.—"*b*" River; Malabar dist., Cottayam tal. Rises in Wynaud and falls into the sea 3 miles north of Tellicherry.—"*c*" Trig. station; Malabar dist., Cottayam tal.; lat. 11° 45' 59·76"; long. 75° 30' 09·82"; height 112 feet; from Tellicherry N.W. 2½ miles; from the sea E. ¼ mile.——*Dharmapoory* (தருமபுரி - tarumappuri, Tam.). See sep. title.——*Dharmaraja cull* (தருமராசாக்கல் - tarumarásákkal, Tam.). From (dharmarájá, san. lord of justice, epithet of booddha + kal, tam. rock). Otherwise Adam's Peak, also called by the Arabs Er-rahoon. Mountain, Ceylon; 7,350 feet above sea. A hollow on the summit is said by Bramins to be foot-step of Shiva; by Booddhists, of Booddha; by Chinese, of Fo; by Mahomedans, of Adam [collam, condaveed]. The peak is visible 60 leagues to seaward. Foot mark on a flat stone near a pool of water is the object of pilgrimage. There are other models of feet in different parts of island. The kadam rasool or foot print of prophet is another foot print on a hill at Secunderabad.——*Dharma rajan* (धर्मराजा - dharmarájá, San.). From (dharma, san. justice + rájá, san. king). A name of Yaman in his beneficent form. He is the king of justice, whose countenance the virtuous only see; the wicked see him as the king of the infernal regions. Pullies worship in temples dedicated to Dharma rajan. In these are found the images of the Pandava Yoodhishtiran or Dharma rajan and his four brothers Bheeman, Arjoonan, Nacoolan, and Sahadevan, of Drowpady, of Krishnan, and occasionally of the really indigenous Potrauz. At the great annual festival in honor of Dharma rajan or the local god or goddess, people walk over burning coals in order to testify their purity of mind. The worship of Dharma rajan is in opposition to Rama the hero among the Bramins. Bramins have nothing to do with these temples. Among rock temples of Mauvellipore [seven pagodas] are the raths or monolithic temples of the five Pandavas and of their wife Drowpady. Dharma rajan was an epithet of Yoodhishtiran the eldest of the five Pandavas of Cashmere or Central asia; hence much confusion in the minds of the people, as above indicated [mahabhaurat, matam].——*Dharma shastram* (धर्मशास्त्र - dharmashástra, San.). From (dharma, san. duty + shástra, san. code). Consisting of text-book, commentaries and digests. A work on the whole body, or on particular subjects, of Hindoo law. The three principal topics of such works are:—auchauram, rules of conduct; vyavahauram, judicature; and prauyaschittam, penance. Forty-seven Dharma shastrams are enumerated by sanscrit authors, and of these the following twenty are known to be still extant:—Angiran, Atry, Aupastamban, Cautyauyanan, Dacshan, Gowtaman, Haureetan, Likhitan, Menoo, Oosbanan, Parausharan, Samvartan, Shankhan, Shautautapan, Vishnoo, Brihaspaty, Vyausan, Vasishtan, Yanyavalcyan, Yaman. Menoo the most important, Yanyavalcyan next [shastram].——*Dharmashaulay* (धर्मशाला - dharmashálá, San.). From (dharma, san. charity + shálá, san. hall). A place of accommodation for travellers and pilgrims [choultry, moosaufer khana].——*Dharmavaram* (ధర్మవరము - dharmavaramu, Tel.). See sep. title.——*Dharna* (دهرنا - dharná, Hind.). From (dhri, san. to restrain). Sitting at the door of a house to compel payment of a debt. The person observes a strict fast, and if the suitor were to perish the consequences of the sin would fall upon the other. There is a similar practice at the door of a temple until attendant priest assures the person his desire will be granted. This mode of harassing is now controlled by law [maryauday].——*Dhauracota* (ధారాకోట - dhárákóta, Tel. dhárákót *). From (dhárá, san. stream + kóta, san. fort). Ancient zemindarry, Village; Ganjam dist., Zemindarry tract; pop. 24,347; square miles 132; lat. of village 19° 38'; long. 84° 37'; from Chetterpore W.N.W. 33 miles; from Russellcondah S. 20 miles. On the Rooshcoolya, adjoining Bodagooda on the north and Goomsoor on the east. Formerly a part of the ancient Khidishingy zemindarry, together with the neighbouring divisions of Sooradah, Bodagooda and Shergadah. The name of the first Rajah of Khidishingy was Sobab chendra sing, who is said to have ruled over the country from A.D. 1168 to 1206. In A.D. 1476 Boliyar sing divided the Khidishingy country. To Damona sing, the son of his eldest son Gangadro pattoo coomonaro, he gave the Bodagooda talook. To his second son Haddoo sing, he gave Dhauracote. To his third son Soonda danoo sing, he gave Sooradah. He kept Shergadah for himself. The zemindarry is divided into the three mittahs [q.v.] of Conoonagodo, Jahada and Sahasrango. The present zemindar [q.v.] is Shree braja soondara sing. Peshcush Rs. 24,462.——*Dhauranay* (धारणा - dháraná, San.). From (dhri, san. to hold). Fixation of thought. One of the eight means of mental concentration practised in Yogam [q.v.]. Sheiva yogies, enumerate nine Dhauranays, viz.:—"*a*" [Nauma dhauranay, name meditation or worship of supreme being in the form of an image under a given name;—"*b*" Mauya dhauranay, mauyay meditation or worship of supreme being who is unlimited and without form, accompanied by entire renunciation of the world;—"*c*" Bhaida dhauranay, change meditation or exercise of the yogy [q.v.] to restrain his bodily affections and by controlling his bodily airs to alter the position of his heart;—"*d*" Muntra dhauranay, spell meditation or worship of shiva by the five-lettered muntram [q.v.] namshivauya;—"*e*" Chatooranga dhauranay, four member meditation or meditation on the supreme being, as when the yogy unites the faculties of his mind with the four constituents of the body, earth, water, fire and wind; this is done when reason and fire, reflection and wind, will and water, are joined with resolution or passion represented by earth, and all co-operate to fix the mind in the air, the seat of bramh [q.v.];—"*f*" Shabda dhauranay, word meditation or continual meditation of the sacred syllable om [q.v.];—"*g*" Vastoo dhauranay, existence meditation or mental perception of bramh;—"*h*" Vajra dhauranay, worship of shiva only in the lingam [q.v.], rejecting the lower passions which represent bramha and vishnoo;—"*i*" Chitra dhauranay or meditation when approaching assimilation to the deity, by gaining a knowledge of the twenty-six properties [tatwam] of the body [shareeram], the soul [autmam] and the supreme being, after this the soul arrives at pure spiritual knowledge [nyaunam] and is emerged in the deity [matam].——*Dhauray* (धारा - dhárá, San.). From (dhri, san. to hold) [dharmam]. Holding. Stream [caulvye, vycaul].——*Dhaurla* (ధార్ల - dhárla, Tel.). Locative plural. Suffix in place names; as Punchadhaurla, meaning five streams.——*Dheiryam* (धैर्य - dhairya, San.). From (dhri, san. to hold) [dharmam]. Courage. Dheirya lutchmy is the goddess thereof. Dheiryanautan, from (nát'ha, san. lord) is Hindoo 2nd or pers. name; common among non-bramins [peyar].

DHARAUPOORAM (தாராப்புரம் - tárappuram, *Tam.* dhárápuram*). From (dhárá, san. stream + pura, san. town) [dhauray]. From the position on the amravatty. Sanscrit name (virátapura), meaning virautan, the mythological king + town.——(1) Talook, Coimbatore district. Tahsildar's pay Rs. 200. Area 830 square miles. Population 249,221. Language Tamul. S. of district, forms part of sub-division. Bounded S. by Pulney talook, Madura district; E. by Caroor; W. by Pulladam and Oodamalpett; and N. by Erode, from which it is separated by Noyil. A peculiarity is the immense inam [q.v.] area. Undulating plain sloping generaly E. towards Cauvery, but with a local water-shed [nadee] near Caungyam falling to Noyil on N. and Amravatty on S. These two rivers, especially Amravatty, drain the talook into the Cauvery. The former is only occasionally in flood, the latter frequently, but at varying heights from May to March. There are two or three petty hills, of which Shivamullay is a landmark and sacred place. The climate is tolerably good, by the end of May S.W. monsoon [q.v.] dispels heat. Being immediately opposite to Palghaut gap, the wind is furious during June and July; but the climate is then healthy and tolerably invigorating. During N.E. monsoon from November to February, heavy mists and chill winds are frequent and fever prevalent. This is also season for cholera. Rainfall inconsiderable. No natural forests or jungles. Talook has only palmyras and the commonest jungle timber. Soils, of low productive power, are gravelly, stony, and sandy, with the usual loams in bottoms. The surface of the south is largely composed of limestone [choonam cull] more or less agglomerated, as especially in the west. Immense fields of calcareous tufa in some places cover the surface in continued masses, the strata being often many feet thick and involving small masses of quartz [ven cull] and other stones. No black-cotton soil [regar]. Aquamarine was found at Padiyore near Caungyam in beginning of century, but mine exhausted. Corundum [q.v.] near Caungyam; and quartz crystals, limpid or amethystine. Caungyam breed of cattle [maud] and ponies are widely known. Chief crops on dry lands are three and four year cotton [q.v.], cumboo [bajrah], cholum [q.v.], gingelly [q.v.], and pulses [dholl]; on garden lands cholum, cumboo, raggy [q.v.] and tobacco [pogauk]; on wet lands paddy [q.v.], raggy, sugar-cane [q.v.], and plantains [q.v.]. In Caungyam division cholum and gingelly are cultivated. Gram grown in N.E. monsoon. Tobacco good, but coarse. Fodder crops in parts especially in Caungyam. Jaggery [q.v.] and toddy [q.v.] produced, especially in Caungyam and Moolanore neighbourhoods. A few pumplemoses [pummelow] near Caungyam. Jaggery and sugar are made and usual local manufactures of cloth, carts, pots [chatty], bricks [shengal], &c. Trade is considerable only at Dharaupooram. Rivers are Amravatty, Noyil, and Ooppaur; the first crossed by six anicuts [q.v.] supplying irrigation channels [q.v.]. Numerous private wells. The channels are apt to fall very low in September and after December. Colinjivaudy channel is divided by a dam near Colinjivaudy into three separate channels, viz., Colinjivaudy, Nelambore, and Veerautchimungalam. Cauttangauny tank, fed from the Noyil by an anicut, gets a supply several times during the year, and is seldom dry; two crops, the first being usually cumboo, are regularly raised. Congore tank in the extreme south is of little importance. Places of archæological interest:—Arsanpolliem, Aulambaudy, Aurtozhvoo, Carcaupolliem, Caudiyore, Caungyam, Cauttangauny, Comarapolliem, Cottanore, Dharaupooram, Ganapatipolliem, Keeranore, Mailmoogam, Marootoray, Maumbaudy, Mettapolliem, Moottore, Mungalaputty, Nandavanampolliem, Nauttaupolliem, Nelaly, Nezhooly, Nuttacaudiyore, Oothiyore, Oottamapolliem, Padiyore, Paranjervaly, Paupiny, Permiyam, Putchapolliem, Shadaiyanpolliem, Shivamullay, Toppanpolliem, Tumbooreddipolliem, Vellacoil, Velliyarsal. Principal trig. stations:—Canappoly, Cautpolliem, Naulcauny, Oothiyore, Putchapolliem, Tirmangaradoo. The leading places, &c., in the talook are the following.——*Amravatty* (அமராவதி - ámarávathi, Tam.). See sep. title.——*Canappoly* (கனப்பொளி - kanappoli, Tam.). From (kanai, tam. closeness + poli, tam. field bank). Otherwise N.W. end, Coimbatore base. Trig. station; lat. 11° 00′ 09·19″; long. 77° 39′ 14·09″; height 1,017 feet; from Dharaupooram N.N.E. 19 miles; from Paupiny W.S.W. 2¼ miles.——*Caungyam* (காங்கயம் - kángayam, Tam.). See sep. title.——*Cautpolliem* (காட்டுப்பாளையம் - káttuppálaiyam, Tam.). From (kádu, tam. forest + pálaiyam, tam. camp). Otherwise S.E. end, Coimbatore base. Trig. station; lat. 10° 56′ 38·65″; long. 77° 43′ 18·55″; height 879 feet; from Dharaupooram N.N.E. 17 miles; from Vailampolliem E.S.E. 1 mile.——*Colinjivaudy* (கொளிஞ்சிவாடி - koliñjivádi, Tam.). From (koliñji, tam. jungle gram, tephrosia purpurea, pers. + vádi, tam. enclosure). Village; pop. 1,437; acres 818; lat. 10° 44′; long. 77° 35′; from Coimbatore E.S.E. 43 miles; from Dharaupooram E. 1 mile. Suburb of Dharaupooram with Shiva temples and inscriptions.——*Coondalam* (குண்டலம் - kundalam, Tam.). Means circle. Village; pop. 2,716; acres 9,517; lat. 10° 50′; long. 77° 30′; from Coimbatore E.S.E. 35 miles; from Dharaupooram N.W. 9 miles. Shiva temple and weekly market.——*Cunnivaudy* (கன்னிவாடி - kannivádi, Tam.). From (kanni, tam. girl + vádi, tam. enclosure). Village; pop. 3,865; acres 8,440; lat. 10° 49′; long. 77° 50′; from Coimbatore E.S.E. 57 miles; from Dharaupooram E.N.E. 18 miles. On road to Caroor. Mud fort in ruin.——*Dalavoyputnam* (தளவாய்ப்பட்டணம் - talaváyppattanam, Tam.). From (talaváy, tam. commander + pattana, san. town). Village; pop. 4,564; acres 6,720; lat. 10° 40′; long. 77° 32′; from Coimbatore S.E. 42 miles; from Dharaupooram S.W. 5 miles. On road to Oodamalpett. Vishnoo temple.——*Dharaupooram* (தாராப்புரம் - tárappuram, Tam.). See below.——*Moolanore* (மூலனூர் - múlanúr, Tam.). From (múla, san. root, epithet of shiva + úr, tam. village). Village; pop. 7,803; acres 18,367; lat. 10° 48′; long. 77° 45′; from Coimbatore E.S.E. 53 miles; from Dharaupooram E.N.E. 13 miles. Shiva temple. Weekly market.——*Naulcauny* (நாலுகாணி - nálugáni, Tam.). From (nál, tam. four + káni, tam. landed estate). Trig. station; lat. 10° 53′ 53·31″; long. 77° 39′ 31·19″; from Cambaliyamputty N.N.E. 1¼ mile; from Dharaupooram N.N.E. 13 miles.——*Noyil* (நொய்யல் - noyyal, Tam.). See sep. title——*Ooppaur* (உப்பாறு - uppáru, Tam.). From (uppu, tam. salt + áru, tam. river). River. Rises in Anamullays, descends in the Vettacauranpoothore frontiers and empties into Auliyaur near Anamullay village. Bridged near Dharaupooram at the junction of the roads from Caungyam, Pulladam, and Tirpore.——*Oothiyore* (ஊதியூர் - úthiyúr, Tam.). From (úthi, tam. to blow the bellows + úr, tam. village). Village; pop. 3,121; acres 7,048; lat. 10° 53′; long. 77° 34′; from Coimbatore E.S.E. 39 miles; from Dharaupooram N. 11 miles. Two old Shiva temples on small hill. Trig. station; lat. 10° 53′ 05·99″; long. 77° 33′ 38·06″; height 1,275 feet; from Dharaupooram N. 11 miles; from Oothiyore S.W. ½ mile.——*Palayacottah* (பழையகோட்டை - pazhaiyagóttai, Tam.). From (pazhaiya, tam. old + kóttai, tam. fort). Village; pop. 2,821; acres 8,656; lat. 11° 04′; long. 77° 44′; from Coimbatore E.N.E. 49 miles; from Dharaupooram N.N.E. 25 miles. Cattle and pony breeding centre.——*Putchapolliem* (பச்சாப்பாளையம் - paççáppálaiyam, Tam.). Means green village or village of shiva the green-haired god. Village; pop. 4,860; acres 12,383; lat. 10° 58′; long. 77° 40′; from Coimbatore E. 45 miles; from Dharaupooram N.N.E. 18 miles. Old Shiva temple. Two dolmens [codaycull]. Trig. station; lat. 10° 59′ 42·55″; long. 77° 39′ 53·80″; height 971 feet; from Dharaupooram N.N.E. 19 miles; from Paupiny S. 2¼ miles.——*Shivamullay* (சிவமலை - shivamalai, Tam.). Means shiva's hill. Hill; lat. 11° 02′; long. 77° 35′; from Coimbatore E. 39 miles; from Dharaupooram N. 20 miles. Two temples. Famous Soobramanya sawmy temple, resorted to by Vellaula.——*Tirmangaradoo* (திருமண்கரடு - tirumangaradu, Tam.). From (tiru, tam. sacred + man, tam. earth + karadu, tam. rough ground). Trig. station; lat. 10° 58′ 25·44″; long. 77° 42′ 12·58″; height 970 feet; from Dharaupooram N.N.E. 18 miles; from Veera cholapooram S. 2 miles.——*Veerautchimungalam* (வீராச்சிமங்கலம் - viráççimangalam, Tam.). From (víra, san. hero + ádchi, tam. possession + mangala, san. prosperity). Means the village given to a hero. Village ; pop. 2,829 ; acres 1,849 ; lat. 10° 46′ ; long. 77° 36′ ; from Coimbatore E.S.E. 43 miles ; from Dharaupooram N.E. 3¼ miles. Vishnoo temple.——*Vellacoil* (வெள்ளக்கோவில் - vellakkóvil, Tam.). From (vellai, tam. white + kóvil, tam. temple). Village ; pop. 6,359 ; acres 13,471 ; lat. 10° 57′ ; long. 77° 46′ ; from Coimbatore E. 51 miles ; from Dharaupooram N.E. 19 miles. On Caroor road with travellers' bungalow. Old Shiva temple with inscriptions and also a dolmen. Four miles north is a temple much frequented. ——**(2)** Town, Talook head-quarters ; Coimbatore dist., Dharaupooram tal. ; pop. 7,680 ; acres 3,597 ; lat. 10° 44′ ; long. 77° 34 ; from Coimbatore E. 42 miles ; from Erode S.S.W. 43 miles ; from Madras S.W. 250 miles ; from Ootacamund S.E. 71 miles ; from Pollachy E.N.E. 35 miles ; from Suttimungalam S.S.E. 56 miles. On left bank of Amravatty, in a fine plateau of open country which stretches nearly to the Pulneys some fifteen miles south. A channel from the river bisects the town. Roads converge from every quarter. In 1667 and again in 1746 taken from Madura by Mysore. In the campaigns with Hyder ally and Tippoo sahib it was a point of strategical importance, being captured by Colonel Wood in 1768 ; retaken by Hyder in the same year ; again occupied by the British in 1783 ; ceded by the treaty of Mangalore, and finally resumed in 1790 by General Meadows. In 1792 the fort was dismantled. The town nearly disappeared, but rebuilt after 1799 and made head-quarters of southern division. Also for a few years seat of Zillah [q.v.] court ; transferred to Coimbatore in 1828. Old Shiva temple with inscriptions. Weekly market. Station of Roman catholic and Wesleyan missions.

DHARMANAM (धर्मण - dharmana, *San.*). From (dhanvá, san. dry soil) [dhan] ; from habitat. Botanically the Grewia genus, tiliaceæ [vricsham, 27]. Shrubs or small trees ; leaves simple, usually serrated ; flowers have five sepals, which are colored on the inside and often hairy outside ; and five petals ; fruit consists of one to four stones, each containing one or two seeds ; leaves of some species eaten by cattle ; many species yield good fibres ; many produce edible fruits ; genus is very scattered in vernacular nomenclature. The species best known to the natives are :—abutilifolia [bird tadda], asiatica [falsah], excelsa [small tadda], hirsuta [bran plant], microcos [abrony], orbiculata [round-leaved tadda], orientalis [female bair], pilosa [dog bran plant], salvifolia [jaurah], tilliæfolia [tadda]. Other s. indian species indigenous or naturalized are :—bracteata, columnaris, diplocarpa, emarginata, lævigata, polygama, populifolia, villosa.

DHARMAPOORY (دھرمپوری - dharampúrí, *Hind.* ; தருமபுரி - tarumappuri, *Tam.* dharmapuri *). From (dharma, san. name of a king + purí, san. town) [dharmam] ; called after local ruler dharma rajah. Ancient name (tagadúr), meaning foliage village.——**(1)** Talook, Salem district. Tahsildar's pay Rs. 175. Most southerly of talooks of Sub-collector's division, and forms portion of ancient province of Baramahaul [q.v.]. Area 941 square miles. W. of district. Between N. lat. 11° 54′ and 12° 26′ and E. long. 77° 43′ and 78° 20′. Extreme length north to south about 35 miles, and extreme breadth east to west about 34 miles ; average being 28 and 26 miles, respectively. Population 18,442. Languages Tamul, Teloogoo, and partly Canarese. Bounded north by Oossoor and Krishnagherry talooks ; west by Oossoor talook and Bhawauny talook, Coimbatore district, the Cauvery dividing it from the latter ; south by Omalore division of Salem talook, from which it is separated by Toppoor river ; and east by Krishnagherry and Ootancaray talooks. Entered from the south by the Toppoor pass. Average elevation, from 1,500 to 1,700 feet. The talook is sparsely wooded towards Pennagaram, but near the hills the jungle grows richer. The talook is not wholly hill-girt, the north-eastern portions being carried on into the plains which mark the Ponniaur valley, and extend into Krishnagherry and Ootancaray talooks. The streams traversing the talook follow for the most part the bases of the hill ranges. Soil is principally ferruginous loam and sand with, in the valleys, black alluvial clay and, in the immediate neighbourhood of Dharmapoory, cotton soil [regar]. Quartzose gravel is commonly found in combination with the inferior classes of sandy soil. In many places the earth is strongly impregnated with saltpetre [shorah] and soda salts [munn cauram]. Principal industries are husbandry, weaving, trade in grains and money dealing, carpentry and the calling of ironsmith and goldsmith. Chief exports are paddy [q.v.], gram [q.v.], gingelly [q.v.] seed, tamarind [q.v.] and cocoanuts [q.v.] ; principally to Bangalore, Madras, Negapatam and Trichinopoly. Imports are salt [ooppoo], jaggery [q.v.], wheat, areca-nut, tobacco [pogauk], pulses [dholl], avaray [country bean], saffron [country saffron], ground-nut [q.v.], and plantains ; principally from Bangalore, Coimbatore and Vellore. Wet crops are paddy, sugar-cane [q.v.], cocoanuts, mostly grown in the valley of the Sanatcomanranuddy near Mauraundahully ; betel [q.v.], areca-nut [q.v.], cholum [q.v.] and saffron to a small extent. In poonjah [q.v.] land raggy [q.v.], cumboo [bajrah], varagoo, [q.v.], shaumay [q.v.], cholum, tovray [common dholl], avaray, cadalay [bengal gram], payar [green gram], oolandoo [black gram], oil [yennay] seeds, nary payar [field gram], horsegram, gingelly, cottamully [cassibor] and tobacco are grown. Wheat [geung] is cultivated on the Vattalamullay ; cotton [q.v.], notwithstanding the abundance of soil suited to its production, is seldom grown, and indigo [q.v.] is unknown. A blue dye resembling the latter in many respects, but much inferior, is prepared somewhat largely from leaves of Veppaulay maram [pwula indigo]. Iron [auhan] ore is the only mineral product. Pennagaram division is noted for Aulambaudy breed of cattle [maud]. Rivers are Cauvery, Chennaur, and Toppoor. Sungambasavan anicut [q.v.] and channel [q.v.], connected with the Chennaur, supply tank of same name. Small tributaries of the Ponniaur and Toppoor traverse the north-east portion and centre of the talook respectively. From the former of these is diverted the Poolamputty caulvye [q.v.]. The chief tanks are the Adamancottah, Annasaugaram, Colagattore, Dharmapoory, Jertalaub, Krishnapooram, Mauthemungalam, Shogattore, Sungambasavan and Yairpully tanks. There are seven ferries in the talook, viz., Bommasamoodram, Congambutty, Cottay sholapaudy, Lakkamputty, Maligay, Naugamaray and Sholapaudy. Camping grounds :—Dharmapoory, Adamancottah, Toppoor choultry, Shogattore, Palcode. Zemindarries :—Baivhully, Belagayapooram, Giddanhully, Gollahully, Hanoomantapooram, Mauraundahully, Mauthehully, Neccoondy, Noolahully, Paneycolam, Paupauraputty, Paupinaickamputty, Pullipatty, Pungoonuttam, Reddihully, Sookkanhully, Tirmalvaudy, Vailamputty, Veppilay. Places of archæological interest. Adamancottah, Cadatore, Caurimungalam, Collaputty, Covilore, Devarmookkoolam, Dharmapoory, Indore, Kerecodihully, Maligay, Mauraundahully, Mothore, Paupauraputty, Pauvily, Pennagaram, Peroombaulay, Pooliyamputty, Shookkamputty. Principal trig. station :—Caradigooddey. The leading places, &c., in the talook are the following.——*Adamancottah* (அதமங்கோட்டை - athamangóttai, Tam.). See sep. title.——*Annasaugaram* (அன்னசாகரம் - annaságaram, Tam.). From (anna, san. food + ságara, san. sea). Village ; pop. 1,812 ; acres 566 ; lat. 12° 07′ ; long. 78° 13′ ; from Dharmapoory S. 1 mile ; from Salem N. 31 miles.——*Baivhully* (ಬೇವುಹಳ್ಳಿ - bévuhalli, Can.). From (bévu, can. neem tree, melia azadirachta, linn. + halli, can. hamlet). Zemindarry, Village ; pop. 216 ; square miles 18½ ; lat. of village 12° 18′ ; long. 78° 03′ ; from Dharmapoory N.W. 16 miles ; from Salem N. 45 miles. Peshcush Rs. 1,605.——*Caradigooddey* (ಕರಡಿಗುಡ್ಡೆ - karadigudde, Can.). From (karadi, can. bear + gudde, can. hill). Trig. station ; lat. 11° 59′ 31·24″ ; long. 77° 55′ 04·51″ ; height 1,984 feet ; from Dharmapoory S.W. 22 miles ; from Donneygooddeyhully S. 1 mile.——*Caurimungalam* (காரிமங்கலம் - kárimangalam, Tam.). From (kári, tam. blackness + mangala, san. prosperity). Canarese name (dandutimmanahalli), meaning army + timmana, proper name + village. Village ; pop. 2,487 ; acres 1,830 ; lat. 12° 19′ ; long. 78° 15′ ; from Dharmapoory N. 12 miles ; from Salem N. 45 miles. On the Krishnagherry road. Inhabitants chiefly Chetties, who trade in grain and oil-seed. Camping ground is indifferent. West is an inscription. Agricultural produce and cattle change hands at the weekly fair.——*Cauvery* (காவேரி - kávéri, Tam.). See sep. title.——*Chennaur* (சென்னாறு - shennáru, Tam.). See sep. title.——*Cottagherry* (கோட்டைகிரி - kóttaigiri, Tam.). From (kóta, san. fort + giri, san. mountain). Hill ; lat. 12° 19′ ; long. 77° 55′ ; from Dharmapoory N.W. 23 miles ; from Salem N.N.W. 49 miles.——*Dharmapoory* (தருமப்புரி - tarumappuri, Tam.). See below.——*Giddanhully* (ಗಿದ್ದನಹಳ್ಳಿ - giddanahalli, Can.). From (gidda, can. proper name + halli, can. hamlet). Zemindarry, Village ; pop. 285 ; lat. of village 12° 15′ ; long. 78° 06′ ; from Dharmapoory N.W. 11 miles ; from Salem N. 41 miles. Peshcush Rs. 293.——*Gollahully* (ಗೊಲ್ಲಹಳ್ಳಿ - gollahalli, Can.). From (golla, can. a cowherd + halli, can. hamlet). Zemindarry, Village ; pop. 254 ; lat. of village 12° 08′ ; long. 78° 04′ ; from Dharmapoory W. 10 miles ; from Salem N.N.W. 34 miles. Peshcush Rs. 255.——*Haleypoora* (ಹಳೇಪುರ - halépura, Can.). From (hale, can. old + pura, san. town). Village ; pop. 120 ; lat. 12° 07′ ; long. 77° 35′ ; from Dharmapoory W. 20 miles ; from Salem N.N.W. 35 miles. A Vishnoo temple with annual festival.——*Hanoomantapooram* (அனுமந்தப்புரம் - anumandappuram, Tam.). From (hanumán, san. the long-jawed monkey chief + pura, san. town). Zemindarry, Village ; pop. 841 ; square miles of village $5\frac{13}{16}$; lat. of village 12° 20′ ; long. 78° 10′ ; from Dharmapoory N.N.W. 14 miles ; from Salem N. 46 miles. Peshcush Rs. 1,455.——*Hogeycull* (ಹೊಗೆನಕಲ್ಲು - hogenakallu, Can.). See sep. title.——*Maudehully* (ಮಾದೆಹಳ್ಳಿ - mádehalli, Can.). From (mádiga, can. chuckler + halli, can. hamlet). Zemindarry, Village ; pop. 507 ; square miles $2\frac{3}{16}$; lat. of village 12° 12′ ; long. 78° 06′ ; from Dharmapoory N.W. 8¼ miles ; from Salem N. 38 miles. Peshcush Rs. 681.——*Mauraundahully* (ಮಾರಾಂಡಹಳ್ಳಿ - márándahalli, Can.). From (máránda, can. proper name + halli, can. hamlet).—"*a*" Zemindarry ; pop. 985 ; square miles $18\frac{1}{16}$; between lat. 12° 20′ and 12° 27′ ; long. 78° 00′ and 78° 04′. Peshcush Rs. 1,744.—"*b*" Village ; lat. 12° 24′ ; long. 78° 03′ ; from Dharmapoory N.N.W. 21 miles ; from Salem N.N.W. 51 miles. Old fort and Shiva temple.——*Neccoondy* (நெக்குந்தி - nekkundi, Tam.). From (ne, tel. good + gondi, tel. narrow pass). Zemindarry, Village ; pop. 324 ; lat. of village 12° 09′ ; long. 77° 56′ ; from Dharmapoory W. 19 miles ; from Salem N.N.W. 38 miles. Peshcush Rs. 2,351.——*Noolahully* (ನುಲಹಳ್ಳಿ - nulahalli, Can.). From (núlu, can. thread + halli, can. hamlet). Zemindarry, Village; pop. 805; square miles $13\frac{3}{8}$; lat. of village 12° 05′; long. 78° 13′; from Dharmapoory S. $3\frac{3}{4}$ miles; from Salem N. 29 miles. Peshcush Rs. 2,498.——*Palcode* (பாலக்கோடு - pálakkódu, Tam. pálakód *). From (pál, tam. milk + kódu, tam. peak). Sanscrit name (kshírapurí), meaning milk town. Ancient name (tambigavundenhalli), meaning tumby gownden, proper name + village. Town; pop. 3,621; acres 441; lat. 12° 18′; long. 78° 07′; from Dharmapoory N.N.W. 14 miles; from Salem N. 45 miles. On the Oossoor road. Water is good and abundant. Public bungalow. Large chuttram [q.v.]. No good camping-ground in the neighbourhood. Fruit, cocoanuts and betel-leaf, the produce of the Sanatcomauranuddy basin, is sold at the weekly market. Large trade in skins [chamrah] and grain.——*Paupauraputty* (பாப்பாரப்பட்டி - páppárappatti, Tam.). From (páppán, tam. bramin + patti, tam. cattle fold).—"*a*" Zemindarry; square miles $5\frac{7}{16}$.—"*b*" Village; pop. 937; lat. 12° 13′; long. 78° 06′; from Dharmapoory N.W. 10 miles; from Salem N.N.W. 39 miles. Bramin village reclaimed, as tradition says, some 500 years ago from the jungles by Hiranya iyer, a Carnatic bramin. Vishnoo temple with inscription. Most of the Bramins, Carnautacas, are reputed descendants of Hiranya iyer. Peshcush Rs. 690.——*Paupinaickamputty* (பாப்பிநாயகம்பட்டி - páppináyagambatti, Tam.). Means paupinaicken's village. Zemindarry, Village; pop. 1,354; square miles $20\frac{9}{16}$; lat. of village 12° 14′; long. 78° 08′; from Dharmapoory N.W. 8 miles; from Salem N. 40 miles. Peshcush Rs. 1,837.——*Pennagaram* (பென்னாகரம் - pennágaram, Tam.). See sep. title.——*Pikkily mullay* (பிக்கிலிமலை - pikkilimalai, Tam.). From (pikili, tel. the hill bulbul + malai, tam. mountain). Hill; lat. 12° 16′; long. 78° 05′; from Dharmapoory N.W. 12 miles; from Salem N. 42 miles.——*Ponautchy bett* (ಪೊನಾಚ್ಚಿಬೆಟ್ಟ - ponáççibetta, Can.). From (ponáççi, can. proper name + betta, can. hill). Hill.——*Pulliputty* (பள்ளிப்பட்டி - pallippatti, Tam.). From (palli, tam. member of the caste, so called + patti, tam. cattle-fold). Zemindarry, Village; pop. 370; lat. of village 11° 58′; long. 77° 58′; from Dharmapoory S.W. 20 miles; from Salem N.W. 27 miles. Peshcush Rs. 306.——*Pungoonuttam* (பங்குநத்தம் - pangunattam, Tam.). From (pangu, tam. portion + nattam, tam. village). Zemindarry, Village; pop. 346; square miles $27\frac{3}{16}$; lat. of village 12° 07′; long. 78° 03′; from Dharmapoory W. 10 miles; from Salem N.N.W. 32 miles. Peshcush Rs. 1,519.——*Reddihully* (ರೆಡ್ಡಿಹಳ್ಳಿ - reddihalli, Can.). From (reddi, can. headman of village + halli, can. hamlet). Zemindarry, Village; pop. 444; square miles $15\frac{1}{8}$; lat. of village 12° 02′; long. 78° 13′; from Dharmapoory S. $6\frac{1}{8}$ miles; from Salem N. 26 miles. Peshcush Rs. 2,478.——*Sungambasavan* (ಸಂಗಮಬಸವ - sangamabasava, Can.). From (sangama, san. junction + basava, can. bull). Village; acres 660; lat. 12° 22′; long. 78° 05′; from Dharmapoory N.W. 18 miles; from Salem N.W. 49 miles. Site of an anicut now broken and damaged. Feeds a tank of same name.——*Tirmalvaudy* (திருமலைவாடி - tirumalaivádi, Tam.). From (tiru, tam. holy + malai, tam. hill + vádi, tam. enclosure). Zemindarry, Village; pop. 336; square miles $18\frac{3}{16}$; lat. of village 12° 19′; long. 78° 01′; from Dharmapoory N.W. 18 miles; from Salem N.N.W. 47 miles. Peshcush Rs. 703.——*Toppoor* (தொப்பூர் - toppúr, Tam.). See sep. title.——*Vailamputty* (வேலம்பட்டி - vélambatti, Tam.). From (vél, tam. acacia tree, acacia arabica, willd. + patti, tam. cattle-fold). Zemindarry, Village; pop. 311; square miles $5\frac{1}{4}$; lat. of village 12° 12′; long. 78° 06′; from Dharmapoory N.W. 8 miles; from Salem N. 37 miles. Peshcush Rs. 180.——*Vattalamullay* (வட்டலமலை - vattalamalai, Tam.). From (vartula, san. circle + malai, tam. mountain). Hill; lat. 12° 02′; long. 78° 16′; from Dharmapoory S.E. 7 miles; from Salem N. 26 miles. A red dye [shauyam] is manufactured for coloring silk [puttoo].——*Veppilay* (வேப்பிலை - véppilai, Tam.). From (vémbu, tam. margosa tree, melia azadirachta, linn. + ilai, tam. leaf). Zemindarry, Village; pop. 282; lat. of village 12° 13′; long. 78° 05′; from Dharmapoory N.W. 10 miles; from Salem N.W. 39 miles. Peshcush Rs. 191.——**(2)** Town, Talook headquarters; Salem dist., Dharmapoory tal.; pop. 7,090; lat. 12° 08′; long. 78° 13′; from Madras W.S.W. 156 miles; from Namcull N. 62 miles; from Oossoor S.S.E. 47 miles; from Salem N. 33 miles; from Tripatore S.W. 37 miles; from Yercaud N.N.W. 25 miles. Healthy. Regularly laid out in a level plain near an old fort formerly one of Tippoo's garrisons. The water is generally brackish. A large circular tank west of the town. Near this is a tank built by Narsiah. Some fine trees line its banks and form a favorite camping-ground. Until 1688 Dharmapoory belonged to the kingdom of Aura, but in that year was annexed by Mysore. In 1768 it was captured by Colonel Wood, but re-occupied by Hyder ally until the signature of peace. For some years residence of Sir Thomas Munro. Two ancient Vishnoo temples, in one of which are two inscriptions. On the banks of the lake near the old town are two carved statues of Rama and Lutchmanan with inscriptions. In Virpautchapooram, a suburb, is an inscription recording a grant of the village by a local chief in the reign of Shreerungan of Vijianugger in A.D. 1619. The town is inhabited chiefly by Mussalmans, trading in skins, and by weavers. Trade in grains and oil-seeds.

DHARMAVARAM * (ధర్మవరము - dharmavaramu, *Tel.*). From (dharma, san. piety + pura, san. city) [dharmam].——**(1)** Talook, Anantapore, tahsildar's pay Rs. 200. Area 1,226 square miles; pop. 118,724; language Teloogoo. Centre of district. Boundaries:—North, Royadroog talook of Bellary west of river Pennair and Anantapore talook from east of river Pennair to near Cuddapah district frontier. East, Anantapore talook, Cadiry talook of Cuddapah district, and Penoocondah talook east of Chitrauvaty river. South, Penoocondah talook between Pennair and Chitrauvaty river, and Pauvoogada talook of Mysore west of Pennair. West, Mysore and Royadroog talook of Bellary. Level, except on the eastern frontier and in the south and west. The highest hill is at Darshimala, about seven miles south of the cusbah [q.v.]. There are other high hills at Calyaundroog and Coondarpy droog. The soil is chiefly red and gravelly, and there is very little regar [q.v.]. The principal crops are horse-gram [q.v.] and paddy [q.v.], and in smaller quantities raggy [q.v.], cholum [q.v.], and castor [aumanac] oil. It is estimated that one-fourth of the paddy grown is sent to Cuddapah and the adjoining black land talooks. Oil-seeds and cholum are received in exchange. Very little industry and commerce, beyond agriculture. Hindoopore extension and Dharmavaram-Tripatty railway pass through the talook. Compared with the size of the talook the irrigation works are few and insufficient. Principal tanks:—Canoomoocla, Coontimaddy, Cumbadore, Dharmavaram, Malyanore, Moolcalaid, Naugasamoodram. Principal camping grounds:—Chennacottapully, Daudalore. Places of archæological interest:—Calyaundroog, Canagaunpully, Canoomoocla, Chennacottapully, Chintarapully, Conaupooram, Coondarpy droog, Cumbadore, Daudalore, Dharmavaram, Garoodapooram, Lutchmanapully, Maurlahully, Mullinayanipore, Narsapooram, Nasancote, Naugasamoodram, Paulore, Rowla cheroo, Togracoonta. Principal trig. stations:—Condapully, Coondarpy, Devaudelbetta, Ooravacondah. The leading places, &c., in the talook are the following.——*Calyaundroog* (కల్యాణదుర్గము - kalyánadurgamu, Tel.). See sep. title.——*Canoomoocla* (కనుముక్కల - kanumukkala, Tel.). From (kanama, tel. pass + mukku, tel. nose); opposite to a pass. Village; pop. 1,781; lat. 14° 18′; long. 77° 48′; from Anantapore S.S.E. 27 miles; from Dharmavaram S. $7\frac{3}{4}$ miles. Contains a tank.——*Chennacottapully* (చెన్నకొత్తపల్లి - chennakottapalli, Tel.). From (chenna, tel. proper name, chennappa + kotta, tel. new + palle, tel. village). Village, travellers' bungalow; pop. 1,611; lat. 14° 16′; long. 77° 40′; from Anantapore S. 28 miles; from Dharmavaram S.W. 12 miles. On Hindoopore railway line.——*Chitrauvaty* (చిత్రావతి - chitrávati, Tel.). See sep. title.——*Condapully* (కొండపల్లి - kondapalli, Tel.). From (konda, tel. hill + palli, tel. village). Trig. station; lat. 14° 31′ 51·62″; long. 77° 26′ 43·35″; height 2,259 feet; from Anantapore S.W. 17 miles; from Dharmavaram W.N.W. 23 miles; from Goontapully N.W. $2\frac{1}{4}$ miles.——*Coondarpy* (కుందర్పి - kundarpi, Tel.). See sep. title.——*Coontimaddy* (కుంటిమద్ది - kuntimaddi, Tel.). From (kunta, tel. tank + maddi, tel. tree, terminalia arjuna, bedd.). Village; pop. 1,242; lat. 14° 20′; long. 77° 38′; from Anantapore S. 23 miles; from Dharmavaram S.W. 10 miles. Contains a tank.——*Cumbadore* (కంబదూరు - kambadúru, Tel.). From (kambadamu, tel. cultivation + úru, tel. village). Village; pop. 1,596; lat. 14° 21′; long. 77° 16′; from Anantapore S.W. 34 miles; from Dharmavaram W. 33 miles. 8 miles west of Peroor bungalow. Has a tank irrigating 900 acres. Four old temples, one built by a Chola king.——*Darshimala* (దరిశిమల - darishimala, Tel.). From (dari, tel. border + mala, tel. hill). Village; pop. 286; lat. 14° 22′; long. 77° 52′; from Anantapore S.E. 25 miles; from Dharmavaram E.S.E. $7\frac{1}{2}$ miles. Among wooded hills.——*Devaudelbetta* (దేవాదులబెట్ట - dévádulabetta, Tel.). From (déva, san. god + ádi, san. etcetera + betta, can. hill); hill of the gods and others. Trig. station; lat. 14° 33′ 38·80″; long. 77° 10′ 04·70″; height 2,434 feet; from Anantapore W.S.W. 34 miles; from Calyaundroog E.N.E. $1\frac{3}{4}$ miles; from Dharmavaram W.N.W. 41 miles.——*Dharmavaram* (ధర్మవరము - dharmavaramu, Tel.). See below.——*Malyanore* (మలియనూరు - maliyanúru, Tel.). From (malliya, tel. jasmine flower, jasminum sambac, ait. + úru, tel. village). Village; pop. 1,831; lat. 14° 15′; long. 77° 01′; from Anantapore W.S.W. 51 miles; from Dharmavaram W.S.W. $51\frac{1}{2}$ miles. Has a large tank.——*Moolcalaid* (ములకలేడు - mulakalédu, Tel.). From (mulaka, tel. brinjaul, solanum ferox, linn. + vídu, tel. town). Village; pop. 3,139; lat. 14° 22′; long. 76° 58′; from Anantapore W.S.W. 50 miles; from Dharmavaram W. 54 miles. Has a tank irrigating 585 acres.——*Nasancote* (నసనకోట - nasanakóta, Tel.). From (narasanna, tel. proper name + kóta, tel. fort). Village; pop. 1,254; lat. 14° 21′; long. 77° 29′; from Anantapore S.S.W. 25 miles; from Dharmavaram W. 19 miles.——*Naugasamoodram* (నాగసముద్రము - nágasamudramu, Tel.). From (nága, san. proper name + samudra, san. ocean). Village; pop. 1,839; lat. 14° 19′; long. 77° 42′; from Anantapore S. $25\frac{1}{2}$ miles; from Dharmavaram S.W. 8 miles. Contains a tank.——*Nyaumadala* (నేమద్దల - némaddala, Tel.). From (néma, san. enclosure + maddi, tel. terminalia arjuna, bedd.). Village; pop. 1,556; lat. 14° 16′; long. 77° 38′; from Anantapore S. $28\frac{1}{2}$ miles; from Dharmavaram S.W. 14 miles. Coarse paper made from aloe [q.v.] fibre.——*Ooravacondah* (ఉరవకొండ - uravakonda,

Tel.). From (urávu, tel. beauty + konda, tel. hill). Trig. station; lat. 14° 15'. 46·62"; long. 77° 38' 57·38"; height 2,193 feet; from Anantapore S. 29 miles; from Dharmavaram S.W. 13 miles; from Nyaumadala E. 1½ miles.——*Pennair* (పెన్నేరు - pennéru, Tel.). See sep. title.——*Peroor* (పేరూరు - pérúru, Tel.). From (péru, tel. large + úru, tel. village). Village, travellers' bungalow; pop. 1,434; lat. 14° 21'; long. 77° 24'; from Anantapore S.W. 28½ miles; from Dharmavaram W. 25¾ miles. On Pennair river and old Bellary road.——*Toomcherla* (తూముచెర్ల - túmucherla, Tel.). From (túmu, tel. sluice + cherla, tel. village). Village; pop. 1,040; lat. 14° 32'; long. 77° 30'; from Anantapore S.W. 14 miles; from Dharmavaram W.N.W. 20 miles. Contains a tank. ——(2) Village, talook head-quarters; Anantapore dist., Dharmavaram tal.; pop. 6,836; lat. 14° 25'; long. 77° 46'; from Anantapore S.S.E. 19½ miles; from Bellary S.E. 73½ miles; from Gooty S. 48 miles; from Madras N.W. 200 miles; from Penoocondah N.N.E. 24¼ miles. On the Chitrauvaty river. Founded by Kriyashacty wodeya, and formerly fortified. Market of importance. Large tank irrigating 1,416 acres. The fort walls have been demolished. Vishnoo temple of great antiquity. Manufacture of silk [puttoo] cloths for women.

DHAU (धा - dhá, *San.*) [dhar]. To support.——*Danaicken* (டணாயக்கன் - tanáyakkan, Tam.). Corruption from (dhannáyaka, san. wealth lord); epithet of coobairan [q.v.], lord of wealth. Proper name.——*Danaicken cottah* (டணாயக்கன் கோட்டை - tanáyakkangóttai, Tam.). Means danaicken's fort. Village; Coimbatore dist., Suttimungalam tal.; acres 275; lat. 11° 26'; long. 77° 7'; from Coimbatore N. 30 miles; from Suttimungalam W.S.W. 13 miles. Formerly gave its name to a talook [q.v.]. Now almost deserted.——*Dhanacataca* (धनकटक - dhanakátaka, San.). From (dhana, san. wealth + kataka, san. hill-village). One of Hwen thsang's nine S. indian kingdoms, his Tonakie-tse-kia. For identification with Dharanicottah, see vol. I (10) [charitram].——*Dhanacoty* (தனக்கோடி - tanakkódi, Tam.). From (dhana, san. wealth + kóti, san. crore). Hindoo 2nd or pers. name. Common among non-bramins [peyar].——*Dhanam* (धन - dhana, San.). From (dhá, san. to nourish) [dhau]. Wealth. Cattle. The plus sign. Female proper name [peyar]. Plant first term; from being valued for usefulness. Ex., where transl. is of second term:—Crotalaria juncea (dhanahári), carrying off; Cyperus rotundus (dhanakúta), heap; Pongamia glabra (dhanavriksha), tree. See gloss. paragrahs.——*Dhananjayan* (தனஞ்சயன் - tanañjayan, Tam.). From (dhana, san. wealth + jaya, san. victory). Conquering booty; epithet of Arjoonan. Hindoo 2nd or pers. name [peyar]. ——*Dhanaujee* (ಧನಾಜಿ - dhanáji, Can.). From (dhana, san. wealth + ji, hind. master). Hindoo 2nd or pers. name [peyar]. ——*Dhanyah* (دھنیا - dhaniyá, Hind.). From (dhánya, san. grain); from grain-like seeds. Coriander [cassibor].——*Dhaun* (دھان - dhán, Hind.). From (dhánya, san. grain). Rice in the husk. Goldsmith's weight. 2 jows = 1 dhaun, 4 dhauns = 1 goomchy [niray, 3 e]. Approximate actual value, 1 dhaun = $\frac{1}{32}$ grain. Same as Can. veesha tookkam, Tam. nelmany. See vol. I, 609.——*Dhaunmady* (دھان مڑی - dhánmarí, Hind.). From (dhánya, san. grain + marí, hind. field). Rice fields.——*Dhaunya cottay* (தானியக்கோட்டை - tániyakkóttai, Tam.). From (dhánya, san. grain + kóttai, tam. a measure). A land measure in Tinnevelly. The extent supposed to require a cottah [q.v.] of seed. It is about 1·62 acres.——*Dhaunyam* (धान्य - dhánya, San.; اناج - anáj, Hind.; ಧಾನ್ಯ - dhánya, Can.; ధాన్యము - dhányamu, Tel.; ധാന്യം - dhányam, Mal.; தானியம் - tániyam, Tam.). From (dhá, san. to support), life-supporter. Hind. from (anna, san. food). San. also (shúkadhánya), meaning awned or bearded grain. Tam. also (kathirdhánya), meaning ear + grain. Equivalent to cereal, otherwise cereal grasses; that is to say the Graminaceæ [vricsham, 156]; cultivated for their seed as food [dry grain, paddy]. Do not include the dholls or pulses [dholl]. Nine principal kinds are enumerated, the Navadhaunyam [q.v.]; small quantities of each of which are given to Bramins at festivals [pundigay]. Dhaunya lutchmy is the goddess of grain.——*Dhautmaulay* (धातुमाला - dhátumálá, San.). From (dhátu, san. root, in grammar + málá, san. garland). List of philological roots. Several works of this name.——*Dhautoo* (धातु - dhátu, San.; معدنیات - madaniyát, *Ar.*; دھات - dhát, Hind.; ಧಾತು - dhátu, Can.; ಧಾತು - dhátu, Too.; ధాతు - dhátu, Tel.; ധാതു - dhátu, Mal.; தாது - táthu, Tam.). Ar. from (madan, ar. mine). Mineral. Any natural production [dravyam] from mine or ore formed by the action of chemical affinities, and organized when becoming solid by the power of crystallization. One class of mineral products are the products of the earth itself; which are brought into use either in the state in which they are found, as colored earths, abruck [q.v.] slates, building stones, &c. [cull, munn]; or are rendered useful after peculiar treatment, such as metals [loham] obtained by smelting, or lime [choonam] obtained by calcination. Another class are the substances distinguished as chemical substances, which are obtained from various minerals, earths, &c., after undergoing chemical processes of sublimation, distillation, solution, &c. [ooppoo, sarakk]. Compare Moolam the vegetable kingdom and Jantoo the animal kingdom.

DHAUMIN (دھامن - dhámin, *Hind.*). Rat-snake [q.v.].

DHAVAM (धव - dhava, *San.*). From (dhav, san. to flow) [dhoby]; from exudation. Botanically the Anogeissus genus, combretaceæ [vricsham, 55]. Trees or shrubs; leaves alternate, entire; flowers in globose heads; fruits small, dry, compressed, containing one seed. The species best known to the natives are:—acuminata [pauchimaun], latifolia [vekkauly].

DHEEMAR (دھیمر - dhímar, *Hind.*). From (dhívara, san. fisherman). A fisherman or one of bearer [boy] caste.

DHER (دھیڑ - dher, *Hind.*). Hindoo of low caste [pariah]. Compare:—Corvus culminatus (dherikavvá), pariah crow; Herodias alba (dherbaglá), pariah crane. See gloss. paragraphs.

DHOBY (دھوبی - dhobí, *Hind.*). From (dháv, san. to wash) [dhavam]. The Hindostany name for the washerman caste [dhoty]. The corresponding terms are:—Tam. vunnaun, Tel. saucala, Can. agasa, Mal. veloottaidan. As forming a caste, various sub-divisions are recognised, which do not eat, drink, or marry together. No Hindoos, even the poorest, ever wash their own clothes; and this operation is always done by the professional caste. Dhobies first steam the clothes by hanging them in a bundle over a cauldron of boiling water; they are then taken to a stream or pond where they are thoroughly washed with the aid of fuller's earth [dhoby's earth]; the dhoby stands in the water, and taking a quantity of clothes by one end into his two hands he raises them aloft in the air and brings them heavily down upon a broad stone slab at his feet; this operation he repeats until the clothes are perfectly clean. There is a Hindostany proverb:—دھوبی کا گدھا نہ گھر کا نہ گھاٹ کا—"Like washerman's ass, neither of the house nor of the washing "ghaut [q.v.];" i.e., from pillar to post. There is a Tamul proverb:—தட்டாரச் சித்து தறிச்சித்து வண்ணாரச் சித்துக்கு வராது—"The skill of a goldsmith and of a weaver are not "equal to the tricks of a washerman;" i.e., substituting clothes. The dhoby is a member of the village corporation of twelve [balootah]; besides being obliged to wash and dry the ryot's cloth, he occasionally spreads a cloth in the choultry [q.v.] when any great man passes for his convenience, and carries links [pandam, masaul] at the religious processions [inam, jauty].——*Dhobin* (دھوبن - dhobin, Hind.). Washerwoman.——*Dhoby boolbool* (دھوبی بلبل - dhobíbulbul, Hind.). Muscicapinæ, muscicapidæ [macsha grauhy], dentirostres, insessores, aves [pacshy, 20], of naturalists [jantoo]. Fly catchers. The species best known to the natives is Erythrosterna leucura. Alias Muscicapa albicilla, parva; Rubecula tytleri; Saxicola rubeculoides; Synornis joulaimus. Resembles in habit the British robin.——*Dhoby's earth* (ऊष - úshá, San.; قلی - kilí, Ar.; طین گازری - tínigázurí, Pers.; سجّی مٹّی - sajjímattí, Hind.; چوڑ کی مٹّی - chaurkimattí, Dec.; ಚೌಳು - chaulu, Can.; సున్నపుచవుడు - sunnaputsavudu, Tel.; உவர்மண் - uvarman, Tam.). Title from being used by washermen in bleaching. San. from (ush, san. to kill); as destroying vegetation. Ar. from (kilí, ar. to cook in a frying pan). Pers. from (tín, ar. earth + gázur, pers. washerman). Hind. from (sajjí, hind. carbonate of soda + mattí, hind. earth). Dec. from (tsavudu, tel. saline earth + mattí, hind. earth). Tel. from (sunnamu, tel. lime + tsavudu, tel. saline earth). Tam. from (uvar, tam. salt + man, tam. earth). Title otherwise Fuller's earth. A whitish grey, sandy efflorescence [sowdoo]; covers country where decayed white granite [caroom cull] forms the surface soil; contains from 13 to 25 per cent. of crude carbonate of soda. Begins to accumulate in the dry weather, and after rains it can be scraped off the surface. By repeated boiling, and the addition of a little quicklime [choonam], the alkali [q.v.] is obtained of considerable strength. Used by dhobies and the lower castes for washing clothes; it has a softening effect on water and removes the dirt. A crude sort of soap in conjunction with lime is produced from this earth, known as choonam [q.v.] soap [saubooh], and sold as sabboo in the bazaars. Weavers and dyers use a solution of the earth as a mordant [cauram] in fixing the red dye [shauyam] of the chironjee [q.v.] bark. It is also employed in the manufactures of glass [cunnaudy, gauzoo] and country soap. In Malabar, where dhoby's earth is not known, the ashes of burnt vegetables [sujjeekhaur], chiefly cocoanut [q.v.] leaves, are used. Same in Ceylon. Dhoby's earth is distinct from Pooneer, which see.——*Dhoby kite* (دھوبی چیل - dhobíchil, Hind.). From bright color. Same as Braminy kite.

DHOLE (अरण्यश्वान - aranyashvána, *San.*; कोळसन - kólasana, *Mahr.*; جنگلی کتا - janglíkuttá, *Hind.*; انجنگتن - anjingutan, *Malay*; ಶೀಳನಾಯಿ - shílanáyi, *Can.*; ಕೆನ್ನಾಯಿ - kennáyi, *Coorg*; రేచుకుక్క - rétsukukka, *Tel.*; ବୋଲିଆକୁକୁର - boliyakukuro, *Oor.*; ചെന്നായ - chennáya, *Mal.*; வேட்டைக்காரன் - véttaikkáran, *Tam.*). San. from (aranya, san. forest + shvána, san. dog). Mahr. from (kólá, mahr. jackal + shuna, san. dog). Hind. from (janglí, hind. wild + kuttá, hind. dog). Malay from (anjing, malay, dog + utan, malay, wild). Can. from (shílu, can. to tear + náyi, can. dog). Coorg from (kem, can. red + náyi, can. dog). Tel. from (rétsu, tel. to set on + kukka, tel. dog); setter-dog. Mal. from (chem, mal. red + náya, mal. dog). Tam. from (véttai, tam. hunting + kri, san. to do). Hind. also (bankuttá), meaning forest dog; (sonkuttá), meaning golden dog; (rámkuttá), meaning beautiful dog. Tel. also (adavikukka), meaning jungle + dog. Tam. also (shennáy), meaning red + dog. Canis [shwaunam] dukhunensis, canidæ [cookooram], digitigrada, carnivora, mammalia [sastanam, 12], of naturalists [jantoo]. Alias Canis primærus; Cuon rutilans. General color bright rusty-red or rufous fawn color, paler beneath; ears erect, rather large, somewhat rounded at the tip; tail moderately brushed, reaching to the heels, usually tipped blackish; limbs strong; body lengthened. The wild dogs prey by night and by day, but chiefly by day. They unite to hunt down their victim, running by smell rather than by the eye. They kill the tiger [pooly].

DHOLL (शमीधान्य - shamídhánya, *San.*; دال - dál, *Hind.*; ಬೇಳೆ - béle, *Can.*; కాయధాన్యము - káyadhányamu, *Tel.*; പയർ - payar, *Mal.*; காய்த்தானியம் - káyttániyam, *Tam.*). Title from hindostany [dalam]. San. from (shamí, san. pod + dhánya, san. grain). Hind. from (dal, san. to split). Tel. from (káya, tel. pod + dhánya, san. grain). Tam. from (káy, tam. unripe fruit + dhánya, san. grain); pod grain. Tam. also (muthirai). The terms may be taken generally for pulses, or leguminous plants. Distinguish from dry grain [q.v]. Properly the pulse Phaseolus mungo, but applied to other kinds, the pea of which, especially when converted into a sort of coarse pease soup, enters largely into the food of the natives. The dholls contain a large proportion of an albuminate called legumin or vegetable casein, which is coagulable like casein; owing to their comparative indigestibility by man they are inferior as food to the flesh of animals and are incapable of being digested in sufficient quantity to support human life by themselves; added in small amount to starchy or fatty foods they are of great value; eaten for instance with rice [q.v.]; they keep well, although becoming harder by time and requiring more careful preparation; they are rich in sulphur [gandhac], potassium and calcium, but inferior to the cereals [dhaunyam] in magnesium and phosphoric acid; they require slow and protracted boiling, and, if old, are steeped and crushed before being cooked for food; when the seeds are fresh, the husk is always removed. There is a Teloogoo proverb:—అరికెలుడికి కందులుడికెను—"If arikey "[khoda millet] fails there will be dholl;" pulse instead of grain. The following are two key-lists in the briefest possible terms of the principal pulses of s. india for which vernacular names are known; further information must be traced in the glossary paragraphs through the small-type cross references at end of this volume; see also vricsham, 7, for the method of expressing the products, &c., of plants in the dravidian languages.—"*a*" Arachis hypogæa, ground nut; Cajanus indicus, common dholl; Canavalia ensiformis, hussar bean; Ceratonia siliqua, carob; Cicer arietinum, bengal gram; Cyamopsis psoralioides, chinese lablab; Dolichos biflorus, madras horse gram; Dolichos lablab, country bean; Ervum lens, lentil; Glycine soja, japanese cow gram; Lathyrus sativus, vetch; Mucuna pruriens, common cowitch; Phaseolus aconitifolius, moorman's gram; Phaseolus adenanthus, wild green gram; Phaseolus lunatus, country french bean; Phaseolus mungo, green gram; Phaseolus mungo, var. radiatus, black gram; Phaseolus trilobus, field gram; Phaseolus vulgaris, french bean; Pisum sativum, garden pea; Vicia faba, broad bean; Vigna catiang, cow gram.—"*b*" Bean, dolichos, vicia; Carob, ceratonia; Cow gram, vigna; Cowitch, mucuna; Dholl, cajanus; French bean, phaseolus; Gram, cicer, dolichos, glycine, phaseolus; Ground nut, arachis; Hussar bean, canavalia; Lablab, cyamopsis; Lentil, ervum; Pea, pisum; Vetch, lathyrus.——*Black dholl* (कालतुवरी - kálatuvarí, San.; ಕಾಡುತೊಗರಿ - kádutogari, Can.; కారుకంది - kárukandi, Tel.; காலியாந்துவரை - káliyánduvarai, Tam.). Title from appearance of seed. San. from (kála, san. black + tuvarí, san. dholl, cajanus indicus, spreng.). Can. from (kádu, can. wild + togari, can. dholl). Tel. from (káru, tel. black + kandi, tel. dholl). Tam. from (káli, tam. point de galle + tuvarai, tam. dholl). Tel. also (nélaolumu), meaning ground + ipomæa angustifolia, jacq.; (chiriulava), meaning small + horse-gram, dolichos biflorus, linn.; (káruchikkudu), meaning wild; (núguchikkudu), meaning downiness; (nallagurigindza), meaning black + abrus precatorius, linn.; (gadichikkudu), meaning paddy field + dolichos lablab, linn.; (karraulava), meaning stick + dolichos biflorus, linn.; (errachikkudu), meaning red + dolichos lablab, linn. Tam. also (káttukkollu), meaning wild + dolichos biflorus, linn.; (karuppukkunri), meaning black + abrus precatorius, linn. Title otherwise Black goomchy, Wild horse-gram. Botanically the Rhynchosia genus, leguminosæ [vricsham, 48]. Herbs or undershrubs, usually with twining stems, and often sprinkled with small yellow resinous or grandular dots; leaves consist of three leaflets, the middle one having a long stalk; flowers yellowish, and disposed in racemes produced from the angles of the leaves; pod flattened, unequal-sided or sickle-shaped, containing two round seeds. The species best known to the natives are:—aurea, cana, cyanosperma, densiflora, heynei, minima, nummularia, rufescens, suaveolens, velutina, viscosa.——*Common dholl* (आढकी - ádhakí, San.; तूर - túra, Mahr.; तोरि - tóri, Conc.; شاخ - sház, Ar.; شاخل - shákhul, Pers.; تور - tuvvar, Hind. and Dec.; ತೊಗರಿ - togari, Can.; ತೊಗರಿ - togari, Too.; కంది - kandi, Tel.; କନ୍ଦୁଲୋ - kandulo, Oor.; തുവര - tumara, Mal.; රතතෝර - ratatóra, Singh.; துவரை - tuvarai; Tam.). Mahr. from (tuvara, san. astringency). Hind., &c., from same. Singh. from (rata, singh. foreign + tóra, singh. cassia). Tam. from (tuvara, san. astringency). San. also (tuvariká), meaning astringent; (súpya), meaning used in making sauce. Hind. also (dál); (barítuvvar), meaning large dholl; (arhar); (pádkátuvvar), meaning wind producing dholl. Can. also (kariuddugida), meaning black pulse plant. Tel. also (peddakondakandi), meaning large + hill + dholl; (pótukandi), meaning male + dholl; (yerrakandi), meaning red + dholl. Tam. also (iyavai), meaning hill dholl. Title otherwise Angola pea, Arhar, Cajan pea, Candy plant, Catjang [q.v.], Congo pea, No-eye pea, Pigeon-pea, Red gram [cow gram], Sauce pea, Togary, Toor, Tovray, Two-colored dholl. Botanically Cajanus indicus, spreng., leguminosæ [vricsham, 48]. Cajanus, from (kachang, malay, pulse). Alias Cajanus bicolor, flavus; Cytisus cajan, pseudocajan. Erect shrub, 3–6 feet, softly pubescent, with tender branches; leaves pinnately trifoliolate; leaves oval, lanceolate, mucronate; calyx campanulate, somewhat bilabiate; lips nearly equal in length, upper one shortly bifid, lower one three-partite; segments slightly curved upwards; apices recurved; corolla papilionaceous; petals equal in length; vexillum broad, bicallous at the base; keel falcate; racemes axillary; pedicels slender, in pairs; legumes hirsutely pubescent, from 2 to 3 inches long and ⅓ to ½ inch broad, three to five-seeded; flowers yellow; native of equatorial africa; cultivated here. Seldom sown alone, but mixed with early zonna [cholum], aurooga [khoda millet], raggy [q.v.], and corra [tinay] crops; cultivated in red soil; ground prepared in south from chittray or april to veiyaushy or may, on coromandel in ashaudham or july and shrauvanam or august, on w. coast from maidom or april to yedavam or may; the land is ploughed up three or four times and manure applied; seed sown in south in chittray or april with cholum or three months later in audy or july with varagoo, on coromandel in ashaudham or july and shrauvanam or august, on w. coast in maidom or april and yedavam or may with rice [q.v.] and in carcatacam [mausam] or july with raggy; sown mixed with the other seed broadcast while under growth; no treatment except weeding; full grown crop bushy, with red pods; cut after six or eight months; the bundles are brought to the threshing floor [calam] and kept under weights; the dry pods are removed from the plants and beaten with sticks to separate the seed; the seeds are then collected, mixed with red earth [shemmunn] to give them a color, and steeped in water till germination takes place; they are then dried in the sun for a couple of days and ground in a mill to break them up, when they are freed of the testa; the cotyledons are now called dholl. Chemical composition of the dholl with husk is water 13·3, albuminoids 17·1, starch 55·7, oil 2·6, fibre 7·5, ash 3·8, phosphoric acid ·9 per cent. Dholl is easily digested and is suitable for invalids; leaves are used in diseases of the mouth. Cattle eat the tender parts of the plant, both green and dry; the green pods are cooked into curries [q.v.]; the dholl also cooked into curries and cakes [poppadam] prepared from it; used by natives as a porridge and by europeans as an ingredient in kitcherry [q.v.]; similar to english split pease. There is a Teloogoo proverb:—పప్పులేని పెండ్లి ఉప్పులేని కూర ఉన్నదా—"Is there a "marriage without dholl or vegetable curry without salt?" The stalks are strong and woody and well adapted for making charcoal [adoopp kary] required in gunpowder manufacture; the dried stem makes good fuel and well adapted for producing fire by friction; stalks also used for roofing, basket-making, &c.; tubular wicker-work fascines of these used to line wells to prevent the earth from falling in. Two chief varieties, Cajanus indicus, var. flavus, dec., with the pea plain yellow, and Cajanus indicus, var. bicolor, dec., with the pea veined with purple. No other species of cajanus here. Dholl greens, title from being cooked with dholl, are the same as Indian purslane. For different peas, compare:—Abrus precatorius, love pea, rosary pea; Adenanthera pavonina, coral pea; Arachis hypogæa, earth pea; Cajanus indicus, angola pea, cajan pea, congo pea, no-eye pea, pigeon pea; Cardiospermum halicacabum, heart pea; Cicer arietinum, chicken pea, egyptian pea, chick pea; Lathyrus odoratus, sweet pea; Pisum arvense, field pea, grey pea; Psophocarpus tetragonolobus, winged pea. See gloss. paragraphs.——*Galle dholl* (காலியாந்துவரை - káliyánduvarai, Tam.). Same as Black dholl.——*Gum dholl* (ಅಂಟುತೊಗರಿ - antutogari, Can.). Title from clammy pubescence like dholl plant. Same as Shittamootty.——*Hill dholl* (پهاڑکا تور - pádkátuvvar, Hind.; కొండకంది - kondakandi, Tel.; மலைத்துவரை - malaittuvarai, Tam.). A variety of Common dholl.——*Jungle dholl* (काडतोरि - kádatóri, Conc.; ಕಾಡುತೊಗರಿಗಿಡ - kádutogarigida, Can.; ಕಾಟುತೊಗರಿದೈ - kátutogaridai, Too.; காட்டுத்துவரை - káttattuvarai, Tam.). Can. from (kádu, can. jungle + togari, can. dholl, cajanus indicus, spr. + gida, can. plant). Too. from (kátu, too. wild + togari, too. dholl + dai, too. plant). Tam. from (kádu, tam. jungle + tuvarai, tam. dholl). Botanically Atylosia candollei, w. and a., leguminosæ [vricsham, 48]. Alias Atylosia major; Collæa trinervia; Odonia trinervia. Erect; branches straight; young parts villous with fulvous hairs; leaflets oval, upper side even, pubescent, under reticulated, shortly tomentose, villous on the nerves and margin; stipules lanceolate-acuminate, spreading; peduncles two-flowered; calyx villous; segments curved upwards; spurs of the vexillum bent inwards, slightly callous; legumes villous; neilgherries. For Atylosia scarabæoides, benth., see Jungle horse-gram.——*Red dholl* (لال تور - láltuvvar, Hind.). Variety of Common dholl.——*Wild dholl* (جنگلی دال - janglídál, Hind.; ಕಾಡುಬಿಳಿಸಜ್ಜಬುಹುಲ್ಲು - kádubilisajjabuhullu, Can.; നീർവള്ളിപ്പുല്ല് - nírvvallippullu, Mal.). Hind. from (janglí, hind. wild + dál, hind. dholl, cajanus indicus, spr.). Can. from (kádu, can. jungle + bili, can. white + sajjabuhullu, can. the plant). Mal. from (nír, mal. water + valli, mal. creeper + pullu, mal. grass); as growing in wet ground. Botanically Leersia hexandra, swz., graminaceæ [vricsham, 156].

DHONY (ڈونی - doní, *Hind.*; డోని - dóni, *Tel.*; തോണി - tóni, *Mal.*; தோணி - tóni, *Tam.*). Literally dug-out trough. A gold washer's trough [julgar]. Distinguish from Doney [q.v.]. A large vessel used on the Coromandel coast, from having been originally dug out of a single tree. This is about seventy feet long, twenty feet broad, and twelve feet deep, with a flat bottom or keel part, which at the broadest place is seven feet; and at the fore and after parts of the vessel it breaks into ten inches, which is the siding of the stem and stern post. The fore and after bodies are similar in form amidships. The draught of water is about four feet, and when loaded about nine feet. Dhonies have only one mast, with a long sail, and are navigated from land to land and coastwise in the fine season only. They have no great sailing qualities:—There is a Tamul proverb:—*கரைகாணாததோணிபோல*—"As a dhony out of sight of land." And another:—*காற்றுக்குத்தோணி எதிர்த்து ஓடாது*—"A "dhony cannot sail against the wind." When they are of a port in a calm, the sailors throw a handful of sand or shells and feathers in the calm sea, and by the drifting of the feathers on the surface, and sinking of the sand or shells, a calculation of the rate of current is formed, and they anchor off the coast accordingly. The anchor is made by lashing together three crooked branches of a tree, which are then loaded with heavy stones, and the cable is formed from coir [q.v.] yarns. They have no deck and are thatched with palm leaves [cadjan]. These vessels trade from Madras and the east coast to the island of Ceylon and Gulf of Manaar. There are various clever contrivances practised by the native mariners of the Coromandel coast, in navigating, sailing and repairing their vessels.—"*a*" The following is an instrument for ascertaining latitude [acsham] when out of soundings. A piece of thin board, oblong in shape, three inches long by one and-a-half wide, is furnished with a string suspended from its centre, eighteen inches long. A number of knots are made in this string indicative of certain previously observed latitudes; in other words, coinciding with the positions of certain well known places on the coast. The position of these knots is obtained in the following manner. The observer elevates the board in his left hand, its longest side being upwards, and draws it backwards and forwards in front of his eye until its upright length exactly corresponds with, or covers the space included between the polar star [dhroovam] and the horizon [cshitijam]. With his right hand he next catches hold of the string and brings it to his nose, he makes a knot at the point where it touches that feature; and if he at the time be abreast of Point palmyra [q.v.], an undeviating index is afforded, which will in future show him when he is off that point, the North star's elevation [avanataumsham] being always fixed, and therefore all the parts of the triangle [mookonam, trikonam] formed by his line of sight, the string, and the distance between the polar star and the horizon, or the length of the board, equally as constant. He makes similar observations at, and a knot is fixed opposite, each conspicuous place, on the length of the string, as far as Dondra head in Ceylon generally. Thus by a simple observation, at any future time the mariner is enabled to ascertain his position with sufficient accuracy for his purposes, anywhere on the coast between Calcutta and the south point of Ceylon.—"*b*" To ascertain the rate of sailing, the procedure is as follows. By previous practice the sailor knows his rate of walking; he throws a piece of wood overboard at the stern of the vessel, and walks towards the stern keeping pace with the wood floating past, then he remembers his rate of walking, to which the progress of the vessel must necessarily be equal.—"*c*" When it is desired to ascertain the direction of the current, this is performed by throwing into the sea during the prevalence of a calm, a ball of ashes kneaded together by water; as it slowly sinks it separates, leaving a long broad tail, like a comet's [dhoomkait], behind it which is wafted away in the run of the current, making a line of direction apparent to an observer standing a little over the surface.—"*d*" The docking of a ship is simple and ingenious. In the first instance, when a ship is to be docked, she is floated into a basin direct from the sea or inlet; then the entrance is closed. The basin is surrounded by a high mud bank which forms it. The level of the water in the basin upon which the vessel now floats, is raised by scarping the mud from the banks into the basin, levelling it at the bottom of the water, and so raising the bottom of the basin which must of consequence elevate its contained water. This process is carried on until the ship is considerably higher than the level of the contiguous sea or inlet, the water is then suffered to run off, two beams are placed transversely under the ship, stem and stern, resting on the new and exposed bottom of the basin. Perpendicular shores are then put to her, and the earth levelled until she is on the same plane as the adjoining ground.—"*e*" For undocking the ship from her elevated position the following is the process. Four sets of cables are used, each one is coiled into the shape of a solid cone, one fake or coil not touching the one beneath it, soft mud and sand being interposed between each layer as well as smeared all over it. One cone is placed under the starboard bulge forward, and another under the same bulge aft, a third and a fourth correspond in position on the larboard side; thus the four solid cones of rope support the ship. She is now gradually lowered by withdrawing from the base of each cone simultaneously a coil or fake, by which the four cones bodily subside, and the vessel along with them, resting as she does upon them. It might be conjectured that by removing the lower coil the superstructure would tumble down, but this is obviated by the solidity of the mass, each layer consisting of a solid flat coil of rope one circle round within another.——*Yautra dhony* (යාත්‍රාඔරුව - yátraoruva, Singh.). From (yátra, san. voyage + oruva, singh. boat). A Ceylon coasting-vessel, with an outrigger.

DHOO (धू - dhú, *San.*). To kindle.——*Dhoomam* (धूम - dhúma, San.). Smoke.——*Dhoom kait* (धूमकेतु - dhúmakétu, San.). From (dhúma, san. smoke + kétu, san. flag), hence sign; whose ensign is marked by smoke. Comet.——*Dhoonah* (دھونہ - dhúnah, Hind.). Dammer [q.v.].——*Dhoopam* (धूप - dhúpa, San.). Means incense. Storax. Botanically the Styrax genus, styraceæ [vricsham, 84]. Trees or shrubs natives of asia and n. america; leaves entire, frequently covered with star-shaped hairs; flowers white, in racemes; fruit globose, one-celled, one-seeded. The species best known to the natives are:—benzoin [q.v.], officinale [true storax]. Compare the compounds, where transl. is of first term:—Ailantus malabarica (gugguladhúpa), dammer; Boswellia serrata (vishéshadhúpa), distinction; Boswellia serrata, var. glabra (kónkanadhúpa), concan, and (yakshadhúpa), demi-god; Canarium strictum (mandadhúpa), slow, (ráladhúpa), resin; Vateria indica (mandadhúpa); slow. See gloss. paragraphs.

DHOOLY (ڈولی - dúlí, *Hind.*). From (dul, san. to swing). A swinging litter for carrying women or sick persons [manjilee]. Consists of a cot [q.v.] or frame, suspended by the four corners from a bamboo [q.v.] pole, and is carried by two or four men. It is lighter and cheaper than a palankeen [q.v.]. Cf. Tonjon.

DHOOP (دھوپ - dhúp, *Hind.*). Sunshine.——*Dhoopchown* (دھوپ چھاؤں - dhúpchháun, Hind.). Means sunshine and shade. A brocaded shot silk with light and shade [puttoo, sheelay].

DHOTY (دھوتی - dhotí, *Hind.*; దోవతి - dóvati, *Tel.*). From (dhoná, hind. to wash); from being washed daily at the time of bathing [dhoby]. Duttee in old trade lists. A plain loin cloth. The end, after a couple of turns round waist, is passed between the legs, and put under the folds which cross behind; so that a festoon of calico [q.v.] hangs down to either knee. Occasionally the end is passed from behind and fastened in front. Amongst Mahomedans, after being folded two or three times round the waist, it is allowed to hang down; not tucked between the legs as with Hindoos. With a Hindoo the dhoty is indispensable. Should he wear drawers or trousers [pyjama], he has a dhoty, large or small, underneath. While at home and at ease, and on the most solemn religious occasions, even royal personages dress in the simplest possible fashion; with only the dhoty wound round the waist and a turban [puggry] on the head. Fine robes and valuable jewelry are reserved for great occasions and for appearance in portraiture. See vol. I (98).

DHOURRA (جواری - javárí, *Hind.*). From (júrna, san. the plant). Same as Cholum.

DHOW (ڈاؤ - dáú, *Hind.*). A sloop on the western coast; applied specially to the old fashioned vessel of Arab build, with a long grab stem, rising at a long slope from the water, and about as long as the keel, usually with one mast and lateen-rig.

DHROOVAM (ध्रुव - dhruva, *San.*). From (dhru, san. fixed). Stationary [dhar]. Dhroova cowle is a permanent lease. Generally the pole of a great circle of the sphere [golam], particularly the Celestial pole [alrooccabah, cootb, meroo]. Also means an epoch to which a computation is referred. Also the twelfth astronomical yogam [q.v.].——**(1)** *Dhroovacam* (ध्रुवक - dhruvaka, San.). Means fixed. Otherwise Nirayanam, meaning without precession [ayanaumsham]. Fixed celestial longitude, measured on the ecliptic [craunty mundalam] from the first point of the fixed Maisham or the beginning of the fixed sidereal zodiac [raushy]. This is a constant arc and not liable to precession error as sauyanam [q.v.] or tropical celestial longitude. Dhroovacams like Sauyanams can be calculated by great circle [mundalam] from the pole of the ecliptic [craunty mundalam], when they are aspootam or invisible or true longitudes; or the same can be done by great circle from the celestial pole only or pole of the earth projected, when they are spootam [q.v.] or apparent. The latter is much the more usual, and hence the difficulty of identifying stars described in the old shastrams.——**(2)** *Dacshina dhroovam* (दक्षिणध्रुव - dakshinadhruva, San.). From (dakshina, san. south + above). The South pole [coo meroo].——*Oottara dhroovam* (उत्तरध्रुव - uttaradhruva, San.). From (uttara, san. north + above). The North pole [soomeroo]. All the fixed stars [nacshatram] revolve about this particular point in the heavens; and near it is star of second magnitude, called Polar star, end of tail of Ursa minor [doobhe asghar]; has no other star of equal brightness near, and always seen in same direction, for circle it describes about pole is too small to be sensible to naked eye [jyotisham].

DHUKKA (دهکا - dhakká, *Hind.*). Shoving.——*Dhukkamhokkhy* (دهکامکهی - dhakkámukkhí, Hind.). From (above + mukkhí, hind. blow). Time of trouble.

DHURRAH (دهرا - dhará, *Hind.*; ధారా - dhara, *Tel.*). Bazaar weight. 2 punchairs = 1 dhurrah; 4 dhurrahs = 1 munn [niray, 2e]. Approximate actual value, 1 dhurrah = 6 lbs. 4 oz. avoirdupois. Same as Can. dhaday. Compare Yeday. See vol. I, 609; II, 513.

DHWAJ (ध्वज - dhvaj, *San.*). To move.——*Dhwajam* (ध्वज - dhvaja, San.; دهجا - dhaja, Hind.). Banner. A pole [dandam] with a strip of cloth tied to the end of it, and erected near a place of worship or elsewhere in satisfaction of a vow.——*Dhwaja stambham* (ध्वजस्तम्भ - dhvajastambha, San.). From (dhvaja, san. banner + stambha, san. pillar). Flag-staff placed in front of a temple [coil].

DIAMPER (ഉദയംപേരൂർ - udayampérúr, *Mal.*). From (udaya, san. rising + pérúr, mal. large village). Sanscrit name (udayapura), meaning rising town. Village; Travancore state, Cottayam division, Wycome talook. Christian town, remarkable as being the scene of the celebrated synod at which Menezes, Portuguese archbishop of Goa, compelled the Syrian christians of St. Thomas in A.D. 1599, to submit to the Pope, and burned their ritual and doctrinal books.

DIBBA (ٹبا - tibbá, *Hind.*; దిబ్బ - dibbá, *Tel.*; திப்பை - tippai, *Tam.*). Mound [tippa]. Suffix in place names, especially in the northern districts; as Frangooladibba, meaning europeans' mound. Olandoodibba, meaning dutch mound [dinney].

DIC (दिक् - dik, *San.*). From (dish, san. to point out) [desham, disay]. Quarter; space. The eight cardinal and intermediate points of the horizon [cshitijam]; but the zenith and nadir [ashata dic, jyotisham] are also called dic.——*Digambaran* (दिगम्बर - digambara, San.). From (above + ambara, san. clothing). Sky-clothed. Also called Nirgrantan, meaning without bond.—"*a*" A mendicant of the Jeina sect. The Jains are divided into two principal divisions, Digrmbarans and Shwetaumbarans. The former have the best pretensions to antiquity and have been most widely diffused. The latter means the white-robed, the teachers being so dressed. In the present day, the Digambaran ascetics do not go abroad naked, but wear colored garments; they confine the disuse of clothes to the period of their meals, throwing aside their wrapper when they receive the food given them by their disciples. The following is a Hindustany proverb:—جہاں نہ جا کوئی لگے تہاں نہ تا کو تہاوں دھوبی بسکر کیا کرے دگمبر کے گاوں—"Let not a man go where his "qualities are not appreciated; what occasion has a washerman "to live in a village of Digambarans?" [matam].—"*b*" Hindoo 2nd or pers. name. Common among Madhwas and Mahrattas [peyar].

DIGOOVA (దిగువ - digoova, *Tel.*). From (digu, tel. to descend). Prefix in place names; as Digoova ahobilam, meaning Lower ahobilam. Cf. Egoova.

DIL (دل - dil, *Hind.*). Heart.——*Dilair* (دلیر - diler, Hind.). Firm in heart. Part of lacab; as Dilair jung, intrepid in war [ism].——*Dilaraum* (دل‌آرام - dilárám, Hind.). From (above + árám, pers. comfort). The comforter. Servant's name [ism].——*Dilawar* (دلاور - diláwar, Hind.). From (above + áwar, pers. having). The brave. Mahomedan servant's name. Prefixed to an alam forms a lacab; as Dilawar ally, the brave ally, taken by Shiahs [ism].——*Dildaur* (دلدار - dildár, Hind.). From (above + dár, pers. keeper). Beloved. Servant's name. Prefixed to an alam forms a lacab; as Dildaur ally, lover of ally. Term of devotion + alam. Taken by Shiahs [ism].——*Dildost* (دلدوست - dildost, Hind.). From (above + dost, pers. friend). Lover. Servant's name. Prefixed to an alam forms a lacab; as Dildost ally, sincere friend of ally. Term of devotion + alam. Taken by Shiahs [ism].——*Diljoo* (دلجو - diljú, Hind.). From (above + jú, pers. seeker). Studious of pleasing. The conciliator. Mahomedan servant's name [ism].——*Dilshaud* (دلشاد - dilshád, Hind.). From (above + shád, pers. joy). The gladdener. Mahomedan servant's name [ism].

DILO OIL (دلوکا تیل - dilokátel, *Hind.*). Title from fiji. Product of Calophyllum inophyllum [common poon].

DIMHUTTY (ದಿಮ್ಹಟ್ಟಿ - dimhatti, *Can.*). From (dimpu, can. below + hatti, can. village). Can. also (úrbetta), meaning village + hill. Hill and village; Neilgherry dist., Paranginaud division; lat. 11° 26′; long. 76° 53′; height 6,903 feet; from Coonoor N.N.E. 7¼ miles; from Ootacamund E.N.E. 11 miles. A short distance N. of approach to Kotagherry. At foot of this the earliest sanitarium stood.

DIMMAM (ದಿಮ್ಮಂ - dimmam, *Can.*). Means mound. Village, Hill; Coimbatore dist., Suttimungalam tal.; lat. 11° 37′; long. 77° 10′; from Coimbatore N.N.E. 45 miles; from Suttimungalam N.W. 11 miles. At head of Hassanore ghaut [q.v.]. Chuttram [q.v.] and bungalow [q.v.]

DIMMAS (درمس - durmus, *Hind.*; دهمس - dhammas, *Dec.*). A pavior's rammer.

DINAM (दिन - dina, *San.*; دن - din, *Hind.*; దినము - dinamu, *Tel.*). From (div, san. to shine) [deva]. Cf. Ahas. A day [naul, pagal, roz].——**(1)** "*a*" In the European system the civil day is divided into two portions of twelve hours each; that from midnight to noon being called Antemeridian, and that from noon to midnight Postmeridian. The astronomical day is reckoned from noon to noon, or often at the present day from midnight to midnight, without the distinction of A.M. and P.M. The civil day commences at the midnight preceding the astronomical day, if the latter dates from noon.—"*b*" The instant of time to which the sun appears on the meridian [raikhay] of a place is apparent noon; and the interval between the departure of the sun from the meridian to its return is an apparent solar day, which is a period of unequal length because the sun moves in the ecliptic [craunty mundalam], and not in the equator [naudy mundalam], and because the diurnal velocity [gaty] varies with earth's distance from sun. But to secure a uniform measure of time, astronomers assume the revolution [bhaganam] of a mean sun; this gives a mean solar day, the length of which is equal to the average or mean of all the apparent solar days in a year. Clocks and chronometers are adjusted to mean solar time [madhyama sowra maunam], while the sun alone keeps apparent time. The difference between mean time and apparent time is the Equation of time.—"*c*" The sidereal day is the interval between the departure and the return of a star [nacshatram] to the same meridian. All the stars give the same exact duration of 23h. 56m. 4·09s. for the sidereal day, instead of 24h.; this acceleration of the sidereal on the solar day produces all the varied aspects seen in the heavens in the course of a year.—— **(2)** The natives have a great variety of ways of considering the day and fixing its duration. The principal are the following:—"*a*" The Sauvanam or natural or civil day is the time between two consecutive sun risings; therefore the Sauvanam days are of various duration even under the equator. According to the ancient shastrams [q.v.], the Sauvanam day is divided into 60 Ghatams or ghaticadandams, the Ghatam into 60 Vinaudicays, the Vinaudicay into 6 Prauna calays, the Prauna calay into 10 Vipalams [caulam].—"*b*" The Sowram day is the time during which the sun describes one degree [bhaugam] of the ecliptic. These days are therefore longer or shorter as the sun is near his apogee or perigee. They are divided in the same proportions as the Sauvanam days but with different names; viz., Dandam, Vicalay or Palam, Prauna calay, Caushta calay. Astronomers sometimes divide these days into minuter parts; thus the Vipalam or Caustha calay into 60 Alipalams, the Alipalam into 3,600 nimishams or twinklings of the eye [caulam, 6].—"*c*" The Nacshatram day, which is also frequently called Sowram with a different meaning from that just mentioned. It is sidereal, being the time between the same point of the ecliptic rising twice; or rather the time between the equinoctial points, called Ayanam [q.v.], rising twice. These days are accounted to be equal to one another throughout the year and are always equal to 60 Ghadiyas, subdivided sexagesimally into Vighadiyas, Params and Soorams [caulam, 5a]. It is to be noted that the measure of time called Ghadiya means also an arc [chaupam] or portion of a Nacshatram of 13° 20′, which is likewise subdivided into Vighadiyas, Params, &c., having no immediate reference to time.—"*d*" The lunar day or Tity [caulam, 4] is divided also sexagesimally like nacshatram day.—"*e*" Deva dinam is equal to a sideral revolution of the sun [varsham].—"*f*" Pitrya dinam is equal to a synodical revolution of the moon [chaundra mausam].—"*g*" Bramha dinam is equal to a calpam, or 4,320,000,000 years; his night being equal to his day [caulam, 2].—"*h*" Yoog dinam is another word for Aharganam [q.v.], meaning the number of days expired from the commencement of a Yoog [q.v.]; or Yoog dinam means the aniversary day of that on which a Yoog began, which is always noticed in the calendar [punchaungam].—— **(3)** *Cary dinam* (కరిదినము - karidinamu, Tel.). From (kari, tel. black + above). A day the morning and previous night of which is considered inauspicious.——*Dinacaran* (தினக்காரன் - tinnakkaran, Tam.). From (above + kara, san doer). Sun, the daymaker [divacaram]. Hindoo 2nd or pers. name. Common among Madhwas and Mahrattas [peyar].——*Dinaurdham* (दिनार्ध - dinárdha, San.). From (above + ardha, san. half). Half the time of sun being above the horizon [cshitijam, jyotisham, nairam].

DINDIGUL * (திண்டுக்கல் - tindukkal, *Tam.*). From (dindu, tel. pillow + kal, tam. rock); from shape. Greek τάγγαλα.—— **(1)** Talook, Madura district. Thasildar's pay Rs. 200. Area 1,121 square miles. Population 370,887. Language Tamul. N. inland part of district. Bounded N. Caroor talook of the Coimbatore district, E. Cooiltalay talook of Trichinopoly district, and Mailore and Madura talooks of Madura district, S. Tirumungalam and Madura talooks, W. Periyacoolam and Pulney talooks. Conquered by Mysore rajahs in 1745 A.D.; captured by the

British in 1783; restored at the peace of 1784; finally ceded to the British by treaty with Tippoo, 18th March 1792 and entered in the schedule as Dindigul and Pulney, two talooks. Mountainous and arid in most parts. Soil consists of grey and dark ferruginous earth, lying upon gneiss, which in some places has decayed into a light grey soft stone, easily dug by a pickaxe or spade. Near wells the soil is about three feet in thickness, and the rock is veined with felspar [mauvayira cull] and sometimes with a soft stratum of clay [calimunn]. For agricultural purposes the inhabitants depend chiefly on the rains, which during six months of the year are abundant, and two crops of dry grain [q.v.] are not unfrequently obtained in the year. The iron works at Coottam and Chilamputty were once considerable. A pearl-bearing mussel is said to have been once found. Tanneries [chamrah] and cheroots [q.v.] manufactured to a great extent in the town. Principal rivers are the Codavanaur, Maungaray, and Vagatchay. The Codavanaur irrigates many villages. Contains 1,542 tanks. There is fine camping ground west of the town of Dindigul, near the rock, the other camping grounds are not very good. Places of archæological interest:—Ahtoor, Anaipputty, Batlagoondoo, Calvaurputty, Dindigul, Keityancottay, Nullamannaurcottay, Ramanautapooram, Raugalaupooram, Taudicomboo, Tavashimaday, Virauliputty. Principal trig. stations:—Caloogoomullay, Cooroomullay, Moodimullay, Rishimullay. The following are the leading places, &c., in the talook.——*Ambatooray* (அம்பத்துரை - ambatturai, Tam. ambaturai *). From (ambá, tam. goddess + turai, tam. ford). Village, Railway station; pop. 4,975; acres 3,255; lat. 10° 17′; long. 77° 58′; height 997 feet; from Dindigul S.S.W. 7½ miles; from Madura N.N.W. 28 miles. Zemindarry resumed by Government.——*Ammayanaickanore* (அம்மயநாயக்கனூர் - ammayanáyakkanúr, Tam.). See sep. title.——*Auttore* (ஆத்தூர் - áttúr, Tam.). From (áru, tam. river + úr, tam. village). Village; pop. 8,565; acres 3,443; lat. 10° 17′; long. 77° 53′; from Dindigul W.S.W. 9¾ miles; from Madura N.W. 31 miles. In the centre of a highly cultivated tract.——*Ayilore* (அயிலூர் - ayilúr, Tam.). From (ayil, tam. plough + úr, tam. village). Village; pop. 4,275; acres 7,637; lat. 10° 29′; long. 78° 13′; height 1,087 feet; from Dindigul N.E. 15 miles; from Madura N. 38 miles. Railway station.——*Batlagoondoo* (வத்திலக்குண்டு - vattilakkundu, Tam.). From (bhaktudu, tel. devotee + gundu, tel. rock); originally the seat of teloogoo bramins. Village; pop. 9,709; acres 6,003; lat. 10° 09′; long. 77° 48′; from Dindigul S.W. 20 miles; from Madura N.W. 29 miles. The Munjalaur flows south of the village. Surrounded by wet lands. Small hills in west and north; the western called Permaul coil caradoo. On main road to Pulneys. In 1768 captured by a Mysore force after a siege of six days and captured a few days later by a reinforced army from Madura.——*Caloogoomullay* (கழுகுமலை - kazhugumalai, Tam.). From (kazhugu, tam. eagle + malai, tam. mountain). Trig. station; lat. 10° 10′ 10·61″; long. 78° 03′ 17·36″; height 4,441 feet; from Coolashekharancottah N.E. 6½ miles; from Dindigul S.S.E. 13 miles; from Shiroomullay S.E. 6 miles.——*Codavanaur* (கொடவனாறு - kodavanáru, Tam.). See sep. title.——*Cooroomullay* (குறுமலை - kurumalai, Tam.). From (kuru, tam. short + malai, tam. mountain). Trig. station; lat. 10° 35′ 21·72″; long. 77° 55′ 00·79″; height 2,527 feet; from Coottam W.N.W. 3½ miles; from Dindigul N.N.W. 17 miles.——*Cunnivaudy* (கன்னிவாடி - kannivádi *, Tam.). From (kanni, tam. plant. aloe socotrina, lamb. + vádi, tam. enclosure). Zemindarry, Village; pop. 3,708; acres 136,218; lat. of village 10° 22′; long. 77° 53′; from Dindigul W. 9¾ miles; from Madura N.W. 37 miles. Peshcush Rs. 38,129. One of the twenty-four polliems of old Dindigul district. Attacked by Hyder ally in 1755, when the poligar [q.v.] offered 3 lakhs of chuckrams [q.v.] and paid down 70,000. Subsequently resumed by Hyder for arrears of revenue [yeriyode].——*Dindigul* (திண்டுக்கல் - tindukkal, Tam.). See below.——*Iyempolliem* (ஐயம்பாளையம் - aiyambálaiyam, Tam.). See sep. title.——*Maroothanuddy* (மருதநதி - maruthanathi, Tam.). From (marutham, tam. terminalia tomentosa, bedd. + nadí, san. river). Sanscrit name (parushanadí), meaning rugged + river. River rises in the Lower pulneys and after a course of about 25 miles joins the Munjalaur.——*Moodimullay* (முடிமலை - mudimalai, Tam.). From (mudi, tam. head + malai, tam. mountain). Trig. station; lat. 10° 24′ 23·60″; long. 78° 13′ 36·95″; height 3,134 feet; from Dindigul E.N.E. 15 miles; from Shengoorchy N.N.E. 2½ miles.——*Moollipaudy* (முள்ளிப்பாடி - mullippádi, Tam.). From (mulli, tam. solanum indicum, linn. + pádi, tam. village). Village; pop. 2,337; acres 2,203; lat. 10° 24′; long. 78° 04′; from Dindigul N.E. 4½ miles; from Madura N.W. 34 miles. The Chandana varadaur flows through village and supplies Periyacoolam tank.——*Munjalaur* (மஞ்சளாறு - mañjuláru, Tam.). See sep. title.——*Nilacottah* (நிலக்கோட்டை - nilakkóttai, Tam.). See sep. title.——*Ramgherry* (இராமகிரி - irámagiri, Tam.). From (ráma, san. the god + giri, san. hill). Village, Hill; lat. 10° 40′; long. 78° 10′; from Dindigul N. 23 miles; from Madura N. 50 miles. Once residence of a poligar; ruined fort and Vishnoo temple.——*Rishimullay* (இருடிமலை - irudimalai, Tam.). From (rishi, san. sage + malai, tam. mountain). Trig. station; lat. 10° 12′ 29·72″; long. 77° 55′ 27·79″; height 1,675 feet; from Dindigul S.S.W. 12 miles.——*Shiroomullay* (சிறுமலை - shirumalai, Tam.). See sep. title.——*Taudicomboo* (தாடிக்கொம்பு - tádikkombu, Tam.). From (tádi, tel. palmyra tree, borassus flabelliformis, linn. + kombu, tam. branch), perhaps from a palmyra with branches. Village; pop. 4,784; acres 9,103; lat. 10° 27′; long. 78° 00′; from Dindigul N. 5½ miles; from Madura N.N.W. 37 miles. Old Vishnoo temple with inscription of Vijianugger dynasty dated 1629.——*Vada madura* * (வடமதுரை - vadamathurai, Tam.). From (vada, tam. north + mathurai, tam. town so called). Village, Railway station; pop. 4,770; acres 7,109; lat. 10° 26′; long. 78° 09′; height 969 R. S.; from Dindigul N.E. 10¼ miles; from Madura N. 37 miles.——*Vagatchay* (வகைச்சை - vagaççai, Tam.). From (vagai, tam. division + shéy, tam. length). River. Rises in the western hills, and running easterly and north-east, crosses the Madura and Nuttam roads. It then divides into the Moollipaudy and Poonganay rivers, which intersect the plain of Dindigul; these being joined by the Cullaur and the Ayilore, two small streams which rise in the low hills to the eastward, again unite, and running north fall into the Codavanaur.——*Vedasundoor* (வேடசந்தூர் - védasandúr, Tam.). See sep. title.——*Veigay* (வைகை - vaigai, Tam.). See sep. title.——*Yeriyode* (எரியோடு - eriyódu, Tam.). From (eri, tam. to burn + ódu, tam. tile). Village; pop. 1,926; acres 3,733; lat. 10° 31′; long. 78° 06′; from Dindigul N.N.E. 12¼ miles; from Madura N. 41 miles. One of the twenty-four polliems of the late Dindigul district. Attacked by Hyder in 1755, when the poligar consented to pay 70,000 chuckrams; subsequently resumed by Hyder for arrears of revenue [cunnivaudy].——

(2) Town, Mountain, Railway station, Head-quarters of Subcollector and Sub-registrar, District moonsiff's station. Madura dist., Dindigul tal.; pop. 20,203; acres 1,280; lat. 10° 22′; long. 78° 00′; height 924; from Kodaykarnal E.N.E. 35 miles; from Madras S.W. 242 miles; from Madura N.W. 30 miles; from Rameshwaram N.W. 114 miles; from Ramnaud N.N.W. 88 miles. On the trunk road from Coimbatore to Pondicherry, at N.E. extremity of valley of same name extending along foot of ghauts [q.v.]. The town is in the middle of an extensive plain, measuring 29 miles from north to south and 30 miles from east to west, entirely surrounded by hills. Formerly capital of an independent province, nominally part of Madura kingdom. As a strategical point of great natural strength, commanding the passes between Madura and Coimbatore, its possession always keenly contested. Between 1623 and 1659 the scene of many encounters between Mahrattas and Mysore and Madura troops, the poligar of Dindigul holding at that time feudatory authority over eighteen neighbouring chieftains. Chundah sahib, the Mahrattas, and Mysore troops, occupied the fort in turn; and during the intervals in which no greater power was in possession, the strongest local chief made it his head-quarters. Attacked by troops of the poligars in the reign of Moottoo veerappanaick of Madura, 1609–1622 A.D. Besieged by an army from Mysore in 1625, during the reign of Trimalnaick, but the assailants were driven back by the Dalavoy saitoopaty. In 1736 stormed by Chundah sahib. In 1745 conquered by the Mysore rajahs. In 1755 garrisoned by Hyder and used by him as the basis of his schemes for subduing the powerful poligars of Madura, and annexing the greater part of that district as well as Coimbatore. As the gate to Coimbatore from the south, the fort proved in the wars with Hyder, a serious obstacle to the operations of the British troops at Trichinopoly and Madura. Taken by the British in 1767, lost again in 1768, retaken in 1783, given up to Mysore by the treaty of Mungalore in 1784, recaptured on the next outbreak of war in 1790, and finally ceded to the Company by the treaty with Tippoo of 18th March 1792. Fort, built on a remarkable wedge-shaped rock 400 feet in length and 300 in breadth, 1,223 feet above the sea, is to the west and in good preservation. It was occupied by British garrison until 1860. At the top of the rock is a ruined temple with an inscription, dated A.D. 1538, recording a gift during the reign of Atchoota deva royel of Vijianugger. Staples of local trade are hides [chamrah], tobacco [pogauk], coffee [q.v.], and cardamoms [q.v.], for the export of which the system of roads radiating from the town afford exceptional facilities. Silks [puttoo] and muslins [mull] manufactured here had once a high repute, as also the blankets [cumbly] made from Cooroombaud [q.v.] wool [pushm]. The following are the travelling distances from Dindigul to different places:—

To	Viâ	Miles and Furlongs.	
Avanashy ...	Dharaupooram	95	0
Bangalore ...	Caroor, Namcull, Salem, Toppoor, Royacottah and Oossoor.	219	4
Caroor	Andiputty	48	1
Caroor	Aravacoorchy	49	0
Coimbatore ...	Dharaupooram and Pulladam	106	7
Cuddalore ...	Trichinopoly	172	3
Dharaupooram.	Pulney	56	4
Madras ...	Trichinopoly and Chingleput!	261	2¼
Madura ...	Sholavandaun	40	1¼
Namcull ...	Aravacoorchy and Caroor	70	0
Oodamalpett ...	Pulney	58	1

To	Viâ	Miles and Furlongs.
Ootacamund ...	Avanashy and Coonoor	152 4¾
Palamcottah ...	Madura and Tirmungalam	135 7½
Palghaut ...	Pulney, Oodamalpett and Pollachy ...	102 7
Periyacoolam ...	Batlagoondoo	30 0
Pulney	......	34 4
Quilon	Madura, Shreevillipoottore, Aryancauv ...	193 6½
Quilon	Goodalore pass	214 6
Rameshwaram.	......	152 1
Salem	Caroor and Nameull	101 4
Seringapatam...	Dharaupooram, Avanashy, Suttimungalam and Hassanore.	212 4
Suttimungalam	Dharaupooram and Avanashy	119 7
Tanjore ...	Trichinopoly	98 1½
Tondy	......	98 4
Trichinopoly ...	Manapauray	60 7½

DINNEY (దిన్నె - dinne, *Tel.*; திண்ணை - tinnai, *Tam.*). Mound. Suffix in place names; as Naugaldinney, meaning Serpent's mound [dibba].

DIRHEM (درهم - dirham, *Hind.*). From Greek δράχμη. An ancient Mahomedan silver coin equivalent to about 10 pence. 20 or 25 equal one deenaur [q.v.]. The deenaur equal to a ducatoon or sequin, about 9 shillings. As a weight, a dirhem is considered equal to 3½ maushams or 52½ grains [damree, daum].

DISAY (திசை - tisai, *Tam.*). From (dish, san. to point out) [desham, dic]. Direction [ashtadic]. Province.——*Disaytchol* (திசைச்சொல் - tisaiççol, Tam.). Provincial words.

DITA (सप्तछद - saptachhada, *San.*; सातवण - sâtavana, *Mahr.*; सान्निरूकु - sánnirúku, *Conc.*; ديت - det, *Hind.*; ಪಾಲೆ - pále, *Can.*; ಪಾಲೆ - pále, *Too.*; ఏడాకులపాల - édákulapála, *Tel.*; ଛତ୍ନିଅ - chhatniya, *Oor.*; ഏഴിലംപാല - ézhilampála, *Mal.*; රුකත්තන - rukattana, *Singh.*; ஏழிலைப்பாலை - ézhilaippálai, *Tam.*). Title from hindostany, name in bombay. San. from (sapta, seven + chhada, san. leaf); from leaves appearing in whorls of seven. Mahr. from (saptaparna, san. seven-leaved). Can. from (pálu, can. milk). Tel. from (édu, tel. seven + áku, tel. leaf + pála, tel. milky plant). Mal. from tamul. Singh. from (ruk, singh. tree + attana, singh. datura fastuosa). Tam. from (ézhu, tam. seven + ilai, tam. leaf + pálai, tam. milky plant). San. also (saptaparna), meaning seven + leaf; (ayngmachhada), meaning having an odd number of leaves; (jivani), meaning life-giver [indian nettle]; (payasyá), meaning milky; (kshatriyá), meaning protecting; (ayngmaparna), meaning having an odd number of leaves; (shárada), meaning flowering in autumn. Can. also (hále), meaning milk; (élelepále). Tel. also (édákulaponna), meaning seven + leaf + calophyllum inophyllum, linn.; (pálagaruda), meaning braminy kite paulay; (édákulaariti), meaning seven + leaf + plantain tree, musa paradisiaca, linn. Mal. also (mukkanpala), meaning three-eyed milk tree; (daivappála), meaning divine milk tree; (mangalappála), meaning auspicious milk-tree; (pála). Tam. also (pálai), meaning milky plant [edible paulay, eve's apple, ground paulay, monkey-face paulay, nakchiknee silk cotton, nauga champak, pauchonty, paula indigo, paulay silk cotton, tellicherry bark]. Title otherwise Devil's tree, Dita-bark tree, Seven-leafed milk plant, Seven-leafed plaintain, Seven-leafed poon. Botanically Alstonia [saptaparnam] scholaris, r. br., apocynaceæ [vricsham, 87]. Alias Alstonia oleandræfolia; Echites scholaris. This tree has obtained the name scholaris from its planks being used as school-boards, on which children trace their letters. Stiff-branched tree, 50 feet; furrowed trunk; leaves five to seven in a whorl, obovate-oblong, obtuse, veins ribbed, approximating the margin; calyx five-parted; corolla salver-shaped, with roundish segments; cymes on short peduncles; limb of corolla a little bearded; flowers greenish-white, follicles very long, slender; flowers emit a sickening smell which pervades air about sunset, flowering in january and february. Stem gives a kind of gutta-percha [q.v.]. The medicinal drug consists of irregular fragments of bark ⅛ to ⅓ inch thick, easily breaking with a short fracture; the external layer fissured, dark grey or brownish, sometimes with black spots; it readily separates when handled; inner substance of a bright buff; it has no smell, is bitter but not disagreeable when chewed. Bark medicinally an astringent tonic, anthelmintic, alterative and antiperiodic; common native medicine in bowel-complaints; gives to pharm. alstoniæ cortex, officinal. Ashes used as mordant [cauram]. Wood white, soft, even-grained, seasons badly, and soon gets mouldy and discolored; not durable, but easily worked.

DITTAM (திட்டம் - tittam, *Tam.*). From (dishta, san. assigned). Rule, agreement; the account in former days of the probable settlement ascertained early in the season, by taking from each ryot [q.v.] a memorandum [cooripp] of what he intended to cultivate [inam].

DITY (दिति - diti, *San.*). One of the wives of Cashyapan [q.v.], whose children were the Deityans [q.v.], as Adity [q.v.] another wife was the mother of the gods and the Sooras [audityan].——*Deityan* (दैत्य - daitya, San.). From (diti, san. wife of kashyapa). Greek τιτᾶς. Oldest Sanscrit word for demoniac giants and enemies of gods [dasyoo, dausan]. At the churning of the ocean they fought with the gods regarding the cup of amritam [q.v.]; when Vishnoo assuming a female form [mohiny], deluded them. The Deityans then plunged into Pantaulam [q.v.]. In the Hebrew genesis the Sons of God and Daughters of Men correspond with males of devas and females of deityans [coormam]. According to European sanscritists the conflict of Devas and Deityans is explained by the solar theory, or daily combat between light and darkness. That legend is also seen in the stories of Vishnoo and Baly, and Indran and Ahalyay. In greek the same exists under form of Theseus, Persephone, and Hades; Heracles, Alcestis, and Hades; Orpheus and Eurydice; and in the later story of Paris and Helen. In latin it exists in the story of Hercules and Cacus, Ceres and Pluto. In the teutonic languages it is told under the names of Odin and Balder, Beowulf and Grendel [matam]. In late sanscrit writings the term deityans is applied to the dark inhabitants of India, such as the Dravidians met by the Aryans. See Asooran, which is a later term; and Raucshasan, which is still later.

DIV (दिव् - div, *San.*). To shine.——*Deva* (देव - déva, San.). See sep. title.——*Dinam* (दिन - dina, San.). See sep. title.——*Divasam* (दिवस - divasa, San.). A day [dinam]. An anniversary commemorative of deceased parents.——*Divaucaram* (दिवाकर - divákara, San.; திவாகரம் - tivágaram, Tam.). From (diva, san. day + kara, san. maker); epithet of the sun, the day maker [dinacaran]. Oldest dictionary [nigantoo] of Tamul language, by Shendan member of the Madura college [q.v.]; twelve chapters.——*Divy* (दिवि - divi, San.). Day time in the calendar [punchaungam]. Thus Tyaujya divy means that the Tyaujyam [q.v.] occurred at day time.

DIVY (దివి - dívi, *Tel.*; ദിവി - divi, *Mal.*). From (dvípa, san. island).—"*a*" Island. Suffix in place names; as Anjidivy, meaning five islands [dweepam, teev].—"*b*" Sanscrit name (hamsadvípa), meaning swan + island. Island, Promontory, Lighthouse; Kistna dist., Bunder tal.; pop. 20; lat. 15° 57′; long. 81° 13′; from Masulipatam S. 16 miles. Low headland surrounded by shoal flats for six miles south and east, the edge of the shoal sometimes extending five or six leagues out to sea. Around the point and between it and Divy false point, several branches of the Kistna fall into the sea. The rise and fall of the tide is seldom more than four or five feet in the springs at the mouths of the rivers; but when a severe gale of wind blows from the sea, the lowland contiguous to it is inundated, causing great destruction of property and lives. The point is 19 miles north-east of the mouth of the Kistna. Formerly belonged to the Noozveed zemindars, but appropriated by the French, who built a fort and cut a canal from the river to Masulipatam. Afterwards included in the Havelly [q.v.] lands of Masulipatam and given to Condregoola jogy puntooloo, as a reward for his services. His brother, Condregoola vencatroyel, doobash [q.v.] under later chiefs in council at Masulipatam, in 1776 took all the Havelly lands on a ten years' lease, which lease was continued to his nephew Jaggappa. In 1807 given on zemindarry [q.v.] tenure to Condregoola gopaul row, who died on 30th April 1812 and was succeeded by his younger brother Jugganauta row. Condregoola gopaul row died on 16th May 1836, leaving authority to his widow to adopt a son. Zemindarry was brought to sale on March 25th, 1853, and purchased for Rs. 25,000 by Government. Divy false point stands 16½ miles south-west by west of Divy point. Light two miles N.W. of Divy point; lat. 15° 59′ 11·79″; long. 81° 10′ 8·15″. White; fixed, 14 miles range. Visible from all directions seaward. Masonry column white. To point out dangerous sands in vicinity.

DIVY DIVY (سماق امريقه - sumákiamríkah, *Ar.* and *Pers.*; امريقه كا سماق - amríkahkásumák, *Hind.* and *Dec.*; ವಿಲಾಯತಿಅಲೆಕಾಯಿಮರ - viláyatíaldekáyimara, *Can.*; கொடிவேலன் - kodivélan, *Tam.*). Title from north american. Ar. from (sumák, ar. sumach + amríkah, ar. america). Pers., &c., from arabic. Can. from (viláyati, hind. foreign + aralekáye, can. gallnut, terminalia chebula, retz. + mara, can. tree). Tam. from (kodumai, tam. crookedness + vél, tam. acacia); from curving legumes. Tam. also (mullillâthavélan), meaning thorn + not having + acacia; (tivithivi); (kónaivél), meaning crooked acacia. Title otherwise American divy divy, American sumach, Diby diby, Liby liby, Sumach. Botanically Cæsalpinia [coobairaucshy] coriaria, willd., leguminosæ [vricsham, 48]. Alias Cæsalpinia thomæa; Poinciana coriaria. Small spreading tree, 25–30 feet, unarmed; leaves bipinnate; pinnæ six to seven pairs; leaflets fifteen to twenty pairs, linear, obtuse; racemes panicled; pedicels shorter than the flowers; calyx cup-shaped at the base, five-lobed; petals five unequal, upper one shorter than the rest; legume tough, oblong, incurved laterally, reddish brown; may be known by its drying into the shape of the letter S.; flowers small yellow fragrant; native of w. indies, naturalised here; now common. Pods contain much tannin like vallonia, and are astringent; powder prepared from them, light yellow color and astringent taste, antiperiodic; decoction of the legume forms injection in bleeding piles; pods are remedy for prolapsus ani in children; mentioned in pharm., but non-officinal. Pods are employed for tanning [chaurah]; superior to all other indian astringents.

DIWAUN (دیوان - díwán, *Hind.*). From (daun, ar. an account).—"*a*" The principal revenue servant under a zemindar [q.v.]. By this title the Company were receivers-general in perpetuity of the revenues of Bengal, Behar, and Orissa, under a grant from the Great moghul. In Persia, a court of justice or of other business. Diwanhy, of or relating to a diwaun; civil as opposed to criminal.—"*b*" Also a collection into one volume of the entire odes of an author, in Persian or Hindostany; in bringing them together they are arranged alphabetically according to the letters in which the verses terminate. There are very many of these current in Madras. See specimens below. ——*Diwaun e dard* (دیوان درد - díwánidard, Hind.). By Dard, takhalloos [q.v.] of Cauja meer of Delhi. Died about 1786. میرا جی هی جبتک تری جستجو می زبان جبتلک هی یهی گفتگو هی * کیا سیر سب همنے گلزار دنیا گل دوستی مین عجب رنگ و بو هی * درد دلسے لوٹتا هون کس کو میرا درد هی هونمین —حرف درد جس پهلو سے اٹهو درد هی * "Live as long as I "may, I shall be ever seeking you; and this will be the subject-"matter of discourse so long as there is a power of speech in "me. I have travelled all over the garden of the world but "I have no where found such wonderful fragrance as that "existing in the clay of friendship. I roll and toss with heart-"ache, and who feels for me? Dard is my name which way you "read and which side I roll and lie." Dard means heart-ache. ——*Diwaun e nausikh* (دیوان ناسخ - díwáninásikh, Hind.). By Nausikh, takhalloos of Sheikh imaum buksh, born at Fyzabad. Died about 1837. زاهدا کیونکر کرونمین ترك یهه دنیا وه هی سیر کو آگے تهے آدم باغ رضوان چهوڑ کر * هوتی هی غربت مین ثروت پر بڑی ایذا کے ساتهه رنج اٹهایا کسقدر یوسف نے کنعان چهوڑ کر * اهل جوهر کو وطن مین رهنے دیتا گرفلك —لعل کیون اس رنگ سے آتا بدخشان چهوڑ کر * "O! monk, how "can I give up this world when Adam forsook Paradise and "came down to enjoy it. Prosperity follows adversity, but "after much hardship; lo! what misery Joseph bore after "leaving Canaan and before attaining prosperity. Had the "envious sky left men of merit to remain in their own country, "why should the ruby have emigrated from its native home." ——*Diwaun e zowk* (دیوان ذوق - díwánizauk, Hind.). By Zowk, takhalloos of Sheikh mahomed ibrahim of Delhi, who was tutor to Bahandur shah, the last king of Delhi. Died about 1853. رکاؤ خوب نهین طبع کی روانی مین که بو فساد کی آتی هے بند پانی مین * نشاه دولت کا بد اطوار کو جس آن چڑها سر په شیطان کے ایك اور بهی شیطان چڑها * آدمیت اور شی هی علم —هی اور چیز کتنا طوطے کو پڑهایا پر وه حیوان هی رها * "It is not well to check the flow of warm passion, for there "comes a fetid smell from stagnant water. When a wicked man "becomes intoxicated with pride of wealth, it is as it were a "second devil exciting the first one. Humanity is one thing "and learning quite another; for if you teach a parrot ever so "much, he will be a parrot [totah] nevertheless."

DO (دو - do, *Hind.*). Two [dwau, dwi].——*Doab* (دو آب - doáb, Hind.). From (above + áb, pers. water). The area between two confluent rivers, or the confluence itself [sangam]. ——*Dofusl* (دوفصل - dofasl, Hind.). From (above + fasl, ar. crop). Raising two crops a year on the same land [iroobhogam]. ——*Dohar* (دوهر - dohar, Hind.). From (above + har, hind. suffix of division). Calico [q.v.] sheet; in cold weather doubled and worn over the shoulders. Cf. Chudder.——*Dohra* (دوهرا - duhrá, Hind.). Double.——*Domoonh* (दुन्दुभ - dundubha, San.; دو منهه کا سانپ - domunhkásámp, Hind.; ಇತ್ತಲೆಹಾವು - ittalehávu, Can.; రెండుతలలపాము - rendutalalapámu, Tel.; മണ്ണണിപ്പാമ്പ് - mannanippámbu, Mal.; இருதலைப்புடையன் - iruthalaippudaiyan, Tam.). San. from (dundu, san. the sound + bhan, san. to utter). Hind. from (domunh, hind. double faced + sámp, hind. snake). Can. from (iru, tel. two + tale, can. head + hávu, can. snake). Tel. from (rendu, tel. two + tala, tel. head + pámu, tel. snake). Mal. from (man, mal. mud + ani, mal. to wear + pámbu, mal. snake). Tam. from (irandu, tam. two + talai, tam. head + pudaiyan, tam. earth snake). Blind snake; two-ended snake. The terms are co-extensive with family Typhlopidæ, ophidii, colubriformes, ophidia [sarpam], reptilia [sarpy, 12], of naturalists [jantoo]. These snakes have the body cylindrical, with very short head not distinct from neck, and with a very short tail; the body and tail are covered with rounded, polished, imbricate scales; jaws scarcely dilatable; rudiments of hinder extremities are hidden below the skin. Live under ground, their rigid body and short curved tail being adapted for burrowing; after showers of rain they occasionally appear above ground; feed on worms and small insects; oviparous; smallest species of snakes belong to this family, some being only half the size of a common earth-worm. The following are the South indian species:—"*a*" Onychocephalus acutus. Alias Onychocephalus lülken, meddel, westermanni; Typhlops russellii. Has the body only a little thicker behind than in front; circumference in middle is contained fourteen times in the total length; tail slightly curved, extremely short; body surrounded by series of scales; light bronze-colored, each scale on the back lighter in the centre; below uniform yellowish.—"*b*" Typhlops braminus. Alias Eryx braminus; Tortrix russellii. Has the body very much thicker behind than in front; circumference in middle one-thirteenth of the total length; tail slightly curved, very short; uniform brown, paler beneath; most common species.—"*c*" Typhlops pammeces. Is closely allied to Typhlops braminus, only half as thick; circumference of body twenty-fourth of total length.——*Doobash* (دو باش - dubásh, Hind.). From (above + básh, hind. language). One who speaks two languages, an interpreter [dragoman]. The doobash in this sense was formerly a usual servant in every household; and there is still one attached to each mercantile house, as the broker [dallaul] transacting business with natives, and corresponding to the Calcutta banyan [q.v.]. Now applied to a dressing boy or other servant with a European.——*Dooggauny* (దుగ్గాణి - duggáni, Tel.; துக்காணி - tukkáni, Tam.). From (duga, tel. two + káni, tel. one sixty-fourth of a tunkam or a pie). A copper coin, variable. At Madras, 2 pies = 1 dooggauny, 2 dooggaunies = 1 doody [naunyam, 2a, b, c]. Same as Hind. adhelah, Tel. yegauny.——*Doogoolam* (ದುಗಲ - dugula, Can.; దుగలము - dugulamu, Tel.).—"*a*" Coin. 2 baidas = 1 doogoolam; 2 doogoolams = 1 chowlam [naunyam, 2b]. Approximate actual value, 1 doogoolam = 4 annas. Nellore and Kistna. Same as Hind. powlah, Can. caul. Compare velly.—"*b*" Goldsmith's weight. Same scale [niray, 3b]. Approximate actual value, 1 doogoolam = 3½ grains. Teloogoo countries. In testaceous scale equal to 2 goorigiujas. Compare Can. adda or manjoty, Tam. munjaudy. See vol. 1, 609. ——*Doopty* (దుప్పటి - duppati, Tel.). Corruption of Doputta [q.v.]. A sheet.——*Doputta* (دوپٹه - dopatta, Hind.). From (above + pata, san. cloth). Literally two breadths. A scarf or loonghee [q.v.] consisting of two pieces or breadths stitched together [doopty, sheelay].——*Doshamba* (دوشنبه - dúshambah, Hind.). From (above + shambah, pers. saturday). Monday; on this day God created the seven firmaments [shamba].——*Doshaula* (دوشاله - doshálah, Hind.). From (above + shál, pers. woollen cloth, so called). Long shawl [q.v.]; invariably manufactured and sold in pairs; production of Cashmere.——*Dosily* (దోసిలి - dósili, Tel.). From (above + li, tel. suffix showing measurement). Two hands joined together, so as to hold anything [prasritam]. Handful, grain as a fee. A single handful is a mooshty [q.v.] or mootty [q.v.].

DODDA (ದೊಡ್ಡ - dodda, *Can.*). Great [hey]. Plant first term. Ex., joining two genera where transl. is of second term:—Amomum subulatum (doddayálakki), elettaria cardamomum; Careya arborea (doddáladamara), ficus bengalensis; Coscinium fenestratum (doddamaradarasina), morinda umbellata; Jatropha curcas (doddaharalu), ricinus communis; Pedalium murex (doddaneggilu), tribulus terristris; Pimpinella anisum (doddajirige), cuminum cyminum; Portulaca oleracea (doddagóni), salvadora persica; Scindapsus officinalis (doddahippali), piper longum; Zea mays (doddajóla), sorghum vulgare. See gloss. paragraphs. ——*Dodabetta* (ದೊಡ್ಡಬೆಟ್ಟ - doddabetta, Can.). From (above + betta, can. hill). Mountain; Neilgherry dist., Todanaud div.; lat. 11° 24′; long. 76° 47′; height 8,647; from Ootacamund E.S.E. 2½ miles. Really a range with Dodabetta peak as its southern and Snowdon as its northern eminence. The distance between these points is 2 miles. Dodabetta peak is highest peak of the Neilgherries, and shuts in valley of Ootacamund on side. Remarkable, even among the mammiform hills so common on Neilgherries, for flattened curve of its summit. The hollows of its slopes are clothed with thick woods; and rhododendron [neilgherry rhododendron] trees, though somewhat stunted, are found even within a few yards of the top, which is covered with thick coarse grass and flowering sub-alpine shrubs and herbs. Numerous small streams which flow into the valleys below take there rise here. During Governorship of Marquis of Tweeddale, an observatory was established on the summit. Observations were begun in 1847 and continued till May 1859. The thermometric observations taken here are not to be relied on. Those of the atmospheric pressure and rainfall though not accurate, are less open to suspicion. A record of the meteorological observations was published at Madras in 1848. There is a tea [q.v.] and cinchona [koinah] estate, on the N. slope of Dodabetta; from Ootacamund E. 3 miles; 184 acres.

DODDY (ದೊಡ್ಡಿ - doddi, *Can.*; దొడ్డి - doddi, *Tel.*; தொட்டி - totti, *Tam.*). From (todu, tam. to bind); enclosure. Cattle pound. Suffix in place names, as Nadimidoddy, meaning middle cattle pen.

DODE (దోడు - dódu, *Tel.*). Connected with (tóda, tel. preposition meaning in company with). Protection. Suffix in place names; as Vendode, meaning rear + protection.

DOG (श्वा - shvá, *San.*; कुत्रा - kutrá, *Mahr.*; ನಾಯಿ - náyi, *Can.*; కుక్క - kukka, *Tel.*; നായ - náya, *Mal.*; நாய் - náy, *Tam.*). San. from (shun, san. to go). Common prefix to plant names, following the Dravidian languages, and denoting an inferior species. Examples are, where translation is of second term:—Cleome viscosa (kukkáválu), brassica juncea; (kukkaváminta), gynandropsis pentaphylla; Grewia pilosa (kukkabudda), grewia hirsuta; Ocimum basilicum (kukkatulasi), ocimum sanctum; Trianthema crystallina (kukkapálakúra), oxystelma esculentum. See gloss. paragraphs [nye].——*Dog bane* (قاتل الكلب - kátilulkalb, Ar.); meaning dog killer. Same as Poison nut.——*Dog prick* (நாயுருவி - náyuruvi, Tam.). Title from curved prickles like dog's teeth. Same as Indian burr.——*Dog's tongue* (श्वरसना - shvarasaná, San.). Title from appearance of leaf. Same as Leafy milk hedge.——*Dog umbrella* (کتے کی چھتری - kuttekí-chhatrí, Hind.). Same as Caulaun.

DOKE (ڈوک - dok, *Hind.*; குறவை - kuravai, *Tam.*). Tam. from (kurumai, tam. shortness). The genus Ophiocephalus, ophiocephalidæ [walking fish], acanthopterygii, teleostei, pisces [matsyam, 29], of naturalists [jantoo]. The species best known to the natives are :—gachua [pariah doke], marulius [murrel], punctatus [spotted doke], striatus [pariah murrel]. Cf. also Rock doke, which is another genus.——*Pariah doke* (ڈھیری ڈوک - dherídok, Hind.; ಮಹಾಕೊರವ - mahákorava, Can.; కొరమట్టు - kóramutte, Tel.; ଚେଙ୍ଗ - chenga, Oor.; കരുവ - kuruva, Mal.; කනාය - kanaya, Singh.; பெருங்குறவை - perunguravai, Tam.). Title from dark color. Hind. from (dherí, hind. pariah + dok, hind. ophiocephalus genus); from its voracity. Can. from (maha, san. great + korava, can. ophiocephalus genus). Tel. from (kóra, tel. fang + mutte, tel. clupea longiceps). Mal. from (kuru, mal. small); small fish. Tam. from (perum, tam. big + kuravai, tam. ophiocephalus genus). Tam. also (kizhátti), siluridæ or cat-fish family. Ophiocephalus [doke] gachua, ophiocephalidæ [walking fish], acanthopterygii, teleostei [matsyam, 29], of naturalists. Alias Ophiocephalus coramota et fuscus, kelaartii, koramotta, limbatus, marginatus, montanus. Coramota from teloogoo; kelaartii from tamul; koramotta from teloogoo. Scales broad and irregular on summit of head; four or five rows between orbit and angle of preopercle; twelve between snout and base of dorsal fin. Those on head roughened by circular lines, which externally are parallel with their outer edge, lines on scales of body are in form of arches. Colors differ materially, according to water in which they reside; usually greenish, lighter beneath; dorsal, caudal, and anal slate-colored, with orange margin; pectoral with black base, transversely barred and having a slight reddish or orange edge. In the young there is often large ocellus with light edge on last five dorsal rays; caudal barred. Occasionally it is spotted white, or even orange. Freshwater; often found thriving at the bottom of wells, and in fact may be taken from the waters of the plains on those in very high elevations. It attains at least 13 inches in length, is very voracious, and may often be captured in little water-courses, into which it has pursued the Haplochili and other small fish.——*Rock doke* (गड - gada, San.; मालव्य - málavya, Mahr.; کورافی کھولی - koráfíkhaulí, Hind.; ಪಂಡಿಪಕ್ಕೆ - pandipakke, Can.; கற்குறவை - karguravai, Tam.). Title from clinging to rocks. Can. from (pandi, can. pig + pakke, can. bird); pig-fish. Tam. from (kal, tam. stone + kuravai, tam. ophiocephalus genus). Hind. also (pattharchátá), meaning stone licker. Title otherwise Hill trout, Stone ophiocephalus. Discognathus lamta, cyprininæ, cyprinidæ, physostomi, teleostei [matsyam, 39], of naturalists. Alias Chondrostoma mullya; Cyprinus gotyla, lamta; Discognathus crenulatus, fusiformis, macrochir, rufus, obtusus; Garra alta, ceylonensis, gotyla, lamta, malabarica; Gonorhynchus bimaculatus, brachypterus, caudatus, gotyla, mcclellandi, rupeculus, stenorhynchus; Lobocheilos caudatus, gotyla, lamta; Platycara lissorhynchus, nasuta, notata. Garra from sanscrit. Air-vessel small, its posterior portion minute; ova small, numerous; greenish, with a bluish-green band along centre of body, and extending along middle of caudal fin; generally dark spot behind gill-opening; abdomen yellowish-green; fins yellowish, stained darker at margins; in malabar and canara some have a dark band along the side, with an orange one above and another below it; at least 8 inches in length; putrifies very rapidly after death, and generally dies almost as soon as removed from the water. No other common species here.——*Spotted doke* (پھولڈوک - phúldok, Hind.; ಬೆಳಿಕೊರವ - belikorava, Can.; ముట్టె - mutte, Tel.; ଗୋରିସ୍ସ - gorissa, Oor.; കരുവ - kuruva, Mal.; குறவை - kuravai, Tam.). Title from black spots. Hind. from (phúl, hind. flower + dok, hind. ophiocephalus genus); from spotted fins. Can. from (bili, can. white + korava, can. ophiocephalus genus). Tel. means snout. Tam. from (kurumai, tam. shortness). Title otherwise Black caboose. Resembles the varaul, but is only a quarter of its size. Ophiocephalus [doke] punctatus, ophiocephalidæ [walking fish], acanthopterygii, teleostei [matsyam, 29], of naturalists. Alias Ophiocephalus affinis, indicus, karrouvei, lata. Karrouvei from tamul. Lower jaw the longer. Scales on summit of head large and irregular; twelve rows between snout and origin of dorsal fin; five rows between eye and angle of opercle. Those on top of head roughened in lines parallel with their outer edges, but on body are more horizontal. Colors vary with water they reside. Back greenish, yellow on sides and abdomen, with dark stripe along side of head; several bands from back pass downwards to middle of body. Fins spotted, caudal and vertical with narrow light edge, and dark basal band; ventrals white or gray. Some have scattered black spots over body and head, and this appears most common near the sea, and in the breeding season, whilst they are absent from the young. Freshwaters, generally in the plains, preferring the stagnant to the running. Foot or a little more in length.

DOLE (ढोल - dhóla, *San.*; ڈھول - dhol, *Hind.*; డోలు - dólu, *Tel.*; തവിൽ - tavil, *Mal.*; தவில் - tavil, *Tam.*). A large drum [paray] both sides covered with leather [chamrah] and played upon with the hands [sangeetam].

DOLPHIN (دلفین - dulfín, *Hind.*). The sea mammal so called [cadalpundry].——*Dolphin fish* (دلفین - dulfín, Ar.; خوک ماهی - khokmáhí, Pers.; سورمچھی - súwarmaçchí, Hind.). Pers. from (khok, pers. hog + máhí, pers. fish). Hind. from (súwar, hind. hog + maçchí, hind. fish). Coryphæna hippurus, coryphænidæ, acanthopterygii, teleostei [matsyam, 18], of naturalists [jantoo]. Alias Coryphæna chrysurus, dolfyn, dorado, japonica; Lampugus pelagica, immaculatus; dolfyn from arabic. Body elongated and compressed; occipital crest well developed. Cleft of mouth oblique, lower jaw longer. Lateral-line curved to opposite end of pectoral, from whence it goes straight to centre of caudal. Back grayish, shot with gold; abdomen golden, covered with blue spots, which become black after death; dorsal fin light blue at base, becoming black towards summit. Sea; 5 feet or more in length; common in Madras, and eaten by natives. No other common species here.——*Dolphin's nose* (డాల్ఫినగ్రము - dálp'hinuagramu, Tel.; மூக்குமலை - múkkumalai, Tam.). From (múkku, tam. nose + malai, tam. hill).—"*a*" Promontory; Vizagapatam dist., Vizagapatam division; lat. 17° 41′; long. 83° 20′; from Vizagapatam S. 1 mile. At southern entrance of Vizagapatam harbour forming, with ruined town on it, a conspicuous landmark to mariners. The light, formerly shown here, was destroyed in the cyclone of 1876 and has not been replaced. A flag is hoisted every morning at 8 A.M. and lowered at 9 A.M. to indicate correct time to the shipping in the roads. The remains of an old Dutch fort exist on its northern face.—"*b*" Hill; Neilgherry dist., Paranginaud division; lat. 11° 22′; long. 76° 54′; from Coonoor E.N.E. 4½ miles. Promontory above Kotagherry gorge. View of Catherine falls and plains of Coimbatore and Salem.

DOMBA (තෙල්දොඹ - teldomba, *Singh.*). Poon [q.v.] oil.

DOMBAR (ڈومرا - domrá, *Hind.*). From (dommi, tel. a multitude). A wandering tribe. Men and women are singers and gymnastic performers; usually possess cattle [maud] and asses [gadhah], but do not engage in the carrying trade; traffic in pigs [soor] and asses, and sell mats [boriyah], baskets [tokrah], and combs; travel with portable huts resembling the top of a country cart; eat all sorts of flesh and usually wear heavy cloths; some are agricultural laborers. They worship Polairamma. Numbers about 12,000 [jauty].

DONA (దొన - dona, *Tel.*). Sacred pool in hills [teertam].

DONEY (దోనె - dóne, *Tel.*; தறிமரம் - tarimaram, *Tam.*). Title from teloogoo. Tam. from (tari, tam. loom + maram, tam. wood). Tam. also (páççutti), meaning warp + roller. Distinguish from Dhony [q.v.]. A wooden revolving bar, round which the woven cloth is wound; opposite of the warp-beam or mady cumboo [nesavoo].

DONKA (దొంక - donka, *Tel.*). From (donku, tel. to be depressed). Pathway.

DOOB (دوب - dúb, *Hind.*). From (durv, san. to hurt); from sharp grass blades [doorvay]. Same as Hurrially. Distinguish from Daub [q.v.].——*White doob* (வெள்ளறுகு - vellarugu, Tam.). Same as Small chiretta.

DOODH (دودھ - dúdh, *Hind.*). From (dugdha, san. milk). Milk [paul]. Very common plant term. Compare:—Holarrhena antidysenterica (dúdhíkílakrí), milk stick; Oxystelma esculentum (dúdhlatá), milk creeper; Tabernæmontana coronaria (dúdhmográ), milk jasmine. See also Euphorbia thymifolia, Ichnocarpus frutescens, Wrightia tomentosa. See gloss. paragraphs.——*Doodhy opium* (دودھی افیم - dúdhiafím, Dec.). Title from large quantity of milky juice. Soft, dark in color and weaker than Malwah opium [aphainam].——*Doogdhyam* (दुग्ध्य - dugdhya, San.). From (duh, san. to milk). Butter. Doogdhya krishnan is an epithet of krishnan in one of his manifestations, when he is induced by his mother Yashoday to eat butter while in the act of crawling.

DOODOOGA (हूम - hûm, *Mahr.*; దుద్దుగ - dudduga, *Tel.*; நெட்டனாரட்டி - nettanáratti, *Tam.*). Tam. from (nedu, tam. tall + nár, tam. fibre). Tel. also (chilakaduduga), meaning parrot + the plant; (chittaduduga), meaning small + the plant. Tam. also (núlilaimaram), meaning thread + leaf + tree. Botanically Polyalthia cerasoides, benth. & h. f., anonaceæ [vricsham, 4]. Alias Guatteria cerasoides; Uvaria cerasoides. Tree; leaves oblong or lanceolate, acute, pubescent beneath; flower bearing shoots almost abortive; lateral ones leafless; peduncles solitary, terminal, with one or two bracteas at their base; calycine lobes nearly as long as the corolla; petals equal, oval, oblong, thick, carpels globose, dark red, size of a cherry [auloo], on stalks nearly twice their length; a moderate-sized tree; flowers in hot months; flowers fragrant, greenish. Wood olive-grey, moderately hard, close-grained. Other species are:—Coffeoides, coffee [q.v.] plant; abundant in wynaud; in flower at all seasons; young leaves come out, brilliant red color; coorumbars make ropes from bark, which when fresh has strong smell of ammonia; soft wood. Fragrans, fragrant doodooga or parrot doodooga, malabar. Korinti, climbing shrub; malabar, tanjore, courtallam. Longifólia [ashocam]. Persicæfolia. Rufescens. Suberosa, tree; flowers small greenish-white; flowering throughout year; wood close, tough, durable.——*Black doodooga* (گیدڑروکھ - gídarrúkh, Hind.; నల్లదుద్దుగ - nalladudduga, Tel.). Hind. from (gídar, hind. jackal + rúkh, hind. tree). Tel. from (nalla, tel. black + dudduga, tel. the plant, polyalthia cerasoides, bth. and hook. f.). Tel. also (peddachilakadudduga), meaning large + parrot + the plant, polyalthia cerasoides, bth. and hook. f. Botanically Miliusa velutina, hook. f. and th., anonaceæ [vricsham, 4]. Alias Uvaria velutina, villosa. Tree, with densely tomentose branches; leaves small, ovate or oblong, acuminated, cordate at the base, densely velvety beneath; peduncles branched; pedicels three to six slender, elongated, densely tomentose, without bracts; sepals tomentose; outer petals resembling the sepals, inner ones broad-ovate, tomentose without, dark-brown and somewhat glabrous within; ovaries velvety; carpels pubescent, short-pedicelled, baccate, black; seeds one to two; flowering in march and april. Wood yellow when fresh cut, grey or greyish-brown when dry; moderately hard. Other common species are:—indica, nilagirica, wightiana.

DOODY (దుడ్డు - duddu, Tel.; துட்டு - tuttu, Tam.). From (dvi, san. two) [do, dwau, dwi]. Ancient copper coin. An old scale is:—10 cash = 1 doody, 8 doodies = 1 fanam, 45 fanams = 1 pagoda. A more modern scale is:—2 dooggaunies = 1 doody, 3 doodies = 1 anna [naunyam, 2 a, b, c]. Approximate actual value, 1 doody = 4 pies. No coin of the name current. At Madras equal to 2 pies and same as dooggauny. Same as Tel. dub. See vol. I, 609.

DOODY (దూది - dúdi, Tel.). Cotton [q.v.] wool [punj]. Distinguish from Doodh.——*Doodeycootam* (దూదేకుల - dúdékula, obl., Tel.). From (above + éku, tel. to clean). A class of Mussalmans who clean cotton [jauty].——*Doody paula* (దూదిపాల - dúdipála, Tel.). Cotton + milk plant. Plant name common to:—Dregia volubilis; Oxystelma esculentum. See gloss. paragraphs.

DOOGARAUZPATAM (దుగరాజపట్నము - dugarájapatnamu, Tel. dugarázpatnam*) [dhroovam]. From (dhruvarádzu, tel. a king + pattana, san. town). Tel. also (svarnamukhidugarája-patnamu), as being near mouth of Swarnamookhy. Sanscrit name (dhruvarájapattana); also (yuvarájapattana), meaning heir apparent + town. Village, Port; Nellore dist.; Goodoor tal.; pop. 2,598; acres 8,313; lat. 13° 59′; long. 80° 12′; from Goodoor E.S.E. 23¾ miles; from Madras N. 61 miles; from Nellore S.S.E. 35 miles; from Poody N.N.W. 9½ miles; from Toopily S.E. 4½ miles. Called Armegam by the English. On the Coromandel coast [q.v.], on the western shore of the northern inlet forming communication between Poolicat lake and the Bay of Bengal, nine miles south of the embouchure of the Swarnamookhy. South-east of the outward or seaward mouth of the inlet is Blackwood harbour. Armegam shoal shelters it in certain directions, while Poody point and shoal and the mainland protect it on other points; so that ships might, if they chose, lie here in safety. It is the only place on the Coromandel coast which offers any real protection to ships during an easterly gale. During the north-east monsoon [q.v.], the sea breaks very high on the shallow ridge of the shoal, rendering the harbour within comparatively smooth. One of the earliest English possessions on the Coromandel coast. In February 1625, the East india company established a factory, the ground being obtained from the Rajah of Vencatagherry by the local Curnum [q.v.] or Canoongo [q.v.] patnaswaumoola, armoogam moodelly, after whom the factory [aurang] was called. On the 24th September 1861 on the removal of the establishment to Chennacooppam [q.v.], the modern Madras, the place was abandoned. On the 31st July 1801 it was ceded with the rest of the Carnatic [q.v.] to the East india company by His Highness Prince Azeem ood dowla, Nawaub [q.v.] soobahdar [q.v.] of Arcot. Old fort. Formerly the chief of a group of small ports lying near Armegam lighthouse, but the export trade by sea has gone down. Trade with Madras, now carried on by canal, consists of grain and firewood and sometimes cured fish. It still possesses a customs station and a travellers' bungalow. The salt manufactured here is of some repute. Armegam lighthouse is five miles distant. Trig. station at the Traveller's bungalow; lat. 13° 59′ 3·51″; long. 80° 12′ 1·13″; from Goodoor E.S.E. 24 miles; from Pambaly N.N.W. 4½ miles; from the sea W. ½ mile. A flagstaff has lately been erected to mark the site of this ancient English settlement.

DOOKKAR (ڈکر - dukkar, Hind.). Corruption of (shúkara, san. hog). Wild hog; term of abuse [soor].

DOOKKY (దుక్కి - dukki, Tel.). From (dunnu, tel. to plough). A ploughing. Rain is measured by this; equivalent to an inch [q.v.] of rain [mazhay]. Padoonoo [q.v.] is more.

DOOMAGOODEM (దుమ్ముగూడెము - dummagúdemu, Tel.). From (dummu, tel. dust + gúdemu, tel. village). Braminical tradition that Rama fought here with Raucshasans and the dust obscured the sky. Zemindarry, Village, Head-quarters of a sub-divisional officer D.P.W.; Godavery dist., Bhadrachellam tal.; pop. 2,475; lat. of village 17° 52′; long. 80° 56′; from Bhadrachellam N. 13 miles; from Cocanada W.N.W. 108 miles. On the Godavery. Until recently head-quarters of the Upper godavery engineering works. The first barrier on the Godavery is here. An account of the anicut [q.v.] works now in abeyance will be found in a foot-note to the article on Public Works, Buildings and Roads, in vol. I, chapter IV. There is considerable timber trade. Branch head-quarter station of Church mission society.

DOOMPA (దుంప - dumpa, Tel.). Tuberous root [gaddah]. Compare:—Dioscorea glabra (éddutókadumpa), ox tail tuber; Dioscorea pentaphylla (pandimukkudumpa), pig's nose tuber; Habenaria platyphylla (tsukkadumpa), spotted tuber; Helmia dæmona (pulidumpa), tiger tuber; Methonica superba (pottidumpa), stunted tuber. See gloss. paragraphs.

DOON (دون - dún, Hind.). A valley [cona].

DOOR (दुर् - dur, San.). Difficult; bad.——*Doorga* (दुर्गा - durgá, San.; துர்க்கை - turkkai, Tam.). From (above + gam, san. to go). Means inaccessible.—"a" δημήτηρ of Greeks; Ceres of Romans; Isis of Egyptians. A Shacty [q.v.] or wife of Shiva, but often identified with the village goddess of this country. She is represented with a sheep's head, standing on the giant Simhamookhasooran or the lion-faced, whom she killed, though as often as his head was severed from his body a new one sprang up. Her head is fiery and adorned with different jewels. On her forehead she wears a crescent made with sacred ashes [vibhooty] of burnt cow-dung [shauny]. In five of her six hands she holds respectively, a ring, a sword, a trident, a goad, and a skull. Doorga was the daughter of the giantess Mahamye and the sage Çashyapan. She has various names, for instance:—Ajomookhy or the sheep-headed, Ayyay or mistress, Bhagavaty or goddess, Neely or the blue one, Showry or heroine, Shooly or she who holds a trident, Soondary or the beautiful, Vaulgeicondole or she who holds a sword, &c. Her pagodas [q.v.] correspond to those of Ayenaur [ayen], and the principal images in them, besides her own, are of Vigneshwaran [q.v.], Veerabhadran [q.v.], and Bhadra cauly [q.v.]. The Poojarry [q.v.] makes offerings every Friday. He receives also offerings brought in fulfilment of vows. The annual festival is like those of other Graumadevatays [q.v.]. She is, like Chamoondy [q.v.], supposed to give valour and to assist in the practice of the black art. Distinguished by her fair complexion from the black Bhadra cauly. See vol. I (73), (78) [matam].—"b" Name common to both sexes especially with Pariahs [peyar]. Similarly Doorgaprasaud, from (prasáda, san. favor), one who has doorga's favor; Doorgauchellam, from (achala san. hill); Doorgojee, from (jí, hind. master).——*Doorgam* (दुर्ग - durga, San.). Means inaccessible. Defile, gorge. Mountain fortress, castle. Common suffix in place names in the form of droog [q.v.].——*Doorga navamy* (దుర్గనవమి - durganavami, Tel.). Means the goddess + ninth day. Lunar festival [pundigay, 3a], subject to intercalation. The ninth lunar day of the waxing moon of the eighth lunar month Caurteecam [mausam], between 25th October and 25th November. Sacred to Doorga. Anniversary of the beginning of the Krityoog. Same as Krityoogaudy.——*Doorga poojay* (దుర్గపూజ - durgapuja, Tel.). Means Doorga worship [pundigay, 6a]. Same as Dusserah.——*Dooryodhanan* (दुर्योधन - duryódhana, San.). From (above + yudh, san. to fight). The eldest son of Dhritaraushtran, who fought with the Pandavas [mahabhaurat].

DOORAST (درست - durust, Hind.). Persian. In repair [shikast].

DOORVAY (दूर्वा - dúrva, San.). From (durv, san. to hurt); from sharp blades of grass [doob]. Same as Hurrially [q.v.].

DOOTAN (दूत - dúta, San.). From (du, san. to go). A messenger of the gods [ganam]. The Gana nautans or Dootans are divided into three classes:—Shivadootans or shiva's messengers; Vishnoo dootans or vishnoo's messengers; Yamadootans or yaman's messengers. The Shivadootans are represented as red, short, and thick, like bhootams; their hair-locks, twisted together, rest on their heads like a cap; from their mouths project two large lion's teeth; they have four hands, in which they hold respectively, a snake, a cord, a trident, and a wine-jug; their body is covered with various ornaments; by these eeshwaran [q.v.] fetches the souls of his devotees at death to keilausam [q.v.] in a pooshpacávimaunam or self-moving chariot. The Vishnoodootans have their hair dressed like the shivadootans, and also like them have lion's teeth; otherwise they resemble vishnoo; that is to say they are of blue color; wear the tirnaumam [q.v.] on their forehead, arms, and breasts; wear round their necks a rosary of toolsimany [q.v.]; and hold in their four hands respectively, a chunk [q.v.], a chuckram [q.v.], a battle-axe, and a club; through these vishnoo fetches his devotees to veicoontam [q.v.]. The Yamadootans are painted quite black, with horrible faces and large teeth; in their hands they carry a trident, a club and ropes; and in their girdles, daggers; their business is to carry the souls of the wicked into naracam [q.v.], where there are two hundred and eighty millions of places of torture; but they cannot lay hold on any one before his fixed period of life is elapsed, and the souls of the pious they cannot touch. When such die as are neither virtuous nor wicked, the messengers of yaman and those of shiva or vishnoo come into conflict with each other, each party claiming the indifferent souls [matam, samsauram].

DOOTTALORE (దుత్తలూరు - duttalúru, *Tel.*). From (dutta, tel. pot + úru, tel. village). Village; Nellore dist., Oodayagherry tal.; pop. 3,459; acres 18,835; lat. 14° 51′; long. 79° 27′; from Nellore N.W. 47 miles; from Oodayagherry E. 7 miles; from Madras N.W. 137 miles. Largest village in the talook [q.v.]. Trade in indigo [q.v.]. Zonna [cholum] cultivated. Soil fertile, black clay [calimunn]. Small hill on west of village. Four tanks in a line.

DORAY (ಧೊರೆ - dhore, *Can.*; దొర - dora, *Tel.*; துரை turai, *Tam.*). Ruler; master [ayyan, iyen]. With the Tamul and Teloogoo races is equivalent to the English words, sir, master, and to the Arabic sahib [q.v.]. Both in its singular and plural forms it is a title of the Conda dora, the chieftains in the mountains of Goomsoor. Suffix and prefix in Tamul proper names [peyar].——*Chinnadoray* (சின்னத்துரை - shinnathurai, Tam.). Young gentleman, term for junior officers.——*Doragauroo* (దొరగారు - doragáru, Tel.). From (above + gáru, tel. honorific plural suffix). Honorific of doray, applied to Europeans especially [sahib].——*Dorasauny* (దొరసాని - dorasáni, Tel.; துரைசானி - turaisáni, Tam.). From (above + sáni, tel. wife). Lady.——*Dorasawmy* (துரைசாமி - turaisámi, Tam.). From (above + svámí, san. lord). Familiarly Doratchy. Hindoo 2nd or pers. name [peyar].——*Doraycunnan* (துரைக்கண்ணன் - turaikkannan, Tam.). From (above + kan, tam. eye); as precious as the master's eye. Hindoo 2nd or pers. name. Common among non-bramins [peyar].——*Dorayraghavan* (துரைராகவன் - turairágavan, Tam.). From (above + rághava, san. ráma of the line of raghu). Hindoo 2nd or pers. name [peyar].

DORIYAH (ڈوریا - doriyá, *Hind.*). From (dorí, hind. string). A striped muslin [charkhauny, sheelay].

DORNAUL (దోరణాల - dóranála, *Tel.*). From (tórana, san. outer entrance of a city) [toranam]. From its being considered one of the entrances of the temple of Srisheilam.—"*a*" Village; Kurnool dist., Marcapore tal.; pop. 1,814; acres 5,979; lat. 15° 55′; long. 79° 08′; from Kurnool E. 69 miles; from Marcapore N.W. 16 miles. At E. entrance of Muntraula canama pass, which is also known under this name. Formerly seat of a poligar [q.v.]. Descendant of the family still resides at Bommalaupooram.—"*b*" Ghaut; Nellore dist., Oodayagherry tal.; lat. 14° 41′; long. 79° 14′; from Nellore N.W. 58 miles; from Oodayagherry S.W. 15 miles. Pass over the Eastern ghauts [q.v.]. The main road to Cuddapah from Nellore and the coast is through it. The road from Nellore to the ghaut [q.v.] is 58 miles in length, and the distance beyond to Cuddapah is 52 miles. Carts are allowed to pass only in the day.

DOROOVOO (درو - darú, *Hind.*; దొరువు - dóruvu, *Tel.*; துரவு - turavu, *Tam.*). From (travvu, tel. to dig) [toorvoo]. A large well [bhauvy] made by excavating the sand [manal]. Seen in casuarina [chowkmaram] plantations. Dorvy is another form.

DOSS (ದಾಸ - dás, *Can.*; దాసుడు dásudu, *Tel.*). From (dása, san. slave) [dausan]. Slave, worshipper. Originally affixed to names of Canyasts and Shoodras, but now common among all castes. Hindoo third name [peyar.]——*Ramdoss* (రామదాసుడు - rámadásudu, Tel.). One who adores Rama [peyar].

DOST (دوست - dost, *Pers.*). Friend. Prefixed to an alam forms a lacab; as Dost ally, friend of ally. Shiah name [ism]. A Dost ally was second Nawaub [q.v.] of the Carnatic [q.v.] from 1732 to 1740; killed in 1740 in an action with the Mahrattas who had invaded the Carnatic [charitram].

DOWGAUM (దవుగాం - davugám, *Tel.*). From (dhau, cor. red soil + gám, cor. village). Village; Ganjam dist., Zemindarry tract tal., Dhauracote estate; lat. 19° 39′; long. 84° 30′; from Chetterpore W.N.W. 40 miles; from Russellcondah S.S.W. 22 miles. Near junction of Sooradah and Shergadah roads at 2 miles from Aska. Rooshcoolya project head-quarters.

DOWLA (دوله - daulah, *Ar.*). Empire. Lacab suffix of Field marshals under the Abbaside caliphs. Since become common; as Itibar ood dowlah, confidant of the empire [ism].——*Dowlat* (دولت - daulat, Hind.). Pers. form of above. Dowlat row a common Mahratta name.——*Dowlatabad* (دولت آباد - daulatábád, Hind.). From (daulat, ar. prosperity + ábád, pers. city). Town, Head-quarters of Tahsildar and Sub-registrar; Salem dist., Krishnagherry tal.; pop. 3,345; acres 306; lat. 12° 31′; long. 78° 16′; from Krishnagherry S.S.E. 1½ miles; from Salem N. 59 miles. Also known as New krishnagherry. The country around is level. Chetties and weavers predominate. Car festival of Navaneeta krishnasawmy [doogdhya krishnan] in May lasts for ten days.

DOWLAISHWERAM (ధవళేశ్వరము - dhavaléshvaramu, *Tel.* dowlaishweram *). From (dhavala, san. white + íshvara, san. lord). Sanscrit name (dhavalagiri), meaning white + mountain. Town, Head-quarters of Superintending Engineer; Godavery dist., Rajahmundry tal.; pop. 10,492; acres 1,869; lat. 16° 56′; long. 81° 49′; from Cocanada W. 30 miles; from Rajahmundry S. 4 miles. At the bifurcation of the Godavery, where the great anicut, 1,400 yards long, was constructed in 1848. Connected with the coast at several points by numerous navigable canals of the Godavery irrigation system and also with Madras through the Kistna system and the Buckingham canal [q.v.]. During the construction of the anicut, Dowlaishweram, as the head-quarters of the Sappers and Miners and a large Engineering staff, was of much importance. Government workshops now. During the wars between the Saitoopaties of Rajahmundry and the Mahomedan rulers of Ellore in the fifteenth and sixteenth centuries, Dowlaishweram was the scene of frequent struggles. Houses of former European residents, built on hills in the neighbourhood, are now in ruins. Quarries of good building stone are worked largely. Close to the town are the ruins of a fort built by the Chalookya vijayauadityan; on the top of a small hill called Dhavalagherry is the temple of Janardana sawmy facing the Godavery.

DOWLE (ڈول - daul, *Hind.*). Mode, manner. An estimate, especially of probable revenue. As applied to abkarry [q.v.] means an agreement between a wholesale renter and his shop-keeper by which the latter agrees to take a certain quantity of spirits for sale each month. Distinguish from Cowle.——*Dowle vasool bauky* (ڈول وصول باقی - daulwasúlbákí, Hind.). Demand, collection, and balance [jumma vasool bauky], the common account rendered of revenue officers.

DOZAK (دوزخ - dozakh, *Hind.*). Hell. The Mahomedans reckon seven hells:—Jahannam a deep pit, destined for such of the worshippers of the true God as are guilty; Lazah or blazing flame, for the Christians; Hootama or intense fire, for the Jews; Saur or flaming fire, for the Sabians; Sakar or scorching heat, for the Magi or Gabars or fire worshippers; Jaheem or large hot fire, for the pagans and idolators; Hauviya or dark bottomless pit, for hypocrites. For heaven see Bheest.

DRAGOMAN (ترجمان - tarjumán, *Hind.*). Title from (tarjamah, ar. to interpret); g is soft. An interpreter [doobash].

DRAGON'S BLOOD (खड्गमृगरक्त - kadgamrigarakta, *San.*; دم الاخوين - dammulakhwain, *Ar.*; خون سیاوشان - khúnisiyáwashán, *Pers.*; دم الاخوين - dammulakhwain, *Hind.* and *Dec.*; ಖಡ್ಗಮೃಗನೆತ್ತರು - khadgamriganettaru, *Can.*; ಖಡ್ಗಮೃಗನೆತ್ತರು - khadgamriganetteru, *Too.*; ఖడ్గమృగం నెత్తురు - khadgamrigamnetturu, *Tel.*; காண்டாமிருகரத்தம் - kándámirugarattam, *Tam.*). Title from size and appearance of tree and color of resin. San. from (khadgamriga, san. sword beast, rhinoceros + rakta, san. blood). Ar. from (damm, ar. blood + akhwain, ar. two brothers). Pers. from (khún, pers. blood + siyáwash, pers. father of cyrus); in allusion to his love for his step-mother. Hind. from arabic. Can. from (khadgamriga, san. rhinoceros + nettaru, can. blood). Too. from canarese. Tel. from (khadgamriga, san. rhinoceros + netturu, tel. blood). Ar. also (dammussubán), meaning dragon's blood; (dammuttinnín), meaning dragon's blood; (káteruddamm), meaning blood-dropping gum. Pers. also (azhdahákhún). Hind. also (indarume); (hírádukhí); (rangbarat). To be distinguished from the Gum dragon or Tragacanth [kateerah]. Greek κιννάβαρι ἰνδικὸν; the mineral cinnabar, with which this vegetable product was thus confounded, is the red sulphuret of mercury [shangarf]. Latin Sanguis draconis. Title otherwise Blood-shedding tree, Brother's blood, Cyrus blood, Rhinoceros blood. The produce of:—Calamus draco, willd., a species of rattan [q.v.] palm [taur] of the eastern archipelago; Pterocarpus draco, linn., allied to the indian kino tree or pterocarpus marsupium, roxb. [common vengay], of south india; Dracæna draco, linn., a liliaceous tree of madeira and the canary islands. An inodorous, insipid resin [gond, raul] or coloring principle, obtained from the surface of the ripe fruit; color in lump is dark-brown-red; in powder, bright red; friable; of shining fracture; contains benzoic acid [saumbrauny poo]; insoluble in water, but readily soluble in alcohol, ether and oils [yennay]. Discarded medicine by european practitioners; veidyans [q.v.], recommend solution in arrack [q.v.] as external application to head and temples in syncope. Employed as a coloring matter [shauyam], as an ingredient in varnishes [rangh] and in the composition of tooth-powder; used for preparing gold lacquer, for staining marble.——*Indian dragon's blood* (గండామృగంనెత్తురుచెట్టు - gándámrigamnetturuchettu, Tel.). Same as Common vengay.——*Madeira dragon's blood* (دم التنين اندلوسی - dammuttinniniandalusí, Pers.). From dracæna draco.——*Socotra dragon's blood* (دم التنين سقوطری - dammuttinnínisokotrí, Pers.). From pterocarpus draco.——*Sumatra dragon's blood* (دم التنين سماترا - dammuttinninisumátrá, Hind.). From calamus draco.

DRAVIDA (द्रविड - dravida, *San.*). The equivalence of the words Drávida and Tamul [q.v.] has been proposed. It is not improbable considering the surd character of the last letter in தமிழ். Both will then be identical with the Διμυρική of Ptolemy. No other etymology is known.—"*a*" Early Sanscrit name for the Tamul people, their language, and their country. In later

Sanscrit a generic name for all South indian peoples, &c., showing that the Aryans then regarded them as allied. Menoo does not realize the aboriginal nature of the Dravidians, but says :—"The following tribes of Cshatriyas have gradually sunk "into the state of Vrishalans from the extinction of sacred rites "and from having no communication with Bramins, viz., "Powndracas, Odras, Dravidas, Cambojas, Yavanas, Shaucas, "Pauradas, Pahlavas, Cheenas, Kirautans, Daradas, and Kha-"shas." Varauha mihirau places the Dravidas in the south-west, but mentions also an eastern half of the Dravidas. The distinction is evidently between the west and east coast civilizations. Dravidam is spoken of in the Brihat samhitay [q.v.] of Varauha mihiran as being divided into Cholam, Paundyam, Keralam, Carnautacam, Calingam, and Andhram. Comaurila bhatt calls the language of the south Andhrádravidabhashay, joining the Teloogoos to the Tamuls [puncha dravidam].—"*b*" Modern authorities make twelve divisions. The four chief being :—Tamul, spoken in paundyam, cholam, and eastern keralam [q.v.], i.e., throughout the central and southern districts of the presidency ; teloogoo, the language of the calingam and andhram countries, or the mahomedan telingana [q.v.], the british northern circars [q.v.] ; malayalam, spoken in western keralam, i.e., malabar, travancore, and cochin ; and canarese, in carnautacam [q.v.], or canara, mysore, and a few tracts of the wynaud and coimbatore. Tooloo is spoken round Mangalore and in Coorg. The other six are uncultivated dialects of hill-tribes. The dravidian languages are distinct in the same way as spanish from portuguese, irish from welsh, hebrew from aramaic, hindee from bengallee.—"*c*" The Dravidian languages have adopted sanscrit words in different proportions. Of the cultivated dravidian languages, the percentage of sanscrit words is smallest in tamul and greatest in malayalam ; the proportion is less in teloogoo than in canarese ; in teloogoo about half the vocabulary consists of sanscrit words, either pure or modified. In the newer Dravidian tongues composition is regarded as refined in language in proportion to the amount of Sanscrit. In Tamul poetry the reverse holds good. In this few Bramins have written anything worthy of preservation. The language has been cultivated and developed with immense zeal and success by Tamulian shoodras, and the highest rank in Tamul literature which has been reached by a Bramin is that of a commentator.—"*d*" The whole of the ethnological portion of this work is devoted to showing that the Dravidians are a totally distinct nationality. See in particular vol. I (33), (42). As illustrating their indifference however to everything lying outside their own sphere and interests, and to comparative philology, it is noticeable that no term belonging to the Dravidian languages themselves has ever been used to designate all the members of the nation [bhaushay].——*Dravida bramin* (द्रविड-ब्राह्मण - dravidabráhmana, San.).—"*a*" Bramins are classed historically or theoretically under two great divisions, named Gowda and Dravida, each of which consists of five tribes. These are mostly separated by geographical boundaries. The following is the Sanscrit shlocam usually quoted :—महाराष्ट्रांध्र द्राविडाः कर्णाटश्चैव गुर्ज्जराः द्राविडाः पंचधा प्रोक्ता विंध्यदक्षिणवासिनः सारस्वताः कान्यकुब्जा गौडोत्कल मैथिलाः गौडाः पंचविधा प्रोक्ता विंध्यादुत्तरवासिनः—Dravidas live south of the Vindhya range and consist of fiv etribes, Maharashtra [mahratta], Andhra [teloogoo], Dravida [tamul], Carnauta [canarese], and Goorjara [goozeratty] ; Gowdas inhabit the north and are divided into Sauraswata of the concans, Caunyacoobja, Gowda, Ootcala [ooriya], Meitila of upper Bengal. The river Nerbudda in Central india is commonly regarded as a geographical line of demarcation between the two. The former are of greater antiquity than the latter.—"*b*" The Gowdas consist of these tribes ; Caunyacoobja, Gowda proper, Meitila, Ootcala, Saraswat. The Dravidas consist of these tribes ; Carnauta, Dravida proper, Goorjara, Maharashtra, Telinga. The Caunyacoobja bramins belong to the old kingdom of Canouj, and are found dispersed over a large portion of the North-western provinces, as far as Benares, where they are very numerous ; the Saraswat bramins are in the North-west of India ; the Gowdas proper are found in the vicinity of Delhi and in Bengal ; the Meitilas inhabit the northern part of Behar ; the Ootcalas have their home in Orissa. The Maharashtras belong to the Mahratta country ; the Telingas to Telingana ; the Dravidas to the tamul-speaking districts ; the Carnautas to the upland Carnatic ; the Goorjaras to Goozerat. Besides these main tribes there are twenty-five supplementary tribes.—"*c*" Although some of these tribes may partake of cooked food together, none intermarry. The five Gowda tribes are entirely distinct from one another, both in regard to marriage and eating food ; and are likewise, in these respects, distinct from the five tribes of Southern bramins. The five Dravidas are not quite so exclusive in their relations to one another. None of them intermarry ; nevertheless four out of the five can eat together, the Maharashtra, Telinga, Dravida, and Carnauta ; none of these however eat with the Goorjara tribe, owing to certain peculiarities in this tribe not found in the rest. Gowdas partake freely of the flesh of many animals, but Dravida bramins do not eat animal food of any kind. The supplementary tribes keep themselves aloof from one another and from all other tribes.—"*d*" The sectarian divisions are practically more operative than any of the above tribal divisions. The following are sects among Dravida bramins, viz. :—Caupaulica or followers of bheiravan a son of shiva, Gaunapatya or followers of ganesh, Shaucta or followers of doorga, Shreeveishnava of ramaunoojan, Smarta, Madhwa, Sowrah or followers of soorya. Caupaulican, Gaunapatyan, Shauctan, and Sowrah, are not to be found at all in a body in Southern india. For the other heads see the heads in this glossary.—"*e*" Also as Dravidas proper, a designation of a branch of Smarta bramins themselves, a division of the general Dravidas. See Bramin [jauty].——*Dravida desham* (द्रविडदेश - dravidadésha, San.). Country of the Dravidian languages. The Southern peninsula of India. One of Hwen Thsang's divisions of S. india, Ta-lo-pi-cha in Chinese writing. Its capital, Kien-chi-pu-lo, or Canchipoora, or Conjeeveram. Regarding the history of the ancient Dravidian dynasties, nothing can be added to what is stated in vol. I (115) to (132) [charitram].——*Dravidam* (द्रविड - dravida, San.). Tamul country.——*Dravida prabandham* (द्राविडप्रबन्ध - drávidaprabandha, San.). From (prabandha, san. composition). Same as Tirvyemozhy, Veishnava work.——*Dravira* (द्राविर - drávira, San.). Bengalee form of Dravida.——*Puncha dravidam* (पञ्चद्राविड - pañchadravida, San.). In opposition to Puncha gowdam ; the five great ancient kingdoms south of the Vindhya mountains, or Dravida, Carnauta, Goozerat, Maharashtra, Telinga. So in languages the colloquial languages of India are divided by the Sanscrit pundits into two classes, each containing five dialects. These dialects are denominated respectively the five Gowdas and the five Dravidas. By the Gowda languages are meant the Bhaushays, or popular dialects of N. india, at the head of which stands the Bengalee, the Gowda proper. The five Dravidas are the Telinga, Carnautaca, Mahratta, Goorjara, and Dravida or Tamul proper. The Mahratta and Goorjara languages are erroneously included in this enumeration, if any attention is to be paid to structural considerations ; in that respect they belong to the northern group [bhaushay].

DRAVYAM (द्रव्य - dravya, *San.*). From (dru, san. to go) [draucshay, drauvacam]. Literally a liquid.—"*a*" Elementary substance, the first category. Nine kinds of Dravyam are usually enumerated, viz. :—pritivy, earth ; ap, water ; tejas, fire ; vayoo, air ; aucausham, ether ; caulam, time ; dic, space ; autman, soul ; manas, mind. The first five of these are the material world. The Jeinas reckon only six dravyams, viz. :—jeevam, soul ; dharmam, virtue ; adharmam, vice ; poodgalam, matter ; caulam, time ; aucausham, space. For category, see Padaurtam ; for elementary substance, see present head ; for matter, see Bhootam ; for organic and inorganic, see Indriyam and Anindriyam ; for organic kingdom, see Ganam [jantoo, vricsham] ; for organic class, see Vargam ; for organic order, see Santaunam ; for organic family, see Coolam ; for organic genus, see Jauty ; for organic species, see Bhaidam. Oopa prefixed to either of the above means a sub-head. For inorganic minerals, see Dhautoo.—"*b*" Wealth. Puncha dravyam are five sources productive of wealth, viz., from mountains, forests, fields, towns, and the sea ; and each of those again yield five kinds.——*Draucshay* (द्राक्षा - drákshá, San.). From (dru, san. to run) [drauvacam, dravyam] ; from juice. Title otherwise Vine. Botanically the Vitis genus, ampelideæ [vriosham, 42]. Sarmentose shrubs ; climbing, usually by means of leaf-opposed tendrils, rarely rooting ; leaves of some simple, undivided or variously lobed ; of others compound ; flowers small greenish and in leaf-opposed panicles ; berry ovoid or globose. The species best known to the natives are :—auriculata [vegetable nerinjy], carnosa [acid naralay], indica [country angoor], latifolia [jungle angoor], lanata [large naralay], lanceolaria [large acid naralay], linnæi [small acid naralay], pedata [naralay], quadrangularis [piranday], setosa [bristly piranday], vinifera [angoor]. Other s. indian species indigenous or naturalized are :—adnata, discolor, elongata, erioclada, himalayana, pallida, repanda, repens, rheedii, roxburghii, tomentosa.——*Drauvacam* (द्रावक - drávaka, San.). From (dru, san. to dissolve) [draucshay, dravyam]. Any strong liquor, especially a mineral acid [poolipp, tezaub]. Pottle ooppoo drauvacam, from (petluppu, tel. nitre) is nitrous acid [shorah]. Swarna drauvacam, from (svarna, san. gold) is Aqua regia, nitro-muriatic-acid ; also called Swarna bhaidy, meaning gold dissolving, and Swarna vaidhay, meaning gold-piercing.

DRICAUNAM (द्रेकाण - drikána, *San.*). From Greek δέκανος. The third of a zodiacal sign [raushy].

DRIK (दृक् - drik, *San.*). Sight.——*Drikmundalam* (दृङ्-मण्डल - drinmandala, San.). Great circle perpendicular to the horizon [cshitijam], and passing through the zenith [ootcham]. Otherwise vertical circle or circle of altitude. The altitude [avanataumsham] of a celestial object is its distance above the horizon ; or it is the arc [chaupam] of a vertical circle intercepted between the object and the horizon. The zenith distance [nataumsham] of a celestial object is its distance from the zenith of the observer ; or it is the arc of a vertical circle contained between the object and the zenith [jyotisham].

DROO (द्रु - dru, *San.*). From (drí, san. to split). Tree, wood. ——*Droomam* (द्रुम - druma, San.). Tree [daur]. Plant second term. Ex., where transl. is of first term :—Alpinia galanga (kapidruma), monkey ; Cordia obliqua (bhútadruma), devil ;

Euphorbia tirucalli (vajradruma), adamantine; Ficus religiosa (bódhidruma), knowledge; Mangifera indica (mádhavadruma), spring; Melia azedarach (himadruma), dew; Securinega leucopyrus (apriyadruma), unliked. See gloss. paragraphs.——*Drowpady* (द्रौपदी - draupadí, San.). From (drupada, san. the king). A patronymic. Wife of the Pandoo princes. The joint wife of the five Pandoos [mahabhaurat]. Cf. Maroomakkatoyem, but the story cannot be in any way S. indian.——*Drowpady's hair* (കുതിരവാൽ - kutiravál, Mal.; துரோபதைக்கூந்தல் - turóbathaikkúndal, Tam.). Mal. from (kutira, mal. horse + vál, mal. tail). Tam. from (draupadí, san. the wife of the five pandavas + kúndal, tam. hair); from twining filiform character. Botanically Porana racemosa, roxb., convolvulaceæ [vricsham, 93]. Alias Dinetus racemosus; Porana dichotoma. Herb; flowers small white.

DROOG (दुर्ग - durga, *San.*; درگ - durg, *Hind.*). From (dus, san. prefix meaning difficult + gam, san. to go) [door]. A mountain fastness [doorgam]. Suffix in place names.

DRUMSTICK TREE (முருங்கை - murungai, *Tam.*). From appearence of pod. Same as Moringa.

DRY GRAIN (خشکاناج - khushkanáj, *Hind.*; మెట్టధాన్యము - mettadhányamu, *Tel.*; പുഞ്ചധാന്യം - puñchadhányam, *Mal.*; புன்செய்தானியம் - punseydániyam, *Tam.*). Hind. from (khushk, pers. dry + anáj, pers. grain). Tel. from (metta, tel. dry land + dhánya, san. grain). Mal. from (puñcha, mal. dry field + dhánya, san. grain). Tam. from (punsey, tam. dry land + dhánya, san. grain). Cereals which do not, like rice [paddy, nunjah], require artificial irrigation, being watered only by the rain. Compare dholl, which is a dry pulse. As a class, dry grains form a more nutritious dietary than rice, and their average composition may be taken as 9 per cent. of nitrogenous aliment, 2·6 of fat, 74 of carbo-hydrates and 2·3 of salts; the ash of the seeds when freed from silica, of which there is a considerable quantity, consists of about 50 per cent. of phosphoric acid in combination with magnesium, potassium and a little sodium; it contains no lime. Most of these grains are prepared for food by removing the outer husk, grinding the remainder into meal and making with this either cakes or a kind of thick porridge. In the case of raggy [q.v.] more especially, complete comminution and careful boiling are necessary to obviate indigestibility leading to diarrhœa and insufficient nutrition. The following is a Hindostany proverb:—دانہ کہا موٹھ کا پانی پی سونٹھ کا—"If you eat millet [q.v.], drink ginger-water;" means, look before you leap. Varagoo [q.v.] is generally cooked in the same manner as rice; that is, boiled carefully and eaten whole. The manufacture of raggy or cholum [q.v.] bread has not yet been tried, though the Italians make their finest bread of the Panicum italicum. The Panicums, Pennisetums, Sorghums, and Eleusines, are called in English millets; there is no generic native term for this. The following are two key-lists in the briefest possible terms of the principal dry grains of s. india for which vernacular names are known; further information must be traced in the glossary paragraphs through the small-type cross references at end of this volume; see also vricsham, 7, for the method of expressing the products, &c., of plants in the dravidian languages.—"*a*" Amarantus paniculatus, brown spinach; Avena sativa, oat; Bambusa arundinacea, common bamboo; Coix lachryma, job's tears; Eleusine coracana, raggy; Hordeum vulgare, barley; Panicum frumentaceum, large shaumay; Panicum glaucum, coraly; Panicum italicum, italian millet; Panicum miliaceum, little millet; Panicum miliare, shaumay; Paspalum scrobiculatum, varagoo; Pennisetum spicatum, spiked millet; Sorghum saccharatum, sweet cholum; Sorghum vulgare, cholum; Triticum vulgare, wheat; Zea mays, maize.—"*b*" Bamboo, bambusa; Barley, hordeum; Cholum, sorghum; Coraly, panicum; Job's tears, coix; Maize, zea; Millet, panicum, pennisetum; Oat, avena; Raggy, eleusine; Shaumay, panicum; Spinach, amarantus; Varagoo, paspalum; Wheat, triticum.

DUB (డబ్బు - dabbu, *Tel.*; இடப்பு - idappu, *Tam.*).—"*a*" Coin. Same as Doody [naunyam, 2b]. Often used for money in general.—"*b*" Goldsmith's weight. 4 pagodas = 1 dub; 16 dubs = 1 tunkam [niray, 3b]. Approximate actual value, 1 dub = 216 grains. Kistna.—"*c*" Alumgheer dub is a copper coin still current in Hyderabad. Rama rajah dub struck by Rama roy, last king of Vijianugger; initial 'ra' occurs on both sides, on one reversed in the centre of a circle. Dubby is a cash-box, kept in temples to receive contributions.

DUBBEER (دبیر - dabír, *Hind.*). Writer, secretary [navees].

DUBBER (ڈبّا - dabbá, *Hind.*). Bottle [cooppy] formed of skins [chamrah] and used for holding and conveying spirits, oil, ghee, &c. These are made of all sizes, from a quart to 10 or 20 gallons. They are formed of untanned goat [vellaud] skins by stretching them when wet over unburned hollow clay forms, the edges being well rubbed down on the lower skin to cause adhesion. The clay core is readily removed after the bottle is dried in the sun. They are of nearly a globular form, roundish at the bottom, so as not to stand well. The aperture end is round like that of the bottom, but large in proportion to their size; the neck is short.

DUFFEDAR (دفعدار - dafadár, *Hind.*). From (dafa, hind. band of policemen + dár, pers. keeper). Head of a Dafa [q.v.]; now of an establishment of daloyets [q.v.] or personal peons [q.v.]. Also a non-commissioned native officer of infantry or cavalry next in rank to a jemadar [q.v.].

DUFTER (دفتر - daftar, *Hind.*; దస్త్రము - dastramu, *Tel.*; தச்த்திரம் - tasttiram, *Tam.*). From (daffat, ar. thick paper). A list, catalogue [daub, zaubitah]. A bundle of written documents [dastavaiz] tied together in a cloth. The place where records are kept, an office. Dufterbund is a record-keeper.

DUGONG (जलनर - jalanara, *San.*; جلمانس - jalmánus, *Hind.*; دويونگ - duyung, *Malay*; ನೀರುಪಿಳ್ಳೆ - nírupille, *Can.*; నీరుపాప - nírupápa, *Tel.*; നീരാളി - nírali, *Mal.*; මුදූරා - múduúrá, *Singh.*; நீர்மனிதன் - nírmanithan, *Tam.*). Title from malay. San. from (jala, san. water + nara, san. man). Hind. from (jal, hind. water + mánus, hind. man). Can. from (níru, can. water + pille, can. child). Tel. from (níru, tel. water + pápa, tel. baby). Mal. from (nír, mal. water + ál, mal. man). Singh. from (múda, singh. sea + úra, singh. hog). Tam. from (nír, tam. water + manithan, tam. man). Halicore dugong, sirenia, mammalia [sastanam, 27], of naturalists [jantoo]. These animals feed entirely on plants, either plucked at the bottom of the sea, or on rocks laid bare by the retreat of the tide, and they do not venture far out to sea, but keep near the shore and the mouths of large rivers. Their pectoral mammæ, and peculiar physiognomy as observed when they raise their bodies partially out of water, led to the accounts by mariners of Tritons, Sirens and Mermaids. The Dugong skin uniform bluish, sometimes blotched with white beneath, or pale fulvous with white under parts; eyes very small; incisors nearly concealed; a few scattered bristles on the body. Up to 9 or 10 feet in length and upwards; usually 5 to 7 feet. The Dugong has been taken on the west coast as high as the coast of Canara. Found along the shore, and in the salt-water inlets of the Concan and South Malabar. Prized for oil [yennay], but not hunted on these coasts. The oil is obtained from the blubber, and is equal to cod-liver oil; a cure for diseases of the ear. The bone of the animal in fineness and hardness of grain, specific gravity, and appearance, approaches nearly to the nature of ivory [dant]. The flesh is often eaten.

DUMMERGUNDY (దుమ్మలగొండి - dummalagondi, *Tel.*). Hyæna [cazhoothay pooly], Anglo-indian term of ridicule.

DUNDORAH (ڈھنڈھورا - dhandorá, *Hind.*). From (dhundhu, san. to search). Proclamation by beat of tom-tom [q.v.].

DUNG KITE (رخمه - rakhamah, *Ar.*; کرگس - kargas, *Pers.*; گوکھاؤچیل - gúkháúchíl, *Dec.*; ಬಿಳಿಹದ್ದು - bilíhaddu, *Can.*; పీతిగద్ద - pítigadda, *Tel.*; மஞ்சட்டிருடி - mañjattirudi, *Tam.*). Title from food. Ar. from (rakham, ar. love); carrion-loving. Dec. from (gú, hind. dung + kháú, hind. eating + chíl, hind. kite). Can. from (bilí, can. white + haddu, can. vulture). Tel. from (piyyi, tel. dung + gadda, tel. vulture). Tam. from (mañjal, tam. turmeric + tirudu, tam. to steal); from yellow face and bill. Ar. also (anúk). Hind. also (kalmurghí), meaning black bird. Tel. also (tellabúraga), meaning white + vulture; (pítirigadda), meaning dung + kite. Tam. also (páppátti), meaning bramin female, contraction of (páppáttikkazhu), meaning bramin female vulture; from yellow face and bill. Title otherwise White scavenger vulture. Neophron percnopterus, neophroninæ, vulturidæ [gridhram], raptores [pacshy, 1], of naturalists [jantoo]. Alias Vultur ginginianus, stercorarius. Pharoah's chicken in Egypt. Adult of a yellowish or creamy white, quills black, feathers of the neck long, face deep, turmeric [country saffron] yellow, tip of bill horny yellow; its chief food, human ordure. No other common species here.

DUNGRY (డంగిడి - dangidi, *Tel.*). Tel. from (dángidi, village so called near bombay). A coarse cotton [q.v.] fabric used by the poorer classes. The stouter kinds are employed in making sails for native sailing vessels and tents [derah]. Dungry is woven with two or more threads together in the web and woof. Superior descriptions are made with the web and woof, or web only, twisted either wet or dry; but this is expensive [nesavoo].

DUNKAH (ڈنکا - danká, *Hind.*). A pair of kettle-drums [paray] carried on a horse [ghorah] or camel [ottagam, sangeetam]. Sign of nobility.

DURBAR (دربار - darbár, *Hind.*; దర్బారు - darbáru, *Tel.*). From (dar, pers. within + bár, pers. courtyard) [dar]. A hall of audience. A levee. Also the executive government of a native state.

DURGAH (درگاہ - dargáh, *Hind.*). From (dar, pers. door + gáh, pers. place) [durree]. A royal court. Here the shrine of a Mahomedan saint; a place of religious resort and prayer [inam].——*Durgamittah* (దర్గామెట్ట - dargametta, Tel.). From (above + metta, tel. high ground). Often wrongly called Doorgamittah. There was formerly a shrine here on edge of the tank. Southern suburb of Nellore where Europeans live.

DURIAN (دورين - duriyan, *Malay*). Title from malay, meaning thorny; from strong prickles over the rind. Title otherwise Civet-cat fruit tree. Botanically Durio zibethinus, dec., malvaceæ [vricsham, 25]. Fruit about size of a man's head; within which is the seed, with edible enveloping pulp of about the size of a hen's egg; pulp pure white, resembling blancmange; bulk of the fruit is offensive, having the smell of putrid animal substance or rotten onions [piyauz]; pulp is edible; seeds, when roasted, have flavor of chestnuts.

DURKHAST (درخواست - darkhást, *Hind.*). From (khástan, pers. to petition). A tender. An application for the cultivation of land; or for farming any branch of the revenue.

DURMA (درما - darmá, *Hind.*). Mat [boriyah] made of the split stalks of Phragmites roxburghii, kunth. [large naunal].

DURREE (دری - darí, *Hind.*). From (dar, pers. door) [durgah]. A small carpet [shatranjee].

DURZEE (درزی - darzí, *Hind.*). A tailor [inam].

DUSSERAH (दशहरा - dashahará, *San.*; دسہرا - dasehrá, *Hind.*). From (dasha, san. ten + hara, san. taking away). Taking away ten sins; epithet of the Ganges; originally a festival in honor of Gungay, but now held in honor of Doorga, especially for her victory over the demon Mahishausooran. The Doorga poojay of N. india. Also commemorates Rama's victory over Ravanan. Particularly a Mahratta festival.—"*a*" Lunar festival [pundigay, 6d], subject to intercalation. Of ten days' duration, beginning with first lunar day [tity] of waxing moon of seventh lunar month Aushweejam [mausam], between September 15th and October 16th at the time of the autumnal equinox [toolauyanam].—"*b*" The nine nights are theoretically a fast, and are called the Navarautry [q.v.]. After Pongal [q.v.], the most celebrated festival. Processions and public ceremonies are made in the pagodas [q.v.] while it lasts. The school boys, finely dressed, walk through the streets, accompanied by their masters, and stopping at the houses of great men sing verses and play colauttam [q.v.], for which they expect a present. It is properly however a domestic festival, when families adore the instruments, tools, and implements by which they gain their livelihood; the farmer his plough, the artisan his hammer and chisels, the barber his razor, the tailor his needle, the writer his pen, teachers and scholars their books, the soldier his sword, shield and gun, &c., the women their baskets, pestle and mortar and household implements. In the course of the poojay [q.v.], several deities also are worshipped; especially Saraswaty, wife of Bramha and goddess of music and letters; and Doorga, Parvaty, or Bhagavaty, formerly propitiated with human sacrifices and offerings of blood. On the ninth day the implements are collected and placed together for adoration. The tenth day is set apart for amusement, and the arms which were exposed the preceding evening are locked up. In the afternoon the gods are carried out of the city or village in procession to hunt, accompanied by the dancing girls and musicians, and fireworks are let off on the occasion if the feast be in the evening.—"*c*" The fifth day is called Saraswaty poojaurambham; the ninth is Saraswaty poojay, or Maharnavamy; the tenth is Ayoodha poojay or Vijaya dashamy or Dusserah day proper. In Malabar the opening day is called Pooja veppoo, and closing day Pooja yedoopp [maryauday].

DUSTER (دستر - dastar, *Hind.*). Table-cloth or towel.

DUSTOOR (دستور - dastúr, *Hind.*). From (dast, pers. hand + bar, pers. to take). Custom.——*Dustoory* (دستوری - dastúrí, Hind.). That which is customary. The commission or percentage on the money passing in any cash transaction which goes to the agent. Ordinary gold coin of Acbar, equal to about nine rupees.

DUTT (दत्त - datta, *San.*). From (dá, san. to give) [dau].—"*a*" Adoption. If a married Hindoo of the upper class is without male issue he is required to procure a son by means of adoption. If he has not a son to perform his obsequies, he will be excluded from happiness after death. The adopted son renounces all claim on the property of his natural father, and acquires an unlimited right of succession to all that belongs to his adopted father. The adopted son is obliged on his part to take care of his acquired parents in their old age, and attend to their funeral when they die. The child adopted may be a relative or not, but must be of the same caste. See vol. I (106), (107). There are four kinds of adoption in Malabar.—"*a*" Adoption by ten hands, i.e., by the hands of the adoptors, male and female, the adoptee, and the adoptee's parents or guardians. In the case of those following the Màroomakkatoyem [q.v.] system of inheritance, the adopters will be the Carnaven [q.v.] and the senior female in the Tarwaud [q.v.], whilst the adoptee's guardians will be his Carnaven and mother. This form of adoption is very rarely used except in Bramin families. The boy selected is usually one on whom the Oopanayanam [q.v.] ceremony has not been performed.—"*b*" Adoption by Chamata, or by burning a pan of sacred grass.—"*c*" Adoption by taking into the family. This is the form commonly adopted by Bramin widows and shoodras for the purpose of perpetuating the family when it is in danger of becoming extinct. There is no limit as to age or number of persons adopted. The only limit is that the person or persons adopted should be of the same Vàmsham [q.v.] or tribe as the adoptor. Among Shoodras, the adoption should be of one or more females, but it is frequently accompanied by the adoption of a male for the purpose of providing for the future management of the adoptor's property. Sometimes a whole family of adults is adopted.—"*d*" Among the Bramins, there is another form of perpetuating the family by the affiliation of the son-in-law which is called Sarwa saudhanam [illatam]. The son-in-law succeeds to the management in trust for the issue of his marriage. If there is no issue, the property reverts to the nearest heirs. This custom seems to be a relic of the Pootrica pootram or son of the appointed daughter and to recall a period when the daughter and the daughter's son were not in the line of heirs [maryauday].—"*e*" Title of a man of the Veisya class, but now common among the Cauyast or writer class. Ramdutt, bestowed by Rama is a common name [payar].

DWAU (द्वा - dvá, *San.*). Two [do, dwi].——*Dwandwam* (द्वन्द्व - dvandva, San.). Couples of qualities or conditions the opposite of one another; as, cold and heat, happiness and misery, honor and dishonor, profit and loss, victory and defeat. Very common in native literature and ordinary parlance.——*Dwaudasham* (द्वादश - dvádasha, San.). From (above + dasha, san. ten). Twelve, twelfth.——*Dwaudashy* (द्वादशी - dvádashí, San.). The twelfth day of a lunar fortnight [pacsham].——*Dwauparam* (द्वापर - dvápara, San.). Literally the age with number two; or second counting from one as zero, or counting backwards. The third age of the world [yoog].——*Dwaupar yoogaudy* (ద్వాపరయుగాది - dváparayugádi, Tel.). From (above + yuga, san. age + ádi, san. beginning). Lunar festival [pundigay, 6d], subject to intercalation. Amavansyay [q.v.] which determines end of eleventh lunar month Maugham [mausam], between 14th January and 12th February, being anniversary of beginning of Dwaupar yoog.

DWAURAM (द्वार - dvára, *San.*). From (dvri, san. to cover). Gate [darwauja].——*Dwaura mantapam* (द्वारमण्डप - dváramandapa, San.). From (above + mandapa, san. hall). Inner portico of temple [coil].——*Dwaura paulacan* (द्वारपालक - dvárapálaka, San.). From (above + pálaka, san. protector). Large sized Yacshas placed at gate of a temple [coil]. Cf. Ashtadicpaulacan.——*Dwaura samoodram* (द्वारसमुद्र - dvárasamudra, San.). From (above + samudra, san. ocean). Capital of the Hoysala ballaulas, marked by the modern Halabeed, about 105 miles N.W. of Seringapatam. Founded in the twelfth century, plundered in 1310 by Malik caufoor [q.v.]; and destroyed in 1326 by Mahomedans when it was abandoned [charitram].——*Dwauravaty* (द्वारवती - dváravatí, San.). From (above + vat, san. suffix of possession). Capital of Krishnan; otherwise called Dwarca. In Goozerat.

DWI (द्वि - dvi, *San.*). Two [do, dwau]. Double. Plant first term. Ex., where transl. is of second term:—Clerodendron serratum, (dvidandi), stick; Lagenaria vulgaris (dvikándiká), melon; Zizyphus jujuba (dviparní), leaf. See gloss. paragraphs.——*Dweepam* (द्वीप - dvípa, San.; தீவு - tívu, Tam.). From (dvi, san. two + ap, san. water).—"*a*" An island [divy, teev]. The seven mythological Dweepams or insular continents are:—Jamboo, meaning eugenia jambolana, lamk. [common jaumoon], surrounded by the sea of salt-water or lavanam; Placsham, meaning ficus arnottiana, miq. [wild peepul], surrounded by the sea of sugar-cane or icshoo; Shaulmaly, meaning bombax malabaricum, dec. [red-cotton tree], surrounded by the sea of wine or soorah; Coosham, eragrostis cynosuroides, retz. [darbhay], surrounded by the sea of ghee or sarpy; Crowncham, meaning the bird, numenius arquata, curlew [deergha chanchoocam], surrounded by the sea of curds or dadhy; Shaucam, meaning vegetables, surrounded by the sea of milk or doogdham; Pooshcaram, meaning nelumbium speciosum, willd. [nelumbo], surrounded by the sea of fresh water or jalam. It is probable that the older pooraunams [q.v.] which give this geography were composed in or near Cashmere [q.v.]. See vol. I (2).—"*b*" Chapter of a book.—"*c*" Foreign. Plant first term. Ex., where transl. is of second term:—Artocarpus incisa (dvípuppilávu), artocarpus integrifolia; Cassia alata (dvípágasti), sesbania grandiflora. See gloss. paragraphs.——*Dweepar* (ദ്വീപര് - dvípar, Mal.). Another name of Teeyar, showing that they came from Ceylon. Cf. Eelavacan, Ilavan.——*Dweitom* (द्वैत - dvaita, San.). From (dvi, san. two). Duality. The special development of Vedauntic philosophy which underlay the religious Veishnavite system of Madhwacharry [q.v.] and his followers. He maintained that the paramautman [q.v.], or divine soul, and the jeevautman [q.v.], or human soul, are two and distinct. This system is opposed to, or distinguished from, the old adweitam [q.v.] of Shuncaracharry [q.v.] and the vishishtaudweitam [q.v.] of Ramaunoojacharry [q.v.]. While the followers of Madhwacharry observe, on the whole, the same rites with other Veishnavas, they have this peculiarity that they place the images of Shiva and his consort as well as that of Ganesh in the same shrine with the forms of Vishnoo, and pay to them adoration as they do to his idols. Madhwacharry having first been a Sheiva, attempted thus to form a kind of alliance between the two sects of the Sheivas and the Veishnavas. The Dweita philosophy is not natural to the south. The Dweita bramins are called Tatwavaudies meaning those who examine the nature of tatwam [q.v.] or truth.——*Dwijan* (द्विज - dvija, San.). From (above + ja, san. born). Twice-born; a Bramin, Cshatriya or Veisya whose investiture [oopanayanam] with the sacred thread [poonool] constitutes religiously and metaphorically his second birth. It is most usually applied to Bramins. See vol. II, 235. There is a stanza—जन्मनाजायतेशूद्रः कर्मणाजायतेद्विजः वेदाध्यायीविप्रस्यात् ब्रह्मज्ञानीचब्राह्मणः—"By birth he is a Shoodra, "by rites a Dwijan, by the reading the scriptures a Vipran, and "by knowledge of the deity a Bramin."——*Dwijyay* (द्विज्या - dvijyá, San.). From (above + jyá, san. sine). The sine; but more properly the chord of an arc [jeevay]. Also the sine of the sun's declination [craunty] when his longitude [sauyanam] is II signs [raushy]. Dwijyah maurgam is a horizontal line. Dwijyah pindam is the sine of 3° 45′ [jyotisham, pindam].——*Dwipada* (द्विपद - dwipada, San.). From (above + pada, san. foot). Couplet.——*Dwiteeyay* (द्वितीया - dvitíyá, San.). The second day [tity] in a lunar fortnight [pacsham].

DYAUNAT (دیانت - diyánat, *Ar.*). From (dána, ar. to obey) [deen]. Honesty. Prefixed to an alam forms a lacab; as Dyaunat ally, faithful to Ally. Term of devotion + alam [ism].

DYE ROOT (சாயவேர் - sháyavér, *Tam.*). Title from use. Commercial term. Same as Chayroot.

E (ए - é, *San.*; ی - ye, *Hind.*; எ - e, ஏ - é, *Tam.*). San. symbol of Vishnoo [q.v.]. Hind. numerically 10; in almanacs [punchaungam] stands for Jupiter [brihaspaty] and sign [raushy] Aquarius [coombham, dalo]. Tam. sign for the numeral 7. Tam. long means an arrow.

EAGLE (عقاب - ukáb, *Hind.*). Prefix [cooralam].——*Eagle stone* (حجرالعقاب - hajarulukáb, Hind.). Found in eagle's nests. A natural concretion of argillaceous oxide of iron, in rounded or ovoidal masses having a concentric structure, often hollow within, with a loose kernel at centre. Varies from size of a walnut [acroot] to that of a man's head. Held to be a specific against disease and a charm against shipwreck and other disasters. Aetiles of the ancients.——*Eagle-stone creeper* (حجرالعقاب - hajarulukáb, Ar.). Title from bearing nuts like Eagle stones. Same as Bonduc.——*Eagle wood* (अगरु - ágaru, San.; شجر عودالطيب - shajariúduttíb, Ar.; عود هندی - údihindí, Pers.; اگر - agar, Hind. and Dec.; كالمبك - kálámbak, Malay; ಅಗರು - agaru, Can.; ಹಗಲ್ಗಂಧ - hagalgandha, Too.; అగరు - agaru, Tel.; അകില്‍ - akil, Mal.; කළුඅගිල් - kaluagil, Singh.; அகில் - agil, Tam.). Title from malayalam, through hebrew ahalím and ahaloth. San. means not heavy [tiger's milk]. Ar. from (shajar, ar. tree + úd, ar. wood + tíb, ar. fragrant). Pers. from (úd, ar. fragrant wood + hindí, pers. indian). Hind., &c., from sanscrit. Singh. from (kalu, singh. black + agil, singh. eagle wood). Tam. from sanscrit [chikrassy, tiger's milk]. San. also (kríshnágaru), meaning black eagle wood; (agnikásht'ha), meaning firewood, from burning as incense. Ar. also (yallanjíy); (údihindí), meaning indian fragrant wood, the black variety. Pers. also (agarihindí), meaning indian fragrant wood; (údikámárí), meaning caumaury wood, the pale colored variety. Hind. also (samandurí), applied to oily variety, from the place where produced. Greek ἀγάλλοχον; later ξυλαλόη. Title otherwise Agallochum, Agar, Agil, Akyaw, Aloes wood, Calambac, Indian scented wood, Lign aloes, Lignum aloes. Botanically Aquilaria agallocha, roxb., thymelæaceæ [vricsham, 114]. Not to be confounded with the medicine bitter aloes, produce of a totally different plant [aloe]. Large tree, sylhet and malayan peninsula; flower small, green; interior part of trunk possesses aroma from oleaginous particles there stagnating and concentrating result of diseased action, yellowish in color. In "all thy garments smell of myrrh [q.v.], aloes, and cassia" of the psalms, aloes means eagle wood. Wood used in decoction [kwautam] in fevers [jwaram]; bark beaten applied externally for rheumatic pains. The resinous extract burnt in temples, chief ingredient of native pastils [oodbutty]. The wood is heavy, yellowish white shaded with green, and resinous; it is very costly, being sold by weight; precious stones [ratnam] frequently set in this wood; also used itself for ornaments and rosary beads [maulay]. A kind of eagle wood is produced by Excæcaria agallocha [tiger's milk].

EAST (مشرق - mashrik, *Hind.*). Prefix.——*East coast canal* (உப்புவாய்க்கால் - uppuváykkál, Tam.). Same as Buckingham canal [q.v.].——*East indian* (مشرقی - mashrikí, Hind.). From (mashrik, ar. east); as opposed to west or Europe. E. indies as distinguished from W. indies include not merely the two great peninsulas of S. Asia, but likewise all adjacent islands from the delta of the Indus to the N. extremity of Philippines. They extend from lat. 35° N. to lat. 10° S. and long. 65° to 130° E. At one time had a wider application including Japan also. Title means also descendants of European fathers and native mothers. Also very common plant term, meaning that the indian plant resembles European one. Ex.:—Bassella rubra, east indian spinach; Cedrela toona, east indian cedar; Flacourtia cataphracta, east indian plum; Hibiscus sabdariffa, east indian sorrel; Holopetala integrifolia, east indian elm; Nerium odorum, east indian oleander; Ocimum gratissimum, east indian basil; Pistacia lentiscus, east indian mastich; Pterocarpus marsupium, east indian kino; Soymida febrifuga, east indian mahogany; Tabernæmontana coronaria, east indian rose-bay; Xylia dolabriformis, east indian iron wood. See glossary paragraphs [indian].

EBONY (آبنوس - ábnús, *Ar.*). From (ében, hebrew, stone); from hard wood. For the indian ebonies see two major heads Indian ebony and Mountain ebony.

EED (عيد - íd, *Hind.*). From (aud, ar. to recur); from periodicity. Festival among Mahomedans. Generally means the two special Eedayeen, which are enjoined by texts of the Koran [q.v.] and are therefore farz [q.v.] or absolute; others being termed soonnat [q.v.] or traditional. The Eedayéen are Eed ool fitr or Ramzaun [q.v.] festival and Eed ooz zoohah or Buckreed [q.v.]. The others are Aukhiry chahaur shamba [q.v.], Baurah wafaut [q.v.], &c.——*Eedayeen* (عيدين - ídaín, Hind.). From Arabic. Dual of Eed; Ramzaun [q.v.] and Buckreed [q.v.].——*Eed e coorbaun* (عيد قربان - ídikurbán, Hind.). From (kurbán, ar. sacrifice). Same as Buckreed.——*Eedee* (عيدی - ídí, Hind.). Plural Eediyaun. A verse or something relating to an eed written by schoolmasters on colored paper, and given to pupils as a method for asking presents from parents. These gifts are principally confined to Aukhiry chahaur shamba [q.v.], Shab e baraut [q.v.], Ramzaun [maheena], Buckreed [q.v.] and Moharram [q.v.].——*Eedgah* (عيد گاه - ídgáh, Hind.). From (above + gáh, pers. place). A place where Mussalmans meet for prayer [namauz, salaut] on holy days. A building generally situated without the walls of a town, erected on a platform three or four feet above the level of the ground, and on an eminence. It consists of a square wall with two or more minarets [meenaur], and having in the centre, on a level with the ground, three steps, which forms the mimbar [q.v.] or pulpit, from which the khootba [q.v.] or sermon is read on particular feast days, such as Buckreed [q.v.] and Ramzaunkee eed [eed ool fitr]. *Eed ool fitr* (عيدالفطر - ídulfitr, Hind.). From (above + fitr, ar. fast breaking). Otherwise Eed oos sagheer, small festival; Ramzaunkee eed, festival of Ramzaun; Eedi sadka, festival of alms; and Chotee eed, small festival. Festival held on the first of Shawaul [maheena], in commemoration of breaking the thirty days' fast of the Ramzaun [q.v.]. Sufficiently described at vol. I (97).——*Eed ooz zoohah* (عيدالضحی - íduzzohá, Ar.). From (above + zohá, ar. forenoon); from time of prayers. Ar. also (ídiazhá), meaning festival of victims. Same as Buckreed.

EEJICA (ईजिक - íjika, *San.*). From (íj, san. to depreciate). Sanscrit corruption of Eelam [q.v.] or Ceylon [eloo].

EELAM (ஈழம் - ízham, *Tam.*). From (izhu, tam. to draw). Toddy; so Ceylon [eejica, eloo]. Cf.:—Plumeria acutifolia (ízhattalari), ceylon oleander; Scindapsus pertusus (ízhattimaravázha), ceylon ivy. See gloss. paragraphs.——*Eelavacan* (ஈழவகன் - ízhavagan, Tam.). From (above + personal suffix). The corresponding terms are:—Tel. idiga, Can. billava, Mal ilava. Same as Ilavan of Malabar [jauty]. Cf. Dweepar.

EENJOO (ஈஞ்சு - íñju, *Tam.*). From (í, tam. to give); useful tree. Same as Small date.——*Eendra* (ఈంద్ర - índra, Tel.). From (ídsu, tel. to make to give, draw). Caste of toddy-drawers [jauty].

EEPOORPOLLEM (ఈపూరుపాలెము - ípúrupálemu, *Tel.* ipurupálem *). From (ípi, tel. dung fly + úru, tel. village + pálemu, tel. fortified village). Village, Port, Head-quarters of Assistant superintendent of Sea customs; Kistna dist., Baupatla tal.; pop. 3,982; acres 8,246; lat. 15° 52′; long. 80° 26′; from Baupatla S.W. 6 miles; from Madras N. 190 miles; from Masulipatam W.S.W. 52 miles; from Nizampatam W. 17 miles. On Golcondah coast [q.v.], 30 miles from mouth of Kistna. Salt marsh.

EESAH (عيسی - isá, *Hind.*). From arabic. Jesus. Mahomedan alam; as Mahomed eesah, double alam [ism].

EESH (ईश - ísh, *San.*). To command, to protect.——*Eeshamaundan* (ஈசமாந்தன் - ísamándan, Tam.). From (ísha, san. shiva + mándan, tam. son). Vigneshwaran.——*Eeshan* (ईश - ísha, San.; ஈசன் - ísan, Tam.). Lord. A name applicable to either of the Trimoorties [eeshwaran]. Suffix in proper names as Ganeshan, Soondreshan [peyar].——*Eesharmool* (ഈശ്വരമൂലി - íshvaramúli, Mal.). Title means lord + root; from medicinal virtue. Same as Screw tree.——*Eeshaunyan* (ईशान्य - íshánya, San.). Shiva, as the regent deity of the north-east quarter. Symbol a crow. Eeshaunya moolay is the north-east quarter [ashta dic].——*Eeshwaram* (ईश्वर - íshvara, San.). From (ísh, san. to protect); medicinal. Botanically the Aristolochia genus, aristolochiaceæ [vricsham, 117]; birthworts. Shrubs erect or straggling; leaves broad and leathery; fruit is a six-celled capsule with numerous seeds. The species best known to the natives are :—bracteata [indian worm-killer], indica [isharmool]. Also suffix in sacred place names, whether dedicated to Shiva or Vishnoo ; as Someshwaram, Rameshwaram.——*Eeshwaran* (ईश्वर - íshvara, San. ; ஈசுரன் - ísuran, Tam.). The supreme being ; mostly Shiva, rarely Vishnoo. May be connected with the Chaldean ashur, and the Egyptian osiris or occidental deity. The Shactibhactans use the term Eeshwaracoil for Amman coil, where the feminine energy is worshipped. In systems of philosophy Eeshwaran is used for spirit, finite or infinite [angamam]. In the Vedauntam [q.v.] system it is the anima mundi. The Jeinas acknowledge no Eeshwaran, creator, or ruling providence [matam]. Hindoo 2nd or pers. name ; also suffix in bramin proper names as Parameshwaran [peyar]. Plant first term ; as Helicteres isora (íshvaramúli), eeshwaran's root.——*Eeshwary* (ईश्वरी - íshvarí, San.). Parvaty [q.v.] ; not applied to Lutchmy [q.v.].

EEYAM (सीस - sísa, *San.* and *Mahr.* ; آنك - ánuk, *Ar.* ; سرب - surb, *Pers.* ; سيسا - sísá, *Hind.* ; شيش - shísh *Dec.* ; تماهتم - timahitam, *Malay* ; ಶೀಸ - shísa, *Can.* ; సీస - sísa, *Too.* ; సీసము - sísamu, *Tel.* ; ഈയം - íyam, *Mal.* ; ඊයම් - íyam, *Singh.* ; ஈயம் - íyam, *Tam.*). Title from tamul. San. from (si, san. to bind). Malay from (timah, malay, tin + itam, malay, black). San. also (sísaka). Lead. Plumbum of chemists ; a soft blue metal [loham] easily scratched, and making a mark on paper ; easily malleable, but slightly tenacious, and not sonorous ; melts at low heat ; alloyed with tin [tagaram] in different proportions it forms solder and pewter [cull eeyam] ; and with antimony [soorma] it constitutes type metal ; generally found as an oxide ; if in contact with water as in water-pipes, lead is liable to be oxidised, and to render the water poisonous ; it also combines with various acids ; carbonate of lead or white lead is a dense white powder commonly employed as a pigment [rangh]. μόλυβδος was exported from Egypt to the west coast according to the Periplus, but for its indigenous distribution see vol. II, 35. Semi-vitrified oxide of lead is moordar sing [q.v.]. White lead or ceruse is moottoovelly [q.v.]. Iodide of lead is seesauroonam from sanscrit. Red oxide of lead is sendoor [q.v.].——**(1)** *Eeya carcand* (ملح الرصاص - milhurrassás, Ar. ; شكرسرب - shakarisurb, Pers. ; سيسا لون - sísálon, Hind. ; شيش كا نمك - shíshká-namak, Dec. ; ஈயக்கற்கண்டு - íyakkargandu, Tam.). Ar. from (milh, ar. salt + rassás, ar. lead). Pers. from (shakar, pers. sugar + surb, pers. lead). Hind. from (sísá, hind. lead + lon, hind. salt). Dec. from (shísh, dec. lead + namak, hind. salt). Tam. from (íyam, tam. lead + kargandu, tam. sugar-candy). Sugar of lead, otherwise Acetate of lead. Plumbi acetas of chemists. Astringent and sedative. In overdoses poisonous. ——*Eeyapaulam* (ஈயப்பாளம் - íyappálam, Tam.). Pig lead. *Eeyatagadoo* (ஈயத்தகடு - íyattagadu, Tam.). Lead sheet.—— **(2)** *Cull eeyam* (கல்லீயம் - kallíyam, Tam.). Meaning stone + lead. Pewter [jas].——*Gandhac kalappeeyam* (கந்தகக்கலப்பீயம் - kandagakkalappíyam, Tam.). Means sulphur mixture + lead. Native sulphide of lead.——*Vediyoopp eeyam* (வெடியுப்பீயம் - vediyuppíyam, Tam.). Means nitre + lead. Nitrate of lead. Plumbi nitras of chemists [ospitry]. Astringent, deodoriser.

EFFENDY (افندی - afandí, *Hind.*). Through turkish from modern greek ἀφέντης, meaning absolute master. Lord ; equivalent to English sir.

EGG PLANT (بينگن - baingan, *Hind.*). Title from appearance of fruit, smooth and somewhat oval like an egg. Same as Brinjaul.

EGOOVA (ఎగువ - eguva, *Tel.*). From (ekku, tel. to ascend). Prefix in place names ; as Egoova ahobalam, or upper ahobalam. Cf. Digoova. Egoomaty is exportation.

EI (ஐ - ai, *Tam.*). Lord. Beauty. Also five, being then a contraction of eindoo below.——*Eindinay* (ஐந்திணை - aindinai, Tam.). From (above + tinai, tam. land). Five species of lands :—Coorinjy, Marootham, Moollay, Neydal and Paulay, or hill, agricultural, wood, maritime, desert [desham].——*Eindoo* (ஐந்து - aindu, Tam.). Five.——*Einganaykizhavan* (ஐங்கணைக்கிழவன் - ainganaikkizhavan, Tam.). From (above + kánai, tam. arrow + kizhavan, tam. lord). Cauman as lord of the five-arrows [cauma baunam], lotus [nelumbo], mango [q.v.], ashocam [q.v.], jasmine [q.v.], and blue indian water-lily [q.v.]. Champak [q.v.] sometimes replaces mango.——*Eingaran* (ஐங்கரன் - aingaran, Tam.). From (above + kara, san. hand). Vigneshwaran, the five-handed god.——*Eivana nel* (ஐவனநெல் - aivananel, Tam.). From (ai, tam. beauty + vana, san. forest + nel, tam. paddy). Mountain paddy [q.v.].——*Eiyaur* (ஐய்யார் - aiyyár, Tam.). From (ai, tam. five + áru, tam. river). River ; Trichinopoly district, Moosiry talook. Jungle stream. Rises in gorge between Putchamullays and Collimullays, and receiving tributaries from both ranges, falls into Cauvery just above upper anicut [q.v.]. Length 30 miles. Principal tributary the Taligay.

EINDAH (آئنده - áindah, *Hind.*). From (ámadan, pers. to come). Future.——*Eindah saul* (آئنده سال - áindahsál, Hind.). From (sál, pers. year). Ensuing year [saul].

EINDRAM (ऐन्द्र - aindra, *San.*). From (indrá, san. the god). The oldest system of Sanscrit grammar. Eight different native schools of grammar are commonly mentioned. Of these, Paniny's system has long superseded all others ; Shaucatauyanan's and Jinendran's are still known by existing manuscripts ; Chundragomin's grammar exists in a Tibetan version ; and four other schools, of Indran, Caushacritsnan, Aupishaly and Amaran, are known by name or by an occasional quotation. The Booddhist canonical works of the north mention the Eindram grammar [vyaucaranam].

EIRAUVATAM (ऐरावत - airávata, *San.*). From (irá, san. water + vat, san. suffix of possession). Indran's elephant [q.v.] produced at the churning of the ocean [coormam]. The elephant of the east quarter [ashta dic]. An image of this divinity made of clay [calimunn] is often worshipped by Canarese women [matam]. As a country, stands for Thibet. Also the northern avastaunam or one-third path of the sun and moon [avastaunam, jyotisham, nacshatram].

EITAREYAM (ऐतरेय - aitaréya, *San.*). From (itará, san. female proper name). An Aranyacam and Oopanishad [q.v.] of the Rig veda, which contains the earliest speculations as to the Braminical ritual [matam].

EIVADZ (عوض - ívaz, *Hind.*). From (ázá, ar. to substitute). Substitute, money. Eivadz nauma is deed of exchange.

EJOO (ايجك - ijuk, *Malay*). A strong black horsehair-looking fibre, obtained from the Arenga saccharifera palm [gomooty]. It is very durable and tenacious, and employed in the countries where the trees are indigenous, for cordage, for nets and seines, for the rigging of vessels, and for cables.

ELEMI (جنگلی بادام کا پیڑ - janglíbádámkáper, *Hind.* ; جنگلی بادام کا جهاڑ - janglíbádamkájhár, *Dec.* ; كانري - kánarí, *Malay* ; ಸಾಂಬ್ರಾಣಿಮರ - sámbránimara, *Can.* ; රටකකුණ - ratakakuna, *Singh.*). Title from philippine language. Hind. from (janglí, hind. wild + bádám, hind. almond, prunus amygdalus, baill. + per, hind. tree). Can. from (sámbráni, can. benzoin + mara, can. tree) ; from smell of oil. Singh. from (rata, singh. foreign + kekuna, singh. canarium zeylanicum). Title otherwise Camnary oil plant, Chinese olive, Java almond, Jungle almond, Manilla elemi plant, Mauritius elemi resin plant, Sambrauny [q.v.] tree. Botanically Canarium [caunary] commune, linn., burseraceæ [vricsham, 35]. Canarium, from (kanari, malay, the tree). Alias Amyris zeylanica ; Balsamodendron zeylanicum ; Bursera paniculata ; Colophonia mauritiana ; Canarium mehenbenthene, zephyricum. Tree, 50 feet ; leaves unequally pinnate ; leaflets seven to ten on long stalks, ovate-oblong, acute, or shortly acuminate, entire, glabrous ; panicles terminal, divaricated ; flowers two to three together, almost sessile at the extremity of the ultimate pedicels ; drupe covered with a thin somewhat fleshy sarcocarp ; calyx three-lobed, externally silky ; petals three ; nut very hard, three-angled ; seed solitary ; flowers white ; flowering in hot season ; introduced into gardens from java, and grown successfully in travancore. The fruit is from 1¼ to 1½ inch long, ovoid, three-angled, pointed at the apex, smooth, purplish, with a thin fleshy epicarp, nut very hard, three-angled, indehiscent, one-celled by abortion of the other two ; the almond consists of a membranous testa, enclosing the oily cotyledons, which are divided into three lobes, folded and twisted together ; the kernels yield 40 per cent. of a semi-solid fat of an agreeable and sweet taste, which keeps very long without turning rancid. Produces resin [raul] so abundantly that it hangs in large pieces and conical tears from the trunk and principal branches. The resin is at first white, liquid and sticky, but afterwards becomes yellowish and of the consistence of wax [mom]. It readily softens when heated. The bark yields a limpid oil with a pungent turpentine [ganda firoza] smell, congealing in a buttery camphoraceous substance, which has the same properties as balsam [q.v.] of copaiba. Gives to pharm. elemi resin, mild terebinthinate stimulant, not administered internally ; officinal ; for british almond oil. The fruit in taste is something like an almond [baudam]. Oil used at table when fresh, for burning when stale ; kernels, mixed with sugar [q.v.], made into cakes and eaten as bread.

ELENGI (ഇലഞ്ഞി - ilaññi, *Mal.*). From (ireyu, mal. to murmur), from the noise produced by the wind upon the tree. Botanical specific name [ilanjy].

ELEPHANT (गज - gaja, *San.* ; हत्ती - hattí, *Mahr.* ; فيل - fíl, *Ar.* ; پيل - píl, *Pers.* ; هاتهی - háthí, *Hind.* ; هاتی - hátí, *Dec.* ; بيرم - beram, *Malay* ; ಆನೆ - áne, *Can.* and *Too.* ; ఏనుగు - énugu, *Tel.* ; ହାତୀ - hatti, *Oor.* ; ആന - ána, *Mal.* ; ඇලියා - aliyá, *Singh.* ; யானை - yánai, *Tam.*). Title from (al, ar. the + ibha, san. elephant + danta, san. tooth). San. from (gaj, san. to roar). Mahr. from (hasti, san. elephant). Ar. from (fayala, ar. bulky). Pers. from arabic. Hind. from (hasti, san. elephant). Can. from (ánu, can. to bear up). Oor. from (hasti, san. elephant).

Mal. from (ántu, mal. to support). Malay also (gajáh). Elephas indicus, elephantidæ, proboscidea, mammalia [sastanam, 20], of naturalists [jantoo]. The Elephantidæ contain two living species only, the Indian and African elephants. The Indian elephant has a head oblong with a concave forehead; crowns of the molars presenting narrow transverse ridges; four toes to the hind feet; ears moderate; tusks large in the male, small in the female. The African elephant is of larger size as a rule, with enormously developed ears, which quite overlap his withers. The forehead recedes, and the trunk is more coarsely ringed; the tusks are larger. Another point of divergence is that the African elephant has only three nails on the hind feet, whereas the Indian has four. The number of pairs of ribs is nineteen in the Indian elephant and twenty-one in the African, and there are thirty-three caudal vertebræ in the Indian and never more than twenty-six in the African. In some males only one tusk is developed; and in Ceylon many male elephants have the tusks very small. Twice round an elephant's foot is his height, of which the maximum is probably 12 feet. The skull of the elephant possesses many striking features quite different from any other animal. The brain in bulk does not greatly exceed that of a man. He is physically incapable of making the smallest spring, either in vertical height or horizontal distance. Thus a trench 7 feet wide is impassable to an elephant, though the step of a large one in full stride is about $6\frac{1}{2}$ feet. The trunk of the elephant is possessed of enormous power. One peculiarity of the elephant is its noiseless tread. Another is the power of withdrawing water from the stomach by the insertion of its trunk into the mouth, which it sprinkles over its body when heated. An old belief was that it had no joints, and that it slept leaning against a tree [mouse deer]. The elephant is one of the oldest known of animals. In the old Sanscrit writings it frequently appears. Eirauvatam [q.v.], which means proceeding from water, is the name of the elephant of Indra, or elephant of the eastern quarter [ashtadic]. At a very early period elephants were used in war by the Indian nati ons. On the west coast the elephant is abundant in many localities from the extreme south, Travancore, to the north latitude 17 or 18 degrees, all along the line of Western ghauts [q.v.], more especially on the Anamullay hills, named from that circumstance; in the Coimbatore hills, Wynaud, the slopes of the Neilgherries, Coorg and parts of Mysore and Canara. The Shevaroys and Collimullays, and other detached ranges to the east, have occasionally small herds of them. Elephants used to be captured by Government establishments near Coimbatore. Some were taken in pit-falls dug for the purpose, others were driven into large enclosures [kheddah]; occasionally they were captured by female decoys taken out for the purpose. A herd of elephants is always led by a female, never by a male. The rarity of the remains of dead elephants has been remarked upon. It is remarkable that a well-trained elephant will stand the charge of a tiger [pooly] without flinching, though naturally one of the most timorous of animals. The Tamul Cooral has the following :—பரியது கூர்ங்கோட்ட தாயினும் யானை வெருஉம் புலிதாக் குறின்—"Although "the elephant has a large body and a sharp tusk, yet it fears "the attack of the tiger." Their chief use here is to assist in the transport of logs of timber from forests to river banks. Of the hair of the elephant's tail, rings, bracelets, and other female ornaments are made. The natives do not speak of it as an intelligent animal, and it does not figure in their ancient literature for its wisdom, as do the fox [lomree], the crow [caurvam], and the monkey [bandar]; but on the other hand Ganesh [q.v.], the god of prudence, is always depicted with the body of a man and head of an elephant. As a badge, the elephant used to represent the Chera and Congoo dynasties. The male elephant is called gendah [q.v.] or tusker [comban] from having large tusks; the female or hine is called maknah [q.v.] and has small tusks [dant]. There is a Tamul proverb :—ஆனி ஆனைவாலொத்த கரும்பு—"In June sugar-cane is like an elephant's tail;" it is a small growth like the shortness of the elephant's tail. And another :—ஆனை தன் தலையில் தானே மண்ணைப்போட்டுக் கொள்ளும்—"The elephant puts sand on its own head;" one who plans his own ruin. And another :—ஆனைக்கவடும் பூனைத் திருடும்—"The deceit of an elephant and the thievishness of "a cat." There is a Teloogoo proverb :—ఏనుగుకు దేశము గుర్రానికి ఒకఊరు బ్రాహ్మణునికి దాసి—"To keep an elephant a whole country "is needed, a village for a horse and a maid-servant for a "buffalo." And another :—ఏనుగుమింగిన వెలగపండువలె—"Like a "wood-apple swallowed by elephant;" elephants are said to swallow wood-apples and pass them out empty but entire and unbroken. The title is also a common prefix to plant names, following the dravidian languages; term denotes a large or coarse species. Cf. Aunay, Cary, Coonjaram, Gajam, Hasty. ——*Elephant apple* (விளாம்பழம் - vilambazham, Tam.). Title from large size of fruit. Same as Wood-apple——*Elephant arrowroot* (ആനക്കൂവ - ánakkúva, Mal.). From large rhizome. Same as Arabian costum.——*Elephant creeper* (ಅಡಿಕೆಬಿಲುಬಳ್ಳಿ - adikebiluballi, Can.; ఆకిఁబూరు - arkebúru, Too.; ആനപ്പരുവ - ánapparuva, Mal.; පොට - pótá, Singh.). Title from size and strength. Can. from (adike, can. areca nut + billu, can. waste land + balli, can. creeper); from oblong red berries. Mal. from (ána, mal. elephant + paruva, mal. creeper). Title otherwise Areca nut creeper. Botanically Pothos scandens, linn., araceæ [vricsham, 152]. Generic name from singhalese. Rooting epiphyte; leaves more or less long-petioled, lanceolate or oblong lanceolate, narrow acuminate, obtusely rounded at the base and there articulated with a winged petiole; spadix axillary, solitary, peduncled, recurved, sub-globose; spathe ovate, acute, boat-shaped, reflexed; malabar, chittagong. Same term for Argyreia speciosa [sea-shore paulay].——*Elephant grass* (रामबाण - rámabána, Mahr.; ಜಂಬುಹುಲ್ಲು - jambuhullu, Can.; జమ్ము - dzammu, Tel.; ஆனைப்புல் - ánaippul, Tam.). Title from food of elephants. Mahr. from (ráma, san. the hero + bána, san. arrow). Can. from (jambu, can. kind of sedge or reed + hullu, can. grass). Tam. from (ánai, tam. elephant + pul, tam. grass). Tel. also (énugadzammu), meaning elephant + the plant. Tam. also (shambu); (ánaikkórai), meaning elephant sedge, cyperus. Title otherwise Bulrush, Cat's tail, Jammoo, Reed mace. Botanically Typha elephantina, roxb., typhaceæ [vricsham, 153]. Culms round, smooth, glossy, jointed at the insertion of the leaves, 6–10 feet; leaves linear, somewhat channelled below, exceeding the flower-bearing stem; male spadix remote from the female, both cylindric; flowering nearly all year; grows in fresh-water tanks, brooks, and slow-stream rivers. The pollen of the flowers is abundant, and if a light be applied to it a flash of fire is produced. Eaten by elephants. Leaves used for making mats [boriyah]; culms tied in bundles and used as buoys to swim with, like sedges in england. Lesser elephant grass, called patar in hindostany, title otherwise eracah, indian reree plant, lesser cat's tail, small bulrush, is typha angustifolia; down of ripe fruit used to wounds and ulcers, like medicated cotton wool [punj]. ——*Elephant lime* (గజనిమ్మ - gajanimma, Tel.). Title from size. Same as Sour lime.——*Elephant palm* (ആനപ്പന - anappana, Mal.). Title from being favorite food of elephants. Same as Bastard sago palm.——*Elephant's ear* (ஆனைச்செவியடி - ánaiççeviyadi, Tam.). Title from resemblance of leaves. Same as Elephant's foot.——*Elephant's foot* (गोजिह्वा - gójihvá, San.; شمدلن - shamdulun, Hind.; ఎద్దునాలుకచెట్టు - eddunálukachettu, Tel.; ആനച്ചുവടി - ánaççóvati, Mal.; ඇත්අඩි - etadi, Singh.; ஆனைச்செவியடி - ánaiççeviyadi, Tam.). Title from resemblance of leaves. San. from (gó, san. cow + jihvá, san. tongue); from resemblance of leaves to cow's tongue. Compare gowzabaun. Tel. from (eddu, tel. bull + náluka, tel. tongue + chettu, tel. tree); from leaf. Mal. from (ána, mal. elephant + chuvata, mal. foot-mark). Singh. from (et, singh. elephant + adi, singh. foot). Tam. from (ánai, tam. elephant + shevi, tam. ear + adi, tam. foot); from resemblance of leaves. Hind. also (gobhí). Tel. also (énugabíra), meaning elephant + elæodendron glaucum, pers.; (hastikarnaka), meaning elephant's ear. Title otherwise Elephant's ear, Rough elephant's foot. Botanically Elephantopus scaber, linn., compositæ [vricsham, 74]. Medicinal herb; stem dichotomous, ramous; leaves scabrous, radical ones crenate, cuneate, alternated at the base; cauline ones lanceolate; floral ones broad cordate, acuminate, canescent; flowers purple; flowering in cold season; common under the shade of trees. Decoction of root and leaves given on west coast in dysuria; good vulnerary; bruised leaves boiled with rice [q.v.] given internally in swellings of body or pains of stomach. No other common species here.——*Elephant thorn* (فیل خار - filkhár, Hind.). From large stout thorn. Same as Coday vail.——*Elephant yam* (कन्द - kanda, San.; کندا - kandá, Hind. and Dec.; ಸುವರ್ಣಗಡ್ಡೆ - suvarnagadde, Can.; కంద - kanda, Tel.; ଓଲୁ - ullo, Oor.; ചേന - chéna, Mal.; கருணை - karunai, Tam.). Title from size. San. means bulbous root. Hind. from sanscrit. Can. from (suvarna, san. gold colored + gadde, can. root). Tel. also (duradakanda), meaning itching + the plant; (surikanda); (suvarnagadda), meaning good + color + root. Tam. also (kárgarunai), meaning to taste acrid + the plant; (kárákkarunai), meaning to taste acrid + negative particle + the plant, a variety. Title otherwise Caroonay [telinga potato, wild telinga potato], Elephant-foot yam. Botanically Typhonium orixense, schott., araceæ [vricsham, 152]. Alias Arum orixense. Stemless; leaves three-lobed; flowers sub-sessile; spathe ample, erect, longer than the spadix; filaments long and often ramous; flowers small. Cultivated in sandy soil; cultivation, dry; no nursery; seeds sown in small plots or else in pits; full grown crop is $1\frac{1}{4}$ yards high; a yard from the root, the stem branches off into smaller stalks, with leaves on all sides and bears a similarity to umbrella held top below; yams dug out after eight months. Roots are exceedingly acrid; used in poultices as a counter-irritant and in snake-bites; pharm. non-officinal. Other common species are :—bulbiferum, cuspidatum, divaricatum. Compare :—Amorphophallus campanulatus (malanchéna), mountain elephant yam; Dracontium polyphyllum (káttuchéna), wild elephant yam. See gloss. paragraphs.

ELIXIR (الاكسير - alaksír, *Hind.*). From (al, ar. particle + aksír, ar. quintessence). The philosopher's stone once supposed to have the power of prolonging life or of transmuting articles into gold [pon]. Hence anything efficacious. Cf. Amritam and Sanjeevy.

ELLIAH (ഇളയ - ilaya, *Mal.*). Young.——*Elliad* (ഇളയതു - ilayatu, obl.; ഇളയത് - ilayatu, pers. sing.; ഇളയതന്മാർ -

iḷétánmár, pers. pl., Mal.). Caste-title in oblique case. A class of Bramins in Malabar lower than Numboory [ardha bramin]. Others are Moossads [q.v.] and Numbies [q.v.]. These do not eat nor keep company with ordinary Bramins, nor however will they eat or associate with Nayar. They officiate as the family priests of Nayar families. In customs they are still Bramins, and their women are strictly gosha [q.v.]. See vol. II, 100 [jauty].——*Elliah rajah* (ഇളയരാജാ - ilayarájá, Mal.). Junior rajah. The nearest heir to the throne on the west coast. He is usually the rajah's next younger brother, or the eldest son of his sister. Should the nephew be older than the brother, the senior is the heir. The next heirs after the Elliah rajah are called first, second, third princes, and so on. When one dies, the next takes the vacant title, so that the third prince will become second, then first, then Elliah rajah. As the succession is continued through sisters' sons [maroomakkatoyem], it is not, as amongst Braminical hindoos, males who are adopted in case of need, but females as sisters to existing heirs, and their sons will succeed. Should there be no sons, or only infants, the mother rules during the minority [baulyam]. The sons of the rajah, who are called tumby [q.v.] or younger brother, reside with him in his palace [covilagam] during their youth, and are provided for while the father is alive, as are their mothers also, by gifts of estates, houses, or money, which they thenceforth enjoy as private property [maryauday].

ELLORE (ఏలూరు - élúru, *Tel.*). From (élu, tel. rule + úru, tel. village). Tel. also (uppuélúru), meaning salt + ellore the place, so called to distinguish it from rye ellore, or vellore of n. arcot. Sanscrit name (vélapura), meaning tide + town; as being on the tammilair.——(1) Talook Godavery district. Tahsildar's pay Rs. 175. Area 729 square miles. Population 171,985. Language Teloogoo. W. of district. Bounded north by the Nizam's territory, south by Goodivauda talook of kistna, Colair lake and Bheemavaram talook, east by Tanookoo and Yernagoodem talooks, and west by Noozveed zemindarry of Kistna district. The greater part is rough and jungly; the southern part, especially in the neighbourhood of the Colair lake, being flat. Soil black cotton [regar] on the Colair side, the rest red sandy. Special industry is the manufacture of fine woollen carpets [cumbly, shatranjee] and saltpetre [shorah]. Trade principally in paddy [q.v.] and other dry grains [q.v.], carpets, saltpetre, and timber from the Nizam's territories. The high-level canal from Vijayeshwaram to Ellore passes through the talook, and is joined by the Bezwada canal at Ellore. Both canals are navigable and there is thus through communication by water between Rajahmundry and Bezwada. Several branch channels supply the villages about Ellore. A few villages are irrigated by the two mountain streams of Ramilair and the Tammilair. Numerous tanks in the upland villages. Camping grounds, Ellore and Raghavapooram. Zemindarries:—Ambarpett, Dooddepoody, Goontoopully, Malacacherla, Shingagoodem, Timmangoodem, Tungellamoody, Vadlaputlanootnam, Vaigavaram, Vasantavauda. Places of archæological interest:—Audamulley, Bheemadvole, Bogole, Caumavarappoocottah, Conijerla, Coppauca, Dendlore, Dharmaujigoodem, Dondapaud, Dwarcatirmalu, Ellore, Gollagoodem, Goontoopully, Koikaram, Moondore, Naugoolapully, Peddapaud, Tadicalpoody. Principal trig. station Bandamcherla, Soodicondah, Yedlagutt. The leading places, &c., in the talook are the following.——*Ambarpett* (అంబరుపేట - ambarupéta, Tel. ambarapet *). From (ambara, san. cloth + péta, tel. suburb). Zemindarry, Village; pop. 2,008; lat. of village 16° 49′; long. 81° 21′; from Cocanada W.S.W. 62 miles; from Ellore N.E. 16 miles. Peshcush Rs. 16,140.——*Bandamcherla* (బందంచెర్ల - bandamcherla, Tel.). From (bandha, san. bund + cheruvu, tel. tank). Trig. station; lat. 17° 03′ 38·94″; long. 81° 06′ 13·46″; height 1,122 feet; from Ponookmaudoo N. 2 miles.——*Caumavarappoocottah* (కామవరపుకోట - kámavarapukóta, Tel.). From (káma, san. cupid + varamu, tel. town + kóta, san. fort). Village; pop. 3,336; lat. 17° 00′; long. 81° 15′; from Cocanada W. 67 miles; from Ellore N.N.E. 22 miles. Old fort dating from time of Reddies. South of village is hill in which is rock-cut cave with sculptures. Above cave are two small temples. At foot of hill are two large statues of Hanooman [q.v.].——*Chintalapoody* (చింతలపూడి - chintalapúdi, Tel.). See sep. title.——*Dendlore* (దెందులూరు - dendulúru, Tel.). From (dvandva, san. double + úru, tel. village). Village; pop. 3,381; acres 7,060; lat. 16° 46′; long. 81° 12′; from Cocanada W.S.W. 72 miles; from Ellore N.E. 5 miles. Once formed part of the ruined city of Vengy [q.v.]. Tradition says that there were 101 temples and 101 tanks. There are still nearly 20 tanks. The fort at Ellore was built by the Mussalmans with materials from the ruined temples of this village. Large statue of Ganesh [q.v.] south of the village. East is a high mound called Bheemalinga dibba, and north is a mound in the centre of a tank with carved stones.——*Dooddepoody* (దుద్దేపూడి - duddépúdi, Tel.). From (dudde, tel. child + púdi, tel. village). Zemindarry, Village; pop. 368; lat. of village 16° 49′; long. 81° 22′; from Cocanada W.S.W. 60 miles; from Ellore E.N.E. 17 miles. Peshcush Rs. 378.——*Dwarcatirmala* (ద్వారకాతిరుమల - dvárakátirumala, Tel.). From (dváraká, san. saint who lived on hill + tiru, tam. holy + mala, tel. hill). Sanscrit name (anantashaila), meaning vishnoo, the eternal + mountain. Village, Place of pilgrimage; pop. 761; acres 1,198; lat. 16° 57′; long. 81° 18′; from Cocanada W. 64 miles; from Ellore N.N.E. 20 miles. Old temple, picturesquely situated on a low rocky hill, considered almost as sacred as Tripatty.——*Ellore* (ఏలూరు - élúru, Tel.). See below.——*Goondagole* (గుండుగొలను - gundugolanu, Tel.). From (gundu, tel. round + kolanu, tel. tank). Village; pop. 2,696; acres 3,545; lat. 16° 47′; long. 81° 17′; from Cocanada W.S.W. 66 miles; from Ellore E.N.E. 9½ miles.——*Goontoopully* (గుంటుపల్లి - guntupalli, Tel.). From (gundu, tel. rock + palli, tel. village). Zemindarry, Village, Place of pilgrimage; pop. 970; lat. 17° 00′; long. 81° 11′; from Cocanada W. 72 miles; from Ellore N. 21 miles. Peshcush Rs. 962. East is a cave temple in a hill, the remains of a rock-cut Booddhist monastery [vihauram] and cheityam [q.v.]. Annual festival at Shivarautry [pundigay, 6a].——*Krishnarowpollem* (కృష్ణారావుపాలెము - krishnarávupálemu, Tel.). From (krishnarávu, tel. proper name + pálemu, tel. fortified village). Village; pop. 153; acres 530; lat. 60° 59′; long. 81° 07′; from Cocanada W.S.W. 74 miles; from Ellore N. 19 miles. Trade registering station.——*Malacacherla* (మలకచెర్ల - malakacherla, Tel.). From (malaka, tel. crooked + cherla, tel. village). Zemindarry, Village; pop. 195; lat. of village 16° 50′; long. 81° 14′; from Cocanada W.S.W. 68 miles; from Ellore N.E. 10 miles. Peshcush Rs. 1,495.——*Raghavapooram* (రాఘవపురము - rághavapuramu, Tel.). From (rághava, san. proper name + pura, san. town). Raghava row was an ancient Zemindar of Zoopully family who lived here. Village; pop. 1,228; acres 6,401; lat. 17° 06′; long. 80° 57′; from Cocanada W.N.W. 86 miles; from Ellore N.N.W. 30 miles. On the boundary between the British and Nizam's territory. Old cantonment. Old European cemetery.——*Shanivaurapettah* (శనివారపుపేట - shanivárapupéta, Tel.). From (shanivára, san. saturday + péta, tel. suburb). Village; pop. 3,598; lat. 16° 43′; long. 81° 07′; from Cocanada W.S.W. 77 miles; from Ellore W.N.W. 2½ miles. Head-quarters of Nidadvole and Baharjully zemindarries. Excellent cloths woven. Noted for betel-leaf [q.v.] gardens.——*Shingagoodem* (శింగగూడెము - shingagúdemu, Tel.). From (shingana, tel. proper name + gúdemu, tel. village). Zemindarry, Village; pop. 475; lat. of village 16° 57′; long. 81° 03′; from Cocanada W. 80 miles; from Ellore N.N.W. 18 miles. Peshcush Rs. 46.——*Soodicondah* (సూదికొండ - súdikonda, Tel.). From (súdi, tel. needle + konda, tel. hill). Trig. station; lat. 16° 57′ 20·75″; long. 81° 14′ 47·19″; height 525 feet; from Vadlaputlanootnam S. 1 mile.——*Tadicalpoody* (తాడికలపూడి - tadikalapúdi, Tel.). From (tadike, tel. screen + púdi, tel. village). Village; pop. 2,538; acres 15,159; lat. 16° 54′; long. 81° 13′; from Cocanada W. 70 miles; from Ellore N.N.E. 14 miles. Old temple of Gungeshwarasawmy, fabled to have been built by Bheeshman, grandfather of the five Pandavas. In the shrine of Ancaulamman are six stone statues bearing inscription.——*Tammilair* (తమ్మిలేరు - tammiléru, Tel. tammilér *). From (tammudu, tel. younger brother + éru, tel. river). According to bramins named after lutchmanan, brother of rama. River. Flows south-east from the Eastern ghauts [q.v.] into Colair lake 3 miles below Ellore town.——*Timmangoodem* (తిమ్మనగూడెము - timmanagúdemu, Tel.). From (timmanna, tel. proper name + gúdemu, tel. village). Zemindarry, Village; pop. 106; lat. of village 16° 50′; long. 81° 16′; from Cocanada W.S.W. 66 miles; from Ellore N.E. 12 miles. Peshcush Rs. 64.——*Tungellamoody* (తంగెళ్లమూడి - tangellamúdi, Tel.). From (tangédu, tel. cassia auriculata, linn. + púdi, tel. village). Zemindarry, Village; pop. 1,846; lat. of village 16° 43′; long. 81° 09′; from Cocanada W.S.W. 75 miles; from Ellore N. ¾ mile. Peshcush Rs. 5,143.——*Vadlaputlanootnam* (వడ్లపట్లనూతనము - vadlapatlanútanamu, Tel.). From (vadlu, tel. paddy + pattu, tel. place + nútana, san. new). Zemindarry, Village; pop. 188; square miles 3⅓; lat. of village 16° 58′; long. 81° 15′; from Cocanada W. 67 miles; from Ellore N.N.E. 19 miles. Peshcush Rs. 84.——*Vaigavaram* (వేగవరము - végavaramu, Tel.). From (véga, san. stream + pura, san. town). Zemindarry, Village; pop. 317; lat. of village 16° 52′; long. 81° 12′; from Cocanada W.S.W. 70 miles; from Ellore N.N.E. 12 miles. Peshcush Rs. 787.——*Vasantavauda* (వసంతవాడ - vasantaváda, * Tel.). From (vasanta, san. spring season + váda, tel. place). Zemindarry, Village; pop. 1,888; lat. of village 16° 37′; long. 81° 03′; from Cocanada W.S.W. 84 miles; from Ellore S.W. 9½ miles. Peshcush Rs. 7,349.——*Yedlagutt* (ఎడ్లగట్టు - edlagattu, Tel.). From (eddu, tel. ox + gattu, tel. hill). Trig. station; lat. 17° 01′ 15·25″; long. 81° 22′ 45·04″; height 571 feet; from Raghavapooram E.S.E. 28 miles.——(2) Town, Municipality, Head-quarters of Head assistant collector and tahsildar; Godavery dist., Ellore tal.; pop. 29,382; acres 5,414; lat. 16° 42′; long. 81° 09′; from Cocanada W.S.W. 75 miles; from Coonavaram S.S.W. 59 miles; from Madras N.N.E. 252 miles; from Narsapore W.N.W. 43 miles; from Rajahmundry W.S.W. 47 miles. The soil of the town is impregnated with saltpetre. On the Tammilair, which divides here into two portions, the town being situated between them. On the right bank are the old barracks and the cantonment hospital, on the left were formerly the officers' houses. The country round is flat, with hills in the distance. Soil chiefly black cotton, and the cultivation paddy. Climate very similar to that of Masulipatam; but, being further inland, hotter and there is less sea-breeze. Originally portion of the Vengy kingdom, it formed part of the Orissa conquests till 1480 when it was occupied by Mahomedans. Under the Vijianugger kingdom it once more became Hindoo. Early in the sixteenth century it was captured by Cootb shah of Golcondah by whom and his successors it was held against the Rajpoots of Rajahmundry and the Reddies and Khonds of surrounding districts, until the Golcondah power was merged in the Mahomedan viceroyalty of the Deccan [q.v.]. It was then in turn possessed by native princes, by the French, and finally by the British. It then became the capital of the Circar [q.v.] of Ellore, which, together with that of Condapully, occupied the whole of the country between the Godavery and Kistna. When the Northern circars [q.v.] were divided into districts, it belonged to Masulipatam district, and was connected with it till 1859, when it was transferred to Godavery district on the redistribution of the districts of Guntoor, Masulipatam, and Rajahmundry. The revenue and magisterial charge of the town and talook was entrusted at first to a Deputy collector, but was transferred to the Head assistant collector in 1867, a portion of the old barracks being converted into his office. A military detachment was stationed at Ellore for many years, but it has now ceased to be a military station. A copper plate inscription [shausanam] discovered here gives the order of precedence in which betel-leaves were served to various chiefs and persons by Ibrahim cootb shah after his conquest of the country in 1566 A.D. In the northern part are the remains of an old fort, built by Mahomedans about the fourteenth century, from the materials of the pagodas [q.v.] in the neighbouring city of Vengy, which were then captured and rifled. A mosque has been built with the materials of a Hindoo temple. The town has benefited greatly by the opening of the canals from Bezwada and Rajahmundry. The carpets [shatranjee] made here are manufactured by Mahomedans, descendants of Persian settlers. Also noted for betel [q.v.] gardens. The Ellore canal is forty miles long from Chettipett to Ellore, where it joins the canal from the Kistna anicut [q.v.] at Bezwada.

ELOO (එළුව - eluva, *Singh.*). Or Heloo. The language of the old Singhalese poetry [ceylon, eelam, eejica, eelavaca].

ELY (मूषिक - múshika, *San.*; گهرکا چوها - gharkáchúhá, *Hind.*; موندوق - munduk, *Malay*; ಮನೆಇಲಿ - maneili, *Can.*; ಎಲಿ - eli, *Too.*; ఎలుక - eluka, *Tel.*; എലി - eli, *Mal.*; ගෙවල්මීයා - gevalmíyá, *Singh.*; எலி - eli, *Tam.*). Title from tamul. San. from (mush, san. to steal); from their sly habits. Hind. from (ghar, hind. house + chúhá, hind. rat). Can. from (mane, can. house + ili, can. rat). Tel. from (illu, tel. house). Singh. from (gé, singh. house + míyá, singh. rat). Tam. means dark one. Hind. also (chúhá). Can. also (ili). Tam. also (vítteli), meaning house rat. Mus [moosham] decumanus, muridæ, rodentia, mammalia [sastanam, 17], of naturalists [jantoo]. Generic name from (músha, san. rat). Alias Mus brunneus, norvegicus. Rat. Title otherwise House rat, Brown rat. Above dusky cinereous brown with a tinge of yellow, the shorter hair being slaty at the base with a yellow tip, and the longer ones dusky-blackish; beneath dirty pale ashy; ears as broad as long, rounded tail naked and scaly. Akin is the Black rat, Mus rattus of naturalists. Grayish black above, dark ashy beneath, tail longer than the body, long piles numerous, somewhat flattened. The muzzle is sharper than that of the brown rat, the ears more oval, and it is lighter in its make, and with much longer hair. This is the black rat of Europe introduced. It is found chiefly in large towns near the coast. Belonging to the same genus also is the striped-bellied field-rat, Mus infralineatus, of naturalists. Above the fur fulvous with the shorter hairs lead colored; throat, breast and belly, pure white, with a central pale fulvous brown streak; tail slightly hairy. Procured in the neighbourhood of Madras and elsewhere. This is distinct from Golunda meltada [varappely]. Indian species not here found are:—Andamanensis or andaman rat, Robustulus or burmese common rat, Rubricosa or small red rat of the kakhyen hills, Sladeni or sladen's rat, Yunnanensis or common house rat of yunnan. The title Ely also forms prefix in many plant names, and then indicates inferiority, or wild habit.——*Maravely* (तरुमूषक - tarumúshaka, San.; جنگلی چوها - janglíchúhá, Hind.; ಹ್ಯಾಡ - hyáda, Can.; మానెలుక - máneluka, Tel.; മരവെലി - maraveli, Mal.; மரவெலி - maraveli, Tam.). Title from tamul. San. from (taru, san. tree + múshaka, san. rat). Hind. from (janglí, hind. wild + chúhá, hind. rat). Can. from (hédi, can. a shy person). Tel. from (mánu, tel. tree + eluka, tel. rat). Tam. from (maram, tam. tree + eli, tam. rat). Title otherwise Tree rat. Mus [moosham] brunneus, muridæ, rodentia, mammalia [sastanam, 17], of naturalists [jantoo]. Alias Mus nemoralis. This belongs to a group of rats having arboreal habits. Above reddish brown, or rusty brown, with a few long bristles intermixed; beneath dull whitish, or pale rusty with a hoary tinge, or pale grayish brown; tail as long as, or a little longer than the head and body; feet pale fleshy; ears rather long, and head somewhat lengthened. Some have the upper parts dark brown, with only a slight rufescent tinge. Found throughout Southern india. It makes a nest in mango [q.v.] trees, or in thick bushes and hedges. Akin is the Rufescent tree rat. Mus rufescens of naturalists. Alias Mus arboreus, brunnensculus, flavescens, kandianus, montanus, tetragonurus. Pale yellowish brown or rufescent brown above, white beneath, with numerous bristles on the back tipped with black. Head long, muzzle pointed; face narrow; eyes large; incisors yellow; ears very large, sub-ovate, nude. Indian species not here found are:—Aquicaudalis, caudatior or chestnut rat, Ceylonus, Concolor or common thatch rat of pegu, Nitidus or shining brown rat, Niveiventer or white-bellied house rat, Palmarum or nicobar tree rat, Plurimammis.——*Moolbely* (शाली - shalí, San.; کانٹےدار چوها - kántedárchúhá, Hind.; ಮುಳ್ಳುಹಂದಿ - mulluhandi, Can.; ಮುಳ್ಳೆಲಿ - mulleli, Too.; ముండ్లపంది - mundlapandi, Tel.; മുള്ളെലി - mulleli, Mal.; முள்ளெலி - mulleli, Tam.). Title from tamul. San. from (shala, san. quill of porcupine). Hind. from (kántá, hind. thorn + dár, pers. possessing + chúhá, hind. rat). Can. from (mullu, can. bristle + handi, can. hog). Tel. from (mullu, tel. bristle + pandi, tel. pig). Tam. from (mullu, tam. bristle + eli, tam. rat). Title otherwise Hedge-hog. Erinaceus micropus, erinacedidæ, insectivora, mammalia [sastanam, 14], of naturalists [jantoo]. Alias Erinaceus nudiventris. Feet pentadactylous or five-toed; legs very short. The tibia and fibula are joined together. The back is clothed with hair intermixed with sharp spines or bristles. Tail short or wanting entirely. Inhabits the low jungles of the extreme south; also obtained on the Neilgherries and on the Western ghauts [q.v.]. Indian species not here found are:—Erinaceus collaris or collared hedge-hog, Erinaceus jerdoni, Erinaceus megalotis or large-eared hedge hog, Erinaceus pictus or painted hedge-hog, Gymnura suilla or short-tailed tree-shrew, Gymnura rafflesii. For porcupine see Kharpoosht.——*Shevvely* (हारिणमूषिक - harinamúshika, San.; يربوع - yarbú, Ar.; موش دشتی - múshidashtí, Pers.; هرناموش - harnámúsh, Hind.; ಬಿಳಿಇಲಿ - biliili, Can.; తెల్లఎలుక - tellaeluka, Tel.; വെള്ളെലി - velleli, Mal.; செவ்வெலி - shevveli, Tam.). Title from tamul. San. from (harina, san. antelope + múshika, san. rat); from activity and size of its eyes. Pers. from (músh, pers. mouse + dasht, pers. forest). Hind. from (haran, hind. antelope + músh, pers. rat). Can. from (bilí, can. white + ili, can. rat); that is, pale colored. Tel. from (tella, tel. white + eluka, tel. rat). Mal. means white rat. Tam. from (shem, tam. red + eli, tam. rat); from the fawn color. Tel. also (erraeluka), meaning red + rat. Tam. also (velleli), meaning white rat. Title otherwise Antelope rat, Jerboa rat, Jumping hare. Gerbillus indicus, muridæ, rodentia, mammalia [sastanam, 17], of naturalists [jantoo]. These field rats have small forelimbs and well-developed hinder limbs. Their form is somewhat slender and their eyes are large. They are extraordinarily agile, and form extensive burrows in plains, especially in sandy districts, and also in sand hills, but not generally in cultivated fields. Above light fulvous brown, or bright fawn color, somewhat paler on the sides, beneath white; eyebrow whitish; whiskers long, black; tail blackish towards the tip, which is clad with a tuft of long blackish hairs; ears large, almost nude. The hairs of the back are light plumbeous at the base with fulvous tips, with some thin black hairs intermixed, most conspicuous on the sides and cheeks. Found over all Southern india, but not at high elevations. Indian species not here found are:—Cryptorbinus or lobe nosed jerboa rat, Erythrurus or red-tailed jerboa rat, Hurrianæ or desert jerboa rat, Nanus or dwarf jerboa rat.——*Varappely* (केदारमूषक - kédáramúshaka, San.; کهیت کا چوها - khetkáchúhá, Hind.; ಕಿರಇಲಿ - kiraili, Can.; ಕಂಡದಎಲಿ - kandadaeli, Too.; మెట్టఎలుక - mettaeluka, Tel.; വരമ്പെലി - varampeli, Mal.; මීවින්නා - mívinná, Singh.; வரப்பெலி - varappeli, Tam.). Title from tamul. San. from (kédára, san. field + múshaka, san. rat). Hind. from (khet, hind. field + chúhá, hind. rat). Can. from (kira, can. small + ili, can. rat). Too. from (kanda, too. field + eli, too. rat). Tel. from (metta, tel. high ground + eluka, tel. rat). Singh. from (mí, singh. rat + vini, singh. forest). Tam. from (varappu, tam. field ridge + eli, tam. rat). Title otherwise Field rat. Golunda meltada, muridæ, rodentia, mammalia [sastanam, 17], of naturalists [jantoo]. With the same generic name as the Bush rat [golandy], but much differs. Above reddish brown with a mixture of fawn, lighter beneath. The fur fine, close and soft, with a few longer hairs projecting. Head short; muzzle sharp; ears large; tail shorter than body. This rat has only been found in Southern india. Lives entirely in cultivated fields making a very slight hole in the root of a bush, or merely harbouring among heaps of stones. Its flesh is eaten by the Woddar or tank-diggers [wodda].

EMBOOREL (இம்பூறல்வேர் - imbúralvér, *Tam.*). From (irumbu, tam. iron + úral, tam. taint + vér, tam. root); because of the red dye from root. Same as Chayroot.

EMETIC NUT (शल्य - shalya, *San.*; جوزالقی - jauzulkai, *Ar.*). Title from use of nut. San. from (shal, san. to cover); protected by thorns. Arabic means same as title. Botanically the Randia genus, rubiaceæ [vricsham, 71]. Shrubs or small trees armed with strong axillary thorns; flowers whitish or yellowish in color; fruit has a dry rind and is internally divided into two compartments, containing numerous seeds; wood smooth, close-grained, hard. The species best known to the natives are shown below. Other s. indian species indigenous or naturalized are :—candolleana, gardneri, speciosa. Compare also Hill emetic nut and White emetic nut which are gardenias.——*Bedaly emetic nut* (బెదలి - bedali, Tel.). Tel. means bad fruit. Tel. also (bedalika); (pedali); (pedayi). Title otherwise Bedaly, Sweet-scented griffithia. Botanically Randia [emetic nut] malabarica, lam., rubiaceæ [vricsham, 71]. Alias Gardenia fragrans, pandaki; Griffithia fragrans; Posoqueria fragrans; Randia fragrans; Stylocoryne malabarica, pandaki. Glabrous shrub, with usually opposite thorns, sometimes unarmed; leaves petioled, from obovate to oblong, cuneate at the base, coriaceous, with concave hairy glands in the axils of the nerves; stipules roundish-ovate, cuspidate, caducous; flowers pedicelled, white, in a short-peduncled umbel-like corymb at the ends of the branches, or on short lateral knobs or leafless young shoots; flowering in june and july; pedicels with two bracts near the base; fruit about the size of a large pea, roundish, red when ripe; common hedge plant. ——*Common emetic nut* (मदन - madana, San.; गेळ - géla, Mahr.; आमार्ले - ámárla, Conc.; جوزالقی - jauzulkaí, Ar. and Pers.; مین پھل - menphal, Hind.; مینڈ پھل - mendphal, Dec.; ಅರೆಮಾದಲು - aremádalu, Can.; ಅರೆಮಾಪಳ - aremápala, Too.; మంగ - manga, Tel.; ପତିର - patira, Oor.; കരളിക്കായ - karalikkáya, Mal.; කුකුරුමාන් - kukurumán, Singh.; மருக்காரை - marukkárai, Tam.). San. from (mad, san. to intoxicate) [white datura]. Mahr. from (garala, san. poison). Ar. from (jauz, ar. nut + kaí, ar. emetic). Hind. and dec. from sanscrit. Can. from (are, can. half + mádala, can. citron, citrus medica, linn.); from fruit. Too. from (are, too. half + mápala, too. citrus medica, linn.). Mal. from (garala, san. poison + káya, mal. fruits). Cf. Indian berry. Tam. from (maru, tam. fragrance + kárai, tam. canthium parviflorum, lam.); from seeds. San. also (maruvaka), meaning causing death, by its poisonous flowers; (karaháṭaka), meaning injuring hand, from thorns. Ar. also (jauzulkausal), meaning physic nut. Hind. also (men). Dec. also (medphal). Can. also (mangari). Tel. also (mranga); (manda). Mal. also (káttunáranna), meaning wild lime is atalantia monophylla, cor. [monkey lime]; from fruit. Singh. also (valkukurumán), meaning wild + the shrub. Tam. also (marukkálam), meaning fragrant poison, from seeds; (mathukkárai), meaning sweet cauray, from seeds; (púngárai), meaning flowering cauray. Title otherwise Bushy gardenia, Manga, Marookkauray, Poison fruit, Sweet cauray. Botanically Randia [emetic nut] dumetorum, lamk., rubiaceæ [vricsham, 71]. Alias Canthium coronatum; Ceriscus malabaricus; Gardenia dumetorum, floribunda, longispina, spinosa; Posoqueria dumetorum, floribunda, longispina; Randia floribunda, longispina, spinosa, tomentosa. Shrub or tree 6–10 feet, armed; spines opposite; leaves almost sessile, oval, cuneate at the base, when young, slightly pubescent; flowers axillary, solitary, terminal on the young shoots, on short pedicels; calyx campanulate, five-parted; lobes oblong; corolla hirsute on the outside; tube with a ring of dense hairs inside near the base; fruit usually globose, sometimes oblong, crowned with the limb of the calyx, two-celled, many-seeded; flowers white; flowering in april. Thorny ramous shrub, or in good soil a small tree, very common in the plains. Size of berry or so-called nut varies from small cherry [auloo] to a walnut [acroot]; generally resembles a small yellow apple [seb]; round and smooth, when ripe yellow, contain large quantity of firm, fleshy pulp; enclosing numerous sweetish-tasted, strong-smelling seeds; the berry has a peculiar sickly smell. The root bark, and fruit are used as emetic; the emetic property of the latter depends on the dry pulp or mucous surrounding seeds, and this pulp can be dissolved in water easily; substituted for british ipecacuanha; quoted in pharm., non-officinal. Pulp roasted and eaten by natives. Whole berry bruised and thrown into ponds to intoxicate fish [indian berry, marotty, round milk hedge, sooptee, walsoora]; they are then easily captured, and fruit does not render them unwholesome. The shrub employed for fences. Wood white or light-brown, compact, hard; used for fuel.——*Gray emetic nut* (पेंढर - péndhara, Mahr.; ಪೇಂಢರಿ - péndharí, Can.; పెద్దమ్రంగ - pedda-mranga, Tel.; ପେଣ୍ଡ୍ର - pendra, Oor.). Title from berry. Mahr. means white. Can. from mahratta. Tel. from (pedda, tel. large + mranga, tel. emetic nut). Tel. also (dévatámalle), meaning divine jasmine, from flowers; (gúáku); (nallamanga), meaning black emetic nut; (nalaika). Title otherwise Divine jasmine, Pindaloo. Botanically Randia [emetic nut] uliginosa, dc., rubiaceæ. [vricsham, 71]. Alias Gardenia uliginosa; Posoqueria uliginosa. Tree; branches straight, four-angled; branchlets decussating, horizontal, bearing one to four thorns and one to three large short-pedicelled white flowers at their extremity; leaves oblong, somewhat cuneate at the base, glabrous, shining; limb of the calyx tubular, bluntly five-toothed or nearly entire, a little shorter than tube of the corolla; corolla villous in the mouth; berry oval, drupaceous, even; flowering in the hot season. Rigid ramous small thorny tree; bears large, white and fragrant flowers in pairs or in threes at the top of the branchlets; berry is about the size of a pullet's egg, ash-colored or olive-grey, and two-celled; the seeds are flattish, nestling in the pulp. Unripe berry, roasted in wood ashes, used as a remedy in diarrhœa and dysentery, the central portion, consisting of the stone and seeds, being rejected; it is astringent. Pulp eaten by natives; unripe fruit employed as a vegetable dye [shauyam]. Wood whitish grey, close-grained, hard, no heart-wood.——*Hill emetic nut* (پاپڑا - pápŕá, Hind.; కొండమంగ - kondamanga, Tel.; କୋଟରଙ୍ଗ - kotaranga, Oor.; கம்பைமரம் - kambaimaram, Tam.). Title from habitat and resemblance. Tel. from (konda, tel. hill + manga, tel. randia dumetorum, lamk.). Hind. also (banpindálú), meaning forest dioscorea globosa, roxb. Tel. also (bikki); (kokkita) [sea-shore paulay]; (kurikiti); (peddakáringuva), meaning large + wild + asafœtida; (chiribikki), meaning small variety; (kákiti); (peddabikki), meaning large variety; (káringuva), meaning wild asafœtida, ferula narthex, boiss. [decamallee]. Title otherwise Broad-leaved gardenia, Cambay. Botanically Gardenia [gandharajah] latifolia, aiton., rubiaceæ [vricsham, 71]. Alias Gardenia enneandra. Unarmed tree; leaves opposite or in threes, very shortly petioled, oval or obovate, glabrous, with a small hairy gland in the axils of the nerves beneath; limb of the calyx campanulate, irregularly divided, hirsute on the inside; coralla hypocrateriform; tube long, hirsute on the outside; limb about nine-cleft, the divisions obliquely obovate, hirsute towards the one margin on the outside; stigma clavate, thick and fleshy, bipartite; segments two-cleft; berry nearly globose, even, crowned with the calyx; nut thin, brittle and bony, with four parietal receptacles; flowers terminal, solitary, very shortly-pedicelled, very large, pure white in the morning, yellow in the evening, fragrant; hills of the circars [q.v.] and carnatic [q.v.]; flowering in april. Leaves, some as much as fifteen inches long and six inches wide. Wood light-yellowish brown, close and even-grained, hard, handsomely mottled, neither warps nor splits; no heart-wood; easy to work, durable, a substitute for box-wood; combs are made of it.——*White emetic nut* (తెల్లమంగ - tellamanga, Tel.). Same as Decamallee.

ENNORE (எண்ணூர் - ennúr, *Tam.*). From (énai, tam. an eel + úr, tam. village). Village just north of Cuttiwaukum [q.v.] backwater; Chingleput dist., Sydapett tal.; pop. 453; acres 1,807; from Madras N. 12 miles; from Ponnairy S.E. 11 miles; from Sydapett N. 17 miles; from sea W. ½ mile. The English settlement at Cuttiwaukum takes this name. Ennore beacon is a trig. station in lat. 13° 13′ 53·06″; long. 80° 22′ 25·58″; from Cadapaukam N.E. 4½ miles; from Sydapett N. 15 miles; from the sea W. 1¼ miles. Ennore D.P.W. bungalow is a trig. station in lat. 13° 13′ 50·20″; long. 80° 22′ 19·41″; from Sydapett N. 15 miles; from the sea W. 1¼ miles.

ERNACOLUM (എറണാകുളം - eranákulam, *Mal.*). From (haranár, mal. the saint, so called + kulam, mal. tank). Sanscrit name (haranágakula), means shiva + serpent + residence; also (rishinábhitatáka), meaning saint + navel + tank. Town, Head-quarters of Diwaun, Appeal court, Zillah court, Moonsif's court and talook, Post and Telegraph office; Cochin state, Canyanore tal.; pop. 3,504; lat. 9° 59′; long. 76° 19′; from Canyanore W.N.W. 10 miles; from Chittoor S.S.W. 59½ miles; from Cochin E.N.E. 2¼ miles; from Madras S.W. 345 miles; from Trichore S. 38 miles; from Tripoontora W.N.W. 5 miles; from the sea E. 3 miles. On the backwater opposite to Cochin town. May be considered the capital of Cochin state. The town itself is insignificant, consisting chiefly of houses of a poor description scattered along the bank of the backwater, the most closely populated portion being inhabited by Black jews [jonaca]. Besides the public offices there is a Durbar [q.v.] hall where the British resident pays his state visit to the Rajah of Cochin. There is a travellers' bungalow [q.v.].

ERODE * (ஈரோடு - íródu, *Tam.*). From (ír, tam. two + ódai, tam. water-course) [ir]; between bhawauny and cauvery. ——(1) Talook, Coimbatore district. Tahsildar's pay Rs. 225. Area 598 square miles. Population 247,008. Language Tamul. N.E. of district. Bounded N. by the Bhawauny; N.E. and E. by the Cauvery which separates it from Trichengode talook of Salem district; S. by the Noyil which separates it from Caroor and Dharaupooram talooks; W. by Pulladam talook; and N.W. and N. by Suttimungalam and Bhawauny talooks respectively. Comprises the old Peroondoray and Erode talooks. The whole talook slopes towards Cauvery, into which all streams eventually fall. A gently undulating plain, broken parallel with the Madras railway by a slight ridge, the peaks of which are Aratchalore, Shennimullay, and Yelmattore. There are also several small isolated hills. The climate of the valley of the Cauvery is hot and close, the south-west monsoon [q.v.] is heated and fitful, and periods of calm alternate with dust storms and gusts of wind [pishauch]. In the west however, where the country is higher, the climate is cooler and healthier, the tracts about Chengampully and Peroondoray being convenient resorts in April, May, June and September. Peroondoray is the locality most favored by rain; towards Erode the fall is somewhat less, while to the west, especially the parts bordering on Pulladam, it is very scanty. Pasture lands are rare. There are no forests or jungles; the country is tolerably provided with common trees. Palmyras [q.v.] are plentiful. Good roads. Soil everywhere largely calcareous, even the disintegrated gneiss yielding lime [choonam] which has infiltrated from above. Excellent felspar [mauvayira cull] suitable for potting is obtainable everywhere. Iron [aurhan] used to be smelted from black sands [manal] of surface streams, especially near Shennimullay, the stones of which are highly ferric. Asbestos [cull naur] is occasionally found and used medicinally. Building stones are good and cheap everywhere; a quarry at Poojarry comanra gowndanore, near Ootcooly railway station, supplies excellent stones for important railway works. Brick [shengal] clays are occasionally good. Potters' clay [calimunn] for ordinary porous earthenware is procurable from tank-beds, &c.; no good potting [chatty] materials, except quartz [vencull] and felspar, exist. Soils are all red; there is no black cotton tract [regar], and the only dark soils are in the beds of tanks and in wet fields where the red soil has changed color owing to continuous manuring with vegetable matter. 80 per cent. of talook is red sand, rest being red loam with 1 per cent. of so called black soils. Except fine wet lands under Calingaroyan and garden lands, talook is of poor soil. The uplands are very poor as a rule, the best part of the soil having been washed into the bottoms and thence largely to Trichinopoly and Tanjore. Trees and crops are those of the ordinary dry lands. Fruit trees, except palmyras and a few cocoanuts near wells, are rare; even tamarinds are scarce. Chillies [q.v.] and tobacco [pogauk], the latter especially in the southern parts of the talook, grow well in gardens in the cold weather; Sunn [q.v.] hemp is grown in the neighbourhood of Tingalore where excellent gunny [q.v.] is made. The chief crops are in dry lands, cumboo [bajrah], cholum [q.v.], pulses [dholl], oil-seeds [yennay], cotton [q.v.] and other fibres; in gardens chillies, raggy [q.v.], cholum, cumboo and tobacco; in wet-lands, paddy [q.v.], raggy and gingelly [q.v.]; sugar-cane [q.v.] and plantains are not extensively grown. Turmeric [country saffron], yams [auloo] and sweet-potatoes [q.v.] are also grown in garden lands, especially near Erode. The only fruits grown are pomegranates [anaur], especially near the railway; cocoanuts [q.v.] on wet lands in topes [q.v.] and in gardens in rows along the water-courses; plantains [q.v.] and tamarinds [q.v.]. Mangoes [q.v.] are very rare. There are also a few pumplemoses [pummelow], oranges [q.v.] and limes [q.v.]. The jujube [q.v.] is plentiful near Coonnatore; there are very few other wild fruits except the prickly-pear [q.v.] which grows in masses. Dry crops are usually poor. For pasture the ryots depend upon the public lands and the grazing of their fallow and cotton lands. Cattle [maud] are not much bred for sale. The chief industries besides agriculture are cart-building, stone-quarrying, well-digging, potting and brick-making, iron-smelting, weaving, choonam-burning and saltpetre-making; there are also the ordinary carpenters and workers in iron, brass [pittalay] and the precious metals [pon]. Cart-building is active in Erode town; it is also found occasionally elsewhere. Stone is quarried in many places, chiefly by Woddar; that for the Cauvery bridge was found near Ootcooly railway station and is of good quality. Common grindstones of gneiss are cut in the Cauvery bed and in many other places. The Woddar are the only well-diggers. Iron smelting is now rare. Only country coarse cloths are woven and the manufacture is on the decline. The saltpetre [shorah] industry once considerable, has now almost died out. A large trade is done in country leather [chamrah]. The trade in raw produce, salt [ooppoo] and cloths is the most important. The oil and hide trades have no special centres, but cotton is largely brought into Erode. The only other product is the bark of the white acacia [velvail] used in distilling, and that of the Cassia auriculata or auvauray [tungaid] largely used for tanning [chamrah]. Rivers are the Bhawauny, Cauvery and Noyil besides numerous drainages, such as the Caroongalpullam crossing the Calingaroyan and Poogalore channels and falling into the Cauvery and Noyil. The various drainages and especially the Caroongalpullam are liable to heavy floods owing to the undulating surface. The Cauvery is somewhat used for traffic from above Bhawauny downwards; passengers and light freight are taken in basket boats when the river is in flood. Ferries are tolerably numerous. Irrigation is either direct from channels [q.v.], from tanks fed by channels, or from tanks supplied by rain-fed surface or jungle streams. Under the first head are the Calingaroyan and Poogalore channels, the latter only irrigating a few acres. In the second class is Vadoogapolliem tank. Cultivation under tanks varies considerably. Under some tanks, as Dalavoypolliem, the ryots do not grow crops unless there is a full supply; in others, as Poothoorpullapolliem, which have not filled for years, the ryots have dug wells and cultivate crops, such as sugar-cane the whole year round. Camping grounds:—Chengampully, Chittore, Erode and Peroondoray. Places of archæological interest:—Circar yairipolliem, Codoomoody, Erode, Nullamputty, Peroondoray. There are small Jeina temples at Arasa mullay, Poondoray, Tingalore, Vellode, Vijiamungalam. Principal Trig. stations:—Shennimullay, Yelmattore, Yettimullay. The leading places, &c., in the talook are the following.——*Aratchalore* (அரச்சலூர் - araççalúr, Tam.). From (arasu, tam. the peepul tree, ficus religiosa, linn. + úr, tam village). Village, Hill; pop. 6,707; acres 14,651; lat. 11° 10′; long. 77° 44′; from Coimbatore E.N.E. 51 miles; from Erode S.S.W. 12½ miles. Four Shiva temples with festivals once a year.——*Bhawauny* (பவானி - paváni, Tam.). See sep. title.——*Calingaroyan* (கலிங்கராயன் - kalingaráyan, Tam.). See sep. title.——*Canacaupooram* (கனகாப்புரம் - kanagáppuram, Tam.). From (kanaka, san. gold + pura, san. town). Village; pop. 1,488; acres 1,897; lat. 11° 15′; long. 77° 44′; from Coimbatore E.N.E. 52 miles; from Erode S.S.W. 7 miles. Cave in rook. Throo Shiva temples. Large market.——*Caunjicoil* (காஞ்சிக்கோவில் - káñjikkóvil, Tam.). From (káñji, tam. holopotala integrifolia, planch. + kóvil, tam temple). Village; pop. 5,417; acres 9,454; lat. 11° 22′; long. 77° 39′; from Coimbatore E.N.E. 51 miles; from Erode W.N.W. 9 miles. Five Shiva temples with festivals.——*Cauvery* (காவேரி - kávéri, Tam.). See sep. title.——*Codoomoody* (கொடுமுடி - kodumudi,* Tam.). From (kodu, tam. rough + mudi, tam. peak). Village, Sub-registrar's station, Railway station; pop. 4,020; acres 3,089; lat. 11° 05′; long. 77° 56′; height 430 feet; from Coimbatore E. 63 miles; from Erode S.S.E. 21½ miles. Thriving wet village. Ancient and well-sculptured Shiva temple. Market much frequented by grain merchants.——*Coonnatore* (குன்னத்தூர் - kunnattúr, Tam.). From (kunram, tam. hill + úr, tam. village). Village; pop. 981; acres 994; lat. 11° 16′; long. 77° 27′; from Coimbatore N.E. 36 miles; from Erode W. 22½ miles. Large market.——*Erode* (ஈரோடு - íródu, Tam.). See below.——*Noyil* (நொய்யல் - noyyal, Tam.). See sep. title.——*Oonjalore* (ஊஞ்சலூர் - úñjalúr, Tam. unjalúr*). From (úñjal, tam. swing + úr, tam. village). From the swinging festival. Village, Railway station; pop. 4,399; acres 3,610; lat. 11° 08′; long. 77° 55′; height 446 feet; from Coimbatore E. 63 miles; from Erode S.E. 17½ miles. Old Shiva temple with inscriptions.——*Passore* (பாசூர் - pásúr, Tam. pásur*). From (pásu, tam. green + úr, tam. village). Village, Railway station; pop. 1,335; acres 1,509; lat. 11° 14′; long. 77° 54′; height 497 feet; from Coimbatore E.N.E. 63 miles; from Erode S.E. 11¼ miles. Irrigated by Calingaroyan channel.——*Peroondoray* (பெருந்துறை - perundurai, Tam.). See sep title.——*Shennimullay* (சென்னிமலை - shennimalai, Tam.). From (shenni, tam. summit + malai, tam. mountain). Village, Hill, Trig. station; pop. 2,656; acres 5,487; lat. 11° 09′ 23·67″; long. 77° 37′ 44·05″; height 1,749 feet; from Coimbatore E.N.E. 44 miles; from Erode S.S.W. 15 miles. Famous Soobramanyan temple much resorted to by Vellaular. Market.——*Yelmattore* (எழுமாத்தூர் - ezhumáttúr, Tam.). From (ezhumai, tam. height + máttúr, tam. village so called). Village; pop. 4,662; acres 8,335; lat. 11° 11′; long. 77° 49′; from Coimbatore E.N.E. 57 miles; from Erode S.S.E. 11½ miles. Shiva and Vishnoo temples on rock. Trig. station; lat. 11° 12′ 02·30″; long. 77° 47′ 27·96″; height 1,342 feet; from Erode S. 10 miles; from Yelmattore village N.W. 2 miles.——*Yettimullay* எட்டிமலை - ettimalai, Tam.). From (etti, tam. the poison-nut tree, strychnos nux-vomica, linn. + malai, tam. mountain). Hill; lat. 11° 03′; long. 77° 53′; from Coimbatore E. 60 miles; from Erode S.S.E. 20¾ miles. Within Vadivoollamungalam village. Trig. station; lat. 11° 03′ 52·68″; long. 77° 53′ 15·10″; height 618 feet; from Erode S.S.E. 20 miles; from Vengambore S.S.W. 3½ miles.——**(2)** Town, Divisional and talook head-quarters, District moonsif's and Sub-registrar's station; it is also the Head-quarters of the Assistant superintendent of Police and of the D.P.W. Sub-divisional officer, Railway station; Coimbatore dist., Erode tal.; pop. 12,330; acres 7,890; lat. 11° 20′; long. 77° 46′; height 543 feet; from Coimbatore E.N.E. 57 miles; from Madras S.W. 212 miles; from Ootacamund E. 69 miles; from Pollachy N.E. 68 miles; from Suttimungalam E.S.E. 35 miles. Close to Cauvery at extreme E. of district. In time of Hyder ally it contained 3,000 houses and a population of 15,000; but in consequence of successive Mahratta, Mysore, and British invasions, it was almost deserted and ruined. Until 1667 it formed part of the Madura kingdom, but in that year fell to Dodda deo, Rajah of Mysore. In 1768, it was taken and lost by the British; and in 1790, it was finally recaptured. As soon as peace was signed, the people returned to a place with so many advantages in position and fertility; and within a year it had 400 houses and a population of over 2,000. The garrison was withdrawn in 1807, and the ruined fort levelled, as a relief work during the famine of 1877. The space enclosed within the ramparts had been long before occupied by cotton presses and saltpetre warehouses. Two old Vishnoo and Shiva temples, both with inscriptions. Trade consists chiefly in the export of cotton, saltpetre, and rice. It is an important railway entrepôt. Besides the Great trunk road from Madras, which passes through Erode; the main lines to Caroor, Peroondoray, and Mysore, one viâ the Hassanore ghaut, the other viâ the Burgoor ghaut, radiate from it. Junction of Madras and S.I. railways. Roman catholic mission. 1½ miles E. is bridge of 22 arches crosses Cauvery, 1,536 feet long.

ETIMAUD (اعتماد - etimád, *Ar.*). From (amada, ar. to support). Right arm. Part of lacab [q.v.]; as Etimaud jung, the support of war [ism].

EUROPE (विलायती - viláyatí, *Mahr.*; ولايتى - viláití, *Hind.*; ಶೀಮೆ - shíme, *Can.*; సీమ - síma, *Tel.*; വിലാത്തി - vilátti, *Mal.*; சீமை - shímai, *Tam.*). Hind. from (viláyat, ar. foreign country). Drav. from (símá, san. border). Common prefix to plant names, following the dravidian languages. Term denotes any foreign article; particularly Arabia, Europe, or Persia. Not used for Chinese, or other countries east of India [faranghee, firangy, foreign, seema, vilauyaty]. Examples joining two genera are, where transl. is of second term:—Adansonia digitata (viláitíamlí), tamarindus indica; Althæa officinalis (shímaittutti), abutilon indicum; Arachis hypogæa (viláitímúng), phaseolus mungo; Baliospermum montanum (shímaiyámanakku), ricinus communis;

Carum carui (viláitízírekáper), cuminum cyminum; Cassia alata (viláitíagtí), sesbania grandiflora; Crotalaria juncea (viláitíakrekánár), calotropis gigantea + fibre; Cydonia vulgaris (shímaimáthalai), punica granatum; Fourcroya gigantea (shímaikkattázhai), aloe indica; Garcinia cambogia (viláitíamlı), tamarindus indica; Hedychium spicatum (shímaikkiççilikkizhangu), curcuma zedoaria; Jatropha multifida (viláyatiharalu), ricinus communis; Lycopersicum esculentum (viláitíbaingan), solanum melongena; Malpighia glabra (shímainelli), phyllanthus emblica; Malva sylvestris, var. mauritiana (viláitíkangíkájhár), abutilon indicum; Myrtus communis (viláitímenhdí), lawsonia alba; Parkinsonia aculeata (símajíluga), æschynomene aspera; Pedilanthus tithymaloides (símachitramúlamu), plumbago zeylanica; Peganum harmala (símagóranta), lawsonia alba; Phaseolus trilobus (shímaiyavarai), dolichos lablab; Pinus longifolia (shímaittévathári), erythroxylon monogynum; Pithecolobium dulce (símachinduga), albizzia odoratissima; Poinciana regia (símatangédu), cassia auriculata; Quisqualis indica (viláitíchaméli), jasminum grandiflorum; Sideroxylon tomentosum (shímaimagizham), mimusops elengi; Stilpnophyllum elasticum (valáitíbarkéjhár), ficus bengalensis; Thevitia nereifolia (shímaiyalari), nerium odorum. See gloss. paragraphs. There are numberless others where the genus is the same.

EVANGELION (എവൻഗലിയോൻ - evangaliyón, *Mal.*). Gospel among Malabar syrian christians.

EYE (چشم - chashm, *Hind.*). Prefix.——*Eye fly* (मशक - mashaka, San.; मुरकूट - murakúta, Mahr.; ڈانس - dáns, Dec.; ಕಣ್ಣುಸೊಳ್ಳೆ - kannusolle, Can.; దోమ - dóma, Tel.; കൊതു - kotu, Mal.; ඝොෂා - ghósha, Singh.; கொசு - kosu, Tam.). Title from getting into the eyes. San. from (mash, san. to hum). Dec. from (damsh, san. to sting). Can. from (kannu, can. eye + solle, can. mosquito). Mal. from tamul by corruption. Singh. from (ghush, san. to sound). Tam. from (ghósha, san. gnat). Belongs to family Muscidæ, diptera, holometabola, insecta [poochy], of naturalists [jantoo]. They form clusters on hanging threads. Avoid rooms in which branches of penny royal [poodeenah], or of walnut tree [acroot] have been suspended.——*Eye powder* (چشمیزج - chashmízaj, Pers.). Title from powdered seed being applied in ophthalmia. Same as Black horse-gram.

EYIL (எயில் - eyil, *Tam.*). Means forest. Ancient division of Tondaimundalam [tonday].

F (ف - fe, *Hind.*). Symbol for 80; in almanacs, the moon [chundran] in her altitude [avanataumsham].

FACE PLANT (ചടമരം - chatamaram, *Mal.*; வட்டிலை - vattilai, *Tam.*). Title from pattern on leaf. Mal. from (chata, mal. hairlock + maram, mal. tree). Tam. from (vadu, tam. scar + ilai, tam. leaf). Title otherwise Caricature plant, Painted justicia, Scar leaf. Botanically Graptophyllum hortense, nees, acanthaceæ [vricsham, 101]. Alias Justicia picta. Low thorny shrub; leaves smooth, elliptical, lanceolate, 3 to 4 inches in length, dull deep green above and dark red below; have yellow marks, supposed to be caricatures of the human face; flower crimson, flowering nearly all year; common in gardens; flower religious; no other species here.

FAKEER (فقیر - fakír, *Hind.*). From (fakr, ar. poverty). Any poor person. So a Mahomedan religious mendicant [calandar]. These are divided first into baushara [q.v.] or with the law, and beshara [q.v.] without the law; and under each head are various distinct brotherhoods, having their own office bearers and special practices. Every new-comer is admitted first as a mooreed [q.v.] or disciple, and may afterwards become a moorshid [q.v.] or teacher [peer]. At the Moharram [q.v.] the term means men disguised as fakeers. The principal Moharram fakeers were originally parties of mourners, and according to Mahomedan law only praying [namauz] and fasting [roza] during the anniversary are recognized. But these have been turned into masquerade [masheikh]. For Hindoo devotees, see Sanyausy and Beiraugy. Term is used in combination with the name of Mahomed, his companions, &c., to form Mahomedan proper names, indicating humility; as Fakeer ahmed, beggar of Ahmed [ism].——*Fakeer's bottle* (अलाबु - alábu, San.; रानभोंपळी - ránabhómpalí, Mahr.; काडदुढी - kádadudhí, Conc.; قرع - kara, Ar.; کدو - kaddú, Pers. and Hind.; هراکدو - harákaddú, Dec.; لبو امبن - labuamban, Malay; ಸೋರೆ - sóre, Can.; ಕಾಟುತುರೆ - kátuture, Too.; సొర - sora, Tel.; ചുര - chura, Mal.; දියලබ්බ - diyalabba, Singh.; சுரை - shurai, Tam.). Title from use by fakeers. San. from (a, san. negative prefix + lamb, san. to sink); serve as buoys. Mahr. from (rána, mahr. wild + bhómpalí, mahr. the pumpkin gourd, benincasa cerifera, savi.). Ar. from (kara, ar. empty). Hind. from persian. Dec. from (hará, hind. green + kaddú, hind. gourd). Too. from (kátu, too. wild + ture, too. gourd). Singh. from (diya, singh. water + labba, singh. long gourd). Drav. mean hollow. San. also (dvikándiká), meaning double melon; (pindap'hala), meaning ball fruit. Hind. also (dilpasand), meaning heart + approved; (golkaddu), meaning round gourd; (janglíkaddú), meaning wild gourd; (kábulí), meaning cabool plant; (kásíphal), meaning benares fruit. Can. also (huççusóre), meaning wild gourd; (kahisóre), meaning bitter + gourd. Tel. also (ánapa), meaning edible; (ánuga), meaning edible; (gubbakáyachettu), meaning plant with round fruit. Mal. also (kaippaççura), meaning bitter gourd; (káttuchura), meaning wild gourd; (vellaççura), meaning white gourd. Tam. also (kinnariççurai), meaning lute gourd [calabash]. Title otherwise Bottle gourd, Calabash, False calabash, Trumpet gourd, White pumpkin [wax gourd]. Botanically Lagenaria vulgaris, sering., cucurbitaceæ [vricsham, 62]. Alias Cucurbita lagenaria; Pepo lagenarius. Stem climbing softly pubescent; calyx campanulate; petals rising from within the margin of the calyx; tendrils three to four-cleft; leaves cordate, nearly entire or lobed, lobes obtuse or somewhat acute, glaucous; flowers fascicled, white; petals very patent; fruit pubescent, at length nearly glabrous and very smooth; seeds numerous, flesh-white, edible; fruit yellow when ripe, having appearance of two oval gourds united endwise, or inflated bladder compressed by a cord around it. Pulp of fruit used in poultices, bitter and purgative, and substitute for colocynth [bitter water melon]; decoction of leaves mixed with sugar [q.v.] given in jaundice; seeds yield oil used for headache. By europeans boiled when young and used as vegetable marrow [q.v.]; by natives sliced and cooked as curry [q.v.]; young shoots and leaves eaten by all classes. Fruit actually used by beggars and others when dried and empty as a bottle [cooppy]; tendril gives a dye; fruit used as buoy for swimming across river and transporting baggage, &c.; the large round kind used for making the stringed instrument kinnary [kingry]; the longer and narrow sort make the wind instruments magady [q.v.], with which snake-charmers entice snakes from holes; when wild the fruit is somewhat poisonous. No other common species here.

FAKR (فخر - fakhr, *Ar.*). From (fakhara, ar. to excel). Glory, pride. Part of lacab; as Fakr ood deen, the pride of religion; Fakr ood dowla, the pride of the empire [ism].

FAKT (فقط - fakt, *Hind.*; ఫకతు - p'hakatu, *Tel.*). From arabic. Only. Written at the end of a document [dastavaiz] to indicate that it is completed.

FALAUNA (فلانه - fulánah, *Hind.*). From (fulán, ar. such a one). A person whose name is not specified.

FALOOS (فلوس - fulús, plural of فلس - *Hind.*). From lat. follis. A copper coin [naunyam] equal to five cash [q.v.]. From arabia and persia.

FALSAH (परुष - parusha, *San.*; फलशि - p'halashi, *Mahr.*; فالسه - fálsah, *Ar.*; پالسه - pálsah, *Pers.*; فالسه - fálsa, *Hind.*; فالسه - fálsa, *Dec.*; పుటికి - putiki, *Tel.*; දමිනිය - daminiya, *Singh.*; பலிசு - palisa, *Tam.*). Title from deccany. San. means rough. Singh. from (damanavá, singh. to tame), devil tamer; from the priest binding the devil he wishes to subdue to this tree [tadda]. Tam. from hindostany. Title otherwise Devil-tamer, Sweet falsah. Botanically Grewia [dharmanam] asiatica, linn., tiliaceæ [vricsham, 27]. Alias Grewia subinequalis. Tree; leaves five-nerved, roundish-cordate, unequally serrated, under side pubescent or hoary; stipules lanceolate-subulate; peduncles two to four, longer than the petiole, three-flowered; sepals oblong-lanceolate, longer than the petals; stigma four-lobed; drupes globose with one to two, one-celled nuts; flowers yellowish-orange. Small, hazel-like tree; cultivated; flowers about end of cold season, and fruit ripens in april and may; fruit a berry, about the size of a pea [calauyam] with a stone in the centre. Fruit medicinally astringent, cooling and stomachic. Fruit eaten; from same a spirit is distilled and a sherbet [q.v.] made. Bark used in rope making. Wood yellowish-white.——*Creeping falsah* (धविपोंसरी - dhavipómsarí, Conc.; ಮೊದಿರಕಣ್ಣಿ - modirakanni, Can.; ಮುಲ್ಲನ್ಕೊಲೆ - mullankole, Too.; తివ్వపుటికి - tivvaputiki, Tel.; മോതിരക്കണ്ണി - mótirakkanni, Mal.; බූගැටියා - búgetiyá, Singh.; மோதிரக்கன்னி - móthirakkanni, Tam.). Title from rambling habit. Can. from malayalam. Tel. from (tivva, tel. creeper + putiki, tel. grewia asiatica, linn.). Mal. from tamul. Singh. from (bú, singh. earth + getiya, singh. the plant). Tam. from (móthiram, tam. ring + kanni, tam. flower-bud); from shape. Tel. also (vudupa); (gatrinta). Singh. also (getiyá); (híngetiyá), meaning low + the plant. Tam. also (agóri). Botanically Hugonia mystax, linn., lineæ [vricsham, 28]. Alias Hugonia obovata. Rambling shrub, 10-15 feet; leaves alternate, or crowded at the ends of the branches, oval, glabrous, entire; sepals distinct, acute, unequal; petals five, alternate with the sepals; styles five, distinct; ovary roundish, five-celled; fruit a drupe, enclosing five distinct one-seeded carpels; peduncles axillary, one-flowered; spines circinate, opposite; flowers yellow; flowering in rainy season. Bruised roots used in reducing inflammatory tumours, in bites of serpents, and as febrifuge and anthelmintic, especially for children.

FANAM (पण - pana, *San.*; فلم - falam, *Hind.*; பணம் - panam, *Tam.*). From (pan, san. to barter). Money in general, so coin.—"*a*" Anciently a small gold coin, the tenth or twelfth part of a calanjy [q.v.]. Somewhere about 1¼ rupee. The ancient gold fanams generally exhibit the same devices as the pagodas [q.v.]. Such are the elephant of the congoos, boar of the chalookyas, fish of the paundyans, tiger of the cholas and of the hoysalas of dwaurasamoodram; some with the lion-looking back, the device of the cadambas; some with a naugam [cobra] serpent called Soobramanyan; the Shreeveishnava three-pronged sectarian mark [naumam], probably struck at Vencatagherry or Tripatty; the Getty fanam with the figure of a dagger identified with the Mahrattas of Tanjore; the bull, which may be related either to Condaveed, Warangal, or perhaps to the later Cholas; the seated Lutchmy fanam connected with the Lutchmy mauda or half pagoda, &c. Latterly the fanam was of silver or base gold. This bore various local values, but according to the old Madras monetary system, prevailing till 1818, 42 fanams went to one star pagoda, and a Madras silver fanam was therefore worth about 2*d*. Silver fanams are still met with on W. coast and as late as 1862 were received at the treasuries of Tellicherry and Calicut; they are generally four chuckrams, and worth about $3\frac{1}{2}$*d*.; like chuckrams [q.v.] they are counted on a board.—"*b*" The following are different kinds of old gold [pon] and silver [velly] Fanam coins:—Cataury, from (kattára, san. dagger); gold, struck by rajahs of negapatam. Chikka deva roya, from the younger devaroya of mysore, silver. Chooly, from (shuli, tam. circle), gold, ramnaud. Gajapaty, from gajapaties of orissa gold. Getty, with figure of dagger, mahrattas of tanjore, gold. Gopooram, from image, gold. Haley, from (halé, can. old), silver. Hydary, copper, issued by hyder. Ikkairy, from place so called, gold. Jhelly fanam, from (shalli, tam. small piece), trichinopoly, 16 to 1 pagoda, gold. Madura, gold, struck by naugama naick. Matsya moodray, from fish stamp, gold. Meily, from (muyyin, can. token), seringapatam, 45 to 1 star pagoda, silver. Moraury row, gold, struck by moraury row, also known as nauga moodray. Mysore, silver. Nangoora; anchor fanam, coimbatore coin, 33 to 1 star pagoda, silver. Nauma moodray, having naumam, gold. Pitchacaul, beggar's fanam, coimbatore, $1,588\frac{3}{8}\frac{1}{4}$ to 100 star pagodas, base gold. Pondicherry, silver. Raja canteroy, coined by canteroy, mysore king, gold. Raushy fanam, from (ráshi, san. a sign of the zodiac); the most ancient of the indigenous fanams; gold, and have fourteen dots; twelve dots are twelve signs [raushy] of the zodiac, and the two separate dots are sun [sooryan] and moon [chundran]. Shambhoo moodray, from (shambhu, san. shiva), gold. Simha moodray, lion stamp, gold, of honnore. Soobbaroya or snake, by poligar of codicondah; gold; four varieties; in one is a snake on a plain field supported by emblems of sun and moon; in a second sun and moon are wanting; in third only upper portion of snake with hood distended appears between sun and moon, on fourth the typical five-headed naugam occurs in usual seated position; on the reverse is the word shree [q.v.] in nagry [q.v.]. Sultauny; a coin of tippoo's, about $3\frac{1}{2}$ to the rupee, silver. Tellicherry, silver, 33 to 1 star pagoda, silver. Trinomallee, gold. Veeroye, by veera royer of coimbatore, gold and silver; malabar, new, 1,225 to 100 star pagodas, old, 1,400 to 100 star pagodas; coimbatore, $1,489\frac{1}{16}$ to 100 star pagodas; some very pure, whence called apuranjy [q.v.] fanams. Vencatramana, from the god, gold. Vrishabha moodray, bull stamp, gold.—"*c*" The following may be taken as a scale for the silver fanam coin:—2 chinnapanams = 1 fanam; $22\frac{1}{2}$ fanams = 1 star pagoda [naunyam, 2a]. Approximate actual value, 1 fanam = 2 annas 6 pies. Compare Can. hana, Tel. baida.—"*d*" Fanam is also a goldsmith's weight. 2 munjandies = 1 fanam; 9 fanams = 1 pagoda weight [niray, 3a]. Approximate actual value, 1 fanam = 6 grains. Same as Can. hana, Tel. chinnam. Compare Chowlam. See vol. I, 609.

FAN PALM (پنکہے کا تاڑ - pankhekátár, *Hind.*). Title from fans being made of the leaves. The usual application of this name is to the palmyra [q.v.], which is the type on which European fans have been formed; but it is also sometimes applied to the talipot [q.v.].

FARAMOOSHY (فراموشی - farámúshí, *Hind.*). From persian. Carelessness.

FARANGHEE (فرنگی - farangí, *Hind.*). Foreign [q.v.] or european [europe, firangy, seema, vilanyaty]. Plant first term. Ex., where transl. is of second term:—Argemone mexicana (frangídhatúra), datura fastuosa; Boswellia serrata, var. glabra (farangíúdkájhár), incense + tree; Sterculia fœtida (farangíbádam), prunus amygdalus. See gloss. paragraphs.

FARASY (فارسی - fársí, *Hind.*). Persian language [pars].

FARAUR (فرار - farár, *Hind.*). From (farra, ar. to run away). Flight.——*Faraury* (فراری - farárí, Hind.). From (farár, pers. flight). A person who has absconded.——*Faraury log* (فراری لوگ - farárlog, Hind.). From (above + log, hind. people). Deserters.

FAREED (فرید - faríd, *Ar.*). From (farada, ar. single). Unique, precious. The name of a Mahomedan saint [walee]. Mahomedan alam. Also part of lacab; as Fareed bee, alam + alaumat; Fareed ood deen, the precious gem of faith [ism].——*Fareedbootee* (فرید بوٹی - farídbútí, Hind.). Means fareed's plant, from a saint of that name having lived on water, rendered mucilaginous with the leaves. Plant name common to Cocculus villosus, Pedalium murex; see gloss. paragraphs.

FARHAT (فرحت - farhat, *Hind.*). From (faraha, ar. to rejoice). Comfort, delight. Part of alam and lacab; as Farhat bee, delightful lady; Farhat ool moolk, joy of the state [ism].

FAROKHT (فروخت - farokht, *Hind.*). From (furokhtan, pers. to sell). Sale [vicrayam].

FAROOK (فاروق - fárúk, *Hind.*). From (faraka, ar. to distinguish). Title of Caliph omar.——*Farooky* (فاروقی - fárúkí, Hind.). A class of Sheikhs named after Caliph omar.

FARSANG (فرسنگ - farsang, *Hind.*). Persian measure of length. Twenty-two furlongs and two-fifths or 2·78 miles [coss].

FARZ (فرض - farz, *Hind.*). From (faraza, ar. to mark), because it is pressed on a man like a mark. God's commands are of two kinds:—Farz or injunction, which in delivering he has repeated thrice and the neglect of which is a mortal sin; Waujib [q.v.] or injunction which in delivering he has repeated twice.

FARZEEN (فرزین - farzín, *Hind.*). Queen in chess [shatranj].

FASEEH (فصیح - fasíh, *Hind.*). Means clear. Eloquent. Part of lacab; as Faseeh ood deen, eloquent in religion [ism].

FATAKREE (پھٹکری - phatakrí, *Hind.*). Alum [padicauram].

FATAUWAH (فتاوی - fatáwá, *Hind.*). From (fatá, ar. decree). Plural. Collection or digest of judicial decisions. The best known is the Fatauwah e alumgheery, compiled by order of Aurungzeeb [futwah].

FATIMAH (فاطمہ - fátimah, *Hind.*). From (fatama, ar. to wean). Name of the prophet's daughter. Female alam, as Fatimah bee, alam + female alaumat [ism].

FAUKHTAH (فاختہ - fákhtah, *Hind.*). A dove [capotam]; term of abuse, meaning simpleton.

FAUSH (فاش - fásh, *Hind.*). From persian. Published.

FAUTIHA (فاتحہ - fátihah, Hind.). From (fataha, ar. to open) [futteh]. The first chapter of the Koran [q.v.] which is recited in prayers [namauz] for dying Mahomedans; hence prayers for defunct [janauza]; at marriages [shaudy], &c., oblations and offerings to saints [walee].

FAZL (فضل - fazl, *Hind.*). From (fazala, ar. to exceed). Grace. Prefixed to an alam forms a lacab; as Fazl hoossain, grace of hoossain; Shiah name [ism].——*Fauzil* (فاضل - fázil, Hind.). From (fazala, ar. to exceed). Excellent. Prefixed to an alam forms a lacab; as Fauzil Mahomed, excellent mahomed. Feminine form is Fauzilah; as:—Fauzilah khanam, with female alaumat added [ism].

FEEL (فیل - fíl, *Hind.*). Elephant [q.v.]. Feel khana are elephant stables [aunesaul].

FEHRIST (فہرست - fehrist, *Hind.*). From persian. Catalogue [daul, zaubitah].

FEISAL (فیصلہ - faislah, *Hind.*). From (fasl, ar. division) [fusl]. Settlement. Feisal teervay is settled land-tax.

FEIZ (فیض - faiz, *Ar.*). From (fáza, ar. to overflow). Bounty. Prefixed to an alam forms a lacab; as Feiz ally, bounty of ally [ism].——*Feiyauz* (فیاض - faiyáz, Ar.). Liberal. Prefixed to an alam forms a lacab; as Feiyauz ally, bounty of ally [ism].——*Feizoo* (فیضو - faizú, Hind.). Graceful. Lacab [ism].

FERISHTA (فرشتہ - firishtah, *Hind.*). From (fristádan, pers. to send). A messenger. An angel. The four recognized angels by Mahomedans are Jibbreel [q.v.], the archangel, Michael [q.v.], of rain; Israfeel [q.v.], of resurrection; and Izraeel [q.v.] of death. Takhalloos [q.v.] of Hindoo shah the historian of the Beejapore court. His work Taureek e ferishta is text-book at Madras.

FEROKHEE (فرخی - farrukhí, *Hind.*). From (farrukh, pers. happy). Tippoo's projected capital near Beypore [furrackabad]. Also his quarter mohur [q.v.].

FEVER (ज्वर - jvara, *San.*). Prefix to many medicinal plants.——*Fever grass* (ज्वराङ्कुश - jvaránkusha, San.). Title from use. Sanscrit means fever goad. Same as Ibharancoosha.——*Fever nut* (జ్వరగత్త - jvaragattsa, Tel.). Title from use. Same as Bonduc.

FI (فی - fí, *Ar.*). Arabic prefix signifying in; as Filjoomla, meaning in + whole, on the whole; Filshad, per cent.

FIDAH (فدا - fidá, *Ar.*). From (fidá, ar. to ransom). Sacrifice. Prefixed to an alam forms a lacab; as Fidah ally, sacrifice of ally; mostly taken by Shiahs [ism].

FIDWY (فدوی - fidwí, *Pers.*). Obedient. So 'your obedient servant,' or 'I.'

FILFIL (فلفل - filfil, *Ar.* and *Pers.*). Chilly [q.v.] or pepper [q.v.]. Cf. Capsicum annuum (filfiliahmar), red chilly; Piper longum (filfilidaráz), long pepper; Piper nigrum (filfilisiyáh), black pepper. See gloss. paragraphs.

FINDAK (فندق - findak, *Hind.*). From (banadík, ar. venice), as coming from there. Filbert.——*Findakihind* (فندق هند - findakihind, Ar.). Indian filbert [bonduc], or soapnut [q.v.].

FIRANGY (فرنگی - farangí, *Hind.*). From (farang, pers. europe). Relating to Europe [europe, faranghee, foreign, seema, vilauyaty]. Portuguese, who settled on the west coast of India, thus known to the natives. Also applied to natives converted by the Portuguese. Now used to denote any European, especially by Mahomedans. Also occurs in some place names, as firangy dibba or portuguese mound.

FIRAUSAT (فراست - firásat, *Hind.*). From (farasa, ar. to discern). Sagacious. Part of lacab ; as Firausat jung, sagacious in war [ism].

FIREWORK PLANT (इंगुदी - ingudí, *San.* ; हिंगण - hingana, *Mahr.* ; هنگن کا پیڑ - hingankáper, *Hind.* ; هنگن کاجهاڑ - hingan-kájhár, *Dec.* ; ಇಂಗಳೀಕ - ingalíka, *Can.* ; గార - gára, *Tel.* ; ഞഞ്ചുണ്ട - nañchunta, *Mal.* ; நஞ்சுண்டான் - nañjundán, *Tam.*). Title from use of nut shells. San. from (ing, san. to move) [baudam, catapang]. Mahr. from sanscrit. Hind. from (hingana, mahr. the tree + per, hind. tree). Can. from sanscrit. Tel. from (gaurí, san. the deity) ; nut shells like grenades used in her worship [portia]. Mal. from tamul. Tam. from (nañju, tam. poison + undai, tam. a ball); destructive ball, from use of nut shells in fireworks. San. also (tápasataru), meaning anchorite's tree ; (munipádapa), meaning anchorite's tree ; because gooroos prepare from the seeds an oil for the lamp which they use in the ceremony of gooroo oopausanay. Hind. also (hingol). Title otherwise Bean caper, Gooroo's tree, Gowry's tree, Hingan, Poison-ball, Zachun-oil tree. Distinguish from Hing [q.v.]. Botanically Balanites roxburghii, planchon, simarubeæ [vricsham, 33]. Alias Balanites ægyptiaca, indica ; Himenia ægyptiaca, americana ; Ximenia ægyptiaca. Tree, 20 feet ; leaves alternate, bifoliate ; spines axillary ; calyx five-parted ; sepals villous ; petals five, lanceolate ; pedicels one-flowered ; flowers aggregate, small, green, fragrant ; flowering in may ; drupe ovoid, acute, one-celled, one-seeded, with a woody five-angled nut ; nut covered with a soft pulpy substance like soap [sauboon], bitter and with an offensive greasy smell ; variety of egyptian plant found in plains of deccan [q.v.]. Unripe drupes are purgative ; seeds given in coughs ; bark and leaves anthelmintic and purgative ; bark used as cattle medicine. Ripe drupes are eaten ; young twigs and leaves browsed by cattle. Seeds give fixed fat oil ; nut very hard and used in fireworks [baunam] ; a hole being made in it, kernel extracted, and shell filled with powder, when on firing it bursts with a loud report. Wood yellowish white, moderately hard, no heart-wood, no annual rings ; used for walking-sticks and for fuel. No other species here.

FIRKAH (فرقہ - firkah, *Hind.*). From (farika, ar. to divide). Division. Portion of a talook [taraf, tookady]. In Canara portion of a hobly [q.v.] ; the charge of one shanbogue [q.v.]. Cf. Vattam.

FIRMAUN (فرمان - farmán, *Hind.*). From (farmúdan, pers. to command). A mandate, charter [sunnud].——*Nahfirmaun* (نافرمان - náfarmán, Pers.). From (ná, pers. against + farmán, pers. order). Title otherwise Dolphin flower, Larkspur, Rocket larkspur. Botanically Delphinium ajacis, linn., ranunculaceæ [vricsham, 1]. The specific name from certain markings on petals, presenting resemblance to letters A I A I ; hence conjectured to be hyacinth of ancients, which had similar markings. Annual with much divided alternate leaves and showy racemes of blue flowers ; seeds very acrid. Stavesacre or Lousewort is from delphinium staphisagria, linn. No other species here.

FIROZE (فیروز - fíroz, *Ar.*). Victorious. Part of lacab ; as a Firoze hoossain, triumph of hoossain [ism].——*Firozah* (فیروزہ - fírozah, Ar., Pers. and Hind. ; నీలమణి - nílamani, Tel. ; நீலக்கல் - nílakkal, Tam.). Drav. means blue gem. From Persia. The stone is opaque, lamellar, and of a fine pale-blue color. It is the tooth of an animal, penetrated with blue calx of copper [ratnam].

FIRYAUD (فریاد - faryád, *Hind.*). From persian. A complaint, entering of a law suit [anyauyam]. Firyaudy is the complainant, plaintiff.

FITR (فطر - fitr, *Hind.*). From (fatara, ar. to break). Breaking a fast [roza] ; especially the meal taken after sunset every day in the month of Ramzaun [q.v.], or the Eed ool fitr when that month [maheena] is complete.——*Fitoor* (فتور - fitúr, Hind.). From (fatara, ar. to slacken). Intrigue, insurrection [baghauvat].——*Fitrah* (فطرہ - fitrah, Hind.). Alms of grain or corn given at Eed ool fitr.——*Fitrat* (فطرت - fitrat, Ar.). Sagacity. Part of lacab, as Fitrat ally, sagacity of ally ; Fitrat jung, sagacious in war [ism].

FLAME TREE (अग्निशिखा - agnishikhá, *San.*). Title from flower. Same as Wild bachnaug and Bastard saffron. Compare flame of the woods [jungle geranium], flame plant [saffron], and fire plant [godaury].

FLORICAN (तनमोर - tanamóra, *Mahr.* ; هوبره - hubarah, *Ar.* and *Pers.* ; چرز - charaz, *Hind.* and *Dec.* ; ಕನ್ನಾವ್ಲು - kannaulu, *Can.* ; నేలనెమలి - nélanemali, *Tel.* ; வரகுக்கோழி - varagukkózhi, *Tam.*). Title from dutch. Mahr. from (tana, mahr. grass + móra, mahr. peacock). Ar. from (hubara, ar. ash-colored). Can. from (kari, can. black + naulu, can. peacock). Tel. from (néla, tel. ground + nemali, tel. peacock). Tam. from (varagu, tam. indian millet, panicum miliaceum, linn. + kózhi, tam. fowl). Hind. also (likh) ; (ghaskámurghí), meaning grass fowl ; (khartítar), meaning grass partridge. Tel. also (chénukódi), meaning field + fowl. Title otherwise Floyerken, Lesser florican, Likh. A small kind of bustard. Sypheotides auritus, otididæ, pressirostres, grallatores [pacshy, 35], of naturalists [jantoo]. Alias Otis fulva. Male, in full breeding plumage, with head, neck, ear-tufts, medial wing-coverts, and whole lower plumage deep black, chin alone being white ; lower part of hind neck and large patch on wing white, rest of plumage fulvous, closely mottled with dark brown ; first three primaries plain dusky brown, remainder both barred and mottled with brown. Down at base of all feathers beautiful pale dull rose-color, quills, when freshly moulted, have beautiful bloom, mingled pink and green, which soon fades. Ear-tufts about 4 inches long, usually three feathers on each side ; with shaft bare, small oval web at the tip, curving upwards. Primaries much acuminated, sometimes ending in point almost as fine as needle. Bill dusky above, edges of upper, and all lower mandible yellowish ; irides pale yellow, clouded with dusky ; legs dirty whitish yellow. Length 18 to 19 inches. Female has prevalent tone of plumage pale fulvus yellow, feathers of head, back, wings and tail, clouded and barred with deep brown, those on head mostly brown ; fore neck with two irregular interrupted streaks, increasing on lower neck and breast, lower plumage thence unspotted and albescent ; hind neck finally speckled brown ; chin and throat white ; first three primaries, as in male, unspotted brown ; wing coverts with only a few bars ; axillaries brown. Bill, legs and irides as in male, but irides generally unclouded yellow. Chiefly found in cold weather ; frequents long grass, but also to be met with in grain fields ; feeds chiefly in morning, then easily raised ; when moving raises its tail ; when flushed suddenly utters sharp note of alarm ; flesh most esteemed of all game birds ; occasionally snared. No other common species here. The Bengal florican is Sypheotides bengalensis.

FLYING FOX (वातुलि - vátuli, *San.* ; वडवागूळ - vadavágúla, *Mahr.* ; خفاش - khaffásh, *Ar.* ; روباه‌پر - rúbáhpar, *Pers.* ; بادر - bádur, *Hind.* ; گدل - gadal, *Dec.* ; ತೊಗಲುಬಾವಲಿ - togalubávale, *Can.* ; ಕೀಚಬಾವೊಲಿ - kíchabávoli, *Too.* ; చీకురాయి - chíkuráyi, *Tel.* ; ଚିମ୍ମୁନିଯା - chimmunia, *Oor.* ; ആവൽ - ával, *Mal.* ; වවුලා - vavulá, *Singh.* ; பழந்தின்வவ்வால் - pazhandinvavvál, *Tam.*). Title from color of hair and length of snout. San. from (váta, san. wind). Mahr. from (vada, corruption of vana, san. forest + valgula, san. flying fox). Ar. from (khafisha, ar. small eye). Pers. from (rúbáh, pers. fox + par, pers. flying). Hind. from sanscrit. Can. from (togalu, can. skin + bávale, can. bat). Too. from (kícha, too. sound + báveli, too. bat). Tel. from (chíku, tel. blindness + váyi, tel. face) ; from small eyes. Tam. from (pazham, tam. fruit + tin, tam. to eat + vavvál, tam. bat). San. also (valgula), meaning handsome. Mahr. also (vágala), from sanscrit. Hind. also (barbagal). Tel. also (síkatyelli), meaning darkness + rat ; (rishipakshi), meaning sage + bird. Singh. also (lokuvavula), meaning large + bat. Title otherwise Large fox bat, Russet fox. Pteropus edwardsi, pteropodidæ, cheiroptera, mammalia [sastanam, 3], of naturalists [jantoo]. Alias assamensis, edulis, medius. Head and nape rufous black ; neck and shoulders golden yellow ; back, dark brown ; chin, dark ; rest of body beneath, fulvous or rusty brown ; interfemoral membrane, brownish black. These are frugivorous bats [vavvaul] of large size, differing so much in their dentition from the insectivorous species that they seem to lead through the flying lemurs [devaunga] directly to the Quadrumana. The dentition is adapted to their diet. They measure sometimes as much as four feet and a half from tip to tip of wing. They have no tail. They are distinguished from the rest of the bats by a claw on the first or index finger, which is short. The tongue is remarkable, being covered with large papillæ, pointing backwards, and each one terminating in a brush or collection of bristly points. It is supposed that they drink toddy [q.v.] from the earthen pots [chatty] on the cocoanut [q.v.] trees. The wild almond [catapang] is their favorite fruit. During the day they roost on trees hanging with their heads down. When disturbed during the day, they fly slowly round and round, with a low screaming noise and soon settle again ; hovering for a moment over a bough, they catch suddenly with the claw at the angle of the wing, and, allowing the body to drop, they swing with a single hold. Towards sunset they move about along the branches, and by ones and twos fly off. If water is at hand, they fly down and touch the water. It is not known whether this is for drinking or for bathing a part of their bodies. It is not for fishing, as by some supposed. About the early dawn they return when a scene of great confusion ensues. Friar Jordanus, the Quilon bishop of the fourteenth century, has the following :—"There be also bats really and truly as big as kites [chillam]. "These birds fly nowhither by day, but only when the sun sets. "Wonderful! By day they hang themselves upon trees by the "feet, with their bodies downwards, and in the daytime they "look just like big fruit on the tree." Marco Polo describes them thus :—" Bald owls [ooloocam] which fly in the night; they "have neither wings nor feathers and are large as an eagle "[cooralam]." The female brings forth only one young one, which adheres firmly to the breast, retaining its position whether the mother be flying or at rest. Many classes eat the flesh. Akin to this is the Fulvous fox bat or Pteropus leschenaultii. Alias seminudus; Xantharpyia seminuda. Fur, of a fulvous ashy, or dull light ashy brown color, paler beneath, the hairs whitish at the base; membranes, dark brown; fur, short and downy. Found at Madras, Pondicherry, Trichinopoly, &c. Again there is the Small fox bat, or Cynopterus marginatus. General color fulvous olivaceous, pale beneath and with an ashy tinge; ears, with a narrow margin of white. It roosts during the day in clusters on the folded leaves of the plantain [q.v.], palmyra [q.v.] palm, and other trees. It is exclusively frugivorous.

FOOZALAH (فضلا - fuzalá, *Ar.*). Plural of (fázil, ar. accomplished). Forms part of lacab; as Malik ool foozalah, king of the accomplished.

FORBIDDEN FRUIT (ثمر ناجایز - samarinájáiz, *Hind.*). Same as Eve's apple and Pummelow.

FOREIGN (ولایتی - viláití, *Hind.*). Very common term for plants introduced to India [europe, faranghee, firangy, seema, vilauyaty]. Cf. :—Acacia ferruginea, foreign velvail; Althæa officinalis, foreign tootty; Carum carui, foreign anise; Cassia alata, foreign agatty; Malva sylvestris, var. mauritiana, foreign marsh mallow. See gloss. paragraphs.

FORT (قلعہ - kilah, *Hind.*). Prefix.——*Fort st. david* (قلعہ سنت ڈیوڈ - kilahisentdevid, Hind.; தேவனாம்பட்டணம் - tévanámbattanam, Tam.). From (tévanáyakkan, tam. proper name + pattana, san. city). Sanscrit name (dévípattana), meaning parvaty + town. Otherwise Tegnapatam by corruption. Town; South arcot dist., Cuddalore tal.; acres 534; lat. 11° 44′; long. 79° 49′; from Cuddalore N.N.E. 2 miles. On left bank of mouth of the Guddilam. Purchased by Company from Rama rajah, a son of Shivajee, for 120,000 chuckrams [q.v.], in 1690. On capture of Madras by French in 1746, Company's agent at this station assumed the control of all the Company's possessions in Southern india and successfully resisted an attack made by Dupleix on the settlement. In 1756 Clive was appointed Governor. In 1758 it was invested by sea and land by the French, and after a short siege, surrendered on June 2, when the fortifications were demolished and were never rebuilt. It was afterwards included in Cuddalore and its dependencies. Ruined houses are still to be seen on the ramparts, and some parts of the fort are in good preservation. Subterranean passages appear to have run completely round under the glacis; while, at short intervals, other galleries striking off at right angles, and terminating in powder chambers, served as mines. At the south-east corner the gallery ran down to the edge of the sea, while on the other three sides the fort was protected by the Ponniaur [q.v.] and two canals. The ruins form a recognised landmark for mariners.——*Fort st. george* (قلعہ سینٹ جارج - kilahisentjárj, Hind.). For a History of fort see vol. II, 279. See also Madras.

FOWJ (فوج - fauj, *Hind.*). From arabic. Army [dandam, pataulam].——*Fowjdar* (فوجدار - faujdár, Hind.). From (above + dár, pers. keeper). Under the Mahomedan governments the chief magistrate of a province.——*Fowjdarry* (فوجداری - faujdárí, Hind.). Criminal, as opposed to diwanny [q.v.] or civil [adawlut].

FOWT (فوت - fáut, *Hind.*). From (fáta, ar. to pass away). Dead. Fowty is one deceased, or legally defunct. Fowtynauma is a list of deaths. Fowty faraury means dead or absconded.

FRANKINCENSE (فرنگی عود - farangíúd, *Hind.*). From (farangí, hind. european + úd, hind. incense). Same as Olibanum.——*Male frankincense* (لوبان - lubán, Dec.). Same as True olibanum.——*White frankincense* (வெள்ளைக்குங்கிலியம் - vellaikkungiliyam, Tam.). Same as White dammer.

FRASERPETT (ಫ್ರೇಜರ್‌ಪೇಟೆ - p'hréjarpéte, *Can.*; fraserpet, *Coorg gov.*). Can. also (kushálanagara), meaning happy + town; named, after birth of tippoo, by hyder. Principal town in Nunjaraputna talook of Coorg. In north lat. 12° 27′; east long. 76° 2′; on the left bank of the Cauvery, on the main road from Seringapatam to Mercara, 20 miles east of the latter. From Mangalore S.E. 81 miles, Bangalore S.W. 117 miles, Madras W. 290 miles. 2,720 feet above sea-level. Population 1,310. Named after General Fraser, first Commissioner in 1834. It is situated close to the ruins of Jafferabad, a fort built by Tippoo. Fort stormed and demolished in 1789 by the Coorgs under Dodda veerarajendra. The ruins supplied materials for the construction of the bridge over the Cauvery finished in 1848. The climate is milder and the rains less severe than at Mercara. The place is the monsoon [q.v.] residence of the Commissioner of Coorg.

FRAUNSEES (فرانسیس - faránsís, *Hind.*). The French.

FRENCH ROCKS (ಹಿರೋಡೆ - hiróde, *Can.*). Hills so called at Hirode, Mysore district. Highest point 2,882 feet [hirode].

FRESH WATER SHARK (میٹھے پانی کی ھورا - míthepáníkíshorá, *Hind.*). Term common to many siluridæ [kizhautty].

FROG FISH (مینڈک مچھی - mendakmacchí, *Hind.*; కప్పచేప - kappachépa, *Tel.*; കടത്തവല - katattavala, *Mal.*). Title from appearance of head and mouth. Tel. means frog fish. Mal. means sea frog. Title otherwise Frog doke, Globe fish, Puff fish. The genus Tetrodon, gymnodontidæ, plectognathi, teleostei, pisces [matsyam, 45], of naturalists [jantoo]. Some are poisonous. The species best known to the natives are lunaris and reticularis. Cf. Plantchy.

FULLAK (فلک - falak, *Hind.*). From (falaka, ar. to become round). The firmament. The bastinado wherein the soles of the feet are turned to the sky [asmaun].

FULWA BUTTER (پھلوا - phalwá, *Hind.*). Product of bassia butyracea [butter mohwah].

FURRAUSH (فراش - farrásh, *Hind.*). From (farsh, pers. floor cloth). A man to spread carpets, &c., a sweeper.

FURRUCKABAD (فرخ آباد - farrukhábád, *Hind.*). From (farrukh, pers. prosperous + ábád, pers. city). Mal. name (paramukk), corruption from hindostany. Title otherwise Ferok. Village, Railway station; Malabar dist., Yernaud tal.; lat. 11° 11′; long. 75° 52′; from Calicut S.E. 6½ miles; from Munjery W.N.W. 20 miles; from the sea E. 2½ miles. The place which Tippoo sahib in 1789 designed to be the capital of Malabar, and whither in that year he removed the inhabitants of Calicut. In the following year fort was captured by British. It still exists in ruin on a hill crowned by a bungalow [q.v.] now used as a dynamite magazine. Railway here crosses Beypore river. Puttimars [q.v.] can come up to it.

FUSL (فصل - fasl, *Hind.*). From (fasala, ar. to divide) [feisal]. A section, season, thence harvest.——*Fusl cummy* (فصل کمی - faslkamí, Hind.). From (above + kamí, pers. deficiency). Remission granted on two-crop land cultivated with only one crop for want of water [teervay cummy]. See vol. I, 134.——*Fusl jausty* (فصل زیادتی - faslziyádatí, Hind.). From (above + ziyádati, hind. addition). A charge for a second crop raised by Government water on land registered as single crop [teervay jausty]. See vol. I, 134.——*Fusl khareef* (فصل خریف - faslikharíf, Hind.). From (above + kharíf, ar. falling of leaves). Autumn season.——*Fusl rabee* (فصل ربیع - faslirabí, Hind.). From (above + rabí, ar. spring). Spring season.——*Fusly* (فصلی - faslí, Hind.). Harvest year. Also called Hindoo year. Instituted by Acbar. In Bengal it begins in September, with the full moon preceding the autumnal equinox [toolauyanam]; its date also varying three years from the Madras fusly; to find this, subtract 593 from the Christian year. Here from 1st July to the 30th June, and it formerly counted from the 12th July. Here 590 years less than the A.D. year. See vol. I, 612; II, 247.

FUTTEH (فتح - fath, *Hind.*). From (fataha, ar. to open) [fautiha]. Victory. Prefixed to an alam forms a lacab; as Futteh ally, ally's victory [ism]. There is a Hindostany proverb :—گانڈ لنگوٹی نام فتح خان—"He has only a strip of rag "between his legs, but his name is Futteh khan, Lord of victory."

FUTWAH (فتویٰ - fatwá, *Hind.*). From (fatá, ar. decree) [fatauwah]. An exposition of the Mahomedan law pronounced by a Moofty [q.v.].

G (ग - ga, *San.*; گ - gáf, *Hind.*). San. indicates Ganesh [q.v.] or Vigneshwaran [q.v.]. Hind. numerically 20.

GA (गा - gá, *San.*). To sing.——*Gandharvacottah* (கந்தருவக்கோட்டை - kandaruvakkóttai, Tam. gandharvakóta *). From (gandharva, san. celestial chorister + kóttai, tam. fort).—"*a*" Zemindarry; Tanjore dist., Tanjore tal.; pop. 1,882; lat. 10° 29′ to 10° 41′; long. 78° 59′ to 79° 17′. The late zemindar [q.v.] was transported for life. Peshcush Rs. 6,577.—"*b*" Village, Head-quarters of zemindar; Tanjore dist., Tanjore tal.; pop. 374; lat. 10° 34′; long. 79° 03′; from Tanjore S.S.W. 17¼ miles. Fairs every Tuesday.——*Gandharvan* (गन्धर्व - gandharva, San.). From (gána, san. song). Celestial chorister. Southey changed this to Glendoveer. The most celebrated Gandharvans are Toombooroo and Nauradan [q.v.]. Also ancient form of marriage depending only on the mutual consent of the parties. Also in modern times an inferior marriage which gives the wife less than full rights. Sometimes applied to a marriage between persons of full age. See vol. I (62), (78) [matam]. Cf. Raucshasam.——*Gaundharva vedam* (गान्धर्ववेद - gándharvavéda, San.). From (gandharva, san. celestial chorister + véda, san. knowledge). Science [shastram] of music [sangeetam].——*Gayatry* (गायत्री - gáyatrí, San.). From (gai, san. to sing). A kind of metre [chandas]. So a particular and specially holy verse of the Veda [q.v.] written therein. The affinity between god [deva] and light [jyoty] is its burden. Bramins [q.v.] repeat it, with certain finger-signs or anganyausam [q.v.], every morning at sunrise; standing in, or near water, which is sipped, and then poured from the hands during the suppressed repetition of the prayer [muntram]. After the trisyllabic om [q.v.], follows an invocation to heaven, earth, and sky, and then a salutation to the sun [sooryan]; probably as a visible representation of deity. Extraordinary powers are attributed to the whole formula; and, like the principal deities, it has its thousand and eight names or epithets, called sahasranaumam [q.v.]. Cf. Chowraushy. The gayatry is also personified as the wife of Bramha [q.v.]. This verse occurs in the tenth hymn of the third Ashtacam, of the Samhitay [q.v.] of the Rig vedam [q.v.]. The following is the original in its common form:—ओंभूर्भुवस्सुवः तत्सवितुर्वरेण्यं भर्गो देवस्यधीमहि धियोयोनःप्रचोदयात्—"Om! earth! air! heaven! We "meditate on that excellent light of the divine sun; may it "illuminate our minds." It admits of two interpretations, one referring to Bramha, and the other to the natural sun. The Vedantists [q.v.] incline to the former, though the latter appears to be more natural. See vol. II, 235 [matam].——*Geeta govindam* (गीतगोविन्द - gítagóvinda, San.). From (gíta, san. song + góvinda, san. vishnu, the cow-protector). By Jayadevan. Erotic poem about twelfth century. To celebrate loves of Krishnan [q.v.] and Raudhay [q.v.]; but is given also a mystical interpretation. See vol. I 74).——*Geetay* (गीता - gítá, San.). From (gá, san. to sing). Short for Bhagavat geeta [q.v.].

GADA (گڑھ - garh, *Hind.*; ଗଡ - gada, *Oor.*). Fort. Suffix in place names, especially in Ganjam and Vizagapatam [ghur, godo, gooda].

GADABAH (గదబ - gadaba, *Tel.*). A tribe in the Northern circars [q.v.]. Some 30,000. The language is Kolarian [bhaushay, jauty, kole]. See vol. I (38).

GADDA (గడ్డ - gadda, *Tel.*). Clod. Mound [goodda, mett, metta, mittah]. Suffix in place names; as Avanigadda, meaning earth + mound. Also lands on high level, bearing favorable assessment [gaddateerwa, inam]. Also means esculent roots [doompa].——*Guddapaur* (గడ్డపార - gaddapára, Tel.; കടപ്പാറ - katappára, Mal.; கடப்பாறை - kadappárai, Tam.). From (gadda, tel. clod + pára, tel. a hoe). Tam. also (párai); also (páraikkól), meaning crowbar + stick. Crowbar.——*Gaddavary* (గడ్డవరి - gaddavari, Tel.). From (gadda, tel. clod + vari, tel. paddy). Sowing paddy [q.v.] without previously flooding the ground; otherwise dry ploughing. Opposite of Coodapa [q.v.]. Same as Veligada [pooldycaul, vellaumay].——*Gaddy* (గడ్డి - gaddi, Tel.). Grass.

GADHAH (गर्दभ - gardabha, *San.* and *Mahr.*; حمار - himár, *Ar.*; خر - khar, *Pers.*; گدها - gadhá, *Hind.*; كالدى - káldi, *Malay*; ಕತ್ತೆ - katte, *Can.* and *Too.*; గాడిదె - gádide, *Tel.*; ଗଧ - gadha, *Oor.*; കഴുത - kazhuta, *Mal.*; කළුඳාවා - kaludává, *Singh.*; கழுதை - kazhuthai, *Tam.*). Title from hindostany. San. from (gard, san. to bray). Hind. from sanscrit. Can. from (kattu, can. to bray). Tel. from sanscrit. Singh. from (kalu, singh. black + dává, singh. burnt); from color. Ar. also (himáriahlí), meaning domestic ass, as opposed to (himárivahshí) or wild ass. Pers. also (ilá). Title otherwise Ass. Domesticated animal. Equus [ashwam] asinus, equidæ, perissodactyla, ungulata, mammalia [sastanam, 21]; of naturalists [jantoo]. Asses are distinguished from horses by their longer head and ears, by the tail being covered with short hairs at the base and furnished with a tuft of long hairs towards the tip and on the sides only, not throughout as in horses. They also want the peculiar hard horny excrescences found on the legs of horses, and have almost invariably a dark longitudinal dorsal stripe. Several species of wild ass are now known to exist, one of which is a native of the western parts of India, Equus onager, but not of this presidency. The domestic ass is small, used only by washermen [dhoby], vagrant Yerkalas [q.v.], and some other wandering tribes. It is unfit for the saddle. The hollow of the ass's foot adapts it for travelling on slippery ground, and its constitution enables it to bear great fatigue in this climate. Pliny describes it as 'animal frigoris maxime impatiens.' Mules are extensively used in this country. There is a Tamul proverb:—என்னைப்போலக் குரலும் என் அக்காளைப்போல ஒயிலும் இல்லை என்கிறதாம் கழுதை—"The ass boasted that there was no voice equal to "his, and no gait equal to that of his elder sister." Generally however the ass is not an object of ridicule. For horse see Ghorah, for mule see Katcher. Indian species not here found are:—Hemionus or kiang or wild ass of Thibet, Onager or wild ass of Cutch.

GAGGARY (گهگری - ghagrí, *Hind.*). From (gharghara, san. the sound). Loose iron fastened to a stick to frighten animals and reptiles [poochy], commonly carried by post-runners.

GAH (گاه - gáh, *Pers.*). Suffix denoting place; as Durgah, meaning threshold + place, any sacred precinct [eedgah].

GAJAM (गज - gaja, *San.*). From (gaj, san. to roar). Elephant [q.v.].——*Gaja mookhan* (गजमुख - gajamukha, San.). From (above + mukha, san. face). Vigneshwaran [q.v.].——*Gajapatinugger* (గజపతినగరము - gajapatinagaramu, Tel.). See sep. title.——*Gajapaty* (گجپتی - gajapatí, Hind.; గజపతి - gajapati, Tel.). From (above + pati, san. master). The lord of the elephants. Proper name [peyar]. A title of the Gungavamsham [q.v.] dynasty [raj] of Orissa [q.v.], 1132—1560, founded by Chorgunga. See vol. I (151); II, 77 [charitram]. The name is now held as a title by a family in N. circars [q.v.].——*Gajendran* (గజేంద్రుడు - gajéndrudu, Tel.). From (above + indra, san. best). Lordly elephant. Indran's elephant. Hindoo 2nd or pers. name [peyar].——*Gajpal* (گج پهل - gajphal, Hind.). From (above + p'hala, san. fruit). Same as Chaab pepper.

GAJAPATINUGGER (గజపతినగరము - gajapatinagaramu, *Tel.* gajapatinagar *). From (gajapati, san. lord of elephants, title of vizianagram dynasty + nagara, san. city) [gajam].——(1) Division; Vizagapatam district; area 348 square miles; population 123,796; language Teloogoo. Boundaries:—north, Bobbily talook; east, Cheepoorpully talook; south, Vizianagram talook; west, Saulore talook. Very irregular in shape; the northern and southern lines of boundaries being respectively 14 and 5 miles, and the eastern and western boundaries being 6 and 14 miles in length. Interspersed with hills of various dimensions and heights. Soil is generally poor; mostly gravelly and sandy. The principal industries are weaving [nesavoo], jewelry and carpentry. The chief exports are gingelly [q.v.], tobacco [pogauk] and jaggery [q.v.]. The Gajapaty nuddy and its tributary Lingaulavalsa gedda are chief sources of irrigation. The rest are shallow rain-fed tanks [q.v.]. Places of archæological interest:—Daivpully, Garbham, Gobaum, Jayanty agrahauram, Regoolavalsa [shikargunj], Vedoollavalsa. Principal Trig. station, Maroopully. The leading places, &c., in the division are the following.——*Andra* (ఆంధ్ర - ándra, Tel.). See sep. title.——*Bheemavaram* (భీమవరము - bhímavaramu, Tel.). From (bhíma, san. the hero + pura, san. town). Zemindarry, Village; pop. 264; from Gajapatinugger E. 21 miles; from Vizagapatam N. 49 miles. The name of the Zemindarry [q.v.] is Saripully bheemavaram.——*Daivpully* (దేవుపల్లె - dévupalle, Tel.). From (dévu, tel. a chief + palle, tel. village). Village; pop. 3,388; lat. 18° 15′; long. 83° 20′; from Gajapatinugger W.S.W. 4 miles; from Vizagapatam N. 37 miles. Former residence of a chief; ruined fort.——*Gajapatinugger* (గజపతినగరము - gajapatinagaramu, Tel.). See below.——*Goommacote* (గుమ్మకోట - gummakóta, Tel.). From (gumma, tel. grain receptacle + kóta, san. fort). Village, Hill; pop. 305. Shiva temple of Mullicarjoona sawmy, resorted to on Shivarautry [pundigay, 6a].——*Gostany* (గోస్తని - góstáni, Tel.). See sep. title.——*Jayity* (జయితి - jayiti, Tel.). Named after the Jeinas who once lived there. Village; pop. 1,576; lat. 18° 21′; long. 83° 18′; from Gajapatinugger N.W. 7½ miles; from Vizagapatam N. 44 miles. Half a mile west are Jeina temples, and near them a Sheiva temple.——*Maradaum* (మరడాం - maradám, Tel.). Village; pop. 1,302; lat. 18° 09′; long. 83° 16′; from Gajapatinugger S.W. 12 miles; from Vizagapatam N. 32 miles. Fine mango [q.v.] tope [q.v.]. Belongs to Saulore zemindar [q.v.]. Substantial choultry [q.v.].——*Maroopully* (మరుపల్లె - marupalle, Tel.). From (maru, tel. barren + palle, tel. village). Village; pop. 1,475; lat. 18° 19′; long. 83° 23′; from Gajapatinugger N. 2½ miles; from Vizagapatam N. 42 miles. Trig. station in lat. 18° 19′ 53·99″; long. 83° 23′ 27·37″; height 1,611 feet; from Gajapatinugger N. 3 miles.——*Sautaumvalsa* (సాతాంవలస - sátámvalasa, Tel.). From (sátu, tel. sack-cloth weaver + valasa, tel. colony). Village, Place of pilgrimage; pop. 1,201; lat. 18° 25′; long. 83° 35′; from Gajapatinugger N.E. 15¾ miles; from Vizagapatam N.N.E. 51 miles. Large cave on the adjoining hill resorted to on feast days. Contains many lingams [q.v.].——*Shikargunj* (شکار گنج - shikárganj, Hind.; శికారుగంజ్ - shikárganj, Tel.). From (shikár, hind. sport + ganj, pers. a granary). Ancient name (régulavalasa), meaning jujube tree, zizyphus jujuba, lam. + village. Village; pop. 1,339; lat. 18° 26′; long. 83° 26′; from Gajapatinugger N.N.E. 11¼ miles; from Vizagapatam N. 50 miles. This is a more recent name given by the late Maharajah of Vizianagram who reserved adjoining jungle for purposes of sport. Old fort.——*Toommicapulley* (తుమ్మికాపల్లె - tummikápalle, Tel.). From (tummika, tel. the tree, diospyros melanoxylon, roxb. + palle, tel. village). Village, Place of pilgrimage; pop. 515; lat. 17° 54′; long. 83° 13′; from Gajapatinugger S.S.W. 27 miles; from Vizagapatam N.N.W. 16 miles. Shiva temple resorted to on Shivarautry [pundigay, 6a] every year. Supposed to have been founded by Balaraman [q.v.], Krishnan's [q.v.] brother. At the junction of two streams.——(2) Deputy tahsildarry; Vizagapatam district. Pay Rs. 70.——(3) Town, Head-quarters of Talook and Deputy tahsildar; Vizagapatam dist., Gajapatinugger division; pop. 2,246; lat. 18° 17′; long. 83° 23′; from Coraputt S.E. 52 miles; from Madras N. 405 miles; from Narsapatam N.E. 63 miles; from Parvatipore S. 34 miles; from Vizagapatam N. 40 miles; from Vizianagram N. 13 miles. Once an important mart for hill produce. Trade declining. On the Champauvaty river, otherwise called the Gajapatinugger river.

GALAM (گلم کا تیل - galamkátel, *Hind.*). The reddish white solid oil [yennay] from Bassia butyracea [butter mohwah].

75

GALANGAL (रास्ना - rásná, *San.*; कोळंजन - kólanjana, *Mahr.*; خولنجان - khulanján, *Ar.*, *Pers.*, *Hind.* and *Dec.*; لنكوس - langkvas, *Malay*; ದುಂಪರಾಸ್ಮಿ - dumparásmi, *Can.*; దుంపరాష్ట్రము - dumparáshtamu, *Tel.*; അരത്ത - aratta, *Mal.*; කළුවා - kaluvá, *Singh.*; அரத்தை - arattai, *Tam.*). Title from arabic. San. from (ras, san. to taste). Ar. from chinese meaning wild ginger. Tel. from (dumpa, tel. root + ráshtamu, tel. galangal). Mal. from tamul. Tam. from (rakta, san. red). San. also (kulanjana), from arabic; (sugandhavachá), meaning fragrant acorus calamus, linn.; (dhúmala), meaning smoke-colored; (kapidruma), meaning monkey tree; (gandhavárunı́), meaning having fragrant juice; (sugandhayóga), meaning sweet smell + union; (nákuli), meaning relating to mongoose, cf. rasnah; (tíkshnamúla), meaning pungent root; (sugandhá), meaning fragrant, cf. marootham; (kórajá); (pátalá), meaning red [pauthiry]; (raktapushpa), meaning red + flower [red-cotton tree]; (aruná), meaning red [munjeet, turbith]; (raktarénu), meaning red powder; (purusha), meaning fragrance; (éláparnı́), meaning cardamom leaved. Ar. also (khulanjánikasabí), meaning reed galangal. Hind. also (kalíjan); (pánkijar), meaning piper betel, linn. + root. Can. also (rásmini); (dumrashta); (sugandhaváchigida), meaning fragrant plant. Tel. also (dumparáshtrakamu), meaning root + galangal. Singh. also (kaluválá). Botanically the Alpinia genus, zingiberaceæ [vricsham, 144]. Plants known by thick, tuber-like, aromatic rhizomes, and by flowers arranged in terminal spikes; fruit is a somewhat fleshy capsule of three many-seeded cells. The species best known to the natives are shown below. Others are:—allughas, khulinjan, rheedii.—"*a*" Greater galangal. Cyperus babylonicus of Pliny. Title otherwise Galangal cardamom, Java galangal, King's drug, Large-flowered alpinia, Loose-flowered alpinia, Mongoose plant, Monkey plant, Tree galangal. Botanically Alpinia [galangal] galanga, willd., zingiberaceæ [vricsham, 144]. Alias Amomum galanga, zedoaria; Galanga major, officinalis; Maranta galanga. Galanga from arabic. Perennial; stem 6–7 feet when in flower, with leafless sheath up to the middle; leaves short-stalked, lanceolate, white, and somewhat callous on the margin, smooth; panicles terminal, spreading, dichotomous, each division with from two to six pale-greenish, fragrant flowers; calyx smooth, white, one-toothed; exterior limb of corolla of three nearly equal recurved divisions; interior one unguiculate, oval, deeply two-lobed, white with reddish specks; capsule size of a small cherry [q.v.], obovate, smooth, deep orange-red, three-celled; seed one, much compressed, deep chestnut color, a little wrinkled, arillate, except at the apex; javanese plant; imported. Brown tuberose root, with a faint aromatic smell and pungent taste, like a mixture of pepper [q.v.] and ginger [q.v.]; radix galangæ majoris of chemists. Root given in infusion in fevers, rheumatism, and catarrhal affections; like ginger; seeds possess similar medicinal properties; substituted for british peppermint [poodeenah]; quoted in pharm. non-officinal. Root used in calico-printing with myrobalans [q.v.].—"*b*" Lesser galangal. Title otherwise Chinese galangal, Root stock galangal. Botanically Alpinia [galangal] officinarum, hance, zingiberaceæ [vricsham, 144]. Alias Alpinia chinensis. Imported from China. Root may be distinguished from greater galangal by its color; on the outside being browner and in the inside reddish, whilst the greater root is brownish on the outside, of a dirty white within, and covered with rings about one-fourth of an inch distant from each other; more warm and fragrant than greater; more highly prized as stimulant and stomachic. Substituted for british peppermint; quoted in pharm. non-officinal; radix galangæ minoris of chemists. There is a smaller variety with still quicker qualities. This article often confounded with the root of the betel-leaf plant, piper betel, linn. [betel pepper], which however is not a tuber; the root of hedychium spicatum, ham. [europe zedoary], also resembles this.—"*c*" Nodding galangal. Title otherwise Drooping galangal, Indian shell-flower, Light galangal. Botanically Alpinia [galangal] nutans, roscoe, zingiberaceæ [vricsham, 144]. Alias Alpinia auriculata; Costus zerumbet; Renealmia nutans; Zerumbet speciosa. Leaves lanceolar, short-petioled, smooth; racemes compound by the lower pedicels being two or three-flowered, drooping; lip large, ovate, cordate, obscurely three-lobed at the base; middle lobe curled on the margin; ovary hairy, oval, three-celled; capsule slightly hairy; flowering in april and may. Drooping compound racemes, about a foot long, of flowers, size and form of fox glove, with bracts and calyces of a pure pearly white, the edges of the flower tinged with pink, and the interior orange; thrives in swampy ground. Rhizome much the same as alpinia galanga, willd.; quoted in pharm. non-officinal.——*Indian galangal* (सुगन्धवचा - sugandhavachá, San.; कचोला - kachólá, Mahr.; कचूर - kaççúru, Conc.; چندر مول - chandarmula, Hind.; ಕಚ್ಚೂರ - kaççúra, Can.; కచోరము - kachóramu, Tel.; കച്ചൂരം - kaççúram, Mal.; கச்சோலம் - kaççólam, Tam). Title from resemblance. San. from (sugandha, san. fragrant + vachá, san. sweet flag, acorus calamus, linn.). Mahr., &c., from (karchúra, san. the plant). Hind. means moon or camphor root. San. also (chandramúlika), meaning camphor + root; (karchúra); (kachhóra), meaning itch-burning. Tam. also (kiççilikkizhangu), meaning citrus aurantium, linn. + root; from aromatic root. Title otherwise Camphor-root plant, Kœmpferian galangal. Botanically Kœmpferia [bhoochampak] galanga, linn., singiberaceæ [vricsham, 144]. Alias Alpinia sessilis; Kœmpferia plantaginea. Rhizome biennial, tuberous; stem none; leaves stalked, spreading flat on the surface of the earth, round, ovate-cordate, margins membranaceous and waved, upper surface smooth, somewhat woolly towards the base; flowers fascicled, six to twelve within the sheath of the leaves, expanding in succession, pure white with a purple spot on the centre of each of the divisions of the inner series; bracts three to each flower, linear, acute, half the length of the tube of the corolla; calyx the length of the bracts; tube of corolla long, filiform, limbs double, both series three-parted; flowering in rains; cultivated in gardens. The round leaves overlap each other, and flowers seem to rest upon them; flowers are scentless; root and leaves when bruised have a fine fragrance; rhizome fleshy, with fleshy fibres. The rhizome reduced to powder and mixed with honey [shahad] is given in coughs and pectoral affections; boiled in oil externally applied in stoppages of the nasal organs; in pharm. non-officinal.

GALBANUM (قنه - kinnah, *Ar.*; بارزد - bárzad, *Pers.*; برجا - baríjá, *Hind.*; برجاگوند - baríjágond, *Dec.*). Title from hebrew, meaning milk, through latin. Greek γαλβάνη. Hebrew khebbenah. Title otherwise Gum galbanum. Gummi-resina galbanum of chemists. Yellowish brown fetid gum-resin [googal, gond] yielded by two plants; Ferula galbaniflua, boiss. and Ferula rubricaulis, boiss., umbelliferæ [vricsham, 67]. Occurs in agglutinated plastic masses; hot, acrid and bitter; in properties resembles asafœtida [q.v.], but weaker. Is in pharm. as a stimulant, antispasmodic, and expectorant; officinal.

GALIYAH (گليا - galiyá, *Hind.*). From (galí, hind. street); i.e., midway. A bullock that lies down in the midst of his work.

GAMBIER (گمبر - gambir, *Malay*; అంకుడు - ankudu, *Tel.*; கத்தக்காம்புச்செடி - kattakkámbuççedi, *Tam.*). Tam. meaning catechu tree. Title otherwise Bastard cutch, Gambier cutch, Japan earth, Pale cutch, Terra japonica. Botanically Uncaria gambier, roxb., rubiaceæ [vricsham, 71]. Specific from malay. Alias Nauclea gambier. A stout climbing shrub, native of straits of malacca. Gambier is the extract by boiling leaves and young shoots; but little soluble in water; is lightish-brown, bitter and powerfully astringent gives a rose-colored precipitate with gelatine, and a deep permanent green with the salts of iron; in chemical composition and qualities strongly resembles cutch [q.v.], and the names catechu and terra japonica are applied to both; this substance is sometimes brought from malay countries to coromandel coast [q.v.]; introduced into european commerce during last century. Used medicinally as astringent; gives to pharm. catechu pallidum, properties similar to catechu nigrum; officinal; properties and uses same as acacia catechu, willd. [catechu]; substituted for british kino [q.v.], oak-galls [mauchicoy] and logwood. The malays chew it with betel [q.v.] leaf, as tamulians chew areca [q.v.] nut. It is employed for tanning and dyeing [shauyam]; gives a soft leather [chamrah].

GAMBOGE (रेवाचिन्निसीरा - réváchinnisírá, *Mahr.*; عصارهٔ ریوند - usárahirewand, *Pers.* and *Hind.*; رونگ - rong, *Malay*; రేవల్‌చిన్నిపాలు - révalchinnipálu, *Tel.*; ගොකටුමෙලියම - gokatumeliyam, *Singh.*; மக்கி - makki, *Tam.*). Title from cambodia [q.v.], the province of that name where produced. Mahr. from (réváchinni, mahr. rhubarb plant + sírá, mahr. vegetable extract). Pers. from (usárah, ar. concrete extract + rewand, ar. rhubarb). Tel. from (revandchíní, hind. rhubarb + pálu, tel. juice). Singh. from (gokatu, singh. gamboge tree + meliyam, singh. gum). Tam. means whitish clay. Tel. also (pasupuvanne); meaning yellow + color. Tam. also (irévalsinippál), meaning rhubarb milk. Product of Garcinia morella, desr. [ceylon gamboge], Garcinia xanthochymus, hk. & f. [yellow mangosteen], Gardenia lucida, roxb. [decamallee]. Yellow resin [raul] imported from Siam, China, or from Ceylon. Occurs in three forms, in rolls or solid cylinders; in pipes or hollow cylinders and in cakes or in masses; inodorous and nearly insipid to taste. One of the most drastic medicinal cathartics. Used as a pigment in miniature painting, and in coloring varnishes [rangh] and lacquers [q.v.]. Argemone mexicana [bramhadand] is gamboge thistle.——*Ceylon gamboge* (तमाल - tamála, San. and Mahr.; वटांब - vatámba, Conc.; ريباس - ribás, Ar. and Pers.; تمال - tamál, Hind.; عصارهٔ ریون کا جہار - usárahirevankájhár, Dec.; درامبا - darámbá, Malay; ಜಾರಿಗೆ - járige, Can. and Too.; రేవల్‌చిన్ని - révalchinni, Tel.; കരുക്കമ്പുളി - karukkampuli, Mal.; ගොකටු - gokatu, Singh.; மக்கிமரம் - makkimaram, Tam.). San. from (tamas, san. dark); from color of bark [cassia cinnamon, karanj, yellow mangosteen]. Dec. from (usárah, ar. extract + revand, pers. rhubarb, rheum + jhár, hind. tree). Tel. from hindostany. Mal. from (karukka, mal. to grow black + puli, mal. tamarind, tamarindus indica, linn.); grows black on drying. Singh. from (go, san. cow + katu, singh. thorn); cattle thorn. Tam. from (makki, tam. whitish clay + maram, tam. tree); from soil where it grows. San. also (tápiñchha), meaning sheltering one oppressed by heat [ceylon cinnamon]. Mahr. also (révalchinní). Ar. also (rubbirevand), meaning rhubarb juice, from its similarity in properties and color; (farfíran). Pers. also (shírevand), meaning rhubarb juice; (usárahirevand), meaning rhubarb extract. Hind. also (ghotághambá), corruption of gummi guttæ. Tel. also (pasupuvannechettu), meaning yellow + color + tree. Mal. also (puliñchakka), meaning sour + jack, artocarpus integrifolia, willd.; cf. country cinnamon and prickly anona; (pinarppuli), meaning stiff tamarind. Singh. also (kanagoraka), meaning eating garcinia cambogia, desr., from oil used as ghee by poor. Tam. also (irévalsinni), from hindostany [indian rhubarb]. Title otherwise Acid jack, Ghotagamba, Indian gamboge, Mysore gamboge, Rhubarb juice tree. Botanically Garcinia [ractaumram] morella, desrous, guttiferæ [vricsham, 22]. Alias Garcinia elliptica, gutta, pictoria; Hebradendron cambogioides, pictorium. Gutta, from (gátah, malay, gum). The principal Indian gamboge. Tree, 60 feet; much branched; bark thick, of deep rust color, with yellow species; leaves opposite, short-petioled, oblong-ventricose, slighty acute, entire, smooth on both sides; hermaphrodite flowers axillary, solitary, sessile; calyx segments obtuse, in two unequal pairs; petals four, oval; berry oval, size of a large cherry [q.v.], smooth, slightly marked with four lobes, and crowned with the sessile verrucose stigma; seeds four, oblong, reniform; calyx and coralla of male flowers as in the female; flowers yellow; flowers in february, and fruit ripens in may and june; native of s. india and ceylon. From tender twigs, and from fissures in the bark exudes a bright yellow juice, which concretes into a hard resinous substance, identical with the best gamboge of commerce; it quickly dries in the sun, is formed at once into rolls, and undergoes no other preparation; in taste it is inodorous, and nearly insipid. Gives to pharm. cambogia indica vel mysoriensis; cambogic acid principal activity; properties identical with siam gamboge; officinal. An oil is procurable in moderate quantities by pounding seeds in stone mortar and boiling mass until oil rises to the surface; chiefly used as a lamp oil [q.v.] by better classes and as a substitute for ghee [q.v.] by the poor; the gamboge is used for coloring [shauyam] cloth. Wood yellow, hard, mottled.——*Malabar gamboge* (रक्तस्राव - raktasráva, San.; ولايتی املی - viláitíamlí, Dec.; ಓಟೆಕಾಯಿಮರ - ótekáyimara, Can.; ఓంటెపులి - óntepuli, Too.; సీమచింత - símachinta, Tel.; കുരുക്കമ്പുളി - kurukkampuli, Mal.; ගොරක - goraka, Singh.; கொறுக்காய் - korukkáy, Tam.). San. from (rakta, san. blood + sru, san. to pour); as yielding red resin. Dec. from (viláití, hind. foreign + amlí, hind. tamarindus indica, linn.). Can. from (ótekáyí, can. stone fruit + mara, can. tree). Tel. from (síma, tel. foreign + chinta, tel. tamarind tree). Mal. from (kuru, mal. short + káya, mal. fruit + puli, mal. tamarind) [corcapilly]. Too. also (esalpuli), meaning leaf + acidity; (karkpuli), meaning sharp + acidity. Tel. also (vádachinta), meaning ship + tamarind tree. Mal. also (kutampuli), meaning pot + tamarind; the dried fruits are preserved in pots; (kotukkáppuli), meaning sharp + fruit + tamarind. Title otherwise Acid leaf tree, Foreign tamarind [corcapilly], Gorga, Malabar tamarind, Pot tamarind. Botanically Garcinia [ractaumram] cambogia, desrous, guttiferæ [vricsham, 22]. Alias Cambogia gutta; Garcinia kydia; Mangostana cambogia. Gutta, from (gátah, malay, gum); mangostana, from (mangusta, malay, garcinia mangostana). Small evergreen tree of w. coast; leaves lanceolate, deep green; flowers terminal or axillary, sessile or subsessile, pedicelled, solitary or several together; male, anthers numerous, on a short, thick androphore, oblong, two-celled, dehiscing longitudinally, introrse; female, staminodes surrounding the base of the ovary in several phalanges, each containing two to three sterile spathulate stamens; stigmas five to ten-lobed, papillose, glandular; ovary six to ten-celled; fruit yellow or reddish, six to ten-furrowed, six to ten-seeded, nearly globular or ovate, furrows broad, with angular edges, the furrows not continued to the apex, which is smooth and depressed, and often nipple-shaped, about size of small orange [q.v.]. A gamboge of fine quality exudes from trunk semi-transparent, very adhesive; is insoluble in water, but soluble in spirits. Fruit used on west coast like tamarinds [q.v.] on coromandel [q.v.]. Gamboge gives usual yellow dye [shauyam]; yields an excellent straight grained lemon colored slightly elastic wood, easily worked. There is a variety conicarpa.——*Siam gamboge* (పసుపువన్నెచెట్టు - pasupuvannechettu, Tel.; மக்கிமரம் - makkimaram, Tam.). Tel. from (pasupu, tel. yellow + vanne, tel. color + chettu, tel. tree); from yellow gamboge. Tam. from (makki, tam. whitish clay + maram, tam. tree); from soil where it grows. Botanically Garcinia [ractaumram] morella, desr., var. pedicellata, guttiferæ [vricsham, 22]. Diœcious tree, with laurel-like foliage and small yellow flowers, found in cambojam [cambodia]; gives the gum resin [googal], true gamboge; substance brittle, fracture shelly, surface opaque, and brownish-yellow with lustre; forms a yellow emulsion when rubbed with water; powder bright-yellow, inodorous, nearly tasteless, but leaving a faintly acrid flavor. Gives to pharm. cambogia, or gummi gambogia, or gummi gutti, valuable hydragogue, cathartic, and anthelmintic. For compound gamboge powder; take of siam gamboge, in powder, three drachms; cream of tartar [draucshaooppoo], in powder, three ounces and one drachm; ginger [q.v.], in powder, two drachms; mix and rub them well together and pass the powder through fine sieve. For compound gamboge pill; take of gamboge, barbadoes or indian aloes [aloe] and compound powder of cinnamon [q.v.], each one ounce; hard soap [sauboon], in powder, two ounces; syrup, a sufficiency; pulverise the gamboge and aloes [q.v.] separately, mix them with the cinnamon powder, and then with the syrup, and beat the whole into a uniform mass. Doses; of compound gamboge powder, from forty grains to one drachm; of compound gamboge pill, from five to ten grains. Siam gamboge is one of the best purgatives in this country and a much stronger drug than jalap [q.v.].

GAN (गण् - gan, *San.*). To count.——*Ganam* (गण - gana, San.). A collection, class. In Mysore, specially Lingayets [q.v.]. A troop of inferior deities [deva], especially those attendant on Shiva [q.v.]. In natural history an organic kingdom. For category in that connection, see Pádaurtam; for elementary substance, see Dravyam; for matter, see Bhootam; for organic and inorganic, see Indriyam and Anindriyam; for organic kingdom, see present head [jantoo, vricsham]; for organic class, see Vargam; for organic order, see Santaunam; for organic family, see Coolam; for organic genus, see Jauty; for organic species, see Bhaidam. Oopa prefixed to either of the above means a sub-head. For inorganic minerals, see Dhautoo.——*Ganapa* (ಗಣಪ - ganapa, Can.). From (gana, san. a class of deities + pá, san. to rule). Ganesh, the ruler of the attendant troops. Hindoo 2nd or pers. name [peyar].——*Ganaparvatam* (गणपर्वत - ganaparvata, San.). From (gana, san. a class of deities + parvata, san. mountain). Keilausam [q.v.].——*Ganapatisoobban* (கணபதிசுப்பன் - kanappathisuppan, Tam.). From (ganapati, san. vighnéshvara, the ruler of gana + subba, can. serpent), meaning ganapaty and soobramanyan, the serpent lord; a compound name. Hindoo 2nd or pers. name [peyar].——*Ganapaty* (गणपति - ganapati, San.). From (gana, san. a class of deities + pati, san. lord). Ganesh, the lord of minor deities attendant on shiva [vigneshwaran]. Hindoo 2nd or pers. name [peyar]. Title of the dynasty [raj] of Warangal [q.v.], said to be descended from the Hastinapooram line. Title otherwise Caucateeya, from the seventh prince of this line. Their first capital was Hanoomacondah. Subsequently Warangal. Chorgunga, the founder of the Gajapaty [q.v.] line said to belong to this line. Prataupa roodra deo and his queen Roodramma who ruled as regent for thirty-eight years after his death, are the most important of the line, which succumbed to Mahomedans about 1323. Vol. I (132) [charitram].——*Ganapaty's lime* (ഗണപതിനാരകം - ganapatinárakam, Mal.). From large size of fruit, referring to his large belly. Same as Citron.——*Ganesh* (गणेश - ganésha, San.). From (gana, san. a class of deities + íśla, san. master); the lord of minor deities [ganapaty]. The North indian name for Vigneshwaran [q.v.]; seldom used here. Ganesha geetay is the Bhagavat geeta [q.v.], but with the name of Ganesh substituted for that of Krishnan [q.v.]; used by the Gaunapatyans. See vol. I (73), (87).——*Ganitam* (गणित - ganita, San.). See sep. title.——*Gaunapatyan* (गाणपत्य - gánapatya, San.). From (ganapati, san. the god). A sect of the Dravida [q.v.] bramins [q.v.]; followers of Ganesh; only occasionally found in this presidency [jauty, matam].

GANDAM (गण्ड - ganda, *San.*). Chief.——*Gandadeva* (गण्डदेव - gandadéva, San.). From (above + déva, san. lord). Name of a Congoo [q.v.] carnautam [q.v.] king; said to have subdued the rajah of Canjy [conjeeveram] and levied tribute upon Dravida [q.v.]. Vol. I (130) [charitram].——*Gandaperandam* (गण्डभेरुण्ड - gandabhérunda, San.; கண்டப்பேரண்டம் - kandappérandam, Tam.). From (above + bhérunda, san. terrible); applied to a bird. Angka of the arabs, γρύπς of the greeks, griffin of european heraldry, gryphon of marco polo. A monstrous, two-headed bird holding elephants in its beak and in its claws, the elephant [q.v.] in the former sometimes replaced by the sharabham [q.v.] or fabulous lion [simham]. Compare the Roc in Sindbad the Sailor and his adventures with the gigantic egg and also with the bird [bheroondam].——*Guntamanaickanore* (கண்டமநாயக்கனூர் - kandamanáyakkanúr, Tam. gandamanáyakanúr*). From (ganda, san. chief + amma, tel. mother, titular affix + náyakkan, tam. titular affix + úr, tam. village). Zemindarry, Village; Madura dist., Periyacoolam tal.; pop. 2,909; Zemindarry pays peshcush of Rs. 13,415. One of the twenty-four polliems resumed by Tippoo sultan in 1788.

GANDH (गन्ध् - gandh, *San.*). To hurt.——*Ganda firoza* (सरलरस - saralarasa, San.; علك البطم - ilakulbutm, Ar.; صمغ پیسته - samaghipistah, Pers.; گنده فیروزه - gandahfírozah, Hind.; కర్పూరతైలము - karpúratailamu, Tel.; തിരുവട്ടപ്പശ - tiruvattappasha, Mal.; கர்ப்பூரத்தைலம் - karppúrattailam, Tam.). Title from hindostany. San. from (sarala, san. pinus longifolius, roxb. + rasa, san. juice). Ar. from (ilak, ar. resin + butm, ar. turpentine tree, pistachia terebinthus, linn.). Pers. from (samagh, ar. gum + pistah, pers. pistachia vera, linn.). Hind. from (gandah, hind. nauseous + baríjá, hind. gum). Tel. from (karpúra, san. camphor + taila, san. oil). Mal. means turpentine + gum. Tam. from (karpúra, san. camphor + taila, san. oil). San. also (shrivása), meaning lutchmy + perfume. Ar. also (ilakulambát), meaning turpentine of nabathæans; (samghussanobar), meaning resin + pinus longifolius, roxb. Hind. also (saralkígond); (chírkígond), meaning pinus resin. Title otherwise Alah of the Old testament. Turpentine. An oleo-resin [teilam], from species of coniferæ; contained in all parts of the trees; thick, viscous, shining, rather transparent, color ranging from white to yellow or amber, odour strong and penetrating, taste bitter and acrid; thickens by age by losing essential oil [attar] and absorbing oxygen [prauna vayoo] from the air. Galipot is the residue of turpentine which has lost its volatile oil [yennay] by spontaneous evaporation; when purified, it is called burgundy pitch; galipot in tears is called false incense. Tar [keel], a liquid or half liquid, tenacious, black; composed of resin [raul], empyreumatic oil, and acetic acid [sirkeyka tezaub]; odour strong and disagreeable, taste bitter and very nauseous; is prepared by the close distillation of the turpentine woods. Smoke black is prepared by the combustion of pitch [zift]; is burned under a dome, within which cloths are suspended to which the soot becomes attached; employed in printer's ink, blacking for shoes, &c. Spirits of turpentine, see Carpoora teilam; this is made by distilling turpentine in a common still; when the oil will be found in the receiver. Common resin or yellow resin is the residue of the distillation of turpentine; when the distillation is performed without addition, it is called common resin, or colophony, but when agitated with about one-eighth of fresh water, while yet fluid, it is named yellow resin. Canada balsam [q.v.] is a transparent resin of honey-like consistence, and of a light straw-color with a greenish tint. For Chian turpentine, see Turpentine pistah.——*Gandhac* (گندك - gandak, Hind.). See sep. title.——*Gandham* (गन्ध - gandha, San.). Smell. Odorous matter pounded for rubbing on the person, or on figures [vigraham] of gods [sandal].—"*a*" Plant first term. Ex., where transl. is of second term:—Alpinia galanga (gandhavárúní), juice; Andropogon schœnanthus (gandhatrina), grass; Cordia obliqua (gandhapushpa), flower; Curcuma zedoaria (gandhamúlí), root; Elettaria cardamomum (gandhakuti), flower-bud; Gardenia florida (gandharája), king; Hibiscus esculentus (gandhamúla), root; Justicia gendarussa (gandharasa), juice; Michelia champaca (gandhap'hala), fruit; Ocimum basilicum (gandhap'hanijjaka), ocimum; Oldenlandia alata (gandhabhadra), auspicious; Pæderia fœtida (gandhálí), bough; Piper cubeba (gandhamenasu), piper nigrum; Santalum album (gandhachekke), wood, (gandhapuchettu), tree, (gandhasára), juice; Saraca indica (gandhapushpa), flower; Vanda roxburghii (gandhanákulí), ichneumon plant alpinia galanga. See gloss. paragraphs.—"*b*" Plant second term. Ex., where transl. is of first term:—Acorus calamus (ugragandha), strong; Allium cepa (ugragandha), strong; Alpinia galanga (sugandha), good; Argyreia speciosa (rikshagandha), bear; Balsamodendron myrrha (rasagandha), juice; Bambusa arundinacea (navágragandhá), new + top; Cæsalpinia pulcherrima (ratnagandhi), gem; Coriandrum sativum (hridyagandhá), agreeable; Evolvulus alsinoides (vishnugandhi), vishnoo; Gynandropsis pentaphylla (ajagandhi), sheep; Hemidesmus indicus (pálasugandhi), milk + good; Hygrophila spinosa (ikshugandha), saccharum officinarum; Ipomæa digitata (ikshugandhá), saccharum officinarum, (rikshagandhá), bear; Myrica sapida (sugandhi), good; Pterocarpus santalinus (agarugandhamu), aquilaria agallocha; Rauwolfia serpentina (sarpagandhá), serpent; Saccharum spontaneum (ikshugandhá), saccharum officinarum; Santalum album (shrígandha), auspicious; Tribulus terrestris (ikshugandhá), saccharum officinarum; Withania somnifera (ashvagandhá), horse. See gloss. paragraphs.—"*c*" Mammal first term. Ex., where transl. is of second term:—Crocidura cærulea (gandhamúshika), rat, mus genus; Viverra civettina (gandhamárjára), cat, felis genus, and (gandhamriga), deer, cervidæ. See gloss. paragraphs.——*Gandharajah* (गन्धराज - gandharája, San.). From (gandha, san. fragrance + rájá, san. king). Title otherwise Cape jasmine, Wild asafœtida. Botanically the Gardenia genus, rubiaceæ [vricsham, 71]. Trees or shrubs, frequently spiny, natives of tropical asia and africa; fruit berry-like; largely cultivated for the fragrance and beauty of the flowers; wood smooth, close-grained, hard; pores small, numerous, and uniformly distributed. The species best known to the natives are:—florida [cape jasmine], latifolia [hill emetic nut], lucida [decamallee], turgida [nunjoondam]. Other s. indian species indigenous or naturalized are:—campanulata, coronaria.——*Gandhaulee* (प्रसारणी - prasárani, San.; चांदवेल - chándavéla, Mahr.; گندھالی - gandhálí, Hind.; సవిరెలచెట్టు - savirelachettu, Tel.). Title from hindostany. San. from (prasri, san. to stretch forth), from relaxing limbs contracted by rheumatism. Mahr. from (chánda, mahr. moon + véla, mahr. creeper). Hind. from (gand, hind. fetid + dhálí, hind. bough). San. also (sáraná), meaning causing to extend; (pratáníní), meaning extending; (katambhará), meaning preserving the hip and loins; (rájabalá), meaning king tonic; (bhadrabalá), meaning good tonic; (gandhabhadrá), meaning fragrant and useful; (bhadraparní), meaning having useful leaves; (chárnparní), meaning having beautiful leaves; (prabhadrá), meaning very useful; (prabalá), meaning very powerful; (balá), meaning powerful [balah]; (rájaparní), meaning having shining leaves; (suprasará), meaning well extending; (sómaráji), meaning moon + brightness [wild jeerah]. Title otherwise Chinese fever plant, Moon creeper [goolancha, somam], Rajaparny, Somraj, Stinking opal berry. Botanically Pæderia fœtida, linn., rubiaceæ [vricsham, 71]. Alias Apocynum fœtidum. Slender climber; leaves opposite, oblong or lanceolate, cordate at the base, glabrous; panicles axillary and opposite, or terminal; flowers sessile along the ultimate divisions; berry ovate, somewhat compressed, two-celled, two-seeded; calyx five-toothed; corolla infundibuliform, hairy inside, five-lobed; stamens almost sessile on the middle of the tube; festoons of small bell-flowers, purple varied with white, emitting fetid odour; flowering in cold season. Whole plant when bruised has same fetid smell; roots emetic; fibre from stalks. No other common species here.——*Gendah* (اقحوان - ukhuván, Ar.; بابونۂ گاؤ چشم - bábúnahigáuchashm, Pers.; گیندا - gendá, Hind.; گیند کا جھاڑ - gendkájhár, Dec.; ಚೆಂಡುಮಲ್ಲಿಗೆ - chandumallige, Can.; బంతిచెట్టు - bantichettu, Tel.; துலுக்கமல்லிகை - tulukkamalligai, Tam.). Title from hindostany. Hind. from (gandha, san. sulphur); from yellow flower. Ar. from (kuhu, ar. to seize). Pers. from (bábúnah, pers. chamomile, anthemis nobilis, linn. + gáu, pers. cow + chashm, pers. eye); from similarity of flowers. Can. from (chendu, can. ball + mallige, can. jasminum). Tel. from (banti, tel. nosegay + chettu, tel. tree), from flowers. Tam. from (tulukkan, tam. mahomedan + malligai, tam. jasmine); from use by mahomedans. Pers. also (gulijafarí), meaning yellow flower. Tam. also (kañjáppúççedi), meaning cannabis sativa, linn. + flower + tree; (kendippúççedi), meaning sulphur + flower + plant; (tulukkappú), meaning mahomedan flower. Title otherwise Marigold, Turk jasmine, Yellow jasmine. Botanically the Tagetes genus, compositæ [vricsham, 74]. Showy annuals largely cultivated for the ornamental compound flowers, which are considered sacred. The species best known to the natives are:—Erecta, african marigold, indian yellow marigold, annual, showy, yellow flowers; whole plant has fœtid smell; medicinally flowers purify the blood, and are remedy for eye diseases. Patula, french marigold; a dwarf plant, with comparatively small flowers.——*Gendarussa* (गन्धरस - gandharasa, San.). See sep. title.

GANDHAC (गन्धक - gandhaka, *San.* and *Mahr.*; كبريت - kibrít, *Ar.*; گوگرد - gogird, *Pers.*; گندك - gandak, *Hind.*; بالی رانگ - bálirang, *Malay*; ಗಂಧಕಾ - gandhaká, *Can.*; ಗಂಧಕ - gandhaka, *Too.*; గంధకము - gandhakamu, *Tel.*; ഗന്ധകം - gandhakam, *Mal.*; ගන්ධක - gandhaka, *Singh.*; கந்தகம் - kandagam, *Tam.*). San. from (gandh, san. injure) [gandh]. Sulphur. Otherwise Brimstone or Burnstone. Occurs in the animal [jantoo] vegetable [vricsham] and mineral [dhautoo] kingdoms, principally the last; elementary combustible solid non-metallic substance of a peculiar yellow color, and very brittle; has neither taste nor smell, though when rubbed it has a faint peculiar odour; very inflammable, burning with a clear flame, and leaving no residuum. As a crude mineral it is chiefly got from volcanic countries, where it is met with in beds; greater part of the sulphur exposed for sale here is imported; it has however been found on west coast in combination with iron [auhan] in the form of pyrites [auhan]; also in godavery; see vol. II, 33. Sublimed sulphur or flowers of sulphur is poo gandhac. Gandhacayooctam, from (yuj, san. to join) is a sulphate, or salt formed by sulphuric acid [gandhac tezaub] in combination with any base, fusible. For different sulphates see Annabhaidy, Mayil toottam, Rasapaspam, Vellay toottam. Sublimed and precipitated sulphur is used medicinally in the form of powder and in ointments; also administered internally; alterative and diaphoretic in small, and mildly aperient in larger doses; used both externally and internally in scabies and other cutaneous affections; pharm. has sulphuris iodidum properties similar to those of iodine, sulphur præcipitatum, sulphur sublimatum. Native sulphur is chiefly employed in the preparation of gunpowder and in making fireworks [baunam] and matches; the fumes of burning sulphur have the effect of whitening raw silk [puttoo]. The following are the different kinds of sulphur.——*Bauna gandhac* (بارودکی گندك - bárúdkígandak, Dec.; బాణగంధకము - bánagandhakamu, Tel.; வாணக்கந்தகம் - vánakkandagam, Tam.). Dec. from (bárúd, hind. gunpowder). Tam. from (vánam, tam. fireworks); as used in fireworks [baunam]. Stick sulphur; also called Roll sulphur, common.——*Dholl gandhac* (دال گندك - dálgandak, Dec.; పప్పుగంధకము - pappugandhakamu, Tel.; പരിപ്പുഗന്ധകം - parippugandhakam, Mal.; பருப்புக்கந்தகம் - paruppukkandagam, Tam.). From resemblance to split dholl. Found in small pieces, some of which are thin and concave, some flat and irregular, and some round like a shot, &c.; bright yellow; form and color resemble half seeds without husk of dholl [common dholl].——*Myrobalan gandhac* (आमलकगन्धक - ámalakagandhaka, San.; आवलागन्धक - áválágandhaka, Mahr.; آنوله سار گندك - áunlahsárgandak, Dec.; ನೆಲ್ಲಿಗಂಧಕ - nelligandhaka, Can.; నెల్లికాయగంధకము - nellikáyagandhakamu, Tel.; ആമലകഗന്ധകം - ámalakagandhakam, Mal.; நெல்லிக்காய்க்கந்தகம் - nellikkáykkandagam, Tam.). From color resembling ripe fruit of myrobalan [q.v.]. Occurs in crystalline pieces like those of alum [padicauram]; bright yellow color with a shade of green; color somewhat like ripe fruit of phyllanthus emblica, linn., or emblic myrobalan [q.v.]; purest of all met with in bazaars.——*Putchay ghandhac* (کچی گندك - kaççígandak, Hind.; పచ్చగంధకము - paççigandhakamu, Tel.; പച്ചഗന്ധകം - paççagandhakam, Mal.; பச்சைக்கந்தகம் - paççaikkandagam, Tam.). Means raw sulphur. Common native sulphur; very impure, hard, and generally whitish yellow in color; the worst in the bazaar [q.v.].——*Yerra gandhac* (रक्तगन्धक - raktagandhaka, San.; तांबडगन्धक - támbadagandhaka, Mahr.; لال گندك - lálgandak, Dec.; ಕೆಂಪು

ಗಂಧಕ - kempugandhaka, Can.; ఎర్రగంధకము - erragandhakamu, Tel.; ചൊവന്നഗന്ധകം - chovannagandhakam, Mal.; கோழித்தலைக்கந்தகம் - kózhittalaikkandagam, Tam.). Title, &c., mean red sulphur. Tam. from (kózhi, tam. fowl + talai, tam. head); from color of cockscomb. Red sulphur. Found in small and highly crystalline, flat or irregular pieces, of purple or brick-dust color; probably a sulphuret of some metal [loham]; it burns with a faint blue flame, and emits a slight smell of sulphur; resorted to by native alchemists, and is the chief ingredient used by them in preparing artificial gold [pon] and silver [velly].

GANDOO (ಗಂಡು - gandu, *Can.*; గండు - gandu, *Tel.*). Male. Plant first term often joining two genera. Ex., where transl. is of second term:—Alstonia venenata (gandugannéru), nerium odorum; Andropogon nardus (gandahanchikhaddi), aristida setacea + spear; Bambusa stricta (gandubiduru), bambusa arundinacea; Memecylon amplexicaule (ganduképala), solanum stramonifolium; Pimenta acris (gandamenasu), piper nigrum. See gloss. paragraphs.

GANITAM (गणित - gánita, *San.*). From (gan, san. to count) [gan]. Arithmetic [shastram]. See vol. II, 245.——*Bhinna ganitam* (भिन्नगणित - bhinnaganita, San.). From (bhinna, san. fraction). Practice; treating of weights [niray] and prices of things.——*Chayyah ganitam* (छायागणित - chháyáganita, San.). Means shadow-reckoning. Explains the method of finding the height and distance of objects by their shadows [shunk].——*Cshetra ganitam* (क्षेत्रगणित - kshétraganita, San.). See sep. title.——*Ghauta ganitam* (खातगणित - khátaganita, San.). From (kháta, san. excavation). Teaches the manner of measuring the extent of tanks [q.v.], and the water they contain; the manner of measuring and making channels [q.v.], fortifications [cottay, kila], embankments [anay, bund]; explains the different measures [alavay] in use, and treats especially of the use of the level, in making channels and tanks.——*Pauvalore ganitam* (పావలూరుగణితము - pávalúruganitamu, Tel.). From the author, one Veeracharry of Pauvalore, village in Baupatla. Treats of weights [niray] and measures [alavay], of the fundamentals of arithmetic, as numeration, addition, the five different ways of multiplying, division, practice, rule of three, rule of five, of seven, of nine, and eleven.——*Prakeerna ganitam* (प्रकीर्णगणित - prakírnaganita, San.). From (prakírna, san. scattered). Algebra [beejaganitam] of the Hindoos.——*Sootra ganitam* (सूत्रगणित - sútraganita, San.). From (sútra, san. rule). Contains rules for solving arithmetical, hydraulical, and algebraical questions, and treats of dry measures, of progression [raushy], &c.——*Swarna ganitam* (सुवर्णगणित - suvarnaganita, San.). From (suvarna, san. gold). The art of assaying gold [pon] and silver [velly] by the touch, and of taking their specific gravities.

GANJ (گنج - ganj, *Hind.*). From persian. Granary. Treasure [golah, gunj].——*Ganjam** (గంజాము - gandzámu, Tel.). From (above + gám, hind. village). Greek παλούρα, the point of departure in crossing Bay of Bengal, there being a place (pálúru) a little north.—"*a*" Revenue district; situated on the Coromandel coast [q.v.] in the north-east corner of the presidency; between 18° 12′ and 20° 26′ N. lat., and between 83° 32′ and 85° 14′ E. long.; bounded N. by Pooree district in Orissa, E. by Bay of Bengal, S. by Vizagapatam district, W. by estates of Calahundy, Patna and Jeypore; square miles 8,370; pop. non-agency 1,589,477, agency 307,326; language Teloogoo, Ooriya, Khond, Sowrah. Contains rivers Langoolya, Rooshcoolya, Vamshadhaura; ports Bapanapaud, Barwah, Calingapatam, Ganjam, Gopalpore, Poondy, Sonapore. The whole area of the district is represented by the following sub-areas, where talook [q.v.] means an ordinary tract administered by a Tahsildar [q.v.], and division means a zemindarry [q.v.] tract administered by a superior Deputy tahsildar:—Berhampore talook, Chicacole talook, Goomsoor talook, Maliah [q.v.] tracts, Zemindarry tracts. For general administrative purposes the district is distributed between the following revenue and magisterial officers, who have their head-quarters at the places shown. The pay set opposite the subordinate officers gives the grade of the corresponding charge:—Collector, Chetterpore; Principal assistant collector, Chicacole, in charge of Chicacole talook, Parlakimedy, Tekkaly and Tarlah zemindarries and the Parlakimedy maliahs; Senior assistant collector, Berhampore, in charge of Berhampore talook, Mundasa, Cheekaty, Pedda kimedy, Soorangy, Jalantra, Boodaurasinghy and Jarada zemindarries, and a portion of the Atagadah zemindarry, the maliahs of Pedda kimedy, Soorangy, Jalantra, Boodaurasinghy, Jarada and Mundasa; General deputy collector, Russellcondah, in charge of Goomsoor talook and a portion of Atagadah, Dhauracote, Shergadah, Chinna kimedy, Aska, Devabhoomy, Coorlah and Bodagooda zemindarries; Special assistant agent, Russellcondah, in the low country and Balligooda in the maliahs, in charge of maliahs of Goomsoor, Chinna kimedy and Bodagooda, and Cuttingia and Chocapaud mittahs of the Goomsoor talook. Tahsildars—Berhampore, Rs. 200; Chicacole, Rs. 175; Goomsoor, Rs. 150. Deputy tahsildars—Aska, Rs. 100, range situated in the north-east of Chinna kimedy; Balligooda, Rs. 250; Ganjam, Rs. 70, range situated in the north-east of Berhampore; Ichapore, Rs. 100, range situated in the south of Berhampore; Narsannapett, Rs. 70, range situated in the north-east of Chicacole; Oodayagherry, Rs. 200, range situated in the north-west of Goomsoor; Parlakimedy, Rs. 100, range situated in the Parlakimedy zemindarry; Poorshottapore, Rs. 100, range situated in the north of Berhampore; Ramagherry, Rs. 200, range situated in the Pedda kimedy maliahs; Sompett, Rs. 70, range situated in the south-west of Berhampore; Sooradah, Rs. 100, range situated in the north-west of Dhauracote; Tekkaly, Rs. 100, range situated in the east of Parlakimedy. Sub-magistrate, Berhampore, Rs. 70, jurisdiction extending over the town of Berhampore. Similarly judicial officers:—Judge, Berhampore; District moonsifs, Berhampore, Chicacole, Tekkaly. District engineer, at Berhampore. Contains Registration sub-districts Aska, Berhampore, Chetterpore, Chicacole, Goomsoor, Ichapore, Narsannapett, Parlakimedy, Poorshottapore, Tekkaly. Contains Forest ranges Berhampore, Cookloobha, Curcholy, Moojagodo, Sooradah. Contains Municipalities Berhampore, Chicacole, Parlakimedy. Contains District board; and Chicacole, Berhampore and Goomsoor talook boards. Chicacole talook board embraces the Chicacole talook, the Parlakimedy zemindarry and some proprietary estates, of which Tekkaly is the principal one. Berhampore talook board embraces the Berhampore talook, and the zemindarries of Mundasa, Jalantra, Jarada, Boodaurasinghy, Soorangy, Cheekaty, Peddakimedy, Hoomma, Biridy, Paulore, Cullicote and Atagadah. Goomsoor talook board comprises Goomsoor talook, Sooradah division, Shergadah and Chinna kimedy zemindarries, Aska and some other proprietary estates. The following general references should be made to the preceding volumes:—general geography, I (1) to (29); general ethnology, I (29) to (109); general history, I (110) to (188); physical geography, II, 1; meteorology, II, 3; geology, II, 8; fauna, II, 21; flora, II, 26; mineralogy, II, 29. The following references in the preceding volumes will furnish details special to the district:—latitudes and longitudes, II, 47; particulars about towns, II, 48; coast survey, II, 167; lighthouses, II, 169; comparative population, II, 172; location of revenue officers, II, 382; revenue settlement of the district, II, 410; registrars' and sub-registrars' stations, II, 421; ports, II, 423; salt factories, II, 426; rain-guage stations, II, 428; police divisions, II, 431; maps published, II, 436; survey topographical lists, II, 443; hospitals and dispensaries, II, 447; head-quarter stations of gazetted officers, II, 461; incidence of taxation, II, 463; weights and measures of the district, II, 510; zemindarries contained, I, 60, and II, 296; agencies contained, I, 71. A special gazetteer account of the whole district is given at II, 77. For the detailed topography of the district, reference should be made to the talook notices in the present volume, Berhampore, Chicacole, Goomsoor; also to the heading Maliah; also to the different zemindarries. The following are the ancient zemindarries and proprietary estates in the district:—Akkavalsa, Aska, Atagadah, Barwah, Belamarapalavalsa, Biridy, Bodagooda, Boodaurasinghy, Bullipully, Caracavalsa, Cheekaty, Chinna kimedy, Chinnaury gocurnapully, Chittivalsa, Consoolacottore, Coorlah, Cullicote, Devabhoomy, Devandy, Dhauracote, Gopalpore, Hoomma, Jalantra, Jarada, Jarjangy, Khallada kimedy, Mundasa, Nowgaum, Nundigaum, Oorlaum, Parlakimedy, Paulore, Pautatekkaly, Pedda kimedy, Penta, Potoolore, Raghoonautapooram, Rajapooram, Saukipully, Saunta lutchmeepooram, Shergadah, Sidibehera cottore, Soorangy, Sowdaum, Talagaum, Talavalsa, Tarlah, Tarlipett, Tekkaly, Temboor, Yellamanchily, Yembaram, Zonnapaud.—"*b*" Deputy tahsildarry; Ganjam district. Pay Rs. 70.—"*c*" Town, Port, Deputy tahsildar's station, Salt factory; Ganjam dist., Berhampore tal.; pop. 4,695; acres 1,535; lat. 19° 23′; long. 85° 06′; from Balligooda S.E. 90 miles; from Berhampore E.N.E. 18¼ miles; from Chetterpore E.N.E. 4 miles; from Chicacole N.E. 105 miles; from Gopalpore N. 5½ miles; from Juggernaut W. 56 miles; from Madras N.E. 530 miles; from Russellcondah S.E. 47 miles. On Orissa coast [q.v.] near the left bank of the Rooshcoolya. The river formerly emptied itself into the sea close to the fort, but its present mouth is nearly three-quarters of a mile farther north. Ganjam was formerly the chief port of the district, but a ship of any size rarely visits the port now. Ships now usually anchor in the roads abreast of the fort in eight or nine fathoms, about two miles from shore. Until 1815 was the head-quarters of the district and a military station when it was visited by an epidemic of fever, which almost depopulated the place and led to its abandonment, the civil and military stations being then moved to Berhampore. The insalubrity has however disappeared. Ganjam used to be remarkable for the magnificence of its European residences. Some of these still exist. There are still to be seen the ruins of a fort in fair condition built in 1768 by Mr. Cotsford, the first Resident, in order to keep the Ooriya zemindars in check, and to resist a threatened invasion by the Mahrattas from Cuttack. There is a mud dock [dhony] for the repair of native vessels. There is some coasting trade by means of the river. The chief trade consists of the export of rice [q.v.]. Important Government salt factory, the manufacture of which forms the principal industry. The salt pans [ooppalam] are situated along the west bank of the canal connecting the Chilka lake with the Rooshcoolya canal. The beds of the pans are on a stratum of black clay. The soil is not so favorable as that at Soorlah and Nowpada factories. Trig. station in lat. 19° 22′ 29·50″; long. 85° 05′ 59·10″; from Berhampore E.N.E. 18 miles; from the sea W. ½ mile. This station is not at Ganjam but on the opposite side of the Rooshcoolya. The following are the travelling distances by road from Ganjam to different places:—

To	Viá	Miles and Furlongs.	
Aska	Poorshottapore	33	0
Berhampore ...	......	19	0
Cuttack ...	Khoordhah	97	5
Cuttack ...	Pooree	114	5
Vizagapatam ...	Berhampore, Chicacole and Chittivalsa.	182	1¼
Vizianagram ...	Berhampore, Chicacole and Chittivalsa.	177	1¼

GANJAH (گانجہ - gánjah, *Hind.*). From (grinjana, san. the plant) [ganjar]. Product of Cannabis sativa, linn. [kinnab].

GANJEEFA (گنجیفہ - ganjífah, *Hind.*). Playing cards [chit]. The pack here is divided amongst eight suits.

GANNAIR (करवीर - karavíra, *San.*; कणेर - kanéra, *Mahr.*; سم الحمار - sammulhimár, *Ar.*; خرزهره - kharzahrah, *Pers.*; کنیر - kaner, *Hind.*; گنیر - ganer, *Dec.*; ಕಣಿಗಿಲು - kanigilu, *Can.*; గన్నేరు - gannéru, *Tel.*; അലരി - alari, *Mal.*; அலரி - alari, *Tam.*). Title from sanscrit through hindostany. San. from (kara, san. hand + víra, san. power), sword; from poisonous root destroying life. Mahr. from sanscrit. Ar. from (samm, ar. poison + himár, ar. ass). Pers. from (khar, pers. ass + zahr, pers. poison). Hind., &c., from sanscrit. Mal. and tam. from (alar, tam. flower). San. also (hayamáraka), meaning horse-killer [paula indigo]; (vishavrikshánka), meaning poisonous tree + body; (pratihása), meaning laughing at, from white flowers; (víra), meaning powerful; (chandáta), meaning powerful; (ashvamáraka), meaning horse-killer. Ar. also (diflí). Hind. also (kanel); (karber). Can. also (biliganagalu), meaning white + oleander; (kempuganagalu), meaning red + oleander; (kanigina); (paddalige). Tel. also (kastúripatte), meaning musk + stripe; (erragannéru), meaning red + the tree. Mal. also (chuvannarali), meaning red alary; (kanavíram), by corruption. Tam. also (asuvalari), meaning horse + gannair; (kattúrippattai), meaning musk + stripe; (irattaisivappalari), meaning double + red + the plant; (irattaivellaiyalari), meaning double + white + the plant; (vellaiyalari), meaning white + the plant; (arali). Greek ῥοδοδένδρον, ῥοδοδάφνη. Title otherwise Horse-killer, Indian oleander, Karaveeram, Oleander, Oleander rosebay, Rosebay, Spurge laurel, Sweet-scented oleander. Botanically Nerium odorum, soland., apocynaceæ [vricsham, 87]. Alias Nerium indicum, odoratum. Large spreading shrub, 6–8 feet; calyx five-cleft; corolla salver-shaped, throat crowned by lacerated segments, segments of the limb twisted, unequal-sided; leaves linear lanceolate, three in a whorl, veiny beneath, with revolute edges; peduncles terminal; flowers ordinarily pale-red, fragrant; follicles cylindrical; near banks of rivers; common in gardens; throws up from ground rod-like stems upon summit of which is borne foliage of the narrow lanceolate leaves; flowers offered to shiva [q.v.] and vishnoo [q.v.]. Roots crooked, bark thick, soft, external surface grey, corky, on young roots the corky layer is very thin, and the interior yellow color of the bark is seen through it, inner surface yellow; the bark when cut or wounded exudes a pale yellow latex, which is resinous and very sticky, odour somewhat acrid, taste acrid and bitter. Bark used externally as a repellent, and made into a paste and applied in cases of ringworm; root taken internally acts as a poison; sometimes taken for suicide; root contains yellow poisonous resin [raul], tannic acid, wax [mom], and sugar [q.v.]; same poison resides in bark and flowers; used in leprosy [cooshtam], eruptions of the skin, and boils; gives to pharm. oleander flowers, non-officinal. An essential oil is distilled from the flowers. Varieties with pink, deep-red, white, and variegated flowers, both single and double; the tamarix gallica, linn. [manna jhow], is sometimes called auttalary or the river alary, but it is no variety. The following is a Hindostany proverb:—جسکے سبب لڑائی هو وہ آدمی نہین کانٹا هی گھر مین سے کایا گل کنیر کا—"Who causes quarrels is not a man, but is like a porcupine [khar-"poosht] quill or an oleander flower in the house;" vapour of flowers being noxious.——*Cluster gannair* (గుత్తిగన్నేరు - gutti-gannéru, Tel.). Tel. from (gutti, tel. cluster + gannéru, tel. nerium odorum, soland.). Botanically Kopsia fruticosa, a. dec., apocynaceæ [vricsham, 87]. Alias Calpicarpum roxburghii; Cerbera fruticosa. Large spreading lanceolate leaves; flower 2½ inches, pale rose, at the base and throat bright red; flowering nearly throughout the year.——*Fragrant gannair* (వాడగన్నేరు - vádagannéru, Tel.). Same as Pagoda tree.——*Water gannair* (நீரலரி - níralari, Tam.). From (nír, tam. water + alari, tam. oleander, nerium odorum, soland.). Knot grass, Red shanks. Botanically the Polygonum genus, polygonaceæ [vricsham, 110]. Annual or perennial herbs, rarely undershrubs; leaves alternate; flowers in spikes or racemes. The species best known to the natives are:—aviculare [hoonrauj], barbatum [alligator's nose], flaccidum [water pepper], roxburghii [wobilinta], tomentosum [river jasmine]. Other s. indian species indigenous or naturalized are:—bishiræ, chinense, donii, glabrum, horridum, lanigerum, minus, misquelianum, nepalense, pedunculare, rivulare, wallichii.——*Wild gannair* (తనికి - taniki, Tel.; കാട്ടലരി - káttalari, Mal.; காட்டலரி - káttarali, Tam.). Title from resemblance of leaf. Mal. and tam. from (kádu, tam. wild + arali, tam. nerium odorum, sol.). Tel. also (shiridamánu). Botanically Homonoya riparia, lour., euphorbiaceæ [vricsham, 118]. Alias Adelia neriifolia; Croton salicifolius; Hæmatospermum javanense. Leaves linear-lanceolate, acuminate, subacute at the base, very often entire, willow-like, beneath sparingly pubescent and scurfy; inflorescences long, many-flowered, erect, slender; segments of the female calyx persistent, ovate-lanceolate; stigmas longer than the capsule, shortish papillose; ovary and capsule here and there muricated, small, pubescent; flowering in the hot season. Large shrub; many-flowered, in beds of rivers; wood grey or greyish-brown, moderately hard, close-grained; there is another species retusa, with varieties cuneata and genuina. The chaltah [q.v.] also is called wild gannair. So also dog bane; botanically alstonia [saptaparnam] venenata, br., apocynaceæ [vricsham, 87]; alias blaberopus venenatus; echites venenata; large tree; flowers largish, pure white; juice of tree poisonous.——*Yellow gannair* (پیلا کنیر - pílákaner, Hind.; پیلا پھول کا گنیر - píláphúlkáganer, Dec.; పచ్చగన్నేరు - pattsa-gannéru, Tel.; പച്ചയരളി - paççayarali, Mal.; பச்சையலரி - paççaiyalari, Tam.). Title from color and resemblance of flowers. Hind. from (pílá, hind. yellow + kaner, hind. oleander, nerium odorum, soland). Tel. from (pattsa, tel. yellow + gannéru, tel. gannair). Tam. from (pattsa, tel. yellow + alari, tam. oleander). Tam. also (tiruváççippú); (shímaiyalari), meaning foreign + oleander; (manjalalari), meaning yellow + oleander. Title otherwise Exile oleander, Exile tree, Foreign oleander, Linear-leaved cerbera, Yellow oleander. Botanically Thevetia nereifolia, juss., apocynaceæ [vricsham, 87]. Alias Cerbera thevetia. Tree, 12 feet; leaves linear, entire, almost veinless, glabrous; calyx five-cleft; segments ovate-lanceolate, acute, three times shorter than the tube of the corolla; peduncles extra-axillary at the tops of the branches, one-flowered; corolla funnel-shaped, tube hairy inside; flowers yellow, fragrant; drupe half orbicular, truncated at the apex, two-celled; cells bipartite. A handsome, spreading tree; constantly in blossom with numerous large, thimble-formed, flowers; fragrant; flowering nearly all year; large almond-like [baudam] nuts; native of west indies; introduced; kernels very bitter, when chewed produce numbness and heat in the tongue; oil is extracted from kernels clear bright yellow. The fresh bark of the young wood, of from ½ to 1 inch in diameter, is green, smooth, and covered by a thin grey epidermis, through which the green color is apparent; it turns black when dry; the bark from the larger stems has a brown suberous coating; the wood is white and soft, with a large central pith; all parts of the plant yield an abundance of acrid milky juice; the fruit is globular, slightly fleshy, green, 1½ to 2 inches in diameter, and contains a hard nut, light brown in color, and triangular, with a deep groove along the edge corresponding to the base of the triangle; each nut contains two pale yellow, slightly winged seeds; the seeds and the inner layer of the bark give, when boiled with hydrochloric acid, a deep blue or bluish-green color. Milk highly venomous; oil from kernels is emetic and purgative; bark antiperiodic, substituted for cinchona [koinah]; gives to pharm. exile bark, non-officinal. Wood worthless.

GANY (కని - gani, *Tel.*; கனி - kani, *Tam.*). From (khan, san. to dig) [kainy]. Mine.

GAON (گانو - gáun, *Hind.*). Corruption of (gráma, san.). Used in Ganjam and Vizagapatam. Village [gaum, graumam].

GAR (گار - gár, *Pers.*). Means doer. Suffix to nouns to denote agent; as Khidmutgar, service + holder [caur, gaur].

GARA (കര - kara, *Mal.*). Shore. So village. Suffix in place names; as Nedoomangara, meaning long + earth + village [cara].——*Garay* (കര - kara, Mal.; கரை - karai, Tam.). Natural bank. Suffix in place names; as Maungaray, meaning mango tree bank [cara, caray].

GARANCHY (گھڑونچی - gharonchí, *Hind.*). From (ghará, hind. pot + unchá, hind. high). A stand on which to place chests, being a bare rectangular frame with legs at the corners.

GARBHAM (गर्भ - garbha, *San.*). From (gribh, san. to hold). Interior.——*Garbhagriham* (गर्भगृह - garbhagriha, San.). From (above + griha, san. house). That part of a temple [coil] in which the idol [vigraham] is placed and where the Bramin officiates.

GARCE (ಗರಸಿ - garasi, *Can.*; గరిసె - garise, *Tel.*; கரிசை - karisai, *Tam.*).—"*a*" Measure of capacity. 400 mercauls = 1 garce [alavay, 3a]. Approximate actual value, 1 garce = 185 cubic feet, 320 cubic inches. As salt measure, 424 mercauls.—"*b*" Superficial measure. In N. circars [q.v.] land which will yield one garce [alavay, 2b]. Compare Mal. parrah, Tam. cottah. See vol. I, 609; II, 506.

GARDAN (گردن - gardan, *Hind.*). Neck.——*Gardan eyengtha* (گردن ایٹھا - gardanaíttá, Hind.; మెడనులిగాడు - medanuligádu, Tel.). Hind. from (gardan, hind. neck + aítta, hind. twirling). Tel. from (meda, tel. neck + nuli, tel. twist + gádu, tel. personal suffix). Title otherwise Wryneck. Yunx torquilla, yunginæ, picidæ [marangotty], scansores, insessores [pacshy, 13], of naturalists [jantoo]. Kestrel-like call; close resemblance of tints to situations on which it alights. No other common species here.

GAROODAN (गरुड - garuda, *San.*). From (garut, san. wing + dí, san. to fly); from swift motion.—"*a*" Mythical bird, prince of birds, the foe of snakes, Vishnoo's vehicle [vauhan], and a son of Cashyapan [q.v.] by Vinatay. Aroonan, the sun's charioteer or the personified dawn, appears as the younger brother of Garoodan. Superior to the common Braminy kite [q.v.], and represented as a being between a man and a bird. On the walls of Veishnava temples and other Veishnava buildings, Garoodan is represented by the figure of a young man seated, with the palms of the hands closed, fingers pointed upwards, a sign denoting reverence; the feet are crossed; the face is that of a man, only with a long, thin, and very aquiline nose; the peculiar cap worn by deities on the head and large wings outstretched from the shoulders. In the Tamul oottara ramayanam [q.v.], the god Vishnoo [q.v.] is represented as going forth to combat, borne by Garoodan; but that is not a usual representation, the quality of mildness or sautwicam [q.v.] being especially ascribed to Vishnoo. The vehicle would seem to be a symbol of swiftness, as the chuckram [q.v.] is an emblem of justice and the mace of power [matam]. Also Hindoo 2nd or pers. name; common among Madhwas [peyar].—"*b*" Plant first term. Generally from being an antidote to poisons, as kite [chillam] is enemy of snakes [sarpam]. Ex., where transl. is of second term: —Aristolochia indica (garudakkodi), creeper; Hydnocarpus venenata (garudap'hala), fruit; Martynia diandra (garudamukku), beak. See gloss. paragraphs.—"*c*" Plant second term, in same sense. Ex., where transl. is of first term:—Alstonia scholaris (pálagaruda), meaning white + tree; Corallocarpus epigæa (ákáshagaruda), sky; Ophiorrhiza mungos (pátálagaruda), nether world; Rauwolfia serpentina (pátalagarudu), pale-red. See gloss. paragraphs.——*Garoodan's beak* (గరుడముక్కు - garudamukku, Tel.). Title from hooked fruit. Same as Tiger claw.——*Garooda ootsavam* (గరుడోత్సవము - garudótsavamu, Tel.; கருடோற்சவம் - karudórchavam, Tam.). Means braminy kite + festival; festival of vishnoo, the braminy kite rider. Otherwise Garooda sairvay. Luni-solar festival [pundigay, 6a]. A local festival at Conjeeveram in second solar month Veiyaushy [mausam], i.e, between 13th May and 12th June. It lasts ten days, during each of which the Vishnoo idol [vigraham] Varadaraja sawmy visits Shiva canjy or Larger canjy on various vauhans [q.v.], for the purpose of permitting the other deities to pay their respects to him. He thus goes down the street [veety] two miles long, which leads from his own temple to the Rajaveety [q.v.], at the foot of which he rests for a while in a mantapam [q.v.]. Varadarajan and Yecaumbara nautan, the Shiva idol, are held to be brothers-in-law, and the evening of sixth day of the feast is occupied by a visit to the Shiva temple. The image is brought down to the front of it, taken thrice round from right to left and the same number of times the opposite way, and then taken away again. This festival is a display of Veishnavism against the old Sheivism. Another Garooda ootsavam takes place at Triplicane on the third day of the lunar month Cheitram [mausam], between 16th March and 15th April, in honor of Paurtasauraty [maryauday, paurtasauraty].——*Garooda punchamy* (గరుడపంచమి - garudapanchami, Tel.). Means braminy kite + fifth lunar day. Same as Nauga punchamy.

GAROOGA (कंकर - kankara, *Mahr.*; توم - túm, *Hind.*; గరుగుచెట్టు - garuguchettu, *Tel.*; ମୋହି - mohi, *Oor.*; കരുവേമ്പു - karuvémbu, *Mal.*; கருவேம்பு - karuvémbu, *Tam.*). Title from teloogoo [fire-work plant]. Hind. from bengalee. Tam. from (karumai, tam. blackness + vémbu, tam. margosa tree, melia azadirachta, linn.); from pinnate leaf [curry-leaf tree]. Hind. also (kharpat). Tel. also (kalugudu). Tam. also (enneykkaraimaram), meaning oil + stain. + tree; from dark brown bark. Title otherewise Black neem, Wing-leaved garooga. Botanically Garuga pinnata, roxb., burseraceæ [vricsham, 35]. Generic name from teloogoo. Medium sized tree; pinnate leaves early take on a yellow shade and fall during the cold season, appear with flowers in the hot season; flowers of a yellowish white, in panicles covered with a mealy kind of white substance; large bunches of smooth fleshy fruits of a pale green color resembling grapes [angoor]; very common. Clear, greenish yellow exudation contains a small proportion of resin [raul] and some oil; it has a terebinthiaceous odour and taste. Fruit eaten both raw and cooked. Leaves used as fodder; bark collected by tanners [chamrah]. Sapwood large, heart-wood reddish, moderately hard.

GARBAR (नान्दिवृक्ष - nandivriksha, *San.*; गरारि - garari, *Mahr.*; گراری - garárí, *Hind.*; ಕಾಡಗರ್ಗರಿ - kádagargari, *Can.*; వొడిశ - vodisha, *Tel.*; କରଡ - karada, *Oor.*; നിലപ്പാല - nilappála, *Mal.*; මදර - madara, *Singh.*; ஒடுகு - odugu, *Tam.*). Title from hindostany. San. from (nandi, san. happiness + vriksha, san. tree). Hind. from mahratta. Can. from (kádu, can. jungle + gargari, can. ocimum). Mal. from (nila, mal. ground + pála, mal. milk-plant). Tam. from (odi, tam. to shine). San. also (indrayava), meaning the plant, holarrhena antidysenterica, wall. + barley, hordeum vulgare, linn., from being antidysenteric and having seeds like barley; (kutaja), meaning the plant, holarrhena antidysenterica, wall. [tellicherry bark]. Can. also (kodasinagida), corruption from (kutaja, san.) the plant, holarrhena antidysenterica, wall. Tel. also (kadisechettu). Tam. also (odu), meaning shining tree. Title otherwise Wodisha. Botanically Lebidieropsis orbicularis, muller, var. collina, euphorbiaceæ [vricsham, 118]. Alias Amanoa collina; Andrachne orbicularis; Bridelia collina; Cluytia collina, patula, retusa. Tree; leaves elliptic or obovate, round-obtuse, obtuse or slightly cordate at the base, pubescent on the rib below; flowers subsessile, softly grey hairy white; sepals oblong triangular ovate; petals very minute glabrous, irregularly rhomboid above; capsules glabrous; seeds globose; flowers in hot season, seed ripens in december and january; the bark or outer crust of capsules is poisonous; wood reddish, very hard and durable.

GAS (ගස් - gas, *Singh.*). Tree.——*Gasambilla* (సామంది - polári, Tel.; ചെറിയകൊട്ടം - cheriyakottam, Mal.; ගස්ඇඹිල්ල - gasambilla, Singh.). Title from singhalese meaning ambilla tree. Mal. from (cheriya, mal. small + kottam, mal. costus speciosus, smith). Singh. from (gas, singh. tree + ambilla, singh. antidesma). Tel. also (dzánapalasheru). Botanically Antidesma [amla shaucam] ghæsembilla, muller, var. genuinum, euphorbiaceæ [vricsham, 118]. Specific name from singhalese. Alias Antidesma paniculatum, pubescens. Small, deciduous tree; flower minute, greenish yellow. Leaves and berries eaten. Bark used for ropes. Wood red, with darker colored heart-wood, smooth, hard, close and even-grained.

GASHT (گشت - gasht, *Hind.*). From (gashtan, pers. to roam). Patrol.——*Gashty* (گشتی - gashtí, Hind.). A patrolling officer.——*Mengasht* (میں گشت - mengasht, Hind.). From (mél, tam. over). Overseer.——*Peigasht* (پیگشت - paigasht, Hind.). From (paí, pers. foot). Foot patrol.

GATLA (గట్ల - gatla, *Tel.*). Corruption of (katta, tel. bank). Locative plural. Suffix in place names; as Daudigatla, meaning army + bank [cutla].

GATY (गति - gati, *San.*). From (gam, san. to go) [go, gungay]. Motion. Specially the diurnal motion of a planet [graham] in its orbit [cacsham]. Madhya gaty is mean motion. Spoota gaty, from (sp'huta, san. true) is true or apparent motion. Vakra gaty, from (vakra, san. bend), is retrograde motion [chauram, cramam, jyotisham].

GAUB (तिन्दुक - tinduka, *San.*; बंदारूकु - bandárúku, *Conc.*; آبنوس هند - ábnúsihind, *Ar.*; آبنوس هندی - ábnúsihindí, *Pers.*; گاب - gáb, *Hind.*; تیندو - tendú, *Dec.*; ಅಂಟಿನಮರ - antinamara, *Can.*; ಹೊಳ್ಳೆತೂಪರ - holletúpara, *Coorg*; ಬಂದದಮರ - bandadamara, *Too.*; తుమికి - tumiki, *Tel.*; ଗୁସ୍ୱକେନ୍ଧୁ - gusvakendhu, *Oor.*; പനിച്ചി - paniççi, *Mal.*; තිඹිරි - timbiri, *Singh.*; பனிச்சை - paniççai, *Tam.*). Title from hindostany. San. from (tij, san. to sharpen); from acidity of glutinous exudation. Ar. from (ábnús, ar. diospyros ebenum, kœnig. + hind, ar. indian). Dec. from sanscrit. Can. from (antu, can. gum + mara, can. tree). Mal. and tam. from (pani, tam. to flow); as yielding juice. San. also (túvara), meaning astringent from fruit; (dautashat'ha), meaning tooth + rogue, from acid fruit [sour auray, wood apple]. Can. also (tumari); (tappasi); (tumaki); (kusharada). Tel. also (tinduki); (tubuki); (nítitumiki), meaning water + the tree, common near backwaters; (gábu); (tummi). Mal. also (vánañchi), by corruption. Tam. also (tumbi). Title otherwise Backwater tree, Glue tree, Malabar garcinia, Malabar mangosteen, Persian mangosteen, Tindooky, Toomiky, Wild mangosteen [malay red wood]. Botanically Diospyros [indian ebony] embryopteris, pers., ebenaceæ [vricsham, 83]. Alias Cavanillea philippensis; Diospyros glutinifera, glutinosa; Embryopteris glutinifera, peregrina; Garcinia malabarica. Evergreen tree, 25–30 feet, forming dense dome of foliage; leaves alternate, linear-oblong, pointed, glabrous shining, short-petioled; male peduncles axillary, solitary, three to four-flowered; stamens twenty; females one-flowered, larger than the male; stamens two to four, short; pistils four; nut globular, size of a small apple [seb], rusty-colored, filled with pulpy-juice and covered with a rusty farina; seeds eight; flowers white; common near backwaters; native of w. coast. Fruit is full of tannin; juice of fruit applied to bruises and sprains; oil from seeds by boiling used in dysentery and diarrhœa; infusion of fruit used as a gargle; substituted for british logwood and rhatany; diospyri fructus officinal in pharm. like catechu [q.v.]. Fruit eaten by natives when ripe, but not palatable; leaves eaten as vegetable [keeray]. Juice of fruit used for paying boat seams, and preparing nets and lines; on malabar coast employed by carpenters [tutchan] as glue; the glutinous pulp surrounding seeds is used in binding books, as obnoxious to insects; fruit and bark give a dye [shauyam]. Wood grey, moderately hard, close-grained; used for building; gives masts and yards to country vessels in ceylon.——*Black gaub* (کالی لکڑی - kálílakrí, Dec.). Same as Malabar black wood.——*Chinese gaub* (ولایتی گاب - viláítígáb, Hind.). Hind. from (viláití, hind. foreign + gáb, hind. diospyros embryopteris.

pers.). Title otherwise Chinese date plum, Japan date plum, Japanese keg-fig. Botanically Diospyros [indian ebony] kaki, linn. f., ebenaceæ [vricsham, 83]. Alias Diospyros chinensis; Embryopteris kaki. Fruit about size of large apple [seb], with twin almond-like [baudam] stones in the centre; rind a rich ruddy crimson in texture resembling, but rougher than, that of the peach [shaft auloo]; rather disagreeable odour; flavor suggestive of over-ripe and very mellow apple, not unpalatable; preserve made from it by the chinese.——*Forest gaub* (तिम्बुराणि - timburani, Mahr.; بن گاب - bangáb, Hind.; ಜಗಳಗಂಟಿ - jagalaganti, Can.; ఎర్రగోడ - erragoda, Tel.; வக்கணைமரம் - vakkanaimaram, Tam.). Hind. from (ban, hind. forest + gáb, hind. diospyros embryopteris, pers.). Can. from (jagala, can. fight + gantu, can. knot). Tel. from (erra, tel. red + goda, tel. the tree); sylvatica being tellagoda. Tam. from (ve, tam. hard + kanai, tam. closeness + maram, tam. tree). Can. also (goindú); (kálagoindú); (balkuniki). Tel. also (kákiulimera), meaning crow + nirvala, cratæva religiosa, forst., from similar bark and wood, but darker; (nallaurimeda), meaning black nirvala; (nallaulimera), meaning same; (muççitanki); (muççitunki); (muççitinki); (michatumnrra); (kondadorus); (vekkana). Title otherwise Goindoo, Mottled ebony, Vuckanay, Yerragoda. Botanically Diospyros [indian ebony] montana, roxb., ebenaceæ [vricsham, 83]. Alias Diospyros cordifolia, goindu, orixensis, punctata, regulosa; goindu from canarese. Leaves ovate-acute, obtuse at the base, smooth, membranaceous; racemes reflexed, nearly twice as long as the petiole; males five to six-flowered, hermaphrodites one-flower; bracts and lobes of the calyx ovate-acute, ciliated; corolla in the males twice as long as the calyx; stamens the length of the tube; ovary globose, smooth; flowers small, green, fragrant; flowering in march and april. Small tree, common in plains and about the foot of mountains in dry localities throughout presidency. Pulp of fruit is edible. Wood dark-brown, mottled, hard and close-grained, small but useful for cabinet work; does not bear exposure.——*Small gaub* (చిట్టితుమికి - chittatumiki, Tel.). Title from size. Same as Sweet gaub.——*Sweet gaub* (काकतिन्दुक - kákatinduka, San.; تومل - túmal, Hind.; میٹھا تیندو - míthátendú, Dec.; ತಿಂಬುರಣಿ - timburani, Can.; చిట్టితుమికి - chittatumiki, Tel.; କେନ୍ଦୁ - kendhu, Oor.). Title from taste of fruit. San. from (káka, san. crow + tinduka, san. diospyros embryopteris, pers.); from jet black heart-wood. Dec. from (míthá, hind. sweet + tendú, hind. diospyros embryopteris, pers.). Tel. from (chitti, tel. small + tumiki, tel. diospyros). Title otherwise Toomal tree. Botanically Diospyros [indian ebony] tomentosa, r., ebenaceæ [vricsham, 83]. Alias Diospyros exsculpta. Branchlets, peduncles and flowers rusty-tomentose; leaves alternate and opposite, broad-elliptic, especially tomentose below; peduncles of the male flowers the length of the petiole, three-flowered at the apex; calyx campanulate, acute at the base, four to six-lobed at the apex; lobes acute, erect; female flowers solitary, short-pedicelled; calyx deeply four to six-cleft; lobes ovate-acute, reflexed at the margin outwards, somewhat winged; tube of the corolla hairy outside; flowers small, whitish; flowering in march and april. Found on western ghauts [q.v.]; when ripe the berries are yellowish, and are filled with a soft, yellow, sweetish, astringent pulp, eaten by natives; gives an ebony [q.v.].

GAUD (గాడు - gádu, *Tel.*). Personal singular suffix, means fellow. Very common bird second term. Ex.:—Yunx torquilla (medanuligádu), neck + twist + fellow. See gloss. paragraphs. ——*Gauroo* (గారు - gáru, Tel.). Plural of gaud. Added to any name as a title of honor [avergal]. Dora gauroo is a gentleman or zemindar [q.v.]. Tally gauroo is a mother [maryauday, peyar, sahib].

GAUD (കാട് - kátu, *Mal.*; காடு - kádu, *Tam.*). Forest. Suffix in place names; as Maungaud, meaning mango forest [caud].

GAUJAR (गर्जर - garjara, *San.*; गासर - gásara, *Mahr.*; جزر - jazar, *Ar.*; زردک - zardak, *Pers.*; گاجر - gájar, *Hind.* and *Dec.*; ಕೆಂಪುಮುಳ್ಳಂಗಿ - kempumullangi, *Can.*; గజ్జరగడ్డ - gaddzaragadda, *Tel.*; மஞ்சள்முள்ளங்கி - mañjalmullangi, *Tam.*). Title from deccany. San. from (garj, san. to call out) [lussoon]. Ar. from sanscrit. Pers. from (zard, pers. yellow); from color of tuber. Hind. from sanscrit. Can. from (kempu, can. red + mullangi, can. raphanus sativus, linn.). Tel. from (gájar, hind. carrot + gadda, tel. root). Tam. from (mañjal, tam. yellow + mullangi, tam. radish); from color of tuber. San. also (griñjana), meaning roaring [ganjah, kinnab, lussoon]; (shikhámúla), meaning top-knot + root; from root having a tuft of leaves. Tel. also (pítikanda), meaning dung + yam, amorphophallus campanulatus, blume, from smell; (pattsamullangi), meaning yellow + radish. Tam. also (kárattukkizhangu), meaning carrot yam; (káççarakkizhangu), from hindostany. Title otherwise Carrot, Dung yam, Hair-knot root. Botanically Daucus carota, linn., umbelliferæ [vricsham, 67]. Seeds are medicinally nervine tonic, roots refrigerant and alterative; seeds boiled with honey [shahad] and fermented, produce spirituous liquor; roots familiar as food; the form here cultivated is hardy and acclimatised, but exceedingly coarse, with almost green roots; no other common species here.

GAULY (గాలి - gáli, *Tel.*). Wind [vayoo]. Suffix in place names; as Yeedagauly, meaning storm + wind.——*Gaulicondah* (గాలికొండ - gálikonda, Tel.). From (above + konda, tel. hill).— "*a*" Mountain; Kurnool dist., Nundiaul tal.; lat. 15° 26′: long. 78° 49′; from Kurnool E.S.E. 54 miles; from Nundiaul E.S.E. 19¾ miles. Highest point of Nundicanama pass. Railway passes under it by tunnel.—"*b*" Hills; Vizagapatam district, Srungavarapoocote division. A long series of lofty humps and saddles forming one of highest portions of Eastern ghauts [q.v.]. The summits are of gneiss and syenite, capped with laterite [q.v.] and black mould. They are easy of access. The two highest peaks reach a height of 5,345 and 5,287 feet respectively. A good cart-road runs up to Anantagherry 6 miles from the top and 19 miles from the plains, where the Maharajah of Vizianagram has a thriving coffee [q.v.] plantation extending over about 700 acres. The climate is temperate all the year round.

GAUM (گاؤں - gáun, *Hind.*). From (gráma, san.). A village [gaon, graumam]. Suffix in place names; as Belgaum, meaning cave + village.

GAUNAM (चक्र - chakra, *San.*; گھانا - ghána, *Hind.*; ಗಾಣ - gána, *Can.*; గానుగ - gánuga, *Tel.*; ചെക്ക് - chekku, *Mal.*; கானம் - kánam, *Tam.*). Title from hindostany. San. from (kram, san. to go); that which goes round. Hind. from (ban, san. to crush) [ghanam, ghantay]. Can., tel. and tam. from hindostany. Mal. from (chakra, san. wheel). Tam. also (shekku), corruption of sanscrit. Oil-mill. The following is the general way of extracting oils [yennay] from the mill:—The seeds, whether gingelly [q.v.], castor [aumanac], ippa [common mohwah], cocoanut [q.v.], margosa [neem], &c., are first sifted, and sand and stones are removed. Then they are thrown into the mill, a large quantity at a time. When the mill has been worked for an hour, and the seeds are crushed so that the husk separates from the seed, jaggery [q.v.] and water are added to the mass. The mill is then worked again for some time, when oil oozes out. When it comes out in large quantities it is baled out by wooden ladles [agappay], and when in small quantities it is removed by brushes made of feathers. Castor seeds are first soaked in hot water for three-quarter of an hour; this and an equal quantity of raw seeds are then thrown into the mill. The cocoanut, if soft, is first dried. Margosa seed is first husked [aulay].——*Gaundla* (గాండ్ల - gándla, obl., Tel.). Corrupt oblique plural form of (gánuga), oil-mill; and so used in anglo-indian for the caste. Oil-monger caste. The corresponding terms are:—Hind. telee, Can. gauniga, Mal. checkaula, Tam. vauniyan. Closely resemble the Tamul, but these use only one bullock to work the mill, while Vauniyar use two. They are therefore usually known as Wonteddoo gaundlas. Numbers some 100,000. See vol. II, 227 [jauty]. Distinguish from gowndla [q.v.].——*Gauniga* (ಗಾಣಿಗ - gániga, Can.). Means oilmill-man. Oil-monger caste. The corresponding terms are:—Hind. telee, Tel. gaundla, Mal. checkaula, Tam. vauniyan [jauty].——*Gaunooga pindy coora* (గానుగపిండికూర - gánugapindikúra, Tel.). Oil-mill + cake + pot herb; from being cooked with oil cakes from cocoanut [q.v.] or sesamum [gingelly]; cf. Tranquebar gendarussa. Plant name common to:—Corchorus acutangulus; Melochia corchorifolia. See gloss. paragraphs.

GAUR (കാര - kára, *Mal.*). From (kri, san. to do). Doer, agent; personal suffix as Altigaur, meaning measurement + doer, measuring officer [caur, gar].

GAUZOO (ಗಾಜು - gáju, *Can.*; గాజు - gádzu, *Tel.*). From (kácha, san. glass). Glass bracelet, substituted by the poor for metallic ornaments [nagay, zewar]. The following is the mode of manufacture. Round pits are dug, and fuller's earth of the particular kind [gauzoo sowdoo, pooneer, valayal oppoo] suitable for making bracelets is heaped near them. Some of the earth is thrown into one of these pits, and water sufficient to stand one span deep is poured over. One or two persons then get into the pit and stir the water and the earth together for half an hour. After two hours the water gets clear, the sand and other heavy substances going to the bottom. This clear water is taken out and poured into the second pit. The same process as in the first pit is repeated in the second and the third pits. The mud which is precipitated between the clear water on the top and the sand at the bottom of the third pit, is taken out and poured upon mats spread near the pits. Some more earth is thrown into the pit and a sufficient quantity of water is mixed with it. The clear brackish water at the top is taken out and mixed with the mud on the mats. It is then left to dry. This last process is done for ten days successively. Four baskets of mud dried in this manner gives ten baskets of dry earth. A large furnace having been previously prepared, numerous earthen pots or crucibles are filled three quarters full with the prepared earth, and placed in piles on the furnace without actually touching it. The crucibles are then closed above with clay. Fire is kept up in the furnace for a night. The earth in the pot melts and turns into a hard black mass, settling down to bulk of half the pot. Over this black mass an incrustation of salt half an inch thick is formed, which is removed. The pots are then taken out of the furnace and broken, and the potsherds are separated from the hard mass. All this is done outside the village. The remaining work is carried on in the village. A small furnace with six openings is prepared, and potsherds are placed above it without touching the fire. The hard mass above referred to is broken into small pieces and thrown into these potsherds. As it melts, it is stirred with a long steel rod, so that some of it sticks round the end of the rod. So much of the substance as is necessary for making one bracelet is taken out by the steel rod in this manner; and the rod is tapped by another iron instrument. By this process a hole is formed in the substance sticking to the rod. This rough bracelet is taken off the rod, attached to a mould, and formed into a bracelet.

GAYAUL (गयाळ - gayála, *Mahr.*). From (gayál, hind. deserted). Land unfit for cultivation [beed, carambay, gheiradah].

GAYETY (గయేతి - gayeti, *Tel.*). A sub-division of the Gond language [bhaushay, gond]. See vol. I (38).

GAZELLE (غزال - ghazál, *Ar.*). Only the Ravine-deer here.

GEER (گیر - gír, *Hind.*). From (giraftan, pers. to seize). Suffix denoting agent; as Jehaungeer, the world seizer.

GELDRIA (பழவேர்க்காட்டுக்கோட்டை - pazhavérkkát-tukkóttai, *Tam.*). Name of the Dutch fort of Poolicat.

GENDAH (गण्ड - ganda, *San.*; گینڈا - gendá, *Hind.*; ఖడ్గమృగము - khadgamrigamu, *Tel.*; വാൾപുലി - válpuli, *Mal.*; காண்டாமிருகம் - kándámirugam, *Tam.*). Tel. from (khadga, san. sword + mriga, san. animal). Tam. from sanscrit. Rhinoceros. Tusker, or male elephant [comban] with long tusks [dant]. Distinguish from Gendah under Gandh.

GENDARUSSA (गन्धरस - gandharasa, *San.*). From (gandha, san. fragrance + rasa, san. juice) [gandh]; from leaves. Botanically the Justicia genus, acanthaceæ [vricsham, 101]. Herbs or shrubs occurring in tropical and sub-tropical regions; flowers red. The species best known to the natives are shown below. Other s. indian species indigenous or naturalized are:—betonica, bivalvis, diffusa, glabra, glauca, montana, nilgherrensis, quinqueangularis, simplex, wynaadensis.——*Common gendarussa* (नीलनिर्गुण्डी - nílanirgundí, San.; कालोनिगुण्डु - kálónigundu, Conc.; اثلق اسود - aslakiaswad, Ar.; پنجنگشت سیاه - panjangashtisiyáh, Pers.; اودی سنبالو - údísambháló, Hind.; کالی سنبالی - kálíshambálí, Dec.; ಕರಿನೆಕ್ಕಿಗಿಡ - karinekkigida, Can.; ಕರುನೆಕ್ಕಿ - karunekki, Too.; నల్లవావిలి - nallavávili, Tel.; വാതങ്കൊടി - vátankoti, Mal.; කළුවරණිය - kaluvaraniya, Singh.; கருநொச்சி - karunoççi, Tam.). San. from (níla, san. blue + nirgundí, san. notchy, vitex negundo, linn.) [water notchy]. Conc. from sanscrit. Ar. from (aslak, ar. vitex negundo, linn. + aswad, ar. black). Pers. from (panjangasht, pers. vitex negundo, linn. + siyáh, pers. black). Hind. from (údí, hind. blue + sambhálú, hind. vitex negundo, linn.). Dec. from (kálí, hind. black + shambálí, hind. vitex negundo, linn.). Can. from (kari, can. black + nekkigida, can. the plant). Too. from (karu, too. black + nekki, too. the plant). Tel. from (nalla, tel. black + vávili, tel. vitex trifolia, l.). Mal. from (vátam, mal. rheumatism + koti, mal. creeper), from leaves and root being prescribed in rheumatism. Singh. from (kalu, singh. black + varaniya, singh. shrub, hedyotis fruticosa, linn.). Tam. from (karumai, tam. blackness + noççi, tam. vitex negundo, linn.). San. also (krishnanirgundí), meaning black notchy; (krishnasurasa), meaning black notchy. Hind. also (nílínargandí), from sanscrit. Can. also (naççukadde); (karelakkigida), meaning black + the plant. Tel. also (nallanoççili), meaning black + the plant, vitex trifolia, linn.; (nélavávili), meaning ground + vitex trifolia, l.; (addasaramu) [adhatoday]. Mal. also (vátankoli), meaning rheumatism destroyer; (karinoççil), meaning black notchy. Tam. also (vádákkodi), meaning ever fresh + creeper; from dark leaf ever green. Title otherwise Black notchy, Willow-leaved justicia. Botanically Justicia [gendarussa] gendarussa, linn., acanthaceæ [vricsham, 101]. Specific name from (gandharasa, san. fragrant juice). Alias Gendarussa vulgaris. Shrub, 3-4 feet; leaves opposite, lanceolate, elongated; branches numerous, long, and straggling; flowers in whorls on terminal spikes; upper lip undivided; flowers pale, greenish white, sparingly stained with purple; flowers during wet season. In gardens it is usually seen in a stunted form, as it is kept closely cut; the young shoots have a smooth green or purple bark; from the joints, which are somewhat tumid, spring secondary shoots; leaves and tender stalks have, when rubbed, a strong, not unpleasant, smell; grows in waste places as well as cultivated; native of malay islands. Leaves in infusion given internally in fevers; also as a bath; externally juice of leaves administered in coughs to children, and mixed with oil as embrocation in glandular swellings of neck and throat; mixed with mustard-seed [rayaun] is a good emetic; natives put leaves in a bag with common salt [ooppoo], and warming them apply externally in diseases of the joints; leaves scattered amongst clothes to preserve from insects [poochy]. ——*Coromandel gendarussa* (ನೆಲಬೇವಿನಗಿಡ - nelabévinagida, Can.; నాగపుట్టచెట్టు - nágaputtachettu, Tel.; මානයි - mánayi, Singh.; நிரைபூத்தி - niraibútti, Tam.). Can. from (nela, can. earth + bévinagida, can. the plant, melia azadirachta, linn.). Tel. from (nága, san. cobra + putta, tel. ant hill + chettu, tel. tree). Tam. from (nirai, tam. completeness + pú, tam. to flower); from flowering all the year. Singh. also (mani). Tam. also (kódagasálai); (áram); cf. mountain ebony. Botanically Justicia [gendarussa] procumbens, linn., acanthaceæ [vricsham, 101]. Alias Justicia ascendens; Rostellularia adenostachya, procumbens. Shrub, 7-8 feet; stem spreading, jointed, five striated, often rooting at the joints; leaves linear-lanceolate, opposite, subsessile, entire, a little downy; spikes terminal, erect, four-sided; flowers opposite, decussate, rose-colored; upper divisions of calyx very minute; tube of corolla short, upper lip erect, two cleft, under lip broad, three-parted; capsule four-seeded, seeds two in each cell; flowering nearly all year; very common on pasture ground on coromandel coast. Juice of leaves squeezed into eyes in ophthalmia; has a faintly bitter, disagreeable taste, and is used as a substitute for fumaria, the true pitpapra [q.v.]. ——*Tranquebar gendarussa* (पिण्डि - pindi, San.; ಕಡ್ಡಿಯರಕಿನಗಿಡ - kaddiyarakinagida, Can.; పిండికొండ - pindikonda, Tel.; தவசுமுருங்கை - tavasumurungai, Tam.). San. from (pinda, san. cake). Can. from (kaddi, can. small stick + eraku, can. to bow + gida, can. plant). Tel. from (pindi, tel. flour + konda, tel. hill). Tam. from (tavasi, tam. devotee + murungai, tam. horse-radish tree, moringa pterygosperma, gærtn.); tavasipillay is a cook boy attending a gooroo [q.v.]. Tam. also (punnákkuppúndu), meaning oil-cake + plant, cooked with sesamum oil-cake [ponnauk]. Title otherwise Pindy conda, Ponnauk poond, Tranquebar adhatoda, Tranquebar justicia. Botanically Justicia [gendarussa] tranquebariensis, linn., acanthaceæ [vricsham, 101]. Alias Adhatoda tranquebariensis; Gendarussa tranquebariensis; Justicia parvifolia. Adhatoda from tamul. Fruticulose, hoary-pubescent; leaves small, roundish; bracts orbiculate, retuse, bracteoles equalling the calyx, linear; flowers axillary, solitary, ascending on a terminal spike, yellowish, purple-dotted. Juice of leaves cooling and aperient, prescribed for children in small-pox; bruised leaves applied to blows and other external injuries.

GENTOO (جنتو - jantú, *Hind.*). From portuguese gentio, a gentile or heathen. The name formerly applied by europeans to the natives of the country, especially to the Teloogoo [q.v.] people, for when the Portuguese arrived the Teloogoo raj [q.v.] of Vijianugger [q.v.] was dominant over great part of the peninsula. Cf. Malabar for tamul.

GERSOPPAH (ಗೇರುಸಪ್ಪೆ - gérusappe, *Can.*; gersoppa, *Mys. Gov.*). From (géru, can. marking-nut plant, semecarpus anacardium, linn. f. + soppu, can. leaf); from the village with the trees. Falls in Shimoga district, Mysore, on the Sharauvaty river [aroovy, sharauvaty].

GEUNG (गोधूम - gódhúma, *San.*; गहूं - gahúm, *Mahr.*; गवु - gavu, *Conc.*; حنطه - hintah, *Ar.*; درخت گندم - darakhtigandum, *Pers.*; گیہوں کا پیڑ - gehúnkáper, *Hind.*; گیہوں کا جھاڑ - gehúnkájhár, *Dec.*; ಗೋಧಿ - gódhi, *Can.*; ಗೋದಿ - gódi, *Too.*; గోధుమ - gódhuma, *Tel.*; ଗୋମ - gómo, *Oor.*; കോതമ്പ - kótampam, *Mal.*; තිරිඟු - tiringu, *Singh.*; கோதுமை - kóthumai, *Tam.*). Title from deccany. San. from (gudh, san. turn, as in a mill); from being used as flour. Mahr. from sanscrit. Ar. from (hanata, ar. red); from color of seeds. Pers., &c., from sanscrit. San. also (mléchhabhójana), meaning barbarian's food; (akshata), meaning unbroken; (sumana), meaning beautiful, pleasant; (dhavala), meaning white; cf. etymology of wheat. Can. also (javegódhi), meaning hordeum vulgare + wheat. Tam. also (várgóthumai), meaning tail + wheat; properly barley [jow]; (kóthi), by corruption. Title otherwise Wheat. Botanically Triticum vulgare, villars, graminaceæ [vricsham, 156]. Alias Triticum æstivum, aristatum, compositum, durum, hybernum, sativum, turgidum. Cereal not much cultivated in s. india. Spike tetragonal, imbricated; rachis tenacious, spikelets usually four-flowered; glumes ventricose, ovate, truncated, mucronate, compressed under the apex, round-convex at the back; nerve prominent; flowers awned or muticous; fruit free. Flour white, heavy; starch or amylum from the seed friable, very white, in an adherent powder, when compressed between the fingers emits a peculiar sound. Wheat is rich in solids, and contain from 1 to 2 per cent. of soluble albumen, 8 to 12 per cent. of gluten, and 60 to 70 per cent. of starch; it is deficient in fat, also in the antiscorbutic salts; when ground it consists of two separable substances, the husk called the bran and the inner starchy portion called flour; the mixture of the two is meal; 504 lb. of wheat should give 392 lb. of flour. Internally flour and water is used as chemical antidote in poisoning by the preparations of mercury [rasam], copper [taumram], tin [tagaram], zinc [tootnaug] and silver [velly], and by iodine. Use of wheat as article of food here chiefly confined to europeans and east indians. There are two varieties classed chiefly according to the consistency of the grain, hard or soft; each of these two classes may be grouped according to the color of the grain in being white or red; and these again may be further sub-divided according to the presence or absence of bristles, which makes them known as bearded or beardless. Cf. Boosam, Rolang, Soojee.

GHAFFAR (غفار - ghaffár, *Hind.*). From (ghafara, ar. to cover). One who pardons; an epithet of God [allah]. Common alam; as Ghaffar ally, double alam; Ghaffar khan, alam +

pataun alaumat [ism].——*Ghafoor* (غفور - ghafúr, Hind.). From (ghafara, ar. to cover). Forgiving; an attribute of God [allah]. Common alam; as Ghafoor beg, alam + moghul alaumat [ism].

GHANAM (घन - ghana, *San.*). From (han, san. to strike) [gaunam]; pressed, dense, heavy. Mass in mathematics. Solid body in geometry. Cube of a number in arithmetic. Ghana moolam is cubic root and ghana palam is contents of a cube or solid [ganitam, shastram].——*Ghanta beejam* (घण्टाबीज - ghantá-bíja, San.; అడవి ఆముదము - adaviámudamu, Tel.). From (ghantá, san. bell + bíja, san. seed); from rattling of dry capsules. Tel. from (adavi, tel. jungle + ámudamu, tel. castor-oil plant, ricinus communis, linn.). Botanically the Croton genus, euphorbiaceæ [vricsham, 118]. Trees or shrubs, rarely herbs; leaves alternate, rarely opposite or whorled; flowers solitary or clustered on the axis of a terminal raceme with small bracts; fruit consists of three carpels separating one from the other, and each containing one seed. The species best known to the natives are:—aromaticus [croton lac tree], oblongifolius [devil's goad], tiglium [jamalgota]. Other s. indian species indigenous or naturalized are:—Cascarilla, bark occurs in short, rolled fragments, tonic; Caudatus, leaves applied as a poultice to sprains; Malabaricus, tree 20–30 feet; Reticulatus, small shrub, western moist forests; Scabiosus, very silvery appearance.——*Ghantaravam* (घण्टारव - ghantárava, San.; గిలిగిజి - giligiji, Can.; గిలిగిత్స - giligittsa, Tel.; கிலுகிலுப்பை - kilugiluppai, Tam.). San. from (ghantá, san. bell + rava, san. sound); from rattle of dry pods. Tel. from (gilaka, tel. rattle + gittsu, tel. to pinch). Tam. from sound of seeds in dry legumen. Can. also (gijigiji). Tel. also (gilakachettu), meaning rattle + tree; (pattsadzanumu), meaning green + hemp, crotalaria juncea, linn.; (telladzanumu), meaning white + hemp; (pillivattatíga), meaning cat + testicle + creeper, from fruit; cf. common cowitch and shakaukool. Tam. also (elippidukkan), meaning rat + testicle, from pod; (elippori), meaning rat + crackle; (mínañju), meaning fish + poison [indian berry]; (míngolli), meaning fish killer; (narimarutti), meaning fox + frightener. Castanet plant, Rattlewort. Botanically the Crotalaria genus, leguminosæ [vricsham, 48]. Herbs or shrubs of very various habit and vestiture; leaves simple or trifoliolate; flowers in terminal or leaf-opposed racemes, often showy; pod sessile or stipulate, straight, linear or oblong, turgid, continuous within, usually many-seeded. The species best known to the natives are:—albida [hill giligitcha], hirsuta [black giligitcha], juncea [sunn], laburnifolia [large giligitcha], linifolia [black hill giligitcha], orixensis [stunted giligitcha], quinquefolia [water giligitcha], retusa [short giligitcha], sericea [silky giligitcha], trifoliastrum [nauga giligitcha], verrucosa [forest giligitcha]. Other s. indian species indigenous or naturalized are:—Barbata, erect; flowers few, yellow; Bifaria, procumbent; Biflora, prostrate; Clavata; Digitata, somewhat shrubby; Evolvuloides, perennial; Formosa, erect; Fulva, shrub, mysore, neilgherries; Globosa, prostrate; Grahamiana, shrub; Heyneana, suffruticose; Hirsuta, perennial; Hirta, suffruticose; Leschenaultii, erect; Lunulata, suffruticose; Madarensis, suffruticose; Medicaginea, suffruticose; Mysorensis, suffruticose; Nana, common, branching from the base; Notonii, shrub; Obtecta, suffruticose, erect; Paniculata, shrub, flowers large; Prostrata, suffruticose; Pulcherrima, flowers large; Pusilla, small annual; Ramosissima, suffruticose; Rigida, sandy soil; Rubiginosa, low shrub; Salicifolia, herbaceous, erect; Semperflorens, herbaceous; Sessiliflora; Speciosa, erect; Subperfoliata, suffruticose; Willdenowiana, shrub.——*Ghantay* (घण्टा - ghantá, San.; گهنٹا - ghantá, Hind.). From (han, san. to strike) [gaunam]. A bell or gong [ghariyaul, ghurry, gong]. European hour [caulam].

GHAR (گهر - ghar, *Hind.*). House [griham].——*Gharbaury* (گهرباری - gharbárí, Hind.). From (above + bár, hind. premises + agent suffix). The head of a house [carnaven].

GHAREEB (غريب - gharíb, *Hind.*). From (ghariba, ar. to retire). Poor. Ghareebnawauz, from (nawáz, pers. protector) is friend of the poor, expression addressed to a European official. Ghareeb parwar salaumat is May you be in peace, O patron of the poor; a phrase in letters.

GHARRY (گاڑی - gárí, *Hind.*). A carriage. Distinguish from Ghurry [q.v.].

GHASSAUL (غسال - ghassál, *Hind.*). From (ghusl, ar. ablution). One who washes the dead before burial [janauza].

GHAT (घट् - ghat, *San.*). To unite.——*Ghadiya* (घटिका - ghatiká, San.; ಘಳಿಗೆ - ghalige, Can.; ఘడియ - ghadiya, Tel.). From (ghata, san. a water-jar).—"*a*" Indian hour; time taken for a jar to fill up and sink. Although the lunar day [tity] is of variable length, its sub-division the Indian hour does not in civil practice vary, but consists precisely of 24 English minutes. Natives measure this by an empty vessel [ghurry] of a certain size placed in water. There is a small hole at the bottom, through which water enters; and the size both of hole and vessel is so proportioned that, if care be taken, the vessel sinks at the termination of every 24 English minutes. The ghadiya is divided sexagesimally into vighadiyas, params and soorams. The following is scale:—60 vighadiyas = 1 ghadiya; 60 ghadiyas = 1 dinam or day [caulam, 4, 5a]. Approximate actual value, 1 ghadiya = 24 English minutes. 2½ Indian hours make one English hour. Same as San. ghaticam [caulam, 3], dandam [caulam 6], naudy, and sometimes calay, Hind. ghurry, Can. ghaligey, Tam. nauzhy [caulam, 1].—"*b*" The ghadiya referring to time must be distinguished from an arc [chaupam] of the same name, which divides a lunar mansion or nacshatram [q.v.] of 13° 20′ into sixty parts, sub-divided likewise sexagesimally into Vighadiya, &c.——*Ghariyaul* (گهڑیال - ghariyál, Hind.). From (ghatí, san. the indian hour of 24′). The plate or gong [q.v.] on which hours are struck with a wooden mallet [ghantay, ghurry].——*Ghatam* (घट - ghata, San.). From (ghat, san. to unite). Means a pot [chatty]. Mud pot used as a drum [paray].——*Ghurry* (घटी - ghatí, San.; گهڑی - gharí, Hind.; ఘడియ - ghadiya, Tel.; கடி - kadi, Tam.). From (ghat, san. to unite); water jar. A floating cup with a small hole in it, adjusted so that it fills and sinks in a fixed time. Also the gong [q.v.] on which the time so indicated is struck. Hence also a clock or watch. Also the sixtieth part of a day and night [ahorautram], same as ghadiya [q.v.] equal therefore to twenty-four minutes, which was in old Hindoo customs the space of time indicated by the clepsydra just mentioned. In Anglo-Indian usage the word is wrongly employed for an English hour. See vol. I, 609 [caulam, ghantay, ghariyaul].

GHATT (గట్టు - gattu, *Tel.*). A mound of earth; suffix in compound as Caraghatt, meaning embankment + mound [gutt].

GHAULIB (غالب - ghálib, *Ar.*). From (ghaliba, ar. to overcome). Powerful. Lacab of Ally [q.v.]. Common alam; as Ghaulib beg, alam + alaumat [ism].

GHAUS (तृण - trina, *San.*; گهاس - ghás, *Hind.*; ಹುಲ್ಲು - hullu, *Can.*; గడ్డి - gaddi, *Tel.*; പുല്ല് - pullu, *Mal.*; புல் - pul, *Tam.*). Fodder [ghiyah, grausam]. There is a considerable number of plants belonging to the Cyperaceæ [vricsham, 155], and a large number of Gramínaceæ [vricsham, 156] consumed by cattle [maud], &c., but as a rule the grasses of s. india are very coarse, and do not contain much nutriment. The native cultivators do not specially cultivate grasses, but give their bullocks [maud] and cows [pashoo] the straw [soppa] of their grain crops, so long as it lasts. For several months in the year the cattle are turned out into bare fields, or driven into the neighbouring jungle. The best grass in s. india, and the one chiefly used for feeding horses [ghorah], is hurrially [q.v.] grass or Cynodon dactylon, pers., graminaceæ. This is capable of withstanding great drought, and when manured and irrigated yields a very large return of green grass or excellent hay. The following are two key-lists of the principal grasses, pulses [dholl] and millets [q.v.] of s. india whose straw, stalks or haulms, are in general use for feeding cattle; further information must be traced in the glossary paragraphs through the small-type cross-references at the end of this volume; see also vricsham, 7, for the method of expressing the products, &c., of the plants in the dravidian languages.—"*a*" Andropogon contortus, spear grass; Andropogon martini, roussa grass; Andropogon muricatus, cuscus; Andropogon schœnanthus, lemon grass; Aristida setacea, broom grass; Chloris barbata, trailing grass; Cynodon dactylon, hurrially grass; Cyperus pangorei, creeping grass sedge; Cyperus rotundus, common sedge; Dolichos biflorus, madras horse-gram; Dolichos lablab, country bean; Eleusine coracana, raggy; Eleusine indica, crab grass; Eragrostis bifaria, basket grass; Eragrostis ciliata, wild coraly; Eragrostis cynosuroides, darbhay; Eragrostis plumosa, shaumay grass; Festuca indica, cleft grass; Hordeum vulgare, barley; Leersia hexandra, wild dholl; Oryza mutica, mountain paddy; Oryza sativa, paddy; Panicum burmanni, wild hurrially; Panicum colonum, matted purple grass; Panicum crus galli, wild darbhay; Panicum egyptiacum, red shaumay; Panicum erucæforme, small raggy; Panicum fluitans, paddy-field grass; Panicum frumentaceum, large shaumay; Panicum glaucum, coraly; Panicum grossarum, stalk grass; Panicum indicum, black tinay; Panicum italicum, italian millet; Panicum javanicum, surprise grass; Panicum jumentorum, guinea grass; Panicum miliaceum, little millet; Panicum miliare, shaumay; Panicum prostratum, wild white shaumay; Panicum remotum, wild varagoo; Panicum repens, ginger grass millet; Panicum stagninum, hedge-hog grass; Panicum verticillatum, sticky grass; Paspalum scrobiculatum, varagoo; Pennisetum, spicatum, spiked millet; Phaseolus mungo, green gram; Phaseolus mungo, var. radiatus, black gram; Phaseolus trilobus, field gram; Pommereulla cornucopiæ, ant grass; Saccharum officinarum, sugar-cane; Saccharum spontaneum, naunal; Sorghum vulgare, cholum; Typha elephantina, bulrush; Zea mays, maize.—"*b*" Ant grass, pommereulla; Barley, hordeum; Basket grass, eragrostis; Bean, dolichos; Broom grass, aristida; Bulrush, typha; Cholum, sorghum; Cleft grass, festuca; Coraly, eragrostis, panicum; Crab grass, eleusine; Cuscus, andropogon; Darbhay, eragrostis, panicum; Dholl, leersia; Ginger grass millet, panicum; Gram, dolichos, phaseolus; Guinea grass, panicum; Hedge-hog grass, panicum; Hurrially, cynodon, panicum; Lemon grass, andropogon; Maize, zea; Millet, panicum, pennisetum; Naunal, saccharum; Paddy, oryza; Paddy-field grass, panicum; Purple grass, panicum; Raggy, eleusine, panicum; Roussa grass, andropogon; Sedge, cyperus; Shaumay, eragrostis, panicum; Spear grass, andropogon; Stalk grass, panicum; Sticky grass, panicum; Sugar-cane, saccharum; Surprise grass, panicum; Tinay, panicum; Trailing grass, chloris; Varagoo, panicum, paspalum.

GHAUT (घट्ट - ghatta, *San.*; گھاٹ - ghát, *Hind.*; ఘాటు - ghátu, *Tel.*). Title from hindostany. San. from (ghatt, san. to go). Steps up from a river; hence a mountain pass [canama, canavye]; hence in particular the mountain ranges themselves parallel to the western and eastern coasts of the peninsula, through which the ghauts lead from the tablelands above down to the coast and lowlands. See also Balaghaut, Talaghaut, and Payeenghaut. Ghautauny, meaning relating to ghauts, is a toll levied on crossing rivers or hill passes.——*Eastern ghauts* (उदयगिरि - udayagiri, San.; مشرقی گھاٹ - mashrakíghát, Hind.; తూర్పుకనములు - túrpukanamalu, Tel.; പൂർവ്വഘട്ടം - púrvvaghattam, Mal.; கீழ்க்கணவாய்மலை - kízhkkanaváymalai, Tam.). Tam. from (kízh, tam. east + kanaváy, tam. pass + malai, tam. mountain). Mal. also (pavizhádri), meaning coral + mountain; (pavizhamala), meaning same. Greek *ὀρούδια ὄρη*, from the sanscrit Veidooryam, which means the northern part of the western ghauts. Ptolemy found in indian topographical lists that the great rivers of the eastern or maesolian, Masulipatam coast rose in the Veidooryam, and having no other clue he placed them near and parallel to that coast; in fact he confused them with the eastern ghauts. The Eastern ghauts at their southern extremity are detached clusters of hills appearing at intervals. About lat. 11° 40′ they assume the character of a continuous chain, and, running along the Coromandel coast [q.v.] in a direction a little north-west of Madras, form a junction at Nagary in lat. 13° 20′, with the main ridge, which crosses the peninsula in a south-west direction to the Neilgherries. Thence they continue a northerly course and terminate in about the same latitude as their counterpart of the opposite coast. Here uniting with the Vindhya zone, which crosses the continent from east to west, they constitute one side of the triangle upon which rests the tableland of the Deccan [q.v.]. In regularity and grandeur the Eastern ghauts bear no comparison with those of Western india; and their average elevation does not exceed 1,500 feet. The intermediate tableland has consequently a gradual slope to the eastward, as indicated by the drainage of the country in that direction. All the principal rivers [aur], the Cauvery, Godavery, Kistna and Pennair, though deriving their sources from the base of the Western ghauts, find their way into the Bay of Bengal through fissures in the Eastern ghauts. With regard to geological structure granite [caroom cull] constitutes the basis of the whole range, and overlying the granite, gneiss, and mica slate that form the sides of the mountains are occasionally found clay-slate, hornblende slate, flinty slate, and primitive or crystalline limestone [choonam cull]. The surface of the level country consists of the débris of granitic rocks, as far north as the Pennair, in approaching which, the laterite [q.v.] or iron clay formation expands over a large surface. From the Kistna northward the granite is often penetrated by injected veins of trap [padicutt cull] and dykes of green stone [putchay cull]. Passing on to Vizagapatam and Ganjam, syenite and gneiss predominate, occasionally covered by laterite. Gaulicondah, 5,346 feet, is the highest peak. The Eastern ghauts form a water shed only in the extreme north. The following are the chief passes through the Eastern ghauts in alphabetical order; reference can be made to glossary titles:—Bijauya, in vizagapatam; from parvatipore to jeypore. Bullipully, on route from madras to bellary. Calingyah, in ganjam; leading from goomsoor to maliahs. Caucoola, in the nullamullays, on route from cumbum to pulnaud, kistna district. Chengam, on route from cuddalore to bangalore. Coorly, in the palcondahs. Cuttingia, in ganjam; from sooradah to cuttingia, in the maliahs. Daumalcheroo, on route from vellore to cuddapah; also called cullore pass. Dopully, in the nullamullays; from endrapully to shreegherrypaud, a roman catholic station in pulnaud; much used by people, four streams across it and a stone-built drinking-water well, not fitted for wheeled traffic. Dornaul, on route from bellary to guntoor; good metalled road. Goolcheroo, in the palcondahs; on route from vellore to cuddapah; also called soorya comauroola canama. Joty, in the nullamullays. Lutchmipore, in vizagapatam; leading from parvatipore to jeypore zemindarry. Mogily, on route from madras to bangalore; good metalled road. Moonshingy; on branch route from kimedy to goomma. Muntraula, in the nullamullays; also known as dornaul pass; from vinoocondah in kistna district to kurnool. Naicknairy, on route from madras to bangalore, near sautghur; now abandoned in favor of synigoonta ghaut. Naugapootla, in the palcondahs, on road from mysore to tripatty. Nundicanama, in the nullamullays; on route from cumbum to bellary. Panchipenta, in vizagapatam; on route from vizianagaram to kamptee. Pippalpunka, in ganjam; from gajellabady to the maliahs. Pooypany, in ganjam, from serangy to cheligodo, in the maliahs. Rampore, in the yerramalas, on route from bellary to cumbum. Raupore; between cuddapah and nellore. Royavalsa, in vizagapatam; on route from vizagapatam to jeypore. Saunipoya, in the palcondahs. Soorya camauroola; otherwise goolcheroo canama. Synigoonta; on route from vellore to bangalore near modicooppam. Taptapauny; otherwise the hot spring; in ganjam from digoopoody to lohogoody in the maliahs. Tautaparty, in vizagapatam; from madgole to jeypore zemindarry. Timmarauzpully, in the yerramalas; on route from cuddapah to kurnool. Vaimlapaud; on route from cumbum to guntoor in good order. Velgoty, in the nullamullays; from nundiaul to cumbum.——*Western ghauts* (अस्तगिरि - astagiri, San.; مغربی گھاٹ - maghrabíghát, Hind.; പശ്ചിമഘട്ടം - pashchimaghattam, Mal.; *மேற்கணவாய்மலை* - mérganaváymalai, Tam.). Tam. from (mél, tam. west + kanaváy, tam. pass + malai, tam. mountain). Mal. also (sahyan). See Sukhein. Greek *ἀδίσαθρος*, in the southern part. The northern limit is the valley of the Tapty, of which a branch from the Sahyadry mountains form the southern inclosing range, about lat. 21° to 21° 15′, long. 73° 45′ to 74° 40′, and is connected with groups which diminish in height towards the east until they sink into the tableland of Berar. The northern side of the valley of the Tapty is inclosed by the Sautpoora range. In lat. 21° 10′, long. 74°, the range turns south nearly at right angles to that which forms the south inclosing range of the valley of the Tapty. Its elevation increases as it proceeds southwards and attains its general maximum towards Coorg. South of this the ghauts join the Neilgherry group by means of the Nedoomullay range, which forms the western buttress of the Neilgherry tableland to lat. 11° 15′, long. 76° 25′, where it rises into the lofty Coondah mountains, and about 25 miles farther south terminates abruptly in high and nearly perpendicular precipices, forming the northern side of that great valley or depression, which affords an uninterrupted communication in this latitude between the eastern and western sides of the peninsula. The length of the Western ghauts, from the northern extremity of the Sahyadry mountains, forming the southern side of the valley of the Tapty, to the southern brow, joining the Coondah mountains on the north side of the Palghaut valley, is about 800 miles. The mountains rising on the south side of Palghaut valley, and which may, with some latitude of expression, be called a continuation of the Western ghauts, have considerable elevation, a spacious tableland, 4,740 feet above the sea, and peaked summits of 6,000 and 7,000 feet. The length of the chain of mountains extending from the Palghaut gap to Cape Comorin is 200 miles [travancore hills]. The Western ghauts within this Presidency range from 3,000 to 5,000 feet above sea-level on the Coorg and Wynaud slopes, with one or two peaks, ranging over 6,000 and up to nearly 8,000 feet. On the Neilgherry coondah face the average height springs up to over 6,000 feet. It falls again to about 4,000 feet and lower on the southern Neilgherry slopes, and again rises to a high altitude in the Vadamullay fringing the northern edge of the Palghaut gap. On the south edge of the gap the Tenmullay, outliers of the lofty Anamullay mountains, commence with an elevation of 4,000 to 5,000 feet above sea-level. In consequence of the excessive moisture the low tract between the ghauts and the sea is traversed by innumerable torrents, which, stagnating as they approach the coast, overspread the depressed levels and form the series of shallow lakes called by the English backwaters [cauyal]. Geologically the great core of the Western ghauts is of primary formation, inclosed by alternating strata of more recent origin, which strata however have been broken up by prodigious outbursts of volcanic rocks. In their more northern parts the overlying rocks are exclusively of the trap [padicutt cull] formation. The face towards the Concan [q.v.] is not uniformly precipitous, but consists of vast terraces with abrupt fronts, such a conformation being characteristic of this kind of rock. The trap formation terminates southward on the sea-coast in about lat. 18° and is succeeded by laterite [q.v.], a ferruginous clay, easily cut when first raised, but by continued exposure to the atmosphere becoming hard as brick [shengal]. This last-mentioned formation extends southwards as the overlying rock almost without interruption to Cape comorin, covering the base of the mountains and the narrow slip of land that separates them from the sea. About the latitude of the Neilgherries there might be expected the divergence of a great connecting cross chain, corresponding with the Himalaya and Vindhya range, and such a range as this may have been at one time above water, connecting the peninsula with the more easterly ridges. The highest hills are usually naked on their summits, and a large portion of their slopes is also free from forest. The ravines and bases of the mountains are covered with dense forest of lofty trees which abound with wild animals. The following are the chief passes through the Western ghauts in alphabetical order; reference can be made to glossary titles:—Agoomby, on route from mangalore to harihar; a good cart road. Aryancauv, on route from palamcottah to quilon, a well-made and easy cart-road. Bisley, leading from south of hassan district of mysore into south canara; an unmade ghaut fit for pack animals only. Bund, on route from mangalore to bellary, leading through the ombatmarady or nine hills; a well-made and good cart road. Carcoor, on route from calicut to seringapatam, a good cart road. Charmaudy, on the old road from vastaura to mangalore; a very steep and rough path fit for pack bullocks only; almost abandoned now in favor of the bund ghaut. Collore, on branch of route from mangalore to harihar, a fair cart road. Coottiyaudy, on route from ootacamund to cannanore; at present only fit for pack animals; a new trace in progress. Goodalore; on route from trichinopoly to quilon, a good cart road. Govardhangherry, overlooking the town of gersoppah in north canara; very steep; a rugged and devious path for pack animals. Hyderghur, on route from mangalore to harihar, a well-made and good cart road. Manaar leading from copanaury in coimbatore district to manaar in malabar; a bad road for pack animals. Manjarabad, on route from bangalore to mangalore, a well-made and good cart road. Mullore; leading from coppa talook in cadoor district of mysore towards mangalore; at present unmade and fit for pack animals only, but it is proposed to improve it. Palghaut; a good cart road. Perambaudy, on route from seringapatam to cannanore; a good cart road. Periya, on route from seringapatam to cannanore, a good cart road. Siskal; leading from the hassan district of mysore into south canara, an unmade path fit for pack animals only. Sisparra, on route from calicut to ootacamund fit for pack animals only. Sumpaujey, on route from bangalore to mangalore, a good cart road. Tamracherry, on route from calicut to seringapatam, a good cart road.

GHAUZY (غازی - ghází, *Ar.*). From (ghazu, ar. to go against an enemy). Hero of the faith. Heroic alam; also Takhalloos; as Ghauzy beg, alam + alaumat [ism].

GHEE (घृत - ghrita, *San.*; گھی - ghí, *Hind.*; ತುಪ್ಪ - tuppa, *Can.*; నెయ్యి - neyyi, *Tel.*; നെയ് - ney, *Mal.*; நெய் - ney, *Tam.*). Title from hindostany. Hind. from (ghrí, san. to sprinkle). Clarified butter. Butter [q.v.] oil. When milk or cream is briskly agitated for some time, the fat globules become aggregated into masses of butter. When boiled and strained, so as to remove the casein and nearly the whole of the water, this constitutes ghee, which has all the advantages of butter for culinary purposes, and which when pure may be kept without rancidity for an unlimited time. It is made from both buffalo's milk and cow's milk [paul]. In veterinary practice a quart bottle full lukewarm is given in colic when nothing else can be procured.

GHEIB (غیب - ghaib, *Hind.*). From (ghába, ar. to be absent). Secret.——*Gayibut* (غیبت - ghaibat, Hind.). From (ghába, ar. to be absent). Out station [mofussil]. Opposed to Huzoor [q.v.].

GHEIR (غیر - ghair, *Hind.*). From arabic. Without.——*Gheiradah* (غیراداء - ghairadá, Hind.). From (above + adá, ar. profit). Uncultivated waste [beed, carambay, gayaul].——*Gheir cutnam* (గైరుకట్నం - gairukatnam, Tel.). From (above + katnamu, tel. present). Extraordinary cutnam [q.v.]; presents levied in zemindarry [q.v.] villages on special occasions at the marriage of the poligar [q.v.] or of his relations; opposed to Mamool cutnam.——*Gheir hauzir* (غیر حاضر - ghairházir, Hind.). From (above + házir, ar. present). Not present; especially non-appearance of the shauvy [q.v.] for the revenue inspection.——*Gheir mahdee* (غیر مهدی - ghairmahdí, Hind.). From (above + mahdí, ar. name of the last imaum). Those who disbelieve that the last imaum [q.v.] will appear at the close of the world with Jesus Christ and hold that he has already appeared and gone [soonnees, mahdee].——*Gheir mookallid* (غیر مقلد - ghairmukallid, Hind.). From (above + mukallid, ar. follower). A non-conformist. A branch of the Soonnee [q.v.] church which claims the right of private judgment in the interpretation of law and exposition of legal doctrines [wahauby].

GHERIA (කිරිය - kíriya, *Singh.*). From (kiri, singh. milk). Same as Tiger's milk.

GHERRY (गिरि - giri, *San.*; گری - girí, *Hind.*). Mountain [giry].

GHIL (گل - gil, *Hind.*). From persian. Earth [khauk, munn].——*Ghil arminy* (حجر ارمنی - hajariarmaní, Ar.; گل ارمنی - giliarmaní, Pers. and Hind.; پھول گیرو - phúlgerú, Dec.; సీమకావిరాయి - símakávirá́yi, Tel.; சீமைக்காவிக்கல் - shímaikkávikkal, Tam.). Ar. from (hajar, ar. stone + armaní, ar. armenian). Pers. from (gil, pers. earth + armaní, ar. armenian). Dec. from (phúl, hind. flower + gerú, hind. ochre). Tam. from (shímai, tam. european + kávi, tam. ochre + kal, tam. stone). Armenian bole [bole]. Bolus armeniæ or Bolus orientalis of chemists. Friable earthy substance of the soap stone [sowcauracull] family; once an article of materia medica; soft, greasy to the touch; yellowish brown color. Brought from Persian gulf. Medicinally astringent; frequent household remedy, with the juice of the coriander [cassibor] plant, in erysipelas, herpes, eczema, &c.; substituted for british plumbi acetas [eeya carcand]. In times of scarcity it has been used as a mechanical substitute for food. With other ingredients, makes a red pigment [rangh]; with seeds of oval-leaved cassia [chakondah] and indigo [q.v.], dyes a nankeen color [shauyam].——*Ghil i bootah* (گل بوتہ - gilibútah, Hind.). From (bútah, pers. a crucible). Fire-clay.——*Ghil i hikmat* (گل حکمت - gilihikmat, Hind.). From (hikmat, ar. artificial). Lute; cement [cauray].——*Ghil i makhtoom* (گل مختوم - gilimakhtúm, Hind.). From (makhtúm, pers. sealed). Sealing wax [lac].——*Ghil i sarshoe* (گل سرشوی - gilisarshoe, Hind.). From (sar, pers. head + shoe, pers. cleansing). Fuller's earth [dhoby's earth].——*Ghil i soofaid* (گل سفید - gilisufed, Hind.). From (sufed, pers. white). Chalk [sheemay choonam].——*Ghil i toorsh* (گل ترش - gilitursh, Hind.). From (tursh, pers. acid). Bi-sulphate of lime.——*Ghil i zard* (گل زرد - gilizard, Hind.). From (zard, pers. yellow). Yellow ochre [cauvy].

GHIYAH (گیاہ - giyáh, *Pers.*). Grass [ghaus]. Plant second term. Ex.:—Nardostachys jatamansi (múigiyáh), hair grass.

GHOOLAUM (غلام - ghulám, *Ar.*). From (ghalima, ar. a beardless lad). Hence a slave. Prefixed to names of the prophet, his companions, and the chief saint to form Mahomedan names. As:—Goolaum ally, the servant of ally, devotional term + alam [ism].——*Ghoolaum mahomed ghouse khan* (غلام محمد غوث خان - ghulámmuhammadghauskhán, Hind). From (above + double alam + title of honor). Last nawaub [q.v.] of the Carnatic [q.v.]. Died without issue. A.D. 1842—1855. See vol. I, 45, 46; II, 252.——*Ghoolaum rasool khan* (غلام رسول خان - ghulámrasúlkhán, Hind.). Alam + pataun suffix. Nawaub of Kurnool, who was deported to trichinopoly in consequence of a conspiracy against british government. See vol. II, 87.

GHORAH (अश्व - ashva, *San.*; घोडा - ghódá, *Mahr.*; حصان - hisán, *Ar.*; اسپ - asp, *Pers.*; گھوڑا - ghorá, *Hind.*; کودا - kuda, *Malay*; ಕುದುರೆ - kudure, *Can.* and *Too.*; గుర్రము - gurramu, *Tel.*; ଘୋଡା - ghódá, *Oor.*; കുതിര - kutira, *Mal.*; අශ්වයා - ashvayá, *Singh.*; குதிரை - kuthirai, *Tam.*). Title from hindostany. San. from (ash, san. to be able); enduring animal. Mahr. from (ghóta, san. horse). Ar. from (hasuna, ar. to defend against). Pers. from sanscrit. Hind. from (ghóta, san. horse). Malay from (ghóta, san. horse). Mal. from (kuti, mal. to jump). Singh. from sanscrit. Tam. from (kuthi, tam. to jump) [coothiray]. Equus [ashwam] vulgaris, equidæ, perissodactyla, ungulata, mammalia [sastanam, 21], of naturalists [jantoo]. Apart from the external differences between the horse and ass [gadhah], they have a structural divergence, that the horse has corns or callosities on the inner side of both fore and hind limbs, whilst the asses have them only on the fore limbs; and there is no common term for the two in the native languages. There is no wild horse in India. The indigenous domesticated animal has degenerated to a pony rarely rising to 13·2 hands in height. In the extreme south it is improbable that there has ever been any horse-breeding at all. There is a want of pasturage [maita], and there is no record of horses being used by the early inhabitants for war. Hyder ally and Tippoo sultan bred horses for their wars with the Mahrattas. The English troops in this country had at first no cavalry. A breeding establishment at Ganjam was removed to Oossoor, with branches at Coongull and Coimbatore. These operations were discontinued in 1850, the Australian import trade supplying what was required. The pony of Southern india is, though small, wiry and capable of great endurance. The improvement of pony-breeding is being undertaken by the Government. There is a Hindostany proverb:—ٹٹو کو کوڑا اور تازی کو اشارہ—"A whip "[chowk] for the pony, a sign for the Arab horse." But on the other hand there is a Tamul proverb:—அரபிக் குதிரையிலும் ஐயம்பேட்டைத் தட்டுவாணி நல்லது.—"An Ay-"yampett pony is preferable to an Arab steed," as to its utility [goorram, tatt].——*Ghorawallah* (گھوڑے والا - ghorewálá, Hind.). From (above + wálá, hind. doer). A groom or horsekeeper; used at Bombay. In Bengal syce [q.v.] is always used. In Madras, horsekeeper.——*Ghorsawaur* (گھوڑ سوار - ghorsawár, Hind.). From (above + sawár, hind. rider). A trooper [sawaur].——*Goda* (ଗୋଡ - góda, Oor.). Horse [coothiray, goorram].——*Godahaddoh* (ଗୋଡାହଡ୍ଡୋ - godáhaddo, Tel.). From (góda, oor. horse + haddoh, oor. bones). River; Ganjam district, Pedda kimedy and Chinna kimedy zemindarries. Tributary of the Rooshcoolya which it joins near Injily. Some tradition of a horse's leap. Has its source in hot springs among Eastern ghauts [q.v.] of Chinna kimedy; is notorious for sudden high floods.

GHOTAGAMBA (گھوٹا غنبہ - ghotaghamba, *Hind.*). Corruption of Gummiguttæ [gumghautty]. Same as Ceylon gamboge.

GHOUSE (घोस - ghósa, *Mahr.*). From (ghush, san. to proclaim). Division of the writer caste [cauyast] in Bengal [peyar].

GHOUSE (غوث - ghaus, *Ar.*). From (ghaus, ar. to aid). The redresser of grievances. Title of the highest of Mahomedan saints [abdool cawder]. Common alam; as Ghouse bee, alam + alaumat. Ghouse khan, alam + alaumat [ism].——*Ghiyaus* (غیاث - ghiyás, Ar.). From (ghaus, ar. to aid). A redresser, aid. Part of lacab; as Ghiyaus ood deen, the aid of religion [ism].

GHOWL (غول - ghaul, *Ar.*). Demon. Plant second term. Ex., where transl. is of first term:—Abutilon indicum (mashtulghaul), comb, from shape of leaves; Adiantum capillus veneris (sharulghaul), hair. See gloss. paragraphs.

GHUR (گڑھ - garh, *Hind.*). Hill-fort [gada, godo, gooda].

GIDDA (గిద్ద - gidda, *Tel.*). Means small. Smallest measure of capacity in use. 4 giddas = 1 sola [alavay, 3b]. Varies. Compare Hind. chittack.——*Giddana* (ಗಿದ್ದನ - giddana, Can.; గిద్దన - giddana, Tel.). 80 rupees' weight or fourteenth part of a canara maund [q.v.].——*Giddauny* (ಗಿದ್ದಾಣೆ - giddáne, Can.). From (above + káni, tel. one-sixty fourth); small cawny. The 256th fraction of a fanam [q.v.] or rupee [q.v.].

GIDH (गृध्र - gridhra, *San.*; गीद - gída, *Mahr.*; رخمه - rakhamah, *Ar.*; مردار خوار - murdárkhwár, *Pers.*; گدھ - gidh, *Hind.*; رنگیت - rangít, *Dec.*; ರಣಹದ್ದು - ranahaddu, *Can.*; గద్ద - gadda, *Tel.*; കഴു - kazhu, *Mal.*; கழு - kazhu, *Tam.*). San. from (gridh, san. to be greedy). Mahr. from sanscrit. Ar. from (rakham, ar. love); carrion loving. Pers. from (murdár, pers. dead body + khwár, pers. eater). Hind. from sanscrit. Dec. from (rana, san. battle-field + gridhra, san. vulture). Can. from (rana, san. battle + haddu, can. vulture). Tel. from sanscrit. Tel. also (pínugulagádu), meaning corpse + fellow. Tam. also (máduppidingi), meaning cattle + devourer. Title otherwise Common brown vulture, White-backed vulture. Gyps bengalensis, vulturinæ, vulturidæ [gridhram], raptores [pacshy, 1], of naturalists [jantoo]. Alias Vultur changoun, leuconotus. Changoun is bengallee corruption, from (shakuna, san. vulture). Above cinereous black, back and rump white; beneath dark-brown; bill horny, dusky on cere; legs dusky black; found in immense numbers.——*Burragidh* (بڑا گیدھ - barágídh, Hind.). Hind. from (bará, hind. large + gridhra, san. vulture). Hind. also (pahárígídh), meaning mountain vulture; (ságún), from sanscrit. Title otherwise Long-billed brown vulture. Gyps indicus, scop., vulturinæ, vulturidæ [gridhram], raptores [pacshy, 1] of naturalists [jantoo]. Alias Vultur tenuiceps, tenuirostris. Pale cinereous brown; albescent on the back and rump; bill and cere bluish horny, dusky at the tip; legs and feet dusky cinereous; young bird is paler, not rare on the neilgherries; breeds on some of the cliffs on their northern face.——*Rangidh* (राजगृध्र - rájagridhra, San.; رنگیت - rangít, Hind. and Dec.; నల్లబూరగ - nallabúraga, Tel.). San. from (rájá, san. king + gridhra, san. vulture). Hind. from (rana, san. battle-field + gridhra, san. vulture). Tel. from (nalla, tel. black + búraga, tel. vulture). San. also (rájashakuna), meaning king vulture. Hind. also (mullágídh), meaning decoy vulture; (lalmatashakuni), meaning red body vulture; (rájgidh), meaning king vulture. Title otherwise Black vulture, King vulture. Otogyps calvus, vulturinæ, vulturidæ [gridhram], raptores [pacshy, 1], of naturalists [jantoo]. Alias Vultur ponticerianus. Adult, dark-brown, black throughout, naked head, neck yellowish red, often more or less black-spotted; legs dull red; young dull brown throughout; usually seen solitary or in pairs hunting over some rocky hill; dreaded by other vultures.

GILIGITCHA (గిలిగిచ్చ - giligittsa, *Tel.*). From rattle of dry pods. A common name for all crotalarias [ghantaravam].——*Black giligitcha* (నల్లగిలిగిచ్చ - nallagiligittsa, Tel.). Title from purple flowers. Tel. from (nalla, tel. black + giligittsa, tel. crotalaria). Botanically Crotalaria [ghantaravam] hirsuta, willd., leguminosæ [vricsham, 48]. Perennial; herbaceous, procumbent, hairy; leaves broad-oval to oblong, often acute, hairy beneath; racemes terminal and leaf-opposite; calyx hairy, cleft almost to the base; vexillum glabrous, purple-spotted; legume sessile, oblong, broader upwards, slightly hairy, twice as long as the calyx, eight to ten-seeded.——*Black hill giligitcha* (నల్లగిరిగిలిగిచ్చ - nallagirigiligittsa, Tel.). Tel. from (nalla, tel. black + giri, san. mountain + giligittsa, tel. crotalaria). Botanically Crotalaria [ghantaravam] linifolia, linn. f., leguminosæ [vricsham, 48]. Alias Crotalaria cæspitosa, montana, tecta. Cæspitose, suffruticose, diffuse, branching from the base, more or less strigose; stipule none; leaves from cuneate to linear oblong, obtuse, strigose beneath; racemes terminal; bracteoles attached to the tube of the calyx, between the lips; calyx densely hairy; upper lip broad, and shortly two-cleft; legume oblique, roundish-ovoid, sessile, glabrous, scarcely as long as the calyx, eight to twelve-seeded.——*Forest giligitcha* (शाणपुष्पी - shanapushpí, San.; بن سن - bansan, Hind.; جھنجھنے کا جھاڑ - jhanjhanekájhár, Dec.; ತನ್ನೆಲೆವುಳುಕಗಿಡ - tannelevulukagida, Can.; ಗಿಜಿಗಿಜಿಡೆ - gijigijide, Too.; గిలిగోరంట - giligóranta, Tel.; പേത്തന്തലക്കൊട്ടി - péttantalakkotti, Mal.; නිල්අඬනහිරිය - nilandanahiriya, Singh.; வட்டக்கிலுகிலுப்பை - vattakkilugiluppai, Tam.). Title from habitat. San. from (shana, san. crotalaria juncea, linn. + pushpa, san. flower). Hind. from (ban, hind. forest + san, hind. crotalaria juncea, linn.). Dec. from (jhanjhaná, hind. castanet + jhár, hind. tree); from rattling noise of seeds in dry pods. Can. from (tanna, can. cool + ele, can. leaf + uluku, can. shining + gida, can. plant). Tel. from (gilaka, tel. rattle + góranta, tel. nail-dye plant, lawsonia alba, lamk.). Mal. from (péy, mal. devil + tantalakkotti, mal. crotalaria retusa, linn.). Singh. from (nil, singh. blue + andanahiriya, singh. crotalaria); from blue flowers. Tam. from (vattam, tam. circle + kilugiluppai, tam. crotalaria); from curled leaf. San. also (bhútagagara), meaning devil + eclipta alba, hassk. Tel. also (allagiligittsa), meaning famous + the plant, crotalaria. Tam. also (pittándalaikkotti), meaning devil + crotalaria; (vellaikkilugiluppai), meaning white + crotalaria; (vattavellaikkilugiluppai), meaning circle + white + the plant. Title otherwise Blue-flowered crotalaria, Fox-frightener, Globe rattle-pod, Rattle nail dye. Botanically Crotalaria [ghantaravam] verrucosa, l., leguminosæ [vricsham, 48]. Crotalaria angulosa, cærulea, flexuosa. Herbaceous, erect; flower large, bright blue and greenish white; flowering in cold season. Slightly bitter, unpleasant-tasted juice of leaves and tender stalks prescribed internally and externally, in scabies and impetigo; juice of leaves efficacious in diminishing salivation.——*Hill giligitcha* (కొండగిలిగిచ్చ - kondagiligittsa, Tel.). Tel. from (konda, tel. hill + giligitsa, tel. crotalaria); found on circar [q.v.] mountains. Botanically Crotalaria [ghantaravam] albida, heyne, leguminosæ [vricsham, 48]. Alias Crotalaria linifolia, montana. Suffruticose, branching from the base, covered all over with silvery hairs; branches procumbent; stipules none; leaves cuneate-oblong, obtuse, or emarginate, mucronate; racemes terminal; bracteoles attached to the tube of the calyx; calyx hairy, the two upper segments lanceolate and longer than the corolla; legume sessile, glabrous, oblong, about twice the length of the calyx, three and four-seeded; flowers drooping.——*Large giligitcha* (مونا - múná, Hind.; పెద్దగిలిగిచ్చ - peddagiligittsa, Tel.; നെല്ലുതന്തലക്കൊട്ടി - nellutantalakkotti, Mal.; கிலுகிலுப்பை - kilugiluppai, Tam.). Tel. from (pedda, tel. large + gilgittsa, tel. crotalaria). Mal. from (nalla, mal. good + tantalakkotti, mal. crotalaria retusa, linn.). Tam. from sound of seeds in dry legume. Tel. also (manne). Title otherwise Laburnum-leaved crotalaria. Botanically Crotalaria [ghantaravam] laburnifolia, linn., leguminosæ [vricsham, 48]. Alias Crotalaria pendula, pedunculosa. An erect, glabrous shrub; stipules wanting; leaves trifoliolate; leaflets broadly oval, usually acute at both ends; racemes terminal and leaf-opposed; bracteoles very minute, below the middle of the pedicel; flowers long-pedicelled; keel acuminated, longer than the vexillum, and twice as long as the wings; legume stalked, glabrous, cylindric-oblong, three times as long as broad; flowers large, yellow; flowering nearly all the year.——*Nauga giligitcha* (నాగగిలిగిచ్చ - nágagiligittsa, Tel.). Tel. from (nága, san. large + giligittsa, tel. crotalaria). Botanically Crotalaria [ghantaravam] trifoliastrum, willd., leguminosæ [vricsham, 48]. Alias Crotalaria medicaginea, stricta. Suffruticose with erect or ascending stems; branches straight and twiggy, tomentose; leaves somewhat distant, trifoliolate, long-petioled; leaflets cuneate, obcordate, slightly hairy beneath; racemes terminal, many-flowered, with occasionally a few-flowered peduncle in the axils of the upper leaves; flowers distant, largish, yellow; flowering in the cold season.——*Short giligitcha* (جھنجھنیا - jhanjhaniyá, Hind.; جھنجھنے کا جھاڑ - jhunjhunekájhár, Dec.; పొట్టిగిలిగిచ్చ - pottigiligittsa, Tel.; തന്തലക്കൊട്ടി - tantalakkotti, Mal.). Hind. from (jhanjhaná, hind. castanet); from rattling noise of seeds when dry pods are shaken. Tel. from (potti, tel. short + giligittsa, tel. crotalaria). Mal. from (tantala, mal. the sound + kottu, mal. to strike), from sound of dry pods. Title otherwise Wedge-leaved crotalaria. Botanically Crotalaria [ghantaravam] retusa, l., leguminosæ [vricsham, 48]. Alias Lupinus cochin-chinensis. Erect, branched, nearly glabrous; stipules and bracts often wanting; leaves cuneate-oblong, retuse or rounded, under sides silky pubescent; racemes terminal, many-flowered; calyx glabrous; legume oblong, broader upwards, sessile, glabrous, many-seeded; flowers yellow; flowering nearly all the year. Fibres of bark for cordage and canvas [gunny].——*Silky giligitcha* (घण्टारव - ghantárava, San.; جھنجھنیا - jhanjhaniyá, Hind.; جھنجھنے کا جھاڑ - jhunjhunekájhár, Dec.). Title from color of pod. San. from (ghantá, san. bell + rava, san. sound). Hind. from (jhanjhaná, hind. castanet); from rattling seeds of dry pods. Botanically Crotalaria [ghantaravam] sericea, retz., leguminosæ [vricsham, 48]. Alias Crotalaria spectabilis. Erect, branched, glabrous; stems obtusely angled; stipules large, semi-sagittate, reflexed; leaves lanceolate, cuneate at the base, mucronate, slightly glaucous and silky pubescent below; racemes terminal, many-flowered; bracts cordate, reflexed, lower ones without flower; calyx smaller than the corolla, glabrous; legume oblong, glabrous, many-seeded; flowers large, bright-yellow; flowering nearly all the year.——*Stunted giligitcha* (ಕಾಡುಬುದ್ದೆಗಿಡ - kádubuddegida, Can.; కూనగిలిగిచ్చ - kúnagiligittsa, Tel.). Can. from (kádu, can. jungle + buddegida, can. the plant). Tel. from (kúna, tel. little + giligittsa, tel. the plant, crotalaria). Botanically Crotalaria [ghantaravam] orixensis, rottl., leguminosæ [vricsham, 48]. Perennial, herbaceous, procumbent; branches, racemes and lower side of the leaves slightly hairy; leaves trifoliolate; leaflets obovate; racemes elongated, leaf-opposed; bracts cordate reflexed; corolla scarcely longer than the calyx; legume stalked, glabrous, short-cylindrical, more than twice the length of the stalk, few-seeded; flowers small, on long filiform pedicels.——*Water giligitcha* (నీరుగిలిగిచ్చ - nírugiligittsa, Tel.; വലിയതന്തലക്കൊട്ടി - valiyatantalakkotti, Mal.). Tel. from (níru, tel. water + giligittsa, tel. the plant, crotalaria); grows in wet rice-fields. Mal. from (valiya, mal. large + tantalakkotti, mal. crotalaria retusa, linn.). Botanically Crotalaria [ghantaravam] quinquefolia, linn., leguminosæ [vricsham, 48]. Alias Crotalaria heterophylla. Annual; erect, branched, pubescent or glabrous; stems hollow; leaves five-foliolate, some of them occasionally trifoliolate; leaflets from lanceolate to narrow-linear, usually longer than the petioles, young ones silky-pubescent beneath; racemes terminal, much elongated; flowers large, rather distant; legumes clavate-oblong, glabrous; seeds very numerous.

GINGELLY (तिल - tila, *San.* ; तीळ - tíla, *Mahr.* ; तीळु - tílu, *Conc.* ; سمسم - simsim, *Ar.* ; كنجد - kunjad, *Pers.* ; تل - til, *Hind.* and *Dec.* ; ಎಳ್ಳು - ellu, *Can.* ; ഖൂരേണ്ണ - úrenme, *Too.* ; నువ్వు - nuvvu, *Tel.* ; ରାଶି - rási, *Oor.* ; എള്ള - ellu, *Mal.* ; තල - tala, *Singh.* ; எள் - el, *Tam.*). Title from (aljuljulán, ar.), the grain in ear. San. from (til, san. to anoint). Ar. from egyptian. Hind from sanscrit. Mal. from (eli, mal. to be slight), what is slight. Singh. from sanscrit. Hind. also (krishnatil), meaning black sesame; (báríktil), meaning slender sesame; (mithátel), meaning sweet oil. Dec. also (sufedtil), meaning white sesamum. Can. also (olleellu), meaning good + gingelly; (úruellu), meaning country gingelly. Tel. also (núgu); (tellanuvvu), meaning white + the plant; (núvu); (mańchinúgu), meaning good + the plant; (telalu), from sanscrit. Mal. also (kárellu), meaning black gingelly; (chittellu), meaning small gingelly. Singh. also (teltala), meaning oil + sesamum. Tam. also (kárel), meaning black gingelly. Greek σήσαμον; Latin sesama. Title otherwise Bennie oil, Georgaline, Indian oily grain, Noovvooloo, Oil plant, Oriental oily grain, Sesame oil, Sesamum, Til oil. Botanically Sesamum indicum, dec., pedalineæ [vricsham, 100]. Generic name from arabic. Alias Sesamum orientale. Annual; leaves ovate-oblong, entire; calyx five-parted; corolla with a short tube and campanulate throat; flowers axillary, solitary; corolla dirty white or pale red; capsule oblong, tetragonal, four-celled; seeds numerous. Stalks straight, herbaceous, hairy, about 2 feet high; bears large, tubular flowers; seeds slightly oval, small, black or red, tasteless and inodorous; native of india, from whence its cultivation was carried in the earliest ages to mesopotamia and egypt, and has now extended to the west indies. Expressed oil from the seeds, met with in all bazaars, known as til or gingelly oil, often dark in color from having been mixed with an inferior oil, or from defective preparation; the plant with black seed is called first sort gingelly, from yielding largest percentage of oil; that with red seed is second sort. In expressing the oil in northern districts, bark of tungaid [q.v.] or babool [q.v.] gum is added to the seed to be pressed, with a view of enhancing the value of the oil cake. Cultivated in sandy soil; the fragrance of the oil is much weaker when the plant has been sown in too moist a soil; cultivation, dry; ground prepared in south in maurgaly or december, on coromandel in pooshyam or january and maugham or february, on w. coast from carcatacam or july till chingom or august; ploughing the soil four or five times and manuring; seed sown in south in maurgaly or december and chittray or april, on coromandel in maugham or february, on w. coast in the early part of chingom [mausam] or august; no nursery; sown broadcast and ploughed in; while under growth, weeded and occasionally watered; four months after sowing plants are pulled up and stacked for seven days; then exposed to the sun for three days, but at night collected again into a heap, and between every two days' drying in the sun it is kept a day in the heap; by this means the capsules burst of themselves and the seed falls to the ground; the cultivators sell the greater part of the seed to the oil-makers; average price twelve imperial seers for one rupee. Oil equal to olive [zeitoon] oil for medicinal purposes, especially for wounds and ulcers; the leaves abound with thick viscid mucilage, serve for emollient poultices; seeds are emollient, nourishing, tonic, diuretic and lactagogue, ground to a paste with water are given with butter in bleeding piles, if taken largely are capable of producing abortion; the plant gives to pharm. gingelly oil, seeds and leaves. The oil will keep for many years without becoming rancid either in smell or taste, after a time it becomes very mild, it is in common use both for the table and for unction; the seed is also made into flour, which is mixed with jaggery [q.v.] and formed into a variety of sweet cakes; cattle are fed with the oil-cake [ponnauk], in some districts the oil-cake mixed with sugar [q.v.] is eaten by the population; the seed is sometimes ground into a chutney [q.v.] to season rice [q.v.] with. Lotion made from leaves is a hair wash; decoction of root has same properties; oil sometimes made the medium for extracting perfume of jasmine [q.v.], tuberose narcissus, camomile [baboona], and yellow rose [gool]; also used to adulterate oil of almonds [baudam]; in europe used for manufacturing soap [sauboon]; for burning in table lamps, in cold climates it is better suited than cocoanut [q.v.] oil, owing to the lower temperature at which it congeals, although the light it gives is not so bright; in s. india it is chiefly used in cooking, for anointing the body, for making soap, for burning in lamps, by the dyer to brighten and fix his colors, &c. [shauyam]; the natives burn it to obtain a species of lamp-black [caujal]; straw used for fuel and for manure. In hindoo medical works, three varieties of gingelly seeds are described, with black, white and red seeds; black kind best suited for medicinal use and in perfumery, the variety with red seed is called as above said second sort gingelly, or bastard gingelly. There is a Tamul proverb :—எள்ளுக்காய் பிளந்தாற்போலப் பேசவேண்டும்—"One ought to speak as evenly as a gingelly-pod splits." And another :—காரியும் வெள்ளையும் கருதிப் பயிரிடு—"Cultivate gingelly and cotton [q.v.] gladly;" both are profitable. And another :—இளைத்தவன் எழு வருஷத்துக்கு எள் விதைக்க வேண்டும்—"A poor man should sow gingelly for "seven years;" as returns are easy and quick. There is a Teloogoo proverb :—నువ్వులకు నూరు రోగాలు—"Hundred diseases to "the gingelly;" these crops are peculiarly liable to attacks of sap worm, blight, &c. And another :—ఓ దౌర్భాగ్యుడా నువ్వులు చల్లుమన్నట్లు—"O unfortunate man! sow gingelly;" advice given to a farmer very unfortunate in his crops. Compare Ramtil. ——*Hill gingelly* (కొండనువ్వు - kondanuvvu, Tel.). Same as Ramtil.——*Peacock gingelly* (तिलक - tilaka, San.; മൈലെള്ള - mailellu, Mal.). Title from color and resemblance of flowers. San. from (tila, san. gingelly, sesamum indicum, dec.), perhaps from similarity to the sesamum plant [country cinnamon, tiroo-tauly]. Mal. from (mayil, mal. peacock + ellu, mal. gingelly). Title otherwise Peacock notchy. Botanically Vitex [sindoocam] alata, heyne, verbenaceæ [vricsham, 102]. Small tree; branchlets with obtuse angles, densely tomentose; leaves trifoliolate, the petiole with a broad wing; leaflets ovate or elliptic-oblong, narrow at both ends, acuminate, quite entire, subcoriaceous, shining above, pubescent or hoary and glandular-dotted beneath, panicle terminal, compound, spreading, pyramidal; flowers pale-yellow, tinged with blue; petioles with a broad veined wing; flowering in april and may. Wood of good quality.——*Wild gingelly* (కారునువ్వు - kárunuvvu, Tel.; കാട്ടെള്ള - káttellu, Mal.; காட்டெள் - káttel, Tam.). Tel. from (káru, tel. jungle + nuvvu, tel. sesamum indicum, dec.). Mal. and tam. from (kádu, tam. forest + el, tam. sesamum indicum, dec.) [ramtil]. Botanically Sesamum prostratum, retz., pedalineæ [vricsham, 100]. Leaves orbiculate, crenated, hispid above, white-tomentose beneath; flowers solitary, peduncled; stem diffuse; sand hills along the sea coast. A prostrate growing plant, bears large deep, rose-colored flowers; sand-binder.——*Wild peacock gingelly* (ಸಂಪಗೆಪಲ - sampagepala, Can.; මිලිල - milila, Singh.; காட்டுமயிலைமரம் - káttumayilamaram, Tam.). Tam. from (kádu, tam. forest + mayilai, tam. black and white + maram, tam. tree); from blue white flowers. Can. also (mirole); (balgai); (nauldi). Singh. also (milla); (sapumilila), meaning michelia champaca, linn. + the tree; (míammilila). Tam. also (mayil-amaram), meaning black and white + tree. Title otherwise Tall chaste tree. Botanically Vitex [sindoocam] altissima, linn. f., verbenaceæ [vricsham, 102]. Large tree with the branchlets quadrangular, compressed, and channelled; petioles and back of the leaf white, with a short, woolly pubescence; leaves long petioled, trifoliolate; leaflets elliptic-oblong, acuminate at both ends, entire; panicle hoary with a dense tomentum, terminal, compound, spreading, pyramidal; cymes interruptedly verticelled; corolla small, lower lip woolly; flowers white, tinged with blue; flowering in april and may. Most valuable timber tree; wood grey with a tinge of olive-brown, hard, close-grained, polishes well.

GINGER (आर्द्रक - árdraka, *San.* ; अलें - além, *Mahr.* ; आलें - állé, *Conc.* ; زنجبيل - zanjabíl, *Ar.* and *Pers.* ; ادرك - adrak, *Hind.* and *Dec.* ; اليا - alya, *Malay* ; ಹಸಿಶುಂಠಿ - hasíshunt'hi, *Can.* ; ಸುಂಟಿ - súnti, *Too.* ; అల్లము - allamu, *Tel.* ; ଓଦ୍ଦା - vodda, *Oor.* ; ഇഞ്ചി - iñchi, *Mal.* ; ඉඟුරු - inguru, *Singh.* ; இஞ்சி - iñji, *Tam.*). Title from sanscrit (shringabéra), through arabic. San. from (árdra, san. wet); sown in ardra caurtey [q.v.]. Ar. from (shringabéra, san. the rhizome). Hind. from sanscrit. Can. from (hasi, can. green + shunthi, can. ginger). San. also (shringabéra), meaning horn + body, from antler-like rhizome; (nagarajá), meaning produced in town; (vishvabhéshaja), meaning universal medicine, specially dried ginger. Hind. also (sont), meaning dried ginger; (sandhí), meaning dried ginger. Malay also (sapádas). Can. also (sontigiua), meaning ginger plant; (vanasunt'hi), meaning dry + ginger. Tel. also (sonti). Greek ζιγγίβερις. Title otherwise Zanzibar root by arabic corruption. Botanically Zingiber [aurdracam] officinale, roscoe, zingiberaceæ [vricsham, 144]. Generic name is from sanscrit through arabic. Alias Amomum zingiber; Zingiber majus. Amomum, from (hamámá, ar. from hamma, ar. to heat); the heating plant; from pungency and aromatic property. Rhizome tuberous, biennial; stems erect and oblique, invested by the smooth sheaths of the leaves, generally 3 or 4 feet high, and annual; leaves sub-sessile on their long sheaths, bifarious, linear-lanceolate, very smooth above and nearly so underneath; sheaths smooth, crowned with a bifid ligula; scapes radical, solitary, a little removed from the stems, 6–12 inches high, enveloped in a few obtuse sheaths, the uppermost of which sometimes end in tolerably long leaves; spikes oblong, the size of a man's thumb; exterior bracts imbricated, one-flowered, obovate, smooth, membranous at the edge, faintly striated lengthwise; interior enveloping the ovary, calyx, and the greater part of the tube of the corolla; flowers small; calyx tubular, opening on one side, three-toothed, corolla with a double limb; outer of three, nearly equal, oblong segments, inner a three-lobed lip, of a dark-purple color; ovary oval, three-celled, with many ovules in each; style filiform. The recent root is tuberous, ash-white externally, rugose, fleshy, yellowish interiorly; when dried it is in fragments of about 2 inches long, grey or ashy with oval knots; the pieces are called races or hands. There are two kinds distinguished, the scraped and the rough or unscraped; the latter or black ginger consists of the inferior roots, which have been immersed in boiling water, previously to being dried; and the former or white ginger of the fairest, roundest, and most delicate roots, picked when fresh, peeled, and dried in the sun. In the young state the rhizome is fleshy, while in its advanced state it becomes woody and starchy. Plant contains a volatile oil [yennay], the source of the aroma of the root, and a resin [raul] on which its acridity depends. The ginger from malabar is reckoned superior to any other; that exported from calicut is the produce of district of chernaud, south of calicut; ginger is chiefly exported even now from malabar, and in earlier times the greeks procured it almost exclusively from that province. For cultivation the only suitable kind of soil is that which, being red earth, is yet free from gravel, and the soil good and heavy; rain is essentially requisite, it is also however necessary that the beds be constantly kept from inundation; cultivated on coromandel wet, on w. coast dry; ground prepared on coromandel in cheitram or april and veishaukham or may, on w. coast in vrishchicam or november; seed sown on coromandel in veishaukham or may and jyeshtam or june, on w. coast in yedavam [mausam] or may; no nursery; small beds are formed, ginger root is buried under earth and manured and watered; a full grown plant attains height of 1½ feet; the leaves and stems then dry and wither away; dug up eight months after sowing; the tubers after gathering are washed and brought to market green or dried; a small quantity is preserved as seed for next year and for medicinal purposes; average price, 1 viss for 1 anna. Gives to pharm. zingiberis radix; activity resides in a volatile oil and in a soft acrid resin; stimulant, stomachic, and carminative; substituted for british peppermint [poodeenah], caraway [q.v.] and aniseed [anise] oils; dried ginger is preferable to green ginger for medicinal use; dried root of plant is used as a masticatory [charvanam] in toothache; essence of ginger is made by steeping ginger in alcohol. Chief use of ginger is as a condiment [chutney]. There is a Tamul proverb:—சுக்கு அறியாத கஷாயம் உண்டா?—"Is there any decoction [kwautam] without dried ginger?"——(1) *Ginger grass* (ಸೊಂಟಿಹುಲ್ಲು - sontihullu, Can.; అల్లపుగడ్డి - allapugaddi, Tel.; சுக்குநாறிப்புல் - shukkunárippul, Tam.). Title from smell; cf. roussa grass. Can. from (sonti, can. dry ginger, zingiber officinale, roscoe + hullu, can. grass). Tel. from (allamu, tel. ginger + gaddi, tel. grass); from smell. Tam. from (shukku, tam. dried ginger + náru, tam. to smell + pul, tam. grass) [indian grass, roussa grass]. Botanically Panicum [priyangoo] repens, linn., graminaceæ [vricsham, 156]. Common about commencement of the rains, on cultivated lands, in gardens, &c., cattle are fond of it. Same name also given to Roussa grass. ——(2) *Amada ginger* (انب سونٹھ - ambahsonth, Hind.). Same as Mango ginger.——*Broad-leaved ginger* (ಅಗಲೆಶುಂಟಿ - agaleshunt'hi, Can.). Same as False ginger.——*Downy-leaved ginger* (زنجبیل بیریشہ - zanjabíliberíshah, Hind.). Same as Cassumunar. ——*False ginger* (स्थूलग्रन्थि - st'húlagrant'hi, San.; بچ - bach, Hind.; ಅಗಲೆಶುಂಟಿ - agaleshunt'hi, Can.; கல்லுசொண்டி - kallusonti, Too.; കാട്ടിഞ്ചി - káttiñchi, Mal.). Title from appearance. San. from (s'thúla, san. stout + grant'ha, san. knot). Hind. means acorus calamus, linn. [vasamboo] from similar aromatic taste. Can. from (agala, can. broad + sunt'hi, can. ginger). Too. from (kallu, too. stone + súnt'hi, too. ginger). Mal. from (kátu, mal. wild + iñchi, mal. ginger, zingiber officinale, roscoe). San. also (víranam), meaning strength, also applied to cuscus [q.v.] andropogon muricatus, retz., from similar fragrance; (kumbhika), meaning pot-like. Hind. also (mahábaribatch), large acorus. Can. also (kallusunt'hi), meaning stone + ginger. Title otherwise Broad-leaved ginger, Wild ginger. Botanically Zingiber [aurdracam] zerumbet, smith, zingiberaceæ [vricsham, 144]. Alias Amomum spurium, sylvestre, zerumbet; Dietrichia major; Zingiber spurium. Stems declinate; leaves sessile, lanceolar; spike long-peduncled, oval, compact, obtuse; bracts broad-obovate obtuse, margins colored; flowers pale sulphur; flowering in august and september.——*Jungle ginger* (جنگلی ادرک - jangliadrak, Hind. and Dec.). Hind. from (janglí, hind. wild + adrak, hind. ginger, zingiber officinale, roscoe). Botanically Zingiber [aurdracam] capitatum, roxb., zingiberaceæ [vricsham, 144]. Stems erect, round, 2–3 feet; leaves narrow-lanceolate, acute, smooth above, slightly hairy beneath; spike terminal, sessile on the mouth of the sheaths of the upper leaves, linear-oblong, somewhat cone-shaped; bracts in pairs, one-flowered, permanent, outer one lanceolate, concave, erect, longer than the corolla tube, inner ovate, shorter, enveloping the ovary, calyx and nearly the whole of the corolla; lip of the corolla three-lobed, middle lobe very large, round, lateral ones expanding; anther with a very long curved beak; flowers large, pure yellow; flowering in the rains.——*Mango ginger* (कर्पूरहरिद्रा - karpúraharidrá, San.; अंबहळदी - ambahaladí, Mahr.; آم هلدی - ámhaldí, Hind.; آم کے بوکی ادرک - ámkebokíadrak, Dec.; మామిడి అల్లము - mámidiallamu, Tel.; കൂവ - kúva, Mal.). Title from smell of root. San. from (karpúra, san. camphor + haridrá, san. turmeric, curcuma longa, roxb.). Mahr. from (amba, mahr. mangifera indica, linn. + halada, mahr. turmeric); from fresh root smelling like green mango [q.v.]. Hind. from (ám, hind. mango + haldí, hind. turmeric). Dec. from (ám, hind. mango, mangifera indica, linn. + bo, hind. smell + adrak, hind. ginger). Tel. from (mámidi, tel. mango + allamu, tel. ginger, zingiber officinale, roscoe). Mal. means crying stem, applies to curcuma generally [coova, malabar arrowroot]. Hind. also (amada) by corruption; (ambahsonth), meaning mango dry ginger. Tel. also (árukandlakachóramu), meaning six + eye + the plant, curcuma zedoaria, roscoe. Title otherwise Amada ginger, Mango turmeric. Botanically Curcuma [haridrah] amada, roxb., zingiberaceæ [vricsham, 144]; amada from hindostany. Tubers palmate, inwardly pale yellow; leaves long-petioled broad-lanceolate, smooth; spikes central, cylindric, crowned with a tuft of pale abortive bracts; flower smallish, white or pale-yellow, with a deeper yellow line running down the middle of the lip; the tuft, pale purple or rose-colored; flowering in rains. The root has smell of a green mango; root carminative and stomachic; in pharm. non-officinal. Root yields a kind of arrowroot [coova].——*Squirrel ginger* (ఉడతల్లము - udatallamu, Tel.; சடைப்புல் - shadaippul, Tam.). Title from bushy roots. Tel. from (udata, tel. squirrel + allamu, tel. ginger, zingiber officinale, roscoe). Tam. from (jatá, san. bushy hair + pul, tam. grass); from creeping roots. Title otherwise Basket grass, Hairy grass. Botanically Eragrostis [coosham] bifaria, vahl., graminaceæ [vricsham, 156]. Alias Poa bifaria. Culms erect, simple, slender, 1–2 feet; leaves keeled and folded, stiff, glaucescent, glabrous; sheaths keeled; spike straight, simple, unilateral, distichous; spikelets sessile, alternate, linear-lanceolate, compressed; lower ones four to eleven, upper fifteen to seventeen-flowered; mountains and dry localities.——*Wild ginger* (కారల్లము - kárallamu, Tel.). Title from taste of stems. Same as Caurallam.

GINGHAM (ಗಿಂಟ - ginta, *Can.*; గింటెన - gintena, *Tel.*; கிண்டன் - kindan, *Tam.*). Vernacular means double-thread texture. Cotton cloth [sheelay].

GIRACAUL (ಗಿರಕಾಲು - girakálu, *Can.*). From (gíra, tel. a line + kálu, can. a fourth); an upright line being a symbol for a quarter, it means a quarter of a quarter. One-sixteenth of a rupee [q.v.].

GIRDLE GRASS (മേഖലപ്പുല്ല് - mékhalappullu, *Mal.*). Used in making bramin's girdle. Same as Moonj grass.

GIRY (गिरि - giri, *San.*). Mountain [gherry].——*Girijay* (गिरिजा - girijá, San.). From (above + já, san. to be born). The mountain-born Parvaty [q.v.].

GIYARWEEN (گیارهوین - giyárwín, *Hind.*). Means eleventh. The 11th of 4th month Rabee oos saunee [maheena], dedicated to Peer e dastgheer [abdool cawder]. Sufficiently described at vol. I (97).

GLUE TREE (ಅಂಟೆನಮರ - antenamara, *Can.*). See Gaub.

GNAT TREE (شجرة البق - shajaratulbakk, *Ar.*). See Bakk.

GO (गो - gó, *San.*). From (gam, san. to go) [gaty, gungay]. Cow, earth, eye, sense, water. In sense of cow a common plant first term. Ex., where transl. is of second term:—Ægle marmelos (góharítakí), terminalia chebula; Barleria longiflora (gókshuraka), hoof; Capparis horrida (góvindí), protecting; Citrullus colocynthis (góvandaní), adorer; Clitoria ternatea (gókarní), ear; Elephantopus scaber (gójihva), tongue, from leaves; Feronia elephantum (gópakarna), protector + ear; Gmelina asiatica (gópabhadra), protector + favorable; Hygrophila spinosa (gókantaka), thorn; Pedalium murex (gókhru), hoof; Plumeria acutifolia (gósampige), michelia champaca; Santalum album (góshírsha), head; Schrebera swietenoides (gólídha), eaten; Tinospora cordifolia (góraksha), protecting; Torenia cordifolia (góróchanam), pleasing; Tribulus terrestris (gokshuraka), hoof; Vitis vinifera (gostaní), teat. See gloss. paragraphs.——*Gajwaun* (گاوزبان - gáuzabán, Hind.). Same as Gowzabaun.——*Gauvada* (ಗಾವದ - gávada, Can.). From (gó, san. cow); distance of cow's lowing being heard. Linear measure. 4 hardauries = 1 gauvada [alavay, 1c]. Approximate actual value, 1 gauvada = 10 miles. Compare San. yojanam, Hind. gow, Tel. aumada, Tam. cautham. ——*Gavyooty* (गव्यूति - gavyúti, San.). From (gó, san. cow + úti, san. delight). Pasture. Linear measure. 2 croshams = 1 gavyooty; 2 gavyooties = 1 yojanam [alavay, 1f]. Approximate actual value, 1 gavyooty = 4½ miles. A smaller gavyooty is half.——*Ghye* (گائی - gáí, Hind.). From (gó, san. cow). Bos indicus. Cf. Gavæus gaurus (gaurgáí), wild cow; portax pictus (nílgáí), blue cow. See gloss. paragraphs.——*Goa* (ಗೋವೆ - góve, Can.). Shepherd country [gova]. The Portuguese town on W. coast in Bombay presidency.——*Goa bean* (چارکونی سیم - chárkonísem, Hind.; දරදඹල - daradambala, Singh.; முறுக்குப்பீன்ச - murukkuppinsu, Tam.). Hind. from (chár, hind. four + koná, hind. corner + sem, hind. bean). Singh. from (dará, singh. earth + dambala, singh. kidney bean, phaseolus vulgaris, linn.). Tam. from (murukku, tam. twist + beans). Title otherwise Chevaux-defrise bean, Square bean, Square-podded dolichos, Winged pea. Botanically Psophocarpus teragonolobus, dec., leguminosæ [vricsham, 48]. Plant large; blue flowers in cold season; bears a curious four-sided pod, 6 or 8 inches long and ¾ an inch wide, with a leafy kind of fringe running along the length of its four corners; indigenous in the mauritius. Pod is cooked whole in the manner of french beans [lobyah], to which it is inferior in flavor. No other species here. ——*Goa potato* (ഗോവാക്കിഴങ്ങ് - góvakkizhannu, Mal.). Same as Goa yam.——*Gobhoomy* (ಗೋಭೂಮಿ - góbhúmi, Can.). From (above + bhúmi, can. land). Pasture land [gomaula, maita]. ——*Gocharmam* (गोचर्म - gócharma, San.). From (above + charma, san. hide); as much as can be comprehended by strips from a cow's hide [chamrah]. Cf. the story of Dido. Superficial measure [alavay, 2 f]. Approximate actual value a parallelogram 300 feet by 10 feet. Considered enough for the range of hundred cows, one bull and their calves; and sufficient to support a man for a year.——*Gochry* (गोचडी - góchadí, Mahr.; طلح - tilh, Ar.; گوچڑی - gochrí, Dec.; توما - tuma, Malay; ಉಣ್ಣೆ - unni, Can.; పిణుజు - pinudzu, Tel.; ഉണ്ണി - unni, Mal.; உண்ணி - unni, Tam.). Title from deccany. Mahr. means cattle louse. Ar. from (talah, ar. to render lean). Can. from (unnu, can. to eat). Tel. from (pidutsu, tel. to wring), from extracting blood from cattle. Tam. from (un, tam. to suck). Tick.——*Gocoolam* (गोकुल - gókula, San.). From (above + kula, san. family). Ancient country of Krishnan [q.v.], the cowherd; supposed to be on the Jumna.——*Gocoolaushtamy* (గోకులాష్టమి - gókuláshtami, Tel.). From (above + kula, san. family + ashtamí, san. eighth). Smarta designation. Same as Krishna jayanty.——*Gocull* (ಗೋಕಲ್ಲು - gókallu, Can.). From (above + kallu, can. stone). Stones set up for cows [pashoo] to rub themselves against.——*Gocurnam* (गोकर्ण - gókarna, San.). From (above + karna, san. ear). Cow's ear. Linear measure. 12 ungoolams = 1 gocurnam; 2 gocurnams = 1 hastam [alavay, 1f]. Approximate actual value, 1 gocurnam = 9 inches. Same as San. vitasty, Hind. bilisht, Can. guenoo, Tel. jena, Tam. jaun. Compare San. pradesham, Tam. adee, wottay.——*Godavery* (గోదావరి - gódávari, Tel. godávari *). Always assumed from (gó, san. water + dá, san. to give + vari, san. stream), and hence here exhibited. The indigenous name however is Goday, which see under Goda. Sanscrit name also (vriddhagangá), meaning old + ganges. ψοάρις of Ptolemy though he wrongly makes it disembogue on west coast.—"*a*" Revenue district; situated on the Coromandel coast [q.v.]; between 16° 18′ and 18° 04′ N. lat., and between 80° 55′ and 82° 38′ E. long.; bounded N. by Central provinces and Vizagapatam district, E. by Vizagapatam district and Bay of Bengal, S. by Bay of Bengal and Kistna district, W. by the Nizam's dominions; square miles 7,857; pop. 1,951,645; language Teloogoo. Contains rivers Godavery, Severy; ports Bendamoorlunka, Cocanada, Coringa, Narsapore, Ooppauda, Peroopollem, Yanam; mountains, Bison range. The whole area of the district is represented by the following subareas, where talook [q.v.] means an ordinary tract administered by a Tahsildar [q.v.], and division means a Zemindarry [q.v.] tract administered by a superior Deputy tahsildar:—Amalaupooram talook, Bhadrachellam talook, Bheemavaram talook, Cocanada division, Ellore talook, Narsapore talook, Peddapore talook, Pittapore division, Rajahmundry talook, Ramchendrapooram talook, Tanookoo talook, Toony division, and Yernagoodem talook. For general administrative purposes the district is distributed between the following revenue and magisterial officers, who have their head-quarters at the places shown. The pay set opposite the subordinate officers gives the grade of the corresponding charge:—Collector, Cocanada; Sub-collector Rajahmundry, in charge of Amalaupooram, Rajahmundry and Ramchendrapooram talooks; Head assistant collector, Ellore, in charge of Tanookoo, Ellore and Yernagoodem talooks; General deputy collector, Narsapore, in charge of Narsapore and Bheemavaram talooks; Special assistant agent, Coonavaram, in charge of Bhadrachellam talook; General duty deputy collector, Cocanada, in charge of Peddapore talook, and the Pittapore, Cocanada and Toony divisions. Tahsildars, Amalaupooram, Rs. 200; Bhadrachellam agency talook, Rs. 120; Bheemavaram, Rs. 175; Ellore, Rs. 175; Narsapore, Rs. 225; Peddapore, Rs. 150; Rajahmundry, Rs. 175; Ramchendrapooram, Rs. 250; Tanookoo, Rs. 200; Yernagoodem, Rs. 150; Deputy tahsildars, Alamore or Ramchendrapooram, Rs. 70, range situated in the west of Ramchendrapooram talook; Chintalapoody, Rs. 70, range situated in the north of Ellore talook; Cocanada division, Rs. 100, Zemindarry division; Cottapettah, Rs. 70, range situated in the north-west of Amalaupooram talook; Cottapully or Gokavaram or Raghoodevapooram, including Rumpa, Rs. 100, range situated in the north of Rajahmundry talook; Pentapaud, Rs. 70, range situated in the west of Tanookoo talook; Pittapore, Rs. 100, Zemindarry division; Polavaram, Rs. 100, range situated in the north-east of Yernagoodem talook; Prodipadoo or Yeleshwaram, Rs. 70, range situated in the north-east of Peddapore talook; Shivacode, Rs. 70, range situated in the south-east of Narsapore talook; Toony, Rs. 100, Zemindarry division; Sub-magistrate, Cocanada town, Rs. 70. Similarly judicial officers:—Judge, Rajahmundry; District moonsifs, Rajahmundry, Peddapore, Cocanada, Tanookoo, Amalaupooram, Narsapore, Ellore. Contains Registration subdistricts Alamore, Amalaupooram, Bheemavaram, Chintalapoody, Cocanada, Coringa, Cottapettah, Ellore, Mamidivaram, Narsapore, Peddapore, Pentapaud, Pittapore, Prattipaud, Rajahmundry, Ramchendrapooram, Shivacode, Tanookoo, Toony, Yernagoodem. Contains Forest ranges Doomagoodem, Rajahmundry. Contains Municipalities Cocanada, Ellore, Rajahmundry. Contains District board and Talook boards, Rajahmundry Talook board embracing Rajahmundry, Amalaupooram and Ramchendrapooram talooks; Cocanada Talook board embracing Peddapore talook, Pittapooram, Cocanada and Toony divisions; Narsapore Talook board embracing Narsapore and Bheemavaram; Ellore Talook board embracing Tanookoo, Ellore and Yernagoodem talooks. The following general references should be made to the preceding volumes:—general geography, I (1) to (29); general ethnology, I (29) to (109); general history, I (110) to (188); physical geography, II, 1; meteorology, II, 3; geology, II, 8; fauna, II, 21; flora, II, 26; mineralogy, II, 29. The following references in the preceding volumes will furnish details special to the district:—latitudes and longitudes, II, 47; particulars about towns, II, 48; coast survey, II, 165; light-houses, II, 169; comparative population, II, 172; location of revenue officers, II, 385; revenue settlement of the district, II, 411; registrars' and sub-registrars' stations, II, 421; ports, II, 423; salt factories, II, 426; rain-guage stations, II, 428; police divisions, II, 431; maps published, II, 436; hospitals and dispensaries, II, 447; missionary stations, II, 455; head-quarter stations of gazetted officers, II, 461; incidence of taxation, II, 463; weights and measures of the district, II, 511; zemindarries contained, I, 57, and II, 297; agencies contained, I, 75; special public works, I, 395. A special gazetteer account of the whole district is given at II, 79. For the detailed topography of the district, reference should be made to the talook notices in the present volume, viz.:—Amalaupooram, Bhadrachellam, Bheemavaram, Cocanada, Coringa, Ellore, Narsapore, Peddapore, Pittapore, Rajahmundry, Ramachendrapooram, Rekapully, Rumpa, Tanookoo, Toony, Yernagoodem.—"*b*" River; Godavery district. Ignored by ancient and mediæval map-makers. Rises on the eastern declivity of the western ghauts [q.v.], at Trimbac in lat. 19° 58′, long. 73° 30′, 16 miles from Nassick, and 50 miles east of the west coast. The traditional site of the source is on a hill behind the village. It is approached by a flight of 690 stone steps, flanked by a low stone wall. At the top of these steps is a stone platform built at the foot of the rock, out of which issues the water of the stream, and an image under a canopy has been so placed that the water trickles through its mouth into a reservoir. From first to last the general direction is south-east. It first flows south-east for 100 miles to the western frontier of the Nizam's dominions in lat. 19° 48′, long. 74° 40′, and continues in the same direction for 90 miles further, forming the boundary between Ahmednugger and the Nizam's dominions to a point in lat. 19° 23′, long. 75° 37′. It then enters the Nizam's dominions and proceeds in a sinuous, but generally easterly course, for 160 miles, receiving on the left side, in lat. 19° 6′, long. 77° 5′, the Doodhna, a considerable stream flowing from the north-west. From that confluence it flows south-east for 85 miles and receives on the right side in lat. 18° 48′, long. 77° 55′, the Manjeerah flowing from the south. From this confluence the course is still sinuous; but generally eastward, for about 170 miles, to lat. 18° 48′, long. 79° 49′, near which the Munnair falls into it. Thence it flows north-east for about 20 miles to lat. 18° 52′, long. 79° 55′, receiving on the left side at Sironchah, the Wurdah, Peingunga and Weingunga, united in one stream called the Pranheeta which discharges the great drainage of the southern declivity of the Vindhyam range. From this junction the river flows south-east, with the Nizam's dominions on the right, and the Upper godavery district of the Central provinces on the left bank, receiving on the left a considerable tributary, the Indrauvaty, the junction of which is concealed by hills. Below this junction low ranges of hills run almost parallel to the left bank of the river till the junction of the Taul is reached. On the right bank the country is more open and cultivated and is marked by the towns of Nagaram and Mungampettah. A short distance below the last place the river enters Godavery district at Purnashaula. It then passes Doomagoodem where is the first anicut and on the opposite bank to which the sacred hill of Ratabgootta rises into view. After passing Doomagoodem, the prominent object on the British side is the small hill of Bhadrachellam, crowned with Hindoo temples. On the opposite side the country is more open and cultivated and thickly dotted with irrigation tanks extending inland for about 250 miles to Warrangal, and the remains of numerous old irrigation works. The river is then joined by the Severy at Coonavaram. Near this junction the whole range of the Eastern ghauts comes into view. Passing Collore in lat. 17° 29′, long. 81° 34′, 170 miles from Sironchah the river forces a passage through that part of the Eastern ghauts [q.v.] known as the Paupicondah range by a precipitous gorge only about 200 yards wide. It again widens out and finally issues into the plains at Polavaram in lat. 17° 15′, long. 81° 42′, 25 miles below Collore. This gorge forms one of the most beautiful pieces of scenery in Southern india. From Polavaram the river continues south-east, widening as it enters the plain, and passes round the island of Pauta pattesham. This island is the first of a series formed or modified by the rapid stream in its future downward course. These islands are exceedingly fertile and are noted for the lunka [q.v.] tobacco [pogauk] grown on them. In December and January many are covered with the relloo or flowering reed [naunal]. Passing the village of Gootaula on the right bank the river reaches Rajahmundry, on the left bank. On approaching the latter place the bank is in many instances cut down precipitously by the action of the stream, so that Tullapoody and other villages

formerly at some distance from the river are now on the very verge of the bank. A short distance below Rajahmundry the river is barred at Dowlaishweram 30 miles from its mouth by the celebrated anicut [q.v.]; see vol. I, 395. Here at Dowlaishweram it divides into two large streams :—the eastern, known as the Gowtamy godavery, flowing past Yanam and Neelapully for 55 miles, and falling into the Bay of Bengal at Cape godavery near Coringa in lat. 16° 48′, long. 82° 23′; and the western or Vasishta godavary flowing nearly due south for 55 miles and entering the bay at Point narsapore in lat. 16° 18′, long. 81° 43′. A few miles above this mouth another large branch, the Veinateya godavery, separates from the river, and falls into the bay near Bendamoorlunka, forming the island of Nagaram. Hindoos assert that there are seven branches by which the river debouches into the sea, the principal of which are the Toolyabhauga, Atreya, Bhauradwaujam, Gowtamy, the Vriddha or the Old gowtamy, the Veinateyam, the Cowshiky, and the Vasishta. The three early English factories [aurang], Injaram, Bendamoorlunka and Madapollem, were situated near the Gowtamy, Vasishta, and Veinateyam mouths. The rich delta [conamoogam], formerly known as Conaseema, spreads out on both sides, extending on the west to the delta of the Kistna at Colair lake, a distance of about 40 miles, and on the east for about 32 miles to Coringa bay. Total length of river 898 miles; estimated area of drainage basin [nadee], 112,200 square miles. The river is navigable from July to November between Rajahmundry and a place called Davadola on the right bank and some six miles below Yenchampully near the second or middle barrier; but beyond Sooraid 30 miles above Doomagoodem, as far as Yedarlapully, 20 miles further up, the navigation is somewhat dangerous, the river-bed being studded with rocks and the level of the water being very variable even in the flood seasons. There is not much boat traffic above Doomagoodem. The main lines of Godavery delta navigable canal are two; from Dowlaishweram anicut to Cocanada, 32 miles, and from Vijayeshwaram anicut to Ellore, 47 miles. The secondary lines of Godavery delta navigable canal are as follows :—1 mile from head of Dowlaishweram main line to Coringa, 36 miles; 4 miles from head of Dowlaishweram main line to Samulcottah and thence round to Cocanada, 38 miles; 6 miles from head of Vijayeshwaram main line to Narsapore, 39 miles; Bobbar lunka anicut to Amalaupooram, 32 miles; Bobbar lunka anicut to Razole, 36 miles; Bobbar lunka anicut to Inapore, 43 miles. The distances of these secondary lines are calculated from the main heads or anicut. Proposed extensions are as follows:—Coringa to Cocanada, by a new canal between tidal locks; Razole canal, extension 8 miles; Amalaupooram canal, extension 10 miles; Amalaupooram canal to Bendamoorlunka, 14 miles. The Godavery is regarded by the natives as peculiarly sacred. It is considered to flow from the same source as the Ganges, but underground, and it is frequently called the Vriddha gungay. In more than one place in the Pooraunams [q.v.], the Ganges proper is described as passing through Calingam [q.v.], which probably means the same thing. Pliny again makes the country of the three Calingams an island in the Ganges. Those who carry the sacred water of the Ganges to the south of India, when they arrive on the banks of the Godavery, invariably replace the water of the Ganges, evaporated on the journey, by water taken from its sister stream. The Gowtamy branch is, if possible, looked on as more holy than the rest of the river. Once every twelve years the Pooshcaram [pundigay, 6d] feast is held on the banks of the Godavery at Cotipully [q.v.] and pilgrims come from all parts to bathe in its waters.——*Gograusam* (గోగ్రాసము - gógrásamu, Tel.). From (above + grása, san. food). Fodder of a cow.——*Gohatyah* (गोहत्या - góhatyá, San.). From (above + han, san. to kill). Killing a cow, a heinous crime. ——*Golla* (ಗೊಲ್ಲ - golla, Can.; గొల్ల - golla, Tel.). From (gó, san. cow). The corresponding terms are :—Hind. dhangar, Mal. yeraudy, Tam. yiday. Canarese and tel. names for the shepherd caste. These were originally the pastoral part of the nation and were engaged in the management of cattle [maud], sheep and goats [aud]. Many now live by cultivation; also employed as confidental servants in public treasuries [inam]. Numbers about a million. See vol. I (67); II, 228.——*Gollapully* (గొల్లపల్లె - gollapalle, Tel.). From (golla, tel. shepherd + palle, tel. village). Village; Kistna dist., Noozveed zemindarry; pop. 1,292; lat. 16° 43′; long. 80° 57′; from Gunnavaram N.E. 15 miles; from Masulipatam N.N.W. 39 miles; from Noozveed S.E. 6 miles. Centre of Golcondah mines.——*Golla's plate* (ಬಂದರೆ - bandare, Can.; గొల్లపుల్లెడ - gollapulleda, Tel.; விராலி - viráli, Tam.). Title from use of leaves. Tel. from (golla, tel. the caste + pulle, tel. plate leaf). Tam. from (viral, tam. strength); heart-wood strong. Can. also (bandargi); (bandrike). Tel. also (pulleda), meaning plate leaf; (bandáru), meaning turmeric, curcuma longa, roxb. [wild anaur, yellow cadamba]; (bandódu), meaning touch wood, from ease with which it burns. Title otherwise Australian native hop, Bog-myrtle, Jamaica switch sorrel. Botanically Dodonæa viscosa, linn., sapindaceæ [vricsham, 43]. Alias Dodonæa angustifolia, burmanniana; dioica; Ptelea viscosa. A stiff, wiry, virgate shrub, with alternate smooth wiry leaves, widening from the stock upwards; foliage resembling arbutus; flowers pale-green and insignificant; covers large meidauns [q.v.]; ascends mountains to 8,000 feet; used for hedges, and for edging in a garden. Leaves viscid and keep green, though dry; taste sour; make poultices. Sapwood white; heart-wood extremely hard and close-grained, dark-brown, with an irregular outline; used for engraving, turning, tool-handles, walking-sticks, &c.; the wood ignites like touch wood, though green. No other common species here.——*Gomantaky* (गोमन्तकी - gómantakí, San.). From (gómantaka, san. cow-possessing, goa). A dialect of Concany [q.v.] used at Goa by Portuguese. See vol. I (60).——*Gomataroya* (ಗೋಮಟರಾಯ - gómataráya, Can.). From (gautama, san. sage so called + ráya, tel. king). Colossal monolithic figures of Booddha [q.v.] among the Jeinas [betta, jeina].——*Gomaula* (ಗೋಮಾಲ - gómála, Can.). From (above + mála, san. village forest). Pasture land [gobhoomy, maita].——*Gomedham* (गोमेध - gómédha, San.). From (above + médha, san. sacrifice). Sacrifice of a cow [pashoo, shiva].——*Gomookhanuddy* (கோமுகநதி - kómuganathi, Tam.). From (above + mukha, san. mouth + nadí, san. river). River; South arcot district, Cullacoorchy and Vriddhauchellam talooks. Rises in the Cullroyen hills and flows for 25 miles through Cullacoorchy talook, joining the Manimooctah nuddy near Nulloor in Vriddhauchellam talook. Several anicuts [q.v.].——*Goomta* (ಗುಮಟ - gumata, Can.). Otherwise Gomaty, Gomátaroya. Corruption of Gowtama. A collossal monolithic figure, probably of Booddha [betta, booddha].——*Gopalpore* (గోపాలపురము - gópálapuramu, Tel. gopálpur*). From (gópála, san. vishnu, the cowherd + pura, san. town). Town, Port, Sea-customs house, Lighthouse; Ganjam dist., Berhampore tal.; pop. 2,865; acres 779; lat. 19° 16′; long. 84° 57′; from Berhampore E.S.E. 8¾ miles; from Chetterpore S.W. 9 miles; from Ganjam S.W. 13 miles; from Madras N.E. 515 miles; from Sonapore N.E. 15 miles. On Orissa coast [q.v.] between Ganjam and Berhampore. Has completely displaced Mansoorcottah a little to the north, formerly chief port of district. A large back-water [cauyal] on the north-east separates it from Mansoorcottah. The intense heat of May is tempered by the sea breeze, and it is a pleasant place of residence for Europeans. Light on mainland sixty yards from low water-mark; lat. 19° 15′; long. 84° 57′. White; fixed. 8 miles range. Visible from all directions seaward. Flag-staff painted white. Guide to the anchorage. Another light at the extreme end of pier. Red; fixed. 3 miles range. Visible from all directions seaward. To point out the sea end of the pier. The port is nothing more than an open roadstead. The depth of water in the anchorage varies from 8½ to 9½ fathoms at low water. The bottom at these depths is sand mixed with stiff mud and is good holding ground. The rise and fall of the tide is about 6 feet. During April, May and October, the surf is frequently so high that communication between the shipping and the shore is interrupted for days together; but it is generally possible to communicate in the early part of the day. The prevailing wind is south to south-east, and for eight months of the year it blows very strongly. The surf is considered more dangerous to boats than at Madras. The current usually runs with the wind. The limit of the port on the north-east or Mansoorcottah side is at a distance of 1,160 yards from the custom-house and on the south-west side at a distance of 600 yards from it. To seaward the boundaries of the port extend to where a depth of 12 fathoms is reached. The anchorage for ships is with the custom-house flagstaff on the beach north-west ½ west; centre of the large white godown [q.v.] on the beach from which the Aska sugars [q.v.] are shipped north, north-west by west; saddlehill entirely detached from the high land and appearing to the south over the beach sand hills west south-west; and Mansoorcottah hill north by west about 1¼ miles from the shore. Coasting steamers call. Considerable export trade to Europe in grain, myrobalans [q.v.], hemp [indian hemp], horns [sing], hides [chamrah], and seeds [cottay, yennay]. Trig. station in lat. 19° 13′ 00·80″; long. 84° 56′ 28·90″; from Berhampore S.E. 8 miles; from the sea E. 1¼ miles; Mr. Boothby's bungalow [q.v.], the highest part of the roof.——*Gopaulan* (गोपाल - gópála, San.). From (above + pála, san. protector). Vishnoo [q.v.] as the cowherd Krishnan [q.v.]. Gopaulsawmy is another form. Familiarly Gopan, Gopoo. Hindoo 2nd or pers. name [peyar].——*Gopinautan* (கோபிநாதன் - kóbináthan, Tam.). From (gópí, san. cowherdess + nát'ha, san. lord). Krishnan. Hindoo 2nd or pers. name. Common among Madhwas and Goozeratties [peyar]. ——*Gopooram* (गोपुर - gópura, San.). From (gó, san. eye + pura, san. town). Feature of architecture [staupatyam] peculiar to the peninsula. A gate, a town gate, but more especially the elevated and ornamented gateway or entrance tower of a Hindoo temple [coil]. Originally for defence [toranam].——*Gopy* (गोपी - gópí, San.). From (above + pá, san. to protect). A cowherdess. Also short for Gopy chandanam.——*Gopy chandanam* (गोपीचन्दन - gópíchandana, San.). Literally shepherdess's sandal [q.v.] paste. Common magnesian clay used by hindoos to make sectarian marks [naumam] on faces, breasts and arms [tirmunn]. Veishnavas employ white earth from Dwarca. Also an aluminous yellow earth brought from Ganges at Hardwar and used by Madhwas. Also a medicine. Cf. Ghil arminy. See vol. I (85), (90).——*Gorochanay* (गोरोचना - góróchaná, San.; حجرالبقر - hajarulbakr, Ar.; گاؤ زهره - gáuzahra, Pers.; گوروچنا - gorochaná, Hind.; گائی رون - gáíron, Dec.; ಗೋರೋಚನ - góróchana, Can.; గోరోచనము - góróchanamu, Tel.; ഗോരോചനം - góróchanam, Mal.; கோரோசனை - kórósanai, Tam.).

San. from (gó, san. cow + róchaná, san. yellow pigment). Ar. from (hajar, ar. stone + bakr, ar. cow). Pers. from (gáú, pers. cow + zahra, pers. bile): Dec. from (gái, hind. cow + róchaná, san. pigment). Ar. also (kharazatulbakr), meaning cow-shell. Bezoar orientale of chemists. Otherwise animal bezoar [q.v.]. One is a concretion found in fourth stomach of capra œgagrus [velland], of persia; it has a smooth glossy surface and is of a dark green or olive color, and about the size of a kidney bean [lobyah], roundish or oblong. Another is biliary concretion of the cow [pashoo] or bullock [maud], calculus cysticus bovis of chemists; contained in a small bag, which holds two or three small bezoars, each about the size of a tamarind [q.v.] stone, or one large one as big as a large marble; bright-yellow color; medicinally cordial and alexipharmic; employed with chebulic myrobalan [q.v.] and galls [mauchicoy] in preparing mixture for cleansing inside of mouths of new-born infants; veidyans [q.v.] prescribe solution in warm ghee [q.v.] to be poured up the nose in cases of headache; much used as a pigment. Camel bezoar found in gall-bladder of the camel [ottagam] is used as a yellow paint [rangh].——*Gosain* (گوسائیں - gosáin, Hind.; గోసాయి - gósáyi, Tel.). From (gó, san. sense + svámí, san. master). A religious mendicant in general. The most respectable are the descendants spiritually of Shuncaracharry, of whom there are ten chief branches, called the Dashnamy [q.v.] or ten named Gosains. These attach to their ordinary Hindoo name one of the terms, Teertam or shrine, Aushramam or an order, Vanam and Aranyam or wood, Saraswaty or goddess of eloquence, Bhauraty or goddess of speech, Poory or city, Giry and Parvatam or hill, Sangaram or ocean. As Anandagiry, Vidyauranyam, Ramaushramam. These are usually assembled in mutts [q.v.], under a superior; particularly at Shringairy, in the Western ghauts, near the sources of the Toongabudra, said to have been founded by Shuncaran [q.v.] himself. The Dashnamy gosains worship Shiva [aundy, jauty]. See vol. I (90).——*Gosangy* (గోసంగి - gósangi, Tel.). From (above + hims, san. to kill); cow-killer. A class of pariah beggars.——*Gosawmy* (गोस्वामी - gosvámí, San.). From (gó, san. sense + svámí, san. master); master of senses or passions. Religious mendicant. ——*Gostanuddy* (గోస్తనది - góstanadi, Tel.). From (gósht'ha, san. cow's abode + nadí, san. river). Sanscrit name (góstanínadí), meaning cow + udder + river; from tradition of the river flowing from the udder of a cow. Canal; Godavery dist., Bheemavaram and Tanookoo tals.; from Bheemavaram N. 4 miles; from Veeravausaram N.W. 11 miles. Natural channel [q.v.] navigable for 28 miles. Converted into a branch of the Western delta main canal. Waters considered sacred by Hindoos, being mentioned in the Vayoo pooraunam [q.v.].——*Gostany* (గోస్తని - góstani, Tel.). From (gó, san. cow + stana, san. udder); named from the form of the basin [angoor].—"*a*" River; Vizagapatam dist., Gajapatinugger, Vizianagram and Bimlipatam divisions. Also called Champauvaty or Conauda. Rises in Pottinghy division, north of Gaulicondah, flows south-east for 48 miles till it enters the sea at Conauda. Principal places on its banks are Gajapatinugger and Andra.—"*b*" Another. Otherwise called Chittivalsa or Bimlipatam river; Vizagapatam dist., Srungavarapoocote and Bimlipatam divisions. Length 65 miles, rises in Pottinghy divisions north of Gaulicondah, near the source of the other river of the same name and disembogues at Bimlipatam.——*Gosye* (గోసాయి - gósáyi, Tel.). Same as Gosain.——*Got* (گوت - got, Hind.). Same as Gotram. ——*Gotram* (गोत्र - gótra, San.). From (above + trai, san. to protect). Literally, a cow-pen; thence an Aryan tribe claiming to be sprung from a particular progenitor. The names of the gotrams have been much confused, particularly in later times, when their number has become considerable. However all Braminic families who have kept the sacred fires are supposed to descend from the seven rishies. These are:—Bhrigoo, Angiran, Vishwamitran, Vasishtan, Cashyapan, Atry, Agastyan. The gotrams which descend from these rishies are again sub-divided into forty-nine gotrams, and these forty-nine branch off into a still larger number of families. The names gotram, vamsham, vargam, pacsham, and ganam are all used in the same sense, to express the larger as well as the smaller families descended from the seven rishies. A Bramin who keeps the sacrificial fire is obliged by law to know to which of the forty-nine gotrams his own family belongs, and in consecrating his own fire he must invoke the ancestors who founded the gotram to which he belongs. Each of the forty-nine gotrams claims one, or two, or three, or five ancestors, and the names of these ancestors constitute the distinctive character of each gotram. See vol. II, 226.——*Gova* (गोव - góva, San.). Meaning cowherd. May imply district of cowherds, that is of nomadic tribes. Ancient name of Southern concan [concan, goa].——*Govardhanan* (கோவர்த்தனன் - kóvarttanan, Tam.). From (above + vardhana, san. increasing). Krishnan, the cowherd. Hindoo 2nd or pers. name [peyar].——*Govindan* (गोविन्द - góvinda, San.). From (above + vind, san. to obtain). Cow-finder, cowherd. Vishnoo as Krishnan. Pilgrims to Tripatty specially invoke this god by this name. Hindoo 2nd or pers. name [peyar]. Otherwise Govindoo.——*Govindrauz* (గోవిందరాజు - góvindarádzu, Tel.). From (góvinda, san. kríshna, the cowherd + rádzu, tel. king). Hindoo 2nd or pers. name [peyar].——*Gow* (گو - gau, Hind.). Mahratta. Distance of cow-lowing being heard. Linear measure. 4 coss = 1 gow [alavay, 1e]. Approximate actual value, 1 gow = 9 miles. In Ceylon it is 4 miles. Compare San. yojanam, Can. hardaury, Tel. aumada, Tam. cantham. See vol. I, 609.——*Gowtaman* (गौतम - gautama, San.). One of the seven rishies and one of the seven stars [nacshatram] forming the small bear [doobhe asghar], near the pole [dhroovam]. His wife's name is Ahalyay; he is celebrated for his curse on Indran [q.v.]. So the surname of the Shakya tribe, from which Booddha shakya moony sprang. See vol. I (75). Another Gowtaman was the author of the Nyauyam [q.v.] philosophy. See vol. I (74) [matam].——*Gowtameeshan* (गौतमीश - gautamísha, San.). From (gautamí, san. durgá + ísha, san. lord). Shiva [q.v.].——*Gowzabaun* (لسان الثور - lisánussaur, Ar.; گاؤ زبان - gáuzabán, Hind.). Title from hindostany. Ar. from (lisán, ar. tongue + saur, ar. bull). Hind. from (gáu, pers. bull + zabán, pers. tongue); from resemblance of leaves [gajwaun]. Greek βούγλωσσον. Title otherwise Bugloss, Bulls' tongue, Gajwaun. Botanically Onosma bracteatum, wall., boragineæ [vricsham, 92]. Alias Onosma macrocephala. Fragmentary leaves covered with curious tuberculated glands, each terminated by a hair. There are other gowzabauns under Echium and Cacalia.

GO (گو - go, *Hind.*). From (guftan, pers. to speak). Suffix denoting agent in compounds; as Canoongo, meaning rule + speak, interpreter of rules.——*Goindah* (گویندہ - goindah, Hind.). From (guftan, pers. to say). A spy.

GODA (గోడ - góda, *Tel.*). Wall.——*Goday* (గోడె - góde, Tel.). Means limit. Dravidian name for the Godavery. A family name also.

GODAURY (धातकी - dhátakí, *San.*; धायटी - dháyatí, *Mahr.*; دھول - dhaval, *Hind.*; గోదారి - gódári, *Tel.*; ଜାତିକୋ - jatiko, *Oor.*). Title from teloogoo. San. from (dhá, san. to hold) Mahr. from sanscrit. San. also (dhátupushpiká), meaning mineral + flower, from the red flowers; (dhátripushpiká), by corruption; (agnijválá), meaning fire flame, from red flowers [flame tree]; (subhikshá), meaning abundance. Tel. also (reyyamánu); (gaddapisinika), meaning root + maba buxifolia, pers.; (gáji); (chiranji) [small dyeing mulberry]; (jargi); (kódára). Oor. also (harwari). Title otherwise Downy grislea, Gummy chiranjy [small dyeing mulberry], Reyya. Botanically Woodfordia floribunda, salisb., lythraceæ [vricsham, 58]. Alias Grislea tomentosa; Lythrum fruticosum; Woodfordia fruticosa, tomentosa. Shrub, 6 feet; branchlets pubescent; leaves opposite, quite entire, lanceolate, somewhat cordate at the base, sessile, hoary underneath; petals usually six; stamens declinate, usually twelve; capsule oblong; peduncles axillary, several-flowered; flowers middle-sized, scarlet, with rose-colored petals, fragrant; flowering from december to march. Gum resembles gum [gond] tragacanth [kateerah] and swells in water. Dried flowers are medicinally stimulant and astringent. Infusion of leaves employed as a tea [q.v.] by hill tribes; a kind of intoxicating drink is extracted from the blossoms with sugar [q.v.]. Flower gives a red dye [shauyam] used in silk [puttoo] dyeing; often used along with morinda [dyeing mulberry]. Wood reddish-white, hard, close-grained. There are two varieties, the white and black, distinguished by the color of the bark, fruit, and shape of the leaves. No other common species here.

GODE (ಕೋಡು - kódu, *Can.*; కోడు - kódu, *Tel.*; കോട്ട് - kótu, *Mal.*; கோடு - kódu, *Tam.*). From (kótu, mal. steep). Summit of a hill. Suffix in place names as Trichengode, meaning sacred + red + summit [code].

GODHICAY (गोधिका - gódhiká, *San.*). From (gudh, san. to envelop); covered with thick skin. Term co-extensive with the european Saurian order of reptiles [sarpy, 5-11]. Distinguished from other reptiles by the presence of legs; some might be taken for snakes [sarpam], but in these are found bones of the shoulder hidden below the skin; the motions of some are slow, while those of others are executed with great but not lasting rapidity; many have the power of changing their colors; this depends on the presence of several layers of cells loaded with different pigments; the animal spreads or compresses these layers by more or less inflating its lungs, whereby the changes in the coloration are effected; the tongue is differently shaped and has different functions affording a character for their subdivision. A key-synopsis connecting european and native terminology will be found included under Sarpy; title heads in this glossary cover each family, and contained genus and species, distinguished by the natives. For insects see poochy; for fishes see matsyam; for batrachians see bhaicam; for reptiles see sarpy; for birds see pacshy; for mammals see sastanam. A general conspectus of the fauna [jantoo] of s. india was given in vol. II, appendix IV.——*Ghorapadey* (ಘೋರಪಡೆ - ghórapade, Can.). From (ghórapada, mahr. iguana). Ancient Mahratta family of Sundoor estate, Bellary district. Identical with Bhonslays of Sattaura. So named from founder Mullojee having scaled an impregnable fort in Concan [q.v.] by fastening a cord round the body of an Iguana [oodoomoo] and sending it up the wall. Originally these were officers of the Beejapore army. Vol I, 42 [charitram].

GODNAH (گودنا - godná, *Hind.*). Puncturing the skin, and rubbing it with the leaves of plants, yielding a dark dye; chiefly by women. Tattooing as a punishment.

GODO (ଗୋଡୋ - gódó, *Oor.*). Fort [gada, ghur, gooda].

GODOWN (گدنگ - gidang, *Hind.*; గిడ్డంగి - giddangi, *Tel.*; കിടങ്ങ - kitaunu, *Mal.*; கிடங்கு - kidangu, *Tam.*). From malay. An out-house, place where household implements or goods are kept [kidang].

GOGLET (کوزه - kúzah, *Hind.*). From portuguese gorgoleta. A water-bottle. Usually earthenware, of globular body with a long neck [cooja].

GOGOO (గోగు - gôgu, *Tel.*). From (góku, tel. to scrape); from fibres being scraped. Same as Hemp bendy.——*Gogoolpully* (గోగులపల్లి - gógulapalli, Tel.). From (above + palli, tel. village). Tel. also (góvulapalli), meaning cow + village. Village; Nellore dist., Canigherry tal.; pop. 2,075; lat. 15° 16′; long. 79° 22′; from Canigherry S.W. 16 miles; from Nellore N.W. 71 miles. Is surrounded by low hills and jungles. Copper [taumram] mining has been attempted. Two ruined forts built by the Batsaly family, who ruled formerly here.

GOGRA (घोगरा - ghôgará, *Mahr.*; బంకెయెద్దు - bankeyeddu, *Tel.*). Tel. from (banka, tel. gum + eddu, tel. bull). Rita pavimentata, silurilæ [kizhautty], physostomi, teleostei [matsyam, 35], of naturalists [jantoo]. Alias Arius pavimentatus; Gogrius sykesii; Phractocephalus gogra. Gogra from mahratta. Freshwater fish; upper jaw longer; upper surface of head smooth, being covered by skin; dull yellowish color, with dark or even black fins; rivers in the deccan [q.v.] and affluents of the kistna, kurnool. No other common species here.

GOKAVARAM (గోకవరము - gókavaramu, *Tel.*). From (kóka, san. wolf + pura, san. town).—"*a*" Deputy tahsildarry, Godavery district. Pay Rs. 100.—"*b*" Village, Deputy tahsildar's station; Godavery dist., Rajahmundry tal.; pop. 1,786; acres 1,962; lat. 17° 16′; long. 81° 53′; from Cocanada N.W. 33 miles; from Coonavaram E. 44 miles; from Ellore N.E. 61 miles; from Madras N.N.E. 300 miles; from Narsapore N.N.E. 57 miles; from Rajahmundry N.N.E. 19 miles. Large tank. A large weekly market for hill people.

GOLANDY (गुल्ममूषक - gulmamúshaka, *San.*; جهاڑی کا چوها - jhárikáchúhá, *Hind.*; ಗುಲಂಡಿ - gulandi, *Can.*; పొరపంజిగాడు - sorapanjigádu, *Tel.*; കാട്ടെലി - kátteli, *Mal.*; කාෆිවත්තිමියා - káp'hivattimíyá, *Singh.*; புதரெலி - puthareli, *Tam.*). Title from canarese. San. from (gulma, san. bush + múshaka, san. rat). Hind. from (jhári, hind. bush + chúhá, hind. rat). Mal. from (kátu, mal. jungle + eli, mal. rat). Singh. means coffee garden rat. Tam. from (puthar, tam. bush + eli, tam. rat). Title otherwise Bush rat. Golunda ellioti, muridæ, rodentia, mammalia [sastanam, 17], of naturalists [jantoo]; generic from canarese. Above olive brown mixed with fulvous, giving a dusky fulvous tint; beneath yellowish tawny or light yellowish gray; the tail somewhat villose; the head long, muzzle blunt, rounded and covered with rough hair, as are the face and cheeks; ears round, hairy; whiskers long and very fine. This rat is found only in S. india and Ceylon. It lives entirely above ground choosing its habitation in a thick bush, among the thorny branches of which, or on the ground, it constructs a nest of elastic stalks and fibres of dry grass, thickly interwoven. Its motion is slow, and it has not the same power of leaping or springing, by which the rats [ely] in general avoid danger. The Yanaudies [q.v.] catch this rat, surrounding the bush and seizing it as it comes out. It is the coffee rat of Ceylon, so destructive to coffee [q.v.] trees. For Golunda meltada see Varappely.

GOLANOO (గొలను - golanu, *Tel.*). Tank. Suffix, place names.

GOLCONDAH (గొలుగొండ - golugonda, *Tel.* golgonda*). From (golugu, tel. glycosmis pentaphylla, corr. + konda, tel. hill).——**(1)** Talook, Vizagapatam district, Tahsildar's pay Rs. 150. Population 118,514. Language Teloogoo. S.W. inland of district. Boundaries:—north, Jeypore zemindarry and Veeravilly talook; east, Sarwasiddhy and Ankapully talooks; south, Sarwasiddhy talook and the Godavery district; west, the Godavery district. Hilly and rugged. Soil sandy, stony, regar [q.v.], loamy and clayey, poor in quality except in a few places in the southern portion. The northern is occupied by a mass of hills consisting of a rugged tableland about 3,000 feet above the sea, with peaks rising to 5,000 feet, almost entirely covered with jungle. This was the scene of part of the Rumpa disturbance of 1879-80. Agriculture is chief industry; cloth weaving to a limited extent. Commerce to a small extent in jaggery [q.v.], oil seeds [yennay] and pulses [dholl] and hill produce such as gallnuts [mauchicoy], tamarinds [q.v.], saffron [country saffron], wax [mom], &c. Chiefly irrigated by rivers Shaurada and Tandaba, a lake, and tanks. Principal trig. stations:—Calingacondah, Cheroocondah, Dhaura, Nullacondah, Pagoolraulloo, Paundavoola condah, Sanjeevy. The leading places, &c., in the talook are the following.——*Balighattam* (బలిఘట్టము - balighattamu, Tel.). From (bali, san. giant so called + ghatta, san. pass). Village, Place of pilgrimage; pop. 2,268; acres 6,295; lat. 17° 39′; long. 82° 39′; from Narsapatam S. 1 mile; from Vizagapatam W. 44 miles. Small rock in vicinity with pagoda [q.v.] to Shiva [q.v.] as Bramheshwar. The idol [vigraham] faces west instead of east as usual. The Varauhanuddy, which washes the rock on which the temple stands, flows from south to north. This combination of directions is particularly auspicious in Hindoo estimation, and the shrine, under the name of Oottara vauhiny, is held in great veneration. On the river bank is a small bed of pulverized shale, which, from its resemblance to ashes, is declared to be the site of a sacrifice performed by Baly [q.v.] chuckravurty [q.v.].——*Bayyavaram* (బయ్యవరము - bayyavaramu, Tel.). From (bayyana, tel. proper name + pura, san. town). Proprietary estate, Village; pop. 909; from Narsapatam S.E. 7 miles; from Vizagapatam W. 38 miles. Peshcush Rs. 851.——*Calingacondah* (కళింగకొండ - kalingakonda, Tel.). From (kalinga, san. ancient kingdom + konda, tel. hill). Trig. station; lat. 17° 49′ 42·31″; long. 82° 21′ 07·75″; height 4,645 feet; from Ghausy village N. 1½ miles; from Golcondah N.W. 15 miles; from Narsapatam W. 22 miles.——*Cheroocondah* (చెరువుకొండ - cheruvukonda, Tel.). From (cheruvu, tel. tank + konda, tel. hill); after the tank on the hill. Trig. station; lat. 17° 52′ 22·72″; long. 82° 11′ 18·24″; height 4,741 feet; from Goodem W. 2¾ miles; from Golcondah N.W. 25 miles; from Narsapatam W. 34 miles.——*Comararole* (కోమరవోలు - kómaravólu, Tel.). See sep. title.——*Dhaura* (ధార - dhárá, Tel.). Means stream. Trig. station; lat. 17° 44′ 01·86″; long. 82° 30′ 55·50″; height 4,095 feet; from Golcondah N. 4 miles; from Narsapatam W. 10 miles.——*Dhauracondah* (ధారకొండ - dhárakonda, Tel.). From (dhárá, san. stream + konda, tel. hill). Hill; lat. 17° 58′; long. 82° 15′; from Narsapatam N.W. 33 miles; from Vizagapatam N. 72 miles.——*Golcondah* (గొలుగొండ - golugonda, Tel.). See below.——*Goodem* (గూడెము - gúdemu, Tel.). Means a hamlet. Village; pop. 480; lat. 17° 52′; long. 82° 14′; from Jeypore S.W. 72 miles; from Narsapatam W. 30 miles; from Vizagapatam W. 72 miles. Ancient capital of the Bhoopaties, former Zemindars of Golcondah.——*Gubbauda* (గబ్బాడ - gabbáda, Tel.). From (gabbu, tel. stench + váda, tel. village). Village; acres 1,585; lat. 17° 43′; long. 82° 38′; from Narsapatam N.N.W. 3 miles; from Vizagapatam W. 44 miles.——*Juggampett* (జగ్గంపేట - jaggampéta, Tel.). From (jaggamma, tel. proper name + péta, tel. suburb). Zemindarry, Village; pop. 1,055; acres 538; lat. of village 17° 34′; long. 82° 30′; from Narsapatam S.W. 12 miles; from Vizagapatam W.S.W. 52 miles. Residence of Ooratla proprietor. Peshcush Rs. 282.——*Narsapatam* (నరసపట్టణము - narasapattanamu, Tel.). See sep. title.——*Nullacondah* (నల్లకొండ - nallakonda, Tel.). From (nalla, tel. black + konda, tel. hill). Trig. station; lat. 17° 44′ 10·51″; long. 82° 48′ 23·45″; height 1,607 feet; from Cottacote E.S.E. 4½ miles; from Golcondah E.N.E. 20 miles; from Narsapatam E. 11 miles.——*Ooratla* (ఉరట్ల - uratla, Tel.). From (úru, tel. village + úta, tel. fountain). Proprietary estate, Village; pop. 2,746; lat. of village 17° 34′; long. 82° 43′; from Narsapatam S.E. 9 miles; from Vizagapatam W. 40 miles. Peshcush Rs. 14,954.——*Pagoolraulloo* (పగులురాళ్లు - pagulurállu, Tel.). From (pagulu, tel. to break + ráyi, tel. stone). Trig. station; lat. 17° 46′ 43·20″; long. 82° 17′ 37·55″; height 3,760 feet; from Bodraulla N. 3½ miles; from Golcondah W. 16 miles; from Narsapatam W.N.W. 25 miles.——*Paidipaula* (పైడిపాల - paidipála, Tel.). From (paidi, tel. gold + pádu, tel. village). Town; pop. 7,010; lat. 17° 38′; long. 82° 46′; from Narsapatam S.E. 8¼ miles; from Vizagapatam W. 37 miles. Attached are five hamlets.——*Pandoor mullavaram* (పండూరుమల్లవరము - pandúrumallavaramu, Tel.). From (pandu, tel. fruit + úru, tel. village + mallavaramu, tel. place so called). Proprietary estate, Village; pop. 1,087; acres 135; lat. of village 17° 39′; long. 82° 31′; from Narsapatam W. 8½ miles; from Vizagapatam W. 52 miles. Peshcush Rs. 1,608.——*Paundavoola condah* (పాండవులకొండ - pándavulakonda, Tel.). From (pándava, san. the pándavás + konda, tel. hill). Trig. station; lat. 17° 40′ 54·88″; long. 82° 15′ 42·06″; height 2,669 feet; from Bodalore S.W. 4 miles; from Golcondah W. 16 miles; from Narsapatam W. 25 miles.——*Sanjeevy* (సంజీవి - sanjívi, Tel.). Trig. station; lat. 17° 31′ 21·44″; long. 82° 43′ 52·00″; height 2,145 feet; from Golcondah S.E. 16 miles; from Ooratla S. 3 miles; from Narsapatam S.S.E. 11 miles.——*Sowdvauda* (చౌడువాడ - tsauduváda, Tel.). From (tsaudu, tel. saline soil + váda, tel. village). Proprietary estate, Village; pop. 682; lat. of village 17° 33′; long. 82° 46′; from Narsapatam S.E. 11 miles; from Vizagapatam W. 37 miles. Peshcush Rs. 952.——*Varauhanuddy* (వరాహనది - varáhanadi, Tel.). See sep. title.——**(2)** Village; Vizagapatam dist., Golcondah tal.; pop. 1,838; acres 11,883; lat. 17° 41′; long. 82° 31′; from Coraputt S.S.W. 78 miles; from Madras N.N.E. 342 miles; from Narsapatam W. 8¾ miles; from Parvatipore S.W. 98 miles; from Vizagapatam W. 56 miles; from Vizianagram W. 68 miles. Formerly belonged to Golcondah zemindarry [q.v.]. In 1836, in consequence of murder of Ranee [q.v.], the estate was sequestrated and zemindar [q.v.] imprisoned. In following year estate was brought by Government at auction. In 1845 chiefs rose in rebellion, and held their ground for three years; and again in 1857–58 it was found neccssary to send troops against thom.

GOLD (सुवर्ण - suvarna, *San.*). Common prefix.——*Gold flower tree* (सुवर्णक - suvarnaka, San.). Same as Common condray.——*Gold mohur tree* (कृष्णचूडा - krishnachúdá, San.; शंकाशूर - shankáshúra, Mahr.; रत्नगंधि - ratnagandhi, Conc.; گل مور - gulmor, Hind.; ರತ್ನಗಂಧಿ - ratnagandhi, Can.; ರತ್ನಗಂಧಿ - ratnagandhi, Too.; పమిడితంగేడు - pamiditangédu, Tel.; ചെത്തിമന്ദാരം - chettimandáram, Mal.; මොනරමල් - monaramal, Singh.; மயிற்கொன்றை - mayirkkonrai, Tam.). Title by corruption from hindostany (gulmor, hind. peacock flower). San. from (krishna, san. the god + chúdá, san. top); krishnan's crest jewel. Conc. from (ratna, san. gem + gandha, san. smell); from variegated flowers. Hind. means peacock flower. Can. from (ratna, san. gem + gandha, san. smell). Tel. from (pamidi, vulgar for paidi, tel. gold + tangédu, tel. cassia auriculata, linn.). Mal. from (chetti, mal. red + mandáram, mal. bauhinia variegata, linn.). Singh. from (monará, singh. peacock + mal, singh. flower); from variegated petals. Tam. from (mayil, tam. peacock + konrai, tam. cassia fistula, linn.); from variegated crimson flowers. Hind. also (guliturrah), meaning tassel + flower. Can. also (kenchige), meaning fair tree. Tel. also (réla); (turáyi), meaning head ornament. Mal. also (teççimandáram); (chekkimandáram), by corruption. Title otherwise Barbadoes flower, Barbadoes pride, Fleurde paradis, Flower-fence, Golden tungaid, Krishna chooran, Peacock condray, Peacock flower, Spanish carnation, Tassel flower, Torye flower. Botanically Cæsalpinia [coobairaucshy] pulcherrima, s.w., leguminosæ [vricsham, 48]. Alias Poinciana alata, bijuga, pulcherrima. Shrub, 8–10 feet, armed; sepals five, obtuse, unequal, lower one vaulted; æstivation imbricative; leaves bipinnate; leaflets obovate-oblong, retuse or emarginate; calyx glabrous on both sides; petals five, fringed on long claws, the upper one shaped differently from the others; racemes terminal, corymbiform; style very long; legume two-valved, several-seeded; flowers orange, variegated with crimson; flowering nearly all year; common in gardens; native of w. indies, here naturalized. The bark is ash-colored, smooth, thickly studded with small elliptic corky warts, the whole of the suber readily separates like birch bark, disclosing a streaky, mottled, green and pink surface, which is marked by numerous small scars corresponding to the warts above mentioned; the substance and internal surface of the bark is of a pinkish tinge; taste rather nauseous, very astringent. All parts are powerfully emmenagogue; roots are acid and tonic and in excess are poisonous; leaves are in decoction purgative, and used for senna [q.v.]; seeds in powder are remedy in colic; flowers and fruit also used medicinally. Flower is offered to shiva; the whole an ornamental hedge-plant. The wood makes good charcoal [adooppkary].——*Gold root* (काञ्चनी - káñchaní, San.). Same as Country saffron.

GOMOOTY (گومتی - gomutí, *Malay*; குமுதிப்பனை - kumuthippanai, *Tam.*). Malay also (aren); (anau). Tam. also (ségóvarisi), meaning sago rice. Title otherwise Ejoo palm, Sago palm, Singapore sago. Botanically Arenga saccharifera, labill., palmaceæ [vricsham, 149]. Generic from malay. Alias Borassus gomutus; Saguerus rumphii. Gomutus from malay. A very large palm [taur]; throws up erect from sides of trunk large shining black-green leaves, which take a plume-like curve towards summit; flower largish yellow, purple. Of importance second only to cocoa palm in the rural economy of the asiatic archipelago from one extremity of it to the other; it takes there the place of the palmyra [q.v.] or borassus flabelliformis of the continent of india. Heart of stem contains large quantities of sago [q.v.]; flower stalks yield a sugary sap made into sugar [jaggery] and palm wine [toddy]. From the black horse-hair-like fibres, or gomooty surrounding the petioles of the leaves, cordage and cables are made; the mid ribs of the side leaves are converted into pens and fine arrows, which malayans blow from long tubes; at the base of the leaves a fine woolly material called baroo [q.v.] is employed in caulking ships, as stuffing for cushions and as tinder. Timber extremely hard and fit for building. No other common species here.

GOND (गोण्ड - gónda, *San.*; گونڈ - gond, *Hind.*; కోడు - kódu, *Tel.*). From (konda, tel. hill). Dravidian language and people; mostly in the N. portion of Central provinces, but also some 8,000 in Ganjam district. A few in Kurnool district also speak the Gayety [q.v.] variety of Gond language. Its chief difference from the other Dravidian dialects consists in its peculiarly elaborate conjugational system. Not to be confounded with Khond [q.v.], though has affinity [bhaushay, coyi, jauty].

GOND (निर्यास - niryása, *San.*; गोंद - gónda, *Mahr.*; صمغ - samagh, *Ar.* and *Pers.*; گوند - gond, *Hind.* and *Dec.*; پولت - pulut, *Malay*; ಗೊಂದು - góndu, *Can.*; ಅಂಟು - antu, *Too.*; బంక - banka, *Tel.*; പശ - pasha, *Mal.*; ලාටු - látu, *Singh.*; பிசின் - pisin, *Tam.*). Title from hindostany. San. from (nis, san. out + yas, san. to exude). Mal. from (pashumai, tam. moistness). Can. also (antu). Gum.——(1) The word gum properly speaking is confined to those natural exudations which solidify on exposure to the air, but are easily redissolved by water; they are often transparent, but vary in tint from white to reddish brown. Under this term however the exudation of a variety of trees is included. When only in part soluble in water, and the rest soluble in alcohol, the exudations bear the name of gum-resins [googal]; these are chiefly used in medicine. When insoluble in water, but soluble in alcohol, ether, and volatile oils, they are resins [raul]; these are used for the most part in preparing dyes [shauyam], varnishes [rangh], lacquers [q.v.], sealing-wax [lac], &c. The resins include also balsams [q.v.] and oleo-resins [teilam]; balsams are semi-solid or liquid exudations from plants, and containing either benzoic acid [sambrauny poo] or an essential oil [attar], or both; oleo-resins are resins combined with volatile oils [yennay]; on distillation the oil passes over, leaving a resin behind. Besides these the elastic gums [pauchonty] belong to the gum class; india rubber and caoutchouc are their types; they come from the indian archipelago. Some gums exude from the fruit and not from the bark [dragon's blood]. There are also some resinous substances as cutch [q.v.], camphor [q.v.], &c., which are artificial decoctions [kwautam] from the bark or wood. The following are two key-lists in the briefest possible terms of the principal indigenous gums of s. india as above defined; further information must be traced in the glossary paragraphs through the small-type cross-references at end of this volume; see also vricsham, 7, for the method of expressing the products, &c., of the plants in the dravidian languages.—"*a*" Acacia arabica, babool, gum; acacia catechu, catechu, cutch and gum; Acacia farnesiana, cassie oil plant, gum; Acacia ferruginea, anasandra, gum; Acacia leucophlæa, white babool, gum; Acacia sundra, sundra, gum; Achras sapota, sapodilla, gum; Adenanthera pavonina, false red sanders, gum; Ægle marmelos, bael, gum; Ailantus exoelsa, coromandel ailanto, gum; Ailantus malabarica, malabar ailanto, resin; Albizzia amara, dark sirissa, gum; Albizzia lebbek, common sirissa, gum; Albizzia odoratissima, fragrant sirissa, gum; Albizzia procera, var. elata, hill sirissa, gum; Albizzia stipulata, stone sirissa, gum; Alstonia scholaris, dita, guttapercha; Altingia excelsa, java storax, resin; Anacardium occidentale, cashew, gum; Anogeissus latifolia, vekkauly, gum; Antiaris saccidora, sack tree, resin and inspissated juice from fruit; Aquilaria agallocha, eagle-wood, resin; Areca catechu, areca, catechu; Argemone mexicana, mexican poppy, sap; Artocarpus hirsuta, anjely, concreted juice; Artocarpus incisa, ratadel, gum; Artocarpus integrifolia, bread-fruit, gum; Artocarpus lakoocha, lakoocha, gum; Balsamodendron berryi, kiloovay, gum-resin; Balsamodendron mukul, mookul bdellium, gum-resin; Balsamodendron myrrha, myrrh, gum-resin; Balsamodendron roxburghii, indian bdellium, gum-resin; Bassia latifolia, wild mohwah, gum; Bassia longifolia, common mohwah, gum; Bauhinia purpurea, purple mountain ebony, gum; Bauhinia racemosa, small-flowered mountain ebony, gum; Bauhinia retusa, nirpa mountain ebony, gum; Bauhinia vahlii, large mountain ebony, gum; Bauhinia variegata, variegated mountain ebony, gum; Bombax malabaricum, red-cotton tree, gum; Borassus flabelliformis, palmyra, gum; Boswellia carterii, true olibanum, gum-resin; Boswellia serrata, yellow dammer, gum-resin; Buchanania latifolia, chironjee, gum and varnish; Butea frondosa, bengal kino, gum; Calamus draco, sumatra dragon's blood, resin; Calophyllum inophyllum, common poon, resin; Calophyllum tomentosum, malabar poon, gum; Calotropis gigantea, mudar, gutta-percha; Canarium commune, elemi, resin and oil; Canarium strictum, black dammer tree, resin; Carapa molucoensis, crab-oil plant, resin; Careya arborea, hindostany slow match, gum; Cassia auriculata, tungaid, resin; Cassia fistula, indian laburnum, gum; Casuarina equisetifolia, whip tree, resin; Cedrela toona, toon, gum and resinous substance; Chickrassia tabularis, chickrassy, gum; Chloroxylon swietenia, satin wood, gum; Cinnamomum camphora, camphor cinnamon, camphor; Citrus aurantium, orange, gum; Citrus decumana, pummelow, gum; Citrus medica, lime, gum; Cochlospermum gossypium, golden silk cotton, gum; Cocos nucifera, cocoanut, gum; Convolvulus scammonia, scammony, gum-resin; Cordia rothii, narrow-leaved sebestens, gum; Cryptostegia grandiflora, paulay silk cotton, caoutchouc; Cycas circinalis, indian sago palm, gum; Dalbergia latifolia, malabar black wood, gum; Dalbergia paniculata, yellow mountain ebony, gum; Dichopsis elliptica, indian gutta-percha, gutta-percha; Diospyros embryopteris, gaub, gum from fruit; Diospyros melanoxylon, coromandel ebony, gum; Elæodendron glaucum, nerija, gum; Eriodendron anfractuosum, silk-cotton tree, gum; Erythrina indica, common coral tree, gum; Eucalyptus globulus, blue gum, gum; Eugenia jambolana, common jaumoon, gum; Euphorbia antiquorum, square milk-hedge, gum-resin; Euphorbia cattimandoo, cement plant, milky sap; Euphorbia tirucalli, round milk-hedge, milky sap; Feronia elephantum, wood-apple, gum; Ferula narthex, asafœtida, gum; Ficus bengalensis, banyan, milky sap; Ficus glomerata, cluster fig, gum prepared from milky juice; Ficus religiosa, peepul, milky juice; Garcinia cambogia, malabar gamboge, gum-resin; Garcinia mangostana, mangosteen, gum-resin; Garcinia morella, ceylon gamboge, gum-resin; Garcinia xanthochymus, yellow mangosteen, gum-resin; Gardenia lucida, decamallee, gum-resin; Garuga pinnata, gargooga, gum-resin; Gossypium herbaceum, indian cotton, gum; Hardwickia binata, yaipy, balsamic oleo-resin; Hopea parviflora, water caung, gum; Jatropha curcas, physic nut, juice; Lagerstrœmia flos-reginæ.

adambo, gum-resin; Lagerstrœmia parviflora, loose strife, gum-resin; Liquidambar orientale, indian storax, resin; Macaranga indica, round-leaved lotus, resin; Mangifera indica, mango, gum-resin; Melia azadirachta, margosa, gum; Melia azedarach, large neem, gum; Mesua ferrea, nauga champak, resin; Mimusops elengi, ilanjy, gum; Mimusops hexandra, monkey-face paulay, gum; Mimusops kauki, edible paulay, gum; Moringa pterygosperma, indian horse-radish, gum; Morus indica, indian mulberry, gum; Odina wodier, wodier, gum; Ougeinia dalbergioides, nemmy, gum; Phœnix sylvestris, wild date, gum; Phyllanthus emblica, emblic myrobalan, gum; Piper cubeba, cubeb pepper, resin; Poinciana elata, indian poinciana, gum; Poinciana regia, flamboyant, gum; Pongamia glabra, indian beech, gum; Prosopis spicigera, shamee, gum; Prunus amygdalus, almond, tragacanth; Prunus communis, bokhara plum, tragacanth; Pterocarpus indicus, andaman red-wood, gum; Pterocarpus marsupium, malabar kino, gum-resin; Punica granatum, pomegranate, gum; Sapindus trifoliatus, soap-nut tree, gum; Schleichera trijuga, ceylon oak, resin; Semecarpus anacardium, marking-nut tree, gum and varnish; Sesbania grandiflora, west indian sesban, gum; Shorea robusta, common saul, resin; Shorea talura, taloora saul, gum; Shorea tumbuggaia, tambaga saul, dammer; Spondias mangifera, hog plum, gum; Sponia wightii, indian nettle, gum; Sterculia urens, false tragacanth, gum; Sterculia villosa, odul tree, gum; Styrax benzoin, gum benjamin, resin; Tectona grandis, teak, resin and oil; Terminalia arjuna, arjoon, gum; Terminalia belerica, belleric myrobalan, gum; Terminalia catappa, country almond, gum; Terminalia chebula, chebulic myrobalan, gum; Terminalia tomentosa, var. typica, black murdah, gum; Thespesia populnea, portia, gamboge from capsule; Vateria indica, piney tree, resin; Ventilago madraspatana, pappily, gum; Woodfordia floribunda, godaury, gum; Wrightia tinctoria, paula indigo, gum; Xylia dolabriformis, burmah iron-wood, resin; Zizyphus jujuba, bair, gum; Zizyphus nummularia, forest bair, gum.—"*b*" Adambo, lagerstrœmia; Ailanto, ailantus; Almond, prunus, terminalia; Anasandra, acacia; Anjely, artocarpus; Arjoon, terminalia; Asafœtida, ferula; Babool, acacia; Bael, ægle; Bair, zizyphus; Banyan, ficus; Bdellium, balsamodendron; Beech, pongamia; Benjamin, styrax; Black-wood, dalbergia; Blue gum, eucalyptus; Bread-fruit, artocarpus; Cashew, anacardium; Cassie, acacia; Catechu, acacia; Caung, hopea; Cement plant, euphorbia; Champak, mesua; Chickrassy, chickrassia; Chironjee, buchanania; Cinnamon, cinnamomum; Cocoanut, cocos; Coral tree, erythrina; Cotton, gossypium; Crab oil, carapa; Cubeb pepper, piper; Dammer, boswellia, canarium; Date, phœnix; Decamallee, gardenia; Dita, alstonia; Dragon's blood, calamus; Eagle-wood, aquilaria; Ebony, diospyros; Elemi, canarium; Fig, ficus; Flamboyant, poinciana; Gamboge, garcinia; Garooga, garuga; Gaub, diospyros; Godaury, woodfordia; Gutta-percha, dichopsis; Horse radish, moringa; Ilanjy, mimusops; Indigo, wrightia; Iron-wood, xylia; Jaumoon, eugenia; Kiloovay, balsamodendron; Kino, butea, pterocarpus; Laburnum, cassia; Lakoocha, artocarpus; Lime, citrus; Loose strife, lagerstrœmia; Lotus, macaranga; Mango, mangifera; Mangosteen, garcinia; Margosa, melia; Marking nut, semecarpus; Mexican poppy, argemone; Milk-hedge, euphorbia; Mohwah, bassia; Mountain ebony, bauhinia, dalbergia; Mudar, calotropis; Mulberry, morus; Murdah, terminalia; Myrobalan, phyllanthus, terminalia; Myrrh, balsamodendron; Neem, melia; Nemmy, ougeinia; Nerija, elæodendron; Nettle, sponia; Oak, schleichera; Odul, sterculia; Olibanum, boswellia; Orange, citrus; Palmyra, borassus; Pappily, ventilago; Paulay, mimusops; Peepul, ficus; Physic nut, jatropha; Piney, vateria; Plum, prunus, spondias; Pomegranate, punica; Poon, calophyllum; Portia, thespesia; Pummelow, citrus; Ratadel, artocarpus; Red cotton, bombax; Red sanders, adenanthera; Red-wood, pterocarpus; Sack tree, antiaris; Sago palm, cycas; Sapodilla, achras; Satin-wood, chloroxylon; Saul, shorea; Scammony, convolvulus; Sebestens, cordia; Sesban, sesbania; Shamee, prosopis; Silk cotton, cochlospermum, cryptostegia, eriodendron; Sirissa, albizzia; Slow match, careya; Soap nut, sapindus; Storax, altingia, liquidambar; Sundra, acacia; Teak, tectona; Toon, cedrela; Tragacanth, sterculia; Tungaid, cassia; Vekkauly, anogeissus; Whip tree, casuarina; Wodier, odina; Wood-apple, feronia; Yaipy, hardwickia.——(2) The gums proper are sometimes divided into three heads, as follows.—"*a*" True gums. Acacia arabica [babool]; Acacia catechu [catechu]; Acacia farnesia [piyvail]; Acacia ferruginea [anasandra]; Acacia sundra [sundra]; Adenathera pavonina [false red sanders]; Ægle marmelos [bael]; Anacardium occidentale [cashew]; Anogeissus latifolia [vekkauly]; Artocarpus integrifolia [jack]; Barleria prionitis [common nail dye]; Bassia longifolia [common mohwah]; Bauhinia racemosa [small-flowered mountain ebony]; Bauhinia retusa [nirpa mountain ebony]; Bauhinia vahlii [large mountain ebony]; Borassus flabelliformis [palmyra]; Buchanania latifolia [chironjee]; Careya arborea [coomby]; Cassia fistula [common condray]; Cedrela toona [toon]; Chickrassia tabularis [chickrassy]; Chloroxylon swietenia [satin-wood]; Citrus decumana [pummelow]; Citrus medica [lime]; Cocos nucifera [cocoanut]; Cordia rothii [narrow-leaved sebestens]; Erythrina indica [common coral tree]; Feronia elephantum [wood-apple]; Garuga pinnata [garooga]; Gossypium herbaceum [indian cotton]; Gyrocarpus jacquini [tanakk]; Heriteira littoralis [soondree]; Holarrhena antidysenterica [tellicherry bark]; Jatropha curcas [wild aumanac]; Melia azadirachta [neem]; Melia azedarach [large neem]; Michelia champaca [champak]; Mimusops elengi [ilanjy]; Mimusops kauki [edible paulay]; Morus indica [indian mulberry]; Odina wodier [wodier]; Phœnix sylvestris [wild date]; Phyllanthus emblica [emblic myrobalan]; Poinciana elata [soonkeswaram]; Poinciana regia [foreign tungaid]; Pongamia glabra [karanj]; Prosopis spicigera [shamee]; Prunus domestica [auloo chah]; Prunus persica [shaft auloo]; Punica granatum [anaur]; Sapindus trifoliatus [soap-nut tree]; Schleichera trijuga [ceylon oak]; Semecarpus anacardium [marking nut]; Soymida febrifuga [soymida]; Spondias mangifera [wild mango]; Sponia wightii [indian nettle]; Tamarindus indica [tamarind]; Tamarix dioica [cypress jhow]; Terminalia arjuna [white murdah]; Terminalia belerica [belleric myrobalan]; Terminalia catappa [catapang]; Terminalia tomentosa [murdah]; Thespesia populnea [portia]; Wrightia tinctoria [paula indigo]; Zizyphus jujuba [bair].—"*b*" Pseudo gums. Ailantus excelsa [coromandel ailanto]; Bombax malabaricum [red-cotton tree]; Cochlospermum gossypium [golden silk cotton]; Cycas circinalis [indian sago palm]; Eriodendron anfractuosum [silk cotton]; Macaranga indica [round-leaved nelumbo]; Moringa pterygosperma [moringa]; Sterculia balanghas [balanghas]; Sterculia colorata [wild papaw]; Sterculia fœtida [bastard poon]; Sterculia urens [false kateerah].—"*c*" Astringent gums. Butea frondosa [palaus]; Sesbania grandiflora [west-indian sesban]; Pterocarpus indicus [padouk]; Pterocarpus marsupium [common vengay].——(3) For gum-resins see Googal; for true resins see Raul; for balsams see Balsam; for oleo-resins see Teilam; for elastics see Pauchonty. For so-called mineral resins see also under Raul; for animal gelatine see Vajram; for vegetable gelatine see Nishastah; for gum as a pharmacographical prefix, see Gum.

GONDY (ಗೊಂಡಿ - gondi, *Can.*; గొంది - gondi, *Tel.*). Lane. Suffix in place names; as Holalgondy, meaning bright street.

GONG (జేగంట - dzáganta, *Tel.*; சேமக்கலம் - shémakkalam, *Tam.*). Title from malay. Tel. from (jaya, san. victory + ghantá, san. bell). Tam. from (kshéma, san. security + kalam, tam. vessel). Formerly beaten by watchmen. Flat and generally circular piece of bell metal [cunts] beaten in temples [coil] at the time of worship [poojah]. A small gong is carried in hand by Dausaries [q.v.] and Pundaurams [q.v.], which they strike in begging alms. It is also used at non-bramin funeral ceremonies. In north of presidency it is used in private houses when worshipping household gods [ghantay, ghurry, griha devatay].

GOOD (கூடு - kúdu, *Tam.*). To join [coodal]. Cf. Coodoo and Coor.——*Gooda* (గూడ - gúda, Tel.; கூடை - kúdai, Tam.). From (kúdu, tam. to unite). Basket [tokrah]. For irrigation used when water to be raised is nearly on a level with the surface of the field to be irrigated; this is made impenetrable with a coating of cowdung [shauny] and clay [calimunn], and is suspended by four cords; two men hold a cord in each hand, draw up the water, and empty it in balancing the basket with a swing [chuckram, yaittam]. Goodoo on Neilgherries is a basket of grain received by the Todahs [q.v.] as fee from the Kotar [q.v.], Iroolar [q.v.], and Badagas [q.v.].——*Goodalore* (ഗൂഡല്ലൂർ - gútalúr, Mal. gúdalúr *). From (kútal, mal. meeting + úr, mal. village).—"*a*" Deputy tahsildarry, Neilgherry district. Pay Rs. 100 + Wynand allowance Rs. 50.—"*b*" Village, Deputy tahsildar's station, Talook head-quarters, Sub-registrar's office, District moonsif's court, Public bungalow; Neilgherry dist., Wynaud S.E. division; lat. 11° 30′; long. 76° 32′; from Coimbatore N.W. 49 miles; from Coonoor W.N.W. 23 miles; from Devaulah E.N.E. 8 miles; from Kotagherry W.N.W. 26 miles; from Madras W.S.W. 280 miles; from Ootacamund W.N.W. 15 miles; from Pundalore E.N.E. 11 miles. At foot of ghaut [q.v.] of same name and at junction of main roads from Mysore and Malabar. Chief town of Numbalagode amshom [q.v.]. Since 1850 the centre of S.E. Wynaud coffee [q.v.] industry, and a place of growing importance. Transferred with surrounding country to jurisdiction of Neilgherry district in 1877. A hospital.—"*c*" Ghaut; Neilgherry dist., Wynaud S.E. division; from Goodalore E. 2¾ miles; from Ootacamund W. 12 miles. So named from village at its base. The old trace was exceedingly rough and steep, the descent being only 4 miles. The new ghaut, which follows mainly the N. face of a spur of the hills, was completed in 1868. From the crest at Nediwuttam near Government cinchona [koinah] plantations to its base distance is 8 miles, and from thence to Goodalore 3 miles. The gradient is easy, being in no case more than one in nineteen. It has eight zigzags. From Goodalore a road runs N.E., and connects this line with Seegore line near Teppacaud, a distance of 11 miles. ——*Goodauram* (గుడారము - gudáramu, Tel.). A tent [derah]. ——*Goodda* (ಗುಡ್ಡೆ - gudde, Can.; గుడ్డ - gudda, Tel.). From (gudi, tel. circle); from being wound round the body. A cloth. The dress of a woman is a single cloth, generally colored [saury, sheelay]. See vol. I (98).——*Goodda* (ಗುಡ್ಡ - gudda, Can.). Hillock [gadda, gootta]. Suffix in place names. Plant first term often joining two genera. Ex., where transl. is of second term:—Careya arborea (guddadaippémara), bassia longifolia; Elæocarpus lancæfolius (guddanérale), eugenia jambolana. See gloss paragraphs.——*Goodem* (గూడెము - gúdemu, Tel.). From (gúdu, tel. nest). Collection of huts. Suffix in place names;

as Gollagoodem, meaning shepherds' hamlet [cooppam].——*Goodicutt* (గుడికట్టు - gudikattu, Tel.). From (gudi, tel. village + kattu, tel. tie). The whole extent of land attached to a village [ayacut].——*Goodivauda* (గుడివాడ - gudiváda, Tel.). See sep. title.——*Goodiyattam* (గుడియాతము - gudiyátamu, Tel.). See sep. title.——*Goodoor* (గూడూరు - gúdúru, Tel.). See sep. title. ——*Goodoovancherry* (گرانچری - guráncharí, Hind.; கூடுவாஞ்சேரி - kúduváñjéri, Tam. gúduváncheri *). From (kúdu, tam. to meet + shéri, tam. village); junction village. Village, Post office, Railway station; Chingleput dist., Chingleput tal.; pop. 831; acres 552; lat. 12° 51′; long. 80° 07′; height 111 feet; from Chingleput N. 12 miles; from Sydapett S.W. 16 miles; from the sea W. 13 miles. Several cairns [maundavar coozhy]. Travellers' bungalow [q.v.]. Suipe [ollaun] east of this.——*Goody* (گڑی - gurí, Hind.; ಗುಡಿ - gudi, Can.; గుడి - gudi, Tel.; കുടി - kuti, *Mal.*; குடி - kudi, Tam.). From (kúdu, tam. to meet).—"*a*" Temple [coil, dewal, pagoda]. Suffix in place names; as Munnargoody, meaning king's temple.—"*b*" Agricultural village. Suffix in place names, especially in Madura and Tanjore, as Maungoody, meaning mango tree + village [coody].——*Goody* (గుడి - gudi, Tel.). From (kúdu, tam. to unite). Round [goondoo].——*Goomidy* (గుమ్మడు - gummadu, Tel.). Means clustering. Same as Cashmere tree.——*Goomma* (గుమ్మ - gumma, Tel.). From (kúdu, tam. to unite). Grain receptacle.——*Goommy* (గుమ్మి - gummi, Tel.). From (kúdu, tam. to unite). Corn-basket. Swamp [parroo]. ——*Goompany* (గుంపెన - gumpena, Tel.). Same as Wodier.——*Goompey* (ಗುಂಪೆ - gumpe, Can.). From (kúdu, tam. to bring together); heap [cooppa]. Hillock.——*Goondaur* (குண்டாறு - kundáru, Tam.). From (kundu, tam. rock + áru, tam. river). Sanscrit name (shanmukhanadí), meaning soobramanyan, the six-faced god + river. River; Madura dist., Tirmungalam tal. and Ramnaud zemindarry. Formed by junction of several streams rising in eastern slopes of Varshanaud and Andiputty ranges above Watrap, Oottapa naickanore, and Doddappa naickanore, and uniting about lat. 9° 36′ N.; long. 78° 12′ E. United stream flows south-east almost parallel to Veigay. Entering Ramnaud zemindarry on north near Cariyaputty, it takes a winding easterly course of about a mile, and thence turns almost south five miles passing by Toppoor and Paranjally, where it receives the Shevericottah flowing from the mountains in Tinnevelly district. It widens considerably at the confluence, and then flows south-easterly between Tirshooly and Pullimadam, washing the western wall of the fort, to Ilooppore. North of Ilooppore it is intersected by a brook from the highlands east of Pillaiyaurnuttam. From Ilooppore it winds eastwardly for six miles and passes by Mundal maunicam, and, flowing south-easterly two miles and a half, turns due south to Camoothy, running between the fort and town. East of this town it is obstructed by a large and massive stone dam, about 170 feet in length and 70 in breadth. A large channel [q.v.] called the Raghoonaut cauvery carries off its waters in an easterly direction to the Calary tank. It issues through the southern portion of the dyke, passes through the salt marshes lying below the village of Veigay, continues from Camoothy towards the south-east for 22 miles, and empties its surplus waters into the Gulf of Manaar at Mookkoorputnam in lat. 9° 8′ N.; long. 78° 33′ 30″ E. Total length 95 miles. The river is narrow and rapid. Its mouth is wide but shallow, and a heavy shoal renders free access of boats at the mouth impracticable.——*Goondla* (గుండ్ల - gundla, Tel.). Locative plural. Suffix in place names; as Gosigoondla, meaning pointed rocks.——*Goondlacumma* (గుండ్లకమ్మ - gundlakamma,* Tel.). From (gundu, tel. rock + kanama, tel. pass). Sanscrit name (gandiká) meaning declivity. River; Kurnool, Kistna, and Nellore districts. Rises in the Nullamalays near Goondlabrambeshwar in lat. 15° 40′ N.; long. 78° 47′ E., and after receiving two mountain torrents, the Zampalair and Yenoomoolair, enters the plains through the gorge of Cumbum, and winding round the town of Cumbum, turns to the north, its easterly course being obstructed by the base of the Veligonda [q.v.] hills. Here it forms western boundary of Podily and south-western boundary of Darshy divisions of Nellore district. In the gap near Cumbum a dam 57 feet in height has been thrown up, and a fine sheet of water known as the Cumbum tank [q.v.] about 4 miles long by three or four broad and fifteen in circumference formed. After a tortuous course through Marcapore of nearly 40 miles, quits Kurnool district entering Kistna district at Moommadivaram, 10 miles from Vinoocondah. Below Moommadivaram it changes its course to the east and then to the south, and, flowing to the south and south-east of Ongole talook, falls into the sea near Pedda devarampaud about 12 miles north of Ongole. Present mouth is a mile south of the old mouth or Pauta goondlacumma, and not far from the villages of Goondaya pollem and Naccavaury pollem, hamlets of Devarampaud. It is always open, 602 yards during monsoons [q.v.] and 256 in hot season. At high tide water in the bar is $1\frac{1}{2}$ yards, and the river may be used for navigation for two miles inland. The fall of its bed is from three to four feet per mile. There are freshes in September, October and November. It has a perennial flow. A full fresh is sometimes 32 feet.——*Goondoo* (గుండు - gundu, Tel.; குண்டு - kundu, Tam.). Round, rock.——*Goondoo colata* (గుండుకొలత - gundukolata, Tel.). From (gundu, tel. round + kolutsu, tel. measure). Finding the area of a village by measuring the perimeter.——*Gooppa* (గుప్ప - guppa, Tel.; குப்பை - kuppai, Tam.). From (kuppintsu, tel. to collect). Heap. Suffix in place names [cooppa].——*Gootta* (ಗುಟ್ಟ - gutta, Can.; గుట్ట - gutta, Tel.). From (kúdu, tam. to unite). A heap of rocks [goodda]. Suffix in place names; as Bollagootta, mean white hill.——*Goottagoodda* (ಗುಟ್ಟ ಗುಡ್ಡ - guttagudda, Can.). A rocky hill.——*Gooty* (గుత్తి - gutti, Tel.). See sep. title.

GOOD (गुड् - gud, *San.*). To preserve, defend.——*Gola deepicay* (கோளதீபிகை - kólathíbigai, Tam.). From (góla, san. globe + dípiká, san. lamp). Modern tract by Sharvana permaul ayyan. Only known Tamul original work on geography [bhoogola shastram]. It consists of Pooraunic geography from the Sanscrit.——*Golah* (گولا - golá, Hind.). From (gol, hind. round); from the typical form. Granary [ganj, gunj]. ——*Golam* (गोल - góla, San.). From (gud, san. to defend). Globe. Golandauz, from (golah, pers. cannon ball + andáz, pers. thrower) is an artilleryman. Bhoogolam is earth [bhoomy] or terrestrial globe; bhagolam or khagolam is heaven or celestial globe. Golaurdham is a hemisphere; dacshina golaurdham is southern and cottara golaurdham is northern hemisphere; andagolam or egg-shaped globe is prolate spheroid, chapatagolam or flattened globe is oblate spheroid.——*Golayantram* (गोलयन्त्र - gólayantra, San.; ذات الحلق - zátulhalk, Ar.). San. means sphere + machine. Ar. from (zát, ar. possessed of + halk, ar. circle); instrument consisting of circles or rings merely and not a globe like the Hindoo instrument [maunam]. Armillary sphere. Vedha valayam is the intersecting circle of declination therein. The Golayantram is placed so that the axis shall point to the pole [dhroovam], and the horizon [cshitijam] be true by a water-level. The instrument being thus placed, the observer is instructed to look at the star Veidhrity [q.v.] through a sight fitted to an orifice at the centre of the sphere; and having found the star, to adjust by it the end of the sign [raushy] Pisces [meenam] on the ecliptic [craunty mundalam]. The observer is then to look through the sight at the yogam [q.v.] star of Ashwiny [q.v.], or at some other proposed object; and to bring the moveable circle of declination over it. The distance in degrees [bhaugam], from the intersection of this circle and ecliptic to the end of Meenam or Pisces, is its fixed longitude or dhroovacam [q.v.] in degrees; and the number of degrees on the circle of declination [craunty], from the same intersection to the place of the star [nacshatram], is its latitude or vicshaipam [q.v.], north or south. When the point measured to is the equinoctial colure [maishauyanamundalam] instead of the end of meenam, dhroovacam becomes sauyanam [q.v.]. It is considered by some that the Greek astronomers reckoned longitudes upon the ecliptic intersected by circles of declination instead of by circles of celestial latitude, in the manner which has been here explained [jyotisham].——*Gordam* (गुड - guda, San.). Treacle [goor].——*Goodauk* (गुडक - gudaka, San.; گڑاکو - gurákú, Hind.; ಗುಡಾಕು - gudáku, Can.; గుడాకు - gudáku, Tel.; ചക്കരപ്പുകയില - chakkarappukayila, Mal.; குடாக்கு - kudákku, Tam.). San. from (guda, san. sugar lump). Hind. from (gur, hind. treacle + áku, tel. leaf). Mal. from (chakkara, mal. jaggery + pukayila, mal. tobacco). Composition for the hookah [q.v.]. Consists of tobacco [pogauk], pounded with jaggery [q.v.], plantain [q.v.] fruit and sandalwood [sandal] powder ,or some other aromatic.——*Googal* (वृक्षनिर्यास - vrikshaniryása, San.; مقل - mukl, Ar.; بوئی جہودان - búijahúdán, Pers.; گگل - gogil, Hind.; گوگل - gúgal, Dec.; ಮರದಂಟು - maradantu, Can.; గుగ్గిలము - guggilamu, Tel.; ഗുല്ഗുലു - gulgulu, Mal.; மரப்பிசின் - marappisin, Tam.). Title through hindostany. San. from (vriksha, san. tree + niryása, san. gum). Pers. from (bú, ar. fragrance + jahúdán, pers. jews), being used by them as fumigatory [bdellium, mookul bdellium]. Hind. from (guggula, san. resin). Can. from (mara, can. tree + antu, can. gum). Tel. from (gud, san. to preserve), useful in nervous diseases. Tam. from (maram, tam. tree + pisin, tam. gum). Ar. also (aflátan). Gum-resin. Tree exudation consisting of true gum [gond] and resin [raul] mixed, so that it requires both water and alcohol to dissolve it entirely. These are chiefly used in medicine and perfumery. The best known googal is indian bdellium [q.v.], product of Balsamodendron roxburghii, arn., burseraceæ. The following however is a complete list of such :—Emulsive; Garcinia cambogia [malabar gamboge]; Garcinia mangostana [mangosteen]; Garcinia morella [ceylon gamboge]; Garcinia xanthochymus [yellow mangosteen]. Foetid; Dorema ammoniacum [ooshak]; Ferula galbaniflua [galbanum]; Ferula narthex [asafœtida]; Gardenia lucida [decamallee]. Fragrant; Balsamodendron mukul [mookul bdellium]; Balsamodendron myrrha [bole]; Balsamodendron roxburghii [indian bdellium]; Mangifera indica [mango]; Styrax benzoin [benzoin]. See gloss. paragraphs. The term googal is popularly confined to the last or fragrant class of gum-resin.——*Goolaca* (గులక - gulaka, Tel.). Shingles for roofings [parookkay cull].——*Goolancha* (गुडूची - gudúchí, San.; गुळवेल - gulavéla, Mahr.; अमृतवेल - amritavéla, Conc.; گلو - gilo, Ar.; گل بیل - gulbel, Pers.; گلنچا - gulanchá, Hind.; گل بیل - gulbel, Dec.; ಅಮೃತಬಳ್ಳಿ - amritaballi, Can.; ಅಮೃತಬೂರು - amritabúru, Too.; తిప్పతీగ - tippatíga, Tel.; ചിറ്റമൃത - chittamritu, Mal.; അമൃതവള്ളി-

rasakinda, Singh.; சிந்தில் - shíndil, Tam.). Title from hindostany. San. from (gud, san. to protect). Mahr. from sanscrit. Ar. from (gudúchí, san. the plant). Pers. from (gul, pers. the plant + bel, pers. creeper). Hind. from sanscrit. Dec. from persian. Can. from (amrita, san. ambrosia + balli, can. creeper). Too. from (amrita, san. ambrosia + búru, too. creeper). Tel. from (tippa, tel. dunghill + tíga, tel. creeper). Mal. from (chiru, mal. small + amritu, mal. nectar, the plant). Singh. from (rasa, san. juice + kinda, singh. the plant). Tam. from (shí, tam. to destroy); medicinal. San. also (amritá), meaning not perishing [chebulic myrobalan, emblic myrobalan, wild bachnaug]; (sómavallí), meaning moon creeper; (góraksha), meaning cow-protecting; (pittaghní), meaning bile destroying; (bhishakpriyá), meaning dear to physicians [chebulic myrobalan]; (nirjará), meaning not perishing; (chhinnaruhá), meaning growing when cut; (vatsádaní), meaning edible to children; (jívantiká), meaning enlivening [indian nettle]; (vishalyá), meaning thornless; (madhuparní), meaning sweet-leaved; refers to sweetish variety. Hind. also (gurach), from sanscrit meaning cow protecting. Can. also (uganiballi); (amaradaballi), meaning nectar + creeper. Tel. also (manapála); (dúyutíga); (galúchi). Mal. also (amritu), meaning nectar; (peyyamritam), meaning raining nectar. Singh. also (kinda). Tam. also (amiruthavalli), meaning nectar creeper; (kaippuçcindil), meaning bitter variety; (narchindil), meaning good + the plant; (porchindil), meaning gold + the plant; refers to sweetish variety in hilly tracts, which is yellow within when broken; (shíndircharkkarai), meaning seendil sugar. the medicinal salt from stem. Title otherwise Amritavully, Bile-killer, Cow protector, Goolbel, Heart-leaved moon seed, Moon Creeper [gandhaulee, somam], Shindie, Somavully. Botanically Tinospora cordifolia, miers, menispermaceæ [vricsham, 5]. Alias Cocculus convolvulaceus, cordifolius; Menispermum cordifolium, glabrum, malabaricum. Twining shrub; bark thick corky, slightly tubercled; leaves alternate, roundish-cordate, with a broad sinus, shortly and sharply pointed, glabrous; racemes axillary or lateral, of male flowers longer than the leaves, pedicels several together, of female ones scarcely so long as the leaves; pedicels solitary; petals unguiculate; unguis linear, slightly margined upwards; limb triangular, ovate, reflexed; drupes two to three globose; flowers small, yellowish; flowering all the year. Runs over the highest trees; from the branches drop fibres, which enter the ground; found in every hedge. Goolancha root consists of dried transverse segments of the woody stem, varying in diameter from one-quarter of an inch to two inches, and from half an inch to two inches in length; they have a shrunken appearance, and are covered with a smooth shrivelled bark, some of the pieces being marked on their surface with warty prominences; inodorous, of a very bitter taste. The roots, stems, and a watery extract are medicinal; alterative, tonic, antiperiodic and antipyretic. Infusion; take of the stem or root, cut into small pieces and slightly bruised, two ounces and a half; boiling water, one pint; macerate in a covered vessel for two hours and strain. Tincture; take of the stem or root, cut into small pieces and bruised, five ounces; proof spirit, one pint; macerate for seven days in a closed vessel, with occasional agitation, filter and add sufficient spirit to make one pint. The watery extract palo [q.v.] is called indian quinine [koinah] by some hakeems [q.v.]; generally adulterated with cheaper substances; the real palo is either tasteless or slightly bitterish in taste, white in color if it is prepared from the roots, and greenish-white or greenish-brown if from the stems; it occurs in powder or loose and flat cake-like pieces; it is prepared easily by cutting the fresh stem into small pieces, which are bruised in a stone or wooden mortar and soaked in water from six to twelve hours; the mass is then rubbed, squeezed and separated from the fluid by straining the latter through cloth; the fluid being evaporated to dryness in the sun, the residue is the palo; the thicker the creeper or its root is, the better; the plant is known to attain sometimes the thickness of a man's arm. Doses; of the infusion, from one to three fluid ounces; of the tincture, from one to two fluid drachms; of the extract, from one to two drachms. Substituted for Jamaica sarsaparilla, Potass. iodid., Quinine and other alkaloids of cinchona [koinah], James powder, Pulv. cinchon. and Pulv. antimonialis. Goolancha when it grows on a margosa [neem] tree is most efficacious as a medicine. At ceremonies plant bruised and put into water, which is drunk by bramins [q.v.]. Cf. Somam. There are other species:—crispa, malabarica, tomentosa; equally tonic. Compare Indian berry.——*Goolican* (குளிகன் - kuligan, Tam.). One of the seven invisible planets [graham]:—Rahoo, kait, goolican, yamacandan, hastapraharan, caulan, arcan. Goolican is called son of saturn [shany]. Goolica caulam is the time when goolican is in motion in a certain fixed direction in each day of the week; this is marked in calendar [punchaungam] and regarded as auspicious [rahoocaulam, vauram].——*Gooligey* (ಗುಳಿಗೆ - gulige, Can.). From (guda, san. ball). Globular. The form ಗು with a numeral is employed in old accounts for expressing pagodas [q.v.]. Also pill in pharmacy.——*Goor* (गुड़ - gur, Hind.; గుడము - gudamu, Tel.). From (gud, san. to preserve). Jaggery [goodam, jaggery].——*Gowda* (गौड - gauda, San.; گور - gaur, Hind.). From (guda, san. sugar), the sugar country. From the province and now ruined city of Gowr, long the capital of Behar and Bengal. Supposed to be the Gangia regia of Ptolemy. One of the two-fold divisions of Bramins [q.v.], into Gowda or Northern and Dravida or Southern. Also as Gowdas proper, a sub-division of the general Gowdas. At present the languages which may be considered Gowda are the Bengalee, Hindee, Hindostany, Punjauby, Goozeratty and Mahratta [bhaushay, jauty]. Distinguish from the canarese form of Gownden [q.v.]. See vol. II, 226.——*Gowdee* (गौडी - gaudí, San.). The Bengal dialect.——*Gowndla* (గౌండ్ల - gaundla, pl. obl., Tel.). From (gaudí, san. spirit from molasses). Caste of toddy [q.v.] drawers. Numbers about 40,000 [jauty]. Distinguish from Gaundla.——*Gowra* (गौर - gaura, San.). Bengalee form of Gowda.

GOODA (ଗଡ଼ - gudá, *Oor.*). Fort [gada, ghur, godo].

GOODIVAUDA (గుడివాడ - gudiváda,* *Tel.*). From (gudi, tel. temple + váda, tel. street) [good]. Sanscrit name (bhíméshvara), meaning bheeman [q.v], the hero + lord.——**(1)** Talook, Kistna district. Tahsildar's pay Rs. 200. Area 595 square miles. Language Teloogoo. Deltaic talook north of Masulipatam and comprising greater part of Colair lake. Bounded north by Ellore talook of the Godavery district, and east by Bheemavaram talook in Godavery district, south by Bunder talook, west by Noozveed zemindarry. Plain low lying. Regar [q.v.] soil. Paddy [q.v.], gunny [q.v.] bags and cumblies [q.v.]. Irrigation by Kistna anicut [q.v.]. Places of archæological interest:—Colair lake, Colleticote, Conoocull, Cowtaram, Culdindy, Goodivauda, Keicalore, Mundapaud, Singanapoody, Vinnacote. The leading places, &c., in the talook are the following.——*Boodamair* (బుడమేరు - budaméru, Tel.). See sep. title.——*Chevendra** (చేవేంద్ర - chévéndra, Tel.). From (ché, tel. field + véndramu, tel. heat). Zemindarry, Village; pop. 1,039; square miles 3·23; lat. of village 16° 21′; long. 81° 09′; from Goodivauda S.E. 10 miles; from Masulipatam N.N.W. 12 miles. Peshcush Rs. 4,728.——*Colair* (కొల్లేరు - kolléru, Tel.). See sep. title.——*Colleticote* (కొల్లేటికోట - kollétikóta, Tel.). See sep. title.——*Conoocull* (కొనుకొల్లు - konukollu, Tel.). From (kona, tel. corner + kollu, tel. pond). Village; pop. 1,329; acres 2,613; lat.; 16° 28′; long. 81° 10′; from Goodivauda E.N.E. 8¾ miles; from Masulipatam N. 19 miles. Fort said to have been built by Reddies [q.v.]. Captured by Captain Macleane of Colonel Forde's army on 3rd March 1759. Mussalman coins are found.——*Cowtaram* (కౌతరము - kautaramu, Tel.). From (gautamu, tel. pasture + pura, san. town). Village, Assistant engineer's head-quarters; pop. 2,414; acres 3,299; lat. 16° 20′; long. 81° 07′; from Goodivauda S.E. 8¾ miles; from Masulipatam N.N.W. 11 miles. Probably Booddhist. Temple built by Reddy chiefs.——*Culdindy* (కల్దిండి - kaldindi, Tel.). From (kallu, tel. stone + dindi, tel. stumps). Village; pop. 2,104; acres 8,780; lat. 16° 30′; long. 81° 21′; from Goodivauda E.N.E. 20¾ miles; from Masulipatam N.N.E. 24 miles. On a large plain of black soil [regar]. Old mud fort built by Mahomedans. Shiva temple of Bhogeshwaraswamy. Festival on Shivarautry [pundigay, 6a] in February. Stone-built reservoir with two perennial springs in front of temple. ——*Goodivauda* (గుడివాడ - gudiváda, Tel.). See below.——*Goorza* (గురజ - guradza, Tel.). From (kuraja, tel. class of shepherds so called). Village; pop. 2,269; acres 1,721; lat. 16° 25′; long. 81° 08′; from Goodivauda E.S.E. 7¼ miles; from Masulipatam N. 16 miles. Residence of family of Caumadauna zemindars.——*Keicalore* (కైకలూరు - kaikalúru, Tel.). See sep. title.——*Paumarroo* (పామఱ్ఱు - pámarru, Tel.). From (pámu, tel. snake + arru, tel. neck of land). Village; pop. 2,949; acres 4,476; lat. 16° 20′; long. 81° 00′; from Goodivauda S.S.W. 7¾ miles; from Masulipatam N.W. 14 miles. Bunder canal sends off branch here to irrigate Goodivauda talook. Lock and bridge. Choultry [q.v.].——*Vinnacote* (విన్నకోట - vinnakóta, Tel.). From (vinna, tel. dilapidated + kóta, tel. fort). Village; pop. 1,942; acres 3,491; lat. 16° 23′; long. 81° 07′; from Goodivauda S.E. 7¼ miles; from Masulipatam N.N.W. 13 miles. Inscription north-east of the village dated A.D. 1438.——**(2)** Town, Tahsildar's head-quarters; Kistna dist., Goodivauda tal.; pop. 4,732; acres 5,066; lat. 16° 26′; long. 81° 02′; from Bezwada E. 25 miles; from Guntoor E.N.E. 37 miles; from Madras N.N.E. 236 miles; from Masulipatam N.N.W. 20 miles; from Vinoocondah E.N.E. 84 miles. Ruined Booddhist [booddha] tope [q.v.] almost demolished. Four caskets found in it. West is a fine Jeina [q.v.] statue, also the site of old village. Andhra coins [naunyam], metal stone and glass beads [munkah] of all kinds of good workmanship, and heaps of massive pottery [chatty] have been found amongst the gravel and earth. Bheemeshwaran temple with inscriptions.

GOODIYATTAM (గుడియాతము - gudiyátamu, *Tel.*; குடியாத்தம் - kudiyáttam, *Tam.* gudiyátam*). From (gudi, tel. temple + yátamu, tel. picottah) [good].——**(1)** Talook, North arcot district. Tahsildar's pay Rs. 175. Area 446 square miles. Length from S.W. to N.E. nearly 50 miles, average breadth 9 miles. Population 176,709. Language Tamul. S. centre of district. Forms a long strip lying upon N. bank of Palaur and opposite Vellore talook. Bounded west by Pulmanair; north by Chittore; its narrow eastern border adjoins Wallajahpet, the

Poyney marking the boundary. The western portion is composed of hills, spurs of the Eastern ghauts [q.v.], interspersed with valleys. The Chittore hills run for a short distance into the north. The strip which borders the Palaur is generally flat. Chief elevations are Codimoocmala, Keilausagherry or Amboor droog, Sautghur hills, and Vandarantaungal hill. About 50 square miles are covered with jungle which produces timber only fit for fuel. Soil is good, being generally a mixture of sand and red clay; in a few parts it is blackish resembling black cotton soil [regar], and more commonly a grey compound of sand and dark clay. Very rich in iron [auhau]. Lime [choonam] and building stone [cull] are also quarried to a large extent. The chief manufacture is that of female cloths [sheelay]. In a few villages coarse cumblies [q.v.] are made by Coorumbar [q.v.]. Superior pottery [chatty] is also made from clay [calimunn]. Besides Palaur and Poyney, which flow along borders, there are small rivers rising in hills and flowing S. into Palaur, as the Cowndinyanuddy or Goodiyattam and the Goddaur or Amboor. Sixty-three spring channels [q.v.]. The Poyney anicut [q.v.] feeds five tanks [q.v.]. Chief tanks are Cautpaudy, Cauvanore, Chervangy, Cumbaroyapooram, Daurapadavaid, Lauttairy, and Veppore. Places of archæological interest:—Amboordroog, Bramhapooram, Caungyanullore, Cauraputt, Cauvanore, Chervangy, Cholamore, Comauramungalam, Coogaynullore, Eeshamputt, Keelputt, Kemparajapooram, Lauttairy, Malayambutt, Malayaputt, Oodayendram, Oolly, Pashoomauttore, Pullaundiputt, Rajacull, Saitoocaray, Sautghur, Tennamputt, Tirmany, Tirvallam, Toottiputt, Veppore. Principal Trig. station:—Sautghur. The leading places, &c., in the talook are the following.——*Amboor droog* (ஆம்பூர்த்துருக்கம் - ámbúrtturukkam, Tam.). See Amboor.——*Caungyanullore* (காங்கயநல்லூரு - kángayanallúru, Tam.). From (gángéya, san. gold + nal, tam. good + úr, tam. village); cf. caungyam. Sanscrit name (gangéshvarapura), means town of gangeshwaran, a deity. Village; pop. 1,707; acres 1,438; lat. 12° 57′; long. 79° 12′; from Chittore S.S.E. 19 miles; from Goodiyattam E. 19¼ miles.——*Cauraputt* (காரப்பட்டு - kárappattu, Tam.). From (kárai, tam. thorny webera, canthium parviflorum, lam. + pattu, tam. village). Village; acres 11,936; lat. 12° 46′; long. 78° 41′; from Chittore S.W. 43 miles; from Goodiyattam S.W. 20 miles. Rock-cut cave with frescoes.——*Cautpaudy* (காட்டுப்பாடி - káttuppádi, Tam. kátpádi *). From (kádu, tam. jungle + pádi, tam. village). Village, Railway station; pop. 2,511; acres 4,105; lat. 12° 58′; long. 79° 11′; height 696 feet; from Chittore S.S.E. 18 miles; from Goodiyattam E. 18¾ miles. Junction of Goontacull and Villoopooram, sections of respectively Madras and S. indian railway lines.——*Cauvanore* (காவனூர் - kávanúr, Tam.). From (ká, tam. grove + van, tam. great + úr, tam. village). Village; pop. 1,681; acres 1,788; lat. 12° 57′; long. 79° 01′; from Chittore S.S.W. 20 miles; from Goodiyattam E. 7½ miles. Jeina [q.v.] remains.——*Codimoocmala* (కోడిముక్కుమల - kódimukkumala, Tel.). From (kódi, tel. fowl + mukku, tel. beak + mala, tel. mountain). Hill; resemblance to fowl's beak.——*Cowndinyanuddy* (కౌండిన్యనది - kaundinyanadi, Tel.). See sep. title.——*Dhaurapadavaid* (தாரப்படவேடு - tárappadavédu, Tam.). From (dhárá, san. stream + padavédu, tam. town so called). Village; pop. 3,323; acres 2,696; lat. 12° 58′; long. 79° 11′; from Chittore S. 17 miles; from Goodiyattam E. 18 miles. Tank. Vellore railway station.——*Goodiyatam* (குடியாத்தம் - kudiyáttam, Tam.). See below.——*Lauttairy* (இலாட்டேரி - ilátteri, Tam.). From (lát, hind. pillar + éri, tam. tank). Village; pop. 1,922; acres 1,698; lat. 12° 58′; long. 79° 07′; from Chittore S. 17 miles; from Goodiyattam E. 14 miles. Jeina remains. Tank.——*Mahadevamullay* (மகாதேவமலை - magáthévamalai, Tam.). From (mahá, san. great + déva, san. god + malai, tam. mountain). Village, Hill; pop. 1,283; lat. 13° 00′; long. 79° 00′; from Chittore S.S.W. 18 miles; from Goodiyattam E.N.E. 7½ miles. Sacred temple of Shiva on hill. The pious place cooked rice [q.v.], ghee [q.v.], and milk [paul] in hollows of rock. Two vultures [gidh] appear exactly at noonday, bathe in the milk, eat the rice and ghee, and fly away. Said never to die, and to come every day from Tircalicoondram in Chingleput district, where they are always seen at 10 A.M. They are the abodes of the spirits of two Bramins, Shambaran and Sampauty.——*Malayambutt* (மலையம்பட்டு - malayambattu, Tam.). From (malayam, tam. mountain + pattu, tam. village). Village; acres 1,237; lat. 12° 46′; long. 78° 42′; from Chittore S.W. 43 miles; from Goodiyattam S.W. 20 miles. Painted rock.——*Oodayendram* (உதயேந்திரம் - uthayéndiram, Tam.). From (udaya, san. rising + indra, san. the god). Village; pop. 2,677; acres 1,356; lat. 12° 42′; long. 78° 40′; from Chittore S.W. 48 miles; from Goodiyattam S.W. 24¼ miles. 1½ north of Vaniyambaudy railway station. Temple with inscriptions.——*Palaur* (பாலாறு - páláru, Tam.). See sep. title.——*Pernambutt* (பெரணம்பட்டு - peranambattu, Tam.). From (pér, tam, great + aranam, tam. jungle fort + pattu, tam. village). Village; pop. 4,639; acres 4,984; lat. 12° 56′; long. 78° 46′; from Chittore S.W. 32 miles; from Goodiyattam W. 10½ miles. Large trading town, a mile from Sautghur. Population chiefly Lubbays [q.v.] trading in jaggery [q.v.], ghee [q.v.], tamarinds [q.v.] and hides [chamrah], which they collect in Pulmanair talook and bring down upon bullocks by the Talapoolla ghaut [q.v.]. Handsome mosque [musjid] of modern date.——*Poyney* (పోయిని - póyini, Tel.). See sep. title.——*Sautghur* (ساتگڑ - sátgarh, Hind.). See sep. title.——*Shengoondram naud* (செங்குன்றநாடு - shengunramnádu, Tam.). From (shem, tam. red + kunram, tam. hill + nádu, tam. country). Pop. 1,548; acres 3,477; lat. 13° 00′; long. 78° 54′; from Chittore south-west 21 miles; from Goodiyattam north 4 miles. Part of Padoovore cottam in the ancient Tondaimundalam [q.v.]. In the present Goodiyattam talook, North arcot district.——*Synigoonta* (శ్యానిగుంట - shyánigunta, Tel.). See sep. title.——*Tirvallam* (திருவல்லம் - tiruvallam, * Tam.). (From tiru, tam. holy + villam, tam. holy bael tree, ægle marmelos, corr.). Sanscrit name (shríbilvakshétra), means holy place of bael trees, ægle marmelos, corr.; also (bílvakshétra), means place of bael trees. Village, Railway station; pop. 1,326; acres 706; lat. 12° 59′; long. 79° 18′; height 629 feet; from Chittore S.E. 20 miles; from Goodiyattam E. 26¾ miles. On the Poyney. Temple to Vilvanauteshwaran. Devotees worship with the leaves of Vilvam [bael]. Large tank.——*Vandarantaungal* (வெண்டரந்தாங்கல் - vendarandángal, Tam.). From (ven, tam. white + taram, tam. hill + tángal, tam. pond). Village; pop. 1,981; acres 4,162; lat. 12° 59′; long. 79° 10′; from Chittore S. 16 miles; from Goodiyattam E. 17¼ miles. Two miles north of Vellore railway station.——**(2)** Town, Tahsildar's station, Railway station; North arcot dist., Goodiyattam tal.; pop. 18,747; acres 704; lat. 12° 57′; long. 78° 55′; height 867 feet; from Arnee W.N.W. 34 miles; from Chittore S.W. 24 miles; from Madras W. 96 miles; from Ranipett W. 31 miles; from Tripatty S.W. 60 miles; from Vellore W. 18 miles. Three miles north of Palaur. Divided into two by Cowndinyanuddy. Includes six suburbs. The town is modern. Temple, built 250 years ago by a Canarese named Holiyappa, in honor of Baula shaurdooleshwaran. Chief industry is weaving. Lubbays [q.v.], Vauniyar [q.v.], and Canarese merchants carry on trade. The first in jaggery [q.v.], hides [chamrah], tamarind [q.v.], tobacco [pogauk], and ghee [q.v.]; the second in grain [dhaunyam] and oil [yennay]; the last keep petty shops and are money lenders. Large cattle [maund] fair every Tuesday which rivals that of Ranipett. The Synigoonta pass [ghaut] leads hence to Mysore.

GOODOOR (గూడూరు - gúdúru, *Tel.* gúdúr *). From (gúdu, tel. hut + úru, tel. village) [good]. Greek for the Kistna village κόδουρα.——**(1)** Zemindarry, Village; Kistna dist., Bunder tal.; pop. 3,580; acres 2,609; lat. of village 16° 13′; long. 81° 07′; from Masulipatam N.W. 3¾ miles; from the sea W. 7½ miles. Peshcush Rs. 35,588. Large village on the Hyderabad road. Fragrant flower plants are grown here.——**(2)** Talook, Nellore district. Tahsildar's pay Rs. 200. S. coast part of district. Bounded:—north by Nellore talook; west by Raupore talook; south in part by Polore division; E. by sea. The Shreeharicote division, the southernmost portion, formerly appertained to Madras district but was transferred in 1865. The climate is healthy except in Shreeharicote. The eastern part contains handsome topes [q.v.] of palmyra [q.v.] and casuarina [chowkmaram] trees and has a good supply of water. Numerous mango [q.v.] and margosa [neem] trees with extensive paddy [q.v.] fields. The western part is dry and the scarcity of water is felt in some years. In the south, comprising Shreeharicote range, there are extensive thick jungles the products of which are largely exported to Madras by the Buckingham canal [q.v.] which runs close by. The soil is fertile for the most part. The western part of the talook is rocky and is suited for cultivation of dry crops. Agriculture forms chief industry; paddy and indigo [q.v.] are largely exported. Weaving to some extent. The north-eastern part is irrigated under Pennair anicut [q.v.]; the rest by tanks [q.v.] and small ponds. Though the Swarnamookhy river is seldom in freshes for more than a few days at a time, it supplies water to tanks in the south. Camping grounds:—Bhairipett, Boodanam, Bramhadevam, Cadivaid, Causipooram, Chendode, Chengalpollem, Chennore, Chintavaram, Chittaid, Chittamore, Cottapatam, Cullore, Doogarauzpatam, Doorgavaram, Eepoor, Goodoor, Goonoopaud, Goorvindapoody, Kistnapatam, Kotah, Lutchmakka khandriga, Manoobole, Metta, Momidy, Mootcore, Moottembauca, Moottiaulpaud, Muddauly, Nellipoody, Pambaly, Pidatapolore, Ponnavole, Poody, Pootsalapully, Reddipollem, Roodravaram, Royadorvoo, Sarwapully, Siddhavaram, Toopily, Toracutla, Vaucaud, Vaulamaid, Venaud, Vencatachellam choultry, Vendode, Vulloor, Wodore, Wojelly, Yairore, Yargautipulley, Yellashiry. Places of archæological interest:—Armegam, Doogarauzpatam, Monapollem, Penoobarty, Shreeharicote. Principal Trig. stations:—Bandaldorvoo, Bullavole, Canoopore, Cottapatam, Doogarauzpatam, Goodaly, Jonangipollem, Kistnapatam, Oottamanellore, Poolinjericooppam beacon, Pootsalapulley. The leading places, &c., in the talook are the following.——*Armegam* (ஆறுமுகம் - árumugam, Tam.). See sep. title.——*Bandaldorvoo* (బండలదొరువు - bandaladoruvu, Tel.). From (banda, tel. rock + doruvu, tel. well). Trig. station; lat. 14° 18′ 11·30″; long. 79° 58′ 40·64″; height 149 feet; from Canoopore S.E. 3 miles; from Goodoor N.N.E. 12 miles; from the sea W. 14 miles.——*Blackwood's harbour* (మోనపాలెమురేవు - monapálemurévu, Tel.). See sep. title.——*Bullavole* (బల్లవోలు - ballavólu, Tel.). From (balu, tel. lofty + prólu, tel. town). Trig. station; lat. 14° 6′ 53·89″; long. 80° 5′ 33·68″;

from Canoopore W. 2 miles; from Goodoor E.S.E. 14 miles; from the sea W. 5 miles.——*Cadivaid* (కడివేడు - kadivédu, Tel.). From (kada, tel corner + vídu, tel. town). Village; pop. 1,749; acres 7,774; lat. 14° 50′; long. 79° 57′; from Goodoor S.E. 6½ miles; from Nellore S.S.W. 27 miles; from the sea W. 15 miles. A ruined fort built before the Mahomedan government by Raivillavaur family.——*Canoopore* (కనుపూరు - kanupúru, Tel.). From (kanapa, tel. a grass, vitis carnosa, wall. + úru, tel. village). Trig. station; lat. 14° 7′ 25·70″; long. 80° 8′ 5·73″; from Bullavole E. 2¾ miles; from Goodoor E.S.E. 16 miles; from the sea W. 2 miles.——*Chella caulwa* (చల్లకాలువ - tsállakálava, Tel.). From (tsalla, tel. cool + kálava, tel. stream). Small river. This is the lower portion of the stream of water called Maumidy caulwa from its source up to its junction with Swarnamookhy at Goodaly, and Chella caulwa from this point to its mouth. It takes its rise in a jungle near Attivaram and flowing through Wojelly, Cooroogonda, Goodaly, and Kotah, falls into the Bay of Bengal at Siddhavaram. ——*Chennore* (చెన్నూరు - chennúru, Tel.). See sep. title.——*Chillacore* (చిల్లకూరు - chillakúru, Tel.). From (chilla, tel. small + úru, tel. village). Village; pop. 675; acres 2,676; lat. 14° 8′; long. 79° 55′; from Goddoor S.S.E. 1½ miles; from Nellore S.S.W. 23½ miles; from the sea W. 18 miles. On route from Madras to Nellore.——*Chintavaram* (చింతవరము - chintavaramu, Tel.). From (chinta, tel. tamarind, tamarindus indica, linn. + pura, san. town); from abundance of tamarind [q.v.] trees in the village. Village; pop. 580; lat. 14° 09′; long. 80° 05′; from Goodoor E. 12 miles; from Nellore S.S.E. 22 miles; from the sea W. 6 miles. Ruined fort built by Reddy royadoo, once a renter under the Zemindar of Vencatagherry.——*Condoor pollem* (కొండూరుపాళెము - kondúrupálemu, Tel.). From (konda, tel. hill + úru, tel. village + pálemu, tel. fortified village). Village, a hamlet of Doogarauzpatam; lat. 14° 00′; long. 80° 12′; from Goodoor E.S.E. 22½ miles; from Nellore S.S.E. 33 miles; from the sea W. ½ mile. The bar is opposite to the Doogarauzpatam travellers' bungalow [q.v.].——*Cottapatam* (కొత్తపట్నము - kottapatnamu, Tel.). From (kotta, tel. new + pattana, san. town). Trig. station at the beacon; lat. 14° 5′ 37·95″; long. 80° 10′ 31·72″; from Goodoor E. 18 miles; from Siddhavarám E. 2 miles; from the sea W. 1 mile.——*Doogarauzpatam* (దుగరాజపట్నము - dugarájapatnamu, Tel.). See sep. title.——*Goodaly* (గూడలి - gúdali, Tel.). From (kúdali, tel. junction), at junction of swarnamookhy and chella caulwa. Village; pop. 1,050; acres 3,386; lat. 14° 01′; long. 80° 04′; from Goodoor S.E. 14½ miles; from Nellore S. 30¼ miles; from the sea W. 9 miles. Built by a Chola tondiman [q.v.]. At the junction of the Swarnamookhy and Chella caulwa. Annual festival of Sangameshwara sawmy about March or April. Fine handkerchiefs [roomaul] made. Trig. station in lat. 14° 01′ 09·45″; long. 80° 03′ 40·54″; height 299 feet; from Chendode S. 1½ miles; from Goodoor S.E. 14 miles; from the sea W. 9 miles.——*Goodoor* (గూడూరు - gúdúru, Tel.). See below.——*Iroocam* (ఇరుకము - irukamu, Tel.). From (iruku, tel. narrow). Island, in Poolicat lake, Goodoor talook; lat. 13° 34′; long. 80° 11′; from Nellore S. 61 miles; from the sea W. 8 miles.——*Jonangipollem* (జోనంగిపాళెము - dzónangipálemu, Tel.). From (dzónangi, tel. mahomedan of lowest order + pálemu, tel. fortified village). Trig. station; lat. 13° 38′ 36·46″; long. 80° 13′ 56·10″; height 31 feet; from Goodoor S.S.E. 42 miles; from Jonangipollem S. 1 mile; from the sea W. 3 miles ——*Kistnapatam* (కృష్ణపట్నము - krishnápatnamu, Tel.). See sep. title.——*Kota* (కోట - kóta, Tel.). See sep. title.——*Manoobole* (మనుబోలు - manubólu, Tel.). From (mannu, tel. wild ox + prólu, tel. town). Village, Railway station; pop. 3,038; acres 13,388; lat. 14° 12′; long. 79° 55′; from Goodoor N.N.E. 3½ miles; from Nellore S.S.W. 19 miles; from the sea W. 17 miles.——*Momidy* (మోమిడి - mómidi, Tel.). After a barber of that name. Village; pop. 2,668; acres 7,610; lat. 14° 12′; long. 80° 05′; from Goodoor E.N.E. 13 miles; from Nellore S.S.E. 18 miles; from the sea W. 5½ miles. Ancient temple to Coota coteshwaraswamy on southern bank of Kistnapatam backwater. ——*Monapollem* (మొనపాళెము - monapálemu, Tel.). See sep. title.——*Mootcore* (ముత్తుకూరు - muttukúru, Tel.). See sep. title. ——*Moottyaulpully* (ముత్యాలపల్లి - mutyálapalli, Tel.). From (muttayya, tel. proper name + palli, tel. village). Village; pop. 977; lat. 14° 07′; long. 79° 56′; from Goodoor S.E. 3¾ miles; from Nellore S.S.W. 24½ miles; from the sea W. 16¼ miles.——*Oottamanellore* (ఉత్తమనెల్లూరు - uttamanellúru, Tel.). From (uttama, san. the best + nellúru, tel. place so called). Trig. station; lat. 14° 3′ 42·35″; long. 80° 7′ 8·62″; from Carlapoody S. 1¾ miles; from Goodoor E.S.E. 17 miles; from the sea W. 4 miles.——*Paumanjy* (పామంజి - pámanji, Tel.). From (pámu, tel. snake + anja, tel. mark). Village, Port; pop. 314; lat. 14° 04′; long. 80° 09′; from Goodoor E.S.E. 18½ miles; from Kistnapatam S. 15¾ miles; from Madras N. 67½ miles; from Nellore S.S.E. 28 miles; from Toopily N. 3½ miles. Near mouth of Swarnamookhy. Exports native ornaments and grain.——*Poody royadoruvoo* (పూడిరాయదొరువు - púdiráyadoruvu, Tel.). From (púdi, tel. place so called + ráyadu, tel. king + doruvu, tel. well). Tel. also (púdi), meaning village. Village, Point; lat. 13° 52′; long. 80° 16′; from Goodoor S.E. 31½ miles; from Nellore S.S.E. 43¾ miles. Chuttram [q.v.] on the beach, and a building erected by the Zemindar [q.v.] of Vencatagherry.——*Poolinjericooppam beacon* (పులింజేరికుప్పందీపస్తంభము - pulinjérikuppamdípastambhamu, Tel.). From (puli, tam. tamarind tree, tamarindus indica, linn. + shéri, tam. village + kuppam, tam. village). Trig. station; lat. 13° 37′ 11·66″; long. 80° 16′ 57·73″; from Goodoor S.E. 45 miles; from Pulleveedhy E. 1½ miles; from the sea W. ¼ mile.——*Pootsalapully* (పుచ్చలపల్లి - puttsalapalli, Tel.). From (puttsa, tel. a kind of melon, cucumis trigonus, roxb. + palli, tel. village). Trig. station; lat. 14° 2′ 25·92″; long. 80° 8′ 51·79″; from Goodoor E.S.E. 18 miles; from Vaulamaid N.W. ¾ mile; from the sea W. 2½ miles.——*Sarwapully* (సర్వపల్లె - sarvapalle, Tel.). See sep. title.——*Shreeharicote* (శ్రీహరికోట - shríharikóta, Tel.). See sep. title.——*Swarnamookhy* (స్వర్ణముఖి - svarnamukhi, Tel.). See. sep. title.——*Tammenupatam* (తమ్మెనపట్నము - tammenapatnamu, Tel.). See sep. title.——*Tayappa chuttram* (తయప్పసత్రము - tayappasatramu, Tel.). From (tayappa, tel. proper name + satramu, tel. choultry). Called after Tayappa moodelly who built the choultry [q.v.]. Village; lat. 14° 02′; long. 80° 11′; from Goodoor E.S.E. 20½ miles; from Nellore S.S.E. 30¼ miles; from the sea W. ⅛ mile.——*Tinnelapoody* (తిన్నెలపూడి - tinnelapúdi, Tel.). From (tunniya, tel. piece + púdi, tel. village); because granted out piece-meal. Village; pop. 392; acres 980; lat. 14° 01′; long. 80° 05′; from Goodoor S.E. 16 miles; from Nellore S.S.E. 31 miles; from the sea W. 7½ miles. On bank of Swarnamookhy south of Kota. A renter called Velama condama naidoo made a grant of portions of land taken from the three villages of Kota, Vaucaud, and Yargautipulley to a bramin, Orooganty anna daunam bhatt, an ancestor of the present curnum [q.v.]. There are some stone idols [vigraham] here, probably belonging to the Jeinas [q.v.].——*Toopily* (తూపిలి - túpili, Tel.). From (túrpu, tel. east + palli, tel. village). Village, Port; pop. 3,245; lat. 14° 01′; long. 80° 09′; from Armegam N.W. 10½ miles; from Goodoor S.E. 19½ miles; from Madras N. 64½ miles; from Nellore S.S.E. 31 miles; from Paumanjy S. 3½ miles. Between the Swarnamookhy river and Armegam. Of little importance and attached to Doogarauzpatam as a subordinate port. Exports native ornaments, &c., and grain in large quantities.——*Vaucaud* (వాకాడు - vákádu, Tel.). See sep. title.——*Vencatachellam choultry* (వెంకటాచలంసత్రము - venkatáchalamsatramu, Tel.). See sep. title.——*Vindoor* (వింధూరు - vindúru, Tel.). From (vindu, tel. feast + úru, tel. village). Village; pop. 1,879; acres 6,825; lat. 14° 11′; long. 79° 52′; from Goodoor N.W. 3¼ miles; from Nellore S.S.W. 21 miles; from the sea W. 20 miles. Good mats [boriyah] and red handkerchiefs [roomaul] are made.——**(3)** Town, Head-quarters of Tahsildar and Special Sub-registrar, Railway station, C.N.S.R.; Nellore dist., Goodoor tal.; pop. 5,749; acres 11,859; lat. 14° 09′; long. 79° 54′; from Madras N.N.W. 77 miles; from Naidoopett N. 16¾ miles; from Nellore S.S.W. 22½ miles; from Ongole S. 95 miles; from the sea W. 18¼ miles. On trunk road. Travellers' bungalow [q.v.] and good choultry [q.v.], dry, and mainly treeless.

GOODRY (گودڑی - gúdrí, *Hind.*). Means tattered clothes. A quilt particularly of a fakeer [q.v.] made up of rags of various cloths sewed together [rizye].

GOOJASTA (گذشته - guzashtah, *Hind.*). From (guzashtan, pers. to pass). Past.——*Saulgoojasta* (سال گذشته - sáliguzashtah, Hind.). From (sál, pers. year + above). Last year [saul].

GOOL (گل - gul, *Hind.*). From persian. Any flower, but especially the rose. Botanically the Rosa genus, rosaceæ [vricsham, 49]. Erect, sarmentose or climbing shrubs, usually prickly; leaves pinnate; leaflets serrate; flowers terminal, solitary or corymbose, white, yellow, or red; cultivated for the beauty of flowers; propagated by cuttings. The species best known to the natives are shown below. They sometimes include under gool, other genera; as gomphrena, hibiscus, nerium, papaver, poinciana.——**(1)** *Cabbage rose* (शतपत्री - shatapatrí, San.; गुलाब - gulába, Mahr.; गुलाबि - gulábi, Conc.; وردالاحمر - vardulahmar, Ar.; گل صد برگ - gulisadbarg, Pers.; گلاب کا پیڑ - gulábkáper, Hind.; گلاب کا جھاڑ - gulábkájhár, Dec.; مور - mawar, Malay; ಗುಲಾಬಿಗಿಡ - gulábigida, Can.; ಗುಲಾಬು - gulábu, Too.; రోజా - rójá, Tel.; പനിനീർപ്പുഷ്പം - paninírpushpam, Mal.; රෝසමල් - rosamal, Singh.; இரோசா - irósá, Tam.). Title from double petals of flowers. San. from (shata, san. hundred + patra, san. petal). Mahr. and conc. from hindostany. Ar. from (vard, ar. rose + ahmar, ar. red). Pers. from (gul, pers. rose + sad, pers. hundred + barg, pers. leaf). Hind. from (guláb, pers. rose + per, hind. tree). Dec. from (guláb, pers. rose + jhár, hind. tree). Malay from (mawur, malay, to scatter); from the application of rosewater. Can. from (guláb, pers. rose + gida, can. plant). Too. from hindostany. Mal from (paninír, mal. rosewater + pushpa, san. flower). Tam. from english. Pers. also (gulisurkh), meaning red rose. Greek ῥόδον ἑκατοντάφυλλον. Title otherwise Hundred-leaved rose, Moss rose, Provence rose. Botanically Rosa [gool] centifolia, linn., rosaceæ [vricsham, 49]. A small shrub, 3–6 feet high, with numerous erect branches, rather densely covered with prickles of various sizes and the larger ones hooked, mixed with glandular setæ; flowers large, mostly very double usually somewhat drooping; peduncles covered with numerous setæ

and glandular hairs, as is also the calyx-tube; petals usually very numerous, large, thin, and delicate, clear rose-pink or white, often passing gradually into stamens through many intermediate organs; fruit oblong or ovoid-oblong, orange-red when ripe. Bears large, double, rose-colored, fragrant flowers; stems profusely covered with small fine spines; native of syria, cultivated; employed for distillation of rosewater, and in the preparation of the essential oil or attar [q.v.]. Petals and the volatile oil obtained from the petal form medicinally officinal parts; petals are mildly laxative, given in syrup; oil or the attar of roses is employed to disguise the unpleasant odour of certain ointments and other external applications. The following preparations made with the petals are used as medicaments:—Doohn-i-ward-i-khaum; a fatty oil made by exposing rose leaves and sweet oil [zeitoon] to the sun and then filtering; the ῥόδινον ἔλαιον of the greeks; considered to be deobstruent, astringent and aperient; also recommended in poisoning by caustic alkalies [cauram]. Doohn-i-ward-i-matbookh; a similar preparation made by heating the petals with sweet oil over the fire. Goolcund; a conserve made from equal parts of rose petals and white sugar [q.v.] beaten together; considered tonic and fattening, and much used by women and old people; cannabis sativa [kinnab] sometimes added. Goolangabeen; a similar preparation made with honey [shahad] and much the same properties. Goolaub; rosewater largely used in native practice as orange [q.v.] flower water by french. Goolaub-ka-attar; otto of roses having properties similar to those of rosewater; made in persia and india, but not in sufficient quantity to supply the indian market; a good deal therefore imported from turkey; the native still is used, a rough form of alembic without a condensing worm, and one hundred thousand roses produced about hundred bottles of rosewater; otto is only made in cold weather; to obtain it the rosewater is exposed to cold in shallow vessels, a thin film forms upon the surface, and is removed with a feather; one hundred thousand roses are estimated to produce about 180 grains of otto; the most reliable tests of the quality of rose oil are its odour, its congealing point, and its crystallization; much of the persian rosewater is diluted with water before it is sold; pure otto is hardly to be obtained; it undergoes adulteration before it is shipped to this country, and on arrival is still further falsified by a large admixture of sandal-wood oil, reducing its value from Rs. 16 to Rs. 2 per tolah [q.v.]; in the preparation of adulterated otto in india sandal-wood chips are added to the roses in the still [attar]. Rosewater is employed as perfume, also for softening flavor of tobacco [pogauk], also in preparing collyria; attar of roses is mixed with sandal [q.v.] and used largely by the natives at the period of festivals and marriages and is profusely distributed to the guests as they arrive and also sprinkled with profusion in the apartments.——*Changeable rose* (گل عجائب - guliajáib, Pers.). Persian means wonderful flower, from constant change of color. Same as Lotus bendy.——*China rose* (جاسون - jásún, Hind.). Same as China rose bendy.——*Corn rose* (لالہ - lálah, Hind.). Same as Corn poppy.——*Damask rose* (तरणी - taraní, San.; गुलाब - gulába, Mahr.; وردالاحمر بستانی - vardulahmaribustání, Ar.; گل سرخ - gulisurkh, Pers.; گل - gul, Hind.; گلاب - guláb, Dec.; ಪನ್ನೀರುಗಿಡ - pannírugida, Can.; రోజా - rójá, Tel.; പനിനീർപുഷ്പം - paninír-pushpam, Mal.; இரோசா - irósá, Tam.). Title from town. San. from (tri, san. to cross); from diffusive smell. Ar. from (vard, ar. rose + ahmar, ar. red + bustán, pers. garden). Pers. from (gul, pers. rose + surkh, pers. red). Hind. and dec. from persian. Can. from (pani, tam. dew + níru, can. water + gida, can. plant). Mal. from (paninír, mal. rosewater + pushpa, san. flower). Tam. from english. Tel. also (gulábipuvvuchettu), meaning rose + flower + plant; (panníruchettu), meaning rosewater + plant. Title otherwise Bussorah rose, Damascus rose, Persian rose. Botanically Rosa [gool] damascena, mill., rosaceæ [vricsham, 49]. Shrubby; prickles numerous, unequal, strong, dilated at the base; leaflets five to seven, ovate, stiffish; flower-bud oblong, sepals deflexed in flower, tube elongated, often dilated at the top, sepals spreading, not inflexed; fruit ovate, pulpy; calyx and peduncles glandulosely hispid, viscous. Same uses as centifolia [cabbage rose]. Very common in S. indian gardens.——*French rose* (وردالجبلی - varduljabalí, Ar.; گل بری - gulibarrí, Pers.; جنگلی گلاب - janglíguláb, Hind. and Dec.). Ar. from (vard, ar. rose + jabal, ar. mountain). Pers. from (gul, pers. rose + barr, pers. forest). Hind. from (janglí, hind. wild + guláb, hind. rose). Title otherwise Provence red rose. Botanically Rosa [gool] gallica, linn., rosaceæ [vricsham, 49]. A small rather compact erect bush, with numerous stems from a creeping root-stock and short stiff branches, the young shoots armed with short nearly equal straight prickles mixed with glandular setæ, but without any large hooked prickles. Native of europe and asia minor; cultivated. Gives to pharm. french rose petals the dried petals of the unexpanded flowers, rosæ gallicæ flores; slightly tonic and astringent.——*Indian rose* (وردصینی - vardisíní, Ar.; گل سفید بری - gulisufídbarrí, Pers.; نسترن - nastaran, Hind. and Dec.; இரோசா - irósá, Tam.). Ar. from (vard, ar. rose + síní, ar. chinese). Pers. from (gul, pers. rose + sufíd, pers. white + barrí, pers. wild). Tam. from english. Title otherwise Bengal rose, China rose [china rose bendy], Monthly rose, Tea rose. Botanically Rosa [gool] indica, linn., rosaceæ [vricsham, 49]. Evergreen, glabrous; stipules very narrow, adnate almost to the top; flowers large on long pedicels rarely single; sepals reflexed.——*Indian white rose* (तरुणी - taruní, San.; وردابیض - vardiabyaz, Ar.; نسرین سفید - nisrínisufíd, Pers.; سفید گل - sufedgul, Hind.; اجلا گلاب - ujlá-guláb, Dec.). San. means (tri, san. to cross), from diffusive smell. Ar. from (vard, ar. rose + abyaz, ar. white). Pers. from (nisrín, ar. dog rose + sufíd, pers. white). Hind. from (sufed, hind. white + gul, pers. rose). Dec. from (ujlá, hind. white + guláb, dec. rose). San. also (sévatí), meaning pleasing. Hind. also (seuntí). Title otherwise Indian white dog rose. Botanically Rosa [gool] alba, linn., rosaceæ [vricsham, 49]. Alias Rosa glandulifera. Germs oblong, shrubby, subscandent, armed; all the tender parts ciliate with glutinous, headed glands; leaflets from five to seven, ovate, doubly-serrate; segments of the calyx sub-ensiform, finely pinnatifid; flowers terminal in large corymbiform panicles. Native of caucasus and afghanistaun; cultivated; flowers a cooling medicine in fever [jwaram]; also used in perfumery.——*Musk rose* (शतपत्री - shatapatrí, San.; نسرین - nisrín, Ar.; گل مشکین - gulimishkín, Pers.; سیوتی - seutí, Hind.). Title from smell. San. from (shata, san. hundred + patra, san. petal). Pers. from (gul, pers. rose + mishk, pers. musk). Hind. from (sévatí, san. the plant). Pers. also (mushkínchah), meaning musk-scented. Botanically Rosa [gool] moschata, mill., rosaceæ [vricsham, 49]. Alias Rosa glandulifera. Tall climber, prickles scattered stout; leaves 2–6 inches, leaflets two to four pair, 1–3 inch, acute or acuminate, serratures very numerous and acute, base rounded, stipules glandular, free part subulate; inflorescence pubescent and usually glandular, but not prickly or bristly, bracts subulate; flower $1\frac{1}{2}$–2 inches diameter, very numerous, pedicels 1–$1\frac{1}{2}$ inches, slender; calyx-tube small, obovoid; lobes $\frac{1}{2}$ inch, lanceolate, caudate-acuminate, entire or cut or pinnatifid, reflexed after flowering, deciduous; petals orbicular-obovate, yellowish-white; fruit $\frac{1}{3}$ inch diameter, dark brown glabrous, styles far exserted.——*Peacock rose* (گل مور - gulmor, Hind.). Same as Gold mohur tree.——*Velvet rose* (گل مخمل - gulimakhmal, Hind.). From softness and appearance. Same as Jaffer goondy.——(2) *Golabjam* (گلابی جام - gulábíjám, Hind.). From (guláb, hind. rose + jám, hind. apple); from color and perfume. Same as Rose apple.——*Goolabash* (گلاباش - gulábásh, Dec.). From (gul, pers. flower + abbás, pers. red), from color of flowers. Same as False jalap.——*Goolaub* (گلاب - guláb, Hind.). Rosewater.——*Goolaub paush* (گلاب پاش - gulábpásh, Hind.). From (above + áb, pers. water + pásh, pers. sprinkler). A long-necked silver bottle perforated with holes at the mouth in the form of a muffineer, out of which rosewater is sprinkled on guests.——*Goolauby* (گلابی - gulábí, Hind.). Means rose-colored. Ex., Pastor roseus (gulábímaina), rosy myna.——*Goolbadan* (گلبدن - gulbadan, Hind.). From (above + badan, ar. body), from its lightness. A striped silk [puttoo] fabric used chiefly by well-to-do-Mahomedan women for trousers [sheelay], &c.; also servant's name.——*Goolchanabad* (گلشن آباد - gulshanábád, Hind.). From (gulshan, pers. garden + ábád, pers. city). The name given by the Mahomedan rulers to a division consisting of Ichapore, Cassimcote, Chicacole, &c., the Poondy river forming its northern boundary [northern circars].——*Goolcheeny* (گل چینی - gulchíní, Hind.). Same as Shaumanty.——*Goolcund* (گلقند - gulkand, Pers. and Hind.; گلقن - gulqan, Dec.; గుల్కండు - gulkandu, Tel.; ഗുൽകന്ത - gulkant, Mal.; குல்கந்து - kulgandu, Tam.). From (above + kand, ar. candy). Candied roses; confection of rose.——*Goolistaun* (گلستان - gulistán, Hind.). From (above + sitán, pers. place). A garden. Oordoo translation in prose, by Meer shere ally afsos, who lived about 1800, of the Persian work of that name by Saady, the moralist. The following is a specimen extract: —اك حکیم اپنے بیٹے کو نصیحت کرتا تھا کہ باباجان علم و
هنر سیکھو کہ ملك و دولت دنیا کی لا یق اعتبار کے نہین جاہ
و رتبہ جاتا رهتا هی روپا سونا بیچ حضر کے - لیکن هنر کا چشمہ
فیض سے مالا مال هی. اور دولت بے زوال اگر هنرمند مفلس
هوجائے کچھ غم نہین هنر بہ ذات خود دولت هی هنرمند جس
جگہ جائے عزت سے رهے *
"A wise man, while advising his "son to acquire knowledge and arts, said that the riches and "sovereignty of the world are not to be trusted, that rank and "dignity fades, and that gold and silver are ever surrounded "with fear, but that the fountain of art is always overflowing, "and is a wealth imperishable. It is no matter for regret should "a man of learning become poor for art itself is a wealth, and "go where a man of learning may, he is honored."——*Goolkesh* (گلکیس - gulkes, Hind.). Means flower + comb; from shape of flower. Same as Moorgha.——*Goolkheir* (گل خیرو - gulikhairo, Dec.). Means handsome flower. Hollyhock [foreign tootty].——*Gool mindie* (گل مہندی - gulmenhdí, Hind.). From (above + mehndí, hind. lawsonia alba, lamk.); from yielding a similar dye. See Mindie.——*Goolrang* (گلرنگ - gulrang, Hind.). From (above + rang, pers. color). Roseate. Servant's name.——*Goolrookh* (گلرخ - gulrukh, Hind.). From (above + rukh, pers. cheek). Rosy cheek. Servant's name.——*Goolzaur* (گلزار - gulzár, Hind.). From (above + zár, pers. place). Rose garden. Servant's name [ism].

GOOLAUL (گلال - gulál, *Hind.*). Red powder thrown in sport on others' clothes at Cauman pundigay [holy] festival. Formed of barley [jow], raggy [q.v.], rice [q.v.] or wheat [geung] flour, or flour of water-nut, Trapa bispinosa [singhaura], dyed red with sappan [q.v.] wood or sanders wood [red sanders]. Used by Mahrattas [q.v.], Bondilies [q.v.] and Rajpoots [q.v.].

GOOLOOM (वृक्षादनी - vrikshádaní, *San.*; गुलूम - gulúma, *Mahr.*; कयावेलिबेंदर्लि - kayávélibéndarli, *Conc.*; باندا - bándá, *Hind.*; ಕಾಸ್ರಕನಬಂದನಿಗೆ - kásrakanabandanige, *Can.*; బదనిక - badanika, *Tel.*; ഇത്തി - itti, *Mal.*; புல்லுருவி - pulluruvi, *Tam.*). Title from mahratta. San. from (vriksha, san. tree + ad, san. to eat); as parasitic on other trees. Mahr. from (gulma, san. bush); from bushy growth. Hind. from (vandá, san. parasite). Can. from (kásarka, can. poison nut, strychnos nux-vomica, linn. + bandanike, can. parasitic plant). Tel. from sanscrit. Mal. from (iru, mal. to drop). Tam. from (pul, tam. any gramineous plant + uruvu, tam. to pierce); as piercing or growing on other tree [pilloory]. San. also (vandá), meaning worshipping, as depending on other plants; (vrikshabhakshá), meaning tree eating; (vriksharuhá), meaning tree grower [rasnah]. Tel. also (velagabadanika), meaning wood-apple, feronia elephantum, corr. + parasite. Mal. also (kāññirattinmélpullunni), meaning parasitical plant on strychnos nux-vomica, linn.; (pullunni), meaning grass eater. Tam. also (kámarísam); (pullúri), meaning parasitic creeper [paushy]; (uççiççedi), meaning top + plant; from habit of overgrowth. Botanically Loranthus longiflorus, desr., loranthaceæ [vricsham]. Alias Loranthus bicolor, falcatus, koenigianus. Parasitic shrub; branches terete; leaves usually opposite, from linear to oblong-lanceolate or ovate, obtuse; racemes axillary, solitary or in pairs, erect or spreading, simple, many-flowered, much shorter than the leaves; bract solitary, concave, oblique; calyx-limb entire, corolla long infundibuliform, gibbous on one side, curved; segments five, linear, recurved, with one of the fissures deeper than the others; anthers linear; fruit oblong; flowers greenish-white, or scarlet-orange with green petals. Common upon the following genera of tree:—albizzia [sirissa], bassia [mohwah], bauhinia [mountain ebony], buchanania [chironjee], diospyros [indian ebony], ficus [atty], melia [neem], mangifera [mango], quercus [belote]. There is a Teloogoo proverb:—పాముకుబదనికచూపినట్లు—"Like showing gooloom "to a snake;" it is said to be an antidote for snake bites. The bark sometimes used in place of betel-nut [q.v.] with choonam [q.v.]; the wood used as a finishing tan stuff in order to give softness to leather [chamrah]. There are numerous other species, as:—amplexifolius, biflorus, blumeanus, buddleioides, capitellatus, cuneatus, elasticus, hookerianus, intermedius, kanneli, lageniferus, lepidophyllus, loniceroides, memecylifolius, neilgherrensis, obtusatus, recurvus, rugulosus, sarcophyllus, tomentosus, trigonus, turbinatus, wallichianus.

GOOLY (കുഴി - kuzhi, *Mal.*; குழி - kuzi, *Tam.*). Lowland. Suffix in place names; as Caroongooly, meaning the black lowland [cooy, coozhy].

GOOMASTA (گماشته - gumáshtah, *Hind.*). From (gumáshtan, pers. to appoint). Agent, clerk, native accountant in the revenue department, substitute for village officers who are minors or otherwise incapacitated from attending to their duties.

GOOMBAZ (گنبذ - gumbaz, *Hind.*). A building with a cupola, a mausoleum.

GOOMCHY (گمچی - gumchí, *Hind.*). From (guñjá, san. abrus precatorius, linn.). From (guj, san. to sound) [goonjana]; from sound of dry pods. Same as Indian liquorice. Same as San. goonjam, Hind. goonj, retty, Can. hauga, Tel. gooriginja, Mal. coonnycooroo, Tam. coondrimany. Small testaceous weight, generally taken as unit. A scale is:—4 dhauns = 1 goomchy; 8 goomchies = 1 mausham [niray, 3e]. Approximate actual value, 1 goomchy = $1\frac{7}{8}$ grains. Seed averages 1·934 grains. Goldsmith's weight called by the name weighs $2\frac{3}{16}$ grains. See vol. I, 609.——*Elephant goomchy* (هاتی گمچی - háthígumchí, Hind.). Title from size and similarity of seeds. Same as False red sanders.——*Wheel goomchy* (బండిగురివెంద - bandigurivenda, Tel.). Title from shape of seed. Same as False red sanders. ——*White goomchy* (श्वेतकाम्बोजी - shvétakámbójí, San.). From whitish small round fruit. Same as White poolah.

GOOMSOOR (ఘుంసరా - ghumsará, *Tel.* goomsur *). From (ghumó, oor. large + soró, oor. ditch).——**(1)** Talook, Ganjam district; Tahsildar's pay Rs. 150; area 1,596 square miles; population 185,870; language Teloogoo and Ooriya. N.E. inland of district. Bounded:—north by Daspalla and Nyagar zemindarries of Cuttack; east by Atagadah zemindarry; south by Bodagooda and Dhauracote zemindarries and Berhampore talook; west by Eastern ghauts [q.v.], which lead up into the Maliahs [q.v.]. Consists of the two ancient zemindarries of Goomsoor and Sooradah, confiscated by Government after rebellion in 1836. One result of annexation was suppression of Meriah [q.v.] among the Khonds [q.v.]. See vol. I, 71, and vol. II, 77. The Sooradah and Goomsoor peiks [q.v.], who hold quit-rent lands in the talook on condition of military service when called out against the Khonds, are a remnant of the old feudal system of Ganjam. The talook contains dense forests, especially on its east and north frontiers; wild beasts and game abound. Towards centre and south it is hilly with well-watered fertile valleys running towards the sea. To the north and east the land is good. Soil generally fertile. The regar [q.v.] soil predominates in the talook, next in quantity the sandy soil. There are no industries worth mentioning. The principal articles of commerce are rice [q.v.], raggy [q.v.], gingelly [q.v.], turmeric [country saffron], hides and skins [chamrah], horns [sing], rape [rara sarsoon] and niger [ramtil] seeds, jaggery [q.v.], hemp [hemp bendy, kinnab] and myrobalans [q.v.]. Rain is plentiful, and artificial irrigation is resorted to, as a rule, only for sugar-cane [q.v.] cultivation. The only important irrigation work is the Bory saugaram tank, near Gungoopooram, constructed by Government in 1861. Camping grounds:—Ballibhadra, Boogoodah, Corcholly, Moojagodoo, Nimmina, Russellcondah. The talook is divided as follows:—Ballibhadra khandam, containing the mittahs of Ballibhadra, Bhavanapooram, Boogoodah, Corcholly and Vishnoochuckram. Boda bora shingy khandam, containing the mittahs of Bondhahgotso, Boottapully, Goondribaudy, Kidica, Kaulo, Noovaugada, Payalpadah, Perdzoo, Poteshingy, Rogodo, and Salingyah. Vonnagherry khandam, containing the mittahs of Biracote, Dacshina godotolo, Darpangya, Doorgaprasaud, Gidipoohully, Jacshabaudy, Padiyah, Pauntso godotolo, Saurangbady and Vonnagherry. Coollauda khandam, containing the mittahs of Cookloobha, Gullary, Juggannaut prasaud, Oottara godotolo, Pasarah and Poorbo godotolo. For the adjoining hill country called the Goomsoor maliahs, see Maliah. Places of archæological interest:—Boudikhole, Boogoodah, Booraga, Coollauda, Goomsoor, Gopinautapooram, Leppah, Maulaty, Rowty. Principal trig. stations:—Khondhobolo, Maulaty, Patarcoomoodah. The leading places, &c., in the talook are the following.——*Ballibhadra* (బల్లిపోతొర - ballipotoro, Tel.). From (balli, oor. sand + potoro, oor. meadow). Tract of country; pop. 46,875. A sub-division of Goomsoor.——*Baugwah* (భాగువా - bháguvá, Tel.). River, Atagadah zemindarry. Rises in the Nyagar hills, and after a winding course of about 50 miles, through parts of Goomsoor and Atagadah zemindarry, joins the Rooshcoolya near Kanjama, a village about 7 miles from Aska.——*Belgoonta* (బెల్లుగుంట - bellugunta, Tel.). From (bello, oor. bael, ægle marmelos, corr. + gunta, tel. pond). Village; pop. 2,235; acres 676; lat. 19° 52′; long. 84° 41′; from Chetterpore N.N.W. 41 miles; from Russellcondah S.S.E. $3\frac{3}{4}$ miles. On high road about 5 miles from Russellcondah, and is greatest mart of barter in the talook. Khonds come to exchange their hill-produce. Manufacture of silver [velly] and brass [pittalay] paundauns [q.v.] and other silver ware of excellent kind.——*Boda bora shingy* (బొడబొరశింగి - bodaborashingi, Tel.). From (bodo, oor. large + boro, oor. banyan tree, ficus bengalensis, linn. + shringa, san. peak). Tract of country; pop. 36,865. A sub-division of Goomsoor.——*Boodanuddy* (బుడానది - budánadi, Tel.). From (buda, oor. old + nadí, san. river). River. Rises in Nyagar hills and flowing southwards drains Goomsoor and joins Mahanuddy near Maudhava boridah. Length about 30 miles.——*Boogoodah* (బుగుడా - bugudá,* Tel.). From (bhú, san. earth + gudá, oor. fort). Village; pop. 1,868; acres 1,067; lat. 19° 48′; long. 84° 50′; from Chetterpore N.N.W. 33 miles; from Russellcondah S.E. 15 miles. About a mile from the Baugwah. Image on a hill called Maulaty representing Virinchy narrainsawmy the sun-god. Finely-carved mantapam [q.v.] erected over it shaped like the chariot [rath] of the sun [sooryan] with seven horses [ghorah]. Old fort with ramparts still remaining. Old temple of Virinchy narrainsawmy largely resorted to.——*Comosorogodo* (కొమొసొరొగొడొ - komosorogodo, Tel.). From (ghumó, oor. large + soró, oor. ditch + gudá, oor. fort). Village; pop. 467; lat. 20° 01′; long. 84° 46′; from Chetterpore N.N.W. 48 miles; from Russellcondah N.E. 10 miles. Near the frontier between Goomsoor talook and Nyagar talook of the Central provinces. Ruined fort situated close to a hill. Scene of a battle during the time of Shreecara bhoonj rajah of Goomsoor between Goomsoor and Nyagar rajahs, in which the former was victorious.——*Cookloobha* (కుక్కులుబ - kukkuluba, Tel.). Village; pop. 554; lat. 20° 07′; long. 84° 45′; from Chetterpore N.N.W. 55 miles; from Russellcondah N.N.E. 14 miles. The chief village in the mittah [q.v.] of that name and is jungly and unhealthy. Contains good saul [q.v.] forest.——*Coollauda* (కుల్లాడ - kulláda, Tel.). See sep. title.——*Doorgaprasaud* (దుర్గాప్రసాదు - durgáprasádu, Tel.). From (durgá, san. párvatí the inaccessible deity + prasáda, san. favor). Village; pop. 210; lat. 20° 07′; long. 84° 30′; from Chetterpore N.W. 62 miles; from Russellcondah N.W. 15 miles. At the foot of the Calingyah ghaut [q.v.] leading to the Maliahs. Formerly one of the principal strongholds of Goomsoor rajahs.——*Ghautigooda* (ఘాటిగుడా - ghátigudá, Tel.). From (ghátí, oor. strong + gudá, oor. fort). Tract of country, Village; pop. 84. Above the ghauts and forms strictly speaking, a part of the Maliahs. Mittah [q.v.] was assessed in 1863 and brought under Goomsoor.——*Girjabaudy* (గిరిజాబాడి - girijábádi, Tel.). Trig. station, Chinna kimedy zemindarry; lat 19° 29′ 44·94″; long. 84° 25′ 18·46″; height 3,399 feet; from Govindapooram W. $2\frac{1}{2}$ miles; from Russellcondah S.S.W. 34 miles; from Chetterpore W.N.W. 42 miles.——*Goomsoor* (ఘుంసరా - ghumsará, Tel.). See below.——*Juggannaut prasaud* (జగన్నాథప్రసాదు - jagannát'haprasádu, Tel.). From (jagannátha, san. vishnu, the lord of the world, god of puri + prasáda, san. favor). Village; pop. 891; acres 1,439; lat. 19° 58′; long. 84° 49′; from Chetterpore N.N.W. 44 miles; from Russellcondah E.N.E. 12 miles. Formerly one of the principal strongholds of Goomsoor rajahs and now the chief village in the mittah [q.v.] of that name. Situated near the Boodanuddy river. ——*Khondhobolo* (ఖొంధొబొలొ - khondhobolo, Tel.). From (konda, tel. hill + palli, tel. village). Trig. station; lat. 19° 51′ 15·78″; long. 85° 00° 45·08″; height 3,115 feet; from Russellcondah E.S.E. 25 miles.——*Loharacundy* (లోహారాకండి - lóharákandi, Tel.). From (lóháró, oor. a caste + gandi, tel. pass). River. Rises in the hills of Doorgaprasaud, flows southwards and joins Mahanuddy and Maudhava boridah about 5 miles from Russellcondah. Length about 30 miles. Spanned at Russellcondah by masonry bridge of five arches.——*Mahanuddy* (మహానది - mahánadi, Tel.). From (mahá, san. great + nadí, san. river). River. Rises among the hills N.W. of Chocapaud and falls into Rooshcoolya at Aska, receiving in its course the waters from surrounding valleys and tributary streams of Boodanuddy from the N.E. and of Loharacundy from N.W. Length about 50 miles.——*Maulaty* (మాలతి - málati, Tel.). See sep. title.——*Patar coomoodah* (పతరకుముదా - patarakumudá, Tel.). From (potoro, oor. meadow + konda, tel. hill). Trig. station; lat. 20° 02′ 31·41″; long. 84° 48′ 58·84″; height 1,778 feet; from Khondhogallery E.S.E. 13 miles; from Russellcondah N.E. 13 miles.——*Pippalpunka* (పిప్పలపంక - pippalapanka, Tel.). From (pippala, san. peepul tree, ficus religiosa, linn. + panka, san. marsh). Ghaut, Village; pop. 111; lat. 19° 49′; long. 84° 22′; from Chetterpore N.W. 54 miles; from Russellcondah W.S.W. 20 miles. Near Rooshcoolya river below ghauts [q.v.]. Overrun with jungles. Pass from Gajellabady to Maliahs [q.v.]. ——*Rooshcoolya* (ఋషికుల్యా - rishikulyá, Tel.). See sep. title. ——*Russellcondah* (రసూలుకొండ - rasúlukonda, Tel.). See sep. title. ——*Salingyah* (సలింగ్యా - salingyá, Tel.). Tract of country. Mittah formerly included in the Maliahs but assessed in 1863. ——*Sooradah* (సురదా - surradá, Tel.). See sep. title.——*Vishnoochuckram* (విష్ణుచక్రము - vishnuchakramu, Tel.). From (vishnu, san. vishnu + chakra, san. wheel weapon). Village; pop. 787; acres 883; lat. 19° 46′; long. 84° 43′; from Chetterpore N.W. 34 miles; from Russellcondah S.S.E. 12¾ miles. Near the Mahanuddy. Ruined fort on an elevated rock.——*Vonnagherry* (వొన్నగిరి - vonnagiri, Tel.). From (vana, san. jungle + giri, san. mountain). Division; pop. 46,955. A sub-division of Goomsoor talook.——*Wolsoogoommah* (ఒలుసుగుమ్మా - olusugummá, Tel.). From (valasa, tel. colony + gummá, oor. fort). Village; pop. 319. Ancient village near the frontier, between Goomsoor and Daspalla zemindarries. Old fort.——**(2)** Village; Ganjam dist., Goomsoor tal.; lat. 19° 50′; long. 84° 40′; from Chetterpore N.W. 40 miles; from Russellcondah S. 6¾ miles. Former cusbah [q.v.] of the talook [q.v.] but now unimportant. Previous to disturbances of 1835-36, was the seat of Goomsoor chiefs, and members of family still reside. Fort in A.D. 832 by Rajah raghoonauta bhoonj, an ancestor of present Goomsoor rajahs.

GOONAM (गुण - guna, *San.*). From (grah, san. to hold) [graham, graumam, griham]. A quality, property, merit, virtue.—"*a*" Metaphysically there are three Goonams:—Satwagoonam, or property of truth, the source of purity and wisdom; Rajogoonam, or property of foulness, the source of passion and error; Tamogoonam, or property of darkness, the source of inertness and ignorance. A happy disposition is Satwagoonam; if in excess it affords light, and produces knowledge and happiness; the person strives to perform good actions [carmam], has patience, is a lover of truth and understanding, has no bad desire; possesses a good memory, is charitable, is devoid of anger, is without avarice; when such a person dies, he becomes a deva [q.v.]. An active disposition or Rajogoonam signifies desire, the love of gain, industry, and commencement of works [carmam], and produces unhappiness when in excess; such a person is unquiet; when a person with such a disposition dies, his soul re-animates another body of an inferior nature. When an inert disposition or Tamogoonam is in excess, it is indicated by a want of energy, secrecy, and distraction of thought; when such a person dies, his soul is conceived again in irrational animals [samsanram]. Deity abstractedly is Nirgoonam, or without any of the three properties. Eight qualities are in turn ascribed to each of the metaphysical Goonams [matam].—"*b*" Goonam is also an attribute of the five elements [bhootam]; each element has its own peculiar quality or qualities as well as organ of sense [indriyam]; thus ether has shabdam [q.v.] or sound for its goonam and the ear for its organ; the air has tangibility and sound for its goonams and the skin for its organ; fire or light has shape, color, tangibility and sound for its goonams and the eye for its organ; water has flavor, shape, tangibility and sound for its goonams and the tongue for its organ; earth has all the preceding goonams with the addition of its own peculiar goonam of smell, and the nose for its organ.—"*c*" Goonam is also one of the six courses of action in foreign politics, viz., peace, war, march, halt, stratagem and recourse to the protection of a mightier king.——*Goonak* (गुणक - gunaka, San.). Multiplier in arithmetic.——*Goonyam* (गुण्य - gunya, San.). Multiplicand in arithmetic [ganitam, shastram].——*Gownam* (गौण - gauna, San.). From (guna, san. quality). Specific. Also unessential, secondary, subordinate. Also for Gowpamausam; opposed to Mookhyam [q.v.].——*Gownamausam* (गौणमास - gaunamása, San.). From (gowna, san. secondary + mása, san. month). The lunar month, from full to full [krishnaudy, maunam, mausam, shooclaudy].

GOONAM (குணம் - kunam, *Tam.*). A corruption of (kunram, tam.). Hill. Suffix in place names; as Vengoonam, meaning the white hill [coonn, coor].

GOONAPORE (గుణుపురము - gunupuramu, *Tel.*). From (ghana, san. great + pura, san. city) [ghanam]. Sanscrit name (ghanapura), meaning same.——**(1)** Division, Vizagapatam district. Languages, Ooriya, Khond, Sowrah and Teloogoo. Boundaries:—E., Ganjam agency; S., Ganjam district and Parvatipore division; W., Royagada division; N., Bissemcuttack division. Physical aspect undulating and hilly. A large plain watered by the Vamshadhaura and surrounded by hills inhabited by the aboriginal Khond [q.v.] and Sowrah [q.v.] tribes. Considerable quantities of grain are exported and much saul [q.v.] wood is floated down the river to Calingapatam. Principal trig. station:—Himagherry. The leading places, &c., in the division are the following.——*Baumany* (బామని - bámani, Tel.). From (bráhmaní, san. bramin lady). Mountain, Trig. station; lat. 19° 32′ 50·40″ N.; long. 83° 49′ 47·50″ E.; height 2,488 feet; from Goonapore N. 32 miles; from Jeypore E.N.E. 92 miles; from Vizagapatam N.N.E. 130 miles. Large weekly market.——*Bijipore* (బిజిపూరు - bijipúru, Tel.). From (vijaya, san. success + pura, san. town). Mittah; pop. 276; lat. 19° 31′; long. 83° 58′; from Goonapore N.N.E. 30 miles; from Jeypore E. 100 miles; from Vizagapatam N.N.E. 130 miles. One of the seven Khond mittahs described by the Meriah [q.v.] agency as addicted to human sacrifice. Consists of nine villages. Separated from Poncaul the next stage by a dense saul jungle nine miles in extent.——*Goodaury* (గుడారి - gudári, Tel.). From (gudáramu, tel. tent). Village; pop. 2,265; lat. 19° 20′; long. 83° 50′; from Goonapore N. 18 miles; from Jeypore E.N.E. 86 miles; from Vizagapatam N.N.E. 116 miles. The Goodaury estate is at present enjoyed by the widows of the Jeypore maharajah's late uncle Cheitanya deo, but will revert to the Maharajah [q.v.] on their death.——*Goomma* (గుమ్మ - gumma, Tel.). Means grain receptacle. Tract of country; pop. 537; lat. 18° 46′; long. 82° 28′; from Goonapore W. 92 miles; from Jeypore W. 11 miles; from Vizagapatam N.W. 90 miles.——*Goonapore* (గుణుపురము - gunupuramu, Tel.). See below.——*Himagherry* (హిమగిరి - himagiri, Tel.). From (hima, san. snow + giri, san. hill). Trig. station; lat. 18° 49′ 30·10″; long. 83° 49′ 34·36″; height 3,710 feet; from Goonapore S. 18 miles; from Merangy E. 15 miles. *Mondemcull* (మొండెంకల్లు - mondemkallu, Tel.). From (mondemu, tel. stump + kallu, tel. stone). Mittah, Village; pop. 637; lat. 18° 55′; long. 83° 45′ 30″; from Goonapore S.W. 14 miles; from Jeypore E. 74 miles; from Vizagapatam N.N.E. 88 miles. Scheduled tract.——*Vamshadhaura* (వంశధార - vamshadhára, Tel.). See sep. title.——**(2)** Deputy tahsildarry. Pay Rs. 200. ——**(3)** Village, Head-quarters of Deputy tahsildar and Ameen [q.v.] of Jeypore maharajah, Superintendent of Hill schools, Vizagapatam dist., Jeypore zemindarry, Goonapore magisterial division; pop. 4,685; lat. 19° 05′; long. 83° 51′; from Coraputt E.N.E. 74 miles; from Jeypore E.N.E. 82 miles; from Madras N. 464 miles; from Narsapatam N.E. 124 miles; from Parvatipore N.E. 32 miles; from Vizagapatam N.N.E. 100 miles; from Vizianagram N.N.E. 71 miles. Village situated on the Vamshadhaura.

GOONCH (मुतंडा - mutańda, *Mahr.*; گونچ - gúnch, *Hind.*; రాతిజెల్ల - rátijella, *Tel.*; ସାଲୁଣ - sálun, *Oor.*). Title from hindostany. Mahr. means large + pendulous filament; from long barbels. Tel. from (ráyi, tel. stone + jella, tel. sphyræna jello). Mahr. also (t'hóróta), meaning large + pendulous filament; (bágariyas), meaning tiger-faced, from markings of lurid colors on face. Hind. also (búnch). Title otherwise Fresh-water shark. Bagarius yarrellii, siluridæ [kizhautty], physostomi, teleostei [matsyam, 35], of naturalists [jantoo]. Generic name from mahratta. Alias Bagarius buchanani; Bagrus yarrellii; Pachypterus luridus; Pimelodus bagarius, carnaticus, platespagon, yarrellii. Upper jaw the longer; skin somewhat scabrous over the summit of the head, and slightly so on the body; colors body gray or yellowish, with large, irregular, brown or black markings and cross bands; black base to all the fins, and generally also a dark band; takes a live bait, but is difficult to kill; it is sluggish, goes to the bottom, and generally escapes by destroying the tackle; large rivers descending to the estuaries; attains 6 feet or more; eaten by poor; very foul feeder. No other common species here.

GOONDAM (कुण्ड - kunda, *San.*; ಗುಂಡ - gunda, *Can.*; గుండము - gundamu, *Tel.*). From (kunda, san. pot, hollow spot). Deep gorge.——*Goonta* (گنٹا - guntá, Hind.; గుంట - gunta, Tel.). From (kunda, san. a vessel of water). Lake, tank. Hollow spot. Also quarry. Suffix in place names, especially in

Anantapore, Arcot north, Bellary, Cuddapah and Kurnool; as Renigoonta, meaning king's tank [coonta]. Also a superficial measure; 16 annas = 1 goonta, 40 goontas = 1 acre [alavay, 2b]; approximate actual value, 1 goonta = 1,089 square feet; but very variable; compare Tel. coonta, Tam. coozhy, gooly. See vol. I, 609; II, 505.——*Goontaca* (గుంటిక - guntike, Can.; గుంటక - guntaka, Tel.). Tel. from (gunta, tel. indentation). Harrow for cleaning land and preparing it for sowing, as well as for covering the seed [gorroo]. Eight-sided frame, on the sides of which weights are put, or if necessary people stand. There is a Teloogoo proverb:—[illegible] "A crop that is not harrowed will be like a man "compelled to go without his midday meal."——*Goontla* (గుంట్ల - guntla, Tel.). Plural locative form of goonta. Tank. Suffix in place names as Nullagoontla, meaning the black tanks [coontla].——*Guntoor* (గుంటూరు - guntúru, Tel.). See sep. title.

GOONGRA (گھنگرو - ghungrú, *Hind.*). Imitative of sound. Bells fastened round the ankles or wrists of children [shalangay].

GOONJANA (గుంజన - gunjana,* *Tel.*). From (gunja, tel. an indistinct sound) [goomchy]. River; Cuddapah dist., Poollampett tal. Rises in the Sheshachellam or Tripatty hills and drains the southern and eastern portions of Poollampett talook. Rapid and deep but narrow. Not navigable.

GOONJAYISH (گنجایش - gunjáish, *Hind.*). From (gunjídan, pers. to hold exactly). Extent or capacity.

GOORBAH (گربه - gurbah, *Pers.*). Cat [poonay]. Cf.:— Lutra vulgaris (gurbahiábí), water cat; viverra civettina (gurbahizabád), musk cat.

GOORGY (گرگی - gurgí, *Hind.*). From (gurgá, hind. knee). Short trousers tight at the knee and full above [sheelay].

GOORJARA (ఘూర్జర - ghúrjara, obl., *Tel.*). The goozerat [q.v.] country. One of the main sub-divisions of Dravida [q.v.] or Southern bramins [jauty]. See vol. II, 226.

GOOROO (गुरु - guru, *San.*). From (grí, san. to teach). A teacher, priest. Also heavy. A gooroo is regarded as a spiritual parent from whom the youth or disciple receives the initiatory muntram [q.v.] or prayer, and who conducts the ceremonies necessary at various seasons of infancy and youth up to the period of investiture with the sacred thread or string [oopanayanam]. This person may be the natural parent or the religious preceptor. A gooroo is to be distinguished from a poorohit [q.v.], who is a sort of domestic chaplain and must be married. The gooroos generally live in celibacy. Epithet of Shiva [q.v.], Brihaspaty [q.v.]. Suffix in proper names as Shivagooroo [peyar].——*Gooroocal* (കുരുക്കൾ - kurukkal, Mal.; குருக்கள் - kurukkal, Tam.). Plural form, and not used in this sense in singular. In malayalam, temple non-bramin servant caste; originally teachers, but their functions, now-a-days are to supply milk [paul], ghee [q.v.], and flowers to temples and to sweep and clean them [inam, jauty]. In tamul priests in shiva temples, always smarta bramins, though considered low in scale, corresponding to numby the veishnava bramin priest, and to poojarry the shoodra priest.——*Gooroo coolam* (குருகுலம் - kurugulam, Tam.). From (above + kula, san. family). A class of priest fishermen.——*Gooroomoorty* (குருமூர்த்தி - kurumúrtti, Tam.). From (above + múrti, san. body). Shiva, the deity in human form as a preceptor [augamam]. Hindoo 2nd or pers. name [peyar].——*Gooroonautan* (குருநாதன் - kurunáthan, Tam.). From (above + nát'ha, san. lord of the preceptor). Scandan; preceptor to Shiva [shivagooroo]. Hindoo 2nd or pers. name [peyar].——*Gooroopaudam* (குருப்பாதம் - kuruppátham, Tam.). From (above + páda, san. foot). Humble appellation. Hindoo 2nd or pers. name [peyar].——*Goorooram* (ಗುರುರಾಮ* - gururám, Can.). From (above + ráma, san. the god), meaning having rama for preceptor. Hindoo 2nd or pers. name [peyar].——*Gooroosawmy* (குருசாமி - kurusámi, Tam.). From (above + svámí, san. lord). Shiva, the lord. Also Soobramanyan, as preceptor to Shiva [shivagooroo]. Colloquially gooroo. Hindoo 2nd or pers. name [peyar].——*Gooroo's tree* (मुनिपादप - munipádapa, San.). From use of oil by ascetics [moony]. Same as Fire-work plant.——*Goorootwam* (गुरुत्व - gurutva, San.). Platinum, as the heaviest metal [loham].——*Gooroovappa* (ಗುರುವಪ್ಪ - guruvappa, Can.). From (above + appa, can. father, titular affix). Compare Shivappa. Hindoo 2nd or pers. name [peyar].——*Gooroo vauram* (गुरुवार - guruvára, San.). From (above + vára, san. day); brihaspaty's day. Thursday [vauram].——*Goorpore* (ಗುರುಪುರ - gurupura, * Can.). From (above + pura, san. town); town of gooroo or priest being a mutt.—"*a*" A hamlet of Moollore village; South canara dist., Mangalore tal.; lat. 12° 56′ N.; long. 74° 58′ E.; from Bombay S.S.E. 425 miles; from Mangalore N.E. 8 miles; from Moolky S.E. 13 miles; from the sea E. 8¼ miles. On river of same name; has an old Jangam mutt [q.v.] with windows of the old zenana [q.v.] elaborately pierced and carved.—"*b*" River; South canara dist., Mangalore tal. Falls into Mangalore backwater and with Netrauvaty forms Mangalore barbour. Takes its source from foot of Western ghauts [q.v.] in Mangalore talook. Is navigable from Mangalore to Goorpore all the year round, and up to seven miles further inland from June to December.

GOORRAM (గుఱ్ఱము - gurramu, *Tel.*). Horse [coothiray, ghorah, goda].——*Goorramcondah* (గుఱ్ఱముకొండ - gurramukonda, Tel. gurramkonda *). From (above + konda, tel. hill); from the appearance. Village, Hill-fort; Cuddapah dist., Voilpaud tal.; pop. 1,674; acres 8,335; lat. 13° 47′; long. 78° 38′; from Cuddapah S.S.W. 50 miles; from Voilpaud N.N.W. 10½ miles. An important fortress in a commanding position on an isolated rock on the summit of a detached and almost inaccessible hill. A portion of the old palace at foot of hill is still used as a traveller's bungalow [moosaufer khana] though very dilapidated. Built or improved by Golcondah kings. Capital of Hyderabad balaghaut [q.v.], one of the five circars [q.v.] of the Carnatic [q.v.] at commencement of eighteenth century. Afterwards held by a poligar [q.v.] under Cuddapah nawaub [q.v.]. The tenure was purely military, and the governor had the privilege of coining money [naunyam]. In 1766 when Meer sahib betrayed Sheerah, he received Goorramcondah, formerly held by his ancestors, as a Mahratta jagheer [q.v.]. In 1768 he made it over to Hyder, his brother-in-law. In 1771 Syed shah, Hyder's general, surrendered it to Trimbac row. Tippoo recaptured it in 1773. In 1791 the Nizam's forces aided by the British captured the lower fort, but the citadel held out till the peace, when the place was ceded to the Nizam. In 1799 it was transferred to the Company with the rest of the Cuddapah district. Near the fort is the tomb of Meer razah ally khan, uncle of Tippoo sultan, with several carved Mussalman buildings. A Persian inscription at the tomb of Razah ally khan consists of an epitaph with the date of his death, A.D. 1780. A Mahomedan religious institution is conducted by Meer mooraud ally khan sahib, a descendant of the Gooramcondah nawaub, who lives in Mahaul [q.v.], thirteen miles distant. He receives a pension of Rs. 60 per mensem from the Mysore government. Twice in the year several hundred fakeers [q.v.] are fed.

GOORTOO (గుర్తు - gúrtu, *Tel.*). Same as Gorroo.

GOORY (గురి - guri, *Tel.*). Means mark. Omen [shacoonam]. Telling one's fortunes by observing marks or lines on face, hands, &c. Soothsaying [coory, samoodricam]. Another name of the Yerkalas [q.v.].——*Goorigínja* (గురిగింజ - gurigindza, Tel.). From (guri, tel. mark + gindza, tel. seed). Same as Coondrimany, Goomchy, Retty.

GOOSEBERRY (تپاری - tipárí, *Hind.*). Plant second term. Cf.:—Averrhoa carambola, country gooseberry, coromandel gooseberry; Melastoma malabathricum, malabar gooseberry; Phyllanthus distichus, country gooseberry, country star gooseberry, hill gooseberry, otaheite gooseberry; Phyllanthus emblica, indian gooseberry; Physalis peruviana, cape gooseberry, peruvian gooseberry; Rhodomyrtus tomentosa, hill gooseberry. See gloss. paragraphs.

GOOTTA (گتا - guttá, *Hind.*). Means lump settlement. Farm; lease. Goottadar is a renter [moostajaur]. For Cauyam goottadar see sep. title.

GOOTY * (గుత్తి - gutti, *Tel.*). From (gutta, tel. a hill) [good]. Sanscrit name (gautamapurí), meaning gowtaman + town.——(1) Talook, Anantapore district. Tahsildar's pay Rs. 200. Area 1,054 square miles; pop. 142,917; languages, Teloogoo, Canarese and Hindostany. N. of district. Boundaries north, Aulore and Patticondah of Kurnool district; east, Tadpatry talook; south, Anantapore; west, Royadroog and Bellary talooks. There are numerous small hills. At Gooty a massive precipitous rock springs abruptly from the plain, which, with the out-lying rocks, is strongly fortified. The other noteworthy hills in the talook are at Conacondla, Goolpollem and Naugasamoodram. At Ooderpidroog and Ooravacondah there are isolated hills about 400 feet in height. In the south of the talook are large unbroken plains of black cotton [regar] soil very thinly wooded. It is almost impossible to grow trees on this soil. A soft limestone [choonamcull] is generally found from 5–10 feet below the surface, partially soluble in water. The trees planted grow well for three or four years, but so soon as the roots strike this limestone strata they wither. In the north of the talook the soil is red and gravelly; in many places rocky and stony. The principal crops on dry soils are cholum [q.v.], cotton [q.v.], corra [tinay] and other pulses [dholl]. Under the tanks [q.v.] and channels [q.v.], paddy; and under wells, paddy [q.v.] and raggy [q.v.] are largely grown. The cotton grown in the south of the talook is sent down to Madras, and the chintzes [q.v.] and dyed cloths of Paumidy are sought for all over the district. A large quantity of cholum and raggy is sent into the Bellary market. Rice [q.v.] is imported from the richer southern talooks, and cattle [maud] in large droves arrive from Nellore through the Kurnool district. There is no special trade in the talook except at Paumidy. In other villages there are looms [tarry], but the cloths produced are of the ordinary kinds. At Nelgonda, Pundicoonta and Ramgherry, glass bangles [gauzoo] are made. At Krishtapaud, good silk [puttoo] cloths are woven. The Pennair is the only river, and it flows along the southern edge of the talook [q.v.]. From it small channels are taken off by excavations in the sand. No anicuts [q.v.] are attempted and these channels require to be renewed year by year. They are kept in order exclusively by the villagers. The usual custom is that for each acre held by him the ryot [q.v.] must contribute a day's labor either in person or by a hired substitute [coody maraumat]. There are forty-five tanks [q.v.] in the talook, but few of these deserve the name. Only five irrigate an area of more than 200 acres, and seven have an irrigable area of between 50 and 200 acres. All the rest have less than 50 acres dependent on them. The five principal tanks are Appecherla, Gooty, Pautacotta cheroo, Ramgherry, and Yerratimrauzcheroo. Camping grounds are at Gooty and Paumidy. Places of archæological interest:—Caroor, Cawderpett, Chetnepully, Chinna vadoogoor, Chintalcheroo, Chitrachaid, Conacondla, Cundla goodoor, Cundlapully, Devarpully, Goondaula, Gooty, Guddecull, Medimacoolapully, Nakkanadoddy, Narimetla, Ooravacondah, Ootcull, Pedda vadoogore, Pennahobalam, Rampooram, Sangaula, Yeddoolapully, Yerragoontla, Yerratimrauzcheroo. Principal trig. stations:—Boglamauricondah, Bolicondah, Chikalgoorky, Gooty, Gooty base north end, Gooty base south end, Guddecull, Gumpamala, Namdabad, Nimbacull, Ooderpidroog, Paumidy. The leading places, &c., in the talook are the following.——*Appecherla* (అప్పెచెర్ల - appecherla, Tel.). From (appa, tel. father + cherla, tel. village). Village; pop. 3,001; acres 7,975; lat. 15° 05′; long. 77° 47′; from Anantapore N.N.E. 29 miles; from Gooty E.S.E. 8 miles. Has a large tank irrigating 206 acres. ——*Aumidella* (ఆమిదేల - ámidéla, Tel.). From (ámudamu, tel. castor oil, ricinus communis, linn. + ila, tel. ground). Village; pop. 3,317; acres 12,239; lat. 14° 51′; long. 77° 18′; from Anantapore W.N.W. 26 miles; from Gooty S.W. 31¾ miles. A large village in the black cotton country in south of the talook. ——*Boglamauricondah* (బొగ్గులమారికొండ - boggulamárikonda, Tel.). From (boggu, tel. charcoal + mári, tel. village deity + konda, tel. hill). Trig. station; lat. 15° 04′ 51·16″; long. 77° 32′ 34·97″; height 2,350 feet; from Anantapore N.N.W. 29 miles; from Gooty W.S.W. 9¾ miles; from Vencatampulley N.E. 13 miles.——*Bolicondah* (బోలికొండ - bólikonda, Tel.). From (bólu, tel. hollow + konda, tel. hill). Trig. station; lat. 15° 10′ 42·57″; long. 77° 33′ 27·65″; height 1,684 feet; from Ameenpully E.N.E. 1¾ miles; from Anantapore N. 35 miles; from Gooty W.N.W. 9½ miles.——*Casaupooram* (కసాపురం - kasápuram, Tel.). From (kasáyi, tel. butcher + pura, san. town). Village, Place of pilgrimage; pop. 1,298; acres 6,603; lat. 15° 12′; long. 77° 26′; from Anantapore N.N.W. 38 miles; from Gooty W.N.W. 17½ miles. Large temple to Hanooman [q.v.].——*Chikalgoorky* (చికలగురికి - chikalaguriki, Tel.). Trig. station; lat. 14° 59′ 07·18″; long. 77° 13′ 34·07″; height 1,521 feet; from Anantapore N.W. 34 miles; from Gooty W.S.W. 31 miles; from Paultore E. 2¼ miles.——*Conacondla* (కోనకొండ్ల - konakondla, Tel.). From (kona, tel. peak + konda, tel. hill). Village, Hill; pop. 4,204; acres 14,382; lat. 15° 6′; long. 77° 24′; from Anantapore N.N.W. 33 miles; from Gooty W. 18 miles. A hill fort in a commanding position.——*Goontacull* (గుంతకల్లు - guntakallu, Tel. guntakal *). From (gunta, tel. quarry + kallu, tel. stone). Village, Railway station; pop. 4,797; acres 9,107; lat. 15° 11′; long. 77° 25′; height 1,412 feet; from Anantapore N.N.W. 35¾ miles; from Gooty W. 19 miles.——*Gooty* (గుత్తి - gutti, Tel.). See below.—— *Guddecull* (గదేకల్లు - gadékallu, Tel.). From (gadda, tel. mound + kallu, tel. stone). Village; pop. 2,320; acres 7,353; lat. 15° 07′; long. 77° 17′; from Anantapore N.W. 38 miles; from Gooty W. 27 miles. The trig. station is in lat. 15° 07′ 18·12″; long. 77° 16′ 53·10″; height 1,823 feet; from Anantapore N.W. 39 miles; from Doneycull E.S.E. 2¾ miles; from Gooty W. 27 miles.—— *Gumpamala* (గంపమల - gampamala, Tel.). From (gampa, tel. basket + mala, tel. hill). Trig. station; lat. 14° 51′ 35·10″; long. 77° 43′ 28·80″; height 2,510 feet; from Anantapore N.N.E. 14 miles; from Chintamaucoolapully S.S.E. 2¾ miles; from Gooty S. 18 miles.——*Hauvaligy* (హావలిగి - hávaligi, Tel.). Village; pop. 2,159; acres 10,747; lat. 15° 01′; long. 77° 10′; from Anantapore N.W. 40 miles; from Gooty W. 35½ miles.——*Krishtapaud* (క్రిష్టపాడు - krishtapádu, Tel.). From (krishna, tel. proper name + pádu, tel. village); built by krishna deva royel. Village; pop. 2,886; acres 5,614; lat. 15° 04′; long. 77° 49′; from Anantapore N.N.E. 28 miles; from Gooty E.S.E. 10¼ miles. Manufacture of silk cloths.——*Namdabad* (నామదాబాదు - námadábádu, Tel.). From (namat, hind. proper name + ábád, hind. city). Trig. station; lat. 15° 05′ 55·10″; long. 77° 38′ 54·61″; height 1,173 feet; from Anantapore N. 29 miles; from Gooty W.S.W. 2½ miles.——*Naugasamoodram* (నాగసముద్రము - nágasamudramu, Tel.). From (nága, san. proper name + samudra, san. ocean). Village, Hill; pop. 2,853; acres 16,958; lat. 15° 03′; long. 77° 33′; from Anantapore N.N.W. 27 miles; from Gooty W.S.W. 10 miles.——*Nelgonda* (నెలగొండ - nelagonda, Tel.). From (néla, tel. ground + konda, tel. hill). Village; pop. 1,685; acres 11,261; lat. 15° 06′; long. 77° 29′; from Anantapore N.N.W. 30½ miles; from Gooty W. 12½ miles. Glass bangles made.—— *Nimbacull* (నింబకల్లు - nimbakallu, Tel.). From (nimba, san. the margosa tree, melia azadirachta, linn. + kallu, can rock). Trig. station; lat. 14° 51′ 55·10″; long. 77° 14′ 19·47″; height 1,570 feet; from Anantapore W.N.W. 29 miles; from Aumidella W.N.W. 3¾ miles; from Gooty W.S.W. 34 miles.——*Ooderpidroog* (ఉదిరిపిదుర్గము - udiripidurgamu, Tel.). From (udiri, tel. gold + durga, san. fort). Trig. station; lat. 14° 49′ 54·24″; long. 77° 23′ 11·81″; height 1,725 feet; from Anantapore W.N.W. 20 miles; from Gooty S.W. 28 miles; from Marootla W. 3¼ miles. Also town; pop. 945; acres 10,926. Isolated hill of 400 feet high in the neighbourhood.——*Ooravacondah* (ఉరవకొండ - uravakonda, Tel.). See sep. title.——*Paumidy* (పామిడి - pámidi, Tel.). See sep. title.——*Pautacottacheroo* (పాతకొత్తచెరువు - pátakottacheruvu, Tel. pátakottacheru *). From (páta, tel. old + kotta, tel. new + cheruvu, tel. tank). Village, Railway station; pop. 852; acres 6,135; lat. 15° 10′; long. 77° 34′; height 1,234 feet; from Anantapore N. 33 miles; from Gooty W.N.W. 8¾ miles. ——*Pedda vadoogore* (పెద్దవడుగూరు - peddavadugúru, Tel.). From (pedda, tel. great + vadugúru, tel. village so called). Village; pop. 2,427; acres 6,638; lat. 15° 01′; long. 77° 43′; from Anantapore N. 23½ miles; from Gooty S.S.E. 7 miles.—— *Pennahobalam* (పెన్నహోబలం - pennahóbalam, Tel.). From (penna, tel. river so called + ahóbalam, tel. place so called). Village, Place of pilgrimage; pop. 4; acres 2,298; lat. 14° 52′; long. 77° 21′; from Anantapore W.N.W. 23¼ miles; from Gooty S.W. 28 miles. On banks of Pennair. Car festival. River narrow and dangerous on account of rocks. Important temple. ——*Pennair* (పెన్నేరు - pennéru, Tel.). See sep. title.——*Pundicoonta* (పందికుంట - pandikunta, Tel.). From (pandi, tel. pig + kunta, tel. pond). Village; pop. 486; acres 9,001; lat. 14° 58′; long. 77° 26′; from Anantapore N.W. 24½ miles; from Gooty W. 19¾ miles. Glass bangles made.——*Ramgherry* (రామగిరి - rámagiri, Tel.). From (ráma, san. proper name + giri, san. mountain). Village; pop. 701; acres 5,127; lat. 14° 57′; long. 77° 31′; from Anantapore N.N.W. 21 miles; from Gooty S.W. 15 miles. Glass bangles made.——*Vajracaroor* (వజ్రకరూరు - vajrakarúru, Tel.). See sep. title.——*Vidoopanacull* (విడుపనకల్లు - vidupanakallu, Tel.). From (vitapa, san. offshoot + kallu, can. rock). Village; pop. 2,790; acres 13,478; lat. 15° 03′; long. 77° 14′; from Anantapore N.W. 38 miles; from Gooty W. 31 miles. ——*Yerratimrauzcheroo* (ఎర్రతిమ్మరాజుచెరువు - erratimmarádzu-cheruvu, Tel.). From (erratimmarádzu, tel. proper name + cheruvu, tel. tank). Village; pop. 1,570; acres 4,566; lat. 15° 09′; long. 77° 36′; from Anantapore N. 32 miles; from Gooty W.N.W. 5½ miles. Large tank, constructed for Krishna deva royel.——**(2)** Town, Divisional and talook head-quarters, District moonsif's station, Traveller's bungalow; Anantapore dist., Gooty tal.; pop. 6,605; acres 5,629; lat. 15° 07′; long. 77° 41′; height, the town 1,200 feet; top of the rock 2,105 feet; from Anantapore N. 30 miles; from Bellary E. 47½ miles; from Madras N.W. 220 miles; from Penoocondah N. 70 miles. Rishy gowtaman selected the rock as his place of abode. Consists of cluster of fortified hills, nearly surrounding a lower fort and native town; and outside the chain of fortified summits are the military cantonment and another pettah [q.v.] or town. The summits of the inclosing rocks are connected by a rampart, and the access to the town within is through two openings, secured by fortified gateways, one on the south-east, the other on the south-west; there are besides two foot-paths, affording communication through sallyports. In the northern part of the circuit of inclosing rocks is an immense smooth rock, which, fortified by gradations surmounted through fourteen gateways, overlooks and commands the whole of the other works. A well near the summit is said to have communication with the Paumidy. On one of the bastions, overlooking a precipice of about 300 feet, is a small building called Moraury row's seat. About half way down the northern side of this huge rock is a projecting shoulder, called Maha gooty, on which are barracks, formerly occupied by part of a European regiment, but now falling to decay. The cantonment has been abandoned. Fort was besieged by Mussalmans in the sixteenth century and fell after siege of twelve years. Afterwards held by Pataups [q.v.] of Cuddapah and Savanoor, from whom it was wrested in 1714 by Ghorapadey [q.v.] family of Mahrattas [q.v.], the most distinguished of whom obtained in 1744 Nizam's recognition of his territory as a Mahratta state. In A.D. 1758 taken by stratagem by Hindoo row, father of Moraury row; and from him by Hyder ally in A.D. 1776 after siege of nine months. The fort passed to English in A.D. 1799. Sir Thomas Munro, who died of cholera on 6th June 1827 at Putticondah, was first buried here, his remains being afterwards taken to Madras. The Railway station is 2 miles from the town. Trig. station here in lat. 15° 06′ 49·02″; long. 77° 41′ 33·38″; height 2,105 feet; from Gooty E.S.E. ¾ mile. Gooty base north end is in lat. 15° 05′ 48·57″; long. 77° 38′ 57·65″; height 1,261 feet; from Anantapore N. 29 miles; from Gooty W.S.W. 2½ miles. Gooty base south end is in lat. 15° 00′ 53·57″; long. 77° 41′ 14·65″; height 1,110 feet; from Anantapore N. 24 miles; from Gajarampulley N.E. 2¼ miles; from Gooty S. 7 miles. The following are the travelling distances by road from Gooty to different places:—

To	Via	Miles and Furlongs.	
Adony	Putticondah	45	1
Anantapore ...	......	32	4
Bangalore ...	Anantapore, Paul samoodram and Chicbullapore.	162	7
Bellary	Goontacull	54	2
Bunganapully ...	Pyaupaly	48	5
Cottacote	Kurnool	100	6
Cuddapah ...	Yaumavaram	97	7
Cumbum	Bunganapully and the Nundicanama ghaut.	120	7½
Jedcherla ...	Kurnool and Cottacote	125	3
Kurnool ...	Veldoorty	60	1
Madras	Yaumavaram, Cuddapah, Kircambaudy, Nagary and Poonamallee.	264	3
Nagary	Yaumavaram, Cuddapah and Kircambaudy.	205	6
Nellore	Cuddapah	205	6
Paul samoodram.	Anantapore	87	6
Penoocondah ...	Anantapore	75	4
Putticondah ...	......	22	0
Pyaupaly	......	9	0
Royachoty ...	Tadpatry and Vempully	122	6
Secunderabad ...	Kurnool, Cottacote and Jedcherla	196	0
Vellore	Tadpatry, Royachoty and Vellore	213	6
Vellore	Anantapore, Cadiry and Poonganore ...	212	5¼

GOOZERAT (गुजरात - gujaráta, *Mahr.*). From (gurjara, san. people so called + ráshtra, san. country) [goorjara]. A province in W. india comprising Surat and other districts round the gulf of Cambay. Goozeratty is the language of Goozerat; see vol. I (61). So here a class of merchants who originally came from Goozerat; numbers about 1,000. Goozeratty bramins are in history one of the five sects of Dravida [q.v.] bramins [bhaushay, jauty].

GOPLA (గొప్పుల - goppula, *Tel.*). From (goppu, tel. threshing floor). Locative plural. Suffix in place names.

GOR (گور - gor, *Pers.*; గోరీ - górí, *Tel.*). Tomb [inam].

GORROO (గొఱ్ఱు - gorru, *Tel.*). From (korru, tel. spike).—"*a*" A seed drill. It consists of a beam with three or six shares [caur] fitted into it, and a corresponding number of bamboos attached to a zaddigam [q.v.] or drill, into which the seed is thrown and is thence carried into the ground by the bamboos. At the lower end of the bamboo [q.v.], just above the beam, is a hole through which seeds, the passage of which may be obstructed by clods, &c., of earth, are thrown out, thus warning the ryot [q.v.] of the obstruction which has to be removed. The gorroo is also used as a plough [calappay]. Palgorroo is a regular harrow [goontaca] with many teeth.—"*b*" Also land which will occupy one plough [yair]. Superficial measure. 50 goontas = 1 gorroo; 8 gorroos = 1 cootchel [alavay, 2b]. Approximate actual value, 1 gorroo = 3⅓ acres. But it rises to 5 acres. Compare Bullah. See vol. I, 609; II, 516.

GOSH (گوش - gosh, *Pers.*). Ear. Cf.:—Felis caracal (siyáhgosh), black ear; Lepus nigricollis (khargosh), donkey ear. See gloss. paragraphs.——*Gosha* (گوشه - goshah, Hind.; గోష - góshá, Tel.). A corner, retirement. Epithet of Mahomedan females of respectability who do not appear in public [zenana]. Many Hindoo women follow the same rule.——*Gosha nisheen* (گوشه نشین - goshahnishín, Hind.). From (goshah, hind. corner + nishín, pers. seated). One who sits in seclusion [purda nisheen].——*Goshparah* (گوشواره - goshwárah, Hind.). From (above + wár, pers. affix of similitude). Aggregate amount, abstract of an account.

GOTAH (گوٹا - gotá, *Hind.*). From (got, hind. the hem of a garment). Narrow gold [pon] and silver [velly] lace [kinaury, sarigay]. Used for female skirts [cholee].

GOTLA (గొట్ల - gotla, *Tel.*). From (gotle, tel. jujube tree). Locative plural. Suffix in place names.

GOURAMY (گورمی - gurami, *Malay*). Fish. Osphromenus olfax, labyrinthidæ, acanthopterygii, teleostei [matsyam, 30], of naturalists [jantoo]. Native of China, where it frequents still places in rivers. Introduced. Attains 20 lb. and is esteemed for flavor. Already naturalized in Mauritius, Cayenne, and Australia. Like all the Labyrinthidæ, is provided with apparatus for retaining water, so that when out of the water it can keep its gills moist, and can run to some distance by means of its fins and tail, and even leap upon neighbouring plants to catch insects [palmyra fish]. No other species here.

GOWNDEN (ಗೌಡ - gauda, *Can.*; கௌண்டன் - kaundan, *Tam.*). From (kavar, tam. to seize); originally life-taker; hunter. Village headman in the Balaghaut [q.v.], where called Gowda, but distinguish from the sanscrit Gowda [q.v.]. The Gownden's province according to old ordinances is to invite and assemble the ryots [q.v.] for the population of a village and cultivation of the lands dependent on it, to settle disputes, bring back and give encouragement to such of the inhabitants as from oppression, caprice, or other cause have deserted the village. If he be not himself a goottadar [q.v.] or renter, it is his duty to make the person who acts in that capacity acquainted with the circumstances of each inferior farmer; that he be not assessed beyond his ability, that the cowle [q.v.] he receives be not infringed, &c. The gownden should be acquainted with all the usages of his village, whether they regard its internal police or the mode of renting out its lands; supposed to have an intimate knowledge of the Shoodamad or ancient customs; he should be able, when applied to either by the ryots or the servants of the Circar [q.v.], to give a satisfactory exposition of every difficult or disputed point. Some of the agricultural classes habitually append the title Gownden as a sort of caste nomenclature after their names [inam, jauty].

GOWRAM (गौर - gaura, *San.*). Reddish.——*Gowr* (गौर - gaura, San.; गवय - gavaya, Mahr.; جنگلی کہلگا - janglíkhulgá, Hind.; سالدڠ - sáladang, Malay; ಕಾಡುಕೋಣ - kádukóna, Can.; ಕಾಟಿ - káti, Too.; కారెనుము - kárenumu, Tel.; ଗୋୟିଲୋ - goyilo, Oor.; കാട്ടി - kátti, Mal.; காட்டுயேனி - káttuyéni, Tam.). Title from sanscrit. San. means pale red. Mahr. from (gava, san. cow). Hind. from (janglí, hind. wild + khulgá, hind. buffalo). Can. from (kádu, can. forest + kóna, can. buffalo). Tel. from (káru, tel. forest + enumu, tel. buffalo). Mal. from (kátu, mal. forest). Tam. from (kádu, tam. forest + éni, tam. young deer). San. also (gaya); (gavala). Hind. also (gaur); (gaurgái), meaning wild ox. Tam. also (káttumádu), meaning forest + ox or cow. Title otherwise Bison. Gavæus gaurus, bovinæ, bovidæ, ruminantia, mammalia [sastanam, 23], of naturalists [jantoo]. Horns pale greenish with black tips, curving outwards upwards and slightly backwards, and finally inwards. General color dark chestnut brown or coffee brown; legs from the knee downwards white. Length 9½ to 10 feet; height at shoulder 6 feet; tail 34 inches. The skull is massive, the frontals large, deeply concave surmounted by a large semi-cylindric crest rising above the base of the horns. The head is square, proportionally shorter than in the ox, the bony frontal ridge is five inches above the frontal plane. The muzzle is large and full, and the eyes small, with a dull pupil of a pale blue color. The whole of the head in front of the eyes is covered with a coat of close short hair of a light grayish-brown color, which below the eyes is darker, approaching almost to black. The muzzle is grayish, and the hair is thick and short. The ears are broad and fan-shaped. The neck is sunk between the head and the back, is short, thick and heavy. Behind the neck, and immediately above the shoulder, rises a fleshy gibbosity or hump of the same height as the dorsal ridge. This ridge rises gradually as it goes backwards and terminates suddenly about the middle of the back. The chest is broad the shoulder deep and muscular, the fore legs short with the joints very short and strong, and the arm exceedingly large and muscular. The hair on the neck and breast and beneath is longer than on the body, and the skin of the throat is somewhat loose giving the appearance of a slight dewlap. The fore legs have a rufous tint behind and laterally, above the white. The hind quarters are lighter and lower than the fore, falling suddenly from the termination of the dorsal ridge. The skin on the neck, shoulders and thighs is very thick, being about 2 inches and more. The cow differs from the bull in having a slighter and more graceful head, a slender neck, no hump, and the points of the horns do not turn towards each other at the tip, but bend slightly backwards; and they are much smaller. The legs too are of a purer white. The very young bull has the forehead narrower than the cow, and the bony frontal ridge scarcely perceptible. The horns [sing] too turn more upwards. In old individuals the hair on the upper parts is often worn off. The skin of the under parts when uncovered is deep ochrey-yellow. The horns are smooth and polished; and in old individuals are generally broken off at both tips. They are slightly flattened at the base. Found in all the large forests of Southern india. On the west coast it is abundant all along the Western ghauts. The Anamullay hills, the Neilgherries, Wynaud, Coorg, and the Bababooden hills, are all favorite haunts. On the eastern side of the peninsula it is found in the Pulney and Dindigul hills, the Shendamungalam range, the Shevaroys, and some of the hill ranges near Vellore and the borders of Mysore. The Gowr is generally driven towards the sportsman by a line of beaters, while he himself remains concealed behind a tree. A wounded Gowr will occasionally charge, but in general he will turn. The flesh of the Gowr is good if not too old. Indian allied species not here found are:—Gavæus frontalis or gayal, Gavæus sondaicus or burmese wild ox, Poephagus grunniens or yak or grunting ox.——*Gowry* (गौरी - gaurí, San.).—"*a*" Parvaty as a maid before she became the wife of Shiva [q.v.]. Gowry was Girijay or mountain-born, that is born in the Himalayas, and she contrasts strongly with the southern Bhadra cauly [bhadra cauly, matam]. Proper name, common to both sexes. Gowripaty is Shiva, the lord of Parvaty; this also pers. name [peyar].—"*b*" Short for Gowry vratam or Gowry pundigay. Otherwise Haritaulica gowry vratam, from yellow image of gowry worshipped on the occasion; also Swarna gowry vratam, from color of image. Precedes Pillaiyaur chatoorty [q.v.]. Distinguish from Kedaury gowry vratam [q.v.]. Lunar festival [pundigay, 6a], subject to intercalation [adhicam], held on the third day [tity] of bright half [shoocla pacsham] of the sixth lunar month Bhaudrapadam [mausam] between 19th August and 18th September and lasting several days. In honor of Shiva's wife Parvaty [q.v.], as

Gowry. The festival is concluded by erecting a statue in each village, composed of paste of grain and intended to represent the goddess. This image is finally placed under a canopy and carried through the streets [maryauday]. See vol. I (93).——*Gowry's fruit* (गौरीफल - gaurip'hala, San.). From (gaurí, san. the goddess + p'hala, san. fruit); red fruit. Hill raspberry, Indian blackberry, Indian bramble, Indian raspberry. Botanically the Rubus genus, rosaceæ [vricsham, 49]. Mostly shrubs trailing or erect, with prickly stems; leaves alternate, simple or compound; flowers white or red; fruit edible. The species best known to the natives are:—Ellipticus, alias rubus flavus, gowreephul, rotundifolius; tall bush; flowers small, white; fruit yellow, flavor of the raspberry; commonly eaten and made into preserves, one of the best of the wild fruits of india; there is a variety hirta. Lasiocarpus, alias rubus albescens, mysorensis, parvifolius, racemosa; large, rambling plant; flowers deep pink; fruits numerous, dry or fleshy, red or orange or a glaucous blue-black color, small, good flavor; white kind of down covers young shoots; very similar to common english blackberry. Moluccanns, the himalayan raspberry; wide-spreading plant; flowers small, white; red edible fruits. Rosæfolius, the mauritius raspberry; fruit very similar in appearance to the english raspberry, but filled with hard seeds; variety produces double white flowers, very like roses [gool].——*Gowry's neem* (گوری نیم - gaurínim, Dec.). Same as Large neem.——*Gowry's tree* (గారచెట్టు - gára-chettu, Tel.). From nut shells used in her worship. Same as Fire-work plant.

GRAB (غراب - ghuráb, *Hind.*). A sloop with long projecting bows, Malabar.

GRÆMESPETT (గిరింపేట - girimpéta, *Tel.*). From (mr. græme, a former collector + péta, tel. suburb). Village; North arcot dist., Chittore tal.; pop. 2,200; acres 2,464; lat. 13° 12′; long. 79° 08′; from Chittore S. 1¼ miles. Suburb of Chittore.

GRAHAM (ग्रह - graha, *San.*). From (grah, san. to seize) [goonam, graumam]; as seizing or influencing destinies of men [griham]. A moveable point in the heavens. With Madhyam and Spootam prefixed, signifies mean and apparent place of such point in the sidereal or fixed zodiac [raushy chuckram]. So a planet [najm]. The following planets give a name to the seven days of the week [vanram]:—Ravy, or sooryan, the sun; Chundran, or soman, the moon; Mungalan, or coojan, mars; Boodhan, mercury; Gooroo, or brihaspaty, jupiter; Shoocran, or bhrigoo, venus; Shany, saturn. Besides these, Rahoo the moon's ascending node, and Kait her descending node, are reckoned as obscure planets [goolican], which occasion the eclipses [grahanam] of the sun and moon. At the large religious festivals a small offering is made to all the planets at once; excepting on these occasions they are never worshipped together. They are however frequently worshipped separately by those who suppose themselves to be under the adverse influence of one or other of them. Sooryan or ravy the sun, and Chundran or soman the moon, belonged to the old Aryan vedic deities. To Sooryan or ravy are offered in burnt sacrifice small pieces of the shrub, calotropis gigantea [yercum]; to Chundran those of butea frondosa [palaus]; to Mungalan or mars those of acacia catechu [catechu]; to Boodhan or mercury those of achyranthes aspera [indian burr]; to Brihaspaty or jupiter those of ficus religiosa [peepul]; to Shoocran or venus those of ficus glomerata [cluster fig]; to Shany or saturn those of the acacia suma [white sundra]; to Rahoo the ascending node blades of cynodon dactylon [hurrially]; and to Kait the descending node blades of eragrostis cynosuroides [darbhay]. The image of Sooryan is a round piece of mixed metal, twelve fingers in diameter; of Chundran, a piece like a half-moon, a cubit from end to end; of Mungalan, a triangular piece six fingers in width; of Boodhan, a golden bow two fingers in breadth; of Brihaspaty, a piece like a lotus [nelumbo]; of Shoocran, a square piece of silver [velly]; of Shany, an iron scimitar; of Rahoo, an iron macaram [q.v.], half stag [mrigam] and half fish [matsyam]; and of Kait, an iron snake [sarpam].——*Graha chauram* (ग्रहचार - grahachára, San.). From (chára, san. motion). Literally planetary motion. Misfortune.——*Grahanam* (ग्रहण - grahna, San.; گرهن - grahan, Hind.). From (grah, san. to take). An eclipse. The popular account of these in S. india of poorannic origin, is that a serpent swallows the sun or moon. Rahoo [q.v.] and Kait [q.v.] as planets stand for the moon's nodes, or dragon's [tinneen] head and tail. Compare Bel and the dragon worshipped at Babylon, where Bel is a name of the sun. The moon in its orbit [cacsham], passing from node to node [craunty pautam], does in effect draw on the line of sun's path [craunty mundalam] the figure of a serpent; and returning fills up the other side so as to produce the figure of a caduceus such as was put into the hands of Mercury by the Greeks having the head, body and tail of a serpent on a straight rod. The duration of an eclipse is considered a sacred, but inauspicious time. Hindoos observe a strict fast and abstain even from water two jaumams [q.v.] or six hours before beginning. They bathe twice both at sparsham or commencement and vimochanam or termination. Tarpanam [q.v.] or sesamum [gingelly] water offered to deceased ancestors is deemed more meritorious then than at other times. The belief is general that a pregnant female seeing the eclipse will bring forth a child with defect of limbs; so she is confined to a dark room. It is held that muntrams [q.v.] acquire unfailing efficacy when learnt or recited during an eclipse [jyotisham, maryauday].——*Grahapatram* (ग्रहपत्र - grahapatra, San.). From (above + patra, san. paper). Horoscopical table showing position and aspects of heavenly bodies at any particular moment, for birth, marriage, &c. [jenmaputtricay].——*Graha poojay* (ग्रहपूजा - grahapújá, San.). From (above + pújá, san. worship). Worship of the planets, to render them propitious.

GRAM (گرام - grám, *Hind.*). From portuguese (grão), meaning grain. Term applied to many pulses [dholl] especially when used for horses [ghorah] or cattle [maud]. Includes the genera:—arachis, atylosia, cajanus, cassia, cicer, dolichos, ervum, glycine, indigofera, malva, osbeckia, phaseolus, rothia, tephrosia, vigna.——*Bengal gram* (चणक - chanaka, San.; चणा - chaná, Mahr.; चणो - chanó, Conc.; حمص - himmas, Ar.; نخود - nakhúd, Pers.; چنے کا پیڑ - chanekáper, Hind.; چنے کا جھاڑ - chanekájhár, Dec; ಕಡಲೆ - kadale, Can.; ಕಡಲೆ - kadale, Too.; శనగ - shanaga, Tel.; ସୁଲୋଚନା - sullochona, Oor.; കടലക്ക - katalakka, Mal.; කඩල - kadala, Singh.; கடலை - kadalai, Tam.). Title from use for horses chiefly in n. india. San. from (chan, san. to give). Mahr., &c., from sanscrit. Mal. from tamul. Tam. from (kadal, tam. sea); foreign plant. San. also (kaláya), meaning causing wind or vayoo [calauyam]; (puta-sañjan), meaning born with a pod; (harimant'ha), meaning eaten by horse. Hind. also (harbarekájhár); (bút). Can. also (kadli). Tel. also (chanakamu). Mal. also (katala). Tam. also (mañjúram), meaning beautiful. Greek ἐρέβινθος, κριός. Title otherwise Bengal horse-gram, Cadalay, Calavanche, Chenna, Chick pea, Columbine, Common gram, Egyptain pea, Garavance, Gram chick-pea, Pea of venus, Shanaga. Botanically Cicer arietinum, linn., leguminosæ [vricsham, 48]. Specific from being like ram's head. Herbaceous, annual plant; height 2 feet or more; calyx five-lobed, scarcely gibbous, segment as long as the alæ of the corolla; leaves unequally pinnated; leaflets ovate, serrated, equal; stipules lanceolate, somewhat toothed; corolla papilionaceous; flowers axillary, bluish purple; legumes hairy, ¾ to 1 inch long, usually contain two seeds. Chemical composition of the gram is water 11·5, albuminoids 21·7, starch 59·0, oil 4·2, fiber 1·0, ash 1·5, phosphoric acid 1·1 per cent. Gives an acidulated exudation or vinegar; not a product of acetous fermentation or destructive distillation, but consists almost wholly of water, oxalic acid, and acid oxalates; it varies in color from pale brown to reddish brown, and has an intense and sharp acid taste, the characteristic of oxalic acid, and a slight and peculiar odour which is different from that of vinegar; its specific gravity is generally between 1·008 and 1·020. Plant cultivated in black loam; dry; ground prepared in south in audy or july or auvany [mausam] or august, on coromandel [q.v.] two or three months later, by ploughing and manuring; seed sown after soaking in water for some hours, broadcast, and soil levelled by harrow [gorroo]; under growth the weeds are cleared if necessary; grown crop is dark green, one foot high; cut after four months with sickles and heaped up; then put in the sun, beaten with sticks, and grain separated; produce brought to market after one month; average price 15 imperial seers [q.v.] for 1 rupee. The vinegar [caudy] above-mentioned is collected in the following manner:—a piece of thin and clean cloth is tied to one of the ends of a stick, and the plants are touched with this early in the morning so as to absorb the dew on them, which is squeezed out in a vessel; sometimes the plants are covered with a cloth during the latter part of the night, which is found wet in the morning and is then wrung out in a vessel, but the liquid in this case is much weaker than in the former case. In medicine seeds are antibilious; vinegar refrigerant, stomachic and tonic, used in atonic dyspepsia; substituted for british diluted acetic acid [sirkey ka tezaub], a common menstruum. When roasted like coffee [q.v.] seeds are aphrodisiac; they are eaten in curries [q.v.] cakes, &c.; very fattening to cattle and horses, but in this case prior to giving it is macerated in cold water till it becomes quite soft and it is not boiled. Varieties, white and red. Bengal gram is also a frequent plant second term. Ex., where transl. is of first term:—Arachis hypogæa (nélashanaga), ground, (vérushanaga), root; Ervum lens (chirishanaga), small; Malva rotundifolia (kátukadale), (káttukatala), and (káttukkadalai), forest; Osbeckia aspera (káttukkadali), forest; Pisum sativum (gundushanaga), round; Sida rhombifolia, var. retusa (kallangadale), stone. See gloss. paragraphs.——*Black gram* (माष - másha, San.; उडीद - udída, Mahr.; उडिदु - udidu, Conc.; اُرد - urud, Hind.; ماش - másh, Dec.; ಉದ್ದು - uddu, Can.; ಉರ್ದು - urdu, Too.; మినుములు - minumulu, Tel.; ବିରି - biri, Oor.; ഉഴുന്ന് - uzhunnu, Mal.; බූමා - búmá, Singh.; உளுந்து - ulundu, Tam.). Title from color of pulse [black horse-gram]. San. from (má, san. to measure); from seed used as weight [niray, 4]. Dec. from sanscrit. Singh. from (bú, singh. earth + má, singh. pulse) [field gram]. Tam. from (uzha, tam. to exert); tonic. San. also (pachélimá), meaning easily cooked; (kasháya), meaning dark-red; (vrishya), meaning aphrodisiac. Can. also (hasaru); (hesaru); (chikuda). Tel. also (uddulu); (káruminumulu), meaning wild + black gram. Title otherwise Maush, Minoomooloo, Oolandoo, Rayed kidney bean. Botanically Phaseolus [moodgam] mungo, var. radiatus, linn., leguminosæ [vricsham, 48]. Alias Phaseolus radiatus, roxburghii. Annual, diffuse; leaves pinnately trifoliolate, hairy; leaflets ovate, acuminated, slightly repand, but not lobed; peduncles erect, shorter than the petioles; flowers somewhat capitate; keel twisted to the left with a very long horn near the base on the left side; legumes very hairy, cylindrical, few-seeded, nearly erect; seeds smooth, somewhat truncated at both ends; flowers yellow; flowering in cold season. Differs from phaseolus mungo [green gram], in having longer and more trailing stems; the plant being much more hairy, the reddish brown pubescence giving the foliage a lighter tint; the seeds being fewer, larger and longer, and usually dark-brown color. Chemical composition of the gram is water 10·1, albuminoids 22·7, starch 55·8, oil 2·2, fibre 4·8, ash 3·3, phosphoric acid 1·1 per cent. This pulse is the origin of the weight mausham, [q.v.], as the seed of abrus precatorius [indian liquorice] is of the weight retty [q.v.]. Cultivated in red loam; dry ground prepared in south from audy or july to poorataushy or september, on coromandel in aushweejam or october and caurteecam or november, on w. coast in mitoonam or june; land ploughed five times, sheep folded; seed sown in south in arpisy or october, on coromandel in caurteecam or november and margashiram or december, on w. coast between 7th and 30th of mitoonam [mausam] or june; sown broadcast and ploughed in; a month after sowing two hoeings; ashes applied; in full grown crop pods are black; three and half months after sowing plants are rooted up; harvesting same as green gram; average price 12 imperial seers for 1 rupee. Root somewhat narcotic; seeds medicinally tonic. Of the meal natives make bread [poppadam] for religious ceremonies; cattle are fond of the straw; mixed with gram reckoned strengthening for horses. Flour detergent. Itself has two distinct sub-varieties, one with large black seeds and the other with smaller green seeds.——*Black horse gram* (कान्कुल्ती - kánkultí, Mahr.; درخت تشميزج - darakhtitashmízaj, Ar.; چشميزج - chashmízaj, Pers.; چاكسو - cháksú, Hind.; چاكوت - chákút, Dec.; చనుపాలవిత్తులచెట్టు - tsanupálavittulachettu, Tel.; കരിങ്കൊള്ള - karinkollu, Mal.; කළුකොල්ලු - kalukollu, Singh.; காட்டுக் கொள் - káttukkol, Tam.). Title because seeds are black and bear a resemblance to the horse-gram [madras horse-gram]; some black seeds are found in real horse-gram itself, and these also are used for medicinal purposes; so that there is some confusion. Mahr. from (kán, mahr. forest + kultí, mahr. horse-gram). Ar. from persian. Pers. from (chashm, pers. eye + zak, pers. tincture). Hind. from (chakshu, san. eye). Tel. from (tsannu, tel. breast + pálu, tel. milk + vittu, tel. seed + chettu, tel. tree); from seed powder applied to eye in breast milk in ophthalmia. Mal. from (kari, mal. black + kollu, mal. horse-gram, dolichos biflorus, linn.). Singh. from (kalu, singh. black + kollu, singh. horse-gram). Tam. from (kádu, tam. forest + kollu, tam. horse-gram). Ar. also (habbussaudán), meaning soudan seeds. Pers. also (chashúm), meaning eye like; (chashmak), meaning small eye. Hind. also (banár). Singh. also (bhútóra), meaning earth + cassia. Tam. also (idikkol), meaning to pound + horse-gram; (karungánam), meaning black + horse-gram; (mulaippálvirai), meaning breast-milk seed; ophthalmic application of seed powder; (kárkkol), meaning black horse-gram. Title otherwise Black-gram [q.v.], Breast-milk seed, Broad-leaved cassia, Chaksoo seed, Eye powder, Four-leaved cassia, Jungle horse-gram [q.v.], Soudan seed. Botanically Cassia [soovarnacam] absus, linn., leguminosæ [vricsham, 48]. Alias Senna absus. Biennial, all over clammy except the leaves; branches diffuse; leaves long-petioled; leaflets two pairs, obovate, obtuse, glabrous or slightly hairy on the under side; lower flowers axillary, solitary, upper ones forming a short raceme; pedicels short, with a bractea at their base, and minute bracteoles about the middle; stamens five, all fertile; legume nearly straight, obliquely pointed, much compressed, sprinkled with rigid hairs, few-seeded; seeds are small, black, and flat, with a projection at one end; flowers small, yellow; flowering all year; common shrub in dry jungles. Chaksoo seeds as occurring are black and polished, flat, of an irregular oval or oblong shape; the end where the hilum is situated is rather more pointed than the other, length and breadth nearly alike, about ⅕ to ⅙ of an inch; testa horny and thick; cotyledons yellow; taste bitter. The seeds are reduced to a fine powder, which is used as a direct application to the conjunctiva in purulent and other ophthalmia, blowing in a few grains from a quill; seeds mentioned in pharm., but non-officinal.——*Cow gram* (निष्पाव - nishpáva, San.; चवळा - chavalá, Mahr.; अलसंदे - alasandé, Conc.; لوبيا - lobiyá, Pers. and Hind.; لوبا - lobá, Dec.; كچنگ - kachang, Malay; ಅಲಸಂದಿ - alasandi, Can.; ಲತ್ತನೆ - lattane, Too.; అలసంద - alatsanda, Tel.; ମାଙ୍କୋଡୋଡାଣ୍ଡି - mamkododandi, Oor.; കോട്ടപ്പയർ - kóttappayar, Mal.; காராமணி - kárámani, Tam.). San. from (nir, san. prefix of intensity + páva, san. winnowing). Tel. from (hasandi, san. cow gram). Mal. from (kóttal, mal. stick for creepers to climb + payaru, mal. leguminous plant). Tam. from (kár, tam. blackness + á, tam. cow + mani, tam. grain). San. also (rájamásha), meaning king's phaseolus mungo, linn., var. radiatus, linn.; (chapala), meaning moving [long pepper]; (shvétarájamásha), meaning white + the plant. Hind. also (sufedlobá), meaning white variety; (chhotálobá), meaning small variety; (ballar) [country bean]; (chaula). Can. also (avade); (bilihesaru); (tadagani); (kursuvpairu). Tel. also (bobbaralu); (dantupesara), meaning stalk + phaseolus mungo, linn.; (kondaalatsanda), meaning hill + the plant; (pesara) [green gram]. Mal. also (mampayar), meaning earth pulse, perhaps from the color; (kantampayar), meaning field pulse; (karkatakappayar), meaning carcatacam, july, the month of fruiting + pulse; (payaru); (arippayar), meaning small pulse. Tam. also (tattaippayaru), meaning flat + pulse [country bean]; (kárámanippayaru), meaning vigna catiang, endl. + pulse; (periyagárámanippayaru), meaning large variety; (payaru) [green gram]; (válavarai), meaning sword + the plant [tambattam]; (perungárámani), meaning large + the plant; (shirugárámani), meaning small + the plant. Greek φακή ἰνδική. Title otherwise Alasanda, Asparagus bean, Cauraumany, Chinese dolichos, Chowlah, Chowlee, Japan lablab, Lentil, Lobyah [q.v.], Red gram [common dholl], Runner bean, Small-fruited dolichos, Tow cok. Botanically Vigna catiang, endl., leguminosæ [vricsham, 48]. Specific name from (kachang, malay, pulses or leguminous plants). Alias Dolichos catjang, cultratus, sinensis, tranquebaricus; Scytalis catjang; Vigna sinensis. Twining annual, glabrous; leaves pinnately trifoliate; leaflets ovate or oblong, acuminated; peduncles longer than the leaves; flowers in an oblong head or short raceme; calyx campanulate, five-toothed; lowest one longer than the rest; legume nearly straight, very long, cylindric, torulose, with a more or less recurved unguiculate beak, six to twelve-seeded; seeds truncated at both ends; flowers largish, pale violet; flowering in june to august. Chemical composition of the gram husked is water 12·5, albuminoids 24·1, starch 56·8, oil 1·3, fibre 1·8, ash 2·5, phosphoric acid 1·0; with husk, water 12·7, albuminoids 23·1, starch 55·3, oil 1·1, fibre 4·2, ash 2·4, phosphoric acid 1·2. Cultivated in sandy soil or black loam; cultivation, dry; ground prepared on coromandel in caurteecam or november and margashiram or december, on w. coast in yedavam or may and mitoonam or june; ploughing the soil four times; seed sown on coromandel in pooshyam or january, on w. coast in mitoonam [mausam] or june; no nursery; broadcast or dibbled in; when the young plant bears three or four leaves ashes are strewn over it; when it is about to climb, boughs of trees of a man's height are given it to climb upon, and mud is heaped round it; pods plucked as they mature; average price, 20 imperial seers for 1 rupee. Seeds considered hot and dry, diuretic and difficult of digestion. Several varieties as to color of flowers and seeds; the most esteemed is the white-seeded. Other common species are pilosa, vexillata.——*Dew gram* (பனிப்பயறு - panippayaru, Tam.). Title from pulse being brought to perfection by dew [pany]. Same as Field gram.——*Dog green gram* (நாய்ப் பயறு - náyppayaru, Tam.). Title from seeds like green gram and wild. Tam. from (náy, tam. dog + payaru, tam. phaseolus mungo, linn.); from pods. Botanically Indigofera [neely] pentaphylla, linn., leguminosæ [vricsham, 48]. Alias Indigofera fragrans, glabra. Suffruticose, decumbent; leaves pinnated; leaflets one to two pair, oval, both sides hoary from white soft hairs; peduncles about the length of the leaves, with two to three rather distant flowers; legumes cylindrical, straight, mucronate, glabrous; seeds ten to twelve, cylindrical, truncated at both ends; flowers small, purple; flowering nearly all the year.——*Field gram* (मुद्गपर्णी - mudgaparní, San.; काकमूग - kákamúga, Mahr.; हर्पुलि - harpuli, Conc.; ترانگلی - tirangulí, Hind.; ಅವರೆ - ávare, Can.; పిల్లిపెసర - pillipesara, Tel.; ചെറുവിതുക്കോൾ - cheruvitukkól, Mal.; බින්මා - binmá, Singh.; வயப் பயறு - vayappayaru, Tam.). San. from (mudga, san. green gram, phaseolus mungo, linn. + parna, san. leaf). Mahr. from (káka, san. crow + múga, mahr. green gram); from inferiority. Hind. from (tin, hind. three + angul, hind. inch); three-lobed. Tel. from (pilli, tel. cat + pesara, tel. green gram). Mal. from (cheru, mal. small + vitukkól, mal. leguminous plant). Singh. from (bin, singh. ground + má, singh. pulse) [black gram]. Tam. from (vayal, tam. field + payaru, tam. pulse); dry pulse. San. also (ajará), meaning not becoming old; (ákulí), meaning filled; (górékha), meaning earth + line; (tryangulí), meaning three-fingered, from trifoliate leaf; (kákamudga), meaning crow's phaseolus mungo, linn.; (sahá), meaning enduring. Mahr. also (ránamúga), meaning wild green gram. Hind. also (kulai), from sanscrit. Can. also (káduhesaru), meaning forest + green gram. Tel. also (madikelu); (mittikelu). Tam. also (narippayaru), meaning fox + pulse, from growing wild [jackal green gram]; (kollaippayaru), meaning garden + pulse; (elippayaru), meaning rat + pulse, a wild variety; (panippayaru), meaning dew + pulse, from being matured by dew; (shímaiyavarai), meaning foreign + dolichos lablab, linn. Title otherwise Crow gram, Dew gram, Fox gram, Rat gram, Three-lobed kidney bean. Botanically Phaseolus [moodgam] trilobus, ait., leguminosæ [vricsham, 48]. Alias Dolichos stipulaceus, trilobatus, trilobus; Glycine triloba; Phaseolus asellus. Herbaceous, procumbent, diffuse; petioles elongated; leaves pinnately trifoliolate; leaves much shorter than the petioles, roundish and entire, three-lobed, middle lobe obovate, narrower towards the base; peduncles elongated, ascending; flowers few, small, capitate, yellow; legume cylindrical, glabrous, or slightly hairy; flowering in cold season; grows wild. Also cultivated; dry; sown broadcast or in small patches; when full grown the leaves become yellow spotted and begin to fall off; three months after sowing pods are plucked by hand, then dried and threshed. Seeds gathered and eaten by the poor; affords good fodder; may be cultivated for hay; leaves and seeds used as famine food. There are several varieties.

——*Forest bengal gram* (കാട്ടുകടലി - káttukadali, Mal. ; காட்டுக் கடலை - káttukkadalai, Tam.). Title from seeds. Mal. from (kátu, mal. forest + kadali, mal. the plant, melastoma malabathricum, linn.). Tam. from (kádu, tam. forest + kadalai, tam. bengal gram, cicer arietinum, linn.), but really a corruption from malayalam; cf. wild bengal gram. Botanically Osbeckia aspera; bl., melastomaceæ [vricsham, 57]. Alias Melastoma asperum. Shrub; branches obscurely four-angled, bristly; leaves short-petioled, oblong-ovate or oblong-lanceolate, acute, three-nerved, upper side bristly, under hirsute on the nerves, and pubescent between them; calyx-tube cup-shaped, rigidly pubescent; segments five, ovate-oblong, obtuse, deciduous; appendages consisting of a tuft of a few bristles; stamens ten; anthers acuminated; style incurved at the apex; ovary crowned with bristles; flowers on short pedicels, terminal, somewhat racemose, purplish-red; flowering nearly all the year. Used medicinally for coughs. Other species are:—cupularis, hispidissima, kotigueda, leschenaultiana, octandra, truncata, wightiana, zeylanica. ——*Fox gram* (நரிப்பயறு - narippayaru, Tam.). Title from pulse growing wild, fox being token of loneliness. Same as Field gram.——*Green gram* (मुद्ग - mudga, San. ; मूग - múga, Mahr. ; मूगु - múgu, Conc. ; مونگ - múng, Hind. and Dec. ; ಹೆಸರು - hesaru, Can. ; ಪಂಡೆಂಗಿ - pandengi, Too. ; పెసర - pesara, Tel. ; ମୁଗ - maggo, Oor. ; ചെറുപയർ - cherupayar, Mal. ; මුං - mum, Singh. ; பயறு - payaru, Tam.). Title from color of pulse. San. from (mud, san. to be glad). Mahr., &c., from sanscrit. Drav. from (pasu, tam. green) [cow gram]. San. also (kámbóji), meaning produced in cambojam [indian liquorice]; (mahásahá), meaning much enduring; (mada), meaning intoxication; (harita), meaning green; (vishaghní), meaning poison destroying [indian heliotrope]. Hind. also (kálimúng), meaning black pulse; (harímúng), meaning green pulse; (kálíurud), meaning black phaseolus mungo, var. radiatus. Can. also (paççehesaru), meaning green + gram; (karehesaru), meaning black + gram; (kádubesaru), meaning wild + green gram; (chikada); (atchayasavu). Tel. also (pattsapesara), meaning green + green gram [tufted green gram]; (nallapesara), meaning black + green gram; (pesalu); (pattsapesalu), meaning green + green gram; (nallapesalu), meaning black + green gram. Tam. also (paççaippayaru), meaning green + pulse; (pásippayaru), meaning green + pulse; (shirubayaru), meaning small + pulse; (karuppuppayaru), meaning black pulse, a dark variety. Title otherwise Hairy-podded kidney bean, Moong bean, Payar, Pesaloo, Small-fruited kidney bean. Botanically Phaseolus [moodgam] mungo, linn., leguminosæ [vricsham, 48]. Specific from hindostany. Alias Phaseolus aureus, hirtus, max, melanospermus. Pulse; annual, nearly erect, hairy; leaves pinnately trifoliolate; leaflets broadly ovate or rhomboid, entire; peduncles at first shorter, afterwards longer than the petioles; racemes axillary; corolla papilionaceous; flowers in a kind of cylindrical head; keel twisted to the left with a short spur near the base on the left; legume horizontal, cylindrical, slender, hairy, six to fifteen-seeded; seeds striated; flowers greenish yellow; flowering in december, january; cultivated in fields. Chemical composition of the gram is water 10·8, albuminoids 22·2, starch 54·1, oil 2·7, fibre 5·8, ash 4·4. Grown generally as subordinate crop with millet [q.v.] or cotton [q.v.]; dry; ground prepared in south in pungoony or march or chittray or april, on coromandel in bhaudrapadam or september and aushweejam or october, on w. coast between 1st and 30th of mitoonam or june; land ploughed five times; sheep folded; seed sown in south in veiyaushy or may, on coromandel in aushweejam or october and caurteecam or november, on w. coast between 7th and 30th of mitoonam [mausam] or june; sown broadcast or by drill [zaddigam]; then ground ploughed once more; a month after sowing two hoeings; crop is dependent on rain; four months or so after sowing plants are rooted up; plant dried in sun ten or fifteen days and then beaten with sticks; stems thus separated from leaves and pods; latter are winnowed and pods separated; pods subsequently trodden by bullocks [mand] and buffaloes [khoolgah]; the grain is then sifted and dried; brought to market at once; average price, 15 imperial seers for 1 rupee. Ripe grain has good taste, is wholesome and nutritious, much esteemed, and commands a comparatively high price; eaten boiled or roasted; cooked into curries [q.v.], for which purpose it is broken up; the flour is substitute for peas [calauyam] in pease pudding; it is ground into meal for the preparation of sweet-cakes, &c.; forms a constituent of poppadams [q.v.]; crushed stalks and leaves prized as fodder for cattle. Flour has detergent properties and is used by native for washing the skin. Several varieties; one has dark-colored seeds, and is called black gram [q.v.]. The small-fruited kidney bean, phaseolus calcaratus, roxb., cultivated and wild, is closely allied to phaseolus mungo; phaseolus tortus, roxb., is a cultivated form of this.——*Horse-gram shrub* (कुलत्थ - kulatt'ha, San. ; کلتهی - kulthí, Hind. ; ಹುರುಳಿಗಿಡ - huruligida, Can. ; ಕುಡು - kudu, Too.). Title from resemblance. San. from (kula, san. cluster + st'há, san. to stand) [madras horse gram]. Can. from (hurali, can. horse gram, dolichos biflorus, linn. + gida, can. plant); from resemblance. Botanically Glycine [manshaparny] tomentosa, pursh., leguminosæ [vricsham, 48].——*Jackal green gram* (ಬೇಳೆ ಕಾಡುಸೊಪ್ಪು - bélakádusoppu, Can. ; ఉబ్బుకాడ - ubbukáda, Tel. ; நரிப்பயறு - narippayaru, Tam.). Title from growing wild. Can. from (béle, can. split pulse + kádu, can. wild + soppu, can. leaves). Tel. from (ubbu, tel. to swell + káda, tel. stem). Tam. from (nari, tam. jackal + payaru, tam. pulse, phaseolus mungo, linn.) [field gram]. Botanically Rothia trifoliata, pers., leguminosæ [vricsham, 48]. Alias Dillwynia trifoliata; Glycine humifusa; Lotus indicus; Trigonella indica; Westonia humifusa. Annual, prostrate, thickly sprinkled with soft, silky hairs; calyx cleft to the middle; leaves petioled, palmately trifoliolate; leaflets nearly sessile, cuneate-oblong, rather fleshy, hairy on the under side; stipules foliaceous; pedicels solitary or twin, leaf opposed; flowers small, sulphur, at last becoming reddish; flowering in february and march. A small procumbent weed, with trifoliate leaves; abundant everywhere; used as greens [keeray].——*Japanese cow gram* (کچنگ جاپون - kachangjápun, Malay). Title from original habitat. Malay from (kachang, malay, pulse, vigna catiang, endl. + jápun, malay, japan). Title otherwise Soja bean, Soy plant, White gram. Botanically Glycine [maushaparny] soja, sieb. & zucc., leguminosæ [vricsham, 48]. Specific name from malay word for a sauce. Alias Soja hispida. Stems sub-erect or climbing upwards, annual, densely clothed with fine ferruginous hairs; leaves long-petioled; leaflets membranous, ovate, acute, rarely obtuse 2–4 inches long, calyx ¼ inch densely hairy; corolla reddish, little exserted; pods usually only two to three-developed in the axil of each leaf, linear-oblong, recurved, densely pubescent 1½–2 inches by ⅓–⅜ inch, three to four-seeded, sub-torulose.——*Jungle gram* (جنگلی کلتهی - janglíkulthí, Hind.). Same as Zanzibar indigo.——*Jungle-horse-gram* (بن کلتهی - bankulthí, Hind. ; కొండఉలవ - kondaulava, Tel. ; காட்டுக்கொள்ளு - káttukkollu, Tam.). Title from appearance [black horse gram]. Hind. means forest horse-gram. Tel. from (konda, tel. hill + ulava, tel. horse-gram, dolichos biflorus, linn.). Tam. from (kádu, tam. forest + kollu, tam. horse-gram). Tel. also (kárulava), meaning jungle + horse-gram. Tam. also (shirugaliyánduvarai), meaning small + black + cajanus indicus, spreng. Botanically Atylosia scarabæoides, benth., leguminosæ [vricsham, 48]. Alias Cajanus scarabæoides; Cantharospermum pauciflorum; Dolichos medicagineus, scarabæoides; Rhynchosia scarabæoides; Stizolobium scarabæoides. Biennial; leaflets obovate, slightly wrinkled and paler on the under side; peduncles shorter than the petiole, about two-flowered; calyx about half the length of the corolla, cleft to the middle; segments lanceolate-acuminate, slightly curved upwards; vexillum recurved; legume linear, velvety or hairy; flowers small, yellow; flowering nearly all year. For atylosia candollei, w. and a., see Jungle dholl.——*Madras horse-gram* (कुलत्था - kulatt'há, San. ; कुळीत - kulíta, Mahr. ; कुळित्थु - kulitu, Conc. ; قلت - kullut, Ar. ; ماش هندی - máshihindí, Pers. ; کلتهی - kulthí, Hind. and Dec. ; ಹುರುಳಿಗಿಡ - huruligida, Can. ; ಕುಡು - kudu, Too. ; ఉలవ - ulava, Tel. ; କୋଳଥ - kulut'ho, Oor. ; മുതിര - mutira, Mal. ; කොල්ලු - kollu, Singh. ; கொள்ளு - kollu, Tam.). Title from seeds feeding horses especially in s. india; cf. bengal gram. San. from (kula, san. group + st'há, san. to stand); from cluster of pods [horse-gram shrub]. Mahr., &c., from sanscrit. Ar. from sanscrit. Pers. from (másh, pers. green gram, phaseolus mungo, linn. + hindí, hind. indian). Hind. from sanscrit. Oor. from sanscrit. Mal. from (mutiru, mal. to grow up). Singh. from tamul. Tam. from (kol, tam. to take, as food). San. also (khalakula), meaning threshing-floor + group; (balakula), meaning strength + group. Mal. also (kollu). Tam. also (kánam); (shengol), meaning red horse-gram. Title otherwise Cooltee, Horse-gram, Madras gram. Botanically Dolichos [shimby] biflorus, linn., leguminosæ [vricsham, 48]. Alias Dolichos tomentosus, uniflorus, waslawa; Glycine uniflorus. Annual vetch; stem erect; branches twining; young shoots and leaves covered with silk hairs; leaves pinnately trifoliolate; leaflets ovate, villous, pubescent when old; corolla papilionaceous; calyx deeply bilabiate; upper lip split at the apex; vexillum longer than the keel, ovate-oblong; alæ cohering with the keel at the base; flowers axillary, one to three together, sulphur-colored; legumes compressed, linear falcate, softly hairy, six-seeded. Chemical composition of the gram with husk is water 11·0, albuminoids 22·5, starch 56·0, oil 1·9, fibre 5·4, ash 2·2, phosphoric acid 1·0 per cent. Cultivated dry in any fair soil; ground prepared by ploughing and manuring; if land cultivated in previous year, soil only gone over with a harrow [gorroo]; seeds sown broadcast and then ploughed in; no weeding or watering; when plant has put forth two or three leaves ashes are sprinkled to promote growth; when crop is full grown the leaves wither and drop off; the stems are then about 2 feet; harvested generally three months after sowing, on w. coast longer; plants rooted out by hand and bundled and dried in the sun for four days; on fifth day brought to threshing floor and trodden under foot by cattle or beaten with sticks; then winnowed in the wind and separated and grain brought to store; average price 20 imperial seers for 1 rupee; largely cultivated here; has never been seen in a wild state; if irrigated, would produce from six to eight crops in the year. Seeds as food used for cattle; when given to horses, must first be boiled; natives use them in curries [q.v.] as substitute for dholl [common dholl] being a very pleasant tasted pulse [dholl]; haulms are good fodder; an oil is expressed from the seeds. There is a variety with jet-black seeds, distinct from so called Black horse-gram.

Madras horse-gram is also a frequent plant first term; ex., where transl. is of second term :—Tephrosia purpurea (kollukkáyvélai), pod + gynandropsis pentaphylla; Teramnus labialis (kollup-púndu), plant. Also plant second term; ex., where transl. is of first term :—Atylosia scarabæoides (káruulava), wild, (kondaulava), hill; Cassia absus (karinkollu), and (kalukollu), black, (idikkol), to pound, (káttukkol), wild; Dolichos falcatus (verriulava), mad; Rhynchosia rufescens (chiriulava), and (siriulava), small; Rhynchosia velutina (karraulava), stick. See gloss. paragraphs.——*Manilla gram* (மணிலாக்கொட்டை - manilákkottai, Tam.). Same as Ground nut.——*Moorman's gram* (मकुष्टक - makushtaka, San.; عدس - adas, Ar.; موٹھ - moth, Hind. and Dec.; కుంకుమపెసర - kunkumapesara, Tel.; துலுக்கப்பயறு - tulukkappayaru, Tam.). Title from original habitat. San. from (mank, san. to adorn); from appearance of matured plant [wild green gram]. Tel. from (kunkuma, tel. red saffron powder + pesara, tel. green gram, phaseolus mungo, linn.). Tam. from (tulukkan, tam. turk + payaru, tam. pulse). San. also (vásanta), meaning produced in spring. Tam. also (piççippayaru), meaning wild + pulse. Title otherwise Aconite-leaved kidney bean, Mutt bean, Saffron gram, Turkish gram. Botanically Phaseolus [moodgam] aconitifolius, jacq., leguminosæ [vricsham, 48]. Alias Dolichos dissectus; Phaseolus trilobus. Annual, diffuse, procumbent, slightly hairy; leaflets deeply and palmately divided into linear-lanceolate lobes; stipules attached below the middle; peduncles nearly as long as the petiole; legumes horizontal, cylindrical; flowers somewhat capitate, small, yellow; flowering in the cold season. Trailing slender-stemmed herb, has a small pleasant-tasted pulse; used like black gram [q.v.]; not considered very wholesome; leaves and stalks given to cattle. Chemical composition of the gram is water 11·2, albuminoids 23·8, starch 56·6, fat 0·6, fibre 4·2, ash 2·8, phosphoric acid 0·8 per cent.——*Mysore gram* (మైసూరుపప్పు - maisúrupappu, Tel.). Title corruption from (masúra, san. the plant). Same as Masoor.——*Rat gram* (எலிப்பயறு - elippayaru, Tam.). Title from small size. Same as Field gram.——*Red gram* (துவரை - tuvarai, Tam.). Title from pulse. Same as Common dholl.——*Saffron gram* (కుంకుమపెసర - kunkumapesara, Tel.). Title from pulse. Same as Moorman's gram.——*Small bengal gram* (చిరిశనగ - chirishanaga, Tel.). Same as Masoor ——*Tufted green gram* (పచ్చపెసర - pattsapesara, Tel.; சடைப்பயறு - shadaippayaru, Tam.). Title from close cluster of pods. Tel. from (pattsa, tel. green + pesara, tel. green gram, phaseolus mungo, linn.) [green gram]. Tam. from (jatá, san. bushy hair + payaru, tam. pulse). Botanically Phaseolus [moodgam] trinervius, heyne, leguminosæ [vricsham, 48]. Alias Phaseolus farinosus. Twining; branches and petioles covered with long spreading hairs; leaflets ovate, acuminated, deltoid or lobed at the base, young ones very hairy, densely ciliated; stipules oblong-lanceolate, attached below the middle; peduncles elongated, straight, hairy, much longer than the leaves; flowers forming a kind of cylindrical head; legumes horizontal, cylindrical, hairy.——*Turkish gram* (துலுக்கப்பயறு - tulukkappayaru, Tam.). Same as Moorman's gram.——*Wild bengal gram* (काडुचण्या - káduchanyá, Conc.; خبازی - khubbází, Ar.; پنیرک - panírak, Pers.; ಕಾಡುಕಡ್ಲೆ - kádukadle, Can.; ಕಾಟುಕಡಲೆ - kátukadale, Too.; త్రికాలమల్లె - trikálamalle, Tel.; കാട്ടുകടലക്ക - káttukatalakka, Mal.; காட்டுக்கடலை - káttukkadalai, Tam.). Title from resemblance of leaf. Conc. from (kádu, conc. forest + chanyá, conc. cicer arietinum, linn.). Ar. from (khubz, ar. bread), from flat round fruit. Pers. from (panír, pers. cheese). Can. from (kádu, can. forest + kadle, can. bengal gram). Too. similar. Tel. from (tri, san. three + kála, san. time + malle, tel. jasminum); flowering morning, noon and evening; and flowers like jasmine. Mal. from (kátu, mal. forest + katalakka, mal. bengal gram). Tam. from (kádu, tam. forest + kadalai, tam. bengal gram, cicer arietinum, linn.) [forest bengal gram]. Pers. also (nánikulágh), meaning crow's bread. Title otherwise Crow's bread mallow, Dwarf mallow. Botanically Malva [khoobauzy] rotundifolia, l., malvaceæ [vricsham, 25]. Alias Malva neglecta, vulgaris. Annual; stems herbaceous, spreading; leaves cordate, roundish, shortly and obtusely lobed, crenated; petioles elongated, sometimes with a line of hairs on their upper side; pedicels several, unequal, axillary, one-flowered; bracteoles three; carpels much wrinkled; flowers middle-sized, pale purple; flowering in february and march. Mucilaginous and emollient leaves used for poultices and also as external application in cutaneous diseases.——*Wild green gram* (वनमुद्ग - vanamudga, San.; काडुमुगु - kádumugu, Conc.; بن بربٹی - banbarbatí, Hind.; ಕಾಡುಹೆಸರು - káduhesaru, Can.; ಕಾಟುಪಡೆಂಗಿ - kátupadengi, Too.; కారలచంద - káralatsanda, Tel.; കാട്ടുപയറു - káttupayaru, Mal.; காட்டுப்பயறு - káttuppayaru, Tam.). San. from (vana, san. wild + mudga, san. green gram, phaseolus mungo, linn.). Conc. means wild green gram. Hind. from (ban, hind. forest + barbat, hind. bean). Can. from (kádu, can. wild + hesaru, can. green gram). Too. from (kátu, too. wild + padengi, too. green gram). Tel. from (káru, tel. wild + alatsanda, tel. vigna catiang, endl.). Mal. and tam. from (kádu, tam. forest + payaru, tam. green gram). San. also (makushta), meaning adorned [moorman's gram]; (mayashtaka), meaning destroying insects; (anup'hala), meaning small fruit. Hind. also (hullundá). Tel. also (adavipesara), meaning wild + green gram. Botanically Phaseolus [moodgam] adenanthus, g. f. meyer, leguminosæ [vricsham, 48]. Alias Phaseolus alatus, amarus, cultratus, rostratus. Perennial, twining; leaflets ovate, acute; stipules reflexed; racemes long-peduncled, few-flowered, shorter than the leaves; flowers in pairs with a gland between them; wings variously twisted; keel with a long spirally-twisted beak; legume pendulous, flat, curved, long-mucronate, many-seeded; flowers large, deep rose-purple; flowering in the cold season. The tuberous roots are eaten by the natives.——*Wild horse gram* (ಕಾಡುಹುರುಳಿಗಿಡ - káduhuraligida, Can.; వెర్రిఉలవ - verriulava, Tel.). Can. from (kádu, can. jungle + hurali, can. horse-gram, dolichos biflorus, linn. + gida, can. plant). Tel. from (verri, tel. mad + ulava, tel. horse-gram). Tel. also (itamungetíga). Botanically Dolichos [shimby] falcatus, klein., leguminosæ [vricsham, 48]. Root perennial, tuberous; stems twining; leaflets somewhat roundish-ovate, acuminated, terminal one more or less three-lobed; stipules sessile, reflexed; peduncles slender, two to eight-flowered at the apex; vexillum broadly-ovate, shortly two spurred at the base, with two long callosities extending half way up the limb and projecting inwards at the apex; keel much falcate; stigma capitate, woolly; legume linear, falcate, glabrous, four to eight-seeded; valves flat; flowers large, bluish-purple; flowering in the cold season.

GRANTAM (ग्रन्थ - grant'ha, *San.*). From (granth, san. to tie). Is the same as tamul nool [q.v.], from which Nunnool [q.v.], a good string. A collection of palm leaves [cadjan] tied together, book. Especially the sacred book of the Sikhs [q.v.], a collection of moral poems. Also an ancient character in the Tamul language, in which Sanscrit is written; called also Arya ezhoot, or bramins' writing; see vol. I (49). The use of several grantam letters, as ஷ sh, ஸ s, ஹ h, ஜ j, &c., is gaining ground among educated Tamulians [bhaushay]. See vol. II, 205.——*Grantavary* (ഗ്രന്ഥവരി - grant'havari, Mal.). From (above + vari, mal. writ). A book formed of the leaves of the Talipot [q.v.] palm in Travancore or S. canara in which Malabar jenmies [q.v.] register their agreements respecting land with their tenants or mortgagees.

GRASS (புல் - pul, *Tam.*). Prefix.——*Grass cutter* (گھاس کاٹا - gháskátá, Hind.). Seems confounded with Hindostany word, the cutter of grass. Servant employed to collect grass [ghaus] for horses [ghorah], one such being usually attached to each horse besides the horsekeeper [q.v.]. In the north the grass cutter is a man; here that office is filled by the horsekeeper's wife.——*Grass oil* (గడ్డినూనె - gaddinúne, Tel.; புல்லெண்ணெய் - pullenney, Tam.). Grass as it begins to flower is cut, bound in small bundles, and thrown into a boiler with water. The oil [yennay] distilling over from this into cold water and thence skimmed is grass oil. The S. indian grass oils are all extremely fragrant, having an odour like a mixture of lemon [q.v.] and rose [gool]. Much esteemed as external application in rheumatism. Internally as carminative. The chief are from Andropogons, viz.:—Martini, roxb., roussa oil grass, giving ginger grass oil; Muricatus, retz., cuscus grass, giving cuscus root oil; Nardus, linn., citronella, giving citronella oil; Schœnanthus, roxb., lemon grass, giving indian melissa oil.

GRAUMAM (ग्राम - gráma, *San.*; ഗ്രാമം - grámam, *Mal.*). From (grah, san. to hold) [goonam, graham, griham]. Holding [cara]. An inhabited but unfortified village in the midst of cultivated fields and where live cultivators, artisans and laborers. A small village has about hundred families; a large village about five hundred. Every village has its grauma devatay [q.v.] or tutelary deity. Graumam is opposed to Aranyam [q.v.] on the one side, and to Pooram [q.v.], Nagaram [q.v.], and Putnam [q.v.] on the other. In Malabar means a Bramin village only, equivalent to agrahauram [q.v.] east of the ghauts [q.v.]. At the time of Parshooraman's gift of the country to the Bramins, sixty-four graumams were established from Goa to Cape comorin, thirty-two being from Cassergode north to Comorin south; to these were attached all the Shoodra villages [keraloputty]. The villages are held by various tenures in the presidency known by different terms according as they are held by one or more persons in common or severally or by fixed determined shares or according as they pay revenue to government or otherwise. The following are the principal tenures which see under their respective heads :—Yecabhogam and palabhogam; Pasancaray, pungoovaly or samoodauyam and aroothicaray; Zemindarry and ryotwarry or amauny; Coroo, sangoroo and shrotriem or inam. See vol. I, 112.——*Graumacurts* (గ్రామఖర్చు - grámakhartsu, Tel.). From (above + kharch, hind. expense). The private expenses of a village contribution among the villagers for the performance of festivals and other purposes which concern the community.——*Grauma devatay* (ग्रामदेवता - grámadévatá, San.). From (above + dévatá, san. deity). Tutelar deities which protect the fields, villages, and towns from evil spirits, and ward off plagues, famine, pestilence, war, conflagration, and inundation. They are regarded as beings who can avert much evil, though not able to bestow positive blessings. These were the gods worshipped by the Tamulians [q.v.] when the Aryan [q.v.] colonists first visited them. The Graumadevatays properly so called are Ayenaur [ayen], with his two wives Pooranay and Poodcalay; and the females Yellamma, Mauriyamman, Ancaulamman, Bhadra cauly, Pidaury, Chamoondy and Doorga. Among the various images that are found in their pagodas [q.v.], together with their own, that of Veerabhadran [q.v.] is the principal. Every township has its Graumadevatay or village goddess, being now under the hindoo system regarded as some form of Cauly [q.v.] or Doorga [q.v.], to whom an annual sacrifice of a living animal is offered [baly]. At Madras town the Graumadevatay is Yegammaul or Yegauttaul [matam]. See vol. I (77).——*Grauma devatay tirnaul* (கிராமதேவதைத்திருநாள் - kirámathévathait-tirunál, Tam.). Means village + deity + festival. This is an annual ceremony [pundigay, 6d], generally after harvest about January, unless interrupted by war or any other cause. Upon this occasion all the inhabitants, of every tribe and description, resort to the temple of the god, each bringing an offering according to his ability. The toty [q.v.] or public crier gives notice of the approaching festival eight days before the time appointed, nor must travellers leave the village till the ceremony has been performed. Famine, pestilence and every public calamity are attributed to the wrath of the sawmy [q.v.], offended either at the neglect of the established rites or at the sins of his votaries. The most devout among the latter deprecate his anger by penance. The Shirry [q.v.] was formerly performed on this occasion. These penances, &c., were generally at the temple of the indigenous village goddess only [maryauday]. Inams were formerly granted for performing village festivals.——*Graumadhicaury* (ग्रामाधिकारी - grámádhikárí, San.). From (above + adhikárí, san. superintendent). The head of a village; either the proprietor, the headman, or the collector of the revenue on government account [monigar].——*Graumahisaub* (గ్రామహిసాబు - grámahissábu, Tel.). From (above + hisáb, hind. accounts). The general demand collection and balance furnished by curnam [q.v.] at the period of settlement.——*Grauma khandam* (గ్రామఖండము - grámakhandamu, Tel.). From (above + khanda, san. part). Village site. A spot of ground in a village allotted free to bonâ fide residents for building houses [grauma nuttam].——*Grauma merah* (கிராமமேரை - kirámamérai, Tam.). From (above + méra, tel. fee). Allowances of a portion of the crop, to the village officers and servants [baluotah, merah].——*Grauma moonsif* (గ్రామమునసపు - grámamunasapu, Tel.). From (above + munsif, hind. judge). The head of a village vested with judicial, criminal and police powers; office created by the British.——*Grauma nuttam* (கிராமநத்தம் - kirámanattam, Tam.). Same as Grauma khandam.——*Graumany* (கிராமணி - kirámani, Tam.). The head man of a village. Title assumed by toddy [q.v.] drawers. In Teloogoo, Canarese, and Malayalam villages it denotes the village barber.——*Grauma pravarticam* (ग्रामप्रवर्तिका - grámapravartiká, San.). From (above + pravartiká, san. judge). Village senate.——*Grauma samoodauyam* (கிராமசமுதாயம் - kirámasamuthâyam, Tam.). From (above + samudáya, san. collection). Property, whether land, topes [q.v.], &c., belonging to and enjoyed by the whole village in common.——*Graumattaun* (கிராமத்தான் - kirámattán, Tam.). In Tamul districts the headman [monigar] of a village.——*Graumyam* (ग्राम्य - grámya, San.). Rustic. Provincialism in grammar [lacshanam]. Barbarisms, including all Hindostany and other corruptions.

GRAUSAM (ग्रास - grása, *San.*). From (gras, san. to swallow) [ghaus, ghiyah]. A mouthful; fodder for cattle.

GREEN HILLS (பச்சமலை - paççamalai, *Tam.*). From (paççai, tam. green + malai, tam. mountain). Range of hills; Salem dist., Salem tal.; lat. 11° 50′; long. 78° 16′; height 5,410 feet; from Salem N. 15 miles. Highest portion of the Shevaroy hills [moottanaud]. Distinguish from Putchamullay range in Ahtoor talook on the south-east.

GRIDHRAM (गृध्र - gridhra, *San.*). From (gridh, san. to be greedy) [gidh]. Vulturidæ family, raptores, aves [pacshy, 1] of naturalists [jantoo]. Vultures. Very large, thick, heavy; head and part of the neck often bare; crop prominent, eye small, wings very long, tail short. Habits sluggish, but not shy of man; devour carcases, &c.; discover food by sight, but have strong sense of smell. Divided into Vulturinæ, true vultures, and Neophroninæ, scavengers. The species best known to the natives are:—Gyps bengalensis [gidh], Otogyps calvus [rangidh], Gyps indicus [burragidh], Neophron peronopterus [dung kite].

GRIHAM (गृह - griha, *San.*). House. From (grih, san. to hold) [ghar, goonam, graham, graumam]. House. Cell excavated in the walls of Booddhist [booddha] caves [staupatyam]. Astronomical mansion [raushy].——*Griha devutay* (गृहदेवता - grihadévatá, San.). From (above + dévatá, san. deity). The household deity; represented by a water-pot, a rude figure, a Shalagram [q.v.] stone, or the Toolsy [q.v.] plant [matam].——*Griha parivritty* (गृहपरिवर्त्ति - grihaparivartti, San.). From (above + parivritti, san. revolution). Name of a cycle [chuckram] of ninety years among the Tamuls, based on the revolution [bhaganam] of the sun and five planets [graham]. The solar year used in this is 365d 6h 12′ 36″ European time, and 365d 15g 31v 30p Indian time [maunam]. The cycle consists of the sum of one revolution of the sun [sooryan], 15 of Mars [coojan], 22 of Mercury [boodhan], 11 of Jupiter [brihaspaty], 5 of Venus [shoocran], and 29 of Saturn [shany]. It was analyzed by Father Beschi [veeramaumoony] in Madura. Its epoch is A.A.C. 24 [jyotisham].——*Grihastan* (गृहस्थ - grihas'tha, San.). From (above + st'há, san. to stand). A householder [aushramam].

GROUND (மனை - manai, *Tam.*). A measure of land 60 × 40 = 2,400 square feet; used at Madras for house-sites. 24 grounds = 1 cawny [alavay, 2a]. Same as Munny. Compare Ancanam. See vol. I, 609; II, 514.——*Ground nut* (भूचणक - bhúchanaka, San.; भुईचणा - bhuíchaná, Mahr.; नेलगडले - nélagadlé, Conc.; ولايتی مونگ - viláitímúng, Hind. and Dec.; کچنگ تانه - kachangtanah, Malay; ನೆಲಕಡಲೆ - nelakadale, Can.; ನೆಲಕಡಲೆ - nelakadale, Too.; వేరుశనగ - vérushanaga, Tel.; നിലക്കടല - nilakkatala, Mal.; රටකජු - ratakaju, Singh.; வேர்க்கடலை - vérkkadalai, Tam.). Title from pod maturing under ground. San. from (bhú, san. ground + chanaka, san. bengal gram, cicer arietinum, linn.). Mahr. from sanscrit. Hind. from (viláití, hind. foreign + múng, hind. phaseolus mungo, linn.). Malay from (kachang, malay, pulse + tanah, malay, earth). Can. from (nela, can. ground + kadale, can. bengal gram). Too. from (nela, too. ground + kadale, too. bengal gram). Tel. from (véru, tel. root + shanaga, tel. bengal gram). Mal. from (nila, mal. ground + katala, mal. bengal gram). Singh. from (rata, singh. country + kaju, singh. cashew nut, anacardium occidentale, linn.). Tam. from (vér, tam. root + kadalai, tam. bengal gram); from legumes appearing about the roots. Mahr. also (bhuímúga), meaning ground + phaseolus mungo, linn. Hind. also (búmúng), meaning ground gram; (múngphallí), referring to pod. Malay also (kachanggoreng), meaning pulse + to fry; (kachangmiñak), meaning pulse + oil. Can. also (nelugalekáyi); (bérukadale), meaning root + bengal gram. Tel. also (nélashanaga), meaning ground + bengal gram. Mal. also (vérkkatala), meaning root + bengal gram. Tam. also (nilakkadalai), meaning ground + bengal gram; (manilákkottai), meaning manilla nut; from original habitat. Greek οὔιγγον, οὔιτον, οὔιτον. Title otherwise American earth nut, Arachis oil plant, Chenee baudam, Country cashew, Earth almond, Earth bengal gram, Earth nut, Earth pea, Grass nut, Katjang, Mandoby, Manilla gram, Manilla nut, Monkey nut, Nut-oil plant, Pea nut, Pindal, Pindar, Underground bean, Teuss oil plant, Underground kidney bean, West indian ground nut. Botanically Arachis hypogæa, linn., leguminosæ [vricsham, 48]. Specific name from the pods burying themselves in the earth, where they ripen their seeds. Alias Arachis africana, americana. Stem hairy; leaves abruptly pinnated; leaflets two-pair; calyx tubular, long; corolla papilionaceous; stamens and petals inserted into the throat of the calyx; pea-like flowers above ground sterile, aggregate, axillary, yellow; legumes long-stalked, to indehiscent, one-celled, two to three-seeded. Annual herb with procumbent branches; presents the appearance of a large clover; its seed-pod perfected under ground, about 2 inches long, and contains two or three pea-like [calauyam] seeds of an earthy flavor; the seeds or nuts abound with starch, oil and a large proportion of albuminous matter; sold in bazaars [q.v.] either parched, with the shell on and put up in paper packets, or shelled and roasted; the cleaned seeds yield about 43 per cent. of a clear straw-colored edible oil possessing a slight bean-like taste and smell. Plant is cultivated in sandy soil; ground ploughed dry in shrauvanam or august; seed sown in bhaudrapadam [mausam] or september, after manuring; no nurseries; watered once a week; height of full grown crop one span; roots are dug after five months, and brought to market immediately; average price 12 imperial seers for one rupee. Oil forms a good substitute for olive [zeitoon] oil; well adapted for the preparation of ointments; gives to pharm. oleum arachis, officinal. The leaf affords food for cattle; nuts, after surplus oil extracted by pressure, yield a good oil cake [poonauk] for manure, &c.; dried kernels of nuts are largely consumed and from the quantity of oil they contain are nutritious; generally toasted before eaten, less wholesome than the cashew-nut [cashew], which much resemble in taste. Seeds are exported to france and elsewhere for the manufacture of oil; oil is used for adulterating gingelly [q.v.] oil; makes a good soap [sauboon]; in fact is good for every purpose for which olive or almond [baudam] oil is used; does not become rancid so quickly as other oils [yennay]; brilliancy of light in lamps is superior to that of olive oil, with scarcely any smoke.

GUAR (गोवारी - góvári, *Mahr.*; वाल्लासांगो - vállásángó, *Conc.*; گوار - guár, *Hind.*; مٹکی کی پھلی کا جھار - matkíkíphallíkájhár, *Dec.*; ಚಪ್ಪರದವರೆ - chapparadavare, *Can.*; ತಂಬಡಬರೆ - tambadabare, *Too.*; గోరుచిక్కుడు - góruchikkudu, *Tel.*; പന്തലമര - pantalamara, *Mal.*; கொத்தவரை - kottavarai, *Tam.*). Title from hindostany. Dec. from (matkí, hind. pot + phallí, hind. pod + jhár, hind. tree). Can. from (chappara, can. shed + avare, can. beans, dolichos lablab, linn.). Tel. from (góru, tel. nail + chikkudu, tel. dolichos lablab, linn.); probably from its being sliced with the nail, being too small to require a knife. Mal. from (pantal, mal. shed + amara, mal. bean, dolichos lablab, linn.). Tam. from (kottu, tam. cluster + avarai, tam. dolichos lablab, linn.). Can. also (góriballi), meaning cyamopsis + creeper; (góvardhanakáyigida), meaning cow + increase + fruit + plant, from use as cattle fodder; (chauvalikáyigida), used in bellary. Tam. also (shíniyavarai), meaning china + dolichos lablab, linn. Title otherwise Chinese lablab, Chupper bean, Cluster bean, Lupin, Nail bean. Botanically Cyamopsis psoralioides, dc., leguminosæ [vricsham, 48]. Alias Dolichos fabæformis, psoralioides; Lupinus trifoliatus; Psoralea tetragonoloba. Robust, hairy, erect, annual herb, 2–3 feet high; flower small, rose-colored; pods thick and from 1½–2 inches long; a sort of gram [q.v.]; cultivated during the cold months; the grain a cattle fodder; small flat pods, used in curries [q.v.] and as french beans [lobyah].

GUAVA (बहुबीजफल - bahubíjap'hala, *San.*; जांबा - jámbá, *Mahr.*; पेर - péra, *Conc.*; امرود کا پیڑ - amrúdkáper, *Hind.*; جام کا جہاڑ - jámkájhár, *Dec.*; جمبو - jambu, *Malay*; ಶೀಬಿ - shíbi, *Can.*; ಪೇರ - péra, *Too.*; జామచెట్టు - jámachettu, *Tel.*; ଜାମୋ - jámó, *Oor.*; പേര - péra, *Mal.*; පේර - péra, *Singh.*; கொய்யா - koyyá, *Tam.*). Title from (guyava, west indian). San. from (bahu, san. many + bíja, san. seed + p'hala, san. fruit); cf. anaur. Hind. means nectar and properly refers to pear [amrood]. Dec. from (jám, hind. guava + jhár, hind. tree). Tel. from hindostany. Mal. from english pear. Tam. from guava by corruption. San. also (amritap'hala), meaning sweet fruit. Hind. also (safríjám), meaning journey + fruit. Can. also (góva); (perala). Tel. also (goyyáchettu); (góvachettu). Mal. also (koyyá). Title otherwise Journey mango. Botanically Psidium guyava, linn., myrtaceæ [vricsham, 56]. Stout-growing shrub, sometimes small tree 15 feet high; begins to bloom during hot season, and bears fruit during rains up to end of cold season; the finest fruit is met with when the general season of bearing is over; the fruit is globose, yellow; an american plant naturalized in india by the portuguese, now universally cultivated, and in some parts of the country has run wild. The external surface of the bark when fresh is smooth and brown, marked by superficial scars indicating the separation of squamous plates of dead bark; these plates sometimes remain partially attached; beneath the brown epidermis the fresh bark is green; its inner surface is marked by longitudinal striæ, and is of a light brown color; the taste is astringent and agreeably acid; the leaves are aromatic, egg-shaped or oblong, short stalked, covered with soft down underneath, and with the principal veins very prominent; the watery extract of bark contains 27·4 per cent. of tannin. For cultivation first sown in nursery in pots; transplanted four months after; fruit plucked after four or five years; average price, 100 per rupee or one fruit per one pie. Bark of the root medicinally astringent; employed in the diarrhœa of children; in form of a decoction young leaves tonic in the diseases of the digestive functions; in pharm. nonofficinal. Fruit has thin bright yellow rind, filled with pulpy yellowish, cream-like or red flesh of pleasantly acid-sweet flavor; natives eat it in its natural ripe state; europeans make it into guava jelly or guava cheese; preferred fresh from the tree in the morning early, as the heat of the day injures its flavor. Wood whitish, moderately hard, even-grained; works well and smoothly; used for wood-engraving and for spear handles and instruments. Two varieties:—Psidium guyava, linn., var. pyriferum, linn., or white guava is pear-shaped; Psidium guyava, linn., var. pomiferum, linn., or red guava is round or ovoid. The difference of color lies only in the seeds; the white guava is the best to eat. No other species of the genus here.——*Dark guava* (کالا جام - kálájám, Hind.). Same as Common jaumoon. ——*Hill guava* (ತವಂಟೆ - tavante, Can.; மலைச்சிறுகொய்யா - malaiççirugoyyá, Tam.). Title from habitat. Can. from (tavudu, can. bran). Tam. from (malai, tam. hill + shiru, tam. small + koyyá, tam. guava, psidium guyava, linn.). Tam. also (tavuttukkoyyá), meaning bran + guava; from similar and tomentose appearance of fruit. Title otherwise Hill gooseberry, Woolly myrtle. Botanically Rhodomyrtus tomentosa, wight, myrtaceæ [vricsham, 56]. Alias Myrtus canescens, tomentosa. Small tree, resembling myrtle; branches downy; leaves opposite, entire, ovate, three-nerved, the lateral nerves near the margin, upper side when young downy, under hoary and tomentose; peduncles one to three-flowered, bearing two ovate bracteoles under the flower; calyx downy, five-cleft; petals slightly downy outside; berry three-celled; seeds compressed, forming two rows in each cell; bears a profusion of pink blossoms somewhat resembling those of peach [shaft auloo]; fruit is a berry of a pale, yellow color. Jelly made from berries, similar to apple-jelly; wood white with pink heart, close-grained, dense, splits in seasoning, good for small turnery purposes.——*Malacca guava* (ملاکہ جام - malákájám, Hind.). Same as Malacca jaumoon.

GUDDEE (گدی - gaddí, *Hind.*). A cushion to sit upon, especially a king's cushion, which is generally a carpet on floor with cushion at head, or throne. Also the pad placed on an elephant's back. Guddee nisheen, from (nishín, pers. who sits) is a sovereign.

GUDDILAM (கடிலம் - kadilam, *Tam.* gadilam *). From (kedilam, tam. a deep gulf). Sanscrit name (garudanadí), meaning braminy kite + river. River; South arcot dist., Cuddalore and Tricalore tals. Rises in Yaigal tank in Cullacoorchy talook. Flows through Tricalore and Cuddalore talooks, and passing close by Fort St. David joins the sea about a mile north of Cuddalore. Length, 59 miles. Principally supplied by the Malattaur, which connects it with the Ponniaur. Three anicuts [q.v.].

GUENOO (ಗೇಣು - génu, *Can.*). A span from the tip of the thumb to that of the little finger. 12 ungoolams = 1 guenoo; 2 guenoos = 1 mola [alavay, 1c]. Approximate actual value, 1 guenoo = 9 inches. Used by Canarese. Same as San. vitasty or gocurnam, Hind. bilisht, Tel. jena, Tam. jaun. Compare San. pradesham, Tam. adee, wottay. See vol. I, 609.

GUENY (ಗೇಣಿ - géni, *Can.*). Tenancy. Guenigar is a tenant. Gueny chit is the agreement executed by a tenant-at-will to the proprietor. Gueny hootwully, from (huttuvali, can. produce), is the portion of produce received by landlord as rent. Moolgueny, from (múla, can. original), is a permanent tenancy.

GUINDY (கிண்டித்தோட்டம் - kindittóttam, *Tam.*). From (kindi, tam. a depression). Village; Chingleput dist., Sydapett tal.; pop. 305; acres 1,269; lat. 13° 00′; long. 80° 17′; from Fort St. George S.W. 6½ miles; from Sydapett S.S.E. 1¼ miles; from the sea W. 3¼ miles. The Governor of Madras [q.v.] has an extensive park and country-house here.

GUINEA (گینی - giní, *Hind.*). Means abounding in gold. The country on W. coast of Africa.——*Guinea cloth* (గినియాగుడ్డ - giniyágudda, Tel.). Old name for piece-goods bought here, especially in Nellore, to be used in West african trade.——*Guinea corn* (گینی کا اناج - ginikáanáj, Hind.). Same as Cholum. ——*Guinea grass* (ರುಸ್ಕಹುಲ್ಲು - ruskahullu, Can.; చామకసవు - tsámakasavu, Tel.; கினிப்புல் - kinippul, Tam.). Tel. from (tsáma, tel. panicum italicum, linn. + kasavu, tel. grass). Tam. means guinea grass. Tam. also (shónaippul), meaning incessant rain + grass. Botanically Panicum [priyangoo] jumentorum, swartz., graminaceæ [vricsham, 156]. Alias Panicum maximum. Tall, hardy, succulent grass; introduced; native of guinea; succeeds even on poor clay soil and on sea sand; when irrigated produces from six to eight crops a year; it should be cut before the flowers appear, as the latter exhaust the nutritive substances of the stem; if planted in rows it allows of interculture by cattle power, by which means the land on which it grows may be easily cleansed; thus it affords an excellent crop for a rotation; much liked by horses [ghorah]; supplies fodder for cattle [maud].——*Guinea pepper* (گینی مرچ - ginímirch, Hind.). Same as Common chilly.——*Guinea sorrel* (گینی چکہ - ginichukkah, Hind.). Same as Red hemp bendy.——*Guinea wheat* (حنطہ رومی - hintahirúmí, Ar.). Same as Mecca cholum.——*Guinea yam* (گینی پنڈالو - ginípindálú, Hind.). Same as Malacca yam.

GULL (గల్లు - gallu, *Tel.*). Corruption of (kallu, tel.). Stone [cull]. Suffix in place names; as Minagull, sky stone.

GUM (گوند - gond, *Hind.*). Prefix in pharmacology [gond]. ——*Gum ammoniac* (اشق گوند - ushshakgond, Hind.). Product of Dorema ammoniacum, don. [ooshak].——*Gum anime* (سندروس - sandrús, Ar. and Pers.; سندرس - sandaras, Hind.; چندرس - chandras, Dec; తెల్లగుగ్గిలము - tellaguggilamu, Tel.; හල්දුම්මල - haldummala, Singh.; வெள்ளைக்குந்துருக்கம் - vellaikkundurukkam, Tam.). Title from many living insects it contains. Tel. from (tella, tel. white + guggalamu, tel. dammer). Singh. from (hal, singh. vateria indica, linn. + dummala, singh. dammer). Tam. from (vellai, tam. white + kunduruka, san. olibanum). Properly resin [raul] of hymenæa courbaril, but generally applied to indian copal [copal] from vateria indica, linn., or piney [q.v.] tree.——*Gum arabic* (صمغ عربی - samaghiarabí, Ar. and Pers.). Ar. from (samagh, ar. gum + arabí, ar. arabic). Greek κόμμι from the egyptian. Product of Arabian acacias. Real gum arabic occurs in roundish morsels, spherical, ovoid, or formless, of variable degrees of whiteness; solid and very hard, rarely friable, diaphanous in some varieties, opaque in others, fractures in plain, shining, glassy surfaces; inodorous, and nearly tasteless; soluble in the mouth, and adherent to the teeth; powder white in proportion to its purity. For Indian gum arabic see Babool, ——*Gum asafœtida* (هنگ - hing, Hind.). Same as Asafœtida. ——*Gum babool* (ببول کا گوند - babúlkágond, Hind.). See Babool, ——*Gum benzoin* (لوبان کا گوند - lobánkágond, Hind.). Same as Benzoin.——*Gum bussorah* (بصرہ کا گوند - basrahkágond, Hind.). Same as Hog gum.——*Gum elastic* (لچیلا گوند - lachílágond, Hind.). India rubber obtained from milky juiced plants [pauchonty].——*Gum elemi* (کانری گا تاہ - kánarígátah, Malay). Gum of Canarium commune, linn. [elemi].——*Gum galbanum* (بریجا گوند - baríjágond, Hind.). Same as Galbanum.——*Gum ghautty* (گہاٹ گوند - ghátgond, Hind.). Title as obtained from above ghauts [q.v.]. Title otherwise Indian gum [q.v.]. Bombay commercial term for mixed gums [gond] from forest trees. Distinguish from Ghotagamba [q.v.].——*Gum kateerah* (کتیرا گوند - katírágond, Hind.). Same as Kateerah.——*Gum kino* (کنیا گوند - kinyágond, Hind.). Same as Kino.——*Gum myrrh* (صمغ مر - simaghimurr, Hind.). Product of Balsamodendron myrrha [bole].——*Gum opopanax* (باس کا گوند - báskágond, Hind.). Hind. means stinking gum. Product of Opopanax chironium, koch.——*Gum sagapenum* (صمغ سکبینج - simaghisakabínaj, Hind.). Same as Sagapenum.——*Gum scammony* (صمغ سقمونیا - simaghisakmúniyá, Hind.). Same as Scammony. ——*Gum styrax* (صمغ اسطرك - simaghiistarak, Hind.). See Storax.——*Gum tragacanth* (کتیرا گوند - katírágond, Hind.). Same as Kateerah.

GUNDY (ಗಂಡಿ - gandi, *Can.*; గండి - gandi, *Tel.*; കണ്ടി - kanti, *Mal.*). Mal. from (khand, san. to cut). Pass. Suffix in place names.——*Gundicote* (గండికోట - gandikóta, Tel. gandikót *). From (above + kóta, tel. fort). Village, Cuddapah dist., Jummalmudoogoo tal.; pop. 1,046; acres 10,569; lat. 14° 49′; long. 78° 20′; from Cuddapah W.N.W. 42 miles; from Jummalmudoogoo W.S.W. 6½ miles. Between Gooty and Cuddapah. Stands inside a large Mahomedan fortress, built on edge of a cliff of Yerramalas forming southern wall of a fissure that cleaves a range of sandstone [manal cull] hills from their summit to their base. The Pennair passes through the gap into the plains of Cuddapah. The strong natural fortress, with its temple endowed by the earliest Vijianugger kings, was formerly a famous stronghold. It was the key to the valley of the Pennair, and must have been impregnable. Built in 1589, it was captured by Golcondah and held by Meer joomla. Later it was the capital of one of the five Circars [q.v.] of the Carnatic [q.v.] hyderabad balaghaut [q.v.], until absorbed by the Pataun [q.v.] nawaub [q.v.] of Cuddapah. It was here that Futteh naick, the father of Hyder, first distinguished himself. Hyder improved and garrisoned the fort, which was taken by the British from Tippoo in 1791. The walls of the fort are in good preservation. The principal buildings still in existence are a fine mosque [musjid], granary, and two old Hindoo temples. The fort was approached by stone steps from two sides. A hill stream in the vicinity was dammed and part of its water turned into a pipe which fed a fountain at the foot of the hill near an old pleasure house. The numerous springs in and near the fort water gardens producing orange [q.v.], lime [q.v.] and custard apple [anona]. Trig. station in lat. 14° 47′ 06·05″; long. 78° 18′ 49·44″; height 1,666 feet; from Gundicote S.S.W. 2¼ miles; from Jummalmudoogoo W.S.W. 8¼ miles.——*Gundypollem* (గండిపాలెము - gandipálemu, Tel.). From (above + pálemu, tel. fortified village). Village; Nellore dist., Oodayagherry tal.; pop. 329; acres 2,517; lat. 15° 00′; long. 79° 21′; from Nellore N.W. 60 miles; from Oodayagherry N. 8½ miles. Ancient tank formed by damming the waters of the Pillapair, an affluent of the Munnair. Breached shortly after completion 500 years ago. Hills on both sides. Bund [q.v.] only one mile long. Sluice is unusually large. A project for its restoration is being considered.

GUNGAY (गङ्गा - gangá, *San.*). From (gá, san. earth + gam, san. to go) [gaty, go]; as having been brought from heaven to earth.—"*a*" Deity of the Ganges. γάγγης of Greeks; Styx of Romans; Nile of Egyptians. The secondary wife of Shiva [q.v.] and goddess of water. She is represented as a siren, half woman and half fish, swimming on the water. Her two hands she folds as if engaged in prayer. On her head she wears a crown, and on her forehead the Shiva mark of sacred ashes [vibhooty]. Her ears, breast, neck, arms, hands, and the rest of her body are adorned with various jewels, and from her shoulders a garland hangs down. There are no books treating especially of Gungay, but various stories are related of her in the great poems and the poorаunams [q.v.]; and all books written for the purpose of showing the efficacy of water in washing away sins, may be regarded as setting forth her praise. For though the river Ganges in Northern india is Gungay especially, there are also other rivers which partake of her sanctity, and whose water is regarded as efficacious in removing sin as that of the Ganges. These are the Godavery, Cauvery, &c. And as all people do not live near those rivers, devotees fetch thence sacred water and sell it. No image of Gungay is found in the pagodas [q.v.]; nor is she, like Parvaty [q.v.] and other goddesses, worshipped with offerings. The Tamulians worship her by bathing in rivers and tanks according to prescribed rules, and with the recitation of certain forms of prayer. Bathing is thought to be particularly meritorious on Monday, Wednesday, and Saturday, but there are also special days on which great merit is attached to bathing. In the river near Mayavaram a great number of people bathe throughout the month of Toolaum [mausam] or October, in order to be purified from sin, and there are many such sacred places. At Combaconam, a great festival called Maumaungam [maha magham], i.e., the great Magham, is celebrated every twelve years. The water of a large tank there is supposed to rise once in twelve years on a certain day and at a certain hour, when thousands of people plunge in, to get rid of their sins. There are also two great festivals, at which many people resort to the sea for bathing. The one occurs once in twenty-five years, and is called Hastodayam; the other annually in May, and is named Magha tirnaul. Every tank near the Shiva temple is regarded and adored as Gungay, and bathing in it is thought to be as efficacious in removing sins as bathing in the Ganges itself. Gungay has various names, of which the following are best known:—Bhageeraty, as brought down from heaven through Bhageeratan; Gungah bhawauny; Gungah devy or gungay goddess; Jauhnavy, as being regarded as the daughter of the giant janoo, who, being disturbed in his penance by her roaring, swallowed her, but emitted her again at the request of bhageeratan; Mandaukiny or the celestial ganges; Soora nuddy or the heavenly river; Tripatagay, as supposed to flow through three worlds; Varanuddy or boon river. She has eight virgins as playmates, which are the following eight rivers:—Cauvay, Cauvery, Godavery, Mannairy, Nerbudda, Saraswaty, Sindhoo or indus, Yamoonay or jumna [matam]. Gungay is a female proper name [peyar]. Gungah toolsy is holy water in which are mixed the leaves of the sacred Toolsy [q.v.]. See vol. I (78).—"*b*" Plant first term often joining two genera, meaning large or excellent. Ex., where transl. is of second term:—Michelia champaca (gangarávi), ficus religiosa; Portulaca oleracea (gangarégu), zizyphus jujuba; Thespesia populnea (gangarávi), ficus religiosa; Trianthema decandra (gangapávili), portulaca quadrifida. See gloss. paragraphs.—"*c*" A dynasty of kings who ruled over congoo [q.v.] country from A.D. 188-894, when they were conquered by the cholas [q.v.]. The founder was Congany vurma. Their capital originally Scandapooram near Guzzelhutty was in third century changed to Talacaud. On the overthrow of their power, one of the family established a kingdom in Orissa [gajupaty] which lasted till 1534 when it succumbed before mahomedans. ——*Ardha gungay* (अर्द्धगङ्गा - ardhagangá, San.). The half Ganges or Cauvery river, having half the merit of the Ganges. ——*Gungamaindan* (கங்கைமைந்தன் - kangaimaindan, Tam.). From (above + maindan, tam. son). Soobramanyan [gungasootan].——*Gungammah* (கங்கம்மா - kangammá, Tam.). From (above + ammá, tam. mother). River-goddess on the Neilgherries. It is a practice there when the rivers are in flood for the herdsman to throw a coin into the rivers before crossing them.——*Gungan* (கங்கன் - kangan, Tam.). Name of a Paundyan king under whose auspices the Nunnool [q.v.] was composed by Pavanandy [q.v.].——*Gungarauz* (గంగరాజు - gangarádzu, Tel.). From (above + rádzu, tel. king). Hindoo 2nd or pers. name [peyar].——*Gunga sootan* (गङ्गासुत - gangásuta, San.). From (above + suta, san. son). Soobramanyan, as born of a lake [gunga maindan, sharvanan].——*Gungaudharan* (गङ्गाधर - gangádhara, San.). From (above + dhri, san. to support). Supporter of the Ganges, Shiva [q.v.]. The river is supposed to proceed from the hair of his head. Similarly the Nile had its source in the tresses of Osiris.——*Gungavamsham* (गङ्गवंश - gangavamsha, San.). From (above + vamsha, san. family). The royal house of Orissa gajapaties. See vol. I (151).——*Gungavenyan* (கங்கைவேணியன் - kangaivéniyan, Tam.). From (above + véni, san. braided hair). Shiva who holds the Ganges on his head.——*Gungavole* (గంగవోలు - gangavólu, Tel.). From (above + prólu, tel. town). Lake; Kistna dist., Repully tal. in Peravaly village; lat. 16° 09′; long. 80° 46′; from Masulipatam W. 28 miles; from Repully N.W. 11 miles; from the sea N. 17 miles. Pearls [moty] were formerly found.——*Gungavully* (ಗಂಗಾವಳ್ಳಿ - gangavalli, Can.). From (above + ávali, san. range). Sanscrit name (pañchagangávali), meaning five + rivers + range. River; South canara dist., Coondapore tal. An estuary formed by the junction of five streams, of which the Collore, Chuckranuddy and Gurgat are the principal.——*Gungaycondapooram* (கங்கைகொண்டபுரம் - kangaigandappuram, Tam.). From (above + konda, tam. obtained + pura, san. town). Place where a Chola king obtained holy water. Village; Trichinopoly dist., Oodayarpolliem tal.; pop. 1,318; acres 930; lat. 11° 13′; long. 79° 30′; height 228 feet; from Ariyalore E.N.E. 25 miles; from Jayancondacholapooram E. 5¼ miles; from Oodayarpolliem E.N.E. 10 miles; from Trichinopoly E.N.E. 57 miles. Also called Gungayconda cholapooram. Capital of Cholas in eleventh century. Ruined Chola temple; the model from which Tanjore temple was constructed. At one time the enclosure was fortified with batteries at four corners, but walls have been demolished and stones used for Coleroon anicut [q.v.]. North of the temple runs an embankment 16 miles long, provided with substantial sluices, and of great strength, which must have formed one of the largest reservoirs in India. This huge tank was filled from the S. end by a channel [q.v.] from Coleroon upwards of 60 miles in length, and from the N. end by a smaller channel from Vellaur. Traces of both channels remain. The tank is in ruins and its bed once almost overgrown with jungle is being gradually brought under cultivation.——*Gungaycondaun* (கங்கைக்கொண்டான் - gangaikkondán, Tam.). From (above + kondán, tam. he who obtained). As maker of a tank [q.v.] or channel [gungaycondapooram]. Name of a Chola king.——*Gungay coolam* (கங்கைக்குலம் - kangaikkular, Tam.). From (above + kula, san. family). Name of the Vellaular [q.v.], as dealing with irrigation.——*Gungayya* (ಗಂಗಯ್ಯ - gangayya, Can.). From (above + ayya, can. master). Hindoo 2nd or pers. name [peyar].——*Gungoola* (గంగుల - gangula, Tel.). From (ganga, tel. proper name). Poligar [q.v.] family, Gungoola gooravayya, principal ancestor of the family, was appointed attsoocauvalgar of the Oodayagberry droog in fusly [q.v.] 1049, and eight villages were granted as Amarams. Under the Mahomedan Government a peshcush [q.v.] of 662 pagodas [q.v.] was imposed on the Amaram [q.v.]. The poliput [q.v.] was enfranchised by the inam [q.v.] commission at an annual quit-rent of Rs. 2,627.——*Gungy* (గంగి - gangi, Tel.). Goddess among sowrahs [q.v.].

GUNJ (گنج - ganj, *Hind.*). A granary. Suffix in place names as Shikargunj [ganj, golah].

GUNNA (గన్న - ganna, *Tel.*). Great.——*Gunnavaram* (గన్నవరము - gannavaramu, Tel.). From (above + pura, san. town).—"*a*" Village, Head-quarters of Deputy tahsildar, Office of Sub-registrar; Kistna dist., Noozveed zemindarry; pop. 1,674; lat. 16° 32′; long. 80° 50′; from Bezwada E. 12 miles; from Guntoor N.E. 29 miles; from Madras N. 240 miles; from Masulipatam N.W. 35 miles; from Noozveed S.S.W. 17¾ miles; from Vinoocondah E.N.E. 77 miles.—"*b*" Canal, Village; Godavery dist., Narsapore tal.; pop. 1,456; acres 1,615; lat. 16° 35′; long. 81° 55′; from Cocanada S.W. 35 miles; from Narsapore N.E. 16 miles; from the sea N. 13 miles. Main canal from the Godavery anicut [q.v.]. Irrigates Amalaupooram and Narsapore talooks. Navigable for 36 miles. Crosses the Veinateyam branch of the Godavery at Gunnavaram by an aqueduct 800 yards long with 49 arches.

GUNNY (गोणी - góní, *San.*; گنی - ganní, *Hind.*; ಗೋಣಿ - góni, *Can.*; గోనె - góne, *Tel.*; கோணி - kóni, *Tam.*). From (gógu, tel. hemp + neyu, tel. weave). Coarse sacking and sacks [borah] made from the fibre [naur] of the jute plant [jute], and sunn [q.v.].

GUNTOOR (గుంటూరు - guntúru, *Tel.* guntúr*). From (gunta, tel. pond + úru, tel. village) [goondam]. Sanscrit name (márkandéyáshrama), meaning marcandeyan the sage + hermit age; also (rámachandrapura), meaning ramchendran, the hero + town.——**(1)** Former British collectorate. Area about 8,413 square miles. Between lat. 15° 37′ and 17° 09′, and long. 79° 15′ to 81° 36′. Bounded north by the Kistna which separated it from the Nizam's dominions and the former district of Masulipatam; south by Nellore and the Bay of Bengal; east by Masulipatam and west by Cuddapah and the Nizam's territory [golcondah coast]. Guntoor, Nizampatam, and Vinoocondah were the principal places. Now represented by Kistna district. ——**(2)** Talook, Kistna district. Tahsildar's pay Rs. 225. Area 500 square miles. Population 143,458. Language Teloogoo. Centre of district. Bounded north by the Kistna; east by Repully talook; west by Narsarowpett and Suttenapully talooks; south by Baupatla talook. Extends south as far as the Condaveed range. To the south the tract adjoining Baupatla talook is a fertile expanse of black soil [regar], very fertile when rainfall is propitious, but extremely desolate in dry weather. Hills of gneiss, more or less granitoid, rise here and there; some of the masses of black rock being bold and picturesque, especially in the line of hills stretching southward from near Amravatty towards Guntoor. The centre of the talook is liable to be submerged by river floods; in July 1882 the Kistna water stood black as far as Taudicondah. This deposit river mud on the land favorable to indigo [q.v.] and other crops, although the low-lying ground is difficult to drain and remains swampy. Irrigation, by rain-fed tanks [q.v.] and Kistna anicut [q.v.]. Places of archæological interest:—Caranootla, Caucauny, Cauza, Condapaud, Coriteypaud, Gaurapaud, Gorantla, Guntoor, Laum, Mandipaud, Marcapore, Mookkaumala, Mungalagherry, Nidmookkala, Nullapaud, Numboor, Oondavully, Paumoolpaud, Penoomauca, Pottoor, Prattipaud, Rauvela, Reddipollem, Royapoody, Shaicore, Sooddapully, Taudicondah, Vejalla, Yanamadala, Zonnalagudda. Trig. stations:—Anantavaram, Gorantla, Guntoor N.E., Guntoor S.W., Mungalagherry, Palcalore. The leading places, &c., in the talook are the following.——*Anantavaram* (అనంతవరము - anantavaramu, Tel.). From (anantayya, tel. proper name + pura, san. town). Trig. station; lat. 16° 30′ 57·95″; long. 80° 27′ 57·29″; height 852 feet; from Guntoor N. 15 miles.——*Caucauny* (కాకాని - kákáni, Tel.). After the person of that name. Tel. also (peddakákáni), meaning large + place so called. Village; pop. 2,082; acres 4,076; lat. 16° 21′; long. 80° 32′; from Guntoor N.E. 4½ miles; from Masulipatam W.N.W. 42 miles. On road to Bezwada.——*Cauza* (కాజ - kádza, Tel.). Village; pop. 1,763; acres 4,493; lat. 16° 24′; long. 80° 35′; from Guntoor N.E. 9½ miles; from Masulipatam W.N.W. 41 miles. Vishnoo temple. Inscriptions.——*Chinna caucauny* (చిన్నకాకాని - chinnakákáni, Tel.). From (chinna, tel. small + kákáni, tel. place so called). Tel. also (kukkakákání), meaning dog + the village, so called; also (shunakákáni), meaning dog + village so called. Village; pop. 876; acres 2,670; lat. 16° 25′; long. 80° 36′; from Guntoor N.E. 11 miles; from Masulipatam W.N.W. 40 miles. Carved figures of a horseman and two dogs commemorate the story of a faithful dog killed through mistake by his master; like Llewellyn's story. Inscription in front of Gopaulsawmy's temple.——*Gorantla* (గోరంట్ల - górantla, Tel.). Means the nail-dye plant, lawsonia alba, lamk. Trig. station; lat. 16° 20′ 41·24″; long. 80° 29′ 01·60″; height 258 feet; from Guntoor N. 3¾ miles.——*Guntoor* (గుంటూరు - guntúru, Tel.). See sep. title.——*Kistna* (కృష్ణ - krishna, Tel.). See sep. title.——*Mootloor* (ముట్లూరు - mutlúru, Tel.). From (mushti, san. alms + úru, tel. village). Sanscrit name (mushtipura), meaning handful of alms + town. Village; pop. 3,127; acres 3,458; lat. 16° 10′; long. 80° 31′; from Guntoor S. 9½ miles; from Masulipatam W. 43 miles. Catholic church and missionary's house. Festival on 3rd December, St. Francis Xavier's day, is largely attended.——*Mungalagherry* (మంగళగిరి - mangalagiri, Tel.). See sep. title.——*Nauracodore* (నారాకోడూరు - nárákódúru, Tel.). From (náráya, tel. proper name + kódu, tel. stream + úru, tel. village). Village; pop. 1,595; acres 2,962; lat. 16° 14′; long. 80° 33′ 39″; from Guntoor S.E. 6 miles; from Masulipatam W. 41 miles. On road from Guntoor to Chebrole ——*Nidamarroo* (నిడమర్రు - nidamarru, Tel.). From (nidivi, tel. long + marri, tel. banyan tree, ficus bengalensis, linn.). Village; pop. 1,391; acres 2,777; lat. 16° 26′; long. 80° 34′; from Guntoor N.N.E. 10½ miles; from Masulipatam W.N.W. 42 miles. Jeina [q.v.] images. ——*Numboor* (నంబూరు - nambúru, Tel.). From (namban, tam. shiva + úru, tel. village). Village; pop. 3,661; acres 7,404; lat. 16° 22′; long. 80° 35′; from Guntoor N.E. 7¼ miles; from Masulipatam W.N.W. 41 miles. Shiva temple with inscription. ——*Oondavully* (ఉండవల్లి - undavalli, Tel.). See sep. title.—— *Palcalore* (పలకలూరు - palakalúru, Tel.). From (palaka, tel. plank + úru, tel. village). Trig. station; lat. 16° 19′ 37·92″; long. 80° 25′ 12·04″; height 675 feet; from Guntoor W.N.W. 5¼ miles. ——*Pedda palcalore* (పెద్దపలకలూరు - peddapalakalúru, Tel.). From (pedda, tel. great + palaka, tel. slab of stone + úru, tel. village). Village; pop. 1,583; acres 4,411; lat. 16° 20′; long. 80° 25′; from Guntoor W.N.W. 5¾ miles; from Masulipatam W. 50 miles. Near is a Jeina image; the right hand grasps a sword and under the foot is an animal resembling a deer [mrigam].—— *Pottoor* (పొత్తూరు - pottúru, Tel.). From (pottu, tel. union + úru, tel. village). Village; pop. 1,267; acres 3,444; lat. 16° 16′; long. 80° 25′; from Guntoor W.S.W. 5¾ miles; from Masulipatam W. 49 miles. Vishnoo temple and inscription south of it.—— *Prattipaud* (ప్రత్తిపాడు - prattipádu, Tel.). From (pratti, tel. cotton + pádu, tel. village). Village, Travellers' bungalow; pop. 3,462; acres 5,552; lat. 16° 11′; long. 80° 23′; from Guntoor S.W. 10½ miles; from Masulipatam W. 53 miles. Former head-quarters of Tahsildar. Shiva temple built by Chola kings. Vishnoo temple built by Condaveed reddies. Former has seven inscriptions. Inscription at the temple of Dandeshwarasawmy and at the temple of Vengopaulsawmy.——*Royapoody* (రాయపూడి - ráyapúdi, Tel.). From (ráyalu, tel. title of ruler + púdi, tel. village). Village; pop. 1,444; acres 3,136; lat. 16° 33′; long. 80° 31′; from Guntoor N. 18 miles; from Masulipatam W.N.W. 49 miles. Temples of Hanooman [q.v.] and Shiva [q.v.]. Several inscriptions.——*Seetanagaram* (సీతానగరము - sítánagaramu, Tel.). From (sítá, san. ráma's wife + nagara, san. city). Village, Railway terminus station, Hills; pop. 1,739; lat. 16° 30′; long. 80° 39′; from Guntoor N.E. 17 miles; from Masulipatam W.N.W. 40 miles. The hills are on the right bank of the Kistna opposite Bezwada and form one base of the great anicut [q.v.]. Near this range are the Oondavully caves.—— *Shaicore* (శేకూరు - shékúru, Tel.). From (shaikh, hind. class of mahomedans + úru, tel. village). Village; pop. 2,355; acres 5,582; lat. 16° 16′; long. 80° 38′; from Guntoor E. 9 miles; from Masulipatam W. 36 miles. Seven inscriptions.——*Taudicondah* (తాడికొండ - tádikonda, Tel.). From (tádi, tel. palmyra tree, borassus flabelliformis, linn. + konda, tel. hill). Village; pop. 4,607; acres 12,689; lat. 16° 25′; long. 80° 29; from Guntoor N. 8¼ miles; from Masulipatam W.N.W. 47 miles. At the beginning of this century four Zemindars [q.v.], Chilcaloorpaud, Repully, Ryechore, and Suttenapully held each one quarter of Taudicondah, and each made his quarter of Taudicondah the head-quarters of a Sammat [q.v.] or circle of villages. Abounds in remains of old temples and inscriptions. One temple contains Jeina figures.——*Veicoomtapooram* (వైకుంఠపురము - vaikunt'hapuramu, Tel.). From (vaikunt'ha, san. abode of vishnu + pura, san. town). Sanscrit name (bandhavirámа), meaning bondage + end; place of emancipation. Village, Place of pilgrimage; pop. 1,059; acres 2,376; lat. 16° 34′; long. 80° 27′; from Guntoor N. 18¼ miles; from Masulipatam W.N.W. 54 miles. On the Kistna. Rajah Vasireddy vencataudry naidoo established Veishnavite bramins and embellished some of the temples with burnished copper [taumram] spires. Previously a sacred place. ——*Yanamadala* (యనమదల - yanamadala, Tel.). From (énuga, tel. elephant + manda, tel. herd). Sanscrit name (vírabhógavasantarájapuri), meaning hero + rule + spring + king + town; town of veerabhadran, the beautiful hero-chief. Village; pop. 2,739; acres 6,111; lat. 16° 14′; long. 80° 22′; from Guntoor W.S.W. 8¾ miles; from Masulipatam W. 51 miles. Formerly important. Inscriptions at temple of Veereshwarasawmy. Festival in April.——**(3)** Sub-Magistracy, Kistna district. Pay Rs. 70.——**(4)** Town, Municipality, Head-quarters of Sub-collector and Talook, Railway station and Travellers' bungalow; Kistna dist., Guntoor tal.; pop. 23,359; acres 8,578; lat. 16° 18′; long. 80° 30′; from Bezwada S.S.W. 19 miles; from Madras N. 220 miles; from Masulipatam W. 44 miles; from Vinoocondah E.N.E. 50 miles. About 18 miles S.W. of the right bank of the Kistna, W. 52 miles from the coast, and about 6 miles east of the Condaveed hills. The town is situated at the junction of ridge of red soil with laterite [q.v.] gravel running east from the last outlier of these hills and a patch of gritty sandstone [manal cull] of the upper Gondwana series. From the end of this ridge the ground falls away to black soil and deltaic alluvium with a considerable slope. The surrounding country is open and flat. The soil is black and produces luxuriant crops of gram [q.v.], cholum [q.v.], and cotton [q.v.]. Divided into the Old town and New town, both irregularly built. Capital of a Circar [q.v.] under the Mahomedans. Came into prominence during French occupation. For military history see vol. I (179). The Judge's court was withdrawn to Masulipatam in 1818, but again restored to Guntoor. Native town burned down in 1823. Famine in 1832. In 1859, on the amalgamation of the old Guntoor and Masulipatam districts, a Sub-collector was stationed at Guntoor. In 1877 the District court was moved from Guntoor to Masulipatam. The village of Ramchendrapooram agrahauram [q.v.], absorbed by Guntoor, is older. Another temple east of red tank with four inscriptions and a sculptured stone many centuries old. A similar stone west of red tank sculptured rudely with a female figure brandishing a sword. Tomb of a Mahomedan priest, Mohee ood deen badshah sahib, who died about 1810. The cemetery contains many reminiscences of the French occupation. Trade in cotton and grain. The former is brought by cultivators and sold to agents who press and despatch it by canal to Cocanada or Madras. American lutheran mission station. Guntoor north-east-end. Trig. station is in lat. 16° 18′ 45·92″; long. 80° 32′ 35·04″. Guntoor south-west-end. Trig. station is in lat. 16° 15′ 41·92″; long. 80° 29′ 22·04″.

GUP (گپ - gap, *Hind.*). Gossip.

GURJAN (कराल - karála, *San.*; گرجن - garjan, *Hind.*; ಗುಗ - guga, *Can.*; හොරගහ - horaguha, *Singh.*). Title from hindostany. San. means opening wide either from deeply cracked bark or open grain in wood. Hind. from bengalee. Title otherwise Borneo vegetable tallow, Indian dipterocarpus, Solid oil, Tallow tree, Wood-oil tree. Botanically Dipterocarpus turbinatus, gærtn., dipterocarpeæ [vricsham, 24]. Alias Dipterocarpus indicus, lævis. Large tree; young branches compressed, two-edged; leaves ovate or oblong-ovate, retuse at the base, acute, shining on both sides, with numerous prominent veins; resembling dillenia [chaltah]; petioles glabrous; tube of enlarged calyx slightly ventricose, two segments expanded into wings when in fruit; capsule ovate, even; flowers white, tinged with red, 3 inches in diameter, appear at beginning of hot season; followed by a nut-like fruit; tree common in all ghaut [q.v.] forests from canara down to cape comorin; the trunk grows to an immense size, bark deeply cracked. The wood oil gurjan balsam is obtained by cutting a notch in the trunk near the earth, where a fire is kept up till the wound is charred, soon after which the liquid begins to ooze out. The freshly-drawn balsam is an opaque, grey fluid, which when placed in the sun gradually separates into two portions; the upper is a thick, viscid fluid of a dark reddish brown color, and transparent when placed between the eye of the observer and the light, but when viewed by reflected light it is opaque, greenish, and florescent; the lower consists of a thick dirty white magma, and is generally rejected; the balsam has a feeble copaiba odour, and a bitter aromatic taste. The balsam [q.v.] in the bazaar generally occurs as a brown, oily looking, semi-transparent liquid, in odour strongly resembling a mixture of balsam of copaiba with a small portion of naphtha [q.v.]; insoluble in water, freely in warm alcohol, and with difficulty in ether; the balsam is shipped to europe. The balsam is in medicine; internally, stimulant, diuretic and alterative; and externally, stimulant; the best way of using it internally is in the form of emulsion with mucilage. Dose, from one to three fluid drachms three times in the 24 hours. Substituted for copaiba, donovan's solution, citrine ointment, chaulmoogra [q.v.] oil. Varieties three, pale-white or grey, red or reddish brown, and black or dark brown; the red or reddish brown and the white or grey are the best for internal medicinal use. Gurjan balsam recently pronounced a specific for leprosy [cooshtam] which is doubtful. Timber very open in the grain, not durable. No other species of dipterocarpus here, but gurjan balsam is also obtained from other species natives of chittagong, tennasserim, burmah, siam, eastern archipelago, philippine islands, andaman islands, and ceylon. Yaipy [q.v.] gives another liquid balsam like copaiba, and called madeiyan sambrauny [q.v.].

GUTT (ಗಟ್ಟು - gattu, *Can.*; గట్టు - gattu, *Tel.*). Bank; hill. Suffix in place names [ghatt].

GUTTA (گات - gáta, *Malay*). Inspissated juice.——*Gutta-percha* گاتپارچا - gátahpárcha, Malay). Malay from (gátah, malay, resin + párcha, malay, the tree, dichopsis gutta, benth. h. f.). Product of Dichopsis gutta, benth. h. f. [pauchonty] a tree of perak; largely adulterated, often consisting of the inspissated saps of some five or six different plants mixed together, of which a fig [atty] and bread-fruit tree [jack], yielding inferior india rubber [q.v.] is chief.

GUZ (गज - gaja, *San.*; گز - gaz, *Hind.*; గజము - gajamu, *Tel.*; கெசம் - kesam, *Tam.*). From persian. A yard, two cubits. In the reign of Acbar [q.v.] there prevailed a great number of measures of this denomination, varying from 18 to 58 inches; to correct which a standard was established in their stead, termed the Ilauhee [q.v.] guz. No standard really preserved, and different measurements made it vary from 29 to 35 inches. 33 inches was assumed as the value. A modern scale is:—2 hauts = 1 guz; 2 guz = 1 baum [alavay, 1e]. Generally guz is translated into the English yard of 36 inches. But it still varies from 26 to 39 inches. In Calicut it is 28 inches. Same as gajam. Compare Tutchacole and Tutchamoolam. See vol. I, 609; II, 505.

GUZZELHUTTY (ಗೆಜಲ್ಹಟ್ಟಿ - gejalhatti, *Can.*). From (guzar, hind. passage + hatti, can. village). Village, Ghaut; Coimbatore dist., Suttimungalam tal.; lat. 11° 33′ N.; long. 77° 3′ E.; from Coimbatore N. 38 miles; from Suttimungalam W. 17 miles. Pass by which foot-passengers and pack-bullocks ascend to Mysore plateau. Formerly principal pass from Coimbatore into Mysore, one track leading from Suttimungalam and another from Coimbatore town through Lanaicken cottah to foot of ghaut [q.v.]. Route usually taken by Tippoo. No longer kept in order, more northern routes being preferred. The head of the pass, 2,800 feet above sea level, is seventeen miles from the Mysore frontier. The valley through which the pass lies is great gorge down the bottom of which flows the Moyaur, and the sides of which are formed towards S.W. by precipitous brow of Neilgherries and towards the N.E. by declivities of mountains rising towards Mysore. The village with an old fort and bridge is situated on left bank of Moyaur. The fort was in 1768 taken from Hyder ally by a British force, but was retaken in the same year.

GYMKHANA (گيند خانہ - gendkhánah, *Hind.*). From (gend, hind. ball + khánah, pers. house). The name usually given to an English racket-court, meeting for sports, &c.

H (ह - ha, *San.*; ہ - he, ح - ḥai, *Hind.*). San. sign for Shiva [q.v.] as Bheiravan [q.v.]. Hind. ہ symbol for 5; denotes Thursday the fifth day of the week [vauram]; the sign [raushy] Virgo [cunyay]; the planet [graham] Venus [shoocran] and the moon [chundran]. Hind. ح symbol for 8, and astronomically Sagittarius [dhanoos]; affixed to royal grants as the initial letter of Huzoor navees [q.v.] or Secretary of state.

HABB (حب - habb, *Ar.*). Seed. Plant first term. Ex., where transl. is of second term:—Baliospermum montanum (habbusalátínibarrí), king + wild; Cassia absus (habbussandán), soudan, the place; Hibiscus abelmoschus (habbulmushk), musk; Ipomæa hederacea (habbunníl), blue; Ipomæa turpethum (habbulzangí), black. See gloss. paragraphs.

HABEEB حبيب - habíb, *Hind.*). From (hubba, ar. to love). Affectionate. Part of lacab; as Habeeb ool lah, friend of God, title of the Prophet [mahomed]. Now a common alam [ism].

HABSHY (حبشی - habshí, *Hind.*). From (habash, ar. abyssinia). Abyssinian; so anything large. Ex., Exacum bicolor (habshícharáitah), abyssinian swertia.

HACKERY (هانكرى - hánkrí, *Hind.*). From (hánkná, hind. to drive). Carriage drawn by bullocks for personal transport.

HAD (هدّ. - had, *Hind.*). Bone.——*Haddah* (هدّا - haddá, Hind.). Spavin or ring bone in horses [ashwarogam, ghorah].

HADEES (حديث - hadís, *Hind.*). From (hadasa, ar. to narrate). Tradition. The traditional sayings and doings of the prophet having for the most part force of law [smrity, soonnat]. These are divided into two classes; Hadees e naboovy or the sayings of the prophet himself, Hadees e coodsy or the holy sayings which the angel Gabriel [jibbreel] brought from heaven. The degree of authenticity to be attached to them has been the subject of differences between the various Mahomedan sects; soonnee [q.v.], shiahs [q.v.], wahaubies [q.v.], mootazalites [q.v.], &c.

HAFEEZ (حفيظ - hafíz, *Hind.*). From (hafaza, ar. to preserve). Guardian; an epithet of God [allah]. Common alam; as Abdool hafeez, slave of the guardian [ism].

HAFT (هفت - haft, *Hind.*). Greek ἑπτά, Latin septem. Seven [saptam].——*Haftah* (هفته - haftah, Hind.). Week [caulam, vauram]. Saturday. Haftah kanakk, a weekly report.

HAGARY (హగరి - hagari, *Tel.*). Assumed from (agha, san. sin. + hari, san. destroyer); but probably a vernacular word. Sanscrit also (védavatí), meaning veda + possessor; holy river. River. Rises in Mysore and flows 125 miles into the Toongabudra near Hatsahully in lat. 15° 44′ N., long. 76° 59′ E. Shallow and broad stream, rarely navigable. On both sides are broad belts of sand [manal]. At Moka, 12 miles from Bellary, where the river is crossed, the sand beds are 2 miles broad. In 1851 the town of Gooliem was washed away by a flood in the river. The Southern mahratta railway crosses the river near Paramadevanhully.

HAJ (حج - hajj, *Hind.*). From (hajja, ar. to tend towards). A pilgrimage by a Mahomedan to Mecca, Medina, &c. Sometimes called Haj ool farz, the ordained haj. It is incumbent on all men who have sufficient means to meet the expenses of the journey and to maintain their families at home during their absence. The day of ceremony is the tenth of Zilhaj [maheena]. The haj to Mecca is to the Caaba [q.v.], round which the pilgrim walks seven times, kissing each time the black stone which is imbedded in the north-east corner of the wall, and which is said to have been given by an angel to Abraham [deen]. The corresponding hindoo term is Yantray.——*Hajee* (حاجى - hájí, Hind.). One who has performed the haj. Taken thereafter as a title. Ism oon nisbat [ism].

HAJAUM (حجام - hajám, *Hind.*). From (hajama, ar. to cup). Name for the barber caste in Hindostany and Canarese. The corresponding terms are:—Tel. mungala, Mal. vilacattravan, Tam. ambatta. One of the village servants [balootah, inam].

HAJR (حجر - hajar, *Ar.*). Stone.——*Hajrdam* (रक्तोपल - raktópala, San.; حجرالدم - hajruddamm, Ar., Pers. and Hind.; உதிரக்கல் - uthirakkal, Tam.). San. from (rakta, san. blood + upala, san. stone). Ar. from (hajar, ar. stone + damm, ar. blood). Pers. and Hind. from arabic. Tam. from (rudhira, san. red + kal, tam. stone). San. also (rudhira), meaning blood. Bloodstone; also called Heliotrope, Oriental jasper. Species of chalcedony [akeek i soofeed] distinguished by red spots like blood. Used for seals [moodray], &c. [ratnam].

HAKEEM (حكيم - hakím, *Hind.*). From (hikm, ar. knowledge). A philosopher, physician [veidyan]. It is also an attribute of God [allah]. No medical tracts in Deccany [q.v.]. Hakeems are well acquainted with Persian and Arabic.——*Haukim* (حاكم - hákim, Hind.). From (hukm, ar. order). A ruler.——*Hikmat* (حكمت - hikmat, Hind.). From (hakama, ar. to know). Knowledge; philosophy [ilm]. Daur ool hikmat is Scientific institute.——*Hookum* (حكم - hukm, Hind.). From (hakama, ar. to restrain). An order. Hookum nauma are standing rules for administration.

HAKKAL (ಹಕ್ಕಲು - hakkalu, *Can.*). A kind of dry cultivation carried on during the rainy season in spots detached from an estate. It differs from Coomry [q.v.] in not requiring to be cleared of large trees, and in being for the most part cultivated annually, although not so regularly as the land included within estates [gaddavary, veligada].

HALAUK (هلاك - halák, *Hind.*). From (halaka, ar. to perish). Disorder; death; in law homicide.

HALAUL (حلال - halál, *Hind.*). From (halla, ar. lawful). Food lawful for Mahomedans, opposed to Haraum [q.v.] or unlawful food. The lawful animals are such as chew the cud and are not beasts of prey; birds that pick up food with their bills and do not seize their prey with their claws or wound them with their bills; fish, but no other marine animals; and locusts [tiddah]. To make halaul is to kill an animal according to prescribed mode.

HALEEM (حليم - halím, *Hind.*). From (hilm, ar. forbearance). Clement; an attribute of God [allah]. Common alam; as Haleem khautoon, alam + pataun female alaumat [ism].——*Haleem khan* (حليم خان - halímkhán, Hind.). Nawaub [q.v.] of Cuddapah. Alam + pataun suffix. Defeated by Hyder and sent to Seringapatam as captive, where he died. Hyder married his sister, subsequently known as Bukshy begum.

HALEEM (चन्द्रशूर - chandrashúra, *San.*; अहळींव - ahalímva, *Mahr.*; رشاد - rashád, *Ar.*; تره تيزك - tarrahtezak, *Pers.*; حالم - hálim, *Hind.*; حليم - halím, *Dec.*; ಕುರ್ತಿಗೆಗಿಡ - kurtigegida, *Can.*; అడలవితల - adalavitala, *Tel.*; ஆளி - áli, *Tam.*). Title from deccany. San. from (chandra, san. moon + shúra, san. heroic plant; medicinal, common to chitramoolam, masoor and monkey jack), as growing at night. Mahr. from deccany. Ar. from (rashada, ar. to take a straight course), from being erect. Pers. from (tarrah, pers. garden herb + tezak, pers. cress). Tam. from (ál, tam. to nourish); used as salad; same as for linseed, linum usitatissimum, linn. [alsee]. San. also (chandriká), meaning moonlight [elephant shoonday, snake root]. Mahr. also (hálímva). Ar. also (hurf). Pers. also (shabkhízak), meaning night + growing. Hind. also (chansar), from sanscrit. Tel. also (ádéli); (ádiyálu). Greek κάρδαμον, Latin nasturtium. Title otherwise Cress, Dittander, Garden cress, Moon cress, Pepper grass, Pepper wort, Tongue grass [darbhay], Town cress. Botanically Lepidium sativum, linn., cruciferæ [vricsham, 10]. Cultivated in cold weather, with mustard [rayaun]; seeds small, ovoid, reddish; seeds a gentle stimulant; substituted for british taraxacum; used as salad; gives oil similar to mustard. Nasturtium officinale, water cress, and Nasturtium palustre, yellow cress, have the same names.

HALEY (ಹಳೆ - hale, *Can.*). Old [pauta, pazha]. Prefix in place names especially.——*Halabeed* (ಹಳೇಬೀಡು - halébídu, Can.). From (above + bídu, can. waste). Village in Bailore talook, Hassan district, Mysore, 10 miles east of Bailore. Marks site of ancient city of Dorasamoodram, Dwaura samoodram [q.v.], or Dwauravatipooram, capital of Hoysala ballaula [q.v.] kings.——*Haleycannada* (ಹಳೆಕನ್ನಡ - halekannada, Can.). Ancient Canarese [bhaushay]. See vol. I (48), (50).——*Haleypeik* (ಹಳೇಪೈಕ - halépaika, Can.). From (above + páik, hind. foot soldier). See vol. I (68). Toddy-drawers in the inland Canarese country. They speak Tooloo. Peiky is the name of the highest class of the Todahs [q.v.] on the Neilgherries [jauty].

HALWAH (حلوا - halwá, *Hind.*). From (halo, ar. sweet). A sweetmeat made of flour [soojee], ghee [q.v.], sugar [q.v.], spices, &c. Halwayee is a confectioner.

HAM (هم - ham, *Hind.*). Particle implying connexion [sa; sam].——*Hama* (همه - hama, *Hind.*). All. Hama baubat is total. Hama cowm is all classes. Hama jins is all articles.——*Hamaisha* (هميشه - hameshah, *Hind.*). From persian. Continually.——*Hamjaut* (همذات - hamzát, Hind.). From (above + zát, ar. caste). Of the same caste.——*Hamsauya* (همسايه - hamsáyah, Hind.). From (above + sáyah, ar. shelter). A neighbour. To be this gives prior claim in the application for lands [durkhast].

HAMEED (حميد - hamíd, *Hind.*). From (hamada, ar. to praise). Praised [hammand, haumid]. An attribute of God [allah]. Common alam; as Hameed khan, alam + alaumat. Also part of lacab; as Hameed ood deen, the glory of religion. Feminine Hameeda, as Hameeda bee, alam + female alaumat [ism].

HAMEEYAT (حميت - hamíyat, *Hind.*). From (hamí, ar. to guard). Honor [himauyat]. Prefixed to an alam forms a lacab as Hameeyat hoossain, honor of hoossain [ism].

HAMMAUD (حماد - hammád, *Hind.*). From (hamada, ar. to praise). Frequent praiser [hameed, haumid]. Part of lacab; as Hammaud ood deen, most praiseworthy of the faithful [ism].

HAMMAUL (حمال - hammál, *Hind.*). From (hamala, ar. to carry). A bearer [boy] of a palankeen [q-v.]. Message-bearer [harcarra].

HAMSAM (हंस - hamsa, *San.*). From (han, san. to go [hanoo, hing]. Cf. latin anser.——(1) Swan. Often translated flamingo and goose. It is really a creature no longer to be found, and might be translated phœnix [hooma]. The swan is supposed to possess the property of extracting milk [paul] from water when both are mixed together. Vemana has the following:—పాల నీరు క్రమము వరక హంస తెలియంగ నీరు పాల క్రమము నెమలి కేల యజ్ఞుడైన వాడు నలశివు నెఱుగునా—"The swan alone "can distinguish water when mingled with milk; how should "the peacock [mayil] distinguish these fluids and how shall the "ignorant man discern the deity from his own works?" The popular notion originates in the color of the bird, and because it seems to extract its food by suction from the water. There is a Tamul proverb:—தன் ஊருக்கு அன்னம் பிற ஊருக்குக் காகம்—"A swan in his own village, a crow [caurvam] "in the next." Hamsa vimshaty from (vimshati, san. twenty) is a poem in five books containing 1,600 stanzas; like vicramarcan [q.v.] tales this is a series of twenty amorous novels, narrated by a hamsam; each tale introduces expressions peculiar to certain castes or trades.——(2) The title is taken here as equivalent of the Anseridæ family, lamellirostres, natatores, aves [pacshy, 49], of naturalists [jantoo]. These divide systematically into:—Plectropterinæ or spurred geese, Nettapodinæ or goose-teal, Tadorninæ or shieldrakes and whistling teal. The species of these three sub-families best known to the natives are shown below. For common teal see Varatam.——*Braminy duck* (चक्रवाक - chakraváka, San.; چکوا - chakwá, Hind.; بهمنی بدک - bahmaníbadak, Dec.; ಚಕ್ರವಕ್ಕಿ - chakkavakki, Can.; బాపనబాతు - bápanabátu, Tel.; சக்கரவாகம் - shakkaravágam, Tam.). Title from marks on forehead resembling caste marks. San. from (chakra, san. the bird so called + vach, san. to speak), known by the name of chuckram. Hind. from sanscrit. Dec. from (bahman, hind. bramin + badak, hind. duck). Tel. from (bápana, tel. bramin + bátu, tel. wild duck). Hind. also (surkháb), meaning water sucker. Tel. also (bápanachiluva), meaning bramin + wild duck. Title otherwise Ruddy goose, Ruddy shieldrake. Casarca rutila, tadorninæ. Alias Anas rubra. Male, forehead and cheeks pale ochreous-yellow or ferruginous; region of eyes, crown and nape, greyish-white; rest of neck ochreous-yellow, tinged orange, surrounded by glossy black collar nearly half inch wide; back and scapulars orange fulvous, some feathers edged paler; upper tail-coverts glossy green-black; lesser and middle wing-coverts white; greater coverts green, glossed purple; primaries black; secondaries glossy green; tertials bright fulvous; chin pale yellowish; breast and lower parts orange fulvous, deepest on breast; bill black; irides dark brown; legs black; length 24 to 25 inches. Female smaller, wants the black collar, more white about forehead, chin and face. Winter visitant; call goose-like, like á-oong. Natives have a legend that two lovers having been transformed into Braminy ducks, they pass the night on opposite banks of the river; the conversation is 'Chakwah, shall I come? No, Chakwy.' 'Chakwy, shall I come? No, Chakwah.' Strong in flavour; seldom brought to table. No other species here.——*Comb-duck* (نكتا - naktá, Hind.; జుట్టుచిలువ - dzuttuchiluva, Tel.). Title from crest. Tel. from (dzuttu, tel. crest + chiluva, tel. wild duck). Title otherwise Black-backed goose. Sarkidiornis melanonotus, plectropterinæ. No other species here.——*Cotton teal* (گری - girí, Hind.; చిలువ - chiluva, Tel.; [illegible] - silechodai, Oor.). Title from white cottony appearance of under parts. Title otherwise White-bodied goose-teal.

Nettapus coromandelianus, nettapodinæ. Alias Bernicla girra; Dendrocygna affinis. No other species here.——*Whistling teal* (سلی - sillí, Hind.; ఎఱ్ఱచిలువ - errachiluva, Tel.; செங்கிலுவை - shengiluvai, Tam.). Title from piping note when on wing. Tel. from (erra, tel. red + chiluva, tel. wild duck). Tam. from (shem, tam. red + kiluvai, tam. teal); from color of plumage. Dendrocygna awsuree, tadorninæ. Alias Anas caryophyllacea; D. arcuata. Not much prized for eating. No other species here.——(3) *Hans* (هنس - hans, Hind.). Swan, cygnus genus:—Grus antigone (sárhans), lake swan; Phœnicopterus roseus (rájhans), royal swan. See gloss. paragraphs.——*Hansroy* (హంసరాయి - hansaráyi, Tam.). From (hamsa, san. swan + rájá, san. king). Hindoo 2nd or pers. name [peyar].

HAMZA (حمزه - hamzah, *Ar.*). Lion [hyder, shere]; name of Mahomet's uncle. Common alam; as Hamza hoossain, double alam [ism].

HANA (ಹಣ - hana, *Can.*; பணம் - panam, *Tam.*). From (pana, san. the coin, from pan, san. to barter).—"*a*" Money; the small coin termed a fanam [q.v.], whether of gold or silver. Canteroyhana, sultaunyhana, gopaulyhana are different kinds of gold fanams, each worth about four silver ones [naunyam].—"*b*" Goldsmith's weight. 2 manjoties = 1 hana; 9 hanas = 1 pagoda weight [niray, 3c]. Approximate actual value, 1 hana = 6 grains. S. canara. Same as Tel. chinnam, Tam. panam or pana tookkam. Compare Chowlam. See vol. I, 609.

HANAK (حنك - hanak, *Hind.*). From arabic. Ceremony of naming a child.

HANEEF (حنيف - haníf, *Ar.*). From (hanafa, ar. to incline). Faithful. The old faith of Abraham, which Imaum aboo haneefa, founder of the Hanafee sect, consolidated [cowm]. Common alam. Feminine Haneefa; as Haneefa bee, alam + alaumat [ism].

HANGAUMA (هنگامه - hangámah, *Hind.*). From persian. Tumult.

HANOO (हनु - hanu, *San.*). From (han, san. to kill) [hamsam, hing]; to destroy and eat. Jaw.——*Hanoomacondah* (హనుమకొండ - hanumakonda, Tel.). From (hanúman, san. the monkey god + konda, tel. hill). The ancient capital of the Warangal [q.v.] kingdom, established south of the Godavery river by the Caucateeya or Ganapaty [q.v.] dynasty, who claimed to be descendants of the old Hastinapooram line. Situated 88 miles east-north-east of Hyderabad in the Deccan [charitram, deccan].——*Hanooman* (हनुमान् - hanumán, San.). From (above + mat, san. affix showing possession). The monkey chief.—"*a*" In early Sanscrit writings the son of the wind, or else an incarnation [avatar] of Vayoo [q.v.] himself. In the Ramayanam [q.v.] story he was the chief general of the monkey-king Soogreevan [q.v.], who assisted Rama [q.v.] in his war with the giant Ravanan [q.v.]. When Rama was in distress at the loss of his wife Seetay [q.v.], Hanooman was employed as a spy; and, after many researches, discovered that Seetay was kept a prisoner in Lunka [q.v.]. Four armies of monkeys and bears [ricsham] were despatched, but only that to the south, under the command of Hanooman, met with any success, and brought back tidings of Seetay. Hanooman is regarded as a demi-god [chiranjeevy] and his whole race as sacred; and because of this monkeys are allowed to multiply indefinitely, no one being willing to interfere with them. The exploits of Hanooman are favourite topics among the Tamulians from childhood to age, and paintings of them are common. He is according to the Ramayanam caumaroopy that is changing his form at will, like Soogreevan, and like all the other monkeys [bandar], his companions.—"*b*" In drawings Hanooman is represented rampant, holding a large fruit in his forepaws, or else a mountain peak with volcanic flames streaming from the summit [humpy]. In the Teloogoo country Hanooman is termed Hanoomanta roya, and in some books Hanoomat deva occurs [matam]. See vol. (63), (72), (86). There is a Tamul proverb:—இராமனைப்போல ராஜா இருந்தால் அனுமானைப்போலச் சேவகனும் இருப்பான்—"If the king be equal to Rama, his servant may "be equal to Hanooman;" both rare.—"*c*" The Sanscrit work Meirauvanan charitram from the Jeiminy bhauratam gives a story of Hanooman prevalent in the south. Abstract is the following. The valour of Hanooman. The sorrow of Ravanan at his defeat by Hanooman. Meirauvanan, a raucshasan, comes to console and point out revenge. Ravanan asks what can be done, against not men but gods. Meirauvanan engages to go down to his kingdom in the inferior world, and offer a sacrifice to the goddess there. The wife of Meirauvanan dissuades him. However he sets out at the head of his army from the inferior world to make war. On the way evil omens [shacoonam] appear. Vibheeshanan, younger brother of Ravanan, knowing the preparations, informs Hanooman and Soogreevan. Rama is then sleeping, and cannot be disturbed. Hanooman assumes a supernatural form; and binds his tail all around the camp of Rama, from the heavens down to the lower regions. He allows only one entrance, at which he keeps guard; and despatching Vibheeshanan as a scout, gives charge of the interior to Soogreevan and others. It is now night. Meirauvanan sends a spy who reports preparations made; adding that Vibheeshanan only is outside, whose form thereupon Meirauvanan assumes, and going to Hanooman, tells him to be on his guard. Being allowed to enter the fortress, he takes Rama and his brother Lutchmanan, both being asleep, and putting them into a box carries them down to his inferior world. Vibheeshanan warned by evil omens; and returning to see the cause, the deception is discovered. Hanooman enquires for directions; and, guided by a particular flower tree, comes to the entrance of the descent to the inferior world. Thither he goes with troops. His proceedings, and the battles which follow. It is not possible to kill Meirauvanan. He is cut into pieces, but the parts of his body come together again. All attempts to put him to death fail; until a relative points out that his life is in a certain cave, in the form of bees [tainee]. These are killed by Hanooman, and Meirauvanan expires. The victor then places the relative of Meirauvanan, who has given the information, in possession of the kingdom of the inferior regions, and takes Rama and Lutchmanan, both still asleep in the box, and knowing nothing of the matter, back to their proper place. Agastyan narrates this tale to Rama in praise of Hanooman. Rama is greatly pleased; and showers down benefits on his successful protector. The whole time of the action of the poem is a single night.——*Hanooman moolamuntram* (हनुमान्मूलमन्त्र - hanumánmúlamantra, San.). From (hanumán, san. the monkey god + múlamantra, san. chief spell). One of the spells [muntram] used by Shactibhactans [q.v.].——*Hanoomantu* (ಹನುಮಂತ - hanumanta, Can.). From (above + mat, san. suffix of possession). Plural form of hanoomat. Hindoo 2nd or pers. name. Common among Madhwas [peyar].——*Hanoomat* (हनुमत् - hanumat, San.). Uninflected form of Hanooman.——*Hanoomatcertam* (ಹನುಮತ್ತೀರ್ಥ - hanumattírtha, Can.). From (hanumán, san. the monkey god + tírt'ha, san. sacred ford). Village, Spring; Salem dist., Ootancaray tal.; pop. 191; acres 405; lat. 12° 11′; long. 78° 36′; from Ootancaray S. by E. 6 miles; from Salem N.E. 44 miles. The water has a copper [taumram] taste, and the masonry has a greenish tinge where the water flows over it.

HAR (هر - har, *Hind.*). Every.——*Harcarra* (هركاره - harkárah, Hind.). From (above + kár, pers. business). Messenger [hammaul].

HARAN (हर - hara, *San.*; அரன் - aran, *Tam.*). From (hri, san. to take away). Shiva, the destroyer, otherwise remover of sin [hary].——*Haram* (हर - hara, San.). From (hri, san. to take off). Divisor in arithmetic [ganitam]. Also called Bhaujak [q.v.].——*Haranidattaval* (அரனிடத்தவள் - aranidattaval, Tam.). From (above + idam, tam. left side + aval, tam. feminine suffix). Parvaty, as being on left of Shiva [ardhanaury].——*Haran magan* (அரன்மகன் - aranmagan, Tam.). From (above + magan, tam. son). Soobramanyan [q.v.], as well as Ganesh [q.v.] and Veerabhadran [q.v.].——*Haran tozhan* (அரன்றோழன் - aranrózhan, Tam.). From (above + tózhan, tam. companion). Coobairan [q.v.], the regent of the north and the god of riches [ashta dicpaulacan].——*Harichendra katay* (हरिश्चन्द्रकथा - barishchandrakat'há, San.). From (harishchandra, san. the king, so called + kat'há, san. story). The tale of Harichendran. Derived from episode in Mahabhaurat [q.v.], put into the mouth of Vasishtan [q.v.]. A tale equally popular among Tamul, Canarese, and Teloogoo authors. Harichendran was a great prince of extreme liberality, and being a Chuckravurty [q.v.] it was not permitted him either to degrade himself as to caste or to tell a lie. One day a mendicant Bramin obtained from him a promise, which involved a very large gift of money. The Bramin did not then take the money; but went away, and returned after many years claiming his money with the interest due thereon. The king unable to liquidate the debt sold his kingdom, and still there was a balance due. The Bramin said that if he would tell a lie, or marry an out-caste woman, the whole of the money should be restored; but the king preferred abandoning his kingdom, and selling himself, his wife, and son, as slaves in order to pay the debt. In pursuance of this design he came to Caushy [q.v.] or Benares, where his wife and child were purchased by a Bramin, and he himself by a Chundaulan [q.v.], whose office was to attend burning-grounds [shood caud]. The Bramin sent the child out one day to gather wood, where being bitten by a snake it died and was by the mother taken to the burning-ground, at which her husband was by this time stationed as Chundaulan. He refused to do what was customary without fees, and the mother had nothing to pay. He said that if she would give him the marriage talee [q.v.] it would suffice. She refused; but conjectured from this demand that the man must be her husband, as no one else knew that she possessed any such thing. At this juncture officers of the king of the country came, and took away the child on suspicion of its being the king's own child that was missing; and, the likeness being great, the king sent instructions that the man at the burning-ground should put the woman to death with a sword. Harichendran struck one blow, when flowers burst forth. He was about striking a second, when Bhagwaun [q.v.] appeared, praised his virtues, and restored him to the possession of his former prosperity.——*Harichendran* (هری چندر - haríchandar, Hind.; హరిశ్చంద్రుడు - harishchandrudu, Tel.). From (hari, san. golden + chandra, san. brilliancy). Refulgent lord. Proper name [peyar].——*Haridoss* (హరిదాస -

haridása, Can.). From (hari, san. vishnu, the attractive + dása, san. slave); Veishnava devotee. Hindoo 2nd or pers. name [peyar].——*Haridrah* (हरिद्रा - haridrá, San.). From (hari, san. yellow + dru, san. go). Title otherwise Turmeric. Botanically the Curcuma genus, zingiberaceæ [vricsham, 144]. Generic name from (kurkum, ar. curcuma longa, roxb.). Stemless herbs; roots perennial, palmately tuberous; leaves herbaceous, petioles sheathing, bifarious; scape simple, lateral or central; flowers yellowish, approximated by threes or fives between each bract; capsule three-celled; seeds arillate. The species best known to the natives are:—amada [mango ginger], angustifolia [malabar arrowroot], aromatica [round zedoary], leucorrhiza [red malabar arrowroot], longa [country saffron], zedoaria [long zedoary]. Other s. indian species indigenous or naturalized are:—neilgherrensis, pseudomontana, reclinata, rutescens.——*Hariharan* (हरिहर - harihara, San.; அரியரன் - ariyaran, Tam.). Vishnoo and Shiva combined. Not connected with Ardhanaury [q.v.]. See vol. I (74), (77) [mohiny]. Hindoo 2nd or pers. name [peyar]. One Hariharan, otherwise Hukka, formed first of the three Vijianugger dynasties [charitram, raj]; see vol. I (148) and II, 251.——*Harihara pootran* (हरिहरपुत्र - hariharapootra, San.). From (hari, san. vishnu + hara, san. shiva + putra, san. son). Ayenaur [ayen] as the son of Shiva [q.v.] by Mohiny [q.v.].——*Haripaulan* (हरिपाल - haripála, San.). From (hari, san. vishnu + pála, san. protector); one who has vishnoo for his protector. Proper name. See vol. I (140).——*Haripootran* (ಹರಿಪುತ್ರ - hariputra, Can.). From (hari, san. vishnu + putra, san. son); applied to bramha [pralayam] and manmatan [q.v.] as the sons of vishnoo [q.v.]. Hindoo 2nd or pers. name [peyar].——*Harishuncaran* (హరిశంకరుడు - harishankarudu, Tel.). From (hari, san. vishnu + shankara, san. shiva, the happiness maker). From of a deity where Vishnoo and Shiva are combined in one [mohiny]. Hindoo 2nd or pers. name [peyar].——*Haritakee* (हरीतकी - harítaki, San.). Means clearing bowels. Same as Chebulic myrobalan.——*Haritam* (हरित - harita, San.). Green. Plant first term. Ex.:—Acalypha indica (haritamañjari), green cluster; Moringa pterygosperma (haritapatra), green leaf. See gloss. paragraphs.——*Haritaulam* (हरिताल - haritála, San.). See sep. title.——*Haritaulica* (హరితాళికము - haritálikamu, Tel.). Means yellow orpiment [hartaul]. From yellow image of gowry set up and worshipped on the occasion. Lunar festival [pundigay, 6d], subject to intercalation [adhicam]. The third tity [q.v.] of the waxing moon of sixth lunar month Bhaudrapadam [mansam] between 19th August and 18th September. An inauspicious day; because Krishnan [q.v.] was falsely accused in his childhood of having stolen a gold gem from Prasainan on that day [gowry, maryauday].——*Hariyanna* (ಹರಿಯಣ್ಣ - hariyanna, Can.). From (hari, san. vishnoo + anna, can. elder brother, titular affix). Hindoo 2nd or pers. name [peyar].——*Haroor* (ಹರೂರು - harúru, Can.). From (hara, san. shiva + úr, tam. village).—"*a*" Deputy tahsildarry, Salem district. Pay Rs. 70.—"*b*" Village; Salem dist., Ootancaray tal.; pop. 2,792; acres 2,187; lat. 12° 03′; long. 78° 32′; from Madras S.W. 140 miles; from Namcull N.N.E. 61 miles; from Oossoor S.E. 62 miles; from Ootancaray S. 16 miles; from Salem N.E. 34 miles; from Tripatore S. 31 miles; from Yercaud N.E. 26 miles. On west bank of Vauniyaur, parcherry [q.v.] being on east bank. West of town towards Morapore and Tencaraycottah extends a vast jungle, chiefly of Toorinjy [dark sirissa]. Healthy and with good water-supply. Between Haroor and Morapore are sculptural remains. Population consists chiefly of Janapars [janapa], trading in grain and cattle [maud] and Lubbays [q.v.] who export Auvauramputtay [tungaid] in considerable quantities to Vaniyambaudy. Shandy [q.v.] on Mondays.——*Harra* (ہڑا - harrá, Hind.; ಅಳೆಗಾರ - alegára, Can.). Title otherwise Citrine myrobalan. Botanically Terminalia [antya parny] citrina, roxb., combretaceæ [vricsham, 55]. Alias Myrobalanus citrina. Large tree; leaves somewhat opposite, oblong, tapering towards the base, smooth, acute, with two small glands on the apex of the petiole; panicles terminal and axillary, composed of several simple erect spikes; drupe oblong-lanceolate, five-cornered, smooth, of a dull orange-yellow; nut oblong, deeply five-grooved; flowers all hermaphrodite, dull-yellow; flowering in april and may; grows in canara. Fruit a gentle purgative; often made into pickle; used in tanning [chamrah]. For the other myrobalans see Tripalam.——*Harsingaur* (ہرسنگار - harsingár, Hind.). From (hára, san. garland + shringára, san. beauty); from use of flowers. Same as Coral jasmine.——*Hartaul* (हरितालक - haritálaka, San.; हरिताली - haritálí, Mahr.; زرنیخ اصفر - zirníkhiasfar, Ar.; زرنیخ زرد - zirníkhizard, Pers.; ہڑتال - hartál, Hind.; ورنگن - warangan, Malay; ಅರದಳ - aridala, Can.; ಅರದಾಳ - aradála, Too.; హరిదళము - haridalamu, Tel.; അരിതാരം - aritáram, Mal.; සිරියල් - siriyal, Singh.; அரிதாரம் - aritháram, Tam.). Title from hindostany. San. from (hari, san. yellow + tála, san. orpiment). Ar. from (zirníkh, ar. arsenic + asfar, ar. yellow). Pers. from (zard, pers. yellow). Hind. from sanscrit. Mal. from sanscrit. Singh. corruption from sanscrit. Tam. from sanscrit. Tel. also (doddapáshánamu), meaning great + arsenic. Mal. also (cháyilyam), corruption of (játilingam), meaning vermilion [shangarf]. Tam. also (elikkúduppasánam), meaning mouse + trap + arsenic, used as rat's bane; (kattarithâram), meaning lump + orpiment; (kallarithâram), meaning stone orpiment, as in lumps. Yellow orpiment or golden pigment or king's yellow. Otherwise Sulphuret of arsenic, Yellow arsenic [paushaunam]. Arsenicum flavum, Arsenicum tersulphuretum, Arsenici trisulphidum of chemists. Of a lemon-yellow color, running often into red and brown; usually got in large angulo-granular distinct concretions, also in concentrate lamellar concretions; it is soft and flexible, but not elastic; looks like yellow talc [q.v.], but is much heavier; when thrown in fire emits blue flame; consists of about 62 parts of arsenic [paushaunam] and 38 of sulphur [gandhac]. Found native, and imported especially from China. There are three kinds in bazaars [q.v.], viz., one in glistening golden scales called workee hartaul and two others in massive lumps of a yellow color, the fracture in one of these latter being dull and in the other resinous. Veidyans [q.v.] use to check obstinate intermittent fevers [jwaram] and in glandular complaints, in apoplectic attacks, and in certain leprous affections [cooshtam]. Used as a yellow dye [shauyam] and pigment [rangh]; used in calico [q.v.] printing, &c.——*Hary* (हरि - hari, San.). From (hri, san. to remove sin).—"*a*" Vishnoo. Compare ἥρα, ἥρως, ἡράκλης in Greek; herth or hertha in German; hur in Chaldean; horus in Egyptian; all solar divinities. Used in the north, as Permaul [q.v.] is in the south. There is a Tamul proverb:—அரி என்றால் ஆண்டிக்குக் கோபம், அரன் என்றால் தாதனுக்குக் கோபம்—"If one says Hary the Sheiva "mendicant is angry, if one says Haran the Veishnava mendicant "is angry" [matam]. Hindoo 2nd or pers. name; common among Madhwas. Also suffix in proper names as Narahary [peyar].—"*b*" Plant first term. Ex., where transl. is of second term:—Methonica superba (haripriyá), meaning liked by vishnoo; Phaseolus mungo (harimúng), meaning green + pulse; Pterocarpus santalinus (harichandana), meaning tawny + santalum album. See gloss. paragraphs.—"*c*" Plant second term. Ex.:—Cassia auriculata (timirahari), ophthalmia + removing; Semecarpus anacardium (shóp'hahari), morbid swelling + removing.——*Hary's plant* (हरिप्रिया - haripriyá, San.). Same as Wild bachnaug.——*Hauram* (हार - hára, San.). From (hri, san. to take off). The denominator of a fraction.——*Hurpanhully* (ಹರಪನಹಳ್ಳಿ - harapanahalli, Can.). See sep. title.——*Hurrially* (ہریالی - hariyálí, Dec.). See sep. title.

HARAUJ (ہراج - haráj, *Hind.*). From (haraja, ar. to run fast). Auction [yailam].

HARAUM (حرام - harám, *Hind.*). From (haruma, ar. to prohibit). Whatever the Mahomedan law disallows; unlawful, such as pork, wine, mushrooms, &c. [halaul].——*Haraumzauda* (حرام زاده - harámzádah, Hind.). From (above + zádah, pers. born). Bastard, scoundrel. Term of abuse.——*Harem* (حرم - haram, Hind.). From (haruma, ar. to forbid). The portion of a house which is reserved for the women of a family; thence the women themselves, the wives and concubines of a Mussalman collectively. Zenana [q.v.] is the word generally used in S. india.

HARCATT (حرکت - harakkat, *Hind.*). From (haraka, ar. to move). A hindrance.

HARE'S EAR (മുയൽചെവി - muyalchevi, *Mal.*; කඩුපාර - kádupára, *Singh.*; முயற்செவி - muyarchevi, *Tam.*). Title from long tubular florets. Mal. from (muyal, mal. hare + chevi, mal. ear). cf. gowzabaun. Botanically Emilia sonchifolia, dec., compositæ [vricsham, 74]. Alias Cacalia glabra, sonchifolia; Crassocephalum sonchifolium; Emilia purpurea; Senecio sonchifolia. Annual; stem herbaceous, branching a little towards the top; leaves lyrate; stem clasping; flowers few, in terminal umbellets, cylindrical, peduncled; flowers small, bright purple; flowering in cold season; is very variable in respect to both stem and leaves. Whole plant used in decoction on west coast as a febrifuge; mixed with sugar [q.v.] the juice is given in bowel-complaints; juice is also as cooling like rosewater [goolaub, panneer], in inflammation of the eyes. No other common species here.

HARITAULAM (हरिताल - haritála, *San.*). From (harit, san. green) [haran]. Treronidæ family, gemitores, aves [pacshy, 28], of naturalists [jantoo]. Sub-divided here into the following sub-families:—Treroninæ, green pigeons; Carpophaginæ, imperial pigeons. The two species best known to the natives are shown below.——*Green pigeon* (ہریال - hariyál, Hind.; ಹಸರುಬಣ್ಣಹಕ್ಕಿ - hasarubannahakki, Can.; పచ్చగువ్వ - pattsaguvva, Tel.; பச்சைப்புறா - paççaippurá, Tam.). Title from color of under parts. Hind. from (hará, hind. green). Can. from (hasaru, can. green + banna, can. color + hakki, can. bird). Tel. from (pattsa, tel. green + guvva, tel. pigeon). Tam. from (paççai, tam. green + purá, tam. pigeon). Crocopus chlorigaster, treroninæ. Alias Treron jerdoni. Whole top of head ashy, devoid in adults of any tinge of green on forehead, whole under parts green; neck and breast less tinged with yellow, shade gradually into green of abdomen; no trace of green upon tail, except at extreme base, which is uniformly ashy above. Length 12 inches. Very abundant. Excellent eating.——*Imperial pigeon* (بڑا ہریال - baráhariyál, Hind.; కాకిరేనిగువ్వ - kákiréniguvva, Tel.; പൊകിന - pokina, Mal.). Title from bright color. Hind. from (bará, hind. large + hariyál, hind. green pigeon). Tel. from (káki, tel. crow + rédu, tel. king + guvva, tel. pigeon). Hind. also (dumkal), meaning black tail; (sonakabutrá), meaning golden pigeon. Title otherwise Fruit pigeon, Gold pigeon. Carpophaga sylvatica, carpophaginæ. Alias Carpophaga œnea, pusilla. Head, neck and whole under parts pearl grey, purer on crown and breast, tinged elsewhere, sometimes on crown, with ruddy vinaceous; back, rump, wings and tail shining coppery green, brightest on tail quills, slaty-grey without, dark blackish grey within; under tail-coverts deep chestnut, with which some feathers of vent and flanks are also sprinkled; chin, orbital feathers, and round the base of the bill white; axillaries buff; bill slaty, red at the base above, and bluish white at the tip; irides and the nude orbits crimson; legs lake red, pale on soles; length 18-19 inches; found in forest countries; call low, deep, moan. The Bronze-backed imperial pigeon is carpophaga insignis, malabar.

HARMAL (حرمل - hurmal, *Ar.*; سپند - sipand, *Pers.*; اسبند - isband, *Hind.* and *Dec.*; సీమగోరంట - símagóranta, *Tel.*; சீமையழவிஞை - shímaiyazhavinai, *Tam.*). Title from arabic. Ar. from syriac. Tel. from (síma, tel. foreign + góranta, tel. nail-dye plant, lawsonia alba, lam.). Tam. from (shímai, tam. foreign + aivanam, tam. nail dye). Title otherwise Foreign henna, Isbund, Lahore seed, Syrian rue. Botanically Peganum harmala, linn., rutaceæ [vricsham, 32]. Specific from arabic. Herbaceous; calyx five-partite; stamens fifteen, shorter than the petals, some abortive; anthers linear; style simple; stigma trigonal; leaves multifid, lobes linear; flowers terminal, white; capsule three-celled, three-furrowed, many-seeded; indigenous plant. The seeds are brown, irregularly triangular, about a line in length; although about six or seven times larger than mindie [q.v.], yet bear great resemblance in their outline, hence one of names of plant. The drug, as found in the bazaar [q.v.], consists of the seeds mixed with a few pedicels surmounted by the five-partite calyx and portions of the three-celled, three-furrowed capsule; the seeds have a heavy narcotic odour when crushed, and a bitter taste. The seeds are one of the commonest drugs in bazaar; physiological actions, narcotic, antispasmodic, hypnotic, anodyne, nauseant, emetic and emmenagogue; preparation, simple powder; doses of the powder, from thirty grains to two drachms, increased gradually; substituted for belladonna, ether, morphia, salicylic acid and its salts, lactuca, conium, squills, lobelia and yellow jessamine; quoted in pharm. non-officinal. Powdered root, mixed with mustard [rayaun] oil, applied to the hair to destroy vermin; the seeds burnt at marriages to drive away evil spirits; also as a charm during forty days of puerperal state; thrown into the fire with benzoin [q.v.] or mustard seed. No other common species here.

HAROON (هارون - hárún, *Ar.*). Means impatient. Aaron. Mahomedan alam; as:—Haroon sait; alam + alaamat [ism].

HASHISH (حشيش - hashísh, *Hind.*; జనుముమొగ్గ - dzanumumogga, *Tel.*). Hind. from (hashsha, ar. dry herbage). Tel. from (dzanumu, tel. hemp plant + mogga, tel. bud). Product of Cannabis [kiunab] sativa, linn. The dried tops and tender parts of the plant collected immediately after inflorescence [mooskiraut].

HASLAR (ಹಸುಲರ - hasulara, *Can.*). From (hasule, can. child from hasur, can. tender). Canarese jungle tribe. A short thick-set race, very dark in color and with curled hair. Their chief employment is felling timber, but they sometimes work in areca [q.v.] nut gardens and gather wild cardamoms [q.v.], pepper [q.v.], &c. They speak a dialect of Canarese [jauty].

HAST (هست - hast, *Pers.*). Is.——*Hastbood* (هست و بود - hastobúd, Hind.). From (above + búd, pers. was). What is and what was; examination into value of land.

HASTAM (हस्त - hasta, *San.*). Means hand. The forearm from the tip of the middle finger to the elbow. Cubit. 2 vitasties or spans = 1 hastam; 4 hastams = 1 dandam [alavay, 1f]. Approximate actual value, 1 hastam = 18 inches. Same as Hind. haut, Tel. moora, Tam. moolam. See vol. I, 609.——*Hasty* (हस्ति - hasti, San.). From the trunk. Elephant [aunay, cary, elephant, gajam]. Plant first term. Ex.:—Cucumis sativus (hastiparní), elephant leaf; Musa paradisiaca (hastivisháni), elephant tusk. See gloss. paragraphs.——*Haut* (هات - hát, Hind.). From (hasta, san. hand). Cubit measured from the tip of the middle finger to the elbow. 2 bilishts or spans = 1 haut; 2 hauts = 1 guz [alavay, 1e]. Approximate actual value, 1 haut = 18 inches. The timber measuring haut is 22 inches. Same as San. hastam, Tel. moora, Tam. moolam. See vol. I, 609.

HASTAMPUTTY (அத்தம்பட்டி - attambatti, *Tam.*). From (aittan, tam. proper name + patti, tam. cattle-fold). Village, Salem dist., Salem tal.; pop. 2,249; lat. 11° 41′; long. 78° 12′; from Salem N. 1½ miles. European settlement.

HASSAN (حسن - hasan, *Hind.*). From arabic. Virtue. Grandson of the prophet [mahomed] through his daughter Fatimah; born about A.D. 622; died 668 A.D. He succeeded his father Ally [q.v.] as the fifth caliph [q.v.] in A.D. 660 and reigned about six months. He resigned the caliphate [q.v.] in favor of Mooauviya. He was eventually poisoned by his wife, who was suborned to commit the deed by Yazeed, son of Mooauviya, so as to succeed to the caliphate [hoossain]. Common alam; as Hassan ahmed, double alam; Hassan khan, alam + alaumat [ism].——*Hassanee* (حسنى - hasaní, Hind.). Lacab of Syeds [q.v.] directly descended from Hassan.——*Hassanore* (ಹಾಸನೂರು - hásanúru, Can.; ஆசனூர் - ásanúr, Tam. hassanúr *). From (hasan, ar. mahomedan proper name + úru, can. village). Village, Ghaut; Coimbatore dist., Suttimungalam tal.; pop. 2,056; lat. 11° 41′; long. 77° 11′; from Coimbatore N.N.E. 49 miles; from Suttimungalam N.N.W. 14 miles. In the Biligherry rungum hills. Ghaut [q.v.] forms a good road for wheeled traffic from Coimbatore through Suttimungalam to Mysore, with an easy gradient for eight miles to a height of 3,000 feet to Dimmam, and thence four miles to Hassanore, where the Collegaul road branches. It is much used.

HAUDY (هادى - hádí, *Hind.*). From (hudá, ar. to guide). Director [hidauyat]; an attribute of God [allah]. Common alam; as Haudy ally, double alam [ism].

HAUFIZ (حافظ - háfiz, *Hind.*). From (hafaza, ar. to preserve). Protector. One who knows koran [q.v.] by heart. Also the takhalloos [q.v.] of a famous Persian lyric poet. Attribute of God. Feminine Haufiza. Ex.:—Haufiza bee, alam + alaumat [ism].

HAUJIB (حاجب - hájib, *Hind.*). From (hajaba, ar. to veil). A door-keeper. Agent. An officer of court similar to that of chancellor, who introduces foreign ambassadors.

HAUL (حال - hál, *Hind.*). From (hála, ar. to turn towards). Present condition.——*Haulatt* (حالت - hálat, Hind.). Unsubstantial, poor condition.——*Haulavaul* (حال احوال - hálahvál, Hind.). State of man's circumstances.——*Haul saul* (حال سال - hálsál, Hind.). Current year [saul].——*Havildar* (حوالدار - havâldár, Hind.). From (havâlah, ar. charge + dár, pers. holder). One holding any office. A non-commissioned officer in a Native regiment subordinate to soobahdar [q.v.] and corresponding to the English sergeant.——*Hawaula* (حوال - hawálah, Hind.). From (hála, ar. to pass from hand to hand). Charge [haul].——*Hully sicca* (حالى سكه - hálísikkah, Hind.). From (hál, pers. modern + sikka, pers. coin); as recently introduced. Coin current in Hyderabad. 100 Government rupees = 114 Hully sicca [q.v.] rupees.

HAUL (ಹಾಳು - hálu, *Can.*; பாழ் - pázh, *Tam.*). Waste land [paul]. Suffix in place names as Hireyhaul, meaning great waste.

HAUMID (حامد - hámid, *Ar.*). From (hamada, ar. to praise). Praiseworthy [hameed, hammaud]. Lacab of the prophet. Common alam; as Haumid hoossain, double alam [ism].

HAURWA (ಹಾರುವ - háruva, *Can.*). From (háru, can. leap). A degenerate class of Bramins who officiate as priests at harvest festivals [jauty]. Connected with Harihara sect, worship both Vishnoo [q.v.] and Shiva [q.v.]. Wear Braminical cord [poonool]. Every second year walk barefoot on burning coal.

HAUSHIM (هاشم - háshim, *Ar.*). Great grandfather of Mahomet. Common alam; as Haushim beg, alam + alaumat [ism].——*Haushimy* (هاشمى - háshimí, Hind.). Title of Mahomet. Lacab of the class of Mahomedans [ism].

HAUZIR (حاضر - házir, *Hind.*). From (hazara, ar. present). Present, ready.——*Hauzir baushy* (حاضر باشى - házirbáshí, Hind.). From (above + búdan, pers. to be). Attendance.——*Hauzir jaumeen* (حاضر ضامن - házirzámin, Hind.). From (above + zámin, ar. security). The person who becomes security for the appearance of another [nagad jaumeen].——*Hazrat* (حضرت - hazrat, Hind.). From (hazara, ar. to be present). Presence, dignity. Title given to a person of rank, equivalent to Your Excellency [samoogam].——*Hazree* (حاضرى - házirí, Hind.). A muster roll; so breakfast. Chota hazree, from (chhotá, hind. slight + háziri, hind. breakfast) is early light breakfast.——*Huzoor* (حضور - huzúr, Hind.). From (hazara, ar. to be present) [samoogam]. The presence, especially of a superior authority. Used generally for a Collector's office. Also used by natives as a respectful way of speaking of exalted personages.

HAVELLY (حويلى - havelí, *Hind.*). From (haul, ar. girt). Environs. The tract of country adjacent to a capital town, and originally annexed to it for the supply of the public establishments; afterwards came to signify lands under direct government management [amauny]. Cf. Home farms.

HAYAM (हय - haya, *San.*). From (hay, san. to go). A horse [coothiray, ghorah].——*Haya greevan* (हयग्रीव - hayagríva, San.). From (above + gríva, san. neck). A centaur. A portion of Vishnoo [q.v.] manifested in the Matsyam avatar [q.v.] as a demon in order to recover the Vedam [q.v.] carried off by the two Deityans [q.v.] Madhoo and Keitabhan. In the south called Somacausooran [matam].

HAYCALAH (ഹയ്ക്ലാ - hayklá, *Mal.*). Nave of a church among Malabar syrian christians.

HAZAUR (هزار - hazár, *Hind.*). Thousand [sahasram]. Plant first term. Ex.:—Andropogon schœnanthus (hazármasálah), thousand ingredients, from aroma; Mollugo cerviana (hazárdánah), thousand seed; see gloss. paragraphs.——*Hazaur danah* (पर्पटक - parpataka, San.; पर्पाटकु - parpátaku, Conc.; تپ جہار - tapjhár, Hind.; ہزاردانہ - hazárdánah, Dec.; ಪರ್ಪಾಟಕ - parpátaka, Can.; ಕೋರಪಂಟಿ - kórapanti, Too.; పర్పాటకము - parpátakamu, Tel.; പര്പ്പടകം - parppatakam, Mal.; පත්පාදගම් - patpádagam, Singh.; பர்ப்பாடகம் - parppádagam, Tam.). Title from numerous seeds. San. from sound of seeds bursting when the shrub is set fire to. Hind. from (tap, hind. fever + jhár, hind. tree); as febrifuge. Dec. from (hazár, hind. thousand + dánah, pers. seed). Tel., &c., from sanscrit. San. also (kavacha), meaning armour, medicinal; (kundalí), meaning annular, from germ [sangcooppy]. Can. also (parpáshtaka). Tel. also (pittsukakálu), meaning sparrow + leg. Title otherwise Fever plant, Sparrow leg. Botanically Mollugo [parpatam] cerviana, sering., ficoideæ [vricsham, 66]. Alias Pharnaceum cerviana, glabrum. Small plant half a foot; stems straightish, ascending, terete; leaves opposite, or alternate by abortion, linear, verticillate, very narrow, bluntish, glaucous; calyx five-parted; petals none; peduncles elongated, bearing three umbellate flowers; stamens usually five, or less by abortion; capsule three-valved, three-celled, many-seeded; calyx white on the inside. Febrifuge, diaphoretic, expectorant, antibilious.——*Hazaur daustaun* (هزار داستان - hazárdástán, Hind.). Means thousand + note. Madras boolbool [q.v.], pycnonotus hæmorhous.——*Hazauree* (هزاری - hazárí, Hind.). The commandant of a thousand men [amaram].——*Hazaur siry* (هزارسری - hazársirí, Hind.). From (above + sirí, hind. step). Flight of stairs to hill forts [kila].

HEENA (हीन - hína, *San.*; هین - hín, *Hind.*). From (há, san. to abandon). Devoid of, low. Heena jauty is of no caste. Heena raushy is that grain which being at the bottom of the heap is mixed with earth. Heenpacshan is an orphan.

HEERADACOON (اژدهاخون - azhdákhún, *Hind.*). From (azhdahá, pers. dragon + khún, pers. blood). Name in Bombay for Dragon's blood.

HEIBAT (هیبت - haibat, *Hind.*). From (hába, ar. to fear). Awe. Component of alam; as Heibat ool lah shah, fear of god, alam + alaumat [ism].

HEIGA (ಹೈಗ - haiga, *Can.*). From (hávu, can. snake); snake land. Ancient name of part of Canara from Bhadragherry river to the Gungavully. See vol. I (128).——*Hyecshetram* (ಹೈಕ್ಷೇತ್ರ - haikshétra, Can.). Another name of Heiga [q.v.] country.

HEIYAT (هیئت - haiyat, *Hind.*). From (haiyá, ar. face or form). Aspect of heavens, astronomy [ilm, nacshatram, najm].

HEMAM (हेम - héma, *San.*). From (hi, san. to go); useful, valuable. Gold [hiranyam, honn, pon, tungam].——*Hemauvaty* (ಹೇಮಾವತಿ - hémávati, Can.; hemavati, Mys. Gov.). From (above + vat, san. suffix of possession).—"*a*" Also in Canarese Yenneholey, oily or shining river. One of chief tributaries of Cauvery. Runs into Cauvery near Hoscote in Atticooppay talook, Hassan district, Mysore.—"*b*" Village, Place of pilgrimage; Anantapore dist., Madaksira tal.; pop. 2,112; lat. 14° 01′; long. 77° 02′; from Anantapore S.W. 62 miles; from Madaksira W.N.W. 20 miles. A celebrated Shiva temple and two others. A car feast in honor of Shiva. Shiva is an image here which is very unusual. There is a tradition that temples are buried underground all round the village and that at one time there was rain of gold in the village. Hence the name.

HENNA (حنا - hiná, *Pers.*). Dye from leaf of Egyptian privet [mindie].——*Foreign henna* (సీమగోరంట - símagóranta, Tel.). Same as Harmal.

HERMIT (तापस - tápasa, *San.*; దాసరి - dásari, *Tel.*). Prefix. ——*Hermit snake* (ದಾಸರಹಾವು - dásarahávu, Can.; దాసరిపాము - dásaripámu, Tel.; தாசரிப்பாம்பு - tásarippámbu, Tam.). Title from marks on head and neck like a dausary's forehead marks. The rock-snake [q.v.].——*Hermit's tree* (तापसप्रिय - tápasapriya, San.). Hermits use oil from seed for burning. Same as Chironjee.

HEY (ಹೆ - he, *Can.*). Abbreviation of hedda in composition. Great [hiree].——*Hebbaura* (ಹೆಬ್ಬಾರ - hebbára, Can.). From (hedda, can. great + háruvá, can. bramin). Title to Canarese veishnava bramins. Hindoo third name [peyar].——*Heggadey* (ಹೆಗ್ಗಡೆ - heggade Can.). Means headman. Title to Bunts. Hindoo third name [peyar].——*Hettey* (ಹೆಟ್ಟೆ - hette, Can.). Great [hiree].——*Hettey coil* (ಹೆಟ್ಟೆಕೋವಿಲ್ - hettekóvil, Can.). From (hette, can. great + kóvil, tam. temple). Principal temple of the Neilgherry badagas.——*Hetteydeva* (ಹೆಟ್ಟೆದೇವ - hettedéva, Can.). From (hette, can. great + déva, can. god). Badaga deity [hiredeva].

HIDAUYAT (هدایت - hidáyat, *Ar.*). From (hudá, ar. to guide). Guidance [haudy]. Prefixed to an alam forms a lacab; as Hidauyat hoossain, guide of hoossain [ism].

HIJJAL (हिज्जल - hijjala, *San.*). Means water-liking [hitam], as growing near water. Same as Small indian oak.

HIJRA (هجری - hijra, *Hind.*; హిజిరి - hijiri, *Tel.*). From (hijr, ar. separation). Flight. The flight of Mahomet the prophet from Mecca to Medina to escape persecution. It took place on the night of Thursday the 15th July, A.D. 622. In the caliphate [q.v.] of Omar, this was constituted the commencement of the Mahomedan era, and the era was called Hijra era. See vol. I, 613. For months see Maheena.

HILL (پہاڑ - pahár, *Hind.*; ಬೆಟ್ಟ - betta, *Can.*; కొండ - konda, *Tel.*; മല - mala, *Mal.*; மலை - malai, *Tam.*). Common prefix. Plant first term in the vernaculars, from place of growth and sometimes indicating large size; often joining two genera. Ex., where transl. is of second term:—Acrocarpus fraxinifolius (malaikkón), king; Agave vivipara (malaikkattázhai), aloe indica; Albizzia procera (kondavágai), albizzia lebbek; Alpinia allughas (malayiñchikkúva), ginger + arrowroot; Alstonia venenatus (kondagannéru), nerium odorum; Amorphophallus campanulatus (malanchéna), yam; Amorphophallus lyratus (kondarákasi), she devil; Andrographis echioides (malakulukki), shaker; Andropogon fascicularis (kondajeri), centipede; Atalantia monophylla (kondanimma), lime; Atylosia scarabæoides (kondaulava), dolichos biflorus; Baliospermum montanum (kondaámudapuchettu), ricinus communis; Balsamodendron roxburghii (kondarégu), zizyphus jujuba; Barleria prionitis (kondagobbi), hygrophila spinosa; Bridelia retusa, var. genuina (malaivéngai), pterocarpus marsupium; Cajanus indicus, var. bicolor (malaittuvarai), cajanus indicus; Caryota urens (kondajílugu), æschynomene aspera; Cassia glauca (kondatantepuchettu), cassia tora; Cassia siamea (kondatangédu), cassia auriculata; Cassia sophera (kondakasinda), cassia occidentalis; Cassia tomentosa (malaiyávárai), cassia auriculata; Cipadessa fruticosa (bettadabévu), melia azadirachta; Cleome aspera (malaivérinbúndu), root + herb; Cochlospermum gossypium (kondagógu), hibiscus cannabinus; Colocasia montana (kondarakkissa), devil; Costus speciosus (malaivasambu), acorus calamus; Croton roxburghii (kondaámudamu), ricinus communis; Cucumis sativus (malaittummatti), cucumis trigonus; Dillenia bracteata (bettadakanigala), nerium odorum; Dillenia indica (bettakanigila), nerium odorum; Eleusine indica (malakkóra), eleusine corocana; Eragrostis punctata (bettadakabuhullu), grass; Ficus tomentosa (kondamarri), ficus bengalensis; Ficus tuberculata (kondadzuvvi), ficus tsiela; Ficus vagans (kondarávi), ficus religiosa; Garcinia xanthochymus (malaippuli), tamarindus indica; Gardenia latifolia (kondamanga), randia dumetorum; Guizotia abyssinica (kondanuvvu), sesamum indicum; Hibiscus collinus (malaivendai), hibiscus esculentus; Hibiscus furcatus (malaippuliççai), hibiscus cannabinus; Hymenodictyon excelsum (malaittanakku), gyrocarpus jacquini; Ipomæa pentaphylla (kondagummudu), ipomæa digitata; Jatropha curcas (kondaámuda), ricinus communis; Kœmpferia rotunda (malankúva), curcuma angustifolia; Macaranga indica (bettadávare), nelumbium speciosum; Manihot utilissima (malaiççakkaraivalli), sugar + ipomæa batatas; Melia azedarach (malavémbu), melia azadirachta; Michrochloa setacea (kondaponuku), gyrocarpus jacquini; Mundulea suberosa (kondavempali), tephrosia purpurea; Polygonum barbatum (kondamalle), jasminum sambac; Protium caudatum (kondamámidi), mangifera indica; (kondarégu), zizyphus jujuba; (malaikkiluvai), balsamodendron berryi; (malaimá), mangifera indica; Protium pubescens (malaikkiluvai), balsamodendron berryi; Psidium guyava, var. pomiferum (malampéra), guava; Sarcostemma brevistigma (kondapála), milky plant; Scleria lithosperma (kondashákatunga), cyperus rotundus; Sida carpinifolia (malatánni), supporter; Smilax ovalifolia (kondadantena), clitoria ternatea; (malaittámarai), nelumbium speciosum; Solanum torvum (malaisundai), solanum pubescens; Sophora glauca (malaiyávárai), cassia auriculata; Sponia wightii (malantutali), scutia indica; Sterculia urens (kondatámara), nelumbium speciosum; Symphorema involucratum (kondatekkali), clerodendron phlomoides; Thespesia lampas (kondapatti), gossypium herbaceum; Toddalia aculeata (kondakasinda), cassia occidentalis; Trichosanthes cucumerina (bettapadavala), trichosanthes anguina; Vaccinium leschenaultii (malaikkilá), carissa; Webera corymbosa (kondapápata), pavetta indica; Xylia dolabriformis (kondatangédu), cassia auriculata; Zizyphus jujuba (malantutali), scutia indica. See gloss. paragraphs. For compounds of Pahaur see Pahaury.——*Hill aloe* (மலைக்கற்றாழை - malaikkattázhai, Tam. Same as American aloe.——*Hill cobra* (پہاڑی سانپ - pahárisámp, Hind.; కొండనాగు - kondanágu, Tel.; കുറിഞ്ഞി - kuriñni, Mal.). Hind. means mountain serpent. Tel. from (konda, tel. hill + nágu, tel. snake). Mal. from (kuriççi, mal. jungle). Tel. also (vairagu). Title otherwise Hamadryad. Ophiophagus elaps, elapidæ [naug], ophidii colubriformes venenosi, ophidia [sarpam], reptilia [sarpy, 27], of naturalists [jantoo]. The genus contains this species only. Alias Hamadryas elaps, ophiophagus; Naja bungarus, elaps, vittata; Trimeresurus ophiophagus. A hooded snake, varying in length, in the adult state, from twelve to fourteen feet. Olive-green above; the shields of the head, the scales of the neck, hinder part of the body and of the tail edged with black; trunk with numerous oblique, alternate black and white bands converging towards the head; lower parts marbled with blackish, or uniform pale greenish. This snake is the most aggressive of all Indian poisonous snakes, but it is nevertheless manageable in captivity. As its Latin name implies, it lives as much as practicable upon other snakes. Inhabits hollow trees. Distinguish from Tree snake.——*Hill corindah* (కొండకోరింద - kondakórinda, Tel.). See Corindah.——*Hill goat* (కొండమేక - kondaméka, Tel.). Same as Jungle sheep.——*Hill gooseberry* (కొండఉసిరిక - kondausirike, Tel.). Same as Brazil cherry and Hill guava.——*Hill guava* (மலைக்கொய்யா - malaikkoyyá, Tam.). See under Guava.——*Hill milk hedge* (மலைக்கள்ளி - malaikkalli, Tam.). Same as Zakhm hayaut.——*Hill neem* (மலைவேம்பு - malaivémbu, Tam.). See under Neem.——*Hill raspberry* (गौरीफल - gauríp'hala, San.). See Gowry's fruit.——*Hill sheep* (కొండగొర్రె - kondagorre, Tel.). Same as Chousinga and Saddle back.——*Hill-station* (ಮಲೆ - male, Can.; కొండ - konda, Tel.; മല - mala, Mal.; மலை - malai, Tam.). Anglo-Indian for stations above level of plains resorted to by Europeans, especially in hot-weather.—"*a*" Principal in presidency are the following [q.v.]:—Bangalore, mysore state; Coonoor, neilgherries; Coothiraymookh, dist. s. canara, tal. ooppinangady; Courtallam, dist. tinnevelly, tal. tencaushy; Cumbum, dist. madura, tal. periyacoolam; Horsleycondah, dist. cuddapah, tal. madanapully; Keilausam, dist. vizagapatam, tal. vizagapatam; Kodaykarnal, dist. madura, tal. pulney; Kotagherry, dist. neilgherry; Oodayagherry droog, dist. nellore, tal. oodayagherry; Ootacamund, dist. neilgherry; Pulmanair, dist. north arcot, tal. pulmanair; Peermaid, dist. travancore state; Ramandroog, dist. bellary, tal. sundoor; Somshaparvat, dist. south canara, tal. mangalore; Talamullay, dist. trichinopoly, tal. moosiry; Wellington, dist. neilgherry; Yercaud, dist. salem, tal. salem.—"*b*" The following is the list reversed:—Arcot north, pulmanair; Bellary, ramandroog; Canara south, coothiraymookh, somshaparvat; Cuddapah, horsleycondah; Madura, cumbum, kodaykarnal; Mysore, bangalore; Neilgherries, coonoor, kotagherry, ootacamund, wellington; Nellore, oodayagherry; Salem, yercaud; Tinnevelly, courtallam; Travancore, peermaid; Trichinopoly, talamullay; Vizagapatam, keilausam.

HILSA (इलीश - ilísha, *San.*; هلسه - hilsah, *Hind.*; పలుస - palusa, *Tel.*; ଇଲିଷ - ilisha, *Oor.*; உல்லம் - ullam, *Tam.*). Title from hindostany. San. from (il, san. to go). Title otherwise Sable fish, Shad. The genus Clupea, clupeidæ, physostomi, teleostei, pisces [matsyam, 40], of naturalists [jantoo]. The species best known is Clupea ilisha. Specific name from sanscrit. Alias Alausa malayana, palasah; Clupanodon ilisha; Clupea palasah. Alausa from sanscrit; palasah from teloogoo. Silvery, shot with gold and purple; no spots in the adult, but a row of them along the upper third of the body in the immature, the most distinct of which is behind the upper third of the opercle, young are usually of a bronze color along the back, with silvery sides and a burnished silvery band going from above the eye to the upper half of the caudal fin, whilst the caudal fin is often deeply edged with black in its entire circumference; main body of these fish swarm up all the larger rivers as soon as the monsoon [q.v.] commences; they are excellent as food until they have deposited their ova, when they become thin and positively unwholesome; their flavor has been compared to a combination of that of the salmon and herring; they are rather heavy of digestion. A west coast sardine is Dussumieria acuta. Clupea fimbriata is sardine of europeans in india; Clupea longiceps is malabar oil sardine; Clupea alba is white-bait; Clupea herengus is herring; Clupea sprattus is sprat.

HIMAM (हिम - hima, *San.*). Snow.——*Heimavaty* (हैमवती - haimavatí, San.). Produced on the Himalayas. Plant name common to:—Acorus calamus; Terminalia chebula; see gloss. paragraphs.——*Himalaya* (हिमालय - himálaya, San.; هماليه - himáliyah, Hind.; இமயமலை - imayamalai, Tam.). From (above + álaya, san. abode).—"*a*" The sacred mountain, the father of Parvaty [q.v.], whence she is called Himayaval.—"*b*" Plant first term. Ex.:—Abies webbiana, himalayan silver fir; Betula bhojpattra, himalayan birch; Cedrus deodara, himalayan cedar; Rubus moluccanus, himalayan raspberry. See gloss. paragraphs.

HIMAUYAT (حمايت - himáyat, *Ar.*). From (hamí, ar. to defend). Defending [hameeyat]. Prefixed to an alam forms a lacab; as Himauyat hoossain, defence of hoossain [ism].

HIN (ಹಿಂ - him, *Can.*). Latter [pin].——*Hingaur* (ಹಿಂಗಾರು - hingáru, Can.). From (above + káru, can. crop). Season and crop of N. east monsoon [q.v.] of September and October. Otherwise Heinoo [caur, parvam, peira, vellaumay].

HIND (هند - hind, *Hind.*). India [q.v.].——*Hindee* (هندى - hindí, Hind.). Indian.—"*a*" The Bengalee form of Hindostany which employs the Devanagry [q.v.] character or varieties of it, and is used chiefly by Hindoos [bhaushay]. See vol. I (60).—"*b*" Plant first term, often joining two genera. Ex., where transl. is of second term:—Cochlospermum gossypium (hindikatérá), tragacanth; Hemidesmus indicus (hindísálsá), sarsaparilla; Terminalia catappa (hindíbádam), prunus amygdalus. See gloss. paragraphs.—"*c*" Plant second term, often joining two genera. Ex., where transl. is of first term:—Ægle marmelos (safarjalihindí), cydonia vulgaris; Carica papaya (anabahihindí), vitis vinifera; Cedrus deodara (sanobarihindí), abies excelsa; Cephalandra indica (kabarihindí), capparis spinosa; Clitoria ternatea (mázariúnihindí), daphne mezereum; Hemidesmus indicus (ushbahihindí), sarsaparilla; Picrorhiza kurrooa (kharbakihindí), helleborus niger; Pinus longifolia (sanobarihindí), abies excelsa; Sapindus trifoliatus (findakihind), corylus avellana; Sorghum vulgare (jávarsihindí), panicum miliaceum; Tamarindus indica (tamarihindí), phœnix dactylifera. See gloss. paragraphs.——*Hindoo* (हिन्दु - hindu, San.; هندو - hindú, Hind.; ಹಿಂದು - hindu, Can.; హిందువు - hinduvu, Tel.; ഹിന്ദു - hindu, Mal.; இந்து - indu, Tam.). From (sindhu, san. the river indus). The Aryans settled in the districts surrounding the streams of the Sindhoo river. The Persians called this Hind. The Greeks, who gained their first conceptions of India from the Persians, changed the hard aspirate into a soft, and named the Hindoos ἰνδοί [india]. The word Hindoo now means any person of Indian religion and race, not being a Mahomedan or foreigner. The Presidency has about 30 million Hindoos under this definition [jauty].——*Hindoopore* (హిందుపురము - hindupuramu, Tel.). See sep. title.——*Hindoo row* (هندو راو - hindúráu, Hind.). From (hindí, san. durgá, the deity + ráu, hind. title). Father of Moraury row, the Mahratta chieftain who played an important part in the affairs of the Carnatic [q.v.] during the last century. The talook [q.v.] of Hindoopore in Anantapore has been called after him.——*Hindostan* (हिन्दुस्थान - hindust'hána, San.; هندوستان - hindústán, Hind.; இந்துஸ்தானம் - indusdánam, Tam.). From (above + st'hána, san. place). Abode of the Hindoos. Properly speaking the late Persian and present Mussalman name for the great plain between the Sutlej and Benares, inhabited by the Hindee [q.v.] speaking people of the modern West bengal or Behar, the North-western provinces, and the East punjab. It is sometimes extended southwards to the country lying as far south as the Nerbudda and Mahanuddy rivers, but even then does not include Bengal. At the present day it is often incorrectly used for the whole of India, including the peninsula [charitram].——*Hindostany* (هندوستانى - hindústání, Hind.). Otherwise Oordoo. As the prevailing language of the south it is a mixture of the Oordoo [q.v.] and the Deccany [q.v.]. See vol. I (60). About 700,000 persons talk Hindostany in Presidency [bhaushay].

HINDASA (هندسه - hindasah, *Ar.*). Geometry [ilm]. The following are some of the common terms.——*Cootr* (قطر - kutr, Hind.). Diameter.——*Cows* (قوس - kaus, Hind.). Arc.——*Dayeera* (دائره - dáirah, Hind.). Circle.——*Khatt* (خط - khatt, Hind.). Line.——*Khatt i moostakeem* (خط مستقيم - khattimustakím, Hind.). Straight line.——*Khatt i mootawauzy* (خط متوازى - khattimutawází, Hind.). Parallel line.——*Markaz* (مركز - markaz, Hind.). Centre.——*Moorabba* (مربع - murabba, Hind.). Square.——*Moosallas* (مثلث - musallas, Hind.). Triangle.——*Moostateel* (مستطيل - mustatíl, Hind.). Parallelogram.——*Mootar* (مطر - mutarr, Hind.). Oblong.——*Satah* (سطح - satah, Hind.). Superficies.——*Shakl* (شكل - shakl, Hind.). Figure.——*Zauviya* (زاويه - záviyah, Hind.). Angle.

HINDOOPORE (హిందుపురము - hindupuramu, *Tel.* hindupur*). From (hinduráva, tel. proper name + pura, san. city) [hindoo]. City of Hindoo row.——**(1)** Talook, Anantapore district. Tahsildar's pay Rs. 150. Area 481 square miles. Population 81,678. Language Teloogoo. S. of district. Boundaries:—North Penoocondah talook, east Cadiry talook of Cuddapah, south Mysore, west Mysore and Madaksira talook. Formerly called the Codicondah talook, and till 1813 a Sub-collector was stationed there. Rocky hills on the east sloping to the Chitrauvaty, west of which there are low hills. Soil gravelly and red. Chief products are grain, wheat [geung], horse-gram [q.v.], saumaloo [shaumay], and castor-oil [lamp-oil]; minor products, cholum [q.v.], cotton [q.v.], saffron [country saffron], sugar-cane [q.v.], and paddy [q.v.]. Agricultural tract. Hindoopore extension railway goes through it. Pennair passes through west of talook [q.v.] close to town of Hindoopore, and Chitrauvaty flows through east. But neither are as yet made use of for irrigation, except by way of supply channels [q.v.] connecting them with some of the tanks [q.v.]. There are large tanks:—Bichaganhully, Cottanore, Hindoopore, Parghy. Camping grounds are Codoor and Paulsamoodram. Places of archæological interest:—Bichaganhully, Chilmuttore, Cholasamoodram, Chowlore, Codigipulley, Codihully, Condoor, Cotmore, Cuggall, Cummavauripully, Gollaupooram, Goodihully, Gorvanahully, Karikera, Lepaucshy, Manasamoodram, Maunepully, Medireddipully, Meidoogolam, Moda, Moolgooroo, Mosalapully, Mullapully, Oolicoonta, Parghy, Salivendla, Shreecuntapooram, Somagutt, Vadigepully, Yerragoontla. Principal trig. station:—Yerracondah. The leading places, &c., in the talook are the following.——*Bichaganhully* (ಬಿಚಗನಹಳ್ಳಿ - bichaganahalli, Can.). From (bichaga, can. proper name + halli, can. village). Village; pop. 1,075; lat. 13° 55′; long. 77° 33′; from Anantapore S. 52 miles; from Hindoopore N. 7 miles. Large tank. Near confluence of Jayamungaly and Pennair.——*Boodaly* (బూడలి - búdali, Tel.).

From (búda, tel. milk pot). Village; pop. 2,228; lat. 13° 56′; long. 77° 47′; from Anantapore S. 51 miles; from Hindoopore E.N.E. 19 miles. Two tanks.——*Chilmuttore* (చిలమత్తూరు - chilamattúru, Tel.). From (chelama, tel. spring + atti, tel. fig, ficus racemosa, linn. + úru, tel. village). Village; pop. 3,185; lat. 13° 50′; long. 77° 45′; from Anantapore S. 57 miles; from Hindoopore E. 15 miles. Inscription A.D. 1367 mentioning Bookka of Vijianugger. Large tank. On left bank of Cooshauvaty.——*Chitrauvaty* (చిత్రావతి - chitrávati, Tel.). See sep. title.——*Codicondah* (కొడికొండ - kodikonda, Tel.). See sep. title. ——*Coodoor* (కోడూరు - kódúru, Tel.). From (kúdu, tel. meeting + úru, tel. village); at the junction of chitrauvaty and cooshauvaty. Village; pop. 1,579; lat. 13° 52′; long. 77° 47′; from Anantapore S. 57 miles; from Hindoopore E.N.E. 16 miles. On Bangalore high road. Large tank.——*Cottanore* (కొత్తనూరు - kottanúru, Tel.). From (kotta, tel. new + úru, tel. village). Village; pop. 1,042; lat. 13° 51′; long. 77° 34′; from Anantapore S. 57 miles; from Hindoopore N.E. 3 miles. Large tank.——*Gorantla* (గోరంట్ల - górantla, Tel.). From (góranti, tel. the nail-dye plant, lawsonia alba, lamk.). Village; pop. 1,569; lat. 13° 59′; long. 77° 49′; from Anantapore S.S.E. 48 miles; from Hindoopore E.N.E. 22 miles. Formerly of importance. The E. gate of Penoocondah fort is called the Gorantla gate. Is on Chitrauvaty river. Two tanks.——*Hindoopore* (హిందుపురము - hindupuramu, tel.). See below.——***Lepaucshy*** (లేపాక్షి - lépákshi, Tel.). From (lépa, san. anointing + akshi, san. eye); epithet of a deity. Village; pop. 2,256; lat. 13° 48′; long. 77° 39′; from Anantapore S. 60 miles; from Hindoopore E. 8 miles. Large stone temple with good carvings. The roof of the hall is supported by 40 pillars. By the roadside is a colossal monolith stone bull [nundy], similar to those at Tanjore and Mysore.——*Ootcore* (ఊటకూరు - útakúru, Tel.). From (úta, tel. spring + úru, tel. village). Village; pop. 1,500; lat. 13° 54′; long. 77° 32′; from Anantapore S. 53 miles; from Hindoopore N. 6 miles. Large tank. Near the confluence of Jayamungaly and Pennair.——*Parghy* (పరిగి - parigi, Tel.). From (parige, tel. gleanings of corn). Village; pop. 4,124; lat. 13° 53′; long. 77° 30′; from Anantapore S. 55 miles; from Hindoopore N.N.W. 5 miles. Large tank irrigating 2,700 acres. Formerly District moonsif's court.——*Paul samoodram* (పాలసముద్రము - pálasamudramu, Tel.). From (pálu, tel. milk + samudra, san. ocean). Sanscrit name (kshírasamudra), meaning the same. Village; pop. 1,027; lat. 13° 57′; long. 77° 43′; from Anantapore S. 50 miles; from Hindoopore N.E. 16 miles. Halting place on Bangalore road, Tank, Travellers' bungalow [q.v.].——*Pidaty* (ಪಿಡತಿ - pidati, Can.). Village; pop. 551; lat. 13° 57′; long. 77° 29′; from Anantapore S.S.W. 51 miles; from Hindoopore N.N.W. 9 miles. Lands irrigated by Parghy tank.——*Salivendla* (చలివెందల - tsalivendala, Tel.). From (tsalla, tel. cool + pandili, tel. shed). Village; pop. 1,278; lat. 13° 53′; long. 77° 39′; from Anantapore S. 54 miles; from Hindoopore E.N.E. 9 miles. Soil suited to growth of date [kharjooram] trees.——*Santebidanore* (సంతేబిదనూరు - santébidanúru, Tel.). From (sante, can. fair + bidanúru, can. place so called). Village; pop. 1,424; lat. 13° 43′; long. 77° 31′; from Anantapore S. 65 miles; from Hindoopore S. 6 miles. Tank fed by Pennair.——*Siracclam* (ಸಿರಕೊಳಂ - sirakolam, Can.). From (sira, can. head + kola, can. tank). Village; pop. 1,243; lat. 13° 54′; long. 77° 28′; from Anantapore S.S.W. 55 miles; from Hindoopore N.W. 7 miles. Is irrigated by Parghy tank.——*Vaunavole* (వానవోలు - vánavólu, Tel.). From (vána, tel. rain + prólu, tel. town). Village; pop. 2,501; lat. 14° 00′; long. 77° 53′; from Anantapore S.S.E. 48 miles; from Hindoopore E.N.E. 27 miles.——*Yerracondah* (ఎర్రకొండ - errakonda, Tel.). From (erra, tel. red + konda, tel. hill). Trig. station; lat. 13° 54′ 58·56″; long. 77° 41′ 36·07″; height 2,820 feet; from Anantapore S. 53 miles; from Hindoopore E.N.E. 12 miles; from Velidadakala S.E. 2 miles.——**(2)** Town, Talook head-quarters; Anantapore dist., Hindoopore tal.; pop. 7,905; lat. 13° 49′; long. 77° 32′; from Anantapore S. 59 miles; from Bellary S.S.E. 97 miles; from Gooty S. 89 miles; from Madras W.N.W. 194 miles; from Penoocondah S.S.W. 19 miles. A large commercial town, the principal market of the talook. Trade in jaggery [q.v.], piece-goods and grain. Founded by Moraury row, and called after his father Hindoo row. Irrigated by tanks and channels from the Pennair, and a commercial centre for agricultural produce. The irrigation project here consists of a channel [q.v.] to be taken from the Pennair river by means of an anicut [q.v.] to be built across the river near Santebidanore. The channel will be nearly 11 miles long by 15 yards broad, and will have an average depth of 4 feet. It will pass above and benefit by sluices the tanks of Basavanhully, Calcoonta, Coolacoonta, Cottanore, Hindoopore, Shreecuntapooram, Yerrakerey, and will finally end in the Ootcore tank. The Hindoopore extension railway passes through the town. Much of the trade is with Bangalore, 62 miles distant by road. The fort has been dismantled and the town is increasing in size. There are good areca [q.v.] nut gardens in the neighbourhood. The talook cutcherry [q.v.] is an old structure, built round a central courtyard. Hand weaving of gunny [q.v.], sacking, common cloth, and blankets [cumbly] is carried on.

HINDRY (హింద్రి - hindri,* *Tel.*). A corruption of indrauvaty, meaning a place frequented by the god indran [q.v.]. Sanscrit name (indrávatí), meaning indran's town. River; Kurnool dist., Putticondah and Ramalcottah tals. Rises in the fields of Maddikera at frontier of Putticondah talook and to S.W. of Kurnool in lat. 15° 16′; long. 77° 27′. It flows through Putticondah and Ramalcottah talooks for a distance of 30 miles, receiving an affluent from the Yerramalas at Ladagiry, and joins the Toongabudra at Kurnool in lat. 15° 50′; long. 78° 06′. Liable to sudden floods. Bed is of yellow sand and rock. Never navigable except by smallest boats. Picottahs [q.v.], but no anicuts [q.v.] Kurnool canal is carried across the bed by aqueduct at Kurnool town. After subsidence in November, sand banks are left, on which vegetables and melons [oorvauroo] are grown.

HING (हिंगु - hingu, *San.*; هنگ - hing, *Hind.*). From (han, san. to kill) [hamsam, hanoo]. Asafœtida [q.v.].——*Hingol* (हिंगुल - hingula, San.; هنگول - hingol, Hind.). From (above + lá, san. to take). That which has the color of asafœtida. Cinnabar [shangarf].

HINGAN (هنگن - hingan, *Hind.*). The Fire-work plant.

HIRA (هيرا - hírá, *Hind.*). Diamond [vajram].——***Hirachund*** (హీరాచందు - híráchandu, Tel.). From (above + chand, hind. moon). Hindoo 2nd or pers. name [peyar].——***Hirakash*** (هيرا كشيش - hírákashísh, Dec.). From (hará, hind. green + kasis, hind. sulphus ferri). Same as Annabhaidy [q.v.].——***Hirasing*** (హీరాసింగు - hírásingu, Tel.). From (above + singh, hind. lion). Hindoo 2nd or pers. name [peyar].——***Hirojee*** (హీరోజి - híróji, Tel.). From (above + ji, hind. master). Hindoo 2nd or pers. name [peyar].

HIRANYAM (हिरण्य - hiranya, *San.*). From (hari, san. yellow) [haran]. Gold [hemam, honn, pon, tungam].——***Hiranya cashipoo*** (हिरण्यकशिपु - hiranyakashipu, San.). From (above + kashipu, san. clothing). A giant [narsimha avatar].——***Hiranya garbham*** (ഹിരണ്യഗർഭം - hiranyagarbham, Mal.). From (above + garbha, san. womb). Originally said to have been a ceremony of being born of, or actually passing through, a golden cow. At present day it is a ceremony performed in Travancore by the rajah [q.v.] of that state in a large golden vessel with a cover of gold. Inside the vessel is placed a mixture of the five products of the cow [punchagavyam]. After preparatory rites the rajah enters the golden tub, the cover is put on, he bathes and offers prayers inside for ten minutes, while the assembled priests continue praying and chanting hymns. After coming out, he is again crowned by the chief priest and is advanced in caste purity. The golden vessel is cut up and distributed amongst the Bramins. ——***Hiranya garbhan*** (हिरण्यगर्भ - hiranyagarbha, San.). From (above + garbha, san. womb). Bramha [q.v.], as born from the golden egg.

HIREE (ಹಿರಿ - hirí, *Can.*). Great [hey]. So senior, as of rulers; for instance Hiree chauma rajah, the elder chauma rajah. ——*Hiredeva* (ಹಿರಿದೇವ - hiridéva, Can.). From (above + déva, can. god). Badaga god [hetteydeva].——*Hirode* (ಹಿರೋಡೆ - hiróde, Can.; hiród, Mys. Gov.). From (above + óde, can. palace). Village and former military station, Mysore district, 4 miles north of Seringapatam, on the Mysore-Naugamungala road [french rocks].

HISAUB (حساب - hisáb, *Hind.*). From (hasaba, ar. to compute). An account [kanak, lekka]; arithmetic [ilm].

HISSA (حصہ - hissah, *Hind.*). From (hissa, ar. to cut). Share [coroo]; astronomical degree [bhaugam], the minute being dakeeka [calay]. For Hissa shrotriem, see Inam.

HITAM (हित - hita, *San.*). From (dhá, san. to hold). Agreeable.——*Hitopadesh* [हितोपदेश - hitópadésha, San.). From (above + upadésha, san. advice). Good advice. Cf. Hoomayoon nauma. Compiled from the larger and older Punchatantram [q.v.].

HIZABR (هزبر - hizabr, *Ar.*). Fierce lion [hamza, hyder shere]. Part of lacab; as Hizabr ood deen, lion of the faith; Hizabr jung, lion of war [ism].

HOBLY (ಹೋಬಳಿ - hóbali, *Can.*; ഹോബളി - hóbali, *Mal.*). Division of a district. In Malabar formerly under Hyder a sub-division of a talook [q.v.] comprehending several Deshoms [q.v.] or villages. It corresponds with Maugauny in Canara, and with Maugaunam [q.v.] on the Eastern coast. See vol. I, 112.

HOG (سیاہ - siyáh, *Hind.*). Prefix.——*Hog gum* (سیاہ گوند - siyáhgond, Hind.). Otherwise Bussorah gum, Hog tragacanth, Kateerah. Group of high-colored gums resembling tragacanth, but inferior. They may be enumerated as follows:— Pale-colored; cochlospermum gossypium [golden silk cotton], sterculia urens [false kateerah]; other species of sterculia [cauvalam]. Dark-colored, decidedly inferior; moringa pterygosperma [moringa], horse-radish tree, gum rapidly decays into a black powder, called mocharas [q.v.] and also false tragacanth; bombax malabaricum [red-cotton tree], yields also a mocharas, superior to the last, but of little commercial value; ailanthus excelsa [coromandel ailanto], resembles moringa gum, but occurs in deep, dark red, large, rounded tears, instead of masses; stereospermum suaveolens [pauthiry], very little known. Odina wodier [wodier], although soluble and not a bussorah gum, is pressed on the market, either as an adulterant for gum arabic, or as a substitute for bussorah and tragacanth [q.v.].——*Hog plum* (امرا - amrá, Hind.). Title from being eaten by hogs. Same as Wild mango.

HOGEY (ಹೊಗೆ - hoge, *Can.*). Smoke [pogay].——*Hogeycull* (ಹೊಗೆನಕಲ್ಲು - hogenakallu, Can.). From (above + kallu, can. rock), from the cloud of spray in the fall. Waterfall; Salem dist., Dharmapoory tal.; lat. 12° 07′; long. 77° 49′; from Dharmapoory W. 25 miles; from Salem N.W. 40 miles. A fall of the Cauvery [q.v.]. The main body of the river here takes a leap of some 80 feet into a deep chasm, and in so doing impinges on an opposing rock. Sacred in Hindoo estimation, being the scene of a yearly festival to which devotees from all parts of India resort. Bramin time of pilgrimage is Arpisy [mausam] or October, and Shoodras and merchants hold a festival called Audy pathinett [pundigay, 2c] on 2nd August [aroovy].

HOLA (ಹೊಲ - hola, *Can.*). Dry land [polam].——*Holeya* (ಹೊಲೆಯ - holeya, Can.). Canarese pariahs. The corresponding terms are:—Tel. maula, Mal. poolaya, Tam. pariah. They believe like all the other pariah tribes that they were once an independent people, and had kings of their own [jauty].——*Holigarna* (होलगेरि - hólagéri, Mahr.; ಹೊಲಗೇರು - holagéru, Can.; കാട്ടുചേർ - káttuchér, Mal.). Can. from (hola, can. dry land + géru, can. marking-nut plant, semecarpus anacardium, linn. f.). Mal. from (kátu, mal. forest + chér, mal. the marking-nut tree); from habitat and similar fruit and nut. Mahr. also (húlagiri). Can. also (kádugéru), meaning wild + marking-nut plant. Title otherwise Jungle marking-nut, Malabar black varnish, Malabar marking-nut. Botanically Holigarna longifolia, roxb., anacardiaceæ [vricsham, 45]. Generic from canarese. Forest tree, 60 feet; leaves alternate, cuneate, oblong or acute; petioles usually with a soft, incurved, thorn-like, deciduous process on each side about the middle; panicles terminal and axillary; styles recurved; calyx five-toothed; petals five, oblong, spreading; stamens five, shorter than the corolla; flower small, whitish; flowers in december and january; ripens fruit in april and may; fruit like a prune [auloochah], at first glaucous and downy, when ripe dark blue and glabrous; nut about size of an olive [zeitoon] contains between the laminæ numerous cells filled with black rather thick, acrid fluid. Fruit and bark are used medicinally. Black oily acrid substance exudes from fruit as in marking-nut tree [q.v.]; used by painters [raugh], and also for fixing indelible colors figured on linen cloths; juice by incision of the stem very acrid, employed in malabar for varnishing shields; small boats are made from the timber. Another variety with a round dark fruit. Another species, Grahamii.

HOLY (هولی - holí, *Hind.*). Title from sound of syllables in songs used on the occasion. Bengal name of Cauman pundigay. Also used in Mysore, Coimbatore, Salem, &c. A festival in honor of Krishnan [q.v.] as Cauman [q.v.] the god of love, held for fifteen days previous to the vernal equinox [meshauyanam], when the hindoos disport themselves; songs are sung in the streets, and performers throw a red powder [goolaul], and splash saffron [country saffron] colored water upon one another. Cf. Dusserah.

HOM (هوم - hom, *Pers.*). Same as Somam [q.v.]. Distinguish from sanscrit Homam [hoo] which is a separate root.

HOME FARMS (حویلی اجاره - havelíijárah, *Hind.*). From (havelí, ar. household + ijárah, ar. farm). Also called Havelly [q.v.] lands. The East india company had, prior to the cession of the Chingleput jagheer [q.v.], become possessed of these, meaning a few villages round the area comprising the original grant for building Fort St. George. They were at first managed by the Board of Revenue, but shortly afterwards placed under a separate officer. The following is a list of the villages:—Arasanore, Auttpollam, Chetput, Egmore, Kilpauk, Mylapore, Nedoombauray, Nungumbaukum, Perambore, Poothoopauk, Pursewaukum, Tondiarpett, Triplicane, Vepery, Vyausarpaudy, and Yiroongoolam. The extent covered by them included the jurisdiction of the former Recorder and present High court.

HONN (ಹೊನ್ನು - honnu, *Can.*). Gold [hemam, hiranyam, pon, tungam]. As a gold coin:—2 dharanams = 1 honn; 2 honns = 1 varahah [naunyam, 2c]. Old coin of Mysore with many prefixes. Not now current [hoon]. Compare Tel. mauda.——*Hangar cutta* (ಹಂಗಾರಕಟ್ಟೆ - hangárakatte, Can.). From (hongara, can. indian coral tree, erythrina indica, lamk. + katte, can. a basin round the trunk of a tree). Part of Coodroo village, Port; South canara dist., Oodipy tal.; from Mangalore N. 42 miles; from Oodipy N. 10 miles. The port of Barcore. At the mouth of the Seetanuddy. Five miles from old Barcore. Considerable export trade in rice [q.v.], &c., principally to Goa, and import trade in cotton [q.v.] piece-goods, cocoanut [q.v.] oil, and salt [ooppoo] from Goa. Goods from the interior and those brought from above the ghauts [q.v.] are taken to it by boats from Cokkarney and Bajey on the Seetanuddy and Swarnanuddy respectively.——*Honiga* (द्वीपी - dvípí, San.; खरडा - kharadá, Mahr.; پلنگ - palang, Pers.; تیندوا - tendwá, Hind.; چیتا باگہ - chítábágh, Dec.; آریموتالپ - arimautálap, Malay; ಹೊನಿಗ - honiga, Can.; చిన్నపులి - chinnapuli, Tel.; କୋରଡପୋତ୍ରିଆ - koradapotriya, Oor.; പുലി - puli, Mal.; කොටියා - kotiyá, Singh.; சிறுத்தை - shiruttai, Tam.). Title from canarese. San. from (dvípa, san. island); island-skinned, or spotted. Mahr. from (kharadané, mahr. to move along upon the buttocks). Dec. from (chítá, hind. spotted animal + bágh, hind. tiger). Malay from (ariman, malay, tiger + tálap, malay, perfume box); variegated. Can. from (honnu, can. gold). Tel. from (chinna, tel. small + puli, tel. tiger). Tam. from (shiru, tam. small). San. also (pundarika), ordinarily means white lotus; as a leopard, may strictly apply to ounce or snow panther. Hind. also (sonáchítá), meaning golden cheetah. Malay also (rimaubintang), meaning tiger + star. Tel. also (ponnáda), meaning gold + dress. Mal. also (karimpuli), meaning black + tiger. Tam. also (peruñjivingi), meaning great + pard. Title otherwise Panther, Puma, Cougnar. Felis [marjauram] pardus, felidæ [deeptauchsham], digitigrada, carnivora, mammalia [sastanam, 9], of naturalists [jantoo]. Alias Felis leopardus. The pard generally, of which the panther is the larger variety, is an animal of a rufous-fawn color, more or less deep, with dark spots grouped in rosettes; tail more or less ringed. Varies greatly in size, from six to eight feet and upwards. The color of the panther is generally pale fulvous yellow, the belly white; whilst some are deeper and more tawny in hue, and others without any white at all beneath. As a general rule the fur of the panther is shorter and closer than that of the leopard. The black panther is merely a variety of the common one. The tiger is tameable, the panther not so. A man-eating panther is more to be dreaded than a tiger [pooly] of the same class. Indian species not here found are:—Nebulosa or macrocelis or clouded panther, Uncia or ounce or snow panther. For the smaller panther or leopard see Kerkal.——*Honnholey* (ಹೊನ್ನುಹೊಳೆ - honnuhole, Can.). From (above + hole, can. river). Sanscrit name (svarnávati), meaning gold + possession. River; Coimbatore district. Tributary of the Cauvery [q.v.]. Formed of two jungle streams, rising in Hassanore ghaut [q.v.] and Taulavaudy hills respectively in Suttimungalam talook, about 45 miles south of the cusbah [q.v.]. It flows through Mysore to a great distance and empties itself into the Cauvery near Humpapore, on its southern bank 2 miles north of the cusbah. The Honnholey valley is fertile, the stream being dammed in its short course by three permanent anicuts [q.v.] as well as by many temporary structures.——*Honzaram* (హొంజరాము - hondzarámu, Tel.). From (above + tsára, tel. vein + gám, hind. village). Estate, Village; Vizagapatam dist., Palcondah tal.; pop. 946; acres 836; lat. of village 18° 26′; long. 83° 51′; from Palcondah S.S.E. 11 miles; from Vizagapatam N.E. 60 miles. Honzaram estate, consisting of thirteen jiroyaty [q.v.] and two shrotriem [q.v.] villages, was purchased by the Collector on behalf of Government for arrears of revenue on the 18th October 1811 and was managed by him up to July 1846, when it was leased with Palcondah to Messrs. Arbuthnot and Co.——*Hoon* (हून - húna, San.; هن - hun, Hind.). From the can. (honnu), meaning gold [honn]. The Mahomedan gold pagoda [q.v.] borrowed from the natives. Equivalent to 3½ rupees [naunyam, 2e]. The company continued the term. Same as Star pagoda, but different from Kurruck pagoda. See vol. I, 609.

HOO (हु - hu, *San.*). To offer to fire.——*Homam* (होम - hóma, San.). From (hu, san. to sacrifice). A fire-offering of butter, oil, grain, &c., not flesh; burnt in small pits consecrated to the planets [graham], or some household god [grihadevatay]. Anciently the homam was the offering peculiar to Agny [q.v.] the god of fire, as the somam [hom, somam] juice was peculiar to Indran [q.v.] the god of rain. The largest homam now kept up in the south is that held annually at Aroonagherry or Trinomallee [q.v.]. It is lighted on the hill by fishermen, at the moment when a signal light appears below [matam].——*Hootaushana powrnamy* (హుతాశనపౌర్ణమి - hutáshanapaurnami, Tel.). From (hutáshana, san. agni, the oblation-eater + paurnami, san. a day of full moon). In commemoration of Cauman's burning on that day. Same as Cauman pundigay.——*Hotra* (होत्र - hótra, San.). From (hu, san. to sacrifice). Oblation.——*Hotry* (होतृ - hótri, San.). Rig veda [q.v.] priest.

HOO (ಹೂ - hú, *Can.*). Flower [poo].——*Hoovinhadgully* (ಹೂವಿನಹಡಗಲ್ಲಿ - húvinahadagalli, Can.). See sep. title.——*Hoovy* (ಹೂವಿ - húvi, Can.). From (húvu, can. flower). Hill-tribe female proper name [peyar].

HOODHOOD (هد هد - hudhud, *Ar.*; مرغ سلیمانی - murghi-sulaimání, *Pers.*; هد هد - hudhud, *Hind.* and *Dec.*; కుక్కురుగువ్వ - kukkuruguvva, *Tel.*; പുഴുകൊത്തി - puzhukotti, *Mal.*). Ar. from its call. Pers. from (murgh, pers. bird + sulaimán, ar. solomon); having shielded him from the sun. Tel. from (kukkuru, tel. the sound + guvva, tel. bird). Mal. from (puzhu, mal. insect + kottu, mal. to peck); from picking up insects for food. Ar. also (aburrabí), meaning father of spring; from its appearing in that season. Tel. also (kondepitta), meaning crest + bird. Upupidæ family, tenuirostres, insessores, aves [pacsby, 18], of naturalists [jantoo]. Hoopoes. European hoopoe is upupa epops; mussalmans venerate it; voice loud, double or treble hoop; found on Neilgherries. Indian hoopoe is upupa nigripennis; alias upupa senegalensis; similar, but smaller, distinguished by generally darker hue of rufous of head and crest, no white on crest; when feeding, crest is depressed; flight undulating and vigorous; call a deep whoot.

HOOKAH (حقه - hukkah, *Hind.*). From arabic. Meaning a receptacle. An apparatus for smoking consisting of a box in which the tobacco [pogauk] burns, a vessel of water through which the smoke passes, and a long pliant pipe through which it is conveyed to the mouth. An elaborated hubble-bubble [q.v.]. The following is a Hindostany proverb:—گنگی جورو بهلی گنگا ناریل نه بهلا—"A dumb wife is better than a dumb pipe;" for unless the hubble-bubble makes a noise it is not worth smoking. Hookah burdar, from (bardár, pers. carrier), is the servant who prepares the pipe for smoking.

HOOLY (ಹುಲಿ - huli, *Can.*). Tiger [pooly].——*Hoolicull droog* (ಹುಲಿಕಲ್ಲುದುರ್ಗ - hulikalludurga, Can.). From (above + kallu, can. rock + durga, san. hill-fort). Sanscrit name (bakásuraparvata), meaning the demon, so called + mountain. Village, Hill; Neilgherry dist., Merkoonaud division; pop. 1,938; lat. 11° 19′; long. 76° 53′; height about 6,000 feet; from Coonoor S.E. 2 miles; from Ootacamund S.E. 11 miles. One of principal eminences on S. side of plateau. Separated from Coonoor ghaut [q.v.] by Coonoor river. Diversified with scarp and crag, relieved with bright green foliage in each hollow. Its base is covered with rich tropical forest, gradually passing into stretches of waving bamboo [q.v.]. Much primeval forest, above the elevation of three or four thousand feet, has been destroyed and its place supplied by coffee [q.v.] plantations. The old fort commands the Coonoor ghaut and the low country. Used by Tippoo sultan, and it is one of the three principal forts of the Neilgherries, with Oodayaroyacottah and Mailcottah [q.v.]. Near this place was a large five-celled dolmen [coday cull], profusely sculptured. Since destroyed. The village near is Nidimund. The village lies at foot of peak. It contains a shrine dedicated to Rama [q.v.] at which Badagas [q.v.] worship. Coffee and cinchona [koinah] estate here, 120 acres.

HOOMA (هما - humá, *Hind.*). Phœnix, a bird of happy omen, as it is supposed that every head it overshadows will wear a crown [hamsam].——*Hoomayoon* (همایون - humáyún, Hind.). From (above + yún, pers. like). Prefixed to an alam forms a lacab; as Hoomayoon ally, ally the auspicious; Hoomayoon jah, auspicious in pomp and dignity [ism].——*Hoomayoon nauma* (همایون نامه - humáyúnnámah, Hind.). From (humáyún, pers. auspicious + námah, pers. work). Turkish edition of Punchatantram [hitopadesh, punchatantram].

HOOMMA (ହୁମ୍ମା - humma, *Oor.*). Means horse [ghorah, goorram]. Ancient zemindarry, Village; Ganjam dist.; pop. 3,862; acres 5,120; lat. of village 19° 26′; long. 85° 07′; from Berhampore E.N.E. 20 miles; from Chetterpore N.N.E. 7 miles; from Russellcondah S.E. 44 miles; from the sea W. 5 miles. Near Ganjam. Smallest zemindarry [q.v.] in district. Contains thirteen villages, some of which are in the Tiroostaunam khandam of Berhampore talook. Formerly in thick jungle. To protect travellers Capilendra deo, king of Orissa, appointed one Madana mohana samanto to be zemindar [q.v.] with the title of Saumanta roya mahapatro, A.D. 1228. Peshcush [q.v.] is Rs. 1,038.

HOONDEE (هندی - hundí, *Hind.*; హుండి - hundi, *Tel.*; உண்டி - undi, *Tam.*). From (hund, san. to collect). Not connected with Hoon [q.v.]. A written order purchased from a sowcar [q.v.] in one place for the payment by a specified sowcar in another place of a specified sum of money; a bill of exchange written in the vernacular.——*Hoondauvany* (هنداونی - hundávaní, Hind.). Commission on a cheque.

HOONRAUJ (هنراج - hunráj, *Hind.*; اندراینی - indráiní, *Dec.*). Dec. from (indráyan, hind. citrullus colocynthis, schrad.); from use of seeds as emetic. Hind. also (drob). Title otherwise Armstrong, Beggar-weed, Common knot grass, Crab grass, Crabweed, Iron grass, Ninety knot [hurrially], North american doorweed, Pink-weed, Sparrow tongue [paula indigo], Swine's grass, Wire grass [wild raggy]. Botanically Polygonum [water gannair] aviculare, linn., polygonaceæ [vricsham, 110]. Root fibrous, long, very tough, and somewhat woody; branched below, simple at the crown; stems several, spreading in every direction, generally prostrate, much branched, round, striated, leafy at the numerous knots or joints; leaves alternate, stalked, hardly an inch long, elliptic or lanceolate, entire, obtuse, single-ribbed, smooth except at the margin, tapering at the base, very variable in width, substance rather coriaceous, color greyish or glaucous; flowers variegated with white, crimson and green; seeds acutely triangular, of a shining black. Dried root anodyne; seeds emetic and purgative.

HOONSOOR (ಹುಣಸೂರು - hunasúru, *Can.*; húnsúr, *Mys. Gov.*). From (hunase, can. tamarindus indica, linn. + úru, can. village). Can. also (gádipálya), meaning cart village. Town in 12° 18′ N. lat., 76° 19′ E. long., on right bank of the Lutchmanateertam, 25 miles west of Mysore. Head-quarters of Hoonsoor talook, Mysore district, Mysore.

HOORMAT (حرمت - hurmat, *Ar.*). From (haruma, ar. sacred). Respect. Prefixed to an alam forms a lacab; as Hoormat hoossain, honor of ally. Also an alam; as Hoormat bauno, alam + alaumat [ism]. Cf. Moharram.

HOOSAUM (حسام - husám, *Hind.*). From (hasama, ar. to cut). Sword. Part of lacab; as Hoosaum ood deen, the sword of the faith; Hoosaum ood dowla, the sword of the kingdom [ism].

HOOSSAIN (حسین - husain, *Hind.*). From (husn, ar. beauty). Common alam; as Hoossain ally, double alam; Hoossain khan, alam + alaumat [ism]. The historical Hoossain was one of the grandsons of Mahomet by his daughter Fatimah and his cousin Ally [q.v.]. It is to commemorate the martyrdom of him and his companions that the moharram [q.v.] anniversary is celebrated. The death occurred on Friday 10th Moharram [maheena], Hijra [q.v.] 61, or 9th of October A.D. 680. His familiar name was Aboo abdoollah, and he is occasionally styled Syed oosh shohdah, the prince of martyrs. Cf. Hassan. Hoossainy are a class of Mahomedans of the syed [q.v.] sect tracing their pedigree to Hoossain. Cf. Cyanecula suecica (husainí piddá), beautiful black robin; Tchitrea paradisi (husainíbulbul), beautiful black boolbool; see gloss. paragraphs.

HOOT (मेदस्तिमि - médastimi, *San.*; حوت - hút, *Ar.*; ಹೆದ್ದಲೆಮೀನು - heddalemínu, *Can.*; తిమి - timi, *Tel.*; തിമിംഗിലം - timinnilam, *Mal.*; பெருந்தலைத்திமிங்கிலம் - perundalaittimingilam, *Tam.*). Title from arabic. San. from (médas, san. fat + timi, san. whale). Can. from (hedda, can. huge + tale, can. head + mínu, can. fish). Tel. from sanscrit. Mal. from (timi, san. whale + gila, san. devourer); large whale. Tam. from (perum, tam. large + talai, tam. head + timingilam, tam. whale). Title otherwise Cachelot, Sperm whale. Euphysetes macrocephalus, physeteridæ, cetacea, mammalia [sastanam, 30], of naturalists [jantoo]. The Hoots have an enormous head with numerous teeth in the lower jaw, the upper teeth being concealed in the gums. The upper part of their huge heads is cellular, and the cavities are filled with the fatty substance, becoming hard when cool, known as spermaceti, for which they are chiefly hunted. The substance called ambergris [meen amber] is a concretion found in their intestines. These are not whale-bone whales [timingilam]. Found in the Bay of Bengal. The hoots are without symmetry, of a prevailing dull black color, occasionally marked with white, especially on the abdomen and tail. They propel themselves round by striking and pulling against the water with the flashes of their tails. They spout a thick watery mist from the nostrils at intervals of 10 or 15 minutes. Spermaceti, the cetaceum of chemists, is white, tasteless, inodorous, crystalline, insoluble in water; it is separated from the oil by filtration and pressure, and afterwards purified and cast into cakes; these are of a white color, have a peculiar lustre, are transparent, brittle, smooth, but not greasy; smell peculiar, but weak; spermaceti makes a soap [sauboon] with potash [jharka namak]. It burns with a brilliant flame. Euphysetes simus is the Great-nosed cachelot; it has less spermaceti. For the fin-whale see Timingilam. For a constellation of this name see Nacshatram.

HOOVINHADGULLY (ಹೂವಿನ ಹಡಗಲ್ಲಿ - húvinahadagalli, *Can.*; హువ్వినహడగలి - huvvinahadagali, *Tel.* huvinahadgalli*). From (húvu, can. flower + hadagalli, can. place so called) [hoo]. So called because flowers were once grown and exported.——(1) Talook, Bellary district. Tahsildar's pay Rs. 150. Area 585 square miles. Population 80,521. Language Canarese. N.W. of district. In shape an irregular parellelogram with an average length of 32 miles and a breadth of 20 miles. Bounded on N. and W. by Toongabudra, on S. by Hurpanhully talook, and on E. by Hospett and Coodligy talooks. The talook is in general flat with a gradual fall to the north. There are a few small and unimportant hills in the south near Adavimullankerey. The soil is chiefly of the red and mixed description, and only about 9 per cent. of the total area is black soil. Very little of it is irrigated. The principal products are cholum [q.v.], raggy [q.v.], sadza [bajrah], corra [tinay], oil-seeds [yennay], cotton [q.v.], gram [q.v.], and other pulses [dholl]. Cholum is the principal crop. The grain exported is sent chiefly to Chitvaudigy, whence it finds its way to the Nizam's territory and to Bellary. The cotton goes to Moondrigy market. Rice [q.v.] from Mysore and wheat [geung] from Dharwar are the only imported grains. Excellent betels [q.v.] and plantains [q.v.] are grown. At Batchigondanahully, Humpasaugar, and Tamrahully, silk cloths [puttoo] are woven. Those made at the last-mentioned place being of superior quality. The only rivers are the Toongabudra and the Hagary, which must be distinguished from the river of the same name which falls into the Toongabudra lower down. There is an anicut [q.v.] across the Toongabudra at Vallabhapooram, and there is a small anicut across the Hagary near Tamrahully. The only large tanks are those of Chintarapully, Hireyhadgully, and Magimauvinahully. There are good camping grounds at Hireyhadgully, Hoovinhadgully, and Tamrahully, and travellers' bungalows at Ballahoonsy and Humpasaugar. Places of archæological interest:—Angore,

Cogaly, Combaly, Cottanacull, Cuttibinnore, Hireyhadgully, Hollal, Hoovinhadgully, Maugalam, Meilaura, Moradagherry, Rungapooram, Sogy, Tamrahully, Vallabhapooram. Principal trig. stations :—Auneycullgoodda, Bettada mullappa, Rameshwarabandy. The leading places, &c., in the talook are the following.——*Auneycullgoodda* (ಆನೇಕಲ್ಲುಗುಡ್ಡ - ánékallugudda, Can.). From (áne, can. elephant + kallu, can. rock + gudda, can. hill). Trig. station; lat. 15° 02′ 35·57″; long. 76° 20′ 44·65″; height 2,378 feet; from Aunecull E. 2 miles; from Bellary W. 41 miles.——*Bettada mullappa* (ಬೆಟ್ಟದಮಲ್ಲಪ್ಪ - bettadamallappa, Can.). From (betta, can. hill + mallappa, can. proper name). Trig. station; lat. 14° 55′ 38·57″; long. 76° 00′ 24·65″; height 3,177 feet; from Bellary W.S.W. 65 miles; from Hoovinhadgully S.S.E. 7 miles.——*Chinna hagary* (చిన్నహగరి - chinnahagari, Tel.). See sep. title.——*Chinturapully* (చింతరపల్లి - chintarapalli, Tel.). From (chintaráya, can. proper name + palli, tel. village). Village; pop. 589; acres 6,877; lat. 15° 02′; long. 76° 16′; from Bellary W.S.W. 47 miles; from Hoovinhadgully E. 20 miles. Contains a large tank.——*Cudlebaul* (ಕಡ್ಲೆಬಾಳು - kadlebálu, Can.). From (kadle, can. bengal gram, cicer arietinum, linn. + bálu, can. growth). Village; pop. 1,176; acres 8,923; lat. 15° 5′; long. 76° 15′; from Bellary W.S.W 48 miles; from Hoovinhadgully E.N.E. 17 miles. On the Hagary.——*Hireyhadgully* (ಹಿರೇಹಡಗಲ್ಲಿ - hiréhadagalli, Can.). From (hiri, can. great + hadagalli, can. place so called). Village; pop. 3,118; acres 5,528; lat. 14° 56′; long. 75° 53′; from Bellary W. 74 miles; from Hoovinhadgully S.W. 9 miles. Beautifully carved blackstone temple of Culleshwara and several large inscribed stones.——*Holalgondy* (ಹೊಲಲಗೊಂದಿ - holalagondi, Can.). From (hole, can. bright + gondi, can. alley). Village; pop. 2,807; acres 11,132; lat. 15° 02′; long. 76° 03′; from Bellary W. 62 miles; from Hoovinhadgully E. 5 miles. Shiva temple on a rock near the village.——*Hollal* (ಹೊಳಲು - holalu, Can.). From (hole, can. brightness). Village; pop. 2,572; acres 7,589; lat. 14° 50′; long. 75° 45′; from Bellary W.S.W. 80 miles; from Hoovinhadgully S.W. 19 miles. Carved statue of Ananta shayana sawmy.——*Hoovinhadgully* (ಹೂವಿನಹಡಗಲ್ಲಿ - húvinahadagalli, Can.). See below.——*Humpasaugar* (ಹಂಪಸಾಗರ - hampaságara, Can.). From (hamparasayya, can. proper name + ságara, san. ocean). The Toongabudra passes by the village. Sanscrit name (pampáságara). Village; pop. 3,713; acres 4,792; lat. 15° 09′; long. 76° 05′; from Bellary W. 58 miles; from Hoovinhadgully N.E. 11 miles. On Toongabudra. Silk cloths woven. Travellers' bungalow.——*Maugalam* (మాగలం - mágalam, Tel.). From (má, tel. great + kallamu, tel. threshing floor). Village; pop. 2,091; acres 10,284; lat. 15° 00′; long. 75° 50′; from Bellary W. 76 miles; from Hoovinhadgully W. 10 miles. On Toongabudra. Temple of Vengopaulsawmy. Another older temple deserted. There is a Jeina temple still used for worship.——*Meilaura* (ಮೈಲಾರ - mailára, Can.). From (malla, san. name of a demon + ari, san. enemy + pura, san. town). Sanscrit name (mallaripura), meaning town of mullaury or shiva, the enemy of mullan [q.v.], the giant. Village, Place of pilgrimage; pop. 2,750; acres 4,087; lat. 14° 48′; long. 75° 44′; from Bellary W.S.W. 85 miles; from Hoovinhadgully S.W. 23 miles. Close to the Toongabudra. An important Shiva temple. 50,000 pilgrims resort at the annual festival in February. There is a special custom at the feast in the utterance of a prophetic sentence annually by a child or man supposed to be inspired by the deity.——*Rameshwarabandy* (ರಾಮೇಶ್ವರಬಂಡಿ - ráméshvarabandi, Can.). From (ráméshavara, san. ráma the lord + bande, can. rock). Trig. station; lat. 15° 12′ 20·57″; long. 76° 12′ 08·65″; from Bellary W. 50 miles; from Hoovinhadgully N.E. 20 miles.——*Tamrahully* (ತಂಬ್ರಹಳ್ಳಿ - tambrahalli, Can.). From (támbra, can. copper + halli, can. village). Copper vessels were once manufactured. Village; pop. 2,492; acres 3,445; lat. 15° 09′; long. 76° 13′; from Bellary W. 48 miles; from Hoovinhadgully E.N.E. 18 miles. Has a large channel and a small anicut across the Hagary. Vishnoo temple on a rock. Silk cloths woven. Fine well called Sooley bhauvy.——*Toongabudra* (తుంగభద్ర - tungabhadra, Tel.). See sep. title.——**(2)** Village, Talook headquarters; Bellary dist., Hoovinhadgully tal.; pop. 4,441; acres 4,890; lat. 15° 01′; long. 75° 59′; from Adony W.S.W. 96 miles; from Bellary W. 64 miles; from Hospett W.S.W. 35 miles; from Hurpanhully N.N.W. 17 miles; from Madras W.N.W. 317 miles; from Tadpatry W. 139 miles. Built on open ground and considered very healthy. Temple of Keshava sawmy. Two temples were discovered, hidden by the walls of the fort, when the latter was dismantled in 1866.

HOPE ISLAND (కోరంగిదివి - kórangidivi, *Tel.*). Vernacular means coringa island. Island, Lighthouse; Godavery dist., tal. Cocanada division; pop. 25 included in Coringa; lat. 16° 49′; long. 82° 22′; from Cocanada S.S.E. 11 miles. A small sand bank above water formed by the discharge of the silt of the Godavery at its mouth. East of Coringa [q.v.] and 2 miles E. of the mouth of Coringa river.

HOPPER (அப்பம் - appam, *Tam.*). Tam. from (appu, tam. to clap with the hand). Unleavened cakes of rice [q.v.] flour and cocoanut [q.v.] milk. Resembling the wheaten choopatties [q.v.] of Upper india.

HORAH (होरा - hórá, *San.*). From the greek. One-twenty-fourth of natural day, European hour [caulam, ghuntay, ghurry].

HORN FISH (سینگی مچھی - síngímaççhí, *Hind.*). Same as Gar-fish [colah].

HORSE (گھوڑا - ghorá, *Hind.*; குதிரை - kuthirai, *Tam.*). Prefix.——*Horse grass* (കുതിരപ്പുല്ല് - kutirappullu, Mal.). Same as Keshinee.——*Horse keeper* (گھوڑےوالا - ghorewálá, Hind.; గుర్రపువాడు - gurrapuvádu, Tel.; குதிரைக்காரன் - kuthiraikkáran, Tam.). From (gurramu, tel. horse + vádu, tel. man). Tam. from (kuthirai, tam. horse + káran, tam. possessor). Term used in Madras and Ceylon for groom. In Northern india, syce [q.v.]. In Bombay ghorawallah [q.v.].

HORSLEYCONDAH (హార్సిలికొండ - hársilikonda, *Tel.* horsley-konda*). From Mr. Horsley, a former Collector. Tel. also (énugamallammakonda), meaning elephant + mullammah, proper name + hill. Hill; Cuddapah dist., Madanapully tal.; lat. 13° 39′; long. 78° 27′; from Cuddapah south 63 miles; from Madanapully N.W. 9 miles to foot. One of the highest peaks in Madanapully talook. There is a valley full of trees, and two bungalows [q.v.] belonging to district officers. The climate is adapted for a sanitarium, being free from fever, and from 10 to 12 degrees cooler than the country below. Well wooded. Cut up into narrow valleys which are but little cultivated. Samber [q.v.], pig [soor] and bears [ricsham] are found in the ravines [hill-station].

HOSA (ಹೊಸ - hosa, *Can.*). New [poothoo]. Prefix in place names; as Hospett.——*Hosangady* (ಹೊಸಂಗಡಿ - hosangadi, Can.). From (above + angadi, can. shop). Hind. name (baidargarh), meaning hyder's fort.—"*a*" Village; South canara dist., Coondapore tal.; pop. 375; lat. 13° 42′; long. 75° 00′; from Coondapore E.N.E. 18 miles; from Mangalore N.N.E. 58 miles; from the sea E. 20 miles.—"*b*" Pass; South canara dist., Coondapore tal.; lat. 13° 43′ N.; long. 75° 1′ E. On route between Bednore and Malabar coast. Much used in the campaigns with Tippoo sultan. Practicable for carts as far as head of water communication with coast. Good road into Mysore.——*Hosdroog* (ಹೊಸದುರ್ಗ - hosadurga, Can.; പുതിയകോട്ട - putiyakótta, Mal.). Can. from (above + durga, san. fort). Mal. means same. A small town in the village of Caunjangaud, Sub-port, Deputy tahsildar's station, Hill; South canara dist., Cassergode tal.; pop. 4,581; lat. 12° 18′; long. 75° 08′; from Cannanore N. 36 miles; from Cassergode S. 15 miles; from Coondapore S.S.E. 95 miles; from Mangalore S.S.E. 41 miles; from Oodipy S.S.E. 75 miles; from Poottore S.S.W. 31 miles; from the sea E. 1½ miles. On route from Cannanore to Mangalore. Large ruined fort built by an Ikkairy [q.v.] rajah [q.v.]. Temple and bungalow [q.v.].——*Hospett* (ಹೊಸಪೇಟೆ - hosapéte, Can.). See sep. title.

HOSPETT (ಹೊಸಪೇಟೆ - hosapéte, *Can.* hospet*). From (hosa, can. new + péte, can. suburb) [hosa].——**(1)** Talook, Bellary district. Tahsildar's pay Rs. 175. Area 540 square miles exclusive of the Sundoor jagheer [q.v.], which contains 145 more. Population 92,512. Language chiefly Canarese. N. of district. Bounded on the north by the Toongabudra and Nizam's territory, east by Bellary talook, south by the Coodligy talook, the Sundoor jagheer and the Mysore territory, on the west by Hoovinhadgully talook. Formerly known as Cumply talook. In 1851 head-quarters were moved from Cumply to Hospett. The Sundoor jagheer, formerly included in Coodligy talook was in 1832 transferred to Hospett talook, and has since been declared to be an independent native state. The principal natural features are the parallel ranges of hills bounding the Sundoor valley, which run through the talook from north to south, finishing abruptly at Hospett. Some of the higher plateau of these ranges have an elevation of 3,000 feet. There are smaller detached ranges, one commencing near Paupinaickhully and going on to Darojee and another starting from Camalaupooram and passing by Bookkasaugaram to Metry. The slopes of these hills are well-wooded and most of the fuel consumed in Bellary is brought from them. The western half of the talook has a more open aspect. The soil is throughout rich. About 4 per cent. is black cotton [regar] soil, but in the west the red predominates. Cholum [q.v.] being the staple food of the agricultural classes, the surplus rice [q.v.] of the talook is very largely exported to Adony, Bellary, and to Moondrigy in the Dharwar district. In return cholum, gram [q.v.] and wheat [geung] are sent into the markets of Chitvaudigy, Cumply, and Narraindevarakery from the Nizam's country and from Hurpanhully and Dharwar. The chief industrial pursuits are the weaving of silk [puttoo] and cotton [q.v.] cloths, known all over the district by their thickness; the manufacture of brass [pittalay] and copper [taumram] vessels at Hospett; and the iron foundaries at Camalaupooram, Hospett and Chilacanhutty, where the caldrons used in sugar-boiling are made. The iron-ore [auban] is procured from the Ramandroog hills. The Toongabudra flows along the northern side of the talook. It is crossed at intervals by anicuts [q.v.] from which six irrigation channels [q.v.] are led off. The only tanks [q.v.] of any size are at Auvinamadoogoo, Camalaupooram, Danaickenkery, and Darojee. Camping grounds:—Antapore, Camalaupooram and Cumply.

Places of archæological interest:—Ananta shayana goody, Caderampooram, Callirampooram, Kishkindyay, Malpangoody, Moopangoody, Nimbaupooram, Odrahully, Sancalaupooram, Timmapooram, Vijianugger. Principal Trig. stations:—Jamboonauta, Timmapooram. The leading places, &c., in the talook are the following.——*Ananta shayana goody* (ಅನಂತಶಯನಗುಡಿ - anantashayanagudi, Can.). Means temple of vishnoo who has anantan, the serpent for his couch. Village; pop. 631; acres 847; lat. 15° 17′; long. 76° 27′; from Bellary W.N.W. 35 miles; from Hospett E.N.E. 1½ miles; from Camalaupooram S.W. 5 miles. Large ruined temple of great architectural interest.——*Antapore* (అంతాపురము - antápuramu, Tel.). From (anantayya, tel. proper name + pura, san. city). Village; pop. 1,333; acres 2,809; lat. 15° 06′; long. 76° 46′; from Bellary W. 14 miles; from Hospett E.S.E. 24 miles. Situated among hills.——*Auvinamadoogoo* (ಆವಿನಮಡುಗು - ávinamadugu, Can.). From (ávu, tel. cow + madugu, can. pond). Village; pop. 1,207; acres 3,287; lat. 15° 05; long. 76° 47′; from Bellary W.S.W. 13 miles; from Hospett E.S.E. 26 miles. Contains a tank.——*Belagodehaul* (ಬೆಳಗೋಡುಹಾಳು - belagóduhálu, Can.). From (bilu, can. white + kódu, can. hill top + hálu, can. waste land). Village; pop. 873; acres 2,197; lat. 15° 26′; long. 76° 39′; from Bellary N.W. 29 miles; from Hospett E.N.E. 19 miles. Contains a channel.——*Bella* (ಬೆಲ್ಲ - bella, Can.). Means jaggery. Channel; one of the Toongabudra channels. Its head is just above the village of Hosoor. It is an old native work of rough stone concave towards the stream, and only extends from the right bank to an island in the river. At the south of this island there is a ledge of rock forming a natural anicut [q.v.].——*Bookkasaugaram* (బుక్కసాగరము - bukkaságaramu, Tel.). From (bhukka, san. name of a king + ságara, san. ocean). Village; pop. 1,124; acres 3,455; lat. 15° 21′; long. 76° 35′; from Bellary W.N.W. 30 miles; from Hospett E.N.E. 12 miles. The Ramsaugar anicut is built near this. It is an old native work of rough stone.——*Callirampooram* (కల్లిరాంపురము - kallírámpuramu, Tel.). From (kalli, can. milk hedge, euphorbia tirucalli, linn. + rámpuramu, tel. place so called). Sanscrit name (rámapura), meaning rama's town. Village built during the reign of Ramrauz of the Vijianugger family; pop. 553; acres 294; lat. 15° 18′; long. 76° 25′; from Bellary W.N.W. 38 miles; from Hospett N.N.W. 2 miles.——*Camalaupooram* (కమలాపురము - kámalápuramu, Tel.). See sep. title.——*Chitvaudigy* (ಚಿತ್ತವಾಡಿಗಿ - chittavádigi, Can.). From (chitti, can. small + vátike, can. garden). Sanscrit name (chitravátiká), meaning beauty + garden. Town; pop. 3,278; acres 607; lat. 15° 17′; long. 76° 25′; from Bellary W.N.W. 37½ miles; from Hospett N.W. 1½ miles. Many of the leading merchants of Hospett town live there. Market of western Bellary talooks and for goods from Nizam's dominions, every Saturday. Roya channel from Toongabudra runs through town.——*Cumply* (ಕಂಪಲಿ - kampali, Can.). See sep. title.——*Danaickenkery* (ಧಣಾಯಕನಕೆರೆ - dhanáyakanakeri, Can.). From (dhanáyaka, can. proper name + kere, can. tank). Village; pop. 1,095; acres 4,975; lat. 15° 08′; long. 76° 21′; from Bellary W. 37 miles; from Hospett S. 9 miles. Large tank.——*Darojee* (ದರೋಜಿ - darójí, Can.). From (darú, hind. tank). Village; pop. 2,620; acres 9,796; lat. 15° 16′; long. 76° 42′; from Bellary W.N.W. 19 miles; from Hospett E. 18 miles. Large tank famous for fish, constructed under Tippoo. The bund [q.v.] breached in 1851, and greater part of village destroyed. Small travellers' bungalow [q.v.] on tank-bund.——*Dhanaupooram* (ధనాపురము - dhanápuramu, Tel.). From (dhana, san. wealth + pura, san. town). Village; pop. 1,245; acres 454; lat. 15° 19′; long. 76° 28′; from Bellary N.W. 34 miles; from Hospett N.E. 5 miles. Near Humpy.——*Hoscote* (ಹೊಸಕೋಟೆ - hosakóte, Can.). From (hosa, can. new + kóte, can. fort). Village; pop. 151; acres 553; lat. 15° 15′; long. 76° 22′; from Bellary W.N.W. 39 miles; from Hospett W. 5 miles. Near the Cooradagudda anicut.——*Hosoor* (ಹೊಸೂರು - hosúru, Can.). From (hosa, can. new + úru, can. village). Village, Place of pilgrimage; pop. 1,574; acres 3,126; lat. 15° 18′; long. 76° 24′; from Bellary W.N.W. 39 miles; from Hospett N.W. 3 miles. Annual festival.——*Hospett* (ಹೊಸಪೇಟೆ - hosapéte, Can.). See below.——*Humpy* (ಹಂಪೆ - hampi, Can.). See sep. title.——*Jamboonauta* (ಜಂಬುನಾಥ - jambunát'ha, Can.). From (jambu, san. the tree, eugenia jambolana, lamk. + nát'ha, san. lord); epithet of a Jeina arhat [q.v.]. Trig. station; lat. 15° 13′ 41·57″; long. 76° 28′ 14·65″; height 2,980 feet; from Bellary W. 33 miles; from Hospett S.E. 4 miles; from Jamboonautanahully S.E. 2 miles.——*Metry* (మెట్రి - metri, Tel.). From (metta, tel. rising ground). Village; pop. 1,333; acres 5,288; lat. 15° 19′; long. 76° 40′; from Bellary W.N.W. 23 miles; from Hospett E. 15 miles.——*Mooddapooram* (ముద్దాపురము - muddápuramu, Tel.). From (mudda, tel. maiden + pura, san. town). Village; pop. 1,535; acres 3,715; lat. 15° 25′; long. 76° 43′; from Bellary N.W. 25 miles; from Hospett E.N.E. 22 miles.——*Narraindevarakery* (ನಾರಾಯಣದೇವರಕೆರೆ - náráyanadévarakeri, Can.). From (náráyanadévaru, can. proper name + kere, can. tank). Town; pop. 4,701; acres 5,878; lat. 15° 11′; long. 76° 21′; from Bellary W. 41 miles; from Hospett S.W. 8 miles. The chief town of a jagheer [q.v.] resumed in 1837. Parts of fort walls remain. Fine tank. District moonsif's court.——*Nimbaupooram* (నింబాపురము - nimbápuramu, Tel.). From (nimba, san. margosa tree, melia azadirachta, linn. + pura, san. town). Village; pop. 94; acres 312; lat. 15° 20′; long. 76° 32′; from Bellary W.N.W. 32 miles; from Hospett N.E. 8 miles. Formerly an Agrahauram [q.v.]. About a mile east lies an oval-shaped heap of calcareous scoria, apparently artificial. Bramins consider it the ashes of bones of giant Vauly [q.v.], killed here by Rama [q.v.] on his expedition to Ceylon.——*Paupinaickhully* (ಪಾಪಿನಾಯಕನಹಳ್ಳಿ - pápináyakanahalli, Can.). From (pápináyaka, can. proper name + halli, can. village). Village; pop. 804; acres 4,624; lat. 15° 14′; long. 76° 32′; from Bellary W.N.W. 29 miles; from Hospett E. 7 miles. Railway station.——*Sanaupooram* (సానాపురము - sánápuramu, Tel.). From (shána, san. grind stone + pura, san. town). Village; pop. 905; acres 1,868; lat. 15° 26′ 30″; long. 76° 41′; from Bellary N.W. 28 miles; from Hospett N.E. 21 miles.——*Suncalaupooram* (సంకలాపురం - sankalápuram, Tel.). From (sankala, san. collection + pura, san. town). Sanscrit name (kótivináyakapura), meaning crore + the belly-god, the obstacle-remover + town. Village; pop. 174; acres 609; lat. 15° 17′; long. 76° 44′; from Bellary W.N.W. 18 miles; from Hospett E. 19 miles.——*Sooganhully* (ಸೂಗನಹಳ್ಳಿ - súganahalli, Can.). From (súganna, tel. proper name + halli, can. village). Village; pop. 557; acres 4,212; lat. 15° 17′; long. 76° 44′; from Bellary N.W. 18 miles; from Hospett E. 20 miles.——*Timmapooram* (తిమ్మాపురము - timmápuramu, Tel.). From (timmaya, tel. proper name + pura, san. town). Trig. station; lat. 15° 20′ 33·57″; long. 76° 36′ 10·65″; height 2,133 feet; from Bellary W.N.W. 27 miles; from Hospett E.N.E. 13 miles; from Canvitimmapooram S.W. 1 mile.——*Toongabudra* (తుంగభద్ర - tungabhadra, Tel.). See sep. title.——**(2)** Town, Talook and Divisional head-quarters, Railway station; Bellary dist., Hospett tal.; pop. 12,878; acres 2,095; lat. 15° 16′; long. 76° 26′; from Adony W.S.W. 65 miles; from Bellary W.N.W. 36 miles; from Hurpanhully N.N.E. 43 miles; from Madras W.N.W. 302 miles; from Tadpatry W.N.W. 110 miles. On high ground. Hill behind town called Joladaraushy, or heap of cholum, from shape. Head assistant collector stationed here. Town improved in 1866 by levelling fort wall and filling up ditch. One fine temple at end of main street. Interesting Mahomedan tombs outside town. Inhabitants chiefly weavers, but brass and copper vessels are made. Ruins of old town Trimaldevipooram are near.

HOURI (حور - húr, *Hind.*). Nymph of paradise, with Mahomedans.

HOWDAH (هودہ - haudah, *Hind.*). From (haudaja, ar. to be high). Seat fixed on elephant [q.v.]. A kind of box with low sides and no top, and holds several persons.

HOWZ (حوض - hauz, *Hind.*). From (háza, ar. to collect water). Reservoir, especially in mosque [musjid] for ablutions.

HOY (ಹೊಯಿ - hoyi, *Can.*). To strike.——*Hoysala ballaula* (ಹೊಯಿಸಲಬಲ್ಲಾಳ - hoyisalaballála, Can.). From (above + sala, can. the founder of the family + ballála, can. the family); from the incident of his killing a tiger [pooly] with an iron staff. See Ballaula.

HUBBLE-BUBBLE (حقہ - hukkah, *Hind.*). Title from sound. Ordinary kind of hookah [q.v.]. The tobacco, or a mixture containing tobacco [pogauk] among other things, is placed with embers in a terracotta chillum [q.v.], from which a reed carries the smoke into a cocoanut [q.v.] shell half full of water, and the smoke is drawn through a hole in the side, either without any kind of mouth-piece, or with a long tube, and making a gurgling sound.

HUDD (حد - hadd, *Hind.*). From (hadda, ar. to prevent). Limit, whether of place or time [avadhy].

HUKK (حق - hakk, *Hind.*). From (hakka, ar. to be right). Truth. A just claim; attribute of God [allah].——*Hakeekat* (حقیقت - hakíkat, Hind.). From (hakk, ar. right). Statement. The final stage of absorption [soofee].——*Hakeeyat* (حقیت - hakíyat, Hind.). From (hakk, ar. right). Right, share, proprietorship.——*Hookook* (حقوق - hukúk, Hind.). Plural from hukk. Rights.

HUKKA (ಹಕ್ಕ - hakka, *Can.*). Short for (hariga), which in turn is colloquial for Hariharan [q.v.]. Proper name.

HULCAUR (اہل کار - ahlikár, *Hind.*). Servant [ahlecaur].

HULDEE (هلدی - haldí, *Hind.*). From (haridrá, san. turmeric) [haran]. Same as Country saffron.

HULLA (ಹಳ್ಳ - halla, *Can.*; பள்ளம் - pallam, *Tam.*). Lowland. Suffix in place names [pullam].——*Hully* (ಹಳ್ಳಿ - halli, Can.; பள்ளி - palli, Tam.). Hamlet. Suffix in place names [milly, pully, villy].

HUMMAUM (حمام - hammám, *Hind.*). From (hamím, ar. hot water). Bath, especially hot or steam bath.

HUMPY (ಹಂಪೆ - hampi, Can.). From (hampu, can. proud); the magnificent city. Sanscrit name (pampákshétra), place of preservation; also (virúpákshapura), meaning the mis-shapen-eyed shiva + town. Village, Place of pilgrimage; Bellary dist.

Hospett tal.; pop. 354; acres 848; lat. 15° 20′; long. 76° 30′; from Bellary W.N.W. 33 miles; from Hospett N.E. 7 miles. On right or south bank of Toongabudra. Main street parallel with river is lined with temples and palaces. Very sacred. For bathing in Toongabudra at a certain conjunction of the planets [graham] vast numbers assemble. Near are ruins of ancient city of Vijianugger [q.v.], covering with Camalaupooram on the south and Anagoondy a space of nearly 9 miles, the most remarkable monument in S. india. During the two and a quarter centuries that the Vijianugger rajahs held the city of Humpy, they extended it and beautified it with palaces and temples. Edoardo Barbessa describes the capital as "of great extent, highly populous, and the seat of an active commerce in country diamonds [vajram], rubies [laul] from Pegu, silks [puttoo] of China and Alexandria and cinnabar [shangarf], camphor [q.v.], musk [custoory], pepper [q.v.], and sandal [q.v.] from Malabar. The palaces of the king and his ministers and the temples are described as stately buildings of stone, but the greater part of the population lived in hovels of straw and mud." In the travels of Cæsar Frederic, the palace is thus spoken of:—"I have seen many kings' courts, yet have never seen anything to compare with the royal palace of Vijianugger, which hath nine gates. First, when you go into that part where the king lodged, there are five great gates, kept by captains and soldiers. Within these are four lesser gates, which are kept by porters, and through these you enter into a very fair court at the end." He describes the city as being 24 miles round, enclosing several hills. The ordinary dwellings were mean buildings with earthen walls, but the three palaces and the pagodas [q.v.] were all built of fine marble [shalavay cull]. Nicolo di Conti A.D. 1420 says it is 60 miles in circumference. Bartema says that it is very like Milan. Of the remains of all this greatness little is now visible. Many of the buildings are so destroyed that it is difficult to say what they were originally meant for. Amongst the ruins however are found particularly fine specimens of Indian architecture. The massive style of architecture and the huge stones that have been employed in their construction specially attract attention. The principal buildings to be noted are the following:—the palace buildings, including council room, concert hall, zenana [q.v.], elephants' stables [aunesaul], three towers, and the queen's bath; the temple of victory or Hazaur rama, so called from containing 1,000 figures of rama, temple of Maulyavanta runganauta sawmy; temple of Vittala; the pagoda [q.v.] at Humpy itself; a small temple west of that of Vittalsawmy, with two historical inscriptions; temple of Shree pampaupatysawmy with fine blackstone sculptures and inscriptions and group of Jeina temples south of same; temple of Krishnasawmy; temples of Atchootanarayanasawmy; large monolithic statue of Narsimhan [q.v.]; temple of Hazaur rama and two pavilions west from same; temple of Gaunagitty and temple of Puttaubhy ramasawmy near Camalaupooram; houses in Humpy bazaar of archæological interest. Veishnava, Sheiva and Jeina temples are found in close proximity, and on many temples sculptures of both the first two mixed together. Some of the Jeina temples are constructed in a northern style. The elephant [q.v.] stables consist of a long row of chambers domed over, the centre one having a double storey over it. The architecture is of the mixed Hindoo and Mahomedan style. The temple of victory is about 300 yards to the south-west of the palace buildings in a quadrangle, 110 feet from north to south and 200 feet from east to west. The bas-reliefs on the exterior of the walls are singularly characteristic, and the long rows of horses [ghorah], elephants, camels [ottagam], soldiers, spirited dancing women, &c., may have led to the name given to the building. The adytum of the interior is supported on four elaborately-carved black basaltic [caroompalingoo cull] columns. The throne consists of a succession of platforms, the outer walls of which are carved in relief with elephants, camels, dancing girls. It is about 600 yards south of the palace buildings. The total height of the platform is 31 feet, and there are signs on its summit of a pavilion having existed. Inside this mound is a staircase which is partly blocked up. It goes by the name of Mahanavamy [q.v.] dibba [q.v.] or Dusserah [q.v.] dibba. The queen's bath about 150 yards south-east of the throne is a building 78 feet 5 inches square in plan, with a reservoir in the centre 50 feet 9 inches square and 6 feet deep. The corridor has an arched ceiling richly carved with foliated ornament in plaster, and over the bath, on each of the four sides, is a projecting window with three openings. The temple of Maulyavanta runganauta sawmy is about 1¼ miles north-east of the travellers' rest-house and stands in a walled enclosure on a rocky hill. There are three gopoorams [q.v.] of the usual Dravidian style of architecture. A mantapam [q.v.] inside is the best architectural feature of the place and is very picturesque with its carved masonry columns. The temple of Vittala or Vittoba is a very fine example of the Dravidian style. In some respects it is as remarkable a specimen as any to be found in Southern india, though less in extent than those at Chidambaram, Rameshwaram and Sheerungam. It is situated on the right bank of the river on a level spot above the reach of any flood, and nearly opposite to the ruins of a bridge, begun but never completed, to connect Vijianugger with Anagoondy. The site of the temple is very picturesque. Behind it are piles of naked granite [caroom cull] rocks of all imaginable forms, stretching westwards to the town of Humpy in a succession of rugged hills. To the north and east are still more lofty eminences of the same formation, all connected with each other, rising into pinnacles of naked tors and loggan stones, and extending down the river to Anagoondy. Immediately in front of the temple, and between it and the river, is a small plain, in part cultivated, and interspersed with trees, which combine with the river and the rocky hills around to form a constant succession of romantic landscapes. Entering by the gateway, which is lofty and in the style peculiar to Vijianugger, is seen an area enclosed by a ruined piazza in the usual monolithic style of construction, intended as shelter for visitors to the shrine. A little to the left of the gateway is a separate smaller temple in the same style of construction as the large one, and between it and the larger edifice is the stone car [rath]. This car is composed of only one stone, most probably a boulder existing on the spot. The upper portion has been restored with a moderate degree of success. A considerable portion of the porch at the each side of the temple was blown away by Tippoo sultan after a vain endeavour to raze the temple by manual labor. A portion of the roof in the centre of the building was also destroyed without however displacing the pillars, or injuring the stability of the edifice. The richness and beauty of the interior is remarkable. In Hindoo temples in general, black hornblende [shalavay cull] rock or green stone [putchay cull] is most usually found as the material of the pillars, which from its color gives a sombre effect to the whole; but in this instance the material is wholly the granite of the locality, which is a creamy, or in some instances a pinkish, white, and as a consequence the interior of this temple, besides having an ample supply of light from without, has a peculiarly cheerful and elegant appearance, while the finish of the figures, flowers, and patterns of all kinds is not less perfect than that of the black stone of other localities. Some of the pillars have been polished with emery or corundum [q.v.], others are prepared for polish and are as smooth as marble. Many have been cut into forms of dragons or lions, with female figures on their backs, interspersed with foliage and smaller figures, ornamented and relieved by rows of separate pillars cut from the same block of stone, which are perfectly unique in design. The larger pillars have four of these columns on each face, others have three or two, the basement they appear to rest on being supported by sitting lions. The heavy eaves are huge blocks of granite, fluted inside and surmounted by a string course of stone, on which is a curious pattern of wolves' [konye] heads in pairs, open mouthed, above which the turrets and other pinnacles are of masonry, plastered. The basement is also peculiarly handsome, and the execution of the stonework and its joints wonderfully perfect. The shrine in this great temple was never filled. The legend of it, which is not an exaggerated one, is that in the plenitude of their power the rajahs of Vijianugger determining to bring the holy image of Krishnan which is at Punderpoor to Vijianugger, built this temple to exceed in beauty everything before created in the Deccan [q.v.], so as to receive it; but the design was never accomplished owing probably to the decadence of the kingdom. Local tradition ascribes the erection of the porch to Atchoota roya, A.D. 1529—1542, or more probably to the usurper Ramrauz during his tenure of power. The pagoda at Humpy itself is dedicated to Viroopaucshan or Shiva, and covers a large area, which is filled by courts containing other shrines, reading rooms, &c., with several Bramins' dwellings. It has only one enclosure and two gateways. Krishna deva royel of Vijianugger is said to have built the edifice in the fifteenth century out of the booty which he obtained on conquering the Chola rajahs of Conjeeveram. The door to the vimaunam [q.v.] has some handsome brass-work with hammered ornament. The temple of Hazaur rama, built in A.D. 1513, has a Jeina figure on the outside of the vimaunam wall. The monolithic statue of the Narsimha avatar [q.v.] close by was hewn, as an inscription states, in A.D. 1529. The Gaunagitty temple, a Jeina shrine, built according to an inscription by Hariharan in A.D. 1385, is in excellent preservation. An interesting group of the Vijianugger ruins is situated in the valley that separates the ground of Humpy proper from Kishkindyay, the sacred land of the Rajah vauly, and of the deeds of the heroes of the Ramayanam [q.v.]. Kishkindyay comprises the area of the hills on the opposite side of the valley, which are a wild congeries of fantastic naked granite rocks, with narrow valleys between, some of these being watered by channels from the main irrigation stream. In one of these is shown the place where the body of Rajah vauly was burned and where his wives performed suttee [q.v.] with him. It is a bed of very white carbonate of lime [choonam], which, as the ashes of the dead, serve to attest the event to all true pilgrims. Here Hanooman [q.v.], of the Ramayanam was born, and here also many of his descendants live in the shape of large grey apes [lungoor], which abound among the rocks and ruins. Here too are believed to be existent evidences of the truth of his feats in the piles of rocks which lie on the plains. These are said to have been brought by his legions from the Himalaya in relays to fill up the sea from Rameshwaram to Ceylon, where the armies of Rama were to cross. There is an outlying line of fortification 8 miles from Humpy on the Bellary road. Anagoondy was formerly a suburb of Vijianugger and was the family dwelling place of the chiefs. It has been identified with the Kongkien-an-pu-lo or Concanapooram of Hwen Thsang. Camalaupooram was another suburb,

HURPANHULLY (ಹರಪನ ಹಳ್ಳಿ - harapanahalli, *Can.* harpanahalli *). From (harappa, can. proper name + halli, can. village) [haran]. Sanscrit name (harapura), meaning shiva's town.——**(1)** Talook, Bellary district. Tahsildar's pay Rs. 150. Area 611 square miles. Population 82,241. Language Canarese. W. of district. Situated in the extreme west of the district. Bounded by Hoovinhadgully talook on the north; Mysore territory on the south; Coodligy talook on the east; Toongabudra river and Mysore province on the west. It is intersected by low ranges of hills. The principal of these runs from Adavimullaukerey to Chigatairy, a distance of 10 miles, and thence is connected by isolated hills with the Mysore tableland. The principal crops are zonna [cholum], raggy [q.v.], corra [tinay], cotton [q.v.] and oil-seeds [yennay], and on irrigated land sugar-cane [q.v.] and paddy [q.v.]. These are exported to Dharwar and Moondrigy in the Bombay presidency and to Hurrihur and Chitaldroog in Mysore. Rice [q.v.] is imported from Dharwar and the better irrigated talooks of Mysore. Most of the people live by agriculture, but there is a small trade in cotton and piece-goods which find a market at Ootchangy droog. At Hurpanhully, copper [taumram], brass [pittalay], and ornamental metal [loham] vessels are made, and the manufacture of wooden toys carried on. The Toongabudra flows along a small part of the western frontier. The largest part of the talook is under dry cultivation. There are only four tanks, Arsikerey, Baugaly, Hagranore and Neelgoonda, capable of irrigating an ayacut [q.v.] of over 200 acres, and no advantage has been taken of the Toongabudra for river channels [q.v.]. There are nine other tanks capable of irrigating between 100 and 200 acres, the largest of which is at Coontsore. Camping grounds:—Arsikerey, Halavaugal and Neelgoonda. Travellers' bungalow [q.v.] at Hurpanhully. Places of archæological interest:—Arsikerey, Baugaly, Bennihully, Chigatairy, Chikka calganacuttey, Chirtahully, Chittenahully, Coolahully, Coorvutty, Doogavutty, Garbhagoody, Goodihully, Goondagutty, Halagilvauda, Halavaugal, Harivy, Hariyammanahully, Hurpanhully, Masalvauda, Mauchahully, Maudalgherry, Munnaira masalvauda, Neelgoonda, Ootchangy droog, Raugy masalvauda. Principal Trig. stations:—Garbhagoody, Narsimha devargoodda. The leading places, &c., in the talook are the following.——*Arsikerey* (ಅರಸೀಕೆರೆ - arasikere, Can.). From (arasi, can. a queen + kere, can. tank). Village; pop. 1,694; acres 4,103; lat. 14° 40′; long. 76° 07′; from Bellary W.S.W. 65 miles; from Hurpanhully S.S.E. 10 miles. Tank.——*Baugaly* (ಬಾಗಳಿ - bágali, Can.). Village; pop. 1,397; acres 3,796; lat. 14° 50′; long. 76° 01′; from Bellary W.S.W. 66 miles; from Hurpanhully N. 4 miles. Tank. Sculptured temple of Cauleshwarasawmy near tank bund.——*Chigatairy* (ಚಿಗಟೇರಿ - chigatéri, Can.). From (chiguru, can. blossom + éri, can. tank). Village; pop. 2,314; acres 8,472; lat. 14° 49′; long. 76° 08′; from Bellary W.S.W. 60 miles; from Hurpanhully E.N.E. 8 miles. Small particles of gold [pon] are found at the foot of a hill.——*Chinna hagary* (చిన్నహగరి - chinnahagari, Tel.). See sep. title.——*Coontsore* (ಕುಂಚೂರು - kunchúru, Can.). From (kuncha, can. a fly brush + úru, can. village). Sanscrit name (chámarapura), meaning chowry + town. Village; pop. 1,524; acres 4,848; lat. 14° 44′; long. 75° 52′; from Bellary W.S.W. 78 miles; from Hurpanhully W.S.W. 12 miles. Large tank.——*Coorvutty* (ಕುರುವತ್ತಿ - kuruvatti, Can.). From (kuri, can. sheep + hatti, can. sheep fold). Sanscrit name (nandikunda), meaning the bull-god + sacred pool. Village, Place of pilgrimage; pop. 1,439; acres 5,524; lat. 14° 47′; long. 75° 45′; from Bellary W.S.W. 84 miles, from Hurpanhully W. 18 miles. Car festival about February. Cattle fair held on the occasion is noted. Fort on bank of Toongabudra.——*Garbhagoody* (ಗರ್ಭಗುಡಿ - garbhagudi, Can.). From (garbha, san. interior + gudi, can. temple). Village; pop. 257; lat. 14° 43′; long. 75° 48′; from Bellary W.S.W. 82 miles; from Hurpanhully W.S.W. 15 miles. Old fort on a hill. Trig. station in lat. 14° 43′ 46·97″; long. 75° 50′ 25·30″.——*Goodihully* (ಗುಡಿಹಳ್ಳಿ - gudihalli, Can.). From (gudi, can. temple + halli, can. village). Village; pop. 257; lat. 14° 39′; long. 76° 07′; from Bellary W.S.W. 65 miles; from Hurpanhully S.E. 11 miles. Formerly the village was built within precints of Shiva temple. Now deserted and village is ½ mile from original site.——*Hagranore* (ಹಗರನೂರು - hagaranúru, Can.). From (hagara, can. proper name + úru, can. village). Village; pop. 590; acres 3,528; lat. 14° 56′; long. 75° 54′; from Bellary W. 72 miles; from Hurpanhully N.W. 13 miles. Large tank.——*Halavaugal* (ಹಲವಾಗಲು - halvágalu, Can.). From (hallu, can. ivory + bágalu, can. door). Sanscrit name (dantadvára), meaning ivory + door. Village; pop. 2,069; acres 10,457; lat. 14° 43′; long. 75° 49′; from Bellary W.S.W. 82 miles; from Hurpanhully W.S.W. 15 miles. Near Toongabudra.——*Hurpanhully* (ಹರಪನಹಳ್ಳಿ - harapanahalli, Can.). See below.——*Narsimha devargoodda* (ನರಸಿಂಹದೇವರಗುಡ್ಡ - narasimhadévaragudda, Can.). From (narasimhadévaru, can. the man-lion god + gudda, can. hill). Sanscrit name (narasimháchala), meaning the same. Trig. station; lat. 14° 40′ 13·57″; long. 76° 05′ 03·65″; height 2,544 feet; from Bellary W.S.W. 67 miles; from Hurpanhully S.S.E. 9 miles; from Timmalaupooram W.N.W. 1½ miles.——*Neelgoonda* (ನೀಲಗುಂದ - nílagunda, Can.). From (níla, can. proper name, nílávati + gunte, can. tank). Sanscrit name (nílávatípattana), meaning neelauvaty's city. Village; pop. 1,161; acres 3,318; lat. 14° 44′; long. 75° 56′; from Bellary W.S.W. 74 miles; from Hurpanhully W.S.W. 7 miles. A flourishing town some centuries ago. Temple of Ananta shayanan and that of Bheemeshwaran on the tank bund [q.v.] are of great antiquity. The latter is profusely sculptured. There is a large tank.——*Ootchangy droog* (ಉಚ್ಚಂಗಿದುರ್ಗ - uççangidurga, Can.). See sep. title.——*Toongabudra* (తుంగభద్ర - tungabhadra, Tel.). See sep. title.——**(2)** Town, Talook head-quarters; Bellary dist., Hurpanhully tal.; pop. 7,842; acres 9,829; lat. 14° 47′; long. 76° 02′; from Adony W.S.W. 104 miles; from Bellary W.S.W. 67 miles; from Hospett S.S.W. 43 miles; from Madras W.N.W. 312 miles; from Tadpatry W. 136 miles. During the last century the seat of a powerful poligar [q.v.]. The founder of the family was a Boy [q.v.] by caste and Taliyary [q.v.] by profession. On subversion of Vijianugger he seized two small districts near Hurpanhully. One of his successors married daughter of Poligar [q.v.] of Chitaldroog, and received as dowry talook of Ootchangy droog. The last of the line was Somashekhara naick, who died without issue in 1766. At this time the poligar was paying peshcush [q.v.] to the Nizam, to Moraury row of Gooty, and the Peshwah [q.v.]. The widow adopted. In 1786 Hurpanhully was taken by Tippoo sultan, and the poligar and his three sons captured and sent to Seringapatam. One of his followers escaped and having joined the army of the Mahratta purseram bhow, was set up by him as poligar. He was expelled in a few days by a detachment sent against him by Tippoo, but he returned during the second Mysore war and made himself master of Hurpanhully. He surrendered in 1800 to General Harris, by whom he was recognised as poligar. This surrender was due to the influence of the Diwaun [q.v.] Hampa. rasayya, who was rewarded with a jagheer [q.v.] in the Hospett talook. The fort has been deserted and is said to be haunted by a late Tahsildar [q.v.], M. Bheema row, who took up arms in 1857 and was killed at the storm of Kopala. A colony of Jeinas has settled in the town.

HURRIALLY (दूर्वा - dúrvá, *San.*; करली - karalí, *Mahr.*; जिर्बांकुर - jirbánkura, *Conc.*; دوب گنیر - dúbganer, *Hind.*; ہریالی - hariyálí, *Dec.*; ಗರಿಕೆ - garike, *Can.*; ಕಡಿಕೆಪಂತಿ - kadikepanti, *Too.*; గరిక - garika, *Tel.*; കറുക - karuka, *Mal.*; හෙළඉතණ - helaítana, *Singh.*; அறுகு - arugu, *Tam.*). Title from deccany [haran]. San. from (durv, san. to injure); as devoured by cattle; also from sharp blades; must not be confounded with darbhay, a synonym of the celebrated coosham [q.v.] grass. Hind. from sanscrit. Dec. from (hará, hind. green). Can. from (gari, can. to fall upon). Mal. from tamul. Tam. from (aru, tam. to cut); from curing virtue. San. also (rasála), meaning juice giving [mango, sugar-cane]; (bhárgaví), meaning pertaining to bhrigoo; (aurva), meaning pertaining to bhaurgavan, born from thigh; (sahasravíryá), meaning very powerful; (anantá), meaning endless [common nail dye, indian sarsaparilla]; (shataparviká), meaning hundred-knotted; (gólómí), meaning earth's hair strictly the white variety [vashamboo]. Hind. also (janíwá); (dúb) to be distinguished from (dáb). Can. also (karike); (ambatíhullu). Tel. also (tellagarika), meaning white + the grass; (garakanattu), meaning garikay, the grass + nutt [q.v.]. Mal. also (muyalpullu), meaning hare + grass; (velikkaruka), meaning sacrificial + the grass. Tam. also (muyarbui), meaning hare + grass, forms food of hares; (angusóli), meaning goad-like, from leaves. Greek ἄγρωστις. Title otherwise Bahama grass, Bent grass, Bermuda grass, Conch grass, Creeping cynodon, Creeping panic grass, Dog grass, Dog's tooth grass, Doob, Doorvay, Hare grass, Hundred-knotted grass [hoonraj], Linear bent grass, Panic grass [purple grass, tinay]. Botanically Cynodon dactylon, pers., graminaceæ [vriesham, 156]. Alias Agrostis bermudiana, cynosurioides, linearis; Chlolis maritima, cynodon; Cynodon linearis, maritimus, occidentalis, portoricensis, stellatus; Dactylon officinale; Digitaria dactylon, linearis, stolonifera; Fibichia umbellata; Milium dactylon; Panicum dactylon, lineare; Paspalum praecox, umbellatum, dactylon; Vilfa linearis. Culms creeping, with flower-bearing branchlets, erect, 6–12 inches high, smooth; leaves small; spikes three to five, terminal, sessile, secund, 1–2 inches long; rachis waved; flowers alternate, single, disposed in two rows on the under side; calyx much smaller than the corolla; exterior valves boat-shaped, keel slightly ciliate. A very nutritious creeping grass; all its stems, which lie near the ground, take root, and by this means, though an annual plant, it spreads; here it constitutes three-fourths of the pasture; it is when cultivated, of most luxuriant growth in the hottest time of the year; with shade, such as light bushes or straw strewed over it, it rises like a creeper 5 or 6 feet high, and when chopped up it will take root. Its merits, its lowly gesture, its spreading quality, give it a frequent place in native poetry; it is sacred to ganesh [q.v.], probably on account of its great tenacity of life. When cultivated, freely manured and irrigated, produces from six to eight crops in the year; like most other meadow grasses, should be cut immediately the flower begins to appear; in this state the juices of the grass are more nutritious, and the hay is superior than when made from the fully-matured plant. The juice of the green grass is a remedy for dysentery; decoction of roots and young leaves is used in fever. The most nutritious fodder for horses [ghorah] and cows [pashoo]. There is a Tamul proverb:—ஆலையும் அறுகம்புல்லினைல் தடைபடும்—

"Even an elephant [q.v.] may be impeded by aroogoo;" that is to say, by a small thing. Other common species are:—gracilis, virgatus.——*Barren hurrially* (ಬಂಜೆಗರಿಕೆ - banjegarike, Can.). Same as Wild hurrially.——*Gum hurrially* (ಅಂಟುಗರಿಕೆ - antugarike, Can.). Same as Small raggy.——*Wild hurrially* (ಬಂಜೆಗರಿಕೆ ಹುಲ್ಲು - banjegarikehullu, Can.; தினை - tinai, Tam.). Can. from (banje, can. barren + garikehullu, can. bent grass, cynodon dactylon, pers.). Tam. from (tin, tam. to eat). Botanically Panicum [priyangoo] burmanni, retz., graminaceæ [vricsham, 156]. Alias Echinochloa hirtella; Oplismenus burmanni; Orthopogon albus, brasiliensis, burmanni, humboldtianus; Panicum album, bromoides, hirtellum. Culms creeping, branched, extremities erect; leaves lanceolate, waved hairy; sheaths half the length of the joints, very hairy; spikes compound, secund, erect; spikelets four to eight, alternate, secund, adpressed; flowers generally paired, one sessile, the other pedicelled; glumes hairy, long-awned; generally found under the shade of trees; cattle eat it, and makes fair hay [ghans].

HUTTY (هٹی - hattí, *Hind.*; ಹಟ್ಟಿ - hatti, *Can.*; பட்டி - patti, *Tam.*). Cattle-pen. Herds man's residence. Suffix in place names [putty].

HYDER (حيدر - haídar, *Ar.*). Lion [hamza, hizabr, safder, shere]. Lacab of ally, the son-in-law and companion of Mahomet. Common alam. Feminine form is Hydary; as Hydary begum, alam + alaumat [ism].——*Hyder ally* (حيدرعلى - haídaralí, Hind.). Double alam. The Mysore ruler; born about 1700; assumed the raj, 1761; negotiated with Council of Bombay, 1763; met the English in battle, September 26, 1767, and November 8; Amboor besieged by Hyder, November 1767; Shingaricottah taken from Hyder on February 12, 1767; Salem on March 20; Krishnagherry on May 2; Vencatagherry on June 10; Moolbaugal on June 28; Oossoor on July 11; Aunecull, July 13; Mangalore, March 1, 1769; Honnore on March 25; advanced on Madras, March 29, 1769; treaty signed with English, April 4, 1769; repeatedly defeated in 1781 and in 1782; died, December 7, 1782 [charitram]. See vol. I (180) to (183), 20. Vol. II, 63, 71, 102.——*Hyderghur* (حيدر گڑھ - haidargarh, Hind.). Means hyder's fort. Fort not now in existence; South canara dist., Coondapore tal.; lat. 13° 43′; long. 75° 03′; from Coondapore E.N.E. 22 miles; from Mangalore N.N.E. 60 miles; from the sea E. 24 miles; from Poottore N.N.W. 67 miles.——*Hyder's tree* (حيدر كا جهاڑ - haidarkájhár, Hind.). Same as Mysore thorn.

HYE (حى - haí, *Hind.*). From (hai, ar. to live). Living. As an attribute of God means deathless [allah]. Common alam; as Abdool hye, slave of the living [ism].——*Hayaut* (حيات - hayát, Ar.). From (hai, ar. to live). Life. Said to be created on the tenth day of Moharram [q.v.].—"*a*" Common alam; as Hayaut bee, alam + alaumat; Hayaut khan, alam + alaumat [ism].—"*b*" Plant second term. Ex., where translation is of first term:—Clitoria ternatea (darakhtibíkhihayát), tree; Sphæranthus indicus (zakhmihayát), wound. See gloss. paragraphs.

I (इ - i, ई - í, *San.*; ا - i, *Pers.*; இ - i, ஈ - í, *Tam.*). San. short, symbol of Cauma devan [cauman]. San. long, symbol of Candarpan, god of love [manmatan]; and of Lutchmy [q.v.]. Sign of the Persian genitive case; as Adawlut i auliya, high court.

IBEX HILL (ಮುಟ್ಟುಬೆಟ್ಟ - muttubetta, *Can.*). From (muttu, can. upright post + betta, can. hill). Hill; Neilgherry dist., Todanaud div.; lat. 11° 21′; long. 76° 35′; from Ootacamund W.S.W. 11 miles. Bluff-like eminence near head of Seegore pass [ghaut].

IBHARANCOOSHA (ज्वरांकुश - jvaránkusha, *San.*; कंर्बलो - kamrbaló, *Conc.*; اذخر - izkhir, *Ar.*; گور گیاه - gorgiyáh, *Pers.*; ابهرن كشا - ibharankushá, *Hind.*; ಕರಿಲಾವಂಚ - karilávancha, *Can.*; ಕರಿಮುಡ್ಯಾಲ - karimudyala, *Too.*; వాసనగడ్డి - vásanagaddi, *Tel.*; കൊടിപ്പുല്ല് - kotippullu, *Mal.*; காமாட்சிப்புல் - kámádchippul, *Tam.*). Title from sanscrit through hindostany. San. from (jvara, san. fever + ankusha, san. goad); febrifuge. Ar. from (zakhara, ar. provision); as forage for camel. Pers. from (gor, pers. camel + giyáh, pers. hay). Can. from (kari, can. black + lávancha, san. andropogon muricatus, retz.). Too. means black cuscus. Tel. from (vásana, san. fragrance + gaddi, tel. grass). Mal. from (koti, mal. creeper + pullu, mal. grass). Tam. from (kámákshí, san. the goddess + pul, tam. grass); really appears to be corruption from (kámanchi, tel. the grass) [indian grass, lemon grass, roussa grass]. San. also (lámajjaka), meaning destroying sap from correcting bad blood [cuscus]. Ar. also (tíbulgharíb), meaning wonderful fragrance. Hind. also (rusá) [roussa grass, stunted jack]. Tel. also (nimmagaddi), meaning lemon, citrus medica, linn., var, limonum, brandis + grass [lemon grass]. Title otherwise Black cuscus, Camel hay, Fever grass. Botanically Andropogon [beard grass] iwarancusa, roxb., graminaceæ [vricsham, 156]. Specific name from hind. Alias Cymbopogon iwarancusa. Root perennial, fibrous; culms erect, 3-6 feet, smooth, filled with a light spongy substance; leaves near the root longer than the culm-points, margins hispid, otherwise smooth; panicles axillary and terminal, consisting of numerous fascicles of pedicelled, thin, five-jointed spikes, with a spathe to each pair of spikes; flowers on the rachis in pairs, one awned, sessile, the other one awnless, male, and pedicelled; the terminal florets are three, one hermaphrodite, two male; glumes two, one-flowered, with which the rachis and pedicels are woolly at the base; native of himalayas. Roots have agreeable aromatic taste, with certain degree of bitterness; medicinally stomachic.

IBN (ابن - ibn, *Hind.*). From arabic. Son. Coonyat [ism].

IBRAHIM (ابراهيم - ibráhím, *Hind.*). From hebrew, father of the multitude. Abraham. Patriarchal alam; as Ibrahim beg, alam + alaumat [ism].——*Ibrampatam* (ఇబ్రహీముపట్టణము - ibrahámupattanamu, Tel.). From (ibráhím, hind. proper name + pattana, san. town). Town; Kistna dist., Bezwada tal.; pop. 1,578; acres 8,480; lat. 16° 35′; long. 80° 33′; from Bezwada N.W. 8 miles; from Masulipatam N.W. 48 miles. On northern bank of the Kistna below Condapully range. Favorite residence of Ibrahim cootb shah of Golcondah, A.D. 1530 to 1580. Many allusions in Ferishta to Ibrahim's gardens. Travellers' bungalow [q.v.].

IBRAT (عبرت - ibrat, *Hind.*). From (ibr, ar. to admonish) [itibar]. Example. Part of lacab; as Ibrat jung, an example in war [ism].

IDREES (ادريس - idrís, *Ar.*). Enoch. Mahomedan alam; generally taken by the Saits; as Idrees sait [ism].

IFTAUR (افطار - iftár, *Hind.*). From (fatara, ar. to break) [fitr]. Breaking fast [roza]. Eating at sunset daily during the Ramzaun month [maheena]. Also the ceremony of breaking the fast at the end of that month [eed ool fitr].

IFTIKHAR (افتخار - iftikhár, *Ar.*). From (fakhara, ar. to glory). Pride. Prefixed to alam makes a lacab; as Iftikhar hoossain, pride of hoossain; Iftikhar ool moolk, ornament of the state [ism].

IJAURA (اجارة - ijárah, *Hind.*). From (ajr, ar. hire). A contract, lease [gootta]. Ijauradar is a contractor [goottadar, moostajar]. There is a hindostany proverb:—اجارة اجاڑ— "farming is famishing."

IJAUZ (اعجاز - ijáz, *Ar.*). From (ajiza, ar. to lack strength); as proving the weakness of the adversary. Miracle. Prefixed to alam makes lacab; as Ijauz hoossain, miracle of hoossain [ism].

IJMAH (اجماع - ijmá, *Hind.*). From (jama, ar. to collect) [jamaut, jumma]. The concordant decisions of the companions of Mahomed and of the general assemblies on matters theological, civil and criminal; received by the Soonnees [q.v.] as a third source of legal authority, after Koran [q.v.] and Soonnat [q.v.].

IKRAR (اقرار - ikrár, *Hind.*). From (karra, ar. to settle) [caraur, istikraur]. Fixing firmly. Ikrarnauma is a deed of acknowledgment.

IKTIAR (اختيار - ikhtiár, *Hind.*). From (khárah, ar. to choose). Choice, will. Doctrine of free will [takdeer] held by the orthodox mahomedans; that man has been endowed with the capacity to understand God's commands, that he is neither the absolute master of his actions [tafweez] nor bound by fixed immutable decrees [jabr]. Iktiar nauma is a power-of-attorney [adhicaura patrica, mooctiar nauma].

ILANG ILANG (النك النك - alangalang, *Malay*). Title otherwise Cananga flower tree. Botanically Cananga odorata, h. f. and t., anonaceæ [vricsham, 4]. Generic name from malay. Alias Uvaria odorata. Tall tree; trunk straight; bark smooth, ashy; shoots glabrous; leaves five to eight by two to three inches, most puberulous on the veins beneath, base rounded, margins waved; petiole $\frac{1}{2}$ inch; flowers three inches long, usually ternate, drooping, yellow, odorous; peduncles solitary or several from old scars; pedicles one inch, recurved, hoary, with a few basal and median scaly bract; petals $\frac{1}{3}$ inch, base broad, silky when young; carpels about twelve, $\frac{1}{2}$ to $\frac{1}{3}$ inch, ovoid or obovoid, black, six to twelve-seeded. An attar [q.v.] prepared from the flowers; frequently blended with pimento [china pepper], orris, rose [gool], tuberose, and jasmine [q.v.] in the preparation of european handkerchief [roomaul] scents.

ILANJY (बकुल - bakula, *San.*; बकुली - bakulí, *Mahr.*; वोव्वलि - vóvali, *Conc.*; مولسرى - molsarí, *Hind.*; گهولسرى - gholsarí, *Dec.*; ಪಗಡೆ - pagade, *Can.*; ರೆಂಜಿ - renji, *Too.*; పొగడ - pogada, *Tel.*; ବାଉଳ - baulo, *Oor.*; ഇരഞ്ഞി - iraññi, *Mal.*; මුනමල් - múnamal, *Singh.*; மகிழம் - magizham, *Tam.*). Title from malayalam. San. from (vak, san. to go crookedly). Mahr. and conc. from sanscrit. Dec. from hindostany. Tel. means coral, from fruit. Oor. from sanscrit. Mal. from (ireyu, mal. to murmur); from murmuring noise produced when wind blows upon the tree. Singh. from (muna, singh. face + mal, singh.

flower); cf. generic name. Tam. from (magizh, tam. to rejoice); from fragrance of flower. San. also (késara), meaning filament [kamela, nauga champak, poison bamboo, saffron]; (simhakésara), meaning lion's mane; (anangaká), meaning pertaining to cupid, from odour of flower; (makura), meaning adorned. Hind. also (bakulmolsarí). Dec. also (bholsarí); (tendu) [coromandel ebony]. Can. also (renji), from malayalam; (mugali); (minjulu). Mal. also (ilaññi), by corruption. Tam. also (vagulam), corruption from sanscrit. Title otherwise Adam's apple [adam's apple, sweet lime], Ape-face flower, Buckool, Elengi, Gholsaree, Kaisaram, Magizham, Mogadam, Molsaree, Monkey-face flower, Pogada, Pointed-leaved mimusops, Taindoo [coromandel ebony], Vacoolam, West indian medlar. Botanically Mimusops [csheericay] elengi, linn., sapotaceæ [vricsham, 82]. Alias Mimusops lucida. Elengi from malayalam. Tree, middling size, of slow growth; leaves alternate, oval-lanceolate or oblong, acuminated, glabrous; pedicels shorter than the petioles, many together, one-flowered; calyx eight cleft, in a double series, segments lanceolate, four exterior ones larger and permanent; corolla-tube very short, fleshy, segments in a double series, exterior ones sixteen, spreading, interior ones eight, generally contorted, and converging, lanceolate, and slightly torn at the extremities; berry oval, smooth, yellow when ripe, usually one-celled; seeds solitary, oblong; produces during hot season small white or pale green fragrant flowers which fall in showers, succeeded by the small, egg-shaped yellow one-seeded berries. Celebrated in pooraunams [q.v.] and placed amongst flowers of paradise [poonyoshadhy]. The substance of the bark is red, it is covered externally by a very thick grey suber on the older branches, which separates in irregular scales, leaving isolated attached portions which consist of five or more distinct suberous layers; the inner surface is red and presents a coarsely striated surface; fracture short, disclosing white specks and stains in the substance of the bark caused by the drying up of the milky juice which it contained when fresh; the taste is bitter, astringent and mucilaginous. Bark medicinally tonic, and antiperiodic; in pharm. non-officinal; water distilled from flowers used in melancholia. Berries have a small quantity of sweetish pulp, sometimes eaten; flowers also eaten. Bark makes a brown color with myrobalans [q.v.]; flowers used as a perfume; grown also for shade; the seed-oil in request by painters [rangh]; an odoriferous water [attar] distilled from the flowers; gives a gum [gond]. Timber close and even-grained, pinkish to reddish brown in color, takes a good polish.——*Foreign ilanjy* (சீமைமகிழம் - shímaimagizham, Tam.). Title from resemblance. Tam. from (shímai, tam. foreign + magizham, tam. mimusops elengi, linn.). Can. also (olay), in use among burghers. Tam. also (pálai), meaning milky tree [dita, edible paulay, eve's apple, ground paulay, monkey-face paulay, nakchiknee silk cotton, naugachampak, pauchonty, paula indigo, paulay silk cotton, tellicherry bark]. Title otherwise Buckool sapota, Bully tree, Iron wood [cassa, chowkmaram, dark vail, deccany deodar, nauga champak, yellow condray]. Botanically Sideroxylon tomentosum, roxb., sapotaceæ [vricsham, 82]. Alias Achras elengioides, tomentosa; Sapota elengioides, tomentosa; Sideroxylon elengioides. Small tree, unarmed; leaves oval, undulated, obtusely narrowed at the apex, younger ones rufous-tomentose; fascicles of flowers axillary, many-flowered; pedicels shorter than the flower and with the calyx silky-pubescent; lobes of the calyx ovate-acute, outer ones broader, corolla twice as long as the calyx; sterile stamens lanceolate-subulate, hispid outside; berry broad ellipsoid, size of an olive [zeitoon], yellow; flowers small, dull white; flowering in the hot season. Fruit made into pickles [chutney] and curries [q.v.]. Wood dull red color, short but straight in the grain and very dense, makes good beams for houses, splits too much to be used for planks; if well seasoned turns well and makes excellent carpenter's planes; sinks in water and corrodes like iron [auban].

ILAUHEE (الہی - iláhí, *Hind.*). From (iláh, hind. god) [allah]. Divine. Title of era [saca] instituted by Acbar [q.v.], commencing with first year of his reign, A.H. 963, A.D. 1556; it did not obtain currency. He embraced what he called Ilauhee mazhab or divine religion of peace with all the world. The Ilauhee was his gold coin, value Rs. 10; also called Laul e jalauly meaning jalaul's ruby, Jalaul [q.v.] being Acbar's name. Ilauhee guz was Acbar's yard of 41 finger breadths [alavay, le]; approximate actual value, 33 inches.

ILAUKA (علاقہ - ilákah, *Hind.*). From (alaka, ar. to hang). Connection, jurisdiction, district [zillah], department.

ILAVA (ഈഴവ - ízhuva, obl.; ഈഴവൻ - ízhuvan, pers. sing.; ഈഴവർ - ízhuvar, pers. pl. *Mal.*). From (ízham, mal. ceylon). Literally Ceylonese [ceylon, eelam]. Tribal-title. These are a branch of a great and wide-spread race of people that occupies South tinnevelly, Travancore, and the Malabar coast as far as the Tooloo country. In the far south on both coasts they are known as Shaunaur [q.v.]; in Central travancore as Ilavar; from Quilon to Paravore as Choganmaur; in Malabar, as far as Calicut, as Teeyar [q.v.]; and still farther north as Billawa [q.v.], a slightly altered form of Ilavar. They immigrated into Malabar from Ceylon, bringing the cocoanut tree along with them. Cf. Dweepar. See vol. II, 99. The Panikkar [q.v.] or artificer is priest of this caste. The special occupation of the Ilavar is the culture of the cocoanut [q.v.] palm, and the manufacture from it of toddy [q.v.] and ardent spirits [arrack]; they are also general agriculturists; some are weavers and boatmen, and a few are petty-traders, teachers, priests, doctors, and such like. Demon worship, especially that of Bhadra cauly [q.v.], is the customary cultus of the tribe, with sacrifices and offerings and devil-dancing like the Shaunaur. Shaustauv [q.v.] and Veerabhadran [q.v.] are also venerated, and the ghosts of ancestors [pitry]. Groves [canv] of trees stand near the temples, and serpent [cobra] images are common, these creatures being accounted favorites of Cauly. The Ilavar who assemble for festival wear the marks of Shiva [q.v.], a dot and horizontal lines on the forehead, and three horizontal lines of yellow turmeric [country saffron] on the chest. The Ilavar proper follow Makkatoyem [q.v.]. Usually the body is buried, either wrapped in mats, or enclosed in a coffin; but if the deceased had been distinguished for wealth, social position, or great age, the remains are burnt. Total numbers about 20,000 [jauty].

ILAY (इला - ilá, *San.*). From (il, san. to go); flow, draught. Libation to the gods [deva]. Food. Earth, source of giving and feeding; also cow, as giving milk. Also the daughter of Menoo, as the thinking man worshipping the gods; she is the goddess of worship and libation, of refreshment and animation; so also of transformation and development. Also in the pooraunams, a son of Veivaswatan [q.v.], the Noah of the Aryans [q.v.], transformed into a woman. On this son a curse from Shiva [q.v.] and Parvaty [q.v.] rested to the effect that he should become a woman for the crime of intruding on their privacy. This resembles the curse from Noah on Ham. Compare the Greek Tiresias. The story is probably a symbol for a change of opinion in religion, by substituting a feminine power [shacty] in creation for a masculine energy.——*Ilauvritam* (इलावृत - ilávrita, San.). From (above + vrita, san. surrounded). One of the central divisions of Jamboo dweepam [q.v.] or asia. See vol. I (3).

ILL (ఇల్లు - illu, *Tel.*; இல் - il, *Tam.*). House.——*Illacoor* (ഇല്ലക്കൂർ - illakkúr, Mal.). From (above + kúr, mal. share). House share. The private property of a w. coast rajah which descends to his heirs. He relinquishes this property to his nephew or next heir [maroomakkatoyem] upon his giving up one official dignity [staunam] for a higher step. Not that he absolutely gives up all control over it, but this arrangement is made to distinguish and separate it from the public property of the official station he has just held, and to prevent its being claimed by his successor in it [maryauday].——*Illam* (ഇല്ലം - illam, Mal.). House. Especially a Numboory bramin's house in Malabar [mana]. A clan among certain tribes [poolaya] for the purpose of prohibiting marriage therein. Cf. Gotram.——*Illaram* (இல்லறம் - illaram, Tam.). Domestic life [aram].——*Illaricam* (ఇల్లరికము - illarikamu, Tel.). From (above + rikamu, tel. suffix meaning state). Connexion by descent from a common ancestor, marked by bearing same family or house name [illatam]. Cf. Gotram among bramins [q.v.].——*Illatam* (ఇల్లటము - illatamu, Tel.). From (above + áta, tel. stage performance, hence life). Residence of son-in-law permanently at father-in-law's house. A son-in-law so living receives in some castes an equal share in the father-in-law's property along with sons [maryauday]. Cf. Dutt.

ILM (علم - ilm, *Hind.*). From (alama, ar. to know). Science [shastram].——*Ilm i ab* (علم آب - ilmiáb, Hind.). Means science of water. Hydraulics.——*Ilm i adab* (علم ادب - ilmiadab, Hind.). Means science of discipline of mind. Science of Polite literature.——*Ilmiakhlauk* (علم اخلاق - ilmiakhlák, Hind.). Means science of manners. Moral philosophy.——*Ilmiaroozy* (علم عروضی - ilmiarúzí, Hind.). Means science of versification. Prosody.——*Ilm i avauz* (علم آواز - ilmiáváz, Hind.). Means science of sound. Accoustics.——*Ilmi balaughat* (علم بلاغت - ilmibalághat, Hind.). Also (ilmibayán). Rhetoric.——*Ilm i basr* (علم بصر - ilmibasr, Hind.). Means science of sight. Optics.——*Ilm i calaum* (علم کلام - ilmikalám, Hind.). Means science of logos. Metaphysics.——*Ilm i coolyaut* (علم کلیات - ilmikuliyát, Hind.). Integral calculus.——*Ilm i falsafee* (علم فلسفی - ilmifalsafí, Hind.). Philosophy.——*Ilm i fikh* (علم فقہ - ilmifikha, Hind.). Jurisprudence.——*Ilmi filzaut* (علم فلزات - ilmifilzát, Hind.). Metallurgy.——*Ilm i havah* (علم ہوا - ilmihavá, Hind.). Means science of air. Pneumatics.——*Ilm i heivanaut* (علم حیوانات - ilmihaivánát, Hind.). Zoology.——*Ilm i heiyat* (علم ہئیت - ilmihaiyat, Hind.). Means the science of outward form of heavens. Astronomy.——*Ilm i hindsa* (علم ہندسہ - ilmihindasah, Hind.). Means science of figures. Geometry.——*Ilm i hindsa biljabr* (علم ہندسہ بالجبر - ilmihindasahbiljabr, Hind.). Analytical geometry.——*Ilm i hisaub* (علم حساب - ilmihisáb, Hind.). Means science of accounting. Arithmetic.——*Ilm i ilauhy* (علم الہی - ilmiiláhí, Hind.). Means science of god. Theology.——*Ilm i imaraut* (علم عمارات - ilmiimárát, Hind.). Means science of building. Architecture.——*Ilm i inshah* (علم انشا - ilmiinshá, Hind.). Belles lettres.——*Ilm i jabromoocaubilah*

(علم جبرو مقابلہ - ilmijabromukábalah, Hind.). Means science of perfective addition and compensative subtraction, because of the frequency of these operations in the reduction of equations. Also (aljabr). Algebra.——*Ilm i jarr i sakeel* (علم جرثقیل - ilmijarrisakíl, Hind.). Means science of heavy base. Mechanics. ——*Ilm i jooghraufiyah* (علم جغرافیہ - ilmijughráfiyah, Hind.). Geography.——*Ilm i joozyaut* (علم جزیات - ilmijuzyát, Hind.). Differential calculus.——*Ilm i keemiyah* (علم کیمیا - ilmikímiyah, Hind.). Alchemy.——*Ilm i kiyaufa* (علم قیافہ - ilmikiyáfah, Hind.). Means science of appearance. Physiognomy.——*Ilm i madaniyaut* (علم معدنیات - ilmimadaniyát, Hind.). Mineralogy. ——*Ilm i mantik* (علم منطق - ilmimantik, Hind.). Means science of speech. Logic.——*Ilm i masauhat* (علم مساحت - ilmimasáhat, Hind.). Mensuration.——*Ilm i moodan* (علم مدن - ilmimudun, Hind.). Means science of cities. Also (ilmisiyásatimudun), meaning science of government of cities. Politics.——*Ilm i moosallas* (علم مثلث - ilmimusallas, Hind.). Means science of trilateral or triangular figures. Trigonometry.——*Ilm i moosiky* (علم موسیقی - ilmimúsíkí, Hind.). Music.——*Ilm i moosowiry* (علم مصوری - ilmimusawwirí, Hind.). Painting.——*Ilm i nabataut* (علم نباتات - ilminabátát, Hind.). Means science of plants. Botany.—— *Ilm i noojoom* (علم نجوم - ilminujúm, Hind.). Means science of stars. Astrology.——*Ilm i raml* (علم رمل - ilmiraml, Hind.). Means science of sand or earth. Also (ilmikhatt) or science of lines. Geomancy.——*Ilm i rasm ool arz* (علم رسم الارض - ilmirasmularz, Hind.). Mathematical geography.——*Ilm i riyauzy* (علم ریاضی - ilmiriyází, Hind.). Means science of learning. Mathematics.——*Ilm i tabaee* (علم طبعی - ilmitabaí, Hind.). Natural philosophy.——*Ilm i tasawoof* (علم تصوف - ilmitasawwuf, Hind.). Mysticism.——*Ilm i tashreeh* (علم تشریح - ilmitashríh, Hind.). Anatomy.——*Ilm i tashreehool arz* (علم تشریح الارض - ilmitashríhularz, Hind.). Means science of anatomy of earth. Geology.——*Ilm i taureek* (علم تاریخ - ilmitárikh, Hind.). Means science of date. History.——*Ilm i tazkira* (علم تذکرہ - ilmitazkirah, Hind.). Means science of memoir. Biography.—— *Ilm i teerandauzy* (علم تیراندازی - ilmitírandází, Hind.). Means science of shooting arrows. Archery.——*Ilm i tibb* (علم طب - ilmitibb, Hind.). Medicine.——*Ilm ool yadd* (علم الید - ilmulyadd, Hind.). Means science of hand. Palmistry.

IMAUD (عماد - imád, *Ar.*). From (amada, ar. to support). Pillar. Part of lacab; as Imaud ood deen, pillar of religion, Imaud ool moolk, pillar of the state [ism]. Imaud shahy was dynasty [raj] which ruled at Berar from 1484 to 1568 [charitram]. See vol. I, (148); II 252.

IMAUM (امام - imám, *Hind.*). From (amma, ar. to preside). Prelate. The title of the four great doctors of the four orthodox Soonnee [q.v.] sects; Shahfayee, Aboo haneefa, Malik and Hambal. Also the title of the twelve leaders of the Shiah [q.v.] sect. Also given to any religious leader in religious matters, whether the head of all Mahomedans as the caliph [q.v.], or the priest of a mosque [musjid] or the leader in the prayers [namauz] of the congregation. In the Koran [q.v.] Abraham, Isaac, and Jacob are called imaums. Common Mahomedan alam; as Imaum ally, double alam [ism].——*Imaumat* (امامت - imámat, Hind.). The office of imaum. The question of imaumat forms a subject of controversy between the followers of the different sects of Mahomedans.——*Imaumiah* (امامیہ - imámiyah, Hind.). The Shiah [q.v.] sect, from their recognizing twelve Imaums in direct hereditary descent from Ally and Fatima, prophet's daughter.

IMAUN (ایمان - ímán, *Hind.*). From the (amn, ar. security) [amaun, ameen]. Faith; according to Mahomedans, interior belief, and exterior confession to six articles of creed, viz., God, angels of god [ferishta], books of God, prophets of God, day of judgment, and predestination [takdeer] to good and evil [islam].

IMAURAT (عمارت - imárat, *Hind.*). From (amara, ar. to dwell). A mansion, public building.

IMMY (இம்மி - immi, *Tam.*). 1,075,200th part of a unit.

IMPERIAL (شاهی - sháhí, Hind.). Prefix denoting superior size and excellence.——*Imperial dove* (رام گهوگهو - rámgghuggú, Hind.; అండిబెల్లగువ్వ - andibellaguvva, Tel.). Hind. from (rám, hind. rama + ghuggú, hind. owl); from cry. Tel. from (andi, tel. kind of metallic vessel + bellaguvva, tel. dove); from brown color of under parts. Hind. also (rájghugghú), meaning king dove. Title otherwise Bronze-winged dove, Ground dove. Chalcophaps indicus, phapinæ, gouridæ, gemitores [pacshy, 30], of naturalists [jantoo]. Alias Columba javanica, superciliaris. Back and wings shining dark emerald green, slightly glossed golden; beneath whole neck, breast and lower parts vinaceous red-brown, paler on lower abdomen; feeds mostly on the ground; flight very rapid; generally seen alone; voice a low plaintive moan. No other common species here.——*Imperial pigeon* (شاهی کبوتر - sháhíkabútar, Hind.). See under Haritaulam.

IMPHEE CANE (ಇಂಪಿಗಿಡ - impigida, *Can.*). Title from canarese, meaning sweet plant. Same as Sweet cholum.

IN (ان - in, *Ar.*). If.——*Insha* (انشا - inshá, Hind.). From (above + shá, ar. please). If it please.——*Insha allah* (انشاءالله - insháalláh, Hind.). If it please God! Ejaculation of Mahomedans.

INAM (انعام - inám, *Hind.*; ఇనాము - inámu, *Tel.*; இனம் - inám, *Tam.*). From (nama, ar. to confer favor). Generally a gift from a superior to an inferior [daunam]. So a grant of land for religious or charitable purposes, made by government. Sometimes given free, sometimes with light quitrent or jody [q.v.]. Same as Maunyam [q.v.]. Technically a Major inam is a whole village [dehaut] or more than one village, and a Minor inam is something less than a village [graumam]. A shrotriem [q.v.] ranks as a major inam; a khandriga [q.v.] as a minor inam. See vol. I, paras. 203 and 204, and the various distinguishing definitions there given. The following is a list of the principal inam tenures past or present of the Presidency, by the names under which they are generally known to the people.——*Acharya pooroosham* (ஆசாரியப்புருடம் - ásáriyappurudam, Tam.). Means priest + man. For the service of head priest [acharry] in a pagoda [q.v.].——*Adhyayanam* (அத்தியயனம் - attiyayanam, Tam.). Means study of sacred books. For reciting Vedas [q.v.] in pagodas [cuttyam, vedavritty].——*Agny poomaun* (அக்கினிப்புமான் - akkinippumán, Tam.). Means fire + man. For dancing before the village goddess with a pot containing fire [gadigey].——*Agrahauram* (அக்கிரகாரம் - akkiragáram, Tam.). A village, or part of a village, occupied by Bramins [q.v.] and held at a favorable rate of assessment [teervay]; sometimes rent-free [bhattavrity, dehaut, kheiraaty, shrotriem]. See sep. title.——*Alavan* (அளவன் - alavan, Tam.). Means measurer. Held by village officer, who measures the grain, where the assessment is paid in kind.——*Amaram* (அமரம் - amaram, Tam.). Means the command of one thousand footmen. A grant of land by a poligar [q.v.] on condition of service, such grants being resumable when the grantee fails to perform service [bissoye, mokhausa, oomblikay]. See sep. title. ——*Ambalacauran* (அம்பலக்காரன் - ambalakkáran, Tam.). Means councilman. Held by the headmen of villages, particularly of villages inhabited by Shoodras [q.v.]. See sep. title.—— *Ambaly* (انبل - ambil, Hind.). For supplying to the poor thick conjee [q.v.].——*Ambicaur* (امبکار - ambikár, Hind.). For ferryman's service.——*Anaicauran* (அணைக்காரன் - anaikkáran, Tam.). Means anicut-man. For preserving anicuts [q.v.] in good order and for keeping off cattle, &c.——*Anakala* (అనకల - anakala, Tel.). Held by cuttoobuddy [q.v.] peons [q.v.] whose duty it was to carry provisions to village and talook officials.—— *Angazaula* (అంగజాల - angadzála, Tel.). Means a sentinel. For distributing water to the fields and collecting ryots [q.v.] for the performance of customary labor [aulotty, coody maraumut].—— *Annacauvady* (அன்னக்காவடி - annakkávadi, Tam.). Means cooked rice + shoulder pole. For collecting boiled rice from door to door and feeding beggars [sadauvritty].——*Anna shrotriem* (அணசுரோத்திரியம் - anásuróttiriyam, Tam.). Inam villages in which the interest of the inamdar is so many annas [q.v.] out of each rupee [q.v.] of revenue, the rest going to the Government [hissa shrotriem].——*Arasoo cauval* (அரசுக்காவல் - arasukkával, Tam.). Means king + police. For performing general police duties [desha cauval, men cauval]. In contradistinction to Grauma cauval [q.v.] or village police.——*Aray* (அறை - arai, Tam.). Means room. For service of storekeeper in pagoda [q.v.].——*Archanay bhaugam* (அருச்சனைப்பாகம் - aruççanaippágam, Tam.). Means worship + portion. For service of poojarry [q.v.] in pagoda [gooroocal, numby].——*Ardha maunyam* (அருத்தமானியம் - aruttamániyam, Tam.). Means half + gift. Land half rent-free.——*Ashoorkhana* (عاشورخانہ - áshúrkhánah, Hind.). Means ten-day + house. For maintenance of building in which bier, banners, and insignia used at Moharram [q.v.] are set up.——*Athirvedy* (அதிர்வெடி - athirvedi, Tam.). Means thundering explosion. For discharging rockets during festivals.——*Atsoocauvaly* (అచ్చుకావలి - attsukávali, Tel.). Means recompense + guard. For guarding a tract with the obligation of making good the value of any property stolen.——*Attar* (عطر - itr, Hind.). From arabic. For supplying perfumes to the poligar [q.v.]. See sep. title.——*Aulotty* (ஆளோட்டி - álotti, Tam.). Means man + driver. For collecting ryots [q.v.] for the performance of customary labor [angazaula, coody maraumut].—— *Aundy samaudhy* (ஆண்டிசமாதி - ándisamáthi, Tam.). Means an aundy's tomb. For support of tomb [gor] of an Aundy [q.v.].——*Ausaudy* (ఆసాది - ásádi, Tel.). Means musician. For beating a drum [paray] before the village deity [davanday, grauma devatay, pambacauran, pambalam, zaumilica].——*Bady baud* (బడిబాడు - badibádu, Tel.). Means petty + fee. Lands held on favorable assessment generally by Rauchavaur [rancha] caste in Godavery and Kistna.——*Badhy* (بڑهئی - barhai, Hind.). For acting as village carpenter [tutchan, vadla].——*Baly* (பலி - pali, Tam.). Means sacrifice. For making sacrifices to village deities [bhoota baly, gauvoo, grauma devatay].——*Bandela* (బందెల - bandela, Tel.). Means a cattle pound. Held by inferior village servants for preventing cattle from straying into the fields [putty].——*Bantoomena* (బంటుమేన - bantuména, Tel.). For doing service as a peon [q.v.].——*Bariky* (బరికి - bariki, Tel.). The same as Toty [boorky].——*Baroot goly* (باروت گولی - bárúdgolí, Hind.). Means powder + bullet. For supplying the poligar [q.v.] with gunpowder and ball.——*Basavy* (బసవి - basavi, Tel.). Means a prostitute. Held by prostitutes who have been married or dedicated to Shiva [q.v.], and who attend upon the idol [cunchany, dausy, vigraham]. See sep. title.——*Baugh maury* (باگھ ماری - bághmárí, Hind.). Means tiger + killing. Granted as a reward for killing tigers [poolicutt, pooly].——*Baunagar* (வாணக்காரன் - vánakkáran, Tam.). For making fire works [baunam] for pagodas [q.v.] or zemindars [q.v.].——*Begaury* (బేగారి - bégári, Tel.). The same as Vetty [maula].——*Beineedy* (బైనీడి - bainídi, Tel.). For singing before the village deity [cuttyam, othoovaun, sooddoola].——*Beldar* (بیلدار - beldár, Hind.). Means pickaxe + holder. For performing bricklayer's work [caumauty, collatt cauran].——*Bhaley log* (بھلے لوگ - bhalelog, Hind.). Means good + people. Rent-free lands to persons of rank.——*Bhatrauz* (భట్రాజు - bhatrádzu, Tel.). Means a bard. For singing praises of poligar [cavy royan, poolavan, sangeetam].——*Bhattavritty* (பட்டவிருத்தி - pattavirutti, Tam.). Means a bramin + profit. For support of Bramins [kheirauty, shrotriem]. See sep. title.——*Bhouraty* (பாரதி - párathi, Tam.). For reading Mahabhaurat [q.v.] in pagodas [q.v.]. Cf. Khateeb and Pooraunam.——*Bhoota baly* (பூதப்பலி - púthappali, Tam.). Means spirit + offering. For making offerings to malignant spirits during festivals of the village deities [baly, gauvoo].——*Bilmacta* (بالمقطع - bilmakta, Hind.). Means with fixed rent. Lands held at a fixed rent below the usual standard. See sep. title.——*Bissoye* (బిస్సాయి - bissáyi, Tel.). Tenure of a class of hill chieftains in Ganjam who used to hold their lands for performing military or police service [amaram, doratanam, mokhausa]. See sep. title.——*Bommalauttam* (பொம்மலாட்டம் - pommaláttam, Tam.). Means puppet + dance. For exhibiting puppet shows at festivals.——*Boorj* (برج - burj, Hind.). Means bastion. For building a bastion for protection of a village [cottah, kota].——*Boorky* (బూర్కి - búrki, Tel.). The same as Toty [bariky].——*Boy* (بھوئی - bhoí, Hind.). For service as a palankeen-bearer [shendhy]. See sep. title.——*Bramhadauyam* (பிரம்மதாயம் - pirammatháyam, Tam.). Means bramin + gift. A general term denoting inams held by Bramins [q.v.] for their personal benefit [kheirauty].——*Calingoo maunyam* (கலிங்குமானியம் - kalingumániyam, Tam.). Means sluice + inam. For having constructed a sluice [calingula] for surplus water of a tank [q.v.].——*Caraiyeed* (கரையீடு - karaiyídu, Tam.). Means boundary + to assign. Tenure under which the lands of a village are exchanged amongst the coparceners periodically [pasancaray].——*Caray maunyam* (கரைமானியம் - karaimániyam, Tam.). Means bank + inam. The same as Coola vett.——*Carpoor deepam* (கர்ப்பூரதீபம் - karppúrattíbam, Tam.). Means camphor + light. For burning camphor [q.v.] in pagodas [coombhauraty].——*Casye* (قصائی - kasáí, Hind.). For support of a butcher.——*Caulvye pannaudy* (కాలువపన్నాడి - kálavapannádi, Tel.). Means channel + servant. For opening and closing irrigation channels [channel, madayvetty, neergunty].——*Caumauty* (کاماتی - kámátí, Hind.). For the support of bricklayer [collatt cauran] attached to pagoda [beldar].——*Caupoo* (కాపు - kápu, Tel.). Same as Peddacaup [dolabehara, gowda, monigar]. See sep. title.——*Caurjy* (కార్జి - kárji, Tel.). Held by a village officer in Ganjam and Orissa.——*Cauvalgar* (காவற்காரன் - kávargáran, Tam.). Means watchman. For the service of a village watchman [taliyary, tookry]. See sep. title.——*Cauyam jody* (కాయంజోడి - káyamjódi, Tel.). Means permanent + rent. An inam held on a fixed quit-rent [jody] not subject to variation with reference to cultivation or produce [hangaumy jody].——*Cauzy* (قاضی - kází, Hind.). From (kaza, ar. decree). For service as Cauzy. See sep. title.——*Cavy royan* (கவிராயன் - kavuráyan, Tam.). Means poet + king. Held by Tamul poets, generally in the service of poligars [bhatrauz, poolavan].——*Cawny maunyam* (காணிமானியம் - kánimániyam, Tam.). Means acre + gift. Same as Grauma maunyam [oor].——*Chamaur* (چمار - chamár, Hind.). For making leather bags [mhote, yaittachaul] for drawing water and other leather [chamrah] work for villages [maudiga].——*Chatoor bhaugam* (சதுர்ப்பாகம் - shathurppágam, Tam.). Means four + part. Inams consisting of one-fourth share of the Government revenue [khirauj, pauticabuddy].——*Chauvady* (சாவடி - shávadi, Tam.). Means choultry [q.v.]. For its support. See sep. title.——*Checkbundy* (چکبندی - chakbandí, Hind.). Means limit + fixing. An inam with defined boundaries as distinguished from one without any fixed locality, such as an Eey [q.v.] or Dittam [q.v.] inam. See sep. title.——*Chinna mailam* (சின்னமேளம் - shinnamélam, Tam.). Means small + band. Granted to a band of musicians with a dancing girl [dausy, mailam].——*Chowdry* (چودھری - chaudhrí, Hind.). Granted to the headman of a trade for settling caste disputes [deshye].——*Chunk coolicauran* (சங்குகுளிக்காரன் - shangugulikkáran, Tam.). Means conch + diver. For diving for chunk [q.v.] shells.——*Chunk naudam* (சங்கநாதம் - shanganátham, Tam.). Means conch + sound. For blowing a conch [q.v.] shell in a pagoda [q.v.].——*Chuttram* (சத்திரம் - shattiram, Tam.). For the support of a chuttram [othookkam]. See sep. title.——*Collan* (கொல்லன் - kollan, Tam.). Means blacksmith. For the service of village blacksmith [cummara, lohaur]. See sep. title.——*Comboo* (கொம்பு - kombu, Tam.). Means horn. For blowing horn before the Tahsildar [q.v.].——*Conda cauvaly* (కొండకావలి - kondakávali, Tel.). Means hill + guard. For watching hills and jungles.——*Cooday vritty* (குடைவிருத்தி - kudaivirutti, Tam.). Means umbrella + profit. For holding an umbrella over the village deity during festivals [godoogoo].——*Coolacauval* (குளக்காவல் - kulakkával, Tam.). Means tank + watch. For guarding tanks [q.v.] and seeing that the ryots [q.v.] do not waste the water.——*Coola vett* (குளவெட்டு - kulavettu, Tam.). Means tank + digging. For the service of collecting work-people to repair tanks [caray maunyam].——*Coombaura* (کمہار - kumhár, Hind.). For the service of village potter [coosavan]. See sep. title.——*Coombhauraty* (கும்பாரதி - kumbárathi, Tam.). Means pot + light. Held by dancing girls [dausy] for the service of carrying a light placed at the top of a water-jar round the principal idol during the performance of poojah [q.v.] in a pagoda [carpoordeepam, panippen]. Distinguish from Cumbhurty. See sep. title.——*Coorooba* (కురుబ - kuruba, Can.). Means a shepherd. For providing sheep [and] for the sacrifices to the village deities. Distinguish from Golla [q.v.]. See sep. title.——*Coosavan* (குசவன் - kusavan, Tam.). Means potter. The same as Coombaura. See sep. title.——*Coottaudy* (கூத்தாடி - kúttádi, Tam.). Means dancer. For dancing before the village deity [devamedy].——*Cotwaul* (کوتوال - kotwál, Hind.). Means fort + master. Held for being the chief police officer of a town. See sep. title.——*Covilagam* (കോവിലകം - kóvilakam, Mal.). Land given for site of residence of a rajah or of Bramins. See sep. title.——*Covil kanak* (கோவிற்கணக்கு - kóvirganakku, Tam.). Means temple + account. For keeping pagoda [q.v.] accounts.——*Cullvailay* (கல்வேலை - kalvélai, Tam.). Means stone + work. For service as sculptor in stone in a pagoda [sangtaraush].——*Cumbamcutty* (కంబంకట్టి - kambamkatti, Tel.). Means pole + fixer. Same as Neergunty.——*Cumbhurty* (کم بھرتی - kambhartí, Hind.). Means deficient + supply. Land granted to village officers in Ceded districts [q.v.] to make up their inams to the standard scale of emolument. Distinguish from Coombhauraty.——*Cummara* (కమ్మర - kammara, Tel.). Means blacksmith. For service of village blacksmith [collan, lohaur]. See sep. title.——*Cumsala* (కంసల - kamsala, Tel.). Means goldsmith. For the service of village goldsmith. See sep. title.——*Cunchany* (کنچنی - kanchaní, Hind.). Land held by dancing girls [basavy, dausy].——*Cundachauram* (కందాచారం - kandácháram, Tel.). Means native militia. Held by cuttoobuddy [q.v.] peons [q.v.] employed in the western talooks of Bellary.——*Cungauny* (கண்காணி - kangáni, Tam.). Means eye + seer. Held for watching crops. See sep. title.——*Curnum* (కరణం - karanam, Tel.). Means accountant. For the service of village accountant [sampraty]. See sep. title.——*Cuttoobuddy* (కట్టుబడి - kattubadi, Tel.). Means settlement. Land granted by poligars [q.v.] to peons [q.v.] on condition of military service [amaram, mootraucha]. See sep. title.——*Cuttoo codigey* (కట్టుకొడిగె - kattukódiga, Tel.). Means fixed + twenty. Same as Dasbandam.——*Cuttyam* (கட்டியம் - kattiyam, Tam.). Means panegyric. For proclaiming the praises of an idol when carried in procession [adhyayanam, beineedy, othoovaun, sooddoola].——*Daiga* (డేగ - déga, Tel.). Means falcon [pattry]. Held by falconers in the service of poligars [q.v.].——*Dandooga* (దండుగ - danduga, Tel.). Means overcharge. Granted by native Governments as a compensation to persons who had suffered from heavy exactions being levied on them for the emergencies of the State.——*Dandya* (దండియ - dandiya, Tel.). Means a bailiff. Held by headmen of Cuttoobuddy [q.v.] peons [q.v.].——*Dasbandam* (దశబంధం - dashabandham, Tel.). Means ten in hundred. An allowance of land, Khanda dasbandam; or of revenue, Shaumilaut [q.v.] dasbandam; given as a compensation for the construction of a tank [q.v.], well, or channel [q.v.]. The grant generally though not invariably, carries with it the condition of keeping the work in repair [cuttoo codigey]. See sep. title.——*Daukkal inam* (داخل انعام - dákhalinám, Hind.). Means entered + inam. Inams entered in any particular register [dufter gardens, gheir daukkal].——*Dausy* (தாசி - tási, Tam.). Means dancing girl. For the service of dancing girl in a pagoda [basavy, cunchany]. For the service of headman of a village. See sep. title.——*Davanday* (தவண்டை - tavandai, Tam.). For beating in pagodas [q.v.] the drum so called [ausaudy, pambacauran, pambalam, zaumilica].——*Dehaut* (دیہات - dehát, Hind.). Means villages. A whole village held as inam [shrotriem]. See sep. title.——*Desha cauval* (தேசக்காவல் - tésakkával, Tam.),

Means district + watch. The same as Mencauval.——*Deshmookh* (దేశముఖం - déshamukham, Tel.). Means district + head. For performing the service of Deshmookh [q.v.], a hereditary native officer under the former governments, exercising chief police and revenue authority over a district and responsible for the revenue. ——*Deshpandya* (దేశపాండ్య - déshapándya, Tel.). Means district + accountant. For performing the service of Deshpandya [q.v.], the hereditary revenue accountant of a district.——*Deshye* (دیسائی - desái, Hind.). Means country. For performing the services of the headman of a talook [q.v.] under the native Government [chowdry].——*Deva dauyam* (தேவதாயம் - tévatháyam, Tam.). Means god + gift. Inam granted for the support of temples [coil, devastaunam].——*Devadiyaul* (தேவடியாள் - tévadiyál, Tam.). Means god + slave. The same as Dausy [basavy].——*Devamedy* (దేవమేడి - dévamédi, Tel.). Means god + friend. Held for dancing before the idol as if under the influence of inspiration [coottaudy].——*Devastaunam* (தேவஸ்தானம் - tévattánam, Tam.). Means god + place. Inam held by pagodas [devadauyam].——*Devatay* (தேவதை - tévathai, Tam.). Means god. Inam granted for worship of village deities [devadauyam]. See sep. title.——*Dharma dauyam* (தருமதாயம் - tarumatháyam, Tam.). Means charity + gift. Inam granted for any charitable purpose.——*Dharmausanam* (தருமாசனம் - tarumásanam, Tam.). Means justice + seat. A village held by Bramins for personal benefit [bramhadauyam].——*Dhoby* (دھوبی - dhobí, Hind.). For the service of village washerman [dhoby, saucala, vunnaun]. See sep. title.——*Dhoorya* (ధూర్య - dhúrya, Tel.). Same as Tandal. ——*Dittam* (దిట్టం - dittam, Tel.). Means settlement. An inam having no locality but consisting of a deduction of a fixed extent of land from the annual cultivation of the village, the proportionate revenue demand on which is paid to the inamdar [eev, checkbundy].——*Dolabehara* (డొలబెహర - dolabehara, Tel.). For support of headman of village [gowda, moliko, monigar, peddacaup].——*Dombar* (ڈومرا - domrá, Hind.). Granted to persons of the Dombar [q.v.] caste [gaurady, nokkan]. See sep. title. ——*Doombauiah* (دنبالہ - dumbálah, Hind.). Means tail. An inam held free of quit-rent [jody].——*Doratanam* (దొరతనం - doratanam, Tel.). Means government. Enjoyed by sirdars [q.v.] in Ganjam for preventing the incursions of hill tribes [bissoye].——*Dufter gardens* (دفتر باغ - daftarbágh, Hind.). Inam gardens entered in the early dufters [q.v.] or records in the district of South arcot and enjoyed as private property without being subject to the ordinary lapse rules [daukkal inam].——*Durgah* (درگاہ - dargáh, Hind.). Means threshold. For service at shrine of Mahomedan saint [gor, pullivausal]. See sep. title.——*Durzee* (درزی - darzí, Hind.). For service of tailor to a zemindar [q.v.] or village community [teiyalcauran].——*Dwaudashy cuttalay* (துவாதசிக்கட்டளை - tuváthasikkattalai, Tam.). Means twelfth day + allotment. For feeding Bramins on the twelfth day [dwaudashy] of each lunar fortnight [pacsham].——*Eev* (ఈవు - ívu, Tel.). Means to give. Same as Dittam [check bundy].——*Gaddateerwa* (గడ్డతీర్వ - gaddatírva, Tel.). Means high level + assessment. Lands on a high level granted on a favorable assessment.——*Gadigey* (గడిగె - gadige, Tel.). Means a pot. For dancing before the village deity, bearing on the head a number of pots, filled some with water and some with fire [agny poomaun].——*Garoodacull* (கருடக்கல் - karudakkal, Tam.). Means kite + stone. For making poojah [q.v.] to the post with bells on the top which is erected before temples [coil, dhwajastambham].——*Gaurady* (గారడి - gáradi, Tel.). Granted to persons skilled in legerdemain [dombar, nokkan].——*Gauvoo* (గావు - gávu, Tel.). Means sacrifice. For offering a sacrifice of a goat [velaud] or fowl [moorghy] at the festivals of the village goddess [baly, bhootabaly].——*Gheir daukkal* (غیر داخلہ - ghairdákhlah, Hind.). Means not + entered. Inams not entered in any particular register [daukkal inam].——*Godoogoo* (గొడుగు - godugu, Tel.). Means an umbrella. For holding an umbrella over the zemindar [cooday vritty].——*Golla* (గొల్ల - golla, Tel.). Means shepherd. For supplying milk [paul] or sheep [aud] to the zemindar [gowda mandey, yidayan]. Distinguish from Coorooba [q.v.]. See sep. title.——*Gooroocal* (குருக்கள் - kurukkal, Tam.). From (guru, san. preceptor). For officiating as a priest in a Sheiva temple [numby, poojarry]. See sep. title.——*Goorrap* (గుర్రపు - gurrapu, Tel.). Means horse. For superintending and breaking in the horses [ghorah] of the zemindar [tabaila]. ——*Gor* (گور - gor, Hind.). Means tomb. For the support of a tomb [durgah, pullivausal]. See sep. title.——*Gowda* (ಗೌಡ - gauda, Can.). For the service of headman of a village [caupoo, dolabehara, monigar, peddacaup]. See sep. title.——*Gowda mandey* (ಗೌಡಮಂಡೆ - gaudamande, Can.). Means village headman + head. For supplying milk [paul] to the zemindar [q.v.] and for manuring the fields of the village by folding sheep [aud, golla, yidayan].——*Grauma bhaugam* (கிராமப்பாகம் - kirámappágam, Tam.). Means village + share. Granted to the Mirassidars [q.v.] of a village in consideration of their having given up their mirassy [q.v.] right to such lands as were granted as inam in their villages.——*Grauma cauval* (கிராமக்காவல் - kirámakkával, Tam.). Means village + watch. For service of a village watchman [arasoo cauval, padicauval, taliyary, vauda cauvaly]. ——*Grauma maunyam* (கிராமமானியம் - kirámamániyam, Tam.). Means village + gift. Inam enjoyed by the whole community of Mirassidars [q.v.] in a village [cawny maunyam, oor].——*Hajaum* (حجام - hajjám, Hind.). For the service of village barber [nauvithan]. See sep. title.——*Hakeem* (حکیم - hakím, Hind.). From (hikm, ar. knowledge). For service of physician [veidyan]. See sep. title.——*Halaulcore* (حلال خور - halálkhor, Hind.). Means lawful + eater. For service of village sweeper [jhaudmauly].——*Hangaumy jody* (హంగామి జోడి - hangámijódi, Tel.). Means temporary + rent. Inam fluctuating from year to year according to the produce or extent of cultivation [cauyam jody].——*Harsaul macta* (ہرسال مقطع - harsálmakta, Hind.). Means every + year + assessment. Land held on a perpetual and invariable rent, generally below the full rent.—— *Hissa shrotriem* (హిస్సాశ్రోత్రియం - hissáshrótriyam, Tel.). Means share + bramin-inam. An inam. Village, the revenue of which is shared between the inamdar and the Government, or the inamdar and the zemindar [q.v.], as the case may be [anna shrotriem].——*Iroomboocutty* (இரும்புக்கட்டி - irumbukkatti, Tam.). Means iron + lump. Granted as an encouragement to manufacture iron [auhan].——*Jagheer* (جاگیر - jagír, Hind.). See sep. title.——*Jeevitam* (ஜீவிதம் - shívitham, Tam.). Means existence. Like Mokhausa [q.v.] in the northern zemindarries, granted by zemindars to their relatives or dependents either for subsistences or on the condition of performing feudal service [amaram].——*Jetty* (جیٹھی - jatthí, Hind.). Held by wrestlers in the service of poligars [q.v.]. See sep. title.——*Joolah hatcar* (جولاھتکار - júláhatkár, Hind.). Granted to weavers to encourage them to settle in a village [pettah gowd].——*Joshy* (جوسی - josí, Hind.). For the service of astrologer and astronomer to the village community. See sep. title.——*Khandriga* (ఖండ్రిగ - khandriga, Tel.). See sep. title.——*Khateeb* (خطیب - khatíb, Hind.). Means preacher. For the service of reading the Koran [q.v.] in a mosque [musjid, pooraunam].——*Khausa* (خاصہ - khása, Hind.). Means own. For domestic service in household of zemindar [q.v.], Northern circars [q.v.].——*Kheirauty* (خیراتی - khairátí, Hind.). Means charity. Inam held for personal benefit by Mahomedans and others not being Bramins [bhattavritty, bramha dauyam, shrotriem].——*Khoolgah* (کھلگا - khulgá, Hind.). Buffalo inam. The same as Potla. See sep. title.——*Kota* (کوٹا - kotá, Hind.). Same as Boorj inam.—— *Lohaur* (لوھار - lohár, Hind.). Same as Cummara [collan]. ——*Lungerkhana* (لنگرخانہ - langarkhánah, Hind.). Means alms + house. For support of alms-house.——*Madavadiyaul* (மடவடியாள் - madavadiyál, Tam.). Means cloister + slave. For sweeper in a temple.——*Madayvetty* (மடைவெட்டி - madaivetti, Tam.). Means sluice + digger. For opening and shutting sluices of a tank and distributing water to the fields [caulvye pannaudy, neergunty].——*Mahsooldar* (محصولدار - mahsúldár, Hind.). Means produce + holder. For preventing clandestine removal of produce of a field before the revenue has been paid. ——*Mahtaud* (مہتاد - mahtád, Hind.). From arabic. For service of village revenue peon [moodaum].——*Mailacar* (மேளக்காரன் - mélakkáran, Tam.). Means bandman. For performing music [sangeetam] in a pagoda [q.v.].——*Mailam* (மேளம் - mélam, Tam.). Means band. For musical band in pagodas [chinna mailam]. See sep. title.——*Maity* (மேட்டி - métti, Tam.). Means chief. Granted to head ryot [q.v.] for encouraging settlement of ryots in the village. See sep. title.—— *Majmoodar* (مجموعہ دار - majmuadár, Hind.). Means total + holder. For district revenue accountant under the native governments.——*Matapaty* (மடப்பதி - madappathi, Tam.). Means choultry + lord. For supplying buttermilk [mor] to public officers, and cooking food for Reddies [q.v.] when they leave village on public duty.——*Maudiga* (మాదిగ - mádiga, Tel.). Same as Chamaur. See sep. title.——*Maula* (మాల - mála, Tel.). Same as Vetty. See sep. title.——*Maulaiyeed* (மாலையீடு - málaiyídu, Tam.). Means garland + give. For keeping in good order burial or burning places [shavacaud, shoodcaud].—— *Maunikkattaul* (மாணிக்கத்தாள் - mánikkattál, Tam.). Means a prostitute. Granted to a dancing girl [dausy] for attending as a mourner in the funeral processions of persons of the Moodelliar [moodelly] caste.——*Maunotty* (மானோட்டி - mánótti, Tam.). Means deer + driver. For driving away deer [mrigam] from crops.——*Mencauval* (மேன்காவல் - méngával, Tam.). Means over + watch. For superior or district watcher under the old native police system [arasoo cauval, desha cauval, maincauvalgar, nautt taliyary].——*Meycauval* (மெய்க்காவல் - meykkával, Tam.). Means body + guard. For guarding the idol [vigraham] in a temple.——*Mohtasib* (محتسب - mohtasib, Hind.). Means calculator. For inspector of weights [niray] and measures [alavay].——*Mokhausa* (مخاصہ - mukhásah, Hind.). See sep. title.——*Moliko* (మొలిక - moliko, Tel.). Same as Dolabehara. ——*Monigar* (மணியக்காரன் - maniyakkáran, Tam.). Means superintendent. Corruption for Maunyacauran. For the service of headman of a village [caupoo, dolabehara, gowda, nauttaumay, pedda caup, potail]. See sep. title.——*Moodaum* (مدام - mudám, Hind.). Same as Mahtaud.——*Moodavan* (முடவன் - mudavan, Tam.). Means a lame man. For the support of a cripple [shappany].——*Mooppauticabuddy* (ముప్పాతికబడి - muppátikabadi, Tel.). Means three-fourths + share. Lands held on three-fourths of usual assessment.——*Mootraucha* (ముత్రాచ - mutrátsa, Tel.). Means the caste. To a man of that caste for service as Cuttoobuddy [q.v.] peon [q.v.].——*Moottallikaun* (متعلقان - mutaallikán, Hind.). Means connected. For dependents of a great man.——*Mootty* (முட்டி - mutti Tam.). Means handful [mooshty]. For carrying balls of rice while treading the boundary line of a village during the festivals of the village goddess and depositing the balls at different points of the line.——*Musjid* (مسجد - masjid, Hind.). Means place for prostrating. For support of a mosque [q.v.]. See sep. title.——*Mutt* (மடம் - madam, Tam.). Means monastery. For a building where Hindoo religious mendicants reside under a superior, or where they halt when travelling [samayacaur]. See sep. title.——*Naidoo* (నాయడు - náyadu, Tel.). For head ryot [q.v.] of a village [nauttambalam]. See sep. title.——*Nakkaura* (نقارہ - nakkárah, Hind.). Means a kettle-drum. For beating a drum at mosques [musjid] or at the gates of nawaubs [q.v.]. See sep. title.——*Nandavanam* (நந்தவனம் - nandavanam, Tam.). Means pleasure + garden. For a garden, the flowers of which are appropriated to the use of a pagoda [q.v.] or of the village community [poondottam, topecaur].——*Nary vetty* (நரிவெட்டி - narivetti, Tam.). Means fox + killer. Reward for having killed a fox [jackal] during a chase.——*Naugaswaram* (நாகசுரம் - nágasuram, Tam.). Means chief clarion. For playing in pagoda [q.v.] on the naugaswaram, a kind of clarionet. See sep. title——*Naunal* (நாணல் - nánal, Tam.). Means reed. For planting reeds for the protection of anicuts [q.v.] and irrigation channels [q.v.]. See sep. title.——*Nauttambalam* (நாட்டம்பலம் - náttambalam, Tam.). Means village + council. For head ryot [q.v.] of more than one village [naidoo.]——*Nauttaumay* (நாட்டாண்மை - náttánmai, Tam.). Means village + rule. For headman of a village [monigar, pedda caup]. ——*Nauttaur* (நாட்டார் - náttár, Tam.). Means a villager. For district revenue officer, whose duty it was under the native administration to superintend cultivation [nauttaun].——*Nautt taliyary* (நாட்டுத்தலையாரி - náttuttalaiyári, Tam.). Means district + watchman. For district watchman under the native police system [desha cauval, men cauval].——*Nauvithan* (நாவிதன் - návithan, Tam.). For village barber [hajaum].——*Neergunty* (నీరుగంటి - níruganti, Tel.). For superintending distribution of water for irrigation [caulvye pannaudy, madayvetty]. See sep. title.——*Neer moonaca* (నీరుమునక - nírumunaka, Tel.). Means water + diving. For diving into the water and opening or shutting the sluice [calingula] of a tank [madayvetty].——*Neer sarhadd* (نيرسرحد - nírsarhad, Hind.). Means water + boundary. Granted to the ryots of a village as a compensation for allowing a channel [q.v.] to be dug through their lands for the benefit of another village.——*Nel goottagay* (நெற்குத்தகை - nerguttagai, Tam.). Means paddy + lease. Villages held on inam tenure on payment of a certain quantity of grain per annum [rokka gootta].——*Nettoorcautt* (నెత్తురుకాటు - netturukátu, Tel.). Means blood + wound. Granted to the family of a person killed in battle, or as a compensation to a person who has been wounded in the public service [oodarapautt, paly cawny, racta caunikkay, racta codigey].——*Netty vailay* (நெட்டிவேலை - nettivélai, Tam.). Means pith + work. For making artificial birds, flowers and toys in pith [solah] work for pagodas [q.v.].——*Nirvauna maunyam* (நிர்வாணமானியம் - nirvánamániyam, Tam.). Means naked + gift. For a Hindoo ascetic.——*Nokkan* (நோக்கன் - nókkan, Tam.). Means a pole dancer. Granted to persons of that caste in the south, who correspond to the Dombars [q.v.] in the Ceded districts [gaurady].——*Nottam* (நோட்டம் - nóttam, Tam.). Means examination of coins, gems, &c. For the service of village shroff [q.v.]. See sep. title. ——*Numby* (நம்பி - nambi, Tam.). For performing poojah in Vishnoo pagodas [gooroocal, poojarry]. See sep. title.——*Oodarapautt* (ఉదరపాటు - udarapátu, Tel.). Means blood flow. Same as Racta caunikkay [nettoorcautt]. ——*Oomblikay* (உம்பிளிக்கை - umbilikkai, Tam.). Same as Amaram.——*Ooppara* (ఉప్పర - uppara, Tel.). Means a digger. Same as Wodda. See sep. title.——*Oor* (ஊர் - úr, Tam.). Means village. Same as Grauma maunyam. See sep. title.——*Oorny* (ఊరణి - urani, Tel.). Means public pond. For maintaining in repair the village ponds for supplying drinking water. ——*Oostaud* (استاد - ustád, Hind.). Means knowing. For teaching the zemindar [q.v.] fencing and gymnastics [vauttiyaur].——*Othookkam* (ஒதுக்கம் - othukkam, Tam.). Means retreat. Same as Chuttram.——*Othoovaun* (ஓதுவான் - óthuván, Tam.). Means a reciter. For a Shoodra attached to Shiva pagodas, whose duty it is to recite Devauram [q.v.], or Tamul divine hymns, during the performance of poojah [beineedy, cuttyam].——*Padicauval* (படிக்காவல் - padikkával, Tam.). Means batta + watch + gift. Same as Grauma cauval.——*Pala vailay* (பலவேலை - palavélai, Tam.). Means miscellaneous + work. For minor duties in a pagoda [q.v.].——*Paly cawny* (பழிக்காணி - pazhikkáni, Tam.). Means strife + acre. Same as Nettoorcautt [racta caunikkay].——*Pambacauran* (பம்பைக்காரன் - pambaikkáran, Tam.). Means drummer. For beating a drum called Pambay at the festivals of village deity [ausaudy, davanday, pambalam, zaumilica].——*Pambalam* (పంబలం - pambalam, Tel.). Means a drum. For beating a drum during festivals of village deity [ausaudy, davanday, pambacauran, zaumilica].——*Panippen* (பணிப்பெண் - panippen, Tam.). Means work + maid. For Coombhauraty [q.v.] service.——*Pany sheyvone* (பணிசெய்வோன் - paniseyvón, Tam.). Means work + doer. Same as Toty.——*Parichauracan* (பரிசாரகன் - parisáragan, Tam.). Means a servant. For servants of pagoda [q.v.] with exception of Archacan or chief priest [swayampaucam].——*Parihaury* (பரிகாரி - parigári, Tam.). Same as Veidyan.——*Parootty* (பருத்தி - parutti, Tam.). Means cotton. For weighing cotton [q.v.] when the Mail vauram [q.v.] of the zemindar [q.v.] on the crop used to be received in kind.——*Paulaputty* (పాలపట్టి - pálapatti, Tel.). Means milk + man. For pouring milk [paul] at particular places on the boundary line of a village on the last day of the procession of the village deity [grauma devatay].——*Pautashaulay* (பாடசாலை - pádasálai, Tam.). Means lesson + hall. For the support of schools where the Vedas [q.v.] are taught [vedavritty].——*Pauticabuddy* (పాతికబడి - pátikabadi, Tel.). Means one-fourth + share. Lands held on one-fourth of usual assessment [chatoor bhaugam].——*Pauttom* (పాటం - pátam, Tel.). Wet lands held on a favorable assessment paid in grain.——*Peddacaup* (పెద్దకాపు - peddakápu Tel.). Means head + caupoo. Headman of a village [caupoo, gowda, monigar, potail].——*Peer* (پیر - pír, Hind.). Means spiritual guide. For the maintenance of the punjas [q.v.] or insignia used during the celebration of the Moharram [q.v.]. See sep. title.——*Peetiperadoo* (పీటిపెరడు - pítiperadu, Tel.) Means dung + yard. Ground within or on the outskirts of the village-site and held free of assessment [teervay].——*Peik* (پائک - páik, Hind.). Held by military peons [q.v.] in Ganjam on condition of service. See sep. title.——*Pellett* (పెల్లెట్టు - pellettu, Tel.). Means clod + to turn. Granted to the person who dug the first clod of earth in constructing a new tank.——*Periya aramanay* (பெரியவரமனை - periyavaramanai, Tam.). Means great + palace. For watching the Zemindar's palace. ——*Pettah gowd* (ಪೇಟೆಗೌಡ - pétegauda, Can.). Granted to the headman of a suburb for encouraging settlement of weavers [joolah hatcar].——*Pidaura veidyan* (பிடாரவைத்தியன் - pidáravaittiyan, Tam.). Means snake catcher + doctor. For the support of a native doctor, who cures snake bites.——*Polimerah* (పొలిమేర - poliméra, Tel.). Means boundary. Same as Yellay inam.——*Polliem* (பாளையம் - pálaiyam, Tam.). Means camp. Villages held by poligars [q.v.].——*Poojarry* (பூசாரி - púsári, Tam.). Means worship + priest. For priest in a pagoda [q.v.], who conducts public worship [gooroocal, numby]. See sep. title.——*Pooluvan* (புலவன் - pulavan, Tam.). Means poet. For composing verses in honor of the zemindar [bhatrauz, cavyroyan].——*Poolicutt* (புலிக்கட்டு - pulikkattu, Tam.). Means tiger [pooly] spell. Granted under the native governments to persons for stopping tigers' mouths by enchantment and rendering them harmless [baugh maury].——*Poondottam* (பூந்தோட்டம் - púndóttam, Tam.). Means flower + garden. Same as Nandavanam [tope caur].——*Poopetty* (பூப்பெட்டி - púppotti, Tam.). Means flower + box. For supplying the zemindar [q.v.] with flowers.——*Pooraunam* (புராணம் - purá̍nam, Tam.). Means antiquity; but here the sacred books so called. For reading the Pooraunams [q.v.] in pagodas [khateeb]. Cf. Bhauraty. See sep. title.——*Poorohit* (புரோகிதன் - purógithan, Tam.). Means before + placed. Same as Punchaungy [vauttiyaur]. See sep. title.——*Pootla cuttoobuddy* (పుట్లకట్టుబడి - putlakattubadi, Tel.). Means pootty, the measure + settlement. Inams held subject to a quit-rent [jody] payable at a certain rate per Pootty [q.v.] of produce.——*Potail* (پٹیل - patel, Hind.). For headman of a village [gowda, monigar, pedda caup]. See sep. title.——*Potla* (పోతుల - pótula, Tel.). Granted to tank-diggers for executing petty repair to tanks and channels caused by cattle treading [khoolgah].——*Potrauz* (పోతరాజు - pótarádzu, Tel.). Means bull + king. For performing poojah [q.v.] to the village deity Potrauz [q.v.].——*Pullan* (பள்ளன் - pallan, Tam.). For measuring lands and the Mail vauram [q.v.] grain. See sep. title.——*Pullicutt* (பள்ளிக்கட்டு - pallikkattu, Tam.). Means village + building. For founding a village.——*Pullivaudy* (பள்ளிவாடி - pallivádi, Tam.). For service of ferryman [teppam].——*Pullivausal* (பள்ளிவாசல் - pallivásal, Tam.). Means temple + door. For maintenance of mosques [musjid] and tombs of Mahomedans [durgah, gor].——*Punchaungy* (பஞ்சாங்கி - pañjángi, Tam.).

For the service of calendar [punchaungam] Bramin, whose duty it is to announce to the villages lucky days for commencing to plough or reap [vellaumay], for celebrating marriages or festivals, or engaging in any business. He is also the village priest, and, as such, performs certain ceremonies connected with births, marriages, and deaths [poorohit, vauttiyaur]. See sep. title.——*Pungoovaly* (பங்குவழி - panguvazhi, Tam.). Means share + way. For the encouragement of cultivation to a body of coparceners holding village in common.——*Punjy curnum* (పంజీకరణం - panjíkaranam, Tel.). Means poor + curnum. Held by certain servants of the Curnum [q.v.] class, who do duty in the Huzoor [q.v.] office of the zemindars [q.v.] in Ganjam. ——*Punt* (పంతులు - puntulu, Tel.). Means teacher. For village schoolmaster [vauttiyaur]. See sep. title.——*Putna chetty* (పట్నసెట్టి - patnasetti, Tel.). Means town + chetty. For settling caste disputes among the Lingayets [q.v.] in Bellary district.——*Puttivaly* (பட்டிவழி - pattivazhi, Tam.). Means register + way. Same as Pungoovaly.——*Putty* (பட்டி - patti, Tam.). Means cattle-fold. For preventing cattle from trespassing and destroying crops [bandela].——*Racta caunikkay* (இரத்தக்காணிக்கை - irattakkánikkai, Tam.). Means blood + present. For the support of the heirs of persons who were killed, while on oath treading boundaries [oodarapautt, yellay].——*Racta codigey* (రక్తకొడిగ - raktakódiga, Tel.). Means blood + twenty. Same as Nettoorcautt.——*Rajbandh* (రాజబంధు - rájabandhu, Tel.). Means king + relative. Held by the relatives of rajahs or zemindars [mokhausa].——*Rayayet mokhausa* (رعایت مخاصه - riáyatmukhásah, Hind.). Means favorable + grant. Mokhausa [q.v.] villages held on a favorable assesment, fluctuating with the cultivation of each year.——*Reddy* (రెడ్డి - reddi, Tel.). Same as Peddacaup. See sep. title.——*Rokka gootta* (రొక్కగుత్త - rokkagutta, Tel.). Means money + rent. Villages held on a fixed money rent, the amount of which is somewhat lower than the standard assessment of Government lands [nel goottagay]. ——*Sadauvritty* (சதாவிருத்தி - shathávirutti, Tam.). Means always + maintenance. For daily distribution of uncooked rice [q.v.] to poor travellers [annacauvady].——*Salivendra* (చలివేంద్ర - tsalivéndra, Tel.). Means water shed. Same as Tunny pandaul [takyah].——*Samayacaur* (சமயக்கார் - shamayakkár, Tam.). Means the follower of a religion. Held by a servant under the Shreeveishnava [q.v.] priest of Shoodras [q.v.]. His duty is to report to the people the movements of the priest [mutt].—— *Sampraty* (சம்பிருதி - shambiruthi, Tam.). Means a public accountant. For service as the accountant [curnum] of a talook [q.v.] in a polliem [q.v.], or of the whole estate when of small extent.——*Samstaunam peon* (సంస్థానంబంటు - samst'hánambantu, Tel.). Means estate + peon. For revenue peons [q.v.] in zemindarries.——*Sangeetam* (சங்கீதம் - shangítham, Tam.). For singing in pagodas [q.v.] or in zemindars' palaces [bhatrauz, cavyroyan, cuttyam, poolavan].——*Sangtaraush* (سنگتراش - sangtarásh, Hind.). Means stone + cutter. For service as a stonemason [cullvailay].——*Santa casivy* (సంతకసివి - santakasivi, Tel.). Means market + sweeper. Held by a female servant of the Chetty [q.v.] caste, who is employed in sweeping, lighting lamps, &c. She is also required to perform similar services for travellers when they halt in the village.——*Sarwa maunyam* (சருவமானியம் - sharuvamániyam, Tam.). Means entire + gift. An inam held free of quit-rent. See sep. title.——*Saucala* (సాకల - tsákala, Tel.). Same as Dhoby.——*Saugbuddy* (சாகுபடி - shágubadi, Tam.). Means cultivation. Granted to head ryots [q.v.] with a view to their encouraging the cultivation of Government lands.——*Seikalgar* (صیقل گر - saikalgar, Hind.). Means polisher. For polishing arms for a zemindar [q.v.].—— *Shappany* (சப்பாணி - shappáni, Tam.). Means a lame person. For the support of a cripple [moodavan].——*Shaunaun* (சாணான் - shánán, Tam.). For supplying cadjan [q.v.] leaves to the zemindar [q.v.] and the village accountants. See sep. title.——*Shavam* (சவம் - shavam, Tam.). Means a corpse. For permitting the dead bodies of persons dying in village to be burnt within the limits of the village.——*Shemmaun* (செம்மான் - shemmán, Tam.). For supplying the zemindar [q.v.] with choonam [q.v.].——*Shendhy* (سیندهی - sendhí, Hind.; சேந்தி - shéndi, Tam.). Held by toddy-drawers for service as bearers [boy], &c.——*Sherveicauran* (சேர்வைக்காரன் - shérvaikkáran, Tam.). Means commander of a body of soldiers. Held for the service of village peon [q.v.].—— *Shilpacharry* (சிற்பாசாரி - shirbásári, Tam.). For the service of architect to a pagoda [q.v.].——*Shroff* (صراف - sarráf, Hind.). Means exchanger. The same as Nottam. See sep. title.—— *Shrotriem* (శ్రోత్రియం - shrótriyam, Tel.). A general term for all favorably assessed whole villages originally held by Bramins [agrahauram, bhattavritty, dehaut, kheirauty]. See sep. title. ——*Shumbah cuttalay* (சம்பாக்கட்டளை - shambákkattalai, Tam.). Means shumbah rice + allowance. For making an oblation in a pagoda [q.v.] with Shumbah [q.v.] rice [q.v.].—— *Siddhy* (సిద్ధి - sidi, Tel.; சித்தி - shitti, Tam.). For performing the swinging festival [shirry] in honor of the village goddess [grauma devatay].——*Sooddoola* (సుద్దుల - suddula, Tel.). Means story. For singing hymns in praise of the village deity [beineedy, cuttyam, othoovaun].——*Stala cauval* (தலக்காவல் - talakkával, Tam.). Means place + watch. Held by the village cauvalgar [q.v.] who performs general duties, such as collecting revenue, watching produce [mahsooldar], &c.——*Staneecam* (தானிகம் - tánigam, Tam.). Held by the director of the ceremonies in a pagoda [q.v.].——*Staunapaty* (தானப்பதி - tánappathi, Tam.). Means place + lord. Held by an officer who acts as the general vakeel [q.v.] or agent of a pagoda [q.v.]. ——*Swayampaucam* (சுவயம்பாகம் - shuvayambágam, Tam.). Means self + cooking. For the service of cooking in a pagoda [parichauracan].——*Tabaila* (طبیله - tabela, Hind.). Means stables. For superintending the stables of a zemindar [goorrap]. ——*Tair vailay* (தேர்வேலை - térvélai, Tam.). Means car + work. For repairing and decorating a car [rath, tair] belonging to a pagoda [q.v.].——*Takyah* (تکیه - takyah, Hind.). Means pillow. For the support of a fakeer [q.v.], whose duty it is to supply Mahomedan pilgrims with water and shelter [salivendra, tunny pandaul].——*Taliyary* (தலையாரி - talaiyári, Tam.). Means bailiff. For the service of village watchman [tookry]. See sep. title.——*Tamalapaukoola* (తమలపాకుల - tamalapákula, Tel.). Means betel-leaf. For supplying betel-leaf to the zemindar [q.v.].——*Tambala* (తంబళ - tambala, Tel.). Means poojarry [q.v.]. For providing leaves, flowers, &c., in honor of the village goddess [tirmaulay].——*Tandal* (தண்டல் - tandal, Tam.). Means collection. Held by a servant employed under the monigar [q.v.] of a village in collecting government revenue. ——*Tarappady* (தரப்படி - tarappadi, Tam.). Means sort + method. Inams granted at the original formation of a village for village purposes, comprising Grauma maunyams [q.v.], the inams enjoyed by the village, revenue, police, and private servants [balootah], and the village pagodas [q.v.]. The term Tarapaddy inam is used in contradistinction to a Sunnud [q.v.] inam, or an inam held under a grant.——*Tauthan* (தாதன் - táthan, Tam.). For singing and beating a drum during matrimonial or funeral ceremonies.——*Tauyif wauly* (طائفه والی - táifahwálí, Hind.). From (táifah, ar. band of musicians + wálí, hind. individual member). Held by dancing girls [cunchany]. ——*Teiyalcauran* (தையற்காரன் - taiyargáran, Tam.). Means tailor. Same as Durzee.——*Teppam* (தெப்பம் - teppam, Tam.). Means raft. For supplying rafts to cross a river [pullivaudy].——*Tirast* (తిరస్తు - tirastu, Tel.). Means alienated village. Held by a description of armed peons [q.v.] maintained by the hill zemindars [q.v.] of Vizagapatam district for preserving the peace of the country.——*Tirmaulay* (திருமாலை - tirumálai, Tam.). Means holy + garland. For supplying garlands of flowers in a pagoda [tambala].——*Tirnaul mantapapuddy* (திருநாள்மண்டபப்படி - tirunálmandabappadi, Tam.). Means festival + temple hall + batta. For celebration of a feast in a Mantapam [q.v.] during the periodical festivals of a pagoda [q.v.].——*Tirpany vailay* (திருப்பணிவேலை - tiruppanivélai, Tam.). Means holy + service + work. For keeping a pagoda [q.v.] in repair [vimauna pratishtam].—— *Tirvanandal cuttalay* (திருவனந்தற்கட்டளை - tiruvanandargattalai, Tam.). Means holy + sleep + portion. For performing the morning oblation in a pagoda [q.v.].——*Toodoomo* (తుడుము - tudumu, Tel.). Means drum. For beating a drum on public occasions, such as the publication of a notice, the arrival at the village of high officials, &c.——*Tookry* (తుక్కుడి - tukkudi, Tel.). Means watchman. For service as head watchman of a village [taliyary].——*Tope* (தோப்பு - tóppu, Tam.). Land consisting of a grove of trees, properly of trees that bear fruit [pazham], as mango [q.v.], tamarind [q.v.], cocoanut [q.v.], &c., held free of assessment. See sep. title.——*Topecaur* (தோப்புக்காரன் - tóppukkáran, Tam.). Means grove-man. For maintaining flower gardens and supplying flowers to temples [nandavanam, poondottam].——*Toranam cutty* (தோரணங்கட்டி - tóranangatti, Tam.). Means festoon + tier. For preparing festoons of leaves [coondal] and tying them across the street during pagoda [q.v.] procession.——*Toty* (தோட்டி - tótti, Tam.). For the service of village Toty, a man of low caste who waits uppon the village officers generally, assists in measuring land, carries letters [tappaul] to the Tahsildar [q.v.], acts as a guide to officers travelling on public duty, &c. [bariky, boorky]. See sep. title.——*Tribhaugam* (திரிப்பாகம் - tirippágam, Tam.). Means three + portion. Inams consisting of one-third share of the Government revenue [trishwaicam].——*Tunny pandaul* (தண்ணீர்ப்பந்தல் - tannírppandal, Tam.). Means water-shed. For maintaining a water-pandaul where water and butter-milk [mor] are distributed gratis to travellers during the hot season [coday, salivendra, takyah].——*Tutchan* (தச்சன் - taççan, Tam.). Means carpenter. Same as Badye [vadla]. See sep. title.——*Vadla* (వడ్ల - vadla, Tel.). Means carpenter. Same as Badye [tutchan].—— *Valaiyan* (வலையன் - valaiyan, Tam.). Means netman. For catching fish for the zemindar [q.v.].——*Vauda cauvaly* (వాడకావలి - vádakávali, Tel.). Means village + guard. Same as Grauma cauval.——*Vauniyan* (வாணியன் - vániyan, Tam.),

For supplying oil [yennay] to a pagoda [q.v.]. See sep. title.——*Vaunpayir ambalam* (வான்பயிரம்பலம் - vánbayirambalam, Tam.). Means sky + crop + village council. For collecting assessment on garden lands [totacaul].——*Vauttiyaur* (வாத்தியார் - váttiyár, Tam.). For support of the village schoolmaster; or for the support of a priest who conducts religious ceremonies in the houses of Bramins [poorohit, punt].——*Vedavritty* (வேதவிருத்தி - véthavirutti, Tam.). Means sacred writing + profit. For reading the Vedas [q.v.] and teaching them to Bramin [q.v.] boys [pautashaulay].——*Veidyan* (வைத்தியன் - vaittiyan, Tam.). For the service of physician [hakeem, parihaury].——*Vetty* (வெட்டி - vetti, Tam.). For performance of the lowest offices in a village, as those of a porter, grain-watcher, scavenger, &c. [begaury, maula].——*Veydan* (வேடன் - védan, Tam.). Granted to a hunter as a reward for display of skill in the chase [veddah].——*Vilvaurchanay* (வில்வார்ச்சனை - vilvárççanai, Tam.). Means bael tree + worship. For the service of performing poojah [q.v.] with the leaves of the vilvam tree [bael], ægle marmelos, corr.——*Vimauna pratishtam* (விமானப்பிரதிட்டம் - vimánappirathittam, Tam.). Means pinnacle + strength. For repairing the Vimaunam [q.v.] or pinnacle of a temple [coil, tirpany vailay].——*Vulloovan* (வள்ளுவன் - valluvan, Tam.). For the service of Vulloovan, who is a Pariah, and is to low-caste persons what the Punchaungy [q.v.] is to the higher classes. See sep. title.——*Vunnaun* (வண்ணான் - vannán, Tam.). Same as dhoby. He is sometimes attached to a temple to wash the cloths of the idol [vigraham] and to supply rags for torches [masaul, saucala]. See sep. title.——*Vycaul* (வாய்க்கால் - váykkál, Tam.). Means place + channel. For preserving channels [q.v.] and other irrigation works in good order. See sep. title.——*Wodda* (ఒడ్డె - odde, Tel.). For repairing tanks [ooppara]. See sep. title.——*Wotta cauran* (ஓட்டக்காரன் - óttakkáran, Tam.) Means runner. For the tappaul [q.v.] runner.——*Yairvauca* (ఏరువాక - éruváka, Tel.). Means commencement of cultivation. Granted to the person who first ploughed the lands of a village.——*Yeediga* (ఈడిగ - ídiga, Tel.). Means toddy drawer. Granted for having planted date [kharjooram] trees for the production of toddy [q.v.].——*Yejmaun* (எசமான் - esamán, Tam.). Same as Grauma maunyam. The inam is called by this name when its holder is the sole mirassidar [q.v.] of the village. See sep. title.——*Yellay* (எல்லை - ellai, Tam.). Means boundary. Granted to a person who settles boundary disputes by treading the boundary line in a solemn manner with a pot of fire on his head, a wet cloth round his waist, and a garland of flowers round his neck [polimerah].——*Yennay vaungy* (எண்ணெய்வாங்கி - enneyvángi, Tam.). Means oil + buyer. For carrying oil [yennay] from the oilmonger to the pagoda [q.v.].——*Yerkala* (ఎరుకల - erukala, Tel.). Granted to persons of tribe for collecting medicinal plants for the use of the zemindar [q.v.]. See sep. title.——*Yidayan* (இடையன் - idaiyan, Tam.). Means middleman. Held by cowherd for the service of taking out the cattle [maud] of the villagers to graze [golla, gowdamandey]. See sep. title.——*Zaumilica* (జామిలిక - dzámilika, Tel.). Means a drum. For playing on the drum so called during the festivals of the village deity [ausaudy, davanday, pambacauran, pambalam].——*Zingaur* (زینگر - zíngar, Hind.). Means saddle + maker. For a saddler in the service of a zemindar [q.v.].

INAUYAT (عنایت - ináyat, *Ar.*). From (ani, ar. to belong to). Gift [inam]. Prefixed to an alam forms a lacab; as Inauyat ally, gift of ally. Devotional term + alam. Generally a Shiah name [ism]. Inauyat nauma is a deed of gift or exemption.

INCH (انچ - inch, *Hind.*). Measure of rain. That is to say, if the rain were to fall on a level surface which did not absorb it, and from which it could not run off or evaporate, it would form a sheet of water one inch in depth [dookky, padoonoo].

INDAH (اندہ - indah, *Pers.*). Suffix added to Persian infinitive to denote agent [dar]; as Naveesindah, writer.

INDIA (هند - hind, *Hind.*; ಇಂಡಿಯಾ - indiya, *Can.*; ఇండియ - indiya, *Tel.*; ഇന്ത്യ - indya, *Mal.*; இந்தியா - indiyá, *Tam.*). From sanscrit Sindhoo or river indus, of which the persians made Hindoo. Greeks called it ἡ ἰνδική, sc. γῆ, Ionian Greeks dropping the aspirate. So latin India. The sanscrit name proper is Bhaurata varsham [jamboo dweepam], divided into khandams [navakhandam]. The holy land of Menoo [q.v.] and the Pooraunams [q.v.] lies between the Drishadwaty and Saraswaty rivers in North-west India. In Hindoo geography fifty-six countries are enumerated [bhoogolashastram]. The principal ancient kingdoms were nineteen, viz., Magadham, Oudh, Indraprastam or the ancient delhi, Canouj or canyacoobjam, Matooray, Vangam or east bengal, Andhram, Ootcalam, Carnautam, Cholam, Paundyam, Cheram, Maharashtram, Coucanam, Malwah, Goozerat, Punjab, Cashmere, Nepaul. The tamul country and language are called Dravida [charitram]. According to Marco Polo there was India the greater, extending from Maabar [q.v.] or Coromandel [q.v.] to Mekran and containing thirteen kingdoms; India the lesser, extending from Champah [cambodia] or Cochin china to Mootfily [motoopully] or Kistna delta [conamoogam] and containing eight kingdoms; and Middle india froming the province of Abash or Abyssinia. Friar Jordanus has similar divisions. From these different plural ideas arose the term Indies.——*Indian* (देशीय - déshíyá, San.; هندی - hindí, Ar., Pers. and Hind.; ناٹ - nát, Dec.; ನಾಡು - nádu, Can.; నాటు - nátu, Tel.; നാട്ടു - nátu, Mal.; நாட்டு - náttu, Tam.). San. from (désha, san. country) [desham]. Ar. from (hind, ar. india). Dec. from tamul. Drav. means country, in the oblique form [naud]. Tel. also (déshapu). Anglo-indian prefix to designate plants or products of india considered to resemble the foreign plant, &c., which follows [country].——*Indian aconite* (بیش هندی - bíshihindí, Hind.). Same as Bachnaug.——*Indian allspice* (ناٹکی سیتل چینی - nátkísítalchíní, *Hind.*). Same as China pepper.——*Indian almond* (هندی بادام کا پیڑ - hindíbádámkáper, Hind.). Same as Catapang.——*Indian aloe* (صبر هندی - sibrihindí, *Hind.*). See under Aloe.——*Indian aristolochia* (زراوند هندی - zaráwandihindí, Hind.). Same as Isharmool.——*Indian barberry* (فیل زهره هندی - filzahraihindí, Hind.). See under Berberry.——*Indian bdellium* (گوگل هندی - gúgalihindí, Hind.). See under Bdellium.——*Indian bead* (ناٹ کا منکا - nátkámanká, Hind.). Same as Indian shot.——*Indian beech* (ولایتی گولر - viláitígular, Hind.). Same as Karanj.——*Indian beet* (पालङ्की - pálankí, San.). Same as Paulak.——*Indian berry* (काकमारी - kákamárí, San. and Mahr.; गड्डफल - gardap'hala, Conc.; مرگ ماهی - margmáhí, Pers.; کاکماری - kákmárí, Hind. and Dec.; توبا - tuba, Malay; ಕಾಗೆಮಾರಿ - kágemárí, Can.; ಚಿಪ್ಪುಲು - chipulu, Too.; కాకిసంప - kákitsampa, Tel.; പൊല്ലക്കായ - pollakkáya, Mal.; තිත්තවැල් - tittaval, Singh.; காக்காய்க்கொல்லி - kákkáykkolli, Tam.). San. from (káka, san. crow + mári, san. killer); as mixed with rice for a lure and poison to crows. Pers. from (marg, pers. death + máhí, pers. fish). Can. from (káge, can. crow + mári, san. destroyer). Tel. from (káki, tel. crow + tsampu, tel. to kill). Mal. from (polla, mal. blister + káya, mal. fruit). Singh. from (titta, singh. bitter + val. singh. creeper); from bitter berry. Tam. from (kákkáy, tam. crow + kol, tam. to kill). San. also (kákanáshiká), meaning crow + destroyer; (kákáhvá), meaning crowplant; compare indian hounds' berry. Mahr. also (kákap'halí), meaning crow + fruit. Can. also (kákísoppugadde), meaning crow + leaf + root. Mal. also (karantakam); (naññinkuru), meaning poison nut; (mínnaññu), meaning fish poison; (naççattinkáya), meaning poison + fruit; (garalap'hala), meaning poison + fruit; cf. common emetic nut. Tam. also (péngottai), meaning louse + seed; destroys vermin. Title otherwise Bacca orientalis, Bitter berry, Caukmaury, Cocculus indicus, Cocques dulevant, Crow berry, Crow-killer, Fish-killer, Fish poison, Jagged moonseed, Louse berry, Meizaragi, Poison berry. Botanically Anamirta cocculus, w. & a., menispermaceæ [vricsham, 5]. Alias Anamirta paniculata, racemosa; Cocculus flavescens, lacunosus, orbiculatus, suberosus; Menispermum cocculus, heteroclitum, lacunosus monadelphum, orbiculatum. A strong climbing shrub, with the bark corky, ash-colored, and deeply cracked into fissures; long trailing branches; stalks shorter than leaves; leaves alternate, slightly cordate, roundish, acute, deep green, whitish beneath, with five digitate ribs; calyx six-sepalled; corolla none; racemes of female flowers, lateral, whitish green; long pendulous bunches of fruit, the size of a large pea [calauyam], pure white in color becoming red and ultimately black as they ripen; resembles tinospora cordifolia [goolancha]. The dried berries as occuring are somewhat kidney-shaped, blackish brown, wrinkled, containing a yellowish, oily, bitter, kidney-shaped kernel inclosed in a two-valved shell; the berries are extremely bitter. Medicinally the berries, fructus cocculi of chemists, are employed powdered for destroying pediculi in the hair, and mixed with warm castor-oil [aumanac] as ointment in cutaneous diseases; the juice of the fresh berry is applied externally to foul ulcers, and in scabies; the kernels contain a large percentage of the virulent principle picrotoxine; the pericarp yields another dangerous alkaloid menispermine, never administered internally; gives to pharm. unguentum cocculi insecticide, officinal, substituted for ung. hydrargy. and ung. hydrarg. nitratis, discarded from british pharmacopœia. Berries added to malt liquors to increase their intoxicating effect; berries formed into paste with moistened rice for intoxicating birds and fish [andaman indian oak, common emetic nut, marotty, round milk-hedge, sooptee, tejbul, walsoora, zanzibar indigo] in order to catch them; oil from berries similar; highly poisonous when in excess. For cocculus genus, see Vausanavully.——*Indian birch* (صنوبر هندی - sanobarihindí, Hind.). Same as Bhoojpattar.——*Indian birthwort* (زراوند هندی - zaráwandihindí, Hind.). Same as Isharmool.——*Indian blood wood* (هندی رکت چندن - hindírakatchandan, Hind.). Same as Adambo.——*Indian burr* (अपामार्ग - apámárga, San.; उत्राणी - utráni, Mahr.; कांटमोग्री - kántamógrí, Conc.; اتکمه - atkumab, Ar.; خارواژگونه - khárivázhgúnah, Pers.; چرچرا - chirchirá, Hind.; اگارا - agárá, Dec.; ಉತ್ತರೇಣಿ - uttaréni, Can.; ಉತ್ತರಣೆ - uttarane, Too.; ఉత్తరేణి - uttaréni, Tel.; കടലാടി - katàláti, Mal.; ගස්කරල්හබ - gaskaralhaba, Singh.; நாயுருவி - náyuruvi, Tam.). Title from prickly flower stalk. San. from (apa, san. away + márga, san. way); as being shunned. Conc. means prickly jasmine. Pers. from (khár, pers. thorn + vázhgún, pers. reversed). Hind. means pungent [surprise grass]. Can. from teloogoo. Tel. from (utta, tel. false + rénu, tel. jujube tree, zizyphus jujuba, lam.). Mal. from (katal, mal. sea + átu, mal. to wave). Tam. from (náy, tam. dog + uruvi, tam. the piercing plant), from its prick. San. also (kharamañjarí), meaning sharp + flower cluster; (dírghamañjarí), meaning long + flower cluster; (apánga), meaning down + limb; (pratyakpushpí), meaning turned downwards + flower; (ghantá), meaning killing; (kíshaparní), meaning monkey + leaf, from leaf hair like that of monkey; (kinihí), meaning one affected with dadroo + to go; (kubja), meaning crooked; (markatí), meaning ape [common cowitch]; (markatapippalí), meaning ape + long pepper, piper longum, linn.; (málákant'ha), meaning wreath + throat; (durabhigraha), meaning difficult to hold; (katumañjariká), meaning sharp + flower cluster; (mayúraka), meaning peacock, from the faint resemblance of the stalk to peacock's feather [indian maiden hair]; (panktikantaka), meaning row + thorn; (shaikharika), meaning produced on mountain tops; (shikhyanga), meaning peacock + limb; (vashira) [elephant long pepper]. Pers. also (khárívázhún), meaning inverted thorn. Hind. also (chikrá); (chirchittá); (latjira). Tel. also (antisa), meaning sticking. Title otherwise Apamaurgam, Chaff-flower, Dog-prick, Monkey-leaf plant, Monkey long pepper, Nyeoorivy, Prickly chaff-flower, Rough chaff-flower. Botanically Achyranthes aspera, linn., amarantaceæ [vricsham, 106]. Alias Achyranthes indica, obtusifolia. Shrub about 6 feet; branches somewhat four-sided; stem erect, pubescent; leaves on short petioles, obovate-rotund, abruptly attenuated at the base, pubescent; spikes virgate, acute, at first horizontal, afterwards reflexed; flowers purplish-green; bracts at first soft, soon becoming rigid and prickle-like; capsules 5-seeded, reddish. The dried plant medicinally astringent and diuretic; has marked diuretic properties in decoction; when burnt the ashes yield potash [jharkanamak], and are administered with ginger [q.v.] for dropsy; the flowering-spikes, rubbed with sugar [q.v.], are made into pills and given to people bitten by mad dogs; the leaves taken fresh and rubbed to a pulp are external remedy for sting of scorpions [tail]; paste of fresh leaves and spikes, with or without turmeric [country saffron] is a remedy in piles; for british digitalis, spiritus ætheris nitrosi and galls; all parts quoted in pharm. non-officinal. Seldom eaten alone, and in general used in calavay keeray [q.v.] or mixed greens; famine food. Used in incantations and sacrifices [yanyam]; used in washing linen; also as a tooth-brush; ashes used as mordant [cauram].—"*a*" There is a species aquatica, called in teloogoo water spinach [maurisham]. Other species are:—bidentata, rubrofusca.—"*b*" Litsæa zeylanica and Panicum javanicum are also called Indian burr; see gloss. paragraphs.—"*c*" Small indian burr, so called in the vernaculars, is Cyathula prostrata, blume, amarantaceæ [vricsham, 106]; alias Achyranthes prostrata; Pupalia prostrata. Stem herbaceous, perennial, prostrate, or ascending; branches subtetragonal, slightly hairy; leaves opposite, obovate, pubescent, glaucous below; spikes virgate, slender, lax; sepals, lanceolate, hairy, interior ones narrower, three-nerved, hispid; staminodes minute, bifid at the apex, glochides fifteen to twenty; unequal, hooked at the apex, hairy below, yellowish; utricle glabrous, greenish; seed ovate-oblong, shining, pale chestnut; flowers greenish-red or purple or whitish-violet; flowering in the cold season.——*Indian bramble* (خسك هندى - khasakihindí, Hind.). See Gowry's fruit.——*Indian buckbean* (باقلة هندى - báklahihindí, Hind.). Same as Floating nelumbo.——*Indian caoutchouc* (ولايتى بر - viláitíbar, Dec.; ಶೀಮೆಆಲ - shímeála, Can.; సీమమఱ్ఱి - símamarri, Tel.; சீமையால் - shímaiyál, Tam.). Vern. means foreign banyan. Title otherwise Elastic fig, Foreign banyan, Indian rubber tree. Botanically Stilpnophyllum elasticum, endl., moraceæ [vricsham, 121]. Alias Ficus elastica; Urostigma elasticum. Tree, 30 to 40 feet; leaves from oval to oblong, pointed, thick, firm, and glossy; fruit in axillary pairs, sessile, oval, smooth, the size of an olive [zeitoon]; stipules nearly as long as the leaves, smooth and rosy; cultivated in malabar. Produces when wounded a quantity of milk which yields about one-third of its weight of caoutchouc [pauchonty]; when the juice is exposed to the air, it separates spontaneously into a fine elastic substance and a fœtid whey-colored liquid; the juice is formed into pear-shaped bottles by being spread over moulds of clay. Caoutchouc furnishes candles and flambeaux; with the milk the insides of vessels and baskets are smeared.——*Indian chamomile* (بابونه هندى - bábúnahihindí, Hind.). Same as Shaumanty.——*Indian cherry* (ولايتى كروندا - viláitíkarondá, Hind.). Same as Bair.——*Indian chickweed* (திராய் - tiráy, Tam.). Same as Tirye.——*Indian china root* (هندى چوب چينى - hindíchobchíní, Hind.). See under China root.——*Indian chrysanthemum* (بابونه هندى - bábúnahihindí, Hind.). Same as Shaumanty.——*Indian copal* (سندروس هندى - sandrúsihindí, Hind.). Product of Vateria indica, linn., Piney.——*Indian coral tree* (ناتكا پانگرا - nátkápángrá, Hind.). See under Coral tree.——*Indian corby* (زاغ هندى - zághihindí, Hind.). Same as Carrion crow.——*Indian cork* (आकाशनिंब - ákáshanimba, San. and Mahr.; آكاس نيم - ákásním, Hind.; ಬೆರಟುಮರ - beratumara, Can.; మానుమల్లె - mánumalle, Tel.; කිරිල්ල - kirilla, Singh.; மரமல்லிகை - maramamalligai, Tam.). San. from (ákásha, san. sky + nimba, san. melia azadirachta, linn.); tall and similar; cf. bhoo nimbam, andrographis genus. Hind. from mahratta. Can. from (birate, can. cork + mara, can. tree). Tel. from (mánu, tel. tree + malle, tel. jasmine). Tam. from (maram, tam. tree + malliká, san. jasminum sambac, ait.); from flower [tree jasmine]. Hind. also (nímchambelí), meaning melia azadirachta, linn. + chambelí, jasminum sambac, ait.; from leaf like margosa and flowers like jasmine. Tam. also (kárkkumaram), meaning cork tree, cf. cork oak; (káttumalli), meaning forest + jasmine [wild jasmine]. Title otherwise Tree jasmine [indian zebra-wood]. Botanically Millingtonia hortensis, linn. f., bignoniaceæ [vricsham, 99]. Alias Bignonia suberosa. Tree, 40–50 feet; leaves opposite, supra-decompound; leaflets acuminated, subcordate, entire; panicles terminal, with horizontal ramifications, the first trichotomous, then dichotomous, with generally a simple flower in the fork; flowers numerous, trumpet shaped, large, pure white, fragrant; ornamental and very rapid grower; flowering in cold season. Flower religious; bark yields an inferior cork; used as an avenue [shaulay] tree; wood is white, firm, and close-grained. Indian cork is also a title given to the Baobab [q.v.].——*Indian corn* (مكه جارى - makkahjárí, Dec.). Title from being introduced from W. indies. Same as Mecca cholum.——*Indian cotton* (قطن - kutn, Ar.). See under Cotton.——*Indian cowhage* (هندى كاچكورى - hindíkáchkurí, Hind.). Same as Common cowitch.——*Indian cuckoo* (कोकिल - kókila, San.). Same as Koel.——*Indian dammer* (هندى ڈامر - hindídámar, Hind.). See Dammer.——*Indian daphne* (مازريون هند - mázariúnihind, Ar.). Same as Crow creeper.——*Indian date* (تمر هند - tamarihind, Ar.). Same as Tamarind.——*Indian dill* (شبت هند - shibitihind, Hind.). Same as Ajwaun.——*Indian ebony* (آبنوس هند - ábnúsihind, Hind.). See sep. title——*Indian elm* (वावळ - vávala, Mahr.; پپڑى - paprí, Hind.; ರಸಬೀಜ - rasabíja, Can.; ತಸ್ಪಿ - taspi, Coorg; నవిలిచెట్టు - navilichettu, Tel.; දඩකිරිල්ල - dadakirilla, Singh.; ஆயா - áyá, Tam.). Can. from (rasa, san. juice + bíja, san. seed). Singh. from (dada, singh. wilderness + kirilla, singh. cork tree, millingtonia hortensis, linn. f.). Tel. also (náli); (návarachettu); (peddanavilieragu). Singh. also (godakirilla). Tam. also (káñji) [caunchy, jow]. Title otherwise Jungle cork tree, Wawalee. Botanically Holoptelea integrifolia, planch., ulmaceæ [vricsham, 120]. Alias Ulmus integrifolia. Large tree; dense dark green foliage; leaves alternate, ovate or cordate, entire, glabrous, shortly petioled, deciduous; flowers hermaphrodite and male mixed; hermaphrodite flowers, calyx four to six-lobed, leaflets spreading, oval; stamens seven to nine; pistils two; capsule one-celled, one-valved, indehiscent; the first part of the flowers that appears is the reddish anthers, next the calyx increases and becomes visible, but is always very minute, and if not looked for may pass unperceived; flowering in cold season. Bruised leaves are applied to boils; leaves lopped for cattle fodder; adapted for avenues [shaulay]; the forks of the branches are used to protect straw heaps against cattle [maud]; oil [yennay] expressed from seed; wood light yellowish-grey, moderately hard, no heart-wood.——*Indian endive* (هندباء برى - hindabáibarrí, Ar.; كاسنى برى - kásníbarrí, Pers.; جنگلى كاسنى - janglíkásní, Hind. and Dec.; காசினிவிரை - kásinivirai, Tam.). Ar. from (hindabá, ar. endive + barr, ar. forest). Pers. from (kásní, pers. endive + barr, ar. forest). Hind. from (janglí, hind. wild + kásní, pers. endive). Tam. from hindostany. Tam. also (shekkiraishivattamullangi), meaning chicory + red + radish plant. Greek κιχώριον. Title otherwise Chicory, Succory, Wild endive, Wild succory, Witloof. Botanically Cichorium intybus, linn., compositæ [vricsham, 74]. The achenes are about the same size as those of the lettuce [kahoo], angled, of a pale, mottled grey color; the root is fleshy and tapering, somewhat branched, longitudinally wrinkled, light brown externally and whitish internally; the bark is rather thin, radially striate from the dark colored milk-vessels, and separated by a brown cambium-line from the finely porous yellow-wood; the taste is bitter and mucilaginous. Seeds are one of the four lesser cold seeds of old writers, and as such are still in use in the east. Tonic, demulcent, and cooling; seeds carminative and cordial; prescribed in bilious complaints much like taraxacum. Young plant used for salad, the leaves being blanched like endive; roots roasted, ground, and mixed with coffee [q.v.] to flavor it. Gives a dye [shauyam]. Garden endive, greek σέρις κηπευτὴ στενοφύλλος, is Cichorium endivia, linn.; two principal varieties of this vegetable, batavian or broad-leaved often used for stews, and the curled called sometimes capuchin's beard used as a garniture for salads.——*Indian fescue* (கமரிப்புல் - kamarippul, Tam.). Same as Cleft grass.——*Indian fig* (ولايتى گولر - viláitígular, Hind.). Same as Banyan and Prickly-pear.——*Indian filbert* (بندق هندى - bundukihindí, Pers.). Seeds like filberts. Same as Bonduc.——*Indian fir* (ناتكا ديودار - nátkádeudár, Hind.). Same as Ashocam.——*Indian frankincense* (ناتكا عود - nátkáúd, Hind.). Same as White dammer.——*Indian gamboge* (ناتكا غوتا غنبا - nátkágbotághambah, Hind.). Same as Ceylon gamboge and Malabar gamboge.——*Indian gazelle* (غزال هندى - ghizálihindí, Hind.). Same as Ravine deer.——*Indian goose-*

berry (ولايتی آنولہ - viláitíáunlah, Hind.). Same as Emblic myrobalan.——*Indian grass* (भूस्तृण - bhústrina, San.; اذخر بری - izkhiribarri, Ar.; سنبل هندی - sumbulihindí, Pers.; گنجنی کا گھاس - ganjníkághás, Hind.; نارنگی کے باس کا گھاس - nárangíkebáskághás, Dec.; ಗಂಧಹಂಚಿಕಡ್ಡಿ - gandahanchikhaddi, Can.; కామంచిగడ్డి - kámanchigaddi, Tel.; ചോറപ്പുല്ല് - chórappullu, Mal.; වතුසවඳරා - vatusavandará, Singh.; சுனறிப்புல் - shunárippul, Tam.). San. from (bhú, san. earth + trina, san. grass). Ar. from (izkhar, ar. andropogon sp. + barr, ar. forest). Pers. from (sumbul, pers. spikenard, nardostachys jatamansi, dec. + hindí, pers. indian). Hind. from (gandh, san. aromatic + ghás, hind. grass). Dec. from (nárangí, hind. orange, citrus aurantium, linn. + bás, hind. smell + ghás, hind. grass); cf. lemon grass. Can. from (gandu, can. male + hanchi, can. long grass of which brooms are made, aristida setacea, retz. + khaddi, can. spear). Tel. from (káru, tel. forest + manchi, tel. good + gaddi, tel. grass) [lemon grass, roussa grass]. Mal. from (chóra, san. fragrance + pullu, mal. grass). Singh. from (vatu, singh. garden + savandará, singh. andropogon muricatus, retz.). Tam. from (shukku, tam. dry ginger + náru, tam. to smell + pul, tam. grass) [ginger grass, roussa grass]. Tel. also (kámákshikasavu) by corruption. Mal. also (kámákshippullu). Singh. also (máná). Tam. also (shukkunárippul), meaning dry ginger + to smell + grass; (vásanaippul), meaning smell + grass; (kámádchippul), by corruption from teloogoo; (mándappul), meaning indigestion + grass; (kávattambul), meaning shed + grass. Title otherwise Citronella, Garden cuscus, Orange grass, Spice grass. Botanically Andropogon [beard grass] nardus, linn., graminaceæ [vricsham, 156]. A large perennial herb, with a long slightly branched, partly aërial rhizome, reaching ½ inch in diameter, and strongly ringed with the closely placed scars of the leaf-sheaths, the remains of which persist on the upper portion, and giving off numerous tough root-fibres. Stem reaching 6 feet or more high, erect, stout, cylindrical, solid, smooth and shining, partially concealed by the leaf-sheaths, scarcely thickened at the nodes, which are approximated below but widely separated above, flat or channelled on one side in the upper portion. Leaves very large and long, numerous, erect, lower ones sometimes reduced to their sheaths; sheaths thick and strong, about 6 inches long, close but not entirely enveloping the stem, quite smooth, striate; ligule short, brown, lacinate, scarious; blade about 2 feet long, linear, very much attenuated at the apex, tapering below, minutely denticulate with forward points on the edges, smooth on both surfaces, pale somewhat glaucous green, lighter beneath. Spikelets very small, arranged in couples, one stalked, containing one male flower, the other sessile, with one hermaphrodite and often one barren flower; the couples, to the number of three or four, articulated on alternate sides of a short, flattened, jointed rachis clothed along the edges with long white silky hairs tufted beneath the spikelets, forming a short acute spike about ½–¾ inch long; the spikes arranged in pairs on a common slender stalk, at the bent basal node of which is a large, erect, acute, leafy, striate, orange-red, shining bract, scarious at the edges, which encloses the pairs of spikes before expansion; the pairs of spikes very numerous, placed on the somewhat zic-zac, elongated, smooth, slender, erect, flattened branches of elongated panicles, which come off in clusters from the axils of the upper leaves, the whole forming a very large, tufted, elongated, somewhat drooping inflorescence, often 2 feet or more in length; glumes nearly equal, acuminate, membranous, smooth, purplish, boat-shaped, the lower one of the sessile spikelet flattened on the back against the rachis and without a midrib, those of the stalked spikelets with several parallel strong veins; pales of the lower spikelet two, or with a third representing a barren flower, very unequal, the lower very small, deeply bifid with two long cusps, from between which comes off a long, slender, slightly kneed purple awn, about twice the length of the glumes, and projecting considerably beyond the spikelet, the upper much larger, acute but without an awn, very delicate and membranous, without veins; in the flower of the upper spikelet there is but a single membranous non-awned pale. Lodicules two, oblong, truncate, longer than the ovary. Stamens three, anthers purple. Stigmas two, spreading, protruded from the flower, plumose, bright red-purple. Fruit not united with the pales. Native of Ceylon. Can be distinguished from other Beard grasses by rufous colour, short spikes, and narrow leaves. On being chewed grass has exactly the flavor of ginger [q.v.]. In infusion is medicinally stomachic; gives to pharm. citronella oil, the volatile oil obtained by distillation from the fresh plant; color is of a light greenish-yellow; officinal; oleum graminis indici, or oleum andropogonis of chemists. Oil used to flavor honey-soap.——*Indian gum* (صمغ هندی - samaghihindí, Hind.). Same as Gum ghautty [q.v.]. Mixture of gums [gond] of:—Acacia arabica, willd. [babool]; Acacia catechu, willd. [catechu]; Acacia farnesiana, willd. [piyvail]; Ægle marmelos, corr. [bael]; Albizzia lebbek, benth. [common sirissa]; Albizza odoratissima, benth. [fragrant sirissa]; Anogeissus latifolia, wall. [vekkauly]; Cassia auriculata, linn. [tungaid]; Feronia elephantum, corr. [wood-apple]; Mangifera indica, linn. [mango]; Melia azadirachta, linn. [neem]; Terminalia belerica, roxb. [belleric myrobalan]; and many other trees.——*Indian gum arabic* (کیکر کا گوند - kikarkágond, Hind.). Gum of the Babool [q.v.].——*Indian gut* (هندی مدن مست - hindímadanmast, Hind.). Product of caryota urens, linn., palmaceæ [bastard sago palm].——*Indian gutta-percha* (ناٹ کا گاٹا پرچا - nátkágátaparchá, Hind.). Hindostany means country guttapercha. Same as Pauchonty.——*Indian heliotrope* (हस्तिशुण्डा - hastishundá, San.; थोरकुरडू - t'hórakuradú, Mahr.; هاتهی شورا - háthíshúrá, Hind.; بچھو کے ڈاک کا پتا - biçchúkedákkápattá, Dec.; ಚೇಳುಬಾಲದಗಿಡ - chélubáladagida, Can.; ಚೇಳಕಡೆ - chélakade, Too.; తేలుమణి - télumani, Tel.; ହାତିସୁରା - hátisurá, Oor.; തേൾക്കൊടുക്ക - télkkotukku, Mal.; தேட்கொடுக்கி - tédgodukki, Tam.). San. from (hasti, san. elephant + shundá, san. trunk); from fruits like elephant's trunk. Mahr. from (t'hóra, mahr. large + kuradú, mahr. ear-ring). Hind. from sanscrit. Dec. from (biçchú, hind. scorpion + dák, hind. sting + pattá, hind. leaf). Can. from (chelu, can. scorpion + bála, can. tail + gida, can. plant). Too. from (chélu, too. scorpion + kade, too. end). Tel. from (télu, tel. scorpion + mani, san. precious stone). Oor. from sanscrit. Mal. from tamul. Tam. from (tél, tam. scorpion + kodukku, tam. sting); from fruits like scorpion's sting. San. also (bhúvrishchikáli), meaning ground + the plant, tragia involucrata, mueller; (nakrári), meaning crocodile's enemy; (vishaghná), meaning poison-destroying; (amaradáru), meaning immortal tree; (nágadantí), meaning serpent's tooth; (shríhastiní), meaning having beautiful elephant's ear-like leaf; (bhúrundi), meaning growing on earth; (vrishchikáli), meaning scorpion + friend [caunjory]. Can. also (chélukondi), meaning scorpion + sting; (chélumani), meaning scorpion + stone. Tel. also (gurugu) [moorgha]. Mal. also (teliyanni), meaning having a clear dye; (télkata), meaning scorpion's end; (vénappaçça), meaning summer green. Tam. also (nakkippú), meaning to lick + flower; (úttiram). Title otherwise Crocodile's foe, Indian turnsole, Scorpion plant, Scorpion sting, Scorpion tail, Wild clary. Botanically Heliotropium indicum, linn., boragineæ [vricsham, 92]. Alias Heliophytum indicum; Heliotropium anisophyllum, cordifolium, hispidum; Tiaridium anisophyllum, indicum. Annual, 1 foot; stem hairy; leaves generally alternate, petioled, cordate, wrinkled, curled at the margins; spikes leaf-opposed, solitary, peduncled, longer than the leaves; flowers sessile, minute, in two rows on the upper sides of the spikes; corolla longer than the calyx, tube gibbous; flowers small, lilac-bluish; flowering in rainy season; common weed, usually found among rubbish. Flowers like those of the garden heliotrope, but smaller; fruit mitreshaped; the plant has a fetid odour like stramonium [europe datura]; taste a little bitter. Whole is medicinally astringent; juice of the leaves applied to gum-boils and pimples on the face and in ophthalmia; in pharm non-officinal. Other common species are:—ovalifolium, paniculatum, polystachyum, scabrum, supinum, zeylanicum.——*Indian hemp* (ناٹ کا سن - nátkásan, Hind.). Fibre of Cannabis sativa, linn., urticaceæ [kinnab]. Extended also to the following fibres:—Crotalaria juncea, linn. [sunn]; Hibiscus cannabinus, linn. [hemp bendy]; Arenga saccharifera, labill. [gomooty palm].——*Indian hibiscus* (انغرای هندی - anghiráihindí, Ar.). Same as China rose bendy.——*Indian hoopoe* (هد هد هندی - hudhudihindí, Hind.). Same as Hood-hood.——*Indian horse radish* (ناٹ کا سہجنا - nátkásahjná, Hind.). Same as Moringa.——*Indian hounds' berry* (काकमाची - kákamáchí, San.; कामुनी - kámuní, Mahr.; عنب الثعلب - anabussalab, Ar.; روباه تربك - rúbáhiturbak, Pers.; مكو - mako, Hind.; كامونى - kámuní, Dec.; ಕರಿಕಾಚಿ - karikáchi, Can.; కాచి - káchi, Tel.; മണത്തക്കാളി - manattakkáli, Mal.; மணத்தக்காளி - manattakkáli, Tam.). San. from (káka, san. crow + má, san. lustre + añch, san. to go); from crow-black berries; compare indian berry. Ar. from (anab, ar. grape + salab, ar. fox). Pers. from (rúbáh, pers. fox + turbak, pers. grape, vitis vinifera, linn.). Dec. from arabic. Can. from (kari, can. black + káchi, can. the shrub). Tel. from sanscrit. Mal. and tam. from (manam, tam. fragrance + takkáli, tam. physalis). San. also (váyasí), meaning crow-like; (kóvidára), meaning small + solanum verbascifolium, linn. [variegated mountain ebony]; (krishnakóvidára), meaning black + the plant; (raktakóvidára), meaning red + the plant. Ar. also (anabussalabiaswad), meaning black fox grape; (anabuzzayib), meaning jackal-grape. Pers. also (rúbáhiturbakisiyáh), meaning black fox grape; (angúrrúbáh), meaning fox grape; (angúrrúbáhisiyáh), meaning black fox grape; (sagangúr), meaning dog grape [dog angoor]; (sagangúrisiyáh), meaning black dog grape. Hind. also (kálámako), meaning black fox grape; (údámako), meaning blue fox grape; (lálmako), meaning red solanum. Dec. also (údíkámuní), meaning blue solanum; (kálíkámuní), meaning black solanum; (lálkámuní), meaning red solanum. Can. also (karikánchi), meaning black + the shrub; (kariganike), meaning black + the shrub; (kempukánchi), meaning red + the shrub; (kempuganike), meaning red + the shrub; (kánchi); (ganiké). Tel. also (kánchi); (nallakánchi), meaning black + the plant; (kámanchi); (nallakámanchi), meaning black + the plant; (errakámanchi), meaning red + the plant; (errakánchi), meaning red + the plant; (gádzuchettu), meaning glass + plant, from fruit. Mal. also (nílaççunta), meaning blue solanum; (karuppumanattakkáli), meaning the black variety; (chovannamanattakkáli), meaning the red variety; (manattankanni). Tam. also (karuppumanattakkáli), meaning black + the plant; (shivappumanattakkáli), meaning red + the plant. Title otherwise Blackberried nightshade, Dog grape [dog angoor], Fox grape, Garden nightshade, Hound-berry, Manatakkauly. Botanically Solanum [cooly] nigrum, linn., solanaceæ [vricsham, 94]. Alias Solanum incertum, roxburghii, rubrum. A small low growing species of nightshade; bears white flowers, producing small berries of a black or red color; annual, if cultivated with care perennial; erect, from $1\frac{1}{2}$ to 3 feet high; branches occasionally and slightly angular and somewhat tubercular at the angles; leaves ovate, soft, slightly wavy, occasionally and partially dentate; petiolate; petiole short and slightly margined; flowers very small and white, drooping, lateral, pedunculate, pedicellate, and three or four form together a kind of umbel; calyx persistent, green, sepals five; corolla white, petals five; stamens five; berries drooping, small purple or black, many-seeded, juicy, and slightly sourish in taste; always found in flower and fruit. In the red variety or rubrum, the berries are red and slightly sweet; leaves generally and distinctly dentate, larger, thicker than that of nigrum, paler in color, not wavy, and possess a slight disagreeable smell; branches more spreading and not distinctly angular or tubercular. In decoction [kwautam] the leaves are bruised and the juice pressed out; this is warmed in an earthen vessel until it loses its green color and becomes reddish brown; when cool, it is strained; the same juice, instead of being warmed, if evaporated on a sand or water bath to the consistence of a soft mass forms an extract. Leaves diuretic, alterative, and laxative; slightly narcotic; used in dropsical affections in decoction and extract; juice of leaves useful in chronic enlargement of liver; substituted for british sweet nitre, cream of tartar and digitalis; in pharm. non-officinal. Berry although reckoned poisonous in europe, is eaten by tamulians with impunity; it is sweetish, but not very palatable; plant itself used as potherb.——*Indian house sparrow* (خان چڑی - khánchurí, Hind.). See Chiriyah.——*Indian hydrocotyle* (ارتا نیام هندی - artániyáihindí, Hind.). Same as Indian pennywort.——*Indian ipecacuanha* (मूलिनी - múliní, San.; انتمول - antamúl, Hind.; پت کاری - pitkárí, Dec.; ನೇಪಾಳ - népála, Can.; ನೇಪಾಳ - népála, Too.; కుక్కపాల - kukkapála, Tel.; വള്ളിപ്പാല - vallippála, Mal.; බින්නුග - binnuga, Singh.; நாய்ப்பாலை - náyppálai, Tam.). San. from (múla, san. root) [country radish]. Hind. from (anta, san. end + múla, san. root). Dec. from (pit, hind. bile + kárí, hind. stick). Can. from (náyi, can. dog + pála, can. milky plant). Tel. from (kukka, tel. dog + pála, tel. plant so called). Mal. from (valli, mal. creeper + pála, mal. milk plant). Singh. from (bin, singh. ground + nuga, singh. milk fig tree, ficus laccifera, roxb.). Tam. from (náy, tam. dog + pálai, tam. milky plant); useful in dog cure. Hind. also also (janglípikván), meaning country ipecacuanha. Can. also (kirumanjiballi), meaning small + hemp + creeper; (ádumuttadagida), meaning goat + not touch + plant; compare adhatoday. Tel. also (verripála), meaning mad + milk plant; (kákapála), meaning crow + milk plant [carook vauly]; (kurinja); (podapatramu), meaning spot + leaf. Tam. also (kurinjá); (sárangam); (naççaruppán), meaning poison + cutter; (nanjumuriççán), meaning poison + breaker; (péyppálai), meaning devil + milk plant; (kodagam). Title otherwise Asthmatic swallow-wort, Coorinjah, Country ipecacuanha, Vomiting swallow-wort. Botanically Tylophora asthmatica, w. & a., asclepiadeæ [vricsham, 88]. Alias Asclepias asthmatica, vomitoria; Cynanchum ipecacuanha, viridiflorum, vomitorium. Twining; leaves opposite, ovate-roundish, acuminated, cordate at the base, glabrous above, downy beneath; peduncles short, with two to three sessile few-flowered umbels; flowers rather large on long pedicels, externally pale green with a faint tinge of purple, internally light purple; corolla five-parted; follicles glabrous, divaricated; leaflets of corona fleshy, clasping the base of the gynostegium. In the dry state the leaves are rather thick and harsh, of a pale yellowish green; they have a not unpleasant herbaceous smell, with but very little taste; the root consists of a short, knotty, descending root stock, about one-eighth of an inch in thickness, emitting two to three aerial stems, and a considerable number of wiry roots; these roots are often six inches or more in length by half a line in diameter, and are very brittle; the whole drug is of a pale yellowish brown; it has no considerable odour, but a sweetish and subsequently acrid taste; in general appearance it is suggestive of valerian, but is somewhat stouter and larger. Root expectorant and diaphoretic in large dose, answers as an emetic; in smaller, often repeated doses, as a cathartic; also as an emetic by rubbing upon a stone 3–4 inches of fresh root, and mixing it with water for a dose; generally purges at the same time; substitute for ipecacuanha; similarly the dried leaf; gives to pharm. dried leaves, tylophoræ folia, emetic, diaphoretic, and expectorant, officinal.—"*a*" Other species of tylophora are:—fasciculata, iphisia, mollissima, pauciflora, tenuis.—"*b*" Small indian ipecacuanha; with the following vernacular names (méshashringí, San.; merásingí, Hind.; parpatrah, Dec.; podapatra, Tel.; binnuga, Singh.; shiruguriñjá, Tam.). San. from (mésha, san. sheep + shringa, san. horn), from fruit like ram's horn; compare wodier and screw-tree. Dec. from teloogoo. Tel. from (poda, tel. spot + patra, san. leaf). Singh. from (bin, singh. ground + nuga, singh. milky fig tree, ficus laccifera, roxb.). Tam. from (shiru, tam. small + kuriñjá, tam. the plant, tylophora asthmatica, w. & a.). Otherwise Small coorinjah; is botanically Gymnema sylvestre r. br., asclepiadeæ [vricsham, 88]; alias Asclepias geminata; Gymnema parviflorum; Periploca sylvestris. Climbing; all, except the upper side of the leaves, softly pubescent; leaves ovate, or ovate-lanceolate, attenuated at both ends, or obscurely cordate at the base; peduncles as long as the petioles; umbels twin, many-flowered; follicles slender, attenuated; flowers crowded, small, yellow; flowering nearly all the year. The leaves are from 4–5 inches long; upper surface dark green shining, under surface pale green; venation transverse and reticulate with a marginal vein; taste saltish and acrid. The root is about the size of the little finger or less, not unlike hemidesmus [indian sarsaparilla]; it has a tough wood, and when fresh a soft spongy bark, which is reddish brown and fissured longitudinally, but loses much bulk in drying, and becomes loose and transversely fissured; the taste is acrid and saltish; the whole plant abounds in milky juice. If chewed the plant destroys the power of the tongue to appreciate the taste of sweets and bitters; sugar [q.v.] tastes like sand, quinine [koinah] like chalk; effect lasts for one or two hours. Leaves a remedy in snake bites; also emetic and expectorant; quoted in pharm., non-officinal.—"*c*" Other common species of Gymnema are:—elegans, hirsutum, tingens, heyneána, lactiferum.——*Indian iron wood* (இருள்மரம் - irulmaram, Tam.). Same as Naugachampak.——*Indian jack* (ചക്ക - chakka, Mal.). Same as Common jack.——*Indian jalap* (جالپ هندی - jálapihindí, Hind.). Same as Turbith.——*Indian jay* (नीलकण्ठ - nílakant'ha, San.; तास - tása, Mahr.; شقراق - shakrák, Ar.; سبزك - sabzak, Pers.; نيل كنٹھ - nílkanth, Hind.; سبزك - sabzak, Dec.; ಕರಸುಂಗನಹಕ್ಕಿ - karasunganahakki, Can.; పాలపిట్ట - pálapitta, Tel.; കാട്ടുകാക്ക - káttukákka, Mal.; கட்டுக்காடை - kattukkádai, Tam.). San. from (níla, san. blue + kant'ha, san. throat). Mahr. corruption from (chásha, san. indian jay). Ar. from (shakara, ar. dusky red). Pers. from (sabz, pers. green). Hind. from sanscrit; cf. neelcunty. Dec. from persian. Can. from (kari, can. black + sunku, can. wrinkle + hakki, can. bird). Tel. from (pálu, tel. milk + pitta, tel. bird); from property of feathers increasing cow's milk when given to eat with grass. Mal. from (kátu, mal. forest + kákka, mal. crow). Tam. from (kattu, tam. to confine + kádai, tam. quail); as a bird of omen. San. also (manikant'haka), meaning beauty + throat; (kiki), imitative from cry; (kikidiva), meaning kiki, the sound + uttering; (chála), meaning sporting. Ar. also (akak). Can. also (goravanka). Tam. also (párguruvi), meaning milk + small bird. Title otherwise Indian roller. Coracidæ family, fissirostres, insessores, aves [pacshy, 8], of naturalists [jantoo]. Rollers. Birds of large size, resembling jays. Adorned, especially on wings, with rich blue colors; noisy and somewhat familiar. The species best known is Coracias indica. Alias Coracias bengalensis; Garrulus naevius. When seated puffs out the feathers of its head and neck; flies not unlike the crow [caurvam], though more buoyant, making sudden darts in the air in all directions; has a harsh grating cry; sacred to shiva [q.v.], who assumed its form; one of the birds on whose movements many omens [shacoonam] depend; if it cross a traveller just after starting it is considered a bad omen [neelcunty].——*Indian kale* (قلقاس - kulkás, Ar.). See Kachvee.——*Indian kino* (دم الاخوين هندی - dammulakhwainihindí, Hind.). Product of Common vengay.——*Indian laburnum* (خيار شنبر هندی - khiyárshambarihindí, Hind.). Same as Common condray.——*Indian leather birch* (चर्मी - charmí, San.). Title from bark. Same as Bhoojpattar.——*Indian lilac* (آزاد درخت هندی - ázáddarakhtihindí, Hind.). Same as Large neem.——*Indian liquorice* (गुञ्जा - guñjá, San.; गुंज - gumja, Mahr.; गुर्गुंजि - gurgumji, Conc.; عين الديك - aínuddík, Ar.; چشم خروس - chashmikhurús, Pers.; گھنگچی - ghungchí, Hind.; گمچی - gumchí, Dec.; ಗುರುಗುಂಜಿ - gurugunji, Can.; గురిగింజ - gurigindza, Tel.; കുന്നി - kunni, Mal.; ඔලිඳවැල් - olindaval, Singh.; குன்றி - kunri, Tam.). Title from appearance and taste of root. San. from (guj, san. to sound); from sound of dry pod. Conc. from canarese. Ar. from (aín, ar. eye + dík, ar. cock); from appearance of seed. Pers. from (chashm, pers. eye + khurús, pers. cock). Hind. from sanscrit. Can. from (guru, san. heavy + gunji, can. the plant); from seed being used as a weight [indian shot]. Tel. similar. Tam. from (kunru, tam. to decrease); from small size of weight. San. also (kákachiñchá), meaning crow + tamarind, tamarindus indica, linn.; (raktiká), meaning slightly red, after the seed. Can. also (gulganji), meaning ball + the plant, as bearing ball-like seeds. Tel. also (gurivenda). Tam. also (kundumani), meaning globular + bead, by corruption. Title otherwise Bead root, Coondrimany, Coral-bead, Country liquorice [tootty], Goomchy, Jamaica wild liquorice, Love pea, Red-bead vine, Rosary-pea, Wild liquorice. Giving Coondry root [q.v.], Retty seeds [q.v.]. Botanically Abrus precatorius, linn., leguminosæ [vricsham, 48]. Alias Abrus minor, pauciflorus; Glycine abrus. Twining woody shrub; young shoots with a few addressed hairs at the apex; leaves alternate, abruptly pinnated; leaflets eight to twenty pair, linear-oval, obtuse at both ends, glabrous or slightly hairy; calyx campanulate, obsoletely four-lobed, upper lobe broadest; racemes axillary, peduncled, many-flowered; flowers pale purple or rose-colored; flowering in cold season; legumes oblong, compressed, four to six-seeded; seeds roundish, distinct;

common in hedges and waste grounds. Root has appearance and taste of liquorice root, product of glycirrhiza glabra, linn., leguminosæ [atimathooram]; note the following distinctions :—"*a*" glycirrhiza glabra, linn.; generally about size of a large goose quill or of the little finger, and sometimes as large as a thumb; color greyish or reddish-brown externally and slightly yellow internally; taste sweet and mucilaginous;—"*b*" abrus precatorius, linn.; generally much smaller than real liquorice and seldom acquires size of a finger; brown externally and white internally; taste generally not distinctly sweet. The seeds of abrus are size of a small pea [calauyam], chiefly black and red, and well known for their polish. Plant is mentioned in sooshrootan. Root yields an extract similar in medicinal properties to liquorice, though somewhat bitter; the leaves yield same even more than root; gives to pharm. indian liquorice root, abri radix; seeds, if eaten, produce headache; powdered and injected hypodermically are poisonous; in the form of paste disperse light and recent swellings, as from bites of poisonous insects; native women swallow seeds, generally the white, every day for some days after each menstruation to prevent conception; for british iodine as a discutient; oil also used in native medicine. In jamaica the leaves are used instead of tea [q.v.], not so known here. The lowest weight in use among the native jewellers and druggists takes its denomination from the seed, though the fictitious weight is nearly double that of the seed; weight of one indian liquorice seed may be a grain and five-sixteenths; the fictitious retty [q.v.] weight is two grains and three-sixteenths nearly; the scarlet seeds, with jet black spot at top, are those generally used thus; the goldsmiths [tattaun] also reduce them to a fine powder, and in this state use them to increase adhesion in the more delicate parts of manufactured ornaments [nagay, zewar]; they are also used for beads [munkah] and rosaries [maulay], whence the specific botanical name of plant. Three principal varieties:—with rose-colored flowers, red seed and black eye; with dark-colored flowers, black seed and white eye; with white flowers, white seed; the first is commonest; also varieties with yellow and purple seeds; abrus fruticulosus, wall., is a species called "small" in all the vernaculars. There is a Tamul proverb:—குன்றி மணிக்கும் குண்டியிற் கறுப்பு—"Even a coondrimany seed has a black spot "on it;" same as no rose [gool] without a thorn. No other common species of abrus here. Compare where transl. is of second term:—Adenanthera pavonina (bandigurigindza), round; Dalbergia volubilis (bandigurigindża), round; Rhynchosia cyanosperma (nallagurigindza), black. See gloss. paragraphs.——*Indian lynx* (سیاہ گوش ھندی - siyáhgoshihindi, Hind.). Same as Caracal.——*Indian madder* (ناتکا منجیت - nátkámanjíth, Hind.). Same as Munjeet and Chayroot.——*Indian mahogany* (ناتکا مہاگنی - nátkámahágani, Hind.). Same as Toon.——*Indian maiden hair* (मयूरशिखण्ड - mayúrashikhanda, San.; घोडाखुरी - ghódákhurí, Mahr.; شعر الجن - sharuljinn, Ar.; پرسیاوشان - parisiyáwashán, Pers.; کالی جھانت - kálíjhánt, Hind.; నెమలిసిగ - nemalisiga, Tel.; மயிற்கொண்டை - mayirgondai, Tam.). San. from (mayúra, san. peacock + shikhanda, san. tail); from resemblance to peacock's tail. Mahr. from (ghódá, mahr. horse + khura, san. hoof); from shape of leaflets and arrangement of spores on under side. Ar. from (shar, ar. hair + jinn, ar. fairy). Pers. from greek meaning chest medicine. Hind. from (kálí, hind. black + jhánt, hind. hair). Tel. from (nemali, tel. peacock + siga, tel. crest). Tam. from (mayil, tam. peacock + kondai, tam. crest); compare trailing grass. San. also (mayúraka), meaning peacock, from beauty [indian burr]. Mahr. also (rájahamsa), meaning flamingo, from beauty; (hamsarája). Ar. also (sharulghaul), meaning demon's hair; (sharuljibál), meaning mountain hair. Hind. also (hansráj), meaning duck + royal; (mubárakah), meaning auspicious. Tel. also (bandanevali), meaning rock + peacock; (bárikí). Tam. also (malaigalakki), meaning mountain shaker; from growing on mountains; compare lance-leaved balah. Greek ἀδίαντον. Title otherwise Capillaire, Dudder grass, Fairy hair, Mountain hair, Peacock's tail, Venus' hair. Compare Foreign tungaid. Botanically the Adiantum genus, filices [vricsham, 157]. Indigenous in himalayas. Leaves sweetish, with slight bitterness and astringency; considered medicinally tonic, given in powder. Forms ingredients in certain dye [shauyam] recipes.——*Indian mallow* (ولایتی کنگوئی - viláitíkangoí, Hind.). Same as Tootty.——*Indian medicago* (शालपर्णी - shálaparní, San; کدالیا - kuddáliyá, جنگلی میتھی - janglímethí, Hind.; ಸೀಗಿಟಿಗಿಡ - sígitigida, Can.; ముంతమందు - muntamandu, Tel.; සාලපර්ණි - shálaparni, Singh.). San. from (shála, san. shorea robusta, gærtn. + parna, san. leaf); from leaves like saul [q.v.] leaves. Hind. from (janglí, hind. wild + methí, hind. trigonella foenum græcum, linn.). Tel. from (munta, tel. pot + mandu, tel. medicine); as healing indolent sores. Singh. from sanscrit. Hind. also (sálpán), from sanscrit. Tel. also (antinta), meaning sticking, of the medicine; (chetenta); (karraantinta); (chepputatta), meaning slipper plate; (gábá); (gítanaramu), meaning line + nerve; (kólákuponna), meaning straight + leaf + the tree, calophyllum inophyllum, linn.; (kokkiti) [sea shore paulay]. Title otherwise Indian trifolium, Sticking plaster plant, Wild fenugreek. Botanically Desmodium [shaulicay] triflorum, dec., leguminosæ [vricsham, 48]. Alias Æschynomene triflora; Hedysarum stipulaceum, triflorum. Stems procumbent, diffuse; leaves trifoliolate; leaflets orbicular, obovate or obcordate, more or less pubescent or hairy; peduncles axillary, solitary, fascicled, one-three flowered, calyx deeply divided; vexillum obovate, long-clawed; style bent acutely near the summit and tumid at the angle; legumes hispidly pubescent, three-six jointed, notched in the middle on the lower margins, even on the other; joints truncated at both ends; flowers small, blue; flowering all year; widely-distributed, springing up in all soils and situations. Natives appply plant fresh gathered to abscesses and wounds that do not heal well [lance-leaved balah]; supplying place of trifolium and medicago in europe.——*Indian millet* (جاورس ھندی - jávarsihindí, Hind.). Same as Varagoo and Cholum.——*Indian mint* (فوتنج ھند - fútanjihind, Ar.). Same as Poodeenah.——*Indian modelwood* (ناتکاھلداو - nátkáhaldáu, Hind.). Same as Yellow cadamba.——*Indian morinda* (ناتکا آل - nátkáál, Hind.). Same as Dyeing mulberry.——*Indian mourner* (अत्यूहा - atyúhá, San.). Same as Coral jasmine.——*Indian mulberry* (شاہ توت - sháhtút, Hind.). From (sháh, pers. king + tút, hind. mulberry). See sep. title.——*Indian myrobalan* (ھلیلہ ھند - halílahihind, Hind.). Same as Chebulic myrobalan.——*Indian nettle* (जीवन्ती - jívantí, San.; کولسے کا جھاڑ - kolse kájhár, Dec.; ಕಿರುಹಾಲೆ - kiruhále, Can.; కాకముస్తె - kákamuste, Tel.; മലന്തുടലി - malantutali, Mal.; பேய்முன்னை - péymunnai, Tam.). San. from (jív, san. to live) [goolancha]. Dec. from (kolsá, hind. charcoal + jhár, hind. tree); from use of wood for charcoal [indian nightshade, neermoolly]. Can. from (kiru, can. small + hále, can. the tree, a species of mimusops). Mal. from (mala, mal. mountain + tutali, mal. scutia indica, brongn.). Tam. from (péy, tam. devil + munnai, tam. premna integrifolia.) San. also (jívaní), meaning living [dita]. Hind. also (chíkun). Can. also (kádubajagida), meaning wild + acorus calamus, linn.; (gorklu). Tel. also (tellakákamuste), meaning white + the plant; (gaddanelli), meaning root + premna latifolia, roxb.; (moralichettu) [chironjee]; (úrakanudzunáluka), meaning domestic + plant, tetranthera pentandra, rox.; (áva); (shékumánu); (budumuru); (priyáluvrikshamu). Mal. also (tíntapparuva), meaning polluting creeper. Tam. also (munnai), meaning shining [moonnay]; (kuttippilá), meaning small jack tree, artocarpus integrifolius, willd. [stunted jack]. Title otherwise Amboyna sponia, Charcoal tree. Botanically Sponia wightii, planch., ulmaceæ [vricsham, 120]. Alias Celtis orientalis; Sponia amboinensis, andaresa, orientalis; Trema orientalis. Small tree, 15 feet; harsh-rough leaves alternate, bifarious, short-petioled, ovate-cordate, acuminated, minutely serrated, scabrous above, villous underneath; flowers axillary, aggregated on short two-cleft diverging peduncles; calyx five-parted; male and female flowers generally on separate trees; drupe small, succulent, black when ripe, nut wrinkled, one-celled, one-seeded; flowers very small, green; common, of rapid growth; flowering all the year. Yields a gum [gond] resembling that of cherry [q.v.] tree. Planted in avenues [shaulay]; the leaves are used for polishing wood and horns [sing]; bark yields fibre [naur], used to tie rafters of houses. Wood is soft and white; makes the best charcoal for gunpowder.—"*a*" Another species of sponia is Velutina.—"*b*" White indian nettle, so called in vernaculars, is Celtis wightii, planch, ulmaceæ [vricsham, 120]. Leaves oblong, abruptly acuminate, somewhat acute at the base, quite entire, three-nerved, lateral pair of nerves extending from the base to the apex; stipules somewhat peltate; cymes about the length of the petioles or sometimes twice as long; berry shortly rostrate, smooth; flowers pale bluish; flowering nearly all the year; subalpine tracts. Wood greyish-white, very hard, close-grained; annual rings indistinctly marked by a narrow belt without pores.—"*c*" There are other species of celtis:—Australis, is european nettle tree, grecian honey-berry, lote tree, lotus tree [bair]; Occidentalis is american nettle tree, hackberry; Roxburghii is a small tree, common on ghauts [q.v.]; Serotina is a tree on neilgherries.—"*d*" Compare also in other genera. Girardina heterophylla, neilgherry nettle; Urtica crenulata, devil's nettle, fever nettle; for which see gloss. paragraphs.——*Indian nightshade* (बृहती - brihatí, San.; कल्लांट - kallánta, Conc.; کولسے کا جھاڑ - kolsekájhár, Dec.; ಕೆಂಪುಗುಳ್ಳಗಿಡ - kempugullagida, Can.; ಕಲ್ಲಂಟೆ - kallante, Too.; తెల్లములక - tellamulaka, Tel.; ചെറുചുണ്ട - cheruchunta, Mal.; තිබ්බටු - tibbatu, Singh.; முள்ளி - mulli, Tam.). San. from (brih, san. to grow) [prickly brinjaul]. Dec. from (kolsá, dec. charcoal + jhár, dec. tree) [indian nettle, neermoolly]. Can. from (kempu, can. red + gullagida, can. the plant, solanum ferox, linn.). Tel. from (tella, tel. white + mulaka, tel. solanum ferox, linn.). Mal. from (cheru, mal. small + chunta, mal. solanum verbascifolium, linn.). Tam. from (mul, tam. thorn). San. also (alpap'balá), meaning having small fruit; (bahupatrí), meaning large-leaved; (dushpradharshiní), meaning not to be touched; (kshudrabhantákí), meaning small brinjaul; (kantálu), meaning adorned with thorn; (kantakiní), meaning thorny; (vanavrintákí), meaning wild brinjaul; (simhí), meaning injuring, from thorns; (dusparshá), meaning not to be touched [caunjory, prickly brinjaul]; (kantakáriká), meaning giving out thorn; (kantatanu), meaning having thorny body; (mahatí), meaning great; (mahatíkrántá), meaning surpassing brinjaul; (ráshtriká), meaning produced in country; (st'húlakantaká), meaning large thorned;

(tóraní), meaning pertaining to gate; (shvétavrihatí), meaning white brinjaul; (asprishí), meaning not to be touched; (vyághrí), meaning tiger-like, from thorns. Can. also (kirigullagida), meaning small + solanum ferox, linn.; (badanegida). Mal. also (nilavazhutina), meaning ground brinjaul, solanum melongena, linn.; (cheruvazhutina), meaning small brinjaul. Tam. also (kuttuççedikkandangattiri), meaning bunch + tree + solanum xanthocarpum, schrad. and wendle; (páppáramulli), meaning bramin + the plant; (vazhuthalai); (karimulli), meaning black + the plant; (shiruvazhuthalai), meaning small + solanum melongena, linn. Title otherwise Bramin moolly. Botanically Solanum [cooly] indicum, linn., solanaceæ [vricsham, 94]. Alias Solanum agreste, canescens, heynei, pinnatifidum, sodomaeum, violaceum. Shrub, armed; prickles of stem compressed, recurved; leaves solitary or twin, oblong or ovate, tomentose, discolored, sinuately lobed, unequal at the base, prickly on both surfaces; racemes interfoliaceous; calyx prickly, segments reflexed; berries globose; corolla deeply five-cleft, blue; berries orange yellow; flowering all year. Root has little sensible taste or smell. Root an ingredient of dashamoolam [q.v.], used in very many diseases; in pharm. non-officinal. There are varieties, differing chiefly in shape of leaves.——*Indian oak* (بلوطالهند - ballútulhind, Hind.). Same as Teak. Also Barringtonia genus, for which see Indian oak, separate title.——*Indian oats* (ولایتی جو - viláitíjau, Hind.). Same as Vilauyaty jow.——*Indian olibanum* (لبان - lubán, Ar.). See under Olibanum.——*Indian olive* (زیتون کاپیر - zaitúnkáper, Hind.; زیتون کاجهاڑ - zaitúnkájhár, Dec.; കരിവെട്ടി - karivetti, Mal.). Hind. from (zaitún, ar. olive, olea europæa, linn. + per, hind. tree) [zeitoon]. Mal. from (kari, mal. black + vetti, mal. a tree of worthless timber). Title otherwise Indian wild olive. Botanically Olea [jita] dioica, roxb., oleaceæ [vricsham, 85]. Moderate sized tree; leaves opposite, oblong, remotely and acutely serrate, acuminate, smooth, on short petioles; panicles axillary and opposite below the leaves; male flowers numerous; calyx four-toothed; corolla tube very short, border four-cleft; female flowers on a separate tree; calyx as in the male; corolla none; drupe nearly round, one-celled, one-seeded, much like english sloe; flowers small, white; flowering in july. A valuable timber.——*Indian paper birch* (صنوبر هندی - sanobarihindí, Hind.). Same as Bhoojpattar.——*Indian pareira* (पाठा - pát'há, San.; वेणीवेल - venívéla, Mahr.; دکھ نربسی - dukhnirbisí, Hind.; పాఠ - páta, Tel.; കാട്ടുവള്ളി - káttuvalli, Mal.; වෙනිවැල් - venival, Singh.; பொன்முசுட்டை - ponmusuttai, Tam.). San. from (pat'h, san. to declare); often quoted in medicine books. Mahr. from (véní, san. braid + véla, mahr. creeper). Hind. from (dukh, hind. pain + nir, san. antidote + visha, san. poison). Mal. from (kátu, mal. forest + valli, mal. creeper). Tam. from (pon, tam. gold + musuttai, tam. ipomæa candicans); from flowers. San. also (ambasht'há), meaning behaving like mother; (vénívallí), meaning braided creeper. Hind. also (hárjorá), meaning bonesetter; cf. piranday. Tam. also (vattattiruppi), meaning circle + to turn; from orbicular sepals. Title otherwise False pareira brava plant, Gravel root, Hair creeper, Ice vine, Velvet leaf, Wild vine. Botanically Cissampelos pareira, linn., menispermaceæ [vricsham, 5]. Alias Cissampelos acuminata, capeba, cocculus, convolvulacea, hernandifolia, hirsuta, mauritiana, microcarpa, orbiculata, tomentosa; Cocculus orbiculatus; Menispermum orbiculatum. Twining shrub; stem pubescent; leaves cordate, usually obtuse or acute, rarely emarginate, sinus narrow or wide, upper side glabrous or slightly pubescent, under more or less pubescent, or even tomentose; petioles inserted at the margin; male racemes 3-4, shorter than the petioles; sepals orbicular, unguiculate; column of stamens longer than the entire and externally hairy cup-shaped corolla; female racemes usually in pairs, sometimes solitary and forked; in flower scarcely so long as, in fruit often longer than, the leaf; drupes hairy; flowers very small, yellowish; flowering all year; habitat, tropical and sub-tropical india from scinde to ceylon. The root is about half an inch in diameter, bark light brown, marked with longitudinal furrows, and transverse constrictions, sometimes very crooked and knotty, from growing in stony ground, seldom branched, fracture fibrous, bark corky, and thick for the size of the root, wood yellowish, in from 10 to 15 wedge-shaped bundles, containing many large vessels, and separated by narrow medullary rays; odour none; taste at first sweetish and aromatic, afterwards very bitter. The bark is brown or greyish-brown, wrinkled longitudinally and crossed transversely by annular elevations; interior woody, porous, and yellowish-white. The root is medicinally demulcent, sedative, and slightly diuretic; active principle, a bitter alkaloid identical with bebeerine. Decoction; take of the root, cut into small pieces and slightly bruised, two ounces and a half; water, one pint and a half; boil on a slow fire till the liquid is reduced to one pint, cool, strain. Dose from one to three fluid ounces. Substituted for pareira root imported from europe. Real pareira brava is from Chondodendron tomentosum of Peru and Brazil. ——*Indian pennywort* (मण्डूकपर्णी - mandúkaparní, San.; एकपानी - ékapání, Mahr. and Conc.; ارتانیاءهندی - artániyáihindí, Ar.; ولّری - vallárí, Dec.; ಒಂದೆಲಗ - ondelaga, Can.; ತಿಮರೆ - timare, Too.; ಪಿನ್ನ ఏలకి - pinnaélaki, Tel.; കുടകം - kutakam, Mal.; හිංගොටුකොළ - híngotukola, Singh.; வல்லாரை - vallárai, Tam.). San. from (mandúka, san. frog + parna, san. leaf) [munjeet]. Ar. from (artániyá, ar. pennywort, antirrhinum cymbalaria, linn. + hindí, ar. indian). Dec. from tamul. Can. from (ondu, can. one + ele, can. leaf). Tel. from (pinna, tel. small + élaki, tel. elettaria cardamomum, maton). Mal. from (kutaku, mal. the hill so called). Singh. means small hydrocotyle. Tam. from (val, tam. strong + árai, tam. marsilea quadrifolia, linn.). San. also (bhékaparní), meaning frog + leaf; (mandúkapatra), meaning frog + leaf; (satyanát'ha), meaning lord of truth; (bráhmí), meaning relating to brahma; (mandukí); (bhékí). Hind. also (bráhmamendki), meaning bramin frog. Dec. also (vallárikápattá), meaning hydrocotyle leaf. Tel. also (mandúkabrambhi); (bokkudu) [prickly coorvitchy]; (bollibúsara), meaning white + physalis peruviana, linn.; (babbasa). Mal. also (muttil), meaning matured gingelly. Title otherwise Asiatic penny-wort, Frog-leaf, Vallauray. Botanically Hydrocotyle asiatica, linn., umbelliferæ [vricsham, 67]. Alias Hydrocotyle thunbergiana, triflora; Trisanthus cochin-chinensis. Herbaceous; leaves attached by the margin, orbicular-reniform, equally crenated, seven-nerved, glabrous or slightly villous below when young; petioles and peduncles fascicled, sprinkled with soft hairs; umbels capitate, short-peduncled, few-flowered; calyx tube slightly compressed; petals ovate, acute, spreading; fruit orbicular, reticulated, with four ribs on each of the flat sides, flowers whitish or purplish red. The plant grows freely all the year round if watered, sending out long runners, which produce leaves, roots and fruit at the joints; the fresh herb has an aromatic somewhat ivy-like odour when crushed and a nauseous bitter taste, but these qualities are to a great extent lost in drying. Gives to pharm. the bitter leaves, hydrocotyles folia; active principle, oil, vellarine; weak alterative tonic, locally applied stimulant; preparations, pulvis hydrocotyles, cataplasma hydrocotyles; officinal. There are other species:—conferta, javanica, rotundifolia.——*Indian peppermint* (فوتنج هندی - fútanjihindí, Hind.). See Poodeenah.——*Indian perch* (ندی کا کٹرنا - naddíkákatarná, Hind.). Same as Cock up.——*Indian pink* (कामलता - kámalatá, San.; ಕೆಂಪುಮಲ್ಲಿಗೆ - kempumallige, Can.; సూర్యరత్నము - súryaratnamu, Tel.; സൂര്യകാന്തി - súryakánti, Mal.; තරුලතා - tarulatá, Singh.; கெம்புமல்லிகை - kembumalligai, Tam.). San. from (káma, san. love + latá, san. creeper); beautiful creeper [quamoclit]. Can. from (kempu, can. red + mallige, can. jasmine). Tel. from (súrya, san. sun + ratna, san. gem) [quamoclit]. Mal. from (súrya, san. sun + kánti, san. lustre) [sooryacaunty]. Singh. from (taru, san. tree + latá, san. creeper). Tam. from (kembu, tam. ruby + malligai, tam. jasmine, jasminum). San. also (tarulatá), meaning tree + creeper; (shvétatarulatá), meaning white + tree + creeper. Hind. also (kámalata); (láltarulata), meaning red + the creeper; (sufedtarulata), meaning white + the creeper. Tam. also (mayirmánikkam), meaning hair ruby; from filiform leaves. Title otherwise American bell-flower, Barbadoes sweetwilliam, China creeper, Crimson cypress-vine, Cupid's flower, Cypress vine, Indian forget-me-not, Star creeper, Wing-leaved convolvulus. Botanically Ipomæa [calamby] quamoclit, linn., convolvulaceæ [vricsham, 93]. Alias Convolvulus pennatus, quamoclit; Quamoclit vulgaris. Climbing annual, 6 feet, pinnate leaves, bright-red, white, or rarely yellow flowers.——*Indian pipeflower* (భారంగి - bhárangí, Tel.). Same as Bhraungy.——*Indian plum* (प्राचीनामलक - práchínámalaka, San.; तालीशपत्रि - tálíshapatri, Mahr.; زرنب - zarnab, Ar.; تالسپتری - tálíspatrí, Hind. and Dec.; ತಾಳೀಸಪತ್ರಿ - tálísapatri, Can.; తాళీసపత్రి - tálísapatri, Tel.; താളീശപത്രം - tálíshapatram, Mal.; රටගුරැස්ස - ratangurassa, Singh.; தாளிசப்பத்திரி - tálisappattiri, Tam.). San. from (práchína, san. east + ámalaka, san. emblic myrobalan tree, phyllanthus emblica, linn.). Hind., &c., from (tálísha, san. the tree + patra, san. leaf) [country cinnamon]. Singh. from (rata, singh. foreign + ugurassa, singh. sweet lovilovi tree, flacourtia ramontchi, l'herit.). Tam. from (tálísha, san. the tree + pattra, san. leaf) [cassia cinnamon]. San. also (tálísha), meaning killing disease like toddy [taulisam]; (tálíshapatra), meaning the tree + leaf; (kálaméshí), meaning black + nardostachys jatamansi, dec. [bawchee, munjeet]; (khadiraparni), meaning having leaves like khadira, acacia catechu, willd; (vidára), meaning tearing asunder. Ar. also (rijluljurád), meaning foot of locust, from shape of leaf. Hind. also (pániaunla), meaning water + phyllanthus emblica, linn.; (paníyála), by corr.; (barhmí). Dec. also (tajpát), meaning cassia leaf, cinnamomum tamala, nees. [country cinnamon]; (barmí). Can. also (goragi); (charichali); (chanchalimara). Singh. also (talis). Title otherwise East indian plum, Many-spined flacourtia, Puneeala plum, Water myrobalan. Botanically Flacourtia [swaudoocantacam] cataphracta, roxb., bixineæ [vricsham, 14]. Middling sized tree, armed with large multiple thorns; leaves oval-oblong, acuminated, serrated; racemes axillary, many-flowered; flowers small, greenish; fruit of the form and size of a cherry [q.v.] or tiparee, slightly compressed into a five or six-sided shape, of a deep dull purplish chocolate color; indigenous in dry forests; flowering in the cold season. Leaves and young shoots taste like rhubarb; astringent and stomachic properties, in diarrhœa, weakness and consumption; infusion of bark in hoarseness; quoted in pharm. but non-officinal. Fruit edible; oil [yennay] from seeds; wood closegrained, hard and durable, but girth small. Compare:—Achras sapota, sapota plum; Cordia myxa, assyrian plum; Diospyros kaki, japanese date plum; Diospyros montana, date plum; Eugenia jambolana, java plum; Eugenia jambos, malabar plum; Flacourtia ramontchi, mauritius plum; Prunus communis, var. insititia, bokhara plum; Prunus triflora, chinese plum; Spondias mangifera, hog plum; Ximenia americana, mountain plum; Zizyphus vulgaris, round plum. See gloss. paragraphs.——*Indian purslane* (लोणी - lóní, San.; بقلة الحمقة - bakalatulhumakah, Ar.; خرفه كلان - khurfahikalán, Pers.; بڑالونيا - baráloniyá, Hind.; خلفه - khulfah, Dec.; ದೊಡ್ಡಗೋಣಿ - doddagóni, Can.; బొద్దుపావిలి - boddupávili, Tel.; കരിച്ചീര - kariççíra, Mal.; හෙගෙන්ද - genda, Singh.; கோழிக்கீரை - kózhikkírai, Tam.). San. from (lú, san. to cut); on account of its acidity. Ar. from (bakalah, ar. purslane, portulaca + humaka, ar. fools); from its growing anywhere regardless of soil. Pers. from (khurfah, pers. purslane + kalán, pers. large). Hind. from (bará, hind. large + loniya, hind. purslane). Dec. from persian. Can. from (dodda, can. large + góni, can. a plant). Tel. from (boddu, tel. navel + pávili, tel. portulaca quadrifida, linn.). Mal. from (kari, mal. black + chíra, mal. greens). Tam. from (kózhi, tam. fowl + kírai, tam. vegetable); from fleshy leaves like cock's crest. San. also (lónámlá), meaning cutting sourness; cf. sour auray. Ar. also (bakalatulmubárik), meaning excellent purslane. Pers. also (turuk). Hind. also (loniya); (núniyah); (luniya-khulfah). Can. also (doddagorai). Tel. also (peddapávili), meaning large + portulaca quadrifida, linn.; (gangapávili), meaning large + the plant; (gangarégu), meaning large + jujube tree, zizyphus jujuba, lam.; (battsali) [heart-leaved malabar night-shade, indian spinach, small indian purslane]; (pappukúra), meaning dholl + vegetable. Tam. also (paruppukkírai), meaning dholl + vegetable, from being cooked with dholl [common dholl]. Greek ἀνδράχνη, Latin porcilaca. Title otherwise Cock's greens, Dholl greens, Fool's purslane, Khoolfah, Lony. Botanically Portulaca oleracea, l., portulaceæ [vricsham, 18]. Annual, herbaceous diffuse; leaves scattered, entire, cuneiform, fleshy, axils and joints naked; flowers sessile; petals five, small, yellow; capsule one-celled; seeds numerous; common weed cultivated by gardeners; flowering in the rainy season. Seeds are medicinally demulcent, slightly astringent and diuretic; leaves refrigerant, astringent, diuretic and emollient; draught made from either; dose of seeds, from thirty grains to one drachm; of juice of leaves, from one to two fluid ounces; substituted for spirit of nitrous ether, pareira-brava, tragacanth [kateerah], elm-bark, rhatany and copaiba. Used as spinach and in curries [q.v.] almost tasteless; leaves used as famine food. Leaf makes green dye [shauyam]. Three varieties of oleracea, the common green, the golden, and the large-leaved golden, grown in gardens.—"*b*" Small indian purslane; with the following vernaculars (upódaki, San.; bhuïkóhalí, Mahr.; baklatulmubárik, Ar.; khurfah, Pers.; chhotáloniyá, Hind.; khulfah, Dec.; baççale, Can.; sannapávili, Tel.; nílaççíra, Mal.; híngenda, Singh.; shirubasalai, Tam.); San. from (upa, san. near + udaka, san. water); Mahr. from (bhuí, mahr. earth + kóhali, mahr. cucurbita pepo, dec.); Ar. from (bakalah, ar. purslane, portulaca + mubárik, ar. auspicious); Hind. from (chhotá, hind. small + loniyá, hind. the purslane, portulaca); Dec. from persian; Can. from (baçça, san. to eat + ele, can. leaf); Tel. from (sanna, tel. fine + pávili, tel. the plant); Mal. from (níla, san. blue + chíra, mal. greens); Singh. from (hín, singh. small + genda, singh. portulaca oleracea, linn.); Tam. from (shiru, tam. small + pasalai, tam. the plant); title otherwise Creeping purslane, Large-flowered purslane, Sun plant, White horse; is botanically Portulaca quadrifida, linn., portulacaceæ [vricsham, 18]; alias Illecebrum verticillatum; Meridiana quadrifida; Portulaca linifolia, meridiana, repens. Annual, diffuse, creeping; joints and axils hairy; moss-like leafage; leaves oblong, fleshy, entire, flat; flowers terminal, nearly sessile, surrounded by four leaves, small, yellow; petals four stamens 8-12; flowering in august and september; the flowers expand at noon and continue open till sunset; medicinal action same as oleracea; fleshy leaves used as greens [keeray]; used as famine food.—"*c*" Other common species of portulaca are:—tuberosa, wightiana.—"*d*" Compare in other genera:—Bergia verticillata (nírupávila), water purslane; Sesuvium portulacastrum, west indian samphire purslane; Trianthema decandra (gangapávili), large purslane; see gloss. paragraphs.——*Indian quince* (سفرجل هندى - safarjalihindí, Ar.). Same as Bael.——*Indian rattel* (भल्लशूकर - bhallashúkara, San.; بجو - bíjú, Hind.; బియ్యఖవర్ - biyakhavar, Tel.; പന്നിക്കരടി - pannikkarati, Mal.; தவக்கரடி - tavakkaradi, Tam.). San. from (bhalla, san. bear + shúkara, san. pig). Mal. from (panni, mal. hog + karati, mal. bear). Tam. from (tavazh, tam. to creep + karadi, tam. bear); from the slow awkward motion. Tam. also (tagasu). Title otherwise Badger, Honey badger. Mellivora indica, melinæ, mustelidæ, semi-plantigrada, carnivora, mammalia [sastanam, 8], of naturalists [jantoo]. Alias Mellivora ratel; Ratelus indicus; Ursitaxus inauritus; Ursus indicus. The badgers and their affines differ from the weasels and martens by their heavy form; stout limbs and more inactive gait, by the decidedly fossorial claws in some, and their harsh coarse hair; and in this group are comprised most of those animals that have the power of diffusing a fetid stench. They are moreover entirely ground animals. They ordinarily erect their tail, and most of them are more are less striped longitudinally. The animal mentioned at head is, above tawny white or light gray, black on the sides and beneath; tail short. Found chiefly in hilly districts, where it has greater facilities for constructing holes and dens. Eats rats [ely], birds [pacshy], frogs [bhaicam], whiteants [q.v.], and various insects, and in the north of India it is known as the grave-digger. It is often destructive to poultry. Its thick and loose skin preserves it from the effects of stings.——*Indian red wood* (ناٹ کا هيشم - nátkáshísham, Hind.). Same as Soymida.——*Indian resin* (ناٹ کا گوند - nátkágond, Hind.). Same as White dammer.——*Indian rhubarb* (रेवलचिनी - révalchinní, Mahr.; راوند هند - rávandihind, Ar.; ريوند هندى - revandihindí, Pers.; هندى ريوند چينى - hindírevandchíní, Hind.; ناٹ کی ريوند چينى - nátkírevanchíní, Dec.; ನಾಡುರೇವುಚಿನ್ನಿ - nádurévuchinni, Can.; నాటురేవల్చిన్ని - náturévalchinni, Tel.; நாட்டுமஞ்சட்சீனக்கிழங்கு - náttumañjadchínakkizhangu, Tam.). Ar. from persian. Pers. from (revand, pers. rhubarb + hindí, pers. indian). Hind. from (hindí, hind. indian + revand, pers. rhubarb + chíní, pers. chinese). Dec. from (nát, hind. country + revan, hind. rhubarb + chíní, hind. chinese). Can. from (nádu, can. country + revan, hind. rhuburb + chíní, hind. chinese). Tel. from (nádu, tel. country + révandchíni, hind. chinese rhubarb). Tam. from (nádu, tam. country + mañjal, tam. yellow + shínam, tam. china + kizhangu, tam. esculent root). Hind. also (révandíchíní), meaning chinese rhubarb. Tel. also (nátupasupuchínagadda), meaning country + yellow + china + root; (révalchinni); (pasupuchínagadda), meaning yellow + china + root. Tam. also (náttuyirévalsinni), meaning country + rhubarb; (mañjadsínakkizhangu), meaning yellow + china root; (irévalsinni) [ceylon gamboge]. Title otherwise Himalayan rhubarb. Product of Rheum emodi, wall., Rheum moorcroftianum, royle, and Rheum webbianum, royle, polygonaceæ [vricsham, 110]. Less active than imported rhubarb, turkey, russian or china; which are officinale. Oxalic acid exists in the juice and crystals of oxalate of lime give grittiness to the roots. The dried root is primarily a mild cathartic; secondarily astringent; in small doses, stomachic and astringent; hakeems [q.v.] use it more than veidyans [q.v.]. The petioles used in cooking.——*Indian roller* (عقعق هندى - akakihindí, Hind.). Same as Indian jay.——*Indian rose* (گل سفيد برى - gulisufídibárrí, Hind.). See under Gool.——*Indian rose-bay* (خر زهرهٔ هندى - kharzahrahihindí, Hind.). Same as Adam's apple.——*Indian rubber* (لبر - labbar, Hind. and Dec.; പാച്ചോറ്റിപ്പശ - páççóttippasha, Mal.). Hind. by corruption. Mal. from (páççótti, mal. the milk-shedding plant, dichopsis elliptica, benth. + pasha, mal. gum). Also known as caoutchouc. Is the thickened milky juice of trees, principally of the breadfruit [jack], mulberry [indian mulberry], dogbane, swallow-wort [yercum], and spurge-wort [milkhedge] families; great quantities obtained from species of hevea, in commerce known as para rubber. Manihot glaziovii, euphorbiaceæ, gives ceara or scraprubber, ceara being province of north brazil. Stilpnophyllum elasticum, endl., moraceæ [indian caoutchouc], gives real east indian. Urceola elastica, roxb., affords a juice that when thickened has all the properties of the caoutchouc. The milky exudations of Artocarpus integrifolia, willd. [common jack], Ficus bengalensis [banyan], and Ficus religiosa, linn. [peepul] possess nearly similar qualities.——*Indian rubber tree* (ناٹ کا لبر - nátkálabbar, Hind.). Same as Indian caoutchouc.——*Indian rubber vine* (பாலை - pálai, Tam.). Same as Paulay silk cotton.——*Indian sacred bean* (श्रीपर्णी - shríparní, San.). Same as Nelumbo.——*Indian sage* (कर्पूरपत्र - karpúrapatra, San.; سفاقس - safákus, Ar.; سالبيه - sálbiyah, Pers.; ولايتى كافور كا پات - viláitíkáfúrkápát, Hind.; ولايتى كافور كا پتا - viláitíkáfúrkápattá, Dec.; சேசி - shési, Tam.). San. from (karpúra, san. camphor + patra, san. leaf); from smell. Hind. from (viláití, hind. foreign + káfúr, pers. camphor + pát, hind. leaf). Hind. also (banbabúrí), meaning forest + acacia arabica, willd. Tam. also (shímaikkarppúrayilai), meaning foreign + camphor + leaf; (káttukkañjángórai), meaning forest + white basil, ocimum basilicum, linn., from similar smell. Title otherwise Camphor leaf, Sage tea plant. Botanically the Salvia genus, labiatæ [vricsham, 103]. Herbs or shrubs distinguished by lipped calyx and two forked stamens; some species considered to have healing properties. The species best known to the natives are:—Gerardiana; with scarlet flowers. Indica, infusion used as gentle tonic. Officinalis, garden, sage, shrubby, dwarfish plant, of somewhat bitter and very hot, aromatic, and slightly astringent flavor; native of south europe; leaves imported; the chinese prize this, and the tea-trade commenced by the dutch exchanging it for tea [q.v.]; leaves are medicinally feeble tonic, astringent, diaphoretic, antispasmodic; their chief use is as a wash for aphthous affections of the mouth and as a gargle in sore-throat and relaxation of the uvula; leaves are macerated to form a drink used in febrile affections to allay nausea. Plebeia, stem herbaceous, erect, branched, pubescent; leaves petioled, oblong, wrinkled; verticels lax, about six-flowered, racemose; racemes paniculate; calyx campanulate, upper lip quite entire, teeth of the lower lip obtuse; corolla scarcely longer than the calyx; flowers purple. Silarea; common clary; greek ὅρμινον and φώρβιον; latin oculus christi.——*Indian sago palm* (ساگودانهٔ هندى - ságúdanahihindí, Hind.). See under Sago.——*Indian salep* (सफेदमुसळी - sap'hédamusalí, Mahr. ; هقاقل هندی - shakákulihindí, Ar., and Pers. ; سفید موسلی - sufedmúslí, Hind. ; هندی هقاقل - hindíshakákul, Dec.). Mahr. from (sap'héda, mahr. white + musalí, mahr. curculigo orchioides, gærtn.). Ar. from (shakákul, ar. wild carrot, asparagopsis floribunda, kth. + hindí, hind. indian). Hind. from (sufed, hind. white + múslí, hind. curculigo orchioides, gærtn.). Dec. from arabic. Hind. also (satávar). Title otherwise Indian shakaukool, Indian wild carrot. Botanically Asparagopsis [shatamooly] ascendens, kunth., liliaceæ [vricsham, 136]. Alias Asparagus ascendens. Herbaceous, erect; spines solitary, straight; leaves fascicled, cylindric; racemes lateral, simple or composite; berries pendulous; flowers white; flowering in october and november; the sprays of minute flowers resemble plumes of silver. Dried tuberous root demulcent and nutrient; substituted for british salep [q.v.]. Is the soofaid moosly of other parts of india, not here; see that head.——*Indian salt-wort* (سجی کهار - sajjíkhár, Hind.; ఉలకూర - ilakúra, Tel.; உமரிக்கீரை - umarikkírai, Tam.). Title from place of growth. Hind. from (sajjí, hind. alkali + khár, hind. saline). Tam. from (uvar, tam. salt + kírai, tam. vegetable). Tel. also (yellakúra). Tam. also (kózhikkásiraikkírai), meaning cock + hibiscus cannabinus, linn.; (kózhippasalai), meaning fowl + the plant, basella. Title otherwise Indian glasswort, Indian salsola, Yellacoora. Botanically Suæda indica, moq., salsolaceæ [vricsham, 108]. Alias Salsola indica. Stems perennial, erect, branching out into many diffuse, alternate ramifications; leaves scattered round the branchlets, erect, approximate, sessile, linear, semi-cylindric, colored in the older plants; spikes terminal, erect, compound or panicled, leafy; flowers minute, greenish, aggregate in the axils of the floral leaves; calyx five-cleft; segments concave within, with a slightly membranaceous margin. Small, procumbent weed, linear shaped leaves having no stalks; with pea green leaves; found in salt marshes, sometimes in gardens. Used in native culinary as spinach [indian spinach]. Yields alkaline ashes, used as mordant [cauram]. There is a Teloogoo proverb :—ఆలుబల్లని మొగుడు ఉలకూరలో ఉప్పు లేదన్నట్టు.—"The carping husband says to "his wife there is no salt in yellacoora."—Sea side indian saltwort; with the following vernaculars (ravakáda, Tel.; nírumari, Tam.); Tam. from (nír, tam. water + umari, tam. the plant, suæda indica, moq.); is Suæda nudiflora, moq., salsolaceæ [vricsham, 108]; alias Salsola nudiflora; stems perennial, many, spreading close upon the ground, and often rooting; extremities of the branches ascending, young parts smooth and colored reddish; leaves alternate, sessile, linear, fleshy; spikes terminal, erect, very long, compound, leafless; flowers very small, greenish, numerous, fascicled; common in salt barren land near sea; very saline taste; yields sujjee [q.v.] for making soap [sauboon] and glass [cunnaudy]; ashes used as mordant [cauram]; natives gather it for fuel.——*Indian sanobar* (صنوبر هندی - sanobarihindí, Ar.). Same as Deodar.——*Indian sarsaparilla* (अनन्ता - anantá, San.; अनन्तमूळ - anantamúla, Mahr.; दुदवालि - dudaváli, Conc.; عشبة مغربية - ushbahimaghribiyah, Ar.; عشبة هندی - ushbahihindí, Pers.; هندی سالسة - hindísálsa, Hind.; ناتکا عشبه - nátkáushbah, Dec.; ಸುಗಂಧಿಬಳ್ಳಿ - sugandhiballi, Can.; ಕನ್ಯಾಬೂರು - kanyábúru, Too.; సుగంధిపాల - sugandhipála, Tel.; നറുനീണ്ടി - naruninti, Mal.; ඉරමසු - iramasu, Singh.; நன்னாரி - nannári, Tam.). Title from similar odour of root. San. from (a, san. negative prefix + anta, san. end); from its value as medicine or from long root [common nail-dye, hurrially]. Mahr. from (ananta, san. endless + múla, san. root). Ar. from (ushbah, ar. sarsaparilla + maghribí, ar. western); from being first known in andalusia in spain. Pers. from (ushbah, ar. sarsaparilla + hindí, pers. indian). Hind. similar. Dec. means country sarsaparilla. Can. from (sugandhi, san. well perfumed + balli, can. creeper). Too. from (kanyá, san. virgin + búru, too. creeper). Tel. from (su, san. good + gandha, san. smell + pála, tel. milk plant). Mal. from (naru, mal. fragrance + nílu, mal. to extend). Tam. from (nal, tam. good + náru, tam. to be fragrant). San. also (sugandhí), meaning sweet-smelling [marootham]; (gopí), meaning protecting; (anantamúla), meaning having endless root; (bhadravallí), meaning happy creeper; (raktashárivá), meaning red + the plant; (shárivá), meaning variegated, from striped leaf [sarsaparilla china root]. Ar. also (ushbatunnár), meaning sarsaparilla + fire; (zaiyán). Pers. also (yásmínibarrí), meaning wild jasmine, from fragrance and acridity. Hind. also (nannáríjar), meaning sarsaparilla root; (kural); (maghrabí), meaning western; (janglíchambélí), meaning wild jasmine. Dec. also (nannárí), from tamul. Can. also (sugandhapáladagida), meaning good smelling + the plant; (námadabéru), meaning sectarian mark + creeper, from white striped leaf; (dúdaváli), meaning milk creeper. Tel. also (nallasugandhipála), meaning black + the plant; (tellasugandhipála), meaning white + the plant; (pálasugandhi), meaning milk + good smelling; (pálatsukkandéru), meaning milk + good smelling; (gadisugandhi), meaning large + the plant; (muttavapulagamu), meaning old + grandmother + pudding [common balah], from medicinal value in household practice. Mal. also (nannári), meaning sweet-smelling; (páravalli), meaning rock + creeper. Tam. also (kiruttinavalli), meaning black + creeper, from dark stems; (párgodi), meaning milk + creeper. Title otherwise Country ooshbah, Country sarsaparilla, False sarsaparilla, Fragrant paulay, Fragrant root, Indian sarsa, Indian sassafras, Sectarian creeper, Wild jasmine [q.v.]. Botanically Hemidesmus indicus, r. br., asclepiadeæ [vricsham, 88]. Alias Asclepias pseudosarsa; Hemidesmus cordatus; Periploca indica. Twining; stem glabrous; leaves from cordate to ovate, cuspidate, passing into narrow linear, acute, often oblong-lanceolate cymes, often sub-sessile, sometimes peduncled; scales of the corolla obtuse, cohering the whole length of the tube; follicles slender, straight; flowers on the outside, pale green, on the inside, dark blood-colored; flowering in rainy season; common in waste ground. The drug is found in commerce in the form of small bundles, which consist of the entire roots of one or more plants, often several feet long, tied up with a portion of the stem. The root is cylindrical, tortuous, from $\frac{2}{10}$ to $\frac{1}{10}$ of an inch in diameter, seldom branched; the bark is transversely cracked and fissured longitudinally, of a dark brown color, sometimes with a slight violet hue when viewed in a strong light; the wood is yellow and porous; the fresh or freshly dried root has a peculiar odour like sassafras or new mown hay, and a sweet but slightly acrid taste. Dried root alterative tonic, diuretic, and diaphoretic; veidyans [q.v.] use it in powder with cow's milk [paul] in gravel and strangury, and in decoction with cumin [jeerah] seeds to purify the blood and correct bile [pittam]; hakeems [q.v.] consider it the best alterative medicine in the country; frequently adulterated with other roots; gives to pharm. hemidesmi radix, crystallizable principle, hemidesmine; preparations, infusum hemidesmi, syrupus hemidesmi; official; like dulcamara, and sarsaparilla; also in british pharm. Gives a dye [shauyam]. Another species is pubescens. Compare the smilax genus [china root], which has real or jamaica sarsaparilla, smilax officinalis.——*Indian scented wood* (عود هندی - údihindí, Pers.). Same as Eagle wood.——*Indian screw-tree* (आवर्तनी - ávartaní, San.). See Screw-tree.——*Indian senna* (سناء هند - sanáihind, Ar.). Same as Tinnevelly senna.——*Indian shot* (सर्वजया - sarvajayá, San.; देवकेळी - dévakélí, Mahr.; केल - kéla, Conc.; نباتعقيق البحر - nabátiakíkulbahr, Ar.; شجر عقيق البحر - shajariakíkulbahr, Pers.; عقیق البحر کا جهاڑ - akíkulbahrkájhár, Dec.; ಕೇಳಹೂ - kélahú, Can.; కృష్ణతామర - krishnatámara, Tel.; കാട്ടുവാഴ - káttuvázha, Mal.; බුත්සරණ - butsarana, Singh.; கல்வாழை - kalvázhai, Tam.). Title from seeds being black and extremely hard, size of swan-shot. San. from (sarva, san. all + ji, san. to conquer). Mahr. from (déva, san. god + kélí, mahr. musa paradisiaca, linn.). Conc. from (kadalí, san. plantain) [plantain]. Ar. from (nabát, ar. tree + akík, ar. cornelian + bahr, ar. sea). Pers. from (shajar, pers. tree + akík, ar. cornelian + bahr, ar. sea). Dec. from (akík, ar. cornelian + bahr, ar. tree + jhár, hind. tree). Can. from (kéla, can. musa paradisiaca, linn. + hú, can. flower). Tel. from (krishna, san. black + támara, tel. nelumbium speciosum, willd.). Mal. from (kátu, mal. forest + vázha, mal. musa paradisiaca, linn.). Singh. means booddha's foot. Tam from (kal, tam. stone + vázhai, tam. plantain, musa paradisiaca, linn.); found among rocks [wild plantain]. San. also (vanakadalí), meaning forest plantain; (shilárambhá), meaning rock plantain. Hind. also (lálsabza), meaning red ocimum basilicum, linn.; Can. also (húdingana). Tel. also (gurigindza), meaning abrus precatorius, linn. + seed; from seeds [indian liquorice]. Tam. also (púvázhai), meaning flower + plantain, musa paradisiaca, linn.; (kunrimaniççedi), meaning seed of abrus precatorius, linn. + plant; from seeds, commonly applied to indian liquorice [q.v.]. Title otherwise Booddha's foot, Cornelian tree, Flowering plantain, Flowering reed, Indian bead, Liquorice plantain, Rock plantain, Stony plantain. Botanically Canna indica, linn., marantaceæ [vricsham, 143]. Alias Canna orientalis, rubra, variabilis; Cannacorus ovatus. Shrub, 2–3 feet; leaves large, ovate-lanceolate, stem-clasping; inner wing of the corolla trifid, segments lanceolate, straight; anther single, attached to the edge of the petal-like filament; style spathulate, growing to the tube of the corolla; capsule bristly, 3-celled, many-seeded; flowers bright scarlet or yellow; constantly in blossom in gardens as ornamental plant; round, hard, black seeds, contained in the hairy pericarp; the root is acrid and stimulant. The root broken up in small pieces and boiled in rice-water [conjee] with pepper [q.v.] is given to cattle [maud] that have eaten any poisonous grass; in ordinary medicine diaphoretic and diuretic in fevers and dropsy. Contains starch in the root-stock, which renders it fit to be used as food after being cooked. The leaves are large and tough, and are sometimes used for wrapping up goods; the natives make necklace [maulay] and other ornaments of the seeds; the leaves yield a purple dye [shauyam] not durable. From Canna edulis comes Tous les mois in w. indies like arrowroot.——*Indian skylark* (வானம்பாடி - vánambádi, tam.). See Vaunambaudy. ——*Indian sloth* (شرمندی بلی - sharmindíbillí, Hind.). See Devaungam.——*Indian sole* (بهینس کی جیب - bhainskíjíb, Hind.; چپل مچهی - chappalmacchí, Dec.; నాలుకచేప - nálukachépa, Tel.; മന്തൽമീൻ - mantalmín, Mal.; நாக்குமீன் - nákkumín, Tam.). Hind. from (bhains, hind. buffalo + jíb, hind. tongue). Dec. from (chappal, hind. slipper + maççhí, hind. fish); from its flat shape. Tel. from (náluka, tel. tongue + chépa, tel. fish). Mal. from (manda, mal. slow + mín, mal. fish). Tam. from (nákku, tam. tongue + mín, tam.

fish). Tam. also (kadalnákkumín), meaning sea + tongue + fish; (erumainákkumín), meaning buffalo + tongue + fish. Title otherwise Flat fish, Naukkmeen. Fish family Pleuronectidæ, anacanthini, teleostei [matsyam, 34], of naturalists [jantoo]. Especially the genera Cynoglossus, Plagusia, Synaptura.——*Indian sorrel* (अम्ललोणिका - amlalóniká, San.). Same as Sour auray.——*Indian spikenard* (سنبل الطيب هندى - sumbuluttíbihindí, Hind.). Same as Jatamansy.——*Indian spinach* (اسفاناخ - isfánákh, Ar.; اسفناج - isfináj, Pers.; پالك - páluk, Hind.; ಬಸಳೆ - basale, Can.; దుంపబచ్చలి - dumpabattsali, Tel.; பசலை - pasalai, Tam.). Ar. from greek. Pers. from greek. Can. from tamul [heart-leaved malabar nightshade]. Tel. from (dumpa, tel. root + battsali, tel. bassella cordifolia, lam.) [red malabar nightshade]. Tam. from (pasumai, tam. greenness) [papaw, small indian purslane]. Hind. also (sagpáluk), meaning dog spinach. Tel. also (mattubattsali), meaning inferior + bassella cordifolia, lam.; (battsali) [heart-leaved malabar nightshade, indian purslane]. Title otherwise Butchaly, Common spinach, Garden spinach, New zealand spinach, Paluck, Spinage. Botanically Spinacea oleracea, linn., salsolaceæ [vricsham, 108]. Alias Spinacia tetrandra. Potherb, native of persia. The plant has large, thick, succulent, deep-green leaves, of a somewhat triangular form, produced on long foot stalks; the stem is erect, large, round and hollow, about two feet high; the male plants are distinguished by their long terminal spikes of green flowers, while those of the females are axillary, sessile and clustered; cultivated in gardens as culinary vegetable [keeray]. Two varieties; prickly-seeded, smooth-seeded.——*Indian squill* (اسقيل هند - iskílihind, Ar.). See Squill.——*Indian swift* (عصفور هند - usfúrihind, Hind.). See Abaubil.——*Indian tailor-bird* (टुण्टुक - tuntuka, San.; پھدکی - phudkí, Hind.; پتپتا - pitpitá, Dec.; ಗಿಜ್ಗ - gijga, Can.; లిక్కుజిట్ట - likkujitta, Tel.; தூக்கணங்குருவி - túkkananguruvi, Tam.). Title from building its nest by sewing leaves together. Tel. from (likki, tel. small sickle + jitta, tel. bird). Tam. from (túnganam, tam. pendant + kuruvi, tam. small bird). Tel. also (rellujitta), meaning reed bird, from haunts. Title otherwise Wren-warblers. Drymoicinæ, sylviadæ [calacuntam], dentirostres, insessores, aves [pacshy, 23], of naturalists [jantoo].—"*a*" The best known is Orthotomus longicauda. Alias Orthotomus bennettii, sphenurus, sutoria; Sylvia guzurata, ruficapila. Ordinary note is to-wee-to-wee-to-wee; when alarmed or angry has a different call. Makes nest with cotton [q.v.], wool [pushm], and various soft materials, sometimes lined with hair, draws together one leaf or more, generally two leaves, on each side, stitches them together with cotton, either woven by itself, or cotton thread [nool] picked up; after passing thread through the leaf, makes a knot at the end to fix. Nest generally built from two to four feet above ground.—"*b*" The dark-ashy wren-warbler is Prinia socialis not seen north of the Godavery. Nest not so neatly sewn together as orthotomus, generally more grass and other vegetable fibres used in construction.—"*c*" Rufous grass-warbler is Cisticola schoenicola. When put up, takes short jerking flight for a few yards and then drops again. Single note jik, jik.—"*d*" The common wren-warbler, called in Teloogoo the hollow eye bird, is Drymoipus inornatus. Rather loud monotonous note twee-twee-twee. Flight feeble. Nest woven with grass, nearly globular, with a hole at the side, lined with soft down, generally that of Calotropis gigantea [yercum].—"*e*" The jungle wren-warbler is Drymoipus sylvaticus.——*Indian tamarisk* (گزانگبين هندى - gazangabínihíndí, Hind.). Same as Manna jhow.——*Indian tea* (ناك كى چاه - nátkíchá, Hind.). Infusion of the leaves of Ocimum canum [white toolsy].——*Indian titlark* (గుర్రపుమారిజిట్ట - gurrapumárijitta, Tel.). See Pilkya.——*Indian tragacanth* (هندى كتيرا - hindíkaterá, Hind.). Product of Cochlospermum gossypium, dec. [golden silk cotton].——*Indian tree spurge* (زقوم هندى - zakkúmihindí, Ar.). Same as Round milk-hedge.——*Indian trout* (ஆற்றுக்கெண்டை - áttukkendai, Tam.). Tam. from (áru, tam. river + kendai, tam. carp, barbus genus). Title otherwise Neilgherry trout, River carp. Barilius gatensis, cyprininæ, cyprinidæ, physostomi, teleostei [matsyam, 39], of naturalists [jantoo]. Alias Barilius rugosus; Leuciscus gatensis; Opsarius gatensis. Silvery gray with about fifteen vertical bars descending from the back, and which become more or less broken up in the adult; dorsal and anal with dark bases and light margins; females and young generally have smooth scales, whereas most of the adult males have one or more rough spots on each; western ghauts of malabar and neilgherry hills, up to about 5,000 feet above the level of the sea; at least six inches in length.——*Indian trumpet flower* (शुकनास - shukanása, San.). Same as Pajanely.——*Indian varnish* (بهلاوينكا جهاڑ - bhíláveukájhár, Hind.). Same as Marking nut.——*Indian walnut* (هندى اكروٹ كا پيڑ - hindíakrotkáper, Hind.). Same as Lumbang nut.——*Indian water lily* (نيلوفر - nílofar, Hind.). See sep. title.——*Indian whiting* (नदादि - nadádi, Mahr.; كلنگان مچهى - kalangánmacçhí, Hind.; సొరంగి - sórangi, Tel.; കതിരാൻ - katirán, Mal.; கிழங்கான் - kizbangán, Tam.). Hind. from tamul. Tel. from (saura, tel. beauty + anga, san. body). Mal. from (katiram, mal. beauty). Tam. from (kizhangu, tam. esculent root). Tel. also (tellasórangí), meaning white + whiting, sillago genus; (aritikáya), meaning plantain; (nettaluchépa), meaning sprat, clupea sprattus + fish. Sillago sihama, trachinidæ, acanthopterygii, teleostei [matsyam, 21], of naturalists [jantoo]. Alias Atherina sihama; Platycephalus sihamus; Sciæna malabarica; Sillago acuta, erythræ, malabarica; Sparus soring. Soring from teloogoo. Upper jaw slightly longer; scales about six rows between lateral-line and last dorsal spine; air-vessel extends posteriorly to opposite first third of anal fin; colors olive-green along back, becoming light on abdomen, the whole having brilliant purple reflection; silvery longitudinal band; minute black points on dorsal and anal fins; sea, ascends tidal rivers. Native women who have young babies are advised to eat it, as it is said to be even more nourishing than shark's [soorah] flesh. The only fish which veidyans [q.v.] allow leprous [cooshtam] patients to eat. Whitings are here smaller than in Europe. Bengal whiting is Sciænoides pama.——*Indian wild pepper* (اثلق آبى - aslakiábí, Hind.). Same as Water notchy.——*Indian wine palm* (سيندى كا جهاڑ - sendíkájhár, Hind.). Same as Wild date.——*Indian willow* (بيدمجنون هندى - bedimajnúnihindí, Hind.). See under Varoonam.——*Indian winter cherry* (टङ्कारी - tankárí, San.; جوزالمرج - jauzulmaraj, Ar.; كاكنج - káknaj, Pers.; مكو - makao, Hind.; ಬುದ್ದೆಹಣ್ಣು - buddehannu, Can.; బూసర - búsara, Tel.; பெரியதக்காளி - periyathakkáli, Tam.). San. from (tam, san. imitative sound + kára, san. doer); from sound with which the leafy cover of fruit bursts on pressure. Ar. from (jauz, ar. nut + maraj, ar. the tree). Can. from (budde, can. swelling + hannu, can. fruit). Tam. from (periya, tam. big + takkáli, tam. physalis angulata, linn.). San. also (agnimanda), meaning fire + to languish. Hind. also (poptá). Tel. also (buddabúsara), meaning bladder + the plant; (pámubudda), meaning snake + bladder; (budama) [country cucumber]. Tam. also (takkáli) [europe brinjaul]. Title otherwise Cape gooseberry, Edible winter cherry [adhatoday, asgand], Peruvian cherry, Poptah cherry, Takkauly. Botanically Physalis [takkauly] peruviana, linn., solanaceæ [vricsham, 94]. Alias Physalis edulis, esculenta. Resembling the next or indigenous article, but stouter, flowers and fruit-calyx larger, usually villous or pubescent; corolla with five large purple spots near the base within; native of tropical america; bears small yellowish flowers; fruit exactly resembles winter cherry of english gardens, to which it is closely allied; is concealed in a dry leafy appendage; is of a bright amber [karbah] color, of the precise size and form of a cherry [q.v.]; the young shoots bear the finest fruit; fruit makes good preserve; cf. brazil cherry. Small indian winter cherry; with the following vernaculars (lakshmídaivatyá, San.; chiriputla, Conc.; bondula, Can.; bondoli, Too.; pínottánotiyan, Mal.; shinnattakkáli, Tam.); San. from (lakshmí, san. the goddess + dévatá, san. goddess). Can. from (bondu, can. hole + hula, can. insect). Too. from canarese. Mal. from (pí, mal. dirty + nottánotiyan, mal. the plant, physalis). Tam. from (shinna, tam. small + takkáli, tam. physalis angulata, linn.); otherwise Small takkauly; is physalis [takkauly] minima, linn., solanaceæ [vricsham, 94]; alias Physalis lagascæ, parviflora; herbaceous, loosely villous with diffuse branches; leaves subcordate or ovate, acuminate, repandly toothed or almost entire, hairy; corolla without spots; anthers yellow; calyx of the fruit ovate, angled, here and there hairy; segments while flowering, triangular acuminate, shorter than the tube; flowers small, pale yellow; flowering nearly all the year; berries eaten by natives. Compare in other genera, where transl. is of first term:—Cardiospermum canescens (chinnabuddabúsara), small + bladder; Hydrocotyle asiatica (bollibúsara), white; Lycopersicum esculentum (erumaittakkáli), buffalo, (péttakkáli), demon, (shímaittakkáli), foreign; Solanum melongena (mulakutakkáli), chilly, capsicum; Solanum nigrum (manattakkáli), fragrance. See gloss. paragraphs.——*Indian wood-cock* (سيمتيتر - símtítar, Hind.; ಕಾಡುಕೋಳಿ - kádukóli, Can.). Hind. from (sím, pers. silver + títar, hind. partridge), from color. Can. from (kádu, can. forest + kóli, can. fowl) [grey jungle-fowl]. Hind. also (tutalar). Scolopax rusticola, scolopacinæ, scolopacidæ [vana cookkootam], longirostres, grallatores [pacshy, 41], of naturalists [jantoo]. Alias Scolopax indicus. Forehead and crown ash-grey, tinged rufous; dusky streak from gape to eyes; occiput, with four broad transverse bars of blackish brown; rest of upper part variegated chestnut brown, ochre yellow and ash-grey, with zigzag lines and irregular spots of black; throat white; rest of under parts yellowish white, passing into rufous on breast and forepart of neck with cross wavy bars of dusky brown; quills barred ferruginous and black; tail black, outer webs edged rufous, tips ash-grey above, silvery white beneath; bill fleshy grey; legs livid; irides dark brown; length 14 to nearly 16 inches; female is larger with colors more dull; a winter visitant to more elevated wooded regions. No other common species here.——*Indian worm-killer* (पत्रभंग - patrabhanga, San.; किडेमारी - kidémárí, Mahr.; كيڑا مار - kírámár, Hind. and Dec.; ಆಡುಮುಟ್ಟದಗಿಡ - ádumuttadagida, Can.; కడపర - kadapara, Tel.; ପନିରି - paniri, Oor.; ആടുതിന്നാപ്പാല - átutinnáppála, Mal.; ஆடுதின்னாப்பாலை - áduthinnáppálai, Tam.). Title from medicinal properties. San. from (patra, san. leaf + bhanga, san. marking); from use in ornamental markings on face. Mahr. from (kidá, mahr. worm + márí, mahr. killer). Hind. from (kírá, hind. worm + már, hind. killing). Can. from (ádu, can. sheep + muttada, can. not touching + gida, can. herb). Mal. from tamul. Tam. from (ádu, tam. goat + tin, tam. to eat + á, negative particle + pálai, tam. milky plant); goats will not eat; cf. adhatoday. Hind. also (gandán), meaning bad smeller; (gandatí). Can. also (kurigida), meaning sheep + plant. Tel. also (gádidegaddapara), meaning ass + the plant. Mal. also (átutodáppála), meaning sheep + not touching + milk-plant. Tam. also (kárirattam), meaning black + blood, from dark purple flowers; (viranam-bókki), meaning ulcer + to cure; cf. zakhmhayaut; (pangam-bálai), meaning mire + milky plant; (puzhukkolli), meaning worm-killer; antidote against all insect poisons [snake jasmine]; (kiruminásam), meaning worm-killer. Title otherwise Black blood plant, Bracteated birth-wort, Floral-leaved birth-wort, Pelican flower, Ulcer plant. Botanically Aristolochia [eesh-waram] bracteata, retz., aristolochiaceæ [vricsham, 117]. Alias Aristolochia microphylla, sempervirens. Trailing; roots perennial, fibrous; stems striated, waved; leaves alternate, petioled, kidney-shaped, curled at the margins, glaucous below; petioles channelled; flowers axillary, solitary, peduncled, drooping; calyx with the upper part of the tube and tongue erect; color dark purple; covered on the inside with purple hairs; capsules ovate; flowering nearly all the year. The drug consists of the whole plant in fruit; the stems are striated, slender, and about as thick as a piece of whip cord; the leaves are of a pale, glaucous green, obtuse, heart-shaped, with wavy edges, about 2 inches long and 1½ inch broad, when dry they are blackish; the capsules are ovate, ¾ of an inch long, ribbed, depressed at the apex, six-celled; each cell contains a column of heart-shaped flat seeds, closely packed; the appearance of the seeds is peculiar, they look as if they had been cut out with a punch; one side is flat, black, and rough from a number of irregular projections; the other is almost entirely occupied by two brown comparatively smooth lobular projections of a soft corky structure; these under the microscope are seen to be entirely compcsed of ovate, empty, dotted cells; the whole plant is nauseously bitter. Plant is medicinally insecticide, anthelmintic, emmenagogue, febrifuge and parturifacient; juice in pharm. non-officinal; natives squeeze juice into wounds to kill worms. Cf. Indian mulberry. ——*Indian worm wood* (افسنتين هندى - afsantínihindí, Ar.). Same as Indian absinth.——*Indian zebra-wood* (हिमपुष्प - hima-pushpa, San.; पन्नीरजांब - pannírajámba, Conc.; پنیرکے پھولکا جھاڑ - panírkephúlkájhár, Hind.; ಬಿಳಿಹೂವಿನಲಕ್ಕಿಮರ - bilihúvinalakki-mara, Can.; పన్నీరుపువ్వుచెట్టు - pannírupuvvuchettu, Tel.; രാവുപൂ - rávupú, Mal.; නිල්පිච්ච - nilpiçça, Singh.; பன்னீர்மரம் - pannírmaram, Tam.). Title from stripes in timber like those of zebra. San. from (hima, san. dew + pushpa, san. flower); flowering in the evening. Hind. from (panír, hind. corruption of tamul meaning dew-water + phúl, hind. flower + jhár, hind. tree). Can. from (bili, can. white + húvu, can. flower + lakkimara, can. vitex negundo, linn.). Tel. from (panníru, tel. rose water + puvvu, tel. flower + chettu, tel. tree). Mal. from (rávu, mal. night + pú, mal. flower). Singh. from (nil, singh. blue + pichha, singh. jasminum sambac, ait.). Tam. from (pannír, tam. dew water + maram, tam. tree); flower on the dew-fall. San. also (hima), meaning dew. Can. also (pannéralu). Tel. also (panníru-pushpachettu), meaning rose-water + flower + tree. Singh. also (valpichha), meaning forest + jasminum sambac, ait. [wild-jasmine]. Title otherwise Dew-flower, Evening flower, Jasmine cadamba, Pigeon wood, Tree jasmine [indian cork]. Botanically Guettarda speciosa, linn., rubiaceæ [vricsham, 71]. Alias Cadamba jasminiflora; Gardenia speciosa; Jasminum hirsutum; Nyctanthes hirsuta. Cadamba, from (kadamba, san. anthocephalus cadamba, miq.). Tree; leaves ovate or obovate, often slightly cordate at the base, obtuse at the apex, pubescent on the under side; cymes peduncled, axillary, velvety, much shorter than the leaf; corolla hypocrateriform, with cylindrical tube; flowers four to nine-cleft; anthers sessile in the throat of the corolla; calyx limb deciduous; stamens four to nine; drupe depressed, marked by the traces of the calyx; cells of the nut curved, one-seeded; flowers white, very fragrant. Coarse shrub frequent in gardens; flowers come out in the evening and have all dropped on the ground by the morning; flower sacred to shiva [q.v.] and vishnoo [q.v.]; in travancore odoriferous water is distilled from the corollas, like rose water [goolaub]; close-grained and durable wood.——*Indian zebu* (ماشيهند - máshiyahihind, Hind.). See Maud.——*Indigo* (نيل - níl, Hind.). See sep. title.

INDIAN EBONY (तिन्दुक - tinduka, *San.*; ಕರಿಮರ - kari-mara, *Can.*; తుమికి - tumiki, *Tel.*). San. from (tij, san. to sharpen); from acid exudation [gaub]. Can. from (kari, can. black + mara, can. tree). Title otherwise Bastard lotus, Date plum. Botanically the Diospyros genus, ebenaceæ [vricsham, 83]. Large, hard-wooded, slow-growing trees, natives of tropical countries; flowers hermaphrodite; fruit pulpy, generally egg-shaped; hard and black heart wood is the ebony of commerce; surrounded by white sapwood. The species best known to the natives are:—ebenum [ceylon ebony], embryopteris [gaub], hirsuta [calaminder wood], kaki [chinese gaub], melanoxylon [coromandel ebony], montana [forest gaub], tomentosa [sweet gaub]. Other species are:—Assimilis, on western ghauts; Candolleana, large tree, glabrous on western ghauts; Chloroxylon, small tree, circars, godavery forests, and western jungles, flower small white, fruit edible, gives a sort of ebony called large collinda; Foliosa, moderate-sized tree, everywhere glabrous, leaves dark shining green; light-colored wood, valuable; Insignis; Microphylla; Nilagirica; Oocarpa; Ovalifolia; Paniculata; Pruriens; Sylvatica, has a whitish, very hard, but small wood. ——*Ceylon ebony* (आबनूस - ábanúsa, Mahr.; آبنوس - ábnús, Ar., Pers., Hind. and Dec.; ಕರಿಮರ - karimara, Can.; తూకి - túki, Tel.; କେନ୍ଦୁ - khendu, Oor.; කළුවර - kaluvara, Singh.; ஆச்சா-áççá, Tam.). Mahr. from arabic. Ar. from hebrew [ebony]. Can. from (kari, can. black + mara, can. tree). Tel. from (túgu, tel. to weigh), from weight. Oor. corruption from (tindu, san. diospyros embryopteris, pers.) [gaub]. Singh. means dark. Tam. from (ár, tam. density, also lustre); from hard wood capable of high polish [atchah, yaipy]. Tel. also (nallaúti), meaning black + maba buxifolia, pers. Tam. also (kákatáli), meaning crow black + palmyra, borassus flabelliformis, linn.; (tumbi). Title otherwise Black palmyra, Black satin-wood, Pomander wood. Botanically Diospyros [indian ebony] ebenum, kœnig., ebenaceæ [vricsham, 83]. Specific name from arabic. Large tree; branchlets glabrous; leaves 4 by 1¾ inches, coriaceous; primary nerves oblique; petiole $\frac{1}{6}$–$\frac{1}{5}$ inch; male flower three to twelve together, almost fascicled on peduncles 0–¼ inch; calyx ⅛ inch, funnel-shaped, nearly glabrous, lobes four, not reaching half-way down, rounded, glabrous or ciliate-pubescent on the margins; corolla-buds ⅓ inch, narrower upwards, lobed half-way down; filaments minutely pilose, anthers linear glabrous, connective long produced; female flower solitary very shortly peduncled; calyx larger than in the male; style one, stigmas four; ovary eight-celled; fruit ¾ inch diameter, globose, glabrous, or adpressedly pubescent; fruiting calyx a sub-hemispheric wooden cup, fitting the base of the fruit; below its margin without spread the four ovate calyx lobes. Found in mountain forests on both sides of presidency; leaves turn very black in drying; flower small, greenish; gives the best looking ebony; wood grey, with irregularly-shaped masses of jet-black ebony [q.v.] near the centre, frequently with lighter-colored streaks; much affected by weather, on which account cabinet-makers seldom use it except in veneer; to prevent splitting, it should be well covered; grain so fine that when polished no trace of woody fibre is perceptible; white when young and darkens with age; wood imported from ceylon.——*Coromandel ebony* (काकतिन्दुक - kákatinduka, San.; آبنوس - ábnús, Ar. and Pers.; سیسم - sísam, Hind.; تیندو - tendú, Dec.; ಕರಿಮರ - karimara, Can.; తుమిద - tumida, Tel.; କେନ୍ଦୁ - khendu, Oor.; കരുവിട്ടി - karu-vítti, Mal.; தும்பிலி - tumbili, Tam.). San. from (káka, san. crow + tinduka, san. diospyros); as yielding black ebony. Dec. from (tindu, san. diospyros embryopteris, pers.) [gaub, ilanjy]. Can. from (kari, can. black + mara, can. tree). Oor. corruption from sanscrit; like deccany. Mal. from (karu, mal. black + vítti, mal. black wood, dalbergia latifolia, roxb.), from purple streaks of heart-wood resembling dalbergia [yooga pattricay]. Tam. from (tumbu, tam. fibre + ili, tam. having not); fruit eatable. Hind. also (sísamkájhár), meaning dalbergia sissoo, roxb. [sissoo]. Can. also (abanási); (bilára); (balaimara). Tel. also (tummika); (tummi). Mal. also (karimaram), meaning black wood. Tam. also (karuppumaram), meaning black tree; (karungáli), meaning black + post [sundra]; (karundumbi), meaning black + the tumby tree. Title otherwise Black ebony, Crow ebony, Taindoo gum. Botanically Diospyros [indian ebony] melanoxylon, roxb., ebenaceæ [vricsham, 83]. Alias Diospyros dubia, exculpta, tomentosa, wightiana. Large tree; young shoots pubescent; leaves nearly opposite, oblong or oblong-lanceolate, acute at the base, coriaceous, entire, obtuse, when young pubescent; calyx and corolla five-cleft; male peduncles axillary, solitary, three to six-flowered; stamens twelve; hermaphrodite flowers rather larger than the male, nearly sessile; styles three to four; berry round, yellow; flowers white; seeds two to eight immersed in pulp; common in most dry forests in remote situations; trees are always small and stunted in the trunk; sheds leaves in cold season, appear again with flowers yearly in the hot season. Bark astringent used in decoction in diarrhœa and dyspepsia as a tonic; in a dilute form used as astringent lotion for eyes; reduced to powder, is applied to ulcerations; mixed with black pepper [q.v.] administered in dysentery; noted in pharm. but non-officinal. Ripe fruit is eatable, but astringent. Wood hard, light-pink color, irregular-shaped masses of ebony [q.v.] in the centre; the ebony is jet black with purple streaks, extremely hard, pores and medullary rays difficult to distinguish; wood used for buildings, shoulder poles, and carriage shafts; ebony for all purposes of fancy work, and carving, though not so good as ceylon ebony.

INDIAN MULBERRY (तूल - túla, *San.*; शातूता - shátútá, *Mahr.*; توت - tút, *Ar.*, *Pers.* and *Hind.*; شاه توت - sháhtút, *Dec.*; كراتو - kratau, *Malay*; ಹಿಪ್ಪಲಿನೇರಳೆ - hippalinérale, *Can.*; కంబళిబూచిచెట్టు - kambalibúchichettu, *Tel.*; கம்பளிப்பூச்சிச்செடி - kambalippúççiççedi, *Tam.*). San. a corruption from persian. Mahr. from persian. Ar. from persian. Pers. from (tutí, pers. parrot), from their fondness for it. Dec. from persian. Can. from (hippali, can. long pepper, piper longum, linn. + nérale, can. nauwal, eugenia jambolana, lamk.). Tel. from (kambalibúchi, tel. caterpillar + chettu, tel. tree). Tam. from (kambali, tam. woollen cloth + púççi, tam. insect + shedi, tam. tree); caterpillar tree. San. also (túda), meaning tormented, from leaves being eaten through by the silk-worms. Ar. also (fisád). Hind. also (tutrí). Malay also (babesaran). Tel. also (kambalichettu), meaning blanket + tree. Singh. also (ratuombilla). Tam. also (musukkattai), meaning large red ant + wood; (kambalikkondán), meaning cumbly + possessor; (kambaliççedi), meaning woollen cloth + tree. Greek συκαμῖνος, not to be confounded with the sycamore. Title otherwise Catterpillar tree, Parrot tree, Silk-worm tree, Sycamine, Toot. Botanically Morus indica, linn., moraceæ [vricsham, 121]. Alias Morus parvifolia. Tree 20 feet; trunk rarely more than the thickness of a man's leg; branches numerous, spreading; bark smooth, ash-colored; leaves deciduous, alternate, petioled, ovate-cordate, long, tapering, entire, pointed, with the lateral margins serrate, and sometimes lobate, and even deeply so, smooth on both sides, very various in size; female aments from the axils of the first leaves or from the scales of the envelope of the bud of the young shoots, solitary, short-peduncled, nearly oval or oval; calyx of four, fleshy cuneate leaflets; style single, half two-cleft; divisions tapering and villous; berry about the size and shape of a small field bean; when ripe black. Flower small, greenish; fruit long and cylindrical resembling a pepper [q.v.] corn, very sweet, but deficient in flavor. Root anthelmintic and astringent; fruit cooling and laxative; juice remedy for sore-throat; consists of sugar [q.v.] and tartaric acid [draucsha ooppoo]; gives to pharm.; juice of the ripe fruit, mori succus, coloring agent, officinal. Fruit and young leaves eaten; the latter are used to feed silk-worms [puttoo]. Gives a gum [gond]. The common mulberry of europe is morus nigra; the red and white mulberries, morus alba and atropurpurea, are natives of persia; the former produces the best fruit, the latter is the handsomer tree.——*Dyeing mulberry* (आच्छुक - áchhuka, San.; आल - ála, Mahr.; آل - ál, Hind. and Dec.; منكدو - mangkudú, Malay; ಹಳದಿಪಾವಟೆ - haladipávate, Can.; మూలుగు - múlugu, Tel.; ଅଚୁ - achu, Oor.; കട്ടപ്പിലാവു - katappilávu, Mal.; අහු - ahu, Singh.; நுணா - nuná, Tam.). Hind. from mahratta. Can. from (haladi, can. yellow + pávate, can. the plant, pavetta indica, linn.). Mal. from (katal, mal. sea + pilávu, mal. jack tree, artocarpus integrifolia, willd.). San. also (achyuta), meaning not fallen. Hind. also (aççí); (ák) [yercum]. Can. also (maddi); (tagachi) [chakondah]. Tel. also (maddi) [murdah]; (togaruchettu), meaning red color + tree; (togarumogali), meaning red color + screw-pine, pandanus odoratissimus, linn.; (mogili) [screw-pine]. Mal. also (maññanátti), meaning turmeric, curcuma longa, rox. + smelling. Tam. also (mañjalbávattai), meaning yellow + the plant, pavetta indica, linn.; (mañjanatti), meaning turmeric, curcuma longa, roxb. + smell; from timber; (tunavu); (periyanuná), meaning large + the tree. Title otherwise Ach, Ach root, Ahoo, Aul, Broad-leaved morinda, Dyeing aul, Morinda root, Muddy, Munjanutty, Noonah, Red screwpine, Sea jack, Togar mogaly, Turmeric timber tree, Yellow pavetta. Botanically Morinda citrifolia, linn., rubiaceæ [vricsham, 71]. Small tree; leaves opposite, oval, alternated at both ends, shining; capituli shortly peduncled, leaf opposed; branchlets four-angled; corolla long infundibuliform five occasionally four to seven-cleft; anthers half hid in the tube; style the length of the tube; berries concrete into an obtuse ovate shining fruit; flowers white; fragrant. Root has a reddish-brown nearly smooth bark, which has a nauseous slightly bitter flavor; the woody portion is hard and of an orange-yellow or reddish-yellow color; the odour of the freshly dug root is acrid and disagreeable. Expressed juice of leaves externally applied in gout; applied fresh to wounds and ulcers; cf. indian worm-killer and zakhm hayaut. Fruits used as famine food. A scarlet dye [shauyam] from bark of root, used for handkerchiefs [roomaul], turbans [puggry], &c.; not equal to that of chayroot [q.v.]; forms an ingredient of various recipes for dyes fixed with alum [padicauram]. The wood is deep yellow, easily worked, and used for common purposes. A variety is citrifolia, linn., var. bracteata; a small tree with large shining leaves; flowers small, white; found in native gardens, temples, &c.; wild in north-east of presidency; root bark yields yellow dye; wood bright, yellow. Another variety is citrifolia, linn., var. citrifolia proper, common; leaves used to wounds and ulcers; internally as tonic and febrifuge; root cathartic; the chief dye-yielding form; wood yellow colored, useful for various purposes. Another variety is citrifolia, linn., var. elliptica; root-bark yields scarlet dye. The separate species tinctoria is by some considered to be citrifolia in its wild state, but the foliage is smaller and never shining; this has fruit, of many drupes, coalescent into a fleshy-globose head, one inch in diameter, insipid; green fruits eaten in curries [q.v.]; the wood hard, very durable, variegated red and white, and employed for gun stocks. The tinctoria, roxb., var. tinctoria proper is a small tree, common; roots have dyeing properties of citrifolia; wood close-grained, light, tough and easily worked, when fresh of bright yellow color, after exposure turning to yellowish brown; used for gun stocks, wooden shoes, &c. The tinctoria, roxb., var. tomentosa is common, in flower a great part of the year; the triplicane burying ground in madras is thickly studded with the tree; root-bark gives a dye; timber yellow. For the umbellata see next head.——*Small dyeing mulberry* (दारुहरिद्रा - dáruharidrá, San.; रुक्कावेलिहलदि - rukkávélihaladi, Conc.; چھوٹا آل - chhotáál, Dec.; چالوب کرتو - chálubkratau, Malay; ಮರದರಸಿನ - maradarasina, Can.; മരമഞ്ഞൾ - maramanjal, Too.; మూలుగుడు - múlugudu, Tel.; നുണാ - nuná, Mal.; කිරිවැල් - kirivel, Singh.; நுணா - nuná, Tam.). Title from size of plant, compared with citrifolia. San. from (dáru, san. wood + haridrá, san. turmeric, curcuma longa, roxb.) [berberry, false calumba]. Dec. from (chhotá, hind. small + ál, dec. the tree, morinda citrifolia, roxb.). Can. from (mara, can. tree + arasina, can. turmeric). Too. from (mara, too. tree + mañjal, too. turmeric, curcuma longa, roxb.). Singh. from (kiri, singh. white + vel, singh. creeper). San. also (pítadáru), meaning yellow tree; (klíbapushpá), meaning having neuter flower; (klíbá), meaning impotent. Dec. also (álkáphúl), meaning morinda flower. Can. also (poppili). Tel. also (maddi); (chiranji) [godaury]. Tam. also (mañjanatti), meaning turmeric + smell, from timber; (matti); (shuriñji). Title otherwise Narrow-leaved morinda, Small ach root. Botanically Morinda umbellata, linn., rubiaceæ [vricsham, 71]. Alias Morinda padavara, scandens. Climbing shrub, glabrous; corolla short infundibuliform; leaves from oblong-lanceolate to cuneate oblong, pointed; stipules membranaceous, united in a truncated sheath; peduncles terminal, three to seven in a sessile terminal umbel about half the length of the leaves; capituli globose; calyx margin entire; limb four occasionally five-cleft; filaments short, inserted into the bottom of the dilated part of the tube among many hairs; anthers exserted; small, delicate flowers, white and extremely fragrant; religious. Fruit when green, used in pickles [chutney]. Compact grained wood yellowish color, made into chairs, &c.

INDIAN OAK (समुद्रफल - samudrap'hala, *San.*; ناتک بلوط - nátkáballút, *Hind.*; මිඩෙල්ල - midella, *Singh.*). Title from resembling oak in branching. San. from (samudra, san. ocean + p'hala, san. fruit). Botanically the Barringtonia genus, myrtaceæ [vricsham, 56]. Trees; natives of india and malayan peninsula; leaves crowded near extremities of branches; flowers in spikes; fruits one-seeded and fleshy; bark narcotic; wood hard and durable. The species best known to the natives are shown below.——*Andaman indian oak* (ಸಮುದ್ರಫಲ - samudrap'hala, Can.; సురపొన్న - suraponna, Tel.; சமுத்திரச்செடி - shamuttiraççedi, Tam.). Can. means sea fruit. Tel. from (sura, san. divine + ponna, tel. tree, calophyllum inophyllum, linn.), from appearance of foliage and flower; cf. common poon. Tam. from (samudra, san. ocean + shedi, tam. plant). Tam also (shamuttiráppazham), meaning sea fruit; (shemmulli), meaning red + moolly plant barleria [common nail dye]. Title otherwise South sea island bottle-brush tree, Tahiti futu tree. Botanically Barringtonia [indian oak] speciosa, forst., myrtaceæ [vricsham, 56]. Tree 30–50 feet, glabrous; leaves often 15 by 7 inches, obtuse, narrowed at the base, quite entire, sessile; raceme short, erect; lower pedicels with a leaf-like bract, upper bracts much smaller; calyx closed over the bud; lobes two, 1½ inch, oblong; petals white; ovary four-celled; ovules about six in each cell; style often exceeding 4 inch; fruit 3 by 3 inch, quadrangular or nearly ovoid by abortion one-seeded. Tree introduced into gardens in s. india, not found in wild state; large foliage, heads of blossom with flowers made up of numerous assemblage of long deep rose-colored filaments. Seeds mixed with bait inebriate fish [common emetic nut, indian berry, marotty, round milk-hedge, sooptee, tejbul, walsoora, zanzibar indigo].——*Common indian oak* (नीप - nípa, San.; समुद्रफल - samudrap'hala, Conc.; ایجل - ijal, Hind.; ಸಮುದ್ರಫಲ - samudrap'hala, Can.; సముద్రపండుచెట్టు - samudrapanduchettu, Tel.; സംസ്തരവടി - samstaravati, Mal.; දියමිඩෙල්ල - diyamidella, Singh.; சமுத்திரக்கடம்பு - shamuttirakkadambu, Tam.). San. from (ni, san. down + ap, san. water); from site of growth [cadamba]. Conc. from (samudra, san. ocean + p'hala, san. fruit). Hind. from (hijjala, san. the tree). Can. from (samudra, san. ocean + p'hala, san. fruit). Tel. from (samudra, san. ocean + pandu, tel. fruit + chettu, tel. tree). Mal. from (samudra, san. ocean + vati, mal. stick). Singh. from (diya, singh. water + midella, singh. barringtonia). Tam. from (samudra, san. ocean + kadambu, tam. the tree, barringtonia acutangula, gærtn.). Hind. also (jauntaríkáphal), meaning mace, myristica fragrans, houtt. + fruit [nutmeg]. Tel. also (kaudangi); (kaniti); (kanapa); (karpa) [cadamba]. Mal. also (samudrappú), meaning ocean flower. Tam. also (kondalamaram), meaning eastern tree; (shamuttiráppazham), meaning sea fruit, said to be brought from eastern islands; (vengadambu), meaning white + indian oak. Title otherwise Canapa, Carpa, Sea side indian oak, White indian oak. Botanically Barringtonia [indian oak] racemosa, blume, myrtaceæ [vricsham, 56]. Alias Eugenia racemosa; Stravadia alba, racemosa; Stravadium coccineum. Stravadia from malayalam. Tree; reddish bark; leaves alternate, short-petioled, cuneate-oblong, acuminated, serrulated, smooth on both sides; racemes terminal, or axillary from the large branches, pendulous; flowers on short pedicels, large, white with a tinge of rose; calyx two to three-cleft; petals four; filaments longer than the petals; style long; fruit size of egg, ovate, drupaceous, bluntly four-angled, smooth, brownish red; endocarp scarcely separating from the epicarp; seed one; flowering in may. Root resembles cinchona [koinah]; slightly bitter, aperient, deobstruent, and cooling; fruit powdered used as snuff medicinally. Wood white, very soft, porous.——*Small indian oak* (हिज्जल - hijjala, San.; समुद्रफल - samudrap'hala, Mahr.; سمندر پهل - samandarphal, Hind.; ಕೆಂಪುಕನಗಿನಮರ - kempukanaginamara, Can.; కనప - kanapa, Tel.;

ಕಿಂಜೋಲ - kinjólo, Oor.; ചെറിയസംസ്തരവടി - cheriyasamstara-vati, Mal.; ඇලමිදෙල්ල - elamidella, Singh.; கடம்பு - kadambu, Tam.). San. from (hita, san. suitable + jala, san. water); as growing near water. Mahr. from hindostany. Hind. from (samandar, hind. ocean + phal, hind. fruit); from growing on banks beyond tidal range. Can. from (kempu, can. red + kanaginamara, can. nerium odorum, soland.). Oor. from sanscrit. Mal. from (cheriya, mal. small + samstaravati, mal. barringtonia racemosa, blume). Singh. from (ela, singh. white + midella, singh. barringtonia). Tam. from (katam, tam. jungle) [abrony]; cf. cadamba. San. also (ambuja), meaning water-born [nelumbo]; (nichula). Hind. also (ijal), from sanscrit; (panniari), meaning water + apart, i.e., beyond tidal influence; (ingar), from sanscrit. Can. also (ganagilatóramara). Tel. also (kanigi); (karpá); (kadimi) [cadamba, water cadamba]. Oor. also (hinjara), from sanscrit. Tam. also (níbamaram), meaning low ground + tree; (kanatti), meaning heavy wood; (shengadambu), meaning red + the tree. Title otherwise Hijjal tree, Red nauclea, Red oleander. Botanically Barringtonia [indian oak] acutangula, gærtn., myrtaceæ [vricsham, 56]. Alias Botryoropis; Eugenia acutangula, racemosa; Meteorus coccineus; Stravadium acutangulum, coccineum, rubum; Stravadium from malayalam. Tree; leaves crowded about the ends of the branches, cuneate-obovate, serrulated; racemes long, pendulous: pedicels very short; calyx four-cleft; ovary two-celled; fruit oblong, four-sided, sharp-angled; flowers small, reddish white, with scarlet filaments; common on banks of rivers or on western coast backwaters [cauyal]; flowering in the hot season. The dry seeds as met with in the shops resemble a nutmeg [jautikye] in size and shape; externally they are somewhat rough, brown, and marked with longitudinal striæ; internally horny, hard and brittle when dry, but easily softened by immersion in water; the bulk of the seed consist of starch; taste sweet at first, afterwards bitter and nauseous. The fruit is one of the best known domestic remedies; when children suffer from a cold in the chest, the seed is rubbed down on a stone with water and applied over the sternum, and if there is much dyspnœa a few grains with or without the juice of fresh ginger [q.v.] are administered internally and seldom fail to induce vomiting and the expulsion of mucus from the air passages; to reduce the enlarged abdomen of children it is given in doses of from 2 to 3 grains in milk [paul]; the roots are used to kill fish. Bark is used in tanning [chamrah]. Wood is hard and of a fine grain, red, and equivalent to mahogany; stands a good polish, greatly in request by cabinet makers.

INDIAN WATER-LILY (उत्पल - utpala, *San.*; కలువ - kaluva, *Tel.*; அல்லி - alli, *Tam.*). San. from (ut, san. up + pal, san. to burst); bursting upwards as a blossom. Tam. from (al, tam. night), from flowering at night; generally applied to white indian water-lily [q.v.] as being the commonest here. San. also (kamala), meaning water adorning; (kuvalaya), meaning earth + bracelet. Tel. also (pankéruhamu), meaning growing in marsh; (kákikaluva), meaning crow + the plant. Greek νυμφαία. Botanically the Nymphæa genus, nymphæaceæ [vricsham, 7]. Water plants found in lakes and rivers; rootstock fleshy or tuberous, sending down rootlets into mud; leaves usually circular, entire or toothed, floating on water; leaf-stalks cylindrical, traversed with air-canals; flower stalks similar to leaf stalks; flowers large, expanded, floating, containing many series of petals; fruit a spongy berry ripening under water. The species best known to the natives are shown below. Distinguish from Egyptian lotus [nelumbo]. Compare also in other genera:—Crinum asiaticum, keel-leaved african lily, poison lily; Fourcroya gigantea, giant mexican lily; Methonica superba, malabar glory lily, superb lily; Phornium tenax, flax lily; Polianthes tuberosa, tuberose white lily. See gloss. paragraphs.——*Blue indian water-lily* (नीलकमल - nílakamala, San.; نیلوفر - nílofar, Ar., Pers., Hind. and Dec.; ಕನ್ನೈದಲು - kannaidalu, Can.; నల్లకలువ - nallakaluva, Tel.; കരിങ്കുവലയം - karinkuvalayam, Mal.; නිල්තෙල්ලු - niltelólu, Singh.; நீலல்லி - nílalli, Tam.). Title from color of flower. San. from (níla, san. blue + kamala, san. nymphæa lotus, linn.). Ar. from (nílótpala, san. blue lily). Can. from (kari, can. blue + naidile, can. water-lily). Tel. from (nalla, tel. black + kaluva, tel. nymphæa). Mal. from (kari, mal. black + kuvalaya, san. water-lily). Singh. from (nil, singh. blue + telólu, singh. water-lily). Tam. from (níla, san. blue + alli, tam. lily). San. also (nílótpala), meaning blue water-lily; (indívara), meaning chief abode of lutchmy; (nílámbujanma), meaning blue lotus. Tel. also (nítikaluva), meaning water + the plant. Mal. also (chittámbal), meaning small water-lily. Title otherwise Star-flowered lily. Botanically Nymphæa [indian water-lily] stellata, willd., nymphæaceæ [vricsham, 7]. Alias Nymphæa cyanea, hookeriana, punctata, versicolor. Perennial creeper; leaves quite entire, margins waved; lobes diverging at the base; petiole attached within the margin; stigma eight to twelve-rayed; flowers blue; flowering all the year; roots and seeds eaten as in red indian water-lily [q.v.].——*Purple indian water-lily* (रक्तोत्पल - raktótpala, San.; செங்கழுநீர் - shengazhunír, Tam.). Title from color of flowers. San. from (rakta, san. red + utpala, san. water-lily, nymphæa genus). Tam. from (shem, tam. red + kazhunír, tam. the plant). Title otherwise American sweet-scented water-lily. Botanically Nymphæa [indian water-lily] odorata, willd., nymphæaceæ [vricsham, 7]. Aquatic perennial, ornamental; leaves cordate, entire, emarginate; lobes divaricating; point obtuse; calyx four-leaved; flowers white; flowering in july. The flower has a smell somewhat like the wall flower.——*Red indian water-lily* (कुमुद - kumuda, San. and Mahr.; तांबडे सालक - támbadésálaka, Conc.; نیلوفر - nílofar, Ar. and Pers.; کنول - kanwal, Hind.; چھوٹا کنول - chhotákanwal, Dec.; ಕೆನ್ನೈದಿಲೆ - kennaidile, Can.; కెంపల్లి - kempalli, Too.; ఎర్రకలువ - errakaluva, Tel.; රංකෛන් - rangkain, Oor.; ആമ്പൽ - ámbal, Mal.; තෙලොලු - telolu, Singh.; செவ்வல்லி - shevvalli, Tam.). Title from color of flower. San. from (ku, san. earth + mud, san. to rejoice). Ar. from (níla, san. blue + utpala, san. water-lily). Pers. from arabic. Hind. from sanscrit [nelumbo, white indian water-lily]. Dec. from (chhotá, hind. small + kamala, san. lotus). Can. from (kem, can. red + naidile, can. water-lily). Too. from (kempu, too. red + alli, too. water-lily). Tel. from (erra, tel. red + kaluva, tel. nymphæa). Mal. from (ám, mal. water + alli, mal. lily) [white indian water-lily]. Tam. from (shem, tam. red + alli, tam. lily). San. also (hallaka), meaning attracting as bees; (shálúka), meaning the root of a lily; (raktótpala), meaning red + water-lily; (kamala), meaning water adorning [nelumbo]; (kalhára), meaning delighted with water; (saugandhika), meaning sweet smelling; (raktasandhyaka), meaning red like twilight; (nílótpala), meaning blue water-lily; (kákótpala), meaning crow's lily; (kandóta), meaning white bulbous water-lily; (varótpala), meaning superior lily; (raktanila), Hind. also (raktachandan), meaning pterocarpus santalinus, linn. f. [red sanders]. Dec. also (alíphúl), from tamul. Can. also (kempudávare), meaning red, nelumbium speciosum, willd.; (bilidávare), meaning white + lotus; (naidele), meaning water-lily; (chennaidile), meaning red + lily; (kóle); (kendávare), meaning red + lotus. Tel. also (chengaluva), meaning red + the plant; (chendova), meaning red + the plant; (kákikaluva), meaning crow + the plant; (koteka). Mal. also (allittámara), meaning lily + lotus; (arakkámbal), meaning red water-lily. Singh. also (ratutelólu), meaning red water-lily; (nelum), meaning lotus, nelumbium speciosum, willd.; (ólu). Tam. also (allittámarai), meaning lily + lotus; (ámbal), meaning water-lily; (shengazhuuír), meaning red + the plant; (shivappalli), meaning red lily; (arakkámbal), meaning red lily; (shivandavallittámarai), meaning red + lily + lotus. Title otherwise Ally, Aumbal, Crow lily, Red lotus, Twilight lily. Botanically Nymphæa [indian water-lily] lotus, linn., nymphæaceæ [vricsham, 7]. Alias Castalia magnifica; Nymphæa edulis, esculenta, rubra. Aquatic; sepals four; petals numerous; leaves peltate, sharply toothed, downy but not spotted beneath; lobes diverging; connectivum not prolonged; petioles inserted very near the margin of the leaf; flowers deep red; torus bottle-shaped; carpels numercus, many-seeded; stigma ten to twenty-rayed; flowering all year; grows in tanks. The dry petals are from 2–3 inches long, broad at the base and lanceolate towards the end, and of pink, crimson or reddish-brown color without any distinct smell or taste; the seeds are small, round, about twice the size of the mustard [rayaun] seeds, pale brown in color, devoid of smell and somewhat mucilaginous in taste; the root is sold in the bazaar in round and flat slices, varying from 1–2 or 2½ inches in diameter, pale or dirty white in color, odourless, and almost insipid with an uneven or irregular and more or less hairy edge. The flowers or rather petals are medicinally cardiac tonic refrigerant and diuretic; the seeds, demulcent and nutrient; the roots, stomachic, demulcent and astringent. The best preparation of the flowers is the syrup; the most convenient way of using the seeds and roots is in simple powder. Doses; of the syrup of flowers, from 2 to 4 drachms; of the powder of the seeds, from 40 grains to 1 drachm; of the powder of the root, from 30 to 50 grains. Substituted; the flowers for digitalis; the seeds for iceland moss, tragacanth [kateerah] and pepsine; the roots for subnitrate of bismuth, pepsine and gallic acid. Root, stalk, leaf, and flower, eaten as vegetables; and the seed as a nut; a kind of arrowroot made from the underground stems and roots.——*White indian water-lily* (सितोत्पल - sitótpala, San.; धवेसालक - dhavésálaka, Conc.; نیلوفر ابیض - nílofariabyaz, Ar.; نیلوفر سفید - nílofarisufíd, Pers.; سفید کنول - sufedkanwal, Hind.; اجلا کنول - ujlákanwal, Dec.; ಬಿಳೇನೈದಿಲೆ - bilénaidile, Can.; తామర - támare, Too.; తెల్లకలువ - tellakaluva, Tel.; വെള്ളാമ്പൽ - vellámbal, Mal.; සුදුතෙලොලු - sudutelólu, Singh.; நெய்தல் - neydal, Tam.). Title from color of flower. San. from (sita, san. white + utpala, san. water-lily, nymphæa genus). Conc. means white lily. Ar. from (nílofar, ar. nymphæa lotus, linn. + abyaz, ar. white). Pers. from (nílofar, ar. nymphæa lotus + sufíd, pers. white). Hind. from (sufed, hind. white + kanwal, hind. nymphæa lotus, linn.). Dec. from (ujlá, dec. white + kanwal, dec. nymphæa lotus). Can. from (bile, can. white + naidile, can. water-lily). Too. from (támare, too. lotus). Tel. from (tella, tel. white + kaluva, tel. the plant). Mal. from (vella, san. white + ámbal, san. water-lily). Singh. from (sudu, singh. white + telólu, singh. water-lily). Tam. from (ney, tam. to be glutinous). San. also (indívara), meaning chief abode of lutchmy; (kairava), meaning liked by swan [hamsam]. Hind. also (kairub); (kanwal) [nelumbo, red indian water-lily]. Can. also (bilitámare), meaning white + lotus. Mal. also (nírámbal), meaning water + water-lily; (ámbal), meaning water-lily [red indian water-lily]. Tam. also (vellámbal), meaning white + lily; (indirávásam), meaning abode of lutchmy. Title otherwise Lutchmy's lily, White aumbal. Botanically Nymphæa [indian water-lily] lotus, linn., var. pubescens, h. f. and t., nymphæaceæ [vricsham, 7]. Alias Castalia pubescens, sacra; Nymphæa lotus, pubescens. Aquatic; leaves oval, quite entire, downy underneath, margin sometimes slightly waved; petiole attached a little within the margin; petals ten to fifteen; stamens thirty, in a double series; stigmas ten to fifteen-rayed; flowers white; connectivum not prolonged; seeds numerous. Has peltate leaves, sharply serrated; the under surface pilose at the nerves and pubescent between them, red at the margins; bears large, white flowers of a vinous smell the root is large, tuberous and eatable like that of the nelumbo [q.v.].

INDIGO (نیل - níl, *Hind.*). Greek *τὸ ἰνδικὸν βαφικόν*. Hence Latin indicum for short, and Portuguese indico. The Sanscrit name appears through the Portuguese anil in "aniline." The Greek *ἰνδικὸν* was also applied to pepper. Indigo is called *ἰνδικὸν μέλαν* in the Periplus. For the botanical indigofera genus see Neely. Besides the various species of that genus, it will be seen from the sub-heads that there are several other so-called indigoes.——*Arabian indigo* (نیل عرب - níliarab, Hind.; இருப்புமுறி - iruppumuri, Tam.). Tam. from (irumbu, tam. iron + muri, tam. to break): from leaves glistening like iron filings. Tam. also (aramuri), meaning file + to break. Title otherwise Silvery-leaved indigo, Wild indigo. Botanically Indigofera [neely] argentea, linn., leguminosæ [vricsham, 48]. Alias Indigofera glauca. The Egyptian and Arabian species, but is also a native here. Allied to Indigofera anil, linn. [west-indian indigo]. Shrub several feet high, with sulcate woody branches; leaves 1–2 inches long; leaflets opposite, sub-coreaceous, persistently argenteous, ½–1 inch long; petiole ½ inch; stipules minute, setaceous; racemes subsessile, twelve to twenty-flowered, shorter than the leaves, ½–1 inch long whilst in flower; calyx 1/24 inch campanulate, argenteous; teeth deltoid, cuspidate, as long as tube; corolla ⅙ inch, reddish yellow, externally canescent; pod ⅜–½ inch by ⅙ inch at first argenteous, finally glabrescent, distinctly torulose. Yields dye, in small quantities, but of superior quality. Cf. Wild indigo.——*Bastard indigo* (கள்ளவுரி - kallavuri, Tam). Dye from Amorpha fruticosa, linn. Ornamental deciduous shrub, 6 feet high; teeth of calyx four blunt, one acuminate, flowers purple.——*British indigo* (ادلميه - idlimeh, Ar.). Woad, Isatis tinctoria, linn. A biennial plant, with oblong crenate root-leaves about a foot in length, on pretty long stalks; an upright, much branched leafy stem, about 3 feet high; small yellow flowers; leaves when cut are reduced to a paste which is kept in heaps for about fifteen days to ferment and then formed into balls which are sun-dried; these balls are subjected to a further fermentation before use.——*Chinese indigo* (نیل خطائی - nílikhatáí, Hind.). Dye from Isatis indigotica, fortune. Small half shrubby plant, with a decumbent stem, bearing at its extremity several long drooping racemes of small yellow flowers, and smooth black and fiddle-shaped pods about half inch long; the lower leaves are rather fleshy, on long stalks oval, lance-shaped, and pointed, with the edges slightly toothed, the upper ones very much narrower and smaller.——*Common indigo* (नीलिनी - níliní, San.; नीली - nílí, Mahr.; نليج - nílaj, Ar.; درخت نیل - darakhtinil, Pers.; نیل کا پیڑ - nílkáper, Hind.; نیل کا جھاڑ - nílkájhár, Dec.; ترم - tarum, Malay; ನೀಲಿಗಿಡ - níligida, Can.; ನೀಲಿ - níli, Too.; నీలి - níli, Tel.; അമരി - amari, Mal.; අවරි - avari, Singh.; அவுரி - avuri, Tam.). San. from (níla, san. blue). Mahr. from sanscrit. Ar. from sanscrit. Pers. from (darakht, pers. tree + níla, san. indigo). Hind. from (níla, san. indigo + per, hind. tree). Dec. from (níla, san. indigo + jhár, hind. tree). Tel. from sanscrit. Mal. from tamul. Tam. from (avi, tam. to boil); from decoction dye. San. also (vanikbandhu), meaning trader's friend; (klítaká), meaning exchanged; (vajranílí), meaning diamond + the plant; (nílí), meaning black; (kálá), meaning black; (shríp'halí), meaning auspicious fruit [bael]; (rañjaní), meaning dyer. Ar. also (annil), meaning the blue. Can. also (ollenili), meaning good + indigo; (hennunili), meaning female + indigo. Tel. also (aviri). Singh. also (nilgaha), meaning indigo + plant; (nilavari). Title otherwise Aviry, Dog-bite shrub, Dyer's indigo, Indian indigo. Botanically Indigofera [neely] tinctoria, linn., leguminosæ [vricsham, 48]. Alias Indigofera emarginata, hawer, indica. Shrub, 2–3 feet, erect, pubescent; branches terete, firm; leaves pinnated; leaflets five to six pairs, oblong-ovate, cuneate at the base, slightly decreasing in size towards the apex of the leaf, darker above than below; racemes shorter than the leaves, sessile, many-flowered; flowers small, approximated at the base of the raceme, more distant and deciduous towards the apex, greenish-rose color, scentless; calyx five-cleft, segments broad, acute; legumes approximated towards the base of the rachis, nearly cylindrical, slightly torulose, deflexed and curved upwards; seeds about ten, cylindrical, truncated at both ends; generally resembles lucerne; flowering in rainy season. The cultivated species of this presidency and of bengal; indigenous in west tropical africa; common here but never far from where cultivated; though naturally a shrub, is grown as an annual or biennial. Indian indigo, as a blue dye, was known in ancient rome; it was first imported into modern europe by the dutch in the year 1660; subsequently by portuguese, french and british traders; it experienced much opposition in europe on account of its interference with woad [british indigo] and was there called the devil's dye. In this presidency indigo cultivation extends along the east coast from kistna to south arcot, and inland to kurnool and cuddapah; cuddapah is the principal district for indigo; next nellore; the crop requires a rich friable soil, neither too moist nor too dry; bright sunshine favors the development of the dye principle, but frequent rains cause a more luxuriant growth; it is generally cultivated as a dry crop; in some parts it is sown mixed with millet [q.v.] crops; then, after the latter are harvested, the indigo shoots up; in dry land as a rule one cutting is obtained in october and a second in january; indigo is also grown however on wet land, here two cuttings are certain, and sometimes there is a third; it is not unfrequently sown in paddy [q.v.] fields a few days before reaping; on whatever soil sown, the crop so far from exhausting is believed to strengthen the soil; the first step in the culture is to plough and manure the ground; a flock of sheep [and] is sometimes enclosed on the ground; at other times the ground is lightly scattered with wood-ashes, cow-dung, &c.; or the refuse of the indigo plant from the steeping vat, or its ashes, are scattered over the fields; the seed is generally sown broadcast; the plant in favorable damp weather, or if lightly irrigated, makes its appearance above ground in four or five days, and ripens in about two months and a half; great care is taken to weed the plantation thoroughly, and to keep the ground moist, but not too wet; when the seedlings attain two or three inches, the fields are weeded; the leaves are cut just before the plant flowers; the first cutting takes place when the crop is three months old, after which the field is lightly ploughed; the other cuttings follow after intervals of two or three months, and are better than the first; the leaves are not gathered after heavy rain, as this washes off from them the farina which constitutes their principal value. Many ryots [q.v.] have their own manufacturing vats, others merely cultivate and sell their leaf to some neighbour who has a vat; large factories for manufacturing the dyes [shauyam] exist at cuddapah, nellore, rajahmundry, salem, tinnevelly, tripassore, vellore, &c. In former years the usual mode of extracting indigo, as practised in southern india, was from the dry leaf; this is now almost superseded by the system of the green leaf manufacture, except in parts of south arcot and salem. The process of green-leaf manufacturing is as follows; the cut bundles of the plant, comprising stalks, leaves, &c., are taken directly after cutting to the factory, and are then at once stacked into the steeping vat, and pressed down by large beams which are firmly bolted to upright iron rods or stone posts buried in the ground; water is then let into the steeping vat, so as to stand a couple of inches above the plant; in this manner it is allowed to macerate for from eighteen to twenty hours, by which time a kind of mucous fermentation will have taken place; the fluid is then let out by the removal of plugs into the beating vat, where it is beaten with oars or paddles for a couple of hours; lime-water [choonam tunny] in proportionate quantity is then thrown in, and the fluid allowed to settle for a couple of hours; during this time the fecula precipitates to the bottom of the vat; the plugs are now opened and the supernatant fluid let out; the fecula is then taken up with flat copper pans and strained through a layer of coarse cloth; it is next placed in a copper boiler with a sufficient quantity of fresh water, and boiled till ebullition freely occurs; the fire is then put out and the contents allowed to cool; the pulpy mass is next collected in bags made of dungry [q.v.] cloth; these are placed in a wooden box having a till, in which it is submitted to pressure by means of a screw in order to expel the whole of the fluid contained in the mass; this is repeated for two or three days; and when the mass has been completely drained, it is cut into square cakes and placed in the shade, and the moisture allowed gradually to evaporate; in about a month the cakes are cleaned or brushed to remove a whitish efflorescence which forms on their surface, and also to give them a glossy appearance; the article is now ready for the market and is styled fresh-leaf indigo; the average quantity of indigo obtained from hundred bundles of the plant is one maund [q.v.]. The dry-leaf process is carried out in the same way, except that the plant is cut, dried and threshed to collect the leaves separately, and these are sold to the manufacturer by weight, or by measure; when kept dry, the leaves undergo, in the course of four weeks, a material change, their green tint turning into a pale blue grey, previous to which they afford no indigo; the dried leaves are infused in the steeping vat, with six times their bulk of water, and allowed to steep for two hours, with continual stirring, till all the floating leaves sink; the fine green liquor is then drawn off into the beater vat; in this method the fermentation of the fresh leaves, often capricious in its course, is superseded by a much shorter period of simple maceration; the following is a Hindostany proverb:—نیل بگڑنا, spoilt indigo, hence to tell lies, because when the vat seems likely to fail, dyers from a curious notion tell lies as a way of charming it; the process of agitation, boiling, &c., are the same as with fresh leaves. Ryots sometimes manufacture on a small scale in large earthenware pots [chatty] about 2½ feet high; this generally with dried leaf; such pots are placed in a range of four, six, or eight, over one fire and slowly boiled; as soon as the boiling has reached a certain point, the indigo leaves are removed and the liquor is poured into earthen vessels and churned for about half an hour; then there is added to it a solution of the bark of the jaumoon tree, eugenia jambolana, lamk. [common jaumoon], for the purpose of separating the dye from the water; the indigo liquor is then allowed to stand until the product deposits itself at the bottom of the vessels, when the water is gently poured off and the deposit poured into moulds to harden; these moulds are simply holes dug in the ground lined with a piece of cloth or gunny; the indigo remains in the mould for one night, by which time it becomes a solid mass, but sufficiently soft to allow of its being cut up into small pieces; after these have been well dried they are packed in chests and are ready for the market. The indigo product does not exist in the raw plant, but is generated by the fermentation from the principle called indican or indigo-blue; the maceration is to produce fermentation and oxydization. Commercially the product is found in cubic cakes of a deep blue color, which when rubbed by a smooth hard body assumes a coppery or bronze hue; commercial indigo only contains from 50 to 60 per cent. pure, the remainder consisting of a number of products; the indigo product is odourless and tasteless when pure; it is insoluble in water, cold alcohol, ether, dilute acids [poolipp, tezaub] and alkalies [cauram], and in cold fixed and volatile oils [yennay]; see later as to its application in dyeing; hot alcohol and fixed oils dissolve indigo in small quantities, but again deposit it on cooling. The indigo plant is reckoned by veidyans [q.v.] as an antidote for poison; leaf considered alterative and prescribed in pakkashoolay [q.v.] or hepatitis; the juice of the young branches mixed with honey [shahad] is used for aphthæ of the mouth in children; manufactured indigo itself is applied to reduce swellings of the body; powdered indigo is employed in epilepsy and erysipelas, and sprinkled on foul ulcers to cleanse them. The chief use is that of the dye product; indigotine or the tinctorial principle, and by consequence the ordinary indigo cake of commerce, is as above mentioned perfectly insoluble in any of the ordinary solvents; when however from any source it takes into its composition two additional atoms of hydrogen it changes to a white color, and then as white or hydrogenised indigo is readily soluble in alkaline compounds, in which state it is applied to textile substances; by subsequent exposure it quickly again oxidises to its blue color, and so becomes a very fast permanent dye; this is the theory of indigo dyeing, the most ancient dye process in the world. The following is the native method; to make a dyeing vat take ten seers of indigo, ground with a little water to a fine powder; put it into a pot capable of containing fifty seers; add a decoction of seed of tagaray or cassia tora, linn. [chakondah], and the boiled seed as well; then add tèn seers of powdered sowdoo [q.v.], or impure soda, twelve seers of quicklime, and two seers of a ley of potash [jharkanamak]; the whole is then stirred with a stick, and the mouth of the pot is covered up; every evening and morning, for four days, three seers more of the ley must be added, and in the last portion must be put about the size of an apple [seb] of quicklime [choonam]; the vat now rests for three days, when four or five seers of boiling water must be added to it, and the vat is then ready for dyeing; the ley of potash above-named is prepared as follows; burn to ashes the branches of the cully or euphorbia tirucalli, linn. [round milk hedge], or of the ootreyena or achyranthes muricata; of these ashes put two seers into a pot, in the bottom of which there is a small hole; the hole is covered with a small inverted cup, and that by some rice husks or chaff; above these are put the ashes, and on them are poured by degrees twenty-five seers [q.v.] of water, which filters through the hole and forms the ley. For every seer weight of cotton [q.v.] thread pass a seer measure of water first through the pot containing the ashes, and in this weak ley dip the seer of cotton; wash it well, and then wring out the water; the thread is next dipped, by seers weight at a time, in the solution of indigo, till the color therein is exhausted; the color given by one dip is called mye, and is a sky blue; that which is given by five dips is nearly approaching to black. The above process with soda, quicklime, and ley of potash are for the purposes of clearing the color; and are not properly mordant [cauram] processes; the mordant is the air, which alone is sufficient to make the blue color perfectly fast; in the simplest native dyeing, the indigo is merely got into solution by the seeds of some plant which produces a ferment, and then the cloth is dipped. The following is a Hindostany by-word :—نیل کا ٹیکا an indigo mark, that is to say an indelible stain on character. Indigo dyes blue with alum [padicauram], green with turmeric [country saffron], and black with iron [auhan]. In concentrated sulphuric acid [gandhac tezaub] it forms a deep blue liquid by name of saxon blue; when submitted to dry distillation it yields a considerable quantity of aniline; these uses are not here known.——*Croton indigo* (सूर्यावर्त - súryávarta, San.). Dye of Crozophora plicata, mueller [round pepper].——*False indigo* (காட்டவுரி - káttavuri, Tam.). Dye of Baptisia tinctoria, h. k., the wild indigo of the United states. Perennial herbaceous deciduous plant, 1½ feet high; leaves ternate, stalked; leaflets roundish ovate; stipules setaceous, obsolete; flowers yellow.——*Large zanzibar indigo* (పెనువెంపలి - penuvempali, Tel.). Tel. from (penu, tel. large + vempali, tel. tephrosia purpurea, pers.). Title otherwise Hairy-leaved indigo plant. Botanically Indigofera [neely] hirsuta, linn., leguminosæ [vricsham, 48]. Erect, covered except the leaves with soft hairs; leaves pinnated; leaflets opposite, two to five pair, oblong-obovate, the terminal one the largest; upper surface slightly, under densely clothed with silky hairs; stipules long, bristly; racemes dense, peduncled, usually longer than the leaves; calyx deeply five-cleft; segment hairy; legumes imbricately reflexed, straight, four-angled, mucronate, villous, four to six-seeded; seeds four-sided, truncated at both ends; flowers small, deep rose-colored; flowering nearly all the year.——*Manilla indigo* (മണിലാനീലം - manilánílam, Mal.). Dye of Anona reticulata, linn. [netted anona].——*Paula indigo* (हयमारक - hayamáraka, San.; काळाकुडा - kálákudá, Mahr.; لسان العصا فير الحلو - lisánulasáfírulhalo, Ar.; درخت اندرجو شیرین - darakhtiindarjavishírín, Pers.; میٹھا اندر جو کا پیڑ - míthaindarjaukáper, Hind.; میٹھا اندر جو کا جھاڑ - míthaindarjaukájhár, Dec.; ಹಲ್ಲುನೋವುಮರ - hallunóvumara, Can.; పాలనీలి - pálanili, Tel.; കൊടകപ്പാല - kotakappála, Mal.; வெட்பாலை - vedbálai, Tam.). Title from white wood yielding indigo. San. from (haya, san. horse + máraka, san. destroyer) [gannair]. Mahr. from (kálá, mahr. black + kudá, mahr. holarrhena antidysenterica, wall.). Ar. from (lisán, ar. tongue + asáfír, ar. sparrows + halo, ar. sweet). Pers. from (darakht, pers. tree + indarjau, hind. holarrhena antidysenterica, wall. + shírín, pers. sweet). Hind. from (míthá, hind. sweet + indarjau, hind. holarrhena antidysenterica, wall. + per, hind. tree), bark and seed being similar to look at, but not bitter. Dec. from hindostany. Can. from (hallu, can. tooth + nóvu, can. pain + mara, can. tree). Tel. from (pála, tel. white + níli, tel. indigo plant). Mal. from (kutaku, mal. coorg + pála, mal. milk plant). Tam. from (vel, tam. white + pálai, tam. milky plant). Ar. also (lisánulasáfír), meaning sparrow's tongue. Pers. also (indarjauishírín), meaning indra's sweet barley, hordeum vulgare, linn.; (darakhtiaharishírín), meaning sweet ash tree; (darakhtizabánikunjashkishírín), meaning tree of sweet sparrow's tongue. Can. also (beppále), meaning white + milky tree. Tel. also (chittiankudu), meaning small + the plant; (tellapála), meaning white + milky plant; (ankudu) [gambier, tellicherry bark]. Tam. also (pálai), meaning milky plant [dita, edible paulay, eve's apple, ground paulay, monkey-face paulay, nakchiknee silk cotton, nauga champak, pauchonty, paulay silk cotton, tellicherry bark]; (pálainílam), meaning milky plant + indigo. Title otherwise Blue dyeing rosebay, Dyer's oleander, Dyer's wrightia, Sparrow's tongue, Sweet inderjow. Botanically Wrightia [veppaulay] tinctoria, r. br., apocynaceæ [vricsham, 87]. Alias Nerium tinctorium. Shrub, 10–15 feet; leaves elliptic-lanceolate or ovate-oblong, acuminated, glabrous; panicles terminal, branches and corymbs divaricate; tube of corolla twice as long as the calyx; follicles distinct, but united at the apex; flowers white, fragrant, 1½ inches in diameter when expanded. The pale green soft leaves deciduous in cold weather; plant flowers in march and april, with white follicles in pairs, from 12–18 inches long, the lower extremities of which unite as they ripen; seeds have pleasant taste, not unlike that of oats [vilauyaty jow], which they also resemble in appearance. Is less dependent than common indigo plants on rain and irrigation. When used to give a blue dye, the leaves are boiled in a pot, and on temperature or consistency becoming suitable the liquid is poured off into another pot and worked with a paddle, a small infusion of naugamaram [common jaumoon], bark being added; when the water clears it is poured off, and the sediment being dried, is fit for the market; manufacture is common in coimbatore. The inert bark and seeds are sold in bazaar [q.v.] for real inderjow [tellicherry bark]; the bark is readily distinguished by its darker color, and by its not exfoliating in patches. The fresh leaves when chewed are pungent, and remove toothache; the coagulated milky juice forms a kind of caoutchouc [pauchonty]. The wood is white and close-grained, somewhat resembling ivory [dant]; it cuts like soap [sauboon] on the lathe, and is much used for ornamental and useful purposes; the turners call it doodhy or milk-wood. There is a glabrous variety more common than the variety with puberulous leaves.——*Sylhet indigo* (نیل سلہٹ - nílsilhet, Hind.). Dye of Marsdenia tinctoria, r. br.——*West indian indigo* (विषशोधनी - vishashódhaní, San.; النيل - annil, Ar.; ولایتی نیل - viláitínil, Hind.; ಶೀಮೆನೀಲಿ - shímenili, Can.; సీమనీలి - símanili, Tel.; சீமைநீலி - shímainili, Tam.). San. from (visha, san. poison + shudh, san. to clear), root reckoned an antidote to poison. Hind. from (viláití, hind. foreign + níl, hind. indigo plant). Can. from (shíme, can. foreign + níli, can. indigo plant, indigofera tinctoria, linn.). Tel. similar. Tam. similar. Title otherwise Foreign indigo. Botanically Indigofera [neely] anil, linn., leguminosæ [vricsham, 48]. Specific name from arabic. Herb or undershrub ever green, biennial; height 3 feet; leaves pinnate, oblong, of three pairs; racemes shorter than leaf; flowering in july-august. Found wild at philip's island in spain and in the west indies; also along the gambia in africa; a larger plant than the indian; its pod sickle-shaped, short, compressed; differs thus also from tinctoria; the spaniards manufactured indigo from this species in mexico and the portuguese in brazil; it was from this plant that aniline, used for the production of the pigments [rangh] mauve and magenta, was first obtained.——*Wild indigo* (कालक्लीतक - kálaklítaka, San.; سرمائی نیل - surmáinil, Hind.; ಕಾರುನೀಲಿ - kárunili, Can.; కారునీలి - kárunili, Tel.; காட்டவுரி -

káttavuri, Tam.). San. from (kála, san. black + klítaká, san. indigo plant, indigofera tinctoria, linn.). Hind. from (surmá, hind. antimony + níl, hind. indigo); from color. Can. from (káru, can. black + níli, can. indigo plant). Tel. from (káru, tel. wild + níli, tel. indigo plant, indigofera tinctoria, linn.). Tam. from (kádu, tam. forest + avuri, tam. indigo plant). Botanically Indigofera [neely] argentea, linn., var. cærulea, leguminosæ [vricsham, 48]. Alias Indigofera cærulea. An erect shrub, covered with whitish pubescence; leaves pinnated; leaflets four to five pair, obovate, the terminal largest; all hairy underneath; racemes solitary, shorter than the leaves; upper flowers deciduous; legumes short, deflexed, and falcate upwards; slightly torulose, three to four-seeded; flowers small, yellowish-red; flowering nearly all the year. Commonly met with on barren and uncultivated ground; a dark green, handsome bush with flowers in large pendulous racemes of delicate pink or rose color; from its leaves, which are about one or two inches long and three-quarters of an inch broad, a light indigo can be extracted in large quantities.——*Zanzibar indigo* (शारपुङ्खा - sharapunkhá, San.; उन्हाळी - unhálí, Mahr.; سر پهونکا - sarphonká, Hind.; جنگلی کلتهی - janglíkulthí, Dec.; ಫಂಕಿಗಿಡ - p'hankigida, Can.; వెంపలి - vempali, Tel.; കോഴിഞ്ഞിൽ - kozhiññil, Mal.; ගම්පිලි - gampili, Singh.; கொள்ளுக்காய்வேளை - kollukkáyvélai, Tam.). San. from (shara, san. arrow + punkha, san. pinion); from pinnate leaf. Mahr. from (unhála, mahr. hot season). Hind. from sanscrit. Dec. from (janglí, hind. wild + kulthí, hind. gram, dolichos biflorus, linn.). Mal. from (kozhi, mal. to wither). Tam. from (kollu, tam. gram, dolichos biflorus, linn. + káy, tam. pod + vélai, tam. gynandropsis pentaphylla, dec.). San. also (punkhá), meaning pinion. Hind. also (hunnálí). Can. also (empaligida). Tel. also (bontavempali), meaning large + the plant; (tellavempali), meaning white + the plant. Title otherwise Fish poison, Galega, Goat's rue, Jungle gram, Purple galega, Purple tephrosia, Vempully, Wild indigo. Botanically Tephrosia purpurea, pers., leguminosæ [vricsham, 48]. Generic from persian. Alias Galega cœrulea, clonila, lanceæfolia, purpurea, sericea, tinctoria; Tephrosia galegioides, lanceæfolia, lanceolata, lobata, stricta, taylorii, tinctoria. A somewhat erect, much-branched shrub; branches glabrous, pubescent or villous; leaflets cuneate-oblong or lanceolate, under side more or less pubescent; racemes leaf-opposed, often longer than the leaves; flowers on pedicels longer than the bracts, two to three together; calyx pubescent; corolla three times as long as the calyx-tube; vexillum silky, bent back from near its base; legumes spreading, linear, slightly falcate, obtuse with a short point, pubescent or glabrous; flowers small, purple; flowering in the rainy season. A small wild shrub with a leaf resembling that of the tamarind [q.v.]; flowers disposed in a loose spike. Roots bitter; a decoction [kwautam] considered good in dyspepsia. There are varieties maxima and pumila. Other species of tephrosia are:—Fusca, whole plant of a dark or dirty grey color; Hookeriana, diffuse shrub; Senticosa, flowers dull-reddish; Spinosa; root, in succulent state, has pleasant taste and somewhat fragrant smell; used in rheumatism; and with ginger [q.v.] in dyspepsia; Tenuis, flowers bluish, in rocky places; Tinctoria, shrub; flowers small dull red; dindigul hills, neilgherries, mysore; flowering in the cold season; gives a dye [shauyam]; there is a variety of this, incana. Compare in other genera where transl. is of first term:—Indigofera hirsuta (penuvempali), large; Mundulea suberosa (kondavempali), hill. See gloss. paragraphs.

INDOO (इन्दु - indu, *San.*). From (und, san. to wet). A name of the moon [chundran], corresponding with Arcan for sun [arcaindoo sangamam, sooryan].

INDRAN (इन्द्र - indra, *San.*). From (íd, san. to possess supreme wealth). Otherwise Devendran [q.v.]. The highest of the Vedic gods, the god of the firmament and the regent of the east [ashtadic]. He presides over Swargam [q.v.], or the hindoo paradise. He is the king of the gods, in many respects corresponding with the grecian Zeus, or the Jupiter fulminator of the romans. The Supreme being, according to the Vedauntam [q.v.]. He possesses the Vajram [q.v.] or thunder-bolt as the god of battle. His wife is Indrauny [q.v.]. He rides on the white elephant Eirauvatam [q.v.]. He is depicted like Argus covered with eyes, the consequence of the curse of the Rishy gowtaman [q.v.], whose wife Ahalyay he seduced [matam]. As lord of clouds, rain, seasons and crops he is still worshipped at the time of sowing and reaping. Compare Pongal. For regent star of the eighteenth lunar mansion see Nacshatram. In composition the title signifies supreme or excellent. Suffix in Canarese and Teloogoo proper names as Raghavendra row. Plant first term; ex., where transl. is of second term:—Holarrhena antidysenterica (indravrikshamu), tree, (indrayava), barley; Terminalia arjuna (indradru), tree; Thunbergia fragrans (indratíga), creeper; Vitex negundo (indrasurasa), basil; see gloss. paragraphs. See vol. I (73), (78), (86).——*Inderjow* (اندر جو - indarjau, Hind.). Means indra's barley. Bitter inderjow is same as Tellicherry bark. Sweet inderjow is same as Paula indigo.——*Indra jaulam* (इन्द्रजाल - indrajála, San.). From (above + jála, san. net). Deception. A stratagem in war. Also a short trance in which a long train of circumstances is supposed to pass.——*Indra locam* (इन्द्रलोक - indralóka, San.). From (above + lóka, san. world). Swargam.——*Indra's creeper* (ఇంద్రతీగ - indratíga, Tel.). Title from showy flowers. Tel. from (indra, san. the god + tíga, tel. creeper). Tel. also (jímandáratíga). Botanically Thunbergia fragrans, r., acantbaceæ [vricsham, 101]. Alias Thunbergia roxburghia. Climbing; leaves oblong, acute, cordate, angular and somewhat hastate at the base, slightly scabrous; calyx twelve-cleft; peduncles axillary, solitary, one-flowered, round downy; capsule flat and beaked; flowers large, pure white, or white with sulphur-colored bottom. Herbaceous plant, with slender stems, and rough, small, heart-shaped leaves; bears nearly always snow-white flowers, size of rupee [q.v.]; very ornamental; there is a variety lævis. Other common species of thunbergia are:—Alata, climbing annual; round, flat flowers of moderate size, and of a great variety of shades of color, white, yellow, buff, and orange, with and without a dark purple eye. Coccinea, climbing shrub; flowers largish, deep red, with a yellow throat; flowering in cold season. Grandiflora, flowers very large, light blue, with a white tube. Hawtayneana, flowers deep purplish blue, with a yellow throat. Mysorensis, flowers large, showy, either of a golden-yellow throughout, or with the limb of an orange or blood-red color. Tomentosa. Wightiana.——*Indrauny* (इन्द्राणी - indrání, San.). The wife of Devendran; represented as an ever blooming virgin, and whilst the dignity of the king of the gods passes from one to another, she remains the wife of every succeeding Devendran. Indrauny is not worshipped, but paintings of her are met with.——*Indravally* (इन्द्रवल्ली - indravallí, San.). See sep. title.——*Indriyam* (इन्द्रिय - indriya, San.). Belonging to indran; what belongs specially to indran as god of all enjoyment. Power of the senses. Faculty of sense.—"*a*" An organ of sense, divided into three classes, Nyaunendriyam, Carmendriyam, and Antarendriyam. The Nyaunendriyam or Punchendriyam are the eye, ear, nose, tongue, and skin. The Carmendriyam are the organs of speech or larynx, hand, foot, anus, and parts of generation. The Antarendriyam are Manas, the mind or organ of thought; Booddhy, the organ of intellect; Ahancauram, the organ of selfishness or emotion; and Chittam, the organ of volition. By mystical interpretation the seven rishies [q.v.] are said to be the seven senses, making Manas or inner sense the sixth, and Vidyay, knowledge or wisdom, the seventh.—"*b*" The organic world of plants and animals. For category, see Padaurtam; for elementary substance, see Dravyam; for matter, see Bhootam; for organic and inorganic, see present head and Anindriyam; for organic kingdom, see Ganam [jantoo, vricsham]; for organic class, see Vargam; for organic order, see Santaunam; for organic family, see Coolam; for organic genus, see Jauty; for organic species, see Bhaidam. Oopa prefixed to either of the above means a sub-head. For inorganic minerals, see Dhautoo.

INDRA VALLY (इन्द्रवल्ली - indravallí, *San.*). From (indra, san. the god + vallí, san. creeper). Water melon. Botanically the Citrullus genus, cucurbitaceæ [vricsham, 62]. Climbing herbs, hispid or scabrous; leaves stalked, palmately lobed, usually deep; flowers tolerably large, solitary; fruit globose or ellipsoid, smooth, fleshy; seeds many, oblong, compressed, smooth. The species best known to the natives are shown below.——*Bitter water melon* (इन्द्रवारुणी - indraváruní, San.; इद्रावण - indrávana, Mahr.; कावंडलि - kávandali, Conc.; حنظل - hanzal, Ar.; هندوانهٔ تلخ - hindavánahitalkh, Pers.; اندراین - indráyan, Hind.; اندراون - indrávan, Dec.; ಹಾವುಮೆಕ್ಕೆ - hávumekke, Can.; ಕಕ್ಕೆಂಡೆಲ್ - kakkendel, Too.; వెఱ్ఱిపుచ్చ - verriputtsa, Tel.; പേക്കുമ്മട്ടി - pékkummatti, Mal.; යක්කොමඩු - yakkomadu, Singh.; பேய்க்கொம்மட்டி - péykkommatti, Tam.). San. from (indra, san. the god + vri, san. to cover); covered with flowers as indran [q.v.] is with eyes, applies to a large variety. Mahr. from sanscrit. Ar. means bitter. Pers. from (hindavánah, pers. water melon, citrullus vulgaris, schrad. + talkh, pers. bitter). Hind. and dec. from sanscrit. Can. from (hávu, can. snake + mekku, can. to eat). Tel. from (verri, tel. mad + puttsa, tel. cucumis trigonus, roxb.). Mal. from tamul. Singh. from (yak, singh. devil + komadu, singh. citrullus vulgaris, schrad.). Tam. from (péy, tam. devil + kommatti, tam. citrullus vulgaris, schrad.). San. also (indráhvá), meaning called indran; (chitrá), meaning variegated, from color of fruit [chitramoolam]; (góvandaní), meaning cow + adorer; (gavákshí), meaning bull's eye, from the flowers; (vishálá), meaning broad is a large variety. Ar. also (alkam). Pers. also (kharbúzahitalkh), meaning bitter water melon; (kabísitalkh), meaning bitter cucumber; (kharbúzahirúbáh), meaning fox's melon; (kharbúzahibújahl), meaning stupid + water melon, meaning the fruit preferred by a stupid person. Hind. also (mákal). Tel. also (chittipápara), meaning small + colocynth; (kárkárukamu); (puttsa); (páparabudama), meaning colocynth + cucumis trigonus, roxb.; (étiputtsa), meaning river + cucumis trigonus, roxb. Mal. also (káttuvellari), meaning forest + cucumis sativus, linn. Singh. also (tiktiká), meaning bitter; (tittakomadu), bitter + citrullus vulgaris, schrad. Tam. also (varikkommatti), meaning stripe + citrullus vulgaris, schrad.; (péthingári), meaning purgative; (áttuttummatti), meaning river + the plant; (péyttummatti), meaning devil + the plant; (tummatti); (varittummatti), meaning stripe + the plant. Greek κολοκυνθὶς ἀγρία. Title otherwise Bitter apple, Bitter cucumber, Bitter gourd, Bull's-eye melon, Colocynth, Colocynth gourd, Coloquintida, Devil water melon, Fox melon, Pakkoth of the bible, River cucumber, River gourd, Striped gourd, Vine of Sodom, Wild gourd. Botanically Citrullus [indravally] colocynthis, schrad., cucurbitaceæ [vricsham, 62]. Alias Cucumis colocynthis. Annual; stems scabrous; leaves smooth above, muricate beneath, with small white tubercles, many-cleft, obtuse-lobed; tendrils short; female flowers solitary; calyx tube globose and hispid; fruits globose, glabrous, streaked; flowers yellow; flowering in the rainy season; common on coromandel in sandy situations in neighbourhood of sea. The fruit is nearly globular, of the size of an orange [q.v.], smooth, marbled with green and yellow when fresh, yellowish brown when dry, and contains a scanty greyish-white pulp in which a number of brown seeds are embedded; this pulp in the fresh fruit is spongy and juicy, and occupies the whole of the interior of the fruit; the seeds are disposed in vertical rows on three thick parietal placentæ, which project to the centre of the fruit, then divide and turn back, forming two branches directed towards one another; the seeds are of flattened ovoid form, 3-10ths of an inch long by 2-10ths broad, not bordered; the testa is hard and thick, with a finely-granulated surface, and is marked on each side of its smaller end by two furrows directed towards the hilum; the leaves are glabrous and nearly smooth above, muricated beneath, with small, white, hair-bearing tubercles, many cleft and lobed, the lobes obtuse; the root is fibrous, tough and stringy, of a yellowish-white color; all parts of the plant are very bitter, and the dust when dry very irritating to the eyes and nostrils. The fruit was familiar to the greeks and romans. Gives to pharm. colocynth pulp, the dried decorticated fruit freed from seeds, colocynthidis pulpa, active principle, a bitter resinoid substance, colocynthin; hydragogue cathartic; officinal; very useful, particularly in combination with other drugs of similar nature, in constipation, hepatic and visceral congestions, dropsical affections and other diseases requiring purgatives; substituted for british jalap [q.v.] and scammony [q.v.]. Sheep [aud], goats [vellaud], jackals [q.v.], and rats [ely] eat colocynth apples readily; they are made into preserves with sugar [q.v.]; the gypsy tribes eat the kernel of the seed, freed from the seed skin by a slight roasting. Oil [yennay] from seeds used in lamps. Cucumis trigonus, roxb. [country cucumber] resembles the colocynth gourd and has been mistaken for it. Cucumis sativus, linn. [common cucumber], hill colocynth, has oval oblong bitter fruits. There is a Hindostany proverb:—اندراین کا پھل دیکھنے ہی کا ھے چکھنے کا نہین— "The fruit of the colocynth is only to look at, not to taste;" said of a person of good appearance, but bad disposition.——*Sweet water melon* (तरम्बुज - tarambuja, San.; तरबूज - tarabúja, Mahr.; बच्चंग - baççanga, Conc.; هندوانه - hindvánah, تربز - tarbuz, Pers., Hind. and Dec.; سامنکا - sámangka, Malay; ಬಚ್ಚಂಗಾಯಿಗಿಡ - baççangáyigida, Can.; ಬಚ್ಚಂಗಾಯಿ - baççangáyi, Too.; దర్బూజ - darbúji, Tel.; വത്തക്ക - vattakka, Mal.; කොමඩු - komadu, Singh.; சர்க்கரைக்கொம்மட்டி - sharkkaraikkommatti, Tam.). San. from persian. Mahr. from hindostany. Pers. from (tar, pers. wet + buz, pers. goat). Tel. from hindostany. Mal. from (pateca, port. water melon). Tam. from (sharkará, san. sugar + kommatti, tam. the plant). Hind. also (samáka); (halinda); (kharbúz), meaning melon. Malay also (mándiki); (pátaka); (támiki). Can. also (karabúju); (kollangadi); (kálenga). Tam. also (piççi); (kommatti); (vattákku), from the portuguese pateca, water melon. Greek πέπων. Title otherwise Goat melon. Botanically Citrullus [indravally] vulgaris, schrad., cucurbitaceæ [vricsham, 62]. Alias Citrullus edulis, pinnatifida; Cucumis citrullus; Cucurbita anguria, citrullus. Flower large yellow; cultivated in river beds and in alluvial deposits of tanks, &c., where abundance of water can be had for; fruit large, ovoid, green, and smooth; flesh whitish yellow or red; seeds compressed and variable in shape and color. The distinction between this and the cultivated form of citrullus colocynthis [bitter water melon] is very small. The four so called cold cucurbitaceous seeds sold in the bazaars are those of cucumis melo, var. utillissimus [country melon], benincasa cerifera [wax gourd], cucumis melo [common melon], and present article; these seeds are in constant demand, and are kept decorticated and ready for use; the natives always use them together, and consider them to be cooling, diuretic, and strengthening. Fruit used as a dessert; though not much flavor, refreshing, and in request amongst natives during hot season; seeds are sometimes dried and the kernels eaten. Oil from seeds.

INDUM PODY (ഇന്തിപ്പൊടി - íntinpoti, *Mal.*; இண்டம்பொடி - indambodi, *Tam.*). From (íntu, mal, cycas + poti, mal. flour). Flour from kernel of Cycas circinalis, linn., cycadaceæ [indian sago palm].

INGRES (انگریز - angrez, *Hind.*). An Englishman.

INK NUT (కరక - karaka, *Tel.*). Title from use. Tel. means black color. Same as Chebulic myrobalan.

INNESPETT (ఇన్నిస్ పేట - innispéta, *Tel.*). Named after Mr. Innes, a former judge. Suburb of Rajahmundry.

INSAUF (انصاف - insáf, *Hind.*). From (nisf, ar. half). Decision of a cause [feisal, teerp].

INTIZAUM (انتظام - intizám, *Ar.*). From (nazama, ar. to arrange) [nizam]. Regulation. Part of lacab; as Intizaum ool moolk, the regulator of the state [ism]. This was title of the third Prince of Arcot from 1879 to 1881.

INZARAM (ఇంజరము - indzaramu, *Tel.*). From (intsu, tel. pleasant + pura, san. town). Zemindarry, Village, Port; Godavery dist., Cocanada division; lat. of village 16° 44′; long. 82° 13′; from Cocanada S.S.W. 15 miles; from Coringa S.S.W. 7 miles; from Madras N.N.E. 278 miles; from Neelapully W. 4 miles. Peshcush Rs. 2,957. Near the mouth of Godavery, on Golcondah coast [q.v.]. Factory founded 1708, established 1722, captured by French under Bussy 1757, part of territory ceded by Nizam's treaty with Colonel Forde 1759, grant confirmed by the Moghul's firmaun [q.v.] 1765. Continued as a mercantile station till 1829. Formerly celebrated for manufacture of long cloth [q.v.] and for its trade in general. An irrigation canal takes its name from town. The place and neighbourhood suffered greatly from a cyclone in 1839.

IPAR (نمام - nammám, *Ar.*; اپار - ípár, *Pers.* and *Hind.*). Title from hindostany. Ar. also (hasha), meaning a garden of palm trees. Greek θύμος. Title otherwise Garden thyme, Thyme. Botanically Thymus vulgaris, linn., labiatæ [vricsham, 103]. Erect plant, sometimes procumbent at the base, or clothed with a hairy pubescence; has a pungent aromatic odour and taste; imported from persia. Oil of thyme stimulant, applied to relieve tooth ache; mixed with olive [zeitoon] oil or spirit, stimulating liniment in chronic rheumatism, sprains, bruises, &c.; chief consumption is however in veterinary practice; the odour and taste of the drug is pleasant, like peppermint [poodeenah], but sweeter. Leaves used for culinary purposes. Thymus serpyllum, linn., is wild thyme.

IR (ಇರು - iru, *Can.*; ఇరు - iru, *Tel.*; இரு - iru, *Tam.*). Two. ——*Ibbady* (ఇబ్బడి - ibbadi, Tel.). From (inu, tel. two + madugu, tel. measure). Double. Prohibitory assessment [teervay].——*Ikkairy* (ಇಕ್ಕೇರಿ - ikkéri, Can.). From (eradu, can. two + kéri, can. street). Village in 14° 07′ N. lat., 75° 04′ E. long., in Saugor talook, Shimoga district, 3 miles south of the cusbah [q.v.]. Formerly a local dynasty [raj], otherwise Bednore rajahs, 1560—1763. Declared themselves independent of Vijianugger sovereigns on the breaking up of that empire. Minted money. The sixteenth and the last died without issue in 1763 when Hyder seized the territories [charitram]. See vol. II, 63.——*Immady* (ಇಮ್ಮಡಿ - immadi, Can.). From (eradu, can. two + madi, can. fold). The second. Specially used with rulers, names as Immady krishna rajah.——*Irasa* (ఇరస - irasa, Tel.). From (iru, tel. two + kuntsamu, tel. the measure). Measure of capacity. 2 coonchams = 1 irasa; 2 irasas = 1 toom [alavay, 3b]. About 1,680 cubic inches. Varies with the cooncham and the toom. ——*Irattaiyar* (இரட்டையர் - irattaiyar, Tam.). Means twins. Two Tamul twin poets, excelled in extempore versification, fourteenth century. The elder was a cripple, younger blind. Younger gave out first two lines of a stanza, the elder last two. Example in praise of Paraucrama paundyan [paraucrama tevan] at the expense of Cholans [q.v.]. The answers to the questions are inserted to make the stanza intelligible:—

குறுமுனிவன் கொல்லியிலோ தமிழ்ப்பிறந்ததம்மானே ஒப்பரிய திருவிளையாட்டுறையூரோவம்மானே திருநெடுமாலவதாரஞ் சிறுபுலியோவம்மானே சிவன்முடிமேலணிவதுவஞ் செங்கதிரோவம்மானே கரையழிந்த காவிரியோ வுரைதெரிந்தவம்மானே கடிப்பகைக்கு வேம்போ கடுக்கையோவம்மானே பரவைபடிந்ததுஞ் சோழன் பதந்தனிலோவம்மானே பராக்கிரமபாண்டியன்புகழைப்பகரொளிதோவம்மானே—"O father! Was "it from the mount Colly [collimullay] the dwarfish sage "Agastyan [q.v.] produced the Tamul [q.v.] language? No, from "the Pothigay [q.v.] in the Paundyam [q.v.] country. O father! "Did the incomparable sports [tirvilaiyaudal] of Shiva [q.v.] "take place at Warriore? No, at Madura, the metropolis of the "Paundyam country. O father! Was Vishnoo [q.v.] ever "metamorphosed into a tiger? No, into a fish, the device on "the banner of the Paundyam kings. O father! Is it the sun "which Shiva wears over the tuft of hair upon the crown of his "head? No, it is the moon [chundrashekharan] the progenitor "of the Paundyam race. O father! Was it the bank destroying "Cauvery which saw the writing of Sambandhan [q.v.] ascend "up against its stream? No, it was Veigay, the river of Madura. "O father! Which is more heroic, the condray [q.v.] or vemboo "garland? The vemboo [neem], worn by the Paundyam kings, "vowing thereby to conquer or die. O father! Was it at the "feet of the Cholan the sea submitted? No, it was at the feet "of Oogra paundyan. O father! Is it then a light thing "to declare the praise of Paraucrama paundyan?"——*Iricore* (ഇരുക്കൂർ - irukkúr, Mal. irikúr*). From (above + kúr, mal. portion). Town; Malabar dist., Chiracal tal.; lat. 11° 59′; long. 75° 36′; from Calicut N.N.W. 52 miles; from Cannanore N.E. 15 miles; from the sea E. 19 miles. Large Moplah town with mosques [q.v.] on high road from coast leading through Poodiyachooram or Heggal pass [ghaut] towards Coorg and Mysore, on right bank of Belliapatam river. During rains timber and bamboos [q.v.] in rafts are floated down to Belliapatam, &c.,

for sale and for construction of small crafts. Scene of Moplah [q.v.] outrages in 1852. Belliapatam river is navigable for boats throughout year up to this place. Considerable entrepôt of trade. ——*Iroobhogam* (இருபோகம் - irubógam, Tam.). Two crops [dofusl].——*Irtalay maniyan* (بالو کا سانپ - bálúkásámp, Dec.; ಹಪ್ಪಟೆಹಾವು - happatehávu, Can.; మొండిపొడ - mondipoda, Tel.; இருதலைமணியன் - iruthalaimaniyan, Tam.). Title from tamul. Dec. from (bálú, hind. sand + sámp, hind. snake). Tel. from (mondi, tel. maimed + poda, tel. spot); stout with blotches. Tam. from (irandu, tam. two + talai, tam. head + maniyan, tam. small black serpent). Dec. also (mattíkásámp), meaning earth snake. Terms co-extensive with the family Erycidæ ophidii colubriformes, ophidia [sarpam], reptilia [sarpy, 25], of naturalists [jantoo]. Sand-snakes. The sand-snakes have the body of moderate length, cylindrical, covered with small, short scales; tail very short, with a single series of subcaudals; head with a broad snout of moderate length, or somewhat elongate; eye rather small, with vertical pupil. Adult individuals with a short conical prominence in a groove on each side of the vent; it is the extremity of a rudimentary hind limb. Show similarity to the Pythons and Boas [rock snake]. More or less arboreal, frequenting marshy places with luxuriant vegetation, burrowing with the greatest facility; their prey consists of mice [shoondely], lizards [chipkalee], and other burrowing snakes. Probably semi-nocturnal, able to see in dark places as well as in the night. The following species are found in Southern india:—"*a*" Eryx johnii. Alias Boa johnii; Clotbonia johnii; Eryx maculatus. Called by the natives Two-headed viper. Body surrounded by longitudinal series of scales; upper parts reddish olive, uniform or with irregular small black spots and dots; lower parts generally marbled with blackish. Young specimens with three or four broad brownish rings round the hinder part of the body. Common in the plains. Never bites. Frequently found in the possession of serpent-charmers, who mutilate the end of the short, thick tail in such a manner that the scarred extremity somewhat resembles the form of the head. Feeds on young mice. Length nearly 4 feet.—"*b*" Gongylophis conicus. Alias Boa conica; Eryx conicus. Called by the natives small Poodeiyan or Wart-snake. Middle of the body surrounded by short-keeled scales; brownish grey, dorsal series of large quadrangular brown blotches edged with dark brown and whitish; spots frequently confluent form a broad zigzag band; irregular smaller brown spots along the side; lower parts white; oblique brown streak on temple proceeding from behind the eye. Attains a length of more than two feet.

IRAUL (अग्निमत्स्य - agnimatsya, *San.*; झिंगा - jhingá, *Mahr.*; جرادالبحر - jarádulbahr, *Ar.*; ملخ دریائی - malakhidaryáí, *Pers.*; جهنگا - jhingá, *Hind.* and *Dec.*; ಬೆಂಕಿಮೀನು - benkimínu, *Can.*; రొయ్య - royya, *Tel.*; ചെമ്മീൻ - chemmín, *Mal.*; இறால் - irál, *Tam.*). Title from tamul. San. from (agni, san. fire + matsya, san. fish). Ar. from (jarád, ar. locust + bahr, ar. sea). Pers. from (malakh, pers. locust + daryá, pers. sea). Can. from (benki, can. fire + mínu, can. fish). Tel. from (royyi, tel. burning ashes). Mal. from (chem, mal. red + mín, mal. fish). Tam. from (iru, tam. to crumble); from the wrinkled appearance. Prawn. The sub-order Macroura of the order Decapoda of crustaceans [kavachiny], of naturalists [jantoo]. Good on Coromandel coast [q.v.]. Considered by veidyans [q.v.] to be stimulating and aphrodisiac, and to possess virtues in diabetes. Makes good curry [q.v.]. A composition of dried prawns pounded up with salt [ooppoo], spices, &c., is much used. The following are the chief kinds.——*Autt iraul* (ஆற்றிறால் - áttirál, Tam.). From (áru, tam. river). Astacus fluviatilis. The craw fish.——*Caul iraul* (காலிறால் - kálirál, Tam.). From (kál, tam. leg). Astacus jamaicensis. Prawn with long legs.——*Coony iraul* (கூனியிறால் - kúniyirál, Tam.). From (kúni, tam. hump-backed). Crangon vulgaris. Shrimp.——*Karvund iraul* (கருவண்டிறால் - karuvandirál, Tam.). From (karu, tam. black + vandu, tam. beetle). Astacus nigricans. Black prawn.——*Shing iraul* (சிங்கிறால் - shingirál, Tam.). From (shringa, san. horn). Astacus marinus. Lobster.——*Vel iraul* (வெள்ளிறால் - vellirál, Tam.). From (vel, tam. white). Cancer setiferus. White prawn.

IRAVA (ഇരവ - irava, obl., *Mal.*). From (irayuka, mal. to scatter); from dispersed numbers. Basket-makers in Malabar [jauty].

IRON (இரும்பு - irumbu, *Tam.*). Prefix.——*Iron-wood* (இருள்மரம் - irulmaram, Tam.). Title from hard dark red wood. Product of nauga champak [q.v.] and yellow condray [q.v.]. Compare also:—Cassa [q.v.], chowkmaram [q.v.], dark vail [q.v.], deccany deodar [q.v.].——*Iron grass* (هنراج - hunráj, Hind.). Same as Hoonrauj.

IROOL (இருள் - irul, *Tam.*). Darkness.——*Iripa* (मधूक - madhúka, San.; نیمنیم - niamniam, Malay; ಕನಕಮರ - kanakamara, Can.; ഇരിപ്പ - irippa, Mal.; ගල්මැන්දෝර - galmandóra, Singh.; நாய்ப்புடுக்கன் - náyppudukkan, Tam.). Title from malayalam. San. from (madhu, san. honey). Can. from (kanaka, san. gold + mara, can. tree). Mal. from (irul, mal. darkness). Singh. from (gab, singh. stone + mandóra, singh. vatica roxburghiana, blume). Tam. from (náy, tam. dog + pidukku, tam. testicle.) Tam. also (irapú). Botanically Cynometra ramiflora, linn., leguminosæ [vricsham, 48]. Tree, 60 feet; leaves composed of two to six opposite leaflets; calyx tube very short, four-partite, segment reflexed; petals five, oblong-lanceolate; stamens distinct, inserted with the petals into a ring lining the calyx tube; peduncle solitary, few-flowered, springing from the branches among the leaves; flowers white; flowering in cold season; malabar and south canara. Root purgative; a lotion is made from the leaves boiled in cow's milk [paul], which, mixed with honey [shahad], is applied externally in scabies, leprosy [cooshtam] and other cutaneous diseases; oil seeds used for same purposes. Chips of wood infused in water give a dark purple dye [shauyam]. Wood red, hard, close-grained. Another species is cauliflora.——*Iroola* (இருளன் - irulan, Tam.). Tribe, mostly on hills. More primitive than Coorumbar [q.v.], akin to the Beydar or hunters of the peninsula. Speak a rude Tamul. The best known are those living at foot of Neilgherry mountains. These are, like the Mysore beydar, worshippers of Vishnoo [q.v.], a remarkable circumstance considering the almost universal Sheivism of the aboriginal tribes of S. india. Near Rungasawmy's peak, and scattered about the slopes and base of the hills to the south and south-east, there are several Iroola mottas. These villages consist of seven or eight split bamboo [q.v.] huts plastered with mud, and generally built round a square. Patches of raggy [q.v.] and tinay [q.v.] surround them. Near their villages they have large gardens of plantain [q.v.] and lime [q.v.] trees, and cultivate the neighbouring ground in the Cautcaud [q.v.] fashion, changing the field every year. They attend the shandy [q.v.] held at Mettapolliem every week, carrying down jungle produce, such as timber, bamboos and game, &c., to exchange for tobacco [pogauk], salt [ooppoo], and cloths. A few mottas are scattered on the northern and western slopes of the hills, but their inhabitants lead a harder life from the severity of the monsoon [q.v.], and their isolated position. They seldom make any provision for the winter, but subsist on a crop of grain as long as it lasts, and trust for seed and what more they may require to the Badagas, with whom they barter wood, honey [shahad], bees' wax [mom], and other forest produce. They will only eat with Badagas [q.v.]. The Iroola temples of the Neilgherries are only circles of rough stones each enclosing an upright one, with iron tridents fixed in the ground. The poojarry [q.v.] or priest is an Iroolan, and he wears the Vishnoo mark on his forehead. Although the Badagas are for the most part Sheivite, they come in large numbers to these temples once a year about sowing time and make offerings of plantains, milk, &c., to the god. No animals are sacrificed. In a cave at Rungasawmy's peak there is earth regarded as holy, which is much valued by worshippers. The neighbours below the ghauts [q.v.] declare that they possess the power of taming tigers, and that Iroola women, when they go into the woods, leave their children to the care of a tiger [pooly]. Apart from the Neilgherries they are most numerous in North arcot, Chingleput, Salem and Coimbatore. They arrange themselves into two clans, the Oorauly and the Cooroo-tauly, meaning rulers and serfs. See vol. I (35); vol. II, 109. Numbers about 36,000 [jauty].——*Iroolan* (இருளன் - irulan, Tam.). A minor deity in Ancaulamman's pagoda [q.v.].——*Iroombily* (இரும்பிலி - irumbili, *Tam.*). From (irumbu, tam. iron); from dark wood. Same as Neilgherry satinwood.

IRSAUL (ارسال - irsál, *Hind.*). From (rasala, ar. to send message). A remittance of anything, especially money. Irsaulnauma is a statement of money or goods remitted.

ISAY (இசை - isai, *Tam.*). Speech.——*Isaimadanday* (இசைமடந்தை - isaimadandai, Tam.). From (above + madandai, tam. woman.). Saraswaty [q.v.].

ISH (इष - ish, *San.*). To desire.——*Ichapore* (ఇచ్ఛాపురము - içchápuramu, Tel. ichápur *). From (içchá, san. desire + pura, san. town).—"*a*" Deputy tahsildarry; Ganjam district. Pay Rs. 100.—"*b*" Town, Head-quarters of Deputy tahsildar and Sub-registrar, Ganjam dist., Berhampore tal.; pop. 5,528; acres 3,716; lat. 19° 07′; long. 84° 44′; from Balligooda S.S.E. 88 miles; from Berhampore S.S.W. 16 miles; from Chetterpore S.W. 26 miles; from Chicacole N.E. 75 miles; from Madras N.N.E. 500 miles; from Russellcondah S.S.E. 56 miles; from the sea W. 6 miles by short cut. On high road between Berhampore and Chicacole, 6 miles N.E. of Bodagherry hills. The Bauhoodah passes near the town and is spanned by a bridge. During Mussalman occupation of Northern circars [q.v.] from 1560 to 1753, Ichapore was head-quarters of a naib [q.v.], In 1768 attached to Ganjam. Mosque [musjid] with Persian inscription [shausanam], built by Nawaub mowlvy moostafah about 200 years ago in the suburb of Laulapett. Betel [q.v.] gardens in the neighbourhood. Trig. station in lat. 19° 06′ 15·40″; long. 84° 43′ 04·50″; from Ichapore W. $1\frac{3}{4}$ miles; from Berhampore S.S.W. 15 miles; from the sea W. 7 miles.——*Ishta devatay* (इष्टदेवता - ishtadévatá, San.). From (ishta, san. favorite + dévatá, san. deity). The patron god selected by any individual.——*Ishtam* (इष्ट - ishta, San.). Desire.

ISHAH (عشا - ishá, *Hind.*). From (ashi, ar. the time of nightfall). Twilight; so prayers [namauz] said at that time.

ISHARMOOL (अर्कमूल - arkamúla, *San.*; सापसंद - sápasanda, *Mahr.*; सांप्सिकडूल - sápsikaddúla, *Conc.*; زراوند - zaráwand, *Ar.* and *Pers.*; اشرمول - isharmúl, *Hind.* and *Dec.*; ಈಶ್ವರೀಬೇರು - íshvaríbéru, *Can.*; ಇಸರಬೇರ್ - isarabér, *Too.*; గోవెల - góvela, *Tel.*; കരൾവേകം - karalvékam, *Mal.*; සක්සඳ - saksanda, *Singh.*; பெருமருந்து - perumarundu, *Tam.*). Title from hindostany. San. from (arka, san. calotropis gigantea, r. br. + múla, san. root). Hind. from (íshvara, san. shiva, the lord + múla, san. root); as an antidote to snake poison. Can. from (íshvarí, san. goddess + béru, can. root). Mal. from (garala, san. poison + véka, mal. to burn); antidote to snake poison. Tam. from (perumai, tam. greatness + marundu, tam. medicine). San. also (sunandá), meaning very + happy plant; (ahigandhá), meaning serpent + smell; (íshvara), meaning protector; (íshvarí); (hari), meaning destroyer. Hind. also (isarbel), meaning lord's creeper; (isharvayal). Can. also (íshvarabéru), meaning god + root. Tel. also (errakalabanda), meaning red + aloe, aloe vulgaris, lam.; (dúlagóvela), meaning itching + the plant. Mal. also (perumarunnu), meaning great medicine; (íshvaramulla), by corr.; (perumkizhannu), meaning big root; (karalékam); (karukappullu), meaning rough grass; (íshvaramúli), meaning divine root. Singh. also (sapsanda). Tam. also (talaiççuruli), meaning head + to curl; (ísuravér), meaning lord + root; (garudakkodi), meaning braminy kite + creeper; (perungizhangu), meaning great + esculent root; (ísura), meaning lord; (íççuramúli), meaning lord root. Title otherwise Braminy kite creeper, Eeshwaran's root, Great medicine, Indian birth wort, Mudar root plant, Raiz de Cobra, Serpent root plant. Botanically Aristolochia [eeshwaram] indica, linn., aristolochiaceæ [vricsham, 117]. Small, shrubby, perennial, twining; leaves stalked, wedge-shaped or obovate three-nerved, pointed, waved; calyx tubular, nearly globose at the base; racemes axillary, shorter than the leaves; flowers erect; corolla purplish; capsule roundish, hexagonal, six-celled, pendulous; seeds numerous; grows in hedges; flowers in rainy season. The drug as sold in the shops consists of the root and stem, the latter in by far the larger proportion; in many parcels the stem only is to be found; it is either in short pieces, or the whole stem may be twisted into a kind of circular bundle; the thickest portion of the stem is $\frac{1}{4}$-$\frac{1}{2}$ an inch or more in diameter, and has a central woody column made up of about ten wedge shaped portions; the bark is thick and corky, marked with longitudinal ridges and numerous small warty projections, it is of a yellowish-brown color, the taste is bitter and camphoraceous, and the odour aromatic and agreeable. Root, leaves, stalks and bark are bitter. Root medicinally stimulant, tonic, emmenagogue, antiperiodic, and antidote to the bites of snakes, &c., internally and externally; expressed juice of leaves the same.

ISHAUK (اسحاق - isḥák, *Hind.*). From hebrew meaning laughter. Isaac. Common Mahomedan alam; as Mahomed ishauk, double alam [ism].

ISKAPULLY (ఇసుకపల్లె - iskapalle,* *Tel.*). From (isaka, tel. sand + palle, tel. village). On Buckingham canal [q.v.]. Village, Port, Salt factory, Head-quarters of Salt and Abkarry inspector and Sea custom assistant superintendent; Nellore dist., Nellore tal.; pop. 3,127; acres 6,259; lat. 14° 44′; long. 80° 09′; from Madras N. 112 miles; from Nellore N.N.E. 21 miles; from Ponnapoody N. 5 miles; from Zoovvaldinney S. 6 miles. Grain and other produce are largely exported. Frequented by large sailing vessels and occasionally by steamers. Anchorage good. The bar of the salt-water channel in the middle of the port has been closed since 1863. Formerly a very large trade in salt [ooppoo]. Granaries on the beach. Bungalow [q.v.] for captains of ships.

ISKH (عشق - iskh, *Hind.*). Love.——*Ishk allah* (عشق الله - ishkalláh, Hind.). From (above + alláh, ar. god). Form of salutation amongst fakeers [q.v.].

ISLAM (اسلام - islám, *Hind.*). From (salama, ar. submission) [salaam]. Submission to the will of God, the Mahomedan religion. Divided into imaun [q.v.] or faith, and deen [q.v.] or practice. The principal tenets of imaun are that there is only one God; that Mahomet is his last and greatest prophet; that there is a paradise [bheest] for the faithful and a hell [dozak] for the ungodly. Adam, Noah, Abraham, Moses, and Jesus are recognized as prophets who introduced in succession new laws and revelations, till all were finally superseded by those of Mahomet. The deen is of five kinds:—to learn the Kalima [q.v.] and repeat it; to pray [namauz] five times a day; to fast [roza] in the month of Ramzaun [maheena]; to give five per cent. of income to charity [zakaut] if wealthy; to go on a pilgrimage [haj] to Mecca, if wealthy.

ISM (اسم - ism, *Ar.*). The composition of Mahomedan proper names, of which the alam [q.v.] or name given at birth forms the basis, has been explained at vol. I (104), footnote. The names appear practically in one or other of the following different forms:—"*a*" A single and simple alam or personal name; as Ahmed.—"*b*" Two of these, or even three, strung together; as Ahmed ally, Ally moosey razah.—"*c*" Lacab or title name, the commonest kind of which are so familiar that they stand for alams, even at birth; as Abd oollah, Shums ood deen, Bahaudur.—"*d*" An alam + a lacab; as Ibrahim siddeeky.—"*e*" An alam + an alaumat or tribal title prefixed or suffixed; as Ally khan.—"*f*" An alam + a coonyat or genealogical surname; as Abool abbaus ahmed. This Arabic style of nomenclature is not in fashion here.—"*g*" An alam + an ism oon nisbat, or functional title; as Cauzy shahaub ood deen; Agha baukir sheerauzy.—"*h*" A takhalloos or name taken for insertion in poetry; as Haufiz, Saady. See all the above heads in this glossary; see also Khitaub and Oorf.——*Ismdar* (اسم دار - ismdár, Hind.). From (above + dár, hind. holder). Permanent office holder.——*Ism oon nisbat* (اسم النسبت - ismunnisbat, Hind.). From (above + nisbat, ar. relation). Names of relation showing origin, quality, functions, &c., not unlike the agnomen of the Latins.——*Ismwar* (اسمواری - ismwárí, Hind.). From (above + distributive suffix). According to the order of names.

ISMAIL (اسماعیل - ismáíl, *Hind.*). From hebrew meaning heard of god. Ismail who according to Mahomedans was the sacrifice to god and not Isaac as Christians believe. Mahomedan alam; as Syed ismail, alaumat + alam [ism].——*Ismailia* (اسماعیلیہ - ismáíliya, Hind.). From (ismáíl, ar. name of son of sixth imaum). A sub-sect of shiahs [q.v.] who acknowledge only seven imaums [q.v.] ending with ismail. Represented in southern india by Khojas [q.v.] and Bohrahs [q.v.]. All the secret societies of Europe, religious and secular, owe their origin to this sect from whom the crusaders borrowed. Hasan bin sabah otherwise Sheikh ool jabal or the Old man of the mountain was the Grand master of this sect, known in Europe as the Assassins.

ISMAUTHY (عصمتی - ismatí, *Hind.*). From (asima, ar. to guard from sin). Chaste. Ismauthy sanyausy was title of Beschi [veeramaumoony].

ISPAGHUL (اسبغول - isbaghol, *Pers.*). Same as Spogel.

ISRAFEEL (اسرافیل - isráfíl, *Hind.*). The angel [ferishtah] who, according to Mahomedan belief, presides over the wind and will sound the last trumpet at the day of resurrection [izraeel].

ISTIAR (اشتہار - ishtihár, *Hind.*). From (shabara, ar. to publish). Act of publication. Istiar nauma is a proclamation.

ISTIFAH (استعفا - istifá, *Hind.*). From (afu, ar. to be absolved). Relinquishing a charge or land, &c.

ISTIKRAUR (استقرار - istikrár, *Hind.*). From (karra, ar. to rest) [caraur, ikrar]. Confirmation.

ISTIMRAR (استمرار - ístimrár, *Hind.*). From (murur, ar. to continue). Permanent. Istimrar graumam is village permanently settled.

ISTREE (استری - istarí, *Hind.*). Smoothing iron. So plain longcloth. Istree wallah is a cloth-ironer associated with the Dhoby [q.v.].

ISVY (عیسوی - ísví, *Hind.*). From (ísá, ar. jesus christ). The Christian era.

ITCHY (இச்சி - iççí, *Tam.*). Same as Tsiela.

ITI (इति - iti, *San.*). Thus, so.——*Itihausam* (इतिहास - itihása, San.). From (above + há, san. indeed + ása, san. it was). Tradition or history [smrity]. The two great Itihausams are Ramayanam [q.v.] and Mahabhaurat [q.v.].——*Ityek* (इत्येक - ityéka, San.). From (above + éka, san. one). Two syllables added to the name of a lunar [chaundramaunam] month [mausam] when it is an intercalary one [adhicam].

ITIBAR (اعتبار - itibár, *Ar.*). From (ibr, ar. to regard) [ibrat]. Faithful. Part of lacab; as Itibar ood dowlah, faithful to the state [ism].

ITIKAUF (اعتکاف - itikáf, *Hind.*). From (akafa, ar. to restrain oneself). Restraining one's senses. Especially spending the month Ramzaun [maheena] in a mosque [musjid] engaged in prayer [namauz] and meditation.

ITISHAUM (احتشام - ihtishám, *Ar.*). From (hashama, ar. to feel ashamed). Glory. Part of lacab; as Itishaum ood dowla, glory of the empire [ism].

ITTY (ഇത്തി - itti, *Mal.*). From (iru, mal. to shed); from milk. The waved-leaved fig tree, ficus infectoria, willd. [stone banyan].——*Itticara* (ഇത്തിക്കര - ittikkara, Mal.). From (above + kara, mal. village).—"*a*" River; Travancore state, Quilon division, Cottaura cara and Quilon tals. Rises from the low hills above Maunore. Course is variable though generally a little to the south or west. Flows through the Paroor lake into the sea. Length 30 miles. Its banks rise boldly from the bed which is generally rocky. It is interrupted by a small cataract in its course. It is a shallow stream not navigable even for floats except in the rainy season. Also called Bhawaunipooram.—"*b*" Village; Travancore state, Quilon division, Quilon talook. Inhabited solely by Nayars of cowherd and shepherd castes. Large Mangalore tiles [wode] are manufactured here. Soil is clayey.

ITWAR (اتوار - itwár, *Hind.*). From (ádityavára, san. sunday). Sunday [shamba]. On this day the angels, especially those supporting the throne of God, were created.

IVICA (അഴിമുഖം - azhimukham, *Mal.*). From (azhi, mal. harbour + mukha, san. mouth) [aye]. Portuguese corruption.—"*a*" Village, Port; Travancore state, Quilon division, Quilon talook; lat. 8° 57′ N., long. 76° 37′ E.; from Bombay S.S.E. 725 miles; from Cauyancollam S. 16 miles; from Quilon N.N.W. 5 miles; from Trivandrum N.W. 41 miles; from Tungacherry N. 4 miles. On the sea-coast, at the mouth of the river of the same name. Large ships must anchor in the open sea, in six or seven fathoms of water, 3 miles off shore. Formerly with export trade in timber, pepper [q.v.], ginger [q.v.], cardamom [q.v.], lac [q.v.] and turmeric [country saffron]; but now superseded by Quilon.—"*b*" River; Travancore state, Quilon division, Quilon talook. Estuary by which the back-water communicates with the sea, but shallow, bar. The bar of the same name is the boundary between the Quilon and Caroonaugapully talooks.

IVORY SEED (दन्ति - danti, *San.*). Same as Jamalgota.

IXORA (बन्धूक - bandhúka, *San.*). Title from (íshvarí, san. párvatí, the deity); flower sacred to her. San. from (bandh, san. to bind); from compact corymbs. Jungle geranium. Wild jasmine of W. indies. Botanically the Ixora genus, rubiaceæ [vricsham, 71]. Shrubs or small trees; leaves opposite; flowers, handsome; scarlet, pink or white in colour; fruit succulent. The species best known to the natives are shown below. Other s. indian species indigenous or naturalized are:—acuminata, barbata, brachiata, lanceolaria, nigricans, notoniana, polyantha, wallichii.——*Jungle geranium* (बन्धूक - bandhúka, San.; पट्कली - patkalí, Conc.; ಕೇಪಲ - képala, Can.; ಕೇಪುಲಡೈ - képuladai, Too.; మన్మథబాణము - manmat'habánamu, Tel.; തെച്ചി - teççi, Mal.; රතඹල - ratambalá, Singh.; வெட்சி - vedchi, Tam.). San. from (bandh, san. to bind), from compact corymbs [mankena]. Tel. from (manmat'ha, san. cupid + bána, san. arrow [arabian jasmine]. Mal. means red, from bright red flowers. Tam. from (vel, tam. to conquer), flowers made conqueror's wreaths in old days. San. also (bhandhujívaka), meaning group + growing; (raktaka), meaning red [mankena]; (pátalí), meaning red one [common bendy, edible paulay, pauthiry, weaver's beam]. Can. also (kisgáragida), meaning red + plant. Tel. also (mankena) [q.v.]. Mal. also (chetti), meaning red; (chekki), meaning red. Singh. also (ratmal), meaning red + flower. Tam. also (shetti); (vetti), meaning victory; from flowers forming a chaplet of victory. Title otherwise Cupid's arrow, Flame of the woods, Scarlet ixora. Botanically Ixora [ixora] coccinea, linn., rubiaceæ [vricsham, 71]. Alias Ixora bhanduca, grandiflora, obovata, propinqua. Bhanduca from sanscrit. Glabrous shrub, 3-4 feet; leaves nearly sessile, oval or oblong or cuneate-obovate, acute or acuminated, mucronate; corymb nearly sessile, thin; calycine lobes acute, connivent in fruit; segments of the corolla ovate-lanceolate or elliptical, acute; style shortly exserted; berry size of a large pea [calauyam], purple when ripe; flowers bright scarlet, in large compact corymbs, nearly always in blossom, but in perfection during rains; without odour; abundant in jungles of western coast near sea. Flower offered to both shiva [q.v.] and vishnoo [q.v.]. Root branched, ½ inch or more in diameter; bark thick, smooth, brown, marked with small warty prominences, it exudes a yellow juice when cut; wood hard, yellowish, odour rancid and disagreeable, porous with strongly marked medullary rays.——*Large jungle geranium* (रायकुरा - ráyakurá, Mahr.; مشعل کا جهار - mashalkájhár, Hind.; ಗೊರವಿಮರ - goravimara, Can.; ಗೊರಿವಿ - gorivi, Coorg; కొరవిపాల - koravipála, Tel.; ତେଲ୍ଲକୁର୍ବନ - tellakurvan, Oor.; මහරතඹල - maharatambalá, Singh.; சூளுந்து - shulundu, Tam.). Hind. from (mashal, hind. torch + jhár, hind. tree). Tel. from (koravi, tel. fire-brand + pála, tel. the milky tree). Singh. from (maha, singh. great + ratambalá, singh. ixora coccinea, linn.). Tam. from (shúl, tam. torch). Mahr. also (lókhandí), meaning iron-like [pappily]. Can. also (hennagorivi), means a long variety; (korgi). Tel. also (puttapála), meaning ant-hill + the tree so called; (teddapála); (kommachettu), meaning branch + tree. Tam. also (kórán); (vellaivedchi), meaning white + jungle geranium; from flowers. Title otherwise Masaul tree, Torch tree. Botanically Ixora [ixora] parviflora, vahl., rubiaceæ [vricsham, 71]. Alias Ixora alba, arborea, decipiens, pavetta; Webera corymbosa. Pavetta from (pávatta, mal. pavetta indica, linn.). Small tree; leaves from linear-oblong to cuneate-obovate, bluntish or short-pointed, coriaceous and hard, shining; stipules with a long subulate point; corymbs or panicles terminal, trichotomous, sessile or peduncled, often with leafy bracts subtending the primary branches; clayx with four small teeth; lobes of the corolla oblong-linear, obtuse, reflexed, forming an oval head during æstivation; style exserted; divisions of the stigma oblong, erect; berry somewhat didymous; flowers very small, numerous white or pink, fragrant; flowering in march and april. Flowers pounded in milk, are given for whooping cough, and at the same time a necklace of the flowers is worn; often planted in gardens, and is ornamental; boughs of the green wood make torches; wood light-brown, smooth, very hard, close-grained; no heart-wood; makes excellent firewood.——*Pink jungle geranium* (சிவப்புவெட்சி - shivappuvedchi, Tam.). Tam. from (shiva, tam. to redden + vedchi, tam. ixora coccinea, linn.). Title otherwise Pink ixora. Botanically Ixora [ixora] stricta, roxb., rubiaceæ [vricsham, 71]. Alias Ixora rosea. Shrub; leaves almost sessile, oblong, acute, contracted at the base and somewhat emarginate, rather downy on the nerves beneath as well as on the branchlets; corymbs terminal, decompound, lax; calycine lobes acute, somewhat ciliated; lobes of the corolla oblong-cuneate, acute; stigma exserted; flowers a pale pink, gradually becomming as they grow old a scarlet-salmon; flowering nearly all the year.——*White jungle geranium* (కోవెలచెట్టు - kóvilechettu, Tel.). Tel. from (kóvela, tel. temple + chettu, tel. tree). Title otherwise White ixora Botanically Ixora [ixora] undulata, r., rubiaceæ [vricsham, 71]. Large ramous shrub; leaves broadly-lanceolate, much waved on the margin; corymbs trichotomous, decompound, open; branches pubescent; calycine-segments short-lanceolate, acute; lobes of the corolla narrow-oblong, reflexed; filaments exserted; style scarcely exserted; divisions of the stigma recurved linear; berries transversely oval; flowers numerous, pure white, fragrant; flowering in march and april.

IYAL (இயல் - iyal, *Tam.*). Natural tamul whether common or poetic, as distinguished from Isay tamul or tamul adapted to music and Nautaca tamul or dramatic tamul; in both of which latter various changes occur in combination, construction, &c. See vol. I (52).

IYAUR (عیار - iyár, *Hind.*). Touch-stone.——*Iyaur e daunish* (عیاردانش - iyáridánish, Hind.). From (above + dánish, pers. wisdom). Persian version of the Punchatantram [q.v.].

IYEN (ஐய்யன் - aiyyan, *Tam.*). From (ai, tam. lord + an, tam. personal termination) [ayen]. Title [peyar] assumed by Smarta [q.v.] and other bramins [q.v.], and by the Sautauny [q.v.]; also adopted by Christian missionaries. Corresponds to Iyengar among Veishnava bramins. In vocative, ayyah, used by a woman to attract her husband's attention, no Hindoo woman ever allowing herself to pronounce her husband's name. Plural form is Iyer [q.v.] and honorific double plural is Iyengar.——*Iyacunn* (ஐய்யாக்கண்ணு - aiyyákkannu, Tam.). From (above + kan, tam. eye); as dear as the master's eye. Cf. Sawimicunu. Hindoo 2nd or pers. name. Common among non-bramins [peyar].——*Iyah* (అయ్య - ayya, Tel.). Same as Iyen in Tamul.——*Iyaloo* (అయ్యలు - ayyalu, Tel.). Plural form of iyah. Non-bramin second name. Common among Balijes [balije, peyar].——*Iyempolliem* (ஐயம்பாளையம் - aiyambálaiyam, Tam.). From (above + pálaiyam, tam. fortified village).—"*a*" Cunnivaudy zameen village, Madura dist., Dindigul tal.; pop. 13,544; lat. 10° 13′; long. 77° 48′; from Dindigul S.W. 18 miles; from Madura N.W. 32 miles. The village is surrounded in the north and west by hills. The northern hill is a small one covered with thorny shrubs. The western hill is largely cultivated with coffee [q.v.], cardamoms [q.v.] and plantain [q.v.]. Coffee and cardamoms are its staple crops and exported.—"*b*" River; Madura district, Dindigul talook. Rises in the Aroongaunal hills. Flows by Tondicoody, when it receives the name of Periyaur. It then winds S. by E., and rushing down the mountains at the head of the Iyempolliem valley is joined by the Shootaur stream. Passing by Poonnacaud, it winds E. by S. in a deep forest to the hamlet of Shadamooppanputty. It passes through an open valley, the banks low, and bed sandy, where it is fringed with cocoanut [q.v.] and mango [q.v.] groves near Iyempolliem. Here a dam crosses it. Thence it runs S.S.E. winding much, with steep banks, through dry cultivation to Iyencottah and Vadiputty. It crosses the high roads N.E. and E. of Batlagoondoo, and passing Tottayan cottay, joins the Veigay river, having a course of twenty-two and a half miles.——*Iyengar* (ஐய்யங்கார் - aiyyangár, Tam.). From (aiyyan, tam. father). Special honorific or double plural of Iyen. Title added to names of Bramins, especially those of the Shreeveishnava [q.v.] or Ramaunoojeeya [q.v.] order. Hindoo 3rd name [peyar].——*Iyer* (ஐய்யர் - aiyyar, Tam.). Honorific plural of Iyen [q.v.].

IZAUFA (اضافه - izáfah, *Hind.*). From (zaifa, ar. to incline); adjunct. Additional charge imposed on areas in inam [q.v.] lands which are found to be in excess of what they were intended to be.

IZAUR (ازار - izár, *Hind.*). From (izar, ar. to cover). Long drawers [pyjauma], worn by Mahomedans [sharayee].

IZRAEEL (عزرائیل - izráíl, *Hind.*). The angel of death amongst Mahomedans [israfeel].

IZZAT (عزت - izzat, *Hind.*). From (izza, ar. to value). Respect.——*Izzat asaur* (عزت آثار - izzatásár, Hind.). From (above + ásár, ar. signs). Greeting. A salutation used at the beginning of letters to subordinates of a higher grade.

J (ज - ja, *San.*; ج - jím, *Hind.*). San. a sign of Vishnoo [q.v.]. Hind. in arithmetic 3; represents Tuesday in almanac [punchaungam], the second day of the week [vauram] and Cancer [carcatacam, sartaun] in astronomy [jyotisham], and is also the contraction of the 6th Mahomedan month [maheena].

JABR (جبر - jabr, *Hind.*). From (jabora, ar. to compel). Doctrine of compulsion held by a few who assert that man has no power and is like the feather suspended in the air with respect to his actions [takdeer].——*Jabbaur* (جبار - jabbár, Hind.). From (jabara, ar. to compel). Superior, overbearing. As attribute of God means unattainable, compeller [allah]. Common Mahomedan alam; as Jabbaur khan, alam + pataun alaumat [ism].

JACK (ചക്ക - chakka, *Mal.*). Title through portuguese. Mal. from (chakra, san. round); from fruit. Title otherwise Bread-fruit. Botanically the Artocarpus genus, artocarpaceæ [vricsham, 122]. Evergreen trees; leaves often very large, alternate, leathery, entire or pinnately lobed; flowers densely crowded on globose or oblong solitary axillary receptacles; fruit a large fleshy oblong cylindric globose or lobed receptacle, clothed with the greatly enlarged fleshy perianths and carpels which have hardened spinous or truncate or pyramidal or plane tips. The species best known to the natives are shown below. Term Jack includes also species from the genera ananas, anona, averrhoa, cinnamomum, epicarpurus, garcinia, morinda and stephegyne, from their having round fruits.——*Acid jack* (പുളിഞ്ചക്ക - puliñchakka, Mal.). From acid round fruit. Same as Ceylon gamboge.——*Black jack* (കരിച്ചക്ക - kariççakka, Mal.). Title from round fruit which turns black when dry. Same as Blimbing.——*Common jack* (पनस - panasa, San.; फणस - p'hanasa, Mahr.; पणसु - panasu, Conc.; کٹہل - kathal, Hind.; پھنس کا جہاڑ - phanaskájhár, Dec.; نڠك - nangka, Malay; ಹಲಸು - halasu, Can.; ಪೆಲ - pela, Too.; పనస - panasa, Tel.; ପଣସ - ponoso, Oor.; പിലാവ് - pilávu, Mal.; කොස් - kós, Singh.; பலா - palá, Tam.). San. from (pan, san. to praise); good fruiting. Dec. from (panasa, san. jack fruit + jhár, hind. tree). Tel. from sanscrit. Mal. from sanscrit. San. also (skandhap'hala), meaning stem + fruit; from fruit issuing from trunk; (kantakip'hala), meaning thorn + fruit; (pashumustá), meaning cow + the grass, cyperus rotundus, linn. Hind. also (chakká). Malay also (támbul), meaning big + jack tree. Can. also (kuvi); (jakamara). Tel. also (vérupanasa), meaning root + jack tree; from fruiting about roots. Mal. also (chakka), cor. of (chakra), meaning round; (varikka), meaning superior fruit. Singh. also (waela). Tam. also (palásam), meaning green, greenish even when ripe; (chírá); (pilá); (vérppila), meaning root + jack tree; from fruiting about roots. Title otherwise Bread-fruit, Bread nut, Chaqui, Hanas, Honey jack, Indian jack, Jaca, Root jack, Trunk fruit, Varaka. Botanically Artocarpus [jack] integrifolia, willd., artocarpaceæ [vricsham, 122]. Alias Artocarpus integrifolius, jaca, heterophylla; Polyphema jaca; Rademachia integra; Sitodium cauliflorum. Jaca from malayalam. Large tree with dense dome of deep dark foliage; young branches hirsute; leaves alternate, petiolate, ovate-oblong, glabrous, pale below and hirsute with stiff hairs; minute flowers male and female on the same branch; peduncle pendulous, arising from the trunk or branches; flower greenish or the male white; amentum of male flowers cylindrical; calyx none; petals two; fruit ovate, muricated. Fruit is produced from the stem and larger branches, and often forms a part of the stem that is covered with earth; it is one of the largest in existence, 12 to 18 inches in length and 6 to 8 inches in diameter, unattractive-looking object; interior of a soft fibrous consistency, with edible portions scattered here and there, possessing rich spicy scent and flavor of the melon [carcauroo]; seeds size and form of a large broad bean; fruit ripens during the rains; kernels contain much oil; gives dark looking true gum [gond], with a resinous fracture. Friar jordanus, the quilon bishop of the fourteenth century, has the following:—"there be always fruits and flowers there, "divers trees, and fruits of divers kinds; for example there "are some trees which bear very big fruit, called chaqui; and "the fruit is of such size that one is enough for five persons; "there is another tree which has fruit like that just named, "and it is called bloqui, quite as big and as sweet, but not of "the same species; these fruits never grow upon the twigs, "for these are not able to bear their weight, but only from the "main branches, and even from the trunk of the tree itself, "down to the very roots;" bloqui is a corruption of varika. In cultivating the jack, red laterite [q.v.] soil near hill sides is most suitable; ground prepared on w. coast in maidom or april and yedavam [mausam] or may, by hand-hoeing, weeding, and pitting; seed first sown in nursery in baskets or bamboo [q.v.] joints filled with soil; when the seedlings are two feet high, transplanted into the pits; watered and manured in south, not necessary on w. coast; yields fruit five years after transplantation; fruit plucked by climbing trees; average price in the south four annas per fruit, on w. coast two annas. Agastyan [q.v.] says that fruit increases secretion of bile [pittam], and in excess produces dyspepsia. Leaves are given to goats [velland] and cattle [maud], very fattening; fruit when unripe cut into small pieces and cooked in curry [q.v.] with shrimps [iraul]; seeds of ripe fruit, when roasted in hot ashes, resemble spanish chestnuts in taste and are eaten by poor. Tree good for avenues [shaulay]; tenacious white juice from fruit makes a good bird-lime and cement [pattoo]; bark yields a fibre [naur]; wood, or its saw-dust, yields on decoction a yellow dye [shauyam], fixed with alum [padicauram] and intensified by turmeric [country saffron]. Wood is like mahogany and makes excellent furniture; heartwood yellow or rich yellowish-brown, darkening on exposure, compact, even-grained, moderately hard, seasons well and takes a fine polish, does not bear great alternations of dryness and moisture.——*Foreign jack* (दीविकाडिगि - dívikadigi, Conc.; نڠك - nangka, Malay; ದೀವಿಹಲಸು - dívihalasu, Can.; ದೀವುದಗುಜ್ಜೆ - dívudagujje, Too.; വിലാത്തിപ്പിലാവ് - viláttipilávu, Mal.; රටදෙල් - ratadel, Singh.; ஈரப்பலா - írappalá, Tam.). Title as brought into ceylon from maldives and south sea islands. Can. from (dívu, can. island + halasu, can. jack tree, artocarpus integrifolia, willd.). Too. from (dívu, too. island + gujje, too. jack fruit). Mal. from (vilátti, mal. europe + pilávu, mal. artocarpus integrifolia, willd.). Singh. from (rata, singh. foreign + del, singh. bread fruit). Tam. from (íram, tam. moisture + palá, tam. jack tree). Mal. also (dvípupilávu), meaning island + jack tree. Tam. also (vázhaikkáy), meaning plantain fruit, musa paradisiaca, linn., common in ceylon; (shímaippalá), meaning foreign + jack tree; (ásini). Title otherwise Ratadel, South sea jack. Botanically Artocarpus [jack] incisa, linn. f., artocarpaceæ [vricsham, 122]. Alias Artocarpus communis; Rademachia incisa. A tree of slow growth; common in cultivated state on the west coast. Fruit is oval, size of a large melon [carcauroo], in general appearance much resembles common jack-fruit; perfectly scentless; without seeds; is composed of carpels agglomerated on a fleshy receptacle; is gathered before it is perfectly ripe, when it consists of a white and farinaceous flesh produced by the united calyces, and is sliced, slightly baked on cinders, and eaten like bread when it resembles the crumb of a new loaf. The stem yields ratadel gum [gond]. A variety of the tree produces fruit containing seed. Foreign jack is the malayalam term for Netted anona [q.v.] and the canarese term for Ananas [q.v.].——*Honey jack* (میٹہا پہنس - míthápanas, Hind.). Same as Common jack.——*Large jack* (ಹೆಬ್ಬಲಸು - hebbalasu, Can.). Same as Wild jack.——*Monkey jack* (लकुच - lakucha, San.; ओंड - omda, Mahr.; بڑہل - barhal, Hind.; لکوچا - lakúchá, Dec.; ಓಟೆಹುಳಿ - ótehuli, Can.; కమ్మరేగు - kammarégu, Tel.; ඇත්හොරලිය - etheraliya, Singh.). Title from inferior fruit. San. from (lak, san. to taste). Dec. from sanscrit. Tel. from (kamma, tel. delicious + régu, tel. jujube tree, zizyphus jujuba, lamk.). San. also (dahu), meaning burning. Tel. also (nakkarénu), meaning fox + zizyphus jujuba, lamk. Title otherwise Lakoocha, Small jack. Botanically Artocarpus [jack] lakoocha, roxb., artocarpaceæ [vricsham, 122]. Specific name from sanscrit. Leaves oval, entire, pointed, smooth above, downy beneath; catkins axillary, male subsessile, female short-peduncled, globular; fruit with a smooth surface, of an irregular roundish form, yellow when ripe. Very large tree, flower minute, internally rose-colored; ill-shapen fruit, size of orange [q.v.], smoothish rind, color of dirty wash leather. Fruit eaten; male spadix acid, astringent, eaten in curries [q.v.]. Whole tree and unripe fruit contain much tenacious, milky juice; stem gives a gum [gond]; root yields a yellow dye [shauyam]. Sapwood large, white, soft, perishable; heartwood yellow, hard; seasons well, takes a good polish; used for furniture and canoes.——*Red jack* (செம்பிலா - shembilá, Tam.). Same as Country cinnamon.——*Sea jack* (കടപ്പിലാവ് - katappilávu, Mal.). Same as Dyeing mulberry.——*Small jack* (குட்டிப்பிலா - kuttippilá, Tam.). Same as Indian nettle.——*Sour jack* (புளிப்பலா - pulippalá, Tam.). Same as Prickly anona and Country cinnamon.——*Stunted jack* (शाखोटक - shákhótaka, San.; سیورا - seurá, Hind.; نکچھلنی - nakchhilní, Dec.; ಮಿಟ್ಲಿಮರ - mitlimara, Can.; చుక్కలిచెట్టు - tsukkalichettu, Tel.; തിണ്ടപ്പരുവ - tíndapparuva, Mal.; ගටනිටුල් - gatanitul, Singh.; குட்டிப்பிலா - kuttippilá, Tam.). Title from appearance. San. from (shákha, san. branch + ótan, san. suffix showing spreading). Mal. from (tíndu, mal. to pollute + paruva, mal. creeper). Tam. from (kuttai, tam. dwarf + pilá, tam. jack tree, artocarpus integrifolia, willd.) [indian nettle]. San. also (pisháchadru), meaning demon tree, the haunt of demons. Hind. also (rúsa) [ibharancoosha, roussa grass]. Can. also (timli). Tel. also (barinika); (barivenka); (barranki); (pakki) [mannajhow]. Tam. also (piráy). Title otherwise Cootty pilah, Demon tree, Pirye, Rough-leaved ramoon, Siamese paper. Botanically Epicarpurus orientalis, bl., moraceæ [vricsham, 121]. Alias Streblus aspera; Trophis aspera. Tree; leaves alternate, short-petioled, obovate, cuspidate, acuminate, serrated towards the apex, very rough above; male flowers capitate, heads axillary, aggregated, short-peduncled; females axillary, one to two together, longish-pedicelled; fruit drupaceous, deep yellow, one-seeded; cotyledons very unequal-sided; flowers small, greenish yellow; a small, rigid, stunted-looking tree; common. Milky juice applied to cracked heels and sore hands; astringent and septic bark in decoction used as a lotion in fevers. Berries eaten by birds; good for hedges; coppices well; twigs are used as tooth-brushes, and the rough leaves to polish wood and ivory [dant]; a fibre [naur] from the stem. Wood white, moderately hard, no heartwood, no annual rings; tough and elastic; sometimes used for cart-wheels.——*Wild jack* (पातफणस - pátap'hanasa, Mahr.; पाच्पणसा - páchpanasá, Conc.; پھنس - phanas, Hind.; ಹೆಬ್ಬಲಸು - hebbalasu, Can.; ಪೆಜ - peja, Too.; పనస - panasa, Tel.; ആഞ്ഞിലി - áññali, Mal.; - aludel, Singh.; அஞ்சலி - añjali, Tam.). Hind. means jack fruit. Can. from (hebbu, can. large + halasu, can. jack tree, artocarpus integrifolia, willd.). Singh. from (alu, singh. ashes + del, singh. wild bread fruit tree). Mahr. also (ránap'hanasa), meaning wild jack. Can. also (kádahalasu), meaning forest + jack tree. Mal. also (ayini); (áyini); (káttupilávu), meaning forest, artocarpus integrifolia, willd. Singh. also (del). Tam. also (akkinimaram); (áyini) [foreign jack]. Title otherwise Anjely, Jungle jack, Large jack. Botanically Artocarpus [jack] hirsuta, lamk., artocarpaceæ [vricsham, 122]. Alias artocarpus pubescens. Large tree; leaves elliptic, obtuse, or rounded at both ends, glabrous, hairy, especially on the nerves beneath; male catkin long, cylindrical, ascending, afterwards pendulous; females oval, size of a hen's egg; fruit globose, echinate, size of large orange [q.v.]; native of malabar forests. Fruit contains a pulpy substance surrounding seeds; also abounds in viscid juice, which flows from the rough rind if touched. The concreted juice forms a waxy, tough, light brown substance, which when melted is used as a cement [pattoo] to join broken earthenware and stoneware; in its simple state is used as bird-lime; the bark gives a brown dye [shauyam]. Wood is strong, tolerably close, evengrained, of a glossy texture, yellowish brown color; much in use for ship-building, house-building, furniture, &c.; stands next to teak [q.v.] with ship-builders. Wild jack is in malayalam same as Water cadamba.

JACKAL (शृगाल - shrigála, *San.*; कोल - kólá, *Mahr*; شغال - shaghál, *Ar.* and *Pers.*; گیدر - gídar, *Hind.*; کولا - kolá, *Dec.*; چکل - chakal, *Malay*; ನರಿ - nari, *Can.*; ಕುಡಿಕೆ - kudike, *Too.*; నక్క - nakka, *Tel.*; ବିଲୁଅ - billuva, *Oor.*; കുറുക്കൻ - kurukkan, *Mal.*; නරියා - nariyá, *Singh.*; நரி - nari, *Tam.*). Title from persian. San. from (asrik, san. blood + lá, san. to take). Pers. from sanscrit. Dec. from mahratta. Mal. from (kuru, mal. small). Tam. means dim color. Ar. also (ibniává), meaning wolf's son. Hind. also (siyál), from sanscrit. Mal. also (nari). Canis [shwaunam] aureus, canidæ [cookooram], digitigrada, carnivora, mammalia [sastanam, 12], of naturalists [jantoo]. Alias Lupus aureus; Oxygoiis indicus; Sacalius indicus. Fur of a dusky yellowish or rufous gray, the hairs being mottled black, gray, and brown, with the under fur brownish yellow; lower parts yellowish gray; tail reddish brown, ending in a darkish tuft; more or less rufous on the muzzle and limbs; tail moderately hairy. The Bengal black variety is not known in the south of India. In the coffee tracts the jackal devours ripe coffee [q.v.] berries; the seeds pass through and are picked up; these are the best for germination. The jackal is easily run down by greyhounds, but gives sport with fox hounds; the fox [lomree] being too small for hunting. The call of the jackal is familiar. The natives assert that they cry after every watch [jaumam] of the night. Called in Europe the lion's provider and here an old jackal is in constant attendance on the tiger [pooly]. The horny substance which grows on the head of some jackals is of great reputed virtue, ensuring prosperity to its possessor. The jackal digs corpses out of shallow graves and devours them. The domestic dog [nye] is supposed to owe its origin to this species, as well as to the wolf [konye]. Pariah [q.v.] dogs which frequent the villages are like jackals, and the two species will interbreed. Jackals are eaten by poor shikarries [q.v.]. Their nasal bones are enclosed in amulets and used as a talisman. There is a Tamul proverb:—அல்லக்காட்டு நரி பல்லெக்காட்டுகிறதுபோல—"Showing his teeth like "a jackal of the ginger [q.v.] fields;", said of one who shows signs of disappointment. And another:—குழியிற் பிள்ளையை நரி சுற்றுகிறாப்போலே—"Like a jackal going "round the grave of a child."

JACKANAIRY (ಜಕ್ಕಲರೆ - jakkalare, *Can.*). From (jakkal, can. shrubby + arai, tam. rock). Village; Neilgherry dist., Paranginand division; pop. 1,138; acres 11,479; lat. 11° 24′; long. 76° 55′; from Coonoor N.E. 7 miles; from Ootacamund E. 12 miles. On hill to W. of Kotagherry new ghaut [q.v.] road. Three miles to the W. is the noted Catherine waterfall [aroovy].

JACKATALLA (ಜಗತಾಳ - jagatálá *Can.*). From (jaggu, can. to sink + tala, can. place). Village, Valley; Neilgherry dist., Paranginaud division; pop. 1,105; acres 4,727; lat. 11° 23′; long. 76° 49′; from Coonoor N.W. 3 miles; from Ootacamund E. 5 miles. Badaga [q.v.] village inhabited by Belly caste. Wellington was till 1860 called after this village.

JADOW (جادو - jádo, *Hind.*). From (yadu, san. the king so called). A tribe which established itself about 1000 A.D. at Devagiry afterwards called by the Mahomedans Dowlatabad. Their crest was a golden kite [chillam, yaudava].

JADWAUR (جدوار - jadwár, *Ar.*; ماه پروین - máhparwín, *Pers.*; نربسی - nirbisí, *Hind.*). Ar. from (zadái, pers. purifying + wár, pers. great), great antidote. Pers. from (máh, pers. moon + parwín, pers. pleiades); from blossoming when pleiades [kritticay, sooreiyah] rise with the dawn, viz., at beginning of summer; cf. wild bachnaug. Hind. from (nir, san. not + bis, hind. poison). Hind. also (máfarfín), being pers. corruption. Greek ζέδοαρ. Generic terms for non-poisonous aconites [bish]; see particularly Atees and Wild bachnaug. For poisonous aconites see Bachnaug and Wolf strangler. Title has no connection with Zedoary [q.v.].

JAFFER (جعفر - jafar, *Ar.*). Yellow. Name of the cousin of Mahomet and of the sixth Imaum [q.v.]. Common alam; as Jaffer beg, alam + alaumat; Jaffer hoossain, double alam [ism]. Jaffery was the two-anna coin [naunyam] of Tippoo sultan.——*Jaffer goondy* (अम्लान - amlána, San.; आबोली - ábólí, Mahr.; گل مخمل - gulimakhmal, Pers. and Hind.; جعفری گنڈی - jafarígundí, Dec.; తెల్లపెద్దగోరంట - tellapeddagóranta, Tel.; വാടാമല്ലിക - vátámallika, Mal.; வாடாமல்லிகை - vádámalligai, Tam.). Title from deccany. San. from (a, san. negative prefix + mlai, san. to fade); ever fresh. Pers. from (gul, pers. flower + makhmal, pers. velvet), from its softness and appearance. Dec. from (jafarí, ar. yellow + gundí, hind. button), from color and shape of flower. Tel. from (tella, tel. white + pedda, tel. large + góranta, tel. nail-dye plant, lawsonia alba, lamk.). Mal. from (vátá, mal. not withering + malliká, mal. jasmine, jasminum sambac, ait.). Tam. means unfading jasmine. San. also (mahásahá), meaning enduring long; everlasting color. Hind. also (lálgul), meaning red flower. Tel. also (peddagóranta), meaning large + nail-dye plant. Tam. also (shivappuvádámalligai), meaning red variety; (vellaivádámalligai), meaning white variety. Title otherwise Batchelor's buttons, Everlasting jasmine, Globe amaranth, Immortal amaranth, Red globe everlasting, Velvet flower, Yellow buttons. Botanically Gomphrena globosa, linn., amarantaceæ [vricsham, 106]. Tall dichotomously branched annual; branches stout obscurely four-angled; leaves 2–4 inches, scaberulous, pale green; petiole 0–1 inch; heads 1–1½ inches diameter, peduncled, terminating the branches; bracts under the head ½–1 inch; flowers densely imbricate; branches ½–¾ inch, scarious, lanceolate, much longer than the perianth; sepals lanceolate, densely woolly, shorter than the staminal tube. Flower heads round of white crimson and yellow colors; ornamental annual. Another species is hispida.

JAGAM (జగము - jagamu, *Tel.*). From (gam, san. to go) [gaty, go, gungay]. World [jehaun].——*Jaconet* (जगन्नाथी - jagannát'hí, Mahr.). Title corruption from juggernaut [q.v.], the city in orissa [q.v.]; from the cloth bearing impression of the idol [vigraham]. Thin cotton [q.v.] fabric between cambric and muslin [q.v.] used for dresses [sheelay], neckcloths, &c. ——*Jagadeeshan* (சகதீசன் - shagathísan, Tam.). From (jagat, san. world + ísha, san. lord). Epithet of Shiva [q.v.], Vishnoo [q.v.] and Bramha [q.v.]. Hindoo 2nd or pers. name [peyar].——*Jaganaick* (జగన్నాయకుడు - jagannáyakudu, Tel.). From (above + náyaka, san. master). Hindoo 2nd or pers. name [peyar].——*Jaganautan* (சகந்நாதன் - shagannáthan, Tam.). From (above + nátha, san. lord). Epithet of Vishnoo. Hindoo 2nd or pers. name [juggernaut, peyar].——*Jagarauz* (జగరాజు - jagarádzu, Tel.). From (above + rádzu, tel. king). Hindoo 2nd or pers. name [peyar].——*Jagaroya* (జగరాయుడు - jagaráyadu, Tel.). From (above + ráyadu, tel. king). Hindoo 2nd or pers. name [peyar].——*Jagat* (जगत् - jagat, San.). Uninflected form of Jagam. World. Jagatcurtah is the creator of the world. Jagatpaty is the lord of the world.——*Jangam* (जङ्गम - jangama, San.). From (gam, san. to go). Moveable, as of property. Name for the Lingayets [q.v.]. The image erected in the Sheiva temples being denominated Stauvara lingam [q.v.] or the stable image, Basava [q.v.] denominated this reliquary the Jangama lingam or locomotive image, a phrase borrowed from the vedas [q.v.], where it is used for living being [jeevam]. Hence he and his followers are denominated Jangams, or living images of the deity.——*Jangamrauzpully* (జంగమరాజుపల్లి - dzangamarádzupalli, Tel.). From (dzangamarádzu, tel. proper name + palli, tel. village). Village, Ghaut; Cuddapah dist., Budwail tal.; pop. 1,302; acres 11,062; lat. 14° 46′; long. 78° 56′; from Budwail W. 13 miles; from Cuddapah N. 20 miles. In a valley, well cultivated with dholl [common dholl], raggy [q.v.] and the castor-oil plant [aumanac]. Good hare [mosal] and partridge [teetar] shooting. Lead [eeyam] ore is found in the hills. In the village are the remains of an old fort. The ghaut [q.v.], west of the village, connects Budwail and Proddootore talooks, and passes across the Nullamullays.——*Jangaula* (జంగాల - dzangála, Tel.). Plural form of Jangam.——*Juggayapett* (జగ్గయ్యపేట - jaggayyapéta, Tel. jaggayapet*). From (jaggayya, tel. proper name + péta, tel. suburb). Tel. also (bétavólu), meaning offshoot of a mountain + town.—"*a*" Deputy tahsildarry, Kistna district. Pay Rs. 70.—"*b*" Town, Deputy tahsildar's station; Kistna dist., Nundigauma tal.; pop. 9,717; acres 8,969; lat. 16° 53′; long. 80° 08′; from Bezwada N.W. 41 miles; from Guntoor N.N.W. 47 miles; from Madras N. 260 miles; from Masulipatam N.W. 83 miles; from

Nundigauma N.W. 15 miles; from Vinoocondah N.N.E. 61 miles. On the Masulipatam road, near Hyderabad border. Rajah Vasireddy vencataudry naidoo, who enclosed it with a wall, called it after his father. Contains Booddhist remains, probably the oldest in Southern india. The stoopam [q.v.], dating B.C., is 66 feet in diameter and has sculptured marbles [shalavay cull] all round. Several stone circles [azhauram] over ancient graves in the neighbourhood, in one of which was found the bones of a horse. Large pots were placed at the four points of the compass. The remains are in the Ashmolean museum at Oxford. Depôt for commerce between Northern circars [q.v.] and Nizam's dominions. Silk [puttoo] cloths are woven from thread brought from Central provinces. Trade in salt [ooppoo], conveyed hither by local merchants. Traders are chiefly Marwar settlers from Hyderabad. The chief staple is opium [aphainam]. Geologically of interest as the extreme north-eastern corner of the Cuddapah-Kurnool rock series, and as the supposed site of a great coal [nilakary] field.——*Juggernaut* (जगन्नाथ - jagannát'ha, San.). From (jagat, san. world + nát'ha, san. lord). A form of Krishnan [q.v.]. Pooree, near Cuttack, is the chief seat of worship, where he is worshipped with his brother and sister Balabhadran and Soobhadray. At the annual car festival, the three idols [vigraham] are placed on cars [rath] and dragged from the temple to a country-temple a mile distant.

JAGGERY (गुड - guda, *San.*; گڑ - gur, *Hind.*; బెల్లము - bellamu, *Tel.*; ചക്കര - chakkara, *Mal*; வெல்லம் - vellam, *Tam.*). Title from malayalam. San. from (gud, san. to preserve) [good]. Hind. from sanscrit. Mal. from (sharkará, san. sugar) [sugar]. Coarse brown or almost black sugar [q.v.], made by boiling down over a slow fire the fresh sap of various palms [taur], borassus [palmyra], caryota [bastard sago palm], cocos [cocoanut], phœnix [kharjooram]; or of sugar-cane [aulay, sugar, sugar-cane]. In the latter case it is equivalent to molasses. The thick syrup is poured into half cocoanut shells, and there hardens into lumps. The boiling is generally done by the toddy-climber's wife [shaunautty]. The wild date tree is that which chiefly supplies it on the Coromandel coast [q.v.]; the palmyra in Tinnevelly. The cocoanut palm is much drawn for toddy [q.v.] on the west coast, and this is occasionally boiled for jaggery. The caryota or kittal [q.v.] is called the jaggery palm, and is especially used for this purpose in Ceylon. Great quantities are produced in Tinnevelly, where the cakes pass as a kind of currency. Jaggery is the sugar chiefly used by the lower orders. Owing to its imperfect preparation, it is inferior in sweetening and nutritive power. It is however often used to stay the stomach, pending food. It is a general practice to employ vegetable matter of some kind in masonry to increase its adhesive quality, and jaggery is among the substances. The indestructibility of the ancient temples [coil] and other buildings is due chiefly to these mixed cements [cauray, pattoo]. Jaggery is also one of the principal ingredients employed in making arrack [q.v.]. For making jaggery candy [q.v.], pots containing jaggery are set out at night, when some of the jaggery crystallises at the bottom.——*Jaggery palm* (ماڑی کا جھاڑ - máríká-jhár, Hind.). Title from product. Same as Bastard sago palm.

JAH (جاہ - já, *Hind.*). Place. Jah e namauz is a place of prayer; term applied to the carpet, mat or cloth on which Mahomedans stand while praying [namauz]. Jah also means dignity [staunam]; in this sense, lacab suffix; as Wallajah, high in dignity [ism].——*Jagheer* (جاگیر - jágír, *Hind.*). Means land + holding. A tenure common under the Mahomedan government, by which the revenues of a certain tract of land were made over to a servant of the state, either unconditionally or on the condition of performing some public service such as the levy and maintenance of troops or other specified duty. The assignment was either for a stated term, or more usually for the lifetime of the holder lapsing on his death to the state, although not unusually renewed to his heir on payment of a nuzrauna [q.v.] or fine, and sometimes specified to be a hereditary assignment. A jagheer was liable to forfeiture on failure of performance of the conditions on which it was granted, or on the holder's incurring the displeasure of the emperor. For the jagheer given to the English east india company by the Nawaub mahomed ally, see Jagheer circar below. The British gave a few jagheers in the early part of the administration. Jagheers were treated by the Inam commission as major inams [inam]. See vol. I, 112.——*Jagheer circar* (جاگیرسرکار - jágírisarkár, Hind.). From (above + sarkár, pers. province). Original name of Chingleput district. Granted to the East india company by nawaub Mahomed ally [q.v.] in return for the espousal of his cause against Razah sahib [q.v.] and was their first important territorial possession in S. india. This grant made in 1760 was not confirmed by the Soobahdar [q.v.] of the Deccan [q.v.] till 1763. On the assumption of the direct management of the jagheer by the East india company, it was placed under the charge of the Committee of Assigned revenues, who had been appointed to manage the other possessions of the Nawaub [q.v.] in the Carnatic [q.v.] on the breaking out of the second war with Hyder ally [q.v.] in 1780. This committee found the country divided into sixteen divisions or pergunnahs [q.v.], containing an aggregate of 2,241 villages. The names of the sixteen pergunnahs were Carangooly, Cauvaly, Cauvitundalam, Chingleput, Covelong, Egmore, Great conjeeveram, Little conjeeveram, Manimungalam, Ootramallore, Peddapolliem, Perambaukam, Ponnairy, Poonamallee, Shaulwaukum and Tripassore. With the exception of Cauvaly, which was soon abolished, this division of the district lasted until it was parcelled out into zemindarries [q.v.]. After the collapse of the zemindarry system in 1807–1820 a division into talooks [q.v.] was introduced. See vol. I (186); II, 66.

JAINY (ചേരി - chéni, *Mal.*). Corruption of (chéri, mal. village). Village. Suffix in place names; as Munnanjainy, meaning king's village [chainy, cherry].

JAIR (زیر - zer, *Pers.*). Below.——*Jairtalaub* (زیر تالاب - zertáláb, Hind.). From (above + táláb, hind. lake). Lands under a large tank [q.v.], especially when registered as double-crop [dofusl, iroobhogam] land.

JAKEERY (ذخیرہ - zakhírah, *Hind.*; ಜಕ್ಕೇರಿ - jakkéri, *Can.*). From (zakhara, ar. to hoard). Means a store; once the military depôt. Village; Salem dist., Oossoor tal.; pop. 363; acres 992; lat. 12° 35′; long. 77° 55′; from Oossoor S.S.E. 10 miles; from Salem N.N.W. 67 miles. Has two old forts, on high ground.

JALAM (जल - jala, *San.*). From (jal, san. to be cold). Water [ab, neer].—"*a*" Plant first term often joining two genera. Ex., where transl. is of second term:—Commelyna salicifolia (jalapippalí), piper longum; Cyperus procerus (jalatunga), cyperus rotundus; Cyperus puncticulatus (jalatunga), cyperus rotundus; Herpestes monniera (jalním), melia azadirachta; Nelumbium speciosum (jalaja), born; Trapa bispinosa (jalakantaka), thorn; Vitex trifolia (jalanirgundí), vitex negundo. See gloss. paragraphs.—"*b*" Mammal first term. Ex., where transl. is of second term:—Delphinus perniger (jalashúkara), pig; Halicore dugong (jalanara), man; Lutra vulgaris (jalamáñjara), cat. See gloss. paragraphs.——*Jalaja lochanan* (जलजलोचन - jalajalóchana, San.). From (above + ja, san. born + lóchana, san. eye). Vishnoo [q.v.], the lotus-eyed.——*Jalajay* (जलजा - jalajá, San.). From (above + ja, san. born). Lutchmy [q.v.]; the water born.——*Jalamundalam* (رتیلا - rutailá, Ar.; دلمہ - dulmah, Pers.; بدمکرو - badmakrú, Hind.; جلمنڈل - jalmandal, Dec.; ಜೇಡರಹುಳ - jédarahula, Can.; புலிமுகச்சிலந்தி - pulimugaççilandi, Tam.). Title from deccany. Hind. from (bad, hind. bad + makrú, hind. large spider). Dec. from (jala, san. water + mandala, san. disc). Can. from (jéda, can. weaver + hula, can. insect). Tam. from (puli, tam. tiger + mukha, san. face + shilandi, tam. spider). A tarantula spider [makree].——*Jalantra* (జలంత్ర - jalantrá, Tel. jalantra *). From (above + antará, san. without). Ancient zemindarry, Village; Ganjam dist., pop. 11,649; pop. of village 1,151; 82 square miles; lat. of village 18° 57′; long. 84° 35′; from Berhampore S.S.W. 29 miles; from Chetterpore S.W. 40 miles. The zemindarry [q.v.] was founded by Shree poorshottama gajapaty deo, who halted in a jungle near the Mahendram [mahendragherry] mountain, when returning to Cuttack after his victory at Conjeeveram. Contains 78 villages. Peshcush Rs. 7,384.——*Jalasand* (जलसन्धि - jalasandhi, San.). From (above + sandhi, san. junction). A strait. The only straits in the Presidency are Palk's strait, a narrow channel between this and Ceylon, so called from a Dutch navigator; and Paumben channel, between Rameshwaram and the mainland.——*Jala tarangam* (जलतरङ्ग - jalataranga, San.). From (above + taranga, san. wave). Thin porcelain [kaolin] cups of sizes, arranged like musical glasses.——*Jaldanky* (జల్దంకి - dzaldaṅki, Tel.). From (above + dá, san. to give + anka, san. mark). Village; Nellore dist., Cauvaly tal.; pop. 3,376; acres 13,729; lat. 14° 52′; long. 79° 57′; from Cauvaly W.S.W. 6 miles; from Nellore N.N.W. 30 miles; from the sea W. 12 miles. Great scarcity of water. Cattle trade. Good tank. Trig. station in lat. 14° 52′ 22·39″; long. 79° 58′ 19·36″; from Bitragoonta N.N.W. 5 miles; from Cauvaly W.S.W. 6 miles; from the sea W. 11 miles.——*Julgar* (ಜಲಗಾರ - jalagára, Can.). From (above + kára, san. personal affix). A caste who sweep streets, or wash refuse, in search of lost money or valuables. A native gold washer.

JALAP (شاطل - shátil, *Ar.*; بیخ جلاب - bíkhijallába, *Pers.* and *Hind.*; جالب - jálab, *Dec.*; భేదిగడ్డ - bhédigadda, *Tel.*; பேதிக்கிழங்கு - péthikkizhangu, *Tam.*). Title from persian; distinguish from salep [q.v.]. Pers. from (bíkh, pers. root + jallába, pers. jalab). Hind. from persian. Tel. from (bhédi, tel. purging + gadda, tel. root). Tam. from (bhédí, san. cathartic + kizhangu, tam. root). Hind. also (jálabkíjar), meaning jalab root; (roshanak). Tam. also (shálappuççedi), meaning jalab plant; (shivathai); properly ipomæa turpethum, r. br., which is a substitute for jalap [indian jalap]. Title otherwise Purgative root, True jalap. Botanically Exogonium purga, benth., convolvulaceæ [vricsham, 93]. Alias Ipomæa purga. Twiner with long crimson flowers; tuberous-rooted; comes from mexico; introduced on neilgherries; root met with in thin transverse slices, solid, hard, weighty, of a blackish color on the outside, and internally of a dark gray, with black circular striæ; taste is nauseous, accompanied by a sweetish bitterness. Gives to pharm. the dried tubercles jalapa; active principle, a resin, jalapæ resina, cathartic, anthelmintic.——*False jalap* (कृष्णकेलि - krishnakéli, San.; आकाशमोग्रि - ákáshamógri, Conc.; زهرالاجل - zahrulajl, Ar.; گل عباس - guliabbás, Pers. and Hind.; گلا باش - gulábásh, Dec.; ಮಧ್ಯಾಹ್ನಮಲ್ಲಿಗೆ - madhyáhnamallige, Can.; ಬೈಯ ಮಲ್ಲಿಗೆ - baiyamallige, Too.; చంద్రకాంత - chandrakánta, Tel.; പൈത്തടിപ്പൂ - paittatippú, Mal.; සෙන්දිරික්කා - sendirikká, Singh.; பத்தராசு - pattarásu, Tam.). Title from supposed origin of true jalap. San. from (krishna, san. black + kéli, san. sport). Conc. means sky jasmine. Ar. from (zahr, ar. poison + ajl, ar. death). Pers. from (gul, pers. flower + abbás, ar. red color), from colors of flowers. Dec. from hindostany by corruption. Can. from (madhyáhna, can. midday + mallige, can. jasmine, jasminum sambac, ait.). Too. from (baiya, too. evening + mallige, too. jasmine). Tel. from (chandra, san. moon + kánti, san. brilliance). Mal. from (paittati, mal. ten feet, evening, from long shadow + pú, mal. flower). Singh. means probably moon plant, as flowering in the evening. Tam. from (bhadram, san. auspicious + aksha, san. eye). San. also (sandhyáràga), meaning evening + color; (bahubhámí), meaning abounding in brilliancy, from various colors of flowers. Hind. also (sanjí). Can. also (nálkughantehúgida), meaning four + hour + flower + plant; (chandramallige), meaning moon + the plant; (gulamáji); (sanjamallige), meaning evening + the plant; (marianmallige); (vibhútigida), meaning ashes + plant. Tel. also (chandramalle), meaning moon + jasmine; (bhadrákshi), meaning auspicious + eye. Mal. also (antimandáram), meaning evening + the tree, bauhinia; (antimalari), meaning evening blossoming. Singh. also (ratusendirikka), meaning red + the plant. Tam. also (andimandárai), meaning evening + the plant, bauhinia; (pattirádcham); (andimalligai), meaning evening + jasmine. Title otherwise Evening jasmine, Four-o'clock-plant, Garden jalap, Goolabash, Marvel-of-peru, Striped marvel-of-peru. Botanically Mirabilis jalapa, linn., nyctagineæ [vricsham, 105]. Alias Jalappa congesta; Mirabilis dichotoma; Nyctago hortensis, jalapa. Large herbaceous plant constantly in blossom with numerous ipomæa-like [calamby] flowers of moderate size, some dark crimson, some pure yellow, some crimson striped with yellow; flowers of each variety frequently upon the same plant. The root of young plants is cylindrical above and tapering below, but in old plants it becomes napiform or subrotund; the external surface is dark brown and marked with numerous circular rings; internally it is dirty white or greyish; when dry, very old roots become hard, compact and heavy, and deepen in color, but younger roots are of a leathery consistence; it has a faintly nauseous odour, and a sweetish, sub-acrid taste; a transverse section of the root shows numerous concentric rings of a darker color than the intervening substance; it shows numerous acicular crystals when magnified. Root purgative, whence plant was once supposed to be true jalap plant; quoted in pharm.; leaves used as poultice in abscess and boils.

JALAUL (جلال - jalál, *Hind.*). From (jalla, ar. to glorify). Glory, majesty. Attribute of God [allah]. Common alam; as Syed jalaul, alaumat + alam. Also part of lacab; as Jalaul ood deen, glory of religion [ism]. Name of Acbar.——*Jalauly* (جلالی - jalálí, Hind.). Called after acbar. A square silver coin [naunyam] almost equivalent to modern rupee [q.v.] in weight and value issued in Acbar's time. On the four sides of it were stamped names of the four companions of the prophet [mahomed].——*Jalaulya* (جلالیه - jaláliyah, Hind.). From syed jalaul ood deen bokhaury. An order of fakeers [q.v.].

JALEE (جلی - jalí, *Hind.*). From (jalá, ar. to be clear). Relief or embossed work.——*Jaloos* (جلوس - jalús, Hind.). From (jalá, ar. displayed). Accession to the throne [takht], the date when a reign commences.

JAM (जम् - jam, *San.*). To eat.——*Jamadagny* (जमदग्नि - jamadagni, San.). From (jamat, san. consuming + agni, san. fire). A rishy [q.v.], father of Parshooraman [q.v.]. His wife was Renoocay. Jaumadagnyan, patronymic, is Parshooraman.——*Jambavan* (जाम्बवान् - jámbaván, San.). The king of the bears [ricsham], an ally of Rama [q.v.]. Now applied to any Nestor. Cf. Maudiga.——*Jambeeram* (जम्बीर - jambíra, San.). Title otherwise Orange. Botanically the Citrus genus, rutaceæ [vricsham, 32]. Shrubs or trees, usually spinous; leaves alternate, one-foliolate, more or less serrate, and gland dotted, stalk often winged; flowers axillary, solitary, in bundles or in small cymes, white or pinkish, sweet-scented; fruit a superior berry, with removable rind and separable sections, packed full of pulpy tissue which is composed of large cells. The species best known to the natives are:—Aurantium [orange], aurantium, var. aurantium proper [sweet orange], aurantium, var. bergamia [bergamot orange], aurantium, var. bigaradia [bitter orange], decumana [pummelow], japonica [cumquot], medica [lime], medica, var. acida [sour lime], medica, var. limetta [sweet lime], medica, var. limonum [lemon], medica, var. medica proper [citron].——*Jambolin* (جمبول - jambúl, Hind.). Form from portuguese. Same as Common jaumoon.——*Jamboo* (जम्बु - jambu, San.). From edible fruit. Title otherwise Eugene myrtle, West-indian myrtle. Botanically the Eugenia genus, myrtaceæ [vricsham, 56]. Trees or shrubs natives of hot and tropical regions; flowers white; berry, one or two-celled, and contains one or two seeds; fruits mostly edible; the species group themselves here into cloves [lavangam], jambolins [common jaumoon] and rose apples [q.v.]. The species best known to the natives are:—alternifolia [moy], aquea [red jaumoon], arnottiana [small jaumoon], bracteata [coromandel jaumoon], caryophyllata [lavangam], jambolana [common jaumoon], jambolana, var. caryophyllifolia [clove-leaved jaumoon], jambos [rose-apple], javanica [java jaumoon], malabarica [malabar jaumoon], malaccensis [malacca jaumoon], munronii [water jaumoon], operculata [cherry jaumoon], uniflora [barbadoes cherry], zeylanica [ceylon jaumoon]. Other s. indian species indigenous or naturalized are:—argentea, calcadensis, calophyllifolia, caryophyllæa, cylindrica, floccosa, gardneri, hemispherica, heyneana, jossinia, laeta, microphylla, montana, mooniana, neesiana, rottleriana, rubicunda, uniflora, wightiana, wynaadensis. Parrot jamboo is the same as Bonduc.——*Jamboo dweepam* (जम्बुद्वीप - jambudvípa, San.). From (jambu, san. rose-apple tree + dvípa, san. island). The Eden of the Hindoos. The centre of the seven great insular continents [dweepam]; contains India [q.v.]. In the centre of Jamboo dweepam is the golden mountain Meroo [q.v.]. Jamboo dweepam has itself nine varshams [q.v.] or sub-divisions:—Bhadraushwam, Bharatam, Harivarsham, Hiranmayam, Ilauvritam, which contains Meroo, Kaitmaulay, Kimpooroosham or kinnaram, Oottara cooroo, Ramyacam. According to the Vishnoo pooraunam [q.v.], Bhaurata varsham or India is again divided into nine dweepams or portions:—Casheroomat, Comauraca, Gabhastimat, Gandharvam, Indra dweepam, Nauga dweepam, Sowmyam, Tamravurnam, Vauroonam [charitram]. See vol. I (2). The title name is used especially by Booddhists [bhoogolashastram].——*Jambookeshwaram* (சம்புகேசுவரம் - shambugésuvaram, Tam.). From (jambu, san. rose-apple tree + íshvara, san. shiva, the lord); in reference to the god being placed under a rose-apple [q.v.] tree. Tamul name (tiruvánaikká), meaning holy + elephant + grove; familiarly (tiruvánaikkával). Town; Trichinopoly dist., Trichinopoly tal.; lat. 10° 51′; long. 78° 46′; from Trichinopoly N. 3 miles. Shiva temple, 400 years old, on Shreerungam island; 1½ miles S.E. of the great Shreerungam temple, but rivalling the latter in architectural beauty and interest, and probably exceeding it in antiquity. It contains the ap lingam, one of the five celebrated lingams worshipped in south; for the other four see Lingam.——*Jamboolingam* (சம்புலிங்கம் - shambulingam, Tam.). From (jambu, san. rose-apple tree + linga, san. phallic emblem of shiva; after the god at jambookeshwaram in trichinopoly. Hindoo 2nd or pers. name. Common among non-bramins [peyar].——*Jaum* (جام - jám, Hind.). Means guava. Plant name common to:—Eugenia jambolana; Psidium guyava. See gloss paragraphs.——*Jaumba* (जांब - jámba, Mahr. and Conc.). Edible. Plant name common to:—Eugenia jambolana; Eugenia jambos; Eugenia malaccensis; Xylia dolabriformis. See gloss. paragraphs.——*Jaumoon* (جامن - jámun, Hind.). See sep. title.——*Jhow* (झावु - jhávu, San.). See sep. title.——*Jumrool* (جمرول - jamrúl, Hind.). Same as Common jaumoon.

JAMAICA (جمیکہ - jameka, *Hind.*). Means land of wood and water. One of the w. indian islands; belongs to Great britain. Plant first term. Ex.:—Abrus precatorius, jamaica wild liquorice; Argemone mexicana, jamaica yellow thistle; Asclepias curassavica, jamaica wild liquorice; Canavalia ensiformis, jamaica horse-bean; Chickrassia tabularis, jamaica cedar; Dodonæa viscosa, jamaica switch sorrel; Lantana camara, jamaica mountain sage; Lawsonia alba, jamaica mignonette; Nerium oleander, jamaica south sea-rose; Pimenta officinalis, jamaica pepper; Zingiber officinale, jamaica ginger. See gloss. paragraphs.

JAMALGOTA (जयपाल - jayapála, *San.*; नेपाळ - népála, *Mahr.*; जाफल - jáp'hala, *Conc.*; درخت حب السلاطین - darakhtihabbussalátín, *Ar.*; درخت بید انجیر خطائی - darakhtibedanjírikhatáí, *Pers.*; جیپال گوٹے کا پیڑ - jepálgotekáper, *Hind.*; جمال غٹے کا جھاڑ - jamálghuttekájhár, *Dec.*; بوری - bori, *Malay*; ಜಾಪಾಳದಮರ - jápáladamara, *Can.*; ಬೇರೆದಮರ - béradamara, *Too.*; నేపాళము - népálamu, *Tel.*; നേർവ്വാളം - nérvválam, *Mal.*; නේපාලය - népálaya, *Singh.*; நேர்வாளம் - nérválam, *Tam.*). Title from deccany [ji]. San. from (jaya, san. victory + pála, san. guardian), from certainty of effect. Ar. from (darakht, ar. tree + habb, ar. seed + salátín, ar. kings). Pers. from (darakht, ar. tree + bedanjír, pers. fruit of ricinus communis, linn. + khatáí, hind. chinese). Hind. from (jayapála, san. the plant + per, hind. tree). Dec. from hindostany by corruption. Can. from sanscrit. Tel. from the country so called. Mal. from (nír, mal. water + vila, mal. to grow). Singh. from (népála, san. the country). Tam. from (népála, san. the country). San. also (népála), meaning the country so called [wild jamalgota]; (danti), meaning ivory-like, from white kernels. Mahr. also (jépála). Ar. also (darakhtidand), meaning purgative tree; (darakhtidátún); (fill), referring to nuts. Pers. also (darakhtihabbikhatáí), meaning the cathay seed tree. Hind. also (jepál). Mal. also (katalávanakku), meaning sea + ricinus communis, linn. Singh. also (jayapála). Title otherwise Chinese castor, Croton oil tree, Ivory seed, King's seed, Molucca grains tree, Nepaul oil tree, Purging croton. Wild aumanac with reference to which see also baliospermum and jatropha. Botanically Croton [ghantabeejam] tiglium, linn., euphorbiaceæ [vricsham, 118]. Alias Croton jamalgota; Tiglium officinale. Jamalgota from deccany. Small tree, 15–20 feet, trunk crooked, bark smooth, ash-colored, with a few spreading branches; leaves alternate, ovate-oblong, smooth, acuminate, three to five-nerved at base, covered when young with minute stellate hairs; petioles channelled; calyx five-cleft; petals five, lanceolate, woolly; racemes erect, terminal; upper flowers male, lower ones female; seeds convex on one side, bluntly angular on the other, enveloped in a thin shell; flowers small, downy, greenish yellow; flowering in hot season; the leaves have a nauseous taste, and the whole tree smells offensively; indigenous, but not common. Seeds are about the size of a grain of coffee [q.v.], oval, rounded, of an imperfectly quadrangular form, with a thin brittle, light-colored shell, containing a yellowish albuminous kernel, enclosing a large leafy embryo; inodorous; taste at first mild, subsequently acrid and pungent. Fatty oil prepared by grinding seed; the oleum crotonis or oleum tiglii of pharmacy; orange yellow color, soluble in alcohol; the active principle of croton oil also exists in the leaves and wood of the plant, but has never yet been obtained thence in a distinct form. Croton seeds and oil are modern introductions in hindoo medicine; they were known in europe in the seventeenth century, but for a long time were not much used in medicine; the revival of their use in english practice in india was due to madras medical officers. The seeds are one of the most drastic purgatives known; ten or twenty seeds have been known to kill a horse [ghorah] by producing violent diarrhœa. A single drop of the oil applied to the tongue is considered sufficient to insure the full results, especially in incipient apoplexy, paralysis of the throat, or difficulty of breathing arising from these causes, even should the patient be insensible at the time; it is also employed in visceral obstruction and occasionally in dropsy; the oil is often adulterated with olive [zeitoon], castor [aumanac], or purging nut oil. The leaves rubbed and soaked in water are also purgative, and when dried and powdered are a good application to snake-bites. Oil externally applied in rheumatism and indolent tumours. If the leaves are chewed they inflame the mouth and lips, and cause them to swell, leaving a burning sensation. The wood which is bitter tasted is gently emetic and powerfully sudorific. Oil now chiefly used in veterinary medicine. Gives to pharm. seeds, crotonis semina, powerful drastic purgative, in over-doses an acronarcotic poison, externally applied stimulant and rubefacient. Wood white and hard.——*Wild jamalgota* (दन्ती - dantí, San.; नेपाळ - népála, Mahr.; حب السلاطين صحرائى - habbusalátíni-sahrái, Ar.; حب السلاطين برى - habbussalátínibarrí, Pers.; جنگلی جمال گوٹہ - janglíjamálgotá, Hind.; جنگلی جمال گھٹہ - janglíjamál-ghuttah, Dec.; ಕಾಡುಹರಳು - káduharalu, Can.; కొండఆముదము - kondaámuda, Tel.; കടലാവണക്ക് - katalávanakku, Mal.; ජයපාල - jápála, Singh.; சீமையாமணக்கு - shímaiyámanakku, Tam.). San. from (danta, san. mountain side); also from seeds like ivory. Mahr. from (népála, san. the country so called). Ar. from (habb, ar. seed + sultán, ar. king + sahrái, ar. wild.). Pers. from (habb, ar. seed + sultán, ar. king + barrí, ar. wild.). Hind. from (janglí, hind. wild + jamálgotá, hind. croton tiglium, linn.). Dec. from hindostany. Can. from (kádu, can. junglo + haralu, can. castor oil seed). Tel. from (konda, tel. hill + ámuda, tel. castor oil tree, ricinus communis, linn.). Mal. from (katal, mal. sea + ávanakku, mal. castor plant), means foreign castor plant. Singh. from (jaya, san. victory + pá, san. to protect). Tam. from (shímai, tam. foreign + ámanakku, tam. castor plant, ricinus communis, linn.). San. also (jayapála), meaning victory + guardian; (népála), meaning produced in nepaul [jamalgota]. Hind. also (jamálghota), meaning croton tree. Tel. also (nélajídi), meaning ground + marking-nut plant, semecarpus anacardium, linn. f.; (erradundiga), meaning red + jatropha glandulifera, roxb.; (adaviámuda), meaning jungle + castor-oil plant; (kanakapáta), meaning gold + cissampelos pareira, linn. Mal. also (shímaávanakku), meaning foreign castor plant; (nága-danti), meaning mountain jamalgota; (nérválam). Tam. also (káttámanakku), meaning wild castor oil plant [wild aumanac]; (nérválam), meaning croton plant; (níradimuttu), meaning water + to strike + pearl; oil from seeds expels serum from body. Title otherwise Foreign castor, Golden pareira, Hydragogue nut, Ivory seed, Lowly marking-nut, Nepaul castor, Red physic nut, Wild castor [aumanac], Wild croton [ghantabeejam], Wild sultan seed. Botanically Baliospermum montanum, muell. euphorbiaceæ [vricsham, 118]. Alias Baliospermum polyandrum; Croton polyandrum, roxburghii; Jatropha montana. Under-shrub; upper leaves lanceolate, acute at the base, lower ones broader, ovate, and often cordate at the base, sinuately toothed or deeply three-lobed, marked with long scattered hairs; inflorescence commonly bisexual, males more loose than the females, and longer peduncled, all shorter than the petioles; fruit bearing pedicels deflexed; sterile bracteoles numerous; segments of the male calyx orbicular-ovate, of the female lanceolate; capsules sub-globose, tridymous, puberulous; seeds smooth, at length marbled, exactly like those of castor oil plant, but much smaller. Roots nearly straight, seldom branched, about as thick as the finger; bark brown, scabrous; wood yellowish-white, soft and tough; the outer layer of the bark consists of several rows of brick-shaped brown cells, mostly empty, but some of them containing a dark reddish-brown resin; within this the parenchyma is so loaded with conglomerate raphides that its structure is with difficulty seen; it has many cells filled with resin as in the suber, and very numerous yellow liber cells; the wood is loaded with starch; the seeds weigh about one and a half grains each, and are exactly similar to very small castor seeds; fixed fat oil expressed from seeds. The seeds are medicinally drastic purgative, in overdoses acronarcotic poison, sometimes substitute for croton tiglium, externally as a stimulant and rubefacient; oil powerful hydragogue cathartic, external application in rheumatism; root cathartic, used in dropsy, anasarca, and jaundice; gives to pharm. seeds and oil, non-officinal [yennay].

JAMALY (జమిలి - dzamali, *Tel.*). From (yamala, san. twin). Two.——*Jamalavoy droog* (జమలవాయిదుర్గము - jamalaváyidur-gamu, Tel.). From (jamali, tel. two + váyi, tel. mouth + durga, san. a hill). Hill, Kistna dist., Vissanapett division; lat. 16° 57′ N.; long. 80° 38′ E.; from Masulipatam N.N.W. 63 miles; from Tirvore S. 11 miles. In Tirvore sub-division. Trig. station in Lat. 16° 57′ 22·17″; long. 80° 38′ 08·19″. Height 1,857 feet.——*Jamdica* (జమలిక - dzamalika, Tel.). From (dzamali, tel. two). A drum [paray], a kind of tabour [sangeetam].

JAMAUDY (جمادى - jamádí, *Hind.*). From (jamad, ar. congealed). Dry month. The fifth and sixth months of Mahomedan year following Rabee [q.v.], distinguished as Jamaudy ool owval, the first, and Jamaudy ool aukhir, the last jamaudy [maheena].——*Jamtee* (पातालगारुडी - pátálagárudí, San.; वासनवेल - vásanavéla, Mahr.; جمتی کی بیل - jamtíkíbel, Hind.; فرید بوٹی کی بیل - farídbútíkíbel, Dec.; ದಾಗಡಿಬಳ್ಳಿ - dágadiballi, Can.; దూసరితీగ - dúsaritíga, Tel.; காட்டுக்கொடி - káttukkodi, Tam.). Title from hindostany. San. from (pátála, san. nether world + gárudí, san. relating to garuda). Mahr. from (vásana, mahr. perfume + véla, mahr. creeper). Hind. from (jamtí, hind. coagulating + bel, hind. creeper), from property of leaves [indian willow]. Dec. from (farid, ar. name of saint + búti, hind. plant + bel, hind. creeper); from his having lived on water rendered mucilaginous by the leaves shaken in it [elephant nerinjy]. Can. from (dágu, can. screened + balli, can. creeper). Tam. from (kádu, tam. forest + kodi, tam. creeper). San. also (vásantitiktá), meaning fragrant bitter plant. Can. also (dúsari); (yadániballi); (sugadigida). Tel. also (chípurutíga), meaning broom + creeper; (katletiga), meaning stick + creeper. Title otherwise Broom creeper, Fareed's creeper, Fragrant creeper, Ink berry, Ink creeper. Botanically Cocculus [vausanavully] villosus, dec., menispermaceæ [vricsham, 5]. Alias Cocculus hastatus, sepium; Menispermum hirsutum, myosotoides, villosum. Twining shrub; leaves on old branches, cordate-orbicular or hastate, three-lobed, obtuse or retuse, mucronulate; on young shoots oblong, cordate or acute at the base, more or less downy; petals about equal to the filaments; racemes axillary, not half the length of the leaves, of male flowers branched and corymbose, of female simple and one to three flowered; nuts of the drupe reniform, compressed; flowers small, greenish; flowering in the rainy season. Root very crooked and twisted upon itself, keeled, seldom branched, but giving off a few thin fibrous rootlets; external surface light brown, nearly smooth, transverse section pale yellow, marked with radiating darker yellow lines; odour peculiar, acrid; taste disagreeable and bitter. Water rendered thick and mucilaginous by agitating briskly the fresh leaves, and sweetened with sugar, is a cool drink; powder of dry leaves mixed with water and sugar [q.v.] has same properties. Dose; of mucilage, from four to eight ounces; of powdered leaves, from one to two drachms. Substituted for pareira brava, sarsaparilla and copaiba. A decoction of fresh root with pepper [q.v.] and goat's [vellaud] milk is given in rheumatism, laxative and sudorific. Natives make curry [q.v.] of leaves. Juice of ripe berries makes a good durable, bluish-purple ink [mashy].

JAMAUL (جمال - jamál, *Ar.*). From (jamala, ar. to become beautiful). Mahomedan common alam; as Jamaul bee, alam + alaumat [ism].——*Jemalabad* (جمال آباد - jamálábád, Hind.). From (jamál, ar. name of tippoo sultan's mother + ábád, pers. city). Can. name (gadekallu), meaning fort + rock. Ancient name (narasimhangadi), meaning narsimhan, proper name + shop. Village; South canara dist., Ooppinangady tal.; lat. 13° 01′; long. 75° 21′; from Beltangady N. 3 miles; from Mangalore E.N.E. 33 miles; from Poottore N.N.E. 19 miles. Founded by Tippoo on site of a ruined city called Narsimhangady. Destroyed by the Coorg rajah in 1799. Many Mussalmans in neighbouring village.

JAMKHANA (جمخانه - jamkhánah, *Hind.*). Cotton carpet [satranjee]; generally in blue and white or red and white stripes. Woollen carpet is cumbly [q.v.].

JAN (जन् - jan, *San.*). To be born.——*Ja* (जा - já, San.). From (jan, san. to be born); produced. Suffix. Especially plant second term, showing natural characteristic, the place of growth, &c. Ex., where transl. is of first term:—Anthocephalus cadamba (nadíja), river; Holarrhena antidysenterica (kutajá), curled; Mollugo spergula (gríshmajá), summer; Nelumbium speciosum (ambujá), water, (jalajá), water, (sarójá) tank; Piper nigrum (véllaja), sea coast; Pterocarpus santalinus (malayaja), malayam mountain; Solanum xanthocarpum (kshétrajá), field; Zingiber officinale (nagarajá), town. See gloss. paragraphs.——*Janacan* (जनक - janaka, San.). A progenitor. The father of Seetay [q.v.] the wife of Ramchendran [q.v.].——*Janacaran* (జనకరుడు - janakarudu, Tel.). From (jana, san. people + kara, san. maker). Creator. Hindoo 2nd or pers. name [peyar].——*Janam* (जन - jana, San.). From (jan, san. to be born). People. ——*Jana padam* (जनपद - janapada, San.). From (jana, san. people + pada, san. place). A community or nation. Also an inhabited region, as graumam [q.v.] or naud [q.v.].——*Janardanan* (జనార్దనుడు - janárdanudu, Tel.). From (jana, san. people + ard, san. to agitate). Krishnan [q.v.], the people-agitator. Hindoo 2nd or pers. name. Common among Madhwas [peyar].——*Janavinodiny* (जनविनोदिनी - janavinódiní, San.). From (jana, san. people + vinódiní, san. that which entertains). Vernacular newspaper. Tamul edition first published 1870, Teloogoo 1874.——*Juntoo* (जन्तु - jantu, San.). From (jan, san. to be born). The most general term for an animal. Faura of a region [desham].—"*a*" For category, see Padaurtam; for elementary substance, see Dravyam; for matter see Bhootam; for organic and inorganic, see Indriyam and Anindriyam; for organic kingdom, see Ganam; for organic class, see Vargam; for organic order, see Santaunam; for organic family, see Coolam; for organic genus, see Jauty; for organic species, see Bhaidam.—"*b*" The kingdom [ganam] of animals [jantoo] is divided into two sub-kingdoms [oopaganam] of invertebrata [nirvamshyam] and vertebrata [vamshyam]. The invertebrata [nirvamshyam] sub-kingdom [oopaganam] includes the classes [vargam] giving the lower forms of animal life. Such as in ascending scale; Sponges [mocabandal], Corals [moongah], Star-fishes [taurah matsyam], Worms [poochy, keerah], Centipedes [kankhajoor], Spiders [makree], Crustaceans [kavachiny], Insects [poochy], Molluscs [chippy]. The vertebrata [vamshyam] sub-kingdom [oopaganam] includes in ascending scale the classes [vargam] of Fishes [matsyam], Batrachians [bhaicam], Reptiles [sarpy], Birds [pacshy], and Mammals [sastanam].—"*c*" A general conspectus of the Fauna of Southern india was given in vol. II, Appendix IV.—"*d*" Compare Vricsham for plants or flora, and Dhautoo for minerals.——*Jaun* (جان - ján, Hind.). Life. Part of lacab; as Jaun bauz jung, intrepid in war [ism.].——*Jaunaky* (சானகி - shánagi, Tam.). Seetay [q.v.], daughter of the king Janacan [q.v.]. Proper name common to both sexes. As a feminine name it is shortened into Shaunoo, Shauny [peyar]. Counterfeit jaunaky is the same as River blatty.——*Jaunee* (جانی - jání, Hind.). In composition makes a lacab; as Jaunee begum, dear lady [ism]. ——*Jaunoo* (جانو - jánú, Hind.). In composition makes a lacab; as Jaunoo miynuu, dear lord [ism].——*Jautacam* (जातक - játaka, San.). Fróm (jan, san. to be born). Astrology applied to nativities [varauha mihiran].——*Jautikye* (சாதிக்காய் - sháthikkáy, Tam.). From (játí, san. nutmeg, myristica fragrans, houtt. + káy, tam. fruit). Nutmeg or nut of myristica fragrans, houtt. [common nutmeg].——*Jauty* (जाति - játi, San.). From (jan, san. to be born). Greek γένος; Latin gens.—"*a*" Originally race. Jauty bhaidam means the distinctions of race. Varnam, an older word used by the Sanscrit writers, originally meant a difference in color. Gradually these two words, jauty and varnam, came to represent not only varieties of race and color, but also numerous original, hereditary, religious, instituted and conventional distinctions; otherwise Caste. The Portuguese word casta, meaning race or quality, was first applied by the Portuguese, when they arrived, to designate the peculiar system of religious and social distinctions which they observed on the west coast. Thus, Camoens:—"A lei da gente toda, rica, e "pobre de fabulas composta se imagina: andam nús, e sómente "hum panno cobre as partes, quea cobrir natura ensina: dous "modos ha de gente; porque a nobre Naires chamados são; e a "menos dina Poleás tem por nome; a quem obriga alei não "misturar a casta antiqua." As stereotyped under Braminical authority, the word jauty is now applied to the distinctions of birth, tribe and occupation, which separate the Hindoos, and preclude their eating, drinking and smoking together; their using the same vessels; their intermarrying; and then reciprocating other relations of social life. The authority of caste rests partly on written laws, partly on legendary fables and narratives, partly on verbal tradition, partly on the injunctions of instructors and priests, and partly on usage.—"*b*" Bramha [q.v.], according to the mythology, produced the Bramins [q.v.] from his mouth, to pray, to read, to instruct; the Cshatriyas [q.v.] from his arms, to draw the bow, to fight, to govern; the Veisyas [q.v.] from his belly or thighs, to nourish, to provide the necessaries of life by agriculture and commerce; the Shoodras [q.v.] from his feet, for subjection, to serve, to labour, to travel. These four higher castes are in Tamul:—Vediyar, bramins; Munnar, cshatriyas; Veisyar, veisyas; and Oozhavar, shoodras. Another division of seven castes is into Bramin, Cshatriya, Veisya, Shoodra, Anooloma [q.v.] or the offspring of a bramin father and cshatriya mother, Pratiloma or that of a cshatriya father and bramin mother, and Sankara or a mixed class of the first four tribes.—"*c*" There is no indigenous word in any dravidian language to signify caste. The dravidians are naturally attached to tribal institutions, and opposed to caste institutions. The last sootram [q.v.] in the Nunnool [q.v.] is as follows:—பழையன கழிதலும் புதியன புகுதலும் வழுவல கால வகையி னானே.—"Lapsing of old and appearance "of new is no error but happens on change of times." There is a Tamul proverb:—கன்மத்தினாற் சாதியன்றிச் சென்மத்தினால் இல்லை—"Caste arises from action [carmam], it is "not from birth [jenmam]." The Tamul cooral [q.v.] has the following:—மழித்தலும் நீட்டலும் வேண்டா உலகம் பழித்தது ஒழித்து விடின்—"There is no need of a shaven "crown, nor of tangled hair, if the world abstain from those "deeds which the wise have condemned."—குடியென்னுங் குன்றா விளக்க மடியென்னு மாசூர மாய்ந்து கெடும்.—"By the darkness of idleness, the indestructible lamp of caste "rank will be extinguished." The following is an apothegm of Sarwanyan:—ಜಾತಿಹೀನರ ಮನೆಯ ಜ್ಯೋತಿ ತಾ ಹೀನವೇ—ಜಾತಿ ವಿಜಾತಿಯನ ಬೇಡ—ದೇವ ವಲಿದಾತನೇ ಜಾತ ಸರ್ವಜ್ಞ—"Is the fire of a man's "hearth polluted, because he is low born? Do not observe "caste distinctions. He is of the best caste, who has won "God's favor."—"*d*" Non-bramin castes are divided popularly into high or low. They are also right-hand and left-hand; this last distinction represents the agricultural classes on the one side and the artizans, &c., on the other [yidangay].—"*e*" The following are the principal Tamul castes; each can be seen under its own head:—Agambadiyaur, Ambalacauran, Ambattan, Berichetty, Bramin, Caraiyaur, Chuckler, Collan, Coorumba, Coosava, Corava, Culla, Cull tutcha, Cummaula, Cunnaura, Devadausy, Eelavaca, Iroola, Kanakan, Keikkila, Mailacaur, Marava, Ooppilya, Padiyautchy, Pariah, Pulla, Pully, Pundaura, Shauliya, Shaunaur, Sheniya, Shreeveishnava, Tattaur, Tautha, Tutcha, Vauniya, Vellaula, Vulloova, Vunnaur and Yiday.—"*f*" The following are the principal Teloogoo castes; each can be seen under its own head:—Aradhyan, Audapaupa, Balije, Besta, Bhogam, Boy, Bramin, Caupoo, Causalnauty, Chentsoo, Comaty, Coommara, Cumbala, Dausary, Gaundla, Golla, Gowndla, Janapa, Jendra, Jetty, Jogy, Maidary, Maudiga, Maula, Moorkinauty, Mootraucha, Mungala, Niyogy, Pauknauty, Rauz, Saucala, Sauley, Sautauny, Telagaunya, Velama, Velnauty, Wodda, Yanaudy, Yeediga and Yerkala.—"*g*" The following are the principal Canarese castes; each can be seen under its own head:—Acasauly, Agasa, Badaga, Badagy, Banajiga, Basavy, Beyda, Billawa, Bramin, Bunt, Coorooba, Coraga, Cullwodda, Gauniga, Haleypeik, Haslar, Haurwa, Hebbaura, Holeya, Jeyda, Julgar, Lingayet, Madhwa, Malaicoody, Maudiga, Okkaliga, Ooppaura and Tooloova.—"*h*" The following are the principal Malayalam castes; each can be seen under its own head:—Agapodwaul, Ambalavausy, Bramin, Chaukyaun, Cherman, Covil tumbooraun, Elíad, Ilava, Irava, Malaiyarasa, Moocwa, Mooshaury, Moossad, Moottad, Nayar, Nayaudy, Numboory, Oorauly, Paniyan, Poolaya, Teeyar and Teeyaudy.—"*i*" The following are other castes; each can be seen under its own head:—Arab, Beiraugy, Bondily, Boodboodikey, Brinjarry, Concany, Deshasta, Dombar, Doodey coolam, Gond, Gosain, Goozeratty, Khond, Lohauro, Lubbay, Lumbaudy, Mahratta, Marwarry, Moplah, Ooriya, Pindarry, Putnool, Rajpoot, Soogauly, Sowrah and Todah.—"*j*" For race, see vol. I (30) to (38), and the following foot-notes, &c.:—scientific localization I (30), south indian race movements I (33), hæckel's gen. synopsis, II, 221.—"*k*" For hindoo caste, see vol. I (61) to (70), and the following footnotes:—history of caste I (61), abbé dubois opinion I (64), punchaular I (67); groups of castes II, 225, hindoo proper names II, 239.—"*l*" In composition Jauty denotes superiority or excellence. Jauticauran is a person of good caste, of unmixed descent; commonly applied to a genuine european as distinguished from Parangicauran or east indian and Shattaicauran or eurasian. Jauty adee is the english foot measure.—"*m*" In natural history Jauty is a genus. For category, see Padaurtam; for elementary substance, see Dravyam; for matter, see Bhootam; for organic and inorganic, see Indriyam and Anindriyam; for organic kingdom, see Ganam [jantoo, vricsham]; for organic class, see Vargam; for organic order, see Santaunam; for organic family, see Coolam; for organic genus, see present head; for organic species, see Bhaidam. Oopa prefixed to either of the above means a sub-head. For inorganic minerals, see Dhautoo.——*Jauty* (जाति - játi, San.). Nutmeg; see sep. title.——*Jauty patry* (जातीपत्री - játípattrí, San.). From (játí, san. nutmeg, myristica fragrans, houtt. + pattri, san. leaf). Mace or pulp of myristica fragrans, houtt. [common nutmeg].——*Jenm* (जन्म - janma, San.; ജന്മം - janmam, Mal.). Means birth. Hereditary freehold proprietorship [cawny, mirass], the Sanscrit form of the Malayalam pair [q.v.]. Jenm property is the highest of Malabar tenures, and corresponds to English fee-simple. It may be sold or mortgaged in various ways, and the right to it passes by descent according to law. It can be left to strangers by will only on failure of heirs; if there be no heirs, nor disposal by bequest, it escheats to the rajah. It cannot be sold without the concurrence of the heir at law. The term is applicable to other than individuals, as there may be the jenm lands of a college [sangham] or temple [coil]. For the transfer of property whereby jenm gradually changes hands, see the theoretical system under Caranam, and the more practical system at vol. II, 104. Compare vol. I, 112, 114; II, 289.——*Jenma bhogam* (ജന്മഭോഗം -

janmabhógam, Mal.). From (janma, san. birth + bhuj, san. to eat). The Jenmy's share.——*Jenma coodiyaun* (ജന്മക്കുടിയാൻ - janmakkutiyán, Mal.). From (janma, san. birth + kutiyán, mal. tenant). The modern Jenmy, who has acquired his property by purchase, in contradistinction to the ancient or hereditary Jenmy.——*Jenma lagnam* (जन्मलग्न - janmalagna, San.). From (janma, san. birth + lagna, san. time). The point of the ecliptic [craunty mundalam] which is on the horizon [cshitijam] at the moment of the birth of a child. See Lagnam.——*Jenmam* (जन्म - janma, San.). From (jan, san. to be born). Birth whether past, present or future; transmigration [samsauram].——*Jenma puttricay* (जन्मपत्रिका - janmapatriká, San.). From (janma, san. birth + patrika, san. letter). Horoscope; or record showing year, lunar day [tity] and the aspects and relative positions of other planets [graham] in the heavens [golam] at the moment of one's birth; also the tablet of fortunes through life composed from these particulars. A man's star is with the Hindoos the lunar constellation in which the moon is found at the moment of his birth; many other accessories are added thereto.——*Jenmauntram* (जन्मान्तर - janmántara, San.). From (janma, san. birth + antara, san. different). Transmigration, prior or posterior [samsauram].——*Jenmcaur* (ജന്മക്കാരൻ - janmakkáran, Mal.). From (janma, san. birth + kár, mal. owner, suffix). Same as Jenmy.——*Jenmpanayam* (ജന്മപ്പണയം - janmappanayam, Mal.). From (janma, san. birth + panayam, mal. mortgage). Sanscrit term for Coodimaneer [q.v.] and Neermoothal [q.v.]. The last mortgage [panayam] before loss of jenm [otty].——*Jenmy* (ജന്മി - janmi, Mal.). The hereditary proprietor.——*Jenmy peimash* (ജന്മിപ്പൈമാശി - janmippaimáshi, Mal.). From (janmi, mal. proprietor of land + paimáish, pers. measure). In M.E. 981, every proprietor of land was called upon to furnish under his signature a detailed account of his landed property. The statements so obtained are known as jenmy peimash and were the basis of the kole peimash [q.v.] of M.E. 983.——*Jinjal* (جنجال - janjál, Hind.; జజాలి - jajáli, Tel.). From (jan, hind. man + jál, hind. net). A small piece of ordnance mounted on a swivel.

JANAPA (జనప - dzanapa, *Tel.*). From (dzanumu, tel. hemp). The flax-dresser caste. Gunny-weavers. Numbers about 15,000 [jauty].

JANAUB (جناب - janáb, *Hind.*). From (janb, ar. side); the people are a side and the prince is a side. Majesty. Used as a respectful term of address to a person of rank and office whether native or european.

JANAUZA (جنازه - janázah, *Hind.*). From (janaza, ar. to gather up). Funeral among Mahomedans. When a Mahomedan is about to expire, the creed and a particular chapter of the koran [q.v.] are read aloud. The moment the spirit departs, the mouth is closed, the toes are brought together and fastened with a thin slip of cloth, and incense [ood] is kept burning. The body is then washed [ghassaul], and wrapped in a winding sheet of calico [q.v.], and powdered camphor [q.v.] is rubbed on the hands, feet, &c. The body is then placed in a box or on a cot [q.v.] and carried on the shoulders of four persons to the mosque [musjid], where the funeral service is read. Those wishing to depart do so then, and the rest proceed to the grave. The corpse is then placed on its back in the grave with the head to the north and feet to the south, the face being turned towards Mecca. Those present take a clod of earth, and repeating the words 'we created you of earth, and return you to earth,' lay it in the grave. After the grave is closed, it is usual to pour a pot of water over it and to plant a twig of the pomegranate [anaur] tree. Then fautihas [q.v.] are offered for the deceased; and later, at a distance of a 40 yards, for all the dead in that burying-ground. Alms are distributed. On the third day the grave is visited in the morning by friends and relations of the deceased, portions of the koran are recited for the benefit of the departed, and alms are distributed [ziyaurat]. On the tenth, twentieth, and fortieth days food is distributed to the poor in the name of the deceased. During the days of mourning the relatives abstain from wearing any new dress [shaudy]. Cf. Hindoo shavacaud.

JANDIRAM (జందియము - dzandiyamu, *Tel.*). Short for (dzannamu, tel. sacrifice + dáramu, tel. thread). The sacred thread [janivaura, jaunwah] of the twice-born [dwijan]; see Poonool and Yanyopaveetam.

JANGADA (ചങ്ങാടം - channátam, *Mal.*). From (samghat, san. to unite). Raft; same as Jungar.

JANIVAURA (ಜನಿವಾರ - janivára, *Can.*). From (janna, can. sacrifice + dára, can. thread). The sacred thread [jandiram, jaunwah] of the twiceborn [dwijan]; see Poonool.

JANNAT (جنت - jannat, *Hind.*). From (janna, ar. to conceal). Garden of trees which by their branches conceal the ground beneath. Heaven [bheest].

JAPAM (जप - japa, *San.*; ஜெபம் - shebam, *Tam.*). From (jap, san. to mutter). Muttering prayers, repeating inaudibly passages from the vedas [q.v.], incantation [muntram].——*Jasoon* (جاسون - jásún, Hind.). From (javásuma, san. shoe flower). Same as China rose bendy.

JAPAN (جاپان - japán, *Hind.*; சப்பங்கி - shappangi, *Tam.*). Means sun-origin-kingdom; so called by the chinese. An empire consisting of four larger and many smaller islands to the east of Asia. Plant first term. Compare:— Cinnamomum camphora, japan camphor plant; Cydonia vulgaris, japan quince; Diospyros kauki, japan date plum; Eriobotrya japonica, japan medlar Rhus succedanea, japan varnish; Vigna catiang, japan lablab. See gloss. paragraphs.

JARADA (జరడ - jarada, *Tel.*). Ancient zemindarry, Village; Ganjam dist., pop. 6,884; square miles 48; lat. of village 19° 05′; long. 84° 33′; from Berhampore S.W. 24 miles; from Chetterpore W.S.W. 38 miles. Small zemindarry [q.v.] adjoining Soorangy and south-west of Cheekaty. Founded in A.D. 1440 by Veerabhadra sing, son of Vishwambhara sing roya toorye, the possessor of a large tract of country in the Mahendram [mahendragherry] maliahs [q.v.]. Hilly but tolerably well watered by small stream that falls into the Bauhoodah. Contains 29 villages. Peshcush [q.v.] Rs. 2,025.

JARALLEA (జాలారి - dzálári, *Tel.*). Specific name from vernacular. Same as Taloora saul.

JARAT (जरत् - jarat, *San.*). From (jrí, san. to grow old). Old.——*Jauradgavam* (जारद्गव - járadgava, San.). From (above + gau, san. cow). The southern avastaunam [q.v.] or one-third path [cacsham] of the sun and moon [eirauvatam, veishwaunary].

JAREEB (جريب - jaríb, *Hind.*). From arabic. A measuring rope. Before Acbar's time it was a simple rope. He directed that it should be made of bamboo [q.v.] with iron joints, as the rope was in itself very imperfect, and also subject to the weather. Europeans have introduced the chain. As a linear measure 60 guz or yards = 1 jareeb [alavay, 1c]. Approximate actual value, 1 jareeb = 55 yards. Compare Puggum. Jareebdar is a surveyor.

JARY (ಜರಿ - jari, *Can.*). From (járu, can. to slide). Precipice.——*Jarimaley* (ಜರಿಮಲೆ - jarimale, Can.). From (jari, can. a precipice + male, can. a hill). Village; Bellary dist., Coodligy tal., pop. 960; acres 6,187; lat. 14° 49′; long. 76° 31′; from Bellary S.W. 37 miles; from Coodligy S.E. 9 miles. Formerly seat of a poligar [q.v.], descended from Penappa naick. The founder of the family received two jagheers [q.v.] from Atchoota royel of vijianugger. These were attacked at various times by Aurungzeeb and the Rajahs of Beejapore, and in 1752 by the Poligar of Chitaldroog. In 1767 the poligar appealing to Hyder for aid, was put to death by the Poligar of Chitaldroog. His son was afterwards reinstated by Hyder. Tippoo resumed the whole district in 1787. The poligar regained possession in 1791, but was expelled again. When Jarimaley was ceded to the Nizam [q.v.] in 1799, the poligar was allowed to rent the district at its full value. Soon after he fell into arrears and fled to Mysore, where he died. In 1801 the country fell under the dominion of the British, a pension being granted to the members of the ruling family for their support. Their family is now extinct. Jarimaley trig. station is in lat. 14° 49′ 07·57″; long. 76° 31′ 42·65″; height 2,743 feet; from Bellary S.W. 36 miles; from Coodligy S.E. 9 miles; from Jarimaley village E.N.E. ¾ mile.

JAS (कांस्य - kámsya, *San.*; جست - jast, *Hind*; جس - jas, *Dec.*; ಸತ್ತು - sattu, *Can.*; సత్తు - sattu, *Tel.*; വെള്ളീയം - vellíyam, *Mal.*; வெள்ளீயம் - vellíyam, *Tam.*). Title from deccany. San. from (kamsa, san. copper) [cumsam, cunts]; from copper as an alloy. Tel. means essence. Tam. from (vel, tam. white + íyam, tam. lead). Tam. also (kallíyam), meaning stone + lead, a hard variety [culleeyam]. Pewter [tagaram].

JASMINE (मल्लि - malli, *San.*; ياسمين - yásamín, *Ar.*; ಮಲ್ಲಿಗೆ - mallige, *Can.*; మల్లె - malle, *Tel.*; മുല്ല - mulla, *Mal.*, සමන් - saman, *Singh*; மல்லி - malli, *Tam.*). Title from arabic. San. from (mall, san. to hold); from use as garlands. Botanically the Jasminum genus, oleaceæ [vricsham, 85]. Shrubs or climbers, natives of warmer regions; leaves pinnate; flowers white or yellow, and scented; propagated by cuttings. The species best known to the natives are shown below. Other s. indian species indigenous or naturalized are:—brevilobum, calophyllum, cordifolium, flexile, malabaricum, rigidum, trichotomum. In anglo-indian usage the term jasmine includes also:—Ægle marmelos, Boerhaavia repens, Gomphrena globosa, Gynocardia odorata, Hemidesmus indicus, Ipomæa quamoclit, Millingtonia hortensis, Mirabilis jalapa, Nyctanthes arbortristis, Polygonum tomentosum, Quisqualis indica, Randia uliginosa, Rhinacanthus communis, Tabernæmontana coronaria, Tagetes sp.——*Arabian jasmine* (मल्लिका - malliká, San.; मोगरा - mógará, Mahr.; मोग्रयाझाड - mógrayájháda, Conc.; ياسمين - yásamín, Ar.; شجرگل سپید - shajarigulisupíd, Pers.; موگرے کا پیڑ - mogrekáper, Hind.; موگرے کا جھاڑ - mogrekájhár, Dec.; ಏಳುಸುತ್ತಿನಮಲ್ಲಿಗೆಗಿಡ - élusuttinamalligegida, Can.; ಮಲ್ಲಿಗೆದ್ಯೆ - malligedai, Too.; మల్లె -

malle, Tel.; മുല്ല - mulla, Mal.; පිච්ච - piçça, Singh.; மல்லிகை - malligai, Tam.). San. from (mall, san. to hold), from the garland made of this flower being extensively used. Mahr. from (mudgara, san. the jasmine). Pers. from (shajar, pers. tree + gul, pers. rose + supíd, hind. white); cf. indian white rose. Hind. from (mográ, hind. jasmine + per, hind. tree). Dec. from (mográ, hind. jasmine + jhár, hind. tree). Can. from (élu, can. seven + suttu, can. turn + mallige, can. jasmine + gida, can. plant). Tel. from sanscrit. Mal. from sanscrit. Tam. from sanscrit. San. also (anangá), meaning relating to cupid; (bhúpadí), meaning earth fixed; (kaushiká), meaning relating to cooshican [indian bdellium]; (trinashákhya), meaning grass + branch; (várshikí), meaning annual; (ásp'hótá), meaning slightly blossoming [wild jasmine, yercum]; (shítabhíru), meaning cold-fearing; flowers in summer. Ar. also (saman); (vardiabyaz), meaning white rose [indian white rose]; (zambak), meaning white lily. Pers. also (zambak), meaning white lily; (champa), meaning michelia champaca, linn., from similar odour. Hind. also (bela), meaning creeper jasmine; (motiyá), meaning pearl-shaped; (banmallika), meaning forest + jasmine; (batmográ), meaning double-flowered variety; (hazáramográ), meaning double-flowered. Can. also (dundumalligegida), meaning round + jasmine + plant; (iruvantige), meaning two-rowed; double-flowered. Tel. also (bondumalle), meaning round + the plant; (gundumalle), meaning round + the plant; (boddumalle), meaning round jasmine; (manmat'habánamu), meaning cupid + arrow [jungle geranium]; (viradzáji), meaning double jasmine. Mal. also (kutamulla), meaning umbrella jasmine, from the large flowers; (cherupiççakam), meaning small + the plant, jasminum grandiflorum, linn.; (nallamulla), meaning good jasmine; (chírakamulla), meaning cuminum cyminum, linn. + jasmine. Singh. also (bhúnimanda), meaning earth + ornament; (desaman). Tam. also (kudamalligai), meaning pot + jasmine; (iruvádi); (iruvádchi), meaning double petalled; (karumugai), meaning black + opening bud; (pérámalligai), meaning large jasmine. Title otherwise Lily jasmine, Mogara jasmine, Sambac jasmine. Botanically Jasminum sambac, ait., oleaceæ [vricsham, 85]. Specific name from arabic. Alias Jasminum fragrans, plenum; Mogorium sambac; Nyctanthes sambac. Mogorium from mahratta. Dwarf-spreading under-shrub; ash-colored branches; leaves opposite, cordate, ovate or oblong, waved, sometimes scolloped, pointed, smooth, downy on the veins on the under side; calyx segments five to nine; flowers terminal, generally in small trichotomus umbellets, white; flowering in the hot season. Flower religious to vishnoo [q.v.]. The leaves if boiled in oil exude a balsam [q.v.] used for anointing the head in eye complaints; an oil is also expressed from the root, used medicinally. Flower gives mahomedan perfume [attar]. There are two varieties; single-flowered and double-flowered.——*Black jasmine* (नीलमल्लिका - nílamalliká, San.). From greenish flowers. Same as Bael. ——*Cat's jasmine* (ಬೆಕ್ಕಿನಅಜ್ಜೆಬಳ್ಳಿ - bekkinaajjeballi, Can.). Same as Tikry.——*Common jasmine* (जाती - játí, San.; चमेली - chamélí, Mahr.; जायचेमोग्रे - jáychémógré, Conc.; ياسمين - yásamín, Ar. and Pers.; چنبیلی - chambelí, Hind. and Dec.; ಜಾಜಿಮಲ್ಲಿಗೆ - jájimallige, Can.; ಜಾಜಿಪೂ - jájipú, Too.; జాజి - dzáji, Tel.; പിച്ചകം - piççakam, Mal.; සමන්පිච්ච - samanpiçça, Singh.; பிச்சி - piççi, Tam.). San. from (jan, san. to be born) [common nutmeg]; meaning well born and so useful. Conc. means jaujy jasmine. Can. from (játi, can. high caste + mallige, can. jasminum sambac, ait.); from good smell. Tel. from sanscrit. Mal. from (piççu, mal. madness + akam, mal. inside). Singh. from (saman, singh. generic name of jasmine + piçça, sing. jasminum sambac, ait.). San. also (málatí), meaning holding fragrance [madablota, wild jasmine, wild nutmeg]. Mahr. also (jái), from sanscrit. Hind. also (játi) from sanscrit. Tel. also (dzádi); (adavimalle), meaning jungle + jasmine. Mal. also (piççakamulla). Tam. also (sháthimalligai), meaning superior jasmine; (kodimalligai), meaning creeper + jasmine; (padarmalligai), meaning to spread + jasmine. Title otherwise Catalonian jasmine, Chambalee, Jaujy, Jauty, Large flowered jasmine, Spanish jasmine. Botanically Jasminum grandiflorum, linn., oleaceæ [vricsham, 85]. Shrub with pinnate foliage, the leaflets less than an inch long; in blossom during both the hot and rainy seasons with middling-sized, white, fragrant flowers; most fragrant species of the genus, and is very generally cultivated; flowers used in garlands on all festive occasions; flowers retain their odour when dried; yields the true essential oil [attar] of jasmine.——*Coral jasmine* (शेफालिका - shép'háliká, San.; पारिजात - párijáta, Mahr.; पारिजातक - párijátaka, Conc.; ھرسنگار - harsingár, Hind.; کیسر - kesar, Dec.; ಪಾರಿಜಾತ - párijáta, Can.; ಪಾರಿಜಾತ - párijáta, Too.; పారిజాతము - párijátamu, Tel.; ଗଙ୍ଗୋ - gongo, Oor.; മഞ്ഞപ്പൂമരം - maññappúmaram, Mal.; සේපාල - sépála, Singh.; பவழமல்லிகை - pavazhamalligai, Tam.). Title from color of flower stalks. San. from (shép'ha, san. sleeping + ali, san. beetle); from fragrant flowers attracting beetles. Mahr. from (pári, san. water + jan, san. to be born); from a tradition of its origin from the ocean [coormam]. Conc. from mahratta. Hind. from (hára, san. garland + shringára, san. beauty). Dec. from (káshmíraja, san. saffron, crocus sativus, linn.); from color of flower tube. Can., &c., from sanscrit like mahratta. Mal. from (maňña, mal. yellow + pú, mal. flower + maram, mal. tree); from orange tube of flowers. Singh. from sanscrit. Tam. from (pravála, san. coral + malliká, san. jasminum sambac, ait.). San. also (párijáta), meaning sea-born, that is celestial [common coral tree]. Hind. also (kesarkáphúl), meaning saffron flower. Can. also (hursing), from hindostany. Tel. also (pagadamalle), meaning coral + jasmine; (krishnavénichettu); (shvétasurasa), meaning white notchy, vitex negundo, linn. [notchy]; (káruchíya); (kirsáru), by gonds. Oor. also (seoli), corruption from sanscrit. Tam. also (shútham), meaning mangifera indica, linn.; perhaps from mango smell of flower; (maňjalbúççedi), meaning yellow flower plant. Title otherwise Beetle's love, Harsingar, Indian mourner, Mango jasmine, Night jasmine, Sad-tree, Sorrowful nyctanthes, Sorrowful tree, Square-stalked nyctanthes, Weeping nyctanthes, White negundo, Yellow flower tree. Botanically Nyctanthes arbortristis, linn., oleaceæ [vricsham, 85]. Alias Nyctanthes pariatica; Parilium arbortristis; Scabrita scabra, triflora. Tree, 15–20 feet, young shoots four sided; leaves opposite, short-petioled, cordate or oblong, pointed, entire or coarsely serrate, scabrous; panicles terminal, composed of smaller six-flowered terminal umbellets; calyx campanulate, slightly five-notched, downy; corolla tube cylindric, as long as the calyx, segments five to seven; involucel of four inverse-cordate, opposite, sessile leaflets; flowers numerous; tube orange-colored; border white, fragrant; flowering nearly all year; cultivated in gardens and near temples; the flowers are fragrant during night only; at sunset they open, and before morning ground is covered with fallen corollas. The fruit is a dry, flat, oblong, mucronate capsule, prominently veined, ¾ inch long by ½ inch broad; it is of a brown color when ripe, and is divided into two cells, each of which contains a flat foliaceous seed of a light brown color; the testa of the seed is thin, the kernel white, bitter and very astringent; the leaves have similar properties, and stain the saliva when chewed. Flower religious. Fresh juice of leaves given with honey [shahad] in chronic fever; decoction of leaves specific for sciatica; powdered seeds for scurfy affections of the scalp; antibilious and expectorant. Native women wear corollas as necklaces [maulay], or twine them in hair; bark yields tanning substances [chamrah]; orange tubes of the flowers dye a fine buff or orange color, sometimes used in combination with turmeric [country saffron], not fast color [shauyam]; an essential oil [attar] from flowers. Wood brown, close-grained, used for fuel.——*Creeper jasmine* (கொடிமல்லிகை - kodimalligai, Tam.). Same as Common jasmine. ——*Divine jasmine* (దేవతామల్లె - dévatámalle, Tel.). From white fragrant flowers. Same as Gray emetic nut.——*Double flowered jasmine* (இருவாட்சி - iruvádchi, Tam.). Meaning double petalled. Same as Arabian jasmine.——*Evening jasmine* (அந்திமல்லிகை - andimalligai, Tam.). From bearing jasmine-like flowers in the evening. Same as False jalap.——*Everlasting jasmine* (வாடாமல்லிகை - vádámalligai, Tam.). From unchanging color. Same as Jaffer goondy.——*Golden jasmine* (हेमपुष्पिका - hémapushpiká, San.; कुसर - kusara, Mahr.; పచ్చఅడవిమొల్ల - pattsaadavimolla, Tel.; പൊന്മല്ലിക - ponmallika, Mal.). Title from flowers. San. from (héma, san. gold + pushpa, san. 'flower), from bright yellow flowers. Tel. from (pattsa, tel. yellow + adavimolla, tel. jasminum auriculatum, vahl.). Mal. from (pon, mal. gold + mallika, mal. jasmine). San. also (suvarnayút'hiká), meaning gold + jasminum auriculatum, vahl. Title otherwise Italian jasmine, Lowly jasmine, Nepaul jasmine, Yellow jasmine. Botanically Jasminum humile, linn., oleaceæ [vricsham, 85]. Alias Jasminum bignoniaceum, chrysanthemum, revolutum, revolutum, var. peninsulare. Erect, not scandent; leaves alternate, pinnated; branches angled; leaflets three, five, seven, eleven-obovate, oblong, narrowed at the base, subacute at the apex; panicles terminal, opposite the leaves, corymbose; calyx acute and acutely denticulate; flowers few, yellow, fragrant; flowering all the year. A stout shrub, from 8–12 feet high, with stems as thick as a man's leg, and foliage of dark green unequally pinnate leaves, bears corymbs of ten to twenty large flowers. Useful in ringworm; wood white, moderately hard, even-grained.——*Large jasmine* (నాగమల్లె - nágamalle, Tel.). Title from size of flowers. Tel. from (nága, tel. large + malle, tel. jasmine). Tel. also (adavimalle), meaning jungle + jasmine. Title otherwise Broad-leaved jasmine. Botanically Jasminum latifolium, r., oleaceæ [vricsham, 85]. Shrubby, climbing; leaves cordate and oblong-acute, glabrous; corymbs terminal, diffuse; calycine lobes five to seven, subulate; lobes of the corolla eight to twelve linear-cuspidate; berries kidney-shaped and oblong; flowers large, white, fragrant; flowering in march and april.——*Lily jasmine* (زنبق - zambak, Ar.). Title from resemblance. Same as Arabian jasmine.——*Mango jasmine* (சூதம் - shútham, Tam.). Title from similar odour of flowers. Same as Coral jasmine.——*Milky jasmine* (دودھ مگرا - dúdhmográ, Hind.). Milky plant with jasmine-like flowers. Same as Adam's apple.——*Moon jasmine* (ಚಂದ್ರಮಲ್ಲಿಗೆ - chandramallige, Can.). From bearing jasmine-like flowers in the evening. Same as False jalap.——*Musk jasmine* (कुन्द - kunda, San.; कस्तूरमोगरा - kastúramógará, Mahr.; कस्तुरिमोग्रे - kasturimógré, Conc.; ಕಸ್ತೂರಿಮಲ್ಲಿಗೆ - kastúrimallige, Can.; ಬೊಳ್ದುಮಲ್ಲಿಗೆ - boldumallige, Too.; గుజరి - gujari, Tel.; കുരുക്കുത്തിമുല്ല - kurukkuttimulla, Mal.; மல்லிகை-

malligai, Tam.). Title from smell. San. from (ku, san. earth + dó, san. to cut) [coo]. Mahr. and conc. from (kastúri, san. musk + mógará, mahr. jasmine, jasminum sambac, ait.). Can. from (kastúri, san. musk + mallige, can. jasmine). Too. from (boldu, too. white + mallige, too. jasmine). Mal. from (kurukka, mal. to sprout + mulla, mal. jasmine, jasminum sambac, ait.). San. also (mághyá), meaning producd in the month of maugham [mausam] or february; (atimuktá), meaning surpassing pearl in whiteness [madablota, nemmy]; (vásanti), meaning produced in spring season. Can. also (doddakádumallige), meaning large + wild jasmine. Mal. also (kuruna); (káttuchírakamulla), meaning wild + cuminum cyminum, linn. + jasmine. Tam. also (magarandam), meaning honey of flower. Title otherwise Downy jasmine, Many-flowered jasmine, Pubescent jasmine. Botanically Jasminum pubescens, wild., oleaceæ [vricsham, 85]. Alias Jasminum hirsutum, multiflorum; Mogorium hirsutum, pubescens; Nyctanthes hirsuta, multiflora, pubescens; mogorium from (mógará, mahr. jasminum sambac, ait.). Shrubby; branchlets hirsute; leaves opposite, short-petioled, cordate, mucronate, below and with the petioles tomentose, above afterwards glabrous; flowers congested in terminal umbels, subsessile; calycine lobes six to nine filiform, hirsute; tube of the corolla a little longer than the calyx; lobes oval, mucronate; flowers white, fragrant; flowering nearly all the year. ——*Needle jasmine* (यूथिका - yút'hiká, San.; जुई - juí, Mahr.; سوئی مگرا - suímográ, Hind.; جوھی - júhí, Dec.; ಸೂಜಿಮಲ್ಲಿಗೆ - sújimallige, Can.; సన్నజాజి - sannadzáji, Tel.; බොලිද - bolidda, Singh; ஊசிமல்லிகை - úsimalligai, Tam.). Title from long slender flower-stalks. San. from (yút'ha, san. multitude), from multitude of flowers. Mahr. from sanscrit. Hind. from (suí, hind. needle + mográ, hind. jasmine, jasminum sambac, ait.). Dec. from sanscrit. Can. from (súji, can. needle + mallige, can. jasmine). Tel. from (sanna, tel. slender + dzáji, tel. jasminum grandiflorum, linn.). Tam. from (úsi, tam. needle + malliká, san. jasmine, jasminum sambac, ait.). San. also (súchimalliká), meaning needle + jasmine; (ambasht'há), meaning sound + abiding, from the sound of beetles crowding round fragrant flowers [sour auray]; (mágadhí), meaning produced in magadham [long pepper]; (gaaiká), meaning attractive like harlot. Hind. also (jutipushpaka), meaning shoe flower. Tel. also (adavimolla), meaning forest + jasminum sp.; (erraadavimolla), meaning red + the plant; (tellaadavimolla), meaning white + the plant; (molla). Title otherwise Eared jasmine, Harlot jasmine, Small jaujy. Botanically Jasminum auriculatum, vahl., oleaceæ [vricsham, 85]. Alias Jasminum ovalifolium. A small, twining shrub, having large, heart-shaped leaves, with a pair of minute leaflets on their foot-stalks, bears numerous middle-sized, white, starlike, very fragrant flowers; flower religious; flower gives mahomedan perfume [attar].——*Night jasmine* (یاسمین شب بو - yásaminishabbo, Hind.). From bearing jasmine-like flowers in the evening. Same as Coral jasmine.——*Rangoon jasmine* (రంగూనుమల్లె - rangúnumalle, Tel.). Same as Rangoon creeper.——*Red jasmine* (ಕೆಂಪುಮಲ್ಲಿಗೆ - kempumallige, Can.). From bright red flowers. Same as Indian pink.——*Rice grain jasmine* (چال موگرا - chálmográ, Hind.). From similar odour and seed like rice grain. Same as Chaulmoogra.——*River jasmine* (ఏటిమల్లె - étimalle, Tel.; සුදුකිඹුල්වැන්න - sudukimbulvanna, Singh.). Title from habitat. Tel. from (éru, tel. river + malle, tel. jasmine). Singh. from (sudu, singh. white + kimbulvanna, singh. polygonum). Botanically Polygonum [water gannair] tomentosum, willd., polygonaceæ [vricsham, 110]. Whole plant covered with adpressed hairs; stem erect, furrowed, thick, glabrescent below; ochreæ long, limb membranaceous, erect, long-bristly-ciliate; leaves oblong-lanceolate, attenuated at both ends; spikes panicled, linear, straight, dense flowered; bracts obtuse; ciliated angles of the achenium not lineate, faces convex; flowers white; flowering in the rainy season.——*Snake jasmine* (यूथिकपर्णी - yút'hikaparní, San.; गजकरण - gajakarana, Mahr.; پالک جوھی - pálakjúhí, Hind.; کبوتر کا جھاڑ - kabútarkájhár, Dec.; ನಾಗಮಲ್ಲಿಗೆ - nágamallige, Can. and Too.; నాగమల్లె - nágamalle, Tel.; പുഴുക്കൊല്ലി - puzhukkolli, Mal.; ඇනිත්ත - anitta, Singh.; நாகமல்லி - nágamalli, Tam.). Title from cure against snake bite. San. from (yút'hiká, san. jasminum auriculatum, vahl. + parna, san. leaf). Mahr. from (gaja, san. elephant + karna, san. ear); epithet for ring-worm; from plant curing ring-worm. Hind. from (pálá, mahr. potherb + júhí, hind. jasminum auriculatum, vahl.). Dec. from (kabútar, hind. pigeon + jhár, hind. tree). Can. and too. from (nága, san. serpent + mallige, can. jasmine). Tel. similar. Mal. from (puzhu, mal. worm + kollu, mal. to kill) [indian worm-killer]. Tam. from (nága, san. serpent + malliká, san. jasminum, sambac, ait.); root cures snake-bite. Hind. also (joípání), meaning river + water, or corrupted from sanscrit. Mal. also (pushpakédal); (nágamalli), meaning serpent's jasmine. Tam. also (uragamalli), meaning snake + jasmine; (aniççai). Title otherwise Nasuta, Nauga mully, Ring-worm root, Tongpangchong, White-flowered justicia. Botanically Rhinacanthus communis, nees, acanthaceæ [vricsham, 101]. Alias Justicia nasuta, scandens. Shrub, 4–5 feet; stem erect, green, shrubby; young shoots jointed; leaves opposite, broad lanceolate, short-petioled, a little downy below, entire; panicles corymbiform, axillary and terminal, trichotomous; peduncels and pedicles short, round, a little downy; corolla with a long slender compressed tube, under lip broad, three-cleft, upper one erect, linear, sides reflected, apex bifid; flowers small, white; flowering nearly all the year. The leaves when chewed have a pungent taste something like cassia [q.v.] bark; their odour when crushed is disagreeable. Fresh root and leaves bruised, mixed with lime-juice, a remedy in ring-worm and cutaneous affections; seeds similar; milk boiled on the roots is with lime [q.v.] juice and pepper [q.v.] a cure for snake bite; quoted in pharm., non-officinal.——*Spanish jasmine* (یاسمین اسپین - yásaminíispen, Hind.). Same as Common jasmine.——*Tree jasmine* (नवमल्लिका - navamalliká, San.; नेवाळी - néválí, Mahr.). Title from size of plant. San. from (nava, san. new + malliká, san. jasmine, jasminum sambac, ait.). Mahr. from sanscrit. San. also (varakunda), meaning superior jasmine; (saptalá), meaning attracting the seven organs of sense including mind and booddhy; (navamáliká), meaning new jasmine. Mahr. also (thóramógar), meaning large jasmine. Botanically Jasminum arborescens, roxb., oleaceæ [vricsham, 85]. Alias Jasminum arboreum; Nyctanthes grandiflora. Shrub or small tree; branches sub-erect, younger ones with the petioles, peduncles, bracteoles and calyx pubescently hirsute; leaves opposite or ternately verticilled, ovate, subcordate, acute, glabrous above, puberulous below; petioles jointed in the middle; calycine lobes five to six, subulate, short; lobes of the corolla ten to twelve, linear-oblong; stigma two-lobed; flowers numerous, arranged in terminal corymbs, large, snow-white, very fragrant; flowering in march and april. Tree jasmine is in dravidian languages the same as Indian cork [q.v.].——*Turk jasmine* (துலுக்கமல்லிகை - tulukkamalligai, Tam.). Title from use by mahomedans. Same as Gendah. ——*Wild jasmine* (अस्फोटा - ásp'hótá, San.; रानमोगरी - ránamógarí, Mahr.; कुसरि - kusari, Conc.; بیل موگرا - belmográ, Hind.; مالتی - málatí, Malay; ಕಾಡುಮಲ್ಲಿಗೆ - kádumallige, Can.; ಎದ್ರೋಳಿ - edróli, Too.; అడవిమల్లె - adavimalle, Tel.; കാട്ടുമല്ലിക - káttumallika, Mal.; වල්පිච්ච - valpiçça, Singh.; காட்டுமல்லிகை - káttumalligai, Tam.). San. from (á, san. prefix showing slightness + sp'hut, san. to blossom) [arabian jasmine, yercum]. Mahr. from (rána, mahr. wild + mógari, mahr. jasmine, jasminum sambac, ait.). Hind. from (bel, hind. creeper + mográ, hind. jasmine). Malay from (málá, san. garland) [common jasmine, madablota, wild nutmeg]. Can. from (kádu, can. wild + malligegida, can. jasmine plant). Tel. from (adavi, tel. jungle + malle, tel. jasminum). Mal. from (kátu, mal. forest + malliká, san. jasmine). Singh. from (val, singh. jungle + piçça, singh. jasminum sambac, ait.). Tam. from (kádu, tam. forest + malliká, san. jasmine, jasminum sambac, ait.) [indian cork]. San. also (supújá), meaning good + adoration; (kánanamalliká), meaning forest + jasmine; (vanamallí), meaning forest + jasmine; (priyá), meaning pleasing. Hind. also (banmallika), meaning forest + jasmine. Malay also (málur); (mánur). Tel. also (chirimalle), meaning small + jasminum. Mal. also (káttupiççakam), meaning forest + jasminum grandiflorum, linn.; (káttupiççakamulla), meaning forest + the plant, jasminum grandiflorum, linn.; (vanamallika), meaning forest + jasmine. Singh. also (valsamanpiçça), meaning wild jasminum grandiflorum, linn. Tam. also (vanamalligai), meaning forest + jasmine; (shirumalli), meaning small + jasmine. Title otherwise Aspotah, Narrow-leaved jasmine. Botanically Jasminum angustifolium, vahl., oleaceæ [vricsham, 85]. Alias Jasminum triflorum, vimineum; Mogorium triflorum, vimineum; Nyctanthes angustifolia, triflora, viminea. Small twining shrub; long twig-like stems; leaves opposite, ovate or oblong, finely pointed, smooth, of a shining deep green; flowers terminal, generally by threes; calycine segments acute; segments of corolla 8–9, lanceolate; berries single, ovate; flowers smallish, white with a faint of red, star-shaped, fragrant; grows wild in woods and differs but little from the common jasmine. Flower religious; the bitter root ground small and mixed with lime-juice and vashamboo [q.v.] root is considered a good remedy in ringworm; well adapted for screening windows and covering arbours. Wild jasmine is in arabic the same as Indian sarsaparilla.

JATAY (जटा - jatá, *San.*; சடை - shadai, *Tam.*). From (jat, san. to become twisted together). Matted hair [lomam] worn by Shiva [q.v.] and his ascetics. Also means Jatamansy which see below. Compare, where transl. is of second term:—Acorus calamus (shadaikkóthan), bushy haired; Celosia cristata (jatádhari), wearing; Cyperus rotundus (shadámáñji), flesh; Cyperus tuberosus (jatámámsí), flesh; Eragrostis bifaria (shadaippul), grass; Nardostachys jatamansi (jatámámsí), flesh; Nardostachys jatamansi (shadámánji), flesh; Phaseolus trinervus (shadaippayaru), phaseolus mungo. See gloss. paragraphs.——*Jadabillay* (జడబిళ్ల - jadabilla, Tel.). From (above + billa, tel. plate). Ornament [nagay] worn on top of head.——*Jatámansy* (जटामांसी - jatámámsí, San.; जटामांवसी - jatámámvasí, Mahr.; سنبل الطیب هندی - sumbuluttíbihind, Ar.; سنبل الطیب هندی - sumbuluttíbihindí, Pers.; جٹاماسی - jatámásí, Hind.; جھٹاماسی - jhatámásí, Dec; ಜಟಾಮಾಂಸಿ - jatámámsí, Can., Too. and Tel.; ജടാമാഞ്ചി - jatámáñchi, Mal.; ජටාමාංස - jatámánsa, Singh.; சடாமாஞ்சி - shadámáñji, Tam.). San. from (jatá, san. matted hair + mámsí, san. the plant); from appearance of root. Mahr. from sanscrit; Ar. from (sumbul, ar. arsenic + tíb, ar. fragrant

+ hind, pers. india); from its properties. Pers. from arabic. Hind., &c., from sanscrit [common sedge]. San. also (jatá), meaning matted hair; (naliká,) meaning fragrant; (lómashá), meaning hairy; (tapasviní), meaning ascetic-like; (mámsí), meaning fleshy. Ar. also (sumbululasáfírihindí), meaning indian sparrow arsenic; (múigiyáh), meaning hair + grass. Hind. also (bálchhar), meaning hair + matted; (chahur), meaning matted; (viláitíjhatámásí), meaning foreign jatamansy; (billílotan), meaning cat + valerian, from fondness of cats; compare cooppamainy [q.v.], cat plant. Can. also (sugandhamuste), meaning fragrant + cyperus rotundus, linn.; (ganigilamuste), meaning oleander, nerium odorum, soland + cyperus rotundus, linn.; (jatámávashi). Tel. also (jatámáshi). Mal. also (máñchi), by corruption. Tam. also (namattam). Greek νάρδος ἰνδική, Latin spica narpi. Title otherwise Cat valerian, Fragrant cyperus, Hair grass, Himalayan valerian, Indian spikenard, Sparrow arsenic, Valerian spikenard. Botanically Nardostachys jatamansi, dc., valerianeæ [vricsham, 72]. Generic from root being shaped like ear of corn. Specific from sanscrit meaning as above. Alias Patrinia jatamansi; Valeriana jatamansi. Rootstalk woody, long, stout, covered with fibres from the petioles of withered leaves; stem 4–24 inches, more or less pubescent upwards, often glabrate below, subscapose; radical leaves 6–8 by 1 inch, longitudinally nerved, glabrous or slightly pubescent, narrowed in the petiole; cauline one or two pairs, 1–3 inches long, sessile, oblong or subovate; flower heads usually 1, 3, or 5; bracts ½ inch, oblong, usually pubescent; corolla-tube ½ inch, long, somewhat hairy within, as are the filaments below; fruit ⅛ inch long, covered with ascending white hairs, crowned by the ovate, acute, often dentate calyx-teeth. A dwarf, unattractive, herebaceous pot-plant; bears small, dirty white flowers in march, on a long erect spike, in much repute for their fragrance; native of mountains of n. india. The drug consists of a short portion of rhizome about as thick as the little finger, of a dark grey color, surmounted by a bundle of fine reddish-brown fibres, the whole forming an object not unlike the tail of a sable or martin; the fibres are produced by an accumulation of the skeletons of the leaves, and are matted together, forming a kind of network; amongst them the remains of flower stalks may be found; the odour of the drug is heavy and peculiar, like a mixture of valerian and patchouli [q.v.], the taste bitter and aromatic; when the central portion is removed and cut across it is seen to consist of a thin cortical portion connected with the central woody column by four medullary bands, between which are situated large canals which contain the fibro-vascular bundles; the central woody column is of a red-brown color, angular and jointed, having a certain amount of resemblance to the vertebræ in the tail of an animal. Root is of a blackish color and resembles bushy tail of the ermine; as met with in bazaar [q.v.], occurs in the form of short pieces of an underground stem, about the thickness of a goose quill, covered towards its tapering extremity, or almost entirely, with coarse, dark, hair-like fibres; odour, peculiar and fragrant; taste, aromatic and bitterish. Spikenard root is stimulant and antispasmodic; much used in treatment of epilepsy, hysteria, and convulsive affections; veidyans [q.v.] prepare from it, in combination with certain oils, a fragrant and cooling liniment for the head; substituted for british valerian root; in pharm. non-officinal. Has the effect of ordinary valerian on cats [poonay]; believed to have power of promoting growth and blackness of hair.——*Jatauyoo* (जटायुस् - jatáyus, San.). From (jatá, san. matted hair). The vulture [gidh] of mythology [garoodan].

JATRAH (यात्रा - yátrá, *San.*; جاترا - játrá, *Hind.*). From (yá, san. to go). A pilgrimage [yautray] to a place of reputed sanctity; a festival in honor of the tutelary goddess of a village [coloopoo]. Jatree is a pilgrim. Compare mahomedan Haj and Hajee.——*Jautrey* (جاترا - játrá, Hind.; జాతర - dzátara, Tel.). From (yá, san. to go). Pilgrimage; processional festival [pundigay, 6d]. A confluence of people at the feast of any holy place [cshetram].

JAUMA (جامه - jámah, *Hind.*). A long gown having a very large quantity of cloth, from eleven to thirty breadths, in the skirt, which at the upper part is folded into innumerable plaits. The body part is tied in two places on each side, being double-breasted [sheelay]. Pyjauma [q.v.] is mussulman trousers.

JAUMAM (याम - yáma, *San.*; జాము - dzámu, *Tel.*; சாமம் - sámam, *Tam.*). From (yáma, san. motion). A watch, as measure of time. 7½ nauzhigays or indian hours = 1 jaumam or watch, 2 jaumams = 1 nairam or half daylight [caulam, 1]. Approximate actual value. 1 jaumam = 3 English hours. Generally applied to the night hours. From 6 to 9 P.M. is Moothalaunjaumam, first. From 9 to midnight is Irandaunjaumam, second. From 12 to 3 A.M. is Moondraunjaumam, third. From 3 to 6 A.M. is Naulaunjaumam, fourth. Midnight is Nadoojaumam, the middle jaumam. Noon is Madhyaunam, or middle day; also Ooroomam [q.v.] or hot hour. Same as San. yaumam, praharam. See vol. I, 609. Jauma cozhy is the cock [moorghy], as indicating the midnight watch by crowing [jackal].

JAUMEEN (ضامن - zámin, *Hind.*). From (ẕamana, ar. to be responsible). Security, bail [zaumin].

JAUMOON (جامن - jámun, *Hind.*). From (jam, san. to eat) [jam]. A common term for several eugenias [jamboo].——*Ceylon jaumoon* (ಗುಡ್ಡಪನ್ನೆರಳು - guddapannéralu, Can.; ଶଗରବଟ୍ନ - sagarabatna, Oor.; വെളുത്തഞാറ - veluttañára, Mal.). Can. from (gudda, can. hill + pannéralu, can. eugenia jambos, linn.). Mal. from (velutta, mal. white + ñára, mal. eugenia jambolana, lamk.). Title otherwise White jaumoon. Botanically Eugenia [jamboo] zeylanica, wight, myrtaceæ [vricsham, 56]. Alias Acmena zeylanica; Eugenia spicata; Myrtus zeylanica; Syzygium bellutta, spicatum, zeylanicum. Belutta from (velutta, mal. white). Arborescent; leaves ovate or oblong, much acuminated, coriaceous, shining on the upper side; flowers shortly pedicillate, forming axillary or terminal compound cymes that are often arranged in a kind of contracted raceme or spike; calyx pruinose, calvate, elongated, repand, five lobed; berry white, globose, one seeded; malabar; affects beds of rivers.——*Cherry jaumoon* (رائی جامن - ráijámun, Hind.; බටදොඹ - batadomba, Singh.). Title from similar fruit. Hind. from (rái, hind. mustard seed, small + jámun, hind. eugenia jambolana, lamk.) [common jaumoon]. Singh. from (bata, singh. bamboo + domba, singh. poon, calophyllum inophyllum). Botanically Eugenia [jamboo] operculata, roxb., myrtaceæ [vricsham, 56]. Alias Eugenia cerasoides, nervosa, paniala; Syzygium angkolanum, costatum, nervosum, nodosum. Angkolanum from (ankólam, mal. alangium lamarckii, thw.). Paniala from (pániaunla, hind. water phyllanthus). Large tree; branches sub-terete or four-gonous; leaves three to eight by 2–4 inches, sub-coriaceous, dots often black, rarely pellucid; primary veins eight to twelve, curving into a rather faint intramarginal vein; petiole ⅓–½ inch; inflorescence often thyrsoidal; peduncles long, acutely angled; flowers small, greenish, in threes, nearly sessile, odorous; calyx campanulate, with short obtuse lobes or nearly truncate; petals united and falling in one piece, calyptra often apiculate; berry ⅓–½ inch, rugose, juicy. Low elevations on mountains on west side; fruit eaten; timber similar to jambolana [common jaumoon], reddish grey, hard.——*Clove-leaved jaumoon* (काकजम्बु - kákajambu, San.; جامن - jámun, Hind. and Dec.; ಜಂಬುನೇರಳೆ - jambunérale, Can.; నేరేడు - nérédu, Tel.; கொட்டைநாகம் - kottainágam, Tam.). San. from (káka, san. crow + jambu, san. eugenia jambolana, lamk.); from dark-purple colour of fruit. Hind. from sanscrit. Tam. from (kottai, tam. seed + nágam, tam. jaumoon tree). San. also (shvétajambu), meaning white jaumoon. Dec. also (ujlájámun), meaning white jaumoon. Tam. also (nárunaruvili), meaning to smell + cordia obliqua, willd.; (vellainával), meaning white jaumoon. Botanically Eugenia [jamboo] jambolana, lam., var. caryophyllifolia, myrtaceæ [vricsham, 56]. Alias Calyptranthes caryophyllifolia; Eugenia caryophyllifolia. Leaves ovate-lanceolate with a long acumen, calyx shortly four-toothed, berry size of a large pea [calauyam], globose. Fruit, when ripe, is of a very dark purple color unpleasantly acid, astringent, not eaten; in taste somewhat resembles the sloe, but sweeter.——*Common jaumoon* (जम्बू - jambú, San.; जाम्ब - jámba, Mahr.; जम्ब - jamba, Conc.; جامن کا پیڑ - jámunkáper, Hind.; جامونکاجہاڑ - jámúnkájhár, Dec.; ನೇರಳೆ - nérale, Can.; నేరొలు - nérolu, Too.; నేరేడు - nérédu, Tel.; ଜାମୋ - jamo, Oor.; ഞാവൽ - ñával, Mal.; මාදං - mádam, Singh.; நாவல் - nával, Tam.). San. from (jam. san. to eat); edible. Mahr., &c., from sanscrit [dark vail, malacca jaumoon, rose apple]. Mal. from tamul. Tam. from (náru, tam. to smell); from fragrant fruit. Hind. also (kálájám), meaning black guava; (jamblá); (ráijámun), meaning small jaumoon [cherry jaumoon]. Can. also (narala); (náyinéralamara), meaning dog + the tree. Tel. also (peddanérédu), meaning large + the tree; (rátsanérédu), meaning royal + the tree; (allanérédu); meaning noted + the tree. Mal. also (kizhakkaññáral), meaning east + the tree; (periññára), meaning large + the tree. Tam. also (nágam); (takkólam); (kottainával), meaning seed + the tree; (kottainágam), meaning seed + the plant. Title otherwise Black plum, Dark guava, Jambolin, Java plum, Jumrool, Myrtle bloom, Nauwal, Neraid. Botanically Eugenia [jamboo] jambolana lamk., myrtaceæ [vricsham, 56]. Specific name corr. from sanscrit. Alias Calyptranthes caryophyllifolia, jambolana; Eugenia corticosa, fruticosa, jambolifera, moorie, obtusifolia; Myrtus corticosa, cumini, cyminum; Syzygium caryophyllifolium, jambolanum. Not to be confounded with the eugenia jambos or rose-apple [q.v.], which has a larger fruit. Tree, 70–80 feet; leaves oval or oblong, more or less acuminated or obtuse, feather-nerved, coriaceous; cymes panicled, lax, usually lateral on the former year's branches occasionally axillary or terminal; calyx shortly turbinate, truncated; berry olive-shaped, often oblique; flowers small, white, honey smelling; flowering in march; tree attains its full size in 40 years; found almost everywhere throughout plains; much planted in topes [q.v.] and avenues [shaulay], ascends mountains to 4,000 feet. The fruit unless improved by cultivation is about the size and shape of a small olive [zeitoon], of a purple color, and very astringent; within it is a thin white papery shell, which encloses a large green kernel, also very astringent; the bark is grey and fissured externally; internally it is red and fibrous; its minute structure is remarkable in having several rows of very large, pitted, oblong-oval cells, which can be easily seen with the naked eye; the odour is like that of oak [belote] bark, and the taste very astringent; the leaves are 3 to 6 inches long, ovate or oblong, obtuse, more or less acuminate, coriaceous, smooth, shining, closely nerved, the numerous nerves uniting within the margin; when crushed they have an agreeable terebinthinate odour, and on distillation yield a bright green oil. The proximate composition of dry jaumoon [q.v.] seeds is:—essential oil, a trace; chlorophyll and fat, 0·37; resin soluble in alcohol and ether, 0·30; gallic acid, 1·65; albumin, 1·25; colored extractive soluble in water, 2·70; moisture, 10·00; insoluble residue, 83·73; total 100·00; the bark of the tree contains 12 per cent. of tannin and affords a kino-like gum [gond]. According to the deerghama sootram it is one of the four colossal mythic trees which mark the four cardinal points [ashtadic], standing to the south of mount meroo [q.v.]; four great rivers rise at its foot; the vishnoopooraunam [q.v.] states that the continent of jamboodweepam [q.v.] takes its name from this tree. A vinegar [caudy] prepared from the juice of the ripe fruit is an agreeable stomachic and carminative, it is also used as a diuretic; a sort of spirituous liquor, called jambauva, is prepared by distillation from the juice; the bark is astringent, and is used, alone or in combination with other medicines of its class, in the preparation of astringent decoctions, gargles and washes; the fresh juice of the bark is given with goat's [vellaud] milk in the diarrhœa of children; the expressed juice of the leaves is used alone or in combination with other astringents in dysentery. Fruit eaten by natives, who also eat kernels in times of famine; fruit improved in taste by being pricked and rubbed with salt [ooppoo] and allowed to stand an hour; unimproved it has flavor something like radish. Bark dyes excellent durable browns [shauyam] of various shades according to the mordant [cauram] employed, or the strength of the decoction; gives a gum [gond]; suited for avenues [shaulay]. Wood used for house-building, cart framing, agricultural implements, &c., resists action of water very well, used for well work, is tolerably close and even grained, not very strong or durable except in water, and in color dirty brown, reddish when fresh. There is a Teloogoo proverb:—నేరేడు పండితే నేలంతా పండును—"If the jaumoon "fruits freely, it foretells a good harvest."——*Coromandel jaumoon* (هجلی مهندی - hijlímhendí, Hind.; అరమండ - aramanda, Tel.; තඹිලිය - tambiliya, Singh.). Tel. also (goragamudi); (aravita). Botanically Eugenia [jamboo] bracteata, j., myrtaceæ [vricsham, 56]. Alias Eugenia roxburghii, zeylanica; Myrtus bracteata, coromandeliana, heynei, latifolia, ruscifolia. Shrub; young parts covered with rusty pubescence; leaves ovate-oblong, tapering or cuneate at the base, obtuse or shortly acuminated, at first slightly downy, afterwards glabrous and shining above; peduncles usually axillary, sometimes terminal, shot, one-flowered, longer than the petioles, one to four-together, with two small bracteoles under the calyx; calyx-segments four, unequal linear-oblong, ciliate; petals four; fruit globose, one to two seeded; flowers white; very common on all the coromandel coast near the sea-shore; flowering nearly all the year.——*Java jaumoon* (جامرول - jámrúl, Hind.). Botanically Eugenia [jamboo] javanica, lamk., myrtaceæ [vricsham, 56]. Alias Jambosa alba. Tree; trunk rarely straight and soon divided, branchlets terete or terete-compressed; leaves 5–6½ by 1¾–2¾ inches, or larger in cultivated examples; nerves indistinct above, slender but prominent beneath and uniting in loops within the margin; calyx-tube turbinate, about ½ inch, slender below; lobes four, rather unequal, membranous at the edges; berry size of the medlar, white or red; flowering in march and april, and fruit ripens in may and june. Berry shining and wax-like [mom]; has a raw, watery, insipid taste, not fit to be eaten.——*Lowly jaumoon* (भूमिजंबु - bhúmijambu, San.; నేలనేరేడు - nélanérédu, Tel.; සිරිබෙක්කු - siribekku, Singh.; பூமிசம்பு - púmisambu, Tam.). San. from (bhúmi, san. ground + jambu, san. eugenia jambolana, lam.). Tel. from (néla, tel. ground + nérédu, tel. eugenia jambolana, lam.). Tam. from sanscrit. Tel. also (gantubhárangi), meaning knotted bhraungy [q.v.]. Tam. also (shiruthékku), meaning small + teak, tectona grandis, linn. f. [knotted bhraungy]. Title otherwise Ground rose-apple. Botanically Premna [jayah] herbacea, roxb., verbenaceæ [vricsham, 102]. Suffruticose, depressed or herbaceous, without a stem; branchlets, cymes and network of the leaves hairy-pubescent; leaves very shortly petioled, obovate or rotund, subacuminate, serratodentate above, villosely ciliated; upper surface at last glabrate, lower somewhat hoary and densely glandular-dotted; cymes terminal and axillary, shorter than the leaf; calyx five cleft, round-lobed, ciliated; flowers small, pale whitish yellow; flowering in february and march. Drupe ½ inch in diameter, globose; roots about as thick as a crowquill with numerous almost globular woody knots. Juice of root given with juice of ginger [q.v.] and warm water in asthma.——*Malabar jaumoon* (നാട്ടുജംബു - náttujambu, Mal.). Mal. from (nátu, mal. country + jambu, san. eugenia jambos, linn.). Botanically Eugenia [jamboo] malabarica, bedd., myrtaceæ [vricsham, 56]. Middling sized tree; branchlets terete; leaves 2–5 by 1–2¾ inches, minutely dotted beneath; petiole ⅓–½ inch; cymes about ½ inch; calyx tube more or less truncate in age, about $\frac{1}{16}$ inch diameter; petals orbicular with a slight claw, pointed, very soon deciduous. Common in Wynaud.——*Malacca jaumoon* (जम्बु - jambu, San.; जांब - jámba, Conc.; ملکا کا جام - malakakájám, Hind.; ಕೆಂಪುಜಂಬುನೇರಳೆ - kempujambunérale, Can.; జంబునేరేళు - jambunérolu, Too.; നാട്ടുജംബു - náttujambu, Mal.; சம்புமலாக்காமரம் - shambumalákkámaram, Tam.). San. from (jam, san. to eat); applies to the edible variety. Conc. from sanscrit [common jaumoon, dark vail, rose apple]. Hind. means malacca + psidium guyava, linn. Can. from (kempu, can. red + jambunérale, can. rose apple tree). Mal. from (nátu, mal. country + jambu, san. eugenia jambos, linn.). Tam. means malacca rose apple tree. Tam. also (shambunával). Title otherwise Kavika, Malacca guava, Malay apple, Malay rose apple, Otaheite cashew. Botanically Eugenia [jamboo] malaccensis, linn., myrataceæ [vricsham, 56]. Alias Eugenia macrophylla; Jambosa domestica, malaccensis, purpurascens; Myrtus macrophylla, malaccensis. Shrub 6–8 feet high, with terete-compressed branchlets; leaves 9-12 by 3½ inches, glossy on both surfaces; dots inconspicuous; nerves indistinct above, the primary ones few prominent beneath and united more or less distinctly within the margin, sometimes in double loopings; petiole stout, channelled above, ¼–½ inch; flowers large, and handsome; calyx-tube ¾ inch; lobes unequal, rounded, with membranous edges, the larger pair ⅜ inch long; petals large, suborbicular, glandular; stamens numerous, about 1 inch in length; style long, persistent, nearly equally the stamens. Small tree, smooth leathery laurel-formed leaves, dense racemes of shortly stalked bright crimson flowers; fruit is of the size and form of a small apple [seb], perfectly smooth, of a pure, translucent white, with a blush of crimson; not worth eating. ——*Red jaumoon* (لال جامرول - láljámrúl, Hind.; වල්ජම්බු - valjambu, Singh.). Title from color of fruit. Hind. from (lál, hind. red + jámrúl, hind. eugenia malaccensis, linn.). Singh. from (val, singh. jungle + jambu, singh. the roseapple tree, eugenia jambos, linn.). Title otherwise Red jumrool, Wild jaumoon. Botanically Eugenia [jamboo] aquea, burm., myrtaceæ [vricsham, 56]. Alias Jambosa aquea. Middling sized tree, 20–30 feet, much branched, variable in the form of its foliage, the shape of the calyx-tube, and the color of the flowers; bark smooth, ash colored; leaves coriaceous, black-dotted, 1⅓–2½ by 1–1½ inch; midrib prominent below, primary nerves 8–10 on each side forming inconspicuous loops near the margin; flowers large, white, red, or pale purple; calyx-tube turbinate or cylindrical, about 1 inch. Brilliant-colored fruit, size of small apple [seb], of waxy appearance, somewhat aromatic taste, but hardly eatable. ——*Small jaumoon* (சிறுநாகம் - shirunágam, Tam.). Title from size of plant. Tam. from (shiru, tam. small + nágam, tam. eugenia jambolana, lamk.); distinguish from nauga champak [q.v.]. Botanically Eugenia [jamboo] arnottiana, wight, myrtaceæ [vricsham, 56]. Alias Syzygium arnottianum, densiflorum. Leaves elliptic-oblong, acuminated, folded, coriaceous, dotted; cyme dense, corymbose; peduncles lateral, general and partial, stout, the partial ones short and bearing at the apex an umbel of eight to twelve almost sessile flowers, subtended by oblong-linear caducous bracts; calyx shortly turbinate; limb shortly and bluntly four-toothed or lobed; petals expanded before falling off; flowering in february and march. Tree of low growth, covered in season with thousands of large clusters of cream-colored flowers; found on neilgherries, pulneys and anamullays. Fruit eaten, very astringent.——*Water jaumoon* (நீர்நாவல் - nírnával, Tam.). Title from being found in moist places. Botanically Eugenia [jamboo] munronii, wight, myrtaceæ [vricsham, 56]. Middling sized tree, 12–20 feet in height; leaves 6–9 by ⅔–3 inches; calyx-lobes somewhat membranous. Flowers white; moist western ghant forests from canara to cape comorin. ——*Wild jaumoon* (වල්ජම්බු - valjambu, Singh.). Same as Red jaumoon.

JAUN (جان - ján, *Hind.*). Means carrier. Small palankeen [q.v.] carriage used by business men in going to their offices.

JAUN (జేన - jéna, *Tel.*; ചാൺ - chán, *Mal.*; சாண் - shán, *Tam.*). Span. Distance between tips of thumb and little finger extended. 12 ungoolams or finger breadths = 1 jaun; 2 jauns = 1 moolam [alavay, 1a]. Approximate actual value, 1 jaun = 9 inches. Same as San. gocarnam, vitasty, Hind. bilisht, Can. guenoo, Tel. jena, Mal. chaun. Compare San. pradesham, Tam. adee, wottay. See vol. I, 609; II, 505.

JAUNWAH (جانوا - jánwá, *Hind.*). From (shana, san. sunn hemp, crotalaria juncea, linn.); originally cshatriyas [q.v.] wore hempen threads. Hindoo sacred thread [jandiram, janivaura, poonool, yanyopaveetam].

JAURAH (జార - jára, *Tel.*; ଧତ୍ତିକି - dhattiki, *Oor.*). Tel. also (putiki); (budamara); (chípudi); (shirijána); (jibilikechettu); (tadakatsuvva). Title otherwise Double-colored grewia, Pootiky. Botanically Grewia [dharmanam] salvifolia, heyne, tiliaceæ [vricsham, 27]. Alias Grewia bicolor, rothii. Leaves oblong, oblique at the base, sharply serrulated, under side hairy with white tomentum; peduncles axillary, solitary, one to three-flowered; pedicels somewhat longer than the peduncle; sepals linear-lanceolate, longer than the petals; drupe globose, two-lobed, glabrous; nuts solitary in each lobe, four-celled. Small tree or shrub, common; leaves very white beneath; fruit small, edible. Wood yellow, heart-wood orange-brown, hard, close-grained, structure similar to grewia tiliæfolia, vahl. [tadda], but medullary rays more numerous, and pores smaller.

JAURY (جاری - jári, *Hind.*). From (jará, ar. to flow). Current. Jaury inam is an inam [q.v.] in actual possession of the inamdar. Jaury mittah is a permanently settled estate, as opposed to amauny [q.v.]. Jaury rupee is a current rupee [q.v.].

JAUSTY (زیادتی - ziyádatí, *Hind.*; జాస్తి - jásti, *Tel.*). From (záda, ar. to augment). Increase, addition. For Fusl jausty see Fusl; for Teervay jausty see Teervay.

JAUTY (जाति - játi, *San.*; जाइफल - jáíp'hala, *Mahr.*). From (játi, san. caste) [jan]; high caste, from grateful aroma. Botanically the Myristica genus, myristiceæ [vricsham, 112]. Lofty tropical trees or shrubs; most of them aromatic and abound in reddish acrid juice; the leaves are entire, flowers very small clustered in the axils of leaves or in panicles; the fruit is fleshy but divides when ripe into two pieces disclosing seed covered by the mace. The species best known to the natives are shown below. Other species are:—Amygdalina, or almond nutmeg, Attenuata, or tapering nutmeg, Farquhariana, or narrow-leaved nutmeg.——*Common nutmeg* (जाति - játi, San.; जाइफळी - jáíp'halí, Mahr.; जायिफल - jáyip'hala, Conc.; شجرة جوزالطيب - shajratijauzuttíb, Ar.; درخت جوز بویه - darakhtijauzbúyah, Pers.; جائے پھل کا پیڑ - jáiphalkáper, Hind.; جاپھل کا جھاڑ - jáphalkájhár, Dec.; پالا - pala, Malay; ಜಾಜಿಕಾಯಿಮರ - jájikáyimara, Can.; ಜಾಜಿಕಾಯಿ - jájikáyi, Too.; జాజికాయచెట్టు - dzájikáyachettu, Tel.; ജാതി - játi, Mal.; ජාති - játi, Singh.; சாதி - sháthi, Tam.). San. from (jan, san. to be born) [common jasmine]. Mahr. and conc. from sanscrit. Ar. from (shajar, ar. tree + jauz, ar. nut + tíb, ar. odorous). Pers. from (darakht, pers. tree + jauz, ar. nut + búyah, pers. odorous). Hind. from (játip'hala, san. nutmeg + per, hind. tree). Dec. from hindostany. Can. from (jájikáyi, can. nutmeg + mara, can. tree). Tel. from (dzájikáya, tel. nutmeg + chettu, tel. tree). Mal. means excellent. Singh. from sanscrit. Tam. from sanscrit. San. also (ghatast'ha), meaning enclosed in a pot. Hind. also (jauntrí), meaning mace; (jauntríkátel), meaning mace oil. Malay also (buwahpala). Tel. also (játíphalamuchettu), meaning nutmeg + tree; (lavangachettu), meaning clove tree, eugonia caryophyllata, willd. [lavangam]. Singh. also (vasávási), meaning mace. Tam. also (sháthikkáymaram), common usage. Title otherwise False aril, Fragrant nut tree, Jaujy tree, Jautikye tree, Mace tree, Nutmeg tree. Botanically Myristica [jauty] fragrans, houtt., myristiceæ [vricsham, 112]. Alias Myristica aromatica, moschata, officinalis. Tree 20–25 feet; leaves ovate, elliptic, acute at the base, acuminate at the apex, lateral, nerves on both sides, eight to nine; peduncles supra-axillary, males few-flowered, females one-flowered; pedicels nearly equalling the peduncle; bracteole under the flower broadly ovate, scale-shaped; flower pale yellow nodding; perigonium ovoid, half three-cleft, nearly equalling the pedicel, strigose externally with adpressed hairs; anthers nine to twelve; fruit ovoid-globose, drooping; aril laciniated, red, aromatic, covering the seed. Has aromatic leaves and peach-like [shaft auloo] fruit; cultivated; native of the moluccas. Nutmeg is the kernel of the seed; large, rounded, obtuse at both ends; the size of a small myrobalan [q.v.] nut, smooth, marked with reticulated chinks, those transversely placed being less evident than the longitudinal, grey externally and reddish internally; taste hot. Mace is the oily, membranous, fleshy, pale yellow-colored pulp, extended over the thin, brittle shell that incloses the nutmeg, itself contained within external covering of fruit first disclosed on fruit ripening and bursting; has spicy, aromatic odour of nutmeg, more pungent and bitter; dried produce of nutmeg consists of two parts of mace, five of shell and eight of nutmeg. Oil of mace, wrongly so called, otherwise nutmeg butter, is a fixed or solid oil or butter, expressed from the nutmeg; there are two sorts of this; one is a soft sebaceous kind of substance, yellowish, sub-aromatic odour, somewhat fatty, pungent, and bitterish taste, little used; the other sort is usually brought from europe in flat square cakes, sometimes called in commerce banda soap, weaker in smell, fainter in color than the former. A white volatile oil [yennay] also resides in the kernel of the fruit; oleum nucis moschatæ of chemists; extensively used for flavoring soaps [sauboon]. For preparation, nutmegs are smoked by slow wood fires for three months before they are fit for exportation; mace requires no such trouble, simple exsiccation in the sun rendering it fit for market. Volatile oil is medicinally stimulant and carminative, and in larger doses narcotic, used in atonic diarrhœa and some forms of dyspepsia, chiefly used as an addition to other remedies; nutmeg butter is a useful application in rheumatism, paralysis, and sprains, diluted with a bland oil; infusion of nutmegs quenches thirst of cholera patients; nutmegs are chewed to improve foul breath; made into a paste they are used in neuralgia, lumbago, &c.; officinal in pharm.; nutmegs and mace are closely allied to cloves [lavangam] and cinnamon [q.v.], for which they may be substituted. Nutmegs are very subject to the attacks of a small insect. Mace much used for culinary purposes; used as a masticatory [charvanam] with betel-leaf [betel pepper]. The refuse nuts ground down, steamed and pressed afford a brown fluid, which cools into the so-called nutmeg soap.——*Jungle nutmeg* (అడవిజాజికాయచెట్టు - adavidzájikáyachettu, Tel.; காட்டுசாதி - káttusáthi, Tam.). Tel. from (adavi, tel. forest + dzájikáyachettu, tel. the nutmeg tree, myristica fragrans, houtt.). Tam. from (kádu, tam. forest + sháthi, tam. nutmeg tree) [wild nutmeg]. Title otherwise Wild nutmeg. Botanically Myristica [jauty] laurifolia, h. f. & t., myristiceæ [vricsham, 112]. Alias Myristigma ceylanica, diospyrifolia. Branches moderately stout; leaves variable, shining above with impressed nerves, pale brown or whitish beneath, base acute rounded or cuneate; nerves sometimes very faint; petiole one to one-and-half; peduncle very stout indeed, ½ inch long or less; flowers densely crowded, sessile or stoutly pedicelled, nearly ¼ inch long, silky pubescent, shortly three-lobed; fruit 2½ inches in diameter, globose, apiculate, with a deep longitudinal furrow; aril deeply cut into linear lacerate lobes, nearly enclosing the seed. The commonest wild nutmeg; a handsome tree; nutmeg and mace here of no value.——*Malabar nutmeg* (ಕನಗಿ - kanagi, Can.; പിണ്ടിക്കായ - pindikkáya, Mal.; பெரியகாட்டுசாதி - periyagáttusáthi, Tam.). Mal. means ball + fruit. Tam. from (periya, tam. big + káttusáthi, tam. the plant). Tam. also (káttusáthi), meaning forest + the nutmeg tree, myristica fragrans, houtt. Title otherwise Bombay mace tree, Poondy oil tree. Botanically Myristica [jauty] malabarica, lamk., myristiceæ [vricsham, 112]. Tree; leaves narrow-oblong or elliptic-lanceolate, acute at both ends or obtuse, quite glabrous, glaucous beneath; in male, inflorescence axillary, dichotomously cymose, many-flowered, longer than the petiole; female few-flowered, alabastrum globose, pubescent externally, bract very broad, embracing the base; fruit oblong, tawny, hairy; aril lacunose; lobes twisted and folded into a cone at the top. The arillus is of a dark brownish-red color, and on the inside has adhering to it a thin papery membrane of a light-brown color; the shell is hard and brittle, and contains an elongated kernel resembling a nutmeg, and from 1¼–2 inches long; when cut in two it is seen to have the same ruminated structure, but the odour is fruity, with hardly any aroma; similarly, the mace is deficient in odour and flavor. This is the ordinary native nutmeg. Kernel, when bruised and subjected to boiling, yields yellowish concrete oil called poondy oil, employed as application to indolent ulcers; for this purpose it requires to be melted down with a small quantity of any bland oil; serviceable as an embrocation in rheumatism; in pharm. non-officinal; like expressed oil of nutmeg. Oil used for burning purposes. Wood reddish-grey, moderately hard; used for building.——*Travancore nutmeg* (ರಾಮನಡಿಕೆ - rámanadike, Can.). From (ráma, san. the hero + adike, can. areca catechu, linn.). Title otherwise Rama's areca. Botanically Myristica [jauty] magnifica, bedd., myristiceæ [vricsham, 112]. Immense gregarious tree, 100 feet high, having buttressed trunks; most allied to myristica laurifolia, h. f. and t. [jungle nutmeg], but very different looking; the leaves and fruit are very much larger.——*Wild nutmeg* (कामुक - kámuka, San.; काडजायिफल - kádajáyip'hala, Conc.; جنگلی جائے پھل کا پیڑ - janglíjáiphalkáper, Hind.; جنگلی جاپھل کا جھاڑ - janglíjáphalkájhár, Dec.; ಕಾಡುಜಾಜಿಕಾಯಿಮರ - kádujájikáyimara, Can.; ಕಾಟುಜಾಕಾಯಿ - kátujákáyi, Too.; అడవిజాజికాయచెట్టు - adavidzájikáyachettu, Tel.; കാട്ടുജാതിക്കായ - káttujátikkáya, Mal.; காட்டுசாதி - káttusáthi, Tam.). San. from (kam, san. to desire). Conc. from (káda, conc. forest + jáyip'hala, conc. the nutmeg tree, myristica fragrans, houtt.). Hind. from (janglí, hind. wild + játip'hala, san. nutmeg + per, hind. tree). Dec. from hindostany. Can. from (kádu, can. forest + jájikáyi, can. nutmeg + mara, can. tree). Too. from (kátu, too. forest + jákáyi, too. nutmeg). Tel. from (adavi, tel. forest + dzájikáyachettu, tel. the nutmeg tree, myristica fragrans, houtt.). Mal. from (kátu, mal. forest + játikkáya, mal. nutmeg). Tam. from (kátu, tam. forest + sháthi, tam. nutmeg tree) [jungle nutmeg]. San. also (málati) [common jasmine, madablota, wild jasmine]; (játip'hala), meaning the plant, myristica fragrans + fruit. Can. also (kádujáyimara). Botanically Myristica [jauty] horsfieldii, blum., myristiceæ [vricsham, 112]. Alias Horsfieldia odorata; Myristica horsfieldia; Pyrrhosia horsfieldii. Tall tree, branches very stout, densely woolly, at length glabrate; leaves 2½–4 inches diameter, pale bright-brown above, rufous at first beneath, or red brown; petiole very stout, ½–1 inch; male panicles 3–6 inches, rachis and branches very stout, heads of flowers ⅛–½ inch diameter, quite globose; perianths subsessile, compacted, glabrous, hardly pedicelled; bracteoles orbicular, retained amongst the flowers, but caducous, densely woolly outside; anthers quite confluent to the tips; female panicles short, few-flowered, ovary tomentose; fruit shortly stoutly peduncled, ovoid, 1 inch long, rusty, tomentose; aril fleshy, entire; the mace has not the same virtues as fragrans [common nutmeg].

JAVA (यवद्वीप - yavadvípa, *San.*; யாவத்தீவு - yávattívu, *Tam.*). One of the East indian archipelago. Colonized by Hindoos from Calingam [q.v.] in B.C. 75. Hindoo government continued till fourteenth century when subverted by Mahomedans. Belongs to Holland. Arabs applied the term to the Archipelago generally.——*Java almond* (بادام جاوی - bádámijávai, Hind.). Same as Elemi.——*Java cedar* (کیئن - kein, Hind.; నలుపుముష్టి - nalupumushti, Tel.; மதகிரிவேம்பு - mathagirivémbu, Tam.). Title from place where first found. Tel. from (nalupu, tel. blackness + mushti, tel. strychnos nux-vomica, linn.). Tam. from (mathagiri, tam. place, so called + vémbu, tam. margosa, melia azadirachta) [chickrassy]. Hind. also (korsa); (iram),

Tam. also (tondi). Title otherwise Black mooshty [q.v.], Red cedar. Botanically Bischoffia javanica, muller, var. genuina, euphorbiaceæ [vricsham, 118]. Alias Andrachne trifoliata, trifoliatus; Bischoffia cumingiana, rœperiana, rœperianus; Micrœlus rœperianus; Stylodiscus trifoliatus. Leaves subelliptic, obtuse at the base, cuspidate-acuminate at the apex; male panicles almost equalling the leaves, large females commonly reduced to a raceme, branched below; segments of the male calyx suborbicular, brown, densely glandular striolate, at length reflex. Timber tree found in western forests generally; wood red, rough, moderately hard, with a small darker-colored heart-wood; one of the best timbers; used by planters in the neilgherries for building; is used for masts, and spars of small vessels.——*Java galangal* (خولنجان جاوي - khulanjánijávai, Hind.). Same as Greater galangal.——*Java honey* (عسل الجاوي - asaluljáwai, Pers.). Same as Benzoin.——*Java pepper* (فلفل جاوي - filfilijávaí, Hind.). Same as Cubeb pepper.——*Java plum* (جامن جاوي - jámunijávaí, Hind.). Same as Common jaumoon.

JAWAUB (جواب - jawáb, *Hind.*). From (jaub, ar. a side). An answer, whether spoken or written [oottaram]. Jawaubdar is a responsible person.

JAWAUDY (జవాది - jevádi, *Tel.*; சவாதி - shaváthi, *Tam.*). Means civet. Hill range; South arcot and Salem districts. For description, see vol. II, 81.

JAWAUN (جوان - jawán, *Hind.*). From (yuvan, san. youth). Literally, a young man. A peon [q.v.]. Same as Buntrote.

JAWAURY (جواری - javárí, *Hind.*). Same as Cholum.

JAWAUSHIR (جواشیر - jawáshír, *Pers.*). Product of Ferula galbaniflua, boiss. and Ferula rubricaulis, boiss. [galbanum]. A yellow or greenish semi-fluid resin [raul], generally mixed with the stems, flower, and fruits of the plant.

JAZAIL (جزایل - jazáil, *Hind.*). From (jazala, ar. to cut). A long matchlock.

JEELAUNY (جیلانی - jîlání, *Hind.*). From (jîlán, ar. town near baghdad); birth-place of the saint. Lacab of the chief Mahomedan saint [abdool cawder]. Common alam; as Jeelauny bee, alam + alaumat; Jeelauny miyaun, alam + alaumat [ism].

JEEN (జీను - jínu, *Tel.*). Anchor.——*Jeenboorra* (జీనుబుర్ర - jínuburra, Tel.). From (jínu, tel. anchor + burra, tel. gourd), from the curved form. A reed musical instrument [magady] used to charm snakes [sangeetam].

JEERAH (जीरक - jíraka, *San.*; जिरे - jiré, *Mahr.*; जीरे - jíré, *Conc.*; كمون - kamún, *Ar.*; زیره - zírah, *Pers.*; زیرا - zírá, *Hind.*; جیرا - jírá, *Dec.*; جنتان - jintán, *Malay*; ಜೀರಿಗೆ - jírige, *Can.*; ಜೀರದರಿ - jíradari, *Too.*; జీలకర్ర - jílakarra, *Tel.*; ജീരകം - jírakam, *Mal.*; දුරු - duru, *Singh.*; சீரகம் - shíragam, *Tam.*). Title from deccany. San. from (jrí, san. to digest); from promoting digestion. Mahr. and conc. from sanscrit. Pers., &c., from sanscrit. San. also (jírana), meaning promoting digestion; (hrasvánga), meaning short + body; (ajájí), meaning natural + overcoming, from curing natural indigestion. Hind. also (jírahisufíd), meaning white cumin. Dec. also (sháhzírá), meaning carum carui, linn. Tel. also (jílakara); (jilakara). Singh. also (sududuru), meaning white cumin. Tam. also (narchíragam), meaning good + cummin; (karunjíragaççedi), meaning black + cumin + plant. Greek κύμινον ἥμερον; Latin cuminum. Title otherwise Common cummin, Cummin, Jilacara, Sheeragam. Botanically Cuminum cyminum, linn., umbelliferæ [vricsham, 67]. Alias Cuminum ægyptiacum; Lygusticum cyminum. Herbaceous; leaves multifid, lobes linear-setaceous, acute; calycine teeth five, unequal, persistent; petals with the point inflexed; umbel with three to five rays, involucre longer than the usually pubescent fruit; seeds slightly concave in front, convex on the back; flowers white; roots acrid; seed has a peculiar heavy, strong odour, and warm bitterish taste; of an ash-gray color, smell. Cultivated, but much of what is used is brought from china; comes also from persian gulf. Both seeds and oil possess carminative properties analogous to coriander [cassibor] and dill [sowa]; in pharm. non-officinal; substituted for british caraways [q.v.]; seed used in veterinary practice. Seeds used to flavor curry [q.v.]; and an ingredient of curry powders; particularly prized by mahomedans. Seeds used for preserving books from insects.——*Armenian jeerah* (كمون ارمني - kamúniarmaní, Ar.). Same as Caraway.——*Black jeerah* (कृष्णजीरक - krishnajíraka, San.; काळाजिरे - kálájiré, Mahr.; कारिजीरे - karijíré, Conc.; شونیز - shúníz, Ar.; سیاه دانه - siyáhdánah, Pers.; کلونجی - kalonjí, Hind.; کالا زیرا - kálázírá, Dec.; ಕರಿಜೀರಿಗೆ - karíjírige, Can.; ಕಪ್ಪಲ್‌ಜೀರದರಿ - kappaljíradari, Too.; నల్లజీలకర్ర - nallajílakarra, Tel.; കരിഞ്ചീരകം - kariñchírakam, Mal.; කළුදුරු - kaluduru, Singh.; கருஞ்சீரகம் - karuñjíragam, Tam.). Title from color and flavor of seeds. San. from (krishna, san. black + jíraka, san. cumin seed, cuminum cyminum, linn.). Mahr. from (kálá, mahr. blackness + jiré, mahr. cumin seed). Conc. from (kari, can. black + jíre, conc. cumin seed). Ar. from persian. Pers. from (siyáh, pers. black + dánah, pers. seed). Hind. from (kála, san. black + jíraka, san. cumin seed, cuminum cyminum, linn.). Drav. all mean black + jeerah. San. also (upakuñchiká), meaning lessening [cardamom]; (kárabhí), meaning coming from camel; (yónishúlaghná), meaning destroying pain in vulva; (káraví), meaning stimulant [oolinja]; (sushaví), meaning stimulant [caraway, carolah]; (musavi). Ar. also (kamúniaswad), meaning black cumin; (habbatussaudá), meaning black seed; (habbatulkhazrá), meaning blue seed. Pers. also (siyáhbiranj), meaning black rice. Dec. also (kulanjan), meaning alpinia galanga, willd. Can. also (jírige). Tam. also (iruli), meaning that which is black; (vizhuttam); (attulákki). Greek μελάνθιον. Title otherwise Black cumin seed, Colinjy seed, Fennel sibthorp, Nigella seed, Small fennel, Sweet fennel. Botanically Nigella sativa, linn., ranunculaceæ [vricsham, 1]. Annual, foot high, white or light blue flowers, five-celled, capsule containing numerous black seeds; from mediterranean countries, cultivated. Seeds resembling coarse gunpowder are triangular, slightly compressed, obtuse above with oblique bases, rugose, black externally, internally of a greenish white hue; the capsules are polyspermous, oblong, and pointed at the side; the seeds are of strong aromatic odour and flavor, resembling sassafras or cubebs [cubeb pepper]; these properties are due to an essential oil, of which the seeds yield from 5 to 10 per cent. called siyah daunah [q.v.]. Seeds carminative and stomachic; substituted for british fennel [sonf] seeds; also prescribed in external application, mixed with gingelly [q.v.] oil in eruptions of skin; seeds in pharm. non-officinal. Seeds used as spice in curries [q.v.]. Seeds if put within folds of woollen cloths, keep them from being worm-eaten. Another species is hispanica.——*Foreign jeerah* (රටදුරු - ratadurn, Singh.). Same as Caraway.——*King jeerah* (දේවදුරු - dévaduru, Singh.). Same as Sonf.——*Large jeerah* (ದೊಡ್ಡಜೀರಿಗೆ - doddajírige, Can.). Same as Anise.——*Royal jeerah* (كمون ملوكي - kamúnimulúkí, Ar.). Same as Ajwaun.——*Turkish jeerah* (كمون رومي - kamúnirúmí, Ar.). Same as Caraway.——*Wild jeerah* (वाकुची - vákuchí, San.; रानजिरें - ránajirém, Mahr.; काळजीरे - kálajíré, Conc.; أطريلال - átrílál, Ar.; اطریلال - itrílál, Pers.; بکچی - bukchí, Hind.; کالی زیری - kálízírí, Dec.; ಕಾಡುಜೀರಿಗೆ - kádujírige, Can.; ಕಾಳಜೀರದರಿ - kálajírdari, Too.; అడవిజీలకర్ర - adavijílakarra, Tel.; കാട്ടുജീരകം - káttujírakam, Mal.; සන්නිනායන් - sanninávan, Singh.; காட்டுச்சீரகம் - káttuççíragam, Tam.). San. from (vá, san. to pierce + kuch, san. to contract); as alleviating piercing diseases as cooshtam [q.v.]; also wind destroyer [bawchee, malkangany]. Mahr. from (rána, mahr. wild + jirém, mahr. cumin, cuminum cyminum, linn.). Pers. from arabic. Hind. from sanscrit. Dec. from (kálí, hind. black + zírí, hind. cumin seed). Can. from (kádu, can. wild + jírige, can. cumin seed). Too. from (kála, too. black + jírdari, too. cumin seed). Tel. from (adavi, tel. forest + jílakarra, cumin seed). Mal. from tamul. Tam. from (kádu, tam. forest + jíraka, san. cumin seed). San. also (avalguja), meaning born of the ugly; (sómarájí), meaning shining with delight [gandbalee]; (agnibíjá), meaning fire-seeded; (kánanajíraka), meaning wild cumin; (atavijíraka), meaning wild cumin; (krishnap'halá), meaning black-fruited; (sahadévi), compare lance leaved balah; (pútip'halí), meaning stinking-fruited. Hind. also (somráj), meaning shining with delight. Dec. also (karvízírí), meaning bitter cumin. Can. also (kálajírige), meaning black + cumin seed; (sahadévi); (karchiudi). Tel. also (vishakantakálu), meaning poison + thorn + esculent root; (nélavávili), meaning ground + vitex trifolia, linn.; (garitikamma). Mal. also (púvánkuruntala), meaning flower + to become + small + head; (kálajírakam), meaning black cumin. Singh. also (náyan); (monarakudimbiya), meaning peacock + crest; (hinmonarakudimbiya). Tam. also (nírnoççi), meaning water + vitex negundo, linn. [water notchy]; (neyççitti), meaning ghee + small, from leaves; (shittılai), meaning small leaved. Title otherwise Flea-bane [indian absinth], Khatzum oil plant, Kinka oil plant, Purple flea-bane, Wild cumin, Worm seed vernonia. Botanically Vernonia anthelmintica, willd., compositæ [vricsham, 74]. Alias Ascaricida anthelmintica, indica; Baccharoides anthelmintica; Chrysocoma anthelmintica; Conyza anthelmintica; Serratula anthelmintica, elegans. Annual; stem erect, roundish, slightly tomentose; leaves alternate, serrate, narrowing at the base into the petioles, calyx ovate; corolla consisting of twenty or more hermaphrodite florets; flowers in panicles at the end of the branches on long peduncles thickening towards the flowers; a solitary peduncle terminates the stalk; flowers purplish; flowering in cold season; varies in the stem and leaves, being more or less hirsute or glabrous; common everywhere. The dried seeds are dark-brown, covered with whitish scattered hairs, cylindrical, tapering towards the base, marked with about ten paler longitudinal ridges, and crowned with a circle of short brown scales; taste, nauseous and bitter. Seeds powerfully anthelmintic; ingredient of compound powder prescribed in snake-bites; infusion of them given on malabar coast for coughs, and against flatulency; reduced to powder and mixed with lime-juice, they are used to expel pediculi from the hair; of great repute in sanscrit materia medica as a medicine in skin diseases; gives to pharm. seeds, non-officinal; like santonin [absinth]; used in leprosy [cooshtam]. Gives a hard coarse fibre [naur]. Seeds by pressure yield valuable solid green oil [yennay]. The species Cinerea is ash-colored fleabane; whole plant, with tasteless flowers, used in decoction, to promote perspiration in febrile affections; seeds powerful anthelmintic; all parts very bitter; eaten as greens [keeray] in famine time. Other common species are:—arborea, bracteata, candolleana, chinensis, divergens, elæagnifolia, indica, pectiniformis, salviæfolia, travaucorica, volkameriæfolia.

JEETAL (جيتل - jítal, *Hind.*). Copper coin equal to about nine daums [q.v.]. Current in Acbar's time.

JEEV (जीव् - jív, *San.*). To live.——*Jee* (جی - jí, Hind.). Contraction of (jíva, san. life). Particle of respect added to names and titles, as Raghoonaut jee, Sahib jee. Forms the termination of most Parsee names, as Jamsetjee, Cowasjee. Used by the Sikhs [q.v.] in the personification of their church as Khaulsajee, and of their chief prayer as Japjee. Also used in conversation as equivalent to the English sir. Also as the affirmative yes.——*Jeetam* (జీతము - jítamu, Tel.). From (jívita, san. livelihood). Wages. Jeetacaur is a paid servant [nowcar].——*Jeeracan* (சீவகன் - shívagan, Tam.). A man of long life. Hero of the Chintaumany, which see.——*Jeevam* (जीव - jíva, San.). From (jív, san. to live). Life.—"*a*" Plant first term. Ex., where translation is of second term:—Acacia catechu (jívamángalya), auspicious; Alstonia scholaris (jívaní), meaning life-giver; Cephalandra indica (jívaka), meaning living; Putranjiva roxburghii (jívanaputra), son, from nuts, used as garland for children; Sponia wightii (jívaní), and (jívantí), meaning living; Tinospora cordifolia (jívantiká), meaning enlivening. See gloss. paragraphs.—"*b*" Plant second term. Ex., where translation is of first term:—Blepharis molluginifolia (purushajívi), man; Ixora coccinea (bandhujívaka), meaning living in group; Pentapetes phœnicea (bandhujívaka), meaning living in group; Polyalthia longifolia (putrajíva), son; Putranjiva roxburghii (putrajíva), son, (sutajíva), son. See gloss. paragraphs.—"*c*" In philosophy individuated spirit, that which pervades the members of the body, and is the cause of life or motion, animated being. Jeevautman is the sentient soul, the emanation of the deity, which is incorporated with the animal body; it is opposed to the abstract state of the soul Paramautman [q.v.], in which by meditating upon its own divine nature and origin, the spirit is set at liberty from human feelings and passions. The following is from a Tamul shastram:—சீவசப்தாவஸ்தைபின் இலக்கணம், தன்னையறியாத அறிவே அஞ்ஞானம், தத்துவபேதந்தெரியாமலமறைத்தது ஆவரணம், விஷயபதார்த்தங்களை சுவதந்தரஞ்செய்தல்விட்சேபம், பிரமமொன்றென்பது பரோட்சஞானம்,அந்தப்பிரமந்தானென்பதே அபரோட்சஞானம், அந்தஞானத்தால் துக்கம் போனதே சோகநிவிர்த்தி, அந்தத்துக்க நிவிர்த்தியால் வந்த ஆநந்தமே தடையற்ற ஆநந்தம்—"The characteristics of the "seven stages [avastay] of personal soul are; anyaunam, "ignorance or knowledge which does not know self; auvarnam, "envelopement or that which prevents knowledge of the real "difference; vieshaipam, projection or causing sensible matter "to appear independent; parotcham or perception of bramh "[q.v.] as the only reality; aparotcham or knowledge that self "is same as that bramh; shocanivritty or emancipation from "sorrow by such knowledge and anandam or the limitless joy "that comes out of freedom from such sorrow." Living things are in natural history classed into:—Jeevacam, viviparous, as man and quadrupeds; Andajam, oviparous, as birds and insects; Swedajam, sweat produced, an insects and vermin; Oodbhijjam, germiniparous, as vegetables. They are also classed into:—spiritual intelligences, men, quadrupeds, birds, aquatics, reptiles, vegetables. There is a Tamul saying:—எறும்புகடை யானைத்தலை யெண்பத்து நான்கு நூறாயிரஞ்சீவ பேதம்—"From "elephant [q.v.] to ant [choomtee] downwards, there are "8,400,000 varieties of living beings."——*Jeevanaumsham* (जीवनांश - jívanámsha, San.). From (jívana, san. livelihood + amsha, san. portion). Provision for a widow or woman separated from husband.——*Jeevanjeevam* (जीवजीव - jívanjíva, San.). Reduplication of (jíva, san. life). Phasianidæ family, rasores, aves [pacshy, 32], of naturalists [jantoo].——*Jeevapootram* (जीवनपत्र - jíyanaputra, Mahr.). From (jíva, san. life + putra, san. child); from necklaces [maulay] of fruits being considered efficacious in preserving health of children wearing the same. Same as Pootran jeeva.——*Jeevautman* (जीवात्मन् - jívátman, San.). From (jíva, san. life + átman, san. soul). The individual soul in the human body [shareeram] as opposed to the supreme soul [paramautman].——*Jeevay* (जीवा - jívá, San.). From (jív, san. to live). The chord of an arc [chaupam, jyotisham].——*Jeevy* (जीवी - jíví, San.). Liver. Suffix in proper names, as Sanjeevy. Familiarly Jeevoo. Hindoo 2nd or pers. name [peyar].

JEHAUD (جهاد - jihád, *Hind.*). From (jahada, ar. to make an effort). A general effort such as Mahomet preached to exterminate unbelievers [caufir]; a holy war against infidels. The Soonnees [q.v.] say a jehaud should be entered on only when there is probability of success; the Shiahs [q.v.] add that the army must be led by the rightful imaum [q.v.].

JEHAUN (جہان - jahán, *Hind.*). World [jagam]. Part of lacab; a Jehaungeer, conqueror of the world; Jehaun shah, king of the world [ism].——*Jehaunabad* (جہانباد - jahánbád, Hind.). From (jahán, hind. shahjahan, the emperor + bád, pers. city). Delhi.——*Jehaungeer* (جہانگیر - jahángír, Hind.). From (jahán, ar. world + gír, pers. seizer). Any emperor. The historical emperor, otherwise known as Selim; fourth Moghul emperor A.D. 1605-1627. Also taken as alam [q.v.], as Jehaungeer shah meaning the king who is the conqueror of the world. Usually taken by fakeers [q.v.] in reference to their ascetic virtues.——*Jehaungeery* (جہانگیری - jahángírí, Hind.). The historic Jehaungeer's silver rupee.——*Jehaungeery tunkam* (جہانگیری تنکہ - jahángírítankah, Hind.). Gold coinage of Jehaungeer with his name on one side and the figure of Zodiacal sign [raushy] corresponding to month of coinage on the other. Various sizes with distinct names. Known also as Selim shahy coinage [naunyam].

JEIMINY (जैमिनि - jaimini, *San.*).—"*a*" Founder of Poorva mimaumsam philosophy [mimaumsam].—"*b*" A more modern poet of thirteenth century. Wrote translation from Sanscrit of Ashwa medha parvam of Mahabhaurat [q.v.], detailing sacrifice of the horse [ashwamedham, ghorah], called Jeiminy bhauratam. Finest specimen of Canarese poetry. 'He has read Jeiminy' is equivalent to he is an accomplished man. The author invented the journey of Arjoonau [q.v.] in Southern india.——*Jeiminy carmam* (जैमिनिकर्म - jaiminikarma, San.). From (above + karma, san. ritual). The ritual philosophy of Jeiminy mimaumsam or Poorva mimaumsam [q.v.].

JELDY (جلدی - jaldí, *Hind.*). From persian. Haste. As an exclamation, quick!

JELLA (जोबन्तोल - jóbantóla, *Mahr.*; జెల్ల - jella, *Tel.*; ചിറാവു - chirávu, *Mal.*). Mal. from (churukku, mal. sharpness). Sphyræna jello, sphyrænidæ, acanthopterygii, teleostei [matsyam, 25], of naturalists [jantoo]. Specific name from teloogoo. Alias Esox sphyræna. Lower jaw the longer; superiorly gray, white on abdomen; on upper part of side festooned band intersects, lateral-line, or a number of short vertical gray bands cross it; ventrals whitish; other fins yellowish with fine black points, most numerous towards margins; sea; 5 feet in length. No other common species here.——*Leaf jella* (ఆకుజెల్ల - ákujella, Tel.; ବଟୁଲି - battuli, Oor.). Title from appearance. Tel. from (áku, tel. leaf + jella, tel. sphyræna jello). Oor. also (bopotassi). Pseudeutropius atherinoides, siluridæ [kizhautty], physostomi, teleostei [matsyam, 35], of naturalists [jantoo]. Alias Bagrus anguis, atherinoides, exodon, urua; Pachypterus atherinoides, trifasciatus; Pimelodus anguis, urua; Silurus atherinoides. Freshwater; upper jaw a little the longer; median longitudinal groove on the head broad; silvery, greenish along the back, and with three or four bands along the sides formed by black spots; occiput and anterior portion of dorsal fin dark colored; not on w. coast; rarely above 4 or 5 inches. For another species see Dog keliroo.——*Mud jella* (బంకజెల్ల - bankajella, Tel.; ଜେଲମ - jellam, Oor.; குளக்கிழாத்தி - kulakkizhátti, Tam.). Title from habitat. Tel. from (banka, tel. gum + jella, tel. sphyræna jello). Tam. from (kulam, tam. tank + kizhátti, tam. siluridæ or cat-fish family). Pangasius buchanani, siluridæ [kizhautty], physostomi, teleostei [matsyam, 35], of naturalists [jantoo]. Generic name is probably from (pankeshaya, san. mud dwelling fish). Alias Pangasius djambal; Pimelodus pangasius. Upper jaw the longer; upper surface of the head smooth in small specimens, rather lineated in large ones; silvery, darkest along back and glossed with purple on sides; cheeks and under surface of head shot with gold; air-vessel large, its anterior portion occupies about ½ the length of the abdominal cavity; large rivers and estuaries; upwards of 4 feet; is a foul feeder. No other common species here.

JELLY (జల్లి - dzalli, *Tel.*; சல்லி - shalli, *Tam.*). From (tsallu, tel. to scatter); means pieces. Same as Kankar [q.v.].

JENDA (جهنڈا - jhandá, *Hind.*). Flag.——*Jendamode* (செண்டாமேடு - shendámédu, Tam.). From (above + médu, tam. high ground). Tract of country; Salem district, Ootancaray talook. So called because the chief standard was raised here in the expedition of Hyder and Nizam ally when they were defeated beyond the Shingaurapett pass by Colonel Smith and were driven back into Ootancaray talook.

JENDRA (జేండ్ర - jéndra, *Tel.*, obl.). From (jádu, tel. to shake) [jeyda]; from plying the loom [tarry]. Also called Devaunga [q.v.]. Teloogoo weavers, who worship Shiva. Numbers about 100,000 [jauty]. See vol. II, 230.

JENTA (జెంట - jenta, *Tel.*). Neighbourhood. Suffix in place names; as Condajenta, meaning hill neighbourhood.

JERBOA (يربوع - yarbú, *Ar.*). Same as Shevvely [q.v.].

JERRY (జెర్రి - jerri, *Tel.*). Centipede.——*Jerripotoo* (జెర్రిపోటు - jerripótu, Tel.). Means centipede's mate. Fish name common to:—Cynoglossus lingua, Plagusia bilineata, Synaptura commersoniana, Synaptura zebra. See gloss. paragraphs.

JETT (செற்று - shettu, *Tam.*). From (sheru, tam. to narrow). Closeness. Suffix in place names; as Veppanjett, meaning margosa close or spinney.

JETTY (جيتى - jatthí, *Hind.*; జెట్టి - jetti, *Tel.*). In Mysore called Mooshtiga, meaning fist-men. Wrestlers and boxers. The jetty itself is a sort of cæstus, worn over first phalanges on the right hand; it is made of buffalo [khoolgah] horn [sing] with four sharp projections like knuckles, and the fifth near the little finger, with a greater prominence than the rest; the hitting is by a sharp perpendicular cut. The combatants are clothed in short drawers [ottootchalladam] only. This class also shampoo and rub ointments in to cure pains. They were formerly sometimes employed as executioners and despatched by a twist of the neck; they are still considered skilful in setting dislocated joints. Numbers not more than 1,000 [jauty].

JEW (جهود - juhúd, *Hind.*). Prefix [jonacu].——*Jew's apple* (వంగ - vanga, Tel.). Same as Brinjaul.——*Jew's scent* (بوى جهودان - búijahúdán, Pers.). Same as Mookul bdellium.

JEYDA (ಜೇಡ - jéda, *Can.*; சேடன் - shédan, *Tam.*). From (jádu, can. to shake) [jendra]; as plying the loom [tarry]. A caste [jauty] of weavers. The corresponding terms are:—Tel. jendra, Mal. chauliyan, Tam. keikkila.

JEYPORE (جيپور - jepúr, *Hind.*; జయపురము - jayapuramu, *Tel.*) [jayam]. From (jaya, san. victory + pura, san. town).——**(1)** Division, Vizagapatam district; population 116,117; language Ooriya. W. inland of district. Boundaries—E., Coraputt division; S., Coraputt and Pottinghy divisions; W., Mulkangberry division and Bustar; N., Nowrungapore division and Bustar. Places of archæological interest:—Borigoomma, Cotepaud, Jayanagaram, Poycapaud, Ramgherry, Singapore. Principal trig. station:—Bardwar, Motigaum. The leading places, &c., in the division are the following.——*Bardwar* (బారాద్వారము - bárádváramu, Tel.). From (bárá, hind. twelve + dvára, san. gate). Trig. station; lat. 18° 50′ 21·09″; long. 82° 17′ 42·00″; height 2,631 feet; from Jeypore W. 20 miles.——*Battigaum* (బత్తిగాము - battigámu, Tel.). From (batti, tel. a still + gráma, san. village). Town; lat. 19° 07′; long. 82° 35′; from Jeypore N. 18 miles.——*Borigoomma* (బొరెగుమ్మ - boregumma, Tel.). From (bhairava, san. the god + gumma, oor. village). Village; lat. 19° 03′; long. 82° 36′; from Jeypore N. 13 miles; from Vizagapatam N.W. 104 miles. One temple near the village; one in the jungle. Situated at intersection of Jeypore, Nowrungapore and Coraputt-Cotepaud roads. Numerous tanks. A large town once existed here.——*Casoomy* (కసుమి - kasumi, Tel.). From (kasemu, tel. fountain). Town; lat. 19° 41′; long. 82° 23′; from Jeypore N.W. 60 miles; from Vizagapatam N.W. 147 miles.——*Coombacote* (కుంబకోట - kumbakóta, Tel.). From (kumbha, san. pot + kóta, san. fort). Town; lat. 19° 07′; long. 83° 17′; from Jeypore N.E. 48 miles; from Vizagapatam N. 97 miles.——*Cotepaud* (కోటపాడు - kótapádu, Tel.). See sep. title.——*Jeypoor* (జయపురము - jayapuramu, Tel.). See below.——*Motigaum* (మోతిగాము - mótigámu, Tel.). From (mótí, pers. pearl + gám, hind. village). Trig. station; lat. 19° 24′ 17·61″; long. 82° 14′ 42·32″; height 2,259 feet; from Jeypore N.N.W. 44 miles; from Motigaum N.N.E. 2 miles.——*Ramgherry* (రామగిరి - rámagiri, Tel.). From (ráma, san. the god + giri, san. mountain). Village; pop. 105; lat. 18° 47′; long. 82° 17′; from Jeypore W.S.W. 22 miles; from Vizagapatam N.W. 99 miles. Rock cut cave with sculptures dedicated to Goopteshwarasawmy, 8 miles distant.——*Singapore* (సింగపురము - singapuramu, Tel.). From (singamu, tel. lion + pura, san. town). Tel. also (bhairavasingapuramu), meaning bheiravan, the god + the village so called. Distinguish from Calyauna singapooram in Royagada. Town; pop. 999; lat. 19° 03′; long. 82° 43′; from Jeypore N.N.E. 16 miles; from Vizagapatam N.N.W. 102 miles. Head-quarters of Maharajah's ameen [q.v.]. Large granary. Several temples.——*Taurapooram* (తారాపురము - tárápuramu, Tel.). From (tára, san. star + pura, san. town).——**(2)** Zemindarry; Vizagapatam dist., Jeypore division. For description see foot-note, vol. I, 60. ——**(3)** Town, Head-quarters of Jeypore zemindarry, Deputy tahsildar's station; pay Rs. 150; Vizagapatam dist., Jeypore division; pop. 4,321; lat. 18° 51′; long. 82° 37′; from Coraputt W.N.W. 11 miles; from Madras N.N.E. 420 miles; from Narsapatam N. 82 miles; from Parvatipore W. 57 miles; from Vizagapatam N.W. 91 miles; from Vizianagram N.W. 73 miles. Contains numerous mutts [q.v.] and temples supported by the zemindar [q.v.]. Two miles north of the northern wall of the upper plateau of the Vizagapatam hills, on the west slope of the Eastern ghauts [q.v.], and on the S.W. frontier of Central provinces. The residence of the Rajah, and a place of rapidly growing importance on route from Central provinces to sea. Excepting one broad main street, consists of a confused mass of mud houses. No building worthy of note, the Rajah's own accommodation being poor. An old rock fort lies within a mile of the town. The Estate manager's head-quarters. See vol. I, 68. The following are the travelling distances by road from Jeypore to different places:—

To	Viâ	Miles and Furlongs.	
Bowdara ...	Padava and Arakoo	93	0
Lamsingy ...	Padava and Padair	108	0
Mulkangherry ...	Cotametla	64	0
Narsapatam ...	Padava, Padair and Lamsingy	124	0
Narsapatam ...	Padava, Padair and Madgole	130	0
Padair ...	Ticarapara and Padava	75	0
Padava ...	Ticarapara	46	0
Vaddigoodem ...	Mulkangherry and Motoo	146	0
Vizagapatam ...	Coraputt, Pauchipenta ghaut and Vizianagram.	138	3
Vizagapatam ...	Daudy, Arakoo and Bowdara	130	4
Vizagapatam ...	Padava, Padair, Lamsingy and Narsapatam.	175	4
Vizagapatam ...	Padair, Bullapollem and Narsapatam ...	181	4
Vizianagram ...	Coraputt and Pauchipenta	101	7
Vizianagram ...	Daudy and Bowdara	113	2½

JHAR (جهاڑ - jhár, *Hind.*). Tree.——*Jharkanamak* (दारुलवण - dárulavana, San.; झाडीचमीठ - jhádíchamít'ha, Mahr.; جوكهار - jaukhár, Hind.; جهاڑ كا نمك - jhárkánamak, Dec.; ಮರದಉಪ್ಪು - maradauppu, Can.; మానుప్పు - mánuppu, Tel.; മരവുപ്പ് - maravuppu, Mal.; மரவுப்பு - maravuppu, Tam.). Title from deccany. San. from (dáru, san. wood + lavana, san. salt). Mahr. from (jhádí, mahr. tree + mít'ha, mahr. salt). Hind. from (yava, san. barley + kshára, san. alkali). Dec. from (jhár, hind. tree + namak, hind. salt). Can from (mara, can. tree + uppu, can. salt). Tel. from (mánu, tel. tree + uppu, tel. salt). Mal. from (mara, mal. wood + uppu, mal. salt). Tam. from (maram, tam. wood + uppu, tam. salt). Hind also (rákkánamak), meaning ashes + salt. Tel. also (búdideuppu), meaning ashes + salt. Mal. also (pappatakkáram), meaning cake + alkali. Tam. also (shámbaluppu), meaning ashes + salt. Potash, Wood ash. Also called Salt of tartar, Salt of worm wood [mara ooppoo]. In one form called Pearl ash. Potassa of chemists. Obtained by the incineration of wood. Natives prepare it from ashes of many burnt vegetables, and call it salt [ooppoo] of each vegetable; thus Vauzhayilay ooppoo, salt of plantain [q.v.] leaf. A Drauvacam [q.v.] or strong liquor, is made by adding certain hot seeds to the potash, and is used as diuretic. On west coast potash is used for bleaching and washing linen, dhoby's earth [q.v.] not being known. Product occurs in hard irregular masses or fragments, of a light bluish gray color, somewhat caustic, alkaline taste, inodorous, and very deliquescent. Carbonate of potash is of great importance in the arts and manufactures, especially in dyeing [shauyam] and bleaching; obtained by passing carbonic acid into a solution of potash, evaporating to dryness, and exposing the dry mass to a red heat. The pharm. has numerous forms and preparations.

JHARTY (جهرتى - jhartí, *Hind.*). Examination [taniky].

JHAUMP (جهانپ - jhánp, *Hind.*). From (jhánpná, hind. to cover). Wicker work or bamboo [q.v.] frame; coarse-matting used as a door [darwauja] or screen [chick].——*Jhampan* (جهپان - jhappán, Hind.). From (jhánp, hind. a cover). Sedan used by travellers in the Himalaya. Something similar here in rural tracts [dhooly, tonjon].

JHAUNJ (جهانجه - jhánjh, *Hind.*). From (jharjhara, san. tingling sound). Cymbals [sangeetam].

JHAURAN ((جهاڑن - jháran, *Hind.*). From (jhárná, hind to sweep). A coarse cloth for wiping furniture.——*Jhaudmauly* (جهاڑنےوالى - jhárnewálí, Hind.). From (jhárná, hind. to sweep + wálí, hind. agent suffix). A sweeper employed in cleaning office rooms.

JHEEL (جهيل - jhíl, *Hind.*). A stream. A lake.

JHINGOOR (तैलपा - tailapá, *San.*; فاسيا - fásiyá, *Ar.*; جعل - jul, *Pers.*; جهينگر - jhíngur, *Hind.*; جهنگور - jhungúr, *Dec.*; ليپس - lipas, *Malay*; ಆತೆಹುಳ - átehula, *Can.*; బొద్దింక - boddinka, *Tel.*; കൂറ - kúra, *Mal.*; කරපොත්ත - karapottá, *Singh.*; கரப்பான்பூச்சி - karappánbúçci, *Tam.*). Title from hindostany. San. from (taila, san. oil + pá, san. to drink). Ar. from (favasa, ar. to emit a noiseless wind). Hind. from (jhinghi, san. cricket). Tam. from (karai, tam. to destroy + púçci, tam. insect). Tel. also (bharanipurugu), meaning casket, which is generally painted red + insect. Tam. also (karappu) in colloquial use. Cockroach. Blatta orientalis, blattidæ, orthoptera, hemimetabola, insecta [poochy], of naturalists [jantoo].

JHOOBBA (جبه - jhubba, *Hind.*). From arabic. A loose garment worn by Mahomedans, reaching down to ankles, having two triangular flaps on each side of the skirt [sheelay].

JHOOL (جهول - jhúl, *Hind.*). From arabic (jull). Body clothing of a horse [ghorah], elephant [q.v.], or other domesticated animal.

JHOOM (جهوم - jhúm, *Hind.*). N. indian for Coomry [q.v.].

JHOOMKAH (جهمكا - jhumká, *Hind.*; சிமிக்கி - shimikki, *Tam.*). Literally a cluster. A bell-shaped golden pendant of an earring, the edges of which are furnished with small pearls [moty, zewar].

JHOW (झावु - jhávu, *San.*). From (jham, san. to consume) [jam]. Title otherwise Tamarisk. Botanically the Tamarix genus, tamariscineæ [vricsham, 19]. Shrubs or small trees; leaves minute, scale-like; flowers small, spiked, white or pink; branches twiggy. The species best known to the natives are shown below.——*Cypress jhow* (पिचुल - pichula, San.; लालझाऊ - lálajháú, Mahr.; لال جهاؤ - láljháú, Hind. and Dec.). San. from (pichu, san. cotton + lá, san. to take). Mahr. from (lála, mahr. red + jháú, mahr. tamarix gallica, linn.); from rose-colored flowers. Hind. from sanscrit. Title otherwise Bastard cypress, Cypress tamarisk. Botanically Tamarix [jhow] dioica, roxb., tamariscineæ [vricsham, 19]. Small under-shrub; young branchlets glabrous; leaves sheathing; flower-bearing branchlets about as long as the terminal spikes; flowers diæcious; styles elongated beyond the corolla; flowers very small, rose-colored; flowering nearly all the year. In beds of rivers, highly ornamental; light feather-branches, resembling casuarina [chowkmaram]. Twigs are used in medicine as astringent. Wood moderately hard, red, outer portion white; used mainly for fuel. but also for the supporting sticks of roofs, and for basket [tokrah] work.——*Garden jhow* ([illegible] - dzáne, Tel.). Tel. also (pabbasachettu). Title otherwise Garden tamarisk, Heath-like trichorus. Botanically Tamarix [jhow] ericoides, rottl., tamariscineæ [vricsham, 19]. Alias Myricaria vaginata; Trichaurus ericoides. Shrub; stems slender, branchlets fastigiate; leaves minute, scale-like, ovate-lanceolate, acuminate; flowers pale rose-pink, in terminal racemes; stamens not exceeding the petals, alternately long and short; capsule ½ inch. Rather large heath-like flowers; beds of rivers; cultivated in gardens.——*Jungle jhow* (جنگلی جهاؤ - janglíjháú, Hind.). Same as Casuarina [chowkmaram].——*Manna jhow* (झावुक - jhávuka, San.; झाऊ - jháú, Mahr.; اثل - asl, Ar.; گز - gaz, Pers.; جهاؤ - jháú, Hind. and Dec.; ప్రక్కె - prakke, Tel.; சிறுசவுக்கு - shiru-savukku, Tam.). Title from saccharine product [manna]. San. from (jham, san. to consume). Mahr. from sanscrit. Ar. from (asala, ar. to have a root). Hind. from sanscrit. Tel. from (prakka, tel. side), from its growing on the sides of rivers. Tam. from (shiru, tam. small + shavukku, tam. casuarina equisetifolia, forst.). Ar. also (tarafá). Pers. also (shorgaz). Hind. also (barímái), meaning the galls. Tel. also (pakke); (pakki) [stunted jack]; (érusaru); (shirisaru); (dzammi) [shamee]. Tam. also (áttuççavukku), meaning river + casuarina equisetifolia, forst.; (kódasavakku), meaning hot season + casuarina equisetifolia, forst. Greek μυρίκη. Title otherwise Burree moy, Indian tamarisk. Botanically Tamarix [jhow] gallica, linn., tamariscineæ [vricsham, 19]. Alias Tamarix articulata, epacroides, indica. Shrub, 6 feet; sepals five; petals five; young branches glabrous; leaves amplexicaul, glabrous; torus ten-toothed, leaves ovate, acute, with white edges; spikes elongated, straight, panicled; capsules attenuated; flowers small, rose-colored; flowering in july-august; sandy beds of rivers especially near sea coast. Feather-like in its growth; numberless spikes of flowers. The galls [mauchicoy] are roundish and very nodular, or knotty excrescences, varying in size from a pea [calauyam] to a soap-nut [q v.]; the knots are often so numerous and prominent with narrow necks that they give the gall the appearance of a cluster; the galls are generally greyish or yellowish brown in color; the quantity of the tannic and gallic acids they contain is smaller than that in oak [belote] galls, and their action is consequently somewhat weaker than that of the latter. The ashes, when tree grows near the sea, contain a quantity of sulphate of soda, and cannot be used as a ley for washing as they coagulate the soap [sauboon]; when the tree grows in sweet soil in the interior the ashes are free from the soda [munucauram]. A saccharine exudation or manna is produced by the puncture of the insect coccus maniparus. The tree was sacred to osiris amongst the ancient egyptians, and to apollo amongst the greeks. Galls are used medicinally as astringent in place of oak galls; action due to tannic and gallic acid; manna [q.v.] is detergent, aperient, and expectorant. Galls and bark employed as a mordant [cauram] in dyeing [shauyam]; baskets [tokrah] made of the twigs. The wood is coarse-grained and often very red; is used for persian wheels [chuckram], in turning, &c.——*Red jhow* (झावुक - jhávuka, San.; लालझाऊ - lálajháú, Mahr.; اثل الاحمر - aslulahmar, Ar.; گز سرخ - gazisurkh, Pers.; لال جهاؤ - láljháú, Hind. and Dec.; ఎఱ్ఱేరుసరు - erraérusaru, Tel.; சிவப்பாற்றுச்சவுக்கு - shivappáttuçça-vukku, Tam.). Title from color of galls. San. from (jham, san. to consume). Mahr. from (lála, mahr. red + jháú, mahr. tamarix gallica, linn.). Ar. from (asl, ar. tamarix gallica, linn. + ahmar, ar. red). Pers. from (gaz, pers. tamarix gallica, linn. + surkh, pers. red). Hind. from (lál, hind. red + jháú, hind. tamarix gallica, linn.). Tel. from (erra, tel. red + érusaru, tel. tamarix gallica, linn.). Tam. from (shivappu, tam. red + áru, tam. river + shavukku, tam. casuarina equisetifolia, forst.). Hind. also (chhotímái), meaning the galls. Tel. also (errashi-risaru), meaning red + tamarix gallica, linn. Tam. also (shivap-pukkódaççavukku), meaning red + hot season + casuarina equisetifolia, forst.; (shivappuççirusavukku), meaning red + small + casuarina equisetifolia, forst. Title otherwise Atlee gall, Choti moy, Red indian tamarix, Red tamarisk. Botanically Tamarix [jhow] articulata, vahl., tamariscineæ [vricsham, 19]. Alias Tamarix orientalis, pharas. Bush or coniferous-looking tree; branchlets fastigiate, elongate, slender, cylindric, jointed; leaves reduced to a very short sheath with a minute tooth; spikes slender, more or less interrupted; bracts sheathing, acute; flowers ⅛ inch in diameter, subsessile; stamens inserted in alternate notches of the ten-lobed disk. Galls smaller than gallica [manna jhow]; not three-angled but round, knotty, of the size of a pea [calauyam], and of a yellowish brown color. Galls employed as an astringent; bark is bitter, astringent and tonic.

JI (जि - ji, *San.*). To conquer.——*Jeina* (जैन - jaina, San.; சைனன் - shainan, Tam.). In the later Booddhist [booddha] system, he who has overcome the eight great crimes is called Jinan. These crimes are eating at night; slaying an animal; eating the fruit of those trees that give milk; tasting honey or flesh; taking the wealth of others; taking by force a married woman; eating flowers, butter, cheese; and worshipping the gods of other religions. The same word as Tsin used by booddhists in china. An older name for the followers of this sect was Nirgrantan meaning destitute of wealth; properly the title of jeina ascetics only or Yaties [q.v.].—"*a*" The Jeinas are divided into two principal divisions, Digambarans [q.v.] and Shwetaumbarans [q.v.]. The former word means sky-clad, or naked, but in the present day ascetics of this division wear colored garments and confine the disuse of clothes to the period of their meals. Shwetaumbaran means one who wears white garments. But the points of difference between these two divisions are far from being restricted to that of dress; they are said to comprehend a list of seven hundred topics, of which eighty-four [chowraushy] are considered to be of paramount importance. Amongst the latter are mentioned the practice of the Shwetaumbarans to decorate the images of their saints with earrings, necklaces, armlets, and tiaras of gold and jewels; whereas the Digambarans leave their images without ornaments. Again, the Shwetaumbarans assert that there are twelve heavens and sixty-four indrans [q.v.]; whereas the Digambarans maintain that there are sixteen heavens and one hundred indrans. Jeinas are divided again into clergy and laity, Yaties and Shramanans [q.v.]; the latter being called by Latin writers Germanes, and now by the Tamuls Shamanar. There are some 25,000 in the Presidency; mostly in Canara, they however have a temple at Conjeeveram. The sixteen nagarams built by Keshavanna in Canara are:—Barcore, Cadama, Moodbidry, Caurcal, Basroor, Bungaudy, Padbidry, Yenoor, Caup, Moodraudy, Sooraul, Nauranvy, Yarmaula, Alauvoo, Moondcoor, Beilangady. The sixteen nagarams formed by Basavanna in Canara are:—Mangalore, Cassergode, Moolky, Vittal, Oollaula, Buntwaul, Manail, Oodipy, Panambore, Nellicaur, Manjeshwar, Neranky, Pauney mangalore, Mordala, Valalunkey, Soolya. The history of Jeinism in this Presidency is sketched at vol. I (57), (63), (75). The system was an offshoot of Booddhism with which it has many leading doctrines in common.—"*b*" The doctrines of Jeinism have been very briefly mentioned at vol. I (95), but the following are further particulars. Booddhists deny the existence of the supreme being, the Jeinas admit of one, but deny his power and interference in the regulation of the universe, and pay their devotion to divine objects of their own creation, viz., the twenty-four beatified sages or Teertancarans [q.v.]. Jeinas deny the divine authority of the vedas [q.v.] and nominally disregard distinctions of caste [jauty]. They admit the images [vigraham] of the gods of the vedantic religion into their temples and it is said worship them to a certain extent. Their priests are called Yaties [q.v.], and the laity are termed Shrauvacans [q.v.]. The novitiate of the Yaties is passed with a Gooroo [q.v.] or teacher and they are then his Chelahs [q.v.] or disciples. They say that the world is eternal, and that there is no deity distinct from the world, and that meditation and renunciation of the world will exalt man to the highest state of bliss or Nirvaunam [q.v.]. They inculcate five duties; mercy to all living creatures, alms-giving, venerating sages, confession of sins and fasting. They prohibit five sins [puncha mahapautacam], killing, lying, stealing, adultery, and worldly-mindedness. Abstinence from killing is the chief part of their system. In their books sixty-three special dispositions are named, being of very high and difficult attainment. Any one who has attained Trishashty, is a man of the sixty-three, a perfect man, and becomes after death a Jinan or a Teertancaran. The Jeinas are sometimes called Syaudvaudies [q.v.], assertors of probabilities, or of what may be. These usually form seven categories, or:—a thing is; it is not; it is and it is not; it is not definable; it is, but is not definable; it is not, neither is it definable; it is, and it is not, and is not definable. Hence the Jeinas are also termed Saptavaudies [q.v.] assertors and oppugners of seven propositions. The Jeinas believe god, the vedam, the world, time, soul, action, and virtue, to be eternal. So the Jeina chintaumany [q.v.]:—"அரியுமல்ல அரனுமல்ல அயனுமல்ல அப்புறங் கருமைவெண்மை செம்மையுங் கடந்துநின்ற காரணம் பெரியதல்ல சிறியதல்ல பெண்ணுமாணு மல்லவே தூரியமுங் கடந்துநின்ற தூரதூர தூரமே"—"On that side it is neither hary [q.v.], nor haran "[q.v.], nor ajan [q.v.], a standing cause removed from black, "white and red; it is not great, it is not small, neither is it male "nor female; beyond even the fourth state of corporeal being, "it is further, further, further still."—"*c*" The principal point in the Jeina créed is as above said the reverence paid to holy men, who by long discipline have raised themselves to divine perfection. The Jinan or conquering saint, who having conquered all worldly desires declares the true knowledge of the Tatwams [q.v.], is with Jeinas what the Booddha [q.v.] or perfectly enlightened saint is with Booddhists. He is also called Jineshwaran, chief of Jinans; Arhat [q.v.], the venerable; Teertacaran or teertancaran, the saint who has made the passage of the world; Sarwanyan, omniscient; Bhagavat, holy one. Time [caulam] with Jeinas proceeds in two eternally recurring cycles [chuckram] or periods of immense duration, defying all human calculation:—the Ootsarpiny [q.v.] or ascending cycle; the Avasarpiny [q.v.] or descending cycle. Each of these has six stages. Those of the Ootsarpiny period are bad-bad, bad, bad-good, good-bad, good, good-good time. In the Avasarpiny period the series begins with good-good and goes regularly backwards. In the first cycle the age and stature of men increases; in the other, decreases. The world is now in the fifth stage of the Avasarpiny, i.e., in bad time. When the two cycles have run out, a Yoog [q.v.] or age is accomplished. Twenty-four Jinans or perfect saints raised to the rank of gods have appeared in the present Avasarpiny cycle, twenty-four have appeared in the past Ootsarpiny, and twenty-four will appear in the future. The idols representing them are always, like that of the Booddha [q.v.], in a contemplative posture, but have different animals, plants, and symbols accompanying them, such as a bull, elephant, horse, ape, a lotus, the moon, to serve as distinguishing characteristics. The first Jinan of the present cycle lived 8,400,000 years, and attained a stature equal to the length of 500 bows [dhanoos]. The age and stature of the second was somewhat less, and so in a descending scale. The last two Jinans, Parshwanautan and Mahaveeran, were probably real persons and are those principally revered by the Jeinas of the present day, the first founder of the sect having been Parshwanautan and its first active propagator, Mahaveeran. In the same cycle there have lived twelve Chuckravurties [q.v.], or universal emperors, nine divine personages called Baladevans, nine called Vausoodevans and nine others called Praty vausoodevans, making a list of sixty-three divine persons in all. With regard to the world, the Jeinas affirm that being formed of eternal atoms [anoo, paramaunoo], it has existed and will exist eternally. They believe that it has three divisions, viz., lower, middle, and upper, and that there are numerous hells and heavens. All existing things are arranged under the two great Tatwams [q.v.] of Jeevam [q.v.], living soul, and Ajeevam, inanimate objects. Of living souls there are three kinds:—Nitya siddhan, ever perfect, as the Jinan; Mooctautman, liberated soul; Baddhautman, bound soul, or one bound by works [carmam] and worldly associations. Material objects are sometimes classed under a Tatwam called Poodgalam, and some make seven, others nine tatwams. There are three gems which together effect the soul's Moosham [q.v.] or liberation, viz.:—right intuition or Samyak darshanam; right knowledge or Samyak nyaunam; right conduct or Samyak chauritram. This last consists in observing five duties or vows of self restraint or vratams [q.v.], thus:—Do not kill or injure; which jeinas carry to such an extreme that they strain water before drinking it, sweep the ground with a brush before treading on it, never eat or drink in the dark, and sometimes wear muslin [q.v.] before their mouths to prevent the risk of swallowing minute insects; moreover, they never eat figs [atty] or any fruit containing seed, nor will they even touch flesh-meat with their hands. Do not tell lies. Steal not. Be chaste and temperate in thought, word, and deed. Desire nothing immoderately.—"*d*" The creed according to its applicability divides itself into the Yaty dharmam and Shramana dharmam. The Yaty dharmam is of ten kinds:—Aurjavam to follow the right way and teach it to others; Maurdavam, to behave with reverence to superiors, and carefully to instruct disciples; Satyam, invariably to speak the truth; Showcham, mentally to renounce hatred, affections, or passion, and evil desire, and outwardly to act with purity; Tyaugam, to renounce all bad conduct; Cshamay, to bear patiently like the earth in time of trouble; Tapas, outward and inward self-mortification; Bramhacharyam, to relinquish all sexual attachment even in word or thought; Akinchanatay, to renounce the darkness of error and to follow the light of truth; Samyamam, duly to celebrate all special periods, festivals, or the like. The Shramana dharmam is of eleven kinds:—Daurshanican, one who relinquishes certain unclean kinds of food, with killing, lying, theft, and all anxious cares; Vratican, one who eats not at night, is faithful to his teacher, to his family, and to his religion; he is self-restrained and keeps silence and zealously renounces the use of all pleasant vegetables; Samaudhican is one, who with the foregoing qualifications, renders homage to the divine being three times a day, morning, noon, and evening; Proshopavausan, one who fasts on certain days, so appointed to be observed; Sanchitavratan, one who, with the foregoing dispositions, renounces certain kinds of food; Rautry bhootan, one who observes mortification during the day only; Brambacharry, one always occupied in contemplation of god; Anaurambhan, one who quits cultivation and all other secular occupations; Aparigrahan, one who renounces all kind of earthly gain; Anoomaty pindavratan, one who forbears to eat even that which he had prepared; Ootchishta pindavratan, one who relinquishes dress, except for mere decency; he carries a pot and lives in a wilderness.—"*e*" The Jeinas say that Yellacharry wrote the Cooral [q.v.], though the Sheivas claim it as theirs. The Jeina scriptures are comprised in fifty different works, collectively called the Sootrams [q.v.], and sometimes the Siddhauntams [q.v.] and classed in two different ways; first, under the two heads of Calpa sootram and Augamam [q.v.], five works coming under the former, and forty-five under the latter head; secondly, under eight different heads, viz., eleven Angams; twelve Oopaungams; four Moola sootram; five Calpa sootram; six Chooddams; ten Payannas; Nundy sootram; Anyoga dwaura sootram. Some of them have a four-fold commentary, under the names Teecay, Niryoocty, Choorny, and Bhaushyam, constituting with the original the five-fold or punchaunga Sootram. They are partly in Sanscrit, partly in Maugadhy pracrit, and the total of the fifty works amounts to 600,000 Shlocams. The authorized books now extant and in use are:—Amaram, Chintaumany, Choodaumany, Dharma pareecshay, Dhavalam, Gomatasauram, Maha dhavalam, Maha pooraunam, Meroo mandara pooraunam, Naya chuckram, Neelakeshy vaudam, Padaurtasauram, Ratna carandacam, Shabdabhangy, Shauctauyanam, Soobodhiny, Trilocasauram, Vijaya dhavalam, &c. Books written in Tamul are:—Chintaumany, Choodaumany, Cooral, Manimekhalay, Meroo mandara pooraunam, Naulady, Neelakeshy vaudam, Nigantoo, Nunnool, &c.—"*f*" The following is Strabo's account of Bramins and Shramanas quoting Megasthenes:—"He makes also another division of the philosophers, saying that there are two races of them, one of which "he calls the Brahmanes, βραχμᾶνες, and the Germanes, γερμᾶνες "[shramanan]. Of these the Brahmanes are the more excellent, "inasmuch as their discipline is preferable; for as soon as they "are conceived they are committed to the charge of men "skilled in magic arts, who approach under the pretence of "singing incantations for the well-doing both of the mother and "child, though in reality to give certain wise directions and "admonitions, and the mothers, that willingly pay attention to "them, are supposed to be more fortunate in the birth. After "birth they pass from the care of one master to that of another, "as their increasing age requires the more superior. The philo-"sophers pass their time in a grove of moderate circumference, "which lies in front of the city, living frugally and lying upon "couches of leaves and skins; they abstain also from animal "food and intercourse with females, intent upon serious dis-"courses and communicating them to such as wish; but it is "considered improper for the auditor either to speak or to "exhibit any other sign of impatience, for, in case he should, "he is cast out of the assembly for that day as one incontinent. "After passing thirty-seven years in this manner they betake "themselves to their own possessions, where they live more "freely and unrestrained; they then assume the linen tunic and "wear gold in moderation upon their hands and in their ears; "they eat also flesh except that of animals which are service-"able to mankind, but they nevertheless abstain from acids and "condiments. They use polygamy for the sake of large families, "for they think that from many wives a larger progeny will "proceed; if they have no servants their place is supplied by "the service of their own children, for the more nearly any "person is related to another, the more is he bound to attend to "his wants. The Brahmanes do not suffer their wives to attend "their philosophical discourses, lest if they should be imprudent "they might divulge any of their secret doctrines to the unini-"tiated, and if they be of a serious turn of mind, lest they "should desert them; for no one who despises pleasure and "pain even to the contempt of life and death, as a person of "such sentiments as they profess ought to be, would voluntarily "submit to be under the domination of another. They have "various opinions upon the nature of death, for they regard "the present life merely as the conception of persons presently "to be born, and death as the birth into a life of reality and "happiness to those who rightly philosophise; upon this "account they are studiously careful in preparing for death. "They hold that there is neither good nor evil in the accidents "which take place among men, nor would men if they rightly "regarded them as mere visionary delusions either grieve or "rejoice at them; they therefore neither distress themselves "nor exhibit any signs of joy at their occurrence. Their specu-"lations upon nature, he says, are in some respects childish: "that they are better philosophers in their deeds than in their "words, inasmuch as they believe many things contained in "their mythologies. However they hold several of the same "doctrines which are current among the Greeks, such as that "the world is generated and destructible and of a spherical "figure, and that the God, who administers and forms it, "pervades it throughout its whole extent; that the principles of "all things are different, water for instance is the first principle "of the fabrication of the world; that after the four elements "there is a certain fifth nature, of which the heaven and stars "are composed; that the earth is situated in centre of the "whole. They add much of a like nature concerning genera-"tion and the soul. They have also conceived many fanciful "speculations after the manner of Plato, in which they maintain "the immortality of the soul and the judgments of Hades and "doctrines of a sirmi description. Such is his account of the "Brahmanes. Of the Germanes he says they are considered "the most honorable who are called ὑλόβιοι, and live in the "woods upon leaves and wild fruits, clothing themselves with "the bark of trees and abstaining from venery and wine. They "hold communication by messengers with the kings who inquire "of them concerning the causes of things, and by their means "the kings serve and worship the deity. After the Hylobii the "second in estimation are the physicians, philosophers, who are "conversant with men, simple in their habits, but not exposing "themselves to a life abroad, living upon rice and grain, which "every one to whom they apply freely gives them and receives "them into his house; they are able by the use of medicines to "render women fruitful and productive either of males or "females, but they perform cures rather by attention to diet "than the use of medicines. Of medicines they approve more "commonly of unguents and plasters, for all others they "consider not free from deleterious effects. These and some "others of this sect so exercise their patience in labors and "trials as to have attained the capability of standing in one "position unmoved for a whole day. There are others also who "pretend to divination and inchantments, and are skilful in "the concerns of the inhabitants and of their laws; they "lead a mendicant life among the villages and towns, but the "better class settle in the cities. They do not reject such "of the mythological stories concerning Hades as appear to "them favorable to virtue and piety. Women are suffered to "philosophise with some of these sects, though they are "required to abstain from venery."——*Jamalgota* (جمال گٹا - jamálghutta, Dec.). See sep. title.——*Jaugatey* (ಜಾಗಟೆ - júgate, Can.; ಜೇಗಂಟ - jéganta, Tel.; சேகண்டி - shégandi, Tam.). From (jaya, san. victory + ghantá, san. bell). Circular gong [q.v.].——*Jaya* (जय - jaya, San.). From (ji, san. to conquer). Victory; used as an exclamation, either singly or with the name or title of a person of distinction, or of a deity, Jaya maharajah, Jayaraman, &c. Epithet of the sun. Hindoo 2nd or pers. name. Common to both sexes. Suffix in proper names as Dhananjayan, Mrityoonjayan [peyar].——*Jayagopaul* (జయగోపాలుడు - jayagópáludu, Tel.). From (jaya, san. victory + gópála, san. cowherd krishna). Hindoo 2nd or pers. name [peyar].——*Jayah* (जया - jayá, San.). From (jí, san. to conquer); useful medicine. Botanically the Premna genus, verbenaceæ [vricsham, 102]. Shrubs or trees with small flowers; fruit is a drupe. The species best known to the natives are:—cordifolia [conjee moonnay], esculenta [curry moonnay], herbacea [lowly jaumoon], integrifolia [moonnay], latifolia [buffalo moonnay], tomentosa [firebrand teak].——*Jayancondacholapooram* (செயங்கொண்டசோளப்புரம் - sheyangondasólappuram, Tam. jayankondacholapuram *). From (jaya, san. victory + konda, tam. achieved + chóla, san. chola king + pura, san. town). Sanscrit name (ámalakavana), meaning emblic myrobalan, phyllanthus emblica, linn. + forest. Town, Tahsildar's head-quarters, General deputy collector's division; Trichinopoly dist., Oodayarpolliem tal.; pop. 3,917; acres 2,824; lat. 11° 13′; long. 79° 26′; from Ariyalore E.N.E. 21 miles; from Oodayarpolliem N.E. 5 miles; from Trichinopoly E.N.E. 53 miles. Two curious Jeina [q.v.] figures. To one outside village on a bund [q.v.], ceremonial observances are performed. It is said, tears drop from its eyes whenever rain is wanted. Superior cloth market every Monday.——*Jayanty* (जयन्ती - jayantí, San.). Means day of success and rejoicing. Originally applied to time of birth of Krishnan [q.v.]; subsequently extended to births of Vishnoo [q.v.] in any of his incarnations [avatar]. Short for Krishna jayanty. Also a form of Canly [q.v.].——*Jayaraman* (சயராமன் - shayaráman, Tam.). From (jaya, san. victory + ráma, san. the god). Hindoo 2nd or pers. name [peyar].——*Jayaramdoss* (జయరామదాసుడు - jayarámadásudu, Tel.). From (jaya, san. victory + ráma, san. the god + dása, san. slave). Hindoo 2nd or pers. name [peyar].——*Jayashunker* (జయశంకరుడు - jayashankarudu, Tel.). From (jaya, san. victory + shankara, san. shiva, the happiness maker). Hindoo 2nd or pers. name [peyar].——*Jayay* (जया - jayá, San.). Victory. Name of the third eighth and thirteenth lunar days [tity] of either half-month [pacsham]. Cf. Nundy.——*Jeypore* (జయపురము - jayapuramu, Tel.). See sep. title.——*Jinan* (जिन - jina, San.). From (ji, san. to conquer). Teacher of the Jeina [q.v.] doctrines, any one of the twenty-four deified teachers of the system; called also a Teertancaran [q.v.].——*Jineshwaran* (जिनेश्वर - jinéshvara, San.). From (jina, san. jaina teacher + íshvara, san. lord). Chief of Jeinas; the Jinan who declares the true knowledge of the tatwams [q.v.]. The same with the Jeinas as Booddha [q.v.] with the Booddhists.——*Jingan* (جنگن - jingan, Hind.). From (jinginí, san. the plant). Same as Wodier.——*Jiyyangar* (జియ్యంగారు - jiyyangáru, Tel.). From (jiyyaru, tel. vaishnava ascetic + gáru, tel. term of respect). High priest [acharry] among the Veishnavas.——*Jiyyar* (சியர் - shiyyar, Tam.). From (ji, san. to conquer); one who has conquered his passions, a monk. Head of a Veishnava mutt [q.v.]. Such mutts are located at Conjeeveram, Shreerungam, Rameshwaram, Totandry, otherwise Vaunamamullay [nangoonairy], and Ahobalam. The mutt at the last place has been transferred to Trivellore in Chingleput district.

JIBBREEL (جبرئیل - jibraíl, *Hind.*). Gabriel, said to have been the medium of revelation to Mahomet. The Mahomedans reckon four great angels:—"*a*" Jibbreel the archangel who is God's messenger, the protector of the Mahomedans.—"*b*" Michael the angel who presides over water and rain, the protector of the Jews.—"*c*" Israfeel or the angel who presides over the wind, and will sound the last trumpet at the resurrection.—"*d*" Izraeel or the angel of death.

JID (ضد - zidd, *Hind.*). From (zidda, ar. contrary). Spite.

JIHWAH (जिह्वा - jihvá, *San.*). From (hvé, san. to call). Tongue. Plant second term. Ex., where transl. is of first term:—Elephantopus scaber (gójihvá), cow; Leea sambucina (karkatajihvá), crab; Methonica superba (ahijihvá), snake. See gloss. paragraphs.

JIMIKY (சிமிக்கிப்பூச்செடி - shimikkippúççedi, *Tam.*). Tam. from (shimikki, tam. the ear ornament + pú, tam. flower + shedi, tam. plant). Tam. also (shirubúnaikkáli), meaning small + mucuna pruriens, dec. Title otherwise Granadilla, Passion-flower. Botanically Passiflora leschenaultii, dec., passifloreæ [vricsham, 61]. Climbing; leaves alternate, half-orbicular, rounded at the base, somewhat truncated and tricuspidate at the apex, pubescent beneath; petioles with two glands about their middle; tendrils simple; calyx without an involucre; petals five; peduncles in pairs, in the same axils as the tendrils, simple, one-flowered; fruit purple when ripe; flowers whitish, with purple filaments; flowering nearly all the year.

JIN (جن - jinn, *Hind.*). From (jinna, ar. conceal). Goblin.

JINJEE (செஞ்சி - shenji, *Tam.* gingee *). Corruption of (shingi, tam. from shringí, san. hill). Sanscrit name (krishnapura), meaning proper name + town. Mahomedan name (nusratgarh), meaning victory + city, after nusrat jung, title of zoolfacar khan.—"*a*" Deputy tahsildarry, South arcot district. Pay Rs. 70.—"*b*" Town; South arcot dist., Tindivanam tal.; pop. 419; acres 953; lat. 12° 15′; long. 79° 27′; from Chidambaram N.N.W. 60 miles; from Cuddalore N.N.W. 44 miles; from Madras S.W. 82 miles; from Tindivanam W. 17 miles; from Tricalore N.E. 24 miles; from Vriddhauchellam N.N.E. 49 miles; from the sea W. 38 miles. On road from Krishnagherry to coast, about half way between Tindivanam and Trinomallee. Site of fine hill fortress. At least six centuries old. Jinjee was once a province. In 1638, Bandoollah khan, the Beejapore general, captured the fort after joining his forces to those of Golcondah, which were then beleaguering the place. The division of the Beejapore army that effected this was commanded by Shahjee, father of Shivajee. In 1677, the fort fell to Shivajee by stratagem, and remained in Mahratta hands for twenty-one years. In 1690, the armies of the Delhi emperor, under Zoolfacar khan, were despatched against Jinjee with a view to the final extirpation of the Mahratta power. The siege was prolonged for eight years, but the fort fell in 1698, and afterwards became head-quarters of standing army in Arcot. In 1750, the French under Bussy captured it by a skilful and daringly-executed night-surprise, and held it with an efficient garrison for eleven years, defeating one attack by the English in 1752. Captain Stephen Smith took the place after five weeks' siege in 1761. In 1780 it was surrendered to Hyder ally, but subsequently it played no part of importance in the wars of Southern india. Jinjee long enjoyed the reputation of being one of the most unhealthy localities in the Carnatic [q.v.]. The french are said by Orme to have lost 1,200 European soldiers during their eleven years' tenancy of it, and their garrison of Europeans rarely exceeded 100 men. The fortress consists of three strongly fortified hills; Chundrayya doorgam, Krishnagherry, and Rajagherry. These are connected by long walls of circumvallation enclosing an area of over 7 miles in circumference. Rajagherry, the highest and most important, is about 600 feet high, and almost impregnable; the only approach being defended by three strong lines of fortification, while the only entrance is by a wooden bridge over a deep natural chasm. It consists of a ridge terminating in an overhanging bluff, facing south. On the summit of the bluff stands the citadel. It is not known who constructed the fort. The site was probably built on by Chola kings. The commencement of the great fort is attributed to a son of Vijayarunga naick, Governor of Tanjore in 1442. The works were completed during the time of the Vijianugger kings. The martello towers and cavaliers show traces of European supervision, and some of the more modern embrasures were the work of the French. The great lines of fortification which cross the valley between the three hills were evidently built at different periods. In their original form, they each consisted of a wall about 5 feet thick, built up of blocks of granite [caroom cull], and filled in with rubbish; but subsequently a huge earthen rampart, about 25 or 30 feet thick, has been thrown up behind these walls, and riveted roughly on the inside with stone, while at intervals in this rampart are barracks or guard rooms. There are several ruins of fine buildings inside the inner fort, two temples, the calyauna [q.v.] mahaul [q.v.], gymkhana [q.v.], granaries, eedgah [q.v.], barracks, mantapams [q.v.], &c., including a great tower of eight storeys. The most noticeable building of all is the Calyauna mahaul [calyauna mantapam]. This consists of a square court surrounded by rooms for the ladies of the Governor's household. In the middle of this court is a square tower of eight storeys, and altogether about 80 feet high, with a pyramidical roof. The first six storeys are all of the same size and pattern, namely an arcaded verandah [q.v.] running round a small room about 8 feet square, and communicating with the storey above by means of small steps. The room on the seventh storey has now no verandah, but there are indications of one having existed formerly. The topmost room is of smaller size than the others. The only other interesting feature in the building is an earthenware pipe leading to the sixth storey, and brought all the way from a tank 600 yards off, outside the walls of the fort, and carried under the wall to the back of the women's quarters, and thence over the roof to the Mahaul [q.v.]. Of curiosities on the hill may be mentioned the great gun; the rajah's bathing-stone, a large slab of granite 15 feet square and 4 or 5 inches thick near the spot where the palace is said to have stood; and a well in rock, into which prisoners were thrown to die of starvation. The latter is a singular boulder about 15 or 20 feet high poised on a rock near the Chuckracoolam and surmounted by a low circular brick wall. It has a natural hollow passing through it and the bottom is blocked up with masonry and the upper edges plastered with choonam [q.v.]. South of Rajagherry is Chuckly droog, also fortified, but separately. Near the Arcot gate of the Jinjee fort is a stone with an inscription. Several of the handsomely carved pillars of the temples on the Rajagherry were carried by the French to Pondicherry, and are still to be seen there. On the summit of a hill, a mile north of Jinjee, called Tirnautar coondroo are twenty-four Jeina figures carved on a rock. There are two perennial springs of excellent water in the top of Rajagherry. At the foot of the ridge of Rajagherry and between it and Chuckly droog are two tanks, and on the western side of the bluff is a third reservoir constructed to catch the surface drainage. Jinjee rock. Trig. station in lat. 12° 14′ 58·39″; long. 79° 26′ 13·98″; height 968 feet; from Jinjee W. 1 mile; from Tindivanam W. 17 miles; from the sea W. 40 miles [carnautaca rajakkal].

JINKA (मृग - mriga, *San.*; हरण - harana, *Mahr.*; كلويت - kalwít, *Hind.*; هرن - haran, *Dec.*; ಚಿಗರಿ - chigari, *Can.*; എറളെ - erale, *Too.*; జింక - jinka, *Tel.*; ହରିଣୋ - horino, *Oor.*; കരിമാൻ - karimán, *Mal.*; கரியமான் - kariyamán, *Tam.*). San. from (mrig, san. to pursue). Mahr. from (harina, san. antelope). Can. from (chigiyu, can. to jump). Tel. from (chimmu, tel. to butt). Mal. from (kari, mal. black + mán, mal. deer). Tam. from (kariya, tam. black + mán, tam. deer). San. also (harina), meaning reddish white; also (krishnamriga), meaning black antelope. Tel. also (irri), meaning butting; also (lédi). Title otherwise Indian antelope. The english Fallow-deer. Antilope bezoartica, antilopinæ, bovidæ, ruminantia, mammalia [sastanam, 23], of naturalists [jantoo]. Alias Antilope cervicapra. Horns long, diverging, with five flexures in old individuals; rings strong at the base, tip smooth; color of adult male rich dark glossy brown color above and on the sides, beneath and inside of the limbs white; hind head, nape, and back of neck hoary yellowish; nose and lips, and a large mark round the eyes white. Length about 4 feet to root of tail which is 7 inches; height at shoulder 32 inches. Horns from 20 to 27 inches long, 9 to 81 inches divergent at tip. The female is somewhat less and is pale yellowish fawn color above, white beneath and inside the limbs, and with a pale streak from the shoulder to the haunch. The buck when adult becomes darker and is called Black buck. Found throughout Southern india in suitable localities, but does not occur in the richly wooded Malabar coast. A large herd is kept in the park round Government house at Madras. Buck-shooting is favorite sport. The venison of this antelope is excellent, that of old bucks is superior to that of young ones. If taken young this antelope becomes very tame. Antelope skins are used by Bramins to sit upon. The skin of the male antelope, in its full shape, is especially valued by performers of yaugams [q.v.]. The intestinal secretion is used in rheumatic pains. The horns [sing] of the male antelope are reduced to powder and used as a medicine for colic and other diseases. The horn-powder is sometimes burnt to keep off scorpions [tail] and mosquitoes [q.v.]. The Jinka is one of the constellations [nacshatram] of the Indian zodiac [raushy] and is sacred to Chundran [q.v.] the moon. Compare :—Gazella bennettii, goat-antelope; Portax pictus, white-footed antelope; Rusa aristotelis (burrajinka), large antelope; Tetraceros quadricornis, four-horned antelope. See gloss. paragraphs.

JINRICKSHAW (جنريكشا - jinrikshá, *Malay*). From japanese meaning man + strength + cart. Japanese chair. Public conveyance of Shanghai introduced into India and now in use at Madras. It is like a small buggy with room inside for one person only; adopted for flat country when roads are good and cooly [q.v.] hire cheap.

JINS (جنس - jins, *Hind.*; దినుసు - dinusu, *Tel.*). From arabic. Kind, sort, article. Hama jins is all articles.

JIROYATY (زراعتى - ziráatí, *Hind.*). From (zara, ar. to sow). Cultivation. Cultivated land. Often used for lands ordinarily assessed, as opposed to inam [q.v.].

JITA (जितवृक्ष - jitavriksha, *San.*). Corruption from arabic (zaitún). Olive tree. Botanically the Olea genus, oleaceæ [vricsham, 85]. Trees or shrubs; leaves evergreen, opposite, entire or toothed; flowers small, whitish, frequently fragrant, in axillary or terminal panicles; fruit has an oily flesh and a bony two-celled stone. The species best known to the natives are :—dioica [indian olive], europæa [zeitoon]. Other s. indian species indigenous or naturalized are :—glandulifera, polygama.

JITTA (జిట్ట - jitta, *Tel.*). Means bird [cooroovy, pitta]. Common bird second term. Ex., where transl. is of first term :—Acrocephalus brunnescens (borrajitta), large; Acrocephalus dumetorum (kampajitta), bush; Calobates sulphurea (mudditippudujitta), rump + turning; Cisticola schænicola (vedurujitta), bambusa arundinacea, bamboo; Corydalla rufula (gurrapumárijitta), horse + keeper; Dicæum concolor (chittujitta), small; Drymoipus inornatus (lottakannujitta), hollow-eyed; Dumetia albogularis (pandijitta), pig; Mirafra affinis (ilajitta), whistling; Nemoricola indica (uyyálajitta), swing; Orthotomus longicaudus (likkujitta), sickle; Pipastes agilis (likkujitta), sickle; Prinia socialis (rellujitta), reed; Pyctorhis sinensis (errakálijitta), red + leg; Tephrodornis pondicerianus (vadambálajitta), mocking. See gloss. paragraphs.

JIZIA (جزيه - jiziyah, *Hind.*). From (jazá, ar. compensation). A poll tax levied by Mussalman rulers from all subjects who were not Mussalmans; thirteen rupees yearly for every two-thousand rupees worth of property possessed.

JO (جو - jo, *Hind.*). Which.——*Jo hookum* (جو حكم - johukm, Hind.). From (above + hukm, ar. order). As ordered.

JODE (جوڑ - jor, *Hind.*; ಜೋಡು - jódu, *Can.*; జోడు - dzódu, *Tel.*). Junction. Suffix in place names.——*Jodah* (جوڑا - jorá, Hind.; జోడు - dzódu, Tel.; சோடி - shódi, Tam.). From (jud, san. to join together). Pair. A pair of shoes. A suit of clothes; especially the Mahomedan ceremonial suit, comprising the duster [q.v.], neemah [q.v.], jauma [q.v.], cummerbund [q.v.] and izaur [pyjauma].——*Jody* (ಜೋಡಿಗೆ - jódige, Can.; జోడీ - jódí, Tel.). From (jódisu, can. to unite); as combining features of a free and a paying grant. Quit-rent, or something less than ordinary assessment [teervay] payable to Government on an Inam [q.v.]. See vol. I, 112.——*Jooree* (جوڑى - jorí, Hind.). From (jorá, hind. a pair). Scarf in pairs, made with a fag between for convenience of separation.——*Jootee* (جوتى - jútí, Hind.; சூத்தி - shútti, Tam.). Slipper. Kowsh are without heels, the back part being flattened down under the foot. Chinauls are without any back-piece, the quarters terminating under the ankles on each side, with raised heels perhaps an inch high. In Nokdars, the toe part is terminated by a long pointed strip, usually of leather [chamrah] lined with cloth, that curls inwards over the toes.

JOG (योग - yóga, *San.*; جوگ - jog, *Hind.*). From (yuj, san. to join). Union. The practice of religious abstraction [yogam], by which the individual may be united with the universal soul [autmam, sauyoojyam], and acquire similar supernatural powers. ——*Jogayya* (ಜೋಗಯ್ಯ - jógayya, Can.). From (jógi, can. sage + ayyá, can. master). Hindoo 2nd or pers. name [peyar].——*Jogy* (योगी - yógí, San.; جوگى - jogí, Hind.). A practiser of Yogam [q.v.]; a pretender to superhuman faculties [siddhy]; in general a religious mendicant, usually sheiva. It is also a caste title.

JOHUR (جوهر - júhar, *Hind.*). From (yóddhri, san. warrior). The practice of Rajpoots of putting their wives and children to death when unable to resist an enemy. It happened at Bobbily in 1758.

JOLLARPETT (சொலார்ப்பேட்டை - sholárppéttai, *Tam.* jalárpet*). From (dzálári, tel. plant, shorea talura, roxb. + péta, tel. suburb). Village, Railway station; Salem dist., Tripatore tal.; pop. 694; acres 579; lat. 12° 34′; long. 78° 37′; height 1,320 feet; from Salem N.N.E. 69 miles; from Tripatore N. 6 miles. Junction of the S.W. line and Bangalore branch lines of the Madras railway; large number of railway employés are resident.

JONACA (జోనంగి - dzónangi, *Tel.*; ജോനക - jónaka, obl., *Mal.*; சோனக - shónaga, obl., *Tam.*). From (yavana, san. greek). The country Shonagam was Sennar or Arabia. Otherwise Yonaca. Greeks, Jews [q.v.].—"*a*" As to the Greeks, India was invaded by Alexander the Great [secunder] three centuries before Christ; and writers of his life and actions, particularly Arrian and Quintus curtius, give an account of the countries he subdued. An ambassador named Megasthenes was sent to the court of Chundragooptan [q.v.] by Seleucus nicator, about three centuries before Christ, some of whose observations have been preserved by the greek geographer, Strabo. The south of India was visited and described by Arrian in the second century B.C., and many geographical notices and names of people and places occur in Ptolemy and Pliny.—"*b*" The Jews of Malabar are of two different denominations; Black jews, natives of the country, and White jews, bearing in their fair complexions evidence of recent emigration from a more temperate climate. The principal settlement of the Jews is in the southern part of the Malabar district. In Cochin are many White jews, the Black jews for the most part inhabiting a suburb on the northern side of the city. There is preserved in Cochin by a Rabbi a grant of Anjoovannam to Joseph Rabban, by the Permaul bhauscara ravy vurman and attested by the chief rajahs of Keralam [q.v.]; as follows in very ancient tamul akin to malayalam :—ஸ்வஸ்தி ஸ்ரீ - கொகோனமை கொணடான்கொ - ஸ்ரீ பார்கரனஇரவிவனமர் பலநூறுயிரதாணடுமசெக

கொல் நடததியாளா நினற யாணடு இரணடாமாண டைகCெக திர்முபபததாருமாணடு - மூயிறிகCொடடு இ ருநதருளிய நாள் பிரஸாதிசசருளியபிரஸாதமாவது-ஈ ஸுப்பு இறவவாஹுககு அஞசு வணணமும் பெடியாதும வாயனத தாலும் பாகுடமும அஞசு வணணப பெறும பகலவிளக குமு பாவாடையும அநதொளகுமகுடை யும—வடுகப பறையுமகாகாளமும இடுபடியும தொர ணமும தொர ணவிதானமும சரவும மிககும எழுபத திரணடுவீடு பெறுமகூடகொடுததொம--உலகுந்துலகக விபுமவிட டொரம-மறறும நகரததிலகுடிகள கொயில்க கு இறுககுமறு இவன இருமைமயும் பெறுமறுபெறவும ஆகச்செபபெட டொடுமசெயது கொததொம—அஞசு வணண முடைய ஈஸுபபு இறவவாஹுககும இவன ஸந ததிஆண் மககள்க குமபெணமககளககும இவன்மருமக கள்ககும் பெண்ம ககளைகொணடமருமககளககும ஸநத திப்பிரதிர்தி—உல குஞசநதிரனும உள்ளவும அஞசு வணணமஸநததிபபி ரகிரிதி—ஸ்ரீ இபபரி அறிவென வெணுடுடைய கொ வர்ததன மாததாணடன இபபரி அ றிவென வெணுவலிநாடுடைய கொதைசிரிதணடன இப பரி அறிவென எருளநாடுடைய மா ன வெபலமாள வீயன இபபரி அறிவென வளளுவநாடுடைய இராயாகு சாததன இபபரி அறிவென தெடுமபுறையூர்நாடுடைய கொதை யிரவி இபபரி அறிவென கிழபபடைநாயகம செயபின றமூர்ககணசாததன வன்றலெசசெரிககணடன குனறபபொழுைய கிழவாய் கCெளடபா னெழுதது—

"Hail! The king who has taken the supreme rule, Permaul shree "bhauscara ravy vurman, wielding the sceptre and ruling for "many 100,000 years in his time, in the thirty-sixth year against "the second cycle, on the day when he was pleased to sit in "Mooyiricode [q.v.], he was pleased to grant this favor. We "have given to Joseph rabban the principality Anjoovannam, "along with the seventy-two Jenmy [q.v.] rights such as going "with elephants and other conveyances, tribute from subordinate "land-holders, and the possession of Anjoovannam, the light by "day, the spreading cloth, the litter, the umbrella, the drum, "the trumpet, the gateway with seats, ornamental arches and "similar awnings and garlands and the rest. We have remitted "to him the tribute due to the supreme government. Given to "Joseph rabban the owner of Anjoovannam, and to his posterity, "sons and daughters, nephews and son-in-law a hereditary "appendage; for the time that earth and moon exist [achan-"draurcam]. Anjoovannam a hereditary appendage."—"*c*" Jonangy nye, from (náy, tam. dog) is a greyhound.

JONNA (జొన్న - dzonna, *Tel.*). Same as Cholum.

JOOGADY (జూగడి - jugadi, *Tel.*). Intoxicating liquor prepared from rice [q.v.] among Ooriyas [mooskiraut, pachwye].

JOOLMAUNA (جرمانہ - jurmánah, *Hind.*). From (jurm, pers. fault). A fine.

JOOLVA (జూల్వ - julva, *Tel.*). A goddess of Sowrahs [q.v.].

JOON (यूक - yúka, *San.*; قمل - kaml, *Ar.*; سپش - supush, *Pers.*; جون - jún, *Hind.* and *Dec.*; كوتو - kutu, *Malay*; ಹೇನು - hénu, *Can.*; ಪೇನ್ - pén, *Too.*; పేను - pénu, *Tel.*; പേൻ - pén, *Mal.*; උකුණා - ukunná, *Singh.*; பேன் - pén, *Tam.*). Title from hindostany. San. from (yu, san. to fasten). Hind. and dec. from sanscrit. Louse. Synonymous with family pediculidæ, hemitera, hemimetabola, insecta [poochy], of naturalists [jantoo].

JOONAH (جونا - júná, *Hind.*). From (guna, san. thread). A rope of twisted grass or twine, made to support a round-bottomed jar.

JOROW (జొరో - joro, *Tel.*). From (jhari, san. torrent). Sanscrit name (sarayu), meaning rapid river. River; Ganjam dist., Bodagooda zemindarry and Sooradah tal. Rises in Bodagooda maliahs [q.v.] and flowing southwards drains Bodagooda zemindarry [q.v.] and part of Sooradah talook [q.v.] and joins the Rooshcoolya near Sooradah. Length about 20 miles.

JOVY (జువ్వి - dzuvvi, *Tel.*). Same as Tsiela.——*Red jovy* (ఎఱ్ఱజువ్వి - erradzuvvi, Tel.). Same as Shilandy.

JOW (यव - yava, *San.*; जव - java, *Mahr.*; बाज्रि - bájri, *Conc.*; شعير - shaír, *Ar.*; جو - jau, *Pers.*, *Hind.* and *Dec.*; ಜವೆಗೋಧಿ - javegódhi, *Can.*; యవలు - yavalu, *Tel.*; பார்லி - párli, *Tam.*). Title from sanscrit through deccany. San. from (yu, san. to attach), grain attached to husk [geung]. Mahr., &c., from sanscrit. Can. from (yave, san. barley + gódhi, can. wheat, triticum vulgare, vill.). Tam. from english. San. also (shita-shúka), meaning having sharp awns. Conc. also (bárli). Can. also (birukánji), meaning beer barley; (mullukánji), meaning spiked barley; (akkikánji), meaning rice barley. Tel. also (dzavabiyyamu), meaning jow + grain; (dzavvubiyyamu), meaning jow + grain; (pattsayava), meaning yellow + jow; (báralibiyyamu), meaning barley + grain. Tam. also (káñji), perhaps conjee grain [caunchy, indian elm]; (várgóthumai), meaning tail + wheat [geung]; (toraigánji), meaning master + barley. Greek κριθὴ λευκή. Title otherwise Barley, Tail wheat. Botanically Hordeum vulgare, linn., graminaceæ [vricsham, 156]. Alias Hordeum cœleste, distichum, hexastichum, hexastochyon, sativum. Cereal; produces many stems, two to three feet high, from a single grain; seeds oval, oblong, straw-colored. Used for manufacture of beer; the corn is first caused to germinate so as to develop sugar [q.v.] at the expense of the starch; the germination is then abruptly checked by turning and heating in a kiln [shoolay]; when dried and ground a mash or infusion is prepared, and this is allowed to ferment till alcohol is formed; the fermented liquor is then strained, and a sufficient quantity of hop is added to impart a bitter flavor; according to the original temperature of the mash, the duration of the fermentation, and the proportion of sugar and hops, are procured pale ale, table beer, and porter. Pearl and scotch barley are formed by the removal of the thin, hard integuments, the grain being hardened by drying. In pharm. pearl barley or the husked seeds, hordeum decorticatum, are officinal; diet for the sick; preparation, decoctum hordei. There are two varieties grown, two-rowed or Distichum and six-rowed or Hexastichum; the last more usual.—"*a*" Jow as the length of a ear of barley is a linear measure. 8 jows = 1 ungoolam [alavay, 1e]. Approximate actual value, 1 jow = ·1 of an inch. Same as San. yavam, Can. yavey, Mal. tora, Tam. nel.—"*b*" Jow as the weight of the same is a goldsmith's weight. 6 zarrahs = 1 jow; 2 jows = 1 dhann [niray, 3e]. Approximate actual value, 1 jow = $\frac{15}{64}$th of a grain. See vol. I, 609.——*Indian jow* (هند کی جو - hindkíjau, Hind.). Same as Varagoo.——*Vilauyaty jow* (ولایتی جو - viláitíjau, Hind.). Hind. from (viláití, hind. foreign + jau, hind. oat, avena). Greek βρόμος. Title otherwise Cultivated oat, Haver, Oat. Botanically Avena sativa, linn., graminaceæ [vricsham, 156]. Seeds cylindrical, covered with a black or white envelope; groats or cuttlings are the bruised oat seeds freed of the pericarp.

JOW (جاؤ - jáu, *Hind.*). Imperative. Be off!

JOWGADA (జౌగడ - dzaugada, *Tel.*). From (dzau, oor. lac + gada, oor. fort), meaning a fort of which the walls are coated with lac [q.v.] and so made slippery and difficult to scale; cf. the story in the mahabhaurat [q.v.]. Village; Ganjam dist., Berhampore tal.; lat. 19° 31′; long. 84° 53′; from Berhampore N. 14 miles; from Chetterpore N.W. 15 miles; from the sea W. 24 miles. On N. bank of Rooshcoolya, close to Pandiyah, amongst the remains of what was once a large city surrounded by a fort wall. An inscribed rock, one of a group inside the fort in N. lat. 19° 13′ 15″, long. 84° 53′ 55″, contains the only Asoca inscription in S. india. It rises vertically and the inscribed surface faces the south-east. Photographs and copies were taken in 1858 and 1871. There are three smoothed places on the rock each close to the other, about 20 feet by 16, and the letters are about 2 inches in length. The first ten edicts of Asoca are found engraved at Capardagiry or Shahbauzgurh, Khalsy, Girnar, Dhowlee and Jowgada, the first two differing from the last three in a portion of the ninth edict. The eleventh, twelfth and thirteenth edicts are found only at Shahbauzgurh, Khalsy and Girnar. The fourteenth is at all five places. Dhowlee and Jowgada have two separate edicts not given at the other places. The following is summary of the contents of the edicts which are found at Jowgada. The first edict prohibits the sacrifice of animals either for food or in religious assemblies. The second edict provides a system of medical aid for men and animals throughout Priyadarshy's dominions and orders trees to be planted and wells to be dug along the sides of the principal public roads. The third edict enjoins a quinquennial humiliation, certain precepts are to be enjoined on the people by their teachers with arguments and examples. The fourth edict draws a comparison between the condition of the country before and during the reign of the kings. The fifth edict records the appointments of missionaries and enumerates some of the countries to which they are to be deputed; in this edict for the first time occurs the name of the celebrated city of Pautalipootram. The sixth edict appoints Pativaidacan, or Custodes morum, who are to take cognizance of the conduct of the people in their meals, their domestic life, their families, their conversation, their general deportment, and their decease; it also nominates magistrates or officers for punishment and gives an indication of the system of moral administration with which Asoca [q.v.] is credited by Greek and Persian historians. The seventh edict expresses desire on the part of the king that all the diversities of religious opinion may be obliterated and that all distinctions in rank and caste may be harmonised into one system of Bhauva shooddhy or peace of mind. The eighth edict contrasts the amusements patronised by former rajahs with the pious enjoyments prescribed by himself; the dharmayautra or festival of religion is set in opposition to the vihaurayautra or festival of amusement, and is stated to consist in the visits to holy people, in alms-giving, in respect to elders, and similar praiseworthy sources of rational gratification. The ninth edict discourses on the sources of true happiness and inculcates the dharma mungalam, or happiness of virtue, which displays itself in benevolence to dependants, reverence to pastors, charity, and so forth, through which alone the blessings of heaven are to be propitiated. The tenth paragraph comments upon the glory of renown. The fourteenth edict sums up the foregoing. It appears from this edict that the whole was engraved at one time from authentic copy, issued, under the royal mandate, by a pundit whose name, however, cannot be deciphered. As at Dhowlee, the letters are all of uniform size and the lines are perfectly straight, and altogether the Ganjam inscriptions are as carefully and neatly engraved as any of the rock edicts. The first tablet contained the first five edicts, but about one-half has been lost by the peeling away of the rock. The second tablet comprised the next five edicts, namely six to ten, to which was added the fourteenth or closing edict of the other versions. About one-third of this tablet has been lost by the peeling away of the rock. The third tablet contained the two separate or additional edicts which are found at Dhowlee. The following is a translation of the second edict and it may be taken as a specimen of this form of composition:—"In "all the subjugated territories of the king Priyadarshy, the "beloved of the gods, and also in the bordering countries, as "Choda, Paundya, Satyapootra, Keralapootra, and Tambapunny, "it is proclaimed, and Antiochus the Yavana [q.v.] ruler, and "those princes who are near to or allied with that monarch, "universally, are apprised that two designs have been cherished "by Priyadarshy, one design regarding men and one relating "to animals; and whatever herbs are useful to men are useful "to animals, wherever there are none, such have been every- "where caused to be conveyed and planted; and roots and fruits "wherever there are none such have been everywhere conveyed "and planted and on the roads wells have been caused to be "dug and trees have been planted for the respective enjoyment "of animals and men." Tambapunny is the island of Ceylon, the Taprobane of the Greeks. Satyapootra has been identified with the Andhras on the Godavery.

JOWHAR (جوهر - jauhar, *Ar.*). Persian gowhar. A jewel. Mahomedan servant's name [ism].——*Jawauhir* (جواهر - jawáhir, Hind.). Plural of (jauhar, ar. jewel). Jewels [zewar]; accompaniment of khilat [q.v.].——*Jowhary* (جوهری - jauharí, Hind.). Jeweller. Geologists, are known as Jowhary sahibs, it being supposed that their investigations have for object discovery of precious stones [ratnam].

JOWLY (జవళి - dzavili, *Tel.*; சவுளி - shavuli, *Tam.*). From (chóli, san. cloths). Cloth, piece-goods.

JOYS (جائی - jái, *Malay*). From the portuguese (joia), a jewel. Jewellery of any kind [nagay, zewar].

JUJUBE (زيزفون - zaizufún, *Ar.*). Same as Bair.

JUMMA (جمع - jama, *Hind.*). From (jama, ar. to collect). Amount, total; the whole revenue [beriz] of a village, or estate. ——*Jamaut* (جماعت - jamáat, Hind.). From (jama, ar. to collect). Mahomedan congregation.——*Jaumy* (جامع - jáme, Hind.). From (jama, ar. to collect). Collection.——*Jemadar* (جمعدار - jamadár, Hind.). From (jama, ar. body of persons + dár, pers. holder). A head peon. An officer in the Native army next below a Soobahdar [q.v.], and corresponding to the English lieutenant.——*Jooma* (جمعه - juma, Hind.). From (jama, ar. to congregate). Congregation. Friday, the day on which Mahomedans assemble in the chief mosque [musjid] for prayers [namauz]. The day on which God created the sun [najm], moon [cumr] and stars and set them in motion; on which he collected the materials of which Adam was created; on which Adam was taken into Paradise [bheest]; and which will be the day of resurrection.——*Joomeraut* (جمعرات - jumarát, Hind.). From (above + rát, hind. night). Friday eve or Thursday [shamba]. The vegetable kingdom was created on this day. ——*Joomla* (جمله - jumlah, Hind.). From (jamala, ar. to collect). Total.——*Jummabundy* (جمعبندی - jamabandí, Hind.). From (above + bandí, pers. a settlement). Annual settlement of fluctuating items in ryotwarry [q.v.] land revenue, coupled with a personal investigation into all manner of subjects connected with the land revenue system. See vol. I, 112.——*Jumma curts* (جمع خرچ - jamakharch, Hind.). From (above + kharch, pers. expense). Account current of receipts and disbursements.——*Jumma kaumil* (جمع كامل - jamakámil, Hind.). From (above + kámil, ar. entire). Standard assessment [kaumil]. Particularly the assessment of the revenue of the Northern circars [q.v.] made about A.D. 1512–1570, or one subsequently made in the reign of Alumgheer, about 1684–1687, for the whole of the Deccan [q.v.].——*Jummamusjid* (جامع مسجد - jámimasjid, Hind.). The principal or congregational mosque [musjid] of prayer [namauz] in a city.——*Jumma vasool bauky* (جمع وصول باقی - jamavasúlbákí, Hind.). From (above + vasúl, ar. collection + bákí, ar. balance). Account of demand, collection and balance [dowle vasool bauky].

JUMMALMADOOGOO (జమ్మలమడుగు - dzammalamadugu,* *Tel.*). From (dzammu, tel. rushes, typha elephantina, roxb. + madugu, tel. pool).——**(1)** Talook, Cuddapah district. Tahsildar's pay Rs. 200. Area 616 square miles. Population 101,296. Language Teloogoo. Occupies N.W. corner of district. Bounded N. and W. respectively by Coilcoontla talook of Kurnool and Tadpatry talook of Anantapore districts, E. and S. by Proddootore and Poolivendla talooks respectively. Two ranges of hills run from east to west through southern division. Bhauncote hills form natural boundary to Poolivendala talook and Yerramala range, starting from near Proddootore reach their highest point at the gorge where the Pennair flows through Gundicote to Jummalmadoogoo. Neither of these ranges much exceed 1,000 feet and are bare of interest and vegetation. The highest point in the Yerramala hills is 1,660 feet above the sea. The whole talook may be included in black cotton soil [regar] district. The soil in the south is red ferruginous to a great extent. The quality varies from excellence in the north and west to mediocrity in the south; but with the exception of Pennair basin, no other system of soil prevails. Agriculture almost entirely dry crops [dry grain]. The open plains of black soil are divided between cholum [q.v.] and cotton [q.v.]. Indigo [q.v.], grain, and oil seeds [yennay] of varieties make up the sum of the crops generally grown, while water is so scarce that rice [q.v.] and raggy [q.v.] are confined to immediate neighbourhood of Pennair and its channels [q.v.]. Cheap turbans [puggry] are made in Jummalmadoogoo and Taulla proddootore and are exported to the Mahratta country. There is a cotton press at Jangaulapully. Thick cotton carpets [jamkhana] are also made and in Jummalmadoogoo there is some trade in dyeing coarse Tadpatry chintzes [q.v.]. The Pennair and Chitrauvaty join near Gandlore, so that the talook is drained by only one stream over the greater portion of its area. The waters of the Pennair are utilised to a slight extent by irrigating channels, but the upward slope of the country from the river banks precludes any great development of river irrigation. The surface water-supply is in many places most deficient, the deepest wells alone retaining water in the dry season. There are thirty tanks [q.v.]. The Cuddapah Kurnool canal runs through the N.E. of the talook but is little used. The talook has been always liable to drought, and from time to time to inundations. There are camping grounds at Gandlore, Shettivaurpulley, Taulla proddootore and Yaumavaram. Places of archæological interest:—Bondalcoonta, Chinna comerla, Codoor, Condasoonkesoola, Digoova calavataula, Dommara nundiaul, Goondlacoonta, Gorigenore, Gundicote, Jummalmadoogoo, Nullapully, Ooppalore, Pedda comerla, Peddandlore, Penikelapaud, Pottipaud, Timmapooram, Toorp soongamanchipulley, Velpoocherla, Yaumavaram, Yenoomoola chintala. Principal trig. station:—Gundicote. The leading places, &c., in the talook are the following.——*Bhauncote* (భానుకోట - bhánukóta, Tel.). See sep. title.——*Bheemagoondam* (భీమగుండము - bhímagundamu, Tel.). From (bhíma, san. shiva + gundamu, tel. a pit). Village; pop. 1,102; acres 2,794; lat. 14° 58′; long. 78° 25′; from Cuddapah N.W. 44 miles; from Jummalmadoogoo N. 8 miles. Four pools in a rock which supply water. Much fever and dysentery.——*Cawderabad* (قادرآباد - kádirábád, Hind.; ఖాదరాబాద - kádarábáda, Tel.). From (kádir, ar. proper name + ábád, ar. city). Village; pop. 2,724; acres 4,710; lat. 14° 50′; long. 78° 21′; from Cuddapah N.W. 41 miles; from Jummalmadoogoo W.S.W. 5 miles. Turbans woven. Two mosques [musjid], a pagoda [q.v.] and the shrine [durgah] of a Mussalman saint [walee].——*Chintacoonta* (చింతకుంట - chintakunta, Tel.). From (chinta, tel. tamarind tree, tamarindus indica, linn. + kunta, tel. pond). Village; pop. 1,023; acres 5,584; lat. 14° 42′; long. 78° 23′; from Cuddapah W.N.W. 35 miles; from Jummalmadoogoo S.S.W. 11 miles. Once head-quarters of a Deputy collector. It is feverish. Temple of Lingameeshwaran on hill by village and inscription in the village. On the route from Cuddapah to Bellary. Former seat of a poligar [q.v.].——*Chitrauvaty* (చిత్రావతి - chitrávati, Tel.). See sep. title.——*Codoor* (కోడూరు - kódúru, Tel. kódúr *). From (kóde, tel. bull + úru, tel. village). Village; pop. 2,232; acres 9,989; lat. 14° 52′; long. 78° 09′; from Cuddapah W.N.W. 54 miles; from Jummalmadoogoo W. 19 miles. Vishnoo temple with inscriptions.——*Condaupooram* (కొండాపురము - kondápuramu, Tel. kondápuram *). From (konda, tel. a hill + pura, san. town). Shrotriem village, Railway station; pop. 299; acres 920; lat. 14° 47′; long. 78° 14′; height 722 feet; from Cuddapah W.N.W. 46 miles; from Jummalmadoogoo W.S.W. 14 miles. Large bridge across Chitrauvaty.——*Coondair* (కుందేరు - kundéru, Tel.). See sep. title.——*Dhodiyam* (ధాడియము - dhodiyamu, Tel.). From (dhadi, can. border). Village; pop. 2,257; acres 10,339; lat. 14° 56′; long. 78° 16′; from Cuddapah N.W. 50 miles; from Jummalmadoogoo W.N.W. 12 miles. On Yerramalas. Several springs.——*Gandlore* (గండ్లూరు - gandlúru, Tel.). From (gandi, tel. gorge + úru, tel. village). Village; pop. 1,044; acres 6,005; lat. 14° 47′; long. 78° 16′; from Cuddapah W.N.W. 45 miles; from Jummalmadoogoo W.S.W. 12 miles. At junction of Pennair and Chitrauvaty.——*Gundicote* (గండికోట - gandikóta, Tel.). See sep. title.——*Jangaulapully* (జంగాలపల్లె - dzangálapalle, Tel.). From (dzangama, tel. the sect + palle, tel. village). Village; pop. 1,584; acres 3,922; lat. 15° 01′; long. 78° 33′; from Cuddapah N.N.W. 42 miles; from Jummalmadoogoo N.E. 15 miles. Thriving village on Kurnool-Cuddapah canal. Cotton press.——*Jummalmadoogoo* (జమ్మలమడుగు - dzammalamadugu, Tel.). See below.——*Mooddanore* (ముద్దనూరు - muddanúru, Tel. muddanúr *). From (muddana, tel. proper name + úru, tel. village). Village, Railway station; pop. 1,292; acres 4,403; lat. 14° 41′; long. 78° 26′; height 619 feet; from Cuddapah W.N.W. 32 miles; from Jummalmadoogoo S. 12 miles.——

Mungaputnam (మంగపట్నము - mangapatnamu, Tel.). From (manga, tel. prickly plant, randia dumetorum, lamk. + pattana, san. town). Village, Railway station; pop. 2,012; acres 12,767; lat. 14° 43′; long. 78° 18′; from Cuddapah N.W. 40 miles; from Jummalmadoogoo S.W. 12 miles.——*Peddamoodiyam* (పెద్దముడియము - peddamudiyamu, Tel.). From (pedda, tel. large + mudiya, tel. bundle of straw). Village; pop. 1,646; acres 4,943; lat. 15° 01′; long. 78° 30′; from Cuddapah N.W. 44 miles; from Jummalmadoogoo N.N.E. 13 miles. Important cotton centre.——*Peddapasapoola* (పెద్దపసుపుల - peddapasupula, Tel.). From (pedda, tel. large + pasupu, tel. turmeric, curcuma longa, roxb.). Village; pop. 2,436; acres 12,732; lat. 14° 53′; long. 78° 29′; from Cuddapah N.W. 37 miles; from Jummalmadoogoo E.N.E. 5 miles. Formerly seat of a poligar. Taken by the Cuddapah nawaub [q.v.] and given to Jamaulooddeen khan who built a fort and mosque which is inscribed with his name. Pagoda [q.v.] to Vishnoo [q.v.] and yearly car festival.——*Pennair* (పెన్నేరు - pennéru, Tel.). See sep. title.——*Talamunchiputnam* (తలమంచిపట్నము - talamanchipatnamu, Tel.). From (tala, tel. head + manchi, tel. good + pattana, san. town). Village; pop. 1,328; acres 4,402; lat. 14° 56′; long 78° 21′; from Cuddapah N.W. 46 miles; from Jummalmadoogoo N.W. 8 miles. Old fort.——*Yaitore* (యేటూరు - yétúru, Tel.). From (yéru, tel. river + úru, tel. village). Village; pop. 1,466; acres 3,444; lat. 14° 47′; long. 78° 11′; from Cuddapah W.N.W. 49 miles; from Jummalmadoogoo W.S.W. 17 miles. Allotted by Vijianugger dynasty as a jagheer [q.v.] to the Gundicote temple but sequestrated by Meer joomla.——*Yerramala* (యెర్రమల - yerramala, Tel.). See sep. title.——(2) Town, Talook head-quarters; Cuddapah dist., Jummalmadoogoo tal.; pop. 5,866; acres 3,395; lat. 14° 51′; long. 78° 25′; from Cuddapah N.W. 38 miles; from Madanapully N. 90 miles; from Madras N.W. 177 miles; from Sidhout N.W. 47 miles. On Pennair, a few miles east of Gundicote hills. The houses are mostly built of blue limestone [choonam cull]. A few are thatched but most have flat roofs covered with Sowdoo [q.v.]. Adjoining bazaar [q.v.] stands a small fort built to command the river. The Diwann [q.v.] khana [q.v.], the place of the Cuddapah patann [q.v.] governors, and the tomb of Syed khan, brother of Haleem khan, Nawaub of Cuddapah, are near. In a tamarind [q.v.] tope [q.v.] N. of town is temple to Narapooreshwaran. Car festival about 22nd May for ten days. Trade centre for indigo [q.v.] and cotton [q.v.]. Local manufacture of cloth. Turbans [puggry] manufactured and exported to Sholapore. S.P.G. mission station.

JUNG (جنگ - jang, *Hind.*). Means war. Hindoo third name [peyar]. Part of Mahomedan lacab; as Moozuffer jung, victorious in war [ism].

JUNGAR (ചങ്ങാടം - channátam, *Mal.*). From (samghat, san. to unite). Jangada [q.v.] in Portuguese. A double platform canoe made by placing a floor of boards across two boats, with a bamboo [q.v.] railing. Used on rivers of Malabar coast [changanda].

JUNGLE (जंगल - jangala, *San.*; جنگل - jangal, *Hind.*; ಕಾಡು - kádu, *Can.*; అడవి - adavi, *Tel.*; കാട് - kátu, *Mal.*; காடு - kádu, *Tam.*). Any tract overrun with bushes or trees, or suffered to be overspread with vegetation.——(1) Plant first term often joining two genera. Ex., where translation is of second term:—Abutilon indicum (adavibenda), hibiscus esculentus; Alstonia venenatus (káttarali), nerium odorum; Amomum subulatum (adaviélaki), ellettaria cardamomum; Amorphophallus lyratus (adavikanda), typhonium orixense; Amorphophallus sylvaticus (adavicháma), colocasia antiquorum; Artemisia vulgaris (kátttuchettippú), chrysanthemum indicum; Atalantia monophylla (káttelumiççai), lime tree; Atylosia scarabæoides (káttukkollu), dolichos biflorus, horse-gram; Baliospermum montanum (káttámanakku), ricinus communis, castor-oil plant; Bauhinia purpurea (adavíavishi), sesbania grandiflora; Bauhinia tomentosa (vanasampagegida), michelia champaca; Blumea lacera (janglíkásní), cichorium endiva, (janglímullí), raphanus sativus; Breynia rhamnoides, var. genuina (kádunuggégida), moringa pterygosperma, horse radish; Buchanania latifolia (káttumá), mangifera indica, mango; Cadaba indica (káttagatti), sesbania grandiflora; Canarium commune (janglíbádam), prunus amygdalus; Canavalia ensiformis, var. virosa (adavichamma), canavalia ensiformis; Canna indica (káttuvázha), musa paradisiaca, plantain; Cassia absus (káttukkol), dolichos biflorus, horse-gram; Casuarina equisetifolia (janglíjháú), tamarix gallica, (janglísaro), cupressus sempervirens; Cerbera odollum (káttarali), nerium odorum, (káttumá), mangifera indica; Chloris barbata (adavigódhuma), triticum vulgare, wheat; Cinnamomum iners (kádulavanga), cloves, eugenia caryophyllata; Citrullus colocynthis (káttuvellari), cucumis sativus; Cleome viscosa (káttukkadugu), brassica juncea, mustard; Clerodendron inerme (vanajai), jasminum auriculatum; Coix barbata (adavigódhuma), triticum vulgare, wheat; Corchorus olitorius (káttuttutti), abutilon indicum; Croton oblongifolius (káttupatólam), trichosanthes anguina; Cryptolepis buchanania (káttupálvalli), chonemorpha malabarica; Curcuma zedoaria (vanárishtá), melia azadirachta; Cycas circinalis (janglímadanmastkájhár), artabotrys odoratissimus; Dillenia indica (kádkanyila), nerium odorum; Dracontium polyphyllum (adavikanda), typhonium orixense, (janglíkandá), colocasia esculenta; Erythroxylon monogynum (adavigóranta), lawsonia alba, nail-dye plant; Fumaria parviflora (kádusabbasige), peucedanum graveolens; Glycine javanica (káduavare), dolichos lablab; Guizotia abyssinica (adavinuvvu), sesamum indicum; Gynandropsis pentaphylla (káttukkatuku), brassica juncea, mustard; Hardwickia binata (káttudugu), acacia pennata; Helmia bulbifera (káttuvalli), dioscorea; Hibiscus abelmoschus (káttupparutti), gossypium herbaceum, cotton; Holigarna longifolia (káttuchér), semecarpus anacardium; Homonoya riparia (káttalari), nerium odorum; Hydnocarpus venenata (janglíbádam), prunus amygdalus; Hymenodictyon excelsum (janglíanár), punica granatum; Jatropha curcas (adaviámuda), ricinus communis; Jatropha multifida (kátttunérválam), croton tiglium; Jussiæa suffruticosa (káttukarayámpú), eugenia caryophyllata; Laggera aurita (adavimullangi), raphanus sativus; Lantana indica (kádujóla), sorghum vulgare, great millet; Lebidieropsis orbicularis, var. collina (kádagargarigida), wedelia calendulacea; Leersia hexandra (janglídál), cajanus indicus; Lepidagathis scariosa (káttuççilandi), ochna squarrosa; Limonia bilocularis (káttelumiççai), lime, citrus; Lippia nodiflora (káttutippali), piper longum; Lobelia nicotianæfolia (adavipogáku), nicotiana tabacum, tobacco; Malva rotundifolia (káttukkadalai), cicer arietinum, bengal gram; Manihot utilissima (kádugenasu), dioscorea aculeata; Melanthesa rhamnoides (káttunírúri), phyllanthus niruri, var. genuinus; Methonica superba (adavinábhi), aconitum ferox; Millingtonia hortensis (káttumalli), jasminum sambac; Mucuna pruriens (kádavare), dolichos lablab; Nasturtium palustre (kádusásive), brassica juncea, mustard; Nauclea purpurea (káttuchakka), artocarpus integrifolia, jack tree; Ormocarpum sennoides (adavimunaga), moringa pterygosperma; Osbeckia aspera (káttukadali), melastoma malabathricum, (káttukkakadalai), cicer arietinum; Panicum crusgalli (kádudabbehullu), eragrostis cynosuroides; Pedalium murex (káttunereñfil), tribulus terrestris; Pithecolobium bigeminum (káttukkonna), cassia fistula; Plumeria acutifolia (adaviganneru), nerium odorum, (kádusampige), michelia champaca; Plumeria alba (adaviganneru), nerium odorum, sweet-scented oleander; Randia dumetorum (káttunáranna), citrus aurantium; Rhizophora mucronata (adaviponna), calophyllum inophyllum; Rhynchosia rufescens (kádutogari), cajanus indicus; Salvia plebeia (káttukañjángórai), ocimum basilicum; Sanseviera lanuginosa (káttukappalkizhannu), ipomæa batatas; Sesselia indicum (vanayamání), carum copticum; Sida rhombifolia, var. retusa (janglímethí), trigonella fœnum-græcum; Sonchus oleraceus (káttumullangi), raphanus sativus, radish; Spondias mangifera (janglíám), mangifera indica; Sponia wightii (kádubajagida), acorus calamus; Sterculia fœtida (janglíbádam), prunus amygdalus; Tabernæmontana dichotoma (káttalari), nerium odorum; Tephrosia purpurea (janglíkulthí), dolichos biflorus; Terminalia belerica (káttiluppai), bassia longifolia; Terminalia catappa (janglíbádam), prunus amygdalus; Terminalia chebula (janglíbádam), prunus amygdalus; Terminalia tomentosa (janglíkaranj), pongamia glabra; Thespesia lampas (adavipatti), gossypium herbaceum, cotton; Toddalia aculeata (kádumenasu), piper nigrum; Trewia nudiflora (kátkumbala), cucurbita maxima; Tribulus terrestris (vanashringáta), trapa bispinosa; Urena lobata (vanabhéndá), hibiscus esculentus; Urena sinuata (janglíkapás), gossypium herbaceum; Urginia indica (janglípíyáz), allium cepa; Vernonia anthelmintica (adavijílakarra), cuminum cyminum. See gloss. paragraphs.——(2) *Jangaly* (ജാംഗലി - jángali, Mal.). Means jungle-dweller. A snake catcher. He professes to cure snake bites [jungle].——*Jungle carp* (वज्रकीट - vajrakíta, San.; कालेमांजर - kálémáñjara, Mahr.; بجرکیٹ - bajrkít, Hind.; پانگولنگ - pángguling, Malay; ಅಲಂಕು - alanku, Can.; ఆలువ - áluva, Tel.; ଗୋଣ୍ଡ - gonda, Oor.; അലങ്കു - alanku, Mal.; කබල්ලෑවා - kaballává, Singh.; அழுங்கு - azhungu, Tam.). Title on account of its arched back in walking. San. from (vajra, san. diamond + kíta, san. reptile); from the dorsal scales. Mahr. from (kála, mahr. black + máñjara, mahr. cat). Hind. from sanscrit. Malay from (guling, malay, to roll); as it rolls itself up in self-defence. Can. from (alanku, can. timid). Tam. means to become dim, from its nocturnal habits. San. also (ghuna), meaning one moving to and fro. Hind. also (banrohú), meaning forest dweller. Title otherwise Indian scaly ant-eater, Pangolin from malay. Manis pentadactyla, manididæ, edentata, mammalia [sastanam, 28], of naturalists [jantoo]. Alias Manis brachyura, laticauda, macroura; Philidotus indicus. Tail shorter than the body, very broad at the base, with sixteen or seventeen scales in each longitudinal line; sixteen scales on the dorsal series in ten or eleven rows; middle nail of the fore feet much stronger than the others. Scales thick, striated at the base, pale yellowish brown or horny clay color; the lower side of the head, body and feet nude, brownish white; nose fleshy; soles of the hind feet blackish; auricles indistinct. The tongue is 12 inches long, flattish or sub-cylindric, extensile, generally covered with a slightly viscid saliva. Most common in hilly districts, but nowhere abundant. It is strictly nocturnal and feeds almost exclusively on white-ants [q.v.]. Its gait in walking is very peculiar, the back arched, the fore feet with their anterior surface bent over and brought into contact with the ground, on which it progresses very slowly. It burrows in the ground in a slanting direction to a depth of from 8 to 12 feet from the surface, at the end of which is a large chamber, about 6 feet in circumference, in which a pair live, and where they may be found with one or two young ones about the months of January, February, and March. The jungle-carp closes up the entrance of the burrow with earth when in it, so that it would be difficult to find it but for the peculiar track it leaves. Indian species not here found are :—Aurita or eared pangolin, Javanica or javan ant-eater.——*Jungle cat* (अरण्यमार्जार - aranyamárjára, San.; मोटलाबनमांजर - mótalábanamáñjara, Mahr.; گربۂ کوهی - gurbahikohí, Pers.; جنگلی بلی - janglíbillí, Hind.; ಮಂಟಬೆಕ್ಕು - mantabekku, Can.; జంగపిల్లి - jangapilli, Tel.; ଭୁବ - bhuva, Oor.; ചെറുപുലി - cheru-puli, Mal.; காட்டுப்பூனை - káttuppúnai, Tam.). Title from frequenting jungles. San. from (aranya, san. wild + márjára, san. cat). Mahr. from (móta, mahr. large + vana, san. forest + máñjara, mahr. cat). Pers. from (gurbah, pers. cat + koh, pers. mountain). Hind. from (janglí, hind. wild + billí, hind. cat). Tel. from (janglí, hind. forest + pilli, tel. cat). Mal. from (cheru, mal. small + puli, mal. tiger). Tam. from (kádu, tam. forest + púnai, tam. cat). Can. also (kádubekku), meaning forest + cat; (vellabekku), meaning white + cat. Tel. also (bávuripilli), meaning mewing + cat. Mal. also (kátanpúççá), meaning wild cat. Common wild cat. Felis [marjauram] chaus, felidæ [deeptaucsham], digitigrada, carnivora, mammalia [sastanam, 9], of naturalists [jantoo]. Alias Chaus lybicus; Felis affinis, catalynæ, erythrotis, jacquemontii, kutas. Yellowish gray, more or less dark and unspotted, approaching to rufous on the sides of the neck and abdomen, where it unites with the white lower parts; a dark stripe from the eyes to the muzzle; ears slightly tufted, rufous black externally, white internally; limbs with two or three dark stripes internally, occasionally faintly marked externally also; tail short, more or less annulated with black, most conspicuously in the young. Frequents alike jungles and the open country and is very partial to long grass and reeds, sugar-cane [q.v.] fields, corn-fields, &c. Larger somewhat than the domestic cat [poonay]; will interbreed with it. Indian species not here found are :—Manul or black-chested wild cat, Ornata or desert cat.——*Jungle fowl* (جنگلی مرغ - janglímurgh, Hind.). See sep. title.——*Jungle hare* (காணமுசல் - kánámusal, Tam.). Title from similar motion. See under Battan.——*Jungle parrot* (جنگلی توتا - janglítotá, Hind. and Dec.; ಕಾಡುಗಿಣಿ - kádugini, Can.; అడవిచిలుక - adavichiluka, Tel.). Title from resort and its red bill. Vernacular means same. Tel. also (puttachiluka), meaning ant-hill + parrot; from frequenting white-ant's nests. Title otherwise Southern sirkeer. Taccocua leschenaultii, centropodinæ, cuculidæ [cokam], scansores, insessores [pacshy, 15], of naturalists [jantoo]. Alias Zandostomus sirkeer. Above pale earthy brown; head ashy; throat whitish; fore neck and breast ashy, tinged with ferruginous; belly dark ferruginous; feathers of the head, neck and breast, with the shafts, black, and bill cherry-red, yellowish at the tip; feet plumbeous; irides reddish brown; length 15 to 15½ inches; frequently seen about white-ants' [q.v.] nests. No other common species here.——*Jungle sheep* (न्यङ्कु - nyanku, San.; भेकर - bhémkara, Mahr.; جنگلی بکرا - janglíbakrá, Hind.; كيجڠ - kijang, Malay; ಕಾಡುಕುರಿ - kádukuri, Can.; కూకగొర్రె - kúkagorre, Tel.; കട്ടമാൻ - katumán, Mal.; காட்டாடு - káttádu, Tam.). Title from its gait. San. from (nyañch, san. to bend down); from its stooping. Hind. from (janglí, hind. wild + bakrá, hind. sheep). Can. from (kádu, can. forest + kuri, tam. sheep). Tel. from (kúka, tel. noise + gorre, tel. sheep), from its bark. Mal. from (katu, mal. fierce + mán, mal. deer). Tam. from (kádu, tam. forest + ádu, tam. sheep). Hind. also (kákur). Malay also (mantják). Tel. also (kondaméka), meaning mountain + goat. Title otherwise Baikree in bombay, Barking-deer in bengal, Muntjack in java, Red hog-deer in ceylon, Rib-faced deer. Cervulus muntjac, cervidæ [mrigam], ruminantia, mammalia [sastanam, 24], of naturalists [jantoo]. Alias Cervus aureus, tamulicus, vaginalis. Color a bright rufous bay; limbs internally, pubic region, and tail beneath, white; chin and lower jaw, whitish; some white spots in front of the fetlocks of all four legs; facial creases dark brown. Average length of male 3½ feet; tail 7; height 26 to 28 inches; horn 8 to 10 inches. The doe is a little smaller, and has bristly black tufts of hair on a knob in the spot where the horns of the buck are. Its tongue is very long and extensile, and it often licks its whole face with it. Abundant in hilly countries, and a forest animal, only coming to the skirts of the woods morning and evening to graze. It is a solitary animal. It carries its head and neck low, and as its hind quarters are high, its action in running is peculiar, somewhat resembling the pace of a sheep [aud], hence its name in Southern india. It is excellent venison, but rarely carries any fat. Its call, which is a kind of short bark, like that of a fox [lomree] but louder, may be heard in the jungles by day and night.

JUNGLE-FOWL (रज्जुवाल - rajjuvála, *San.*). San. from (rajju, san. rope + vála, san. tail). The sub-family Gallinæ, phasianidæ [jeevanjeevam], rasores, aves [pacshy, 32], of naturalists [jantoo]. The species best known are shown below.——*Grey jungle-fowl* (جنگلی مرغ - janglímurgh, Hind. and Dec.; ಕಾಡುಕೋಳಿ - kádukóli, Can.; అడవికోడి - adavikódi, Tel.; കാട്ടുകോഴി - káttukózhi, Mal.; காட்டுக்கோழி - káttukkózhi, Tam.). Title from color of head and neck. Hind. from (janglí, hind. wild + murgh, hind. fowl). Can. from (kádu, can. forest + kóli, can. fowl) [indian woodcock]. Tel. from (adavi, tel. jungle + kódi, tel. fowl). Mal. from tamul. Tam. from (kádu, tam. forest + kózhi, tam. fowl). Can. also (kukkuta); (pugulakki), meaning note of a cuckoo + bird. Tam. also (shambangózhi), meaning shamboo sedge, typha angustifolia, linn. + fowl, from feeding on its seeds. Gallus sonneratii, gallinæ [jungle-fowl], phasianidæ [jeevanjeevam], rasores [pacshy, 32], of naturalists. Alias Phasianus gallus. Whole head and neck, with hackles, blackish grey, yellow spots, each feather blackish, with shaft white and two spots, terminal one somewhat square form, as if a drop of yellow sealing-wax [lac]; the other whitish, passing on wing-coverts into oblong spots of glistening wood-brown; ear-coverts pale rufous; rest of plumage above and below blackish grey, feathers white shafted, those on flanks broadly centered and tipped with wood-brown; outermost primaries dusky, with shaft and narrow edge pale; others black, faintly glossed; upper tail-coverts glossy purple; central tail-feathers glossy green, gloss diminishing on lateral feathers; vent dirty brownish; under tail-coverts glossy black, with white shafts. Bill yellowish horny; comb, face and wattles red; irides orange brown; legs and feet horny yellowish. Length 24 inches and upwards. Hen mottled brown above, pale shafts on wing-coverts; beneath blackish brown, feathers broadly centered, pure white passing into plain dull brown on flanks, thigh-coverts, vent, and under tail-coverts; head and neck rufous brown, paler on chin, and throat somewhat yellowish; primaries dark brown, secondaries mottled brown; tail blackish brown, edged mottled brown. Length about 17 inches. Found in S. india only, extending on east coast to a little north of the Godavery, and on west coast to Rajpipla hills, where it meets the Red jungle-fowl [q.v.]. Very abundant on Malabar coast, especially in more elevated districts; constantly brought for sale to Madras market. Particularly partial to bamboo [q.v.] jungles. Call of cock a broken and imperfect kind of crow, quite unlike that of the Red jungle-cock. The principal source of the domestic fowl [moorghy].——*Painted spur-fowl* (ನವಿಲುಬಣ್ಣದಹಕ್ಕಿ - navilubanna-dahakki, Can.; జిట్టకోడి - jittakódi, Tel.). Title from appearance. Can. from (navilu, can. peacock + banna, can. color + hakki, can. bird). Tel. from (jitta, tel. small + kódi, tel. fowl). Galloperdix lunulosus, gallinæ [jungle-fowl], phasianidæ [jeevanjeevam], rasores [pacshy, 32], of naturalists. Alias Francolinus nivosus. Male, head, face and neck variegated black and white, feathers black with white streaks and triangular spots, head mostly black; upper plumage and wings rich chestnut, with white spots on back, sides of neck, shoulders and wing-coverts; primaries earthy brown; tail dark sepia brown, glossed green in old birds; beneath throat and neck, variegated black and white, changing on breast to ochreous buff, with small triangular black marks, which disappear on abdomen; flanks, thigh-coverts and under tail-coverts dull chestnut. Bill blackish; orbits red; irides red brown; legs horny brown. Length 13 inches. Female has top of head dusky, with forehead, over eye, and nape tinged with chestnut; pale ruff and moustachial line; rest of plumage dull olive brown, changing to ochreous-olive on breast and abdomen. Length 12½ inches. Male has generally two spurs on each leg, occasionally three, hen bird has almost always one, frequently two. Not found on Malabar coast; common along Eastern ghauts [q.v.]; partial to rocky jungles and tangled coverts. Very difficult to flush, short and rapid flight; males have a cackling call like fowls [moorghy].——*Red jungle-fowl* (بن مرغ - banmurgh, Hind.; جنگلی مرغ - janglímurgh, Dec.; అడవికోడి - adavikódi, Tel.; ବନକୁକ୍କୁଡ଼ - bonokukkuda, Oor.). Title from color of body. Hind. from (ban, hind. forest + murgh, hind. fowl). Dec. from (janglí, hind. wild + murgh, hind. fowl). Oor. means jungle-fowl. Male bird is :—Tel. (geragogor). Tel. also (kuru), from ghond; female bird. Gallus ferrugineus, Gallinæ [jungle-fowl], phasianidæ [jeevanjeevam], rasores [pacshy, 32], of naturalists. Alias Gallus bankiva. Male, colors as in typical Barn-door fowl, viz., rich golden hackles on head, neck, throat and breast, paler on sides of neck and posteriorly; ear-coverts white; back purplish brown in middle, rich orange brown on sides; upper tail-coverts lengthened, also bright orange; wings with lesser and greater-coverts black, glossed green; median-coverts rich dull maroon; primaries dusky with pale edges; secondaries chestnut externally, dusky within; tertiaries glossy black; tail with central feathers rich glossy green-black, gloss diminishing on lateral feathers; beneath, from breast, unglossed black; thigh-coverts the same. Bill slaty brown; irides orange red; face, comb and wattles red; legs slaty black. Length about 26 inches; the jungle hen has general color yellowish brown, minutely mottled with dark brown; some feathers, especially of upper back and wing-coverts having conspicuously pale shafts; head dusky above, passing into short hackles of dark brown, edged bright yellow on neck and sides of breast; quills and tail dark brown; central rectrices edged mottled brown; ear-coverts yellowish; line down throat deep bright red-brown ending in point below, and passing up in a line behind the ears to join small supercilium of same hue; breast pale rufous brown, with central pale streaks, lighter on middle of belly and becoming dull brown on flanks, vent, thigh-coverts, and under tail-coverts ; wants the comb and wattles, and has only a small nude red space. Length 16 or 17 inches ; tail 7. Partial to bamboo jungle [q.v.], and lofty forests ; crow morning and evening, all the year round, but especially at the pairing season, is like that of Bantam cock, but shorter, and never prolonged as in domestic cocks ; after breeding season neck hackles of male sometimes fall off, replaced by short blackish grey feathers.——*Red spur-fowl* (چھوٹا جنگلی مرغ - chhotájanglímurgh, Hind. and Dec. ; ఎర్రకోడి - errakódi, Tel. ; ବନକୁକ୍କୁଡ - bonokukkuda, Oor. ; சிறகுக்கோழி - shiraguk-kózhi, Tam.). Title from color and spurs. Hind. from (chhotá, hind. small + janglí, hind. wild + murgh, hind. fowl). Tel. from (erra, tel. red + kódi, tel. fowl). Oor. means wild fowl. Tam. from (shiragu, tam. wing + kózhi, tam. fowl) ; from flight. Tel. also (errajittakódi), meaning red + small + fowl. Galloperdix spadiceus, gallinæ [jungle-fowl], phasianidæ [jeevanjeevam], rasores [pacshy, 32], of naturalists. Alias Polyplectron narthiæ. Male, head and nape dusky olive-brown ; forehead and round eye pale whity brown, somewhat buff in some ; chin, throat and sides of neck pale brown ; rest of body, both above and below, rich brown-chestnut or bay ; each feather pale edged ; primaries brown ; secondaries and tertiaries minutely mottled ; tail with central feathers chestnut, others dark-brown, more or less mottled, disappearing with age ; lower abdomen, vent and under tail-coverts olivaceous. Bill dusky-horny ; orbits red ; irides orange brown ; legs and feet vermillion red. Length 14 to 14½ inches. Female has crown dusky blackish, neck olive brown, rest of upper plumage pale rufous-brown, each feather with two or three blackish bands, minutely speckled, tip pale ; rump and upper tail-coverts minutely freckled ; tail mostly blackish, with mottled rufous bars, tending to become obsolete ; primaries, coverts and winglet spotless dusky brown ; throat albescent ; neck olive brown, the feathers becoming rufous in centre, and tipped black ; breast and flanks bright ferruginous, with narrow black tips ; belly dusky brown ; under tail-coverts freckled rufous brown. Length 13 inches. Male bird has usually two spurs on each tarsus, sometimes three on one, occasionally two on one leg and one on another, often long and sharp ; hen bird has usually one on each leg, sometimes absent on one leg ; occasionally two on one leg and one on the other. Common. Most abundant in Malabar jungles, difficult to obtain without dogs [nye], as it runs before the sportsmen or beaters. Runs with its tail raised.

JUNKAMEER (ചുങ്കക്കാരൻ - chunkakkáran, *Mal.*) [choongam]. From (chunkam, mal. custom + káran, mal. personal suffix). Old Anglo-Indian for a collector of customs [sayer].

JUTE (कालशाक - kálashåka, *San.* ; پٹ - patt, *Hind.* ; ಸಣಬು - sanabu, *Can.* ; జనుము - dzanumu, *Tel.* ; பிண்ணாக்குச்செடி - pinnákkuççedi, *Tam.*). Title from (jhóto, ooriya), from sanscrit (jhat), meaning to be tangled. San. from (kála, san. black + sháka, san. herb). Hind. from sanscrit. Tam. from (pinnákku, tam. oil-cake + shedi, tam. plant) ; from being cooked with sesamum oil cakes. San. also (patta), meaning cloth, perhaps from sackcloth made of fibre. Hind. also (títápát), meaning bitter leaf. Tel. also (gánugapindikúra), meaning oil-cake + greens ; (chittontakúra), meaning small + cooking + greens. Greek κόρχορος. Title otherwise Capsular corchorus, Gunny-bag plant, Heart-leaved corchorus, Jews' mallows, Pat fibre. Botanically Corchorus capsularis, linn., tiliaceæ [vricsham, 27]. Slender-stemmed annual, 5–10 feet ; calyx deeply five-cleft ; petals five ; leaves alternate, oblong-acuminate, serrated, two lower serratures terminating in narrow filaments ; peduncles short ; flowers whitish-yellow in clusters opposite the leaves ; capsules globose, truncated, wrinkled and muricated, five-celled ; seeds few in each cell, without transverse partitions ; in addition to the five-partite cells there are other five alternating, smaller and empty ; native of india ; flowering in rainy season. Extensively cultivated for the sake of its fibres [naur] ; these are soft and silky, and may be used as a substitute for flax [alsee] ; are very perishable. Crop takes four or five months to mature ; fit for harvesting as soon as flowers appear ; fibre of plants in fruit is stronger, though coarse ; the plants are cut, bundled, and stacked for two or three days, though this process discolors the fibre ; the bundles are then submerged either in rivers, or, as is usually done, in tanks or roadside pools, with sods placed on their tops ; the period of maceration lasts from two to twenty-five days, during which time, the bundles are carefully watched, so that they may not become rotten, and thus useless for commercial purposes ; the fibre is then separated from the stalks, cleaned, and dried ; great care is observed in watching the immersed jute until it almost putrefies, to preserve its silky character. The reeds or dried stems after the bark has been removed are used for a variety of purposes ; they are straight, brittle, and readily combustible ; largely consumed in the preparation of the charcoal [adoopp kary] used for gunpowder and in the manufacture of fireworks [baunam] ; used as tinder in the preparation of native matches ; one of the most useful purposes to which the jute cane is put is the burning or charring of the hulls of native boats to destroy or expel the insects which may have commenced their depredations upon the timber ; tied in bundles, they are also used for torch-light [masaul, pandam] processions ; europeans use them as pea-stakes.——*Wild jute* (नाडीक - nádika, San. ; పెరింటకూర - périntakúra, Tel. ; ନାଲିତା - nálitá, Oor. ; பெராட்டிக்கீரை - perattikkírai, Tam.). San. from (nála, san. tube). Oor. from sanscrit. San. also (patta), meaning cloth. Tel. also (parinta). Tam. also (pinnákkuççedi), meaning oil cake + plant ; (káttuttutti), meaning forest + mallow, abutilon indicum, g. don. ; (perumbunnákkukkírai), meaning big + the plant ; (kónippattai), meaning gunny bark. Title otherwise Bristly-leaved jews' mallow. Botanically Corchorus olitorius, linn., tiliaceæ [vricsham, 27]. Alias Corchorus decemangularis. Annual, 5–6 feet, erect ; leaves alternate, ovate-acuminated, serrated, the two lower serratures terminated by a slender filament ; peduncles one to two-flowered ; calyx five-sepalled ; petals five ; capsules nearly cylindrical, ten-ribbed, five-celled, five-valved ; seeds numerous, with nearly perfect transverse septa ; flowers small, yellow ; flowering in the rainy season. Fresh or dry herb, after being toasted and reduced to ashes, mixed with honey [shahad], given in obstructions of the viscera ; leaves used in infusion as a domestic medicine, being tonic and slightly febrifuge, and hence used as a fever drink. Leaves and tender shoots eaten [keeray]. Fibres, like those of capsularis [jute], substituted for flax [alsee] ; makes cloth, gunny [q.v.] bags, and rope.

JUTKAH (جھٹکا - jhatká, *Hind.*). Means quick. The native conveyance of mofussil [q.v.] towns in this presidency ; it consists of a box with venetian windows, on two wheels, and drawn by a pony [shigram, tattoo].

JWARAM (ज्वर - jvara, *San.* ; சுரம் - shuram, *Tam.*). From (jvar, san. to be hot). Fever [veidyan]. There are seven different classes of fevers according to natives :—Ajeernajwaram, from indigestion ; Astijwaram, of the bones ; Bhootajwaram, caused by evil spirits ; Dinajwaram, daily fever or quotidian ; Pittajwaram, that proceeds from pittam [q.v.] ; Sheetajwaram, that proceeds from sheetam [q.v.] ; Vautajwaram, that proceeds from vautam [q.v.].——*Jwara hary* (ज्वरहारि - jvarahari, San.). From (above + hri, san. to take away). Febrifuge.

JYAH (ज्या - jyá, *San.*). From (jyá, san. to overpower). Bow string. Sine or chord [chaupam, jeevay]. For Cramajyay and Paramaupama cramajjay see Cramam.——*Jyah pindam* (ज्यापिण्ड - jyápinda, San.). The sines of the twenty-four Pindams of 3° 45′ each into which the quadrant [paudam] is divided.——*Jyeshta* (ज्येष्ठ - jyésht'ha, San.). From (jyá, san. to become old). Eldest. Greatest. y in the algebraic form $ax^2 + b = y^2$.——*Jyeshtaumsham* (ज्येष्ठांश - jyesht'hámsha, San.). From (above + amsha, san. part). Primogeniture.——*Jyeshtay* (ज्येष्ठा - jyésht'há, San. ; சேட்டை - shéttai, Tam.). Elder sister, otherwise Moodevy [q.v.] ; younger sister being Lutchmy [q.v.].

JYOTY (ज्योतिस् - jyótis, *San.* ; சோதி - shóthi, *Tam.*). From (jyut, san. to shine). Splendour. Luminary or star. Epithet of Shiva. Light, one of the five gross elements [bhootam] ; the other four being, aucausham or ether, vayoo or air, aupas or water, pritivy or earth.——*Joshy* (ज्योतिषी - jyótishí, San. ; जोशी - jóshí, Mahr. ; జోసి - jósi, Tel. ; சோதிடன் - shóthidan, Tam.). An astronomer, astrologer [jyotisham]. Often a village servant remunerated by inam [q.v.] land. Bramin by caste, and duties are to prepare the calendar [punchaungam], caste nativities [jautacam], and announce the time propitious for any act. He is also the Hindoo artist and paints the idols [vigraham] and pictures of the gods.——*Joty canama* (జోతికనమ - jótikanama, Tel.). From (jyóti, san. brightness + kanama, tel. ravine). Pass ; Kurnool district, Nundicotcore talook. In Nullamullays [ghaut].——*Jyotisham* (ज्योतिष - jyótisha, San.). Astronomy.—"*a*" This was title of sixth and last Vedaungam [q.v.], object being to fix the most auspicious days for commencing sacrifices [yaugam]. Among the ancient astronomical ideas there shown are the measure of a day by thirty moohoortams [q.v.] or hours of forty-eight minutes, division of zodiac [raushy chuckram] into twenty-seven parts or lunar asterisms [nacshatram], the first of which is kritticay [q.v.], and a location of the solstitial points [ayanam] differing widely from present. Compare Maunam for some ancient views about the sidereal and solar years. Also Mausam regarding the history of the months. Also Nacshatram for the general theories of sidereal astronomy. The solar signs of the zodiac and much of the later astronomy, with many astronomical terms, such as horah = ὥρα, caindram = κέντρον, dricaunam or the third of a zodiacal sign = δέκανος, liptah or the minute of a degree = λεπτός ; were borrowed from the Greeks.—"*b*" The earliest Hindoo astronomer whose name has come down is Aryabhatta [q.v.], who lived about fifth century of the Christian era. He is the author of three works, Arya bhatteeyam, Dasha geeticay, and Aryaushta shatam. He asserted a diurnal revolution [bhaganam] of the earth [bhoomy] on its axis, knew the true theory of the causes of lunar and solar eclipses [grahanam], and noticed the motion of the solstitial and equinoctial points [ayanam]. After Aryabhatta came Varauha mihiran [q.v.] who lived about sixth century of christian era and was born at Oojjein. He wrote a work on nativities called Brihad jautacam, an astrological work called Brihat samhitay, and a summary of the five original siddhauntams [q.v.] called Puncha siddhaunticay. After Aryabhatta and Varauha mihiran lived Bramha gooptan, towards the end of the sixth century, who wrote the Bramha siddhauntam, containing chapters on arithmetic and algebra [ganitam]. Fourth and last of celebrated astronomers and mathematicians came Bhascaracharry [q.v.], who lived in the twelfth century and composed the Siddhaunta shiromany, containing treatises on algebra and arithmetic.— "*c*" The following are the elements of the old astronomy proper :—Shunk; the gnomon. Chauyay; its shadow. Palabhay or vishama chauyay; the shadow of the gnomon at midday, when the sun is in the equinoctial points. Vishama carnam; the hypothenuse of a right-angled triangle formed by the shunk and the two sides of its shadow under the preceding circumstances. Madhyama chauyay; the midday shadow at any other time of the year. Sama mundala chauyay; the shadow when the sun is east or west of the gnomon. Craunty mundalam; the ecliptic. Craunty bhaugam; the declination of a point of the ecliptic. Naudy mundalam; the equator. Sauyanam; celestial longitude considered in the same manner as that of the europeans, with reference to the pole of the ecliptic. Vicshaipam; celestial latitude. Swadesha paridhy; a circle of longitude in any given latitude. Agram; the amplitude. Nataumsham or nata bhaugam; zenith distance. Cshitijam; the horizon. Lagnam; the arc of the equator which passes over the meridian in the same time with each sign of the ecliptic; answering to right ascension. Madhyama lagnam; mean ditto; that of lunka [q.v.], the same arc which rises above the horizon with each sign of the ecliptic. Oollagnam; the lagnam of any particular place, being the arc of the equator which rises above the horizon of that place in the same time that each sign of the ecliptic rises. Dinaurdham; half the day. Rautryardham; half the night. Jyah; when connected with the name of any element means its sine. Paramaupama cramajyay; the sine of the greatest declination of a planet; as the hindoos take the obliquity of the ecliptic to be constantly 24°, the above term when referred to the sun means the sine of the obliquity.— "*d*" The following extract from Varauha mihiran's Brihatsamhitay summarizes the functions of an astronomer-astrologer of his time. "The Jyotishacan is one who is versed in " Samhitay [q.v.] or Astronomy and Horoscopy. He must be " of noble birth and of agreeable appearance; meek, truthful " and without jealousy; of proportional limbs; of joints well " built and of good growth; have no physical defects; be of fine " hands, feet, nails, eyes, chin, teeth, ears, forehead, eye-brows " and head; of fine physique and of high, sonorous voice; " generally speaking do not virtues and vices follow the body? " The virtues:—He must be of cleanly habits, able, noble-minded, " eloquent and of originality and imagination; must possess " a knowledge of place and time; be meek and without nervous- " ness; must be difficult of conquest by his fellow students; must " be able and devoid of vices; must be learned in matters of " expiatory ceremonies [prauyaschittam], of hygiene, of occult " magic and of ablutions; must be a worshipper of the devas " and an observer of fast and penance [oopavausam, vratam]; " must be of remarkable genius and capable of solving any diffi- " culties save in matters of direct divine interference; and " finally he must be learned in astronomy, natural astrology and " horoscopy. In Astronomy:—He must have studied the " works of poolishan, romacan, vasishtan, sooryan and pitau- " mahan; he must have a correct knowledge of a yoog [q.v.], " varsham [q.v.], ayanam [q.v.], ritoo [q.v.], mausam [q.v.], " pacsham [q.v.], ahorautram [q.v.], yaumam [q.v.], moohoortam " [q.v.], naudy, vinaudy [q.v.], praunam [q.v.], trooty [q.v.] and " parts of a trooty and other divisions of time [caulam] and also " of divisions of space; he must have a clear knowledge of the " causes of solar, sauvanam [q.v.], sidereal and lunar months " as well as of intercalary lunations [maunam, mausam] and " intercalary [adhicam] days [dinam, tity]; he must have a " knowledge of the beginning and end of shashtyaubdam, yoog, " varsham, mausam, dinam [q.v.] and horah [q.v.] and of their " lords; he must know the solar and other divisions of time " [caulam], their similarity and dissimilarity and must be capable " of propounding the fitness or unfitness of each for particular " purposes; these divisions of time are, of men, of devas, of " jupiter, of pitries, of star, of the sun, of the moon, of the " earth and of bramha; if the methods of calculation given in " the five astronomical works mentioned above should produce " different results he must be able to calculate correctly the " places of the sun [sooryan] and planets [graham] by actual " observation, by means of shadow and water level and with the " help of astronomical instruments, of the termination of their " ayanam or northward and southward course, of their being due " east to the observer after rising and of their altitude [avana- " taumsham] at any time; he must know the reason for the " correction required for the conversion of the heliocentric into " geocentric longitude and vice versâ; the causes of the ayanam " of the sun and planets and of their slow and rapid movements " at different times; in solar and lunar eclipses [grahanam], he " must be able to calculate the times of the commencement and " end of the eclipses, the places of first and last contact, the " magnitude and duration of the eclipse; in total eclipses, he " must be able to calculate the time between middle eclipse and " the beginning or end of total phase or vimardam; he must " also know the color of the eclipsed lunar disc; he must be able " to calculate beforehand the times of the moon's conjunction " with the planets as well as of planetary conjunctions; he " must know the length, in yojanams [q.v.], of the daily motion " of each planet in its orbit [cacsham] and of the orbit itself, " and generally the length, in yojanam, in every case; he " must know the earth's revolution [bhaganam] round the sun " and its rotation round its axis, its shape, size and the like, the " latitude [acsham] of a place and its complement, the nature " of the hour circle, the chaura dala calam, the times of the " rising of the zodiacal signs [raushy]; he must also be able to " calculate time from shadow [chauyay] and shadow from time " and to convert longitude into right ascension and right ascension " [lagnam] into longitude [dhroovacam, sauyanam]; he must " be able to meet objections and questions in clear and distinct " language and must be capable of explaining the science in " its purity in just the same way as separating the pure gold " from dross and making it capable of retaining its value " when submitted to the touch stone, to the fire and to the " hammer; how can one, who is incapable of entrapping others " with a hard question or of answering any that is put to " himself or of explaining his views to his students, expect to " become an astronomer? In Horoscopy:—He must know such " divisions of space as raushy [q.v.], horah [q.v.], dricaunam " [q.v.], navaumshacam, dwaudashaumshacam, trimshaumsha- " cam, and their strength or weakness considered horoscopically; " he must know the horoscopic strength of the planets with " respect to their dic [q.v.], staunam, caulam [q.v.], chaishtay " [q.v.]; he must know the temperament of the planets and the " parts of the body lorded over by each; the mineral division of " each; the caste, sex and authority of each and the like; he " must be able to state, from the time of conception or birth of a " person, particulars connected with these occasions so as to " insure belief; he must be able to say in what cases a child will " die in infancy, and to calculate the period of one's existence; " he must be able to divide one's life into planetary divisions " and sub-divisions; he must be able to use the ashtacavargam " tables to a given horoscope; he must know how the several " raja, chundra, dvigraha, and nabhasa yogams affect the for- " tunes of men; he must also know how the fortunes of men are " affected by the position and look of planets; he must be able " to calculate the cause of one's death and discover his future " life; he must be able to discover auspicious periods for " marriages and the like. In Yautray [q.v.]:—he must know " the fitness or unfitness of a tity [q.v.], vauram [q.v.], caranam " [q.v.], nacshatram [q.v.], moohoortam [q.v.], and lagnam [q.v.] " and yogam [q.v.] for particular purposes. He must be able to " interpret natural gestures and dreams; he must be able to " state when a prince ought to start for battle to secure success " in war; he must be learned in rules relating to ablutions and " sacred fire ceremonies in honor of the planets and offerings to " evil spirits; he must be able to interpret phenomena connected " with such sacred fires and with elephants [q.v.] and horses " [ghorah] while mounting the same. A true astrologer is also " one who has thoroughly mastered the science of samhitay; it " treats of the effects of agastya [q.v.] chauram and saptarishy " [q.v.] chauram on particular parts of india, corresponding to " particular portions of the ecliptic [craunty mundalam]; of the " stellar divisions of every substance, animal and plant, and of " their increase or decrease according to the motion of the " planets among the stars; of the formation and interpretation of " various figures presented by the planets when meeting together; " of planetary conjunctions; of planetary years; of indications of " the weather [caulam, caurtey]; of the moon's conjunction with " rohiny [q.v.], swauty [q.v.] and the two ashaudhams [q.v.], on " particular week days of the month of ashaudham and of " predicting the nature of the coming weather and crops [vellau- " may] from the same; it treats of the prediction of immediate " rain [mazhay] from surrounding phenomena; of judging the " nature of the future crops from the growth of plants and " flowers; of the halos round the sun and moon; of lines of " clouds crossing the solar disc at rising and setting; of the " winds; of meteoric falls; of false fires; of earthquakes; of the " red sky immediately before sunrise and after sunset; of the " fanciful shapes of clouds; of dust storms; of thunderbolts; of " the price of food grains; of gardening; it treats of indradhwa- " jam, of the rainbow and of architecture; of the prediction of " events from casual words and gestures and from the cawing of " crows; of the formation of zodiacal circles for purposes of " horary astrology; it treats of the prediction of future events " from phenomena connected with the deer [mrigam], the dog " [nye] and the motions of the wind; of the construction of " temples [coil], towers and palaces; of the casting of images " [vigraham] and of founding the same; of the growth of plants " and trees; of under currents; of certain annual ceremonies to " be performed by princes for success in war; it also treats of " the prediction of events from the flight of the khanjan bird " and from the appearance of various abnormal phenomena, of " expiatory ceremonies; of miscellaneous planetary phenomena; " of ghrita cumbalam; of the royal sword; of puttam [q.v.]; " of the features of a house, cock [moorghy], a cow [pashoo], " a sheep [and], a horse, an elephant, a man and a woman; it " also treats of the treatment of women; of moles in the body; " of injuries to shoes and clothes; of hairy fans; of walking " sticks; of beds and seats; of lamplight; of tooth-brush and " the like. That bramin jyotishacan who has mastered both " the text and the purport of the entire science deserves to be " respected and fed first on occasions of shrauddham [q.v.] and " he purifies the party of diners; even the mlechas [q.v.] and " the yavanas [q.v.] who have well studied the science are

" respected as rishies; such being the case, if the jyotishacan " should happen to be a bramin, who will deny him respect? " that service, which a single jyotishacan, having a knowledge " of place and time can render to a prince, cannot be rendered " to him by a thousand elephants or by four thousand horses."—"*e*" At present day even astronomy is made the foundation of a vast system of astrology. The real movements and the relative positions of the planets [graham] are wrought into a systematic connection with a great variety of arbitrary divisions of the signs [raushy] of the zodiac, and of the twenty-seven lunar mansions [nacshatram]. To these bodies are added various mythological appendages, as beasts, birds, trees, &c. The astrological dogmas have an important bearing on all the domestic arrangements and practices of the people. This is seen in the lucky and unlucky months, days and other divisions of time, in the horoscope [jenma puttricay] which has a powerful controlling influence in marriage, and in other matters relating to the settlement of families and in the more general prognostics for the year as given in the hindoo calendar [punchaungam]. See vol. I (108).—"*f*" The following is a list of the different European astronomical terms with the corresponding native terms [najm]:—Algebra; beejaganitam, catapayaudy, coottacam, prakeerna ganitam. Altitude; avanataumsham. Amplitude; agram. Anomaly; mandam. Aphelion; mandotcham. Apparent; spootam. Apsis of planet's orbit; ootcham. Arc; bhoojam. Arc of circle; chaupam. Arc of one minute; calay. Armillary sphere; golayantram. Ascensional difference; chauracoomoodam. Astronomical table; patacam. Astronomy; jyotisham. Azimuth; agracoty. Chord; chaupam, jeevay. Circle; chuckram, valayam. Circle, centre of; caindram. Circle, great; bhaganam, mundalam. Circle, vertical; drikmundalam. Circumference; paridhy. Circumference of great circle; mundalam. Comet; dhoomkait. Complement of arc; coty. Conjunction; crauntam, sangamam, yoog. Conjunction or opposition of sun and moon; mahacalay. Constellation; nacshatram. Cosine; cotijyay. Cube; ghanam. Culmination of celestial object; oordhwa samcramanam. Cycle, jovian; brihaspaty chuckram. Day; ahas, dinam. Day time; divy. Declination; craunty. Declination, northern of sun; eirauvatam. Declination, southern of sun; jauradgavam. Degree; bhaugam. Denominator; hauram. Diameter; vyausam. Dividend; bhaujyam. Divisor; bhaujak. Earth; bhoo. East; prauchy. Eclipse; grahanam. Ecliptic; craunty mundalam. Elevation; oonnatam. Epicycle; paridhy. Equation, argument of; caindram. Equator, celestial; naudymundalam. Equatorial parts; niracshadesham. Equator, radius of; bhoocarnam. Equator, terrestrial; bhoochuckram, bhooparidhy, niracsham. Equinoctial points; craunty pautam. Equinox; vishoo. Equinox, autumnal; toolauyanam. Equinox, vernal; maishauyanam. Fixed stars, sphere of; bhamundalam, nacshatra chuckram. Fortnight; pacsham. Fortnight, waning; bahoolam. Fortnight, waxing; shooclam. Full moon; poornimay; powrnimay. Geometry; cshetraganitam. Gnomon; shunk. Horizon; cshitijam. Horoscope; grahapatram, jenma puttricay. Hour; horah. Hour-angle; natanaudicay. Hypothenuse; carnam. Inclination; natam. Intercalary; adhicam. Jupiter; brihaspaty. Latitude, celestial; vicshaipam. Latitude, terrestrial; acsham. Line, horizontal; dwijjyah maurgam. Longitude, celestial; dhroovacam, sauyanam. Longitude, terrestrial; deshauntaram, raikhauntaram. Lunar time; chaundra maunam. Lunation; chaundra mausam, pitry dinam. Mansion; griham. Mars; bhowman, coojan, mungalan. Mean; madhyam. Mean solar time; madhyama sowra maunam. Mercury; bhoodhan. Meridian; raikhay. Minus; rinam. Minute; calay. Moon; chundran, indoo, soman. Moon's node, ascending; rahoo. Moon's node, descending; kait. Motion, diurnal; gaty. Multiplicand; goonyam. Multiplier; goonak. New moon; amavausyay, darsham. Night; rautry. Node of planet's orbit; pautam. North; oottaram. Orbit; cacsham. Parallax; acshavalanam, sheeghram. Perehelion; chalotcham, sheeghrotcham. Perpendicular; lambam. Phase of moon; calay. Planet; graham. Plus; dhanam. Pole; dhroovam, meroo. Pole, south; asoora dhroovam, coomeroo. Precessional variation; craunty pautagaty. Precession of equinox; ayanaumsham. Quantity, known; roopam. Quantity, unknown; caulak, neelak. Quotient; labdham. Reduction; shodhanam. Remainder; shaisham. Revolution; bhaganam. Right ascension; lagnam. Rule of three; treiraushy. Saturn; shany. Series; raushy. Series, infinite; anantaraushy, bhauga anoobandham. Shadow; chauyay. Sine; jyah. Solid; ghanam. Solstice, northern; dacshinauyanam. Solstice, southern, oottaranyanam. South; dacshinam. Sphere; golam. Square; vargam. Square root; vargamoolam. Star; nacshatram. Sun; arcan, bhaunoo, ravy, sooryan. Sun's course; ayanam. Terrestrial orb; bhoo golam, meroo. Triangle; mookonam, trikonam. True; spootam. Twilight; sundhyay. Venus; bhrigoo, shoocran. Versed sine; oottarajyay. West; pashchimam. Zenith; ootcham. Zenith distance; nataumsham. Zodiac; raushy chuckram. Zodiac, signs of; raushy.—"*g*" The following is the above list reversed:—Acsham; terrestrial latitude. Acshavalanam; parallax. Adhicam; intercalary. Agracoty; azimuth. Agram; amplitude. Ahas; day. Amavausyay; new moon. Anantaraushy; infinite series. Arcan; sun. Asooradhroovam; south pole. Avanataumsham; altitude. Ayanam; sun's course. Ayanaumsham; precession of equinox. Bahoolam; waxing fortnight. Beejaganitam; algebra. Bhaganam; great circle, revolution. Bhamundalam; sphere of fixed stars. Bhauga anoobandham; infinite series. Bhaugam; degree. Bhaujak; divisor. Bhaujyam; dividend. Bhaunoo; sun. Bhoo; earth. Bhoocarnam; radius of equator. Bhoochuckram; terrestrial equator. Bhoogolam; terrestrial orb. Bhoojam; arc. Bhooparidhy; terrestrial equator. Bhowman; mars. Bhrigoo; venus. Boodhan; mercury. Brihaspaty; jupiter. Brihaspaty chuckram; jovian cycle. Cacsham; orbit. Calay; arc of one minute, minute, phase of moon. Caindram; argument of equation, centre of circle. Carnam; hypothenuse. Catapayaudy; algebra. Caulak; unknown quantity. Chalotcham; perehelion. Chaundra maunam; lunar time. Chaundramausam; lunation. Chaupam; arc of circle, chord. Chaura coomoodam; ascensional difference. Chauyay, shadow. Chuckram; circle. Chundran; moon. Coojan; mars. Coomeroo; south pole. Coottacam; algebra. Cotijyay; cosine. Coty; compliment of arc. Crauntam; conjunction. Craunty; declination. Craunty mundalam; ecliptic. Craunty pautagaty; precessional variation. Craunty pautam; equinoctial points. Dacshinam; south. Dacshinauyanam; northern solstice. Darsham; new moon. Deshauntaram; terrestrial longitude. Dhanam; plus. Dhoomkait; comet. Dhroovacam; celestial longitude. Dhroovam; pole. Dinam; day. Divy; daytime. Drik mundalam; vertical circle. Dwijjyah maurgam; horizontal line. Eirauvatam; northern declination of sun. Gaty; diurnal motion. Ghanam; cube, solid. Golam; sphere. Golayantram; armillary sphere. Goonak; multiplier. Goonyam; multiplicand. Graham; planet. Grahanam; eclipse. Grahapatram; horoscope. Griham; mansion. Hauram; denominator. Horah; hour. Indoo; moon. Jauradgavam; southern declination of sun. Jeevay; chord. Jenmaputtricay; horoscope. Jyah; sine. Jyotisham; astronomy. Kait; moon's descending node. Labdham; quotient. Lagnam; right ascension. Lambam; perpendicular. Madhyam; mean. Madhyama sowra maunam; mean solar time. Mahacalay; conjunction or opposition of sun and moon. Maishauyanam; vernal equinox. Mandam; anomaly. Mandotcham; aphelion. Meroo; pole, terrestrial orb. Mookonam; triangle. Mundalam; circumference of a great circle, great circle. Mungalan; mars. Nacshatram; constellation, star. Nacshatra chuckram; sphere of fixed stars. Natam; inclination. Natanaudicay; hour-angle. Nataumsham; zenith distance. Naudy mundalam; celestial equator. Neelak; unknown quantity. Niracshadesham; equatorial parts. Niracsham; terrestrial equator. Oonnatam; elevation. Oordhwa sancramanam; culmination of celestial object. Ootcham; apsis of planet's orbit, zenith. Oottarajyay; versed sine. Oottaram; north. Oottarauyanam; southern solstice. Pacsham; fortnight. Paridhy; circumference, epicycle. Paschimam; west. Patacam; astronomical table. Pautam; node of planet's orbit. Pitry dinam; lunation. Powrnimay; full moon. Prakeernaganitam; algebra. Prauchy; east. Rahoo; moon's ascending node. Raikhauntaram; terrestrial longitude. Raikhay; meridian. Raushy; series, signs of zodiac. Raushy chuckram; zodiac. Rautry; night. Ravy; sun. Rinam; minus. Roopam; known quantity. Sangamam; conjunction. Sauyanam; celestial longitude. Shaisham; remainder. Shany; saturn. Sheeghram; parallax. Sheeghrotcham; perehelion. Shodhanam; reduction. Shooclam; waxing fortnight. Shoocran; venus. Shunk; gnomon. Soman; moon. Sooryan; sun. Spootam; apparent, true. Sundhyay; twilight. Toolauyanam; autumnal equinox. Treiraushy; rule of three. Trikonam; triangle. Valayam; circle. Vargam; square. Vargamoolam; square root. Vicshaipam; celestial latitude. Vishoo; equinox. Vyansam; diameter. Yoog; conjunction.——*Jyoty shastram* (ज्योतिश्शास्त्र - jyótishshástra, San.). From (above + shástra, san. science). A comprehensive term. May be classified under the following four heads:—"*a*" Mathematics, algebra, astronomy, and general treatises. Soorya siddhauntam is the best-known manual [siddhauntam].—"*b*" Judicial astrology, horoscopes, divination [jautacam].—"*c*" Omens. Punchapacshy shastram is a well-known book on omens from birds, a popular superstition in S. india [shacoonam].—"*d*" Palmistry and physiognomy. These are old arts here. The peculiar marks attributed to Booddha [q.v.] are an early example of this superstition. Samoodricam is the principal title to such works [samoodricam].

K. (क - ka, का - ká, *San.*; ك - káf, ق - káf, *Hind.*; க - ka, கா - ká, *Tam.*). San. for the who or the unknown; any chief god [deva]. Arabic ending for the second person singular; as Aleik, on + thee. Diminutive ending in persian words; as in Dastak. Similar in sanscrit. Hind. ك in arithmetic symbol for 20. Hind. ق symbol for 100. Tam. short sign for the numeral 1.

KACHVEE (कच्वी - kachví, *San.*; अळू - alú, *Mahr.*; वेंटि - vénti, *Conc.*; قلقاس - kulkás, *Ar.*; کچو - kachú, *Hind.*; اروی - arví, *Dec.*; ಶಾಮೆಗಡ್ಡೆ - shámegadde, *Can.*; ಕೆಸು - kesu, *Coorg*; ತೇವು - tévu, *Too.*; చేమ - chéma, *Tel.*; ସରୁ - saru, *Oor.*; ചേമ്പ - chémpu, *Mal.*; ගහල - gahala, *Singh.*; சேம்பு - shémbu, *Tam.*). San. from (kachhu, san. itch); from property. Ar. from lat. colocasia. Hind. from sanscrit. Can. from (sháma, can. black + gadde, can. root). Mal. from tamul. Tam.

from (shé, tam. redness + pai, tam. green). San. also (mánaka), meaning garden plant. Conc. also (téró). Ar. also (kur). Hind. also (arvi); (gorikachú), meaning white + yam; (bíshkachú), meaning poison colocasia; (mánkachú). Can. also (késhava-nagadde), meaning water-lying root; (kádakesugida), meaning wild + colocasia. Too. also (kádutévu), meaning wild + colocasia. Tel. also (balurakkasi), meaning plumpness + she-devil, a large variety [bastard aloe]; (tótabalurakkasi), meaning garden + colocasia; (kondarakkisa), meaning hill + devil, wild variety; (tsárakanda), meaning stripe + yam. Mal. also (nírççémbu), meaning water colocasia; (veli), meaning white one. Singh. also (kandala). Tam. also (shémbai), meaning reddish green; (shagudam); (nírççémbu), meaning water + the plant. Greek ἄρον from egyptian. Title otherwise Indian kales. Botanically the Colocasia genus, araceæ [vricsham, 152]. Herbs with tuberous, or stem-like root-stocks; leaves peltate; scapes somewhat solitary or many in the same axil, shortened, sheathed; closely allied to caladium.—"*a*" The species best known is the Bread-and-butter plant, Cocco, Coco, Cocoa root, Eddoes, Egyptian arum, Egyptian gudger, Egyptian wake lobbin, Egyptian yam, Indian kale, Kachvee, Kolcas, Scratch-coco, Tara plant, Tarow plant. Botanically Colocasia antiquorum, schott. Alias Arum colocasia. Herb, stemless; large heart-shaped leaves, borne on long foot-stalks, rising from a short farinaceous corm; flowering in rainy season; cultivated in wet marshy grounds; tubers resembling jerusalem artichoke [sooryacaunty]; in flavor not unlike salsify. Pressed juice of the petioles styptic, in pharm. non-officinal. Young leaves eaten like spinach [maurisham], but, like the root, require to be well cooked in order to destroy the acridity peculiar to aroideous plants, used as famine food. Ashes used as mordant [cauram]. Many varieties, the outer marks of distinction resting upon the different tinge observable in the corm, leaf, stalks, and ribs of the leaves, white, yellowish, purple.—"*b*" Another is Colocasia indica, roxb. Alias Arum indicum. Cultivated for esculent stems and small pendulous tubers, these being eaten in curries [q.v.]; requires to be cooked, being acrid in the raw state.—"*c*" Another is Colocasia montana, kunth. Alias Arum montanum. Stemless; mountainous parts of the northern circars [q.v.]; root poisonous; flowering in rains; root employed to poison tigers [pooly].—"*d*" Another is the Saura cunda, Water-lily-leaved arum. Botanically Colocasia nymphæifolia, kunth. Alias Arum nymphæifolia; Caladium nymphæifolium. Stemless; malabar; tubers are given in gonorrhœa; leaves used as famine food, and require cooking being acrid in the raw state.——*Water kachvee* (நீர்ச்சேம்பு - nírççémbu, Tam.). Same as Pit nelumbo.——*Wild kachvee* (جنگلی کندا - janglíkandá, Hind.). Same as Wild telinga potato.

KADAM (قدم - kadam, *Hind.*) [cautham]. A foot, linear measure [adee]. Also footstep [dharmarajacull].

KADAR (காட - káda, obl.; காடன் - kádan, pers. sing.; காடர் - kádar, pers. pl., *Tam.*). From (kádu, tam. forest) [caud]. A hill race, occupying the Anamullay hills. They are strong-built and active with woolly hair and something of the African features, and file their front teeth to a point. The women wear enormous circles of pith [solah] in the lobes of their ears, which they distend down to their shoulders. A small number are employed by Government in forest conservancy and in felling timber. Others collect forest produce, which they barter for grain. They also cultivate patches of raggy [q.v.], which they supplement as a food-supply with roots [doompa, gadda], herbs, &c., found on the hills [jauty]. See vol. I (35); II, 52.

KADR (قدر - kadr, *Ar.*). From (kadara, ar. to measure). The power of directing one's own actions without restraint or irresistible fate [jabr].——*Cazah o kadr* (قضا و قدر - kazáwakadr, Hind.). Divine decree existing from all eternity [takdeer]. The belief of the generality of the Mahomedans is that men's actions depend partly on their own free will [ikhtiar], and partly on exterior causes [tafweez], these being due to general laws of nature the sequence of which God alone knows.

KAFFAUSH (काकपिशाच - kákapishácha, *San.*; خفاش - khaffásh, *Ar.* and *Pers.*; گدل - gadal, *Hind.*; کلونگ - kalong, *Malay*; ಕೀಚಪಾಲ - kíchapála, *Can.*; రక్తకాట్రేడు - raktakátrédu, *Tel.*; പാറയാത്തൻ - párayáttan, *Mal.*; உதிரமாகாளி - uthiramágáli, *Tam.*). Title from arabic. San. from (káka, san. crow + pishácha, san. demon); terror of crows. Ar. from (khafisha, ar. small eye). Can. from (kíchu, can. to squeak + bávala, can. bat). Tel. from (rakta, san. blood + kádu, tel. forest + rédu, tel. king). Mal. from (pára, mal. rock + chàttan, mal. demon). Tam. from (uthiram, tam. blood + má, tam. great + kálí, san. the goddess durgá). Tam. also (kákkáviriççi), meaning crow terror. Family Vampyridæ, cheiroptera, mammalia [sastanam, 4], of naturalists [jantoo]. Vampires. These are bats with a nose leaf either simple or complicated.—"*a*" The first of family is the large-eared Vampire bat, Megaderma lyra. Of a slaty blue or pale mouse-color, albescent or yellowish ashy beneath. Nasal appendage, large, oblong, free at the tip, reaching to the base of the ears with a fold down the centre; muzzle, truncated; under lip, cleft. Frequents old buildings, pagodas [q.v.], caves, roofs of houses, &c. It sucks the blood from other bats, fixing on them behind the ear, sucking the blood during flight, and then devouring the body. It also eats frogs [bhaicam] and fish [matsyam].—"*b*" The next is the Allied leaf bat, Rhinolophus affinis. Ears, large, pointed, emarginate externally, anti-helix well developed; upper leaf triangular, emarginate at the tip, reaching above the base of the ears; varies much in color—above, bright rufous, or ferruginous brown, or brown; paler beneath. Most abundant on the west coast.—"*c*" The next is the Rufous leaf bat, Rhinolophus rouxi. Ears, large, pointed, externally notched; tip of upper nose-leaf triangular, with its sides well emarginate, reaching above the base of the ears; fur short, crisp; color above, smoky brown in some, red-brown in others, and golden rufous in some; beneath, paler. Found near Tellicherry.—"*d*" Next is the Indian horse-shoe bat, Hipposideros speoris. Alias Hipposideros apiculatus, penicillatus; Phyllorhina speoris; Rhinolophus dukhunensis, speoris. Ears, large, erect, acuminate, rounded at the base, emarginate on the outer margin; facial membrane complicated; muzzle short; interfemoral membrane, narrow, square, enclosing the tail, the half of the last joint alone free; body short, thick of variable color; sometimes light mouse color, beneath; at times, fulvous-brown; at other times, bright rufo-ferruginous or golden fulvous. It inhabits old buildings, wells, &c.—"*e*" Next is the Little horse-shoe bat, Hipposideros murinus. Alias Hipposideros fulvus; Phyllorhina aurita, fulva; Rhinolophus fulgens, murinus. Ears, large, erect, rounded; muzzle, short; a transverse frontal leaf and sac; in front a simple membrane round the nostrils; interfemoral membrane, large, including the tail all but the extreme tip; body short and thick; color, dusky brown or mouse color, sometimes light fawn or ferruginous; wing membranes blackish. Almost peculiar to Southern india.—"*f*" The last is the Long-tailed leaf bat, Rhinopoma hardwickii. Muzzle, long, thick, truncated, and surmounted by a small leaf tragus, oblong, biacuminate; forehead, concave, with a fossa or channel down the centre; fur, soft and very fine, dull brown throughout; face, rump, and part of the abdominal region naked. Frequents old ruins, caves, clefts in rocks, &c. This species is very closely allied to R. microphylla, from Egypt, on which the genus was founded.—"*g*" Indian species not here found are:—Cœlops frithii or frith's tail-less bat; Hipposideros armiger or large horse-shoe bat, blythii, cineraceus or ashy horse-shoe bat, larvatus, vulgaris or common malayan horse-shoe bat; Megaderma spasma, spectrum or cashmere vampire; Phyllorhina armigera, bicolor, diadema, galerita, leptophylla, masoni, nicobarensis; Rhinolophus andamanensis, cœlophyllus, garoensis, macrotis or large-eared leaf-bat, minor, mitratus or mitred leaf-bat, pearsonii or pearson's leaf-bat, perniger or luctus or large leaf-bat, petersii, rammanika, sub-badius or day leaf-bat, tragatus or ferrum equinum or dark-brown leaf-bat, trifoliatus.—"*h*" For vespertilions see Vavvaul; for noctules see Chamgadal.

KAH (کاه - káh, *Hind.*). Straw.——*Kahoo* (خس - khass, Ar.; کاهو - káhú, Pers., Hind. and Dec.; ಸಲಾಡಿ - saládi, Can.; కావుచెట్టు - kávuchettu, Tel.; சல்லாத்து - shallàttu, Tam.). Title from persian. Ar. from (khassa, ar. slender); from long corymbose flower-stems. Pers. from (káh, pers. straw); from dingy brown color of leaves. Can. and tam. are english salad. Tel. from hindostany. Tam. also (kaççu), meaning bitter plant. Greek θρίδαξ. Title otherwise Cabbage lettuce, Drumhead lettuce, Garden lettuce, Lettuce. The long upright kind is Cos lettuce, which is best. Botanically Lactuca scariola, linn., var. sativa, clarke, compositæ [vricsham, 74]. Alias Lactuca sativa. Succulent, quite smooth, leaves spreading pinnatifid or entire, branches of panicle short, with numerous bracts, achenes black. From the sap is prepared a resinous, dry juice known as lactucarium, a quasi substitute for opium [aphainam]; gives to pharm. extractum lactucæ, mild sedative, officinal; young leaves with mild, narcotic, soothing action, used as food chiefly as salad; a clear, transparent, sweet oil, from seeds.——*Karbah* (तृणमणि - trinamani, San.; قرن البحر - karnulbahr, Ar.; کهربا - kahrubá, Pers., Hind. and Dec.; عنبر - ambar, Malay; ತೃಣಗ್ರಾಹಿ - trinagráhi, Can. and Too.; కర్పూరపూస - karpúrapúsa, Tel.; പൊന്നമ്പർ - ponnambar, Mal.; අඹර - ambara, Singh.; கர்ப்பூரமணி - karppúramani, Tam.). Title from persian. San. from (trina, san. grass + mani, san. gem); straw attracting gem. Ar. from (karn, ar. horn + bahr, ar. sea). Pers. from (káh, pers. straw + rubá, pers. attracting). Can. from (trina, san. grass + gráhi, san. attractor). Tel. from (karpúra, san. camphor + púsa, tel. gem) by corrupt analogy. Mal. from (pon, mal. gold + amber). Tam. from (karpúra, san. camphor + mani, san. gem) by corrupt analogy. Ar. also (mistáhurrúm), meaning light of turkey. Tam. also (ponnambar), meaning gold + amber; as distinguishing from (mínambar), meaning fish + amber or ambergris. Amber. Succinum or electrum of chemists. A fossil [cull poo] of the resin [raul] yielded by trees chiefly pines [devadauram] which grew during the cretaceous period of geologists; a brittle, light, hard substance, generally almost transparent; commonly yellow; when bruised, exhales aromatic odour; when rubbed becomes electrical. Occasionally met with in alluvial soil in Travancore. The greater part brought from Japan. Copal [q.v.] is occasionally sold in the bazaars [q.v.] under the name of amber; and a substance known as false amber, possibly fossil copal, is exported hence into China. Distilled amber yields the succinic acid, and with it comes over the oil of amber, a valuable stimulant and antispasmodic. Not employed here as in Europe in preparing varnishes [rangh], but is made into beads [munkah] and other ornaments. The natives generally mean ambergris by Amber [q.v.], that being the most common [ratnam].

KAID (കേട് - kétu, *Mal.*). From (ketu, mal. to be spoilt). Bad.——*Kaid vellam* (കേട്ടവെള്ളം - kétuvellam, Mal.). From (above + vellam, mal. water). Stinking condition of water in seas and backwaters [cauyal] on Malabar coast [q.v.], at various periods of year, chiefly towards close of rains. Fatal to fishes [matsyam].——*Kedmaney* (ಕೇಡುಮನೆ - kédumane, Can.; கேடு மனை - kédumanai, Tam.). From (kédu, tam. misfortune + manai, tam. house). Funeral house among Todahs [q.v.].——*Kerd* (கேடு - kédu, Tam.). From (kedu, tam. to perish). A Todah [q.v.] funeral, of which there are two kinds:—the Hasy kerd, or green funeral, which is special for each todah, and takes place as soon as possible after death; and the Barla kerd, or dry funeral, which takes place some months later, and may include all the members of the tribe who have died during the year. See vol. II, 237.

KAINY (கேணி - kéni, *Tam.*). From (khan, san. to dig) [gany]. Tank or public well [kinar].

KAIT (केतु - kétu, *San.*). From (chi, san. to observe); appearance, brightness. A ray. Descending node [pautam] of the moon [chundran], or point where the moon in its southward course cuts the ecliptic [craunty mundalam]; ರಾ [rahoo]. Represented in arts sometimes by a dragon's tail. Sometimes by the headless trunk of Rahoo riding on a vulture [gidh]. It is imagined to be an actual heavenly body or planet [graham], and to cause the eclipses [grahanam] of the sun [sooryan] and the moon, especially the latter, by seizing them in their course [jyotisham].——*Kaitmaulay* (केतुमाला - kétumálá, San.). From (above + málá, san. succession). One of the nine divisions of Jamboo dweepam [q.v.]. See vol. I (3). It was situated between Gandhamaudanam, not identified, and the sea. Its principal river Chacshoo was the Oxus. The Vayoo pooraunam [q.v.] states that it is inhabited by barbarians of a black complexion, their women being of complexion of lotus [nelumbo]. Romacam according to sooryasiddhauntam [q.v.] is in this region. Kaitmaulay refers plainly to regions west of India.

KAITY (ಕೇರಿ - kéti, *Can.*) [kery]. Village, Valley; Neilgherry dist., Merkoonaud div.; pop. 3,513; acres 8,115; lat. 11° 22′; long. 76° 47′; from Coonoor W.N.W. 5 miles; from Ootacamund S.E. 3 miles. Badaga village in valley of same name below road from Ootacamund to Coonoor. One of the earliest settlements on the Neilgherries. Mr. John Sullivan, Collector of Coimbatore, opened out a Government experimental farm here in 1832. Tea [q.v.] was planted in 1835. The farm was abandoned about 1838. The bungalow [q.v.] was afterwards occupied for some time by the Governor of Pondicherry. In March 1840 Lord Elphinstone, Governor of Madras, fixed his residence here, taking possession of the Government farm buildings. He expended considerable sums of money in building and furnishing a large country house and laying out the grounds ornamentally. The property was subsequently purchased by Mr. Casamajor of the Civil Service, formerly Resident at Mysore, for Rs. 1,50,000. This gentleman established a school for Badaga [q.v.] children. On his death in 1849 he left the greater portion of his property to the Basel mission, who subsequently purchased the houses. Since then this has been the head-quarters of the mission on the Neilgherries and a convalescent depôt for other agents. The mission has three missionaries, and an orphanage and boarding school. The Kaity valley, which forms the upper basin of the Kartairy river, lies to south of Dodabetta range, and is enclosed to N. and W. by that branch of the same range which runs out towards Devasholah. It contains numerous thriving Badaga villages, the greater portion being under cultivation. The soil is so well-suited for the growth of the staple hill crops that even the steepest hill-sides are utilised by the ryots [q.v.].

KAJAUWAH (کجاوہ - kajáwah, *Hind.*). Camel's [ottagam] litter or panier, formed of wooden frames covered with cloth or leather [chamrah].

KAJO (काजू - kájú, *Mahr.*). From brazilian through portuguese. Same as Cashew.

KAKRONDAH (ککروندا - kakrondá, *Hind.*). Plant name common to:—Blumea lacera; Laggera aurita. See gloss paragraphs.

KAL (கல - kal, *Tam.*). To mix.——*Kalabanda* (కలబంద - kalabanda, Tel.). Mixed with mud. Plant name common to:—Aloe indica, Aloe vulgaris, Phaseolus trilobus. Compare where transl. is of first term:—Agave cantala (pítikalabanda), dung; Aloe indica (chinnakalabanda), small and (errakalabanda), red; Aloe littoralis (chinnakalabanda), small; Aristolochia indica (errakalabanda), red. See gloss. paragraphs.——*Kalipauk* (களிப்பாக்கு - kalippákku, Tam.). From (kali, tam. thick paste + pákku, tam. areca-nut). Boiled areca-nut [q.v.] covered with thick paste [pauk].——*Kaly* (களி - kali, Tam.). Thick paste; water in which areca [q.v.] nut has been boiled.

KALADANAH (حب‌النیل - habbunníl, *Ar.*; گیاہ تخم نیل - giyáhitukhmiuíl, *Pers.*; کالدانہ کی بیل - kalahdánahkíbel, *Hind.*; کالی زرکی کی بیل - kálízirkíkíbel, *Dec.*; కొల్లి - kolli, *Tel.*; கொடிக்காக்கட்டான் - kodikkákkattán, *Tam.*). Title from hindostany. Ar. from (habb, ar. seed + níl, ar. blue). Pers. from (giyáh, pers. creeper + tukhm, pers. seed + níl, hind. blue), from color of flowers. Hind. from (kálá, hind. black + dánah, pers. seed + bel, hind. creeper). Dec. from (kálá, hind. black + zirkí, hind. the seed + bel, hind. creeper). Tam. from (kodi, tam. creeper + kákkattán, tam. clitorea ternatea, linn.). Hind. also (mirchai), meaning pepper plant, from its acridity [pepper]; (nílkalmí), meaning indigo quill from the stems. Tel. also (jiriki). Tam. also (shirikki), from deccany; (kákkattán), clitoria ternatea, linn. [crow creeper]. Title otherwise Black seed creeper, Gay bine, Kaladanah resin plant, Morning glory, Pale blue ipomæa, Smaller morning glory. Botanically Ipomæa [calamby] hederacea, jacq., convolvulaceæ [vricsham, 93]. Alias Convolvulus hederaceus, nil; Ipomæa cœrulea, nil; Pharbitis cœrulea, hederacea, nil. Annual, 6 to 12 feet long, twining, hairy; stems as thick as crow's quill; leaves alternate cordate, three-lobed, intermediate lobe dilated at the base, downy; peduncles axillary, two to three-flowered, usually longer than the petioles; sepals ovate-lanceolate, hispid at the base; flowers pale blue, expanding in the morning and closing during the day; flowering in rainy season; cultivated and seeds also imported; common. Seeds are black, angular, a quarter of an inch or more in length, weighing on an average about half a grain each, having the form of the segment of an orange [q.v.]; of a sweetish and subsequently rather acrid taste and heavy smell; powder of a grey color. Their use in medicine not known to hindoos in remote times; known however to arab physicians. Gives to pharm. kaladanah seeds, pharbitis semina, active principle, a resin, pharbitisin; safe and effectual cathartic, closely resembling in properties and uses officinal jalap [q.v.], for which it forms substitute, though not so active in operation; officinal. Compare Laldanah.——*False kaladanah* (باریك بھوری - báríkbhaurí, Hind.; කළුඅලංගා - kaluálangá, Singh.; காட்டுத்தாளி - káttuttáli, Tam.). Title from use as adulterant. Hind. from (bárík, hind. less + bhaurí, hind. porana racemosa); from similarity of calyx. Singh. from (kalu, singh. black + álangá, singh. ipomæa bonanox, linn., var. grandiflora). Tam. from (kádu, tam. forest + táli, tam. convolvulus). Botanically Ipomæa [calamby] muricata, jacq., convolvulaceæ [vricsham, 93]. Alias Calonyction bonanox, var. muricata, muricatum; Convolvulus muricatus; Ipomæa bonanox. Annual herbaceous, climbing; root small, tapering, with many slender rootlets; stem branched, covered with soft prickles, not hairy; leaves broadly cordate, acuminate, smooth, on long petioles; flowers axillary, two to four, on long peduncles having prickles like the stem; pedicels large, fleshy and club-shaped, of a light green color, $1\frac{1}{2}$ inches long; calyx divided; sepals five, broadly ovate, mucronate, smooth, persistent; corolla purple, about 2 inches in diameter, expanding at sunset, and closing before sunrise; capsule two-celled, composed of four segments, which separate from the central partition; cells two-seeded; seeds dark brown, smooth, the same shape as those of kaladanah, about $\frac{1}{3}$ of an inch in length, and $\frac{1}{4}$ in breadth; weight about 3 grains each; they can easily be distinguished from kaladanah by their greater size, lighter color and thick testa; their medicinal properties are identical.

KALEELA (کلیلہ - kalílah, *Hind.*). From (karataka, san. name of a jackal in pañchatantra). A jackal [q.v.] so named.——*Kaleela damna* (کلیلہ دمنہ - kalílahdamnah, Hind.). From (above + damanaka, san. name of a jackal in pañchatantra). Arabic version of Punchatantram [q.v.].

KALIMA (کلمہ - kalimah, *Hind.*). From (kalm, ar. a word). The Mahomedan confession of faith:—"There is no God but God, and Mahomet [q.v.] is his prophet." The shiahs [q.v.] add:—"Ally is the caliph of God." Its recital is the first of five pillars of practical religion [deen] in Islam; and when any one is converted to Islam [q.v.] he is required to repeat this formula.

KALY (कलि - kali, *San.*; கலி - kali, *Tam.*). From (kal, san. to do) [cal]. Misery personified as a deity. The ace in dice, and a personification of ill luck [calathy, moodevy]. A name of Shany [q.v.], or regent of the planet [graham] Saturn; as considered to be of malignant influence.——*Kaliyoog* (कलियुग - kaliyuga, San.). See Yoog.——*Kaliyoogaudy* (కలియుగాది - kaliyugádi, Tel.). From (kaliyuga, san. the fourth age + ádi, san. beginning). Lunar [chaundramaunam] festival [pundigay, 6d], subject to intercalation [adhicam]. The thirteenth lunar day [tity] of the waning moon [krishna pacsham] of sixth lunar month Bhaudrapadam [mausam] between 15th September and 13th October; commemorates the beginning of the Kaliyoog.

KAMELA (काम्पिल्लक - kampillaka, *San.*; शेंदरी - shéndarí, *Mahr.*; उंडीरूकु - undírúku, *Conc.*; قنبیل - kinbíl, *Ar.*; کنبیلا - kambelá, *Pers.*; کمیلا - kamelá, *Hind.*; کمود کا جہاز - kamúdkájhár, *Dec.* ; ಕುಂಕುಮದಮರ - kunkumadamara, *Can.* ; ಪೊಂನೆ - ponne, *Too.* ; వసంతగుండము - vasantagundamu, *Tel.* ; ବୋସୋଂତୋଗୁଣ୍ଡି - bosontogundi, *Oor.* ; പുന്ന - punna, *Mal.* ; කම්පිලිය - kampiliya, *Singh.* ; கமேலாமாவுமரம் - kamélámávumaram, *Tam.*). Title from sanscrit through hindostany. San. from (kamp, san. to shake) ; see below for getting the farina. Mahr. from (sindúra, san. red lead) ; of the color of sendoor [q.v.], from red scarlet dye. Ar., &c., from sanscrit. Can. from (kunkuma, san. saffron, crocus sativus, linn. + mara, can. tree). Too. from (ponnu, too. gold) [common poon, soora poon]. Tel. from (vasanta, san. spring + gandha, san. fragrance). Oor. like teloogoo. Mal. from (pon, mal. gold) ; from scarlet dye [common poon, malabar poon, wild mohwah]. Singh. from sanscrit. Tam. from (kamélá, tam. the drug + mávu, tam. flour + maram, tam. tree). San. also (madhuka), meaning sweet [atimathooram, common mohwah] ; (punnáma), meaning named poomaun ; (punnágakésara), meaning male + messua ferrea, linn. ; (kapila), meaning tawny colored [wild date] ; (punnága), meaning male, messua ferrea, linn. [common poon, soora poon] ; (késara), meaning messua ferrea, linn. [ilanjay, nauga champak, poison bamboo, saffron] ; (réchanaka), meaning brightening. Hind. also (kamúd) ; (kapílá), from sanscrit. Can. also (honne), meaning gold ; (punnága), meaning male + messua ferrea, linn. ; (munnága), meaning front + messua ferrea, linn., from early flowering ; (purushatungamara), meaning male + lofty + tree ; (korangumúnji), meaning monkey's face ; (suvarnakésari), meaning gold filament ; (hulichellu). Tel. also (chendúrapuchettu), meaning red powder + tree ; (kunkumapuvvuchettu), meaning saffron + tree ; (veligárapuchettu), meaning borax + tree ; (kápilapodichettu), meaning the drug + the tree ; (tungavrikshamu), meaning tall tree ; (peyyarodda), meaning female + the tree. Oor. also (komalagundi) ; (sundorogundi). Mal. also (ponnakam), meaning gold holding ; (pípponnakam), meaning dirty + the tree. Tam. also (kabilappodimaram), meaning the drug + tree ; (kámbósam) ; (shuvarnagésari), meaning gold + filament ; (kurangumúñjimaram), meaning monkey-face tree ; cf. ilanjy. Title otherwise Capilapody, Dyer's rottlera, Mallata, Monkey's face tree, Ponnagam, Scarlet croton. Botanically Mallotus philippensis, muell., euphorbiaceæ [vricsham, 118]. Alias Croton coccineus, montanus, philippensis, punctatus ; Echinus philippensis ; Rottlera aurantiaca, tinctoria. Mallotus from nepaulese mallata. Small tree or under-shrub ; younger branchlets, petioles, and inflorescences rusty-tomentose ; leaves rhomb-ovate, acuminate, acute at the base, entire or slightly toothed, clothed with scarlet tomentum beneath, glabrous above ; spikes of either sex axillary and terminal, rusty-tomentose ; male bracts three-flowered, female one-flowered ; bracts triangular-ovate, acute ; segments of the female calyx ovate-lanceolate ; stamens twelve to fifteen ; ovary densely scarlet ; capsules slightly three-cornered, globose, covered with scarlet dust ; flowers in cold season ; near banks of rivers ; common. Kamela is the powder rubbed off the capsules, found to a smaller extent on the leaves and stalks ; it has a heavy odour, nearly tasteless ; the fine grains consist of a red substance enclosed in a membranous sac ; water does not act on this envelope, but it is readily ruptured by alcohol or an alkaline fluid ; hence the powder communicates its color to alcohol or an alkaline menstruum, but not to water ; alum [padicauram] added to the alkaline infusion renders the color more bright and permanent. For production, the ripe capsules are gathered in march and rubbed together or shaken in bags till the farina separates ; exported from malabar. Kamela is medicinally anthelmintic, vermifuge and purgative ; the vermifuge action depends on the minute stellate hairs found in the powder ; substituted for british santonin [absinth] ; gives to pharm. tinctura kamalæ, officinal, also in british ; fruit and leaves rubbed with honey [shahad] applied to bites of poisonous animals. Kamela gives an orange dye [shauyam], chiefly to silk [puttoo] ; bark used for tanning [chamrah] ; powdered bark of casearia tomentosa, roxb. [anavinga] is used as adulterant ; also found mixed with red sand [manal] ; kamela like lycopodium is inflammable. Wood smooth, grey to light red, hard, close-grained ; no heartwood ; warps and shrinks ; used only for fuel. Other common species are :—albus, atrovirens, aureo-punctatus, barbatus, distans, lawii, muricatus, repandus, rhamnifolius, stenanthus.

KAMMAL (کمل - kammal, *Hind.*). From (kambala, san. blanket) [cumbly]. Blanket.——*Kammalposh* (کمل پوش - kammalposh, Pers.). From (above + posh, pers. wearer). A fakeer [q.v.].

KANAK (கணக்கு - kanakku, *Tam.*). From (gan, san. to count) [gan]. Accounts or the art of accounting [hisaub, lekka].——*Kanakan* (கணக்கன் - kanakkan, Tam.). An accountant especially village accountant [curnum, shanbogue].——*Kanak choornay* (கணக்குச்சுருணை - kanakkuççurunai, Tam.). From (above + shurunai, tam. scroll). A bundle of accounts kept on palmyra [q.v.] leaves [cadjan] by a village accountant.——*Kanaksauram* (കണക്കുസാരം - kanakkusáram, Mal.). From (above + sára, san. essence). Ancient Malabar work on arithmetic and weights and measures [alavay] ; differs materially from Ganita shastram [q.v.]. Author Neelacuntan. Six chapters. First treats of fractions, literally what is below one ; second of decimals, what is above one ; third Yidangazhy [q.v.], measures of capacity ; fourth Cautham [q.v.], measures of length ; fifth Calanjy [q.v.], weights ; sixth, Caulam [q.v.] or time.

KANAKA (കണക്ക - kanakka, obl. ; *Mal.*). From (kanam, mal. grain). Means a tribe on the West coast, till lately in a state of slavery. The Kanakar live together in small clans, each hamlet under the patriarchal rule of headman. They cultivate by Coomry [q.v.]. In the south they speak Tamul, and further north Malayalam [jauty].

KANDAL (کندل - kandal, *Hind.*). From (kanda, san. root) ; meaning root-colored or whitish brown. Same as Sagapenum. Distinguish from Candel [q.v.].

KANGAN (کنگن - kangan, *Hind.*). From (kankana, san. a wrist ornament). An ornament worn on the wrist [pownchee]. The tying and untying of the Kangan are important parts of marriage [shaudy] ceremonies [zewar].

KANJILY (خنجری - khanjarí, *Hind.*). From (khál, hind. hide + jarí, hind. covered). Small tambourine with bells [sangeetam].

KANNY (കണ്ണി - kanni, *Mal.*). From (kalam, mal. square). A plot of land from eight to fourteen feet long, and five to eight broad, set apart for evaporating or manufacturing salt [alam, ooppoo].

KAOLIN (گل چینی - gilichíní, *Pers.* ; කිරිමැටි - kirimati, *Singh.*). Title is a chinese word, meaning high ridge, from the mountain where it is obtained. Pers. from (gil, pers. earth + chín, pers. china). Singh. means milk clay. Cf. Ghil arminy. Fine porcelain clay, derived from the decomposition of felspar [khauk i cheeny, mauvayiracull].

KAPOK (کپوک - kapuk, *Malay*). Fibre of Red-cotton tree.

KAR (کار - kár, *Hind.*). Work [car, caur, kri].——*Kardaur* (کاردار - kárdár, Hind.). From (above + dár, pers. holder). Manager [carbaury].——*Karkhana* (کارخانہ - kárkhánah, Hind.). From (above + khánah, pers. house). A workshop, arsenal [caurgah].

KARAFS (अजमोदा - ajamódá, *Mahr.* ; کرفس - karafs, *Ar.* ; کرفش - karafsh, *Pers.* ; اجمود - ájmúd, *Hind.* ; اجموده اجوان - ájmúdahajwán, *Dec.* ; சல்லரி - shallari, *Tam.*). Title from syriac through persian. Mahr. from (aja, san. goat + móda, san. smell) [ajmood, ajwaun]. Pers. from syriac. Dec. from (ajmúdá, hind. carum roxburghianum, benth. + ajwán, hind. ajowan, carum copticum, benth.). Tam. from english celery. Greek σέλινον. Title otherwise Celery, Small edge. Botanically Apium graveolens, linn., umbelliferæ [vricsham, 67]. Biennial ; stem 1–8 feet, erect branched ; peduncle 0–$\frac{1}{4}$ inch, leaf-opposed ; rays of the umbel five to ten, $\frac{1}{2}$–$1\frac{1}{2}$ inches ; ridges narrow, vittæ broad, occupying the whole breadth of the furrows ; flower, smallish white. Root aromatic, bitter, acrid, aperient. When wild, poisonous ; when cultivated, nutritious. The root and blanched petioles are used for food, have exciting qualities. Apium petroselinum, willd., is Parsley. For the carum genus, also called Ajmood in hindostany, see Ajmood.

KARANJ (नक्तमाल - naktamála, *San.* ; करंज - karanja, *Mahr.* ; कारिंजेर - karinjér, *Conc.* ; کرنجھ - karanjh, *Hind.* ; کرنج - karanj, *Dec.* ; ಹೊಂಗೆ - honge, *Can.* ; ಪುಂಗು - pungu, *Too.* ; కానుగ - kánuga, *Tel.* ; କରଂଜ - koranja, *Oor.* ; പുന്നു - punnu, *Mal.* ; මගුල්කරඬ - magulkaranda, *Singh.* ; புங்கு - pungu, *Tam.*). Title from sanscrit through hindostany. San. from (nakta, san. night + al, san. to decorate). Mahr. from (karañja, san. the plant). Conc., &c., like mahratta. Can. like tamul. Tel. means hard tree [caunooga]. Mal. from tamul. Singh. from (magul, singh. auspicious + karanda, singh. the plant, pongamia sp.). Tam. from (pon, tam. gold + agam, tam. inside) ; from yellow wood [caunooga, malabar poon]. San. also (karañja), meaning reddening water ; (tamála), meaning liked, for shade [cassia cinnamon, ceylon gamboge, yellow mangosteen] ; (dhanavriksha), meaning riches + tree, useful tree ; (hastijá), meaning born of elephant, a large variety ; (mátrivriksha), meaning mother tree ; (karaja), meaning reddening water ; (chiribilva), meaning curing long standing disease [roodrauck]. Can. also (huligilimara), meaning tiger + threatening + tree ; (kanaga) ; (biti) ; (thodagatti) ; (pong). Tel. also (kránuga), meaning hard tree ; (kaggera) ; (króvichettu). Mal. also (unnu), by corruption [variegated mountain ebony] ; (mínnári), meaning fish-smelling. Tam. also (karunduvarai), meaning black + dalbergia ; (tattaippungu), meaning flat + the tree, from flat pods. Title otherwise Caunooga, Indian beech, Poongam, Smooth-leaved pongamia, Woody dalbergia. Botanically Pongamia glabra, vent., leguminosæ [vricsham, 48]. Pongamia adaptation from tamul. Alias Dalbergia arborea ; Dolichos arboreus ; Gadelupa arborea, indica, pongam ; Pongamia gadelupa ; Robinia mitis. Leaves unequally pinnated ; leaflets opposite, two to three pairs, ovate, acuminated, glabrous ; racemes axillary, many-flowered, about half the length of the leaves ; pedicels in pairs ; vexillum with two callosities at the base of the limb and decurrent along the claw ; legume oblong, nearly sessile, thick and somewhat woody, with a short recurved beak, tumid along both sutures ; calyx cup-shaped, red ; corolla papilionaceous, white. Erect tree or climber abundant on banks of streams or near water; generally sheds its leaves at end of cold season; flowers mixture of white and purple produced in hot season; seed ripens towards end of year. Seed compressed, of the shape and size of a broad bean; testa thin, smooth, veined, light-red; cotyledons very oily, bitter. The bark has a thin ashy-grey outer layer, which readily peels off; when this is removed, the surface is seen to be green with white transverse marking; the substance of the bark is tough with a white granular fracture; odour mawkish; taste bitter and somewhat aromatic, with a peculiar pungency; starch and rhomboid crystals are observed under the microscope; the root bark is of a rusty-brown externally, yellow within. All parts of the plant when crushed afford a yellow juice. Poultice of leaves applied to ulcers; juice of root used as wash for sores; oil used medicinally for skin diseases. Leaves eaten by cattle; used as manure to fields. Oil used in lamps; gives fibre; gives also a thick, black, opaque gum [gond]; the dense foliage affords grateful shade. Wood light, tough and fibrous, coarse and even-grained, of light yellowish brown color, not easily worked nor giving a smooth surface; improved in strength and color by being seasoned in water; readily eaten by insects [poochy]. Compare where transl. is of first term:—Derris scandens (kodippungu), creeper; Sapindus trifoliatus (manippungu), bead; see gloss. paragraphs.

KARIVIA (കരിവിവള്ളി - karivivalli, *Mal.*). Meaning waste-land + creeper. Generic. Same as Rama's caper.

KARKAM (कर्क - karka, *San.*). From (kri, san. to injure). Hardness. Crab [carcam].——*Kakrasinghy* (कर्कटशृंगी - karkatashringí, San.; काकडाशिंगी - kákadashingí, Mahr.; کاکڑا سینگی - kákrásíngí, Hind.; کاکڑ سنگی - kákarsingí, Dec.; కాకరశింగి - kákarashingi, Tel.; காக்கடசிங்கி - kákkadasingi, Tam.). San. from (karkata, san. crab + shringa, san. horn), from horn-like galls [red lac sumach]. Mahr., &c., from sanscrit. Tel. also (dushtupuchettu), meaning hair-knot plant [hedge cotton]. Title otherwise Crab's horn, Zebra-wood tree [indian zebra wood]. Botanically Pistacia [pistah] integerrima, stewart, anacardiaceæ [vricsham, 45]. Alias Rhus kakrasinghee, specific from hindostany. Nearly glabrous tree, 40 feet and upwards; leaves 6–9 inches, with or without a terminal leaflet; petiole terete, puberulous; leaflets sub-opposite, petiolulate, coriaceous, quite entire, base oblique; nerves many, arched; panicles lateral; male flower compact, pubescent; female flower lax, elongate; flowers pedicelled, with two ovate bracts; stamens five to seven, filaments short; anthers large, dark red; female flower, sepals four, linear, and bracts deciduous; style almost three-partite; drupe ¼ inch, broader than long, glabrous, rugose, grey. Has horn-like excrescences, formed by the deposition of the ova of an insect; these galls [mauchicoy] are generally single, but sometimes lobed, of a purse-like form, and vary much in size; the external surface is of a pale greenish grey, and has a fimbriated appearance; the taste is strongly astringent and slightly bitter; they are tonic, expectorant, and useful in cough, phthisis, asthma, fever, want of appetite, and irritability of stomach. Compound powder; take of the galls of pistacia integerrima, terminalia chebula [chebulic myrobalan], and pistacia terebinthus [turpentine pistah], and of fenugreek seeds [maitee] and cinnamon [q.v.] bark, all in powder and of each five ounces; opium [aphainam], in powder, one ounce; gum [gond] acacia [babool], in powder, six ounces; and prepared chalk [sheemay choonam], eight ounces; mix them well, pass the compound powder through a fine sieve, rub it lightly in a mortar and keep it in a stoppered bottle. Doses; of simple powder, from fifteen to thirty grains; of compound powder, from thirty to sixty grains. Substituted for gummi-rubrum, hæmatoxylum, krameria, pul. cretæ aromaticus cum opio, and pulv. ipecac. compositus. The wood is handsome, yellowish brown, darkly veined, hard, heavy, fine-grained, very durable, takes a good polish and is much esteemed for furniture, &c.——*Kakree* (ککڑی - kakrí, Hind.). From (karkatí, san. the plant). Same as Country melon.——*Kankar* (कंकर - karkara, San.; کنکر - kankar, Hind.; کریکل - karikil, Malay; కంకర - kankara, Tel.; ചരൽ - charal. Mal.; பருக்கைக்கல் - parukkaikkal, Tam.). San. means hard. Tam. from (parukkai, tam. gravel + kal, tam. stone). Tam. also (shukkángal), meaning fragment + stone; (murambu); (shalli), meaning pieces. Otherwise Sookkaun. Indian gravel. A coarse kind of limestone [choonam cull] found in the soil. Material for road metal. There are two varieties, white and red. The white consists of carbonate of lime, silica, alumina, and sometimes magnesia and protoxide of iron. The red contains a large proportion of peroxide of iron. Kankar is sometimes found in thick stratified beds like the travertine near Rome, and seems in this case to have been formed by calcareous springs. More generally it is met with in clay [calimunn] or alluvial soil, in the shape of small pieces from the size of peas [calauyam] or filberts [findak] to that of the hand. In the blue clay which stretches along the shores it is found in vast abundance, generally assuming the most fantastic forms; indeed it abounds in every rice [q.v.] field and open soil all over the country. The more recent varieties seem to be formed by the agency of the rains [mazhay]. When the earth abounds with vegetation, the tepid waters are charged with fixed air, and dissolve the lime [choonam] prevailing in the soil everywhere around, the mineral being again thrown down as the advancing season dispels the excess of gas. It in this state absorbs the clayey matter around and cements it into kankar. It contains usually about 70 per cent. of carbonate of lime, 2½ per cent. of carbonate of magnesia, a trace of oxide of iron, and 10 to 20 per cent. of sand and clay. Mixed with half its weight of river sand [manal], it makes an excellent mortar [cauray]. Burnt in pieces of a cubic inch or so in size, and then powdered without slaking, it forms a good water cement [pattoo], setting in a few minutes, and becoming as hard as stone. The finer varieties of kankar are burnt with charcoal [adoopp kary] all throughout the country, in neat pigmy-looking kilns [shoolay], 2½ feet high and about as much in diameter at the base. These hold about a cubic foot of material, or about 36 lb. of charcoal and kankar in equal parts. When burnt and slaked, it is then made up into bricks [shengal], which are sold in the bazaar [q.v.] for whitewashing. The following legend is told of several hillocks of white pebbles in different parts of the country. Two Raucshasans [q.v.], named Vautaupy and Ilvalan, lived there and were accustomed to feast foot travellers. Ilvalan first slew his younger brother Vautaupy, and then cooked him in pots [chatty], out of which he fed the traveller. The meal being finished Ilvalan called on his brother by name, who came forth alive, rending the guest, who died in consequence, and then both giants feasted on his body. Agastyan [q.v.] came by and was given the usual meal. On its being finished Ilvalan called his brother, but Agastyan took up the words, and a Sanscrit muntram [q.v.], in consequence of which the body of Vautaupy dissolved, and passed away without doing Agastyan any mischief. He then cursed Ilvalan who died. The bones of these two Raucshasans having fallen to pieces, and becoming petrified, are now present as white pebbles. The hills are really ancient kankar. Hard particles of matter of yellowish color found imbedded in sores on body of horse [ghorah], which break out in Bursauty [q.v.], are also called Kankar [jelly].

KARNAM (कर्ण - karna, *San.*). From (kri, san. to do), useful. Ear [carnam].——*Kankhajoor* (शतपदी - shatapadí, San.; اربع - arba, Ar.; هزار پا - hazárpá, Pers.; کنکهجور - kankhajúr, Hind.; ಜರಿ - jari, Can.; కాళ్లజెర్రి - kállajerri, Tel.; പൂരം - púram, Mal.; பூரான் - púrán, Tam.). Title from hindostany. San. from (shata, san. hundred + pada, san. foot). Ar. means forty. Pers. from (hazár, pers. thousand + pá, pers. foot). Hind. from (karna, san. ear + kharjúra, san. scorpion), as entering the ear. Can. from (jari, can. to slide). Tel. from (kálu, tel. leg + jerri, tel. worm). Tam. from (púra, san. full), as full of legs. Centipede [poochy].——*Kaniyaur* (कर्णिकार - karnikára, San.; کنیار - kaniyár, Hind.; మచ్చకంద - mattsakanda, Tel.; வெண்ணாங்கு - vennángu, Tam.). Title from hindostany. San. means resembling an earring [hemp bendy, tirauna]. Hind. from sanscrit. Tel. corruption from (muchukunda, san. the tree). Tam. from (ven, tam. white + nángu, tam. tree, polygala). Hind. also (katháchampá). Title otherwise Maple-leaved pterospermum. Botanically Pterospermum [moch coondam] acerifolium, willd., sterculiaceæ [vricsham, 26]. Alias Pentapetes acerifolia. Tree; leaves entire or coarsely toothed, usually more or less peltate, the underside covered with rough tomentum; pedicels axillary, much shorter than the petiole; involucel leaves very caducous; petals linear-revolute; capsule long, five-angled, covered with scurfy pubescence on the outside; flowers large white, fragrant; flowering from march to may. Dark brown timber as strong as teak [q.v.] or oak [belote].

KARTAIRY (ಕಾಟೇರಿ - kártéri, *Can.*). From (kádu, can. jungle + éri, can. bank).—"*a*" Village, Peak; Neilgherry district, Merkoonaud division; acres 1,434; lat. 11° 20′; long. 76° 46′; from Coonoor W. 5 miles; from Ootacamund S.S.E. 5 miles. A small but rising Badaga [q.v.] village which has sprung up on saddle to the south of the waterfall near junction of roads from Ootacamund, Coonoor, &c. Considerable trade in grain. Group of sculptured cromlechs [paundoocull] on an estate in the neighbourhood.—"*b*" *River*; Neilgherry dist., Merkoonaud division. Rises near Ootacamund. After flowing through the rich coffee-growing tract of Kartairy, at an elevation of about 6,000 feet, it descends upon the plains in a series of waterfalls near Kartairy village and finally falls into the Bhawauny near Mettapolliem in lat. 11° 20′ N. and long. 76° 47′ E. The principal waterfall is 180 feet in depth [aroovy].—"*c*" Coffee [q.v.] and cinchona [koinah] estates, Merkoonaud, Neilgherries. Below the waterfall. 170 acres.

KARY (अङ्गार - angára, *San.*; कोळसे - kólasé, *Mahr.*; فحم - fahm, *Ar.*; زغال - zughál, *Pers.*; کوئلہ - koilah, *Hind.*; کولسا - kolsá, *Dec.*; ارانگ - aráng, *Malay*; ಇದ್ದಲು - iddalu, *Can.*; ಮಜಿ - maji, *Too.*; బొగ్గు - boggu, *Tel.*; കരി - kari, *Mal.*; අඟුර - angura, *Singh.*; கரி - kari, *Tam.*). Title from tamul. San. from (agni, san. fire). Tam. from (kari, tam. to be burnt). Tel. also (poyiboggu), meaning hearth + charcoal. Mal. also (muttikkari), meaning wood + charcoal. Carbon of chemists. Elementary combustible substance, existing pure and crystallized in the diamond [vajram]. The following are the three kinds of Kary. Carbonic acid is Karipoolipp. For Carbonates see Choornam.——*Adoopp kary* (काष्ठाङ्गार - kásht'hángára, San.;

लकडीकोळसे - lakadíkólasé, Mahr. ; فحم الخشب - fahmulkhashb, Ar. ; زغال چوبی - zughálichobí, Pers. ; كوئلا - koelá, Hind. ; كولسا - kolsá, Dec. ; ارانگ برا - arángbara, Malay ; ಕಟ್ಟಿಗೆಇದ್ದಲು - kattigeiddalu, Can. ; ಕನಕುಮಜಿ - kanakumaji, Too. ; కట్టెబొగ్గు - katteboggu, Tel. ; അടുപ്പുക്കരി - atuppukkari, Mal. ; ලිපඅඟුරු - lipaangura, Singh. ; அடுப்புக்கரி - aduppukkari, Tam.). Title from tamul. San. from (kásht'ha, san. wood + angára, san. charcoal). Mahr. from (lakadí, mahr. wood + kólasé, mahr. charcoal). Ar. from (fahm, ar. charcoal + khashb, ar. wood). Pers. from (zughál, pers. charcoal + chob, pers. wood). Malay from (aráng, malay, charcoal + bara, malay, live coal). Can. from (kattige, can. firewood + iddalu, can. charcoal). Too. from (kanaku, too. fuel + maji, too. charcoal). Tel. from (katte, tel. firewood + boggu, tel. charcoal). Singh. from (lipa, singh. hearth + angára, san. charcoal). Tam. from (aduppu, tam. hearth + kari, tam. charcoal). Wood charcoal. Carbo ligni of chemists. Artificial coal; consisting of wood charred by exposure to a red heat without access of air; in black brittle porous masses without taste or smell, very light, and retaining the shape and texture of the wood from which it was obtained; easily pulverized; when burned at a high temperature with free access of air, it leaves not more than two per cent. of ash. Manufactured as follows; firewood is cut in the forest and piled in a heap; the heap is then set on fire, and allowed to burn well; when it ceases to burn with a blaze, and burns only with a small flame, the heap is covered 2 inches thick with earth or sand, so that the flame does not penetrate the covering; it is left in that condition for a whole night; when it has cooled, the charcoal is raked out with a long pole. That from particular trees is best suited for particular purposes; goldsmiths [tattaun] in the south prefer it from biswool [q.v.] and tungaid [q.v.]; blacksmiths [collan] in the northern circars [q.v.] take it from sundra [q.v.]; in the south they take it from babool [q.v.] tamarind [q.v.] and satin-wood [q.v.]; for pharmaceutical purposes, that of the shrub yercum [q.v.] is always employed; gunpowder requires charcoal from woods of a hard close grain. Medicinally wood charcoal is antiseptic, deodorizing, and disinfectant; for purifying water an effectual plan is to boil it with a large-sized piece of freshly prepared wood charcoal; also forms an excellent filter, placed in alternate layers with river sand [manal]; charcoal, especially that of the areca [q.v.], forms the best tooth-powder. In the absence of coal [nilakary] all ore-smelting and other processes are dependent on wood charcoal, as well as the goldsmiths' and various other ornamental and useful trades; also used as a common domestic fuel [lukdy]; also in the manufacture of gunpowder.——*Nilakary* (నేలబొగ్గు - nélaboggu, Tel. ; കല്ക്കരി - kalkkari, Mal. ; நிலக்கரி - nilakkari, Tam.). Title and tam. from (nilam, tam. earth + kari, tam. charcoal). Tel. from (néla, tel. earth + boggu, tel. charcoal). Mal. from (kal, mal. stone + kari, mal. charcoal). Tam. also (vilaigari), meaning natural charcoal. Coal. Result of the mineralization of vegetable remains. That is to say vegetable tissue converted into a substance proportionally poorer in water and volatile ingredients, and richer in carbon. The different kinds are brown coal, pitch or just coal, glance or anthracite coal [cullcary], and others. Lignite is fossil wood, carbonised and altered, but still containing a much larger proportion of volatile ingredients than true coal. ——*Yeloomboo kary* (अस्थ्यङ्गार - ast'hyangára, San. ; هڈی کا کوئلہ - haddíkákoelah, Hind. ; هڈ کا کولسا - hadkákolsá, Dec. ; ಎಲುವುಇದ್ದಲು - eluvuiddalu, Can. ; ఎముకబొగ్గు - emukaboggu, Tel. ; അസ്ഥിക്കരി - ast'hikkari, Mal. ; எலும்புக்கரி - elumbukkari, Tam.). Title and tam. from (elumbu, tam. bone + kari, tam. charcoal). San. from (ast'hi, san. bone + angára, san. charcoal). Tel. from (emuka, tel. bone + boggu, tel. charcoal). Mal. from (ast'hi, san. bone + kari, mal. charcoal). Animal charcoal. Otherwise Bone ash, Bone black, Ivory black. Carbo animalis of chemists; alias Os ustum. The residue of bones which have been burned to a white ash in contact with air. Consists chiefly of phosphate of lime, with some carbonate of lime, &c. Is deodorizing and antiseptic. Employed as an antidote in poisoning cases.

KASR (کسر - kasr, *Hind.*). From (kasara, ar. to exceed). Surplus, profit in the exchange of coins [naunyam].

KATAY (कथा - kat'há, *San.* ; کتھا - kathá, *Hind.* ; கதை - kathai, *Tam.*). From (kat'h, san. to relate). The following is a fair specimen of a Tamul story of the extended class. Veera dhoorandhara rajah ruled in Vijianugger [q.v.]. He had a muntry [q.v.] named Tatwa pracausha pillay. One day when the king, accompanied by his minister, went out to hunt in the forest, he came to a spring of water named the looking-glass, near which was a writing cut in a stone to the effect that the king who listened to the counsels of his minister would perish. The king consulted with his minister concerning the writing. The minister took counsel within himself, that his own life was in danger. In order therefore to avert such a result, he seized the king, threw him into the spring, and returning to the city usurped the kingdom. The late king's wife Chinnamma devy privately made her escape, being pregnant, went to Chundragherry, and there subsisted in a miserable manner by gathering and selling firewood. The king of Chundragherry designing evil towards her, she left that place, and went to Arsanaupoory where a native chief named Ragha sing treated her hospitably and had a small cottage built for her reception. A child was born to her named Veeramauran. This child, being well instructed, early distinguished himself by killing a tiger [pooly]. Next come in the story details of a literary or poetical contest with the daughter of Veeraraman, king of Cosala [q.v.] desham; by skill in which contest Veeramauran gained her in marriage. These literary disputations are never-ending themes with the story-tellers. The forces of the father being now at the prince's disposal he with them dispossessed and killed the usurping muntry, and then proceeded to the place where his own father had been made away with. He there offered a great sacrifice, as the result of which the celestials [deva] descended and brought with them his father restored to life, who remained with his son while the latter ruled the kingdom.——*Katah munjary* (कथामञ्जरी - kat'hámañjarí, San.). From (above + mañjarí, san. series). A book of fables in Tamul by Villapaukam taundavaroya moodelliar teacher in the College of Fort St. George, Madras. Modern text-book.——*Katah sangraham* (कथासंग्रह - kat'hásangraha, San.). From (above + samgraha, san. collection). Canarese selections. A modern compilation.——*Katah sarit saugaram* (कथासरित्सागर - kát'hásaritságara, San.). Means ocean of rivers of stories. A large collection of tales compiled from Brihat katay [q.v.] by Somadeva bhatt of Cashmere about the commencement of twelfth century. For a smaller collection of tales see Punchatantram.

KATCHAY (कक्ष - kaksha, *San.* ; کاچھا - káchhá, *Hind.* ; ಕಚ್ಚೆ - kaçço, *Can.* ; കച്ച - kaçça, *Mal.* ; கச்சை - kaççai, *Tam.*). From (kach, san. to bind). Waist belt; the end of any lower garment gathered up behind and tucked into the part that girds the waist.

KATCHER (वेसर - vésara, *San.* ; بغل - baghl, *Ar.* ; استر - astar, *Pers.* ; خچر - khaççar, *Hind.* ; ಹಾಸರಕತ್ತೆ - hásarakatte, *Can.* ; కంచరగాడిద - kantsaragádide, *Tel.* ; കോവർകഴുത - kóvarkazhuta, *Mal.* ; கோவேறுகழுதை - kóvérugazhuthai, *Tam.*). Title from hindostany. San. from (véga, san. rapidity + sri, san. to go). Ar. from (baghula, ar. to affect stupidity). Hind. from sanscrit. Can. from (sanscrit + katte, can. ass). Tel. from (kantsaramu, tel. a sort of carriage + gádide, tel. ass). Tam. from (kó, tam. king + éru, tam. to ride + kazhuthai, tam. ass). Can. also (khachara). The mule; offspring of female horse [ghorah] and male ass [gadhah].

KATEERAH (कतेर - katéra, *Mahr.* ; كثيرا - kasírá, *Ar.* ; كتيرا - katerá, *Pers.* and *Hind.* ; كتيرا گوند - katerágond, *Dec.* ; ಬಾದಾಮಿಗೊಂದು - bádámigóndu, *Can.* ; ಬಾದಾಮಿಅಂಟು - bádámiantu, *Too.* ; బాదంబంక - bádambanka, *Tel.* ; வாதுமைக்கொட்டைப்பிசின் - váthumaikkottaippisin, *Tam.*). Title from arabic. Can. from (bádámi, can. almond + góndu, can. gum). Tel. from (bádamu, tel. almond tree, prunus amygdalus, baill. + banka, tel. gum). Tam. from (váthumaikkottai, tam. almond + pisin, tam. gum). Ar. also (samaghimiswákulabbás), meaning gum of red tooth-brush tree; (samaghulkattád), meaning gum of the tragacanth tree. Pers. also (samaghikon), meaning gum of astragalus verus, oliv. Title otherwise Baudam gum, Gum dragon to be distinguished from Dragon's blood, Gum of almonds, Gum tragacanth, Tragacanth, True milk vetch, True tragacanth. Product of Astragalus verus, oliver, leguminosæ [vriesham, 48]. Gummy exudation from the stem [gond]; is pale, yellowish or reddish, semi-transparent, smooth, horny, light, brittle, of every shape, in compressed or twisted fragments, often straight, or in vermicular tears, inodorous, tasteless, and unalterable by time; in water it swells very much, and forms a soft mucilage; occasionally found in bazaars [q.v.], brought from alexandria by red sea; more costly than gum arabic [q.v.]. Gives to pharm. tragacantha, emollient and demulcent; ingredient for imparting firmness to lozenges and pill masses. Used in the arts as a substitute for glue [vajram]; also in dyeing [shauyam]. The following gums are used as substitutes for kateerah:—Cochlospermum gossypium, dec., bixineæ [golden silk cotton]; Sterculia urens, roxb., sterculiaceæ [false kateerah]; Prunus amygdalus, baill., rosaceæ [baudam], hog tragacanth [hog gum], imported from Persia. For sarcocolla of the astragalus genus see Anzeroot.——*Almond kateerah* (بادام كتيرا - bádamkatírá, Hind.). Product of Baudam or bitter almond.——*Babool kateerah* (ببول كتيرا - babúlkatírá, Hind.). Product of Velvail.——*False kateerah* (कावळी - kávalí, Mahr. ; بلی - balí, Hind. ; ಕೆಂಪುದಾಳೆ - kempudále, Can. ; కవిలె - kavile, Tel. ; வெள்ளைப்பூத்தாளி - vellaippútáli, Tam.). Can. from (kempu, can. red + táli, can. borassus flabelliformis, linn.). Tam. from (vellai, tam. white + pú, tam. flower + táli, tam. borassus flabelliformis, linn.); from soft white wood. Hind. also (guler), meaning wild fig [cluster fig]; (katírá) [golden silk cotton, kateerah]. Tel. also (errapuniki), meaning red + gyrocarpus jacquini, roxb.; (tanukumánu); (tabase); (kondatámara), meaning hill + lotus, nelumbium speciosum, willd. [oval-leaved china root]. Title otherwise Country tragacanth, False tragacanth. Botanically Sterculia [cauvalam] urens, roxb., sterculiaceæ [vricsham, 26]. Alias Cavallium urens; cavallium from malayalam [cauvalam]. Tree; leaves palmately five-lobed, soft, velvety beneath, lobes acuminate, entire; calyx campanulate; panicles terminal; carpels ovate, hispid, with rigid bristly hairs, pubescent within; seeds several in each carpel; flowers small, yellow; flowering in the cold season. Trunk erect, very straight, top large and shady, bark light ash-colored, very smooth; deciduous in cold weather, flowers appear before the leaves; native of coromandel, but common everywhere. The bark yields a gum [gond] resembling tragacanth, and formerly substituted for it; this occurs in large light brown transparent tough masses which immersed in water swell like a jelly, but do not dissolve except by protracted boiling; the solution is not adhesive; the bark is very astringent, and tinges the saliva reddish; leaves and tender branches steeped in water yield a mucilaginous extract; fruits or rather capsules contain each from three to five oblong, chestnut-colored seeds. Gum used in medicine; seeds cathartic; extract from branches is useful in pleuropneumonia in cattle. Seeds roasted and eaten with chestnut flavor; kind of coffee [q.v.] made from them; gum used in making sweetmeats [halwah]. Liber yields a good fibre. Native zithers and toys made of the wood [moochee wood], which is soft and spongy.——*Indian kateerah* (هندی کتیرا - hindíkatírá, Hind.). Product of Golden silk cotton.

KAUMIL (کامل - kámil, *Hind.*). From (kamala, ar. to be complete). Complete. So standard assessment [jumma kaumil]. Also the whole sum raised by a village for the total of its expenses, including the Government demand. See vol. I, 112.

KAV (कव् - kav, *San.*). To paint, to describe.——*Kavay* (कवयी - kavayí, San.). Means clever. Palmyra fish.——*Kavy* (कवि - kavi, San.). From (kav, san. to describe). Means poet [cavy]. Title of the rulers of Calyaunapooram [q.v.]. Cherma permaul made Kavy simha royer of Calyaunapooram chief ruler of Tooloovam [q.v.].——*Kawy* (کوی - kawí, Hind.). Literally narrative. The ancient language of Java [q.v.] and Baly [q.v.]. In Baly it is still the language of law and religion, as it was in Java until the adoption of the Mahomedan religion in the fifteenth century.

KAVACHAM (कवच - kavacha, *San.*). Armour [vurman].——*Kavachiny* (कवचिनी - kavachiní, San.; گهونگا - ghúngá, Hind.; ಚಿಪ್ಪುಹುಳ - chippuhula, Can.; గుల్లపురుగు - gullapurugu, Tel.; ഓട്ടുമത്സ്യം - óttumatsyam, Mal.; ஓட்டுமீன் - óttumín, Tam.). Title from sanscrit. San. from (kavacha, san. armour); from crust-like shell covering body and legs. Hind. from (kambuka, san. shell). Can. from (chippu, can. shell + hula, can. worm). Tel. from (gulla, tel. shell + purugu, tel. worm). Mal. from (ótu, mal. shell + matsya, san. fish). Tam. from (ódu, tam. shell + mín, tam. fish). Crustaceans generally [iraul, nundoo, taurahmatsyam]. Crabs, cray fish and prawns are regularly collected as food; generally caught in lagoons [cauyal] or fresh water lakes; there are some land-crabs.

KAVIKAH (کویکا - kaviká, *Hind.*). Same as Malacca jaumoon.

KAWAH (قهوه - kahwah, *Hind.*). Same as Coffee [q.v.].

KAYA (کیا - kaya, *Malay*). Wood.——*Kayoo manis* (کیومنس - kayúmanis, Malay). From (kayú, malay, wood + mains, malay, sweet). Cinnamon.

KAYAM (കയം - kayam, *Mal.*). From (kasi, tam. to ooze). Deep pool in a river [casham, madoogoo]. Suffix in river names; as Anakkayam, meaning elephant + deep pool.

KECHWAH (भूनाग - bhúnága, *San.*; خراطین - kharátín, *Ar.* and *Pers.*; کیچوه - kechwah, *Hind.* and *Dec.*; چچینگ - chaching, *Malay*; ಮಣ್ಣುಹುಳ - mannuhula, *Can.*; నక్కురు - nakkuru, *Too.*; ఎఱ్ఱ - erra, *Tel.*; ഞാഞ്ഞൂൽ - ñáññúl, *Mal.*; நாக்குப்பூச்சி - nákkuppúççi, *Tam.*). Title from deccany. San. from (bhú, san. earth + nága, san. serpent). Ar. from (khará, ar. worm + tín, ar. earth). Hind. from (kiñchilika, san. earth-worm). Can. from (mannu, can. earth + hula, can. insect). Tel. means red. Mal. from (nánguzhu, tam. belly worm). Tam. from (nángu, tam. to shrink + púççi, tam. insect); from shrinking when moving. Earth-worm. For worms generally see Keerah.

KEDAMANAIR (కేతామన్నేరు - kétámannéru, *Tel.*). From (géde, tel. buffalo + mannu, tel. sand + éru, tel. river). River; Nellore dist., Atmacore and Oodayagherry tals. Rises in the Eastern ghauts [q.v.] near Dornaul pass, and falls into the Anantasaugaram tank [aroovy].

KEDAURAM (केदार - kédára, *San.*). From (ka, san. water + dhri, san. to hold) [cam]. A particular part of the Himalayas. Called also Kedaurnath in Garhwal. Has a shrine dedicated to Shiva [q.v.] and a lingam considered one of twelve [lingam].——*Kedaura gowry vratam* (కేదారగౌరీవ్రతము - kédáragaurivratamu, Tel.). From (above + gaurí, san. párvatí, the brilliant goddess + vrata, san. vow); vow to parvaty. Lunar [chaundramaunam] festival [pundigay, 6b], subject to intercalation [adhicam]. Occurs at new moon [amavausyay] of seventh lunar month Aushweejam [mausam] between 15th October and 14th November. One of the three great feasts, which after once celebrated obliges the person to continue the celebration every year [ananta chatoordashy, vara lutchmy vratam]. Women worship Parvaty [q.v.] in their houses, and ask for offspring. Those who keep it observe the demi-fast and tie a yellow string on their right arm. Different from Gowry vratam [q.v.].——*Kedauran* (केदार - kédára, San.). Epithet of Shiva [q.v.].——*Kedaura vanam* (केदारवन - kédáravana, San.). From (above + vana, san. forest). A waste place in the neighbourhood of any town, where a stone lingam [q.v.] is placed.

KEDDY (କେଡ଼ି - keddi, *Oor.*). Meriah [q.v.] sacrifice.

KEDGEREE (کهچڑی - khichrí, *Hind.*). Otherwise Kitcherry. A mess of rice [q.v.] cooked with butter [q.v.], dholl [common dholl], and flavored with spice, shred onion [piyauz], &c.

KEEKAR (کیکر - kíkar, *Hind.*). Acacia [cantalam].

KEEL (قیر - kír, *Ar.*; قیل - kíl, *Pers.*, *Hind.* and *Dec.*; ಕೀಲು - kílu, *Can.*; ಟಾರು - táru, *Too.*; తారు - táru, *Tel.*; കീൽ - kíl, *Mal.* and *Singh.*; கீல் - kíl, *Tam.*). Ar. also (difl). Pers. also (kitrán). Tam. also (kisil). Tar. Pix liquida of chemists. Obtained by burning pine and fir trees in a close smothering heap, with a channel through which the tar exudes [dammer, zift]. For pitch see Zift.

KEEL (കീഴ് - kízh, *Mal.*; கீழ் - kízh, *Tam.*). Below, or east. Suffix in place names; as Cherankeel, meaning village below the tank. Prefix in place names; as in Keelcherry, meaning eastern village.——*Keelakaray* (கீழக்கரை - kízhakkarai, Tam. kílakarai *). From (kízh, tam. east + karai, tam. coast). Town, Port; Madura dist., Ramnaud zemindarry tal.; pop. 12,396; lat. 9° 14′; long. 78° 50′; from Madras S.S.W. 280 miles; from Madura S.E. 66 miles; from Moottoopett W.S.W. 10 miles; from Ramnaud S.S.W. 10 miles; from Yervandy E. 5 miles. On the Gulf of Manaar. Chiefly inhabited by Mussalmans. The houses and granaries are finely built on the shore. Small Roman catholic church, contiguous to which are ruins of a Dutch factory. Several Mussalman mosques [musjid] and tombs [gor]. Ancient Shiva temple built by Varagoona paundyan. Thick groves of palmyra [q.v.] trees. Large trade in pathaneer [q.v.], which Mussalmans drink, and in manufacture of fine and coarse long cloths. The port has upwards of 100 boats. The coast abounds with low rugged rocks, which are only seen above water at low tide.——*Keel goottagay* (கீழ்க்குத்தகை - kízhkkuttagai, Tam.). Sub-tenure, under-contract.——*Keel maday* (கீழ்மடை - kízhmadai, Tam.). From (above + madai, tam. channel). Land most distant from the sluice [maday].——*Keelpaloorore* (கீழப்பழூர் - kízhappaluvúr, Tam. kílpaluvúr *). From (kízh, tam. east + pazhu, tam. banyan tree, ficus bengalensis, linn. + úr, tam. village). Sanscrit name (vatavana), meaning banyan tree, ficus bengalensis, linn. + forest.—"*a*" Deputy tahsildarry, Trichinopoly district. Pay Rs. 70.—"*b*" Village, Deputy tahsildar's station, General deputy collector's division; Trichinopoly dist., Oodayarpolliem tal.; pop. 2,219; acres 3,814; lat. 11° 03′; long. 79° 08′; from Ariyalore S. 7 miles; from Jayancondacholapooram S.W. 23 miles; from Laulgoody N.E. 21 miles; from Madras S.S.W. 160 miles; from Moosiry E. 41 miles; from Oodayarpolliem S.W. 19 miles; from Shreerungam E.N.E. 28 miles; from Trichinopoly E.N.E. 29 miles. Good camping ground. Former head-quarters of talook [q.v.]. Deputy tahsildar [q.v.] transferred from Rajendraputnam in 1873. Old Shiva temple elaborately sculptured and with a Chola inscription.——*Kelamungalam* (ಕೆಳಮಂಗಲ - kelamangala, Can.). From (kéla, can. underneath + mangala, san. prosperity); from its hollow situation. Village; Salem dist., Oossoor tal.; pop. 2,277; acres 1,297; lat. 12° 36′; long. 77°; from Oossoor S. 9 miles; from Salem N.N.W. 68 miles. In a hollow near the crossing of the roads to Dencanicottah, Oossoor and Royacottah. Good camping-ground. Frequently mentioned in the wars with Mysore. The weekly fair is the largest in the district. Large trade in grain and oil-seeds [yennay]. Cloths are manufactured.——*Kilanelly* (கீழாநிலை - kízhánilai, Tam.). From (kízh, tam. low + nilai, tam. site). Village; Trichinopoly dist., Foodoocottah state; lat. 10° 10′; long. 78° 54′; from Ariyalore S.S.W. 67 miles; from Madras S.S.W. 219 miles; from Moosiry S.S.E. 60 miles; from Poodoocottah S.E. 14 miles; from Shreerungam S.S.E. 49 miles; from Trichinopoly S.E. 45 miles; from Trimayam S.E. 9 miles. Fort of local importance. Made over in 1830 by Clive to the rajah as a reward for his fidelity to British government. Temple dedicated to Arya nautchy amman. On south bank of Pambaur.——*Kizhakk* (கிழக்கு - kizhakku, Tam.). From (kízh, tam. downward). East.

KEENA (කීන - kína, *Singh.*). Nut of Small poon.

KEERAH (कृमि - krimi, *San.*; कीड - kída, *Mahr.*; دود - dúd, *Ar.*; کرم - kirm, *Pers.*; کیرا - kírá, *Hind.* and *Dec.*; ಹುಳ - hula,

Can.; ಪುರಿ - puri, *Too.*; పురుగు - purugu, *Tel.*; പുഴു - puzhu, *Mal.*; කීට - kíta, *Singh.*; புழு - puzhu, *Tam.*). Title from hindostany. San. from (kram, san. to move) [cramam, craunty]. Mahr. from (kíta, san. worm). Pers. from sanscrit. Hind. from (kíta, san. worm). Tel. from (pulaka, san. insect). Singh. from (kíta, san. worm). Worm. Any insect without wings [poochy]. For earth-worms see Kechwah.

KEERAM (कीर - kíra, *San.*). From (kí, san. the sound + rá, san. to give); imitative word. Psittacidæ family, scansores, insessores, aves [pacshy, 12], of naturalists [jantoo]. Parrots. Divided into sub-families as follow:—Psittacinæ, or true Parrots; Loriinæ or lories [lory]; Palæorninæ or parrakeets [totah]; Platycercinæ, or australian parrakeets; Arainæ or maccaws; Cacatuinæ, or cockatoos of australia.

KEERAY (शाक - sháka, *San.*; بهاجی - bhájí, *Hind.*; ಪಲ್ಯ - palya, *Can.*; కూర - kúra, *Tel.*; ചീര - chíra, *Mal.*; கீரை - kírai, *Tam.*). Terms synonymous with greens of all sorts. Most greens are made by natives into curries [q.v.] and other dishes. Some are made into decoctions [kwautam] or teas [q.v.]. A description of all the plants eaten as vegetables by natives would include nearly the whole of the weeds, except those absolutely poisonous, that are to be met with in the country. The following however are two key-lists of the most common culinary vegetables indigenous or introduced for which vernacular names are known. Further information must be traced in the glossary paragraphs through the small type cross-references at end of this volume; see also vricsham, 7, for the method of expressing the products, &c., of the plants in the dravidian languages.—"*a*" Achyranthes aspera, indian burr; Ærua lanata, woolly ærua; Æschynomene aspera, solah; Agaricus campestris, mushroom; Allium cepa, onion; Allium sativum, garlic; Amarantus atropurpureus, red spinach; Amarantus blitum, var. oleraceus, common spinach; Amarantus campestris, field spinach; Amarantus gangeticus, garden spinach; Amarantus paniculatus, brown spinach; Amarantus spinosus, thorny spinach; Amarantus tenuifolius, wild spinach; Amarantus viridis, stunted spinach; Amorphophallus campanulatus, telinga potato; Anisochilus carnosus, country lavender; Apium graveolens, celery; Artocarpus integrifolia, bread-fruit; Bambusa arundinacea, common bamboo; Bambusa stricta, male bamboo; Basella cordifolia, heart-leaved malabar night-shade; Basella rubra, red malabar night-shade; Basella rubra, var. alba, white malabar night-shade; Bauhinia purpurea, purple mountain ebony; Bauhinia vahlii, large mountain ebony; Benincasa cerifera, wax gourd; Beta vulgaris, indian beet; Bœrhaavia repens, var. diffusa, spreading hog-weed; Bombax malabaricum, red-cotton tree; Borassus flabelliformis, palmyra; Brassica alba, white mustard; Brassica campestris, sub-sp. campestris, colza; Brassica campestris, sub-sp. rapa, turnip; Brassica oleracea, cabbage; Canavalia ensiformis, hussar bean; Canthium parviflorum, thorny webera; Capparis aphylla, common caper; Capparis zeylanica, ceylon caper; Capsicum annuum, common chilly; Capsicum frutescens, shrubby chilly; Capsicum minimum, bird's eye chilly; Carica papaya, papaw; Carthamus tinctorius, safflower; Cassia sophera, stinking casoudy; Cassia tora, chakondah; Cephalandra indica, indian caper; Citrullus vulgaris, sweet water melon; Cocos nucifera, cocoanut; Commelyna communis, calf's grass; Corchorus olitorius, wild jute; Coriandrum sativum, coriander; Cucumis melo, common melon; Cucumis sativus, common cucumber; Cucumis trigonus, country cucumber; Cucurbita maxima, great pumpkin; Cucurbita ovifera, vegetable marrow; Curcuma longa, turmeric; Cyamopsis psoralioides, chinese lablab; Cynodon dactylon, hurrially; Daucus carota, carrot; Dillenia indica, chaltah; Dioscorea aculeata, goa potato; Dioscorea alata, wing-stalked yam; Dioscorea globosa, humped yam; Dioscorea pentaphylla, five-leaved yam; Dioscorea purpurea, pondicherry yam; Dioscorea sativa, common yam; Dolichos lablab, country bean; Dregea volubilis, nakchiknee silk cotton; Emilia sonchifolia, hare's ear; Ficus glomerata, cluster fig; Ficus racemosa, country fig; Flacourtia ramontchi, var. sapida, ceylon plum; Fœniculum vulgare, indian fennel; Gisekia pharnaceoides, sand greens; Gynandropsis pentaphylla, dog mustard; Helmia bulbifera, malacca yam; Hibiscus cannabinus, hemp bendy; Hibiscus esculentus, common bendy; Hibiscus sabdariffa, red hemp bendy; Hydrocotyle asiatica, indian pennywort; Ipomæa aquatica, creeping bind-weed; Ipomæa batatas, sweet potato; Ipomæa reniformis, rat's ear; Ipomæa sepiaria, laldanah; Lactuca scariola, var. sativa, lettuce; Lagenaria vulgaris, bottle gourd; Lepidium sativum, cress; Leucas indica, wild toombay; Luffa acutangula, common luffa; Luffa ægyptiaca, oil-giving luffa; Lycopersicum esculentum, tomato; Mangifera indica, mango; Manihot utilissima, tapioca; Mentha piperita, peppermint; Mentha viridis, spearmint; Meriandra bengalensis, bengal sage; Momordica charantia, balsam apple; Morinda umbellata, small ach root; Moringa pterygosperma, indian horse radish; Mucuna nivea, white cowitch; Murraya kœnigii, curry-leaf tree; Musa paradisiaca, plantain; Mussænda frondosa, moossanda; Nasturtium officinale, water cress; Nelumbium speciosum, sacred lotus; Nymphæa lotus, red indian water-lily; Ocimum basilicum, sweet basil; Ocimum sanctum, var. hirsuta, rough basil; Origanum vulgare, marjoram; Oxalis corniculata, sorrel; Pandanus odoratissimus, screw-pine; Pteroselinum sativum, parsley; Peucedanum graveolens, dill; Phaseolus adenanthus, wild green gram; Phaseolus lunatus, country french bean; Phaseolus vulgaris, french bean; Phyllanthus emblica, emblic myrobalan; Pisum sativum, garden pea; Portulaca oleracea, indian purslane; Portulaca quadrifida, small indian purslane; Premna integrifolia, moonnay; Raphanus sativus, country radish; Rothia trifoliata, jackal green gram; Rumex vesicarius, country sorrel; Sesbania grandiflora, west-indian sesban; Solanum melongena, brinjaul; Solanum nigrum, indian hound's berry; Solanum torvum, hill shoonday; Solanum trilobatum, prickly shoonday; Solanum tuberosum, potato; Solanum verbascifolium, shoonday; Spinacia oleracea, garden spinach; Spondias mangifera, hog plum; Suæda indica, indian salt-wort; Tamarindus indica, tamarind; Trianthema monogyna, shauranay; Tribulus terrestris, land caltrops; Trichodesma indicum, donkey toombay; Trichosanthes anguina, common snake gourd; Trichosanthes dioica, palwal snake gourd; Trigonella fœnum-græcum, fenugreek; Vicia faba, broad bean; Vigna catiang, cow gram; Vitis quadrangularis, piranday; Zea mays, maize; Zingiber officinale, ginger; Zizyphus jujuba, bair.—"*b*" Ach root, morinda; Bair, zizyphus; Balsam apple, momordica; Bamboo, bambusa; Basil, ocimum; Bean, dolichos, vicia; Beet, beta; Bendy, hibiscus; Bind-weed, ipomæa; Bread-fruit, artocarpus; Brinjaul, solanum; Burr, achyranthes; Cabbage, brassica; Calf's grass, commelyna; Caltrops, tribulus; Caper, capparis, cephalandra; Carrot, daucus; Casoudy, cassia; Celery, apium; Chakondah, cassia; Chaltah, dillenia; Chilly, capsicum; Cocoanut, cocos; Colza, brassica; Coriander, coriandrum; Cowitch, mucuna; Cress, lepidium; Cucumber, cucumis; Curry-leaf tree, murraya; Dill, peucedanum; Fennel, fœniculum; Fenugreek, trigonella; Fig, ficus; French bean, phaseolus; Garlic, allium; Ginger, zingiber; Gourd, lagenaria; Gram, phaseolus, rothia, vigna; Hare's ear, emilia; Hog plum, spondias; Hog-weed, bœrhaavia; Horse radish, moringa; Hound's berry, solanum; Hurrially, cynodon; Hussar bean, canavalia; Jute, corchorus; Lablab, cyamopsis; Laldanah, ipomæa; Lavender, anisochilus; Lettuce, lactuca; Lotus, nelumbium; Maize, zea; Mango, mangifera; Marjoram, origanum; Melon, cucumis; Moonnay, premna; Mountain ebony, bauhinia; Mustard, brassica, gynandropsis; Mushroom, agaricus; Myrobalan, phyllanthus; Night-shade, basella; Onion, allium; Palmyra, borassus; Palwal, trichosanthes; Papaw, carica; Parsley, pteroselinum; Pea, pisum; Pennywort, hydrocotyle; Peppermint, mentha; Piranday, vitis; Plantain, musa; Plum, flacourtia; Potato, amorphophallus, dioscorea, ipomæa, solanum; Pumpkin, cucurbita; Purslane, portulaca; Radish, raphanus; Rat's ear, ipomæa; Red cotton, bombax; Safflower, carthamus; Sage, meriandra; Saltwort, suæda; Sand greens, gisekia; Screw-pine, pandanus; Sesban, sesbania; Shauranay, trianthema; Shoonday, solanum; Silk cotton, dregia; Snake gourd, trichosanthes; Solah, æschynomene; Sorrel, oxalis, rumex; Spearmint, mentha; Spinach, amarantus, spinacia; Tamarind, tamarindus; Tapioca, manihot; Tomato, lycopersicum; Toombay, leucas, trichodesma; Turmeric, curcuma; Turnip, brassica; Vegetable marrow, cucurbita; Water cress, nasturtium; Water-lily, nymphæa; Water melon, citrullus; Wax gourd, benincasa; Webera, canthium; Yam, dioscorea, helmia.

KEERTY (कीर्ति - kírti, *San.*). From (krít, san. to mention). Fame. Common in royal names [peyar].——*Keertanay* (கீர்த்தனை - kírttanai, Tam.). From (krít, san. to praise). A species of Tamul verse. It consists of four stanzas, the first of which is preceded by a short intercalary line, which is repeated before each of the others. It is reckoned a lower order of poetry, and is much used in dramatic composition.——*Keerty lutchmy* (कीर्तिलक्ष्मी - kírtilakshmí, San.). From (above + lakshmí, san. the goddess). The goddess of fame [ashta lutchmy].

KEET (கீற்று - kíttu, *Tam.*). From (kíru, tam. to split). Line. Half of a cocoanut [q.v.] leaf, generally plaited for thatching and screening [cadjan].——*Keet naumam* (கீற்றுநாமம் - kíttunámam, Tam.). From (above + námam, tam. vaishnava mark). Veishnavite tridental mark [naumam].

KEEYAH (قياس - kiyás, *Hind.*). From (kása, ar. to compare). Means analogy. Conclusions drawn by analogy from the Koran [q.v.], the traditions [hadees], and the Ijmah [q.v.].

KEI (ಕೈ - kai, *Can.*; కై - kai, *Tel.*; കൈ - kai, *Mal.*; கை - kai, *Tam.*). From (shey, tam. to do); cf. chey. Hand [caram, hastam].——*Kei badil* (ಕೈಬದಲು - kaibadalu, Can.). From (above + badala, ar. to change). A loan of money for a short time.——*Keicalore* (కైకలూరు - kaikalúru, Tel.). From (kaikóla, tel. a weaver + úru, tel. village). Sanscrit name (kainkaryapura), meaning service + town.—"*a*" Deputy tahsildarry, Kistna dist. Pay Rs. 70.—"*b*" Village, Deputy tahsildar's station; Kistna dist., Goodivauda tal.; pop. 1,278; acres 2,097; lat. 16° 33′; long. 81° 15′; from Bezwada E. 39 miles; from Goodivauda E.N.E. 16 miles; from Guntoor E.N.E. 52 miles; from Madras N.N.E. 246 miles; from Masulipatam N. 26 miles; from Vinoocondah E.N.E. 103 miles. Near Colair lake. Vencateshwaran temple with inscription. Also Ramalingeshwaran temple with inscriptions.——*Kei caunom* (കൈക്കാണം - kaikánam, Mal.). From (above + kánam, mal. property). Property in hand, personal property.——*Keicauran* (கைக்காரன் - kaikkáran,

Tam.). From (above + káran, tam. possessor). Artificer.——*Keicooly* (കൈക്കൂലി - kaikkúli, Mal.). From (above + kúli, mal. wages). Fee paid by lessee to proprietor upon renewal of lease; also a bribe.——*Keicutty* (கைக்கட்டி - kaikkatti, Tam.). From (above + kattu, tam. to tie). From tyeing red silk or other cord on the upper arm. The accountant caste [kanakan].——*Keikkila* (కైకోల - kaikóla, Tel.; கைக்கிள - kaikkila, Tam.). From (above + kizhavan, tam. master). Weavers. The corresponding terms are:—Can. jeyda, Tel. sauley, Mal. chaulyan. About half the men are employed in the construction of textile fabrics and dress, in which they are aided by their families. Most of the southern weavers profess the Sheiva religion but worship village deities and demons. The women and children all work at the loom [tarry]. Some allow widows to remarry. The weavers of the Chingleput district devote their eldest daughter to the service of the temple [devadausy]. See vol. II, 230. In every large town there are colonies of silk-weavers, Putnool caurar, whose ancestors originally came from Goozerat, their chief men dealing in raw silk [nesavoo, puttoo].——*Keimal* (കൈമൾ - kaimal, Mal.). From (kaima, mal. power). Honorific term applied by lower castes to Nayars.——*Keimany* (കൈമണി - kaimani, Mal.). From (above + mani, mal. bell). Cymbals.——*Keimoothal* (കൈമുതൽ - kaimutal, Mal.). From (above + mutal, mal. capital). Personal property.——*Keipanam* (കൈപ്പണം - kaippanam, Mal.). From (above + panam, mal. money). Ready money.——*Keipidy* (கைப்பிடி - kaippidi, Tam.). From (above + pidi, tam. to catch). A handful [mooshty].——*Keivayipp* (കൈവായ്പ - kaiváypa, Mal.). From (above + váypa, mal. borrowing). Borrowing for a short time on a verbal promise to pay.——*Keividooga otty* (കൈവിടുകഒറ്റി - kaivitukaotti, Mal.). Full form of Keividotty [otty].——*Keiyiroopp* (കയ്യിരിപ്പ് - kayyirippu, Mal.). From (above + iri, mal. to be). Balance in hand.——*Keiyoppam* (கையொப்பம் - kaiyyoppam, Tam.). From (above + oppu, tam. to agree to). Signature [daskat].——*Valangay* (வலங்கை - valangai, Tam.). Right hand. See sep. title.——*Yidangay* (இடங்கை - idangai, Tam.). Left hand. See sep. title.

KEID (قيد - kaíd, *Hind.*). From arabic, meaning a shackle. Imprisonment.——*Keidy* (قيدى - kaídí, Hind.). A prisoner.

KEIDA (കൈത - kaita, *Mal.*). From (kétakí, san. screw-pine). Same as Screw-pine.

KEILAUSAM (कैलास - kailása, *San.*). From (kélása, san. crystal).—"*a*" The residence of Coobairan [q.v.], and favorite heaven of Shiva [q.v.]; supposed amongst the Himalaya mountains. Called also Ganaparvatam and Rajata parvatam. Shiva here holds his court attended by ganams [q.v.] or hosts of celestials. In this situation Parvaty [q.v.] is the name of his consort, not Devy [q.v.] or Doorga [q.v.]. The lake Maunasa sarovaram, deemed sacred, lies near the foot of the mountain, and is the birth place of Soobramanyan [q.v.]. The locality is evidently connected with some early events in the history of mankind [matam].—"*b*" Hindoo 2nd or pers. name. Common among non-bramins [peyar].—"*c*" Hill; Vizagapatam dist., Vizagapatam tal. Suggested at one time as a sanitarium for Bengal; and with that view one or two houses were built, the Maharajah of Vizianagram assisting the project with much liberality. The houses are falling into ruins. The project failed chiefly owing to Waltair, the European station on the coast being itself very cool all the year round. There is an average difference of about 8 degrees between the temperature of Keilausam and that of Vizagapatam and owing to its proximity to the sea, within 3 miles, and the absence of forest growth, the site is singularly free from fever. It is easy of access, and the climate is bracing [hill station].——*Keilausa nautan* (कैलासनाथ - kailásanát'ha, San.). From (above + nát'ha, san. lord). Shiva.

KEISAR (قيصر - kaisar, *Hind.*). Corruption of cæsar. Emperor.——*Keisarehind* (قيصر هند - kaisarihind, Hind.). Emperor or Empress of India.

KEIYOOM (قيوم - kaiyúm, *Ar.*). From (kauma, ar. to stand). Eternal. Attribute of God [allah]. Common alam; as Keiyoom ally, double alam [ism].

KEKUI (കകണ - kakuna, *Singh.*). Same as Lumbang nut.

KELIROO (கெளிறு - keliru, *Tam.*). From (keli, tam. greediness). The genus Macrones, siluridæ [kizhautty], physostomi, teleostei, pisces [matsyam, 35], of naturalists [jantoo]. Freshwater fish; employed as food by poor, but insipid. The species best known to the natives are:—black, fiddler, golden, snouted, white. Cf. also cat, dog, slippery, variegated, in other genera.——*Black keliroo* (കരി - kari, Mal.). Mal. means black. Macrones [keliroo] armatus, siluridæ [kizhautty], physostomi, teleostei [matsyam, 35], of naturalists. Alias Hypselobagrus armatus. Freshwater; a considerable rise from snout to base of dorsal fin; upper surface of the head roughened, shoulder-bone roughened in lines; leaden or brown superiorly, lighter beneath, with or without a brown band along the side, and a dark blotch at the base of the caudal fin; upper half of dorsal fin darkish, and a dark band along the anal; malabar and wyuaud range of hills.——*Cat keliroo* (பூனைக்கெளிறு - púnaikkeliru, Tam.). Title from appearance of face. Tam. from (púnai, tam. cat + keliru, tam. macrones genus). Osteogeniosus militaris, siluridæ [kizhautty], physostomi, teleostei [matsyam, 35], of naturalists [jantoo]. Alias Ageniosus militaris; Arius militaris; Osteogeniosus cantoris; Silurus militaris. Upper surface of head almost or quite smooth, few granulations generally present; silvery, darkish superiorly, fins tinged with red; sea, estuaries and tidal rivers; no other common species here.——*Dog keliroo* (நாய்க்கெளிறு - náykkeliru, Tam.). Title from appearance of face. Tam. from (náy, tam. dog + keliru, tam. macrones genus). Pseudeutropius sykesii, siluridæ [kizhautty], physostomi, teleostei [matsyam, 35], of naturalists [jantoo]. Alias Pseudeutropius mitchelli; Schilbe sykesii. Freshwater; upper jaw slightly the longer; median longitudinal groove on upper surface of the head reaches to base of occipital process, which latter is narrow; bluish-silvery along back, silvery-white on sides and below; dorsal and caudal gray, the other fins white; western coast attains about 6 inches; for another species see Leaf jella.——*Fiddler keliroo* (كترنا - katarná, Hind. and Dec.; సాకుజెల్ల - sákujella, Tel.; କୁଣ୍ଟିଆ - kuntiyá, Oor.; கெளிறு - keliru, Tam.) Title from noise when irritated. Tam. from (keli, tam. greediness). Macrones [keliroo] vittatus, siluridæ [kizhautty], physostomi, teleostei [matsyam, 35], of naturalists. Alias Bagrus affinis; Macrones tengara; Pimelodus carcio, indicus; Silurus vittatus. Tengara from bengalee. Freshwater. Upper surface of head roughened in tubercles hardly forming lines. Colors silvery or golden, old specimens have a light bluish band along middle of side, and narrow light one above and below it, dark shoulder spot, and sometimes another near base of caudal fin. Sometimes these fish appear to be dark. Tips of fins usually dark. When touched on the wet ground, it appears to become very irate, erecting its dorsal fin and making a noise resembling the buzzing of a bee [tainee], evidently a sign of anger. 7 or 8 inches.——*Golden keliroo* (نیلاکترنا - nílákatarná, Hind.; മണലേട്ട - manalétta, Mal.). Title from color. Hind. from (nílá, hind. blue + katarná, hind. the fish, macrones vittatus). Mal. from (manal, mal. sand + étta, mal. the fish, polyacanthus cupanus). Macrones [keliroo] chryseus, siluridæ [kizhautty], physostomi, teleostei [matsyam, 35], of naturalists. Alias Pseudobagrus chryseus. Freshwater; upper jaw slightly longer; upper surface of head, opercles and humeral process with smooth ridges; back greenish-yellow, sides golden; a large round black mark on shoulder surrounded by light yellow ring; dorsal and anal fins yellowish orange, stained with darker at margins; caudal yellow, with black base and dark edges; rivers in canara and malabar, preferring the deepest pools; wounds from their spines are deemed venomous by natives.——*Slippery keliroo* (शिलिन्द - shilinda, San.; వంజు - vandzu, Tel.; ଝିଲଙ୍ଗ - jillang, Oor.; வழுக்கைக்கெளிறு - vazhukkaikkeliru, Tam.). Title from mucous secretion. Tel. from (vandza, tel. stem of the lotus); probably from its being slippery. Tam. from (vazhukku, tam. to slip + keliru, tam. macrones genus). Tam. also (púnattai), meaning flower + snail. Silundia gangetica, siluridæ [kizhautty], physostomi, teleostei [matsyam, 35], of naturalists [jantoo]. Generic name from sanscrit. Alias Pimelodus silondia; Silonia lurida. Lower jaw the longer, snout rather broad; air-vessel small, with its lateral edges protected by a short osseous process from either side; the air-vessel itself, when opened, is found to consist of two oval chambers, having a communicating canal, and in the young is almost surrounded by high osseous sides; colors bluish along the back, becoming silvery on the sides, fins stained with gray; estuaries, ascending high up larger rivers to nearly their sources; attains 6 feet or more in length, and is called a shark [soorah] by the natives; very voracious; another common species is sykesii.——*Snouted keliroo* (शिंगाळा - shingálá, Mahr.; ముక్కుజెల్ల - mukkujella, Tel.; ଅଲ୍ଲି - alli, Oor.; கொம்புக்கெளிறு - kombukkeliru, Tam.). Mahr. means horned. Tel. from (mukku, tel. snout + jella, tel. sphyræna jello). Tam. from (kombu, tam. tusk + keliru, tam. macrones genus); cf. hammer-headed shark. Macrones [keliroo] aor, siluridæ [kizhautty] physostomi, teleostei [matsyam, 35], of naturalists. Specific name from bengalee. Alias Bagrus aor, aorides, aorinus; Pimelodus aor. Freshwater; snout broad, depressed, upper jaw the longer; air-vessel large and pyriform; colors bluish-leaden superiorly, becoming white beneath; fins yellowish, stained with dark externally in both dorsal and caudal; black spot about equal to diameter of eye on soft dorsal on its posterior and inferior portion; common.——*Variegated keliroo* (नारशिंगाळा - nárashingálá, Mahr.; இரங்குக்கெளிறு - irangukkeliru, Tam.). Mahr. from (nára, san. water + shingálá, mahr. macrones genus). Tam. from (rangu, tel. color + keliru, tam. macrones genus). Plotosus canius, siluridæ [kizhautty], physostomi, teleostei [matsyam, 35], of naturalists [jantoo]. Alias Plotosus cæsius, horridus, unicolor, viviparus et multiradiatus. Brown, the vertical fins edged with black; estuaries; attains 3 feet and upwards in length; no other common species here.——*White keliroo* (शिंगटी - shingatí, Mahr.; ముదిజెల్ల - mudijella, Tel. ଗୁଣ୍ଟିଆ - guntiyá, Oor.; வெள்ளைக்கெளிறு - vellaikkeliru, Tam.). Mahr. means horned. Tel. from (mudi, tel. old + jella, tel. sphyræna jello). Tam. from (vellai, tam. white + keliru, tam. macrones genus). Macrones [keliroo] cavasius, siluridæ [kizhautty], physostomi, teleostei [matsyam, 35], of naturalists. Specific name from bengalee. Alias Bagrus cavasius; Hypselobagrus cavasius; Pimelodus cavasius, seengtee. Seengtee from mahratta. Freshwater; snout rather obtuse, upper jaw a little the longer; upper surface of head slightly roughened; leaden superiorly, yellowish along abdomen and cheeks; maxillary barbels, dorsal and caudal fins dusky; pectoral, ventral, and anal dull white; usually a black spot covering basal bone of dorsal fin; occasionally a bluish band along lateral-line; common, at least 18 inches.

KELVAN (கேள்வன் - kélvan, *Tam.*). From (kél, tam. regard); the husband. Vishnoo [q.v.].

KEMPA (ಕೆಂಪ - kempa, *Can.*). Red [chem, shem]. Common in composition. Kempoo is ruby [laul].

KENDAY (रोहितक - róhitaka, *San.*; بنی - bunní, *Ar.*; سہری - sahrí, *Hind.*; గండుచేప - ganduchépa, *Tel.*; തമ്പര - tambara, *Mal.*; கெண்டை - kendai, *Tam.*). Title from tamul. San. from (róhita, san. red). Tel. from (gandu, tel. male + chépa, tel. fish). Mal. means copper-like. Tam. from (kan, tam. eye + tai, tam. to beautify); from beautiful eyes. Title otherwise Barbel, Carp. The genus Barbus, cyprininæ, cyprinidæ, physostomi, teleostei, pisces [matsyam, 39], of naturalists [jantoo], &c. The largest genus in s. india. The species differ greatly in size, from mahseer [q.v.], 80 lb. to barbus gelius of an inch in length; the mouth opens forwards, the lips are clean, without fringes, or inner folds, or horny covering; the lateral line runs along the middle of the body and tail. The genus may be divided into three groups; having four barbels, having two barbels, without barbels. The species best known to the natives are shown below. Other S. indian species are:—amphibus, dubius, lithopidos, micropogon, pulchellus, stiquia, ticto. The term includes also the Crow carp, Large-eyed carp, and Rock carp, which are separate genera.——*Bitter carp* (शफर - shap'hara, San.; चवळ - chavala, Mahr.; کچا کڑوا - kaççákarwá, Hind. and Dec.; చేదుపరిగె - chéduparige, Tel.; ପିତ୍ତାକେରୁଣ୍ଡି - pitt'hákerundi, Oor.; പെരളി - perali, Mal.; கருங்கெண்டை - karungendai, Tam.). Title from taste. San. from (shap'ha, san. hoof). Mahr. from (chámara, san. the tail of bos grunniens used to whisk off flies); from white color. Hind. from (kaççá, hind. raw + karvá, hind. bitter); quite bitter. Tel. from (chédu, tel. bitter + parige, tel. sprat, clupea sprattus). Oor. means bitter carp. Tam. from (karumai, tam. blackness + kendai, tam. carp, barbus genus). Mahr. also (kapótachavala), meaning pigeon white. Barbus [kenday] chola, cyprininæ, cyprinidæ, physostomi, teleostei [matsyam, 39], of naturalists. Specific name from mahratta. Alias Barbus liacanthus, sophoroides, thermalis; Capoeta chola; Cyprinus chola; Puntius perlee; Systomus chola, immaculatus, sophore. Perlee from malayalam; sophore from sanscrit. Freshwater; jaws equal anteriorly; silvery, opercles shot with purple and gold; dark blotch is usually present on the side of the free portion of the tail from the twenty-third to the twenty-fifth scales of the lateral-line; dark mark along base of anterior of the dorsal rays, and a row of dark spots along its centre; from malabar and the wynaad, through madras, orissa; about 5 inches; as food bitter; in burmah oil obtained from it during breeding season.——*Carnatic carp* (گیدھی کھولی - gídhíkhaulí, Hind. and Dec.; ಗಿಡ್ಡಪಕ್ಕೆ - giddapakke, Can.; అడుసుగెండె - adusugende, Tel.; பூரிக்கெண்டை - púrikkendai, Tam.). Dec. from (gídhí, dec. dwarf + khaulí, dec. barbus ticto). Can. from (gidda, can. dwarf + pakke, can. bird). Tel. from (adusu, tel. mud + gende, tel. carp, barbus genus). Tam. from (púri, tam. gold + kendai, tam. carp, barbus genus). Tam. also (shérgendai), meaning red carp; (shél), meaning red fish. Barbus [kenday] carnaticus, cyprininæ, cyprinidæ, physostomi, teleostei [matsyam, 39], of naturalists. Alias Puntius carnaticus. Freshwater; upper jaw the longer; greenish-brown along the back, becoming dull white glossed with gold on the sides and beneath; fins grayish; eyes golden; rivers along the bases of the neilgherries, wynaad, and south canara hills; 25 lbs. in weight; some introduced into ootacamund lake.——*Crow carp* (പള്ളത്തി - pallatti, Mal.; රැල්ලියා - rallia, Singh.; காக்கைச்சேல் - kákkaiççél, Tam.). Title from leaden color of body. Mal. from (pallam, mal. low ground). Tam. from (kákkai, tam. crow + shél, tam. carp, barbus genus). Tam. also (iralliya), from singhalese. Etroplus maculatus, chromides, acanthopterygii, teleostei [matsyam, 33], of naturalists [jantoo]. Alias Chætodon maculatus; Etroplus coruchi; Glyphisodon kakaitsel. Kakaitsel from tamul. Freshwater; profile rises abruptly to dorsal; lower jaw rather longer; yellowish, with greenish back, and about seventeen horizontal lines of deep golden spots; occasionally a few along dorsal fin, back, and abdomen, also on anal; between dorsal spines and rays there are more spots, some being brown and others yellow; along the lateral-line are three black finger marks, central being largest, and darkest; ventral and anal fins stained deep black; common along the coasts in every paddy [q.v.] field, tank [q.v.], or piece of freshwater, and even occasionally found in backwaters [cauyal]; exists some distance inland; eaten by natives; exceedingly pugnacious; it readily takes a worm [keerah]; very small, not exceeding 3 inches. Another species is suratensis.——*Flying carp* (کچا کڑوا - kaççákarwá, Hind. and Dec.; പാറപ്പെരളി - parapperali, Mal.). Hind. from (kaççá, hind. raw + karvá, hind. bitter) or quite bitter. Mal. from (para, mal. flying + perali, mal. the fish barbus chola); from jumping into air. Barbus [kenday] parrah, cyprininæ, cyprinidæ, physostomi, teleostei [matsyam, 39], of naturalists. Specific name from (para, mal. flying). Alias Puntius parrah. Freshwater; back greenish, divided from a silvery abdomen by a dark-bluish line; cheeks golden red; pectoral, ventral, and anal tinged with yellow; dorsal and caudal dusky; a diffused black spot on the lateral-line extending from the twentieth to the twenty-second scales; eyes golden; malabar, mysore, and madras, at least 6 inches.——*Golden carp* (മണ്ടത്തി - mandatti, Mal.; பூங்காலா - púngálá, Tam.). Title from fins. Mal. from (mandu, mal. to run). Tam. from (pú, tam. flower + kálá, tam. sturgeon, polynemus genus); from golden fins. Barbus [kenday] chrysopoma, cyprininæ, cyprinidæ, physostomi, teleostei [matsyam, 39], of naturalists. Alias Barbus polydori; Systomus chrysopoma. Freshwater; height of head almost equals its length; profile of back elevated; dark silvery, lightest beneath, opercles shot with purple and gold; dark vertical band behind opercles and a dull spot on the lateral-line just anterior to the base of the caudal fin; upper and lower margins of the caudal grayish; the other fins golden; freshwaters along coasts.——*Gray carp* (कोलशि - kólashi, Mahr.; నిలుసు - nilusu, Tel.). Mahr. from (kólasa, mahr. charcoal). Mahr. also (kapótakólasa), meaning pigeon white + charcoal black. Barbus [kenday] kolus, cyprininæ, cyprinidæ, physostomi, teleostei [matsyam, 39], of naturalists. Specific name from mahratta. Alias Barbus guentheri; Capoeta kolus; Hypselobarbus kolus; capœta kolus from mahratta. Freshwater; body compressed, considerable rise in the profile; upper jaw the longer, overlapping the lower; silvery, with a tinge of yellow; dorsal, caudal, and anal tipped with gray; deccan, and throughout the kistna, toongabudra, and godavery rivers; upwards of a foot.——*Large-eyed carp* (గుండిగ - gundiga, Tel.; ପୁନ୍ନିକାଉଁ - punnikaun, Oor.; കണ്ണൻ - kannan, Mal.; மோதக்கெண்டை - móthakkendai, Tam.). Tel. means a broad-mouthed vessel. Mal. from (kan, mal. eye). Tam. from (móda, san. pleasure + kendai, tam. carp, barbus genus). Megalops cyprinoides, clupeidæ, physostomi, teleostei [matsyam, 40], of naturalists [jantoo]. Alias Clupea cyprinoides; Cyprinodon cundinga; Elops apalike, cundinga; Megalops cundinga, curtifilis, filamentosus, indicus, macropterus, macrophthalmus, oligolepis, setipinnis. Lower jaw prominent; caudal deeply lobed; the lobes rather more expanded in the immature than in the adult fish; summit of head dark olive, back bluish-green in the adult, lighter in the immature; abdomen silvery, with bluish reflections; the margins of the scales of a brilliant silver, as are also the lateral-line and the sides of the head; the centre of the jaws black; dorsal and caudal grayish, minutely dotted with black, and the margins blackish, as is also the last elongated dorsal ray; pectoral, ventral, and anal diaphanous, with some black dots, the last anal ray dark; eyes silvery, with the orbital margin having a dark tint; the pupils are oval pointing downwards; freshwaters and estuaries; occasionally captured in rivers, but much more commonly found in tanks. No other common species here.——*Mahseer carp* (मास्ता - mástá, Mahr.; مہاسر - mahásir, Hind.; ಹಳ್ಳಮೀನು - hallamínu, Can.; ಪೆರುವಳ್ - peruval, Too.; മെരുവാൾ - meruvál, Mal.; ලේලු - lélu, Singh.; பூமீன்கெண்டை - púmíngendai, Tam.). Title from hindostany. Hind. from (mahá, hind. large + sir, hind. head). Can. from (halla, can. watercourse + mínu, can. fish); as frequenting perennial rivers. Mal. from (meruku, tam. lustre + vál, mal. sword). Tam. from (pú, tam. flower + mín, tam. fish + kendai, tam. carp, barbus genus). Mahr. also (khádchi), meaning beard fish, from developed lips; (másalí), meaning large scaled; (tóvarí), meaning tender sprout from appearance; (pútitóvarí), meaning small tor. Hind. also (naharam). Can. also (haralemínu); (peruval). Too. also (heragulu). Singh. also (lélukúriyá), meaning mahaseer fish. Tam. also (pommín), meaning gold + fish. Called the salmon of india; a large fish of the carp species, common to all mountain streams. Barbus [kenday] tor, cyprininæ, cyprinidæ, physostomi, teleostei [matsyam, 39], of naturalists. Specific name perhaps from mahratta. Alias Barbus hamiltonii, macrocephalus, macrolepis, mosal, mussulah, progeneius, megalepis; Cyprinus tor, mosal, putitora; Labeobarbus macrolepis, progenius, tor. Mosal, mussulah, putitora from mahratta. Freshwater; snout pointed; jaws of about the same length; lips thick, with an uninterrupted fold across the lower jaw; lips are largely developed; free portion of the tail longer than high; silvery or greenish along the upper half of the body, becoming silvery shot with gold on the sides and beneath; lower fins reddish yellow. The Red mahseer is barbus thomassi. ——*Red carp* (ಕೆಮ್ಮೀನು - kemmínu, Can.; ಚಮ್ಮೀನು - chammínu, Too.; തമിൻ - tamín, Mal.). Title from fins. Can. from (kem, can. red + mínu, can. fish). Too. from (channa, too. red + mínu, too. fish). Barbus [kenday] jerdoni, cyprininæ, cyprinidæ, physostomi, teleosti [matsyam, 39], of naturalists. Freshwater; height of head nearly equals its length; body compressed; mouth narrow; upper jaw the longer; lower labial fold interrupted; silvery, fins which have an orange tint, tipped with black; rivers in canara below the ghauts [q.v.], attaining 18 inches.——

Rock carp (پتھرچاٹا - phattarchátá, Hind.; கற்கெண்டை - kargendai, Tam.). Title from being found in rocky streams. Hind. from (phattar, hind. stone + chátá, hind. licker). Tam. from (kal, tam. stone + kendai, tam. carp, barbus genus). Homaloptera brucei, cyprininæ, cyprinidæ, physostomi, teleostei [mastyam, 39], of naturalists [jantoo]. Alias Balitora brucei; Platycara australis. Snout broad and depressed; scales absent from chest and as far as the posterior margin of base of ventrals; colors dark brown with darker blotches; caudal banded; wynaud and bhawauny rivers; no other common species here.——*Sarana carp* (कद्‌लि - kadali, Mahr.; گیدھی کھولی - gídhíkhaulí, Hind. and Dec.; ಗಿಡ್ಡಪಕ್ಕೆ - giddapakke, Can.; కన్నాకు - kannáku, Tel.; ଶରଣ - sarana, Oor.; பூங்காலா - púngálá, Tam.). Title from bengalee. Hind. from (gidbí, hind. dwarf + khaulí, barbus ticto). Can. from (gidda, can. short + pakke, can. bird). Tel. from (kannu, tel. eye + áku, tel. leaf), from compressed form of body. Tam. from (pú, tam. flower + kálá, tam. sturgeon, polynemus genus). Mahr. also (pitale), meaning brass-like. Hind. also (darhí); (potah). Barbus [kenday] sarana, cyprininæ, cyprinidæ, physostomi, teleostei [matsyam, 39], of naturalists. Specific name from bengalee. Alias Barbus caudimarginatus, deliciosus, duvancelli, gardonides, immaculatus, kadoon, kakus, russellii; Cyprinus kadoon, kakoo, kunnamoo, macclellandi, sarana; Puntius sarana; Systomus chrysostomus, immaculatus. Fresh-water; profile of back elevated; silvery, darkest superiorly, opercles shot with gold; mostly some dark spots behind the opercle; fins whitish or yellowish-white, and externally stained with gray; at least a foot in length.——*Shell carp* (لمبی کھولی - lambíkhaulí, Hind. and Dec.; ಮರಪಕ್ಕೆ - marapakke, Can.; சேற்கெண்டை - shérgendai, Tam.). Title from tamul. Hind. from (lambí, hind. long + khaulí, hind. fish, barbus ticto). Can. from (mara, can. tree + pakke, can. bird). Barbus [kenday] dorsalis, cyprininæ, cyprinidæ, physostomi, teleostei [matsyam, 39], of naturalists. Alias Barbus tetraspilus, layardi; Systomus dorsalis, tristis. Freshwater; head conical anteriorly, snout pointed, upper jaw the longer; uniform silvery, frequently the scales in upper two-third of the body with dark bases; a black spot at the posterior portion of the base of the dorsal, which more or less disappears after maceration; found as far south as the cauvery and coleroon; not large.——*Spotted carp* (പാറ്റപ്പെരലി - páttapperali, Mal.). Title from dorsal spots. Mal. from (pátta, mal. moth + perali, mal. the fish, barbus chola). Barbus [kenday] punctatus, cyprininæ, cyprinidæ, physostomi, teleostei [matsyam, 39], of naturalists. Alias Puntius punctatus; Systomus conchonius. Freshwater; olive-green superiorly, becoming white on the abdomen; a diffused black spot on twentieth and twenty-first scales of lateral-line; anterior half of third or fourth scale from the opercle, in the row next below the lateral-line, black; fins yellowish, dorsal and anal tipped with orange; dorsal with two rows of black spots; malabar and coromandel coasts; does not exceed 3 inches.

KEORA (کیوڑا - keurah, *Hind.*). Same as Screw-pine.

KERAM (केर - kéra, *San.*; കേരം - kéram, *Mal.*). W. coast mode of pronouncing Cheram [q.v.]. The cocoanut [q.v.] fruit. ——*Keracalpam* (കേരകല്പം - kérakalpam, Mal.). From (above + kalpa, san. law). Sanscrit work written in Malayalam. Old institutions about the four oobhayams, viz., cocoanut [q.v.], betelnut [q.v.], jack [q.v.] tree, and pepper [q.v.] vine.——*Kerala anauchauram* (കേരളഅനാചാരം - keralaanácháram, Mal.). From (above + anáchara, san. irregular custom). Sixty-four rules constituting the irregular Braminical customs of Keralam. One tradition alleges that Shuncaracharry [shuncaran] promulgated them at Collam on 25th August 825 A.D., the first day of the first year of the Collam [q.v.] era [saca].——*Keralam* (केरल - kérala, San.; കേരളം - kéralam, Mal.). Sanscrit form for Chera, but applied specially to the coast part of that kingdom or the country between Gocurnam and Cape comorin. This coast is also called Parshoorama cshetram, or Parshooraman's country. It is also called Carma bhoomy, the land of salvation by works; the opposite coast being called in contradistinction Nyauna bhoomy, land of salvation by faith. The term Shooddhy or pure is applied to the portion lying south of Neeleshwar. The portion from the river Canyarote poya [payashwany], the original southern boundary of Canara to Travancore inclusive, is now called Malayalam, or the country below the ghauts [q.v.] and by the English generally the Malabar coast [q.v.]. There is little to be added to what is said at vol. I (13), (127); II, 100. Keralam was originally divided into sixty-four graumams [q.v.] by Parshooraman [q.v.]. These were subsequently distributed by Aryapermaul into four rajyams [q.v.] or provinces, viz., Tooloovam, Coopam, Keralam proper, and Mooshicam. Further subdivision into seventeen nauds [q.v.] also made by Aryapermaul. The nauds are :—Bettatnaud, Colatnaud, Cooroombranaud, Mooringanaud, Nedoonganaud, Parapnaud, Perimpadappnaud, Polnaud, Pooravyenaud, Ravananaud, Tirmaunicherrynaud, Tooloonaud, Valavanaud, Venaud, Venganaud, Wonanaud, Yernaud. He erected eighteen forts or Cottapadies.——*Kerala mahautmyam* (കേരളമാഹാത്മ്യം - kéralamáhátmyam, Mal.). From (above + máhátmya, san. greatness). History of Malabar. Written in indifferent Sanscrit; contains traditions current among the people regarding the ancient history of the Malabar province. See vol. II, 103.——*Keralapootran* (केरलपुत्र - kéralaputra, San.). From (above + putra, san. son). Greek κηροβόθρος. Title of the Chera ruler.——*Keraloputty* (കേരളോല്പത്തി - kéralólpatti, Mal.). From (above + utpatti, mal. origin). History of Malabar. Written in modern prose Malayalam [q.v.]. As an historical work it is of little use, but as a mine of half-forgotten native usages and customs it is valuable. Ascribed to Shuncaracharry [shuncaran]. It is the only work of the kind in the Dravidian languages. The following is a digest. Parshooraman was born in the family of Bhrigoo in Tretayoog [q.v.]. His father Jamadagny [q.v.] was murdered by the sons of Caurtaveeryan, and Parshooraman to satisfy his widowed mother defeated and slew the Cshatriyas twenty-one times. He then made a gift of the whole world to Bramins as an expiation for the sin committed. Having no place to live he obtained from Varoonan [q.v.] the strip of land from Gocurnam to Comorin. This land was afterwards called Keralam. He then introduced into his new land Bramins from various parts, but they did not remain there from fear of serpents. He then brought Bramins afresh from Aryapooram, divided the country into sixty-four graumams [q.v.] and presented them to these. Some shoodras were also introduced, and changes were made in their social customs that they might not go back to their native place. Among these changes were the introduction of poorvashikhay or front wearing of the coodoomy [q.v.] and maroomakkatoyem [q.v.]. He also built many temples, chiefly dedicated to Bhagavaty [q.v.]. He divided the people into various classes and settled what occupation each was to follow. Having ruled over the country for 50,000 years, he disappeared. Then ensued discord among the Bramins who were entrusted with the government of the country, and they agreed to have a king. Accordingly Keya permaul was brought from Keyapooram and was installed king in A.D. 216. He ruled over them for eight years. Fourth in succession from him was Keralan from Chola mundalam, who ruled for twelve years. He was one of the best of kings and the province was called after him. Then followed others, one of whom Baunapermaul became a convert to the Booddhist faith. He convened a congregation of the Bramins and said to them that they must unite with the Booddhists and follow their system. The bramins were greatly alarmed, and incensed; and on their consulting with a leading individual among them at Tricaroor, he promised to remove their difficulties. Following his advice, the Bramins went to the king, and remonstrated with him, calling for a public disputation, when if they the Bramins were vanquished, their tongues should be cut out, and the like done to the Booddhists if these should be overcome. The dispute was held; terminating favorably to the Bramins, in consequence of a magical influence emanating from the head Bramin at Tricaroor. The tongues of the Booddhists were cut out, and they were banished the country. The king who had adopted their system was dethroned, and some lands were set apart for his support. He is not the Cherma permaul who went to Mecca. His son was crowned; and an oath was taken from him, never to permit the Booddhists or people of any other religion to obtain public sanction. Other details of some subsequent matters are given. At later periods, when the above ban had fallen into desuetude, the Booddhists obtained some footing in different places. The system of Bhattacharry [samayam] obtained in the Malayalam country; and the Vedantists of that class received some endowments in lands. At an assembly of the Bramins of the sixty-four villages, it was determined that only the Bramins of eleven village districts should possess the right of offering a particular species of yaugam [q.v.] or sacrifice, and of performing some other special ceremonies. In process of time the rule of kings had become extinct and some Bramins went to Krishnaroya inviting him to take the rule of the country. He sent two persons named Audy raja permaul and Paundyaraja permaul as his viceroys, each for a period of twelve years. After them Cherma permaul was sent, who was welcomed by some distinguished persons, safely conducted, and duly installed. He ruled thirty-six years, being three times the appointed period, on account of his good qualities. The Royel however was not satisfied with this extension of the term, and determined on hostilities. Cherma permaul took counsel as to the best means of meeting the invasion. In the first place two Bramin ambassadors were sent to the Royel to endeavour to pacify him; but he refused to listen to them. A story is narrated of the manner in which the messengers acquired a magical quill, by looking through which the real nature of any being would be discerned. The Chermaun in connexion with the Calicut rajah, and other subordinates, assembled a great army, and while the multitudes were asleep, by looking at them through the quill it was perceived that 10,000 were men, 30,000 gods, and the rest asoorans. To the 10,000 a distinctive mark was affixed; and with them the Royel was encountered and defeated. The birth of Shuncaracharry is then narrated, with his proceedings as to the different castes of people, and the regulations established by him, accounted for in rather a fanciful manner; but it is stated that his regulations continued to be observed. Cherma permaul continued to rule. A Nayar was killed, who, after death, is represented as instructing the king to attend to the lessons of a Jonaca [q.v.] teacher, according to whose advice he might embark on board ship, and would thereby attain a partial beatification. This is the Cherma permaul who adopted the Mahomedan religion, and went to Mecca. He divided his whole dominions into eighteen portions, which he gave over to the charge of different chiefs. The two ambassadors by whose means the Royel had been conquered, each received portions of country. He specially gave a shield to the Calicut rajah. Cherma permaul then went away by sea to the country termed Asoo supposed to designate Arabia. The Calicut rajah afterwards waged war with the various petty chieftains, conquering some of them and acquiring superiority. The arrival of the Portuguese at Calicut is noticed, and the Calicut rajah is said to have fought with the captain. The rajah ruled over eighteen forts and seventeen districts. He fought continually with his neighbours, the Travancore and Tellicherry rajahs being excepted; he subdued many countries. He acquired pre-eminence above other kings. The customs of the Calicut kingdom are then narrated with laws regulating interest and profit. The commencement of the Collam era is thus accounted for. The rule of the viceroys of Vijianugger had been fixed at twelve years, corresponding with the revolution [bhaganam] in orbit [cacsham] of the planet [graham] Jupiter [brihaspaty]. But as Cherma permaul exceeded the prescribed time, this mode of reckoning fell into disuse. In a period of great scarcity and drought, when a large reservoir of Collam had become quite dry, the Bramins in a body went to the Calicut rajah, and represented that the cause was his withholding the customary largesses to the gods and the Bramins; the rajah acknowledged his fault and promised to repair it. As a commencement a great number of Bramins were fed in the dry bed of the tank, and before they had finished eating, the water rushed in with such rapidity, that they were obliged to make their escape without having time to take away the leaves on which their food had been eaten. An era was begun to commemorate this event, being the Collam era. Matters relating to the cultivation of cocoanut [q.v.] trees, betel-vines, &c., customs in dealings, buying, selling, &c., rules to regulate hunting. Origin of the Nayars; also of a kind of divinity derived from the fable in the Mahabhaurat [q.v.] of Shiva's appearing to Arjoonan [q.v.] during his penance near Himalaya mountains. The origin of the Ayenaur [ayen] born from Shiva [q.v.] and Mohiny [q.v.]. The names of various local numina in the Malayalam country are given. Names of various fanes in that country. Besides which the thirty-three crores of inferior gods [deva], and the sixty-six thousand asoorans [q.v.], are all said to have been in Malayalam; together with the superior gods, protecting the country. Afterwards the names of the Calicut rajahs and other inferior chiefs are given. The story of a Jonaca who came to this country; the cause of which is narrated, the foreigner extended the dominion of the Calicut rajah. Magnificent things are stated as to the conquests of the Calicut rajah, originating in his devotedness to Shree bhagavaty, and her gifts to him. Notwithstanding the foreign Europeans came and took possession of Calicut; whom however in the end the rajah defeated. The Coorumbar of the hilly district greatly helped and had districts given in consequence. Disputes between this Cooruniba chief and the Cochin rajah. Details of the number of Nayars belonging to different parts of the country. Reference to the regulations made by Parshooraman, and confirmed by Shuncaracharry, as to the distance which must be observed by different castes in their approach one towards another, the distance in feet being minutely stated. Bramins and cows are of good birth; other classes of men and other animals not so. With these regulations as to personal distinctions, and caste observances, the account concludes [charitram]. See vol. I (127); II, 103.——*Kelappan* (കേളപ്പൻ - kélappan, Mal.). From (kéralan, mal. native of malabar + appan, mal. father). Hindoo 2nd or pers. name [peyar].——*Keya* (കേയ - kéya, Mal.). Keralam.——*Keya permaul* (കേയപ്പെരുമാൾ - kéyapperumál, Mal.). From (above + perumál, mal. chief). Same as Cherma permaul.——*Keyapooram* (കേയപുരം - kéyapuram, Mal.). Ancient name for Coimbatore.

KEREY (ಕೆರೆ - kere, *Can.*). Tank [cheroo, chira].

KERKAL (श्वव्याघ्र - shvavyághra, *San.*; بوربچّہ - borbaçça, *Hind.*; ಕೇರಕಾಲ - kérakála, *Can.*; కరింగోల - karingóla, *Tel.*; പട്ടിപ്പുലി - pattippuli, *Mal.*; சிறுசிவிங்கி - shirusivingi, *Tam.*). Title from canarese; distinguish from caracal, the lynx. San. from (shvá, san. dog + vyághra, san. tiger). Mal. from (patti, mal. bitch + puli, mal. tiger). Tam. from (shiru, tam. small + shivingi, tam. pard). Can. also (chiratéhuli), meaning small tiger. Title otherwise Leopard; small variety of Panther [honiga].

KERY (ಕೇರಿ - kéri, *Can.*). Hamlet [cherry, kotah].

KESHAM (केश - késha, *San.*). From (ka, san. head + shí, san. to rest); produced from the head. Hair of head in particular. Hair of body is romam, otherwise lomam [q.v.]; braided hair is vainy [q.v.]; clotted or matted hair is jatay [q.v.]; hair on the neck or mane is kesharam. For wool of animals see Pushm.——*Kesary* (केसरी - késarí, San.; కేసరి - késari, Tel.). From (késara, san. hair); lion, the maned animal.—"*a*" Title of the rulers of Orissa [q.v.] previous to the Gungavamsha line [charitram].—"*b*" also means crocus sativus, linn., saffron [q.v.]. Also a yellow four-month paddy in Godavery, Kistna, Nellore, Anantapore, &c. Pedda kesary is a large variety, Potty kesary a short [paddy].——*Keshavan* (केशव - késhava San.). From (késha, san. hair); long-haired. Vishnoo. Hindoo 2nd or pers name. [peyar]. Common among Madhwas.——*Keshavanna* (ಕೇಶವಣ್ಣ - késhavanna, Can.). From (késhava, san. vishnoo + anna, can. brother, suffix of respect). The name of a learned Jeina [q.v.] said to have built Barcore, &c., in Canara.——*Keshinee* (केशिनी - késhiní, San.; सांखवेल - sánkhavéla, Mahr.; چورکانٹا - chorkántá, Hind.; కట్లెచెట్టు - katlechettu, Tel.; കുതിരപ്പുല്ല - kutirappullu, Mal.; යක්බෙරිය - yakbériya, Singh.). San. from (késha, san. hair); from tuft of hair on the flower; also from supposition that it promotes growth of hair. Mahr. from (shankha, san. conch + véla, mahr. creeper). Hind. from (chor, hind. thief + kántá, hind. thorn). Tel. from (katte, tel. stalk + chettu, tel. plant). Mal. from (kutira, mal. horse + pullu, mal. grass). Singh. from (yak, singh. devil + bériya, singh. lumnitzera racemosa, willd.). San. also (chórapushpí), meaning thief + flowering; (shankhiní), meaning having conch-like flower. Tel. also (katlegaddi), meaning stalk + grass; (shankhapushpi), meaning conch + flower. Title otherwise Conch flower, Horse grass, Thief-flower. Botanically Andropogon [beard grass] aciculatus, retz., graminaceæ [vricsham, 156]. Alias Chrysopogon acicularis. Culms erect, rooting at the base, simple or branched, 1–2 feet; nodes, sheaths and leaves smooth, the last somewhat radical and abbreviated, lanceolate, margins rough and prickly; panicle terminal, linear-oblong, branches sub-verticelled, simple, hirsute towards the apex; glumes of the hermaphrodite floret almost equal, upper two-cleft with the awn about twice the length of the floret. Small, coarse spear grass [q.v.], not liked by cattle.

KETAKY (केतकी - kétakí, *San.*). From (kéta, san. desire); from flower in request. Same as Screw-pine.

KETT (കെട്ട് - kettu, *Mal.*). Tie [cutt].——*Kettoovallam* (കെട്ടുവള്ളം - kettuvallam, Mal.). From (above + vallam, mal. boat). Distinguish from Kaidvellam. Sewed boats. Baggage boats which ply on Malabar inland navigable waters. They are built of planks sewn together with coir [q.v.] cordage through holes drilled in the edges; the seams also being caulked to make them water-tight with coir fibre and yarn, round and over which the stitching goes. The general outline is the same as that of a canoe, but they can be made of much larger size.

KETTAY (கேட்டை - kéttai, *Tam.*). From (jyésht'há, san. elder). Moodevy [q.v.]; the goddess of ruin [kaly, calathy]. The elder sister of Lutchmy [q.v.], the goddess of prosperity. Also the eighteenth lunar mansion [nacshatram] in astronomy [jyotisham]. Cf. Jyeshtay.

KHADEEJAH (خديجه - khadíjah, *Ar.*). From (khadajah, ar. deformed). Name of Prophet's wife. Common female alam; as Khadeejah bee, alam + alaumat [ism].

KHAJOOR (كهجور - khajúr, *Hind.*). Means cleansing. Same as Arabian date.

KHALEEL (خليل - khalíl, *Hind.*). From (khalla, ar. to penetrate). A true friend. Part of lacab; as Khaleeloollah, friend of god, title of Abraham. Now an ordinary alam [ism].

KHALSA (خالصه khálisah, *Hind.*). From (khális, ar. pure). Revenue department under Mahomedans. Khalsa lands are those in Government amauny [q.v.]. Cf. Havelly.——*Khoolausa* (خلاصه - khulásah, Hind.). From (khalasa, ar. deliverance). Release.——*Khoolausat* (خلاصة - khúlasat, Ar.). From (khalasa, ar. to purify). Essence. Part of lacab; as Khoolausat ool moolk, the essence of the state [ism].

KHAN (خان - khán, *Pers.*). Lord. Title of Tartar kings. Now a Pataun [q.v.] title and title of honor; as Mahomed khan, alam + pataun alaumat; Bahaudur beg khan, alam + title of honor [ism].——*Khanam* (خانم - khánam, Hind.). Any lady of rank. An ordinary Mahomedan suffix for a Pataun lady, as Khadeejah khanam. Khanam, Khautoo, Bee, Begum, Beeby, Nissa are honorific suffix appellations for Mahomedan women. Among Moghuls [q.v.] the title is commonly added to the names of all women; as Hameeda khanam, alam + female alaumat [ism].——*Khandauny* (خاندانی - khándání, Hind.). From persian meaning a family. A title borne by Mahomedan nobles, especially when of Persian or Pataun [q.v.] descent. Applied especially to members of the Carnatic [q.v.] family [anwarooddeen].——*Khan sahib's canal* (கான்சாயப்புவாய்க்கால் - kánsáyappuváykkál, Tam.). From (khánsáhib, hind. name of the constructor of the canal + váykkál, tam. canal). Channel; South arcot district, Chidambaram talook. Flows into Vellaur at its mouth. Connects the Coleroon and the Vadavaur channel with the Vellaur at Porto novo viâ Chidambaram. Length about 25 miles. Irrigates about 7,000 acres. To facilitate the carriage of the iron [auhan] ores, which were brought by water from Salem to Porto Novo, the old canal was made navigable in 1804 by the construction of three locks, one where the canal debouches into the Vellaur, nearly opposite the town of Porto novo; the second where it leaves the Veeraunam tank; and the third a little lower down. Deepened and rendered navigable for small boats in 1854.

KHANA (خانه - khánah, *Pers.*). House. Suffix denoting place [gah], as Lungerkhana, alms + house.——*Khana shoomaury* (خانه‌شماری - khánahshumárí, Hind.). From (above + shumárí, pers. calculation). Census.——*Khankah* (خانقاه - khánkáh, Hind.). Arabic form of (khánah, pers. house + gáh, pers. place). A monastery; a rest-house.——*Khan saumah* (خانسامان - khánsámán, Hind.). From (above + sámán, pers. effects). A house steward or butler [compradore].——*Tauh khana* (ته خانه - tahkhánah, Hind.). From (tah, pers. floor + khánah, pers. room). A cellar in Mahomedan houses used during midday.

KHANAH (کهانا - khánah, *Hind.*). From (khád, san. to eat). A meal. Mussalmans use three meals a day:—Naushta [q.v.] or Hazree [q.v.] or breakfast, at 9 or 10 A.M.; Khanah or dinner, which they partake of at 3 or 4 P.M., the lower orders generally at 1 P.M.; Rautkah khanah or supper, at 7 or 8 P.M.

KHANCHAH (کهانچا - kháncha, *Hind.*). A marsh.

KHAND (ఖండి - khandi, *Tel.*). Means mountaineer. Another form of Khond [q.v.].

KHAND (खण्ड - khand, *San.*). To cut.——*Khadgam* (खड्ग - khadga, San.). From (khand, san. to cut). A sword. Khadga mrigam is rhinoceros; also tusker or male elephant [elephant, gendah]. Khadga mriga ractam is Dragon's blood [q.v.]——*Khandak* (خندق - khandak, Hind.). Ditch of a fort [kila].——*Khandam* (खण्ड - khanda, San.). From (khand, san. to cut). Section.——*Khandriga* (ఖండ్రిగ - khandriga, Tel.). Means a small hamlet. A large block of land granted as inam, less than a village but much larger than an ordinary inam [q.v.]. See vol. I, 112.——*Khind* (खिंड - khinda, Mahr.). Mountain pass [cundy, ghaut].

KHAR (खर - khara, *San.*; خر - khar, *Pers.*). Means hard, sharp. Also means a thorn. Also an ass.——*Kharam* (खर - khara, San.). Sharp, rough, pungent, hot, hard. Plant first term. Ex.:—Achyranthes aspera (kharamñjari), meaning sharp + flower cluster; Acorus calamus (kharasára), meaning pungent + juice; Celosia cristata (kharáshvá), meaning heat + accumulating; Ficus clenia (kharapatra), meaning rough + leaf; Sanseviera roxburghiana (kharabusa), meaning hard + thread. See gloss. paragraphs.——*Kharboja* (خربوزه - kharbuzah, Hind.). Means large + sweet fruit. Same as Common melon.——*Khargosh* (خرگوش - khargosh, Hind.). Means donkey + ear. Same as Mosal.——*Kharmoosh* (خرموش - kharmúsh, Hind.). Means ass + mouse. Same as Bandicoot.——*Kharpoosht* (शल्यकण्ठ - shalyakant'ha, San.; सलेंद्र - saléndra, Mahr.; دلج - dula, Ar.; خارپشت - khárpusht, Pers.; سیہی - síhí, Hind.; لندک - landak, Malay; ಎದು - édu, Can.; ಮುಳ್ಳುಪಂಜಿ - mullupanji, Too.; ఏదుపంది - édupandi, Tel.; ଝିଙ୍କୋ - jhinko, Oor.; മുള്ളൻപന്നി - mullanpanni, Mal.; හිතාව - hitava, Singh.; முள்ளம்பன்றி - mullambanri, Tam.). Title from persian. San. from (shalya, san. thorn + kant'ha, san. throat). Mahr. from (shalya, san. thorn + undura, san. rat). Pers. from (khár, pers. thorn + pusht, pers. back). Hind. from (shallakí, san. porcupine). Tel. from (édu, tel. quill + pandi, tel. pig). Tam. from (mullu, tam. bristle + panri, tam. hog). Pers. also (rúbáhiturkí), meaning turkish fox. Hind. also (siyál). Can. also (mulluhandi), meaning thorn + hog. Title otherwise Porcupine. Hystrix leucura, hystricinæ, hystricidæ, rodentia, mammalia [sastanam, 18], of naturalists [jantoo]. Alias Crista indica; Hystrix hirsutirostris, zeylanensis. Procupines are rodents which take their name, signifying spiny-pig [soor], from their large size and grunting voice. The peculiar open tubes of the tail are supported on slender stalks, and they make a rattling noise when shaken. The genus given above is the Indian porcupine. Muzzle clad with short stiff bristly hairs, and a few white spines on the face; spines on the throat short, grooved, some with white points forming a demi-collar; crest full, long, chiefly of black bristles, a few of them only with long white points; the larger quills on the back black; many annulated with white at base and middle, and some with white points; the long thin quills mostly white at tip; the quills on the loins mostly all white, the pedunculated quills of the tail yellowish-white; some of the quills of the sides and lumbar regions flat and striated; whiskers long black, a few tipped white. It forms extensive burrows, often in societies, in the sides of hills, banks of rivers and nullahs [q.v.], and very often in the bunds of tanks, and in old mud walls, &c. Very destructive to crops, potatoes [q.v.], carrots [gaujar], and other vegetables. It never issues forth till after dark. Dogs [nye] take up the scent of the porcupine. It charges backwards at enemies erecting spines at the same time. The porcupine can be eaten. The intestines are used in medicine for dropsy or coughs. Indian allied species not here found are:—Atherura fasciculata or brush-tailed porcupine, Hystrix bengalensis or bengal porcupine, Hystrix longicauda or crestless porcupine, Hystrix yunnanensis. For hedge-hog see Moollely.——*Khaudee* (کہادی - khádí, Hind.). Coarse cloth.

KHAR (کہار - khár, *Hind.*). From (kshára, san. from kshar, san. to flow). Any alkali [cauram].——*Khary matty* (क्षारीलवण - kshárílavana, San.; کہاری‌نون - khárínún, Hind.; کہاری مٹی - khárímattí, Dec.). From (kshára, san. saline earth + lavana, san. salt). Impure sulphate of soda. Glauber's salt. Cf. Sujjee matty.——*Paparkhar* (پپڑ کہار - papparkhár, Dec.). Dec. from (pappar, hind. thin crisp cake + khár, hind. alkali). Same as Appalacauram.

KHAREEF (خریف - kharíf, *Hind.*). From (kharf, ar. to pluck fruit). Autumnal harvest.

KHAREETA (خریطہ - kharítah, *Hind.*). From (kharata, ar. to render fast). A bag; the ornamental bag used as an envelope for a letter from or to a person of high rank; thence the letter itself.

KHARJOORAM (खर्जूर - kharjúra, *San.*). From (kharj, san. to cleanse); from supposition that it is useful in purifying blood and bile. Date palms. Botanically the Phœnix genus, palmaceæ [vricsham, 149]. Leaves pinnate; some species have scarcely any trunk, while in others the trunk is thickly covered with the scars of fallen leaves; fruit fleshy and one-seeded. The species best known to the natives are shown below. Under term date come also some species of cycas, tamarindus and zizyphus genera.——*Arabian date* (पिण्डखर्जूर - pindakharjúra, San.; खजूर - khajúra, Mahr.; نخل - nakhal, Ar.; درخت خرما - darakhti-khurmá, Pers.; سندولے کا پیڑ - sandolekáper, Hind.; سندولے کا جہاڑ - sandolekájhár, Dec.; خرما - khurma, Malay; ಖರ್ಜೂರ - kharjúra, Can.; ಗಜ್ಜಿರ - gajjira, Too.; ఖర్జూరము - kharjúramu, Tel.; ଖଜୁରି - khójiri, Oor.; ഈന്ത - ítta, Mal.; ඉඳි - indi, Singh.; ஈச்சமரம் - íççamaram, Tam.). San. from (pinda, san. ball, a morsel + kharjúra, san. phœnix), meaning edible variety. Mahr. from sanscrit. Pers. from (darakht, ar. tree + khurma, ar. date). Hind. from (sandolá, hind. date + per, hind. tree). Dec. from hindostany. Malay from arabic. Tel. and oor. from sanscrit. Tam. from (ínju, tam. date + maram, tam. tree). Ar. also (tamar); origin of tamarind [q.v.]. Hind. also (chuhárá); (khajúr), meaning raw date. Dec. also (pendkhajúr), meaning raw date. Tel. also (íta); (muddakarjúramu), meaning mass + date tree; (péríta), meaning large + phœnix sylvestris, rox. Mal. also (téníçça), meaning honey + the tree. Tam. also (ínju), meaning beneficent tree; (périnju), meaning large date tree. Wherever the palm is mentioned in the bible, the date palm is meant; the greeks called the tree φοίνιξ from phœnicia, distinguishing the female as ἡ φοίνιξ βαλανηφόρος and the male as ὁ φοίνιξ ἔρσην; the male flowers they called ἐλάτη and σπάθη, and the fruit φοινικοβάλανος; hebrew tamar. Title otherwise Common date, Edible date, Large date, True date. Botanically Phœnix [kharjooram] dactylifera, linn., palmaceæ [vricsham, 149]. Diœcious tree; tall; usually unbranched stems, pinnate or fan-shaped leaves, flowers growing on a single or branched spadix, covered by a spathe, fruit being a nut, drupe, or berry, and seeds containing cartilaginous or hard albumen, with a small embryo in a cavity remote from the hilum; the stem exhibits endogenous growth, hardest part being outside. The trees that grow here are very inferior to those brought from persia and arabia; the fruit consists more of seed than of pulp, and altogether is only about one-fourth the size of the arabian kind. Fruits imported dried; these are cylindrical, drupe twelve to eighteen lines long, covered with a thin, smooth, deep brown pellicle, enclosing a rich pulp and bony nut; the pulp is nearly inodorous, the taste sweet, mucilaginous and agreeable. A persian poem celebrates the arabian date and its 360 uses. Fruits used medicinally as demulcents and expectorants; continued use produces soreness of gums. Edible uses of fruit well known.——*Barren date* (ಗೊಡ್ಡುಈಚಲು - godduíchalu, Can.). From giving neither fruit nor toddy. Same as Indian sago palm.——*Chinese date* (چین کا سندولا - chínkásandolá, Hind.). Same as Bair.——*Indian date* (خرماہ ہندی - khurmahihindí, Hind.). Same as Tamarind.——*Marsh date* (हिन्ताल - hintála, San.; గిరుకతాటి - girukatáti, Tel.). San. from (hi, san. to grow + tála, san. palm). Tel. from (giraka, tel. short + táti, tel. palmyra tree, borassus flabelliformis, linn.). Title otherwise Dwarf palmyra, Hintaul. Botanically Phœnix [kharjooram] paludosa, roxb., palmaceæ [vricsham, 149]. Stem straight, 6–16 feet, sub-arboreous; pinnæ solitary, ensiform, flaccid, bifarious; embryo in the base of the seed; flowering in the hot season; fruit sessile, on thick knobs pointing downwards, first yellow then red, lastly black purple, oval. The leaves serve for thatch; gives no toddy [q.v.]. The trunks of the smaller trees serve for walking-sticks, and the natives have an idea that snakes get out of the way of any person having such a staff; the larger trees serve for rafters to houses [taur].——*Small date* (सानुइच्लारूकु - sánuichlárúku, Conc.; سندولے کا جہاڑ - sandolekájhár, Dec.; ಸಣ್ಣಈಚಲು - sannaíchalu, Can.; చిట్టీత - chittíta, Tel.; ഈന്ത - ínta, Mal.; சிறுயீஞ்சு - shiruyínju, Tam.). Conc. like canarese. Dec. from (sandolá, hind. wild date + jhár, hind. tree). Can. from (sanna, can. small + íchalu, can. wild date, phœnix sylvestris, roxb.). Tel. from (chiru, tel. small + íta, tel. phœnix sylvestris, roxb.). Tam. from (shiru, tam. small + ínju, tam. phœnix sylvestris, roxb.). Can. also (íchal). Mal. also (chittíntal), meaning small + phœnix dactylifera, linn. Tam. also (ínju), meaning beneficent tree; (índu), meaning beneficent tree. Title otherwise Eenjoo, Eetcha maram. Botanically Phœnix [kharjooram] farinifera, roxb., palmaceæ [vricsham, 149]. Alias Phœnix pusilla, pygamæa. Shrub, 2–3 feet; leaves pinnate; leaflets long, narrow, pointed; spathe axillary, one-valved; spadix erect, much ramified; branches simple, spreading; male flowers, calyx three-toothed; petals three; stamens six; female flowers, petals three; berry black, shining; flowers in january and february, fruit ripens in may. A dwarf species; small almost stemless palm of sandy lands. Stem gives a sago [q.v.]; in order to separate it from the numerous white fibres in which it is enclosed, the stem is split into six or eight pieces, dried, beaten in mortars, and then sifted; this is then boiled to a thick gruel; it is not so nutritive as common sago, and it has a bitter taste. Fruit has a small quantity of pulp, sweet and mealy, eaten by natives. The leaf stalks are used for making baskets [tokrah] and for other purposes; the plant also contains a fibre; gives no toddy [taur]. ——*Stemless date* (جنگلی کھجور - janglíkhajúr, Hind.; پنڈ کھجور - pendkhajúr, Dec.; பேரீஞ்சு - pérínju, Tam.). Hind. from (janglí, hind. wild + khajúr, hind. date). Dec. from (pinda, san. morsel + kharjúra, san. phœnix); edible variety. Tam. from (pér, tam. large + íñju, tam. phœnix). Title otherwise Wild date. Botanically Phœnix [kharjooram] acaulis, roxb., palmaceæ [vricsham, 149]. Fronds radical pinnate, pinnæ plicate, ensiform, arranged in sub-opposite fascicles, lower ones thorny; flowering in november and december; is not absolutely stemless; fruit small, eaten by natives; gives no toddy [taur].——*Wild date* (खर्जूर - kharjúra, San.; खजूर - khajúra, Mahr.; سندولے کا پیڑ - sandolekáper, Hind.; سندولے کا جہاڑ - sandolekájhár, Dec.; ಈಚಲು - íchalu, Can.; ಈಚಲು - íchilu, Too.; ఈత - íta, Tel.; കാട്ടീന്ത - káttínta, Mal.; காட்டீஞ்சு - káttíñju, Tam.). San. from (kharj, san. to cleanse), supposed to purify blood and bile. Mahr. from sanscrit. Hind. from (sandolá, hind. wild date + per, hind. tree). Dec. from hindostany. Mal. from (kátu, mal. wild + ínta, mal. date tree, phœnix dactylifera, linn.). Tam. from (kádu, tam. wild + íñju, tam. date). San. also (kharjúrí), meaning cleaning; (róshana), meaning angry; (kapilá), meaning tawny-colored [kamela]; (parushaka), meaning rough. Mahr. also (shindí). Hind. also (khajúr), meaning date; (sendíkájhár), meaning toddy tree. Can. also (kalluíchalu), meaning stone + the tree. Tel. also (peddaíta), meaning large + the tree. Mal. also (ínta). Tam. also (íççambanai), meaning date + palmyra tree, borassus flabelliformis, linn.; (madal); (karavam). Title otherwise Cautt eenj, Indian wine palm, Khajoor, Saudolah, Shendhy. Botanically Phœnix [kharjooram] sylvestris, roxb., palmaceæ [vricsham, 149]. Alias Elate sylvestris. Height 30–40 feet; fronds 10–15 feet long; petioles compressed towards the apex with a few short spines at the base; pinnæ numerous, densely fascicled, ensiform, rigid; male spadix 2–3 feet long; spathe of the same length, separating into two valves; spikes numerous towards the apex of the peduncle, 4–6 inches long, slender, very flexuose; calyx cup-shaped, three-toothed; petals longer than the calyx, ridged and furrowed on the inside; female spikes 1½ feet long, not bearing flowers throughout, the lower 4–6 inches; flowers distant; petals three, very broad; style recurved; fruit scattered on long pendulous spikes, roundish; wild and cultivated; appears in all soils and situations; flowers at beginning of hot season. When not stunted in its growth by the extraction of its sap or toddy, it is a very handsome tree, with a dense crown of leaves spreading in a hemispherical form on its summit; the leaves are composed of numerous leaflets or pinules about 18 inches long; the fruit is only about one-fourth the size of the arabian variety; when ripe, small, oval-shaped; dark-colored; the palm has the general characteristics of the family, but is inferior to the palmyra [q.v.], cocoanut [q.v.], &c.; a tree is fit for being cut for toddy [q.v.] when ten years old and lasts for this purpose about twenty years more. Natives chew the fruit in the same manner as they do the areca-nut [q.v.] with the betel-leaf [q.v.] and choonam [q.v.]. The juice is extracted as follows:—the lower leaves and their sheaths are removed, a notch is cut into the pith of the tree close to the remaining leaf sheaths, and a thin channelled slip of wood or piece of the date or palmyra leaf is inserted into the notch; the juice issues from the notch, is conducted by the channel and falls into an earthen pot which is tied on to receive it; in the cold season from the end of october to february, the trees are thus tapped in the evening, and the juice is taken before sunrise. It is used in its unfermented fresh state, or in its fermented state. In its fresh state it is used in two ways. In a small proportion it is sold in the early mornings as khajoorras, it is then the sweet juice and is drunk by the natives as such. In a larger proportion, also in the early morning, the sweet juice is collected, generally under some shady tree, in large, open earthen vessels and boiled over wood fire until the juice becomes thick; it is then taken off the fire, and dried by exposure; the substance obtained is jaggery [q.v.] or goor [q.v.], or raw date sugar [q.v.]; the quantity of raw sugar thus made every year is large. A certain quantity of the juice, instead of being used in the two ways above described, is exposed to the sun's influence and soon ferments, and is then known as toddy; toddy is used as an intoxicating drink, and as yeast in making bread. Fibrous leaflets and fibre from petiole made into mats [boriyah], ropes, and baskets [tokrah]; gives gum, little known. Wood light brown, the outer portion hard and durable; sometimes used for building, water conduits, and temporary bridges. There is a Tamul proverb:—ஈச்சங்கள்ளு எதிலும் குளிர்ச்சி—"Date-"palm toddy is the coolest of all beverages [taur]."

KHARNOOB (خرنوب - kharnúb, *Ar.*). Same as Carob.

KHARWAH (کھاروا - khárwá, *Hind.*). From (kahár, hind. member of the boy caste); generally used by them. Coarse red cotton cloth, used to wrap up books, parcels, &c.

KHAS (خاص - khás, *Hind.*). Own, private [khood]. Honorifically for the possessive of the second person.——*Khausa* (خاصہ - khásah, Hind.; ఖాసా - khásá, Tel.). From (khás, ar. own). A slave; hereditary bondsman in the families of Teloogoo rajahs.——*Khawaus* (خواص - khawás, Hind.). Plural of (khás). Attendants.

KHASKAS (خشخش - khashkhash, *Dec.*). Seeds of Papaver somniferum [aphainam]. Oil expressed is demulcent and used in cookery.

KHAT (خط - khatt, *Hind.*). From (khatta, ar. to make a mark). An entry in a book; also a letter, especially as used in zemindarry correspondence; also a figure drawn by exorcists. ——*Khautadar* (کھاتادار - khátadár, Hind.). A mercantile correspondent.

KHATEEB (خطیب - khatíb, *Hind.*). From (khataba, ar. to read) [khitaub, khootba]. The reader of khootba in a musjid [inam, musjid], who delivers the same standing on the second step of the mimbar [q.v.] with wooden staff in his right hand.

KHATIAN (ختیان کا گوند - khatiyánkágond, *Hind.*). Gum of Silk-cotton tree.

KHATPAT (کھٹ پٹ - khatpat, *Hind.*). Literally wrangling. Intrigue and corruption.

KHATWAM (खट्वा - khatvá, *San.*). From (khatt, san. to screen). Bedstead.——*Khatwaungam* (खट्वाङ्ग - khatvánga, San.). From (khatvá, san. bedstead + anga, san. limb). A club, shaped like the foot of a bedstead, with a skull at the top; the weapon of Shiva [q.v.] and carried by ascetics.

KHATZUM (کالی زیری - kálízírí, *Dec.*). Means black cummin. Same as Wild jeerah.

KHAUDIM (خادم - khádim, *Hind.*). From (khadama, ar. to serve). A servant, slave, specially person in charge of tombs [goombaz] mosques [musjid], &c. Prefixed to an alam makes a lacab; as Khaudim hoossain, slave of hoossain; mostly Shiah [q.v.] names [ism].

KHAUK (خاک - khák, *Hind.*). From persian. Earth [munn]; clay. Khauk i cheeny, from (chín, pers. china) is Kaolin [q.v.]. Khauk i kirmiz, from (kirmiz, pers. red) is Potter's clay [calimunn]. Khauk i shifah, from (shifá, pers. cure) is earth of the plain of carbalah in arabia, made into rosaries and venerated especially by shiahs [q.v.]. Khauk i zighaul, from (zighál, pers. live-coal) is coal-dust.——*Khauky* (خاکی - khákí, Hind.). A light drab or chocolate colored cloth. Produced by boiling myrobalans [q.v.], gall-nuts [mauchicoy], and sulphate of iron [annabhaidy] together; in many parts of the country, a natural earth is used. Also one of the Veishnava sects of modern origin; they smear the body with ashes, whence the name; they add the worship of Hanooman [q.v.] to that of Vishnoo [q.v.].

KHAUKSEE (خاکشی - khákshí, *Hind.*). Retty seed [indian liquorice].

KHAULY (خالی - khálí, *Hind.*). Vacant.——*Khauly zameen* (خالی زمین - khálízamín, Hind.). From (above + zamín, pers. land). Lands remaining uncultivated.

KHAUM (خام - khám, *Hind.*). Raw, unsettled as an account, gross revenue as distinguished from nett revenue of a village. The settlement made with ryots directly without intervention of at hird party [ryot, ryotwarry, zemindar]. Khaum lekka is a rough account. Khaum vasool are gross collections.

KHAURIJ (خارج - khárij, *Hind.*). From (kharaja, ar. to extract). Dues excluded from the gross crop.——*Khaurjee* (خارجی - khárjí, Ar.). Separatists. A sect of Mahomedans who hold that any man may be promoted to the dignity of caliph [q.v.] even though he be not of the Koresh [q.v.] tribe [soonnee]. They do not reckon Ally [q.v.] among the legal successors of the prophet [mahomed] and consider him as the assassinator of his predecessor Osman [q.v.]; they are therefore opponents of Shiahs [q.v.]. They are strict predestinarians [tafweez]. Their own chiefs according to them are the lawful imaums [q.v.] after Omar.

KHAUTOO (خاتو - khátu, *Hind.*). Female pataun suffix [khanum]; as Fatimah khautoo, alam + alaumat [ism].

KHAUVIND (خاوند - khávand, *Hind.*). From (khudáwand, ar.). Meaning god-like or master.

KHEDDAH (کھیدا - khedá, *Hind.*). From (khedná, hind. to chase). Enclosure to entrap wild elephants [q.v.]. It is made in thick jungle near an elephant cover; it is about a hundred yards in diameter; surrounded by a ditch except at one point, where a chain-and-log gate is suspended between two t rees two guiding trenches converge from the cover to this entrance.

KHEIR (خیر - khair, *Ar.*). From (khára, ar. to be favorable). Excellent. Part of lacab; as Kheir ood deen, excellent in religion [ism].——*Kheirauty* (خیراتی - khairátí, Hind.). Charity [inam].——*Kheir khah* (خیرخواہ - khairkhwáh, Hind.). From (above + khwáh, pers. wisher). A well-wisher, a common signature to an anonymous petition [arzee]. Cf. Aucausha ramayya.——*Kheiroo* (خیرو - khairú, Hind.). Charitable. In composition make a lacab; as Kheiroo bee, charitable lady [ism].

KHEIR (کہیر - khair, *Hind.*). From (khadira, san. acacia). Acacia [cantalam]. Plant second term. Ex.:—Acacia ferruginea (pándhrákhair), white acacia; Acacia sundra (lálkhair), red acacia. See gloss. paragraphs.

KHES (کہیس - khes, *Hind.*). Cotton diaper used by natives as a dress; in demand by Europeans for table-linen purposes.

KHET (کہیت - khet, *Hind.*). From (kshétra, san. field) [cshetram]. Field.——*Khetry* (ఖత్రి - khetri, Tel.). Corruption of cshatriya. Title in zemindarry [q.v.] families in Vizagapatam.

KHETACAM (खेटक - khétaka, *San.*). From (khé, san. to consume). Club of Doorga [q.v.].

KHIDMAT (خدمت - khidmat, *Hind.*). Service. Khidmatgar is a personal servant.

KHILAT (خلعت - khilat, *Hind.*). From (khala, ar. robe of honor). A dress of honor presented by superior authority as a mark of distinction. A complete khilat may include arms [sillah], or a horse [ghorah], or an elephant [q.v.].

KHIRAD (خرد - khirad, *Hind.*). Understanding.——*Khirad afroz* (خرد افروز - khiradafroz, Hind.). From (above + afroz, pers. kindle). Oordoo [q.v.] version of Punchatantram [q.v.] by Hafeez ood deen ahmed published in 1803.

KHIRAUJ (خراج - khiráj, *Hind.*). From (kharaja, ar. to pass out). Tax; applied originally especially to the tribute levied by Mahomedans upon infidels [caufir] after conquest, afterwards to the general land revenue [lakhiraj].

KHIRNY (کهیرنی - khírní, *Hind.*). From (kshíra, san. milk). Same as Monkey-face paulay.

KHITAUB (خطاب - khitáb, *Hind.*). From (khataba, ar. to address) [khateeb, khootba]. Honorific surname, expressive of zeal for faith, political importance, &c., conferred by Caliphs [q.v.] and Mahomedan sovereigns. Ex.:—Ameen ool moolk, Ameen ool oomara, Ameer ood dowla, Asaf jung, Azeem jah, Badrool islam, Cootb ool aulam, Goozaurish khan, Hoomayoon jah, Shums ool oolamah [alam, lacab], Tauj oosh shareeyat. Distinguish from Kitaub.

KHODA (कोद्रव - kódrava, *San.*; کودرو - kodro, *Hind.* and *Dec.*; ಆರಕೆ - árike, *Can.*; ఆరికె - árike, *Tel.*; ଖୋଡ଼ି - khoddi, *Oor.*; വരക - varaku, *Mal.*; අමු - amu, *Singh.*; சிறுகூவரகு - shiruguvaragu, *Tam.*). Title from hindostany. San. from (ku, san. prefix of deficiency + udra, san. water); requiring little water, as a dry crop. Hind. and dec. from sanscrit. Mal. from (varaka, san. desirable). Tam. from (shiru, tam. small + kúvaragu, tam. raggy). San. also (kóradúsha), meaning blood spoiling. Hind. also (kodrocháwal), referring to millet rice. Can. also (hárakahullu), meaning panicum semi-verticillatum, rott. + grass. Tel. also (áriga); (állu), pl.; (níráruga), meaning water + the plant; (pátiárige), meaning high ground + the plant; (asakalu); (nallaasakalu), meaning black + the grain. Title otherwise Arikey, Hurreek, Kodo millet, Kora millet, Little millet, Punctured paspalum, Small varagoo. Botanically Paspalum scrobiculatum, linn., graminaceæ [vricsham, 156]. Alias Paspalum commersonii, frumentaceum, kora, orbiculare. Kora from hindostany. Root fibrous; culm branched, erect, 1–2 feet; sheaths glabrous or hirsute at the base, ciliated; ligula very short rounded; leaves linear, sub-acuminate, glabrous; racemes two to three approximated, alternate; spikelets biserial, short-pedicelled, oblong-roundish, acutish; glumes five to seven-nerved, upper one scrobiculate at the sides. A millet found near water edges; grain minute, black and globular; five-month crop; produces a sort of intoxication; straw given as fodder to cattle, whether green or dry; the poorest of millets [q.v.], and only cultivated by those living in the most barren parts of the country; when cooked it tastes somewhat like rice [q.v.]. There is a Teloogoo proverb:—అరుద్రానాటేసిన అరికె ఆకుల వేసిన అన్నముతోటి సమానము—"A crop of arikey sown in ardray "[caurtey] is as safe as food served on a leaf," that being its best season. Paspalum distichum, burm., is silt grass [ghaus].

KHOJA (خوجہ - khojah, *Hind.*). From (khwájah, pers. master). Tribe of Mahomedans, mostly of the Shiah [q.v.] sect; they have a separate religion of their own consisting of the ten incarnations [avatar] of the Hindoos grafted on the Shiah tenets. They do not go to the Musjid [q.v.], but have a separate place of worship [namauz]. There are some reformers of late among them who have become Soonnees [ismailia].

KHOND (కోడు - kódu, *Tel.*). From (konda, tel. hill). English name for the Kooi [q.v.] dravidian language and people. Also spelt in english Khand. An aboriginal tribe, whose principal habitat now lies in Orissa [q.v.], the eastern parts of the Central provinces, and the northern hill districts of this presidency. Allied to the Gonds [q.v.]. Khonds are wiry and active, have an upright gait, carry their heads erect, have straight noses, narrow nostrils, full but not thick lips, black eyes, cheek-bones somewhat prominent, slightly projecting lower jaw, white and regular teeth, with oval faces, as if of a mixed caucasian and mongolian origin. The eye is quick and brilliant, the general expression of the face intelligent, determined, and good-humoured; the skin is clear and glossy, and it varies little in color from a light bamboo to deep copper; they have little or no beard; the men are of medium height, stout, strong, and not uncomely, with aquiline noses, high cheek-bones, and receding foreheads; the women are short-statured and coarse-featured; they wear a scanty kilt-like piece of cloth reaching from the waist to the middle of the thigh; both men and women wear a profusion of brass rings and armlets. The religion of the Khonds is special to themselves. Their supreme god is called Boorapennoo, the god of light; who created for himself a consort, the earth-goddess, called Taripennoo, the source of evil in the world. They believe that the worship of the earth-goddess by human sacrifice is necessary for their agricultural prosperity. This [meriah] and the destruction of female infants formerly prevailed. The Cottiya or upland Khonds on the Calahundy and Jeypore borders are the most martial. The tribes occupying the hills bordering on Ganjam, with the exceptiom of the Simily khond tribe of Bodagooda, are somewhat more civilized; and in the Goomsore maliahs [q.v.] where many of them speak Ooriya [q.v.], there is not much perceptible difference between the Khond tribes of the hills and those living in the jungle villages at the foot of the ghauts [q.v.]. The Khonds dwell in villages in the forests. Each village consists of two streets composed of a double row of huts, well-built of timber, daubed with mud, and having thatched roofs. In some cases the villages are stockaded. Their agriculture is of the rudest kind; a piece of forest is marked out and the ground cleared by fire; small holes are then chopped in the earth by axes and the seeds are dropped in; after a year or two this is deserted for a fresh piece of forest land cleared in like manner. The family is the basis of their society, and khond sons have no property during their father's life; on failure of male issue, the land passes to the village. Numbers about 250,000 in presidency, almost all in Ganjam and Vizagapatam. See vol. I (36); II, 141.

KHONGAR (ఖొంగర - khongara, *Tel.*). From (khaja, san. killing). A class of professional robbers once employed by the Jeypore chiefs [jauty].

KHOOBAUZY (خبازی - khubází, *Hind.*). From (khubz, ar. bread); from flat round fruit. Mallow. Botanically the Malva genus, malvaceæ [vricsham, 25]. Herbaceous plants, annual or perennial and shrubs of variable height; they all possess tough fibre and abundance of mucilage; flowers frequently showy but of short duration; mainly tropical. The species best known to the natives is rotundifolia [wild bengal gram]. Others are:—sylvestris, verticillata.

KHOOD (خود - khud, *Hind.*). From persian. Self, own [khas]. Honorifically for the possessive of the second person.——*Khoodadad circar* (خداداد سرکار - khudádádsarkár, Hind.). The God-given-rule; the title assumed by Tippoo sultan.——*Khoodah* (خدا - khudá, Hind.). From (khud, pers. self + á, pers. come). God. A Mahomedan alam when followed by suffix denoting devotion; as, Khoodah buksh, alam + alaumat [ism].——*Khoodawund* (خداوند - khudáwand, Hind.). From (khudá, pers. god + wand, pers. like). Lord. A form of address to superiors, like your worship.——*Khoodkasht* (خود کاشت - khudkásht, Hind.). From (above + kásht, pers. sown). Self-sown; not let out to a farmer. Also ryots [q.v.] cultivating in their own village, as opposed to strangers [pykasht].

KHOOLFAH (خلفا - khulfá, *Dec.*). Corruption of pers. (khurfah). Same as Indian purslane.

KHOOLGAH (महिष - mahisha, *San.*; جاموس - jámús, *Ar.*; گاؤمیش - gáúmesh, *Pers.*; کہلگا - khulgá, *Hind.*; کارباو - kárbau, *Malay*; ಕೋಣ - kóna, *Can.*; ಎರ್ಮೆ - erme, *Too.*; దున్న - dunna, *Tel.*; എരിമ - erima, *Mal.*; මීමා - mímá, *Singh.*; எருமை - erumai, *Tam.*). Title from hindostany. San. from (mah, san. to value highly). Ar. from persian. Pers. from (gáú, pers. cow + mesh, pers. sheep). Tel. from (dunnu, tel. to plough). Singh. from (mi, singh. buffalo + má, singh. great). Tel. also (barre), from bellowing. Title otherwise Buffalo [q.v.]. The earlier Anglo-indians gave this name to the common Indian ox [maud], and then present species was called the water-buffalo. Bubalus arni, bovinæ, bovidæ, ruminantia, mammalia [sastanam, 23], of naturalists [jantoo]. Specific is from sanscrit (aranya), wild. The wild buffalo inhabits Thibet, but is domesticated in India. It is the only indigenous ruminant of Ceylon. There is scarcely an animal upon which domesticity has made so little impression, the wild being only larger and fiercer. Of the Mysore buffalo there are three varieties, the Hoolloo, the Gowzry or Goozerat, and the Chokkatoo [q.v.] which comes from the country bordering the river Kistna; of these the Hoolloo is by far the most common, and is the native breed of the country. The Todah buffalo is well known on the Neilgherry hills, where each Todah [q.v.] mund [q.v.] possesses a herd; they come from Mysore; differ from the kind generally met with on the plains. The common domestic buffalo is extensively used both for draught and milk, and milk is richer than that of the cow [pashoo]. The male buffalo is frequently sacrificed by the aboriginal races. The following is the description. Forehead convex, rounded; horns large, black; general color dark blackish-slaty; hair scanty, black. Length 10½ feet and upwards from snout to root of tail which is short, not exceeding lower than the hock; tuft of hair on the forehead, over the eyes, and on the knees. Height at shoulder up to 6½ feet. The horns [sing] are of two kinds; the one very long, nearly straight, well thrown back; the other much shorter and well curved, more directed upwards. The horns of the bull are thicker than those of the cow, but the horns of the cow are larger. Alone perhaps of all wild animals in India, the buffalo will charge unprovoked. There is a Tamul proverb:—அவனுக்கும் இவனுக்கும் எருமைச் சங்காத்தம்—"The intimacy of these two persons is that of "the buffalo," referring to its gregariousness. And another:—எட்டு வருஷத்து எருமைக்கடா ஏரிக்குப்போக வழி தேடுகின்றது—"A buffalo eight years old is at a loss to "find its way to the tank;" derisive. And another:—எருமைக் கோமயம் எக்கியத்திற்கு ஆகுமா—"Will the dung of the "buffalo serve for sacrificial purposes?" it is never so used. And another:—வீட்டுக்கு வாய்த்தது எருமை, மேட்டுக்கு வாய்த்தது போர்—"A buffalo makes a house prosper, a "corn-stack makes high ground conspicuous;" referring to its utility. There is a Teloogoo proverb:—తల్లినిచూచి పిల్లను, పాడిని చూచి బఱ్ఱెను తీసుకోవలెను—"As you look at the mother before "taking the daughter, so inquire how a buffalo milks before you "purchase."

KHOON (خون - khún, *Pers.*). Blood.——*Khoony* (خونی - khúní, Hind.). Murder [colley].

KHOOR (خر - khur, *Hind.*). Sun.——*Khoorsheed* (خورشید - khurshíd, Pers.). Part of lacab; as Khoorsheed bee, sun of ladies; Khoor sheed jah, high as sun [ism].

KHOORD (خرد - khurd, *Ar.*). Small. Plant second term. Ex.:—Alpinia officinarum (khusravidárúikhurd), small king's drug; Bambusa stricta (banskhurd), small bamboo. See gloss. paragraphs.

KHOOSH (خوش - khush, *Pers.*). Happy. Part of lacab; as Khoosh kadam, happy gift. Female servant's name [ism].——*Khooshbaush* (خوش باش - khushbásh, Hind.). From (above + básh, pers. remain). One who lives at ease; a cultivator who occupies nuttam [q.v.] lands free or on easy rent [sookhavausy].

KHOOSROW (خسرو - khusrau, *Pers.*). King. Plant first term. Ex., where transl. is of second term:—Alpinia galanga (khusravidárúikalán), drug + large; Alpinia officinarum (khusravidárúikhurd), drug + small. See gloss. paragraphs.

KHOOTBA (خطبه - khutbah, *Hind.*). From (khataba, ar. to discourse) [khateeb, khitaub]. A discourse delivered every Friday [shamba] after the forenoon service in the principal mosque [musjid], when the ruling power is prayed for. Also on the two great festivals [eed] in the morning after sunrise. The right of being named in the khootba and that of coining money are two of the principal privileges of the sovereign.

KHORASSAN (خراسان - khurásán, *Hind.*). Country between the Caspian and Afghanistaun.——*Khorassan mint* (حبق خراسانی - habakikhurásání, Ar.). Same as Country sorrel.——*Khorassan omam* (కురాసానిఓమము - kurásániómamu, Tel.). Plant name common to:—Hyoscyamus niger, Seseli indicum. See gloss. paragraphs.

KHOW (کهو - khaú, *Hind.*). Underground granary [gunj], common in hill forts.

KHUBBER (خبر - khabar, *Hind.*). From (khabura, ar. to know). News; especially as a sporting term, news of game.

KHUD (کهڈا - khaddá, *Hind.*). A precipitous hill-side.

KHUN (کهن - khan, *Hind.*). A day of Mahomedan lunar fortnight. For a day of Hindoo fortnight or pacsham [q.v.] see Tity.

KIBLA (قبله - kiblah, *Hind.*). From (kabala, ar. opposite). The direction in which all Mahomedans must pray, whether in their public or in their private devotions [namauz], namely towards Mecca. The direction is known and kibla constructed in mosques [musjid] according to the position of the pole-star [alrooccabah, nacshatram] by means of an astrolabe [q.v.] for finding the bearing of Mecca.

KIDANG (گڑنگ - garang, *Hind.*; கிடங்கு - kidangu, *Tam.*). Store-house; suffix in place names [godown].

KIDDY (கிட்டி - kitti, *Tam.*). From (kittu, tam. to approach). Finger-pincher made by two slips of bamboo [q.v.], &c., for torturing.

KIFAUYAT (کفایت - kifáyat, *Hind.*). From (kafá, ar. to suffice). Profit, gain resulting from lands held at reduced rates, surplus.

KILA (قلعه - kila, *Hind.*). A fortress [cottay]. Killadar is the governor of a fort. Cf. Cotwaul.

KILKILAH (मत्स्यरङ्ग - matsyaranga, *San.*; کلکلا - kilkilá, *Hind*, and *Dec.*; బుచ్చిగాడు - buççigádu, *Tel.*; പൊന്മ - ponma, *Mal.*; மீன்கொத்தி - míngotti, *Tam.*). Title from hindostany. San. from (matsya, san. fish + ranga, san. love), fish loving. Hind. and dec. from chirping. Tel. from (buççi, tel. little + gádu, tel. personal suffix). Mal. from (pon, mal. gold + váya, mal. mouth). Tam. from (mín, tam. fish + kottu, tam. to peck). San. also (kuttaka); (suchitraka), meaning variegated. Hind. also (chhotákilkila), meaning small king-fisher; (chhotámachrangá), meaning small + white-breasted king-fisher. Tel. also (lakumuki), meaning small + face; (nílabuççigádu), meaning blue king-fisher. Mal. also (malapponma), meaning hill + king-fisher. Tam. also (viççuli), meaning swift bird; (shaççili), meaning beaked, from the long beak. Halcyonidæ family, fissirostres, insessores, aves [pacshy, 9], of naturalists [jantoo]. King-fishers. Divided into Halcyoninæ and Alcedininæ. Brown-headed king-fisher is halcyon leucocephalus, halcyoninæ; alias halcyon brunniceps, capensis, gurial, javana. White-breasted king-fisher is halcyon fuscus, halcyoninæ, alias alcedo fusca, halcyon smyrnensis. Black-caped purple king-fisher is halcyon atricapillus, gmel.; alias alcedo brama, pileata. Ruddy king-fisher is halcyon coromandelianus, alias halcyon coromander, schlegelii, lilacina, calipyga; very rare here in spite of name. White-collared king-fisher is todiramphus collaris, scop.; alias alcedo chlorocephala, sacra. Three-toed purple king-fisher is ceyx tridactyla; alias alcedo erythaca, purpurea, microsoma; a coast bird. Common indian king-fisher is alcedo bengalensis, alcedininæ; alias alcedo ispidioides; head and hind neck dusky feathers edged with pale blue; rufous band from base of nostrils to end of ear-coverts, below this dark band, back, rump and upper tail-coverts pale-blue, wings and tail dull green-blue; wing-coverts speckled with pale-blue; chin and throat white, rest of lower plumage bright ferruginous; in young bluish-green tinge is the prevalent tint, in adults a pure blue; blackish above, orange beneath; irides dark brown, legs orange red; length 6½ to 7 inches; a diminutive of the european bird. Pied king-fisher, cowryaula kilkilah in hindostany, is ceryle rudis, alcedininæ; alias ceryle varia; ispida bicincta, bitorquata; very common on banks of rivers and tanks.

KILOOVAY (கிளுவை - kiluvai, *Tam.*). From (kilai, tam. to ramify); from many branches and branchlets. Botanically Balsamodendron [balsam] berryi, arn., burseraceæ [vricsham, 35]. Alias Amyris gileadensis; Balsamodendron gileadense; Protium gileadense. Distinct however from Balm of gilead [q.v.]. Ultimate branches spinescent, with small short abortive branchlets bearing the leaves and flowers at their extremities; leaves palmately three-foliolate; leaflets roundish-obovate, obtuse, obscurely crenulate, glabrous; peduncles one-flowered, shorter than the petioles. Shrub or tree, covered with flower and fruit in february and march. Very common as a hedge plant but seldom flowering in that state, as the inflorescence is either attacked when young by some insect or rendered abortive from a successive propagation from cuttings. The whole tree has a grateful fragrance, gum-resin [googal] exuding. Useless wood.——*Hill kiloovay* (ಕೊಂಡಮಾಮಿಡಿ - kondamámidi, Can.; వేటపత్రి - vétapatri, Tel.; மலைக்கிளுவை - malaikkiluvai, Tam.). Can. from (konda, tel. hill + mámidi, tel. mango, mangifera indica, linn.). Tam. from (malai, tam. mountain + kiluvai, tam. the plant). Tel. also (kondamámidi), meaning hill + mango tree, mangifera indica, l.; (kondarégu), meaning hill + jujube tree, zizyphus jujuba, lam. Tam. also (karppúrakkiluvai), meaning camphor + the plant; (malaimá), meaning mountain mango. Title otherwise Hill jujube, Hill mango. Botanically Protium caudatum, w. & a., burseraceæ [vricsham, 35]. Leaves long-petioled with short lateral leaflets, the terminal one with a long petiolule, ovate entire; cymes bracteate at the branches, the bracteoles beneath the flowers very minute; flowers polygamous, small; calyx lobes deltoid, acute, as long as broad; petals about twice as long as calyx lobes; drupe about the size of a pea [calauyam], nearly globular, subtended by the persistent calyx. Green barked tree, common as avenue [shaulay] tree, though bare of leaves for some months towards end of cold season and beginning of hot; whole tree very odoriferous, leaves and bark having fragrance something like mangoes [q.v.]. Bark and all tender parts on being wounded discharge pale, whey-colored liquid, fragrant something like orange [q.v.] leaf; wood very brittle and full of sap, of no value. Another species is pubescens.

KILTAUN (കില്ത്താൻ - kiltán, *Mal.*). Island; pop. 790. One of the Laccadive group attached to South canara.

KIM (किं - kim, *San.*). What.——*Kimpoorooshan* (किम्पुरुष - kimpurusha, San.). From (above + purusha, san. man). Same as Kinnaran.——*Kingry* (کنگری - kingrí, Hind.; கின்னரி - kinnari, Tam.). From (kiunara, san. a divine chorister). A musical instrument something like but smaller than the veenay [q.v.], having only two steel strings and three or four pumpkins [carcauroo] as sounding boards; fixed frets [sangeetam].——*Kinnaran* (किन्नर - kinnara, San.). From (above + nara, san. man). Beings with the form of a man and the head of a horse [ghorah] dwelling on Keilausam [q.v.]. They are also called Ashwa mookha, Toorangavactra and Mayoo. Celestial choristers [gandharvan, matam]. See vol. I (78).

KIMEDY (కిమెడి - kimedi, *Tel.*). From (akhimundo, oor. eye-headed). Epithet of an aboriginal ruler. Zemindarry tract; Ganjam dist. On western border of district. Contains three estates:—Parlakimedy; Pedda kimedy or Boda kimedy, also called Vizianagram; and Chinna kimedy or Prataupagherry. Each estate consists of two distinct divisions, a lowland and an upland tract; the former held as an ordinary zemindarry [q.v.] under the regular district officers, and the latter under the supervision of a special Government agency. The whole country was ruled from a remote date by a descendant of the royal house of Orissa [q.v.]. In 1607 the Kimedy rajah allotted Vizianagram and Prataupagherry to his younger son Ananga bheema deo kesary, whose descendants divided the estate into two zemindarries, though they were temporarily reunited under Bheema deo. The latter proving troublesome, his fort at Coorlah was taken in 1769. The following year, in consequence of his suspected intrigues with Seetaram raj of Vizianagram and the Mahrattas, Prataupagherry his principal stronghold was seized. On this the Rajah accepted the terms offered him; but in 1772 it was again found necessary to enter the country. The British gained possession of all his forts, and the estate was divided between his two sons. The brothers ravaged one another's territory and burnt one another's villages, till in 1800 they were both thrown into jail in Ganjam for disturbing the peace. They were replaced by their respective sons, and the feud was carried on until very recently. The country is now peaceful and flourishing, and connected by road with the coast. The principal towns are Digoopoody, Parlakimedy and Poodamary.

KINAR (കിണറ് - kinaru, *Mal.*; கிணறு - kinaru, *Tam.*). From (khan, san. to dig). Well [kainy].

KINAURAH (کنارا - kinárá, *Hind.*). From persian. Side, bank, shore.——*Kinaury* (کناری - kinárí, Hind.). From (kinárah, pers. edge). Gold and silver lace [gotah, sarigay].

KINCOB (کمخاب - kamkháb, *Hind.*). From (kam, pers. privative + kháb, pers. soft down). Brocade. Silk [puttoo] stuff interwoven with gold or silver thread [sarigay].

KING (شاهی - sháhí, *Hind.*). Prefix.——*King-crow* (भृङ्गराज - bhringarája, San.; هزاردستان - hazárdástán, Pers.; کولسا - kolsá, Hind. and Dec.; ಭರದ್ವಾಜ - bharadvája, Can.; పసలపోలిగాడు - pasalapóligádu, Tel.; കാക്കത്തമ്പുരാട്ടി - kákkattampurátti, Mal.; கரிக்குருவி - karikkuruvi, Tam.). Title from habit of pursuing crows [caurvam], hawks [shyainam], and kites [chillam], to drive them away from its nest. San. from (bhringa, san. bee + rája, san. king) [bhangrah]. Pers. from (hazár, pers. thousand + dástán, pers. tale); from variety of its notes. Hind. and dec. means charcoal, from color. Tel. from (pashuvu, tel. cattle + póli, tel. proper name + gádu, tel. personal suffix), from being seen perched on cattle. Mal. from (kákka, mal. crow + tampurátti, mal. queen). Tam. from (kari, tam. black + kuruvi, tam. bird). Hind. also (kotwál), meaning guard; (buchangá); (dhapri); (paharíbuchangá), meaning hill drongo; (chaptiyá), meaning flat; (chhotákesráj), meaning small + drongo; (bhímráj); (kishanráj), meaning black king; (kesráj). Tel. also (bháradvájamu); (étrinta); (kondapasalapóligádu), meaning hill drongo; (nallapasalapóligádu), meaning black drongo; (tókapasalapóligádu), meaning long-tailed drongo; (hati), from ghond; (ventrukapasalapóligádu), meaning hairy drongo. Tam. also (karikkarumá), meaning black bird. Drongo shrikes. Dicrurinæ, laniadæ [pingalam], dentirostres, insessores, aves [pacshy, 19], of naturalists. Common drongo shrike is Dicrurus macrocercus; alias buchanga albirictus; dicrurus balicussius, indicus. Long-tailed drongo is Dicrurus longicaudatus; alias dicrurus cineraceus, intermedius, macrocercus, pyrrhops. White-bellied drongo is Dicrurus cœrulescens; called by natives mountain drongo; alias lanius fingah. Bronzed drongo is Chaptia ænea; generic from hindostany; alias dicrurus æratus; chaptia muscipetoides. Large racket-tailed drongo is Edolius paradiseus; called by the natives tailed drongo; alias chibia malabaroides; edolius dentirostris, grandis; lanius malabaricus; peculiar call, beginning with harsh chuckle, ending in peculiar metallic creaking cry 'tse-rung tse-rung;' often caught and tamed; will imitate all sorts of sounds, as of dogs, cats, sheep and goats, poultry, and the notes of many birds; hence called by some hazaurdaustaun, or the bird with a thousand tales; will eat raw meat, lizards [chipkalee], and almost any kind of animal food that is offered to it. Malabar racket-tailed drongo is Edolius malabaricus; alias dicrurus retifer; edolius cristatellus, paradiseus. Hair-crested drongo is Chibia hottentota; called by natives hairy drongo; alias chibia casia; criniger splendens; dicrurus criniger; edolius barbatus, krishna; frequently tamed by mussalmans.——*King fish* (شیر ماهی - shermáhí, Hind.). Hind. from (sher, pers. corruption of portuguese serra, saw + máhí, pers. fish), from serrate appearance of rows of finlets. Anglo-indian name given to several species of Cybium [seer], and Polynemus [robaul].

KINKA (کنکا - kinká, *Dec.*). Same as Wild jeerah.

KINNAB (भङ्गा - bhangá, *San.*; भांग - bhánga, *Mahr.*; भांगि - bhángi, *Conc.*; نبات القنب - nabátulkinnab, *Ar.*; درخت کنب - darkhtikinnab, *Pers.*; گانجے کا پیڑ - gánjekáper, *Hind.*; گانجے کا جہاڑ - gánjekájhár, *Dec.*; گنجہ - ganja, *Malay*; ಭಂಗಿ - bhangi, *Can.*; ಬಂಗಿ - bangi, *Too.*; గంజాయిచెట్టు - gandzáyichettu, *Tel.*; കഞ്ചാവ് - kañchávu, *Mal.*; කංසාගහ - kanságaha, *Singh.*; கஞ்சா - kañjá, *Tam.*). Title from arabic. San. from (bhañj, san. to break); in allusion to process of debarkation by which the fibres were separated from stem [hemp bendy]. Mahr. from sanscrit. Ar. from (nabát, ar. plant + kinnab, ar. hemp). Pers. from (darakht, pers. plant + kinnab, pers. hemp). Hind. from (gánjah, hind. intoxicating drug + per, hind. tree). Dec. from (gánjah, hind. the drug + jhár, hind. tree). Tel. from (gánjah, hind. the drug + chettu, tel. tree). Mal. and tam. from hindostany. San. also (vijayá), meaning victorious, from giving success to its votaries; (shana), meaning giving [sunn]; (siddhapatra), meaning saint's leaf; (aláta), meaning firebrand; (vajradru), meaning adamantine tree; (griñjana), meaning grumbling [gaujar, lussoon]; (mátuláni), meaning unequalled [datura]; (indráshana), meaning eaten by indran; (ánandá), meaning the gladdener; (harshiní), meaning delighter; (madiní), meaning intoxicator; (ganjá), meaning the noisy; (ganjiká), meaning small variety. Mahr. also (gánjá), meaning the dried leaves of the plant. Ar. also (kinnab), meaning hemp. Pers. also (darakhtiwarakulkhiyál), meaning intoxicating leaf tree; (darakhtihashísh), meaning hashish tree; (darakhtibhang), bhang tree. Hind. also (bhangkájhár), meaning bhang tree. Can. also (kusuvugida); (ganjá); (ganjáyi). Tel. also (jadagandzáyi), meaning plaited + the plant; (bangichettu), meaning bhang + tree; (kalpamu), meaning wishing tree. Mal. also (cherukañchávu), meaning small variety; (vakkuççana), meaning bark + crotalaria juncea, linn. Singh. also (ganjágaha); (matkansá), meaning head opium. Tam. also (pangi); (kórakkarmúli), meaning siddhan so called + plant; (kalbam), meaning useful preparation; (shanappu); (mathamattagam), meaning intoxication + head. *νήπενθες* of Homer. Later greek *κάνναβις* from the Arabic kinnab, whence English hemp. Title otherwise Carl hemp, Corakkan's drug, Fimble, Gallow grass, Giddy plant, Indian hemp, Victory plant, Wishing plant. Giving Bhang, Charas, Ganjah, Hashish, Majoon, Sabjee, Siddhee. Botanically Cannabis sativa, linn., urticaceæ [vricsham, 119]. Cannabis, from (kinnab, ar.). Alias Cannabis indica; Polygonum viridiflorum. Annual, 4–6 feet covered all over with an extremely fine rough pubescence; stem erect, branched, green, angular; calyx five-parted; leaves alternate or opposite, on long petioles, digitate, with linear-lanceolate, sharply-serrated leaflets, tapering to a long, smooth point; flowers in spikes, axillary clustered, small, greenish white; males lax, and drooping; females erect, leafy at the base; flowering all the year; cultivated; the whole plant has a strong aromatic and heavy odour. In certain seasons a resinous juice exudes and concretes on the leaves, slender stems, and flowers; this resin [raul] when separated and formed into small masses or lumps constitutes charas [q.v.] which is the type or basis of all hemp preparations; the resin in its purest form called cannabin is very soluble in alcohol and ether, partially soluble in alkaline, insoluble in acid solutions; when pure, of a blackish grey color; hard at 90°; softens at higher temperatures and fuses readily; soluble in the fixed and in several volatile oils [yennay]; odour fragrant and narcotic; taste slightly warm, bitterish and acrid. The dried plant which has flowered and from which the resin has not been removed is called simply ganjah [q.v.]; stems, leaves, and petioles pressed together is the form in which it is found in commerce; the bundles of ganjah are about 2 feet long and 3 inches in diameter, and contain twenty-four plants; the color is dusky green, the odour agreeably narcotic, the whole plant resinous, and adhesive to the touch; the natives cut the plant when in flower, allow it to dry for three days, and then lay it in bundles averaging one seer [q.v.] weight, which are distributed to the license-dealers; the ganjah itself is sold for smoking chiefly; ganjah yields to alcohol twenty per cent. of resinous extract, composed of the resin and green coloring matter, or chlorophylle; distilled with a large quantity of water, traces of essential oil pass over, and the distilled liquor has the powerful narcotic odour of the plant. The large leaves and capsules, macerated in water, without the stalks, are called bhang [q.v.]; they are used for making an intoxicating drink; bhang is cheaper than ganjah. The above make also a confection called majoon [q.v.]; the chief ingredients of this are ganjah leaves, milk [paul], ghee [q.v.], poppy seeds [khaskas], flowers of the thorn apple [datura], the powder of the nux vomica [poison nut], sugar [q.v.]. Hashish is a confection prepared from the tender parts of the plant dried. The hemp plant is cultivated in europe for fibre, but here for narcotic properties; it requires an elevated exposure and a cool climate; it thrives from 3,000 to 7,000 feet; cultivated in sandy soil and red loam; ground prepared on coromandel in aushweejam or october and caurteecam or november; on w. coast in maidom or april to yedavam or may; seed sown on coromandel in caurteecam or november, on w. coast in macaram [mausam] or january; when the plant is full grown the leaves drop; cut ten months after sowing; the plant is cut just above the root or pulled up; the plant so cut is hung for about fifteen days, not exposing it to severity of sun; then the large stem is removed and the remaining parts are packed in small bundles, which should be exposed to the dew for three days and subsequently brought into store. Medicinally almost every part of the plant is useful; but especially the flowering-tops, the leaves, the milky juice or resin, and the seeds; with natives aphrodisiac, particularly in the majoon; leaves prescribed in diarrhœa, or in conjunction with turmeric [country saffron], onions [piyauz] and warm gingelly [q.v.] oil, made into unction for piles; the seeds in emulsion are prepared for gonorrhœa; substituted for british chloral hydras, bromide of potash, henbane and belladonna; in pharm. officinal; also in british pharm.; indian hemp is medicinally much more potent than that grown in europe. For smoking ganjah [q.v.] the dried article and some tobacco [pogauk] are rubbed together in the palm of the hand with a few drops of water; simple tobacco is placed in the pipe first, then a layer of the prepared ganjah, then more tobacco, and the fire above all; the hookah [q.v.] is passed round, and generally each person takes a single draught; intoxication ensues almost instantly. The bhang [q.v.] is not smoked, but pounded up with water into a pulp, so as to make a drink; it is considered highly conducive to health; same effects as opium [aphainam], but more agreeable. The fibre [demon plantain, sunn] is hemp, of which ropes and door mats are made, when woven known as canvas; the hemp plant destroys caterpillars and other insects [poochy], which prey upon vegetables; oil obtained by expression from the seed, not well known. Compare:—Abroma augusta, perennial indian hemp; Calotropis gigantea, bow-string hemp; Crotalaria juncea, bengal hemp, bombay hemp, brown hemp, concany hemp, deccany brown hemp, false hemp, indian hemp, jubbulpore hemp, madras hemp, salsette hemp, sunn hemp, taag hemp; Eupatorium cannabinum, agrimony hemp, water hemp; Hibiscus cannabinus, bombay hemp, brown hemp, deccany hemp, indian brown hemp, indian hemp; Musa textilis, manilla hemp; Sanseviera roxburghiana, bow-string hemp; Tragia cannabina, hemp-leaved tragia; Vitex trifolia, hemp tree. See gloss. paragraphs.

KINNY (ಚಿನ್ನಿ - kinni, *Can.*). Means small [chinna]. Pariah proper name [peyar].

KINO (کنیا گوند - kinyágond, *Hind.*; సీమగాండామృగము నెత్తురు - símagándámrigamnetturu, *Tel.*; சீமைக்காண்டாமிருகரத்தம் - shímaikkándámirugarattam, *Tam.*). Title from (kína, san. flesh); from red color. Tel. from (síma, tel. foreign + gándámrigamunetturu, tel. dragon's blood). Tam. from (shímai, tam. foreign + kándámirugam, tam. rhinoceros + rakta, san. blood). A gum [gond] from genera butea, eucalyptus, eugenia, pterocarpus; generally occurs in shining grains; of a rich ruby red color, of bitter, styptic taste, nearly all soluble in alcohol and readily pulverisable between the fingers; medicinally astringent; used to dye cotton cloth of a nankeen yellow [shauyam].——*Amboyna kino* (کنیا گوند انبونہ - kinyágondiambúnah, Hind.). Product of Common vengay.——*Bengal kino* (کنیا گوند بنگالہ - kinyágondibangálah, Hind.). Otherwise Butea kino. Product of Palaus tree.——*Malabar kino* (کنیا گوند ملیبار - kinyágondimalebár, Hind.). Product of Common vengay.——*Nemmy kino* (نیمی کنیا - nemmikinyá, Hind.). Product of Nemmy tree.——*Rangoon kino* (کنیا گوند رنگون - kinyágondirangún, Hind.). Product of Padouk.

KIOSK (کوشک - kúshak, *Hind.*). From turkish through (khushk, pers. dry). An open summer house supported by pillars [staupatyam].

KIRAUNY (കിരാണി - kiráni, *Mal.*). Writer. In Malabar used exclusively for Portuguese and half-caste writers.

KIRAUTAN (किरात - kiráta, *San.*). From (krí, san. to throw); arrow-thrower, bowman. Mountaineers mentioned in ancient Sanscrit as living in the mountains east of Hindostan. They are described in the Ramayanam [q.v.] as islanders, who eat raw fish, live in the waters, and are men-tigers, or men below and tigers [pooly] above. Their females are gold-colored and pleasant to behold, and have sharp-pointed hair knots. The word indicates probably the inhabitants of Orissa [q.v.]. According to Arrian, the coast before coming to the mouths of the Ganges is occupied by the κιρράδαι, a savage race [jauty].——*Chiretta* (چرائیتہ - charáitah, Hind.). See sep. title.——*Kariyat* (کریات - kiriyát, Hind.). From (kiráta, san. mountaineer); from use by them. Same as Chiretta.

KIRMAUN (کرمان - kirmán, *Pers.*). A province in S.E. of Persia. Latin name Caramania. Shawls [q.v.] and carpets are made.——*Kirmauny* (کرمانی - kirmání, Hind.). From (kirmán, pers. a place in babylonia). Lacab of a class of Mahomedans tracing their descent from a Koord clan on the frontiers of Persia [ism].

KIRMIZ (लाक्षा - láksha, *San.*; किरमीज - kiramíja, *Mahr.*; قرمز - kirmiz, *Ar.*; کرم رنگریزان - kirmirangrízán, *Pers.*; قرمز - kirmiz, *Hind.* and *Dec.*; ఇంద్రగోపపురుగు - indragópapurugu, *Tel.*; கிருமிஞ்சிப்புழு - kirumiñjippuzhu, *Tam.*). Title from arabic. San. from (rañj, san. to dye). Mahr. from arabic. Ar. from (kirm, pers. insect + kíz, pers. silk). Pers. from (kirm, pers. insect + rangríz, pers. dyer). Hind. from arabic. Tel. from (indragópa, san. the beerboty insect + purugu, tel. insect). Tam. also (shappáttippuzhu), meaning prickly pear [q.v.] worm, as feeding on leaves of opuntia dillenii, haw. Cochineal insect. Coccus cacti, coccidæ, hemiptera, hemimetabola, insecta [poochy], of naturalists [jantoo]. Cochineal is the dried female insect. Imported. Useful for imparting red color [shauyam] to liquid medicines. Native use, aphrodisiac, astringent and anodyne; substituted for British phosphorus. Pharm. preparation is tincture of cochineal, tinctura cocci officinal. Distinguish the native article Lac [q.v.].

KIRRET (కడితము - kaditamu, *Tel.*). Book made of a long slip of cotton cloth, from eight inches to a foot wide, and from 12 to 18 feet long, covered on each side with a compost of paste and powdered charcoal [adoopp kary]. When dry, it is folded up, without cutting, in leaves of equal dimensions. To the two end folds are fixed ornamented plates of wood, painted and varnished, resembling the sides of a book, and the whole is put into a case of silk [puttoo] or cotton [q.v.], or tied with a tape. Those in use with the lower classes are tied up by a common string. The book opens at either side, and if unfolded and drawn out is still a long slip of the original length of the cloth. The writing is similar to that on a slate [cull palagay], and may be in like manner rubbed out and renewed. In Mysore Tippoo prohibited its use in recording the public accounts. This is the linen cloth described by Arrian as being written on by the Indians.

KISHK (किष्क - kishk, *San.*). To kill.——*Kishkindyay* (किष्किन्ध्या - kishkindhyá, San.). Ancient city. Capital of Soogreevan [q.v.], an ally of Rama [q.v.], the hero of Ramayanam [q.v.]. Site supposed to be in the north of Mysore about the source of the Pumpah river [charitram, rishyamoocam].

KISM (قسم - kism, *Hind.*). From (kasama, ar. to divide). Kind, sort, share.——*Kismat* (قسمت - kismat, Hind.). From (kasama, ar. to divide). Share of prosperity, hence fate [takdeer].

KISMIS (کشمش - kishmish, *Hind.*). Stoneless raisins from Persia [draucshay].

KIST (قسط - kist, *Hind.*). From (kasata, ar. to apportion equitably). Stated payment, instalment of rent.——*Kistbundy* (قسطبندی - kistbandí, Hind.). From (above + bandí, pers. settlement). Settlement of instalments of kist, both as to time and amount. See vol. I, 112.

KITAUB (کتاب - kitáb, *Hind.*). From (kataba, ar. to write). Book. Koran [q.v.] of mahomedans, Old testament of jews, New testament of christians. Distinguish from Khitaub.

KITCHAUN (കിളാൻ - kíççán, *Mal.*; கிச்சான் - kíççán, *Tam.*). From (kíru, tam. streak); from bands. The genus Therapon, percidæ, acanthopterygii, teleostei, pisces [matsyam, 1], of naturalists [jantoo]. Marine fishes feeding on carrion, but eaten by poor. Color usually silvery, with longitudinal bands. The species best known to the natives are:—jarbua, puta, theraps.

KITTAIRY (கித்தேரி - kittéri, *Tam.*). Catherine. Native christian proper name [peyar].

KITTAL (කිතුල් - kitul, *Singh.*). Bastard sago palm.

KIYAUM (قیام - kiyám, *Ar.*). From (kauma, ar. to stand). Prop. Part of lacab; as Kiyaum ood dowla, prop of empire [ism].

KIZHAMAY (கிழமை - kizhamai, *Tam.*). Means ownership. A fraction of a week, a day [ahas, dinam, naul]; also a week [vauram].——*Kizhavan* (கிழவன் - kizhavan, Tam.). From (kizhamai, tam. propriety). Proprietor, lord, old man.——*Kizhavan saitoopaty* (கிழவன்சேதுபதி - kizhavanséthuppathi, Tam.). Old man + title. Title of Raghoonaut tevar saitoopaty, the sixth Marava [q.v.] ruler of Ramnaud. Murdered the Jesuit missionary John De Britto; changed his capital from Pogalore to Ramnaud, the present seat of Government; wrested all the territories south of the Amboor river from the ruler of Tanjore; created the Poodoocottah state and appointed his brother-in-law of the Cullan [q.v.] family as Tondiman [charitram, tondiman]. See vol. I (120), (124), 56.

KIZHAUTTY (జెల్ల - jella, *Tel.*; கிழாத்தி - kizhátti, *Tam.*). Siluridæ [matsyam, 35] or Cat-fish family of fishes. Otherwise Fresh-water sharks.

KLING (کلنگ - kling, *Malay*). Malay term. Name given by Burmese, Malays and Javanese to Teloogoos, being a corruption of Calingam [q.v.]. The trade and intercourse of the Teloogoo coast with the Indian archipelago is of great but unascertained antiquity, and still goes on. Many Teloogoos have from time to time settled in Sumatra and the Malay peninsula, and their mixed descendants are numerous. In Singapore they form one-tenth of the population, and in Penang [q.v.] they are even more numerous. Malays sometimes mean the whole of india by Kling.

KOBEE (كرنب - karnab, *Ar.*; كوبى - kobí, *Hind.*; كرمكى بهاجى - karamkíbhájí, *Dec.*; ಮುದ್ದೆಕೋಸು - muddekósu, *Can.*; గోసుకూర - gósukúra, *Tel.*; கோவிசு - kóvisu, *Tam.*). Title from hindostany. Canarese from (mudde, can. lump + kósha, san. egg). Hindostany also (karamkallá), meaning cabbagewort. Dec. also (karamkáság), meaning cabbage leaf. Greek ῥάφανος and κράμβη ἥμερος. Title otherwise Cabbage, Domestic colewort. Botanically Brassica [sarshapam] oleracea, linn., cruciferæ [vricsham, 10]. Produced by cultivating the european wild colewort; when perfect consists of solid masses formed by the leaves compactly enveloping one another. Cabbage was introduced into s. india by europeans at an early date of their occupation; it is now grown on the hills. Seeds diuretic, laxative, stomachic, and anthelmintic; leaves form application in gout and rheumatism. The following are the chief varieties:— Capitata, linn., white cabbage; Rubra, linn., red cabbage; Sabauda, linn., savoy; Sabauda gemmifera, brussels sprouts; Sabellica, linn., borecole or scotch kale; Botrytis, linn., cauliflower; Botrytis cymosa, brocoli; Caulorapa, knol-khol. Rubra is only eaten in pickle; Sabauda instead of forming one single head, produces numerous small heads, of about the size of a pullet's egg, with blistered leaves; Sabellica is remarkable for its crimped and plume-like leaves; Botrytis heads [phool kobee], are a malformation of the inflorescence, forming a white conglomeration of imperfect buds; Caulorapa replaces the turnip in this country, as it endures heat; knol-khol being dutch for turnip cabbage; the stalk at one point expands into a globular mass resembling a turnip, and this is the edible part; originally imported into s. india from the cape.——*Phool kobee* (پهول كوبى - phúlkobí, Hind.). From (phúl, hind. flower + kobí, hind. cabbage). Cauliflower.

KODA (ಕೋಡ - kóda, *Can.*). Monkey [bandar].——*Kodanaud* (ಕೋಡನಾಡು - kódanádu, Can.). From (above + nádu, can. tract).—"*a*" Village, Hill; Neilgherry dist., Paranginaud div.; pop. 1,126; acres 8,170; lat. 11° 30′; long. 76° 56′; height 6,740 feet; from Coonoor N.N.E. 13 miles; from Ootacamund E.N.E. 15 miles. Three cairns [paundoocull, raucshasagoondloo] of rubble stones have been discovered containing pottery and jewelry.—"*b*" Tea estate, Paranginaud, Neilgherries, 6 miles N. of Kotagherry. Is the largest tea [q.v.] estate in Paranginaud division.

KODAYKARNAL (கொடிக்கானல் - kodikkánal, *Tam.* kodaikánal *). From (kodi, tam. creeper + kánal, tam. forest).—"*a*" Hills, Deputy tahsildarry, Madura district; pay Rs. 100.—"*b*" Hill, Sanitarium, Village, Deputy tahsildar's station; Madura dist., Pulney tal.; pop. 1,743; lat. 10° 14′; long. 77° 32′; from Dindigul W.S.W. 35 miles; from Madras S.W. 270 miles; from Madura W.N.W. 48 miles; from Pulney S. 17 miles; from Rameshwaram W.N.W. 140 miles; from Ramnaud W.N.W. 110 miles. For description see vol. II, 84 [hill station].

KOEL (कोकिल - kókila, *San.*; كوكو - kúkú, *Ar.*; كويل - koyal, *Hind.* and *Dec.*; ಕೋಗಿಲೆ - kógile, *Can.*; కోకిలము - kókilamu, *Tel.*; മുളകുപൊട്ടി - mulakupótti, *Mal.*; குயில் - kuyil, *Tam.*). Title from hindostany. San. from the sound of the bird. Hind., &c., from sanscrit. Mal. from (mulaku, mal. pepper + póttu, mal. to bring up); as feeding on pepper. Tam. from (kuyil, tam. to utter). Tel. also (kóvela). Cuculinæ, cuculidæ [cokam], scansores, insessores, aves [pacshy, 15], of naturalists [jantoo]. Bill broad, flattened at base, sides compressed to tip; wings long; tail long; tarsi short, feathered and scaled. There is a Tamul proverb:—குயிற் குரலும் மயில் அழகும் போல—"Like the voice of the cuckoo, and the beauty of "the peacock [mayil]." There is a Hindostany proverb:— كويل كالے كوے كى جورو—"The cuckoo is the black crow's wife." The species best known to the natives are shown below.——*Banded koel* (పచ్చకాటిపిట్ట - pattsakátipitta, Tel.; வரிக்குயில் - varikkuyil, Tam.). Title from markings. Tel. from (pattsa, tel. green + kátipitta, tel. bird, hierococcyx varius, vahl.). Tam. from (vari, tam. stripe + kuyil, tam. cuckoo). Cuculus sonneratii. Alias Cuculus himalayanus, pravatus, rufovittatus, venustus. Above greenish-dusky, numerously cross-barred with rufous.——*Common koel* (कोकिल kókila, San.; كويل - koyal, Hind. and Dec.; కోకిల - kókila, Tel.; കോകിലം - kókilam, Mal.; குயில் - kuyil, Tam.). Hind., &c., from sanscrit. Tam. from (kuyil, tam. to utter). Male bird is:—Tel. (nallapakki), meaning black + bird, from color. Female bird is:—Hind. (kauriyálá), meaning spotted. Tel. (podapakki), meaning spotted + bird, from spots. Eudynamys orientalis. Alias Cuculus maculatus, mindanensis, niger, scolopaceus. Male glossy greenish black throughout; bill pale-greenish, inside of the mouth reddish, irides fine crimson; legs slaty blue; length 15½ inches. Female glossy dusky-green, spotted with white above, wings and tail banded with white, beneath white, with black spots, longitudinal on throat and neck, somewhat heart-shaped or arrow-shaped on breast, transverse on abdomen, thigh-coverts, and under tail-coverts; length 7½ inches. About the breeding season the Koel is very noisy, its well-known cry 'ku-il-ku-il;' the male bird has also another note 'ho-whee-ho;' female deposits her eggs almost exclusively in the nest of the common crow [q.v.], more rarely in that of the carrion crow; mostly destroys the eggs of the crow at the time of depositing her own; flight not so quiet and gliding as that of the true cuckoos, performed with more numerous strokes of the wings.——*Hawk koel* (زكات - zakát, Hind.; కాటిపిట్ట - kátipitta, Tel.; ഇറലൻ - iralan, Mal.). Title from resemblance. Hind. means alms bird or customs bird. Tel. from (kádu, tel. forest + pitta, tel. a bird). Mal. a corruption of (iravullálan), from (ira, mal. roof + ul, mal. inside + álu, mal. to possess), from building nests under the eaves. Hind. also (kúpak). Hierococcyx varius. Alias Cuculus ejulans, fugax, lathami, tenuirostris. The common cuckoo of the plains; loud crescendo notes to be heard in the breeding season, april to july; very fond of the fig of the banyan [q.v.] and other fici [atty]; flight rapid; lays its eggs in the nest of the shikrah [q.v.]; excellent eating, being very fat.——*Shepherd koel* (پپيها - papíhá, Hind.; ಗೊಲ್ಲಕೋಗಿಲೆ - gollakógile, Can.; గొల్లకోకిల - gollakókila, Tel.). Title from following cattle. Hind. from (pika, san. indian cuckoo). Can. from (golla, can. shepherd + kógile, can. cuckoo). Hind. also (chatak), meaning bright colored. Can. also (jádige). Tel. also (tangédugóranki), meaning cassia auriculata, linn. + myna. Coccystes melanoleucos. Alias Oxylophus ater, edolius, serratoides, serratus. Above uniform black, under-parts dull white; peculiar call, a high pitched wild metallic note; flight not rapid.——*Small hawk koel* (చిన్నకాటిపిట్ట - chinnakátipitta, Tel.). Tel. from (chinna, tel. small + kátipitta, tel. hierococcyx varius, vahl.). Polyphasia nigra. Alias Cuculus flavus, niger.

KOH (كوه - koh, *Hind.*). Mountain.——*Kohistaun* (كوهستان - kohistán, Hind.). From (above + sitán, pers. place). Hill districts.——*Kohkauf* (كوه قاف - kohkáf, Hind.). From (above + káf, hind. the range of that name). A mountainous chain supposed to surround the world [locaulocam]; abode of the demons and genii, of the fairies, and of the famous simurgh or great griffin; identified by some with mount caucasus. Cf. Cashyapan.

KOHL (كحل - kohl, *Ar.*). Collyrium.

KOINAH (كنا كن - kinákin, *Hind.* and *Dec.*; జ్వరపట్టచెట్టు - jvarapattachettu, *Tel.*; സിങ്കൊയിനാ - sinkoyina, *Mal.*; கொயினா - koyiná, *Tam.*). Title from the american indian. Tel. from (jvara, san. fever + patta, tel. bark + chettu, tel. tree). Tam. also (shurappattaisattu), meaning fever + bark + essence; applies to quinine. Title otherwise Cosmibuena, Fever bark, Kinah, Kinkin, Peruvian bark plant, Quinine plant. Botanically Cinchona species, rubiaceæ [vricsham, 71].—"*a*" The genus includes trees of varying size, some reaching an altitude of 80 feet and upwards, with evergreen leaves and deciduous stipules; the flowers are arranged in panicles, white or pinkish in color, with a pleasant odour, the calyx being five-toothed superior, and the corolla tubular, five-lobed, and fringed at the margin; the stamens are five, almost concealed by the tubular corolla, and the ovary terminates in a fleshy disk; the fruit is an ovoid or sub-cylindrical capsule, splitting from the base, and held together at the apex; the numerous seeds are flat and winged all round; natives of peru; cultivated here on mountain lands.—"*b*" The following is the botanical description of cinchona officinalis, linn., the commonest of the species here cultivated:—tree reaching 35 feet or more in height, with a naked stem, or two to four stems, and an ovoid rather tapering leafy head, with spreading or even drooping branches; or a mere bush, four feet to eight feet high; leaves four to five inches long, varying from broadly oval or even sub-rotund to lanceolate, acute at both ends, usually smooth on both sides, shining full green above, paler beneath, with glandular hairy depressions in the angles of the lateral veins; capsule oblong-ovate, about ¾ inch long, and about twice as long as broad; flowers rose colored; calyx-teeth triangular acuminate; flower buds not inflated at the end. The principal varieties of officinalis are:—Uritusinga, pav., characterised by its broad large leaves, wavy or undulated at the margin, and very prominent leaf-veins; a large forest tree; original type of the species; Condaminea, howard, scarcely differs from the last in its smaller and non-wavy leaves, with less strongly marked veins, and a more lax inflorescence; Crispa, taf., the thick texture of the narrow leaves, and the very strongly marked and conspicuous scrobicules, are the characteristics of this form, which is generally little more than a shrub in habit; its name is derived from the short fracture of the bark. The following is the botanical description of cinchona calisaya, wedd., which is slightly cultivated:—very tall tree with a straight bare stem and leafy crown, or a shrub; leaves oblong, ovate-oblong, or lanceolate-obovate, usually obtuse at the apex, attenuate at the base, or rarely acute at both ends, two to seven inches long, smooth on both surfaces or pubescent beneath, with or without scrobicules, on short petioles; capsule small ovate, flower-buds usually much enlarged at the ends. The following is the botanical description of cinchona succirubra, pavon., which is cultivated here nearly as much as officinalis:— tree reaching 50 to 80 feet, head rounded-pyramidal; leaves large, rounded-ovate or ovate, obtuse, usually acute or even tapering at the base, margin wavy, bright apple green, paler beneath, becoming when withering a fine red or orange-pink, upper surface usually with fine scattered short hairs, or smooth, the veins deeply impressed, under surface with the veins, especially the midrib, very thick, prominent and pubescent, the leaf itself smooth, and forming deep concavities between the veins, no scrobicules.—"*c*" The spanish colonists of peru were the first to ascertain the nature of cinchona barks generally; the american indians regarded it as a poison, they called it kinkin or kinah, hence title; introduction into europe took place in 1640; jesuits were the first to import it on a large scale, hence jesuit's bark; all knowledge however was uncertain until the voyage of de la condamine in 1738, hence condaminea; the first were discovered in the neighbourhood of loxa, hence that name; botanists also discovered the species lancifolia, cordifolia, oblongifolia, and ovalifolia, the barks of which were orange-colored, amarilla, rosy, white, &c.; pelletier and caventou in 1820 made the discovery of the two alkalies cinchonine and quinine. The idea of cultivating cinchonas in other parts of the world than their native country was suggested by ruiz in 1792, by fée in 1824, and royle in 1839; in 1848 weddell brought cinchona seeds to the jardin des plantes, and in june 1850 seedlings raised there were sent to algeria, and in 1852 to java; prior to this in 1849 cinchona plants had been sent to algeria by the jesuits of cusco; the dutch were the first to carry on cinchona culture to any great extent, and the enterprise was conducted in java; the next large experiment was instituted by the english government on the neilgherry hills and it has been eminently successful.—"*d*" The tree is cultivated in friable loam with loose sub-soil and good drainage; ground prepared in cold season, jungle being felled and burnt and pits 18 inches cube dug four to six feet apart; seed sown in nursery usually during latter half of year, but varies according to variety; after transplanting the plant is left to itself for several years, ground only being kept clear of weeds and suckers removed; no species can be successfully grown under the shade of other trees; the calisaya alone requires a certain degree of shade; this can be secured by placing the plants close together, so that they may shade each other. The bark is usually removed about the fourth to sixth year; may be coppiced, shaved with a spokeshave, or uprooted; the three methods of harvesting bark are practised according to circumstances. On the neilgherries the bark is chiefly harvested by what is called the mossing process; in this the bark is removed from the stem in vertical strips each from 2 to 3 inches wide, a strip of bark of the same width being left intact between each two denuded surfaces; in removing the strips great care is taken to avoid injuring the cambium; when the requisite number of strips of bark has been removed, the stem of the tree is enveloped in a thick covering of moss [pausy], under which the bark speedily renews more or less perfectly; the chief advantage of this process is a great increase of alkaloids in the renewed bark, but it is doubtful whether this increase is not gained at the expense of the bark on other parts of the tree; bark harvested in this way is called mossed bark, and bark taken from trees which have not been covered with moss, unmossed bark. The following is the mode of preparing the bark after removal; the bark is placed to dry before the sun; if the pieces are thin they roll up longitudinally into thin cylinders like quills, the larger pieces may retain their original form; thus the old distinction of quill, round and flat barks, as characteristic of species, are delusive; as however the bark of moderately grown trees is the richest in the powerful alkalies, too great quilling or its total absence, are unfavorable characters of barks, as showing that the branches were either too young or too old. In the market root bark from all kinds of cinchona is in the form of short recurved or twisted pieces, thicker and lighter in color than the stem bark; shavings consist of the outer or cellular portion of the bark, and are consequently thin and brittle, and are easily crushed in packing; mossed bark has a dark surface, is usually free from lichen [cull pausy], and occurs in thick, half or single quills; renewed bark is light in color, easily fractured on account of the absence of much liber, and is known by the peculiar uniform smoothness of its external surface.—"*e*" Quinine is the product of the cinchona alkaloids; other products similar are quinidine or conquinine, cinchonine, cinchonidine, quinamine. Quinine is a light-colored, amorphous, brittle substance in an anhydrous state, but may be obtained in a crystalline condition; it is soluble in ether, alcohol, chloroform, and very slightly in water; the quinine salt mostly used in medicine is the sulphate, the theoretical composition of which is:—quinine, 74·31; sulphuric acid, 11·23; water of crystallization, 14·45; cinchona bark is sold by the unit of sulphate of quinine; the unit is the price in pence per pound of bark containing one per cent. of sulphate of quinine. A cheap quinine is manufactured at the plantations on the neilgherries. For european quinine manufacture the bark of officinalis, is best suited, being rich in quinine; though perhaps in total yield succirubra, is the richest; after those two calisaya is the most important. With the exception of opium [aphainam], no single remedy has a wider range of therapeutic uses than quinine; dried bark and powder form the official parts, being powerfully antiperiodic, tonic, and astringent; the two former properties are due to the presence of quinine; leaves also possess tonic and antiperiodic properties.—"*f*" The following are the principal species known here, but it is to be observed that practically cultivation is limited to Officinalis, Succirubra, and the hybrids between these two. Calisaya, wedd., yellow bark, bolivian bark, calisaya bark, with a well known variety called ledgeriana. Lancifolia, mutis., columbian bark. Micrantha, r. et p., huanoco or lima bark, grey bark. Nitida, r. & p., genuine grey bark, huanoco or lima bark. Officinalis, linn., the most frequently grown, crown bark, loxa bark, pale bark; with varieties; uritusinga, original loxa bark; condaminea, select crown bark; crispa, fine crown bark. Peruviana, how., huanoco or lima bark, finest grey bark. Succirubra, pav., next most frequent to officinalis; red bark, new granada bark.—"*g*" The color of the leading barks found in the druggists' shops are pale, yellow, and red. Pale or grey bark occurs in solid pieces with clear or deep grey epidermis; inner surface pale yellow or reddish; powder deep brown, contains but minute quantities of the active alkalies; comes from officinalis, nitida, micrantha, and peruviana, but here practically only from the first. Yellow bark or royal bark was brought to spain in 1789, and monopolized for the spanish royal family; the inner bark of this has a yellow color passing into orange; comes from calisaya. Red bark is frequently warty; the color of the fine quills is faint red brown; in thick pieces this darkens to chestnut, sometimes with a purple tinge; the red barks stain the fingers red, and are bitter and astringent to an extreme degree; come from succirubra.—"*h*" The following are the commercial names of the different barks, and the species to which they belong:—Bogota, lancifolia; Bolivian, calisaya; Calisaya, calisaya; Caqueta, lancifolia; Carthagena, lancifolia; Columbian, lancifolia; Coquetta, lancifolia; Crown, officinalis; Fine crown, officinalis, var. crispa; Finest grey, peruviana; Genuine grey, nitida; Grey, micrantha; Huanoco, micrantha, nitida, peruviana; Lima, micrantha, nitida, peruviana; Loxa, officinalis; New granada, succirubra; Original loxa, officinalis, var. uritusinga; Pale, officinalis; Red, succirubra; Select crown, officinalis, var. condaminea; Silver, micrantha; Yellow, calisaya.—"*i*" For cinchona planting in s. india, see vol. I, 304.

KOK (गर्ताश्रय - gartáshraya, *San.*; کور موش - kormúsh, *Pers.*; ಕೊಕ್ಕು - kokku, *Can.*; అడవిఎలుక - adavieluka, *Tel.*; പെരിച്ചാഴി - periççázhi, *Mal.*; அகழெலி - agazheli, *Tam.*). Title from canarese. San. from (garta, san. hollow + áshraya, san. resort). Pers. from (kor, pers. blind + músh, pers. mouse). Tel. from (adavi, tel. forest + eluka, tel. rat). Tam. from (agazh, tam. to dig out + eli, tam. rat); as living in holes. Tel. also (golattakokku). Title otherwise Mole-rat. Nesokia indica, muridæ, rodentia, mammalia [sastanam, 17], of naturalists [jantoo]. Alias Arvicola indica; Mus dubius, indica, kok, providens, pyctoris, rattoides. Fur long and somewhat harsh, brown mixed with fawn, the short fur softer and dusky; paler beneath and tinged gray; the color generally being like that of the common rat [ely], but with more fawn or red intermixed, and lighter beneath; head short and truncated; ears small, nearly round, covered with a fine down or small hairs; tail naked, nearly as long as the body without the head; whiskers long and full; incisors orange yellow. This is a large field-rat [varappely]; is found throughout Southern india, ranging up to a considerable altitude, above 7,000 feet. The Woddar [q.v.] or tank-diggers capture this animal in great numbers as an article of food, and during the harvest they plunder their earths of the grain stored up for their winter consumption, as to subsist almost entirely upon it, during that season of the year. The kok abounds in the richly cultivated black plains or cotton ground [regar]. A variety found in the red soil is much redder in color. This rat is occasionally destructive to tea [q.v.] trees, biting the roots just below the surface; more probably because they come in the way of their burrows than to feed on them. Indian species not here found are:—Elliotanus or elliot's field-rat, Barclayiana or barclay's field-rat, Blythiana or bengal field-rat, Hardwickii or hardwick's field-rat, Huttoni or hutton's field-rat, Scullyi or scully's field-rat.

KOLCAS (قلقاس - kulkás, *Ar.*). Latin colocasia. See Kachvee.

KOLE (कोल - kóia, *San.*; کول - kol, *Hind.*). Tribe inhabiting mountain tracts in South behar and Chota nagpore; akin to Gonds [q.v.]. There is a distant affinity to Dravidians.——*Kolaria* (कोलराज्य - kólarájya, San.). Means kola kingdom. Ancient name of India from the Koles of Central india. See vol. I (42).

KOLE (கோல் - kól, *Tam.*). Stick, measuring rod [colauttam, kole peimash]. Staff. A linear measure. 3 adees = 1 kole [alavay, 1d]. Approximate actual value, 1 kole = 28 inches. Another kole measures 6 feet, land measure. Compare Tutchacole, Tutchamoolam. See vol. I, 609; II, 515.——*Kolecauran* (கோல்காரன் - kólgáran, Tam.). The village toty [q.v.], who, as a badge of office, carries a hard bamboo [q.v.] blackened by age and fire, and shod with iron; from the end hang one or more small heart-shaped pieces of iron.——*Kolezhoot* (കോലെഴുത്ത് - kólezhuttu, Mal.). From (above + ezhuttu, mal. writing). The primitive dravidian character still in use on w. coast. See vol. I (44), (49), (128). Vattezhoot [q.v.] is better known, as a title, but in reality kolezhoot alone survives [bhaushay].

KOOCHLAH (کچلہ - kuchlah, *Hind.*). From (kuchíla, san. the tree). Same as Poison nut.——*Climbing koochlah* (کچلا لتا - kuchlálatá, Hind.). Same as Snake-wood tree.

KOOI (కోయి - kóyi, *Tel.*). Original form of Khond [coo].

KOOL (کول - kul, *Hind.*). From (kólí, san. the tree). Bair.

KOOM (کم - kum, *Ar.*). Arabic ending for second person plural; as Aleikoom, on + you.

KOOST (قسط - kust, *Ar.*). Means bad spot. Same as Costum.

KORAN (قران - kurán, *Hind.*). From (kara, ar. to read). Holy book of the Mahomedans. Distinguished in the text of the book by fifty-five special titles. Contains revelations made to the prophet [mahomed], delivered by him orally, collected and commited to writing by the caliph Omar.

KORESH (قریشی - kuraishi, *Hind.*). From (karasha, ar. to trade). A tribe of Arabs to which the prophet [mahomed] belonged and of which, according to Mahomedans, the caliph [q.v.] should also be. The Shareef [q.v.] of Mecca is always of this tribe; and to this tribe will belong also the last of the imaums [q.v.], Mahdee [imaumat].

KORKAY (கொற்கை - korgai, *Tam.*). From (kol, tam. to slay + kai, tam. hand) [col]. Arm of slaughter; poetical name for a military camp or Government head-quarters. Greek κόλχοι ἐμπόριον. Village; Tinnevelly dist., Tencaray tal.; pop. 2,289; acres 1,294; lat. 8° 39′; long. 78° 08′; from Shreeveicoontam E. 12 miles; from Tinnevelly E.S.E. 27 miles; from the sea W. 5 miles. Close to the modern Mauramungalam. Ancient seaport well known to early European geographers. It was formerly at the mouth of the Tamrapurny, but the silt of the river has spread seawards. Succeeded as a port by Cauyal, this in its turn left inland. Capital of the early Paundyans [q.v.] and one of the most important trading-marts in India. Megasthenes mentions it B.C. 302. The author of the Periplus mentions it as a celebrated place for pearl-fishery [moty]. In the Peutinger tables it is called "Colchis Indorum" to distinguish it from the Colchis in the Black sea. The Greeks named the Gulf of Manaar from this place, Colchic gulf. It was the first port visited by the Greeks after rounding Cape comorin and the first place on the Tinnevelly coast whose name was recorded by them. Excavations have been made and quantities of remains discovered in the shape of ruined houses, sepulchral urns, pottery of all kinds, Chinese and Arabian included, and coins [aursham]. The remains extend for many miles round. At the great Shiva pagoda [q.v.] at Tinnevelly the earth used in the ceremonies at the annual festivals is brought from Korkay as having been the habitation of Vamsha coolashekhara paundyan, who built temple [charitram]. See vol. I (6), (119); II, 130.——*Korkay auly* (கொற்கையாளி - korgaiyáli, Tam.). From (above + áli, tam. ruler). Title of the Paundy king.

KOS (කොස් - kós, *Singh.*). Gum from jack in Ceylon.

KOTA (कोट - kóta, *San.*; کوٹ - kotá, *Hind.*; కోట - kóta, *Tel.*). Fort [cote, cottah, cottay].—"*a*" Deputy tahsildarry, Nellore district, situated east of Goodoor. Pay Rs. 70.—"*b*" Village, Head-quarters of Deputy tahsildar; Nellore dist., Goodoor tal.; pop. 5,203; acres 8,501; lat. 14° 02′; long. 80° 05′; from Goodoor E.S.E. 15 miles; from Madras N. 69 miles; from Naidoopett N.E. 14 miles; from Nellore S. 29 miles; from Ongole S. 103 miles; from the sea W. 7 miles. Celebration in honor of Cotamma once every five years; formerly with swinging festival [shirry]. The temple of Cotamma was built by Tondiman [q.v.] kings. Supplies betels [q.v.] to Nellore market. Large tank.

KOTAH (ಕೋಟ - kóta, *Can.*). A hill tribe of Neilgherries.—"*a*" Language an old and very rude canarese; the chief difference between todah [q.v.] and kotah lies in the deep guttural pronunciation of the todahs, the kotahs' pronunciation being more dental; the dialects are mutually understood; in kotah language an unusual number of words end in (*é*).—"*b*" Probably next to Todahs as to length of residence on hills. They have a settlement at foot of western slopes near Goodalore, and, like the Todahs, their oldest village or street is in the western highlands of the Todanaud. There is a tradition among them that they once lived on a mountain in Mysore called Collimullay after which they named the first village they built on the Neilgherries. The Todahs say that they were brought from the plains to work for them, which is probably true. They occupy seven villages on the hills, each called Kotagherry.—"*c*" Their color is lighter than other tribes and inclined to copper. They are better-looking and of stronger physique than Coorumbar [q.v.] or Iroolar [q.v.], having well formed heads and well shaped noses. Their cheek-bones are high and prominent, and they have generally an air of decision. The men wear their hair, which is black, straight and long, parted down the middle, either loose or tied in a knot behind. In the men the forehead is inclined to be prominent. In the women this defect is more marked, and they are generally less good-looking. The noses of the women are shorter and inclined to a snub, and the chin is short and angular. The dress of the men consists of the usual coarse unbleached cloth. The women have a similar one, which is worn over one shoulder and under the other arm, and forms a kind of petticoat reaching just below the knees. They are fond of rude ornaments, bracelets, armlets, and necklaces of seeds and wire. The dress of the dancers who attend festivals is peculiar; it is a loose ill-made gown of calico [q.v.], with a skirt gathered very full round the waist and reaching to the ankles; this is ornamented with country red cloth sewn on in patterns, a bright-colored girdle or scarf, and a handkerchief [roomaul] round the neck; trousers of colored cotton [q.v.] stuff and a turban [puggry] complete the costume; it is evidently borrowed in part from the mahomedans and so far cannot be very ancient; their national dance requires six or eight performers, who stand in a row, their motions being uniform; the effect of these dresses when the dancers twirl together from one side to the other is singular; the main characteristic of the dance in fact is the way in which their draperies swing to and fro with the measure.—"*d*" The Kotahs have one special deity Caumataroya, but they also worship his wife Kalikay; each is represented by a silver plate. These are sometimes supposed to be Shiva [q.v.] and Parvaty [q.v.]. Their temples are mere pent-houses of thatch, open at both ends, and supported by square stone pillars sculptured after the same fashion as the pillars of their verandahs [q.v.], but on a larger scale; there is no image of any kind; there are two or more of these temples in each village. Of their two great annual festivals one is in honor of caumataroya; it lasts for a fortnight in february and gives them an opportunity for decorating themselves in any dresses, ornaments, &c., that they can borrow, and of performing their national dance to the music of their drums [paray] and horns [comboo] accompanied by singing; on the day appointed they collect together, bringing shaumay [q.v.] rice with them, which is boiled in front of the temple, and offered with other articles to the idol, with dancing, singing, and music, which is continued for two days; a piece of tobacco [pogauk] is given to each person present. The other feast is in honor of the dead who have died during the year, and answers in some respects to the Todah green funeral [kerd]. Occasionally a kotah becomes possessed by a god; he then yells, dances, rolls about and performs the most frantic gestures until at last he falls down in a kind of fit. Kotahs are not allowed to enter a Badaga [q.v.] temple or to join in their annual feast to Hettey [q.v.], to which the Todahs are invited.—"*e*" Kotahs recognise no caste among themselves; the divisions are keries or streets, though these now appear to have little to do with locality; they always seek their wives from another kery [q.v.]. The kotahs are the artizans of the hills and are necessary to all the other tribes as their blacksmiths, carpenters, tanners, rope-makers, umbrella-makers, potters, musicians, and workers in gold and silver; consequently their villages have sprung up in the localities which enabled them to pursue their handicrafts and to find a ready sale for their wares. Every Badaga village has a number of Moottkotahs or attached kotahs living in the nearest Kotagherry. Each Badaga also has a particular individual among the Moottkottahs who works for him and who is repaid in grain at harvest time. The Kotahs work in the same way for the other tribes, who pay them in the produce they possess. Todahs pay them in dead buffaloes [khoolgah] and ghee [q.v.], the Coorumbar in grain, and the Iroolar in plantains [q.v.] and grain. They are also well paid for their music, and often receive ¼ rupee each for playing at a feast. On their part they pay the usual tribute in grain or goodoo [q.v.] to the Todahs. The Kotahs always attend the funerals and obsequies of the Todahs, &c., and receive from them the carcases of the buffaloes that are offered in sacrifice, allowing from a half to a quarter of a rupee for some, if they cannot give payment in service. The Kotahs burn their dead [shoodcaud], collect the bones on the following day, and bury these in a hole, marking the spot where they have done so. This they do in order to the performance of the obsequies. On the night of the first Monday after the first new moon [amavausyay] in the month of March, all the friends of the deceased assemble, and, preceded by music, go to the place of burning. Kotah villages are large and generally contain sixty houses or more; the houses are of mud and thatch, not so regularly arranged as those of the badagas and only saved from a squalid appearance by the patches of cultivation which surround them; though the houses are devoid of ornament, the pillars of the verandah are sometimes of stone sculptured by cutters from the low country. Kotahs are on the whole intelligent and hardworking, and their monogamous customs seem likely to ensure their rapid increase in numbers. The customs of marriage, divorce, &c., are the same as those of the Badagas. Those in lower circumstances are in a state of servitude, and are employed in cutting wood, making charcoal [adoopp kary], &c.—"*f*" See vol. I, (51); II, 109.——*Kotagherry* (ಕೋಟಗಿರಿ - kótagiri, Can. kotagiri *). From (above + giri, san. hill). A hill occupied by Kotar.—"*a*" Village; Neilgherry dist., Paranginaud div.; pop. 4,284; acres 7,660; lat. 11° 25′; long. 76° 54′; height 6,500 feet; from Coimbatore N. 32 miles; from Coonoor N.E. 7 miles; from Devaulah E.S.E. 32 miles; from Madras W.S.W. 258 miles; from Ootacamund E.N.E. 12 miles; from Pundalore E.S.E. 36 miles. Every Kotah village on the hills is called Kotagherry by the natives. There are two such in Paranginaud, two in Todanaud, one in Merkoonaud, and one in the Coondahs. The Kotagherry above is the largest colony of Kotahs.—"*b*" Ghaut; Neilgherry dist., Paranginaud div.; from Coonoor E. 10 miles; from Ootacamund E. 17 miles. There are two lines known as the Old and New kotagherry ghauts [q.v.]. For description see vol. II, 85. There was once an anicut [q.v.] from Devanaickencottah to Dimhutty by Tainaud and Keel kotagherry below Rungasawmy's peak and Nedoongoolam; the distance being 20 miles [hill station].

KOTIYEH (കോട്ടിയ - kóttiya, *Mal.*). Ceylon word. A fast-sailing vessel, with two masts and lateen sails, employed on the Malabar coast.

KOTODY (کوٹھری - kothrí, *Hind.*). From (kósht'ha, san. apartment). Room, gymnasium.

KOYFUL (کائی پھل - káiphal, *Hind.*). From (katu, san. sharp + p'hala, san. fruit). Wild nutmeg.

KRAIT (کریت - karait, *Hind.*; ಕಡಬಲಕೆ - kadabalake, *Can.*; తుట్టెపురుగు - tuttepurugu, *Tel.*; പനയൻ - panayan, *Mal.*; பனைவிரியன் - panaiviriyan, *Tam.*). Tel. from (tutte, tel. rubbish + purugu, tel. reptile); from its resort. Mal. from (pana, mal. palmyra tree, borassus flabelliformis, linn. + an, mal. personal suffix). Tam. from (panai, tam. palmyra tree + viriyan, tam. viper). Hind. also (társámp), meaning palmyra snake. Tel. also (gaddiparugudu), meaning grass + runner. Title otherwise White-arched bungaur. Bungarus cæruleus, elapidæ [haug], ophidii colubriformes venenosi, ophidia [sarpam], reptilia [sarpy, 27], of naturalists [jantoo]. Compare Bungaur, which is Bungarus fasciatus. Alias Boa krait, lineata; Bungarus arcuatus, candidus, lineatus, lividus; Pseudoboa cærulea. Lower parts uniform white; upper parts bluish or brownish-black, uniform, or with more or less numerous very narrow white cross streaks, not quite as broad as a scale, and generally radiating from a white vertebral spot. No collar. It varies in size from two feet to four and a half. The fangs are smaller than those of the cobra [q.v.]. It is found in fields, huts, houses, in book-cases, ledges of windows, and venetians. It is often mistaken for the Lycodon aulicus, which is an innocent snake. In the krait the hexagonal scales on back and its fangs are sufficient to distinguish it from the Lycodon aulicus. It is also darker than Lycodon. This is next to the cobra, the snake most destructive to human life. Terrestrial snake; feeding on small mammals, lizards [chipkalee], small snakes [sarpam], and toads [bhaicam]; diurnal, yet prefers the shade to the sun. Shy and attempts to escape, but when attacked defends itself fiercely.

KRAYAM (क्रय - kraya, *San.*). From (krí, san. to sell). Sale. Kraya shausanam is a bill of sale.

KRI (कृ - kri, *San.*). To do [car, caur, kar].——*Kritam* (कृत - krita, San.). From (kri, san. to do). Done. The side of the die marked with four points. The first or golden age [yoog].——*Krita yoogaudy* (కృతయుగాది - kritayugádi, Tel.). From (kritayuga, san. the age + ádi, san. beginning). The same as Doorga navamy.——*Krity* (కృతి - kriti, Tel.). Writing of books; one of the seven meritorious acts.——*Kriyah lopam* (क्रियालोप - kriyálópa, San.). From (kriyá, san. rite + lópa, san. omission). Neglect of essential ceremonies involving loss of caste [jauty].——*Kriyay* (क्रिया - kriyá, San.). From (kri, san. to do). Action in general; religious ceremony. The second of the four stages of progress towards union with deity [yogam].

KRISH (कृष् - krish, *San.*). To draw, to plough; to attract.——*Kistna* (కృష్ణ - krishna, Tel.); means dark-blue; from color of the waters.—"*a*" Revenue district; situated on the Coromandel coast [q.v.]; between 15° 36′ and 17° 09′ lat., and between 79° 17′ and 81° 36′ E. long.; bounded N. by Nizam's dominions and Godavery district, E. by Godavery district and Bay of Bengal, S. by Bay of Bengal and Nellore district, W. by Kurnool district and Nizam's dominions; square miles 8,397; pop. 1,855,582; language Teloogoo. Contains rivers Kistna, Moonair, Naugilair and Palair; ports Cottapollem, Eepoorpollem, Gungadipollem, Masulipatam, Mortota, Motoopully, Naugayalunka, Nizampatam and Penoomoody; mountains Bellamcondah, Condapully, Condaveed, and Jamalavoy droog; sanitarium Dindey. The whole area of the district is represented by the following sub-areas, where talook [q.v.] means an ordinary tract administered by a Tahsildar [q.v.], and division means a Zemindarry [q.v.] tract administered by a superior Deputy tahsildar:—Baupatla talook, Bezwada talook, Bunder talook, Goodivauda talook, Guntoor talook, Krittivenn zemindarry, Lingagherry zemindarry, Meilavaram zemindarry, Moongaula zemindarry, Narsarowpett talook, Noozveed division, Nundigauma talook, Pulnaud talook, Repully talook, Sullapully zemindarry, Suttenapully talook, Valloor zemindarry, Vinoocondah talook, Vissanapett division. For general administrative purposes the district is distributed between the following revenue and magisterial officers, who have their head-quarters at the places shown. The pay set opposite the subordinate officers gives the grade of the corresponding charge:—Collector, Masulipatam; Sub-collector, Guntoor, in charge of Baupatla, Guntoor, Suttenapully and Repully talooks; Head assistant collector, Bezwada, in charge of Bezwada and Nundigauma talooks and Vissanapett and Noozveed divisions; General deputy collector, Vinoocondah, in charge of Pulnaud, Narsarowpett and Vinoocondah talooks. Tahsildars; Baupatla, Rs. 225; Bezwada, Rs. 150; Bunder, Rs. 175; Goodivauda, Rs. 200; Guntoor, Rs. 225; Narsarowpett, Rs. 200; Nundigauma, Rs. 150; Pulnaud, Rs. 200; Repully, Rs. 250; Suttenapully, Rs. 175; Vinoocondah, Rs. 150. Deputy tahsildars; Avanigadda, Rs. 70, range situated in the south of Bunder talook; Juggayapett, Rs. 70, range situated in the north-west of Nundigauma talook; Keicalore, Rs. 70, range situated in the north-east of Goodivauda talook; Mungalagherry, Rs. 70, range situated in the north of Guntoor talook; Noozveed, Rs. 100, range conterminous with the zemindarry; Ponnore, Rs. 70, range situated in the north of Baupatla talook; Tenally, Rs. 70, range situated in the north of Repully talook; Toomaracote, Rs. 70, range situated in the west of Pulnaud talook; Vissanapett, Rs. 100, range conterminous with the zemindarry. Sub-magistrate, Bunder town, Rs. 70, jurisdiction extending over the municipal town of Masulipatam. Port officer and Special first-class magistrate, Bunder fort, Rs. 300, jurisdiction extending over the fort of Masulipatam. Sub-magistrate, Guntoor, Rs. 70; jurisdiction extending over the town of Guntoor. Similarly judicial officers:—Judge, Masulipatam. District moonsifs; Baupatla with jurisdiction extending over portions of Repully, Baupatla and Narsarowpett talooks; Bezwada with jurisdiction extending over Keicalore division in Goodivauda talook, Bezwada and Nundigauma talooks, Noozveed and Vissanapett divisions. Coochipoody agrahauram, Bunder talook; Ellore sub-judge division, Caurampoody with jurisdiction extending over Pulnaud and Vinoocondah talooks and portions of Narsarowpett and Suttenapully talooks; Guntoor with jurisdiction extending over Guntoor talook, portions of Repully, Baupatla and Narsarowpett talooks; Masulipatam with jurisdiction extending over Bunder talook, except Coochipoody agrahauram, and Goodivauda talook except Keicalore division. Similarly Public works officers:—District engineer, Bezwada; Superintending engineer, Bezwada, Executive engineers, Dooggiraula, Bezwada, Goodivauda. Sub-divisional officers Baupatla, Dooggiraula, Masulipatam, Bezwada and Cowtaram. Contains Registration sub-districts:—Avanigadda, Baupatla, Bezwada, Bunder, Dauchepully, Goodivauda, Guntoor, Juggayapett, Narsarowpett, Noozveed, Nundigauma, Ponnore, Repully, Suttenapully, Tenally, Toomaracote, Vinoocondah. Contains Forest ranges:—Baupatla, Bezwada, Bunder, Crossoor, Guntoor, Pulnaud, Vinoocondah. Contains Municipalities:—Bezwada, Guntoor and Masulipatam. Contains district board and talook boards; Bunder, embracing Bunder and Goodivauda talooks including Zemindarries; Bezwada, embracing Bezwada and Nundigauma talooks and Noozveed and Vissanapett divisions; Guntoor, embracing Guntoor and Suttenapully talooks; Repully, embracing Baupatla and Repully talooks; Vinoocondah, embracing Vinoocondah, Narsarowpett and Pulnaud talooks. The following are the zemindarries:—Balliparroo, Calagara, Capileshwarapooram, Chevendra, Chinna gollapollem, Chintalapauty vantoo, Chitty goodoor, Comirey, Condore and Cumbampaud, Coochipoody, Devarcote, Devarpully, Goodoor pergunnah, Gumpalagoodem, Inagadapa, Kokilampand, Krittivenn samoot, Lingagherry, Medore, Meilavaram mittah, Mirjapooram, Mooncoolla, Moongaula pergunnah, Narsayyagoodem, Ootcore, Pengolloo, Pingoodoor lunka, Pootraila, Royavaram, Sanoobunda, Tailaprole, Tirvore, Valloor samoot, Ventrapragada, Vissanapett, Vooyyoor. The following general references should be made to the preceding volumes:—general geography, I (1) to (29); general ethnology, I (29) to (109); general history, I (110) to (188); physical geography, II, 1; meteorology, II, 3; geology, II, 8; fauna, II, 21; flora, II, 26; mineralogy, II, 29. The following references in the preceding volumes will furnish details special to the district:—latitudes and longitudes, II, 47; particulars about towns, II, 48; coast survey, II, 164; light-houses, II, 169; comparative population, II, 172; location of revenue officers, II, 386; revenue settlement of the district, II, 412; registrars' and sub-registrars' stations, II, 421; ports, II, 423; salt factories, II, 426; rain-guage stations, II, 428; police divisions, II, 431; maps published, II, 436; survey topographical lists, II, 443; hospitals and dispensaries, II, 447; missionary stations, II, 455; head-quarter stations of gazetted officers, II, 461; incidence of taxation, II, 463; weights and measures of the district, II, 511; zemindarries contained, I, 59, and II, 298; special public works, I, 396. A special gazetteer account of the whole district is given at II, 82. For the detailed topography of the district, reference should be made to the talook notices in the present volume, viz.:—Baupatla, Bezwada, Bunder, Goodivauda, Guntoor, Krittivenn, Lingagherry, Meilavaram, Moongaula, Narsarowpett, Noozveed, Nundigauma, Pulnaud, Repully, Sullapully, Suttenapully, Valloor, Vinoocondah, Vissanapett.—"*b*" River; Kistna dist., Bunder tal. The μαίσωλος of Ptolemy is often taken for the Godavery; but in these pages it is taken for the Kistna; compare Masulipatam. In maps down to those of the sixteenth, seventeenth, and even eighteenth century, the Godavery was omitted altogether. The Booddhist [booddha] civilization on the Kistna absorbed attention, being the prototype of the later Bramin civilization on the Cauvery. The river rises at Mahableshwar, on the eastern brow of the Western ghauts [q.v.], 4,500 feet above sea level and in lat. 18° 00′, long. 73° 44′, 40 miles east of the western coast of the peninsula. Here stands an ancient temple of Mahadeo, at the foot of a steep hill. In the interior is a small tank, into which a stream of pure water ever pours out of a spout fashioned into the image of a cow's mouth. This is the traditional fountain-head of the river, which is likened to the deity in a female form, and called Krishna bye. Pilgrims in large numbers crowd to the sacred spot, which is embowered in trees of dark foliage and flowering shrubs. Like the Godavery and Cauvery the Kistna flows almost across the peninsula from west to east. Taking a south-easterly course of about 145 miles through the territory of Sattaura, and thence dividing that province from the jagheers [q.v.] of the Southern mahratta country for a further distance of 10 miles, in lat. 16° 45′, long. 74° 34′, on the right side, it receives the Warna, flowing from the west. From that confluence flowing south-east for 158 miles, alternately between and through the jagheers of the southern Mahratta country, Sattaura, and the British district of Belgaum and Caladgy, it on the right side receives the Ghautprabha, and thence holds a similar course for 35 miles, separating the collectorates of Sholapore and Belgaum, to lat. 16° 10′, long. 76° 17′, where it arrives at the territory of the Nizam [q.v.]. During this part of its course, besides the Ghautprabha, it receives on the right side, 22 miles lower down, the Maulprabha, besides several small torrents on the right and left. All these, like the main stream, are characteristic rivers of the plateau of the Deccan [q.v.]. They run in deep channels, from which it is almost impossible to lead off channels [q.v.] for irrigation. In the rainy season they swell into brimming torrents, but during the remaining eight months of the year they shrink to mere threads of water, straggling through a sandy waste. The river, skirting the territory of the Nizam for about 10 miles, passes into it, and holds through it a course north-east for about 60 miles, to lat. 16° 33′, long. 77° 02′ where it turns south-east, and, flowing in that direction 25 miles, on the left side receives, in lat. 16° 24′, long. 77° 20′, the Bheema, a large tributary from the north-west. Continuing to flow in a south-easterly direction 80 miles farther, it receives on the right side, at Sangam in lat. 15° 58′, long. 78° 18′, the Toongabudra, from the south-west. At this point it enters British territory. On entering the Nizam's dominions the Kistna drops from the tableland of the Deccan proper down to the alluvial Doabs [q.v.] of Sharapore and Ryechore. The fall is as much as 408 feet in about 3 miles. The first of the Doabs mentioned above is formed by the confluence of the Bheema, which brings down the drainage of Ahmednugger, Poona, and Sholapore; the second by the confluence of the Toongabudra, which drains the north of Mysore and the districts of Bellary and Kurnool. Flowing north-easterly for 180 miles through an uninhabited tract in the wilds of the Nullamullays, a zigzag course across the plateau on which the famous Srisheilam or Parvatam pagoda [q.v.] stands, in a wide and steep sided trench of nearly 1,000 feet in depth, it reaches Rauvairila in lat. 16° 50′, long. 80° 08′. During this part of its course it receives the Bhavanausy. After passing through the Nullamullays the river turns south-east, and enters Kistna district at Chintapully, near its confluence with the Palair. Between the confluence of the Toongabudra and Chintapully, it receives on the left side, from the territory of the Nizam, the Dindy, the Moosy; on whose banks stands Hyderabad, the Palair, the Seena, and the Neema; and a few miles below its entrance into the plain, the Moonair, flowing in a southerly direction. On the right it receives the S. Wardhah and Hagary. During its course through the mountains, its tributaries, though numerous, are all unimportant. From the confluence of the Toongabudra to that of the Palair, it forms the boundary between the territory of the Nizam and the districts of Kurnool and Kistna; thus giving the general boundary between this Presidency and the Nizam's dominions. From Chintapully, the river holds a course of 70 miles south-east to Bobbar lunka in Kistna district, lat. 16° 5′, long. 80° 56′, where it parts into two arms, the one flowing south-east 30 miles, and falling into the Bay of Bengal at Point divy, in lat. 15° 57′, long. 81° 13′; the other flowing south 25 miles, and falling into the Bay of Bengal, in lat. 15° 45′, long. 80° 53′; inclosing between them a delta [conamoogam] traversed by a third branch sent off from the southern arm, and by some water courses from the main branches. The delta is traversed by others of less magnitude, which are numerous during inundations. The total length of the river is about 1,000 miles and the total area of its catchment basin [nadee] about 97,050 square miles. As a great part of the course of the Kistna and its tributaries flow through alluvial soil [vandal munn], the flood-water is heavily charged with silt [adaimunn]. When it reaches Bezwada, it is confined between two gneissic hills, the width of the gorge being about 1,300 yards. At this point the velocity of the river in flood is rather more than 6·5 miles an hour, and the maximum flood discharge is 761,000 cubic feet per second. The solid matter carried by the flood-water past Bezwada is $\frac{1}{232}$ of the bulk. It follows that the Kistna in high flood carries past Bezwada daily enough detritus to form a deposit one foot deep over a surface of 5 square miles. Below Bezwada to the sea, the fall of the river is only 0·66 foot per mile, and the bed widens out to 3 or 4 miles, so that in the course of ages an extensive deltaic tarct has formed between Bezwada and the coast. This delta slopes away on either side, with a fall of about 18 inches per mile from the elevated river bed; hence all that is not protected by embankments is submerged whenever a high flood occurs, and the deposition of fluviatile alluvium still continues. The colair lake represents the work still to be done by this alluvium in levelling up the land wrested from the sea by the rivers. The actual mouths of the rivers have thrown out low promontories far into the sea. The river is subject to two periodical inundations annually. The first and principal, caused by the south-west monsoon [q.v.] precipitating its heavy rains on the Western ghauts, Mysore, and other elevated tracts about the upper parts of the river's course, takes place about June; the other, and much smaller one caused by the local rains brought by the north-east monsoon, occurs about October. In consequence of the rapid declivity of its water way and rockiness of channel, the river may be said to be almost entirely useless for navigation. From Juggayapett down to the Bezwada anicut [q.v.], about 50 miles, the river is navigable for about six months of the year by sea-going dhonies [q.v.], which are brought up either by the Bunder or the Ellore canal. The mode of crossing at the ferries is by wide circular baskets, made of hides [chararah] stretched over a framework of bamboos [q.v.]. Near Ryechore, the main stream is crossed by an iron girder bridge of the Great indian peninsula railway. In utility for irrigation the Kistna is inferior to the Godavery or the Cauvery. Throughout the whole upper portion of its course it runs in a deep bed, with high, very steep, almost perpendicular banks rising from 30 to 50 feet above its ordinary level. Here it drains rather than waters the surrounding country. As to its tributaries, the head-waters of the Bheema are dammed up at Kharakwasla to furnish Poona with a water-supply; and the Madras irrigation company expended large sums of money to water Kurnool from the floods of the Toongabudra. On the main stream, a small work has been constructed high up in Sattaura district, called the Kistna canal. A dam has here been thrown across the bed of the river, from which a canal is taken parallel to the left bank, capable of irrigating an area of 1,825 acres. But the greatest irrigation work on the Kistna is the Bezwada anicut, for description of which see vol. I, 396. In the Kistna delta there are several lines of canals. The principal line of navigable canal are as follows:—Bezwada to Ellore, 39 miles; Bezwada to Masulipatam creek, 48 miles; Kistna anicut to Nizampatam creek, 41 miles; Dooggiraula, at 12th mile of No. 3 Nizampatam canal, to Santaravore near Incolloo to which point the Buckingham canal [q.v.] is opened, 50 miles. The secondary lines of navigable canal are as follows:—Paumarroo, 31st mile of Masulipatam canal, to Vinzarampaud near Keicalore, 26 miles; Revendrapaud 8th mile of Nizampatam canal to Collore, 20 miles. Proposed lines of navigable canal are as follows:—Cowtaram to Ooppootair below Colair lake *viâ* Buntoomilly, 25 miles; Cowtaram to Ooppootair below Colair lake near Aucveed, continuation of No. 5, 26¼ miles; Yenamala coodroo 4th mile, Masulipatam canal to Pooligedda in Divy island, 36 miles; Revendrapaud 8th mile, Nizampatam canal to Gungadipollem near mouth of Kistna, continuation of No. 6, 45¾ miles. The Kistna, though less sacred than the Godavery and Cauvery, is a very sacred river. Nivritty sangam, or the junction of the river with the Bhavanausy, is considered a holy place of pilgrimage. Once in twelve years it is said that the river attains a peculiar sanctity when Jupiter [brihaspaty] enters the Canyay [q.v.] sign [raushy] of the zodiac [raushy chuckram] and that all sins are then washed away from the bather. Cf. Mahamagbam and Pooshcaram. Near this place is a lingam [q.v.] said to have been originally made of wood and established by Dharmarajan [q.v.], the chief hero of the Mahabhaurat [q.v.]. Delay having occurred in the receipt of a stone lingam from Benares, Dharmarajan, when the auspicious hour arrived, established a wooden lingam which in process of time has been petrified. A short distance below the junction is a whirlpool called Chuckra teertam, regarded as having been caused by the discus [chuckram] weapon of Krishnan [q.v.], being thrown there.——*Kistnapatam* * (కృష్ణాపట్నము - krishnápatnamu, Tel.). From (krishna, tel. proper name + pattana, san. town). Named after krishna deva royel. Greek *σωπάτμα*. Title otherwise Calitore. Village, Port, Salt factory, Backwater; Nellore dist., Goodoor tal.; pop. 2,807; acres 7,142; lat. 14° 17′; long. 80° 10′; from Goodoor E.N.E. 21 miles; from Madras N. 82 miles; from Meipaud S. 15 miles; from Nellore S.E. 15 miles; from Paumanjy N. 16 miles. On the Buckingham canal [q.v.], connected by road with Nellore. The canal basin is generally called the Mootcore basin from the village on road 3 miles distant. Anchorage outside the bar is unsafe, not being a good holding ground; but within the bar there is a fine backwater with great depth of water. The entrance to the backwater is always open, and the channel by which ships come in is 40 yards wide, and on the bar ordinarily 9 feet deep at mean tide, at high tide 11 feet. The whole width of the mouth is 500 or 600 yards. The channel shifts its position with the season of the year. A place of shelter for native craft during the monsoons [q.v.] and in the stormy months of April and May. Dhonies [q.v.] are sometimes taken into dock and repaired at this port. There used to be trade in salt; chief trade now is grain. It has been proposed to make the irrigation canal from Nellore to Kistnapatam navigable. Trig. station at the Beacon; lat. 14° 17′ 51·75″; long. 80° 11′ 1·11″; from Goodoor N.E. 22 miles; from Mootcore E. 3 miles; from the sea W. ¼ mile. For Collector's bungalow here see Conamoola.——*Krishna* (कृष्ण - krishna, San.). From (krish, san. to attract); originally applied to an attractive dark-blue. Black [calam, car, caulam, caur]. Plant first term, often joining two genera. Ex., where transl. is of second term:—Canna indica (krishnatámara), nelumbium speciosum; Justicia gendarussa (krishnanirgundi), vitex negundo; Murraya kœnigii (krishnanimba), melia azadirachta; Phyllanthus multiflorus (krishnakámbhójí), abrus precatorius. See gloss. paragraphs.——*Krishna ashtamy* (కృష్ణాష్టమి - krishnáshtami, Tel.). From (krishna, san. the god + ashtami, san. eighth lunar day). The eighth lunar day [tity] of the waning moon [krishna pacsham] of fifth lunar [chaundra maunam] month Shrauvanam [mausam] as having been the birth-day of Krishnan. Same as Krishna jayanty.——*Krishna bhoomy* (కృష్ణభూమి - krishnabhúmi, Tel.). From (krishna, san. black + bhúmi, san. soil). Means black soil. Same as regar.——*Krishna chooday* (कृष्णचूडा - krishnachúdá, San.). Means Krishnan's hair jewel, from flower. Same as Gold mohur tree.——*Krishnadeva roya* (కృష్ణదేవరాయ - krishnadévaráya, Tel.). From (krishna, san. the god + déva, san. lord + rájá, san. king). Otherwise Krishnaroya. Rajah of Vijianugger of the Narsimha dynasty. A.D. 1509–1530. Extended his dominions to the north as far as the Kistna, defeating the Adil shahy sultan of Beejapore; to Warangal and Cuttack in the east, whose daughter he married as bond of peace; to Salsette in the west; on the south to Mysore, Madura and Trichinopoly. A great patron of Sanscrit and Teloogoo literature; the eight Ashta diggajams [q.v.] flourished in his Court. His minister was Timmarajah, the Hem rajah of the Mahomedan historians [charitram]. See vol. I (150), (153); II, 80, 250.——*Krishna dosham* (कृष्णदोष - krishnadósha, San.). From (krishna, san. black + dósha, san. disorder). From attendant symptoms of dark spots and dark tongue and lips and teeth. Typhus fever [veidyan].——*Krishnagherry* (கிருட்டிணக்கிரி - kiruttinakkiri, Tam.). See sep. title.——*Krishna jananam* (కృష్ణజననం - krishnajananam, Tel.). From (krishna, san. the god + janana, san. birth). Same as Krishna jayanty.——*Krishna jayanty* (కృష్ణజయంతి - krishnajayanti, Tel.). Means krishnan's day of rejoicing. Otherwise Shree jayanty [q.v.]. Lunar [chaundra maunan] festival [pundigay, 6c], subject to intercalation [adhicam]. The eighth day of waning moon [krishna pacsham] of fifth lunar month Shrauvanam [mausam] between 8th August and 7th September. Anniversary of Vishnoo's incarnation [avatar] as Krishnan [q.v.]. Celebrated in houses and in Vishnoo [q.v.] pagodas [q.v.]. Natives form figures out of clay representing Krishnan and his family, and worship them during the night, observing a fast. In pagodas the festival is celebrated for nine days, during which the image of Vishnoo is carried in procession through the streets. The festival is particularly observed by shepherds [yaudava] in commemoration of Krishnan having been brought up amongst them [maryauday].——*Krishnamma* (కృష్ణమ్మ - krishnamma, Tel.). From (krishna, san. the god + amma, tel. mother). Hindoo 2nd or pers. name. Common to both sexes. Taken by males among Veishnava bramins, Comaties, and Shoodras [peyar].——*Krishnan* (कृष्ण - krishna, San.; கிருட்டிணன் - kiruttinan, Tam.). Means black, from color of person. ἀπόλλων of Greeks; Apollo of Romans; Osiris or occident deity or setting luminary of Egyptians. Eighth avatar [q.v.] of Vishnoo [q.v.].—"*a*" Krishnan's life is related at length in the Vishnoo pooraunam [q.v.] and other books. Krishnan was the son of Vasoodevan by his wife Devaky, a sister of Cumsan, a king who from jealousy ordered the child to be destroyed. This was attempted by Pootanay his nurse. The parents therefore gave their son in charge to Nundan [q.v.], a shepherd, who was in turn ordered by the king to kill the child. But as the shepherd's wife Yashoday had taken a fancy to the child they adopted him instead of a child which they had lost. Thus Krishnan grew up as Gopaulan [q.v.], a cowherd among cowherds. His favorite mistress was Raudhay. The Geeta govindam [q.v.] is a poem on their amours. He exchanged however soon the life of a shepherd for that of politician and warrior, joining the five Pandavas [pandoo] his relatives, and becoming their ambassador and a charioteer of Arjoonan [q.v.] whence his epithet Partasauraty [q.v.], in their war with Dooryodhanan [q.v.]. Throughout the war which he advocated, his was the presiding mind, while Arjoonan was the principal hero and Dharma rajan the nominal head of the confederacy. The war ended in the defeat of Dooryodhanan [mahabhaurat]. Krishnan was vulnerable in his sole only. One day when he sat in a forest, engaged in thought and resting his foot upon his knee, a hunter named Jaray came, and beholding from a distance the foot of Krishnan mistook it for the foot of a deer [mrigam], and shooting his arrow lodged it in the sole. Krishnan then abandoned his mortal body, and was in the language of the Vishnoo pooraunam united with his own self, or the universal spirit.—"*b*" There is a considerable coincidence between the account of the infancy of Cyrus, as stated by Herodotus, and the infancy of Krishnan, as narrated in the tenth book of the Bhangavatam [q.v.]. The avatar of Krishnan was outside of India proper. The Pandavas were probably rulers in Cashmere. Partasauraty, or the car-driver of the Paurtan, is the name by which Krishnan is worshipped at the great pagoda [q.v.] at Triplicane, Madras.—"*c*" Krishnan is generally represented as a man standing on one leg and playing a flute [pillangrovy]. The separate scenes of his life however are represented in the arts. One is krishnan with his chief wife raudhay, daughter of the shepherd nundan and krishnan's foster sister. Another is ponna maunoo krishnan; when the gopicays or milk-maids were bathing in the jumna, krishnan removed their cloths and climbed a ponna maunoo tree or alexandrian laurel [common poon]. Another is chemboo krishnan or krishnan as a child carrying a pot. The scene of cauliya krishnan represents him jumping into the tank of cauliya, the king of snakes, then standing on the head of the snake and playing the flute. Murry aukoo krishnan represents him floating on a banyan [q.v.] leaf in the water. Another scene represents krishnan seated on a five-headed cobra [q.v.], keeping his right toe in his mouth and surrounded with ten avatars or incarnations of himself. Baulakrishnan is the infant krishnan seated on a five-headed cobra, his right toe in his mouth and his mother standing by with a peacock [mayil]. Doogdhya krishnan is krishnan being induced by his mother yashoday to eat butter when in the action of crawling. In the scene of govardhana krishnan he as a boy of seven years old lifts up the mountain govardhanam to protect the gopas [q.v.] and gopicays from a storm sent by indran [q.v.]. See vol. I (74). Gopaulkrishnan is krishnan grown up as a cowherd [matam].—"*d*" Hindoo 2nd or pers. name [peyar]. Familiarly corrupted into Kittan, Kittoo, Kittah and Kitty and sometimes Keelan. In Tel. and Can. it becomes Kishta, Kishtoo and Kishty.——*Krishna pacsham* (कृष्णपक्ष - krishnapaksha, San.). Means dark fortnight. The half of a lunar month [mausam] from full [powrnimay] to new moon [amavausyay] when the moon [chundran] is on the wane. First styled Apara pacsham or latter half and Apacsheeyamauna pacsham or waning half; subsequently Krishnam, Taumisram or Vadyam. In tamul Tey piray [q.v.] or decrescent moon [jyotisham, pacsham].——*Krishna rajah wodeyar* (ಕೃಷ್ಣರಾಯಒಡೆಯರು - krishnaráyaodeyaru, Can.). Name + title. Adoptive father of the present ruler of Mysore. Succeeded when a minor with Poornayya as minister. Ill-government of the Maharajah after Poornayya's resignation forced his subjects into open revolt, and led to British management, which continued till Maharajah's death in 1868. See vol. I, 20; II, 250.——*Krishna's arrow* (कृष्णबाण - krishnabána, San.). Same as Poison nut.——*Krishnasawmy* (கிருட்டிணசாமி - kiruttinasámi, Tam.). From (krishna, san. the god + svámí, san. lord). Hindoo 2nd or pers. name [peyar].——*Krishnaudy* (कृष्णादि - krishnádi, San.). From (krishna, san. dark + ádi, san. beginning). The n. indian mode of reckoning [maunam] a month [mausam] by beginning with the Krishnapacsham or moon-waning half, making the day following the full moon [powrnimay] to be the first day of the month [gownam], and the day of the full moon to be the thirtieth. For the s. indian method see Shooclaudy.——*Krishnavenay* (कृष्णवेणा - krishnavéná, San.). From (krishna, san. the river so called + véní, san. stream). Tributary of the Kistna; see vol. I (3).——*Krishy* (कृषि - krishi, San.; കൃഷി - krishi, Mal.). From (krish, san. to plough). Cultivation [vellaumay]. Krishicauran is the cultivator [coody, ryot].

KRISHAM (कृश - krisha, *San.*). From (krish, san. to become thin). Lean.——*Krishaungy* (कृशाङ्गी - krishángí, San.). From (krishánga, san. thin-limbed). Rails. Rallidæ family, latitores, grallatores, aves [pacshy, 44], of naturalists [jantoo]. Most characteristic points of this family, which includes the water hens, coots, and rails, are the large feet, and the short stout and compressed beak; head is small and compressed, neck short, body also compressed; general aspect, and partially vegetable diet, give them appearance of gallinaceous birds [moorghy]; some are furnished with membranes or webs on toes, and swim well. Divided into two sub-families, Gallinulinæ, the coots and water hens; and Rallinæ, the true rails. The species best known are:—Purple coot, porphyrio poliocephalus, gallinulinæ; loud and somewhat fowl-like call. Bald coot called in tel. (bollikódi) or white fowl, from white beak and frontal disc; fulica atra, gallinulinæ. Water cock called in persian (zághiábí) or water raven, and in hindostany (pankavvá) or water crow; gallicrex cristatus, gallinulinæ; very noisy bird; partially nocturnal; male birds fight, and natives keep them for that purpose; excellent eating. Water hen or moor hen called in hindostany (pánikíbadak) or water duck; gallinula chloropus, gallinulinæ; head dusky grey; upper plumage deep olive; wing dusky; edge of wing white; throat, neck and breast dusky grey, rest of under parts deep bluish-grey; feathers edged whitish, flanks with large streaks of white; under tail-coverts pure white, with few black feathers intermixed; bill red at base, yellow at tip; irides red; legs and feet pale olive green, with orange garter above knee; length 12 to 13 inches; female larger and somewhat richer colored; swims freely, but when approached always retreats to the shore, and conceals itself among shrubs, which it climbs or among thick reeds; it runs with the tail erect. White-breasted water hen; gallinula phœnicura, gallinulinæ. Spotted rail; porzana maruetta, rallinæ. Pigmy rail; porzana pygmæa, rallinæ. Ruddy rail; porzana fusca, rallinæ. Banded rail; porzana ceylonica, rallinæ. Blue-breasted rail; rallus striatus, rallinæ. Indian water rail; rallus indicus, rallinæ.

KRISHNAGHERRY (کشنگری - kishnagirí, *Hind.*; கிருட்டிணக்கிரி - kiruttinakkiri, *Tam.* krishnagiri*) [krish]. From (krishna, san. black + giri, san. mountain). After a Krishna row of Chundragherry, who built the fort.——**(1)** Talook, Salem district, Tahsildar's pay Rs. 150. Area 659 square miles. N. of district. Between N. lat. 12° 14′ and 12° 42′ and E. long. 78° 00′ and 78° 32′. Extreme length and breadth about 32 miles each way. Bounded north by Oossoor talook, Baitmungalam talook of Mysore and the Cungoondy zemindarry in North arcot; west and south-west by Oossoor and Dharmapoory talooks; south by Dharmapoory and Ootancaray talooks, and east by Ootancaray and Tripatore talooks. The talook is in the border land between the Mysore plateau and the Carnatic [q.v.]. The whole country is a series of small plains and valleys overlooked on all sides by droogs [q.v.] of greater or less size. It is the centre of the true Baramahaul [q.v.], the fortresses of which are scattered all round. In the amphitheatre of hills which skirt the talook the chief outlet is that through which the Ponniaur flows. It is also traversed very equally by numerous streams rising in the surrounding hills and all finally becoming tributary to the Ponniaur. Of these the Mullapaudyaur, the Muttooraur and the Rendaur are almost perennial, the latter two being much utilised for irrigation. The centre is occupied by a range of hills jutting out from the Mysore plateau the passes to which they command, about ten miles in extent bearing no particular name and including amongst its peaks four or five of the Droogs from which the Baramahaul takes its name; of these the chief are the Eiyyagownden mullay or Gaganaghurmullay, visible for miles on every side and the Juggadevyghurmullay. Red soils predominate, earth containing large quantities of saltpetre [shorah] and soda salts [munn cauram] is prevalent in positions suited for wet cultivation. Trap dyke exists in several places and whole mountains of trap [padicutt cull] may be seen near Vepanahully. On the road from Maharajghur there is a large tract of torrent mounds. Iron [auhan] ore of excellent quality is found in several of the hills and worked for local consumption. Fresh water nodular limestones [choonam cull], also easily obtainable. Chief products are cumboo [bajrah], cholum [q.v.], raggy [q.v.], varagoo [q.v.], tinay [q.v.], avaray [country bean], dholl [common dholl], horse-gram [madras horse-gram], oolandoo [black gram], cadalay [bengal gram], putchay payar [green gram], vaircadalay [ground nut], castor-oil [aumanac] and gingelly-oil [gingelly] seeds and paddy [q.v.]; sugar-cane [q.v.] and tobacco [pogauk] are cultivated in small quantities; cocoanuts [q.v.] are largely grown along the banks of rivers, and grapes [angoor] of excellent quality are produced in Krishnagherry and its vicinity. Palmyra [q.v.] jaggery [q.v.] also is manufactured in large quantities. Chief jungles are Bellaurapully, Canavyeputty, Kadireesha vriddhy, Maharajghur, Oppattavaudy, Tobbagutty. The hills are, generally speaking, covered with wood fit only for fuel and agricultural implements. On the Maharajghur hills are a few valuable timber [maram] trees. In the eastern part of the talook a large extent of land is covered with palmyras, much used for building purposes. The whole talook abounds in tamarind [q.v.] trees in the fruits of which there is a large trade. Exports are chiefly rice [q.v.], cumboo and other grains, ghee [q.v.], tamarind and hides [chamrah], grapes, shoes and black cloth. Imports are chiefly silk [puttoo], indigo [q.v.], cloths, salt [ooppoo], spices, raggy [q.v.], wheat [geung], bengal gram [q.v.] and betel nuts [q.v.]. The talook is remarkable for the number of ancient breached tanks [q.v.], some very large. Anicuts [q.v.] and river channels [q.v.] are small. Chief anicuts are those of Agaram, Bandaurapully, Baroor, Chandaupooram, and Punnandore. Important tanks are Badetalaub near Krishnagherry, Attipullam and Baroor in the south-eastern portion, and Pennagondapooram tank. Camping grounds:—Coorumbarpully, Juggadevy, Krishnagherry. Mahendramungalam, Mattore, and Mullapaudy. Zemindarries:—Atchamungalam, Auvatvaudy, Bellaurapully, Bellaurcooppam, Coondaurapully mittah, Coorumbarpully, Eelagam, Eicondamcottapully, Juggadevy, Mahendramungalam, Nammaundahully, Nulloor, Oolagam, Payanapully, Penneshwaramutt, Poorshottamapooram, Royacottah, Shandaurapully, Shaumandamullay, Shooligoonta, Talihully, Tippanapully. Places of archæological interest:—Agaram, Chikka timmanhully, Coorumbarpully, Krishnagherry, Royacottah, Shappauniputty. The leading places, &c., in the talook are the following.——*Atchamungalam* (அச்சமங்கலம் - açcamangalam, Tam.). From (açcam, tam. tree, sesbania grandiflora, pers. + mangala, san. prosperity). Zemindarry, Village; pop. 645; square miles 5; lat. of village 12° 31′; long. 78° 22′; from Krishnagherry E. 7 miles; from Salem N.N.E. 61 miles. Peshcush Rs. 631.——*Auvatvaudy* (ஆவத்துவாடி - ávattuvádi, Tam.). From (ávattu, tam. from ápad, san. distress + vádi, tam. enclosure). Zemindarry, Village; pop. 1,135; sq. miles 5; lat. of village 12° 20′; long. 78° 19′; from Krishnagherry S.S.E. 14 miles; from Salem N.N.E. 47 miles. Peshcush Rs. 1,946.——*Baramahaul* (بارا محل - báramahal, Hind.). See sep. title.——*Baroor* (ಬಾರೂರು - bárúru, Can.). See sep. title.——*Bellaurapully* (பெள்ளாரப்பள்ளி - pellárappalli, Tam. pallárapallimitta *). From (ballála, can. dynasty so called + palli, tam. village). Zemindarry, Village; pop. 101; square miles 60; lat. of village 12° 30′; long. 78° 11′; from Krishnagherry W.S.W. 4 miles; from Salem N. 58 miles. Peshcush Rs. 5,711.——*Cauveryputnam* (காவேரிப்பட்டணம் - kávérippattanam, Tam.). See sep. title.——*Coondaurapully* (குந்தாரப்பள்ளி - kundárappalli, Tam.). From (kunru, tam. hill + áru, tam. river + palli, tam. village). Zemindarry, Village; pop. 773; square miles 31; lat. of village 12° 34′; long. 78° 13′; from Krishnagherry N.W. 4 miles; from Salem N. 62 miles. Peshcush Rs. 312.——*Coorumbarpully* (குறும்பர்ப்பள்ளி - kurumbarppalli, Tam.). From (kurumban, tam. member of the caste + palli, tam. village). Zemindarry, Village; pop. 318; lat. of village 12° 36′; long. 78° 10′; from Krishnagherry N.W. 8 miles; from Salam N. 65 miles. Peshcush Rs. 2,488.——*Dowlatabad* (دولت آباد - daulatábád, Hind.). See sep. title.——*Eelagam* (ஈலகம் - ílagam, Tam.). From (ízham, tam. toddy + agam, tam. place). Zemindarry, Village; pop. nil; square miles 14; lat. of village 12° 34′; long. 78° 04′; from Krishnagherry W.N.W. 14 miles; from Salem N.N.W. 63 miles. Peshcush Rs. 1,275.——*Eicondamcottapully* (ஐக்கொந்தம்கொத்தப்பள்ளி - aikkondamgottappalli, Tam.). From (aiyyakkavundan, tam. proper name + kotta, tel. new + palli, tel. village). Zemindarry, Village; pop. 985; square miles 6; lat. of village 12° 27′; long. 78° 22′; from Krishnagherry S.E. 9 miles; from Salem N.N.E. 55 miles. Peshcush Rs. 720.——*Gaganaghur* (گگن گڑھ - gagangarh, Hind.; ககனக்கடை - kaganakkadai, Tam.). From (gagan, hind. sky + garh, hind. hill fort); hill reaching the sky. Sanscrit name (gaganagiri), meaning the same. Tam. also (aiyyakkavundanmalai), meaning ayya gownden, proper name + mountain. Hill; lat. 12° 26′; long. 78° 20′; from Krishnagherry S.S.E. 8 miles; from Salem N.N.E. 54 miles. One of the Baramahauls.——*Juggadevy* (ಜಗದೇವಿ - jagadévi, Can.; சகதேவி - shagathévi, Tam.). From (shagathévaráyan, tam. proper name). Zemindarry, Village, Hill; pop. 979; acres 9,846; lat. of village 12° 29′; long. 78° 22′; from Krishnagherry E.S.E. 7 miles; from Salem N.N.E. 58 miles. The hill is one of the Baramahauls. It was the fortress of Juggadeva royer, who with his eleven brothers ruled the surrounding country in the sixteenth century. Peshcush Rs. 1,890.——*Krishnagherry* (கிருட்டிணக்கிரி - kiruttinakkiri, Tam.). See below.——*Maharajghur* (مہاراج گڑھ - mahárájgarh, Hind.; மகாராசக்கடை - magárásakkadai, Tam.). From (mahá, san. great + rájá, san. king + garh, hind. hill fort). Sanscrit name (mahárájagiri), meaning same. Village, Hill; pop. 719; acres 290; lat. 12° 38′; long. 78° 18′; from Krishnagherry N.N.E. 7 miles; from Salem N. 67 miles.——*Mahendramungalam* (மகேந்திரமங்கலம் - magéndiramangalam, Tam.). From (mahá, san. great + indra, san. the god + mangala, san. prosperity). Zemindarry, Village; pop. 596; square miles 42; lat. 12° 25′; long. 78° 06′; from Krishnagherry S.W. 14 miles; from Salem N.N.W. 52 miles. Peshcush Rs. 4,398.——*Mullapaudy* (மல்லப்பாடி - mallappádi, Tam.). From (malla, san. a wrestler + pádi, tam. village). Village; pop. 852; acres 1,226; lat. 12° 32′; long. 78° 25′; from Krishnagherry E. 10 miles; from Salem N.N.E. 62 miles. One of the Baramahauls.——*Nammaundahully* (ನಮ್ಮಾಂಡಹಳ್ಳಿ - nammándahalli, Can.). From (nam, tam. our + ándai, tam. ruler + halli, can. village). Zemindarry, Village; pop. 477; square miles 13; lat. of village 12° 28′; long. 78° 01′; from Krishnagherry W.S.W. 18 miles; from Salem N.N.W. 57 miles. Peshcush Rs. 1,360.——*Nulloor* (நல்லூர் - nallúr, Tam.). From (nal, tam. good + úr, tam. village). Zemindarry, Village; pop. 225; square miles 9; lat. of village 12° 32′; long. 78° 03′; from Krishnagherry W. 14 miles; from Salem N.N.W. 61 miles. Peshcush Rs. 1,432.——*Payanapully* (பைய்யணப்பள்ளி - paiyyanappalli, Tam.). From (painá, tel. high + palli, tam. village). Zemindarry, Village; pop. 232; lat. of village 12° 32′; long. 78° 19′; from Krishnagherry E. 4 miles; from Salem N.N.E. 60 miles. Peshcush Rs. 278.——*Pennagondapooram* (பென்னக்கொண்டப்புரம் - pennakkondappuram, Tam.). From (penu, tel. great + konda, tel. mountain + pura, san. town). Village; pop. 6; lat. 12° 21′; long. 78° 27′; from Krishnagherry S.S.E. 18 miles; from Salem N.N.E. 50 miles. Irrigation project.——*Penneshwaramutt* (பெண்ணேசுவரமடம் - pennésuvaramadam, Tam.). From (pennésuvaran, tam. the local god + mat'ha, san. cloister). Zemindarry, Village; pop. 679; square miles 7; lat. 12° 24′; long. 78° 17′; from Krishnagherry S.S.E. 10 miles; from Salem N.N.E. 51 miles. There is Penneshwarasawmy temple here. Peshcush Rs. 2,006.——*Ponniaur* (பெண்ணையாறு - pennaiyáru, Tam.). See sep. title.——*Poorshottamapooram* (புருசோத்தமப்புரம் - purusóttamappuram, Tam.). From (purushóttama, san. proper name + pura, san. town). Zemindarry, Village; pop. 56; square miles 8; lat. of village 12° 30′; long. 78° 23′; from Krishnagherry E.S.E. 8 miles; from Salem N.N.E. 59 miles. Peshcush Rs. 598.——*Royacottah* (ರಾಯಕೋಟೆ - ráyakóte, Can.). See sep. title.——*Shandaurapully* (சந்தாரப்பள்ளி - shandárappalli, Tam.). From (shandam, tam. beauty + áram, tam. garden + palli, tam. village). Zemindarry, Village; pop. 860; square miles 11; lat. of village 12° 29′; long. 78° 21′; from Krishnagherry E.S.E. 6 miles; from Salem N.N.E. 58 miles. Peshcush Rs. 706.——*Shaumandamullay* (சாமந்தமலை - shámandamalai, Tam.). From (sámanta, san. a tributary prince + malai, tam. mountain). Zemindarry, Village; pop. 229; lat. of village 12° 35′; long. 78° 14′; from Krishnagherry N.N.W. 3 miles; from Salem N. 63 miles. Peshcush Rs. 709.——*Shooligoonta* (ಸೂಳೆಗುಂಟೆ - súligunta, Can.). From (súle, can. dancing girl + gunta, can. property). Zemindarry, Village; pop. 131; lat. of village 12° 33′; long. 78° 06′; from Krishnagherry W. 11 miles; from Salem N. 62 miles. Peshcush Rs. 555.——*Talihully* (ತಲಿಹಳ್ಳಿ - talihalli, Can.). From (tale, can. head + halli, can. hamlet). Zemindarry, Village; pop. 809; square miles 12; lat. of village 12° 24′; long. 78° 17′; from Krishnagherry S.S.E. 9 miles; from Salem N.N.E. 52 miles. River Ponniaur passes by. Peshcush Rs. 1,890.——*Tippanapully* (திப்பணப்பள்ளி - tippanappalli, Tam.). From (tippa, tel. proper name + palli, tam. village). Zemindarry, Village; pop. 383; lat. of village 12° 36′; long. 78° 13′; from Krishnagherry N.N.W. 6 miles;

from Salem N. 65 miles. Peshcush Rs. 729.——*Tuttacull* (தட்டைக்கல் - tattaikkal, Tam.). From (tattai, tam. flat + kal, tam. rock). Village; pop. 515; acres 1,010; lat. 12° 22′; long. 78° 20′; from Krishnagherry S.S.E. 12 miles; from Salem N.N.E. 50 miles.——(2) Town, Hill, Talook and District moonsif's head-quarters; Salem dist., Krishnagherry tal.; pop. 5,314; acres 317; lat. 12° 32′; long. 78° 16′; from Madras W.S.W. 143 miles; from Namacull N. 90 miles; from Oossoor E.S.E. 30 miles; from Salem N. 60 miles; from Tripatore W. 24 miles; from Yercaud N. 52 miles. On the Madras-Bangalore road at the foot of the Droog, from which it takes its name. Consists of two portions, old and new Krishnagherry, the latter known as Dowlatabad. Said to have been built by Juggadeva royer, a relative of Krishna row, the chief of Chundragherry. The ascent to the hill is difficult. In 1767, and again in 1791, British troops attempted to take this fort by assault, but failed to do so. On the 2nd May 1768 it surrendered to a blockading force under Colonel Smith and was held by a British garrison for some years until restored by treaty. The fortification, as well as the reservoirs of water, were dismantled during the mutiny, and remains of these in fair preservation may be seen about half way up to the north-west and north-east. Great loss of life is said to have ensued amongst European troops quartered on the rock by the explosion in 1803 of one of the magazines which was struck by lightning. From the summit of the Droog many of the forts of the Baramahaul can be seen. On the summit are a few ruined magazines and the cutcherry [q.v.] of the Killadar [q.v.]. The latter is a remarkable structure. A huge rocking stone spreads out from a columnal centre, being supported partly by rocks in situ and partly by masonry, thus making a sort of circular room, entered by narrow doors, and having this columnal mass in the centre. The measurement round the central mass is 24½ fathoms and that of the outer wall 30⅓ fathoms; the height is from 6 to 8 feet. A Krishna temple formerly stood on the Droog. Two tombs on the hill are regarded by Mussalmans with much veneration, being waited on by a fakeer [q.v.] who levies fees from visitors. North of the town is a picturesque tank, and beyond this are the tombs of former residents.

KRITTY (कृत्ति - kritti, *San*). From (krit, san. to divide). Elephant's skin.——*Krittivenn* (కృత్తివెన్ను - krittivennu, Tel.). From (above + vat, san. suffix of possession), meaning shiva, the elephant-skin wearer. Sanscrit name (krittivásapura), meaning shiva, the skin-covered deity + town.—"*a*" Zemindarry talook, Kistna district. In Bunder goverment talook.—"*b*" Zemindarry; Kistna dist., Bunder tal.; pop. 3,627; square miles 32. The estate formerly belonged to Jampany family. In 1811 Malrauz vencata goonda row zemindar [q.v]. of Narsarowpett purchased it in revenue sale and transferred it to Poolloory pedda vencatareddy naidoo, who still holds it.—"*c*" Village; Kistna dist., Krittivenn zemindarry tal.; pop. 417. Old temple [pondrauca].

KULLAUR (கல்லாறு - kalláru, *Tam.*). From (kal, tam. stone + áru, tam. river) [cull].—"*a*" Village; Coimbatore dist., lat. 11° 20′; long. 76° 55′; from Coonoor E.S.E. 5 miles; from Ootacamund E.S.E. 13 miles. At foot of Coonoor ghaut [q.v.].—"*b*" River; Neilgherry and Coimbatore districts. Tributary of the Bhawauny. Flows close to base of hills, below Coonoor ghaut. As it brings down water from the Coonoor and Kotagherry side only of the hills, it is not much affected by S.W. monsoon [q.v.], but is nevertheless capricious. Wet cultivation carried on by means of the Allauvaly and Maroothauvaly channels [q.v.].

KULSY (ಕಳಸಿ - kalasi, *Can.*). Measure of capacity. 14 seers = 1 kulsy; 3 kulsies = 1 mooda [alavay, 3c]. Approximate actual value, 1 kulsy = 980 cubic inches. South canara. Same as moonta of Nellore. Compare:—Nowt, Toom of Godavery; Mercaul of Madras, North arcot, Chingleput. See vol. 1, 609; II, 508.

KURNOOL* (కర్నూలు - karnúlu, *Tel.*). From (kandena, tel. a mixture of lamp oil and burnt straw used in greasing cart wheels + prólu, tel. village). When the temple of Alampore was under construction the carts [bandy] for carrying stones had wheels greased here, which made a settlement. Tel. also (kandenavólu), meaning same. Colloquially (kandanólu).—"*a*" Revenue district; situated inland; between 14° 54′ and 16° 18′ N. lat., and between 77° 23′ and 79° 37′ E. long.; bounded N. by Toongabudra and Kistna rivers and Kistna district, E. by Kistna and Nellore districts, S. by Cuddapah and Anantapore districts, W. by Bellary district; square miles 7,768; pop. 817,811; language Teloogoo but Hindostany is extensively spoken. Contains rivers Bhavanausy, Coondair, Goondlacumma, Kistna, Saglair, Toongabudra; mountains Nullamullays, Veligonda hills, Yerramalas. The whole area of the district is represented by the following sub-areas:—Bunganapully Native state, Coilcoontla talook, Cumbum talook, Marcapore talook, Nundiaul talook, Nundicotcore talook, Putticondah talook, Ramalcottah talook, Sirwail talook. For general administrative purposes the district is distributed between the following revenue and magisterial officers, who have their head-quarters at the places shown. The pay set opposite the subordinate officers gives the grade of the corresponding charge:—Collector, Kurnool; Head assistant collector, Nundiaul, in charge of Nundiaul and Sirwail talooks; General deputy collector, Cumbum, in charge of Cumbum and Marcapore talooks; General deputy collector, Pyaupaly, in charge of Coilcoontla and Putticondah talooks; General deputy collector, Kurnool, in charge of Ramalcottah and Nundicotcore talooks. Tahsildars; Coilcoontla, Rs. 225; Cumbum, Rs. 150; Marcapore, Rs. 150; Nundiaul, Rs. 200; Nundicotcore, Rs. 175; Putticondah, Rs. 175; Ramalcottah, Rs. 200; Sirwail, Rs. 150. Deputy tahsildars; Atmacore, Rs. 70, range situated in the east of Nundicotcore talook; Caulwa, Rs. 70, range situated in the west of Nundiaul talook; Kurnool, Rs. 70, range situated in the north of Ramalcottah talook; Owk, Rs. 70, range situated in the west of Coilcoontla talook; Pyaupaly, Rs. 70, range situated in the south of Putticondah talook. Similarly judicial officers:—Judge, Kurnool; District moonsifs, Cumbum with jurisdiction extending over Cumbum and Marcapore talooks, Kurnool with jurisdiction extending over the talooks of Ramalcottah, Nundicotcore, Putticondah, and a portion of Nundiaul talook, Nundiaul with jurisdiction extending over Coilcoontla, Sirwail and a portion of Nundiaul talooks. Similarly Public works officers:—District engineer, Kurnool; Sub-divisional officers, Nundiaul and Kurnool. Contains Registration sub-districts Atmacore, Caulwa, Coilcoontla, Cumbum, Giddalore, Kurnool, Marcapore, Nundiaul, Nundicotcore, Owk, Putticondah, Pyaupaly, Ramalcottah, Sirwail. Contains Forest ranges Cumbum, Nundiaul, Nundicotcore, Marcapore, Sirwail, Yerramalas. Contains Municipality Kurnool. Contains District board; and Talook board, Nundiaul embracing Nundiaul and Sirwail talooks. The following general references should be made to the preceding volumes:—general geography, I (1) to (29); general ethnology, I (29) to (109); general history, I (110) to (188); physical geography, II, 1; meteorology, II, 3; geology, II, 8; fauna, II, 21; flora, II, 26; mineralogy, II, 29. The following references in the preceding volumes will furnish details special to the district:—latitudes and longitudes, II, 47; particulars about towns, II, 48; comparative population, II, 172; location of revenue officers, II, 387; revenue settlement of the district, II, 413; registrars' and sub-registrars' stations, II, 421; rain-guage stations, II, 428; police divisions, II, 431; maps published, II, 436; survey topographical lists, II, 443; hospitals and dispensaries, II, 447; missionary stations, II, 455; head-quarter stations of gazetted officers, II, 461; incidence of taxation, II, 463; weights and measures of the district, II, 513; special public works, I, 397. A special gazetteer account of the whole district is given at II, 85. For the detailed topography of the district, reference should be made to the talook notices in the present volume, viz.:—Bunganapully, Coilcoontla, Cumbum, Marcapore, Nundiaul, Nundicotcore, Putticondah, Ramalcottah, Sirwail.—"*b*" Deputy tahsildarry, Kurnool district. Pay Rs. 70.—"*c*" Town, Municipality, Head-quarters of Collector, District judge and tahsildar; Kurnool dist., Ramalcottah tal.; pop. 24,376; acres 797; lat. 15° 50′; long. 78° 06′; height 815; from Cumbum W.N.W. 72 miles; from Madras N.W. 240 miles; from Nundiaul N.W. 37 miles; from Pyaupaly N.N.E. 46 miles. A hot town, on a tongue of land composed chiefly of limestone [choonamcull] and shale rocks, at the junction of the Hindry and Toongabudra. The temperature is high in April, May, and June, and in July variable, ranging from 75° to 87°. In August showers are usual and heavy rains occasional. September and the first half of October are cloudy and hazy in the mornings; evenings still, and oppressive, and the thermometer ranges from 76° to 88°. November and December cold and bracing, thermometer falling to 64°. The heat increases from January to April. The prevailing winds are west and north-east. The population is half Hindoo and half Mussalman; this unusual proportion marking the long rule of the Pataun [q.v.] nawaubs [q.v.]. In 1799, after fall of Seringapatam, when Mysore territories were divided between English and Nizam [q.v.], Kurnool fell to share of latter. In 1800 it passed with the other Ceded districts [q.v.] to British. Besides fort [kila] and pettah [q.v.] the town comprises Newpettah, Boodhavaurampett, Roja and Zorahpore. Europeans reside in Newpettah which belongs to Culloor. Roja lies N. of Newpettah and is a jagheer [q.v.] village. Boodhavaurampett is a small rural village between Hindry and Collector's office. Zorahpore lies on S. bank of the Hindry. Formerly populous and noted as scene of conflict between the foreign soldiers of the late Nawaub and the British regiment sent to take possession of the country in A.D. 1839. The name is derived from Zorah, sister of Abd ool wahaub, the first Beejapore Governor of Kurnool. The following are the travelling distances by road from Kurnool to different places:—

To	Viâ	Miles and Furlongs.	
Adony	Aspry	81	0
Anantapore ...	Gooty	92	5
Bangalore	Gooty, Anantapore and Paul samoodram.	223	0
Bellary	Aspry	92	0
Bezwada	Guntoor	204	5
Bezwada	Sooryapett	248	5
Bhadrachellam ...	Devarcondah and Sooryapett	266	7
Chittore	Cuddapah and Royachoty ... --	224	3
Cuddapah	Nundiaul and Chaugulmurry	123	0

To	Viâ	Miles and Furlongs.	
Cumbum	Nundiaul and Nundicanama ghaut ...	101	3½
Devarcondah ...	Pentelly	101	1
Goolburga	Ryechore	152	5
Gooty	Pyaupaly	50	1
Guntoor	Ootcore, Dornaul pass and Vinoocondah.	184	4½
Kamptee	Secunderabad and Nirmal	453	5
Lingusagoor ...	Ryechore	112	3
Madras	Cuddapah and Nagary	289	4
Masulipatam ...	Guntoor	232	4½
Masulipatam ...	Sooryapett and Bezwada	292	4½
Nellore	Cumbum and Canigherry	219	3½
Nundiaul	Jarimoley	45	0
Paul samoodram ...	Gooty and Anantapore	147	7
Ryechore	Jeej	55	1
Secunderabad ...	Cottacote and Janampettah	135	7
Sooryapett	Devarcondah	165	5
Vellore	Cuddapah and Royachoty	246	3
Vellore	Gooty, Anantapore and Pulmanair ...	272	4½

KURRUCK (కరుకు - karuku, *Tel.*). Rough, as in bas-relief. Kurruck hoon [q.v.] or rough pagoda [star pagoda] was a gold coin [naunyam] by Hyder worth four rupees; also called Bahaudry [q.v.].

KUSHNEE (کشنیز - kishníz, *Hind.*). Coriander [cassibor].

KWAUTAM (क्वाथ - kvát'ha, *San.*). From (kvat'h, san. to boil). Decoction [veidyan].——*Kath* (کتھا - katthá, Hind.; കത്തു - kattu, Mal.). Hind. from (kvát'ha, san. decoction). The purest or crystallized form of cutch [catechu, cutch]; but the term is merely the general Hindostany for that article.——*Kwauta shastram* (क्वाथशास्त्र - kvát'hashástra, San.). From (above + shástra, san. science). A botanical vocabulary in Sanscrit with Teloogoo synonyms [shastram].

KYABOCA (کیبوکا - kaiboká, *Burm.*). Moch coondam [q.v.].

KYDAH (قاعدہ - káidah, *Hind.*). From (kada, ar. to sit). Rule, custom [mamool].

KYFIYAT (کیفیت - kaífiyat, *Hind.*). From (kaif, ar. how). Particulars [tafseel], statement [vaukmoolam].

KYLE (کیل - kail, *Ar.*). From (kálá, ar. to measure). Measurement. Amount of grain on the threshing floor [calam] after thrashing and before sharing it. So experiment as to produce.

L (ल - la, *San.*; ل - lám, *Hind.*). San. name of indran [q.v.]; also Paniny's technical term for all the tenses and moods. Hind. denotes 30 in arithmetic; saturn [shany]; and the opposite aspect in astrology [jyotisham]; abbreviation of the tenth mahomedan month [maheena].

LA (لا - lá, *Ar.*). Negative prefix.——*Lakhiraj* (لاخراج - lákhiráj, Hind.). From (above + khiráj, ar. revenue). Land that does not pay revenue [khirauj] to Government [inam]. In contradistinction to maulgoozarry [q.v.]. See vol. I, 112.

LABBAR (لبر - labbar, *Hind.*; సాగుబంక - ságubanka, *Tel.*; மார்ச்சனி - márççani, *Tam.*). Hind. from english rubber. Tel. from (ságu, tel. to be stretched + banka, tel. gum). Tam. from (márj, san. to rub). Title otherwise Caoutchouc, Gum elastic. See Indian rubber.

LABDHAM (लब्ध - labdha, *San.*). From (labh, san. to obtain). Quotient [palam] in arithmetic [pauty ganitam, shastram].

LABLAB (لبلاب - lablâb, *Ar.*). Same as Country bean.

LAC (लाक्षा - lákshá, *San.*; लाख - lákha, *Mahr.*; لك - luk, *Ar.*; لاك خام - lákikhám, *Pers.*; لاکھ - lákh, *Hind.* and *Dec.*; امبلو - ambalu, *Malay*; ಅರಗು - aragu, *Can.*; ಅರಕ್ - arak, *Too.*; లక్క - lakka, *Tel.*; അരക്ക - arakku, *Mal.*; ලාකඩ - lákada, *Singh.*; அரக்கு - arakku, *Tam.*). Title from sanscrit through hindostany. San. from (laksha, san. one hundred thousand) [lacsh, lakh]; from the great number of insects. Pers. from (láksha, san. lac + khám, pers. raw). Tam. from sanscrit by corruption. Greek κάγκαμον. Product of Coccus lacca, hemiptera, of naturalists [poochy]. Improperly been called a gum [gond]. The female of this insect punctures the bark of certain trees in order to lay its eggs in the orifice; the incrustation thereon called lac is formed by the insects being crowded so densely on the branches as to leave no spaces, and to exude from their bodies this resinous substance; the parent lac insect, after laying her eggs, becomes a lifeless bag, of an oval shape, containing a small quantity of the red liquid; the young insects feed on this, and their bodies also assume the same hue; the tree itself is at length destroyed by the incrustation. Previous to the discovery of the mexican cochineal [kirmiz], coccus cacti, the coloring matter of the lac insect was universally employed for dyeing red [shauyam]. λάκκος χρωμάτινος or colored lac was according to the Periplus exported from the north Malabar coast. Efforts were made by the east india company to introduce cochineal from mexico into india in 1799, but an inferior variety coccus cacti sylvestris was the one brought, not the variety coccus cacti grana fina; the lac product still holds its ground locally. Lac is used in the preparation of certain red paints [rangh] and of native ink [mashy]; chucklers [q.v.] use it in conjunction with the milky juice or yercum paul, of the gigantic swallow-wort, calotropis gigantea, r. br. [yercum], and some other ingredients, when they dye leather [chamrah] red; a mixture of lac, alum [padicauram], and tamarind [q.v.] water is the dye for silk [puttoo] or cotton [q.v.] cloth of a crimson color; also used in the preparation of varnishes [rangh]; with seed lac [q.v.] in conjunction with powdered flint [teetatty cull], grind stones are made; with shell lac [q.v.], beads [munkah], ornamental rings, necklaces [maulay], sealing-wax [q.v.], &c., are made; a peculiar acid [poolipp, tezaub] resides in lac called laccic acid. Veidyans [q.v.] prescribe lac medicinally in old bowel-complaints; also mixed with gingelly [q.v.] oil, as external application for the head, in debility from continued fever [jwaram]; tincture of lac favorite medicine amongst hakeems [q.v.] in preparing cleansing washes, they call it mahauwar [q.v.]; decoction [kwautam] of stick lac [q.v.] in mustard [rayaun] seed oil, to which is added some pounded root of morinda citrifolia, linn. [dyeing mulberry], used as unguent for anointing body in cases of general debility. Lac burns with a pleasant odour. The following are two key-lists of the trees of s. india on which the insect settles; further information must be traced in the glossary paragraphs through the small type cross-references at end of this volume:—"*a*" Acacia arabica, babool; Acacia concinna, soap-pod; Anona squamosa, sweet sop; Bombax malabaricum, red-cotton tree; Butea frondosa, bengal kino; Dichrostachys cinerea, ashy babool; Eriodendron anfractuosum, silk cotton; Erythrina indica, common coral tree; Feronia elephantum, wood-apple; Ficus bengalensis, banyan; Ficus infectoria, stone banyan; Ficus religiosa, peepul; Pithecolobium dulce, corcapilly; Schleichera trijuga, ceylon oak; Shorea talura, taloora saul; Stilpnophyllum elasticum, indian caoutchouc; Terminalia tomentosa, murdah; Zizyphus jujuba, bair.—"*b*" Babool, acacia, dichrostachys; Bair, zizyphus; Banyan, ficus; Caoutchouc, stilpnophyllum; Coral tree, erythrina; Corcapilly, pithecolobium; Kino, butea; Murdah, terminalia; Oak, schleichera; Peepul, ficus; Red cotton, bombax; Saul, shorea; Silk cotton, eriodendron; Soap-pod, acacia; Sweet sop, anona; Wood-apple, feronia.——(1) The following are the different varieties of the product distinguished.——*Gum lac* (کچالاکھ - kaççálákh, Hind.; ಅಂಟುಅರಗು - antuaragu, Can.; బంకలక్క - bankalakka, Tel.; പച്ചയരക്ക് - paççayarakku, Mal.; துப்பு - tuppu, Tam.). Hind. from (kaççá, hind. raw). Tel. from (banka, tel. gum). Mal. from (paçça, mal. raw). The lac when first gathered is called cutcha lac, gum lac, or raw lac. This is treated with water, and thus the coloring matter is extracted.——*Lac dye* (अलक्तकरस - alaktakarasa, San.; لاکھی رنگ - lákhírang, Hind.; ಅರಗುಛಾಯೆ - araguchháye, Can.; അരക്കച്ഛായം - arakkuççáyam, Mal.; அரக்குச்சாயம் - arakkuççáyam, Tam.). The coloring matter extracted from the stick lac or gum lac. Used instead of cochineal [kirmiz]. A varnish [rangh] with lac as its basis.——*Lacquer* (ಮೆರುಗೆಣ್ಣೆ - merugenne, Can.; బచ్చెన - baççena, Tel.; மெருகெண்ணெய் - merugenney, Tam.). Can. from (merugu, can. polish + enne, can. oil). Tel. from (prachhanna, san. covered). Tam. from (merugu, tel. lustre + enney, tam. oil). A varnish either for wood or brass made with shell lac and spirits of wine.——*Lake* (ಕೆಂಪರಗು - kemparagu, Can.; చెంగావి - chengávi, Tel.; അരക്കരങ്ക് - arakkuranku, Mal.; செம்பரக்கு - shembarakku, Tam.). Can. from (kempu, can. red + aragu, can. lac). Tel. from (chem, tel. red + kávi, tel. tint). Mal. from (arakku, mal. lac + ranku, mal. color). Tam. from (shem, tam. red + arakku, tam. lac). By pouring warm water on stick lac, a crimson coloring matter is obtained, which is made into square cakes for sale, and then called lac dye, lake, or cake lake. These cakes, when broken, are dark-colored, shining, and compact, but when scraped they yield a bright red powder approaching carmine.——*Lump lac* (ಮುದ್ದೆಅರಗು - muddearagu, Can.; ముద్దలక్క - muddalakka, Tel.; അരക്കിൻകട്ടി - arakkinkatti, Mal.; கட்டியரக்கு - kattiyarakku, Tam.). Seed lac melted up into masses.——*Sealing wax* (مہرکی لاکھ - muharkilákh, Hind.; ಮುದ್ರೆ ಅರಗು - mudrearagu, Can.; മുദ്രയരക്ക് - mudrayarakku, Mal.; முத்திரையரக்கு - muttiraiyarakku, Tam.). Tam. also (shemmezhugu), meaning red wax. Gum lac, melted and incorporated with resin [raul], and afterwards colored with vermillion [shangarf], ivory-black [yeloomboo kary], &c.——*Seed lac* (بینج لاکھ - bínjlákh, Hind.; ಪುಡಿಅರಗು - pudiaragu, Can.; ಪರೆಲರಕ್ - parelarak, Too.; లక్కబియ్యము - lakkabiyyamu, Tel.; അരക്കരി - arakkari, Mal.; அரக்கரிசி - arakkarisi, Tam.). Title from appearance. Hind. from (bínj, hind. seed + lákh, hind. lac). Can. from (pudi, can. powder + aragu, can. lac). Too. from (parel, too. a grain of sand + arak, too. lac). Tel. from (lakka, tel. lac + biyyamu, tel. grain). Mal. from (arakku, mal. lac + ari, mal. rice). Tam. from (arakku, tam. lac + arisi, tam. rice). The stick lac separated from the twigs, appearing in a granulated form and deprived of its resinous matter and part of its coloring matter by boiling.

When melted over a fire and squeezed through a long sack [gunny] into troughs, spreads out into thin flakes known as shell lac. If dropped into rounded masses, it is button lac. If into larger pieces, it is sheet lac or piece lac.——*Shell lac* (چپڑا لاکھ - chaprálákh, Hind.; ಬಿಲ್ಲೆಅರಗು - billearagu, Can.; ಲಾಕ್ಷ - láksha, Too.; అటుకులక్క - atukulakka, Tel.; அவலரக்கு - avalarakku, Tam.). Title from appearance. Hind. from (chaprá, hind. liquid + lákh, hind. lac). Can. from (bille, can. cake + aragu, can. lac). Tel. from (atuku, tel. flattened rice + lakka, tel. lac). Tam. from (aval, tam. bruised flat rice + arakku, tam. lac). Seed lac melted, strained, and run into thin layers. The most common form in which lac is generally known. A decoction [kwautam] of this is used in the preparation of several medicinal oils.——*Stick lac* (بتی کی لاکھ - battíkílákh, Hind.; ಕಡ್ಡಿಅರಗು - kaddiaragu, Can.; కొయ్యలక్క - koyyalakka, Tel.; കോലരക്ക് - kólarakku, Mal.; கொம்பரக்கு - kombarakku, Tam.). Title from its covering the small twigs of tree [croton-lac tree]. All mean stick + lac. The substance in its natural state, before its separation from the twigs which it incrusts, being gathered before the insects have left their cells; and the best is of a red purplish color. Decoction [kwautam] of this given to suppress hæmorrhage.——(2) *Croton-lac tree* (కొమ్మలక్క - kommulakka, Tel.; වැල්කැප්පිටිය - valkappitiya, Singh.; கொம்பரக்கு - kombarakku, Tam.). Tel. from (komma, tel. branch + lakka, tel. lac). Singh. from (val, singh. creeper + kappitiyá, singh. the plant). Tam. from (kombu, tam. branch + arakku, tam. lac); from lac formed on branches [stick lac]. Tel. also (siribilla). Singh. also (kappitiyá). Botanically Croton [ghanta-beejam] aromaticus, linn., euphorbiaceæ [vricsham, 118]. Alias Croton lacciferus. Tree; branches, petioles, and leaves roughish, with stellate hairs; leaves long-petioled, bearing stalked glands at the base, ovate, acute, cordate at the base, denticulate, glands yellowish; racemes lax, spiked; bracts broadly subulate, males one-flowered, equalling the flowers; petals snowy-woolly at the margin; disc hypogynous, urceolar, sub-entire; filaments about thirty, bearded near the base, glabrous, shining brown; ovary hispid with stellate hairs; styles once two-cleft, divisions sub-spathulate entire or two-lobed or cleft; capsules ellipsoid or obovoid sub-globose, scabrous; seeds very minutely puberulous.——*Gum-lac tree* (کچا لاکھ کا جھاڑ - kaççálákhkájhár, Hind.). Same as Ceylon oak.——*Taloora-lac tree* (தளூர - talúra, Tam.). Same as Taloora saul.

LACAB (لقب - lakab, *Ar.*). Name of honor. Attached as title, generally at the end of a proper name [alam, ism, khituab]. Some lacabs originally belonged to prophets, to the household of Mahomet [q.v.], to his companions, or to the Imaums [q.v.]. They appear both as simple and compound terms; but at present date many compound lacabs have passed into use as simple alams. Specimens of lacabs originally pertaining to prophets are:—Caleem ool lah, speaker to god, to Moses; Rooh ool lah, spirit of god, to Jesus christ; Habeeb ool lah, friend of god, to Mahomet. Of lacabs originally pertaining to Mahomet's household:—Syedat oon nissa, prince of women, to daughter Fatimah; Asad ool lah, lion of god, to Ally, prophet's son-in-law, fourth caliph [q.v.]; Zoon noorein, possessor of two lights, to Osman, third caliph, from prophet having married two of his daughters. Of lacabs originally belonging to Mahomet's companions:—Siddeek, the true, to first caliph, Aboo bakr; Farook, the distinguisher, to caliph omar, second caliph. Of lacabs originally belonging to the Imaums:—Saudic, the true, to sixth Imaum; Cauzim, the restrainer of anger, to seventh Imaum, on account of his patience under sufferings; Takee, pious, to ninth Imaum; Nakee, pure to tenth. The following are some of the simple lacabs generally current:—Alavee, Faurooky, Hasanee, Haushimy, Hoossainy, Kirmauny, Koreishy, Madanee, Mehkary, Moohaujir, Moortazavee, Siddeeky, &c. The lacabs given as relating to prophets illustrate compound lacabs. See vol. I (104).

LACSH (लक्ष - laksh, *San.*). To see, mark, distinguish [lac].——*Laccadives* (لکها دیپ - lakhádíp, Hind.; ಲಕ್ಷದ್ವೀಪ - laksha-dvípa, Can.; ലക്ഷദ്വീപു - lakshadvípu, Mal.). From (laksha, san. hundred thousand + dvípa, san. island). Islands; South canara and Malabar dists.; pop. 10,637; lat. 8° 20′ to 13° 50′; long. 71° 47′ to 74° 03′. Barbosa, in 1516, calls the laccadives Malandiva, and the maldives Palandiva. The Tohfat ool moojauhideen calls the laccadives the Islands of malabar. The latin Maniolae are the Maldives, not the Laccadives. The Laccadives were discovered by De gama in his first voyage. For description see vol. II, 89. For the Malabar islands proper see the heads:—Agatty, Andrott, Calpeny, Cavarathy, Soohely. For the S. canara islands see Amindivy. See also Minicoy for the southernmost island near Maldives.——*Lacsha deepam* (ലക്ഷദീപം - lakshadípam, Mal.). From (laksha, san. a lakh + dípa, san. light). Solar festival [pundigay, 6d]. Celebrated at Trivandrum once in six years on the first of tenth solar [madhyama sowra maunam] month Macaram [mausam] or 12th January. This closes moorjapam [bhadradeepam, maryauday].——*Lacsham* (लक्ष - laksha, San.). From (laksh, san. to see). A recognized mark; object to aim at; a prize, a great number. Lakh [q.v.]. Cf. Lac.——*Lacshanam* (लक्षण - lakshana, San.; இலக்கணம் - ilakkanam, Tam.). Distinguishing quality or characteristic. Elegance, philology, the institutes of grammar [vyaucaranam].—"*a*" For Sanscrit grammar see Paniny.—"*b*" In Tamul a highly developed study and almost wholly separate from sanscrit grammar. Agastyan [q.v.] wrote the first grammar of the Tamul [q.v.] language, which was called Agastya nool. He had twelve disciples, whom he instructed in the language; one of these was Tolgauppyan. Soon after, Tolgauppyan prepared another grammatical work called Tolgauppya nool [tolgauppyam], of which the Agastya nool was the basis. The former gradually sunk into oblivion, and is now lost excepting the fragments contained in Tolgauppyan's work. Some time after, Pavanandy vidwaun, a learned man of the Jeina [q.v.] sect, abridged the Tolgauppya nool and called it Nunnool [q.v.]. Of the five parts into which the Tolgauppyam was divided, viz., Yezhoot adhicauram, the chapter of letters or orthography, Sboll adhicauram, the chapter of words or etymology, Porool adhicauram, the chapter of matter, Yaup adhicauram or Sheyyool adhicauram, the chapter of poetry, and Alancanraudhicauram, the chapter on beauty or rhetoric; and into which Pavanandy also divided his work; only the two first chapters have been preserved. The rest are lost, though they were afterwards supplied by other persons. After Pavanandy was a learned man of the Shamana [q.v.] or Jeina sect, who wrote an explanation of the Nunnool. About the same time arose a learned Shiva bhacticauran, named Veidya nauta pundauram, and pretending to find errors in the text of the Nunnool, wrote a grammatical work called Ilakkana vilakkam, or the light of rules, in which he changed some parts of the Nunnool, and added others at his discretion, but retained the before-mentioned division in five parts. About the year 1770, there was a poet in Tinnevelly, named Shuncara namashivauya poolavan. Upon the request of the Ootoomullay poligar [q.v.], Marootbappa tevan, he wrote an explanation of the text of the Nunnool made by Pavanandy. About the same time, Shivanyauna tumbiraun, a learned sanyausy [q.v.], wrote a work, in which he exposed the errors of the Ilakkana vilakkam made by the above-mentioned Veidyanauta pundauram. This work he called Ilakkana vilakka shoorauvaly, i.e., the blast or strong wind on the light of grammar. He wrote also the Sootra vriddhy, in which he explained the Tolgauppyam. Moreover he undertook to examine and compare the former three works, viz., Ilakkana cott, Ilakkana vilakka shoorauvaly, and Sootra vriddhy; made the necessary extracts; and embodied them in the Nunnool prepared by Shuncara namashivauyan. The thus enriched Nunnool is now in use among the Tamulians and held in high estimation as the best classical work. It is called Nunnool ooray, or an exposition of the Nunnool.—"*c*" The most ancient Teloogoo grammarian, of whom mention is made in the native books is the sage Canwa. His work is not now to be found. All the treaties on Teloogoo grammar at present extant consist of Sanscrit commentaries on an ancient series of concise apothegms originally written in Sanscrit by a Bramin named Nannayya bhatt but not now extant [bhaushay]. Teloogoo grammar is excessively modern compared with Tamul.——*Lacshyam* (लक्ष्य - lakshya, San.; இலக்கியம் - ilakkiyam, Tam.). Marked, defined; example in illustration of grammatical rules; classical writings according to grammatical rules. Includes all approved poetical compositions, whether original or translated. Under this head the Dravidians have epic, lyric, ethic, dramatic, scientific and philosophic pieces; but of these by far the most important are the ethic [bhaushay].——*Lakh* (لاکھ - lákh, Hind.). From (laksh, san. to see), a recognized mark; object to aim at; a prize, a great number. A hundred thousand [lacsham]. Generally 100,000 rupees. The Hindoo method of writing and reading high numbers is by thousands, lakhs, and crores; thus, 1,02,30,000 or one crore [q.v.], two lakhs, thirty thousand.——*Lutcham* (लक्ष - laksha, San.). From (laksh, san. to see). Mark.——*Lutchman* (लक्ष्मण - lakshmana, San.). Brother of Rama [q.v.].——*Lutchmanan* (இலட்சுமணன் - iladchumanan, Tam.). One who bears auspicious marks. Familiarly atchanna. Hindoo 2nd or pers. name [peyar].——*Lutchmanateertam* (ಲಕ್ಷ್ಮಣತೀರ್ಥ - lakshmanatírt'ha, Can.; lakshmantírtha, Mys. Gov.). River. Rises in Western ghauts on southern frontier of Coorg, flows north-east and falls into Cauvery near Sagarcuttey village in Yedatorey talook, Mysore [aroovy].——*Lutchmicauntan* (இலட்சுமிக்காந்தன் - iladchumikkándan, Tam.). From (lakshmí, san. the goddess of fortune + kánta, san. husband). Vishnoo. Hindoo 2nd or pers. name [peyar].——*Lutchminarrain* (இலட்சுமிநாராயணன் - iladchumináráyanan, Tam.). From (lakshmí, san. wife of vishnu + náráyana, san. vishnu, the water wanderer). Hindoo 2nd or pers. name [peyar].——*Lutchminarsoo* (లక్ష్మీనరసు - lakshminarasu, Tel.). From (lakshmí, san. the goddess of fortune + narasu, tel. familiar contraction of narasimha, san. vishnu, the man-lion deity). Hindoo 2nd or pers. name [peyar].——*Lutchmipaty* (लक्ष्मीपति - lakshmípati, San.). From (lakshmí, san. the goddess + pati, san. husband). Vishnoo [q.v.].——*Lutchmipore* (లక్ష్మీపురము - lakshmípuramu, Tel.). From (lakshmí, san. goddess of fortune + pura, san. town). Ghaut; Vizagapatam district, Parvatipore division; from Parvatipore N.W. 35 miles; from Vizagapatam N.N.W. 123 miles.——*Lutchmivallabhan* (இலட்சுமிவல்லபன் - iladchumivallaban, Tam.). From (lakshmí, san. wife of vishnu + vallabha, san. husband). Hindoo 2nd or pers. name [peyar].——*Lutchmy*

(लक्ष्मी - lakshmí, San.; இலக்குமி - ilakkumi, Tam.). From (laksha, san. mark); of good sign or luck. ἀφροδίτη of greeks; venus of romans; isis or orient luminary deity of egyptians. The goddess of prosperity and wealth; in the later mythology identified with Shree [q.v.], appearing in Tamul as Tiroo [q.v.] and made the shacty [q.v.] or wife of Vishnoo [q.v.]. Lutchmy was one of the products from churning the milk sea and agrees specially with the sea-born Venus [coormam]. It is possible that the idea of a shacty to Vishnoo was suggested by the success of the Sheivas. Lutchmy and Bhoo devy with Veishnavites counterbalance Parvaty [q.v.] and Gungay [q.v.] with Sheiveites. There exists in the literature much less of romance with reference to Vishnoo and Lutchmy than with reference to Shiva and Parvaty. On the other hand the stories of Rama [q.v.] and Seetay [q.v.], and of Krishnan [q.v.] and his wives, make up the deficiency. Lutchmy is represented in Southern india as a woman in a sitting posture, with four arms and hands, two of which she has empty and as it were ready to give blessings; the other two she raises, holding in each a lotus [nelumbo] flower. On each side of her stands a white elephant [q.v.], holding with his trunk a water pot from which he waters the flowers in Lutchmy's hands. The color of her body is yellow, and her forehead is marked with a red paste, called Tirchoornam [q.v.], which is also worn by the women of the country. Her ornaments are the same with those of other goddesses. Her seat is a little elevated, and behind her lies a cushion. Thus she is found in pagodas [q.v.] as well as in many houses; for of all the images in the pagodas miniatures of metal, stone or wood are made and worshipped in the private dwellings. Lutchmy has no pagodas of her own, but she is, thrice every day, worshipped with offerings in those of Vishnoo, where she has a temple, and she is also adored in those of Shiva [q.v.] where she has a small chamber of her own. There are no special festivals celebrated in her honor, but she is carried about with Vishnoo at his festivals; and Friday is set apart as a special fast in her honor. There are no books separately written about her, but many stories are told of her in the books on Vishnoo. Of her many names the following may be mentioned:—Alar magal or the flower-daughter; Aukkam or wealth; Indray or the supreme female; Jalajay or the lotus-born; Jaunaky or Seetay; Maheadal piranda cothay or that was born in the great ocean [coormam]; Mungala devy or goddess of luck; Narayany or water goddess; Patniyammay or the chaste or faithful; Pon or Ponam or gold; Porool shelvy or the rich one; Samoodra devy or sea-goddess; Seeta lutchmy; Sheyyaul or the red or beautiful one; Shree or Shree devy or the divine, or the goddess of fortune; Taukkanang or she whose beauty excels all others; Tirmagal or the divine or illustrious daughter; Tirvengadamoodeiyal or possessor of tripatty; Yileiyaul or the younger one. Lutchmy, whose presence is a guarantee for happiness and prosperity, is said to dwell in the face of a horse [ghorah] of superior caste, with the wise and good, in all fragrant flowers, in the tree of paradise [calpacam] that bestows whatever its votaries may desire, in beauty of a good and obedient wife, in the ocean, in the portal of a house where a marriage is being celebrated, in a well governed country, in grain [dhaunyam], in brilliant lamps [deepam] and flaming torches [masaul], in the words of the great, with truth-speaking men, in the arrows of cupid [cauma baunam], and in vessels of milk [paul]. For the eight lutchmies or deities of prosperity see Ashta lutchmy. For Lutchmy vratam, or worship in honor of lutchmy, see Vara latchmy vratam. There is a Tamul proverb:—நடந்தவன் காலிலே சீதேவி, இருந்தவன் காலிலே மூதேவி—"The goddess of fortune "dwells in the feet of the industrious; the goddess of misfortune "[moodevy] dwells in the feet of the sluggard" [matam]. See vol. I (74), (79). As a female name, Lutchmy is shortened into Yatchy, Yatchmy, Yatchoo, Latchy [peyar].——*Lutchmy's lily* (इन्दीवर - indívara, San.). From (indirá, san. lakshmí, the goddess + vara, san. choice); from tradition that the goddess issued at the creation from the petals [cauma baunam]. Same as Blue indian water-lily.

LADOW (लदाव - ladáu, *Hind.*). From (ládná, hind. to load). Vault or arched roof [staupatyam].

LAG (लग् - lag, *San.*). To adhere.——*Lagna bhoojam* (लग्नभुज - lagnabhuja, San.). From (lagna, san. right ascension + bhuja, san. arm). Ascensional difference in sunrise.——*Lagnam* (लग्न - lagna, San.). From (lag, san. to adhere); contact. Point of contact or intersection of two lines. The point or arc [chaupam] of the equator [maudy mundalam] which corresponds to a given point or arc of the ecliptic [craunty mundalam]; the division of the equator which rises in succession with each sign [raushy]; the right ascension of european astronomers. This is more technically the arc of the equinoctial, or angle at the pole [dhroovam], intercepted between the celestial meridian [raikhay] passing through the object and that passing through the tropical [ayanaumsham, maunam] first point of aries [maisham]; it is reckoned eastward, in the order of the signs [raushy], to 360° or 24h; it is generally expressed in time, 1 hour for 15°, being the rate at which the heavens appear to revolve round the pole; as the equinoctial is merely the projection of the terrestrial equator [niracsham], right ascension corresponds with terrestrial longitude [deshauntaram]; distinguish from celestial longitude, dhroovacam or sauyanam as the case may be. Lagnam is also the rising of a sign of the zodiac [raushy chuckram] above the horizon [cshitijam], astrologically indicative of good or evil [jyotisham, noojoom].——*Langoolya* (లాంగూలియ - lángúliyá, Tel. lángulya*). From (lángala, san. plough); according to legend it was dug by the plough of balaraman [q.v.], elder brother of krishnan [q.v.]. Sanscrit name (lángalí), meaning plough; also (nágávali), meaning serpent + line. River; Vizagapatam and Ganjam districts, Bobbily, Chicacole, Palcondah, Parvatipore and Saulore talooks. Formed by the junction of three streams rising in the Gondwana mountains near Calahundy in the Central provinces. Flows south-east across the territory of Jeypore and into the plains of the presidency where it is joined by important tributaries draining the eastern slopes of the ghauts [q.v.] from Gaulicondah to Royagada and the Saulore, Bobbily, Parvatipore and Palcondah divisions. Bridged at Chicacole. In the last 30 miles of its course, forms the boundary between Vizagapatam and Ganjam districts, entering the sea below Chicacole. Total length, 140 miles. On its banks are Nagore, Palcondah, and Chicacole. Principal tributaries are the Saulore and Makkoova. Its rapid current makes navigation impossible.——*Lingadhaury* (లింగధారి - lingadhári, Tel.). From (linga, san. phallic emblem of shiva + dhári, san. wearer). Same as Lingayet.——*Lingagherry* (లింగగిరి - lingagiri, Tel.). From (linga, san. symbol of shiva + giri, san. hill).—"*a*" Zemindarry talook, Kistna district.—"*b*" Zemindarry; Kistna dist., Nundigauma tal.; pop. 4,947; square miles 30. The territory lies detached in the Nizam's dominions. The zemindars are bramins. They trace their descent from Muntry preggada muilapa rauz, who resided at Lingagherry two centuries ago. Peshcush Rs. 486.—"*c*" Village; Kistna dist., Lingagherry zemindarry, pop. 1,133; lat. 16° 53′; long. 79° 52′; from Bezwada W.N.W. 60 miles; from Guntoor N.W. 59 miles; from Madras N. 260 miles; from Masulipatam W.N.W. 100 miles; from Vinoocondah N. 56 miles. Inscription dated A.D. 1174 records grant of land to the temple.——*Lingam* (लिङ्ग - linga, San.). From (lag, san. to fasten); mark to lay hold of. The phallic emblem of Shiva [q.v.], under which form alone he is worshipped in S. india. It is represented by a cylindrical stone rounded off at the top, and at the other end inserted in masonry or in the ground, but transfixing another horizontal and flat stone named yony [q.v.]; the two sections thus indicating the two sexes; this is the original meaning, but it is not recognized by the people, who merely worship the symbol of shiva; the emblem is placed in the open field, on the way side, and in shiva temples. In temples the figure is worshipped daily three times, with drink-offering, food-offering, and burning of incense, by a certain class of bramins [gooroocal]; none but these bramins are allowed to perform the lingam worship before that lingam which stands in the innermost and most holy part [garbhagriham] of the pagodas [q.v.]; but this class of bramins is less esteemed than other classes; they wear a string of the holy roodraucsham [q.v.] beads on their necks and another on their heads, which they have always uncovered; they wear also in common with all bramins [q.v.] the poonool [q.v.]. The lingam has several names:—Audhaura lingam or fundamental lingam; Auvoodeiyaur lingam or the life possessor; Moola lingam or original or chief lingam; Paurtivalingam or earth lingam; Pautaula lingam or hell lingam; Prauna lingam or life lingam; Shiva lingam, &c. Some, when about to bathe in a river and intending to perform religious ceremonies, make a figure of earth, representing a lingam, worship it, and then throw it into the water; this is the Paurtivalinga poojay. Some lingams are held to have grown spontaneously out of the earth, and these cannot be dug out, because they have no end below; they go down into the lowest world; these are the Pautaula lingam; pilgrims often flock to the places where such lie. The Prauna lingam is that specially worshipped and worn by lingayets [q.v.]. The twelve great and renowned lingams of India are or have been at:—Somnaut in goozerat; Mullicarjoonan or srisheilam in kurnool; Maha caulan in oojjein; Omcauram on the nerbudda; Amareshwaram in oojjein; Veidya nautan at deogarh in bengal; Rameshaṁ at saitoobandham or the island of rameshwaram between ceylon and this presidency; Bheema shuncaram, at draucsharaumam near rajahmundry; Vishweshwaran at benares; Triyambacan on the banks of the goomty; Gowtameeshan site uncertain; Kedaureshan or kedaur nautan in the himalayas. Many of these were destroyed by the mahomedans. The Srisheilam and Rameshwaram, lingams are to this day much resorted to. In the old augamam [q.v.] philosophy of s. india there are five lingams:—Streelingam, properly the organ entire, male and female, with its functions; it is a figure, the only one of the five which has form; the charitay or popular pooraunic course of worship belongs to this roopam. Poollingam or the male lingam, defined to the perception; to this belongs the kriyay course of worship, the second great stage. Napoomsaca lingam or neuter lingam, the stage of darkness or of doubt and neutrality and as a course of worship is included in the succeeding stage. Parama lingam or supreme lingam, under the domain of mauyeshwaran the concealer and is called maraippoo lingam; the course of worship here is that of yogam [q.v.], the third great stage. Mahalingam, symbol of enlightenment; and the course of worship is nyaunam [q.v.] or knowledge, the last stage which exempts from births and secures absorption into the supreme essence [bramh]. Puncha lingam are again the imaginary forms of the five elements:—Lingam of earth, worshipped at conjeeveram; Lingam of water, worshipped at tirvanna-cauval or jambookeshwaram; Lingam of fire, worshipped at trinomallee; Lingam of wind, worshipped at calastry; Lingam of ether, worshipped at chidambaram [matam]. An historical account of phallic worship in connection with Southern india has been given in the foot-note on the History of Hindoo religion, at vol. I (72), (83), (84), (88). The word is a suffix in Tamul and Teloogoo proper names; Mahalingam, Ramalingam, &c. [peyar].——*Linga shareeram* (लिङ्गशरीर - lingasharíra, San.). From (linga, san. mark + sharíra, san. body). A higher development of the material body [shareeram, stoola shareeram].——*Lingavant* (ಲಿಂಗವಂತ - lingavanta, Can.). From (linga, san. phallic emblem of shiva + vat, san. suffix of possession). Deccan canarese for Lingayet.——*Lingayet* (ಲಿಂಗಾಯತ - lingáyata, Can.). From (linga, san. phallic emblem + vat, san. suffix of possession). Corruption of Lingavant. Title otherwise Jangum, Lingadhaury, Lingavant, Veerasheiva. The ascetics of the sect are called Tumbiraun [q.v.]. Not a caste, but a religious designation embracing many castes. See vol. I (57), (68), (77) and (84). The sect wear as a reliquary a miniature of the lingam, made of stone or crystal, in a small casket of silver or gold either on the breast secured by means of a string round the neck, or fastened to the right arm, or to the tuft of hair on the head. Some never remove it from their bodies, and are buried with it; this is the Prauna lingam or life lingam. The worship of the Lingam and Yony marks the Sheivas; the worship of the Lingam alone denotes the Lingayets. The latter attach a further meaning to the word indicating various heavens or locams [q.v.] in the invisible world; the uppermost is the Bramha [q.v.], or sometimes Shiva lingam, concerning which metaphor is extensive. In the south the Lingayets are very numerous, and the officiating priests of Sheiva shrines are commonly of this sect, when they bear the designations of Aradhya [q.v.] and Pundauram [q.v.]; such priests claim to be descendants of Sheivite bramins, and between them and the Smartas [q.v.] there is a certain degree of reluctant intercourse, founded upon the rites of initiation or oopanayanam [q.v.], which both parties use. The history of this sect from its foundation by basava [q.v.] in the inland Canarese country, has been given in the foot-note on the History of Hindoo religion at vol. I (77). They adore shiva as the one god and wear his image hung on their breasts; they call themselves primitive worshippers and look upon others as idolators; they deny the authority of the bramins, by whom they therefore are detested as heretics; basava abolished caste [jauty], pilgrimage [jatrah], and penance [tapas]. Though the lingayets generally deny the sanctity of any particular place, the aradhyar have yielded to the hindoo propensity to worship in certain places as peculiarly holy; one of these at conjeeveram, one at jambookeshwaram near trichinopoly, one at arnagiry trinomallee, one at calastry, and one at chidambaram; these are respectively called the lingams of earth, water, fire, air, and ether. No case is known of the image having been voluntarily laid aside; and lingayets declare that no one of their brotherhood has ever embraced the christian or the mahomedan faith. Lingayets differ from other hindoos with regard to a future state; other men are liable to transmigration [samsauram]; they depart either to heaven or hell, and that state is eternal; the prayers of lingayets are addressed to the image they wear, which they salute as basaveshwaran; the daily prayers usually are in the mother tongue. Lingayets receive and return the salutation of every woman. In common with the sheivas generally, the lingayets smear their foreheads with vibhooty [q.v.] or ashes and wear necklaces [maulay] and carry rosaries [maulay] made of the roodrauksham [q.v.] seed; the clerical members of the sect usually stain their garments with red ochre [cauvy]. Lingayets desist from:—Apasavyam, Tila tarpanam [q.v.], Sacred grass or darbhay [q.v.], Burnt sacrifice [homam], Parvam [q.v.] at the new [amavausyay] and full moon [powrnimay], Arghyam, Paudyam; which list is intended to sum up all the Braminical rites. The dress of Lingayets differs from that of other Hindoos only in the rite of wearing the image. An analogy exists between pythagoreans and lingayets; pythagoras call the four principles by numerical names, the monad, duad, triad and tetrad; the lingayets call them by specific names, viz., the lingam, bhactan, gooroo, and sheivam, i.e., the deity, the disciple, the teacher, and supreme spirit, which pervades and unites all three; the lingam and the sheivam, being the first and fourth principles, are one and the same. The basava pooraunam in canarese is the chief work on the religion of the sect; but there are many other canarese works, such as the chenna basava pooraunam, prabhoolinga leelay, sharanaleelaumritam, viractara-cauvyam, and others, containing legends of jangam saints; lingayets have no objection to read any part of the braminical books, but they refuse to accept them as authoritative. Lingayets generally are of two classes; Ayets, who do not take animal food nor the food prepared by bramins; and Ganayets who eat flesh and food prepared by other castes. Aradhyar, or braminical lingayets, are of three classes; Rigvaidies, Yajooryaidies, Saumavaidies, according to the vedams [q.v.] which they follow. Lingayets also class themselves as Saumaunyans and Vishaishans. The Saumaunya or ordinary lingayet is bound by no vow; he can eat flesh excepting that of the cow [pashoo], drink wine [angoor], use betel-nut [q.v.], and eat in any one's house; only he is obliged to marry in his own caste. The higher grade opposed to this is the Vishaisham or extraordinary, being the gooroo [q.v.] or teacher, commonly called Mataudhipaty or spiritual guide; all the rest are his disciples; he taking a vow, the greater vow. Among lingayets at all solemnities whether marriage, birth, initiation or funerals, four vases of water are solemnly placed in the name of the four Aradhyar or prophets. In four ages, it is said, these four successively appeared as precursors of the divine Basava. They are analogons to the four peers [q.v.] of the Mussalmans [q.v.]. The latter play the same part in the ceremony of making a Mussalman mooreed [q.v.] that the four Aradhyar do in that of making a Jangam [jauty, matam]. Numbers about 120,000 in presidency. It is to be observed that the Lingayet creed has never had followers in Malabar.——*Lingayya* (లింగయ్య - lingayya, Tel.; இலிங்கய்யன் - ilingayyan, Tam.). From (linga, san. phallic emblem of shiva and so shiva + ayyan, tam. father, title of respect). Common proper name.——*Loonghee* (لنگی - lungí, Hind.). From (lung, pers. a cloth worn between the legs). A cotton [q.v.] cloth wrapt once or twice round the hips and tucked in at the upper edge; not tucked between the legs like a dhoty [q.v.]. When large and of plain material, it acts not only as a clothing during the day, but as a sheet [chudder] at night. Some loonghees are made with checks and stripes or with a figured diaper body. A common variegated form is plain with colored borders and gold in ends. In another style, color is employed in the body of the piece, as well as in the ends and borders. Sometimes a cotton [q.v.] loonghee has silk [puttoo] in borders and ends.——*Lungoor* (हनुमान् - hanúmán, San.; वानर - vánara, Mahr.; قرد - kird, Ar.; بوزنه - búzinah, Pers.; هنومان - hanúmán, Hind.; لنگور - langúr, Dec.; ಮುಸ್ಯ - musya, Can.; కొండముచ్చు - kondamuttsu, Tel.; കരിങ്കുരങ്ങൻ - karinkurannan, Mal.; වඳුරා - vandurá, Singh.; கொண்டைமுசுறு - kondaimusuru, Tam.). Title from deccany. San. from (hanu, san. jaws + mat, san. suffix of possession). Mahr. from (vana, san. forest + nara, san. man). Ar. from (karida, ar. submissive); from docility. Pers. from (bú, ar. father + zannah, ar. suspicion); from vigilance. Dec. from (lángúla, san. tail); long-tailed. Tel. from (konda, tel. hill + muttsu, tel. thief). Mal. means black monkey. Tam. from (kondai, tam. crest + musuru, tam. black ape). Equivalent to sub-family of Apes; or Semnopithecinæ, cercopithecidæ, quadrumana, mammalia [sastanam, 1], of naturalists [jantoo]. Cf. Baboon for the sub-family Cercopithecinæ. The superior apes of India, the genus Hylobates or gibbon, which possess the callosities of true monkeys [bandar], but differ from them in having neither tail nor cheek pouches, are not represented in Southern india. The genus Semnopithecus which gives the apes of the south is characterised by slender bodies and long limbs and tails. By some they are called Slim-apes. Another peculiarity of this genus is the absence of cheek pouches, which, if present, are but rudimentary. They are also to be distinguished by the peculiar structure of the stomach, which is singularly complicated, almost as much so as in the case of ruminants, which have four divisions. They are long and loose-limbed, with a prodigious tail, black face, and overhanging brows of long stiff black hair, projecting like a penthouse. The Lungoors can take enormous leaps, twenty-five feet in width, with thirty to forty in a drop, and never miss a branch. But generally speaking their progress is not made so much by leaping as by swinging from branch to branch, using their powerful arms alternately. Strychnine has no effect on Lungoors. It is possible that in the forests they eat the fruit of the strychnos nux-vomica [poison nut], which is also the favorite food of the pied hornbill [sooliman moorghy]. The Sanscrit and mythological name for a Lungoor is Hanooman [q.v.]. In Braminical history Hanooman, the meaning of which is long jaw, was one of the rulers of the monkey kingdom of Southern india, who aided Rama [q.v.] in his conquest of Ceylon by forming a bridge of rocks [adam's bridge] opposite Manaar [q.v.]. His figure is often found in Hindoo temples [coil] in the guise of a man, with a black monkey face and a long tail. He is not however actually worshipped.—"*a*" The ordinary Madras lungoor is the Semnopithecus priamus of naturalists; alias Presbytis priamus; Semnopithecus albipes, pallipes. Otherwise called Black-faced monkey. It is of an ashy-gray color with a pale reddish tint overlaying the whole back and head; sides of the head, chin, throat and beneath, pale yellowish; hands and feet, whitish; face, palms and fingers, and soles of the feet and toes, black; a high compressed vertical crest of hairs on the top of the head; hairs long and straight, not wavy; tail of the color of the darker portion of the back, ending in a whitish tuft. This species inhabits the Eastern ghauts and southern portion of the tableland of Southern india, not extending however to the Malabar coast. It is found both in forests and large groves of trees and has the usual habits and call of its tribe. It is often domesticated at Madras and other places.—"*b*" On the west coast there is a Malabar lungoor called Semnopithecus hypoleucus; alias Presbytis johnii. Above, dusky brown, slightly paling on the sides; crown, occiput, sides of head and beard, fulvous, darkest on the crown; limbs and tail, dark brown, almost black; beneath, yellowish white. A somewhat small variety. This monkey is found from about latitude 14° or 15° to Cape Comorin, that is to say in South canara, Malabar, Cochin, and Travancore. It does not ascend the mountains to any great height above the sea. It does not occur on the wooded tableland of the Wynaud. It is not confined to the forests, but frequents gardens and the belt of cultivated wooded land that extends all along the sea coast of Malabar. It varies a good deal in the intensity of its color, and especially in the blackness of its limbs and tail, and the young are throughout of a sooty brown.—"c" On the hill ranges there is the Neilgherry lungoor, Semnopithecus johnii of naturalists; alias Semnopithecus cucullatus. Of a dark glossy black throughout, except the head and nape, which are reddish brown, the hair very long; in old individuals, a grayish patch on the rump. This monkey is found not only on the Neilgherry hills, but also in the Anamullays, the Pulneys, the Wynaud, and all the higher parts of the range of ghauts [q.v.] as low as Travancore. It does not descend lower than from 2,500 to 3,000 feet. It is shy. The fur is fine and glossy, and is much prized.—"d" Indian species of Semnopithecus not here found are:—Senex or white lungoor, Barbei or tipperah lungoor, Cephalopterus or ceylon lungoor, Entellus or bengal lungoor, Obscurus or dusky-leaf monkey, Phayrei or silvery leaf monkey, Pileatus or capped lungoor, Schistaceus or himalayan lungoor.——*Lungooty* (لنگوٹی - langotí, Hind.). From (linga, san. male organ + addana, san. shield). A piece of cloth about two feet long and six or eight inches broad, passed between the legs and the end tucked in before and behind to the dawauly [q.v.] or tusma [q.v.].——*Oollagnam* (उल्लग्न - ullagna, San.). From (ut, san. upper + lagna, san. right ascension). The Lagnam of a particular place, answering to the oblique ascension of the stars, in any place which has latitude [acsham, jyotisham].

LAHNGAH (لہنگا - lahangá, *Hind.*). Skirt or petticoat.

LAHOOT (لاهوت - láhút, *Ar.*). Means extinction or absorption. The last stage of the mystic journey [soofee].

LAHORE (لاهور - láhor, *Hind.*). Means fort of loh [lavan]. Chief town of Punjaub.——*Lahore carrot* (زردک لاهوری - zardakiláhorí, Pers.). Same as Sweet potato.——*Lahore seed* (لاهوری حرمل - láhoríhurmul, Hind.). Same as Harmal.

LAHSAN (لہسن - lahsan, *Hind.*). From (lashuna, san. garlic). Garlic [lussoon].——*Lahsanyah* (वैदूर्य - vaidúrya, San.; عين الهر - aínulhirr, Ar.; لہسنیا - lahsaniyá, Hind.; పిల్లికన్రత్నము - pillikanratnamu, Tel.; വൈഡൂര്യം - vaidúryam, Mal.; பூனைக்கண்கல் - púnaikkangal, Tam.). San. from (vidúra, san. name of a mountain). Ar. from (aín, ar. eye + hirr, ar. cat). Hind. from (lahsan, hind. garlic, allium sativum, linn.); from color. Tel. from (pilli, tel. cat + kannu, tel. eye + ratna, san. precious stone). Mal. from sanscrit. Tam. from (púnai, tam. cat + kan, tam. eye + kal, tam. stone). Cat's eye. A variety of quartz [vencull] having the appearance of an eye. A pseudo opal [csheeraspaticam], common in Ceylon. Its composition is nearly the same as that of the common opal [ratnam].

LAINA (لینا - lená, *Hind.*). To take.——*Laina dainah* (لینادینا - lenádená, Hind.). From (above + dená, hind. to give). Also in the aorist, Laivadaivy. Traffic. Money transactions.

LAKLAK (لکلک - laklak, *Hind.*). From imitation of its chattering. White stork. Bird name common to:—Ciconia alba; Ciconia leucocephala. See gloss. paragraphs.

LAKOOCHA (लकुच - lakucha, *San.*). From (lak, san. to taste). Same as Monkey jack.

LALONG GRASS (बर्हिस् - barhis, *San.*; النكالنك - alangalang, *Malay*; మొదవ - modava, *Tel.*). Title from malay. San. from (vrih, san. to pluck up). Botanically Imperata kœnigii, nees., graminaceæ [vricsham, 156]. Culm erect, simple; leaves linear, attenuately plaited at the base, short acuminated at the apex; sheaths densely hairy at the margins; panicle spiked, elongated, cylindric; pedicels scarcely dilated at the apex; glumes colored, four times shorter than the involucrating hairs; styles rather longer than the glume. Small grass; used by teloogoos in marriage ceremonies; not of much use as fodder; used for thatching houses; no other species here.

LAMB (लम्ब् - lamb, *San.*). To hang.——*Lambacam* (लम्बक - lambaka, San.; இலம்பகம் - ilambagam, Tam.); means pendent. A chapter in works of history and fiction [chintaumany].——*Lambajyay* (लम्बज्या - lambajyá, San.). From (lamba, san. co-latitude + jyá, san. sine). Sine of the co-latitude [lambam] or cosine [cotijyay] of the latitude [jyotisham, vicshaipam].——*Lambam* (लम्ब - lamba, San.). Perpendicular. The co-latitude, or the arc [chaupam] between the Pole [dhroovam] and Zenith [oordhwam, ootcham] of a given place.

LAMP OIL (एरण्डतैल - érandataila, *San.*; بڑی ارنڈ کا تیل - baríarandkátel, *Hind.*; چراغ کا تیل - charághkátel, *Dec.*; ದೀಪಯಣ್ಣೆ - dípayanne, *Can.*; ఆముదం - ámudam, *Tel.*; വിളക്കെണ്ണ - vilakkenna, *Mal.*; விளக்கெண்ணெய் - vilakkenney, *Tam.*). San. from (éranda, san. castor plant + taila, san. oil). Hind. means large + castor-plant oil. Tel. from (ámanda, san. castor plant). Mal. and tam. from (vilakku, tam. lamp + enney, tam. oil). Product of the large-seeded castor-oil plant [aumanac]. This called specially lamp oil, though many other oils used in lamps. For oils generally see Yennay.

LAND WIND (مغربی هوا - maghribíhawá, *Hind.*; انگن دارت - angindárat; *Malay*; ಕರೆಘಾಳಿ - kareghálí, *Too.*; పడమటిగాలి - padamatigáli, *Tel.*; மேல்காற்று - mélgáttu, *Tam.*). Title as blowing from the land. Hind. from (maghribí, ar. western + hawá, ar. air). Malay from (angin, malay, wind + dárat, malay, land). Too. from (kare, too. land, as opposed to water + ghálí, too. wind). Tel. from (padamara, tel. west + gáli, tel. wind). Tam. from (mél, tam. west + káttu, tam. wind). Tam. also (kódai), meaning wind of the hot season. Portuguese Terrenho. Westerly winds prevailing mainly during day-time to the east of the western ghauts [q.v.] especially in Carnatic [q.v.]. See vol. II, 5, for causes. They are always preceded by a long calm, and carry before them a cloud of dust [pishauch]; the atmosphere while they blow is hazy and thicker than in common, and the sun when rising appears as if involved in mist or dust. In most parts they set in about ten or eleven o'clock in the forenoon, and increase in violence and heat till they are stopped by the easterly sea breeze; the sea breeze is preceded by a short lull or calm; if the sea breeze fail, as sometimes happens, the land wind continues blowing, but gradually decreases in strength, and finally dies away in the beginning of the night, having slowly veered round to the south-west; about morning a little motion of the air is perceptible; but it is very weak, until at the usual time the wind sets in stronger and hotter than on the preceding day. The land winds are said to be dry, and on that account productive of an uneasy sensation all over the body, with a dryness of the skin as if the perspiration had been suddenly stopped; this sensation is peculiarly felt in the eyes, which must frequently be shut while walking in this wind, as the lids become stiff; these wind can destroy men and animals if exposed to them too long; it is not very uncommon to see large kites [chillam] and crows [caurvam], while on the wing, drop down at once as if they had no life in them; at the setting in of the wind, when people are caught unprepared, pains of the bones and general lassitude are felt, and paralytic or hemiplectic affections are common. Nightly illuminations of the ghauts [q.v.] or of the hills in their neighbourhood are seen at this season, after it has continued for some time without rain; these appear always about the middle of the mountain, seldom or never reaching the top; the natives account for these spontaneous combustions by the friction of the bamboos [q.v.] against each other. The natives use no other means of securing themselves against the effects of the land winds than shutting up their houses and bathing in the morning and evening; Europeans cool their apartments by means of wetted tatties [tatty], made of straw or grass, and sometimes of the roots of the cuscus [q.v.] or vettivair or andropogon muricatus, retz., which when wetted exhales a pleasant but faint smell [longshore wind, monsoon, sea breeze].

LANSEH (لنگست - langsat, *Malay*). Title otherwise Langsat. Botanically Lansium anamalayanum, bedd., meliaceæ [vricsham, 36]. Moderate sized tree; leaves 6–9 inches; leaflets 3–4½ by 1½–2 inches; petiole 1–⅜ inch; hermaphrodite flowers sessile, about ⅛ inch diameter; fruit the size of a large grape [angoor]; produced in bunches; succulent aril in fruit eaten by monkeys [bandar] and birds [pacshy].

LARIN (لاری - lárí, *Hind.*). From (lár, pers. province on the north of the persian gulf). Coin usually in shape of a fish-hook, formed of two pieces of silver wire welded together and doubled round into this shape [naunyam]. A rarer form is straight [ridy].

LASCAR (لشکر - lashkar, *Hind.*). From persian. An army, camp, cantonment, gang, crew. Thence a single member of such; as a sailor, tent-pitcher [calassy], inferior artillery man. Proper form of latter would be Lascary.

LATEEF (لطیف - latíf, *Hind.*). From (latafa, ar. slender). Exquisite. An attribute of God [allah]. Common alam. Also part of lacab, as Lateefa bauno, alam + pataun female alaumat. Lateef ood deen, the most exquisite of the faithful [ism]. Feminine Lateefa, subtle.

LATERITE (سلی کا پتھر - sillíkápatthar, *Hind.*; کالا پتھر - káláphattar, *Dec.*; ಮುರಕಲ್ಲು - murakallu, *Too.*; బొంతరాయి - bontaráyi, *Tel.*; വെട്ടുകൽ - vettukal, *Mal.*; சொறிக்கல் - shorikkal, *Tam.*). Title from latin, from brick-like red color. Hind. from (sillí, hind. whet stone + patthar, hind. stone). Dec. from (kálá, hind. black + phattar, hind. stone). Tel. from (bonda, tel. fissure + ráyi, tel. stone). Mal. from (vettu, mal. to cut + kal, mal. stone), because soft when first dug. Tam. from (shori, tam. roughness + kal, tam. stone). Hind. also (muram); (kírekápatthar), meaning worm stone; from worm-eaten appearance. Mal. also (charakkal), meaning gravelly stone; (ishtakakkallu), meaning brick + stone, from color and use. Tam. also (vettukkal), meaning cut + stone; (shembúrángal), meaning red + centipede + stone, from color of common centipede; (tavalaikkal), meaning frog stone, from roughness of surface. Cabook of Ceylon. Anglo-indian term. Irony red or brick dust colored clay iron [auhan] ore peculiar to India. It covers the western coast almost continuously, and for the most part up to the very foot of the ghauts [q.v.]; it is found in detached beds along the coromandel coast [q.v.], near madras and nellore, rajahmundry and samulcottah, extending into cuttack; it caps the loftiest summits of the eastern and western ghauts [q.v.], and some of the isolated peaks in the tableland in the interior; it occurs in mysore, salem, coimbatore, south arcot, the carnatic [q.v.] and tanjore; it rarely if ever contains either crystals [palingoo cull] or organic remains [cull poo], is never stratified or columnar, and generally spreads out in vast sheets over the surface of the plutonic or volcanic rocks; the origin is regarded as modified volcanic matter, the low-level having undergone a further re-arrangement and deposition. Laterite is chemically a porous, argillaceous rock, much impregnated with iron peroxide, which is irregularly distributed throughout the mass, some forms of the rock containing as much as from 25 to 35 per cent. of metallic iron; this iron exists either entirely in a state of hydrated peroxide or limonate, or else partly as hydrated and partly as anhydrous peroxide; the surface after exposure is usually covered with a brown or blackish brown crust of limonite, but the rock when freshly broken, is mottled with various tints of brown, red and yellow, and a considerable portion sometimes consist of white clay [calimunn]; the difference of tint is due to the segregation of the iron in the harder portions, the pale-yellow and white portions of the rock, which contain little or no iron, being very much softer and liable to be washed away on exposure; the exposed surface, whether vertical or horizontal, is extremely irregular, being pitted over with small hollows caused by the washing away of the softer portions. The laterites of this country contain manganese [q.v.], silica, alumina, and lime [choonam] with traces of magnesia, soda and potash; they differ from the conglomerates of other countries in containing more manganese and ochrey clay. The surface of the country composed of the more solid forms of laterite is usually very barren, the trees and shrubs growing upon it being thinly scattered and of small size. The rock is so porous that all water sinks into it; when the upper surface of laterite is cleared away, the rock below is found soft and easily cut into blocks of any form, whence malayalam name; it quickly hardens and darkens in hue by exposure to the air, and is then not at all liable to decomposition or injury from the weather. It is much used on the Western coast and about Madras for building and road-making, as kankar [q.v.] is used in the north. When ground into clay mixed with jaggery [q.v.], it makes a good water-proof cement [cauray] for the roofs of houses. The proportions for laterite road-making at Madras are:— 15 laterite, $\frac{3}{4}$ gravel [parookkay cull], 2 clay, $2\frac{3}{8}$ sand [manal].

LATORAH (भृङ्ग - bhringa, *San.*; लटोरा - latórá, *Mahr.*; اخيل - akhyal, *Ar.*; کاسکينہ - káskínah, *Pers.*; لٹورا - latorá, *Hind.*; బెలంచి - belanchi, *Tel.*; கிச்சாங்குருவி - kíççánguruvi, *Tam.*). Title from hindostany. San. from (bhri, san to sound). Ar. (khaila, ar. having moles). Tam. from (kíççu, tam. chirping + kuruvi, tam. small bird). Hind. also (dúdhiyálatorá), meaning milky shrike; (mattiyálatorá), meaning earth-colored shrike; (kachkachlatorá), meaning talkative shrike; (kájallatorá), meaning lamp-black shrike; (pachrang), meaning five colored. Dec. also (sufedlatorá), meaning white shrike; (mattíkerangkálatorá), meaning earth-colored shrike. Tel. also (shenkubelanchi), meaning conch or white shrike; (peddakiritigádu), meaning large + crested + fellow; (errabelanchi), meaning red shrike; (chinnabelanchi), meaning small shrike; (vennadéga), meaning butter hawk; (bhattigádu), meaning a song fellow; (bhattikirítigádu), meaning a crested song fellow. Title otherwise True shrikes. Lanianæ, laniadæ [pingalam], dentirostres, insessores, aves [pacshy, 19], of naturalists [jantoo]. The indian grey shrike is lanius lahtora; alias lanius burra; pale blue grey narrow frontal streak; affects low, thin, jungle; sits on top of some low tree, on the watch for a cricket, locust, &c., to come near; usually harsh grating cry, but imitates the song of other birds to bring them near; captures small birds. The rufous-backed shrike is lanius erythronotus; alias lanius caniceps; call a shrill single sound, generally repeated with one high and one low note, like peek peek. The black-headed shrike is lanius nigriceps; alias antiguanus, tricolor. The bay-backed shrike is lanius hardwickii. The brown shrike is lanius cristatus; alias lanius ferrugiceps, phænicurus, superciliosus; peculiarly harsh chattering.——*Hill latorah* (धूम्राट - dhúmráta, San.; پہاڑی لٹورا - pahárílatorá, Hind. and Dec.; ఈలపిట్ట - úlapitta, Tel.). San. from (dhúmra, san. dark red + ata, san. wanderer). Hind. from (pahár, hind. mountain + latorá, hind. shrike). Tel. from (úla, tel. whistle + pitta, tel. bird). Tel. also (vadambálajitta), meaning imitation + bird. Wood shrikes. Malaconotinæ, laniadæ [pingalam], dentirostres, insessores, aves [pacshy, 19], of naturalists [jantoo]. The malabar wood shrike is tephrodornis sylvicola. The common wood shrike is tephrodornis pondicerianus; alias keroula indica; lanius griseus, muscicapoides, sordidus; muscicapa philippensis; tenthæa leucura; tephrodornis superciliosus; common in thin jungle; found in small flocks, in general, pleasing mellow whistling note; occasionally caged for its song.

LATTA (లాత్త - látta, *Tel.*). From (látamu, tel. a stick). Means struck. Astrological element. There are two sorts of Lattas, eastern and western; those of the Sun [sooryan], Mars [coojan] and Saturn [shany], being accounted east, and those of Rahoo [q.v.] and Kait [q.v.] west. Whenever the sun is in XII Nacshatrams [q.v.] counted eastward from that in which the moon [chundran] happens to be, then he is Latta or struck, &c. The planets [graham] have each a different scale [jyotisham].

LAUDA (ಲಾಡ - láda, *Can.*). From (láta, san. south goozerat). Traders in the Mahratta country. Smartas [q.v.] and followers of Shuncaracharry [shuncaran]. Worship god at Tripatty. Customs do not differ from Rauchavaur [q.v.].

LAUL (माणिक्य - mánikya, *San.*; لعل - lal, *Ar.*, *Pers.* and *Hind.*; ಕೆಂಪು - kempu, *Can.*; కెంపు - kempu, *Tel.*; ചുവപ്പുകല്ലു - chuvappukkallu, *Mal.*; சேப்பு - sheppu, *Tam.*). San. from (manika, san. town, so called). Ar. means red. Can. and tel. mean red. Mal. means red stone. Tam. means redness, short for (shivappu). Tam. also (kembu), meaning red. Ruby. This variety of perfect corundum [q.v.] can be procured in Ceylon, but is more abundant and of a much finer kind in Burmah. It is properly a red sapphire [neelam]; and when perfect its color is cochineal [kirmiz] red.——*Laldanah* (لال دانہ - láldanah, Hind.; మెట్టతూటి - mettatúti, Tel.; തിരുതാളി - tirutáli, Mal.; රසතැල්ල - rasatella, Singh.; தாளி - táli, Tam.). Title from hindostany, meaning red seed. Tel. from (metta, tel. high ground + túti, tel. ipomæa aquatica, forsk.). Mal. from (tiruku, mal. to twist + táli, mal. creeper). Botanically Ipomæa [calamby] sepiaria, kœn., convolvulaceæ [vricsham, 93]. Alias Convolvulus marginatus, maximus. Twining; leaves cordate oblong; peduncles many-flowered; heads of flowers dense; sepals oblong, ovate acute or obtuse; corolla pinkish, tubular, funnel-shaped. A climbing perennial plant with rose-colored flowers found in hedges; leaves eaten as greens.——*Laulah* (لالا - lálá, Hind.). Literally a writer. A Hindostany speaking caste; follow trade; some of them held high offices under the Nawaubs [q.v.] of the Carnatic [q.v.]. So a mere Hindoo third name [peyar]. Also used as an address in speaking to a respectable person, not of high rank, especially with jee [q.v.] annexed, as Laulah jee, sir [jauty, maryauday].——*Laul baugh* (لال باغ - lálbágh, Hind.). From (above + bágh, pers. garden). Name of a garden in more than one town; specially one in Bangalore, first laid out by Hyder ally [q.v.].——*Laulbye* (లాలు బాయి - lalubáyi, Tel.). From (above + bái, mahr. woman). Hindoo 2nd or pers. name [peyar].——*Laul e jalauly* (لعل جلالی - lalijalálí, Hind.). Means jalaul's gem. Acbar's gold coin [ilauhee, jalaul].——*Laulgoody* (இலாலுக்குடி - ilálukkudi, Tam. lálgudi*). From (lálá, mahr. caste so called + kudi, tam. village).—"*a*" Deputy tahsildarry, Trichinopoly district. Pay Rs. 100.—"*b*" Town, Deputy tahsildar's station, Assistant collector's division; Trichinopoly district, Trichinopoly talook; pop. 4,830; lat. 10° 52′; long. 78° 53′; from Ariyalore S.W. 25 miles; from Madras S.S.W. 179 miles; from Moosiry E.S.E. 27 miles; from Shreerungam E. 9 miles; from Trichinopoly E.N.E. 9 miles. Taken from French in 1752. In 1861 the old Laulgoody and Conaud talooks were amalgamated and formed into the present talook of Trichinopoly. Old Shiva temple. Richly sculptured. On left side of road to Poollambaudy, is old Jeina [q.v.] statue.

LAUT (لاٹ - lát, *Hind.*). Also called stambham [q.v.]. Pillar, obelisk. These are common to all the styles of Indian architecture [staupatyam]. With the Booddhists [booddha] they were employed to bear inscriptions on the shafts, with emblems or animals on the capitals. With the Jeinas [q.v.] they were generally deepdandams [q.v.], or lamp-bearing pillars. With the Veishnavas [q.v.] they bear statues of Garoodan [q.v.] or Hanooman [q.v.]. With the Sheivas [q.v.] they are flagstaffs [dhwajastambham]. Whatever their destination, they are always in a superior style of art.

LAVANGAM (लवङ्ग - lavanga, *San.*; قرنفل - karanful, *Ar.*; ميخك - mekhak, *Pers.*; لونگ کا جہاڑ - longkájhár, *Hind.* and *Dec.*; چڠکي - chángke, *Malay*; ಲವಂಗಮರ - lavangamara, *Can.*; లవంగము - lavangamu, *Tel.*; കരയാമ്പൂ - karayámbú, *Mal.*; වරාල - varála, *Singh.*; இலவங்கம் - ilavangam, *Tam.*). San. from (lú, san. to cut) [cassia cinnamon, ceylon cinnamon, country cinnamon, loo]. Pers. from (mekh, pers. nail + diminutive suffix). Hind. from (lavanga, san. clove + jhár, hind. tree). Can, from (lavanga, san, cloves + mara, can. tree). Tel. from sanscrit. Mal. from (kara, mal. blackness + áku, mal. to become + pú, mal. flower), from flower blackening when dried. Tam. from sanscrit. San. also (dévakusuma), meaning divine flower. Singh. also (karábu). Tam. also (kirámbu); (karuvá) [ceylon cinnamon]. Greek καρυοφύλλον, from tamul (karuvá). Title otherwise Clove tree, Nail-fruit tree. Giving Cloves, Clove oil, Mother cloves. Clove from resemblance of fruit to nail. Botanically Eugenia [jamboo] caryophyllata, willd., myrtaceæ [vricsham, 56]. Alias Caryophyllus aromaticus. Tree, habitat moluccas, cultivated in malabar, resembles the laurel; 15–40 feet high; leaves large; ovate-oblong, acuminated at each end, evergreen; flowers small, produced in great profusion in cymes; the calyx has a cylindrical tube and four-cleft border corolla consists of four petals united by their tips; the stamens are in four clusters; the fruit an oblong dry berry with one or two cells and as many seeds; leaves, flower and bark have an aromatic odour. Cloves are the unexpanded flowers of the tree quickly dried in the sun; as occurring they should be large, heavy, brittle, brown externally, red within, and when compressed or rasped allowing a volatile oil [yennay] to exude; their odour is aromatic, very sweet; taste aromatic, strong, hot, and acrid, almost to burning, slightly bitter; the ripe fruits dried before the sun are clove berries, or mother cloves, their properties feebler, but these are in hindostany narlaung or male cloves; oil above-mentioned is deep red, flavor of the clove, comparatively milder, sinks in water. The clove tree is indigenous only in the five small islands which constitute the moluccas proper, afterwards introduced into other neighbouring islands, where it is now cultivated, and at a later period into zanzibar and pemba on the east coast of africa; introduced into india, and mentioned by characan, the oldest sanscrit medical writer. The product, cloves, have been much prepared by the dutch at amboyna; they have been known in china and india as an introduced article from time immemorial. The flowers of the clove grow as above said in cymes and when fit for gathering the calyx tube is of a bright red color; the collection is by hand, each clove being picked singly; they are afterwards dried upon mats in the sun, which takes about three days; very inferior samples of cloves are sold in bazaars; good cloves are plump and of fair size, and should leave an oily stain when pressed between the thumb nails; the essential oil should be 16 to 18 per cent.; cloves are stronger than cinnamon [q.v.] for all uses; the oil of cloves of the indian bazaars [q.v.] is made by steeping cloves in sweet oil; no essential oil is manufactured in the country. A paste of cloves is applied to the forehead and nose as a remedy for colds; a clove roasted in the flame of a lamp and held in the mouth is a popular remedy for sore throat; gives to pharm. the clove, caryophyllum; active principles, a volatile oil and a resinous crystalline principle, caryophyllin; aromatic stimulant and carminative; preparations, infusum caryophylli, oleum caryophylli; officinal. Much used as a spice in cooking; also with betel-leaf [q.v.] for chewing; the oil easily combines with grease, soap and spirit, and is extensively used in the manufacture of perfumery.——*Jungle lavangam* (అడవిలవంగ - adavilavanga, Tel.). Same as Country cinnamon.——*Lowly lavangam* (भूलवङ्ग - bhúlavanga, San.; पाणीलवङ्ग - pánílavanga, Mahr.; بن لونگ - banlaung, Hind.; ಕಾವಾಕುಲಗಿಡ - kávákulagida, Can.; నీరుఅగ్నివేంద్రము - níruagnivéndramu, Tel.; കാട്ടുകരയാമ്പൂ - káttukarayámpú, Mal.; நீர்க்கிராம்பு - nírkkirámbu, Tam.). Title from habitat and resemblance. San. from (bhú, san. ground + lavanga, san. cloves, eugenia caryophyllata, willd.), aromatic plant. Mahr. means water clove, referring to habitat. Hind. from (ban, hind. forest + laung, hind. clove). Tel. from (níru, tel. water + agnivéndramu, tel. ammannia baccifera, linn.). Mal. from (kátu, mal. forest + karayámpú, mal. cloves). Tam. from (nír, tam. water + kirámbu, tam. cloves, eugenia caryophyllata, willd.). Can. also (kávakúlagida). Mal. also (karámbu). Singh. also (hamargo). Tam. also (kirámbuppúndu), meaning cloves + plant; (káttukkirámbu), meaning wild clove plant. Title otherwise Primrose willow, West-indian loose strife, Wild clove tree. Botanically Jussiæa suffruticosa, linn., onagraceæ [vricsham, 59]. Alias Epilobium fruticosum; Jussiæa exaltata, fruticosa, villosa. Perennial, herbaceous, 1½ feet, erect, more or less pubescent or villous; leaves from broadly lanceolate to linear acuminate, tapering at the base into a short petiole; flowers almost sessile; calyx lobes four or five, broadly lanceolate or ovate, three to five-nerved, much shorter than the roundish-ovate petals; capsule nearly cylindrical, elongated, tapering at the base into a short pedicel; flowers largish, yellow, evening-primrose-like; flowering in rainy season. The plant, ground small, and steeped in butter-milk [mor], is considered good in dysentery; also in decoction as a vermifuge and purgative. A smaller species is repens.——*Wild lavangam* (قرنفل بری - karanfulibarri, Hind.). Same as China pepper.

LAVAUJAMAH (لوازمہ - lawázimah, *Hind.*). From (lazama, ar. to be necessary). Necessary things, baggage.

LAYAK (لایق - láik, *Hind.*). From (laika, ar. to do right). Fit. Layak bunjar is waste land fit for tillage.

LEAF INSECT (پتے کا کیرا - pattekákirá, *Dec.*; ಎಲೆಹುಳ - elehula, *Can.*; గొల్లభామ - gollabháma, *Tel.*; ഇലപ്പുഴു - ilappuzhu, *Mal.*; இலைக்கிளி - ilaikkili, *Tam.*). Title from haunt and appearance. Dec. from (pattá, hind. leaf + kírá, hind. worm). Can. from (ele, can. leaf + hula, can. insect). Tel. from (golla, tel. shepherd caste + bháma, tel. woman); the posture of sitting suggesting the posture of a shepherd woman while churning. Mal. from (ila, mal. leaf + puzhu, mal. insect). Tam. from (ilai, tam. leaf + kili, tam. locust); leaf-winged locust. Terms synonymous with the family Phasmidæ, orthoptera, hemimetabola, insecta [poochy], of naturalists [jantoo]. Of varied shapes. Called spectres, phantoms, devils' horses, walking sticks, walking leaves, &c. They mostly are inoffensive leaf-eating creatures, some being broad and leaf-like, while others are long and cylindrical, so as to resemble sticks or bits of withered grass. The Mantidæ however, so called because of their habit of sitting with their long fore feet held up as if in prayer, are carnivorous, taking that position in wait for their prey.

LEELAY (लीला - lílá, *San.*). From (lal, san. to play). A pastime. Also avatar [q.v.]. Shiva's miracles at Madura. See the Tamul tirvilaiyaudal.——*Leelaudhar* (లీలాధరుడు - líládharndu, Tel.). From (above + dhara, san. assumer). Vishnoo [q.v.] who assumes incarnations. Hindoo 2nd or pers. name [peyar].——*Leelaudharvilaus* (లీలాధర విలాసుడు - líládharavilásudu, Tel.). From (above + dhara, san. assumer + vilása, san. shining). Shining like Vishnoo. Hindoo 2nd or pers. name [peyar].

LEIL (لیل - laíl, *Hind.*). Night [shab].——*Leilat ool kadr* (لیلۃالقدر - laílatulkadr, Hind.). From (above + kadr, ar. power). The night of power, when the Koran [q.v.] descended from heaven [bheest] to the fourth firmamont [asmaun], generally held to have been on the twenty-seventh Ramzaun [q.v.]. Anniversary observed with reverence by Mahomedans. The devout sit up all night burning frankincense pastiles, repeating nafeelen, reciting the praises of the deity, reading the Koran, &c.——*Leilat ool mirauj* (لیلۃالمعراج - lailatulmiráj, Hind.). From (above + miráj, ar. ladder). The night of Mahomed's ascent to heaven. Held to be the fifteenth or sixteenth or twenty-seventh of seventh month Rajab [maheena]. The angel Gabriel [jibbreel] then conveyed the prophet [mahomed] mounted on the boorauk [q.v.] to the Almighty. People commemorate the night by sitting up all night, reading narratives written concerning it, and next day keep fast [roza]. The custom is peculiar to the learned and devout.——*Leilat ool moobaurak* (لیلۃالمبارك - laílatulmubárak, Ar.). From (above + mubárak, ar. blessed). Same as Shab e baraut [q.v.].——*Leilee* (لیلی - lailí, Hind.). Name of the celebrated mistress of mujnoon [q.v.], the subject of many poems.

LEKKA (లెక్క - lekka, *Tel.*). From (likh, san. to write). An account [hisaub, kanak].

LEMON GRASS (गन्धतृण - gandhatrina, *San.*; हिर्वेच - hirvacha, *Mahr.*; ताकातण - tákkátana, *Conc.*; اذخر - izkhar, *Ar.*; چاہ کشمیری - cháikashmírí, *Pers.*; اکیا گھاس - akiyághás, *Hind.*; ہزار مصالح - hazármasálah, *Dec.*; ವಾಸನೆಹುಲ್ಲು - vásanehullu, *Can.*; ಚಾತಪ್ಪು - chátappu, *Too.*; నిమ్మగడ్డి - nimmagaddi, *Tel.*; സംഭാരപ്പുല്ല് - sambhárappullu, *Mal.*; පෙංගිරිමාන් - pengirimán, *Singh.*; கற்பூரப்புல் - karbúrappul, *Tam.*). Title from scent. San. from (gandha, san. perfume + trina, san. grass). Conc. means curd grass, from use to flavor curd. Pers. from (chá, pers. tea + kashmír, pers. cashmere); from fragrance. Hind. from (agiya, hind. bird, alauda genus + ghás, hind. grass). Dec. from (hazár, hind. thousand + masálah, ar. ingredient); referring to aroma. Can. from (vásane, can. fragrance + hullu, can. grass). Tel. from (nimma, tel. lemon, citrus medica, linn., var. limonum, brandis + gaddi, tel. grass). Mal. from (sambháram, mal. diluted butter-milk + pullu, mal. grass); from grass used to flavor butter-milk. Singh. from (pengiri, singh. acid + mán, singh. having). Tam. from (karpúra, san. camphor + pul, tam. grass). San. also (bhústrina), meaning earth grass; (málátrinaka), meaning wreath + grass; (takratrina), meaning curd grass; (dévajagdhaka), meaning eaten by gods. Mahr. also (olancha). Hind. also (gandbel), meaning aromatic creeper; (ganjnikághás) by corruption from sanscrit meaning fragrant grass. Can. also (kámanchahullu); (kávanchehullu); (káchihullu); (majjigehulla), meaning butter-milk grass; (purvalihullu). Tel. also (kámanchigaddi), meaning forest + good + grass; (kámákshikasuvu); (vásanagaddi), meaning good smell + grass; (chippagaddi). Mal. also (vásanappullu), meaning fragrant grass; (cháyappullu), meaning color grass; (rámaççam). Tam. also (vásanaippul), meaning fragrant grass; (kávattambul), meaning shed + grass; (mándappul), meaning dullness + grass; (kámádchippul), meaning goddess + grass; really corruption from teloogoo. Greek σχοίνου ἄνθος. Title otherwise Butter-milk grass, Camel's hay, Camphor grass, Cashmere tea, Fragrant grass, Indian melissa oil grass, Masaulay grass, Sour grass, Sweet rush, Verbena oil grass. Botanically Andropogon [beard grass] schœnanthus, roxb., graminaceæ [vricsham, 156]. Alias Andropogon aromaticus, bicornis, citratum, citriodorus, nardus, pruinosus; Cymbopogon citratum, citriodorus, schœnanthus; Lagurus schœnanthus; Trachypogon schœnanthus. Root perennial; panicles somewhat secund; spikes conjugate, ovate-oblong; rachis pubescent; floscules sessile, awnless; culms 5–7 feet, erect, smooth; leaves many near the root, bifarious, soft, pale green, 3–4 feet long; spikelets in pairs, on a common pedicel furnished with a spathe; rachis articulated, hairy; flowers in pairs, one hermaphrodite and sessile, the other male and pedicelled. Sweet-smelling, bitterish, aromatic grass much cultivated in w. coast gardens. Oil by distillation, pale sherry color owing to resin contained, transparent, extremely pungent taste and lemon-like odour. Infusion of leaves medicinally tonic and stimulant; mixed with butter-milk [mor], leaves used in ring-worm; rhizomes and flowers have similar qualities; lemon-grass oil is substituted for british chamomile [baboona], caraway [q.v.], peppermint [poodeenah], and cajeput [q.v.] oils; gives to pharm. the volatile oil, oleum andropogi citrati, stimulant, carminative, antispasmodic, and diaphoretic; locally applied, rubefacient; officinal. Leaves used for tea [q.v.] and curries [q.v.] like roussa grass [q.v.]. Oil used as a perfume. Compare :—Andropogon martini (doddabilikáchihullu), large white lemon grass; Apluda aristata (sannakarikáchihullu), small black lemon grass. See gloss. paragraphs.

LEMURIA (ليموريه - limoriyah, *Malay*). From the Lemur found both in Madagascar and Southern india. A continent which from soundings is supposed to have formerly extended from Madagascar to Ceylon, India, and the Malay islands, from the Permian to the end of the Miocene geological period.

LIFAUFAH (لفافه - lifáfah, *Hind.*). From (lafa, ar. to wrap). Envelope.

LIMBOLEE (ليمبولى - limbolí, *Hind.*). Oil of Murraya kœnigii, spr., Curry-leaf tree.

LIME (करुणा - karuná, *San.*; اترج - utraj, *Ar.*; ترنج - turanj, *Pers.*; ليمو - límú, *Hind.*; نينبو - nímbú, *Dec.*; ಹೇರಳೆ - héralo, *Can.*; డబ్బ - dabba, *Tel.*; கொம்மட்டிமாதளை - kommattimáthalai, *Tam.*). Title from arabic (límú), through portuguese lima. Hind. from arabic. Dec. from hindostany. Can. from (híru, can. great). Tam. from (kommatti, tam. water-melon, citrullus vulgaris, schrad. + máthalai, tam. pomegranate, punica granatum, linn.). San. also (bíjapúra), meaning filled with seed [anaur, guava]; (mátulunga), meaning unequalled. Tel. also (lungamu); (mádíp'halamuchettu); (pulladabba), meaning sour + the tree; (peddanimma), meaning large + lime tree, citrus medica, linn., var. acida, brandis. Botanically Citrus [jambeeram] medica, linn., rutaceæ [vricsham, 32]. The typical lime, native of Sikkim and Koomaon. The "e" in specific name is long; in ancient times it derived its name from media; was the median apple introduced into greece and italy from persia and asia; greek μῆλον μηδικὸν. Shrub or small tree; leaflets 3 to 6 inches, elliptic ovate or ovate-lanceolate; petiole naked or winged; flowers five to ten in a raceme, small or middle-sized; stamens twenty to forty.——**(1)** All four varieties mentioned below [citron, lemon, sour lime, sweet lime] are cultivated to a limited extent in gardens.——*Citron* (फलपूर - p'halapúra, San.; मावळंग - mávalanga, Mahr.; मावलिङ्ग - mávalinga, Conc.; اترج - utraj, Ar.; ترنج - turanj, Pers., Hind. and Dec.; ಮಾದಳದಗಿಡ - mádaladagida, Can.; మాపల - mápala, Too.; నారదబ్బ - náradabba, Tel.; ഗണപതിനാരകം - ganapatinárakam, Mal.; ලප්නාරං - lapnáram, Singh.; துரிஞ்சி - turiñji, Tam.). Title from greek. San. from (p'hala, san. kernel + púra, san. full). Mahr. from (mátulunga, san. the plant). Conc. from (mátulunga, san. the plant). Ar. from syriac (atrogha). Pers. from arabic. Can. from (mádala, can. citron + gida, can. plant). Tel. from (nára, tel. fibre + dabba, tel. citrus medica, linn.). Mal. from (ganapati, san. the deity + nárakam, mal. lime, citrus). Tam. from persian. San. also (mátulunga), meaning unequalled; (jambíra), meaning eatable; (bíjapúra), meaning seed-filled. Ar. also (utranj). Hind. also (barálímú), meaning large lime. Can. also (maháp'halagida), meaning great + fruit + plant; (máduválagida). Tel. also (mádíp'halamu); (lungamu); (májíp'halamu); (pulladabba), meaning sour + the tree. Mal. also (mátalanárakam), meaning pomegranate, punica granatum, linn. + lime, citrus. Singh. also (sedaran). Tam. also (kommattimáthalai), meaning water-melon, citrullus vulgaris, schrad. + pomegranate, punica granatum, linn.; (kodimáthalai), meaning creeper + pomegranate. Title otherwise Cedrat, Creeper lime, Ganapaty's lime, Giant lime, Large lemon, Melon lime, Ootraj, Pomegranate lime, Tooranj. Botanically Citrus [jambeeram] medica, linn., var. medica proper, brandis, rutaceæ [vricsham, 32]. Alias Citrus fructu maximo, limon, solaniana, tuberosa; Limona racemosum, spinosum, vulgare. Shrub; young branches rigid; leaves oblong, pointed; petioles simple; flowers white, tinged with red; flowering in hot season; fruit great size, obovoid, deeply furrowed and wrinkled, with thick spongy rind, terminated by a knob, and juice only slightly acid; found wild along base of himalayas; at the present day no where cultivated extensively, the more prolific lemon [q.v.] and sour lime [q.v.] having generally taken its place. Citron rind is hot, dry and tonic; pulp cold and dry; seeds, leaves, and flowers hot and dry; juice refrigerant and astringent; the juice as sherbet is substituted for british citric and tartaric acids. The fruit itself seldom eaten, but made into confections and preserved; the rind very fragrant from quantity of aromatic oil. ——*Lemon* (महाजम्बीर - mahájambíra, San.; थोरनिंबू - t'hóranimbú, Mahr.; قلنبق - kalambak, Ar. and Pers.; بڑا ليمو - barálímú, Hind.; بڑا نينبو - baránímbú, Dec.; ದೊಡ್ಡನಿಂಬೆಗಿಡ - doddanimbegida, Can.; పెద్దనిమ్మ - peddanimma, Tel.; വലിയചെറുനാരകം - valiyacherunárakam, Mal.; ලොකුදෙහි - lokudehi, Singh.; பெரியவெலுமிச்சை - periyavelumiççai, Tam.). Title from sanscrit (nimbuka), so hindee (nimbu) and (limbu), so arabic (limun), so english lemon; the natives rightly consider it a mere variety of lime. San. from (mahá, san. great + jambíra, san. sweet lime, citrus medica, linn., var. limetta, brandis). Mahr. from (thóra, mahr. large + nimbú, mahr. lemon). Hind. from (bará, hind. large + límú, hind. lime). Dec. from hindostany. Can. from (dodda, can. large + nimbe, can. lime + gida, can. plant). Tel. from (pedda, tel. large + nimma, tel. lime, citrus medica, linn.). Mal. from (valiya, mal. large + cherunárakam, mal. sweet lime). Singh. from (loku, singh. large + dehi, singh. sweet lime). Tam. from (periya, tam. big + elumiççai, tam. lime). Dec. also (pahárínimbú), meaning mountain lime. Malay also (pahárîkághazí), meaning mountain paper-like lime. Tam. also (kodiyelumiççai), meaning creeper + lime. Title otherwise Creeper lime, Large lime, Mountain lime. Botanically Citrus [jambeeram] medica, linn., var. limonum, brandis, rutaceæ [vricsham, 32]. Alias Citrus limonum, medica. Small tree 10 to 15 feet; young branches flexible; leaves oval-oblong, usually toothed; petioles simply margined; flowers white tinged with red, fragrant; flowering in hot season. Fruit middle-sized, ovoid oblong, nippled at top, external skin thin, smooth, highly odoriferous, pale yellow, marked all over by small cells filled with essential oil; rind thin; juice very acid. Real lemons are rarely met with in madras. Gives to pharm. the outer part of the rind of the ripe fruit, limonis cortex; again the essential oil of the rind, limonis oleum; again the expressed juice of the ripe fruit, limonis succus. Yellow peel is an aromatic oil from rind used in perfumery; citric acid made of the fruit.——*Sour lime* (जम्बीर - jambíra, San.; निंबू - nimbú, Mahr.; ليمو حامض - límúihámiz, Ar.; ليمو ترش - límúitursh. Pers.; ليمو - límú, Hind.; نينبو - nímbú, Dec.; جارك كرباو - járukkarbau, Malay; ನಿಂಬೆಗಿಡ - nimbegida, Can.; నిమ్మ - nimma, Tel.; ଲିମ୍ବୁ - limbo, Oor.; ചെറുനാരകം - cherunárakam, Mal.; දෙහි - dehi, Singh.; எலுமிச்சை - elumiççai, Tam.). Title from taste of all parts. San. from (jam, san. to eat + víra, san. strong). Mahr. from (nimbúka, san. the plant). Ar. from (límú, ar. lime + hámiz, ar. sour). Pers. from (límú, ar. lime + tursh. pers. sour). Hind. from arabic. Dec. from sanscrit. Malay from (járuk, malay, citrus sp. + kárbau, malay, buffalo). Can. from (nimbe, can. lime + gida, can. plant). Tel. from sanscrit. Oor. from sanscrit. Mal. from (cheru, mal. small + nárakam, mal. lime, citrus). San. also (nimbúka); (mátulunga), meaning unequalled; (limpáka), meaning stainer, from removing stains on garments. Ar. also (límún), meaning lime. Pers. also (límú), meaning lime. Malay also (járuknipis), meaning thin orange; (limau), from persian. Can. also (gajanimbegida), meaning elephant + lime + plant. Title otherwise Acid lime, Buffalo lime, Elephant lime, Small lemon, Thin orange. Botanically Citrus [jambeeram] medica, linn., var. acida, brandis, rutaceæ [vricsham, 32]. Alias Citrus acida. Leaflet elliptic oblong, petiole many times shorter than the leaflet linear or obovate, racemes short, flowers small, petals usually four, fruit usually small globose or ovoid, with a thick or thin rind, pulp pale sharply acid. As the true lemon [q.v.] is scarce here, the fruit of this is universally used as a substitute; differs considerably in appearance from lemon; smaller, quite round or nearly so, smooth rind thinner than lemon; much more acid than lemon; to a certain degree acrid; in natural qualities otherwise the same; color, when the fruit arrives at a perfect state of maturity, is a fine bright yellow; much more common than the lemon; is like the w. indian lime. The fruit contains free citric acid, combined malic and phosphoric acids, and potassium, the first being the essential constituent; the juice can be prepared for market either by boiling or by adding 10 per cent. of a strong spirit, brandy or whisky, to it. For cultivation best soil is sandy clay; ground prepared at any time, being turned up manured with dung [shauny] and alluvial soil and pitted; seed sown in nursery [nauttangaul] in pots and transplanted at rains; plant requires frequent watering, and occasional manuring; plants will come to full bearing after 7 years; price 5 annas per 100 fruits. The juice of fruit is medicinally antalkaline, antiscorbutic, refrigerant, astringent, stomachic and tonic; diluted with water and sweetened, forms a refrigerant drink; used in pharm. for the officinal lemon [q.v.]; the dried rind of fruit used as a vegetable drug. Dried limes are used to fasten and improve colors; lime-juice is used by dyers in dyeing yellow [shauyam], by washermen [dhoby] for taking stains out of linen, and with borax [vengauram] in preparation of the tirchoornam [q.v.]. The best of this variety are called by the natives paper-lime and leaf-lime, on account of thinness of the rind.——*Sweet lime* (निम्बूक - nimbúka, San.; मिठानिंबू - mit'hánimbú, Mahr.; ليمو حلو - límúihalo, Ar.; ليمو شيرين - límúishírín, Pers.; ميٹھا ليمو - míthálímú, Hind.; ميٹھا نينبو - míthánímbú, Dec.; ನಿಂಬೆಗಿಡ - nimbegida, Can.; నిమ్మ - nimma, Tel.; ചെറുനാരകം - cherunárakam, Mal.; දෙහි - dehi, Singh.; எலுமிச்சை - elumiççai, Tam.). Title from taste of pulp. Mahr. from (mit'há, mahr. sweet + nimbú, mahr. lemon). Ar. from (límú, ar. lemon, citrus medica, linn., var. limonum, brandis + halo, ar. sweet). Pers. from (límú, ar. lemon + shírín, pers. sweet). Hind. from (míthá, hind. sweet + limú, pers. lemon). Dec. from hindostany. Can. from (nimbe, can. lime + gida, can. plant). Mal. from (cheru, mal. small + nárakam, mal. lime, citrus). San. also (madhukarkatí), meaning sweet + cucumis melo, linn. Hind. also (amritphal), meaning sweet fruit. Tel. also (tiyyanimma), meaning sweet lime. Tam. also (tittippuyelumiççai), meaning sweet lime. Title otherwise Adam's apple, Limetta, Pear lemon, Sweet lemon. Botanically Citrus [jambeeram] medica, linn., var. limetta, brandis, rutaceæ [vricsham, 32]. Alias Citrus limetta. Leaves and flowers as in sour lime, fruit globose 3–5 inches diameter, rind thin smooth, juice abundant, sweet not aromatic. Native of northern india; has smooth, laurel-like leaves, and fruits similar to the orange [q.v.], but of an oval form, and the apex depressed, forming a hollow; very smooth, pale-green rind, scarcely any flavor perceptible besides that of sweetness; flower white fragrant. Cultivation same as Sour lime; average price one fruit for six pies. Fruit is used somewhat as an orange.——(2) The following are limes so called in other genera.——*Manilla lime* (چینی نارنگی - chínínárangí, Dec.). Same as Musk lime.——*Monkey lime* (माकडनिंबूण - mákadanimbúna, Mahr.; चोर्निंबुवे - chórnimbuvé, Conc.; جنگلی نیمبو - janglínimbú, Dec.; ಕಾಡುನಿಂಬೆ - kádunimbe, Can.; କୈପେରିପୁଳି - kaipéripuli, Too.; కొండనిమ్మ - kondanimma, Tel.; ନର୍ଗୁନି - narguni, Oor.; മലനാരകം - malanárakam, Mal.; காட்டெலுமிச்சை - káttelumiççai, Tam.). Title from exterior appearance of fruit. Mahr. from (mákada, mahr. monkey + nimbú, mahr. lemon, citrus medica, linn., var. limonum, brandis). Conc. means thief lime or false lime. Dec. from (janglí, hind. wild + nimbú, dec. lime). Can. from (kádu, can. forest + nimbe, can. lime tree). Too. from (kaipéru, too. bitter + puli, too. acidity). Tel. from (konda, tel. hill + nimma, tel. lime). Mal. from (mala, mal. mountain + nárakam, mal. lime). Tam. from (kádu, tam. forest + elumiççai, tam. lime, citrus medica, linn., var. acida, brandis); from berry-like lime. Mahr. also (rânanimbúna), meaning wild lemon. Can. also (kádulimbi), meaning wild + lime tree; (dodlihuligida), meaning large + sour + orange, citrus aurantium; (náyibéladamara), meaning barber + bael tree, ægle marmelos, corr. [wild lime] Tel. also (adavinimma), meaning jungle + lime. Mal. also (káttukurunnu), meaning forest shoot; (káttunárakam), meaning forest lime. Tam. also (káttuk-kurundu), meaning wild shoot. Title otherwise Bitter orange, Dog-wood apple, Hill lime, Indian wild lime, Jungle lime, Monkey lime, Thorny trichilia. Botanically Atalantia monophylla, corr., rutaceæ [vricsham, 32]. Alias Atalantia floribunda, platystigma; Limonia monophylla, rotunda; Trichilia spinosa; Turæa virens. Shrub, 8 feet; thorns small; leaves ovate or oblong, more or less emarginate at the apex; calyx four-toothed; petals four; racemes short, sessile; pedicels long, slender; berry globose, size of a nutmeg [jautikye] or small lime, three to four-seeded; flowers axillary and terminal, small, white; flowering in november; native of s. india. Warm, pleasant-smelling oil prepared by veidyans [q.v.] from the berry; application in chronic rheumatism and paralysis. Wood yellow, very hard and close-grained; substitute for box. Other common species are:—missionis, racemosa.——*Musk lime* (چینی نارنگی - chíninárangí, Dec.; கத்தூரியெலுமிச்சை - kattúriyelumiççai, Tam.). Title from flavor. Dec. from (chín, hind. china + nárangí, hind. orange, citrus aurantium, linn.). Tam. from (kastúri, san. musk + elumiççai, tam. lime, citrus). Tam. also (shinnakkozhunji), meaning small + orange. Title otherwise China limboo, China orange, Manilla lime. Botanically Triphasia trifoliata, dec., rutaceæ [vricsham, 32]. Alias Triphasia aurantiola. Glabrous spinous shrub, with straggling evergreen branches and leaves; spines slender, straight; leaflets thick and soft, crenulate, coriaceous, almost nerveless, the terminal shortly petioled, ⅝–1¼ inch, ovate with a cuneate base, and rounded notched tip; lateral smaller, more rounded, oblique; flowers very shortly peduncled, nearly ½ inch long, white, fragrant; petals linear-oblong; fruit ½ inch long, fleshy, apiculate, gland-dotted. A small thorny shrub; bears small, white, fragrant flowers; the fruit about the size of a large black currant; encloses a stone which fills nearly the whole of the centre, leaving room for a small quantity of juicy pulp of an agreeable aniseed [anise] like flavor. No other common species here.——*Wild lime* (नैबेल - naibéla, Mahr.; بیلی - belí, Hind.; ನೈಬೆಲ - naibela, Can.; అడవినిమ్మ - adavinimma, Tel.; ଭେଣ୍ଟ - bhenta, Oor.; ചെറുകാട്ടുനാരകം - cherukáttunárakam, Mal.; காட்டெலுமிச்சை - kátteluniççai, Tam.). Mahr. means barber's bael; from fruit used by barbers for soap. Hind. from (bel, hind. bael tree, ægle marmelos, corr.). Can. from mahratta. Tel. from (adavi, tel. forest + nimma, tel. citrus medica, linn., var. acida, brandis). Mal. from (cheru, mal. small + káttunárakam, mal. atalantia monophylla, corr.). Tam. from (kádu, tam. forest + elumiççai, tam. lime tree, citrus medica, linn., var. acida, brandis); berries resemble lime. Tel. also (tórelaga), meaning strong + wood-apple, feronia elephantum, corr. Tam. also (kuttivilá), meaning small + wood-apple tree, feronia elephantum, corr. Title otherwise Barber's bael, Musk-deer plant. Botanically Limonia acidissima, linn., rutaceæ [vricsham, 32]. Alias Limonia crenulata. Limonia, from (limú, ar. lime). Armed shrub, orange family, 6–10 feet; leaves pinnate, with two to three pairs of leaflets and an odd one; leaflets oblong, retuse, crenated; spines solitary; petioles broadly winged; flowers corymbose; corymbs umbelliform, two to three together from the axils of the fallen leaves; petals four; fruit globose, size of a nutmeg [jautikye], yellowish, but red when perfectly ripe; flowers small, white, fragrant; flowering in april and may. Root purgative, sudorific, and used in colic pains; the dried fruits are tonic and antidote to various poisons; wood very hard, close-grained, yellowish-white; used for turning. Other species are alata and bilocularis.

LINGO WOOD (لنگوکا جہار - lingokájhár, *Hind.*). Same as Moch coondam.

LISAUN (لسان - lisán, *Ar.*). Tongue. Plant first term. Ex., where transl. is of second term:—Holarrhena antidysenterica (lisánulasáfírulmurr), sparrow + bitter; Onosma bracteatum (lisánussanr), bull; Wrightia tinctoria (lisánulasáfír), sparrow; (lisánulasáfírulhalo), sparrow + sweet. See gloss. paragraphs.

LITCHY (لیچی - líchí, *Hind.*; لچی - liççí, *Malay*). Title from chinese through malay. Malay also (kálengkeng). Title otherwise Lee-chee. Botanically Nephelium litchi, camb., sapindaceæ [vricsham, 43]. Specific name from malay. Alias Scytalia litchi. Fine tree of moderate height, with spreading branches; leaves 3–9 inches; leaflets 1½–6 by ½–1¾ inches; petiolules $\frac{1}{12}$–¼ inch; inflorescence tawny-puberulent; flowers greenish-white, $\frac{1}{12}$–⅛ inch wide; anthers shorter than the filaments; disk glabrous ovary two to three-celled, ferruginous-hairy; style two to three-lobed, lobes recurved; fruit two to one-lobed, globose, about 1 inch diameter; pericarp dry, at length brittle; tubercles angular; aril fleshy, whitish, edible. Conspicuous with spreading branches, compound alternate extipulate leaves, very small white flowers; introduced into gardens; most celebrated native fruit of china; fruit size and form of a large plum [auloochah], with rough, thin, scale-like rind, which, while the fruit is hanging ripe upon the tree, is of a red tinge, but gradually becomes of a dull brown color short time after gathered; pulp of the fruit resembles white of a plover's egg; contains in its centre a stone; in the best fruit the stone is very small. The chinese dry the fruit, when it becomes black like a prune; the pulp has a sub-acid flavor when eaten fresh. Wood red, hard, heavy. Nearly allied to the Rambutan [q.v.] and Longan [q.v.].

LITTLE MOUNT (சின்னமலை - shinnamalai, *Tam.*). As distinguished from St. Thomas' mount which is the Great mount. Village. Chinglepnt district, Sydapett talook; being a portion of Guindy; lat. 13° 01′; long. 80° 17′; from Fort St. George S.S.W. 6 miles; from St. Thomas' mount E. 2 miles; from Sydapett S.E. ¾ mile; from the sea W. 4 miles. Traditionary site of St. Thomas' martyrdom. There is a cave in a rock and a natural spring. It is asserted that St. Thomas took refuge here from his pursuers. A church is erected over the spot. Two stones below are pointed out as bearing impress of his foot and marks of his knees, while another is said to be stained with his blood. At the foot of the steps leading up to the church is a slab with an inscription in Armenian characters. The spring is said to have been miraculously created to supply the saint with water when attacked by thirst in the cave in which he had taken refuge. The legend regarding this is still current in Syria.

LO (లో - ló, *Tel.*). Within.——*Locoony* (లోకుని - lókuni, Tel.). From (above + kuni, tel. piece of land). Patch of ground within a field, as distinguished from Veloocoony or patch on the side of a field. Used in field measurement [cshetram, pramaunam].——*Loloom* (లోదుము - lodumu, Tel.). Tel. from (lodugu, tel. fallen in). Hollow; natural stream.——*Lona* (లోన - lóna, Tel.). Interior; suffix in place names.——*Lopaly soonkam* (లోపలిసుంకము - lópalisunkamu, Tel.). From (lópala, tel. inside + sunkamu, tel. duty). Import duty.

LOBAUN (لوبان - lobán, *Hind.*). Ar. from (laban, ar. juice). Stands for either Benzoin or Olibanum.

LOBYAH (باقلا - báklah, *Ar.*; لوبیا - lobiyá, *Pers.*; لوبیا - lobaya, *Hind.*; لوبا - lobá, *Dec.*; ಹುರಳಿಗಿಡ - huraligida, *Can.*; දඹල - dambala, *Singh.*). Title from hindostany [cow gram]. Ar. from (bákil, ar. ground producing herb). Title otherwise French bean, Haricot bean, Kidney bean. Botanically Phaseolus [moodgam] vulgaris, linn., leguminosæ [vricsham, 48]. Alias Phaseolus manus, vulgaris. Sub-glabrous annual; stems low and sub-erect, or twining to a height of 6–10 feet; racemes much shorter than the leaves; pedicels finally ¼–½ inch long; bracteoles ovate or roundish, persistent; pod 4–6 inches by ⅓ inch, glabrous, rostrate, turgid. Bears middle-sized, white flowers; stems low or sub-erect, twining; cultivated in gardens. Green pod and its immature beans are cut up into slices, boiled, and eaten. Two kinds, first runners, second dwarfs which require no sticks for their support. For the different grams see Gram, and for beans see Shimby.——*Country lobyah* (کہرسنبل - kharsambal, Hind.). Title otherwise Country french bean, Country haricot, Duffin bean, Hibbert bean, Lima bean, Scymitar-podded kidney bean, Sugar bean. Botanically Phaseolus [moodgam] lunatus, linn., leguminosæ [vricsham, 48]. Alias Phaseolus maximus. Biennial, usually twining, glabrous or pubescent; leaflets ovate, acuminated; stipules reflexed; racemes shorter than the leaves, the flowering part elongated; pedicels in pairs; bracts narrow, much shorter than the calyx; legumes pendulous, scimitar-shaped, long mucronate, not torulose, two to four-seeded; flowers small greenish; flowering in the cold season. The pods are rather coarse looking and are not eaten; the large, flat, ivory-like [daut] beans are shelled, laid in a pan of cold water and boiled till they are quite soft; they are then exceedingly agreeable, having a mealy roast chestnut-like flavor; not much used however by natives. Six varieties are cultivated for the table.

LOCAM (लोक - lóka, *San.*). From (luk, san. to see). World, sometimes divided into three [trilocam]. Generally means seven upper worlds allotted for the residence of different species of animated beings, including Bhoo locam the earth as the first; Bhoovar locam is the space between the earth and the sun; Swar locam is the heaven of indran [q.v.] between the sun and the polar star [dhroovam]; Maharlocam, the abode of bhringy and other rishies; during the conflagration of these lower worlds the saints ascend to the next, or Jana locam, the abode of bramha's sons; above this is the Tapolocam, where the deified sages reside; the seventh world Satya locam is the abode of bramha [q.v.], and translation to this world exempts beings from further birth [samsauram]. The seven regions below the earth are called stalam [q.v.]; the habitations of the snake gods, and are named in the order of their talam [q.v.] or descent:—Atalam, Vitalam, Sootalam, Rasautalam, Talautalam, Mahautalam, and Pautaulam. Both the written and popular views regard the inferior worlds as places of punishment, and the superior worlds as ascending in the scale of sanctity and happiness. Sectaries have also invented locams or regions of their own, as:—Veicoontam, the sphere of vishnoo; Golocam, the region of krishnan, &c. [matam].——*Locachundran* (உலோகச்சந்திரன் - ulógaççandiran, Tam.). From (above + chandra, san. the moon). Hindoo 2nd or pers. name [peyar].——*Loca mautah* (लोकमाता - lókamátá, San.). From (above + mátá, san. mother). Saraswaty [q.v.].——*Locan* (உலோகன் - ulógan, Tam.). Short for any of the compounds. Hindoo 2nd or pers. name [peyar].——*Locanautan* (உலோகநாதன் - ulóganáthan, Tam.). From (above + nát'ha, san. lord); epithet of any of the superior gods, shiva [q.v.], krishnan [q.v.], vishnoo [q.v.], &c. Hindoo 2nd or pers. name [peyar].——*Loca paulacan* (लोकपालक - lókapálaka, San.). From (above + pálaka, san. protector). Sovereign. Also any one of the eight regent deities of the quarter [ashtadic paulacan].——*Locaulocam* (लोकालोक - lókálóka, San.). Means visible and not visible; world and not world. The mountain range encircling the world and separating it from the non-world. In the Shiva tantram it is said that the gods had their play-ground at the foot of the Locaulocam mountain. The Mahomedans have a mountain in their legends, called Koh kauf [q.v.], a girdle of stone surrounding the world.——*Locauyatam* (लोकयत - lókáyata, San.). From (above + áyata, san. extended); world-extending or material. The system of atheistical philosophy [chaurvaucan, samayam, shastram].——*Locayyan* (உலோகய்யன் - ulógayyan, Tam.). From (above + aiyyan, tam. master, titular affix). Hindoo 2nd or pers. name [peyar].——*Log* (لوگ - log, Hind.). From (lóka, san. world). People. Suffix in compounds; as Sahib log, meaning master + people, gentle folk.——*Lowkica* (लौकिक - laukika, San.). From (lóka, san. world). Secular, as opposed to Veidica or priestly.

LOCMAUN (لقمان - lokmán, *Hind.*). Arabian author of fables, the Æsop of the east.

LOCUST TREE (خرنوب - khurnúb, *Hind.*). Same as Carob.

LODH (लोध्र - lódhra, *San.*; لودھ - lodh, *Hind.*; عبیر کا جھاڑ - abírkájhár, *Dec.*; ಬಲಲೊಡ್ಡಿ - balaloddi, *Can.*; లొద్దుగ - lodduga, *Tel.*; പാച്ചോറ്റി - páççótti, *Mal.*; ලොත්සුඹුල - lotsumbula, *Singh.*). Title from hindostany. San. from (rudhira, san. red); from red dye. Hind. from sanscrit. Dec. from (abír, hind. red powder used in hóli festival + jhár, hind. tree); from being made of this bark. Can. from (bala, can. strong + loddi, can. the tree). Tel. from sanscrit. Mal. from (pál, mal. milk + chori, mal. to shed) [pauchonty]. San. also (shábara), meaning pertaining to shabaras; (shrímat), meaning propitious; (tilaka), meaning caste mark, as being used for it. Can. also (loddi). Tel. also (erralodduga), meaning red + the tree. Title otherwise Californian cinchona, China nora, Lotur bark. Botanically Symplocos racemosa, roxb., styraceæ [vricsham, 84]. Alias Symplocos hamiltoniana, theæfolia. Tree, 10–12 feet; leaves oblong-lanceolate, acuminate, acute at the base, quite glabrous sub-denticulate, shining above; racemes simple, axillary, nearly equalling the petiole, hairy; sepals and bracteoles ovate, obtuse, ciliated; ovary free at the apex; flowers small, yellow. The bark is very soft and friable, of a light fawn color; the external surface corky and much fissured transversely; the internal of a lighter color and fibrous texture; on making a transverse section a middle layer of a red color is seen between the corky and fibrous portions; microscopic examination shows that the colored layer is chiefly composed of oblong cells containing red coloring matter; the inner layer of the bark consists almost entirely of woody fibre; the taste is faintly balsamic and astringent. Bark medicinally cooling, astringent, like cinchona [koinah]; decoction of wood used as gargle. Bark gives a red dye [shauyam]; ashes used as mordant [cauram]. Wood small, white or yellowish, hard and durable, suitable for turnery. Other common species are:—acuminata, anamallayana, ferruginea, foliosa, gardneriana, macrophylla, microphylla, monantha, nervosa, obtusa, oligandra, pendula, pulchra, rosea, spicata.

LOMAM (लोम - lóma, *San.*). Later form of romam [q.v.]. From (ruh, san. to grow). Short hair on the body of men and animals; less properly applied to long hair of head [kesham] and beard or to that on the mane [kesharam] or tail of animals. Braided hair is Vainy [q.v.]; clotted or matted hair is Jatay [q.v.]. For hair of animals or wool see Pushm. Cf. Anooloma.——*Lomree* (किखि - kikhi, San.; खोकड - khókada, Mahr.; ثعلب - salab, Ar.; روباه - rúbáh, Pers.; لونبڑی - lonbrí, Hind.; لومڑی - lomrí, Dec.; ಚನ್ನಂಗಿನರಿ - channanginari, Can.; గుంటనక్క - guntanakka, Tel.; କୋଙ୍କିବିଲୁଅ - konkibilluva, Oor.; കുറുനരി - kurunari, Mal.; වල්නා - valná, Singh.; குழிநரி - kuzhinari, Tam.). Title from deccany. Ar. from (salaba, ar. cowardly). Hind. from (lómasha, san. fox). Dec. from hindostany. Can. from (channa, can. red + anga, can. body + nari, can. jackal). Tel. from (gunta, tel. hole + nakka, tel. jackal). Mal. from (kuru, mal. small + nari, mal. jackal). Tam. from (kuzhi, tam. hole + nari, tam. jackal). Ar. also (abulhusain), meaning father of the inaccessible; (abulhiyal), meaning father of stratagems. Can. also (konk); (kempunari), meaning red + jackal. Tel. also (pottinakka), meaning short + jackal; (konkanakka), meaning timid + jackal. Tam. also (kullanari), meaning short + jackal. Title otherwise Fox. Vulpes bengalensis, canidæ [cookooram], digitigrada, carnivora, mammalia [sustanam, 12], of naturalists [jantoo]. Alias Canis bengalensis, kokree, rufescens; Cynalopex bengalensis; Vulpes hodgson, indicus. Kokree from mahratta. The Indian fox is reddish gray, rufous on the legs, muzzle, reddish white beneath; ears long, dark brown externally; tail long, bushy with a broad black tip; muzzle very acute; chin and throat whitish. Rare in the forest, abundant in open country. It burrows in the open plains. Coursed with grey hounds. It runs with great speed, doubling like a hare [mosal]; but instead of stretching out at first like that animal and trusting to its turns as a last resource, it turns more at first and if it can fatigue the dogs [nye], it then goes straight away. Its numerous earths in this country prevent its being hunted with fox hounds, and the scent is poor. See Jackal. Indian species not here found are:—Ferrilatus or thibetan grey fox, Alopex or persian fox, Leucopus or desert fox, Canna or hoary fox.

LONGAN (لونگن - longan, *Malay*; ಮಲಹಕೋಟ - malahakota, *Can.*; මොර - mora, *Singh.*; பூவத்தி - púvatti, *Tam.*). Title from malay. Tam. from (pú, tam. flower + atti, tam. fig tree, ficus). Tam. also (pirappinmaram). Title otherwise Dragon's-eye. Botanically Nephelium longana, camb., sapindaceæ [vricsham, 43]. Specific name from malay. Alias Dimocarpus longan; Euphorbia longana; Scytale longana; Scytalia longana. Leaflets two to four pair, entire, somewhat glaucous beneath; panicles lax, terminal; calyx deeply five-partite; petals five, narrow-oblong, hairy, without a scale; stamens hairy; ovary two to three-lobed; stigmas two to three, linear; berries usually solitary or in pairs, rarely three, globose, slightly scabrous; flowers white; flowering in february and march. Handsome tree, similar to litchy [q.v.], but smaller; fruit the size and form of a marble, of a russet color, and borne in bunches like grapes [angoor]; fruit smaller than litchy; pulp edible, resembles that of litchy in flavor, but vapid and inferior. Wood hard and close-grained.

LONG CLOTH (گاڑھا - gárhá, *Hind.*; ಪರಕಾಳಿ - parakáli, *Can.*; పరకాళ - parakálá, *Tel.*; കുപ്പായശ്ശീല - kuppáyashshíla, *Mal.*; சட்டைத்துணி - shattaittuni, *Tam.*). Hind. means thick as opposed to mull [q.v.] which is thin. Can. from (paraka, can. fine + ele, can. thread). Tel. from canarese. Mal. from (kuppáyam, mal. coat + shíla, mal. cloth). Tam. from (shattai, tam. coat + tuni, tam. cloth). Tam. also (shattaiççámbu), coat + piece. Anglo-indian name for Lancashire white cotton [q.v.] shirtings, because it is made of length unusual in India; cloth for native use being ordinarily made in pieces sufficient only to clothe one person [poonjam].

LONGSHORE WIND (దక్షిణపుగాలి - dakshinapugáli, *Tel.*; தென்றல் - tenral, *Tam.*). Tel. from (dakshina, san. south + gáli, tel. wind). Tam. means south wind. Damp wind that blows on the Coromandel coast [q.v.], July to September, from the south [land wind, monsoon, tennal]. See vol. II, 5.

LONTAR (لونتر - lontar, *Malay*). Same as Palmyra.

LOO (लु - lu, *San.*). To cut.——*Lavaly* (लवली - lavalí, San.). From (lu, san. to cut); from sour taste of fruit. Botanically the Averrhoa genus, geraniaceæ [vricsham, 31]. Small trees cultivated throughout india; leaves evergreen, alternate, pinnate; flowers small, purplish, in racemes; fruit is like a gherkin in shape, very acid, but pleasant when made into syrup, candied, or pickled; leaves are slightly sensitive. The species best known to the natives are:—bilimbi [blimbing], carambola [coromandel gooseberry].——*Lavan* (लव - lava, San.). From (lú, san. to cut). The younger of the twin sons of Rama [q.v.] by Seetay [q.v.]. The elder was Cooshan [q.v.].——*Lavangam* (लवङ्ग - lavanga, San.). See sep. title.——*Loham* (लोह - lóha, San. and Mahr.; حدید - hadíd, Ar.; آهن - áhan, Pers.; لوها - lohá, Hind.; لهوا - lhauvá, Dec.; لابرن - láburan, Malay; ಲೋಹ - lóha, Can.; ଲୋହା - lóhá, Too.; లోహము - lóhamu, Tel.; ലോഹം - lóham, Mal.; ලෝහ - lóha, Singh.; உலோகம் - ulógam, Tam.). San. from (lú, san. to cut + há, san. to avoid), not easily cut. Ar. from (hadda, ar. to binder); from its resistance. Malay from (labur, malay, to melt); thing melted. Metal, one form of minerals [dhautoo]. Cf. Col and Pon. The following are all the south indian metals:—Antimony [soorma], Brass [pittalay], Calamine [madaltoottam], Chromium [cooroom], Copper [taumram], Gold [pon], Iron [auhan], Lead [eeyam], Manganese [q.v.], Mercury [rasam], Pinchbeck [tambauk], Platinum [goorootwam], Pyrites [teecull], Silver [velly], Steel [wootz], Tin [tagaram], Zinc [tootnaug]. Simple metals are the following:—Copper, Gold, Iron, Lead, Mercury, Platinum, Silver, Tin, Zinc. Note that carbon [kary] and sulphur [gandhac] are non-metallic substances. Water vessels or lotahs [q.v.], dishes, bowls, candlesticks, images of the gods [vigraham], temple bells, sacrificial spoons, censers, and other sacred and domestic utensils in brass and copper are made all over the country, and of the same patterns as are found in representations on the oldest Booddhist [booddha] sculptures [staupatyam] and cave-paintings. These metal vessels in a native Indian household supply the place of the porcelain [kaolin], glass [cunnaudy] and silver plate in a European family. Hindoos use brass vessels, and Mahomedans copper, except for drinking-cups, which are generally of silver. The metal work of Madura and Tanjore is the finest in India. In its bold forms and elaborately inwrought ornamentation the latter recalls the descriptions by Homer of the work of the artists of Sidon. Some designs are simply etched, and others deeply cut in mythological designs, and others are diapered all over with crustæ of the leaf pattern seen in Assyrian sculptures, copper on brass, or silver on copper, producing an effect often of quite regal grandeur. The temple bells of Southern india are distinguished by their stately architectural forms. The handles are generally crowned with a group of the Pooraunic gods, sculptured in full relief. The sacrificial vases also are often very beautifully designed and wrought. See vol. II, 29.——*Lohauro* (لوهار - lohár, Hind.; [illegible] - loháro, Tel.). From (lóha, san. metal). The corresponding terms are:—Tam. collan, Tel. cummara. Ironsmith caste among the Ooriyas.——*Loniyah* (لونيا - loniyá, Hind.). Means cutting; from acidity. Same as Indian purslane.

LOOCSAUN (نقصان - nuksán, *Hind.*). From (nuks, ar. defect). Loss.

LOOT (لوٹ - lút, *Hind.*). From (lut'h, san. to plunder). Plundering. Also the booty carried away.——*Lootcher* (لچا - luççá, Hind.). A libertine. A common term of abuse.

LOQUAT (لكوٹا - lakotá, *Hind.*; ಲಕ್ಕೊಟೆಗಿಡ - lakkotegida, *Can.*; நோக்கட்டாமரம் - nókkattámaram, *Tam.*). Title from chinese through hindostany. Title otherwise Japan medlar. Botanically Eriobotrya japonica, lindl., rosaceæ [vricsham, 49]. Alias Mespilus japonica. Branchlets as thick as the little finger; leaves 6–8 by 1½–3 inches, thick and stiffly coriaceous; base obtuse or narrowed into the very short stout woolly petiole; nerves twelve to fifteen very prominent beneath; panicles 3–6 inches long and broad; branches very stout; flowers ½ inch diameter, crowded, fragrant; calyx-tube short; lobes ovate, sub-acute; petals broadly ovate; fruit 1–1½ inch long, rather narrower, yellow, rarely as many as five-seeded. Tree of apple [seb] class; introduced from china; cultivated for fruit; handsome foliage and large leaves; flower smallish white, fragrant; fruit grows in clusters, small, yellow, 1–1½ inches long, thin skin, luscious pulp, and brown seeds; resembles a very small pear [amrood]; no distinct varieties, but great difference in fruits from different trees; esteemed for desserts and preserves.

LORY (نوری - nuri, *Malay*; பச்சைக்கிளி - paççaikkili, *Tam.*). Title corrupted from the malay. Malay from (núr, hind. light) [noor]; shining. Tam. from (paççai, tam. green + kili, tam. parrot). Brilliantly-colored variety of parrot found in the Moluccas. Loriinæ, psittacidæ [keeram], scansores, incessores, aves [pacshy, 12], of naturalists [jantoo]. Bill compressed, small or moderate, slightly curved; lower mandible much longer than high; tongue in most is furnished with a protrusile tuft of elongated papillæ, enabling them to draw the nectar from flowers, which with soft fruits constitutes their sole food; they appear to have a delicate sense of taste. ——*Lorikeet* (بهورا - bhorá, Hind.; ಪಂಚವರ್ಣಗಿಣಿ - panchavarnagini, Can.; പഞ്ചവർണ്ണക്കിളി - pañchavarnnakkili, Mal.; பஞ்சவன்னக்கிளி - pañjavannakkili, Tam.). Title means small lory. Can. means five-colored parrot. Mal. and tam. from (pañcha, san. five + varna, san. color + kili, tam. parrot). Hind. also (latkan), meaning pendent; from sleeping head downwards suspended by claws. Title otherwise Love-bird. Loriculus vernalis, loriinæ [lory], psittacidæ [keeram], scansores, insessores [pacshy, 12], of naturalists. Alias Psittacus pendulus. Above grass-green, darker on wing-coverts and scapulars; paler and yellowish beneath wings and tail blue-green; rump and upper tail-coverts dull deep red; wings and tail beneath pale-bluish; chin and throat in the male tinged with verdigris-blue; bill dark-yellow, irides pale-yellow; feet leaden; w. coast, found in small flocks; keeps up continual chirping when feeding, which it does on fruit and flower-buds; fond of toddy [q.v.] of cocoanut [q.v.] palm and sometimes taken stupified at toddy-pots; occasionally caged, become very tame, sleeping with head downwards.

LOTAH (لوٹا - lotá, *Hind.*). Small spheroidal brass [pittalay] pot [chatty], which the natives of all classes use for drinking and sometimes for cooking.

LOTUS (لوٹس - lotas, *Hind.*). Greek λωτός. Originally egyptain term for the nile water-lily, a nelumbium or nymphæa [nelumbo, indian water-lily]; the former has edible pith and root, the latter has edible pod. Sacred plant there as here. The lotus of the lotophagi in Homer's odyssey, otherwise the cyrenean lotus, was a north african shrub of the nature of zizyphus jujuba, lam. [bair]; also called in arabic the fruit of paradise. The plant has also been ascribed to Celtis australis, linn. [indian nettle], and Diospyros [indian ebony] lotus, linn. For Hill lotus see China root; for Black lotus see Makhanah.

LOUSE BERRY (பேன்கொட்டை - péngottai, *Tam.*). Title from use of powdered berries in destroying lice in hair. Same as Indian berry.

LOVEDALE (ಮಂಜನಕೊರೈ - manjanakorai, *Can.*). From (manju, can. dew + korai, can. small shola). Hill, Station; Neilgherry district, Merkoonaud division; lat. 11° 22′; long. 76° 44′; height 7,330 feet; from Coonoor W.N.W. 7 miles; from Ootacamund S. 2 miles. The Lawrence asylum is situated here.

LOVI-LOVI (ලොවිලොවි - lovilovi, *Singh.*). Tomi tomi.

LOWH (لوح - lauh, *Ar.*). From (láha, ar. to shine). A light which appears to angels showing them the things they are commanded to do.

LUBBAY (لبے - labbe, obl. *Hind.*; లబ్బి - labbí, *Tel.*; இலப்பை - ilappai, *Tam.*). Dravidian corruption of (arabí) [choliya]. A race, Mussalmans in creed, but speaking Tamul. Supposed to be, like the Moplahs [q.v.] of the West coast, the descendants of Arab immigrants by intermarriage with native women. They are found in large numbers on the eastern coast, chiefly between Poolicat on the north and Negapatam on the south, their head-quarters being at Nagore near Negapatam, the burial-place of their patron saint Nagore meeraun sahib [cawderwally], to whose shrine numerous pilgrimages are made by the tribe. Physically they are good-looking, tall, well-made, robust, sometimes inclined to obesity, of light complexion and with well-developed limbs, not unlike the Moplah in their general configuration. The cranium is singularly and strikingly small; the eyes are slightly oblique, and not wanting in expression; cheek-bones prominent; lower jaw large and heavy; beard in some instances full and long, but in most cases decidedly spare. They generally wear the loonghee [q.v.], a cloth loosely wrapped round the waist and extending below the knees; they also wear bright-colored jackets, occasionally turbans [puggry]; the most frequent head-gear being a skull-cap, fitting closely to a shaved head. They live freely on animals and vegetables, making use of all kinds of flesh meats, saving pork for which Mahomedans have a religious abhorrence. They are exceedingly industrious and enterprising in their habits and pursuits, there being hardly a trade or calling in which they do not succeed. They make persevering fishermen and good boatmen. They are lapidaries, weavers, dyers, matmakers, jewellers, gardeners, bazaar men, grocers, boatmakers, boat and ship owners, and merchants, and as regards the leather [chamrah] and horn [sing] trade they excel as merchants. There are few classes of natives in Southern india, who, in energy, industry, and perseverance, can compete with the Lubbay. They have translated the Koran [q.v.] into Tamul. In Travancore they are called Maittan and Jonacan [q.v.]; the former word meaning a convert. They belong chiefly to the Soonnee [q.v.] sect. By the Mussalmans they are looked down upon. There are some 30,000 in presidency [jonangy]. See vol. I (37), 493; II, 233.

LUFFA (لف - laff, *Ar.*; பீர்க்கு - pírkku, *Tam.*). Ar. from (laffa, ar. to involve); from reticulate fruit. Tam. from (pír, tam. pale green). Botanically the Luffa genus, cucurbitaceæ [vricsham, 62]. Climbing gourd; pepo is ovate and oblong, fibrous within, containing many compressed seeds; natives of tropical asia and africa. The species best known to the natives are shown below.——*Bitter luffa* (कोशातकी - kóshátakí, San.; राणतुरई - ránaturaí, Mahr.; नागतालि - nágatáli, Conc.; كڑوی ترائی - karvíturáí, Hind. and Dec.; ಕಹಿಹೀರೆ - kahihíre, Can.; చేదుబీర - chédubíra, Tel.; കൊട്ടപ്പീരകം - kottappírakam, Mal.; பேய்ப்பீர்க்கு - péyppírkku, Tam.). Title from taste of fruit. San. from (kósha, san. sheath, cocoon + at, san. to go); from disposition of seeds in the fibrous fruit. Mahr. from (rána, mahr. wild. + turaí, mahr. the plant). Hind. from (karví, hind. bitter + turáí, hind. luffa acutangula, roxb.). Can. from (kahi, can. bitter + híre, can. the creeper). Tel. from (chédu, tel. bitterness + bíra, tel. the plant, luffa acutangula, rox.). Mal. from (kotta, mal. seed + pírakam, mal. the plant, luffa acutangula, roxb.). Tam. from (péy, tam. devil + pírkku, mal. the plant). San. also (jáliní), meaning having a net; from reticulate fruit; (raktakóshátakí), meaning red + the plant; (katukí), meaning pungent; (dálika), meaning bursting; (ghóshaka), meaning noisy, alluding to the rattling sound of seeds in dry fruits. Hind. also (bindál); (karelá), meaning momordica charantia, linn. [carolah]. Can. also (nágadáliballi), meaning prickly-pear creeper. Tel. also (adavibíra), meaning jungle + luffa acutangula, rox.; (chétibíra), meaning bitter + luffa acutangula, rox.; (verribíra), meaning mad + the plant, luffa acutangula, rox. Title otherwise Bindaul luffa, Net fruit, Wild luffa. Botanically Luffa acutangula, roxb., var. amara, roxb., cucurbitaceæ [vricsham, 62]. Alias Cucumis acutangulus;

operculata; Luffa amara, bindaal, plukenetiana. Bindaal from hindostany. Climbing; stems slender; leaves a little scabrous, roundish-cordate, slightly five to seven-lobed; calyx five-toothed; petals five, distinct; male racemes long peduncled; fruit oblong, tapering towards each end, acutely ten-angled; seeds blackish grey, marked with elevated minute black dots; margin turned, two-lobed at the base; flowers large, yellow, flowering in rainy season; bitter in every part; hedges and dry uncultivated places. Fruit violently carthartic and emetic; juice of the young roasted fruit applied to cure headache; seeds in substance or infusion, used as an emeto-cathartic; quoted in pharm., non-officinal. Chebeera [q.v.] also is called Bitter luffa.——*Common luffa* (झिङ्गाक - jhingáka, San.; घोसाळी - ghósálí, Mahr.; घोसाले - ghósálé, Conc.; خيار - khiyár, Pers.; ترائی - turáí, Hind. and Dec.; جنجی - jinjí, Malay; ಹೀರೆ - híre, Can.; ಪೀರೆ - píre, Too.; బీర - bíra, Tel.; ଜହ୍ନି - janhi, Oor.; പീച്ചകം - píççakam, Mal.; වැටකොළු - vatakolu, Singh.; பீர்க்கு - pírkku, Tam.). San. from rattling fruit when dry. Mal. from (piççu, mal. bile + akam, mal. inside). Tam. from (pír, tam. pale green). San. also (damargava); (jhinginí); (jhingi). Mahr. also (jinga). Hind. also (jinga), from mahratta. Can. also (kádukahihíre), meaning jungle + bitter + the creeper. Mal. also (cherupírakam), meaning small + the plant. Singh. also (dáravatakolu). Tam. also (karukkuppírkku), meaning rough edge + the plant, luffa; from four-edged form of fruit; (píram); (pír); (shálini), domestic plant. Title otherwise Gourd plant, Marvellous apple, Strainer vine. Botanically Luffa acutangula, roxb., cucurbitaceæ [vricsham, 62]. Alias Cucurbita acutangulus; Luffa fœtida. Climbing; stems glabrous; leaves five-angled or five-lobed; male racemes long peduncled; stamens distinct; calyx segments of the female flowers covered with glands; fruit, about 1 foot long and 2–3 inches thick, clavate, obtuse, or shortly pointed, tolerably smooth, ten-angled, the angles sharp and smooth; seeds black irregularly pitted, two-lobed at the base; flowers large, yellow, flowering nearly all year. Seeds purgative and emetic; half-grown fruit is excellent vegetable, much used in curries [q.v.]; pickled, boiled, and dressed with butter, pepper [q.v.] and salt [ooppoo] is little inferior to green peas [calauyam]; oil from seed.——*Oil-giving luffa* (राजकोषातकी - rájakóshátakí, San.; घोंसाळी - ghónsálí, Mahr.; لف - laff, Ar.; خيار - khiyár, Pers.; گهی ترائی - ghíturáí, Dec.; ತುಪ್ಪದಹೀರೆ - tuppaduhíre, Can.; నేతిబీర - nétibíra, Tel.; കാട്ടുപീരകം - káttupírakam, Mal.; நுரைப்பீர்க்கு - nuraippírkku, Tam.). San. from (rája, san. radiant + kóshátakí, san. luffa acutangula, roxb., var. amara, roxb.); from whitish color of fruit. Ar. from (laffa, ar. to involve). Dec. from (ghí, hind. ghee + turáí, hind. luffa acutangula, roxb.), from oil-giving properties. Can. from (tuppa, can. ghee + híre, can. the plant). Tel. from (neyyi, tel. ghee + bíra, tel. luffa acutangula, roxb.). Mal. from (kátu, mal. forest + pírakam, mal. luffa acutangula, roxb.). Tam. from (nurai, tam. butter + pírkku, tam. the plant); from whitish fruit. San. also (dírghapatólika), meaning long + luffa acutangula, roxb. Tel. also (guttibíra), meaning cluster + luffa acutangula, roxb.; (núnebíra), meaning oil + luffa acutangula, roxb. Tam. also (párbírkku), meaning white + the plant. Title otherwise Long luffa, Towel gourd, Washing gourd. Botanically Luffa ægyptiaca, müller, cucurbitaceæ [vricsham, 62]. Alias Luffa pentandra, racemosa. Extensively climbing hairy; tendrils two to three fid; leaves 4 inches diameter, reniform-orbicular, five-angled or somewhat five-lobed, dentate, usually scabrous, punctate on both surfaces, pubescent on the nerves beneath; petiole 2 inches; male peduncle 6 inches, flowers often approximate near the summit; pedicels short, each carrying a small ovate viscid entire bract sometimes obsolete; petals five, $\frac{3}{4}$–1 inch, yellow, often with elevated hairy green veins; stamens five; female flower solitary, peduncle 1–3 inches; fruit 5–12 inches; seeds $\frac{3}{8}$ by $\frac{1}{4}$ inch, usually black, very narrowly winged, smooth or very sparingly tubercled. Flower large, yellow; oblong fruit thickening at the lower end and without ridges. Seeds used as cooling medicine. Commonly used in curry [q.v.]. Gives an oil; ashes used as mordant [cauram].——*Snake luffa* (देवदाली - dévadálí, San.; పాముబీర - pámubíra, Tel.; நுரைப்பீர்க்கு - nuraippírkku, Tam.). Title from use as an antidote. San. means divine luffa, from medicinal property. Tel. from (pámu, tel. snake + bíra, tel. luffa acutangula, roxb.). Tam. from (nurai, tam. butter + pírkku, tam. the plant), from whitish fruit. San. also (ákhuvishahá), meaning rat-poison-destroying. Tam. also (péyppírkku), meaning devil + the plant. Botanically Luffa echinata, r., cucurbitaceæ [vricsham, 62]. Stems herbaceous, scandent, five-sided, slightly hairy; tendrils two-cleft; leaves generally five-lobed, somewhat hairy, margins scallop-toothed; petioles as long as the leaves, ribbed; fruit oval, the size of a nutmeg [jautikye], armed with numerous long, rather soft, diverging bristles, obscurely divided into three cells by a network of dry fibres, and opening at the top with a perforated stopple, which falls off when the seeds are ripe; seeds about eighteen, ovate, compressed, black and scabrous; testa very hard; kernel white; the fibrous substance in which the seeds are enclosed is intensely bitter. Pulp of fruit a frequent ingredient in the compound decoctions which are prescribed for bilious fevers; and given in snake bite. Fruit an abortifacient.

LUGHAEE (لگهائی - laghái, *Hind.*). Thug who buries victim.

LUKDY (काष्ठ - kásht'ha, *San.*; لکڑی - lakrí, *Hind.*; ಕಟ್ಟಿಗೆ - kattige, *Can.*; కట్టె - katte, *Tel.*; മുട്ടി - mutti, *Mal.*; கட்டை - kattai, *Tam.*).—"*a*" Firewood. The indigenous fuel-producing trees are too numerous to mention. In the plains of the southern districts, the introduced Casuarina equisetifolia, forst. [chowkmaram], is the best. On Neilgherry hills the Australian eucalyptus globulus, labill. [blue gum], has produced astonishing results. The two Australian acacias, Acacia melanoxylon, r. br. [australian blackwood], and Acacia dealbata, link., are also both useful, and of quick growth.—"*b*" Plant second term. Ex., where transl. is of first term:—Acorus calamus (gankílakrí), scent; Dalbergia latifolia (kálílakrí), black; Glycirrhiza glabra (míthílakrí), sweet; Holarrhena antidysenterica (dúdhíkílakrí), milk; Tetranthera laurifolia (maidálakrí), flour; Tetranthera monopetala (maidálakrí), flour. See gloss. paragraphs.

LUMBANG NUT (अक्षोट - akshóta, *San.*; अखोड - akhóda, *Mahr.*; شجرجوزبری - shajarijauzibarrí, *Ar.*; درخت چهار مغزهندی - darakhtichahármaghzihindí, *Pers.*; هندی اخروٹ کا پیڑ - hindíakhrotkáper, *Hind.*; جنگلی اکروٹ کا جهاڑ - jangliakrotkájhár, *Dec.*; ನಾಟುಅಕ್ರೋಡು - nátuakródu, *Can.*; నాటుఅక్రోటు - nátuakrótu, *Tel.*; കാരങ്കോലം - kárankólam, *Mal.*; කකුණ - kakuna, *Singh.*; நாட்டக்கரோட்டு - náttakkaróttu, *Tam.*). Title from malay. San. from (aksh, san. to pervade), from spreading roots. Mahr. from sanscrit. Ar. from (shajar, ar. tree + jauz, ar. walnut + barr, ar. forest). Pers. from (darakht, pers. tree + chahár, four + maghz, pers. kernel + hindí, pers. indian). Hind. from (hindí, pers. indian + akhrot, pers. walnut + per, hind. tree). Dec. from (janglí, hind. forest + akrot, hind. walnut + jhár, hind. tree). Can. from (nádu, can. country + akhrot, pers. walnut). Tel. like canarese. Mal. from (kár, mal. black + ankólam, mal. alangy tree, alangium lamarckii, thw.). Tam. like canarese. Ar. also (khasafihindí). Pers. also (girdagán), meaning round thing [acroot]. Hind. also (hijlíbádam), meaning cashew nut; (akóla) [alanjy]. Tel. also (úduga), meaning serviceable tree. Mal. also (akrótt); corruption of (akshóta). Title otherwise Belgaum walnut, Bencoolen nut, Bengal walnut, Candle nut, Country walnut, Indian walnut, Kekui-oil plant, Kekune-oil plant, Molucca nut, Otaheite walnut. Botanically Aleurites triloba, forst., euphorbiaceæ [vricsham, 118]. Alias Aleurites moluccana; Camirium cordifolium; Jatropha moluccana; Juglans camirium. Large tree; leaves petioled, very large, cordate, with entire or scalloped margins, three to five-lobed; panicles terminal; small white flowers succeeded by sub-globose, fleshy, smooth, olive-colored fruit containing hard seeds, rich in oil and with a furrowed testa, resembling a walnut [acroot]. Oil from kernels a mild purgative. In pharm. non-officinal, like castor [anmanac] oil. Kernels eatable, tasting like fresh walnuts. An oil cake for cattle and manure. Oil used for food and for burning. The nuts themselves burn like a candle. Timber of no value. The ordinary walnut is Juglans regia, linn. [acroot].

LUMBAUDY (لمباڑا - lambárá, *Hind.*; లంబాడి - lambádi, *Tel.* and *Tam.*). From (lampata, san. greedy). A tribe who wander about as gypsies. Their occupation is grain-carrying. They speak a dialect of Hindostany [q.v.]. Closely resembling Brinjarries [q.v.] and Soogaulies [q.v.]. About 20,000 in presidency [jauty]. See vol. I (69), 195; II, 113.

LUNGAR (لنگر - langar, *Hind.*). From persian. Alms; also an anchor.——*Lungarbaudy* (لنگرواڑی - langarwárí, Hind.). An anchorage.——*Lungar curts* (لنگرخرچ - langarkharch, Hind.). From (above + kharch, pers. expense). A dole.——*Lungarkhana* (لنگر خانه - langarkhánah, Hind.). From (above + khánah, pers. house). A poor-house, where some reside and to others food is dispensed [inam].

LUNKA (लङ्का - lanká, *San.*; లంక - lanka, *Tel.*; இலங்கை - ilangai, *Tam.*). From (ilangu, tam. to shine). One of the four cities supposed in sanscrit science to lie under the equator [niracsham] at 90° distance from each other, viz., Yavacoty, Lunka, Romacam, and Siddhapoory. Lunka is considered by all Indian astronomers to give the first meridian [raikhay], to which all computations should be referred; though several and particularly Teloogoo astronomers refer instead to Rameshwaram. Towards the north, and under the same meridian as Lunka, the shastrams [q.v.] state that there are two other cities and a great mountain; viz., Avanty supposed to be the same as Oojjein, and Sannihita saras, which in former times were the seats of colleges, observatories, and Rohitacam the mountain. The meridian of Lunka lies in 75° 53′ 15″ or 5h 3′ 33″ east of Greenwich; and 73° 33′ or 4h 54′ 12″ east of Paris [jyotisham]. Lunka is also the island of Ceylon [q.v.], where the war between Rama [q.v.] and Ravanan [q.v.] is supposed to have taken place [charitram]. Also an islet in a river. Also a kind of cheroot [q.v.] so called from being made of tobacco [pogauk], grown in islands of Godavery delta [conamoogam].——*Lunkamala* (లంకమల - lankamala, Tel.). From (lanka, san. island + mala, tel. hill); probably from the position between two rivers, pennair and saglair. Range of hills; Cuddapah dist., Budwail, Cuddapah, Sidhout tals.; between lat. 14° 27′ and 14° 43′ and long. 78° 50′ and 79° 05′; from Cuddapah N.N.E. 5 miles. Form a block nearly square, one half being situated in Budwail and the other in Sidhout talook. Cease about the point where the talooks of Cuddapah, Proddootore, Budwail, and Sidhout meet. Here the Nullamullays commence. Average elevation 2,000 feet. Many old pagodas [q.v.] in the valleys, almost all deserted and in ruins, for the range is haunted by a deadly fever. The only inhabitants are Yanaudies [q.v.]. Two water-falls; Matsyalunka and Saulunka. Trig. station in lat. 14° 39′ 43·05″; long. 78° 57′ 23·44″; height 2,871 feet; from Budwail W.S.W. 12 miles; from Regoolacoonta S. 5 miles.

LUSSOON (रसोनक - rasónaka, *San.*; लसूण - lasúna, *Mahr.*; लसुण - lasuna, *Conc.*; ثوم - súm, *Ar.*; سیر - sír, *Pers.*; لہسن - lahsan, *Hind.*; لسن - lassan, *Dec.*; بونگ پتح - buvangputih, *Malay*; ಬೆಳ್ಳುಳ್ಳಿ - bellulli, *Can.*; ಬೊಳ್ಳುಳ್ಳಿ - bollulli, *Too.*; తెల్లగడ్డ - tellagadda, *Tel.*; ଲୋସୋନୋ - losono, *Oor.*; വെളുള്ളി - vellulli, *Mal.*; සුදුළූනු - sudulúnu, *Singh.*; வெள்ளைப்பூண்டு - vellaippúndu, *Tam.*). Title from hindostany. San. from (rasa, san. taste + úna, san. deficient), wanting sourness out of the six tastes in medicine. Mahr. and conc. from sanscrit. Malay from (bavang, malay, an onion + putih, malay, white). Can. from (beli, can. white + ulli, can. garlic). Too. from (bollu, too. silver + ulli, too. garlic). Tel. from (tella, tel. white + gadda, tel. root). Mal. from (vel, mal. white + ulli, mal. onion, allium cepa, linn.). Singh. means white onion. Tam. from (vellai, tam. white + púndu, tam. small plant). San. also (lashuna), meaning eaten; (arishta), meaning harmless [neem, soap-nut tree]; (griñjana), meaning roaring [gaujar, kinnab]; (shvétakanda), meaning white root; (mahaushadha), meaning great remedy. Ar. also (fúm). Tel. also (tellaulli), meaning white + onion, allium cepa, linn.; (vellulli), meaning white + onion; (ellulli), meaning white + onion; (velligadda), meaning white + root. Tam. also (vellaivengáyam), meaning white + onion; (vellulli), meaning white + garlic; (írulli), meaning moisture + garlic; (púndu), meaning small plant. Title otherwise Garlic, Poorman's treacle, White onion. Botanically Allium sativum, linn., liliaceæ [vricsham, 136]. Alias Porrum sativum. Stem 2 feet, unbranched, bearing at the top an umbel of a few whitish flowers, mixed with small bulbs; upper part of stem before flowering rolled into a ring; leaves grass-like, obscurely keeled, not fistulous like those of the onion [piyauz]; three alternate stamens are three-pointed, the middle point bearing the anther; bulb consists of about twelve to fifteen ovate oblong cloves or subordinate bulbs, which are axillary buds of its scales thus developed. Flower small, white; native of sicily, cultivated here; volatile oil obtained by distilling the bruised bulbs, when purified, colorless. Cultivated in black loam; wet; ground prepared in chittray or april for caur [q.v.] and in poorataushy [mausam] or september for pishaunam [q.v.] crop, by ploughing and sheep folding; ground divided into small plots by banks; seed sown two months after; dibbled in; irrigation water let in once a week, while under growth; harvested same as onion [piyauz]; average price 50 imperial seers for 1 rupee. The juice is applied to the ears for deafness and pain; oil from seed is medicinal; oil mixed with vinegar [caudy] is astringent in sore throat, &c.; supposed to prevent the hair turning grey when applied externally; bulb given in confection for rheumatism. In veterinary practice, when made into paste with two-thirds of its weight of wheat [geung] flour, forms a very powerful blister which should be removed fifteen minutes after application; the part to be blistered should be shaved. As food, garlic promotes digestion; forms constant ingredient in curries. The onion is Allium cepa, linn. [piyauz].

LUTCHAH (لچھا - laçchá, *Hind.*). A necklace, having a semi-lunar ornament in the centre [zewar]. Same as Hindoo talee [q.v.].

M (म - ma, मा - má, *San.*; م - mím, *Ar.* and *Hind.*; மா - má, *Tam.*). San. short, name of the fourth note of the musical scale [swara graumam]. San. short symbol of bramha [q.v.], shiva [q.v.], and vishnoo [q.v.] combined. San. long, name of lutchmy [q.v.]. Adverbial prefix used with Arabic verbs to denote place; as in musjid, meaning place of prostration. Also a suffix denoting feminine gender; as in begum, meaning beg + feminine suffix. Hind. numerically 40. Countersignature of diwaun [q.v.] under moghul [q.v.] government on imperial grants of revenue. Sunday. Contraction of the first Mahomedan month [maheena]. Tam. long, the fraction $\frac{1}{20}$ [mah].——*Maumandore* (மாமண்டூர் - mámandúr, Tam.). From (má, san. lakshmí, the goddess + vindu, tam. vishnu + úr, tam. village). Sanscrit name (lakshmínarasimhapura), because founded by lutchmy narsimha iyer. Also (lakshmínáráyanapura), meaning lutchmy + vishnoo, the mover on the waters + town. Village; North arcot dist., Arcot tal.; pop. 1,942; acres 1,536; lat. 12° 45′; long. 79° 43′; from Arcot E.S.E. 25 miles; from Chittore S.E. 50 miles. Rock-cutting similar to those in Puncha pandava mullay. Caves now used as cattle-pens. Large tank [q.v.] exceeding Cauverypauk, supply lasting fifteen months. Below bund [q.v.] are kistvaens [paundicoozhy] of flat boulders evidently not quarried. On verge of tank, and within Doosy village, is large rock with inscription in Tamul [q.v.] and Grantam [q.v.]. Vencataudry naidoo, Poligar [q.v.] of Calastry, named the tank Chennasamoodram after his father Chennappa naidoo. When granting the English a settlement at Madras, he similarly stipulated that that town should be called Chennappa putnam [madras]. Trig. station in lat. 12° 44′ 40·27″; long. 79° 42′ 27·20″; height 431 feet; from Arcot E.S.E. 25 miles; from Narsamungalam N.W. ½ mile.

MA (ما - má, *Ar.*). That which.——*Mashallah* (ماشاالله - másháalláh, Hind.). From (above + shá, ar. pleased + alláh, ar. god). Expression of admiration.

MAABAR (معبر - mabar, *Hind.*). From (ubr, ar. to cross). Means the place of crossing over, that is from Madura to Ceylon, but applies to the whole coast of Madura north from Rameshwaram. Not to be confounded with Malabar. Friar jordanus, the Quilon bishop of the fourteenth century, in the following passage clearly distinguishes between these two words:—"In this Greater india [q.v.] are twelve idolatrous "kings, and more. For there is one very powerful king in the "country where pepper [q.v.] grows, and his kingdom is called "Molebar. There is also the king of Singuyli and the king "of Columbum, the king of which is called Lingua, but his "kingdom Mohebar. There is also the king of Molephatam, "whose kingdom is called Molepoor, where pearls [moty] are "taken in infinite quantities." The very powerful king is the Zamorin [q.v.]. Molebar is Malabar. Singuyli may be Cauyancollam, an old port a few miles north of Quilon and formerly a small kingdom. Columbum is Quilon. Lingua is perhaps a name derived from the Lingayet religion. Mohebar is Maabar. Molephatam and Molepoor are probably near Cauyal [charitram]. See vol. I (12).

MAAD (معاد - maád, *Hind.*). From (maada, ar. to travel). The doctrine of return to God [allah] or the conception of future existence. The belief of the Mahomedans in general is that the soul when freed from the body will exist as a self-conscious entity, and that pleasure and pain in a future existence will depend on the use or misuse of a man's powers [mabdah] here. Compare Carmam and Samsauram of the Hindoos.

MABDAH (مبدا - mabdá, *Hind.*). From (bida, ar. to produce something new). The doctrine of origin or the coming from God [allah]. The belief is that the primal absolute cause created the active intelligence, from which sprung the abstract soul [nafs], out of which was evolved primary matter, which was made capable of taking shapes and forms. Thus the abstract soul individualized in man strives to attain by self-discipline and purity of life the goal of perfection, and to return to the source from which it emanated [maad]. Compare Srishty of the Hindoos.

MACLEOD SEER (ഇടങ്ങഴി - itannazhi, *Mal.*). As introduced by Mr. Macleod. Measure of capacity. 4 nauzhies = 1 Macleod seer; 10 Macleod seers = 1 parrah [alavay, 3d]. Approximate actual value, 1 Macleod seer = 113¾ cubic inches. Introduced in 1802, and contains when liberally heaped 130 tolahs [q.v.] of rice [q.v.]. Used in Chiracal, Cottayam, Cooroombranaud, Valavanaud and Palghaut. In Calicut and Ponnany Macleod's half seer liberally heaped and containing 65 tolahs [q.v.] is used. Same as Mal. yidangazhy. See vol. I, 609; II, 516.

MACSHAM (मक्ष - maksha, *San.*). From (maksh, san. to collect). Fly.——*Macsha grauhy* (मक्षग्राहि - makshagráhi, San.). From (above + grih, san. to catch). Muscicapidæ family, dentirostres, insessores, aves [pacshy, 20], of naturalists [jantoo]. Flycatchers. Divided into:—Myiagrinæ, true flycatchers, live chiefly on soft-winged insects, which they almost always capture in the air, often with a loud snap of their mandibles, occasionally picking one off a leaf or a branch [shah boolbool, mynautty]; and Muscicapinæ [dhoby boolbool]; bill rather wide, depressed, shallow; the culmen straight, distinctly hooked and notched at the tip; rictal bristles numerous and strong; wings moderate, tail generally rather short or moderate; tarsus short, weak; feet moderately small, feeble.——*Makkhee* (मक्षिक - makshika, San.; माशी - máshí, Mahr.; ذباب - zubáb, Ar.; مگس - magas, Pers.; مکھی - makkhí, Hind. and Dec.; للت - lalat, Malay ನೊಣ - nona, Can.; ಕಿಲೆಂಜಿ - kilenji, Too.; ఈగ - íga, Tel.; ഈച്ച - íçça, Mal.; මැස්සා - makshi, Singh.; ஈ - í, Tam.). Title from hindostany. San. from (maksh, san. to collect); as collecting honey. Ar. from (zabba, ar. in constant motion). Pers. from sanscrit. Hind. from sanscrit. Musca domestica, muscidæ, diptera, holometabola, insecta [poochy], of naturalists [jantoo]. There is a Tamul proverb:—ஈக்கு விடம் தலையில், தேளுக்குக்கொடுக்கில்—"In a fly the head is the seat of poison, in a "scorpion [tail] the tail." Tamul (máttí) is the cattle-fly or gad-fly.

MAD (मद् - mad, *San.*). To intoxicate, gladden.——*Madablota* (माधवी - mádhaví, San.; مدھ مالتی - madhmáltí, Hind.; వడ్లయారాల - vadlayárála, Tel.; ବୋରୋମଲି - borómali, Oor.; குரிந்தை - kurindai, Tam.). Title corruption from hindostany. San. from (madhu, san. spring season); flowers in spring. Hind. from sanscrit. Tel. from (vadla, tel. corruption of vedala, tel. flower + yárála, tel. putranjiva roxburghii, wall.). San. also (atimuktá), meaning surpassing pearls [musk jasmine, nemmy]; (málatí), meaning beautiful flowered [common jasmine, wild jasmine, wild nutmeg]. Tel. also (mádhavitíga), meaning spring creeper; (pótuvadla), meaning male + the tree; (vedala-chettu), meaning flower + tree. Tam. also (shiruguriñjá), meaning small + the plant [small indian ipecacuanha]; (kuriñjá) [indian ipecacuanha]; (kurukkatti), meaning white + fig plant, ficus; cf. musk jasmine. Title otherwise Clustered gærtnera, Delight-of-the-woods, Spring creeper. Botanically Hiptage madablota, gærtn., malphigiaceæ [vricsham, 29]. Specific name from (mádhavílatá, san. spring flower creeper), through (madúbúlúta, beng.). Alias Banisteria bengalensis, unicapsularis; Gærtnera racemosa; Molina racemosa. Tall climber, glabrous except the young parts and inflorescence which are hoary and appressed-tomentose; leaves 3–6 inches, coriaceous, petioled, shining above; racemes 1–6 inches, axillary, usually forming a leafy panicle; flower $\frac{1}{2}$–$\frac{3}{4}$ inch diameter, fragrant, white; sepals obtuse; petals twice as long, fimbriate, fifth petal yellow at the base; wings of carpels oblong, coriaceous inner 1–2 inches, linear-oblong outer narrower shorter spreading. Large shrub, scandent; lanceolate pointed leaves, 7 inches long; profuse trusses of white and yellow fragrant flowers, somewhat resembling horse-chestnut. Leaves useful in cutaneous diseases; wood red in centre, yellowish-white in outer portion, moderately hard. There is another species, parvifolia.——*Madak* (مدك - madak, Hind.). Intoxicating pill made of chopped betel leaves [q.v.], and opium [aphainam] to be swallowed or smoked in a pipe [chandoo, mookhadiraut].——*Madaksira* (మడకశిర - madakasira, Tel.). See sep. title.——*Madanaghanta* (मदनघण्ट - madanaghanta, San.; घंटी - ghantí, Mahr.; మదనగ్రంథి - madanagrandhi, Tel.; താർത്താവൽ - tárttával, Mal.; நத்தைச்சூரி - nattaiççúri, Tam.). Title from sanscrit. San. from (madana, san. cupid + ghantá, san. bell); from aphrodisiac seeds. Mahr. from (ghantá, san. bell). Tel from (madana, san. cupid + grant'hi, san. knot); from aphrodisiac seeds. Mal. from (tár, mal. flower + távu, mal. to spread). Tam from (nattai, tam. oyster + shúri, tam. knife); for explanation see below. Tel. also (madana), meaning cupid; (modina); (madanabudatakáda), meaning cupid + short + stem. Tam also (nattaiççundi), meaning oyster pincher. Title otherwise Bristly button weed, Button weed, Shaggy button weed. Botanically Spermacoce hispida, linn., rubiaceæ [vricsham, 71]. Alias Spermacoce articularis, scabra. A procumbent, scabrous, or hirsute herb; root fibrous, annual or perennial; leaves obovate spathulate, oblong or elliptic, obtuse or acute, coriaceous, $\frac{1}{2}$–$1\frac{1}{2}$ by $\frac{1}{6}$ to $\frac{2}{3}$ inches; flowers four to six in a whorl, blue or white; capsules hispid or pubescent; seeds oblong, granulate, opaque; in some forms of the plant the leaves have cartilaginous edges. There is a Hindoo myth that an oyster [auly] will open its shell if touched by the plant. Seeds aphrodisiac, plant prescribed to cure hæmorrhoids; alterative and purifier of the blood like sarsaparilla, and is prescribed in decoction.——*Madanam* (மதனம் - mathanam, Tam.). Silence. There is a Tamul proverb:— மதனம் மலைக்கு ஒப்பிடலாம்—"Silence is comparable to "a mountain;" being as irresistible.——*Madanan* (मदन - madana, San.). Manmatan [q.v.], called in Northern india and in literature Cauman [q.v.].——*Madanapully* (మదనపల్లె - madanapalle, Tel.). See sep. title.——*Madapollem* (మాధవాయపాలెం - mádhaváyapálem, Tel.). From (mádhavayya, tel. proper name + pálemu, tel. fortified village). Town, Port, Head-quarters of General duties deputy collector; Godavery dist., Narsapore tal.; pop. 1,862; acres 852; lat. 16° 26'; long. 81° 44'; from Cocanada S.W. 50 miles; from Coonavaram S.S.E. 82 miles; from Ellore E.S.E. 43 miles; from Madras N.N.E. 248 miles; from Narsapore N.E. 1 mile; from Rajahmundry S. 39 miles. On the Godavery. Part of present town of Narsapore, English factory established, 1679; withdrawn in 1688; resettled, 1698; captured by French in 1757; ceded by Nizam's treaty with Colonel Forde, 14th May 1759; grant confirmed by Moghul's firmaun [q.v.], 12th August 1765. The sites of the old buildings have been carried away by successive encroachments of the river. Trade declined since the abolition of the Company's factory [aurang] in 1827. A fine kind of white piece-goods intermediate between calico [q.v.] and muslin [q.v.] manufactured here, and well known in trade.——*Madaur* (مدار - madár, Hind.). From (mandára, san. the plant, specially the white variety). Same as Yercum.——*Madh* (مدھ - madh, Hind.). Honey. Caulee madh means black honey; same as Poolah. Soofaid madh means white honey; same as White poolah.——*Madhoo* (मधु - madhu, San.). Sweetness, spring, honey, intoxicating liquor [shahad, tain, tem]. Plant first term in the sense of sweet. Ex., where transl. is of second term:— Celosia cristata (madhuchhada), cover; Dioscorea aculeata (madhválu), esculent root; Dregea volubilis (madhumálati), jasmine; Glycirrhiza glabra (madhuyashtika), stick; Mangifera indica (madhudúta), meaning spring + servant; Tinospora cordifolia (madhuparní), leaf. See gloss. paragraphs.——*Madhoocam* (मधुक - madhuka, San.). Sweet. Plant name common to:— Glycirrhiza glabra; Mallotus philippensis. See gloss. paragraphs. ——*Madhoopaty* (मधुपति - madhupati, San.). From (madhu, san. spirits + pati, san. master). Mistress of ardent spirits; Bhadra cauly [q.v.].——*Madhooram* (मधुर - madhura, San.). Sweet. Plant first term. Ex., where transl. is of second term:—Citrus decumana (madhuranárakam), lime; Ipomæa batatas (madhurakkizhanna), esculent root; Zizyphus jujuba (madhurap'hala), fruit. See gloss. paragraphs.——*Madhoo sakhan* (मधुसख - madhusakha, San.). From (madhu, san. spring + sakha, san. friend). Companion of the spring. Manmatan [q.v.].—— *Madhwa* (मध्व - madhva, San.). From (madhu, san. sweet). Otherwise Madhwacharry. Also called Ananta teertan, Ananda teertan and Poornapranyan. A Bramin, native of Tooloovam [q.v.], in the twelfth century. He was a worshipper of Vishnoo and as a religious philosopher he promulgated the doctrine of Dweitam [q.v.] or dualism, according to which the supreme soul [paramautman] of the universe and the human soul [autmam], jeevautman are distinct; as against the old and now still orthodox doctrine of Adweitam or non-duality, according to which god and soul, spirit and matter, are one. See Adweitam, Shuncaracharry [shuncaran]. Also for the nearly contemporaneous Veishnavite doctrine Vishishtaudweitam, see that head and Ramaunoojan. The history of Madhwa's religious and philosophic efforts has been given in the foot-note on the History of Hindoo religion at vol. I (76), (85), (90). The sect which follows Madhwa is not a numerous one, perhaps 60,000 in all. They are called also Bramha sampradayees. Their tenets are fully described at vol. I (76). Madhwa bramins hold the ninth day of the eleventh lunar month as a festival. Distinguish from Maudhavan.——*Madhwam* (माध्व - mádhva, San.). Dweitam philosophy promulgated by Madhwa. See vol. I (74).—— *Madmaunty* (हरचंपक - harachampaka, San.; विलायतीचांपा - viláyatíchámpá, Mahr.; مدن مانتی - madanmántí, Hind.; مدن مست - madanmast, Dec.; ಮನೋರಂಜನಬಳ್ಳಿ - manóranjanballi, Can.; మనోరంజితము - manóranjitamu, Tel.; മദനകാമേശ്വരി - madanakámésharí, Mal.; மனோரஞ்சிதம் - manórañjitham, Tam.). Title from hindostany. San. from (hri, san. to captivate + champaka, san. michelia champaca, linn.). Mahr. from (viláyatí, mahr. foreign + chámpá, mahr. michelia champaca, linn.). Hind. from (madana, san. cupid + mántí, hind. subservient). Dec. from (madan, hind. cupid + mast, hind. intoxicated). Can. from (manas, san. mind + rañj, san. to please + balli, can. creeper). Tel. from (manas, san. mind + rañj, san. to be pleased). Mal. from (madana, san. lustful + káma, san. cupid + íshvarí, san. goddess). Tam. from (manas, san. mind + rañj, san. to be pleased). Tel. also (p'halasampenga), meaning fruit + michelia champaca, linn.; (sakalap'halasampenga), meaning all + fruit + michelia champaca, linn.; from flowers having the mixed flavor of many fruits. Mal. also (manórañjitam), meaning heart + ravishing. Title otherwise Cupid's plant, Foreign champak, Fruited champak, Heart's joy. Botanically Artabotrys odoratissimus, br., anonaceæ [vricsham, 4]. Glabrous, branches long; leaves 2 to 8 by 1 to 2 inches; flowers yellow, solitary or gemmate; petals 1 to $1\frac{3}{4}$ inches, nearly equal, young pubescent, especially at the base; carpels obovate-oblong, yellow, odorous. Large shrub; lanceolate, glossy, pure green leaves; moderate-sized irregular-formed flowers similar to custard-apple [anona], of a heavy, pale yellow color, perfume somewhat like over-ripe apples [seb]: small, golden, pear-like [amrood] fruit. Flowers are narcotic.——*Madrantacam* (மதுராந்தகம் - mathurándagam, Tam.). See sep. title.——*Madura* (மதுரை - mathurai, Tam.). See sep. title.——*Madyam* (मद्य - madya, San). Any intoxicating liquor [mooskiraut].——*Mahoor* (مہور - mahúr, Hind.). Same as Bachnaug.——*Mandam* (मन्द - manda, San.). Slow. Astronomical anomaly. Mandotcham is the apsis of a planet's [graham] orbit [cacsham], Toonga mandotcham being the higher apsis [ootcham]. Manda caindram, from (kéndra, san. centre), is argument of anomaly. Manda jyay, from (jyá, san, sine) is equation to the centre. Manda palam, from (p'hala, san. equation) is anomalistic equation of a planet [graham].——*Mandaram* (मन्दर - mandara, San.). From (mand, san. to rejoice). The mountain used by the gods in churning the ocean [coormam].——*Mandaukiny* (मन्दाकिनी - mandákiní, San.). From (manda, san. slow + aka, san. going). Name of the celestial Ganges.——*Mandiram* (मन्दिर - mandira, San.). From (mand, san. to halt). The adytum of a temple [coil].——*Mantapam* (मण्डप - mandapa, San.; منڈپ - mandaf, Hind.). From (mand, san. to adorn). Any square or rectangular hall with a flat roof supported by pillars, open at the sides. Particularly the porch [toranam] of a temple [coil]. Cf. Chauvady.——*Mathy* (மதி - mathi, Tam.). From (mad, san. to rejoice). Moon [chundran]. Niraymathy is full moon [powrnimay].——*Matsyam* (मत्स्य - matsya, San.). See sep. title.——*Maudhavan* (माधव - mádhava, San.).—"*a*" Manmatan [q.v.], the god of spring season. Also Vishnoo [q.v.].— "*b*" Name of an author. Otherwise Maudhavacharry or Vidyauranyan, the latter designation giving rise to Vidyaunagaram or Vijianugger [q.v.] as he was chiefly instrumental in its foundation. He belonged to the adweitic school of Shuncaracharry [shuncaran] and was the Jagat gooroo of shringairy about the middle of the fourteenth century. Though apparently an original author, he is best known in literature by his Sarwa darshana sangraham or critical review of the principal systems of philosophy [darshanam] current down to his time. These systems are arranged in a progressive series, beginning with the Chaurvaucam [q.v.] as being the furthest removed from, and gradually ascending to the Saunkhyam [q.v.] and Yogam [q.v.] the systems nearest approaching to, Maudhavan's own [matam]. Maudhavan was priest and minister of Bookka roya and Harihara of Vijianugger, in the fourteenth century as his father Mayana had been of their father Sangama. Distinguish from Madhwa. ——*Maudhoo row* (माधुराव - mádhurávu, Mahr.). Mahratta chief. Contested with Hyder; invaded Mysore, captured Sheerah;

appointed Hyder's brother-in-law as Governor of Goorramcondah. Died in 1772 [charitram].——*Maundavair* (మాండవేరు - mándavéru, Tel.). From (mándavya, san. the sage + éru, tel. river). Sanscrit name (mándavyanadí), meaning maundavyan, the sage, so called + river. River; Cuddapah dist., Royachoty tal. Drains the greater part of Royachoty talook, flowing through the centre of the talook and joining Pinchahnuddy, at foot of hills. Has little water and a wide sandy bed.——*Mendphal* (مینڈ پھل - mendphal, Dec.). Means intoxicating fruit. Same as Common emetic nut.——*Mohwah* (مھوا - mohwá, Hind.). See sep. title.——*Mom* (موم - mom, Hind.). See sep. title.——*Mowloo* (ماوآلو - máuálú, Hind.). Means sweet esculent root. Same as Goa yam [auloo].——*Mudar* (مدار - mádár, Hind.). Common spelling of Madaur or Yercum [q.v.].——*Mundalam* (मण्डल - mandala, San.; منڈل - mandal, Hind.). From (mand, san. to adorn). A circle, especially great circle; also any elliptical figure; a division of a country; as Toudaimundalam, Paundy mundalam, Cholamundalam. In medicine and ritual applied to a period of forty days. Mundalaubbishaicam is a daily anointing of an idol [vigraham] for forty days after the Coombhaubhishaicam or other ceremonies. Mundaleshan or Mundaleshwaran is an independent sovereign, especially one who governs a country forty yojanams [q.v.] in length and forty in breadth and containing over 100,000 hamlets. Mundalaurdham is a semi-circle. A division of the Rig vedam [q.v.]. Craunty mundalam, from (kránti, san. going) is the ecliptic. Naudy mundalam, from (nádi, san. indian hour) is the celestial equator [niracsham]; the circle in the heavens [bhagolam], equally distant from the poles [dhroovam] of the celestial sphere, is the equinoctial or celestial equator, which is merely the projection of the terrestrial equator [niracsham] to the sphere of the fixed stars [jyotisham, maunam, nacshatram].——*Must* (مست - mast, Hind.). From (mad, san. to be drunk). Drunk or lustful; especially applied to an elephant [q.v.] or camel [ottagam] in a state of periodical excitement.——*Mutchly* (مچھلی - machhlí, Hind.). Means fish or sinew. Also same as Tanner's sumach. Mutchly bunder, from (bandar, hind. port) is Masulipatam.

MADA (మడ - mada, *Tel.*; മട - mata, *Mal.*; மடை - madai, *Tam.*). From (madu, tam. to hold). Irrigation channel [q.v.]; small sluice. Also means den.——*Madaiyaun* (மடையான் - madaiyán, Tam.). Means keeper of sluice. A village servant who distributes water for irrigation [inam, maday vetty, neer gunty].——*Madakara* (മടക്കര - matakkara, Mal.). From (mata, mal. den + kara, mal. village). Island; Malabar district, Chiracal talook. On north side of Belliapatam river. Obtained from Rajah of Chiracal as a trading post on rent in 1669. Formally ceded by rajah, 1749. Permission granted by rajah for erection of a fort, 1759. Fort blown up and island given back to the Vice-regent of Chiracal in 1762. Abandoned in 1762 after the fall of Pondicherry and Mahé in 1761. Ceded by Tippoo with the rest of Malabar, 18th March 1792.——*Madal* (மடல் - madal, Tam.). Means turning; branch channel. Channel [q.v.].——*Madavay* (بوری - búrí, Ar.; پڑھن - parhan, Hind.; عربی مچھی - arabímaçchí, Dec.; బొంత - bonta, Tel.; மடவை - madavai, Tam.). Ar. from (búrah, ar. town in egypt); where frequent. Dec. from (arabí, ar. arabian + maçchí, hind. fish). Tel. means large. Tam. from (madai, tam. channel). Name for the family Mugilidæ [matsyam, 26] of fishes.——*Madoogoo* (مڑوگ - marug, Hind.; మడుగు - madugu, Tel.). From (madu, tam. to contain). Pool. Distinguish from Mathagoo.

MADAGASCAR (مدغاسقر - madagháskar, *Ar.*). The island to east of Africa, once joined to southern india, as is supposed, by the now submerged Lemuria [q.v.].——*Madagascar palm* (مدغاسقر کا تاڑ - madagháskarkátár, Hind.). Same as Traveller's palm.

MADAKSIRA (మడకశిర - madakasira, *Tel.* madakasíra *). From (madaka, san. raggy, eleusine coracana, gærtn. + sirá, san. stream) [mad].——**(1)** Talook, Anantapore district. Tahsildar's pay Rs. 150. Area 439 square miles. Population 67,993. S.W. of district. Languages Teloogoo and Canarese. Surrounded by Mysore except on the east where it joins Hindoopore talook. In the south the talook is very hilly and rocky, the two highest peaks being at Madaksira and Ratnagherry, both of which are strongly fortified. Towards the west the country is more level and fertile. The soil is chiefly red. The principal products are paddy [q.v.], raggy [q.v.], cholum [q.v.], cumboo [bajrah], oil-seeds [yennay] and gram [q.v.]. The largest market in the talook is at Amrapore. Grain is imported from the Mysore country and exported to the Hyderabad country and Hindoopore. Agricultural tract, no manufactures. There are eighty-six spring channels [q.v.] and about 2,560 wells, most of which are the private property of the ryots [q.v.]. There are altogether 158 tanks [q.v.] in the talook, the largest being Agaly, Amrapore, Harisamoodram, Madaksira, Morabaugal, Shivaram. Camping ground at Madaksira. Places of archæological interest:—Agaly, Amrapore, Doddairy, Hemauvaty, Madaksira, Madhoody, Poyalbunda, Shivaram, Toommadihully. Principal Trig. station:—Cariyacull. The leading places, &c., in the talook are the following.——*Agaly* (అగళి - agali, Tel.). From (aga, san. tree + ilá, san. ground). Village; pop. 1,629; lat. 13° 47′; long. 77° 05′; from Anantapore S.S.W. 72 miles; from Madaksira S.W. 18 miles. Contains numerous areca, &c., gardens. Large tank irrigating 873 acres. River Swarnamookhy runs by.——*Amrapore* (అమరాపురము - amarápuramu, Tel.). From (amara, san. god, the immortal + pura, san. town). Ancient name (nadimipalli), meaning middle village. Village; pop. 3,805; lat. 14° 08′; long. 77° 01′; from Anantapore S.W. 56 miles; from Madaksira N.W. 23 miles. On the old route from Chitaldroog to Chittore. The ancient name was as lying midway between the Pyaulagherry and Cottacote towns built by Hottal naidoo. The old site of the town is about half a mile to the west. A large weekly market. It contains good areca [q.v.] and other gardens and orchards. Tank irrigating 602 acres.——*Cariyacull* (కరియకల్లు - kariyakallu, Tel.). From (kari, can. black + kallu, tel. rock). Trig. station; lat. 13° 55′ 14·57″; long. 77° 05′ 07·65″; height 2,646 feet; from Anantapore S.W. 65 miles; from Cholagherry W. 4 miles; from Madaksira W. 16 miles.——*Halcore* (హల్కూరు - halkúru, Can.). From (halaku, can. to climb + úru, can. village). Village on the slope. Village; pop. 1,628; lat. 14° 05′; long. 77° 02′; from Anantapore S.W. 57 miles; from Madaksira W. 21 miles. Situated on road to Amrapore. Contains superior areca gardens. Tank irrigating acres 511.——*Harisamoodram* (హరిసముద్రం - harisamudram, Tel.). From (hari, san. proper name + samudra, san. ocean). Village; pop. 1,756; lat. 13° 54′; long. 77° 20′; from Anantapore S.S.W. 57 miles; from Madaksira S.E. 2½ miles. Has a large tank irrigating acres 894.——*Hemauvaty* (హేమావతి - hémávati, Tel.). See sep. title.——*Madaksira* (మడకశిర - madakasira, Tel.). See below.——*Madhoody* (మధూడి - madhúdi, Tel.). From (madhu, can. proper name + hudi, can. dam). Village; pop. 1,692; lat. 13° 49′; long. 77° 03′; from Anantapore S. 71 miles; from Madaksira W.S.W. 19 miles. Tank irrigating 532 acres. Contains numerous areca [q.v.] and cocoanut [q.v.] gardens. River Swarnamookhy runs by.——*Manoor* (మనూరు - manúru, Tel.). From (mani, san. gem + úru, tel. village). Village; pop. 1,821; lat. 13° 51′; long. 77° 23′; from Anantapore S.S.W. 59 miles; from Madaksira S.E. 8 miles. Has a tank irrigating acres 468. Produces tobacco [pogauk].——*Morabaugal* (ಮೊರಬಾಗಲು - morabágalu, Can.). From (murári, can. proper name + bágalu, can. door). Village; pop. 1,745; lat. 13° 57′; long. 77° 05′; from Anantapore S.W. 62 miles; from Madaksira W. 16 miles. Large tank.——*Ratnagherry* (రత్నగిరి - ratnagiri, Tel.). From (ratna, san. gem + giri, san. mountain). Village; pop. 1,378; lat. 13° 49′; long. 77° 10′; from Anantapore S.S.W. 68 miles; from Madaksira S.W. 13 miles. A strongly fortified hill. Poligar [q.v.] was deprived of office by Sir Thomas Munro. Present poligar draws a small pension [madaksira].——*Shivaram* (శివరాము - shivaramu, Tel.). From (shrí, san. the goddess + pura, san. city). Sanscrit name (shrípura), meaning lutchmy's city. Village; pop. 1,061; lat. 14° 02′; long. 77° 04′; from Anantapore S.W. 59 miles; from Madaksira W.N.W. 18 miles. Large tank.——*Shunkercull* (శంకరగల్లు - shankaragallu, Tel.). From (shankara, san. shiva, the pleasure giver + kallu, tel. stone). Village; pop. 1,719; lat. 13° 59′; long. 77° 16′; from Anantapore S.S.W. 52 miles; from Madaksira N.W. 5 miles. Formerly Poligar's station. Contains a few areca and cocoanut gardens. Situated amidst hills.——**(2)** Talook head-quarters, Anantapore dist., Madaksira tal.; pop. 4,896; lat. 13° 56′; long. 77° 19°; from Anantapore S.S.W. 56 miles; from Bellary S.S.E. 86 miles; from Gooty S.S.W. 85 miles; from Madras W.N.W. 215 miles; from Penoocondah W.S.W. 24 miles. Situated at foot of a rock. Built on a forest clearing in A.D. 1520 by a chief, Ratnagherry sarjappa royappa rajah, who also built the temple of Anjaneyan [hanooman]. Hirey wodeya, the founder of the poligar family, formerly established here, served the Vijianugger Government with 1,000 peons [q.v.], for the support of whom twelve villages in the Chitaldroog talook were given to him in jagheer [q.v.]. This jagheer was afterwards augmented by the incorporation of adjacent districts bearing a rent of one lakh [q.v.] of pagodas [q.v.]. One of the family built the fort at Sheerah in Mysore, Much of the country was taken from the poligar by the Sultan of Beejapore early in the seventeenth century. The two chief forts which remained in his possession were Madaksira and Ratnagherry. The former of these was at one time resumed but afterwards restored. In 1728 the place fell under the Mahrattas and in 1741 it was captured by Moraury row who imposed a chowt [q.v.] of Rs. 8,000. He also built a fort and palace. In A.D. 1762 the Mussalmans seized the place, but were ejected two years later. Hyder ally took it in 1769 and demanded from the poligar a peshcush [q.v.] of Rs. 15,000, and as this was not punctually paid, he captured the poligar and his five sons in 1776 and sent them prisoners to Seringapatam. The eldest son was taken by the English troops at the siege of Seringapatam in 1792 and set at liberty. He returned to Ratnagherry and captured the place, but was again driven out and died a year or two afterwards without issue. His brothers were all hanged by Tippoo sultan and the family became extinct. The Mussalmans regained possession in A.D. 1774 and held it till 1799 A.D., when the country fell under the English on the defeat of Tippoo sultan. There are some fine wells with steps of cut-stone. Large tank.

MADANAPULLY (మదనపల్లె - madanapalle,* *Tel.*). From (madana, san. the god of love + palle, tel. village) [mad]. Probably a corruption from name of the ruler maryauda ramanna. Sanscrit name (madanapuri), meaning cauman, the god of love + town.——**(1)** Talook, Cuddapah district. Tahsildar's pay Rs. 175. Area 837 square miles. Population 127,352. Language Teloogoo. S.W. of district. Contains 93 Government and 17 inam [q.v.] villages, but all of these have hamlets attached to them, and some as many as 80, 90, or 100, separated many miles from the village to which they belong. The principal ryot's house is enclosed by a mud-wall, and the hamlet is named by the original proprietor. Bounded east by Voilpaud and north by Royachoty and Cadiry talooks of the district, south by Poonganore zemindarry of North arcot, and west by Mysore and Cadiry talook. Very hilly, except in the south-western part where the land meets Mysore plateau. Climate pleasant and favorable to Europeans; though a low kind of fever is prevalent. Soil good, especially in valleys. Sugar-cane [q.v.] noted. Tanks [q.v.] very small, and the majority are dasbandam [q.v.]. The principal tanks are—Pedda tippasamoodram, Rungasamoodram, and Vyausasamoodram, situated within a few miles of each other, all receiving supply from the Mysore water-shed. The supply diminishes from year to year, as fresh works of irrigation are constructed in Mysore. Two other large tanks are Badicauyalapully and Chinna tippasamoodram. There are two rivers, Paupughny and Bauhoodah nuddy. The former runs greater part of year, the latter only during monsoon [q.v.]. Another stream, Peddapollem wunka, formed by surplus water of Pedda tippasamoodram tank is generally dry. Many jungle streams, some of which are utilised. No anicuts [q.v.]. Tanks trust to the scanty rainfall only. Talook is rich in natural springs which open out with every shower of rain. These springs are in reality often nothing more than surface drainage, but they run for three months after the heavy monsoon [q.v.]. The two largest spring head channels [q.v.] are the Battala caulwa and the Cottapully caulwa, both at Madanapully. Places of archæological interest :—Badicauyalapully, Basnicondah, Batlanootigadda, Beerangy, Boorracauyalacote, Cadinaudhoonicote, Calicherla, Chadam, Chinnatippasamoodram, Chippily, Cokkunty, Cosoovaurpulley, Cottacote, Cottaula, Cundoocore, Gollapully, Gootlastalam, Gutt, Madanapully, Marellagadda, Moodivaid, Moolcalcheroo, Nadigadda, Paupayapully, Pedda tippasamoodram, Sompully, Tamballapulley, Tavalam, Veligull, Vempully. Principal trig. stations :—Adavy auvoolapully, Canoogonda. The leading places, &c., in the talook are the following.——*Adavy auvoolapully* (అడవిఆవులపల్లి - adaviávulapalli, Tel.). From (adavi, tel. forest + ávu, tel. cow + palli, tel. village). Village; lat. 13° 28′; long. 78° 26′; from Cuddapah S.S.W. 75 miles; from Madanapully S.W. 9 miles. Trig. station in lat. 13° 28′ 22·05″; long. 78° 26′ 36·44″; height 3,850 feet; from Maulepaud S.W. 3 miles.——*Badicauyalapully* (బడికాయలపల్లి - badikáyalapalli, Tel.). From (badikáya, tel. school boy + palli, tel. village). Village; pop. 1,795; acres 9,125; lat. 13° 37′; long. 78° 19′; from Cuddapah S.S.W. 70 miles; from Madanapully W. 16 miles. Ramasawmy temple. Tank.——*Basnicondah* (బసినికొండ - basinikonda, Tel.). From (basava, can. bull + konda, tel. hill). Village, Hill; pop. 1,394; acres 5,432; lat. 13° 33′; long. 78° 34′; from Cuddapah S.S.W. 67 miles; from Madanapully E. 1½ miles. Rock 660 feet above the town of Madanapully. On the summit a pagoda [q.v.] to Vencatesha sawmy, who placed one foot here while travelling to Tripatty the other foot resting on Gundicote. Three inscriptions.——*Canoogonda* (కనుగొండ - kanugonda, Tel.). See sep. title.——*Cheyair* (చెయ్యేరు - cheyyéru, Tel.). See sep. title.——*Chinnatippasamoodram* (చిన్నతిప్పసముద్రం - chinnatippasamudram, Tel.). From tipparasayya, name of the constructor of the tank; as opposed to pedda tippasamoodram. Village; pop. 2,642; acres 6,246; lat. 13° 38′; long. 78° 36′; from Cuddapah S.W. 60 miles; from Madanapully N.N.E. 8 miles. Large tank seldom full. At opposite corner of talook from other of same name. Feeds channel which irrigates 60 acres near Voilpaud.——*Cottaula* (కోటహాల - kot'hála, Tel.). From (kottamu, tel. thatched house). Village; pop. 1,293; acres 7,710; lat. 13° 55′; long. 78° 27′; from Cuddapah S.W. 48 miles; from Madanapully N.W. 26 miles. Inscription on rock N. of village.——*Cundoocore* (కండుకూరు - kandukúru, Tel.). From (kandu, tel. black + úru, tel. village). Village; pop. 2,432; acres 7,405; lat. 13° 45′; long. 78° 12′; from Cuddapah S.S.W. 66 miles; from Madanapully W.N.W. 27 miles. Among paddy [q.v.] fields, and water of town is impregnated with their drainage. Village given as a gift to a priest by Krishna rajah of Vijianugger. Two old Vishnoo [q.v.] temples. Vyausasamoodram tank is close by.——*Gutt* (ఘట్టు - ghattu, Tel.). Means hill. Village; pop. 3,101; acres 18,309; lat. 13° 39′; long. 78° 22′; from Cuddapah S.S.W. 65 miles; from Madanapully W.N.W. 14 miles. Hill-fort, the poligar [q.v.] of which at one time, possessed considerable power. A pension is paid to his descendants who reside at Cottapettah. Fort in ruins; also ancient palace. Two ruined temples and inscriptions.——*Horsley condah* (హర్సిలికొండ - hársilikonda, Tel.). See sep. title.——*Madanapully* (మదనపల్లె - madanapalle, Tel.). See below.——*Moodivaid* (ముదివేడు - mudivédu, Tel.). From (mudi, tel. old + vídu, tel. town). Village; pop. 2,529; acres 7,470; lat. 13° 42; long. 78° 33′; from Cuddapah S.W. 57 miles; from Madanapully N. 11 miles. Four inscriptions.——*Moolcalcheroo* (ములకలచెరువు - mulakalacheruvu, Tel.). From (mulaka, tel. brinjal, solanum ferox, linn. + cheruvu, tel. tank). Village; pop. 1,073; acres 3,178; lat. 13° 49′; long. 78° 19′; from Cuddapah S.W. 59 miles; from Madanapully N.W. 2 miles. Inscriptions.——*Paupayapully* (పాపేపల్లి - pápépalli, Tel.). From (pápaya, tel. proper name + palli, tel. village). Village; pop. 942; acres 7,129; lat. 13° 57′; long. 78° 35′; from Cuddapah S.W. 41 miles; from Madanapully N. 28 miles. Once residence of a poligar.——*Paupughny* (పాపఘ్ని - pápaghni, Tel.). See sep. title.——*Peddapollem* (పెద్దపాళెము - peddapálemu, Tel.). From (pedda, tel. large + pálemu, tel. fortified village). Village; pop. 95; acres 4,505; lat. 13° 46′; long. 78° 20′; from Cuddapah S.W. 61 miles; from Madanapully N.W. 21 miles. Former residence of a poligar.——*Pedda tippasamoodram* (పెద్దతిప్పసముద్రం - peddatippasamudram, Tel.). From (tipparasayya, tel.); name of the constructor of the tank [chinna tippasamoodram]. Village; pop. 3,009; acres 3,073; lat. 13° 42′; long. 78° 15′; from Cuddapah S.W. 67 miles; from Madanapully W.N.W. 23 miles. Old temples and forts. Near hamlet of Poollaygootvauripully is an inscription; another on a rock called Boyabunda, south-west of village; others on boulders near the chauvady [q.v.]; others in a temple on the road from Poollaygootvauripully, and in the forts. Chiefly remarkable for its large tank. This lies close to Mysore frontier, from water-shed of which it receives supply.——*Rungasamoodram* (రంగసముద్రం - rangasamudram, Tel.). From (ranga, san. vishnu + samudra, san. ocean). Village; pop. 2,704; acres 7,348; lat. 13° 42′; long. 78° 18′; from Cuddapah S.W. 65 miles; from Madanapully N.W. 20 miles. Large tank, ayacut [q.v.] 1,917 acres, assessed at Rs. 8,318. Pays low assessment, land being on high level. Supply precarious and it leaks.——*Sompully* (సోంపల్లి - sómpalli, Tel.). From (sompu, tel. excellent + palli, tel. village). Village, Place of pilgrimage; pop. 3,135; acres 11,707; lat. 13° 50′; long. 78° 18′; from Cuddapah S.W. 57 miles; from Madanapully N.W. 25 miles. Residence of a poligar. Old Vishnoo temple with frescoed roof, in front of which stands a sculptured monolithic pillar [stambham] 50 feet high. Bangles [gauzoo] manufactured from an earth similar to iron earth. One and-a-half miles east is fort of Causincote, at least 830 years old.——*Tettoo* (తెట్టు - tettu, Tel.). Means fort-gate. Village, Place of pilgrimage; pop. 1,117; acres 11,896; lat. 13° 38′; long. 78° 28′; from Cuddapah S.S.W. 64 miles; from Madanapully N.W. 7 miles. Former residence of a poligar [q.v.]. Ancient temple.——*Vyausasamoodram* (వ్యాసనముద్రము - vyásasamudramu, Tel.). See sep. title.——**(2)** Town, Talook and divisional head-quarters; Cuddapah dist., Madanapully tal.; pop. 6,527; acres 6,626; lat. 13° 33′; long. 78° 32′; from Cuddapah south 68 miles; from Madras 126 miles W. & by N.; from Bangalore north-east 74 miles; from Sidhout S.S.W. 71 miles. Once the residence of a poligar. The family now extinct. Two inscriptions in Goondlapully hamlet. Remains of an old fort. Has a number of spring head channels. The favorite resort of pensioned officials of the district.

MADAUR (مدار - madár, *Ar.*). From (dára, ar. to move in a circle). A centre, pivot. Common alam; as Madaur bee, alam + alaumat [ism].——*Madauriya* (مداریہ - madáriyah, Hind.). From (madár, ar. title of the founder). His full name was Shah badee ood deen zinda shah madaur. A class of Fakeers [q.v.].

MADDALAM (मर्दल - mardala, *San.*; மத்தளம் - mattalam, *Tam.*). From (mard, san. to strike). Double drum [paray, sangeetam].

MADEENA (مدینہ - madínah, *Ar.*). From (madana, ar. to build or settle in a place). City. Particularly the holy city of the Mahomedans in Arabia, where Mahomet is buried. Taken as alam; as Madeena sahib [ism].——*Madanee* (مدنی - madaní, Hind.). Lacab of Mahomet. Title of a class of Mahomedans [ism].

MADHYAM (मध्य - madhya, *San.*). Latin medius. Middle, interior, centre [caindram]. Meridian [raikhay]. Middle term or mean of a progression [raushy]. Madhyama graham is the mean place of a planet [graham]. Madhyamam is mean; in contradistinction to spootam [q.v.], or true, apparent in astronomy [jyotisham]. Madhyama sowra maunam, from (saura, san. solar), is mean solar reckoning of time [maunam]. Madhyastan is a mediator; in Malabar arbitrator; corresponds with Punchayetdar [q.v.] in other places. Madhyaunam, from (ahan, san. day), is noon [ooroomam].——*Madhya desham* (मध्यदेश - madhyadésha, San.). From (above + désha, san. region). In Sanscrit literature the central region or the land lying between the Himalayas on the north, the Vindhya mountains on the south, Vinaushanam on the west, and Prayaugay on the east [charitram]. See vol. I (2).——*Madhyaushtamy* (మధ్యాష్టమి - madhyáshtami, Tel.). From (above + ashtamí, san. eighth day). Lunar [chaundramaunam] festival [pundigay, 3e], subject to intercalation [adhicam]. The eighth lunar day [tity], in middle of the waning moon [krishna pacsham] of the sixth lunar month Bhaudrapadam [mausam] between 8th September and 8th October. Otherwise Mahaulya pacsham [q.v.]. A day on which it is meritorious to observe the Shrauddham [q.v.], which, when done, produces the same effect as if that ceremony had been performed during every other day of the Pacsham [maryauday, pacsham].

MADOOBBAH (മദ്ബഹ - madubbá, *Mal.*). Chancel among Malabar syrian christians.

MADRANTACAM (مدنات - madnát, *Hind.*; மதுராந்தகம் - mathurándagam, *Tam.* madurántakam *). From (mathurai, tam. town, so called + antaka, san. end) [mad]; indicating the northern limit of the kingdom of madura. Sometimes called Vada madura, or northern madura.——(1) Talook, Chinglepnt district. Tahsildar's pay Rs. 225. The largest and most important talook in the district. Area 696 square miles. Population 263,137. Language Tamul, Teloogoo. Bounded west by Arcot and Wandiwash talooks of North arcot district; south by Tindivanam talook of South arcot district; east by the sea; and north and north-west by the Cheyaur and Palaur. The surface is generally undulating. The northern portion is studded with a few low conical or ridged hills, the former predominating; towards the south run two long ridges, seven miles apart, rising here and there into peaks. A strip of land running down the coast and separated from the mainland by backwaters [cauyal] is called the Yidakkay naud [q.v.]. Tradition points to its separation by an irruption of the sea. This tract is covered with cocoanut [q.v.] trees, which yield the best nuts of any in these parts, the produce being exported to Madras. The soil is generally red ferruginous loam, but becomes sandy as the sea is approached. Its fertility is however fair. Paddy [q.v.] of the usual sort is the principal crop raised on the wet area [nunjah]. The dry [poonjah] ayacut [q.v.] is chiefly occupied by varagoo [q.v.]. Weaving is carried on to a small extent, principally for local requirements. The Palaur and Cheyaur irrigate a large acreage. The water is either stored in tanks [q.v.], being brought down by channels from the rivers when in fresh, or flows directly into the fields from spring channels [q.v.], whose heads are excavated in the beds of the rivers after the floods have run off. The Kiliyaur irrigates a few villages in the western portions. The only large tank besides Madrantacam tank is that of Ootramallore, which is filled through a long channel of about 7 miles from the Cheyaur. Camping grounds, Acharapaukam and Carangooly. Petty zemindarries:—Agaram, Aneicutt, Aumayamputt, Aundaurcooppam, Boothore, Carimbaukam, Cayanullore, Cayapaukam, Chinnakilacaudy, Chinnavelicaud, Chittore, Choonampett, Cokkantaungal, Colattanullore, Colattore, Collambaukam, Comauracooppam, Coomily, Cullputt, Cuttiwaukum, Eesore, Illaid, Iroombaid, Keelcanday, Keelcauranay, Keeralvaudy, Madavilaugam, Maroovalam, Maumbaukam, Mogaiyore, Moodelliarcooppam, Nariyore, Neerpair, Neinaurcooppam, Nercoonaputt, Noogambal, Olavetty, Orangauvaly, Othiyore, Ottivilaugam, Panayore, Pavanjore, Perively, Periyakilacaudy, Periyavelicaud, Pilancooppam, Pondore, Poothoocooppam Poothooputt, Poroor, Saulore, Sheyoor Shirvambaukam, Shirmeilore, Shiroocalattore, Shiroonugger, Shiroopinayore, Tattamputt, Taudauncooppam, Tondamanullore, Tonnaud, Toondamvellairy, Toorayore, Velanganore, Vembanore, Venmaulaharam, Vettoor, Vilangaud, Vitchoor, Vunniyanullore, Yendatore. Places of archeological interest:—Acharapaukam, Alamparva, Cadambarcoil, Carangooly, Keenore, Madrantacam, Ootramallore, Pernugger, Peroombayore, Pondore, Shaulwaukum, Sheettancherry, Tirmacoodal, Tirpoolivanam, Tirvancoil, Villivaukam. Principal trig. stations:—Avirimode, Carangooly, Vilangaud. The leading places, &c., in the talook are the following. ——*Acharapaukam* (அச்சரவாக்கம் - açcaravákkam, Tam. acharapákam *). From (açcuram. tam. a thorny plant, tribulus terrestris. linn. + pákkam, tam. village). Sanscrit name (akshéshvarapura), meaning soul + lord + town, or town of shiva, lord of souls. Village, Railway station; pop. 1,272; acres 1,626; lat. 12° 25′; long. 79° 53′; height 135 feet; from Madrantacam S.S.W. 8 miles; from Sydapett S.W. 50 miles; from the sea W. 20 miles. Travellers' bungalow [q.v.] on great southern trunk road. Old Shiva temple. Five inscriptions of Chola and Paundy dynasties [raj] on temple of Aesheshwarasawmy.——*Alamparva* (ஆலம்பறை - álambarai, Tam.). See sep. title.——*Avirimode* (அவிரிமேடு - avirimódu, Tam.). From (avíri, tam. indigo plant, indigofera tinctoria, linn. + módu, tam. high ground). Trig. station: lat. 12° 27′ 13·49″; long. 79° 57′ 08·32″; height 490 feet; from Madrantacam S. 4 miles; from Yendatore W. 2 miles; from the sea W. 16 miles.——*Carangooly* (கருங்குழி - karunguzhi, Tam.). See sep. title.——*Cauvitundalam* (காவித்தண்டலம் - kávittandalam, Tam.). From (kávi, tam. red earth + tan, tam. cool + talam, tam. place). Village; pop. 187; acres 1,155; lat. 12° 43′ 35″; long. 79° 59′; from Madrantacam N.N.W. 16 miles; from Sydapett S.W. 28 miles; from the sea W. 20 miles. N.E. of Ootramallore. Its mud fort was scene of struggles between English and French.——*Cayapaukam* (கயப்பாக்கம் - kayappákkam, Tam.). From (kayam, tam. tank + pákkam, tam. village). Zemindarry, Village; pop. 1,294; square miles 2; lat. of village 12° 21′; long. 79° 54′; from Madrantacam S. 11 miles; from Sydapett S. 52 miles; from the sea W. 13 miles. Peshcush Rs. 2,120.——*Cheyaur* (செய்யாறு - sheyyáru, Tam.). See sep. title.——*Cheyoor* (செய்யூர் - sheyyúr, Tam. cheyúr *). From (sheyya, tam. red + úr, tam. village). Zemindarry, Town; pop. 5,364; acres 8,802; lat. of town 12° 21′; long. 80° 03′; from Madrantacam S.E. 13 miles; from Sydapett S. 17 miles; from the sea W. 4 miles. Temple of Keilansanautan with inscriptions, temple of Soobramanyan [q.v.]; inscription at the temple of Valmeekeshwaran. The inscriptions belong to the Chola dynasty. Extensive salt pans [ooppalam].——*Choonampett* (சுணாம்பேடு - shúnámbattu, Tam. chúnámpet *). From (shunnámbu, tam. lime stone + pattu, tam. village). Zemindarry; pop. 4,306; lat. 12° 16′; long 79° 58′; from Madrantacam S. 17 miles; from Sydapett S.S.W. 56 miles; from the sea W. 7 miles. Peshcush Rs. 1,996.——*Choonampett villivaukam* (சுணாம்பட்டுவில்லிவாக்கம் - shúnámbattuvillivákkam, Tam.). From (shúnámbattu, tam. village so called + villivákkam, tam. vilage so called); villivaukam in choonampett. Village; pop. 3,779; acres 4,718; lat. 12° 16′; long. 79° 59′; from Madrantacam S. 17¼ miles; from Sydapett S. 56 miles; from the sea W. 6 miles. Chief place of Choonampett zemindarry. Salt pans. An old Shiva temple.——*Keelcauranay* (கீழ்க்காரணை - kízhkkáranai, Tam.). From (kízh, tam. east + kár, tam. black + anai, tam. dam). Zemindarry, Village; pop 535; lat. of village 12° 24′; long. 79° 58′; from Madrantacam S. 8 miles; from Sydapett S. 47 miles; from the sea W. 12 miles. Peshcush Rs. 396.——*Kiliyaur* (கிளியாறு - kiliyáru, Tam.). From (kili, tam. a grasshopper + áru, tam. river). River; Tributary of Palaur. Rises in Wandiwash hill, and after supplying a few villages in western portion of the talook, runs into Madrantacam tank, after flowing over calingula [q.v.] of which it runs between high banks in a course at first due east, and afterwards north-east till it joins the Palaur, about 10 miles from sea.——*Madrantacam* (மதுராந்தகம் - mathurándagam, Tam.). See below.——*Mogaiyore* (முகையூர் - mugayúr, Tam.). From (mugai, tam. a bud + úr, tam. village). Zemindarry, Village; pop. 1,356; square miles 3; lat. of village 12° 24′; long. 80° 08′; from Madrantacam S.E. 16 miles; from Sydapett S. 43 miles; from the sea W. 1 mile. Peshcush Rs. 1,732.——*Nedoombauray* (நெடும்பறை - nedumbarai, Tam.). From (nedum, tam. long. + párai, tam. rock). Otherwise Nedoomaram. Village; pop. 928; acres 1,522; lat. 12° 26′; long. 80° 08′; from Madrantacam S.E. 15 miles; from Sydapett S. 41 miles; from the sea W. 3 miles. Formed part of the Home farms [q.v.].——*Ootramallore* (உத்திரமேரூர் - uttiranmérúr, Tam.). See sep. title. ——*Ottivilaugam* (ஒத்திவிளாகம் - ottivilágam, Tam.). From (otti, tam. a plant, pupalia atropurpurea, moq. + világam, tam. battle field). Zemindarry, Village; pop. 137; square miles 3¼; lat. of village 12° 17′; long. 80° 01′; from Madrantacam S. 16 miles; from Sydapett S.W. 54 miles; from the sea W. 5 miles. Peshcush Rs. 233.——*Palaur* (பாலாறு - páláru, Tam.). See sep. title.——*Panayore* (பனையூர் - panaiyúr, Tam.). From (panai, tam. palmyra tree, borassus flabelliformis, linn. + úr, tam. village). Zemindarry, Village; pop. 1,741; square miles 2⅜; lat. of village 12° 19′; long. 80° 04′; from Madrantacam S.E. 16 miles; from Sydapett S. 50 miles; from the sea W. 1¼ miles. Peshcush Rs. 168.——*Pattaulam* (பட்டாளம் - pattálam, Tam.). Means regiment. Village, Railway station; pop. 869; acres 641; lat. 12° 36′; long. 80° 00′; height 86 feet; from Madrantacam N.E. 7 miles; from Sydapett S. 34 miles; from the sea W. 16 miles.——*Perively* (பெருவேலி - peruvéli, Tam.). From (peru, tam. large + véli, tam. fence). Zemindarry, Village; pop. 807; square miles 2 $\frac{1}{16}$; lat. of village 12° 26′; long. 79° 57′; from Madrantacam S. 5 miles; from Sydapett S. 45 miles; from the sea W. 15 miles. Peshcush Rs. 488.——*Pernugger* (பெருநகர் - perunagar, Tam.). From (peru, tam. large + nagara, san. city). Village; pop. 2,233; acres 3,535; lat. 12° 39′; long. 79° 42′; from Madrantacam W.N.W. 18 miles; from Madras S.W. 52 miles; from Sydapett S.W. 45 miles; from the sea W. 36 miles. Ancient Shiva temple, elaborately sculptured and containing many inscriptions. Old Vishnoo temple. East of village is a ruined jeina temple, stones of which were used in building Vishnoo temple. In bed of tank are three cairns [paundicoozhy]. ——*Pondore* (போந்தூர் - póndúr, Tam.). From (póndu, tam. palmyra tree, borassus flabelliformis, linn. + úr, tam. village). Zemindarry, Village; pop. 213; square miles 1¼; lat. of village 12° 20′; long. 79° 58′; from Madrantacam S. 13 miles; from Sydapett S. 52 miles; from the sea W. 8 miles. Peshcush Rs. 3,627. Old Vishnoo temple.——*Shaulwaukum* (சாலவாக்கம் - shálavákkam, Tam.). From (shálai, tam. avenue + vákkam, tam. village). Village; pop. 1,922; acres 1,081; lat. 12° 40′; long. 79° 56′; from Madrantacam N. 11 miles; from Sydapett S.W. 33 miles; from the sea W. 22 miles. Between Ootramallore and Chingleput. Being conveniently situated in the centre of a fertile country it was always the head-quarters both of Hindoo and Mahomedan revenue officers. The fort, a Hindoo work, was maintained by Mahomedans when they occupied country. ——*Tonnaud* (தொன்னாடு - tonnádu, Tam.). From (tol, tam. old + nádu, tam. country). Zemindarry, Village; pop. 654; square miles 1¼; lat. of village 12° 24′; long. 79° 58′; from Madrantacam S. 8 miles; from Sydapett S.W. 47 miles; from the sea W. 13 miles. Peshcush Rs. 238.——*Vilangaud* (விளாங்காடு - vilángádu, Tam.). From (vilá, tam. wood-apple tree, feronia elephantum. corr. + kádu. tam. forest). Zemindarry, Village; pop. 474; square miles 2 $\frac{1}{16}$; lat. of village 12° 21′; long. 79° 58′; from Madrantacam S. 11 miles; from Sydapett S.W. 51

miles; from the sea W. 24 miles. Peshcush Rs. 297. Trig. station in lat. 12° 20′ 34·18″; long. 79° 58′ 31·18″; from Madrantacam S.S.E. 12 miles; from Villivaukam N. 6 miles; from the sea W. 8 miles.——*Yendatore* (எண்டத்தூர் - endattúr, Tam.). From (vendu, tam. to grow dry + úr, tam. village). Zemindarry, Village; pop. 1,134; square miles $3\frac{1}{16}$; lat. of village 12° 27′; long. 79° 59′; from Madrantacam S. E. 5 miles; from Sydapett S. 44 miles; from the sea W. 14 miles. Peshcush Rs. 1,599.——*Yidakkay naud* (இடக்கைநாடு - idakkainádu, Tam.). From (idam, tam. left + kai, tam. hand + nádu, tam. country). A strip of land running down the coast of the talook and separated from the mainland by backwaters.——**(2)** Town, Railway station, Talook head-quarters; Chingleput dist., Madrantacam tal; pop. 5,143; acres 4,451; lat. 12° 30′; long. 79° 56′; height 91 feet; from Chingleput S.S. W. 14 miles; from Conjeeveram S.E. 26 miles; from Madras S.W. 47 miles; from St. Thomas' mount S.W. 39 miles; from Sydapett S. 41 miles; from the sea W. 18 miles. On great southern trunk road, at fiftieth stone from Madras. Vishnoo temple of Codandaramasawmy with inscriptions. Chola inscription at Shiva temple of Vencateshwaran mostly in Grantam [q.v.] and Nagry [q.v.] character. The large tank is formed by damming up the Kiliyaur. Bund [q.v.] is 1½ miles long and circumference when full 7 miles. The calingula, one of the finest works of its kind in the country, is built in the form of a waved line, the height from the crest to the bed of the river below being 30 feet. The southern portion is a curious and beautiful specimen of masonry. Instead of being built in steps, the descent is formed to imitate the curve which the flood water takes in a fresh, and huge blocks of granite [caroomcull] have been hewn into this shape and are bound with lead [eeyam].

MADRAS (मन्दराजपट्टन - mandarájápattana, *San.*; مدراس - madrás, *Hind.*; ಮದರಾಸು - madarásu, *Can.*; చన్నపట్టణం - channapattanam, *Tel.*; മദിരാശി - madiráshi, *Mal.*; சென்னப்பட்டணம் - shennappattanam, *Tam.*). Hind. and can. from (mandarádzu, tel. name of a local telugu royer) [mund]. Tel. and tam. from (channappa, tel. name of a local poligar + pattana, san. town) [maumandore]. Colloquially (pattanam) or city by eminence.——**(1)** Revenue district comprising the city. Area 29 square miles. The Revenue district as originally comprised was conterminous with the present Municipal limits with the exception of some outlying portions of the Perambore division. In 1877 for administrative convenience certain portions of Aminjicaray, Aroombaukam, Maumbalam, Pooliyore and Shirvallore, villages of the Chingleput district which are all parts of tank beds, comprising an area of 1,040 acres, were added to the district. Bounded north, south, and west by Chingleput district; east by the sea. Population 452,518. Tamul, Teloogoo, and Hindostany are the principal languages; but Goozeratty, Marwarree, Canarese and Mahratta are spoken. Contains rivers Adyar and Cooum. General administration is conducted by Collector of Madras, who is also Collector of Sea customs, Protector of Emigrants, Superintendent of Stamps and Stationery and chairman of the Harbour trust board; assisted by two Deputy collectors in charge respectively of the Sea customs and the Quit-rent and Income-tax departments, and a Tahsildar, Rs. 150, whose duties are the supervision of the quit-rent and ground-rent, immediate charge of the Talook treasury, sale of stamps, &c. The Revenue local jurisdiction of the Collector and the Deputy collector is concurrent. For purposes of quit-rent collections, the town is divided into the following 15 divisions, to each of which are attached a conicopoly [q.v.] and an attender:—1 and 2 Mylapore, 3 Nungumbaukum, 4 Egmore, 5 Pursewaukum, 6 Perambore, 7 Vepery, 8 and 9 Tondiarpett, 10 and 11 Moottiaulpett, 12, 13 and 14 Peddanaickenpett, 15 Triplicane. The High court with the Orignal and Appellate branches, and the Small cause court, administer civil justice; while the two Presidency magistrates' courts of Egmore and Black town, with the High court, Original side, conduct the administration of criminal justice. Public works are administered by the Municipality, with the exception of bridges, roads over them, and Government buildings; all of which are in charge of the Executive engineer, Presidency. The tanks [q.v.] are supervised by a technical department called Tank maintenance department, supervised by the same officer. The following are the zemindarries [q.v.] and shrotriems [q.v.] in the district:—Chintaudripett, Maumbalam, Pooliyore, Trivateeshwarampett.——**(2)** City. Lat. 13° 06′; long. 80° 21′. The Madras observatory, in Nungumbaukam is lat. 13° 04′ 05·93″; long. 80° 17′ 22·17″. The city is an aggregate of sixteen hamlets, viz., Chetput, Chintaudripett, Comaleshwarampett, Egmore, Moottiaulpett, Nadoombauray, Nungumbaukam, Peddanaickenpett, Perambore, Pursewaukum, St. Thomé, Tondiarpett, Triplicane, Vepery, Vyausarpaudy, and Yeroongoondam. Lighthouse on esplanade, north of the fort Lat. 13° 05′; long. 80° 20′. White; flashing. Light has five faces and every minute one face flashes towards the same spot, but three faces are presented seaward at one time. 20 miles range. Visible from all directions seaward. Granite column. To guide vessels clear of the Poolicat shoal and into the roadstead. Mariners should not bring this light to southward of S.S.W. ½ W. to avoid Poolicat shoal. Also a leading Light at the Pier T. head. Lat. 13° 06′; long. 80° 21′. Red. Fixed; 5 miles; visible from all directions seaward; wooden post; to guide vessels leaving the harbour or making the anchorage at night. Another leading light on the Port office terrace. Lat. 13° 06′; long. 80° 21′. Green. Other particulars as the last. Map directions and distances from different places:—Anantapore E.S.E. 207 miles; Arcot E. 67 miles; Bangalore E. 185 miles; Bellary S.E. 270 miles; Bombay S.E. 640 miles; Calcutta S.W. 835 miles; Calicut N.E. 330 miles; Cannanore E. 343 miles; Chetterpore S.W. 530 miles; Chittore E. 80 miles; Cocanada S.S.W. 292 miles; Coimbatore N.E. 270 miles; Cuddalore N. 96 miles; Cuddapah S.E. 136 miles; Ernacolum N.E. 346 miles; Hyderabad S.E. 320 miles; Kurnool S.E. 240 miles; Madura N.N.E. 261 miles; Mangalore E. 370 miles; Masulipatam S. 220 miles; Nagpore S. 557 miles; Nellore S.S.E. 96 miles; Ootacamund E.N.E. 266 miles; Pondicherry N. 85 miles; Poona S.E. 570 miles; Salem N.E. 174 miles; Sydapett N.E. 6 miles; Tanjore N. 178 miles; Tinnevelly N.N.E. 245 miles; Trichinopoly N.E. 191 miles; Trivandrum N.E. 386 miles; Vizagapatam S.S.W. 369 miles. Travelling distances by road to different places:—

To.	Viá	Miles and Furlongs.
Amboor	Ranipett and Vellore	115 0
Bangalore ...	Ranipett, Pulmanair and Colaur ...	205 7½
Bangalore	Ranipett, Vaniyambaudy, Krishnagherry and Oossoor.	214 0
Bangalore	Ranipett, Goodiyattam, Naicknairy ghaut and Colaur.	203 4
Bangalore	Ranipett, Pullicondah, Synigoonta ghaut, Pulmanair and Colaur.	211 0
Bellary	Nagary, Cuddapah and Gooty	318 5
Bellary.	Ranipett, Chittore, Royachoty, Tadpatry and Gooty.	336 6½
Bellary	Ranipett, Pulmanair, Cadiry and Anantapore.	324 2
Bellary	Ranipett, Pulmanair, Colaur, Chedalpore and Anantapore.	362 6½
Berhampore ...	Nellore, Bezwada and Chicacole ...	645 5
Bezwada	Nellore, Ongole and Guntoor	272 4½
Calicut	Ranipett, Pulmanair, Bangalore, Seringapatam and the Tamracherry ghaut.	418 7½
Calicut	Ranipett, Salem, Coimbatore, Palghaut and Malapooram.	422 4
Cannanore... ...	Bangalore, Seringapatam and the Perambaudy ghaut.	403 6½
Cannanore... ...	Ranipett, Vaniyambaudy, Bangalore, Seringapatam and the Perambaudy ghaut.	411 7
Carangooly ...	Chingleput	48 0
Chetterpore ...	Nellore, Bezwada, Chicacole and Berhampore.	660 0
Chicacole ...	Nellore, Bezwada and Rajahmundry ...	546 4½
Chingleput ...	Pullavaram	34 7
Chittore	Ranipett and Shercaud	100 6½
Cocanada	Nellore, Ongole and Masulipatam ...	379 1
Cocanada	Nellore, Ongole, Bezwada and Rajahmundry.	404 6½
Cochin	Ranipett, Salem, Coimbatore, Palghaut and Trichore.	424 0
Coimbatore ...	Ranipett, Tripatore, Munjavaudy ghaut, Salem and Erode.	308 1
Coimbatore ...	Ranipett, Tripatore, Toppoor ghaut and Bhawauny.	312 2
Coimbatore ...	Ranipett, Toppoor ghaut, Salem and Bhawauny.	310 0
Combaconam ...	Chingleput, Vicravaundy and Panrooty	172 6
Cuddalore ...	Chingleput, Tindivanam and Pondicherry.	114 0
Cuddapah ...	Chittore and Royachoty	202 1½
Cumbum	Nellore, Caligherry and Canigherry ...	225 6
Cumbum	Nellore, Singaroyacondah and Canigherry.	236 2
Cuttack	Nellore, Bezwada, Chicacole, Berhampore and Khoordhah.	762 2
Dindigul	Chingleput, Oolandoorpett and Trichinopoly.	261 2½
Ellore	Nellore, Ongole and Bezwada	311 5½
Erode	Ranipett, Tripatore, Munjavaudy pass and Salem.	247 1
French rocks ...	Ranipett, Bangalore and Closepett ...	283 0½
French rocks ...	Vellore, Bangalore and Closepett ...	291 1
Ganjam	Nellore, Bezwada and Chicacole ...	664 5
Goodiyattam ...	Ranipett	105 1
Gooty	Nagary, Cuddapah and Tadpatry ...	264 3
Gooty	Ranipett, Chittore, Royachoty and Tadpatry.	270 0
Guntoor	Nellore, Ongole and Maurtore... ...	252 4
Guntoor	Nellore, Ongole and Incolloo	249 7
Hoonsoor	Ranipett, Colaur, Bangalore and Seringapatam.	317 1½
Kamptee	Ongole, Secunderabad and Nirmal ...	707 6
Kamptee	Cuddapah, Kurnool, Secunderabad and Nirmal.	743 1
Kurnool	Cuddapah and Nundiaul	289 4
Madura	Chingleput, Oolandoorpett, Trichinopoly and Dindigul.	301 4
Madura	Chingleput, Oolandoorpett and Trichinopoly.	281 3
Mangalore	Ranipett, Colaur, Bangalore and Manjarabad.	426 7½
Mangalore	Ranipett, Bangalore, Seringapatam and Mercara.	448 3½
Masulipatam ...	Nellore, Ongole and Baupatla	279 3
Masulipatam ...	Nellore, Ongole and Guntoor	300 4½
Masulipatam ...	Nellore, Ongole and Bezwada	316 3
Mercara	Ranipett, Bangalore and Seringapatam	362 5½
Mysore	Ranipett, Bangalore, Maddore and Seringapatam.	294 6½
Nagary	Poonamallee and Tripassore	58 5
Negapatam ...	Chingleput, Cuddalore and Tranquebar	194 4
Nellore	Sooloorpett	107 6
Ongole	Sooloorpett and Nellore	184 1
Oossoor	Ranipett, Vellore and Krishnagherry...	188 3
Palamcottah ...	Chingleput, Trichinopoly, Dindigul and Madura.	407 3
Palamcottah ...	Chingleput, Trichinopoly and Madura.	377 1

To		Via	Miles and Furlongs.	
Palghaut ...	...	Ranipett, Munjavaudy ghaut, Salem, Erode and Coimbatore.	338	0
Paumben ...	...	Chingleput, Negapatam, Tondy and Ramnaud.	373	4
Point calimere	...	Chingleput, Cuddalore and Negapatam	232	1
Point calimere	...	Chingleput, Cuddalore and Mayavaram	233	5
Pondicherry	...	Chingleput and Kilyanore	102	1
Pondicherry	...	Chingleput and Meilum	105	6
Poonamallee	...	......	12	4
Pooganore	...	Ranipett and Pulamunair	140	3
Pullavaram	...	St Thomas' mount	12	0
Pulmanair	...	Ranipett	121	5½
Pulmanair	...	Vellore and Synigoonta ghaut	126	6
Quilon	...	Ranipett, Coimbatore, Palghaut and Cochin.	517	2
Quilon	...	Chingleput, Trichinopoly, Madura and Palamcottah.	508	5
Quilon	...	Chingleput, Trichinopoly, Dindigul, Goodalore ghaut and Peermaid.	470	0½
Quilon	...	Chingleput, Trichinopoly, Madura and the Aryancauv ghaut.	435	0
Rajahmundry	...	Nellore, Ongole and Bezwada	366	6½
Ramnaud	...	Chingleput, Cuddalore, Negapatam and Tondy.	336	4
Ranipett	...	Shreepermatore	70	5
Sadras	...	Chingleput	54	3
Salem	...	Ranipett, Tripatore and the Munjavaudy ghaut.	209	4
Salem	...	Ranipett, Tripatore and the Toppoor ghaut.	220	6
Samulcottah	...	Nellore, Ongole, Bezwada and Rajahmundry.	396	6½
Secunderabad	...	Nellore, Ongole, Pondakholl, and Haitipamla.	390	0
Secunderabad	...	Cuddapah, Kurnool and Janampettah.	425	3
Tanjore	...	Chingleput, Vieravaundy and Combaconam.	196	2
Tanjore	...	Chingleput, Pondicherry, Chidambaram and Combaconam.	210	6
Tranquebar	...	Chingleput and Cuddalore	172	2
Trichinopoly	...	Chingleput, Oolandoorpett and Volcondapooram.	200	3
Trichinopoly	...	Chingleput, Tindivanam and Govindrajpett.	218	3
Trichinopoly.	...	Chingleput, Pondicherry, Cuddalore and Combaconam.	239	6
Trichore	...	Ranipett, Munjavaudy pass, Salem, Coimbatore and Palghaut.	380	1
Trivandrum	...	Chingleput, Trichinopoly, Madura and Palamcottah.	466	6
Trivandrum	...	Chingleput, Trichinopoly, Madura and the Aryancauv pass.	476	7
Vaniyambaudy	...	Ranipett and Vellore	125	4
Vellore	...	Shreepermatore and Ranipett	84	3
Vencatagherry	...	Ranipett and Shereaud	110	2½
Vizagapatam	...	Nellore, Ongole, Bezwada, Rajahmundry and Cassimcote.	489	6½
Vizianagram	...	Nellore, Ongole, Bezwada, Rajahmundry and Soobaraum.	513	1½

The following general references should be made to the preceding volumes :—general geography, I (1) to (29); general ethnology, I (29) to (109); general history, I (110) to (188); physical geography, II, 1; meteorology, II, 3; geology, II, 8; fauna, II, 21; flora, II, 26; mineralogy, II, 29. A general gazetteer account of the city is given at II, 90. For the Municipality, see I, 219.——**(3)** The leading places, &c., in the city are the following.——*Adyar* (அடையாறு - adaiyáru, Tam.). From the fort S.S.W. 5 miles. European suburb on banks of river. For river see sep. title.——*Ameer mahaul* (امیرمحل - amírmahal, Hind.; அமீருமகால் - amírumagál, Tam.). From the fort S.W. 2 miles. Residence of the Princes of Arcot after Prince Azeem jah. Constructed by Government on the site of the old Police Royapettah Court house when the Shaudy mahaul was sold at auction as the property of the mother of Prince Azeem jah.——*Anderson pettah* (ஆண்டர்சன்பேட்டை - ándarsanbéttai, Tam.). Named after Dr. James Anderson of the madras medical service. Is a large block of land at Nungumbaukum, more than eighty cawnies [q.v.] in extent. Granted rent free to the abovementioned by the Court of Directors at the end of the last century.——*Armenian street* (அறமனிக்காரத்தெரு - aramanikkáratteru, Tam.). From the fort N. ½ mile. Begins at the southern end of Black town [q.v.] opposite the Lighthouse esplanade and ends at its northern limit in Moottiaulpett. Towards the end of seventeenth century, wealthy Armenian merchants settled here. Important thoroughfare and contains houses of agency, Roman catholic cathedral, Armenian church and Agra bank.——*Basin* (மூலைக்கொத்தளம் - múlakkottalam, Tam.). From (múlai, tam. corner + kottalam, tam. rampart). From the fort N.N.W. 2 miles. A canal basin in north-west corner of Black town outside north rampart wall, where it is spanned by basin bridge. About 300 yards long and 80 broad. There formerly existed, at a distance of 2 miles from the sea and almost parallel to it, numerous detached portions of backwater, which were soon after Hyder's invasion in the latter part of the eighteenth century lengthened and deepened to facilitate carriage of materials for the construction of the north rampart wall of Black town. Subsequently an enterprising merchant named Cochrane continued the excavation and united the several detached portions and improved the basin, and the canal thus formed was named after him Cochrane's canal [q.v.]. The basin and canal belonged to Messrs. Arbuthnot and Co. until 1820, when they were purchased by Government. It now forms part of Buckingham canal [q.v.]. There is a wharf where dues are collected from boats passing up and down the canal, and the basin itself is used as a place of anchorage. Cargoes of firewood [lukdy], grain, salt [ooppoo], fish, condiments [chutney], cocoanuts, gram [q.v.], plantains [q.v.], palmyra [q.v.], and cocoanut [q.v.] fibre [coir] carried over the canal are loaded or unloaded at the wharf.——*Beach* (دریا کنارا - daryákinárá, Hind.; சமுத்திரக்கரை - samuttirakkarai, Tam.). Madras town has 9 miles of sea-coast. The beach throughout is flat and sandy. For the first half mile from the shore the bed of the sea slopes from 6 to about 7 fathoms or 42 feet in depth. After this the slope becomes very gradual, for, at the distance of 3½ miles from the shore, the depth is only 10½ fathoms or 63 feet. The difference of level between high and low tide is about 3 feet only. The two principal currents along shore both flow parallel to the coast. The first, from the north sets in about middle of October, and continues till February, or till such time as the long shore winds [q.v.] begin to blow, when the second current sets in from the south. This current ceases about August, when variable currents and calms set in and continue till the burst of the north-east monsoon [q.v.] in the middle of October. The two principal currents, must be caused by the winds. The velocity at full strength is computed at 3 miles per hour.——*Beach road* (சமுத்திரக்கரைவழி - shamuttirakkaraivazhi, Tam.). Runs along the sea beach for a distance of over 5 miles, from the old town north rampart wall on the north to St. Thomé on the south. Divided into North and South beach roads. The former skirts Black town on its eastern side and is of great commercial importance. It is bounded by the new harbour bounds for some distance on the east, and it contains the Custom house, High court, Stamp office, General post and Telegraph buildings, Houses of Agency, &c. The southern section is the resort of those seeking the evening sea breeze generally from the southern end of the fort to the old Ice house. On this are the Senate house, old Chepauk palace which is now Revenue board office, Public works department offices, and Presidency college. A broad promenade or Marina has been lately constructed from the Cooum bridge on the north to St. Thomé on the south, a distance of three miles.——*Black town* (پٹن - patan, Hind.; பட்டணம் - pattanam, Tam.). Title is name given by earlier English settlers because occupied by the natives, in contradistinction to their own quarters called White town, which latter name however is no longer used. Area about 1,000 acres. From the fort N. ½ mile. Bounded north by Tondiarpett; south by Fort St. George from which it is separated by the esplanade; east by the sea; and west by the Buckingham canal. A low-lying tract, being in some places only 6 inches above the level of the sea at spring-tides. Crowded with houses and narrow streets. Is the centre of trade. Divided into two pettahs [q.v.]; Peddanaickenpett the western half, and Moottiaulpett the eastern. The water pipes from the Red hills [q.v.] reservoirs have considerably improved the health of Black town and form the chief source of water-supply. Before these were laid, the Seven wells [q.v.] and a few wells dug on the esplanades gave a meagre supply. Three broad streets, running north and south divide the town into four nearly equal parts. Mint street is occupied by wealthy sowcars [q.v.] and merchants. Popham's broadway has some of the chief shops and firms. The houses are generally built of clay [calimunn], overlaid with cement [cauray] of choonam [q.v.], and roofed with tile [wode]; and for the most part they consist of continuous rooms, arranged round a small quadrangular court. There is no cultivation, space not being available. Black town possesses some fine buildings, such as Patchiappah's hall, the Madras christian college, the Agra bank, the Evangelistic hall and Church, the Students' home, the late Mint, and the store-houses of the principal European merchants. The drainage, still defective, is being attended to.——*Buckingham canal* (உப்புவாய்க்கால் - uppuváykkál, Tam.). See capital title.——*Burra bazaar* (بڑا بازار - barábázár, Hind.; மார்க்கட்டு - márkkattu, Tam.). From (bará, hind. great + bázár, hind. market). Otherwise General market. From the fort N.N.W. ¾ mile. The largest market of the city, whence supplies for the European residents are chiefly drawn. In the heart of Black town north of Oakes & Co., adjoining Popham's broadway.——*Cassimode* (காசிமேடு - kásimédu, Tam.). From (kási, tam. proper name + médu, tam. high ground). From the fort N.N.E. 3 miles. A straggling village, adjacent to Tondiarpett on the north, and lying along the sea coast. Originally a high sand bank with a few fishermen's huts, but latterly has become thickly populated, and there are some bungalows [q.v.] on the west tenanted by Europeans and wealthy natives, chiefly Mahomedans. The soil is only fit for the growth of casuarina [chowkmaram]. There are a few good roads. The water-supply is not abundant, the chief source being the municipal water pipes and wells. With the exception of the European portion, the whole village presents a poor appearance. Owing to erosions, partly in consequence of the construction of the Madras harbour, the sea is slowly but steadily encroaching, and more than two streets have already been submerged. To obviate further claims for damages, the Government have purchased a belt of land likely to yield to further erosions, and this comprises nearly half the village.——*Chepauk* (بڑا باغ - barábágh, Hind.; சேப்பாக்கம் - shéppákkam, Tam.). Hind. from (bará, hind. large + bágh, hind. garden). Tam. from (shé, tam. beautiful + pákkam, tam.

village). From the fort S.S.W. 1 mile. Originally the whole site now occupied by the Marine villa, the Senate house, the Revenue board's office, the Civil engineering college, the Public works office and the Presidency college, comprised this village; to the back of which lay a large garden. Nothing now left of the village but a few houses occupied by Mahomedans.——*Chetput* (சேத்துப்பட்டு - shéttupputtu, Tam.). From (shéru, tam. marshy ground + pattu, tam. village). From the fort W.S.W. 3¾ miles. Small village in the westernmost part of the district consisting of about fifty insignificant huts principally occupied by Vellaular [q.v.], who migrated from the south and took to cultivation and sale of paddy [q.v.], flowers and vegetables [keeray]. Bounded north by Kilpauk, south by the Cooum, east by Egmore, and west by Sydapett talook of Chingleput district. In the northern and western parts are fine houses and gardens, chiefly occupied by Europeans. The locality is marshy, but healthy.——*China bazaar* (چینی بازار - chíníbázár, Hind.; பீங்கான்கடை - píngángadai, Tam.). From the fort N.W. ¾ mile. Between Patchiyappah's hall and Tumboo chetty street. European miscellaneous articles retailed here by natives.——*Chintaudripett* (چنتهادری - chinthádárí, Hind.; చింతాద్రిపేట - chintádripéta, Tel.; சிந்தாதிரிப்பேட்டை - shindáthirippéttai, Tam.). From (chintádri, tel. proper name + péta, tel. suburb). From the fort W.S.W. 1 mile. Nearly surrounded by the Cooum river which separates it from Vepery except a slight portion abutting on Mount road. Formerly a mere jungle; now a flourishing densely-populated and fairly well-laid-out little town. Chiefly inhabited by artizans, many of whom are wealthy. Some East indian quarters are springing up. In the centre are two well-built temples of Shiva and Vishnoo, called Audipooreeshwaran and Audikeshava permaul, after Audiyappa naick founder of the village. In the vicinity is a small park called Napier's park after Lord Napier, a former governor. To this the well-to-do classes of this densely-populated locality generally resort in the evenings. Chintaudripett is a shrotriem [q.v.] village conferred in 1787 on Goday mungapaty naidoo and Vencatroyel naick, the descendants of Audiyappa naick, founder of the village, on an annual jody [q.v.] of 30 pagodas [q.v.] or Rs. 105. Audiyappa received the village as a gift in perpetuity from the Golcondah dynasty [raj]. He built the two temples in its centre and also residences for the temple servants. About 1734 Chintaudry and Narrain, head-weavers of Madras and descendants of Audiyappa naick, were granted a cowle [q.v.] permitting them to settle in this village in consideration of their engaging to supply all the cotton [q.v.] that the Company might require. In course of time, this arrangement fell through, and about 1787 two rival parties set up a claim to the soil, one representing the family of Audiyappa naick, and the other alleging that it was Government property available to the public at large. A commission of enquiry recommended that, in consideration of the large outlay incurred in the erection of the temples and the houses, as also of the resumption, on the change of dynasty to Mahomedan rule, of Cadapaukam village which was a free gift to Audiyappa naick, Chintaudripett might be given as shrotriem to his family. This was done under a cowle issued that year in favor of G. Mungapaty naidoo and Vencatroyel naick and with power to raise the rents on the houses, shops, and lands for the upkeep of the temple.——*Choultry plain* (சாவடிமைதானம் - shávadimaithánam, Tam.). From the fort S.W. ½ mile. Shortly after Fort St. George was built, there was a large sandy plain to the south of the fort, extending from the sea on the east to the Cooum on the west, and from Government house bridge on the north to St. Thomé on the south. This tract, the four corners of which are now denotable by the bridge over Cooum, Colonel Law's bridge, Munro bridge and Capper house hotel, was called Choultry plain from a large choultry [q.v.] which then existed. The villages of Chepauk, Triplicane, Chintaudripett, Royapettah, Nungumbaukum and Teynampett now occupy its site. The ground so called began about 2,000 yards south-west of Fort St. George, from which it was separated by the Triplicane river and another stream coming from the north-west passing near the western side of Black-town and ultimately joining the mouth and bar of Triplicane river. The low ground included by the channels of the two rivers and the canal, called the island, was about 3,000 yards in circumference. 1,200 yards from the strand of the sea was a long bridge leading from the island over the Triplicane river to a road, which continued south to St. Thomé. Another bridge over the canal led to the west towards Egmore. All the ground between the St. Thomé road and the sea was filled with villages and enclosures; and so was that on the left for half a mile towards the Choultry plain, from which a road and several smaller passages led through them to the St. Thomé road. The Choultry plain extended two miles to the west of the enclosures which bounded the St. Thomé road and terminated on the other side at the Mylapore tank, behind which ran with deep windings the Triplicane river. The road from the Mount passed two miles and a half under the bund [q.v.] of the tank [q.v.], and at its issue into the Choultry plain was a kind of defile, formed by the mound on the one hand and buildings with thick enclosures on the other. From a very early date, the Madras troops not required to garrison the fort usually encamped on this plain, and the Commander-in-chief living on a part of it dated his orders from Choultry plain. The fiction of the latter name was kept up till quite recently. The plain has long since been covered with buildings of every description, and, at the present time, upwards of 70,000 people form its population.——*Cochrane's canal* (காக்குரேன்வாய்க்கால் - kákkurénváykkál, Tam.). Named after Mr. Basil Cochrane who stood security to the contractor on the canal. Part of the present Buckingham canal [q.v.].——*Comaleswarampett* (கோமளேசுவரம்பேட்டை - kómlésuvarambéttai, Tam.). From (kómalésuvaran, tam. the handsome lord shiva + péttai, tam. suburb). From the fort W.S.W. 1½ miles. Temple dedicated to Comaleswaran. Is a hamlet of Egmore and the Egmore villagers claim a mirassy [q.v.] right over the hamlet which is disputed. Is situated on the banks of the Cooum, and the Harris road formed in 1853-54 runs through it. The village contain the residences of a few wealthy natives.——*Cooum* (کہاری - khárí, Hind.; கூவம் - kúvam, Tam.). See capital title.——*Cotton's canal* (காட்டன்வாய்க்கால் - káttanváykkál, Tam.). Named after Col. Cotton, R.E. In the north-western part of Madras district, being in the northern part of Vyausarpaudy division and touching the boundary line of Madras and Chingleput districts. Excavated about sixty years ago. Carries off the surplus water of the Vyausarpaudy tank and the drainage of the surrounding lands. Empties itself into the part of Buckingham canal once known as Cochrane's canal after running a distance of two miles due east. It has been abandoned, and is becoming so silted up that ere long there will be no trace of it left [buckingham canal].——*Egmore* (எழும்பூர் - ezhumbúr, Tam.). From (ezhu, tam. seven + úr, tam. village). The village had originally six hamlets attached to it:—Chintaudripett, Comaleshwarampett, Narraingaud parcherry, Sawmyreddy parcherry, Seetapett, Soorammaulpett. From the fort W. 2 miles. Important suburb and Revenue division. Bounded north by Pursewaukum; south by the Cooum; east by the same river, Chintaudripett and Vepery; and west by Chetput. Contains many good residences. Some cultivation. South indian railway terminus is built near its eastern extremity. Other places of interest are Government central museum, Lying-in Hospital, Police Commissioner's office, Southern division presidency magistrate's court, Revenue survey office, and Scotch kirk, the last an edifice of considerable architectural importance.——*Evening bazaar* (گذری - guzrí, Hind.; குச்சிலி - kuççili, Tam.). Hindostany means road-side market. Called sometimes Thieving bazaar, a corruption from title. From the fort W.N.W. ¾ mile. Originally petty sowcars [q.v.] sold sundry articles in the street at this locality, in the evening. Now a large bazaar [q.v.]. Is between the south-eastern extremity of Mint street and the Ordnance lines on the Esplanade. On its western side there is a Hindoo temple to Cundasawmy. The Memorial hall is a little to its south-east.——*Fort st. george* (قلعہ - kila, Hind.; கோட்டை - kóttai, Tam.). Named after the patron saint of England, Saint George. Lat. 13° 5′; long. 80° 21′. On the sea-shore, between Black town on the north and Triplicane division on the south. Originally a small factory constructed by the East india company as a place of defence and refuge for the few merchants and other Europeans then in Madras. The site was a marshy plain where the Cooum and what was known as the North river met. It was gradually enlarged and improved until it reached its present dimensions. It has six gates, two of which face the sea and the others inland. The fort is in form an irregular polygon, somewhat in the form of a semi-circle of which the sea face is nearly a diameter, running north and south, and presenting a clear front on that side of 500 yards. On the land side the fort is defended by a double line of fortifications, both bombproof; its sea face is well armed with heavy guns. The inner inclosure is so constructed as to afford accommodation to a large body of troops. It is protected by a moat and bastions and is garrisoned by a battery of artillery and a wing of British infantry. See vol. II, 279. Contains offices civil and military, including Government offices, Council chamber, Government arsenal, St. Mary's, the oldest church in Madras.——*Goojelly bazaar* (گذری - guzrí, Hind.; குச்சிலி - kuççili, Tam.). From (guzrí, hind. road-side market + bázár, hind. shop). Same as Evening bazaar.——*Guindy* (గిండి - gindi, Tel.; கிண்டி - kindi, Tam.). Means basin. From the fort S.W. 6½ miles. The country residence of the Governor of Madras. See capital title.——*Hamilton's bridge* (حجام کا پل - hajámkápul, Hind.; அம்பட்டன்வாராவதி - ambattanvárávathí, Tam.). Hind. and tam. mean barber's bridge, from barbers being usually seated there. Connects Mylapore and Royapettah.——*Island* (கோட்டைமைதானம் - kóttaimaithánam, Tam.). Vernacular from (kóttai, tam. fort + maithánam, tam. plain). From the fort S.W. ½ mile. Formed by the two arms of the Cooum encircling it, and lies between Fort st. george and the Governor's bridge, the Mount road running through it. It lies low and is partially under water during the monsoons [q.v.]. Used as a parade ground for troops. In 1886, the local gymkhana [q.v.] club erected a handsome stand which is used for races and sports. The Governor's Body guard is at one end with the Camp equipage depôt, St. Mary's, St. Andrew's and St. Patrick's cemeteries, all lying close together. The equestrian statue of Sir Thomas Munro, a former Governor of Madras, occupies the centre. The water surrounding it is crossed by three bridges; St. Mary's, Wallajah, and Governor's.——*Kilpauk*

(கீழ்ப்பாக்கம் - kízhppákkam, Tam.). From (kízh, tam. low + pákkam, tam. village). In contradistinction to Medapauk or high village, adjacent. From the fort W. 3½ miles. Bounded north by Pursewaukum, south by Chetput, east by Pursewaukum, and west by Sydapett talook of Chingleput district. As in Chetput, a few straggling Vellaula families settled here. It now consists of about fifty tiled huts, the inhabitants living by cultivation, although the soil is poor. Possesses fine gardens, good houses with grounds, and good roads. Its situation is low, but it is healthy. Buildings of interest are former and present lunatic asylums. Has small tank with one month's supply and 20 acres of cultivation.——*Krishnampett* (கிருட்டிணாம்பேட்டை - kiruttinámbéttai, Tam.). Named after krishnayya a bramin minister of nawaub [q.v.] wallajah [q.v.]. From the fort S.S.W. 2½ miles. A small hamlet at the northern end of Mylapore to the back of the old Ice house, and consisting of a few straggling tiled huts.——*Long tank* (மைலாப்பூரேரி - mailáppúréri, Tam.). Tam. from (mailáppúr, tam. mylapore + éri, tam. tank). From the fort S.W. 3½ miles. Also called Mylapore tank. Lies in the south-west part of Madras and was excavated in the time of the Gentoo [q.v.] kings. When full it contains five months' supply of water and the cultivation of 812 acres of land, on which paddy [q.v.], betel [q.v.], plantains [q.v.], &c., are raised, depends on it. There is a Tamul proverb:— மயிலாப்பூர் ஏரி உடைந்துபோகிறது என்றால், வருகிற கமிட்டிக்கு ஆகட்டும் என்றாற்போல—"Like saying it may "be deferred to the next committee, on hearing that the "Mylapore tank has given way." Its principal source of supply is the Nungumbaukum tank situated immediately to the north of it, and from which it is separated by the Codambaukam road. The bund [q.v.] lies partly in Madras district and partly in Sydapett talook of Chingleput district. Mount road touches it at the third mile stone, and then runs parallel to its bund for a distance of a mile and a half, until the limits of Chingleput district are reached. Maumbalam, a zameen [q.v.] village in Sydapett talook, is situated in the bed. For conservancy arrangements it is in charge of the Collector of Madras.——*Luz church* (தலைவெட்டிக்கோயில் - talaivettikkóyil, Tam.). Title from Portuguese. From the fort S.W. 3¼ miles. European suburb between Mylapore and Teynampett.——*Marmalong* (மாம்பலம் - mámbalam, Tam.). From (má, tam. plant, mangifera indica, linn. + ambalam tam. open space). Village near Sydapett, which gives name to bridge. The latter spans Adyar river 410 yards; long but narrow; has 29 arches; on the hither side is a square building 14 feet high with pillars at each corner and an inscription in English, Latin and Persian, recording legacy by Adrian Fourbeck, a Madras merchant, for expenses of bridge built from plan and under direction of Lieut.-Col. Patrick Ross, Chief engineer, in 1786; about 6 miles S.W. of Fort; leads to Guindy park, and is often called Guindy bridge.——*Monegar choultry* (மணியக்காரஞ்சாவடி - maniyakkáraññjávadi, Tam.). From the fort N.N.W. 2 miles. The oldest charitable institution of Madras, founded in 1808 A.D. Supported by public contributions aided by Government. A lying-in hospital and a surgery ward recently added. Situated to the north of Black town, adjoining the north rampart wall. ——*Moor's pettah* (میر صاحب پیٹھ - mírsáhibpeth, Hind.; மீர் சாயப்புப்பேட்டை - mírsáyappuppéttai, Tam.). Vernacular from (mírsáhib, hind. proper name + péttai, tam. suburb). Village in Mylapore revenue division. From the fort S. 3 miles. Called after a high official of the former Carnatic [q.v.] court. On the Royapettah high road. Bounded north by Triplicane, south by Mylapore, east by Krishnampett, and west by Royapettah. It stands high and its water-supply is indifferent. There is little cultivation beyond cocoanut [q.v.] and betel [q.v.] gardens. There are about two hundred tiled houses originally occupied entirely by Mahomedans, but now by various castes.——*Moottiaulpett* (ముత్యాలపేట - mutyálapéta, Tel.; முத்தியாலப்பேட்டை - muttiyálappéttai, Tam.). From (mutyálu, tel. proper name + péta, tel. suburb). Village. Acres 345. From the fort N. ½ mile. This and Peddanaickenpett form Black town.——*Mount road* (மலைச்சாலை - malaiçálai, Tam.). From being the main road leading from Fort st. george to Saint thomas' mount. Ten miles in length. Begins at the Wallajah gate. The broadest and the most important road in Madras. The portion of it lying in Madras district measures about four miles, the remainder is in Chingleput district. A good portion of the road runs in south-westerly direction, but near Teynampett it takes a turn to the south and runs for some distance parallel to the bund of the long tank. There are many shops and other important buildings and objects of interest on both sides of the Madras portion of it. The chief of these are Government house, the Banqueting hall, the Vizianagram maharajah's water-fountains, statues of Sir Thomas Munro and General Neil, Thousand lights, St. George's cathedral, Government agrihorticultural gardens, and the Government bakery. Wheel traffic of all kinds is heavy.——*Munnady* (மண்ணடி - mannadi, Tam.). From (man, tam. sand + adi, tam. bottom). From the fort N. 1 mile. Name of a street connecting Popham's broadway on the west, and Lingachetty street on the east. When Popham's broadway was the bed of a river separating Peddanaickenpett from Moottiaulpett, the only ford was at this spot.——*Museum* (موری کالج - maríkálij, Hind.; விநோதக்காலேசு - vinóthakkálésu, Tam.). Hind means dead animal's college. From the fort S.W.W. 2 miles. In Egmore, established by Government in 1851. Contains a natural history section, a herbarium, collection of coins, &c. Attached to it is a reading room, a general and a scientific library. Open gratuitously to the public daily and to gosha [q.v.] ladies on the first Saturday of every month.——*Mylapore* (மயிலாப்பூர் - mayiláppúr, Tam.). From (mayil, tam. peacock + pura, san. city). Referring according to bramins to the tradition that parvaty [q.v.] worshipped her husband shiva [q.v.] here in the form of a peacock [mayil]. Sanscrit name (mayúrapurí), means the same; also (vámanát'hapura), meaning shiva + lord + town. From the fort S.S.W. 3¾ miles. Bordering the sea and near the open suburbs of the Adyar and the Luz. Bounded north by Nungumbaukum, Poodoopauk, and Triplicane; south by the Adyar river; east by the sea; and west by Sydapett talook of Chingleput district. Former residence of the Gentoo [q.v.] rulers. In the fifteenth century, the Portuguese formed a commercial settlement and built a fort here, of which no trace remains. The Cooral [q.v.] was written here. Also the principal scene of the labors of St. Thomas [q.v.] in India. The shrine regarded as the tomb of the apostle was visited by travellers in the twelfth and thirteenth century. There is a Shiva temple dedicated to Capauleshwaran with a fine tank in front approached by flights of steps. This tank has a mantapam [q.v.] in the centre of the water and is surrounded on all sides by substantially built houses of well-to-do natives. The place has no commercial importance now, but is a favorite Bramin residence. The soil is a fertile reddish loam, and plantains [q.v.], betel [q.v.], sugar-cane [q.v.] and paddy [q.v.] are cultivated to a limited extent. A little pot-making [chatty] and cloth-making is carried on, but chiefly for local supply. For Mylapore tank, see Long tank.——*Nedoombaray* (நெடும்பறை - nedumbarai, Tam.). From (nedu, tam. long + parai, tam. pariah caste). In the middle of the last century a number of Pariah families settled in it, and called the place Clive's pettah, after the then Governor of Madras, Lord Clive. Village in Perambore revenue division. From the fort N.W. 2 miles. In the north-western part of the district. Bounded north by Vyausarpaudy and Perambore divisions, south by Pursewaukum, east by Vepery division, and west by Perambore. It lies low, being covered with water during the monsoons [q.v.], and is considered unhealthy. The soil is so saline that there is no cultivation. There are about fifty tiled houses, occupied by pot-makers [coosavan] and Pariahs [q.v.] employed in the municipal slaughter-house close by. ——*Nungumbaukum* (நுங்கம்பாக்கம் - nungambákkam, Tam.). From (nungamudu, tel. proper name + pákkam, tam. village). Tel. name (bommarádzupuram). One of the Revenue divisions. From the fort W.S.W. 3½ miles. Bounded north by the Cooum and Sydapett talook; south by Mylapore division; east by the Cooum and Poodoopauk; and west by Sydapett talook. The Teloogoo name was after a Carvetnugger zemindar named Bomarauz, to whom the village and the surroundings originally belonged. He divided this whole tract of land into 100 parts, four of which he dedicated to the local temples of Shiva and Vishnoo, and the remaining ninety-six were divided equally among twenty-four Bramin families. One Noongama naick, who was appointed by the zemindar to look after these charitable grants, excavated the tank in this village, which is now the third largest in the district, and called the village after his own name. Being more than 3 miles from the crowded parts of the town and having very good drinking water, it is about the healthiest part of the city and much sought after as a place of residence by well-to-do classes. On September 25th, 1708, a purwanna [q.v.] was received by the British from Davood khan, Nawaub [q.v.] of the Carnatic [q.v.] portion of the Golcondah [q.v.] soobah [q.v.], granting the towns of Vyausarpaudy and Nungumbaukum. In October 1713, these towns were resumed by Nawaub saadat ool lah khan. On January 5th, 1716, firmaun [q.v.] was received from the Emperor, Ferokshere, cancelling this resumption and confirming the grant. On September 10th, 1746, the town surrendered with the city of Madras to the French. On August 15th, 1749, delivered up as part of the city of Madras by the French under the operation of the treaty of Aix-la-chapelle, dated 7th October 1748. In 1765, the old grants were confirmed by firmaun of the Moghul. The College hall and the Government observatory are the only places of interest. There are many fine bungalows [q.v.] with extensive compounds and gardens, chiefly occupied by European gentlemen. Products are paddy [q.v.], betel [q.v.], plantain [q.v.], sugar-cane [q.v.], and ordinary vegetables [keeray]. The soil is fertile, being a rich black loam. 161 acres depend on the tank.——*Partasaurathy coil* (பார்த்தசாரதிக்கோவில் - párttasárathikkóvil, Tam.). From the fort S. 2 miles. In Triplicane. Principal Vishnoo temple in the city. Festival in Chittray [mausam] or april.——*Patchiappah's hall* (பச்சையப்பாசாலை - paççaiyappásálai, Tam.). North of the Esplanade.——*Peddanaickenpett* (పెద్దనాయనిపేట - peddanáyanipéta, Tel.; பெத்தநாயக்கன்பேட்டை - pettanáyakkanbéttai, Tam.). From (peddanáyakudu, tel. proper name + péta, tel. suburb). From the fort W.N.W. ¾ mile. This and Moottiaulpett form Black town.——*Perambore* (பெரம்பூர் - perambúr, Tam.). From (pirambu, tam. cane + úr, tam. village). The site having been a cane [rattan] jungle in which families of Vellaulas [q.v.], who had migrated from Madura and Tinnevelly, were allowed to build huts in the time of the Tondiman [q.v.] rulers. From the fort N.W. 3½ miles. Chief village of the revenue division of that name. Bounded north by Vyausarpaudy, south by Pursewaukum, east by Nedoombaray, and west by Sydapett talook of Chingleput district. Since the opening of the Madras railway, thirty years ago, the place has risen greatly in importance. The Madras railway company's work-shops being situated there, a very large number of its employés, European, Native, and Eurasian, live in the neighbourhood.——*Periamett* (بڑی میٹ - barímet, Hind.; பெரியமெட்டு - periamettu, Tam.). Hind. from (barí, hind. large + mettu, tam. toll-gate). Tam. from (periya, tam. great + mettu, tam. a toll-gate). From the fort W. 1½ mile. Within a mile of Black town and in a somewhat elevated situation on the northern bank of the Cooum. Bounded north and west by Vepery division, of which it forms a part for revenue administration; east by the People's park; and south by the Poonamallee road. During Mahomedan rule the chief station where moturfa [q.v.] was collected on articles brought into the town. The inhabitants are for the greater part either laborers, or keepers of stores from which oils and condiments, imported wholesale, are supplied to all the bazaars [q.v.] in Madras.——*Pier* (دریا کا پل - daryákápul, Hind.; சமுத்திரவாராவதி - shamuttiravárávathi, Tam.). Vernacular means sea-bridge. From the fort N. 1¼ miles. Screw-piled pier, 40 feet broad and jutting out 1,000 feet into the sea. Has stairs down to the water. Landing and shipping effected by lighters to the pier-head and thence conveyed to Customs-house by railway. Opposite Sea customs house.——*Pooliyore* (புலியூர் - puliyúr, Tam.). From (puli, tam. tiger + úr, tam. village). From the fort W.S.W. 4¾ miles. Is in the Sydapett talook of the Chingleput district, but a small portion was transferred to Madras district in 1877 for tank conservancy purposes. Occupied mostly by Vellaulas [q.v.].——*Poonamallee road* (پھولمری کا روڈ - phulmarikárod, Hind.; பூந்தமல்லிரோட்டு - púndamalliróttu, Tam.). Traverses Madras nearly through its centre from east to west for a distance of about 4 miles and connects it with the military cantonment of Poonamallee and hence its name. One of the general system of military roads constructed by the British prior to railways.——*Poothoopauk* (புதுப்பாக்கம் - puthuppákkam, Tam.). Etym. from (puthu, tam. new + pákkam, tam. village). From the fort S.W. 1 mile. See Trivateeshwarampett.——*Poothoopett* (புதுப்பேட்டை - puthuppéttai, Tam.). From (puthu, tam. new + péttai, tam. suburb). From the fort W.S. W. 1¾ miles. Almost in the centre of district on the north bank of the Cooum. Bounded north and west by Egmore division, of which it forms a part for revenue purposes, and south and east by the Cooum. A low-lying tract. Poor Mahomedans and Native christians are its chief inhabitants. The site formerly belonged to a member of the Nawaub wallajahs' family, but became through the owner's embarrassments the property of a sowcar [q.v.], who divided it into small blocks, which he sold as house sites about half a century ago. The town which sprang up was called Poothoopett or New town, in contradistinction to the Black or Old town. Chief industries are jewel-making, clock-repairing, and type-casting, conducted chiefly by Native christians.——*Popham's broadway* (மார்க்கட்டுத்தெரு - márkkattutteru, Tam.). Title from Mr. Popham, a merchant, and from its being the broadest street in the town at that time. Tamul means market-street. Runs from north to south and divides Black town into two parts, the western being styled Peddanaickenpett and the eastern Moottiaulpett. Begins opposite the north glacis of Fort st. george and runs due north, ending with the north rampart wall of Black town. About 1½ miles in length and bordered by shops and places of business, the general market and civil debtors' jail being also situated in it. Several streets cross it at right angles, and there is a continual stream of traffic. From its site having originally been the bed of what was formerly known as the north river, the situation is low and liable to being flooded during heavy rains.——*Pully teynampett* (பள்ளித்தேனாம்பேட்டை - pallitténámbéttai, Tam.). From (palli, tam. cultivating caste + ténámbéttai, tam. place so called). From the fort S.W. 3¾ miles. Portion of Teynampett, which see.——*Pursewaukum* (புரசவாக்கம் - purasavákkam, Tam.). From (purasu, tam. bastard teak, butea frondosa, roxb. + pákkam, tam. village). There was a close jungle here in the days of the Gentoo [q.v.] rulers. One of the Revenue divisions. From the fort W. 2 miles. Bounded north by Perambore, south by Egmore, east by Vepery, and west by Kilpauk and Chetput. Connected with Fort st. george by several good roads. A large number of Vellaula [q.v.] families migrated from Madura and Tinnevelly districts and this porasam [palaus] jungle was assigned to them as the site for a settlement. It has since increased in size and importance and now forms a separate revenue division of the Madras district on its western side. It lies high and has good drainage. Its climate is healthy, water-supply good, and soil fertile, being black sandy clay. Inhabited by persons of all classes and possesses some fine terraced houses with gardens. Too closely built over to allow of cultivation. Shiva temple in the middle of this suburb, erected soon after the formation of the Vellaula settlement.——*Quibble island* (குவிபில்தீவு - kuvibildívu, Tam.). So called because a portion of the high lying land in its centre changed hands owing to a quibble in a court of law. This is the derivation usually given. Area 47½ acres. From the fort S.S.W. 4¼ miles. At the mouth of the Adyar river, in the extreme south-east district. It is not strictly speaking an island, but when the bar of the Adyar river is open at high tide, and during the heavy rains, it is nearly surrounded by water. A portion is high lying and covered with cocoanut [q.v.] and casuarina [chowkmaram] trees, but the greater portion is marshy and during many months of the year an unwholesome and unsightly swamp. A project is under consideration for draining it and converting it into a public park.——*Robertson's pettah* (இராபர்ட்டுசன்பேட்டை - irábarttusanbéttai, Tam.). Named after Mr. Robertson, a european merchant. From the fort S. 4 miles. Consists of about fifty tiled houses and lies on the east of Brodie's road in Mylapore in the south of Madras. Bounded north and west by Mylapore, east and south by the Adyar. The site is low and marshy during the monsoons [q.v.], not very healthy, and water-supply indifferent. Inhabitants are chiefly laborers, weavers, and servants of Europeans living in the Adyar. The site of the pettah [q.v.] was originally a grant of land from Government, with an area of 20 acres, and belonged to a Portuguese named D'Frouze in 1804. There is no cultivation or trade.——*Royapettah* (రాయపేట - ráyapéta, Tel.; இராயப்பேட்டை - iráyappéttai, Tam.). From (ráyadu, tel. king + péta, tel. suburb). After Krishna deva roya the last of the Gentoo [q.v.] kings, who ruled the country surrounding Madras. Village in Mylapore Revenue division. From the fort S.W. 2 miles. In the south-west part of Madras. Bounded north by Poothoopauk, south by Mylapore, east by Meersahibpett, and west by Nungumbaukum. Connected with the fort by several good roads, of which the principal is Royapettah high road. It lies fairly high and its climate and water-supply are good. Formerly a favorite place of residence with wealthy Hindoos. It is all built over, so there is no cultivation. Lord Harris' school, the Madras club, and the Government hospital popularly known as Royapettah hospital are situated in this suburb.——*Royapooram* (రాయపురం - ráyapuram, Tel.; இராயப்புரம் - iráyappuram, Tam.). From (ráyappa, tel. proper name + pura, san. town). So called by the original teloogoo inhabitants after St. Peter, whom they called royappan. Village in Tondiarpett Revenue division. From the fort N. 2 miles. On the south-east of the division, bordering the sea, north of Black town. Bounded north by Cassimode, south by the north rampart wall, east by the sea, and west by Attapolliem village. Stands on low sandy soil, unfit for cultivation. Its water-supply is not good, but the neighbourhood is considered fairly healthy on account of the open ground surrounding it. Inhabitants are chiefly poor Native christian fishermen or boatmen. St. Peter's church, one of the largest Roman catholic churches in Madras, built in 1790, is situated here. The Madras railway company's terminus was originally erected here; but since the opening of the Central station, the fine building has been chiefly used as offices. The Southern india spinning and weaving mills, Robinson park, and Arcot armoogam moodelliar's fernery contribute to its importance.——*Salt cotaur* (ఉప్పుకొటారు - uppukot'háru, Tel.; உப்புக்கொட்டாரம் - uppukkottáram, Tam.). From the fort N.W. 1½ miles. Salt store. Close to Madras salt depôts and N. of People's park. Terminal goods station of the Madras railway, about a mile from the Central station.——*Seven-wells* (سات باوڑی - sátbáurí, Hind.; ஏழுகிணறு - ézhuginaru, Tam.). From having originally been seven in number. From the fort N.N.W. 2 miles. Sunk between 1772 and 1782. When finished they were purchased by the East india company at a cost of about 4 lakhs [q.v.] of rupees [q.v.] in order to supply the troops in Fort st. george with good drinking water. As demand increased, fresh wells were sunk in the neighbourhood, and there are now about 30. They are situated to the north of Black town, adjacent to the north rampart wall. The water is conveyed to the fort by iron pipes under ground, and it is considered to be purer even than that brought from Red hills [q.v.] tank.——*Shoolay* (சூளை - shúlai, Tam.). Means a kiln. From having originally been the site of numerous kilns constructed for the manufacture of bricks when Fort st. george was built. From the fort W.N.W. 1½ miles. Densely populated suburb of Black town. Bounded north by Nedoombaray village, east by Sydenham's road, south by Periamett and Vepery, and west by Pursewaukum. Still the abode of many potters [cosavan] and brickmakers, although the kilns themselves have been removed to more outlying parts. Has Shoolay market, otherwise new market.——*Spur tank* (எழும்பூரேரி - ezhumúréri, Tam.). Title from the tank being like a spur in shape. Tam. from (ezhumúr, tam. egmore + éri, tam. tank). From the fort W. 2½ miles. Almost in the centre of the city. Bounded north by Poonamallee road, east by Egmore village, south by Spur tank road, and on the west by Chetput. It is of moderate size, and the extent of cultivation depending on it is only 25 acres. It is rain-fed and holds only six months' supply of water. The South indian railway runs right through it from east to west. It was at one time proposed to close the tank and sell the bed as building sites, but this idea was abandoned in consequence of its usefulness to the neighbouring villages, to whose healthiness it contributes in no small degree.——*St. thomé* (மயிலாப்பூர் - mayilāppúr, Tam.). Title from St. Thomas the apostle, who landed here and converted the inhabitants to christianity. Lat. 13° 2′ N.; long. 80° 19′ E. From the fort S.S.W. 3¾ miles. Forms the extreme north-eastern part of Mylapore, and the natives have no separate name for it. Bounded north by Triplicane, south and west by Mylapore, and east by the sea. It lies on the seashore and is cool and healthy. There are a good many residences of Europeans and well-to-do Eurasians, but the bulk of the population consists of poor Native christians who make their living by fishing. This soil is sandy and unfit for cultivation, and water, though abundant, is brackish, except that supplied in pipes from the Red hills. The place was taken in 1547 by the Portuguese, who gave it its name. It was one of their most important stations on the Coromandel coast [q.v.]. It subsequently belonged successively to the French, the Dutch, the king of Golcondah, the Nawaub of Arcot. On October 2nd, 1749, Mahomed ally [q.v.], Nawaub [q.v.] of the Carnatic [q.v.], granted the English by a firmaun [q.v.] the town of Mylapore or St. Thomé. The English immediately after the restoration on 15th August 1749 of Madras by the French, under the treaty of Aix-la-Chapelle, took possession of St. Thomé, for fear of its falling into the hands of the French. On August 12th, 1765, the grant was confirmed by the Moghul's firmaun. From time immemorial, this town has been crowded every year with pilgrims from various parts of Asia, including Syria, Palestine, and Armenia, eager to visit the spot where, according to tradition, St. Thomas the Apostle suffered martyrdom on 21st December A.D. 58. The generally alleged scene of the martyrdom is a small mount near the petty fort. Others maintain that the apostle was martyred at St. Thomas' mount. According to the traditions of the Native christians, St. Thomas having preached Christianity in Arabia, the island of Socotra, and Malabar, proceeded to the Coromandel coast, and, having succeeded in making many proselytes at Mylapore, excited the violent jealousy and resentment of the Bramins, at whose instigation he was stoned to death by the populace and buried on the mount.——*Teynampett* (தேனாம்பேட்டை - ténámbéttai, Tam.). From (teyvavináyagan, tam. proper name + péttai, tam. suburb). Village in Mylapore division. From the fort S.W. $3\frac{1}{2}$ miles. Bounded north by Nungumbaukum and Poothoopauk; east and south by Mylapore, and west by the Mylapore long tank. It is low-lying. Divided into Vellaula and Pully Teynampett. The climate is fairly healthy. The water-supply is abundant, and is drawn from the long tank. Mount road runs through it. Productions are paddy [q.v.], betel [q.v.], plantain [q.v.], sugar-cane [q.v.], and other vegetables for local consumption. It has no trade and its inhabitants are chiefly gardeners and cultivators. Objects of interest are St. George's cathedral, the Agri-horticultural gardens, and the Government bakery.——*Thousand lights* (نقشه - nakshah, Hind.; ஆயிரம் விளக்கு - áyiramvilakku, Tam.). Hind. means picture. Tam. means same as title. From the fort S.W.W. $2\frac{3}{4}$ miles. Suburb of Madras, called after the building of that name constructed by Oomdat ool omrah, in which the Shiah [q.v.] mahomedans assemble during the Moharram [q.v.] to bewail the martyrdom of the grandsons of the prophet [hoossain]. Situated S.W. of the Madras club, at the acute angle formed by the Mount road with Peter's road, west of Mackay's gardens and north of Saint George's cathedral.——*Tondiarpett* (தண்டையார்ப்பேட்டை - tandaiyárppéttai, Tam.). From (tándavaráyan, tam. proper name + péttai, tam. village). Village, Revenue division. From the fort N. $1\frac{3}{4}$ miles. On the sea-shore immediately north of Black town. It has an extensive sea-board on the east, and the Buckingham canal [q.v.] skirts it on the west. Towards the sea, the tract is an uninteresting sandy plain, with fishermen's and boatmen's hamlets scattered here and there. Owing to the sandy soil it is ill-adapted for cultivation. Towards the north however there are cocoanut [q.v.] topes [q.v.] with good bungalows [q.v.], the summer retreats of well-to-do natives. A fine metalled road runs through the village leading on to Trivettore. On February 10th, 1693, Asad khan, Aurungzeeb's grand vizier, granted the English the three towns of Tondiarpett, Pursewaukum and Egmore. On September 10th, 1746, these were surrendered to the French under Labourdonnais. Ransom fixed by him at 11 lakhs [q.v.] of pagodas [q.v.]; but the stipulation disregarded by Dupleix. On August 15th, 1749, delivered up, as part of the city of Madras, by the French under the operation of the treaty of Aix-la-Chapelle, dated 7th October 1748. On August 12th, 1765, original grant confirmed by a firmaun [q.v.] from the Moghul [q.v.].——*Triplicane* (ترملکهری - tirmulkharí, Hind.; திருவல்லிக்கேணி - tiruvallikkéni, Tam.). From (tiru, tam. holy + alli, tam. white lotus + kéni, tam. tank). Sanscrit name (kairaviní), meaning tank of white lotus. Village, Revenue division. From the fort S.S.W. $1\frac{3}{4}$ miles. Bounded by the Cooum on the north, Mylapore on the south, Nungumbaukum on the west, and the sea on the east. It has a long sea-board, which presents a fine aspect owing to its numerous public buildings. The chief of these are the Marine villa, Senate house, Chepauk palace, Public works office buildings, and the Presidency college. It is densely populated and unhealthy. Water-supply is derived from the Red hills [q.v.] water supplied through municipal pipes. Ancient and richly endowed Vishnoo temple. The presiding deity is Partasauraty [q.v.] of the Pandoos [q.v.]. The temple is mentioned in the Prabandhams [q.v.]. The ancient temple tank is Vedavully pooshcarny. Triplicane is also spoken of in the Stala pooraunams [q.v.]. First formed by detaching portions of Egmore, Poothoopauk and St. Thomé and appropriating them to the temple service and servants. It continued in the enjoyment of the temple authorities till the conquest of the south by the Sultan [q.v.] of Golconda. The East india company subsequently sent a Hindoo ambassador to the Golcondah court to procure a confirmation of the grant of Madras. The latter obtained a free sunnud [q.v.] for the Triplicane pagoda and then recommended that the village should remain under the protection of the company, but that the company's merchants should pay to the pagoda [q.v.] a subsidy of 50 pagodas a year, and that the whole of the revenues that accrued from the village should be enjoyed by the temple. This arrangement was acceded to. During the administration of Mr. Pitt, the company interfered with the revenues and charged the gardens of Triplicane with rents amounting to 151 pagodas and 24 fanams [q.v.], which the company received for many years. The Nawaub of the Carnatic, who was, in virtue of a treaty with the company, compelled to settle in Triplicane, afterwards purchased some of these gardens. The inams [q.v.] granted for the maintenance of the temple have been resumed and in lieu an annual allowance of 1,050 rupees deducted from the gross demand of the village is granted. When the Nawaubs of Carnatic took up their abode at Chepauk, Triplicane became the centre of the Mahomedan population. The residence of the present Princes of Arcot, a fine building called Ameer mahaul, is in the centre of the town. There is no cultivation as the land is all built over.——*Trivateeshwarampett* (திருவட்டீசுவரன் பேட்டை - tiruvattísuvaranbéttai, Tam.). From (tiru, tam. holy + vatéshvara, san. shiva, lord of the baynan tree + péttai, tam. village). From the fort S.W. $1\frac{1}{2}$ miles. About two centuries ago this village was a sandy tract through which a small water-course ran. A Shiva [q.v.] lingam [q.v.] being discovered here by Samoodra moodelly, head conicopoly [q.v.] in the Sea customs house, he erected a small shed over it and appointed a Bramin for its service. Subsequently he obtained from the Nawaub [q.v.] of the Carnatic [q.v.] a grant of land of 12 cawnies [q.v.] for this lingam free of rent, then built from his private resources the fine temple which at present renders the place sacred to Hindoos, marked out the four streets surrounding it and built houses for the pagoda [q.v.] attendants. The revenues from this grant were appropriated for the upkeep of the temple, but the houses in which the pagoda servants lived were rent free and remain so to this day. Some time after Samoodra moodelly purchased $155\frac{1}{2}$ cawnies of land in the neighbourhood from the Mahomedan killadar [q.v.] of Poonamallee for the support of the temple, and had the sale ratified by the then Nawaub of the Carnatic. This land, together with that granted by the Nawaub, was converted into a shrotriem [q.v.] and conferred, free of jody [q.v.], on Samoodra moodelly and his heirs in perpetuity as wardens of the temple. The additional block of land of $155\frac{1}{2}$ cawnies is now known as Poothoopauk. A great portion of this shrotriem land is now in the occupation of private proprietors, and the present shrotriem of Trivateeshwarampett and Poothoopauk does not measure more than 30 cawnies. Houses multiplied in both the villages, and in course of time all, except those occupied by the pagoda servants were charged a monthly rent of 2 annas and 6 pies per house. The present total amount of rent collected per annum, viz., Rs. 700, is spent on the pagoda. In 1795 the present shrotriem of Trivateeshwarampett and Poothoopauk was charged with an annual jody of Rs. 105, which the shotriemdar still continues to pay to Government.——*Vellaula teynampett* (வெள்ளாளத் தேனாம்பேட்டை - vellálatténámbéttai, Tam.). From (vellálan, tam. member of that caste + tenámbéttai, tam. place, so called). From the fort S.W. $3\frac{1}{4}$ miles. Part of Teynampett.——*Vepery* (வேப்பேரி - véppéri, Tam.). From (vémbu, tam. margosa tree + éri, tam. tank). Its site having been originally the bed of a large tank surrounded by veppam [neem] trees. Village, Revenue division. From the Fort W.N.W. $1\frac{1}{2}$ miles. Almost in the heart of Madras. Bounded north by Pursewaukum, east by Periamett and Shoolay, south by Poonamallee road and Periamett, and west by Pursewaukm. Now a large and densely populated locality and one of the most important suburbs of the city. Inhabited by all classes. Nawaub Saadat ool lah khan, Soobahdar of Arcot, granted by way of inam [q.v.] to the company this and villages now included in the city of Madras on November 4th, 1742. Surrendered, as part of the city of Madras, to the French under Labourdonnais on September 10th, 1746. Delivered up, as part of the city of Madras, by the French on August 15th, 1749, under the operation of the treaty of Aix-la-Chapelle, dated October 7th, 1748. Original grant confirmed by firmaun [q.v.] of the Moghul [q.v.] on August 12th, 1765.——*Vyausarpaudy* (வியாசர்ப்பாடி - viyásarppádi, Tam.). From (vyása, san. the sage so called + pádi, tam. village). Vyausan [q.v.] worshipped from this place the tyaugaraja sawmy of trivettore close by, but would not go there, as the tradition was that even the sand of that place was so many shiva lingams [q.v.] which should not be trodden over. Village, in Perambore revenue division. From the fort N.W. $2\frac{3}{4}$ miles. In the north-western part of the district. Bounded north and west by Sydapett talook of Chingleput district, south by Perambore, and east by the Buckingham canal. Consists of about 100 houses. The soil is black clay, but, as it contains much saline matter, it is ill-adapted for cultivation and very little grain is produced. The situation is very low, and, although far away from Black town and possessing a large tank, it is not healthy.

The Madras railway traverses it. The Gun powder factory lies in the precincts.——*Wallajah road* (والاجاه رود - wálájáhrod, Hind.; வாலாசாரோட்டு - válásáróttu, Tam.). After the nawaub of that name. From the fort S.W. 1¼ miles. About two furlongs in the length. Commences from the Mount road near the old Round tannah, now called the Vizianagram maharajah's fountain, and runs from west to east to the entrance of the Chepauk palace buildings. To its south lies Triplicane, while Government house and grounds form its northern boundary. Of little commercial importance, but forms one of the chief approaches to the Marina and the Government offices.——*Wall-tax road* (நெல்லுமண்டித்தெரு - nellumanditteru, Tam.). Vern. from (nellu, tam. paddy + mandi, tam. warehouse + teru, tam. street). After Hyder's invasion in the eighteenth century, the East india company built rampart walls except on the east and the south, where the town is protected by the sea and Fort st. george, respectively. Numerous cells were formed in the rampart walls, and they were occupied by families, who paid a tax for the privilege of living in them. Gradually a road was formed along the wall, which was called Wall-tax road. This road is two miles long and runs from south to north parallel with the Buckingham canal [q.v.], beginning at the General hospital and ending at the north rampart wall of Black town. The wall was demolished in 1859 and its site sold in convenient lots as freehold building blocks. Between 1866 and 1872, the whole site was re-purchased and the Madras railway company's Central station built on it. There is good deal of traffic on the southern portion of road, as large grain bazaars [q.v.] exist in the neighbourhood; but the northern portion is not much used. There are houses on the east side up to the Elephant gate in the southern section, while gardens and the Madras salt cotaurs [q.v.] skirt it on both sides in its northern section.——*Washermanpett* (دهوبی پیٹھ - dhobípeth, Hind.; வண்ணாரப்பேட்டை - vannárappéttai, Tam.). Vernacular means the same thing. From the fort N. 2 miles. South of Tondiarpett. When Fort st. george and the East india company's factory were established and when people began to settle in the present Black town and Moottiaulpett, the washermen and dyers, not finding the accommodation and water-supply necessary for their avocation, settled in the outlying parts, and hence the name. Subsequently, when Black town grew more populous, men of other races and profession went to Washermanpett to the gradual exclusion of the original settlers. The village now contains some excellent bungalows [q.v.] owned by natives of position.——*Yedapolliem* (இடைப்பாளையம் - idaippálaiyam, Tam.). From (idai, tam. the yiday caste + pálaiyam, tam. fortified village). Originally a shepherd settlement. From the fort N.W. 1 mile. Part of Peddanaickenpett.——**(4)** *Madras cloth* (పట్నంరుమాలు - patnamrumálu, Tel.). Generally shortly called a Madras. This was formerly a large bright-colored handkerchief [roomaul], of silk [puttoo] warp and cotton [q.v.] woof, made in Nellore, &c., exported from Madras, and used by the negroes in the West indies as a headdress. The word is still preserved in French, but is obsolete in English [nesavoo].

MADRISSA (مدرسہ - madrasah, *Hind.*). From (dars, ar. lesson). A place for reading, a school [maktab].——*Madrissa i azam* (مدرسۂ اعظم - madarsa-i-azam, Hind.). From (azam, ar. poetical appellation of the last nawaub of the carnatic). Principal Mahomedan school of S. india. Begun by last Nawaub of Carnatic [ghoolaum mahomed ghouse khan], and taken over by British in 1859.

MADURA (மதுரை - mathurai, *Tam.*). From (madhura, san. attractive) [mad]. Tam. also (álaváy), meaning poison + mouth; as held to be encircled by a coiled serpent whose mouth and tail are joined; also (kúdal), meaning place of meeting and shelter; also (tengási), meaning south + benares. Sanscrit name (hálásya), meaning serpent, the poison-mouthed; also (kadambavana), meaning the tree, authocephalus cadamba, miq. + forest. Greek μόδουρα. Muttra [matooray] in N. india, which is a different word, was with the Greeks μεθόρα.——**(1)** Revenue district; situated on the Coromandel coast [q.v.]; between 9° 06′ and 10° 50′ N. lat., and between 77° 15′ and 79° 29′ E. long.; bounded N. by Coimbatore, Trichinopoly and Tanjore districts; E. by the sea; S. by the sea and Tinnevelly district; W. by Travancore state; square miles 8,813; pop. 2,608,404; language Tamul. Contains rivers, Goondaur, Varshaleiyaur, Veigay; ports, Attangaray, Caurangaud, Damodaraputnam, Deviputnam, Keelakaray, Mantapam, Marcauyaputnam, Moodiapatam, Moottoopett, Numboodalay, Paumben, Paushiputnam, Pillaymadam, Poothooputnam, Rameshwaram, Tirpaulancoody, Tondy, Vaulimookham, Vedaulay, Yemanangoondoo, Yervaudy; mountains, Alagar hills, Carandamullay, Nuttam hills, Pulney hills, Shiroomullays, Travancore hills; sanitarium, Kodaykarnal. The whole area of the district is represented by the following sub-areas:—Dindigul talook, Madura talook, Mailore talook, Periyacoolam talook, Pulney talook, Ramnaud zemindarry, Shivagunga zemindarry, Tirmungalam talook. For general administrative purposes the district is distributed between the following revenue and magisterial officers who have their head-quarters at the places shown. The pay set opposite the subordinate officers gives the grade of the corresponding charge:—Collector, Madura; Sub-collector, Dindigul, in charge of Dindigul and Pulney talooks; Head assistant collector, Ramnaud, in charge of Ramnaud and Shivagunga zemindarries; Assistant collector, Deputy collector of Mailore division, Madura, in charge of Mailore talook and Madura town; General deputy collector, Madura, in charge of Madura and Tirmungalam talooks. Tahsildars—Dindigul, Rs. 200; Madura, Rs. 225; Mailore, Rs. 175; Periyacoolam, Rs 150; Pulney, Rs. 150; Tirmungalam, Rs. 200. Deputy tahsildars—Oottamapolliem, Rs. 70, range situated in the south of Periyacoolam talook; Kodaykarnal hills, Rs. 100, range situated in the south of Pulney talook; Madura, Rs. 100, range situated in the east of Madura talook; Deputy tahsildar of Madura has virtually no revenue charge. Moothoocoolatore, Rs. 70, range situated in the south of Ramnaud zemindarry; Nilacottah, Rs. 70, range situated in the south of Dindigul talook; Oosilamputty, Rs. 70, range situated in the north of Tirmungalam talook; Ramnaud, Rs. 100, range situated in the east of Ramnaud zemindarry; Shivagunga, Rs. 100, range situated in the south of Shivagunga zemindarry; Tirshooly, Rs. 100, range situated in the west of Ramnaud zemindarry; Tripatore, Rs. 100, range situated in the north of Shivagunga zemindarry; Tirvadaunay, Rs. 70, range situated in the north of Ramnaud zemindarry; Vedasundoor, Rs. 70, range situated in the north of Dindigul talook. Town sub-magistrate of Madura is in charge of a portion of Madura talook and Shivagunga zemindarry. Similarly judicial officers:—Judge, Madura. District munsifs, Dindigul, Madura, Paramacoody, Tirmungalam, Shivagunga. Contains Registration sub-districts, Aroopoocottah, Chinnammanore, Dindigul, Kodaykarnal, Madura, Mailoor, Moothoocoolatore, Nilacottah, Oosilamputty, Paumben, Periyacoolam, Ponmainy, Pulney, Ramnaud, Shivagunga, Sholavandaun, Tirmungalam, Tirparacoondram, Tirshooly, Tirvadaunay, Tripatore, Tullacoolam, Vedasundoor. Contains Forest ranges, Chinnammanore, Dindigul, Madura, Mettooputty, Periyacoolam, Poyyacarayputty. Contains Municipalities, Dindigul, Madura, Periyacoolam, Pulney. The following general references should be made to the preceding volumes:—general geography, I (1) to (29); general ethnology, I (29) to (109); general history, I (110) to (188); physical geography, II, 1; meteorology, II, 3; geology, II, 8; fauna, II, 21; flora, II, 26; mineralogy, II, 29. The following references in the preceding volumes will furnish details special to the district:—latitudes and longitudes, II, 47; particulars about towns, II, 48; coast survey, II, 157; lighthouses, II, 169; comparative population, II, 172; location of revenue officers, II, 387; registrars' and sub-registrars' stations, II, 421; ports, II, 423; salt factories, II, 426; rain-gauge stations, II, 428; police divisions, II, 431; maps published, II, 436; survey topographical lists, II, 443; hospitals and dispensaries, II, 447; missionary stations, II, 455; head-quarter stations of gazetted officers, II, 461; incidence of taxation, II, 463; weights and measures of the district, II, 515; zemindarries contained, I, 56, and II, 298; special public works, I, 408. A special gazetteer account of the whole district is given at II, 95. For the detailed topography of the district, reference should be made to the talook notices in the present volume, viz.:—Dindigul, Madura, Mailore, Periyacoolam, Pulney, Ramnaud, Shivagunga, Tirmungalam.——**(2)** Talook, Madura district. Tahsildar's pay Rs. 225. Area 446 square miles. Population 261,195. Language Tamul. Central inland part of district. Bounded:—N. Dindigul and Mailore talooks, E. Mailore talook and Shivagunga zemindarry, S. Tirmungalam talook and Shivagunga zemindarry, W. Tirmungalam and Dindigul talooks. Madura talook is chiefly a plain broken by a few isolated hills and masses of rocks towards the north, west and south. The most important of these are Alagarmullay, Cutchaicutty hills, Elephant rock, Kiloovamullay, Nangamullay, Pasoomullay, Scandamullay, and Vagathoomullay. The principal soils are sand [manal], clay [calimunn], loam, gravel and lime [choonam]. The Veigay valley is the most fertile part. Madura town is the most important centre of trade and industries for the talook. Weaving [nesavoo] and dyeing [shauyam] are the chief industries while trade is carried on in cloths, agricultural produce, and metal [loham] vessels. The rivers Kritamaula, Sathiyaur and Veigay, and numerous tanks [q.v.] are the sources of irrigation. The Veigay has two anicuts [q.v.], viz., Chittanay and Pairanay within the limits of the talook. Camping grounds for troops are available at Chittamputty, Tirparacoondram, Tirvaidagam, and Tullacoolam. Places of archæological interest:—Anoopaunady, Codimungalam, Coonnatore, Coosavaputty, Covilcoorvittoray, Cuttacoolam, Madura, Maudacoolam, Maungoolam, Moollippullam, Nileiyore, Paravay, Pooliyangoolam, Rajaukkalputty, Shengottay, Shileiyoomaun, Sholaicoorchy, Sholavandaun, Tainore, Tirmoogore, Tirparacoondram, Tirvoypcodeiyaurcoil, Vadapalanjy, Velleiyamputty, Vilacherry. Principal trig. stations:—Naugamullay, Scandamullay. The leading places, &c., in the talook are the following.——*Anamullay* (ஆனைமலை - ánaimalai, Tam.). See sep. title.——*Chittanay* (சிற்றணை - shittanai, Tam.). From (shiru, tam. little + anai, tam. bund). Anicut, Village; lat. 10° 04′; long. 77° 56′; from Madura N.W. 19 miles. Site of an anicut across the Veigay constructed by Vishwausa naick, ruler of Madura in the sixteenth century [veigay].——*Goripolliem* (கோரிப்பாளையம் - kórippálaiyam, Tam.). From (gor, pers. tomb + pálaiyam, tam. fortified village). Village, Place of pilgrimage; pop. 843; acres 549; lat. 9° 56′; long. 78° 10′; from Madura N.E. 1½ miles. North of the Veigay. Mosque [musjid], called Syed sultan allah ood deen durgah, with inam [q.v.] of nine villages, originally granted by Coon paundyan for 14,000 gold pieces. Principal place of Mussalman worship.——*Madura* (மதுரை - mathurai, Tam.). See below.——*Maungoolam* (மாங்குளம் - mángulam, Tam.). From (má, tam. mango tree, mangifera indica, linn. + kulam, tam. tank). Village; pop. 2,355; lat. 10° 02′; long. 78° 17′; from Madura N.E. 12 miles. A mile east is a hill called Caloogoomullay in which is a rock-cut cave and inscriptions. Another rock is known as the Puncha pandava padookye. In the village is a sculptured stone elephant [q.v.], and in the neighbourhood dolmens [coday cull] are found.——*Naugamullay* (நாகமலை - nágamalai, Tam.). See sep. title.——*Pairanay* (பேரணை - péranai, Tam.). From (pér, tam. great + anai, tam. bund). Village; lat. 10° 05′; long. 77° 54′; from Madura W.N.W. 22 miles. Site of the anicut across the Veigay. So named in contradistinction to Chittanay. It is two miles higher up the river than Chittanay [q.v.]——*Scanda mullay* (கந்தமலை - kandamalai, Tam.). From (skanda, san. subrahmanya, the god + malai, tam. hill). Tam. also (tirupparakkunram), meaning holy + god + hill. Sanscrit name (skandagiri), meaning the same. Otherwise Secunder mullay by corruption by Mahomedan fakeers [q.v.]. Village, Hill, Place of pilgrimage; lat. 9° 53′; long. 78° 07′; height 471 feet; from Madura S.W. 4 miles. Celebrated temple. Trig. station in lat. 9° 52′ 34·03″; long. 78° 06′ 40·21″; height 1,048 feet; from Madura S.W. 4 miles; from Tirparacoondram S.W. ¼ mile.——*Sholavandaun* (சோழவந்தான் - shózhavandán, Tam. sholavandán*). From (shózhan, tam. chóla ruler + vandán, tam. he who came). Sanscrit name (chólapura), meaning chola town. Town, Railway station, Subregistrar's office; pop. 2,885; acres 2,799; lat. 10° 01′; long. 78° 01′; height 547 feet; from Madura W.N.W. 13 miles. On the Veigay. Old fort commanding a pass on main road from Dindigul to Madura. Occupied by Mahomed yoosoof in 1757 to cover the operations of Calliaud against Madura. In the same year, captured by Hyder ally and retaken by British. Two temples and a musjid [q.v.]——*Siroopaulay* (சிறுப்பாலை - shiruppálai, Tam.). From (shiru, tam. small + pálai, tam. desert tract). Zemindarry, Village; pop. 1,109; square miles 3; lat. of village 10° 02′; long. 78° 07′; from Madura N.N.W. 8 miles. Peshcush Rs. 903.——*Veigay* (வைகை - vaigai, Tam.). See sep. title.——*Velliyacoondam* (வெள்ளியக்குண்டம் - velliyakkundam, Tam.). From (vel, tam. white + íyam, tam. lead + kunram, tam. hill). Zemindarry, Village; pop. 1,072; square miles 5½; lat. of village 10° 01′; long. 78° 14′; from Madura N.E. 8 miles. Peshcush Rs. 2,183.——**(3)** Ancient kingdom, the Paundy mundalam of the Tamuls. μόδουρα βασίλειον πανδίονις of Ptolemy's tables; showing that the Paundyans [q.v.] had transferred their capital from Korkay on the Tamrapuruy to Madura on the Veigay before the Christian era. Between 8° and 11° of N. lat. and 95° to 97° of E. long. Bounded north by the Cauvery; east by the Bay of Bengal and Manaar straits; south by Cape comorin and the Indian ocean; and west by the ghauts. In 1324 the Mussalmans occupied the province and held it for fifty years. It subsequently became a province of the empire of Vijianugger kings under whom the Naick [q.v.] dynasty [raj] reigned in Madura from 1559 to 1623. In 1740 it fell into the hands of Chundah sahib and was subsequently under the nominal rule of the Nawaubs of the Carnatic. It came into British possession in the beginning of the nineteenth century. For further information regarding history, &c., see vol. I (120), (154), &c.——**(4)** Deputy tahsildarry, Madura district. Pay Rs. 100.——**(5)** Town, Railway station, Head-quarters of division, Talook, Collector, Deputy tahsildar, Judge, Place of pilgrimage, Madura dist., Madura tal.; pop. 87,428; acres 1,217; lat. 9° 55′ long. 78° 10′; height 440 feet; from Dindigul S.S.E. 32 miles; from Kodaykarnal E.S.E. 48 miles; from Madras S.S.W. 264 miles; from Rameshwaram W.N.W. 92 miles; from Ramnaud N.W. 60 miles. Locally known as Tencaushy on the Veigay. From time immemorial the political and religious capital of the extreme south. Also seat of ancient Dravidian college [madura college] consisting of the great Tamul scholars known as Sangattaur [q.v.]. Capital of the Paundyan kings for many centuries. Mentioned by classical writers and well known to the Greeks and Romans. Many Roman copper coins found in river bed. Great Shiva temple, best preserved in S. india. The invasion of S. india by Malik caufoor in A.D. 1310 caused the destruction of the original temple, built probably many centuries before Christ. The present temple is formed on the model of most others in Southern india, the small shrine in the centre being the oldest; while the courts with their towers, increasing in size and grandeur with their distance from the shrine, are newer. The present edifices were for the most part built by Trimal naick [q.v.] in the first half of the seventeenth century. The enclosure is a rectangle, 847 feet long by 744 feet wide. There are two temples in the centre; one dedicated to Shiva [q.v.] and the other to Meenautchy [q.v.]. These sanctuaries are said to date from A.D. 1520. The enclosure possesses four large gopoorams [q.v.] and five of less importance; the beautiful teppacoolam tank by the name of Pottaumaray [q.v.] surrounded by a handsome colonnade; and a hall of 1,000 pillars with sculptures of singular merit unequalled elsewhere in India. This building, called the Poothoo mantapam, or Vasanta mantapam, contains statues of Trimal naick and his nine predecessors and their wives. Outside the principal enclosure of the temple to the east is the mantapam [q.v.] built by Trimal naick for the reception of the deity of the temple. It is 333 feet long by 105 feet wide and consists of four ranges of columns all elaborately sculptured, some with the rampant Yaulies [q.v.] and others with human figures. The effigy of Trimal naick, in the central corridor with a canopy over it, is brilliantly painted. At one end of the central corridor is a handsome black basaltic stone canopy. At the east end of the hall is an unfinished gateway commenced by Trimal naick; it measures 174 feet by 107 feet, and if completed would have been the most important gopooram [q.v.] in Southern india. The great gopooram, which is the principal entrance to the temple, has an elaborately carved stone base, and a superstructure of masonry and plaster nine storeys in height, covered with intricate ornaments and figures. The plaster is painted in brilliant colors, but at a distance the general tone is neutral and not inharmonious. The entrance to Meenautchy's temple is to the south of this gate, and its elaborately painted façade of plaster ornamentation and figures is a most picturesque object, although grotesque in detail. The teppacoolam [q.v.] tank measures 995 feet long by 742 feet broad, and has a central garden with a vimaunam [q.v.] in the centre and four pavilions at the corners. About one and a half mile from the station is the palace of Trimal naick, the builder of the Madura pagoda [q.v.] and palaces. The pillars which carry the arches are of masonry, and the foliated brick arches are of choonam [q.v.]. The height of the massive columns gives great dignity to the building, and the plaster enrichments both inside and outside are very remarkable and effective specimens of their class. This palace was destroyed in A.D. 1666 by Trimal naick's grandson Chokkalingam. The tamkam [q.v.] or summer-house is a palace building of the same period erected by Trimal naick for wild beast fights. The old Permaul [q.v.] temple is another object of interest. The following are the travelling distances by road from Madura to different places:—

To	Viâ	Miles and Furlongs.	
Adiramputnam ...	Arantaungy	107	3
Allinagaram ...	......	46	6½
Arantaungy ...	Tripatore	71	4
Aryancauv ...	Shreevillipoottore	103	5
Bangalore ...	Dindigul, Namcull and Salem	259	5
Bellary	Dindigul, Salem and Bangalore... ...	447	0½
Calicut	Dindigul, Palghaut and Malapoorum ...	227	4
Cannanore ...	Dindigul, Palghaut and Calicut ...	286	5
Caroor	Dindigul and Andiputty	88	2
Caroor	Dindigul and Aravacoorchy	89	1
Cochin	Dindigul, Palghaut and Trichore ...	229	0½
Coimbatore ...	Dindigul, Dharaupooram and Pulladam	147	0½
Cuddalore ...	Trichinopoly	192	3½
Cuddalore ...	Tripatore and Tanjore	199	0
Dindigul	Sholavandaun	40	1½
Madras	Trichinopoly and Chingleput	281	3
Madras	Dindigul and Trichinopoly	301	4
Nagarcoil ...	Palamcottah and Aramboly	143	3
Negapatam ...	Tripatore, Puttoocottah and Munnargoody.	155	5
Oodamalpett ...	Dindigul and Pulney	98	1½
Palamcottah ...	Trimungalam and Viroothooputty ...	95	6
Palghaut ...	Dindigul and Pulney	143	0½
Paumben	Ramnaud	97	7
Point calimere ...	Arantaungy and Adiramputnam ...	150	7
Puttoocottah ...	Arantaungy	102	1
Quilon	Palamcottah, Aramboly, and Trivandrum.	227	2
Quilon	Shreevillipoottore and Aryancauv ghaut.	153	5
Quilon	Allinagaram, Goodalore ghaut, and Peermaid.	216	4½
Rameshwaram ...	Ramnaud and Paumben	105	4
Ramnaud ...	Paramacoody	68	4
Salem	Dindigul, Caroor and Namcull	138	5½
Shivagunga ...	......	27	5
Shreevillipoottore	Tirmungalam	46	3
Tanjore	Tripatore and Poodoocottah	102	0
Tinnevelly ...	Shreevillipoottore and Shuncaraneinarcoil.	98	7
Tondy	Shivagunga	69	1
Tripatore	Mailore	38	4
Trichinopoly ...	Mailore and Toovarancoorchy	81	0
Trichinopoly ...	Dindigul	101	1
Trivandrum ...	Palamcottah and Nagarcoil	185	3
Tuticorin	Aroopoocottah and Yettiyaupooram ...	83	0

——**(6)** *Madura college* (மதுரைக்கல்விச்சங்கத்தார் - mathuraikkalviççaugattár, Tam.). From (kalvi, tam. learning + sangha, san. assemblage). Anglo-indian; native name is Sangattaur [q.v.]. Not a teaching institution, but association of poets, who gave their imprimatur to works they considered classical by giving the writer a place on the board on which they sat. The ruler Vamshashekhara paundyan first founded the College. His son Vamshachoodaumany completed it. There were forty-nine professors; the chief before the appearance of Cooral being Nakkeeran [q.v.], and the chief after being Capilan and Paranan. In the early history a dispute arose between the professors and the Sheiva bramin priests. The priests proved more powerful. This is the meaning of the legend of Nakkeeran the chunkcutter, incurring the wrathful glance of Shiva, and only escaping from being burnt to ashes in the flames emanating from the eye in the forehead of the god, by plunging into the holy pool pottaumaray, and there composing the Antaudy panayam, a poem in honor of Shiva. It was after this that Shiva presented to the professors a diamond [vajram] bench to sit on, which contracted if an unworthy person offered to sit on it, and expanded to receive a worthy one. The abolition of the Sangattaur is narrated in the following manner. A candidate for a seat appeared in the person of the pariah priest Tirvulloovan, author of Cooral [q.v.]. His book itself when placed on the seat began to expand and continued to do so till all the professors were ejected therefrom. The latter drowned themselves in a neighbouring pool. In consequence the establishment was abandoned. This indicates a Tamul revival against Sanscrit. The following works are the most celebrated which received sanction of college, and they are all by writers of Jeina [q.v.] faith :—Auchaura covay, Calavazhy naurpath, Caurnaurpath, Cooral, Innah naurpath, Inyahnaurpath, Moothoo mozhy caunjy, Nauladiyaur, Naunmany cadigay, Pazhamozhy, Shiroo puncha moolam, Togay, Tricatoocam, Yelauthy. The forty-nine professors were as follows :—Accauracany nutchman, Alangoody vangan, Arisilkizhaur, Aushriyar nullandoovan, Bhauratampaudiya peroondevan, Calattorekizhaun, Capilan, Cauvery poomputnatt cauricunnan, Cavisaugara peroondevan, Codinyanlan mannipoothan, Coolapatinayanaur, Covoorkizhaun, Cullaudan, Gotaman, Gownyan, Iraiyan, Keerandaiyan, Marootwan damodaran, Mathooray balausiriyan, Mathooray permaroothan, Mathooray tamul nayaganaur, Maumoolan, Maungoody maroothan, Mosikeeran, Nakkeeran, Nalgoor velviyaun, Nappaulattan, Nariveroottalaiyaun, Naugandevan, Nutchman, Nuttattan, Oogra pervazhoothiyaun, Paranau, Peroom sheettanaur, Pokkiyaur, Pounmoodiyaur, Roodrajenman, Sheettalay shauttanaur, Shengoonroorkizhaur, Sheyalore codoom shengannan, Sheyircauveriyaur maganaur shauttanaur, Shrimethauviyaur, Tainicoody keeran, Todittalay vizhoottandinaur, Vannakkam shauttanaur, Velliveetiyaur, Warriore moothoocoottan, Yerichelore malandanaur, Yilavettan [bhaushay].——*Madura veerappen* (மதுரைவீரப்பன் - mathuraivírappan, Tam.). A deified person, to whom a small temple has been built at Madura. He cut off his own head before the shrine of Meenautchy [q.v.]. He is the subject of a poem termed Veerappan ammaunay.

MADY (ಮಡಿ - madi, *Can.*; మడి - madi, *Tel.*; மடி - madi, *Tam.*). Literally means to turn; also to die. Lap cloth. Field. ——*Mady cathir* (மடிக்கதிர் - madikkathir, Tam.). From (madi, tam. lap + kathir, tam. an ear of corn). A perquisite belonging to the women engaged in reaping the crops.——*Mady moottaur tauzhy,* (மடிமூத்தார்த்தாழி - madimúttárttázhi, Tam.). From (madi, tam. to die + múttán, tam. an elder + tázhi, tam. urn). Large globular sepulchral urns found in the old Dravidian burial places. They are generally pyriform like the gravid human uterus, and with a process at the small end like the cervix uteri. The uterine shape of the urn may have been intentional. The body was placed in a crouching position, and such conceptions are very common among the Tamuls [aursham, paundicoozhy].——*Mercara* (ಮಡಿಕೇರಿ - madikéri, Can.; mercara, Coorg Gov.). From (madi, can. paddy field + kéri, can. street). Can. also (mádapéte), corruption of (mahádévípéte), meaning great queen + suburb, after the principal queen of dodda veera rajendra; also (madhukéri), meaning madhoo, the king + street; also (shukravárasante), meaning friday + market.—"*a*" Talook in the centre of Coorg. Head-quarters at Mercara. Contains the following nauds :—Caggodloo, Hoodikery caunta more, Hooroor noorokal, Mercara, Oolgooly moodgairy. Principal places :—Carnangerey, Catigerey, Maudey.—"*b*" Naud in Mercara talook.—"*c*" Town; capital of Mercara talook; in 12° 26′ north lat., 75° 47′ east long., on plateau 3,809 feet, 128 miles S.W. of Bangalore, 48 miles N.E. of Cannanore, 70 miles E. of Mangalore by the great trunk roads. Population 6,227. Founded in 1681 by Madhoo rajah first Coorg rajah. The original seat of the family had been at Haulairy. Built in 1773 by Hyder. Hyder's garrison driven out in 1782, and Tippoo's general capitulated to Dodda veera rajendra in 1790. Given to the Rajah by the British after the peace of 1792. Occupied by a British force in 1834, the Rajah being deposed and deported to Benares and the present British establishments formed. The palace erected in 1812 by Linga rajendra wodeyar, a large substantial castellated building with numerous windows, is now occupied as a treasury. The principal buildings in the native quarter are the mausoleums of Dodda veera rajendra, the hero of Coorg independence, Linga rajendra and their favorite queens. The central school occupies the site of a handsome building erected by Dodda veera rajendra as a reception house for English visitors. Mercara has now ceased to be a military station. The climate, though it is cold and damp compared with the plains, is favorable to the European constitution. Average annual temperature in May 72° F., in September 64°. Average annual rainfall 139·8 inches. Tiles [wode] similar to those of Mangalore are manufactured. Consists of native town of Mahadevapett, of Fort, and Military cantonment.——*Mulla* (మళ్ల - malla, Tel.). From (madi, tel. field). Locative plural. Suffix in place names; as Sooddamulla, meaning pipe-clay fields.

MAGADHAM (मगध - magadha, *San.*). From (maga, san. sin + dhá, san. to generate); braminical name for boodhist [booddha] country. South behar [charitram]. See vol. I (116).

MAGADY (மகடி - magadi, *Tam.*). Wind-instrument with which snakes are enticed from their holes [jeenboorra, tootty].

MAGAZINE (مخزن - makhzan, *Ar.*). From (khizana, ar. to lay up). A store.

MAGHAM (మఘ - magha, *Tel.*; മഖം - makham, *Mal.*; மகம் - magam, *Tam.*). Means gift; wealth. The tenth lunar mansion; hence the feast held on that day of Cunny on which the moon's position is in Magham lunar mansion [nacshatram]. Luni-solar [maunam] festival [pundigay, 5c] in sixth solar month Cunny [mausam], i.e., between 15th September and 15th October, a little after Wonam [q.v.] in memory of Bhadracauly [q.v.]. The ceremonies are the same as that of Wonam [maryauday]. ——*Makhrauz* (మఖరాజు - makharádzu, Tel.). Maghay, star + king. Founder of the present line of Carvetnugger zemindars [q.v.]. See vol. I, 58.——*Maushimagham* (மாசிமகம் - másimagam, Tam.). From (máshi, tam. the eleventh tamul solar month + magha, san. the tenth lunar asterism). Luni-solar [maunam] festival [pundigay, 5b]. On the day of full moon [powrnimay] or on the next day thereto, when the moon [chundran] is in the constellation [nacshatram] Magham [q.v.] in the eleventh solar month of Maushy [mausam], i.e., between 12th February and 11th March. This happens each year. It consists in performing ablutions in sacred water. The orthodox fast and make Tarpanam [maryauday, tarpanam].——*Maushy* (மாசி - mási, Tam.). The eleventh tamul solar month [mausam].

MAGIZH (மகிழ் - magizh, *Tam.*). Means rejoicing, from fragrant flowers. Same as Ilanjy.——*Magizhady saivay* (மகிழடிசேவை - magizhadisévai, Tam.). From (above + adi, tam. foot + shévai, tam. worship). Worship under the fragrant flower tree so called. Local festival [pundigay, 6d] at Trivettore, 6 miles north of Madras. On this occasion the two celebrated birds of Tircalicoondram, which were once rishies [q.v.], said to be thousands of years old, visit the temple. Occurs in the eleventh solar month of Maushy [mausam], i.e., between 12th February and 11th March [maryauday]. See vol. I (94).——*Mogadam* (மகிழம் - magizham, Tam.). Same as Ilanjy.

MAH (ما - má, *Hind.*). A termination of female names amongst Sheikhs; as Shareefa mah, alam + alaumat [ism]. Cf. Maujoo.

MAH (மா - má, *Tam.*). Otherwise Mow. Means one-twentieth. Superficial measure. 100 goolies = 1 mah; 20 mahs = 1 vaily [alavay, 2a]. Variable. Approximate actual value, 1 mah = 14,400 square feet. Tanjore. See vol. I, 609; II, 518.——*Maugauny* (மாகாணி - mágáni, Tam.). From (má, tam. one-twentieth + káni, tam. one-eightieth); meaning a measure of a mah [q.v.] and cawny [q.v.]. Distinguish from the teloogoo maugauny [q.v.]. One-sixteenth, or anna [q.v.], or veesam [q.v.].

MAHA (महा - mahá, *San.*). From (mah, sad. to grow). Greek μέγα. Great. Plant first term. Ex., where transl. is of second term :—Ægle marmelos (mahákapitt'ha), feronia elephantum; Ailanthus excelsa (maháním), melia azadirachta, (maharukha), tree; Ailanthus malabarica (mahánimba), melia azadirachta; Allium sativum (mahaushadha), medicine; Andrographis paniculata (mahátiktá), bitter; Carissa carandas (mahakaramba), carissa; Cedrela toona (mahaním), melia azadirachta; Citrus decumana (mahanáran), orange, (mahánímbú), lime; Citrus medica, var. limonum (mahájambíra), lime, (maháp'halagida), fruit tree; Datura fastuosa (mahát'ha), wicked; Ipomæa digitata (maháshvétá), white; Ixora parviflora (maharatambalá), ixora coccinea; Lycopersicum esculentum (mahára-tatámatti), foreign tomato; Melia azedarach (mahánimba), melia azadirachta; Phaseolus mungo (mahásahá), enduring; Pimpinella anisum (mahaduru), cumin; Pterocarpus indicus (mahákutaja), holarrhena antidysenterica; Saccharum officinarum (mahárasa), juice; Sida rhombifolia, var. rhomboidea (mahábalá), sida rhombifolia, var. retusa; Solanum ferox (mahaushadhí), medicine; Solanum indicum (mahatíkrántá), surpassing brinjaul; Trichosanthes palmata (mahakála), black; Zizyphus jujuba (mahadebara), zizyphus. See gloss. paragraphs. ——*Macheen* (مہا چین - maháchín, Hind.). From (mahá, hind. large + chín, hind. china). China [cathay]. Generally used pleonastically coupled with cheen [q.v.] to denote the same country.——*Mahabhaurat* (महाभारत - mahábhárata, San.). See sep. title.——*Maha bhootam* (महाभूत - mahábhúta, San.). From (above + bhúta, san. being). Gross element as opposed to subtle element or tanmautram [q.v.]. The gross elements are five, viz., ether, fire, air or light, water, and earth [bhootam]. ——*Maha calay* (महाकला - mahákalá, San.). From (kalá, san. phase of moon). The conjunction [amavausyay] or opposition [powrnimay] of the sun [sooryan] and moon [chundran]. ——*Mahacauvyam* (महाकाव्य - mahákávya, San.). See sep. title.——*Maha cshetram* (महाक्षेत्र - mahákshétra, San.; മഹാക്ഷേത്രം - mahákshétram, Mal.). From (above + kshétra, san. temple). Temple of first order.——*Mahadevan* (महादेव - mahádéva, San.). From (above + déva, san. god). The great god. Always Shiva [q.v.]. See vol. I (**73**). **There** is a Tamul proverb :—மழையும் பிள்ளைப்பேறும் மகாதேவருக்கும் தெரியாது—"Even Mahadevan does not "know when it will rain [mazhay], nor when a child will be "born," Hindoo 2nd or pers. name [peyar]; familiarly Manthoo,

——*Mahadevy* (महादेवी - mahádéví, San.). The great goddess. Always cauly [q.v.].——*Mahajan* (مہاجن - mahájan, Hind.). From the sanscrit (above + jana, san. person). A great man; a banker; Bramin land owner.——*Mahalingasawmy* (மகாலிங்கசாமி - mágalingasámi, Tam.). From (above + linga, san. phallic emblem + svámí, san. master). Deity, especially among Badagas [q.v.] on the Neilgherries.——*Mahalutchmy* (மகாலச்சுமி - magálaççumi, Tam.). From (above + lakshmí, san. the goddess of fortune). Female proper name. Familiarly contracted into Mauchy, Maulutchmy [peyar].——*Maha magham* (महामघ - mahámagha, San.; మహామఘం - mahámagham, Tel.; മഹാമഖം - mahámakham, Mal.; மகாமகம் - magámagam, Tam.). From (above + magha, san. tenth nacshatram). Means the great magham; so called to distinguish it from Maushy magham occurring once every year, in Maushy. Colloquially Maumaungam. Luni-solar [maunam] festival [pundigay, 5c]. The great Magham feast occurs in 11th solar month Maushy [mausam], i.e., between 12th February and 11th March, once in twelve years, when Jupiter [brihaspaty, gooroo] joins Simham [q.v.], and the full moon [powrnimay] is in or about the asterism [nacshatram] Magham. This time is auspicious for bathing. At Combaconam there is a large tank, the water of which rises once in twelve years, on the above occasion, and when people in great numbers assemble from distant places to bathe and obtain remission of sins. Similar to the Godavery pooshcaram [cotipully] or Krishna [kistna] pooshcaram [q.v.]. A similar festival used formerly to be held every twelfth year at Tirnavoya temple in Ponnany talook, Malabar; this was always the occasion for a Cootam [q.v.] or assembly of all Keralam [q.v.]. There is a Tamul proverb:—மகாமகம் பன்னிரண்டு வருஷத்திற்கு ஒரு விசை—"Maha magham festival is celebrated every "twelfth year." On this occasion certain holy rivers are believed to receive an under current from the Ganges. Special services to Shiva [q.v.] are then performed. There is a proverb:—மாமாங்கமாற்றுப் பார்க்கக்கூடாது—"Brothers and sisters "when they have not visited each other for twelve years, should "not meet without a propitiatory offering." A cycle of Jupiter [brihaspaty chuckram] is, roughly speaking, twelve years; more accurately 4,332 days [bhaganam, maryauday].——*Maha mauyay* (महामाया - mahámáyá, San.). From (above + máyá, san. illusion). The illusory nature of wordly objects personified, and identified with Doorga [q.v.].——*Maha moony* (மகாமுனி - magámuni, Tam.). From (above + muni, san. sage). Usually limited to Agastyan [q.v.].——*Mahamye* (మహామాయి - mahámáyi, Tel.). From (mahá, san. great + máyí, mahr. mother). Village deity.——*Maha naud* (மகாநாடு - magánádu, Tam.). From (above + nádu, tam. country). Council of a nation. In former times composed of the chief landed proprietors of a naud [q.v.], or district, who met to consider agricultural interests.——*Mahanavamy* (महानवमी - mahánavamí, San.; మహానవమి - mahánavami, Tel.). From (above + navamí, san. ninth day of the lunar fortnight). A feast [pundigay, 3e] observed on the ninth day of the waxing moon [shoocla pacsham] of the seventh lunar month aushweejam [mausam]; the last day but one of the Dusserah [q.v.], on which arms are worshipped [saraswaty poojay].——*Mahant* (महन्त - mahanta, San.; మహంతు - mahantu, Tel.). From (mahán, san. great). The head of a religious establishment of mendicants. According to the mitaucsharam [q.v.] a mahant is succeeded on his death by his virtuous disciple; if no such person is qualified, the mahants of neighbouring mutts [q.v.] meet and elect a successor. The best known mahant in the south is the manager of the pagoda [q.v.] at Tripatty.——*Maha nyaunam* (महाज्ञान - maháñána, San.). From (above + ñána, san. knowledge). Knowledge of the supreme deity [bramh, paramautman].——*Maha peroondevy* (மகாப்பெருந்தேவி - magápperundévi, Tam.). From (above + perum, tam. great + déví, san. goddess). Name of Mauriyamman [q.v.], the small-pox [ammay] goddess.——*Maha pooraunam* (महापुराण - mahápuráṇa, San.). From (above + purána, san. history). Great pooraunam [q.v.], applied to the Bhagavat and Vishnoo. ——*Maha pralayam* (महाप्रलय - maLápralaya, San.). From (above + pralaya, san. dissolution). The entire destruction or dissolution of all things after a period commensurate with the life of Bramha [q.v.], when the seven locams [q.v.] and their inhabitants, together with all the saints, gods, and Bramha himself, are annihilated [calpam]. See Pralayam.——*Maharajah* (महाराज - mahárájá, San.; مہاراجہ - mahárájah, Hind.). A supreme king; applied in courtesy to every rajah [q.v.], or to any person of high rank or deemed holy. The religious heads of the Vallabhacharries [q.v.] take this title [peyar].——*Maharany* (مہارانی - mahárání, Hind.). A queen, either in her own right or as wife of a rajah [q.v.]. The term is applied also in courtesy to Hindoo ladies of lesser rank [peyar].——*Maharashtram* (महाराष्ट्र - mahárāshtra, San.). From (above + ráshtra, san. kingdom). Mahratta language and country. Capital anciently at Deogarh. About the middle of the twelfth century, the reigning sovereigns were a family of Yadoos [q.v.]. One of Hwen Thsang's nine divisions of S. india, in Chinese Mobo-lo-cha. The old Tamul name is Maraudam [bhaushay, charitram]. See vol. I (10). Maharashtram is one of the main sub-divisions of Dravida [q.v.] or Southern bramins [jauty].——*Maharauz* (مہاراج - mahárāj, Hind.; మహారాజు - mahárádzu, Tel.). The great king. Proper name [peyar].——*Maha sancraunty* (महासंक्रान्ति - mahásankránti, San.). The great Sancraunty [q.v.], or sun's entrance into Capricorn [macaram], the winter solstice [oottarauyanam]. The Pongal [q.v.] festival [pundigay, 2b].——*Maha shivarautry* (మహాశివరాత్రి - mahàshivarátri, Tel.; மகாசிவராத்திரி - magásivaráttiri, Tam.). Lunar [chaundramaunam] festival [pundigay, 6a], subject to intercalation [adhicam]. Correct name for the yearly Shivarautry [q.v.]; as opposed to monthly. Fourteenth of waning moon [krishna pacsham] of eleventh lunar month of Maugham [mausam] between 11th February and 11th March. When the gods churned the ocean to obtain the water of immortality [amritam], a deadly poison was emitted in the process. To save gods and men from destruction, Shiva [q.v.] drank the poison; but he lay insensible for a time from its effects, in memory of which his followers fast [neelacuntan]. In Egypt there was a similar commemoration for a night of the distress of Osiris. This, in the estimation of the followers of Shiva, is the most sacred of all their observances, expiating all sins, and securing the attainment of all desires during life, and union with Shiva, or final emancipation [mocsham] after death. The three essential observances of Shivarautry are fasting during the whole Tity [q.v.], holding a vigil during the night and worshipping the lingam [q.v.] at the same time. But the ritual is loaded with directions, not only for the presentation of offerings to the lingam, but for gesticulations to be employed, and prayers to be addressed to subordinate divinities connected with Shiva, and to Shiva himself in a variety of forms. After bathing in the morning the worshipper recites his Sancalpam [q.v.], or pledges himself to celebrate the worship. He repeats the ablution in the evening, and going afterwards to a temple of Shiva renews his pledge. Those modes of adoration which are at all times addressed to the different forms of Shiva, and those articles which are peculiarly enjoined to be presented to the lingam, necessarily form part of the observances of Shivarautry. Amongst the forms is the Japam [q.v.], or muttered recitation of his different names, as the worshipper turns between his fingers the beads of a rosary [maulay] made of the seeds of the Roodraucsham [q.v.] or Eleocarpus [roodrauck]; the fullest string contains one hundred and eight [chowraushy] beads, for each of which there is a separate appellation, as Shiva, Roodran, Haran, Shuncaran, Eeshwaran, Maheshwaran, Shoolapauny, Pashoopaty, and others. The feast is particularly observed at Calastry in North arcot district [maryauday]. See vol. I (94).——*Mahat* (महत् - mahat, San.). From (mah, san. to increase). Intellect, first production of Pradhaunam [moola pracrity]. There is a Tamul saying:—மகத்து, தன்னிலும் அதிகமான வஸ்துவில்லாதவர்—"Mahat, besides which there "is nothing great [matam]."——*Mahaty* (महति - mahati, San.). Greater in mathematics [ganitam].——*Mahaulya amavausyay* (మహాలయ అమావాస్య - mahálayaamávásya, Tel.). Lunar [chaundramaunam] festival [pundigay, 3e], subject to intercalation [adhicam]. The new moon day in Mahaulya pacsham [q.v.].——*Mahaulyam* (महालय - mahálaya, San.). From (above + álaya, san. dwelling); place of refuge. Bramha's abode. Offerings made to the spirits of departed ancestors, fifteen days prior to Dusserah [q.v.]. ——*Mahaulya pacsham* (మహాలయపక్షము - mahálayapakshamu, Tel.). From (álaya, san. abode + paksha, san. lunar fortnight). Lunar [chaundramaunam] festival [pundigay, 6d], subject to intercalation [adhicam]. The fortnight of waning moon [krishna pacsham] in sixth lunar month Bhaudrapadam [mausam] between 1st September and 15th October, sacred to the world of Bramha [q.v.], the highest heaven. Commonly Mahaulyam. The fortnight is intended to provide for failures in the due performance of the anniversary or annual ceremony or the Paurvana shrauddham or Tarpanam [q.v.] every new moon day [amavausyay]. It is likewise intended for cases, in which individuals have either forgotten the dates of deaths of their ancestors or for ancestors on whose behalf the anniversary or the annual ceremony is not observed. The principal days in the fortnight on which Bramins are bound to perform this ceremony are Mahabharany, Madhyaushtamy, and Vyateepautam. See vol. I (93).——*Mahaulyaurambham* (మహాలయారంభం - mahálayárambham, Tel.). The beginning of Mahaulya pacsham [maryauday].——*Mahautmyam* (माहात्म्य - máhátmya, San.). Means greatness; or the greatness of the place named. Same as Stala pooraunam.——*Mahavanso* (महावंश - mahávamsha, San.). From (above + vamsha, san. lineage). A metrical chronicle in Pali [q.v.] of the dynastic history of the island of Ceylon from B.C. 543 to A.D. 1750. This and other Ceylonese scriptures were reduced to the present form by Booddhaghoshan in the beginning of the fifth century A.D. The 17th chapter is entitled, Arrival of Relics, and details the acquisition to Ceylon of the collar bone and other relics of Booddha [booddha, charitram, rajaratnaucary, rajauvaly]. See vol. I (110).——*Mahavaucyam* (महावाक्य - mahávákya, San.). From (above + vákya, san. saying). High passages in Vedauntam [q.v.], which deal with the subject matter of the origin, modification and extinction of the lord of existence [pralayam, srishty].——*Maha veera charitam* (महावीरचरित - mahávíracharita, San.). From (mahávírá, san. ráma, the great hero + charita, san. story). The adventures of the great hero. Sanscrit Indian drama in seven acts by Bhavabooty [q.v.]. An abstract of Ramayanam [q.v.].——*Mahavindam* (महाविन्द - mahávinda, San.). From (above + vind, san. to obtain). A book which relates the history of the Puncha pandavas [q.v.] getting their kingdom.——*Maha yanyam* (महायज्ञ - maháyaña, San.). Any great sacrifice or act of worship. Five such are recognized:—Bramha yauyam, study of bramha [q.v.] or the veda [q.v.]; Pitry yanyam, offering to the manes; Deva yanyam offering to the gods; Baly yanyam or bhoota yanyam, worship of all existing things, also of mischievous spirits, by offerings of food scattered in the air; Nri yanyam, worship of man, hospitality [maryauday].——*Maha yoog* (महायुग - mahá-yuga, San.). From (above + yuga, san. period of time). A grand period of general astronomical conjunction, containing 4,320,000 solar sidereal years, and comprehending the four lesser yoogs [q.v.]. The following is the scale:—12,000 devavarshams or years of the gods = 1 Mahayoog or great age, 1,000 mahayoogs = 1 calpam or bramha's day light [caulam, 2]. The distribution and reckoning [maunam] in divine years of the four yoogs with their morning and evening crepuscules, the two latter equalling in each case one-sixth of the total quaternary division, is as follows:—Krityoog [q.v.] 4,000, Sundhyay [q.v.] 400, Sundhyaum-sham [q.v.] 400, Total 4,800; Tretayoog [q.v.] 3,000; Sundhyay 300, Sundhyaumsham 300, Total 3,600; Dwaupar [q.v.] yoog, 2,000, Sundhyay 200, Sundhyaumsham 200, Total 2,400; Kaliyoog [q.v.] 1,000, Sundhyay 100, Sundhyaumsham 100, Total 1,200; grand total 12,000. If these divine years are converted into years of mortals, by multiplying them by 360, a year of men being a day of the gods, the following figures are given:—

$4,800 \times 360 = 1,728,000$ years
$3,600 \times 360 = 1,296,000$,,
$2,400 \times 360 = 864,000$,,
$1,200 \times 360 = 432,000$,,

Thus a Maha yoog = 4,320,000 years. So that these periods resolve themselves into the conception of four ages in a deteriorating series expressed by descending arithmetical progression, as 4, 3, 2, 1; the conversion of units into thousands; and the belief that these are divine years, each composed of 360 years of men. The following are some astronomical elements of a Maha yoog:—"*a*" The sun [sooryan] performs 4320000 bhaganams [q.v.] or sidereal revolutions in a Maha yoog; and in the same period of time there are 1577917828 natural or Bhoomy sauvana days [dinam].—"*b*" The moon [chundran] makes 57753336r in the same period.—"*c*" The sun's upper Apsis [mandotcham] makes 387r in a Calpam or 1000 Maha yoogs which Calpam [q.v.] therefore contains 1577917828000 Bhoomy sauvana days.—"*d*" The moon's apogee [chundra mandotcham] makes 488203r in a Maha yoog, with an additive Beejam [q.v.] or correction of four revolutions in the same space of time.—"*e*" The Ayanams [q.v.] or equinoctial points, called sometimes Craunty pautams [q.v.], or Nodes of the ecliptic [craunty mundalam] make 600 revolutions, or librations, if that view is taken of the Hindoo precessional variation [craunty pauta gaty], in a Maha-yoog.—"*f*" The Maha yoog is an anomalistic period of the sun and moon, at the end of which the latter, with her apogee and ascending node, is found together with the sun in the first degree of Aries [maisham]; the planets [graham] also deviating from that point only as much as is their latitude [vicshaipam] and the difference between their mean and true anomaly [jyotisham, mandam]. See vol. I, 609.——*Mahbaly* (மாபலி - mábali, Tam.). From (má, tam. great + bali, san. a king). The great Baly [q.v.] giant, probably a very ancient Coorumba [q.v.] ruler.——*Mahcadalpiranda cothay* (மாகடற்பிறந்தகோதை - mágadar-birandagóthai, Tam.). From (má, tam. great + kadal, tam. sea + pira, tam. to be born + kóthai, tam. woman). Lutchmy [q.v.] as born out of the ocean when it was churned by gods [deva] and asoorans [q.v.]. Venus Anadyomene [coormam].——*Mahendragherry* (మహేంద్రగిరి - mahéndragiri, Tel.; மகேந்திரகிரி - magéndiragiri, Tam.). From (mahá, san. great + indra, san. indra + giri, san. mountain).—"*a*" Malli quorum Mons maleus, of Pliny. Hill; Ganjam dist., Berhampore tal.; Mundasa zemindarry; lat. 18° 58′; long. 84° 24′; from Berhampore S.W. 36 miles; from Chetterpore W.S.W. 50 miles; from the sea W. 21 miles. An outlying spur of the Eastern ghauts [q.v.]. The highest mountain in the district. See vol. II, 98. Trig. station, Boodaurasinghy zemindarry; lat. 18° 58′ 00·37″; long. 84° 24′ 29·94″; height 4,923 feet; from Boodurasinghigodo W. 5 miles; from Berhampore S.W. 36 miles; from Chetterpore S.W. 50 miles.—"*b*" Hill; Tinnevelly dist., Nangoonairy tal.; lat. 8° 23′; long. 77° 32′; height 5,370 feet; from Nangoonairy W.S.W. 14 miles; from Tinnevelly S.S.W. 27 miles; from the sea N. 22 miles. Peak of the Coolacaul hills. Said to be the hill from which Hanooman [q.v.] jumped to Ceylon. Southernmost peak of Travancore ghauts. Tea [q.v.] largely grown.——*Mahendratanaya* (మహేంద్రతనయ - mahéndratanaya, Tel.). From (mahéndra, san. a mountain + tanayá, san. daughter).—"*a*" River; Ganjam dist., Sompett tal., Deputy tahsildar's range. Boodaurasinghy and Mundasa zemindarries and Barwah estate. Rises in Mahendragherry and flowing eastwards drains Boodaurasinghy, Mundasa and Barwah zemindarries and falls into the sea near Barwah.—"*b*" River; Ganjam dist., Parlakimedy zemindarry. Rises in Mahendragherry and flowing south into Parlakimedy zemindarry where it fills several important reservoirs for irrigation and passing Parlakimedy town joins the Vamshadhaura.——*Maheshwaran* (மகேசுவரன் - magésuvaran, Tam.). From (above + íshvara, san. lord). Shiva [q.v.]. Hindoo 2nd or pers. name [peyar].——*Maheshwary* (माहेश्वरी - máhéshvarí, San.). From (above + íshvarí, san. goddess). One of the seven divine mothers [mautah].——*Mahilauropyam* (महिलारोप्य - mahilárópya, San.). From (máhilá, san. female proper name + áropya, san. fixed); founded by mahilay. City where the Punchatantram [q.v.] stories were narrated according to the southern version; evidently Mylapore.——*Mahisham* (महिष - mahisha, San.). Buffalo [khoolgah]. Ancient name for Mysore.——*Mahisha-mardiny* (महिषमर्दिनी - mahishamardiní, San.). From (mahisha, san. asura, so called + mardini, san. crusher). Doorga [q.v.], the crusher of Mahishausooran. See Dusserah.——*Mahishan* (महिष - mahisha, San.). Means powerful. An Asooran buffalo-headed, slain by Doorga; the subject of a piece of sculpture at Mauvellipore [seven pagodas].——*Mahout* (مہاوت - mahávat, Hind.). From (mahá, san. great + mátra, san. measure); great in measure; high official. Elephant-driver. He sits on the neck, makes the animal move forward by pressing the pointed end of the goad [ancoosham], stops it by the butt end, and turns it by pressing his leg to the neck. The same man tends the elephant [q.v.].——*Mahratta* (مہراٹا - mahrátá, Hind.). From (above + ráshtra, san. kingdom). Language and race. The southern limit of the present Mahratta language runs from Goa through Kolhapore and Beedar to Chundah. Its eastern line follows the Wurdah to the chain of hills north of the Nerbudda. Those hills are its northern limit as far west as Nandode near the Nerbudda; and its western will be shown by a line from Nandode to Damaun continued along the sea to Goa. Compare Maharashtram [bhaushay, jauty, mullarashtram]. There are many descendants of the Mahrattas who settled themselves in South india during their invasion of the Tamul country; they are regarded as a distinct caste, and they number many castes amongst them. Maharatta bramins [q.v.] are a large branch of the great Dravida [q.v.] division. They embrace the following castes:—Deshastas, to be found in Tanjore; Concanastas; Carandigar; Canwas; Maudhyandinas; Padyas; Hoossainies, half converts to the Mahomedan faith; and others. Mahratta bramins were extensively employed in the public service during the existence of the Mahomedan kingdoms of the Deccan [q.v.]. See vol. I (169).——*Mahratta buds* (మరాటిమొగ్గ - marátimogga, Tel.). As originally brought from mahratta country. These are very young and tender fruits of either bombax malabaricum [red-cotton tree] or eriodendron anfractuosum [silk-cotton tree], but more frequently the former; in some places the buds of poisonous plants, datura alba [white datura] and datura fastuosa [purple datura], are sold under the same name; and in a few the buds of artabotrys odoratissimus [madmaunty]. The young fruits of bombax malabaricum, when separated from their stalks vary in their length from one to three quarters of an inch, and in their thickness from one to two lines; and are five angled or roundish, and conical or tapering; they are brown or dark-brown when old, and grey when new; odourless and slightly aromatic in taste; young as they are they contain minute black seeds, and are distinctly five-celled; the stalks are about the same length as the fruits, one to three quarters of an inch, but somewhat less in thickness paler in color, rough and often knotty or bent in the centre; the fruits, with their stalks attached to them, particularly when fresh, bear a great resemblance to flower buds. In eriodendron anfractuosum the fruit stalk is round, about the thickness of a pin and two or three times longer than the fruit; the fruits are always round without any ridge near the hilum, and somewhat larger and darker in color than those of bombax malabaricum. Medicinally sedative and slightly intoxicant; chiefly used by natives as electuary or in milk in diarrhœa and dysentery to stop purging and to ease pain.——*Mahratta ditch* (مہراٹی خندق - mahrátíkhandak, Hind.). Originally applied to an excavation on the landward-side of calcutta, made to protect the settlement from the mahrattas in 1742. Name given in this presidency to a defensive earthwork round Saint thomas mount [q.v.] raised about the close of the eighteenth century.——*Mahtaud* (مہتاد - mahtád, Hind.). A village peon [q.v.] for watching crops.——*Mahy campam* (महीकम्प - mahíkampa, San.). From (mahí, san. the great earth + kampa, san. quake). Earthquake. Varauha mihiran has the following:—"Some say "that earthquake is caused by huge water monsters and some "that it is caused by the elephants [ashtadic gajam] supporting "the earth, resting for a time from their labor. According to "some earthquake is caused by the violent collision of winds and "their striking the earth in consequence, and according to others "the cause is some invisible and unknown agency. Once upon "a time, in the days gone by, the earth, being shaken by the "rising and falling of winged mountains, addressed Bramha "[q.v.] the creator in the court of Indran [q.v.], as follows, and "with feelings of shame. Lord, I was named by thee as the "unmoving. This character has now suffered, and I am unable "to bear the troubles caused by moving mountains. Bramha, "perceiving her broken speech, trembling lips, bent head and "weeping eyes, spoke as follows:—O Indran, relieve the "earth of her grief; throw thy weapon—the Vajrauyoodham "[vajram]—to destroy the wings of mountains."——*Maitary* (మేతరి - métari, Tel.). From (mehtar, hind. headman). A headman amongst palaukeen [q.v.] bearers [boy], washermen [dhoby], cowherds [golla, yiday], &c. [mehtar].——*Manantoddy* * (മാനന്തവാടി - mánantaváti, Mal.). From (má, mal. large + ananta, san. endless + váti, san. garden). Town, Deputy collector's and tahsildar's and North Malabar district forest officer's head-quarters; Malabar dist., Wynaud tal.; lat. 11° 48′; long. 76° 03′; from Calicut N.N.E. 40 miles; from Cannanore E.S.E. 43 miles; from Madras W.S.W. 300 miles; from Malapooram N. 51 miles; from Palghaut N.N.W. 82 miles; from Ponnany N.N.E. 68 miles; from Tellicherry E. 34 miles. Principal town of Talook. Was one of the chief towns of Wynaud coffee [q.v.] tract. The coffee has been largely replaced by lantana, wild cholum [q.v.]. Early in the century a military out-post. In 1802 the garrison was massacred by the Cotiote rebels. Travellers' bungalow [q.v.]. Centre of some trade. Weekly market on Sundays. Government botanical gardens. Formerly a cantonment.——*Maraudam* (மராடம் - marádam, Tam.). Mahratta country.——*Maul* (மால் - mál, Tam.). Greatness. Name of Vishnoo [q.v.]; especially used in combination with other words, as Permaul [q.v.].——*Mauloondivandone* (மாலுந்திவந்தோன் - málundivandón, Tam.). From (mál, tam. vishnu + undi, tam. navel + vandón, tam. one who came). Bramha [q.v.], who is sprung from Vishnoo's navel according to Veishnava poorannams [poorannam, pralayam].——*Maumoondiyaur* (மாமுண்டியார் - mámundiyár, Tam.). From (má, tam. great + mundu, tam. to be unruly + áru, tam. river). River; Trichinopoly dist., Coolitalay tal. Rises in Cadavore and Maroongapoory hills, and flows into Wyacondaun channel just above Trichinopoly, where it causes damage by high floods. Known also at different stages as Ariyaur, Coraiyaur, and Ponnanayaur.——*Mausticull* (ಮಾಸ್ತಿಕಲ್ಲು - mástikallu, Can.). From (mahá, san. great + satí, san. a virtuous wife + kallu, can. stone). A slab of stone, about four feet high, bearing the sculpture of a pillar [stambham] or post with a human arm projecting from it and underneath a rude sculpture of a man and his wife. These stones mark the spots where widows became suttee [aursham, paundoocull].——*Mauthoo* (மாது - máthu, Tam.). Familiar contraction of Mahadevan, the great god Shiva. Also of Maudhava or vishnoo. Hindoo 2nd or pers. name [peyar].——*Mauvelicara* (മാവേലിക്കര - mávélikkara, Mal.). From (mávélan, mal. subrahmanya, the great spear-god + kara, mal. village).—"*a*" Talook; Travancore state, Quilon division. Contains 145 caras or villages; pop. 111,731. Its greatest length N. to S. is 10 miles, and its greatest breadth E. to W. is 17 miles. It is sub-divided into 8 praverties [q.v.]. Bounded N. by Chengancre talook, E. and S. by Coonnatore talook, and W. by Caroonaugapully and Caurtigapully talooks.—"*b*" Town, Head-quarters of Talook and Tahsildar; Travancore state, Quilon division, Mauvelicara tal.; pop. 13,218; lat. 9° 14′; long. 76° 35′; from Alleppey S.E. 22 miles; from Cauyancollam N.E. 5 miles; from Cottayam S. 24 miles; from Madras S.W. 367 miles; from Nagarcoil N.W. 93 miles; from Paravore S.S.E. 65 miles; from Quilon N. 25 miles; from Trivandrum N.N.W. 58 miles; from the sea E. 9 miles. Former capital of Mauvelicara principality. At present the residence of the Mauvelicara rajahs, from whose family the Travancore royal family usually make their adoptions [dutt] whenever there is an occasion of so doing. Contains the remains of a Dutch fort. Centre of the Church missionary society. It is situated on the Coolacudda river and contains a large Nayar [q.v.] population.——*Mauvellipore* (மாவலிப்புரம் - mávalippuram, Tam.). Seven pagodas [q.v.].——*Mauvilingam* (மாவிலங்கை - mávilangai, Tam.). From (má, tam. large + villam, tam. bael, ægle marmelos, corr. + kai, tam. bitter); fruit like that of bael but bitterish. Same as Nirvala.——*Mauvratam* (மாவிரதம் - mávíratham, Tam.). From (má, tam. great + vrata, san. vow). One of the six divisions of orthodox Sheivism [ootchamayam].——*Mehtar* (مہتر - mehtar, Hind.). From persian meaning great. A head or chiefman; honorific title of sweepers, &c. [maitary], perhaps in irony.——*Moplah* (മാപ്പിള - máppilla, Mal.; மாப்பிள்ளை - máppillai, Tam.). From (ma, mal. great + pilla, mal. child, title). A bridegroom, son-in-law. Also honorary title given to colonists from the West, perhaps at first only to their representatives. The name now applies in native usage to Mahomedans, Christians and Jews. Mahomedans are sometimes called Jonaca [q.v.] moplahs, to distinguish them from the christian moplahs who are Nasrauny [q.v.] moplahs. By the English the term is always used as meaning the West coast mahomedans, mostly a mixed race of original Arab fathers with native women. The settlement of Mahomedans in Malabar goes back to ninth century A.D. The Moplahs have numerous mosques [musjid]. Their spiritual chief, denominated Tangal [q.v.], resides at Ponnany and is maintained by lands which have been allotted for the purpose. The Moplahs are active and enterprising, and possess much landed property. They have been restless under British rule and have repeatedly risen in insurrections, but these have been local. Under the influence of religious excitement, they are reckless of their own lives or those of others, and the presence of European troops in the district has always been considered necessary to secure peace. There have been several outbreaks. They all speak Malayalam, but they use a modified form of the Arabic alphabet to write it in. The Moplah women are secluded. The Moplahs of N. malabar follow Maroomakkatoyem, those of S. malabar, with few exceptions, follow ordinary Mahomedan law. Among those who profess Maroomakkatoyem [q.v.], the practice frequently prevails of treating the self-acquisitions of a man as descendible to his wife and children under the Mahomedan law. Among those who follow the ordinary Mahomedan law, it is not unusual for a father and sons to have community of property and for the property to be managed by the father and, after his death, by the eldest son. The Lubbays [q.v.] of the South-east coast, the Moors [q.v.] of Ceylon, and a large proportion of the Maldive islanders in the Atolls [q.v.] have sprung from an origin similar to that of the Moplahs of Malabar. See vol. I (17), (37), (51); II, 103,233 [jauty]. Moplahs number some 500,000 [arab, turk, yavana].——*Mysore* (ಮೈಸೂರು - maisúru, Can.). See sep. title.

MAHABHAURAT (महाभारत - mahábhárata, *San.*). From (mahá, san. great + bhárata, san. relating to bharata, the hero) [maha]. Otherwise Bhauratam. The great epic poem of Hindoos. Later than Ramayanam [q.v.]. Corresponds to Greek Iliad. The longest in the world. Divided into 18 parvams [q.v.] and contains about 220,000 lines. Reputed compiler Krishna dweipauyanan, otherwise Vyausan [q.v.] or the fitter together. There are several great wars indicated in Hindoo story; as:—Soobramanyan against asoorans; Parshooraman against cshatriyas; Rama against ravanan and other raucshasans; Doorga against mahishausooran; Pandavas against cowravas or mahabhaurat. The original legend of the Pandavas is properly Cashmerian. The leading subject of Mahabhaurat is the war between them and the Cooroos. The object of the struggle was the kingdom whose capital was Hastinapooram, the ruins of which are traceable fifty-seven miles north-east of Delhi, on an old bed of the Ganges. The following table shows the genealogy:—

Bharatan.

Dhritaraushtran. | Pandoo—Coonty.

A hundred sons, the Cooroos or Cowravas; the eldest son was Dooryodhanan. | Yoodhishtiran. Bheeman. Arjoonan. Nacoolan. Sahadevan.

Drowpady was their joint wife.
These were the Pandoos or Pandavas.
Their tutor was Dronan.

Bharatan was the head of one branch of the great Lunar race [aryan, vamsham]. Pandoo, though he was the younger son, succeeded Bharatan, but abdicated the kingdom in favor of Dhritaraushtran, and retired to the Himalayas, where he died. His sons returned, and Yoodhishtiran was installed as his uncle's coadjutor and successor. The jealousy of Dooryodhanan and his brothers procured at length from their blind old father the banishment of the Pandoos. These latter won Drowpady, daughter of Droopadan, king of Paunchaulam by their skill in archery, displayed at the Swayamvaram [q.v.], and building Indra prastam became powerful kings. But Yoodhishtiran lost everything at the gambling table to his rival Dooryodhanan; and with difficulty the Pandavas and Drowpady were permitted to go into the forest as exiles. After twelve years of wandering, with Krishnan [q.v.] as their powerful ally, the Pandoos met their rivals on the field of Coorooo cshetram or the Cooroos' field and the great battle, which lasted eighteen days, and in which all the chivalry of India was engaged, was fought. The issue was that only three of the Cooroos and the five Pandavas with their wife survived. In the hour of their triumph the latter retired to the Himalayas, unable to survive the death of their kindred. The leading story occupies only a fourth part; numerous episodes and legends, chiefly didactic, and interpolations of a later date, make up the other three-fourths. The whole forms a collection of the traditions of the early history of the Aryan people prior to and during their first settlement in India. There are some analogies between the Iliad and the Bhauratam; and it is not impossible that some very early tradition was carried by colonists in different directions, and made use of by two races. Dhritaraushtran answers to Priam; Dooryodhanan to Paris; Drowpady to Helen; Dharma rajan agrees with Menelaus; Achilles combines something of Krishnan and Arjoonan, for like the first, he is vulnerable only in his heel; Ajax agrees with Bheeman; Diomedes has a counterpart in Sahadevan. Mahabhaurat records the first eclipse [grahanam] of the sun mentioned in any shastram [q.v.]. European commentators say its date is 25th October in 945 B.C., and therefore anterior to that transmitted from Chaldeans, which was observed on the 19th March in 720 B.C. There is an entry in Mahabhaurat which describes the shape of India as an equilateral triangle, divided into four smaller equal triangles [trikonam]. The apex of the triangle is Cape comorin and the base is formed by the line of the Himalaya mountains. No dimensions are given and no places are mentioned. However, by drawing a small equilateral triangle on the line between Dwarca in Goozerat and Ganjam on the eastern coast, and by repeating this small triangle on each of its three sides, to the north-west, to the north-east, and to the south, there are obtained the four divisions of India in one large equilateral triangle. The shape corresponds very well with the general form of the country, if the limits of India are extended to Ghuznee on the north-west, and the other two points of the triangle are fixed at Cape comorin and Sadiyah in Assam. The Javanese have, both in their ancient and modern language, an epitome of Mahabhaurat under the name of the Bratayooda [q.v.]. They have transferred the locality to the province of Pakalongan in their own island. The Tamul version of Mahabhaurat was written at Shreevillipoottore, by a Veishnava bramin called Saurwa bhowma iyengar. It is only part of the whole. It was not equal to the Tamul ramayanam of Cumban [q.v.], which stands, with the Chintaumany [q.v.] and the Cooral [q.v.], in the first rank of Tamul poems. There is a Teloogoo version. The first three parvams by Nannaya bhatt [q.v.] and his associate Yerra pragada [q.v.]. Remaining fifteen by Ticcana [q.v.]somayaujy. These authors unitedly are called Cavy [q.v.] trayam the three bards. The 19 sections are as follows.——"*a*" *Audy parvam* (आदिपर्व - ádiparva, San.). From (ádi, san. first + parva, san. chapter). Introductory book. Describes how the two brothers, Dhritaraushtran and Pandoo, are brought up by their uncle Bheeshman, and how Dhritaraushtran, who is blind, has 100 sons, commonly called Cooroo princes, by his wife Gaundhaury, and how the two wives of Pandoo, Pritay or Coonty and Maudry have five sons, called the Pandoo princes.——"*b*" *Sabha parvam* (सभापर्व - sabháparva, From (sabhá san. assembly). Describes the great assembly of princes at Hastinapooram, when Yoodhishtiran, the eldest of the five Pandavas, is persuaded to play at dice with Shacoony and loses his kingdom. The five Pandavas and Drowpady, their wife, are required to live for twelve years in the woods.——"*c*" *Vana parvam* (वनपर्व - vanaparva, San.). From (vana, san. forest). Narrates life of Pandavas in Caumyacam forest. This is one of the longest books and full of episodes, such as the story of Nalan [q.v.] and that of the Kirautarjooneeyam [q.v.].——"*d*" *Virauta parvam* (विराटपर्व - virátaparva, San.). From (viráta, san. the country, so called). Describes 13th year of exile and adventures of Pandavas while living disguised in service of King virautan.——"*e*" *Oodyoga parvam* (उद्योगपर्व - udyóga-parva, San.). From (udyóga, san. employment). Preparations for war.——"*f*" *Bheeshma parvam* (भीष्मपर्व - bhíshmaparva, San.). From (bhíshma, san. the person so called). Both armies join battle on Cooroo cshetram, a plain north-west of Delhi. The Cowravas are commanded by Bheeshman, who falls transfixed with arrows by Arjoonan [q.v.].——"*g*" *Drona parvam* (द्रोणपर्व - drónaparva, San.). From (dróna, san. the person so called). Cooroo forces are commanded by Dronan and numerous battles take place. Dronan falls in a fight with Dhrishtadyoomnan, son of Droopadan.——"*h*" *Carna parvam* (कर्णपर्व - karnaparva, San.). From (karna, san. the person so called). Cooroos are led by Carnan. Other battles are described. Arjoonan kills Carnan.——"*i*" *Shalya parvom* (शल्यपर्व - shalya-parva, San.). From (shalya, san. the person so called). Shalyan is made general of Cooroo army. The concluding battles take place, and only three of the Cooroo warriors, with Dooryodhanan, are left alive. Bheeman and Dooryodhanan then fight with clubs. Dooryodhanan, chief and eldest of the Cooroos, is struck down.——"*j*" *Sowptica parvam* (सौप्तिकपर्व - sauptika-parva, San.). From (supti, san. sleeping). The three surviving Cooroos make a night attack on the camp of the Pandavas and kill all their army, but not the five Pandavas.——"*k*" *Stree parvam* (स्त्रीपर्व - stríparva, San.). From (strí, san. woman). Lamentation of queen Gaundhaury and the other women over bodies of slain heroes.——"*l*" *Shaunty parvam* (शान्तिपर्व - shánti-parvam, San.). From (shánti, san. peace). Yoodhishtiran is crowned in Hastinapooram. To calm his spirit, troubled with the slaughter of his kindred, Bheeshman still alive instructs him at great length in the duties of kings, Raja dharmam 1995–4778; rules for adversity, Aupatt dharmam 4779–6455; rules for attaining final emancipation, Mocsha dharmam 6456 to end.——"*m*" *Anooshausana parvam* (अनुशासनपर्व - anushásanaparva, San.). From (anushásana, san. instruction). Instruction is continued by Bheeshman, who gives precepts and wise axioms on all subjects, such as the duties of kings, liberality, fasting, eating, &c., mixed up with tales, moral and religious discourses, and metaphysical disquisitions. At the conclusion of his long discourse Bheeshman dies.——"*n*" *Ashwa medha parvam* (अश्वमेधपर्व - ashva-médhaparva, San.). From (ashvamédha, san. horse-sacrifice). Yoodhishtiran having assumed government, performs an Ashwa medham [q.v.] or horse sacrifice in token of his supremacy.——"*o*" *Aushrama vausica parvam* (आश्रमवासिकपर्व - áshramavásika-parva, San.). From (áshrama, san. hermitage + vas, san. to dwell). The blind king Dhritaraushtran, with his queen Gaundhaury and with Coonty, mother of the Pandavas, retires to a hermitage in the woods. After two years a forest conflagration takes place, and they immolate themselves in the fire to secure heaven and felicity.——"*p*" *Mowsala parvam* (मौसलपर्व - mausalaparva, San.). From (musala, san. club). Death of Krishnan [q.v.] and Balaraman [q.v.], their return to heaven, the submergence of Krishnan's city Dwarca by the sea, and the self-slaughter in the fight with clubs of Krishnan's family, the Yaudavas [q.v.] through the curse of some Bramins.——"*q*" *Maha prastaunica parvam* (महाप्रस्थानिकपर्व - maháprast'hánikaparva, San.). From (mahá, san. great + prast'hána, san. departure). Renunciation of their kingdom by Yoodhishtiran and his four brothers, and their departure towards Indra's heaven in Mount meroo [q.v.].——"*r*" *Swargarohanica parvam* (स्वर्गारोहणिकपर्व - svargáróhanika-parva, San.). From (svarga, san. heaven + áróhana, san. ascending). Ascent and admission to heaven of the five Pandavas, their wife Drowpady, and kindred.——"*s*" *Harivamsah parvam* (हरिवंशपर्व - harivamshaparva, San.). From (hari, san. vishnu + vamsha, san. family). A later addition, recounting the genealogy and birth of krishnan and the details of his early life.

MAHA CAUVYAM (महाकाव्य - mahákávya, *San.*). From (mahá, san. great + kávya, san. poem) [maha]. Six great Sanscrit poems, great not with reference to length, but to subjects. Generally enumerated as follows.——*Comaura sambhavam* (कुमारसम्भव - kumárasambhava, San.). From (kumára, san. son + sambhava, san. birth). By Calidass [q.v.], on the birth of Coomaran or Caurtikeyan [q.v.], god of war, son of Shiva [q.v.] and Parvaty [q.v.]; originally in sixteen cantos, of which seven are usually edited, and nine more have been printed.——*Kirautarjooneeyam* (किरातार्जुनीय - kirátárjuníya, San.). From (kiráta, san. mountaineer + arjuna, san. one of the pándavás + íya, san. suffix, meaning belonging to). The battle of the Kirautan [q.v.] and Arjoonan [q.v.], by Bhauravy, in eighteen cantos, on a subject taken from the third chapter of Mahabhaurat [q.v.]. Penance performed by Arjoonan, one of the Pandava princes, and his combat with Shiva disguised as a Kirautan or wild mountaineer.——*Maigha dootam* (मेघदूत - méghadúta, San.). From (mégha, san. cloud + dúta, san. messenger). By Calidass. A poem of 116 verses in the Mandaucrauntam metre, describing a message sent by a banished Yacshan [q.v.] to his wife in the Himalayas, a cloud being personified and converted into the messenger. Called also Maigha sandaisham. Two parts, Poorvam and Oottaram.——*Neishadam* (नैषध - naishadha, San.). From (nishadha, san. the country so called). Otherwise Neishadheeyam. By Shreeharshan, on a subject from an episode in sixth chapter of Vana parvam of Mahabhaurat [q.v.], viz., the history and adventures of Nalan [q.v.], king of Nishadham [neidatham].——*Raghoo vamsham* (रघुवंश - raghuvamsha, San.). From (raghu, san. the king so called + vamsha, san. race). In nineteen chapters, by Calidass, on same subject as Ramayanam [q.v.], viz., history of Ramchendran [q.v.], but beginning with a longer account of his ancestors.——*Shishoopaula vadham* (शिशुपालवध - shishupálavadha, San.). From (shishupála, san. baby-protector, the king of chédí + vadha, san. killing). Destruction of Shishoopaulan [q.v.]. Otherwise Maugham. In twenty cantos, by Maughan, on a subject taken from the seventh chapter of the Sabha parvam of the Mahabhaurat [q.v.], viz., the slaying of the impious Shishoopaulan by Krishnan at a Rajasooya sacrifice performed by Yoodhishtiran [q.v.].

MAHAR (مهر - mahar, *Hind.*). Mahomedan dowry. A large sum far beyond the capacity of the bridegroom whose gift it is to the bride is often arranged for, the object being to prevent a divorce. The dowry is the property of the bride unless she waives her claim to it; which she often does, sometimes at the point of death, in order to prevent her children claiming it from their father. For Hindoo dowry see Stree dhanam.

MAHAUL (محال - mahál, *Hind.*). Properly the plural of (محل), but used as a singular noun, with a plural of its own, or mahallaut.—"*a*" Apartment, palace, district, department. Distinguish from maul, property.—"*b*" Village; Cuddapah dist., Voilpaud tal.; acres 1,428; lat. 13° 47′; long. 78° 51′; from Cuddapah S. 48 miles; from Voilpaud N.E. 16 miles. Important place of trade. Heratty merchants, settled here for several generations, import elephants [q.v.], horses [ghorah], shawls [q.v.], pearls [moty], &c. Residence of representative of nawaubs [q.v.] of Goorramcondah.——*Mahallaut* (محلات - mahallát, Hind.). Women's apartments [zenana]. Figuratively, women.

MAHBOOB (محبوب - mahbúb, *Hind.*). From (hubba, ar. to love). Beloved. Title of the chief saint of the Mahomedans [dastgheer]. Common alam; as Mahboobally, double alam; Mahboob bee, alam + alaumat; Mahboob shah, alam + alaumat of fakeer [ism].

MAHDEE (مهدی - mahdí, *Hind.*). From (hudá, ar. to guide). Guide. Name of the twelfth and last Imaum [q.v.], who according to the belief of Soonnee [q.v.] mahomedans will appear again on the second coming of Jesus christ and is not born yet. The Shiahs [q.v.] believe that he has already appeared and remains concealed. Gheir mahdevites believe that he was on and has disappeared from earth. Common alam; as mahdee ally, double alam [ism].——*Mahdivy* (مهدوی - mahdiví, Hind.) From (mahdí, ar. name of the last imaum). A sect of Mahomedans who believe in the reappearance of Mahdee, the twelfth and last Imaum [q.v.], towards the close of this world.

MAHÉ (മയ്യഴി - mayyazhi, *Mal.*). Title from the french. Mal. from (mai, mal. black + azhi, mal. river mouth). Mahé was the first name of Labourdonnais.—"*a*" French town and tract of country, Port; Malabar dist., Cooroombranaud tal.; lat. 11° 42′; long. 75° 35′; from Badagara N.N.W. 8 miles; from Bombay S.S.E. 516 miles; from Calicut N.N.W. 35 miles; from Cannanore S.E. 16 miles; from Chombye N.W. 3 miles; from Cullye W. 3 miles; from Tellicherry S.E. 4 miles. The only

French settlement on west coast. Now of little importance. South of mouth of the river Mahé, and possesses a roomy harbour whose rocky bar admits vessels up to 70 tons. The town overlooks the river. The French first settled here with a view to acquiring a share in the pepper [q.v.] trade in 1722, having obtained the grant of a plot of ground for a factory [aurang] from the rajah of Cadatnaud about the same time they obtained the grant of a piece of land at Calicut from the Zamorin [q.v.]. In 1752 they acquired by purchase from the rajah of Chiracal the ports of Ramatody, Cauvaly, Neeleshwar and Mattalye; and in 1754 Mount delly from the same. But with surrender of Mahé in February 1761, all these possessions fell into hands of English; and with exception of the fort at Mount delly, all other fortifications were razed to the ground. Mahé was restored to French in 1765; but with surrounding dependencies, was recaptured by English in 1779 and dismantled, to be once more restored in 1785. It was for a third time taken in 1793, and was restored to French with small factory at Calicut in 1815. In 1853 four outlying aldées [q.v.] were restored increasing the area to 5 square miles. The desboms [q.v.] constituting the settlement are Chaulacara, Chembra, Chooticottah, Manchacull, Mattaummal, Moondokkil, Pandacull, Pauracull, Pooliyil, Pullore, Valappinagam, Valavil, Valiyangaudy, Wodattinagam. Of the four outlying aldées restored in 1853, Chaulacara, Pullore and Chembra formed the demesne of the Numbiyaurs of Iroovalinaud and Pandacull of Coorangote nayar, and the four villages together constituted the amshom [q.v.] of Naultara in Cottayam talook. The settlement is in charge of a chef-de-service subordinate to Pondicherry. The Carmelites have a church and missionary establishment. A long wooden bridge maintained by British government gives access to British territory on right bank. The coast road from Beypore running northward through Tellicherry and Cannanore, passes through Mahé.—"*b*" River; Malabar district, Cooroombranaud talook. Rises in heavy forests of Wynaud ghauts, and after 34 miles falls into sea at Mahé, of the main portion of which territory it forms northern and eastern boundary for two miles. Navigable for small country craft for half a mile, and for boats as far as Pauracadavoo, 12 miles.—"*c*" Light on the south side of the entrance to the river at the foot of the flagstaff; lat. 11° 42′; long. 75° 34′. Red. Fixed. 7 miles. Visible from all directions seaward. Small white pyramid. As a guide to the anchorage.

MAHEENA (شهر - shahr, *Ar.*; ماه - máh, *Pers.*; مهينا - mahíná, *Hind.*). Month [mau, mausam]. 4 haftahs or weeks = 1 maheena; 12 maheenas = 1 saul or year [caulam, 7]. The months of the Mahomedan year [hijrah] and the number of days [dinam, roz] in each, are the following.——"*a*" *Moharram* (محرم - muharram, Ar.). From (haruma, ar. sacred). 30 days. See sep. title.——"*b*" *Safar* (صفر - safar, Hind.). From (sifr, ar. empty); because in this month the Arabians went to war and left their homes empty. The most unlucky, for in it Adam was turned out of Eden and the prophet was taken ill [aukhiry chahaur shamba, teyrah teyzee]. 29 days. ——"*c*" *Rabee ool owval* (ربيع الاول - rabíulavval, Ar.; باراوفات - báráwafát, Hind.). Ar. from (rabí, ar. spring season + awwal, ar. first). Hind. from the prophet's anniversary. 30 days [vilaudat e shareef].——"*d*" *Rabee ool aukhir* (ربيع الاخر - rabíulákhir, Ar.; دستگير - dastgír, Hind.). Ar. from (rabí, ar. spring season + ákhir, ar. last). Hind. from the anniversary of the saint [abdool cawder]. 29 days.——"*e*" *Jamaudy ool owval* (جمادى الاول - jamádiulawwal, Ar.; مدار - madár, Hind.). Ar. from (jamádí, ar. winter + awwal, ar. first); being first of the winter months. Hind. from saint's anniversary [shah badee ood deen]. 30 days.——"*f*" *Jamaudy ool aukhir* (جمادى الاخر - jamádiulákhir, Ar.; قادر - kádir, Hind.). Ar. from (jamádí, ar. winter + ákhir, ar. last). Hind. from the anniversary of the saint [cawder wally]. Otherwise Jamaudy oos saunee. 29 days. ——"*g*" *Rajab* (رجب - rajab, Ar. and Hind.). From (rajiba, ar. to revere). 30 days. War was not permitted during this month. Mahomet's nocturnal journey to heaven occurred in it [leilat ool mirauj].——"*h*" *Shabaun* (شعبان - shabán, Ar. and Hind.). From (shaaba, ar. to separate); because the arabs used to disperse for predatory expeditions. 15th of this month is Shab e baraut [q.v.]. 29 days.——"*i*" *Ramzaun* (رمضان - ramazán, Hind.). 30 days. See sep. title.——"*j*" *Shawaul* (شوال - shauvál, Ar.; دودھ كا مهينا - dúdhkámahíná, Hind.). Ar. from (shaul, ar. vacant), the arabs having left their homes vacant for hunting excursions. Hind. from (dúdh, hind. milk + mahíná, hind month); from ramzaun feast when milk is used to break the fast. Hind. also (khálímahíná), meaning empty month, in that it has no feast. The first day is the Eed ool fitr [q.v.].——"*k*" *Zoolcada* (ذوالقعده - zulkadah, Ar.; بنده نواز - bandahnawáz, Hind.). Ar. from (zu, ar. lord + kadah, ar. sitting); sitting month; no war or pilgrimage allowed. Hind. from saint's festival [bunda nawauz]. 30 days.——"*l*" *Zool hijja* (ذوالحجه - zulhijjah, Ar.; بكرعيد - bakríd, Hind.). Ar. from (zú, ar. lord + hij, ar. pilgrimage); pilgrimage month. Hind. from the festival which occurs in this. 29 days; except in the intercalary years [nasee], when this last month also has 30 days.

MAHIMALORE (మహిమలూరు - mahimalúru, *Tel.*). From (mailumallayya, tel. proper name + úru, tel. village); from mayil mullareddy, the founder. Village; Nellore dist., Atmacore tal.; pop. 3,377; acres 11,562; lat. 14° 38′; long. 79° 33′; from Atmacore W. 7 miles; from Nellore W. 37 miles. Village and temple established or rebuilt by Mayil mullareddy, from Hyderabad. His brothers Bheema reddy and Nundan who accompanied him established the villages of Bheemavaram and Nandavaram in Oodayagherry talook. Traces of an old fort, which formerly had five killadars [q.v.] when it was held by the zemindar [q.v.] of Vencatagherry's ancestors. Pagoda [q.v.] to Shiva as Gopaulsawmy, with inam [q.v.] of acres 63·96. Extensive indigo [q.v.] trade. Large tank. A bramin of this village, Pautoolayya, was a well-known poet [cavy].

MAHOE (مهو - maho, *Hind.*). W. indian for Cork wood bendy.

MAHOMED (محمد - muhammad, *Ar.*). From (hamada, ar. to praise). Praised. Name of the prophet of the Mahomedans. Common alam; as Syed mahomed, alaumat + alam; Mahomed acbar, double alam [ism].——*Mahmood* (محمود - mahmúd, Ar.). From (hamada, ar. to praise). Praiseworthy. Name of the prophet. Common alam; as Mahmood ally, double alam; Mahmood bee, alam + alaumat [ism].——*Mahomed ally* (محمد علی - muhammadalí, Hind.). Double alam. Nawaub of the Carnatic. Styled Wallajah [q.v.]. Second son of Anwar ood deen [q.v.], died, aged 78, on 13th October, A.D. 1795. Escaped from the field of Amboor on death of his father, to Trichinopoly, where he was besieged by the French who had espoused Chundah sahib's [q.v.] claims to Carnatic [q.v.] throne. Relieved by Clive by an attack on Arcot. Succeeded by his son Oomdat ool oomrah [charitram]. Vol. I (122), (177), 44; II, 252.——*Mahomedan* (محمدی - muhammadí, Hind.). From (muhammad, ar. prophet's name). English formation from mahomet. A Mussalman. There are nearly two millions in the Presidency. Malabar has the greatest number [moplah], next Tanjore, and next Bellary. In Trichinopoly they are important. Ganjam has very few. Mahomedans are divided into four great classes, Syed [q.v.], Sheikh [q.v.], Moghul [q.v.], and Pataun [q.v.]. The Pataans are sometimes also termed Afghauns.——*Mahomedan's lime* (ജോനകനാരകം - jónakanárakam, Mal.). Same as Bergamot orange.——*Mahomed cassim* (محمد قاسم - muhammadkásim, Hind.). Otherwise Ferishta [q.v.], author of Taureek e ferishta, historical work published in Acbar's reign.

MAHSOOL (محصول - mahsúl, *Hind.*). From (hasúla, ar. to obtain). That which is produced. Mahsooldar is crop watcher, for whom inam [q.v.] was formerly allowed.

MAHWAL (ماهول - máhwal, *Hind.*). Same as Large mountain ebony.

MAHZAR (محضر - mahzar, *Hind.*). From (hazara, ar. to be present) [hauzir]. Otherwise Mahzar nauma. A certificate signed by several. Especially award of a punchayet [q.v.].

MAIDARY (మేదరి - médari, *Tel.*). From (méda, can. basket). Mat and basket makers. The corresponding terms are:—Tam. corava; Can. maidara; Mal. cavara. Their wares are made of bamboo [q.v.] only. Date [kharjooram] mats [boriyah] and baskets [tokrah] are made by Coorchar [coorchar, jauty].

MAIL (ಮೇಲೆ - méle, *Can.*; మేలు - mélu, *Tel.*; മേൽ - mél, *Mal.*; மேல் - mél, *Tam.*). Over, above [mett]. Also in tamul, west. Prefix in place names; as Mailore, meaning west village; Mailcote, meaning high fort.——*Mailcaunom* (മേല്ക്കാണം - melkánam, Mal.). Mortgage upon mortgage. See Caunom.——*Mailcoondah* (ಮೇಲ್ಕುಂದ - mélkunda, Can.). From (mél, can. upper + kunda, can. hill). Village, Mountain; Neilgherry dist., Coondah div.; pop. 233; acres 8,200; lat. 11° 15′; long. 76° 41′; height 6,924 feet; from Ootacamund S.S.W. 13 miles. One of principal eminences overlooking Bhawauny valley, near S.W. extremity of Neilgherries. Village inhabited by Badagas [q.v.], Large sculptured cromlech [paundoocull] surrounded by others unsculptured.——*Mailcooray* (மேற்கூரை - mérgúrai, Tam.). From (above + kúrai, tam. thatched roof). Thatched roof, upper part of a house.——*Mailcottah* (மேலக்கோட்டை - melakkóttai, Tam.). From (mél, tam. west + kóttai, tam. fort). Mahomedan name (hussainábád), meaning beautiful city. Hill; Neilgherry district, Todanaud division; from Ootacamund N.W. 5 miles. One of the three principal old forts of the Neilgherries, near the Seegore pass. Utilized by Tippoo sultan who called it Hoossainabad.——*Mailcoyma* (മേൽകോയ്മ - mélkkóyma, Mal.). From (above + kóyma, mal. power). The right of the ruler, especially over temples. See vol. II, 104.——*Mailezhoott pillay* (മേലെഴുത്തുപ്പിള്ള - mélezhuttuppilla, Mal.). From (above + ezhuttu, mal. writing + pilla, mal. accountant). Head village accountant.——*Mailore* (மேலூர் - mélúr, Tam.). See sep. title.——*Mailpady* (மேற்படி - mérppadi, Tam.). From (above + padu, tam. to occur). Aforesaid.——*Mail vauram* (மேல்வாரம் - mélváram, Tam.). From (above + vára, san. quantity). Rent of landlord. The Circar [q.v.] share of the produce of a field, either in kind or money;

as distinguished from Coodivauram [q.v.], or tenant's share [maiticore]. Cf. Sawmibhogam. See vol. I, 112.——*Main cauvalgar* (மேன்காவற்காரன் - méngávargáran, Tam.). From (above + kával, tam. guard + káran, tam. agent). A petty chief, a poligar [q.v.], the superior guardian or protector of the country [deshacauvalgar].——*Maiticore* (మేడికోరు - médikóru, Tel.). From (above + kóru, tel. share). The landlord's share of the crop [mail vauram, sawmibhogam].——*Maittan* (മേത്താൻ - méttan, Mal.). From (above + st'ha, san. to stand). Travancore name for Lubbay [q.v.].——*Maity* (ಮೇಟಿ - méti, Can.; మేటి - méti, Tel.; മേട്ടി - métti, Mal.; மேட்டி - métti, Tam.). From (mél, tam. high). The post in a threshing-floor [calam]. Also lord; head of a body of persons, especially of inferior cultivators [inam]. A menial servant, in Anglo-indian establishments, who washes dishes, &c., always of the pariah [q.v.] tribe; probably this last is the sailors' phrase maity for mate.——*Melagherry* (ಮೇಲಗಿರಿ - mélagiri, Can.). From (mél, tam. west + giri, san. mountain). Hill range; Salem dist., Oossoor tal.; pop. nil; lat. between 12° 12′ and 12° 26′; long. 77° 52′ and 78° 00′; from Oossoor S.S.E. 21 miles; from Salem N.N.W. 43 miles. The hills extend northwards, more or less unbroken, to a point south-east of Kelamungalam where they are hardly distinguishable from the Punchabully hills, and similarly to the bank of the Cauvery on the south, while they merge more or less in the Pikkily mullay in the Dharmapoory talook on the east. Practically they may be held to commence on the north in the valley of the Sanatcomauranuddy and to end southwards in Gootroyen, the highest peak. This gives an approximate length of 20 miles from north to south, with an average breadth of 5 miles from east to west. They are most easily reached from Dencanicottah viâ Irdoocottay, whence access is obtained to Siddhapore, by a ghaut [q.v.] practicable for horses [ghorah]. The plain at the foot is about 3,000 feet above sea-level and the ghaut is about 1,000 more. In places somewhat stony, after about two-thirds of its length, the steep path is succeeded by a series of grassy undulations and terraces; the plateau at the top is therefore about 4,000 feet high, and the average height is about 3,500 or 3,800 feet. The summit is fairly level and abounds in grassy lawns, fringed with forest and bamboos [q.v.]. About half a mile south of Siddhapore is Glenshaw, a picturesque plateau, where coffee [q.v.] has been unsuccessfully tried. The most striking feature of the hills is the superabundance of white ants [q.v.]. The Malayaulies [q.v.] are chiefly Lingayets [q.v.], but there are numbers of Gollar [q.v.], Iroolar [q.v.], Pullies [q.v.], and other classes. The sandalwood [sandal] reserves are valuable, and other timbers and bamboos are found in abundance. The hills are reputed feverish. The great want is drinking water. ——*Menaud* (மேனாடு - ménádu, Tam.). Highland.——*Menon* (മേനോൻ - ménón, Mal.). From (above + an, mal. personal suffix); means over man, supervisor. The corresponding terms are:—Can. shanbogue, Tel. curnum, Tam. kanaka. The village or district accountant in Malabar. A frequent third name there. ——*Merkk* (மேற்கு - mérgu, Tam.). From (mél, tam. above). West. Prefix in place names; as Merkoonaud, meaning west country.——*Merkoonaud* (மேற்குநாடு - mérgunádu, Tam. merkunád *). From (mérgu, tam. west + nádu, tam. country). Division, Neilgherries; acres 63,891; pop. 42,798; divided from Paranginaud by S. spur of Doddabetta range and Kartairy river; from Todanaud on N.W. by a spur of Doddabetta range, and E. branch of Coondah river, which flows through Lovedale and Nunjenaud valleys to the main stream; the same stream separates it from the Coondah division on S.W. Included in the jurisdiction of the Deptuy tahsildar and Sub-magistrate of Coonoor, and forms the charge of a Revenue inspector.——*Meroovey* (ಮೇರುವೆ - méruve, Can.). From (mél, tam. above, high). An inclined plane up which blocks of stone are rolled for the upper parts of a building.——*Methonica* (മേത്തോന്നി - méttónni, Mal.). Title corruption from malayalam meaning superior lily. A genus [wild bachnaag].——*Meyjodoo* (پائتابہ - páitábah, Hind.; میجور - mejor, Dec.; మేజోడు - médzódu, Tel.; மேசோடு - mésódu, Tam.). Hind. from (pái, pers. foot + tábah, pers. support). Tel. from (mél tam. upper + dzódu, tel. shoe). Tam. from teloogoo. Socks.

MAILAM (ಮೇಳ - méla, *Can.*; మేళము - mélamu, *Tel.*; മേളം - mélam, *Mal.*; மேளம் - mélam, *Tam.*). From (mil, san. to join); means an assemblage of instruments [sangeetam]. Drum [paray].——*Maula* (మాల - mála, Tel.). From (mélam, tam. drum). The corresponding terms are:—Tam. pariah, Can. holeya, Mal. poolaya. The teloogoo pariah [q.v.] caste. Numbers about 1½ millions [jauty]. Compare, where name given on account of dingy habit:—Corvus culminatus (málakáki), pariah crow; Herodias alba (málakonga), pariah crane; Milvus govinda (málagadda), pariah kite.——*Melah* (میلہ - melá, Hind.). A fair [chunda, santa, santey, shandy].

MAILORE (ಮೇಲೂರು - mélúru, *Can.*; மேலூர் - mélúr, *Tam.* melúr *). From (mél, tam. upper + úr, tam. village) [mail].——**(1)** Village; Neilgherry dist., Merkoonaud division; pop. 2,578; acres 14,169; lat. 11° 18′; long. 76° 45′; from Coonoor W.S.W. 7 miles; from Ootacamund S. 7 miles. Badaga village. Contains one of the principal Badaga [q.v.] temples. There is a large group of cromlechs [paundoocull] and sculptured memorial stones.——**(2)** Pass; Neilgherry dist., Merkoonaud division, from Ootacamund S.W. 15 miles. Constructed next in order to the Kotagherry ghaut, about 1828, and at one time much used by passengers from S. and W. districts. Westwards from Shoondaputty at its foot the ancient track to Munnarcaud and Calicut runs up Bhawauny valley crossing ridge near Silent valley, which lies between two spurs of the Coondahs. E. a path runs down left bank of Bhawauny to Mettapolliem, thence to Coimbatore from Shoondaputty. The pass reaches the summit of the ghaut [q.v.] below the Shoondabetta, near Mailore. It was once much used by tobacco [pogauk] smugglers. W. is the Tullapoya pass [ghaut].——**(3)** Coffee [q.v.] estate, Merkoonaud, Neilgherries; from Coonoor S.W. 8 miles. 283 acres.——**(4)** Talook, Madura district. Tahsildar's pay Rs. 175. Area 484 square miles. Population 148,656. Language Tamul. North centre inland part of district. Bounded:—N. by the Coolitalay talook of Trichinopoly district, E. by the Shivagunga zemindarry and Coolitalay and Poodoocottah in Trichinopoly district, S. by the Shivagunga zemindarry and the Madura talook, W. by Madura and Dindigul talooks. Contains mountains, Alagar hills, Carandamullay, Nuttam hills. Red soil generally. Rain-fed tanks and two streams Tirmany moottaur and Palaur in Nuttam firkah [q.v.]. There are spots where tents [derah] may be pitched in the following places:—Mailore, under a large banyan [q.v.] tree within the compound of the travellers' bungalow [q.v.]; Nauviniputty near Mailore; Pullaputty near Cottaumputty, a large tope [q.v.] by the side of the stream Palaur; Nuttam, a large tope by the side of the stream Tirmany moottaur. Places of archæological interest:—Ambalacauranputty, Cottaumputty, Cotteinoottputty, Covilputty, Cullivailiputty, Keel valaivoo, Mailore, Poothacoody, Tirchoonay, Tirvathore, Vilamputty. The leading places, &c., in the talook are the following.——*Alagar hills* (அழகர்மலை - azhagarmalai, Tam.). See sep. title.——*Carandamullay* (கரந்தமலை - karandamalai, Tam.). From (karandai, tam. sweet basil, ocimum basilicum, linn. + malai, tam. hill). Hill; trig. station; lat. 10° 19′ 03·64″; long. 78° 15′ 18·92″; from Madura N.N.E. 29 miles; from Mailore N.N.W. 22 miles.——*Caroongaulacoody* (கருங்காலக்குடி - karungálakkudi, Tam.). From (karumai, tam. blackness + kála, san. death + kudi, tam. village). Village; pop. 2,708; acres 3,479; lat. 10° 10′; long. 78° 25′; from Madura N.E. 23 miles; from Mailore N.N.E. 8 miles. Weekly market.——*Cottaumputty* (கொட்டாம்பட்டி - kottámbatti, Tam.). From (kottán, tam. blacksmith's hammer + patti, tam. village). Village; pop. 2,332; acres 1,728; lat. 10° 13′; long. 78° 26′; from Madura N.E. 28 miles; from Mailore N.N.E. 13 miles. On high road to Trichinopoly. Large choultry [q.v.].——*Mailore* (மேலூர் - mélúr, Tam.). See below.——*Nuttam* (நத்தம் - nattam, Tam.). See sep. title.——**(5)** Town, Talook head-quarters, Sub-registrar's office. Madura district, Mailore talook; pop. 5,858; acres 5,753; lat. 10° 02′; long. 78° 23′; from Dindigul S.E. 35 miles; from Kodaykarnal E.S.E. 57 miles; from Madras S.S.W. 246 miles; from Madura E. 18 miles; from Rameshwaram N.W. 81 miles; from Ramnaud N.N.W. 55 miles. Former stronghold of the Cullar [q.v.] of Mailore nand. Old Shiva temple with inscriptions. Large and richly endowed choultry [q.v.]. Mission station.

MAISTRY (మేస్త్రి - méstri, *Tel.*; மேஸ்த்திரி - mésttiri, *Tam.*). From portuguese. Head workman.

MAITEE (मेथिका - mét'hiká, *San.*; मेथी - mét'hí, *Mahr.*; मेत्ति - métti, *Conc.*; حلبه - hulbah, *Ar.*; شنبلید - shambalíd, *Pers.*; میتھی کا پیر - methíkáper, *Hind.*; میتھی کا جہار - methíkájhár, *Dec.*; ಮೆಂತ್ಯ - mentya, *Can.*; ಮೆತ್ತೆ - mette, *Too.*; మెంతి - menti, *Tel.*; ମେଥି - meti, *Oor.*; ഉലുവ - uluva, *Mal.*; උලුවා - uluvá, *Singh.*; வெந்தயம் - vendayam, *Tam.*). Title from mahratta. Mahr. from sanscrit. Ar. from (huluba, ar. to increase flow of milk). Hind., &c., from sanscrit. Mal. from arabic. San. also (mét'hí). Pers. also (shamlít); (shamlíz). Mal. also (ventayam). Greek βουκέρας, τῆλις. Its mucilaginous seeds in latin are Siliquæ. Title otherwise Fenugreek, Vendayam. Botanically Trigonella fœnum-græcum, linn., leguminosæ [vricsham, 48]. Annual, robust, erect, sub-glabrous; stipules not laciniated; leaflets toothed, ¾–1 inch long, oblanceolate-oblong; flowers one to two, sessile in the axils of the leaves; calyx ¼–⅓ inch, teeth linear; corolla much exserted; pod 2 to 3 inches long, ten to twenty-seeded, with a long persistent beak, often falcate. Small, herbaceous plant; pod horn-shaped; seeds oblong, cylindrical, a little compressed, truncated at both ends, covered with small hollow and yellow points; internally their color is yellow; the odour is strong and peculiar on chewing; the seed is mucilaginous, and the taste is analogous to the smell; an unctuous farinaceous taste, accompanied with a degree of bitterness; containing the principle called coumarin, which imparts the smell to hay. Seeds are medicinally diuretic, emmenagogue, demulcent, astringent, emollient and suppurative; externally employed in poultice and fomentation; used in veterinary practice in cordial preparation. Seeds aromatic and stimulant in curries [q.v.]; also used as coffee [q.v.] after roasting; the plant is eaten fresh as a vegetable. Seed yields a yellow dye [shauyam]; fresh seed yields small percentage of oil [yennay]. There is a Tamul proverb :—வெந்தயம் போடாத கறியும் கறி அல்ல, சந்தை இல்லாத ஊரும் ஊர் அல்ல—"A curry made without vendayam is not a curry, a village "without a market is not a village." And another :—வெந்தயம் இட்ட கறிக்கு சந்தேகம் இல்லை—"A curry with vendayam "in it needs not be questioned." The species corniculata is Horseshoe fenugreek.

MAJAL (ಮಜಲ - majala, *Can.*). Second sort of rice land in South canara and Mysore, producing annually one crop of rice [q.v.] and one of vegetables or dry grain [q.v.].

MAJD (مجد - majd, *Ar.*). From (majada, ar. to excel in glory). Glory. Part of lacab; as Majd ood deen, glory of religion; Majd ood dowla, glory of the empire [ism].——*Majeed* (مجيد - majíd, Hind.). From (majada, ar. to excel in glory). Lord of glory. Epithet of God [allah]. Common alam; as Majeed khan, alam + alamaut. Sometimes part of lacab; as Majeed ood deen, glory of the faith; Majeed ood dowlah, glory of the state [ism].

MAJIL (منزل - manzil, *Hind.*). From (nazala, ar. to descend). A stage [makaum, tappaul] in travelling [manjilee]. Cf. Manzil.

MAJMOO (مجموع - majmúa, *Ar.*). Total.——*Majmoodar* (مجموعه دار - majmúadár, Hind.). From (above + dár, pers. keeper). The head accountant in the talook [q v.] cutcherry [q.v.].

MAJOON (معجون - majún, *Hind.*). From (ajín, ar. kneaded). Product of Cannabis sativa [kinnab]. Electuary used by Mahomedans. The chief ingredients are ganjah [q.v.] leaves, milk [paul], ghee [q.v.], poppy seeds [opium poppy], flowers of the thorn apple [datura], the powder of the nux vomica [poison nut], and sugar [q.v.]. Two similar aromatic compounds, containing hemp [janam], are well known among the Tamulians, and are frequently ordered by the veidyans [q.v.]; one of them is composed of twenty-one, the other of thirty-five ingredients [mookhadiraut].

MAKAUM (مقام - makám, *Hind.*). From (káma, ar. to stand). Station. Halting place [majil].——*Maugaunam* (மாகாணம் - mágánam, Tam.). From (makán, ar. a place). A division of a revenue district, usually consisting of six or seven villages. See vol. I, 112. Distinguish from Maugauny.

MAKBARAH (مقبره - makbarah, *Hind.*). From (kabr, ar. grave). Mausoleum [goombaz].

MAKBOOL (مقبول - makbúl, *Hind.*). From (kabala, ar. to receive favourably). Approved. Prefixed to an alam forms a lacab; as Makbool hoossain, accepted of Hoossain. Generally taken by Shiahs [ism].

MAKDOONAS (مقدونس - makdúnas, *Ar.*; فطراساليون - fitrásálíún, *Pers.*). Title means of macedon. Ar. also (kussah); (yukhsis). Pers. also (karafsimakduní), meaning macedonian apium graveolens, linn. Greek πτεροσέλινον, Latin apium. Title otherwise parsley. Botanically Pteroselinum sativum, wight, umbelliferæ [vricsham, 67]. The leaf used as a garnish.

MAKHAM (मख - makha, *San.*). From (mah, san. to worship). Sacrifice.——*Makhanah* (मखान्न - makhánna, San.; مکهانا - makhanah, Hind.; నల్లనిపద్మము - nallanipadmamu, Tel.; କୁଣ୍ଟପଦେନ - kuntapudena, Oor.). San. from (makha, san. sacrifice + anna, san. food); from use of seed during yaugam [q.v.] or sacrifices. Tel. from (nalla, tel. black + padma, san. nelumbium speciosum, willd.). Hind. also (machaná), meaning sacrifice food; (makhúrch). Title otherwise Black lotus, Gorgan plant, Machnah, Prickly water-lily. Botanically Euryale ferox, salisb., nymphæceæ [vricsham, 7]. Alias Anneslea spinosa. Specific from bristling foliage. Stemless floating plant; sepals four; petals numerous in four to seven series; leaves peltate, about 1 to 4 feet each way from orbicular to oval, entire, dark green above, with ferruginous veins, armed, with few slender prickles above, spinous beneath; petioles armed; calyx covered with recurved spines on the outside; carpel size of a pea [calauyam]; flowers bluish purple; flowering nearly all year. Seeds are deemed powerful tonics. Seeds are farinaceous and eaten after having been heated in sand and husked. No other common species here.

MAKHDOOM (مخدوم - makhdúm, *Hind.*). From (khadama, ar. to serve). Lord. Prefixed to an alam forms a lacab; as Makhdoom ally, ally the master [ism], one of Hyder's generals in Malabar defeated by Colonel Humberstone in 1782 near Calicut.

MAKKAL (ಮಕ್ಕಳು - makkalu, *Can.*; മക്കൾ - makkal, *Mal.*; மக்கள் - makkal, *Tam.*). From (maga, tam. child). Children [moga].——*Makkala santauna* (ಮಕ್ಕಳಸಂತಾನ - makkalasantána, Can.). Same as Makkatoyem in Malabar. The system of inheritance [dauyam] in which the property descends to the son or succession in the line of sons [aliya santauna].——*Makkatoyem* (മക്കത്തായം - makkattáyam, Mal.). From (above + táyam, mal. portion). The right of a man's sons to inherit as distinguished from Maroomakkatoyem, the right of his sisters' sons to inherit [maroomakkatoyem]. The following are the principal castes who follow the Makkatoyem system of inheritance [dauyam] :—Adigal, Chaukky, Cheroonan, Comaty, Cummaulan, Eeramcolly, Elliad, Ilavan, Moossad, Mootta chettiyaun, Numbeeshan, Numbidy, Numboory, Pidauran, Podwaul, Puttan, Tandaun, Tangal, Teeyan in Cadatnaud and Travancore, Veisya, Vilacattravan, Yembraun [maryauday].

MAKKAMAH (محكمه - mahkamah, *Hind.*) [hookum]. From (hukm, ar. order). A tribunal [adawlut].

MAKMULL (مخمل - makhmal, *Hind.*). From (khaml, ar. nap). Velvet [sheelay].

MAKNAH (مکهنا - makhná, *Hind.*; പിടി - piti, *Mal.*). Hine or female elephant [q.v.].

MAKREE (ऊर्णनाभ - úrnanábha, *San.*; عنکبوت - ankabút, *Ar.*; کارتنه - kártinah, *Pers.*; مکڑی - makrí, *Hind.*; ಜೇಡಹುಳ - jédahula, *Can.*; సాలెపురుగు - sálepurugu, *Tel.*; എട്ടുകാലി - ettukáli, *Mal.*; சிலந்தி - shilandi, *Tam.*). Title from hindostany. San. from (úrna, san. wool + nábhi, san. navel). Hind. from (markata, san. a spider). Can. from (jéda, can. weaver + hula, can. worm). Tel. from (sále, tel. weaver + purugu, tel. worm). Mal. from (ettu, mal. eight + kálu, mal. leg). Spider [poochy].

MAKTAB (مکتب - maktab, *Hind.*). From (kataba, ar. to write) [kitaub]. Mahomedan school [madrissa]. According to Muslim law [shareeyat], all education should be carried on in connection with religious instruction in the first instance; and consequently schools are generally attached to mosques [musjid], where the Koran [q.v.] and other branches of learning [ilm] are taught. The teacher seats himself on the ground, with his bearers all seated round him in a ring. Instruction is usually given in the early morning after the morning prayer [namauz], and continues some 3 or 4 hours. It is again renewed for a short time after the midday prayer. Also schooling ceremony amongst Mahomedans when a child has attained the age of four years four months and four days.

MAL (മാൽ - mál, *Mal.*; மால் - mál, *Tam.*). Black [meilam].——*Mahl* (മാൽ - mál, Mal.). Language of Minicoy of the Laccadives, with a mixture of corrupt Malayalam [bhaushay]. See vol. I (51).——*Maldives* (مالديپ - máldíp, Hind.; മാലദ്വീപ് - máladvípu, Mal.). From (mál, mal. black + dvípa, san. island); from the dark soil. Sanscrit name (máládvípa), meaning garland + island; from configuration. Latin Maniolæ. Islands extending southwards from lat. 7° 6′ 30″ N. to 0° 42′ S. About 12,000 in number. Have been colonized from Arabia. The ruler is styled Sultan [q.v.] of the thirteen atolls [q.v.] and 12,000 isles. Upon the acquisition of Ceylon by the British in 1766, the supreme authority over the Maldives accompanied. The present sultan sends an ambassador to the Governor of Ceylon annually. These islands belong to Ceylon, not India; excepting the most northern or Minicoy, which detached from the rest is part of the Cannanore island dominions, and is thus administered as part of the Malabar district. Mahomedanism has been the accepted religion of the Maldivians for at least six centuries, but side by side with it there has continued to exist an older creed in demons. Maldive cocoanut is same as Sea cocoanut.——*Malkangany* (वह्निरुचि - vahniruchi, San.; मालकांगोणि - málakángóni, Mahr.; مال کنگنی - málkangní, Hind. and Dec.; ಕಂಗೊಂಡಿಬಳ್ಳಿ - kangondiballi, Can.; గుండుమెడ - gundumeda, Tel.; പാലുഴവം - páluzhavam, Mal.; කටුපිල - katupila, Singh.; வாலுளுவை - váluluvai, Tam.). Title from hindostany. San. from (vahni, san. fire + ruchi, san. taste); from its acrid and stimulating properties. Hind. from (mál, tam. black + kangu, san. panicum italicum); from black oil and seeds like tinay [large chintoo]. Can. from (kanga, san. crooked + ondu, can. unite + balli, can. creeper). Tel. from (gundu, tel. round + meda, tel. neck). Mal. from tamul [oolinja]. Singh. from (katu, singh. thorny + pila, singh. nerium). San. also (jyótishmatí), meaning light possessing, in allusion to its supposed property of stimulating intellectual powers and sharpening memory [oolinja]. Tel. also (peddachinta), meaning large + tamarindus indica, linn.; (bávanji); (erikata); (maneru); (málaerikata), meaning pariah + the tree; (máyalaerikata), meaning deceit + the tree. Singh. also (lavaná); (duhudu). Tam. also (athiparíççam), properly the seed; (málganguni). Title otherwise Black-oil tree, Intellect tree, Malkangany oil tree, Spindle tree [large chintoo], Staff tree. Botanically Celastrus paniculatus, willd., celastrineæ [vricsham, 40]. Alias Ceanothus paniculatus; Celastrus nutans, rothiana. Climbing shrub, unarmed; young shoots and flower-bearing branches pendulous; leaves alternate, broadly oval, or ovate, or obovate, usually with a sudden short acumination, slightly serrated, glabrous; racemes terminal, compound or supra-decompound, elongated, much longer than the uppermost leaves; petals five; calyx five-partite; lobes rounded, ciliated; capsule globose, three-celled, three to six-seeded; seeds with a complete arillus; flowers small, greenish; grows in dry elevated jungles. The fruit is a three-celled, globose green capsule, containing from three to six seeds enclosed in a complete arillus of a rich orange colour and sweet taste; the seeds are about the size of millet [q.v.], of a reddish-brown colour, oily, angular like the section of a sphere; the testa is hard, and the kernel which is white has an acrid taste. The expressed oil has a deep reddish-yellow colour, derived from the adhering arillus; it deposits a quantity of solid fat after it has been kept for a short time. Oleum nigrum or black oil is a compound and empyreumatic oil obtained by a destructive distillation of the seeds with several other ingredients, and is generally manufactured in northern circars [q.v.]; there are several varieties, those in vizagapatam, ellore and masulipatam are best. The following is description of the preparation of oleum nigrum:—into an earthen pot, the bottom of which is perforated by a number of small holes, are put the seeds ℔. iss., benzoin [q.v.], cloves [lavangam], nutmegs [jauty], and mace [jauty] aa ʒ ss; the mouth is closed, and the pot, placed over another, is luted to it; they are then placed in a pit three feet deep and nearly as wide, and surrounded by cakes [bratty], of dry cow dung, which are set on fire; and when they are consumed, about ℥ vi of the oil is found in the under vessels, ready for use; it should be kept in well-closed vessels; sp. gr. 0·975. The seeds, fixed oil and compound empyreumatic oil, are medicinally diuretic, diaphoretic, stimulant and nervine tonic; the seeds long been in repute with vaidyans [q.v.] for stimulating intellectual powers; the oils are substituted for juniper, sp. æther. nit., buchu, broom, phosphates, hypophosphites and strychnia, a popular remedy in beri-bery [q.v.], administered in doses of a few drops daily in emulsion. Oil also burnt in lamps and employed in religious ceremonies. Wood pinkish-yellow, soft. Same title given to Gymnosporia montana [chintoo].

MALA (ಮಲೆ - male, *Can.*; మల - mala, *Tel.*; മല - mala, *Mal.*; மலை - malai, *Tam.*). Mountain [maley, mullay].——*Malabar* * (മലയാളം - malayálam, Mal.) [mala]. Title is an arabic corruption from (mala, mal. mountain + vára, san. slope). Mal. from (mala, mal. mountain + ázham, mal. depth). Sanscrit name (malayavára), meaning malaya mountain + slope. Greek μαλέ. Distinguish from Maabar. The term Malabar was transferred by the Portuguese as a name for the Tamul language and so continued till a much later date by Anglo-Indians. The fisherman's Tamul on the coast is very like Malayalam. Cf. Gentoo for teloogoo. Revenue district. This is situated along the coast; between 10° 15′ and 12° 18′ N. lat. and between 75° 13′ and 76° 54′ long.; bounded N. by South canara, E. by Coorg, Mysore, Neilgherries and Coimbatore, S. by Cochin, W. by Arabian sea; square miles 5,584; pop. 2,652,565; language Malayalam. Rivers:—Agalapoya, Anjarcundy, Belliapatam, Beypore, Bhawauny, Cadaloondy, Chetwye, Cotta, Cubbany, Cullye, Delly, Mahé, Ponnany, Ramapore, Taliparamba, Tellicherry, Yelattore. Ports:—Attacooy, Auttpooram, Badagara, Belliapatam, Beypore, Cadaloondy, Calicut, Cannanore, Caupautt, Cavvye, Chombaula, Collam, Coorcooy, Cootye, Cottacull, Cuddalore, Cullye, Dharmapatam, Mahé, Maudye, Molancadav, Moottangal, Parpanangaudy, Ponnany, Poothiyangaudy, Quilandy, Talye, Taunore, Tellicherry, Tricody, Velliangode, Yelara, Yellatore, Yetticoolam. Mountains:—Western ghauts and Anamullay hills. The whole area of the district is represented by the following talooks:—Calicut, Chiracal, Cochin, Cooroombranaud, Cottayam, Palghaut, Ponnany, Valavanaud, Wynaud, Yernaud. For departmental purposes the district is distributed between the following revenue and magisterial officers, who have their head-quarters at the places shown. The pay set opposite the subordinate officers gives the grade of the corresponding charge:—Collector, Calicut. Sub-collector, Tellicherry, in charge of Chiracal, Cooroombranaud and Cottayam talooks. Head assistant collector, Palghaut, in charge of Palghaut and Valavanaud talooks. Special assistant collector, Malapooram, in charge of Yernaud and Calicut talooks. General deputy collector, Ponnany, in charge of Ponnany talook. General deputy collector, Manantoddy, in charge of Wynaud talook. General duty deputy collector, Cochin, in charge of Cochin talook. Tahsildars, Calicut, Rs. 175. Chiracal, Rs. 175. Cooroombranaud, Rs. 200. Cottayam, Rs. 175. Palghaut, Rs. 200. Yernaud, Rs. 200. Valavanaud, Rs. 200. Ponnany, Rs. 225. Wynaud, Rs. 200 plus Rs. 50, Hill allowance. Deputy tahsildars, Aulatore, Rs. 70; range situated in the south of Palghaut talook. Calicut, Rs. 70; range situated in the western coast of Calicut talook. Cannanore, Rs. 100; range situated in the western coast of Chiracal talook. Cherpalcherry, Rs. 70; range situated in the south of Valavanaud talook. Chowghaut, Rs. 70; range situated in the south of Ponnany talook. Coottooparamba, Rs. 70; range situated in the north-east of Cottayam talook. Quilandy, Rs. 70; range situated in the south of Cooroombranaud talook. Taliparamba, Rs. 70; range situated in the north of Chiracal talook. Tiroorangaudy, Rs. 70; range situated in the west of Yernaud talook. Bettatt poothiyangaudy Rs. 70; range situated in the north of Ponnany talook. Vythery, Rs. 100 plus Rs. 50, Hill allowance; range situated in the south of Wynaud talook. Sub-magistrates, Anjengo, Rs. 70. Jurisdiction extending over Anjengo, situated to the north of Trivandrum, in Travancore. Tungacherry, Rs. 70; jurisdiction extending over Tungacherry, situated to the north of Anjengo. Similarly judicial officers:—Judges, Calicut and Tellicherry; Sub-judges, Calicut, Palghaut and Tellicherry. District moonsifs, Angaudipooram, with jurisdiction extending over thirty-one amshoms of Valavanaud talook; Aulatore, with jurisdiction extending over twenty-nine amshoms in Palghaut talook; Badagara, with jurisdiction extending over fourteen amshoms in Cooroombranaud talook; Bettatnand, with jurisdiction extending over twenty-six amshoms in Ponnany talook; Calicut, with jurisdiction extending over thirty-eight amshoms in Calicut talook; Cannanore, with jurisdiction extending over twenty-one amshoms in Chiracal and seven in Cottayam talook; Chowghaut, with jurisdiction extending over twenty-one amshoms in Ponnany talook; Munjery, with jurisdiction extending over twenty-six amshoms in Yernaud, one in Calicut and three in Valavanaud talook; Nadaupooram, with jurisdiction extending over twenty amshoms in Cooroombranaud talook; Nedoonganaud, with jurisdiction extending over twenty-nine amshoms in Valavanaud and three in Palghaut talook; Palghaut, with jurisdiction extending over twenty-four amshoms in Palghaut, and one in Valavanaud talook; Parpanangaudy, with jurisdiction extending over twenty-six amshoms in Yernaud talook and five in Ponnany talook; Ponnany, with jurisdiction extending over twenty-one amshoms in Ponnany talook; Quilandy, with jurisdiction extending over twenty-three amshoms in Cooroombranaud talook; Taliparamba, with jurisdiction extending over twenty-two amshoms in Chiracal talook; Tellicherry, with jurisdiction extending over twenty-one amshoms in Cottayam talook; Vythery, with jurisdiction extending over Wynaud and two amshoms in Calicut talook; Similarly Public works officers:—District engineer, Calicut; Divisional officers, Palghaut, Tellicherry, Valavanaud, Wynaud. Contains Registration sub-districts:—Andattode, Anjarcundy, Anjengo, Aulatore, Badagara, Bettattpoothiyangaudy, Cannanore, Cherpalcherry, Chevayore, Chowghaut, Cochin, Codevauyore, Condotty, Coottiyaudy, Coottooparamba, Malapooram, Manantoddy, Mungara, Munjery, Munnarcaud, Nadaupooram, Nadoovannore, Palghaut, Pannore, Payoly, Payyangaudy, Perindalman, Ponnany, Quilandy, Taliparamba, Tamracherry, Taunore, Tiroorangaudy, Tripriaur, Trittaula, Tungacherry, Vandoor, Vythery. Contains Forest ranges:—Nelambore, Palghaut and Wynaud. Contains Municipalities:—Calicut, Cannanore, Cochin, Palghaut, Tellicherry. Sultan ally, Rajah of Cannanore, resides in Malabar district. Leading Jenmies [q.v.] are:—Amarambalatt edavanna tirmalpaud, Collangode vengoonattil valiya numbidy, and Nelambore tutcharacauvil tirmalpaud. The following general references should be made to the preceding volumes:—general geography, I (1) to (29); general ethnology, I (29) to (109); general history, I (110) to (188); physical geography, II, 1; meteorology, II, 3; geology, II, 8; fauna, II, 21; flora, II, 26; mineralogy, II, 29. The following references in the preceding volumes will furnish details special to the district:—latitudes and longitudes, II, 47; particulars about towns, II, 48; coast survey, II, 148; lighthouses, II, 168; comparative population, II, 172; location of revenue officers, II, 388; registrars' and sub-registrars' stations, II, 420; ports, II, 424; rain-gauge stations, II, 428; police divisions, II, 431; maps published, II, 436; hospitals and dispensaries, II, 447; missionary stations, II, 455; head-quarter stations of gazetted officers, II, 461; incidence of taxation, II, 463; weights and measures of the district, II, 515; zemindarries, II, 298. A special gazetteer account of the whole district is given at II, 99. For the detailed topography of the district, reference should be made to the talook notices in the present volume, viz.:—Calicut, Chiracal, Cochin, Cooroombranaud, Cottayam, Laccadives, Minicoy, Palghaut, Ponnany, Valavanaud, Wynaud, Yernaud.——*Malabar almond* (நாட்டுவாதுமை - náttuváthumai, Tam.). Same as Catapang.——*Malabar arrowroot* (तवखीर - tavakhíra, Mahr.; कुव्याझाड - kúvyájháda, Conc.; تیکھر - tíkhar, Hind.; جو کے آٹے کا گڈہ - jaukeátekágaddah, Dec.; ಕೂವೆಗಿಡ - kúvegida, Can.; ಕೂವೆ - kúve, Too.; పాలగుండ - pálagunda, Tel.; ପଲୁ - palu, Oor.; കൂവ - kúva, Mal.; கூகை - kúgai, Tam.). Title from habitat. Mahr. from (tvakkshírá, san. bamboo milk) [tabasheer]. Dec. from (jau, hind. barley, hordeum vulgare, linn. + átá, hind. flour + gaddah, hind. tuber). Can. from (kúvalu, can. cry). Tel. from (pálu, tel. milk + kunda, tel. pot). Mal. from (kúvu, mal. to cry + kai, mal. stem); from hollow stems through which children blow out bubbles. Tam. from malayalam. Hind. also (kuvvekágaddah), meaning coova root; (viláitíátekágaddah), meaning foreign flour tuber; (kuvvekenishastekágaddah), meaning coova + starch + tuber. Tel. also (támaravalli), meaning lotus, nelumbium speciosum, willd. + creeper; (mettatámara), meaning dry land + lotus. Tam. also (kúvaikkizhangu), meaning arrowroot. Title otherwise Coova [q.v.], Indian arrowroot, Milk-pot root, Narrow-leaved turmeric, Tikhar, Wild arrowroot. Botanically Curcuma [haridrah] angustifolia, roxb., zingiberaceæ [vricsham, 144]. Bulbs oblong, with pale oblong pendulous tubers; leaves petioled, narrow lanceolate, most acute, striated with fine parallel veins; flowers longer than the bracts; petioles 6–10 inches long, lower half sheathing; spike radical, 4–6 inches long, crowned with an ovate purple tuft; flower large, bright-yellow, with a purple tuft, expanding at sunrise and decaying at sunset; grows without cultivation, especially in travancore. Farinaceous substance procured from roots; like arrowroot both in appearance and virtues; commonly eaten boiled in water and mixed with tyre [q.v.] and salt [ooppoo]. Red malabar arrowroot from color of root, otherwise Large malabar arrowroot, or Kempa coova, is Curcuma leucorrhiza, roxb.; bulbs ovate; palmate tubers long and far-spreading; leaves broad-lanceolate, smooth, spikes lateral, few-flowered; flowers the length of the bracts, outer border slightly tinged with pink, inner yellow; flowering in the rains. Compare also in other genera:—Alpinia allughas (malaiyiñchikkúva), hill ginger arrowroot; Costus speciosus (channakkúva), violent arrowroot; Kœmpferia rotunda (malankúva), hill arrowroot; Manihot utilissima, brazilian arrowroot; Tacca pinnatifida, mergui arrowroot, tahiti arrowroot, and south sea arrowroot. See gloss. paragraphs.——*Malabar black varnish tree* (കാട്ടുചേര് - káttuchér, Mal.). Title from acrid juice from wood used as black varnish in malabar. Mal. means wild marking nut tree, from similar juice. Same as Holigarna.——*Malabar blackwood* (शिसव - shisava, Mahr.; बीटी - bítí, Conc.; سیسم - sísam, Hind.; کالی لکڑی - kálílakrí, Dec.; ಬೀಟಿ - bíti, Can.; విరుగుడు - virugudu, Tel.; ସିସ୍ସା - sissa, Oor.; വീട്ടി - vítti, Mal.; ஈட்டி - ítti, Tam.). Dec. from (kálí, hind. black + lakrí, hind. wood). Tel. from (virugu, tel. to break); wood splits lengthwise. Mal. from (vítu, mal. freehold property); one of the privileges of jenmies [q.v.] to use the wood. Tel. also (iruvudu); (jillagechettu); (irugudu); (jittégi), meaning small + the vaigy tree, pterocarpus marsupium, roxb. Tam. also (tóthagatti), meaning closeness + interior, from hard heartwood; (núkkam), meaning slackening, from weakening diseases; (karunduvarai), meaning black + diospyros embryopteris, pers. Title otherwise Beety, Black gaub, Bombay blackwood, Eety, Indian blackwood, Indian ebony, Indian rosewood, Ironwood, Jittaigy, Lesser vengay, Nookmaram, Sheesham, Todacutty, Veety. Botanically Dalbergia [yooga pattricay] latifolia, roxb., leguminosæ [vricsham, 48]. Alias Dalbergia emarginata. Tree 40 to 50 feet; leaves pinnate; leaflets alternate three to seven, generally five, orbicular, emarginate, above glabrous, beneath somewhat pubescent when young; panicles axillary, branched, and divaricating; corolla papilionaceous; calyx segment oblong; stamens united in a sheath open on the upper side; ovary stalked, five-ovuled; legumes stalked, oblong-lanceolate, one-seeded; flowers small, white, on short slender pedicels; flowering in hot season. Found throughout presidency; grows to immense size on mountains, particularly on west of presidency to nearly 4,000 feet; chiefly in dry deciduous forests with teak [q.v.], and in the moist evergreen sholahs [q.v.], and is often associated with the bamboo [q.v.] of very slow growth; especially when young; difficult to rear from the ravages of insects on the sprouting seeds. Seeds yield an oil; stem gives a gum [gond]. Sapwood yellow, small; heartwood extremely hard, dark purple, with black longitudinal streaks; no distinct annual rings; coppices well; valuable furniture wood, exported to europe from the forests of canara and malabar; also used here for cart wheels, agricultural implements, gun-carriages, sleepers, carving and fancy work; planks 4 feet wide, after removing the outer white wood, are procurable; the cut wood is heavy and close-grained, and admits of a very fine polish, having appearance then of rosewood; the oil in the wood makes it difficult to paint; the planks split longitudinally, when not well seasoned; an earthy deposit is frequently found embedded in the largest logs, a great defect in what would otherwise be fine planks; malabar blackwood generally fetches a higher price than teak; a variety sissoides, common in Coimbatore, Palghaut, Anamullays, Madura and Tinnevelly, smaller tree, wood redder, is called in tamul dark eety.——*Malabar cardamom* (ملیواری الایچی - malewárkíiláchí, Hind.). Same as Cardamom.——*Malabar catmint* (ओष्टफल - ósht'hap'hala, San.; चोधरा - chódhará, Mahr.; कालोतुम्बो - kálótumbó, Conc.; مگبیرے کا جھاڑ - mogbírekájhár, Dec.; ಕರಿತುಂಬೆಗಿಡ - karitumbégida, Can.; మొగబీర - mogabíra, Tel.; കരിന്തുമ്പ - karintumba, Mal.; பேய்மருட்டி - péymarutti, Tam.). San. from (ósht'ha, san. lip + p'hala, san. fruit); flowers resemble lip. Can. from (kari, can. black + tumbégida, can. the plant, leucas). Tel. from (moga, tel. male + bíra, tel. elæodendron glaucum, pers.). Mal. from (kari, mal. black + tumba, mal. leucas indica, r. br.); from flowers. Tam. from (péy, tam. devil + maruttu, tam. to threaten). San. also (bhútánkusha), meaning demon goad; (vaikunt'ha), meaning not blunt. Tel. also (mábhéri); (chinaranabhéri), meaning small + war + drum; (mogabhéri), meaning male + drum. Mal. also (péymeratti), meaning demon driver; (perumtumba), meaning large + the plant, leucas indica, r. br. Tam. also (péyverutti), meaning devil + to frighten; (irattaippéymarutti), meaning two + devil + to frighten. Title otherwise Black toombay, Devil frightener, Large toombay. Botanically Anisomeles malabarica, r. br., labiatæ [vricsham, 103]. Alias Ajuga fruticosa; Anisomeles intermedia; Nepata malabarica; Stachys mauritiana. Shrub, 2 to 5 feet; branches tomentose; leaves ovate-lanceolate, crenately serrated at the upper part, entire below; calyx five cleft, thickly covered with long, white, somewhat viscid pubescence; upper lip of corolla entire, white, under one three cleft, with the lateral divisions reflexed; anthers deep purple; whorls disposed in simple racemes; flower faintly fragrant. A clear reddish oil is distilled, of heavy odour, acrid and slightly bitter. Leaves are bitter and medicinally astringent; juice in infusion given in colic, indigestion, &c.; perspiration produced by inhalation from infusion of whole plant; oil is external application in rheumatism. Anisomeles ovata, br., is similar.——*Malabar convolvulus* (കാട്ടുകിഴങ്ങ് - káttukizhannu, Mal.). Same as Malabar creeper.——*Malabar creeper* (കാട്ടുകിഴങ്ങ് - káttukizhannu, Mal.; பேய்முசுட்டை - péymusuttai, Tam.). Mal. from (kátu, mal. forest + kizhannu, mal. root). Tam. from (péy, tam. devil + musuttai, tam. ipomæa candicans, bot. mag.). Title otherwise Malabar convolvulus. Botanically Argyreia [ajauntry] malabarica, choisy, convolvulaceæ [vricsham, 93]. Alias Convolvulus malabaricus; Ipomæa malabarica. Twining shrub; stem downy; leaves roundish-cordate, acute, furnished with a few scattered hairs on both surfaces, paler below; corolla campanulate; peduncles as long as the leaves, many-flowered at the apex; sepals five; exterior ones clothed with hoary villi with revolute edges; petioles and peduncles villous; flowers small, cream-colored, with deep purple eye; native of malabar. The root is cathartic with farriers [naulbund].——*Malabar glory* (മേത്തോന്നി - méttónni, Mal.). Title from habitat and shining flower. Same as Wild bachnaug.——*Malabar kino* (വേങ്ങ - vénna, Mal.). Same as Common vengay.——*Malabar nightshade* (उपोदिका - upódiká San.; پوی - poí, Hind.; بچلا - bachlá, Dec.; ಬಸಳೆ - basale, Can.; బచ్చలి - battsali, Tel.; പച്ചല - pachala, Mal.; නිවිති - niviti, Singh.; பசளை - pasalai, Tam.). San. from (upa, san. near + udaka, san. water); from moist habitat. Hind. from sanscrit. Drav. from (pasai, tam. stickiness). Botanically the Basella genus, basellaceæ [vricsham, 109]. Generic from tamul. One of the Indian spinaches; cf. Maurisham. Climbing plant with succulent stems and leaves; grown over trellis-work for protection from sun; flowers white or red and hermaphrodite; fruit, a single seed with an embryo coiled up like a watch-spring. The species best known to the natives are shown below.—"*a*" Heart-leaved malabar nightshade with the following vernaculars; (upódiká, San.; poí, Hind.; hiribasale, Can.; battsali, Tel.; pachala, Mal.; mápatniviti, Singh.; kottuppasalai, Tam.); San. from (upa, san. near + udaka, san. water); Can. from (hiri, can. large + basale, can. basella); Mal. from (pasalai, tam. the plant); Singh. from (mápata, singh. large + niviti, singh. malabar nightshade); Tam. from (kottu, tam. cluster + pasalai, tam. basella); Can. also (basale), (doddabasaleballi), meaning large + green + creeper; Tel. also (pottibattsali), meaning short + the plant, (allubattsali), meaning spreading + the plant, (peddabattsali), meaning large + the plant, (tigabattsali), meaning creeper + the plant; Mal. also (pótika); title otherwise Small malabar night shade; is botanically Basella [malabar nightshade] cordifolia, lam., basellaceæ [vricsham, 109]. Climbing, stem variegated green and purple; leaves cordate, entire, undulated; spikes much shorter than the leaves, long-peduncled; flowers purplish without, whitish-green within; berries dark purple; flowering in the cool season; cultivated as pot-herb. Succulent shoots and leaves eaten like spinach [maurisham]. Yields purple dye [shauyam].—"*b*" Red malabar nightshade with the following vernaculars; (pútika, San.; vála, Mahr.; támbadiválí, Conc.; poí, Hind.; lálbachlá, Dec.; kempubasale, Can.; kempubasale, Too.; peddamattu, Tel.; chuvannapachala, Mal.; shivappukkodippasalai, Tam.); Title from color of stem and leaves; San. from (púti, san. putrid); Conc. from (támbada, mahr. red + váli, conc. creeper); Dec. from (lál, hind. red + bachlá, hind. spinach, basella); Can. from (kempu, can. red + basale, can. basella); Too. from canarese; Tel. from (pedda, tel. large + mattu, tel. plant basella); Mal. from (chuvanna, mal. red + pachala, mal. the herb, basella cordifolia, lamk.); Tam. from (shivappu, tam. red + kodi, tam. creeper + pasalai, tam. basella); is botanically Basella [malabar nightshade] rubra, linn., basellaceæ [vricsham, 109]; alias Basella nigra. The commonest species. Stem scandent, 3–4 feet, angular, brownish purple; leaves ovate, acuminate, purplish, spikes nearly equalling the leaves, long-peduncled; flowers purple; outer divisions of the calyx oblong-elliptic; berries dark purple, obsoletely four-lobed, greenish and purple at the apex before ripening; seeds pale brown. Juice of leaves used in catarrh of children. Leaves dressed and eaten like spinach; infusion of leaves used as tea [q.v.]. Yields a very rich purple dye [shauyam], but this is difficult to fix.—"*c*" White malabar nightshade with the following vernaculars; (upódiká, San.; dhaviváli, Conc.; sufedpoí, Hind.; sufedbachlá, Dec.; bilibasale, Can.; boldubasale, Too.; allubattsali, Tel.; vellappachala, Mal.; niviti, Singh.; vellaikkodippasalai, Tam.); Title from color of stem; San. from (upa, san. near + udaka, san. water); Conc. from (dhava, mahr. white + váli, conc. creeper); Hind. from (sufed, hind. white + poí, hind. basella); Dec. from (sufed, hind. white + bachlá, hind. basella); Can. from (bili, can. white + basale, can. basella); Too. from (boldu, too. whiteness + basale, too. basella); Tel. from (allu, tel. to spread + battsali, tel. the plant, basella); Mal. from (vella, mal. white + pachala, mal. the herb, basella cordifolia, lam.); Tam. from (vellai, tam. white + kodi, tam. creeper + pasalai, tam. basella); title otherwise Field basella; is botanically Basella [malabar nightshade] rubra, linn., var. alba, basellaceæ [vricsham, 109]; alias Basella alba. Deciduous biennial trailer; cultivated; leaves ovate, wavy; peduncles simple, longer than the leaf; flowers white, flowering in july and november. Climber in damp regions. Succulent leaves dressed and eaten.——*Malabar nut*

(അടലോടകം - átalótakam, Mal.). Same as Adhatoday.——*Malabar nutmeg* (ملیوار کا جاپھل - malewárkájáphal, Hind.). See under. Jauty.——*Malabar oil* (मत्स्यतैल - matsyataila, San.; دهن السمك - dhonussamak, Ar.; روغن ماهی - raughanimáhí, Pers.; مچھلی کا تیل - machhíkátel, Hind.; ಮೀನೆಣ್ಣೆ - mínenne, Can.; చేపనూనె - chépanúne, Tel.; മീനെയ്യി - mínneyi, Mal.; மீனெண்ணெய் - mínenney, Tam.). Vernacular means fish + oil. Oleum piscis of chemists [yennay]. Made on W. coast from livers of sharks [soorah], skates [tenky], saw fishes, rays [tenky], oil-sardines [hilsa], &c. The oil-sardine is the basis. This is a migratory fish, and very capricious as to times of arrival and departure; hence supplies of fish-oil vary. The oil exported is sent to Europe for tanning leather [chamrah] and other purposes, taking the place of Train-oil. When properly made it is of a fine amber color; the smell and taste similar to cod-liver oil, but more strongly marked and more disagreeable. It is usually rancid, owing to the livers being exposed to the sun and allowed to putrify in the process of extraction. This oil is used by native painters in preparing coarse pigments [rangh]; it is also rubbed on the large beams and small wood work employed in house-building to preserve them from the weather and white-ants [q.v.].——*Malabar plum* (ജംബു - jambu, Mal.). Same as Rose apple.——*Malabar sago palm* (ഈറമ്പന - írampana, Mal.). Same as Bastard sago palm.——*Malabar squirrel* (پہاڑی گلہری - pahárígilehri, Hind.; ಕೆಂಪಳಿಲು - kempalilu, Can.; മലയണ്ണാൻ - malayannán, Mal.). Can. from (kempu, can. red + alilu, can. squirrel). Hind. and Mal. mean mountain squirrel. Sciurus [anil] malabaricus, sciuridæ [chamarapootcham], rodentia, mammalia [sastanam, 16], of naturalists [jantoo]. Ears, nape, back of neck, the back and sides of the body, bright maroon chestnut; the posterior part of the back, rump, and upper portion of all the limbs, and the tail, back, forehead and interocular regions brownish; muzzle and cheeks rufous; neck, breast, and lower parts dingy-yellow; feet rufous in front, yellow internally; ears small, rounded, very hairy. This large squirrel inhabits the southern portions of Malabar, the Wynaud, slopes of the Neilgherries, Travancore, &c.—"*a*" Allied is Bombay red squirrel, Sciurus elphinstonei. Ears and the whole upper surface of the body, and half way down the tail, outside the hind legs, and half-way down the forelegs outside, of an uniform rich reddish chestnut; the whole under surface of the body from the chin to the vent, inside of the limbs and lower part of the forelegs, crown of head, cheeks and posterior half of the tail, of a fine reddish-white, the two colors being separated by a defined line, and not merging into each other; feet light red; forehead and nose reddish brown, with some white hairs intermixed. Ears tufted. It is found in the northern portion of the Western ghaut [q.v.] extending into north Malabar.—"*b*" Also the Grizzled hill squirrel, Sciurus macrourus. Head and neck, basal half of tail, and limbs externally, dull maroon black, much grizzled with white, especially on the haunches, sides, croup and tail, the apical end of which is brown with a whitish grizzle; lips, cheeks, neck in front and on the sides, belly, and limbs internally, yellow or yellowish white. Ears ovate, acuminate, with short hair, not tufted, or whitish externally with a very small black tuft. The fur here is coarse, slightly waved, and varies from maroon black to rufous brown.—"*c*" Indian species of Sciurus akin to the above and not here found are:—Atrodorsalis or black-backed squirrel, Blanfordii or blanfords' squirrel, Caniceps or golden-backed squirrel, Erythræus or assam red-bellied squirrel, Ferrugineus or rusty-colored squirrel, Giganteus or black hill squirrel, Gordoni or gordon's squirrel, Hipparis or chestnut-bellied assam squirrel, Lokriah or orange-bellied grey squirrel, Lokroides or hoary-bellied grey squirrel, Maximus or central indian red squirrel, Phayrei or laterally banded or phayre's squirrel, Pygerythrus, Sladeni or sladen's squirrel.—"*d*" The large forest squirrels just mentioned inhabit lofty tree jungle, making their nests on the tops of the tallest trees. They are awkward on the ground. They are to be distinguished from the ordinary Striped squirrel [anil pillay].——*Malacoota* (मलकूट - malakúta, San.). From (malaya, san. the mountain + kúta, san. summit). Hwen thsang's mo-lo-kiu-cha. The modern districts of Tanjore and Madura on the east, with Coimbatore, Cochin, and Travancore on the west. In the Chino-Japanese map of India, the alternative name of Malacoota is Hai-an-men, Ptolemy's ἀΐοι [charitram]. See vol. I (10), (13).——*Malaicoody* (ಮಲೆಕುಡಿ - malekudi, Can.; മലക്കുടി - malakkuti, Mal.). From (above + kuti, mal. house). A hill-tribe living in the jungle tracts of South canara, Ooppinangady talook, in the cardamom [q.v.] forest tracts, &c., bordering on the ghauts [ghaut, jauty]. See vol. II, 63. General term for hill-tribes.——*Malaimadanday* (மலைமடந்தை - malaimadandai, Tam.). From (above + madandai, tam. woman). Parvaty [q.v.].——*Malainaud* (மலைநாடு - malainádu, Tam.). Any hilly country, term used in many parts. The hilly forest tract in Mysore bordering on Western ghauts [q.v.].——*Malaiyarasa* (മലയരശർ - malayarashar, Mal.; மலையரச - malaiyarasa, obl., Tam.). From (above + arachan, mal. chief). Aboriginal race of ancient traditions, found among the hills of Canara, Coimbatore, and Malabar. They live in small communities of five or six families, and probably do not exceed 500 in all. Their huts consist of a few sticks covered with bark and thatch. They live on wild forest products, and have a few fowls [moorghy] and dogs [nye]. As a race they are diminutive; with crania small, and pear-shaped [amrood], rising to a point about the junction of the occipital bone and the sagittal suture; a low retreating forehead, long, tangled, black hair, flat nose, and small eyes. They are averse to intercourse with strangers. They catch wild animals with pits and traps and use bows and arrows. They collect drugs for the trade. They burn the dead. They speak corrupt Malayalam in the north and corrupt Tamul in the south. They have a tradition giving them special permission to eat the black monkey [bandar]. From this they are by the low county people called Corangootinnies. The inhabitants of the plains regard them as in alliance with demonolatry, and presents are bestowed in order to prevent their curses producing ill effects. Each village has its priest, who when required calls on the demon resident in the hill. If he obtains the necessary encouragement he appears possessed and gives out answers with yells and gestures. The Malaiyarasar have sacred groves in which they will not fire a gun or speak above a breath [jauty]. See vol. I (111).——*Malaiyaraya* (മലയരയൻ - malayarayan, Mal.). Travancore form of Malaiyarasa.——*Malapaty* (மலைப்பதி - malaippathi, Tam.). From (above + pati, san. master). Refers to Tripatty deity. Hindoo 2nd or pers. name [peyar].——*Malapooram* (മലപ്പുറം - malappuram, Mal. malapuram *). From (mala, mal. mountain + puram, mal. side). Town, Special assistant collector's head-quarters, Telegraph office, Assistant superintendent of Police; Malabar dist., Yernaud tal.; lat. 11° 03′; long. 76° 06′; from Calicut S.E. 24 miles; from Cannanore S.E. 72 miles; from Madras W.S.W. 320 miles; from Manantoddy S. 51 miles; from Munjery S.W. 6 miles; from Palghaut W.N.W. 44 miles; from Ponnany N.N.E. 20 miles; from Tellicherry S.E. 61 miles; from the sea E. 15 miles. Centre for many years of Moplah [q.v.] fanatical outbreaks. In consequence of two such risings in 1841 and 1843, native troops were stationed here; but as they proved useless during the outbreaks of 1849 and 1851, a detachment of European troops has since been quartered. Since 1873 the soldiers have been three times called out to deal with Moplah fanatics. A special police force, consisting of one European inspector, four European head constables and eighty constables is now stationed here. They are relieved from ordinary Police duty and only deal with local outbreaks. Public bungalow [q.v.], barracks for European troops. Tippoo [q.v.] had a fort here, now in ruins.——*Malasa* (மலச - malasa, obl., Tam.). Short form of tamul Malaiyarasa [mulcer].——*Malavauram* (മലവാരം - malavάram, Mal.). From (above + váram, mal. tax). Tax on hill land cleared.——*Malayalam* (മലയാളം - malayálam, Mal.). From (malai, tam. mountain + ázham, tam. depth). From the abrupt slope. Also in old books Malayarma. No such word known to earlier Greeks. In Cosmas Indicopleustes writing especially about Ceylon, the adjacent country of μαλέ whence the pepper [q.v.] comes is mentioned. This is Tamul மலை a hill, probably from Tamul settlers in Ceylon.—"*a*" The country lying between Neeleshwar river and Cape comorin and the sea and ghauts. Compare Keralam, which is a wider term. See vol. I (51). The whole space was geographically divided into four parts Colanaud, Yairaud, Perimpadapp, Vainaud.—"*b*" The Malayalam language is, like Codoon tamul, an immediate dialect of Shen tamul [q.v.]. Has lost all its verb personal terminations. Written in three characters, Aryam, Kolezhoot [q.v.], and Vattezhoot [q.v.]. The first is a variety of the Grantam [q.v.] and expresses the Nagry [q.v.] alphabet [varnamaulay]; the second is the character in which public grants are drawn up; and the third, the clipped or abbreviated letter, is only a modification of the second. Both the latter differ little from Tamul, except in the mode of joining the vowels to the consonants and in the manner of writing. There is a large intermixture of Sanscrit in the vocabulary. See vol. I (50), (51), (52), (58); II, 110.——*Malayam* (मलय - malaya, San.). The travancore hills.——*Malayamaun* (மலையமான் - malaiyamán, Tam.). From (above + mán, tam. suffix showing possessor). Epithet of any king of the Chera [q.v.] race, as lord of a hilly country.——*Malayauly* (മലയാളി - malayáli, Mal.; மலையாளி - malaiyáli, Tam.). From (above + áli, tam. ruler).—"*a*" A native of Malabar.—"*b*" Also a tribe inhabiting the hill ranges of North and South arcot and Salem districts, especially the Shevaroys; engaged chiefly in pastoral and agricultural pursuits. According to traditions these originally emigrated from Conjeeveram about 600 years ago, on account of religious persecution. They tenaciously cling to their common origin and shrink from alliances with the people of the plains. In features and physical appearance and dress they scarcely differ from inhabitants of the adjoining country, and speak Tamul somewhat corrupted. The chief deity is Cauly [q.v.], in whose honor they celebrate a feast once a year lasting fifteen days. During this time no one from the plains approaches them. Marriage ceremonies are performed without the intervention of Bramins [q.v.]. The traces of ancient polyandric institutions still survive. In certain localities it is imperative on a widow to marry again. Even at 80 years of age a widow is not exempted from this rule. The houses are long, low, thatched structures, with the roofs secured by long bamboos pegged down at intervals. Each hut stands in a yard surrounded by a palisade of wattled bamboos. The village precincts are regarded as sacred; and even Bramins are desired to walk barefoot along their alleys. In certain districts villages resemble clusters of enlarged beehives, houses being circular and raised on wooden piles about two feet high. The walls are of split bamboo [q.v.] coated with mud; roof conical and thatched with long coarse grass [cooray]. Numbers about 70,000 [jauty]. See vol. II, 82,124.——*Maldaivy* (మాలదేవి - maldévi, Tel.). From (mala, tel. mountain + dévi, tel. goddess). Sanscrit name (malat'ha), meaning sin-taker. River; Nellore dist., Nellore tal. Takes its rise in the calingula [q.v.] of Caligherry reservoir [sangam]. Pearls [moty] were found formerly.——*Maley* (ಮಲೆ - male, Can.; మల - mala, Tel.; மலை - malai, Tam.). Hill; suffix in place names [mullay].——*Maliah* (మాలియ - máliya, Tel.). From (mala, tel. mountain). High lands in Ganjam district formed by the irregular chain of the Eastern ghauts [q.v.]. In the Ganjam maliahs there are three plateaux. One is from the Boad frontier to a line drawn from Oodayagherry in the Goomsoor maliahs and Sarangada of Chinna kimedy. This is flat and uninteresting and differs but little in appearance and produce from the plains near the foot of the hills. The second is considerably higher with fine hills and valleys intersecting it in every direction, and extends from this line to a line drawn from Noovaugada in the Parlakimedy maliahs to Mahendragherry. The third, from this to the Vizagapatam frontier, is again lower than the central one and less picturesque. The mean elevation of the central plateau is 2,000 feet, that of the other two is considerably less. Balligooda is 2,200 feet, Soobarnagiry 2,445 feet, and Dosragaum a little more above sea-level. The chief peaks are Dodosoro, near Reikyah, 3,800 feet, in the Goomsoor maliahs; Singarauz 4,976 feet, and Mahendragherry 4,923 feet, in the Soorangy maliahs; and Deodangar or Ojjeigodo 3,941 feet, in Parlakimedy. The chief passes [ghaut] into the Ganjam maliahs are as follows. To begin with the easiest, that from Russellcondah by Doorgaprasaud known as the Calingyah ghaut, is a bandy [q.v.] road quite practicable for carts. Proceeding southward, the next ghaut is Pippalpunka by Gajellabady to Daringabaudy, a long and stony road. After that the Cuttingia ghaut from Sooradah viâ Meercote to Cuttingia. The next is the Hot spring or Taptapauny ghaut from Digoopoody to Lohogoody. Further south is the Pooypauny ghaut from Serangy viâ Noovaugada to Cheligodo. Last is the Moonshingy ghaut in Parlakimedy from Kimedy to Goomma. These are all passable by loaded elephants [q.v.] and horses [ghorah] and men. There are other paths used by the hill-people. From Calingyah, the top of the first ghaut named, besides the Boad road there is a road completely bridged to Balligooda, and an alternative road to the same place viâ Sarangada and Coortely. From Balligooda there are roads to Baracoma and Toomaribund, and one which traverses the length of the Maliah country from Balligooda towards Goomma known as the Grand military road. The more important Maliahs of Ganjam are given below; they take their names from the contiguous tracts in the plains. The Goomsoor maliahs, population 49,750, Khonds [q.v.] chiefly, containing the following mittahs [q.v.]:—Baurah, Chocapaud, Coradah, Hodogodo, Lanipoda, Oteero, Tentooligodo. The Daringabaudy maliahs, population 6,761, Khonds chiefly, containing the mittahs of Cuttingia and Daringabaudy. The Bodagooda maliahs, population 16,810, Khonds chiefly, containing the following mittahs:—Boodooly, Corchobady, Gondogoto, Govindapooram, Jhiliky, Jorow, Kondhoodoba, Lohogoody, Meercote, Moheno, Odoba. Chinna kimedy maliahs, population 46,264, Khonds chiefly, containing the following mittahs:—Balligooda, Baracoma, Bodagooda, Codootooly, Comonkolla, Coortumgar, Cotgodo, Gadapore, Mahashingy, Mirikyah, Moondigar, Panigonda, Poosangyah, Roomisy, Sarangada, Toomaribund. Pedda kimedy maliahs, population 29,512, chiefly Sowrahs [q.v.] containing the following mittahs:—Bodopoda, Cotodesho maliah, Jalarshingy goomah, Keradango goomah, Kojiripoda, Noovaugada, Oodayagherry, Ramgiry goomah. Parlakimedy maliahs, population 19,201, chiefly Sowrahs, containing the following mittahs:—Boomulshingy, Geiba, Gondahutty, Goomma, Jirango, Koniporo, Lohkniyagodo, Narayanaporo, Naumangoro, Ojoyogodo, Ryegodo, Serangy. The Boodaurasinghy, Jalantra, Jarada, Mundasa and Soorangy maliahs are comparatively small and of little importance. Their inhabitants are chiefly Sowrahs. The several mittahs have always formed part of the zemindarries [q.v.] whose name they bear, but in 1875 special hill sunnuds [q.v.] were granted for them to the Zemindars [q.v.] concerned; under these sunnuds, their alienation by sale or otherwise was forbidden. For the administrative arrangements, see volume I, 71.——*Mulcer* (மலசர் - malasar, Tam.). English corruption for Malaiyarasa [malasa].——*Mullay* (ಮಲೆ - male, Can.; మల - mala, Tel.; മല - mala, Mal.; மலை - malai, Tam.). Mountain [mala, maley]. The principal mountains in this Presidency are the Western ghauts, or Sahyadry range, running for 800 miles along the shore of the Arabian sea. The range increases to 6,000 feet in height along the borders of Mysore and joins the Neilgherries; highest summit, Dodabetta, 8,760 feet, the highest point but one [anamoody] in Southern india. South of the Neilgherries, and separated from them by the Palghaut valley, a gap 20 miles broad, lies an unnamed range, continuing the Western ghauts for 200 miles to Cape comorin. From the eastern parts of the Neilgherry mountains extend several ranges towards north-east as far as the Godavery, with an average elevation of about 1,500 feet. These ranges are called the Eastern ghauts. There are several detached groups as the Shevaroy hills, north of Salem; highest summit, Moottanaud [green hills], 5,260 feet high. Besides the principal mountains mentioned above there are the Nagary hills in North arcot; the Varauhagherry or Pulney hills in Madura; and the Cuddapah hills between Cuddapah and Nellore [ghaut].——*Mullay chaurp* (மலைச்சார்பு - malaiççárbu, Tam.). Hilly country.——*Mullay poonam* (மலைப்புனம் - malaippunám, Tam.). Rocky soil.——*Mulnaud* (ಮಲನಾಡು - malanádu, Can.). Any hilly country. Especially western part of Mysore.

MALABATHRUM (तमालपत्र - tamálapatra, *San.*). From (tamála, san. cassia cinnamon + pattra, san. leaf). Title from sanscrit, omitting first syllable. Greek *μαλάβαθρον*. In former days this was the dried leaf of various wild species of cinnamomum [cinnamon]. Classical export from India.

MALACA (మలక - malaka, *Tel.*). Bullock load [pothy].——*Malacapootty* (మలకపుట్టి - malakaputti, Tel.). From (above + putti, tel. a grain measure). Measure of capacity. 2½ pullepootties = 1 malacapootty; 3 malacapootties = 1 garce [alavay, 3b.] Approx. actual value, 1 malacapootty = 32 cubic feet and 704 cubic inches. Godavery. Also sub-divided into 20 tooms.

MALACCA (ملاكا - malakka, *Malay*; மலாக்கா - malákká, *Tam.*). Means emblic myrobalan, phyllanthus emblica, linn., plant being abundant there. Town and territory on western side of Malay peninsula, washed by straits which bear its name. The town is in lat. 2° 20′ N.; long. 102° 00′ E., at mouth of small river. Malacca was taken by the Portuguese under Albuquerque in 1511; became a Dutch possession in 1642; fell in 1795 into the hands of the British, to whom it was finally ceded in 1824. Part of the Indian empire till 1867, when transferred to the colonial office and since a crown colony. Term also applied to the whole of the Malay peninsula. Distinguish from Moluccas. See vol. I, 31.——*Malacca bean* (ملاکہ کی پھلی - malákahkíphalli, Hind.). Marking-nut.——*Malacca benzoin* (மலாக்காசாம்பிராணி - malákkásámbiráni, Tam.). Same as Benzoin.——*Malacca cane* (ملاکہ کی بید - malákahkíbed, Hind.). The cane of Calamus scipionum, lour. Stems are thicker than Calamus rotang [country rattan]. Prized as walking sticks. Some are of a uniform rich brown color, others are variously mottled. Imported from Singapore and Malacca.——*Malacca jamboo* (ملاکہ کا جام - malákakájam, Hind.). Same as Malacca jaumoon [q.v.]——*Malacca yam* (زمینی کندا - zamínikandá, Hind. and Dec.; మలాకాకాయపెండలము - malákákáyapendalamu, Tel.; കാട്ടുകാച്ചിൽ - káttukáççil, Mal.; පනුකොන්දොල් - panukondol, Singh.; காட்டுவள்ளி - káttuvalli, Tam.). Hind. from (zamín, hind. ground + kandá, hind. root) [telinga potato]. Tel. from (maláká, tel. malacca + káya, tel. fruit + pendalamu, tel. dioscorea). Mal. from (kátu, mal. forest + káççil, mal. dioscorea alata, linn.). Singh. from (panu, singh. living + kondol, singh. yam). Tam. from (kádu, tam. forest + valli, tam. dioscorea). Tam. also (káyvalli), meaning fruit + dioscorea, from bulbous yams; (shíragavalli), meaning cumin seed, cuminum cyminum, linn. + dioscorea, from similar smell of plant; (káttukkáyvalli), meaning wild + fruit + dioscorea; (káttuççíragavalli), meaning wild + cumin + dioscorea. Title otherwise Bulbous-rooted yam, Cummin yam, Granada yam, Guinea yam, Zameen cundah. Botanically Helmia bulbifera, kth., dioscoreaceæ [vricsham, 132]. Alias Dioscorea bulbifera. Shrub, leaves alternate, deeply cordate, acuminate, seven-nerved; the exterior nerves two-cleft; transverse veins reticulated; stem bulbiferous; male spikes fasicled; west coast. Root applied to ulcers after being dried and powdered; bulb on stem and roots used as vegetables; the latter are bitter, but after process of being covered over with ashes and steeped in cold water, they become eatable. Other common species are:—Dæmona, called tiger-root, nauseous even boiled; Hirsuta; Tomentosa. For the dioscorea genus see Auloo.

MALATTAUR (மலட்டாறு - malattáru, *Tam.*). From (maladu, tam. barren + áru, tam. river). River; South arcot dist., Tricalore and Cuddalore tals. An offshoot from the Ponniaur, which it leaves eight miles east of Tricalore, falling into the Guddilam three miles west of Panrooty.

MALAY (ملی - male, *Malay*). Race of people inhabiting the Malayan peninsula and the Western islands of the Archipelago. Also their language.——*Malay almond* (ملے کا بادام - malekábádam, Malay). Same as Catapang.——*Malay apple* (ملے کا میوہ - malekámewah, Hind.). Same as Malacca jaumoon.——*Malay camphor* (ملے کا کافور - malekákáfúr, Hind.). Product of Dryobalanops aromatica, colebr., dipterocarpeæ [vricsham, 24].——*Malay earth gall* (ملے کا ماجو پھل - malekámájúphal, Hind.). Same as Mongoose snake root.——*Malay red wood* (چندن کا جھاڑ - chandankájhár, Dec.; سنتور - santur, Malay; చేవమాను - chévamánu, Tel.; சேவமரம் - shévamaram, Tam.). Dec. from (chandan, dec. redwood, santalum album, linn. + jhár, dec. tree). Tel. from (chéva, tel. red heart-wood + mánu, tel. tree) [soymida]. Tam.

from teloogoo. Tam. also (sháyamaram), meaning color + tree. Title otherwise False mangosteen, Santoór, Wild mangosteen. Botanically Sandoricum indicum, cav., meliaceæ [vricsham, 36]. Generic name from malay. Alias Mella koetjape; Trichilia nervosa, venosa. Lofty tree; leaves 6–18 inches; leaflets 3–8 by 1¼–4⅜ inches; common petiole 1½–6 inches; flowers ⅓ inch long; calyx about $\frac{1}{16}$ inch; stigmas truncate; fruit about 3 inches diameter; pulp fleshy acid, with a peculiar smell. Small or middling-sized tree; flowers numerous, small, yellow; berry nearly round, size of small orange [q.v.], slightly villous when ripe, yellow; has a fleshy acid pulp. Root bitter and used medicinally. The fruit is eaten and made into jelly. Sapwood grey; heart-wood red, moderately hard, close-grained, takes good polish; used for carts and boat-building.——*Malay sandal* (سنتور - santur, Malay). Same as Malay red wood.——*Malay upas* (چنڈال - chandál, Hind.). Same as Sack tree.——*Moley* (மலாய் - maláy, Tam.). A kind of curry [q.v.] corruption of Malay.

MALDA (مالدا - máldá, *Hind.*). A district of Bengal north of Ganges noted for the manufacture of silk [puttoo] and indigo [q.v.]. Had an English silk factory, now known as English bazaar.——*Malda dye* (پنڈالو - pindálú, Dec.; ಕಾಡುಗೆಣಸು - kádugenasu, Can.; మానుపెండలము - mánupendalamu, Tel.; മരക്കിഴങ്ങ് - marakkizhannu, Mal.; மரவள்ளி - maravalli, Tam.). Dec. from sanscrit meaning ball-like yam. Can. from (kádu, can. wild + genasu, can. dioscorea). Tel. from (mánu, tel. tree + pendalamu, tel. dioscorea). Mal. from (maram, mal. wood + kizhannu, mal. root). Tam. from (maram, tam. tree + valli, tam. the plant, ipomœa batatas, lamk); from fleshy root. Hind. also (rotíálu), meaning bread potato. Dec. also (pindalam). Can. also (maragenasu), meaning tree + the plant; (kanagala). Tel. also (karrapendalamu), meaning stick + the plant; dioscorea. Mal. also (maravélikkizhannu), meaning wood + hedge + root; (marachinikkizhannu), meaning wood + foreign root; (vélikkizhannu), meaning hedge + root, from being planted as hedgestakes; (púlakkizhannu), meaning bombax malabaricum, dec. + root [long zedoary]; (chinakkantal), meaning chinese root; (ézhilakkizhannu), meaning seven leaves + root, from the palmate leaves. Tam. also (álvalli), meaning useful yam + the plant; (malaiççarkkaraivalli), meaning mountain + ipomœa batatas, lamk. Title otherwise Brazilian arrowroot, Cassareep, Cassava, Cipips, Mandioc, Manioc, Maravully tree, Mountain sweet potato, Mousache, Sweet potato, Tapioca. Botanically Manihot utilissima, pohl., euphorbiaceæ [vricsham, 118]. Alias Janipha manihot; Jatropha manihot. Stems white, crooked, 6–7 feet, smooth, covered with protuberances from the fallen leaves; branches crooked; leaves palmate, divided nearly to their base into five lanceolate, entire lobes, attenuated at both extremities, dark green above, glaucous beneath; midrib prominent below, of a yellowish-red color; panicles axillary and terminal, 4–5 inches long; male flowers smaller than the female; calyx purplish on the outside, brownish within, segments five, spreading, divided nearly to the base; female flowers deeply five-parted, with lanceolate-ovate segments; root oblong, tuberous; capsule ovate, triangular, tricoccous; seeds elliptical, black, shining; flowers small, reddish; shrub of tropical america, introduced here by portuguese; thrives on most barren soil. The large fleshy root is full of venomous juice, chemically hydrocyanic acid, which if taken internally produces death; in manufacture the root is rasped, and pulp well bruised and thoroughly washed, after which the mass is placed on iron plates and heated; in this way the venom is driven off, and the residue or fecula becomes cassava flour or cassava starch; lumps of this again are heated, and by agglutination form cakes fit for consumption; tapioca is the same substance differently treated and broken into small grains for use; extract made from the concentrated juice of the root called cassareep is a powerful antiseptic. From the juice red indians in south america prepare mandioc poison to tip arrows. Cassava flour is eaten with fish curry [q.v.] when rice [q.v.] is scarce; natives also cook the raw root for curries; tapioca is the well-known food; the expressed juice is sometimes fermented with treacle into an intoxicating fluid. Leaf gives here dye called green dye of malda [shauyam]. Wood soft.

MALEEDA (ملیدہ - malídah, *Hind.*). From (malídan, pers. to rub). A meal formed of pounded bread or cakes mixed with ghee [q.v.], sugar [q.v.], milk [paul].

MALFOOF (ملفوف - malfúf, *Hind.*). From (lafa, ar. to wrap). Enclosure in a cover.

MALIK (مالک - málik, *Hind.*; മാലിക - málika, *Mal.*). From (milk, ar. property) [maul, milk]. Proprietor, king. Attribute of god [allah]. Forms composite alam; as Abd ool malik, slave of god [ism]. Part of lacabs; as Malik oosh shorah, king of poets. Also a house title; as Malik ghoolaum dastgheer, alaumat + name; Malik ool masheikh, chief of the priests; Malik ool toojar, chief of the merchants [ism].——*Malik aslam khan* (ملک اسلم خان - malikaslamkhán, Hind.). Royal title + alam + honorific title. Fowjdar [q.v.] of Nellore from 1765 to 1772 and nephew of Nawaub [q.v.] wallajah [q.v.].——*Malikhana* (مالکانہ - málikána, Hind.; മാലിഖാന - málikhána, Mal.). Subsistence allowance granted to zemindars [q.v.], poligars [q.v.], and others, dispossessed of their estates, usually at the rate of ten per cent. on the collections actually made from their estates.——*Mulkangherry* (ملکنگری - mulkangiri, Hind.). See sep. title.——*Mullika* (ملکہ - malikah, Ar.). Queen. Part of lacab; as Mullikai jehaun, queen of the world [ism].

MALLOTUS (ملاتا - mallata, *Hind.*). From nepaulese. A genus [kamela].

MALPAUN (മല്പാൻ - malpán, *Mal.*). Syrian word, meaning doctor of divinity. Archdeacon with Malabar syrian christians.

MALPEY (ಮಾಲ್ಪೆ - malpe, *Can.*). Village; Port South Canara dist., Oodipy tal.; pop. 3,125; lat. 13° 21′; long. 74° 45′; from Mangalore N. 34 miles; from Oodipy W. 3 miles. Port of Oodipy. Small fishing village at mouth of Oodipy river. Daryah bahaudur ghur, an island off Malpey, forms sheltered anchorage. As regards trade one of the most important towns in the district. light close to the entrance of the river; Lat. 13° 20′; long. 74° 44′; white; fixed; 5 miles range; flagstaff; guide to vessels making the port; exhibited 1st October to 31st May.

MALWA (मालव - málava, *San.*). A table-land in Central india, north of Vindhya mountains. Governed in prehistoric times by Hindoo rajahs, one of whom was the celebrated Vicramadityan [q.v.], it passed into the hands of Mahomedans about the commencement of fourteenth century and continued in their possession till conquered by Mahrattas in eighteenth century. Now consists of many native states, the more important being Gwalior and Indore. Large quantity of opium is produced and exported.——*Malwa opium* (مالوی افیم - málví-afím, Dec.). Occurs in round or slightly flattened balls, weighing about ten ounces each; consistence like that of smyrna opium; appearance of section homogeneous; colour almost rusty brown, odour very powerful, taste intensely bitter and lasting [aphainam].

MAMIRAUN (ماميران - mámírán, *Ar.*; درخت ماميران - darakhtimámírán, *Pers.*; ماميران كا پير - mámíránkáper, *Hind.*; ماميران كا جهاڑ - mámíránkájhár, *Dec.*; පීතකරෝහිණී - pítakarosan, *Singh.*). Title from arabic. Greek μαμιρâς. Title otherwise Assamese golden-thread root, Coptis root, Huldy bachnaug, Mishmee bitter, Mishmi teeta. Botanically Coptis teeta, wall., ranunculaceæ [vricsham, 1]. Specific through assamese from san. (tikta), bitter. Rootstalk horizontal, golden yellow, woody, densely fibrous, very bitter; leaves glabrous; petioles 6–12 inches; leaflets 2–3 inches, ovate-lanceolate, pinnatifid, lobes incised, terminal largest; scape slender, equalling the leaves; flowers one to three-pedicelled, bracts leafy; sepals ¼ inch, oblong-lanceolate, acute; petals narrow, ligulate, obtuse, ⅔ shorter than the sepals. Creeping-rooted, three-leaved, low plant, native of assam; the roots are nearly cylindrical and uneven, scabrous, more or less curved, of a greyish brown color externally, internally bright yellow, varying in thickness from the size of a crow quill to double that diameter; taste intensely and purely bitter, very lasting, with only a slight aroma; on mastication the root tinges the saliva yellow. Sold in bazaars [q.v.] as a bitter tonic; substituted for british gentian [chiretta] calumba [q.v.] and cinchona [koinah]; gives to pharm. mishmi tita, coptidis radix; officinal.

MAMODEESA (മാമോദീസ - mámódísa, *Mal.*). Baptism with the Malabar syrian christians.

MAMOOL (معمول - mamúl, *Hind.*; மாமூல் - mámúl, *Tam.*). From (aml, ar. action) [amal]. Custom. Immemorial custom is declared by Menoo [q.v.] to be the root of all law. It is the vital spirit of the Hindoos and the immediate cause of the permanence of their institutions. Cf. Auchauram, Maryauday.

MAN (मन् - man, *San.*). To think.——*Manas* (मनस् - manas, San.). From (man, san. to think). Mind, sign of Mahat [q.v.], an organ of action and of perception and action. The heart, the will, the seat of desire and consciousness. According to Vishnoo pooraunam [q.v.], manas is that which considers the consequences of acts to all creatures, and provides for their happiness.——*Manmatan* (मन्मथ - manmat'ha, San.). From (manas, san. mind + mat'h, san. to agitate). The god of love. The Cauman of the north. Manmatan is represented in the south as a natural man, with a crown on his head; and his ears, neck, breast, arms, hands, feet, and the remaining part of his body, are adorned with various ornaments of pearls [moty], precious stones [ratnam], gold [pon], and silver [velly]. On his shoulders he wears a Bauhoo puttay or shoulder girdle. In one of his hands he holds a bow of sugarcane [q.v.], with a string of insects; and in the other an arrow, ready for discharge. On his back he carries a quiver, with the Puncha baunam [caunia baunam] or five sorts of arrows, consisting of five kinds of flowers. His standard is a fish [matsyam]; his vehicle is a parrot [totah]; and the color of his body is yellow. Raty [q.v.] his wife is represented as a female with long black hair braided into a pig tail that reaches to the ground. Like her husband she wears a crown, and is on the whole adorned and equipped similar to him. Manmatan has no pagodas [q.v.] and is not worshipped, but the poets make much use of his name. Books specially devoted to his praise are:—Nellaimaulay, Manthoonool, Viralividoo tooth. Among his numerous epithets may be specified:—Anangan or bodiless;

Angajan or body-born; Carootliya caroop villy or the designing sugar-cane-man; Caumy or the lustful; Chittajan or mind-born; Einganaykizhavan or the lord of the five flower arrows; Madanan or the wanton; Madhoo sakhan or the friend of spring; Manoblavan or mind-born; Manojan or mind-born; Mauran or killer; Meenoorcodiyooyurttone or bearer of the fish-standard; Mohan or the lustful; Oorvilly or beautiful bow-man; Poovauly or he with the flower arrow; Raticauthalan or raty's husband; Shambaraury or destroyer of shambaran; Shengan maul meindan or vishnoo's son; Tenraltairone or he whose chariot is the south wind; Tirmagalmaindan or the son of the divine daughter; Villy or the bow-man. Manmatan creates love both in mortals and celestials, but more especially in the female sex, whilst his wife Raty causes love in the male sex [matam]. ——*Manobhavan* (मनोभव - manóbhava, San.). From (manas, san. mind + bhú, san. to be). Mind-born or created by fancy or imagination; Manmatan.——*Manojan* (मनोज - manója, San.). From (manas, san. mind + jan, san. to be born). Mind-born; like manobhavan. Manmatan.——*Manoshilay* (मनश्शिला - manashshilá, San.; زرنيخ احمر - zirníkhiahmar, Ar.; زرنيخ سرخ - zirníkhisurkh, Pers.; منسل - mansal, Hind.; لال هرتال - lálhartál, Dec.; ورنگن - warangan, Malay; ಮಣಿಶಿಲೆ - manishile, Can.; మణిశిల - manishila, Tel.; മനോല - manóla, Mal.; රත්සිරියල් - ratsiriyal, Singh.; மனோசிலை - manósilai, Tam.). San. from (manas, san. orpiment + shilá, san. stone). Ar. from (zirníkh, ar. arsenic + ahmar, pers. red). Pers. from (zirníkh, ar. arsenic + surkh, pers. red). Hind. from sanscrit. Dec. from (lál, hind. red + hartál, hind. orpiment). Mal. from sanscrit. Singh. from (rat, singh. red + siriyal, singh. arsenic). Tam. from sanscrit. Hind. also (lálsumbul), meaning, red arsenic. Tam. also (kuthiraipparbásánam), meaning horse-tooth arsenic. Realgar. Otherwise Red arsenic [paushaunam], Impure bisulphate of arsenic, Sulphuret of arsenic, Red orpiment. Arsenicum rubrum, bisulphuretum, disulphidum, of chemists. Aurora-red color, which passes through scarlet red, and hyacinth-red; lighter in weight than yellow orpiment [hartaul], contains less sulphur [gandhac]; internally shining, otherwise soft, brittle, and frangible; tasteless, and insoluble in water. Imported from China. Purified by being rubbed with the juice of lemons [q.v.] or of ginger [q.v.]; used internally in fever, skin diseases, cough, asthma, &c., externally in skin diseases; in fever, it is generally used in combination with mercury [rasam], orpiment [hartaul], &c. Used as a coloring substance [shauyam] as well as in pyrotechnical compounds [baunam].——*Manwantaram* (मन्वन्तर - manvantara, San.). From (manu, san. sovereign of earth + antara, san. interval). The period or age of a Menoo [q.v.]. A period equal to seventy-one times the number of years contained in the four yoogs [q.v.], with some additional or sundhyay [q.v.] years. This is the duration of the Menoo, the attendant divinities, and the rest, which is equal to 852,000 divine years, or to 306,720,000 years of mortals, independent of the additional period. Fourteen times this period constitutes a Bramha day [dinam], that is a day light of Bramha [q.v.] or a Calpam [q.v.]. Total 308,448,000 solar sidereal years [maunam]. The seven past manwantarams, agree in number with seven successive periods or Yomim of creation, recorded in the 1st chapter of Genesis, in the seventh of which periods the world now is. Cf. the epistle of St. Jude, in the expression "Enoch, the seventh from Adam."——*Matam* (मत - mata, San.; மதம் - matham, Tam.). From (man, san. to think).—"*a*" Religion, principle. The development of the Hindoo religion took place in three periods, the Vedic, Epic, and Pooraunic. The knowledge of the first is derived from the Veda [q.v.]; of the second from the Ramayanam [q.v.] and the Mahabhaurat [q.v.]; of the last from the Pooraunams [q.v.] and Tantrams [q.v.]. For the Dravidian religion as found, see vol. I (70) to (94), and the following foot notes:—history of rel. and phil. I (70), consp. of pantheon I (77), devil worship I (80), serpent worship I (82), sectarian marks I (85), existing hindoo sects I (88), jeinas I (95).—"*b*" The seven matams or principles of authorship are according to Nunnool:—agreement or acquiescence; rejection or refutation; conditional adoption and rejection of other tenets; establishing and maintaining an hypothesis; inclining to, and adopting, one or other of two contrary opinions; exposing the faults of other works; unyielding and positive adherence to one's own opinions. ——*Maumsam* (मांस - mámsa, San.). From (man, san. to think); what makes one feel strong. Flesh. Eaten freely by lower orders when they can procure it. To Bramins it is forbidden food. Many medicinal uses. Flesh of tiger [pooly], boiled in mustard seed [rayaun] oil, used as an unguent for the body, is remedy for emaciation. Flesh of elephant [q.v.], boiled in mustard seed oil, is a remedy for Cochin leg [q.v.]. Bear's [ricsham] flesh is used for affections of the eyes, especially cataract. Flesh of jackal [q.v.], boiled in oil and rubbed on the loins, in use for hæmorrhoids. Flesh of male camel [ottagam] employed in diabetes. Flesh of buffalo [khoolgah], dog [nye], musk-deer [mrigam], monkey [bandar], black partridge [teetar], peacock [mayil], have all specific properties attached to them by veidyans [q.v.].——*Maumsicay* (मांसिका - mámsiká, San.). From (mámsa, san. worm); worm-killer. Title otherwise Copper-leaf, Three-seeded mercury. Botanically the Acalypha genus, euphorbiaceæ [vricsham, 118]. Shrubs, undershrubs, perennial or annual herbs, found in tropical and sub-tropical regions; leaves alternate, toothed or crenate, and nettle-like; flowers minute, usually green or reddish, and disposed in erect or drooping spikes; capsule three sided, three-celled and of the size of a pea [calanyam]. The species best known to the natives are:—fruticosa [chinny], indica [cooppamainy], spiciflorus [vuttatauly]. Other s. indian species indigenous or naturalized are:—alnifolia, brachystachya, capitata, ciliata, fallax, malabarica, paniculata.——*Maunam* (मान - mána, San.). Honor. Distinguish from Maunam, a measure [mau].——*Maunasam* (मानस - mánasa, San.). Conducive to mental contemplation; a lake in the Himalaya mountains, a lake in the world of Bramha [q.v.]; also name of a snake goddess.——*Maunavedan* (മാനവേദൻ - mánavédan, Mal.). From (mána, san. honor + véda, san. knowledge). Hindoo 2nd or pers. name [peyar].——*Mauna vicrama* (മാനവിക്രമ - mánavikrama, Mal.). From (mána, san. pride + vikrama, san. prowess). Name of the Zamorin [q.v.] to whom Calicut was given by Chermaun on his retirement to Mecca.——*Maunoosham* (मानुष - mánusha, San.). From (man, san. to think). Propitious to man. Epithet of certain signs of the zodiac [raushy]. ——*Maunyam* (मान्य - mánya, San.). From (mánya, san. respectable). Privilege. A land exempt from tax [teervay] in whole or in part. Generally land given to village servants [balootah]. Corresponds to the foreign word inam [maniyam, monigar]. Ardha maunyam is where the holder has a claim only to the government revenue [khiranj, teervay]. Sarwa maunyam is where the holder is entitled not only to the revenue of the state, but the rents of the cultivators.——*Mautangy* (मातङ्गी - mátangí, San.). From (mata, san. will + gam, san. go). The young woman; Bhadra cauly [q.v.] or Mauriyamman [q.v.].——*Menoo* (मनु - manu, San.; మనువు - manuvu, Tel.). From (man, san. to think). Thought; man. Compare μίνως in Greek, Manes in Lydian, Mannus the early Teutonic leader and legislator, the Cretan minos, the Egyptian menes, &c. In the Vedic legend of the flood [pralayam] the man saved by the fish is called Menoo. Title of 14 patriarchs who preside successively over the same number of Manwantarams of which with sundhyays [q.v.] the Calpam [q.v.], bright-half of Bramha's day [dinam] is composed. Each rules during seventy-one Mahayoogs [q.v.], amounting altogether to 994 Mahayoogs for the fourteen. Besides these, in order to complete the bright-half of Bramha's day, are required six more Mahayoogs which are the Sundhyay. There are seven Menoos past and seven others to come. The Jeinas [q.v.] have 14 Menoos, to whom they give names different from those found in Hindoo pooraunams [q.v.]. The calpam formerly consisted only of nine manwantarams. Five have been interpolated. Festivals are held for the commemoration of the patriarchs according to the following table compiled from the Vishnoopooraunam [q.v.]:—

No.	Name of Menoo.	Lunar month.	Pacsham.	Tity.	
				Numeral.	Name.
1	Swauyambhoovan	Caurteecam	Shooclam.	12	Dwaudashy.
2	Swarochishan ...	Aushweejam	Do. ..	9	Navamy.
3	Oottaman	Cheitram ...	Do. ...	3	Triteeyay.
4	Taumasan ...	Bhaudrapadam.	Do. ...	3	Triteeyay.
5	Reivatan	Pooshyam ...	Do. ...	11	Yecaudashy.
6	Ieshwauk	Ashaudham.	Do. ...	10	Dashamy.
7	Veivaswatan ...	Maugham ...	Do. ...	7	Saptamy.
8	Bramha sauvarny.	Phaulgoonam	Do. ...	15	Powrnimay.
9	Roodra sauvarny.	Ashaudham.	Krishnam	8	Ashtamy.
10	Dacsha sauvarny.	Caurteecam	Do. ...	8	Ashtamy.
11	Agny sauvarny ...	Shrauvanam.	Do. ...	30	Amavausyay
12	Soorya sauvarny.	Bhaudrapadam.	Do. ...	8	Ashtamy.
13	Rowchyan ...	Cheitram ..	Shooclam.	15	Powrnimay.
14	Bhowtyan ...	Jyeshtam ...	Do. ...	15	Powrnimay.

The name is most commonly met with now in connection with the Maunava dharma shastram [dharma shastram], which purports to have been uttered by the first Menoo, the son of Bramha [q.v.]. The compilation is an irregular compendium of rules and maxims by different authors, which existed unwritten for a long period of time, and were then handed down orally. The contents of the twelve books may be ranged under six principal heads:—Veda, sacred knowledge and religion; Vedauntam, philosophy in general; Auchauram, social duties; Vyavahauram, civil and criminal law; Prauyaschittam, penance;

Carmapalam.——*Mimaumsam* (मीमांस - mímámsa, San.). See sep. title.——*Moony* (मुनि - muni, San.). See sep. title.

MANA (മന - mana, *Mal.*). House of Bramins and Numboories. Different names for houses in Malabar according to castes are the following:—Mana, numboodripaud; Illam, numboory; Covilagam, cottauram, rajah; Yidam, naudvauly; Coottaula, naudvauly; Veed, nayar; Pooshpacam, ambalavausy; Pishauram, ambalavausy; Vauryam, ambalavausy; Mutt, chaukyaur, puttar; Coody, chaulyar; Peedica, moplah; Poora, teeyan; Chaula, cherooman; Poora, blacksmith, goldsmith, silversmith, carpenter, brazier.——*Manay* (निवेशन - nivéshana, San.; ಮನೆ - mane, Can.; மனை - manai, Tam.). A house; house-site. So land measure equal to 2,400 coozhies, or square feet, or the 24th part of a cawny [q.v.]; the proper form is a parallelogram of 60 feet by 40 [ground]. Cf. Tel. ancanam. Manay chit is a title-deed; Manay vary is house-tax; Manay veed, from (vídu, tam. house) is a house and grounds; also building site [nuttam]. See vol. I, 609; II, 514.——*Munny* (మన్ని - manni, Tel.). Tel. form of manay [q.v.] and ground [q.v.].

MANAM (மணம் - manam, *Tam.*). Fragrance, marriage. ——*Manatakkauly* (மணத்தக்காளி - manattakkáli, Tam.). From (manam, tam. fragrance + takkáli, tam. physalis). Same as Indian hound's berry.——*Manavaula maumoony* (रम्यजामातृ मुनि - ramyajámátrimuni, San.; மணவாளமாமுனி - manaválamámuni, Tam.). From (manaválan, tam. marriage ruling man, hence husband or male person + má, tam. great + muni, san. sage). The opponent of Vedauntacharry at Conjeeveram and head of the Tengalays [q.v.] or conservative party among the Shreeveishnavas [q.v.], otherwise Ramaunoojeeyans. See vol. I (85).

MANAUKIB (مناقب - manákib, *Hind.*). From (nakaba, ar. to retail misfortunes). Hymns sung in the Moharram [q.v.].

MANCHAM (मञ्च - mañcha, *San.*). Platform; bedstead. ——*Machaun* (مچان - machán, Hind.). From (mañcha, san. platform). A scaffolding erected to watch for a tiger [pooly] to guard a field, &c.——*Manchua* (മഞ്ചി - mañchi, Mal.). From (mañcha, san. cot). Portuguese usage; also Munjy. A large cargo-boat, with a single mast and a square sail, used on the Malabar coast, from 10 to 40 tons [munjy].——*Manjeshwar* (ಮಂಜೇಶ್ವರ - manjéshvara, Can.; മഞ്ചിശ്വരം - mañchíshvaram, Mal.). From (above + íshvara, san. the lord). A Jeina [q.v.] deity. Village, Port, South canara dist., Cassergode tal.; pop. 2,608; lat. 12° 43′; long. 74° 56′; from Bombay S.S.E. 432 miles; from Cassergode N.N.W. 16 miles; from Coombla N.N.W. 7 miles; from Madras W. 360 miles; from Mangalore S. 12 miles; from Oolaul S.S.E. 9 miles. At mouth of a small stream on an inlet of Arbian sea. A large straggling town. The southern portion stands on a plain, and the northern on a steep bank that overhangs the river. These two portions were held by the petty Jeina [q.v.] bungar rajah and the Vittala rajah respectively, until Tippoo [q.v.] hanged the former and forced the latter to take refuge with the English at Tellicherry.——*Muncheel* (മഞ്ചൽ - mañchal, Mal.). From (mañcha, san. a bedstead). Hammock-litter on West coast, substitute for a palankeen [q.v.] or dhooly [q.v.]. Consists of a long and broad strip of canvas suspended at each end to a stout pole.——*Munjy* (മഞ്ചി - mañchi, Mal.). See sep. title.

MANCOOHA (منكوحه - mankúhah, *Hind.*) [nicka]. From (nikáh, ar. marriage). A woman married by the simple Nicka [q.v.] ritual. Takes a lower social place here than a wife married by Shaudy [q.v.] ceremony.

MANDEY (మండె - mande, *Tel.*). Title from teloogoo. Tel. from (mandu, tel. medicine). Tel. also (manchimande), meaning good medicine. Botanically Ceropegia bulbosa, roxb., asclepiadeæ [vricsham, 88]. Root tuberous, a little flattened like a turnip, with several fibres from its base; it is about as large as a small apple [seb]; stems twining, herbaceous, smooth, succulent; from 2 to 4 feet long; leaves opposite, short petioled, obovate with small point, entire, fleshy; size various; umbels lateral, length of the leaves, peduncled, few-flowered; flowers pretty large, erect, tube greenish, border purple; follicles two, slender, singly, about 3 or 4 inches long. Every part is eaten by natives, either raw or stewed in curries [q.v.]; the tubers when boiled lose their bitterness, and pulped with milk form a sweet mucilaginous mixture not unlike salep [q.v.], which is highly nutritious.

MAN EATER (வேங்கை - véngai, *Tam.*). Tam. from (vé, tam. to heat); impetuous animal. Old tiger or panther which has lost its teeth, or whose teeth are worn out, so that it takes human food by preference. See Pooly.

MANEY (منی - mane, *Hind.*). Highland.——*Maneysultan* (منی سلطان - manesultán, Hind.). Title of the Maharajah of Vizianagram. Also of Travancore rulers.

MANGALORE * (ಮಂಗಳೂರು - mangalúru, *Can.*; മംഗലാപുരം - mangalápuram, *Mal.*). From (mangalá, san. local deity + úru, can. village) [mungalam]. Sanscrit name (mangalápura), meaning same. Hind. name (kauriyálbandar). Greek νίτρα'ἐμπό-ριον; also μαγγάνουρ in Ptolemy. Mandegora of Arrian.——(1) Talook, South canara district. Tahsildar's pay Rs. 225. Area 620 square miles. Centre coast of district. Boundaries:—on the north, the Oodipy talook; on the south Cassergode talook; on the east, Ooppinangady talook and Mysore territory; on the west, Arabian sea. A hilly country intersected by rivers and streams. Soil mostly laterite [q.v.]. Principal industry is agriculture. Among minor industries are to be classed the manufacture of machine-made tiles [wode] and bricks [shengal], earthern-ware [chatty], coir [q.v.] and coir mats, brass [pittalay], tin [tagaram] and copper [taumram] vessels, weaving, printing, book-binding, coffee-curing, iron-casting. Imports consist of cloths, twist, salt, kerosine oil, oils, grains, dried fruits, porcelainware, hardware, spices, drugs, spirits, and wines. Exports coffee [q.v.] of Mysore and Coorg, rice [q.v.], other grains, arecanuts [q.v.], sandalwood, sandalwood [sandal] oil, jaggery [q.v.], cocoaunts [q.v.], pepper [q.v.], cardamoms [q.v.], sundry spices, &c. Irrigation mainly dependant upon rains, and in the dry season upon supplies of water drawn from rivers and streams and private wells and reservoirs. Camping grounds:—Buntwaul, Farangipett, Goorpore, Mangalore, Moodbidry, Moolky, Soortacull. Places of archæological interest:—Adyapaudy, Adyaur, Aladangady, Amataudy, Amoonajey, Balanja, Bangra cooloor, Banpanaud, Belina, Belvye, Bondamtilla, Cajeycaur, Cancanaudy, Cauntauvara, Caurandore, Caushiputna, Cauvala moodore, Cauvore, Chitraupoora, Conaja, Coodoopoo, Coonjatta byle, Cuddry, Goorpore, Haleynilla, Inna, Inoovully, Irveil, Kellapoottigay, Kempoonaja, Mangalore, Mauntraudy, Mogar, Moodbidry, Moodoo, Moondcoor, Moondore, Munchy, Nauraavy, Nellicaur, Nelliteerta, Niddody, Oolaul, Oolipaudy, Padoo, Padoocody, Padoo panambore, Panambore, Poottigey, Prauntya, Savanaul, Simantooroo, Someshwaram, Tirvyle, Woolaibett, Yeed, Yenoor. Principal trig. stations:—Anjaragoodda, Cunnore, Mangalore, Mijarra. The leading places, &c., in the talook are the following.——*Anjaragoodda* (ಅಂಜರಗುಡ್ಡ - anjaragudda, Can.). From (anjúra, can. fig, ficus carica, linn. + gudda, can. hill). Trig. station; lat. 13° 01′ 14·68″; long. 75° 04′ 17·08″.——*Ass' ears* (ಕೊಣಜದಕಲ್ಲು - konajadakallu, Can.). See sep. title.——*Balmatta* (ಬಳ್ಮಠ - balmat'ha, Can.). See sep. title.——*Bolore* (ಬೋಳೂರು - bólúru, Can.). From (bólu, can. hollowness + úru, can. village). Village; pop. 1,256. In Mangalore town. On bank of Goorpore river. Battery constructed by Tippoo [q.v.] sultan [q.v.] of granite [caroomcull] rock.——*Buntwaul* (ಬಂಟ್ವಾಳ - bantvála, Can.). See sep. title——*Cuddry* (كدری - kadrí, Hind.; ಕದ್ರಿ - kadri, Can.). Sanscrit name (kadali), meaning plantain. Village; pop. 1,677; from Mangalore N.E. 2½ miles; from the sea E. 3 miles. Old temple of Shree munjoonauta and a Jogy [q.v.] mutt [q.v.]. Just above the temple are nine tanks for bathing.——*Cunnore* (ಕಣ್ಣೂರು - kannúru, Can.). Trig. station; lat. 12° 51′ 56·68″; long. 74° 56′ 11·08″.——*Farangipett* (فرنگی پیٹھ - farangípeth, Hind.). From (farangí, hind. european + péte, can. town); from the portuguese having settled here. A hamlet, being portions of Arcoola and Pooda villages; lat. 12° 52′; long. 74° 59′; from Mangalore E. 7 miles; from the sea E. 9 miles. On north bank of Netrauvaty; has a traveller's bungalow [q.v.], a military encamping ground, and an old church and convent built during Portuguese settlement.——*Goorpore* (ಗುರುಪುರ - gurupura, Can.). See sep. title.——*Jappoo* (ಜಪ್ಪು - jappu, Can.). A hamlet of Mogar cusbah [q.v.] village. A suburb of Mangalore on northern bank of Netrauvaty; tile and brick factories, a coffee-curing establishment and a large seminary newly built by Jesuit mission.——*Manail* (ಮನೇಲು - manélu, Can.). Sanscrit name (pulinapura), meaning river-bank + town. Village. On N.E. bank of Goorpore river. Temple called Rajah rajeshwary ammanavara devastauna.——*Mangalore* (ಮಂಗಳೂರು - mangalúru, Can.). See below——*Mijarra* (ಮಿಜಾರು - mijáru, Can.). Village; pop. 2,608; lat. 13° 01′; long. 74° 59′; height 694 feet; from Mangalore N.N.E. 13 miles; from the sea E. 11 miles. Gold found on a hill called Moondabett in neighbouring village of Yedapadavoo. Trig. station in lat. 13° 03′ 23·00″; long. 74° 58′ 39·98″; from Mijarra N. 3 miles; from Mangalore N.N.E. 14 miles; from the sea E. 10 miles.——*Moodbidry* (ಮೂಡಬಿದ್ರಿ - múdabidri, Can.). See sep. title.——*Moolky* (ಮೂಲ್ಕಿ - múlki, Can.). See sep. title.——*Moondcoor* (ಮುಂಡ್ಕೂರು - mundkúru, Can.). Village; pop. 2,179; lat. 13° 07′; long. 74° 55′; from Mangalore N. 26 miles; from the sea E. 10 miles. Temple.——*Naurauvy* (ನಾರಾವಿ - nárávi, Can.). From (nára, can. water + ávi, can. vapour). Village; pop. 1,292; lat. 13° 08′; long. 75° 11′; from Mangalore N.E. 28 miles; from the sea E. 25 miles. Temple of Sooryanarrain, car festival in February.——*Netrauvaty* (ನೇತ್ರಾವತಿ - nétrávati, Can.). See sep. title.——*Nireshaulya* (ನಿರೆಶ್ವಾಲ್ಯ - nirashválya, Can.). From (nere, can. full + shalya, can. cloth). Village. Part of Mangalore; contains Collector's office.——*Oolaul* (ಉಳ್ಳಾಲ - ullála, Can.). Village, Port; pop. 5,703; acres 3,840; lat. 12° 50′; long. 74° 53′; from Bombay S.S.E. 422 miles; from Mangalore S. 2 miles; from Manjeshwar N. 10 miles. On south bank of Netrauvaty river. A ferry connects the south coast road with Mangalore. Former residence of a petty Jeina prince. Jeina [q.v.] basty [q.v.] of uncertain age. ——*Panambore* (ಪಣಂಬೂರು - panambúru, Can.). From (panambu, can. arrow + úru, can. village). Village; pop. 2,658; lat. 12° 56′; long. 74° 51′; from Mangalore N. 5 miles; from the sea E. 1 mile. Nundeeshwaran temple.——*Premeira* (ಮೂಲ್ಕಿಬಂಡೆ - múlkibande, Can.). See sep. title.——*Shumbavaty* (ಶಂಭವತಿ - shambhavati, Can.). See sep. title.——*Soortacull* (ಸುರ್ತಕಲ್ಲು - surtakallu, Can.). From (surata, san. great enjoyment + kallu, can. rock). Village; pop. 2,770; lat. 13° 00′; long. 74° 50′; from Mangalore N.N.W. 9 miles; from the sea E. ½ mile. Camping ground. Temple on a high rock on sea-shore, car festival at end of December.——*Valalunkey* (ವಳಲಂಕೆ - valalanke, Can.). A sub-division of talook comprising seven villages; pop. 3,871.——*Yenoor* (ಯೇಣೂರು - yénúru, Can.). See sep. title. ——**(2)** Sub-magistracy, South canara district. Pay Rs. 100. ——**(3)** Town, Cantonment, Head-quarters of Collector, Judge, Tahsildar, Deputy tahsildar, South canara dist., Mangalore tal.; pop. 40,922; lat. 12° 52′; long. 74° 53′; from Bombay S. 418 miles; from Coondapore S.S.E. 54 miles; from Goorpore S.W. 8 miles; from Madras W. 370 miles; from Moolky S.S.E. 16 miles; from Oodipy S.S.E. 38 miles; from Oolaul N. 2 miles; from Poottore W.N.W. 25 miles; from Seringapatam W. 130 miles; from Soobramanyam W.N.W. 53 miles. Light on a hill above the town, and near some high trees. Lat. 12° 52′; long. 74° 53′. White; fixed. 14 miles range. Visible from all directions seaward. Small white masonry tower. Guide to the anchorage. Town is on the backwater [cauyal] formed by the convergent mouths of Netrauvaty and Goorpore rivers. Connected with Mercara by a good road. Also with Mysore. Has water on three sides of it. Arabian dhonies [q.v.] and country craft enter harbour. Also steamers of light draught. The bar is impassable during monsoon [q.v.]. Boats of large size are carried as far as Buntwaul up the Netrauvaty. Mangalore is buried in groves of cocoanut [q.v.] trees. The monsoon sets in between May and June. The climate has a relaxing and debilitating effect. In 1547 Mangalore was desolated by the Portuguese. Being rebuilt in 1555, it was again destroyed by the same. It once more fell into the hands of the Portuguese, who destroyed every living being and burned the town. In 1567 finally occupied by the Portuguese, who built the fort St. sebastian and a church. In 1617 the Portuguese governor defeated the rajah of the small territory in the vicinity and compelled him to cede a portion of his possessions. In 1640 Mangalore was still in the hands of the Portuguese, but subsequently wrested from them by the Rajah of Bednore. Occupied by Hyder ally in 1763. All his and Tippoo's ships built here. Taken by the British, 1768; retaken by Hyder ally, 1768; a second time surrendered to the English, 1783; yielded to Tippoo sultan, 1783. In 1784 was concluded the treaty of Mangalore between the East india company and Tippoo sultan. In 1799 Mangalore became British territory. Since that time the only disturbance has been during the Coorg insurrection in 1837, when the rebels entered the town, burnt the cutcherry [q.v.], and then retired. The East india company held a monopoly from the rajah of the magazines here for sandalwood growing on the Mysore hills. Mangalore is at present garrisoned. The cantonment is north of the town on a level space, gently elevated, well-drained, and open to the sea breezes; and from these circumstances is healthy. The Mungala devy temple, which gives its name to the town, is an old one. There is a large native Roman catholic population with a European bishopric. Has two colleges, one maintained by Government, the other recently established by Jesuit mission. A few miles north is found a deposit of porcelain clay, closely resembling that of which Sevres ware is formed. Mangalore clears and exports all the coffee of Coorg and a great deal of that produced in the neighbouring plantations in Mysore, and trades directly with Arabia and the Persian gulf. The Basel lutheran mission has its head-quarters here. Good cloth is woven at their establishment; the making of roof-tiles, printing, and binding are also taught. Rice [q.v.] is the great article of export, more than three-fourths of the whole produce being sent to Muscat, Goa, Bombay, and Malabar. Betel-nut [q.v.], coffee [q.v.], black pepper [q.v.], sandal-wood [sandal], cassia [q.v.] and turmeric [country saffron] are also exported. Salt [ooppoo] is not manufactured but imported from Bombay and Goa. Raw silk [puttoo] for the use of the manufactures above the ghauts [q.v.], and sugar [q.v.] are imported from Bengal and China and oil and ghee [q.v.] from Surat. In Hyder's reign, the principal merchants were Moplahs and Concanies. Many men of property have however come since then from Surat, Cutch, Bombay and other places to the north. These persons are chiefly of the Veisya [q.v.] caste, but there are also some Parsees [q.v.], and the vessels employed in trade generally belong to other ports. Good water is only procurable in the dry season, and even then it is always more or less impregnated with iron [auhan] from the laterite [q.v.] through which it percolates. The small tanks in the neighbourhood are seldom dry, though in the hot weather the surface of the water becomes covered with slimy vegetable matter. Trig. station in lat. 12° 52′ 17·25″; long. 74° 53′ 10·48″; height; 196 feet; from Mangalore S. ½ mile; from the sea E. ¼ mile. The following are the travelling distances by road from Mangalore to different places:—

To	Via	Miles and Furlongs.	
Agoomby ...	Moodbidry	63	2
Bangalore ...	Sumpaujey ghaut, Mercara, Hoonsoor and Seringapatam.	242	4
Bangalore ...	The Manjarabad ghaut, Hassan and Coongal.	221	0
Bellary	Boond ghaut, Vastaura, Tarikerey and Chitaldroog.	285	7
Bellary	Manjarabad ghaut, Hassan, Bailore, Hooliyoor and Hurrihur.	301	6
Bellary	Agoomby ghaut, Shimoga and Hurrihur.	278	2
Bellary	Agoomby ghaut, Shimoga and Chitaldroog.	297	7
Bellary	Hyderghur ghaut, Hurrihur and Hospett.	235	0
Calicut	Cassergode, Cannanore and Tellicherry ...	145	2
Calicut	Puttoor and Cannanore	182	1
Cannanore ...	Cassergode	86	1
Cannanore ...	Puttoor and Pauney mangalore	123	0
Cassergode ...	......	29	0
Chikmagalore ...	Codicull ghaut and Vastaura	94	6
Cochin	Calicut and Cannanore	243	0
Coomtah ...	Oodipy and Honnore	123	3¼
Dharwar	Hyderghur ghaut and Hurrihur	265	1½
Dharwar	Agoomby ghaut, Shimoga and Hurrihur.	258	3½
French rocks ...	Sumpaujey ghaut, Mercara and Seringapatam.	169	5
Gersoppah falls...	Oodipy and Honnore	150	6½
Goa	Honnore and Coomtah	217	4
Hassan	Manjarabad ghaut	106	2
Honnore ... • ...	Oodipy and Coondapore	113	1¼
Hoonsoor ...	Sumpaujey ghaut and Mercara	131	2
Hurrihur ...	Agoomby ghaut and Shimoga	166	2
Hurrihur ...	The Hyderghur ghaut and Einore ...	173	0
Madras	Manjarabad ghaut, Bangalore and Ranipett.	426	7½
Madras	Sumpaujey ghaut, Mercara, Bangalore and Ranipett.	448	3½
Manjarabad ...	Pauney mangalore	78	4
Mercara	Sumpaujey ghaut	85	6
Mysore	Sumpaujey ghaut and Hoonsoor	160	1
Nugger	Hyderghur ghaut	90	0
Oodipy	Moolky	37	6
Quilon	Cannanore, Calicut and Cochin	331	1
Sadaushivaghur.	Honnore and Coomtah	163	6¾
Seringapatam ...	Sumpaujey ghaut and Hoonsoor	163	1
Shimoga	Agoomby ghaut	118	2
Shimoga	Hyderghur ghaut	141	1½
Trichinopoly ...	Cannanore, Palghaut, Coimbatore and Caroor.	389	4
Trichinopoly ...	Sumpaujey ghaut, Mysore and Caroor ...	370	1
Vastaura ...	Boond ghaut	88	5
Vellore	Manjarabad ghaut, Bangalore and Krishnagherry.	349	5
Yelwaul	Sumpaujey ghaut and Hoonsoor	150	6

MANGANESE (منغنيس - manghanís, *Hind.*). From arabic Manganesium of chemists. For local distribution, see vol. II, 36. No native uses known.

MANGO (आम्र - ámra, *San.*; अंब - amba, *Mahr.*; आंबो - ámbó, *Conc.*; شجرة الانبج - shajaratulambaj, *Ar.*; درخت انبه - darakhtiambah, *Pers.*; آنبک پیڑ - ámbkáper, *Hind.*; آم کا جھاڑ - ámkájhár, *Dec.*; مم پالم - mampálam, *Malay*; ಮಾವು - mávu, *Can.*; ಕುಕ್ಕು - kukku, *Too.*; మామిడి - mámidi, *Tel.*; ଅମ୍ବୋ - ambó, *Oor.*; മാവ് - mávu, *Mal.*; අඹ - amba, *Singh.*; மா - má, *Tam.*). Title by portuguese from malay through tamul (mángáy), the fruit. San. from (am, san. to afflict with sickness); generates disease. Mahr. and conc. from sanscrit. Ar. from (shajar, ar. tree + ambaj, ar. mango). Pers. from (darakht, pers. tree + ambah, pers. mango). Hind. from (ámb, hind. mango + per, hind. tree). Dec. from (ám, hind. mango + jhár, dec. tree). Malay from tamul. Can. from tamul. Oor. from sanscrit. Mal. from tamul. Singh. from sanscrit. San. also (chúta), meaning trickling juice; (madhukara), meaning honey producing; (mákanda), meaning sweet mango tree; (bhringábhíshta), meaning liked by bees; (chakralatámra), meaning circular leaved mango; (kámánga), meaning cupid's limb; (kámáyudha), meaning cupid's weapon; (káméshta), meaning liked by cupid; (kámap'hala), meaning desire + fruit; (kámashara), meaning cupid's arrow [cauma baunam]; (kámavallab'há), meaning cupid's beloved; (kíréshta), meaning liked by parrots; (kókilánanda), meaning cuckoo's joy; (kókilávása), meaning cuckoo's abode; (kókilótsava), meaning cuckoo's feast; (mádhavadruma), meaning tree of spring; (madhudúta), meaning harbinger of spring; (nílakapitt'ha), meaning dark + wood-apple tree, feronia elephantum, corr.; (rasála), meaning juice-giver [hurrially, sugar cane]; (sahakára), meaning fragrant mango; (nripapriyá), meaning king's beloved. Pers. also (darakhtinaghzak). Malay also (ampálam); (pálam). Tel. also (mávi); (tiyyamámidi), meaning sweet + mango; (guddzumámidi), meaning juice + mango; (rátsamámidi), meaning king + mango; (elamávi), meaning delicate + mango. Oor. also (ám). Mal. also (muççi), meaning old. Tam. also (ottumá), meaning grafted mango; (kilimúkkumá), meaning parrot + beak + mango [dil pasaud]. Title otherwise Amba, Common mango, Cuckoo's joy, Cupid's favourite, Harbinger of spring, Spring tree. Botanically Mangifera [mango] indica, linn., anacardiaceæ [vricsham, 45]. Alias Mangifera amba, domestica, montana. Amba from mahratta.——**(1)** Tree, 40 feet; leaves alternate, lanceolate, acuminated, glabrous; calyx five-cleft; petals five; panicles terminal, much branched, pubescent, erect; drupe obliquely-oblong or somewhat reniform; seed solitary; flowers small, greenish-yellowish. Evergreen tree of a rounded form, with dense foliage; blossoms according to situation, from february to april; fruit ripens from may to july; grows very large in mountain forests up to 4,000 feet, generally in ravines and on banks of streams; most variable in the length and breadth of its leaves and form of its panicles. Its fruit is the apple [seb] of the tropics; this also differing in shape, size, color, and flavor; the most usual form is an oval, somewhat flattened, and with a kind of heel near the apex; of a yellow or yellow-and-red color when ripe; the inferior kinds are terebinthaceous in flavor; the fruit contains a large stone; the blue stain produced on a knife cutting the fruit results from presence of gallic acid in the pulp, which likewise contains citric acid and gum. Gum resin [googal] obtained from the bark with a hot and bitter taste and bearing with a pleasant odour; only partially soluble in water; occurs in small and irregular masses, some of which consist of very small tears sticking to each other; this is generally reddish-yellow or reddish-brown in color, with a bland mucilaginous taste. Friar jordanus, the quilon bishop of the fourteenth century, has the following:—"there is another tree which has fruit like a plum [auloochah] "but a very big one, which is called amba; this is a fruit so "sweet and delicious as it is impossible to utter in words." Flower religious, and celebrated in poetry; with it one of the five arrows of cauman [q.v.] is tipped. The mango tree is best propagated by grafting, though it will readily grow from seeds; really good fruit is seldom found except on grafted trees; for cultivation garden soil is most suited; ground prepared by digging pits one cubic yard in contents and filling and manuring them; seed sown in jyeshtam or june in nursery; transplanted in caurteecam or november and margasbiram [mausam] or december when plants are about 2 feet high; while under growth the plant is watered for the first month every alternate day, for the first year once a week and afterwards occasionally; gives fruit five to eight years after; fruits picked by a long stick with net attached or by climbing trees; unripe fruits buried in straw till ripe; the price varies from one fruit per one pic to one for two annas according to the quality. The kernel is medicinally astringent, demulcent, and nutrient; the gum, demulcent, and slightly stimulant; the pulp of the ordinary mango laxative, and that of the grafted variety very nutrient. The kernel should be removed from young or half-grown mangoes in their fresh state and cut into small pieces and dried in the sun immediately; in the case of ripe mangoes, the seed or kernel must also be separated from the shell as soon as possible, and if not already dry, it should be dried in the sun in the same manner. Compound powder; take of the kernel of young or half-grown mangoes, in powder, three ounces; cuminum cyminum, [jeerah], piper nigrum [black pepper], zingiber officinale [ginger], in powder, each one ounce and two drachms; the gum of mangifera indica, in powder, five drachms; opium [opium poppy], in powder, one drachm; mix them thoroughly, pass the powder through a fine sieve, rub lightly in a mortar. Doses; of simple powder, from forty to eighty grains; of compound powder, from ten to sixty grains; there is one grain of opium in every drachm of the compound powder. Substituted; the simple powder, for creta præparata and pulv. cretæ aromat., and compound powder, for pulv. ipecac. compositus, pulv. kino compositus, and pulv. cretæ aromat. cum opio. The kernels dried and powdered, are useful in expelling common round worm; the fruit acts as a diaphoretic and refrigerant; the resin [raul] mixed with lime-juice or oil is used externally in cutaneous affections; the resin mixed with white of egg and opium [aphainam], is a specific on malabar coast for diarrhœa and dysentery; the stalks, powdered and calcined, are used to take away warts; the bark is administered in infusion in menorrhagia and leucorrhœa; gives to pharm. the kernels, non-officinal, like santonin [absinth]. The cultivated fruit is one of the best in the world, that of the wild tree however is uneatable; mangoes when eaten in excess heat the blood and produce exanthematous affections. When fruit is green, the stone is extracted, and the fruit cut into halves or slices, and treated in following ways:—put into curries [q.v.]; made into pickle with salt [ooppoo], mustard [rayaun] oil, chillies [q.v.], and other ingredients; made into chutney [q.v.]; made into presrves and jellies by being boiled and cooked in syrup; boiled, strained, and with milk [paul] and sugar [q.v.] made into a custard known as mango phool; dried and made into the native ambchoor, used for adding acidity to certain curries. When fruit is ripe it is treated in following ways:—made into curry which has a sweet acid not unpleasant taste; cut into small pieces, and made into salad with vinegar [caudy] and chillies; the juice squeezed out, spread on plates and allowed to dry, and made to form the thin cakes known as ambsath. The flower also is edible. The leaves are tied up in a row in front of houses on festive days; cf. margosa leaves hung up for small-pox; natives use the leaves as tooth brushes; dry unripe fruit is largely used in dyeing with safflower [bastard saffron]; bark and leaf also yield a yellow dye [shauyam]; from wounds in the bark issues a soft reddish brown gum-resin [googal], hardening by age and much resembling bdellium [q.v.], burnt in the flame of a candle, it emits a smell like that of cashew [q.v.] nuts when roasting; oil from seeds [yennay]. The timber is soft, of a dull grey color, porous, soon decaying if exposed to wet, but useful for common purposes; in large old trees the wood acquires a light chocolate color towards the centre of the trunk and larger branches, and is then hard, close-grained and somewhat durable; the wood, burnt with sandal-wood [sandal], is used for burning corpses. There is a Tamul proverb:—பொங்கும் காலம் புளி பூக்கும், மங்கும் காலம் மாபூக்கும்—"In times of plenty the tamarind [q.v.] tree "blossoms, in times of scarcity the mango bears in abundance." There is a species sylvatica, called in sanscrit (kóshámra) or sheath mango; (ghanaskandha), meaning having heavy trunk; (jantupádapa), meaning insect tree, cf. cluster fig; (kshudrámra), meaning inferior mango tree; (raktámra), meaning red mango tree; (suraktaka), meaning very red; (vanámra), meaning wild mango.——**(2)** There are no recognized scientific varieties of Indica but the following different fruits are produced in this presidency.——*Ameer golah* (امیر گولہ - amírgolah, Hind.). From (amír, ar. proper name + golah, hind. ball). Round and whitish yellow; insipid.——*Caula pahaur* (کالا پہاڑ - kálápahár, Hind.). From (kálá, hind. black + pahár, hind. mountain). Green; red inside, sweet.——*Cawder pasand* (قادرپسند - kádirpasand, Hind.). From (kádir, ar. proper name + pasand, pers. approved). Kidney-shaped; reddish yellow when ripe; fleshy and of milky flavor; largely eaten.——*Dil pasand* (دل پسند - dilpasand, Hind.). From (dil, pers. heart + pasand, pers. approved). Parrot-beak shaped larger than cawder pasand; yellow when ripe; sweet.——*Haufiz pasand* (حافظ پسند - háfizpasand, Hind.). From (háfiz, ar. proper name + pasand, pers. approved). Round and yellow; sweetish.——*Malghobah* (ملغوبہ - malghobá, Hind.). From (marghúb, ar. lovely). Round; yellowish green; fleshy.——*Peter pasand* (پیٹر پسند - pítarpasand, Hind.). From (petre, eng. judge + pasand, pers. approved). Similar to cawder pasand in size and color but slightly compressed; sweetish sour.——*Roommauny* (رومانی - rummání, Hind.). From (rummán, pers. pomegranate). Round and reddish; not luscious.——*Wallajah pasand* (والاجاہ پسند - wálájáhpasand, Hind.). From (wáláját, pers. wallajah + pasand, pers. approved). Round; greenish-yellow when ripe.——**(3)** *Mango bird* (हरित - harita, San.; पावशा - pávashá, Mahr.; پیلک - pílak, Hind. and Dec.; వంగపండు - vangapandu, Tel.; മാന്നാക്കിളി - mánnákkili, Mal.; மஞ்சக் கொழுப்பன் - mañjakkozhuppan, Tam.). Title from yellow colour. San. from (hari, san. yellowish green). Hind. from (pílá, hind. yellow). Tel. from (vanga, tel. brinjaul, solanum melongena, linn. + pandu, tel. fruit), from the color. Mal. from (máuna, mal. mango + kili, tam. bird). Tam. from (mañjal, tam. turmeric + kozhuppu, tam. fat). Indian oriole. Oriolinæ, brachypodidæ [boolbool], dentirostres, insessores, aves [pacsby, 22], of naturalists [jantoo].—"*a*" The most familiar is Oriolus kundoo. Alias Oriolus aureus, galbula, galbuloides. Feeds especially on figs of banyan [q.v.]. Call loud mellow whistle, resembling peeho.—"*b*" The black-naped indian oriole is Oriolus indicus; black horse-shoe mark extending from base of bill through eyes to nape.—"*c*" The southern black-headed oriole, called in teloogoo hill oriole, is Oriolus ceylonensis.——*Mango fish* (انبہ مچھی - ámbahmaçchí, Hind.). From colour. Title otherwise Tupsee. Same as Robaul.——*Mango ginger* (మామిడిఅల్లము - mámidiallamu, Tel.). From smell. See under Ginger.——*Mango shower* (மாசிமழை - másimazhai, Tam.). From (mási, tam. month so called + mazhai, tam. rain). Showers which fall in March and April, when the mangoes begin to ripen.——**(4)** *Bald mango* (బొడమామిడి - bodamámidi, Tel.). Same as Devil fig.——*Black beetle mango* (తుమ్మెదమామిడి - tummedamámidi, Tel.). Same as Marking nut.——*Christian's mango* (പാതിരിമാവു് - pátirimávu, Mal.). Same as Cashew.——*Eeshwara's mango* (ఈశ్వరమామిడి - íshvaramámidi, Tel.). Same as Yellow mangosteen.——*Female pot mango* (ఆడఅటికమామిడి - ádaatikamámidi, Tel.). Same as Tikry.——*Fibre mango* (నారమామిడి - náramámidi, Tel.). Same as Meidalukdy.——*Fig mango* (బొడ్డమామిడి - boddamámidi, Tel.; நிகோடா - nigódá, Tam.). Title from shape of frnit. Tel. from (bodda, tel. fig, ficus glomerata, miq. + mámidi, tel. mango tree, mangifera indica, linn.). Tam. corruption from (ney, tam. ghee + kottai, tam. seed); ghee-seeded tree. Can. also (kaluyette). Tel. also (murumámidi), meaning beauty + mango tree, mangifera indica, linn.; (koravi), meaning firebrand; (égisa) [common vengay]; (kottaichettu). Tam. also (karadipungam). Title otherwise Four-leaved soap-nut, Nicotah. Botanically Hemigyrosa canescens, thw., sapindaceæ [vriesham, 43.]. Alias Cupania canescens; Molinæa canescens; Sapindus tetraphyllus. Tree; leaflets two pair, obovate or oblong, quite entire, glabrous; racemes simple or panicled, from the old leafless shoots; sepals roundish; petals four-fifth deficient, flat, the claw silky at the back; scale woolly in front, two-cleft, with a crested appendage at its back below the cleft; stamens eight, on one side, opposite from the disk; ovary ovate; style simple, elongated; stigma three-toothed; capsule ovoid, three-sided; flowers small, white; flowering in february and march. Resembles soap-nut [q.v.] tree, but differs in its irregular flowers and unilateral disk and in its inflorescence being lateral instead of terminal. Wood of average quality, white, does not bear exposure.——*Forest mango* (காட்டுமா - káttumá, Tam.). Same as

Chironjee and Odallam.——*Gummy mango* (சிகிடிமா - shigidimá, Tam.). Same as Cashew.——*Hill mango* (కొండమామిడి - kondamámidi, Tel.; மலைமா - malaimá, Tam.). Same as Hill kiloovay.——*Journey mango* (سفری آم - safaríám, Hind.). Otherwise (supáríám), by corr. meaning areca mango. Same as Guava.——*Juicy mango* (చారుమామిడి - chárumámidi, Tel.). Same as Chironjee.——*Jungle mango* (காட்டுமா - káttumá, Tam.). Same as Odallam.——*Papaw mango* (പപ്പായമ്പഴം - pappáyampázham, Mal.). Title from yellow pulp of fruit. Same as Papaw.——*Portuguese mango* (പോർത്തുകിമാവ് - pórtukimávu, Mal.). Same as Cashew.——*Pot mango* (అతికమామిడి - atikamámidi, Tel.). From being cooked as potherb. Same as Tikry.——*Red mango* (कोकंबि - kókambi, Mahr.). Same as Mate mangosteen.——*Saffron mango* (ஆவிமா - ávimá, Tam.). Same as Coomby.——*Ship mango* (കപ്പൽമാവ് - kappalmávu, Mal.). Title from being a foreign tree. Same as Cashew.——*Stone mango* (ಕಲ್ಲುಮಾವು - kallumávu, Can.). From hard wood and shape of leaf. Same as Alanjy.——*Wild mango* (आम्रातक - ámrátaka, San.; अंबाडा - ambádá, Mahr.; आंबाडो - ámbádó, Conc.; درخت مريم - darakhtimaryam, Ar.; درخت مريم - darakhtimaryam, Pers.; امرا - amrá, Hind.; مريم كا جهاڑ - maryamkájhár, Dec.; ಅಮಟೆ - amate, Can.; అడవిమామిడి - adavimámidi, Tel.; അമ്പഴം - ampázham, Mal.; ඇඹරැල්ල - ambaralla, Singh.; காட்டுமா - káttumá, Tam.). San. from (ámra, san. mangifera indica, linn. + at, san. to go), resembling mango. Mahr. and conc. from sanscrit. Ar. from (darakht, ar. tree + maryam, ar. mary). Pers. from arabic. Hind. from sanscrit. Dec. from (maryam, ar. mary + jhár, hind. tree). Tel. from (adavi, tel. forest + mámidi, tel. mango, mangifera indica, linn.). Mal. from sanscrit. Tam. from (kádu, tam. forest + má, tam. mango, mangifera indica, linn.). San. also (pítana), meaning making yellow; (kapítana), meaning gladdening monkeys with fruits; (kánanámra), meaning wild mango; (adhvagabhógya), meaning traveller's comfort, cf. journey mango; (pittavriksha), meaning bile tree, from being used in bilious dyspepsia. Mahr. also (ránaámba), meaning wild mango. Hind. also (ambodhá); (ranámb), meaning wild mango tree. Dec. also (janglíamkájhár), meaning wild mango tree. Can. also (ambate); (pullile); (pundi). Tel. also (ivurumámidi), meaning tender leaf + mango tree, mangifera indica, linn. [yellow mangosteen]; (ambálamu); (pítavrikshamu); (sítavrikshamu). Mal. also (káttampázham), meaning wild + the tree. Tam. also (marimá), meaning devil + mango, mangifera indica, linn. [chironjee]; (pullile), of kaders. Title otherwise Bile tree, Greens mango, Hog-plum, Traveller's delight, Yellow mango. Botanically Spondias [amrautam] mangifera, willd., anacardiaceæ [vricsham, 45]. Alias Baldingera glandulosa; Evia amara; Mangas paniculata; Mangifera pinnata; Poupartia mangifera; Spondias amara. Large tree; calyx small, five-cleft; petals five, spreading; leaves alternate, unequally pinnated; leaflets four to five pairs, ovate or elliptic-oblong, oblique at the base, entire, glabrous; panicles axillary and terminal, diffuse; drupe fleshy, oval, yellow; nut oblong, woody, outwardly fibrous, five-celled, very hard; flowers small, white. Deciduous tree, wild and cultivated; leaves are agreeably acid; fruit, when largest, is of the size of a goose's egg, of a rich olive green, mottled with yellow and black, with but a trifling degree of scent, and none of the quince-like [bedauna] odour of the other species of the genus. When very large and old the tree throws out occasionally a large quantity of gum mixed with a resinous substance through an old wound or crack; the gum [gond] and resin [raul] collect on the ground in the form of a thick, flat, oblong or irregular mass; in addition to the above occasional flow, a small quantity is often found on the stem, generally in small and transparent tears; this latter is quite soluble in water and resembles the indian gum-arabic in many other characters. The young fruit is medicinally stomachic and tonic, and the gum demulcent and emollient. Preparation is simple powder; select the young fruits before their nut is hard and fully developed, remove the nut, cut the fleshy portion into small pieces and dry them in the sun, when quite dry reduce them to a fine powder in the usual manner. Dose; from thirty grains to one drachm or more, three or four times in the 24 hours. Substituted; the young fruit for gentian [chiretta] and calumba [q.v.], and the gum for indian gum-arabic [q.v.]. Pulp of fruit is astringent; bark is a refrigerant; juice of leaves applied to ear-ache. The inner part of fruit nearest the rind is rather acid, but that being removed, the part nearest the stone is sweet and eatable; leaves used in chutneys [q.v.]. Wood soft, light-gray.——*Yellow mango* (पीतन - pítana, San.). Same as Wild mango.

MANGOSTEEN (منگوستان - mangústán, *Hind.* and *Dec.*; منگستا - manggusta, *Malay*; ശൂലമ്പുളി - shúlampuli, *Mal.*; சூலம்புளி - shúlambuli, *Tam.*). Title from malay; no connection with mango. Hind. and dec. from malay. Mal. from tamul. Tam. from (shúla, san. trident + puli, tam. tamurind tree, tamarindus indica, linn.). Malay also (manggis). Title otherwise Common mangosteen. Botanically Garcinia [ractaumram] mangostana, linn., guttiferæ [vricsham, 22]. Specific name from malay. Branches many, decussate; leaves 6–10 by $2\frac{1}{2}$–$4\frac{1}{4}$ inches, very coriaceous; nerves regular, close, in arching with the intermarginal one; male flower in three to nine-flowered terminal fascicles; pedicels short; sepals orbicular, concave, persistent; petals broad, ovate, fleshy; stamens indefinite; hermaphrodite flower 2 inches diameter, solitary or geminate at the tips of the young branches; pedicels $\frac{1}{2}$ inch, thick, woody; sepals and petals as in the male; stamens many, filaments slender, connate below; ovary four to eight-celled; stigma sessile, eight-rayed; ovules solitary; berry as large as an orange, smooth, dark, purple; pericarp firm, spongy; seeds large, flattened; aril very fleshy, white, juicy. A small, conical tree, 20 to 30 feet, evergreen, with leathery leaves; the flowers are followed by fruit as large as an orange [q.v.], which is smooth, dark purple, with a firm covering having a spongy layer, and containing large flattened seed having a white fleshy and juicy growth from the seed stalk which is the part eaten; native of molucca. Gives to pharm. fleshy pericarp of the fruit, non-officinal, for diarrhœa and dysentery; fruit to eat is between a strawberry and a grape [angoor]; to taste the fruit in perfection it must be eaten as it is gathered from the tree; gum [gond] from rind and bark; flower gives a dye [shanyam].——*False mangosteen* (جهوٹا منگو ستان - jhútámangústán, Hind.). Same as Malay red wood.——*Mate mangosteen* (भिरंड - bhiranda, Mahr.; बीरंड - birunda, Conc.; كوكم - kúkam, Hind. and Dec.; ಮುರುಗಿನಹುಳಿ - murginahuli, Can.; ಪುನರಪುಳಿ - punarapuli, Too.; പുനമ്പുളി - punampuli, Mal.). Title means cook-room mangosteen; ship term. Hind. and dec. from (kókambi, mahr. red mango). Can. from (murige, can. twisted + huli, can. tamarind, tamarindus indica, linn.). Mal. from (pinar, mal. stiff + puli, mal. tamarind). Mahr. also (rátambi), meaning red mango, mangifera indica, linn.; (kókambi), meaning red mango; (támbudaámbá), meaning red mango. Can. also (murghulimara). Mal. also (pinampuli), stiff tamarind. Title otherwise Brindones, Cokum butter tree, Moorgana tallow tree, Red mango. Botanically Garcinia [ractaumram] indica, chois., guttiferæ [vricsham, 22]. Alias Brindonia indica; Garcinia celebica, purpurea; Stalagmites cowa. Brindonia from concany. Small tree of upright, conical habit; drooping branches; leaves lanceolar, obtuse, of a bright coppery color while young, and dark green smooth and leathery when mature; native of west coast; flowers are inconspicuous, and are followed by globular purple fruit the size of a small orange [q.v.], containing several large seeds, from which a concrete oil is obtained by crushing and boiling the seed in water; this oil, or cokum butter [q.v.], preserves its solidity to 98° fahr. [yennay]. Cokum butter is found in bazaars [q.v.] in the form of egg-shaped or oblong lumps about 4 inches long by 2 inches in diameter, and weighing about a quarter of a pound; it is a whitish substance, at ordinary temperatures, firm, dry, and friable, yet greasy to the touch; when long kept it acquires an unpleasant rancid smell and brownish hue, and an efflorescence of shining tufted crystals appears on the surface of the mass. The butter and dried fruit are medicinally demulcent, nutrient and emollient; used in substance with or without sugar. Doses; as a nutrient or remedy for phthisis pulmonalis and scrofulous diseases, from half to one ounce, or more; as remedy or adjuvant to other medicines in dysentery and mucous diarrhœa, from one to two drachms. Substituted for cod-liver and fish oils, cetaceum and wax. Gives to pharm. cokum butter, garciniæ purpureæ oleum, used in preparation of ointments, suppositories, and for other pharmaceutical purposes, local application to ulcerations, fissures of the lips, hands, &c., officinal; in canara cokum used medicinally as cure for cattle wounded by tigers [pooly]. Fruit, agreeable acid flavor; syrup made from it; cokum [q.v.] used to adulterate ghee [q.v.]; workers in iron [auhan] use the acid juice as a mordant [cauram].——*Wild mangosteen* (جنگلی منگو ستان - janglímangustán, Hind.). Same as Gaub.——*Yellow mangosteen* (तमाल - tamála, San.; دمپل - dampal, Hind. and Dec.; ಹಿರೇಕಾನಿಗಿನಮರ - hirekaniginamara, Can.; చీకటిమాను - chíkatimánu, Tel.; സമുദ്രപ്പച്ച - samudrappaçça, Mal.; ගොරක - goraka, Singh.; தமாலம் - tamálam, Tam.). Title from color of fruit. San. from (tamas, san. dark), from dark leaves and bark [cassia cinnamom, ceylon gamboge, karanj]. Hind. and dec. from sanscrit. Can. from (hiri, can. superior + kaniginamara, can. nerium odorum, sol.). Tel. from (chíkati, tel. darkness + mánu, tel. tree) [nanga champak]. Mal. from (samudra, san. sea + paçça, mal. green). Tam. from sanscrit. San. also (kálaskandha), meaning having black trunk; (tápiñchha), meaning allaying one oppressed by heat. Tel. also (ivurumámidi), meaning tender shoot + mango tree, mangifera indica, linn. [wild mango]; (íshvaramámidi), meaning god + mango tree; fruit is like a mango. Tam. also (malaippuli), meaning mountain tamarind tree, tamarindus indica, linn.; (kulavi); (malaippaççai), meaning mountain + greenness. Title otherwise Cheekaty, Eeshwara's mango, Hill green, Hill tamarind, Painter's xanthochymus. Botanically Garcinia [ractaumram] xanthochymus, hook. f., guttiferæ [vricsham, 22]. Alias Stalagmites pictorius; Xanthochymus tinctorius, pictorius. Tree, 40 feet; leaves linear-lanceolate, shining; calyx of five unequal sepals; petals five, deciduous, alternating with the sepals; flowers lateral, fascicled, all bisexual; ovary five-celled; fruit ovate pointed, yellow, one to four-seeded; flowers small, white. Fruit like a mango [q.v.], but flatter; the seeds or stones like jack [q.v.] stones. Fruit eaten by natives. Yields an indifferent gamboge [q.v.].

MANGROVE (منگی منگی - mangimangi, *Malay*). Title is corruption. Applied to the genera Rhizophora and Avicennia, shrubs or small trees growing on low coasts. Extended to Bruguiera, Carallia, Kandelia, Lumnitzera, Manihot. The barks are generally a valuable tan [chamrah].——*Candel mangrove* (ରସୁରିୟ - rasuriya, Oor.; ചെറുകണ്ടൽ - cherukantal, Mal.; கண்டல் - kandal, Tam.). Title from tamul. Mal. from (cheru, mal. small + kantal, mal. bulb-like). Tam. means bulb-like. Mal. also (kantal), meaning bulb-like. Tam. also (púkkandal), meaning flower + candel tree. Title otherwise Candel [q.v.]. Botanically Kandelia rheedii, w. & a., rhizophoreæ [vricsham, 54]. Generic from malayalam. Alias Rhizophora candel. Shrub; leaves quite entire, linear-oblong, obtuse, two to three chotomous, four to nine-flowered; inflorescence axillary; calyx tube campanulate, segments linear, persistent; petals as many as the segments of the calyx, membranaceous, cleft to below the middle into numerous capillary segments; fruit oblong, longer than the tube of the calyx; germinating embryo subulate-clavate, acute; flowers largish, white and green; s. canara and malabar tidal backwaters. Bark mixed with dried ginger [q.v.] or long pepper [q.v.] and rose-water [goolaub, panneer] is cure for diabetes. Bark used for tanning [chamrah]; gives a dye [shauyam]. Wood soft, close-grained; used for fire-wood.——*Caurally mangrove* (फणसी - p'hanasí, Mahr.; ಅಂಡಿಪುನಾರುಮರ - andipunáru-mara, Can.; ಅಂಡಿಪುನಾರ್ - andipunár, Too.; కారల్లి - kéralli, Tel.; വങ്കണ - vankana, Mal.; දවට - davata, Singh.). Title from teloogoo; distinguish from caurallam [q.v.]. Mahr. from (p'hanasa, mahr. artocarpus integrifolia, willd.), from resemblance. Can. from (anda, can. handsome + punáru, can. the tree, so called). Tel. from (káru, tel. forest + alli, tel. memecylon edule, rox., var. capitellata). Mal. from (van, mal. large + kana, mal. knot). Can. also (punselu). Tel. also (káravalli), meaning forest + memecylon edule, rox., var. capitellata. Title otherwise Davata, Wild cassa. Botanically Carallia integerrima, dec., rhizophoreæ [vricsham, 54]. Generic from teloogoo. Alias Carallia corymbosa, lucida, octopetala, sinensis, timorensis, zeylanica; Marallia zeylanica; Pootia cereopsifolia. Tree; leaves oval, acuminated, finely serrated; petals six to seven, roundish, entire, waved on the margin, much larger than the segments of the calyx; stigma concave, three-lobed; peduncles short, axillary, bifid; flowers small, greenish-white; flowering in the hot season; it is only the younger trees that have the leaves serrated; in old ones they are perfectly entire and vary in shape and size. Timber is ornamental reddish, used in s. canara for furniture and cabinet purposes, it is tough and not easily worked, has a wavy appearance, is peculiar in structure, having a great deal of cellular tissue. Another species is lancæfolia; bark giving dye [shauyam].——*China mangrove* (ചീനക്കണ്ടൽ - chínakkantal, Mal.). Same as Malda dye.——*Madagascar mangrove* (مدغاسقر منگی منگی - madagháskarmangimangi, Hind.; കടക്കണ്ടൽ - katakkantal, Mal.; බෙරිය - bériya, Singh.). Mal. from (katal, mal. sea + kantal, mal. kandelia rheedii, w. and a.). Mal. also (karakkantal), meaning shore + the plant. Title otherwise Cadal candel. Botanically Lumnitzera racemosa, willd., combretaceæ [vricsham, 55]. Alias Bruguiera madagascariensis; Jussieua racemosa; Petaloma alternifolia; Pyrrhanthus albus. Shrub; calyx five-cleft; segments rounded; petals five, acute, inserted on the calyx and longer than it; leaves alternate, cuneate obovate, alternated at the base into a short petiole, glabrous, thick and somewhat fleshy; spikes axillary, five stamens longer than the other alternating ones, and about the length of the petals; drupe clove-shaped, ovate-oblong, bluntly angled, crowned with the calyx; nut linear-oblong, angled one-seeded; flowers small white; found in salt marshes on the coast; wood remarkably strong and durable.——*Ooppata mangrove* (तिवर - tivara, Mahr.; మడ - mada, Tel.; ഉപ്പുകുറ്റി - uppukutti, Mal.; உப்புக்குட்டி - uppukutti, Tam.). Title from malayalam. Mal. from (uppu, mal. salt + kutti, mal. stump); from growing near salt-water. Tam. from malayalam. Tel. also (nallamada), meaning black + the tree. Mal. also (uppútti), by corruption. Title otherwise Common indian mangrove, Downy-leaved avicennia, New zealand mangrove, Nulla mada, White mangrove. Botanically Avicennia officinalis, linn., verbenaceæ [vricsham, 102]. Alias Avicennia alba, resinifera, tomentosa; Mangium album; Oepata; Secura marina. Oepata is malayalam. Small tree; leaves opposite, obovate or oval, slightly tomentose beneath; flowers terminal, small, dingy yellow; seeds germinate in the fruit, while still hanging on the tree and produce a root, 3 or 4 feet long, which ultimately falls into the mud and forms a new centre; grows on lagoons [cauyal] and tidal rivers; the plant sends up, in a wide radius all round its stem, a dense crop of shoots from 1½ to 2 feet high; these catch mud and débris of plants, and thus gradually form a sort of peninsula which protects the land from erosion by the water; plant contains a juice which is very tenacious. The bark contains a red coloring matter striking a greenish color with ferric chloride, but giving no precipitate with gelatine; the coloring matter is precipitated by acids [poolipp, tezaub] and redissolved by alkalies [cauram]; the ash of the air-dried bark amounts to 11·4 per cent., and is deliquescent. Roots aphrodisiac; unripe seeds are used as poultice to hasten suppuration of boils. Kernels bitter but edible. Bark used for tanning [chamrah]; a preparation is made from ashes of wood which dhobies [q.v.] use for cleaning cotton cloths and painters use with colors to make them adhere; juice used for sealing letters. Wood grey, with a darker heartwood, hard, heavy, consisting of numerous, narrow, well marked, concentric layers; very brittle; used for fire-wood.——*Tree mangrove* (കണ്ടൽ - kantal, Mal.). Mal. from (kanta, mal. bulbous root). Botanically Bruguiera gymnorhiza, lamk., rhizophoreæ [vricsham, 54]. Alias Bruguiera australis, rheedii, rumphii, wightii; Rhizophora gymnorhiza. Tree; leaves ovate-oblong, acuminated at both ends; calyx about twelve-cleft; segments linear, acuminated, triquetrous towards the point; petals two-lobed, with about five short bristles; ovary three to four-celled; germinating embryo somewhat cylindric, tapering towards each end; flowers largish, red; peduncles one-flowered, solitary, drooping; common on the sea-coast; flowering in the hot season. Bark gives a dye [shauyam] and used in tanning [chamrah]. Wood yellowish hard and durable, used for house-building and for fuel. Other species are:—caryophylloides, eriopetala, parviflora.——*White candel mangrove* (منگی منگی - manggimanggi, Malay; అడవిపొన్న - adaviponna, Tel.; വെങ്കണ്ടൽ - venkantal, Mal.; කඩොල් - kadol, Singh.; கண்டல் - kandal, Tam.). Title from flowers. Tel. from (adavi, tel. forest + ponna, tel. calophyllum inophyllum, linn.). Mal. from (ven, mal. white + kantal, mal. kandelia rheedii, w. & a.). Malay also (kayuapiapi), meaning fire-fly tree. Tel. also (uppuponna), meaning salt + calophyllum inophyllum, linn. Tam. also (péykkandal), meaning devil + kandelia rheedii, w. & a. Title otherwise Candelaria mangrove, Demon candel, Kunro bark tree, Mangle. Botanically Rhizophora mucronata, lamk., rhizophoreæ [vricsham, 54.]. Alias Rhizophora candelaria, mangle. Candaleria from malayalam. Small tree; leaves oval, long-cuspidate; segments of the calyx triangular-ovate; peduncles three to six-flowered; germinating embryo subulate-clavate, acute; flowers largish, white, fragrant; flowering in hot season; abounds in tidal backwaters [cauyal]; has aerial roots, which descend into the mud and raise the stem of the plant upwards. Fruit is sweet and edible, and juice when fermented forms a light wine; salt extracted from aerial roots. Bark used for tanning [chamrah]; has been exported to europe; leaf gives a dye [shauyam]. Wood dark reddish, hard and durable. Another species is conjugata.——*White mangrove* (ഉപ്പുക്കുറ്റി - uppukutti, Mal.). Title from color of wood. Same as Ooppata mangrove.

MANILLA (மணிலா - manilá, *Tam.*). The chief town in the Philippine islands and head-quarters of Spanish government in the East.——*Manilla cauray* (മണിലക്കാര - manilakkára, Mal.). Same as Edible paulay.——*Manilla hemp* (منلا كا نار - manillakánár, Hind.). Same as Demon plantain.——*Manilla lime* (منلا كا ليمو - manillakálimú, Hind.). Same as Musk lime.——*Manilla nut* (மணிலாக்கொட்டை - manilákkottai, Tam.). Title from original habitat. Same as Groundnut.——*Manilla tamarind* (خرنوب - kharnúb, Ar.). Title otherwise Algaroba [carob], Aloja, Cashew [q.v.] tree, Paray of peru. Botanically Prosopis [shivah] dulcis, kunth., leguminosæ. By spaniards introduced to philippine islands, and thence here; sweetish, succulent pods, 20 to 24 inches long, enclosing black seeds embedded in white pulp; pods used for feeding cattle; planted along railway lines. Manilla tamarind. Term is also applied to Corcapilly [q.v.].

MANJILEE (منزلی - manzilí, *Hind.*). From (manzil, ar. a journey). A litter at Goa [majil].

MANKENA (बन्धूक - bandhúka, *San.*; तांबडीदुपारी - támbadídupárí, *Mahr.*; دوپہریا - dopahariyá, *Hind.*; మంకెన - mankena, *Tel.*; നാഗപ്പൂ - nágappú, *Mal.*). Title from teloogoo. San. from (bandh, san. to bind), attracting on account of its beauty [jungle geranium]. Mahr. from (támbadá, mahr. red + duparí, mahr. the plant). Hind. from (do, hind. two + pahar, hind. measure of time); or noontide; from time of flowering. Tel. from (manku, tel. obstinate), from obstinate growth [jungle geranium]. Mal. from (nága, san. serpent + pú, mal. flower). San. also (bandhujívaka), meaning living in group; (raktaka), meaning red, on account of crimson flowers [jungle geranium]; (arkavallabhá), meaning beloved of the sun; (pushparakta), meaning red-flowered. Mahr. also (duparí), from hindostany. Title otherwise Bandhoocam, Doopaury, Scarlet-flowered plant, St. helena red wood. Botanically Pentapetes phœnicea, linn, sterculiaceæ [vricsham, 26]. Alias Dombeya phœnicea; Pentapetes angustifolia. Annual; leaves linear-lanceolate, hastate, serrated; peduncles one to two-flowered, axillary, drooping, red; flowering in the rainy season. Has an erect stem about two feet high, common weed of rice-fields, bearing spike of middle-sized flowers, deep carmine color; also a white variety.

MANNA (من - mann, *Ar.*; شیرخشت - shírkhisht, *Pers.* and *Hind.*; ಮನ್ನಾ - manná, *Can.*; ಮನ್ನ - manna, *Too.*; మేనా - méná, *Tel.*; மன்னா - manná, *Tam.*). Title from arabic through hebrew, meaning to bestow. Pers. from (shír, pers. juice + khushk, pers. dry). Pers. also (turanjabín), meaning persian manna; (gazangabín), meaning tamarisk. Saccharine exudation obtained from several plants naturally, and from others on the bark or epidermis being incised. Eaten in its natural condition, or prepared into paste, mixed with other ingredients and made into sweetmeats [halwah]. Purgative, given to children and delicate women.——*Alhagi manna* (شیرخشت الحاج - shírkhish-tulháj, Hind.). Same as Arabian manna.——*Arabian manna* (شیرخشت - shírkhist, Hind.). See sep. title.——*Australian manna* (شیر خشت فرنگ - shírkhishtifarang, Hind.). From Eucalyptus manifera, moudic.——*Khorassan manna* (شیرخشت خراسانی - shírkhishtikhurásání, Hind.). From olive [zeitoon]. *Oak manna* (شیرخشت زیتون - shírkhishtizaitún, Hind.). Product of two species of quercus [belote], vallonea and persica. These trees are visited by immense number of a small white coccus, from puncture of which a saccharine fluid exudes and solidifies in small grains.——*Persian manna* (ترنجبین - taranjabín, Hind.). Same as Arabian manna.——*Sicilian manna* (شیرخشت - shírkhisht, Hind.). Title from place of growth. Title otherwise Calabrian manna, Flowering ash, Manna ash. Botanically Fraxinus ornus, linn., oleaceæ [vricsham, 85]. Alias Ornus europæa. Inhabitant of Sicily. A manna from this appears in tears, length of a finger, uneven, wrinkled, brittle, resembling stalactites, light, porous, and pulverizable, white, with traces of bark on one side; is devoid of odour, of sweet, mild, and rather heavy taste, dissolves entirely in the mouth; it is a concrete saccharine exudation from the stem obtained by incisions; a mild purgative in pharm.——*Tamarind manna* (شیرخشت تمرهندی - shírkhishtitamarihindí, Hind.). Product of Tamarind.——*Tamarisk manna* (گزانگبین - gazangabín, Hind.). Product of Tamarix gallica [manna jhow], arabian manna.——*Turkish manna* (عسل اللبنن - asalullibanan, Hind.). From (asal, ar. honey + libanan, ar. lebanon). Product of Pistacia lentiscus [mastic], manna of lebanon.——*Yercum manna* (سکرالعشر - sakkarulushr, Hind.). From (sakkar, hind. sugar + ushr, ar. calotropis). Product of Calotropis procera [yercum].

MANOO (మనవి - manavi, *Tel.*; மனு - manu, *Tam.*). A request, petition [arzee, durkhast].

MANSAB (منصب - mansab, *Hind.*). From (nasaba, ar. to fix). Dignity. A military title conferred by the Moghul [q.v.]. Government of Delhi, and regulated by the supposed number of horse [ghorah] the holder of the title could if required bring into the field. Jagheers [q.v.] were assigned for the maintenance of this force. In many cases the title was nominal, and often it was assumed without warrant. Title is still current in Nizam's dominions.

MANSOOR (منصور - mansúr, *Ar.*). From (nasara, ar. to conquer). Victorious. Name of a great Mahomedan saint. Taken as alam; as Mansoor ally, double alam; Mansoor beg, alam + alaumat [ism].——*Mansoorcottah* (మనసూరుకోట - manusúrukóta, Tel.). From (mansúr, ar. maho. proper name + kóta, san. fort). Village, Port; Ganjam dist., Berhampore tal.; pop. 250; acres 982; lat. 19° 17′; long. 84° 57′; from Berhampore E. 8 miles; from Chetterpore W.S.W. 7 miles; from Ganjam W.S.W 12 miles; from Gopalpore N. 2 miles; from Madras N.N.E. 520 miles. Under Mahomedan rule an administrative centre. Aska sugar [q.v.] is exported largely [gopalpore].

MANTIK (منطق - mantik, *Hind.*). From (nataka, ar. to speak). Logic [ilm].

MANUEL COTTAH (മനുയൽകോട്ട - manuyalkótta, *Mal.*). Means fort of manuel, king of portugal. Otherwise Cotchy cottah. Also called Fort manuel. Portuguese fort built at Cochin in 1503. Francisco de albuquerque superintended its construction. The first European fort in India [cochin].

MANY (मणि - mani, *San.*; மணி - mani, *Tam.*). Beauty, gem [ratnam] or pearl [moty]. A bead; corn grain. Blackness. A bell or gong [ghantay]; the hour of the day, maninairam being european hour. Also a golden bell presented for distinction by kings; hence royal insignia, a badge of honor, office or authority. Also applied to poison stone [bezoar]. Suffix in proper names as Devashikhaumany, Naugamany. Proper name common to both sexes. Also familiar contraction of Soobramanyan [peyar].——*Manimooctah* (மணிமுத்தா - manimuttá, Tam. manimukta *). From (mani, san. crystal + muktá, san. pearl). River; South arcot dist., Cullacoorchy and Vriddhauchellam talooks. Tributary of Vellaur. Rises in Cullroyen hills and flows through Cullacoorchy and Vriddhauchellam into Vellaur, 12 miles west of Bhoovangherry. Several anicuts [q.v.]. Of equal sanctity with Ganges at Benares, and its junction with the Gomookhanuddy is known as Prayaugay, a name also given to Allahabad.——*Manipooram* (मणिपुर - manipura, San.). From (mani, san. gem + pura, san. city). Name occurring in the Mahabhaurat [q.v.]. Also ancient city, Mysore district, Mysore, three miles south-east of Chaumrajnugger.——*Maniyam* (ಮಣಿಯ - maniya, Can.; മണിയം - maniyam, Mal.; மணியம் - maniyam, Tam.). Bearing royal insignia. Applied to office of superintendence in a palace or temple and in modern times in a village. An office of this name existed once for clearing the way for persons of distinction. Management of affairs. A subordinate revenue-officer; as well as the holder of the office of monigar [q.v.].——*Maniyauchy* (மணியாச்சி - maniyáççi, Tam. maniyáchi *). From (mani, tam. corn-grain + ádchi, tam. possession). Zemindarry, Village, Railway station; Tinnevelly dist., Ottapidauram tal.; pop. of village 1,396; acres 8,587; lat. of village 8° 52′; long. 77° 56′; height 206 feet; from Ottapidauram W.S.W. 9 miles; from Tinnevelly E.N.E. 17 miles; from the sea W. 18 miles. It is the junction station between Tinnevelly, Madura and Tuticorin. Peshcush Rs. 1,808.——*Maunicam* (మాణిక్యము - mánikyamu, Tel.; மாணிக்கம் - mánikkam, Tam.). Means ruby. Hindoo 2nd or pers. name. Common among non-bramins, applied to both sexes; also taken by Native christians [peyar].——*Maunica vauchacan* (மாணிக்கவாசகன் - mánikkavásagan, Tam.). From (mánikya, san. ruby + váchaka, san. speaker). Sheiva devotee and poet. Minister of Arimardana paundyan, a very early king of Madura. Bramin caste. When sent to buy horses [ghorah] for the king, spent the money in founding Sheiva temple at Tirperoondoray, and was put into prison. At this moment a great flood occurred in the Veigay and the king, considering it a retribution by Shiva released Maunicam. He then established himself at Chidambaram, where he defeated Booddhist priests from Ceylon, as related in the Tirvauthavoorar pooraunam [q.v.]. Author of Tamul grammar [lacshanam], Coovalayaunandam, besides two works Chittambala covay and Tirvauchacam. Chittambala covay of 400 stanzas is an epithalamium of Shiva [q.v.] and Parvaty [q.v.]. Tirvauchacam, a series of hymns to Shiva [tirvauchacam]. In the Devashikhaumany paudal, a Tamul work of W. coast, it is stated that a sorcerer Maunica vauchacan came to Malayalam and induced the king to kill his state minister, a Roman catholic named Devashikhaumany. The native Roman catholics still exhibit a drama on this. Maunica vauchacan died at Chidambaram, aged 32.——*Monigar* (ಮಣಿಯಗಾರ - maniyagára, Can.; మణికాడు - manivakádu, Tel.; மணியக்காரன் - maniyakkáran, Tam.). From (maniyam, tam. superintendence) [maniyam]. The headman of a village, employed as a revenue officer of the Circar [q.v.], for which he holds a maunyam [q.v.] or receives payment. Potail in mahratta, Peddacaup in teloogoo, Adhicaury in malayalam.

MANZIL (منزل - manzil, *Ar.*) [majil, manjilee]. From (nazala, ar. to alight). Place of alighting. A stage. In astronomy, mansion of the moon [chundran]. The Hindoo asterisms [nacshatram] generally consist of nearly the same stars as the Arabian manzils, but in a few instances they essentially differ. See Nacshatram for list.

MAPHRIAN (മെപ്രിയാൻ - mép'hrián, *Mal.*). Archbishop of the Syrian church of Malabar next in rank to the patriarch.

MAR (मर - mar, *San.*). To die.——*Maranam* (मरण - marana, San.). From (mri, san. to die). Death; one of the effects of Cauman's arrows [cauma baunam].——*Marcandeyan* (मार्कंडेय - márkandéya, San.). From (mrikandu, san. the sage); a patronymic. Ancient sage. One of the chiranjeevies [q.v.]. Also a pooraunam [q.v.] of this name.——*Marcapore* (మార్కాపురము - márkápuramu, Tel.). See sep. title.——*Mard* (مرد - mard, Hind.). Man.——*Mardaun* (مردان - mardán, Pers.). Manly. Prefixed to an alam forms a lacab; as Mardaun ally, manliness of ally [ism].——*Mardoom giyah* (استرنج - ustaranj, Ar.; مردم گیاه - mardumgiyáh, Pers.; لکهمنی - lakhmuní, Hind.; لفاها - lufáha, Malay; காட்டுசுட்டி - káttusútti, Tam.). Title from pers. meaning man + grass. Hind. from (lákh, hind. lakh + muni, hind. sage). Tam. from (kádu, tam. forest + shuttu, tam. forehead ornament). **Ar.** also (laffáh); (yabrúh); (sirájulkutráb), meaning fairy's lamp; from use in magic rites. Pers. also (mihrgiyáh), meaning love grass, from the fact of those possessing the root being liked by others; (yabrúz). Greek μανδραγόρας μέλας, Latin mandragora or circeium. Dudaim of the bible. Venus was often styled Mandragorites. Title otherwise Devil's apple, Love apple, Mandrake. Botanically Mandragora officinarum, wight, solanaceæ [vricsham, 94]; generic from μάνρα cattle-fold, and in spite of the persian and english associations has nothing to do with the word man. A perennial plant, with a long, thick, fusiform, light brown root, which often bifurcates; the leaves are all radical, petioled and humifuse, broad, acute, with undulating edges; flowers numerous, on peduncles shorter than the leaves; fruit a yellow berry, ovoid; plants when fresh have a nauseous acrid taste. Has fetid root like parsnip in shape, with fancied resemblance to human form; nearly allied, in appearance and structure, to Atropa belladonna, linn. [dog angoor]. Formerly an article of materia medica. Smell of plant induces drowsiness; root narcotic and antispasmodic. The root is worn as a charm.——*Maroot* (मरुत् - marut, San.). From (mri, san. to die); agent of destruction. God of the wind [vayoo] in the Aryan mythology.——*Marwah* (मरुवक - maruvaka, San.; मरवा - maravá, Mahr.; مرزنجوش - marzanjúsh, Ar.; مرزنگوش - marzangúsh, Pers.; مروا - marwá, Hind. and Dec.; మరువము - maruvamu, Tel.; மரு - maru, Tam.). Title from sanscrit through hindostany. San. from (maru, san. desert); from habitat. Mahr. from sanscrit. Ar. from persian. Pers. from (marz, pers. mouse + gosh, pers. ear). Hind. from sanscrit. Tel. from sanscrit. Tam. means fragrance. San. also (p'hanijjaka), meaning serpent + holy basil, ocimum sanctum, linn. Ar. also (marzanjúnash); (bakalatulghizál), meaning gazelle herb; (habakulfíl), meaning elephant basil; (habakulkaná), meaning spear ocimum; (surmuk). Pers. also (ávíshan). Hind. and dec. also (dauná), cf. absinth. Tel. also (mridumaruvamu), meaning soft + the plant. Greek ἀμάρακον and σαμψύχον. Latin amaracus. Title otherwise Marjoram, Organy. Botanically the Origanum genus, labiatæ [vricsham, 103]. Aromatic herbs or under shrubs; leaves entire or toothed; flowers in cylindrical or oblong spikes; they give the hill-side on which they grow a gay appearance and hence the generic name.—"*a*" The best known species is botanically Origanum marjorana, linn., labiatæ [vricsham, 103]; alias Majoranum hortense; ornamental and aromatic shrub, native of portugal and palestine, here cultivated, brown fibrous root, flower odorous, sacred to soobramanyan [q.v.]. Seeds astringent, leaves eaten with gynandropsis pentaphylla, dc. [vailay], for colic; essential oil from leaves used as a perfume. Leaves used for flavoring sauces, &c.—"*b*" Another species is vulgare. Bears small, rose-colored or purple flowers; yields oil of thyme [ipar], a remedy for toothache. Esteemed by mahomedans as tonic; the dried leaves used as tea [q.v.].—"*c*" Pot marjoram is onites. ——*Marwarry* (ماروڑی - márwárí, Hind.). From (maru, san. desert); from the arid tract of marwah, their country. A caste from marwah in central india, the members of which follow the business of banker, broker and merchant. They are mostly of Jeina [q.v.] religion. They are spread over all towns in the peninsula. Numbers about 500 [jauty].——*Maur* (मार - már, San.). To kill.——*Mauran* (मार - mára, San.; மாறன் - máran, Tam.). Means killer. Manmatan [q.v.]. Pariah proper name [peyar].——*Mauraun* (മാരൻ - márán, Mal.). From being originally employed in maury or bhagavaty temples. Sweepers and musicians in temples.——*Mauriyamman* (மாரியம்மன் - máriyamman, Tam.). From (mári, tam. death + amman, tam. goddess). The best known of the South indian tutelary village goddesses. Literally the mother of death, or of contagious diseases, more especially of the small-pox [maury]. She is supposed to inflict these diseases, and also to deliver from them. Mauriyamman is represented in the arts in a sitting posture, with four hands, in which she holds the same weapon as Yellamma. Her pagodas [q.v.] are to be found everywhere, usually at some distance from the villages in groves. Many of them are somewhat large, and surrounded by a wall, within which there is a vaulted stage, containing figures of wood, on which she is carried at festivals; and in front of all of them stands an altar of stone. In the pagoda stands her image of stone, together with that of Vigneshwaran [q.v.]. But her image is also made of metal; and small images of wood or stone, representing all the different Graumadevatays [q.v.], are sometimes found in the houses of the Tamulians [q.v.]. Opposite to her pagoda stands a small temple, in which are the following images:—Chettippen or the daughter of a merchant, stolen by Cauttaun; Cauttaun or a chief among the demons, of whom the people are more afraid than of mauriyamman; Mautangy; Pauppautty the daughter of a bramin, stolen by cauttaun; Shookmauttadicaurar or wearers of a staff called shookmauttady, her door-keepers; Veerabhadran; Yidaippen or shepherd woman. Besides these images, there are many more figures of clay, both within and without the enclosure of the pagodas, all of which are presented in fulfilment of vows by people who recover from the small-pox. These however are not worshipped, but regarded simply as ornaments. In those pagodas, which have a sufficient income, Mauriyamman receives an offering daily, in the lesser pagodas only on Friday. Besides the ordinary offerings that are made to her by the priest, she receives also extraordinary offerings, consisting of eatables which are laid before the pagoda by women; and these offerings belong to the priest [poojarry] and other servants of the pagoda. Moreover in her honor an annual festival is celebrated, which lasts eight days, when her image is carried every morning and evening. On the last and principal day, many thousands of people, more especially women, gather together near her pagoda, kindle fires, boil rice, &c., and make offerings therewith to her. The men bring goats [velland], and cocks [moorghy], and beheading them before the pagoda, ask the goddess to protect them in the coming year from evil. They have at the same time dancing and sports of kinds. This festival is not celebrated at a fixed time, but whenever it is convenient to the people of a place. There are no books written specially about Mauriyamman, but a few stories are told of her in various books relating to other deities. She has a variety of names:—Candcaul amman, the forest-goddess; Comala vully, the beautiful female; Cotty, the valiant female; Maha peroondevy, the very great goddess; Maury, death, small-pox; Mautangy, the wilful pariah woman; Mody, show, enchantment; Shoory, heroine; Vadoogantye, vadoogan's or bheiravan's mother, &c. To propitiate Mauriyamman, hook-swinging was once practised, many persons making a vow to swing in her honor every year. As a rule however the hook-swinging [shirry] was done by professional devotees [matam]. See vol. I (78), (82). Mauriyannan and Mauriyappan are common names among non-bramins [peyar]. ——*Mauriyaye* (மாரியாயி - máriyáyi, Tam.). Proper name [peyar].——*Maurthy* (மாருதி - máruthi, Tam.). Son of Maroot. Epithet of Hanooman [q.v.]. Hindoo 2nd or pers. name [peyar].——*Maury* (मारी - márí, San.; மாரி - mári, Tam.). Means killer. Same as Mauriyamman. See vol. I (71). Pariah proper name [peyar]. Common to both sexes.——*Mirch* (مرچ - mirch, Hind.). Means killing, from burning sensation [mar]. Pepper. Cauly mirch is black pepper. Laul mirch is red pepper; same as Common chilly.——*Miriyaul* (మిరియాలు - miriyálu, Tel.). Means killing, from burning sensation. Same as Black pepper. ——*Moordar* (مردار - murdár, Hind.). Dead. ——*Moordar sing* (مردا سنج - murdásanj, Ar.; مردا سنگ - murdásing, Pers.; مردار سنگ - murdársing, Hind. and Dec.; ಮುದದಾರಶಿಂಗಿ - mudadárashingi, Can.; ముదారసింగు - murdárasingu, Tel.; മുദാരശിങ്ങു - mudárasingu, Mal.; மிருதாரசிங்கி - miruthárasingi, Tam.). Pers. from (murdah, pers. dead + sang, pers. stone). Hind. from (murdár, hind. dead + sang, pers. stone). Can., &c., from hindostany. Litharge. Otherwise Impure oxide of lead. Plumbi oxidum of chemists. A semi-vitrified oxide of lead in the form of small shining heavy scales, or more or less agglutinated masses; usually produced in the purification of silver [velly] from lead [eeyam]. Medicinally irritant; inhalation of vapour poisonous; veidyans [q.v.] use as ingredient of plasters; natives generally employ mixed with vinegar [caudy] to remove pimples from face. Also used by painters [rangh].

MAR (മാർ - már, *Mal.*). Lord. Ecclesiastical title among the Malabar syrian christians.

MARABOU (مرابو - marabu, *Hind.*). From javanese. Under-tail coverts of the Adjutant [q.v.] crane. The feathers are very light, and are much worn for head-dresses, the white kinds being exceedingly valuable.

MARAM (दारु - dáru, *San.*; لکڑی - lakrí, *Hind.*; ಮರ - mara, *Can.*; మాను - mánu, *Tel.*; മരം - maram, *Mal.*; மரம் - maram, *Tam.*). Tree.——**(1)** The influence of trees on climate is to prevent the too rapid withdrawal of moisture from the soil, a point of great importance in this country where the heat of the sun is intense and the supply of water is dependant only upon periodical falls of rain [mazhay, monsoon]. Wood and timber are not only applied here to the usual economic uses, but they also furnish fuel [lukdy] to all classes, supplying the place of coal [nilakary], which has not yet been found in any quantity within the limits of the presidency.——**(2)** The following are two key-lists of the timber trees of s. india for which vernacular names are known; further information must be traced in the glossary paragraphs through the small-type cross references at end of this volume; see also vricsham, 7 for the method of expressing the products, &c., of the trees in the dravidian languages.—"*a*" Acacia arabica, babool; Acacia catechu, catechu; Acacia farnesiana, cassie-oil plant; Acacia ferruginea, anasandra; Acacia intsia, corindah; Acacia leucophlæa, white babool; Acacia melanoxylon, australian blackwood; Acacia pennata, rusty mimosa; Acacia planifrons, arrow thorn tree; Acacia suma, white sundra; Acacia sundra, sundra; Acacia tomentosa, umbrella thorn; Acrocarpus fraxinifolius, shingle tree; Adansonia digitata, baobab; Adenanthera pavonina, false red sanders; Adhatoda vasica, malabar nut; Adina cordifolia, model wood; Ægle marmelos, bael; Ailanthus excelsa, coromandel ailanto; Ailanthus malabarica, malabar ailanto; Alangium lamarckii, ancola; Albizzia amara, dark sirissa; Albizzia lebbek, common sirissa; Albizzia odoratissima, fragrant sirissa; Albizzia procera, var. elata, hill sirissa; Albizzia stipulata, stone sirissa; Aleurites triloba, lumbang nut; Alstonia scholaris, dita; Amoora rohituka, rohitacam; Anacardium occidentale, cashew; Anogeissus acuminata, pauchimaun; Anogeissus latifolia, vekkauly; Anona muricata, sour sop; Anona reticulata, bullock's heart; Anona squamosa, sweet sop; Anthocephalus cadamba, cadamba; Antiaris saccidora, sack tree; Antidesma bunius, chinese laurel; Antidesma ghæsembilla, var. genuinum, gasambilla; Aquilaria agallocha, eagle wood; Areca catechu, areca; Artocarpus hirsuta, anjely; Artocarpus incisa, ratadel; Artocarpus integrifolia, bread fruit; Artocarpus lakoocha, lakoocha; Atalantia monophylla, monkey lime; Averrhoa bilimbi, blimbing; Averrhoa carambola, coromandel gooseberry; Avicennia officinalis, ooppata mangrove; Balanites roxburghii, fire-work plant; Balsamodendron berryi, kiloovay; Balsamodendron mukul, mookul bdellium; Bambusa arundinacea, common bamboo; Bambusa stricta, male bamboo; Bambusa vulgaris, striped bamboo; Barringtonia acutangula, small indian oak; Barringtonia racemosa, common indian oak; Bassia latifolia, wild mohwah; Bassia longifolia, common mohwah; Bauhinia anguina, snake-like mountain ebony; Bauhinia malabarica, malabar mountain ebony; Bauhinia purpurea, purple mountain ebony; Bauhinia racemosa, small-flowered mountain ebony; Bauhinia retusa, nirpa mountain ebony; Bauhinia tomentosa, wild mountain ebony; Bauhinia vahlii, large mountain ebony; Bauhinia variegata, variegated mountain ebony; Berberis aristata, berberry; Berrya ammonilla, trincomalee tree; Bischoffia javanica, var. genuina, javanese cedar; Bixa orellana, monkey turmeric; Bombax malabaricum, red cotton tree; Borassus flabelliformis, palmyra; Boswellia serrata, yellow dammer; Boswellia serrata, var. glabra, white dammer; Breynia rhamnoides, var. genuina, poolah shrub; Bridelia retusa, var. genuina, thorny vengay; Bruguiera gymnorhiza, candel mangrove; Buchanania latifolia, chironjee; Butea frondosa, bengal kino; Cæsalpinia bonducella, bonduc; Cæsalpinia coriaria, divy divy; Cæsalpinia sappan, sappan; Cæsalpinia sepiaria, mysore thorn; Calamus draco, sumatra dragon's blood; Calamus rotang, country rattan; Calophyllum angustifolium, narrow-leaved poon; Calophyllum bracteatum, bracteate poon; Calophyllum inophyllum, common poon; Calophyllum tomentosum, malabar poon; Calophyllum wightianum, small poon; Calotropis gigantea, mudar; Calycopteris floribunda, white wodala; Camellia theifera, tea; Canarium strictum, black dammer; Canthium didymum, black cauray; Capparis grandis, raghota caper; Capparis horrida, thorny caper; Carallia integerrima, caurally mangrove; Carapa moluccensis, crab-oil plant; Careya arborea, hindostany slow match; Carissa carandas, carondah; Caryota urens, bastard sago palm; Cassia auriculata, tungaid; Cassia fistula, indian laburnum; Cassia glauca, tree senna; Cassia marginata, horse cassia; Cassia siamea, sumatra senna; Cassia tora, chakondah; Casuarina equisetifolia, whip tree; Cedrela toona, toon; Celastrus paniculatus, malkangany; Celtis wightii, white indian nettle; Ceratonia siliqua, carob; Cerbera odollam, odallam; Chickrassia tabularis, chickrassy; Chloroxylon swietenia, satin wood; Cinnamomum zeylanicum, ceylon cinnamon; Citrus aurantium, var. aurantium proper, sweet orange; Citrus decumana, pummelow; Cochlospermum gossypium, golden silk cotton; Cocos nucifera, cocoanut; Coffea arabica, coffee; Corchorus capsularis, jute; Corchorus olitorius, wild jute; Cordia myxa, small sebestens; Cordia obliqua, large sebestens; Cordia rothii, narrow-leaved sebestens; Corypha umbraculifera, talipot; Cratæva religiosa, garlic pear; Croton oblongifolius, devil's goad; Cynometra ramiflora, iripa; Dæmia extensa, hedge cotton; Dalbergia lanceolaria, caunooga; Dalbergia latifolia, malabar blackwood; Dalbergia paniculata, yellow mountain ebony; Dalbergia sissoo, sissoo; Dendrocalamus tulda, bengal bamboo; Dichopsis elliptica, indian guttapercha; Dichrostachys cinerea, ashy babool; Dillenia indica, chaltah; Dillenia pentagyna, small chaltah; Diospyros ebenum, ceylon ebony; Diospyros embryopteris, gaub; Diospyros hirsuta, calaminder wood; Diospyros melanoxylon, coromandel ebony; Diospyros montana, forest gaub; Diospyros tomentosa, sweet gaub; Dodonæa viscosa, bog myrtle; Dolichandrone crispa, flowering pauthiry; Dolichandrone falcata, wody; Dolichandrone rheedii, long-leaved wody; Ehretia lævis, smooth coorvitchy; Elæodendron glaucum, nerija; Epicarpurus orientalis, stunted jack; Eriodendron anfractuosum, silk cotton; Erioglossum edule, rusty soapnut; Erythrina indica, common coral tree; Erythrina ovalifolia, devil coral tree; Erythrina stricta, thorny coral tree; Erythrina suberosa, white coral tree; Erythroxylon monogynum, deccany deodar; Eucalyptus globulus, blue gum; Eugenia alternifolia, moy; Eugenia arnottiana, small jaumoon; Eugenia jambolana, common jaumoon; Eugenia jambolana, var. caryophyllifolia, clove-leaved jaumoon; Eugenia operculata, cherry jaumoon; Euphorbia antiquorum, square milk-hedge; Euphorbia cattimandoo, cement plant; Euphorbia nereifolia, leafy milk-hedge; Euphorbia tirucalli, round milk-hedge; Eurya japonica, wild tea; Excœcaria agallocha, blinding tree; Excœcaria sebifera, china tallow; Feronia elephantum, wood-apple; Ficus bengalensis, banyan; Ficus excelsa, tall fig; Ficus glomerata, cluster fig; Ficus infectoria, stone banyan; Ficus racemosa, country fig; Ficus religiosa, peepul; Ficus tomentosa, hill banyan; Ficus tsiela, tsiela; Filicium decipiens, pehimbia; Flacourtia inermis, tomi-tomi; Flacourtia montana, attack; Flacourtia ramontchi, mauritius plum; Flacourtia ramontchi, var. sapida, ceylon plum; Garcinia cambogia, malabar gamboge; Garcinia indica, mate mangosteen; Garcinia mangostana, mangosteen; Garcinia morella, ceylon gamboge; Garcinia xanthochymus, yellow mangosteen; Gardenia latifolia, hill emetic nut; Gradenia lucida, decamallee; Gardenia turgida, nunjoondam; Garuga pinnata, garooga; Givotia rottleriformis, white tanakk; Gluta travancorica, red carany; Gmelina arborea, cashmere tree; Gossypium arboreum, tree cotton; Gossypium barbadense, var. acuminatum, peruvian cotton; Grewia asiatica, falsah; Grewia orbiculata, round-leaved tadda; Grewia pilosa, dog-bran plant; Grewia salvifolia, jaurah; Grewia tiliæfolia, tadda; Guazuma tomentosa, roodrauck tree; Guettarda speciosa, indian zebra wood; Gymnosporia emarginata, small chintoo; Gymnosporia montana, large chintoo; Gyrocarpus jacquini, tanakk; Hardwickia binata, yaipy; Helicteres isora, screw tree; Hemigyrosa canescens, fig mango; Heritiera littoralis, looking glass plant; Hibiscus tiliaceus, cork-wood bendy; Hiptage madablota, delight of the woods; Holarrhena antidysenterica, telicherry bark; Holigarna longifolia, holigarna; Holopetala integrifolia, indian elm; Homonoya riparia, wild gannair; Hopea parviflora, water caung; Hopea wightiana, common caung; Hydnocarpus venenata, fish-poison tree; Ixora parviflora, torch tree; Jasminum humile, golden jasmine; Jatropha curcas, physic nut; Jatropha glandulifera, adul oil; Jatropha multifida, small physic nut; Kandelia rheedii, candel mangrove; Lagerstrœmia flos-reginæ, adambo; Lagerstrœmia lanceolata, venteak; Lagerstrœmia parviflora, loose strife; Lawsonia alba, henna plant; Lebedieropsis orbicularis, var. collina, garrar; Limonia acidissima, wild lime; Loranthus longiflorus, gooloom; Lumnitzera racemosa, madagascar mangrove; Maba buxifolia, neilgherry satin-wood; Macaranga indica, round-leaved lotus; Mallotus philippensis, kamela; Mangifera indica, mango; Melanthesopsis patens, large neeroory; Melia azadirachta, margosa; Melia azedarach, large neem; Melia dubia, hill neem; Melocanna rheedii, berry-bearing bamboo; Memecylon edule, cassa; Mesua ferrea, naugachampak; Michelia champaca, champak; Miliusa velutina, black doodooga; Millingtonia hortensis, indian cork; Mimusops elengi, ilanjy; Mimusops hexandra, monkey-face paulay; Mimusops kauki, edible paulay; Morinda citrifolia, ach root; Moringa pterygosperma, indian horse radish; Murraya exotica, andaman satin-wood; Murraya kœnigii, curry leaf tree; Myristica malabarica, malabar nutmeg; Nephelium litchi, litchy; Nephelium longana, longan; Ochna squarrosa, shilandy; Ochrocarpus longifolius, soora poon; Odina wodier, wodier; Olea dioica, indian olive; Ougeinia dalbergioides, nemmy; Pavetta indica, pavetta; Persea nan-muh, nan-muh; Phœnix sylvestris, wild date; Phyllanthus distichus, brazil cherry; Phyllanthus emblica, emblic myrobalan; Phyllanthus polyphyllus, forest nelly; Pimenta officinalis, pimento; Pithecolobium bigeminum, venezuela soap-bark; Pithecolobium dulce, corcapilly; Pithecolobium saman, zamang; Plecospermum spinosum, cority; Poinciana elata, indian poinciana; Poinciana regia, flamboyant; Polyalthia cerasoides, doodooga; Pongamia glabra, indian beech; Premna integrifolia, moonnay; Premna latifolia, buffalo moonnay; Premna tomentosa, fire-brand teak; Prosopis glandulosa, mesquit; Prosopis spicigera, shamee; Protium caudatam, hill kiloovay; Psidium guyava, guava; Psidium guyava, var. pyriferum, white guava; Pterocarpus indicus, andaman red wood; Pterocarpus marsupium, malabar kino; Pterocarpus santalinus, red sanders; Pterospermum suberifolium, velanga; Punica granatum, pomegranate; Putranjiva roxburghii, wild olive; Randia dumetorum, common emetic nut; Randia uliginosa, gray emetic nut; Rhododendron arboreum, neilgherry rhododendron; Ricinus communis, castor-oil; Salix tetrasperma, indian willow; Salvadora oleoides, large tooth-brush tree; Salvadora persica, tooth-brush tree; Samadera indica, niepa bark; Sandoricum indicum, malay red wood; Santalum album, sandal; Sapindus trifoliatus, soap-nut; Saraca indica, bengal ashocam; Schleichera trijuga, ceylon oak; Schrebera swietenioides, weaver's beam; Securinega leucopyrus, white honey shrub; Semecarpus anacardium, marking nut; Sesbania ægyptiaca, common sesban; Sesbania grandiflora, west-indian sesban; Shorea robusta, common saul; Shorea talura, taloora saul; Shorea tumbuggaia, tambaga saul; Sideroxylon tomentosum, foreign ilanjy; Sonneratia acida, blatty; Soymida febrifuga, rohan tree; Spondias mangifera, hog plum; Sponia wightii, indian nettle; Stephegyne parvifolia, water cadamba; Sterculia balanghas, edible sterculia; Sterculia colorata, wild papaw; Sterculia fœtida, bastard poon; Sterculia guttata, dung tree; Sterculia urens, false tragacanth; Sterculia villosa, odul; Stereospermum chelonoides, pauthiry; Stereospermum xylocarpum, valencoorny; Stilnophyllum elasticum, indian caoutchouc; Strychnos nux-vomica, poison nut; Strychnos potatorum, clearing nut; Symplocos racemosa, californian cinchona; Tabernæmontana coronaria, adam's apple; Tabernæmontana dichotoma, eve's apple; Tamarindus indica, tamarind; Tamarix dioica, cypress tamarisk; Tectona grandis, teak; Terminalia arjuna, arjoon; Terminalia belerica, belleric myrobalan; Terminalia catappa, country almond; Terminalia chebula, chebulic myrobalan; Terminalia paniculata, flowering murdah; Terminalia tomentosa, var. coriacea, leathery murdah; Terminalia tomentosa, var. typica, black murdah; Tetranthera monopetala, meida lukdy; Thespesia populnea, portia; Thevetia nereifolia, exile tree; Toddalia aculeata, lopez root; Trewia nudiflora, river portia, Vateria indica, piney; Ventilago madraspatana, pappily; Vitex alata, peacock gingelly; Vitex altissima, wild peacock gingelly; Vitex leucoxylon, field notchy; Vitex negundo, notchy; Vitex pubescens, tall notchy; Webera corymbosa, tirauna; Woodfordia floribunda, godaury; Wrightia tinctoria, paula indigo; Wrightia tomentosa, ground paulay; Xylia dolabriformis, burmah iron wood; Zanthoxylum rhetsa, rhetsa; Zizyphus glabrata, carook vauly; Zizyphus jujuba, bair; Zizyphus nummularia, forest bair; Zizyphus œnoplia, jackal bair; Zizyphus xylopyrus, nutty bair.—"*b*" Ach root, morinda; Adambo, lagerstrœmia; Adam's apple, tabernæmontana; Adul oil, jatropha; Ailanto, ailanthus; Almond, terminalia; Anasandra, acacia; Ancola, alangium; Anjely, artocarpus; Arjoon, terminalia; Arrow thorn, acacia; Ashocam, saraca; Attack, flacourtia; Babool, acacia, dichrostachys; Bael, ægle; Bair, zizyphus; Bamboo, bambusa, dendrocalamus, melocanna; Banyan, ficus; Baobab, adansonia; Bdellium, balsamodendron; Beech, pongamia Bendy, hibiscus; Berberry, berberis; Blackwood, acacia, dalbergia; Blatty, sonneratia; Blimbing, averrhoa; Blinding tree, excœcaria; Blue gum, eucalyptus; Bog myrtle, dodonia; Bonduc, cæsalpinia; Bran plant, grewia; Brazil cherry, phyllanthus; Bread fruit, artocarpus; Bullock's heart, anona; Cadamba, anthocephalus, stephegyne; Calaminder wood, diospyros; Caoutchouc, stilpnophyllum; Caper, capparis; Carany, gluta; Carob, ceratonia; Carondah, carissa; Carook vauly, zizyphus; Cashew, anacardium; Cashmere tree, gmelina; Cassa, memecylon; Cassie, acacia; Castor-oil, ricinus; Catechu, acacia; Caung, hopea; Caunooga, dalbergia; Cauray, canthium; Cedar, bischoffia; Cement plant, euphorbia; Chakondah, cassia; Chaltah, dillenia; Champak, mesua, michelia; Chickrassy, chickrassia; China tallow, excœcaria; Chinese laurel, antidesma; Chintoo, gymnosporia; Chironjee, buchanania; Cinchona, symplocos; Cinnamon, cinnamomum; Clearing nut, strychnos; Cocoanut, cocos; Coffee, coffea; Coorvitchy, ehretia; Coral tree, erythrina; Corcapilly, pithecolobium; Corindah, acacia; Cority, plecospermum; Cork, millingtonia; Cotton, dæmia, gossypium; Crab oil, carapa; Curry-leaf tree, murraya; Dammer, boswellia, canarium; Date, phœnix; Delight of woods, hiptage; Deodar, erythroxylon; Devil's goad, croton; Dita, alstonia; Divy divy, cæsalpinia; Doodooga, miliusa, polyalthia; Dragon's blood, calamus; Dung tree, sterculia; Eagle wood, aquilaria; Ebony, bauhinia, diospyros; Elm, holopetala; Emetic nut, gardenia, randia; Eve's apple, tabernæmontana; Exile tree, thevetia; Falsah, grewia; Fig, ficus; Fire-work plant, balanites; Fish poison, hydnocarpus; Flamboyant, poinciana; Gamboge, garcinia; Gannair, homonoya; Garlic pear, cratæva; Garooga, garuga; Garrar, lebedieropsis; Gasambilla, antidesma; Gaub, diospyros; Gingelly, vitex; Godaury, woodfordia; Gooloom, loranthus; Gooseberry, averrhoa; Guava, psidium; Gutta-percha, dichopsis; Henna, lawsonia; Hog plum, spondias; Horse radish, moringa; Ilanjy, mimusops, sideroxylon; Indigo, wrightia; Iripa, cynometra; Ironwood, xylia; Jack, epicarpurus; Jasmine, jasminum; Jaumoon, eugenia; Jaurah, grewia; Jute, corchorus; Kamela, mallotus; Kiloovay, balsamodendron, protium; Kino, butea, pterocarpus; Laburnum, cassia; Lakoocha, artocarpus; Lime, atalantia, limonia; Litchy, nephelium; Longan, nephelium; Looking-glass plant, beritiera; Loose strife, lagerstrœmia; Lopez root, toddalia; Lotus, macaranga; Lumbang, aleurites; Malabar nut, adhatoda; Malkangany, celastrus; Mango, hemigyrosa, mangifera; Mangosteen, garcinia; Mangrove, avicennia, bruguiera, carallia, kandelia, lumnitzera, rhizhophora; Margosa, melia; Marking-nut, semecarpus; Meidalukdy, tetranthera; Mesquit, prosopis; Milk-hedge, euphorbia; Mimosa, acacia; Modelwood, adina; Mohwah, bassia; Moonnay, premna; Mountain ebony, dalbergia; Moy, eugenia; Mudar, calotropis; Murdah, terminalia; Myrobalan, phyllanthus, terminalia; Nan-muh, persea; Neem, melia; Neeroory, melanthesopsis; Neipa bark, samadera; Nelly, phyllanthus; Nemmy, ougeinia; Nerija, elæodendron; Nettle, celtis, sponia; Notchy, vitex; Nunjoondam, gardenia; Nutmeg, myristica; Oak, barringtonia, schleichera; Odallam, cerbera; Odul, sterculia; Olive, olea, putranjiva; Orange, citrus; Palmyra, borassus; Papaw, sterculia; Pappily, ventilago; Pauchimaun, anogeissus; Paulay, mimusops, wrightia; Pauthiry, stereospermum; Peepul, ficus; Pehimbia, filicium; Physic nut, jatropha; Pimento, pimenta; Piney, vateria; Plum, flacourtia; Poison nut, strychnos; Pomegranate, punica; Poolah, breynia; Poon, calophyllum, ochrocarpus, sterculia; Portia, thespesia, trewia; Ratadel, artocarpus; Rattan, calamus; Red cotton, bombax; Red wood, pterocarpus, sandoricum; Rhetsa, zanthoxylum; Rohan, soymida; Rohitacam, amoora; Roodrauck, guazuma; Sack tree, antiaris; Sago palm, caryota; Sandal, santalum; Sanders, adenanthera, pterocarpus, Sappan, cæsalpinia; Satin-wood, chloroxylon, maba, murraya; Saul, shorea; Screw tree, helictores; Sebestens, cordia; Senna, cassia; Sesban, sesbania; Shamee, prosopis; Shilandy, ochna; Shingle tree, acrocarpus; Silk cotton, cochlospermum, eriodendron; Sirissa, albizzia; Sissoo, dalbergia; Slow match, careya; Soap bark, pithecolobium; Soap nut, erioglossum, sapindus; Sour sop, anona; Sundra, acacia; Sweet sop, anona; Tadda, grewia; Talipot, corypha; Tamarind, tamarindus; Tanakk, givotia, gyrocarpus; Tea, camellia, eurya; Teak, premna, tectona; Tellicherry bark, holarrhena; Thorn, acacia, cæsalpinia; Tirauna, webera; Tomi-tomi, flacourtia; Toon, cedrela; Tooth brush tree, salvadora; Torch tree, ixora; Tragacanth, sterculia; Trincomalee, berrya; Tsiela, ficus; Tungaid, cassia; Turmeric, bixa; Valencoorny, stereospermum; Vekkauly, anogeissus; Velanga, pterospermum; Vengay, bridelia; Venteak, lagerstrœmia; Weaver's beam, schrebera; Whip tree, casuarina; White honey shrub, securinega; Willow, salix; Wodala, calycopteris; Wodier, odina; Wody, dolichandrone; Woodapple, feronia; Yaipy, hardwickia; Zamang, pithecolobium; Zebra wood, guettarda.——(3) *Maracaur* (മരക്കാർ - marakkár, Mal.). From (marakkalam, mal. boat + kár, mal. plural termination showing possession). Titular appellation of the Moplah [q.v.] mahomedans on the south-west coast [peyar].——*Maramairy* (மரமேறி - maraméri, Tam.). From (maram, tam. tree + éru, tam. to ascend). Another name for Shaunaur [q.v.].——*Marungotty* (दार्वाघाटकुल - dárvághátakula, San.; نقارالخشب - nakkárulkhashb, Ar.; کتھ پھوڑ - kathphor, Hind.; لکڑ پھوڑ - lakarphor, Dec.; پالتك - pálatuk, Malay; ಮರಕುಟಕ - marakutaka, Can.; వడ్లంగిపిట్ట - vadlangipitta, Tel.; മരങ്കൊത്തി - marankotti, Mal.; மரங்கொத்தி - marangotti, Tam.). Title from tamul. San. from (dáru, san. wood + ághat, san. to strike). Ar. from (nakkár, ar. constant pecker + khashb, ar. wood). Hind. from (kath, hind. wood + phor, hind. breaker). Dec. from (lakar, dec. wood + phor, hind. breaker). Can. from (mara, can. wood + kutaka, can. pecker). Tel. from (vadlangi, tel carpenter + pitta, tel. bird). Mal. and tam. from (maram, tam. tree + kottu, tam. to peck). Ar. also (akhyal); (surad). Tel. also (mánutolachi), meaning wood borer; (chirutapakshi), meaning castanet bird from rapid rapping on trees. Tam. also (marandulaiççi), meaning wood borer. Picidæ family, scansores, insessores, aves [pacshy, 13], of naturalists [jantoo]. Wood-peckers. Divide into:—Picinæ, Campephilinæ, Gecininæ, Yunginæ or wrynecks.——*Marcalan* (മരക്കലൻ - marakkalan, Mal.). From (marakkalam, mal. boat). Title among fishermen. Hindoo third name [peyar].——*Marcam* (మరకము - marakamu, Tel.). From (marakkál, tam. the measure). Measure of capacity. 12 pucka seers = 1 marcam [alavay, 3b]. Approximate actual value:—1 marcam = 840 cubic inches. Same as Tam. paunay. Compare Mercaul, Parrah of malabar. See vol. I, 609; II, 511.——*Marcauyar* (மரைக்காயர் - maraikkáyar, pers. pl., Tam.). Tamul form of Maracaur; applied to Lubbays [q.v.] honorifically.——*Marotty* (कडूकवंठ - kadúkavant'ha, Mahr.; गडेफल - gardap'hala, Conc.; جنگلی بادام کا پیڑ - janglíbádámkáper, Hind.; جنگلی بادام کا جھاڑ - janglíbádamkájhár, Dec.; ಗರುಡಫಲ - garudap'hala, Can.; ಸೂರಂಟೆ - súrante, Too.; నీరుడుచెట్టు - níruduchettu, Tel.; മരോട്ടി - marótti, Mal.; මකුලු - makulu, Singh.; நீரடிமுத்து - níradimuttu, Tam.). Title from malayalam. Mahr. from (kadú, mahr. bitter + kavant'ha, mahr. wood-apple, feronia elephantum, corr.). Conc. from canarese. Hind. from (janglí, hind. wild + bádám, hind. prunus amygdalus, baill.). Dec. from hindostany. Can. from (garuda, san. braminy kite + p'hala, san. fruit). Tel. from (níru, tel. water + údu, tel. to drop out + chettu, tel. tree); from its drawing out bad water from blood in skin diseases. Mal. from (maram, mal. tree + vattu, mal. ball); fruits resembling wooden balls. Tam. from (nír, tam. water + adi, tam. to strike + muttu, tam. pearl) [wild jamalgota]. Tel. also (adavibádamchettu), meaning wild almond tree, prunus amygdalus, baill. Mal. also (níralam). Singh. also (ratakakuna), meaning foreign canarium zeylanicum. Tam. also (maravattai), (nírettimuttu), meaning water + to reach + pearl-like seed. Title otherwise Fish-poison tree, Jungle almond, Makooloo, Maravetty, Neeradimoot, Soorty-oil tree, Tamana-oil tree. Botanically Hydnocarpus venenata, gærtn., bixineæ [vricsham, 14]. Alias Chilmoria pentandra; Hydnocarpus inebrians; Munniksia laurifolia. Tree, 50 feet; leaves glabrous, crenately serrated, alternate; sepals five, two outer ones ovate, three inner ones larger, very concave; petals five, fringed with soft white hairs; fruit globose, very hard, as large as an apple [seb], crowned with the undivided portion of the stigma; seeds numerous; flowers small, white; malabar. Kernel of seed has nauseous smell, and tastes unctuous and a little acrid. Oil got by expression resembles in appearance almond oil but much thicker; in effects resembles chaulmoogra [q.v.], giving a green reaction with sulphuric acid [gandhac tezaub]. Oil in great repute as a drastic, and externally for leprosy [cooshtam] and other cutaneous complaints; in pharm. non-officinal; kernels and thin shells sometimes ground together, mixed with castor-oil [aumanac] applied externally to cure itch. Fruit, if eaten, occasions giddiness; seeds act as a poison to fish [common emetic nut, indian berry, indian oak, round milk-hedge, sooptee, tejbul, walsoora, zanzibar indigo], but render them unfit for use as food. There are species alpina and wightiana.——*Mercaul* (మరకము - marakamu, Tel.; மரக்கால் - marakkál, Tam.). From (maram, tam. wood + kalam, tam. vessel).—"*a*" Measure of capacity. 8 puddies = 1 mercaul; 12 mercauls = 1 calam [alavay, 3a]. Approximate actual value, 1 mercaul = 800 cubic inches. But very various in the districts. Same as cooroony. Compare Tel. marcam, coonchum, toom. See vol. I, 609; II, 506, 507, 509, 513, 515, 518, 519. Penday mercaul means split bamboo mercaul; it contains $2\frac{1}{2}$ Madras measures or puddies.—"*b*" Superficial measure. 8 puddies = 1 mercaul; 21 mercauls = 1 dhaunya cottay [alavay, 2a]. Approximate actual value, 1 mercaul = 3,362 square feet. Used in Tinnevelly. Land requiring a mercaul of seed. Same as Cooroony. Compare Tel. coonchum, Mal. parrah.——*Mercaunum* (மரக்காணம் - marakkánam, Tam.). From (maram, tam. wood + kánam, tam. horse gram, dolichos biflorus, linn.).—"*a*" Deputy tahsildarry, South arcot district. Pay Rs. 70.—"*b*" Town, Port, Deputy tahsildar's station. South arcot dist., Tindivanam tal.; pop. 5,690; acres 9,716; lat. 12° 12′; long. 79° 59′; from Chidambaram N.N.E. 56 miles; from Cuddalore N.N.E. 34 miles; from Madras S.S.W. 64 miles; from Pondicherry N.N.E. 19 miles; from Sadras S.S.W. 25 miles; from Tindivanam E. 20 miles; from Tricalore E.N.E. 51 miles; from Vriddhauchellam N.N.E. 61 miles. Village by a backwater. Salt [ooppoo] manufactured. Cocoanut [q.v.] keets [q.v.] manufactured.

MARAM (மறம் - maram, *Tam.*). Bravery.——*Marava* (மறவ - marava, Tam.). Means warrior. The Marullo of Cosmas indicopleustes. A race allied to the Cullar [q.v.], found in Madura, Tinnevelly, Ramnaud, and Shivagunga. Ramnaud is the Greater marava country and Shivagunga the Smaller marava country. Their early history is very obscure, and it is only known that they are very ancient. At least two centuries before the Christian era, Kirautan their ruler made war with Coola bhooshana paundyan, and overran the whole of his country. Nothing else is known till the invasion of the country by the Mahomedans, which terminated the Paundyan dynasty. The Maravar then threw off their old allegiance to the ruler of Madura, and during the administration of the Naickar continued practically independent. The origin of the title Saitoopaty [q.v.] held by their leader in Ramnaud, and their latter history will be found described at vol. I (124). To this class belonged most of the southern poligars [q.v.] who disputed with the English the possession of Tinnevelly during the latter half of the last and the first years of the present century. The tribe constituted themselves the protectors of more peaceable tribes in times when no central authority existed. Hence arose the systems of Desha cauval [q.v.] and Stala cauval [q.v.], or the guard of a tract of country comprising a number of villages against open marauders in armed bands, and the guard of separate villages, their houses and crops, against secret theft. The feudal chief received a contribution from the area around his fort in consideration of protection afforded against armed invation. His servants of the same caste, spreading themselves among the villages, received fees and sometimes rent-free land for undertaking to protect the property of the villagers against theft, or to restore an equivalent in value for anything so lost. Claims to Desha cauval fees as well as to Village cauval fees are of common occurrence to the present day [inam]. The Maravar resemble in this respect the Ramoosy of Sholapore and Bombay. Maravar are a dark-skinned race, of moderate height, the cranium rounded, narrow in front, forehead low, eyes large and full; the men do not wear turbans [puggry]; they wear their hair long; the women wear very long cloths folded in plaits, which they fasten behind; this is unlike other women of southern india, whose cloth is fastened on the right side in front; men and women wear ear-rings, and by pulling elongate the lobes of the ears. They worship the usual local deities and demons; on the occurrence of a small-pox or cholera epidemic devil-dances are common. The tribes that pay outward respect to the authority of the Saitoopaty are the eighteen chiefs of the Tanjore country, Wodeya tevar the chief of shivagunga, and the Tondiman of Poodoocottah. Deva [tevar] is the caste-title of all Maravar. The chief of Ramnaud however prefers to be called by his special hereditary title of Saitoopaty, lord of Rama's bridge. Numbers about 300,000. They have, at different times and in various proportions, been spread through the Tanjore, Madura, and Tinnevelly provinces; but properly speaking they inhabit a strip of land on the coast, from Cape comorin to some distance north of Ramnaud, the principal town. There are seven sub-divisions in the tribe, respectively denominated Shemboonautt marava, Condaiyan cottay marava, Appanore naud marava, Agatha marava, Worore naud marava, Oopcottay marava and Coorchicutt marava. Among these sub-divisions that of the Shemboonautt maravas is the principal. See vol. I (124); II, 52, 97, 230, 236.——*Mauramungalam* (மாறமங்கலம் - máramangalam, Tam.). From (máran, tam. pándya title + mangala, san. prosperity); Village; Tinnevelly dist., Tencaray tal.; pop. 1,108; acres 677; lat. 8° 39′; long. 78° 07′; from Shreeveicoontam E. 11 miles; from Tinnevelly E. 27 miles; from the sea W. 4 miles. Former name of a portion of Korkay [q.v.].——*Mauran* (மாறன் - máran, Tam.). Means brave man. Native title of the Paundy kings while at Korkay. A portion of Korkay was called Mauramungalam, 'the good fortune of the Mauran.' See vol. I (118), (120).

MARAUMUT (مرمت - marammat, *Hind.*). From (rama, ar. to mend). Repairs, small or large [doorast].——*Maraumut tafreek* (مرمت تفریق - marammattafrík, Hind.). From (above + tafrík, ar. distribution). Charge made upon ryots [q.v.] for preservation of tank [q.v.] bunds [q.v.], &c. They are required to furnish so many days' labour [amanjy] and so many loads of earth for filling in goolies [coozhy], &c. This is now often commuted to a money charge. See vol. I, 112.

MARAY (மறை - marai, *Tam.*). From (marai, to hide), hidden or secret knowledge. Vedam [q.v.].——*Maraimoothal* (மறைமுதல் - maraimuthal, Tam.). From (above + muthal, tam. first). The first in the Vedas. Shiva [q.v.]. Cf. Marayone for bramha [q.v.].

MARCAPORE (మార్కాపురము - márkápuramu, *Tel.* markápur*). From (márika, tel. a devotee of chennakéshavasvámi who built village + pura, san. town) [mar].——**(1)** Talook, Kurnool district. Tahsildar's pay Rs. 150. Area 1,117 square miles. Population 99,971. Language Teloogoo. N.E. of district. Bounded N. by Pulnaud talook of Kistna district, E. by Vinoocondah talook of same district and Darshy zemindarry of Nellore, S. by Cumbum talook, and W. by Nullamullays, which separate it from Nizam's territories and Nundicotcore talook. Very hilly and largely covered with jungle. Some hills are dome-shaped and crowned with pagodas [q.v.]. Some in N.W. corner contain extensive pasture lands to which cattle from coast resort for grazing. The W. half near Nullamullays is very unhealthy, fever being almost endemic. Soil is generally rocky. 89·58 per cent. of the soil is classed as red and is generally impregnated with sowdoo [q.v.]. Except in Dornaul valley and in neighbourhood of Marcapore, very little regady [regar]. The general poverty of soil is compensated by facilities which exist for construction of tanks [q.v.] and wells and the short depth, 8 yards, at which water is usually found. Several hills like Inooparauty condah contain iron [auhan] ore. Products are paddy [q.v.], cholum [q.v.], sadza [bajrah] the staple food here, corra [tinay], arikeloo [varagoo], candooloo [common dholl], castor-oil seeds [aumanac], cotton [q.v.], horse-gram [q.v.] and indigo [q.v.]. The paddy crop is generally raised by transplantation [nautt nadavoo]. Indigo cultivation has lately decreased. Rice [q.v.] and salt [ooppoo] are imported by the Lumbaudies [q.v.] and Yerkalas [q.v.] on pack-bullocks. Earth salt was formerly manufactured extensively and used for cattle Saltpetre [shorah] is also manufactured from salt earth found in streets and near the walls of houses. Rivers are Candlair, Doovvalair, Goondlacumma, Raullavaugoo, and Teegalair. Places of archæological interest:—Doddanaula, Marcapore, Millampully, Rajampulley, Tripoorauntacam, Vaimlacote, Vencataudripollem, Yerragondapollem. Principal Trig. stations:—Doorgapoocondah, Inooparautycondah. The leading places, &c., in the talook are the following.——*Bhoopatipully* (భూపతిపల్లి - bhúpatipalli, Tel.). From (bhúpati, san. earth-lord, epithet of a king + palli, tel. village). Village, B.K.S. railway station; pop. 1,533; acres 4,768; lat. 15° 40′; long. 79° 14′; from Kurnool E. 76 miles; from Marcapore S.W. 7 miles. On S. banks of Goondlacumma.——*Bommalaupooram* (బొమ్మలాపురం - bommalápuram, Tel.). From (bomma, tel. wooden toy + pura, san. town). Village; pop. 2,153; acres 3,906; lat. 15° 57′; long. 79° 11′; from Kurnool E. 72 miles; from Marcapore N.W. 17 miles. Residence of descendants of Dornaul poligar [q.v.].——*Calanootla* (కలనూతుల - kalanútula, Tel.). From (kalla, tel. hedge + núyi, tel. well). Village; pop. 1,591; acres 6,057; lat. 15° 49′; long. 79° 11′; from Kurnool E. 72 miles; from Marcapore W.N.W. 11 miles. In the hills. At temple of Cautamrauz annual festival on Teloogoo new year's day [pundigay, 4].——*Caukoola canama* (కాకులకనమ - kákulakanama, Tel.). See sep. title.——*Chaupalmadoogoo* (చాపలమడుగు - chápalamadugu, Tel.). From (chápa, tel. fish + madugu, tel. pond). Village; pop. 3,225; acres 5,740; lat. 16° 05′; long. 79° 25′; from Kurnool E.N.E. 89 miles; from Marcapore N.N.E. 24 miles. Former head-quarters of Deputy tahsildar. Also formerly seat of a poligar.——*Doopaud* (దూపాడు - dúpádu, Tel.). From (duppi, tel. spotted deer + pádu, tel. waste). Village; pop. 2,896; acres 8,497; lat. 15° 55′; long. 79° 25′; from Kurnool E.N.E. 89 miles; from Marcapore N.N.E. 14 miles. Former head-quarters of talook of same name. Ruins of fort built in Prattauparoodran's time. Large tank.——*Doorgapoocondah* (దుర్గపుకొండ - durgapukonda, Tel.). From (durga, san. fort + konda, tel. hill). Trig. station; lat. 16° 03′ 45·46″; long. 79° 08′ 09·04″; height 2,958 feet; from Marcapore N.N.W. 25 miles; from Vencataudripollem W. 8 miles.——*Doovvalair* (దువ్వలేరు - duvvaléru, Tel.) From (duvva, tel. dust + éru, tel. river). River. Tributary of the Goondlacumma.——*Dornaul* (దోరనాల - dóranála, Tel.). See sep. title.——*Gadzalacondah* (గజ్జలకొండ - gaddzalakonda, Tel.). From (ghizál, hind. antelope + konda, tel. hill). Village; pop. 2,416; acres 6,877; lat. 15° 45′; long. 79° 26′; from Kurnool E. 89 miles; from Marcapore E. 8 miles. Bilamboodoo cave in the vicinity has sacred spring. Hilly and rocky. Railway station.——*Goondlacumma* (గుండ్లకమ్మ - gundlakamma, Tel.). See sep. title.——*Inooparautycondah* (ఇనపరాతికొండ - inaparátikonda, Tel.). From (inumu, tel. iron + ráyi, tel. stone + konda, tel. hill). Trig. station; lat. 15° 59′ 39·81″; long. 79° 10′ 34·74″; height 2,372 feet; from Bommalaupooram N. 4 miles; from Marcapore N.N.W. 19 miles.——*Marcapore* (మార్కాపురము - márkápuramu, Tel.). See below.——*Muntraula canama* (మంత్రాలకనమ - mantrálakanama, Tel.). See sep. title.——*Murrivaimla* (మర్రివేముల - marrivémula, Tel.). From (marri, tel. banyan tree, ficus bengalensis, linn. + vému, tel. margosa tree, melia azadirachta, linn.). Village; pop. 1,553; acres 2,755; lat. 16° 14′; long. 79° 36′; from Kurnool E.N.E. 103 miles; from Marcapore N. 39 miles. Former seat of a poligar. A collateral scion of the family now draws small pension.——*Nullagoontla* (నల్లగుంట్ల - nallaguntla, Tel.). From (nalla, tel. black + gunta, tel. pond). Village; pop. 505; acres 1,653; lat. 15° 52′; long. 78° 58′; from Kurnool E. 57 miles; from Marcapore W.N.W. 25 miles. In the Nullamullays. Former seat of poligar whose ancestor served under the Vijianugger royel. On the decline of the power he seized nine villages, but was expelled by the Hyderabad kings and Aurungzeeb. The present representative, a widow, draws small pension. Deity of this village Mantraulammah, worshipped by Chentsoos [q.v.], gives name to Muntraula canama pass [ghaut].——*Nullamullay* (నల్లమల - nallamala, Tel.). See sep. title.——*Rollapenta* (రోళ్ళపెంట - róllapenta, Tel.). From (rólu, tel. the pounding mortar + penta, tel. heap). Village, Hill, Trig. station; lat. 15° 52′ 02·60″; long. 78° 51′ 09·09″; height 2,455 feet; from Kurnool E. 50 miles; from Marcapore W. 32 miles. Half-way over the Muntraula canama pass. Brinjarry [q.v.] camping ground. Grove of wild mangoes [q.v.]. Fine watering place.——*Teegalair* (తీగలేరు - tígaléru, Tel.). From (tíga, tel. creeper + éru, tel. river). River. Rises in Nullamullays, flows in E. direction and joins Goondlacumma near Doopaud. Runs from September to February.——*Tripoorauntacam* (త్రిపురాంతకం - tripurántakam, Tel.). From (tripura, san. name of the three-citied giant + antaka, san. destroyer). Epithet of shiva [q.v.] who is said to have destroyed the giant of that name to save mankind. Sanscrit name (tripurántakapura), meaning tripooran, the giant + destroyer + town. Village, Place of pilgrimage; pop. 1,410; acres 4,044; lat. 16° 00′; long. 79° 30′; from Kurnool E. 93 miles; from Marcapore N.E. 22 miles. Considered one of the gates of Srisheilam. Temple to Tripoorauntaceshwara sawmy on the top of hill. S.W. is temple of Tripoora soondary in a tank. Annual festivals for Tripoorauntaceshwaran on Shivarautry [pundigay, 6a] and for Tripoora soondary on Dusserah [pundigay, 6d].——*Veligonda* (వెలిగొండ - veligonda, Tel.). See sep. title.——*Vencataudripollem* (వెంకటాద్రిపాలెం - venkatádripálem, Tel.). From (venkatádri, tel. proper name + pálemu, tel. fortified village). Sanscrit name (venkatádripura), meaning vishnoo + hill + town. Village; pop. 3,452; acres 8,032; lat. 16° 03′; long. 79° 16′; from Kurnool E.N.E. 78 miles; from Marcapore N. 22 miles. Seat of a poligar with a small pension. N. is old Vishnoo [q.v.] temple with annual festival in February.——*Yandrapully* (ఎండ్రపల్లి - yandrapalli, Tel.). From (endri, tel. a crab + palli, tel. village). Village; pop. 1,154; acres 4,877; lat. 16° 07′; long. 79° 22′; from Kurnool E.N.E. 86 miles; from Marcapore N. 26 miles. Residence of ancient poligar in the hills.——*Yerragondapollem* (ఎఱ్ఱగొండపాలెం - erragondapálem, Tel.). From (erragondu, tel. proper name + pálemu, tel. fortified village). Named after yerragondoo, builder of the tank in the village. Village; pop. 2,890; acres 7,287; lat. 16° 03′; long. 79° 21′; from Kurnool E.N.E. 84 miles; from Marcapore N. 21 miles. Former seat of poligar. Large tank. Stone slab, lies in a field, on which the ancient rulers took their seat when administering justice.——**(2)** Village, Tahsildar's station; Kurnool dist., Marcapore tal.; pop. 3,276; acres 7,238; lat. 15° 44′; long. 79° 19′; from Cumbum N.E. 16 miles; from Kurnool E.S.E. 81 miles; from Madras N.N.W. 194 miles; from Nundiaul E. 55 miles; from Pyaupaly E.N.E. 107 miles. Large Vishnoo temple, with annual festival in April and allowance of Rs. 175. Copperplate grant [shausanam] dated A.D. 1542, records grant by Sadaushiva deva roya of Vijianugger. An officer of Gajapaty rajah named Teloogoo royadoo built the tank here as well as the large Teloogoo royady cheroo in the Nullamullay valleys in N.W. corner of talook [q.v.].

MARJ (मार्ज - márj, *San.*). To cleanse.——*Marjauram* (मार्जार - márjára, San.). From (márj, san. to cleanse); from habit of constantly cleaning itself. Cat. The genus Felis, felidæ [deeptaucsham], digitigrada, carnivora, mammalia [sastanam 9], of naturalists [jantoo]. The species known to the natives are:— bengalensis [shivingy poonay], caracal [q.v.], chaus [jungle cat], domestica [poonay], pardus [honiga], rubiginosa [poolly poonay], tigris [pooly], viverrina [meencolly poonay].

MARKING-NUT (भल्लातक - bhallátaka, *San.*; बिबी - bibí, *Mahr.*; बिब्बयि - bibbayi, *Conc.*; شجر حب القلب - shajarihabbulkalb, *Ar.*; درخت بلادر - darakhtibaládur, *Pers.*; بھیلے کا پیڑ - bhelekáper, *Hind.*; بھلاوین کا جھاڑ - bhilávenkájhár, *Dec.*; ಗೇರು - géru, *Can.*; ತೇರೆದಮರ - téredamaru, *Too.*; జీడిచెట్టు - jídichettu, *Tel.*; ଭଲ୍ଲିଆ - bhalliya, *Oor.*; ചേർ - chér, *Mal.*; බඩුල්ල - badulla, *Singh.*; சேரான் - shérán, *Tam.*). Title from juice of nut used to mark cotton cloth. San. from (bhall, san. to hurt); vesicant. Ar. from (shajar, ar. tree + habb, ar. nut + kalb, ar. heart), from shape of nut; cf. specific name. Pers. from (darakht, pers. tree + baládur, pers. marking nut). Hind. and dec. from sanscrit. Can. from tamul. Tel. from (jídi, tel. corrosive sap + chettu, tel. tree). Oor. from sanscrit. Mal. from tamul. Tam. from (shér, tam. to fit + á, tam. negative particle), disagreeable, from caustic juice. San. also (arushkara), meaning producing sores; (agnimukhí), meaning fire-faced; (vranakrit), meaning wounding, a vesicant; (kshatáksha), meaning wound seed; (vírataru), meaning heroic tree, from caustic juice. Ar. also (inkardiyá), from greek anacardia; (shajarihabbulfahm), meaning intellect nut tree. Hind. also (bhiláma), from sanscrit. Can. also (karigéru), meaning black + the tree; (kéru). Too. also (gérkáyi). Tel. also (nallajídi), meaning black + the tree; (tummedamámidi), meaning black beetle + mango tree, mangifera indica, linn. Mal. also (kampíra); (ténprákku). Singh. also, (shénkotte) from tamul. Tam. also (shé), meaning red; (tagilimá); (vírasági), meaning heroic tree; (erimugi), meaning burning face. Greek ξανθοβάλανον. Title otherwise Bhilawaun, Black beetle mango, Black varnish, Fire-face tree, Indian varnish, Intellect nut, Jeedy, Malacca bean, Malacca kidney bean, Marking fruit tree, Marknut tree, Marsh-nut, Singhalese varnish, Sore plant, Sylhet varnish. Botanically Semecarpus anacardium, linn. f., anacardiaceæ [vricsham 45]. Alias Anacardium latifolium, officinarum. Tree, 50 feet; leaves entire, cuneate-obovate, rounded at the apex, whitish beneath, but not downy; calyx flat, five-cleft; petals five, sessile, spreading; flowers panicled, terminal, branched; fruit sessile, cordate-ovate, with a slight notch on one side under the apex; flowers small, green; flowering in may to july; trunk straight, covered with grey scabrous bark; common in dry elevated jungles. Nut is described in arabic works as resembling the heart of an animal, the fleshy stem representing the auricles, and the fruit the ventricles; it is black, smooth, shining, and flattened on both sides; it contains between the laminæ of shell an acrid juice of a pale milk color till perfectly ripe, when juice becomes black; when dry the juice has all the appearance of a bitumen [shilajit], being brittle, translucent, and very inflammable; the juice is not soluble in water; it unites perfectly with oils; should be cautiously handled. Like cashew-nut, the marking-nut is a fruit and not a seed or nut as its name implies; but it is commonly known as a nut in contradistinction to the fleshy torus, to which it is attached, and which is considered by the natives of this country as a fruit. The fruit and its acrid oil are in medicine; internally, sedative, antispasmodic, nervine and alterative tonic; externally, stimulant, rubefacient and vesicant. Oil is generally prepared by natives by aid of heat; the nuts being slightly cut or broken at each of their ends, they are put in an earthen pot, the bottom of which is perforated by three or four small holes; the pot's mouth, well closed with an earthen plate, is placed over another and smaller vessel, and the two luted together, and then placed in a pit about 2½ feet deep and nearly as wide, with a smaller pit at its bottom just sufficient to hold the smaller vessel; the pot is finally surrounded with cakes of dry cow-dung [bratty], which are set on fire till they are consumed; on removing the vessels when cool, the smaller one at the bottom will be found to contain a thick, black, very acrid and smoky oil in proportion to the quantity of the nuts used in the process; the oil is to be strained through thin muslin [q.v.] if it is intended for internal use. The oil can however be got by compression, and thus prepared is more pure and quite free from smoke. An electuary is prepared as follows; take by weight one part of the marking-nut, six parts of the kernel of cashew-nut without the testa or skin in coarse powder, and one part of clarified honey [shahad]; bruise and rub well separately the marking-nut in a stone mortar, add gradually the cashew-nut powder and the honey, and rub them all into a uniform mass. Doses; of the acrid oil, from 60 to 150 minims; of the electuary, from 60 to 150 grains. Substituted; internally, for salicylate of soda, salicylic acid, colchicum, ether, belladonna, iodide of potassium, perchloride of mercury, aconite root, valerianate of zinc, and strychnia; externally, for cantharides. An oil is also made by boiling entire nut; with much the same properties. Juice employed to remove rheumatic pains, aches, and sprains; a powerful vesicant; employed for making fictitious bruises; employed in every kind of venereal complaint; also given internally in small doses in leprous and scrofulous affections [cooshtam]. Oil used externally. The farina of anthers of flowers is narcotic and irritating; people of a peculiar habit sleeping under tree when in blossom, or even going near the flowers are stupefied, and have their faces and limbs swollen. Bruised nut applied by native women to procure abortion. Gives to pharm. juice between laminæ of shell, non-officinal; used in veterinary practice. The yellow mature corolla and receptacle are fleshy and of a sweetish sour taste, and are eaten roasted; seeds also eaten, supposed to stimulate the mental powers and especially, the memory. The whole nuts are used as a mordant [cauram]; the black juice is used to mark cotton cloth; by the mixture of quicklime [choonam] and water the color is improved, prevented from running, and fixed; juice also used as a varnish [rangh]; in caulking ships; the bark mildly astringent gives out in decoction a deep color, which dyes brown of various shades [shauyam]; the bark wounded yields a dirty looking, brownish, soft gum [gond]; the green nuts, well pounded into a paste, make good bird lime; the dark tenacious oil from seeds is used as a preventive against the attacks of white-ants [q.v.]. Wood greyish-brown, often with yellow streaks; contains like the nut an acrid juice which causes swelling and irritation, and timber-cutters object to felling; sometimes used for charcoal [adoopp kary].——*Jungle marking nut* (കാട്ടുചേർ - káttuchér, Mal.). Same as Holigarna.——*Lowly marking nut* (నేలజీడి - nélajídi, Tel.). Same as Wild jamalgota.

MARLEMUND (ಮಾಲೇಮಂದು - málémandu, *Can.*). From (mále, can. recess in a wall + mandu, can. todah village).—"*a*" Village, Hill; Neilgherry dist., Todanaud division; lat. 11° 26′; long. 76° 44′; from Ootacamund N. 3 miles. With large tank and plantation.—"*b*" Tea [q.v.], cinchona [koinah], and gum [blue gum] estates. Todanaud, Neilgherries; from Marlemund tank N. ½ a mile. 142 acres.

MAROO (മറു - maru, *Mal.*). Next, other.——*Maroomakkal* (മരുമക്കൾ - marumakkal, Mal.). From (above + makkal, mal. children). Sister's sons.——*Maroomakkatoyem* (മരുമക്കത്തായം - marumakkattáyam, Mal.). From (above + makkal, mal. children + táyam, mal. portion). The right which accrues to a man's sisters' sons of inheriting whatever may belong to that man, as distinguished from Makkatoyem [q.v.], the right of his sons to inherit it. This custom prevails among the Nayars [q.v.] and other classes in Malabar and Canara. In the latter district it is called Aliya santauna [q.v.]. The rule is otherwise known in English as nepotism in the female line. Under this rule of descent, a man's sons are not anywhere in the list of his heirs. His property goes to his sisters, sister's sons, sister's daughters, sister's daughter's sons and daughters, mother, mother's sisters, their children, and to his maternal grandmother, her sisters, and their children. Failing these and their stock in the same way of descent, it goes, as in the other parts of the Presidency, to the man's disciple, and fellow-student, and then escheats. The origin of the rule is said by the Bramins [q.v.] to have been thus. Parshooraman [q.v.], the first king of Malabar, introduced Bramins into the district, and gave them possesions there, and, to prevent these properties from being split up, decreed that they should vest in the elder brothers, whom alone he permitted to contract marriage. The sons of these were to be accounted as sons for the whole family. The junior brothers being without wives were allowed to consort with females of lower castes. The offspring of these unions not being legitimate could not take rank as Bramins, or inherit from their fathers. Their inheritance was hence made to follow from their mothers. The lower castes fell into the same system of promiscuous intercourse among themselves. Though the fact about the Bramins however may be so, it will not sufficiently account for a domestic custom among a large race of people; and it is quite certain that the Bramins utilized the custom [auchanram] only and did not invent it. Friar Jordanus, who resided at Quilon, and wrote his description of the wonders of the East some five centuries and a half ago, states as follows the reasons for the nepotistic law:— "In this India, never do even the legitimate sons of great kings, "or princes, or barons, inherit the goods of their parents, but "only the sons of their sisters; for they say that they have no "surety that those are their own sons; but 'tis not so with the "sister, for whatever man may be the father, they are certain "that the offspring is of their sister, and is consequently thus "truly of their blood." The nepotistic method of inheritance is known to exist also among the aborigines of Hispaniola and tribes of New granada and Bagota; among negro tribes of the Niger; among certain sections of the Malays of Sumatra; in the royal family of Tipperah and among the Kasias of the Sylhet mountains; in a district of Ceylon adjoining Bintenne; in Madagascar; in the Fiji islands; and among the Hurons and Natchez of North america. In fact it is a not unnatural result of polyandry other than that which is restricted to brothers. For the consideration of this see what is set out at vol. I (106) and (107) in the text. The polyandry of the west coast is explained in some detail at vol. I (111), foot-note. See also vol. II, 100. Under this law of succession, the sister being the mother of the heirs becomes a person of great importance, daughters are desired, and sons are treated as of less account. The whole arrangement tends to give Nayar women much influence, admits of their being to some extent educated, and saves them from the privations of Braminical widowhood. The castes that follow this rule of Maroomakkatoyem are all excepting Bramins; Agapodwauls a class of pagoda [q.v.] servants; the artisans, namely carpenters, brasssmiths, blacksmiths and goldsmiths; and some of the lowest denominations, such as the Cheroomar, the Malayar and the Paniyar. The Teeyar or toddy-drawers and the Moocwas or fishermen of North malabar follow Maroomakkatoyem, while those to the south observe Makkatoyem. In North malabar most of the Moplahs, although Mahomedans, follow the rule of Maroomakkatoyem, in this respect having conformed to Hindoo usage. The above regards the rule of descent or inheritance [dauyam]. As to the rights which descend or are inherited, these can be seen for the higher castes under the head tarwaud, which is the undivided family of these castes; in the case of the lower castes the rights are the ordinary rights in movable and immovable property [maryauday].——*Mautt* (മാററ - máttu, Mal.; மாற்று - máttu, Tam.). From (máru, tam. change). Touch or fineness of the precious metals [loham]. Very pure gold is said to be of 9 mautt, inferior gold of 5 or 6 mautt; the figures being in inverse proportion to amount of alloy [carat]. Distinguish from Mautt [q.v.], ambuscade.

MAROO (மரு - maru, *Tam.*). Fragrance.——*Marookkauray* (மருக்காரை - marukkárai, Tam.). From (above + kárai, tam. canthium parviflorum, lam.). Same as Common emetic nut.——*Maroothum* (कटफल - katp'hala, San.; कायफळ - káyap'hala, Mahr.; ازوری - azúrí, Ar.; درخت هیشعان - darakhtishísháan, Pers.; کائی پھل کا پیڑ - káíphalkáper, Hind.; کائی پھل کا جھاڑ - káíphalkájhár, Dec.; కైదర్యము - kaidaryamu, Tel.; മരുതു - marutu, Mal.; மருதம் - marutham, Tam.). Title from tamul. San. from (katu, san. pungent + p'hala, san. fruit). Mahr. from sanscrit. Hind. from (katap'hala, san. the tree + per, hind. tree). Dec. from hindostany. Tam. from (maru, tam. fragrance); from aromatic bark [black murdah]. San. also (kaidarya), meaning juice + praised, from medical properties of juice [curry-leaf tree]; (sugandhí), meaning fragrant, from slightly aromatic bark [indian sarsaparilla]. Ar. also (audulbark), meaning fragrant + lightning; (kandol). Title otherwise Box myrtle, Marootham bark tree. Botanically Myrica sapida, wall., myricaceæ [vricsham]. Tree; leaves lanceolate, acuminate or obtuse at the apex, quite entire, glabrous, coriaceous; aments cylindric, alternate, remote, with a pubescent rachis; male flowers with an ovate puberulous bract; stamens three to five, longer than the bract; anthers glabrous; female flowers with a pear-shaped [amrood] granular fruit; nut very hard, attenuated at both ends. Bark aromatic stimulant, rubefacient and sternutatory; similar in action to kino [q.v.]; quoted in pharm., non officinal; powder of bark mixed with ginger [q.v.] and camphor [q.v.] used for rubbing on body of cholera patients to promote reaction; combination with gingelly [q.v.] oil a remedy in aphthæ; milky juice escharotic, powerful application for removing warts and other excrescences. Bark gives a dye [shauyam]. Another species is integrifolia. Marootham, with the same ultimate root, means also agricultural land [desham].——*Maroothaud naud* (மருதாநாடு - maruthádunádu, Tam.). From (marutham, tam. agricultural land + kádu, tam. forest + nádu, tam. country); country of forest and agricultural land. Part of Vengoondra cottam [q.v.] in the ancient Tondaimundalam [q.v.]. In the present Wandiwash talook, North arcot district.——*Maroothiyaur* (மருதையார் - maruthaiyár, Tam.). From (marutham, tam. tree, terminalia alata, don. + áru, tam. river). River; Trichinopoly dist. Drains Perambalore and Oodayarpolliem talooks and falls into Coleroon.——*Maroothoo* (மருது - maruthu, Tam.). From (maru, tam. fragrance). Tree, Terminalia alata. At the temple of Neinaurcoil, in Ramnaud zemindarry, Shiva [q.v.] is in shape of a lingam [q.v.] at foot of a Maroothoo tree [murdah]. Family name of the Sherogars [q.v.] of Shivagunga in last century.

MAROOL (मूर्वा - múrvá, *San.*; घोणसकांडें - ghónasakándém, *Mahr.*; مرغابی - murghábí, *Hind.*; مرگابی - murgábí, *Dec.*; మంజినారు - manjináru, *Can.*; చాగ - chága, *Tel.*; കരുമ്പ - kurumpa, *Mal.*; නියද - niyada, *Singh.*; மருள் - marul, *Tam.*). Title from tamul. San. from (murv, san. to bind); from fibres making bowstrings. Mahr. from (ghónasa, mahr. the snake); antidote to bite of that snake. Hind. and dec. from sanscrit. Can. from (manji, can. hemp plant + náru, can. fibre). Tel. from (ságu, tel to be elastic). Tam. means devil from strength of fibre; properly (maral). San. also (kharabusa), meaning hard thread; (déví), meaning shining; (madhurasá), meaning honey juice; (móratá), meaning entwining; (téjaní), meaning kindling; (sravá), meaning shedding; (madhúliká), meaning having honey; (madhushréní), meaning collection of honey; (gókarní), meaning having leaves like cow's ear; (píluparní), meaning having leaves like peeloo, salvadora persica, linn. Mahr. also (múra). Can. also (maruva). Tel. also (sága), meaning elastic; (chéga); (chámakáda), meaning colocasia antiquorum, schott. + stalk; (vishamakonda); (vishamangalapuchettu). Mal. also (perunkurumpa), meaning large + the plant. Singh. also (niyanda); (mahaniyanda), meaning large + the plant. Tam. also (aralai); (malaimañji), meaning mountain + the plant, crotalaria juncea, linn. Title otherwise Bowstring hemp, Ceylon sanseviera, Hyacinth aloe, Munchy naur. Botanically Sanseviera roxburghiana, schult., liliaceæ [vricsham, 136]. Alias Aletris hyacinthoides, zeylanica; Aloe hyacinthoides, zeylanica; Sanseviera æthiopica, zeylanica. Stemless; roots perennial; leaves radical, exterior ones shorter, spreading, and more broad, interior ones nearly erect, 1–4 feet long, semi-cylindric, grooved on the upper side, sharply acuminated at the apex, somewhat striated, smooth; scapes rising from the centre of the leaves, 1–2 feet long, erect, with four or five alternate sheaths between the raceme or flower-bearing part and the base; racemes erect, about as long as, or longer than, the scape below the flowers, striated, smooth; flowers greenish white, erect, fascicled, four to six together; pedicels short, one-flowered; corolla one-petalled, funnel-shaped; calyx none. Flowers somewhat fragrant; abundant along coasts; fleshy creeping root warm to taste, unpleasant odour. Fibre ordained by menoo [q.v.] to form the sacrificial zone [jandiram] of the military classes. The method of preparing the fibres [naur] is to steep the leaves, which are 3 or 4 feet long, in water for several days, in order that the pulpy part may rot; the fibres are then easily separated, but putting them in water is apt to discolor them; in other cases they are first beaten to separate the fibres more easily, and placed on a board and scraped with a piece of rough stick or iron till all the pulp is removed. The root is electuary in chronic cough and consumption; juice of tender shoots given to children as expectorant. The fibre from leaves is very soft silky, and pliant, resembling that of pine-apple [ananas]; used for ropes, twine, thread, bowstrings, cord and paper manufacture. Another species is lanuginosa.

MARSIYA (مرثیہ - marsiyah, *Hind.*). From (rasa, ar. to bewail). A funeral eulogium; a Moharram hymn [manaukib].

MARTABAN (مرتبان - martabán, *Hind.*). Port in Lower burmah formerly of great trade, but in decay. Large glazed jars are exported from this port.——*Martaban camphor* (مرتبان کا کافور - martabánkákáfúr, Hind.). Same as Martaban cinnamon.——*Martaban cinnamon* (مرتبان کا دارچینی - martabánkádárchíní, Hind). See under Cinnamon.

MARTEES (सौगन्धिक - saugandhika, *San.*; جبلقوم - jabalkúm, *Ar.*; مرطیس - martís, *Hind.*; మాణిక్య - mánikya, *Can.*; కురివిందరాయి - kurivindaráyi, *Tel.*; செவ்வந்திக்கல் - shevvandikkal, *Tam.*). Title from hindostany. San. from (sugandha, san. sweet scent); epithet of blue water-lily, nymphæa stellata, wild. Tel. from (kurivindamu, tel. ruby + ráyi, tel. stone). Tam. from (shevvandi, tam. chrysanthemum indicum, linn. + kal, tam. stone). Amethyst. Quartz or rock crystal of a pink or purple color, the color being due to the presence of manganese [q.v.] or iron [auhan]. Those found in the bed of the Godavery are only purple colored mountain crystals [palingoo cull]. A gem however of this name is imported from Burmah. which is a variety of perfect corundum [q.v.] and the real oriental amethyst [ratnam].

MARYAH (मर्या - maryá, *San.*). Limit [avadhy].——*Maryauday* (मर्यादा - maryádá, San.; മര്യാദ - maryáda, Mal.). From (above + dá, san. to give). In Tamul means honor, respect; in Malabar, the customary respect due to any status, and so custom [auchauram, maumool]. See vol. I (97) to (109), and the following foot-notes :—clothing I (98), wearing hair I (99), arms I (100), habitations I (100), dietary I (101), occupations I (102), iron industry I (103), music I (103), mode of address I (104), mahomedan proper names I (104), family life I (107), ceremonies I (107), magic I (109), special tribes I (109) ; ceremonies II, 235.

MARYAM (مریم - maryam, *Ar.*). From (ráma, ar. to love). Mary. Common female alam ; as Maryam bee, alam + alaumat [ism].——*Mariyamma* (மரியம்மா - mariyammá, Tam.). Mary, the virgin ; used by the Romanists. Native christian-female proper name [peyar]. Distinguish from Mauriyamman.

MASAB (మసబు - masabu, *Tel.*). Clay soil [munn].

MASAUL (مشعل - mashal, *Hind.*). From (shola, pers. flame). Torch. A torch made of rags wrapt round a stick and fed at intervals with oil from an earthen pot [pandam].——*Masaul chory* (مشعل چوری - mashalchorí, Hind.). From (above + chorí, hind. theft). Torch robbery [dacoity].——*Masaulchy* (مشعلچی - mashalchí, Hind.). A torch-bearer ; also domestic servant for lamps.——*Masaul tree* (مشعل کا جھاڑ - mashalkájhár, Hind.). Means torch tree ; boughs of the tree used for torches. Same as Large jungle geraninm.

MASAULAY (مصالح - masálah, *Hind.*). Materials, drugs, curry-stuffs.——*Masaulay grass* (هزار مصالح - hazármasálah, Dec.). Title as used to flavour curries [q.v.]. Same as Lemon grass.

MASAUT (مساحت - masáhat, *Hind.*). From (masáh, ar. to measure). Survey of lands [peimash].

MASEEH (مسیح - masíh, *Ar.*). From (masaha, ar. to anoint). Anointed, Messiah. Part of lacab ; as Maseeh ood dowla, messiah of the empire [ism].

MASHEIKH (مشایخ - masháikh, *Hind.*). Plural of masheekha, which is again the plural of sheikh. Mahomedan elders or holy persons ; mostly hold Soofee [q.v.] doctrines. Alias Peers [q.v.], Moorshids [q.v.]. They are of two kinds, Jaddee and Khoolfaee. Jaddee means ancestral, i.e., family in which the system of making mooreeds [q.v.] has been hereditary. Khoolfaee means deputed, i.e., family which acquired right by deputy. Some of them, independently of making mooreeds, gain additional subsistence by fortune-telling, composing amulets and charms, practising medicine, pronouncing blessings, or exercising incantations. Fakeers who are Masheikhs have necessarily at the commencement or in the middle of their names the word shah, and at the termination the words cawdiry, chishty, tabacauty, or shoottaury ; thus, Shah abdool lah cawder cawdiry, Hameed ool lah shah chishty ; tabacautiya and shoottauriya are rare [fakeer].

MASHY (मसि - masi, *San.* ; మసి - masi, *Tel.* ; മഷി - mashi, *Mal.* ; மசி - masi, *Tam.*). Ink. The Tamulians occasionally make ink on nearly the European system. But that which is used by native writers in cutcherries [q.v.] is prepared by the following process. First, burnt rice-water is made. Half a seer of rice [q.v.], burnt black, is well boiled in a seer-and-a-half of water till but one seer [q.v.] remains ; then strain off the dregs. To this seer of burnt rice-water is added two pollums of lac [q.v.] ; boil them well together, and strain off the dregs. Half a seer [q.v.] of lamp black [caujal] and half a pollum [q.v.] of gum arabic [q.v.] are then well rubbed into a fine powder and gradually added to the decoction of lac and burnt rice-water, when the whole are rubbed together and well shaken at different intervals for three days. The Mahomedans prepare their ink [shirah, shye] in the following manner. Take of lamp black and gum arabic equal quantities, and pound together to very fine powder. This powder is then moistened with the juice of the pulp of the cuttaulay or small aloe [q.v.] and well rubbed at intervals for two days together ; after which it is formed into small cakes which are put on plantain [q.v.] leaves and dried in the sun. The Tamulians prepare red ink by adding water to shempunjy or red cotton [q.v.].——*Mashicauran* (മഷിക്കാരൻ - mashikkáran, Mal.). From (above + kára, san. doer). A conjurer, who detects theft by applying a black powder to his eyes, or by rubbing it on his hand, or on a plate, and viewing in it the person of the thief.

MASILAUMANY (மாசிலாமணி - másilámani, *Tam.*). From (másu, tam. stain or spot + il, tam. not + mani, san. gem) ; spotless gem. Hindoo 2nd or pers. name. Common among non-bramins [peyar].

MASOOM (معصوم - masúm, *Hind.*). From (asama, ar. to guard against sin). Innocent. Infant or sinless. A necessary qualification for an imaum [q.v.] according to shiahs [q.v.]. Prefixed to an alam forms a lacab ; as Masoom ally, infant of ally. Mostly taken by Shiahs [ism].

MASOOR (मसूर - masúra, *San.* ; عدس - adas, *Ar.* ; مرجومک - marjúmak, *Pers.* ; مسور - masúr, *Hind.* and *Dec.* ; చిరిశనగ - chirishanaga, *Tel.* ; മസൂര - masura, *Singh.* ; மைசூர்ப்பருப்பு - maisúrpparuppu, *Tam.*). San. from (mas, san. to ripen). Tel. from (chiru, tel. small + shanaga, tel. bengal gram, cicer arietinum, linn.). Tam. means mysore pulse but really from sanscrit. San. also (mangalyaka), meaning auspicious. Greek φακὸς ; latin Lens. The lentil of scriptures, of which Esau's pottage was made. Revalenta arabica is Lentil flour, the name being a corruption of Ervum lens. Title otherwise Lentil, Lentil tare, Red pottage, Small bengal gram. Botanically Ervum lens, linn., leguminosæ [vricsham, 48]. Alias Cicer lens ; Vicia lens. Weak, pea-like [calauyam], wing-leaved, annual ; flower small, pale blue ; a mysore pulse ; highly esteemed as article of food, containing 27·96 per cent. of nitrogenous matter and 56·36 of starch ; meal also used by natives as substance for washing ; no other species here. Same title is given to Vicia hirsuta, koch., or tare [dholl].

MASTIC (रूमीमस्तकी - rúmímastakí, *Mahr.* ; شجر مصطکی - shajarimastakí, *Ar.* ; درخت کندر رومی - darakhtikundurirúmí, *Pers.* ; مصطکی کا پیڑ - mastakíkáper, *Hind.* ; رومی مصطکی کا جھاڑ - rúmímastakíkájhár, *Dec.* ; పిల్లికండ్లగుగ్గిలము - pillikandlaguggilamu, *Tel.* ; பூனைக்கண்குங்கிலியம் - púnaikkangungiliyam, *Tam.*). Title from arabic ; hence english mastication. Mahr. from deccany. Ar. from (shajar, ar. tree + mastakí, ar. mastich). Pers. from (darakht, pers. tree + kundur, pers. olibanum + rúmí, pers. turkish). Hind. from (rúm, hind. turkey + mastakí, ar. mastich + per, hind. tree). Dec. from hindostany. Tel. from (pilli, tel. cat + kannu, tel. eye + guggilamu, tel. dammer). Tam. from (púnai, tam. cat + kan, tam. eye + kungiliyam, tam. resin) ; from glossy pale yellow like cat's eye. Ar. also (shajarimastakírúmí), meaning turkish mastic tree. Pers. also (kinnah) [galbanum]. Greek σχῖνος. Title otherwise Cat's eye resin, Lentisk, Manna of lebanon, Turkish mastic, Turkish olibanum. Botanically Pistacia [pistah] lentiscus, linn., anacardiaceæ [vricsham, 45]. Diœcious evergreen shrub ; leaves evergreen, fruits very small, pea shaped [calauyam], reddish when ripe ; flower small green, imported. Yields by incision of its trunk an aromatic resin called mastic ; this occurs in oval tears, smooth diaphanous, brittle, breaking with plane brilliant, glassy, and pale yellow surfaces, and owing to its brittleness being usually covered with its own dust ; odour agreeable ; flavor balsamic ; melts at a moderate heat, and then exhales a sweet odour ; insoluble in water. Softening in the mouth, medicinally slightly tonic and astringent, and much used here to perfume the breath and strengthen the gums ; officinal in pharm. ; diuretic and astringent ; dentists employ it dissolved in alcohol, ether, or chloroform for filling carious teeth. It is employed in europe to flavour wines and for varnishing pictures ; its place is generally supplied here in the arts by less costly resins [raul], such for example as dammer [q.v.], together with gum sandrach [q.v.], gum elemi [q.v.], lac [q.v.], alcohol, and in conjunction with turpentine [ganda firoza] ; jewellers lay it under the diamond [vajram] to add to lustre.

MASULAH (مچھلی - macchlí, *Hind.* ; మసూలా - masúlá, *Tel.*). Hind. means fish, as frequently used by fishermen [mad]. Cf. Masulipatam. A boat used for crossing the surf on the Coromandel coast [q.v.]. It is formed with a flat bottom, for the purpose of taking the beach in the surf when European boats cannot approach it. 30 to 35 feet long, 10 to 11 feet broad, and 7 to 8 feet in depth. The planks are sewed together with coir yarns, crossing the seams over a wadding of coir [q.v.], which presses on the joints and prevents leakage. By this the boat remains as pliable as a basket, and yields to the shock which it receives on taking the ground. Takes cargo and passengers from ships outside surf. Rowed by twelve men in double banks, with paddles or boards about ten inches broad and fourteen inches long fixed at the end of a pole. Steered by a tindal or cockswain, and one or two men constantly bale out the water. The steersman gives time by a song. Eight or ten passengers can be carried, and great quantities of goods can lie in the well of the boat, being supported and kept out of the wet by dunnage.——*Masulipatam** (మచిలీపట్టణము - machilípattanamu, Tel.). From (machhlí, hind. fish + pattana, san. town), from an old tradition of a whale stranding on shore ; greek μαισωλία in ptolemy, μασαλία in periplus. Sanscrit name (matsyapura), meaning fish + town. Hind. name (machhlíbandar), meaning fish + port.—" *a* " A former district of the British government named from its principal town. Area about 514 square miles. Between lat. 15° 45′—16° 26′, long. 80° 52′—81° 36′. Bounded north by the territory of the Nizam ; north-east and east by the district of Rajahmundry ; south-east by the Bay of Bengal ; and south-west by the Kistna, which divided it from the district of Guntoor. Masulipatam, Condapully, and Ellore were the principal places. For history see under next head. Masulipatam district is represented now by Bezwada, Bunder, Goodivauda, Noozveed, Nundigauma and Tirvore talooks of the Kistna district and Ellore, Pentapaud and Relangy talooks of the Godavery district.—" *b* " Town, Port, Municipality, Headquarters of Collector, Judge, talook and division ; Kistna dist., Bunder tal. ; pop. 38,809 ; acres 11,219 ; lat. 16° 11′ ; long. 81° 10′ ; from Bezwada E.S.E. 40 miles ; from Guntoor E. 44 miles ; from Madras N.N.E. 218 miles ; from Nizampatam E.N.E. 36 miles ; from Vinoocondah E. 92 miles. The town is on Golcondah coast [q.v.], north of mouth of a branch of Kistna, in an unhealthy situation, and in an extensive plain stretching westwards to the ghauts [q.v.]. It is still the principal port of Kistna district though it has few natural advantages, and suffers in addition from competition with Cocanada with which the Kistna delta [conamoogam] has inland communication by water. Large ships cannot anchor nearer than five miles from the shore; and during the north-east monsoon [q.v.], all communication is suspended. Light in the fort; lat. 16° 10′; long. 81° 12′. White; fixed, 6 miles range. Visible from all directions seaward. Flagstaff. Guide for vessels to the anchorage. The Chinnacaupooram canal communicates with the sea about a mile and a half south-east of the fort, and passing close on the south side of its rampart, is navigable up to it for small craft. It joins the Kistna, about 15 miles farther to the north-west. It can be entered from the sea, even by boats, only at high water. Barges and native craft come up the river and go on by canal to Bezwada. The port was founded in the 14th century by Arabs. The first reliable date is 1425 when the Hindoo rajahs of the Carnatic [q.v.] gave permission for the erection of a Mahomedan mosque [musjid]. In 1478, the Bahmany [q.v.] king Mahomed II entered Masulipatam. An English agency was established in 1611. Factory established 1621; removed to Armegam 1628; reestablished under the Firmaun [q.v.] of the King of Golcondah, 1632. The station then became the centre of English trade in these parts and was managed by a chief and council. Factory established by Dutch in 1660 and by French in 1669. In 1686 Dutch took possession of the town forbidding the English to trade. Factory seized by the local Governor owing to the rupture between Aurungzeeb and the Company, 1689. Cowle [q.v.] for the factory renewed, firmaun dated 28th December 1690, from Zoolfacar khan, the Moghul [q.v.] general. Captured by the French in 1750; formally ceded to France by the Nizam with the rest of the Circar [q.v.], 1753; retaken from the French by Colonel Forde, 7th April 1759; bestowed on the English company as an inam [q.v.] together with the whole of the Circar of Masulipatam and eight districts, the Circars of Nizampatam and the districts of Condaveed and Acoolamannaud, by Nizam salaubut jung, 14th May 1759; grant confirmed by the Moghul's firmaun, 12th August 1765. The small Circar of Masulipatam is not to be confounded, with the extensive district afterwards so called. For details regarding the territory ceded by the foregoing treaty see vol. II, 277. The family of the Masulipatam nawaubs [q.v.] trace their descent from the Ameer yauwar ahmed najm e sauny, Commander-in-Chief of the armies of Shah ismail safavee, Emperor of Persia, about three centuries ago. His son, Baukir khan najm e sauny, came to Delhi and rose high in the service of the Emperor Jehaungeer. He married a niece of the famous Noor jehaun and his name is perpetuated in Baukirabad near Mooltaun. His only son Feiyauz khan najm e sauny left two sons. The elder, Ally coolee khan, was Aurungzeeb's vizier. The vizier's younger son, Yoosoof khan, died in his father's lifetime, leaving an infant son Mahomed takee khan, who left the protection of his uncle, Mahomed beg khan, and obtained from the Nizam of Hyderabad a Jagheer [q.v.] in the Godavery district which his descendants hold to this day. Mahomed takee khan had two sons, Hoossain ally khan, who died childless, and Hassan ally khan, whose name is conspicuous in early records. Hassan ally khan entered the service of the Nizam, and after distinguishing himself in the province of Aurungabad became the Soobahdar [q.v.] of the Northern circars [q.v.]. He suggested to the Madras government the idea of taking the Condapully and Ellore circars from Nizam ally khan and he fought by the side of the English troops at Rajahmundry and elsewhere. In the arrangements necessary when the Circars were taken over he administered the provinces of Condapully, Ellore, and Rajahmundry for three years. He subsequently was compelled to disband his troops, and to content himself with the life-rent of the Jagheer. He died in 1771 and the Jagheer was at once resumed, an annual allowance of one lakh [q.v.] of rupees [q.v.] being granted for the maintenance of his numerous family. Masulipatam is the centre of missionary labour in Teloogoo country. A storm wave in 1864 swept over the entire town at night and destroyed 30,000 lives. A similar calamity happened during Dutch occupation. The fort has fallen into decay since the withdrawal of the garrison in 1865. A large square in the native town, in which the markets are held, bears the name of Mr. Robertson. In the Native quarter is the sight of the French lodge. An interesting memorial is Eliza's tree, so called from Mrs. Draper, the correspondent of sterne. In the centre of the native quarter, stands a collection of 33 upright slabs, of compact limestone [choonamcull], carved with figures in alto-relievo. They were brought from the ruins of a pagoda [q.v.] 7 miles from the town and are Jeina [q.v.] relics. Weavers form a large portion of the inhabitants. Their operations, besides weaving, include printing, bleaching, washing and dressing. In former days the chintzes [q.v.] of Masulipatam had a great reputation and there is still a small demand for them in Burmah, the Straits, and the Persian gulf. Another speciality was madapollems [q.v.]; but this industry was ruined by the refusal of the West indian negroes to wear these kerchiefs after their emancipation. Tartans, ginghams [q.v.], towels, and table linen are still manufactured to a small extent. The export trade is partly to Europe; imports are chiefly local. Trig. station is in Lat. 16° 8′ 55·41″; long. 81° 11′ 39·35″. From Masulipatam S.E. 3 miles. From the sea W. 1½ miles. The following are the travelling distances from Masulipatam to different places:—

To	Viâ	Miles	Furlongs
Bangalore	Baupatla, Nellore and Chittore	407	4
Bellary	Guntoor, Cumbum and Gooty	331	0
Berhampore ...	Mogultoor, Rajahmundry and Chicacole.	369	1½
Berhampore ...	Ellore, Rajahmundry and Chicacole ...	378	6
Bezwada ...	......	43	6½
Chanda	Ellore, Dammapett and Chinnore ...	350	4½
Chicacole	Ellore and Rajahmundry	279	5½
Chicacole	Mogultoor and Rajahmundry	260	1
Chingleput	Baupatla, Nellore and Madras	314	2
Chinnore	Ellore, Dammapett and Mungapett ...	248	3½
Chinnore	Bezwada and Khamamet	256	7½
Chinnore	Ellore, Jangamreddygoodem, Dammapett and Mungapett.	261	4½
Chittore	Baupatla, Nellore and Tripatty	297	2
Cocanada	Mogultoor	99	6
Cocanada	Rajahmundry	128	3
Cuddapah	Bezwada, Guntoor and Cumbum ...	161	4
Cuddapah	Guntoor and Cumbum	145	5½
Cumbum	Baupatla and Ongole	163	7½
Cumbum	Guntoor and Vinoocondah	160	7½
Cuttack	Ellore, Rajahmundry, Chicacole and Berhampore.	495	3
Dammapett ...	Ellore and Chintalapoody	88	5½
Dammapett ...	Ellore and Ashwarowpett.	101	6½
Ellore	......	44	6½
Ganjam	Ellore, Chicacole and Berhampore ...	386	1½
Guntoor	Bezwada	63	7
Guntoor	Ayyaloor	48	0½
Haitipamla	Bezwada and Sooryapett	145	5
Haitipamla	Guntoor and Pondakholl	156	7½
Kamptee ...	Ellore, Dammapett, Chinnore and Chanda.	455	7½
Kamptee	Ellore, Jangamreddygoodem, Dammapett, Chinnore and Chanda.	469	0½
Kamptee	Bezwada, Khamamet, Chinnore and Chanda.	464	3½
Khamamet	Bezwada	106	6½
Kurnool	Guntoor	232	4½
Kurnool	Bezwada and Sooryapett	292	4½
Madras	Baupatla, Ongole and Nellore	279	3
Madras	Guntoor, Ongole and Nellore	300	4½
Madras	Bezwada, Guntoor and Nellore	316	3
Mungapett	Ellore and Dammapett	176	4½
Nellore	Baupatla and Ongole	171	5
Nellore	Guntoor,and Ongole	192	6½
Nellore	Bezwada, Guntoor and Ongole	208	5
Ongole	Baupatla	95	2
Ongole	Guntoor	116	3½
Ongole	Bezwada and Guntoor	132	2
Pondakholl	Guntoor	110	1½
Rajahmundry ...	Mogultoor	90	3
Rajahmundry ...	Ellore	99	7½
Samulcottah ...	Mogultoor and Cocanada	107	6
Secunderabad ...	Bezwada, Sooryapett and Haitipamla ..	210	5
Secunderabad ...	Guntoor, Pondakholl and Haitipamla.	221	7½
Sironchah	Ellore, Dammapett and Chinnore ...	263	2½
Sironchah	Ellore, Jangamreddygoodem, Dammapett and Chinnore	276	3½
Sironchah	Bezwada, Khamamet, Warangal and Chinnore.	271	6½
Sooryapett	Bezwada	126	6½
Vizagapatam ...	Ellore, Rajahmundry, Toony and Cassimcote.	222	7½
Viziananagram ...	Ellore, Rajahmundry, Toony and Soobaraum.	246	2½

MATHAGOO (மதகு - mathagu, *Tam.*). A covered gutter or channel [mada].——*Mathagoo moolgy* (மதகுமுழுகி - mathagumuzhugi, Tam.). From (above + muzhugu, tam. to dive). One whose business it is to dive and stop cracks in bund [q.v.] of a tank [q.v.], or mend the sluices [inam, maday, madayvetty].

MATHIL (மதில் - mathil, *Tam.*). The wall that encloses a temple [coil, pagoda, praucauram].

MATOORAY (मथुरा - mat'hurá, *San.*). From (mat'h, san. to kill), place where madhoo, an asooran [q.v.] was killed. Muttra in n. india, sacred to Krishnan [charitram, krishnan, madura]. Greek μεθόρα. Distinguish from Madura [q.v.].

MATSYAM (मत्स्य - matsya, *San.*). From (mad, san. to be lively) [mad]. Fish. Pisces of naturalists [jantoo]. Cold-blooded animals with a two-chambered heart, which breathe by means of gills, and have their limbs developed in the form of fins.——(1)—"*a*" Fish are classified into six sub-classes as follows. First Teleostei, or fishes with a complete bony skeleton, which includes all the most perfectly organised forms; by far the greater number of existing fishes are included in this sub-class. Secondly Dipnoi, of which only two species are known. Thirdly Ganoidei, in which are the sturgeons and a few other forms. Fourthly Chondropterygii, fishes with a cartilaginous skeleton, which includes all the sharks [soorah] and rays [tenky]. Fifthly Cyclostomata, round-mouthed or sucking fishes, including the lampreys [aural] and their allies. Sixthly Leptocardii, only one species known.—"*b*" The next division is into orders. The first sub-class or Teleostei, which is practically the only one of any consequence, is divided into five orders, as follows. Acanthopterygii or spiny-finned. This order comprises those fishes of which the perch [calavye] may be taken as a type. They have usually a number of sharp spines forming part of the fin on the back, and some of the other fins. They have frequently two dorsal fins, but both of them are composed of rays, and the adipose or gristly fin does not appear in this order. When there are two dorsal fins, the first is composed entirely of spinous rays, or the two fins may be united.

The acanthopterygian fishes do not exist in any numbers in the inland freshwaters of S. india, being mostly confined to either within, or but a short distance removed from, tidal influence, or above the sea level. The larger the river, the greater is the probability of their extending their range up it. The hard-rayed fishes captured in the fresh-waters mostly belong to one of the following genera :—Lates, Ambassis, Nandus, Badis, Pristolepis, Sciæna, Equula, Gobius and allied genera, Mugil, members of the Labyrinthiform and Ophiocephaloid families, as well as the spined eels, and the Etropli. Anacanthini or spineless. This order have all their fin rays soft and flexible, such as the cod-fish and the soles. The order has been divided into sub-orders, thus :—Anacanthini gadoidei, the two sides of the head symmetrical; Anacanthini pleuronectoidei, the two sides of the head apparently unsymmetrical. Physostomi. This order contains the greater number of freshwater fishes. The fishes of this order have frequently one strong bony ray in front of the back fin, but the remaining rays of that fin are soft and branched. Lophobranchii. This order is unimportant. The fishes which comprise it normally swim in a vertical position, the dorsal fin being the principal propeller, and which while in motion it rapidly undulates from end to end. Plectognathi. This order is unimportant, mostly oceanic. Mouth narrow, the bones of the upper jaw united, sometimes produced into the form of a beak. The second and third sub-classes do not require special mention. The fourth sub-class Chondropterygii as at present constituted is divided into two orders, the first of which has not any representatives in India, thus :—Holocephala, with only one external gill-opening and a rudimentary cartilaginous gill-cover; four branchial clefts inside gill-cavity; the palatal and maxillary apparatus coalescent with the skull. Plagiostomata, with five to seven external gill-openings and no cartilaginous gill-cover; jaws distinct from the skull. The order of Plagiostomata has been sub-divided as follows :—First sub-order, Selachoidei or Sharks; trunk gradually passing into the tail; gill-openings lateral. Second sub-order, Batoidei or Skates and Rays; gill-openings ventral; body depressed, forming, due to largely-developed pectoral fins, a more or less flat disk, and having usually a thin and slender tail; dorsal fin, when present, in the caudal portion of the body; anal absent. The fifth and sixth sub-classes require no special mention.—"*c*" The next division is that of families, and these form the most natural of the groups into which fishes can be divided, each making generally a well-defined congregation.—"*d*" A genus of fishes is a group which closely resemble one another in all important details of their structure, and differ from all other genera in one or more essential points.—"*e*" As to species all the individuals of a species resemble each other both in structure and habits; they breed freely together and their progeny resemble themselves.—"*f*" Sea-fishes are properly speaking divisible into real marine fish, and marine fish which ascend within or even above tidal influence to deposit their ova in suitable localities, or to obtain sustenance. In some of the real marine forms also the fry are hatched along the coast, and subsequently pass into small estuaries, creeks, rivers and streams, in order to find security and food suitable to their condition.—"*g*" Nearly every fish either salt water or fresh water is eaten by natives. Even sharks [soorah] are valued. In the bazaars [q.v.] it would be possible to obtain some two or three hundred different kinds of dried fish, including different preparations of the same species. The fish most in repute for European tables are the seer [q.v.], Cybium commersonii, the pomfrets [q.v.], species of stromateus, and mullets [q.v.]. The first-named of these, the seer, is sold in cuts like salmon in Europe. The gouramy [q.v.] was introduced lately from the Mauritius and is as yet confined to a few private ponds. The fresh-water fishes fit for European tables are few in number, and embrace some carps [kenday], the hilsa [q.v.] or Clupea ilisha, the murrel [q.v.] or Ophiocephalus, and some siluroid [keliroo] species. The fish which afford the best sport with rod and line are a large barbus [carp], the mahaseer [q.v.], which rises to the fly and runs like salmon; and the murrel, which may be caught with live-bait or gorge-tackle.——**(2)** The following is a key synopsis of the s. indian fishes, marine and freshwater, ranged down to species, connecting the european and native terminology; the small capitals indicate the sub-class, the small capitals in inverted commas indicate the order, the italics indicate the family, the italics in inverted commas indicate the sub-family, and the ordinary type indicates the genus and species :—TELEOSTEI. "ACANTHOPTERYGII."—1 *Percidæ.*—Lates calcarifer [cock-up]. Serranus hexagonatus [spotted perch], flavo-caeruleus [yellow perch], lanceolatus [sore-headed perch], malabaricus, salmoides, bœnack [striped perch], sonnerati [red perch]; Lutjanus sebæ, bengalensis, rivulatus, marginatus [bride fish], erythropterus, sillago, johnii, jahngarah, argentimaculatus [red-rock cod], roseus, fulviflamma, lineolatus; Ambassis gymnocephalus [white chandwah], nama [striped chandwah], ranga [red chandwah], thomassi; Therapon [kitchaun] puta, jarbua, theraps; Pristipoma furcatum [pyekeely], maculatum [caratchy], hasta [caukkan], dussumieri, guoraca; Lobotes surinamensis; Scolopsis vosmeri; Synagris japonicus, tolu; Gerres filamentosus.—2 *Squamipinnidæ.*—Heniochus macrolepidotus; Holacanthus impérator, annularis; Scatophagus argus; Ephippus orbis; Drepane punctata.—3 *Mullidæ.*—Upeneus indicus [red mullet].—4 *Nandidæ.*—Badis buchanani, dario; Nandus marmoratus.—5 *Sparidæ.*—Lethrinus carwa; Pagrus spinifer; Chrysophrys sarba, berda [black rock cod]; Pimelepterus cinerascens.—6 *Cirrhitidæ.*—Cirrhitichthys aureus.—7 *Scorpænidæ.*—Pterois volitans [flying toomby], miles [black toomby]; Apistus carinatus; Minous monodactylus.—8 *Teuthididæ.*—Teuthis java, vermiculata.—9 *Berycidæ.*—Myripristis murdjan, botche; Holocentrum rubrum.—10 *Kurtidæ.*—Kurtus indicus; Pempheris mangula.—11 *Polynemidæ.*—Polynemus indicus [screwpine robaul], tetradactylus [golden robaul].—12 *Sciænidæ.*—Umbrina russellii, dussumieri; Sciæna maculata [striped cuttalay], diacanthus, miles [white cuttalay], coitor [black cuttalay], belangeri [rusty cuttalay], ancus, albida [gray cuttalay]; Sciænoides pama; Otolithus maculatus, argenteus.—13 *Xiphiidæ.*—Histiophorus immaculatus [peacock fish], gladius.—14 *Trichiuridæ.*—Trichiurus haumela [moorman's vaulay], savala.—15 *Acanthuridæ.*—Acanthurus matoides, triostegus.—16 *Carangidæ.*—Caranx rottleri [shark pauray], kurra, gymnostethoides, djeddaba, leptolepis [rama pauray], affinis, kalla [thief pauray], melampygus, hippos, ire [black-headed pauray], jarra, carangus, malabaricus, sansun, atropus [striped pauray], armatus [golden pauray], nigrescens [gray pauray]; Seriolichthys bipinnulatus; Chorinemus sancti-petri, moadetta, lysan [thick skin pauray], tala, toloo; Trachynotus baillonii, ovatus; Psettus argenteus, falciformis; Platax vespertilio, teira; Equula edentula, fasciata, insidiatrix, bindus, splendens, daura; Lactarius delicatulus.—17 *Stromateidæ.*—Stromateus cinereus [white pomfret], sinensis [bat-faced pomfret], niger [black pompfret].—18 *Coryphænidæ.*—Coryphæna hippurus [dolphin fish]; Mene maculata [barber pauray].—19 *Scombridæ.*—Scomber microlepidotus; Thynnus thunnina; Cybium guttatum, commersonii [seer]; Elacate nigra [sea murrel]; Echeneis neucrates.—20 *Uranoscopidæ.*—Ichthyscopus inermis.—21 *Trachinidæ.*—Sillago domina, sihama [indian whiting].—22 *Cottidæ.*—Platycephalus insidiator [false bummelo], scaber, tuberculatus.—23 *Gobiidæ.*—Gobius giuris [river goby], malabaricus, striatus [ringed goby], viridipunctatus [scorpion goby]; Apocryptes lanceolatus [black ramah], bato; Eleotris fusca, butis, amboinensis; Gobioides anguillaris [eating ramah], cæculus [crooked ramah]; Trypauchen vagina.—24 *Rhynchobdellidæ.*—Rhynchobdella aculeata [aural]; Mastacembelus pancalus, armatus [rock aural], guentheri.—25 *Sphyrænidæ.*—Sphyræna jello [jella].—26 *Mugilidæ.*—Mugil cunnesius, seheli [gray mullet].—27 *Aulostomatidæ.*—Fistularia serrata.—28 *Centriscidæ.*—Amphisile scutata.—29 *Ophiocephalidæ.*—Ophiocephalus marulius [murrel], micropeltes, striatus [pariah murrel], gachua [pariah doke], punctatus [spotted doke].—30 *Labyrinthidæ.*—Anabas scandens [palmyra fish]; Polyacanthus cupanus; Osphromenus olfax [gouramy]; Trichogaster fasciatus.—31 *Glyphidodontidæ.*—Glyphidodon sordidus, cælestinus.—32 *Labridæ.*—Cossyphus diana, axillaris; Platyglossus dussumieri; Pseudoscarus rivulatus.—33 *Chromidæ.*—Etroplus suratensis, maculatus [crow carp].—"ANACANTHINI."—34 *Pleuronectidæ.*—Plagusia bilineata [jerripotoo]; Cynoglossus lingua.—"PHYSOSTOMI."—35 *Siluridæ.*—Plotosus canius [variegated keliroo]; Clarias magur; Silurus wynaadensis; Saccobranchus fossilis [scorpion fish]; Wallago attu [vaulay]; Callichrous bimaculatus [two-spotted shark], malabaricus [malabar shark]; Ailia coila; Pseudeutropius taakree, skyesii [dog keliroo], atherinoides [leaf jella], garua; Pangasius buchanani [mud jella]; Silundia gangetica [slippery keliroo], skyesii; Macrones aor [snouted keliroo], chryseus [golden keliroo], carcio, punctatus, cavasius [white keliroo], vittatus [fiddler keliroo], malabaricus, armatus [black keliroo], oculatus; Rita pavimentata [gogra]; Osteogeniosus militaris [cat keliroo]; Bagarius yarrellii [goonch].—36 *Scopelidæ.*—Saurida tumbil [false bummelo]; Harpodon nehereus [bummelo].—37 *Scombresocidæ.*—Belone annulata [green pike], strongylurus [stork pike]; Hemiramphus far, limbatus; Exocœtus pœcilopterus [flying pike].—38 *Cyprinodontidæ.*—Haplochilus melastigma, lineatus, rubrostigma.—39 *Cyprinidæ.* "*Cyprininæ.*"—Homaloptera brucei [rock carp]; Discognathus lamta [rock doke]; Labeo fimbriatus [fringed labeo], calbasu [black labeo], nigrescens, gonius, kontius [red labeo], dussumieri [scaled labeo], ariza, bata, boga; Cirrhina cirrhosa, reba; Catla buchanani; Thynnichthys sandkhol; Amblypharyngodon mola [streaked robaul], melettinus; Barbus sarana [sarana carp], pinnauratus, dubius, micropogon, carnaticus [carnatic carp], jerdoni [red carp], tor [mahseer carp], neilli, pulchellus, melanampyx, dorsalis [shell carp], chrysopoma [golden carp], chola [bitter carp], parrah [flying carp], mabicola, kolus [gray carp], curmuca, lithopidos, thomassi, denisonii, amphibius, arulius, ambassis, ticto, punctatus [spotted carp], gelius, stigma, filamentosus, vittatus; Nuria danrica; Rasbora daniconius, buchanini; Aspidoparia morar; Rohtee vigorsii, ogilbii; Barilius bendelisis, bakeri, canarensis, gatensis [indian trout]; Danio rerio, albolineatus, neilgherriensis; Chela gora, untrahi, argentea, clupeoides, phulo, bacaila.—"*Cobitidinæ.*"—Lepidocephalichthys thermalis; Jerdonia maculata; Nemacheilus semiarmatus, sinuatus, striatus, notostigma, denisonii, triangularis, guentheri, rubidipinnis.—40 *Clupeidæ.*—Clupea brachysoma, longiceps, fimbriata, ilisha [hilsa], toli; Pellona motius, indica, brachysoma, megaloptera; Chatoessus nasus, chacunda; Engraulis malabaricus, kammalensis, setirostris, indicus, purava; Coilia dussumieri; Dussumieria acuta; Elops saurus; Megalops cyprinoides [large-eyed carp]; Chanos salmoneus [white mullet].—41 *Notopteridæ.*—Notopterus kapirat [barber vaulay].—42 *Murænidæ.*—Muræna punctata, polyzona; Anguilla bengalensis, bicolor; Murænesox talabon [talabone].—"LOPHOBRANCHII."—43 *Syngnathidæ.*—

Syngnathus serratus [whip fish]; Ichthyocampus carce; Doryichthys cunculus, bleekeri; Hippocampus guttulatus.—"PLECTOGNATHI."—44 *Sclerodermidæ.*—Triacanthus brevirostris, strigilifer; Balistes mitis, conspicillum; Monacanthus setifer, monoceros, scriptus; Anacanthus barbatus [bottle-nosed pike]; Ostracion turritus [bony plautchy], cubicus, cornutus [bull plautchy].—45 *Gymnodontidæ.*—Tetrodon patoca, cutcutia, lunaris, sceleratus, fluviatilis, reticularis; Diodon hystrix [prickly plautchy].—DIPNOI.—Not represented.—GANOIDEI.—Not represented.—CHONDROPTERYGII. "PLAGIOSTOMATA. SUB-ORDER SELACHOIDEI."—46 *Carchariidæ.*—Carcharias laticaudus [white shark], acutus [red shark], macloti [gray shark], menisorrah [black shark], gangeticus; Galeocerdo rayneri [yellow shark]; Zygæna malleus, blochii [hammer-headed shark]; Mustelus manazo [dun shark].—47 *Scylliidæ.*—Stegostoma tigrinum [zebra shark]; Chiloscyllium indicum [fawn-colored shark].—"PLAGIOSTOMATA. SUB-ORDER BATOIDEI."—48 *Pristidæ.*—Pristis cuspidatus, zysron [great white shark].—49 *Rhinobatidæ.*—Rhynchobatus djeddensis, ancylostomus [ground goby]; Rhinobatus granulatus.—50 *Trygonidæ.*—Urogymnus asperrimus [bristly tenky]; Trygon uarnak [tiger tenky], zugei, sephen [shark tenky]; Pteroplatea micrura [large tenky].—51 *Myliobatidæ.*—Myliobatis nieuhofii [banded tenky]; Ætobatis narinari [black-tail tenky]; Rhinoptera adspersa [flat tenky]; Dicerobatis eregoodoo; Ceratoptera ehrenbergii.—CYCLOSTOMATA.—Not represented.—LEPTOCARDII.—Not represented.——(3) The following is a list of the principal families alphabetically arranged, with the Sanscrit equivalent, references to the key-synopsis, and brief description.——*Acanthuridæ* (कण्टकवालकुल - kantakaválakula, San.). Means spine + tail. Acanthopterygii, 15. Body oblong or elevated and compressed; eyes of moderate size and lateral.——*Aulostomateidæ* (नालीमुखकुल - nálímukhakula, San.). Means pipe + mouth. Acanthopterygii, 27. Form of body elongated; the anterior bones of the skull produced, forming a long tube and having a small mouth at its anterior extremity.——*Carangidæ* (रुक्ममत्स्यकुल - rukmamatsyakula, San.). Means bright fish. Acanthopterygii, 16; the horse mackerel [pauray] family; body oblong, elevated, or subcylindrical and compressed; eyes lateral; scales usually small, unless absent; contains the cobbler fish [golden pauray], equula, and others.——*Carchariidæ* (कर्करमकरकुल - karkaramakarakula, San.). From (karkara, san. hard + makara, san. shark). Selachoïdei, plagiostomata, 46. The snout may be produced longitudinally or laterally [soorah].——*Centriscidæ* (आयतास्यकुल - áyatásyakula, San.). Means long-mouthed. Acanthopterygii, 28. Form of body oblong or elevated and compressed; the anterior bones of the skull produced, forming a long tube and having a small mouth at its anterior extremity.——*Chromidæ* (रुचिरमत्स्यकुल - ruchiramatsyakula, San.). Means shining fish. Acanthopterygii, 33. Body oblong or elevated; fresh-water fishes [kenday].——*Cirrhitidæ* (शुक्रमत्स्यकुल - shukramatsyakula, San.). Means resplendent fish. Acanthopterygii, 6. Body oblong and compressed; mouth in front of snout having a lateral cleft; eyes of moderate size.——*Clupeidæ* (इलीसकुल - ilísakula, San.). From (il, san. to go). Physostomi, 40; herring family; this is a large family; differs from carp [kenday] in being essentially marine; there are however several freshwater species; body covered with scales, which are generally thin, and often easily detached; berbels none; abdomen generally compressed into an edge which is often serrated; dorsal fin rather short; adipose fin none; anal fin often very long [hilsa, kenday, mullet, poorva].——*Coryphænidæ* (चित्रमत्स्यकुल - chitramatsyakula, San.). Means variegated fish. Acanthopterygii, 18. Dolphin fish [q.v.] family. Body oblong or elevated and compressed; eyes lateral [dolphin fish, pauray].——*Cottidæ* (गोशीर्षकुल - góshírshakula, San.). From (gó, san. bull + shírsha, san. head). Acanthopterygii, 22. Body oblong, compressed or sub-cylindrical; eyes lateral or partly directed upwards and outwards; some bones of the head armed [bummelo].——*Cyprinidæ* (शफरकुल - shap'harakula, San.). From (shap'hara, san. carp). Physostomi, 39. Carps [kenday]. Body oblong or elongated; head scaleless, body scaled or scaleless, never covered by osseous plates; freshwater. By far the greater number of S. indian fresh-water fish belong to this family. The Carp [kenday], Barbel [kenday], Roach, Bream, &c., are english representatives [chilwah, doke, indian trout, kenday, rohitam]. The family are not such foul feeders as the siluroides [keliroo]; and enter largely into the diet of the indigenous population. But Indian carps do not restrict themselves so much to a vegetable diet as do those in Europe.——*Cyprinodontidæ* (दन्तशफरकुल - dantashap'harakula, San.). From (danta, san. tooth + shap'hara, san. carp). Physostomi, 38. Eyes lateral; scales on head and body; have been sub-divided into Cyprinodontidæ carnivoræ and C. limnophagæ.——*Glyphidodontidæ* (कर्षदन्तकुल - karshadantakula, San.). From (karsha, san. furrowed + danta, san. tooth). Acanthopterygii, 31. Eyes lateral; body more or less short and compressed; bones of head armed or smooth.——*Gobiidæ* (चित्रवाजीकुल - chitravájíkula, San.). Means variegated + fin. Acanthopterygii, 23. Body elongate. Two dorsal fins, the spinous portion being always the less developed, and composed of flexible spines. The Gobies [ooloovay] are carnivorous fishes, living in the freshwaters and off the coasts of temperate and tropical regions. They reside mostly at the bottom of the water [ooloovay, ramah].——*Gymnodontidæ* (नग्नदन्तकुल - nagnadantakula, San.). From (nagna, san. naked + danta, san. tooth). Plectognathi, 45. Body more or less short. Some possess the means of dilating an elastic portion of the œsophagus, or an abdominal sac, with air. Most of the forms are highly indigestible as food or even virulently poisonous [frog fish, plautchy].——*Kurtidæ* (कुटिलकुल - kutilakula, San.). From (kutila, san. curved); from form of body. Acanthopterygii, 10. Body oblong and compressed; eyes large; lower jaw prominent.——*Labridæ* (ओष्ठीयकुल - ósht'híyakula, San.). From (ósht'ha, san. lip); from lip form. Acanthopterygii, 32. Body oblong or elongated. Many adorned with gorgeous colors, generally abundant in the neighbourhood of rocks and coral reefs [atoll]. Some provided with excessively strong teeth to enable them to crush the shells of marine molluscs [chippy].——*Labyrinthidæ* (मण्डलगात्रकुल - mandalagátrakula, San.). From (mandala, san. coil + gátra, san. body). Acanthopterygii, 30. The Climbing perch [palmyra fish] family; freshwater; body compressed, oblong, or elevated; eyes lateral; freshwater and estuary fishes; capable of living a considerable period out of their natural element; good for eating. Some reputed to have medicinal stimulating properties. These fishes are remarkable for the length of time they are able to live without water, their gills being especially adapted to breathe the air direct. Even when in water they are obliged to ascend to the surface constantly to breathe, otherwise they are soon drowned. Anabas scandens [palmyra fish] and Trichogaster fasciatus are common examples [gouramy, palmyra fish].——*Mugilidæ* (श्वेतमल्लकुल - shvétamallakula, San.). From (shvéta, san. white + malla, san. the fish). Acanthopterygii, 26. Grey mullets [q.v.]. Body oblong, compressed; the head and anterior portion may be depressed; eyes lateral; marine forms, some ascending tidal rivers or estuaries; freshwater forms, confined to the larger rivers; esteemed as food. Mullets putrefy very rapidly in hot climates [mullet].——*Mullidæ* (मल्लकुल - mallakula, San.). From (malla, san. the fish). Acanthopterygii, 3. Red mullet or Wood-cock of the seas. Body rather elongate; eyes of moderate size, lateral; mouth in front of snout rather small; sea fish. Many young and some adults have been captured in rivers; excellent as food [mullet].——*Murænidæ* (कुञ्चीयकुल - kuñchíyakula, San.). From (kuñchí, san. eel). Physostomi, 42. Eels [vilaung]. Body elongated, cylindrical, or band-shaped. Eels have by some authors been considered as hermaphrodites [talabone, vilaung]. Very common at Madras. The natives catch them just at the edge of the surf by bruising a crab [nundoo] in their hands and throwing it into the surf, then walking about over the spot and when they feel the eel about their feet, stoop down and suddenly dash it on to the sand with both hands. If placed on the moist sand they burrow themselves, tail foremost, almost instantaneously.——*Myliobatidæ* (समुद्रपिशाचकुल - samudrapisháchakula, San.). From (samudra, san. sea + pishácha, san. devil). Batoïdei, plagiostomata, 51. Devil fishes, Eagle rays, Sea devils. Fins are not present on the sides of the head, but appear at the end of the snout [tenky].——*Nandidæ* (नन्दकुल - nandakula, San.). Acanthopterygii, 4. Body oblong and compressed; scales covering the body; some are marine, others freshwater. The colors are liable to variations; carnivorous fishes.——*Notopteridæ* (नितंबपत्रकुल - nitambapatrakula, San.). From (nitamba, san. back + patra, san. wing). Physostomi, 41. Barber's knife [barber vaulay] family. Strange-shaped fishes; body oblong, or more or less elongated and compressed; tail prolonged and tapering; head and body with small scales; fresh and brackish waters [vaulay].——*Ophiocephalidæ* (अहिकपालकुल - ahikapálakula, San.). Means serpent + head. Acanthopterygii, 29. Walking fish [q.v.] family or Snake-headed fishes [doke, murrel, walking fish]. Are found only in the East indies. Are a fresh-water family, and of carnivorous habits. Like the labyrinthici, they are able to exist for a long time out of the water; they afford a light and wholesome but rather insipid diet; they are long in shape, with a large mouth, the head and body being covered with scales; they have long dorsal and anal fins, without any spines, teeth in the jaws, and on the palate. Jugglers exhibit these fishes walking on the land. Some grow to a large size. Rather voracious, but appear to consider a frog [bhaicam], mouse [shoondely], or rat [ely] as luscious a morsel as a fellow fish; keep water pure by destroying either animal or vegetable substances which may come in their way. These fishes may be conveyed long distances alive; inhabit both ponds and rivers; able to change their place of abode by traversing moist pieces of ground between one piece of water and another. Those which inhabit rivers are better flavored than the others which live in sluggish or stagnant water. Some of them bury themselves in the mud, when the waters of the tank or ditches are dried up; and are enabled to live for sometime in a torpid state, till a fresh supply of water calls them into renewed existence.——*Percidæ* (श्यामाकुल - shyámákula, San.). From (shyáma, san. dusky). Acanthopterygii, 1. Perch [bride fish, calavye, caratchy, caripey, caukkan, chandwah, cock up, kitchaun, pyekeely, rock cod, taumbam]. Are carnivorous fishes, and are found in the seas and freshwaters of all parts of the globe. The only representatives of real perch in South indian freshwaters are small fishes belonging to the genus Ambassis [chandwah]. They are all small fishes, with the body deep and compressed, more or less transparent. The so called Climbing perch, anabas scandens, belongs to the family Labyrinthici [palmyra fish]. The Red perch of the west coast, called Kembairy by the natives, is an estuary fish frequenting the rocks.——*Pleuronectidæ* (पार्श्वप्लवकुल - párshvaplavakula, San.). From (párshva, san. side + plava, san. swimming). Anacanthini, 34. Flat fishes [indian sole]. Common both on Coromandel and Malabar coasts; in last particularly large. Should more correctly be termed deep or thin fishes than flat fish, as they rest on one side, either left or right. They carry both eyes on one side of the head, the right or left side, whichever is uppermost; when young their eyes are placed as in other fish, but become twisted round as they grow larger. The upper side is always dark and the under side light-colored. The Turbot, Brill, and Flounder are English similar fish.——*Polynemidæ* (बहुतन्तुकुल - bahutantukula, San.). From (bahu, san. many + tantu, san. thread); from free thread like appendages below pectoral fin. Acanthopterygii, 11. Body oblong, somewhat compressed; eyes large, lateral, more or less covered by an adipose membrane; mouth on the lower side of a prominent snout and having a lateral cleft [robaul].——*Pristidæ* (क्राकचिककुल - krákachikakula, San.). From (krákachika, san. sawyer). Batoidei, plagiostomata, 48. Saw fishes. Snout much produced, flattened, and having a saw-like appearance. Great injuries are inflicted by these fishes, which strike sideways with their formidable snouts. Large ones have been known to cut a bather entirely in two. Sea fish [soorah].——*Rhinobatidæ* (खरत्वक्कुल - kharatvakkula, San.). From (khara, san. rough + tvak, san. skin). Batoidei, plagiostomata, 49. Tail thickened, moderately elongated, and with a longitudinal fold along either side. Very destructive amongst marine crustacea [kavachiny] and molluscs [chippy]; said to live in large droves. Sea fish [oloovay].——*Rhynchobdellidæ* (कण्टककुञ्चिकाकुल - kantakakuñchikákula, San.). From (kantaka, san. thorn + kuñchika, san. eel). Acanthopterygii, 24. Spiny eels. Body elongated, eel-shaped; fresh and brackish waters; found far inland and often at great elevations; excellent as food, although owing to their resemblance to eels or snakes [sarpam] some people object to them. They salt well, but their flesh is reputed to be slightly heating [aural].——*Sciænidæ* (घर्घरमत्स्यकुल - gharghāramatsyakula, San.). Means gurgling fish. Acanthopterygii, 12. The Maigre family. This family has several representatives. Some species, such as the Maigre, have the power of producing a drumming or grunting sound beneath the surface of the water. Body somewhat compressed and rather elongate; eyes lateral, of moderate or small size; mouth in front of or below the snout; scales covering the head and snout, placed in oblique and often sinuous rows on the body. Afford isinglass [meen vajram] which is exported to China and elsewhere. As food their flesh is rather tasteless whilst young and coarse when large. Throughout the seas they are numerous, many entering estuaries and rivers [cuttalay].——*Sclerodermidæ* (कठिनत्वक्कुल - kat'hinatvakkula, San.). From (kat'hina, san. hard + tvak, san. skin). Plectognathi, 44. Body compressed or angular; snout somewhat produced; skin rough or spinate; marine fishes [colah, plautchy].——*Scombresocidæ* (उड्डीनमत्स्यकुल - uddínamatsyakula, San.). Means flying fish. Physostomi, 37. Mackerel pike family. Scales present, frequently a keeled row along either side of the free portion of the tail. The genus Exocœtus, or Flying-fish, belongs to this family [colah].——*Scombridæ* (चित्रांकमत्स्यकुल chitránkamatsyakula, San.). Means variegated fish. Acanthopterygii, 19. Mackerel family. Are well-known on account of their importance as an article of food. Marine fishes. The family includes the common Mackerel, the Tunny, the Albacore, the Bonito, the Pilot fish, the Remora or Sucking fish, the Seer [q.v.], the John dory, and the Coryphene or dolphin fish [q.v.] of sailors [murrel, seer].——*Scopelidæ* (कूपकीयकुल - kúpakíyakula, San.). From (kúpaka, san. rock). Physostomi, 36. Are deep sea fishes, among them is included Harpodon nehereus, the Bombay duck [bummelo], a well-known article of food on the other coast when dried and smoked. They have an adipose fin but no barbels, and sometimes are covered with scales, entirely, or partially [bummelo].——*Scorpænidæ* (वृश्चिकीयकुल - vrishchikíyakula, San.). From (vrishchika, san. scorpion). Acanthopterygii, 7. Body oblong, compressed or sub-cylindrical; eyes lateral; cleft of mouth lateral; body scaled or scaleless [toomby].——*Scylliidæ* (विनयनपुटमत्स्यकुल - vinayanaputamatsyakula, San.). Means without eyelid. Selachoidei, plagiostomata, 47. Eye without any nictitating membrane; teeth small, several rows being generally in use [soorah]. *Siluridæ* (शृङ्गीयकुल - shringíyakula, San.). From (shringí, san. shad). Physostomi, 35. Cat-fish family [butter fish, gogra, goonch, jella, keliroo, scorpion fish, soorah, vaulay]. The family is a large one, and very numerously represented in s. indian waters. It is, like the carp [kenday] family, essentially a freshwater group of fishes; but some few species belonging to it are also found in salt water keeping however near the coast. Many are credited with causing poisonous wounds; in which respect they may be divided into two classes, those in which the wounds are of a distinctly venomous description, and those in which their jagged spines occasion intense inflammation often of a dangerous character. They are eaten by the poorer classes. They are forbidden to Jews and Mahomedans. They are very foul feeders. The Siluridæ family are to be distinguished chiefly by the absence of scales; but they have sometimes bony plates on certain parts of the body. They are provided with barbels, often of great length, and generally numerous. They have frequently a second dorsal fin which is gristly, or adipose, and without rays, and their mouths are furnished with teeth, which however, vary much in form and disposition. ——*Sparidæ* (नासाग्रास्यमत्स्यकुल - náságrásyamatsyakula, San.). Means nose + front + mouthed. Acanthopterygii, 5. Seabreams. Body oblong and compressed; eyes of moderate size, lateral; mouth in front of snout. Sea fish; some entering fresh waters [rock cod].——*Sphyrænidæ* (मौद्गरीयकुल - maudgaríyakula, San.). From (mudgara, san. hammer). Acanthopterygii, 25. Body elongated, sub-cylindrical; eyes lateral; carnivorous fishes; not much esteemed for the table [jella].——*Squamipinnidæ* (शल्कवाजकुल - shalkavájakula, San.). From (shalka, san. scale + vája, san. fin). Acanthopterygii, 2. Scaly finned fish family. Body elevated and compressed; eyes lateral and of moderate size; mouth generally small, with a lateral cleft and situated in front of snout; are, as a rule, marine. This family consists mostly of bright-colored fishes, with bodies very deep in comparison to their length and very narrow with small mouths. It is distinguished by the scales extending over a large portion of the dorsal and anal fins.——*Stromateidæ* (बहुवर्णकुल - bahuvarnakula, San.). From (bahu, san. many + varna, san. color). Acanthopterygii, 17. Body oblong or slightly elongated and compressed; eyes lateral; sea fish [pomfret].——*Syngnathidæ* (हनुमत्कुल - hanumatkula, San.). From (hanu, san. jaw). Lophobranchii, 43. Gill-openings small, round [whip fish].——*Teuthididæ* (विदरीमुखमत्स्यकुल - vidarímukhamatsyakula, San.). Means cleft-mouth. Acanthopterygii, 8. Body oval and strongly compressed; eyes of moderate size, lateral; mouth slightly cleft. ——*Trachinidæ* (परुषकुल - parushakula, San.). Means rough. Acanthopterygii, 21. Body more or less elongated, posteriorly compressed; head often large; eyes more or less lateral. Body scaleless, scaled, or with a single series of plate-like scales. The fishes of this family are generally of a long shape and inhabit salt water [varawa].——*Trichiuridæ* (रोमवालकुल - rómaválaku, San.). Means hairy tail. Acanthopterygii, 14. Hair-tails [moorman's vaulay]. Body elongated and compressed. Along the coasts of India esteemed mostly, because being thin or ribbon-shaped they can be dried without salting. Afford very delicate eating when fresh though never brought to the table of Europeans [vaulay].——*Trygonidæ* (शंकुवालकुल - shankuválakula, San.). From (shanku, san. sting + vála, san. tail). Batoidei, plagiostomata, 50. Electric rays; tail long and slender without any lateral folds; the forms with armed tails occasion exceedingly dangerous injuries; sea fish [tenky]. Skates and rays [tenky] generally exist in enormous numbers in these seas, where they attain to a great size, and some are dreaded by fishermen because of the wounds inflicted by their caudal spines, while others cause great injury to the oysters [auly]. Skates are gregarious. Rays lie concealed in the sand, and are able to suddenly encircle fish or prey swimming above them with their long whip-like tails, and then wound them with their serrated tail spine. Their skins were formerly valuable as shagreen, being considered superior to those of sharks [soorah], owing to the scales being of somewhat larger dimensions. Irrespective of being employed for shagreen, they are occasionally used as rasps or sand-paper, to give the first surface to wood or horn [sing] which it is desired to polish. Their fins are exported along with those of the sharks to China, where they are used for soups, while from their livers an oil [malabar oil, yennay] is extracted. The thin horny cases, inside which are the fœtal rays, are more square in form and comparatively smaller than what are observed among the sharks. Many of these cases are square, with a horn-like projection from each corner.——*Xiphiidæ* (खड्गमत्स्यकुल - khadgamatsyakula, San.). From (khadga, san. sword + matsya, san. fish). Acanthopterygii, 13. Sword fish. Sea fish. Eyes lateral; body compressed; upper jaws produced into a long, sword-shaped process. Sword-fishes [macaram] are known to occasionally attack vessels [peacock fish].——**(4)** The following is a list of the principal genera alphabetically arranged, with the family in which contained:— Acanthurus, acanthuridæ, 15; Ætobatis, myliobatidæ, 51; Ailia, siluridæ, 35; Ambassis, percidæ, 1; Amblypharyngodon, cyprinidæ, 39; Amphisile, centriscidæ, 28; Anabas, labyrinthidæ, 30; Anacanthus, sclerodermidæ, 44; Anguilla, murænidæ, 42; Apistus, scorpænidæ, 7; Apocryptes, gobiidæ, 23; Aspidoparia, cyprinidæ, 39; Badis, nandidæ, 4; Bagarius, siluridæ, 35; Balistes, sclerodermidæ, 44; Barbus, cyprinidæ, 39; Barilius, cyprinidæ, 39; Belone, scombresocidæ, 37; Callichrous, siluridæ, 35; Caranx, carangidæ, 16; Carcharias, carchariidæ, 46; Catla, cyprinidæ, 39; Ceratoptera, myliobatidæ, 51; Chanos, clupeidæ, 40; Chorinemus, carangidæ, 16; Chatœssus, clupeidæ, 40; Chela, cyprinidæ, 39; Chiloscyllium, scyllidæ, 47; Chrysophrys, sparidæ, 5; Cirrhina, cyprinidæ, 39; Cirrhitichthys, cirrhitidæ, 6; Clarias, siluridæ, 35; Clupea, clupeidæ, 40; Coilia, clupeidæ, 40; Coryphæna, coryphænidæ, 18; Cossyphus, labridæ, 32; Cybium, scombridæ, 19; Cynoglossus, pleuronectidæ, 34; Danio, cyprinidæ, 39; Dicerobatis, myliobatidæ, 51; Diodon, gymnodontidæ, 45; Discognathus, cyprinidæ, 39; Doryichthys, syngnathidæ, 43; Drepane, squamipinnidæ, 2; Dussumieria, clupeidæ, 40; Echeneis, scombridæ, 19; Elacate, scombridæ, 19; Eleotris, gobiidæ, 23; Elops, clupeidæ, 40, Engraulis, clupeidæ, 40; Ephippus, squamipinridæ, 2; Equula, carangidæ, 16; Etroplus, chromidæ, 33; Exocætus, scombresocidæ, 37; Fistularia, aulostomateidæ, 27; Galeocerdo, carchariidæ, 46; Gerres, percidæ, 1; Glyphidodon, glyphidodontidæ, 31; Gobioides, gobiidæ, 23; Gobius, gobiidæ, 23; Haplochilus, cyprinodontidæ, 38; Harpodon, scopelidæ, 36; Hemiramphus, scombresocidæ, 37; Heniochus, squamipinnidæ, 2; Hippocampus, syngnathidæ, 43; Histiophorus, xiphiidæ, 13; Holacanthus, squamipinnidæ, 2; Holocentrum, berycidæ, 9; Homaloptera, cyprinidæ, 39; Ichthyocampus, syngnathidæ, 43; Ichthyscopus, uranoscopeæ, 20; Jerdonia, cyprinidæ, 39; Kurtus, kurtidæ, 10; Labeo, cyprinidæ, 39; Lactarius, carangidæ, 16; Lates, percidæ, 1; Lepidocephalichthys, cyprinidæ, 39; Lethrinus, sparidæ, 5; Lobotes, percidæ, 1; Lutjanus, percidæ, 1; Macrones, siluridæ, 35; Mastacembelus, rhynchobdellidæ, 24; Megalops, clupeidæ, 40; Mene, coryphænidæ, 18; Minous, scorpænidæ, 7; Monacanthes, sclerodermidæ, 44; Mugil, mugilidæ, 26; Muræna, murænidæ, 42; Murænesox, murænidæ, 42; Mustelus, carchariidæ, 46; Myliobatis, myliobatidæ, 51; Myripristis, berycidæ, 9; Nandus, nanaidæ, 4; Nemacheilus, cyprinidæ, 39; Notopterus, notopteridæ, 41; Nuria, cyprinidæ, 39; Ophiocephalus, ophiocephalidæ, 29; Osphromenus, labyrinthidæ, 30; Osteogeniosus, siluridæ, 35; Ostracion, sclerodermidæ, 44; Otolithus, sciænidæ, 12; Pagrus, sparidæ, 5; Pangasius, siluridæ, 35; Pellona, clupeidæ, 40; Pempheris, kurtidæ, 10; Pimelepterus, sparidæ, 5; Plagusia, pleuronectidæ, 34; Platax carangidæ, 16; Platycephalus, cottidæ, 22; Platyglossus, labridæ, 32; Plotosus, siluridæ, 35; Polyacanthus, labyrinthidæ, 30; Polynemus, polynemidæ, 11; Pristipoma, percidæ, 1; Pristis, pristidæ, 48; Psettus, carangidæ, 16; Pseudeutropius, siluridæ, 35; Pseudoscarus, labridæ, 32; Pterois, scorpænidæ, 7; Pteroplatea, trygonidæ, 50; Rasbora, cyprinidæ, 39; Rhinobatus, rhinobatidæ, 49; Rhinoptera, myliobatidæ, 51; Rhynchobatus, rhinobatidæ, 49; Rhynchobdella, rhynchobdellidæ, 24; Rita, siluridæ, 35; Rohtee, cyprinidæ, 39; Saccobranchus, siluridæ, 35; Saurida, scopelidæ, 36; Scatophagus, squamipinnidæ, 2; Sciæna, sciænidæ, 12; Sciænoides, sciænidæ, 12; Scolopsis, percidæ, 1; Scomber, scombridæ, 19; Seriolichthys, carangidæ, 16; Serranus, percidæ, 1; Sillago, trachinidæ, 21; Silundia, siluridæ, 35; Silurus, siluridæ, 35; Sphyræna, sphyrænidæ, 25; Stegostoma, scylliidæ, 47; Stromateus, stromateidæ, 17; Synagris, percidæ, 1; Syngnathus, syngnathidæ, 43; Tetrodon, gymnodontidæ, 45; Teuthis, teuthididæ, 8; Therepon, percidæ, 1; Thynnichthys, cyprinidæ, 39; Thynnus, scombridæ, 19; Trachynotus, carangidæ, 16; Triacanthus, sclerodermidæ, 44; Trichiurus, trichuiridæ, 14; Trichogaster, labyrinthidæ, 30; Trygon, trygonidæ, 50; Trypauchen, gobiidæ, 23; Umbrina, sciænidæ, 12; Upeneus, mullidæ, 3; Urogymnus trygonidæ, 50; Wallago, siluridæ, 35; Zygæna, carchariidæ, 46.——(5) Title heads in this glossary cover each genus, and contained species, clearly known to be distinguished by the natives. When all the aliases are taken into account, the majority of known S. indian fishes have attached to them a generic or specific name derived from the vernaculars. These are however chiefly from the Bengalee aud the Marhatta, the observers having been residents of the more northern provinces. Further-more in the case of those scientific terms which can be connected with the S. indian vernaculars, the terms themselves, borrowed as they have been from a fisherman's patois, are so corrupt as to be almost beyond recognition. On these two grounds the number of fish items may be found comparatively inconsiderable.——(6) For insects see Poochy; for batrachians see Bhaicam; for reptiles see Sarpy; for birds see Pacshy; for mammals see Sastanam. A general conspectus of the fauna [jantoo] of s. india was given in vol. II, appendix IV.——(7) *Matsya avatar* (मत्स्य - matsya, San.). From (mad, san. to rejoice); the gay one. The first or fish avatar [q.v.] of Vishnoo [q.v.]. Statements concerning it appear in the Matsya, Bhagavat, and Agny pooraunams [q.v.]; in the Narayana oopanishad; and in the Mahabhaurat [q.v.]. The substance as taken from South indian literature is that in a time of great wickedness Satyavratan [q.v.] was doing penance in the Dravida [q.v.] country; that he took up a small fish in his water vessel which increasing in bulk he put it into another; that after constant increase of bulk in different vessels he transferred it to the ocean; that it then announced to him an approaching great flood, and warned him to take refuge with his wife and the seven rishies [q.v.] and their wives, in a machine to be provided, directing him also to take pairs of all living things with necessary provision of food; that soon after torrents began to pour down, and the sea began to swell, when a vessel appeared floating on the waves, into which Satyavratan entered accompanied as above; that when the deluge had ceased, the god who had accompanied and towed the vessel in his fish-like form appointed Satyavratan, the seventh Menoo [q.v.], by name of Veivaswatan [q.v.] child of the sun, whence the solar line of kings [soorya vamsham]. The correspondence with the Noachian deluge is very exact [matam].

MATTAM (മട്ടം - mattam, *Mal.*). Level.——*Matagherry* (ಮತ್ತಗಿರಿ - mattagiri, Can. matigiri *). From (matta, can. flat + kere, can. bund). Town; Salem dist., Oossoor tal.; pop. 782; acres 1,048; lat. 12° 42′; long. 77° 51′; from Oossoor S.S.W. 3 miles; from Salem N.N.W. 75 miles. The Government Remount depôt was removed here from Coongal in 1828. All indents for horses for the cavalry and artillery in the presidency are supplied from here. Weekly fair with much traffic especially in oil and garden produce.——*Mattancherry* (മട്ടാഞ്ചേരി - mattáñchéri, Mal.). From (mattam, mal. level + chéri, mal. village). Village, Cochin state; pop. 3,987; lat. 9° 57′; long. 76° 17′; from Ernacolum W.S.W. 3 miles; from the sea E. ¼ mile. Suburb of Cochin. The Rajah has a palace used on state occasions. Immediately adjoining the palace is the synagogue of the Jews [jonaca], with a belfry, with rude clock more than 200 years old. The floor of the synagogue is paved with neat porcelain [kaolin] tiles [wode].——*Mattigay* (மட்டிகை - mattigai, Tam.). From (matti, tam. to affix). Seal impressed on cow-dung [shauny], &c., and put upon a heap of rice-corn in the threshing floor [calam], or upon sacks.

MAU (मा - má, *San.*). To measure, form, make.——*Macaram* (मकर - makara, San.). From (máyá, san. illusion + kri, san. to do). A monster in dolphin [cadal pundry, punrimeen] form, perhaps derived from the whalebone whale [timingilam]. Also called Asita damshtram or black-teethed, and Jala roopam or water formed. It is the vauhan [q.v.] or vehicle of Varoonan [q.v.], the god of the ocean, and is on the banner of Manmatan [q.v.], god of love. Also the tenth sign [raushy] of the solar zodiac [raushy chuckram] corresponding to Capricorn ♑. Winter solstice or oottarauyanam [q.v] occurs at present when the sun [sooryan] enters this sign. The macaram is represented in sculpture with the head and forelegs of an antelope [jinka] and the body and tail of a fish [matsyam]. As a modern term is the sword fish family xiphiidæ [matsyam, 13], of naturalists.——*Macara sancramanam* (మకరసంక్రమణము - makarasankramanamu, Tel.). Means the tenth sign of zodiac + passage; entrance of the sun [sooryan] into macaram about the 12th of january when the pongal [q.v.] feast is observed, a solar [maunan.] festival [pundigay, 2a]. Otherwise Macara sancraunty. The period from this day till the arrival of the sun at the N. point [carcatacam] of the zodiac [raushy chuckram], or oottarauyanam [q.v.] is lucky and from that time till he returns to Macaram or Dacshinauyanam [q.v]. is unlucky [jyotisham, maryanday, mausam].——*Maderpauk* (மாதர்ப்பாக்கம் - mátharppákkam, Tam.). From (máthu, tam. woman + pákkam, tam. village).—"*a*" Sub-magistracy, North arcot district. Pay Rs. 70.—"*b*" Village, Deputy tahsildar's station; North arcot dist., Calastry zemindarry, Maderpauk division; pop. 636; lat. 13° 27′; long. 80° 03′; from Arnee N.E. 72 miles; from Calastry S.E. 30 miles; from Chittore E.N.E. 64 miles; from Madras N.W. 31 miles; from Ranipett N.E. 59 miles; from Tripatty E.S.E. 42 miles; from Vellore E.N.E. 70 miles. 3 miles from Suttivaid in Chingleput district. Rude stone implements have been found. A great many Jendravar [q.v.] live here and export cloths to Madras.——*Mah* (मा - má, San.; ماه - máh, Pers.). Means measurer. Moon [cumr]. Month [maheena].——*Maheena* (مهينا - mahíná, Hind.). See sep. title.——*Mahtaub* (ماهتاب - máhtáb, Hind.). From (máh, pers. moon + táb, pers. splendour). Fireworks. Bengal light [baunam].——*Mahwar* (مهوار - mahwár, Hind.). Monthly [maugwar].

——*Mauchicoy* (मायाफल - máyáp'hala, San.; عفص - afs, Ar.; مازو - mázú, Pers.; ماپهل - máphal, Hind.; ماجو پهل - májúphal, Dec.; ಮಾಚಿಕಾಯಿ - máchikáyi, Can.; మాచికాయ - máchikáya, Tel.; മാചിക്ക - máchikka, Mal.; மாச்சக்காய் - máççakkáy, Tam.). San. from (máyá, san. illusion + p'hala, san. fruit); unreal fruit. Drav. from sanscrit through hindostany (májúphal). Galls. Gallæ chinenses and Gallæ japonicæ of chemists. Spherical concretions and other tubercular excrescences, made by the puncture of female gall flies, provided with ovipositors, by means of which they pierce bark or leaves of trees with a view of having a nidus for their ova, causing an unnatural growth that becomes a gall and contains the pupa of the future insect. If the insect has escaped they are yellow and inferior, and are called white galls. Oak galls are from the dyer's oak [q.v.], quercus infectoria, oliv. Tamarix galls are from the indian tamarix, tamarix gallica, linn. [manna jhow]; these are small. Terminalia galls are from the myrobalan [q.v.] trees; chiefly from leaves and twigs of terminalia chebula, retz. [chebulic myrobalan]. In veterinary practice, for cancer and thrush, take finely powdered galls, rub over the part with a spatula, dropping lime [q.v.] juice while rubbing. Galls are used in dyeing, ink-making, &c. [cauram, chamrah, mashy, myrobalan, shauyam, shye]. Compare:—Ophiorrhiza mungos, malayan earth gall; Quercus infectoria, oak galls; Quercus robur, oak galls; Rhus succedania, sumach galls; Tamarix articulata, atlee galls; Tamarix gallica, indian tamarix galls. See gloss. paragraphs [moy].——*Maudicoty* (ಮಾದಿಕೋತಿ - mádikóti, Can.). From (mádi, can. female + kóti, can. monkey). Hill-tribe female proper name [peyar].——*Maudry* (ಮಾದ್ರಿ - mádri, Can.; మాదిరి - mádiri, Tel.; மாதிரி - máthiri, Tam.). A pattern [muster].

——*Maudy* (ಮಾಡಿ - mádi, Can.). Means a female. Hill-tribe female proper name [peyar].——*Maugwar* (ماہوار - mahwár, Hind.). From (máh, pers. month). Month by month [mahwar]. ——*Maujoo* (ماجو - májú, Hind.). Means mother's soul. In composition makes a lacab; as Maujoo bee, soul of mother [ism]. Cf. Mah.——*Maulaty* (మాలతి - málati, Tel.). Means jasmine flower. Tel. also (késaripalli), meaning lion + village. Village, Hill; Ganjam dist., Goomsoor tal.; pop. 387; acres 485; lat. 19° 44′; long. 80° 40′; from Chetterpore N.W. 36 miles; from Russellcondah S. 15 miles. Ancient village 4 miles from Gungoopooram. Old fort at the foot of the hill. Gold coins and fragments of golden images have been found. On the hill is a lamp carved in stone which holds 250 seers [q.v.] of oil. The oil-pan is turned upside down and set on the stone pedestal of the lamp. Old temple excavated from the foot of the hill. The image of Sooryanarrain moorty, the sun-god, was carried to Boogoodah, where it was consecrated in a new temple built in its honor in the shape of the sun-car [rath]. In former times a Kesary rajah lived here, and carved stones and unusually large bricks [shengal] are shown on the hill. Several images, probably either Jeina [q.v.] or Booddhist [booddha] have been removed from the hill. Trig. station in lat. 19° 44′ 54·35″; long. 84° 39′ 35·97″; height 1,719 feet; from Kesarpully W.N.W. 4 miles; from Gungoopooram S. 3 miles; from Russellcondah S. 13 miles; on Aska Russellcondah road.——*Maulay* (माला - málá, San.; مالا - málá, Hind.; ಸರ - sara, Can.; దండ - danda, Tel.; മാല - mála, Mal.; தாழ்வடம் - tázhvadam, Tam.). From (má, san. to arrange). Tam. from (tázh, tam. to hang down + vadam, tam. string). Necklace. These are made of various seeds; as of :—Elæocarpus ganitrus, roxb. [roodrauck], Leucæna glauca, benth. [large chakondah], Nelumbium speciosum, willd. [nelumbo], &c. Also of wood of toolsy, Ocimum sanctum, linn. [common toolsy]. Also of pearls [moty], corals [moongah], gold beads [munkah], &c. Maulay means also a group, series, vocabulary [acarauthy] dictionary [nigantoo]. Also a kind of elegy consisting of couplets. For the inam called maulaiyeed see under Inam.——*Maulee* (आरामिक - árámika, San.; مالی - málí, Hind.; ತೋಟದವ - tótadava, Can.; తోటవాడు - tótavádu, Tel.; തോട്ടക്കാരൻ - tóttakkáran, Mal.; தோட்டக்காரன் - tóttakkáran, Tam.). Anglo-indian for a gardener. The following are two key-lists of the garden trees and plants of s. india for which vernacular equivalents are with certainty known; further information must be traced in the glossary paragraphs through the small type cross-references at end of this volume; see also vricsham, 7, for the method of expressing the products, &c., of the plants in the dravidian languages.—"*a*" Achras sapota, sapodilla; Adansonia digitata, baobab; Ægle marmelos, bael; Albizzia lebbek, common sirissa; Albizzia odoratissima, fragrant sirissa; Alpinia nutans, nodding galangal; Amarantus caudatus, red stem spinach; Amarantus gangeticus, garden spinach; Amoora rohituka, rohitacam; Anacardium occidentale, cashew; Anona muricata, sour sop; Anona reticulata, bullock's heart; Anona squamosa, sweet sop; Areca catechu, areca; Argemone mexicana, mexican poppy; Artabotrys odoratissimus, foreign champak; Artocarpus incisa, ratadel; Artocarpus integrifolia, breadfruit; Bauhinia variegata, variegated mountain ebony; Beta vulgaris, indian beet; Bombax malabaricum, red-cotton tree; Boswellia serrata, yellow dammer; Butea frondosa, bengal kino; Calophyllum inophyllum, common poon; Camellia theifera, tea; Canavalia ensiformis, hussar bean; Capsicum frutescens, shrubby chilly; Capsicum grossum, caffrie chilly; Capsicum minimum, bird's eye chilly; Cardiospermum halicacabum, balloon vine; Caryota urens, bastard sago palm; Cassia fistula, indian laburnum; Cassia siamea, sumatra senna; Cedrela toona, toon; Celosia cristata, cock's comb; Chickrassia tabularis, chickrassey; Chloroxylon swietenia, satin-wood; Citrus aurantium, var. aurantium proper, sweet orange; Citrus decumana, pummelow; Citrus medica, var. acida, sour lime; Citrus medica, var. limetta, sweet lime; Cocos nucifera, cocoanut; Coffea arabica, coffee; Coleus aromaticus, country borage; Corchorus olitorius, wild jute; Costus speciosus, arabian costus; Cryptostegia grandiflora, paulay silk cotton; Cupressus sempervirens, cypress; Curcuma longa, turmeric; Cynodon dactylon, hurrially; Dalbergia sissoo, sissoo; Delphinium ajacis, lark spur; Dillenia indica, chaltah; Dodonæa viscosa, bog-myrtle; Eriobotrya japonica, loquat; Eriodendron anfractuosum, silk cotton; Eugenia jambolana, common jaumoon; Feronia elephantum, wood-apple; Ficus carica, european fig tree; Filicium decipiens, pehimbia; Garcinia indica, mate mangosteen; Gardenia florida, cape jasmine; Gardenia lucida, decamallee; Garuga pinnata, garooga; Gomphrena globosa, bachelor's buttons; Graptophyllum hortense, face plant; Grewia asiatica, falsah; Helianthus annus, sun flower; Hibiscus esculentus, common bendy; Hibiscus mutabilis, lotus bendy; Hibiscus rosa-sinensis, china rose bendy; Hibiscus sabdariffa, red-hemp bendy; Hibiscus syriacus, thorny-hemp bendy; Hibiscus tiliaceus, cork-wood bendy; Ipomæa batatas, sweet potato; Ipomæa quamoclit, indian pink; Ixora coccinea, flame of the woods; Jatropha multifida, small physic nut; Lagerstrœmia indica, china privet; Lawsonia alba, henna plant; Linum usitatissimum, flax; Lobelia nicotianæfolia, wild tobacco; Lycopersicum esculentum, tomato; Mangifera indica, mango; Melia azadirachta, margosa; Melia azedarach, large neem; Meriandra bengalensis, bengal sage; Mesua ferrea, nauga champak; Methonica superba, wild bachnaug; Michelia champaca, champak; Millingtonia hortensis, indian cork; Mimusops elengi, ilanjy; Mirabilis jalapa, false jalap; Murraya exotica, andaman satin-wood; Musa paradisiaca, plantain; Musa superba, wild plantain; Myrtus communis, common myrtle; Nelumbium speciosum, sacred lotus; Nephelium litchi, litchy; Nephelium longana, longan; Nerium odorum, oleander; Nyctanthes arbor-tristis, coral jasmine; Nymphæa lotus, red indian water-lily; Nymphæa stellata, blue indian water-lily; Ocimum basilicum, sweet basil; Ocimum sanctum, holy basil; Papaver somniferum, opium poppy; Parkia biglandulosa, nitta; Phœnix acaulis, stemless date; Phœnix dactylifera, arabian date; Physalis peruviana, indian winter cherry; Plumeria acutifolia, pagoda tree; Pogostemon patchouli, patchouli; Poinciana regia, indian poinciana; Polyalthia longifolia, ashocam; Portulaca oleracea, indian purslane; Prunus persica, peach; Psidium guyava, red guava; Pterospermum acerifolium, maple-leaved pterospermum; Pterospermum suberifolium, velanga; Punica granatum, pomegranate; Pyrus malus, apple; Ricinus communis, castor oil; Saccharum procerum, wild sugar-cane; Saraca indica, bengal ashocam; Sesbania grandiflora, west-indian sesban; Solanum melongena, brinjaul; Solanum tuberosum, potato; Soymida febrifuga, rohan tree; Tabernæmontana coronaria, adam's apple; Tabernæmontana dichotoma, eve's apple; Tamarindus indica, tamarind; Terminalia catappa, country almond; Thespesia populnea, portia; Thymus vulgaris, thyme; Viola odorata, violet; Vitis vinifera, grape vine; Zingiber officinale, ginger.—"*b*" Adam's apple, tabernæmontana; Almond, terminalia; Apple, pyrus; Ashocam, polyalthia, saraca; Bachelor's buttons, gomphrena; Bachnaug, methonica; Bael, ægle; Balloon vine, cardiospermum; Baobab, adansonia; Basil, ocimum; Beet, beta; Bendy, hibiscus; Bog myrtle, dodonia; Borage, coleus; Bread-fruit, artocarpus; Brinjaul, solanum; Bullock's heart, anona; Cape jasmine, gardenia; Cashew, anacardium; Castor oil, ricinus; Chaltah, dillenia; Champak, artabotrys, mesua, michelia; Chickrassy, chickrassia; Chilly, capsicum; Cock's comb, celosia; Cocoanut, cocos; Coffee, coffea; Cork, millingtonia; Cypress, cupressus; Dammer, boswellia; Date, phœnix; Decamallee, gardenia; Eve's apple, tabernæmontana; Face plant, graptophyllum; Falsah, grewia; Fig, ficus; Flame of the woods, ixora; Flax, linum; Galangal, alpinia; Garooga, garuga; Ginger, zingiber; Guava, psidium; Henna, lawsonia; Hurrially, cynodon; Hussar bean, canavalia; Ilanjy, mimusops; Jalap, mirabilis; Jasmine, nyctanthes; Jaumoon, eugenia; Jute, corchorus; Kino, butea; Laburnum, cassia; Larkspur, delphinium; Lime, citrus; Litchy, nephelium; Longan, nephelium; Loquat, eriobotrya; Lotus, nelumbium; Mango, mangifera; Mangosteen, garcinia; Margosa, melia; Mexican poppy, argemone; Mountain ebony, bauhinia; Myrtle, myrtus; Neem, melia; Nitta, parkia; Oleander, nerium; Orange, citrus; Pagoda tree, plumeria; Patchouli, pogostemon; Peach, prunus; Pehimbia, filicium; Physic nut, jatropha; Pink, ipomæa; Plantain, musa; Pomegranate, punica; Poon, calophyllum; Poppy, papaver; Portia, thespesia; Privet, lagerstrœmia; Pummelow, citrus; Purslane, portulaca; Ratadel, artocarpus; Red cotton, bombax; Rohan, soymida; Rohitacam, amoora; Sage, meriandra; Sago palm, caryota; Sapodilla, achras; Satin-wood, chloroxylon, murraya; Senna, cassia; Sesban, sesbania; Silk cotton, cryptostegia, eriodendron; Sirissa, albizzia; Sissoo, dalbergia; Sour sop, anona; Spinach, amarantus; Sugar-cane, saccharum; Sun-flower, helianthus; Sweet potato, ipomæa; Sweet sop, anona; Tamarind, tamarindus; Tea, camellia; Thyme, thymus; Tobacco, lobelia; Tomato, lycopersicum; Toon, cedrela; Turmeric, curcuma; Velanga, pterospermum; Vine, vitis; Violet, viola; Water-lily, nymphæa; Winter-cherry, physalis; Wood-apple, feronia.——*Mauligay* (मालिका - máliká, San.; മാളിക - málika, Mal.; மாளிகை - máligai, Tam.). Buildings arranged as flowers are in a garland. Palace.——*Mauliny* (मालिनी - máliní, San.). Bhadra cauly [q.v.]; the garland wearer.——*Maulipooram* (മാലിപ്പുറം - málippuram, Mal.). From (máli, mal. coir net + pura, mal. house). Village, Port; Cochin state, Cochin tal.; pop. 316; lat. 10°; long. 76° 17′; from Bombay S.S.E. 660 miles; from Cochin N. 2 miles; from Ernacolum W. 3 miles; from Naracal S. 3 miles. Small port between British Cochin and Naracal, to which pertains a flagstaff of the Cochin native state. Used in fine weather by native craft.——*Mauly* (మాలి - máli, Tel.). From (mála, san. garland). A class of Poojarries [q.v.] in Ganjam. ——*Maunam* (मान - mána, San.). Measure. See sep. title.——*Maunasauram* (मानसार - mánasára, San.). From (mána, san. measure + sára, san. essence). The essence of proportion. Ancient Sanscrit treatise on the building of sacred edifices, of great celebrity in S. india. The first chapter treats of the measures [alavay] used in architecture, sculpture, carpentry, &c. The second describes the qualification of a Shilpy [q.v.], and gives a brief account of the origin of the five different classes of artists said to have been descended from Vishwacarman and to have followed respectively the occupations of sculptors, joiners, braziers, jewellers, and blacksmiths [punchaula]. The third, fourth, and fifth chapters explain the nature and qualities of the soil [desham, munn] on which buildings should be erected; such as temples, palaces, and private dwelling-houses for the several classes of people. The sixth contains directions for constructing a gnomon [shunk], for the purpose of determining the several points of the compass [ashtadic]. The seventh treats of the parts into which the ground plan of the cities, towns, temples, palaces and houses should be divided. The eighth chapter gives a minute description of sacrifices and other devotional rites to be performed on various occasions in the building of temples, houses, &c. The ninth chapter treats of villages and towns, and prescribes rules for the formation of streets [veety], and the allotment of fit places for the erection of temples, and for the residence of the different classes of people [oor, veed]. The tenth contains a description of the different sorts of cities. The eleventh treats of the dimensions of the several sorts of edifices; the twelfth of the garbha vinyausam or laying the foundation-stone in the centre of the intended building; the thirteenth of oopapeetam or pedestals; the fourteenth of adhishtaunam [q.v.] or basements; the fifteenth of the several species of pillars [stambham], with their respective dimensions; the sixteenth of prastaram [q.v.] or entablature; the seventeenth of the junction of the several parts of timber work with reference to their points; the eighteenth of vimaunams [q.v.], temples, or palaces in general. Twelve successive chapters, from the nineteenth to the twenty-eighth, contain descriptions of temples surmounted by pyramidal domes, consisting of from one to twelve storeys, with their respective dimensions. The twenty-ninth chapter treats of praucaurams [q.v.] or outer courts of temples; the thirtieth of the attendant deities, and the parts respectively assigned to each within the walls of the temple; the thirty-first of gopoorams [q.v.] or pyramidal buildings raised over the gateways leading into temples; the thirty-second of mantapams [q.v.] or porticos, or resting places for the deity; the thirty-third of shaulays [q.v.] or halls; the thirty-fourth of cities; the thirty-fifth of private dwelling-houses; the thirty-sixth and thirty-seventh of gates and doorways, with their dimensions; the thirty-eighth and thirty-ninth of the palaces and their appendages; the fortieth of princes with their titles; the forty-first of the building of cars [rath] and other vehicles [vauhan] of the gods; the forty-second of couches, cushions, and the like; the forty-third of the thrones [simhausanam] for the gods and for princes; the forty-fourth of ornamental arches [toranam]; the forty-fifth of the calpa taroo [calpacam] or the all-productive tree, which is planted in Indra's heaven and supplies all the wants of those who take shelter under it. The forty-sixth chapter treats of abhishaicams [q.v.] or ablutionary rites, by which images are sanctified; the forty-seventh of jewels and ornaments worn by the gods and mortals; the forty-eighth of statues [vigraham] of Bramha [q.v.] and other deities; the forty-ninth of the lingam [q.v.], the emblem of Shiva [q.v.]; the fiftieth of seats and forms raised for the reception of images; the fifty-first of the form of Shacty [q.v.], the goddess of nature; the fifty-second and fifty-third of the images worshipped by the Booddhists [booddha] and Jeinas [q.v.]. The fifty-fourth describes the statues of Yacshans [q.v.], Vidhyaudharans, and other choristers; the fifty-fifth those of the saints or holy men; and the fifty-sixth and fifty-seventh those of the Devas [q.v.] or gods, with their respective vehicles. The fifty-eighth concludes with rules for chiselling the eyes of a statue and the ceremonies to be performed on the occasion. A stapaty, architect; a sootra grauhy, measurer; a vardhaky, joiner; and tutchan, carpenter; are indispensably necessary to the building of an edifice. Among other moral qualities enumerated as requisite in the architect is "sincerity." The Hindoo orders consist of four principal parts: the oopapeetam or pedestal, the adhishtaunam or base, the stambham or pillar, and the prastaram or entablature. The writers invariably treat of a pedestal and base as separate bodies, as they are sometimes employed without pillars. The parts of the orders are compared to the several parts of the human body [shareeram]. The difference in the orders consists chiefly in the proportion between the thickness and height of pillars. The columns are diminished gradually in their diameter from the base to the summit of the shaft. The general rules adopted by the architects, in this respect, is that the thickness at the bottom, being divided into as many parts as there are diameters in the whole height of the column, one of these parts is invariably diminished at the top. The plan of the columns admits of every shape, and is frequently found in the quadrangular and octangular form, and richly adorned with sculptured ornaments. The capitals are varied at pleasure, though not without regard to the diameter and length of the shaft. The entablature of the order admits of little variety. The massiveness of the entablature offers a striking contrast to the lightness of the Grecian. Various examples are to be met with in which human figures, as well as representations of animals, are employed in relief in the sides of pillars in temples and porticos. Compare the Greek Atlantes and Caryatides [coil, pagoda, staupatyam].——*Maund* (من - man, Hind.; మణుగు - manugu, Tel.; மணங்கு - manangu, Tam.). Title is the old english word for basket, applied by corruption as an equivalent of the hindostany munn. Hind. from (mána, san. measure); Drav. from (mánaka, san. measure). Compare the Hebrew maneh, the Greek μνᾶ, and the Roman mina.—"*a*" A measure of weight, and principal standard thereof. 8 visses = 1 maund; 20 maunds = 1 bhauram or candy [niray, 2 a, b, c, e]. Approximate actual value, 1 maund = 960 tolahs or 25 lbs. avoir. Used in every district except Malabar, Trichinopoly, and Tinnevelly. In Bellary it is 25 lbs. 14 oz. 12 drs. avoir. in South canara 28 lbs. 12 oz. 12⅔ drs. avoir., in South Arcot 25 lbs. 11 oz. 6⅘ drs. avoir., and in every other district 25 lbs. avoir.—"*b*" The above is usually called the Madras maund. The Indian maund consists of 40 seers of 80 tolahs each and is equal to 82⅔ lbs. 27 Indian maunds are equal to a ton. Used on railways. Bombay maund is 28 lbs. That of Surat 41 lbs. The smallest Indian maund is that of Colachel in Travancore and = 18 lbs. 12 oz. 13 drs.—"*c*" Compare Toolaum. See vol. I, 609; II, 505–519.——*Maunica* (మానిక - mánika, Tel.). From (má, san. to measure).—"*a*" Liquid measure. 2 coodavams = 1 maunica; 2 maunicas = 1 prasta [alavay, 4b]. Approximate actual value, 1 maunica = 52½ cubic inches. Obsolete. Same as San. sharauvam.—"*b*" Measure of capacity. 2 tavvas = 1 maunica; 4 maunicas = 1 coöncham [alavay, 3b]. Approximate actual value, 1 maunica = 140 cubic inches, but very variable. Used in Vizagapatam, Kistna, Kurnool, and Nellore. In Vizagapatam a maunica is equal to 2 seers [q.v.] of 90 tolahs [q.v.] or 157½ cubic inches. In Kurnool very variable. In Vizianagram it is equal to 1 seer of 90 tolahs or 78¾ cubic inches. In Nellore a maunica is equal to 122½ cubic inches. In Kistna there are three maunicas measuring 140, 131¼ and 122½ cubic inches, respectively. Same as Adda in Kistna. Compare Puddy. See vol. I, 609; II, 512–520. ——*Mausam* (मास - mása, San.). Month. See sep. title.——*Maush* (माष - másha, San.; ماشه - máshah, Hind.; ماش - másh, Dec.; మాషము - máshamu, Tel.). Means black gram. Goldsmith's weight, 8 goomchies = 1 mausham; 4 maushams = 1 miscal [niray, 3e]. Approximate actual value, 1 maushm = 15 grains. Used by Mahomedans, and in medical books by Hindoos. There is a Hindostany proverb:—گهڑی مین تولہ گهڑی مین ماشہ—"A tolah [q.v.] one hour, and a mausham the next"; said of a capricious person. See vol. I, 609; II, 507.——*Mausha parny* (माषपर्णी - máshaparní, San.). From (másha, san. phaseolus bean + parna, san. leaf); from leaves and pods like phaseolus. Title otherwise Kidney-bean tree. Botanically the Glycine genus, leguminosæ [vricsham, 48]. Slender twining herbs; leaves made up of three to seven dissimilar leaflets; flowers small, yellow or violet; legume linear, cylindrical, nearly straight, many-seeded, with partitions. The species best known to the natives are:—javanica [javanese country bean], soja [japanese cow gram], tomentosa [horse-gram shrub].——*Mautah* (माता - mátá, San.). See sep. title.——*Mautray* (मात्रा - mátrá, San.). From (má, san. to measure). Measure of time. 60 mautrays or indian seconds = 1 vinaudicay or indian minute [caulam]. Approximate actual value, 1 mautray or indian second = ·4 english seconds. Same as caushtacalay [caulam, 6], vipalam [caulam, 6], param [caulam, 5]. See vol. I, 609. ——*Mauyan* (மாயன் - máyan, Tam.). Vishnoo [q.v.].—— *Mauyay* (माया - máyá, San.). From (má, san. to form). Illusion personified. The visible world regarded as only a phantom, and so the vanities of the world that lead men astray. Mythologically, the shacty [q.v.] or female energy of Bramha [q.v.] as creator; in this sense nearly synonymous with pracrity [q.v.], matter. In all Hindoo documents of a religious or philosophical kind, not founded on the oopanishads [q.v.], matter is regarded as inseparable from the notion of deity, as a creative power; and the office of creator was to mould pre-existent matter into shape and form. Mauyam, in the neuter gender, is used more extensively for power or form [matam]. A Tamul shastram [q.v.] says:—மாயாவடீசணம் (ரு) அசத்து, சடம், துக்கம், அநித்தம், கண்டம். மாயை யின்வித்து (ச) தேகம், மனம், மனஅசைவு, வருணனை— "The properties of Mauyay are five:—unreality, matter, distress, "transiency and division. The seeds of Mauyay are four:— "body, mind, emotions of mind and knowledge of motions."—— *Mauyone* (மாயோன் - máyón, Tam.). Vishnoo.——*Mauyone maroogan* (மாயோன்மருகன் - máyónmarugan, Tam.). From (máyón, tam. vishnu + marugan, tam. nephew). Soobramanyan, as son of Parvaty [q.v.] sister of Vishnoo in the Krishnan [q.v.] avatar [q.v.].——*Mayavaram* (மாயவரம் - máyavaram, Tam.). See sep. title.——*Mitam* (मित - mita, San.). From (má, san. to measure). Measured.——*Mitaucsharam* (मिताक्षर - mitákshara, San.). From (mita, san. measured + akshara, san. syllables). Commentary by Vinyauneshwaran [q.v.] on the Code of Yaunyavalcyan [q.v.]. This work is the chief authority of the Benares school of laws, which is the prevailing one in Middle india.——*Mugger* (नक्र - nakra, San.; تمساح - timsáh, Ar.; نهنگ - nahang, Pers.; مگرمچھ - magarmachh, Hind.; مگر - magar, Dec.; ಮೊಸಳೆ - mosale, Can.; మొసలి - mosali, Tel.; മുതല - mutala, Mal.; කිඹුලා - kimbulá, Singh.; முதலை - muthalai, Tam.). Title from hindostany. San. from (na, san. not + kram, san. so move), slow in motion; cf. coormam. Hind. from (makara, san. alligator + matsya, san. fish). Dec. from (makara, san. alligator). Mal. from (mun, mal. front + tala, mal. head); from its head being prominent. Terms co-extensive with family Crocodilidæ, sauria [godhicay], reptilia [sarpy, 5], of naturalists [jantoo]. These are generally called here alligators. Alligator from Spanish lagarto, a lizard. Friar Jordanus, the Quilon Bishop of the fourteenth century, has the following:— "There be also coquodriles, which are vulgarly called calcatix.

"Some of them be so big that they be bigger than the biggest "horse [ghorah]. These animals be like lizards [chipkalee], and "have a tail stretched over all, like unto a lizard's; and have a "head like unto a swine's, and rows of teeth so powerful and "horrible that no animal can escape their force, particularly in the "water. This animal has, as it were, a coat of mail; and there is "no sword nor lance nor arrow which can anyhow hurt him, on "account of the hardness of his scales. In the water, in short, "there is nothing so strong, nothing so evil, as this wonderful "animal." In the word calcatix, crocodile and cockatrice, the fabulous serpent [cobra, naugam], appear to be confounded. Have head with the snout produced; body depressed, covered above and below with square shields arranged in longitudinal and transverse series. Are thoroughly aquatic. Their short limbs are limbs of secondary use for locomotion in the water. Being more or less webbed, these prevent the animals from sinking in the mud when walking on the shore. The tail is not only the principal organ for locomotion, but, at the same time, a powerful weapon. The armour, which protects the body also serves as ballast, by aid of which the animal can sink instantaneously on being disturbed. The gullet is too narrow to allow of the passage of the entire body of the victim. The teeth being adapted for seizing and holding fast only and not for biting, they are obliged to mangle the carcase of their prey, tearing off single pieces by sudden strong jerks. They live much on fish. Alligators are found in the Kistna, Godavery and Cauvery. In calm weather they float two or three miles out to sea. Some bury themselves in the mud and remain in a state of torpor during the time of the drought; during that period, after they have been released from the state of enforced fasting, they are most formidable. A man seized by an alligator has only one way of saving his life, namely to force his fingers into the eyes; it then immediately lets go its victim. All alligators are oviparous; young alligators are of rather rapid growth. There is a Tamul proverb:—ஆனையைத் தண்ணீரில் இழுக்கிற முதலை பூனையைத் தரையில் இழுக்குமா—"Can an alli- "gator, which draws an elephant [q.v.] in water, drag a cat "[poonay] on dry ground?" There is a Hindostany proverb:— دریا میں رهنا اور مگر مچھ سے بیر—"to live in the river and be at "enmity with the crocodile," or to be on bad terms with him under whose authority one is placed. The following are the species known in Southern india:—"*a*" Crocodilus palustris. Alias Bombifrons trigonops; Crocodilus biporcatus, bombifròns, trigonops, vulgaris. Upper surface of snout covered with numerous small, rounded, irregular prominences; Malabar.—"*b*" Crocodilus porosus. Alias Crocodilus biporcatus; Oopholis porosus. Common species along all rivers; grows to the size of 30 feet.

MAU (மா - má, *Tam.*). Animal.——*Maud* (पशु - pashu, San.; مواشی - mavàshí, Ar. and Pers.; گائی گورو - gáigorú, Hind.; جوی - jawi, Malay; ದನಕರು - danakaru, Can.; ಕೈಕಂಜಿ - kaikanji, Too.; పశువు - pashuvu, Tel.; ସନ୍ଧ - sandha, Oor.; കാലി - káli, Mal.; மாடு - mádu, Tam.). Title from tamul. San. from (pash, san. to bind); as bound to the stake during sacrifice. Ar. and pers. from (máshiya, ar. quadruped). Hind. from (gáí, hind. cow + gorú, hind. horned cattle). Can. from (dana, can. cattle + karu, can. calf). Tel. from sanscrit. Mal. from (kál, mal. leg). Tam. from (má, tam. animal). Title otherwise Indian ox, Indian zebu. The bull is called Braminy bull [q.v.]. Bos indicus, bovinæ, bovidæ, ruminantia, mammalia [sastanam, 23], of naturalists [jantoo]. Comprises several varieties, all of which are remarkable for having long pendulous ears and a fatty elevated hump on their withers. The upper castes of natives consider it a sin to kill them, and pollution to eat their flesh. The bull is worshipped under the name of Nundy [q.v.], being the vehicle of Shiva [q.v.]. Cattle vary much in the districts as to size and form, and as to the growth of their horns. The cattle of Mysore are celebrated as draught cattle; they are quick in their paces, somewhat firey in disposition. The height of the Mysore bullock varies from 12 to 15 hands, the horns are straight and long, extending from 2–3 feet in length. The principal breeds of horned cattle in Mysore are the Amrit mahaul, Maudeshwarabetta, the Cancanhully, and the village cattle. Almost all other cattle seen in the country are importations or crosses between these. The Amrit mahaul, literally milk department, is a breeding establishment. The Amrit mahaul cattle comprise three varieties, called the Hullicaura, Haugalvaudy and Chitaldroog, from the districts which originally produced them. Maudeshwarabetta cattle come from the jungles and hills near Biligherry runga mullay on the south-eastern frontier of Mysore. They are larger than the Amrit mahaul cattle. They are very slow animals. Cancanhully cattle come from Cancanhully in the south-east of Mysore; they are very like the Maudeshwarabetta breed, but are generally smaller than the Amrit mahaul breed. Nellore cattle are the best breed within this Presidency, especially for milking purposes. A good specimen of the Nellore breed stands from 15 to over 17 hands in height. Their powers of draught and spirit of endurance are great. The horns are short, barely 3–6 inches in length, inclined outwards, tapering to a blunt point. Countenance, dull; eyes, large, prominent and heavy-looking; face, short with greater breadth of forehead and muzzle; large lop ears; eye, hoof and tail-tuft black; head, erect and well carried on a short stout-neck rising over the withers into a huge hump which frequently inclines to one side; back, short and straight; tail, high and well-set, a fair depth and width of chest; carcase, compact and solid-looking, with a large heavy dewlap; legs, clean but massive, straight and fairly apart to support the carcase. Skin, fine and covered with soft short hair; prevailing color, white. From their docility the nose string is seldom used. The influence of this breed extends north as far as the Kistna district. In Vizagapatam, Godavery, Ganjam, and Orissa, an inferior breed of cattle exists. They are small, under 12 hands in height, with small short horns never exceeding 6–12 inches in length. Their chief value is as pack animals, being well adapted to the hilly districts. About the Kimedy hills in Ganjam there is a more diminutive breed with short and frequently crumpled horns. Cuddapah and Bellary districts import their cattle chiefly from Nellore. North arcot cattle or Mysore are bred chiefly in the Poonganore zemindarry, this estate being a continuation of the Mysore tableland. Cattle are also bred in the hilly villages in the vicinity of Vellore, Canyambaudy, Goodiyattam, and Cungoondy. They are small, rarely exceeding 12–14 hands in height, and having much of the appearance of the Mysore breed, with long straight horns about 2 feet in length. They are of all colors, white, brown, black, &c.; and are chiefly used for agricultural purposes, to draw the cart [bandy] or plough [calappay, yair], or to act as pack animals to export and import produce. Among them are to be found some bullocks of fair size, which are good trotters. South arcot cattle are bred in the villages of Maumandore, Shirpaukam, and Shuncaraupooram. They are the usual small description, with horns of from 10–18 inches in length. Tanjore cattle are small and diminutive, and among them is a small variety which has a peculiar look from the complete absence of horns. Most of the latter have a small osseous protuberance in the centre of the forehead between the parts where the horns are usually found. Trichinopoly cattle are chiefly reared in the villages of Volcondapooram, Runjengoody, &c. They are small and useful, with horns from 10–15 inches long. Salem district is a good cattle-breeding country. The cattle are of small size and resemble the Mysore breed. They are very active and spirited and trot well when used to draw a carriage. They are chiefly bred in the villages of Abtoor, Namcull, Dharmapoory, Krishnagherry, Oossoor, Ootancaray, Tripatore, and Vaniyambaudy, the hills in the vicinity affording good pasturage. The prevailing color is white, with moderately-sized horns from 15–18 inches in length. The face short, eyes expressive and prominent, of rather spare make of carcase, quick and active in their movements. Bullocks of this breed are exported from Salem and Palghaut to Madura and Tinnevelly. There is a very superior breed of cattle raised in the jungles reaching down from Aulambaudy, along the banks of the Cauvery. The Trichengode cows are also famous as good milkers. In the plains of Coimbatore district there is a small and sturdy breed of cattle. They are generally much tamer than most cattle. There is quite a different breed in the hilly parts of Coimbatore district, between which and the plains considerable trade is carried on. Coimbatore hill cattle are of light build and show something of the Mysore breed, having long horns, somewhat of a pendant dewlap, and a graceful figure. The prevailing color is white. Malabar is not a good cattle-producing country. The chief working cattle are imported thither from either Mysore or Salem, but there is a small breed indigenous to the coast, and these extend through Malabar and South canara. The prevailing color is black; in form and shape they would resemble English cattle but for their diminutive size. They have fine thin necks, a small well-shaped head, and prominent sparkling eyes. Between the Bos taurus or English cattle, and the Bos indicus alias Bos zebu or Indian cattle, a cross-breed has been obtained, but these have been continued by successive breeding. The cross-bred cows are mostly appreciated. Of English cattle, the North devon bulls are the best for obtaining crosses. The hump on the shoulder which distinguishes the Indian ox is when dressed extremely delicate and tender. The Mahomedans are fond of beef and know well how to make its various preparations, beef tea, &c. In the Padaurta chintaumány also beef is included and recommended as a proper diet in cases of jaundice [caumalay], dyspepsia and when the body requires to be strengthened. The ancient Aryans [q.v.] probably ate beef [maumsam]. Candles are seldom made of tallow here. For vegetable tallow see Piney. The yak or Bos gruniens is common in Nepaul and Thibet, the bushy tail of which called Chowry [q.v.] is here in use. For curd see Tyre. For cow's milk see Paul. For other species of the family bovidæ, see Gowr, Khoolgah. For the festival of Mautt pongal after the harvest see Pongal.——*Maun* (மான் - mán, Tam.). Deer [mrigam].——*Maunidamendy* (மானிடமேந்தி - mánidaméndi, Tam.). From (mán, tam. deer + idam, tam. left side + éndi, tam. one who holds). Shiva [q.v.].

MAUCHY (माची - máchí, *San.*). From (mánksh, san. to desire), useful plant. Same as Absinth.

MAUCHY (ಮಾಚಿ - máchi, *Can.*). Means an unmarriageable woman. Hill-tribe female proper name [peyar].

MAUD (മാടു - mátu, *Mal.*). Raised ground [mail, mett, mode]; hillock.——*Maudqm* (മാടം - mátam, Mal.). Hut of the Paniyar [q.v.] mountaineers in Malabar. Also means royal palace.——*Maudambimaur* (മാടമ്പിമാർ - mádampimár, Mal.). From (mátam.

mal. palace + nambi, mal. the caste + már, mal. honorific plural suffix). West coast title, equivalent to lord of the manor. See vol. II, 135, 289.——*Maudan* (மாடன் - mádan, Tam.). Devil, imp. Coomily maudan, from (kumizhi, tam. bubble) is the Bubble-devil of running water. There are many other devils similarly called. See vol. I (80).——*Maudye* (മാടായി - mátáyi, Mal.). From (mádan, mal. the ruler so called + ézhi, mal. the place so called), maudan's yezhy to distinguish from yezhy or delly, a few miles north. Mal. also (pazhayannáti) old + bazaar. Sanscrit name (nasamípapura), meaning the ruler so called + city. Portuguese maravia. Village, amshom, Port; Malabar dist., Chiracal tal.; pop. 7,825; lat. 12° 02″; long. 75° 19′; from Belliapatam N.W. 9 miles; from Bombay S.S.E. 491 miles; from Calicut N.N.W. 62 miles; from Cannanore N.N.W. 14 miles; from Yetticoolam E.N.E. 4 miles. Ancient Moplah [q.v.] town in Mount delly bay. A place of trade. Boats of large size come up to it. Small redoubt, bungalow [q.v.] for travellers, and handsome mosque [musjid]. In hamlet of Payyangaudy is an old tank called the Jewish tank, near which stands the old Yezhy palace of the Colattiry rajahs. Two cave sepulchres.

MAUDA (మాడ - máda, Tel.). Also known as Camala mauda. Silver coin; half pagoda. Also goldsmith's weight. 4 chowlas = 1 mauda; 2 maudas = 1 pagoda weight [naunyam, 2b]. Approximate actual value, 1 mauda = 27 grains. Compare Sanscrit mausham. See vol. I, 609.

MAUDIGA (మాదిగ - mádiga, Can. and Tel.). From (mátanga, san. self-willed); as being beyond the caste pale. The corresponding terms are:—Tam. chuckler, Mal. tolcollan. The Chamaur of Upper india. The Maudigar are the lowest of the whole left-hand faction. They are therefore also called Yedagay [yidangay]. They are divided into two tribes, the Canarese and the Teloogoo. They are looked upon as a very low caste. They dress hides, make shoes, and some of them cultivate the ground. They are divided into small tribes of ten or twelve houses and intermarry with the daughters of these houses only, in order to be certain of the purity of their race. Some of them take two or more wives. Wives are only divorced for adultery. They eat carrion and animal food and drink spirits. At marriages the bridegroom has to provide thirty-five new pots and a sum of Rs. 5, which is spent in drink consumed by the guests. The ceremony is performed by their own priests, for no Bramin [q.v.] will approach their haunts. They are the drummers and horn-blowers of their village, their horn being called 'banka' and their drum 'tappattay'. They claim the privilege of taking free of payment the hides [chamrah] of all animals dying in the village. They have a priestly tribe called Jumboo [q.v.], who never intermarry with the laity, and live entirely on their contributions. There is a Mutt [q.v.] of Jumboos at Cuddapah, and the office of high priest there is hereditary. This official takes frequent rounds through the country, collecting money and admonishing his followers. Their tradition refers to one Aroondhaty [q.v.], a Maudiga girl, whom they say the rishy [q.v.] Agastyan [q.v.] made his wife. Proud of this distinction, the Maudigar often call themselves Aroondhaty's caste. Numbers in Presidency about 130,000; mostly in Kistna and Nellore [jauty].——*Madgole* (మాడుగుల - mádugula, Tel.). From (mádiga, tel. chuckler caste).—"*a*" Zemindarry; Vizagapatam dist., Veeravilly division; pop. 56,512. Contains 139 villages. Partly under the Agency administration of Vizagapatam. The zemindars [q.v.] claim descent from the rulers of Matsya desham who were closely connected with the Pandavu [q.v.] race. They state that they established themselves first at Padair above the ghauts [q.v.] to the north of Madgole. There is a rocky pool in the Matsyair in the hill mittahs [q.v.] of the zemindarry [q.v.] called Matsya goondam, containing numbers of sacred fish [matsyam] specially under the protection of the family. Before signing their names the Zemindars of Madgole inscribe the figure of a fish on the document, and the same is borne on their flags [dhwajam]. Another account is that they came into the country with the founder of the Jeypore family, whose cousins they are, and who gave them the Madgole country with the title of Bhoopaty. Linga bhoopaty of Madgole, joining in the general insurrection of the hill chiefs against Vizianagram, was in 1770 dispossessed by Poosapauty seetaram rauz with the aid of the Company's troops. He fled to Jeypore, where he died and where his family remained in exile till the death of Vijaya ram rauz in 1794, when they were recalled and sunnud [q.v.] for their ancient estate was given to Linga bhoopaty's eldest paternal nephew, Juggernaut bhoopaty. There have been numerous changes but the estate has reverted to the old family. Peshcush Rs. 30,099. The estate is now under mortgage to Jeypore and is likely to escheat to Government in a few years.—"*b*" Town; Vizagapatam dist., Veeravilly division; pop. 7,612; lat. 17° 55′; long. 82° 51′; from Chodavaram N.W. 9 miles; from Coraputt S. 60 miles; from Madras N. 368 miles; from Narsapatam N.E. 22 miles; from Parvatipore S.W. 70 miles; from Vizagapatam N.W. 34 miles; from Vizianagram S.W. 41 miles. Near the foot of the ghauts and on the road from Ankapully into the Jeypore country. Old temple of Bheemeshwaran.

MAUF (معاف - muáf, *Hind.*). From (afú, ar. pardon). Exemption, pardon, remission. Mauf saucshy is an approver.

MAUFOOZ (محفوظ - mahfúz, *Hind.*). From (hafiza, ar. to preserve). Safe. Proper name.——*Maufooz bunder* (محفوظ بندر - mahfúzbandar, Hind.; మాపూసుబందరు - mápúsubandaru, Tel.). From (mahfúz, ar. mahomedan name + bandar, pers. port); after mahfooz khan, son of anwarooddeen [q.v.], first of the carnatic [q.v.] nawaubs. Chicacole.——*Maufooz khan* (محفوظ خان - mahfúzkhán, Hind.). Alam + honorific title. Brother of Nawaub [q.v.] wallajah [mahomed ally]. Taken prisoner at Amboor, where his father was killed, and subsequently released and appointed governor of Madura. A suburb of Black town in Madras city is still called after him [charitram]. See vol. I (122).

MAUGAUNY (మాగాణి - mágáni, *Tel.*). From (mágu, tel. to ripen well + káni, tel. land). Wet cultivation [nunjah]. Distinguish from the tamul maugauny [mah].

MAUJID (ماجد - májid, *Hind.*). From (majada, ar. to glorify). The glorious, attribute of God [allah]. Common alam; as Maujid ally, double alam [ism].

MAUL (مال - mál, *Hind.*). Property [milk], revenue therefrom [khirauj].——*Mauldar* (مالدار - máldár, Hind.). From (above + dár, pers. holder). A rich man.——*Maulgoozarry* (مالگذاری - málguzárí, Hind.). From (above + guzár, pers. pay). Land liable to pay revenue [khirauj] to Government in contradistinction to Lakhiraj [q.v.].——*Maul jaumeen* (مال ضامن - málzámin, Hind.). From (above + zámin, ar. security). Money security [nagad jaumeen].

MAULIM (معلم - muallim, *Hind.*). From (ilm, ar. knowledge) [ilm]. Pilot [maunjhee].

MAULISH (مالش - málish, *Hind.*). From (málídan, pers. to rub). Rubbing; the hand-grooming of a horse [ghorah]; also the threshing and treading out of corn.

MAUMAH (ماما - mámá, *Hind.*). From portuguese. Confidential female attendant [ayah].

MAUMLUT (معاملت - muámalat, *Hind.*) [amal]. From (amala, ar. to act). State affairs, revenue business.——*Maumlutdar* (معاملت دار - muámalatdár, Hind.). From (above + dár, pers. holder). Collector or farmer of revenues [khirauj, maul].

MAUN (مان - mán, *Pers.*). Suffix meaning like; as Asmaun mill-stone + like.

MAUNAM (मान - mána, *San.*; మాన - mána, *Tel.*; மானம் - mánam, *Tam.*). From (má, san. to measure) [mau]. Generally a measure or computation. Instrument for measuring, rule, standard. Proportion or ratio. Also proof, demonstration, means of proof. Compare Pramaunam.——**(1)** Superficial measure. 25 coontas = 1 maunam [alavay, 2b]. Approximate actual value, 1 maunam = 18,225 square feet or ·4,184 acres. Ganjam.——**(2)** Teloogoo measure of capacity. 4 solgas = 1 maunam; 4 maunams = 1 bullah [alavay, 3b]. Approximate actual value, 1 maunam = 1,120 cubic inches. Bellary. Compare Kulsy, Coончam of Nellore, Toom of Godavery. See vol. I, 609; II, 508, 510.——**(3)** Tamul measure of capacity. 2 maunams = 1 puddy [alavay, 3a]. Approximate actual value, 1 maunam = 50. cubic inches. Used in Salem. Same as Chinnapuddy.——**(4)** In astronomy a system of reckoning the duration of the year; for instance Sowram, Chaundram, Sauvanam, Nacshatram, Baurhaspatyam, Bramhyam, Pitryam, or Prajaupatyam. Cf. Siddhauntam which is a treatise on the same. The principal mode of reckoning the year as now practised in S. india is either solar or luni-solar.—"*a*" The solar [madhyama sowra maunam] is the time which the sun [sooryan] takes to perform a complete revolution [bhaganam] round the heavens [bhagolam], beginning from a star [nacshatram] and returning to the same; this is therefore sidereal, but even thus it is taken to be of various durations, according to the systems and authorities which are followed [siddhauntam]. Whilst all the northern astronomers reckon the solar year to be of 365d. 6h. 12′ 34″, agreeably to the doctrines of the Soorya siddhauntam, those who reside south of the Nerbudda make it by Arya siddhauntam only 365d. 6h. 12′ 30″. From this last, however, must be excepted a certain sub-division of the Siddhauntics who belong to the southern-most part of the peninsula and whose year differs only one second of time in minus from that of the northern astronomers.—"*b*" The luni-solar year in most general use, or the common Chaundra maunam [q.v.], consists of 12 or 13 lunar months [chaundra mausam]; it commences with the new moon [amavausyay] at or next before the time when the sun enters the first sign [raushy] of the solar sidereal ecliptic [craunty mundalam]; its months are called Mookhyam [q.v.] or primary. The Baurhaspatya chaundra maunam, to be distinguished from Brihaspaty [q.v.] maunam though name is of same root, is another luni-solar year, which begins at the full moon [powrnimay] next preceeding the sun's entrance [sancramanam] into the sidereal ecliptic; its months are called Gownam [q.v.], or secondary. The Teloogoo luni-solar year [samvatsaram] rests on the calculations of the Soorya siddhauntam.—"*c*" The Brihaspaty maunam [q.v.], or Jupiter reckoning is properly based on the time during which that planet [graham] describes one sign [raushy] or 12th part of its orbit [cacsham]; however in S. india it is taken by corruption to be equal to the solar year, and in present times serves only to give a specific name in a cycle [brihaspaty chuckram] of 60 years to each solar and luni-solar year.—"*d*" For Deva maunam and Bramha maunam see under Caulam, 2.——*Chaundra maunam* (चान्द्रमान - chándramána, San.). From (chandra, san. moon + above). Lunar measure of time. The luni-solar year [samvatsaram] of the Teloogoos. As the so called solar year here is really soli-sidereal, so the lunar year is really luni-solar. Accordingly the solar calender [punchaungam] must first be constructed, at least to a certain extent, according to the rules laid down in Madhyama sowra maunam [q.v.], before anything can be done with Chaundra maunam; such a document being indispensable at every step of the luni-solar problems.—"*a*" The elements which are required for computing the articles of the luni-solar calendar are principally as follows:—The sun's mean place in the hindoo ecliptic [craunty mundalam] called ravy madhya graham [q.v.]. The moon's mean place in the hindoo ecliptic called madhyama chundra graham. The place of the sun's apogee in the hindoo ecliptic called generally his upper apsis, or ravy toonga mandotcham [q.v.]. The moon's apogee in the hindoo ecliptic called chundra mandotcham. The ayanaumsham [q.v.] or ayana bhaugam; meaning the arc comprised between the vernal equinoctial point [maishauyanam] and the first point in the hindoo sidereal ecliptic; this latter element is required for referring all the computations made on the fixed, sidereal, to the movable or tropical sphere. The obliquity of the ecliptic which the hindoos take to be constantly 24°. There are also certain quantities and expressions which are constantly required in the processes. Such are the names of the Hindoo signs [raushy] of the zodiac [raushy chuckram], with their numerical succession, both current and complete; the absolute number of days which the sun takes to move through each sign, the number of complete natural days [sauvana dinam] in each solar month [mausam], both civil and sidereal; and lastly, the numbers which are to be added to the solar, or luni-solar Aharganams [q.v.] on the beginning of the proposed year, for obtaining the epochs of recurrence of mean conjunctions during the whole of its duration.—"*b*" The luni-solar year is ordinarily accounted to begin at the true instant of conjunction [arcaindoo sangamam], or new moon, which precedes the commencement of the solar year [varsham], with which it is mainly to concur; but see Gownam for another method. The Chaundra maunam year [samvatsaram] is divided into twelve months [mausam], subject by intercalation [adhicam] to a thirteenth month. The Chaundra maunam month [chaundra mausam] is divided into two parts of fifteen Tities [q.v.] each, called Pacsham [q.v.], the first fortnight being denominated Shooclam [q.v.] the lightening, the second Krishnam [q.v.] or Bahoolam the darkening half of the month. The instant of true conjunction which determines the commencement of the lunar month is called Arcaindoo sangamam, literally meaning conjunction of the sun and moon [amavausyay, darsham]. Although the instant of conjunction is that which determines the commencement of the year or months; yet the day on which it occurs, and which on that account is called the Amavausyay tity, is always reckoned in the calendar [puchaungam], as well as in account, as the 30th Tity of the lunar month, because it ends on that instant. The Pratamay [q.v.] or first Tity of the ensuing month is always accounted to be the next, for the same reason. The day of opposition is called Powrnimay [q.v.] tity, and is always the 15th of the first Paosham [q.v.]. The lunar day [tity] of the Hindoo calendar is thus independent of sunrise or sunset, and means the time occupied by the moon [chundran] in traversing a thirtieth part of its circuit [cacsham]. In the Punchaungam [q.v.] the days are numbered no farther than fifteen, but in computations the series is followed up to thirty.—"*c*" In dating, notation will be as follows:—Chittrabaun samvatsaram, Adhica aushweejam, Shooddha dwiteeyay, Mungala vauram, Kaliyoog 4924, Saca 1745; in the year Chittrabaun the 16th of the cycle of 60 [brihaspaty chuckram], of the intercalary month Aushweejam the second day of waxing moon of bright fortnight; Tuesday; Kaliyoog 4924, and Saca 1745.—"*d*" For lunar mansion see Nacshatram.—"*e*" The moon with her phases [calay, piray] is of great importance with the Hindoos; nearly all their feasts [pundigay] and fasts [vratam] are regulated by the moon. Regarding the phases of the moon the Pudma pooraunam [q.v.] explains that Dacshan [q.v.], the son-in-law of Bramha [q.v.], and of the nine progenitors of mankind, gave twenty-seven of his daughters as wives to the moon [chundran] who is in Indian mythology of the masculine gender, expecting that he would attach himself to all equally. But the moon lived with Rohiny [q.v.], the Hyades [aldebaran], more than the others for which conduct Dacshan cursed him with the sickness of consumption. And he grew less and less till he disappeared. On this the gods [déva] asked Dacshan to remove his curse; but he would not revoke it altogether, and only consented to mitigate it if the moon lived equally long with every one of his wives. The moon dwells now with all his twenty-seven wives equally long, but always for one fortnight [pacsham] grows, and for another wanes.—"*f*" The following is an eleven year chronological table showing the principal circumstances of the common Luni-solar year [samvatsaram] and the concurring Vicramadityan [q.v.] and Fusly [q.v.] years:—

1	2	3	4	5	6	7	8	9	10	11	12
Christian years.	Years expired of the Kali yoog [q.v.].	Character of the year.	Last feria in the Luni-solar year.	Date of the last mean conjunction in the Luni-solar year.	Date in Cheitram of Solar year.	Sidereal duration of Cheitram.	Civil duration of Cheitram.	Solar Aharganam [q.v.], or Yoog dinam [q.v.], to be counted from Friday.	Luni-solar Aharganam to be counted from Thursday.	Years of Æra [saca] Vicramadityan.	Fusly years expired.
					Syd.			DAYS. G. V. P.	DAYS.		
1890	4991	A	Friday	21 Mar.	—10	30	30	1823003 55 37 30	1822983	1947	1299
1891	4992	...	Thursday	9 April	—29	31	30	1823369 11 8 45	1823367	1948	1300
1892	4993	...	Monday	28 Mar.	17	30	30	1823734 28 40 0	1823721	1949	1301
1893	4994	A	Saturday	17 Mar.	6	30	31	1824099 42 11 15	1824075	1950	1302
1894	4995	...	Thursday	6 April	—25	30	30	1824464 57 42 30	1824459	1951	1303
1895	4996	A	Tuesday	26 Mar.	—15	31	30	1824830 13 13 45	1824814	1952	1304
1896	4997	...	Saturday	14 Mar.	3	30	30	1825195 28 45 0	1825168	1953	1305
1897	4998	...	Friday	2 April	22	30	31	1825560 44 16 15	1825552	1954	1306
1898	4999	A	Tuesday	22 Mar.	—11	30	30	1825925 59 37 30	1825906	1955	1307
1899	5000	...	Monday	10 April	—30	31	30	1826291 15 18 45	1826290	1956	1308
1900	5001	...	Saturday	31 Mar.	19	30	31	1826656 30 50 0	1826645	1957	1309

A = Adhicam [q.v.]; the year contains one intercalary lunar month [mausam], and is of 384 solar days, against 354 solar days ordinary.

——*Madhyama sowra maunam* (मध्यमसौरमान - madhyamasauramána, San.). From (madhyama, san. middle + saura, san. solar). Means solar measure of time. The mean solar year [samvatsaram, varsham] used by the Tamuls and forming the foundation of the luni-solar year of the Teloogoos. It should much more properly be called sidereal. It contains that space of time during which the sun departing from a star [nacshatram] returns to the same.—"*a*" The actual point of time at which a solar or sidereal year may be held to begin, viewed as marking a physical fact or a certain conjunction of the heavenly bodies in space, is a matter upon which many others both in science and general chronology depend, and the subject may here be suitably set out. The best means for obtaining an initial datum of this sort is to mark the instant when the sun in his apparent path [cacsham] or ecliptic [craunty mundalam] seems to touch the equinoctial [naudy mundalam] or prolongation of the earth's equator [niracsham] which happens twice a year. On the days when this happens the sun approximately seems to travel round the earth in the line of the equator, and day is the same length as night all over the world; hence the vernal and autumnal equinoxes [maishauyanam, toolauyanam]. Modern European astronomers accept this method as an ultimate fact for such practical purposes as calculating celestial longitude [sauyanam], regulating the calendar [punchaungam], &c.; and disregard other consequences. Of the latter class are the effects of precession [craunty pauta gaty], whereby the equinoctial points [ayanam] owing to the earth's oblate figure [andagolam], &c., move all round the heavens in a westerly direction against the order of the zodiacal signs [raushy] in 25,868 years, and the appearance of the heavens in relation to the sun, moon and earth and even to a small extent in respect of the mutual relations of the fixed stars themselves is changed in a corresponding manner. But another method is possible. At the point of the equinox in any year the heavenly bodies must be in a certain position relatively to each other. This conjunction in say the vernal equinox [maishauyanam] of any year may be taken as the fixed datum, and all further and subsequent calculations of chronology may be made by the mere application of tables and without either observation or corrections for precession [craunty pauta gaty].—"*b*" General history shows the employment of both these methods. But that of a fixed vernal equinox retained after it has ceased to be true to the facts and so with a new year's day always getting later and later in relation to the seasons [ritoo] is the ancient method; while that of a vernal equinox shifting with precession, and a new year's day consequently having always the same relation to the seasons is the modern method.—"*c*" The earliest indication of an Indian epoch dependent on the facts of the equinoxes is that derived from the month terminology of the Hindoo soli-lunar calendar. The moon's constant daily path in the heavens for the period of a lunar month [chaundramausam] is mapped out by twenty-seven constellations [nacshatram, 7], whose names were as far as at present appears assigned fancifully. When the luni-solar [chaundra maunam] method of reckoning time was instituted, or at any rate when a year of twelve lunar months began to be recognized, twelve out of these twenty-seven mansions were chosen to give the names to the months; the moon being always in the period of those months full in those or approximately in those mansions [nacshatram]; reference to the diagram at Raushy [q.v.] will show that while the sun occupies one and the same zodiacal sign [raushy] in any given month in each year, the moon which to be full must be opposite or at six signs distance has a choice of only 2¼ mansions to be full in; the selection of 1 out of these 2¼ to make into a month-name may have been arbitrary, or may have arisen from the moon actually being full in those particular mansions in the year when the Chaundra maunam [q.v.] was arranged. Now at the present day for the purposes of the hindoo soli-lunar calendar the equinoctial colure [maishauyanamundalam] is or is assumed to be among the stars in the same meridian [raikhay] with the beginning of the mansion Ashwiny [q.v.], or near hamel [q.v.] in the head of the ram [maisham], while the first month of the year speaking for india generally is Veishaukham, named after the mansion vishaukham [q.v.] six signs distant from ashwiny; the shastrams state that at a previous date the colure was at Oottarabhaudram [q.v.] or near aldebaran [q.v.] in the eye of the bull [vrishabham], and the first month was Cheitram, named from the mansion chitta [q.v.] six signs distant from oottarabhaudram; the shastrams similarly state that yet earlier the colure was at Shatabhishay [q.v.] or near betelgeux [q.v.] in the right shoulder of orion [ardray, jabbaur], and the first month was Phaulgoonam, named from the mansion poobbam [q.v.] six signs distant from shatabhishay; so shravanam, maugham, magham; so poorvashaudham, pooshyam, pooshyam; so jyeshtay, margashiram, mrigashiras; so vishaukham, caurteecam, kritticay; so chitta, aushweejam, ashwiny. There can be no doubt about the meaning of these statements. The matter is expressed in the shastrams by saying that the line of the Rishies [q.v.] intersected the first points of the mansions [nacshatram] first-named, which is the same thing as saying that the equinoctial colure [maishauyanamundalam] was there. The line of the Rishies is a great circle [mundalam] drawn through the pole [dhroovam] of the ecliptic [craunty mundalam], that is to say through a point one-third way between the head of the dragon and polaris, and the equinoctial colure; it cut in its course the square of the Great bear [doobhe acbar] about 5,000 years B.C., and the shastrams contain reference to this; some commentators indeed write as if it was still cutting the Bear when the colure was in Raivaty [q.v.] or within the christian era, which is probably a simple error, for consideration of the longitudes [sauyanam] will show such to have been impossible. Even supposing ayanaumsham [q.v.] to be under some definition or other libratory, as appears advanced in one or two native writers, this cannot affect the above plain statement of the shastrams as to the eight successive stages of the line of the Rishies, &c., for there are not two methods by which the sun and moon could respectively and simultaneously travel into the named mansions; they could only do so by constant westerly precession [crauntypanta gaty] as defined by european science. The earliest conjunction according to this month nomenclature history, or the point of time when the month Aushweejam headed the soli-lunar year, would have been at or earlier than 15291 B.C., at about $\frac{7}{12}$ths of the distance of one entire precessional course. It is open to those who disbelieve in very high antiquity for history to consider that the earlier of the above month datings were not in fact at any time used by the hindoos or other races, and were merely inferred backwards from the known facts of the later month datings. It is equally possible however to believe that the above are bonâ fide human traditions; throughout these pages it is held that hindoo antiquities involve much more distant dates than is generally supposed. Varauha mihiran [q.v.] of the sixth century christian era opens one of his chapters with an allusion to the time when the sun was recorded to have had its summer solstice [dacshinauyanam] a month and a half earlier than it was in his time, which would be an event considerably prior to the kaliyoog [q.v.], and the aldeberan [q.v.] epoch. The European scholar Bentley has made a theory that because 3,056 lunations [chaundra mausam] make 247 years + 1 month, therefore the bramins changed the name of the first month of the year every 247 years; doing this from 1192 B.C. to 538 A.D., and there stopping, as the last date brought them to a coincidence with the constellation of ashwiny [q.v.]. But there is no foundation whatever for this in the shastrams, and the dates are brought in to suit the theory. Probably Bentley had not heard of the traditions of the line of the Rishies. It was said above that the month veishaukham was the first month of the year for india generally; southern india has for some reason not yet explained stopped in its nomenclature at the penultimate stage when cheitram month headed the year and the bull [vrishabham] headed the zodiac [raushy chuckram], and has not adopted the last correction to veishaukham; this makes no difference to the conclusions to be drawn as above shown from the whole series of first month titles.—"*d*" The adoption of the months later than Aushweejam to head the soli-lunar year indicates approximate epoch dates as follows:—Caurteecam, 13143 B.C.; Margashiram, 10995 B.C.; Pooshyam, 8847 B.C.; Maugham, 6699 B.C.; Phaulgoonam, 4551 B.C.; Cheitram, 2403 B.C.; Veishaukham, as at present for India generally, 255 B.C.—"*e*" The present Kaliyoog destined according to hindoo authorities to last altogether 432,000 years began in 3101 B.C. The shastrams say that there was in that year no ayanaumsham [q.v.]. This means that that year was made into an epoch beginning with the point in the heavens occupied by the vernal equinox [maishauyanam] of the year. The vernal equinox was then about at Aldeberan [q.v.] in the eye of the bull, or at the position assigned above for the epoch designated by cheitram as first month of the soli-lunar year.—"*f*" According to the solar, as opposed to soli-lunar, division of the hindoo year, the months are named not from mansions [nacshatram] but from zodiacal signs [raushy]; that is to say from the same stars of the zodiacal region, but with these differently grouped according to the well-known division of the bull, the ram, &c. Here also the astronomical year has always begun with the vernal equinox, and the month taken to head the year is that having the name of the constellation [nacshatram] where the sun at the vernal equinox of the epoch year was residing. An epoch recognized in many shastrams, equally with many Greek and Latin writings, as having existed within historical times, is that when the sign of the bull [vrishabham] headed the zodiac [raushy chuckram] and so the year. This epoch may be taken as co-incident more or less with that last named, as well as with the Cheitram epoch.—"*g*" Under the nomenclature for solar months now current in this as in most other countries, the ram [maisham] heads the year. The real commencement of this epoch may be supposed to have been when the vernal equinox was somewhere in a line with the bright star Hamel [q.v.] in the head of the ram, or at about 274 B.C. Hipparchus who is said to have determined the then existing place of the equinoxes among the stars, and to have discovered the true nature of their precession, lived at the beginning of the following century. This epoch has made such an impression on history and science, that, where as in the case of modern European astronomy the idea of a fixed sidereal starting point has been abandoned and the epoch changes every year with the precessional motion of the vernal equinox, the old nomenclature of the ram is nevertheless still retained. In that case the first 30 degrees of the sun's course after leaving the vernal equinox are still called the sign of the ram, though the constellation of the ram has long since been left behind, to the extent indeed of a full sign [raushy]. The astronomical name for the vernal equinox is still the first point of Aries, with sign of ram's horn ♈, though this is a movable point in the heavens and has now nothing to do with the constellation of the ram. The zodiacal signs which follow the ram are similarly shifted. The Hindoos do the same as this in their higher astronomy, having a movable or tropical Maisham, &c., like the European movable or tropical ram, &c. The movable epoch will be considered at the close of these remarks, and is only mentioned here to show that it bears the old names of the Hamel epoch.—"*h*" As above indicated the epoch designated by Veishaukham as first month of the soli-lunar year must have been about identical with the Hamel epoch; calculating back by intervals of 30° it comes to about 255 B.C. It seems probable that from this time onwards Greek astronomy greatly influenced Hindoo astronomy. This nomenclature too has remained constant during subsequent epochs.—"*i*" The present date for the new year in India, wherever the new year plainly is intended to represent the vernal equinox, as among the Tamuls, is 12th April, Gregorian reckoning. This is twenty-two days behind the real present vernal equinox, or 21st March, Gregorian reckoning. Calculating back these twenty-two days by the precession rate of European science, or 50″ per annum, there would have been an epoch at about 317 A.D., when the vernal equinox stood at the point which is now R.A. 1h. 28′, or nearly in a line with the comparatively bright star in the tail of the eastern fish, η Piscium [meenam].—"*j*" According to the more modern shastrams there is a distinct record of an epoch having been made at 3600 kaliyoog, or 499 A.D. The tradition is that this was the epoch, and that it was reduced to table subsequently in 4070 kaliyoog, or 969 A.D. The vernal equinox was in 499 A.D. at the point which is now R.A. 1h. 18′, but there is still no principal star nearer to that point than η Piscium.—"*k*" Raivaty is in the lunar mansion [nacshatram] or lunar constellation [nacshatram] scheme the last of the twenty-seven; while Ashwiny [q.v.] is the next, beginning the series again. Raivaty [q.v.] consists of thirty-two stars in the Fishes [meenam], Ashwiny is the head of the Ram [maisham]. The last point of Raivaty and first of Ashwiny is in many of the more modern shastrams said to mark the position of the vernal equinox for the most recent of the epochs. Then according to some authorities the yogam [q.v.] star of a mansion is at the exact limit between it and the next. This is impossible for the whole twenty-seven for non-telescopic stars; however Veidhrity [q.v.] the yogam of Raivaty is said to have been such a limiting star between Raivaty and Ashwiny, to have been the southernmost star in the mansion, and to have had no latitude [vicshaipam] or little latitude. Adopting these definitions as authoritative, Veidhrity has been held to represent ζ Piscium in the string of the Fishes, whose R. A. is now 1h. 7′, and whose declination is now 7° N. If this star had to be taken with precision as marking by its longitude a vernal equinox, that would have to be put at about 692 A.D. But nothing further is known of such a date.—"*l*" If the system of the modern European precessional year be called an epoch in the above sense, then that epoch begins at the present date at a point not far from the longitude of Alpheratz [q.v.], α Andromedæ, whose R. A. is 0h. 3′. The Hindoos use this year for the higher astronomical purposes, and they call the distance along the ecliptic between this position of the vernal equinox and its position assumed for their old and unchanging sidereal starting point, the ayanaumsham [q.v.]. The value of the ayanaumsham is a matter of constant discussion, on account of the embarrassing ambiguities which exist among the native writers as to the date of epoch, rate of precession, and precision or otherwise of a sidereal starting-point.—"*m*" To sum up this matter as far as the modern fixed epoch is concerned. The most natural epoch to take is that given by the evidence of the Hindoo new year date brought out in Gregorian style, viz., 12th April. This, as above seen, gives an epoch date, with the 50″ rate of precession, of about 317 A.D. and an ayanaumsham of about 20°. But if with an initial date of 499 A.D. which is the date fixed by the native authorities the 54″ or native rate of precession is adopted, 12th April will still be reached as the present new year's day; the ayanaumsham being then 19° 28′, and this is a figure often quoted. It appears then that this last is the truth as to the origin of the present Hindoo new year. 499 A.D. was the epoch, and some star of the fishes which may have been either η or ζ Piscium was the sidereal starting-point, though inexact. ζ Piscium happens to tally exactly in longitude [sauyanam] with a position calculated back by the European rate of precession, but need not necessarily have had anything to do with the matter. In the absence of proof against ζ Piscium having been the star observed in 499 A.D., for this and η Piscium are about equally distant in longitude from the true vernal equinox of that date on two opposite sides, the custom of the last century has been followed in these pages in inserting it in the tables as the equivalent of Veidhrity or yogam star of the mansion Raivaty.—"*n*" The following statement shows the above information tabularly and in detail. The rate taken for precession is the true rate of 1° in 71·6 years or about 50″:—

Serial number of epoch.	Name and nature of epoch.	Year of Christian era.	Year of Kaliyoog [q.v.].	How many years ago from present date.	How many degrees back from present position of vernal equinox, by the march of precession [craunty pauta gaty]; in other words the value of Ayanaumsham [q.v.]; precession at 50″ per annum.	The same in Right ascension [lagnam].	The nearest principal star, with its present Right ascension and Declination; + means north declination, and — means south declination.
1	2	3	4	5	6	7	8
1	Epoch with month Aushweejam at head of year.	15291 B.C.	12190 B. ky.	17184	240°	16^{h}	α Serpentis, Oonuk [oonuk], 15^{h} 39′, + 6° 46′ α Scorpii, Antares [alkalb, vareeyas], 16^{h} 23′, — 26° 11′
2	Epoch with month Caurteecam at head of year.	13143 B.C.	10042 B. ky.	15036	210°	14^{h}	α Bootis, Arcturus [haursool samah, vajram], 14^{h} 11′, + 19° 45′ α Virginis, Spica [harshanam, simauk ool azal], 13^{h} 19′, — 10° 35′
3	Epoch with month Margashiram at head of year.	10995 B.C.	7894 B. ky.	12888	180°	12^{h}	β Leonis, Denebola [denebola, dhroovam], 11^{h} 43′, + 15° 11′
4	Epoch with month Pooshyam at head of year.	8847 B.C.	5746 B. ky.	10740	150°	10^{h}	α Leonis, Regulus [gandam, zoobra], 10^{h} 3′, + 12° 30′
5	Epoch with month Maugham at head of year.	6699 B.C.	3598 B. ky.	8592	120°	8^{h}	β Geminorum, Pollux [alzirah, soocarmam], 7^{h} 39′, + 28° 17′
6	Epoch with month Phaulgoonam at head of year.	4551 B.C.	1450 B. ky.	6444	90°	6^{h}	α Orionis, Betelgeux [atigandam, betelgeux], 5^{h} 49′, + 7° 23′
7	Epoch of commencement of present Kaliyoog [q.v.]	3101 B.C.	0	4994	69°45′	4^{h} 39′	α Tauri, Aldeberan [aldeberan, sowbhaugyam], 4^{h} 30′, + 16° 17′
8	Epoch with month Cheitram at head of year.	2403 B.C.	698 Ky.	4296	60°	4^{h}	α Tauri, Aldeberan [aldeberan, sowbhaugyam], 4^{h} 30′, + 16° 17′
9	Epoch by taking the vernal equinox at the constellation of the Ram defined by α Arietis [hamel, vishcambham].	274 B.C.	2828 Ky.	2166	30°15′	2^{h} 1′	α Arietis, Hamel [hamel, vishcambham], 2^{h} 1′, + 22° 57′
10	Epoch with month Veishaukham at head of year.	255 B.C.	2846 Ky.	2148	30°	2^{h}	α Arietis, Hamel [hamel, vishcambham], 2^{h} 1′, + 22° 57′
11	Epoch deduced back from date of present Tamul new year's day [tamul new year].	317 A.D.	3149 Ky.	1575	22°	1^{h} 28′	η Piscium [veidhrity], 1^{h} 25′, + 14° 47′
12	Epoch of 3600th year of Kaliyoog.	499 A.D.	3600 Ky.	1394	19°28′	1^{h} 18′	η Piscium [veidhrity], 1^{h} 25′, + 14° 47′
13	Epoch by taking the vernal equinox at the constellation Raivaty defined by Veidhrity held equivalent to ζ Piscium.	692 A.D.	3794 Ky.	1200	16°45′	1^{h} 7′	ζ Piscium [veidhrity], 1^{h} 7′, + 7°
14	Modern European astronomy and Hindoo tropical astronomy.	1893 A.D.	4994 Ky.	0	0	0	α Andromedae, Alpheratz [alpheratz, eindram], 0^{h} 3′, + 28° 29′

"*o*" To avoid confusion mention has been omitted above of the yearly date of commencement of the Teloogoo luni-solar year [teloogoo new year], which happens at the new moon [amavausyay] prior to the opening of the solar year, and so has a range of twenty-nine days; it is from the present point of view merely a variant of the solar year, and was probably devised in part to increase the complexity of the calendar [punchaungam] in the interests of astrology [jyotisham]. Similarly the fact that the Parshoorama era [saca] on the W. coast begins its year with the autumnal [toolauyanam] instead of the vernal equinox [maishauyanam] indicates nothing new regarding the astronomical epoch. The European civil year begins in midwinter on 1st January, but is none the less regulated astronomically by the vernal equinox.—"*p*" An every day manner of determining the commencement of the solar year consists in observing the passage [sancramanam] over the meridian [raikhay] of some yogam [q.v.] star the position of which is given in the hindoo tables. Thus Harshanam [q.v.], the yogam of and only star in the lunar mansion [nacshatram] Chitta [q.v.], is accounted to be exactly six signs [raushy] in longitude [sauyanam] from the beginning of the solar zodiac [raushy chuckram]. It is taken in these pages to be Spica virginis [simauk ool azal]. When it is observed to pass over the meridian at midnight anywhere, the mean hindoo solar year ought to begin. Veidhrity, the yogam star of the lunar mansion Raivaty, taken in these pages to be either η or ζ Piscium, is the last point of the sign Meenam [q.v.], the Indian pisces; or what comes to the same thing, the first of Maisham [q.v.], the Indian aries.

So that when it is observed to pass the meridian anywhere at midnight, it should mark the mean sidereal beginning of the Tamul month Arpisy [q.v.], from which that of the year may be deduced. But from the above remarks it will be seen that this opposition of Harshanam and coincidence of Veidhrity to and with the commencement of the Hindoo solar zodiac, must necessarily be a somewhat rough one.—"*q*" For purposes of calculating the almanac [punchaungam] observation is not attempted, but figures are projected from the commencement of an epoch [kaliyoog]. The rule for finding the mean epoch of the commencement of the Tamul solar year will be seen under Aharganam [q.v.]. It is to be observed that Tamul astronomers have adopted the details of the Arya siddhauntam [q.v.] treatise, in preference to that of the Soorya siddhauntam, using the Vaukyam [q.v.] process of calculation in their operations. The general element to be ascertained is the Aharganam or time elapsed from the beginning of the kaliyoog to that of any proposed year. This includes the initial feria of the year, called Shooddha dinam [q.v.]. After this has to be determined the beginning and duration of the twelve months [mausam] of the year.—"*r*" Each solar month [mausam] contains as many days and parts of days as the sun [sooryan] actually stays in each zodiacal sign [raushy]. The portion of time assigned to each month, is affected by the time occupied by the sun in moving through the northern and southern signs of the ecliptic [craunty mundalam], the time for the former being 186 days 21 hours 38 minutes and 24 seconds, and for the latter 178 days 8 hours 34 minutes and 6 seconds. The odd hours and minutes of this are applied to the beginning of the year and months; and being so distributed there is no need for leap or bissextile years, because the astronomical beginning of each year is reckoned from the hour and minute over 365 days when the last year and month expired. The civil differs from the astronomical account only from its rejecting fractions of days, each year and month being accounted to begin at sunrise, instead of the time of his mean entrance into the respective signs; observing that if the said fraction exceeds 30 Indian hours [ghadiya] which lapse of time is conceived to be the mean half of the day [dinam] then the civil year, or month, are accounted to begin one day later than the astronomical ones; whereas if the time falls below that quantity, both coincide. It results from this arrangement that civil time is sometimes longer, sometimes shorter, than the astronomical.—"*s*" The following is an eleven year chronological table referring to various solar styles and years; and showing the numerals or names, and the epoch of the commencement of the latter according to European account:—

1	2	3	4		5	6	7		8		9
Christian years.	Years expired of the kaliyoog [q.v.].	Years expired from the birth of Shalivahanan [q.v.].	Expired years of the 4th cycle of the era [saca] par-shooraman. Years of the Cycle.	Initial date in September.	Years of the 22nd Cycle of Graha parivritty [q.v.].	Years of the S. indian Brihaspaty cycle [chuckram] of 60 years. Name and Numeral.	Initial feriæ of Tamul civil year.	Date in April.	Initial feriæ of Tamul sidereal year.	Date in April.	Point in time of beginnings of Tamul years counted from Sunday [caulam]. D. G. V. P.
1890	4991	1812	66	15	24	Vicrit 24	Sat	12	Fri	11	(5) 55 37 30
1891	4992	1813	67	16	25	Kharum ... 25	...	...	Sun	12	(0) 11 8 45
1892	4993	1814	68	15	26	Nandanam ... 26	...	...	Mo	11	(1) 26 40 0
1893	4994	1815	69	15	27	Vijayam ... 27	We	12	Tu	11	(2) 42 11 15
1894	4995	1816	70	15	28	Jayam 28	Th	12	We	11	(3) 57 42 30
1895	4996	1817	71	16	29	Manmatum ... 29	...	...	Fri	12	(5) 13 13 45
1896	4997	1818	72	15	30	Doonmookhy ... 30	...	...	Sat	11	(6) 28 45 0
1897	4998	1819	73	15	31	Hevilamby ... 31	Mo	12	Sun	11	(0) 44 16 15
1898	4999	1820	74	15	32	Vilamby ... 32	Tu	12	Mo	11	(1) 59 47 30
1899	5000	1821	75	16	33	Vicaury 33	...	...	We	12	(3) 15 18 45
1900	5001	1822	76	16	34	Shaurvary ... 34	Fri	13	Th	12	(4) 30 50 0

MAUNAM (மானம் - mánam, *Tam.*). Sky [vaun].——*Maunavaury* (மானவாரி - mánavári, Tam.). From (above + vári, san. water). Land of which the cultivation depends solely upon rain [mazhay].

MAUNJHEE (مانجهی - mánjhí, *Hind.*). The steersman of any native river craft [maulim].

MAUNOO (మాను - mánu, *Tel.*). Tree. Suffix in place names; as Caukamaunoo, meaning crow's tree.——*Maurella* (మారేళ్ల - márélla, Tel.). From (márédu, tel. tree, ægle marmelos, corr.). Village; Nellore district, Canigherry talook. Belongs to Vencatagherry and gives name to Zemindarry talook.

MAUR (മാറു - máru, *Mal.*). A fathom. Distance between the finger tips of either arm extended sideways. Linear measure. 4 moolams or cubits = 1 maur; 2,000 maurs = 1 crosham [alavay, la, d]. Approximate actual value, 1 maur = 6 feet. In Madura it is 6½ feet. In Salem there are two maurs, one of 6 feet 4½ inches, and another of 8 feet. Same as San. vyaumam, dandam, Hind. baum, Can. bauroo, Tel. niloovoo, Tam. bauham. See vol. I, 609.

MAURISHAM (मारिष - márisha, *San.*). From (mrish, san. to endure). Title otherwise Amaranth, Spinach, Velvet flower. Botanically the Amarantus genus, amarantaceæ [vricsham, 106]. Cf. Malabar nightshade. Tropical annual plants; leaves alternate; flowers small; in axillary or spiked clusters; fruits one-seeded, splitting circularly round when ripe; seeds orbicular, compressed; several cultivated for their ornamental, bright-colored leaves. The species best known to the natives are shown below.——*Brown spinach* (حبق بستانی - habakibustání, Ar.; بستان افروز - bustánafroz, Pers.; لال ساگ - lálság, Hind.; راج گیرا - rájgírá, Dec.; ಕಿಲುಹರಿವೆ - kiluharive, Can.; රණතම්පලා - ranatampalá, Singh.; பூங்கீரை - púngírai, Tam.). Title from foliage. Ar. from (habak, ar. mentha pulegium, linn. + bustán, pers. garden). Pers. from (bustán, pers. garden + afroz, pers. illuminator). Hind. from (lál, hind. red + ság, hind. pot-herb). Can. from (kilu, can. inferior + harive, can. the greens). Singh. from (rana, singh. forest + tampalá, singh. greens). Tam. from (pú, tam. flower + kírai, tam. vegetable), from red color. Pers. also (tájikhurús), meaning cock's comb, celosia cristata, linn. Can. also (kiresoppu), meaning small + greens. Tam. also (shánini), by corruption from (shákini), meaning vegetable. Title otherwise Cock's-comb greens, Flowering greens, Prince's feather. Botanically Amarantus [maurisham] paniculatus, linn., amarantaceæ [vricsham, 106]. Alias Amarantus frumentaceus. A large species 4 to 6 feet, leaves of a reddish brown color. Stem herbaceous, erect; leaves long-petioled, broad-lanceolate, acute; panicles terminal, erect; sepals subulate, acute; stamens five; stigmas three; seed sub-compressed, smooth; utricles wrinkled. Extensively cultivated in coimbatore and neilgherries. Cultivated by hill tribes for the seeds, which are ground into flour, and form a principal article of diet; leaves used as greens. ——*Common spinach* (मारिष - márisha, San.; तांबडीमाठ - támbadímát'ha, Mahr.; भाज्जि - bhájji, Conc.; ماٹ کی بہاجی - mátkíbhájí, Dec.; ಹರಿವೆಸೊಪ್ಪು - harivésoppu, Can.; ಪಡ್ಪೆ - padpe, Too.; తోటకూర - tótakúra, Tel.; සුදුතම්පලා - sudutampalá, Singh.; தண்டுக்கீரை - tandukkírai, Tam.). San. from (mrish, san. to endure). Mahr. from (támbadá, mahr. red + mát'ha, mahr. pot-herb). Dec. from sanscrit. Can. from (hari, can. to cut + soppu, can. greens). Tel. from (tóta, tel. garden + kúra, tel. herb). Singh. from (sudu, singh. white + tampalá, singh. greens). Tam. from (tandu, tam. stem + kírai, tam. vegetable). Mahr. also (bhájí), meaning esculent vegetable. Hind. also (dat); (datkíbhájí). Can. also (chivikesoppu), meaning to chew + greens; (kunambavugida). Tel. also (perugutótakúra), meaning plucking + the plant; (mokkatótakúra), meaning stump + the plant; (erratótakúra), meaning red + the plant; (perugukúra), meaning plucking + herb; (tellatótakúra), meaning white + the plant; (peddatótakúra), meaning large + the plant. Singh. also (sulukúra). Tam. also (tandangírai), meaning stem + vegetable; (kullattandukkírai), meaning short + the plant; (vellaittandukkírai), meaning white + stem + greens. Title otherwise Garden greens. Botanically Amarantus [maurisham] blitum, var. oleraceus, linn., amarantaceæ [vricsham, 106]. Alias Euxolus oleraceus. Stem erect or ascending, striated, glabrous, whitish; leaves petioled, ovate, very obtuse, emarginate, rather wrinkled, pale green; spikelets axillary, shorter than the petiole, a little branched; spikes terminal, erect, abbreviated, thickish, rather obtuse, dense, rigid; flowers closely clustered, pale green; calyx twice the length of the bracts; utricles ovate, rather acute, smooth. Superior stems are peeled and eaten as asparagus.——*Field spinach* (अल्पमारिष - alpamárisha, San.; چری کی بہاجی - churíkíbhájí, Dec.; ಗಿರಕಸಾಲೆ - gírakasále, Can.; చిర్రికూర - chirrikúra, Tel.; ചെറുചീര - cheruchíra, Mal.; சிறுகீரை - shirugírai, Tam.). San. from (alpa, san. small + márisha, san. amarantus blitum, var. oleraceus, linn.). Dec. from tamul. Can. from (gíru, can.

small + kasále, can. herb). Tel. from (chiru, tel. small + kúra, tel. herb). Mal. from (cheru, mal. small + chíra, mal. greens). Tam. from (shiru, tam. small + kírai, tam. vegetable). San. also (ghanarava), meaning cloud + roar; (méghanáda), meaning cloud + roar. Can. also (kírakasále), meaning parrot + herb; (handikíre), meaning pig + greens. Tam. also (kammai), meaning that which is dark. Title otherwise Pig's greens. Botanically Amarantus [maurisham] campestris, willd., amarantaceæ [vricsham, 106]. Of rapid growth; root demulcent.——*Garden spinach* (لال ساگ - lálság, Hind. and Dec.; ಬಿಳಿದಂಟು - bílidantu, Can.; కొయ్యతోటకూర - koyyatótakúra, Tel.; அறைக்கீரை - araikkírai, Tam.). Hind. from (lál, hind. red + ság, hind. greens). Can. from (bili, can. white + dantu, can. stalk). Tel. from (kóyu, tel. to cut + tótakúra, tel. amarantus blitum, var. oleraceus, linn.). Tam. from (aru, tam. to cut + kírai, tam. vegetable); from leaves being plucked for use; as distinguished from (mulaikkírai), where the whole plant is pulled out with roots for use. Can. also (kempudantu), meaning red + stalk. Tel. also (tótakúra), meaning garden + herb. Tam. also (kuppaikkírai), meaning dung hill vegetable. Title otherwise Flower gentle, Joseph's coat, Round-headed amaranth, Three-colored amaranth, Tricolor. Botanically Amarantus [maurisham] gangeticus, linn., amarantaceæ [vricsham, 106]. Stem erect, furrowed and striated, glabrous, dark red, or greenish; leaves long-petioled, ovate or lanceolate-ovate, somewhat obtuse, dark green, sometimes purple below; spike terminal, very short, ovate, stiff; glomerules axillary, ovate; flowers thick, reddish-green; calyx shorter than the bracts; utricles enclosed in the calyx, two to three-toothed at the apex, smooth; flowering in the rains. Varieties many, differing chiefly in color from green to bright red.——*Red spinach* (ఎర్రతోటకూర - errarótakúra, Tel.; செந்தண்டுக்கீரை - shendandukkírai, Tam.). Title from foliage. Tel. from (erra, tel. red + tótakúra, tel. herb, amarantus blitum, var. oleraceus, linn.). Tam. from (shem, tam. red + tandu, tam. stem + kírai, tam. vegetable). Title otherwise Purple spinach. Botanically Amarantus [maurisham] atropurpureus, roxb., amarantaceæ [vricsham, 106]. Erect; leaves lanceolate, reddish-purple above, dark purple beneath; sepals four to five, cuspidate; stamens eight; spike terminal; glomerules axillary; utricles shorter than the calyx, wrinkled.——*Rose spinach* (گل تاش - gulitásh, Dec.; ఎర్రకాడతోటకూర - errakádatótakúra, Tel.). Tel. from (erra, tel. red + káda, tel. stem + tótakúra, tel. amarantus blitum, var. oleraceus, linn.). Title otherwise Floramor, Florimer, Lovelies-bleeding, Thrumwort, Velvet flower. Botanically Amarantus [maurisham] caudatus, linn., amarantaceæ [vricsham, 106]. Alias Amarantus cruentus. Difficult to distinguish from brown spinach; plant smaller, with the leaves obtuse at the tip; more globose softer masses of smaller red-green or white flowers on the thryse, the terminal spike of which is very long, thick and drooping; acicular bracts shorter and not squarrose; sepals shorter, broader, more obtuse and usually obovate-oblong; utricle and seeds smaller; drooping tail-like flower-stems of crimson flowers.——*Stunted spinach* (ದಗ್ಗಿಸೊಪ್ಪು - daglisoppu, Can.; చిలకతోటకూర - chilakatótakúra, Tel.; குள்ளத்தண்டுக்கீரை - kullattandukkírai, Tam.). Title from size. Can. from (taggu, can. sort + soppu, can. greens). Tel. from (chilaka, tel. parrot + tótakúra, tel. amarantus blitum, var. oleraceus, linn.). Tam. from (kullam, tam. shortness + tandu, tam. stem + kírai, tam. vegetable). Tel. also (chilakalakúra), meaning parrot + herb. Title otherwise Parrot spinach. Botanically Amarantus [maurisham] viridis, linn., amarantaceæ [vricsham, 106]. Alias Amarantus fasciatus; Euxolus caudatus. Stem erect, angularly striated, glabrous, green; leaves long-petioled, ovate or rhomb-ovate, narrowing at both ends, bluntish, emarginate, glabrous, green; spikes ascending, somewhat interrupted below, more compact and sub-cylindrical above; flowers sessile, aggregated in dense glomerules, green; bracts longer than the sepals; utricle globose, pointed very rough; sepals three; in waste ground. ——*Thorny spinach* (कण्टकशाकिनी - kantakashákiní, San.; कांटेमाठ - kántémát'ha, Mahr.; کانٹے ماٹ - kántemát, Hind. and Dec.; ಮುಳ್ಳುದಂಟು - mulludantu, Can.; ముండ్లతోటకూర - mundlatótakúra, Tel.; മുള്ളഞ്ചീര - mullañchíra, Mal.; කටුතම්පලා - katutampalá, Singh.; முள்ளுக்கீரை - mullukkírai, Tam.). Title from spines on leaves. San. from (kantaka, san. thorn + sháka, san. greens). Mahr. from (kántá, mahr. thorny + mát'ha, mahr. amarantus gangeticus, linn.). Hind. from (kantá, hind. thorn + mát, hind. amarantus gangeticus, linn.). Can. from (mullu, can. thorn + dantu, can. stalk). Tel. from (mullu, tel. thorn + tótakúra, tel. amarantus blitum, var. oleraceus, linn.). Mal. from (mullu, mal. thorn + chíra, mal. greens). Singh. from (katu, singh. thorny + tampalá, singh. greens). Tam. from (mullu, tam. thorn + kírai, tam. vegetable). Mahr. also (kántébhájí), meaning thorny pot-herb. Hind. also (kántárájgírá), meaning thorny amaranth. Can. also (mulluharive), meaning thorn + amarantus gangeticus, linn. Tel. also (nalladoggali), meaning black + amarantus polygamus, linn.; (erramulugórinta), meaning red + barleria prionitis, linn. Title otherwise Prickly spinach, Red nail-dye. Botanically Amarantus [maurisham] spinosus, l., amarantaceæ [vricsham, 106]. Erect-1–3 feet, somewhat striated, glabrous, reddish; leaves long, petioled, rhomb-ovate, or lanceolate-oblong, with two spines in the axils; panicles sparingly branched; spikes erect, cylindric, acute, terminal ones long, stiffish, lateral ones middle-sized; flowers dense, green; utricles two to three-cleft at the top, somewhat wrinkled; bracts unequal, bearded; seed lenticular, polished, black; troublesome to gather on account of thorns. Poultices made of bruised leaves. Makes tolerable spinach. Ashes used as mordant [cauram].——*Wild spinach* (காட்டுச்சிறுகீரை - káttuççirugírai, Tam.). Tam. from (kádu, tam. forest + shiru, tam. small + kírai, tam. vegetable). Title otherwise Fine-leaved amaranth. Botanically Amarantus [maurisham] tenuifolius, willd., amarantaceæ [vricsham, 106]. Alias Mengea tenuifolia. Herbaceous; stem erect, angled, striated, green; leaves lanceolate-linear or linear, much attenuated at the base, glabrous, glaucous-green; nerves prominent below; glomerules shorter than the petiole, subternate, few-flowered, rather lax; bracts lanceolate, green, nerved; sepal lanceolate, pale-greenish; stamens one rarely two; ovary obovate; utricle five-ribbed, smooth, green; seed lenticular, polished, black; flowers green; flowering in the rainy season. A weed, with clusters of green flowers proceeding from the axils of the leaves; stem much branched; found everywhere.

MAURITIUS (موريش - moras, *Hind.*; மோரிசு - mórísu, *Tam.*). Known also as Isle of France. An island in the Indian ocean belonging to Great Britain. Used by the lower orders as synonym for transportation.——*Mauritius elemi* (موريش كانرى - moraskánari, Malay). Same as Elemi.——*Mauritius plum* (पहार - pahára, Mahr.; موريش كا پهل - moraskáphal, Hind.; కానరేగు - kánarégu, Tel.; ବଳିବଇଁଚ - balibainoho, Oor.; උගුරැස්ස - ugurassa, Singh.; சொத்தைக்களா - shottaikkalá, Tam.). Title from habitat Tel. from (kána, tel. forest + régu, tel. jujube tree, zizyphus jujuba, lamk.). Tam. from (shottai, tam. worm eaten + kalá, tam. the plant, carissa genus) [forest bair, tomi tomi]. Oor. also (bonicha). Title otherwise Batoko plum, Shining-leaved flacourtia. Botanically Flacourtia [swaudoocantacam] ramontchi, l'her., bixineæ [vricsham, 14]. Alias Flacourtia sapida; Stigmarota africana. Tree; thorns few, naked; leaves roundish-ovate or oblong; flowers diœcious; stigmas five to nine; racemes terminal; flowers minute, greenish; flowering in the cold season. Fruit roundish, pulpy, edible; hard and close-grained wood.

MAURY (மாரி - mári, *Tam.*). Rain [mazhay]. There is a saying of Avvay:—மாரியல்லது காரியமில்லை—"Without "rain there is no doing;" nothing succeeds.——*Maury caulam* (மாரிக்காலம் - márikkálam, Tam.). From (above + kála, san. time). Monsoon [q.v.] season.——*Maury caur* (மாரிக்கார் - márikkár, Tam.). From (above + kár, tam. the crop). Caur crop growing and maturing during rains [caur, paddy].

MAUSAM (मास - mása, *San.*; మాసము - másamu, *Tel.*). From (má, san. to measure) [mau]. Month [caulam]. Primarily the time in which the moon [chundran] revolves round the earth [bhoomy]. But according to the details of astronomical calculation [maunam] there are several varieties even of this. There is also the artificial month formed by dividing the time of the earth's revolution [bhaganam] round the sun [sooryan] into twelve more or less equal portions. There is also the civil month formed by counting one of the other forms of month by sunrises only.——(1) For purposes of the S. indian calendar [punchaungam] the month may be regarded under five principal heads:—the synodical in its simplest relations; the soli-sidereal, generally called for short solar; the synodical in its special relations to the Hindoo luni-solar year; the luni-sidereal; the tropical.—"*a*" The synodical month is that from new moon to new [amavausyay, shooclaudy]. It appears in its simple form in the year of the Hijra [q.v.] era [saca] only. This is a purely lunar event; so much so that it is reckoned from the time of actually seeing the new crescent moon [piray], allowing however not more than a day's variation to occur for this [maheena]. The mean value of the synodical month is 29 days 12 hours 44 minutes 2·8 seconds.—"*b*" The solar, otherwise soli-sidereal, month here in use is the twelfth part of the period during which the sun makes a complete apparent circuit [bhaganam] round the heavens [bhogolam] from star to star, such being a mean period allowing for nutation of 365 days 6 hours 9 minutes 9·6 seconds [madhyama sowra maunam]. The twelfth part is however not an exact duodenary division, but the period during which the sun so apparently travelling traverses an arc equal to a twelfth or 30° of the great circle [mundalam] described; and that owing to the varying rate of progress in northern and southern declination [ayanam] is a variable quantity. The following are the durations of the solar months, according to the computations [maunam] of Soorya siddhauntam:—

Month.				Absolute duration of each.	The same collectively.
No.	Solar Names.	Soli-lunar names.	Zodiacal sign.	D. G. V. P. S.	D. G. V. P. S.
1	Maisham ...	Chittray ...	♈	30 55 32 2 39	30 55 32 2 39
2	Vrishabham...	Veiyaushy ...	♉	31 24 12 2 41	62 19 44 5 20
3	Mitoonan ...	Auny ...	♊	31 36 38 2 44	93 56 22 8 4
4	Catacam ...	Audy ...	♋	31 28 12 2 42	125 24 34 10 46
5	Simham ...	Auvany ...	♌	31 2 10 2 40	156 26 44 13 26
6	Canyay ...	Pooratanshy.	♍	30 27 22 2 38	186 54 6 16 4
7	Toolaum ...	Arpisy ...	♎	29 54 7 2 35	216 48 13 18 39
8	Vrishchicam...	Caurtigay ...	♏	29 30 24 2 33	246 18 37 21 12
9	Dhanoos ...	Maurgaly ...	♐	29 20 53 2 31	275 39 30 23 43
10	Macaram ...	Tye ...	♑	29 27 16 2 32	305 6 46 26 15
11	Coombham ...	Maushy ...	♒	29 48 24 2 33	334 55 10 28 48
12	Meenam ...	Pungoony ...	♓	30 20 21 2 36	365 15 31 31 24

The duration of these months, which is that used by Telinga astronomers, differs from those of the Arya siddhauntam only in the ratio of 365 d., 15 g., 31 v., 31 p., 24 s., to 365 d., 15 g., 31 v., 15 p. The strictly orthodox Tamul astronomers however prefer the Arya siddhauntam reckonings even in their lunar computations. These solar months are used in the year of the Bengalee san, Tamul saca, and Malayalam parshoorama eras; see description of the solar reckoning at vol. I, 610 [maunam]. The original theory of the solar year and months was that the year began with the vernal equinox [maishauyanam], and that the months represented the sun's path in certain fixed tracts of the visible fixed stars [nacshatram] mapped out from the vernal equinox as a starting point. But this assumed a permanent correspondence between the equinoctial points [ayanam] and the sphere of stars which does not exist, the equinoctial points really travelling round the earth's equator [niracsham] against the stars at a rate giving a complete revolution in 25,868 years, sufficient to cause complete dislocation within the period of astronomical observations. The present Indian nomenclature of solar months, which this country shares with several other nations, must have had its origin when the sun stood somewhere in the constellation or tract of stars designated Maisham [q.v.] or the Ram, the European aries, at the same time that he was at the vernal equinox; and probably when he was about in the same longitude with Hamel [q.v.] the brightest star in the Ram. This was so about 250 years B.C. The first arc of 30° of the sun's course in the ecliptic [craunty mundalam] dating from the vernal equinox continues to be called Maisham, but the stars which were then the first constellation [nacshatram] of the solar zodiac [raushy chuckram] continue also to be called Maisham, though they have now receded so as to be about 30° of space or a month in time behind the real solar zodiac. Hence a double system of astronomy; one part allowing for precession [crauntypauta gaty] and following the sun [sooryan] in its relation to the earth [bhoomy] and the seasons [ritoo], the other not allowing for precession and following the sun in its relation to the stars alone. As a further complication the present Sowra maunam or computation of solar or soli-sidereal years from a fixed sidereal starting-point, though still retaining the Maisham terminology, had its epoch or epochs later than the above. See the whole matter set out in detail under Madhyama sowra maunam [maunam]. These sidereal starting-points are very obscure, there having been no observations in correction for a long time past, and the present calendar [punchaungam] depending solely on tables giving the number of revolutions [bhaganam] of heavenly bodies [graham] in assumed periods. The most definite epoch is that given by working back from the present retarded date of the new year, which is at 12th April, while the real vernal equinox is at 21st March. The net result of all the above circumstances is represented in the three following propositions:—Indian astronomers for the finer portions of astronomy [jyotisham] and astrologers recognize precession [ayanaumsham] and consequently the moveable character of the true solar and lunar zodiacs [raushy chuckram]; for the purposes of the calendar [maunam, punchaungam], the year is held to begin when the sun is in the meridian of some fixed point in the anciently conceived fixed sidereal zodiac, and owing to precession begins now about 12th April or twenty-two days behind the true vernal equinox; the names of the months in astrology follow the nomenclature instituted when the equinox coincided with the beginning of the stars Maisham, and are called Maisham [q.v.], Vrishabham [q.v.], &c., or in other words adopt the nomenclature of the old Chaldean solar zodiac. The soli-sidereal month varies in length, as above said, with declination [ayanam, craunty]; its period being that during which the sun stays in each sign [raushy]. Its mean theoretic length is thirty days ten hours twenty-nine minutes four seconds. For ordinary civil purposes the duration of the above months are modified in the following way:—if the sun enters a new division between sunrise and midnight, the day of his entrance is the 1st of the month; if he enters a new division between midnight and sunrise, the month commences at the following sunrise. Before leaving the question of the soli-sidereal year and months, it may be repeated here, as was said under Madhyama sowra maunam [q.v.], that there was an ancient period when the bull and not the ram was the first constellation even of the solar zodiac; and this fact is recognized alike in Hindoo, Greek, and Roman literature. Indeed it will appear from certain inference, to be mentioned later on, that the luni-solar year of southern as opposed to northern india had its epoch during this period.—"*c*" The synodical month of the Hindoo luni-solar year, Chaundra maunam [q.v.], is the month adopted to make up the luni-solar N. indian year of the Samvat [q.v.] era [saca], and similarly to make up the luni-solar Teloogoo and Canarese year of the Vicramadityan [q.v.] era; the two eras here being the same under different names. See description of the lunar reckoning at vol. I ,611. It is the same in length with the synodical lunar month first mentioned. It is in S. india the lunar month from new to new, mathematically computed [amavausyay, mookhyam, shooclaudy]. Owing however to the peculiar grafting of the lunar principle on the solar year, it has special features as to its commencement, its liability to intercalation [adhicam], and its nomenclature. The first month of the luni-solar year in S. india begins with the moment of true conjunction between sun and moon [arcaindoo sangamam] next preceding the beginning of the solar year [tamul new year] as above computed by either Soorya or Arya siddhauntam [q.v.]. This gives a date varying by about twenty-nine days before 12th April, Gregorian style, at the present period. In some parts of N. india as a variation the year begins with the full moon which precedes the beginning of the solar year as above computed by the Soorya or Arya siddhauntam [gownam, krishnaudy], and gives similarly a date varying by about twenty-nine days before 12th April, Gregorian style, at the present period. Twelve of these months fall short of the soli-sidereal year by about eleven days each year, and require an intercalary month about every three years; for mode of intercalation see Adhicam and Chaundra maunam. For nomenclature a selection has been made of twelve names from the twenty-seven fixed constellations of the lunar zodiac [nacshatram]. In those months the moon is held to be full in those nacshatrams; probably this was so in the year when the Chaundra maunam was arranged. It may be noted that, under such system of nomenclature, the sidereal division [raushy, sancraunty], which gives the name to the solar month, owing to the sun being therein, will be exactly opposite in the heavens to this sidereal division [nacshatram] which gives its name to the coincident luni-solar month, owing to the full moon being therein; for the full moon [powrnimay] must always be in an opposite part of the heaven sidereally to the sun. For civil purposes the same practical arrangement is made as above said for the soli-sidereal year. For divisions of the synodic month, see Pacsham and Tity.—"*d*" The luni-sidereal month is the period of the return of the moon from star to star. It has a mean length of 27 days 7 hours 43 minutes 11·5 seconds. It is used only by astrologers [nacshatram, chaundra mausam].—"*e*" The tropical month is the month of the moveable lunar zodiac abovementioned, and is from the moon passing the equinox till her return thereto. Its value is 27 days 7 hours 43 minutes 4·7 seconds. It is used here by astrologers and for the finer parts of astronomy.—**(2)** The following table shows certain astronomical data, and the nomenclature of the months according to seven different styles beginning in each case with about 12th April.—"*a*" As to the astronomical data which precede the month nomenclature columns. Columns 1 and 2 show the time divisions of the Hindoo year exhibited in terms of the European reckoning; the Hindoo year is supposed to date from the vernal equinox, but from having neglected precession for about 1400 years it begins now in European reckoning not on 21st March which is the true vernal equinox but on 12th April [madhyama sowra maunam]. Column 3 is the list of the corresponding real arcs of the sun's path, which allows for precession, is adopted by Europeans for all purposes, and is adopted by Hindoos for scientific calculations [ayanaumsham, madhyama sowra maunam]. Column 4 is the list of corresponding zodiacal constellations in which the sun at the periods named in column 1 now stands; it will be seen that as the Hindoo year begins nearly a month late, so the sun is at that later period about among the original stars which gave their names to the solar month. This comparative agreement in the nomenclature is claimed by the Hindoo system as an advantage, but it is of course at the expense of any agreement in respect of the seasons [ritoo]. Column 5 is the list of constellations originally designed to map out the moon's path, one to a day; but used also to indicate the corresponding stages of the sun's path, dividing the year into twenty-seven [caurtey]. Column 6 is the list of constellations on the opposite side of the heavens from those just mentioned, being those in one of which with slight variations the full moon always stands at the present day in that particular solar month; shown here as being the origin of the names in columns 11, 12 and 13.—"*b*" As to the month nomenclature columns. The solar columns are placed

Month-names. See Mausam (2) page 495.

Number of the month.	Astronomical Data.					Solar nomenclature. Used for purposes of astrology all through presidency. Used for purposes of civil calendar [punchaungam] in Malabar, where Parshooraman [q.v.] era [saca] employs them.				Soli-lunar nomenclature. Used for purposes of civil calendar except in Malabar and N. of presidency. Brihaspaty [q.v.] cycle and Shalivauhanan [q.v.] Saca [q.v.] employ them.		Lunar nomenclature. Used for all purposes of the civil calendar in N. of presidency. Vicramadityan [q.v.] era employs them.	Number of the month.
	Period in terms of Gregorian calendar.	Approximately corresponding monthly arc of sun's path [cacsham] in ecliptic or moveable solar zodiac [craunty mundalam] beginning with vernal equinox [maishauyanam]. Latin, Sanscrit, English, number in european system, and sign.	Sidereal constellation [nacshatram] of the fixed Hindoo soli-sidereal zodiac [raushy] in which the sun now stands; being about 1 month later than column 3. Sanscrit, English, number, and sign.	Sidereal constellation [nacshatram] of the fixed lunar zodiac [bhamundalam] in which the sun now stands. Called for this purpose in Tel. and Can. countries Caurtey [q.v.].	Sidereal constellation of same in one of which full moon [powrnimay] now stands; being 6 months different from col. 5; hence titles in cols. 11—13.	Coorg fixed solar months.	Tooloo fixed solar months.	Malayalam fixed solar months.	General fixed solar months.	General Dravidian fixed solar months borrowing lunar names. Here called soli-lunar names.	N. indian fixed solar months; same as in column 11, shown here because names are shifted one month forward.	Approximately corresponding Teloogoo and Canarese moveable lunar months.	
1	2	3	4	5	6	7	8	9	10	11	12	13	14
1	April 12-May 12.	Taurus, vrishabham, bull (2) ♉	Maisham, ram (1) ♈	Ashwiny. Bharany.	Chitta. Swauty. Vishaukham.	Yadamyaur, 31.	Pagg, 31.	Maidom, 31.	Maisham, 31.	Chittray, 31.	Beisaukh, 31.	Cheitram, 30.	1
2	May 13-June 12.	Gemini, mitoonam, twins (3) ♊	Vrishabham, bull (2) ♉	Kritticay. Rohiny. Mrigashiras.	Vishaukham. Anooraudhay. Jyeshtay.	Caudyaur, 31.	Baisha, 31.	Yedavam, 31.	Vrishabham, 31.	Veiyaushy, 31.	Jaith, 31.	Veishaukham, 29.	2
3	June 13-July 14.	Cancer, carcatacam, crab (4) ♋; real summer solstice, dacshinauyanam on 21st June.	Mitoonam, twins (3) ♊	Ardray. Poonarvas.	Moolam. Poorvashaudham. Oottarashaudham.	Audrey, 32.	Cartail, 32.	Mitoonam, 32.	Mitoonam, 32.	Auny, 32.	Ashaudh, 32.	Jyeshtam, 30.	3
4	July 15-Aug. 14.	Leo, simham, lion (5) ♌	Carcatacam, crab (4) ♋	Pooshyam. Aushlaisham.	Oottarashaudham. Shravanam. Dhanishtay.	Cakkada, 32.	Auty, 32.	Carcatacam, 32.	Catacam, 32.	Audy, 32.	Sauwan, 32.	Ashaudham, 29.	4
5	Aug. 15-Sep. 14.	Virgo, canyay, virgin (6) ♍	Simham, lion (5) ♌	Magham. Poobbam.	Dhanishtay. Shatabhishay. Poorva bhaudram.	Chingyaur, 30.	Sona, 31.	Chingom, 31.	Simham, 31.	Auvany, 31.	Bhaudon, 31.	Shrauvanam, 30.	5
6	Sep. 15-Oct. 15.	Libra, toolaum, balance (7) ♎; real autumnal equinox, toolauyanam, being on 23rd September.	Canyay, virgin (6) ♍	Oottaram. Hastam.	Poorva bhaudram. Oottara bhaudram. Raivaty.	Cunnyaur, 31.	Nirnaula or coony, 30.	Cunny, 30.	Canyay, 30.	Poorataushy, 30.	Ausin, 30.	Bhaudrapadam, 29.	6
7	Oct. 16-Nov. 14.	Scorpio, vrishchicam, scorpion (8) ♏	Toolaum, balance (7) ♎	Chitta. Swauty. Vishaukham.	Ashwiny. Bharany. Kritticay.	Toleyaur, 30.	Bontail, 30.	Toolaum, 30.	Toolaum, 30.	Arpisy, 30.	Caurtik, 30.	Aushweejam, 30.	7
8	Nov. 15-Dec. 13.	Sagittarius, dhanoos, archer (9) ♐	Vrishchicam, scorpion (8) ♏	Anooraudhay. Jyeshtay.	Kritticay. Rohiny. Mrigashiras.	Britchiyaur, 29.	Jaurdey, 30.	Vrishchicam, 30.	Vrishchicam, 30.	Caurtigay, 30.	Aghan, 30.	Caurteecam, 29.	8
9	Dec. 14-Jan. 11.	Capricornus, macaram, goat (10) ♑; real winter solstice; oottarauyanam on 21st December.	Dhanoos, archer (9) ♐	Moolam. Poorvashaudham.	Mrigashiras. Ardray. Poonarvas.	Darmeyaur, 29.	Perardey, 29.	Dhanoo, 29.	Dhanoos, 29.	Maurgaly, 29.	Poosh, 29.	Margashiram, 30.	9
10	Jan. 12-Feb. 11.	Aquarius, coombham, waterman (11) ♒	Macaram, goat (10) ♑	Oottarashaudham. Shravanam.	Poonarvas. Pooshyam. Aushlaisham.	Maulyaur, 30.	Pooyintel, 29.	Macaram, 29.	Macaram, 29.	Tye, 29.	Maugh, 29.	Pooshyam, 29.	10
11	Feb. 12-Mar. 11.	Pisces, meenam, fishes (12) ♓	Coombham, waterman (11) ♒	Dhanishtay. Shatabhishay. Poorva bhaudram.	Magham. Poobbam. Oottaram.	Coombyaur, 30.	Mye, 30.	Coombham, 30.	Coombham, 30.	Maushy, 30.	Phaugoon, 30.	Maugham, 30.	11
12	Mar. 12-April 11.	Aries, maisham, ram (1) ♈; real vernal equinox, maishauyanam, being on 21st March.	Meenam, fishes (12) ♓	Oottara bhaudram. Raivaty.	Oottaram. Hastam. Chitta.	Meenyaur, 30.	Sooggy, 30	Meenam, 30.	Meenam, 30.	Pungoony, 30.	Cheit, 30.	Phaulgoonam, 29.	12

first, for though there may have been in S. india an anterior lunar reckoning, for which sêe vol. I, 609, it has not left any trace that is yet known in the nomenclature; and the original indigenous nomenclature is the solar held in common with such nations as the Chaldeans, followed in point of time by the luni-solar borrowed from the Aryans. Column 7 are the old Coorg solar months, the names being mainly from the Sanscrit names of solar zodiacal signs [raushy]. Column 8 or the old Tooloo solar months, the names being mostly original. Columns 9 and 10 are the general old solar months, with names corrupted from the Sanscrit names of the solar zodiac [raushy chuckram]; see the heading for usage. Column 11 are for period identically the same months as column 10, but the lunar names have been borrowed and attached; see the heading for usage. Column 12 is explained by the heading, and see below. Column 13 are pure lunations [chaundramausam] and are for period variable differing from the other columns by from ten to thirty days, and being kept from going beyond that by the triennial intercalations [adhicam]; it is on account of the great inconvenience of this month system that the Teloogoo and Canarese use caurteys [q.v.], otherwise solar residences in the lunar mansions [nacshatram], for purposes of agriculture [vellaumay] and the seasons [ritoo]; see column 5.—"c" The singular fact should finally be noticed that though the N. india year begins at the same time as in S. india, there is an advance by one, in the names merely, of the months in the soli-lunar nomenclature, as per column 12; Veishaukham in that case being first month of year in N. india, and Chittray being first month in S. india. It is evident that this terminology arose when the Bull [vrishabham] headed the zodiac [raushy chuckram], and has not since been corrected. For this see the remarks under Madhyama sowra maunam:—[*See page* 494].

——(3) The following are particulars about each of the above named months showing the derivation of the names.——*Aghan* (اگہن - aghan, Hind.). From (agra, san. front + háyana, san. year). So called as being first month of a most ancient style when this or Margashiram headed the list [madhyama sowra maunam]. Eighth N. indian soli-lunar.——*Alpisy* (ஐப்பசி - aippasi, Tam.). Corruption of eippásy.——*Arpisy* (ஐப்பசி - aippasi, Tam.). Corruption of eippasy.——*Ashaudh* (اساڑہ - asárh, Hind.). From (ashádha, san. invincible, epithet of twentieth and twenty-first nacshatram); from the full moon occurring in that month in or near that nacshatram. Third N. indian soli-lunar.——*Ashaudham* (आषाढ - áshádha, San.). See Ashaudh. Fourth lunar.——*Audrey* (ಆದ್ರೆ - ádre, Coorg). From (árdrá, san. sixth lunar mansion). Third Coorg solar.——*Audy* (ஆடி - ádi, Tam.). Corruption of ashaudham. Fourth Dravidian soli-lunar.——*Auny* (ஆனி - áni, Tam.). From (háni, san. loss). Third Dravidian soli-lunar. This refers to S.W. monsoon [q.v.]. Also applied in Tamul to Jyeshtay, the eighteenth nacshatram.——*Aushweejam* (आश्वयुज - áshvayuja, San.). From (ashva, san. horse + yuj, san. to join); from the full moon joining the nacshatram Ashwiny [q.v.] in that month. Otherwise Aushwinam. Seventh lunar.——*Aushwinam* (आश्विन - áshvina, San.). From (ashvini, san. the first and horse-headed nacshatram); from the full moon occurring in that month in or near that nacshatram. Otherwise Aushweejam. Seventh lunar.——*Ausin* (آسن - ásin, Hind.). Corruption of aushwinam. Sixth N. indian soli-lunar.——*Auty* (ಆಟಿ - áti, Can.). Corruption of ashaudham. Fourth Tooloo solar.——*Aurany* (ஆவணி - ávani, Tam.). Corruption of shraurvanam. Fifth Dravidian soli-lunar. Cf. Auny.——*Baisha* (ಬೇಶ - bésha, Can.). Means sultry. Second Tooloo solar.——*Beisaukh* (بیساکھ - baisákh, Hind.). Corruption of veishaukham. First N. indian soli-lunar.——*Bhaudon* (بہادوں - bhádún, Hind.). Corruption of bhaudrapadam. Fifth N. indian soli-lunar.——*Bhaudram* (भाद्र - bhádra, San.). Short for bhaudrapadam. Sixth lunar.——*Bhaudrapadam* (भाद्रपद - bhádrapada, San.). From (bhadrapadá, san. auspicious-footed; epithet of the twenty-fifth and twenty-sixth nacshatram); from the full moon of the month occurring about that nacshatram. Sixth lunar.——*Bontail* (ಬೊಂತೆಲ್ - bontél, Can.). Seventh Tooloo solar.——*Britchiyaur* (ಬ್ರಿಚ್ಚಿಯಾರು - briççiyáru, Coorg). From (vrishchika, san. the month so called + ñáyar, mal. month). Eighth Coorg solar.——*Cakkada* (ಕಕ್ಕಡ - kakkada, Coorg). Corruption of carcatacam. Fourth Coorg solar.——*Canyay* (कन्या - kanyá, San.). From (kanyá, san. virgin); as the sun stands in that zodiacal constellation. Sixth general solar.——*Carcatacam* (कर्कटक - karkataka, San.). Means crab; as sun stands in that zodiacal constellation. Otherwise Catacam. Fourth general solar.——*Cartail* (ಕಾರ್ತೆಲ್ - kártél, Can.). Third Tooloo solar.——*Catacam* (கடகம் - kadagam, Tam.). Corruption of carcatacam. Fourth general solar.——*Caudyaur* (ಕಾಡ್ಯಾರು - kádyáru, Coorg). Second Coorg solar.——*Caurteecam* (कार्तिक - kártika, San.). From (krittiká, san. the pleiades or third nacshatram); from the full moon of the month occurring in or near that nacshatram. Eighth lunar.——*Caurtigay* (கார்த்திகை - kárttigai, Tam.). Form of caurteecam. Eighth Dravidian soli-lunar.——*Caurtik* (کارتک - kártik, Hind.). Form of caurteecam. Seventh N. indian soli-lunar.——*Cheit* (چیت - chait, Hind.). Form of cheitram. Twelfth N. indian soli-lunar.——*Cheitram* (चैत्र - chaitra, San.). From (chitrá, san. the fourteenth nacshatram); from the full moon of the month occurring in or near that nacshatram. First lunar.——*Chingom* (ചിങ്ങം - chinnam, Mal.). Corruption of simham; means lion. Fifth Mal. solar.——*Chingyaur* (ಚಿಗ್ಞಾರು - chignyáru, Coorg). From (simha, san. the month, so called + ñáyar, mal. month). Fifth Coorg solar——*Chittray* (சித்திரை - shittirai, Tam.). Form of cheitram. First Dravidian soli-lunar. There is a Tamul proverb:—சித்திரை மாதத்திற் செல்வன் பிறந்தால் சீரும் சிறப்பும் கெடும்—"If a son is born in Chittray, "the state and reputation of the family will be ruined."——*Coombham* (कुम्भ - kumbha, San.; കുംഭം - kumbham, Mal.). Means water-pot; as the sun stands in that zodiacal constellation. Eleventh general solar.——*Coombyaur* (ಕುಂಬ್ಯಾರು - kumbyáru, Coorg). From (kumbha, san. the month so called + ñáyar, mal. month). Eleventh Coorg solar.——*Coony* (ಕೂನಿ - kúni, Can.). Corruption of canyay. Sixth Tooloo solar. Otherwise Nirnaula.——*Coony* (கூனி - kúni, Tam.). Short for Pungoony in poetry. Twelfth Dravidian soli-lunar. There is a Tamul proverb:—ஆனி அடியிடாதே கூனி குடிபோகாதே—"Do not begin to build in Auny, nor set out to occupy "a house in Coony."——*Cunny* (കന്നി - kanni, Mal.; கன்னி - kanni, Tam.). Corruption of canyay. Sixth Malayalam solar.——*Cunnyaur* (ಕನ್ನ್ಯಾರು - kannyáru, Coorg). From (kanyá, san. the month so called + ñáyar, mal. month). Sixth Coorg solar.——*Darmeyaur* (ದರುಮೆಯಾರು - darumeyáru, Coorg). From (dhanus, san. the month so called + ñáyar, mal. month). Ninth Coorg solar.——*Dhanoo* (ധനു - dhanu, Mal.). Means bow. Ninth Malayalam solar.——*Dhanoos* (धनुस् - dhanus, San.; ധനു - dhanu, Mal.). Means bow; as the sun stands in that zodiacal constellation. Ninth general solar.——*Eippasy* (ஐப்பசி - aippasi, Tam.). From (asuvathi tam. corruption of ashvayuj, san. ashvini, the first nacshatram); from the full moon occurring in that month in or near the nacshatram ashwiny. Otherwise Arpisy. Seventh Dravidian soli-lunar.——*Jaith* (جیٹھ - jeth, Hind.). Corruption of jyeshtam. Second N. indian soli-lunar.——*Jaurdey* (ಜಾರ್ದೆ - járde, Can.). Eighth Tooloo solar.——*Jyeshtam* (ज्येष्ठ - jyésht'ha, San.; జ్యేష్ఠము - jyéshtamu, Tel.). From (jyésht'há, san. eldest, the name of the eighteenth nacshatram); from the full moon occurring in that month in or near that nacshatram. Third lunar.——*Macaram* (मकर - makara, San.; മകരം - makaram, Mal.). Means dolphin; as the sun stands in that zodiacal constellation. Tenth general solar.——*Maidom* (മേടം - métam, Mal.). Corruption of maisham. First Malayalam solar.——*Maisham* (मेष - mésha, San.; மேடம் - médam, Tam.). Means ram; as the sun stands in that zodiacal constellation. First general solar.——*Margasheersham* (मार्गशीर्ष - márgashírsha, San.). From (mrigashiras, san. the fifth deer-headed nacshatram); from the full moon occurring in that month in or near that nacshatram. Also called Agrahayanam, as beginning old style solar year. Ninth lunar.——*Margashiram* (మార్గశిరము - márgashiramu, Tel.). Ninth lunar.——*Maugh* (ماگھ - mágh, Hind.). Form of maugham. Tenth N. indian soli-lunar.——*Maugham* (माघ - mágha, San.). From (maghá, san. tenth lunar asterism); from the full moon occurring in that month in or near that nacshatram. Eleventh lunar.——*Maulyaur* (ಮಾಲ್ಯಾರು - mályáru, Can.). From (mágha, san. the month). Tenth Coorg solar.——*Maurgaly* (மார்கழி - márgazhi, Tam.). Corruption of margasheersham. Ninth Dravidian soli-lunar. There is a Tamul proverb:—ஐப்பசிமாதத்தில் எருமைக்கடாவும் மார்கழி மாதத்து நம்பியாரும் சரி—"A buffalo in Arpisy and a Veishnava bramin in Maurgaly are "alike."——*Maushy* (மாசி - mási, Tam.). Corruption of maugham. Eleventh Dravidian soli-lunar.——*Meenam* (मीन - mína, San.; മീനം - mínam, Mal.). Means fish; as the sun stands in that zodiacal constellation. Twelfth general solar.——*Meenyaur* (ಮೀನ್ಯಾರು - mínyáru, Coorg). From (mína, san. the month so called + ñáyar, mal. month). Twelfth Coorg solar.——*Mitoonam* (मिथुन - mit'huna, San.; മിഥുനം - mit'hunam, Mal.). Means the twins; as the sun stands in that zodiacal constellation. Third general solar.——*Mye* (ಮಾಯಿ - máyi, Can.). Corruption of maushy. Eleventh Tooloo solar.——*Nijaushwinam* (निजाश्विन - nijáshvina, San.). From (nija, san. real + áshvina, san. the month). The proper month of Aushwinam in contradistinction to Adhica aushwinam, the intercalated lunar month.——*Nirnaula* (ನಿರ್ನಾಲ - nirnála, Can.). Otherwise Coony. Sixth Tooloo solar.——*Pagg* (ಪಗ್ಗು - paggu, Can.). First Tooloo solar.——*Perardey* (ಪೆರಾರ್ದೆ - perárde, Can.). Ninth Tooloo solar.——*Phaugoon* (پھاگن - phágun, Hind.). Corruption of phaulgoonam. Eleventh N. indian soli-lunar.——*Phaulgoonam* (फाल्गुन - p'hálguna, San.). From (p'halguní, san. the eleventh and twelfth nacshatrams); from the full moon occurring in that month in or near that nacshatram. Twelfth lunar.——*Poorataushy* (புரட்டாசி - purattási, Tam.). From (prósht'hapáda, san. bench-footed; epithet of the twenty-fifth nacshatram); from the full moon occurring in that month in or near the nacshatram Prosbtapadam, more commonly Bhaudrapadam. Sixth Dravidian soli-lunar.——*Poosh* (پوس - pús, Hind.). Corruption of pooshyam. Ninth N. indian soli-lunar.——*Pooshyam* (पुष्य - pushya, San.). Means flower, epithet of the eighth nacshatram; from the full moon occurring in that month in or near that nacshatram. Otherwise Powshnam or Powshyam. Tenth luuar.——*Pooyintel* (ಪುಯಿಂತೆಲ್ - puyintél, Can.). Corruption of pooshyam. Tenth Tooloo solar.——*Powshnam* (पौष्ण - paushna, San.). Form of pooshyam. Tenth lunar. Otherwise Pooshyam.——*Pungoony* (பங்குனி - panguni, Tam.). From (p'halguni, san. name of the eleventh and twelfth nacshatrams); from the full moon occurring in that month in or near that nacshatram. Twelfth Dravidian soli-lunar.——*Sauwan* (ساون - sávan, Hind.). Corruption of shrauvanam. Fourth N. indian soli-lunar.——*Shrauvanam* (श्रावण - shrávana, San.). From (shravana, san. the twenty-second nacshatram); from the full moon occurring in that month in or near that nacshatram. Fifth lunar.——*Simham* (सिंह - shimha, San.; சிங்கம் - shingam, Tam). Means lion; as the sun stands in that zodiacal constellation. Fifth general solar.——*Sona* (ಸೋಣ - sóna, Can.). Corruption of shrauvanam. Fifth Tooloo solar.——*Sooggy* (ಸುಗ್ಗಿ - suggi, Can.). Means the spring season. Twelfth Tooloo solar.——*Toleyaur* (ತೊಲೆಯಾರು - toleyáru, Coorg). From (tulá, san. the month so called + ñáyar, mal. month). Seventh Coorg solar.——*Toolaum* (तुला - tulá, San.; തുലാം - tulám, Mal.). From (tulá, san. balance); as the sun stands in that zodiacal constellation. Seventh general solar.——*Tye* (தை - tai, Tam.). From (taisha, san. ancient name for pausha, san. the tenth month); from the full moon occurring in that month in or near the nacshatram Tishyam or Pooshyam. Tenth Dravidian soli-lunar. There is a Tamul proverb:—தை ஈனைப் புல்லும் இல்லை, மாசி ஈனை மரமும் இல்லை—"There is no grass that does not grow in January, nor tree "that does not sprout in February."——*Veishaukham* (वैशाख - vaishákha, San.). From (vishákhá, san. the forked, sixteenth nacshatram); from the full moon occurring in that month in or near that nacshatram. Second lunar.——*Veiyaushy* (வைகாசி - vaigási, Tam.). Corruption of veishaukham. Second Dravidian soli-lunar.——*Vrishabham* (वृषभ - vrishabha, San.). Means bull; as the sun stands in that zodiacal constellation. Second general solar.——*Vrishan* (वृषन् - vrishan, San.). Form of vrishabham. Second general solar.——*Vrishchicam* (वृश्चिक - vrishchika, San.; വൃശ്ചികം - vrishchikam, Mal.). Means scorpion; as the sun stands in that zodiacal constellation. Eighth general solar.——*Yadamyaur* (ಯೆಡಂಯಾರು - yadamyáru, Coorg). From (edam, can. good + ñáyar, mal. month). First Coorg solar.——*Yedaram* (ഇടവം - itavam, Mal.). Corruption of vrishabham. Second Malayalam solar.——**(4)** The following are different kinds of mausam in astronomy or theology.——*Adhica mausam* (अधिकमास - adhikamása, San.). Means additional + month. An intercalated lunar month [adhicam, chaundra maunam].——*Brahma mausam* (ब्रह्ममास - brahmamása, San.). From (brahma, san. the god + mása, san. month). Thirty of Bramha's days [caulam, 2].——*Chaundra mausam* (चान्द्रमास - chándramása, San.). Means moon + month. Tingal [q.v.]. Ordinary lunar month, the synodical month [shooclaudy]. Under the exceptional Krishnaudy method, the period taken is from full moon to full moon [powrnimay], instead of from new moon [amavausyay] to new moon [caulam, 4, maheena].——*Cshaya mausam* (क्षयमास - kshayamása, San.). From (kshaya, san. destruction + mása, san. month). An expunged lunar month.——*Deva mausam* (देवमास - dévamása, San.). From (déva, san. god + above). Thirty sidereal years [caulam, 2].——*Gowna chaundra mausam* (गौणचान्द्रमास - gaunachándramása, San.). From (gauna, san. secondary + chándramása, san. lunar month). Otherwise Gownam. The lunar month, when reckoned as beginning at full moon instead of new.——*Mookhya chaundra mausam* (मुख्यचान्द्रमास - mukhyachándramása, San.). From (mukhya, san. principal + chándramása, san. lunar month). Otherwise Mookhyam. The lunar month, when reckoned in the ordinary way from new moon to new moon [shooclaudy].——**(5)** The following are the Tamulians' views about the weather in the different months. Cf. Caurtey, Caulam and Caur:—Chittray or april; சித்திரைக்குறுப்பம்—"rough "weather or storm in chittray"—fore-runner of the s.w. monsoon [q.v.]; ஆருமீன்றவோட்டம்—"the transit of the sun "through the pleiades;" regarded by seamen, as a critical or disastrous season, when rough weather is to be looked for. Veiyaushy or may; சோகாசிமின்னல்—lightning in n.e. before s.w. monsoon; வைகாசிமாதம் ஆற்றில் தண்ணீர்—"in "veiyaushy the river is in flood." Auny or june; ஆனித்தூக்கம்—"auny sleep;" calms in june; ஆனியளையாறு ஆவணிமுழு ஆறு—"in auny half river, in auvany full river." Audy or july; ஆடிக்கரு—"audy clouds;" indicative of plentiful rain in ensuing monsoon; ஆடிக்கருவழிந்தால் மழை குறைந்துபோம்—"if the teeming clouds in audy fail, rains will decrease "in the ensuing season;" ஆடிக்காற்றில் அம்மி ஆகாயத்தில் பறக்கும்—"in audy wind the grindstone roller will fly "in the air." Auvany or august; ஆவணி அழுகற்றூற்றல்—"in auvany incessant drizzling." Arpisy or october; ஐப்பசி மாதத்து வெய்யலில்அன்று உரித்ததோல் அன்றுசாயும்—"in heat of arpisy the skin dries, the day it is stript off;" ஐப்பசிமாதம் அழுகற்றூறல், கார்த்திகைமாதம் கனமழை;—"in arpisy drizzling; in caurtigay heavy rains;" ஐப்பசிக்கும் கார்த்திகைக்கும் மழை யில்லாவிட்டால் அண்ணனுக்குஞ்சரி தம்பிக்குஞ்சரி—"if the rains of arpisy "and caurtigay fail, the elder and younger brother will be "on a par;" that is, all labour is in vain. Caurtigay or november; கார்த்திகைக்குமேல் மழையுமில்லை கர்ணனுக்குமேல் கொடையுமில்லை—"no rain after caurtigay and "no gift after carnan [q.v.]." Maurgaly or december; கருப்பவோட்டம்—the southern passage of the clouds, from about december 13th till december 27th, carrying away the surplus water as a reserve for the following months. Tye or january; தையும் மாசியும் வையகத்துறங்கு—"in tye and maushy, "sleep under thatch." Pungoony or march; பங்குனிமாதம் பகல்வழி நடந்தவன் பெரும்பாவி—"he who travels by "day in pungoony is a great sinner;" the sun is so hot [mazhay].

MAUTAH (माता - mátá, *San.*; மாதா - máthá, *Tam.*). From (má, san. to cause) [mau]. A mother.——**(1)** The seven great mautahs or mothers are the following. Cauvery and Chamoondy are sometimes included.——*Brahmy* (ब्राह्मी - bráhmí, San.). The shacty [q.v.] of bramha [q.v.].——*Cauly* (काली - kálí, San.). The black deity.——*Cowmaury* (कौमारी - kaumárí, San.). The shacty of soobramanyan or the son-god.——*Eindry* (ऐन्द्री - aindrí, San.). The shacty of indran [q.v.].——*Maheshwary* (माहेश्वरी - máhéshvarí, San.). The shacty of shiva [q.v.] the great lord.——*Narayany* (नारायणी - náráyaní, San.). The shacty of vishnoo [q.v.].——*Varauhy* (वाराही - váráhí, San.). The shacty of vishnoo in the form of a boar [varauham].——**(2)** *Oolagamautah* (लोकमाता - lókamátá, San.; உலகமாதா - ulagamáthá, Tam.). From (lóka, san. world + máthá, tam. mother). Saraswaty [q.v.]; also lutchmy [q.v.].

MAUTT (మాటు - mátu, *Tel.*). Tel. means screen or covering. An ambuscade for shikar [q.v.].

MAUZY (ماضی - mází, *Hind.*). From (mazú, ar. to precede). Late, former.

MAYAVARAM (மாயவரம் - máyavaram,* *Tam.*). From (máyá, san. goddess kálí + áviram, tam. shepherd village) [mau]. Sanscrit name (mayúrapura), meaning peacock + town; also (shrímushna), meaning holy excellent city. Commonly Mauyooram or Gowry mauyooram.——**(1)** Talook, Tanjore district. Tahsildar's pay Rs. 225. Area 282 square miles; pop. 244,835; language Tamul; N. coast of district. Bounded on the south by Nunnilam talook and the French settlement of Caricaul, on the west by Combaconam talook, and on the east by Shiyally talook and the Bay of Bengal, on the north by Shiyally and Chidambaram talooks of South arcot district. The land slopes from west to east. The lands cannot be classed as very fertile. The western portion is best. Soil, western portion clay, eastern portion near the sea sandy. Cloths worn by Hindoo females [sheelay], form the chief article of manufacture. The Cauvery and its branches and the Rajah vycaul branching from the Coleroon furnish irrigation. Camping grounds:—Aukkore, Coottaulam, Illooppaputt, Mayavaram, Perambore, and Tircadayore. Places of archæological interest:—Auttore, Coottaulam, Illooppaputt, Korkay, Manamode, Mayavaram, Moovalore, Nadoocaray, Nullauday, Peroomullay, Tairezhandore, Tirnandriyore, Tirvaudootoray, Tirvaulolipoottore, Tranquebar, Trivengaud, Vazhoovore. Principal trig. stations, &c.:—Tircadayore, Tranquebar tower. The leading places, &c., in the talook are the following.——*Antaundavapooram* (ஆனைதாண்டவப்புரம் - ánaithándavappuram, Tam. antándavapuram *). Title from sanscrit. Sanscrit name (ánandatándavapura), meaning town of shiva, the delightful dancer. Village, Railway station; pop. 1,617; acres 1,369; lat. 11° 09′ 14″; long. 79° 42′; height 27 feet; from Mayavaram N. 3 miles; from Tanjore N.E. 42 miles; from the sea W. 14 miles.——*Cadalangoody* (கடலங்குடி - kadalangudi, Tam.). From (kadalan, tam. a fisherman + kudi, tam. village). Village; pop. 1,326; acres 1,136; lat. 11° 11′; long. 79° 36′; from Mayavaram N.W. 8 miles; from Tanjore N.E. 39 miles; from the sea W. 20 miles.——*Cauvery* (காவேரி - kávéri, Tam.). See sep. title.——*Coleroon* (கொள்ளடம் - kolladam, Tam.). See sep. title.——*Comal* (கோமல் - kómal, Tam.). From (kó, tam. greatness + mal, tam. fertility). Village; pop. 4,036; acres 3,080; lat. 11° 01′; long. 79° 38′; from Mayavaram S.S.W. 7 miles; from Tanjore N.E. 33 miles; from the sea W. 17 miles.——*Conairirajapooram* (கோனேரிராசப்புரம் - kónérirásappuram, Tam.). From (kónéri, tam. proper name + rájá, san. king + pura, san. town); conairirajan's town. Village; pop. 2,097; acres 2,028; lat. 10° 59′; long. 79° 35′; from Mayavaram S.W. 12 miles; from Tanjore E. 30 miles;

from the sea W. 22 miles. Name given originally by Tirmalayya cholan to a tract of country made over to Bramins as a gift at the request of Conairiyappan, one of his ministers. ——*Coottaulam* (குற்றாலம் - kuttálam, Tam.). Title from sanscrit. Sanscrit name; ancient (drutikshétra), meaning sacred place of a sage drooty; modern (kuddála), meaning mountain ebony, bauhinia variegata, linn.; from the tree in shiva temple. Village, Railway station; pop. 3,537; acres 1,628; lat. 11° 04′; long. 79° 36′; height 53 feet; from Mayavaram W.S.W. 7 miles; from Tanjore N.E. 34 miles; from the sea W. 20 miles. Old Shiva temple with inscriptions. Weaving centre.——*Mayavaram* (மாயவரம் - máyavaram, Tam.). See below.——*Munjalaur* (மஞ்சளாறு - manjaláru, Tam. manjayár *). From (mañjal, tam. saffron, curcuma longa, roxb. + áru, tam. river); so called as it is munjal cawny or saffron property, i.e., female property [streedhanam], having been dug by poligar [q.v.] shivanauta naick for his daughter to bathe in. Sanscrit name (haridránadí), meaning the same. River.——*Oolava mungalam* (உழவன்மங்கலம் - uzhavanmangalam, Tam.). From (uzhavan, tam. ploughman + mangala, san. prosperity). Village; pop. 2,249; acres 1,373; lat. 11° 02′; long. 79° 52′; from Mayavaram E.S.E. 12 miles; from Tanjore E. 49 miles; from the sea W. 2 miles.——*Perambore* (பெரம்பூர் - perambúr, Tam.). From (pirambu, tam. cane + úr, tam. village). Village; pop. 720; acres 1,088; lat. 11° 02′; long. 79° 46′; from Mayavaram S.S.E. 6 miles; from Tanjore E. 41 miles; from the sea W. 11 miles.——*Porayaur* (பொறையார் - poraiyár, Tam.). From (porai, tam. a mountain + áru, tam. river). Town; pop. 5,725; acres 2,287; lat. 11° 01′; long. 79° 53′; from Mayavaram E.S.E. 13 miles; from Tanjore E. 49 miles; from the sea W. 1¼ miles. Suburb of Tranquebar. Weaving centre. S.P.G. mission station. ——*Tillayaudy* (தில்லையாடி - tillaiyádi, Tam.). From (tillai, tam. a tree, excæcaria agallocha, mueller, var. camettia + vádi, tam. enclosure). Village; pop. 3,695; acres 1,461; lat. 11° 03′; long. 79° 51′; from Mayavaram E.S.E. 11 miles; from Tanjore E. 48 miles; from the sea W. 3 miles.——*Tircadayore* (திருக்கடையூர் - tirukkadaiyúr, Tam.). From (tiru, tam. sacred + kadai, tam. last + úr, tam. village); the last place of worship by marcandeyan, before made immortal. Sanscrit name (amritaghatapura), meaning nectar + pot + town. Village; pop. 2,689; acres 1,976; lat. 11° 05′; long. 79° 51′; from Mayavaram E. 10 miles; from Tanjore E. 48 miles; from the sea W. 4 miles. Trig. station in lat. 11° 04′ 23·72″; long. 79° 50′ 51·12″; from Manamode N. ½ mile; from Mayavaram E. S.E. 11 miles; from the sea W. 4 miles.——*Tirvaudootoray* (திருவாடுதுறை - tiruváduthurai, Tam.). From (tiru, tam. sacred + ádu, tam. sheep + turai, tam. ford). Tam. also (ávaduthurai), meaning cow + liberation + place. Sanscrit name (gómuktipura), meaning cow + absolution + town; also (kshírinívana), meaning forest of csheeriny, the moon-plant, sarcostemma brevistigma, w. and a. [somam]. Village; pop. 3,115; acres 1,348; lat. 11° 02′; long. 79° 34′; from Mayavaram W.S.W. 10 miles; from Tanjore E. 31 miles; from the sea W. 23 miles. Wealthy Shoodra mutt [q.v.].——*Tranquebar* (தரங்கம்பாடி - tarangambádi, Tam.). See sep. title.——*Vicramanaur* (விக்கிரமனாறு - vikkiramanáru, Tam.). Means vicraman's river. Canal; Canal from the Cauvery, constructed by Vicraman, a Chola king.——**(2)** Town, Municipality, Railway station, Talook and Moonsif's head-quarters and place of pilgrimage; Tanjore dist., Mayavaram tal.; pop. 23,765; acres 1,434; lat. 11° 06′; long. 79° 42′; height 47 feet; from Combaconam E.N.E. 21 miles; from Madras S.S.W. 141 miles; from Munnargoody N.N.E. 33 miles; from Negapatam N.N.W. 26 miles; from Tanjore E.N.E. 40 miles; from the sea W. 14 miles. On the Cauvery. Coranaud is a suburb. Has a large temple, Mayooranauta sawmy, and is one of the chief seats of Braminical religion in the district. Parvaty [q.v.] in the form of a peacock [mayil] is said to have worshipped Shiva [q.v.] here. The Toolah cauvery [q.v.] festival, extends over thirty days of the Tamul month of Arpisy [mausam], October and November. During this time ablutions in the river are considered to confer special spiritual benefit; and on the more important days there is an immense gathering from all parts of the district. Station of German lutheran mission and Pondicherry roman catholic mission.

MAYIL (मयूर - mayúra, *San.*; मोर - móra, *Mahr.*; طاؤس - táús, *Ar.*; مور - mor, *Pers.*; مہر - muhr, *Hind.* and *Dec.*; ನವಿಲು - nevilu, *Can.*; నెమలి - nemali, *Tel.*; ମୟୂରୋ - moyuro, *Oor.*; മയിൽ - mayil, *Mal.*; மயில் - mayil, *Tam.*). Title from tamul. San. from (mí, san. to injure). Ar. from (tásá, ar. beautiful). Pers., &c., from sanscrit. Oor. from sanscrit. Mal. from (mayi, mal. black). Tam. from (mai, tam. black). Ar. also (sarrákh), meaning vehement crier. Hind. also (manjír). Can. also (navilu). Title otherwise Common peacock. Pavo cristatus, pavoninæ, phasianidæ [jeevanjeevam], rasores [pacshy, 32], of naturalists [jantoo]. Frequents forests especially in mountainous districts; domesticated; venerated by natives; many temples have large flocks; easily caught in snares; in confinement they destroy snakes [sarpam] and other reptiles; common in jungles resorted to by tigers [pooly]; on the islands of chilka lake, there are great numbers; young pea-hens at certain seasons are not inferior to turkeys [feel moorghy], as food; by natives they are preferred. Native practitioners [veidyan] consider peacock's fat valuable external application in cases of rigid joints, and in certain paralytic affections. As early as days of Solomon imported into Judea by the fleets which traded to Malabar. Mayil is a common plant first term. Ex., where transl. is of second term:—Actiniopteris dichotoma (mayirchikki), crest; Adiantum caudatum (mayirgondai), crest; Apluda aristata (mayirgondaippul), crest + grass; Cæsalpinia pulcherrima (mayirgonrai), cassia fistula; Chloris barbata (mayirgondaippul), crest + grass; Lawsonia alba (mayiláñchi), to stretch; Poinciana regia (mayirgonrai), cassia fistula; Sida rhombifolia, var. retusa (mayilumánikyamu), ruby; Vitex altissima (mayilmaram), tree. See gloss. paragraphs.——*Mayil vauhanan* (மயில்வாகனன் - mayilvábanan, Tam.). From (above + váhana, san. vehicle). Soobramanyan [q.v.], whose vehicle [vauhan] is a peacock.

MAYOORAM (मयूर - mayúra, *San.*). Peacock. Mayoora vurman, from (above + varman, san. coat, title), was regal title among Cadambas [q.v.].——*Mor* (مور - mor, Hind.). Peacock. ——*Morah* (मोर - móra, Mahr). Peacock, pavo cristatus. Compare:—Aquila fulvescens (móraghára), peacock vulture.——*Morpankhy* (मयूरशिखा - mayúrashikhá, San.; मोरशिखा - mórashikhá, Mahr.; مور پنکھی - morpankhí, Hind.; నెమలిజుట్టు - nemalidzuttu, Tel.; மயிற்சிக்கி - mayirchikki, Tam.). Title from hindostany. San. from (mayúra, san. peacock + shikhá, san. crest). Mahr. from sanscrit. Hind. from (mor, pers. peacock + pankhá, hind. fan); from appearance of tree. Tel. from (nemali, tel. peacock + dzuttu, tel. crest). Tam. from (mayil, tam. peacock + shikhá, san. crest). Tel. also (nemalishikha), meaning peacock + crest. Title otherwise Peacock crest [moorgha], Peacock fan. Botanically Actiniopteris dichotoma, forsk., filices [vricsham, 157]. A fern like a miniature palm [taur]. Medicinally anthelmintic and styptic.

MAZHAR (مظہر - mazhar, *Ar.*). From (zahara, ar. apparent). A place where any spectacle is represented; manifestation. Prophet's lacab. Common alam; as Mazhar ally, double alam [ism].

MAZHAY (वर्ष - varsha, *San.*; مطر - matarr, *Ar.*; باران - bárán, *Pers.*; مینھ - menh, *Hind.*; برسات - barsát, *Dec.*; اوجن - újan, *Malay*; ಮಳೆ - male, *Can.*; ବର୍ଷା - barsa, *Too.*; వాన - vána, *Tel.*; മഴ - mazha, *Mal.*; වැසි - wesi, *Singh.*; மழை - mazhai, *Tam.*). San. from (vrish, san. to shower). Pers. from (vári, san. water). Hind. from (mégha, san. cloud). Dec. from sanscrit. Mal. from (mazhu, mal. to grow dim). Singh. from sanscrit. Rain [maury]. The Tamul Cooral [q.v.] has the following:—வானின்றுலகம்வழங்கிவருதலாற் றானமிழ்த மென்றுணரற் பாற்று. துப்பார்க்குத் துப்பாய துப் பாக்கித் துப்பார்க்குத் துப்பாய தூஉமழை. விண் ணின்று பொய்ப்பின் விரிநீர் வியனுலகத் துண்ணின் றுடற்றும் பசி. ஏரி னுழாஅ ருழவர் புயலென்னும் வாரி வளங்குன்றிக் கால். கெடுப்பதூஉங் கெட்டார்க் குச் சார்வாய்மற் றாங்கே யெடுப்பதூஉ மெல்லா மழை. விசும்பிற் றுளிவீழி னல்லான்மற் றாங்கே பசும்புற் றலைகாண் பரிது. நெடுங்கடலுந் தன்னீர்மை குன்றுந் தடிந்தெழிலி தானல்கா தாகி விடின். சிறப்பொடு பூசனைசெல்லாது வானம் வறக்குமேல் வானோர்க்கு மீண்டு. தானந் தவமிரண்டுந் தங்கா வியனுலகம் வானம் வழங்கா தெனின். நீரின் றமையா துல கெனின் யார்யார்க்கும் வானின் றமையா தொழுக்கு—

"By the continuance of rain the world is preserved in existence; "it is therefore worthy to be called ambrosia [amritam]; rain "produces good food, and is itself food; if the cloud [maigham], "withholding rain, deceive, hunger will long distress the "sea-girt spacious world; if the abundance of wealth-imparting "rain diminish, the labor of the plough [calappay, vellaumay] "must cease; rain by its absence ruins men; and by its "existence restores them to fortune; if no drop falls from the "clouds, not even the green blade of grass will be seen; even "the wealth of the wide sea will be diminished, if the cloud "that has drawn up gives not back again; if the heaven dry "up, neither yearly festivals [pundigay], nor daily worship will "be offered in this world, to the celestials; if rain fall not, "penance [tapas] and alms-deeds [dharmam] will not dwell "within this spacious world; if it be said that the duties "of life cannot be discharged by any person without water, "so without rain there cannot be the flowing of water [neer]." There is a Teloogoo proverb:—వానరాకడ ప్రాణంపోకడ తెలియదు— "When rain [vaun] comes, when life goes, no one knows." The natives hold that clouds which appear in certain seasons of the year are pregnant clouds and yield rain later at particular times and places. The following are Varauha mihiran's remarks thereon. Note that his month names are all north indian names as per column 12 of the month table under Mausam, and he means one month earlier in each case than would be understood by the same names here:—"As food is the support of life and food "depends upon rain, it is important to discover the laws of rain "by any means; the predictions of an astronomer who pays

" exclusive attention both day and night to the indications of
" rain afforded by pregnant clouds [maigham], will as little fail
" of success as the words of rishies [q.v.]; what science can
" possibly excel in interest the science relating to the prediction
" of rain, by a thorough study of which one though ignorant in
" other matters passes for a great astrologer in this iron age
" [kaliyoog]. The days on which clouds are to be deemed preg-
" nant commence from the day when the moon [chundran]
" reaches the asterism [nacshatram] of poorvashaudham [q.v.] or
" the first quarter of oottarashaudham [q.v.] on any of the lunar
" days [tity], from the first, of the bright half [shooclapacsham]
" of the lunar month of margashiram [q.v.]. If pregnant clouds
" appear when the moon is in a certain asterism the delivery
" of rain will occur 195 days after. Clouds conceiving originally
" during the bright half [shooclapacsham] will be delivered
" eventually during the dark half [krishnapacsham] of a lunar
" month [chaundramausam] and clouds conceiving during the
" dark half will be delivered during the bright half; also clouds
" conceiving during the day will be delivered at night and clouds
" conceiving at night will be delivered during the day; also clouds
" conceiving in the twilight of the morning will be delivered
" in the twilight of the evening and clouds conceiving in the
" twilight of the evening will be delivered in the twilight of the
" morning. Clouds that conceive in the bright and dark halves of
" the month [mausam] of margashiram [q.v.] and in the bright
" half of pooshyam [q.v.] will be delivered of rain respectively
" in the dark half of jyeshtam [q.v.] and in the bright and dark
" halves of ashaudham [q.v.]; but the fall of rain in these cases
" will only be moderate; and clouds that conceive in the dark
" half of pooshyam will be delivered of rain in the bright half
" of shrauvanam [q.v.]. Clouds that conceive in the bright half
" of maugham [q.v.] will be delivered of rain in the dark half of
" shrauvanam and those that conceive in the dark half of mau-
" gham will be delivered in the bright half of bhaudrapadam [q.v.].
" Clouds that conceive in the bright half of phaulgoonam [q.v.]
" will be delivered of rain in the dark half of bhaudrapadam
" and those that conceive in the dark half of phaulgoonam will
" be delivered in the bright half of aushweejam [q.v.]. Clouds
" that conceive in the bright half of cheitram [q.v.] will be
" delivered of rain in the dark half of aushweejam and those that
" conceive in the dark half of cheitram will be delivered in the
" bright half of caurteecam [q.v.]. Clouds that conceive in the
" east will be delivered in the west and clouds that conceive in
" the west will be delivered in the east; the same rule holds
" with regard to the other directions and also with respect to the
" winds that appear both at the times of conception and delivery.
" If gentle and agreeable winds blow from the north, north-
" east and east, if the sky should be clear, if the sun [sooryan]
" and moon [chundran] should appear surrounded by bright,
" white, thick halos; if the clouds should appear huge, bright,
" dense, or shaped like a needle or a sword and red, if the sky
" should appear dark as the crow's egg, if the moon and stars
" should appear white; if the twilight [sundhyay] should be
" marked by the rainbow, by the low rumbling roar of thunder,
" by lightning, by the mock-sun, if it be of agreeable appearance,
" if groups of birds and animals should sound sweet music from
" the north, north-east and east; if the planets [graham]
" should appear of large bright disc, if their course should lie to
" the north of the constellations [nacshatram], if they should be
" free from abnormal affections, if the trees should grow well
" and be free from disease; if men and cattle should be happy;
" these are indications of a healthy pregnancy, and in such
" cases the clouds will yield abundance of rain. We will now
" proceed to state the indications of a healthy pregnancy of rain-
" clouds in the several seasons [ritoo] of the year. In the
" months of margashiram [q.v.] and pooshyam [q.v.], if the sky
" should appear very red just before sunrise and just after
" sunset; if the clouds should appear surrounded by halos; if the
" month of Margashiram should be found to be very cold and if
" the fall of snow should be excessive in the month of pooshyam;
" in the month of maugham [q.v.], if strong winds should blow,
" if the discs of the sun and moon should be dimmed by the fall
" of snow, if at rising and setting the sun should be hid by
" clouds and it be then exceedingly cold; in the month of
" phaulgoonam [q.v.] if strong and violent winds should blow, if
" fine clouds should be found marching from place to place, if
" broken or imperfect halos should appear in the sky, if the sun
" should appear of the color of gold or red; in the month of
" cheitram [q.v.] if the sky should be marked by winds, clouds,
" rain and halos; in the month of veishaukham [q.v.] if there
" should be rain, lightning and thick clouds; in all these cases
" it may be concluded that the pregnancy of the clouds is a
" healthy one. If the pregnant clouds should be of the color of
" pearls or silver or of the color of the bark of the tamaulam
" [yellow mangosteen] tree or of the blue lotus [blue nelumbo]
" or of collyrium, they will yield abundance of rain. If the
" pregnant clouds should be exposed to the hot rays of the sun,
" if they should be accompanied by gentle winds and appear as
" if covered by drops of rain, they will yield abundance of rain.
" If the appearance of the pregnant clouds should be marked by
" meteoric falls, by thunder-bolts, dust-storms and the appear-
" ance of mock-fires about the horizon; or if at the time of such
" appearance, clouds should present the shape of cities and
" towers and if spots should appear in the solar disc or if there
" should be planetary conjunctions at the time; or, if there
" should be a shower of blood, if halos or rainbows should
" appear in the sky, if there should be a solar or lunar eclipse
" [grahanam] at the time; in all these cases the pregnancy will
" miscarry. If the symptoms of a healthy pregnancy assigned
" for the several seasons [ritoo] of the year should fail, the
" pregnancy will miscarry and the clouds will yield little or no
" rain. Clouds that conceive when the moon is in the asterisms
" of poorvabhaudram [q.v.], oottarabhaudram [q.v.], poorva-
" shaudham [q.v.] and oottarashaudham [q.v.] and rohiny [q.v.]
" will yield abundance of rain. Clouds that conceive when the
" moon is in the asterism of shatabhishay [q.v.], aushlaisham
" [q.v.], ardray [q.v.], swauty [q.v.] and magham [q.v.]
" will yield rain continuously for several days unless the preg-
" nancy should have suffered in any of the ways stated above.
" Clouds that conceive when the moon is in any one of the five
" asterisms referred to in the last stanza in the six months from
" margashiram to veishaukham, will yield rain respectively for
" eight, six, sixteen, twenty-four, twenty, and three days
" continuously. If either the sun or moon should be attended
" by a malefic planet at the time of conception, the subsequent
" rainfall will be marked by hail, thunder, and fish; if on the
" other hand either the sun or moon should be attended by or
" within view of a benefic planet at the time of conception the
" rainfall will be abundant. If there should be fall of heavy rain
" at the time of conception, the pregnancy will miscarry and
" there will be no rain; this will be the case only when the
" quantity of rainfall exceeds one-eighth of a dronam. If, owing
" to adverse planetary influences, the pregnant clouds should fail
" to yield rain at the seasons described, they will do so at the
" period of the next conception and in such a case the rain will
" be marked by a shower of hail. If milch animals should
" remain unmilked for a long period, the milk will become solidi-
" fied; so the rain which the clouds fail to yield at the proper
" season becomes congealed after a time in the sky. If a healthy
" pregnancy should be established in the five ways given below,
" the rainfall will extend to 100 yojanams [q.v.] all round; if
" one of the five indications be wanting, the extent will be
" reduced to one-half; if two should be wanting, to one-fourth,
" and so forth. If the pregnancy should be marked by all the
" five indications, the quantity of subsequent rainfall will be a
" dronam; if in such a case the rain should be attended by strong
" winds, the quantity will only be 3 audaks [q.v.]; an audak is
" one-fourth of a dronam or 50 pollums; if by lightning, the
" quantity will be 6 audaks; if then the sky should be overcast
" by clouds, the quantity of rainfall will be 9 audaks; if there
" should be the roar of thunder then 12 audaks of rain will fall.
" The signs of a healthy pregnancy are winds, rain, lightning,
" roar of thunder, and the appearance of clouds at the time of
" conception; in such a case the subsequent rainfall will be
" abundant; but if the rainfall should be excessive at the time of
" conception, there will only be a poor drizzling shower during the
" rainy season." Certain days again are considered Dharanam
or rain support days. The following is what Varauha mihiran
says of these :—" The four days commencing from the eighth day
" in the light half [shooclapacsham] of the month of jyeshtam
" [q.v.] are known as vayoo dharanam days, that is to say days
" from the winds that blow on which the nature of the health of
" the pregnancy of the rainclouds might be determined; if the
" winds should be gentle and agreeable, and then if the sky
" should be covered by fine bright clouds, there will be good
" rain; but if, in the said light half of jyeshtam, there should
" be a fall of rain in the four days when the moon passes through
" the asterism of from swauty [q.v.] to jyeshtay [q.v.], there
" will be rain in the rainy season, from shrauvanam [q.v.] to
" caurteecam [q.v.]; if the four dharanam days should be exactly
" alike in their indications, there will be happiness in the land;
" if different from one another, there will be misery and there
" will also be fear from robbers; if on the dharanam days the
" sun and moon should be covered by wet clouds attended by
" lightning and dust-storm, there will be good rain; if on the
" dharanam days the sky should be marked by beautiful light-
" ning alternately appearing in opposite benefic quarters, every
" species of crop [dhaunyam] will thrive; if on the same days
" there should fall a shower of rain attended by dust-storm
" [pishauch] or if children should in play blow through their
" mouths or birds sing or play in the dust or in water; if the
" halos round the sun and moon should appear bright and not
" much disfigured there will be rain and all crops will thrive;
" if, on the dharanam days, the clouds should appear beautiful
" and collected together with their course from left to right,
" there will be immediate rain and such rain will be exceedingly
" useful to the crops." The following are Varauha mihiran's
remarks on the connection between rain and the celestial
phenomena :—" Judging from the rain that falls on the days
" when the moon passes from the asterism of poorvashau-
" dham [q.v.] to that of moolam [q.v.] in the lunar month of
" jyeshtam and after the full-moon [powrnimay], an astronomer
" should predict the agricultural condition of the country
" as well as the quantity of rainfall in the coming rainy season.
" Falling rain should be collected in a vessel with a circular
" mouth, a cubit in diameter and the collected rain should be
" measured with a vessel whose capacity is an audak [q.v.],
" which is equal to 50 pollums [q.v.]; paraushavan defines an
" audak to be the capacity of a vessel with a circular mouth 20
" inches in diameter and whose depth is 8 inches. There will be

"continuous rain for as many days of the moon's course from poorvashaudham [q.v.] onwards as the number of asterisms, through which, when the moon passes, a shower of rain occurs just marking the earth, from the same asterism of poorvashaudham in the lunar month of jyeshtam [q.v.]; or there will be rain for as many days as there are number of rain drops sticking to the edge of the blades of grass; the quantity of subsequent rainfall can also be ascertained from such rain; if such first shower should be excessive there will be no rain in the rainy season; some writers say that the subsequent rainfall will be confined to the spot where the first shower falls; others say that the extent of the subsequent rainfall will be 10 yojanams all round. If there should be rain when the moon passes through certain asterisms from poorvashaudham to moolam in the lunar month of jyeshtam then there will also be rain when the moon passes through the same asterisms in the rainy season; if there should be no rain in the month of jyeshtam, there will be no rain in the rainy season; if there should be a fall of rain when the moon passes through the asterisms of hastam [q.v.], poorvashaudham [q.v.], mrigashiras [q.v.], chitta [q.v.], raivaty [q.v.] and shravishtam [dhanishtay] in the month of jyeshtam, there will fall 16 dronams of rain in the coming rainy season; if there should be a fall when the moon passes through shatabhishay [q.v.], jyeshtay [q.v.] and swauty [q.v.], in the month of jyeshtam, the subsequent rainfall will be 4 dronams; if there should be a fall when the moon passes through kritticay [q.v.], the quantity of subsequent rainfall will be 10 dronams; if there should be a fall of rain when the moon passes through shravanam [q.v.], magham [q.v.], anooraudhay [q.v.], bharany [q.v.] and moolam [q.v.], the quantity of subsequent rainfall will be 14 dronams; if when through poorva phalgoony [poobbam], the quantity will be 25 dronams; if when through poonarvas [q.v.], the quantity will be 20 dronams; if there should be a fall of rain, when the moon passes through the asterisms of vishaukham [q.v.] and oottarashaudham [q.v.] in the lunar month of jyeshtam, the quantity of subsequent rainfall will be 20 dronams; if when through aushlaisham [q.v.], the quantity will be 13 dronams; if when through oottarabhaudram [q.v.], oottaraphalgoony [ottaram] and rohiny [q.v.], the quantity will be 25 dronams; if there should be a fall of rain when the moon passes through the asterisms of poorvabhaudram [q.v.] and pooshyam [q.v.] in the lunar month of jyeshtam, the quantity of rainfall in the coming winter will be 15 dronams; if when through ashwiny [q.v.], the quantity will be 12 dronams; if when through ardray [q.v.], it will be 18 dronams; in all the above cases the subsequent rainfall depends upon the asterisms remaining unaffected by comets, meteors and the like from the month of jyeshtam to the rainy season. If the asterisms should suffer by the meeting together in them of the sun [sooryan], saturn [shany] and kait [q.v.], or by the course of mars [coojan] through them or by meteoric falls comets [dhoom kait] or planetary conjunctions, there will be neither rain nor prosperity in the land; but if benefic planets should pass through the asterisms or if the asterisms should remain unaffected in any of the ways described above, mankind will be happy." Aday mazhay, from (adai, tam. to shut) is continual rain. Alaungatty mazhay, from (álangatti, tam. hail) is a hailstorm. Caur mazhay, from (kár, tam. blackness) is rain in rainy season [caur] proper. Cautt mazhay, from (káttu, tam. wind + mazhai, tam. rain) is a storm. Coday mazhay, from (kódai, tam. hot season) is rain in the hot season, deemed pernicious. Munn maury mazhay, meaning mud rain, is a shower of sand or dust; cf. Pishauch. Toottal mazhay, from (túru, tam. to drizzle) is drizzling rain. Yidy mazhay, from (idi, tam. thunder) is a thunder storm.

MAZHOO (மழு - mazhu, *Tam.*). Means blunt. A battle-axe [parshoo]; weapon of Shiva [q.v.].

MAZRAH (مزرع - mazra, *Hind.*). From (zara, ar. to sow). A detached hamlet. A smaller division of Mowza [q.v.].

McDONALD'S CHOULTRY (மகுடன்சாவடி - magudansávadi, *Tam.*). Village, Railway station; Salem dist., Trichengode tal.; pop. 250; lat. 11° 33′; long. 78° 02′; height 786 feet; from Salem W.S.W. 14 miles; from Trichengode N.N.E. 14 miles. Named after Colonel Macdonald who built a choultry [q.v.] when he was stationed with troops at Shunkerrydroog.

M. E. (കൊല്ലമാണ്ടു - kollamántu, *Mal.*). Mal. from (kollam, mal. the place + ántu, mal. year). Abbreviation of Malabar era. Otherwise Quilon era, Parshooraman era [collam, mausam, saca]. See vol. I, 611.

MEADOW GRASS (مرغزار - marghzár, *Hind.*; నక్కతోకగడ్డి - nakkatókagaddi, *Tel.*). Tel. from (nakka, tel. fox + tóka, tel. tail + gaddi, tel. grass. Title otherwise Fox-tail grass. Botanically Poa species, graminaceæ [vricsham, 156]. The inflorescence in spreading or close panicles, the spikelets mostly several-flowered and without awns; outer glumes unequal, generally keeled, many-nerved; lower pales keeled, five-nerved, sometimes with three intermediate nerves; upper pales shorter and narrower, with inflexed membranous margins.

MECCA (مكه - makkah, *Ar.*). The capital of Arabia and sacred city of Mahomedans. Celebrated as the birth-place of Mahomed [q.v.] and the site of Caaba [q.v.]. Prefixed to plant names as having been introduced by pilgrims from mecca.——*Mecca hay* (كاه مكه - káhimakkah, Pers.). Title from food of cattle. Same as Roussa grass.——*Mecca wheat* (گندم مكه - gandumimakkah, Pers.). Same as Mecca cholum.

MEEN (मीन - mína, *San.*; மீன் - mín, *Tam.*). From (mí, san. to move). A fish [matsyam].——*Meenachel* (മീനച്ചിൽ - mínaççil, Mal.). From (mín, mal. fish + chál, mal. channel).—"*a*" Talook; Travancore state, Cottayam division. Contains ninety caras [q.v.] or villages; pop. 57,102; sub-division. Subdivided into six praverties [q.v.]. Its greatest length N. to S. is 14 miles and the greatest breadth E. to W. is 11 miles. Bounded N. and E. by Todoopoya talook, S. by Tungacherry, Cottayam and Yaittmanore talooks, and W. by Mooatpoya talook. Hilly; soil very fertile. Areca-nut [q.v.] forms an important article of trade in this part of the country, as the soil is peculiarly adapted to its growth. Pepper [q.v.] dry ginger [q.v.] and turmeric [country saffron] are also produced. The soil is irrigated by the Meenachel river.—"*b*" Village; Travancore state, Cottayam division, Meenachel tal.; pop. 8,669; lat. 9° 41′; long. 76° 44′; from Laulam S.S.E. 3 miles; from Trivandrum N.N.W. 82 miles; from the sea E. 27 miles. Consists of a few straggling Nayar [q.v.] habitations and a pagoda [q.v.].—"*c*" River; Travancore state, Cottayam division, Meenachel, Cottayam and Yaittmanore talooks. Formed by the union of several mountain streams which descend from the Codiyattore and Coodamoorty mountains and unite at Yirattipettah. On passing Cottayam the waters dispersed in minor channels unite with the Vembanaud lake by several embouchures. Pullykidangore and Cottayam are on its banks. Length 35 miles. 26 miles are navigable for small boats during a considerable portion of the year; they cannot ascend beyond Yirattipettah, although timber is floated down from some distance above that place. While passing through Meenachel talook, both banks are well planted with areca-nut trees.——*Meenautchy* (மீனாட்சி - minádchi, Tam.). From (above + ádchi, tam. rule). The name is often considered to mean fish-eyed on the analogy of Caumautchy or wanton-eyed, Vishaulautchy or large-eyed. The true meaning is fish rule. Goddess worshipped especially at Madura and regarded as a form of Parvaty [q.v.]. Hindoo 2nd or pers. name. Applied to males and females. As a female name it is shortened into meena and meenoo, otherwise meenaumbah [peyar]. This was the name of widow of Chokkanautan, twelfth Naick [q.v.] ruler of Madura, 1731–1736, who killed herself when Chundah sahib conquered Madura. See vol. I (121); II, 137.——*Meenavan* (மீனவன் - mínavan, Tam.). Means fish-flag man. Title of Paundy [q.v.] rulers. The fish was their special cognizance [meenautchy]. The particular fish is a carp [kenday] or barbel found in the larger rivers, mahseer [mahseer carp] of English sportsmen. Same is used in heraldry of N. india.——*Minicoy* (മെനക്കായത്ത് - menakkáyat, Mal.). From (mín, mal. fish + kayam, mal. deep pool). Island; Malabar dist.; lat. 8° 20′ to 8° 24′ N.; long. 72° 58′ to 73° 03′ E.; from Calicut S.W. 272 miles. Between the Laccadives and Maldives. Though nominally one of the Laccadives as being Cannanore property, it belongs ethnologically to the Maldives which are attached to Ceylon. Separated from the head of the Maldives proper by the Eight-degree channel, 68 miles in breadth, which is adopted by vessels bound to the Malabar coast or Ceylon during the south-west monsoon [q.v.]. The island is a narrow strip of low land, seven miles long, and less than a mile in width, in direction N.E. and S.W. From its N.W. face an irregular coral [moongah] reef projects; on the S.E. side there is no reef [atoll]. Within 100 yards of the reef no bottom is found. The reef encloses a large lagoon [cauyal], which has three entrances from the sea, one with a depth of two fathoms. It abounds in turtle [aumay] and fish [matsyam]. The soil is coarse powdered coral with a little vegetable matter. The island is flat, and no part is destitute of vegetation; the south side is thickly covered with tall cocoanut [q.v.] trees, visible from a vessel 10 or 12 miles; the north inhabited by a people of Maldive race and language. Formerly under the Maldive sultans but since the seventeenth century it has been subject to the rajahs of Cannanore, and is at present the personal property of Ally rajah. The islanders export fish, coir [q.v.] and cocoanuts to Goa, the Malabar ports, Ceylon and Bengal; bringing home chiefly rice [q.v.], salt [ooppoo], spices and cotton cloth. To south of the main island and separated from it by a channel about one-fourth of a mile wide, is the small island of Viringilly, to which small-pox patients are transported. The island is demarcated into nine large blocks;—the great north Pundauram; north Mowlood grant, leper settlement; south Mowlood land; Malikhana land; central Pundauram; Attiry pundauram, containing most of the village site; eastern block, containing rest of the village Tottams; and Pundauram plots and great southern Pundauram. The village is divided, for purposes of administration, into Attiries [q.v.], *i.e.*, sea-shore or male assemblies; and Varaungies [q.v.] or female assemblies. Of the latter, there are ten. The land is the property of the community and is managed by the Pundauram. Private property in the soil is unknown, but improvements, such as houses, cocoanut and other trees, &c., belong to the persons who make them. Every tree in the inhabited part of the island has the mark of its owner cut upon it. The inhabitants are divided into four classes, viz., Malikhanas, corresponding to Carnaver [q.v.] of the other islands; Maulims [q.v.] or pilots; Takkar or sailors and boatmen; Melacherries or tree-climbers. In personal appearance and in their dress, manners and customs they differ considerably from the inhabitants of the other islands. They are much smaller in stature, darker, and have very round faces. In disposition they are quiet and obliging. The customs are in many respects remarkable. One without parallel amongst any society of Mussalmans is that the men are monogamous. The women appear in public freely with their heads uncovered and take the lead in almost everything except navigation. Every woman in the island is dressed in silk. Their gowns fit closely round the neck and reach to the ankles. The upper classes wear red silk and earrings of peculiar fashion. The Melacherry women are restricted to the use of a dark-striped silk [puttoo] of a coarser quality. The language spoken is Mahl [q.v.]. The inhabitants are exclusively Mahomedans. The cultivation is almost entirely the cocoanut palm. Marine product is the maas fish, of which large quantities are annually cured and exported chiefly to Ceylon. Cattle cannot be bred in the island, as they are killed by mosquitoes [q.v.] and a kind of poisonous grass. The few to be found on the island are imported for slaughter at religious ceremonies. The manufactures are the same as those of other islands. Coir is a little dark in color, but much finer in quality. One-sixth of the adults perished in a cyclone in 1867. A light-house was erected in 1885. See vol. I (51), 53.

MEENAUR (مینار - mínár, *Hind.*). Tower of a mosque [musjid]. Cf. Minaret.

MEER (میر - mír, *Pers.*). Contraction of ameer, lord, chief or head of a department. Tribal prefix attached to the names of Mahomedans of the Syed [q.v.] class. Also part of lacab; as Meer aulam, lord of world [ism].——*Meeraun* (میران - mírán, Hind.). From (mír, ar. lord). Lacab of the chief saint [abdool cawder]. Taken as alam; as Meeraun hoossain, double alam [ism].——*Meeraun sahib* (میران صاحب - míránsáhib, Hind.). Name of saint buried at Nagore. Also known as Cawder wally [q.v.].——*Meer moonshee* (میر منشی - mírmunshí, Hind.). Chief secretary.——*Meer zauda* (میرزاده - mírzádah, Hind.). From (mír, ar. lord + zádah, pers. born). Tribal surname of the children of Moghuls [q.v.].——*Mirzah* (مرزا - mirzá, Hind.). From (mír, ar. lord + zah, pers. offspring). A prince. Moghuls [q.v.] prefix this title to their names and add Beg after them, as Mirzah mahomed beg.——*Mirzayee* (مرزائی - mirzaí, Hind.). From (mirzá, pers. lord); moghul title. A cotton [q.v.] or muslin [q.v.] jacket, with long loose sleeves and open cuffs; worn under the cabah [q.v.].

MEHKARY (مہکری - mehkarí, *Hind.*). From (mehkr, ar. place in arabia); whence emigrated. Lacab of a class of Mahomedans [ism]. Of the sect of nivayats [q.v.].

MEHMAN (میمن - maiman, *Hind.*). From (momin, ar. true believer). Converts from Hindooism. They are Soonnee [q.v.] mahomedans, and wear a peculiar Scinde hat. Have settled themselves in Madras as traders and merchants.

MEHR (مہر - mehr, *Pers.*). Sun, love. Prefixed to an alam forms a lacab; as Mehr ally, ally's love [ism].

MEIDA (میدا - maidá, *Hind.*). Flour.——*Meida lukdy* (गजपिप्पली - gajapippalí, San.; मैदालकडी - maidálakadí, Mahr.; مغاث هند - mughásihind, Ar.; کلز - kilz, Pers.; میدا لکڑی - maidálakrí, Hind. and Dec.; నారమామిడి - náramámidi, Tel.; முசைப்பேயெட்டி - musaippéyetti, Tam.). Title from deccany. San. means elephant long pepper [q.v.]. Mahr. from hindostany. Hind. from (maidá, hind. flour + lakrí, hind. wood). Tel. from (nára, tel. fibre + mámidi, tel. mango tree, mangifera indica, linn.). Mahr. also (ránaámbá), meaning wild mango, properly spondias mangifera, willd. Tel. also (narrachettu), meaning fibre + tree; (meda); (narramámidi), meaning fibrous mango. Tam. also (maithálagadi); (pisinbattaiççedi), meaning gum + bark + tree. Title otherwise Fibre mango, Wild mango. Botanically Tetranthera monopetala, roxb., lauraceæ [vricsham, 111]. Tree, middling size; dark-greenish, rusty-colored smooth bark; leaves alternate, short-petioled, oblong, entire, smooth on the upper surface, pubescent beneath; smell like cinnamon [q.v.]; flowers male and female; peduncles axillary, numerous, short; flowers small, yellowish green. Bark mildly astringent, balsamic, used by hill people in diarrhœa, also applied to wounds and bruises. Leaves are given to silk [puttoo] worms; berries yield an oil, used for ointment and candles. Wood olive-grey, soft, not durable; is readily attacked by insects; aromatic. Other common species are:—Cordifolia, small tree; Glabrata, willow-leaved laurel; Glauca; Læta; Laurifolia; tree; many-flowered; one of the best known and most popular of native drugs, used internally, demulcent in diarrhœa and dysentery, externally emollient application to bruises, &c.; oil from berries used in rheumatism; bark triturated in water or milk or dry applied to bruises; wood greyish-brown or olive-grey, moderately hard, shining, close and even-grained, seasons well, durable, and is not attacked by insects; there are varieties citrifolia and platyphylla. Laurifolia, var. roxburghii; small tree; many-flowered; bears small, greenish, yellowish flowers; comes from chittagong, cochin-china, and java; the fruit is globose, black, and about the size of a pea [calauyam]; fruit yields a kind of greasy exudation, from which the chinese manufacture candles of a bad quality; Ligustrina, small tree; many-flowered; there is a variety celastroides; Oleoides; Panamonja; Tomentosa, or ganapaty tree; many-flowered; found in all the western forests; wood soft greyish-yellow with an unpleasant odour when fresh cut; there is a variety glabrescens; Venulosa; Wightii.

MEIDAUN (میدان - maidán, *Hind.*). From the persian. An open space, parade ground.

MEILAM (మైల - maila, *Tel.*). Pollution [mal].——*Meilavaram* (మైలవరము - mailavaramu, Tel.). From (maila, tel. pollution + pura, san. city).—"*a*" Zemindarry; Kistna dist., Bezwada tal.; square miles 135. Comprises the greater portion of the old Havelly [q.v.] lands of Condapully pergunnah [q.v.]. The Soorinainy family came to this neighbourhood about A.D. 1670 as cultivators, and rented villages from the Killadar [q.v.] of Condapully. Later Soorinainy veucatapaty assumed the title of Moostaujar and his son, Soorinain narayanan, took the title of zemindar [q.v.], claimed to be independent of Condapully, and built the fort at Meilavaram.—"*b*" Village; Kistna district, Meilavaram zemindarry; pop. 4,481; lat. 16° 46′; long. 80° 41′; from Bezwada N. 17 miles; from Guntoor N.N.E. 35 miles; from Madras N. 253 miles; from Masulipatam N.W. 51 miles; from Vinoocondah N.E. 75 miles.

MEIPAUD (మైపాడు - maipádu, *Tel.*). From (mai, tel. sidewise + pádu, tel. village). Village, Port; Nellore dist., Nellore tal.; pop. 2,151; acres 2,212; lat. 14° 30′; long. 80° 12′; from Kistnapatam N. 15 miles; from Madras N. 96 miles; from Nellore E.N.E. 13 miles; from Varny S.S.E. 10 miles. On the coast on Buckingham canal [q.v.] and near mouth of Pennair. Open roadstead. Visited by many vessels. Grain is the chief article of export. Is the market for grain grown in the Pennair delta [conamoogam]. Formerly trade in cloths, &c.

MEL (மெல் - mel, *Tam.*). Soft.——*Mellinam* (மெல்லினம் - mellinam, Tam.). From (mel, tam. soft + inam, tam. class). Soft letter. One of the three Tamul classes of consonants [mey]. ங், ஞ், ண், ந், ம், ன். Each letter is the corresponding nasal to the strong class. Only ஞ், ந், and ம் are initial. All except ங் may be final. See vol. I (52); II, 205, 209.

MELLORPETTAH (మిల్లరుపేట - millarupéta, *Tel.*). From (name of a former collector + péta, tel. suburb). Suburb of Bellary included in Brucepettah.

MELOE (میلو - mílo, *Hind.*). Same as Telini fly.

MELON TREE (കൎമ്മൂസ് - karmmós, *Mal.*). Title from fleshy fruit. Same as Papaw.

MERAH (ಮೇರೆ - mére, *Can.*; మేర - méra, *Tel.*; மேரை - mérai, *Tam.*). Boundary, limit. A portion of the crop given as a perquisite to the holders of a proprietary right [cawnyautchy, mirass] in the village lands, or to the hereditary village officers and servants [balootah], out of the common stock from the threshing-floor [calam].——*Merangy* (మేరంగి - mérangi, Tel. merangi *). From (méra, tel. boundary + angu, tel. beauty). Zemindarry, Village; Vizagapatam dist., Parvatipore division; pop. 3,867; acres 695; lat. of village 18° 49′; long. 83° 36′; from Parvatipore E. 9 miles; from Vizagapatam N.N.E. 78 miles. When Vishwambhara deo reigned in Jeypore, the Zemindar of Merangy rebelled and fled to Parlakimedy, whence he was given up on Jeypore agreeing to cede Buttaly talook to Kimedy. He was then put to death, his estate being made over to Jugganath rauz, who was required to marry his widow. Jugganath rauz was then styled Shatricherla. The estate was later incorporated with Cooroopaum and brought under Vizianagram, but in 1795 restored to old family. There were numerous disputes and disturbances in the family in early part of century, one Veerabhadra rauz being specially concerned. This man was in 1821 imprisoned in Chingleput where he lately died. The estate was bought in by Government for arrears in 1833. At this time the three principal leaders in the Palcondah rebellion known as the Attsapavalsa brothers were still at large. The Diwaun of Merangy attacked the rebels near the village of Gorye. After a desperate conflict, all three brothers were killed, and their forces scattered. For this service Government restored Merangy to young Jugganath rauz, the son of the last Zemindar. The family belongs to the Condarauz tribe, of the same branch as the Cooroopaum and Andra zemindars. Ooriya [q.v.] is their vernacular, but they cultivate Teloogoo [q.v.].

MERAKA (మెరక - meraka, *Tel.*). From (mirru, tel. elevation). High ground. Suffix in place names.

MERGUI (مرگوئی - marguí, *Hind.*). Southernmost district of Lower burmah.——*Mergui arrowroot* (காறாக்கருணை - kárákkarunai, Tam.). Same as Otaheite salep.

MERIAH (మెరయ - meraya, *Tel.*). A human victim. The rite among the Khonds [q.v.] of sacrificing human beings to the earth god. The practice was put a stop to in 1836; see vol. I (51).

MEROO (मेरु - méru, *San.*). From (mi, san. to fix). Otherwise Maha meroo or great meroo, Soomeroo or good meroo. The terrestrial orb [golam]; yolk of the mundane egg [bramhaundam]. Indian Olympus. Supposed centre of earth [bhoomy] in far north, having on one of its summits the paradise Keilausam [q.v.], from whence the seven patriarchs [rishy] came. The form of the mountain is that of the seed-cup of the sacred lotus flower [nelumbo]. The sun [sooryan] turns round it, hence resembles north pole [oottara dhroovam]. Its height is 84,000 yojanams [q.v.], 16,000 of which are below the surface of the earth. See vol. I (2), (11). There is a Tamul proverb:—பூர்வோத்தரம் மேரு காத்திரம்போல் இருக்கிறது—"His pedigree is the size of Mount meroo." Meroo is sometimes held to mean the highland of Tartary, immediately to the north of the Himalaya mountains.

MEROOGENNEY (कुकुभ - kukkubha, *San.*; روغن - raughan, *Pers.*; وارنس - várnas, *Dec.*; ಮೆರುಗೆಣ್ಣೆ - merugenne, *Can.*; ರೋಗಣೆಣ್ಣೆ - róganenne, *Too.*; మెరుగునూనె - merugunúne, *Tel.*; மெருகெண்ணெய் - merugenney, *Tam.*). Title from tamul. Can. from (merugu, can. polish + enne, can. oil). Too. from (róganu, too. polish + enne, too. oil). Tel. from (merugu, tel. glitter + núne, tel. oil). Tam. from (merugu, tel. glitter + ennéy, tam. oil). Varnish [gond, rangh]. Various substances used in solution with spirit, or in the natural condition, or liquified by heat. Of the commercial varnishes the following are the more important here in use:—Lac or spirit varnish [lac]; Singhalese varnish, semecarpus anacardium, linn. f. [marking-nut]; Japanese varnish, rhus succedanea, linn. [red-lac sumach].

MESHAMSHANA (മെശംശന - meshamshana, *Mal.*). Deacon with the Malabar syrian christians [syrian].

MESQUIT (مسقیط - miskít, *Mexican*). Title otherwise Texas algaroba, Texas mesquit. Botanically Prosopis [shivah] glandulosa, tor., leguminosæ [vricsham, 48]. Introduced. Interior of pods filled with sweet pulp; this by fermentation and boiling, makes a pleasant drink; seeds or beans, powdered and mixed with water, forms a paste, which, on being dried in the sun, makes an article of food, and keeps for a considerable time. Wood exceedingly hard and durable, with a fine grain; used for furniture, picket poles, and charcoal [adoopp kary].——*Screw mesquit* (مسقیطپیچدار - miskítipechdár, Hind.). Title from shape of pods. Title otherwise Californian screw-bean mesquit, Screw bean, Tornillo bean, True mesquit bean. Botanically Prosopis [shivah] pubescens, bth., leguminosæ [vricsham, 48]. Introduced. Beans or pods, screw-shaped, contain much saccharine and nutritious matter from which molasses [jaggery] is made by boiling; pods form important article of food to natives; largely devoured by cattle; great caution required in their use as fodder for horses [ghorah].

METHEL (میتهل - methal, *Hind.*). Same as Poison nut.

METRAUN (മെത്രാൻ - metrán, *Mal.*). From syriac, corruption of metropolitan. Bishop of the Syrian church in Malabar.

METT (మెట్ట - metta, *Tel.*; மேட்டு - mettu, *Tam.*). From (médu, tam. high ground) [mail, maud, mode]. Ground not capable of irrigation [gaddu, moott]. So a custom-house [chowky], as placed high for supervision.——*Metla* (మెట్ల - metla, Tel.). From (metta, tel.). Locative plural. Mound. Suffix in place names; as Narimetla, meaning the mound of the women.——*Metta* (మెట్ట - metta, Tel.). Dry land. Plant first term. Ex., where transl. is of second term:—Cassia alata (mettatámara), nelumbium speciosum; Curcuma angustifolia (mettatámara), nelumbium speciosum; Ipomæa digitata (mettapálatíga), milk + creeper; Ipomæa sepiaria (mettatúti), ipomæa aquatica; Ocimum adscendens (mettatulasi), ocimum sanctum. See gloss. paragraphs.——*Mettapolliem* (மேட்டுப்பாளையம் - méttuppálaiyam, Tam. mettupálaiyam *). From (médu, tam. high ground + pálaiyam, tam. fortified village).—"*a*" Deputy tahsildarry, Coimbatore district. Pay Rs. 70.—"*b*" Village, Deputy tahsildar's station, Railway station; Coimbatore dist., Coimbatore tal.; pop. 614; acres 1,178; lat. 11° 18′; long. 76° 59′; height 1,070 feet; from Coimbatore N. 22 miles; from Erode W. 53 miles; from Madras W.S.W. 256 miles; from Ootacamund E.S.E. 18 miles; from Pollachy N. 44 miles; from Suttimungalam S.W. 25 miles. Terminus of Neilgherry branch of Madras railway, and starting of Neilgherry ghaut [q.v.]. Railway projected from here to Coonoor. Hot and unhealthy. Bhawanny runs by and gives fishing. Game of all sorts abundant. 100 dolmens [coday cull] in fields in neighbourhood, showing existence of old population at foot of Neilgherries.——*Mettavazhy* (മേട്ടുവഴി - méttuvazhi, Mal.). From (métu, mal. high + vazhi, mal. way). A path through a mountain [ghaut].——*Mettoocauran* (மெட்டுக்காரன் - mettukkáran, Tam.). From (above + káran, tam. possessor). Means custom house man. One who examines persons entering or leaving a village.——*Mettoocherry* (மேட்டுச்சேரி - méttuççéri, Tam.). From (médu, tam. high ground + shéri, tam. village). Village; Neilgherry dist., Todanaad division; lat. 11°24′; long. 76° 44′; from Ootacamund W. ½ a mile from the bazaar. Hamlet forming part of Ootacamund, and site of the Roman catholic church. The first church was near Nediwuttam. The next was at Caundal. The present is the third. There is a convent of the Society of Marie Réparatrice in a building adjoining the church, established in January 1875, and bearing the name of Nazareth.——*Mitta* (మిట్ట - mitta, Tel.). Mound [mode]. Distinguish from Mittah.

MEY (மெய் - mey, *Tam.*). Means the body. A consonant. Also truth. In Tamul there are eighteen consonants, divided into three classes:—"*a*" Vallinam [q.v.] or hard consonants are க், ச், ட், த், ப், ற்;—"*b*" Mellinam [q.v.] or soft consonants are ங், ஞ், ண், ந், ம், ன்;—"*c*" Yidaiyinam [q.v.] or middle consonants are ய், ர், ல், வ், ழ், ள் [bhaushay]. See vol. II, 205.——*Menaricam* (మేనరికము - ménarikamu, Tel.). From (ménu, tel. body + rikamu, tel. suffix meaning state). State of being connected through the body of the parents. The relationship between a man's son and the man's sister's daughter. First cousins. Among the Comaties [q.v.] these are usually married to each other.——*Meynyaunapooram* (மெய்ஞானபுரம் - meyñánappuram, Tam. megnánapuram *). From (mey, tam. true + ñána, san. knowledge + pura, san. town). Village, Post office; Tinnevelly dist., Tencaray tal.; pop. 2,049; acres 1,181; lat. 8° 28′; long. 78° 03′; from Shreeveicoontam S.S.E. 13 miles; from Tinnevelly S.E. 28 miles; from the sea W. 8 miles. Early Protestant mission station. Fine church built in 1837, the spire of which is a landmark.

MEZ (میز - mez, *Hind.*). Table. Corr. of English 'mess.'

MHOTE (उद्घाटन - udghátana, *San.*; موٹھ - moth, *Hind.*; ಕಪಲಿ - kapali, *Can.*; మోటు - mótu, *Tel.*; ഏത്തക്കൊട്ട - éttakkotta, *Mal.*; கவலை - kavalai, *Tam.*). Title from hindostany. San. from (ud, san. prefix meaning up + ghat, san. to move). Mal. from (éttam, mal. rising + kotta, mal. basket). The large bucket of a draw well [capiley, picottah, yaittachaul].

MIDDEY (మిద్దె - midde, *Tel.*; மெத்தை - mettai, *Tam.*). From (mída, tel. above). A house with an upper story, with a flat or terraced roof.

MIH (मिह् - mih, *San.*). To sprinkle.——*Maigham* (मेघ - mégha, San.). From (mih, san. to sprinkle). Cloud. According to ancient shastrams, clouds are known by particular names which are either seven or nine in number; and special characters, meteorological and astrological are predicated of each by ancient writers.——*Maigha recoola poda* (మేఘరేకులపొడ - megharékulapoda, Tel.). From (mégha, san. cloud + réku, tel. scale + podu, tel. spot). Cynophis helena, colubridæ [paumb], ophidii colubriformes, ophidia [sarpam], reptilia [sarpy, 17], of naturalists [jantoo].——*Maisham* (मेष - mésha, San.). From (mish, san. to sprinkle). Ram.—"*a*" The first sign [raushy] of the solar zodiac [raushy chuckram] whether fixed or moveable [mausam]. European Aries.—"*b*" The month in which the sun [sooryan] enters the fixed Maisham, or April-May [ayanam, maunam] as assumed by the Hindoos.—"*c*" The first arc of 30° in any circle [chuckram].——*Maishauyanam* (मेषायन - mésháyana, San.). From (mesha, san. aries + ayana, san. equinoctial point). Vernal equinoctial point [ayanam, vishoo]. Maishauyana mundalam is the equinoctial colure.——*Meetah* (میٹھا - míthá, Hind.). From (mishta, san. sweet). Sweet. Plant first term. Ex., where translation is of second term:—Aconitum ferox (mítházahar), poison; Citrus medica, var. limetta (míthálimba), (míthálímú) and (míthánímbú), lime, citrus; Diospyros tomentosa (míthátendú), diospyros embryopteris, from berries; Glycirrhiza glabra (míthílakrí), stick; Ipomæa batatas (míthálú), potato; Sesamum indicum (míthátel), oil; Wrightia tinctoria (míthaindarjaukájhár), holarrhena antidysenterica + tree. See gloss. paragraphs.——*Mihiran* (मिहिर - mihira, San.). From (mih, san. to rain down moisture). An epithet of the sun [sooryan, varauha mihiran].——*Mithie* (مٹھائی - mithái, Hind.). From (míthá, hind. sweet). An intoxicating sweetmeat [halwah].

MIHRAUB (محراب - mihráb, *Hind.*). From (harb, ar. fight); a person praying is said to war with the devil. Niche in a mosque [musjid] where the priest [imaum] prays before the congregation [jamaut] with his face towards Mecca. Also any niche.

MILK (ملک - milk, *Hind.*). Property [maul].——*Milkiyat* (ملکیت - milkiyat, Hind.). Proprietary right [cawnyauchy, mirass, sawmyam].——*Milkyat i istimrar* (ملکیت استمرار - milkiyatiistimrár, Hind.). From (milkiyat, hind. proprietary right + istimrár, ar. continued). Proprietary right in perpetuity.

MILK-HEDGE (वज्री - vajrí, *San.*). Title from milky juice of plant. San. from (vajra, san. adamant); from hard spines. Title otherwise Devil's milk, Gum thistle, Spurge, Wolf's milk. Cf. Tiger's milk. Botanically the Euphorbia genus, euphorbiaceæ [vricsham, 118]. Herbaceous in temperate regions but shrubby or tree-like here; these plants resemble in having a milky juice and in the arrangement of flowers, which are monœcious, collected into heads, surrounded by bracts, constituting an involucre ; fruit consists of three single-seeded carpels. Distinguish from opuntia [prickly pear]. The species best known to the natives are :—antiquorum [square milk-hedge], cattimandoo [cuttimandoo], indica [ammaun putcharisy], nereifolia [leafy milk-hedge], tirucalli [round milk-hedge], tortilis [twisting milk-hedge]. Other s. indian species indigenous are :—acaulis, bracteolaris, corrigioloides, dracunculoides, elegans, erythroclada, fimbriata, halophila, notoptera, oreophila, pulcherrima, pycnostegia, sanguinea, serpens, trigona, zornioides. There is a Tamul proverb :—கள்ளிபெருத்து என்ன ? காய் உண்டா நிழல் உண்டா ?—"What if the cully grow large ? "has it any fruit or any shade ?" There is another :—கள்ளிக் கொம்புக்கு வெள்ளிப்பூண் கட்டினது போல—"Like "attaching a silver ferule to a cully stick." And another :—கரும்பிலும் தேன் இருக்கும் கள்ளியிலும் பால்இருக்கும்—"There is honey [shahad] in sugar-cane [q.v.], there is "sap in milk-hedge." Term Milk-hedge includes also Cacalia, Echium, Opuntia, and Sarcostemma species.——*Buffalo tongue milk-hedge* (ఎనుబోతునాలుకజెముడు - ennbótunálukajemudu, Tel.). Same as Gowzabaun.——*Creeping milk-hedge* (கொடிக்கள்ளி - kodikkalli, Tam.). Same as Somam.——*Leafy milk-hedge* (स्नुहि - snuhi, San. ; निवडुंग - nivadunga, Mahr. ; पानानिवलि - pánánivali, Conc. ; سيج - síj, Hind. ; کتےکی جیب کا پتا - kuttekíjibkápattá, Dec. ; ಎಲೆಕಳ್ಳಿ - elekalli, Can. ; ಇರೆಕಳ್ಳಿ - irekalli, Too. ; ఆకుజెముడు - ákujemudu, Tel. ; ഇലക്കള്ളി - ilakkalli, Mal. ; පතුක් - patuk, Singh. ; இலைக்கள்ளி - ilaikkalli, Tam.). Title from leaves on toothed shoots. San. from (snuh, san. to vomit), from being an emetic. Hind. from sanscrit. Dec. from (kuttá, hind. dog + jíb, hind. tongue + pattá, hind. leaf). Can. from (ele, can. leaf + kalli, can. milk-hedge). Too. from (ire, too. leaf + kalli, too. milk-hedge). Tel. from (áku, tel. leaf + jemudu, tel. milk-hedge plant). Mal. from tamul. Tam. from (ilai, tam. leaf + kalli, tam. euphorbia tirucalli, linn.). San. also (pattrasnuk), meaning leaf + euphorbia antiquorum, linn. ; (shvarasaná), meaning dog's tongue. Dec. also (kuttékejíbkísendh), meaning dog-tongue-shaped milk-hedge. Title otherwise Dog's tongue, Five-angled spurge, Holy milk-hedge, Leafy tree spurge, Oleander-leaved spurge. Botanically Euphorbia [milk-hedge] nereifolia, linn., euphorbiaceæ [vricsham, 118]. Alias Euphorbia ligularia. Tree, 20 feet ; young shoots five-sided, somewhat spirally disposed, and armed with large teeth, each of which supports a leaf, and a pair of short, black, stipulary thorns ; leaves alternate about the ends of the branches, wedge-shaped, waved, fleshy ; peduncles solitary between the serratures of the angles of the branchlets, one to three dichotomous, with a larger sessile flower in the forks ; petals five, fringed with a ragged margin inserted into the calyx ; flowers greenish yellow ; cultivated near villages ; has a whitish dead appearance, except during the rains ; every part abounds with the acrid milky juice. Plant is sacred to snake [naugam] deities ; natives offer milk and sugar, praying to be delivered from snake-bites. Root mixed with black pepper [q.v.] employed medicinally in snake-bites, both internally and externally ; on the western coast bark of root boiled in ricewater and arrack [q.v.] considered useful in dropsy ; root quoted in pharm., but non-officinal. Juice used to remove warts and cutaneous eruptions ; also as purge and deobstruent, in visceral obstructions and dropsical affections ; also mixed with margosa [neem] oil, as external application in cases of contracted limb. Leaves simply warmed in the fire will promote urine, while their juice warmed is a good remedy in ear-ache, and is occasionally rubbed over the eyes to remove dimness of sight. The pulp of the stem, mixed with green ginger [q.v.] is given to persons who have been bitten by mad dogs, previous to the appearance of hydrophobia. Veidyans [q.v.] purify arsenic [paushaunam] as follows :—they make a hole in the trunk of this tree, filling it up with solid arsenic ; then after being covered with the bark of the same plant, the whole is exposed to a strong fire, until the external parts of the trunk are completely charred, when the arsenic is taken out and is fit for use. Forms a good fence round fields ; gives ashes used as mordant [cauram].——*Round milk-hedge* (दण्डस्नुहा - dandasnuhá, San. ; वज्रदुह - vajraduhá, Mahr. ; बड्डिनिवलि - baddinivali, Conc. ; زقوم هند - zakkúmihind, Ar. ; زقو نیاه هندی - zakúniyáihindí, Pers. ; کونپل سینڈھ - konpalsondh, Hind. ; کاڑی کی سینڈھ - káríkísendh, Dec. ; ಕಳ್ಳಿಮರ - kallimara, Can. ; ಕೋಡುಕಳ್ಳಿ - kódukalli, Too. ; జెముడు - jemudu, Tel. ; ଲୋଧୋକସିଜୁ - lodhokasiju, Oor. ; കോൽക്കള്ളി - kólkalli, Mal. ; නවහන්දි - navahandi, Singh. ; கள்ளி - kalli, Tam.). Title from branches not being angular, but round and polished. San. from (danda, san. stick + snuhá, san. euphorbia antiquorum, linn.). Mahr. from (vajra, san. diamond + dugdha, san. milk) ; hard, milky plant. Ar. from (zakkúm, ar. a thorny tree + hindí, hind. indian). Pers. from arabic. Hind. from (konpal, hind. tender shoot + sendh, hind. milk-hedge). Dec. from (kárí, hind. stick + sendh, hind. milk-hedge). Can. from (kalli, can. milk-hedge + mara, can. tree). Too. from (kódu, too. branch + kalli, too. milk-hedge). Tel. from (simhunda, san. milk-hedge plant). Mal. from (kól, mal. stick + kalli, mal. milk-hedge). Singh. from (nava, san. nine + handi, singh. joint). Tam. compare prickly pear. San. also (trikantaka), meaning three-thorned. Hind. also (sehnd), meaning milk-hedge ; (síj), from sanscrit ; (shirthohar), meaning milk-hedge plant. Dec. also (bárkísend), meaning hedge euphorbia. Can. also (mundukalli), meaning joint + milk-hedge ; (kódukalli), meaning branch + milk-hedge ; (bontekalli), meaning entangled + milk-hedge. Tel. also (kádajemudu), meaning stick + milk-hedge plant. Mal. also (tirukkalli), meaning twisted milk-hedge ; properly euphorbia tortilis, rottl. ; (kátterumakkalli), meaning wild buffalo + milk plant. Tam. also (kombukkalli), meaning stick + euphorbia tirucalli, linn. ; from cylindrical branches. Title otherwise Common tree spurge, Round tree spurge. Botanically Euphorbia [milk-hedge] tirucalli, linn., euphorbiaceæ [vricsham, 118]. Specific name from tamal ; really applies to Euphorbia tortilis. Alias Tithymalus tirucalli. Tree unarmed, 20 feet ; leaves alternate, remote, sessile, linear, smooth ; flowers at the end of the twigs and in the divisions of the branchlets, crowded, sub-sessile, pale yellow ; calyx campanulate, with three to five flat peltate horizontal segments ; capsule villous, five-lobed, three-celled ; seeds solitary ; common hedge plant ; branches round, polished, very lactescent, leaves small ; milk sap is like that of antiquorum [square milk-hedge], evaporated, resembles indian rubber [q.v.]. Fresh juice is vesicatory ; juice mixed with butter is given as a purgative on west coast ; juice quoted in pharm., but non-officinal ; decoction of tender branches is given in colic. Goats [vellaud] eat this plant. The whole used as manure ; fish are destroyed by placing pieces in water [common emetic nut, indian berry, marotty, sooptee, tejbul, zanzibar indigo] ; the bark and small branches are employed in dyeing leather [chamrah] black ; much planted as a hedge ; hung up in rooms keeps off eye-flies ; burnt ashes are used for preparing dye [shauyam]. When found of sufficient size the wood is used for tile [wode] and terrace dunnage ; wood is white, close grained, and rather hard ; also used for veneering and for toys. The root of old shrubs is adapted for gun-stocks, but plants of sufficient age are seldom met mith.——*Snake milk-hedge* (నాగజెముడు - nágajemudu, Tel.) From leaves like cobra hood. Same as Prickly pear.——*Square milk-hedge* (वज्री - vajrí, San. ; निवलि - nivali, Mahr. ; निवलि - nivali, Conc. ; زقو نیاه هندی - zakúniyáihindí, Pers. ; تدهارا سینڈھ - tidhárásendh. Hind. ; ಜೆಡೆಕಳ್ಳಿ - jedekalli, Can. ; ದಾರೆಕಳ್ಳಿ - dárékalli, Too. ; బొంతజెముడు - bontajemudu, Tel. ; ଦୋକାନାସିଜୁ - dokánásiju, Oor. ; ചതുരക്കള്ളി - chaturakkalli, Mal. ; දළුක් - daluk, Singh. ; சதுரக்கள்ளி - shathurakkalli, Tam.). Title from branches being angular instead of round. San. from (vajra, san. hard) ; from large piercing thorns of branches which make good fences against elephants [q.v.] and wild buffaloes [khoolgah]. Pers. from (zakkúm, ar. thorn tree + hindí, ar. indian) [round milk-hedge]. Hind. from (tidhárá, hind. triple edged + sendh, hind. euphorbia tirucalli, linn.). Dec. from (tin, hind. three + dhárí, hind. edged + send, hind. euphorbia). Can. from (jede, can. matted + kalli, can. milk-hedge). Too. from (dare, too. sharp + kalli, too. milk-hedge). Tel. from (bonta, tel. large + jemudu, tel. milk-hedge plant). Mal. from tamul. Tam. from (chaturashra, san. quadrangular + kalli, tam. euphorbia tirucalli, linn.). San. also (vajrakantaka), meaning having adamantine thorns ; (snuhi), meaning causing vomiting, being an emetic ; (simhunda), meaning lion-faced ; (tridháraka), meaning three-edged ; from triangular branches. Mahr. also (shéranivadanga), meaning euphorbia tirucalli, linn. + prickly-pear bush, opuntia dillenii, haw. ; (tidharinivadunga), meaning three-edged + prickly-pear. Hind. also (tidhárá), meaning three-edged ; (nárásej), meaning fibrous milky hedge ; (sihand), meaning causing cut ; (sendkájhár), meaning milk-hedge tree. Dec. also (tidhárísendh), meaning three-edged euphorbia. Can. also (bontekalli), meaning entangled + milk-hedge. Tel. also (bommajemudu), meaning god + milk-hedge plant ; (bhúmijemudu), meaning earth + milk-hedge plant ; (múdumúlajemudu), meaning three + corner + milk-hedge plant ; (bontachemudu), meaning large + milk-hedge plant. Mal. also (katakkalli), meaning sea milk-hedge. Tam. also (shutháççi) ; (keníravam) ; (tirugukkalli), meaning to twist + euphorbia tirucalli, linn. Title otherwise Ancient spurge, Euphorbium plant, Triangular spurge. Botanically Euphorbia [milk-hedge] antiquorum, linn., euphorbiaceæ [vricsham, 118]. Alias Tithymalus antiquorum. Bush ; stems jointed, erect, ramous, three to four or more angled ; angles furnished with numerous protuberances, each armed with two short spreading stipularly spines ; joints straight ; peduncles solitary or in pairs, usually three-flowered a little above the axils of the stipules ; flowers greenish yellow ; very common in waste places ; distinguishable from other species by the straight untwisted stems, and by peduncles being one or two only from each bud ; milky gum reisn [googal] which flows from the wounded stems is an acrid poison and is collected in leather bags. Plaster, prepared from roots and mixed with asafœtida [q.v.] applied externally to the stomachs of children suffering from worms ; bark of root is purgative ; stem is given in decoction in gout. Juice from the branches used in rhoumatism, in toothache, and internally when diluted as a purgative in cases of obstinate constipation ; it has acrid, narcotic, drastic, and emetic qualities ; it is used in dropsy and as an errhine in chronic affections of the ears, eyes, or brain ; it is quoted in pharm., but non-officinal. The inspissated juice was at one time considered to be the Euphorbium of medicine ; this really gum of Euphorbia resinifera.——*Twisting milk-hedge* (वज्रतुण्ड - vajratunda, San. ; پیلی سینڈھ - pílisendh, Hind. ;

తిరుగుజెముడు - tirugujemudu, Tel.; සිනුක් - sínuk, Singh.; திருகுக்கள்ளி - tirugukkalli, Tam.). Title from spiral stems. San. from (vajra, san. adamant + tunda, san. stem). Hind. from (pílí, hind. yellow + sendh, hind. + euphorbia tirucalli, linn.). Tel. from (tirugu, tel. screw + jemudu, tel. milk-hedge plant). Tam. from (tirugu, tam. to twist + kalli, tam. euphorbia tirucalli, linn.); from spiral stems. Tam. also (áttángalli), meaning goat + euphorbia tirucalli, linn.; goats [vellaud] eat the plant, though other animals do not touch the plant for the acrid juice. Title otherwise Spiral spurge, Twisted spurge. Botanically Euphorbia [milkhedge] tortilis, rottler, euphorbiaceæ [vricsham, 118]. Shrubby, three to four-cornered; branches spirally twisted, angles compressed, repandly toothed; prickles diverging; cymes fascicled in the sinuses of the ribs, short-peduncled, three-headed; floral leaves oblong, minute; involucres campanulate; styles very short, united at the base, dilated at the apex, two-lobed; common. Milky juice very similar to euphorbia antiquorum, linn.; drastic, cathartic and deobstruent; prescribed in conjunction with palmyra [q.v.] jaggery [q.v.]; undiluted acts as vesicatory; when mixed with castor-oil [lamp-oil] forms embrocation in palsy and chronic rheumatism.

MILLAT (ملت - millat, *Ar.*). Religion. Part of lacab; as Taujool millat, crown of the faith.

MILLET (موٹا اناج - motáanáj, *Hind.*). Means coarse grain as opposed to rice [q.v.]. Common name for various species of small seed corn, especially panicum miliaceum [varagoo] and panicum miliare [shaumay].——*Bulrush millet* (باجرا - bájrá, Hind.). Same as Bajrah.——*Chenna millet* (چینا - chíná, Hind.). Same as Varagoo.——*Coix millet* (रानजोंधला - ránajóndhalá, Mahr.). Same as Coratty pausy.——*Common millet* (باجرا - bájrá, Hind.). Same as Varagoo.——*German millet* (ولايتی باجرا - viláitíbájrá, Hind.). Same as Tinay.——*Great millet* (جواری - javárí, Hind.). Same as Cholum.——*Guinea-corn millet* (گینی کا اناج - gíníkáanáj, Hind.). Same as Cholum.——*Horse-tail millet* (குதிரைவாற்சாமை - kuthiraivárchámai, Tam.). Same as Sticky grass.——*Indian millet* (جوار هندی - jawárihindí, Hind.). Same as Cholum and Varagoo.——*Italian millet* (ولايتی باجرا - viláitíbájrá, Hind.). Same as Tinay.——*Juar millet* (جواری - javári, Hind.). Same as Cholum.——*Kangnee millet* (کنگنی - kangní, Hind.). Same as Tinay.——*Khoda millet* (کودو چاول - kodocháwal, Hind.). See Khoda.——*Little millet* (अणु - anu, San.). Same as Shaumay.——*Marua millet* (منروی - manraví, Hind.). Same as Raggy.——*Sanwa millet* (سانوا - sánwá, Dec.). Same as Shaumay.——*Spiked millet* (باجرا - bájrá, Hind.). Same as Bajrah.——*Sugar millet* (शर्कराजूर्ण - sharkarájúrna, San.). Same as Sweet cholum.

MILLY (మల్లి - milli, *Tel.*). Small hamlet. Suffix in place names [hully, pully, villy].

MIMAUMSAM (मीमांस - mímámsa, *San.*; மீமாஞ்சை - mímáñjai, *Tam.*). From (man, san. to think). Mental reflection [man].——*Oottara mimaumsam* (उत्तरमीमांसा - uttaramímámsá, San.). From (uttara, san. latter). System of philosophy, commonly called Vedauntam [q.v.], founded by Baudarauyanan. It is so called as being founded on the Oopanishad [q.v.] or latter part of the Vedas [q.v.]. It is also called Brahma mimaumsam, as regarding knowledge of Bramh [q.v.].——*Poorva mimaumsam* (पूर्वमीमांसा - púrvamímámsá, San.). From (púrva, san. first). Inquiry into the first or ritual portion of the Vedas. Hence also Carma mimaumsam. It is attributed to Jeiminy [q.v.]. It is usually called Mimaumsam simply, in opposition to Oottara mimaumsam of Baudarauyanan, which is called Vedauntam [matam]. See vol. I (74), (87).

MIMBAR (منبر - mimbar, *Hind.*). From (nabar, ar. raised). The pulpit in a mosque [musjid] from which the sermon [khootbah] is recited. It consists of three steps and is sometimes a movable wooden structure and sometimes a fixture of brick and stone built against the wall. The sermon is usually preached from the middle step.

MIN (மின் - min, *Tam.*). To flash.——*Minnal* (तडित् - tadit, San.; برق - bark, Ar.; بجلی - bijlí, Hind. and Dec.; کلت - kilat, Malay; ಮಿಂಚು - minchu, Can.; ಮೆಂಚಿ - menchi, Too.; మెరుపు - merupu, Tel.; മിന്നൽ - minnal, Mal.; மின்னல் - minnal, Tam.). San. from (tad, san. to shine). Ar. from (baraka, ar. to flash) [boorauk]. Hind. from (vidyut, san. lightning). Tel. from (meriyu, tel. to flash). Lightning. According to the Champoo ramayanam the following predictions may be formed from the color of the lightning. If it is of an impure green color, it precedes strong wind; if red, the weather will be afterwards hot; if yellow, strong thunder and rain will follow; and if white, or black, it presages a season without rain and dearth [caur, caurtey, maigham, mazhay].——*Moonnay* (முன்னை - munnai, Tam.). See sep. title.

MINCHERRY (మించేరి - minchéri, *Tel.*). From (mintsu, tel. abundant + éri, can. tank).—"*a*" Village; Bellary dist., Bellary tal.; pop. 602; acres 2,805; lat. 15° 04′; long. 76° 57′; from Bellary S. 5 miles.—"*b*" Range of hills; Bellary dist., Bellary tal. Highest peak, the Copper mountain [q.v.].

MINDIE (मेन्धिका - méndhiká, *San.*; मेंधी - méndhí, *Mahr.*; मेत्येझाड - métyéjháda, *Conc.*; حنا - hinná, *Ar.*; حنا - hiná, *Pers.*; مهندی - mhindí, *Hind.*; مهندی - mhendí, *Dec.*; حانا - hána, *Malay*; ಗೋರಂಟೆ - góranti, *Can.*; ಮದಿರೆಂಗಿ - madirengi, *Too.*; గోరంట - góranta, *Tel.*; ମଞ୍ଜୁତି - manghati, *Oor.*; മയിലാഞ്ചി - mayiláñchi, *Mal.*; මරිතොන්ඩි - maritondi, *Singh.*; மருதாணி - maruthání, *Tam.*). Title from sanscrit through hindostany. Ar. from (haná, ar. to become green); from pale greenish flowers. Malay from arabic. Too. from (mada, san. intoxication + ranga, san. colour); from soporific and dye-giving properties. Tel. from (góru, tel. nail + antu, tel. to stick). Mal. from (mayil, mal. peacock + áñchu, mal. to stretch). Tam. from (maru, tam. fragrance + tónri, tam. blood); from fragrant red dye. San. also (sahachara), meaning accompanying, useful companion as a medicine; properly a nail dye [q.v.]. Ar. also (yuranná). Can. also (madarangi), meaning intoxication + dye. Tel. also (maida), meaning deceitful. Mal. also (poytalaççi), corr. of (púttalaççi), meaning flower + head. Tam. also (aivanam), meaning beautiful; (maruthónri). Greek κύπρος. Title otherwise Camphire, Egyptian privet, Fragrant nail dye, Henna plant, Jamaica mignonette, Mendhee, Sweet-smelling camphire. Botanically Lawsonia alba, lamk., lythraceæ [vricsham, 58]. Alias Alcanna spinosa; Lawsonia inermis, spinosa. Shrub, 6–10 feet; calyx four-partite; petals four, unguiculate, alternate with the lobes of the calyx, obovate, spreading; stamens in pairs alternating with the petals; small neat foliage resembling myrtle; leaves opposite, oval-lanceolate, quite entire, glabrous; flowers panicled; ovary sessile, four-celled; capsule globose, three to four-celled; seeds numerous; large compact panicles of small greenish-white flowers, fragrant; flowering nearly all year; a hedge plant, resembling english privet; indigenous on coromandel coast; flowers religious. Has vulnerary and astringent properties; decoction of leaves used to purify the blood, applied externally in ulcers and other sores and skin diseases; leaves used for disease called burning-of-hands and feet to which madras sepoys [q.v.] in burmah are very subject; they are then reduced to pulp, made into a poultice with vinegar [caudy], and applied to soles of feet; flowers used as a sodorific, being placed in a pillow; oil and essence are rubbed over the body to keep the body cool; seeds and roots tonic gives to pharm. henna leaves, non-officinal. Very common in gardens as a hedge plant. From leaves red henna dye is prepared; this is used by women to stain the palms of the hands and the soles of the feet, and the tips of the fingers and toes; for this purpose the freshly gathered leaves are pounded with catechu [q.v.] or lime [choonam]; mussalmans use it also to dye their beards, the orange color being afterwards turned to a deep black by application of indigo [q.v.]; as a dye [shauyam] for fabrics it is very fleeting and therefore rarely used; a fragrant volatile otto [attar] is distilled from the flowers; wood grey, hard, close-grained. There is a variety with red flowers; the species called spinosa is the same plant growing in a dry sterile oil.——*China mindie* (چینی حنا - chíníhiná, Pers. and Hind.; చీనాచెట్టు - chíná-chettu, Tel.; சீனப்பூ - shínappú, Tam.). Title as being a privet brought from china; mindie, from resembling lawsonia alba, lamk. Hind. from (chíní, hind. chinese + hiná, pers. lawsonia alba, lamk.). Tel. means china tree. Tam. from (shínam, tam. china + pú, tam. flower). Title otherwise China privet, Tsjinkin. Botanically Lagerstrœmia [cadaly] indica, linn., lythraceæ [vricsham, 58]. Shrub showy in flower; leaves 2 inches, glabrous, elliptic or oblong, sessile, acute or somewhat obtuse at each end, never acuminate; panicle not condensed, minutely pubescent or glabrous; petals bright pink; calyx-teeth on the fruit long-triangular, erect, but distant, thin not woody; seed ¼ inch including its wing. Erect-growing shrub, three feet high; smooth oval leaves; large panicles of rather small, fringe-petalled, flowers ranging from pale rose to dark crimson; also white and lilac; flowers religious.——*Foreign mindie* (آس - ás, Ar.; مورد - múrad, Pers.; ولايتی مهیندی - viláitímenhdí, Hind.). Hind. from (viláití, hind. foreign + mhendí, hind. lawsonia alba, lamk.). Ar. also (hakas). Greek μυρσίνη. Title otherwise Common myrtle. Botanically Myrtus communis, linn., myrtaceæ [vricsham, 56]. Shrub; white flowers succeeded by blue black berries in cold season; dark-green foliage, pleasant odour; introduced. Leaves useful in cerebral affections; fruit carminative and emetic; gargle of leaves used in aphthæ; paste of seeds applied to scorpion bites. Buds and berries used as spices. Seeds ground down and mixed with antimony [soorma] used to color eyelids. Compare:—Dodonæa viscosa, bog myrtle; Eugenia caryophyllæa, clove myrtle; Myrica sapida, box myrtle; Rhodomyrtus tomentosa, woolly myrtle. See gloss. paragraphs.——*Gool mindie* (दुष्पत्रि - dushpatri, San.; तेरडा - téradá, Mahr.; گل مهیندی کا جهاڑ - gulmhendíkájhár, Dec.; ಕಾಡುಕರ್ಣಕುಂಡಲಗಿಡ - kádukarnakundalagida, Can.; కాశితుమ్మి - káshitummi, Tel.; ହରଗାର - haragára, Oor.; കാശിത്തുമ്പ - káshittumpa, Mal.; காசித்தும்பை - kásittumbai, Tam.). Title from deccany. San. from (dus, san. bad + patra, san. leaf); from bursting on slight contact. Dec. from (gul, pers.

flower + mhendí, hind. lawsonia alba, lamk. + jhár, hind. tree), from its yielding a similar dye. Can. from (kádu, can. wild + karnakundala, san. earring + gida, can. plant). Tel. means benares toombay. Mal. from tamul. Tam. from (kási, tam. benares + tumbai, tam. leucas). San. also (divipatra), meaning divine leaf; (dvipatra), meaning double-leaved. Title otherwise Balsam flower, Snapweed, Touch-me-not. Botanically the Impatiens genus, geraniaceæ [vricsham, 31]. Glabrous herbs, with thick succulent stems enlarged at the joints, where the alternate undivided leaves are given off; flowers axillary, often handsome; capsule oblong, sub-cylindrical or with five blunt angles; largely cultivated in gardens for the beauty of the flowers, which are rose-pink, white, blue or variegated; ripe capsules on being touched, fly open and scatter their seeds. Hence generic name. The S. indian species indigenous or naturalized are:—acaulis, auriculata, balsamina, campanulata, chinensis, crenata, dasysperma, diversifolia, elegans, fruticosa, gardneriana, goughii, grandis, inconspicua, jerdoniæ, kleinii, latifolia, leschenaultii, ligulata, maculata, modesta, munronii, mysorensis, oppositifolia, parvifolia, pendula, racemosa, repens, rivalis, scabriuscula, scapiflora, setosa, stocksii, tangachee, tenella, tomentosa, umbellata, uncinata, verticillata, viridiflora, viscida, viscosa, wightiana.

MINHAH (منہا - minhá, *Hind.*; మినహా - minahá, *Tel.*). From (min, ar. from + há, ar. that). Deduction; as from the assessed revenue of a village, on account of uncultivable tracts of wood or water, wilderness or waste, &c.——*Ashalminhah* (حشو منها - hashominhá, Hind.; అసల్మినహా - asalminahá, Tel.). From (hasho, ar. credit side of account + minhái, ar. deduction). Deductions from the total revenue [beriz, jumma] entered on the credit side of the account with government. The term is therefore applied to rent-free [inam] and other favorably assigned lands [jody]. Commonly used for unoccupied and unassessed land. See vol. I, 112.

MINTAKA (منطقہ - mintaka, *Hind.*). From (niták, ar.) Zone. ——*Mintaka i mabrooda* (منطقہ مبرودہ - mintakahimabrúdah, Hind.). From (above + mabrúd, ar. cold). Frigid zone.—— *Mintaka i mahrooca* (منطقہ محروقہ - mintakahimahrúkah, Hind.). From (above + mahrúk, ar. hot). Torrid zone.——*Mintaka i mooaddila* (منطقہ معتدلہ - mintkahimuaddilah, Hind.). From (above + muaddil, ar. moderate). Temperate zone.——*Mintakat ool boorooj* (منطقة البروج - mintakatulburúj, Hind.). The Zodiac [nacshatram, noojoom, raushy].

MIRASS (میراث - mírás, *Hind.*). From (irs, ar. to inherit). Right derived from inheritance [cawnyautchy, milkyat, sawmyam]. Mirassy is hereditary, and mirassidar is hereditary proprietor or landholder. See vol. I, 112, 125.

MIS (مس - mis, *Pers.*). Copper [taumram].——*Missee* (مسی - missí, Hind.). An oxide of copper used against toothache and to stain teeth black.

MISBAH (مصباح - misbáh, *Ar.*). Lamp. Lacab of the prophet. Prefixed to allah makes a lacab; as Misbah ool lah, lamp of allah [ism].

MISCAL (مثقال - miskál, *Hind.*). From (sikal, ar. weight). Goldsmith's weight. 4 maushams = 1 miscal; 3 miscals = 1 tolah [niray, 3e]. Approximate actual value, 1 miscal = 60 grains troy. Compare Varauhaniday, Cutlay pagoda. See vol. I, 609.

MISHAMMAH (మిస్సమ్మ - missamma, *Tel.*). Native term for a female missionary or zenana [q.v.] lady.

MISHMEE (مشمی - mishmí, *Hind.*). A tract of land at the head of Assam valley from which the best mamiraun [q.v.] comes.——*Mishmee teeta* (مشمی تیتا - mishmítíta, Hind.). From (above + títá, hind. bitter). Same as Mamiraun.

MISHMISH (مشمش - mishmish, *Ar.*; زرد آلو - zardálú, *Pers.*, *Hind.* and *Dec.*). Pers. from (zard, pers. yellow + álú, pers. plum, prunus). Ar. also (tuffáhiarmaní), meaning armenian apple; (kashmírípistah), meaning cashmere pistachio. Hind. also (khúbání), meaning dried plum; (chúari) [cherry]. Title otherwise Apple of the bible, Apricot, Armenian apple, Cashmere pistachio, Moon of the faithful, Yellow plum. Botanically Prunus [auloo] armeniaca, linn., rosaceæ [vricsham, 49]. Deciduous fruit tree, 15 feet high; leaves sub-cordate; flowers sessile, white, flowering in february and march; introduced on Neilgherries; a gum [gond] exudes from wounds in bark.

MISL (مثل - misl, *Hind.*). From arabic. Similitude, appointment.——*Misl bundy* (مثل بندی - mislbandí, Hind.). From (above + bandí, dec. binding). Register containing the names of persons holding village offices [balootah] in each village.——*Misl curnum* (మిసల్కరణము - misalkaranamu, Tel.). From (above + karanamu, tel. curnum). The regularly appointed Curnum [q.v.].

MISR (مصر - misr, *Hind.*). Egypt.——*Misry* (مصری - misrí, Hind.). From (misr, ar. egypt); the original source of supply. Sugar-candy [candy].——*Salep misry* (ثعلب مصری - salabmisrí, Pers.). From being exported from egypt. Same as Salep.—— *Shaulah misry* (ثعلب مصری - salabmisrí, Hind.; సాలామిసిరి - sálámisiri, Tel.; சாலாமிசிரி - shálámisiri, Tam.). Means Egyptian salep. From being exported from Egypt. See Salep.

MISWAUK (مسواک - miswák, *Hind.*). A twig of a tree, of which several kinds are in use, as that of the margosa [neem] tree, used as a substitute for a tooth brush. It is about a span long, split at one end and chewed to render it softer.

MITCHAM (മിച്ചം - miççam, *Mal.*). From (miru, tam. to remain). Surplus.——*Mitchauram* (മിച്ചാരം - miççáram, Mal.). From (above + váram, mal. rent). Remaining share. Rent due to Jenmy [q.v.] after deducting the interest of the cannom advanced by the tenant [cannom].

MITHY (తొక్కుడుకర్ర - tokkudukarra, *Tel.*; മെതി - meti, *Mal.*; மிதி - mithi, *Tam.*). Title from tamul. Tel. from (tokku, tel. to tread + karra, tel. stick). Tam. means to tread. Treadle [nesavoo].

MITTAH (مٹھا - mitthá, *Hind.*). From (makta, ar. fixed). Sub-division of a district. A small polliem [q.v.] or zemindarry [mootah, zemindarry].——*Mittahdarny* (مٹھداری - mitthadární, Hind.). A female mittahdar.——*Mootah* (مٹھا - mutthá, Hind.). A sub-division.

MIYAUN (میاں - miyán, *Pers.*). From arabic. A term of respectful address amongst Mahomedans; like title 'father' given to monks. A schoolmaster. Also term of endearment for a boy.

MIYAUNAH (میانہ - miyánah, *Hind.*). From (miyán, pers. waist). A litter used at marriage ceremonies of Mahomedans.

MLECHA (म्लेच्छ - mléçça, *San.*). Onomatopoeic. From (mlichh, san. to speak indistinctly). Impure [neecha]. A foreigner, one who is not a Hindoo [q.v.]. The term is as old as the Mahabhaurat [q.v.], in which the tribes of Southern india are called by this name, and also Nishaudan [q.v.]. See vol. I (2).

MOBALAG (مبلغ - mablagh, *Hind.*). From (balagha, ar. to attain the utmost point). Sum of money. Total.

MOCHA (یمن - yaman, *Ar.*). Fortified sea-port near the strait of Babelmandeb, 130 miles north-west of Aden. Principal export is coffee [q.v.].——*Mocha aloes* (صبر یمنی - sibriyamaní, Hind.). Same as Bombay aloe.——*Mocha senna* (سناء یمنی - sanáiyamaní, Hind.). Same as Tinnevelly senna.

MODAM (मोद - móda, *San.*). From (mud, san. to rejoice). Glad.——*Modacam* (मोदक - módaka, San.). From (mud, san. to rejoice). A small round sweetmeat made of rice flour, sugar, &c.——*Modaca priyan* (मोदकप्रिय - módakapriya, San.). From (módaka, san. the cake + priya, san. loving). Vigneshwaran [q.v.], who is fond of rice-flour cake.——*Moodgam* (मुद्ग - mudga, San.). From (mud, san. to be glad).——Botanically the Phaseolus genus, leguminosæ [vricsham, 48]. Annuals or herbaceous perennials; leaves have three leaflets; flowers often showy; pod straight or slightly curved containing several seeds. The species best known to the natives are:—aconitifolius [moorman's gram], adenanthus [wild green gram], lunatus [country lobyah], mungo [green gram], mungo, var. radiatus [black gram], semi-erectus [needle chacondah], trilobus [field gram], trinervius [tufted green gram], vulgaris [lobyah].——*Moong* (مونگ - múng, Hind.). Same as Green gram. Ground nut is Foreign moong.

MODE (മേട് - métu, *Mal.*; மேடு - médu, *Tam.*). High ground [maud, mett, mitta]. Suffix in place names.——*Modan* (മോടൻ - mótan, Mal.). From (métu, mal. high land). A hill paddy in Malabar. Carroottary modan is a black, and Veloottary modan is a white variety [paddy].——*Mody* (மோடி - módi, Tam.). From (módu, tam. height). A forest deity [caudcaul].—— *Mootpily* (మోటుపల్లె - mótupalle, Tel.). Corr. from tel. meaning uneven village [motoopully]. Ancient province, now part of Baupatla talook.——*Moott* (முட்டு - muttu, Tam.). Rising ground [mett].——*Moottam* (മുട്ടം - muttam, Mal.). From (métu, mal. high ground). Town, Port, Rocky promontory; Travancore state, Pudmanaubhapooram division, Yerraneel tal.; lat. 8° 07'; long. 77° 22'; from Yerraneel S. 6 miles; from Bombay S.S.E. 795 miles; from Cadiapatam S. E. 1¼ miles; from Colachel S.E. 5 miles; from Shaunaurgoody W. 16 miles; from Trivandrum S.E. 35 miles. On the coast near Colachel. Abounds with palmyras [q.v.]. The soil is red and the promontory shows red. London mission bungalow [q.v.]. Resorted to by Europeans. Light in lat. 8° 07'; long. 77° 21'. White; fixed. 16 miles range. Visible from all directions seaward. Dark grey granite column. Intended to mark the vicinity of the Crocodile rock, ¾ miles off Cadiapatam.——*Moottanaud* (முட்டநாடு - muttanádu, Tam.). From (muttu, tam. high ground + nádu, tam. country). Village, Hill; Salem dist., Salem tal. Highest summit on the Shevaroy hills [green hills].——*Moottaul* (முட்டாள் - muttál, Tam.). From (muttu, tam. impediment + ál, tam. person). A dunce; term of abuse.——*Mott* (மோடு - módu, Tam.). High ground. Prefix in place names; as Mottore, meaning high village.

MOEEN (معين - muín, *Ar.*). From (ána, ar. to aid). Aider. Part of lacab; as Moeen ood deen, support of religion; Moeen ool moolk, support of the kingdom [ism].

MOFUSSIL (مفصل - mofassal, *Hind.*). From (fasl, ar. division). Separated, detailed. The subordinate divisions of a district, in contradistinction to the sudder [q.v.] or chief seat of government. So the country in general, including large towns, as distinct from the capital of a province.

MOGA (మొగ - moga, *Tel.*). Male [makkal]. Plant first term; as Anisomeles malabarica (mogabíra), male elæodendron glaucum.

MOGALINGAM (மொகலிங்கம் - mogalingam, *Tam.*). From (magga, can. loom + vilangu, tam. to shine); wood polishes well and used for weaver's beam. Same as Weaver's beam.

MOGALY (మొగలి - mogali, *Tel.*). Screw-pine [q.v.].——*Mogultoor* (మొగలితుర్రు - mogaliturru, Tel. mogaltur*). From (mogali, tel. fragrant screw-pine, pandanus odoratissimus, linn. + turru, tel. village). Sanscrit name (kétakipura), meaning same. Town, Head-quarters of Rajah of Mogultoor; Godavery dist., Narsapore tal.; pop. 5,970; acres 7,463; lat. 16° 25′; long. 81° 39′; from Cocanada S.W. 55 miles; from Narsapore W. 5 miles; from the sea N. 4 miles. In 1758, the Rajah of estate of this name assisted in expelling French from Narsapore. In 1763, the Rajah was defeated by Seetaram row of Vizianagram. In 1787, estate was taken under management, Zemindar having fallen into arrears. In 1791 an insurrection raised by one Jagaranz was quelled and a company of sepoys [q.v.] was stationed here. The Rajah, Culdindy tripatty rauz, died on the 28th of August 1791. He had adopted a very distant relative as his successor, but the child was not permitted to succeed, and the estate was annexed to the Company's dominions, and became a portion of the Government lands of Masulipatam. About 1794 the town was the head-quarters of the second division, comprising the old Rajahmundry and Masulipatam districts. The town is at present noteworthy for its salt [ooppoo] manufacture. The Narsapore canal is connected at this place with the Ooppooteroo. Old fort. Protestant mission. Trig. station in lat. 16° 25′ 38·06″; long. 81° 40′ 4·12″; from Mootyaulapully N.E. 3 miles.

MOGHUL (مغل - mughal, *Hind.*). From (mongol, turk. native of mongolia). Name given by Hindoos to the Mahomedan dynasty [raj] founded by Baber and made paramount in India by Acbar. The race to which these rulers belonged was mixed Mongolian and Caucasian. Mahomedans now called Moghuls in S. india are those bearing tribal adjuncts of Aghah [q.v.] and Beg [q.v.]. They are very poor. All soonnees [q.v.]. About a thousand all told in the presidency, of which North arcot has the most [mahomedan]. Moghul, as the name of a period of a Mahomedan school of architecture, is applied only to the time of Acbar and Jehaungeer [staupatyam]. See vol. II, 204.

MOGRAH (موگرا - mográ, *Hind.*). Jasmine, jasminum sambac. Plant second term. Ex., where transl. is of first term:—Gynocardia odorata (chálmográ), bark; Jasminum auriculatum (suímográ), needle; Jasminum grandiflorum (jáychémógré), jasminum; Jasminum pubescens (kastúrimógré), musk; Tabernæmontana coronaria (dúdhmográ), milk. See gloss. paragraphs.

MOHAM (मोह - móha, *San.*). From (muh, san. to stupify). Bewilderment; one of the effects of Manmatan's arrows [cauna baunam]. Spiritual ignorance which leads men to believe in the reality of worldly objects, and to addict themselves to mundane or sensual enjoyment.——*Mohan* (मोह - móha, San.). Manmatan [q.v.].——*Mohiny* (मोहिनी - móhiní, San.). A female form assumed by Vishnoo [q.v.] at the time of the Coorma [q.v.] avatar [q.v.]. Shiva [q.v.] became enamoured of Mohiny, who bore him a son, named in the north Hariharan [q.v.]; in the south Ayenaur [ayen]. See vol. I (77).

MOHARRAM (محرم - muharram, *Hind.*; పీర్లపండుగ - pírlapanduga, *Tel.*; அல்லாப்பண்டிகை - allâppandigai, *Tam.*). From (haruma, ar. prohibited and so sacred); cf. latin sacer. First month of Mahomedan lunar year [hijra, maheena]. Also the commemorative function celebrated by Mussalmans on the first ten days of that month [hoossain]. The latter has been sufficiently described at vol. I (96). In certain traditional works it is stated that it was on the tenth day of Moharram that the following events took place:—"*a*" the first fall of rain;—"*b*" Adam and Eve's descent on earth and the establishment of the propagation of the species;—"*c*" divine mission granted to the souls of ten thousand prophets;—"*d*" the creation of Arsh, the ninth heaven or the empyrean throne of the divine glory and majesty; and—"*e*" Coorchy, the eighth or crystaline heaven, supposed to be the judgment seat of god;—"*f*" Bheest, or the seven heavens;—"*g*" Dozak, or hell;—"*h*" Lowh, or the tablet on which the decrees of the deity are inscribed;—"*i*" Calam, the pen wherewith they are written;—"*j*" Takdeer, fate or destiny;—"*k*" Hayaut or life;—"*l*" Mamaut or death.

MOHEE (محي - muhí, *Hind.*). From (hai, ar. to live). The restorer. An attribute of God [allah].——*Mohee ood deen* (محي الدين - muhíuddín, Hind.). The reviver of the faith. Lacab of the chief Mahomedan saint [abdool cawder]. Assumed as ordinary alam at present [ism].

MOHIB (محب - muhib, *Ar.*). From (hubba, ar. to love). Attached. Prefixed to an alam forms a lacab; as Mohib ally, friend of ally [ism].

MOHIRY (మోహిరి - móhiri, *Tel.*). From (móharamu, tel. battle-array). Tel. also (kerandimala), whence called Kerandy hills. Village, Talook, Hills; Ganjam dist., Berhampore tal.; acres 17,920; lat. 19° 18′; long. 84° 43′; from Berhampore W. 8 miles; from Chetterpore W.S.W. 22 miles; from the sea W. 17 miles. The name given to the Government talook [q.v.] under the direct jurisdiction of the Tahsildar [q.v.], Berhampore. Formerly a zemindarry [q.v.]. The last zemindar [q.v.] was of unsound mind and without issue. He fell into arrears and the estate was brought in by Government for Rs. 100 fifty years back. The hills lie in the centre of the Senior assistant's division and occupy about 20 square miles of territory. They separate the Government lands from the Pedda kimedy and Cheekaty zemindarries. The boundary line between the Government and zemindarry lands runs through the centre of the range. The range is about 2,500 feet high and contains some thirty hamlets inhabited by Tinka khonds [q.v.]. The more remote hills and valleys contain fair bamboo [q.v.] jungle and a few forest trees, but the more accessible slopes have been almost denuded for the supply of fuel to Berhampore town and the neighbourhood. The station of Sircote in the hills was occupied during the disturbances of 1818 by the Collector's sibbundy [q.v.] corps.

MOHSAL (محصل - mohassil, *Ar.*). From (hasula, ar. to remain over and above). A guard placed over a person to enforce payment of a demand.

MOHTASIB (محتسب - muhtasib, *Hind.*). From (hasiba, ar. to calculate). A superintendent of markets and police [inam].

MOHUR (مهر - muhr, *Hind.*; మొహరీ - moharí, *Tel.*; மோரா - mórá, *Tam.*). From persian. A seal [moodray]. A gold coin equal in Bengal, to sixteen sicca [q.v.] rupees [q.v.]; in Madras, to fifteen Arcot rupees; in Bombay, to fourteen soonnat rupees. From 4 to 5 pagodas [q.v.], called otherwise gold mohur. A gold rupee similar to a mohur was coined under the reign of the Emperor Shah alam, which began in 1770. There was also the mohur of Tippoo. Cf. Nishkam.——*Charyauree mohur* (چهار یاری مهر - chahâryárímuhr, Hind.). From (chahár, hind. four + yár, pers. companion). A gold mohur of Shah jehaun; reverse his name, obverse Mahomedan creed and the four companions, viz., aboo bakr, oomr, osman, ally.——*Chinnamaila mohur* (சின்னமேளமோரா - shinnamélámógará, Tam.). From (shinna, tam. small + mélam, tam. a musical instrument + above). Tinnevelly coin, equal to 3 pagodas 34 fanams 7 cash.——*Shree ram mohur* (ಶ್ರೀರಾಮಮೊಹರ - shrírámamohará, Can.). From (shrírâma, san. holy ráma). Cup-like form stamped in three different ways; one with figure of Rama [q.v.] on concave side, another with figure of Rama and Seetay [q.v.] on concave side and of Rama yantram on convex, and third with figure of Hanooman [q.v.] on convex. See vol. I, 609.

MOHURRER (محرر - muharrir, *Hind.*). From (harra, ar. to write). A clerk.

MOHWAH (مهوا - mohwá, *Hind.*). From (madhuka, san. sweet) [mad]. Botanically the Bassia genus, sapotaceæ [vricsham, 82]. Trees; inhabitants of india and malay islands; alternate, silky leaves; flowers whitish, with fleshy corolla; fruit pulpy with three or four one-seeded cells. The species best known to the natives are shown below. Other species are:—malabarica, microphylla. The vernacular term includes also Achras sapota and Terminalia belerica.——*Butter mohwah* (پهلوارا - phalwárá, Hind.). Title from semi-solid oil from seeds. Hind. from (phalwá, hind. the oil). Title otherwise Butter tree, Epie oil plant, Fulwa butter, Indian butter. Botanically Bassia [mohwah] butyracea, roxb., sapotaceæ [vricsham, 82]. Deciduous tree, 30–40 feet; leaves obovate, tomentose beneath; corolla eight-cleft; stamens thirty to forty on longish filaments; pedicels aggregate, and, as well as the calyx, woolly; drupes oval; flowers smallish, white. By pressure seeds yield a semi-solid oil [yennay], which thickens and becomes like lard; used for culinary purposes, for soap [sauboon], and for anointing the body; in pharm. non-officinal. The flowers abound in honey, scarcely differing in the raw state from hive honey [shahad], except that it is more limpid; it is manufactured into sugar [q.v.], in every respect equal to that of the sugar-cane [q.v.]. Pulp of fruit eaten.——*Common mohwah* (मधूक - madhúka, San.; मोह - móha, Mahr.; درخت گل چکان - darakhtigulchakán, Pers.; مهوا - mahuá, Hind.; موها - mohá, Dec.; ಇಪ್ಪೆ - ippe, Can. and Too.; ఇప్ప - ippa, Tel.; ഇരിപ്പ - irippa, Mal.; මීගස - mígasa, Singh.; இலுப்பை - ilúppai, Tam.). San. from (madhu, san. sweet); from flowers. Mahr. from (muh, san. to intoxicate); from flowers [atimathooram, kamela]. Pers. from (darakht, pers. tree + gul, pers. flower + chakán, pers. shedding). Hind. from (muh, san. to intoxicate). Dec. from sanscrit. Can.

from (impu, can. sweetness). Too. from canarese. Tel. from (impu, tel. sweetness). Mal. from tamul. Singh. from (mí, singh. honey + gasá, singh. tree). Tam. from (irumbu, tam. iron), iron-like. Tel. also (pinnaippa), meaning small + the tree. Singh. also (telmí), meaning oil + bassia. Tam. also (iruppai). Title otherwise Flower-dropping tree, Honey tree, Ilooppay, Ilpa, Ippa, Long-leaved bassia, Wild sapota. Botanically Bassia [mohwah] longifolia, linn., sapotaceæ [vricsham, 82]. The species generally found in southern districts, but also found in circars [q.v.]. Oak like [belote] umbrageous tree, 40 feet; trunk 6 or 7 feet in circumference, leaves 4–8 inches long, 2–4 inches broad; ovate-lanceolate, entire, crowded about the ends of the branchlets, immediately above the peduncles; young shoots and petioles slightly villous; calyx of two opposite pairs of leaflets; corolla eight-cleft; filaments scarcely any; pedicels axillary, drooping, crowded, one-flowered; stamens sixteen to twenty, within the gibbous tube of the corolla; flowers whitish; fruit olive-shaped, yellowish when ripe, eight to nine-seeded; seeds solitary; flowers in hot weather. Bassia bark is thick and red colored, with a rough brown surface and astringent taste. The dried flowers at a little distance have the appearance of raisins, on closer inspection they are seen to be fleshy, sticky, compressed, hollow bodies, about $\frac{6}{10}$ of an inch long, and nearly as broad, with an aperture at both ends, the upper being much the larger and serrated; upon being soaked in water they assume an almost globular form, and the numerous anthers are seen attached by very short filaments to the inside of the corolla; the taste is acid and sweet; the fleshy substance of the corolla, which is about $\frac{1}{10}$ of an inch in thickness and translucent, consists of a parenchyma which may be divided into two portions: an outer or cortical, consisting of smaller cells, and an inner consisting of large cells; it is traversed by numerous bundles of spiral vessels; some of the cells contain crystalline masses of sugar [q.v.]; all of them granular matter; there is no starch. The seeds are from 1–2 inches long, and enclosed in a chestnut colored thin shell; they have a peculiar odour and bitter aromatic taste; the seeds yield a fatty oil, greenish yellow in color, which concretes immediately it is expressed and is used as butter [q.v.]. The latex of these trees is a milky liquid, sticky to the touch, when kept it develops a rancid sour odour; it contains, besides the guttapercha [q.v.], some starch and about 88 per cent. of water. Not found at great elevation; cultivated in topes [q.v.] and elsewhere on account of its oil; where cultivated, soil most suitable, red and black loam or sandy soil; planted in pits; after five years the trees fruit; on w. coast not cultivated; the wild tree produces fruits after twenty years; a bad mohwah harvest has never been known; the flowers are produced in enormous quantities in march and april, after the old leaves have fallen and before the new leaves have appeared; the flowers fall off and cover the ground beneath the trees, and are gathered by the natives; the flowers when dried have somewhat the odour and appearance of sultauna raisins; so distributed over this country like dried grapes in europe; from the quantity of sugar contained, the flowers yield when fermented a large quantity of vinous juice; the flavor of the spirit roughly distilled from juice is very similar to that of irish whisky; strong, smoky, and rather mouse-like [shoondely] odour and flavor; this latter disappears with age; this spirit is distilled in southern districts. Gummy juice employed by veidyans [q.v.] in rheumatic affections; the bark used in decoction as an astringent and emollient and as a remedy in itch; flowers used in coughs in the form of a decoction; gives to pharm. fixed concrete oil and spirit distilled from the flowers; non-officinal; whole plant is stimulant, demulcent, and emollient, heating, astringent, tonic, and nutritive; seeds yield thick concrete oil, applied to the head in cephalalgia; residuum or cake left after the expression of the oil is employed as an emetic. Flowers are eaten raw; jackals [q.v.] are fond of them; they have a sickly sweet taste resembling marma [q.v.]; the flowers also dried and preserved; the part eaten is the succulent corollas; the flowers are again roasted and eaten; also bruised and boiled to a jelly, and made into small balls, which are exchanged by the natives for fish [matsyam] and rice [q.v.]. In ganjam, mohwah spirit [arrack] is largely used by the gonds [q.v.] and others; the fresh spirit is, owing to the quantity of aromatic or empyreumatic oil which it contains, very deleterious; the fresh refuse or marc after the extraction of the spirit is attractive to animals; the flower is exported to france for the manufacture of liqueurs [mooskirant, sharaub]. Oil is to the common people a substitute for ghee [q.v.]; cakes are made of it; sold as ilooppay butter; oil also used in lamps especially in temples [coil], and to make soap [sauboon]; the oil cake [pounauk], is used for washing the head, and carried as a small article of trade to those countries where the tree is not to be found; gum [gond] is not turned to any use. Wood is hard, and nearly as durable as teak [q.v.], but not so easily worked, nor is it procurable of such length for beams and planks; it is not liable to be deteriorated by immersion in water, or to suffer from the attacks of the teredo navalis; it is not much used; not being of sufficient value to compensate for the loss of the flower and fruit, tree is seldom cut down. There is a Tamul proverb:—இலுப்பைப்பூவைத் திருப்பினால் இரு புறமும் பொத்தல்—"If the flower of ilooppay be turned, it "will be found hollow on both sides;" it looks like a globule; character needs close examination.——*Foreign mohwah* (سپوتے کا جہاز - sapotekájhár, Hind.; సీమఇప్ప - símaippa, Tel.; മനിലക്കാര - manilakkára, Mal.; சீமையிலுப்பை - shímaiyiluppai, Tam.). Title from being introduced from america and from taste and flavor of fruit like that of mohwah. Hind. from english. Tel. from (síma, tel. foreign + ippa, tel. bassia longifolia, linn.). Mal. from (manilla, mal. manilla, the place + kára, mal. canthium) [edible paulay]. Tam. from (shímai, tam. foreign + iluppai, tam. bassia longifolia, linn.). Hind. also (chakchakotíkájhár). Title otherwise American bully, Australian cranberry, Bully, Mazeberry, Naseberry, Neesberry, Nisberry, Rough chaff, Sapodilla, Sapota, Sapotilla. Botanically Achras sapota, linn., sapotaceæ [vricsham, 82]. Sapota from Mexican through Spanish. Alias Mimusops manilkara; from (manilakkára, mal. manilla canthium, mimusops kauki). Evergreen fruit tree, 30 feet high; leaves lanceolate-ovate; flowers solitary, white. Of low growth; from jamaica; fruit size and form of an orange [q.v.], with a rough, brown, dark-looking, but thin and tender rind; interior, containing black almond-formed [baudam] seeds, consists of a pale-brown juicy pulp. Gives a gum [gond].——*Jungle mohwah* (காட்டு இலுப்பை - káttiluppai, Tam.). Same as Belleric myrobalan.——*Wild mohwah* (अटाविमधूक - atavimadhúka, San.; मोह - móha, Mahr.; درخت گل چکان صحرائی - darakhtigulchakánisahráí, Pers.; مہوا - mahuá, Hind.; موھا - mohá, Dec.; ಕಾಡಿಪ್ಪೆ - kádippe, Can.; ಇಪ್ಪೆ - ippe, Too.; అడవిఇప్ప - adaviippa, Tel.; ମୋହ - moha, Oor.; കാട്ടിരിപ്പ - káttirippa, Mal.; காட்டு இலுப்பை - káttiluppai, Tam.). San. from (atavi, san. forest + madhúka, san. bassia). Mahr. from sanscrit. Pers. from (darakht, pers. tree + gulchakán, pers. bassia longifolia, linn. + sahráí, pers. wild). Hind. from sanscrit. Dec. from hindostany. Can. from (kádu, can. wild + ippe, can. bassia). Tel. from (adavi, tel. forest + ippa, tel. the tree). Oor. from sanscrit. Mal. from (kátu, mal. forest + irippa, mal. the mohwah tree). Tam. from (kádu, tam. forest + iluppai, tam. plant, bassia longifolia, linn.) [belleric myrobalan]. San. also (priyála), meaning desired [chironjee]; (lóddhrapushpá), meaning symplocos racemosa, roxb. + flower; perhaps from similarity in flowers. Hind. also (múva), from sanscrit. Can. also (honge); (ippemara). Tel. also (ippa). Mal. also (irippa); (punna), meaning golden [common poon, kamela, malabar poon]. Title otherwise Broad-leaved bassia, Piyal, Quindah, Yallah oil plant. Botanically Bassia [mohwah] latifolia, roxb., sapotaceæ [vricsham, 82]. Alias Madhura indica. Madhura from sanscrit. The species usually found in northern india and circars [q.v.]. Tree, 40 feet; leaves alternate, oblong or elliptic, crowded about the extremities of the branches, smooth above, somewhat whitish below; stamens twenty to thirty within the gibbous tube of the corolla, on short filaments; corolla thick, fleshy, with a more than eight-lobed limb; lobes cordate; sepals four; pedicels drooping, terminal; flowers white, with a tinge of green and cream color, numerous, crowded from the extremities of the branchlets, peduncled, and bent with the mouth of the flowers directly to the ground; flowering in march and april; berry size of a small apple [seb], one to four-seeded. Flowers used as famine food; mohwah spirit [arrack] distilled as in longifolia.

MOIZ (معز - muiz, *Ar.*). From (azza, ar. to strengthen). Dear, honored. Attribute of God [allah]. Common alam. Also part of lacab; as Moiz ood deen, dear to religion [ism].

MOKADDAM (مقدم - mukaddam, *Hind.*). From (kidama, ar. to go before). Placed above. The head of a village or caste.——*Mokaddamah* (مقدمہ - mukaddamah, Hind.). A subject matter, case, law-suit.——*Mokaddim* (مقدم - mukaddim, Hind.). The bringing forward. Attribute of God [allah]. Common alam; as Mokaddim hoossain, double alam [ism].

MOKARRER (مقرر - mukarrar, *Hind.*). From (karra, ar. to settle) [caraur]. Appointed, fixed.

MOKEEM (مقیم - mukím, *Hind.*). From (kauma, ar. to stand). Steadfast. Used as alam; as Mahomed mokeem, double alam [ism].

MOKHAUBILA (مقابلہ - mukábalah, *Hind.*). From (kabala, ar. opposite). Examination. Compared with the original draft and found to agree.

MOKHAUSA (مخاصہ - mukhásah, *Hind.*). From (khassa, ar. to particularize). Private. Grant of land by zemindar [q.v.] for support of relatives, followers, and dependents, or for military service [inam].

MOKKA (మొక్క - mokka, *Tel.*). Stump. Plant first term often joining two genera. Ex., where transl. is of second term:—Andropogon bladhii (mokkadzanumu), crotalaria juncea; Bignonia sp. (mokkavépa), melia azadirachta; Stereospermum chelonoides (mokkavépa), melia azadirachta; Zea mays (mokkadzonna), sorghum vulgare. See gloss. paragraphs.

MOKOOP (موقوف - maukúf, *Hind.*). From (vakafa, ar. to stop). Dismissed [bartarf, tagheir]. Suspended.

MOLUCCAS (ملوک - mulúkah, *Hind.*). Means royal islands. Otherwise Spice islands. Strictly the five clove islands, Batjan, Makian, Motir, Ternate and Tidore, lying to the west of Gilolo and washed by the Moluccas strait which separates Gilolo from

Celebes. But term extended to all islands over nearly 11 degrees of latitude and longitude now under Dutch rule, between Celebes and N. guinea. The islands are divided into four residencies:—Amboyna, Banda, Manado and Ternate. Distinguish from Malacca.——*Molucca bean* (ملوک کا منکا - mulúkahká-manká, Hind.). Same as Bonduc.——*Molucca bramble* (ملوک کا گوری پہل - mulúkahkágauríphal, Hind.). See Gowry's fruit.——*Molucca grain* (حب الملوک - habbulmulúkah, Hind.). Same as Jamalgota.——*Molucca nut* (جوز ملوک - jauzimulúkah, Hind.). Same as Bonduc.

MOM (मधुज - madhuja, *San.*; मेण - ména, *Mahr.*; شمع - shama, *Ar.*; موم - mom, *Pers.*, *Hind.* and *Dec.*; للن - lilin, *Malay*; ಮೇಣ - ména, *Can.*; ಮಾಯಣ - máyana, *Too.*; మైనము - mainamu, *Tel.*; മെഴുക - mezhuku, *Mal.*; ඉටි - míiti, *Singh.*; மெழுகு - mezhugu, *Tam.*). Title from hindostany. San. from (madhu, san. honey + já, san. to be born). Mahr. from (madana, san. bees' wax). Singh. from (mí, singh. honey + iti, singh. wax). Tam. means to spread. Wax. Substance secreted by the bee [tainee] and used in the construction of the comb. The ordinary yellow wax, cera flava of chemists, is a solid substance, moderately heavy, and of yellow color. In odour it resembles honey. It is obtained by draining off or pressing out the honey from honey-combs and then giving repeated boilings and strainings. The wax skimmed off is eventually put into moulds. For the greater number of uses to which bees' wax is appropriated, it is however necessary that the wax should be rendered perfectly white. This is effected by exposing it in thin ribands on a bleaching ground, where it is subjected to the action of light, air, and moisture, and loses both color and odour. It there becomes white wax, cera alba of chemists. Waxes are worth more than greases, on account of their very high melting points. Their relative values depend upon color, transparency, and freedom from resinous matter. Resin [raul] may be easily detected by lighting a small piece of the wax; the more smoke, the greater proportion of resin, and therefore less value. The paler and more transparent the wax, the better. Medicinally wax is emollient and demulcent; ingredient in ointments, plasters and suppositories. Medicinally no difference between white and yellow. For honey see Shahad.——*Mom jauma* (موم جامہ - momjámah, Hind.). Wax cloth, used for covering packages in rainy weather, &c.——*Vegetable wax* (ಎಣ್ಣೆಮೇಣ - enneména, Can.; గూటిమైనము - gútimainamu, Tel.; എണ്ണക്കൂടി - ennakkúti, Mal.; எண்ணெய்மெழுகு - enneymezhugu, Tam.). Can. from (enne, can. oil + ména, can. wax). Tel. from (gúdu, tel. niche + mainamu, tel. wax); as found beneath lamp niches. Mal. from (enna, mal. oil + kútu, mal. to join). Tam. from (enney, tam. oil + mezhugu, tam. wax). Anglo-Indian term applied to solidified oil produced from oils [yennay], generally from the common lamp oil [q.v.] or castor [aumanac] oil of the country. Ilooppay oil [mohwah] also produces a perfectly white substance of the consistency of good tallow and is mixed with castor oil for the manufacture of vegetable wax. Margosa [neem] oil, the oil of Melia azadirachta, produces a vegetable wax as hard as any made from the best lamp oil and of a light saffron [q.v.] color.

MOMIN (مومن - momin, *Hind.*). From (amn, ar. peace). A true believer. Orthodox mahomedan.

MOMIREE (पशुमारण - pashumárana, *San.*; مومیری - momírí, *Hind.*; پیلی جڑی - pílíjarí, *Dec.*). Title from hindostany. San. from (pashu, san. cow + márana, san. death). Dec. from (pílí, hind. yellow + jarí, hind. root). Hind. also (piyárangá), meaning lovely color. Title otherwise Cow-killer, Feathered columbine, Meadow rue, Meadow spice root, Piyaranga root, Yellow root. Botanically Thalictrum foliolosum, dc., ranunculaceæ [vricsham, 1]. Herbaceous, erect, branched; leaves large, supra-decompound, leaflets very numerous, small, oval, cut and lobed; petioles auricular at the base; sepals oblong, obtuse, five to seven-nerved, pale green or brownish purple; stamens numerous; filaments filiform; anthers mucronate; panicles much branched, leafless; bracts small; achenia few, oval-oblong, acute at both ends, narrowly ribbed; flowers yellowish. Root fibrous, fasciculate, about the thickness of a crow quill, dark-brown externally, internally yellow, rather difficult to pulverize, bitter to the taste; yields to water 25 per cent. of a yellow bitter extract, to alcohol 15 per cent. In pharm. non-officinal; preparations, powder, tincture, and extract. Thalictrum flavum in france is called Poor man's rhubarb. There is another indian species, javanicum.

MONDAN (மொந்தன் - mondan, *Tam.*). From (mottam, tam. bulk); from large fruit. Same as Plantain.

MONDY (మొండి - mondi, *Tel.*). Bare. Suffix in place names, as Yadoormondy, meaning bamboo waste.——*Mondem* (మొండెము - mondemu, Tel.). A salt heap part of which has been sold. Distinguish from Mundem.

MONGOOSE (नकुल - nakula, *San.*; मुंगूस - mungúsa, *Mahr.*; ابن عرس - ibniirs, *Ar.*; راسو - rású, *Pers.*; نیولا - neulá, *Hind.*; منگوس - mungús, *Dec.*; ಮುಂಗುಲಿ - munguli, *Can.*; ಕೀರ - kíra, *Coorg*; ಮುಂಗಿಲಿ - mungili, *Too.*; ముంగిస - mungisa, *Tel.*; ନେଉଳ - nevulo, *Oor.*; കീരി - kíri, *Mal.*; මුගටියා - mugatiyá, *Singh.*; கீரிப்பிள்ளை - kírippillai, *Tam.*). Title from deccany. San. from (na, san. negative particle + kula, san. family). Ar. from (ibn, ar. son + irs, ar. lioness). Hind. from sanscrit. Oor. from sanscrit. Mal. from (kíru, mal. to squeak). Tam. from (kíri, tam. mongoose + pillai, tam. diminutive suffix of birds and animals). Can. also (mungisi). Tel. also (yentawa). Title otherwise Indian ichneumon, Pharoah's cat. Herpestes mungo, viverrinæ, viverridæ, digitigrada, carnivora, mammalia [sastanam, 11], of naturalists [jantoo]. Alias Herpestes ferrugineus, frederici, griseus, malaccensis, pallidus; Ichneumon griseus; Mangusta grisea, mungo, nyula; Viverra mungo. Nyula, from hindostany. The mongoose is a well-defined genus of animals, with long vermiform bodies, clad with long, harsh grizzled hair, long muscular tails, thick at the base, and tapering to a fine point; semi-plantigrade feet with five toes, and partially retractile claws; the eyes are small, but glittering and snake like; the tongue rough like a cat's [poonay]. Their extreme agility prevents their being bitten, and the stiff rigid hair, which is excited at such times, and a thick loose skin, are an additional protection. If the poison of a snake [sarpam] is injected into the veins of a mongoose it proves fatal. The cry of the mongoose is a mew. When angry it growls.—"*a*" The species mentioned at head is tawny yellowish gray, the hairs ringed with rufous and yellowish, the general result being an iron gray tinge, with less of the yellow tint than in the next species from Northern india, which it otherwise much resembles in size and form, whilst in the character of its fur it is more like Herpestes nipalensis. The muzzle is concolorous with the body, as is the tail, which is not tipped with black, and is nearly equal in length to the body. Frequently domesticated.—"*b*" Akin is the Long-tailed mongoose or the ruddy mongoose. Herpestes smithii of naturalists. Colors much as in Griseus, but somewhat more yellow in its general tone; tail longer, tipped with maroon and black, and more hairy; feet dark reddish-brown; muzzle not dark, slightly tinged with reddish. Larger than Griseus. Tail nearly equal in length to the head and body. Procured from the Eastern ghauts inland from Nellore, where it inhabits forests among the hills.—"*c*" Also the Brown Neilgherry mongoose. Herpestes fuscus of naturalists. General color brown, the hair being ringed black and yellow, and tawny at the base; throat dusky yellowish; tail nearly equal in length to head and body. Procured on the Neilgherries, probably in other elevated hill regions of Southern india.—"*d*" Lastly the Stripe-necked mongoose. Herpestes vitticollis of naturalists. Of a grizzled gray color more or less tinged with rusty reddish, especially on the hinder part of the body and tail; a dark stripe from the ear to the shoulder; tail rufous black at the tip. Found on the Western ghauts and in Travancore.—"*e*" Indian species of Herpestes not here found are:—Auropunctatus or gold-speckled, Burmanicus, Fulvescens, Pallidus, Urva or crab-eating.—"*f*" There is a Tamul proverb:—நன்றிசெய்த கீரிப்பிள்ளையைக் கொன்றகதைப்போல—"Like the story of killing a mongoose "that had done well"; the story being the same as Llewellyn's dog.——*Mongoose plant* (नाकुली - nákulí, San.). Same as Greater galangal.——*Mongoose snake root* (सर्पाक्षि - sarpákshi, San.; गडैपातालि - gardapátáli, Conc.; ಪಾತಾಳಗರುಡ - pátálagaruda, Can.; ಪಾತಾಳಗರುಡೆ - pátálagarude, Too.; సర్పాక్షి - sarpákshi; Tel.; അവില്പൊരി - avilpuri, Mal.; දත්කටියා - datkatiyá, Singh.; கீரிப்புரண்டான் - kírippurandán, Tam.). Title because the mongoose has recourse to the plant when bitten by cobra; cf. greater galangal. San. from (sarpa, san. serpent + akshi, san. eye). Conc. from (garuda, san. braminy kite + pátála, san. nether-world). Can. from (pátála, san. low regions + garuda, san. braminy kite). Too. like canarese. Tel. from sanscrit. Mal. means rice bruised and dried. Singh. from (dat, singh. sharp edged + katiya, singh. pittosporum ceylanicum). Tam. from (kíri, tam. mongoose + pural, tam. to roll over). San. also (sarpári), meaning serpent's enemy; (garudaputa), meaning garoodan's shoot; (pátálabhédi), meaning dividing the nether-world. Can. also (garudapátála). Singh. also (ekávériya), meaning rauwolfia serpentina, benth. (nágavalli), meaning serpent creeper, being considered a specific for bite of ribband snake. Tam. also (kírippúndu), meaning mongoose + plant. Title otherwise Indian snake root, Malayan earth gall, Mongoose plant, Pautaula garoodan, Sarpaury, Snake eye. Botanically Ophiorrhiza mungos, linn., rubiaceæ [vricsham, 71], specific from singhalese meaning mongoose. Perennial 1 to ½ foot; stem when old, suffruticose; leaves opposite, elliptic-lanceolate, acuminated at both ends, glabrous, very thin, unequal in size; calyx tube turbinate, limb five-cleft; corolla tube infundibuliform, short, hairy within, limb five-lobed; stamens enclosed; capsule compressed, crowned with the calycine segments, two-celled, two-valved; seeds numerous, somewhat hexagonal; cymes peduncled, terminal, branched; flowers nearly sessile white. The root consists of several hard, woody, contorted branches, about six inches in length, covered with a thin brown bark; the lower portions of the stem are generally collected along with the root. Root intensely bitter, used as a tonic, believed to be a remedy against the bites of venomous snakes, mad dogs, &c.; in pharm.

non-officinal. Several varieties slightly differ in form of inflorescence. Other common species are :—brunonis, eriantha, grandiflora, harrisiana, roxburghiana.

MONKEY (कपि - kapi, *San.*). Plant first name, either from fruits being eaten by monkeys [bandar], or from leaves and stalks being covered with hairs like those of the lungoor [q.v.], or from red seeds resembling face of white monkey.——*Monkey fruit* (कपित्थ - kapitt'ha, San.). Monkeys eat it. Same as Wood-apple.——*Monkey-leaf plant* (कीशपर्णी - kíshaparní, San.). Title from hairy leaf. Same as Indian burr.——*Monkey turmeric* (കുരങ്ങുമഞ്ഞൾ - kurannumaññal, Mal.). Same as Monkey country saffron.

MONSOON (वर्षाकाल - varshákála, *San.*; موسم - mausim, *Ar.* and *Pers.*; موسم - mosam, *Hind.* and *Dec.*; موسم - musim, *Malay*; ಮೋಸುಮಾ - mósumá, *Can.*; ಮರ್ಯಾಳ - maryála, *Too.*; వర్షాకాలము - varshákálamu, *Tel.*; വർഷം - varsham, *Mal.*; වැසිකල - vasikala, *Singh.*; மழைகாலம் - mazhaigálam, *Tam.*). Title from arabic through portuguese. San. from (varsha, san. rain + kála, san. time). Ar. from (vasama, ar. sign). Mal. from (vrish, san. to shower). Tam. from (mazhai, tam. rain + kálam, tam. time). Malay also (kutika); (kátika). Can. also (malekála), meaning rainy season. Tam. also (márigálam), meaning rainy season [maury]. Nothing can be added to what is said at vol. II, 5. Monsoons are not understood by Dravidians whose observation is too local. See Caulam, Caur, Mausam, Mazhay and Caurtey for their views on rainfall [land wind, longshore wind, sea breeze].

MOO (மூ - mú, *Tam.*). Forward, prominent, old.——*Macoorty* (ಮುಕುರ್ತಿ - múkurti, Can.). From (múgu, can. nose + aru, can. to cut + ti, can. feminine suffix); from a badaga tradition that a woman whose nose was cut off transformed herself into the mountain. Mountain; Neilgherry dist., Todanaud division; lat. 11° 22′ 05″; long. 76° 33′ 37″; height 8,330 feet; from Ootacamund W.S.W. 12 miles. One of highest peaks of Neilgherries; at junction of latter with Western ghauts [q.v.], about 10 miles behind Culcoodiyore. Commands a good view. Pycarrah river rises here. The ascent is by a zigzag path cut on E. face. Its western is an almost unbroken wall-like precipice, several thousand feet in depth. There was formerly a Todah [q.v.] boa [q.v.]; now in ruins. The spirits of men and buffaloes [khoolgah] are supposed by the Todahs to take a leap together into the next world from this peak.——*Minnal* (முன்னல் - munnal, Tam.). From (mun, tam. antiquity + il, tam. place). Title otherwise Menil. Village, Railway station; North arcot dist., Wallajahpett tal.; pop. 2,652; acres 3,564; lat. 13° 03′; long. 79° 37′; height 351 feet; from Chittore E.S.E. 33 miles; from Wallajahpett E.N.E. 17 miles. Station to which the Madras railway was first projected. Old Vishnoo temple.——*Molay* (മുള - mula, Mal.; முளை - mulai, Tam.). A young plant first springing from the ground. Bamboo [q.v.]. Prefix in place names; as Molaucadav, meaning bamboo ford.——*Monagooddaly* (మొనగుద్దలి - monaguddali, Tel.). From (mona, tel. point + guddali, tel. spade). Pickaxe.——*Monapollem* (మొనపాలెము - monapálemu, Tel.). From (mona, tel. end + pálemu, tel. fortified village); as bordering on the sea. Title otherwise Armegam. A hamlet of Poody royadorvoo belonging to Vencatagherry zemindarry; Nellore dist., Goodore tal.; pop. 1,861; lat. 13° 53′; long. 80° 15′; from Goodoor S.E. 29 miles; from Nellore S.S.E. 41 miles. Fishing village on one of the islands of the Poolicat lake. Lighthouse has been erected inside of the Armegam shoal [armegam, blackwood's harbour, doogarauzpatam].——*Monay* (మొన - mona, Tel.; முனை - munai, Tam.). Point. A cape. Principal capes of presidency are :—Cape comorin, most southern point of peninsula; Point calimere, south of Tranquebar and opposite Ceylon. For other headlands, &c., see Coast survey at vol. II, 146.——*Moodbidry* (ಮೂಡಬಿದ್ರಿ - múdabidri, Can.). From (mudu, can. east + bidu, can. vishnu + adri, san. mountain). Sanscrit name (púrvavénupura), meaning east + bamboo + town. A hamlet composed of portions of Prauntya and Pothigay villages; South canara dist., Mangalore tal.; pop. 921; lat. 13° 04′; long. 75° 03′; from Mangalore N.E. 18 miles; from the sea E. 14 miles. Ruined town. Once contained many thousands of inhabitants. Formerly subject to Jeina [q.v.] rajahs of the Chowtara family, whose descendants have still a palace here. Subsequently subject to the rajahs of Ikkairy until these were overthrown by Hyder. Still an important Jeina centre and visited by pilgrims even from Goozerat and other distant places. There are eighteen basties or Jeina temples, and a Mutt [q.v.] occupied by one of the chief gooroos [q.v.] of that sect. The basties illustrate the attempt to copy wooden forms which characterizes all Hindoo stone workings, especially those on the west coast. There are also several tombs of Jeina priests, lofty erections of several storeys, and interesting as being some of the few Hindoo tombs in Southern india. Their forms are quite unlike any other building now known to be standing in India. The rajah's old palace has an insignificant appearance as the roof is made only of thatch, but the stone sculptures inside are of a superior order. There is a handsomely carved wooden roof. The walls are covered with paintings. There is an old bridge near the Jeina basty, illustrating the efforts of Hindoos to bridge a stream while still ignorant of the principal of the arch. On the road to Caurcal, north of Moodbidry, is another ancient Jeina basty [q.v.].——*Moodelliar* (முதலியார் - muthaliyár, Tam.). Honorific form of Moodelly. Used in the Tamul districts of Ceylon, and formerly here also, for a native headman [peyar].——*Moodelly* (முதலி - muthali, Tam.). From (muthal, tam. first). The first one. Hindoo third name. Common among Vellaular [q.v.], and Keikkilar [q.v.]; also taken by males of the Devadausy [q.v.] class [peyar]. There is a Tamul proverb :—ஆழாக்கு அரிசி மூழாக்குப்பானை முதலியார் வருகிற வீருப்பைப்பாரும்— "With an olluck [q.v.] of rice in hand "and a pot that will suffice to boil 3 ollucks, look at the ostentation the Moodelliar displays [jauty];" they are considered to have this quality.——*Moodevy* (மூதேவி - múthévi, Tam.). From (mú, tam. old + déví, san. goddess, elder goddess). As poverty often precedes wealth, so Moodevy is poverty personified. The elder sister of Lutchmy [q.v.] and the goddess of unhappiness. She is said in literature to have her habitation with the glutton, the irascible, with liars and other abandoned characters, with those clothed in rags, with vicious women, in a flock of sheep [aud], and in the face of the dead. No special books are written about her, but the poets mention her here and there, and give her various names, viz., Calathy or she who confuses; Indreik moottaul or the elder sister of indray, or lutchmy; Jyeshtay or the elder sister; Kettay or she who ruins; Moogady or poverty; Tavvay or elder sister. She receives no offerings, nor is she worshipped in any pagoda [coil]. The Tamul cooral [q.v.] has the following :—ஔவித்தழுக்கா றுடையானைச்செய்யவ டௌவையைக்காட்டி விடும்— "Lutchmy envying the prosperity of the envious man will depart "and introduce her sister to him." And again :—மடியுளாள் மாமுகடி யென்பமடியிலான் றாளுளாடாமரையினாள்— "They say that the black Moodevy dwells with laziness and that "Lutchmy dwells with the labor of the industrious [matam]." See vol. I. (79).——*Moodiyootty* (ಮುದಿಗುಟ್ಟಿ - mudigutti, Can.). From (mudi, can. old + gutti, can. grave). Hill-tribe proper name [peyar].——*Moodroo* (ముదురు - muduru, Tel.). Means mature; hot season. Season and crops under S.W. monsoon. Same as Poonausa [caur].——*Moody* (ಮುಡಿ - mudi, Can.). Old.——*Moogady* (முகடி - mugadi, Tam.). Means misfortune. Moodevy.——*Mookk* (மூக்கு - múkku, Tam.). From (mú, tam. prominent). Nose.——*Mookkala* (ముక్కల - mukkala, Tel.). From (mukka, tel. portion). Locative pl. Suffix in place names; as Donimookkala, meaning boatmen's portions.——*Mookkan* (மூக்கன் - múkkan, Tam.). From (múkku, tam. nose); large-nosed. Pariah proper name [peyar].——*Mookkootty* (മൂക്കുത്തി - múkkutti, Mal.; மூக்குத்தி - múkkutti, Tam.). From (múkku, tam. nose + kuttu, tam. to pierce). Ornament worn on alæ of nose [nagay].——*Moolapett* (మూలపేట - múlapéta, Tel.). From (múla, san. corner + péta, tel. suburb). Tel. also (múlast'hánéshvarapéta), meaning shiva, the lord of the principal sacred place + suburb. Village; lat. 14° 27′; long. 80° 01′; from Nellore W.S.W. ½ mile; from the sea W. 14 miles. Suburb of Nellore.——*Moolay* (మూల - múla, Tel.; மூலை - múlai, Tam.). Corner.——*Mooll* (ಮುಳ್ಳು - mullu, Can.; ముల్లు - mullu, Tel.; മുള്ള - mullu, Mal.; முள் - mul, Tam.). Thorn.—"*a*" Plant first term, often joining two genera. Ex., where transl. is of second term :—Barleria prionitis (mullugórante), lawsonia alba; Berberis aristata (mullukkilá), carissa species; Bombax malabaricum (mullilavu), eriodendron anfractnosum; Bridelia retusa, var. genuina (mulvéngai), pterocarpus marsupium; Erythrina indica (mullumurikku), butea frondosa; Opuntia dillenii (mullukalli), euphorbia. See gloss. paragraphs.—"*b*" Plant second term. Ex., where transl. is of first term :—Acanthus illicifolius (kazhuthaimulli), ass, (kózhimulli), fowl; Barleria cristata (nílasemmulli), black + red, (úthámulli), brown; Barleria cuspidata (vellaimulli), white; Barringtonia speciosa (shemmulli), red; Cæsalpinia mimosoides (tímullu), fire; Dædalacanthus nervosus (nílamulli), blue; Flacourtia sepiaria (kurumulli), small; Hygrophila spinosa (nírmulli), water; Opuntia dillenii (nágamullu), cobra; Pedalium murex (kákkamullu), crow; Polycarpæa corymbosa (páramullu), rock; Zizyphus œnoplia (túrimullu), meaning piercing. See gloss. paragraphs.—"*c*" Fish first term. From spines. Ex., where transl. is of second term :—Ambassis thomasis (mullujubbu), globe; Chirocentrus dorab (mulluválai), wallago attu; Diodon hystrix (mullambiláççai), sea frog, ostracion genus; Urogymnus asperrimus (mullaudirukkai), stinging ray or thorn back, trygon genus. See gloss. paragraphs.——*Moon* (முன் - mun, Tam.). Before. Front.——*Moonair* (మునేరు - muniyéru, Tel. muniyur *). From (muni, tel. point + éru, tel. river). River; Kistna dist., Nundigauma tal. The largest tributary of Kistna in district. Rises in Nizam's dominions; crosses Hyderabad road at Keesara, 25 miles N.W. by W. of Bezwada, being there called the Keesara; and joins the main stream about 20 miles above the anicut [q.v.] at Bezwada. Fordable except for a few days in the rainy season.——*Moondlapaud* (ముండ్లపాడు - mundlapádu, Tel.). From (mullu, tel. thorn + pádu, tel. village). Sanscrit name (mundéshvara), meaning shiva, the shaven-headed + lord. Village; Kurnool dist., Cumbum tal.; pop. 3,047; acres 8,159; lat. 15° 20′; long. 78° 57′; from Cumbum S.W. 22 miles; from Kurnool S.E. 66 miles. On the Yenoomoolair. Built by shepherd, Caumana boyanna and held by his family till the downfall of the Vijianugger dynasty [raj] when it was seized by a Naidoo chief of Velgode, the ancestor of the present Vencatagherry rajah [velgode]. In 1659, it passed into the hands of the Golcondah king. A Pataun [q.v.] obtained Talapully, a hamlet, in jagheer [q.v.]. In 1696 Chalchalmala narsimha reddy of Nossam obtained Bramhanapully, Moondlapaud, Vaimlapaud, and two other villages in jagheer. In 1749 his son Runga reddy built a fort in the fields of Tallapully, calling it Cottacote [q.v.]. Deserted temple to Bheiravan [q.v.]. Temple of Bhawauny shuncarasawmy. Ruined fort. At Tallapully is an old mosque [musjid].——*Moongaur* (ಮುಂಗಾರು - mungáru, Can.). From (munde, can. before + káru, can. crop). Season and crop of S.W. monsoon [caur, poonausa].——*Moonnadiyaur* (முன்னடியார் - munnadiyár, Tam.). From (mun, tam. before + adiyán, tam. slave). Head-servants; the two door-keepers [dwaura paulacan] standing at the entrance of the temple of Ayenaur [ayen].——*Moonnone* (முன்னோன் - munnón, Tam.). Means the first. Vigneshwaran [q.v.], the elder son.——*Mooppan* (மூப்பன் - múppan, Tam.). An elder, the headman of a class or business, especially among agriculturalists.——*Mooppapanam* (മൂപ്പപ്പണം - múppappanam, Mal.). From (múppan, mal. head man + panam, mal. money). A premium made to an owner by tenant.——*Moopp cazhivoo* (மூப்புக்கழிவு - múppukkazhivu, Tam.). From (múppu, tam. seniority + kazhivu, tam. exemption). Dues payable to the headman of a village.——*Moopp staunam* (മൂപ്പസ്ഥാനം - múppust'hánam, Mal.). From (múppu, mal. seniority + st'hána, mal. place). Headship.——*Moosaliyaur* (മുസലിയാർ - musaliyár, Mal.). From (mutaliyár, mal. headman). Moplah [q.v.] title.——*Moosiry* (முசிரி - musiry, Tam.). See sep. title.——*Moossad* (മൂസ്സത - mússatu, Mal.). See sep. title.——*Mootchy* (മൂച്ചി - múççi, Mal.). From (múkka, mal. to grow). An old mango [q.v.] tree.——*Moothal* (മുതൽ - mutal, Mal.; முதல் - muthal, Tam.). Means first [moodelly]; hence capital, property.——*Moothalady* (முதலடி - muthaladi, Tam.). From (muthal, tam. first + adi, tam. to thresh). First crop.——*Moothalaulan* (മുതലാളൻ - mutalálan, Mal.). From (mutal, mal. property + álu, mal. to own). The native term for Jenmy [q.v.].——*Moothalavacausham* (മുതലവകാശം - mutalavakásham, Mal.). From (mutal, mal. property + avakásha, san. right). Right to property.——*Moothal cadan* (முதற்கடன் - mutharгadan, Tam.). From (muthal, tam. capital + kadan, tam. debt); loan of capital. Advance of money to ryots [q.v.] for bullocks and seed to enable them to cultivate [tuccauvy].——*Moothal maday* (முதல்மடை - muthalmadai, Tam.). A field first watered from a tank [q.v.].——*Moothal palisha* (മുതൽപലിശ - mutalpalisha, Mal.). From (mutal, mal. property + palisha, mal. interest). Principal and interest.——*Moothal sambandham* (മുതൽസംബന്ധം - mutalsambandham, Mal.). From (mutal, mal. property + sambandha, san. relationship). Community of property. On the West coast those who are members of the same family are said to be connected by Moothal sambandham, whilst those who were once of the same family and have separated from one another are said to be connected by Poolasambandham [q.v.] or community of pollution. In questions of inheritance [dauyam], on failure of the former class who are termed Auandraven [q.v.], the latter inherit and are termed Attaladakkam heirs [maryauday].——*Moothoo* (முது - muthu, Tam.). Ancient.——*Moothoocoolatore* (முதுக்குளத்தூர் - muthukkulattúr, Tam. mutukulatur *). From (muthu, tam. old + kulam, tam. tank + úr, tam. village).—"*a*" Deputy tahsildarry, Ramnaud zemindarry, Madura district. Pay Rs. 70. Subregistrar's office.—"*b*" Village; Madura dist., Ramnaud zemindarry; pop. 3,172; lat. 9° 20′; long. 78° 34′; from Dindigul S.S.E. 79 miles; from Kodaykarnal S.E. 93 miles; from Madras S.S.W. 282 miles; from Madura S.S.E. 48 miles; from Rameshwaram W. 56 miles; from Ramnaud W. 22 miles. Head-quarters of a Zameen [q.v.] talook [q.v.] of the same name. Weekly market on Thursday.——*Moothoomullay* (മുതുമല - mutumala, Mal.). From (mutu, mal. old + mala, mal. mountain). Tract of country. Forest; Neilgherry dist., Wynaud S.E. division; square miles 73; lat. between 11° 32′ and 11° 42′; long. 76° 29′ and 76° 40′; from Goodalore N. 8 miles; from Ootacamund N.W. 19 miles. On the Goodalore-Mysore road. Consists principally of teak [q.v.], vengay [q.v.] and bamboo [q.v.]. In the forests is a deserted temple in good preservation.——*Moothooray* (முதுரை - múthurai, Tam.). From (múthu, tam. old + urai, tam. speech). One of Avvay's [q.v.] five aphoristic works taught in schools [auttisoody, calvy oloocam, condray vendan, nalvazhy].——*Moottad* (മൂത്തത് - múttatu, obl.; മൂത്തവൻ - múttavan, pers. sing.; മൂത്തവർ - múttavar, pers. pl., Mal.). From (mútta, mal. old). Caste-title. Class of ambalavausies [q.v.]; cf. Moossads, who are however brauins.——*Moottan* (முத்தன் - muttan, Tam.), Pariah proper name [peyar].——*Moottaul* (முத்தாள் - múttál, Tam.). Means the elder. Moodevy.——*Mooyiricode* (മുയിരിക്കോട്ട - muyirikkótta, Mal.). From (mutiru, mal. to grow old + kótta, mal. fort). Greek μούζιρις. Old name of Krishnamcottah opposite to Cranganore [q.v.].

MOO (ము - mu, *Tel.*; மு - mu, *Tam.*). Three.——*Mooatpoya* (മൂവാറ്റുപുഴ - múváttupuzha, Mal.). From (mú, mal. three + áru, mal. river + puzha, mal. river); literally river formed of three rivers.—"*a*" Talook, Travancore state, Cottayam division. Population 95,460. Sub-divided into eight praverties [q.v.] and containing 162 caras [q.v.] or villages. Greatest length N. to S. is 30 miles, and greatest breadth E. to W. is 18 miles. Bounded N. by Aulangaud talook, E. by Todoopoya and Meenachel talooks, S. by Yaittmanore talook and W. by Coonnatnaud and the Cochin territory. Hilly. Areca nut [q.v.] is principal produce and is exported. Mooatpoya river irrigates.—"*b*" Town; Travancore state, Cottayam division, Mooatpoya tal.; pop. 11,874; lat. 9° 59′; long. 76° 37′; from Cottayam N. 27 miles; from Madras S.W. 330 miles; from Nagarcoil N.N.W. 134 miles; from Paravore E.S.E. 27 miles; from Quilon N. 73 miles; from Trivandrum N.N.W. 105 miles; from the sea E. 23 miles. Agreeably situated at junction of two rivers, and in neighbourhood of a third. Small town inhabited by Christians and Lubbays [q.v.].—"*c*" River; Travancore state, Cottayam division, Todoopoya, Mooatpoya, and Wycome talooks. The three branches rise in the mountainous tract stretching eastward of the village of the same name, uniting immediately in its vicinity. These streams pass through a wild country, but their joint flood proceeds over a sandy bottom and between banks which gradually diminish as river approaches the town of Wuddiyaur, where its water separating into a variety of channels [q.v.] are discharged into Vembanaud lake 28 miles below Mooatpoya. The river runs a course north-west generally of sixty-two miles, forty-three of which are navigable during the rains. Boats ascending to Codamungalam and Todwully at this period float a greater distance.——*Mooccanty* (ముక్కంటి - mukkanti, Tel.). From (múdu, tel. three + kannu, tel. eye). An epithet of Shiva [q.v.]. See vol. I (129); II, 112. Mookkanteshwaran is the same.——*Mooccoty yecaudashy* (ముక్కోటేకాదశి - mukkótékádashi, Tel.). Means three crores + eleventh lunar day; from tradition that all the gods [deva] visit the place on the occasion. Otherwise Swarga dwaura yecaudashy, Swarga vausal yecaudashy, Veicoonta yecaudashy. Lunar [chaundramaunam] festival [pundigay, 3e], subject to intercalation [adhicam]. The eleventh tity [q.v.] of the waxing moon [shooclapacsham], of ninth lunar month Margashiram [mausam] between 26th November and 25th December. A general fast observed in honor of Vishnoo [q.v.], and kept all day and night; no one should indulge in sleep during the whole of the tity. The day of the great festival of the Vishnoo pagoda [q.v.] at Shreerungam [cottye ootsavam, maryauday]. See vol. I (92).——*Mooccunnan* (முக்கண்ணன் - mukkannan, Tam.). Three-eyed. Epithet of Shiva.——*Mooccunny* (முக்கண்ணி - mukkanni, Tam.). Bhadra cauly; the three-eyed goddess. Also cocoanut, the three-eyed fruit.——*Moocooppey* (ಮೂಕುಪ್ಪೆ - múkuppe, Can.). From (above + kuppe, can. heap). Mode of cultivation by which crop is divided into three parts, one for rent, one for labor, third for seed and implements.——*Moommay* (மும்மை - mummai, Tam.). From (above + mai, tam. suffix of condition). The three different states of existence, viz.:—Oommay the former birth, Inmay the present birth, and Ammay futurity [tritwam].——*Moommoorty* (மும்மூர்த்தி - mummúrtti, Tam.). From (above + múrtti, san. body). The Hindoo triad [trimoorty]. See vol. I (74).——*Moonanaud* (മൂന്നാട് - múnnanátu, Mal.). From (múnnu, mal. third + nádu, mal. country); country of third chief. Amshom; Neilgherry dist., Wynaud S.E. division; pop. 1,243; acres 38,784; lat. between 11° 28′ and 11° 39′; long. between 76° 19′ and 76° 30′; from Goodalore N.W. 6 miles; from Ootacamund W. 20 miles. Prior to consolidation of Keralam [q.v.] into one empire under Cherma permaul [q.v.], divisions were held by chieftains. Moopnaud was country of First chief; Moonanaud tract held by Third chief. This amshom [q.v.] consists of the three deshoms [q.v.] of Moonanaud, Nelacottah, and Nelliyaulam. The temple of Ponnairy is of great repute. Its present trustee is the Vandoor numboodripaud. The Phœnix, Glenrock, and Consolidated are gold mines.——*Moonneer* (முந்நீர் - munnír, Tam.). From (above + nír, tam. water). Three kinds of water [neer], viz., spring, rain, and river.——*Moopparah* (മൂപ്പറ - múppara, Mal.). From (above + para, mal. a measure). Three measures, that is to say three in ten. Assessment of three-tenths of the average of full tax on paddy [q.v.] lands.——*Mooppath* (முப்பது - muppathu, Tam.). From (above + pattu, tam. ten). Three tens or thirty. Title of numerous poems.——*Mooppow* (ముప్పావు - muppávu, Tel.). From (above + pávu, tel. a quarter). Three-quarters of any coin.——*Mootchundy moopan* (முச்சந்திமூப்பன் - muççandimúppan, Tam.). From (above + shandi, tam. meeting + múppan, tam. president). The president of the three periods of the day. One of the Tamulian devils [pey],

MOOABAUDAL (जलशोषणी - jalashóshaní, *San.*; اسفنج - isfanj, *Ar.*; ابر مرده - abrimurdah, *Pers.*; مواباڈل - muábádal, *Hind.*; ಸಮುದ್ರದಪಾಚಿ - samudradapáchi, *Can.*; సముద్రపుపాచి - samudrapupáchi, *Tel.*; നീരൊപ്പി - níroppi, *Mal.*; கடற்காளான் - kadargálán, *Tam.*). Title from hindostany. San. from (jala, san. water + shush, san. to dry). Pers. from (abr, pers. cloud + murdah, pers. dead). Hind. from (muá, hind. lifeless + bádal, hind. cloud). Can. from (samudra, can. sea + páchi, can. moss). Tel. ditto. Mal. from (nír, mal. water + oppu, mal. wipe). Tam. from (kadal, tam. sea + kálán, tam. fungus). Ar. also (sahábulbahr), meaning sea-cloud. Pers. also (abrikuhan), meaning old cloud. Sponge. A skeleton of cells and pores, secreted by numerous associated gelatinous animalcules. The animal matter is removed by soaking in salt water. This leaves the skeleton. Found by divers attached to bottom of rocks. When properly prepared, very porous, light, soft and brownish yellow.

MOOAZZAZ (معزز - muzzaz, *Ar.*). From (azzu, ar. to strengthen). Honored. Part of lacab; as Mooazzaz ood dowlah, honor of the empire [ism].

MOOAZZIN (موذن - muazzin, *Hind.*). From (izn, ar. permission). The herald of the mosque [musjid] who calls persons to prayers [azaun, namauz].

MOOBAUDALAH (مبادله - mubádalah, *Hind.*). From (badl, ar. exchange) [budl]. Sums lent and paid on running accounts without the use of receipts.

MOOBAURAK (مبارک - mubárak, *Ar.*). Propitious. Prefixed to an alam forms a lacab; as Moobaurak ally, blessed of ally [ism].

MOOCARRAM (مکرم - mukarram, *Ar.*). From (karuma, ar. to respect). Venerable; respected. Prefixed to an alam forms a lacab; as Moocarram jung, venerable in war [ism].

MOOCH (मुच - much, *San.*). To liberate.——*Mocha* (मोच - mócha, San.). From (much, san. to liberate). Same as Red-cotton tree. Ch is soft; distinguish from Arabian town, where ch is hard.——*Mocharas* (मोचरस - mócharasa, San.; موچرس - mocharas, Hind.; ಬೂರಗದಅಂಟು - búragadaantu, Can.; బూరగబంక - búragabanka, Tel.; പൂളപ്പശ - púlappasha, Mal.; ඉඹුල්ලාටු - imbullátu, Singh.; இலவம்பிசின் - ilavambisin, Tam.). Ch is soft. Title from hindostany. San. from (mócha, san. the tree, bombax malabaricum, dec. + rasa, san. juice). Hind. from sanscrit. Can. from (búraga, can. bombax malabaricum, dec. + antu, can. gum). Tel. from (búraga, tel. bombax malabaricum, dec. + banka, tel. gum). Mal. from (púla, san. the tree, bombax malabaricum, dec. + pasha, mal. gum). Singh. from (imbul, singh. silk-cotton tree + látu, singh. gum). Tam. from (ilavu, tam. silk-cotton tree + pisin, tam. gum). The gum of Bombax malabaricum, dec. [red-cotton tree]. Also stands for that of Moringa pterygosperma, gærtn. [moringa]. Both occur in very irregular nodular, smooth, and shell-like pieces, opaque and dark-brown in color; the moringa mocharas is very hard and broken with difficulty, and the red-cotton mocharas is brittle and easily broken and less astringent in taste. The latter is the inferior of the two.——*Mochcoondam* (मुचुकुन्द - muchukunda, San.). From (much, san. to abandon + kunda, san. jasminum pubescens, willd.); from white fragrant flowers excelling jasmine. Botanically the Pterospermum genus, sterculiaceæ [vricsham, 26]. Trees or shrubs; leaves alternate, entire or toothed, and usually very oblique; flowers usually large, white and fragrant; capsule woody containing many winged seeds; wood reddish, moderately hard. The species best known to the natives here are:—acerifolium [kaniyaur], suberifolium [velanga]. Some species in Moluccas give Amboyna wood, Kyaboca wood, or Lingo wood.——*Mocsham* (मोक्ष - móksha, San.). From (much, san. to set free). Emancipation. Especially of the soul, and its exemption from further transmigration [samsauram]. Mocsha dharmam is rules for attaining final emancipation.——*Mooc* (मुकु - muku, San.). Liberation.——*Moocoondan* (मुकुन्द - mukunda, San.). From (muku, san. liberation + dá, san. to give). Vishnoo [q.v.].——*Moocoondapooram* (മുകുന്ദപുരം - mukundapuram, Mal.). From (mukunda, san. vishnu, the giver of absolution + pura, san. town).—"*a*" Talook, Cochin state; area 418¼ square miles; pop. 115,212. Divided into Arippaulam, Codacherry, Coratty, Maupraunam, Moocoondapooram, Patinettarayaulam, Paulatingal, Poothoocaud and Taulacaud divisions. Principal places:—Adoor, Annamanada, Caroopadanna, Chaulacoody, Codacherry, Coondoor, Coratty, Irinyaulacode, Keeyoor, Maupraunam, Poothoocaud, Rappaul, and Tirvanjicoolam.—"*b*" Village; Cochin state, Moocoondapooram talook.——*Moocty* (मुक्ति - mukti, San.). From (much, san. to deliver). Final beatitude, exemption from further transmigration, re-absorption of the emancipated spirit [autmam], into its great primary source, identification with God. Moocty is of two kinds, partial and complete deliverance. There are three impediments to Moocty, viz., ignorance, doubt, and perversion [matam, samsauram].——*Moty* (موتی - motí, Hind.). See sep. title.

MOOCHEE (موچی - mochí, *Hind.*). One who works in leather [chamrah], either as shoemaker, book-binder or saddler. Also employed in painting [rangh], gilding, and upholsterer's work, &c. One who serves out paper, quills, &c., in a public office; the duftery of N. india.——*Moochee wood* (ముచ్చికఱ్ఱ - muççikarra, Tel.). Product of Erythrina [coral tree] indica, lam., leguminosæ [vricsham, 48]. Among timber trees the following also are found with soft light wood, but they are not specifically called moochee-wood:—Bombax malabaricum [red-cotton tree]; Eriodendron anfractuosum [silk cotton]; Euphorbia tirucalli [round milk-hedge]; Givotia rottleriformis [white tanakk]; Hymenodictyon excelsum [wild anaur]; Sesbania ægyptiaca [common sesban]; Sterculia urens [false kateerah].

MOOCHILKA (مچلکه - muchalkah, *Hind.*). From turkish. An agreement in writing. Generally the counterpart of a lease executed by the tenant to the landlord. See vol. I, 112.

MOOCTIAR (مختار - mukhtár, *Hind.*). From (khára, ar. to choose). Principal, independent. An attorney; not allowed in general to plead, which is the function of the vakeel [q.v.]. Mooctiar nauma is a power-of-attorney [iktiarnauma]. Part of lacab; as Mooctiar oon nissa, chief of ladies; Mooctiar ool moolk, absolute lord of the kingdom [ism].

MOOCWA (ಮುಕ್ಕವ - mukkava, *Can.*; മുക്കുവർ - mukkuvar, *Mal.*). From (muzhugu, tam. to dive); as diving for pearls. Fishermen in Canara and Malabar, said to be immigrants from Ceylon, and are probably allied to the Ilavar [q.v.]. The corresponding terms are:—Tam. shembadava, Tel. besta. Their proper business is that of fishermen, or palankeen-bearers [boy] for persons of low birth or of no caste; but they serve also as boatmen. In some places they cultivate the cocoanut [q.v.]. In the southern parts of the coast most of them have become Mahomedans, but continue to follow their usual occupations. These are held in contempt by those of the north. They have hereditary chiefs called Aryan [q.v.], who settle disputes, and, with the assistance of a council, punish by fine or excommunication those who transgress the rules of the caste. Some of the Moocwas marry, which ceremony consists in a feast without any religious rite. In this case, the marriage can only be dissolved on account of the woman's infidelity. They have another kind of marriage called Parastry, in which the man and woman may separate whenever they please; the children always go along with their mother. The Moocwas can eat all kinds of animal food, except beef and may lawfully drink intoxicating liquors. They have no gooroo [q.v.], nor poorohit [q.v.]. The deity of the caste is the goddess Bhadra cauly [q.v.], who is represented by a log of wood, which is placed in a hut that is called a temple. Four times a year the Moocwas assemble, sacrifice a cock, and make offerings of fruit to the log. One of the caste acts as poojarry [q.v.], but his office is not hereditary. They are not allowed to enter any of the temples of the great gods, worshipped by the Bramins [q.v.], but they sometimes stand at a distance and send their offerings by more pure hands. They know nothing of a state of future existence, but believe in pishauch, or evil spirits, who inflict diseases and occasion other evils. A class of men called Caniyaun are employed to drive away pishauch [q.v.]. They bury the dead [jauty, shavacaud]. Among these and among the corresponding class of Paravar [q.v.] on the East coast, Xavier's most noted labors in India occurred. See vol. I (16), (68); II, 100.

MOODA (മൂട - múta, *Mal.*). From (mútu, mal. to cover).—"*a*" A fastening package. Especially the packages in a circular form, like a Dutch cheese, fastened with wisps of straw, in which rice is made up in Malabar and Canara.—"*b*" A measure of capacity. $2\frac{1}{2}$ parrahs = 1 mooda [alavay, 3c]. Approximate actual value, 1 mooda = 1 cubic foot and 1,116 cubic inches. In South canara, it is equal to 3 kulsies. Same as Robin. See vol. I, 609; II, 508.——*Moody* (ಮುಡಿ - mudi, Can.). From (mútu, mal. to cover). See vol. I, 609; II, 508.—"*a*" Measure of capacity. 3 kulsies = 1 moody; 42 moodies = 1 corjy [alavay, 3c]. Approximate actual value, 1 moody = 2,940 cubic inches. South canara. Varies. A moody of grain weighs about one Indian maund. Same as Robin. Compare Toom of Kistna, and Calam of Tanjore.—"*b*" Superficial measure [alavay, 2c]. Land requiring a moody of seed. Standard measure of S. canara. In measuring land a moody is taken at 60 pucka seers. The extent for wet land about an acre. Compare Cawny. See vol. I, 609; II, 508.

MOODAUM (مدام - mudám, *Hind.*). Constant. Moodaum sibbundy is a fixed establishment. In the eastern districts they are a kind of extra peon [q.v.] placed in villages for general service.

MOODAY (முடை - mudai, *Tam.*). To plait.——*Moodasal* (முடைசல் - mudasal, Tam.). From (mudai, tam. to plait). A screen formed with bamboos [q.v.] and cocoanut [q.v.] or palmyra [q.v.] leaves for protection of banks of rivers from action of stream.——*Moodipp* (ముడుపు - mudupu, Tel.; முடிப்பு - mudippu, Tam.). A tie; money wrapt in a cloth and tied up. Moodippcauran is a person who makes or holds the purse, collector of revenue in primitive village arrangements [tandalgar].——*Moody* (முடி - mudi, Tam.). A knot, especially bundle of young rice tied in small bundles for transplanting [nautt moody, paddy].

MOODRAY (मुद्रा - mudrá, *San.*; முத்திரை - muttirai, *Tam.*). From (mud, san. to unite). Intertwining of the fingers practised in religious worship and symbolical. Also a seal.——(1) *Moodracurta* (முத்திராக்கர்த்தா - muttiraikkarttá, Tam.). From (above + kartá, san. doer). Bramin sheivites are under the religious supervision of high priests [acharry]. These religious heads make their pastoral visitation according to their convenience once in five, ten or fifteen years. But they have deputies or Moodracurtas, generally one for each talook, to look after the people and report from time to time any irregularity on their part in the observance of religious rites or caste rules. These Moodracurtas, who are always of the same persuasion as the high priest, are not paid any fixed salaries. They rent the privileges and perquisites of the high priest for a fixed number of years. At the close of the period they are either reappointed or superseded by others at the discretion of the high priest. Sometimes the appointment of Moodracurta is hereditary. The religious or moral offences of which the high priest or his agents take cognizance are the following :—Disobedience to shreemookhams or orders of the priest; Disregard of the local sabhay or assembly of bramins; Co-habitation with a shoodra woman; Drunkenness; Non-observance of annual ceremony to the deceased; Bramin widows of more than twenty years of age not shaving their heads; Omission to perform the ceremonies prescribed in the case of a somayaujee's death; Eating flesh; Illicit intercourse by a widow or a married woman; Other minor offences. The penalties imposed for any of these offences are fine and excommunication from caste. Besides Shrotriems [q.v.] and minor Inams [q.v.] in various parts of the country possessed by the priest, he is entitled by custom to receive the following fees and perquisites :—Varshaushanam or annual tax, payable by a bramin according to a list originally prepared, from 4 annas upwards; House-tax at 4 annas, payable by the comaties and merchants; a marriage fee, payable by bramins and comaties, the fee varying according to the circumstances of the family; Agrapoojay paid in acknowledgment of priest's title for precedence; Yeda paid by comaties on the occasion of funeral ceremonies, consisting of money, rice and sundries; Badimauda or schoolmaster's fee at two rupees paid by pyall masters in expiation of the sin committed by them by selling learning, almost obsolete. Besides these, the priest receives large sums on his pastoral visitation [matam]. Cf. Jiyyangar.——*Moodrah dhauranam* (मुद्राधारणा - mudrádháraná, San.). From (above + dhri, san. to bear). Bearing an indelible mark on some part of the body made with a hot iron, representing the insignia of a deity, as the shell of Vishnoo [q.v.], as a sectarial indication.——*Moodray munn* (முத்திரைமண் - muttiraiman, Tam.). From (above + man, tam. mud). The earth seal affixed to a grainheap, and stamped with some mark.——*Moodray palagay* (முத்திரைப்பலகை - muttiraippalagai, Tam.). From (above + p'halaka, san. board). A wooden stamp for sealing a heap of corn.——*Moodrola* (മുദ്രോല - mudróla, Mal.). From (above + óla, mal. cadjan). Stamped cadjan [q.v.].——*Mothiram* (மோதிரம் - móthiram, Tam.). From (mudrá, san. stamp). Finger-ring.——(2) *Matsya moodray* (మత్స్యముద్ర - matsyamudra, Tel.). From (matsya, san. fish). Hindoo gold coin struck by Paundy kings.——*Nauga moodray* (ನಾಗಮುದ್ರೆ - nágamudre, Can.). From (nága, san. snake). Hindoo gold coin struck by Moraury row; also known as Moraury row hana.——*Padava moodray* (పడవముద్ర - padavamudra, Tel.). From (padava, tel. ship). Old Hindoo copper coin [naunyam].

MOOFTY (مفتی - muftí, *Hind.*). From (fatá, ar. to decide). Pronounced Mufty by Anglo-indians. In former times the officer who assisted the Cauzy [q.v.] or judge, and supplied him with decisions on legal points. The word is commonly used also to denote the civilian dress worn by a military or naval officer when off duty.

MOOHAUJIR (مهاجر - muhájir, *Hind.*). From (hijr, ar. separation). A class of Mahomedan sheikhs, descendants of the exiles and refugees who accompanied the prophet [mahomed] in his flight from Mecca to Medina.

MOOHOO (मुहु - muhu, *San.*). In a moment.——*Moohoorta caul* (முகூர்த்தக்கால் - mugúrttakkál, Tam.). From (muhúrta, san. auspicious moment + kál, tam. pillar). The first pillar put to a marriage pandaul. It is ornamented with alternate stripes of white and red, either in paper or in choonam [q.v.] and red ochre [cauvy]. To the top is tied a bunch of mango [q.v.] leaves. The pillar is fixed in an auspicious moment, decided on by the poorohit [q.v.].——*Moohoortam* (मुहूर्त - muhúrta, San.). From (muhus, san. often). Measure of solar time. 30 calays = 1 moohoortam; 30 moohoortams = 1 dinam or day [caulam, 2]. Approximate actual value, 1 moohoortam = 48 English minutes. Same as San. cshanam. Moohoortam is also taken as equal to 3¾ ghaticams or 1½ English hours. Distinguish from Moortam [caulam, 3]. See vol. I, 609.

MOOJAUHID (مجاهد - mujáhid, *Ar.*). From (jahada, ar. to strive after truth). Persevering in religious cause. Part of lacab; as Moojauhid ood deen, the hero of faith [ism].

MOOJAUWIR (مجاور - mujávir, *Hind.*). From (javar, ar. near). An attendant at a Mahomedan shrine [durgah], hermitage, or other consecrated spot [goombaz].

MOOJEEB (مجيب - mujíb, *Hind.*). From (vajaba, ar. to approve). Acceptor of supplications. Attribute of God [allah] part of common alam; as Abdool moojeeb [ism].

MOOJTABAH (مجتبی - mujtabá, *Hind.*). From (jába, ar. to choose). Approved. Lacab of the prophet. Common alam; as Moojtabah hoossain, double alam [ism].

MOOJTAHID (مجتهد - mujtahid, *Hind.*). From (jihada, ar. to strive after truth). Doctor of law, whose exposition of doctrines is accepted and followed by the orthodox moslems [soonnee] without the exercise of private judgment [takleed].

MOOKHADIRAUT (مخدرات - mukhaddirát, *Hind.*). From (khadira, ar. to become languid). Narcotics; substances which are either anodyne in their action or sodorific. For intoxicants see Mooskiraut. The following are two key-lists of the principal narcotic substances used by the natives of s. india; further information must be traced in the glossary paragraphs through the small type cross-references at end of this volume; see also vricsham, 7, for the method of expressing the products, &c., of the plants in the dravidian languages.—"*a*" Aconitum ferox, indian aconite, root; Anamirta cocculus, indian berry, berry; Cannabis sativa, indian hemp, whole plant, except large stem; Cerbera odollam, odallam, nut; Cinnamomum camphora, camphor cinnamon, camphor; Datura fastuosa, purple datura, seed; Hydnocarpus venenata, fish poison tree, seeds; Nicotiana tabacum, tobacco, leaf; Papaver somniferum, opium; Solanum melongena, brinjaul, leaf; Solanum nigrum, indian hound's berry, leaf; Strychnos nux-vomica, poison nut, seed; Withania somnifera, asgand, root.—"*b*" Aconite, aconitum; Asgand, withania; Brinjaul, solanum; Camphor, cinnamomum; Fish poison, hydnocarpus; Hemp, cannabis; Hound's berry, solanum; Indian berry, anamirta; Odallam, cerbera; Opium, papaver; Poison nut, strychnos; Tobacco, nicotiana.

MOOKHAM (मुख - mukha, *San.*). Face.——*Mookhyam* (मुख्य - mukhya, San.). From (mukha, san. face). Front, chief [mookhya mausam].——*Mookhyastan* (മുഖ്യസ്ഥൻ - mukhyast'han, Mal.). From (mukhya, san. chief + st'ha, san. stand). A modern term, introduced since Hyder's invasion of Malabar, meaning Tarwaudcaurar. See vol. I, 117.

MOOKHAUTIB (مخاطب - mukhátib, *Hind.*). From (khataba, ar. to converse with) [khitaub]. In person.

MOOLAINAGHERRY (ಮುಲ್ಲೈನಗಿರಿ - mulainagiri, *Can.*; mulaingiri, *Mys. Gov.*). From (muluku, can. arrow or arrow-head + giri, san. hill). Mountain. Highest point in the Bababooden range, 6,317 feet, and is the loftiest mountain between the Himalayas and the Neilgherries.

MOOLAM (मूल - múla, *San.*). From (múl, san. to be rooted). Original. Root. Vegetable; organic body destitute of sense and motion, but furnished with pores and vessels, by the help of which it draws nourishment from other bodies; natives consider that it has sense and partial motion.——*Moola dhanam* (मूलधन - múladhana, San.). From (above + dhana, san. property). Capital [moothal].——*Moola lingam* (मूललिङ्ग - múlalinga, San.). From (above + linga, san. emblem of shiva). Chief lingam [q.v.].——*Moola muntram* (मूलमन्त्र - múlamantra, San.). From (above + mantra, san. hymn). The five-lettered incantation [punchauesharam]. The foundation of all spiritual wisdom and religion, and the means prescribed for obtaining emancipation from births [jenmam] and all the evils thereunto belonging, and union [mooety] with the supreme [muntram. samsauram]. There is however a Tamul proverb :—அரிது அரிது அஞ்செழுத்து உணர்தல்—"It is difficult indeed to comprehend the purport "of the five letters."——*Moola poorooshan* (मूलपुरुष - múlapurusha, San.). From (above + purusha, san. person). Original ancestor.——*Moolapracrity* (मूलप्रकृति - múlaprakriti, San.). From (above + prakriti, san. cause). Germ out of which all apparent forms are evolved. See Pracrity and Poorsham.——*Moola staunam* (मूलस्थान - múlast'hána, San.). From (above + st'hána, san. place). The sanctuary of a temple [coil].——*Moolgueny* (ಮೂಲಗೇಣಿ - múlagéni, Can.). From (above + géni, can. rent). A permanent, unchangeable rent [gueny].——*Moolwurg* (ಮೂಲವರ್ಗ - múlavarga, Can.). Original proprietary right in land [cawnyautchy, milkyat, mirass, sawmyam].

MOOLAM (മുഴം - muzham, *Mal.*; முழம் - muzham, *Tam.*). Cubit measured from the elbow to the tip of the middle finger. Linear measure. 2 jauns = 1 moolam; 4 moolams = 1 bauham [alavay, 1, a.d]. Approximate actual value, 1 moolam = 18 inches. But it is often up to 20 inches. Same as San. hastam, Hind. haut, Can. mola, Tel. moora. See vol. I, 609; II, 505.

MOOLAUM (ملمع - mulamma, *Hind.*). From (lama, ar. to shine). Plating with gold [pon] and silver [velly].

MOOLK (ملك - mulk, *Ar.*). Means empire. Part of lacab, as Nizam ool moolk, regulator of the empire.——*Moolkgeery*

(ملك گیری - mulkgírí, Hind.). From (above + girí, pers. taking). The periodical incursion of a military force for collection of tribute or revenue.——*Moolky* (ملکی - mulkí, Hind.; ముల్కి - mulki, Tel.; ಮುಲ್ಕಿ - múlki, Can.). Means pertaining to civil administration. Town, consisting of Baupanaud, Cusbah bazaar and a portion of Manampady village, Port; South canara dist., Mangalore tal.; pop. 3,776; lat. 13° 05′; long. 74° 50′; from Bombay S.S.E. 420 miles; from Goorpore N.W. 14 miles; from Madras W. 370 miles; from Mangalore N. 16 miles; from Padbidry S. 4 miles; from the sea E. 1 mile. On an inlet of the sea receiving the Shumbavaty. Opposite the mouth of the inlet is a group of islets known as the Moolky or Premeira rocks [premeira]. Formerly seat of a petty kingship subdued by the Bednore rajah in the beginning of the seventeenth century. Considerable trade in rice [q.v.]. Seat of Basel mission. Here the New testament was translated into Tooloo [q.v.]. A weekly fair is held here every Saturday. There is a Jeina [q.v.] basty [q.v.] besides two Hindoo temples belonging to the Concany and Shivully bramins, respectively. Has a military encamping ground.

MOOMTAUZ (ممتاز - mumtáz, *Ar.*). From (máza, ar. to separate). Select, distinguished. Part of alam, as Moomtauz hoossain, distinguished hoossain, double alam. Also part of lacab, as Moomtauz ool oomrah, the illustrious of nobles [ism].

MOON (चन्द्र - chandra, *San.*). Prefix. Plant first name; from round leaves, or from shining white flowers, or from flowers opening at night.——*Moon creeper* (चांदवेल - chándavéla, Mahr.). Same as Gandhaulee.——*Moon flower* (मन्दवल्ली - mandavallí, San.; गुलचांदणी - gulachándaní, Mahr.; चन्द्रकान्ति - chandrakánti, Conc.; گل چاندنی - gulichándní, Hind. and Dec.; ಚಂದ್ರಕಾಂತಿ - chandrakánti, Can.; పండితివంకాయ - panditivankáya, Tel.; മുണ്ടവള്ളി - mundavalli, Mal.; ඇලංගා - álangá, Singh.; நாக முக்கொற்றி - nágamúkkotti, Tam.). Title from flowering after sunset. Mahr. from (gula, mahr. flower + chandra, san. moon). Hind. from (gul, pers. flower + chándní, moon-light); from opening at night. Tel. from (pandili, tel. pandal + vankáya, tel. brinjaul, solanum melongena, linn.). Mal. from (munda, san. branchless + valli, mal. creeper). Tam. from (nága, san. cobra de capello + múkkotti, tam. inula indica); as antidote against snake-bites. Tel. also (nagaramukkatte), by corruption from tamul. Mal. also (mandavalli). Title otherwise Good-night flower, Moon creeper, Paudaul brinjaul. Botanically Ipomæa [calamby] bonanox, linn., convolvulaceæ [vricsham, 93]. Alias Calonyction speciosum; Convolvulus muricatus, roxburghii; Ipomæa grandiflora, longiflora, roxburghii. Herb; stem climbing to a great extent; leaves large, quite smooth, cordate, pointed; peduncles very long, one to five-flowered; flowers very large, pure white, opening at sunset, fading next morning, flowering in rainy season. Contains in its roots resin, fatty matter, volatile oil, albumen, starch, fibre, malic acid, and various salts. Bark of root used as purgative; seeds eaten when young. Ipomæa grandiflora, roxb., is another species. A well-known variety is Ipomæa bonanox, linn., var. grandiflora; large climber with soft thorns on the stems; cordate, ovate, acute, entire smooth leaves; pure white circular flowers 3 to 4 inches in width, opening in the evening and fading next morning; the peduncle is club-shaped and supports a membraneous fruit enclosing four large seeds, white, red, or black in color; as a creeper for trellis work in gardens, has a very striking appearance; dried these capsules and seeds as well as flowers, leaves and root, supposed to have virtues in snake-bites; the seeds are eaten when young.——*Moon leaf* (इन्दुपर्णी - induparní, San.). Title from round white back of leaf. Same as Country lavender.

MOONAGA (మునగ - munaga, *Tel.*). Same as Moringa.——*Moonagavalsa* (మునగవలస - munagavalasa, Tel.). From (munaga, tel. horse-radish tree, moringa pterygosperma, gærtn. + valasa, tel. colony).—"*a*" Zemindarry, Ganjam dist., Chicacole tal.; pop. 4,125; acres 3,054. Peshcush Rs. 3,948.—"*b*" Village; Ganjam dist., Chicacole tal.; pop. 495; acres 3,054; lat. 18° 28′; long. 83° 57′; from Chetterpore S.W. 92 miles; from Chicacole N. 12 miles; from the sea N. 18 miles. Remains of extensive mud fort of Danta vactran, a giant killed by Vishnoo [q.v.]. Old gold and silver coins found.——*Moongaula* (మునగాల - munagála, Tel.). From (munaga, tel. horse radish, moringa pterygosperma, gærtn.).—"*a*" Zemindarry talook, Kistna district.—"*b*" Zemindarry; Kistna dist., Nundigauma tal.; pop. 17,360; sq. miles 100. This family are Reddies [q.v.] and claim centuries of uninterrupted residence at Moongaula, going back to the days when another Reddy family left Hanoomacondah and established themselves at Condaveed. Moongaula lies out in the Nizam's territory in the track of Mahratta and other freebooters, so has been sacked often. Peshcush Rs. 4,527.—"*c*" Village; Kistna dist., Moongaula zemindarry tal.; pop. 1,439; lat. 17° 3′; long. 79° 53′; from Bezwada N.W. 61 miles; from Guntoor N.W. 66 miles; from Madras N. 273 miles; from Masulipatam N.W. 101 miles; from Vinoocondah N. 67 miles. Zemindar's station.

MOONDAM (मुण्ड - munda, *San.*). From (mund, san. to be pure). Skull [capaulam].——*Moonda* (മുണ്ട് - muntu, Mal.). Means anything short. The cloth worn round the waist by natives of both sexes in Malabar.——*Moondagampaula* (മുണ്ടകംപാല - muntakampála, Mal.). From (muntam, mal. dwarf + pála, mal. milky paddy). A Malabar paddy. Carootta moondagampaula is black; Chonna moondagampaula, from (chukanna, mal. red) is red; Veloötta moondagampaula is white [paddy].——*Moondagan* (മുണ്ടകൻ - muntakan, Mal.). From (muntam, mal. dwarfish); from absence of tail to ear. A Malabar paddy. Of slow growth, yields best straw. Caroo moondagam is black; Chempan moondagam, from (chempu, mal. copper) is red; Cheroo moondagam is small; Chouna moondagam, from (chukanna, mal. red) is red [paddy].——*Moondamaulay* (मुण्डमाला - mundamálá, San.). From (above + málá, san. garland). A necklace of skulls worn by Shiva [capauly].——*Moondappa* (ಮುಂಡಪ್ಪ - mundappa, Can.). From (above + appa, can. father). Hindoo 2nd or pers. name [peyar].——*Moondavully* (മുണ്ടവള്ളി - mundavalli, Mal.). Means branchless creeper. Same as Tooty coora.——*Moondy* (முண்டி - mundi, Tam.). A bald-headed person. Hill-tribe proper name [peyar]. Also botanically the Sphæranthus genus, compositæ [vricsham, 74]. Low annuals with spreading branches; leaves alternate, toothed, decurrent, oblong or lance-shaped; flower-heads in dense spherical clusters; florets pink; nut oblong, smooth or downy, containing a single seed. The species best known to the natives are:—amaranthoides [fever toolsy], indicus [seed toolsy].——*Mottay* (மொட்டை - mottai, Tam.). Means bald-head. Proper name among the lower caste. Common to both sexes [peyar].

MOONEEB (منیب - muníb, *Hind.*). From (naub, ar. to supply one's place). The principal who sends out his goomastas [q.v.].

MOONEER (منیر - munír, *Ar.*). From (nára, ar. to shine). Lacab of the prophet. Common alam; as Mahomed mooneer, double alam. Also part of lacab; as Mooneer ood dowla, splendour of the empire [ism].

MOONGA (ముంగ - munga, *Tel.*). Plant crotalaria [ghantaravam] sessiliflora, linn.——*Moongamore* (ముంగమూరు - mungamúru, Tel.). From (above + úru, tel. village). Village; Nellore dist., Cauvaly tal.; pop. 2,110; acres 3,724; lat. 14° 48′; long. 80° 04′; from Cauvaly S.S.E. 8 miles; from Nellore N. 25 miles; from the sea W. 5 miles. Wealthy village. Soil fertile. Good tank. Large trade in grain and cattle. Trig. station in lat. 14° 48′ 46·56″; long. 80° 3′ 39·70″; from Cauvaly S.S.E. 7 miles; from Gavaravaram S.E. 2 miles; from the sea W. 5 miles.

MOONGAH (विद्रुम - vidruma, *San.*; مونگا - múngá, *Hind.*; ಹವಳ - havala, *Can.*; పగడము - pagadamu, *Tel.*; പവിഴം - pavizham, *Mal.*; பவழம் - pavazham, *Tam.*). Title from hindostany. San. from (vi, san. prefix of excellence + druma, san. tree). Tel. and tam. from (pravála, san. sprout). Coral. Corallium of naturalists. The stony skeletons of zoophytes. These live in sea attached to rocks, and grow by process of budding and fissure, whereby a branching organism is produced. Off the south-west coast numerous islands and reefs are formed of the debris of the coral [atoll]. The stem of the zoophyte is divisible into two distinct parts, a central axis, hard and brittle like stone, which is the part used in commerce, and a soft epidermis which easily yields to the nail when it is fresh, but is friable or brittle when dry. Natives have a preference for so-called worm-eaten beads from a belief that gods dwell in the recesses. Veidyans [q.v.] prescribe calcined coral in cases of diabetes and bleeding piles. Coral is made by natives into personal ornaments, knobs, buttons, bracelets, necklace, &c., and worn by people of all classes. Compare:—Abrus precatorius, coral bead; Adenanthera pavonina, coral pea-tree; Erythrina indica, coral tree; Jatropha multifida, coral plant. See gloss. paragraphs. Moongah means also sore-throat in horses [ashwarogam, ghorah].

MOONJ (मुञ्ज - muñja, *San.*; मुंज - munja, *Mahr.*; مونج - múnj, *Hind.* and *Dec.*; ಮುಂಜಿ - munji, *Can.*; ముంజగడ్డి - munjagaddi, *Tel.*; മുഞ്ഞ - muñja, *Mal.*; முஞ்சி - muñji, *Tam.*). Title from deccany. San. from (muj, san. to sound); from sound when wind blows through a plot of the long grass. Mahr., &c., from sanscrit. Hind. also (sarpatá). Tel. also (ponika). Mal. also (mékhalappullu), meaning girdle grass; used in making bramin's girdle. Title otherwise Edible pith, Girdle grass. Botanically Saccharum [sharam] munja, roxb., graminaceæ [vricsham, 156]. Specific name from sanscrit. Kind of reed; culms straight, 8–12 feet, smooth; leaves channelled, long, linear, white-nerved, hispid at the base inside; panicles large, oblong, spreading; ramifications verticilled; flowers hermaphrodite; corolla two-valved. Leaves give fibre [naur].

MOONNAY (अग्निमन्थ - agnimant'ha, *San.*; चाम्हारी - chámhárí, *Mahr.*; هشت بندہ - hashtbandah, *Hind.*; పిన్న నెల్లి - pinnanelli, *Tel.*; മുഞ്ഞ - muñña, *Mal.*; මිඩි - midi, *Singh.*; முன்னை - munnai, *Tam.*). Title from tamul. San. from (agni, san. fire + mant'h, san. to churn); the wood serves to produce fire by attrition. Hind. from (hasht, pers. eight + band, pers. tie); from nature of root. Tel. from (pinna, tel. small + nelli, tel. premna latifolia, rox.). Mal. from tamul. Tam. from (min, tam. flash) [min]; from shining leaves [indian nettle]. San. also (ganikáriká), meaning attractive as a courtezan; (kaniká), meaning having sparks of fire; (shríparna), meaning having beautiful leaves. Tel. also (gabbunelli), meaning stinking + the tree, premna latifolia, rox.; (karnika). Singh. also (mahamidi), meaning large + the plant. Tam. also (pasumunnai), meaning greenness + the plant. Title otherwise Entire-leaved premna, Indian headache tree. Botanically Premna [jayah] integrifolia, linn., verbenaceæ [vricsham, 102]. Alias Premna hircina, integrifolia, serratifolia, spinosa. A large shrub or small tree, blossoming in the rainy season; trunk short; branches numerous, often procumbent and rooting; bark smooth, dark brown, leaves opposite, petioled, cordate, serrate on the anterior margins, acute pointed, smooth on both sides, from 1–6 inches long and from 1–3 inches broad; flowers in corymbs, terminal or between two branchlets, primary divisions opposite, the last two-forked, flowers minute, numerous, of a pale greenish-white; berries black, the size of a pea [calauyam]; the plant has an agreeable aromatic odour and an acidulous and astringent taste. Root used medicinally in decoction [kwautam] as a cordial and tonic; leaves rubbed along with pepper [q.v.], administered in colds and fevers; whole plant used in form of decoction in rheumatism and neuralgia; root bitter, stomachic, useful in fever; anasarca, urticaria, &c.; soup made of the leaves, occasionally used as a stomachic and carminative; root forms an ingredient of dasha moolam [q.v.] preparation often prescribed by the native physicians in obstinate fevers. Leaves used by natives in soups and curry [q.v.], in spite of odour; also for feeding cattle. Wood white with purple streaks, moderately hard, close-grained; used for fire-wood.——*Buffalo moonnay* (పెద్దనెల్లి - peddanelli, Tel.; ଗନ୍ଧଣା - gondhona, Oor.; මහමිදි - mahamidi, Singh.; எருமைமுன்னை - erumaimunnai, Tam.). Title from large size. Tel. means large moonnay. Singh. from (maha, singh. large + midi, singh. premna integrifolia, linn.). Tam. from (erumai, tam. buffalo + munnai, tam. premna integrifolia, linn.). Tel. also (nelli) [curry moonnay, tirootauly]; (navuru). Title otherwise Broad-leaved premna. Botanically Premna [jayah] latifolia, roxb., verbenaceæ [vricsham, 102]. Tree; leaves round, cordate, entire, smooth; corymbs axillary and terminal; throat of corolla woolly; flowers dirty yellow; drupe size of a pea [calanyam], erect, wrinkled, four-celled; generally near coast; particulars same as integrifolia [moonnay].——*Conjee moonnay* (கூழ்முன்னை - kúzhmunnai, Tam.). Title from use. Tam. from (kúzh, tam. thick gruel + munnai, tam. premna integrifolia, linn.). Botanically Premna [jayah] cordifolis, roxb., verbenaceæ [vricsham, 102]. Shrubby; branchlets, cymes and petioles of the younger leaves, villous; leaves short-petioled, cordate, or cordate-ovate, acuminate, entire, bullate, glabrous on both sides, shining above, dull and pale beneath; panicles terminal, small, contracted-corymbose; flowers greenish white; flowering in may and june.——*Curry moonnay* (కూరనెల్లి - kúranelli, Tel.). Tel. from (kúra, tel. curry + nelli, tel. premna latifolia, roxb.). Tel. also (nelli). Title otherwise Coora nelly. Botanically Premna [jayah] esculenta, r., verbenaceæ [vricsham, 102]. Shrub; branchlets and cymes thinly mealy-puberulous; leaves very shortly petioled, oblong, acuminate, somewhat narrowed at the base, glabrous, coarsely and sharply toothed above, glaucescent below; cyme terminal, small, contracted; calyx two-lipped, unequally five-toothed; tube of the corolla greenish-yellow.——*Devil moonnay* (பேய்முன்னை - péymunnai, Tam.). Same as Indian nettle.

MOONSHEE (منشی - munshí, *Hind.*). From (nishá, ar. to educate). A secretary, teacher, interpreter [jawaub navees]. Meer moonshee is chief secretary.——*Moonshee grass* (शर - shara, San.; سینٹھی - senthí, Hind.; ಲೇಖಿನಿಹುಲ್ಲು - lékhinihullu, Can.; గుండ్ర - gundra, Tel.; ശരപ്പുല്ല് - sharappullu, Mal.; எழுதுகிறநாணல் - ezhuthugiranánal, Tam.). Title from use as pens. San. from (shrí, san. to split in pieces). Hind. from (senth, hind. merchant); as used by them. Can. from (lékhini, can. pen + hullu, can. grass). Tel. from (gundra, san. the plant). Mal. from (shara, san. the plant + pullu, mal. grass). Tam. from (ezhuthu, tam. to write + nánal, tam. reed, saccharum spontaneum, linn.). San. also (gundra), meaning sounding, as when wind blows through it; (téjanaka), meaning resisting. Title otherwise Moonshee-reed, Moonshee's pen, Pen-grass, Pen-reed. Botanically Saccharum [sharam] sara, roxb., graminaceæ [vricsham, 156]. Specific name from sanscrit. Culms perennial, erect, 6–16 feet, smooth, very strong; lower leaves 4–8 feet long, narrow, upper ones shorter, broader, tapering from the base to a fine acumination, concave above, with hispid margin; sheaths 12–18 inches long, with a tuft of hair above their mouths on the inside; panicles dense, open when in flower, condensed when in seed; ramification decompound, the inferior ones alternate, superior ones sub-verticilled, generally with their sharp angles armed with stiff bristles and covered with white silky hairs; flowers paired, one sessile, the other pedicelled; calyx two-valved, clothed with long silky hairs; corolla three-valved, fringed. Root burned near women after delivery and near burns and scalds, its smoke being considered beneficial. Fibre inferior to moonj [q.v.] grass; reeds used for matting, thatching, chairs, &c.; flower tops may be used as a paper material; leaves sometimes made into mats [boriyah], and bundles of the stems used for floating heavy timber on the rivers. Species fuscum also is used for pens.

MOONSIF (منصف - munsif, *Hind.*; మునసపు - munasapu, *Tel.*; முனிசிப்பு - munisippu, *Tam.*). From (nisf, ar. half). Just. A minor native judge. Certain headmen of villages have been constituted village moonsifs by the British, and given police, magisterial, and civil court powers in a small degree. When there is a monigar [q.v.] or peddacaup [q.v.] in a village in addition to a moonsif, the latter takes precedence [balootah]. The headman of a village is always the moonsif now, where there is a moonsif.

MOONTA (ముంత - munta, *Tel.*). Vessel. See vol. I, 609; II, 508, 516.—"*a*" Measure of capacity. 4 solas = 1 moonta; 16 moontas = 1 toom [alavay, 3b]. Approximate actual value, 1 moonta = 245 cubic inches. In Bellary moonta is 4 seers of 84 tolahs or 294 cubic inches. Same as solga. Compare Cooncham of ganjam and godavery, Mercaul of tanjore, Bullah of salem and coimbatore.—"*b*" Liquid measure [alavay, 4b] = 70 cubic inches. Used in Bellary for toddy [q.v.].

MOONY (मुनि - muni, *San.*). From (man, san. to think) [man]. Any great sage. In Southern india they are reckoned as forty-eight thousand. These are holy persons who by different kinds of austerities have acquired power to bless and curse effectually. They need neither sleep nor rest, eating nor drinking; and yet perform severe penance before god continually. Distinguish from risby [q.v.] who is rather an ancient patriarch. In common usage moony is used also to denote a demon. In the lower castes it is a name applied to males and females. Also suffix in proper names, as Nauthamoony [peyar].——*Mahamoony* (महामुनि - mahámuni, San.). From (mahá, san. great + muni, san. sage). Thirty-one in number, viz., Agastyan, Atry, Angeerasan, Hiranyan, Roman, Herandan, Calaicottan, Caushyapan, Gowtaman, Shattacoon, Satchidaunandan, Jamadagny, Sanacan, Sanatcomauran, Shoocan, Dadheechy, Doorvausan, Nauradan, Patanjaly, Bharadwaujan, Parausharan, Pudman, Bhrigoo, Pinauky, Poolastyan, Maurcandan, Vasishtan, Vaulmeeky, Vishwaumitran, Vyaughrapaudan, and Vyausan.——*Mooniyammah* (முனியம்மா - muniyammá, Tam.). From (above + ammá, tam. mother). Hindoo female proper name [peyar].——*Mooniyan* (முனியன் - muniyan, Tam.). Pariah proper name [peyar].——*Moonoosawmy* (முன்னுசாமி - munnusámi, Tam.). From (above + svámi, san. lord). Hindoo 2nd or pers. name [peyar].

MOOR (मुर् - mur, *San.*). To bind.——*Mooraleedharan* (मुरलीधर - muralídhara, San.). From (murali, san. flute + dhara, san. bearer). Krishnan [q.v.].——*Mooraly* (मुरली - muralí, San.). Flute.——*Mooran* (मुर - mura, San.). Asooran, so called.——*Mooraury* (मुरारि - murári, San.). From (mura, san. the asura, so-called + ari, san. enemy). Vishnoo [q.v.].——*Moraury row* (मुरारिराव - murárirávu, Mahr.). Of the Sundoor ghorapadey [q.v.] family and chief of Gooty in 1743. Helped Mahomed ally against Chundah sahib. Joined the English against Hyder. See vol. I (122), 42.——*Mowrya* (मौर्य - maurya, San.). Matronymic, from (murá, san. mother of chandragupta). The name of a dynasty [raj] which began with Chundragooptan, the Sandracottus of the Greeks, about three centuries before Christ, and included Asoca [q.v.], the patron of the Booddhists [booddha]. Their capital was Palibothra, the present Patna [charitram]. See vol. I (132).

MOOR (துலுக்கன் - tulukkan, *Tam.*). Title from portuguese. Properly means a Mauritanian. Formerly used here for Mussalmans.

MOORA (മുറ - mura, *Mal.*). Custom.——*Moray* (முறை - murai, Tam.). Custom [moora].——*Morayneer* (முறைநீர் - murainír, Tam.). From (above + nír, tam. water). Water allowed to flow in turn, for a fixed term, to the fields of each cultivator. Settled by the village headman who gives orders to the neergunty [q.v.]. The matter very rarely requires adjustment by any higher authority, but if so the enquiry is confined to what is customary. In the minor tanks and water-works of the country the village headman regulates the whole water flow beginning with the tank sluice itself; but in the larger works the head sluices and vents are kept in the hands of the government engineering department.——*Moorjapam* (മുറജപം - murajapam, Mal.). From (above + japa, san. prayer). A feast in Travancore celebrated every sixth year in Dhanoo or december and Macaram [mausam] or january. Numboories [q.v.] assemble from all parts of the country and offer prayers for the maharajah [q.v.] and state. Three times a day some hundred of them stand immersed in water and repeat muntrams [q.v.]. Festival lasts for eight weeks during which time they are supplied with food and lodgings at the cost of circar [q.v.] and are then dismissed with liberal presents [daunam]. It is believed to be conducive to defence of kingdom and regular supply of rain [mazhay].

MOORAUD (مراد - murád, *Ar.*). From (arada, ar. to desire). Object of desire. Prefixed to an alam forms a lacab; as Mooraud ally, desire of ally [ism].

MOORDHAN (मूर्द्धन् - múrddhan, *San.*). From (múrv, san. to bind); that which binds all organs of body. Head.——*Moordhanyam* (मूर्द्धन्य - múrddhanya, San.). Cerebral. In all the languages and dialects of India, whether they belong to the Aryan [q.v.] or to the Dravidian [q.v.] families, much use is made of a series of consonants—ṭ ḍ, with their aspirates, and ṇ—pronounced far back in the mouth, with a hard, ringing sound. The following letters are considered cerebral for purposes of Tamul transliteration:—ட ண ள ழ. Similarly in Teloogoo:—ట డ ణ ళ ఱ. Similarly in the other Dravidian languages. See vol. II, 186, 206.

MOOREED (مريد - muríd, *Hind.*). From (arada, ar. to intend). Amongst Mahomedans a disciple, particularly of a moorshid [q.v.] or the head of order of dervishes [peer]. He is initiated by secret signs and words. The mooreeds have their own rules and customs [masheikh].

MOORGANA TALLOW (ಮುರಿಗನಹುಳಿಬೆಣ್ಣೆ - murginahuli-benne, *Can.*). Means mate mangosteen + butter. Same as Cokum butter [mate mangosteen].

MOORGH (مرغ - murgh, *Hind.*). Cock.——*Moorgha* (मयूरशिखा - mayúrashikhá, San.; मोरशिखा - mórashikhá, Mahr.; تاج خروس - tájikhurús, Pers.; مرغ كيس - murghkes, Hind.; ಶಿಖಾವಳ - shikhávala, Can.; కోడిజుట్టుతోటకూర - kódidzuttutóta-kúra, Tel.; അടക്കമണിയൻ - atakkamaniyan, Mal.; කිරිහෙන්ද - kirihenda, Singh.; பண்ணை - pannai, Tam.). Title from hindostany. San. from (mayúra, san. peacock + shikhá, san. crest). Mahr. from sanscrit. Pers. from (táj, ar. crown + khurús, pers. cock). Hind. from (murgh, hind. cock + kes, hind. comb). Tel. from (kódi, tel. cock + dzuttu, tel. crest + tótakúra, tel. amarantus blitum, var. oleraceus, linn., pot-herb). Mal. from (atakka, mal. closed fruit + mani, mal. globule). Singh from (kiri, singh. white + henda, singh. plant.). Tam. from (pan, tam. agricultural land); from place of growth. San. also (dípya), meaning promoting digestion; (shikhálu), meaning peacock's crest; (sahasránghri), meaning thousand rooted; (nílakant'hashikhá), meaning peacock's crest; (mayúra), meaning peacock; (mayúrachúdá), meaning peacock's crest; (lóchamastaka), meaning tears + head; (madhuchhada), meaning sweet cover; (kékishikhá), meaning peacock's crest; (barhi-chúdá), meaning peacock's crest; (kharáshvá), meaning heat + accumulating; (lóchamarkata), meaning tears + monkey. Hind. also (pílámurghá), meaning yellow cock; (lálmurghá), meaning red cock; (dabkútí), meaning stunted stump; (sarpankhí), meaning head fan; (safedmurghkes), meaning white cockscomb. Can. also (shikhi); (shikhini); (annesoppu), meaning strong leaf. Tel. also (errakódidzuttutótakúra), meaning red + the plant; (gurugu) [indian heliotrope]; (panchechettu). Mal. also (cheri-yaatakkamaniyan), meaning small var.; (veluttaatakkamaniyan), meaning the white var. Tam. also (shávalgondaiççedi), meaning cock + crest + plant; (shévarbannai), meaning cock + pannay plant; (shembannai), meaning red + pannay plant. Title otherwise Cockscomb, Goolkeah, Peacock's crest [morpankhy]. Botanically Celosia cristata, linn., amarantaceæ [vricsham, 106]. Ornamental annual. Five or six varieties:—α bears numerous heads of bloom resembling so many golden sponges; β heads of flowers bright crimson; γ leaves as well as flower-heads bright crimson; δ dwarf variety, sponge-like heads of tawny-orange colored flowers. Leaves and young shoots are used as greens. Other common species are:—argentea, polygonoides, pulchella. ——*Moorghy* (कुक्कुट - kukkuta, San.; دجاج - dajjáj, Ar.; مرغ خانگی - murghikhánagí, Pers.; ککڑی - kukrí, Hind.; مرغی - murghí, Dec.; కోడి - kódi, Tel.; കോഴി - kózhi, Mal.; கோழி - kózhi, Tam.). Title from deccany. San. from the sound. Ar. from (dajja, ar. to walk leisurely). Pers. from (murgh, pers. fowl + khánah, pers. house). Tel. from the sound. Mal. from tamul. Tam. from (kózhai, tam. timidity). Gallus domesticus, Gallinæ [jungle fowl], phasianidæ [jeevanjeevam], rasores [pacshy, 32], of naturalists [jantoo]. House or domestic hen. Feel moorghy, from (píl, pers. elephant) is the Turkey, Meleagris genus, meleagridæ, rasores.——*Mooryhbyeza* (مرغ بيضه - murgh-baizah, Hind.). From (murgh, pers. hen + baizah, pers. egg). Windgalls or soft puffy swellings, size of hen's egg on fetlock of horses [ashwarogam, ghorah].

MOOROO (முரு - muru, *Tam.*). Beauty——*Mooroogan* (முருகன் - murugan, Tam.). From (murugu, tam. beauty or tenderness). Youth. Scandan [q.v.]. Non-bramin proper name [peyar].——*Mooroogappan* (முருகப்பன் - murugappan, Tam.). (murugan, tam. skanda + appan, tam. father, titular affix). Hindoo 2nd or pers. name. Common among non-bramins [peyar]. ——*Moorkinauty* (ముఱికినాటి - murikináti, obl., Tel.). From (murikinádu, tel. country so called in kistna). A section of Smarta [q.v.] bramins. They profess the White yajoor vedam [q.v.]. Numbers about 1,000 [jauty].——*Moorkham* (முருக்கம் - murukkam, Tam.). From (murugu, tam. beauty). Same as Common coral tree.——*Mooroogesham* (முருகேசம் - muru-gésam, Tam.). From (murugan, tam. skanda + ísha, san. lord, soobramanyan, the lord). Hindoo 2nd or pers. name. Common among non-bramins [peyar].

MOORSHID (مرشد - murshid, *Hind.*). From (rushd, ar. to be in the right way). A religious teacher [peer]. He initiates disciples, styled mooreed [q.v.], into his sect [masheikh].

MOORTAM (मूर्त - múrta, *San.*). From (murchh, san. to settle into form); real. The practical division of time [caulam], 3]; as opposed to the imaginary division, Amoortam [q.v.]. Distinguish from Moohoortam.——*Moommoorty* (மும்மூர்த்தி - mummúrtti, Tam.). Means three deities. The Hindoo trinity [trimoorty].——*Moortiyappan* (மூர்த்தியப்பன் - múrttiyappan, Tam.). From (múrti, san. deity + appan, tam. father, titular affix). Hindoo 2nd or pers. name [peyar].——*Moorty* (मूर्ति - múrti, San.). From (múrchh, san. to take form). Manifestation, incarnation [avatar]. Greek μορφή. Image, and so deity. Hindoo 2nd or pers. name. Suffix in proper names as Krishna-moorty, Ramamoorty [peyar]. The eight forms of shiva are Ashtamoorty; which includes sun [sooryan], moon [chundran] and soul [autmam] besides the five elements [bhootam].——*Trimoorty* (त्रिमूर्त्ति - trimúrtti, San.). Means three deities. The Hindoo trinity [moommoorty].

MOORTEZAH (مرتضىٰ - murtazá, *Ar.*). From (razá, ar. to be pleased). Approved. A title of Ally. Common alam; as Moortezah beg, alam + alaumat. Moortezah hoossain, double alam [ism].——*Moortezah ally* (مرتضیٰ علی - murtazáalí, Hind.). Double alam. Otherwise Ghoolaum moortezah ally khan. Married a daughter of Dost ally, nawaub of the Carnatic from 1732–1740. Murdered his brother-in-law, Sufder ally. Proclaimed Nawaub [q.v.] of the Carnatic [q.v.] by Dupleix in 1753 as a rival to Anwarood deen khan [q.v.] supported by the English. See vol. I (177).——*Moortezavee* (مرتضوی - murtazaví, Hind.). From (murtuzá, ar. lacab of ally). Title of a class of Mahome-dans tracing their pedigree to Ally [ism].

MOORY (మూరి - múri, *Tel.*; മുറി - muri, *Mal.*). From (muri, mal. to cut). A hamlet. Also a leaf, a bond. Blue cloth; principally manufactured in Nellore district, otherwise there called Salampore [q.v.]; also at Coonnatore in Chingleput; once largely exported to Straits.

MOOSA (موسیٰ - músá, *Hind.*). Hebrew, drawn out of water. Moses. Common alam; as Moosa bee, alam + alaumat [ism].

MOOSADDY (مصدی - musaddí, *Hind.*). From (sada, ar. to come before). Writer in a public office. Distinguish from the Tel. moosaddy [moosh].

MOOSALLAS (مثلث - musallas, *Hind.*). From (suls, ar. three). Trigonometry. The following are the principal terms- ——*Fasala* (فصله - fasala, Hind.). From (fasl, ar. to divide). Segment.——*Hammarkaz* (هم مركز - hammarkaz, Hind.). From (ham, ar. same + markaz, ar. centre). Concentric circle.——*Jeb* (جيب - jeb, Hind.). From (jába, ar. to cut). Sine.——*Jeb i moostavee* (جيب مستوی - jebimustaví, Hind.). Cosine.——*Moomaus* (مماس - mumás, Hind.). From (massa, ar. to touch). Tangent.——*Saham* (سهم - sahm, Hind.). From (sahama, ar. to cut). Secant [ilm].

MOOSAMBAR (مصبر - musambar, *Hind.*). Bitter aloes [aloe]. To be distinguished from scented aloe wood or eagle wood [q.v.].

MOOSAUFER (مسافر - musáfir, *Hind.*). From (safr, ar. journey). Traveller. Moosaufer khana is a place for the accom-modation of travellers, especially those who are not caste Hin-doos [chuttram, dharmashaulay].

MOOSAUHIB (مصاحب - musáhib, *Ar.*). From (sahiba, ar. to accompany). Associated. Attaché.

MOOSH (मुष् - mush, *San*). To steal, break, kill.——*Moosaddy* (ముసడి - musadi, Tel.). Same as Mooshty.——*Moosha* (മൂശ - músha, Mal.). From (mush, san. to break), as used for melting. Mould.——*Moosham* (मूष - músha, San.). From (mush, san. to steal); from sly habits. Mouse. The genus Mus, murinæ, rodentia, mammalia [sastanam, 17], of naturalists [jantoo]. The species best known to the natives are:—bandicota [bandicoot], brunneus [maravely], cervicolor [varappoo shoondely], decumanus [ely], oleraceus [mara shoondely], urbanus [shoondely]. Other S. indian species are crassipes, infralineatus, nilagiricus, rattus, rufescens, terricolor.——*Mooshawry* (മൂശാരി - músári, Mal.). From (músha, mal. mould + kári, mal. doer). Brass and coppersmiths in Malabar [jauty]. ——*Mooshicam* (मूषिक - múshika, San.). From (mush, san. to steal). Means rat. One of the four divisions of Keralam, extending from Cullada to Comorin. Comprises S. travancore. Other divisions are Coopam, Keralam proper, and Tooloovam. See vol. I (5).——*Mooshty* (मुष्टि - mushti, San.). From (mush, san. to steal), from what is stolen being concealed in closed hand. Handful. Measure of capacity. 12 mooshties = 1 coodavam [alavay, 3f]. Approximate actual value, 1 mooshty = $2\frac{1}{2}$ tolahs weight of grain or $2\frac{3}{16}$ cubic inches. See vol. I, 609. For Strychnos genus see sep. title.——*Mootthy* (مٹھی - mutthí, Hind.). Means the fist. Linear measure. 4 ungools = 1 mootthy; 3 mootthies = 1 bilisht [alavay, le]. Approximate actual value, 1 mootthy = 3 inches. See vol. I, 609.

MOOSHEER (مشیر - mushír, *Ar.*). From (shára, ar. to point out). Minister. Part of lacab; as Moosheer ool moolk, regulator of the state [ism].

MOOSHRIK (مشرك - mushrik, *Hind.*). From (shirk, ar. to go in partnership). A polytheist; wide term for an infidel, [caufir] including moslem [q.v.], christian and jew [jonaca].

MOOSHTARY (مشتری - mushtarí, *Ar.*; برجیس - birjís, *Pers.*; برسپت - biraspat, *Hind.*). The planet Jupiter, the Hindoo brihaspaty [q.v.]. Also called (káziifalak), meaning celestial judge. An auspicious star; one born under its influence being supposed to distinguish himself [najm]. Tippoo's copper coin [naunyam].

MOOSHTY (मुष्टि - mushti, *San.*). From (mush, san. to kill); poison nut [moosh]. Title otherwise Nux-vomica, Vomit-nut tree. Botanically the Strychnos genus, loganiaceæ [vricsham, 89]. Scandent shrubs with short tendrils, or trees, natives of tropical regions; leaves entire, strongly-nerved, opposite; flowers white or yellowish; fruit a globose or oblong berry with many seeds, which are flattened disk-like and silky, surrounded by pulp. The species best known to the natives are:—colubrina [snake-wood tree], ignatii [papeeta], nux-vomica [poison nut], potatorum [clearing nut]. Other S. indian species indigenous or naturalized are:—axillaris, cinnamomifolia. Includes also species in bischoffia and tiliacora.——*Black mooshty* (నలుపుముష్టి - nalupumushti, Tel.). Title from color of heart-wood. Same as Java cedar.——*Creeper mooshty* (بگلوٹا - baglútá, Hind.; నాగముషడి - nágamusadi, Tel.; വള്ളിക്കാഞ്ഞിരം - vallikkáññiram, Mal.). Tel. from (nága, san. snake + musadi, tel. strychnos nux-vomica, linn.). Mal. from (valli, mal. creeper + káññiram, mal. strychnos nux-vomica, linn.). Tel. also (tigamushini), (tivvamusidi), (tígamushti), all meaning creeper + strychnos nux-vomica, linn.; (kappatíga), meaning frog + creeper [chebulic myrobalan]; (pátavéru); (pátéru). Title otherwise Frog creeper, Nauga mooshty, Snake mooshty. Botanically Tiliacora racemosa, colebr., menispermaceæ [vricsham, 5]. Generic name from bengalee. Alias Cocculus acuminatus, radiatus; Menispermum acuminatum, polycarpum, radiatum; Tiliacora acuminata. Twining shrub; leaves ovate, acuminated, acute or truncate, or slightly cordate at the base, glabrous; racemes axillary, usually about half the length of the leaf; pedicels in the males, one or two from each bractea, two to three-flowered, in the females solitary, one-flowered; petals much shorter than the filaments; flowers small, cream-colored, fragrant; drupes numerous; common in hedges. Used as antidote to snake-bites, being rubbed between two stones and mixed with water; also in elephantiasis [cochin leg]; decoction of leaves applied externally in ulcers, &c.——*Snake-wood mooshty* (నాగముషడి - nágamusadi, Tel.). Same as Creeper mooshty.

MOOSHY (ముశి - mushi, *Tel.* múshi*). From (musí, tel. falsehood); from its being a treacherous river. River; Nellore district, Podily and Darshy divisions and Cundoocore and Ongole talooks. Rises near Dokkalashaula in the Veligondas and flowing first easterly and then southerly through Podily and Darshy divisions of Vencatagherry zemindarry and Cundoocore talook and forming the S.E. boundary of Ongole talook falls into the sea near Anantavaram. It is a dangerous river. There are freshes in September, October and November.

MOOSIRY (முசிறி - musiri,* *Tam.*). From (mú, tam. old + shirai, tam. place) [moo]. Sanscrit name (gópálakrishnapura), meaning cowherd + krishnan, the god + city.——**(1)** Talook, Trichinopoly district. Tahsildar's pay Rs. 225; pop. 282,619; language Tamul. Area 762 square miles. Lies entirely north of Cauvery. W. of district. Bounded N. by Ahtoor talook, and W. by Namcull talook of Salem district, S. by Coolitalay and Trichinopoly talooks, and E. by Perambalore talook. The surface is generally flat, the only range of hills being the Putchamullays which separate the talook from Perambalore talook. The Collimullays form boundary at N.W. corner, but they are entirely in Salem district. S.W. of the Collimullays is Talamullay, which forms the boundary of the district at one point, although it lies entirely outside it. The portion of the talook lying along the N. bank of Cauvery possesses a fertile soil and excellent means of irrigation. The country N. of valley of Cauvery and S. of Putchamullay hills is very uniform in character. Soil is black in the hollows and red on the higher levels and in neighbourhood of hills. Water is found, as a rule, near the surface, and both tanks and wells abound, especially in Toorayore zemindarry. Principal grains are paddy [q.v.], cholum [q.v.], cumboo [bajrah], raggy [q.v.], and horse-gram [q.v.]; varagoo [q.v.] is found but not extensively cultivated. The staple food of the people in villages along the Cauvery is paddy. Further north dry grains [q.v.] especially cholum, raggy and cumboo, are largely consumed. Turbans and cloths in Toorayore and Manamode villages. Mats [boriyah] in Varadarajapooram. Cotton [q.v.] trade on a small scale in the Toorayore division and plantain [q.v.] trade in Cautpoottore. The principal sources of irrigation are the Caraypottanaur, Cauvery and Eiyaur. The following are the more important of the channels [q.v.] from the Cauvery:—Nautt vycaul, Sheelapillapottore, Shreenivasa nullore, Tottiyam chinna vycaul, and Tottiyam periya vycaul. There are fifty-three tanks [q.v.] of which the most important are Jambairy, the large irrigation tank in Toorayore zemindarry. Tirtalaiyore tank, and Mooroonga calattore. The centre and northern portions are, as a rule, unirrigated. There is one zemindarry in the talook that of Toorayore. Cautpoottore mittah is in the south-western corner. Camping grounds:—Cautpoottore, Chetticoolam, Cunnanore, Harikrishnavary, Ooppoolyapooram, Shirooganore, Shobhanapooram, Toorayore, Tottiyam, Yeragoody. Places of archæological interest:—Caraypottanaur, Caumautchipooram, Moosiry, Naugaya nallore, Pauleiyore, Tirvenginautamullay, Toorayore, Tripatore, Yedoomullay, Yeragoody. The leading places, &c., in the talook are the following.——*Caraypottanaur* (கரைப் பொட்டாறு - karaippottánáru, Tam.). See sep. title.——*Cautpoottore* (காட்டுப்புத்தூர் - káttupputtúr, Tam. kátuputtúr*). From (kádu, tam. forest + puthu, tam. new + úr, tam. village). Mittah, Village; pop. 5,152; acres 2,519; lat. 10° 59′; long. 78° 16′; from Moosiry W.N.W. 16 miles; from Trichinopoly W.N.W. 34 miles. The only mittah in Trichinopoly district. Created by Government in 1802, and given to Sarwotama row, Head sheristadar of Salem collectorate. He sold the estate in 1810 to Goonnamareddy, who sold it to Annayyar and Sapta rishy reddy in 1813. These men are ancestors of present owners, and estate has always been enjoyed by two joint proprietors, one Bramin and the other Reddy. The mittah [q.v.] was transferred from Salem district to Trichinopoly in 1851. The village is well-built and prosperous. The country in the vicinity contains some of the best irrigated lands in the district. Peshcush Rs. 15,901.——*Cauvery* (காவேரி - kávéri, Tam.). See sep. title.——*Cunnanore* (கண்ணனூர் - kannanúr, Tam.). From (kannan, tam. krishna, the god + úr, tam. village). Sanscrit name (bhujabalarájapattana), meaning the strong armed king + town; named after bhoojabala royen who built there a temple for cunnan [q.v.], or krishnan [q.v.]. Village; pop. 2,645; acres 3,093; lat. 11° 05′; long. 78° 37′; from Moosiry N.E. 12 miles; from Trichinopoly W. by N. 21 miles. Head-quarters of the old Toorayore talook. Weekly market on Thursdays.——*Eiyaur* (ஐய்யார் - aiyyár, Tam.). See sep. title.——*Keerambore* (கீரம்பூர் - kírambúr, Tam.). Village; pop. 4,714; lat. 11° 10′; long. 78° 41′; from Moosiry N.E. 19 miles; from Trichinopoly N. 25 miles. In Toorayore zemindarry.——*Moosiry* (முசிறி - musiri, Tam.). See below.——*Naugaya nallore* (நாகயநல்லூர் - nágayanallúr, Tam.). From (nágayya, tel. proper name + nal, tam. good + úr, tam. village). Village; pop. 3,740; acres 4,782; lat. 11° 01′; long. 78° 18′; from Moosiry W. 16 miles; from Trichinopoly W.N.W. 34 miles.——*Ooppoolyapooram* (உப்புலி யப்புரம் - uppuliyappuram, Tam.). From (uppiliyan, tam. member of that caste + pura, san. city). Village; pop. 3,648; acres 1,606; lat. 11° 16′; long. 78° 34′; from Moosiry N.N.E. 22 miles; from Trichinopoly N. 33 miles. Originally founded by Ooppilyars [q.v.] or salt makers.——*Putchamullay* (பச்சை மலை - paççaimalai, Tam.). See sep. title.——*Shikkitambore* (சிக்கித்தம்பூர் - shikkittambúr, Tam.). Village; pop. 4,144; lat. 11° 12′; long. 78° 37′; from Moosiry N.N.E. 19 miles; from Trichinopoly N.N.W. 28 miles. In Toorayore zemindarry.——*Shreenivasa nullore* (சீனிவாசநல்லூர் - shínivásanallúr, Tam.). From (shríniváša, san. proper name + 'nal, tam. good + úr, tam. town). Village; pop. 1,019; acres 638; lat. 10° 58′; long. 78° 26′; from Moosiry W.N.W. 5 miles; from Trichinopoly W.N.W. 25 miles. Gives its name to a channel from the Cauvery.——*Talamullay* (தலைமலை - talaimalai, Tam.). See sep. title.——*Tirpangaly* (திருப்பங்கலி - tiruppangali, Tam.). From (tiru, tam. holy + pangu, tam. portion + kali, tam. clay); holy place with clayey soil. Devastaunam inam [q.v.] village; pop. 3,243; acres 5,366; lat. of village 10° 57′; long. 78° 42′; from Moosiry E. 14 miles; from Trichinopoly N.N.W. 9 miles.——*Toorayore* (துறையூர் - turaiyúr, Tam.). See sep. title.——**(2)** Town, Head-quarters of Talook and Division; Trichinopoly dist., Moosiry tal.; pop. 4,516; acres 2,489; lat. 10° 57′; long. 78° 30′; from Ariyalore W.S.W. 44 miles; from Madras S.W. 189 miles; from Shreerungam W.N.W. 18 miles; from Trichinopoly W. by N. 19 miles. On the Cauvery, almost exactly opposite to Coolitalay. Since 1867 head-quarters of the Head assistant collector. Very old Shiva temple. Peramore estate choultry [q.v.]. Weekly market on Wednesdays. Imposing-looking Roman catholic chapel built in 1876. In 1875 three flights of steps leading down to the Cauvery were built by local subscriptions, &c. Old bridge with Chola inscriptions.

MOOSKIRAUT (مسکرات - muskirát, *Hind.*). From (sakara, ar. to become intoxicated). Intoxicant. For narcotics see Mookhadiraut. The following are two key-lists of the principal intoxicating substances used by the natives of S. india; further information must be traced in the glossary paragraphs through the small type cross-references at the end of this volume; see also vricsham, 7, for the method of expressing the products, &c., of the plants in the dravidian languages.—"*a*" Anamirta cocculus, indian berry, seed ; Cannabis sativa, indian hemp, whole plant except stem ; Datura fastuosa, purple datura, seed ; Eleusine coracana, raggy, fermented drink ; Grewia asiatica, falsah, fruit ; Manihot utilissima, tapioca, juice ; Papaver somniferum, opium, capsule infusion ; Sarcostemma brevistigma, somam, juice ; Sorghum valgare, cholum, fermented drink ; Strychnos nux-vomica, poison nut, seed ; Vitis vinifera, grape vine, wine ; Woodfordia floribunda, godaury, drink from blossom.—" b " Cholum, sorghum ; Falsah, grewia ; Godaury, woodfordia ; Grape vine, vitis ; Hemp, cannabis ; Indian berry, anamirta ; Opium, papaver ; Poison nut, strychnos ; Raggy, eleusine ; Somam, sarcostemma ; Tapioca, manihot.

MOOSLY (موسلی - músli, *Hind.*). Asparagopsis genus [shatamooly].——*Cauly moosly* (तालमूली - tálamúlí, San. ; मुसळी - musalí, Mahr. ; भुयिमाड्डि - bhúyimáddi, Conc. ; سیاہ موسلی - siyáhmúslí, Hind. ; کالی موسلی - kálímúslí, Dec. ; ನೆಲತಾಳೆ - nelatále, Can. ; ನೆಲಮುಂಡ - nelamunda, Too. ; నేలతాడి - nélatádi, Tel. ; ତାଲ୍ମୂଲି - tálmúlí, Oor. ; നിലപ്പന - nilappana, Mal. ; හිංබිංතල් - hinbintal, Singh. ; நிலப்பனை - nilappanai, Tam.). Title from black root. San. from (tála, san. palm, borassus flabelliformis, linn. + múla, san. root). Hind. from (siyáh, pers. black + múslí, hind. asparagopsis sarmentosa, kunth.). Dec. from (kálí, hind. black + múslí, hind. asparagopsis sarmentosa, kunth.). Can. from (nela, can. ground + tále, can. palmyra, borassus flabelliformis, linn.). Tel. from (néla, tel. ground + tádi, tel. palmyra, borassus flabelliformis, linn.). Mal. from (nila, mal. ground + pana, mal. palm). Singh. from (hín, singh. low + bintal, singh. curculigo). Tam. from (nilam, tam. ground + panai, tam. palmyra tree, borassus flabelliformis, linn.) ; from leaf. San. also (bhúmitála), meaning ground palm ; (bahulavalkala), meaning having thick bark ; (bhúta), meaning existing ; (váráhí), meaning hoggish ; (musalí), meaning pestle-like, from cylindrical form of fresh roots. Hind. also (safedmúslí), meaning asparagopsis ascendens, kunth. Can. also (nelatátigadde) ; (neladáli). Tel. also (nallatádi), meaning black + palmyra, borassus. Tam. also (tirakkattáru), meaning wrinkled rooted palm ; (talattádu), meaning ground palm. Title otherwise Black palm, Ground palm, Hog palm, Narrow-leaved curculigo, Nilapanay, Weevil root. Botanically Curculigo orchioides, gærtn., hypoxidaceæ [vricsham, 146]. Alias Hypoxis orchioides. Stemless ; root tuberous, with many spreading fibres ; leaves narrow-lanceolar, nerved, slender ; petioles channelled, sheathing below ; racemes solitary, axillary ; flowers hermaphrodite, yellow ; flowering nearly all year ; apices of the leaves are viviparous and will produce young plants if allowed to rest on ground ; grows in moist forests ; tuberous and wrinkled root about 4 inches long ; slightly bitter and mucilaginous to the taste. The root is used in gonorrhœa and has tonic qualities ; in pharm. non-officinal. Other common species are :—brevifolia, malabarica, recurvata.——*Semul moosly* (موسلی سیمل - múslísemal, Dec.). Aphrodisiac preparation from young root of Red-cotton tree [q.v.]. This root is like the tap-root of many other young plants, tapering, and varies a great deal in its size according to the age of plant ; if the age is two years the tap-root is generally about the size of long radish ; when fresh it is tuberous and cuts easily, grey, reddish-brown or brown externally, and white internally ; taste mucilaginous, smell none ; when dry, the root is much shrivelled, shrunken and wrinkled longitudinally, the epidermis is reddish-brown, brown or slightly ash-colored and generally loose and peels off easily, beneath the epidermis the root is reddish brown but white or pale-white internally, odourless and tasteless ; the dry root is not easily powdered, but the dry slices of the fresh root are reduced to a fine powder without difficulty. There is no drug in this country which enjoys a greater reputation as an aphrodisiac and tonic in native medical works.——*Soofaid moosly* (शतावरि - shatávari, San. ; शतावली - shatávalí, Mahr. ; شقاقل - shakákul, Ar. and Pers. ; سفید موسلی - sufedmúslí, Hind. ; شقاقل - shakákul, Dec. ; ಹಲವುಮಕ್ಕಳಬಳ್ಳಿ - halavumakkalaballi, Can. ; ಉದುರಿಬೂರು - uduriburu, Too. ; చల్లగడ్డ - tsallagadda, Tel. ; ശതാവരി - shatávari, Mal. ; හාතාවාරිය - hátáváriya, Singh. ; தண்ணீர்விட்டான் - tannírvittán, Tam.). Title from hindostany and white root. San. from (shata, san. hundred + ávri, san. to cover) ; from shaggy root. Mahr. from sanscrit. Hind. from (safed, hind. white + múslí, hind. asparagopsis genus). Can. from (halavu, can. many + makkalu, can. children + balli, can. creeper) ; useful tonic to children. Too. from (uduru, too. hanging down + búru, too. creeper). Tel. from (tsalla, tel. butter milk + gadda, tel. root). Mal. from sanscrit. Singh. from sanscrit. Tam. from (tannír, tam. water + vidu, tam. to leave) ; holds cool water. Hind. also (shakákul) [shakaukool] ; (satwárí). Can. also (majjigegadde), meaning butter milk + lump ; (shíbáribéruballi), meaning broom + root + creeper ; (shahávaliballi) ; (áhéruballi), meaning asparagopsis floribunda + creeper. Tel. also (pillipítsara), meaning cat + the plant. Mal. also (shatávali), by corruption. Tam. also (tannírmuttán), by corruption ; (sathámulam), meaning hundred + root ; (sháttiravéri), hundred + root ; (kilávarí), meaning branched root, from appearance of root in thin, long narrow pieces. Title otherwise Climbing asparagus. Botanically Asparagopsis [shatamooly] sarmentosa, kunth., liliaceæ [vricsham, 136]. Alias Asparagus sarmentosus. Malabar climber ; stems woody, climbing, very much branched ; branches grooved, ribbed, branchlets rather rough ; thorns subulate, straight, turned downwards ; leaves linear mucronulate ; racemes many-flowered, flowers white, berries red. When a plant is dug out with roots, has appearance as if many large round worms were attached to it ; the fresh root is very fleshy and succulent, about a foot or foot and a half in length, generally of the thickness of a finger smooth and round, tapering to a very narrow and long point at both ends, of dull white or pale grey color, no smell, and taste slightly demulcent. Soofaid moosly of commerce is the fresh root dried and split longitudinally ; this occurs in thin and long pieces like strings, curled upon itself once or twice, varies in length from three or four inches to a span or more, of pale-grey or dirty-white color, and devoid of any particular taste or smell. Root medicinally like shakaukool [q.v.] ; specially boiled with oil, applied to cutaneous diseases. Soofaid moosly of other parts of india is the root of Asparagopsis ascendens, kunth. [indian salep], a substitute for salep [q.v.].

MOOSSAD (മൂസ്സതു - mússatu, obl. ; മൂസ്സ് - mússu, pers. sing. ; മൂസ്സന്മാർ - mússémár, pers. pl., *Mal.*). From (múkku, mal. to grow old) [moo]. Caste-title. A subordinate class of Bramins in Malabar. See vol. II, 100. Others are Elliads and Numbies. The following are the principal Moossads.——*Aulatore numby* (ആലത്തൂർനമ്പി - álattúrnampi, Mal.). Ponnany.——*Cheerattmana* (ചിരട്ടമന - chírattumana, Mal.). Valavanaud.——*Coottancherry* (കുട്ടഞ്ചേരി - kuttañchéri, Mal.). Ponnany.——*Plaundole* (പ്ലാന്തോൾ - plántól, Mal.). Valavanaud.——*Tycaut* (തൈക്കാട്ട - taykkáttu, Mal.). Cochin.——*Yeledat tycaut* (എളേടത്തു തൈക്കാട്ട - elétattutaikkáttu, Mal.). Cochin [jauty].

MOOSSANDA (बेल्लोटि - béllóti, *Conc.* ; بیبینا - bebíná, *Hind.* ; ಬೆಳ್ಳೊಟ್ಟಿ - bellotti, *Can.* ; ಬೊಳ್ಳೆತಪ್ಪು - bolletappu, *Too.* ; വെള്ളില - vellila, *Mal.* ; මුස්සැන්ද - mussanda, *Singh.* ; வெள்ளிமடந்தை - vellimadandai, *Tam.*). Title from singhalese. Can. means white plant. Too. from (bolle, too. white + tappu, too. leaf). Mal. from (vel, mal. white + ila, mal. leaf), from white leaves. Tam. from (vel, tam. white + madandai, tam. lady). Singh. also (valbutsarana), meaning creeper + canna indica, linn. Tam. also (vellilai), meaning white leaf. Title otherwise Creeping indian shot, Velilla, White lady, White-leaf plant, White-rag plant. Botanically Mussænda frondosa, l., rubiaceæ [vricsham, 71]. Generic name from singhalese. Alias Mussænda dorinia, flavescens, formosa, glabra, velilla, zeylanica. Velilla from malayalam. Erect shrub ; leaves oval, acuminated, from villous or hirsute to nearly glabrous ; branches and corymbs when young pubescent or tomentose ; calyx-segments subulate, much longer than the ovary, hirsute, one of them in some of the axillary flowers of the corymb produced into a large pubescent or villous leaf ; corolla externally hirsute ; style the length of the tube ; fruit at first hairy, afterwards glabrous, obovoid ; flowers middle-sized, gold-colored ; common ; flowering nearly all the year. Used as a charm against demons. The root is given with cow's urine as a remedy for jaundice ; the juice of the leaves and fruit, which is very mucilaginous, is used as an eye-wash ; the flowers are attenuant and diuretic, and are used in cough, asthma, ague, and flatulence ; externally applied they clean foul ulcers, and cure skin eruptions. Leaves boiled and eaten as a vegetable [keeray]. Other common species are :—corymbosa, tomentosa.

MOOSTAFAH (مصطفی - mustafá, *Ar.*). From (safu, ar. pure). Lacab of Mahomed. Common alam ; as Moostafah ally, double alam ; Moostafah beg, alam + alaumat [ism].——*Moostafahnugger* (مصطفی نگر - mustafánagar, Hind.). From (above + nagar, hind. town). One of the five Circars [q.v.] obtained by the English from the emperor of Delhi [charitram]. See vol. I (179). Modern name is Condapully.

MOOSTAJARY (مستاجری - mustájirí, *Hind.*). From (ajr, ar. hire). Renting system as opposed to Ryotwarry [q.v.] tenure. Moostaujar is a farmer of revenue [goottadar].

MOOSTAKEEM (مستقیم - mustakím, *Ar.*). From (kauma, ar. to stand). Resolute. Part of lacab ; as Moostakeem jung, resolute in war [ism].

MOOSTOWFY (مستوفی - mustaufí, *Ar.*). Auditor of accounts. Part of lacab ; as Moostowfy ood dowla, comptroller of the empire [ism].

MOOTAH (متعه - mutah, *Hind.*). Literally enjoyment. Temporary marriages allowed by Shiah [q.v.] code, but, considered illegal by Soonnees [q.v.].

MOOTALIK (متعلق - mutaallik, *Hind.*). From (alaka, ar. to hang) [talook]. Dependent.

MOOTAMAD (معتمد - mutamad, *Ar.*). From (amada, ar. to confide). Faithful. Prefixed to an alam forms a lacab ; as Mootamad hoossain, faithful to hoossain [ism].

MOOTAZALA (معتزل - mutazála, *Hind.*). From (azala, ar. to separate one's self). A dissenter ; from the founder of this sect, Wausil, having seceded from his master Imaum hassan basree on a question of dogma. The society of Ikhwaun oos safah or Brothers of purity, from which issued about the tenth century treatises on every department of human study, was founded by the members of this school. Rationalism was put down during the Abbaside period.

MOOTT (முட்டு - múttu, *Tam.*). Joint.——*Moottpoochy* (முட்டுப்பூச்சி -múttuppúççi, Tam.). Bug. See Poochy.

MOOTTOO (முத்து - muttu, *Tam.*). Pearl [moty]. As an affix in proper names it is common among the lower castes, as Showrimoottoo, Maurimoottoo. Also as prefix, as Moottookrishnan, Moottoosawmy. Also familiar contraction of all names which it begins [peyar].——*Atimooctah* (अतिमुक्ता - atimuktá, San.). Surpassing + pearl, alluding to flowers or wood. Plant name common to:—Chrysanthemum indicum; Hiptage madablota; Ougeinia dalbergioides. See gloss. paragraphs.——*Mootcore* (ముత్కూరు - muttukúru, Tel.). From (muttayya, tel. proper name + úru, tel. village); after moottayya, relative of krishna deva royel. Village; Nellore dist., Goodoor tal.; pop. 2,011; acres 2,933; lat. 14° 17′; long. 80° 08′; from Goodoor E.N.E. 19 miles; from Nellore S.E. 14 miles; from the sea W. 3 miles. Rising into importance as close to the basin of the Buckingham canal [q.v.] and the road to Nellore. Good private choultry [choultry, kistnapatam].——*Moottammah* (முத்தம்மா - muttammá, Tam.). From (above + ammá, tam. mother). Familiarly Moottoo. Hindoo female proper name [peyar].——*Moottauraммah* (முத்தாரம்மா - muttárammá, Tam.). From (above + áram, tam. pendant + ammá, tam. mother). A Tamulian demoness.——*Moottayyan* (முத்தய்யன் - muttayyan, Tam.). From (above + aiyyan, tam. master). Epithet of Soobramanyan [q.v.]. Hindoo proper name [peyar].——*Moottiaul* (ముత్యాలు - mutyálu, Tel.). Means pearls. Hindoo 2nd or pers. name. Common among non-bramins [peyar].——*Moottiaulpaud* (ముత్యాలపాడు - mutyálapádu, Tel.). From (muttayya, tel. proper name + pádu, tel. village).—"*a*" Zemindarry; Nellore dist., Cundoocore tal.; square miles 20. Peshcush Rs. 2,000. Consists of three villages and ten hamlets in the Cundoocore talook.—"*b*" Village; Nellore dist., Cundoocore tal.; pop. 2,926; lat. 14° 59′; long. 79° 51′; from Cundoocore S.S.W. 16¼ miles; from Nellore N.N.W. 39 miles; from the sea W. 17 miles. Principal village of the Moottiaulpaud estate held by Bauley row [q.v.]. The founder of the Bauley row family obtained this jagheer [q.v.] from the Nizam [q.v.] of Hyderabad as a reward for his services in reducing the rebellious jagheerdars of Anama condah, Veligonda, &c. Large tank [q.v.]. Betel [q.v.] gardens. Two old temples of Vishnoo and Shiva. Festivals in November and December.——*Moottoocomauran* (முத்துக்குமாரன் - muttukkumáran, Tam.). From (above + kumára, san. son). Epithet of Soobramanyan [q.v.], the beautiful son-god. Hindoo 2nd or pers. name. Common among non-bramins [peyar].——*Moottookrishnan* (முத்துக்கிருட்டிணன் - muttukkiruttinan, Tam.). From (above + krishna, san. the god); beautiful krishnan [q.v.]. Hindoo 2nd or pers. name [peyar].——*Moottoo krishnappa* (முத்துக்கிருட்டிணப்பன் - muttukkiruttinappan, Tam.). From (above + krishnappan, tam. proper name). Naick ruler of Paundyam, in whose reign Robert de Nobilibus preached at Madura. A.D. 1602–1609. See vol. I (121); II, 250.——*Moottoomaury* (முத்துமாரி - muttumári, Tam.). From (above + mári, tam. the goddess of small-pox). Village deity. Maury presiding over small-pox, white pearl-like variety. The other and more dreaded form is the dark variety.——*Moottoopett* (முத்துப்பேட்டை - muttuppéttai, Tam. mutupet*). From (muttu, tam. pearl, proper name + péttai, tam. village). Town, Port, Sea-customs office; Tanjore dist., Tritrapoondy tal.; pop. 5,381; acres 1,453; lat. 10° 23′; long. 79° 32′; from Calimere point N.W. 27 miles; from Adirampatnam N.E. 9 miles; from Madras S.W. 191 miles; from Tanjore S.E. 36 miles; from Tritrapoondy S.W. 14 miles. On Coraiyaur in bay to west of Point caliniere. Though but a mere boat harbour, upwards of 100 vessels, with an aggregate of 6,000 tons, annually frequent the port. Large Lubbay [q.v.] community trading with Ceylon and other places. Paddy [q.v.] largely exported to Ceylon.——*Mootton ramalinga saitoopaty* (முத்துராமலிங்கசேதுபதி - muttuarámalingaséthuppathi, Tam.). Name + title. Ruler of Ramnaud. Twice deposed and sent to Madras as state prisoner. It was at this time that the English becoming virtual rulers of the Carnatic [q.v.] the revenues of Ramnaud had to be assigned to them by Nawaub wallajah [charitram]. See vol. I (124).——*Moottoosawmy* (முத்துசாமி - muttusámi, Tam.). From (above + svámi, san. lord). Hindoo 2nd or pers. name [peyar].——*Moottoovail* (முத்துவேலு - muttuvélu, Tam.). From (above + vél, tam. spear). Epithet of Soobramanyan, the beautiful lance-holder. Hindoo 2nd or pers. name. Common among non-bramins [peyar].——*Moottoo veerappan* (முத்துவீரப்பன் - muttuvírappan, Tam.). From (above + vírappan, tam. proper name). Naick ruler of Paundyam. A.D. 1609–1623. See vol. I (121); II, 250.

MOOTTY (बाल - bála, *San.*; முட்டி - mutti, *Tam.*). San. from (val, san. to cover). Tam. from (muttu, tam. to oppose); medicinal. Botanically the Pavonia genus, malvaceæ [vricsham, 25]. Small shrubs or herbs, natives of america; leaves various in form. The species best known to the natives are shown below.——*Peramootty* (बाल - bála, San.; काळावाळा - kálávála, Mahr.; سگہند بالا - sughandbálá, Hind.; ಬಲರಕ್ಕಸಿಗಿಡ - balarakkasígida, Can.; ముత్తవపులగముచెట్టు - muttavapulagamuchettu, Tel.; பேராமுட்டி - pérámutti, Tam.). Title from size of plant. San. from (val, san. to cover), medicinal. Mahr. from (kála, san. black + válá, mahr. andropogon muricatus, retz.). Hind. from (sughandha, san. odour + bálá, hind. andropogon); from its resemblance to stimulating and carminative action of musk. Can. from (bala, can. strong + rakkasi, san. giantess + gida, can. plant). Tel. from (mutta, tel. old + avva, tel. grandmother + pulagamu, tel. pudding + chettu, tel. plant) [common balah, lance-leaved balah, shoondy, shrubby balah], familiar household medicine. Tam. from (peru, tam. great + mutti, tam. pavonia). San. also (hrívéra), meaning shy + body. Tel. also (chittibenda), meaning small + hibiscus esculentus, linn.; (errakúti), meaning red + pulp. Title otherwise Chittibenda, Fragrant pavonia. Botanically Pavonia [mootty] odorata, willd., malvaceæ [vricsham, 25]. Alias Hibiscus chittlebenda, moriforius, odoratus; Pavonia sidoides. Chittlebenda from teloogoo. Shrub, 2–3 feet; calyx five-cleft; involucel twelve-leaved, ciliated, longer than the calyx; stems viscidly hairy; leaves cordate, roundish-ovate, upper one three-lobed, toothed, more or less hairy and viscid, lower ones sometimes entire; pedicels axillary, one-flowered; carpels five, two-valved, one-seeded, not prickly; flowers rose-colored; fragrant; flowering nearly all year. Roots 7–8 inches long, more or less twisted, not more than ¼ inch in diameter at the thickest part; giving off numerous thin fibres and having a delicate musk odour; bark light brown, nearly smooth, wood hard, yellowish; seeds brown, oily, not musky. Flower religious; one of the flowers with which arrows of cauman [cauma baunam] are tipped. Infusion of roots is a diet drink in fevers. Yields a fibre [naur].——*Shittamootty* (बाल - bála, San.; ಚಿಟ್ಟಾಮುಟ್ಟಿ - chittámutti, Can.; చిన్నముత్తవపులగముచెట్టు - chinnamuttavapulagamuchettu, Tel.; ഗസ്ബവില - gasbavila, Singh.; சிற்றாமுட்டி - shittámutti, Tam.). Title from size of plant. San. from (val, san. to cover), covering the earth with roots, also medicinal. Can. from tamul. Tel. from (chinna, tel. small + muttavapúlagamuchettu, tel. pavonia odorata, willd.). Tam. from (shiru, tam. small + mutti, tam. pavonia sp.). Can. also (antutogarigida), meaning gum + cajanus indicus, spr. Tel. also (peramutti). Title otherwise Ceylon pavonia. Botanically Pavonia [mooty] zeylanica, cav., malvaceæ [vricsham, 25]. Alias Hibiscus zeylanicus. Annual; lower leaves somewhat roundish-cordate, crenated, upper ones deeply three to five-lobed, coarsely toothed; pedicels axillary, one-flowered; involucel leaves ten, ciliated, longer than the calyx; carpels unarmed; flowers middle-sized, whitish; flowering in the rainy season. Root has little taste or smell. An infusion of the root is given in fevers. Yields a fibre [naur].

MOOTWULLEE (متولی - mutawallí, *Hind.*). From (vilá, ar. near). A person appointed to the management of a religious building and endowment [dharmacurta, musjid].

MOOZUFFER (مظفر - muzaffar, *Ar.*). From (zafr, ar. victory). Victorious. Lacab of the prophet. Common alam; as Moozuffer hoossain, victorious hoossain, double alam [ism].——*Moozuffer jung* (مظفر جنگ - muzaffarjang, Hind.). Victorious in war. Alam + khitaub title. Grandson of the first Nizam. Disputed his uncle, Nausir jung's title to the throne, and, on his assassination became Nizam under the French protection. Killed in a mutiny of his troops [charitram]. See vol. I (177) and 9; II, 252.

MORABBA (مربا - murabba, *Hind.*; ಗೊಜ್ಜು - gojju, *Can.*; గుజ్జు - guddzu, *Tel.*; പാവ് - pávu, *Mal.*; பாகு - págu, *Tam.*). Tel. from (gudzuru, tel. the pulp of fruits). Mal. from (pach, san. to cook). Tam. from (páka, san. boiling). Jelly. The principal fruit [pazham] jellies used by natives of s. india are:—Wood-apple jelly, from fruit of feronia elephantum, corr. wood-apple [q.v.] tree; has a peculiar flavor; agreeable and somewhat astringent. Rozelle jelly, from hibiscus sabdariffa, linn., red sorrel plant [red-hemp bendy]; contains a wholesome acid. Guava jelly, from psidium guyava, linn., var. pomiferum, linn., round-fruited guava [q.v.] tree; much used and exported to europe.

MORAH (موڑہا - morhá, *Hind.*). A foot stool. The usual form of the cane [rattan] morah is that of two truncated cones meeting at the smaller ends.

MORCHANG (مرچنگ - murchang, *Hind.*). From (munh, hind. mouth + chang, pers. lute). Jew's harp [sangeetam].

MORINDA (مورندا - morindá, *Hind.*). Same as Dyeing mulberry.

MORINGA (शोभाञ्जन - shóbhánjana, *San.*; शेगवा - shégavá, *Mahr.*; मशिंगु - mashingu, *Conc.*; سہجنا - shajná, *Hind.*; مونگے کا جھاڑ - múngekájhár, *Dec.*; کیلور - kelor, *Malay*; ನುಗ್ಗೆ - nugge, *Can.*; ನುರ್ಗೆ - nurge, *Too.*; మునగ - munaga, *Tel.*; ମୁନିଘ - munigha, *Oor.*; മുരിങ്ങ - murinna, *Mal.*; മുരുംഗാ ,

murungá, *Singh.*; முருங்கை - murungai, *Tam.*). Title from tamul through malayalam. San. from (shóbhá, san. brightness + añj, san. to clear); improves brightness. Mahr. from (shigru, san. the tree). Oor. from teloogoo. Mal. from (muram, mal. rough + káya, mal. fruit). Tam. from (murungu, tam. to perish); from soft wood. San. also (shigru), meaning sharp; (sanámaka), meaning with stripe; (dvishigru), meaning double moringa, from fruiting in pairs generally; (móchaka), meaning liberating, from gum; (haritapatra), meaning having green leaves; (kákshívaka), meaning stimulant; (janapriya), meaning liked by people; (chákshushya), meaning eye medicine; (murangí); (damshamúla), meaning pungent root; (ugragandhaka), meaning pungent odour; (madhushigru), meaning honey + the plant, is the red variety; (shvétamarícha), meaning white pepper, piper nigrum, linn., is the seed. Pers. also (moriaban). Hind. also (segwá); (ban). Dec. also (mungekíbhájí), meaning moringa greens; (múngekáphúl), meaning moringa flower; (mungekíjhárkíjar), meaning moringa root; (mungekíphallí), meaning moringa pod; (mungekágond), meaning moringa gum. Can. also (móchaka), meaning deliverer. Tel. also (adavimunaga), meaning forest + the tree; (kárumunaga), meaning wild + the tree; (erramunaga), meaning red + the tree; (tellamunaga), meaning white + the tree. Tam. also (úgadan), meaning stimulant; (shuligai), meaning stimulant; (karuñjanam). Greek βάλανος. Title otherwise Ben nut, Ben-oil tree, Country horse radish, Drumstick tree, Glans unguentaria, Indian horse radish, Segwah, Shajnah, Smooth horse radish. Botanically Moringa pterygosperma, gærtn., moringeæ [vricsham, 46]. Alias Anoma moringa; Guilandina moringa; Hyperanthera moringa; Moringa nux eben, oleifera, polygama, zeylanica. Generic from dravidian. Tree 30–35 feet; leaves two to three pinnate with an odd leaflet; calyx five-cleft; petals five, nearly equal, the upper one ascending; filaments hairy at the base; racemes panicled; five stamens without anthers; seeds numerous, three-angled, the angles expanding into wings; flowers small yellowish white, irregular; flowering in hot season. Common about villages but wild in some jungles; easily raised from seed; fruit is a long whip-like bean, hence called drumstick; roots have flavor of horse radish, hence that term. The fruit is light brown when ripe, a foot or more in length, triangular, ribbed, and composed of three valves containing a soft white pith, and a single row of from twelve to eighteen seeds, which are dark brown, roundish, the size of a pea [calauyam] and furnished with three membranaceous wings; the kernel is white, oily and bitter. The fresh root of a large and well-grown tree varies in its diameter, in the thickest part, from 1–4 inches, and in its length, from 1–3 feet, tapering gradually towards its end; it is pale and yellowish-white internally and externally, porous, soft, slightly aromatic and disagreeable in smell, and pungent in taste; it is covered with a root bark, which has the same color, smell and taste, and is about one or two lines in thickness. The bark of the trunk is about ½ inch thick, and its taste and smell are similar to those of the root-bark, but somewhat weaker; it is covered with a rough and scaly epidermis, which is generally of a brown or greyish-brown color, and is easily removed; the inner bark is externally of a greenish, yellowish or pale white color, and its color internally is pale or yellowish white. The bark of the root has a reticulated light brown external surface; it is thick, soft, and internally white, and has a pungent odour and taste, exactly like horse radish; the wood of the root is soft, porous, and yellowish, and has the same properties in a less degree. The gum from bark, when it first exudes, is opaque and white; from exposure to the air it soon becomes pink, and finally of a dull red color on the surface, the interior remaining white; it occurs in pieces of considerable size, generally more or less vermicular in form, and is only produced upon trees which have been injured by insects; the taste is bland and mucilaginous; in dry air the gum becomes very friable, but in a damp climate it is tough and holds 20 per cent. of its weight of water; it resembles tragacanth [kateerah], for which it may be a substitute; one of the gums often called mocharas [q.v.]. From seeds comes a clear, limpid, almost colorless oil, called ben oil. The large branches planted in the ground root freely and soon become small trees, but produce from seedling plants is the best. Flowers, bark, root-bark and root are medicinal. The fresh root is stimulant, carminative, stomachic and stimulant-diuretic; the flowers slighly stimulant; the bark and root-bark, used externally, are rubefacient and vesicant. Compound spirit of moringa; take of the root, sliced, twenty ounces; orange [q.v.] peel, ten ounces; nutmegs [jautikye], bruised, two drachms and a half; proof-spirit, four pints; water, one pint and a half; mix and distil four pints; dose from one to four fluid drachms. Internally, the compound spirit of moringa is a good substitute for spirit. ammon. arom., tinct. cascarillæ, tinct. valerianæ, tinct. moschi, tinct. cardamom comp., and spirit armoraciæ comp. Externally, the root-bark and the bark, particularly the former, is a fair substitute for the mustard flour imported from europe and for emplastrum cantharidis. Oil from seeds is used externally for pains in the limbs, gout, and rheumatism. Juice of the leaves mixed with pepper [q.v.] applied over the eyes in vertigo, mixed with common salt [ooppoo] given to children in flatulency; also used to hasten suppuration in boils. Bark, rubbed up in rice-water mixed with cummin seed [jeerah], is a cure for gum-boils and toothache. Leaves simply warmed applied in hydrocele, and also good for ulcers and guinea worm [naudy vranam]. The gum [gond] is used in headache, mixed with milk and externally rubbed on the temples, also locally applied to buboes and venereal pains in the limbs. Root quoted in pharm., but non-officinal, like armoracia. The leaf, flower, and long pod eaten as vegetables [keeray]; after the beans are taken off the tree, branches are lopped off and leaves given to cattle; scraped root furnishes horse radish for table; flower pickled; every part indeed is turned to some culinary account; root used in adulterating country mustard [rayaun]. Ben oil is used by watch-makers and jewellers, as it neither grows rancid nor freezes readily; also used by perfumers as an absorbent for some of the more delicate odours; bark yields coarse fibre [naur]; wood gives a dye [shauyam]; used as avenue [shaulay] tree. Timber very soft and useless, not even fit for fuel. There is a variety with red flowers, called red in vernaculars. Another species is aptera; native of palestine. Another is concanensis; very abundant on the hills in n. arcot district; like a variety of pterygosperma, but has much larger and rounder leaflets.——*Jungle moringa* (काननशेखर - kánanashékhara, San. - جنگلی منگے کا جہاڑ - janglímungekájhár, Hind.; ಕಾಡುನುಗ್ಗೆ - kádunugge, Can.; అడవిమునగ - adavimunaga, Tel.; കാട്ടുമുരിങ്ങ - káttumurinna, Mal.; காட்டு முருங்கை - káttumurungai, Tam.). Title from similarity of pods. San. from (kánana, san. forest + shékhara, san. the plant, moringa). Hind. from (janglí, hind. wild + mungá, hind. moringa pterygosperma, gaert. + jhár, hind. tree); from similarity of pods. Can. from (kádu, can. wild + nugge, can. the moringa). Tel. from (adavi, tel. wild + munaga, tel. moringa). Mal. from (kátu, mal. forest + murinna, mal. the plant moringa). Tam. from (kádu, tam. forest + murungai, tam. moringa pterygosperma, gært.). San. also (kánanashigru), meaning wild + the plant, moringa. Tel. also (nallakáshana), meaning black + bauhinia acuminata, linn. Mal. also (punamurinna), meaning forest + the plant, moringa. Title otherwise Senna-leaved french honey-suckle. Botanically Ormocarpum sennoides, dec., leguminosæ [vricsham, 48]. Alias Hedysarum nallakashina, sennoides. Nallakashina from teloogoo. Shrub; young shoots, petioles, peduncles and calyx covered with glutinous hairs; leaves unequally pinnated; leaflets alternate, four to six pair, obovate, retuse; stamens equally diadelphous, five and five; legume two to five-jointed, covered with prickly warts; flowers yellow, fragrant; racemes short, axillary, flowering in the rainy season. Root stimulant and tonic; bark of root with gingelly [q.v.] oil makes liniment for lumbago.——*Wild moringa* (ಕಾಡುನುಗ್ಗೆ - kádunugge, Can.). Same as Poolah coral tree.

MORMASSY (मोडमस - módamasa, *Mahr.*; چلا - chillá, *Hind.*; కొండజుంగురు - kondadzunguru, *Tel.*; වල්වරික - valvarika, *Singh.*). Title from mahratta. Mahr. from (móda, mahr. pile + mashí, san. soft tumour); from curing piles. Tel. from (konda, tel. hill + dzungamu, tel. rivea hypocrateriformis, chois.). Hind. also (chilara), (bairí). Botanically Casearia esculenta, roxb., samydaceæ [vricsham, 60]. Alias Casearia championi, varians; Vareca zeylanica. Vareca from singhalese. Large shrub; leaves alternate, oblong, entire, smooth; flowers axillary, greenish-yellow; stamens eight. The root is from ½ to 2 inches in diameter, often very crooked, forming angular bends; it consists of a central red woody column, having seven or a less number of dark concentric rings; the bark is of a deep dull-red color, thick, and extremely hard, covered with a thin papery suber of an ochre-yellow color; the taste is astringent; the root yields to water an abundant dark reddish-brown extract; the powder has a cobweb-like character due to the length and silkiness of the liber cells. In western india the root has a great reputation as a remedy for hepatic enlargements and for piles; used here as a remedy for diabetes, for which disease it is considered specific. For tomentosa see Anavinga.

MORTT (ಮೊರ್ಟ್ - mort, *Can.*). Todah village [mund, todah].

MOSAL (शश - shasha, *San.*; ससा - sasá, *Mahr.*; ارنب - arnab, *Ar.*; خرگوش - khargosh, *Pers.* and *Hind.*; ಮೊಲ - mola, *Can.* and *Too.*; కుందేలు - kundélu, *Tel.*; ଖୁତୁରୋ - khuturo, *Oor.*; മുയൽ - muyal, *Mal.*; හාවා - haba, *Singh.*; முசல் - musal, *Tam.*). Title from tamul. San. from (shash, san. to jump); moves swiftly by leaps. Mahr. from sanscrit. Pers. from (khar, pers. donkey + gosh, pers. ear). Mal. from (muyal, tam. to be active). Hind. also (sussá), from sanscrit. Tam. also (muyal). Title otherwise Hare. Lepus nigricollis, leporidæ, rodentia, mammalia [sastanam, 19], of naturalists [jantoo]. Alias Lepus melanauchen. The habits of hares are well known; their timidity, watchfulness, increased by the situation of their eyes, which are so placed that they can see all round, and their great speed. The young are born, unlike the case of rabbits, with their eyes open. The hare lives in the open, and its lair or form is merely a slight depression in some secluded spot. It has been noticed that the hare always returns to its form, no matter to what distance it may have wandered or have been driven. There are no rabbits or burrowing hares in India. As the spots in the moon resemble the form of a hare, she is called in Sanscrit shashy [chundran]; but the Tamulians say that an old woman is seated in the moon spinning cotton. The Indian animal is much fleeter than in Europe. As food often dry; veidyans prescribe it for incontinence of urine. The gall of this animal is used in medicine. Its blood is given to children suffering from cough.—" *a* " The species named at head is usually called the black-naped hare, and is the chief representative here of the family. Upper part grayish rufescent, slightly mottled with black; large nuchal spot extending to near the shoulders velvety black; ears grayish brown internally, dusky posteriorly, black at the base, and white fringed at the apex; lower neck yellowish, chin and abdomen white; tail grizzled black and yellowish-gray above, white beneath. The black-naped hare is found throughout the South of India, extending north to the Godavery river on the east, and on the west coast as high as the Tapty river and perhaps further. It is the hare of Ceylon also, and has been introduced into Java and the Mauritius. The black-naped hare of the Neilgherries is the same as that of the plains, only larger from the effect of climate.—" *b* " Akin is the common Indian hare of Upper india. Lepus ruficaudatus of naturalists. General hue rufescent mixed with blackish on the back and head; ears brownish anteriorly, white at the base and the tip brown; neck, breast, flanks and limbs, more or less dark sandy rufescent unmottled; nape pale sandy rufescent; tail rufous above, white beneath; upper lip, small eye mark, chin, throat, and lower parts, pure white. This hare is found southwards to the Godavery river.—" *c* " Indian species not here found are:—Craspedotis or large-eared hare, Hispidus or hispid hare, Hypsibius or mountain hare, Pallipes or pale-footed hare, Pamirensis or pamir hare, Peguensis or pegu hare, Stoliczkanus or stoliczka's hare, Tibetanus or thibet hare, Yarkandensis or yarkund hare.—" *d* " The rabbit is Lepus cuniculus, not here found.

MOSMOOSKY (अहिलेखन - ahilékhana, *San.*; चिराति - chiráti, *Mahr.*; اگمکی - agamaki, *Hind.*; ಮಡುತೊಂಡೆ - madutonde, *Can.*; ನುರ್ತೆಂಗಿ - nurtengi, *Too.*; నూగుదోస - núgudósa, *Tel.*; മുക്കാപ്പീര - mukkáppira, *Mal.*; முசுமுசுக்கை - musumusukkai, *Tam.*). Title from tamul. San. from (ahi, san. snake + lékhana, san. mark); from vertical white stripes upon the fruit. Can. from (madu, can. hollow in river + tonde, can. cephalandra indica, naud.). Tel. from (núgu, tel. down + dósa, tel. cucumis melo, linn., var. utilissimus, roxb.). Mal. from (mukkál, mal. three-quarters + píra, mal. luffa). Tam. from (musumusu, tam. to feel a sensation like crawling of insects); from itching bristly fruit. San. also (ghantáli), meaning bell + row, from the vertical marks on the fruit resembling slits on bells worn by dancing girls. Tel. also (putribudama), meaning daughter + country cucumber, cucumis trigonus, roxb.; from being frequently given to children. Title otherwise Bryony, Bristly bryony, Globe-fruited bryony, Rough bryony. Botanically Mukia scabrella, arn., cucurbitaceæ [vricsham, 62]. Alias Bryonia althæoides, madraspatana, rottleri, scabra, scabrella; Cucumis madraspatanus. Plant hispid and scabrous; tendrils simple; leaves cordate, lobed or angled; flowers short-peduncled, male numerous, fascicled; female, one to four, small, campanulate, yellow; berry globular, size of a pea [calauyam], scarlet when ripe, marked with white vertical lines, smooth or sprinkled with a few bristly hairs; plant and fruit bitter; the fruits ripen in october to december. Gently aperient and stomachic, frequently given to children.

MOSQUE (مسجد - masjid, *Hind.*; మసీదు - masídu, *Tel.*; மசூதி - masúthi, *Tam.*). An English form derived through the Spanish mezquita. A Mahomedan church [musjid].

MOSQUITO (मशक - mashaka, *San.*; मच्छर - machhara, *Mahr.*; بق - bakk, *Ar.*; پشه - pashshah, *Pers.*; مچهر - maççhar, *Hind.* and *Dec.*; ناملك - námuk, *Malay*; ಸೊಳ್ಳೆ - solle, *Can.*; ಉಮಿಲ್ - umil, *Too.*; దోమ - dóma, *Tel.*; കൊതു - kotu, *Mal.*; මශක - mashaka, *Singh.*; கொசு - kosu, *Tam.*). Title from portuguese; diminutive of mosca, a fly. San. from (mash, san. to hum). Mahr. from (matsara, san. gnat). Ar. from (bakka, ar. to bring forth many children). Pers. from sanscrit. Hind. from (matsara, san. gnat). Mal. from tamul. Tam. from (ghósha, san. gnat). Malay also (agas). Tel. also (chíkatíga), meaning darkness + fly. The genus Culex, culicidæ, diptera, holometabola, insecta [poochy], of naturalists [jantoo]. Species known are Circumvolens, Regins, Laniger, Fuscanus. Abound near stagnant water. Have three stages of existence, in two of which they are a water insect, and in the third a winged insect. Preventatives are sprigs of worm-wood [absinth], the aloe [q.v.] indica [common indian aloe] suspended root upwards with an incision in each leaf so as to eject the aroma, branches of penny royal [poodeenah], pastilles containing sulphate of copper [toottam], &c.

MOTABAR (معتبر - mutabar, *Ar.*). From (ibr, ar. to regard). Trusted, confidential. Part of lacab; as Motabar jung, trusted in war [ism].

MOTRAH (موتهرا - mothrá, *Hind.*). Bog-spavin in horses [ashwarogam, ghorah].

MOTTAM (மொத்தம் - mottam, *Tam.*). Total. Mottafeisal, from (faisal, hind. settlement), a lump money assessment not liable to variation fixed on a village; prevails in Tanjore. Motta puttah is a lease of a whole village or district.

MOTURFA (محترفه - muhtarafah, *Hind.*). From (hirfah, ar. handicraft). Taxes formerly levied on the manufacturing and trading community, as loom tax, cooly tax, &c.; or on artizans, as weavers, cotton-cleaners, shepherds, goldsmiths, braziers, ironsmiths, carpenters, stone cutters, &c. See vol. I, 163.

MOTY (मुक्ता - muktá, *San.*; لولو - lúlú, *Ar.*; مرواريد - marwáríd, *Pers.*; موتی - motí, *Hind.*; ಮುತ್ತು - muttu, *Can.*; ముత్యము - mutyamu, *Tel.*; മുത്ത് - muttu, *Mal.*; முத்து - muttu, *Tam.*). Hind. and drav. from sanscrit. San. from (much, san. to set free) [mooch]. Homer's ἕρματα τρίγληνα μορόεντα are pearl earrings. Theophrastus and the Latin writers call a pearl μαργαρίτης and margarita, whence the French Marguerite, the Daisy; this is by error from Sanscrit (marakata), which is an emerald, not a pearl. Pearl [chippy]. A small, round or oval concretion, of bright translucent whiteness, found in the inside of the pearl oyster [sadaf] or mother-of-pearl fish, of great value when of the best quality. The most desirable color is a silver-like brightness, and with this quality the largest is of course the most valuable. The most beautiful shape is round; but the larger pearls have in very many cases the figure of a pear [amrood]. Seed pearls are those of smallest size. The pearl oyster is Meleagrina margaritifera, lamarck, of naturalists; alias avicula margaritifera, meleagrina, radiata; Margarita sinensis; Mytilus margaritiferus. Does not belong to same genus as edible oyster [auly] although in its internal structure it has a resemblance to it. It is found at a considerable depth at the bottom of the sea; is very coarse, and forms no part of the food of the natives. It resembles more the mussel tribe, more particularly as it has a byssus or cable by which it attaches itself to foreign substances or to others of its kind. It has no eyes. About one and a quarter inch from the rim of the shell is a pair of gills. The stomach is very small. It lives on minute algæ or weeds, animalcules, and shells called foraminifera. The native divers say that there are male and female pearl oysters. The large flat ones they call males, and those that are thick concave and vaulted they call females. The animal cannot detach the byssus from the rock to which it is attached, but it has the power of casting it off its own body and leaving it behind, in order to make another byssus, either on the same rock or on any other convenient place. It is highly tenacious of life. It can live even in brackish water, and in places so shallow that it must be exposed for three or four hours daily to the sun and other atmospheric influences. It will move about in search of food, if the locality in which it is originally placed is not rich in its natural supplies. It can live for a long time without forming a byssus. Taking the foregoing facts into account, there appears to be no reason why pearl oysters should not be translated from their native beds and made to colonize other parts of the sea. The young as well as the old are in spawn from March to September, and probably there is no stated period for spawning. The production of the pearl within some suppose to be an accretion within the animal of the super-abundant matter called mother-of-pearl [sadaf] which coats over the inside of the shell; others consider it a disease of the fish, similar to bezoar [q.v.]. Tinnevelly has long been celebrated for its pearl fisheries. The Periplus states that pearls, μαργαρῖτης or πίνικον, were exported in considerable quantity and of superior quality from μούζιρις and νελκύνδα. A pearl fishery, πινικοῦ κολύμβησις, was conducted in the neighbourhood of Korkay, in the kingdom of Pandyan, near the island of Epidorus; the produce transported to the interior of the country, where muslin robes with pearl inwoven or μαργαριτιδες σινδόνες were fabricated. The modern fishery is very uncertain. This is due to the migrating habits of the pearl oyster. When there is any prospect of a fishery the custom is to send out vessels in different directions to test the localities [par], and from each vessel a few divers are let down, who bring up some thousands of oysters, which are heaped upon the shore and opened and examined. If the pearls found in each heap are found by appraisers to be sufficiently valuable it is publicly announced that there will be a fishery that year. Great crowds of people assemble on the coast on the day appointed for the commencement of the fishery; and traders come there with wares of all kinds. The fishery is conducted as a Government monopoly. When a vessel containing the divers reaches its place, the divers plunge into the sea, each with a heavy stone tied to his feet to make him sink rapidly, and furnished with a net in which to put his oysters, and having a rope tied round his body, the end of which is passed round a pully and held by some of the boatmen. On reaching the bottom the diver fills his net with oysters until his breath fails, when he pulls a string, and the signal being perceived he is hauled up. No artificial appliances of any kind are used to enable the men to stay under water for long periods. The diving over, the vessels return to the coast and discharge their cargoes, and the oysters are all thrown on to the ground and left for two or three days, at the end of which time they open. The pearls having been extracted from the shells and carefully washed, are placed in a metal receptacle containing some five or six colanders of graduated sizes, which are fitted one into another so as to leave a place between the bottoms of every two, and are pierced with varying sizes, that which has the largest holes being the topmost colander, and that which has the smallest the undermost. When dropped into colander No. 1, all but the very finest pearls fall through to No. 2, and most of them pass to Nos. 3, 4 and 5, whilst the smallest of all the seeds are strained off into the receptacle at the bottom. When all have stayed in their proper colanders, they are classified and valued accordingly. The largest or those of the first class are the most valuable, and the value of any given pearl is appraised almost exclusively with reference to its size, and is held to be affected but little by its shape and lustre. The native belief is that pearls are produced by the pearl oyster drinking in the drops of rain; and that these and other precious stones [ratnam] cannot be formed, nor fish spawn, without rain [mazhay]. Vemana has the following:—ఆల్చిప్పలోనఁ బడ్డ చినుకు ముత్యంబాయె నీటబడ్డ చినుకు నీళ్లఁగలసె ప్రాప్తముకలచోట ఫలమేల దప్పురా— "The drop that falls into the oyster shell becomes a pearl; "while the drop that falls into the wave turns to water; if the "situation be suitable, the fruit shall not fail." There is a Tamul proverb:—சிப்பியிலே விழுந்த மழைத்துளி முத்தாகும்; அது போல, நல்லவர்க்குச் செய்த உதவி நிலைநிற்கும்— "A rain drop that falls on an oyster shell will become a pearl, "so a benefit conferred on the virtuous will endure." The Tamulians also suppose pearls to be formed in the elephant's tusk [dant], bamboo [q.v.], sugar-cane [q.v.], &c. Hakeems [q.v.] suppose powder of pearl to have virtues in weak eyes, palpitations, nervous tremors, atrabilious affections, and hæmorrhage. They hold, that when applied externally, while in its embryo state in the shell, it cures leprosy [coostam]. Veidyans [q.v.] give it calcined, in typhus fever [krishnadosham]. These prescriptions are for the affluent. Pearls are valued by two kinds of weights, real and nominal. By the former they are weighed, and by the latter sold. The real weight formerly used at Madras was the mangelin [q.v.] which was divided into sixteen parts, and is equal to six English grains. The nominal weight was the chow [q.v.], which was divided into sixty-four parts; and was deduced from the mangelin. Moty mahaul, the palace of pearls, is a common name for a palace. Moty is a common proper name [peyar].

MOULMEIN (مولمین - molmín, *Hind.*). The chief town of Tenasserim division of Lower burmah.——*Moulmein cedar* (صنوبر مولمین - sanobarimolmín, Hind.). Same as Toon.

MOUNTAIN EBONY (काञ्चन - káñchana, *San.*; ஆரை - árai, *Tam.*). San. from (káñch, san. to shine); beautiful tree. Tam. from (ár, tam. splendour). Botanically the Bauhinia genus, leguminosæ [vricsham, 48]. Trees or climbers found throughout tropics; leaves two-lobed; flowers showy; seeds albuminous; several yield dark colored heavy and durable timber. The species best known to the natives are shown below. Other species are:—cannabina, diphylla, macrostachya, richardiana, scandens. Term includes also one species of Dalbergia.——*Large mountain ebony* (चांबूळी - chámbúlí, Mahr.; ماهول - máhwal, Hind.; چمبولی - chambúlí, Dec.; అడ్డ - adda, Tel.; ଶିୟୋଳି - shiyóli, Oor.). Title from extent of branches. Title otherwise Chehoor, Mahwal Yaipy. Botanically Bauhinia [mountain ebony] vahlii, w. & a., leguminosæ [vricsham, 48]. Alias Bauhinia racemosa. One of the commonest species. Shrub, climbing to an immense extent, even 300 feet over highest trees; young shoots, petioles, peduncles, and tendrils covered with thick rusty-colored tomentum; leaves roundish, deeply cordate at the base, upper side nearly glabrous, under tomentose; leaflets oval, obtuse, united to a little above the middle, four to six-nerved; nerves covered with rusty tomentum; tendrils opposite, below the leaves, spiral; racemes terminal corymbiform; pedicels elongated, and with the calyx densely villous; calyx ovate, splitting to the base of the limb into two reflexed segments; petals densely clothed on the back with silky hairs, the three upper a little larger than the others; fertile stamens three, villous at the base; ovary densely villous, its stalk cohering on one side with the calyx tube; legumes pendulous, long, linear, compressed eight to twelve-seeded; flowers largish, white, gradually becoming cream-colored; flowers appear in march and april. Ripe seeds eaten raw, tasting like cashewnut [cashew]. Very useful wild plant; stems form natural ropes, used in the construction of huts; ropes are also made from the bark, boiled and beaten, but rot if kept too long in the water; leaves, often a foot each way, firm, tough, durable, sold in bazaars for plates, lining baskets, covering packets, thatching houses, &c.; a copious gum [gond] of little use. Wood porous, broad, irregularly broken concentric layers, alternating with red, juicy, bark-like tissue; the pith is cross-shaped.——*Malabar mountain ebony* (कोरळ - kórala, Mahr.; املی - amlí, Hind.; ಬಸವನಪಾದ - basavanapáda, Can.; పులిచింత - pulichinta, Tel.; ଗଉରୁବତି - gaurubati, Oor.; புளியாரை - puliyárai, Tam.). Hind. from (amla, san. sour). Can. from (basava, can. an ox + páda, san. foot). Tel. from (pulla, tel. sour + chinta, tel. tamarind tree, tamarindus indica, linn.), from taste of leaves [sour auray]. Tam. from (puli, tam. sour + árai, tam. the tree, bauhinia). Hind. also (amlosa). Can. also (cheppura). Tel. also (pulladonda), meaning sour + cephalandra indica, naud. Title otherwise Cheppoora, Sour covay, Sour mountain ebony, Sour tamarind, St. Thomas' tree. Botanically Bauhinia [mountain ebony] malabarica, roxb., leguminosæ [vricsham, 48]. Large tree; leaves transversely broad, oval, cordate at the base; leaflets rounded, united far above the middle, four-nerved, parallel; calyx funnel-shaped, regular, five-cleft, pubescent; corolla regular; petals spathulate; stamens ten, all fertile, very slightly monadelphous at the base, alternately shorter; racemes axillary, corymbiform, almost sessile; legume long-stalked, linear, slightly falcate, marked longitudinally with waved lines; flowers white; flowering in october and november. Leaves very acrid. Wood moderately hard; numerous narrow wavy white, concentric bands of softer tissue alternate with bands of harder and red-colored wood of equal width, in which the numerous, fine, uniform and equidistant medullary rays are distinctly visible.——*Nirpa mountain ebony* (کندلا - kandlá, Hind.; నిర్ప - nirpa, Tel.). Hind. also (kanall); (kanlas); (kúayral); (semla). Title otherwise Semla gum [q.v.] tree. Botanically Bauhinia [mountain ebony] retusa, ham., leguminosæ [vricsham, 48.] Middling sized tree; leaves cordate at the base, emarginate or retuse at the apex, coriaceous, glabrous; leaflets almost connected to the top, five-nerved, broadly semi-ovate; panicle lax, terminal; petals ovate, unguiculate; anther-bearing stamens three, the rest sterile; flowers small, pale yellow, purple-dotted; flowering nearly all the year. Gives a clear gum [gond], resembling gum arabic [q.v.]; used medicinally. Wood reddish-white with irregularly shaped, darker masses near the centre, hard.——*Purple mountain ebony* (वनराजा - vanarájá, San.; देवकांचन - dévakánchana, Mahr.; جنگھورا - jinghorá, Hind.; ಕಂಚಿವಾಳ - kanchivála, Can.; పెద్దఆరె - peddaáre, Tel.; මෛල - maila, Singh.; நீலத்திருவாத்தி - nílattiruvátti, Tam.). Title from color of flowers. San. from (vana, san. forest + rájá, san. king). Mahr. from (déva, san. god + kánchana, san. bauhinia acuminata, linn.). Tel. from (pedda, tel. large + áre, tel. bauhinia racemosa, lam.). Tam. from (níla, blue + tiru, tam. holy + átti, tam. bauhinia racemosa, lam.). Can. also (sárulmara); (aupta). Tel. also (bódantachettu); (adaviavishi), meaning forest + sesbania grandiflora, pers.; (kánchanamu), meaning gold [champak, toddaly, white mountain ebony]. Tam. also (periyavátti), meaning large mountain ebony; (shegappumandárai), meaning red + bauhinia, from rose-colored flowers. Title otherwise Large mountain ebony, Shaurool autty, Wild sesban. Botanically Bauhinia [mountain ebony] purpurea, linn., leguminosæ [vricsham, 48]. Alias Bauhinia coromandeliana, triandra. Tree; leaves roundish, cordate at the base, coriaceous, glabrous; leaflets oval, obtuse, parallel, united to the middle, the free parts sometimes overlapping, four five-nerved; racemes terminal, panicled; calyx usually cleft to the base of the limb into two reflexed segments, the one emarginate, the other three-toothed, sometimes all cohering at the apex and spathaceous; petals oblong-lanceolate, attenuated at the base; fertile stamens three, sometimes four, long, ascending; legume long, linear, six to twelve-seeded; flowers very large, deep rose-color; flowering in the cold season. A large stout tree, 20–30 feet; found in jungles; cultivated in gardens. Medicinally bark is astringent, root carminative, flowers laxative. Flowers used as pot-herb [keeray] in curries [q.v.], also made into pickles; leaves given to cattle as fodder. Fibre from bark; gives one of the Sem gums [q.v.]. Wood pinkish-white, turning dark-brown on exposure, moderately hard, serviceable.——*Saffron mountain ebony* (पिवालाकांचन - piválákánchana, Mahr.). From pale sulphur flower. Same as Wild mountain ebony.——*Small-flowered mountain ebony* (वनराजा - vanarájá, San.; अपटा - apatá, Mahr.; کچنار - kachnár, Hind.; آرے کا جھاڑ - árekájhár, Dec.; ఆరె - áre, Tel.; ଅମ୍ଭୋଟ - ambhóta, Oor.; මයිල - mayila, Singh.; ஆத்தி - átti, Tam.). San. from (vana, san. forest + rájá, san. king). Hind. means bauhinia acuminata, linn. Dec. from (árai, tam. bauhinia + jhár, hind. tree). Tam. from (ár, tam. brightness), shining tree [west-indian sesban]. San. also (shvétakáñchana), meaning white bauhinia. Tel. also (adaviavishi), meaning forest + tree, sesbania grandiflora, pers.; (yépi) [yaipy]; (ápa) by corruption. Tam. also (ár), meaning beautiful tree; (arikkámaram); (arinár); (árchi), meaning shining tree; cf. coromandel gendarussa. Title otherwise Autty, Great-leaved mountain ebony, Vana rajah, Wild sesban. Botanically Bauhinia [mountain ebony] racemosa, lam., leguminosæ [vricsham, 48]. Alias Bauhinia parviflora, stricta; Piliostigma racemosa. One of the commonest species. Small crooked very ramous tree, unarmed, bushy; branchlets drooping; leaves cordate at the base, upper side glabrous, under villous, or pubescent, or nearly glabrous; leaflets roundish or broadly ovate, united to about the midde, three-nerved; racemes solitary, terminal or leaf-opposed, leafless, much longer than the leaves; flowers scattered, small, white; calyx spathaceous, at length reflexed, five-toothed, pubescent; petals linear, lanceolate, slightly hairy outside; stamens all fertile, united at the base; filaments and anthers bearded; style none; stigma flat sessile; legumes linear, straightish or curved, scarcely dehiscent, many-seeded; flowering in may and june. Bark when stripped off, is of a reddish brown color. Gum [gond] used medicinally, one of the Sem gums [q.v.]. Leaves eaten by elephants [q.v.] and buffaloes [khoolgah]; ripe seeds eaten by the people raw, tasting like cashewnuts [cashew]. The fibre [naur] from bark makes very strong ropes, but it is not durable and rots if kept constantly in water; from bark, matchlockmen make their matches [coomby], burning long and slowly without any substance being mixed with it; leaves sometimes used for making native cigars [cheroot]. Wood light-brown, hard, with irregularly shaped masses of darker-colored and harder wood near the centre; good, but not used.——*Snake-like mountain ebony* (नागवल्ली - nágavallí, San.). Title from peculiar foldings. San. means snake creeper. Title otherwise Snake-charm, Snake-climber. Botanically Bauhinia [mountain ebony] anguina, roxb., leguminosæ [vricsham, 48]. Climbing; leaves cordate, glabrous; leaflets three-nerved, half-ovate, acuminated, united on the young plants to the middle, on the older ones to the apex; tendrils simple or bifid; racemes long, simple, many-flowered, forming a terminal panicle; calyx cup-shaped, obtusely five-lobed; petals obovate; stamens three, all fertile; legume oblong, glabrous, one to two-seeded; flowers very small, white; flowering in the rainy season. Large climber; malabar; very destructive to trees; stems are bent generally in alternate folds and with a straight thick margin. Bark used in rope-making. Wood soft and porous.——*Variegated mountain ebony* (कोविदार - kóvidára, San.; कांचन - kánchana, Mahr.; तांबडेमन्दार - támbadémandára, Conc.; سونا - soná, Hind.; ಬಿಳಿಕಂಚಿವಾಳ - bilikánchivála, Can.; దేవకాంచనము - dévakánchanamu, Tel.; ବୋରର - borara, Oor.; ചുവന്നമന്ദാരം - chuvannamandáram, Mal.; செம்மந்தாரை - shemmandárai, Tam.). Title from color of flowers. San. from (ku, san. earth + vidri, san. to split) [indian hounds' berry]. Mahr. from (káñch, san. to shine). Can. from (bili, can. white + kanchivála, can. the tree). Tel. from (déva, san. divine + kánchanamu, tel. bauhinia acuminata, linn.). Mal. from (chuvanna, mal. red + mandára, san. bauhinia). Tam. from (shem, tam. red + mandárai, tam. bauhinia acuminata, linn.). San. also (káñchanára), meaning splendour giving; (yugapatra), meaning double-leaved, from two-lobed leaf; (kuddála), meaning earth-splitting; (támrapushpi), meaning copper-flowered. Mahr. also (raktakáñchana), meaning red bauhinia. Hind. also (kanchár), meaning bauhinia. Can. also (kempumandára), meaning red + bauhinia; (karalbogi); (irkumbalithumara); (kanchivála). Tel. also (peddaáre), meaning large + bauhinia racemosa, lamk. Mal. also (unnu) [karanj]. Tam. also (shegappumandárai), meaning red + mandauray tree; (vellaippúvátti), meaning white + flower + bauhinia. Title otherwise Variegated St. Thomas' tree. Botanically Bauhinia [mountain ebony] variegata, linn., leguminosæ [vricsham, 48]. Alias Bauhinia candida, purpurea. One of the commonest species. Tree, 20–30 feet; unarmed; leaves roundish, upper side glabrous, under when young villous, cordate at the base; leaflets oval, obtuse, five-nerved, united far beyond the middle; petals oblong, nearly sessile, the upper one somewhat larger and on a rather longer claw than the others; fertile stamens five, all shortly united at the base; racemes axillary and terminal; calyx spathaceous, five-toothed at the apex; legumes straight five to twelve-seeded. Flower larger; for color see below; plant, becomes one entire mass blossom, the large handsome flowers in february-march; seeds ripen two months later; indigenous having a strong resemblance to those of a pelargonium or geranium; flowers in many jungles, also extensively planted in gardens, &c. The bark is grey, tolerably smooth, compact, fracture granular, reddish brown, the external surface is covered thickly with small elliptic warts of a darker color than the rest of the bark; the internal surface is white; the taste is feebly astringent. Gives a brown colored gum [gond], one of the sem gums [q.v.]; swells in water, very little only being soluble. Bark medicinally tonic in fevers; dried buds astringent in diarrhœa and worms. Buds eaten as vegetables when prepared with animal food. Bark is used for tanning [chamrah] and dyeing [shauyam]; bark for making rope; leaves used for packing; oil from seeds. Wood grey, moderately hard, with irregular masses of darker and harder wood in the centre. Two botanical varieties:—Purpurascens, four petals reddish and varied with purple, fifth variegated with purple brown and yellow, malabar, coromandel; Candida, four petals whitish fifth variegated on inner side with yellow and green.——*White mountain ebony* (काञ्चन - káñchana, San.; धवेमन्दारु - dhavémandáru, Conc.; کچنار - kachnár, Hind.; کچنال - kachnál, Dec.; ಬಿಳೆಮಂದಾರ - bilémandára, Can.; కాశనము - káshanamu, Tel.; വെള്ളമന്ദാരം - vellamandáram, Mal.; வெள்ளை மந்தாரை - vellaimandárai, Tam.). Title from color of flowers. San. from (káñch, mal. to shine); beautiful tree [champak, purple mountain ebony, toddaly]. Conc. from (dhava, mahr. white + mandáru, mahr. bauhinia). Hind. and dec. from sanscrit. Can. from (bile, can. white + mandára, san. bauhinia). Tel. from sanscrit. Mal. from (vella, mal. white + mandára, san. bauhinia). Tam. from (vellai, tam. white + mandárai, tam. the tree). Tel. also (dévakánchanamu), meaning divine + the tree. Tam. also (kokkumandárai), meaning crane + the plant; (kokkiragumandárai), meaning crane + feather + the plant, from acuminate lobes of leaves; (mandárai), meaning beautiful bauhinia. Title otherwise Crane's feather, Taper-pointed mountain ebony. Botanically Bauhinia [mountain ebony] acuminata, linn., leguminosæ [vricsham, 48]. Alias Bauhinia candida. Large erect shrub; leaves cordate at the base, young ones slightly pubescent beneath; leaflets ovate, acute or acuminated, united to above the middle, parallel, four-nerved; calyx spathaceous, splitting at the apex into five setaceous teeth; stamens ten, all fertile and united at the base, alternately shorter; racemes solitary, leaf-opposed, or terminal, few-flowered; legumes eight to twelve-seeded, obliquely linear-lanceolate, the seed-bearing suture with three prominent ribs; flowers large, pure white; flowering all the year. Flowers offered at shrine of shiva [q.v.]. Flowers rubbed up with pepper [q.v.] applied to forehead in headache. Gives an oil.——*Wild mountain ebony* (फल्गु - p'halgu, San.; पिवळाकांचन - pivalákánchana, Mahr.; काडरुम्बाडिरूकु - kádarumbádirúku, Conc.; کچنار - kachnár, Hind.; ಕಾಡತ್ತಿ - kádatti, Can.; ಕಾಟರ್ತಿಮರ - kátartimara, Too.; అడవిమందారము - adavimandáramu, Tel.; കാഞ്ചനപ്പൂ - káñchanappú, Mal.; පෙතං - petam, Singh.; திருவாத்தி - tiruvátti, Tam.). San. from (p'hal, san. to split). Mahr. from (pivalá, mahr. yellow + káñchana, san. bauhinia); from pale sulphur flower. Can. from (kádu, can. wild + atti, can. the tree, ficus glomerata, miq.). Tel. from (adavi, tel. forest + mandáramu, tel. tree, bauhinia). Mal. from (káñchana, san. gold + pú, mal. flower). Tam. from (tiru, tam. sacred + átti, tam. bauhinia racemosa, lamk.), used in worship. San. also (úshmadughá), meaning heat giving. Can. also (vanasampige), meaning forest + michelia champaca, linn.; (kallatti), meaning stone + fig tree. Tel. also (kánchini), meaning gold-like tree. Mal. also (káttátti), meaning wild bauhinia. Singh. also (kahapetam), meaning curcuma longa, roxb. + the plant. Tam. also (káttátti), meaning wild bauhinia; (káttumandárai), meaning forest + bauhinia acuminata, linn. Title otherwise Downy mountain ebony, Golden flower, Holy mountain ebony, Saffron mountain ebony, St. Thomas' tree, Tomentose mountain ebony, Yellow mountain ebony, Wild champak. Botanically Bauhinia [mountain ebony] tomentosa, linn., leguminosæ [vricsham, 48]. Upright growing shrub, 6 to 12 feet; ash colored smooth bark; one of the commonest species, unarmed; leaves ovate or roundish at the base, under surface villous as well as the petioles, branches, peduncles and calyx; leaflets connected beyond the middle, oval, obtuse, three-nerved; peduncles two-flowered, leaf-opposed; pedicels each with three bracteas at the base; calyx spathaceous, five-toothed; petals oval; stamens all fertile; legumes flat, lanceolate, five to six-seeded. Flowers large, pale sulphur, drooping; one petal usually with a dark purple spot inside; flowering in july, august; all the tender part except the upper surface of the leaves, covered with a soft down; common on hills on eastern side of presidency, rarer on western; cultivated in gardens and about native temples; a native of ceylon, malabar, and coromandel. Seeds are medicinally tonic and aphrodisiac; seeds made into a paste with vinegar [candy], applied to poisoned wounds; young leaves in powder given in dysentery; decoction of root of bark given in inflamed liver. Seeds are eaten. With the tough stringy fibres [naur] of the small branches a coarse rope is prepared; gives an oil. Wood very tough, heart often quite black.——*Yellow mountain ebony* (ಹಸರುಗುನ್ನಿ - hasarugunni, Can.; పచ్చారి - pattsári, Tel.; പിയങ്ങണി - piyangáni, Mal.; பச்செலைமரம் - paççelaimaram, Tam.). Title from color of wood. Can. from (hasaru, can. green + gunni, can. the tree, so called). Tel. from (pattsa, tel. yellow + áre, tel. bauhinia racemosa, lam.). Tam. from (paççai, tam. green + ilai, tam. leaf + maram, tam. tree). Can. also (paççári). Tel. also (porilasápara), meaning layer + tree, so called; (jálári), meaning net + bauhinia racemosa, lam.; (tellapattsári), meaning white variety. Title otherwise Jaulary, Pattsaury. Botanically Dalbergia [yooga pattricay] paniculata, roxb., leguminosæ [vricsham, 48]. Large tree; leaflets five to six pair, alternate, obovate-oblong or oval, usually emarginate, glabrous; petioles and peduncles pubescent; panicles terminal or axillary, compound; calyx pubescent or hairy, five-cleft, lowest segment long and narrow; vexillum without callosities; stamens ten, equally diadelphous; legume lanceolate, one to two-seeded; flowers small, bluish-white; flowering in the hot season; plains and subalpine dry forests throughout presidency. Gives a gum [gond]. Wood yellowish or greyish-white, soft, perishable; no heartwood; structure is remarkable, broad concentric masses of wood alternate with narrow, dark-colored belts of a fibrous substance, resembling the inner bark; planks cut out of old trees fall to pieces; wood not durable, subject to attacks of insects; but used by natives for building and other purposes.

MOUSE DEER (गिरिकामृग - girikámriga, *San.*; पिसोरा - pisórá, *Mahr.*; پسوری - pisúrí, *Hind.*; پالندوك - pálandok, *Malay*; ಹುಲ್ಲೆ - hulle, *Can.*; కురుపంది - kurupandi, *Tel.*; ଗଣ୍ଡବ - gandava, *Oor.*; ചെറുമാൻ - cherumán, *Mal.*; මීමින්නා - míminná, *Singh.*; சிறுப்புள்ளிமான் - shiruppullimán, *Tam.*). Title from its size. San. from (giriká, san. mouse + mriga, san. deer). Tel. from (kuru, tel. small + pandi, tel. pig). Mal. from (cheru, mal. small + mán, mal. deer). Tam. from (shiru, tam. small + pulli, tam. spot + mán, tam. deer). Tel. also (jarinipandi); (podapandi), meaning spotted pig. Singh. also (valmiyá), meaning wild + deer or rat. Memimna indica, moschidæ, ruminantia, mammalia [sastanam, 25], of naturalists [jantoo]. Generic name from singhalese. Alias Memimna edwardsii; Moschus memimna; Tragulus memimna. The smallest of the deer tribe [mrigam]. Above olivaceous mixed with yellow gray; white below; sides of the body with yellowish white lines formed of interrupted spots, the upper rows of which are joined with those of the opposite side by some transverse spots; ears reddish-brown. Length of body about 22 to 23 inches; tail 1¼; height 10 to 12 inches; weight 5 to 6 lb. Much more abundant in the south of India than towards the north. Abounds in the forests of Malabar, and also occurs in some of the denser portions of the woods of the Eastern ghauts [q.v.]. The animal walks on the tips of its hoofs, which gives the legs a rigid appearance, and the natives say that it has no knee-joint, and that in order to rest it is obliged to lean against a tree [elephant]. Easily domesticated. Compare Hog-deer, under head Cheetal.

MOWDA (مودا - maudá, *Hind.*). Same as Chironjee.

MOWDOOD (مودود - maudúd, *Hind.*). From (vadda, ar. to love). Endeared. Suffixed to an alam forms a lacab; as Mahomed mowdood, endeared to mahomed [ism].

MOWLAH (مولی - maulá, *Hind.*). From (vilá, ar. to befriend). Lord. Prefixed to an alam forms a lacab; as Mowlah hoossain, the lord [ism].——*Mowlauna* (مولانا - mauláná, Hind.). From (maulá, ar. lord + ná, ar. possessive suffix). The highest title given to the learned amongst Mahomedans.——*Mowlvy* (مولوی - maulaví, Hind.). From (maulá, ar. a lord). Learned; a teacher of Arabic; an expounder of Mahomedan law. Used as a prefix to the names of learned men and professors of Mahomedan law and literature. Cf. Pundit.——*Moollah* (ملا - mullá, Hind.). Corruption of mowlah [q.v.]. The same as Mowlvy [q.v.]. Mahomedan learned man, judge, school-master who also has charge of the village mosque [musjid]. Prefixed to names of learned men; as Moollah abd oor rasool, prefix + lacab [ism].

MOWLOOD (مولود - maulúd, *Hind.*). From (valada, ar. born). Anniversary of a birth.——*Mowlood shareef* (مولود شریف - maulúdisharíf, Hind.). From (above + sharíf, ar. noble). Anniversary of the birth of the prophet.——*Mowloody* (مولودی - maulúdí, Hind.). From (maulúd, ar. born). An era [saca] instituted by Tippoo, reckoned from 1,200 hijra [q.v.], when a special faith was founded; did not survive.

MOWROOSY (موروثی - maurúsí, *Hind.*). From (irs, ar. to inherit). Hereditary [mirass].

MOWRY (موری - maurí, *Hind.*). Anise [q. v.] seed.

MOWZA (موضع - mauza, *Hind.*; మవుజె - mavuje, *Tel.*). From (vaza, ar. settlement). A village, understanding by that term one or more clusters of habitations and all the lands belonging to their proprietary inhabitants. The lands may sometimes have outlying portions intermixed with those of other villages.

MOY (مائی - máí, *Hind.*). Gall [mauchicoy].——*Burree moy* (بڑی مائی - barímáí, Hind.; జమ్మికాయ - dzammikáya, Tel.; வன்னிக்காய் - vannikkáy, Tam.). Same as Manna jhow.——*Choti moy* (چھوٹی مائین - chhótimáin, Hind.; چھوٹی مائی - chhótímáí, Dec.). Same as Red jhow.

MOY (మోయిచెట్టు - móyichettu, *Tel.*). Botanically Eugenia [jamboo] alternifolia, wight., myrtaceæ [vricsham, 56]. Alias Syzygium alternifolium. Leaves alternate, suborbicular, thick, and coriaceous, feather-nerved; calyx truncated, entire; petals calyptriated; cymes lateral, longish-peduncled, corymbose, dense, sometimes congested near the apex of year-old branches. Tree common in kurnool, cuddapah and north arcot; not on west coast; timber used.

MOY (மொய் - moy, *Tam.*). Elephant [aunay, cary, elephant, gajam, hasty].——*Moyaur* (ಮೋಯಾರು - móyáru, Can.; மொய் யாறு - moyyáru, Tam.). From (above + áru, tam. river). Can. also (badigihole), meaning north + river. River; Neilgherry dist., Todanaud division. Rises in Macoorty peak in lat. 11° 22′ N.; long. 76° 33′ E. and receiving the drainage waters of Pitchal and Pycarrah valleys, flows past Pycarrah and Nediwuttam, descending the hills at the north-west angle by a fall near Nediwuttam. After reaching plains it turns due east and flowing round base of Neilgherries on north and east faces, joins Bhawauny in lat. 11° 28′; long. 77° 08′, near Danaicken cottah.——*Moygarashcory* (முயகராசூரி - muyagarasúri, Tam.). From (above + kara, san. trunk + shúrí, san. heroine); heroine with the strength of an elephant's trunk in her arm. One of the seven matrons [mautah] in the temple of Ayenaur [ayen].

MOYEN (معین - muaiyan, *Hind.*). From (ána, ar. to keep a sharp look out). Fixed. Moyen zaubitah is the sanctioned establishment of an office, as opposed to temporary establishment [angaumy sibbundy].

MOZHY (மொழி - mozhi, *Tam.*). Word [shol].——*Mozhipeyarpp* (மொழிப்பெயர்ப்பு - mozhippeyarppu, Tam.). Means word + change. Translation [tarjooma].—"*a*" For the translation of English scientific terms into the vernaculars the following may be considered useful rules. In ordinary translation, either give a simple dictionary vernacular equivalent, or compound a vernacular word by uniting roots or a root and a particle. In a compound English word translate and join its several members. If the word cannot be satisfactorily rendered by the vernacular seek a term in the Sanscrit, with the same procedure. In an English compound if there be for any member of the compound a satisfactory Tamul word, combine it with the Sanscrit. Finding no term in the Tamul or Sanscrit transfer the English in the following way. Write the word preserving its accent and the sounds of its radical portion and terminate it in ordinary Tamul form. Modify it, when requisite, by the addition of an appropriate particle. In compounds, if there be for any member as satisfactory Tamul word, combine it with the English word. The following are examples. Tamul:—dome, தூபி; anthelmintic, இருமிகொல்லி; tin-stone, தகரக்கல். Sanscrit:—febrifuge, சுரக்கினம்; forearm, சயம்; atmospheric electricity, நபமின்சாரம். English:—ether, ஈதர்; gum acacia, அகசிப்பிசின்.—"*b*" As regards grammar [lacshanam], the following can be observed. Introduce each term as a noun; make it as brief as possible consistent with the preservation of its radical sounds and accent, and so end it in some ordinary form that it may easily turn to the adjective or verb.—"*c*" The following rules are general. Among several terms designating the same thing, choose the one which will enter the Tamul most easily. As far as practicable, differentiate the term from any pre-existing Tamul word. Transpose syllables, when so doing favors cadence and termination. Chemical terminations show special difficulty. Some may be rendered thus. The first two forms are the English and Latin, respectively:—Ate, as, அசு; etted, eus, ஏற்று; id, idum, இரம்; ic, icum, இக்; ite, is, இசு; ous, osum, ஓசு. Similarly:—ated or ata, சு; bi or deut, துவி; gen, ஜ; hyper or super, அதி; hypo or sub, அத; per, பிர; prot, புர; sesqui, சார்த்த [bhaushay].

MRIDANGAM (मृदङ्ग - mridanga, *San.*; مردنگ - mirdang, *Hind.*). From (mrid, san. to strike). Same as Maddalam; double drum [paray, sangeetam].

MRIG (मृग - mrig, *San.*). To pursue.——*Maurgaly* (மார்கழி - márgazhi, Tam.). The ninth tamul solar month [mausam].——*Maurgaly tirmanjanam* (மார்கழித்திருமஞ்சனம் - margazhittirumañjanam, Tam.). Means ninth Tamul solar month + ablution, of idol. Same as Ardrah darshanam.——*Maurgam* (മാർഗ്ഗം - márgam, Mal.). Means way; hence religion.——*Maurga cauran* (മാർഗ്ഗക്കാരൻ - márgakkár, Mal.). From (márgam, mal. way + kár, mal. doer). Literally, follower of law. So one of foreign religion, as Christian or Mahomedan, mostly the latter or Moplahs [q.v.]. But distinguish from Marcauyar [q.v.].——*Mrigam* (मृग - mriga, San.; هرن - haran, Hind.; ಜಿಂಕೆ - jinke, Can.; ఉర - are, Too.; జింక - jinka, Tel.; മാൻ - mán, Mal.; මුව - múva, Singh.; மான் - mán, Tam.). San. from (mrig, san. to pursue). Hind. from (harina, san. deer). Tel. from (chimmu, tel. to butt). Singh. from sanscrit. Tam. from (mâ, tam. animal) [maud, maun]. Title otherwise Deer.—"*a*" Equivalent to family Cervidæ, ruminantia, mammalia [sastanam, 24], of naturalists [jantoo]. Deer are remarkable for their fine horns [sing], or osseous prominences, which are shed and renewed annually, more or less contemporaneously with the renewal of the hair, and are called antlers. In the reindeer alone of all the family the females possess horns normally, though very rarely old and barren females of other species have been known to assume them. The feet touch the ground only at the extremity of the two principal toes, and there are usually two rudimentary toes with small hoofs at the back of the foot. The end of the muzzle is bare in almost all deer, and is sometimes called the muffle. When the horns first appear they are covered with a hairy skin, commonly called the velvet, which becomes dry and is thrown off; and at each successive renewal of the horns, they become larger and more developed, getting additional branches in some, till excessive age, when they diminish at each renewal. In their early condition the horns are soft and yielding. As development goes on, progressive ossification takes place. The envelopes shrivel up and fall off, and the animals perfect the desquamation by rubbing their horns against trees, technically called burnishing. The rutting season immediately follows the development of the antlers. The sub-family Cervinæ comprises the true stags; the Red-deer of Scotland is the type of this group. The Sub-family Rusinæ have one basal tine and no median tine; summit more or less branched, generally with only one subterminal tine; muffle high; this group, which includes the Samber [q.v.], the spotted deer [cheetal], and the Jungle sheep [q.v.], is peculiar to the tropical and sub-tropical regions of Asia and its archipelago. There is a Tamul proverb:—மான் கண்ணிலும் அழகு விரைவிலும் விரைவு—"The deer is beautiful in eye, and rapid in speed."—"*b*" Mrigam stands also for the genus Cirrhina, cyprininæ, cyprinidæ, physostomi, teleostei, pisces [matsyam, 39], of naturalists [jantoo]. From beauty of color. Large handsome fish, of importance as food. They are long in shape, elegantly formed, and of a brilliant golden, bronze, or silvery appearance. The lips are thin and clean, neither of them being fringed; there is a small knob on the centre of the lower jaw, at the junction of the two mandibular bones. The best known species are:—cirrhosa, reba.—"*c*" For Hindoo constellation so called see Mrigashiras under Nacshatram.——*Mrigsaul* (مرگ سال - mrigsál, Hind.). From (mirg, hind. deer); from the year commencing in the month of Ashaudham [maunam, mausam] or june when the sun is in mriga shiram [caurtey]. The fusly [q.v.] year [saul] so called in the north. See vol. I, 609.

M.R.RY. (महाराजराजश्री - mahárájarájashrí, *San.*). From (mahá, san. great + rájá, san. king + rájá, san. king + shrí, san. prosperity); royal majesty of the great king. Title of address among Hindoos. Compare Sahib with mahomedans; and Mr. in english. See vol. I (104).

MUCKNA (مقنع - makna, *Hind.*). A veil worn by Mahomedan females over the head and reaching almost to the ground [boorca].

MUCTA (مقطع - makta, *Hind.*). From (kita, ar. to cut). Fixed. A contract. A special form of assessment fixed on the village as a whole, in vogue in the early period of Revenue settlement. See vol. I, 112.

MUD BAY (മഞ്ചിറ - mañchira, *Mal.*). From (man, mal. mud + chira, mal. reservoir). Otherwise Mud bank. Found at Northern collam near Quilandy, at Calicut, at Naracal in Cochin state, at Alleppey in Travancore. These are caused by subterranean passages communicating with rivers and backwaters [cauyal]; such become more active after heavy rains, particularly at the commencement of the monsoon [q.v.], and carry off the accumulating water and with it vast quantities of soft mud. The mud is unctuous and sticky; possibly indicating subjacent lighitiferous deposits.

MUDDY (మద్ది - maddi, *Tel.*). Same as Dyeing mulberry.——*Black muddy* (నల్లమద్ది - nallamaddi, Tel.). Same as Common saul. ——*Maddikera* (మద్దికెర - maddikera, Tel.). From (maddi, tel. a tree, terminalia arjuna, bedd. + kere, can. tank). Town; Railway station; Kurnool dist., Putticondah tal.; pop. 7,504; acres 22,591; lat. 15° 15′; long. 77° 28′; from Kurnool S.W. 58 miles; from Putticondah S.S.W. 12 miles. At foot of a granite [caroom cull] hill at source of the Hindry 2½ miles east of Nuncherla railway station. Most elevated town in the district. Former seat of a powerful poligar [q.v.]. Remains of poligar hill-fortress and old temple. Saltpetre [shorah] manufactories. Roman catholic chapel. Weekly market on Friday.

MUGHRIB (مغرب - maghrib, *Hind.*). From (gharaba, ar. to set). West.——*Mughriby* (مغربی - maghrabí, Hind.). Westerns, i.e., western Arabs, or Moors of Morocco.

MUJNOON (مجنون - majnún, *Pers.*). From (jinn, ar. demon). Insane. Name of a celebrated eastern lover, whose amours are the subject of many poems. Now applied to any true lover. There is a Hindostany proverb :—لیلی کو مجنون کے آنکھون سے دیکھو—"One must look at Leilee [q.v.], with Mujnoon's eyes;" for she is said to have been plain. Mahomedan proper name.

MUKKY (மக்கி - makki, *Tam.*). Tam. means whitish clay, from soil where the tree grows. Same as Gamboge [q.v.].

MUL (मल् - mal, *San.*; മൽ - mal, *Mal.*). To hold; to be strong.——*Malhary* (ಮಲ್ಹರಿ - malhari, Can.). From (malla, san. boxer, the asura, so called + ari, san. enemy). Krishnan [q.v.] or Vishnoo [q.v.] or Shiva [q.v.]. Madhwa second name. Familiarly Mullaury [peyar].——*Molla* (మొల్ల - molla, Tel.). Means a kind of jasmine, multiflorum or pubescens. A poetess of Coommara or potmaker caste. She lived in Padoogoopaud of the Nellore talook, and translated the Ramayanam [q.v.] into Teloogoo. This work is called after her name and known as Molla ramayanam.——*Mulla* (ಮಲ್ಲ - malla, Can.). Means a wrestler; title to certain later Chalookya [q.v.] kings as well as Concany [q.v.] bramins. Hindoo third name [peyar].——*Mullagashetty* (மல்லகசெட்டி - mallagasetti, Tam.). From (malla, san. athlete + shetti, tam. wrestler caste). Wrestler and boxer. Name of a minor deity.——*Mullam* (மல்லம் - mallam, Tam.). Strength.——*Mullammah* (மல்லம்மா - mallammá, Tam.). From (malla, san. athlete + ammá, tam. mother). Village deity.——*Mullappan* (மல்லப்பன் - mallappan, Tam.). From (malla, san. boxer + appan, tam. father, titular affix). Hindoo 2nd or pers. name [peyar].——*Mullarashtram* (मल्लराष्ट्र - malláráshtra, San.). From (malla, san. wrestler + ráshtra, san. kingdom). Pooraunic name for Mahratta [q.v.] country. ——*Mulliah* (ಮಲ್ಲಯ್ಯ - mallayya, Can.). From (malla, can. a wrestler + ayya, can. father). Hindoo third name [peyar]. ——*Mullicah* (मल्लिका - malliká, San.). Jasmine flower.——*Mullicarjoonan* (மல்லிகார்ச்சுனன் - mallikkárççunan, Tam.). From (malliká, san. jasmine + arjuna, san. proper name); epithet of Shiva. Hindoo 2nd or pers. name [peyar]. Familiarly Mulloo. Title of the lingam [q.v.] at Srisheilam and formerly at Vijianugger; a book relating to this deity and his shacty [q.v.] exists in Teloogoo. Name of a Teloogoo astronomer, supposed to have flourished in 4279th year of the Kaliyoog [q.v.] or 1100 Saca [q.v.]; and who like Baulaudityacau referred his computations [maunam] to meridian [raikhay] of Rameshwaram.——*Mully* (மல்லி - malli, Tam.). From (mall, san. to hold); from jasmine garlands being largely in use. Jasmine [q.v.].

MULKANGHERRY (మలకనగిరి - malakanagiri, *Tel.*). From (malik, ar. proper name + giri, san. hill) [malik].——**(1)** Division; Vizagapatam district; population 28,277. Boundaries:—E. Pottinghy, Jeypore, Golcondah and Padair divisions; S. Godavery district; W. Central provinces; N. Bustar. A wild forest-clad region, watered by the Severy and Sillair, and sloping from the Toolsy toongaury which separate it on the north from the Ramgherry tannah [q.v.] to the Godavery. Average elevation 1,200 feet. There are fine saul [q.v.] and teak [q.v.] forests, and the whole tract abounds with large game. Places of archæological interest:—Anantapully, Condacambair, Garshipully, Mulkangherry, Nullacottah. Principal trig. stations:—Baly, Moonasa, Pantsa, Singanauma. The leading places, &c., in the division are the following.——*Baly* (బలి - bali, Tel.). Means sacrifice. Trig. station; lat. 18° 25′ 07·50″; long. 82° 19′ 30·49″; height 3,533 feet; from Gocarapaurya S.S.W. 2 miles; from Mulkangherry S.E. 26 miles.——*Moonasa* (మునస - munasa, Tel.). Means water-lift. Trig. station; lat. 18° 20′ 27·24″; long. 82° 00′ 08·19″; height 2,311 feet; from Mulkangherry E.S.E. 5 miles.——*Motoo* (మోటు - mótu, Tel.). Means the place where two rivers meet. Villages; lat. 17° 50′; long. 81° 26′; from Jeypore S.W. 103 miles; from Mulkangherry S.W. 49 miles; from Vizagapatam W. 124 miles. Trading station at confluence of Sillair and Severy rivers. Some trade in timber and forest produce.——*Mulkungherry* (మలకనగిరి - malakanagiri, Tel.). See below.——*Pantsa* (పంస - pantsa, Tel.). Means a porch. Trig. station; lat. 18° 04′ 19·42″; long. 81° 57′ 58·67″; height 3,591 feet; from Bijikwaura S.E. 2 miles; from Mulkangherry S. 20 miles.——*Sillair* (సిల్లేరు - silléru, Tel.). See sep. title.——*Singanauma* (సింగనామ - singanáma, Tel.). From (singamu, tel. lion + náma, san. name). Trig. station; lat. 18° 04′ 22·28″; long. 81° 35′ 08·46″; height 1,576 feet; from Mulkangherry S.W. 30 miles; from Naudagherry S.W. 1½ miles. *Toolsy toongaury* (తులసితుంగారి - tulasitungári, Tel.). See sep. title.——**(2)** Deputy tahsildarry, Vizagapatam district. Pay Rs. 150.——**(3)** Village, Head-quarters of Deputy tahsildar and Ameen [q.v.] of Jeypore maharajah; Vizagapatam dist., Jeypore zemindarry, Mulkangherry magisterial division; pop. 855; lat. 18° 22′; long. 81° 56′; height 641 feet; from Coraputt S.W. 62 miles; from Jeypore S.W. 56 miles; from Madras N.N.E. 372 miles; from Narsapatam N.W. 67 miles; from Parvatipore W.S.W. 104 miles; from Vizagapatam N.W. 102 miles; from Vizianagram W.N.W. 100 miles. Old mud fort.

MULL (ململ - malmal, *Hind.*). Anglo-indian. Fine muslin [q.v.].

MULLAGATAWNY (چار - chár, *Hind.*; చారు - cháru, *Tel.*; ചാറു - cháru, *Mal.*; மிளகுத்தண்ணீர் - milaguttannír, *Tam.*). Tel., Mal. from (sára, san. essence). Tam. from (milagu, tam. pepper + tannír, tam. water). A soup with the ordinary ingredients of curry [curry, masaulay].

MULLET (బొంత - bonta, *Tel.*). Mugil genus, mugilidæ [madavay], acanthopterygii, teleostei [matsyam, 26], of naturalists. Includes also species of chanos, serranus and upeneus. ——*Gray mullet* (ମଗି - magi, Oor.; മാലാൻ - málán, Mal.). Title from color. Mal. from (mála, san. garland). Mugil seheli, mugilidæ [madavay], acanthopterygii, teleostei [matsyam, 26], of naturalists [jantoo]. Alias Mugil axillaris, cylindricus, parsia. Scales twenty-one or twenty-two between the snout and base of first dorsal fin. Colors silvery, with bluish-green tinge along head and back black mark in axilla. Ventrals white. Sea; a foot in length. No other common species here. ——*Red mullet* (రాతిగులివింద - rátigulivinda, Tel.; மணலை - manalai, Tam.). Title from color. Tel. means stone + seed of abrus precatorius, probably from color. Tam. from (manal, tam. sand); from frequenting shores. Title otherwise Indian sur-mullet. Upeneus indicus, mullidæ, acanthopterygii, teleostei [matsyam, 3], of naturalists [jantoo]. Alias Mullus barbatus, indicus, malabaricus; Parupeneus indicus, russellii; Upeneus malabaricus, russellii, waigiensis. Snout somewhat pointed. Air-vessel present; colors purplish-red, with large oval shining golden blotch on lateral-line opposite interspace between two dorsal fins, which usually disappears after death; purplish-black mark, lightest in centre, on either side of free portion of tail between end of dorsal and base of caudal fins; yellow lines or spots on abdomen. Light violet lines on upper surface of head; broad purple band from eye to snout, having a narrow violet one on either side; cheeks pink, variegated with yellow and tortuous blue lines; dark spot at corner of mouth. Dorsal purplish streaked with blue; a few yellow bands on anal, fins pinkish except caudal, which has rays purplish, membrane has greenish tinge. Sea; 16 inches in length. No other common species here. Upeneoides vittatus is English mullet, Striped red mullet, Sur mullet.——*Stone mullet* (రాతిబొంత - rátibonta, Tel.). Same as Striped perch.——*White mullet* (ಹೂಮೀನು - húmínu, Can.; ପୂମିନୁ - púmínu, Too.; పాలబొంత - pálabonta, Tel.; துளிர்க்கெண்டை - tulirkkendai, Tam.). Title from color. Can. from (hú, can. flower + mínu, can. fish). Too. from (pú, too. flower + mínu, too. fish). Tel. from (pála, tel. white + bonta, tel. mullet). Tam. from (tulir, tam. tender sprout + kendai, tam. carp, barbus genus); from brilliant gloss of head and back. Title otherwise Milk fish. Chanos salmoneus, clupeidæ, physostomi, teleostei [matsyam, 40], of naturalists [jantoo]. Alias Butirinus argenteus, maderaspatensis; Chanos arabicus, chanos, chloropterus, indicus, mento, nuchalis, orientalis, pala, tolo; Cyprinus palah bontah, tooleloo; Leuciscus salmoneus, zeylonicus; Lutodeira chanos; Mugil chanos, salmoneus; palabontah from teloogoo. Body elongated; upper surface of head flat; upper jaw over-hanging the lower. Scales small, covering the body; there are some rows of enlarged ones over the nape. Summit of head and back of a brilliant glossy blue, fading into silvery on the abdomen; snout light brown. Dorsal and caudal rays grayish, which, as well as the membranes, are dotted with light brown, and both these fins are margined with black. Caudal semi-lunar laminæ of scales pale slate color, the pectorals and ventrals white, with the anterior halves of their external surfaces minutely dotted with dark brown, their elongated appendages bright silvery. The anal white, with the anterior half dotted with black. Iris silvery, orbital half pale brownish. Seas; attains 3 feet at least. In South canara Hyder ally introduced it from the sea into tanks of fresh and brackish water, where it still thrives. No other common species here.

MULLEY (మల్లె - malle, *Tel.*). Corruption of (palle, tel.) [pully]. Village. Suffix in place names, as Zargoomulley, meaning shifting village.

MUNCHY (మంచి - manchi, *Tel.*). From (mañju, san. beautiful). Goodness. Suffix in place names; as Caurmanchy, meaning season goodness. Plant first term. Ex.:—Aloe littoralis (manchikattáli), best aloe; Sesbania procumbens (manchijíluga), best æschynomene aspera. See gloss. paragraphs.

MUND (ಮಂದೆ - mande, *Can.*; మంద - manda, *Tel.*; மந்தை - mandai, *Tam.*).—"*a*" Cattle-herd. Suffix in place names. [manda].—"*b*" A Todah [q.v.] village. The individual Todah hut is oval-shaped usually 10 feet broad, presenting a striking resemblance to the raths [q.v.] of Mauvellipore. The entrance or doorway measures 32 inches in height and 18 in width, and is not provided with any door or gate; but the entrance is closed by means of a solid slab or plank of wood from 4 to 6 inches thick and of sufficient dimension to entirely block up the entrance. This sliding door is inside the hut, and so arranged and fixed on two stout stakes buried in the earth and standing to the height of 2½ to 3 feet as to be easily moved to and fro. There are no openings or outlets of any kind either for the escape of smoke or for free ingress and egress of atmospheric air. The doorway itself is of such small dimensions that to effect an entrance those who enter must go down on all fours. Each building has an end wall before and behind, composed of solid blocks of wood, which slopes down to the ground. The inside is sufficiently high in the middle to admit of a tall man moving about with comfort. On one side there is a raised platform or pyall [q.v.] formed of clay, about two feet high and covered with samber [q.v.] or buffalo [khoolgah] skins, or sometimes with a mat. This platform is used as a sleeping-place. On the opposite side is a fire-place and a slight elevation on which the cooking utensils are placed. In this part of the building faggots of firewood are piled up from floor to roof, and secured in their places by loops of rattan [q.v.]. Here also the rice-pounder and pestle are fixed. The mortar is formed by a hole dug in the ground 7 to 9 inches deep and rendered hard by constant use. The other household goods consist of three or four brass dishes or plates, several bamboo [q.v.] measures, and sometimes a hatchet. Each cluster of huts is surrounded by an enclosure or wall formed of loose stones piled up from 2 to 3 feet high and includes a space or yard measuring 13 by 10 feet. A cluster of five or six of these houses, with a cattle kraal [q.v.], forms a mund or village. One hut is always used as a dairy, or paultchy [q.v.], and one or two give shelter to the calves. The rest are simply dwelling-houses. The presence of the buffaloes, seldom driven far away when pasture can be found near at hand, ensures a patch of short green velvet sward, sloping down to the stream which supplies the mund with water, or terminating in a marsh where the animals wallow. The inhabitants of a mund are generally related to one another, and although each household has its head, the whole together forms but one family. The practice of polyandry however tends to make the relationships confusing.——*Munda* (منڈا - mandá, Hind.; మంద - manda, Tel.; மந்தை - mandai, Tam.). Herd. Suffix in place names; as Yellamunda, meaning boundary herd [mund].——*Mundapauty* (మందపాటి - mandapáti, Tel.). From (mandapádu, tel. village in kistna), meaning herd village. Zemindarry family of the Ongole district. Ayyapparauz, the founder of the family, obtained from the nawaub of Hyderabad a grant of three villages, Conijaid, Mangamore, Pairanamitta, for the administration of the police. During the time of Raghoopatyrauz, sixth in descent from the founder, the estate comprised the whole of the Ongole talook. The estate was divided during the time of one Peddabhadrarauz. One Ramachendrarauz of this family was authorized by the Governor of Madras to keep an armed force of 5,000 men. When the district came under the British rule in 1792, the Zemindar was pensioned as his military services were no longer required; and the pension itself was stopped in 1842.——*Mundapett* (మందపేట - mandapéta, Tel.). From (manda, tel. cattle herd + péta, tel. suburb). Sanscrit name (mándavyapura), meaning maundavyan, the sage + town. Village, Canal; Godavery dist., Ramchendrapooram tal.; acres 5,301; lat. 16° 51′; long. 81° 58′; from Cocanada W.S.W. 21 miles; from Ramchendrapooram W.N.W. 7 miles. Village is one mile south of the canal which connects the Coringa and Cocanada canals.——*Mundarauz* (మందరాజ - mandarája, Tel.). From (above + rájá, san. king). A Hindoo ruler of the lunar race [chundra vamsham], according to Sanscrit legends, from whom the town of Madras takes its name, through the Teloogoo. See vol. I (161).——*Mundarauzputnam* (مندراج - mandráj, Hind.). Madras [q.v.].——*Mundasa* (మందస - mandasá, Tel. mandasa). Ancient zemindarry, Town; Ganjam dist., Sompett tal., Deputy tahsildar's range; pop. 35,532; pop. of village 5,240; acres 82,899; lat. of village 18° 51′; long. 84° 30′; from Berhampore S.S.W. 37 miles; from Chetterpore S.W. 49 miles; from the sea W. 8 miles. Separated from Parlakimedy by the Mahendragherry. The paddy [q.v.] is best in Ganjam. Founder, Punchendra bommana sing, from the Punjaub. Number of villages, 166. Peshcush Rs. 14,035. Ten temples built by former zemindars. Contains Dandraushy [q.v.] and Maula [q.v.] trig. stations.——*Mundey* (ಮಂಡೆ - mande, Can.). Subdivision of a hobly [q.v.] corresponding to a firkah [q.v.].

MUNDEM (మండెము - mandemu, *Tel.*). From (mandi, tam. warehouse). Factory. Distinguish from Mondem [mondy].

MUNGALAM (मङ्गल - mangala, *San.*). From (mang, san. to go); speed, good speed. Good fortune. Village in a rich agricultural tract. Hindoo proper name. Applied to males and females. Also Native christians [peyar].——*Mangalore* (ಮಂಗಳೂರು - mangalúru, Can.). See sep. title.——*Mungal* (منگل - mangal, Hind.). From (mangala, san. happiness). Tuesday. On this day the seven strata of the earth were created.——*Mungala* (మంగల - mangala, Tel.). Teloogoo barbers' caste. The corresponding terms are:—Hind. hajaum, Tam. ambattan, Can. nayinda, Mal. vilakkataravan. It is divided into the Reddy bhoomy, Moorkinauty, and Coorchy nauty sub-castes. Most are Veishnavites. They consider Tamul barbers as lower than themselves, because these consent to shave the whole body, while they only shave the upper portions. Besides their ordinary occupation, the members of this caste engage in surgery and their females practise midwifery. They are also employed as musicians on the occasion of marriages, funerals or other ceremonies. Flesh-eating is allowed, but not widow-marriage. Numbers about 350,000; mostly in Tel. districts, but there are many in Madura. See vol. II, 232.——*Mungala devy* (मङ्गलादेवी - mangaládévi, San.). From (above + dévi, san. goddess). Lutchmy [q.v.]; the goddess of good luck [shree devy].——*Mungalagherry* (మంగళగిరి - mangalagiri, Tel.). From (mangala, san. auspiciousness + giri, san. hill).—"*a*" Deputy tahsildarry, kistna district. Pay Rs. 70.—"*b*" Town, Place of pilgrimage, Deputy tahsildar's head-quarters, Travellers' bungalow; Kistna dist., Guntoor tal.; pop. 6,426; acres 2,002; lat. 16° 26′; long. 80° 37′; from Bezwada S.S.W. 7 miles; from Guntoor N.E. 12 miles; from Madras N. 232 miles; from Masulipatam W.N.W. 40 miles; from Vinoocondah E.N.E. 60 miles. On the high road between Bezwada and Guntoor. In the last century old Mungalagherry, half a mile to south, belonged to Suttenapully zemindar; while Mungalagherry proper, the town close to the pagoda [q.v.] under the hills, was part of Nizampatam circar [q.v.]. Plundered by Hyder's cavalry in 1780, also by Pindarries [q.v.] in 1816. Up the hill is a rock-cut platform with Narsimhasawmy temple, behind which is a cave said to communicate with those near Oondavully. Large and deep square reservoir in the town, in which 9,840 matchlocks and forty-four iron bullets were found when it ran dry in 1832. Festival at full moon [powrnimay] in March. Trig. station. in lat. 16° 26′ 19·92″; long. 80° 36′ 55·04″.——*Mungalan* (மங்கலன் - mangalan, Tam.). From (mangala, san. prosperity). The planet Mars [coojan]. Identical with Caurtikeyan [q.v.]. In the arts, he is represented as a red man [shevvye] with four arms riding on a sheep [aud]. He wears a red necklace and cloths of the same color. The Hindoo astrologers say:—if a person be born under the planet Mungalan, he will be full of anxious thoughts, wounded with offensive weapons, imprisoned, oppressed with fear of robbers, fire, &c., and will lose his land, trees, and good name. The motions of mungalan are greatly relied upon in astrology. The following are Varauha mihiran's remarks on that head:—"The "retrograde motion [vakra gaty] of mungalan is of five kinds, "known technically as ooshnam, ashroomookham, vyaulam, "lohitaunanam and nistrimsha moosalam. If mungalan should "begin to retrograde from the seventh, eighth or ninth constel-"lation from that in which he reappears after his conjunction "[crauntam] with the sun, such retrograde motion is technically "known as ooshnam; when mungalan should reappear after his "next conjunction with the sun [sooryan], persons who live by "fire will be afflicted with disease; mungalan disappears when "within 17 degrees [bhaugam] from the sun and reappears "when beyond that; if mungalan should begin to retrograde "from the tenth, eleventh, or twelfth constellation [nacsha-"tram] from that of his reappearance, such retrograde motion "is known as ashroomookham; when mungalan should reappear "after his next conjunction with the sun, juice will be injured "and there will be disease and drought; if he should begin to "retrograde from the thirteenth or fourteenth constellation "from that of his reappearance, such retrograde motion is "known as vyaulam; when he should disappear before his next "conjunction with the sun, wild boars and fierce animals will "be afflicted with distress; if mungalan should begin to retro- "grade from the fifteenth or the sixteenth constellation from "that of his reappearance, such retrograde motion is known as "Roodhiraunanam; at the time of such reappearance mankind "will be afflicted with disease in the face and with various "fears, but there will be prosperity in the land; if he should "begin to retrogade from the seventeenth or the eighteenth "constellation from that of his reappearance such retrograde "motion is known as Asimoosalam; when mungalan is in his "re-retrograde motion, bands of robbers will be afflicted with "distress and there will be drought and wars in the land; if "mungalan should reappear in the constellation of Poorvaphal- "goony [poobbam] or in that of oottaraphalgoony [oottaram] "retrograde in the constellation of oottarashaudham [q.v.] and "disappear in the constellation of rohiny [q.v.] he will afflict "the three worlds with miseries; if mungalan, after his reappear- "ance in the constellation of Shravanam [q.v.], should retro- "grade in that of Pooshyam [q.v.], anointed monarchs will be "afflicted with miseries; those countries and these persons will "suffer in whose nacshatram [q.v.], mungalan should begin to "reappear; if he should pass through middle of the constellation "of Magham [q.v.] and retrograde back through the same, the "ruler of the Paundyan [q.v.] country will perish and mankind "will suffer from wars and drought; if mungalan should, after "cutting through the constellation of magham [q.v.], approach "the middle of vishaukham [q.v.], there will be famine in the "land; if he should cut through the constellation of rohiny "[q.v.], there will be fearful deaths in the land; if mungalan "should pass to the south of the constellation of rohiny, rulers "will suffer, prices will rise and there will be little rain; if "mungalan should appear enveloped in smoke or with a pointed "flame, the people of pauriyautram will perish; if mungalan "should pass through the constellation of rohiny [q.v.], shrava- "nam [q.v.], moolam [q.v.], oottaraphalgoony [q.v.], oottara- "shaudham [q.v.], oottarabhaudram [q.v.], and jyeshtay [q.v.], "he will destroy clouds charged with rain; if mungalan should "pass through the constellations of shravanam [q.v.], magham "[q.v.], poonarvas [q.v.], hastam [q.v.], moolam [q.v.], poorva- "bhaudram [q.v.], ashwiny [q.v.], vishaukham [q.v.], and rohiny "[q.v.] there will be prosperity in the land; if mungalan should "appear with a large and clear disc or red like the flower of "kimshoocam [palaus] or of ashocam [bengal ashocam] or of "clear and fine rays or like molten gold or if he should pass "through the northern path [avastaunam], rulers will be happy "and there will be prosperity in the land." Mungalavauram is Tuesday [vauram].——*Mungala sootram* (मङ्गलसूत्र - mangala-sútra, San.). From (above + sútra, san. thread). The lucky thread, the talee [q.v.].——*Mungala veety* (मङ्गलवीथी - mangala-vít'hí, San.). From (above + vít'hí, san. street). Street [veety] round a village [oor].

MUNGAY (மங்கை - mangai, *Tam.*). Woman. Lutchmy [q.v.].——*Mungammah* (மங்கம்மா - mangammá, Tam.). From (above + ammá, tam. mother). Lutchmy. Hindoo female proper name [peyar].——*Mungammaul* (மங்கம்மாள் - mangammál, Tam.). From (mangai, tam. woman + ammál, tam. mother). Grandmother and queen regent of Vijaya runga chokkanaúta naick, ruler of Madura [charitram]. See vol. I (121).——*Mungay bhaugan* (மங்கைபாகன் - mangaibágan, Tam.). From (above + bhága, san. portion). Shiva [ardhanaury].——*Mungayya* (ಮಂಗಯ್ಯ - mangayya, Can.). From (above + ayya, can. master). Vishnoo [q.v.], lord of Lutchmy. Non-bramin. Hindoo 2nd or pers. name [peyar].——*Mungeshan* (ಮಂಗೇಶ - mangésha, Can.). From (above + ísha, san. lord). Vishnoo, lord of Lutchmy. Hindoo 2nd or pers. name. Common among Madhwas and Mahrattas [peyar].——*Mungimadoss* (ಮಂಗಿಮದಾಸ - mangi-madás, Can.). From (above + dása, san. slave). Adherent of Lutchmy. Hindoo 2nd or pers. name [peyar].

MUNJAL (മഞ്ഞ - maññа, *Mal.*; மஞ்சள் - mañjal, *Tam.*). Yellow. Same as Country saffron. Plant first term often joining two genera; meaning yellow. Ex., where transl. is of second term:—Adina cordifolia (maññakkadamba), anthocephalus cadamba; Crossandra undulæfolia (maññakkuriññi), barleria genus; Daucus carota (mañjalmullangi), raphanus sativus, radish; Morinda citrifolia (mañjalbávattai), pavetta indica; Thevetia nereifolia (mañjalalari), nerium odorum. See gloss. paragraphs.——(1) *Mangelin* (ಮಂಜಾಳಿ - manjáli, Tel.). Same as Munjaudy. Cf. Carat.——*Manjarabad* (ಮಂಜರಾಬಾದ - manjarábád, Can.). From (manjaramani, can. seed of adenanthera pavonina, linn. + ábád, hind. town). Pass; South canara dist., Oppinangady tal. Between Mysore and Canara.——*Munja-cooppam* (மஞ்சக்குப்பம் - mañjakkuppam, Tam.). From (mañjal, tam. saffron, curcuma longa, roxb. + kuppam, tam. village). Tam. also (kuppam), meaning maritime village. South arcot dist., Cuddalore tal.; acres 1,297; lat. 11° 46'; long. 79° 48'; from Cuddalore N. 3 miles; from the sea W. 2 miles. Suburb of Cuddalore.——*Munjalaur* (மஞ்சளாறு - mañjaláru, Tam.). From (mañjal, tam. saffron, curcuma longa, roxb. + áru, tam. river). Sanscrit name (haridránadí), meaning the same. River; Madura district, Dindigul and Periyacoolam talooks. Rises in Lower pulneys, and passing villages of Devaudanaputty and Gengoovaurputty of Periyacoolam talook and Batlagoondoo, Vunnambutty of Dindigul, flows into Veigay at Coonvaran cottay in Dindigul talook. Length 30 miles.——*Munjanutty* (மஞ்சணத்தி - mañjanatti, Tam.). From (mañjal, tam. turmeric, curcuma longa, roxb. + náru, tam. to smell); from timber. Same as Dyeing mulberry.——*Munjaudy* (മഞ്ചാടി - mañcháti, Mal.; மஞ்சாடி - manjádi, Tam.). From (manju, san. beautiful). Title otherwise Mangelin, Manjoty. Seed of Adenanthera pavonina [false red sanders].—"*a*" One of the earliest measures of weight. Of a bright scarlet color, hard, durable, and tolerably uniform in size and weight. For ordinary purposes place of the munjaudy has been taken by its representative the copper fanam [q.v.].—"*b*" Artificial goldsmiths' munjaudy weights are made of brass in the form of an octahedron, the primitive crystal [palingoo cull] of the diamond [vajram]. The following is scale:—2 coondrimanies or goonj seeds = 1 munjaudy; 2 munjaudies = 1 pana tookkam [niruy, 3a, d]. Approximate actual value, 1 munjaudy = 3 grains. But this is less than its usual actual weight. Same as Can. adda, manjoty. Compare Carat, Doogoola. Compare also coondrimany which is about half. See vol. I, 609; II, 518.——**(2)** *Custoory munjal* (கஸ்தூரிமஞ்சள் - kattúrimañjal, Tam.). From similar fragrance. Same as Long zedoary.——*Maramunjal* (மரமஞ்சள் - maramañjal, Tam.). From yellow wood. Same as False calumba.

MUNJAN (منجن - manjan, *Hind.*). From (mánjaná, hind. to scrub). Dentifrice. Gen. powdered charcoal [adooppkary].

MUNJEET (मञ्जिष्ठा - mañjisht'há, *San.*; मंजिष्ठ - manjisht'ha, *Mahr.*; فوة الصباغين - fuvvahussabbághín, *Ar.*; روناس - rúnás, *Pers.*; دارهلد - dárhald, *Hind.*; منجيت - manjít, *Dec.*; ಮಂಜಿಷ್ಠ - manjisht'ha, *Can.* and *Too.*; మంజిష్ఠ - manjisht'ha, *Tel.*; മഞ്ചെട്ടി - mañchetti, *Mal.*; වැල්මදට - valmadala, *Singh.*; மஞ்சிட்டி - mañjitti, *Tam.*). Title from sanscrit through deccany. San. from (mañju, san. beautiful + isht'ha, san. superlative affix). Mahr. from sanscrit. Ar. from (fuvvah, ar. madder + sabbágh, ar. dyer). Pers. from (rú, pers. color + nás, ar. man). Hind. from (dár, hind. wood + hald, hind. turmeric, curcuma longa, roxb.) [berberry, false calumba]. Dec., &c., from sanscrit. Singh. from (val, singh. creeper + maddata, singh. munjeet). Tam. from sanscrit [monkey-country saffron]. San. also (chitravallí), meaning many-colored creeper [chitramoolam]; (kálaméshiká), meaning black + the plant, nardostachys jatamansi, nees.; (gandári), meaning boils + enemy; (mandúkaparní), meaning frog-leaved [indian pennywort]; (samangá), meaning going or spreading in all direction; (vikasá), meaning blooming; (aruná), meaning red [nodding galangal, turbith]; (yójanavallí), meaning league + creeper; (bhándí); meaning mentioned; (bhandíri), meaning mentioned; (jingi), meaning spreading. Ar. also (fuvvah), meaning madder. Pers. also (royan). Hind. also (manjít). Can. also (manjettibíja), meaning madder + seed; (isht'hamadhúka), meaning desirable + honey. Tel. also (mánipasupu), meaning wood + turmeric, curcuma longa, roxb.; (tâmbravallí), meaning copper + creeper. Mal. also (púvattu), meaning flower + inside. Tam. also (shevvalli), meaning red creeper; (shávalgodi), meaning cock + creeper. Title otherwise Bengal madder, Copper creeper, Frog-leaf, Heart-leaved madder, Indian madder, Ulcer-killer. Botanically Rubia cordifolia, linn., rubiaceæ [vricsham, 71]. Alias Rubia cordata, manjith, munjista. Manjith from deccany; munjista from sanscrit. Herbaceous; stem rough, with prickles on the angles, rarely smooth; leaves in fours, long-petioled, oblong or ovate, acute, more or less cordate, three to seven-nerved, margins, middle nerve, and petioles rough with minute prickles; calyx tube ovate-globose; panicles in the upper axils peduncled, trichotomous; bracts opposite, not forming an involucre; flowers usually five-cleft, whitish; berries red or black; grows in elevated jungles. Root consists of a short stock, from which numerous cylindrical roots about the size of a quill diverge; these are covered by a thin brownish suber which peels off in flakes, disclosing a red-brown bark marked by longitudinal furrows; the taste is sweetish at first, afterwards acrid and bitter; fibres of root not so thick or succulent as those of european madder, rubia tinctorum, linn. Infusion of root used in medicine as a coloring agent; also as an astringent in external inflammations, ulcers, and skin diseases; made into a paste with honey [shahad], forms application to freckles and discolored skin; in pharm. non-officinal. The root has in a minor degree the same dyeing properties as the european madder; dyes pink, lake, purple, orange, yellow and brown [shauyam]; for calico [q.v.], linen [alsee], or wool [pushm]; used alone, or, in conjunction with the emboorel root [chayroot].

MUNJOOR (منظور - manzúr, *Hind.*). From (nazr, ar. sight). Acceptance. Approved.

MUNJY (മഞ്ചി - mañchi, *Mal.*). From port. manchua. Large boat on W. coast used for navigating a river and for coasting. Manned by Moplahs [q.v.]; are always laid up in the monsoon [masulah]. The following are different kinds.——*Bottell munjy* (ബൊത്തെല്ലമഞ്ചി - bottellamañchi, Mal.). Title is portuguese. Navigates the Gulf of Manaar and the Southern coasts. Is about 50 to 60 feet in length, 16 to 18 feet in breadth, and 8 to 10 feet in depth. Has more of the European form than any of the others. The afterpart shows the construction to be of Portuguese origin. Has a deck fore and aft, and is built with jungle wood in a rough manner, and fastened with nails and bolts. Has one mast, which inclines forward, and a square lug-sail; also a small bowsprit, at about 45°, with a sort of jib foresail, one pair of shrouds, and a backstay, which completes the rigging.——*Bunder munjy* (ബന്തർമഞ്ചി - bantarmañchi, Mal.). From (bandar, hind. port + mañchi, mal. boat). Harbour boat for goods.——*Calicut munjy* (കോഴിക്കോട്ടുമഞ്ചി - kózhikkóttumañchi, Mal.). Like the Mangalore munjy, but has a raking stem, for the purpose of taking the beach, as the port of Calicut is open to the coast and there is no river. These boats are propelled by the paddle and sail, and generally carry eight men.——*Cochin bunder munjy* (കൊച്ചിവഞ്ചി - koççivañchi, Mal.). Canoe of burthen, cut from the largest timber. From 20 to 50 feet in length; breadth and depth being proportioned to the full size of the tree, so as to reduce its dimensions as little as possible. Carries about 18 tons burden.——*Mangalore munjy* (മംഗലപുരംമഞ്ചി - mangalapurammañchi, Mal.). A flat-bottomed boat of burden, about 25 to 35 feet long, 6 to 7 feet broad, and 4 to 5 feet deep. It is formed to suit the Mangalore river, which is shallow. Sewed together similar to the masulah [q.v.] boat of the East coast. Poled by bamboo [q.v.] poles.——*Paumban munjy* (പാമ്പൻമഞ്ചി - pámpanmañchi, Mal.). From (pámbu, mal. snake + mañchi, mal. boat). The snake boat of Cochin, a canoe used for conveyance on the rivers and backwaters [cauyal], particularly on that between Cochin, Alleppey and Quilon. These boats are from 30 to 60 feet in length, worked from the solid tree.——*Ponnany munjy* (പൊന്നാനിമഞ്ചി - ponnánimañchi, Mal.). A coasting boat of about 50 feet long, 10 to 12 feet broad, and 5 to 7 feet deep. It is framed with timbers and planks, which are sewed together. The timbers are about 4 feet asunder, and on them inside some few planks are placed as bands and clamps, which are nailed to the frame. These are very rudely put together, and not of much importance either in form or construction. Have generally from eight to ten men.

MUNKAH (अक्ष - aksha, *San.*; منکا - manká, *Hind.*; ಮಣಿ - mani, *Can.*; ಮಣಿ - mani, *Too.*; పూస - púsa, *Tel.*; മണി - mani, *Mal.*; மணி - mani, *Tam.*). Bead. The seeds of various plants are used as beads. In some cases wood is cut into small globular bodies, as in the case of bael [q.v.], and toolsy [q.v.], and these answer the purpose of beads. The commonest beads in economic use are from:—Abrus precatorius, linn. [indian liquorice]; Adenanthera pavonina, linn. [false red sanders]; Areca catechu, linn. [areca]; Cæsalpinia bonducella, flem. [bonduc]; Canna indica, linn. [indian shot]; Caryota urens, linn. [bastard sago palm]; Coix lachryma, linn. [coratty pausy]; Corypha umbraculifera, linn. [talipot]; Elæocarpus lanceolatus [roodrauck]; Melia azedarach, linn. [large neem]; Ocimum sanctum, linn. [common toolsy].

MUNN (भूमि - bhúmi, *San.*; خاك - khák, *Pers.*; مٹی - mittí, *Hind.*; مٹی - mattí, *Dec.*; تنا - tanah, *Malay*; ನೆಲ - nela, *Can.*; ಮಣ್ಣು - mannu, *Too.*; మన్ను - mannu, *Tel.*; മൺ - mań, *Mal.*; மண் - man, *Tam.*). San. from (bhú, san. to be) [bhoo]. Hind. from (mrit, san. earth). Malay from (st'hána, san. place). Earth, soil.——(1) Dividing soils according to their most general characteristics the scientific classification is as follows:—alluvial and exceptional soils, black-cotton soil, red ferruginous, white and grey cretaceous, arenaceous. The alluvial and exceptional series, includes the rich lunka [q.v.] or island soils deposited from rivers, and also provides for the garden and other soils, which have been permanently improved, and rank above the ordinary cultivation [adaimunn, vandalmunn]. The second series is the regar, or as it termed commonly the black-cotton soil [regar]; its character may be easily distinguished from that of other series, even when mixed with large proportions of sand, as in the case of the masab [q.v.] which is included in the general head of regar; the great fertility of the regar is ascribed to its containing, besides a large proportion of organic matter, to which it probably owes its color, much mineral matter in a fine comminuted state, so as to be available for the supply of nourishment to vegetation by the ordinary processes of chemical affinity and mechanical action, which are constantly going on. The red ferruginous series [shemmunn] is also easily distinguished, and has its origin mostly from ferruginous sandstone [manal cull], laterite [q.v.], or other rocks; the red color is generally the result of iron [auhan], and is separable from the reddish brown belonging to some of the regar soils, with which this series forms a contrast in its want of natural fertility, arising probably from the smaller proportion of organic matter, and of the richer constituent elements, and its general dryness. The color of the white and grey cretaceous series [sookkaunmunn] is chiefly dependent on the chalk or lime in the soil, and sometimes verges into a dark shade; this derives its character from a substratum of lime [choonam], the properties of which in the surface soil may be partially or wholly removed by influence to which it is exposed from the air, moisture, &c. The characteristic of the arenaceous series [vandal munn] is the seashore or flinty sand which forms the basis of the soil in littoral tracts of country; vegetation and cultivation have contributed much by introducing fertile elements, but even there the original character is easily discernible.——(2) The principal ingredients of all soils are clay, sand, lime, and vegetable or other organic matter, in varying proportions; there are smaller ingredients, such as potash [jharkanaunak], soda [munn cauram], magnesia [caunta munn], phosphoric acid, oxide of iron, sulphuric acid [gandhac tezaub], chlorine, &c. The chief ingredients are derived from minerals and stones, which are gradually dissolved, or rather reduced to powder or grains by potash, and other small, but powerful ingredients above described, as well as by the action of the air and moisture; in some cases also decayed vegetable deposit forms or combines with soils; a portion of the soil is thus in a state of fine impalpable powder, while the remainder is hard and insoluble as the grains of sand, pebbles, &c. It is only from the fine portion or powder that the crops derive their nourishment; and, as a rule, the greater proportion of it, ceteris paribus, that a soil contains, the greater will be the source of fertility. Some of the richest regar soils are almost entirely composed of this impalpable powder. For the purpose of scientific classification this impalpable powder is called clay, though it includes vegetable matter, and the remainder is termed sand. The grades of minor classification are then for each series of soil as follows:—Clayey, containing more than $\frac{2}{3}$ of clay. Mixed or loamy, containing from $\frac{1}{3}$ to $\frac{2}{3}$ of clay; sandy or gravelly, containing not more than $\frac{1}{3}$ of clay. The saline ingredients of soils have to be considered in determining its value. Five kinds of saline ingredients are recognized by the natives of the country. These are in Teloogoo where the distributions are best recognized:—Gauzoo sowdoo [q.v.] or bangle salt; Paula sowdoo [q.v.] or carbonate of soda; Ooppoo sowdoo [q.v.], or common salt; Soonnapoo sowdoo [q.v.], or washerman's earth; and Sooracaurapoo sowdoo [q.v.], or saltpetre, or potash with its nitrate [sowdoo]. The soda is not injurious, unless in excess, when however it may be easily removed by irrigation; in small quantities it is a very valuable ingredient; the common salt cannot be removed easily, and it often takes many years before the character of this soil changes; the excess of soda in the fifth kind is not so hurtful as the last, and yields more readily to the influence of water; the potash is a useful ingredient, particularly for several garden crops to which it is applied as a manure, and its excess is rapidly removed by irrigation. Very stony and gravelly soils come at the end of the classification; but small stones and gravel scattered over the fields are not necessarily at all hurtful to vegetation. In the calcareous series, the value of the soil may in a measure be determined according to the lime being only in moderation, that is to say not more than 15 per cent.; or in excess, that is to say above that quantity.——(3) The darker-colored soils, as the black, brown and dark-red, absorb more heat than the white, grey and yellow, and are consequently hotter; while the light-colored soils reflect or throw back more heat than the dark soils, and thus tend more to scorch up the crops growing upon them; though, on the other hand, the moisture is less rapidly evaporated from them than from the dark soils. Color has also a great influence upon soils in their comparative retention of heat as opposed to its first absorption; a dark soil gives out or radiates the heat much more quickly than a light colored one in the absence of the sun's rays; thus sand will cool more slowly than clay, and clay more slowly than a dark soil with vegetable matter; the consequence is that the latter in dry weather begins to absorb the dew before the sandy soil, and thus may be enabled to sustain vegetation while the crops in the sandy soil languish for want of moisture; generally speaking the power of soils to retain heat is in proportion to their weight or specific gravity.——(4) Excepting hard sand, all kinds of soil have the property of absorbing moisture from the air, and this is greatest in the clay soils, especially when containing much vegetable matter, which is a powerful absorbent; the absorption of all soils greatest at first, and less as they become more saturated with moisture; a portion is again evaporated by the heat of the sun, and this is again absorbed during the night; some soils, such as sands, have more than others the property of drawing up to the surface by capillary action the moisture which lies below.——(5) The power of retaining moisture as opposed to its first absorption is a very valuable property of soils in this part of the country, where there are long intervals without rain; sands have the least power of containing water, and vegetable matter has the greatest power of holding it; clays also will hold a large quantity when they are fully saturated; but some of the soils give out the moisture they contain much more quickly than do others; the degree of porosity or consistency of the ground affects the rapidity of drying; vegetable matter which is loose in texture gives off more moisture in the same time than clay and thus dries sooner, though in the first instance it holds more water than clay, when both are saturated.——

(6) Soils when moist have the power of absorption of oxygen, in different degrees; vegetable matter in the greatest, next the clays, and the last the sandy earths. When dry the soils lose the property of absorbing oxygen from the air [vayoo].——**(7)** A subsoil is that which immediately underlies the culturable surface soil; about one yard in depth may be considered as the proper surface soil, which is ample for the roots of all kinds of crops, and below this is the subsoil. Subsoils may consist of the same earthy substance as the soil itself, or it may be of similar character, differing only in degree or in kind, or it may be of quite an opposite character, or may consist of hard rock; thus soils and subsoils sometimes take their character from the underlying rocks of the country. The red soils are extensively found over ferruginous sandstone and laterite, and partake of the same elements. The regar soil is found sometimes over large tracts of country of which the volcanic, the gneiss, and other primeval rocks are the characteristic basis; at other times it is found overlying large tracts of limestone [choonam cull], chalk [sheemay choonam], and other rocks of different characters. The subsoil has generally a considerable influence on the condition and agriculture of the soil lying above it. If it is clay it is impervious to water, and tends to keep the upper soil wet or moist; on the other hand, a sandy, gravelly, or a calcareous subsoil will, from its porous nature, allow the moisture of the surface soil to drain through it. A porous soil on a porous subsoil will rarely suffer from excess of water except during the period of a long submergence. A tenacious soil, such as clay upon a similar subsoil, will generally suffer comparatively much from inundation, and the injurious effects of excess of moisture will be of longer continuance. The tenacious or retentive character of subsoils is an important consideration in irrigation, as some of the superjacent soils owing to these differences require very much more water than others. Rock may form either a retentive or porous subsoil; according as it is a massive structure, or as it is stratified so as to admit of the water percolating through it. The soil will not always be of one kind to the depth of one yard prescribed for the proper or surface soil; and gravel, sand, rock, or other substances may be found at the depth of a few inches below a more fertile surface.——**(8)** The following is the native classification of soils according to the Calpastaunam. There are five kinds:—"*a*" Soil in which the earthy principle prevails. Very fertile, shining brown yellowish, or black color, and very stiff. All large trees and grass and every kind of crop come to perfection in it.—"*b*" Soil in which there is much water. Is cold and has a whitish color, but its surface is covered with luxuriant plants and trees. Its tanks are constantly filled.—"*c*" Fire soil. It is light and has a greyish color. Trees have a sterile grey appearance. It produces climbing plants in abundance.—"*d*" Soil in which air prevails. It has an ash color. The trees are usually rotten inside. Its crops are thin, and it produces only such as grow in cold weather.—"*e*" Ether ground. Its color is blackish; it is stony and produces trees that yield resins [raul] and oil [yennay]. It will be perceived that the names and divisions of soils here are derived from the five elements [bhootam] of the Indian philosophy, namely, earth, water, fire, air, and ether. The following is a favorite Tamul classification:—Pottal, Vandal, Manal, Sevval, Carisal and Veppal. Pottal is a granular earth, very free from stones, with a small residue of granite and quartz; vandal is ordinary clay capable of retaining moisture and of a light red color; manal is arenaceous somewhat stony and of a light brown color; carisal is a black-cotton soil quite free from anything like stone; sevval is of a light red-color containing a considerable amount of quartz; veppal is a light greyish brown earth, lumpy, free from stones.——**(9)** *Manaar* (மன்னார் - mannár, Tam.). From (man, tam. sand. + áru, tam. river). Village; Tinnevelly dist., lat. 8° 58′; long. 79° 53′; from Tinnevelly E. 148 miles.——*Manaar gulf* (மன்னார்க்குடாக்கடல் - mannárkkudákkadal, Tam.). Greek κόλπος κηλχικός. A portion of the Indian ocean, bounded west by the coast of Tinnevelly and Madura districts, north by Adam's bridge, and east by the coast of Ceylon. Extreme breadth from Cape comorin to Point de galle is about 200 miles. The length of the Tinnevelly and Madura coast is 135 miles. A current sets into the gulf during the south-west monsoon [q.v.]. During December and January the north-east monsoon blows strong out of the gulf. A bank has been formed in the gulf by the accumulation of sand carried out from the Malabar coast; due south of Comorin it stretches 45 miles off shore. Pearl-fisheries [moty] are carried on in the gulf both along the coast of Ceylon and off Tinnevelly and Madura. Its survey resulted in the formation of the Paumben passage. Though little frequented by large vessels in consequence of the obstruction northwards, it has on its north-west side the road-stead of Tuticorin, where ships may anchor throughout the year in considerable safety.——*Manaar island* (மன்னார்த்தீவு - mannárttívu, Tam.). Greek ἠπιοδώροςνῆσος. Island; Madura dist.; lat. 9° 03′; long. 79° 48′; from Madura E.S.E. 136 miles; from Ramnaud E.S.E. 75 miles. Off the coast of Ceylon, and at eastern extremity of Adam's bridge. It is 14 miles long and 3¼ broad, and with Rameshwaram island nearly connects the peninsula with Ceylon. Seat of the pearl fishery [chunk, moty].——*Manacoody* (മനക്കുടി - manakkuti, Mal.). From (manal, mal. sand + kuti, mal. dwelling).—"*a*" Village, Port; Travancore state, Pudmanaubhapooram division, Agasteeshwaram tal.; lat. 8° 5′; long. 77° 32′; from Sooshindram S. 5 miles; from Bombay S.S.E. 794 miles; from Comorin W. 4 miles; from Shaunaurgoody W.S.W. 5 miles; from Trivandrum S.E. 45 miles. Distinguished by its churches. Situated on edge of lake of same name.—"*b*" Lake; Travancore state, Pudmanaubhapooram division, Agasteeshwaram talook. Receives the Palayaur in its passage to the sea. Near Cape comorin salt pans at Taumara coolam and Vauriyore.——*Manal* (वालुका - váluká, San.; رمل - raml, Ar.; ریگ - reg, Pers.; بالو - bálú, Hind.; پسر - paser, Malay; ಉಸುವು - usuvu, Can.; ಪೊಯ್ಯೆ - poyye, Too.; ఇసుక - isuka, Tel.; മണൽ - mañal, Mal.; වැලි - vali, Singh.; மணல் - manal, Tam.). Title from tamul. Hind. from sanscrit. Mal. from (man, mal. earth). Sand. Particles of stone. A common soil is pure river or shore sand with a comparatively insignificant proportion of argillaceous matter, often impregnated with salt [ooppoo] or lime [choonam]. This description of soil [munn] is generally barren; and when cultivated it requires a considerable amount of manure to make it productive. The sand-binding plants of the Coromandel [q.v.] beach are a remarkable peculiarity of that coast. The wide-spreading roots and under-ground stems of these extend themselves in quest of food and thus become interwoven together, so as to sustain the soil in a sort of basket-work and consolidate the sands thrown up by the waves of the ocean. If it were not for the subterranean stems of these sea-side plants, which can vegetate amidst dry and drifting sand, the banks which man heaps up as a barrier against the sea would be blown away by the first hurricane. The following is a key-list of the plants arranged under the botanical names:—Ipomæa biloba, goat's foot; Ipomæa pestigridis, tiger's foot; Launea pinnatifida, style plant; Pandanus odoratissimus, screwpine; Pedalium murex, elephant nerinjy; Pupalia orbiculata, auday otty; Sesamum prostratum, wild gingelly; Spinifex squarrosus, ravanan's whiskers. For sandstorms, see Pishauch. For sandstone, see Manal cull [cull]. Caroomanal is black sand; used in sprinkling over wet writing to dry it. Irooppoo manal, from (irumbu, tam. iron) is sand containing iron [auhan]. Mergoo manal, from (merugu, tel. glitter) is red sand used by goldsmiths [tuttaun] in washing jewels to give them a glitter. Paroo manal, from (paru, tam. big) is coarse sand. Pody manal, from (podi, tam. powder) is fine sand. Pon manal, from (pon, tam. gold) is sand containing gold [pon]. Shemboo manal, from (shembu, tam. copper) is sand containing copper [taumram]. Shem manal is red sand. Shory manal, from (shori, tam. to scatter) is blown sand. Tootnaug manal is sand containing zinc [tootnaug]. Vellay manal is white sand.——*Manaly* (بالو کا ساگ - bálúkáság, Hind.; بالو کی بھاجی - bálúkíbhájí, Dec.; ఇసుకదాసరికూర - isukadásarikúra, Tel.; අත්තිරිල්ලපාල - attirillapála, Singh.; மணலி - manali, Tam.). Title from tamul. Hind. from (bálú, hind. sand + ság, hind. greens). Dec. from (bálú, hind. sand + bhájí, hind. greens). Tel. from (isuka, tel. sand + dásari, tel. vaishnava mendicant + kúra, tel. pot-herb). Tam. from (manal, tam. sand); from habitat [shiva's neem]. Tel. also (isukadontikúra), meaning sand + pile + pot-herb. Title otherwise Chickweed-like gisekia, Sand-greens, Trailing gisekia. Botanically Gisekia pharnaceoides, linn., ficoideæ [vricsham, 66]. Herbaceous; leaves short-petioled, elliptic lanceolate, very obtuse, scarcely mucronulate, pale green above, glaucous white beneath; cymes sub-sessile, shorter than the leaf, ball-shaped, simple, five to ten-flowered, somewhat loose; flowers nearly equalling the pedicel, pale green; common weed in pasture grounds, flowering especially during rains. Seeds blackish, smooth, minutely glandular-punctate; embryo curved less than a semi-circle. Powerful anthelmintic in cases of tænia; fresh plant including leaves, stalks, and capsules is employed in doses of about an ounce with sufficient water to make a draught; quoted in pharm. but non-officinal. Leaves are used by natives in preparation of dholl [q.v.].——*Manapaud* (மணப்பாடு - manappádu, Tam.). From (manal, tam. sand + pádu, tam. place). Village, Cape; Tinnevelly dist., Tencaray tal.; pop. 1,648; lat. 8° 23′; long. 78° 06′; from Cape comorin E. 41 miles; from Shreeveicoontam S.S.E. 20 miles; from Tinnevelly S.E. 35 miles. Hamlet of Coolashekharaputnam. South-west of estuary of river Nauttaur. Portuguese settlement in 1542, subsequently a Dutch station. Demolished in 1782. Now inhabited entirely by Roman catholic fishermen. Some finely carved Dutch tombstones. A light here in lat. 8° 22′ 30″; long. 78° 6′ 30″; red; fixed; 6 miles; visible from all direction seaward; white masonry tower. Is intended to warn vessels off the dangerous shoal in the vicinity. The cape itself is a high sandy promontory, based on rock, jutting boldly into the sea and having a small white-washed church on its summit, visible in clear weather for 12 or 13 miles. The breakers extend 3 or 4 miles to the north-east of this point and about one mile to the south-east. The port of Coolashekharaputnam may be known by the ruins of a large church half-buried in sand and the mouth of a small river, too shallow for internal navigation, opening into the bay to the north of Manapaud point. The shoal above-mentioned has its nearest part five miles south-west from Manapaud point. A depth of twelve fathoms is found all round this extensive shoal. It extends east-north-east and west-south-west 10 miles, having an average breadth of one mile, from its centre a tongue projects in a northerly direction. There are other dangerous shoals and rocks to the east and it is altogether a hazardous place for shipping.——*Manapauray* (மணப்பாறை - manappárai, Tam. manapárai *). From (manal, tam. sand + párai, tam. rock).—"*a*" Deputy tahsildarry, Trichinopoly district. Pay Rs. 70.—"*b*" Village, Deputy tahsildar's station, Railway station, Head assistant collector's division; Trichinopoly dist., Coolitalay tal.; pop. 3,158; lat. 10° 36'; long. 78° 29'; height 512 feet; from Aryalore S.W. 56 miles; from Coolitalay S. 22 miles; from Madras S.W. 208 miles; from Moosiry S. 23 miles; from Shreerungam S.W. 25 miles; from Trichinopoly S.W. 23 miles. Hamlet of Shivalore. A talook called after this town was in 1861 with old talook of Vetticooty made into Coolitalay talook. Public bungalow [q.v.] not built by English. Has lofty circular dome, and resembles large hall in Nawaub's palace in Trichinopoly. Built by Mungammaul as a chuttram [q.v.]. Weekly market, largest in the district, every Wednesday. Also cattle fair. Old Vishnoo temple. Seven miles N.E. are remains of a small military station.——*Manarchaul* (മാന്നാർചാല - manárççála, Mal.). From (mannan, mal. king + chála, mal. palace). Village; Travancore state, Quilon division, Caurtigapully talook. The village is the principal seat of the serpent-worship in Travancore. It contains the largest temple dedicated to the snake-god, with an extensive cauv [q.v.] or sacred enclosure consisting of a thick shady grove, which many living cobras [q.v.] infest. The temple contains thousands of images of the snake-god and attracts many worshippers.——*Momatty* (खनित्र - khanitra, San.; پھاورا - pháurá, Hind.; ಡೊಕುಬಾರಿ - dokubári, Can.; పార - pára, Tel.; കൈക്കോട്ട - kaikkóttu, Mal.; மண்வெட்டி - manvetti, Tam.). Title from tamul. San. from (khan, san. to dig). Hind. from (p'hala, san. blade of a weapon). Can. from (dóku, can. to grub + páre, can. crowbar). Mal. from (kai, mal. hand + kóttu, mal. digging instrument). Tam. from (man, tam. earth + vetti, tam. cutter); is digging tool; not in the shape of a spade, but in that of a hoe, with the helve at an acute angle with the blade.——*Munjery* (മഞ്ചേരി - mañchéri, Mal. manjeri *). From (man, mal. loose earth + chéri, mal. village). Town, Talook and Moonsif's head-quarters; Malabar dist., Yernaud tal.; pop. 9,840; lat. 11° 06'; long. 76° 10'; from Calicut E.S.E. 26 miles; from Cannanore S.E. 72 miles; from Madras W.S.W. 310 miles; from Malapooram N.E. 6 miles; from Manantoddy S.S.E. 47 miles; from Palghaut N.W. 42 miles; from Ponnany N.E. 25 miles; from Tellicherry S.E. 61 miles; from the sea E. 20 miles. A Moplah gooroocal family of this place rose in rebellion in 1785-86 A.D. against Arshed beg khan, Tippoo's principal officer. Scene of one of the worst Moplah outrages in 1849. Large dolmens [coday cull]. Public bungalow [q.v.]. Weekly market.——*Munnair* (మన్నేరు - mannéru, Tel. mannér *). From (mannu, tel. sand + éru, tel. river). River; Nellore dist., Canigherry, Oodayagherry, Cauvaly and Cundoocore. Rises in Veligondas near Chundrashekharapooram in Canigherry talook, and after traversing Canigherry, Oodayagherry and Cauvaly talooks in a south-easterly direction and Cundoocore in a north-easterly direction, falls into sea near Binginipully, in the last talook. Runs between August and December. A dangerous river. Feeder to Caraid tank. Not navigable. A causeway near Shingaroyacondah.——*Munnan* (മന്നൻ - mannan, Mal.; மன்னன் - mannan, Tam.). From (mannu, mal. earth). Means a king. Also a pariah proper name [peyar]. Also a tribe of mountaineers in travancore; hardy and very black, speaking bad tamul, employed by the circar [q.v.] to collect cardamoms [q.v.], keep watch, &c.; they cultivate raggy [jauty].——*Munnargoody* (மன்னார்குடி - mannárgudi, Tam.). See sep. title.——*Munnpully* (മണ്ണപ്പള്ളി - manppalli, Mal.). From (mannan, mal. king + palli, mal. village). Greek βαλῖτα. Village; Travancore state. Trivandrum division, Cherankeel talook. A little north of Anjengo.——*Muttipaul* (மட்டிப்பால் - mattippál, Tam.). Title from (matti, tam. coarse + pál, tam. milk). Impure juice from trunk of Malabar ailanto.——*Mutty* (మట్టి - matti, Tel.). Earth.——*Mutty paumb* (میٹھی پانی کا سانپ - míthepáníkásámp, Hind.; మట్టిపాము - mattipámu, Tel.; മണ്ണൻ - mannan, Mal.). Title from teloogoo. Hind. from (míthá, hind. sweet + pání, hind. water + sámp, hind. snake). Tel. from (matti, tel. earth + pámu, tel. snake). Mal. from (man, mal. earth + an, mal. personal suffix). Tel. also (allipámu), meaning plant, nymphæa alba, linn. + snake; from likeness of body to stem of the indian water-lily [q.v.]. Terms co-extensive with the family Homalopsidæ ophidii colubriformes, ophidia [sarpam], reptilia [sarpy, 18], of naturalists [jantoo]. Fresh-water snakes; have the body of moderate length, cylindrical or slightly compressed; head rather thick, broad, not very distinct from neck; tail strong, of moderate length, tapering, more or less prehensile and compressed at its root, especially in the males; all have a grooved fang at the hinder extremity of the maxillary bone. Easily recognized by position of nostrils on the top of the snout, which enables them to breathe by raising but a very small part of their head out of the water; the same arrangement as that in the crocodiles [mugger], sea-snakes, and other aquatic animals; many have a distinctly prehensile tail, by means of which they hold on to projecting objects; food consists entirely of fish [matsyam], and, in a few species, of crustacea [kayachiny] also; all appear to be viviparous; do not grow to any size; gentle disposition, bite not dangerous, will not feed in captivity. Several of them enter the sea, and in several points approach the truly marine snakes. The following are the two South indian species:—"*a*" Cerberus rhynchops. Alias Cerberus boæformis, cinereus, obtusatus; Elaps boæformis; Homalopsis rhynchops, schneideri; Hurria schneideriana; Hydrus rhynchops. Upper parts blackish ash, with irregular, more or less distinct black cross bars; two or three outer series of scales yellowish; lower parts whitish, with numerous black blotches; labials spotted with black; attains nearly 4 feet.—"*b*" Hypsirhina enhydris. Alias Coluber aeydoux; Homalopsis aer, enhydris, olivaceus; Hydrus enhydris; Hypsirhina aer, bilineata et furcata, trilineata. Brownish olive above, outer series of scales and the belly whitish; blackish line along each margin of the belly. May be seen in rivers as well as in irrigated fields and estuaries, preying upon fishes which, however, it refuses in a state of captivity. Of timid and peaceful habits.——(10) *Adaimunn* (पुलिन - pulina, San.; వండ - vanda, Tel.; அடைமண் - adaiman, Tam.). Title and Tam. from (adai, tam. to settle + man, tam. mud). San. means river bank. Tel. from (vattu, tel. to dry up). Tam. also (vandal), meaning sediment; also (vandalman), meaning sediment earth. Alluvium. Clay [calimunn], silt [vandalmunn], sand [manal], and gravel [kankar] deposited from water, especially from rivers, lakes, and seas still existing, or which existed in very late geological times. The commonest case is of deposits formed by rivers overflowing their banks.——*Ayacaly munn* (அயக்களிமண் - ayakkaliman, Tam.). From (ayas, san. iron + kali, tam. clay + man, tam. mud). Clay ironstone. A mixture of carbonate of iron and clay [calimunn], found in beds and nodules, and especially common in the coalmeasures.——*Calar munn* (களர்மண் - kalarman, Tam.). From (kalar, tam. brackish ground + man, tam. mud). Alkaline earth.——*Calimunn* (कृष्णमृत्तिका - krishnamrittiká, San.; چکنی مٹی - chiknímattí, Hind.; బంకమన్ను - bankamannu, Tel.; കളിമണ്ണ - kaliman, Mal.; களிமண் - kaliman, Tam.). Title and Tam. from (kali, tam. thick glutinous mass + man, tam. mud). San. from (krishna, san. black + mrittiká, san. mud). Hind. from (chikni, hind. plastic + mattí, hind. earth) [chicken mutty]. Tel. from (banka, tel. gum + mannu, tel. earth). Clay. Argilla of chemists. Clays of every description are found in S. india, including all the varieties of tough plastic ball clays, fire clays, aluminous shales or slate clays, common potter's brown, yellow, grey and black clays, marls, and porcelain earths or kaolins [q.v.]. They are found chiefly amongst the primitive granite [caroomcull] and felspar [mauvayiracull] rocks or amongst the sedimentary and tertiary deposits at the base of granite hills, from the decay of which they are formed. The decaying felspars yield either the white plastic clays, or when mixed with iron and vegetable matter the darker colored varieties. Those granites which contain much mica [abruck], yield very soapy smooth clays in decaying. The pure white felspars [mauvayira cull] and pegmatitis produce the porcelain [káolin] earths. These occur of the best qualities in Madura, Cuddapah, North arcot, the Neilgherries, and Travancore. In Salem they are accompanied by magnesian clays and armenian bole. The commoner clays are to be found in almost every district. Potter's clay [chicken mutty] is greasy to touch, and adheres to the tongue; the finer kind, a sort of pipe clay [naumam], is used for the forehead marks [tirmunn]. Other varieties of clay, used in medicine by veidyans are Armenian bole [ghilarminy], Shilajit [q.v.] of nepaul, and Gopy [q.v.]. Alumina consists of pure clay; in its crystalline form it is the base of corundum [q.v.], emery, and other hard polishing substances used in the arts; combinations of it yield fuller's earth [dhoby's earth], pipeclay [tirmunn], ochres [cauvy], &c.; a dye for calico-printers is procured from it, and it enters into the manufacture of porcelain [kaolin].——*Carisal munn* (கரிசல்மண் - karisalman, Tam.). From (karisal, tam. darkness + man, tam. mud). Dark humus in Tamul districts; much resembles the regar [q.v.] or black-cotton soil of the Ceded districts [q.v.], and is soft and plastic when wet. It ranks next to Tamul sevval [sevval munn] in productive power.——*Caunta munn* (காந்தமண் - kándaman, Tam.). Magnesia. See sep. title.——*Jaidy munn* (ചേടിമണ്ണ - chétiman, Mal.). Mal. from (chéti, mal. glutinous earth + man, mal. soil). White clay mixed with small pieces of quartz [vencull], with which, in conjunction with the ashes of the Muddy tree [murdah], the natives of Malabar prepare a whitewash for their houses.——*Morapa munn* (మొరపమన్ను - morapamannu, Tel.). From (moramu, tel. gravel + mannu, tel. earth). Gravelly soil.——*Oovar munn* (ऊषरभूमि - úsharabhúmi, San.; ریہ مٹی - rehmittí, Hind.; ಚೌಳುಮಣ್ಣು - chaulumunnu, Can.; చవిటిమన్ను - tsavitimannu, Tel.; ഓരുമണ്ണ - órman, Mal.; உவர்மண் - uvarman, Tam.). Title and Tam. from (uvar, tam. saltishness + man, tam. mud). San. from (úshara, san. saline + bhúmi, san. soil). Hind. from (reh, hind. impure carbonate of soda + mitti, hind. earth). Tel. from (tsavudu, tel. fuller's earth + mannu, tel. earth). Mal. from sanscrit. Dhoby's earth [q.v.].——*Pasalay munn* (பசலைமண் - pasalaiman, Tam.). From (pasalai, tam. sallowness + man, tam. mud). Loam. A soil composed of clay [calimunn] and fine sand [manal].——

Pashima munn (പശിമമൺ - pashimman, Mal.). From (pashima, mal. softness + man, mal. soil). A deep, clayey soil. ——*Pashimaraushy munn* (പശിമരാശിമൺ - pashimaráshiman, Mal.). From (pashima, mal. softness + ráshi, san. heap + man, mal. soil). Loam with an admixture of sand [manal].——*Raushy munn* (രാശിമൺ - ráshiman, Mal.). From (ráshi, san. heap + man, mal. soil). Soil formed by the decomposition of heaped up substances. Sandy soil.——*Sevval munn* (ಎರೆಭೂಮಿ - erebhúmi, Can.; ఎర్రభూమి - errabhúmi, Tel.; செவ்வல்மண் - shevvalman, Tam.). Title and Tam. from (shevval, tam. red soil + man, tam. mud). Tel. from (erra, tel. red + bhúmi, san. soil). Reddish loam soil. Its chief constituent is ferruginous red sand [manal]. It is plastic when wet but friable when dry.——*Shavatt munn* (சவட்டுமண் - shavattuman, Tam.). Any earth containing sowdoo [q.v.].——*Shemmunn* (ఎఱ్ఱమన్ను - erramannu, Tel.; ചെമ്മൺ - chemman, Mal.; செம்மண் - shemman, Tam.). Title and Tam. from (shem, tam. red + man, tam. mud). Tel. from (yerra, tel. red + mannu, tel. earth). Ruddle.——*Sooddy munn* (ಸುದ್ದಿಮಣ್ಣು - suddimannu, Can.; సుద్దమన్ను - suddamannu, Tel.). From (shuddha, san. pure + mannu, can. mud). A kind of white pipe clay [tirmunn] used in terracing mud houses in cold countries.——*Sookkaun munn* (कर्करभूमि - karkarabhúmi, San.; சுக்கான்மண் - shukkánman, Tam.). Title and Tam. from (shukkán, tam. limestone + man, tam. mud). San. from (karkara, san. hard, nodular stone + bhúmi, san. earth). Otherwis kankar [q.v.] soil. Largely impregnated with carbonate of lime [sheemay choonam] and exhibits a whitish calcareous incrustation on its surface. This description of soil is exceedingly barren and unproductive.——*Tirmunn* (श्वेतमृत्तिका - svétamrittiká, San.; کھری - kharí, Hind. and Dec.; ನಾಮ - náma, Can.; ನಾಮ - náma, Too.; నామము - námamu, Tel.; നാമം - námam, Mal.; මකුල් - makul, Singh.; திருமண் - tiruman, Tam.). San. from (shvéta, san. white + mrittiká, san. clay). Can. means mark on forehead, from use [naumam]. Tam. from (tiru, tam. sacred + man, tam. mud). Singh. also (makulmati), meaning bright + pipe clay. Tam. also (námam), meaning mark on the forehead; (námakkatti), meaning forehead mark + lump. Pipe-clay. With this Veishnavites prepare white tirchoornam [q.v.], with which they mark their foreheads perpendicularly. Of this natives make also white and finer kind of earthenware. It is in use amongst painters and is employed by the sepoys [q.v.] in cleaning their belts.——*Valayal munn* (வளையல்மண் - valaiyalman, Tam.). Bangle earth [gauzoo].——*Vandal munn* (ಎಕ್ಕಲುಗದ್ದೆ - ekkalugadde, Can.; వండ - vanda, Tel.; வண்டல்மண் - vandalman, Tam.). Title and Tam. from (vandal, tam. sediment + man, tam. mud). Silt. Fine sediment from water, especially from rivers. Alluvial soil [adaimunn]. This is a somewhat pulverized form of the soil called Sevval, which see. This soil produces good garden crops.

MUNNARGOODY (மன்னார்குடி - mannárgudi, *Tam.* mannárgudi *).——**(1)** From (mannan, tam. king + kudi, tam. town) [munn]. Sanscrit name (víranáráyanapura), meaning hero + vishnoo, the mover on the waters + town. Otherwise Munnaurcoil, or Cautt munnaurcoil to distinguish it from rajah munnaurcoil or munnargoody in Tanjore.—"*a*" Deputy tahsildarry, Chidambaram talook, South arcot district. Pay Rs. 70.—"*b*" Deputy tahsildar's station; pop. 1,936; acres 569; lat. 11° 16′; long. 79° 36′; from Chidambaram S.W. 13 miles; from Cuddalore S.S.W. 34 miles; from Madras S.S.W. 132 miles; from Tindivanam S.S.W. 67 miles; from Tricalore S.E. 53 miles; from Vriddhauchellam S.E. 23 miles; from the sea W.S.W. 22 miles. Former head-quarters of talook of same name. Large tank and Vishnoo temple. French grain depôt was destroyed by the English in 1754. Weekly fair.——**(2)** From (mannan, tam. king + gudi, tel. temple); called after raghoonaut naick, the king who built the temple. Tam. also (mannárkkóyil), meaning king + temple. Sanscrit name (champakáranya), meaning champák tree, michelia champaca, linn. + forest; also (dakshinadváraká), meaning southern dwarca. Otherwise Rajah munnaurcoil to, distinguish it from cautt munnaurcoil near chidambaram. Talook, Tanjore district; Tahsildar's pay Rs. 200; area 801 square miles; pop. 187,434; language mostly Tamul. Inland S. central. Boundaries N. Nunnilam and Combaconam talooks; E. Negapatam and Tritrapoondy talooks; S. Tritrapoondy and Puttoocottah talooks; and W. Puttoocottah and Tanjore talooks. Flat country. Soil, chiefly black clay, red soil in the west. Chiefly agricultural. Coarse mats; vessels of brass and other metals; rough paper; country cloth and paddy [q.v.] are the main articles of commerce. Irrigation by the Ayenaur, Coraiyaur, Harichendranuddy, Moollaiyaur, Paumaniyaur, and Vennaur and some tanks. Places of archæological interest:—Abhishaicacuttalay, Agravelacoody, Annaumalaynautancoil, Atchaulpooram, Caloovattore, Carappookilaur, Cazhappaul, Coilvunny, Coonniyore, Manacaray, Munnargoody, Narvalikilappaul, Nautyattaungoody, Needamungalam, Palashillaraytottam, Paulacoorchy, Paumany, Poothootevangoody, Poovanore, Pothoocoody, Shauttanore, Tircalary, Tirchattimoottam, Tirnellicauval, Trimacottah, Trirameshwaram, Trivandootoray, Tunneercoonnam, Veloocoody, Vicrapaundyam. Principal trig. station:—Moovanullore. The leading places, &c., in the talook are the following.——*Coilvunny* (கோவில்வன்னி - kóvilvanni, Tam.). From (kóvil, tam. temple + vanni, tam. prosopis spicigera, linn.). Village; pop. 1,953; acres 2,048; lat. 10° 47′; long. 79° 24′; from Munnargoody N.W. 11 miles; from Tanjore E. 15 miles. On the road from Needamungalam to Tanjore, two miles east of Ammapett railway station. Old Shiva temple.——*Cootanullore* (கூத்தாநல்லூர் - kúttánallúr, Tam.). From (kúttan, tam. a dancer + nal, tam. good + úr, tam. village). Village; pop. 3,266; acres 478; lat. 10° 42′; long. 79° 34′; from Munnargoody E.N.E. 5 miles; from Tanjore E.S.E. 27 miles. On the Vennaur. Old Shiva temple, betel [q.v.] vines largely cultivated. Mussulmans [q.v.] and Lubbays [q.v.] emigrate to Burmese ports.——*Coraiyaur* (கோரையாறு - kóraiyárú, Tam.). See sep. title.——*Cotore* (கோட்டூர் - kóttúr, Tam.). From (kódu, tam. bank + úr, tam. village). Village; pop. 1,653; acres 1,263; lat. 10° 37′; long. 79° 36′; from Munnargoody E.S.E. 8 miles; from Tanjore E.S.E. 30 miles. On the Adappaur, between Munnargoody and Tritrapoondy.——*Mahadevaputnam* (மகாதேவப்பட்டணம் - magáthévappattanam, Tam.). From (mahádéva, san. shiva, the great god + pattana, san. town). Village; pop. 1,325; acres 2,092; lat. 10° 36′; long. 79° 27′; from Munnargoody S.W. 6 miles; from Tanjore S.E. 22 miles. On the trunk road from Munnargoody to Puttoocottah. Captured by Hyder ally in the latter part of the eighteenth century; recaptured by the English under Colonel Brathwaite. Tomb of a Mahratta ranee [q.v.] and a Vishnoo [q.v.] temple. Fort in ruins and a small chuttram [q.v.]. Weekly fair on Thursday.——*Mailnuttam* (மேலநத்தம் - mélanattam, Tam.). From (mél, tam. west + nattam, tam. village). Village; pop. 1,047; acres 750; lat. 10° 32′; long. 79° 29′; from Munnargoody S. 9 miles; from Tanjore S.S.E. 27 miles. Wesleyan mission station.——*Moovanullore* (மூவாநல்லூர் - múvánallúr, Tam.). From (múváy, tam. three ways + nal, tam. good + úr, tam. village). Lat. 10° 41′; long. 79° 28′; from Munnargoody W.N.W. 3 miles.——*Munnargoody* (மன்னார்குடி - mannárgudi, Tam.). See below.——*Needamungalam* (நீடாமங்கலம் - nídámangalam, Tam.). See sep. title.——*Peinganaud* (பைங்காநாடு - paingánádu, Tam.). From (pai, tam. green + ká, tam. grove + nádu, tam. country). Village; pop. 1,923; acres 5,018; lat. 10° 35′; long. 79° 30′; from Munnargoody S. 5 miles; from Tanjore S.E. 24 miles.——*Peroovaundaun* (பெருவாழ்ந்தான் - peruvázhndán, Tam.). From (peruga, tam. prosperously + vázhndán, tam. one who lives). Village; pop. 4,075; acres 5,622; lat. 10° 30′; long. 79° 32′; from Munnargoody S. 13 miles; from Tanjore S.E. 31 miles. Between the Coraiyaur and the Paumaniyaur. Four small temples, two Vishnoo and two Shiva.——*Poovanore* (பூவனூர் - púvanúr, Tam.). From (pú, tam. flower + vana, san. garden + úr, tam. village). Sanscrit name (pushpavana), meaning flower garden. Village; pop. 1,299; acres 1,516; lat. 10° 45′; long. 79° 28′; from Munnargoody N.N.W. 6 miles; from Tanjore E. 17 miles. On the Paumaniyaur, on the road from Munnargoody to Needamungalam, two miles south of Needamungalam railway station. Old Shiva temple.——*Trimacottah* (திருமக்கோட்டை - tirumakkóttai, Tam.). From (tirumal, tam. proper name + kóttai, tam. fort), trimal's fort. Sanscrit name (brahmapura), meaning bramha's city. Village; pop. 993; acres 3,300; lat. 10° 32′; long. 79° 30′; from Munnargoody S. 9 miles; from Tanjore S.E. 27 miles. Two well-endowed temples, one Shiva and the other Vishnoo. Weekly market on Sunday.——*Vadivore* (வடிவூர் - vadivúr, Tam.). From (vadivu, tam. beauty + úr, tam. village). Sanscrit name (dakshináyódhyá), meaning southern ayodhyay. Village; pop. 5,031; acres 1,474; lat. 10° 42′; long. 79° 22′; from Munnargoody W. 9 miles; from Tanjore E.S.E. 14 miles. On the road from Tanjore to Munnargoody. Old Vishnoo temple frequented by pilgrims. Large tank in the vicinity.——*Vicrapaundyam* (விக்கிரப்பாண்டியம் - vikkirappándiyam, Tam.). From (vikramapándya, san. a pándya king). Village; pop. 1,158; acres 1,424; lat. 10° 39′; long. 79° 38′; from Munnargoody E.S.E. 9 miles; from Tanjore E.S.E. 31 miles. On the southern bank of the Harichendranuddy. Two temples of Shiva and Vishnoo.——**(3)** Same etymologies. Town, Municipality, Head-quarters of Deputy collector, Tahsildar, District moonsif and D.P.W. Sub-division; Tanjore dist., Munnargoody tal.; pop. 20,395; acres 1,342; lat. 10° 40′; long. 79° 30′; height 196 feet; from Combaconam S.S.E. 20 miles; from Madras S.S.W. 173 miles; from Mayavaram S.S.W. 32 miles; from Negapatam W.S.W. 27 miles; from Tanjore E.S.E. 24 miles. On the southern bank of the Paumaniyaur, a branch of the Vennaur which irrigates the western portion of the talook. Considerable bramin population. Contains a bathing tank called Haridranuddy, 1,158 feet long, 837½ feet broad. There are nine old temples, four Vishnoo and five Shiva. Rajagopaulsawmy temple, the largest and most important, built by rajah Ragoonaut naick. Annual festival in March. Old Jeina [q.v.] temples in good order, and a mile west a ruined fort belonged to Ballaula raja. Car [rath] festival in connection with the pagoda [q.v.]. In the hamlets of Keilausanautapooram and Melamadapooram are two old Shiva temples; in the hamlet of Ashaisham three old temples of Shiva, Vishnoo, and Ganesh; and in the hamlet of Toondan cuttalay an old Shiva temple. Considerable trade in country goods, paddy [q.v.], chiefly metal-ware of local manufacture. Chief seat of the Wesleyan mission. Weekly market every Tuesday.

MUNTJAC (منتجاك - mantják, *Malay*). Jungle sheep.

MUNTRAM (मन्त्र - mantra, *San.*; منتر - mantar, *Hind.*). From (mantr, san. to speak indistinctly). A prayer or charm. As distinguished from tantram [q.v.], it is the invocation only; tantram being the form or ritual or rubric. A muntram is either good or bad, from its nature and its intent. It is distinguishable from shaunty [q.v.], a litany; the latter being long and poetical, while the muntram is usually restricted to a few letters, syllables or words. The muntram is the simple original form; the maulay muntram is a string of comments, or paraphrases founded on the simple form. The good muntrams are few; the evil and malignant muntrams especially among the Sheivas and Shactibhactans [q.v.] are numerous. The tauntric system is founded on them, and the atarvanam vedam [q.v.] teaches them. The tri-literal (aum) or om [q.v.] is a primitive muntram, having extraordinary power [gayatry]. The Sheiva muntram is of five letters, representing the five elements (na ma si va ya); this also has miraculous power [moola muntram, punchaucsharam]. Another form is (om nama shivaya), six-lettered, used by the votaries of Soobramanyan [q.v.]. The veishnava muntram is eight-lettered, (om na mo na ra ya na ya) [matam]. Muntram also stands for the art of magic generally. The Tamuls enumerate sixty-four arts and sciences and of these twenty are connected with magic as follows:—the art of summoning by enchantment; exorcism; exciting hatred between parties by magical spells; libidinous fascinations produced by enchantment; the art of subduction by magic; charms against poison; information respecting anything concealed in the palm of the hand; the art of entering into the air and becoming invisible; the art of walking in the air; the power of leaving one's own body and entering another lifeless body or substance at pleasure; the power of making one's self invisible; the art of conjuring; the art of performing wonders in heaven and earth; restraining the action of fire; counteracting the yielding quality of water so as to be able to walk on its surface; the art of restraining the power of the mind; the art of fascinating the eyes; the art of fascinating the mouth; the art of preventing the discovery of things concealed; the art by which the power of the sword or any other weapon is nullified. For the nature of the magical rites used by the Tamulians see the foot-note on vol. I (109). By Mahomedans, incantation is held lawful only when the help of God is invoked in practising it, and when no one is associated with him; and is practised for good purposes. This science is generally resorted to, to establish friendship, to cause the cure of a certain person, to secure the accomplishment of one's wishes, to obtain victory in battle.——*Muntraula canama* (మంత్రాలకనమ - mantrálakanama, Tel.). From (mantrálamma, tel. a goddess + kanama, tel ravine). From muntraulammah, a wooden idol at the eastern foot, chiefly worshipped by lumbaudies [q.v.]. Also known as the Dornaul pass from dornaul, a village at the eastern entrance. Pass; Kurnool dist., Nundicotcore and Marcapore tals.; lat. 15° 54′; long. 78° 55′; from Cumbum N.W. 28 miles; from Kurnool E. 51 miles; from Nundicotcore E. 37 miles; from Madras N.N.W. 215 miles; from Nundiaul N.E. 34 miles; from Pyaupaly N.E. 55 miles. Northernmost pass on the Nullamullays, between Nundicotcore and Marcapore talooks, about 15 miles in length. Chiefly used by Brinjarries [q.v.], who export salt from the coast of Kistna district to inland districts on pack bullocks and asses. Wheeled traffic generally prefers the Nundicanama pass which is provided with a good road. About half-way is Rollapenta.——*Muntraulammah* (మంత్రాలమ్మ - mantrálamma, Tel.). From (above + amma, tel. goddess). Goddess of charms.——*Muntry* (मन्त्री - mantrí, San.). A minister [vizier]. In old South indian governments, the first of the three regular ministers. The Muntry is the prime minister, the king's adviser in matter, of state; especially in matters of internal government, and externally of peace or war. The Pradhauny [q.v.] is the Lord high treasurer; office often usurped by the Muntry. The Dalavoy [q.v.] is the commander of the forces. In modern, and weak governments, the latter sometimes assumed the other two offices, the king being in virtual confinement, and shown as a puppet occasionally to the people. The Tamul Cooral has the following:—எற்றென் றிரங்குவ செய்யற்க செய்வானேன் மற்றன்ன செய்யாமை நன்று—"Let a minister "never do acts of which he would have to grieve saying, What "is this I have done? but should he do them, it were good that "he grieved not."—தொக்ச்சொல்லித் தூவாத நீக்கி நகச்சொல்லி நன்றி பயப்பதாந்தூது—"He is an ambassador "who, in the presence of foreign rulers, speaks briefly, avoids "harshness, talks so as to make them smile, and thus brings "good."—கூறாமை நோக்கிக் குறிப்பறிவானெஞ் ஞான்று மாறாநீர் வையக் கணி—"The minister who by looking at "the king understands his mind without being told of it, will "be perpetual ornament to the world which is surrounded by a "never-drying sea." Muntry mahanaud is the minister and council of the nation. Muntry also means Coobairan [q.v.] as prime minister of Shiva [q.v.].

MUNTSOO (మంచు - mantsu, *Tel.*). Dew [pany].——*Muntsoocaur* (మంచుకారు - mantsukáru, Tel.). Dewy season [caurtey].

MURDAH (آسن - ásan, *Hind.*; جنگلی کرنج - janglíkaranj, *Dec.*; ಮತ್ತಿ - matti, *Can.*; మద్ది - maddi, *Tel.*; ସହାଜ - sahajo, *Oor.*; മരുതു - marutu, *Mal.*; කුඹුක් - kumbuk, *Singh.*; மருதம் - marutham, *Tam.*). Title from malayalam. Hind. from (asana, san. black murdah). Dec. from (janglí, hind. wild + karanj, hind. pongamia glabra, vent.). Tam. from (maru, tam. fragrance), from a fragrant species. Can. also (banipu); A common term for certain Terminalias.——*Black murdah* (असन - asana, San.; असणा - asaná, Mahr.; मत्तीरूकु - mattírúku, Conc.; آسن - ásan, Hind.; جنگلی کرنج - janglíkaranj, Dec.; ಕುದುರೆಕಿವಿಗನಮರ - kudurekiviganamara, Can.; నల్లమద్ది - nallamaddi, Tel.; କାଳାସହାଜ - kálásahajo, Oor.; കരിമരുതു - karimarutu, Mal.; කුඹුක් - kumbuk, Singh.; கருப்புமருதம் - karuppumarutham, Tam.). Title from color of wood. San. from (as, san. to drive away). Mahr. from sanscrit. Hind. from sanscrit. Dec. from (janglí, hind. wild + karanj, hind. pongamia glabra, vent.). Can. from (kudure, can. horse + kivi, can. ear + mara, can. tree). Tel. from (nalla, tel. black + maddi, tel. terminalia arjuna, bedd.). Oor. from (kálá, hind. black + sahajo, oor. terminalia). Mal. from (kari, mal. black + marutu, mal. terminalia tomentosa, bedd.). Tam. from (karuppu, tam. blackness + marutham, terminalia tomentosa, bedd.). San. also (pítasálaka), meaning yellow, shorea robusta, gærtn. Hind. also (sadrí); (arjan), meaning terminalia. Can. also (karimatti), meaning black + the tree; (sóhoune). Tel. also (inumaddi), meaning iron + terminalia arjuna, bedd. [common saul]. Oor. also (saháju). Mal. also (marutu). Tam. also (marutham) [maroothum]; (karimatti), meaning black + terminalia paniculata, rottl. Title otherwise Ashanam, Black maroothum, Negroe's olive, Sahajo, Winged terminalia. Botanically Terminalia [antya parny] tomentosa, bedd., var. typica, combretaceæ [vricsham, 55]. Alias Chunco tomentosa; Pentaptera tomentosa; Terminalia alata. Large tree; bark deeply cracked; leaves nearly opposite, linear-oblong, somewhat cordate at the base, pubescent, but finally glabrous above, tomentose or pubescent beneath, with thick-stalked turbinate glands on the midrib near the base; fruit glabrous; spikes disposed in a brachiate panicle; flowers small, greenish white. Bark is reddish brown, unpleasant astringent taste. A sacred tree [poonyoshadhy]. Gives to pharm. bark, non-officinal, astringent and febrifuge; used both externally and internally; juice of leaves poured into ears for earache. Ashes from burnt bark produce a kind of choonam [q.v.] eaten with betel [q.v.] leaf [white murdah]; plant yields a gum [gond] used as an incense and cosmetic; bark imparts the characteristic red color to native leather [chamrah], gives a black dye [shauyam], with iron [auhan]; bark is used for tanning [chamrah]. Sap-wood reddish-white, heart-wood dark-brown, hard, variegated with streaks of darker color, showing on a radial section as dark streaks which are generally wavy or undulating; durable, seasons well, and takes a good polish; the wood splits however unless thoroughly seasoned; an excellent fuel, and makes good charcoal [kary]; used for the wheels [nemmy] of the heavy idol carts at the pagodas; when well polished resembles walnut [acroot].——*Flowering murdah* (किंजल - kinjala, Mahr.; ಹುಲುವೆ - huluve, Can.; నిమిరి - nimiri, Tel.; പൂമരുതു - púmarutu, Mal.; பூமருதம் - púmarutham, Tam.). Mal. from (pú, mal. flower + marutu, mal. terminalia). Tam. from (pú, tam. flower + marutham, tam. terminalia). Can. also (honal); (kírijul); (kondul); (marwah). Tel. also (maddi). Mal. also (pullamarutu), meaning yellowish + terminalia. Tam. also (pillamarutham), meaning yellow murdah, common in anamullays and malabar. Title otherwise Poo murdah. Botanically Terminalia [antya parny] paniculata, roth., combretaceæ [vricsham, 55]. Alias Pentaptera paniculata. Tree with diverging branches; leaves nearly opposite, linear-oblong, cordate at the base, acute or obtuse at the apex, coriaceous, rugose above, with umbilicate glands beneath near the base; spikes forming a compound panicle; drupe with one large and two small wings; flowering in november and december. Flowers used, pounded with the root of cissampelos pareira [indian pareira], as a remedy in cholera; the juice of the flowers along with that of guava [q.v.] bark is administered as an antidote in poisoning by opium [aphainam]; if the flowers are not obtainable the bark may be used; the juice of the flowers or bark, with melted butter [q.v.] and rock salt [sendah namak], is applied externally in parotitis. Bark contains tannin; fruit brown-red, used in dyeing. Wood grey, with dark heart-wood, very hard, not equal to tomentosa; improved by being kept under water.——*Leathery murdah* (बणपु - banapu, Conc.; آسن - ásan, Hind.; ಬನಪು - banapu, Can.; ಬನ್ಪು - banpu, Too.; கருமருதம் - karumarutham, Tam.). Title from leaves. Hind. from (asana, san. black murdah). Tam. from (karumai, tam. blackness + marutham, tam. the tree, terminalia tomentosa, bedd.). Can. also (matti); (marthu). Tam. also (shathagam), properly terminalia bellerica, roxb. Title otherwise Banapoo. Botanically Terminalia [antya parny] tomentosa, bedd., var. coriacea, combretaceæ [vriesham, 55]. Alias Pentaptera coriacea; Terminalia coriacea. Tree; bark deeply cracked; leaves nearly opposite, short-petioled, coriaceous, oval, cordate at the base, hard above, hoary and soft beneath, one to two sessile glands at or near the base of the midrib; spikes panicled; nut hoary; flowers small, dull yellow; flowering in july. Strong, hard, and heavy timber.——*White murdah* (अर्जुन - arjuna, San. and Mahr.; ارجن - arjan, Hind. and Dec.; ಬಿಳಿಮತ್ತಿ - bilimatti, Can.; తెల్లమద్ది - tellamaddi, Tel.; ହଂଜଳ - hanjal, Oor.; പുല്ലമരുത - pullamarutu, Mal.; කුඹුක් - kumbuk, Singh.; வெள்ளைமருதம் - vellaimarutham, Tam.). Title from color of wood. San. means white. Hind. from sanscrit. Can. from (bili, can. white + matti, can. terminalia tomentosa, bedd., var. typica). Tel. from (tella, tel. white + maddi, tel. the tree). Mal. from (pulla, mal. yellowish + marutu, mal. terminalia). Tam. from (vellai, tam. white + marutham, tam. terminalia). San. also (nadisarja), meaning river + shorea robusta, gærtn.; (indradru), meaning indran's tree, as growing near water; (kakubha), meaning distinguished tree. Can. also (toramatti), meaning river + terminalia tomentosa, bedd., var. typica; (banipu). Tel. also (maddi); (erramaddi), meaning red + the tree; (érumaddi), meaning river + the tree. Oor. also (karedha). Mal. also (vellamarutu), meaning white + terminalia. Tam. also (vellaimatti), meaning white + the tree so called; (karumarutham), meaning black + terminalia. Title otherwise Arjoon tree, Mutty tree, River saul. Botanically Terminalia [antya parny] arjuna, Bedd., combretaceæ [vricsham, 55]. Specific name from san. Alias Pentaptera angustifolia, arjuna, berryi, glabra; Terminalia berryi, crenulata, glabra. Gigantic tree; bark smooth; leaves nearly opposite, narrow-oblong, obtuse or acute at the apex, glabrous on both sides, often reddish beneath, with some nearly sessile glands near the base of the midrib; spikes terminal; drupe ovate, with five to seven equal longitudinal wings; flower small, greenish white; flowering in may, april; common near banks of rivers. The bark is generally sold in short half quills, from ¼–½ of an inch thick, and several inches long; it has a pinkish color, which is seen through the thin grey epidermis; its substance is fibrous and gritty under the teeth; it breaks with a short fracture, the internal surface being of a lighter color and finely striated; the taste is agreeably astringent; the ash amounts to 34 per cent. of almost pure calcium carbonate, watery extract is 23 per cent., 16 per cent. of tannin. Bark is medicinally a tonic internally, and a vulnerary externally. Ashes from burnt bark produce a kind of choonam [q.v.] which is eaten with betel [q.v.] leaf [black murdah]. Largely planted as an avenue [shaulay] tree, particularly in south; bark is astringent and used for dyeing black [shauyam] and for tanning [chamrah]; gives a brown translucent gum [gond]. Sap-wood reddish white; heartwood brown, variegated with darker-colored streaks; the wood is apt to split in seasoning and is not easy to work; boats are often made from it; inferior to tomentosa, but a valuable timber [maram]. There is a variety angustifolia.

MURREL (پھول مرل - phúlmaral, *Hind.*; مرل - maral, *Dec.*; ಹುವ್ವಿನಮರಳು - huvvinamaralu, *Can.*; పూచేప - púchépa, *Tel.*; ചൗരിവരാൽ - chaurivarál, *Mal.*; பூவிரால் - púvirál, *Tam.*). Title from deccany. Hind. from (phúl, hind. flower + maral, hind. murrel); from spots on body. Can. from (huvvu, can. flower + maralu, can. murrel). Tel. from (puvvu, tel. flower + chépa, tel. fish). Mal. from (chauri, mal. courageous + varál, mal. ophiocephalus genus). Tam. from (pú, tam. flower + virál, tam. caboz, ophiocephalus genus). Mal. also (kuruva), meaning small fish. Title otherwise Walking fish. Ophiocephalus [doke] marulius, ophiocephalidæ [walking fish], acanthopterygii, teleostei [matsyam, 29], of naturalists [jantoo]. Specific name from deccany. Alias Ophiocephalus aurolineatus, theophrasti. Scales on head are roughened by raised lines, which surround in an angular course a central spot, on the body the outer edge of the scales are smooth. Colors vary both with age and the water they reside in. Back grayish green, immature with brilliant orange band passing from eye to middle of caudal fin, but in more mature there are five or six cloudy bands descending to below lateral-line; abdomen orange, bases of each scale darkest; on posterior third of body, on dorsal, anal, and caudal fins are pearly-white spots, generally a large black ocellus at upper part of base or first third of caudal fin, which latter is gray, ventrals orange. Freshwaters, principally rivers; four feet in length. Very savage, protecting their young with great boldness. Take a live bait pretty well.——*Pariah murrel* (शाल - shála, San.; डाखु - dákhu, Mahr.; ڈھیری مرل - dherímaral, Hind.; ಕುಚ್ಚಿನಮುರಳು - kuççinamuralu, Can.; సవార - savára, Tel.; ସୋଲ - sola, Oor.; വരാൽ - varál, Mal.; ලූලා - lúlá, Singh.; வரால் - varál, Tam.). Title from dark gray color. Mahr. means dark stained. Hind. from (dheri, hind. pariah + maral, hind. murrel). Can. from (kuççu, can. bunch + maralu, can. murrel). Tel. means beauty. Oor. from sanscrit. Mal. from (vara, mal. stripe). Tel. also (korramínu), meaning dart + fish; (púchépa), meaning flower + fish. Mal. also (kuruntala), meaning depressed head; (vrál). Singh. also (hálpatmálu). Tam. also (karuppuvirál), meaning blackness + caboz, ophiocephalus genus. Ophiocephalus [doke] striatus, ophiocephalidæ [walking fish], acanthopterygii, teleostei [matsyam, 29], of naturalists [jantoo]. Alias Chena sola; Ophiocephalus chena, wrahl. Sola from sanscrit; wrahl from tamul. Lower jaw longer. Scales plate-like on summit of head large and irregularly shaped, from eighteen to twenty rows between snout and origin of dorsal fin; nine rows between eye and angle of preopercle. Scales on head are roughened in lines parallel to margins, on body they are arched towards centre of each. Colors dark grayish or blackish superiorly, dirty-white or yellowish white beneath; cheeks and lower surface of mouth streaked and spotted with gray; bands of gray or black from sides to abdomen. Spots and bars at posterior end of dorsal fin; ventrals and anal grayish, with whitish lines or spots along base of latter. In the young there is occasionally a large black ocellus at the end of base of dorsal fin, and the body may be destitute of any marks. Freshwaters throughout the plains, especially delighting in swamps and grassy tanks; attain 3 feet or more in length. They take bait very readily, especially a frog, and rise to the salmon fly.——*Sea murrel* (शाकुल - shakula, Mahr.; పెద్దముత్తె - peddamutte, Tel.; கடல்விரால் - kadalvirál, Tam.). Title from habitat. Tel. from (pedda, tel. large + mutte, tel. fish, clupea longiceps). Tam. from (kadal, tam. sea + virál, tam. caboz, ophiocephalus genus). Elacate nigra, scombridæ, acanthopterygii, teleostei [matsyam, 19], of naturalists [jantoo]. Alias Centronotus gardenrii; Elacate bivittata, canada, malabarica, motta, pondiceriana; Meladerma nigerrima; Scomber niger, peddah mottah. Motta, from (mutte, tel. clupea longiceps); peddahmottah from teloogoo. Upper surface of head flat; olivaceous brown, having dark band along back below base of dorsal fin and another along centre of side. Fins brownish, with dark or black edges. Outer edges of caudal lobes white. Sea; 13½ inches in length. No other common species here.

MURRY (మఱ్ఱి - marri, *Tel.*). From (marugu, tel. shelter). Banyan tree. Suffix in place names.——*Marla* (మర్ల - marla, Tel.). From (marri, tel banyan tree). Locative plural. Suffix in place names; as Collimarla, meaning river banyans. Or prefix; as Marlapaud, banyan spot.——*Murry aukoo krishnan* (మఱ్ఱియాకుకృష్ణుడు - marriákukrishnudu, Tel.). From (above + áku, tel. leaf + krishna, san. the god). Krishnan [q.v.] in one of his manifestations, where he is represented floating on a banyan [q.v.] leaf in the water [aulileimail pullicondone].

MURRY (మరి - mari, *Tel.*). Again.——*Murry caur* (మరికారు - marikáru, Tel.). From (above + káru, tel. crop). A second crop. Distinguish from Mauricaur [caur].

MURSOOL (مرسول - marsúl, *Hind.*). From (rasúla, ar. to send) [irsaul]. Forwarded, especially with a letter.

MUSANG (ميوسڠ - músang, *Malay*). Toddy cat [q.v.].

MUSHNY (ಮಶಿನಿ - mashini, *Can.*). From (mashi, can. black); black goddess [cauly, parvaty]. Wife of shiva [q.v.] among the Oorumbar [q.v.] of neilgherries.——*Mushnigoody* (ಮಶಿನಿಗುಡಿ - mashinigudi, Can. masingudi *). From (masini, can. the goddess of that name + gudi, can. temple). Village; Todanaud division, Neilgherry dist.; pop. 1,361; acres 33,120; lat. 11° 34′; long. 76° 41′; from Ootacamund N.N.W. 12 miles. On the Seegore road. Most populous village in feverish Seegore valley.

MUSHROO (مشروع - mashrú, *Hind.*). From (shara, ar. law); from being permitted at prayers, where pure silk is prohibited. Fabric of satin with cotton back, used by well-to-do classes for trouserings of both sexes, for covering cushions, &c. Very strong and durable, washes well and preserves color. Manufactured at Madras, Trichinopoly, &c. Now going out of fashion [sheelay].

MUSJID (مسجد - masjid, *Hind.*; మసీదు - masídu, *Tel.*; പള്ളി - palli, *Mal.*; மசூதி - masúthi, *Tam.*). From (sajada, ar. to bow). The mosque or place of Mahomedan public prayer [namauz]. Mosques are generally built of stone or brick, in the form of a square, in the centre of which is an open courtyard, surrounded with cloisters for students. In the centre of the wall facing Mecca is the mihraub [q.v.] or niche, which marks the direction of the Caaba [q.v.] at Mecca, and on the right of this niche is the mimbar [q.v.] or pulpit from which the Friday oration [khootbah] is recited. In the centre of the open court-yard, there is usually a large tank [howz], in which the worshippers perform their ablutions, and adjoining the mosques are lavatories in which the legal washings can be performed. Along the front, within the doorway is a low barrier, a few inches high, which denotes the sacred part of the mosque, at which the Mahomedan stops, takes off his shoes, carries them in his left hand sole to sole, and puts his right foot first, as he passes into the square devoted to prayer. If he have not previously performed the ablution, he repairs to the tank to perform the necessary duty. Round each mosque there are either two or four high towers. These are called minarets [meenaur], and from them, instead of a bell, the people are called to prayers [azaun]. Most mosques have a kind of hospital belonging to them, in which travellers, of what religion soever, are entertained during three days. Each mosque has also a spot which is the burying-place of its founder. Women are forbidden in the Koran [q.v.] to go into the public mosques; therefore the wealthy have frequently a mosque in their own compound where females perform their devotions. The different officers attached to large mosques are :—the cauzy or ecclesiastical judge, the khateeb or priest, the moollah or schoolmaster, two naibs or deputies, a furraush or sweeper called also moojauwir or devoutly employed, the ghassaul whose business is to wash the bodies of the dead ; two rahbardaur, guides or messengers. In inferior mosques there are only a moollah [q.v.] and a mooazzin [q.v.]; and the latter has no pay, but lives upon what he can earn by carrying messages of invitation, or acting as a servant at marriage [shaudy] ceremonies. In mosques there are no sermons, no common prayer, and no singing. At the principal mosques no public service is held except there be forty persons present, exclusive of strangers, slaves, and the deformed. The first musjid was built on the spot where Mahomet's camel of its own accord stopped on his arrival at Medina after his flight from Mecca.

MUSK (مشك - mushk, *Hind.*). A secretion of Muskdeer, Moschus moschiferus of Himalayas [custoory]. Prefix in animal names as Musk duck, Musk ox, from musky smell ; also in plant names, from smell. Compare :—Cucurbita moschata, musk melon ; Hibiscus abelmoschus, musk mallow ; Limonia acidissima, musk-deer plant ; Rosa moschata, musk rose, musk scented rose. See gloss. paragraphs.——*Musk-rat* (गन्धमूषिक - gandhamúshika, San. ; خلد - khuld, Ar. ; موش كور - múshikor, Pers. ; چھچوندر - chhachúndar, Hind. ; چچوندری - chichundarí, Dec. ; تكس كستوری - tikuskasturí, Malay ; ಸುಂಡಿಲಿ - súndili, Can. ; ಕಿಚ್ಚಿಲಿ - kiççili, Too. ; చుంచెలుక - tsuncheluka, Tel. ; ଚଲାମୁଷା - chalomussa, Oor. ; കണ്ടെലി - kandeli, Mal. ; කුනමීයා - kunamíyá, Singh. ; மூஞ்சூறு - múnjuru, Tam.). Title from its smell. San. from (gandha, san. fragrance + múshika, san. rat). Pers. from (múshi, pers. musk + kor, pers. blind). Hind. from (chhuchhundara, san. musk rat). Malay from (tikus, malay, mouse + kastúri, san. musk). Can. from (shundu, tam. small + eli, tam. rat). Tel. from (tsuntsu, tel. the sound produced by the animal. + eluka, tel. rat). Mal. from (gandha, san. smell + eli, mal. rat). Singh. from (kuna, singh. dirt + míyá, singh. rat). Tam. from (mó, tam. to smell + shúran, tam. shrew). Ar. also (fáratulmask), meaning musk mouse ; (fáratulbísh), meaning poisonous mouse. Pers. also (múshbíshá), meaning poison + mouse. Can. also (múgili), meaning nose + rat. Tel. also (tsúreluka), meaning eaves + rat, from its inhabiting the eaves of houses. Title otherwise Grey musk shrew, Indian musk rat as opposed to those of america and pyrenees. Crocidura cærulea, sorecidæ, insectivora, mammalia [sastanam, 13], of naturalists [jantoo]. Alias Crocidura cærulescens, fulvosinera, sindensis, waldemarii ; Sorex cærulescens, caeruleus, capensis, giganteus, indicus, murinus, myosurus, pilorides, sonneratii. The Shrews comprise a large number of small animals, which, from their general appearance and nocturnal habits, are popularly confounded with rats [ely] and mice [shoondely] known by a sharp shrill cry. Emit a musky odour. Food, chiefly insects [poochy]. Snakes [sarpam] are said to avoid the neighbourhood of the shrew. In Jeypore the body of a small musk rat is regarded as a powerful talisman.—"*a*" The animal specified at head is the common small musk shrew. Of an uniform bluish ash or pale gray color, very slightly tinged with ferruginous, and most so on the under parts ; naked parts flesh-colored. The tail thick and tapering.—"*b*" Next is the Large musk rat. Crocidura murina of naturalists. Brownish, or dark brownish-gray above, grayish-brown beneath, the fur longer and coarser than in cærulescens ; ears larger tail nearly equal in length to the body, rounded thick at the base, nearly nude with a few longish hairs scattered over it ; feet and tail, fleshy. Found especially on the Malabar coast, where its bite is considered venomous. The odour is less powerful than in Cærulescens.—"*c*" Next is the Neilgherry wood shrew. Sorex niger of naturalists. Blackish brown with a rufescent shade on the upper parts ; abdomen, dusky-grayish ; tail, equal in length to the body, gradually tapering to a point ; snout, much attenuated. The odour is of a very faint musky nature.—"*d*" Last is the Neilgherry pigmy shrew. Crocidura perroteti of naturalists. Back deep blackish brown ; belly pale ; limbs and feet brown, palms and plantæ clad with hairs ; ears large conspicuous. A very small animal.—"*e*" Indian species of the sorecidæ not here found are :—Anurosorex assamensis or assam burrowing shrew, Chimarrogale himalayica or himalayan water-shrew, Crocidura macropus or large-footed shrew, Nyctogale elegans or thibet water-shrew, Soriculus caudatus or long-tailed shrew, Crocidura hodgsoni, or small-clawed pigmy-shrew, Soriculus nigrescens or mouse-tailed shrew, Crocidura fuliginosa or Blyth's shrew.—"*f*" The Madras tree shrew, Tupaia ellioti, tupaiidæ, insectivora, mammalia [sastanam, 15], is known in Tamul by prefixing the term (mara) to the above. The tree-shrews, are diurnal in their habits, live on trees, and feed both on fruit and insects, which they hold in their paws like squirrels. At one time confounded with squirrels [anil]. The eyes are large and prominent, and the tail bushy ; the toes are five in number, with strong claws ; the shank-bones are not united as in the hedgehogs [moollely]. The Madras tree-shrew is above pale rufescent or reddish-brown, the hairs being grizzled red and brown ; chin, throat, breast, and lower parts yellowish white ; which is continued in a narrow line along the underside of the tail. Found on the hills west of Madras, the continuation of the Eastern ghauts.

MUSKET TREE (துப்பாக்கிமரம் - tubákkimaram, *Tam.*). From seeds resembling shot. Same as Roodrauck tree.

MUSLIM (مسلم - muslim, *Hind.*). From (salama, ar. submission). One who has received Islam ; a Mahomedan believer [moslem].——*Moslem* (مسلم - muslim, Hind.). From (islám, ar. resignation to will of god). Mahomedan [muslim].——*Mussalman* (مسلمان - musalmán, Hind.). From (salama, ar. submission) [islam] ; (muslim) is the name given by mahomed to the faithful ; the persian plural of this is (muslimán), which was adopted as a singular, and the word (musalmán) thus formed. A follower of Islam [q.v.]. According to religion, Mussalmans are divided into Soonnees [q.v.] and Shiahs [q.v.], besides a few minor sects. The division dates from the death of Mahomet, though the leadership of both parties was for a short time united in the hands of Ally, who was fourth caliph [q.v.] of the Soonnees and first imaum [q.v.] of the Shiahs. According to origin; Indian mussalmans are of three classes :—"*a*" the descendants of foreign Mussalmans, who came with their families into India, such as the Syeds [q.v.], Sheikhs [q.v.], Moghuls [q.v.] and Pataans [q.v.] ;—"*b*" the descendants of Arabs and Persians, who came by sea and settled on the coast and took native wives, such as the Moplahs [q.v.] and Nivayats [q.v.] ;—"*c*" the descendants of converts from Hindooism ; as a Mussalman of even the highest stock may take a wife from any other class, there are now few if any Mussalmans, who are not at least in part of Hindoo descent. See vol. II, 233 [jonacan, lubbay].

MUSLIN (अंशुक - amshuka, *San.* ; ململ - malmal, *Hind.* ; ರವೆಶಲ್ಲ - raveshallá, *Can.* ; రవశల్లా - ravashallá, *Tel.* ; ശല്ല - shallá, *Mal.* ; கவணி - kavani, *Tam.*). Title from Mosul on the Tigris. San. from (amshu, san. filament). Can. from (rave, can. fine grain + shallá, can. cloth). The finest class of cotton goods. ὀθόνιον ordinary muslin and κάρπασος or fine muslin were according to Periplus exported from Southern india to Egypt. The finest is Mulmul khas or king's muslin ; the second, Abrawaun or running water ; the third, Shabnam or evening dew. Other muslins are :—Sullah, fine quality found in Cuddapah and Arnee ; Doriyah, or striped muslin, from each thread in the stripes being composed of two threads twisted together ; Charkhanah, or chequered muslin ; Jamdauny, or loom-figured muslin, the highest work of the weaver [mull, sheelay].

MUSNUD (مسند - masnad, *Hind.*). From (sanada, ar. to lean against). A cushion [guddee]. The large cushion, &c., used by native princes in place of a throne [takt].

MUSTER (మోస్తరు - móstaru, *Tel.*). Portuguese for pattern [maudry].

MUTT (मठ - mat'ha, *San.*). From (mat'h, san. to dwell). Cloister. A species of college where a celibate Hindoo priest lives with disciples making the same profession, one of whom becomes his successor. Generally comprehends a set of huts or chambers for the mahant [q.v.] or superior and his permanent pupils ; a temple sacred to the deity whom they worship, or the samaudhy [q.v.] or shrine of the founder of the sect, or some eminent teacher ; and a dharmashaulay [q.v.], viz., one or more sheds or buildings for the accommodation of the mendicants or travellers who are constantly visiting the mutt. Most mutts have endowments of land, generally of small extent. Besides lands, the monks receive presents from lay votaries, ask alms daily in their neighbourhoods, and sometimes traffic [inam]. The mutt at Shringairy, founded by Shuncaracharry [shuncaran], was once famous. A mutt of Veerasheivas at Madura was lately in repute for Tamul learning. For Jiyyar mutts see Jiyyar.

MUTT (موٹھ - moth, *Hind.*). Same as Moorman's gram.

MUTTY (दुर्नामा - durnámá, *San.* ; سیپی کا کیڑا - sípíkákírá, *Hind.* ; ఆలిపురుగు - álipurugu, *Tel.* ; കക്ക - kakka, *Mal.* ; மட்டி - matti, *Tam.*). San. from (dur, san. bad + náma, san. name). Hind. from (sípí, hind. shell + kírá, hind. worm). Tel. from (áli, san. ridge + parugu, tel. worm). Mal. from (kal, mal. stone + káya, mal. fruit). Cockle [chippy]. Cardium edule of naturalists.

MUZCOOR (مذكور - mazkúr, *Hind.*). From (zikr, ar. mention). Before-mentioned [mailpady].

MUZMOON (مضمون - mazmún, *Hind.*). From (zamana, ar. to include). Contents of letter, &c.

MYNA (مينا - mainá, *Dec.*). Sturnidæ family, conirostres, insessores, aves [pacshy, 26], of naturalists [jantoo]. Starlings. Divided here into Sturninæ, starlings and mynas ; Lamprotorninæ, glossy mynas, or grakles. The species best known to the natives are shown below.——**(1)**. *Braminy myna* (بهمنی مینا - bahmanímainá, Hind. ; پپائی مینا - papaímainá, Dec. ; పాపటిగోరంకి - pápatigóranki, Tel. ; വെള്ളക്കാരൻ - vellakkárán, Mal. ; பாப்பாத்திமைனா - páppáttimainá, Tam.). Title from bright yellow legs, as if by use of saffron [country saffron] which bramin women use daily. Hind. from (bahman, hind. bramin + mainá, hind. starling). Dec. from (papaí, hind. fruit of carica papaya, linn. + mainá, hind. myna) ; from color of beak. Tel. from (pápata, tel. the parting of the hair on the forehead

+ góranki, tel. bird, acridotheres tristis, linn.). Mal. from (vella, mal. white + kárán, mal. the bird, edolius malabaricus, scop.). Tam. from (páppátti, tam. bramin women + mainá, tam. myna). Hind. also (papaia). Tel. also (pápataparige), meaning having parted hair on the head + ortolan. Tam. also (vellimainá), meaning silver + myna; (rawanati). Beng. also (monghyrpawi). Title otherwise Blackheaded myna. Temenuchus pagodarum, sturninæ. Alias Maina sylvestris; Pastor nigriceps. Frequently caged. No other common species here.——*Bush myna* (جهوندی مینا - jhúndímainá, Hind. and Dec.; நானவந்தான் - nánavandán, Tam.). Title from resort. Hind. from (jhúndí, hind. bush + mainá, hind. starling). Tam. from (nánu, tam. to be shy + vá, tam. to come), from habit. Hind. also (pahárímainá), meaning hill myna; (jhontisálik), meaning bush myna. Acridotheres fuscus, sturninæ, Alias Acridotheres griseus; Gracula cristatella; Maina cristatelloides. No other common species here.——*Common myna* (सारिका - sáriká, San.; शालुंकी - shálunkí, Mahr.; زوزر - zuzúr, Ar.; سار - sár, Pers.; مینا - mainá, Hind. and Dec.; ಗೊರವಂಕ - goravanka, Can.; గోరంక - góranki, Tel.; ചിത്ര - chitra, Mal.; மயினா - mayiná, Tam.). From (shára, san. variegated). Can. from teloogoo. Tel. from (góru, tel. claw + vanka, tel. curved). Mal. means variegated. Hind. also (desímainá), meaning country myna; (sálik), from sanscrit; (bhatsálik), meaning bramin myna. Can. also (sárike), from sanscrit; (gorwantera). Tam. also (karuppumayiná), meaning black myna. Title otherwise Indian starling. Acridotheres tristis, sturninæ. Alias Gracula gryllivora; Maina tristoides. Whole head with moderate occipital crest, neck and breast glossy black; rest of plumage quaker or snuff brown, darkest on back and wing-coverts, lightest beneath; primaries black with white spot at base, forming conspicuous wing-spot; tail black with white tip, successively broader from centre pair; lower abdomen, vent and under tail-coverts white; bill and orbits deep yellow; legs dull yellow; irides red brown with white specks. Length about 10 inches. Very common. Roosts in large numbers in a tree, and morning and evening keeps up a noisy chattering; has a great variety of notes. Household bird, breeding almost exclusively in nooks and eaves of houses, under the roofs, in holes in walls, pots hung out for that purpose by the natives. Very commonly caged and domesticated, learns to pick up words and sentences. The following is a Hindostany proverb:— مینا جو میں نہ کہے دودھ بہات نت کہائے بکری جو میں—میں کہے اوسکی کہال کہچائے "The Myna cries 'not I' and eats milk and rice for ever," "The goat cries 'I, I' and loses his skin." Said to a boaster. "Main "ná" is "not I"; "I, I," stands for the bleating of the goat. The humble Myna is well treated and the boastful goat is killed. No other common species here.——*Hill myna* (کوکنی مینا - kokníminá, Hind.; కొండగోరంక - kondagóranki, Tel.; മലച്ചിത്ര - malaççitra, Mal.). Title from resort. Hind. from (kokní, hind. tiny + mainá, hind. starling). Tel. from (konda, tel. hill + góranki, tel. myna, acridotheres tristis, linn.). Mal. from (mala, mal. hill + chitra, mal. myna). Eulabes religiosa, lamprotorninæ. Alias Eulabes indicus; Gracula minor. No other common species here.——*Pied myna* (ابلق مینا - ablakmainá, Hind.; వెండిగోరంక - vendagóranki, Tel.). Title from variegated color. Hind. from (ablak, hind. piebald + mainá, hind. starling). Tel. from (vendi, tel. silver + góranki, tel. myna, acridotheres tristis, linn.). Sturnopastor contra, sturninæ. Alias Sturnus capensis. Often taken young and caged. No other common species here.——*Rosy myna* (گلابی مینا - gulábímainá, Dec.). From color of lesser plumage. See Cholúm bird.——(2) *Mynautty* (مچھریا - maççhariyá, Hind.; దాసరిపిట్ట - dásaripitta, Tel.; മൈനാത്തി - mainátti, Mal.; விசிறிக்குருவி - visirikkuruvi, Tam.). Title from malayalam. Hind. from (maççhar, hind. mosquito); from food. Tel. from (dásari, tel. vaishnava mendicant + pitta, tel. bird); from white band on face resembling caste mark of the mendicant [dausary]. Mal. means female myna. Tam. from (visiri, tam. fan + kuruvi, tam. small bird); from fan-like tail. Hind. also (shámchurí), meaning evening bird. Title otherwise White-browed fantail. Leucocerca albofrontata, myiagrinæ, muscicapidæ [macsha grauhy], dentirostres, insessores [pacshy, 20], of naturalists [jantoo].

MYROBALAN (त्रिफल - trip'hala, *San.*). Title from greek, meaning sweet juice acorn. San. means three fruits; referring to Emblic myrobalan, Chebulic myrobalan and Belleric myrobalan [tripalam].

MYRRH (مر - murr, *Ar.*). Gum resin [googal] obtained from Balsamodendron myrrha, nees. [bole]. Also similar product from other allied plants.——*Buffaloe myrrh* (بهینسا بول - bhainsábol, Hind.). Same as Indian bdellium.——*East india myrrh* (بهینسا بول - bhainsábol, Hind.). Hind. means buffalo myrrh. Same as African bdellium [q.v.].——*False myrrh* (گوگل - gúgal, Dec.). Any googal [q.v.].——*Turkey myrrh* (بول رومی - bolirúmí, Hind.). Title as being shipped from turkish ports. Same as Balm of gilead. Also the best myrrh of commerce.

MYSORE (महिषमण्डल - mahishamandala, *San.*; میسور - maisúr, *Hind.*; ಮೈಸೂರು - maisúru, *Can.*; మైసూరు - maisúru, *Tel.*; മൈസൂർ - maisúr, *Mal.*; மைசூர் - maisúr, *Tam.*). From (máhisha, san. buffalo + úru, can. town) [maha]. Ancient name for the province is Carnautam or Carnautacam [q.v.]; ancient name for the town is Pooragerey or place of tanks and streams. Protected state under the Government of India, but occupied entirely by a Dravidian race. For general description of the province see vol. I, 20. The following are the principal rivers:—Arcauvaty, Badary, Bauvaly, Bhadra, Bhrigoo, Cadamba, Cauvery, Chitrauvaty, Chuckrateertam, Coomadwaty, Coondaur, Cooshauvaty, Csheera, Cubbany, Dandauvaty, Goondlooholey, Haridrauvaty, Hemauvaty, Honnholey, Janagihulla, Jayamungaly, Locapauvany, Lutchmana teertam, Naliny, Nandiny, Netrauvaty, Paupughny, Pennair, Sharauvaty, Sharmanauvaty, Sheeta, Shimsha, Shunkhateertam, Somauvaty, Southern pinaukiny, or Ponniaur, Swarnamookhy, Swarnauvaty, Toonga, Toongabudra, Varada, Vedavaty, Yenneholey. The following are the large tanks:—Ayyankerey, Jogoo, Madagadkerey, Motitalaub, Samoodrakerey, Soolekerey, Vishnoo. The following are the principal hills and ghauts:—Agoomby ghaut, Ambaujidroog, Auvany betta, Bababooden, Baswanbetta, Beirandroog, Bellibetta, Bhasmaungy, Biligherryrunganbetta, Bramhagherry, Cabbaul droog, Careycullgoodda, Carigaut, Chamoondibetta, Chennakeshavabetta, Chennaroyandroog, Chitaldroog, Chundragootty, Coda sahyadry, Colaurbetta, Coloorghaut, Coordoomullay, Coothiraymookh, Devaroydroog, Dibbagherry, Doccalcondah, Doreygoodda, Gersoppah, Gungamoola, Harihareshwarabetta, Haimadevarbetta, Himad gopaulsawmybetta, Hoolaganmoradibetta, Hooliculldroog, Hooliyoordroog, Hoottaridroog, Hyderghurghaut, Madgherry, Mahacaulydroog, Mailcotebetta, Malecullfripatty, Mauvinkereybetta, Midagesby betta, Moolbaugal betta, Moolainagherry, Moorgamullay, Mungalabetta, Nundidroog, Oottanhullybetta, Pauvoogada, Rungasawmybetta, Savandroog, Scandagherry, Shivagungey, Shravanabelgola, Soonnacullbetta, Tyancull, Vakkalairy. The following are the places of pilgrimage, or places where great fairs are held:—Auvany, Bannairghatt, Bellauvy, Biligherryrunganbetta, Boppagondanpooram, Calaghatta, Carigatt, Chamoondibetta, Choonchaucutty, Choonchangherry, Chundragootty, Coodaly, Cullhully, Devanhully, Devaroydroog, Ghauty soobramanyam, Goobby, Harihar, Hindiginaul, Hiriyore, Holalore, Mailcotebetta, Mailore, Moodookdorey, Moogore, Munchenahully, Mungalabetta, Naickanhutty, Nullore, Nundidroog, Oottanhully betta, Santekesalagherry, Shiby, Shravanabelgola, Shringairy, Tiptore, Tirmullay, Togarshy, Vasantapooram, Yedabetta, Yediyore. The following are the places of historical interest, or places where remarkable works of nature or art exist:—Auvaty, Bailore, Bangalore, Baswancote, Belganvy, Bellibetta, Bhasmaungy, Cabbaul droog, Chamoondibetta, Chaumrajnugger, Chikkanaickenhully, Chitaldroog, Colaur, Devaroydroog, Goobby, Halabeed, Hassan, Hauranhully, Hebbore, Holoovanhully, Hoolicull, Hoscote, Jaumagal, Jogoo, Keidala, Kelady, Madgherry, Maharajandroog, Manjarabad, Moogore, Muddore, Mysore, Narsapore, Sargore, Seringapatam, Sharauvaty, Sheerah, Shravanabelgola, Somnautpore, Talacaud, Togarshy, Toorvekerey, Yelahunka, Yelwaul. The following are the towns, the population of which amounts to 5,000:—Aunecull, Bangalore, Chennaputna, Chikbullapore, Chikmagalore, Chintaumany, Closepett, Colaur, Dauvangerey, Devanhully, Dodbullapore, Hassan, Hoonsoor, Malvully, Nanjangode, Seringapatam, Shidlaghatt, Shimoga, Tarikerey, Toomcore. The following are places, &c., mentioned in connection with the history of this Presidency, the vernacular identifications being shown.——*Achalabetta* (ಅಚಲಬೆಟ್ಟ - achalabetta, Can.). Means immoveable + hill. Mountain in Malvully talook, Mysore district, near Closepett.——*Agoomby* (ಅಗುಂಬಿ - águmbi, Can.; agumbe, Mys. Gov.). Ghaut [q.v.], town in Teertahully talook, Shimoga district.——*Ajimpoora* (ಅಜಿಂಪುರ - ajimpura, Can.; ajjampur, Mys. Gov.). Means (azím, proper name + town). Town in Tarikerey talook Cuddore district, on the Tarikerey, Hosdroog road, 12 miles east of the cusbah [q.v.]. Weekly fair Tuesday.——*Ambaujidroog* (ಅಂಬಾಜಿದುರ್ಗ - ambájidurga, Can., Mys. Gov.). Means (ambáji, proper name + fort). Hill in Chintaumany talook, Colaur district, 4,399 feet; summit fortified by Tippoo. Until 1873 the surrounding hoblies formed Ambaujidroog talook, head-quarters Chintaumanipett.——*Anantapoora* (ಅನಂತಪುರ - anantapura, Can.; anantapur, Mys. Gov.). Means (andásura, proper name + town). Sanscrit name (ánandapura), meaning pleasure + town. Town in 14° 5′ N. lat., 75° 17′ E. long., in Saugar talook, 15 miles south-south-east of the cusbah, on the Shimoga-Gersoppah road. In 1838 included in Nugger talook, but till 1875 again the head-quarters of a talook bearing its own name, Shimoga district.——*Antargunga* (ಅಂತರಗಂಗ - antaraganga, Can.). Means interior + ganges. River. Rises in the Shatashringa hill, north-west of the town of Colaur in the Colaur district. Signifying the subterranean Ganges is esteemed sacred.——*Arcauvaty* (ಅರ್ಕಾವತಿ - arkávati, Can.). See sep. title.——*Arkalgode* (ಅರ್ಕಲಗೋಡು - arkalagódu, Can.; arkalgód, Mys. Gov.). Means sun + hill-top. Sanscrit name (arkapuri), meaning sun + town, as gowtaman worshipped the sun here.—"*a*" Talook in the south, Hassan district. Head-quarters, Arkalgode. Contains the hoblies:—Arkalgode, Baswaputnam, Conanore, Kesavattore, Krishnarajcutty, Marore, Mulliputnam, Ponnatpore. Principal places:—Arkalgode, Baswaputnam, Cadaly, Carlapooram, Conanore, Hosahully, Hoscote, Roodraputnam.—"*b*" Town, Hassan district, in 12° 46′ N. lat., 76° 7′ E. long., 17 miles south of Hassan. Talook head-quarters and municipality. Present town founded about 1568 by Krishnappa naick. Captured by canteroy narsa rajah of Mysore in 1647 and subsequently by Shivappa naick of Ikkairy. Again besieged by Chikka deva rajah in 1694 and finally annexed to Mysore.——*Arsikerey* (ಅರಸೀಕೆರೆ-arashikere, Can.). Means queen + tank. Talook in the north Hassan district. Head-quarters Arsikerey. Contains the hoblies :—Arsikerey, Coorvanka, Cullyaudy, Gandashy, Hauranhully, Kittanakerey. Principal places :—Hauranhully, Kenkerey.——*Ashtagram* (ಅಷ್ಟಗ್ರಾಮ - ashtagráma, Can. ; ashtagram, Mys. Gov.). Means eight + village. Former division and talook [seringapatam].——*Atticooppey* (ಅತ್ತಿಕುಪ್ಪೆ - attikuppe, Can. ; attikupa, Mys. Gov.). Means fig tree + heap.—"*a*" Talook in the south-east, Hassan district. Head-quarters, Atticooppey. Contains the hoblies :—Akkihebbaul, Atticooppey, Bookinkerey, Chincooraly, Cunnambaudy, Kikkairy, Santebauchhully, Sindhoogatt. Principal places :—Atticooppey, Bookinkerey, Cunnambaudy, Goommanhully, Hosaholáloo, Kikkairy, Sindhoogatt.—"*b*" Town, Hassan district, in 12° 41′ N. lat., 76° 33′ E. long., 41 miles south-east of Hassan, on the Seringapatam-Chenroyputnam road. Talook head-quarters and municipality.——*Aulore* (ಆಲೂರು - álūru, Can.). Means banyan tree + village. Hobly, Village, Channel. In Hassan talook, Hassan district, 7 miles west of Hassan. Fair Wednesdays, rice market.——*Aunecull* (ಆನೆಕಲ್ಲು - ánekallu, Can. ; anekal, Mys. Gov.). Means hailstone.—"*a*" Talook of Bangalore district. In the south-east. Head-quarters at Aunecull. Contains the hoblies :—Attibeley, Aunecull, Bidargooppey, Haurguddey, Iggalore, Jigany, Sarjapore. Principal places :—Attibeley, Aunecull, Dommasundra, Jigany, Sarjapore.—"*b*" Town in 12° 42′ N. lat., 77° 43′ E. long., 20 miles south-east of Bangalore. Talook head-quarters and municipality. Founded in 1603 by Chikka timma gowda, descendant of original Soogatore chief and continued in possession of his descendants till annexed to Mysore by Hyder.——*Ayyankerey* (ಅಯ್ಯನಕೆರೆ - ayyanakere, Can. ; ayyankere, Mys. Gov.). Means master + tank. Also called Dodda madagadkerey. Town, lake. Four miles north-west of Sakroyputnam, Cuddore district.——*Bailore* (ಬೇಲೂರು - bélūru, Can.). Means shore + town.—"*a*" Talook in the north-west, Hassan district. Head-quarters, Bailore. Contains the hoblies :—Adagore, Andaley, Areyhully, Bailore, Halabeed, Lakkoonda, Melpaul, Naurvey. Principal places : Adagore, Bailore, Halabeed. "*b*" Town. On right bank of the Yegachy, 23 miles north-west of Hassan. Talook head-quarters and municipality.——*Baitmungalam* (ಬೇತಮಂಗಲ - bétamangala, Can. ; betmangala, Mys. Gov.). Means hunt + village. Town, Colaur district, on the right bank of the Palaur, said to have been founded in the time of the Chola kings, 18 miles south-east of Colaur. Former talook [bowringpett].——*Ballaulroyendroog* (ಬಲ್ಲಾಳರಾಯನದುರ್ಗ - ballálaráyanadurga, Can. ; belredurga, Mys. Gov.). Means (ballálaráya, proper name + fort). Hill in the Western ghaut range in 13° 8′ N. lat., and 75° 29′ E. long., in the old Vastaura talook, Cuddore district.——*Bangalore* (ಬೆಂಗಳೂರು - bengalūru, Can.). See sep. title.——*Bannairghaut* (ಬನ್ನೇರುಘಟ್ಟ - bannérughatta, Can. ; bannirgatta, Mys. Gov.). Means forest + plough + hill pass. Sacred hill and place of pilgrimage in Bangalore talook, Bangalore district, 10 miles south of Bangalore. Height 3,271 feet.——*Baswaputna* (ಬಸವಾಪಟ್ಣ - basavápatna, Can.). Means bull god + town. Town in 14° 12′ N. lat., 75° 52′ E. long., in the north of the Chennagherry talook, Shimoga district, 16 miles north-west of the cusbah [q.v.].——*Baugeypully* (ಬಾಗೆಪಲ್ಲಿ - bágepalli, Can.). Means beauty + village.—"*a*" Talook in north, Colaur district. Head-quarters, Baugeypully. Contains the hoblies :—Baugeypully, Billore, Chaukvail, Cheelore, Goolore, Mittemary, Paulya, Yellampully. Principal places :—Baugeypully, Chaukvail, Mittemary, Yellampully.—"*b*" Town on the right bank of the Chitrauvaty, about 60 miles north-west of Colaur, on the old Bangalore-Bellary road. Head-quarters of the Baugepully talook, Colaur district.——*Baunauvar* (ಬಾಣಾವರ - bánávara, Can. ; banavar, Mys. Gov.). Means arrow + town. Town, Cuddore district, in 13° 24′ N. lat., 76° 14′ E. long., nearly 30 miles east of Chikmagalore, on the Bangalore-Shimoga road.——*Beerore* (ಬೀರೂರು - bírūru, Can. ; birur, Mys. Gov.). Means hero + village. Trading town in Cuddore talook, Cuddore district, on the Bangalore-Shimoga road, 19 miles north-west of the cusbah [q.v.].——*Beirandroog* (ಭೈರನದುರ್ಗ - bairanadurga, Can. ; bairandurga, Mys. Gov.). Means shiva + fort. Hill in the north-west of the Maugady talook, Bangalore district, near Coodoor, formerly fortified.——*Belgauvy* (ಬೆಳಗಾವಿ - belagáve, Can.). Means (bali, the giant + village). Also called Balgaumy. Village in 14° 24′ N. lat., 75° E. long., in Shikarpore talook, Shimoga district, 18 miles north-west of the cusbah [q.v.]. Remarkable for its antiquities.——*Belgootty* (ಬೆಳಗುತ್ತಿ - belagutti, Can.). Means white + hillock. Village in 14° 12′ N. lat., 75° 35′ E. long., in Honnauly talook, Shimoga district, 5 miles north-west of Nyaumty.——*Bellawvy* (ಬೆಳ್ಳಾವಿ - bellávi, Can. ; bellavi, Mys. Gov.). Means jaggery + steam. Town, Place of pilgrimage. A town in Toomcore talook, Toomcore district, 9 miles north-west of Toomcore. Municipality, fair Mondays.——*Bettadpore* (ಬೆಟ್ಟದಪುರ - bettadapura, Can. ; bettadpur, Mys. Gov.). Means hill + town.—"*a*" Village in Hoonsoor talook, Mysore district, 20 miles north-west of the cusbah, [q.v.] on the Periyapptna-Hassan road.—"*b*" Mountain. Height 4,350 feet.——*Bettore* (ಬೆತ್ತೂರು - bettūru, Can.). Means cane + village. Village in Dauvangerey talook, Chitaldroog district, 2 miles north of the cusbah. Old capital of a principality.——*Bhasmaungy* (ಭಸ್ಮಾಂಗಿ - bhasmángi, Can. ; bhasmangi, Mys. Gov.). Means shiva, the ash-besmeared. Fortified hill in Madgherry talook, Toomcore district, 26 miles north of Toomcore.——*Bileshwarbetta* (ಬಿಳೇಶ್ವರಬೆಟ್ಟ - biléshvarabetta, Can.). Means cave + lord + hill. Also called Agastya parvat. Hill near Hoomcha, in Nugger talook, Shimoga district, from which several streams spring, namely, the Coomadwaty, Cooshauvaty, Haridrauvaty, Sharmanauvaty.——*Biligherryrunganbetta* (ಬಿಳಿಗಿರಿರಂಗನಬೆಟ್ಟ - biligirirangana-betta, Can. ; biligirirenganbetta, Mys. Gov.). Means biligiriranga, the god + hill. Sanscrit name (shvétádri), meaning white + mountain. Mountain. Place of pilgrimage [balli-rungam].——*Boodicote* (ಬೂದಿಕೋಟೆ - būdikóte, Can.). Means ashes + fort. Village in Bowringpett talook, Colaur district. 8 miles south-west of the cusbah [q.v.], between the two branches of the Maurcanda near their point of junction. The birth place of Hyder ally.——*Boodihaul* (ಬೂದಿಹಾಳು - būdihálu, Can. budihal, Mys. Gov.). Means ashes + waste. Ruinous town, Chitaldroog district, 9 miles west-north-west of Hooliyaur. Formerly head-quarters of a talook.——*Bowringpett* (ಬಾರಿಂಗಪೇಟೆ - bauringapéte, Can. ; bowringpet or maramutlu, Mys. Gov.). Means mr. bowring, chief commissioner + suburb.—"*a*" Talook in the south-east, Colaur district. Head-quarters at Bowringpett. Contains the hoblies :—Baitmungalam, Boodicote, Cummasundra, Dausarhoshully, Hoolibeley, Kyasambully, Ramsaugar, Soolicoontey, Tayalore. Principal places :—Baitmungalam, Boodicote, Bowringpett, Ooriga, Tayalore.—"*b*" Town situated at the Colaur road station of the Bangalore branch railway. Includes the formerly existing villages of Marmatloo and Hosingerey, established in 1864, being named after Mr. Bowring, then Chief commissioner. Lies 10 miles south of Colaur. Head-quarters of the talook.——*Bramhagherry* (ಬ್ರಹ್ಮಗಿರಿ - bramhagiri, Can.). Means the deity + hill. Hill of the Nundidroog range, reputed source of the Arcauvaty, Colaur district. To the south-west of Nundidroog.——*Cadaba* (ಕಡಬ - kadaba, Can. ; kadaba, Mys. Gov.). Means the sage, cadamban. Sanscrit name (kadambapura), meaning cadamban, the sage + town. Town on right bank of the Shimsha, 18 miles south-west of Toomcore, formerly head-quarters of a talook, Toomcore district.——*Calaley* (ಕಳಲೆ - kalale, Can.). Means threshing floor + field. Hobly. Village in Nanjangode talook, Mysore district, 3 miles south-west of Nanjangode, close to the Mysore-Ootacamund road.——*Calasha* (ಕಲಶ - kalasha, Can.). Means a cupola. Village in Chikmagalore talook, Cuddore district, in 13° 14′ N. lat., 75° 26′ E. long., near the right bank of the Bhadra, 30 miles west-south-west of the cusbah [q.v.].——*Calavardroog* (ಕಳವರದುರ್ಗ - kalavaradurga, Can. ; kalavarabetta, Mys. Gov.). Means bustle + fort. Also called Scandagherry Hill-fort, Prominent height, Colaur district, 5 miles north of Nundidroog. Source of Paupughny.——*Cancanhully* (ಕಾನಕಾನಹಳ್ಳಿ - kánakánahalli, Can. ; kankanhalli, Mys. Gov.). Means (kánakána, proper name + village).—"*a*" Talook in the south, Bangalore district. Head-quarters at Cancanhully. Contains the hoblies :—Cancanhully, Codihully, Haurohully, Maralvaudy, Moodvaudy, Ooyambully, Somanhully, Toongauny. Principal places :—Aulhully, Cancanhully, Chikkamaralvaudy, Codihully, Haurohully, Hevandyavappanahully, Moolahully, Nalahully.—"*b*" Town on the right bank of the Arcauvaty in 12° 33′ N. lat., 77° 29′ E. long., 36 miles south of Bangalore, Bangalore-Malvully road. Talook head-quarters and municipality. Weekly fair Thursday.——*Cancooppa* (ಕಣಕುಪ್ಪ - kanakuppá, Can. ; kankuppa, Mys. Gov.). Means thrashing-floor + heap. Formerly cusbah [q.v.] of Jagalore talook.——*Cauvery* (ಕಾವೇರಿ - kávéri, Can.). River. See sep. title.——*Cavaledroog* (ಕವಲೇದುರ್ಗ - kavalédurga, Can. ; kavaledurga, Mys. Gov.). Means two + fort. Hill in the west of Cavaledroog talook, Shimoga district, 3,058 feet. Formerly gave name to a talook.——*Chámoondibetta* (ಚಾಮುಂಡಿಬೆಟ್ಟ - chámundibetta, Can. ; chamundibetta, Mys. Gov.). Means the deity + hill. Mountain, Place of pilgrimage. Mysore district, two miles south-east of the fort of Mysore, 3,489 feet above the level of the sea.——*Chaumrajnugger* (ಚಾಮರಾಜನಗರ - chámarájanagara, Can. ; chamrajnagar, Mys. Gov.). Means (chámarája, proper name + city).—"*a*" Talook in the south-east, Mysore district. Head-quarters, Chaumrajnugger. Contains the hoblies :—Aulore, Bedarpore, Caugalvaudy, Chaumrajnugger, Cottalvaudy, Dausanore, Devanore, Hardanhully, Honganore; Oommatore, Ooyambully, Santemarahully, Sarwamaunya kittore. Principal places :—Aulore, Bangaly, Bendravaudy, Caugalvaudy, Caurya, Chaumrajnugger, Choondacavaudy, Coodair, Coodlore, Cottalvaudy, Devanore, Haravey, Hardanhully, Honganore, Jotigondanapooram, Mungalam, Naugavully, Oodigaula, Oommatore, Ramasamoodram, Sargore, Sarwamaunya kittore, Saugerey, Somahully, Tagdore, Tamadhully, Vataloo.—"*b*" Town, Mysore district, in 11° 55′ N. lat., 77° E. long., 36 miles south-east of Mysore, on the Hassanore ghaut road. Talook head-quarters and municipality.——*Chellakerey* (ಚೆಳ್ಳಕೆರೆ - chellakere, Can.). Means tree, cordia latifolia + tank.—"*a*" Talook in the north-east, Chitaldroog district, head-quarters at Chellakerey. Contains the hoblies :—Chellakerey, Doddairy, Jaujore, Naickanhutty, Parshoorampore. Principal places :—Bomaghatta, Chellakerey, Conasaugaram, Devasamoodram, Doddairy, Ghataparty, Jaupore.—"*b*" Town. Head-quarters of the Chellakerey talook, Chitaldroog district, in 14° 18′ N. lat., 76° 43′ E. long., on the Bangalore-Bellary road, 18 miles east-north-east of Chitaldroog and municipality.——*Chenna-*

gherry (ಚೆನ್ನಗಿರಿ - chennagiri, Can.; channagiri, Mys. Gov.). Means beautiful + hill.—"*a*" Talook in the east, Shimoga district. Head-quarters, Chennagherry. Contains the hoblies:—Baswaputna, Chennagherry, Nullore, Santebennore. Principal places:—Baswaputna, Chennagherry, Coolamby, Devarhully, Hodigerey, Nullore, Santebennore, Tyauvanigey, Vadanahaul.—"*b*" Town, Shimoga district, 14° 1′ N. lat., 75° 59′ E. long., 25 miles north-east of Shimoga on the Benkipore-Chitaldroog road. Talook head-quarters and municipality.——*Chennakesharabetta* (ಚೆನ್ನಕೇಶವಬೆಟ್ಟ - channakéshavabetta, Can.; channakeshavanbetta, Mys. Gov.). Means (chennakéshava, god + hill). Hill and source of the northern and southern Pennair, 5 miles west of Chikbullapore, Colaur district.——*Chennaputnam* (ಚೆನ್ನಪಟ್ಟ - channapatna, Can.; channapatna, Mys. Gov.). Means beautiful + town. Town in the Closepett talook, Bangalore district, in 12° 38′ N. lat., 77° 13′ E. long., 37 miles south-west of Bangalore, on the Bangalore-Seringapatam road; till 1873 head-quarters of a talook, of the same name. The industrial portion is called Shoocravaurapett, Friday bazaar.——*Chennároyandroog* (ಚೆನ್ನರಾಯನದುರ್ಗ - channaráyanadurga, Can.; channaraydurga, Mys. Gov.). Means (channaráya, proper name + fort). Deserted hill fort in Madgherry talook, Toomcore district, midway between Cortagherry and Madgherry. Formerly head-quarters of a talook.——*Chenroyputna* (ಚೆನ್ನರಾಯಪಟ್ಟ - channaráyapatna, Can.; channaraypatna, Mys. Gov.). Means (channaráya, proper name + town).—"*a*" Talook in the north-east, Hassan district. Head-quarters, Chenroyputna. Contains the hoblies:—Anaty, Annekerey, Baugore, Chenroyputna, Didaga, Hireysauvey, Nooggihully, Shravanabelgola, Yerganahaul. Principal places:—Baugore, Chenroyputna, Hireysauvey, Nooggihully, Shravanabelgola.—"*b*" Town, Hassan district, in 12° 54′ N. lat., 76° 26′ E. long., 20 miles east of Hassan, on the Bangalore-Hassan road. Talook head-quarters and municipality.——*Chikbullapore* (ಚಿಕ್ಕಬಳ್ಳಾಪುರ - chikkaballápura, Can.; chikballapur, Mys. Gov.). Means (small + ballápura, place so called).—"*a*" Talook in the west, Colaur district. Head-quarters at Chikbullapore. Contains the hoblies:—Auvaty, Chikbullapore, Manchanabeley, Munchenahully, Nundy, Pereysundra, Poornasaugaram. Principal places:—Auvaty, Chikbullapore, Manchana beley, Munchenahully, Nundy, Shaumpore.—"*b*" Town, Colaur district, 36 miles north-west of Colaur, on the old Bangalore-Bellary road. Talook head-quarters and municipality. Founded about 1479 by Mulla beira gowda.——*Chikkanaickenhully* (ಚಿಕ್ಕನಾಯಕನಹಳ್ಳಿ - chikkanáyakanahalli, Can.; chiknayakanhalli, Mys. Gov.). Means (chikkanáyaka, proper name + village).—"*a*" Talook in the west, Toomcoor district. Head-quarters, Chikkanaickenhully. Contains the hoblies:—Chikkanaickenhully, Dandinashivara, Haugalvaudy, Kibbanhully, Nittore. Principal places:—Agálagutta, Chikkanaickenhully, Haugalvaudy, Kotey, Nittore, Settikerey.—"*b*" Town, Toomcore district, in 13° 25′ N. lat., 76° 41′ E. long., 40 miles west-north-west of Toomcore. Talook head-quarters and municipality. Prosperous town surrounded by cocoanut [q.v.] and areca [q.v.] palm plantations. Their produce together with coarse cotton cloths locally manufactured are largely sold at the weekly fair.——*Chikmagalore* (ಚಿಕ್ಕಮಗಳೂರು - chikkamagalúru, Can.; chikmagalur, Mys. Gov.). Means younger + daughter + village.—"*a*" Talook in the centre, Cuddore district. Head-quarters, Chikmagalore. Contains the hoblies:—Cadagullnaud, Calása, Chikmagalore, Lakya, Maurley, Melbangaudy, Sakroyputna, Vastaura. Principal places:—Ambaley, Auldore, Baswanhully, Calasapooram, Chikmagalore, Chikkanhully, Coorvangy, Coovey, Devaroypett, Hireymagalore, Hullicaura, Indavaura, Malalore, Matavara, Maurley, Mauvinkerey, Moogalvully, Sakroyputnam, Talihully, Vastaura.—"*b*" Town, Municipality and head-quarters of the Cuddore district in 13° 18′ N. lat., 75° 51′ E. long., on the Hassan-Shimoga road, 130 miles west-north-west of Bangalore. Weekly fair is held here on Wednesday.——*Chintaumanipett* (ಚಿಂತಾಮಣಿಪೇಟೆ - chintámanipéte, Can.; chintamani, Mys. Gov.). Means (chintámaniráya, proper name + suburb). Town in the Chintaumany talook, Colaur district, 25 miles north-north-west of Colaur, on the Shreenivasapore-Chikbullapore road. Head-quarters of the talook of the same name.——*Chintaumany* (ಚಿಂತಾಮಣಿ - chintámani, Can.). Means (chintámaniráya, proper name). Talook in the north-east, Colaur district. Head-quarters, Chintaumany. Contains the hoblies:—Adagull, Chintaumany, Dalsanore, Moorgamullay, Nelavanky, Numbihully, Ronore, Royalpaud, Shreenivasapore, Somayaujoolapully, Yeladore. Principal places:—Chintaumany, Digavacote, Moorgamullay, Shreenivasapore, Yeladore.——*Chitaldroog* (ಚಿತ್ರದುರ್ಗ - chitradurga, Can.; chitaldroog, Mys. Gov.). Means picturesque + fort.—"*a*" District sub-divided into the following seven talooks:—Chellakerey, Chitaldroog, Dauvangerey, Hiriyore, Holalkerey, Jagalore, Molacaulmooroo.—"*b*" Talook in the centre and west, Chitaldroog district. Head-quarters at Chitaldroog. Contains the hoblies:—Bheemasamoodram, Chitaldroog, Chitrahully, Kyausapooram, Shiddavvanhully, Taulya, Toorvanore. Principal places:—Bailgutt, Chikkanaickenhully, Chitaldroog, Coonabaiv, Dyamappanhully, Hayicull, Jauncondа, Jempalnaickenpaulya, Kelakotey, Nunnivala, Shiddavvanhully, Sonore, Taulya, Toorvanore.—"*c*" Chief town of Chitaldroog district in 14° 14′ N. lat., 76° 27′ E. long., on the Bangalore-Harihar road, 126 miles north-west of Bangalore. Once garrisoned by British troops but given up for unhealthiness.——*Chitrauvaty* (ಚಿತ್ರಾವತಿ - chitrávati, Can.). Means picturesque. River. Affluent of the N. pinaukiny, Colaur district. Affluent of the Toongabudra, Shimoga district. Runs into the Toongabudra at Moodanore.——*Chundrabetta* (ಚಂದ್ರಬೆಟ್ಟ - chandrabetta, Can.). Means moon + hill. Mountain in Shravanabelgola village, Hassan district with numerous Jeina temples. At the summit of Indrabetta close by 3,250 feet above the level of the sea, is the colossal statue of Gomateshwaran, 60 feet high and surrounded with numerous sacred buildings [betta].——*Chundragootty* (ಚಂದ್ರಗುತ್ತಿ - chandragutti, Can.; chandragutti, Mys. Gov.). Means moon + cover.—"*a*" Mountain, Place of pilgrimage. In Soraba talook, Shimoga district. Formerly fortified 2,836 feet.—"*b*" Village at the foot of the hill. Former residence of one of the Cadamba [q.v.] kings of Banavausy.——*Closepett* (ಕುಲೀಸ್ಪೇಟೆ - kulíspéte, Can.). See sep. title.——*Colaur* (ಕೋಲಾರ - kólára, Can.; kolar, Mys. Gov.). Means (kóláhala, shouting).—"*a*" District. Is sub-divided into the following talooks:—Bowringpett, Baughepully, Chikbullapore, Chintaumany, Colaur, Goribidnore, Maulore, Moolbaugal, Shidlaghaut.—"*b*" Talook in the centre towards the south, Colaur district, head-quarters, Colaur. Contains the hoblies:—Colaur, Coorbore, Haraty, Holore, Hoottore, Moodavaudy, Soogatore, Vakkalairy, Vemagull. Principal places:—Colaur, Devaroysundra, Vakkalairy.—"*c*" Chief town of the Colaur district in 13° 6′ N. lat., and 78° 7′ E. long., 43 miles east-north-east of Bangalore by road, but connected with it by rail. The tomb of Hyder ally's father is one of the principal buildings.——*Colaurbetta* (ಕೋಲಾರಬೆಟ್ಟ - kólárabetta, Can.; kolarbetta or shatashringaparvata, Mys. Gov.). Means shouting + hill. Hills. Also bear the name of Shatashringa parvat, hundred peaked hills. Colaur district. Extends along the north-west of the town Colaur; highest point 4,026 feet.——*Coongull* (ಕುಣಿಗಲ್ಲು - kunigallu, Can.; kunigal, Mys. Gov.). Means dancing + stone.—"*a*" Talook in the south-east, Toomcore district. Head-quarters, Coongull. Contains the hoblies:—Amritore, Bedarhully, Coongull, Coppa, Cottagerey, Hooliyoordroog, Hootry droog, Yediyore. Principal places:—Amritore, Cauvooley, Coongal, Hooliyoordroog, Oojjayiny.—"*b*" Town, Toomcore district, in 13° 2′ N. lat., 77° 5′ E. long., 22 miles south of Toomcore, on the Bangalore-Hassan road. Talook head-quarters and municipality.——*Coppa* (ಕೊಪ್ಪ - koppa, Can.; koppa, Mys. Gov.). Means a suburb.—"*a*" Talook in the north-west, Cuddore district. Head-quarters, Hariharpore. Contains the hoblies:—Baggoonjy, Belarey, Coppa, Hoskerey, Kigga, Megoonda, Shringairy. Principal place:—Shringairy.—"*b*" Mountain.—"*c*" Town.——*Cortagherry* (ಕೊರಟಗಿರಿ - koratagiri, Can.; koratagere, Mys. Gov.). Means robber + hill. Town, Toomcore district, on the left bank of the Swarnamookhy, in 13° 31′ N. lat., 77° 17′ E. long., 16 miles north of Toomcore, on the Toomcore-Madgherry road. Lately a talook head-quarters.——*Cubbinadagoodda* (ಕಬ್ಬಿಣದಗುಡ್ಡ - kabbinadagudda, Can.). Means iron + hill. Mountain in Teertahully talook. Shimoga district. Iron stone of a superior quality obtained here; the iron [anhan] made from which is considered to be as good as steel [wootz].——*Cuddore* (ಕಡೂರು - kadúru, Can.; kadur, Mys. Gov.). Means (kadave, elk + village).—"*a*" District in the west of Mysore. Sub-divided into the following talooks:—Chikmagalore, Coppa, Cuddore, Moodgerey, Tarikerey.—"*b*" Town in Cuddore talook, Cuddore district, 15 miles north-west of the cusbah [q.v.], on the Bangalore-Shimoga road. Municipality.——*Cullhully* (ಕಲ್ಲಹಳ್ಳಿ - kallahalli, Can.; kalhalli, Mys. Gov.). Means rock village. Place of pilgrimage. Village in Nanjangode talook, Mysore district.——*Cullhuttygherry* (ಕಲ್ಲುಹತ್ತಿಗಿರಿ - kalluhattigiri, Can.). Means stone + climb + hill. Mountain. One of the heights of the Bababooden range in the Cuddore district, 6,155 feet.——*Dauvangerey* (ದಾವಣಗೆರೆ - dávanagere, Can.; dauvangerey, Mys. Gov.). Means purifying + tank.—"*a*" Talook in the north-west, Chitaldroog district. Head-quarters at Dauvangerey. Contains the hoblies:—Anagode, Anajy, Bharmasaugar, Condajjy, Dauvangerey, Hadady, Harihar, Malebennore, Mayacondah. Principal places:—Anajy, Aulore, Baulvaly, Bettore, Codaganore, Coonchenhully, Dauvangerey, Hadady, Harihar, Melebennore, Mayacondah, Narsanhully, Sirgery.—"*b*" Seat of trade; Chitaldroog distrct, 14° 28′ N. lat., 75° 59′ E. long., 40 miles north-west of Chitaldroog. Talook head-quarters and municipality.——*Devanhully* (ದೇವಂದಹಳ್ಳಿ - dévandahalli, Can.; devanhalli, Mys. Gov.). Means (déva, the headman + village).—"*a*" Talook in the north-east, Bangalore district. Head-quarters at Devanhully. Contains the hoblies:—Boodigerey, Calaley, Chenroyputna, Coondauna, Devanhully, Jangamcote, Jaula, Vadagenhully. Principal places:—Bettahalsore, Boodigerey, Devanhully, Kyaulnore, Vadagenhully.—"*b*" Town and place of pilgrimage in 13° 15′ N. lat., 77° 44′ E. long., 23 miles north of Bangalore on the old Banglore-Bellary road. Talook head-quarters and municipality. Weekly fair.——*Devaroydroog* (ದೇವರಾಯದುರ್ಗ - déváráyadurga, Can.; devarayadurga, Mys. Gov.). Means (dévaraya, proper name + fort). Hill-fort, Place of pilgrimage. Toomcore district, 9 miles east of Toomcore.——*Dodbullapore* (ದೊಡ್ಡಬಳ್ಳಾಪುರ - doddaballápura, Can.; dodballapur, Mys. Gov.). Means (large + ballápurá, place so called).—"*a*" Talook in the north-west, Bangalore district. Head-quarters at Dodbullapore. Contains the hoblies:—Caucole, Codihully, Dodbullapore, Honnavaura, Hoolicoontey, Rajghatta, Tippore, Toobgerey. Principal places:—

Dodbullapore, Toobgerey.—"*b*" Town on the right bank of the Arcauvaty, situated 13° 18′ N. lat., 77° 26′ E. long., 27 miles north-west of Bangalore. Talook head-quarters and municipality. Weekly fair. Cotton cloths in great variety made here.——*Doddairy* (ದೊಡ್ಡೇರಿ - doddéri, Can.; doderi, Mys. Gov.). Means large + tank. Lately cusbah of Chellakerey talook.——*French rocks* (ಹಿರೋಡೆ - hiróde, Can.). See Hirode.——*Goobby* (ಗುಬ್ಬಿ - gubbi, Can.; gubbi, Mys. Gov.). Means sparrow.—"*a*" Talook in the south, Toomcore district. Head-quarters Goobby. Contains the hoblies :—Cadaba, Chitnahully, Culloor, Dabbegatt, Goobby, Hebbore, Mayasundra, Toorvekerey. Principal places :—Cadaba, Chitnahully, Goobby, Hebbore, Toorvekerey.—"*b*" Trading place, Place of pilgrimage in 12° 19′ N. lat., 77° E. long., 13 miles west of Toomcore, on the Bangalore-Shimoga road. Head-quarters of Goobby talook, Toomcore district.——*Goodibundey* (ಗುಡಿಬಂಡೆ - gudibande, Can.; gudibanda, Mys. Gov.). Means temple + rock. Town, Colaur district, in Nundidroog range, 55 miles north-west of Colaur. Lately a talook head-quarters. Municipality.——*Goomma naicken pollicm* (ಗುಮ್ಮನಾಯಕನಪಾಳ್ಯ - gummanáyakanapálya, Can.; gumnayakanpalya, Mys. Gov.). Means (gummanáyaka, proper name + camp). Village in talook of the same name, Colaur district, and formerly the head-quarters. Ten miles east of Baugepully.——*Goondloopett* (ಗುಂಡ್ಲುಪೇಟೆ - gundlupéte, Can.; gundlupet, Mys. Gov.). Means (gundalu, river so called + suburb).—"*a*" Talook in the south, Mysore district. Head-quarters, Goondloopett. Contains the hoblies :—Cootanore, Goondloo, Hangala, Kelasore, Raghavapooram, Tircanaumby. Principal places :—Coteykerey, Cubbahully, Devanagarapett, Hangala, Horiyala, Kelasore, Padagore, Tircanaumby, Vijayapooram.—"*b*" Town, Mysore district, in 11° 49′ N. lat., 76° 45′ E. long., near the left bank of the Goondal river, 36 miles south of Mysore, on the Mysore-Ootacamund road. Talook head-quarters, municipality.——*Goribidnore* (ಗೋರಿಬಿದನೂರು - góribidanúru, Can.; goribidnur, Mys. Gov.).—"*a*" Talook in the north-west, Colaur district. Head-quarters, Goribidnore. Contains the hoblies :—Bommasundra, Goribidnore, Hosoor, Tondebhauvy, Varavany. Principal places:—Bommasundra, Goribidnore, Gungasundra, Hosoor, Moodgerey, Tondebhauvy, Varavany.—"*b*" Town, Colaur district, on the left bank of the North pinaukiny, 56 miles north-west of Colaur, on the Dodbullapore-Hindoopore road. Stated to have been in ancient times the residence of Vidooran, an uncle of the Pandavas. Talook head-quarters and municipality.——*Gowrihulla* (ಗೌರಿಹಳ್ಳ - gaurihalla, Can.). Means deity + pool. River rising near Moolainagherry, flows eastward and is embanked at a gorge near Shaknigherry, expanding into the Ayyankerey lake, the stream on leaving which takes the name of the Vedah.——*Gungamoola* (ಗಂಗಮೂಲ - gangamúla, Can.; gangamula, Mys. Gov.). Means ganges + source. Mountain in the Varauha parvata, Western ghauts and source of the Toonga and Bhadra. Cuddore district, in 13° 15′ N. lat., 75° 14′ E. long.——*Halsore* (ಹಲಸೂರು - halasúru, Can.). Means jack-tree + village. Otherwise Ulsoor [q.v.].—"*a*" Town. One of the suburbs of Bangalore, north-east of the cantonment, close to the large tank of the same name. Contains two temples, one unfinished, and is a prosperous village.—"*b*" Hobly in Bangalore district.——*Harihar* (ಹರಿಹರ - harihara, Can.; harihar, Mys. Gov.). Means the deity. Ancient town, Place of pilgrimage, Chitaldroog district, in 14° 31′ N. lat., 75° 51′ E. long., on the Mysore and Dharwar frontier. Till 1875 head-quarters of a talook of the same name.——*Hassan* (ಹಾಸನ - hásana, Can.; hassan, Mys. Gov.). Means (hasanamma, smiling goddess).—"*a*" District, sub-divided into seven talooks as follows :—Arkalgode, Arsikerey, Bailore, Chenroyputna, Hassan, Manjarabad, Narsapore.—"*b*" Talook towards the centre, Hassan district. Head-quarters, Hassan. Contains the hoblies :—Attavar, Aulore, Canaghaul, Chikkanagaul, Cowshica, Graumam, Hassan, Honnavaura, Maudihully, Paulya, Sauligamey. Principal places :—Graumam, Handanakerey, Hassan.—"*c*" Chief town of the Hassan district in 13° N. lat., 76° 9′ E. long., 114 miles west of Bangalore.——*Hauranhully* (ಹಾರನಹಳ್ಳಿ - háranahalli, Can.; harnhalli, Mys. Gov.). Means shiva + village. Town, Hassan district, in 13° 15′ N. lat., 76° 17′ E. long., 19 miles north of Hassan, on the Hassan-Arsikerey road. Lately a talook head-quarters. Municipality. Contains ruined temples and monuments.——*Heggadadevancote* (ಹೆಗ್ಗಡದೇವನಕೋಟೆ - heggadadévanakóte, Can.; heggaddevankote, Mys. Gov.). Means (heggadadéva, proper name + fort).—"*a*" Talook in the south-west, Mysore district. Head-quarters, Sargore. Contains the hoblies:—Antarsantey, Heggadadevancote, Jinahully, Nemmanhully, Sargore. Principal places :—Beltore, Bidagal, Hebbelcooppey, Heggadadevancote, Malaly, Nerley, Sargore.—"*b*." Formerly chief town of the talook, Mysore district, 36 miles south-west of Mysore, on the Sargore-Hoonsoor road.——*Hireymagalore* (ಹಿರೇಮಗಳೂರು - hiremagalúru, Can.). Means eldest + daughter + village. Village, Cuddore district, 1 mile south-east of Chikmagalore.——*Hiriyore* (ಹಿರಿಯೂರು - hiriyúrn, Can.; hiriyur, Mys. Gov.). Means great + town.—"*a*" Talook in the south-east, Chitaldroog district. Head-quarters at Hiriyore. Contains the hoblies :—Dharmapooram, Eimungalam, Hiriyore, Javangondanhully, Muttode. Principal places :—Barampooram, Dharmapooram, Eimungalam, Harty, Hiriyore, Maradibully, Muttode, Tavanandy.—"*b*" Town, Place of pilgrimage, Chitaldroog district, in 13° 57′ N. lat., 76° 40′ E. long., on the right bank of the Vedavaty. Talook head-quarters and municipality. Ancient temples.——*Hiróde* (ಹಿರೋಡೆ - hiróde, Can.). See sep. title.——*Holalkerey* (ಹೊಳಲ್ಕೆರೆ - holalakere, Can.). Means bright + tank. Talook in the south-west, Chitaldroog district. Head-quarters at Holalkerey. Contains the hoblies :—Baugore, Bharmanaickendroog, Holalkerey, Hosdroog, Jaunacull, Ramgherry. Principal places :—Baugore, Holalkerey, Hosdroog, Jaunacull, Ramgherry.——*Holey narsapore* (ಹೊಳೆನರಸಾಪುರ - holenarasápura, Can.). Means (bright + narasimba náyaka + town).—"*a*" Talook in the south, Hassan district. Head-quarters, Holey narsapore. Contains the hoblies :—Gunny, Maudapoor, Mauvinkerey, Narsapore, Nidoovany. Principal place :—Holey narsapore.—"*b*" Town, Hassan district, on the right bank of the Hemauvaty, in 12° 47′ N. lat., 76° 18′ E. long., 21 miles south-east of Hassan, on the Mysore-Hassan road. Talook head-quarters and municipality. Cloth of good quality made here.——*Honnauly* (ಹೊನ್ನಾಳಿ - honnáli, Can.; honnali, Mys. Gov.). Means gold + village. Sanscrit name (bháskarakshétra), meaning shiva, the resplendent + sacred place.—"*a*" Talook in the north-east, Shimoga district. Head-quarters, Honnauly. Contains the hoblies :—Belgootty, Coomshy, Honnauly, Sasiveyhully. Principal places :—Belgootty, Coomshy, Coonagalgutty, Hauranhully, Honnauly, Nyaumty.—"*b*" Town, Shimoga district, in 14° 15′ N. lat., 75° 42′ E. long., on the left bank of the Toongabudra, 24 miles north of Shimoga, on the Shimoga-Harihar road.——*Honvully* (ಹೊನ್ನವಳ್ಳಿ - honnavalli, Can.; honnavalli, Mys. Gov.). Means (honnamma, deity + village). Town on the Gandashy-Hiriyore road, in Tiptore talook, Toomcore district, 8 miles to the north-east of Tiptore. Lately a talook cusbah.——*Hoonsoor* (ಹುಣಸೂರು - hunasúru, Can.). Means tamarind + village. Talook in the north-west, Mysore district. Head-quarters, Hoonsoor. Contains the hoblies :—Bettadpore, Bilikerey, Chilcoonda, Cuggoondy, Gauvadagerey, Hauranhully, Heggandore, Kirajaujy, Periyaputna, Rauvandore. Principal places :—Bettadpore, Bilikerey, Bunnoocooppey, Chammaroyencote, Cottavully, Cullacoonikey, Gauvadagerey, Dodda hoonsoor, Kampelaupooram, Kittore, Malalvaudy, Mancode, Periyaputna, Pyantagraumam.——*Hoottaridroog* (ಹುತ್ತರಿದುರ್ಗ - huttaridurga, Can.; hutridurga, Mys. Gov.). Means (uttara, north + fort). Fortified hill in Coongal talook, Toomcore district. The fort was taken by Lord Cornwallis in 1792.——*Hoscote* (ಹೊಸಕೋಟೆ - hosakóte, Can.; hoskote, Mys. Gov.). Means new fort, hoscote, new fort, to distinguish it from colaur.—"*a*" Talook in the east, Bangalore district. Head-quarters at Hoscote. Contains the hoblies :—Caudgoody, Goobby, Hoscote, Hoollore, Moogalore, Nandagoody, Soolibeley, Vangata. Principal places :—Hoscote, Soolibeley.—"*b*" Town on the left bank of the S. pinaukiny in 13° 4′ N. lat., 77° 48′ E. long., 18 miles east-north-east of Bangalore on the Bangalore-Colaur road. Talook head-quarters and municipality. Place of pilgrimage.——*Hosdroog* (ಹೊಸದುರ್ಗ - hosadurga, Can.; hosdurga, Mys. Gov.). Means new fort. Town, Chitaldroog district, in 13° 48′ N. lat., 76° 21′ E. long., 30 miles south by west of Chitaldroog. Lately a talook cusbah [q.v.].——*Jagalore* (ಜಗಳೂರು - jagalúru, Can.). Means duel + village. Talook in the north-west, Chitaldroog district. Head-quarters at Jagalore. Contains the hoblies :—Bilchode, Jagalore, Sokkey. Principal places :—Anagode, Baswancote, Bidarkerey, Bilchode, Jagalore, Sokkey.——*Jayamungaly* (ಜಯಮಂಗಳಿ - jayamangali, Can.). Means victor + prosperity. River. Affluent of the North pinaukiny, Toomcore district.——*Keidala* (ಕೈದಳ - kaidala, Can.). Means hand + restoration. Sanscrit name (krídápura), meaning sport + town. Village, Toomcore district, 3 miles south of Toomcore, appears to have been formerly the capital of a state, also reported to be the native place of Jakanacharry, the sculptor, to whom is attributed all the finest temple-carving in the province, as at Halabeed, Bailore, &c.——*Kengairy* (ಕೆಂಗೇರಿ - kengéri, Can.; kengeri, Mys. Gov.). Means south + street. Kengairy or Tengairy, southern street. Town in Bangalore talook, Bangalore district, 9 miles south-west of Bangalore, on the Bangalore-Seringapatam road. Municipality. Once the head-quarters of a talook of the same name.——*Lakvully* (ಲಕ್ಕುವಳ್ಳಿ - lakkuvalli, Can.; lakvalli, Mys. Gov.). Means plant, vitex negundo + village. Town, Tarikerey talook, Cuddore district.——*Madgherry* (ಮಧುಗಿರಿ - madhugiri, Can.; maddagiri, Mys. Gov.). Means honey + hill.—"*a*" Talook in the north-east, Toomcore district, Head-quarters, Madgherry. Contains the hoblies :—Chennaroyandroog, Codigenhully, Cortagherry, Doddairy, Holoovanhully, Humpasundra, Madgherry, Midgaishy, Pooravaram, Raptavalal, Taridal, Teriyore, Totlagerey, Yitagadibbanhully. Principal places :—Bramhasundra, Byaula, Cadagattore, Codigenhully, Coordy, Cortagherry, Doddairy, Haroody, Holoovanhully, Madgherry, Midgaishy, Paulgoonda, Rampore, Sheetacull, Taroor, Totlagerey, Yedagore, Yitagadibbanhully.—"*b*" Town, Toomcore district, in 13° 39′ N. lat., 77° 16′ E. long., 24 miles north of Toomcore, on the Toomcore-Panvoogada road. Talook head-quarters and municipality. Two large temples. Extensive trade in brass [pittalay], copper [taumram] and silver [velly] vessels.—"*c*" Hill.——*Mailcote* (ಮೇಲುಕೋಟೆ - mélukóte, Can.). Means superior + fort. Sanscrit name (yádavagiri), meaning vishnoo + hill, also (náráyanagiri), meaning vishnoo + hill. Celebrated sacred town in Seringapatam talook, Mysore district, in 12° 40′ N. lat., 76° 43′ E. long., 12 miles north of the cusbah [q.v.], built on the rocky hills named Yadoogiry overlooking the Motitalaub and Cauvery valley towards Seringapatam.——*Malvully* (ಮಳವಳ್ಳಿ - malavalli, Can.; malvalli, Mys. Gov.). Means hill + village.—"*a*"

Talook in the east, Mysore district. Head-quarters, Malvully. Contains the hoblies :—Codambully, Coolagerey, Cubbaula, Doddarshinkerey, Gaudagerey, Kiragauval, Malvully. Principal places :—Arsinkerey, Halgore, Kiragauval, Malvully.—" *b* " Town, Mysore district, in 12° 23′ N. lat., 77° 7′ E. long., 28 miles east of Mysore, at the intersection of the Mysore-Cancanhully and Muddore-Shivasamoodram roads. Talook head-quarters and municipality.——*Mandya* (ಮಂಡ್ಯ - mandya, Can. ; Mys. Gov.). Sanscrit name (vishnupura), meaning vishnoo + town.—" *a* " Talook in the north-east, Mysore district. Head-quarters, Mandya. Contains the hoblies :—Aney, Autcore, Basaraul, Coodargoondy, Cottatty, Doodda, Mandya, Muddore, Moottegerey, Tippore, Yeleyore. Principal places :—Besagarhully, Boodanore, Goottal, Holalore, Honnalgerey, Kelsagerey, Keregode, Mandya, Muddore, Sautnore, Tippore, Yelchaukanhully.—" *b* " Town, Mysore district, in 12° 32′ N. lat., 76° 57′ E. long., 25 miles north-east of Mysore, on the Bangalore-Seringapatam road. Talook head-quarters and municipality.——*Manjarabad* (ಮಂಜರಾಬಾದ್ - manjarábád, Can. ; manjarabad, Mys. Gov.). Means fog + abode.—" *a* " Talook in the west, Hassan district. Head-quarters, Sakleshpore. Contains the hoblies :—Banacull, Bauloo, Beikerey, Belgode, Bellore, Bisley, Hettore, Manjarabad, Ooggihully, Yesalore. Principal place :—Sakleshpore.—" *b* " Town in Manjarabad talook, Hassan district.—" *c* " Hill pass. ——*Maugady* (ಮಾಗಡಿ - mágadi, Can. ; magadi, Mys. Gov.). Means the jasmine plant.—" *a* " Talook in the west, Bangalore district. Head-quarters at Maugady. Contains the hoblies :—Bidady, Coodoor, Goodeyamauranhully, Hoolicull, Maudabal, Maugady, Narasundra, Sautanore, Solore, Tauvarkerey, Tipsundra. Principal places :—Bidady, Cuddore, Goodeyamauranhully, Hoolicull, Maugady, Motagondahully, Solore, Taulya, Tauvarkerey, Tipsundra, Tirmullay.—" *b* " Town in 12° 57′ N. lat., 77° 17′ E. long., 28 miles west of Bangalore. Talook head-quarters and municipality.——*Maulore* (ಮಾಲೂರು - málúru, Can. ; malur, Mys. Gov.). Means village forest + village. Sanscrit name (mallikápura), meaning jasmine plant + town.—" *a* " Talook in the south-west, Colaur district. Head-quarters, Maulore. Contains the hoblies :—Coodyanore, Hooladenhully, Lakkore, Maulore, Mausty, Narsapore, Tyaucull. Principal places :—Lakkore, Maulore, Mausty, Narsapore.—" *b* " Town, Railway station, Colaur district, 18 miles south-west of Colaur, on the Bangalore branch railway. Talook head-quarters and municipality. ——*Molcaulmooroo* (ಮೊಳಕಾಲ್ಮೂರು - molakálmuru, Can.). Means knee + fracture. Talook of Chitaldroog district. Head-quarters at Molcaulmooroo. Contains hoblies :—Devasamoodram, Gowrasamoodram, Molcaulmooroo, Siddhapooram. Principal places :—Devasamoodram, Molcaulmooroo, Rampore, Siddhapooram.——*Moolainagherry* (ಮುಲ್ಲೈನಗಿರಿ - mulainagiri, Can.). See sep. title. ——*Moolbaugal* (ಮುಳಬಾಗಲು - mulabágalu, Can. ; mulbagal, Mys. Gov.). Means (múdla, east + gate).—" *a* " Talook in the east, Colaur district. Head-quarters, Moolbaugal. Contains the hoblies :—Auvany, Beiracore, Dooggasundra, Moolbaugal, Mullinaickenhully, Nangly, Oottanore. Principal places :—Agara, Moolbaugal, Nangly.—" *b* " Eastern gate. Town, Colaur district, 18 miles east-north-east of Colaur, on the old Bangalore-Madras road by the Mogily pass. Talook head-quarters and municipality. Old temples and tomb of Mahomedan saint.—" *c* " Hill.——*Muddore* (ಮದ್ದೂರು - maddúru, Can. ; maddur, Mys. Gov.). Means tree, terminalia arjuna, bedd. + village. Sanscrit name (arjunapura), meaning arjoonan, the hero + town. Town, Mandya talook, Mysore district, on the Shimsha, 36 miles north-east of Mysore on the Bangalore-Seringapatam road. Once the head-quarters of a talook of the same name. ——*Muttode* (ಮತ್ತೋಡು - mattódu, Can.). Village in Hiriyore talook, Chitaldroog district, 20 miles south-west of the cusbah [q.v.]; celebrated for glass [cunnaudy] works. Seat of a line of poligars [q.v.].——*Naicknairy* (ನಾಯಿಕನೇರಿ - náyikanéri, Can.). Means naick + street. Hill-pass on the east of Colaur district leading to the plains of the Carnatic [q.v.].——*Nanjangode* (ನಂಜನಗೂಡು - nanjanagúdu, Can. ; nanjangúd, Mys. Gov.). Means (nanjundéshvara, shiva the poison devouring lord + abode). Sanscrit name (garalapura), meaning poison + town.—" *a* " Talook in the centre southwards, Mysore district. Head-quarters, Nanjangode. Contains the hoblies :—Badangooppey, Calaley, Hadanaur, Hedataley, Hoora, Nanjangode. Principal places :—Badanavaul, Calaley, Coodlapooram, Hadanaur, Haginavaul, Haleypooram, Hedataley, Hemargaula, Hoollahully, Nanjangode, Nirley, Toombanirley.—" *b* " Town, Mysore district, 12° 7′ N. lat., 76° 45′ E. long., on right bank of the Cubbany, 12 miles south of Mysore, at the point where the trunk road from Mysore branches to Ootacamund and to the Hassanore ghaut [q.v.]. Talook head-quarters and municipality. Large temple and place of pilgrimage.——*Naugamungala* (ನಾಗಮಂಗಲ - nágamangala, Can. ; nagamangala, Mys. Gov.). Means serpent + village.—" *a* " Talook in the north, Mysore district. Head-quarters, Naugamungala. Contains the hoblies :—Bellore, Bheemanhully, Bindiginavaley, Manhully, Naugamungala, Naugatihully, Yeldahully. Principal places :—Bellore, Canagonahully, Naugamungala.—" *b* " Town, Mysore district, in 12° 49′ N. lat., 76° 49′ E. long., on the Seringapatam–Sheerah road, 61 miles south-east of Hassan. Talook head-quarters and municipality. Remains of fine temples and royal buildings.——*Nelamungala* (ನೆಲಮಂಗಲ - nelamangala, Can. ; Mys. Gov.). Means ground + village.—" *a* " Talook in the west, Bangalore district. Head-quarters at Nelamungala. Contains the hoblies :—Begore, Dodbeley, Melnahully, Nelamungala, Nijagull, Sondacoppa, Tyaumgondloo. Principal places :—Dodbeley, Hesarghatt, Nelamungala, Sondacoppa, Tyaumgondloo.—" *b* " Town in 13° 6′ N. lat., 77° 27′ E. long., 17 miles north-west of Bangalore on the Bangalore-Toomcore road. Talook head-quarters and municipality. Weekly fair.——*Nirgoonda* (ನಿರಗುಂದ - niragunda, Can.). Village. Sanscrit name (nílávatípattana), meaning neelauvaty's city. Village in Hosdroog talook, Chitaldroog district, 7 miles west of the cusbah [q.v.]. Ancient city. Capital of a Jeina principality.——*Noogoo* (ನೂಗು - núgu, Can.). Means foam. River. Also called the Bhrigoo, affluent of the Cubbany, Mysore district. Joining it near the village of Humpapore on the Mysore-Manantoddy road.——*Nugger* (ನಗರ - nagara, Can. ; nagar, Mys. Gov.). Means city.—" *a* " Talook in the south-west, Shimoga district. Head-quarters, Colloorcuttay. Contains the hoblies :—Haritala, Hoomcha, Jaula, Kerahully, Mavinahole, Nugger, Patgooppey. Principal place :—Nugger.—" *b* " Town, Shimoga district, 13° 50′ N. lat., 75° 6′ E. long., on the Anantapoora-Hyderghur road. Head-quarters of the talook.——*Nyaumty* (ನ್ಯಾಮತಿ - nyámati, Can. ; nyamati, Mys. Gov.). Town in 14° 9′ N. lat., 75° 38′ E. long., on the Honnavully-Einore road. Shimoga district. ——*Paulhully* (ಪಾಲಹಳ್ಳಿ - pálahalli, Can. ; palhalli, Mys. Gov.). Means milk + village. Town, Mysore district, the right bank of the Cauvery, 7 miles north of Mysore and 3 miles west of Seringapatam on the Seringapatam-Mercara road.——*Pauvoogada* (ಪಾವುಗಡ - pávugada, Can. ; pavugada, Mys. Gov.). Means snake + hill.—" *a* " Talook, in the north-east, Toomcore district. Head-quarters at Pauvoogada. Contains the hoblies :—Goomguttey, Hoscote, Moogdaulbetta, Nidgull, Pauvoogada, Ponnasamoodram, Raucharloo. Principal places :—Aralikerey, Byaudanore, Goomguttey, Hoscote, Palavully, Pauvoogada, Raucharloo, Ryauvatey, Syatacaunacherloo, Vencataupooram, Vullore.—" *b* " Town, Toomcore district, in 14° 6′ N. lat., 77° 21′ E. long., 60 miles east of Chitaldroog. Talook head-quarters and municipality.—" *c* " Mountain, 3,026 feet.——*Periyaputna* (ಪೆರಿಯಾಪಟ್ಣ - periyápatna, Can. ; periyapatna, Mys. Gov.). Means (periyavodeya, proper name + town). Town, Mysore district, in 12° 21′ N. lat., 76° 9′ E. long., on the Mysore-Mercara road, 13 miles west by north of Hoonsoor. Formerly head-quarters of a talook. According to tradition was visited in the mythological ages by Agastyan.——*Rahmanghur* (ರಹಿಮಾನಘಡಿ - rahimánaghadi, Can.). See sep. title.——*Ramagherry* (ರಾಮಗಿರಿ - rámagiri, Can.). Means (ráma the god + hill). Hill fort on the left bank of the Arcauvaty, in the Closepett talook, Bangalore district ; formerly gave its name to the talook.——*Sakleshpore* (ಸಕಲೇಶಪುರ - sakaléshapura, Can.). Means (sakaléshvara, shiva + town). Town, on the right bank of the Hemauvaty, in 12° 57′ N. lat., 75° 51′ E. long., 23 miles west of Hassan, on the Bangalore-Mangalore road. Head-quarters of the Manjarabad talook, Hassan district.——*Sargore* (ಸರಗೂರು - saragúru, Can. ; saragur, Mys. Gov.). Means merchandise + village. Town, Mysore district, in 12° N. lat., 76° 28′ E. long., on right bank of the Cubbany, 36 miles south-west of Mysore. Head-quarters of Heggadadevancote talook and municipality.——*Sarjapore* (ಸರ್ಜಾಪುರ - sarjápura, Can. ; sarjapur, Mys. Gov.). Means (sarója, san. tank-born, lotus + pura, san. town). Town in the Aunecull talook, Bangalore district, 12 miles north-east of the cusbah [q.v.]. Till 1873 head-quarters of a talook of the same name.——*Saugar* (ಸಾಗರ - ságara, Can.). Means ocean.—" *a* " Talook in the west, Shimoga district. Head-quarters, Saugar. Contains the hoblies :—Anantapoora, Baurangy, Ikkairy, Saugar, Talgooppey. Principal places :—Kelady, Saugar.—" *b* " Town, Shimoga district, on the left bank of the Varada near its source, in 14° 10′ N. lat., 75° 5′ E. long., 40 miles west-north-west of Shimoga, on the Shimoga-Gersoppah road. Talook head-quarters and municipality. One of the chief depôts for the areca nut [q.v.] trade.——*Sauvandroog* (ಸಾವನದುರ್ಗ - sávanadurga, Can. ; savandurga, Mys. Gov.). Means death + fort. Hill fort. In the Maugady talook, Bangalore district, 7 miles south-east of the cusbah [q.v.], 4,024 feet.——*Seringapatam* (ಶ್ರೀರಂಗಪಟ್ಟ - shrírangapatna, Can.). Means (holy + vishnu + town). Talook in the north, Mysore district. Head-quarters at Seringapatam. Contains the hoblies :—Arakerey, Baivinhully, Balgoola, Bannore, Chundagaul, Coora, Haravoo, Kirangore, Kyautanhully, Paulhully, Shatthully, Trimalsaugar. Principal places :—Arakerey, Balgoola, Bannore, Culloocoony, Gaumanahully, Haurohully, Hirode, Kirangore, Mahadevapooram, Nagonahully, Ookkada, Paulhully, Seringapatam [q.v.].——*Sharmanauvaty* (ಶರ್ಮನಾವತಿ - sharmanávati, Can. ; sarmanavati, Mys. Gov.). Means pleasure + possessing. River springs from the Bileshwarbetta in Nugger talook, Shimoga district, and flows into the Haridrauvaty.——*Sheerah* (ಶಿರಾ - shirá, Can.). Means head.—" *a* " Talook in the north-west, Toomcore district, transferred from the Chitaldroog to the Toomcore district in 1866. Head-quarters, Sheerah. Contains the hoblies :—Agrahauram, Bargore, Baunagerey, Bookkaputnam, Cullamballa, Nandore, Sheerah. Principal places :—Bookkaputnam, Chengavaur, Chirtahully, Cullamballa, Halenhully, Hanjanaul, Madalore, Mailcoontey, Maugode, Naudore, Sheerah, Yaldabaugey.—" *b* " Town, Toomcore district, in 13° 44′ N. lat., 76° 58′ E. long., 33 miles north-north-west of Toomcore, on the Toomcore-Chitaldroog road. Talook head-quarters and municipality. Contains a fort, well built of stone, surrounded with a moat and a fine glacis,

——*Shiby* (ಶಿಬಿ - shibi, Can.; shibi, Mys. Gov.). Means a king so called. Village, Place of pilgrimage. In Sheerah talook, Toomcore district, 15 miles north of Toomcore, on the Toomcore-Chitaldroog road. Temple of Narsimhan, annual festival in Maugham [mausam] or february.——*Shidlaghatt* (ಶಿಡ್ಲಘಟ್ಟ - shidlughatta, Can.; sidlagatta, Mys. Gov.). Means ruined + defile.—"*a*" Talook in the centre towards the north, Colaur district. Head-quarters, Shidlaghatt. Contains the hoblies:—Bashtihully, Bhaktarbully, Chilcullnerpoo, Corlapurty, Gunjigoontey, Iragampully, Keivaura, Mullore, Moonganahully, Sandaly, Shidlaghatt. Principal places:—Booradagoontey, Chilcullnerpoo, Keivaura, Malemauchanahully, Saudaly, Shidlaghatt, Yegavacote.—"*b*" Town, Colaur district, 30 miles north-west of Colaur, on the Shreenivasapore-Chikbullapore road. Talook head-quarters and municipality.——*Shikarpore* (ಶಿಕಾರಿಪುರ - shikáripura, Can.; shikarpur, Mys. Gov.). Means hunter + town.—"*a*" Talook in the north, Shimoga district. Head quarters, Shikarpore. Contains the hoblies:—Bellandore, Hosoor, Moogalgerey, Oodagany, Shikarpore, Taulagoonda.—"*b*" Town, Shimoga district, near the right bank of the Chorady or Coomadvaty, in 14° 16′ N. lat., 75° 25′ E. long., on the Honnauly-Soraba road, 28 miles north-west of Shimoga. Talook head-quarters, and municipality.——*Shimoga* (ಶಿವಮೊಗ್ಗ - shivamoggá, Can.; shimoga, Mys. Gov.). Means sweet + dish or shiva's face.—"*a*" District in the north-west, sub-divided into eight talooks:—Teertahully, Chennagherry, Honnauly, Nugger, Saugar, Shikarpore, Shimoga, Soraba.—"*b*" Talook in the south, Shimoga district. Head-quarters, Shimoga. Contains the hoblies:—Benkipore, Bidarey, Holalore, Holey, Honnore, Shimoga. Principal places:—Benkipore, Coppa, Holalore, Holey, Honnore, Moottore, Nadkerey, Shimoga.—"*c*" Chief town of the Shimoga district, situated in 13° 55′ N. lat., 75° 38′ E. long., on the left bank of the Toonga, 171 miles north-west of Bangalore, on the Bangalore-Gersoppah road.——*Shimsha* (ಶಿಂಶಾ - shimshá, Can.; shamsha, Mys. Gov.). Means (shimshapa tree, dalbergia sissoo). River. Sanscrit name (kadamba), meaning cadamban, the sage who lived on its banks. Also called Shimshoopa, Cadabacola, Cadaba or Cadamba [q.v.], Mysore and Toomcore districts, tributary of the Cauvery, enters the Cauvery a few miles below the Falls at Shivasamoodram. ——*Somauvaty* (ಸೋಮಾವತಿ - sómávati, Can.; somavati, Mys. Gov.). Means the moon plant + possessing. River. Tributary of the Hemauvaty, one of the chief tributaries of the Cauvery. ——*Somavauhiny* (ಸೋಮವಾಹಿನಿ - sómavâhini, Can.). Means the moon plant + river. River. Tributary of the Bhadra which it joins in Lakvully talook. Cuddore district.——*Soraba* (ಸೊರಬ - soraba, Can.; sorab, Mys. Gov.). Means the mythological cow of plenty.—"*a*" Talook in the north-west, Shimoga district. Head-quarters, Soraba. Contains the hoblies:—Anavutty, Chundragootty, Kyasanore, Soraba, Tavanandy, Telaguddey. Principal places:—Coobatore, Cooppagady, Moody, Oodry, Soraba.—"*b*" Town, Shimoga district, on the right bank of the Dandauvaty, in 14° 23′ N. lat., 75° 10′ E. long., on the Shikarpore-Soraba road, 46 miles north-west of Shimoga. Talook head-quarters and municipality. Principal residence of the sandalwood [sandal] carvers, whose delicate and elaborate workmanship is generally well-known.——*Swarnamookhy* (ಸುವರ್ಣಮುಖಿ - suvarnamukhi, Can.). Means gold + mouth. River. Toomcore district, after a course of about 15 miles, runs into the Jayamungaly.——*Talacaud* (ತಲಕಾಡು - talakádu, Can.; talkad, Mys. Gov.). Means (tala + kádu, two hunters, so called), otherwise Dalavanapuram. Town, Mysore district, in 12° 11′ N. lat., 77° 5′ E. long., on the left bank of the Cauvery, 28 miles to the south-east of Mysore and 10 miles to the south-east of Narsapore. Lately a talook cusbah.——*Tarikerey* (ತರೀಕೆರೆ - tarîkere, Can.; tarikere, Mys. Gov.). Means tree, acacia catechu + tank.—"*a*" Talook in the north-east, Cuddore district. Head-quarters, Tarikerey. Contains the hoblies:—Ajimpoora, Amritapoora, Coodlore, Lingadhully, Oobrauny, Shivaney, Tarikerey. Principal places:—Ajimpoora, Coodlore, Dornaul, Lingadhully, Shivaney, Tarikerey, Tauvarkerey.—"*b*" Town, Cuddore district, in 13° 42′ N. lat., 75° 52′ E. long., on the Bangalore-Shimoga road, 30 miles north of Chikmagalore. Talook head-quarters and municipality.——*Teertahully* (ತೀರ್ಥಹಳ್ಳಿ - tírt'hahalli, Can.). Means sacred water + village.—"*a*" Talook in the south-west, Shimoga district. Head-quarters, Teertahully. Contains the hoblies:—Agoomby, Agrahauram, Auraga, Mandaguddey, Moottore. Principal place:—Teertahully.—"*b*" Town in 13° 41′ N. lat., 75° 17′ E. long., on the left bank of the Toonga, 30 miles south-west of Shimoga, on the Shimoga-Agoomby road. Head-quarters, Teertahully talook, Shimoga district.——*Tiptore* (ತಿಪಟೂರು - tipatúru, Can.; tiptur, Mys. Gov.). Means (tippe, hillock + village). Town, Place of pilgrimage.—"*a*" Talook in the west, Toomcore district. Head-quarters, Tiptore. Contains the hoblies:—Handlagerey, Haulacoorky, Honvully, Itchanore, Nonavinkerey, Tiptore. Principal places:—Aralgooppey, Handlagerey, Honvully, Nonavinkerey, Sauratahully, Tiptore.—"*b*" Trading place, in 13° 15′ N. lat., 76° 32′ E. long., 46 miles west of Toomcore, on the Toomcore-Shimoga road. Head-quarters of Tiptore talook, Toomcore district.——*Tirmacoodloo narsapore* (ತಿರುಮಕೂಡ್ಲು ನರಸಾಪುರ - tirumakúdlunarasápura, Can.).—"*a*" Talook in the east, Mysore district, Head-quarters, Narsapore. Contains the hoblies:—Moogore, Narsapore, Poorigauly, Rungasamoodram, Sosiley, Talacaud, Tayore. Principal places:—Algoonjy Belakvaudy, Benakanhully, Bilgull, Caliyore, Chidravully, Dodda abaugil, Gaunaganore, Hemmigey, Holesaul, Hosa alsore, Kempanapooram, Kerey hully, Kiragoonda, Moogore, Nilasoghey, Somnautpore, Sosiley, Talacaud, Tayore.—"*b*" Town in 12° 13′ N. lat., 76° 58′ E. long., at the confluence of the Cauvery and the Cubbany, 18 miles south-east of Mysore, on the Mysore-Talacaud road. Since 1868 head-quarters, Talacaud talook, Mysore district.——*Tirmullay* (ತಿರುಮಲೆ - tirumale, Can.; tirumale, Mys. Gov.). Means sacred + hill. Village, Place of pilgrimage, two miles east of Maugady in Maugady talook, Bangalore district.——*Toyarshy* (ತೊಗರ್ಷಿ - togarshi, Can. togarshi, Mys. Gov.). Means split pulse + heap. Village, Place of pilgrimage in Shikarpore talook, Shimoga district.——*Toomcore* (ತುಮಕೂರು - tumakúru, Can.; tumkur, Mys. Gov.). Means drum + village.—"*a*" District. Sub-divided into the following talooks:—Chikkanaickenhully, Coongull, Goobby, Madgherry, Pauvoogada, Sheerah, Tiptore, Toomcore.—"*b*" Talook in the centre eastwards, Toomcore district. Head-quarters, Toomcore. Contains the hoblies:—Bellauvy, Cheelore, Colala, Goolore, Honnoodikey, Kora, Oordoogerey, Toomcore, Tovinkerey. Principal places:—Bellauvy, Bidarey, Cheelore, Goolore, Honnoodikey, Kestore, Kyautasundra, Oordoogerey, Toomcore, Tovinkerey.—"*c*" Chief town, Toomcore district, in 13° 20′ N. lat., 77° 9′ E. long., 43 miles north-west of Bangalore.——*Varada* (ವರದ - varada, Can.; Mys. Gov.). Means boon + give. River. Tributary of the Toongabudra, Shimoga district. Rises at Varadamoola near Ikkairy, and running north past Chundragootty and Banavausy turns north-east.——*Vayooparvata* (ವಾಯುಪರ್ವತ - váyuparvata, Can.). Means wind + hill. Mountain. One of the Bababoodens 6,214 feet. Also called Bababoodengherry and Marootsheila.——*Vedah* (ವೇದಾ - védá, Can.). Means sacred writing. River. Its immediate source is the Gowrihulla, which is embanked at a gorge near Shaknigherry expanding into the Ayyankerey lake, the stream on leaving which takes the name of the Vedah. ——*Yedatorey* (ಎಡತೊರೆ - edatore, Can.; yedatore, Mys. Gov.). Means left + river.—"*a*" Talook in the north, Mysore district. Head-quarters, Yedatorey. Contains the hoblies:—Byaudarhully, Hallimysore, Hardanhully, Mirley, Shalagram, Tippore, Yedatorey. Principal places:—Ballore, Byaudarhully, Chundagaul, Cooppey, Haliyore, Hebbaul, Humpapore, Jeerya, Kestore, Mailore, Mirley, Moondore, Shalagram, Sigavully, Tippore, Yedatorey.—"*b*" Town, Mysore district, in 12° 28′ N. lat., 75° 27′ E. long., on the right bank of the Cauvery 24 miles north-west of Mysore. Talook head-quarters and municipality.——*Yelandore* (ಎಳಂದೂರು - elandúru, Can.; yelandur, Mys. Gov.). Means (elache, jujube tree + village).—"*a*" Talook in the south-east, forming the estate of a Jagheerdar, Mysore district. Head-quarters, Yelandore. Contains the hoblies:—Agara, Muddore, Yelandore, Yereyore, Yergampully. Principal places:—Agara, Ambaley, Honnore, Kestore, Muddore, Yelandore, Yereyore, Yergampully.—"*b*" Town in 12° 3′ N. lat., 77° 5′ E. long., on the Honnholey. Cusbah of the Yelandore jagheer, Mysore district. Prosperous town. Contains temple and inscription.——*Yennëholey* (ಎಣ್ಣೆಹೊಳೆ - ennehole, Can.; yennehole, Mys. Gov.). Means oil + river. River. Tributary of the Sharauvaty which it joins near Baurangy in Saugar talook, Shimoga district.——*Yettinhulla* (ಎತ್ತಿನಹಳ್ಳ - ettinahalla, Can.). Means ox + pit. River in Manjarabad talook, Hassan district.——**(2)** The southernmost portion of Mysore and of the former Ashtagram division. Sub-divisions consist of eleven talooks and one jagheer:—Ashtagram, Chaumrajnugger, Goondloopett, Heggadadevancote, Hoonsoor, Malvully, Mandya, Mysore, Nanjangode, Tirmacoodloo narsapore, Yedatorey, Yelandore jagheer.——**(3)** Talook towards the centre, Mysore district. Head-quarters, Mysore. Contains the hoblies:—Anandore, Coodloohully, Lingamboodhy, Mysore, Navashahar, Sindhoovully, Vaurcode, Yilvaula, Principal places:—Ayravutty, Bhandipaulya, Cadacola, Degore, Dhanagahully, Mysore, Oodabore, Rampore, Sindhoovully, Vajamungalam, Vaurcode, Yedacola, Yilvaula.——**(4)** Capital of the province and residence of the Maharajah; situated in 12° 18′ N. lat. and 76° 42′ E. long, at the north-western base of the Chamoondy hill, Mysore district. Contains three suburbs and covers an area of about 3 square miles.——**(5)** *Mysore thorn* (चिलार - chilára, Mahr.; حیدرکا جہاڑ - haídarkájhár, Hind. and Dec.; ಕುರುಡುಗಜ್ಜಿಗಗಿಡ - kurudugajjigagida, Can.; புலித்தடுக்கி - pulittadukki, Tam.). Hind. from (haidar, hind. ruler + jhár, hind. tree); planted by hyder in defence of his forts. Can. from (kurudu, can. black + gajjigagida, can. cæsalpinia bonducella, flem.); from color of seeds which are oblong, smooth and dark and variegated, of the size of a large pea [calauyam]. Tam. from (puli, tam. tiger + tadukku, tam. to obstruct); from prickles said to obstruct passage of tiger. Mahr. also (chilhári). Hind. also (chillur). Can. also (hotsige). Tam. also (pulittodakki), by corruption. Title otherwise Bahama braziletto, Bahama sappan, Black bonduc, Hyder's tree, Tiger stopper. Botanically Cæsalpinia [coobairaucshy] sepiaria, roxb., leguminosæ [vricsham, 48]. Alias Reichardia decapetala. Scandent shrub with powerful thorns and small-leaved foliage; branches and petioles armed with short, strong, sharp, recurved prickles; pinnæ of the leaves six to ten pair; leaflets eight to twelve pair, linear-oblong, obtuse; petioles pubescent; stipules broad, semi-sagittate; racemes axillary, solitary; calyx colored, the segments soon reflexed;

legumes linear-oblong, glabrous, with a long cuspidate point, four to eight-seeded; flowers bright-sulphur; flowering nearly all the year; indigenous to mysore, but now generally diffused. When kept closely clipped, forms impenetrable hedges [vaily].

N (न - na, *San.*; ن - nún, *Hind.*; நா - ná, *Tam.*). San. means booddha [q.v.] and ganesh [q.v.]. Hind. symbol for numeral 50; conjunct aspect of stars [nacshatram, noojoom].

NA (न - na, *San.*). Not.——*Nagaram* (नगर - nagara, San.; نگر - nagar, Hind.). From (above + gam, san. to go); a fixed habitation. Large city, especially ancient and fortified. Once applied by pre-eminence to Ahmednugger in the north and Vijianugger in the south. Compare Putnam. Suffix in place names, especially in Bellary and the northern districts; as Poothoonagaram, meaning new + city [graumam, nugger]. Specially used of the seven [saptam] sacred cities which confer eternal happiness:—Avanticay or Oojjein, Ayodhyay, Canjy, Caushy, Dwarca, Matooray, Maya. Caushy is Benares; Maya is Gayay; Canjy is Conjeeveram in this presidency. Gandharvanagarams are Cloud castles.——*Nagary* (नगरी - nagarí, San.; نگری - nagarí, Hind.; నగరి - nagari, Tel.).—"*a*" Small city. Suffix in place names; as Alwar tirnagary, meaning alwar + holy + city [nugger]. Nagary nilam is unassessed cultivable land, so called in contradistinction to Putcut nilam, or land in private puttahs [q.v.].—"*b*" Sanscrit name (kushast'halí), means wild tract of coosham [q.v.] grass. Village, Range of hills, Railway station, River; North arcot dist., Carvetnugger zemindarry, Narrainavaram division; pop. 3,196; lat. 13° 20′; long. 79° 38′; height 397 feet; from Arcot N.E. 33 miles; from Carvetnugger S.E. 12 miles; from Chittore E.N.E. 34 miles; from Narrainavaram S. 8 miles; from Poottore S.S.E. 8 miles. Village is on the Cooshastaly, 5 miles south of Nagary nose. One and-a-half miles N.E. of Railway station. Once a large city. Busy trading place. Fair on Fridays. The range forms the extreme S.E. spur of Eastern ghauts [q.v.]. It runs N. from Carvetnugger along eastern side of Swarnamookhy as far as Calastry. Geological formation is similar to that of Table mountain at the Cape of Good hope, near which coal [nila kary] and diamond [vajram] conglomerates have been found. Among the hills are caves which, by means of rough stone walls, have been turned into habitable chambers. Braminical tradition ascribes the work to the five Pandavas [q.v.]. The conas [q.v.] are wooded and stocked with game.——*Nagary nose* (ముక్కుకొండ - mukkukonda, Tel.). From (mukku, tel. nose + konda, tel. mountain). Hill; North arcot dist., Carvetnugger zemindarry, Narrainavaram division; lat. 13° 23′; long. 79° 38′; height 2,824; from Carvetnugger E.S.E. 10 miles; from Chittore E.N.E. 36 miles; from Narrainavaram S. 3 miles. Highest peak in Nagary hills. Forms the summit of a small range, which rises gradually from the east and then terminates in a sheer precipice about 200 feet high, up to the base of which the ground from the west rises. Landmark for ships from N. ports. 50 miles from coast, but first piece of land sighted. Vigneshwaran [q.v.] temple on the summit. On each full moon [powrnimay] night a bonfire is kindled at the top, and early in January the local idols [vigraham] make their circuit of the hill. Trig. station in Narrainavaram division; lat. 13° 22′ 47·88″; long. 79° 38′ 14·26″; from Narrainavaram S. 3 miles; from Poottore S.E. 5 miles.——*Nagry* (नागरी - nágarí, San.). From (nagara, san. a town). Sanscrit character. Otherwise Devanagry, or the divine city character. With more or less of modification is used also for the Hindee, Bengalee, Mahratta, and other Aryan [q.v.] derived languages. See vol. I (48).——*Naregamia* (നാരകം - nárakam, Mal.). Title from malayalam. Generic term [shrub orange].——*Naustican* (नास्तिक - nástika, San.). From (above + asti, san. exists); non-existence. An atheist. As Chaurvaucan [q.v.], &c. Bowddhans [booddha] are thus designated, or any one who denies the divine authority of the Vedams [q.v.], or doubts the legends of the Pooraunams [q.v.].——*Nugger* (नगर - nagara, San.; نگر - nagar, Hind.). Town [nagaram].

NABEE (نبی - nabí, *Ar.*). Way. Lacab of the prophet [mahomed]. Common alam; as Nabee khan, alam + alaumat [ism].

NACODAH (ناخدا - nákhudá, *Hind.*). From (náu, pers. ship + khudá, pers. master). Captain of a ship [serang, tindal].

NACSHATRAM (नक्षत्र - nakshatra, *San.*; نچھتر - nachhattar, *Hind.*). From (naksh, san. to ascend).——**(1)** A star in general. The fixed sidereal year [maunam], month [mausam], and day [dinam], are called Nacshatra samvatsaram, N. mausam, and N. dinam respectively.—"*a*" The following abstract with glossary terms bracketed will enable a comparison to be made of the European and native systems [siddhauntam] of astronomy [golayantram, jyotisham]. Terrestrial longitude [deshauntaram] is measured on the equator [niracsham], terrestrial latitude [acsham] on the meridian [raikhay] of a place; as is also co-latitude [lambam], the elevation [oonnatam] of the equator [niracsham] equal to the co-latitude [lambam], and the elevation [oonnatam] of the pole [dhroovam] equal to the latitude [acsham]. Right ascension [lagnam] and the hour angle [nata naudicay] are measured on the equinoctial [nandy mundalam]; declination [craunty], and polar distance or co-declination [crauntycoty], on circles of declination or the celestial meridians [raikhay]. Altitude [avanataumsham], and zenith distance [nataumsham] are measured on vertical circles [drik mundalam]; the amplitude [agram] and azimuth [agracoty] of a celestial body, on the horizon [cshitijam]. The meridian altitude [oordhwaavanataumsham] and the meridian zenith distance [oordhwanataumsham] are measured on the celestial meridian [raikhay] of the place. The angles at the pole [dhroovam] are hour angles [nata naudicay]; and the angles at the zenith [oordhwam, ootcham] are azimuth [agracoty] angles. In celestial latitude [vicshaipam] and longitude [dhroovacam, sauyanam] there is practically a difference between the two systems. In European astronomy use is made of great circles [mundalam] drawn perpendicular to the ecliptic [craunty mundalam] from the poles [dhroovam] thereof, called circles of celestial latitude; then the latitude of a celestial body is the arc of such a circle of celestial latitude intercepted between the object and the ecliptic; and the longitude of a celestial body is the arc of the ecliptic intercepted between the first Point of Aries [craunty pautam, maishauyanam] and the circle of celestial latitude passing through the object, being reckoned in the order of the signs [raushy]. In native practical astronomy the poles [dhroovam] of the ecliptic [craunty mundalam] are disregarded; then the vicshaipam [q.v.] or celestial latitude is an arc of the terrestrial meridian [raikhay] which intersects the star and the ecliptic [craunty mundalam]; and first the sauyanam [q.v.] or tropical [ayanaumsham, craunty pautagaty, maunam, mausam] celestial longitude is the portion of the ecliptic which is intersected by the same meridian and the equinoctial colure [craunty pautam, maishauyanamundalam]; while secondly the dhroovacam [q.v.] or fixed [ayanaumsham, maunam, mausam] celestial longitude is the same, substituting the origin [maunam, mausam, rishy raikhay, veidhrity] of the Hindoo sidereal zodiac [raushy chuckram] for the equinoctial colure [maishauyanamundalam, vishoomundalam]. There have been anciently real celestial latitudes and longitudes here, but they are now quite out of use [sauyanam].—"*b*" As regards nomenclature of the stars it has always been customary in the east to distinguish the brightest stars by proper names, as Aldebaran [q.v.], Rigel [q.v.], Fomalhaut [q.v.], &c.; and the position of any such star is referred to as being in some part of a constellation. Thus, Aldebaran, in the eye of the Bull [sowr]; Rigel, in the foot of Orion [jabbaur], &c. Europeans have adopted the plan of using small letters of Greek and Roman alphabets; α being generally or at least according to the original idea the brightest star, β the next, and so on; to which is added the name of the constellation in genitive case. Aldebaran becomes α Tauri, Rigel becomes β Orionis, &c. When Greek letters are exhausted, recourse is had to Roman, as a, b, c, &c. When Greek and Roman letters are exhausted, numerals are brought into use. Though the system is not always as rigorously observed as is here set out.—"*c*" The following are approximate mean places, with hours of rising [oodayam] and period of being above horizon [cshitijam] in lat. 13°, of the principal fixed stars for which native names are known, arranged according to their Right ascension [lagnam]. In the early part of any month given in columns 8–19, in the case of stars whose declination does not differ very largely from 13° N, if observing at 6 p. m. [sooryan], 6 hours stands roughly for being on the western horizon, 9 for being midway in the western arch of the heavens, 12 for culmination, 15 for being midway in the eastern arch of the heavens, and 18 for being on the eastern horizon. If observing at 7 p. m., add 1 to all the hour figures; if at 9 p. m., add 3; if at midnight, add 6; and so on. Taking the eye down the month column between those limits the stars in a very broad central belt can be traced from west to east. To suit the visible span of heavens north and south when observing in this latitude, plus declinations must be decreased by 13, and minus declinations must be increased by 13. The following 12 considerable stars culminate almost vertically in this latitude:—Aldebaran [q.v.], α Tauri; Algenib [q.v.], γ Pegasi; Arcturus [haursool samah], α Boötis; Denebola [q.v.], β Leonis; Markab [q.v.], α Pegasi; Nautih [q.v.], γ Tauri; Regulus [kalb ool asad], α Leonis; Roomhool simauk [q.v.], η Boötis; Rasalgethy [q.v.], α Herculis; Rasal hague [q.v.], α Ophiuchi; Shoobham [q.v.], α Delphini; Shoolam [q.v.], α Cancri. In the case even of stars whose period above the horizon differs much from 12 hours, such as Canopus [sooheil], α Argûs or Doobhe [q.v.], α Ursæ majoris, and these are few in the arabian or hindoo systems, the above calculations can first be suitably modified by consulting column 20, and then applied. If the points of the compass [tisay] are not known, a very rough N. and S. bearing can be taken from the Polar star [alrooccabah] α Ursæ minoris to the bottom of the southern cross the un-named α Crucis [trishunkoo], or to the conspicuous star α Centauri [hazaur], or to Achernar [q.v.] α Eridani, whichever of the last three is visible. By the manipulation of this table, and especially with the help of the cross-references shown in column 4, all main fixed stars appearing on a starry night can be traced and identified without a star map. Beyond 30° S. hindoos recognize only one star, Canopus; and its name Agastyan [q.v.] shows that it was a late discovery after bramins had reached S. india. The Arabian system recognizes Fomalhaut [q.v.], Canopus [sooheil], Achernar [q.v.] and α and β Centauri [hazaur, wazn]:—

Principal fixed stars for which native names are known.

No.	Arabic name. See section 8.	Sanscrit name. See section 8.	Scientific and popular european name. For cross-references see section 8.	Magnitude.	Approximate Right Ascension [lagnum], hours and minutes.	Approximate Declination [craunty], degrees and minutes, + is north, − is south.	Approximate time of rising [oodayam] in latitude 13°, hours and minutes of Madras mean time reckoning from midnight, on date Jan. 1.	Feb. 1.	Mar. 1.	Apr. 1.	May 1.	June 1.	July 1.	Aug. 1.	Sept. 1.	Oct. 1.	Nov. 1.	Dec. 1.	Approximate period during which it is above horizon [cshitijam], hours and minutes of mean time.	No.
							8	9	10	11	12	13	14	15	16	17	18	19	20	21
1	2	3	4	5	6	7														
1	Alpheratz ...	Rindram ...	α Andromedæ [miratimoosalsila].	2	0 3	+ 28 29	10 53	8 50	6 59	4 57	2 59	0 57	22 58	20 56	18 54	16 56	14 53	12 55	12 56	1
2	Algenib ...	Mahendram ...	γ Pegasi [faras ool azam].	3·0	0 8	+ 14 35	11 13	9 10	7 19	5 17	3 19	1 17	23 18	21 16	19 14	17 16	15 13	13 15	12 26	2
3	Deneb kyetos ...	......	β Ceti [kyetos] ...	2	0 38	− 18 35	12 15	10 12	8 21	6 19	4 21	2 19	0 20	22 18	20 16	18 18	16 15	14 17	11 23	3
4	Batn ool hoot ...	......	β Andromedæ [miratimoosalsila].	2·2	1 4	+ 35 3	11 45	9 42	7 52	5 49	3 51	1 49	23 50	21 48	19 46	17 48	15 45	13 47	13 14	4
5	......	Veidhrity ...	ζ Piscium [hoot] ...	5·4	1 7	+ 7 0	12 16	10 9	8 20	6 22	4 23	2 22	0 24	22 22	20 21	18 18	16 16	14 18	12 10	5
6	Al rooccabah ...	Dhroovam ...	α Ursæ minoris or Polaris [doobhe asghar].	2·2	1 19	+ 88 44	Circumpolar.													6
7	Achernar ...	......	α Eridani [nahr] ...	1	1 34	− 57 47	14 23	12 20	10 29	8 27	6 29	4 27	2 28	0 26	22 24	20 26	18 23	16 25	9 5	7
8	Batn kyetos ...	......	ζ Ceti [kyetos] ...	3·8	1 46	− 10 52	13 16	11 13	9 22	7 20	5 22	3 20	1 21	23 20	21 17	19 19	17 16	15 18	11 38	8
9	Shartein ...	......	β Arietis [hamel] ...	2·8	1 49	+ 20 16	12 49	10 46	8 55	6 53	4 55	2 53	0 54	22 52	20 50	18 52	16 49	14 51	12 36	9
10	Hamel ...	Vishcambham ...	α Arietis [hamel] ...	2	2 1	+ 22 57	12 58	10 55	9 4	7 2	5 4	3 2	1 3	23 1	20 59	19 1	16 58	15 0	12 42	10
11	......	Preety ...	35 Arietis [hamel] ...	5·0	2 37	+ 27 15	13 25	11 18	9 28	7 31	5 32	3 30	1 33	23 31	21 29	19 27	17 25	15 27	12 52	11
12	Algol ...	......	β Persei [haumili rausool ghowl].	Var 2·3 to 4	3 0	+ 40 32	13 33	11 30	9 39	7 37	5 39	3 37	1 38	23 36	21 34	19 36	17 33	15 35	13 30	12
13	Mirfak ...	......	α Persei [haumili rausool ghowl].	2	3 17	+ 49 28	13 33	11 30	9 40	7 37	5 39	3 37	1 38	23 36	21 34	19 36	17 33	15 35	14 4	13
14	......	Ayooshmat ...	η Tauri or Alcyone [sowr].	3	3 41	+ 23 46	14 37	12 34	10 43	8 41	6 43	4 41	2 42	0 40	22 38	20 40	18 37	16 39	12 44	14
15	Nautih ...	......	γ Tauri [sowr] ...	4	4 14	+ 15 22	15 18	13 15	11 24	9 22	7 24	5 22	3 23	1 21	23 18	21 21	19 18	17 20	12 26	15
16	Aldebaran ...	Sowbhaugyam ...	α Tauri [sowr] ...	1	4 30	+ 16 17	15 33	13 30	11 39	9 37	7 39	5 37	3 38	1 36	23 34	21 36	19 33	17 35	12 28	16
17	Oyook ...	Bramhahridayam	α Aurigæ or Capella [mausik oolinaun].	0·2	5 9	+ 45 53	15 32	13 29	11 38	9 36	7 38	5 36	3 37	1 35	23 33	21 35	19 32	17 34	13 28	17
18	Rigel ...	......	β Orionis [jabbaur] ...	0·3	5 9	− 8 20	16 34	14 31	12 40	10 38	8 40	6 38	4 39	2 37	0 35	22 37	20 34	18 36	11 44	18
19	Mirzam ...	......	γ Orionis or Bellatrix [jabbaur].	2	5 19	+ 6 14	16 29	14 26	12 35	10 33	8 35	6 33	4 34	2 32	0 30	22 32	20 29	18 31	12 10	19
20	Nath ...	Agny ...	β Tauri [sowr] ...	2	5 19	+ 28 31	16 8	14 5	12 14	10 13	8 14	6 12	4 13	2 11	0 8	22 11	20 8	18 10	12 56	20
21	Nitauk ool jowzah	......	ε Orionis [jabbaur] ...	1·8	5 31	− 1 16	16 50	14 47	12 56	10 54	8 56	6 54	4 55	2 53	0 51	22 53	20 50	18 52	11 56	21
22	Fakaur ool jowzah	......	ζ Orionis [jabbaur] ...	2	5 35	− 2 0	16 56	14 53	13 2	11 0	9 2	7 0	5 2	2 59	0 57	22 59	20 56	18 58	11 54	22
23	Betelgeux ...	Atigandam ...	α Orionis [jabbaur] ...	0·9 to 1·5	5 49	+ 7 23	17 1	14 58	13 8	11 5	9 7	7 5	5 6	3 4	1 2	23 4	21 0	19 3	12 11	23
24	......	Prajaupaty ...	δ Aurigæ [mausik ool inaun].	4·0	5 51	+ 54 17	15 48	13 46	11 52	9 54	7 56	5 54	3 56	1 55	23 53	21 50	19 49	17 51	14 32	24
25	Sooheil ...	Agastyan ...	α Argûs or Canopus [sufeenah].	1	6 22	− 52 38	18 56	16 53	15 2	13 0	11 2	9 0	7 1	4 59	2 57	0 59	22 56	20 58	9 30	25
26	Shira ...	Mrigavyaudham...	α Canis majoris or Sirius [kalbiacbar].	1·4	6 40	− 16 34	18 14	16 11	14 20	12 18	10 20	8 18	6 19	4 17	2 15	0 17	22 14	20 16	11 27	26
27	Ghoomeisah ...	......	α Canis minoris or Procyon [kalbiasghar].	1	7 34	+ 5 30	18 47	16 44	14 53	12 51	10 53	8 51	6 52	4 50	2 48	0 50	22 47	20 49	12 9	27
28	Alzirah ...	Soocarmam ...	β Geminorum or Pollux [jowzah].	1·1	7 39	+ 28 17	18 28	16 25	14 34	12 32	10 34	8 32	6 33	4 31	2 29	0 31	22 28	20 30	12 56	28
29	......	Dhrity ...	δ Cancri [sartaun] ...	4·5	8 39	+ 18 33	19 36	17 33	15 43	13 46	11 43	9 41	7 44	5 42	3 40	1 42	23 36	21 38	12 32	29
30	......	Shoolam ...	α Cancri [sartaun] ...	4·3	8 53	+ 12 16	19 56	17 53	16 3	14 6	12 7	10 1	8 4	6 2	4 0	1 58	23 56	21 58	12 20	30
31	Alphard ...	......	α Hydræ [shoojah] ...	2	9 22	− 8 11	20 47	18 44	16 53	14 51	12 53	10 51	8 52	6 50	4 48	2 50	0 47	22 49	11 44	31
32	Kalb ool asad ...	Gandam ...	α Leonis or Regulus [asad]	1·4	10 3	+ 12 30	21 9	19 6	17 15	15 13	13 15	11 13	9 14	7 12	5 10	3 12	1 9	23 11	12 21	32
33	Alkes ...	......	α Crateris [bautiya].	4	10 54	− 17 43	22 28	20 25	18 34	16 32	14 34	12 32	10 33	8 31	6 29	4 31	2 28	0 30	11 24	33
34	Alanak ...	......	β Ursæ majoris [doobheacbar].	2·6	10 55	+ 56 58	20 49	18 46	16 55	14 53	12 55	10 53	8 54	6 52	4 50	2 52	24 50	22 51	14 46	34

Principal fixed stars for which native names are known—continued.

No.	Arabic name. See section 8.	Sanscrit name. See section 8.	Scientific and popular european name. For cross-references see section 8.	Magnitude.	Approximate Right ascension [lagnam], hours and minutes.	Approximate Declination [craunty], degrees and minutes. + is north, — is south.	Approximate time of rising [oodayam] in latitude 13°, hours and minutes of Madras mean time reckoning from midnight, on date: Jan. 1.	Feb. 1.	Mar. 1.	Apr. 1.	May 1.	June 1.	July 1.	Aug. 1.	Sept. 1.	Oct. 1.	Nov. 1.	Dec. 1.	Approximate period during which it is above horizon [cshitijam], hours and minutes of mean time.	No.
1	2	3	4	5	6	7	8	9	10	11	12	13	14	15	16	17	18	19	20	21
35	Doobhe	......	α Ursæ majoris [doobhe acbar]	2	10 57	+ 62 20	20 34	18 31	16 40	14 38	12 40	10 38	8 39	6 37	4 35	2 37	0 34	22 36	15 28	35
36	Zoobra	Vriddhy	δ Leonis [asad]	2·3	11 8	+ 21 7	22 1	19 59	18 9	16 11	14 13	12 11	10 9	8 8	6 6	4 3	2 2	0 4	12 38	36
37	Denebola	Dhroovam ...	β Leonis [asad]	2·2	11 43	+ 15 11	22 46	20 43	18 52	16 50	14 52	12 50	10 51	8 49	6 47	4 49	2 46	0 48	12 26	37
38	Algoreb	......	α Corvi [ghooraub] ...	4·5	12 3	— 24 8	23 38	21 35	19 44	17 42	15 44	13 42	11 43	9 41	7 39	5 41	3 38	1 40	11 12	38
39	......	Vyaughautam ...	δ Corvi [ghooraub] ...	3·0	12 24	— 15 43	23 52	21 49	20 0	18 2	16 3	14 2	12 0	9 58	7 57	5 54	3 52	1 55	11 28	39
40	......	Aupas	δ Virginis [soomboola] ...	3·7	12 50	+ 3 59	0 7	22 4	20 13	18 11	16 10	14 11	12 12	10 10	8 8	6 10	4 7	2 9	12 6	40
41	Simauk ool azal ...	Harshanam ...	α Virginis or Spica [soomboola].	1·2	13 19	— 10 35	0 50	22 47	20 56	18 54	16 56	14 54	12 55	10 53	8 51	6 53	4 50	2 52	11 40	41
42	Benetnasch ...	......	η Ursæ majoris [doobhe acbar].	2	13 43	+ 49 51	0 0	21 57	20 6	18 4	16 6	14 4	12 5	10 3	8 1	6 3	4 0	2 2	14 8	42
43	Roomhool simauk.	......	η Boötis [awwah]	3	13 49	+ 18 57	0 52	22 49	20 58	18 56	16 58	14 56	12 57	10 55	8 53	6 55	4 52	2 54	12 34	43
44	Haurs ool samah...	Vajram	α Boötis or Arcturus [awwah].	1	14 11	+ 19 45	1 13	23 10	21 19	19 17	17 19	15 17	13 18	11 16	9 14	7 16	5 13	3 15	12 36	44
45	Ghafr	......	ε Boötis [awwah]	2·6	14 40	+ 27 32	1 33	23 30	21 39	19 37	17 39	15 37	13 38	11 36	9 34	7 36	5 33	3 35	12 54	45
46	Zubenesch ...	Siddhy	α Libræ [meezaun] ...	3·0	14 45	— 15 36	2 12	0 9	22 19	20 22	18 23	16 21	14 23	12 22	10 16	8 14	6 12	4 14	11 30	46
47	Kochab	......	β Ursæ minoris [doobhe asghar].	2	14 51	+ 74 36	22 18	20 15	18 24	16 22	14 24	12 22	10 23	8 21	6 19	4 21	2 18	0 20	19 36	47
48	Alphacca	......	α Coronæ Borealis [yikleeli shoomauly].	2	15 30	+ 27 5	2 25	0 22	22 31	20 29	18 31	16 29	14 30	12 28	10 26	8 28	6 25	4 27	12 50	48
49	Oonuk	......	α Serpentis [hooweiyah] ...	2·7	15 39	+ 6 46	2 54	0 51	23 0	20 58	19 0	16 58	14 59	12 57	10 55	8 57	6 54	4 56	12 10	49
50	......	Vyateepautam ...	δ Scorpii [akrab]	2·4	15 54	— 22 19	3 28	1 26	23 36	21 33	19 40	17 38	15 46	13 39	11 33	9 30	7 29	5 31	11 14	50
51	......	Parigham	ν Scorpii [akrab]	4·5	16 4	— 19 5	3 32	1 30	23 40	21 42	19 44	17 42	15 44	13 43	11 37	9 34	7 33	5 35	11 26	51
52	Alkalb	Vareeyas	α Scorpii or Antares [akrab].	1·1	16 23	— 26 11	4 9	2 6	0 15	22 13	20 15	18 13	16 14	14 12	12 10	10 12	8 9	6 11	11 6	52
53	Rauks	......	μ Draconis [tinneen] ...	5·2	17 3	+ 54 38	3 6	1 3	23 12	21 10	19 12	17 10	15 11	13 9	11 7	9 9	7 6	5 8	14 30	53
54	Rasalgethy ...	......	α Herculis [jausy]	3 to 4	17 10	+ 14 31	4 17	2 14	0 23	22 21	20 23	18 21	16 22	14 20	12 18	10 20	8 17	6 19	12 25	54
55	Ras al hague ...	......	α Ophiuchi [heiyah] ...	2·2	17 30	+ 12 38	4 39	2 36	0 45	22 43	20 45	18 43	16 44	14 42	12 40	10 42	8 39	6 41	12 21	55
56	Etenin	......	γ Draconis [tinneen] ...	2·3	17 54	+ 51 30	4 6	2 3	0 12	22 10	20 12	18 10	16 11	14 9	12 7	10 9	8 6	6 8	14 14	56
57	......	Shivam	δ Sagittarii [kows] ...	2·8	18 14	— 29 53	5 56	3 53	2 4	0 6	22 7	20 6	18 8	16 6	14 4	11 58	9 56	7 59	10 58	57
58	Nasr ool wauky ...	Abhijit	α Lyræ or Vega [shalyauk.	0·2	18 33	+ 38 41	5 15	3 12	1 21	23 19	21 21	19 19	17 20	15 18	13 16	11 18	9 15	7 17	13 24	58
59	......	Siddham	τ Sagittarii [kows] ...	3·6	19 0	— 27 53	6 40	4 37	2 47	0 50	22 51	20 49	18 52	16 50	14 48	12 46	10 40	8 42	11 2	59
60	Altair	Saudhyam ...	α Aquilæ [ookaub] ...	1·0	19 46	+ 8 35	6 57	4 54	3 3	1 1	23 3	21 1	19 2	17 0	14 58	13 0	10 57	8 59	12 14	60
61	......	Shoobham	α Delphini [doolfeen] ...	4	20 35	+ 15 32	7 41	5 38	3 47	1 45	23 47	21 45	19 46	17 44	15 42	13 44	11 41	9 43	12 27	61
62	Deneb	......	α Cygni [dajjajah]	1·5	20 38	+ 44 53	7 5	5 2	3 11	1 10	23 11	21 9	19 10	17 8	15 6	13 10	11 5	9 7	13 44	62
63	Fomal fars ...	......	ε Pegasi or Enif [faras ool azam].	2·3	21 39	+ 9 23	8 50	6 47	4 57	2 54	0 56	22 54	20 55	18 53	16 51	14 53	12 50	10 51	12 15	63
64	Denebalgedy ...	......	δ Capricorni [jaddy] ...	3	21 41	— 16 37	9 17	7 14	5 23	3 21	1 23	23 21	21 32	19 20	17 18	15 20	13 17	11 19	11 27	64
65	......	Shoobhram ...	λ Aquarii [dalo]	4	22 47	— 8 10	10 13	8 10	6 19	4 17	2 19	0 17	22 18	20 16	18 14	16 16	14 13	12 15	11 44	65
66	Fomalhaut ...	......	α Piscis australis [hoot i joonooby].	1·2	22 52	— 30 12	10 42	8 39	6 49	4 46	2 48	0 46	22 47	20 45	18 43	16 45	14 42	12 44	10 56	66
67	Mankib	......	β Pegasi or Scheat [faras ool azam].	2·0 to 2·5	22 58	+ 27 26	9 49	7 47	5 55	3 53	1 55	23 53	21 54	19 52	17 50	15 52	13 49	11 51	12 54	67
68	Markab	Bramham ...	α Pegasi [faras ool azam]...	2·6	22 59	+ 14 37	10 5	8 2	6 11	4 9	2 11	0 9	22 10	20 8	18 6	16 8	14 5	12 7	12 25	68

——(2) The following is the approximate time of the culmination [oordhwasancramanam] of the First point of Aries [maishauyanam], in hours and minutes of Madras mean time from midnight. The Right ascension [lagnam] of any fixed star, though not in above table, reduced to mean time added to these figures will give the hour of the culmination of the fixed star. Near the equator [niracsham]; subtracting 6 hours again from the latter figure, the time of the star's rising [oodayam] will be given; or adding 6 hours to the same figure the time of the star's setting will be given. For latitude 13° a star not in the equator rises one minute earlier for each degree of N. declination, and one minute later for each degree [bhaugam] of S. declination [craunty]:—

Month.	1st.		10th.		20th.	
January	17	13	16	37	15	57
February	15	11	14	36	13	56
March	13	21	12	45	12	6
April	11	19	10	43	10	4
May	9	20	8	46	8	6
June	7	19	6	44	6	4
July	5	21	4	45	4	6
August	3	19	2	44	2	5
September	1	17	0	42	0	3
October	23	15	22	40	22	0
November	21	14	20	38	19	59
December	19	16	18	40	18	1

——(3)—"a" The following stars are of the first magnitude, and the cross-references show those known to the natives. North, of the equator, 9:—α Aurigæ, capella, 46° n. [oyook]; α Lyræ, vega, 39° [nasr ool wauky]; β Geminorum, pollux, 28° [alzirah]; α Boötis, arcturus, 20° [haurs ool samah]; α Tauri, 16° [aldebaran]; α Leonis, regulus, 13° [kalb ool asad]; α Aquilæ, 9° [altair]; α Orionis, 7° [betelgeux]; α Canis minoris, procyon, 6° [ghoomeisah]. South of the equator, 10:—β Orionis, 8° s. [rigel]; α Virginis, spica, 10° [simauk ool azal]; α Canis majoris, sirius, 17° [shira]; α Scorpii, antares, 26° [alkalb]; α Piscis australis, 30° [fomalhaut]; α Argûs, canopus, 53° [sooheil]; α Eridani, 58° [achernar]; β Centauri, 60° [wazn]; α Centauri, 60° [hazaur]; α Crucis, 62°.—"b" The following stars are of second magnitude, with similar remark. North of the equator, 29:—α Ursæ minoris, polaris, 89° n. [al rooccabah]; β Ursæ minoris, 75° [kochab]; α Ursæ majoris, 62° [doobhe]; α Cassiopeæ, schedir, 56°; γ Ursæ majoris, megrez, 54°; γ Draconis, 52° [etenin]; η Ursæ majoris, 50° [benetnasch]; α Persei, 49° [mirfak]; β Aurigæ, 45°; α Cygni, deneb or aridad [q.v.], 45° [deneb]; β Persei, 40° [algol]; β Andromedæ, mirack, 35° [batn ool hoot]; α Geminorum, castor, 32°; ε Boötis, 28° [ghafr]; β Tauri, 28° [nath]; α Andromedæ, 28° [alpheratz]; β Pegasi, scheat, 27° [mankib]; α Coronæ borealis, gemma, 27° [alphacca]; α Arietis, 23° [hamel]; γ Leonis, 21° [algeiba]; δ Leonis, 21° [zoobra]; γ Geminorum, 17° [alhena]; β Leonis, 15° [denebola]; α Pegasi, 14° [markab]; α Ophiuchi, 13° [rasal hague]; ε Pegasi, enif, 9° [fomal fars]; α Serpentis, 7° [oonuk]; γ Orionis, bellatrix, 6° [mirzam]; α Ceti, menkar, 4° [menkar]. South of equator, 20:—δ Orionis [nazm], 0° s.; ε Orionis, 1° [nitauk ool jowzah]; α Hydræ, cor hydræ, 8° [alphard]; β Libræ, 9° [zubenelg]; α Libræ, 15° [zubenesch]; β Ceti, 19° [deneb kyetos]; β Scorpii, 19°; β Corvi, 23°; ε Canis majoris, 29°; α Columbæ, 34°; γ Argûs, 47°; α Gruis, 48°; γ Crucis, 56°; α Pavonis, 57°; ι Argûs, 59°; β Crucis, 59°; η Argûs, 59°; θ Argûs, 63°; β Argûs, 69°; α Trianguli australis, 69°.—"c" The following are of 3rd magnitude, with similar remark. North of equator, 37:—γ Cephei, 77° n. [al royee]; β Cephei, 70°; δ Ursæ majoris, phegda, 68°; α Draconis, 65° [thuban]; α Cephei, alderamin [q.v.], 62°; η Draconis, 62°; β Cassiopeæ, 58° [cuff ool khazeeb]; β Ursæ majoris, merak, 57° [alanak]; ε Ursæ majoris, 57° [alioth]; ζ Ursæ majoris, mirzar, 56°; β Draconis, rastaban, 52° [alwaida]; θ Ursæ majoris, 52°; ι Ursæ majoris, 49°; γ Andromedæ, alanak [q.v.], 42°; 12 Canum venaticorum, cor caroli, 39°; ι Aurigæ, 33°; β Lyræ, 33°; ζ Herculis, 32°; ζ Cygni, 30°; μ Herculis, 28°; ε Leonis, 24°; η Tauri, 24° [ayooshmat]; μ Geminorum, 23°; δ Geminorum, 22°; β Arietis, 20° [shartein]; η Boötis, 19° [roomhoolsimauk]; α Herculis, 15° [rasalgethy]; γ Pegasi, 14° [algenib]; ζ Aquilæ, 14°; γ Aquilæ, 10°; ζ Pegasi, 10°; κ Ophiuchi, 10°; ε Hydræ, 7°; δ Aquilæ, 3°; γ Ceti, 3°; ζ Virginis, 0°; η Virginis, 0°. South of equator, 13:—ε Virginis, vindemiatrix, 1° s.; α Aquarii, 1°; δ Ophiuchi, 3°; β Aquarii, 6°; θ Ceti, 9°; α Capricorni, 13°; δ Hydræ et crateris, 14°; γ Eridani, 14°; α Leporis, 18° [arsh ool jowzah]; ε Corvi, 22°; 15 Argûs, 24°; θ Ophiuchi, 25°; β Hydri, 78°.——(4) The following 9 fixed stars are those whose lunar distances are tabulated in English Nautical almanac, for finding Greenwich date, and thence longitude [dhroovacam, sauyanam]:— α tauri, aldebaran [q.v.]; α scorpii, antares [alkalb]; α aquilæ, altair [q.v.]; α arietis, hamel [q.v.]; α piscis australis, fomalhaut [q.v.]; α pegasi, markab [q.v.]; β geminorum, pollux [alzirah]; α leonis, regulus [kalb ool asad]; α virginis, spica [simauk ool azal].——(5) Secondly Nacshatram means generally a constellation. The following are the principal constellations for which native names are known arranged according to present european R.A. [lagnam], with their leading stars [yogam] and references; for tracing at night see last column and (1) "c" above:—

Constellations for which native names are known.

Arabic const., lun. mansion or sign. See sec. 8.	San. name, ditto. See sec. 8.	How made up on Eur. system. For cross-ref. see sec. 8.	Scientific, &c., name of principal star [yogam], with its no. on star table.	Ditto of other stars contained.	Present R.A. of col. 4.	Present Decl. of col. 4.
1	2	3	4	5	6	7
Mirat i moosalsila.	......	Andromeda [mirat i moosalsila].	α Andromedæ, alpheratz, eindram, 1.	β Andromedæ, mirack, batn ool hoot, 4; γ Alanak.	0-3	+ 28-29
Mooakhar, 27th.	Oottara bhaudram, 26th.	Pt. of An. [mirat i moosalsila] and Peg. [farasoolazam].	α Andromedæ, lpheratz, eindram, 1.	γ Pegasi, algenib or janah ool faras, mahendram, 2.	0-3	+ 28-29
Zant ool coorsy.	Caushyapy ...	Cassiopea [zantoolcoorsy] ...	α Cassiopeæ	β Cassiopeæ, cuff ool khazeeb.	0-34	+ 55-56
Kyetos ...	.. ...	Cetus [kyetos]	β Ceti, deneb kyetos, 3	α Ceti, menkar or cuff ool jazmah; ζ batn kyetos, 8; o mira.	0-38	— 18-35
Alrishah, 28th...	......	String of pisces [hoot] ...	ε Piscium	δ Piscium	0-57	+ 7-19
......	Raivaty, 27th.	32 stars in pisces [hoot] ...	ζ Piscium, veidhrity, 5	Many others	1-7	+ 7- 0
Hoot, XII ...	Meenam, XII	Pisces [hoot]	η Piscium	ζ Piscium, veidhrity, 5; ι ...	1-26	+ 14-47
Nahr	......	Eridanus [nahr.]	α Eridani, achernar, 7	β γ Eridani	1-34	— 57-47
Shartein, 1st ...	Ashwiny, 1st.	Horns of aries [hamel] ...	α Arietis, hamel, 10	β Arietis, shartein, 9	2- 1	+ 22-57
Hamel, I ...	Maisham, I ...	Aries [hamel]	α Arietis, hamel, 10	β Arietis, shartein, 9; γ ...	2- 1	+ 22-57
......	Bharany, 2nd.	Part of Aries [hamel] or Musca.	35 Arietis, preety, 11	39, 41 Arietis	2-37	+ 27-15
Bootein, 2nd ...	......	Part of Aries [hamel]	ε Arietis	π υ Arietis	2-53	+ 20-55
Haumil i raus ool ghowl.	......	Perseus [haumil i raus ool ghowl].	α Persei, mirfak, 13	β Persei, algol, 12	3-17	+ 49-28
Sooreiyah, 3rd...	Kritticay, 3rd.	Pleiades [sowr]	η Tauri, alcyone, ayooshmat, 14.	......	3-41	+ 23-46
Aldebaran, 4th.	Rohiny, 4th ...	Hyades [sowr]	α Tauri, aldebaran, sowbhaugyam, 16.	β Tauri, nath, agny, 20; γ nautih, 15; δ ε θ.	4-30	+ 16-17
Sowr, II... ...	Vrishab., II.	Taurus [sowr]	α Tauri, aldebaran, 16	β Tauri, nath, agny, 20 ...	4-30	+ 16-17
Mausik ool inaun.	......	Auriga [mausik ool inaun] ...	α Aurigæ, capella, oycok or rakeeb, bramhahridayam, 17.	δ Aurigæ, prajaupaty, 24; ε alanaz; β γ ζ η ι θ.	5- 9	+ 45-53
Jabbaur ...	......	Orion [jabbaur]	β Orionis, rigel, 18	α Orionis, Betelgeux, 23; γ bellatrix, mirzam, 19; ε nitauk, 21; ζ fakaur, 22; &c.	5- 9	— 8-20
Arnab	......	Lepus [arnab]	α Leporis, arsh ool jowzah ...	......	5-28	— 17-54
Hakah, 5th ...	Mrigash., 5th.	Head of Orion [jabbaur] ...	λ Orionis, shobhanam	Two others	5-29	+ 9-52
Fakaur ool jowzah.	......	Belt of Orion [jabbaur] ...	ε Orionis, nitauk ool jowzah, 21.	δ Orionis, mintaka, nazm; ζ fakaur ool jowzah, 22.	5-31	— 1-18
Hanah, 6th ...	Ardray, 6th ...	Shoulder of Orion [jabbaur].	α Orionis, betelgeux, 23 ...	......	5-49	+ 7-23
Safeenah ...	......	Argo navis [safeenah] ...	α Argus, canopus, sooheil, 25 ...	β γ δ ε ζ θ η, 6 Argûs ...	6-22	— 52-38
Kalb i acbar ...	......	Canis major [kalbi acbar]. ...	α Canis majoris, dog star or sirius, 26.	β Canis majoris, mirzam; ε.	6-40	— 16-34
Kalb i asghar ...	......	Canis minor [kalbi asghar]....	α Canis minoris, procyon, 27 ...	β Canis minoris, mirzam ...	7-34	+ 5-30
Jowzah, III ...	Mitoonam, III.	Gemini [jowzah] ...	β Geminorum, pollux, alzirah, soocarmum, 28.	α Geminorum, castor; γ, alhena; ξ alzirr.	7-39	+ 28-17
Zirah, 7th ...	Poonarvas, 7th.	Head of Gemini, [jowzah] ...	Ditto.	α θ τ Geminorum	7-39	+ 28-17

Constellations for which native names are known—continued.

Arabic const., lun. mansion or sign. See sec. 8.	San. name, ditto. See sec. 8.	How made up on Eur. system. For cross-ref. see sec. 8.	Scientific, &c., names of principal star [yogam], with its no. on star table.	Ditto of other stars contained.	Present R.A. of col. 4.	Present Decl. of col. 4.
1	2	3	4	5	6	7
Sartaun, IV ...	Carcatac., IV.	Cancer [sartaun]	β Cancri, præsepe, milaf ...	α Cancri, shoolam; δ dhrity; γ &c.	8-11	+ 9-31
Nasara, 8th ...	Pooshyam, 8th.	Nebula, &c., in Cancer [sartaun].	δ Cancri, dhrity, 29	β Cancri, milaf; γ.	8-39	+ 18-33
Tarafa, 9th ...	......	Part of Leo [asad] and Cancer [sartan].	α Cancri, shoolam, 30	λ Leonis	8-53	+ 12-16
......	Aushlai., 9th.	Part of Cancer [sartaun] ...	α Cancri, shoolam, 30	4 others	8-53	+ 12-16
Shoojah	......	Hydra [shoojah]	α Hydræ, corhydræ, alphard, 31.	......	9-22	— 8-11
Asad, V	Simham, V ...	Leo [asad]	α Leonis, cor leonis or regulus, kalbool asad, gandam, 32.	β Leonis, denebola, dhroovam, 37; γ algeiba; δ vriddhy, 36.	10-3	+ 12-30
Jabaha, 10th ...	......	Part of Leo [asad]	α Leonis, cor leonis, 32	γ algeiba; ζ η Leonis... ...	10-3	+ 12-30
......	Magham, 10th.	Part of Leo [asad]	α Leonis, cor leonis, 32	γ algeiba; s μ ν Leonis ...	10-3	+ 12-30
Zoobra, 11th ...	P. phalgoony, 11th.	Part of Leo [asad]	δ Leonis, vriddhy, 36	θ Leonis	11-8	+ 21-7
Bautiya	......	Crater [bautiya]	δ Crateris	α Hydræ et crateris, alkes, &c	11-14	— 14-12
Sarafa, 12th ...	O. phalgoony, 12th.	Part of Leo [asad]	β Leonis, denebola, 37	....	11-43	+ 15-11
Ghooraub ...	......	Corvus [ghooraub]	α Corvi, algoreb, 38	β Corvi; δ vyaughautam, 39.	12-3	— 24-8
Arsh ool simauk.	......	Part of Virgo [soomboola] ...	η Virginis	δ Virginis, aupas, 40; γ ε.	12-14	— 0-3
......	Hastam, 13th.	Part of Corvus [ghooraub] ...	δ Corvi, vyaughautam, 39 ...	α Corvi, algoreb, 38; β γ ε.	12-24	— 15-43
Doobhe acbar ...	Maha ricsham.	Ursa major [doobhe acbar].	ε Ursæ majoris, alioth or jaddy ool far kad.	α Ursæ majoris, doobhe, 35; β alanak, 31; η benetnasch or kauyid or alkaid, 42; γ, ζ.	12-49	+ 56-32
Awwah, 13th. ...	......	Part of Virgo [soomboola] ...	δ Virginis, aupas, 40	γ η Virginis; ε vindemiatrix.	12-50	+ 3-59
Simauk ool azal, 14th.	Chitta, 14th ...	Spike of Virgo [soomboola] ...	α Virginis, spica, harshanam, 41.	......	13-19	— 10-35
Soomboola, VI.	Canyay, VI ...	Virgo [soomboola]	Ditto.	δ Virginis, aupas, 40; ε vindemiatrix.	13-19	— 10-35
Ghafr, 15th ...	......	Part of Virgo [soomboola] ...	ι Virginis	κ λ Virginis	14-10	— -29
Awwah	Swauty, 15th.	Boötes [awwah]	α Boötis, arcturus, haurs ool samah or simauk &c., vajram, 44.	η Boötis, alroomh, roomhool simauk, 43; ε izaur.	14-11	+ 19-45
Cantooras ...	......	Centaurus [cantooras] ...	α Centauri, hazaur	β wazn; ζ θ Centauri ...	14-32	— 60-23
Saboo	......	Lupus [saboo]	α Lupi	......	14-35	— 46-55
......	Vishauk., 16th.	Part of Lib. [meezaun], & Sc. [akrab].	α Libræ, siddhy, 46	ι ν Libræ; λ Scorpii	14-45	— 15-36
Doobhe asghar.	Cshoodra ricsham.	Ursa minor [doobhe asghar].	β Ursæ minoris, kochab, 47 ...	α Ursæ min., polaris, alrooccabah, dhroovam, 6; γ δ ε ζ η.	14-51	+ 74-36
Farkdaun ...	......	Watches of U. m. [doobhe asghar].	β Ursæ minoris, kochab, 47 ...	γ Ursæ minoris	14-51	+ 74-36
Meezaun, VII ...	Toolaum, VII.	Libra [meezaun]	β Libræ, zubenelg	α Libræ, siddhy, zubenesch ...	15-11	— 8-59
Zoobannah, 16th.	......	Part of Libra [meezaun] ...	β Libræ, zubenelg	α Libræ, siddhy, 46; γ ...	15-11	— 8-59
Yikleel i shoomauly.	......	Corona borealis [yikleeli shoomauly].	α Coronæ borealis, gemma, alphacca, 48.	......	15-30	+ 27-5
Hooweiyah ...	......	Serpens [hooweiyah]	α Serpenti, oonuk, 49	......	15-39	+ 6-46
Yikleel, 17th ...	Anoora, 17th.	Part of Scorpio [akrab] ...	δ Scorpii, vyateepautam, 50 ...	β υ π ρ Scorpii	15-54	— 22-19
Akrab, VIII ...	Vrishchic., VIII.	Scorpio [akrab]	α Scorpii, antares, 52	β Scorpii &c.	16-23	— 26-11
Kalb, 18th ...	Jyeshtay, 18th.	Part of Scorpio [akrab] ...	α Scorpii, antares, 52	σ τ Scorpii	16-23	— 26-11
Jausy	......	Hercules [jausy]	β Herculis	α Herculis, rasalgethy, 54; ζ.	16-25	+ 21-43
Kyekows ...	......	Triangulum aust. [kyekows].	α Trianguli australis	β γ Trianguli australis ...	16-37	— 68-49
Mijmarah ...	......	Ara [mijmarah]	β Aræ	α γ Aræ	17-16	— 55-25
......	Moolam, 19th.	Part of Scorpio [akrab] ...	λ Scorpii	ε μ &c. Scorpii	17-26	— 37-2
Showla, 19th ...	......	Part of Scorpio [akrab] ...	λ Scorpii	ν Scorpii, parigham, 51 ...	17-26	— 37-2
Heiyah	......	Ophiuchus [heiyah]	α Ophiuchi, rasalhague, 55 ...	......	17-30	+ 12-38
Tinneen ...	......	Draco [tinneen]	γ Draconis, etenin, 56	α Thuban; β alwaida; μ rauks, 53.	17-54	+ 51-30
Nauyim, 20th ...	P. ashau., 20th.	Bow of Sagittarius [kows] ...	δ Sagittarii, shivam, 57	ε Sagittarii	18-14	— 29-53
Balda, 21st ...	Dhanoos ...	Bow of Sagittarius [kows] ...	δ Sagittarii, shivam, 57	ε μ χ Sagittarii	18-14	— 29-53
Kows, IX ...	Dhanoos, IX.	Sagittarius [kows]	ε Sagittarii	λ Sagttariii, royinauyim; ν uyeen, &c.; δ μ θ σ τ ζ.	18-17	— 34-26
Shalyauk ...	Abhijit, 21st, α	Lyra [shalyauk]	α Lyræ, vega, 58	β γ Lyræ	18-33	+ 38-41
......	O.ashau., 21st.	Body of Sagittarius [kows] ...	τ Sagittarii, siddham, 59 ...	ζ Sagittarii	19-0	— 27-53
Yikleelijoonooby.	......	Corona aus. [yikleel i joonooby].	θ Coronæ australis	......	19-2	— 39-33
Ookaub	Shravan., 22nd.	Aquila [ookaub]	α Aquilæ, altair, 60...	β alshain; γ η Aquilæ ...	19-45	+ 8-35
Saham	......	Sagitta [saham]	γ Sagittæ	......	19-53	+ 19-12
Jaddy, X ...	Macaram, X...	Capricornus [jaddy]	α Capricorni	β δ Capricorni	20-12	— 12-52
Zaubih, 22nd ...	......	Horns of Capricornus [jaddy].	α Capricorni	β Capricorni	20-12	— 12-52
Doolfeen ...	Dhanisht. 23rd.	Delphinus [dool feen]. ...	α Delphini, shoobham, 61 ...	β γ δ Delphini	20-35	+ 15-32
Dajjajah ...	......	Cygnus [dajjajah]	α Cygni, aridad, deneb, 62 ...	γ Cygni, sadr ool dajjajah; ζ.	20-38	+ 44-53
Kita ool faras ...	......	Equuleus [kita ool faras]. ...	α Equulei	......	21-10	+ 4-48
Boola, 23rd ...	......	Part of Aquarius [dalo] ...	β Aquarii	ε μ Aquarii...	21-26	— 6- 2
Dalo, XI ...	Coombham, XI.	Aquarius [dalo]...	β Aquarii	λ υ ζ Aquarii	21-26	— 6- 2
Sood, 24th ...	......	Part of Aquarius [dalo] ...	β Aquarii	ξ Aquarii	21-26	— 6- 2
Faras ool azam	......	Pegasus [faras ool azam] ...	ε Pegasi, enif, fomal fars or sad ool hoomaum, 63.	α Pegasi, markab, 68; β mankib, 67; γ algenib, 2; δ.	21-39	+ 9-23
Akbee, 25th ...	......	Part of Aquarius [dalo] ...	γ Aquarii	ζ η π Aquarii	22-16	— 1-56
......	Shatabhishay, 24th.	Right leg of Aquarius [dalo].	λ Aquarii, shooclam or shoobhram, 65.	......	22-47	— 8-10
Hoot i joonooby.	......	Piscis aus. [hoot i joonooby].	α Piscis australis, fomalhaut, 66.	......	22-52	— 30-12
Mokaddam, 26th.	P. bhaudram, 25th.	W. sq. of Peg. [faras ool azam].	α Pegasi, markab, 68	β Pegasi, scheat, mankib, 67; ζ.	22-59	+ 14-37
Farghaun ...	......	Sq. of Peg. [faras ool azam]...	α Pegasi, markab, 68	β Pegasi, scheat, 67; γ algenib, 2; δ.	22-59	+ 14-37

Hindoo Lunar Mansions. See Nacshatram (7), page 546.

No.	Name.	Sign used in native astronomy.	Approximately corresponding European constellation.	Index star [yogam] and corresponding European scientific and popular name, with number on fixed star table, and present R.A.	Presiding deity.	Quality in nativities; *i.e.*, when the moon stands in this constellation at time of a birth.	Character of each nacshatram, and favorite animals, &c., in astrology [jyotisham, vaunashastram]. Gunam.	Animal.	Tree.	Bird.	Corresponding section of the Solar zodiac [raushy chuckram], sign [raushy], and Solar month [mausam].	Veety [q.v.].	Avastaunam [q.v.].	No.
1	2	3	4	5	6	7	8	9	10	11	12	13	14	15
1	Ashwiny ...	Horse's head	Part of Aries [hamel].	Vishcambham, α Arietis, Hamel (10), 2 h. 1 m.	Twin-gods.	Good. Shaunty.	Devam.	Horse [ghorah].	Yetty [poison nut].	Rajauly [shyninam].	Maisham, ♈, Chittray.	Naugam.		1
2	Bharany ...	Yony, triangle, or fire place.	Musca [hamel] ...	Preety, 35 Arietis (11), 2 h. 37 m ...	Yaman ...	Bad ...	Maunoosham.	Male elephant [q.v.].	Nelly [emblic myrobalan].	Crow [caurvam]				2
3	Kritticay ...	Razor	Pleiades [sowr]. ...	Ayooshmat, η Tauri, Alcyone (14), 3 h. 41 m.	Agny ...	Very bad. ...	Raucsham.	Ewe [aud] ...	Atty [q.v.] ...	Mayil [q.v.] ...				3
4	Rohiny ...	Cart	Hyades [sowr] ..	Sowbhaugyam, α Tauri, Aldebaran (16), 4 h. 30 m.	Prajaupaty.	Good	Maunoosham.	Male cobra [q.v.].	Nauval [jaumoon].	Owl [ooloocam].	Vrishabham, ♉, Veiyaushy.	Gajam ...	Eirauvatam.	4
5	Mrigashiras.	Antelope's head	Head of Orion [jabbaur].	Shobhanam, λ Orionis, 5 h. 29 m. ...	Soman ...	Good	Devam.	Female ratsnake [q.v.].	Caroongauly [sundra].	Cock [moorghy]				5
6	Ardray ...	Gem, coral, or burning coal.	Part of Orion [jabbaur].	Atigandam, α Orionis, Betelgeux (23), 5h. 49 m.	Roodran.	Bad	Maunoosham.	Male dog [nye]	Red caroongauly.	Anril	Mitoonam, ♊, Auny.			6
7	Poonarvas...	House, bow, or large sea boat.	Part of Gemini [jowzah].	Soocarmam, β Geminorum, Pollux (28), 7 h. 39 m.	Adity ...	Good	Devam.	Female cat [poonay].	Bamboo [q.v.]	Hamsam [q.v.].		Eirauvatam.		7
8	Pooshyam...	Arrow, string, or looking glass with handle.	Part of Cancer [sartaun].	Dhrity, δ Cancri (29), 8 h. 39 m. ...	Brihaspaty.	Good. Shaunty.	Devam.	Ram [aud] ...	Peepul [q.v.].	Water crow [jala caukkay].	Catacam, ♋, Audy.			8
9	Aushlaisham	Potter's wheel, serpent, or sloping stone.	Part of Cancer [sartaun].	Shoolam, α Cancri (30), 8 h. 53 m.	Sarpam ...	Bad	Raucsham.	Male cat [poonay].	Poon [q.v.] ...	Shitchily [kilkilah].				9
10	Magham ...	House, palanqueen, or yoke.	Part of Leo [asad] ...	Gandam, α Leonis, Regulus (32), 10 h. 3 m.	Pitri ...	Good. Shaunty.	Raucsham.	Male rat [ely].	Banyan [q.v.].	Male vulture [gidh].	Simham, ♌, Auvany.	Arshabhoo.		10
11	Poobbam ...	Couch, two small squares, or legs of bedstead.	Part of Leo [asad] ...	Vriddhy, δ Leonis (36), 11 h. 8 m. ...	Bhagam ...	Medium ...	Maunoosham.	Female rat [ely].	Palaus [q.v.].	Female vulture [gidh].				11
12	Oottaram ...	Bed, two small squares, or legs of bedstead.	Part of Leo [asad] ...	Dhroovam, β Leonis, Denebola (37), 11 h. 43 m.	Aryamay.	Medium ...	Maunoosham.	Bull [maud].	Araly [ganmair].	Shil vandoo ...				12
13	Hastam ...	Hand	Part of Corvus [ghooraub].	Vyaughautam, δ Corvi (39), 12 h. 24 m.	Savitry ...	Good	Devam.	Female buffalo [khoolgah].	Autty [mountain ebony].	Kite [chillam].	Canyay, ♍, Pooratau-shy.	Go ...	Veishwaunary.	13
14	Chitta ...	Pearl	Part of Virgo [soomboola].	Harshanam, α Virginis, Spica (41), 13 h. 19 m.	Twashtay.	Bad. Shaunty.	Raucsham.	Male tiger [pooly].	Bael [q.v.] ...	Marangotty. [q.v.].				14
15	Swauty ...	Coral bead, ruby, or small brinjaul.	Part of Boötes [awwah].	Vajram, α Boötis, Arcturus (44), 14 h. 11 m.	Vayoo ...	Good	Devam.	Male buffalo [khoolgah].	Marootham [murdah].	Tainee [q.v.] ...	Toolaum, ♎, Arpisy.			15
16	Vishaukham	Circle, gateway or arch ...	Pt. of Lib. [meezaun] and Sc. [akrab] ..	Siddhy, α Libræ (46), 14 h. 45 m. ...	Indran and Agny.	Bad. Shaunty.	Raucsham.	Female tiger [pooly].	Wood apple [q.v.].	Shevvaul coorvy or red tail bird.		Jauradgavam.		16
17	Anooraudhay.	Row of oblations, umbrella in hand, or bow.	Part of Scorpio [akrab].	Vyatcepautam, δ Scorpii (50), 15 h. 54 m.	Mitran ...	Good	Devam.	Female deer [mrigam].	Magizham [ilanjy].	Chautacam [koel].	Vrishchicam, ♏, Caurtigay.			17
18	Jyeshtay ...	Ring, umbrella in hand, or spear.	Part of Scorpio [akrab].	Vareeyas, α Scorpii, Antares (52), 16 h. 23 m.	Indran ...	Bad. Shaunty.	Raucsham.	Male deer [mrigam].	Pirye [stunted jack].	Chuckravaucam [bram. duck].				18
19	Moolam ...	Lion's tail, leaping lion, or trumpet.	Part of Scorpio [akrab].	Parigham, λ Scorpii 17 h. 26 m. ...	Prajaupaty.	Very bad. Shaunty.	Raucsham.	Female dog [nye].	Marah ...	Shempottoo [cr. pheasant].	Dhanoos, ♐, Maurgaly.	Mrigam.		19
20	Poorvashaudham.	Elephant's tooth, two double squares, or legs of bedstead.	Part of Sagittarius [kows].	Shivam, δ Sagittarii (57), 18 h. 14 m. ...	Aupas ...	Medium ...	Maunoosham.	Male monkey [bandar].	Vanjy [goolancha].	Paganday [teetar].				20
21	Oottarashaudham.	Elephant's tooth, two double squares, or legs of bedstead.	Part of Sagittarius [kows].	Siddham, τ Sagittarii (59), 19 h. 0 m.	Vishwedevah.	Good	Maunoosham.	Barren cow [maud].	Pilah [jack].	Valiyan [king crow].				21
21a	Abhijit ...	Triangle	Part of Lyra [shalyauk].	Abhijit, α Lyræ, Vega (58), 18 h. 33 m.	Bramha ...	......	......	......	......	......				21a
22	Shravanam.	Triangle or three foot-steps.	Part of Aquila [ookaub].	Saudhyam, α Aquilæ, Altair (60), 19 h. 45 m.	Vishnoo ...	Good	Devam.	Female monkey [bandar].	Yercum [q.v.].	Nauray [blue heron].	Macaram, ♑, Tye.	Ajam ...	Jauradgavam.	22
23	Dhanishtay.	Drum	Part of Dolphin [dooleen].	Shoobham, α Delphini (61), 20 h. 35 m.	Vasoo ...	Bad. Shaunty.	Raucsham.	Female lion [simham].	Vanny [shamee].	Pon vandoo [zeerangy].				23
24	Shatabhishay.	Circle	100 stars of Aquarius [dalo].	Shooclam, λ Aquarii (65), 22 h. 47 m.	Varoonan.	Bad	Raucsham.	Mare [ghorah].	Cadamba [q.v.].	Andam caukkay [carrion crow].	Coombham, ♒, Maushy.			24
25	Poorva bhaudram.	Couch, double headed figure, two double squares, or legs of ravanan's bedstead.	Part of Pegasus [faras ool azam].	Bramham, α Pegasi, Markab (68), 22 h. 59 m.	Ajeicapaud.	Medium ...	Maunoosham.	Male lion [simham].	Taimah [mango].	Oollaun [q.v.].		Dahanam.		25
26	Oottara bhaudram.	Couch, double headed figure, two double squares, or legs of ravanan's bedstead.	Part of Andromeda [mirat i moosal si lah] and Pegasus [faras ool azam].	Eindram, α Andromedæ, Alpheratz (1), 0 h. 3 m.	Ahirboodnay.	Medium ...	Maunoosham.	Cow [maud].	Vaimboo [neem].	Cottaun [ooloocam].	Meenam, ♓, Pungoony.			26
27	Raivaty ...	Tabor, or fish	32 Stars in Pisces [hoot].	Veidhrity, ζ Piscium (5), 1 h. 7 m. ...	Pooshan.	Good. Shaunty.	Devam.	Female elephant [q.v.].	Hooppay [common mohwah].	Vallooroo [shyainam].				27

(6)—"*a*" The following are the constellations north of the zodiac [raushy chuckram]:—Andromeda [mirat i moosalsila]; Aquila, the eagle [ookaub]; Auriga, the charioteer [mausik ool inaun]; Boötes, the herdsman [awwah]; Camelopardus, the giraffe; Canes venatici, the greyhounds; Cassiopea [zaut ool coorsy]; Cepheus [zaut ool coorsy]; Coma berenicis, berenice's hair; Corona borealis, the northern crown [yikleel i shoomauly]; Cygnus, the swan [dajjajah]; Delphinus, the dolphin [doolfeen]; Draco, the dragon [tinneen]; Equuleus, the little horse [kita ool faras]; Hercules [jausy]; Lacerta, the lizard; Leo minor, the little lion; Lynx, the lynx; Lyra, the harp or lyre [shalyauk]; Monoceros, the unicorn; Ophiuchus, or serpentarius, the serpent bearer [heiyah]; Pegasus, the winged horse [faras ool azam]; Perseus [haumil i rausoolghowl]; Sagitta, the arrow [saham]; Serpens, the serpent [hooweiyah]; Triangulum, the triangle; Ursa major, the great bear [doobhe acbar]; Ursa minor, the little bear [doobhe asghar]; Vulpecula, the fox.—"*b*" The following are the constellations of the zodiac. Northern:—Aries ♈, the ram [hamel]; Taurus ♉, the bull [sowr]; Gemini ♊, the twins [jowzah]; Cancer ♋, the crab [sartaun]; Leo ♌, the lion [asad]; Virgo ♍, the virgin [soomboola]; Southern:—Libra ♎, the balance [meezaun]; Scorpio ♏, the scorpion [akrab]; Sagittarius ♐, the archer [kows]; Capricornus ♑, the goat [jaddy]; Aquarius ♒, the water-bearer [dalo]; Pisces ♓, the fishes [hoot].—"*c*" The following are the constellations south of the zodiac:—Antlia pneumatica, the air pump; Apparatus sculptoris, the sculptor's tools; Apus, the bird of paradise; Ara, the altar [mijmarah]; Argo navis, the ship argo [safeenah]; Canis major, the great dog [kalb i acbar]; Canis minor, the little dog [kalb i asghar]; Cela sculptoris, the engraver's tool; Centaurus, the centaur [cantooras]; Cetus, the whale [kyetos]; Chameleon; Circinus, the pair of compasses; Columba, the dove; Corona australis, the southern crown [yikleel i joonooby]; Corvus, the crow [ghooraub]; Crater, the cup [bautiya]; Crux, the cross [trishunkoo]; Dorando, the sword fish; Equuleus pictorius, the painter's easel; Eridanus, the river eridanus [nahr]; Fornax, the furnace; Grus, the crane; Horologium, the clock; Hydra [shoojah]; Hydrus, the water snake; Indus, the indian; Lepus, the hare [arnab]; Lupus, the wolf [saboo]; Microscopium, the microscope; Mons mensæ, the table mountain; Musca, the fly [bharany]; Norma, the square; Octans, the quadrant; Orion [jabbaur]; Pavo, the peacock; Phœnix; Piscis australis, the southern fish [hoot i joonooby]; Piscis volans, the flying fish; Reticulum, the net; Sextans, the sextant; Telescopium or tubus, the telescope; Toucanus, the toucan; Triangulum australe, the southern triangle [kyekows].——**(7)** Thirdly nacshatram means the special form of constellation called an asterism in the moon's path [cacsham], otherwise a lunar mansion, in which the moon [chundran] happens to be each day [tity], this being one of the important entries in the native calendar [punchaungam]. Of these according to the earlier reckoning twenty-seven are enumerated, but in the later astrology [jyotisham] more usually twenty-eight [abhijit], distinct in name, figure and number of stars.—"*a*" In the vedams [q.v.], the asterisms are considered to be the abodes of the gods or the visible forms of pious persons after death [samsauram]. In the later mythology they are regarded as wives of moon [chundran] and daughters of Dacshan [q.v.]. Note that Bel of Chaldea meant the sun; and the Chaldean serpent or dragon was the moon's course through these asterisms; the effect of which, in connexion with ecliptic [craunty mundalam], is to form a serpentine figure like the Caduceus of the Greeks. Compare Kait and Raboo. A modern notion is that the nacshatrams of the moon are human beings who have been exalted to that honor, but that when their stock of merit is exhausted they again descend to earth as shooting stars [samsauram].—"*b*" An ordinary lunar mansion contains an arc of 13° 20′ of the circumference [paridhy] of the zodiac [raushy chuckram], 27 × 13° 20′ being = 360°; therefore a solar zodiacal sign [raushy] contains 2¼ Nacshatrams, 30° ÷ 13° 20′ being = 2¼. There are a fixed and a movable lunar zodiac, as well as a fixed and movable solar zodiac [raushy chuckram]; therefore there are fixed and movable Nacshatrams, the motion of the latter being equal to the progress of the Ayanaumsham [q.v.], or 54″ per annum according to Soorya siddhauntam [maunam, mausam], against the 50″ about of european science. The number of stars in the constellations from ashwiny [q.v.] are according to Varauha mihiran [q.v.]:—3, 3, 6, 5, 3, 1, 5, 3, 6, 5, 8, 15, 5, 1, 1, 5, 4, 3, 11, 2, 8, 3, 5, 100, 15, 8 and 32; these numbers also represent the various stellar periods of astrology; in matters connected with marriage these numbers represent years after which the effects indicated will be felt; recovery from fever and the like will begin after so many days. Authorities vary as to the numbers; those given in these pages are based on a collation of several. In the 6 lunar mansions beginning from Raivaty [q.v.] the 27th, the stars are towards the east; and in the 12 beginning from Ardray [q.v.] the 6th, they are in the centre; and in the 9 beginning from Jyeshtay [q.v.], the 18th, they are in the west of the several mansions; the moon's conjunction [sangamam] with the lunar mansions is said to take place when the moon is in the middle of these mansions. For Abhijit see that head, and for the stars supposed to lie at the junction between different nacshatrams see Yogam. Each mansion is itself divided into 60 ghadiyas, the ghadiay into 60 vighadiyas, &c., so that 1 ghadiya is equal to 13′ 20″, a vighadiya to 13″ 20‴, and a para to 13‴ 20⁗; which denominations must not be confounded with the measures of time of the same names [caulam]. The mansions are in more common usage divided into four quarters, called Paudams [q.v.], giving to the whole ecliptic 108 paudams.—"*c*" The astrologers make lunar mansions of great practical consequence from their assumed good or evil influence; not only at time of birth, but during life. They are spoken of as quasi-deities, whose favor needs to be propitiated, and whose frown is fatal to health and life. The test of application is the situation of the moon [chundran] in this or that Nacshatram at the moment of an event occurring. Thus the so called star of a person through life is that nacshatram or mansion in which the moon was at the moment of his or her birth. There is no question that the nacshatrams are a source of infinite terror to natives of all castes. They are consulted at births and marriages and in all times of difficulty, sickness, and anxiety. Journeys are begun under their direction [rijaul ool gheib], and, according to their decision days and events become lucky or unlucky. The consultation of the nacshatrams is in fact part of an orthodox native's life, and is as important in his eyes as the institution of caste [jauty] or the worship [poojah] of the gods. The nacshatrams are classified into ganams, as devam divine, maunoosham human, raucshasam savage; see table of hindoo lunar mansions opposite; if two parties to be married are born in the same class according to this arrangement, it is well; if one asterism be divine, the other human, it may pass; but divine and savage is a cross that may not be permitted [zyecha]. In the list below it will be observed that 'shaunty' is affixed to names of mansions; it means rest and shows that the ill-natured deity, to whom it refers, requires a ceremony of pacification to be performed in the event of a child being born at the time of their rising, in order that calamities and dangers which it threatens to send upon the child or its parents or other relatives, or on its friends, or on its caste, may be averted. Modern astrologers consider the nacshatrams as good, bad, and indifferent, according as they are male, female, or neuter. Natives observe anxiously the course of the moon [chundran] with respect to the four stars of the tenth constellation, magham [q.v.], when the sun [sooryan] is in the sign coombham [q.v.], i.e., from about february 10th to march 10th with a view to ascertain the future agricultural [vellaumay] prospects of the land; the market price [agavilay] of food-grains [dhaunyam] is at once lowered or raised according as the moon's course lies to south of the four stars or more and more to north of Regulus, the southernmost star; it is also stated in shastrams that if the moon should pass to the north of all the four stars the world would be at an end; similarly if saturn [shany] should enter the fourth constellation, rohiny [q.v.]. Cf. Calky, Calpam, Caulam. Oottaraphalgoony [oottaram], Oottarashaudham [q.v.], and Oottarabhaudram [q.v.], together with Rohiny [q.v.], are in astrology known as Dhroovam or stable asterisms. Moolam [q.v.], Ardray [q.v.], Jyeshtay [q.v.], and Aushlaisham [q.v.], are known as Teecshnam or sharp asterisms. Poorvaphalgoony [q.v.], Poorvashaudham [q.v.], Poorvabhaudram [q.v.], Bharany [q.v.], and Magham [q.v.], are known as Oogram or severe asterisms. Hastam [q.v.], Ashwiny [q.v.], and Pooshyam [q.v.], are known as Laghoo or light asterisms. Anooraudhay [q.v.], Chitta [q.v.], Raivaty [q.v.], and Mrigashiras [q.v.], are known as Mridoo or soft asterisms. Kritticay [q.v.] and Vishaukham [q.v.] are known as Mridoo teecshnam, or soft and sharp asterisms and they produce effects of mixed character. Shravanam [q.v.], Shravishtay [dhanishtay], Shatabhishay [q.v.], Hastam [q.v.] and Swauty [q.v.] are asterisms through which when the moon passes should be commenced works of a moving character. The following are varauha mihiran's [q.v.] dogmas regarding lunar asterisms in simple nativity [jenma puttricay]:—"a person born at the moment "when the moon [chundran] passes through ashwiny [q.v.] "will be fond of ornaments, will be of fine appearance, will "be popular, skilled in work and intelligent; when the moon "passes through bharany [q.v.] will be successful at work, "truthful, free from diseases, able and free from grief; when "the moon passes through kritticay [q.v.] will be a glutton, "fond of the wives of other men, of bright appearance and "of wide-spread fame; when the moon passes through rohiny "[q.v.] will be truthful, will not covet the property of other "men, will be of cleanly habits, of sweet speech, of firm "views, and of fine appearance; when the moon passes through "mrigashiras [q.v.] will be of no firm principles, will be able, "timid, of good speech, of active habits, rich and will indulge "in sensual pleasures; when the moon passes through ardray "[q.v.] will be insincere, of irascible temper, ungrateful, "troublesome and addicted to wicked deeds; when the moon "passes through poonarvas [q.v.] will be devout and of patient "habits, will live in comfort, will be good-natured, quiet, of "wrong views, sickly, thirsty and pleased with trifles; when the "moon passes through pooshyam [q.v.] will have a control over "his desires, will be generally liked, learned in the shastrams "[q.v.], rich, and will be fond of acts of charity; when the moon "passes through aushlaisham [q.v.] will not be attentive to the "work of other men, will be a promiscuous eater, will be sinful, "ungrateful and skilled in cheating other men; when the moon "passes through magham [q.v.] will have numerous servants, "will worship the devas [q.v.] and pitries [q.v.] and will be "engaged in important works; when the moon passes through

" poorvaphalgoony [poobbam] will be of sweet speech, will " be liberal in his gifts, of wandering habits, and will serve " under kings; when the moon passes through cottaraphalgoony " [oottaram] will be generally liked, will earn money by his " learning, and will live in comfort; when the moon passes " through hastam [q.v.] will be of active habits, full of resources, " shameless, merciless, and a thief and a drunkard; when the " moon passes through chitta [q.v.] will wear cloths and flowers " of various colors and will have beautiful eyes and limbs; when " the moon passes through swauty [q.v.] will be of a mild and " quiet nature, will control his passion, will be skilled in trade, " will be merciful, unable to bear thirst, of sweet speech, and " disposed to do acts of charity; when the moon passes through " vishaukham [q.v.] will be jealous of another's prosperity, will " be a niggard, of bright appearance, of distinct speech, skilled " in earning money, and disposed to bring about quarrels among " men; when the moon passes through anooraudhay [q.v.] will " be rich, will live in foreign lands, will be unable to bear " hunger, and disposed to wander from place to place; when the " moon passes through jyeshtay [q.v.] will have few friends, " will be very cheerful, virtuous, and of irascible temper; when " the moon passes through moolam [q.v.] will be haughty, rich, " happy, not disposed to injure other men, of firm views and will " live in luxury; when the moon passes through poorvashaudham " [q.v.] will have an agreeable wife, will be proud and attached " to friends; when the moon passes through oottarashaudham " [q.v.] will be obedient, will be learned in the rules of virtue, " will possess many friends, will be grateful and return favors " received, and will be generally liked; when the moon passes " through shravanam [q.v.] will be prosperous and learned, will " have a liberal-minded wife, will be rich and of wide-spread " fame; when the moon passes through dhanishtay [q.v.] will " be liberal in gifts, rich, valiant, fond of music, and will be a " niggard; when the moon passes through shatabhishay [q.v.] " will be harsh in his speech, will be truthful, will suffer grief, " will conquer his enemies, will thoughtlessly engage in work, " and will be of independent ways; when the moon passes " through poorvabhaudram [q.v.] will suffer from grief, will " place his wealth at the disposal of his wife, will be of distinct " speech, will be skilled in earning money, and will be a niggard; " when the moon passes through oottarabhaudram [q.v.] will be " an able speaker, will be happy, will possess children and " grandchildren, will conquer his enemies, and will be virtuous; " when the moon passes through raivaty [q.v.] will possess " perfect limbs, will be liked by all the people, will be deeply " learned, will never covet the property of other men, and will " be rich."—"*d*" For the application of the lunar mansion series on the full moon [powrnimay] principle to the month nomenclature see Mausam, and for their application on the solar residence [sancramanam, sancraunty] principle to the 27 seasonal divisions of the year see Caurtey; it is owing to this three-fold use of the mansion names for the daily stations [tity] of the moon [chundran], for the monthly stations of the full moon [powrnimay], and for the 27 stations [caurtey] of the sun [sooryan], that the whole of the complexity of the luni-solar [chaundramaunam] calendar [punchaungam] nomenclature arises.—"*e*" The following is the list of Nacshatrams. They reckon from the beginning of the solar zodiac [raushy chuckram] whether that is movable or fixed [craunty pautam, maishauyanam, maunam, mausam, rishy raikhay, veidhrity]. The numbers run from west to east, so that the lower number rises before the higher:—[*See page* 544].—"*f*" The 28 Arabian lunar mansions or manzils [q.v.] can be readily seen from the Constellation Table on pages 542, 543.——**(8)** The following is an alphabetical list of all the fixed stars and constellations for which native names are known, showing their derivation, and the scientific or European equivalents with a few particulars. The Arabian and European constellations largely correspond; the Hindoo constellations rarely exceed limits of solar or lunar zodiac [raushy chuckram]. The figures appended to star-names or star-letters show where the corresponding fixed stars are to be found in the Table of Fixed Stars at pages 540, 541.——*Abhijit* (अभिजित् - abhijit, San.). From (abhiji, san. to conquer). Otherwise Nasr ool wauky [q.v.], 58. Intercalary [adhicam] hindoo lunar mansion, between 21st and 22nd. Figured as a triangle or as the nut of the floating trapa [singhaura]. Does not occupy an equal portion of the ecliptic [craunty mundalam] with the other nacshatrams, but is taken out of the contiguous divisions; is very remote from the zodiac [raushy chuckram]. Principal star is Vega, α Lyræ [shalyauk], 58. 1st magnitude. Cf. Asaufy, Azfaur.——*Achernar* (اخرالنهر - ukhrunnahar, Ar.). From (ukhr, ar. end + nahar, ar. river). Star of first magnitude in the southern hemisphere. α Eridani [nahr], 7. Not known to Hindoos.——*Agastyan* (अगस्त्य - agastya, San.). Means the sage so called.—"*a*" Otherwise Coombha yony [q.v.]. Same as Sooheil [q.v.], 25; or Canopus. Only known to Hindoos after coming to s. india.—"*b*" Also Atry [q.v.] in maharicsham [q.v.]. His wife Atreyee [q.v.] or Anoosya [q.v.] is κ Draconis [tinneen].——*Agny* (अग्नि - agni, San.). Means fire; from brightness. Otherwise Nath [q.v.]. Star of second magnitude, β Tauri [sowr], 20; which star is also known as γ Aurigæ [mausik oolinaun]. Title is also name of 3rd hindoo lunar mansion Kritticay [q.v.].——*Ajooz ool asad* (عجزالاسد - ajúzulasad, Hind.). From (ajúz, ar. rump + asad, ar. leo). Same as Arsh ool simauk.——*Akbee* (اخبيه - akhbíh, Ar.). From (khibá, ar. grain of barley); from the circular figure of the constellation. Otherwise Sad ool akbee [q.v.]. ζ, η, β, γ, π, Aquarii [dalo]. 25th arabian lunar mansion. Compare hindoo mansion Shatabhishay. It is said that when it rises aurorally reptiles which are under ground by reason of cold come forth.——*Akhzar* (اخضر - akhzar, Ar.). Means verdant, fresh; being a rainy star. Same as Fomal haut.——*Akrab* (عقرب - akrab, Ar.). From (akaraba, ar. to twist). Scorpio [vrishchicam]. Eighth constellation of the ancient zodiac [raushy chuckram]. Distinguished by a remarkable star of a reddish color, having two small stars close to it; this is α Scorpii or Antares, 52 [alkalb, vareeyas]. From it a line of small stars of the 3rd and 4th magnitude trends first to the S. and then E. into Milky way [kahkashaun]; these mark the tail of Scorpion, where is to be traced the yogam [q.v.] star [parigham] of 19th hindoo mansion, λ, ν or υ. To the W. of Antares is another line of small stars, ranged nearly W. and S., which show the claws; among them is β Scorpii. On a line drawn from Vega, 58 [abhijit, nasr ool wauky] through α Ophiuchi [heiyah], 55 [rasalhague], and produced rather more than the same distance, lies Antares. Or, a line produced to the southward from α Coronæ borealis [yikleel i shoomauly], 48 [alphacca], through α Serpentis [hooweiyeh], 49 [oonuk], leads to the stars forming the head of the Scorpion; the principal star of the group is β Scorpii, to the south-eastward of which is Antares. Arcturus, 44 [haurs ool samah, vajram], Spica, 41 [harshanam, simauk ool azal], and Antares, 52, form a right-angled triangle, Spica being at the right angle. Antares passes meridian at midnight about end of May. For Kalb ool akrab or heart of scorpio, see Alkalb and Kalb. For claw of scorpio, see Zubenelg and Zubenesch. For δ Scorpii, 50, see Vyateepautam. For λ or ν Scorpii, 51, see Parigham. For arabian extension of scorpio into Libra see Zoobaunah. For other stars see Anooraudhay, Jyeshtay, Moolam, Showla, Yikleel.——*Alanak* (العناق - alanák, Ar.). From (unuk, ar. neck) [oonuk].—"*a*" Star of third magnitude, β Ursæ majoris [doobhe acbar, maharicsham], 34. Is Poolahan in hindoo system.—"*b*" Also (anákularz). γ Andromedæ [mirat i moosalsila].——*Alanaz* (العنز - alanz, Ar.). From (anaza, ar. to turn away); being on the left elbow of the constellation. Star, ε Aurigæ [mausikoolinaun]. Cf. Alinauz.——*Alasah* (العصا - alasá, Hind.). Means staff. Orion's belt [fakaur ool jowzah].——*Aldebaran* (الدبران - aldabarán, Ar.). From (al, ar. the + dabarán, ar. follower); also called Towbee [q.v.] or follower, from its following pleiades; Handy oon najm [q.v.], meaning urger of the asterism or pleiades; Taulyoon najm [q.v.], meaning the follower of pleiades [kritticay, sooreiyah]; Kalb oos sowr [q.v.], meaning heart of taurus. As a constellation it corresponds to Hyades, and is α, β, γ 15, δ, ε Tauri [sowr]; 4th Arabian lunar mansion; compare hindoo mansion Rohiny. As a star it is α Tauri [sowr], 16 [ayeen ool sowr, sowbhangyam], of the first magnitude. This is about longitude of equinoctial colure at commencement of present Kaliyoog [madhyama sowramaunam].——*Alderamin* (الدرامين - aldaramin, Ar.). Star of third magnitude, α Cephei [caushyapy, zaut ool coorsy].——*Alfirk* (الفرق - alfirk, Ar.). Star. β Cephei [caushyapy, zautool coorsy].——*Alfoorood* (الفرود - alfurúd, Ar.). Means apart from other stars. Certain bright stars round pleiades [kritticay, sooreiyah]. Cf. Alphard.——*Algeiba* (الجابه - aljába, Ar.). From (al, ar. diminutive + jába, ar. lion). Star, γ Leonis [asad].——*Algenib* (الجناح - aljanáh, Ar.). From (al, ar. the + janáh, ar. wing). Otherwise Janah ool faras [q.v.], meaning wing of the horse; also Mahendram [q.v.]. Star of third magnitude, γ Pegasi [faras ool azam], 2.——*Algol* (الغول - alghúl, Ar.). From (al, ar. the + ghúl, ar. goblin); from its variations in light, fading and brightening at intervals. Star usually of second magnitude but changes to fourth every third day. β Persei [haumil i rausool ghowl], 12. Also known as β Medusæ, in the head of Medusa held in Perseus's hand.——*Algoreb* (الغراب - alghuráb, Ar.). From (al, ar. the + ghuráb, ar. corvus). Otherwise Alchiba. Star, α Corvi [ghooraub], 38. 4th or 5th magnitude.——*Alhena* (الهنعه - alhana, Ar.). From (al, ar. diminutive + hana, ar. group in orion). Star, γ Geminorum [jowzah]. Cf. Hanah, the mansion.——*Alinauz* (العناز - alináz, Ar.). Pl. of (alanz). Two stars on the left wrist of the charioteer, η ζ Aurigæ [mausik ool inaun], together with α Aurigae or Oyook [q.v.], 17. Cf. Alanaz.——*Alioth* (الجدى - aljadí, Ar.). From (al, ar. diminutive + jadí, ar. kid). To be distinguished from constellation Jaddy [q.v.] or capricornus. Compare also the same word Aljaddy as synonym of Alrooccabah. The present star is otherwise Jaddy ool farkad [q.v.] or the kid of the small bear guards. Is Angiran in hindoo system. Star of third magnitude, ε Ursæ majoris [doobhe acbar, maharicsham], the one in the tail next body.——*Alkaid* (القائد - alkáid, Hind.). From (al, ar. the + káid, ar. mourner); from stars in tail being taken as mourners accompanying the bier formed by 4 stars of Bear's body [naash]. η Ursæ majoris [doobhe acbar, maharicsham], at the end of tail, 42. Also called Benetnasch [q.v.], and Kauyid [q.v.]. Is Mareechy in hindoo system.——*Alkalb* (القلب - alkalb, Ar.). From (al, ar. the + kalb, ar. heart). Otherwise Kalb ool akrab [q.v], meaning heart of scorpio. Star of first magnitude, α Scorpii [akrab], 52; otherwise Antares and

Vareeyas [q.v.]. See also Kalb, the arabian mansion.——*Alkes* (الكاسه - alkásah, Ar.). From (al, ar. the + kásah, ar. the cup). Star of 4th magnitude, α Hydræ et crateris [bautiya], 33. Compare the terms in Casat ool masaukeen and Causa i darvishaun.——*Alnitak* (النطاق - alniták, Ar.). From (al, ar. diminutive + nitak, ar. belt). Star, ζ Orionis [jabbaur]; at eastern end of belt [alasah, fakaur ool jowzah].——*Alphacca* (الفكه - alfakkah, Ar.). From (fakka, ar. opening), from semi-circular shape of the constellation of which this is the leading star. Otherwise Gemma. Star of second magnitude, α Coronæ borealis [yikleel i shoomauly], 48.——*Alphard* (الفرد - alfard, Ar.). Means single, being apart from other visible stars. Cf. Alfoorood. Otherwise Oonuk shoojah [q.v.], meaning neck of hydra. Star of second magnitude, α Hydræ [shoojah], 31, or Cor hydræ.——*Alpheratz* (الفرس - alfaras, Ar.). From (al, ar. the + faras, ar. horse). Star of 2nd magnitude, α Andromedæ [miratimoosalsila], 1; also known as δ Pegasi [faras ool azam]. This is about the longitude of the present equinoctial colure [madhyama sowra maunam].——*Alrishah* (الرشاء - alrishá, Ar.). From (al, ar. the + rishá, ar. cord). Also called Kalb ool hoot [q.v.], meaning heart of the fish; also Batn ool hoot [q.v.], meaning belly of the fish. δ ε Piscium [hoot, meenam], with some neighbouring stars in the form of a fish with tail towards the south and head towards the north. 28th Arabian lunar mansion. Compare hindoo mansion Raivaty.——*Al riyaul* (الريال - arriyál, Ar.). Plural of (rál), meaning young of an ostrich. Certain small stars in the neighbourhood of Naayim [q.v.] the ostriches, regarded as their young ones.——*Al rooba* (الربع - alrubaa, Ar.). Means a fourth. Small star in middle of Awoyiz [q.v.] in head of Draco [tinneen].——*Al rooccabah* (الرقبه - alrukabah, Ar.). Means the guardian. Also Aljaddy meaning the kid; compare Alioth. Star of second magnitude, α Ursæ minoris [cshoodra ricsham, doobhe asghar], 6; otherwise Polaris the present pole star [dhroovam], a little less than 1½° from the north pole of the equator [naudy mundalam]. Round this the other stars appear to revolve in the course of a day. For past and present pole-stars see under Doobhe asghar, where also see pointers to Alrooccabah. There is no bright star near south pole [dacshina dhroovam]; the only star near about it being of the sixth or last visible magnitude. For pointers of the south pole see Trishunkoo.——*Alroomh* (الرمح - alrumh, Hind.). From (al, ar. the + rumh, ar. spear). Same as Roomh ool simauk.——*Al royee* (الراعى - arrái, Hind.). Means a watcher. Star. Term for both α Ophiuchi [heiyah], 55 [rasalhagne] and γ Cephei [zaut ool coorsy]. Cf. Kalb ool royee for the attendant dog in each case.——*Alsamak* (السمك - assamak, Hind.). Means the fish. Same as Hoot.——*Alshain* (الشاهين - alsháhín, Ar.). From (al, ar. diminutive + sháhín, ar. falcon). Star, β Aquilæ [ookaub].——*Altahauyee* (التحاى - altaháyí, Ar.). From (hayá, ar. rain); from its setting aurorally in midwinter when there is much rain. Small constellation. Three stars over against Hanah [q.v.] between milky way [kahkashaun] and capella, 17 [bramhahridayam, oyook].——*Altair* (الطائر - attáir, Ar.). From (al, ar. the + táir, ar. bird); with wings expanded as if to fly. Otherwise Nasrooltair [q.v.]. Star of the first magnitude, α Aquilæ [ookaub], 60 [saudhyam].——*Alwaida* (العوائذ - alawáiz, Ar.). From (al, ar. diminutive + awáiz, ar. group in draco). Cf. Awoyiz. Star, β Draconis [tinneen].——*Alzirah* (الذراع - alzirá, Ar.). From (al, ar. the + zirá, ar. foreleg); cf zirah, leo's foreleg being here in the old arabian configuration. Otherwise Pollux. Star of the first magnitude, β Geminorum [jowzah], 28 [soocarmam].——*Alzirr* (الزر - alzirr, Ar.). Means a button. Star, ξ Geminorum [jowzah].——*Angiran* (अङ्गिर - angira, San.). From (ang, san. to go round). One of the seven stars [sapta rishy] of Maharicsham [q.v.], at end of tail next body, ε Ursæ majoris [doobhe acbar]. Is Alioth in arabian system.——*Anooraudhay* (अनुराधा - anurádhá, San.; അനിഴം - anizham, Mal.; அனுடம் - anudam, Tam.). From (anu, san. along + rádh, san. to succeed); causing welfare. 17th hindoo lunar mansion. Described as a row of oblations; also as umbrella in hand, or bow. Four stars, β, δ 50, π and ρ Scorpii [akrab]. For δ Scorpii see Vyateepautam. Cf. arabian mansion Yikleel.——*Anoosham* (அனுடம் - anudam, Tam.). Corruption of Anooraudhay [q.v.].——*Anoosya* (अनुस्या - anusyá, San.). Otherwise Atreyee [q.v.]. Wife of Agastyan [q.v.] or Atry [q.v.] in Maharicsham [q.v.]. κ Draconis [tinneen].——*Antacan* (अन्तक - antaka, San.). From (anta, san. end), from yaman [q.v.] or death, the presiding deity. Same as Bharany.——*Arcabhay* (अर्कभा - arkabhá, San.). From (arka, san. sun + bhá, san. to shine). Same as Hastam.——*Ardray* (आर्द्रा - árdrá, San.; ஆதிரை - áthirai, Tam.). Means wet or fresh. Tam. also (tiruváthirai), meaning holy + ardray. Otherwise Rowdray [q.v.]. Sixth hindoo lunar mansion, made up of a single bright star; described as a gem, coral, a burning coal. The star in the shoulder of Orion, α Orionis [jabbaur], 23 [atigandam, betelgeux]. 1st magnitude. Compare arabian mansion Hanah.——*Aridad* (الردف - arridf, Hind.). From (ridf, ar. hinder part). Star of second magnitude, α Cygni [dajjajah], 62 [deneb].——*Arnab* (ارنب - arnab, Ar.). Means a hare. Twelve stars. Lepus in S. hemisphere. Small constellation to the south of Orion [jabbaur]. Its principal star, α Leporis [arsh ool jowzah], of third magnitude, is about same distance or 17° west of Sirius, 26 [loobdhacam, mrigavyandham, shira] that it is south of the middle star [nitauk ool jowzah] of Orion's belt [fakaur ool jowzah]; the three stars form a right-angled triangle, α Leporis being at the right angle.——*Aroondhaty* (अरुन्धती - arundhatí, San.). From (a, san. negative prefix + rudh, san. to stop); not to be interfered with, chaste. A star near Maharicsham [q.v.] said to be wife of Vasishtan [q.v.]; α Draconis [tinneen] or Thuban [q.v.].——*Arsh ool jowzah* (عرش الجوزا - arshuljauzá, Ar.). Means throne of orion [jabbaur]. Four stars; two on forelegs and two on hind legs of Lepus [arnab]. Also specially applied to the single star α Leporis.——*Arsh ool simauk* (عرش السماك - arshussimák, Ar.). Means throne of boötes [awwah]. Otherwise Ajoozool asad [q.v.]. Certain stars in advance of simauk ool azal [q.v.], 41; probably γ, δ 40, ε, η Virginis [soomboola]. For δ Virginis, 40, see Aupas. Compare Awwah the 13th arabian mansion.——*Arsh ool sooreiyah* (عرش الثريا - arshussuraiyah, Ar.). Means throne of pleiades [kritticay, sooreiyah]. Certain small stars near them. Cf. Alfoorood.——*Asad* (اسد - asad, Ar.). Means a lion [simham]. Leo. Fifth constellation of ancient zodiac [raushy chuckram]. South of Great bear [doobhe acbar, maharicsham], on opposite side of it to Polaris, 6 [alrooccabah, dhroovam]. Its four principal stars, α, β, γ, δ, form a quadrilateral figure. To find α Leonis, 32 or Regulus [gandam, kalb ool asad], and β Leonis, 37 or Denebola [q.v.]; a line drawn from Polaris through the Pointers [alanak, doobhe] of the Great bear, and continued rather more than the same distance, will pass between these two stars, Regulus [gandam, kalbool asad], 32 being on the west and β Leonis [denebola, dhroovam], 37 on the east. A line drawn from Vega, 58 [abhijit, nasr ool wauky] through Cor caroli [doobhe acbar] and produced, leads to δ Leonis, 36 [vriddhy, zoobra], and then passes near Regulus, 32. Again, δ [atry] and γ Ursæ majoris [poolastyan], the two stars of the body next tail of Great bear, are nearly in the same line with γ Leonis [algeiba] and Regulus. Again a line drawn from middle star [nitauk ool jawzah] of Orion's belt [alasah, fakaur ool jowzah] through Procyon, 27 [ghoomeisah], in the Little dog [kalb i asghar], will lead directly to Regulus, 32. A line drawn from η Ursæ majoris, 42 [benetnasch], the last star in the tail of the Great bear, through Cor caroli [doobhe acbar], and produced about twice the distance, will lead to β Leonis, 37 [denebola, dhroovam]. It is the most conspicuous star on a line drawn from Arcturus, 44 [haurs ool samah, vajram] to Regulus, 32, but situated nearer the latter. γ Leonis [algeiba] is north, a little easterly and distant about 8° from Regulus. δ Leonis is N.W. of β Leonis, distant about 10°. α Leonis or Regulus is sometimes from its position called Cor leonis or the Lion's heart; Denebola [q.v.] is in tail. Regulus passes the meridian at midnight towards the end of February. Leo minor or the Little lion is a small constellation between Leo and Ursa major [doobhe acbar, maharicsham]. The old arabian Asad extended far west over Cancer [sartaun] and into Gemini [jowzah]. For Ajooz ool asad or rump of leo see Arsh ool simauk. For Jabhat ool asad or forehead of leo see Jabaha. For Kalb ool asad or heart of leo see sep. title. For Oorkoob ool asad or hock of leo see Awwah. For Coonb ool asad see sep. title. For Anfool asad or nose of leo see Nasara. For Zirah ool asad or foreleg of leo see Zirah. Compare arabian mansion Sarafa. Compare also Zirah, Zirah ool mabsoot, and Zirah ool makbooz for the extended arabian Asad. See also Jabaha, Magham, Oottaram, Poobbam, Tarafa, and Zoobra.——*Asaufy* (اثافى - asáfí, Hind.). From (asfiya, ar. one of the three stones on which a cooking pot is placed). A trivet. σ, τ, ν, Draconis [tinneen]. Also the three chief stars in Lyra [shalyauk]. Cf. Azfaur.——*Ashaudham* (आषाढ - áshádha, San.). From (ashádha, san. invincible). Epithet of 20th and 21st hindoo lunar mansions [oottarashaudham, poorvashaudham]. Also name of 4th luni-solar [chaundramaunam] month [mausam].——*Ashraut* (اشراط - ashrát, Ar.). Plural of Sharat. 3 stars in Aries [hamel], two bright [shartein] and one small towards the north of them.——*Ashwiny* (आश्विनी - ashviní, San.; அசுவதி - asuvathi, Tam.). Title and san. from (ashva, san. horse). Tam. from (ashva, san. horse + pati, san. master). The hindoo Dioscuri, horsemen. Probably originally the two twilights. Now first hindoo lunar mansion. Obtained its present situation at head of asterisms, when zodiac [raushy chuckram] started from first degree of the fixed Maisham [q.v.]. For the ancient zodiac headed by Kritticay [q.v.] see remarks under Maunam. Figured as a horse's head. Comprises three bright stars in the head of Aries [hamel], α β and γ; in conformity with Shartein [q.v.], the first lunar mansion of the arabs. For α Arietis, 10 see Hamel and Vishcambham; for β Arietis, 9 see Shartein.——*Atigandam* (अतिगण्ड - atiganda, San.). From (ati, san. prefix of intensity + ganda, san. prominent). Yogam star of sixth hindoo lunar mansion. α Orionis [jabbaur], 23 [betelgeux]. 1st magnitude.——*Atreyee* (अत्रेयी - átréyí, San.). Descendant of Atry. Same as Anoosya.——*Atry* (अत्रि - atri, San.). Means devourer. Otherwise Agastyan [q.v.]. One of seven stars [sapta rishy] in Maha ricsham [q.v.], in square, δ Ursæ majoris [doobhe acbar].——*Aupas* (आपस् - ápas, San.). Means water.

Otherwise (apámvatsa), meaning water + child. Star δ Virginis [canyay, soomboola], 40. 4th magnitude.——*Aushlaisham* (आश्लेष - áshlésha, San.; ஆயில்லியம் - áyilliyam, Tam.). From (á, san. intensive prefix + shlish, san. to cling). Embrace. Otherwise Ayilliyam [q.v.], and Sarpam [q.v.]. Ninth hindoo lunar mansion. Figured as a potter's wheel, serpent, or sloping stone. Contains five stars of which the principal or eastern is the bright star in the southern claw of Cancer, α Cancri [sartaun], 30 [shoolam]. Compare arabian mansion Tarafa.——*Avittam* (அவிட்டம் - avittam, Tam.). Corruption from shravishtay [q.v.] the 23rd hindoo lunar mansion. Same as Dhanishtay.——*Awoyiz* (عوائذ - awáiz, Ar.). Four stars in the head of Tinneen [q.v.]; between Zeebaun [q.v.] and Nasr ool wauky, 58 [q.v.]. β Draconis is Alwaida [q.v.] or small Awoyiz.——*Awwah* (عوا - awwá, Ar.). Means a barking dog; also called Seiyyah meaning clamorous constellation; also called Tarood al bard meaning driver of cold, from rising in evening at close of cold weather.—"*a*" Constellation consisting of two and twenty stars within the figure and one without it; the figure being that of a man having in his right hand a staff, between the stars alphacca [q.v.], 48 and benetnasch [q.v.], 42; and the one without the figure is the red bright star between his thighs, Arcturus, 44 [haurs ool samah, vajram]. This is in the european system the herdsman Boötes, who in rising immediately follows Great bear [doobhe acbar, mahariesham], in early times figured as an ox. Arcturus, or α Boötis, 44 [haurs ool samah, vajram], is the brightest star in N. hemisphere. To find it, continue curve formed by the three stars in tail [banaut] of Great bear to about twice its length, and it will lead to it. η Boötis, 43 is Alroomh [q.v.] or Roomhoolsimauk [q.v.]. ε Boötis, 45 is Izar [q.v.], or Ghafr [q.v.]. Boötes was later called by greeks Arctophylax or the bear-watcher. For Zauviyat ool awwah or angle of boötes see sep. title.—"*b*" As 13th arabian mansion it consists of five stars in the wing of Virgo [canyay, soomboola]. Compare Hastam, 13th hindoo mansion.——*Ayeen ool faras* (عين الفرس - ainulfaras, Ar.). Means eye of the horse, pegasus. Otherwise Markab [q.v.], 68. Star of second magnitude, α Pegasi [faras ool azam], 68 [bramham]. Compare also Farghaun.——*Ayeen ool raumy* (عين الرامى - ainurrámí, Ar.). Means eye of sagittarius [kows]. Star, ν Sagittarii.——*Ayeen ool sowr* (عين الثور - ainussaur, Ar.). Means bulls' eye. Otherwise Kalb ool sowr [q.v.]. Star of first magnitude, α Tauri [sowr], 16 [aldebaran, sowbhaugyam]. ——*Ayilliyam* (ஆயில்லியம் - áyilliyam, Tam.). Corruption from aushlaisham [q.v.] the ninth hindoo lunar mansion.——*Ayooshmat* (आयुष्मत् - áyushmat, San.). From (áyus, san. life + mat, san. suffix of possession). Yogam star of third hindoo lunar mansion. Otherwise Alcyone. η Tauri [sowr], 14. 3rd magnitude.——*Azfaur* (اظفار - azfár, Hind.). From (zafr, ar. talon). Three small stars before α Lyræ [shalyank], 58 [abhijit, nasr ool wauky], forming the vulture's talon. Cf. Asaufy.——*Azfaur oolzeib* (اظفار الذيب - azfáruzzíb, Ar.). From (azfár, ar. claws + zíb, ar. wolf); cf. saboo. Certain stars before those called Zeebaun [q.v.] and near Farkdaun [q.v.].——*Balda* (بلدة - baldah, Ar.). Means breast, as in front of the archer. Six stars in Sagittarius [kows], including ε δ χ μ forming the bow. 21st arabian lunar mansion. Compare hindoo mansion Oottarabhaudram.——*Banaut* (بنات - banát, Ar.). Plural of (bint), daughter. Three stars in the tail of Ursa major [doobhe acbar]. ——*Batn kyetos* (بطن قيطس - batnkítas, Ar.). From (batn, ar. belly + kítas, ar. whale). Star of the third magnitude, ζ Ceti [kyetos], 8.——*Batn ool hoot* (بطن الحوت - batnulhút, Ar.). From (batn, ar. belly + hút, ar. fish). Otherwise Mirack [q.v.]. Bright star of the second magnitude above the drapery round the waist of Andromeda [miratimoosalsila]. β Andromedæ, 4. Also applied to Alrishah [q.v.].——*Bautiya* (باطية - bátiyah, Ar.). Means a cup. Constellation. Seven stars [milaf]. In the european system the Hydra and Goblet, S. hemisphere; is south of the Lion's tail [denebola]. The two principal stars, magnitude 3 and 4 are δ Hydræ et Crateris, and α Hydræ et Crateris, 33, sometimes called Alkes [q.v.], and are about 6° apart in N.E. and S.W. direction. They lie E.S.E., distant about 25° from Cor hydræ [alphard, 31], and south, a little westerly distant 30° from Denebola, 37 [q.v.] in the Lion's tail [asad]. ——*Benetnasch* (بنات النعش - banátunnaash, Ar.). From (banát, ar. daughters + naash, ar. dead body); cf. banaut. Means daughters of the dead following the bier. Same as Alkaid.——*Betelgeux* (ابط الجوزا - ibtuljauzá, Ar.). Title also written Betelgeuse; comes through french. From (ibt, ar. armpit + jauzá, ar. orion). Otherwise Mankib ool jowzah [q.v.], meaning orion's shoulder; also Yadd ool jowzah [q.v.], meaning arm of orion. Star of first magnitude. α Orionis [jabbaur], 23 [ardray, atigandam]. Variable, but variability extends over many years. ——*Bharany* (भरणी - bharaní, San.; பரணி - parani, Tam.). From (bharana, san. nourishing). Also called Antacan [q.v.], from yaman the presiding deity. 2nd hindoo lunar mansion. Figured by yony, triangle, or fire place; comprises three stars in Musca or the fly, forming a triangle almost equilateral. Midway between ram's horn [shartein] and Pleiades [kritticay, sooreiyah]. Its influence is generally bad; but when at the nadir [q.v.] it is held to be a good time to begin to dig a foundation, a well, or a tank. Compare arabian mansion Bootein.——*Bhaudram* (भाद्र - bhádra, San.). Short for Bhaudrapadam [q.v.].——*Bhaudrapadum* (भाद्रपदा - bhádrapadá, San.). From (bhadra, san. auspicious + pada, san. foot), from being represented by legs of a bedstead. The 25th [poorvabhaudram] and 26th [oottarabhaudram] hindoo lunar mansion. For luni-solar [chaundramaunam] month so called see Mausam. Compare Fargh ool dalo.——*Boola* (بلع - bula, Ar.). Means voracious; so close that one of them swallows the other; cf. Zaubih. Otherwise Sad i boola. Two stars, ε, μ Aquarii [coombham, dalo]. 23rd arabian lunar mansion. Cf. hindoo mansion Dhanishtay.——*Bootein* (بطين - butain, Ar.). Diminutive of (batn, ar. belly). ε. π, υ Arietis [hamel]. 2nd arabian lunar mansion. Cf. hindoo mansion Bharany.——*Bramhahridayam* (ब्रह्महृदय - brahmahridaya, San.). From (brahma, san. the deity + hridaya, san. heart). Otherwise Capella, or Oyook [q.v.]. Star. α Aurigæ [mausik ool inaun], 17. 1st magnitude.——*Bramham* (ब्रह्म - brahma, San.). From (brahma, san. the deity). Otherwise Markab [q.v.]. Yogam star of 25th hindoo lunar mansion. α Pegasi [faras ool azam], 68. 2nd magnitude.——*Cantooras* (قنطورس - kuntúras, Ar.). From greek κένταυρος. Constellation of 37 stars. Centaurus, S. hemisphere. Begins 20° south of Spica, 41 [harshanam, simauk ool azal], and extends as far as Southern cross [trishunkoo]. It contains three principal stars, α. β and θ Centauri. α [hazaur] and β [wazn] Centauri are east, a little south, of the eastern arm of the Cross [trishunkoo]. β Centauri being distant about 9½°, and α Centauri 4½° more easterly still. θ Centauri, in the shoulder of Centaur, is south-westerly of α Libræ, 46 [siddhy, zubenesch], the chief star in Balance [meezaun, toolaum], and these two stars form with Spica, 41 [harshanam, simauk ool azal] a right-angled triangle. ζ Centauri, a star in the body of Centaur, is 13° northward of β [wazn] Centauri. α [hazaur] Centauri is the nearest fixed star to the earth, 20 billions of miles away; has parallax of $\frac{93}{100}$ ths of a second; light travelling 191,500 miles per second comes in 3⅓ years.——*Canyay* (कन्या - kanyá, San.). Means virgin. 6th sign [raushy] of the zodiac [raushy chuckram]. Virgo, ♍ [soomboola].——*Carcatacam* (कर्कटक - karkataka, San.). Means crab. 4th sign [raushy] of zodiac [raushy chuckram]. Cancer, ♋ [sartaun].——*Casat ool masaukeen* (قصعة المساكين - kasatulmasákín, Hind.). From (kasa, ar. bowl + masákín, ar. pauper); cf. alkes; from configuration. Same as Yikleel i shoomauly.——*Causa i darvishaun* (كاسه درويشان - kásahidarwíshán, Hind.). From (kásah, pers. bowl + darwísh, pers. pauper); cf. alkes; from configuration. Same as Yikleel i shoomauly.——*Caushyapy* (काश्यपी - káshyapí, San.). From (kashyapa, san. the sage). Constellation. Cassiopea, wife of Cepheus or Cashyapan [zaut ool coorsy].——*Chitta* (चित्रा - chitrá, San.; చిత్త - chitta, Tel.). Means bright. Figured as a pearl. 14th hindoo lunar mansion; consists of single star of Virgin's spike, α Virginis [soomboola], 41, spica [harshanam, simauk ool azal]. 1st magnitude.——*Coombham* (कुम्भ - kumbha, San.). Means pot. 11th sign [raushy] of the zodiac [raushy chuckram]. Aquarius, ♒ [dalo]. See also Sood.——*Coombha yony* (कुंभयोनि - kumbhayóni, San.). From (kumbha, san. pot + yóni, san. origin); from traditional origin out of a water jar. Otherwise Agastyan [q.v.]. Same as Sooheil [q.v.], 25, or Canopus.——*Coonb ool asad* (قنب الاسد - kumbulasad, Hind.). From (kumb, ar. sheath + asad, ar. leo). Star of second magnitude. Otherwise Denebola [q.v.]; also Dhroovam [q.v.]. β Leonis [asad], 37. Compare Sarafa, the arabian mansion.——*Cratoo* (क्रतु - kratu, San.). From (kri, san. to do). One of the seven stars [sapta rishy] of Mahariesham [q.v.], in square; α Ursæ majoris [doobhe acbar], 35. Doobhe [q.v.] in arabian system.——*Cshoodra ricsham* (क्षुद्रऋक्ष - kshudrariksha, San.). From (kshudra, san. little + riksha, san. bear). Constellation. Ursa minor [doobhe asghar].——*Cuff ool jazmah* (كف الجذماء - kaffuljazmá, Hind.). From (kaff, ar. hand + jazmá, ar. amputated); being a less distance from pleiades [kritticay, sooreiyah] in opposite direction than cuff ool khazeeb [q.v.]. Refers to some ancient figure. Otherwise Menkar [q.v.]. α Ceti [kyetos].——*Cuff ool khazeeb* (كف الخضيب - kaffulkhazíb, Hind.). From (kaff, ar. hand + khazíb, ar. extended); being farther off from pleiades [kritticay, sooreiyah] in opposite direction than cuff ool jazmah [q.v.]. Otherwise Chaph. β Cassiopeæ [caushyapy, zaut ool coorsy]. At the culmination [noojoom] of this the mahomedans believe every prayer to be favorably heard; this was recently the longitude of the equinoctial colure.——*Dajjajah* (دجاجه - dajjájah, Ar.). Means a domestic fowl. Also (attáir), meaning a bird. Constellation. Nineteen stars in the figure and two outside, of which four stars [fawauris] lie in Milky way [kahkashaun]. Cygnus, the Swan. The principal star is α Cygni, 62, or Deneb [q.v.] or Aridad [q.v.]. A line passing between last two stars of body [naash] of Great bear [doobhe acbar], γ [poolastyan] and δ Ursæ majoris [atry], thence between guards [farkdaun] of Little bear, β, 47 [kochab] and γ Ursæ minoris [cshoodra ricsham, doobhe asghar], and produced, will lead to α Cygni, or Deneb [q.v.]. A line drawn from α Persei, 13 [mirfak] through middle of Cassiopea [caushyapy, zaut ool coorsy] will lead to it. ζ Cygni is a few degrees north of a line drawn from Alpheratz, 1 [q.v.], through Scheat, β Pegasi, 67 [mankib], and produced rather less than twice their distance; the double star, 61 Cygni, is 9° to north of ζ Cygni. γ Cygni is Sadr ool dajjajah; which see. For Zanab ool dajjajah or tail of cygnus see Deneb. See also Fawauris.——*Dalo* (دلو - dalo, Ar.). Means a bucket. Aquarius [coombham], the water-bearer. 11th constellation of ancient zodiac [raushy chuckram]. Contains a very great number of small stars situated to the south of Markab, 68 [q.v.] and Enif, 63 [fomalfars] in Pegasus [faras ool azam]. β Aquarii passes the meridian at midnight during the middle of August. λ Aquarii is Shoobhram [q.v.] or Shooclam [q.v.]. For others see Akbee, Shatabhishay, Sood. For Fargh ool dalo or side of dalo, see sep. title.——*Deneb* (الذنب - azzanab, Ar.). From (al, ar. the + zanab, ar. tail). Otherwise Zanab ool dajjajah [q.v.], 62, meaning the tail of cygnus; from resembling the tail of a horse; also Aridad [q.v.]. Star of first magnitude. α Cygni [dajjajah], 62.——*Denebalgedy* (ذنب الجدی - zanabuljadí, Ar.). From (zanab, ar. tail + jadí, ar. capricornus). Star of third magnitude. δ Capricorni [jaddy], 64. See also Sood.——*Deneb kyetos* (ذنب قیطس - zanabkitas, Ar.). From (zanab, ar. tail + kítas, ar. cetus). Star of second magnitude. β Ceti [kyetos], 3.——*Denebola* (ذنب الاسد - zanabulasad, Ar.). From (zanab, ar. tail + asad, ar. leo). Otherwise Coonb ool asad [q.v.]; also Dhroovam [q.v.]. Star of second magnitude. β Leonis [asad], 37. Compare Sarafa, the arabian mansion.——*Dhanishtau* (धनिष्ठा - dhanisht'há, San.; அவிட்டம் - avittam, Tam.). Means very rich. Otherwise Shravishtay [q.v.] or Avittam [q.v.]. 23rd hindoo lunar mansion. Represented by a drum or tabor. Four stars, α, β, γ and δ Delphini [doolfeen]. For α Delphini, 61 see Shoobham. Compare arabian mansion Sood.——*Dhanoos* (धनुस् - dhanus, San.). Means bow. Ninth sign [raushy] of the zodiac [raushy chuckram]. Sagittarius ♐ [kows].——*Dhrity* (धृति - dhriti, San.). Means holding fast. Yogam star of eighth hindoo lunar mansion. δ Cancri [sartaun], 29. 4th magnitude.——*Dhroovam* (ध्रुव - dhruva, San.). From (dhru, san. to be fixed).—"*a*" Otherwise Polaris, or Alrooccabah [q.v.]. For other pole stars see under Doobhe asghar. For south pole see Trishunkoo. Star of second magnitude. α Ursæ minoris [cshoodraricsham, doobhe asghar], 6.—"*b*" Yogam star of 12th hindoo lunar mansion, β Leonis [asad], 37. Same as Denebola [q.v.].——*Doobhe* (دب - dubb, Ar.). Means the bear. Star of second magnitude. α Ursæ majoris [doobhe acbar, maharicsham], 35; the european N. pointer, the S. pointer being β Ursæ majoris or alanak, 34 [q.v.]. Is Cratoo in hindoo system. ——*Doobhe acbar* (دب اکبر - dubbiakbar, Ar.). From (dubb, ar. bear + akbar, ar. great). Also (banátunnaashikubrá). Constellation. 27 stars. The Great bear, Ursa major [maharicsham], most conspicuous constellation of N. hemisphere. In European system distinguished by seven stars between first and third magnitudes; called from figure, when seen below the pole which is not the case here, Plough, Waggon, Charles's wain, Butcher's cleaver, &c. Four of these stars, α 35, β 34, γ, and δ Ursæ majoris, form a quadrilateral figure [naash], called Square of great bear [maharicsham]. They are in body of the animal; and because a line from two of the stars of this group, α and β Ursæ majoris, nearly falls into the Polar star, 6 [al rooccabah, dhroovam], these two are called pointers; the N. pointer, α Ursæ majoris, is Doobhe, 35 [q.v.] or the hindoo Cratoo [q.v.]; the S. pointer, β Ursæ majoris is Alanak, 34 [q.v.] or the hindoo Poolahan [q.v.]. δ Ursæ majoris [atry] has diminished in brightness during present century. The three stars ε, ζ, and η, are tail [banaut] of the Bear [ricsham]; the first, or that next body, is ε Ursæ majoris, or Alioth [q.v.], the hindoo Angiran [q.v.]; that at end of tail is η or Benetnasch, 42 [q.v.], the hindoo Mareechy [q.v.]. The middle of tail is ζ, the hindoo Vasishtan [q.v.]. Canes venatici, Hunting dogs or Grey-hounds, are not represented in the arabian system; these lie between Boötes [awwah] and Great bear [doobhe acbar, maharicsham], to south of tail; contain 12 Canum venaticorum, or Cor caroli. To find Cor caroli, a line from Arcturus, 44 [haurs ool samah, vajram] to β Ursæ majoris, 34 [alanak] is bisected by Cor caroli; or a line, from α Ursæ majoris, 35, Doobhe [q.v.], through γ Ursæ majoris [poolastyan], and produced nearly twice their distance, will point it out. Cor caroli, ε Ursæ majoris, and the S. pointer, β Ursæ majoris, 34 [alanak], form a triangle. See also Soohah. Cf. Ricsham, Rishy.——*Doobhe asghar* (دب اصغر - dubbiasghar, Ar.). From (dubb, ar. bear + asghar, ar. minor). Also (banátunnaashisughrá). Constellation. The Little bear, Ursa minor [cshoodraricsham], N. hemisphere. Seven principal stars, not unlike Great bear, but smaller; the tails of the two bears are in reversed directions. The quadrilateral figure is formed by β, γ, ζ, and η; in the tail are ε, δ, and α. α Ursæ minoris, 6, called Polaris, or the Pole star, or Al rooccabah [q.v.], or Dhroovam [q.v.], is of second magnitude, at end of tail. β 47, and γ of Little bear are used by sailors to mark hours of night; called guards, from the spanish meaning the night watches [farkdaun]. Polaris, 6 [al rooccabah] is found by pointers [alanak, doobhe] of Great bear, being first bright star on a line produced from β, 34 through α Ursæ majoris, 35 [doobhe]. North pole of heavens [oottaradhroovam] may be found by a line from ε Ursæ majoris [alioth], the first star in the tail, to Polaris, 6 and producing that line about 1½°. When ε Ursæ majoris [alioth] is 6 hours from meridian, Polaris is at its greatest distance from meridian [raikhay], and its altitude [avanataumsham] in that position will be nearly same as elevation [oonnatam] of pole [dhroovam]; which is equal to latitude [acsham] of the observer. At present Polaris is approaching the pole, and about A.D. 2100 will be only 28′ off it, after which it will recede. Then the pole will pass from the Little bear to Cepheus [zaut ool coorsy] and then over the borders of the Swan [dajjajah]. 4,200 years ago α Draconis [tinneen] or Thuban [q.v.] or Aroondhaty was pole star, being at that time distant from pole only 10′. 2,000 years ago, β Ursæ minoris, 47 or Kochab [q.v.], was nearest the pole. In 6000 A.D. γ Draconis [tinneen], 56 [etenin] will be pole star. After 12,000 years, Vega, α Lyræ [shalynuk], 58 [abhijit, nasr ool wauky], will be the only pole star within about 5° of the pole [dhroovam]. Similarly Canopus, α Argûs [safeenah], 25 [agastyan, sooheil] will hereafter be bright star near south pole [dacshina dhroovam]. For pointers of south pole at present see Trishunkoo. These changes are connected with precession of equinoxes [ayanaumsham, craunty panta gaty, maunam, rishy].——*Doolfeen* (دلفین - dulfín, Ar.). Means dolphin. Constellation. Ten stars. Delphinus [dhanishtay]. For α Delphini, 61 see Shoobham. See also Saleeb.——*Eindram* (ऐन्द्र - aindra, San.). Otherwise Alpheratz, 1 [q.v.]. Yogam star of 26th Hindoo lunar mansion, α Andromedæ [mirat i moosalsila], 1. 2nd magnitude. Compare Mahendram [q.v.] and Mankib [q.v.].——*Etenin* (تنین - tinnín, Ar.). Means a dragon. Star of third magnitude. γ Draconis [tinneen], 56.——*Fakaur ool jowzah* (فقار الجوزا - fakáruljauzá, Ar.). From (fakár, ar. spine + jauzá, ar. orion). Star of second magnitude. ζ Orionis [jabbaur], 22. Also as constellation the three bright stars δ, ε 21, ζ 22 disposed obliquely in the midst of jabbaur [q.v.], otherwise called warrior's belt or belt of orion [jabbaur]; also alasah [q.v.]. ζ Orionis, 22 is the eastern end of the belt [alnitak]; ε Orionis, 21 or nitauk ool jowzah [q.v.] is the centre, and δ Orionis or nazm [q.v.] or mintaka [q.v.] is the western end of the belt. The belt is known in english by various names as Golden yard, Jacob's staff and Three kings.——*Fakkah* (فكہ - fakkah, Hind.). From (fakk, ar. opening); from shape. Same as Yikleel i shoomauly.——*Faras ool azam* (فرس الاعظم - farasulazam, Ar.). From (faras, ar. horse + azam, ar. highest). Otherwise Faras ool acbar, meaning the greater horse. Constellation. Nineteen stars. Pegasus, the Winged horse. To south-westward of Andromeda [mirat i moosalsila], and south-eastward of Cygnus [dajjajah]; four remarkable stars, α, β, γ, δ of the second and third magnitudes, form the square [farghaun] of Pegasus, on opposite side of pole [dhroovam] to square of Great bear [doobhe acbar, maharicsham]; one constellation passes the meridian about 12 hours after the other. α Pegasi, 68 [ayeen ool faras, bramham] or Markab [q.v.], and β Pegasi, 67 [mankib] or Scheat, form the western side of the square, and pass the meridian [raikhay] first. α Pegasi, 68 is at the south-west angle of the square; β Pegasi, 67 is at the north-west angle, and distant about 13° from Markab, 68 [q.v.]. γ Pegasi, 2 [algenib, mahendram] is 14° south of α Andromedæ [mirat i moosalsila], 1 [alpheratz, eindram], and 16° east of Markab, 68 [q.v.]; it forms the south-east angle of the square [farghaun]. ε Pegasi, 63 [fomal fars, sad ool hoomaum] or Enif, a star between the second and third magnitude, lies about W. by S. from α Pegasi, 68, distant about 20°. Or a line drawn from β 4 to α 1 Andromedæ, and produced about twice their distance, will lead to it. Seven conspicuous stars in Pegasus, Andromeda [mirat i moosalsila], and Perseus [humiliraus ool ghowl], resemble the seven stars in the Great bear [doobhe acbar, maharicsham], but smaller. For others see Sad ool baury, Sad ool bihaum, Sad ool matar. For Ayeen ool faras or eye of horse see Markab. For Fomal fars or mouth of horse see sep. title. For Janah ool faras or wing of horse see Algenib. For Kita ool faras or small horse see sep. title. For Mankib ool faras or shoulder of horse see Mankib. For Matn ool faras or middle of horse see Mankib. See also Mokaddam, Mooakhar, Oottarabhaudram, Poorvabhaudram.——*Farghaun* (فرغان - farghán, Ar.). From (fargh, ar. width); from forming a square. Also (aldalo), the bucket. Constellation. Four stars α 68, β 67, γ 2, δ Pegasi [faras ool azam], forming a square, the apparent distance between each pair being the measure of a spear. Compare arabian mansion Fargh ool dalo, Fargh ool owwal, Fargh ool sauny, Mokaddam, and Mooakhar. ——*Fargh ool dalo* (فرغ الدلو - farghuddalo Ar.). Means the breadth of a bucket. Name of the two arabian lunar mansions, 26th and 27th, distinguished by Mokaddam [q.v.] and Mooakhar [q.v.]. Compare hindoo mansions Poorvabhaudram and Oottarabhaudram.——*Fargh ool owwal* (فرغ الاول - farghulawwal, Hind.). From (fargh, ar. width of a bucket + awwal, first). Westernmost or first rising side of square. Same as Mokaddam. Compare hindoo mansion Poorvabhaudram.——*Fargh ool sauny* (فرغ الثانی - farghussání, Hind.). From (fargh, ar. breadth + sání, ar. latter). Easternmost or later rising side of square. Same as Mooakhar. Compare hindoo mansion Oottarabhaudram.——*Farkdaun* (فرقدان - farkdán, Ar.). From (farkad, ar. calf + ar. dual sign). Small constellation. β 47 and γ Ursæ minoris [cshoodra ricsham, doobhe asghar]; by which one directs one's course by sea and by land. Called 'guards' by sailors. For β Ursæ minoris, 47 see Kochab.——*Fawauris* (فوارس - faváris, Hind.). Constellation. Four stars in Cygnus [dajjajah] lying across the Milky way [kahkashaun].——*Fomal fars* (فم الفرس - fammulfaras, Ar.). From (famm, ar. mouth + faras, ar. horse). Otherwise Enif, 63. Star of second magnitude. ϵ Pegasi [faras ool azam], 63 [sad ool hoomaum]. See also Akhzar.——*Fomalhaut* (فم الحوت - fammulhút, Ar.). From (famm, ar. mouth + hút, ar. pisces). Star of first magnitude. α Piscis australis [hoot i joonooby], 66. See also Akhzar.——*Gandam* (गण्ड - ganda, San.). Means chief. Otherwise Regulus, 32. Yogam star of first magnitude of tenth hindoo lunar mansion. α Leonis [asad], 32 [kalb ool asad].——*Ghafr* (غفر - ghafr, Ar.). Means belly. Constellation. Three stars ι, κ, λ, of Virgo [soomboola]. 15th arabian lunar mansion. Compare hindoo mansion Swauty. Also a star of third magnitude, ϵ Boötis [awwah], 45 or Izar [q.v.].——*Ghoomeisah* (غميصاء - ghumaisáh, Ar.). From (ghamasa, ar. a flux from the eyes); from being affected with constant weeping. Otherwise Shiralghoomeisah [q.v.], meaning the shira with weeping eye on account of her separation from her sisters sirius, 26 [mrigavyandham, shira] and canopus 25 [agastyan, sooheil]; also Shiralshaumiyah [q.v.] meaning the syrian or northern shira; also Roomeisah [q.v.], meaning having weeping eye. The european Procyon. Star of first magnitude. α Canis minoris [kalbiasghar], 27 [shira]. Compare Shiriyaun, the two sisters Shira [q.v.], and Ghoomeisah and Sooheil [q.v.].——*Ghooraub* (غراب - ghuráb, Ar.). Means crow. Constellation. Seven stars. The Crow, S. hemisphere, near the tail of Hydra [shoojah]; has four principal stars of the third magnitude in the form of a small quadrilateral figure, distant 15° to 20° in a S.W. direction from Spica, 41 [harshanam, simaukoolazal] in the Virgin [soomboola]. The northernmost star is δ Corvi, 39 [vyaughautam] and the southernmost star is β Corvi. Algoreb [q.v.] is α Corvi, 38. Compare Hastam. ——*Hakah* (هقعه - hakaah, Ar.). Three stars in Orion [jabbaur]. Fifth arabian lunar mansion. Compare hindoo mansion Mrigashiras.——*Hamel* (حمل - hamal, Ar.). Means lamb. The star α Arietis, 10 [hamel, vishcambham]. Also Aries, the Ram [maisham], the first constellation in the ancient zodiac [raushy chuckram]. This contains two principal stars, α 10 and β Arietis, 9 [shartein]; which mark the base of the horns [shartein] of the ram, and are about 4° apart. To find α Arietis, 10, or Hamel, and β Arietis, 9, or Shartein [q.v.], a line drawn from Polaris, 6 [alrooccabah, dhroovam] through ϵ Cassiopeæ [caushyapy, zautool coorsy], the nearest to the Great bear [doobhe acbar, maharicsham] of the five stars, and produced thence through Alanak [q.v.], γ Andromedæ [mirat i moosalsila], leads to them nearly. Or, a line joining the Pleiades [kritticay, sooreiyah], and Algenib, 2 [q.v.], or γ Pegasi [faras ool azam], 2 [mahendram], is bisected by β Arietis, 9 [shartein]. β is to the south-westward of α Arietis, 10 [hamel] and close to β, about 1½° to the southward, is a star of the fourth magnitude, γ Arietis. The three stars are near each other, and in a line. Musca [bharany], the fly, is a group of small stars in the northern part of Aries not represented in arabic, and now called 35, 39, and 41 Arietis even in europe. See also Bootein [nowroz].——*Hanah* (هنعه - hanaah, Ar.). Means a mark on camel's neck. Five stars in Orion [jabbaur]. Sixth arabian lunar mansion. Compare hindoo mansion Ardray.——*Harshanam* (हर्षण - harshana, San.). From (hrish, san. to gladden). Yogam star of 14th hindoo lunar mansion. α Virginis [soomboola], 41. Spica [simauk ool azal]. 1st magnitude [madhyama sowra maunam, p].——*Hastam* (हस्ता - hastá, San.; அத்தம் - attam, Tam.). From (hasta, san. hand). 13th hindoo lunar mansion. Figured as a hand; contains five stars, α, β, γ, δ, ϵ Corvi [ghooraub]. For α Corvi, 38 see Algoreb. For δ Corvi, 39 see Vyaughautam. Compare arabian mansion Awwah.——*Haudy oon najm* (حادی النجم - hádiyunnajm, Hind.). From (hádí, ar. urger + najm, ar. pleiades). Same as Aldebaran.——*Haumil i rausool ghowl* (حامل راس الغول - hámilirásulghúl, Ar.). From (hámil, ar. carrier + rás, ar. head + ghúl, ar. goblin). Otherwise Parisiyawash [q.v.], meaning maiden's hair. Constellation. Twenty-six stars. Perseus, slayer of Medusa. Contains two principal stars, α Persei, 13 or Mirfak [q.v.], and β Persei, 12 or Algol [q.v.]; the latter is also known as β Medusæ, being in head of Medusa, which in european figure of constellation Perseus holds in his hand. A line drawn from γ Ursæ minoris, the southernmost guard [farkdaun] of Little bear [cshoodra ricsham, doobhe asghar] through Polaris, 6 [al rooccabah, dhroovam], and produced twice their distance, leads to α Persei, 13, which is the brightest of several stars forming an arc of a circle, the concave part of which is turned towards Great bear [doobhe acbar, maharicsham]: β Persei, 12 or β Medusæ lies to the south-west of α Persei, at distance of about 10°; it is also called Algol, 12 [q.v.], and is one of the variable stars, being usually of the second magnitude, and continuing so for 2 days 13½ hours; then it suddenly dims, and in 3½ hours is reduced to fourth magnitude, at which it continues for 15 minutes; it then increases, and in 3½ hours more returns to usual magnitude, going through all changes in 2d. 20h. 48m. 58s. A line drawn from Orion's belt [fakaur ool jowzah] through Aldebaran, 16 [q.v.] in the Bull [sowr], and produced twice their distance, will lead to Algol, 12 [q.v.]. Algol forms a triangle with Capella, 17 [bramhahridayam, oyook] and the Pleiades [kritticay, sooreiyah]. ——*Haurs ool samah* (حارس السماء - hárisussamá, Ar.). From (háris, ar. guardian + samá, ar. sky); from its being seen always in the sky; also Haurs ool shimaul meaning guardian of the north; also Simauk ool raumih [q.v.], from its position with η boötis [awwah], 43 [roomhool simauk]; also Simauk ool mirzam [q.v.], the cold star, as distinguished from Simauk ool azal [q.v.] or spica virginis [soomboola], 41 [harshanam]. Otherwise Arcturus, and Vajram [q.v.]. Star of first magnitude. α Boötis [awwah], 44.——*Hazaur* (حضار - hazár, Ar.). From (hazara, ar. to be present). α Centauri [cantooras]. Compare Moohlifaun and Wazn.——*Heiyah* (حيه - haiyah, Ar.). Means a serpent. Constellation. Also (alhawwá). Eighteen stars. Ophiuchus, the serpent-bearer. N. hemisphere. To the south of Hercules [jausy], and west of Aquila [ookaub]. α Ophiuchi, 55 [alroyee, rasalhague] and α Herculis, 54 [rasalgethy] are about 5° apart, or the same distance as the Pointers [alanak, doobhe] of the Great bear [doobhe acbar, maharicsham]; α Ophiuchi being south-eastward of α Herculis. They are in a line between Arcturus, 44 [haurs ool samah, vajram] and Altair, 60 [q.v.], but nearer the latter; α Ophiuchi, 55, Altair 60, and Vega, 58 [abhijit, nasr ool wauky], form an equilateral triangle. α Ophiuchi is called Rasal hague [q.v.]; and α Herculis, Rasalgethy [q.v.]. For Hydrus the water snake see under Nahar. For Serpens the serpent see Hooweiyah. For Oonuk ool heiyah or neck of serpent see Oonuk.——*Hoot* (حوت - hút, Ar.). Means a fish. Otherwise Alsamak [q.v.]. Pisces [meenam]. 12th constellation of ancient zodiac [raushy chuckram]; two fishes linked together by a string [alrishah] tied to their tails; one is due south of Mirack [q.v.], or β Andromedæ [miratimoosalsila], 4 [batn ool hoot], the other is south of the square [farghaun] of Pegasus [farasoolazam]; ι Piscium in the latter fish passes the meridian at midnight during the middle of September; η Piscium [maunam], the principal star in the former fish, and situated to the S.W. of α Arietis, 10 [hamel, vishcambham], passes the meridian at midnight about the middle of October. For α Piscium see Ookda. For η and ζ Piscium see Raivaty and Veidhrity. For Batn ool hoot or belly of the fish see Alrishah. For Kalb ool hoot or heart of the fish see Alrishah.——*Hoot i joonooby* (حوت جنوبی - hútijunúbí, Ar.). From (hút, ar. fish + junúbí, ar. southern). Constellation. Eleven stars. Piscis australis, the Southern fish. S. hemisphere. Southward of Aquarius [coombham, dalo], and contains one principal star, α Piscis australis, 66, or Fomalhaut [q.v.]. A line drawn from β Pegasi [faras ool azam], 67, Scheat [mankib] through α Pegasi [faras ool azam], 68, Markab [q.v.], the two stars forming the west side of the square [farghaun] of Pegasus [faras ool azam] and produced three times their distance, will lead to Fomalhaut [q.v.]. Menkar [q.v.], Mira, and Deneb kyetos [q.v.], 3, in the Whale [kyetos], and Fomal haut in the southern fish, are nearly in a line running N.E. and S.W., Fomal haut being at the S.W. end.——*Hooweiyah* (حويه - huwaiyah, Ar.). Means a serpent. Constellation. Serpens. N. hemisphere. A long, winding constellation, which, commencing close to α Corona borealis [yikleel i shoomauly], 48 [alphacca,], passes to the southward on the west side of Ophiuchus [heiyah], and then turning to the eastward, through the latter, is found again on its east side stretching toward Aquila [ookaub]. It contains one principal star, α Serpentis, 49 [oonuk]. This is about 20° nearly due south, a little easterly, from Gemma, 48, the principal star of Corona borealis [yikleelishoomauly]; it is also about 25° S.E. from Arcturus, 44. The three stars, α Serpentis, 49, Gemma, 48 [alphacca], and Arcturus, 44 [haurs ool samah, vajram] form a conspicuous triangle. For Hydrus the water-snake see under Nahr.——*Izar* (ایسار - ísár, Hind.). From (yusr, ar. left). Star, ϵ Boötis [awwah], 45 [ghafr].——*Jabaha* (جبهه - jabahah, Ar.). Means forehead; also (jabhatulasad), meaning forehead of leo. Tenth arabian lunar mansion. Four stars, ζ, γ, η, α of Leo [asad, simham]; some say five including ν Leonis. For α Leonis, 32 see Gandam and Kalb ool asad. For γ Leonis see Algeiba. Compare hindoo mansion Magham.——*Jabbaur* (جبار - jabbár, Ar.). Means haughty and inaccessible; represented as a crowned king upon a throne. Otherwise Jowzah, or middle constellation, this largely entering into compounds for which see below; though Jowzah [q.v.] is also Gemini. No hindoo name for the whole. Constellation of 38 stars. Orion, lover of Diana. S. hemisphere. Lies to the south of Auriga [mausikoolinaun] and S.E. of Taurus [sowr]. Four bright stars, α, β, γ and κ, form a great quadrilateral; Betelgeux, 23 [q.v.], or α Orionis, the chief star, is at the north-east angle in the right shoulder of Orion; Rigel [q.v.], or β Orionis, 18, at the opposite angle, is in the left foot, compare Rigel ool jowzal yoosrah under Rigel; Bellatrix, or γ Orionis, 19 [mirzam], situated the same distance on one side of Aldebaran, 16 [q.v.] that Pleiades [kritticay, sooreiyah] are on the other side, is in left shoulder; κ Orionis [rigel ool jowz al yoomnah] is in right knee. In the middle of the quadrilateral, are three conspicuous stars, δ [mintaka, nazm], ϵ, 21 [nitauk ool jowzah], and ζ, 22 [alnitak, fakaur ool jowzah], ranged N.W. and S.E.; these are called the belt of Orion [alasah] or Fakaur ool jowzah [q.v.], whence to the southward there is a luminous train of small stars forming the sword, and among these are some nebulæ. For λ Orionis see Shobhanam. See also Hakah and

Hanah, Mrigashiras and Ardray, the arabian and hindoo mansions. For Arsh ool jowzah or throne of orion see sep. title. For Rigel ool jowzal yoomnah or right leg of orion see sep. title. For Rigel ool jowzal yoosrah or left leg of orion see Rigel. For Taujool jowzah or crown of orion see sep. title. For Zawauyib ool jowzah or pendent forelock of orion see sep. title. For arm of orion see Betelgeux and Yaddooljowzah. For belt of orion see Fakaur ool jowzah. For shoulder of orion see Betelgeux and Mankibool jowzah. For spine of orion see Fakaur ool jowzah.——*Jaddy* (جدی - jadí, Ar.). Means a kid. Capricornus, the Goat [macaram]. Tenth constellation of ancient zodiac [raushy chuckram], distinguished by its two principal stars, α and β Capricorni, being in a line produced from Vega, 58 [abhijit, nasr ool wauky] through Altair, 60 [q.v.] or Saudhyam [q.v.]. The star δ Capricorni, 64, or Deneb algedy [q.v.], is nearly due south of Enif, 63 [fomal fars], in Pegasus [faras ool azam], at the distance of 26°. α Capricorni, which is in the horn of the Goat, passes the meridian at midnight towards the end of July. See also arabian mansion Zaubih; also Sadinaushira.——*Jaddy ool farkad* (جدی الفرقد - jadíulfarkad, Hind.). From (jadí, ar. kid + farkdán, ar. the guards of small bear). Same as Alioth.——*Janah ool faras* (جناح الفرس - janáhulfaras, Hind.). From (janáh, ar. wing + faras, ar. horse). Same as Algenib.——*Jausy* (جاثی - jásí, Ar.). Means a strong man. Constellation. Twenty-eight stars. Hercules. N. hemisphere. South of the two principal stars in Draco [tinneen] west of Lyra [shalyauk], and east of Boötes [awwah] and Corona borealis [yikleelishoomauly]. α Herculis, 54, or Rasalgethy [q.v.] is one of the variable stars, going from 3 to 4 in 66 days. β Herculis is midway on a line between α Herculis, 54 and α Coronæ borealis, 48 [alphacca]. ζ Herculis is on a line between α Coronæ borealis [yikleelishoomauly], 48 and α Lyræ [shalyauk], 58 [abhijit, nasr ool wauky], but nearer the former star; it is a double star, with the shortest period known, viz. 36 years.——*Jowzah* (جوزا - jauzá, Ar.). From (jauz, ar. middle); from its culminating vertically in arabia. Gemini [mitoonam]. Third constellation of ancient zodiac [raushy chuckram]. To E. of Taurus [sowr], and S.E. of Auriga [mausikoolinaun], contains three principal stars, α Geminorum or Castor, β Geminorum, 28 [alzirah, soocarmam] or Pollux, and γ Geminorum [alhena]. α Geminorum, or Castor, and β Geminorum, 28 or Pollux [alzirah, soocarmam], form the heads of the Twins [mitoonam], and are about 5° apart, Castor to the N.W., Pollux to the S.E. A line drawn from the Pleiades [kritticay, sooreiyah] through β Tauri [sowr], 20 [agny, nath], and produced the same distance beyond, leads to them; as does also a line drawn from Rigel, 18 [q.v.], the bright star in the heel of Orion [jabbaur], through the middle star of his belt [fakaur ool jowzah]. Several small stars in a line running N.W. and S.E. form the feet of the Twins [mitoonam]; the brightest, γ Geminorum [alhena], is due east of Aldebaran, 16 [q.v.] at the distance of 28°; this star also bisects the line drawn from the centre of Orion's belt [alasah, fakaurool jowzah] to Castor. Castor and Aldebaran are the base of an isosceles triangle of which Capella, 17 [bramhahridayam, oyook] is the apex. Castor is a double star, period about 1,000 years. Pollux, 28 [alzirah, soocarmam] passes the meridian at midnight about middle of January. For ξ Geminorum see Alzirr. See also the arabian lunar mansion Zirah, which takes the heads of the twins.——*Jyeshtay* (ज्येष्टा - jyéshtá, San.; തൃക്കേട്ട - trikkétta, Mal.; கேட்டை - kéttai, Tam.). Means the eldest. Otherwise Kettay [q.v.], by corruption. Eighteenth hindoo lunar mansion; figured as a ring, umbrella in hand or spear; three stars, α, σ and τ Scorpionis [akrab]. α scorpii, 52 is Antares or Alkalb [q.v.] or Vareeyas [q.v.]. Compare arabian mansion Kalb.——*Kahkashaun* (شرج - sharaj, Ar.; کہکشان - kahkashán, Pers.; பால்வீதிமண்டலம் - pálvíthimandalam, Tam.). Ar. from (sharaja, ar. to collect together). Pers. from (káh, pers. straw + kashán, pers. drawn); from resemblance to trace of such in a sandy tract. Otherwise Oomoon noojoom [q.v.], meaning mother of stars; also Majarra [q.v.], place where anything runs; also (darví ásmám), meaning gate of heaven. The Milky way, Galaxy, or Via lactea. A whitish, luminous band, of irregular form, which stretches across the heavens from one side of the horizon [cshitijam] to the other, containing nine-tenths of visible stars; nearly a great circle inclined at an angle of about 63° to the equinoctial [naudy mundalam], and cutting that circle twice in R. A. 10h 47m and 12h 47m, so that its northern and southern poles respectively are situated in R. A. 12h 47m N P D 63° and R. A. 0h 47m N P D 117°. If traced in order of R.A., the milky way is found traversing Cassiopeia [caushyapy, zaut ool coorsy], its brightest part passing about two degrees to north of δ in about 62° of N.D. or 28° N P D. Passing thence between γ and ε it sends off a branch to the south-preceding side, towards α Persei [haumili rausool ghowl], 13 or mirfak [q.v.], very conspicuous, so far prolonged faintly towards ε of ditto, and traceable towards Hyades [sowr] and Pleiades [kritticay, sooreiyah] as remote outlyers. The main stream passes on through Auriga [mausik ool inaun], over the three stars, ε [alanaz], ζ [alinauz], η [alinauz], preceding Capella [bramhahridayam, oyook] called the Hœdi, between the feet of Gemini [jowzah, mitoonam] and horns [nath, nautih] of Bull [sowr, vrishabham], where it intersects the ecliptic [craunty mundalam] nearly in the present solstitial colure [yaumyottara vrittam], and thence over the club [alasah, fakaurool jowzah] of Orion [jabbaur] to the neck of Monoceros, intersecting the equinoctial [naudy mundalam] in R. A. 6h 54m. Thence it passes over the head of Canis major [kalbiacbar] and enters the prow of Argo [safeenah], nearly on the southern tropic. Here it again subdivides, about *m* Puppis, sending off a narrow and winding branch on the preceding side as far as γ Argûs [safeenah], where the branch terminates abruptly. The main stream pursues its southward course to the 123rd parallel of N P D, where it diffuses itself broadly and again sub-divides, opening out into a wide fan-like expanse, nearly 20° in breadth, formed of interlacing branches, all which terminate abruptly in a line drawn nearly through λ and γ Argûs [safeenah]. At this place the continuity is interrupted by a wide gap, and where it recommences on the opposite side it is by a somewhat similar fan-shaped assemblage of branches, which converge upon the bright star η Argûs [safeenah]. Thence it crosses the hind feet of the Centaur [cantooras], and enters the Cross [trishunkoo] being here at its narrowest. After this it expands into a broad and bright mass, enclosing α and β Crucis [trishunkoo], and β Centauri [cantooras] or wazn [q.v.], and extending almost up to α Centauri or hazaur [q.v.]. In the midst of this bright mass occurs a dark pearshaped vacancy, called the coal-sack. This is the place of nearest approach to the South pole [dacshina dhroovam]. At α Centauri [cantooras], it again subdivides, sending off a great branch at an angle of about 20° with its general direction towards the preceding side, to η and *d* Lupi [saboo], beyond which the branch loses itself. The main stream passes on increasing in breadth to γ Normæ, where it makes an abrupt elbow, and again subdivides into one principal and continuous stream on the following side, and a complicated system of interlaced masses on the preceding. The main stream, making an abrupt bend to the following side, passes over the stars ι Aræ [mijmarah], θ and ι Scorpii [akrab, vrishchicam], and γ Tubi, to γ Sagittarii [dhanoos, kows], where it collects into an oval mass, about 6° in length and about 4° in breadth. Northward of this mass the stream crosses the ecliptic [craunty mundalam] in about longitude [sauyanam] 276°, and proceeds along the bow of Sagittarius [dhanoos, kows] into Antinous [ookaub]. Crossing the equinoctial [naudy mundalam] at R. A. 19h, it next runs through Aquila [ookaub], Sagitta [saham], and Vulpecula up to Cygnus [dajjajah], at which point is a vacuity, like the southern coal-sack, occupying space between ε, α, 62 [aridad, deneb] and γ Cygni [dajjajah]. Hence it proceeds irregularly to the point in Cassiopeia [caushyapy, zaut ool coorsy] whence it began.——*Kalb* (قلب - kalb, Ar.). Means the heart. Otherwise Kalb ool akrab [q.v.], meaning heart of scorpio. Three stars in Scorpio [akrab], α scorpii and two small stars close to it. 18th arabian lunar mansion. Compare hindoo mansion Jyeshtay.——*Kalbaun* (کلبان - kulbán, Ar.). Also (kulyatán). Two stars ν, κ Tauri [sowr].——*Kalb i acbar* (کلب اکبر - kalbiakbar, Ar.). From (kalb, ar. dog + akbar, ar. great). Constellation. Eighteen stars. Canis major, the Great dog. S. hemisphere. S.E. of Orion [jabbaur]. Three principal stars, one of which, α Canis majoris, or Sirius, or the Dog star [mrigavyaudham, shira], is the brightest in the firmament. α Canis majoris, 26, or Sirius, lies in the line of Orion's belt [fakaur ool jowzah], being as far to the S.E. of it as Aldebaran, 16 [q.v.] is to the N.W. Sirius, 26, Procyon, 27 [ghoomeisah] and Betelgeux, 23 [q.v.] or Atigandam [q.v.] form an equilateral triangle, Sirius being at the southern apex. Procyon and Sirius, the stars of the 2 dogs, are on opposite sides of the Milky way [kahkashaun]. β Canis majoris [mirzam, mirzamaun] lies 5° west, a little southerly, from Sirius; and a line drawn from Betelgeux, 23 [atigandam], passing between these two stars, will lead to ε Canis majoris in the flank of the Dog; Sirius, 26 is at the nose.——*Kalb i asghar* (کلب اصغر - kalbiasghar, Ar.). From (kalb, ar. dog + asghar, ar. minor). Otherwise Kalb ool mootakaddim [q.v.], meaning the foremost or easternmost dog, but as to rising it comes up last not first. Canis minor, the Little dog. S. hemisphere. Small constellation to the south of Gemini [jowzah, mitoonam]; contains two principal stars. α Canis minoris, 27, or Procyon [ghoomeisah], is very conspicuous; it is nearly due south of Pollux, 28 [alzirah, soocarmam], the brightest of the Twins [jowzah, mitoonam], and east of Betelgeux, 23 [q.v.] in Orion [jabbaur]; and thus Pollux, 28, Procyon, 27 and Betelgeux, 23 [atigandam] form a right-angled triangle, Procyon being at the right angle. β Canis minoris [mirzam, mirzamaun] lies N.W. of Procyon, nearly in the same position from that star that Castor is from Pollux, but the latter two, may be distinguished from the former, since Castor and Pollux are 1st and 2nd magnitude, whereas Procyon and β Canis minoris are 1st and 3rd magnitude. See also Zirah ool makbooz.——*Kalb ool akrab* (قلب العقرب - kalbulakrab, Hind.). From (kalb, ar. heart + akrab, ar. scorpio). Same as Alkalb and Kalb.——*Kalb ool asad* (قلب الاسد - kalbulasad, Ar.). Means heart of leo. Also (alasad). Star of first magnitude. Cor leonis or Regulus, α Leonis [asad], 32 [gandam].——*Kalb ool hoot* (قلب الحوت - kalbulhút, Ar.). Means heart of pisces [hoot]. Same as Alrishah.——*Kalb ool mootakaddim* (کلب المتقدم - kalbulmutakaddim, Hind.). From (kalb, ar. dog + mutakaddim, ar. going before). Same as Kalb i asghar [q.v.].——*Kalb ool royee* (کلب الراعی - kalburráyí, Ar.). From (kalb, ar. dog + arráí, hind., α ophiuchi); from being in attendance on α Ophiuchi [alroyee], 55, rasalhague. Star; α Herculis, 54 Rasalgethy, third magnitude. Same title applies to κ Cephei [zaut ool coorsy], as attending on γ Cephei [alroyee] similarly.——*Kalb ool sowr* (قلب الثور - kalbussaur, Ar.). Means heart of taurus [sowr]. Otherwise Ayeen ool sowr [q.v.]. Same as Aldebaran.——*Kauyid* (قائد - káid, Hind.). From (kaud, ar. to mourn). Same as Alkaid or Benetnasch.——*Kettay* (கேட்டை - kéttai, Tam.). By corruption from jyeshtay [q.v.]. The 18th hindoo lunar mansion.——*Kita ool faras* (قطع الفرس - kitaulfaras, Ar.). From (kita, ar. piece + faras, ar. horse). Constellation of 4 stars just west of the head of Pegasus. Equuelus. For the great horse or Pegasus see Fars ool azam.——*Kochab* (قطب - kutb, Ar.). Means axis. Star of second magnitude. β Ursæ minoris [cshoodra-ricsham, doobheasghar], 47.——*Kows* (قوس - kaus, Ar.). Means a bow. Also (arrámí), meaning the thrower. Sagittarius, the Archer [dhanoos]. Ninth constellation of ancient zodiac [raushy chuckram], lies to S. of Ophiuchus [heiyah] and Aquila [ookaub]. To the east of Antares, 52 [alkalb, vareeyas], four stars, ε δ λ [royinauyim], and μ Sagittarii, form a curve in the milky way [kahkashaun]; these are the bow; and immediately beyond are four others, θ, σ, τ, and ζ, in the figure of a quadrilateral, forming the body of the Archer. μ Sagittarii passes the meridian at midnight towards the end of June. For ν Sagittarii see Ayeen ool raumy. For λ Sagittarii see Royinauyim. See also the lunar mansions Balda, Nauyim, Oottarashaudham and Poorvashaudham. For Sagitta the arrow see Saham.——*Kritticay* (कृत्तिका - krittiká, San.; கார்த்திகை - kárttigai, Tam.). From (krit, san. to cut); a dagger, because of Configuration. Also called Agny [q.v.], because of regent. Third hindoo lunar mansion [maunam]. The six stars of Pleiades, formerly seven, in the shoulder of Taurus [sowr]; hence called Seven virgins. Represented as a flame or as a knife. Kritticay's influence is particularly evil; and when the moon [chundran] is near the Pleiades but especially when she is so in the mouth of Caurtigay [mausam] this is a time of fasting and prayer; children do not attend school on that day, and others if possible avoid doing anything of importance. The six stars were nymphs who nursed Soobramanyan [q.v.], or Scandan [q.v.] god of war, thence called Caurtikeyan [q.v.], each nurse suckling one of his six mouths. The Greeks called the Pleiades stormy, because of being orient in the evening in the winter season. Compare arabian mansion Sooreiyah. The principal star of the group is Alcyone, or η Tauri [sowr], 14; otherwise Ayooshmat [q.v.]. See also Alfoorood and Arsh ool sooreiya.——*Kyekows* (قيقاؤس - kaikáús, Ar.). Means a triangle. Constellation. Eleven stars. Triangulum australe, the Southern triangle. S. hemisphere. South-eastward of the two bright stars, α [hazaur] and β [wazn], in Centaurus [cantooras]; α and γ Trianguli australis are in the same line with γ and β Crucis [trishunkoo], α Trianguli australis being the most easterly; β and γ Trianguli australis are on the opposite side of the Milky way [kahkashaun] to α Centauri [cantooras] or hazaur [q.v.]; β Trianguli australis is the northern apex of the triangle, at the distance of about 8° from α and γ Trianguli australis. α Trianguli australis is of the second magnitude; β and γ of third and fourth magnitudes. Pavo, the Peacock, eastward of Triangulum australe is not represented in Arabic; its principal and northernmost star, α Pavonis, of second magnitude, is in a line to the eastward with γ and β Crucis [trishunkoo], and γ and α Trianguli australis. α Pavonis, Achernar 7 [q.v.], and Fomal haut 66 [q.v.], form an equilateral triangle.——*Kyetos* (قيطس - kítas, Ar.). Constellation. Twenty-two stars. Cetus, the Whale. S. hemisphere. South of Aries [hamel, maisham], and Pisces [hoot, meenam], and S.W. of Taurus [sowr, vrishabham]. Contains two principal stars, α Ceti [cuff ool jazmah], or Menkar [q.v.], and β Ceti, 3, or Deneb kyetos [q.v.]; in it is also the variable star ο Ceti, otherwise Mira. A line drawn through β Andromedæ [miratimoosalsila], 4 [batn ool hoot], through α Arietis, 10 [hamel], and produced rather more than the same distance, leads to α Ceti [cuffool jazmah]; or, it lies a little to the south of a line drawn from Procyon or α Canis minoris, 27 [ghoomeisah], through Bellatrix, 19 [mirzam], in Orion [jabbaur], and produced about an equal distance. Menkar [q.v.], α Arietis 10 [hamel], and the Pleiades [kritticay, sooreiyah], form an equilateral triangle, Menkar being at the southern apex. About 7° to the eastward of a line drawn from α Andromedæ [miratimoosalsila], 1 or Alpheratz [q.v.], through γ Pegasi [faras ool azam], 2 [algenib, mahendram], and produced nearly twice their distance, is β Ceti, 3 [deneb kyetos]; or, it is a little to the southward of a line produced from Aldebaran, 16 [q.v.] through Menkar [q.v.] to about twice their distance. Menkar is in the head of the Whale and Deneb kyetos [q.v.] at the tail; between the two, but nearer the latter, are four stars of the third magnitude in the form of a quadrilateral figure, the easternmost of which is ζ Ceti, 8, or Batn kyetos [q.v.], in the centre of the body. Between Batn kyetos and Menkar, but nearer the former, is the variable Mira, or ο Ceti; this when brightest is of the second magnitude in which state it remains for a fortnight; during the three following months it diminishes to the fourth, fifth, &c., magnitude, and then for five or six months is completely invisible to the naked eye, after which it reappears; the exact period of its changes is 331 d 15 h 7 m; or it is seen as of the second magnitude about twelve times in eleven years.——*Loobdhacam* (लुब्धक - lubdhaka, San.). From (lubh, san. to covet); means hunter. Otherwise Mrigavyaudham [q.v.]. So called from a legend which narrates that shiva [q.v.] transformed himself into a hunter in order to shoot an arrow, represented by the three stars in the belt [fakaur ool jowzah] of orion [jabbaur] lying in a direct line with sirius, 26, at bramha [q.v.] transformed into a deer [mrigam] and pursuing his own daughter metamorphosed into a doe for the purpose of committing incest with her. Same as Shira [q.v.], or Sirius, the Dog star; α Canis majoris [kalbi acbar], 26.——*Macaram* (मकर - makara, San.). Means sea-monster, so called. Tenth sign [raushy] of the zodiac [raushy chuckram]. Capricornus, ♑ [jaddy]. See arabian mansion Zaubih; also Sadinaushira.——*Magham* (मघा - maghá, San.; மகம் - magam, Tam.). From (maghá, san. gift). Otherwise Pitryah. Tenth hindoo lunar mansion. Figured as a house, palankeen or yoke. α, γ, s, μ and ν Leonis [asad, simham]. The principal or southern one is Regulus or α Leonis, 32 [gandam, kalb ool asad]. Mahamagham [q.v.] is the occurrence of the full moon in or about this asterism along with other astronomical incidents, which event happens once in twelve years and gives a time auspicious for bathing, especially at Combaconam. Compare arabian mansion Jabaha.——*Maharicsham* (महाऋक्ष - mahá-riksha, San.). From (mahá, san. great + riksha, san. bear). Also called Sapta rishy [q.v.], meaning seven sages. Same as Doobhe acbar [q.v.] or Ursa major. The first three form the tail [banaut]; the last four make up the square of the bear [naash]. Varauha mihiran has the following regarding Maharicsham [doobhe acbar]; his notion about the stars of the constellation having a proper motion independent of precession [ayanaumsham, craunty pauta gaty] appears to be an error of confusion arising out of the question of the line of the rishies [rishy raikhay]:—"The seven rishies [q.v.] form as it were "a garland of the white lotus [nelumbo] to the maiden of "the northern quarter or look like her smile or seem to be "her masters; or by the direction of her lord the pole star "[alrooccabah, dhroovam], the maiden of the northern quarter "appears to dance round as the seven rishies move in their "course; during the reign of yoodhishtiran 2526 years before "the commencement of vicrama [q.v.] saca [q.v.] the seven "rishies were at the constellation of magham [q.v.]; the "rishies take a period of 100 years to go over each of the 27 "asterisms; they rise in the north-east and are accompanied by "the chaste aroondhaty [q.v.], the consort of vasishtan [q.v.]; "the easternmost of the group is bhagavan mareechy [q.v.]; "the next to him is vasishtan; the next is angiran [q.v.] and "the next two are atry [q.v.] and poolastyan [q.v.]; the next "in order are the rishies poolahan [q.v.] and cratoo [q.v.]." The identification of the stars will be seen from the references; easternmost in the quotation means when the Bear is above the pole.——*Mahendram* (महेन्द्र - mahéndra, San.). From (mahá, san. great + indra, san. the deity). Yogam star of the 26th hindoo lunar mansion. 2nd magnitude. Eindram, 1 [q.v.] or Alpheratz α andromedæ [miratimoosalsila], 1 [alpheratz, eindram]. 2nd magnitude. Otherwise Algenib [q.v.], γ Pegasi, 2. 3rd magnitude. Almost the longitude of present equinoctial colure.——*Maisham* (मेष - mésha, San.). Means ram. First sign [raushy] of the zodiac [raushy chuckram]. Aries, ♈ [hamel]. See also Ashwiny, Bharany, Bootein and Shartein.——*Majarra* (مجرة - majarrah, Hind.) From (majarr, ar. a place along which a thing has been dragged); resembling such trace on sand. Same as Kahkashaun——*Mankib* (منكب - mankib, Ar.). Otherwise Mankib ool faras meaning horse's shoulder; Matn ool faras, meaning middle of the horse; also Scheat. Star of magnitude 2 to 2·5. β Pegasi [faras ool azam], 67. See also Farghaun.——*Mankib ool jowzah* (منكب الجوزا - mankibuljauzá, Hind.). From (mankib, ar. shoulder + jauzá, ar. orion). Same as Betelgeux.——*Mareechy* (मरीचि - maríchi, San.). Means luminous. One of the seven stars [sapta rishy] of Maharicsham [q.v.], at end of tail, η Ursæ majoris [doobhe acbar] or Benetnasch [q.v.].——*Markab* (مركب - markab, Ar.). Means a saddle; also called Ayeen ool faras [q.v.] meaning horse's eye; also Bramham [q.v.]. Star of second magnitude. α Pegasi [farasoolazam], 68. See also Farghaun.——*Mausik ool inaun* (ماسك العنان - másikulinán, Ar.). From (másik, ar. holder + inán, ar. reins). Constellation. Fourteen stars. Auriga, the Charioteer, contains five principal stars, α, β, δ, γ, and ι Aurigæ which form a large irregular pentagon. The most conspicuous star, and one of brightest stars in N. hemisphere, is Capella, α Aurigæ, 17 [bramhahridayam, oyook]. A line drawn from δ [atry] to α Ursæ majoris [doobhe acbar], 35 [doobhe], the two northernmost stars in square of Great bear [doobhe acbar, maharicsham], and produced, leads to Capella, which is also distinguished by having close to it three small stars, ε [al anaz], η, and ζ Aurigæ [al inauz], forming isosceles triangle. In brilliancy Capella ranks next to Arcturus, 44 [haurs ool samah, vajram]. β Aurigæ is the star of the pentagon nearest Capella; from which it is distant above 13° to E. γ Aurigæ, the S. star of pentagon, is also β Tauri [sowr], 20 [agny, nath], being at the horn of the Bull [sowr], on which the foot of the Charioteer rests; it is also on the edge of the Milky way [kahkashaun]. For δ Aurigæ, 24, see Prajaupaty. For ε Aurigæ see Alanaz. For η and ζ Aurigæ see Alinauz. See also Tawaubyool oyook.——*Meenam* (मीन -

mína, San.). Means fish. Twelfth sign [raushy] of the zodiac [raushy chuckram]. Pisces, ♓ [hoot].——*Meezaun* (میزان - mízán, Ar.). Means a balance. Libra, the Balance [toolaum], ♎. Seventh constellation of ancient zodiac [raushy chuckram]. Contains two principal stars of second magnitude, α and β Libræ [zoobaunah]. β Libræ, or Zubenelg [q.v.], in the Northern balance, is east, a little northerly, from Spica, 41 [harshanam, simauk ool azal], with which and Arcturus, 44 [haurs ool samah, vajram], it forms an isosceles triangle, Arcturus being the apex. About 9° south-westerly from β Libræ is α Libræ, or Zubenesch, 46 [q.v.], in the Southern balance; it passes the meridian at midnight about the beginning of May. For hindoo synonym of zubenesch see Siddhy. See also mansions Vishaukham and Zoobaunah.——*Menkar* (منکر - minkar, Ar.). Otherwise Cuff ool jazmah [q.v.]. Star of second magnitude. α Ceti [kyetos].——*Mijmarah* (مجمرة - mijmarah, Ar.). Means a furnace. Constellation. Seven stars. Ara, the Altar. S. hemisphere. Lies to north-eastward of Triangulum australe [kyekows]. Its principal stars, α, β, γ Aræ, are between third and fourth magnitude; α is the northernmost; and at the distance of 6° to the southward are β and γ Aræ, close together.——*Milaf* (معلف - milaf, Ar.). Means a manger. The nebula in Cancer [sartaun]. See also Nasara and Pooshyam.——*Mintaka* (منطقه - mintakah, Ar.). Means belt. Star, δ Orionis [jabbaur]; western star in belt [fakaur ool jowjah, nazm].——*Mirack* (مراة - mirat, Hind.). Means a lady. Otherwise Batn ool hoot [q.v.]. Star of second magnitude. β Andromedæ [mirat i moosalsila], 4.——*Mirat i moosalsila* (مراةمسلسله - miratimusalsila, Ar.). From (mirat, ar. lady + musalsilah, ar. chained). Constellation. Twenty stars. N. hemisphere. Andromeda, daughter of Cepheus and Cassiopea [caushyapy, zaut ool coorsy], bound to a rock, exposed to a sea monster, rescued by Perseus [haumil i rausool ghowl]. To southward of Cassiopea and westward of Perseus, and is on a line produced from Polaris, 6 [al rooccabah, dhroovam], through Cassiopea. Three principal stars, α Andromedæ, 1 [alpheratz, eindram], β Andromedæ, 4, or Mirack [batn ool hoot], and γ Andromedæ, or Alanak [q.v.]. To find β Andromedæ, 4 or Mirack [q.v.]; a line drawn from α Pegasi [faras ool azam], 68 [bramham, markab] to α Andromedæ, 1 [alpheratz, eindram], and produced about the same distance, will lead a little to the northward of β Andromedæ, 4. To find γ Andromedæ, or Alanak [q.v.]; in the same north-easterly direction that α Andromedæ, 1 is from α Pegasi, 68, the star γ Andromedæ lies from α Andromedæ at the distance of about 13°; it is also about 13° in a westerly direction from Algol, 12 [q.v.], in Perseus [haumil i rausool ghowl]. To find α Andromedæ, or Alpheratz; this star, also known as δ Pegasi, is at the north-eastern angle of the square [farghaun] of Pegasus [faras ool azam]; it is also on a line drawn from δ Ursæ majoris [doobhe acbar, maharicsham], and produced through Polaris, 6 [alrooccabah, dhroovam], to the distance of 61°. See also Mooakhar and Oottarabhaudram.——*Mirfak* (مرفق - mirfak, Ar.). Means elbow. Star of second magnitude. α Persei [haumil i rausool ghowl], 13.——*Mirzam* (مرزم - mirzam, Ar.). From (ruzama, ar. cold); being rainy stars. γ Orionis [jabbaur], 19 or Bellatrix. Same term applied to β Canis minoris [kalbiasghar], and β Canis majoris [kalbiacbar]. See also Mirzamaun, Zirah ool makbooz.——*Mirzamaun* (مرزمان - mirzamán, Hind.). Means two mirzams. Also (mirzamashshirain) [shiriyaun]. The pair of stars, β Canis majoris [kalbiacbar] and β Canis minoris [kalbiasghar], Procyon and Sirius. See also Mirzam, Zirah ool makbooz. ——*Mitoonam* (मिथुन - mit'huna, San.). Means twins. Third sign [raushy] of the zodiac [raushy chuckram]. Gemini, ♊ [jowzah].——*Mokaddam* (مقدم - mukaddam, Ar.). Means going before. Otherwise Farghool owval [q.v.], being the foremost or westernmost pair of the four stars forming a square [farghaun], thus rising first. Two stars, α, β Pegasi [faras ool azam]. 26th arabian lunar mansion. For α Pegasi, 68 see Bramham and Markab. For β Pegasi, 67 see Mankib. Compare hindoo mansion Poorvabhaudram. See also Fargh ool dalo.——*Mooakhar* (موخر - muakkhar, Ar.). Means the last. Otherwise Fargh ool sawny [q.v.], the latter fargh, being the hindermost or easternmost or last rising pair of the four stars forming square [farghaun]. Two stars, α Andromedæ [miratimoosalsila], 1 [alpheratz, eindram] and γ Pegasi [faras ool azam], 2 [algenib, mahendram]. 27th Arabian lunar mansion. Compare hindoo mansion Oottarabhaudram. See also Fargh ool dalo.——*Moohlifaun* (محلفان - muhlifán, Ar.). From (halafa, ar. to swear); beholders swearing one against another as not able to distinguish them from canopus [agastyan, sooheil]. α [hazaur] and β [wazn] centauri [cantooras], rising at a different part of the year from Canopus, 25, which in general appearance they resemble.——*Moolam* (मूल - múla, San.; மூலம் - múlam, Tam.). Means root. Otherwise called Nirrity. 19th hindoo lunar mansion. It is of bad or malignant influence; next so to Kritticay [q.v.], to which it is nearly opposite. Represented by a lion's tail, leaping lion, or trumpet; ten stars, ε, μ, ζ, η, θ, ι, κ, λ, υ and ν, Scorpionis [akrab]. For λ or ν Scorpii, 51 see Parigham. Compare arabian mansion Showla.——*Mrigashiras* (मृगशिरस् - mrigashiras, San.; മകീരം - makíram, Mal.; மிருகசீரிடம் - mirugasíridam, Tam.). From (mriga, san. deer + shiras, san. the head). Fifth hindoo lunar mansion. Containing three stars in head of Orion jabbaur], the principal of which is λ. Compare arabian mansion Hakah.——*Mrigavyaudham* (मृगव्याध - mrigavyádha, San.). From (mriga, san. deer + vyádha, san. hunter). Otherwise Loobdhacam [q.v.], or hunter. Same as Sirius or Shira [q.v.], the Dog-star. α Canis majoris [kalbiacbar], 26.——*Naash* (نعش - naash, Ar.). Means dead body. Four stars forming the square in body of Ursa major [alkaid, benetnasch, doobhe acbar, maharicsham].——*Nahr* (نهر - nahr, Ar.). Means a river. Constellation. Thirty-four stars. Eridanus. S. hemisphere. Southward of Taurus [sowr] and south-eastward of Cetus [kyetos]; winds over considerable space extending between 4° and 60° S. Contains one principal star, Achernar [q.v.], or α Eridani, 7. This is on a line joining Fomalhaut, 66 [q.v.], or α Piscis Australis [hootijoonooby] and Canopus, α Argûs [safeenah], 25 [agastyan, sooheil], about midway between the two. β Eridani is a small star 3° northward of Rigel, 18 [q.v.], or β Orionis [jabbaur]. γ Eridani is on a line drawn from Procyon or α Canis minoris [kalbiasghar], 27 [ghoomeisah] to Rigel or β Orionis, 18 and extended to about half its length. Hydrus, the Water-snake, not represented in arabic, lies to the S. and S.E. of Achernar, 7, the principal star in Eridanus, from which α Hydri, mag. 3, is distant about 5°. β Hydri, mag. 3, lies S. by W. from Achernar, 7, distant about 21°, and is the most conspicuous star near the South pole [dacshina dhroovam], from which it is distant about 12°. For Hydra, feminine, the Snake, see Shoojah. For Ophiuchus or serpent-bearer see Heiyah. For Serpens or the serpent see Hooweiyah.——*Nasara* (نثرة - nasarah, Ar.). Means the nose. Also (anfulasad) or nose of the lion [asad]. Eighth arabian lunar mansion. Two stars in Cancer [sartaun], including the Nebula. The arabian Leo was once projected further westward. Compare hindoo mansion Pooshyam. See also Milaf.——*Nasrein* (نسرين - nasrain, Ar.). Means two vultures. Constellations Aquila [ookaub] and Lyra [shalyauk].——*Nasr ool tair* (نسرالطائر - nasrultáir, Hind.). From (nasr, ar. vulture + táir, ar. flying). The flying vulture. Same as Altair.——*Nasr ool wauky* (نسرالواقع - nasrulwáki, Ar.). From (nasr, ar. vulture + wáki, ar. to contract wings as if to alight upon a thing). The swooping vulture. Otherwise Vega. Star of first magnitude, with parallax of ¼ second. α Lyræ [shalyauk], 58 [abhijit]. See also Azfaur [q.v.].——*Nath* (نطح - nath, Ar.). Means a horn. Otherwise Agny [q.v.]. Star of second magnitude, β Tauri [sowr], 20; also known as γ Aurigæ [mausik ool inaun]. For the other horn see Nautih. For the horns of the ram [hamel] see Shartein.——*Nautih* (ناطح - nátih, Ar.). Means a horn. Star of fourth magnitude. γ Tauri [sowr], 15. For the other horn see Nath. For the horns of the ram [hamel] see Shartein. ——*Nauyim* (نعايم - naáim, Ar.). Plural of (naím, ar. ostrich). 20th arabian lunar mansion. Two stars in Sagittarius [kows]. Royinauyim meaning guardian of nauyim is λ Sagittarii. Compare hindoo mansion Poorvashaudham. See also Alriyaul. ——*Nazm* (نظم - nazm, Ar.). From (nazama, ar. to join in a row). Star. δ Orionis [jabbaur]. Westernmost of three stars forming orion's belt [fakaur ool jowzah]; the other two being ε Orionis, 21 or Nitauk ool jowzah [q.v.], and ζ Orionis, 22 or Fakaur ool jowzah [q.v.].——*Nitauk ool jowzah* (نطاق‌الجوزا - nitákuljauzá, Ar.). From (niták, ar. girdle + jauzá, ar. orion). Star of second magnitude. ε Orionis [jabbaur], 21. Middlemost of three stars forming orion's belt [fakaur ool jowzah]; the other two being δ Orionis or Nazm [q.v.] and ζ Orionis or Fakaur ool jowzah [q.v.].——*Ookaub* (عقاب - ukkáb, Ar.). Means an eagle. Constellation. Nine stars. Aquila. N. hemisphere. To the southward of Lyra [shalyauk] and south-westward of Pegasus [faras ool azam]; three principal stars, close together, and in a straight line, α, β, and γ Aquilæ; the centre is α Aquilæ, 60, or Altair [q.v.], on edge of Milky way [kahkashaun]. A line drawn from Polaris, 6 [al rooccabah, dhroovam] so as to pass between α Lyræ [shalyauk], 58 [abhijit, nasr ool wauky] and α Cygni [dajjajah], 62 [deneb], and produced an equal distance beyond them, will lead to α Aquilæ, 60 [altair, saudhyam]. Or it can be found by drawing a line from between the two bright stars of Draco [tinneen] to α Lyræ, 58, and continuing it twice that distance. For β Aquilæ see Alshain. η Aquilæ is variable, going from 3·4 to 4·5 in 7 days 4 hours. See also Nasrein and Shravanam.——*Ookda* (عقده - ukdah, Ar.). Means a knot, being in the place of the knot of the two strings of the fishes. α Piscium [hoot].——*Oom oon noojoom* (ام‌النجوم - ummunnujúm, Hind.). From (umm, ar. mother + nujúm, ar. stars). Same as Kahkashaun.——*Oonuk* (عنق - unuk, Ar.), cf. alanak. Otherwise Oonuk ool heiyah, meaning neck of serpent or Unakalkay by corr. Star of second magnitude. α Serpentis [hooweiyah], 49.——*Oonuk shoojah* (عنق الشجاع - unukushshujá, Ar.). From (unuk, ar. neck + shujá, ar. hydra). Otherwise Alphard [q.v.]. Star of second magnitude. α Hydræ [shoojah], 31.——*Oorkoob ool asad* (عرقوب‌الاسد - urkúbulasad, Hind.). From (urkúb, ar. hock + asad, ar. leo). Same as Awwah, the lunar mansion.——*Oottara bhaudram* (उत्तरभाद्रपदा - uttarabhádrapadá, San.; உத்திரட்டாதி - uttirattáthi, Tam.). From (uttara, san. second + bhadra, san. prosperous + pada, san. foot). Otherwise Oottarattauthy [q.v.]. The second or later rising or inferior Bhaudram [q.v.]. Cf. Poorva bhaudram.

26th hindoo lunar mansion. Figured by a couch, double headed figure, two double squares, or legs of ravanan's bedstead and comprehending two stars; the most northerly is the bright star in the head of Andromeda [mirat i moosalsila], α Andromedæ, 1 [alpheratz, eindram], and the other is the star in the extremity of the wing of Pegasus [faras ool azam], γ Pegasi, 2 [algenib, mahendram]. See also Proshtapadam. Compare arabian mansion Mooakhir.——*Oottaram* (उत्तरफल्गुनी - uttarap'halguní, San.; உத்திரம் - uttiram, Tam.). The second or later rising Phalgoony [q.v.]; 12th hindoo lunar mansion, containing two stars, figured by a bed, two small squares, or legs of bedstead. Northernmost indicates β Leonis [asad], 37 [denebola, dhroovam]. Compare arabian mansion Sarafa.——*Oottarashaudham* (उत्तराषाढा - uttaráshádhá, San.; உத்திராடம் - uttirádam, Tam.). From (uttara, san. second + ashádha, san. invincible). Otherwise Oottaraudam [q.v.]. The second or later rising of the two Ashaudhams [q.v.]; 21st hindoo lunar mansion. Represented by a couch or by an elephant's tooth, two double squares, or legs of bedstead. Two stars, ζ and τ Sagittarii [kows]. For τ Sagittarii, 59 see Siddham. Compare arabian mansion Balda.——*Oottarattauthy* (உத்திரட்டாதி - uttirattáthi, Tam.). By corruption from oottara proshtapadam [q.v.]. The 26th hindoo lunar mansion [oottara bhaudram]. ——*Oottaraudam* (உத்திராடம் - uttirádam, Tam.). By corruption from oottarashaudham [q.v.]. The 21st hindoo lunar mansion.——*Oyook* (عيوق - aiyyúk, Ar.). From (áka, ar. to impede); impeding aldebaran, 16 [q.v.] from meeting pleiades [kritticay, sooreiyah], though it is not between them; also called Rakeeb [q.v.], meaning watcher from its rising shortly after pleiades; also Bramhahridayam [q.v.]. European Capella. Star of first magnitude. α Aurigæ [mausik ool inaun], 17. Compare Tawauby ool oyook.——*Parigham* (परिघ - parigha, San.). Means iron club. Yogam star of 19th hindoo lunar mansion. λ or ν Scorpii [akrab], 51. 4th magnitude.——*Parisiyawash* (پرسیاوش - parisiyáwash, Hind.). From (par, pers. hair + siyáwash, pers. maiden). Same as Haumil i rausool ghowl. ——*Phalgoony* (फल्गुनी - p'halguní, San.). Means red. 11th or 12th hindoo lunar mansion. For Poorva phalgoony, the 11th, see Poobbam; for Oottara phalgoony, the 12th, see Oottaram. Compare arabian mansions Sarafa and Zoobra.——*Poobbam* (पूर्वफल्गुनी - púrvap'halguní, San.; పుబ్బ - pubba, Tel.; பூரம் - púram, Tam.). From (púrva, san. first + p'halguna, san. the star). Otherwise Pooram [q.v.]. 11th hindoo lunar mansion. Represented by a couch, two small squares, or legs of bedstead. Two stars, δ, 36 [zoobra] and θ Leonis [asad, simham]. For δ Leonis, 36 see Vriddhy and Zoobra.——*Poolahan* (पुलह - pulaha, San.). From (pul, san. to be high). One of the seven stars [sapta rishy] of Maharicsham [q.v.], in square; β Ursæ majoris [doobhe acbar] or Alanak [q.v.].——*Poolastyan* (पुलस्त्य - pulastya, San.). From (pul, san. to be high). One of the seven stars [sapta rishy] of Maharicsham [q.v.], in square; γ Ursæ majoris [doobhe acbar].——*Poonarvas* (पुनर्वसु - punarvasú, San.; പുണർതം - punartam, Mal.; புனர்பூசம் - punarppúsam, Tam.). From (punar, san. afresh + vasu, san. goods). Restoring goods. 7th hindoo lunar mansion. Part of Gemini [jowzah, mitoonam]. Represented by a house, or a bow, or a large sea boat. Name is properly dual, implying two stars; four are now assigned to it. Comprises stars in the heads of the twins [jowzah, mitoonam], α, β, Geminorum; to which, θ and τ may be added to complete the four. For β Geminorum, 28 or Pollux see Alzirah and Soocarmam. Compare arabian mansion Zirah ool mabsoot.——*Pooram* (பூரம் - púram, Tam.). By corruption from (púrva, san. first). Same as Poobbam.——*Poorattauthy* (பூரட்டாதி - púrattáthi, Tam.). From (prósht'hapada, san. the 25th lunar asterism). Same as Poorvabhaudram. Compare Pooorattaushy [proshtapadam].——*Pooraudam* (பூராடம் - púrádam, Tam.). Corruption from poorvashaudham [q.v.]. The 20th hindoo lunar mansion.——*Poorva bhaudram* (पूर्वभाद्रपदा - púrvabhádrapadá, San.; பூரட்டாதி - púrattáthi, Tam.). Otherwise Poorattauthy [q.v.]. 25th hindoo lunar mansion. Represented by a couch or else by a double-headed figure, or two double squares, or legs of ravanan's bedstead; two stars α and ζ Pegasi [faras ool azam]. For α Pegasi, 68 see Brambam and Markab. Compare arabian mansion Mokaddam. ——*Poorvashaudham* (पूर्वाषाढा - púrváshádhá, San.; பூராடம் - púrádam, Tam.). From (púrva, san. first + áshádha, san. the lunar mansion). Otherwise Pooraudam [q.v.]. 20th hindoo lunar mansion. Figured as an elephant's tooth or as a couch, two double squares, or legs of bedstead; two stars, δ and ε Sagittarii [kows]. There is a Tamul proverb:—பூராடக்காரர் ஜெயிப்போராட முடியாது—"one cannot strive with a man "born under the star pooraudam." For δ Sagittarii, 57 see Shivam. Compare arabian mansion Nauyim.——*Poosham* (பூசம் - púsam, Tam.). By corruption from pooshyam [q.v.]. The eighth hindoo lunar mansion.——*Pooshyam* (पुष्य - pushya, San.; പൂയം - púyam, Mal.; பூசம் - púsam, Tam.). From (push, san. to increase); a blossom. Also called Tishyam; also Poosham [q.v.]. Eighth hindoo lunar mansion. Described as an arrow, string, or looking glass with handle; consists of three stars, β, γ and δ in the body and claws of Cancer [sartaun], or the nebula [milaf] in Cancer. For δ Cancri, 29 see Dhrity. Compare arabian mansion Nasara.——*Powshnam* (पौष्ण - paushna, San.). From (púshan, san. sun). 27th hindoo lunar mansion, so called from the regent deity Pooshan or sun. It is also called Raivaty [maunam, raivaty, veidbrity].——*Prajaupaty* (प्रजापति - prajápati, San.). From (prajá, san. creature + pati, san. lord). Star δ Aurigæ [mausik ool inaun], 24. 4th magnitude.——*Preety* (प्रीति - príti, San.). Means happiness. Yogam star of second hindoo lunar mansion. 35 Arietis [hamel, maisham], 11. 5th magnitude.——*Proshtapadam* (प्रोष्ठपद - prósht'hapada, San.). From (prósht'ha, san. bench + pada, san. foot); from being represented by the legs of a bedstead. Epithet of the 25th and 26th hindoo lunar mansion, more commonly Bhaudrapadam [q.v.]. Gives rise to the tamul name of the asterism Poorattauthy [q.v.] and the month [mausam] Pooorataushy [q.v.]. Cf. Oottarattauthy.——*Raivaty* (रेवती - révatí, San.; இரேவதி - irévathi, Tam.). Otherwise Powshnam [q.v.]. From (rayi, san. wealth, prosperity + vat, san. possessing). 27th hindoo lunar mansion. Figured as a tabor, or fish. Thirty-two stars; the principal marks according to some the star close to the ecliptic [craunty mundalam] in the string of the Fishes, ζ Piscium [hoot, meenam], 5 [veidhrity] of 6th magnitude. Or it may mean η Piscium at the tail of the eastern fish. As beginning the solar year see remarks under Madhyama sowra maunam [maunam]. Compare arabian mansion Alrishah. ——*Rakeeb* (رقيب - rakíb, Hind.). From (rakaba, ar. to watch). Same as Oyook.——*Rasalgethy* (راس الجاثي - rásuljásí, Ar.). From (rás, ar. head + jásí, ar. hercules). Star of magnitude 3 to 4, going from 3 to 4 in 66 days. α Herculis [jausy], 54.——*Rasalhague* (راس الحيه - rásulhaiyah, Ar.). From (rás, ar. head + haiyah, ar. ophiuchus). Otherwise Alroyee [q.v.], meaning the guardian of α Herculis [jausy], 54. Star of second magnitude. α Ophiuchi [heiyah], 55.——*Rauks* (راقص - rákis, Ar.). From (raks, ar. dance). Star of fifth magnitude. μ Draconis [tinneen], 53.——*Rigel* (رجل - rijl, Ar.). Contraction of rigel ool jabbaur, meaning leg of orion; also Rigel ool jowzal yoosrah, meaning upon the left foot of orion. Star of 1st magnitude. β Orionis [jabbaur], 18.——*Rigel ool jowz al yoomnah* (رجل الجوز اليمنى - rijluljauzalyumná, Hind.), meaning upon the right leg of orion. Star. κ Orionis [jabbaur].——*Rohiny* (रोहिणी - róhiní, San.; உரோகிணி - urógini, Tam.). Red one; from color of aldebaran, 16 [q.v.]. Fourth hindoo lunar mansion. Personified as a daughter of Dacshan [q.v.], and the favorite wife of the moon [chundran]. In astrology auspicious. Krishnan [q.v.] was born with the moon in Rohiny. See Krishna jayanty. Figured as a wheeled carriage. Comprises five stars, out of the seven which the Greeks named the Hyades; they probably are α, β, γ, δ, ε Tauri [sowr]. The Arabs agree. Compare arabian mansion Aldeberan. For α Tauri, 16 see Aldeberan and Sowbhaugyam. For β Tauri, 20 see Agny and Nath. For γ Tauri, 15 see Nautih. Rohiny yogam is the period of a day when the moon [chundran] passes through the asterism of rohiny in the dark half [krishna pacsham] of the lunar month [mausam] of Jyeshtam [q.v.] or june; it is part of an astronomer's duty to examine the weather [monsoon] indications on this day and to predict scientifically the future condition of the land [swauty yogam].——*Roomeisah* (رميصاء - rumaisá, Hind.). From (ramasa, ar. matter that collects in the eye). Same as Ghoomeisah.——*Roomh ool simauk* (رمح السماك - rumhussimák, Ar.). From (rumh, ar. spear + simák, ar. star arcturus). Otherwise Airoomh [q.v.], meaning the spear, from its position in relation to arcturus, 44 [haurs ool samah, vajram] which is just east of it. Star of third magnitude. η Boötis [awwah], 43.——*Rowdray* (रौद्रा - raudrá, San.). Belonging to roodran [q.v.] or shiva [q.v.]. Otherwise Ardray [q.v.]. Sixth hindoo lunar mansion, so called because the presiding deity of the mansion is Roodran. Compare arabian mansion Hanah. ——*Royiljowzah* (راعي الجوزا - ráyiljauzá, Ar.). Means guardian of orion. Same as Rigel.——*Royinauyim* (راعي النعايم - ráyinnaáim, Hind.). Means guardian of nauyim. λ Sagittarii [kows]. See also Nauyim.——*Saboo* (سبع - sabu, Ar.). Means a wolf; cf. azfaur ool zeib and zeebaun, two wolves. Constellation. Nineteen stars; Lupus.——*Sad i boola* (سعد بلع - sadibula, Ar.). Same as Boola.——*Sad i naushira* (سعد ناشره - sadináshira, Hind.). Means constellation of verdant herbage. Two stars in the tail of capricornus [jaddy, macaram].——*Sad ool akbee* (سعد الاخبيه - sadulakhbíh, Hind.). From (sad, ar. auspicious + akhbíh, ar. the constellation). The 25th arabian lunar mansion. See Akbeé.——*Sad ool baury* (سعد البارع - sadulbári, Hind.). Means excellent constellation. Small constellation. Two stars μ and λ in the breast of Pegasus [faras ool azam].——*Sad ool bihaum* (سعدالبهام - sadulbihám, Hind.). Means constellation of the kids. Small constellation. ε, θ Pegasi [faras ool azam]. For ε Pegasi, 63 see Fomal fars.——*Sad ool hoomaum* (سعد الهمام - sadulhumám, Hind.). Means a magnificent constellation. Same as Fomal fars [q.v.], ε Pegasi [faras ool azam], 63.——*Sad ool malik* (سعد الملك - sadulmalik, Hind.). Means a royal constellation. Small constellation α, ο Aquarii [coombham, dalo].——*Sad ool matar* (سعد المطر - sadulmatarr, Hind.). Means a rainy constellation. Small constellation. η, ο Pegasi [faras ool azam].——*Sad ool sood* (سعدالسعود - sad us suúd, Ar.). Same as Sood——*Sadr ool dajjajah* (صدر الدجاجه - sadruddajjájah, Hind.). From (sadr, ar. breast + dajjájah, ar. swan). Star. γ Cygni [dajjajah].——*Safeenah* (سفينه - safínah, Ar.). Means a ship. Constellation. Forty-five stars. Argo navis. S. hemisphere. South-eastward of Canis major [kalb i acbar]. Extensive area. Besides the principal stars, α Argûs, 25 [agastyan, coombhayony, sooheil] or Canopus, and η Argûs which is variable in magnitude, it contains several others, β, γ, δ, ε, ζ, θ, and star 6, of the second and third magnitudes. α Argûs, 25 or Canopus [agastyan, sooheil], next to Sirius, 26 [loobdhacam, mrigavyaudham, shira], is brightest in the heavens; nearly on a line drawn from Rigel, 18 [q.v.], in Orion [jabbaur], through α Columbæ and produced half the distance. β Argûs is the southernmost of the conspicuous stars in this constellation, and lies nearly midway between Canopus, 25 and α Crucis [trishunkoo], the southernmost and brightest star in the Southern cross [trishunkoo]. η Argûs is as far to the westward of α Crucis [trishunkoo] as β Centauri [cantooras] is to the eastward; it goes from 1 to 4, but irregularly. θ Argûs is 5° due south of η Argûs. θ, 6, δ, γ and ζ Argûs are nearly in a straight line, γ Argûs being as far to the westward of θ Argûs as α Centauri [cantooras] is to the eastward. ε Argûs is nearly midway between β and γ Argûs. Grus, the Crane, opposite side of South pole [dacshina dhroovam] to the group, of bright stars in Argo navis, is not represented in Arabic; α Gruis, of the second magnitude, is on a line drawn from α Centauri [cantooras] through α Trianguli australis [kyekows], and produced about three times their distance; it is also distant from Fomalhaut, 66 [q.v.] 20° in a S.S.W. direction, when η and θ Argûs are on the meridian [raikhay] above the South pole [dacshina dhroovam], β Gruis is very near the meridian below the pole [dhroovam], but at about twice the distance. Phœnix, not represented in Arabic, lies between Grus and Eridanus [nahr]; its principal star, α Phœnicis, is midway between Achernar, 7 [q.v.]; and Fomalhaut, 66 [q.v.]; when the two principal stars of the Southern cross [trishunkoo] are on the meridian below the pole, α Phœnicis is on the meridian above the pole.——*Saham* (سهم - saham, Ar.). Means arrow; also (sahamurrámí), meaning arrow of the archer. Constellation; five stars; Sagitta. For Sagittarius, the archer, see Kows.——*Saleeb* (صليب - salíb, Ar.). Means a cross. Small constellation of four stars in delphinus [doolfeen] behind Altair, 60 [q.v.].——*Sarafa* (صرفه - sarafah, Ar.). From (sarafah, ar. to turn away); from its driving away cold at its auroral setting, and heat at its auroral rising. Otherwise Coonboolasad [q.v.], meaning sheath of leo, from its position; also Denebola [q.v.]; also Dhroovam [q.v.]. β Leonis [asad], 37. Stands for 12th arabian lunar mansion. Compare 12th hindoo mansion Oottaram.——*Sarpam* (சர்ப்பம் - sharppam, Tam.). From (srip, san. to creep). Serpent. Otherwise Aushlaisham [q.v.], or Ayilliyam [q.v.]. Ninth hindoo lunar mansion. Compare 9th arabian mansion Tarafa.——*Sartaun* (سرطان - sartán, Ar.). Means a crab. Cancer [carcatacam]. Fourth constellation of ancient zodiac [raushy chuckram], with no star greater than fourth magnitude; lies to east of Gemini [jowzah, mitoonam]. Centre of constellation passes meridian at midnight about end of January. For α cancri, 30 see Shoolam. For δ cancri, 29 see Dhrity. For the nebula in cancer see Milaf. See also Aushlaisham and Pooshyam.——*Saudhyam* (साध्य - sádhya, San.). From (sádh, san. to accomplish). Yogam star of 22nd hindoo lunar mansion. Otherwise Altair [q.v.]. α Aquilæ [ookaub], 60. 1st magnitude.——*Sauk ool asad* (ساق الاسد - sákulasad, Hind.). From (sák, ar. shank + asad, ar. leo). Same as Simauk ool azal.——*Shalyauk* (شلياق - shalyák, Ar.). Also called (assulahfát), meaning a tortoise. Constellation. Ten stars. Lyra, the Lyre or Harp. Opposite side of the pole [dhroovam] to Auriga [mausik ool inaun]. One principal star, α Lyræ, 58, or Vega [abhijit, nasr ool wauky]. This is somewhat more than an equal distance on opposite side of pole with respect to Capella or α Aurigæ [mausik ool inaun], 17 [bramhahridayam, oyook]. It is also 24° in a W.S.W. direction from α Cygni [dajjajah], 62 [deneb]. In brilliancy, Vega, 58 is next to Capella, 17. The variable star β Lyræ lies south-east of Vega, at distance of 6°, and close to it is γ Lyræ; they are not far from the edge of the milky way [kahkashaun]. β Lyræ changes from 3·4 to 4·5 in 12 days 21¾ hours. See also Asaufy, Azfaur and Nasrein.——*Shartein* (شرطين - sharatain, Ar.). Means two marks. Otherwise Sheratan. Two stars α 10, β 9 Arietis which are its two horns. Also applied to the single star β Arietis, 9. First arabian lunar mansion. For α Arietis, 10 see Hamel and Vishcambham. Compare hindoo mansion Ashwiny. For the horns of the bull [sowr] see Nath and Nautih.——*Shatabhishay* (शतभिषा - shatabhishá, San.; சதயம் - shathayam, Tam.). From (shata, san. hundred + bhishaj, san. physician); one struck with disease when moon is in this mansion requires 100 physicians to cure him. Otherwise Shata tauracam, meaning hundred stars. Also Shathayam [q.v.]. 24th hindoo lunar mansion containing hundred stars. Figured by a circle. These may be sought in the stream from the Jar, and in the right leg of Aquarius [coombham, dalo]. Compare arabian mansion Akbee.——*Sheratan* (شرطان - sharatán, Ar.). Same as Shartein.——*Shira* (شعرى - shira, Ar.). Means a bitch. Otherwise Shiralaboor [q.v.], the crossing Sirius, from its having crossed the milky way [kahkashaun] following its sister Sooheil, 25 [q.v.] when the latter descended into the south. Whence also Shiralyamaniyah [q.v.], meaning yemenian or southern shira, as opposed to shiral shaumiyah [q.v.] which remained in its place. Otherwise Sirius; also Loobdhacam [q.v.]; also Mrigavyaudham [q.v.]. Star of first magnitude, with parallax of ¼ second. α Canis majoris [kalbiacbar], 26. See also Shiriyaun.——*Shiral aboor* (شعر العبور - shiralabúr, Hind.). From (shira, ar. sirius + abúr, ar. crossing). Same as Shira.——*Shiral ghoomeisah* (شعرى الغميصاه - shiralghumaisá, Hind.). From (shira, ar. sirius + ghumaisá, ar. with eye affected). Same as Ghoomeisah.——*Shiral shaumiyah* (شعرالشاميه - shiralshámmiyah, Hind.). From (shira, ar. sirius + shámmiyah, ar. syrian); from remaining where it was and not accompanying sirius, 26 when the latter followed sooheil, 25 to the south. Same as Ghoomeisah.——*Shiral yamaniyah* (شعراليمانيه - shiralyamániyah, Hind.). From (shira, ar. sirius + yamániyah, ar. yemenian). Same as Shira.——*Shiriyaun* (شعريان - shiriyán, Hind.), meaning two shiras, viz., shira, 26 [q.v.] and ghoomeisah, 27 [q.v.]. These two together are called the sisters of Sooheil, 25 [q.v.]. When Sooheil [agastyan, coomba yony] descended into the south, Sirius followed it crossing the milky way [kahkashaun], and Procyon or ghoomeisah remained in her place weeping for the loss of the two others.——*Shivam* (शिव - shiva, San.). Means deity. Yogam star of 20th hindoo lunar mansion. δ Sagittarii [kows], 57. 3rd magnitude.——*Shobhanam* (शोभन - shóbhana, San.). From (shubh, san. to shine). Yogam star of fifth hindoo lunar mansion. λ Orionis [jabbaur].——*Shoobham* (शुभ - shubha, San.). From (shubh, san. to shine). Yogam star of 23rd hindoo lunar mansion. α Delphini [doolfeen], 61. 4th magnitude.——*Shoobhram* (शुभ्र - shubhra, San.). From (shubh, san. to shine). Yogam star. λ Aquarii [coombham, dalo], 65. Same as Shooclam. 4th magnitude.——*Shooclam* (शुक्ल - shukla, San.). Means white. Otherwise Shoobhram, 65 [q.v.]. Yogam star of 24th hindoo lunar mansion. λ Aquarii [coombham, dalo], 65. 4th magnitude.——*Shoojah* (شجاع - shujá, Ar.). Means a snake. Constellation. Twenty stars. Hydra, the Snake. S. hemisphere. Beginning near Procyon. 27 [ghoomeisah], trends to the eastward in a serpentine form along the south of Cancer [carcatacam, sartaun], Leo [asad, simham], and Virgo [canyay, soomboola], and terminates near Libra [meezaun, toolaum]. It is represented in European system carrying on its back a goblet or cup, Crater [bautiya], and on its tail a crow, Corvus [ghooraub, bastam], and from its great length is divided into three parts; Hydra, at the head; Hydra et Crater, the middle part; and Hydra et Corvus, at the tail. It contains one principal star, α Hydræ, 31, or Alphard [q.v.], sometimes called Cor hydræ or Oonuk shoojah [q.v.]. A line drawn from γ Leonis [asad] through Regulus, 32 [gandam, kalb ool asad] and produced to the south-westward; or a line through Castor and Pollux, 28 [alzirah, soocarmam], produced to the south-eastward for a considerable distance, will pass through no brighter star than α Hydræ, 31, which may be known by its dark ruddy appearance. For Hydrus, the water-snake see under Nahr.——*Shoolam* (शूल - shúla, San.). Means pointed weapon. Yogam star of ninth hindoo lunar mansion. α Cancri [sartaun], 30. 4th magnitude.——*Shothy* (சோதி - shóthi, Tam.). By corruption from swauty [q.v.]. The 15th hindoo lunar mansion.——*Showla* (شول - shaulah, Ar.). From (shaul, ar. tail). Two stars λ and ν 51 in Scorpio [akrab]; 19th arabian lunar mansion. For λ or ν Scorpii, see Parigham. Compare hindoo mansion Moolam.——*Shravanam* (श्रवण - shravana, San.; திருவோணம் - tiruvónam, Tam.). From (shru, san. to hear). Otherwise Wonam [q.v.] by corruption; also Tirwonam [q.v.]. 22nd hindoo lunar mansion presided over by Vishnoo [q.v.], whence represented by three foot-steps containing three stars, α, β and γ Aquilæ [ookaub]. For α Aquilæ, 60 see Altair and Saudhyam. Compare arabian mansion Boola.——*Shravishtay* (श्रविष्ठा - shravisht'há, San.; அவிட்டம் - avittam, Tam.). Most famous. 23rd hindoo lunar mansion. Same as Dhanishtay.——*Siddham* (सिद्ध - siddha, San.). Means accomplished. Yogam star of 21st hindoo lunar mansion. τ Sagittarii [kows], 59. 3rd magnitude.——*Siddhy* (सिद्धि - siddhi, San.). Means accomplishment. Yogam star of 16th hindoo lunar mansion. Same as Zubenesch [q.v.].——*Simauk ool azal* (سماك الاعزل - simákulazal, Ar.). From (simák, ar. star, arcturus + azal, ar. one without a weapon); so called from its having no stars near it, which is unlike the neighbouring arcturus, 44 [haurs ool samah, vajram]; or from its rising aurorally unaccompanied by cold or wind. Otherwise Sauk ool asad [q.v.], meaning shank of leo [asad], which the arabs had considerably extended; also Spica; also Harshanam [q.v.]. Star of first magnitude. α Virginis [soomboola], 41. Stands for 14th arabian lunar mansion. Compare hindoo mansion Chitta.——*Simauk ool mirzam* (سماك المرزم - simákulmirzam, Hind.). From (simák, ar. star + mirzam, ar. cold); from its rising aurorally with the first of the rains [mazhay]. Same as Haurs ool samah.——*Simauk ool raumih* (سماك الرامح - simákurrámih, Hind.). From (simák, ar. star + rámih, ar. spear); from its position with η Boötis [awwah], 43 [roomh ool simauk]. Same as Haurs ool samah.——*Simham* (सिंह - simha, San.). Means lion. Fifth sign [raushy] of the zodiac [raushy chuckram]. Leo, ♌ [asad].——*Soocarmam* (सुकर्मन् - sukarman, San.). From (su, san. good + karma, san. action). Otherwise Alzirah, 28 [q.v.]; also Pollux, 28. Yogam star of seventh hindoo lunar mansion. β Geminorum [jowzah, mitoonam], 28. 1st magnitude.——*Sood* (سعد - suud, Ar.). Meaning auspicious; also (sadussood), meaning the most approved of the sad. Two stars, β Aquarii [coombham, dalo] and δ Capricornii [jaddy, macaram], 64 [denebalgedy]; by some β and ξ Aquarii [coombham, dalo]. 24th arabian lunar mansion. Compare hindoo mansion Shatabhishay.——*Soohah* (سها - suhá, Ar.). A dim star by the side of Alanak [q.v.] by looking at which persons try their powers of sight. 80 Ursæ majoris [doobhe acbar, maharicsham].——*Sooheil* (سهيل - suhail, Ar.). From (sahala, ar. smooth); distinguish from sahely [q.v.]. Otherwise Agastyan [q.v.], Coombhayony [q.v.], Canopus. Star of first magnitude, α Argûs [safeenah], 25. Known to hindoos only after coming to S. india [agastyan]. Friar Jordanus, the Quilon Bishop of the fourteenth century, has the following:— "From the place aforesaid, namely Indran [ashtadic], is seen "continually between the south and the east a star of great size "and ruddy splendour, which is called Canopus, and which from "these parts of the world is never visible." See also Ghoomeisah, Shira and Shiriyaun.——*Soomboola* (سنبلة - sumbulah, Ar.). From (sumbula, ar. ear of wheat); figure being a girl having a ear of corn in her right hand raised to the level of shoulder while the left hand hangs down. Virgo [canyay]. Sixth constellation of ancient zodiac [raushy chuckram]. Contains one very conspicuous star, α Virginis, 41, or Spica [chitta, harshanam, simauk ool azal], with no other near it. α Virginis, 41 or Spica, is distant from β Leonis [asad], 37, or Denebola [q.v.], about 35° in a south-easterly direction, and may be recognised by forming the southern angle of an equilateral triangle, of which Arcturus, 44 [haurs ool samah, vajram] and Denebola, 37 [q.v.] or Dhroovam, 37 [q.v.] are the northern angles. Again Arcturus, 44, Regulus, 32 [gandam, kalb ool asad], and Spica, 41 form a right-angled triangle, having Spica at the right angle. Spica passes the meridian at midnight about the beginning of April. ϵ Virginis, or Vindemiatrix, is a star of the third magnitude within the triangle just mentioned; this star is south of Cor caroli [doobhe acbar], and on a line drawn from γ to β Leonis [asad], 37 and produced half their distance. γ Virginis is a double star with 174 year period 15° to the N.W. of Spica, 41; or, it is a little to the south of a line drawn from Spica, 41 to Denebola, 37 or β Leonis, 37, but nearer the former star; γ Virginis, Spica, and Vindemiatrix form an obtuse angled triangle, γ being at the obtuse angle. For δ Virginis, 40 see Anpas. For the claw of soomboola see Zubenesch. See also Awwah, Ghafr, Simauk ool azal.——*Sooreiyah* (ثريا - suraiyá, Ar.; پروین - parvín, Pers.). Means beneficent or plentiful; on account of its influence on weather [monsoon] of all the mansions of the moon [chundran]; hence called also (annajm) or the asterism. Six or seven conspicuous stars together with many small ones altogether twenty-four constituting the Pleiades in the shoulder of the Bull [sowr, vrishabham]. See also Alfoorood and Arsh ool sooreiyah. Compare Taulyoon najm. Third arabian lunar mansion. Compare hindoo mansion Kritticay.——*Sowbhaugyam* (सौभाग्य - saubhágya, San.). From (su, san. good + bhágya, san. fortune). Otherwise Aldeberan [q.v.]; also Ayeen ool sowr [q.v.]. Yogam star of fourth hindoo lunar mansion. α Tauri [sowr], 16. 1st magnitude.——*Sowr* (ثور - saur, Ar.). Means a bull. Taurus [vrishbham]. Second constellation of the ancient zodiac [raushy chuckram], to southward of Perseus [haumiliraus ool ghowl] and Auriga [mausik ool inaun], and north-westward of **Orion** [jabbaur]. Contains two principal stars, α, 16 [aldebaran, sowbhaugyam] and β, 20 Tauri [agny, nath]. Taurus is also recognised by the two clusters of small stars called the Pleiades [kritticay, sooreiyah], and Hyades [aldebaran], in the latter of which is the bright ruddy star α Tauri, 16 or Aldebaran [q.v.]. A line drawn from Polaris, 6 [al rooccabah, dhroovam], and passing between Capella, 17 [bramhahridayam, oyook] and α Persei [haumilirausoolghowl], 13 [mirfak], will lead to no conspicuous star until it reaches Aldebaran, 16. β Tauri, 20, or Nath [q.v.] or Agny [q.v.] is also γ Aurigæ [mausik ool inaun]; it bisects a line drawn from Capella, 17 to Betelgeux, 23 [q.v.], the principal star of Orion [jabbaur]. It is at the extremity of the Bull's horn. The Pleiades [kritticay, sooreiyah], in the Bull's shoulder, are generally said to be seven in number, but only six stars are visible to the naked eye; the telescope reveals multitudes more; with Aldebaran, 16 and β Tauri, 20, they form an isosceles triangle, having Aldebaran at the apex. η Tauri, 14 or Alcyone or Ayooshmat [q.v.] is the brightest of the Pleiades, and is the star around which, as their common centre, the whole firmament revolves. The Hyades [aldebaran, rohiny] form the forehead and Aldebaran the eye of the Bull [ayeen ool sowr], while γ Tauri, 15 [nautih] is near the nose; they are arranged like the letter V, of which γ is the angular point, α and ϵ Tauri being at the extremities; θ between α and γ Tauri; and δ between ϵ and γ. Aldebaran, 16 [q.v.] passes the meridian at midnight towards the end of November. For Kalb ool sowr or heart of bull see Aldebaran. For others see Kalbaun.——*Swauty* (स्वाति - sváti, San.; ചോതി - chóti, Mal.; சுவாதி - shuváthi, Tam.). From (su, san. well + at, san. to walk). Otherwise Shothy [q.v.], by corruption. 15th hindoo lunar mansion. Represented by a coral bead, ruby, or small brinjaul. Contains a single star of first magnitude, Arcturus, 44 [haurs ool samah, vajram]. Swauty yogam is the period of a day when the moon [chundran] passes through the asterism of swauty in the month of jyeshtam [q.v.] or june [rohiny, yogam]. Compare arabian mansion Ghafr.——*Tarafa* (طرف - tarafah, Ar.). Means the eyes; being regarded as two eyes of Leo [asad, simham]. λ Leonis in the face of the lion and α Cancri [sartaun], 30 [shoolam]. Ninth arabian lunar mansion. Compare hindoo mansion Aushlaisham.——*Tauj ool jowzah* (تاج الجوزا - tájuljauzá, Ar.). Meaning crown of orion [jabbaur]. Otherwise Zawauyib ool jowzah [q.v.], or hanging forelock of orion. Nine stars disposed in a curved form in the sleeve of orion.——*Tauly oon najm* (تالی النجم - tálíunnajm, Hind.). From (tálí, ar. follower + najm, ar. pleiades). Aldebaran, 16 [q.v.], or following or rising later than the pleiades [kritticay, sooreiyah]. See also Sowr.——*Tawauby ool oyook* (توابع العيوق - tawábiulaiyyúk, Hind.). From (tawábi, ar. follower + aiyyúk, ar. capella); β, θ, ϵ Aurigæ [mausik ool inaun]. For Capella, 17 see Oyook.——*Thuban* (ثعبان - subán, Ar.). Means a dragon. Star, α Draconis [tinneen]. Aroondhaty of the hindoos [maharicsham]. Once the brightest in the constellation now of 3rd magnitude. 4,200 years ago it was the pole star being then about 10′ near the pole [dhroovam]. For more details see under Doobhe asghar.——*Tinneen* (تنين - tinnín, Ar.). Means a dragon. Constellation. Thirty-seven stars. Draco, winding constellation, commences between Ursa major [doobhe acbar, maharicsham] and Ursa minor [cshoodraricsham, doobhe asghar], runs almost half way round the latter, and then turns towards Lyra [shalyauk]. Contains three principal stars, α, β, and γ. To find β [alwaida] and γ Draconis, 56 [etenin]; a line through the guards [farghdaun], from β, 47 to γ Ursæ minoris [doobhe asghar], passes through the head of the Dragon, in which they are placed; or a line from Polaris, 6 [al rooccabah, dhroovam], produced through δ Ursæ minoris [doobhe asghar] and extended 38°, leads to them, nearly; they are also nearly on a line joining α Ursæ majoris, 35 [doobhe] and Vega, α Lyræ [shalyauk], 58 [abhijit, nasr ool wauky], but not far from the latter. A line drawn from ζ Ursæ majoris [doobhe acbar], the last star but one in the tail, to the nearest star in δ Ursæ minoris will be bisected by α Draconis [aroondhaty, thuban]. If a line be drawn from λ Draconis to Polaris, 6, the pole [dhroovam] of the ecliptic [craunty mundalam, sauyanam] will be on this line at about the same distance from γ Draconis, 56 [etenin] that this star is from Vega, α Lyræ [shalyank], 58. For μ Draconis, 53 see Rauks. For other stars in the group see Alrooba, Asaufy, Awoyiz and Zeebaun.——*Tirvauthiray* (திருவாதிரை - tiruváthirai, Tam.). Means holy ardray. Same as Ardray.——*Tirwonam* (திருவோணம் - tiruvónam, Tam.). Means holy Wonam [q.v.]. Same as Shravanam.——*Tisyham* (तिष्य - tishya, San.). Same as Pooshyam.——*Toolaum* (तुला - tulá, San.). Means balance. Seventh sign [raushy] of the zodiac [raushy chuckram]. Libra, ♎ [meezaun].——*Towbee* (توبيع - taubí, Hind.). Means follower. Aldebaran [q.v.] is so called from following or rising later than the pleiades [kritticay, sooreiyah]. See also Sowr.——*Trishunkoo* (त्रिशंकु - trishanku, San.). From (tri, san. three + shanku, san. spoke of a wheel). A modern name, not in the shastrams. The southern cross in the southern hemisphere [golam]. Crux or the Cross is a remarkably well defined constellation, about 30° from the South pole [dacshina dhroovam], and due south from Corvus [ghooraub, hastam]; a line from Arcturus, 44 [haurs ool samah, vajram] through spica, 41 [harshanam, simauk ool azal] also leads to it. The four principal stars are α, β, γ and δ Crucis, of which α is the brightest and most southern star; at a distance of 6° to the north of α is γ Crucis which is also 47° S. by W. from spica, 41 [harshanam, simauk ool azal]; about $4\frac{1}{2}$° N.E. of α is β Crucis, the eastern arm of the Cross, and δ the western arm is $4\frac{1}{2}$° from β. All the stars of the Southern cross are within the Milky way [kahkashaun]. None of them recognized either in Hindoo or in Arabian system [achernar, agastyan]. The northernmost and southernmost stars are pointers to the S. pole [dacshina dhroovam]. For pointers of north pole [oottara dhroovam] see Alanak and Doobhe and Doobhe asghar.——*Tyaujyam* (त्याज्य - tyájya, San.). See sep. title.——*Vajram* (वज्र - vajra, San.). Means a cross. Otherwise Haurs ool samah [q.v.]; also Arcturus. Yogam [q.v.] star of swauty [q.v.], the 15th hindoo lunar mansion. α Boötis [awwah]. 44. 1st magnitude.——*Vareeyas* (वरीयस् - varíyas, San.). Means more excellent. Otherwise Alkalb, 52 [q.v.]; also Antares, 52. Yogam star of 18th hindoo lunar mansion. α Scorpii [akrab], 52. 1st magnitude.——*Varjyam* (वर्ज्य - varjya, San.). From (vrij, san. to abandon). The unlucky portion of a nacshatram. See Tyaujyam.——*Vasishtan* (वसिष्ठ - vasisht'ha, San.). Means most patient. One of the seven stars [sapta rishy] of Maharicsham [q.v.]; at arch of tail; ζ Ursæ majoris [doobhe acbar].

——*Veidhrity* (वैधृति - vaidhriti, San.). From (vi, san. suffix of separation + dhrita, san. held), stop; opposition. Yogam star of 27th hindoo lunar mansion of Raivaty [q.v.]. η or ζ, 5 Piscium [hoot, meenam]. It is the last point of Raivaty [q.v.] and the first point of Ashwiny [q.v.] in the lunar constellation scheme, and marks the beginning of the fixed hindoo ecliptic [ayanaumsham, craunty pautagaty, maunam, mausam, rishy], at any rate approximately. See Madhyama sowra maunam, for full account of the last-named matter.——*Vishaukham* (विशाखा - visháklhá, San.; விசாகம் - viságam, Tam.). From (vi, san. spreading + shákhá, san. branches). 16th hindoo lunar mansion. Figured by a decorated gateway or arch, and containing four or originally two stars placed under the regency of a dual divinity, Indran and Agny. The four are α, ν, ι Libræ [meezaun, toolaum] and λ Scorpii [akrab]. For α Libræ, 46 see Siddhy and Zubenesch. Compare arabian mansion Zoobaunah.——*Vishcambham* (विष्कम्भ - vishkambha, San.). From (vishkambh, san. to fix firmly). Yogam star of first hindoo lunar mansion. α Arietis, 10 [hamel]. 2nd magnitude.——*Vriddhy* (वृद्धि - vriddhi, San.). Means increase. Otherwise Zoobra, 36 [q.v.]. Yogam star of 11th hindoo lunar mansion. δ Leonis [asad, simham], 36. 2nd magnitude.——*Vrishabham* (वृषभ - vrishabha, San.). Means bull. Second sign [raushy] of the zodiac [raushy chuckram]. Taurus, ♉ [sowr].——*Vrishchicam* (वृश्चिक - vrishchika, San.). Means scorpion. Eighth sign [raushy] of the zodiac [raushy chuckram]. Scorpio, ♏ [akrab].——*Vyateepautam* (व्यतीपात - vyatípáta, San.). From (vyati, san. to pass away + páta, san. falling). Yogam star of 17th hindoo lunar mansion. δ Scorpii [akrab], 50. 2nd magnitude. See also Yikleel.——*Vyaughautam* (व्याघात - vyágháta, San.). Means impediment. Yogam star of 13th hindoo lunar mansion. δ Corvi [ghooraub], 39. 3rd magnitude. See also Hastam.——*Wazn* (وزن - wazn, Ar.). From (wazana, ar. to weigh exactly). Also (alwazn). β centauri [cantooras]. Cf. Hazaur for α. The pair are Moohlifaun [q.v.].——*Wonam* (ഓണം - ónam, Mal.; ஓணம் - ónam, Tam.). By corruption from Shravanam [q.v.], the 22nd hindoo lunar mansion. For feast so called see sep. title.——*Yadd ool jowzah* (يدالجوزا - yadduljauzá, Hind.). From (yadd, ar. arm + jauzá, ar. orion). Same as Betelgeux.——*Yikleel* (اكليل - iklíl, Ar.). Means a crown. Four stars in Scorpio [akrab]; β, δ, υ, π Scorpii. 17th arabian lunar mansion. For δ Scorpii, 50 see Vyateepautam. Compare hindoo mansion Anooraudhay.——*Yikleel i joonooby* (اكليل جنوبى - iklílijunúbí, Ar.). From (iklíl, ar. crown + junúbí, ar. southern). Constellation. Thirteen stars. Corona australis, Southern crown. For Northern crown see Yikleel i shoomauly.——*Yikleel i shoomauly* (اكليل شمالى - iklílishumálí, Ar.). From (iklíl, ar. crown + shumálí, ar. northern). Otherwise (fakkah), meaning gap; cf. alphacca, 48; from its semi-circular position; also Casat ool masaukeen [q.v.], meaning pauper's bowl; also Causa i darvishaun [q.v.], meaning beggar's bowl, from its similarity. Constellation. Corona borealis, the Northern crown. N. hemisphere. Is east of Boötes [awwah], stars disposed in small semi-circle; at same distance from last star of tail of Great bear [doobhe acbar, maharicsham], η Ursæ majoris, 42 [benetnasch], that this star is from Doobhe, 35 [q.v.], the northernmost of the Pointers [alanak, doobhe], and on the same line. Or, it lies to the northward of a line drawn from Vega, 58 [abhijit, nasr ool wauky] to Arcturus, 44 [haurs ool samah, vajram], one-third the distance from the latter. The principal star is Gemma, or Alphacca, 48 [q.v.]. For Southern crown see Yiklee li joonooby.——*Zanab ool dajjajah* (ذنب الدجاجه - zanabuddajjájah, Hind.). From (zanab, ar. tail + dajjájah, ar. cygnus). Same as Deneb.——*Zaubih* (ذابح - zábih, Ar.). From (zabah, ar. to slaughter); two stars close together one bright and the other obscure so that one of them is represented as slaughtering the other; cf. Boola. Also (saduzzábih). Two stars α β Capricorni [jaddy, macaram]. 22nd arabian lunar mansion. Compare hindoo mansion Abhijit.——*Zaut ool coorsy* (ذات الكرسى - zátulkursí, Ar.). From (zát, ar. lady + kursí, ar. chair). Constellation. N. hemisphere. Thirteen stars. Cassiopea [caushyapy], wife of Cepheus. Several stars of third and fourth magnitudes, grouped like chair; otherwise Cassiopea's chair, or the chair only, or lady's chair. For the chained lady or Andromeda see Mirat i moosalsila. The five principal stars resemble a distorted M or W. A line drawn from any one of the three stars of tail of Great bear, ε, ζ, or η, 42 Ursæ majoris [doobhe acbar, maharicsham], through Polaris, 6 [alrooccabah, dhroovam], will lead to this; Great bear [doobhe acbar] and Cassiopea are opposite sides of pole [dhroovam]. A line drawn from δ Ursæ majoris through Polaris, 6 [al rooccabah, dhroovam], leads to β Cassiopeæ [cuff ool khazeeb]; the two stars are nearly equidistant from Polaris, 6. When above the pole, β Cassiopeæ [cuff ool khazeeb] is westernmost star of group. When above the pole, α is a few degrees S.E. of β Cassiopeæ; when below the pole, a few degrees S.W. of it. α Cassiopeæ or schedir is a variable star, generally fainter than β but sometimes brighter. Cepheus, husband of Cassiopea, is not separately noticed as a constellation in Arabian system; between Draco [tinneen] and Cassiopea, on opposite side of pole to Ursa major [doobhe acbar]; the principal star, α Cephei [alderamin] is only of magnitude 3, and is nearly midway between α Cassiopeæ and β Draconis [tinneen] or alweida [q.v.]; β Cephei [alfirk] also of magnitude 3 is 8° north of α Cephei [alderamin], on a line leading towards Polaris, 6 [alrooccabah, dhroovam]. For κ Cephei see Kalb ool royee. For γ cephei see Alroyee.——*Zauviyat ool awwah* (زاوية العوا - záviyatulawwá, Ar.). From (záviyah, ar. angle + awwá, ar. the lunar mansion). γ Virginis [soomboola], from being so disposed in awwah [q.v.], the 13th arabian mansion.——*Zaw auyib ool jowzah* (ذوائب الجوزا - zawáibuljauzá, Hind.). From (zawáib, ar. hanging cluster + jauzá, ar. orion). Same as Tauj ool jowzah.——*Zeebaun* (ذئبان - zíbán, Ar.). Means two wolves; cf. saboo, a wolf. Two white stars, ξ, η Draconis [tinneen] between awoyiz [q.v.] and farkdaun [q.v.]. Compare Azfaur oolzeib.——*Zirah* (ذراع - zirá, Ar.). Means a forearm; cf. alzirah. Short for zirah oolasad or forearm of Leo [asad].——*Zirah ool mabsoot* (ذراع المبسوط - ziráulmabsút, Ar.). From (zirá, ar. foreleg + mabsút, ar. stretched); foreleg extended. Two stars α, β Geminorum [jowzah, mitoonam], forming the heads of the twins. Seventh arabian lunar mansion. β Geminorum, 28 is Pollux or Alzirah [q.v.] or Soocarmam [q.v.]. Compare hindoo mansion Poonarvas.——*Zirah ool makbooz* (ذراع المقبوض - ziráulmakbúz, Hind.). From (zirá, ar. foreleg + makbúz, ar. contracted); the retracted foreleg of leo; the ancient arabs had projected leo [asad] far beyond the limits now assigned to it. Two stars, α, β Canis minoris [kalb i asghar]. For α Canis minoris, 27 Procyon see Ghoomeisah. See also Mirzam and Mirzamaun.——*Ziraun* (ذراعان - ziráán, Ar.). Dual of zirah. Applied to both zirah ool mabsoot and zirah ool makbooz.——*Zoobaunah* (زبانا - zubáná, Ar.). Means claw. Short for zoobaunah ool akrab, meaning claw of scorpio, which the arabs projected into Libra. Two stars in the claws of Scorpio [akrab]; by some, α, β, by some α, γ, of Libra [meezaun, toolaum] according to the auroral rising or setting. 16th arabian lunar mansion. For α Libræ, 46 see Siddhy and Zubenesch. For β Libræ see Zubenelg. Compare hindoo mansion Vishaukham.——*Zoobra* (زبره - zubrah, Ar.). Means the part where the neck is joined to the back-bone. Also (zubratulasad); (kharátán). Two stars δ θ Leonis [asad, simham], two whips length apart. 11th arabian lunar mansion. For δ Leonis, 36 see Vriddhy. Zoobra is also applied to single star δ Leonis. Compare hindoo mansion Poobbam.——*Zubenelg* (زبانيا العقرب - zubániyalakrab, Ar.). From (zubániya, ar. claw + akrab, ar. scorpio); according to some this is in Scorpio [akrab] which the arabs had considerably enlarged to include a portion of Libra [meezaun, toolaum]. Otherwise Zubenel chamauly or northern claw. Star of second magnitude. β Libræ.——*Zubenesch* (زبانيا السنبله - zubániyassumbulah, Ar.). From (zubániya, ar. claw + sumbulah, ar. virgo). Otherwise Zubenel joonooby or southern claw. Star of second magnitude. α Libræ [meezaun, toolaum], 46 [siddhy]. See also Soomboola.——(9) The following are the regents of the Hindoo lunar mansions.——*Adity* (अदिति - aditi, San.). Death. Of 7th.——*Agny* (अग्नि - agni, San.). Fire. Of 3rd.——*Ahirboodnay* (अहिर्बुध्न्य - ahirbudhnya, San.). Serpent of the deep. Of 26th.——*Ajeicapaud* (अजैकपात् - ajaikapát, San.). Single-legged driver. Of 25th.——*Aryamay* (अर्यमा - aryamá, San.). Playfellow. Of 12th.——*Aupas* (आपस् - ápas, San.). Water. Of 20th.——*Bhagam* (भग - bhaga, San.). Bestower of wealth. Of 11th.——*Bramha* (ब्रह्म - brahma, San.). Creator. Of 21a.——*Brihaspaty* (बृहस्पति - brihaspati, San.). Priest of gods. Of 8th.——*Indran* (इन्द्र - indra, San.). Lord of gods. Of 18th.——*Indran and agny* (इन्द्राग्नी - indrágni, San.). Of 16th.——*Mitran* (मित्र - mitra, San.). A friend. Of 17th.——*Pitries* (पितृ - pitri, San.). Spirits of the departed. Of 10th.——*Pooshan* (पूषन् - púshan, San.). Nourisher, Sun. Of 27th.——*Prajaupaty* (प्रजापति - prajápati, San.). Creator. Of 4th and 19th.——*Roodran* (रुद्र - rudra, San.). Destroyer. Of 6th.——*Sarpam* (सर्प - sarpa, San.). Serpent. Of 16th.——*Savitry* (सवितृ - savitri, San.). Generator, sun. Of 13th.——*Soman* (सोम - sóma, San.). Moon. Of 5th.——*Twashtay* (त्वष्टा - twashtá, San.). Architect of gods. Of 14th.——*Twin-gods* (अश्विनौ - ashvinau, San.). Of 1st.——*Varoonan* (वरुण - varuna, San.). God of waters. Of 24th.——*Vasoo* (वसु - vasu, San.). Wealth. Of 23rd.——*Vayoo* (वायु - váyu, San.). Wind. Of 15th.——*Vishnoo* (विष्णु - vishnu, San.). The preserver. Of 22nd.——*Vishwedevah* (विश्वेदेवाः - vishvédéváh, San.). All gods. Of 21st.——*Yaman* (यम - yama, San.). Lord of the nether world. Of 2nd.——(10) Nacshatram is also used for meteors. These are considered appearances of those who, having enjoyed in the higher worlds the effects of their Poonyacarmam [carmam, samsauram] or good deeds, fall down to the earth. These meteors are of five sorts known technically as Ashany, Vidyoot, Dhishnyam, Taurah, and Oolcay. Varauha mihiran says of them:—"Ashany is a meteoric substance, "circular in shape; it strikes with a loud report men, elephants, "horses, deer, rocks, houses, trees and sheep and passes into the "earth. Vidyoot is a large bent fiery substance and strikes, "with a loud and fearful sound, living creatures and collection

" of wood. Dhishnyam is a blazing fiery meteoric appearance, " thin and with a small tail, and visible beyond a distance of 40 " cubits; its length is two cubits. Taurah is a meteoric sub- " stance, a cubit in length, and of white or copper color, or of the " color of the stem of the lotus [nelumbo]; it will appear to move " either horizontally or vertically downwards or upwards as if " by some invisible force. Oolcay is an appearance with a large " head, a very small tail and of the length of a man's body; as it " falls it increases in length; this appearance is of several " kinds." A common term for the ordinary comet is Vaul nacshatram or tailed-star [dhoom kait].

NAD (नद् - nad, *San.*). To sound.——*Nadaupooram* (നാദപുരം - nádápuram, Mal.). From (náda, san. noise + pura, san. town). Town, District moonsif's head-quarters; Malabar dist., Cooroombranaud tal.; lat. 11° 41′; long. 75° 42′; from Badagara N.E. 7¾ miles; from Calicut N.N.W. 30 miles; from the sea E. 8 miles. Rising Moplah [q.v.] town.——*Nadee* (नदी - nadí, San.). From (nad, san. to sound). Common termination for Sanscrit names of rivers, especially principal rivers forming what are called in English river-basins. Properly speaking Nadam, a male river, is a river flowing to the north or west, as meeting aryan immigrants; and Nadee, a female river, is a river flowing to the east or south [aur], as running away from the same. Generally appears in anglo-indian terminations as Nuddy.——*Nadee mautricam* (नदीमातृक - nadímátrika, San.). From (nadí, san. river + mátrika, san. having for mother); river-nourished. Land irrigated by a river as opposed to devamautricam or land nourished by the skies, i.e., dependent on rains [mazhay].

NADEEM (نديم - nadím, *Ar.*). From (nudama, ar. to be in confidence). Companion. Part of lacab; as Nadeem ood dowla, companion of the empire [ism].

NADIR (نظير - nazír, *Ar.*). From (nazara, ar. to see). Otherwise (nazírussamt), meaning opposite to zenith. Point in the heavens [bhagolam] directly opposite to the zenith [q.v.].

NADOO (നടു - natu, *Mal.*; நடு - nadu, *Tam.*). Middle. Equity. Prefix in place names; as Nadoovuttam, meaning middle circle.——*Nadoojaumam* (நடுச்சாமம் - naduççámam, Tam.). From (above + yáma, san. watch of three hours). Midnight [jaumam].——*Nadoovan* (നടുവൻ - natuvan, Mal.). From (above + an, mal. personal suffix). An arbitrator [madhyastan]. The impartial one; Yaman [q.v.], god of death.——*Nediwuttam* (നടുവട്ടം - natuvattam, Mal.). From (nadu, tam. middle + vattam, tam. valley); place being midway between the wynaud and the neilgherries. Village; Neilgherry dist., Todanaud div.; pop. 1,713; acres 26,030; lat. 11° 29′; long. 76° 36′; from Ootacamund W.N.W. 12 miles. At the head of the Goodalore pass. Public bungalow [q.v.]. Good carriage road to Ootacamund. Cinchona [koinah] estate close to the village on the north; 683 acres.——*Needamungalam* (நீடாமங்கலம் - nídámangalam,* Tam.). From (nadu, tam. middle + áru, tam. river + mangala, san. prosperity). Sanscrit name (yamunámbápura), meaning yamoonay, the queen + town.—"*a*" Deputy tahsildarry, Tanjore district. Pay Rs. 70.—"*b*" Inam village, Head-quarters of Deputy tahsildar, Railway station; Tanjore dist., Munnargoody tal.; pop. 2,806; acres 723; lat. 10° 46′; long. 79° 28′; height 78 feet; from Combaconam S.S.E. 13 miles; from Madras S.S.W. 167 miles; from Mayavaram S.S.W. 27 miles; from Munnargoody N.N.W. 8 miles; from Negapatam W. 28 miles; from Tanjore E. 19 miles. Two old Shiva [q.v.] temples, with inscriptions [shausanam]. Old Vishnoo [q.v.] temple [coil, pagoda]. Largely endowed chuttram [q.v.] built in 1761 by rajah Prataup sing in honor of his Ranee, Yamoonah bye sahiba. Lies between the Vennaur and the Coraiyaur.

NAFAR (نفر - nafar, *Hind.*). From persian. An individual. Nafargaty feisal is an individual settlement [ryotwarry]. Nafar jaumeen is personal security as opposed to money security [nagad jaumeen, rokka jaumeen].

NAFEEL (نفل - nafil, *Ar.*). From (nafala, ar. to present). Prayers not enjoined. Voluntary devotion [namauz, salaut].

NAGAD (نقد - nakd, *Hind.*). Money, cash. Nagad jaumeen is money security [rokka jaumeen]. Nagady chittah is a cash receipt. Nagady goomasta is a treasury clerk. Nagady jummacurts is an account of cash receipts and disbursements. Nagady is bullion or uncoined gold [pon] and silver [velly] in the mass.

NAGAY (நகை - nagai, *Tam.*). From (nagu, tam. to shine) [nangay]. Ornament. See vol. I (98). See Zewar for Mahomedan ornaments.

NAH (நா - ná, *Tam.*). Tongue.——*Naugaswaram* (நாகசுரம் - nágasuram, Tam.). From (nákku, tam. tongue or mouth-piece of a musical instrument + shuram, tam. tube), corrupted. Tam. also (náyagasuram), meaning chief clarion; also (náyagasinnam), meaning chief clarion; the latter corrupted into (náyanam), the form by which familiarly known. Native clarionet [mookhaveenay] used in temples [coil, pagoda] in daily worship [poojah] and indispensable on festive occasions in houses. Also gives name to a reed used in making it; see Large naunal.——*Naumagal* (மநாகள் - námagal, Tam.). From (above + magal, tam. daughter). Saraswaty [q.v.]. Naumagal ilambam is title of a chapter in Jeevaca Chintaumany [q.v.].

NAHAH (نہا - nahá, *Mahl.*). Master; captain [nacodah].

NAIB (نائب - náib, *Hind.*). From (naub, ar. to be near) [nawaub]. A deputy. The word is prefixed, like the English 'sub-,' to the titles of officers; as naib rissaldar, a lower grade of rissaldar; naib diwaun, a sub-treasurer.——*Nawaub* (نواب - navváb, Hind.). From (naub, ar. to be near). Portuguese nababo. The plural of (náib, ar.), but used honorifically in the singular [naib]. Originally a viceroy or governor of a province under Moghul [q.v.]; these often became independent, whence title for a Mahomedan ruler. The title also conferred upon a person of high rank without office being attached to it.——*Nawaubpett* (నవాబుపేట - navábupéta, Tel.). From (naváb, hind. mahomedan ruler + péta, tel. suburb). Village; lat. 14° 28′; long. 80° 03′; from Nellore E.N.E. 1¾ miles; from the sea W. 12 miles. Suburb of Nellore.

NAICHA (نيچه - nechah, *Hind.*). Hookah [q.v.] tube.

NAIL DYE (झिण्टी - jhintí, *San.*; గోరంట - góranta, *Tel.*; കുറിഞ്ഞി - kuriññi, *Mal.*; කරඬු - karandu, *Singh.*; முள்ளி - mulli, *Tam.*). Title from use of leaves. Tel. from (góru, tel. nail + antu, tel. paste); leaves made into paste and used to dye nails and extremities. Tam. from (mul, tam. prickle). Botanically the Barleria genus, acanthaceæ [vricsham, 101]. Spiny under-shrubs; leaves entire and opposite; fugaceous flowers of various hues and showy; fruit a capsule bursting elastically with two valves; seeds roundish. The species best known to the natives are shown below. Other species are:—bispinosa, buxifolia, courtallica, cuspidata, gibsoni, involucrata, longiflora, montana, mysorensis, noctiflora, pilosa, tomentosa. Compare in other genera, where transl. is of first term:—Amarantus spinosus (erramulugóranta), red thorn; Crotalaria verrucosa (giligóranta), rattle; Erythroxylon monogynum (adavigóranta), forest; Gomphrena globosa (peddagóranta), large; Peganum harmala (símagóranta), foreign. See gloss. paragraphs.——*Blue nail dye* (नीलझिण्टी - nílajhintí, San.; నీలాంబరము - nílámbaramu, Tel.; നീലക്കുറിഞ്ഞി - nílakkuriññi, Mal.; நீலாம்பரம் - nílámbaram, Tam.). Title from flowers. San. from (níla, san. blue + jhintí, san. barleria cristata, linn.), from blue flowers. Tel. from (níla, san. blue + ambara, san. sky). Mal. from (níla, san. blue + kuriññi, mal. barleria). Tam. from (níla, san. blue + ambara, san. sky). San. also (dásí), meaning wounding plant, from prickles; (vana), meaning wounding plant. Tam. also (mañjalsemmulli), meaning yellow + red + thorny shrub. Title otherwise Neelaumbram [q.v.], Sky-blue barleria. Botanically Barleria [nail dye] strigosa, willd., acanthaceæ [vricsham, 101]. Alias Barleria cærulea. Undershrub; stem strigose; leaves elliptic-oblong, decurrent into the petiole, lineolate above, glabrous; spikes axillary, subsessile, short, dense; bracts elliptic, somewhat attenuated at the apex, mucronulate-ciliated; upper segment of the calyx emarginate; tube of the corolla elongated; flowers pale-blue; flowering in the cold season. There is a variety terminalis.——*Common nail dye* (कुरुण्टक - kuruntaka, San.; कोरांटी - kóránti, Mahr.; गोरटि - gorati, Conc.; كٹسريا - katsariyá, Hind.; لال پھول كے كولسے كا پتا - lálphúlkekolsekápattá, Dec.; ಮುಳ್ಳುಗೋರಂಟೆ - mullugórante, Can.; ಗೋರಂಟೆದೈ - górantedai, Too.; ములుగోరంట - mulugóranta, Tel.; ചെമ്മുള്ളി - chemmulli, Mal.; කටුකරඬු - katukarandu, Singh.; செம்முள்ளி - shemmulli, Tam.). San. from (ku, san. earth + ram, san. to delight). Mahr. from sanscrit. Dec. from (lál, hind. red + phúl, hind. flower + kolsá, hind. charcoal + pattá, hind. leaf). Can. from (mullu, can. thorn + górante, can. the plant). Tel. like canarese. Mal. from (chem, mal. red + mulli, mal. thorny plant). Singh. from (katu, singh. thorn + karanda, singh. the plant). Tam. from (shem, tam. red + mulli, tam. thorny shrub) [andaman indian oak]. San. also (sairéyaka), meaning turned up by the plough; (anantá), meaning endless [hurrially, indian sarsaparilla]; (kóranta). Mahr. also (vajradantí), meaning diamond + tooth. Hind. also (kántajantí), meaning thorn + barleria cristata, linn. Can. also (mullumadarangi), meaning thorn + henna plant, lawsonia alba, lamk.; (kurantakagida), meaning yellow amaranth. Tel. also (pattsamulugóranta), meaning yellow + the plant; (kondagobbi), meaning hill + plant, hygrophila spinosa, t. & andr. Mal. also (kollattuvettila), meaning betel of collam; (vettilakkodi), meaning betel creeper, piper betel, linn. [betel pepper]. Tam. also (varalmulli), meaning to dry + thorny shrub; (kodippasalai), creeper + the plant, basella. Title otherwise Collam betel leaf, Thorny nail dye. Botanically Barleria [nail dye] prionitis, linn., acanthaceæ [vricsham, 101]. Alias Barleria hystrix; Justicia appressa. Shrubby weed, 2 feet; stem herbaceous; deep green leaves opposite, entire, lanceolate-ovate; between the branch and the leaf there is a spine with four sharp rays from the same centre; flowers sessile, axillary, orange colored; flowering nearly all the year; root woody, perennial, with numerous lateral rigid rootlets. Hindoo poets compare its yellow flowers to a flash of lightning. Juice of leaves, which is rather bitter, mixed with sugar and water, given to children in fevers and catarrh, diaphoretic and expectorant; also applied to soles of feet to prevent cracking; the ashes of burnt plant, mixed with water and rice conjee [q.v.], employed in dropsy, anasarca and coughs; a paste is made of the root which is applied to disperse boils and glandular swellings, and a medicated oil, made by boiling the leaves and stems with sweet oil [zeitoon] until all the water has been driven off, is used as a cleansing application to wounds. Plant grown as hedge.——*Large nail dye* (झिण्टी - jhintí, San.; పెద్దగోరంట - peddagóranta, Tel.; କୈଲେକ - kóiléka, Oor.; ஊதாமுள்ளி - úthámulli, Tam.). Tel. from (pedda, tel. large + góranta, tel. nail-dye plant, barleria). Tam. from (údá, hind. brown + mulli, tam. thorny shrub). San. also (kuruvaka), meaning sounding; applied to purple or yellow barleria; (sairéyaka), meaning produced in saira or turned up by plough. Tel. also (errapúlapeddagóranta), meaning red flower + large + nail-dye plant; (tellanílámbari), meaning white + plant, barleria strigosa, willd.; (nallapeddagóranta), meaning black + large + nail-dye plant. Tam. also (nílasemmulli), meaning black + red thorny shrub, barleria prionitis, linn.; (vellainílámbaram), meaning white + barleria strigosa, willd. Title otherwise Crested barleria, Purple barleria. Botanically Barleria [nail dye] cristata, linn., acanthaceæ [vricsham, 101]. Alias Barleria ciliata, dichotoma. Herbaceous, strigose with adpressed hairs; leaves elliptic, attenuated at both ends, petioled; peduncles axillary, very short, few-flowered; bracts linear-subulate, ciliated; larger calycine segments unequal, elliptic-oblong, ciliated and serrated; flowers blue. Ornamental bushy shrub, 3 feet high, blossoms in cold season with numerous, rather large bright flowers. Seed an antidote for snake-bite; roots and leaves used to reduce swellings, an infusion given in coughs.

NAIR (നേർ - nér, *Mal.*). Correct, just.——*Nairpalisha* (നേർപ്പലിശ - nérppalisha, Mal.). From (above + palisha, mal. interest). Ten per cent. per annum.——*Nery* (நேரி - néri, Tam.). From (nér, tam. straight). Ancient mountain in the chola [q.v.] country. See vol. I (125). Neriyan or Nery verpan is chola king as lord of that mountain.

NAJEEB (نجيب - najíb, *Ar.*). From (najaba, ar. to be generous). Noble. In composition makes an alam; as Najeeb ood dowlah, nobility of the empire [ism]. Now used for militia or police.——*Najeeb oollah khan* (نجيب الله خان - najíbulláhkhán, Hind.). Alam + honorific title. Brother of Nawaub wallajah [q.v.] and governor of Nellore. See vol. II, 112.

NAJM (نجم - najm, *Ar.*). From (najama, ar. to rise). Also called (kowkab); (saiyárah), meaning wandering star [noojoom]. A planet [graham]. The following are the names, &c., of the planets.——*Cumr* (قمر - kamr, Ar.; ماه - máh, Pers.; سوم - som, Hind.). Called also (kásidifalak), meaning celestial messenger. Moon [chundran]. In the first heavens, propitious.——*Mirreek* (مریخ - mirríkh, Ar.; بهرام - bahrám, Pers.; منگل - mangal, Hind.). Also called (jalládifalak), meaning celestial executioner. Mars [coojan, mungalan]. In the fifth heaven. Inauspicious.——*Mooshtary* (مشتری - mushtarí, Ar.; برجیس - birjís, Pers.; برسپت - biraspat, Hind.). Also called (káziifalak), meaning celestial judge. Jupiter [brihaspaty]. In the sixth heaven. Auspicious.——*Ootaurid* (عطارد - utárid, Ar.; تیر - tír, Pers.; بدھ - budh, Hind.). Also (dabírifalak), meaning celestial teacher. Mercury [boodhan]. In the second heaven. Propitious.——*Shums* (شمس - shams, Ar.; خورشید - khurshíd, Pers.; آدت - ádit, Hind.). Also (mutbikhifalak) or celestial cook. Sun [sooryan]. In the fourth heaven. Indifferent.——*Zohra* (زهره - zuhara, Ar.; ناهید فلک - náhídifalak, Pers.; سکر - sukr, Hind.). Also (mutribifalak) or celestial prostitute. Venus [shoocran]. In the third heaven. Propitious.——*Zoohal* (زحل - zuhal, Ar.; کیوان - kaiwán, Pers.; سنیچر - saníchar, Hind.). Ar. from (zuhala, ar. to retire); being remote in seventh heaven. Also (mukhannasifalak), meaning celestial eunuch. Saturn [shany]. In the seventh heaven. Unpropitious.

NAKAL (نقل - nakl, *Hind.*). From (nakala, ar. to transcribe). A copy.

NAKCHIKNEE (चिक्कणी - chikkaní, *San.*; नाकशिंकणी - nákashinkaní, *Mahr.*; نك چھکنی - nakchhikní, *Hind.*; نك چھینکنی - nakchhínkní, *Dec.*). Title from hindostany. San. means sneezing. Mahr. from hindostany. Hind. and dec. from (nák, hind. nose + chhikní, hind. sneezing) [nakchiknee silk cotton]. Hind. also (nágdauna) [indian absinth]. Title otherwise Small-seeded absinth, Sneeze-wort. Botanically Centipeda orbicularis, lour., compositæ [vricsham, 74]. Alias Artemisia minima, sternutatoria; Centipeda minuta; Cotula minuta, minuta et cuneifolia; Dichrocephala schmidii; Grangea cuneifolia, decumbens, minuta; Myriogyne minuta. Herb; decumbent ascending; slightly glabrous or somewhat velvety at the apex; leaves oblong, cuneate at the base, serrated at the apex, somewhat obtuse or sub-acute; flowering in february and march; flowers small, yellow; in moist places. Minute seeds are sternutatory, also the powdered herb. No other species here.

NAKEE (نقی - nakí, *Ar.*). Pure, excellent. Lacab of the tenth Imaum [q.v.]. Common alam; as Nakee ally, double alam [ism].

NAKKAURA (نقاره - nakkárah, *Hind.*; ನಗಾರು - nagáru, *Can.*). A large kettle drum [paray, sangeetam]. Nakkaurkhanah is a chamber where state drums are sounded; usually an open alcove over the gateway [darwauja, dwauram].

NAKSHA (نقشه - nakshah, *Hind.*). From (naksh, ar. impression). A map.

NAL (नल - nal, *San.*). To shine.——*Nalam* (नल - nala, San.; بڑا جواری - barájawárí, Hind.; ಕಾಡುಗುಂಡುಹುಲ್ಲು - kádugunduhullu, Can.; కుశతుంగ - kushatunga, Tel.). San. from (nal, san. to shine). Hind. from (bará, hind. large + jawárí, hind. sorghum vulgare, pers.). Can. from (kádu, can. forest + gundu, can. round + hullu, can. grass). Tel. from (kusha, san. sacred grass, eragrostis cynosuroides, retz. + tunga, tel. cyperus rotundus, linn.). Can. also (bettadausumánihullu), meaning hill + the sedge grass, cyperus compressus, linn.; (gaddegunduhullu), meaning field + round + grass. Tel. also (murukashabi). Tam. also (kórai) [common sedge, straight sedge]. Botanically Fimbristylis genus, cyperaceæ [vricsham, 155]. Grasses, mostly natives of warm countries, having the inflorescence in spikes, solitary, in pairs, or in crowded heads, many-flowered; style compressed and fringed. The s. indian species indigenous or naturalized are:—Æstivalis, culms leafy at the base; Albicans, compressed culm; Argentea, glaucous, culms leafy at the base; Bispicata, culms leafy at the base; Capillacea, culms erect; Chætorhiza, culm compressed and three-cornered, straight; Communis, cæspitose, glaucous; Complanata, culms compressed, leafy at the base; Dichotoma, glaucous, culms leafy at the base; Glabra, culms erect; Latifolia, culm furrowed and angular, slender; Miliacea, culms leafy at the base; Monticola, culms erect; Polytrichoides, culms one-leaved at the base; Quinquangularis, culms leafy at the base, sometimes leafless; Scaberrima, culms compressed; Schænoides, culms leafy at the base; Tenera, culm angular; Torta, rhizome creeping; Uliginosa, root fibrous, culms leafy at the base.——*Nalan* (नल - nala, San.). From (nal, san. to shine). Means king. Generally with the addition of chuckravurty [q.v.] or rajah [q.v.]. A king, whose adventures form an episode in the Mahabhaurat [q.v.] and are specially the subject of the Neishadam [q.v.]. Small poems and poetical allusions in other works are also numerous.——*Nalavenbah* (நளவெண்பா - nalavenbá, Tam.). From (nala, san. the king + venbá, tam. the verse). Considered the most refined Tamul poem, written by Poogazhendy [q.v.] about the eleventh century. The following extracts will furnish an idea of the style of the poem:—வெஞ்சிலையே கோடுவன மென்குழலே சோருவன அஞ்சிலம்பே வாய்விட் டரற்றுவன—கஞ்சம் கலங்குவன மாளிகைமேற் காரிகையார் கண்ணே விலங்குவன மெய்ந்நெறியை விட்டு—"The only curved things in this city are the cruel bows; the "only thing which gets loose is the soft hair of females; the "only things which open their mouths and lament are the ankle "ornaments; the only thing which trembles is water; the only "things which go astray from the right path are the eyes of the "maidens who sit on the terraces of houses."—கானுந் தடங் காவுங் காமன் படைவீடு வானுந்தேர் வீதி மறிகடலும்-மீனக் கொடியாடை வையமெல்லாம் கோதண்டசாலை, பொடிபாடி கொன்றதெல்லாம் பொய்—"The forest and "the extensive groves constitute the arsenal of the god of "love, the heavens are the highways upon which his chariot "rolls, the wave-bounded ocean is his banner marked with the "insignia of a fish, the whole earth is a depository for his "arrows; therefore it is false to assert that he has been "destroyed by Shiva [q.v.]."—சேலுற்ற வாவித் திருநாடு பின்னொழியக் காவிற்போய்த் தேவியொடுங் கண்ணுற் றான்—ஞாலஞ்சேர், கள்ளிவே கத்தரவின் கண்மணி கடாம் பொடியாய்த், துள்ளிவேகின்ற சுரம்—"Leaving "behind him his beautiful country, in which the shell-fish glide "in the tanks, Nalan, walking with his wife, saw the desert in "which the gems on the heads of snakes were burnt to ashes by "intense heat of the Cully [q.v.] plants, and the reptiles "themselves writhed in agony."—காரிகைதன் வெந்துயரங் காணமனீத்தந்தக், கூரிருளிற் போவான் குறித்தெ ழுந்து—நேரோ, இருவர்க்கு மோருயிர்போ லெய்தியதோ ராடை, அரிதற் கவனினைந்தா னங்கு—"Wishing to "desert Damayanty [q.v.] in her great sorrow and separate "from her in that dense darkness, he rose, and contemplated "dividing into halves the garment which was to them as their "common life."—எண்ணிய வெண்ணண முடிப்ப விகல்வேந் தன், கண்ணணி யதையறிந்து காய்கலியும்—பண்ணினுக் க்குக், கேளான தேமொழியை நீக்கக் கிளரொளி சேர், வாளாய் மருங் கிருந்தான் வந்து—"Knowing the thoughts "of the valiant king, the angry Caly [q.v.] came and attached "himself to the waist of Nalan, in the form of a bright knife, to "enable him to fulfil his design of deserting the maiden whose "speech was as pleasant as the flow of music."—ஒற்றைத் துகிலு முயிரு மிரண்டாக முற்றுந்தன் னன்னை முதலோடும்—பற்றி அரிந்தா னரிந்திட்டவணிலைமை நெஞ்சில் தெரிந்தா னிருந்தான் றிகைத்து—"Nalan then "divided the garment, as if he were separating the two lives and "rooting up his affections. And having done this he brooded "over Damayanty's state, and swooned."—அழல்வெஞ் சிலை வேடனம்புருவ வாற்று துழலுங் களி யில்போ லோடிக்—குழல்வண் டெழுந்தோட வீழ்ந்தாளிருகுழை?மற் கண்ணீர்க்கொழுந்தோட வீமன்கொடி—"As the joyous "peacock [mayil], which, when it is pierced by the arrow of the "huntsman, who bends a bow as destructive as fire, unable "to endure the agony, rushes about from place to place, so "Damayanty ran from one place to another, falling down at "times, so that the bees flew away from her plaited tresses, and "the tear-drops moistened her ear."—செய்தபிழை யேதென் னுந் தேர்வேந்தே யென்றழைக்கும், எய்துதுய ரக்கரை காணே னென்னும்—பையவே, என்னென்று தென் னென்னு மிக்கானின் விட்டேகு, மன்னென்றுவாடு மயர்ந்து—"Then Damayanty would ask, What fault have I "done? she would call out O king that possessest great chariots! "And exclaim, I cannot see the shore terminating the sea of "sorrow to which I have now attained and fainting, would ask, "why do you not reply to my cries? O king, who deserted me "in that forest! Thus exclaiming she would continue sorrowing "and swoon away."——*Nargeel* (نارجيل - nárjíl, Hind.). From (nárikéla, san. cocoanut). Cocoanut.——*Naudy* (नाडी - nádí, San.). Means tubular stalk of any plant, reed, lotus, &c. Tube inserted in hole at bottom of clepsydra. Indian hour. Measure of solar time. 60 vinaudies or indian minutes = 1 naudy; 60 naudies = 1 dinam or day [caulam]. Approximate actual value, 1 naudy = 24 English minutes. Same as San. ghaticam [caulam, 3b], dandam [caulam, 6], Hind. ghurry [caulam], Tel. ghadiya [caulam, 4, 5], Tam. nauzhigay [caulam, 1]. See vol. I, 609. Naudy mundalam is celestial equator, for which see under Mundalam.——*Naurail* (نارېل - nárel, Dec.). From (nárikéla, san. coocoanut tree). Same as Coooanut.——*Naurikelam* (नारिकेल - nárikéla, San.). From (nádí, san. tube + ka, san. water + ír, san. to raise). Persian Nargeel. Greek ἀργέλλιον. Properly the cocoanut; thence the hubble-bubble [q.v.], or hookah [q.v.], in its simplest form.——*Nauzhigay* (നാഴിക - názhika, Mal.; நாழிகை - názhigai, Tam.). Indian hour [nauzhy].——*Nauzhigay vattil* (நாழிகைவட்டில் - názhigaivattil, Tam.). From (názhigai, tam. hour + vattil, tam. a brass tray). A small vessel for determining time, which having holes in the bottom and floating on water, sinks at the end of twenty-four minutes.——*Nauzhy* (നാഴി - názhi, Mal.; நாழி - názhi, Tam.). From (nála, san. tube). Measure. See vol. I, 609; II, 516.—"*a*" A measure of capacity. 2 oories = 1 nauzhy; 4 nauzhies = 1 yidangazhy, whether naudan or McLeod's [alavay, 3d]. Approximate actual value, 1 nauzhy = 28 cubic inches. W. coast. Used chiefly in measuring rice. In Tanjore $\frac{1}{8}$th of a mercaul, about 30 cubic inches. Compare oyak of Madras.—"*b*" Superficial measure. 8 nauzhies = 1 cooroony [alavay, 2a]. Approximate actual value, 1 nauzhy = $420\frac{1}{4}$ square feet. Tinnevelly. Equal to 1 square rod of $7\frac{1}{2}$ tutcha coles or $20\frac{1}{2}$ feet to the side. Compare goonta, coozhy.—"*c*" Indian hour, as being the time for the vessel of clepsydra to sink. Measure of solar time. 60 vinaudies or indian minutes = 1 nauzhy; 60 nauzhies = 1 dinam or day [caulam, 1]. Approximate actual value, 1 nauzhy = 24 English minutes. Same as Sanscrit ghaticam [caulam, 3b], dandam [caulam, 6], naudy [caulam], Hind. ghurry [caulam], Tel. ghadiya [caulam, 4, 5].—"*d*" Otherwise Nauzhivazhy in Tamul. Distance that can be walked in one Indian hour. Linear measure. $7\frac{1}{2}$ nauzhivazhies = 1 cantham [alavay, 1a]. Approximate actual value, 1 nauzhivazhy = $1\frac{1}{2}$ miles.——*Nelumbo* (නෙළුං - nelum, Singh.). See sep. title.

NAM (नम् - nam, *San.*). To bow, bend.——*Namas* (नमस् - namas, San.). From (nam, san. to bow down). Salutation.——*Namascauram* (नमस्कार - namaskára, San.). From (namas, san. salutation + kri, san. to make). Uttering the exclamation namas and bowing with two hands raised to the forehead. Appropriate to a deity, and proper between equals. An inferior should make Pranaumam [q.v.], which a superior will acknowledge by Ausheervaudam or pronouncing benediction.——*Namashivauya* (नमशिवाय - namashshiváya, San.). From (namas, san. salutation + shiva, san. the god). Salutation to Shiva! the five-lettered muntram [q.v.] or mystic prayer of the Sheiva sect [moola muntram, punchauosharam]. If the syllable om [q.v.] be prefixed to Namashivauya, then it is called shadacshary or six-syllabled. Namashivauyam is a Hindoo 2nd or pers. name; common among non-bramins [peyar].——*Natam* (नत - nata, San.). Means bent. Descent. The arc [chaupam] of distance of any planet [graham] from the zenith [oordhwam, ootcham]. Nata naudicay is Hour-angle. Nataumsham is Zenith distance [jyotisham].

NAMAK (نمك - namak, *Hind.*). Salt [ooppoo].——**(1)** Namak chasy, from (chashí, pers. tasting), is the ceremony of feeding a child for first time when six months old. Namak halaul, from (halál, ar. lawful), is true to his salt. Namak haraum, from (harám, ar. untrue), is ungrateful. Namak angoor, from (angúr, pers. grape), is cream of tartar [drauosha ooppoo]. Namak i frang, from (farang, pers. english), is glauber's salt or sulphate of soda. Namak i mooshil, from (mushil, ar. purgative), is epsom salt [bhaidy ooppoo]. Namak i saug, from (sang, pers. stone), is rock salt [sondah namak]. Namak i sheeshah, from (shíshah, pers. glass), is glass-gall. Namak i siyah, from (siyáh, pers. black), is bitloban [q.v.]. Namak khaur, from (khuár, pers. eater), is a dependent. Namak mahaul, from (mahál, ar. department), is the salt department. Namak naujoyiz, from (nájáiz, pers. not permissible), is contraband salt.——**(2)** *Chowd ka namak* (چوڑ کا نمك - chaurkánamak, Hind.). Impure carbonate of soda [sowdoo].——*Rauk ka namak* (راك كا نمك - rákkánamak, Hind.). From (rák, hind. ashes + namak, pers. salt). Impure carbonate of potash [jhar ka namak].

NAMAUZ (نماز - namáz, *Hind.*). From persian. Daily prayers. The Mussalmans have five principal devotional acts. They are:—"*a*" prayer or namauz five times a day, reduced by shiahs [q.v.] to three times, morning midday, and evening;—"*b*" almsgiving or zakaut [q.v.];—"*c*" fasting, especially keeping the great fast [roza] during the ninth month [maheena], Ramzaun [q.v.] once a year;—"*d*" the haj [q.v.] or pilgrimage to Mecca once in a lifetime;—"*e*" confession of faith or shahaudat [q.v.], repeating the towheed [q.v.] or declaration of faith in the unity of God, there is no god but God [allah], and Mahomet is the apostle of God. The five namauz are:—at sunrise; between one and four; between four and sunset; just after sunset; and when the night has closed in. Besides the above, there are also three voluntary prayers, and prayers at a funeral [janauza, nafeel].

NAMCULL (நாமக்கல் - námakkal, *Tam.* námakal *). From (náma, san. mark + kal, tam. rock) [naumam]. Rock of the vishnoo mark. Sanscrit name (námádripura), meaning sacred mark + hill + town; also (námagiri), meaning sacred mark + hill.——**(1)** Talook, Salem district. Tahsildar's pay Rs. 225. Area 715 square miles. Population 300,047. Language Tamul. Between 11° 01′ and 11° 25′ N. lat. and 77° 54′ and 78° 32′ E. long. Extreme length from north to south 22 miles, breadth from east to west 39 miles. Most southerly talook of the district. Bounded north by Trichengode, Salem and Ahtoor talooks; west by Erode talook in Coimbatore and Trichengode talook; east by Perambalore talook in Trichinopoly; and south by Caroor and Moosiry talooks in Coimbatore and Trichinopoly districts respectively. The north-eastern portions are mountainous and its south-western area is flat. Beyond Namcull to the south-east are the Talamullays. South and south-east is the Cauvery. The soil, owing to the alluvial deposits of the Cauvery and the detritus of the Collimullays, is exceedingly rich on the west, south, and eastern borders. Black loam prevails towards the east. Other soils are red soil mixed with sand, red soil mixed with gravel, soil composed almost entirely of sand and gravel, and light and sandy soils [munn]. The formation is gneissic with red soil on the surface. Alluvial deposits skirt the Cauvery and granite [caroomcull] is plentiful, especially towards the south-east corner. The usual trap [padicutt cull] dykes and magnetic iron [cauntamunn] beds appear. Magnesite is found at Powtram south of the Collimullays, and chlorite schists to the south-east of Tautayyengarpett. Blown sand hills [tairy] have been formed on a small scale on the north bank of the Cauvery a few miles west of Moganore. The great sigmoid curve of the strata at Mahadevy hill is illustrative of the bedding. The speciality of the talook is its cotton [q.v.] crop classed as Ookkam parootty [ookkam] or annual, and Naudam parootty [naudam] or the crop which lasts three years. Both are indigenous, the Ookkam parootty [ookkam] being the staple article. The staple crop under the Cauvery channels [q.v.] is rice [q.v.], which is produced far in excess of local demand, half of the crop being exported. As a rule two crops, and sometimes three, are produced within the year, under favorable circumstances five crops being gathered in two years. Principal dry crops are cumboo [bajrah], cholum [q.v.], horse-gram [q.v.], black-gram [q.v.], green-gram [q.v.], bengal-gram [q.v.], varagoo [q.v.], raggy [q.v.], gingelly-oil [gingelly] seed, tovray [common dholl], shaumay [q.v.], tinay [q.v.], tobacco [pogauk], cotton [q.v.], turmeric [country saffron], chillies [q.v.], &c. Wheat [geung], is confined to the Collimullays. Iron [auhan], chiefly in the form of black sand, is found in the Neinamullays and is smelted at Shendamungalam. Domestic and agricultural implements for local use are manufactured from the ore. Coarse cloth is woven in most villages. Trade in hides [chamrah] is carried on at the Neinamullay fair. Cotton is a considerable item of commerce. Jaggery [q.v.] is manufactured at Cannoorputty, Cathiranullore, Moganore, Nunjay yideiyaur, Vengaray and Yeddayaur. Saltpetre [shorah] is made at Coomaripolliem, Manapully, Moganore, Nunjay yideiyaur, Oravandore, Pettapolliem and Yeddayaur. The whole crop of wheat and three-quarters of the other produce of the Collimullays, including some coffee [q.v.], are exported to Trichinopoly. Hides find their way to the coast through Vaniyambaudy or Salem. Cotton [q.v.] and saltpetre [shorah] are exported to Madras. A brisk trade is carried in cotton cloths with Mysore, Salem, and Trichinopoly. Plantains [q.v.] are exported in large quantities to Bangalore, Madras, Salem, Tripatore, and Vellore. The principal imports are raw silks [puttoo], areca nut [q.v.]

pepper [q.v.] and salt [ooppoo]. Chief rivers are the Carvauttaur, Eiyaur, and Tirmany moottaur. The Cauvery is, to the centre of its bed, considered as belonging to the district. Tanks [q.v.] are few; the chief are Mahadevy, Powtram, Tautayyengarpett, Toosore and Idoomban coolam tanks. Anicuts [q.v.] are mostly of earth, and are thrown across jungle streams and hill torrents from the Collimullays and other hill ranges. During heavy rains the bed of the Cauvery is impassable for traffic, and ferries are established at Coonnatore, Moganore, Pandamungalam, Sholasiraumany, Veloor and Vengaray. There are also minor ferries at Jedarpolliem, Manapully and Vadacarayauttore. Camping grounds:—Moganore, Namcull, Valayaputty. Zemindarries:—Agrahaura valavendy, Circarvalavendy mittah, Condisettiputty, Conoor, Coodacherry, Coopericapolliem, Dindamungalam, Dommancoorchy, Keerambore, Laddivaudy, Maroorputty, Mettooputty, Moottakkaputty, Moottanchetty mittah, Mothalaputty, Namcull, Palayapolliem, Periyapullambauray, Perooncoorchy, Pilloor, Ponnairy, Poodoocottah, Pottanam, Powtram, Shailore, Shendamungalam, Sholasiraumany, Taulambaudy, Tidoomal, Tippara mahadevy, Tolore, Toosore, Tottamoodeiyamputty, Vailcoorchy, Yermayputty. Places of archæological interest:—Capilamullay, Carvauttaur, Caurcoody, Coonnamullay, Moganore, Namcull, Neinamullay, Nunjay Yideiyaur, Pandamungalam, Paramatty, Pilloor, Shendamungalam, Tautayyengarpett, Valappore, Vassalore, Yermayputty. The leading places, &c., in the talook are the following.——*Agrahaura valavendy* (அக்கிரகாரவாளவந்தி - akkiragáraválavandi, Tam.). From (agrahára, san. bramin quarter + válavandi, tam. village, so called). Zemindarry, Village; pop. 1,089; square miles $18\frac{13}{16}$; lat. of village 11° 05′; long. 78° 18′; from Namcull S.S.E. 12 miles; from Salem S.S.E. 41 miles. Peshcush Rs. 2,629.——*Arautchy* (ஆராச்சி - áráççi, Tam.). From (ár, tam. cassia tree, cassia fistula, linn. + ádchi, tam. possession). Village; pop. 1,051; acres 2,145; lat. 11° 06′; long. 78° 31′; from Namcull E.S.E. 22 miles; from Salem S.S.E. 44 miles.——*Capilamullay* (கப்பிலமலை - kappilamalai, Tam.). From (kapila, san. brown + malai, tam. mountain). Tam. also (kavalaikkuriççi), meaning picottah + village. Sanscrit name (kapilagiri), meaning the sage, so called + mountain. Village; pop. 1,188; lat. 11° 09′; long. 78° 00′; from Namcull S.W. 15 miles; from Salem S.S.W. 38 miles. Old and well-sculptured Shiva temple with inscriptions, and surrounded by several fine mantapams [q.v.] erected by the Madura Naicks [q.v.]. Local centre of trade. Festival in Tye [mausam] or january.——*Carvauttaur* (கருவாட்டாறு - karuváttáru, Tam.). From (karai, tam. embankment + váttam, tam. slope + áru, tam. river). Otherwise Caraypottanaur in Trichinopoly. River. There is said to have been an embankment here marking the boundary between the Paundyan [q.v.], Chola [q.v.], and Congoo [q.v.] kingdoms. Rises in the Collimullays and empties in the Cauvery. Running only in the rainy season.——*Cauvery* (காவேரி - kávéri, Tam.). See sep. title.——*Circarvalavendy mittah* (சர்க்கார்வாளவேந்திமிட்டா - sharkkárválavéndimittá, Tam. sarkárvalavendimittá *). From (sarkár, hind. government + válavandi, tam. village so called + mittah, hind. estate). Zemindarry, Village; pop. 646; square miles $13\frac{3}{8}$; lat. of village 11° 07′; long. 78° 08′; from Namcull S.W. 9 miles; from Salem S.S.W. 38 miles. Peshcush Rs. 6,260.——*Collimullay* (கொல்லிமலை - kollimalai, Tam.). See sep. title.——*Condisettiputty* (கொண்டிசெட்டிப்பட்டி - kondisettippatti, Tam.). From (kondisetti, tam. proper name + patti, tam. cattle-fold). Zemindarry, Village; pop. 619; square miles 6; lat. of village 11° 12′; long. 78° 12′; from Namcull S. $1\frac{3}{4}$ miles; from Salem S. 32 miles. Peshcush Rs. 1,843.——*Conoor* (கோனூர் - kónúr, Tam.). From (kón, tam. shepherd + úr, tam. village). Zemindarry, Village; pop. 1,223; square miles 8; lat. of village 11° 10′; long. 78° 07′; from Namcull W.S.W. 7 miles; from Salem S.S.W. 34 miles. Peshcush Rs. 3,247.——*Coodacherry* (கூடச்சேரி - kúdaççéri, Tam.). From (kúdal, tam. meeting + shéri, tam. village). Zemindarry, Village; pop. 831; square miles $8\frac{1}{16}$; lat. of village 11° 13′; long. 78° 04′; from Namcull W. 10 miles; from Salem S.S.W. 32 miles. Peshcush Rs. 3,546.——*Coopericapolliem* (குப்பெரிக்காப்பாளையம் - kupperikkáppálaiyam, Tam.). From (kopparikkáy, tam. dried kernel of the cocoanut + pálaiyam, tam. fortified village). Zemindarry, Village; pop. 190; square miles $3\frac{1}{4}$; lat. of village 11° 16′; long. 77° 56′; from Namcull W.N.W. 19 miles; from Salem S.W. 32 miles. Peshcush Rs. 2,026.——*Dindamungalam* (திண்டமங்கலம் - tindamangalam, Tam.). From (dindu, can. strength + mangala, san. prosperity). Zemindarry, Village; pop. 419; square miles $16\frac{7}{8}$; lat. of village 11° 13′; long. 78° 05′; from Namcull W. 9 miles; from Salem S.S.W. 31 miles. Peshcush Rs. 7,283.——*Dommancoorchy* (தொம்மங்குறிச்சி - tommanguriççi, Tam. dommankurchi *). From (domba, can. pole-dancer + kuriççi, tam. village). Zemindarry, Village; pop. 385; square miles $9\frac{3}{8}$; lat. of village 11° 14′; long. 78° 09′; from Namcull W. 4 miles; from Salem S.S.W. 30 miles. Peshcush Rs. 5,438.——*Eiyaur* (ஐய்யாறு - aiyyáru, Tam.). See sep. title.——*Idoomban coolam* (இடும்பங்குளம் - idumbangulam, Tam.). From (idumban, tam. from hidimba, san. a rákshasa, so called + kulam, tam. tank). Village; pop. 210; acres 1,648; lat. 11° 08′; long. 78° 06′; from Namcull S.W. 10 miles; from Salem S.S.W. 37 miles. Tank.——*Keerambore* (கீரம்பூர் - kírambúr, Tam.). From (kír, can. little + ambúr, tam. place so called). Zemindarry, Village; pop. 1,315; square miles $8\frac{7}{16}$; lat. of village 11° 12′; long. 78° 08′; from Namcull W.S.W. 6 miles; from Salem S. 33 miles. Peshcush! Rs. 3,632.——*Laddivaudy* (இலத்திவாடி - ilattivádi, Tam.). From (ilatti, tam. dung of horse + vádi, tam. enclosure). Zemindarry, Village; pop. 1,104; square miles $8\frac{7}{16}$; lat. of village 11° 10′; long. 78° 13′; from Namcull S. 4 miles; from Salem S. 34 miles. Good cumblies [q.v.] are made here. Peshcush Rs. 3,179.——*Maroorputty* (மரூர்ப்பட்டி - marúrppatti, Tam.). From (maru, tam. the plant, origanum majorana, linn. + úr, tam. village + patti, tam. cattle-fold). Zemindarry, Village; pop. 688; square miles $4\frac{3}{8}$; lat. of village 11° 16′; long. 78° 14′; from Namcull N.N.E. 3 miles; from Salem S. 27 miles. Peshcush Rs. 1,784.——*Mettooputty* (மேட்டுப்பட்டி - méttuppatti, Tam.). From (médu, tam. high ground + patti, tam. cattle-fold). Zemindarry, Village; pop. 612; square miles $5\frac{1}{2}$; lat. of village 11° 06′; long. 78° 17′; from Namcull S.S.E. 10 miles; from Salem S. 39 miles. Peshcush Rs. 1,667.——*Moganore* (முகவனூர் - mugavanúr, Tam.). From (mugavan, tam. proper name + úr, tam. village). Sanscrit name (bilvádripura), meaning bael tree, ægle marmelos, corr. + mountain + town. Village; pop. 3,247; acres 1,513; lat. 11° 03′; long. 78° 17′; from Namcull S. 12 miles; from Salem S. 42 miles. On the Cauvery. Old Shiva temple. Paddy [q.v.] and plantains [q.v.] exported to Neinamullay bazaar and Salem.——*Moottakkaputty* (முத்தக்காப்பட்டி - muttakkáppatti, Tam.). From (muttakká, tam. proper name + patti, tam. village). Zemindarry, Village; pop. 2,533; square miles $11\frac{9}{16}$; lat. of village 11° 15′; long. 78° 17′; from Namcull E.N.E. 5 miles; from Salem S. 29 miles. Peshcush Rs. 4,929.——*Moottanchetty mittah* (முட்டாஞ்செட்டிமிட்டா - muttánjettimittá, Tam. mutanchettimitta *). Means moottanchetty's mittah [q.v.]. Zemindarry, Village; pop. 1,179; square miles $13\frac{7}{16}$; lat. of village 11° 08′; long. 78° 21′; from Namcull S.E. 11 miles; from Salem S.S.E. 38 miles. Peshcush Rs. 7,507.——*Morputty* (மோருப்பட்டி - móruppatti, Tam.). From (mór, tam. butter milk + patti, tam. cattle-fold). Village; pop. 5,746; acres 2,181; lat. 11° 10′; long. 78° 30′; from Namcull S.E. 19 miles; from Salem S.S.E. 39 miles. Paddy [q.v.] exported to Salem and Trichinopoly.——*Mothalaputty* (மொதலைப்பட்டி - mothalaippatti, Tam. modalaipati *). From (muthalai, tam. crocodile + patti, tam. cattle-fold). Zemindarry, Village; pop. 2,307; square miles $9\frac{5}{8}$; lat. of village 11° 15′; long. 78° 12′; from Namcull N.N.W. 2 miles; from Salem S. 28 miles. Peshcush Rs. 5,431.——*Namcull* (நாமக்கல் - námakkal, Tam.). See below.—*Palayapolliem* (பழயப்பாளையம் - pazhayappálaiyam, Tam.). From (pazhaiya, tam. old + pálaiyam, tam. fortified village). Zemindarry, Village; pop. 1,665; square miles $5\frac{7}{16}$; lat. of village 11° 13′; long. 78° 17′; from Namcull E. 5 miles; from Salem S.S.E. 31 miles. Peshcush Rs. 3,150.——*Pandamungalam* (பாண்டமங்கலம் - pándamangalam, Tam.). From (pandai, tam. antiquity + mangala, san. prosperity). Village; pop. 1,756; acres 757; lat. 11° 06′; long. 78° 01′; from Namcull S.W. 16 miles; from Salem S.S.W. 41 miles. Shiva and Vishnoo temples with inscriptions.——*Paramatty* (பரமதி - paramathi, Tam.). See sep. title.——*Periyapullambauray* (பெரியப்பள்ளம்பாறை - periyappallambárai, Tam.). From (periya, tam. large + pallam, tam. low land + párai, tam. rock). Zemindarry, Village; pop. 85; square miles $12\frac{3}{16}$; lat. of village 11° 17′; long. 78° 20′; from Namcull E.N.E. 9 miles; from Salem S.S.E. 28 miles. Peshcush Rs. 3,465.——*Perooncoorchy* (பெருங்குறிச்சி - perunguriççi, Tam.). From (perum, tam. large + kuriççi, tam. village). Zemindarry, Village; pop. 164; square miles $5\frac{13}{16}$; lat. of village 11° 17′; long. 77° 57′; from Namcull W.N.W. 18 miles; from Salem S.S.W. 32 miles. Peshcush Rs. 3,340.——*Pilloor* (பில்லூர் - pillúr, * Tam.). From (pul, tam. grass + úr, tam. village). Zemindarry, Village; pop. 1,339; square miles $11\frac{3}{16}$; lat. of village 11° 12′; long. 78° 04′; from Namcull W. 10 miles; from Salem S.S.W. 33 miles. Peshcush Rs. 4,514.——*Ponnairy* (பொன்னேரி - ponnéri, Tam.). From (pon, tam. beauty + éri, tam. tank). Zemindarry, Village; pop. 1,216; square miles $3\frac{1}{16}$; lat. of village 11° 09′; long. 78° 19′; from Namcull S.E. 8 miles; from Salem S.S.E. 36 miles. Peshcush Rs. 2,135.——*Poodoocottah* (புதுக்கோட்டை - puthukkóttai, Tam.). From (puthu, tam. new + kóttai, tam. fort). Zemindarry, Village; pop. 964; square miles $7\frac{1}{8}$; lat. of village 11° 10′; long. 78° 18′; from Namcull S.E. 7 miles; from Salem S.S.E. 35 miles. Peshcush Rs. 4,943.——*Pottanam* (பொட்டணம் - pottanam, Tam. potanam *). From (pottal, tam. arid tract + nattam, tam. village). Zemindarry, Village; pop. 2,025; square miles $3\frac{3}{8}$; lat. of village 11° 17′; long. 78° 15′; from Namcull N.N.E. 5 miles; from Salem S. 26 miles. Peshcush Rs. 1,989.——*Powtram* (பவித்திரம் - pavittiram, Tam.). Means sacred; called after a person of that name. Zemindarry, Village; pop. 1,563; square miles $13\frac{9}{16}$; lat. of village 11° 08′; long. 78° 24′; from Namcull E.S.E. 14 miles; from Salem S.S.E. 38 miles. Peshcush Rs. 4,034.——*Shailore* (சேலூர் - shélúr, Tam.). From (shél, tam. carp fish + úr, tam. village). Zemindarry, Village; pop. 336; square miles $8\frac{1}{4}$; lat. of village 11° 07′; long. 77° 57′; from Namcull W. 19 miles; from Salem S. 41 miles. Peshcush Rs.

4,340.——*Shendamungalam* (சேந்தமங்கலம் - shéndamangalam, Tam.). From (shéndan, tam. the god skanda + mangala, san. prosperity). Zemindarry; pop. 13,354; square miles 6$\frac{1}{16}$. Peshcush Rs. 4,306. Also town; pop. 13,354; lat. 11° 17′; long. 78° 17′; from Namcull N.E. 6 miles; from Salem S.S.E. 26 miles. On the right bank of the Carvauttaur, from which and the Yetticoolam its water-supply is derived. Two old Shiva and Vishnoo temples. Iron [auhan] ore is smelted.——*Sholasiraumany* (சோளசிராமணி - shólasirámani, Tam. sólasirámani, *). From (chóla, san. chóla king + shirómani, san. crest jewel). Zemindarry, Village; pop. 685; square miles 11$\frac{3}{16}$; lat. of village 11° 14′; long. 77° 55′; from Namcull W. 21 miles; from Salem S.W. 36 miles. Peshcush Rs. 5,347.——*Talamullay* (தலமலை - talamalai, Tam.). From (talai, tam. head + malai, tam. mountain). Hill; lat. 11° 05′; long. 78° 22′; from Namcull S.E. 15 miles; from Salem S.S.E. 42 miles.——*Taulambaudy* (தாளம்பாடி - tálambádi, Tam.). From (tázhai, tam. fragrant screw-pine, pandanus odoratissimus, linn. + pádi, tam. village). Zemindarry, Village; pop. 854; square miles 5$\frac{3}{4}$; lat. of village 11° 18′; long. 78° 12′; from Namcull N.N.W. 5 miles; from Salem S. 25 miles. Peshcush Rs. 1,486.——*Tautayyengarpett* (தாத்தையங்கார்ப்பேட்டை - táttaiyyangárppéttai, Tam.). Means tauttayyangar's village. Village; pop. 2,081; acres 953; lat. 11° 07′; long. 78° 29′; from Namcull E. 20 miles; from Salem S. 20 miles. About 2 miles from the right bank of the Eiyaur. Includes the hamlet of Pillatoray. Old Shiva temple. White cloths, similar to those manufactured at Namcull, are produced and exported to Salem, Trichinopoly and Bangalore. ——*Tidoomal* (திடுமல் - tidumal, Tam.). From (tidal, tam. high land + mal, tam. fertility). Zemindarry, Village; pop. 484; square miles 11; lat. of village 11° 12′; long. 77° 58′; from Namcull W. 17 miles; from Salem S.S.W. 36 miles. Peshcush Rs. 5,237. ——*Tippara mahadevy* (திப்பரமகாதேவி - tipparamagáthévi, Tam.). From (tripura, san. the three cities destroyed by shiva + mahá, san. great + dévi, san. deity). Zemindarry, Village; pop. 952; square miles 3$\frac{11}{16}$; lat. of village 11° 08′; long. 78° 17′; from Namcull S.E. 7 miles; from Salem S.S.E. 37 miles. Peshcush Rs. 2,356.——*Tirmany moottaur* (திருமணிமுத்தாறு - tirumanimuttáru, Tam.). See sep. title.——*Tolore* (தோழூர் - tólúr, Tam.). From (tózham, tam. cattle-fold + úr, tam. village). Zemindarry, Village; pop. 1,462; square miles 9$\frac{1}{16}$; lat. of village 11° 08′; long. 78° 10′; from Namcull S.S.W. 6 miles; from Salem S.S.W. 36 miles. Peshcush Rs. 3,556.——*Toosore* (தூசூர் - túsúr, Tam.). From (túsi, tam. dust + úr, tam. village). Zemindarry, Village; pop. 1,239; square miles 10$\frac{13}{16}$; lat. of village 11° 12′; long. 78° 16′; from Namcull E.S.E. 4 miles; from Salem S.S.E. 32 miles. Peshcush Rs. 6,191.——*Vailcoorchy* (வேளுக்குறிச்சி - vélukkuriççi, Tam. velukurchi *). From (vélu, tam. proper name + kuriççi, tam. village). Zemindarry, Village; pop. 2,191; square miles 21$\frac{1}{4}$; lat. of village 11° 23′; long. 78° 18′; from Namcull N.N.E. 13 miles; from Salem S.S.E. 20 miles. Peshcush Rs. 7,894.——*Valappore* (வலப்பூர் - valappúr, Tam.). From (valapu, tel. fragrance + úr, tam. village). Village, Hill; pop. 2,797; lat. 11° 16′; long. 78° 27′; from Namcull E. 17 miles; from Salem S.S.E. 31 miles. On the Collimullays. In the neighbourhood is the Arapulleshwara sawmy temple at the head of a ravine opening from the central plateau basin towards the Toraiyore valley. It is called the fish temple, a large number of tame fish being preserved in a pool made by damming the river. They are fed daily to the sound of a bell. The temple is covered with inscriptions [shausanam], according to one of which it dates from A.D. 1350.——*Valayaputty* (வலயப்பட்டி - valayappatti, Tam.). From (valaya, san. boundary + patti, tam. cattle-fold). Sanscrit name (dévarájapura), meaning devarajan + town. Village; pop. 2,222; acres 2,665; lat. 11° 08′; long. 78° 16′; from Namcull S.E. 8 miles; from Salem S. 37 miles. Formed the southern extremity of the ancient Mysore kingdom.——*Veloor* (வேலூர் - vélúr, Tam.). From (vél, tam. acacia tree, acacia arabica, willd. + úr, tam. village). Village; pop. 1,579; acres 967; lat. 11° 06′; long. 78° 03′; from Namcull S.W. 13 miles; from Salem S.S.W. 40 miles. On the Cauvery. Paddy [q.v.] and plantains [q.v.] are exported.——*Vengaray* (வெங்கரை - vengarai, Tam.). From (ven, tam. white + karai, tam. bank). Village; pop. 4,499; acres 2,883; lat. 11° 05′; long. 78° 00′; from Namcull S.W. 16 miles; from Salem S.S.W. 42 miles.——*Yermayputty* (எருமைப்பட்டி - erumaippatti, Tam. erumaipati *). From (erumai, tam. buffalo + patti, tam. cattle-fold). Zemindarry; square miles 7$\frac{3}{8}$. Peshcush Rs. 4,296. Also Village; pop. 3,591; lat. 11° 09′; long. 78° 20′; from Namcull S.E. 10 miles; from Salem S.S.E. 36 miles. Inscription of Madura naicks [q.v.], dated A.D. 1652.——**(2)** Town, Head-quarters of Deputy collector, District moonsif and Tahsildar, Zemindarry; Salem dist., Namcull tal.; pop. 6,341; acres 11,924; lat. 11° 13′; long. 78° 13′; from Madras S.W. 191 miles; from Oossoor S.S.E. 106 miles; from Salem S. 30 miles; from Tripatore S.S.W. 91 miles; from Yercaud S. 39 miles. At the foot of a rounded mass of gneiss on the summit of which is a hill fort. Divided into two portions, the Cottay and Pettah. Place held in honor by Hindoos, local tradition marking it as the present abode of Vishnoo [q.v.]. The rock itself is some 200 feet in height and nearly half a mile in circumference. Its sides contain many cup-like hollows, generally in pairs, one above the other. From the supposed virtues of these cavities, the natives scale the steep scarps of the hill to bathe and wash their cloths in them. On the south-east side of the rock is the Camalaulayam tank, sacred to Naumagiry ammaul. The teertams [q.v.] are known as Camalaulayam, Chuckra teertam, Lutchmana teertam, Narsimha teertam and the Rama teertam. The visit of Hanooman [q.v.] is commemorated by a colossal statue in the Cottay, representing him as worshipping towards the Naumagiry ammaul coil. On the eastern slope is a temple of Runganautasawmy. A serpentine marking in the rock enters the temple, and is reputed to be the great snake Caurcotacan. On the north side, at the base of the rock, is a temple of Narsimhasawmy. The fort, on the summit of the rock, is accessible most easily on the south-west by a flight of narrow steps. On the north is a Trittoo vausal or secret gate designed for flight or as a sally-port. On the lower slope of the hill, to the south and south-west, are the remains of a first line of fortifications, but the revetment has given way in many places and the earthwork is rapidly following it. The outer walls of the true fort above are in almost perfect preservation. These are made of well-cut blocks of the same stone as the rock itself and secured to the rock by mortar [cauray]. No mortar has been used in the higher courses. The whole is surmounted by a parapet of strong brick-work, some 2$\frac{1}{2}$ or 3 feet thick, serrated by machicolations and pierced in every direction for musketry. Round the interior of the ramparts runs a masonry structure about one yard broad and sufficiently high to enable the marksmen to reach the loop-holes. These are so skilfully made that there is no ground all round the fort which could not be raked by musketry. In one or more places the brickwork has the appearance of having been removed to make embrasures for cannon. The ramparts are irregular in shape, following the outlines of the natural rock, with here and there projecting bastions and salient angles. They enclose an area of about an acre and a half, and contain a roofless brick building said to have been used as a treasury, but more probably as the granary of the garrison. There is also a ruined bomb-proof chamber and a small Vishnoo temple with an inscription. The fort is one of great natural strength. It was captured by the English in 1768, but retaken by Hyder a few months afterwards. It is said to have been built by Ramchendra naick, Poligar of Shendamungalam and Namcull. Old inhabitants however state that it was built by Lutchmy narsimha ayyar a harcarra [q.v.] under the Mysore rajah, at a period variously stated to be from 200 to 500 years ago. In the time of Hyder and Tippoo a killadar [q.v.] held the fort for the Mysore government, whose possessions then extended as far south as Valayaputty. In the Company's time, it was held by a guard of sepoys [q.v.]. Public bungalow [q.v.] here. White cloths of superior description are manufactured, part being exported to Bangalore, Mysore, Salem and Trichinopoly. Some brass and coppersmiths supply the local demand. The chief source of water-supply is the Camalaulayam.

NAMOOD (نمود - namúd, *Hind.*). From (namúdan, pers. to show). Particularized.——*Namoona* (نمونه - namúnah, Hind.). From (namúdan, pers. to show). A specimen.

NANGAY (நங்கை - nangai, *Tam.*). From (nagu, tam. to shine) [nagay]. Milk-wort, Rattle-snake root. Botanically the Polygala genus, polygaleæ [vricsham, 16]. Herbaceous plants or shrubs, with entire leaves, and very irregular flowers; capsule flat, two-celled, with a seed in each compartment; seeds downy; increase the lacteal secretion of animals that feed on them; all the species have handsome, showy flowers, chiefly pink, scarlet, red or white. The species best known to the natives are shown below. Other s. indian species indigenous or naturalized are:— arillata, crotalarioides, elongata, erioptera, javana, rosmarinifolia.——*Common nangay* (மிளகுநங்கை - milagunangai, Tam.). Tam. from (milagu, tam. pepper, piper nigrum, linn. + nangai, tam. polygala, sp.). Title otherwise Pepper nangay. Botanically Polygala [nangay] chinensis, linn., polygaleæ [vricsham, 16]. Alias Polygala arvensis, brachystachya, procumbens, tranquebarica. Stems herbaceous, procumbent, branched from the base, pubescent, angled; leaves glabrous, pubescent along the margin, upper ones oblong-linear, narrow, lower ones oblong, or narrow-obovate; racemes three to five-flowered, about half as long as the leaves; wings with a membranaceous margin, ovate, glabrous, ciliated below the length of the capsule; keel crested; capsule roundish, oblique, glabrous, ciliated, not margined; flowers yellow; flowering in july and august.——*Large nangay* (பெரியாணங்கை - periyánangai, Tam.). Tam. from (periya, tam. big + nangai, tam. the plant, polygala sp.). Botanically polygala [nangay] telephioides, willd., polygaleæ [vricsham, 16]. Alias Polygala serphyllifolia. Stems herbaceous, diffuse, pubescent; leaves succulent, glabrous, oval-oblong, narrow at the base; racemes four to five-flowered, scarcely half as long as the leaves; wings leafy, oval, very sharp, a little longer than the capsule; keel crested; capsule nearly orbicular; flowers very small, greenish; flowering in the rainy season. Used medicinally in catarrhal affections; in pharm. non-officinal.——*Senegal nangay* (செனகநங்கை - shenaganangai, Tam.). Title otherwise Seneca. Botanically polygala [nangay] senega, linn., polygaleæ [vricsham, 16]. Ornamental, deciduous, perennial, and herbaceous plant; stem erect, herbaceous, quite simple; spike terminal, filiform; leaves oblong, lanceolate; flowers beardless; flowering in july. Gives to pharm. the dried root, senegæ radix; acrid principle, polygalic acid; stimulant, expectorant, diuretic, and emmenagogue, in large doses emetic and cathartic; officinal.

NANGOONAIRY (நாங்குநேரி - nánguneri, *Tam.* nanguneri*). From (nángu, tam. four + kún, tam. bending + éri, tam. tank) [naul]. Tam. also (nágálañjéri), meaning four + poison-nut tree, strychnos nux-vomica, linn. + village; also (vánamámalai), meaning sky + great + mountain. Sanscrit name (tótádri), meaning praise + hill.——**(1)** Talook, Tinnevelly district. Tahsildar's pay Rs. 200. Aea 730 square miles. Population 174,418. Language Tamul. South of district. Bounded east by Tencaray talook and south by the sea, west by ghauts and Travancore, and north by Tencaray, Tinnevelly and Ambasamoodram talooks. Where the talook adjoins Ambasamoodram the ghauts, known in this portion as the Coolacaul hills, rise to 5,000 feet and are densely forested to the top. Near the mountains the country rises and falls in long easy slopes, following the drainage lines chiefly north-east and south-west. There are numerous tamarind [q.v.] and mango [q.v.] topes [q.v.] as well as good avenues [shaulay] along the main roads in this portion. East and south palmyra [q.v.] and babool [q.v.] abound, and occasionally in avenues are single specimens of banyan [q.v.]. Soil is mostly red clay, loams and sands, excepting for a strip parallel with the sea and extending some three to ten miles inland, where white sands and soil having an excess of sand as well as portions of the blown sand tracts called Tairy [q.v.] prevail. In the latter the palmyra [q.v.] prevails, being there almost the sole produce of the soil and subsistence of the inhabitants. Towards the centre of the talook are found numerous tanks [q.v.] both rain-fed and supplied by channels [q.v.] from mountain streams, innumerable wells under which small patches are cultivated, and dry cultivation, poor and interrupted by fallows sometimes for two years out of three. The well lands produce chillies [q.v.], brinjauls [q.v.] and other vegetables, raggy [q.v.] and cholum [q.v.]; dry lands, shanmay [q.v.] and horse-gram [q.v.]; tank land, rice [q.v.] and occasional gardens of plantains [q.v.] and betel-nuts [q.v.]. The salt pans [ooppalam] at Cootangooly and Vijayapathy supply the villages of this talook and of Ambasamoodram. There are no large sea-ports along the coast. Cauyalputnam and Coolashekharaputnam afford an outlet for jaggery [q.v.] manufactured in the talook, and supply the talook with paddy [q.v.], rice [q.v.], cocoanuts [q.v.] and betel [q.v.]. Calacaud, Panagoody, and Tircooroongoody are well supplied during both monsoons [q.v.] with water from the mountains, and much of the irrigation of the talook is direct from the channels which divert the waters of those streams almost as soon as they reach the plains. The tanks at Nangoonairy, Vijianarayanam and Vulliyore are the finest in the whole district. Places of archæological interest:—Calacaud, Chittoor, Cottaycaroongoolam, Dalapatysamoodram, Nangoonairy, Panagoody, Pauppaungoolam, Ponnacoody, Pudmanairy, Puttay, Rajakkal mungalam, Raudhaupooram, Shenbagaramanullore, Tircooroongoody, Vijayapathy, Vijianarayanam, Vulliyoor, Yervaudy. Principal trig. stations:—Codangoolam observatory, Cunnimaurpottay, Maunpottay, Parameshwarapooram, Punnay observatory, Raudhaupooram, Shanganairy, Vijayapathy. The leading places, &c., in the talook are the following.——*Calacaud* (களக்காடு - kalakkádu, Tam. kalakád*). From (kalam, tam. threshing ground + kádu, tam. closeness); from the many threshing floors. Town; pop. 3,346; acres 2,406; lat. 8° 31′; long. 77° 35′; from Nangoonairy W.N.W. 8 miles; from Tinnevelly S.W. 18 miles; from the sea N. 26 miles. Large Shiva temple with inscriptions. Festival in Veiyaushy [mausam], May-June. Ruins of fort. Weekly fair Thursday.——*Codangoolam* (கோடங்குளம் - kódangulam, Tam.). From (kódu, tam. hill + kulam, tam. tank). Trig. station; lat. 8° 10′ 24·19″; long. 77° 43′ 54·51″; height 159 feet; from Nangoonairy S. 22 miles; from Vijayapathy W.S.W. 4 miles; from the sea N. ¾ mile.——*Coolacaul hills* (குளக்கால்மலை - kulakkálmalai, Tam.). See sep. title.——*Cunnimaurpottay* (கன்னிமார்ப்பொத்தை - kannimárppottai, Tam.). From (kannimár, tam. virgin deities + pottai, tam. hillock). Trig. station; lat. 8° 30′ 22·00″; long. 77° 39′ 53·38″; height 678 feet; from Nangoonairy W.N.W. 3 miles; from the sea W. 34 miles.——*Hanoomanuddy* (அநுமாநதி - anumánathi, Tam.). From (hanumán, san. the monkey god + nadí, san. river). River. Drains the south portion of the southern ghauts.——*Mahendragherry* (மகேந்திரகிரி - magéndiragiri, Tam.). See sep. title.——*Maunpottay* (மான்பொத்தை - mánbottai, Tam.). From (mán, tam. deer + pottai, tam. hillock). Trig. station; lat. 6° 15′ 55·94″; long. 77° 37′ 06·22″; height 507 feet; from Nangoonairy S.S.W. 17 miles; from Vijayapathy W.N.W. 13 miles; from the sea N. 9 miles.——*Nangoonairy* (நாங்குநேரி - nánguneri, Tam.). See below.——*Numbiyaur* (நம்பியாறு - nambiyáru, Tam.). From (nambi, tam. vaishnava devotee + áru, tam. river). River. Drains southern portion of southern ghauts [q.v.].——*Panagoody* (பணக்குடி - panakkudi, Tam.). From (panai, tam. palmyra, borassus flabelliformis, linn. + kudi, tam. village). Village; pop. 4,244; acres 4,001; lat. 8° 19′; long. 77° 37′; from Nangoonairy S.S.W. 13 miles; from Tinnevelly S.S.W. 29 miles; from the sea N. 12 miles. On road to Cape comorin. Large Shiva temple. Festival in Pungoony [mausam], March-April.——*Parameshwarapooram* (பரமேசுவரப்புரம் - paramésuvarappuram, Tam.). From (paraméshvara, san. shiva, the supreme lord + pura, san. town). Trig. station; east end of base; lat. 8° 14′ 31·02″; long. 77° 44′ 20·40″; from Nangoonairy S. 17 miles; from Vijayapathy N.W. 5 miles; from the sea N. 5 miles.——*Peroongoody* (பெருங்குடி - perungudi, Tam.). From (perum, tam. great + kudi, tam. village). Town; pop. 6,651; acres 9,072; lat. 8° 17′; long. 77° 39′; from Nangoonairy S.S.W. 15 miles; from Tinnevelly S. 31 miles; from the sea N. 9 miles.——*Punnay* (பண்ணை - pannai, Tam.). Means field. Trig. station; lat. 8° 09′ 30·42″; long. 77° 40′ 03·59″; height 40 feet; from Nangoonairy S. 23 miles; from Vijayapathy W.S.W. 9 miles; from the sea N. ½ mile.——*Putchayaur* (பச்சையாறு - paççaiyáru, Tam.). From (paççai, tam. green + áru, tam. river). River. Affluent of the Tamrapurny.——*Puttay* (பத்தை - pattai, Tam.). From (pattai, tam. low shrubbery). Village; pop. 1,301; acres 853; lat. 8° 32′; long. 77° 37′; from Nangoonairy W.N.W. 8 miles; from Tinnevelly S.W. 17 miles; from the sea W. 20 miles.——*Raudhaupooram* (இராதாப்புரம் - iráthappuram, Tam.). See sep. title.——*Shanganairy* (சங்கனேரி - shanganéri, Tam.). From (shangu, tam. plant, azima tetracantha, lamk. + éri, tam. tank). Trig. station; lat. 8° 13′ 03·06″; long. 77° 44′ 11·18″; from Nangoonairy S.S.E. 19 miles; from Vijayapathy W.N.W. 4 miles; from the sea N. 4 miles.——*Soovishaishapooram* (சுவிசேடப்புரம் - shuvisédappuram, Tam.). From (suvishésha, san. gospel + pura, san. town). Village; pop. 293; acres 558; lat. 8° 23′; long. 77° 54′; from Nangoonairy E.S.E. 15 miles; from Tinnevelly S.S.E. 27 miles; from the sea N. 8 miles. Mission station.——*Terkk vulliyore* (தெற்குவள்ளியூர் - terguvalliyúr, Tam.). From (tergu, tam. south + valli, tam. the village deity + úr, tam. village). Village; pop. 2,970; acres 6,403; lat. 8° 21′; long. 77° 39′; from Nangoonairy S.S.W. 10 miles; from Tinnevelly S.S.W. 26 miles; from the sea N. 15 miles.——*Tircooroongoody* (திருக்குறுங்குடி - tirukkurungudi, Tam.). From (tiru, tam. holy + kurumai, tam. littleness + kudi, tam. village). Sanscrit name (kuranganagara), meaning antelope + town. Village; pop. 1,816; acres 1,987; lat. 8° 26′; long. 77° 36′; from Nangoonairy W.S.W. 7 miles; from Tinnevelly S.S.W. 22 miles; from the sea N. 22 miles. Large and important Vishnoo temple. Chuttram [q.v.] at which 60,000 travellers are annually fed. Car festival in Pungoony [mausam], March-April. Place of pilgrimage. Jeermutt [jiyyar] or Hindoo monastery.——*Vijayapathy* (விசயாப்பதி - visayáppathi, Tam.). From (vijaya, san. victory + pathi, tam. village); called after vijaya a paundy king. Town; pop. 4,833; acres 17,438; lat. 8° 12′; long. 77° 47′; from Comorin E.N.E. 16 miles; from Madras S.S.W. 374 miles; from Nangoonairy S.S.E. 21 miles; from Ootangoody S.W. 3 miles; from Tinnevelly S. 37 miles. On Gulf of Manaar, at mouth of a small creek. Ancient Shiva temple. Trig. station in lat. 8° 12′ 10·99″; long. 77° 49′ 03·83″; height 84 feet; from Nangoonairy S.S.E. 22 miles; from Vijayapathy W. 1½ miles; from the sea N. ¼ mile.——*Vijianarayanam* (விசயநாராயணம் - visayanáráyanam, Tam.). From (vijaya, san. victory + náráyana, san. vishnu, the mover on the waters). Town; pop. 4,068; acres 13,542; lat. 8° 25′; long. 77° 50′; from Nangoonairy E.S.E. 10 miles; from Tinnevelly S.S.E. 22 miles; from the sea N. 13 miles. Three very ancient temples with inscriptions in old Tamul. South are traces of a mud fort.——*Vulliyore* (வள்ளியூர் - valliyúr, Tam.). From (valli, tam. the village deity, consort of subrahmanya + úr, tam. village). Tam. also (vadakkuvalliyúr), meaning north + place, so called. Village; pop. 4,907; acres 11,236; lat. 8° 23′; long. 77° 39′; from Nangoonairy S.S.W. 8 miles; from Tinnevelly S.S.W. 24 miles; from the sea N. 16 miles. Large Shiva temple, built by Coolashekhara paundyan. Old fort built by a Paundyan [q.v.] king. Rock-cut temple. Large tank, the stones in the revetment of which were procured from a Jeina [q.v.] temple in the village then completely destroyed.——*Yidayangoody* (இடையங்குடி - idaiyangudi, Tam.). See sep. title.——*Yidindacaray* (இடிந்தகரை - idindagarai, Tam.). From (idinda, tam. broken + karai, tam. bank). Village; pop. 1,345; acres 867; lat. 8° 11′; long. 77° 47′; from Nangoonairy S.S.E. 22 miles; from Tinnevelly S. 38 miles. On seashore.——**(2)** Town, Talook head-quarters; Tinnevelly dist., Nangoonairy tal.; pop. 3,548; acres 11,135; lat. 8° 29′; long. 77° 42′; height 397 feet; from Madras S.S.W. 360 miles; from Palamcottah S.S.W. 17 miles; from Shermadevy S.S.E. 15 miles; from Shreevillipoottore S. 69 miles; from Tinnevelly S. 16 miles; from Tuticorin W.S.W. 40 miles; from the sea N. 23 miles. Large and richly endowed ancient temple with inscriptions. Weekly fair on Monday. Jeermutt [jiyyar] in which are valuable jewels. Car [rath] festival in Chittray [mausam], April-May.

NAN MUH (نمو - nanmuh, *Hind.*). Botanically Persea nanmuh, oliv., lauraceæ [vricsham, 111]. Tree. Wood soft to moderately hard, with pleasant aromatic scent when fresh cut; even-grained, of an olive-brown color, shining; the wood used in china by persons of wealth for coffins. For gratissima see Alligator pear.

NARACAL (ഞാറക്കൽ - ñárakkal, *Mal.*). From (nára, mal. a crane, tantalus ibis + kal, mal. stone). Town, Port; Cochin state, Cochin tal.; pop. 4,254; lat. 10° 2′ N.; long. 76° 16′ E.; from Bombay S.S.E. 659 miles; from Chittoor S.S.W. 59 miles; from Cochin N.W. 5 miles; from Ernacolum N.W. 4 miles; from Maulipooram N. 3 miles; from Paliport S. 8 miles; from Madras S.W. 340 miles; from Trichore S. 33 miles; from Tripoontora N.W. 11 miles. Chief port of the state. Church, small palace and pagoda [q.v.]. The seat of a considerable Christian population. During the south-west monsoons [q.v.] a curious mud bank [q.v.], stretching about 2½ miles seaward and about 4 miles in length, is formed within a couple of miles of the shore. On it and between it and the shore there is smooth water during the heaviest weather, in which vessels can anchor safely and discharge cargo throughout the monsoon whilst Cochin is unapproachable. The most probable theory is that the superabundant fresh water caused by the heavy rains forces its way under a sort of crust which forms the shore, and rising at some distance to sea mixed with exceedingly fine mud particles forms a greasy substance on which waves cannot break. Coasting steamers call here regularly. Light on the beach at mouth of creek, 5 miles to the northward of Cochin; lat. 10° 03′ 0″; long. 76° 12′ 0″; white; fixed; 10 miles' range; visible from all directions seaward; flagstaff; is exhibited only during the south-west monsoon [caur], viz., from 15th May to 30th September, when Cochin port is avoided by shipping.

NARALAY (गोधापदी - gódhápadí, *San.*; घोरपडवेल - ghórapadavéla, *Mahr.*; ఏడాకులమండులమారి - édákulamandulamári, *Tel.*; വെളുത്തചൊറിവള്ളി - veluttachorivalli, *Mal.*; நறளை - naralai, *Tam.*). Title from tamul [naroo]. San. from (gódhá, san. iguana + pada, san. foot); from a fancied resemblance of leaves to the foot of that reptile. Mahr. from (ghórapada, mahr. iguana + véla, mahr. creeper). Tel. from (édu, tel. seven + áku, tel. leaf + mandulamári, tel. vitis carnosa, wall.). Mal. from (velutta, mal. white + chorivalli, mal. vitis carnosa, wall.). Tam. from (narumai, tam. fragrance). San. also (suvahá), meaning enduring. Tel. also (kániápatíga), meaning yoke + bearing + creeper, cf. acid naralay; (pulimáda); (kánnem). Title otherwise Ghorapadey creeper, Iguana's foot. Botanically Vitis [draucshay] pedata, vahl., ampelidæ [vricsham, 42]. Alias Cissus heptaphylla, pedatus. Young parts softly pubescent; stipules cordate, acute; leaves petioled, pedate; leaflets six to eleven, three to five placed pedately on each of the lateral, secondary petioles, and one on the terminal, stalked, oblong-lanceolate, acuminated, serrated; peduncles with bract about the middle, axillary or leaf-opposed, half as long as the petioles, with two divaricating branches, each bearing a compound cyme; petals distinct; fruit flattened at the top, usually four-lobed, and four-seeded; flowers small, green; flowering in the rainy season. ——*Acid naralay* (अंबटवेल - ambatavéla, Mahr.; گیدڑ دراکھ - gídardrákh, Hind.; امل بیل - amalbel, Dec.; మండులమారితీగ - mandulamáritíga, Tel.; ചൊറിവള്ളി - chorivalli, Mal.; புளி நறளை - pulinaralai, Tam.). Title from taste of roots. Mahr. from (ambata, mahr. acid + véla, mahr. creeper). Hind. from (gídar, hind. jackal + drákh, hind. grape, vitis vinifera, linn.). Dec. from (amlí, hind. tamarind, tamarindus indica, linn. + bel, hind. creeper); from acidity. Tel. from (mandu, tel. medicine + mári, tel. personal suffix + tíga, tel. creeper). Mal. from (chori, mal. itch + valli, mal. creeper). Tam. from (puli, tam. acid + naralai, tam. vitis lanata, roxb.). Hind. also (kasar). Tel. also (mékamettanichettu), meaning goat + not trodden + plant; (kádépatíga), meaning yoke + bearing + creeper, from being applied to sores on the necks of bullocks caused by the yoke; (kanapatíga); (kániáputíga), meaning yoke + bearing + creeper; (kurudinne); (édakulamandulamáritíga), meaning seven + leaf + the plant; (pulimáda). Title otherwise Fleshy vine, Fox grape, Itching creeper, Medicinal creeper, Sour creeper. Botanically Vitis [draucshay] carnosa, wall., ampelideæ [vricsham, 42]. Alias Cissus carnosa, cinerea, crenata, obtusifolia. Young parts densely pubescent; older, glabrous; stem striated; stipules oblong; leaves trifoliolate, long-petioled; leaflets ovate, crenate-serrated; cymes peduncled, compound; petals distinct; berries black, two to four-seeded; flowers small, green; flowering in the rainy season; common in hedges; acrid roots used in medicine. ——*Large acid naralay* (తెల్లగుముడు - tellagumudu, Tel.; വലിയ ചൊറിവള്ളി - valiyachorivalli, Mal.). Tel. from (tella, tel. white + gumudu, tel. gmelina asiatica, linn.). Mal. from (valiya, mal. large + chorivalli, mal. + vitis carnosa, wall.). Botanically Vitis [draucshay] lanceolaria, roxb., ampelideæ [vricsham, 42]. Alias Cissus muricata; Vitis muricata. Unisexual; glabrous, except the inflorescence which is densely pubescent; stem woody; branches with muricated bark; leaves petioled, trifoliolate; leaflets stalked, somewhat coriaceous, serrated, oblong-acuminate, lateral ones unequal-sided; umbels axillary, with bracts at the base, not so long as the petiole twice compound; petals distinct; style very short and thick; stigma large, somewhat lobed; fruit globose, size of a large cherry [q.v.], white when ripe, two to four-seeded; flowers greenish; flowering in the hot season.——*Large naralay* (பெருநறளை - perunaralai, Tam.). Tam. from (perum, tam. large + naralai, tam. the plant). Tam. also (naralai), meaning fragrant creeper. Title otherwise Heart-leaved vine. Botanically Vitis [draucshay] lanata, roxb., ampelideæ [vricsham, 42]. Alias Cissus vitiginea; Vitis cordifolia, heyneana, pallida. Stems, petioles and peduncles woolly; leaves cordate-ovate, serrated, underside tomentose with rusty-colored wool; racemes elongated; flower-bearing peduncles often tendrilled; flowers bisexual; petals united at the apex; stamens much longer than the ovary; fruit globose, one-seeded, size of large pea [calauyam]; flowers small, green; flowering in april and may.——*Small acid naralay* (చిన్నమండులమారి - chinnamandulamári, Tel.). Tel. from (chinna, tel. small + mandulamári, tel. vitis carnosa, wall.). Tel. also (bankabaddu), meaning gum + male organ; (tígagummudu), meaning creeper + gmelina asiatica, linn. Botanically Vitis [draucshay] linnæ, wall., ampelideæ [vricsham, 42]. Alias Cissus angulata. Stems and leaves sub-fleshy; branches cylindric or very obtusely angled; cymes slender, about as long as the leaves; flowers small; fruit oblong, bluish, pruinose; pedicels recurved.

NARD (نرد - nard, *Pers.*). From persian. Greek νάρδος. Name among ancients for any Indian essence. Cf. Jatamansy.

NAROO (நறு - naru, *Tam.*). Fragrant.——*Naralay* (நறளை - naralai, Tam.). See sep. title.——*Naroovily* (நறுவிலி - naruvili, Tam.). Means fragrant tree. Same as Sebesten.——*Naugalaupooram* (நாகலாப்புரம் - nágaláppuram, Tam.). From (nával, tam. jamboo tree, eugenia jambolana, lamk., var. caryophyllifolia + pura, san. town). Village, Hills; Chingleput dist., Trivellore tal.; pop. 3,992; acres 7,917; lat. 13° 23′; long. 79° 52′; from Sydapett N.W. 37 miles; from Trivellore N.N.W. 18¼ miles. Old Vishnoo temple in village. Krishna devan repaired the temple. Three days in the year the rays of the sun, passing through the gopooram [q.v.] entrance, fall on the idol in the vimaunam [q.v.], and this is considered an act of adoration by the sun. The hills lie between 13° 24′ and 13° 28′ N. lat. and between 79° 49′ and 79° 52′ E. long. and are connected with the Suttivaid hills on north and the Nagary group on west. Average height 1,800 feet. Highest peak Cambaukum droog. The character of these hills is bluff ridge and beetling crag, here and there starting up into sharp tapering peaks. The tops are generally bare, and the sloping sides clothed with coarse grass and jungle. There are three principal ghauts [q.v.].——*Nauval* (நாவல் - nával, Tam.). From (náru, tam. to smell); from fruit. Same as Jaumoon.

NARSAPORE (నరసాపురము - narasápuramu, *Tel.* narsápur *). From (narasanna, tel. proper name + pura, san. town) [nee].——**(1)** Talook, Godavery district. Tahsildar's pay Rs. 225. Area 437 square miles. Language Teloogoo. S. coast of district. Bounded:—North by Tanookoo and Bheemavaram talooks; east by the Veinateyam branch of the Godavery and Amalaupooram talook; west by Bheemavaram talook; and south by the sea. The river Vasishta divides the talook into two blocks Narsapore proper and Nagaram island. The latter is very fertile and abounds in cocoanut [q.v.] and areca [q.v.] gardens. Sulpherous earth [gandhac] has been found in some places. Soil sandy towards the sea, and regar [q.v.], loamy and clayey in the interior. Special industry is the manufacture of toys at Narsapore. Palcole is noted for its orchards. The trade is chiefly in paddy [q.v.], pulses [dholl], jaggery [q.v.], oil seeds [yennay], cloths and cotton [q.v.] twist, which are largely exported. Cotton twist is also imported from England for sale to the weavers, who form a large proportion of the population. The Vasishta branch of the Godavery fertilises the islands in its course. Well supplied with the means of irrigation by three main canals, also used for navigation, namely, the Narsapore canal, the Gunnavaram canal, and the Mooccaumala canal. There are also numerous minor irrigation channels branching off from the above. The Narsapore canal is connected with the Godavery by a lock. This affords excellent facilities for the carriage of goods from the interior of the district for exportation. Zemindarries:—Chinchinauda, Chinnamaumidipully, Neredoomilly, Varidhanam, Yellamanchily. Places of archæological interest:—Antarvedhy, Atsanta, Cadalay, Cadamy, Codamanchily, Lutcheshwaram, Madapollem, Maumidycoodoor, Nadoopoody, Nagaram, Narsapore, Palcole, Rameshwaram, Roostoombada, Tautipauca. Principal trig. stations:—Antarvedhy, Beinapollem, Chintamoola, Goganamett, Gondy, Keshanapully, Mogultoor, Shuncaragooptam. The leading places, &c., in the talook are the following.——*Antarvedhy* (అంతర్వేది - antarvédi, Tel.). See sep. title.——*Atsanta* (అత్సంట - átsanta, Tel.). From (tsannu, tel. female breast); from tradition that shiva appeared to a worshipper here from the breast of a woman. Town; pop. 7,047; acres 5,180; lat. 16° 36′; long. 81° 50′; from Cocanada S.W. 37 miles; from Narsapore N.N.E. 14 miles; from the sea N. 16 miles. Formerly belonged to Pittapore estate. Temples and inscriptions.——*Beinapollem* (బయ్యన్నపాలెము - bayyannapálemu, Tel.). From (bayyanna, tel. proper name + pálemu, tel. fortified village). Trig. station; lat. 16° 23′ 22·04″; long. 81° 42′ 50·59″; from Linganaboyanacherla S.E. 1 mile.——*Boorgapully* (బూరుగపల్లి - búrugapalli, Tel.). From (búraga, tel. silk-cotton tree, bombax malabaricum, dec. + palli, tel. village). Village; pop. 1,074; acres 535; lat. 16° 32′; long. 81° 53′; from

Cocanada S.W. 38 miles; from Narsapore N.E. 12 miles; from the sea N. 10 miles.——*Chinchinauda* (చించినాడ - chinchináda, Tel.). From (chincha, tel. tamarindus indica, linn. + nádu, tel. country). Zemindarry, Village; lat. of village 16° 28′; long. 81° 49′; from Cocanada S.W. 44 miles; from Narsapore N.E. 6 miles; from the sea N. 8 miles. Peshcush Rs. 1,627.——*Chinnamaumidipully* (చిన్నమామిడిపల్లి - chinnamámidipalli, Tel.). From (chinna, tel. small + mámidi, tel. mango, mangifera indica, linn. + palli, tel. village). Zemindarry, Village; square miles 2½; lat. of village 16° 27′; long. 81° 44′; from Cocanada S.W. 50 miles; from Narsapore N. 1¼ miles; from the sea N. 10 miles. Peshcush Rs. 235.——*Chintamoola* (చింతమూల - chintamúla, Tel.). From (chinta, tel. tamarind, tamarindus indica, linn. + múla, tel. corner). Trig. station; lat. 16° 22′ 42·38″; long. 81° 51′ 59·38″; from Antarvedhy N.E. 7 miles.——*Godavery* (గోదావరి - gódávari, Tel.). See sep. title.——*Goganamett* (గోగనమెట్టం - góganamattam, Tel.). From (gógu, tel. plant, hibiscus cannabinus, linn. + metta, tel. mound). Trig. station; lat. 16° 24′ 50·26″; long. 81° 58′ 28·48″; from Cautrenipaud E. 2 miles.——*Gondy* (గొంది - gondi, Tel.). Means an alley. Trig. station; lat. 16° 21′ 47·21″; long. 81° 46′ 14·28″; from Rameshwaram S. 2½ miles. ——*Gunnavaram* (గన్నవరము - gannavaramu, Tel.). See. sep title. ——*Keshanapully* (కేశనపల్లి - késhanapalli, Tel.). From (késhana, tel. proper name + palli, tel. village). Trig. station; lat. 16° 24′ 19·59″; long. 81° 56′ 58·95″; from Goodapully S.E. 3 miles.—— *Madapollem* (మాధవాయపాలెము - mádhaváyapálemu, Tel.). See sep. title.——*Mogultoor* (మొగలితుర్రు - mogaliturru, Tel.). See sep. title.——*Narsapore* (నరసాపురము - narasápuramu, Tel.). See below.——*Neredoomilly* (నేరేడుమిల్లి - nérédumilli, Tel.). From (nérédu, tel. eugenia jambolana, lamk. + palli, tel. village). Zemindarry, Village; square mile 1; lat. of village 16° 31′; long. 81° 49′; from Cocanada S.W. 42 miles; from Narsapore N.E. 9 miles; from the sea N. 12 miles. Peshcush Rs. 445.—— *Palcole* (పాలకొల్లు - pálakollu, Tel.). See sep. title.——*Paserlapoody* (పాశర్లపూడి - pásharlapúdi, Tel.). From (pasaramu, tel. cattle + púdi, tel. village). Village; pop. 2,929; acres 1,881; lat. 16° 31′; long. 18° 58′; from Cocanada S.W. 36 miles; from Narsapore E.N.E. 17 miles; from the sea N. 6 miles.—— *Penoomadam* (పెనుమడం - penumadam, Tel.). From (penu, tel. great + médha, san. sacrifice). Village; pop. 3,414; acres 4,613; lat. 16° 33′; long. 81° 48′; from Cocanada S.W. 42 miles; from Narsapore N.N.E. 9 miles; from the sea 14 miles. Janamejayan grandson of Arjoonan [q.v.] is said to have performed here Ashwamedham [q.v.] or horse sacrifice [yanyam].—— *Peroopollem* (పెరుపాలెము - perupálemu, Tel.). From (peru, tel. great + pálemu, tel. fortified village). Village, Port; acres 6,589; lat. 16° 22′; long. 81° 36′; from Cocanada S.W. 59 miles; from Madras N.N.E. 240 miles; from Narsapore S.W. 9 miles.—— *Rameshwaram* (రామేశ్వరము - rámeshvaramu, Tel.). From (ráma, san. the god + íshvara, san. lord). Village; pop. 1,878; acres 3,861; lat. 16° 24′; long. 81° 46′; from Cocanada S.W. 50 miles; from Narsapore S.E. 3 miles; from the sea N. 5 miles. Ancient temple of Ramaligeshwaran with inscriptions.——*Shivacode* (శివకోడు - shivakódu, Tel.). See sep. title.——*Shuncaragooptam* (శంకరగుప్తము - shankaraguptamu, Tel.). From (shankara, san. shiva, the pleasure giver + gupta, san. protected). Trig. station; lat. 16° 23′ 25·76″; long. 81° 53′ 32·47″; from Keshanapully W.S.W. 3 miles.——*Vasishta godavery* (వశిష్ఠగోదావరి - vashisht'hagódávari, Tel.). See sep. title.——*Veinateyam* (వైనతేయము - vainatéyamu, Tel.). See sep. title.——*Yellamanchily* (యెలమంచిలి - yelamanchili, Tel.). From (ella, tel. boundary + manchi, tel. good). Zemindarry, Village; square miles 7; lat. of village 16° 29′; long. 81° 49′; from Cocanada S.W. 44 miles; from Narsapore N.E. 7 miles; from the sea N. 9 miles. Peshcush Rs. 8,804.——**(2)** Town, Port, Head-quarters of Tahsildar; Godavery dist., Narasapore tal.; pop. 7,464; acres 659; lat. 16° 26′; long. 81° 44′; from Antarvedhy N.N.W. 7 miles; from Cocanada S.W. 50 miles; from Coonavaram S.S.E. 82 miles; from Ellore E.S.E. 43 miles; from Madras N.N.E. 248 miles; from Peroopollem N. E. 9 miles; from Rajahmundry S. 39 miles. Near the mouth of Vasishta branch of the Godavery on the Golcondah coast [q.v.]. Former head-quarters of Sub-collector, but since his removal to Rajahmundry, the station of a Deputy collector. The Dutch had an iron foundry in 1665. The English occupied the northern suburb Madapollem in 1677 and maintained their factory for 150 years. French had a factory in 1758. Fine market place. On the west near the canal, which communicates with Rajahmundry, is a well-laid suburb named after a former Sub-collector, Taylorpett. Many native crafts are built and repaired. Noted for the manufacture of toys and for cloth dyeing. A handsome and conspicuous obelisk [laut], 75 feet high, stands near Narsapore point to the east of the bar. There is a basin in the river opposite the town, inaccessible on account of the sandy bar at the mouth of the river.

NARSAROWPETT (నరసారావుపేట - narasárávupéta, *Tel.* narsaraopet *). From (narasárávu, tel. proper name + péta, tel. suburb) [nee]. Tel. also (atlúru), meaning cake + village.—— **(1)** Talook, Kistna district. Tahsildar's pay Rs. 200. Area 712 square miles. Population 156,377. Language Teloogoo. S. inland part of district. Lies to the west of Guntoor, and forms part of the division of the Deputy collector of Vinoocondah. Bounded on the north by Suttenapully talook, on the east by Guntoor and Baupatla talooks, on the south by Ongole talook, of Nellore district, on the west by the Vinoocondah talook. The water-shed runs from the Condaveed hills along the north of the talook near its boundary with Suttenapully, and from this ridge the country slopes down towards the sea. Generally dry crops and an occasional patch of irrigation under a rain-fed tank [q.v.]. There are several bold hills, such as Cotappa condah, and the country is intersected by water courses, dry for the greatest part of the year, and torrents during the rains. The first object that meets the eye on entering this talook is the conspicuous hill fortress of Condaveed. Soil rocky, partly red, partly black cotton [regar] mixed with limestone [choonamcull]. Industries are indigo [q.v.] manufacture, country paper-making at Condaveed, but on the decline. Oil-press in Narsarowpett. Commerce chiefly in agricultural produce. Rain-fed tanks Cooncalgoonta, Copparam, Goontoopully, Santa mauglore, Vipparla, Yelchore, being the most important. Camping grounds:— Copperapaud, Nekaricull, Rompicherla, Yelchore. Places of archæological interest:—Annavaram, Appaupooram, Babbeypulley, Bookkapooram, Boppoody, Canooparroo, Caucauny, Caumcpully, Caurbolo, Challagoondla, Chaugal, Cheemalmurry, Chejerla, Chennoopulley, Chirmaumilla, Commalpaud, Condacauvore, Condaveed, Conidena, Cooncalgoonta, Copparam, Cotappa condah, Daigaramoody, Dronaudoola, Ganapavaram, Gunnavaram, Goontey garlapaud, Gogoolapaud, Gorizavole, Govindapooram, Ikkoor, Irlapaud, Jaggaupooram, Keshanapully, Lingamgoonta, Maurtore, Moolacalore, Moorkipoody, Mullayyapollem, Mydavole, Nadendla, Narsarowpett, Naugarauzpulley, Nekaricull, Ooppalapand, Ooppoo mauglore, Pamidipaud, Paumarroo, Polore, Poorshottapatam, Rajapett, Rauvipaud, Rompicherla, Roopenagoontla, Santa goodipaud, Santa mauglore, Sautlore, Sooravarapulley, Timmaupooram, Toobaud, Toorimilla, Tungedpulley, Vaimavaram, Vancauyalpaud, Vayidana, Velpoor, Vipparla, Vipparlapulley, Vishwanautoony khandriga, Yadavully, Yadlapaud, Yanamadala, Yeddanapoody, Yelchore, Yellamunda, Zaulaudy, Zonnalagudda, Zonnatauvy. Trig. stations:—Adamsahib, Babbeypulley, Condaveed, Cotappacondah, Daunapa, Yellamunda. The leading places, &c., in the talook are the following. ——*Adam sahib* (آدم صاحب - ádamsáhib, Hind.; ఆదంసాహేబు - ádamsáhebu, Tel.). From the person so called. Trig. station; lat. 16° 15′ 15·59″; long. 80° 19′ 48·48″; height 1,680 feet; from Condaveed E. 1¾ miles; from Narsarowpett E. 15 miles.—— *Babbeypulley* (బబ్బేపల్లి - babbepalli, Tel.). From (bábu, tel. gentleman + palli, tel. village). Trig. station; lat. 15° 56′ 52·79″; long. 80° 10′ 20·71″; height 669 feet; from Babbeypulley W. 1 mile; from Narsarowpett S.S.E. 20 miles.—— *Bugglecondah* (బొగ్గులకొండ - boggulakonda, Tel.). See sep. title. ——*Chejerla* (చెజెర్ల - chejerla, Tel.). See sep. title.——*Chilcaloorpaud* (చిలకలూరుపాడు - chilakalúrupádu, Tel.). From (chilaka, tel. parrot + úru, tel. village + pádu, tel. village). Zemindarry, Village; lat. of village 16° 05′; long. 80° 13′; from Narsarowpett S.E. 13 miles. To south of Condaveed on banks of Vaugair. A member of the Manore family of zemindars lives here. They were for some time zemindars [q.v.] of Suttenapully and this place.——*Commalpaud* (కొమ్మాలపాడు - kommálapádu, Tel.). From (komma, tel. branch + pádu, tel. village). Village; pop. 1,561; lat. 16° 02′; long. 79° 59′; from Masulipatam W. 77 miles; from Narsarowpett S.S.W. 16 miles. On the Ongole road. Graves of soldiers. Vishnoo temple, 400 years old. Ruined stone fort, 300 years old. Travellers' bungalow [q.v.]. Irrigation tank.——*Condacauvore* (కొండకావూరు - kondakávúru, Tel.). From (konda, tel. hill + kávi, tel. red ochre + úru, tel. village). Village; pop. 630; acres 3,174; lat. 16° 08′; long. 80° 04′; from Masulipatam W. 71 miles; from Narsarowpett S. 8 miles. Inscriptions near temple of Hanooman [q.v.] and in the highly sculptured Vishnoo [q v.] temple south of fort. Contains Cotappa condah.——*Condaveed* (కొండవీడు - kondavídu, Tel.). See sep. title.——*Conidena* (కొనిదెన - konidena, Tel.). From (kóna, tel. corner + dona, tel. mountain spring). Ancient name (kottiyadona), meaning village + mountain spring. Village; pop. 3,108; acres 9,176; lat. 16° 01′; long. 80° 06′; from Masulipatam W. 72 miles; from Narsarowpett S. 15 miles. Irrigation tank. Some very old temples and inscriptions. A town in olden times.——*Cooncalgoonta* (కుంకలగుంట - kunkalagunta, Tel.). From (kunka, tel. worthless person + gunta, tel. pond). Village; pop. 3,795; acres 8,525; lat. 16° 18′; long. 79° 55′; from Masulipatam W. 82 miles; from Narsarowpett W.N.W. 12 miles. Three deserted temples with inscriptions. Connected with the Chejerla legend.——*Coondoorroo* (కుందుర్రు - kundurru, Tel.). From (kundu, tel. to sink + turru, tel. place). Village; pop. 2,321; acres 9,535; lat. 16° 01′; long. 79° 57′; from Masulipatam W. 81 miles; from Narsarowpett S.W. 18 miles. Two irrigation tanks. Ruins of an ancient fort and several ancient temples. A poligar [q.v.] Mootoomah naidoo once reigned here. Date not known.——*Cotappa condah* (కోటప్పకొండ - kótappakonda, Tel.). See sep. title.——*Daigaramoody* (డేగరమూడి - dégaramúdi, Tel.). From (déga, tel. hawk + múdi, tel. village). Village; pop. 1,658; acres 2,977; lat. 16° 00′; long. 80° 10′; from Masulipatam W. 67 miles; from Narsarowpett S. 16 miles. Two old temples. Inscription.——*Daunapa* (దానప్ప - dánappa, Tel.). Trig. station; lat. 15° 56′ 02·91″; long. 79° 58′ 35·12″; height 1,015 feet; from Gorrepaud E. 2 miles; from Narsarowpett S.S.W. 22 miles.——*Govindapooram* (గోవిందపురము - góvindapuramu, Tel.). From (góvindu, tel. proper name + pura, san. town). Village; pop. 2,498; acres 4,868; lat. 16° 09′; long. 80° 09′; from Masulipatam W. 68 miles; from Narsarowpett S.S.E. 6 miles. West is a temple with inscriptions, built by a Chola [q.v.] rajah. Vishnoo temple. Also a deserted temple.——*Maurtore* (మారుటూరు - márutúru, Tel.). From (máruti, san. son of the god of the winds, epithet of hanumán + úru, tel. village). Sanscrit name (márutipura), meaning hanooman + town. Village; pop. 1,474; acres 5,855; lat. 15° 59′; long. 80° 09′; from Masulipatam W.S.W. 67 miles; from Narsarowpett S. 17 miles. Old Vishnoo temple with inscription.——*Nadendla* (నాదెండ్ల - nádendla, Tel.). Village; pop. 3,564; acres 9,904; lat. 16° 11′; long. 80° 14′; from Masulipatam W. 60 miles; from Narsarowpett E.S.E. 9 miles. Two ancient temples with inscriptions. ——*Narsarowpett* (నరసారావుపేట - narasárávupéta, Tel.). See below.——*Nekaricull* (నెకరికల్లు - nekarikallu, Tel.). From (nekkaru, tel. tree, cordia myxa, linn. + kallu, tel. stone). Village; pop. 1,894; acres 2,210; lat. 16° 22′; long. 79° 59′; from Masulipatam W. 80 miles; from Narsarowpett N.W. 12 miles. On the high road. Travellers' bungalow [q.v.]. Soldiers' graves. A tope [q.v.]. An irrigation tank. Temples with sculptured figures and inscriptions.——*Pasoomarroo* (పసుమఱ్రు - pasumarru, Tel.). From (pasi, tel. cattle + marri, tel. banyan tree, ficus bengalensis, linn.). Village; pop. 2,559; acres 7,343; lat. 16° 04′; long. 80° 14′; from Masulipatam W. 62 miles; from Narsarowpett S.E. 14 miles. Pasoomarroo and Poorshottapatam are about one mile apart; between them lies Chilcaloorpaud. Temple with sculptured figures and inscriptions. Hamlet of this village, Comarivullipaud on bank of Vaugair, is coolest place in the division.——*Poorshottapatam* (పురుషోత్తమపట్టణము - purushóttamapattanamu, Tel.). From (purushóttama, san. proper name + pattana, san. town). Village; pop. 5,250; acres 4,158; lat. 16° 05′; long. 80° 13′; from Masulipatam W. 62 miles; from Narsarowpett S.E. 13 miles [pasoomarroo]. Chilcaloorpaud, is hamlet of Poorshottapatam. Fortress of mud walls with bastions at angles. Two roads, the Great northern road and the Peraula nekaricull road, cross here. Trade in cloths, &c.——*Rajapett* (రాజాపేట - rájápéta, Tel.). From (rájá, san. king + péta, tel. suburb). Village; pop. 2,394; acres 4,710; lat. 16° 06′; long. 80° 09′; from Masulipatam W. 68 miles; from Narsarowpett S.S.E. 11 miles. Formerly gave name to the talook. Ruined sculptured temple. West of the village is an inscription. Old fort. 17 dolmens [coday cull].——*Rauvipaud* (రావిపాడు - rávipádu, Tel.). From (rávi, tel. the peepul tree, ficus religiosa, linn. + pádu, tel. village). Village; pop. 1,335; acres 5,276; lat. 16° 16′; long. 80° 03′; from Masulipatam W. 74 miles; from Narsarowpett N.W. 4 miles. Catholic mission station chiefly Cumma [q.v.] cultivators. Old temple of Hanooman [q.v.]. Shiva temple with inscription.——*Rompicherla* (రొంపిచెర్ల - rompicharla, Tel.). From (rompi, tel. bog + cherla, tel. village). Village; pop. 2,750; acres 6,929; lat. 16° 13′; long. 79° 57′; from Masulipatam W. 80 miles; from Narsarowpett W. 10 miles. Temple of Suncareshwara sawmy with three inscriptions near the Dhwaja stambham [q.v.]. Temple in the fort with two inscriptions; built by Trimal devy, sister of Prataupa roodran [q.v.]. Travellers' bungalow [q.v.]. Soldiers' graves on the Hyderabad road. ——*Sautlore* (సాతులూరు - sátulúru, Tel.). From (sátu, tel. company of travellers + úru, tel. village). Village, Railway station; pop. 2,087; acres 5,357; lat. 16° 15′; long. 80° 10′; from Masulipatam W. 67 miles; from Narsarowpett E.N.E. 4 miles. Tank and large tamarind [q.v.] tope [q.v.]. Inscriptions.——*Vipparla* (విప్పర్ల - vipparla, Tel.). From (vippa, vulg. for ippa, tel. tree, bassia longifolia, linn. + parra, tel. swamp). Village; pop. 2,995; acres 8,672; lat. 16° 18′; long. 79° 59′; from Masulipatam W. 79 miles; from Narsarowpett W. 9 miles. Two large irrigation tanks. Several inscriptions. Saltpetre [shorah] pans. ——*Yelchore* (యేల్చూరు - yéltsúru, Tel.). From (élche, tel. kind of snipe + úru, tel. village). Village; pop. 1,710; acres 6,889; lat. 16° 05′; long. 79° 58′; from Masulipatam W. 80 miles; from Narsarowpett S.W. 13 miles. A large irrigation tank. An inscription. An astrological diagram on a stone.——*Yellamunda* (ఎల్లమంద - ellamanda, Tel.). From (ella, tel. boundary + manda, tel. herd of cattle). Village; pop. 2,427; acres 10,534; lat. 16° 11′; long. 80° 06′; from Masulipatam W. 70 miles; from Narsarowpett S. 5 miles. Ancient temple of Ramalingasawmy with eight inscriptions, dates ranging from A.D. 1131 to 1555. On the summit of a hill, 2½ miles south of the village, is a small temple with carved figures and mantapam [q.v.] and five inscriptions. Trig. station in lat. 16° 09′ 09·73″; long. 80° 04′ 47·49″; height 1,588 feet; from Narsarowpett S. 6 miles; from Yellamunda S.W. 3 miles.——**(2)** Village, Talook head-quarters, Railway station; Kistna dist., Narsarowpett tal.; pop. 5,309; acres 3,641; lat. 16° 14′; long. 80° 06′; from Bezwada W.S.W. 41 miles; from Guntoor W.S.W. 27 miles; from Madras N. 216 miles; from Masulipatam W. 69 miles; from Vinoocondah E.N.E. 25 miles. Formerly called Atlore. Present name from a zemindar who enlarged the fine tank west of the fort. On death of Narsarow his territory was divided between two zemindars Pedda vencata goonda row and Chinna vencata goonda row, one of whom took the fortress of Vinoocondah and the other Bellamcondah. In 1803 one of these resigned his share in favor of the other, and the zemindarry was reunited. In 1846 it was sold and purchased for Government. Vencata narsimha row, the last zemindar, resides in the fort at Narsarowpett, and is the hereditary custodian of the shrine of Cotappa condah. The palace resisted an attack of the Pindarries [q.v.] in 1816. Mango [q.v.] orchards, south of the town. Shiva temple built by Jeinas [q.v.]. Temple of Bheemeshwaran, with an inscription. Temple of Puttaubhy ramasawmy with inscription. American baptist mission station.

NARVEL (नर्वेल - narvala, *Mahr.*; ನರುವಲ್ - naruval, *Can.*). Botanically Viburnum fœtidum, wall., caprifoliaceæ [vricsham]. A shrub, leaves variable, usually ovate-lanceolate, serrated, length 1½ to 2 inches, flowers small, greenish white, berries small, ovoid, and of a vivid red color; all parts of the plant have a powerful unpleasant odour like that of premna integrifolia, linn. [moonnay]; native of burmah found in cultivation throughout western india. Two Viburnums are garden shrubs in europe, Viburnum opulus, linn. and Viburnum tinus, linn.; the former is the Gueldres rose, in which the flowers form a white ball, whence called snow-ball tree; the latter is the Laurestine.

NARY (நரி - nari, *Tam.*). From (narai, tam. greyness). Fox. Plant first term, often joining two genera, indicating wildness. Ex., where transl. is of second term:—Crotalaria verrucosa (narimarutti), threatener; Ledebouria hyacinthoides (narivengáyam), allium cepa; Phaseolus mungo, var. radiatus (narippayaru), pulse; Rothia trifoliata (narippayaru), pulse; Urginia indica (narivengáyam), allium cepa. See glossaries paragraphs.

NASEE (نسی - nasí, *Hind.*). From (nasa, ar. to omit). Intercalary correlation amongst the ancient arabs of the lunar year [saul] with the solar. This was by the addition of a month every third year. Owing to various heathen rites which came to be observed during the intercalary year, this calculation was abolished; consequently the mahomedan names of the months [maheena] have now no relation to the seasons [ritoo]. For intercalation among Hindoos see Adhicam and Maunam.

NASEEB (نصیب - nasíb, *Hind.*). From (nasab, ar. what is fixed). Fate [takdeer].

NASH (नश् - nash, *San.*). To perish.——*Nashtam* (नष्ट - nashta, San.). Loss.——*Nausan* (நாசன் - násan, Tam.). From (násha, san. ruin). Means the god of death [yaman]. Pariah proper name [peyar].

NASL (نسل - nasl, *Hind.*). Lineage. Nasleharaum, from (harám, ar. unlawful), is a villain; a term of abuse [haraumzauda].

NASOOT (ناسوت - násút, *Ar.*). The first of the four stages of a soofee [q.v.] in which a disciple must strictly conform to shureeyat [q.v.] and which is said to be lowest form of spiritual existence.

NAT (नट् - nat, *San.*). To dance.——*Natan* (नट - nata, San.). Dancer.——*Natarajan* (நடராசன் - nadarásan, Tam.). From (nata, san. dancer + rájá, san. king). Epithet of Shiva [q.v.], the king of dancers. Hindoo 2nd or pers. name [peyar].——*Natcheny* (नाचणी - náchaní, Mahr.). Same as Raggy.——*Nateshan* (नटेश - natésha, San.). From (nata, san. dancer + ísha, san. lord). Shiva the lord of dancers. Hindoo 2nd or pers. name [peyar].——*Nautacam* (नाटक - nátaka, San.). From (nat, san. to dance). Acting, dancing, or any public performance. Also one of the three varieties of Tamul [q.v.], used in dramas. See vol. I (52).——*Nautch* (ناچ - nách, Hind.). From (nat, san. to dance). An exhibition given by dancing-girls [dausy]. Usually a combination of singing and slow dancing and gesticulating with an accompaniment of music [sangeetam] played by two or three men standing behind. Two or three words are repeated over and over again till the dancer has exhausted every means of expression; the words are sung by the attendants behind, and the dancer now and then joins in with the song.

NAU (نا - ná, *Hind.*). Without. Naudaur, from (dár, pers. property or house), is having nothing, insolvent. Naumard, from (mard, pers. man), is a coward.

NAUD (ناٹ - nát, *Hind.*; నాడు - nádu, *Tel.*; നാട് - nátu, *Mal.*; நாடு - nádu, *Tam.*). From (nadu, tam. to plant). Country where planting corn, plants or trees is done [graumam, m
Ootham]. Rural and agricultural tract as distinguished from a city [nagaram, putnam] or a forest tract [caud]. A range of country, as Mulnaud, Wynaud. The plateau of the Neilgherry hills is arranged into three nauds, Paranginaud, Merkoonaud, and Todanaud. Naudautchy is the management of a naud, as ooraütchy is that of a village. Naud curts are collections made to meet the expenses of persons deputed in the general interests of a village. Nautamcar is a village headman. Nautcootam is country assembly. Nautkanakan is a village accountant. Nautpooram is country in opposition to town. Nauttavan is the headman of a naud. Malainaud is hilly country. Valanaud is fertile country of which there were formerly five in southern

india :—chola, congoo, malayalam, paundya and tonday.——*Nauda* (నాడ - náda, Tel.). From (nádu, tel. country). Country. Locative singular. Suffix in place names ; as Conauda meaning corner country.——*Naudan* (നാടൻ - nátan, Mal.). Belonging to a locality. Cf. Yidangazhy.——*Naudaun* (நாடான் - nádán, Tam.). Title among toddy-drawers. Hindoo third name [peyar].——*Naudava* (ನಾಡವ - nádava, Can.). The same as Nayar.——*Naudiga* (ನಾಡಿಗ - nádiga, Can.). Village accountant in the inland Canarese country. With hardly an exception they are of the Bramin [q.v.] caste. The office is hereditary in common with those of all the other village officials [baloota h].——*Naudvauly* (നാടുവാഴി - nátuvázhi, Mal.). See sep. title.——*Nautt* (நாட்டு - náttu, obl., Tam.). Country [q.v.], as opposed to foreign [q.v.] or sheemay [seema].——*Nauttaun* (நாட்டான் - náttán, Tam.). From (nádu, tam. country). The headman of any caste invested with the civil jurisdiction of a tract under the native administration. This title is now-a-days assumed by people of the Shaunaur [q.v.] caste [jauty].

NAUDAH (त्रसर - trasara, *San.* ; نلی - nalí, *Hind.* ; కొమ్ము - kommu, *Tel.* ; ഓടം - ótam, *Mal.* ; நாடா - nádá, *Tam.*). Title from tamul. San. from (tras, san. to shake). Hind. means a tube. Tel. means horn. Mal. from (óta, mal. hollow bamboo). Weaver's shuttle ; commonly a small hollow bamboo [nesavoo].

NAUDAH (نارا - nárá, *Hind.*). Country twist.

NAUDIR (نادر - nádir, *Ar.*). From (nadara, ar. to remain alone). Singular. Prefixed to an alam forms a lacab ; as Naudir ally, wonder of ally [ism].

NAUDVAULY (നാടുവാഴി - nátuvázhi, *Mal.*). From (nátu, mal. country + vázhuka, mal. to rule) [naud].——**(1)** The chief of a Naud or province. He was not considered a Naudvauly who had not at least 100 Nayars [q.v.] attached to his range; any number below that ranked a person as a Deshavauly [q.v.]. See vol. II, 104, 144.——**(2)** The following are the principal Naudvaulies in North malabar, with the talook indicated.——*Avinyaut nayar* (അവിഞ്ഞാട്ട് നായർ - aviññáttunáyar, Mal.), Cooroombranaud.——*Cakkautt vayoonnavar* (കക്കാട്ടുവാഴുന്നവർ - kakkáttuvázhunnavar, Mal.), Cooroombranaud.——*Caumbratt numbiyaur* (കാമ്പ്രത്ത് നമ്പ്യാർ - kámprattunampyár, Mal.), Cottayam.——*Cauracautt edattil numbiyaur* (കാരക്കാട്ടെടത്തിൽനമ്പ്യാർ - kárakkáttetattilnampyár, Mal.), Chiracal.——*Cauryautt numbiyaur* (കാര്യാട്ട് നമ്പ്യാർ - káryáttunampyár, Mal.), Cottayam.——*Chandrote numbiyaur* (ചന്ത്രോത്ത് നമ്പ്യാർ - chantróttunampyár, Mal.), Cottayam.——*Chedicherry yedattil numbiyaur* (ചെടിശ്ശേരി എടത്തിൽ നമ്പ്യാർ - chetishshérietattilnampyár, Mal.), Chiracal.——*Choyaly yedattil numbiyaur* (ചുഴലിയെടത്തിൽനമ്പ്യാർ - chuzhaliyetattilnampyár, Mal.), Chiracal.——*Coonnoommail numbiyaur* (കുന്നുമ്മേൽ നമ്പ്യാർ - kunnummélnampyár, Mal.), Cottayam.——*Coorangote nayar* (കുരങ്ങോട്ട് നായർ - kúrannóttunáyar, Mal.), Cottayam.——*Coottauly nayar* (കൂത്താളിനായർ - kúttálináyar, Mal.), Cooroombranaud.——*Cundote yedattil numbiyaur* (കണ്ടോത്ത് എടത്തിൽ നമ്പ്യാർ - kantóttuetattilnampyár, Mal.), Chiracal.——*Eetticherry yedattil numbiyaur* (ഈറ്റിശ്ശേരിഎടത്തിൽനമ്പ്യാർ - íttishshérietattilnampyár, Mal.), Chiracal.——*Kizhakk edatt numbiyaur* (കിഴക്കേടത്ത് നമ്പ്യാർ - kizhakkétattunampyár, Mal.), Cottayam.——*Naurangoly chiracal numbiyaur* (നാരങ്ങോളിചിറക്കൽനമ്പ്യാർ - nárannólichirakkalnampyár, Mal.), Cottayam.——*Padinyauredattil numbiyaur* (പടിഞ്ഞാറെടത്തിൽ നമ്പ്യാർ - patiññáretattilnampyár, Mal.), Chiracal.——*Poothiyedatt edattil numbiyaur* (പുതിയെടത്ത് എടത്തിൽനമ്പ്യാർ - putiyetattuetattilnampyar, Mal.), Chiracal.——**(3)** The following are similarly the principal Naudvaulies in South malabar.——*Alliyil edattil nayar* (അല്ലിയിലെടത്തിൽനായർ - alliyiletattilnáyar, Mal.), Calicut.——*Amarambalatt tirmalpaud* (അമരമ്പലത്ത് തിരുമുല്പാട് - amarampalattutirumulpátu, Mal.), Yernaud.——*Ayyayira prabhoo cartauv* (അയ്യായിരപ്രഭുകർത്താവ് - ayyáyiráprabhukarttávu, Mal.), Yernaud.——*Blahayil nayar* (ബ്ലാഹയിൽനായർ - bláhayilnáyar, Mal.), Ponnany.——*Cannambara nayar* (കണ്ണമ്പ്ര നായർ - kannampranáyar, Mal.), Palghaut.——*Cauppil nannambara tirmalpaud* (കാപ്പിൽനന്നമ്പറാതിരുമുല്പാട് - káppilnannamparatirumulpátu, Mal.), Yernaud.——*Cavalpaura nayar* (കവളപ്പാറനായർ - kavalappáranáyar, Mal.), Valavanaud.——*Chenautt nayar* (ചേനാട്ട് നായർ - chenáttunáyar, Mal.), Palghaut.——*Chikkote tirmalpaud* (ചീക്കോട്ട് തിരുമുല്പാട് - chíkkóttutirumulpátu, Mal.), Yernaud.——*Congauttil nayar* (കോങ്ങാട്ടിൽ നായർ - kónnáttilnáyar, Mal.), Palghaut.——*Coothiravuttat nayar* (കുതിരവട്ടത്ത് നായർ - kutiravattattunáyar, Mal.), Valavanaud.——*Dharmote panikkar* (ധർമ്മോത്ത് പണിക്കർ - dharmóttupanikkar, Mal.), Valavanaud.——*Malapooratt pauranumby* (മലപ്പുറത്ത് പാറനമ്പി - malappurattupáranampi, Mal.), Valavanaud.——*Mandamoye tirmalpaud* (മണ്ടമ്മുയി തിരുമുല്പാട് - mantammuyitirumulpátu, Mal.), Yernaud.——*Mappooratt tirmalpaud* (മപ്പുറത്ത് തിരുമുല്പാട് - mappurattutirumulpátu, Mal.), Yernaud.——*Moolanyore nayar* (മുലഞ്ഞൂർനായർ - mulaññúrnáyar, Mal.), Valavanaud.——*Moothoovilatt nayar* (മുതുവിലത്ത് നായർ - mutuvilattunáyar, Mal.), Valavanaud.——*Mungara nayar* (മങ്കരനായർ - mankaranáyar, Mal.), Palghaut.——*Mungaut atchan* (മണ്ണാട്ടച്ചൻ - mannáttaççan, Mal.), Calicut.——*Munjery caurnavapaud* (മഞ്ചേരി കാരണവപ്പാട് - mañchérikáranavappátu, Mal.), Yernaud.——*Munnarçaud nayar* (മണ്ണാരക്കാട്ട് നായർ - mannárakkáttunáyar, Mal.), Valavanaud.——*Munnil yedattil nayar* (മണ്ണിൽ എടത്തിൽ നായർ - manniletattilnáyar, Mal.), Calicut.——*Munnore mootta nayar* (മണ്ണൂർമൂത്തനായർ - mannúrmúttanáyar, Mal.), Palghaut.——*Nadoovatt edattil nayar* (നടുവത്തെടത്തിൽനായർ - natuvattetattilnáyar, Mal.), Calicut.——*Naricote nayar* (നരിക്കോട്ട് നായർ - narikkóttunáyar, Mal.), Palghaut.——*Nelambore tutcharacauvil tirmalpaud* (നിലമ്പൂർതച്ചറക്കാവിൽതിരുമുല്പാട് - nilampúrtaççarakkávilirumulpátu, Mal.), Yernaud.——*Parappore yedattil nayar* (പറപ്പൂരെടത്തിൽ നായർ - parappúretattilnáyar, Mal.), Calicut.——*Poonnattore numbidy* (പുന്നത്തൂർനമ്പിടി - punnattúrnampiti, Mal.), Ponnany.——*Rekanutt kyemal* (രക്കണത്ത് കയ്മൾ - rakkanattukaymal, Mal.), Palghaut.——*Taracull menon* (തറക്കൽമേനോൻ - tarakkalménón, Mal.), Valavanaud.——*Tenayancherry elliad* (തെനയഞ്ചേരി എളയത് - tenayañchérielayatu, Mal.), Yernaud.——*Teningal edattil nayar* (തേനിങ്ങൾ എടത്തിൽനായർ - téninnaletattilnáyar, Mal.), Calicut.——*Tricadeery nayar* (തൃക്കടീരിനായർ - trikkatírináyar, Mal.), Valavanaud.——*Vadagara moottaur* (വടകരമൂത്താർ - vatakaramúttár, Mal.), Valavanaud.——*Vagayil nayar* (വാകയിൽ നായർ - vákayilnáyar, Mal.), Ponnany.——*Vengoonauttil numbidy* (വെങ്ങനാട്ടിൽനമ്പിടി - vennunáttilnampiti, Mal.), Palghaut.——*Venmaniyore nayar* (വെണ്മണിയൂർനായർ - venmaniyúrnáyar, Mal.), Palghaut.——*Yedattara nayar* (എടത്തറനായർ - etattaranáyar, Mal.), Palghaut.——*Yelamboolacherry nayar* (എളമ്പുലാശ്ശേരി നായർ - elampulashsherináyar, Mal.), Valavanaud.——*Yelayautt nayar* (എളയാട്ട് നായർ - elayáttunáyar, Mal.), Valavanaud.

NAUG (नाग - nága, *San.* ; ناگ - nág, *Hind.*). From (naga, san. naked). Serpent [sarpam] in general.——*Nagarcoil* (നാഗർകോവിൽ - nágarkóvil, Mal.). From (nága, san. serpent + kóvil, mal. temple). Town, District judge's head-quarters ; Travancore state, Pudmanaubhapooram division, Agasteeshwaram tal. ; pop. 16,534 ; lat. 8° 11′ N. ; long. 77° 29′ E. ; from Alleppey S.E. 115 miles ; from Cottayam S.E. 113 miles ; from Madras S.S.W. 390 miles ; from Paravore S.S.E. 156 miles ; from Quilon S.E. 76 miles ; from Trivandrum E.S.E. 38 miles ; from the sea E. 13 miles. Suburb of Cottaur. Former seat of Travancore government. Still head-quarters of a district with courts and offices. Centre of a large Christian population. London mission society has a school and printing-press. A centre of snake-worship. Pagoda [q.v.] dedicated to serpent god. The principal image of Naugamma or the snake mother, of copper-gilt, in form of a serpent is carried in procession in a car [rath] once a year. From behind the image for six months a large quantity of black sand is thrown up. For the other six months white sand is thrown up. These are distributed as prasaudam [q.v.] to the devotees. Inside the temple and without are numerous stone images of snakes. People assemble on Sundays and other special days, bringing milk [paul], sugar [q.v.], and cocoanuts [q.v.] to worship the serpent goddess, and for the living cobras [q.v.]. It is said that within a circuit of a mile from the temple no snake bite will be mortal [manarchaul]. Nagarcoil has a reputation for fine lace works [sarigay] done by the Mission converts.——*Nagore* (நாகூர் - nagúr, Tam.). From (nága, san. serpent + úr, tam. village). Sanscrit name (nágapurí), meaning snake town. Town, Port ; Tanjore dist., Negapatam tal. ; lat. 10° 49′ ; long. 79° 53′ ; from Caricaul S. 7 miles ; from Madras S.S.W. 157 miles ; from Negapatam N. 4 miles ; from Tanjore E. 47 miles. On an outlet of the Coleroon. Included in Negapatam municipality. Convenient harbour at the mouth of the Vettaur. Light on bastion ; lat. 10° 45′ 43·25″ ; long. 79° 53′ 27·85″ ; white ; fixed ; 14 miles range. Visible from all directions seaward. Masonry column, white. Guide to the anchorage. The town is easily distinguished at sea by pagodas [q.v.] rendered conspicuous by their white color. Chiefly inhabited by Lubbays [q.v.]. Vessels of two or three hundred tons burthen belong to this place, and are navigated by natives, who conduct them to the coast of Sumatra, Acheen, Malacca strait, and other parts on the east side of the Bay of

Bengal, where they have a constant trade. The port with a small territory adjoining was sold by the Rajah of Tanjore to the Dutch at Negapatam in 1771; subsequently taken from them by the Nawaub [q.v.] of the Carnatic [q.v.] with the aid of the English; sacked by Lally in 1758; acquired by the English by a grant of the Rajah in 1776. In 1780-81 food supplies were obtained hence for the British troops. Hyder ceded the place to the Dutch from whom it passed to the English in 1788. In 1868 the port was incorporated with that of Negapatam. Old Shiva temple, celebrated mosque [musjid], with a minaret [q.v.], 90 feet high resorted to during its annual festival by pilgrims from all parts of India. Wesleyan mission station. Oors [q.v.] of Cawder wally [q.v.] about February.——*Nahor* (نہور - nahor, Assamese). Same as Nauga champak.——*Naugabhooshanam* (நாகப்பூசணம் - nágappúsanam, Tam.). From (above + bhúshana san. ornament). Epithet of Shiva. Hindoo 2nd or pers. name. Common among non-bramins [peyar].——*Naugacull* (நாகக்கல் - nágakkal, Tam.). From (above + kal, tam. stone). Stone with serpent figures.——*Naugadonda* (నాగదొండ - nágadonda, Tel.). From (nága, san. serpent + donda, tel. cephalandra indica, naud.). Title from antidote to snake bite. Same as Braminy kite caper.——*Nauga dweepam* (नागद्वीप - nágadvípa, San.). Means serpent island or continent, from prevalence of serpents. One of the nine divisions of Bhaurnta varsham or Northern india [bhaurata varsham].——*Naugaisar* (ناگیسر - nágesar, Hind.). From (nága, san. serpent + késara, san. filament); from resort of serpents. Nauga champak, Soora poon, &c.——*Naugalingam* (நாகலிங்கம் - nágalingam, Tam.). From (above + linga, san. phallic emblem of shiva). Hindoo 2nd or pers. name. Commom among non-bramins [peyar].——*Naugam* (नाग - nága, San.; நாகம் - nágam, Tam.). The cobra snake.—"*a*" Serpent worship as belonging to Southern india is fully described at vol. I (82). It is not a primary form of belief among the Dravidians, but has obtained some currency, coming probably from the north-east. Various places in Southern india are named after the serpent, as Nagore, Negapatam, and Nagarcoil. At Nagarcoil the principal images of Naugamma, or the snake mother, of copper-gilt, and in the form of a serpent, is carried in procession in a car like other idols once a year. Inside the temple and without are numerous stone images of snakes. Perhaps the principal seat of this superstition in Travancore is at Manarchaul in Caurtigapully district. Natives are careful not to speak disrespectfully of the naugam; as the Malayaulies of the Shevaroy hills while hunting the tiger [pooly] only speak of it as a dog [nye], so the cobra [q.v.] is called nulla Tumbiraun, the good lord, or nulla paumb, the good snake.—"*b*" In mythology there are the snake gods. These have human heads and the bodies of serpents and wear jewels in their heads. They are the sons of Cashyapan [q.v.] and Cadroo, subject to Vishnoo's bird Garoodan [q.v.], and inhabiting part of Pautaulam [q.v.] called Naugalocam, the capital of which is Bhogavaty. The king of the serpent race, Anantan [q.v.], is superior in wisdom and intelligence, having one thousand heads, on one of which he supports the world. He forms both the couch and canopy of Vishnoo [q.v.]. Snake-worshippers expect after death to go to Naugalocam. Shiva wears a snake as an ornament in the hair of his head; and it is worn as a ring by his wife. Legends are told of the gods churning the sea to recover the elixir of immortality [amritam], with a mountain [mandaram] for a churning stick, and the five-headed serpent Vausooky for a rope, the poison issuing from whose mouth was drunk up by Shiva [q.v.], and made his neck blue. He is hence called Neelacuntan [coormam].—"*c*" A people bearing this name are historical and have left many traces behind them. There were mountains so called, and Nauga dweepam was one of the seven divisions of Bhaurata varsham. The naugas were a race distinct from the ordinary natives of India. They probably obtained their name from worshipping serpents. Certain Sheiva sanyausies [q.v.] who go nearly naked are called Naugas to this day.—"*d*" Plant first term meaning large, usefulness in snake bite, or resort of snakes; often joining two genera. Ex., where transl. is of second term:—Artemisia vulgaris (nágadamaní), subduing; Baliospermum montanum (nágadantí), tooth; Bauhinia scandens (nágavalli), creeper; Calophyllum inophyllum (nágachámpá), michelia champaca; Canthium parviflorum (nágabalá), strength; Crinum asiaticum, var. toxicarium (nágadavana), subduing; Corallocarpus epigæa (nágadonda), cephalandra indica; Crotalaria trifoliastrum (nágagiligittsa), crotalaria; Heliotropium indicum (nágadantí), tooth; Jasminum latifolium (nágamalle), jasminum sambac; Justicia procumbens (nágaputtachettu), ant-hill + tree; Luffa acutangula, var. amara (nágadáli), creeper; Mesua ferrea (nágachampa), michelia champaca, (nágakésara), filament, (nágappú), flower, (nágapushpá), flower; Murraya exotica (nágagolugu), glycosmis pentaphylla; Opuntia dillenii (nágp'haná), hood, from leaf resembling cobra's hood, (nágadáli), creeper, (nágajemudu), euphorbia tirucalli, (nágamullu), thorn, (nágatáli), creeper; Piper betel (nágavallí), creeper; Rhinacanthus communis (nágamalle), jasminum sambac; Rhynchocarpa fœtida (nágadonda), cephalandra indica; Roxburghia gloriosoides (nágapotti), shortness; Ruta graveolens, var. angustifolia, (nágadálisoppu), lustre + vegetable; Strychnos colubrina (nágamusadi), strychnos nux-vomica. See gloss. paragraphs.—"*e*" May be taken as the general term for the important family Elapidæ, ophidii colubriformes venenosi, ophidia [sarpam], reptilia [sarpy, 27], of naturalists [jantoo]. The Elapidæ are thus defined. Body cylindrical or sub-cylindrical; tail rather short, tapering; head with the normal number of shields above; loreal constantly absent; nostril lateral; eye rather small, with round pupil. The venom-fang shows a distinct groove along its front, and the canal in its interior terminates in a slit at its extremity. The following are the South indian species:—Bungarus cæruleus [krait], Bungarus fasciatus [bungaur], Callophis nigrescens, Naja tripudians [cobra], Ophiophagus elaps [hill cobra].——*Naugamany* (நாகமணி - nágamani, Tam.). From (above + mani, san. gem). Hindoo 2nd or pers. name. Applied to males and females. Common among non-bramins [peyar].——*Naugamma* (ನಾಗಮ್ಮ - nágamma, Can.). From (above + amma, can. mother). Serpent goddess worshipped at Nagarcoil and other centres of serpent worship. Otherwise Pudmauvaty, queen of Bijjnla [q.v.].——*Naugamullay* (நாகமலை - nágamalai, Tam.). From (above + malai, tam. hill). Sanscrit name (nágashaila), meaning the same. Hill; Madura dist., Madura tal.; lat. 9° 59′; long. 77° 58′; height 1,021 feet; from Madura W.N.W. 14 miles. An offshoot of the Andiputty and Varshanaud ranges, themselves a continuation of the Travancore hills. About 15 miles in length. Trig. station in lat. 9° 59′ 55·72″; long. 77° 58′ 45·79″; height 1,021 feet; from Madura W.N.W. 14 miles; from Poodoocottah W.S.W. 66 miles.——*Naugamully* (నాగమల్లె - nágamalle, Tel.; நாகமல்லி - nágamalli, Tam.). Root antidote to snake bite. Same as Snake jasmine.——*Naugan* (நாகன் - nágan, Tam.). Proper name among the lower castes [jauty]. Familiarly shortened into Naugoo, which is applied to males and females [peyar].——*Naugannan* (நாகண்ணன் - nágannan, Tam.). From (above + annan, tam. elder brother). Hindoo 2nd or pers. name [peyar]. Naugappan similar.——*Nauga punchamy* (నాగపంచమి - nágapanchami, Tel.). Means snake + fifth lunar day. Lunar [chaundramaunam] festival [pundigay, 3a], subject to intercalation [adhicam]. Fifth day in the waning moon [krishnapacsham] of fourth lunar month Ashandham [mausam] between 5th July and 4th August. Or again fifth day of waxing moon [shoocla pacsham] in fifth lunar month Shrauvanam between 21st July and 20th August. Otherwise Garooda punchamy. On both of these serpent deities are worshipped. Offerings are made to snakes; milk, grain, and other articles being taken to the holes in which they live.——*Naugauttammah* (நாகாத்தம்மா - nágáttammá, Tam.). From (above + áttál, tam. mother + ammá, tam. mother). Hindoo 2nd or pers. name. Common among non-bramins [peyar].——*Naugdown* (ناگدون - nágdaun, Hind.). From (nág, hind. snake + damana, san. subduing). Title otherwise Common asparagus. Botanically Asparagopsis [shatamooly] officinalis, linn., liliaceæ [vricsham, 136]. Cultivated by English, but does not thrive in Carnatic [q.v.]. The title naugdown is also applied to:—Artemisia vulgaris; Centipeda orbicularis; see gloss. paragraphs.——*Naugeshwaran* (நாகேசுவரன் - nágésuvaran, Tam.). From (above + íshvara, san. lord). Hindoo 2nd or pers. name [peyar].——*Naugilair* (నాగేలేరు - nágiléru, Tel.). From (nága, san. serpent + éru, tel. river). Sanscrit name (sarpanadí), meaning same. River; Kistna dist., Pulnaud tal. Perennial stream. Rises near Caurempoody and passing Dauchepully, enters the Kistna after a course of about 20 miles. A massive embankment, once dammed up its waters between the Savaditola hill of Caurempoody and the Podily hill of Shingarootla agrahauram. The water is raised into wells on the banks similar to those in Vinoocondah talook on the banks of the Goondlacumma. At Dauchepully, Gaumalpaud, and Shuncaraupooram, huge stone dams have been raised whence small irrigation channels [q.v.] are led.——*Naugojee* (ನಾಗೋಜಿ - nagóji, Can.). From (above + jí, hind. sir). Hindoo 2nd or pers. name. Common among Madhwas and Mahrattas [peyar].——*Naugoola chavity* (నాగులచవితి - nágulatsavati, Tel.). Means serpent + fourth. Lunar [chaundramaunam] festival [pundigay, 3a], subject to intercalation [adhicam]. The fourth day of the waxing moon [shoocla pacsham] in the eighth lunar month of Caurteecam [mausam] between 20th October and 19th November; set apart for the worship of the cobra [q.v.] capella snake by pouring milk into its hole. Also the fourth day of the increasing moon in the fifth lunar month Shrauvanam between 20th July and 19th August; similar observance.——*Naugoovayyan* (நாகுவய்யன் - náguvayyan, Tam.). From (above + aiyyan, tam. master). Hindoo 2nd or pers. name [peyar].——*Negapatam* (நாகப்பட்டணம் - nágappattanam, Tam.). See sep. title.

NAUL (نعل - naal, *Hind.*). Horse-shoe. Naulbund, from (band, pers. fastener) is a farrier.

NAUL (നാൾ - nál, *Mal.*; நாள் - nál, *Tam.*). A solar day and night [ahorautram, nyauyir]. A natural day [sauvana dinam]. Also a lunar asterism [nacshatram].——*Naulvazhy* (നാൾവഴി - nálvazhi, Mal.). From (above + vazhi, mal. way). Day-book.

NAUL (നാല് - nál, *Mal.*; நாலு - nálu, *Tam.*). Four.——*Nangoonairy* (நாங்குநேரி - nángunéri, Tam.). See sep. title.

——*Naulady* (நாலடி - náladi, Tam.). From (above + adi, tam. foot). From the class of stanza. A book containing 400 verses or epigrams on morals. The production of some of the Jeina [q.v.] literati of the Madura college [q.v.], and is of equal authority with the Cooral [q.v.], though inferior in sentiment and language. There is a Tamul proverb :—ஆலும்வேலும் பல்லுக்குறுதி நாலுமிரண்டுஞ் சொல்லுக்குறுதி—"As "the splint of the banyan [q.v.] and vail [q.v.] trees gives "strength to the teeth by rubbing them, so naulady and cooral "give strength to the speech." Example of Naulady:—ஆகாதெனினுமகத்து நெய்யுண்டாகிற் போகாதெறும்பு புறஞ்சுற்றும் ; யாதுங் கொடா அரெனினு முடையாரைப் பற்றிவிடா அருலகத்தவர்—"If there be ghee [q.v.] "in the vessel although they cannot get at it, the ants [choomtee] "will creep round the outside; though the rich give nothing, "the world will tenaciously cling to them."——*Naulauyira prabandham* (நாலாயிரப்பிரபந்தம் - nálâyirappirabandam, Tam.). From (above + áyiram, tam. thousand + prabandha, san. work). Same as Tirvyemozhy, Veishnava work.——*Naul mookhan* (நாலுமுகன் - nálumugan, Tam.). From (above + mukha, san. face). The four-faced god; Bramha [q.v.].

NAULKY (نالکی - nálkí, *Hind.*). State palankeen [q.v.].

NAUMA (نامه - námah, *Pers.*). From (navishtan, pers. to write) [nasindah, navees]. Writing. Suffix in compounds; as Mooctiarnauma, agent + writing. Rauzeenauma is a deed of assent.

NAUMAM (नाम - náma, *San.*). From (ñá, san. to know) [nyaunam]. Literally name. The tridental mark which the Veishnavas wear on the forehead. Also called Tirnaumam, or holy name. It consists of two white lines, extending from the hair to the eyebrows, and then leading to the nose where they meet, and a yellow or red perpendicular line between them from the nose to the hair. The two white side lines represent the feet of Vishnoo [q.v.] and the centre red line is the symbol for Lutchmy [q.v.]. It is sometimes worn also on the two shoulders and on the breast. The Vadagalay [q.v.] sub-division of the Shreeveishnavas [q.v.] use the mark as above-mentioned, but with the Tengalays [q.v.] the central line is produced to the bridge of the nose. The naumam in very large size is marked on sacred buildings, and of a smaller size on the street-door of ordinary habitations. The mark on forehead is put on after ablution in a sacred tank; with the use of invocations and anganyausam or finger signs in the case of Bramins [q.v.]. See vol. I (85). Naumam also stands for the clay used for the above purpose [matam]. Plant first term as being striped; ex., Hemidesmus indicus (námadabéru), striped creeper. For Sheiva marks see Tilacam, Tripoondram, Vibhooty.——*Namcull* (நாமக்கல் - námakkal, Tam.). See sep. title.——*Naumadhaury* (నామధారి - námadhári, Tel.). From (above + dhri, san. to wear). General name for non-braminical Veishnavas.

NAUN (نان - nán, *Hind.*). Bread; pension. Nauncaur, from (kár, pers. business), is subsistence allowance [malikhana]. Naun parvarish, from (parvarish, pers. protection), is maintenance allowance to a child.——*Nankah* (نانخواه - nánkháh, Pers.). From (nán, pers. bread + kháh, pers. demanding); appetiser. Same as Ajwaun.

NAUNAL (काश - kásha, *San.*; खंगर - khangara, *Mahr.*; کاگرا - kágará, *Hind.*; ಹೊಡಕೆಹುಲ್ಲು - hodakehullu, *Can.*; కాకివెదురు - kákiveduru, *Tel.*; ഞാങ്ങണ - ñánnana, *Mal.*; நாணல் - nánal, *Tam.*). Title from tamul. San. from (kásh, san. to shine); from silvery racemes of flowers. Mahr. and hind. from (khaggara, san. the plant). Can. from (hodaku, can. to destroy + hullu, can. grass). Tel. from (káki, tel. crow + veduru, tel. bamboo, bambusa arundinaceæ, willd.); inferior bamboo. Mal. from (náya, mal. dog + kana, mal. bamboo, bambusa arundinaceæ, willd.). Tam. from (nán, tam. bashfulness); from drooping head. San. also (khaggara), applies to the large var.; (ikshugandhá), meaning smelling like sugar-cane [nerinjy, neermoolly]. Hind. also (kás), from sanscrit. Can. also (darbhe) [darbhay]. Tel. also (rellu); (billugaddi); (verricheruku), meaning mad + sugar-cane, saccharum officinarum, linn. Tam. also (korukkai), from crackling sound; (péykkarumbu), meaning devil's sugar-cane; (eruvai), meaning buffalo reed. Title otherwise Buffalo reed, Crow bamboo, Dog bamboo, Thatch grass [darbhay], Wild sugar-cane. Botanically Saccharum [sharam] spontaneum, linn., graminaceæ [vricsham, 156]. Root perennial; culms annual, erect, leafy, round; leaves sheathing, remarkably long and narrow; margins hispid; mouths of the sheaths woolly; panicles terminal, spreading, erect, 1–2 feet long, composed of verticelled, filiform, simple ramifications, except the lower verticel or two, spiked as racemes; flowers paired, one-pedicelled and the other sessile; calyx two-leaved, margins ciliate, surrounded with soft silvery hairs; corolla one-valved, ciliate, membranaceous; stigma feathery, purple. A very tough grass; grows on the banks of rivers, in hedges, and on moist uncultivated lands; the immense quantity of long-bright silver-colored wool which surrounds the base of the flowers gives it a conspicuous appearance; the poets say that it gives a plain at a distance the appearance of a broad river. Eaten by buffaloes [khoolgah]; village cattle take to it during seasons of scarcity. The culm is made into rafts for passing rivers; also much used for thatching; some of the larger stalks are occasionally used as pens for writing. Compare Moonshee grass.——*Large naunal* (नल - nala, San.; نال - nál, Hind.; برو - barú, Dec.; ಹುಲುಗಿಲಹುಲ್ಲು - hulugilahullu, Can.; పెద్దరెల్లు - peddarellu, Tel.; ഞാങ്ങണ - ñánnana, Mal.; பெருநாணல் - perunánal, Tam.). San. from (nal, san. to shine). Hind. from sanscrit. Dec. from sanscrit. Can. from (hulu, can. insect + gili, can. fear + hullu, can. grass). Tel. from (pedda, tel. large + rellu, tel. reed). Mal. from (náya, mal. dog + kana, mal. bamboo, bambusa arundinaceæ, willd.). Tam. from (perumai, tam. greatness + nánal, tam. reed, saccharum spontaneum, linn.). San. also (dhamana), meaning blowing; (nada), meaning sounding; (pótagala), meaning clasped to the mouth and made to move. Hind. also (durma). Can. also (hulugalagu); (hulugilu). Tel. also (puvvuguttigaddi), meaning flower + cluster + grass; (nágasaramuchettu), meaning musical instrument + plant; (kikkasagaddi), meaning dense grass; from thick growth. Title otherwise Baroo, Dog bamboo, Naugaswaram [q.v.]. Botanically Phragmites roxburghii, kunth., graminaceæ [vricsham, 156]. Alias Amphidonax karka; Arundo karka. Reed; culms erect, 8–12 feet, round, smooth, covered with the sheaths of the leaves; leaves approximate, ensiform, smooth; mouths of the sheaths bearded; panicles erect, oblong, composed of many filiform, sub-verticelled ramifications, bowing to the wind; rachis of the branches angular and hispid; florets alternate; calyx three to five-flowered; glumes unequal. From the split stalks are made the common durma mats of bengal; the fibres also are made into ropes; pipes [pillangrovy] are made of the culms, by people carrying about dancing snakes [sarpam]; the stalks in bulk are a common dunnage for ships and boats. No other common species here.

NAUNJIL (நாஞ்சில் - náñjil, *Tam.*). From (ñengu, corr. for ñemungu, tam. to sink + kól, tam. stick); grooving or furrowing instrument. Plough.——*Naunjinaud* (നാഞ്ചിനാട് - náñchanátu, Mal.). From (náñjil, tam. plough + nádu, tam. country). Tamul portion of South travancore, lying south-west of Tinnevelly and north-west of Cape comorin.

NAUNYAM (नाणक - nánaka, *San.*; நாணயம் - nánayam, *Tam.*). From (nah, san. to bend); impressed metal. Coinage. That is to say pieces of metal, mostly of a round, and flat shape stamped by authority with certain impressions, which give them a legal and current value, and also serve as a guarantee for their weight and fineness; of gold [pon], silver [velly], and copper [taumram]. In each there is a certain proportion between the quantity of pure metal and its alloy. The alloy of silver is mostly copper and that of gold, both silver and copper. In the computation of coins, the alloy is never reckoned of any value. Besides the standard fineness [carat] of coins, there is also a standard weight fixed for them.——(1) There is a rough history of coinage in S. india at vol. I, 615; the following is more detailed.—"*a*" Punch coins, or irregularly-shaped pieces of metal stamped with rude symbols, preceded die coins in this as in other countries; known to sanscrit writers as Pooraunams, meaning ancient; also called Chaupahs or punches. The oldest form of a copper coin observed is a round ingot or spherule, somewhat depressed by the impact of an obscure sign above, with an occasional mark of the anvil or support beneath. Silver punch-coins have been found in the Paundicoozhies [q.v.], but are foreign coins placed there for their special value; silver is quite a foreign metal in S. india.—"*b*" Along the Coromandel coast [q.v.], a class of thin copper die-struck coins are found as antiquities. They are found in considerable numbers in or near dunes and sandknolls in the vicinity of the cooppams [q.v.] or fishing hamlets that stud the shore. These are collected by the wives and children of the fishermen after gales of wind or heavy rains, and purchased from them by the itinerant Lubbays [q.v.] and Marcauyar [q.v.] in exchange for useful necessaries; and by these they are sold to braziers and coppersmiths [cunnaun]. Indicate considerable maritime trade in former times. They bear generally the device of a bull, with occasionally some letters in the cave character on the obverse; and on the reverse a tree, ship, star, crab, fish, &c. A few specimens are between the size of a six pence and a shilling, rather thicker, of some white metal containing tin [tagaram]; and bear on the obverse, some the figure of a bull, others of horse, of the same elegant design as those of the copper. These early die-struck coins belonged to either the Coorumbar [q.v.] or the Pullavas [q.v.].—"*c*" The most distinctive coin-devices of the three great Dravidian early dynasties [raj] are as on their flags; Paundyans [q.v.] a fish, Cholans [q.v.] a tiger, Cherans [q.v.] a bow. The Paundyan fish appears sometimes singly in the centre of a coin with a sun and moon in the field, while in others two fish are represented with either a sceptre or inscription between. Sometimes the fish appears crossed, and in later issues it occupies the exergum, with a dancing figure of Vishnoo [q.v.] or Garoodan [q.v.] in the field. Paundyan issues usually bear an inscription, but rarely decipherable. Commonest name is Soondra paundyan. Other names are Korkay andaun, Coolashekharan, Veera paundyan, Bhootaulan, Samara colauhalan, Cunchy vazhangoom permaul or the king who gave back Conjeeveram, &c. Another type round Madura bears the lingam [q.v.] on one side, sometimes plain, sometimes surrounded by a row of dots, which may be intended to represent a wreath of flowers; and sometimes in a vimaunam [q.v.] or shrine; while the reverse has two standing figures. At other times the lingam appears on the back of a bull; and occasionally on a bird, possibly in connection with Meenautchy [q.v.], Shiva's wife. The Naicks [q.v.] followed the two fish and sceptre device of the Paundyans. Cholan coins are often distinguishable by the rude figure of a man standing upright, with head thrown back, and apparently holding in front of his face a flower. In his pendant right arm he holds a weapon. A straight line between his legs, and a waving one on either side, mark his flowing cloth, and under his left arm usually appear five dots. The reverse bears a similar figure curled up with legs crossed, his right hand resting on his right leg. This figure is technically called the raucshasan. Beneath the left arm is usually found the name of the king, or rarely some other emblem, such as the Paundyan fish. Cholan type issues in bolder relief, the letters being in a squarer type of Nagry [q.v.], were struck by the kings of Ceylon; known as Lunkeshwaran. The Cheran type shows on one side the Cataury or native long-handled dagger, and on the other the bow. These coins are thin and in appearance not unlike those of the Coorumbas.—"*d*" The early coins of the Andhra [q.v.] monetary system in the north differ from those in the more southern districts. The prevailing metal there is lead [eeyam]. A few occur of copper [taumram], and some of alloy of copper [taumram] and tin [tagaram], but none of gold [pon] or silver [velly]. The lead is generally very pure. They are stamped with symbols of a Booddhist [booddha] character. The obverse has figures of a lion [simham] or horse [ghorah] with the name of the sovereign, but never his effigy. The reverse has often the Booddhist cross or wheel, to which the name of Oojjein symbol has sometimes been given. The pieces vary greatly in size; they are generally round, sometimes square. Some are only struck on one side, the reverse being plain or exhibiting marks of the substance on which they had rested, wood or stone, to receive the impact of the upper die. Many of the smaller pieces appear to have been cast in moulds, with the figure of an elephant rudely represented by three convexities with or without legs. On some specimens, the elephant [q.v.] is sharp and symmetrical, facing mostly to the right, the trunk pendant or raised over the head. On the larger lead pieces is a stately maneless lion, the reverse with Booddhist emblems, or plain; while on the thicker alloyed specimens the animal has an ample mane, is short-legged, one paw uplifted, and on the reverse a vase, the Dronam, between two candelabra.—"*e*" The Vijianugger copper issues bear the figure of some deity, while the reverses vary. Those of Deva royel bear with his name the figure of a bull [rishabham] or elephant [q.v.], or the Ganda bheroondam [q.v.] or double-headed bird familiar on palampores [q.v.] and tapestries. Tirmula has on the obverse of his pieces Hanooman [q.v.]. Krishna devan takes Garoodan [q.v.].—"*f*" The oldest specimens of die-struck gold coinage are spherules quite plain and smooth, save for a single very minute punch mark too small to be identified, by the impress of which they have been slightly flattened. They weigh about fifty-two grains. Their original name being pon [q.v.], which simply means gold in Tamul, becoming hoon in Canarese, and the origin of the Mahomedan hoon [q.v.]. The second step in advance from the primitive form of gold coinage is that of very thin, almost circular pieces, nearly an inch and-a-half in diameter, weighing about sixty-six grains. These were succeeded by flat, round, thicker pieces of superior workmanship, which have received the name of Pudma tunkams [q.v.], from having what is called a lotus [nelumbo] in the centre, a favorite emblem amongst the Jeinas [q.v.]. These are from fifty-five to sixty-five, or even seventy grains. The superior execution of the Pudma tunkams ruled for a considerable time with many variations, until the adoption of the double die led to the final and complete disuse of the punch. The earliest design on the reverses of these coins is that of an elegant floral or arabesque pattern. It is found on the Chalookya, Cheran, &c., coins. Next after the Pudma tunkam is a gold piece with four transverse horizontal bars, two and two, in contact with each other, and between the pairs a considerable space, in which are four smaller vertical bars curved at the bottom, and some indistinct marks above and below the tranverse bars. The reverse is not figured, and may therefore be considered to have been plain. The last to be noticed is a gold pagoda [q.v.] with perfect obverse and reverse. The figure on the obverse may be described as a heart-shaped symbol, from the upper lobes of which two-pointed lines rise, often truncated by the margin, and between them a dot; sometimes to the left of these are another dot and a curved line. The figure on the reverse resembles a flat dish in which are two rounded forms like balls. Gradually the gold coinage came to exhibit more definite devices, with the legends in Haleycannada [q.v.] or old Canarese [q.v.] and Nagry [q.v.] characters. The coins themselves became narrower and thicker, but without any alteration of the standard weight, and this continued to be the prevailing character down to 1833. They were also coined in halves under various names, as prataupa, mauda, &c., having the same device as the full-sized piece.—"*g*" Antique die-struck pieces of silver are rarely to be met with. The absence of all mention of silver money is conspicuous in the narratives of the plunder of the Deccan [q.v.]. The currency continued to be mainly of gold until the Mahomedans came to be permanently established in the south. Their preference for the rupee [q.v.] led to the introduction of a silver currency, without however displacing the gold previously in circulation. The substitution of silver money increased with the intercourse of European traders. Single and double silver fanams [q.v.] were coined at the different factories of the English, French, and Danish settlements; the French distinguished by the fleur-de-lis, and afterwards by a cock; the Danish by the cipher of King Christian. The same practice was adopted in Mysore after the fall of Seringapatam, and the Travancore state issues large numbers of silver chuckrams [q.v.] to the present day. In the English factory at Madras, in 1811, a silver pagoda coin was introduced about the size of a half-crown, having a rude representation of a goddess on the obverse, and the gate tower, or gopooram [q.v.] of a temple [coil, pagoda], on the reverse, with the monetary designation of the piece in English, Tamul, and Teloogoo characters. At the same time the authorities issued a large supply of single and double, half and quarter rupees, and silver fanams of an improved form, in pieces of one, two, three, four, five fanams; the silver rupee of 180 grains being convertible at the rate of 350 rupees for 100 pagodas of account.—"*h*" During the two past centuries many zemindars [q.v.], poligars [q.v.] and district chiefs, taking advantage of the weakness of the paramount power, assumed the right of issuing money coined by themselves. Such were the rajahs of Sunda, the Beedar chiefs of Shorapore and Bednore or Nugger, the Reddies [q.v.] of Condaveed, the Poligars [q.v.] of the Ceded districts [q.v.], the zemindars [q.v.] of Ramnaud and Shivagunga, the nawaubs [q.v.] of Savanore, Jinjee, and Cuddapah, the naicks [q.v.] of Tanjore, Trichinopoly, and Madura, &c. Hence an endless variety of copper coins is still met with in the bazaar.—"*i*" After the introduction of his new system of dates, Tippoo invented a series of new names; for his gold mohur [q.v.] is called Ahmedy [q.v.], his half gold mohur Siddeeky [q.v.], his pagoda Farooky [q.v.]. His silver coins are the double rupee or Imaumy, the half rupee or Aubidy, the quarter rupee or Baukiry, the two-anna piece or Jaffery, the one-anna piece or Cauzimy, and the half-anna piece or Khizry. Among the silver coins each refers to name of one of the Imaums [q.v.]. The Aubidy after Zein ool abideen or Aubid i beemaur; the Baukiry after Mahomed, Baukir; the Jaffery after Jaffer i saudik; and the Cauzimy after Moosah cauzim. The gold coins refer to Mahomedan saints. The Ahmedy is from Ahmed, one of the designations of the prophet himself; Siddeeky from Aboo bakr siddeek, the first caliph; and the Farooky from Omar farook, the second caliph. The largest of Tippoo's copper coins is the double peisa [q.v.]. It bears two names Oosmauny and Mooshtary. The first derived from Oosmaun bin affaun, the third caliph [q.v.]. When in the Mowloody year 1221 Tippoo started a series of names for his smaller copper coins, derived from those of different stars, the designation Oosmauny did not agree with the rest. Accordingly the double peisas of Mowloody year 1222 and following bear denomination, Mooshtary, the Arabic name of the planet Jupiter [brihaspaty, najm]. The name of the peisa is zohrah and that of the half-peisa bahraum. These are the Persian designations of the planets Venus [shoocran] and Mars [coojan, mungalan]. The quarter peisa is known as Akhtar, which in Persian signifies a star. The Nawaubs [q.v.] of the Carnatic [q.v.] had gold and copper issues struck in Arcot. Mussalman coins have clear cut impressions and legible superscriptions. Unlike coins of Hindoos, they bear a date.—"*j*" The Portuguese issued money in gold [pon], silver [velly], copper [taumram], and tootnaug [q.v.], in Goa and Cochin. A new stamp usually marking the rule of each successive governor. In no instance do Indo-portuguese coins bear any word in a native language. The following are the relative values of the various Portuguese coins that have found currency in India:—

30	Reis	= 1	Meia tanga.
60	Reis	= 1	Tanga.
2½	Tangas	= 1	Meia pardao.
2	Meia pardaos	= 1	Pardao.
2	Pardaos	= 1	Rupia.

The Venetian sequin, the Shaunaur [q.v.] cash [q.v.] of the natives, was current in Goa and neighbouring parts; a thin gold coin. The issues of the Danish mint at Tranquebar consisted chiefly of four-cash pieces in copper and far more rarely of ten cash in silver and copper. All bear on one side the monogram of the reigning monarch. French coins struck locally are comparatively few; on obverse either the cock or fleur-de-lis, on the reverse date. The Dutch quarter stiver, known as duits, or challies, are met with in great quantities. Contemporaneous with these is a series of thick and roughly-formed medals, with letters to denote town of mintage. The former were made in a European mint, while the latter were country-made.—"*k*" There are Mahomedan coins of the different dynasties [raj], Arabic, Persian, Pataun, Moghul, &c., and sometimes of the Caliphs who reigned previously to the first Mahomedan invasion. They are distinguished by inscriptions in Arabic or Persian, and few of them, except the zodiacal coins, have figures of any living creature. They are either round or square. Ancient Persian or Parthian coins, with inscriptions in the Pahlava character, and sometimes in Greek are now and then found and generally represent the fire worship on one side. Chinese coins are found on the coast. Roman aurei have been unearthed in a perfect state of preservation. Some small Roman copper pieces are said to have been struck locally, but this is doubtful. Commonest type of reverses in these bears the figures of three Roman soldiers standing and holding spears in their hands.—"*l*" The indigenous monetary system of Southern india is based on rude seminal and testaceous exponents of value, which have been exchanged for definite metallic counters, regulated by artificial skill, their original names and the numerous changes and variations in which exhibit a certain affinity, indicative of their common origin; but the discrepancies are common throughout, the simple word being all that can be identified as having survived the changes of system. While the Moghul power prevailed the monetary system was very simple. There was current one principal coin of silver, denominated the sicca rupee. It was of a certain weight called the sicca [q.v.], which served also as a standard for weighing other articles. There were gold coins minted, but their price was not fixed, silver being the only standard of value. The principal piece of gold was the mohur; it was of the same weight as the sicca rupee, and both are supposed to have been originally coined without any alloy.—"*m*" The East india company kept as near to this method as the necessary firmness of coin allowed. According to the system in S. india at the early part of British administration, accounts were kept in star pagodas [q.v.], fanams [q.v.], and cash [q.v.]; 80 cash equal to 1 fanam, and 42 fanams equal to 1 pagoda. The East india company and other European merchants kept their accounts at 12 fanams the rupee, and 42 fanams or 3½ rupees the star pagoda; but the natives reckoned the rupee at 12 fanams 60 cash, and the star pagoda at 44 fanams 50 cash. The bazaar exchange fluctuated from 35 to 45 fanams. The gold coins were star or current pagodas, and the silver coins Arcot rupees. Double and single fanams [q.v.] and copper pieces of 20 cash [q.v.], called pie [q.v.], were current; also pieces of 10 and 5 cash, called doody [q.v.] and half doody; and single cash pieces. These copper coins were struck in England, and the value was marked upon each. The star pagoda weighed 52·56 English grains, and the gold was 19¼ carats fine; it contained, therefore, 42·048 grains of fine gold, and was worth 7s. 5¼d. sterling; but it was commonly valued at 8s. The Arcot rupee, which was also coined at the Fort st. george mint, weighed 176·4 grains and contained 166·477 grains of fine silver; its sterling value was, therefore, 23¼d. It was divided into 16 annas or 192 pies like the other rupees. Many other coins then circulated on the Coromandel coast [q.v.], of which the following were the most generally current:—The old pagoda, with three sawmy [q.v.] or figures, coined at Madras and Negapatam, which was about 20⅞ carats [q.v.] fine, and which generally bore a batta [q.v.] of 10 per cent. against the new coins of the same places. The new pagoda of Negapatam and Tuticorin which was 18¼ carats fine and was reckoned about 4 per cent. worse than the star pagoda. The Porto novo pagoda, which was 17¾ carats fine, and was about 20 per cent. worse than the star pagoda. The Pondicherry pagoda, which was originally equal in value to the star pagoda, but its standard was lowered to 17 carats and even less. All these different pagodas were nearly of the same weight.—"*n*" In 1811 a coinage from Spanish dollars took place, consisting of double rupees, single rupees, halves and quarters, and pieces of 1, 2, 3, and 5 fanams. One rupee weighed 186·70 grains troy and contained 166·477 grains pure silver, which was the same quantity as was contained in the Arcot rupee. It was therefore worth 23·247d. sterling. A silver coinage of half and quarter pagodas, of dollar silver fineness, also took place then. The silver half-pagoda weighed 326·73 grains troy and was equal to 1¾ Arcot rupee.—"*o*" By a proclamation, dated 7th January 1818, the silver rupee was made to constitute the standard coin of this presidency. The public accounts were in consequence converted from the star pagoda into the Madras rupee at the exchange of 350 rupees for 100 pagodas, and all engagements of the Government became negotiable in the same rupees. The new coinage of silver consisted of rupees weighing 7½ dwts. and 11/12 fine. Thus the rupee contained 165 grains of pure silver and 15 grains of alloy, making together 180 grains, with half rupees, quarters, eighths, and sixteenths in proportion. The sixteenth was the anna, and the eighth, the double anna. The new coinage of gold consisted of rupees, halves, and quarters of the same weight and fineness as the silver rupee. Thus the former contained 165 grains of pure gold and 15 grains of alloy. The new gold rupee, valued at the mint price of gold in England, was worth £1 9s. 2·42d.; and the new silver rupee, valued at the old mint price of silver in England, was 1s. 11·04d.; but, as the fifteenth part of the gold rupee, it was worth 1s. 11·36d. The coinage of the pagoda was at this time discontinued. The charge for coining at the Madras mint was 3 per cent. for gold and 4 per cent. for silver, including the charge for refining.——**(2)** The following is an attempt to reduce to an average table and a standard value the modern but strictly native coins of the presidency, taking them under five divisions according to nationality of the populations using, and adding Sanscrit:—"*a*" Average table of money in Tamul districts:—2 cash or pies = 1 dooggauny or farthing, 2 dooggaunies = 1 doody, 3¾ doodies = 1 chinnapanam or single fanam, 2 chinnapanams = 1 panam or double fanam, 22½ panams = 1 varauhan or star pagoda. Extras:—5 chinnacash = 1 cash, 2 cash = 1 doody. Approximate actual value:—1 panam = 2 annas 6 pies.—"*b*" Average table of money in Teloogoo districts:—2 roowas or pies = 1 dooggauny or farthing, 2 dooggaunies = 1 dub, 6 dubs = 1 baida, 2 baidas = 1 doogoolam, 2 doogoolams = 1 chowlam, 4 chowlams = 1 mauda, 2 maudas = 1 kurruck varahah. Approximate actual value:—1 varahah = 4 rupees.—"*c*" Average table of Canarese money:—2 cash or pies = 1 dooggauny or farthing, 2 dooggaunies = 1 doody, 3 doodies = 1 haunga, 2 haungas = 1 adda, 2 addas = 1 caul. Extras:—3 haungas = 1 mooppauga. Approximate actual value:—1 dooggauny or farthing = 2 pies.—"*d*" Average table of money of Malabar:—2 reis = 1 cash or pie, 4 cash = 1 peisa, 14 peisa = 1 veeroye fanam, 3½ veeroye fanams = 1 rupee. Extras:—10 peisa = 1 velly, 5 vellies = 1 rupee. Cochin state:—10 cash = 1 poottan, 5½ poottans = 1 veeroye fanam, 3½ veeroye fanams = 1 rupee. Extras:—2 poottans = 1 retta poottan. Travancore state:—16 cochin cash = 1 chuckram, 4 chuckrams = 1 caly fanam, 2 caly fanams = 1 anandrye fanam, 3½ anandrye fanams = 1 rupee.—"*e*" Average table of Mahomedan money:—12 damrees or pies = 1 anna, 16 annas = 1 rupee, 3½ rupees = 1 hoon or pagoda. Extras:—1 adhelah = 1, 2, 3 or 4 damrees or pies; 4 damries or pies = 1 peisa or pice; 4 annas = 1 powlah; 16 rupees = 1 ashrafee.—"*f*" Average table of Sanscrit money:—16 panams = 1 dharanam or pagoda, 16 dharanams = 1 nishcam. Approximate actual value:—1 dharanam = 3½ rupees.——**(3)** The following is the recognized table under the English administration:—

12 pies = 1 anna.
16 annas = 1 rupee.
3½ rupees = 1 pagoda.
15 rupees = 1 gold mohur.

A lakh [q.v.] of rupees is 100,000; a crore [q.v.] of rupees 100 lakhs, or 10 millions. Taking the rupee [q.v.] at 2 shillings, an anna will be equal to one and half pence, a pie to half farthing. ——**(4)** The heads of this glossary can be consulted for the different terms for money and coins.

NAUR (तन्तु - tantu, *San.*; ناڑ - nár, *Hind.*; ನಾರು - náru, *Can.*; నార - nára, *Tel.*; நார் - nár, *Tam.*). **Fibre of any sort.** Especially the hempen fibres of various plants. Vegetable fibres are used:—in making ropes, cables and strings, which require strong fibres, capable of flexibility; in making yarns finer than ropes or strings, which should possess the spinning quality or a glossy surface to slide smoothly, parallelism of the fibres being necessary; in making paper, which is produced by felting together, while they are in a wet state, fibres generally very thin and short, and having a curly disposition, so that they become entangled. Fibres produced by dicotyledons are contained in the bark; chief orders are:—linaceæ, malvaceæ, tiliaceæ, leguminosæ, urticaceæ, cannabinaceæ, moraceæ, thymelaceæ, salicaceæ. Fibres produced by the monocotyledons are generally contained in the leaves; chief orders are:—graminaceæ, bromeliaceæ, liliaceæ, juncaceæ, amaryllidaceæ, musaceæ, palmaceæ. Third sort of fibres found are hairs that surround the seed; cotton [q.v.] is the most remarkable of this class. Fibrous plants abound in every hedge row and waste place in the presidency, and many of them contain fibre in large quantity and of excellent quality. Palms [taur] yield strong materials for cordage and mats [boriyah], or bast. Coarse strong fibres are given by plants of the aloe [q.v.] tribe. Those of the American aloe [q.v.] vary from 3–4 feet; of the Fourcroya [foreign aloe], from 6–9 feet; and of Agave vivipara, linn. [bastard aloe], from 3–5 feet. Their thickness is about that of stout pack thread, and they are nearly white and possess considerable strength, but a little stiffness. The fibres of the Yuccas [adam's needle] are much shorter, varying from 1–2 feet; they are however more pliant and finer, resembling human hair. Nearly allied to the aloes and yielding a fibre are many species of Musa [plantain]. For flax see under Linum usitatissimum, linn. [alsee]. For hemp see Cannabis sativa, linn. [kinnab], and Crotolaria juncea, linn. [sunn]. For jute see that head. Besides these there are many miscellaneous. The large hill-nettles give fibre. Jungle tribes make fibres from various barks. The obstacle to the utilisation of this source of wealth has been the want of a simple and efficient means of extracting the fibre, so as to admit of its being sold at a cheap rate while not impairing its quality. The native method of preparing fibre is by maceration in water and beating and scraping; a process slow, expensive, and prejudicial to the quality of the product. The following are two key-lists of the principal indigenous fibres of s. india for which vernacular names are known; further information must be traced in the glossary paragraphs through the small type cross-references at end of this volume; see also vricsham, 7, for the method of expressing this and other products of the plants in the dravidian languages.—"*a*" Abutilon indicum, indian mallow, stem; Acacia arabica, babool, bark; Acacia latronum, buffalo thorn, bark; Acacia leucophlœa, white babool, bark; Adansonia digitata, baobab, bark; Æschynomene aspera, solah, outer bark; Agave americana, american aloe, leaf; Agave vivipara, bastard aloe, leaf; Aloe indica, common indian aloe, leaf; Aloe vulgaris, barbadoes aloe, leaf; Althæa rosea, english hollyhock, stem; Ananas sativus, pine-apple, leaf; Andropogon contortus, spear grass, leaf; Andropogon muricatus, cuscus, leaf; Andropogon schœnanthus, lemon grass, leaf; Anona reticulata, bullock's heart, bark; Antiaris saccidora, sack tree, bark;

Antidesma bunius, chinese laurel, bark ; Antidesma ghæsembilla, var. genuinum, gasambilla, bark ; Areca catechu, areca, leaf and spathe ; Arenga saccharifera, sago palm, fibre round petioles ; Artocarpus integrifolia, bread-fruit, bark ; Bambusa arundinacea, common bamboo, stem ; Bambusa stricta, male bamboo, stem ; Bauhinia purpurea, purple mountain ebony, bark ; Bauhinia racemosa, small-flowered mountain ebony, bark ; Bauhinia tomentosa, wild mountain ebony, bark of small branches ; Bauhinia vahlii, large mountain ebony, bark ; Bixa orellana, monkey turmeric, bark ; Bombax malabaricum, red cotton tree, inner bark ; Borassus flabelliformis, palmyra, leaf ; Butea frondosa, bengal kino, inner root bark ; Calamus rotang, country rattan, stem ; Calotropis gigantea, mudar, bark ; Cannabis sativa, indian hemp, stem ; Careya arborea, hindostany slow match, bark ; Caryota urens, bastard sago palm, sheathing petiole ; Cerbera odollam, odallam, bark ; Cocos nucifera, cocoanut, fibre covering nut ; Corchorus capsularis, jute, bark ; Corchorus olitorius, wild jute, bark ; Cordia myxa, small sebesten, bark; Cordia obliqua, large sebesten, bark ; Cordia rothii, narrow-leaved sebesten, inner bark ; Corypha taliera, talura palm, leaf ; Corypha umbraculifera, talipot, leaf ; Crotalaria juncea, sunn, bark ; Crotalaria retusa, short giligitcha, bark ; Cryptostegia grandiflora, paulay silk cotton, bark ; Cyperus corymbosus, indian matting sedge ; Cyperus exaltatus, fox-tail sedge, leaf ; Cyperus iria, tail sedge, leaf ; Dæmia extensa, hedge cotton, stem ; Dolichandrone falcata, wody ; Dolichandrone rheedii, long-leaved wody, branches and roots ; Dregea volubilis, nakchiknee silk cotton ; Epicarpurus orientalis, stunted jack, stem ; Eragrostis cynosurioides, darbhay, leaf ; Eriodendron anfractuosum, silk cotton, wool of fruit ; Erythrina indica, common coral tree, bark ; Eucalyptus globulus, blue gum, bark ; Ficus bengalensis, banyan, bark ; Ficus infectoria, stone banyan, bark ; Ficus oppositifolia, devil fig, bark ; Ficus racemosa, country fig, bark ; Ficus religiosa peepul, bark ; Ficus tsiela, tsiela, bark ; Fourcroya gigantea, great aloe, leaf; Girardina heterophylla, neilgherry nettle, bark ; Gossypium barbadense, var. acuminatum, peruvian cotton, wool of fruit ; Gossypium herbaceum, indian cotton, wool of fruit ; Grewia asiatica, falsah, bark ; Grewia excelsa, small tadda, bark ; Grewia tiliæfolia, tadda, bark ; Guazuma tomentosa, roodrauck tree, bark ; Hardwickia binata, yaipy, bark ; Helicteres isora, screw tree, bark ; Hibiscus abelmoschus, musk bendy, stem ; Hibiscus cannabinus, hemp bendy, stem ; Hibiscus collinus, hill bendy, stem ; Hibiscus esculentus, common bendy, stem ; Hibiscus ficulneus, spreading bendy, stem ; Hibiscus mutabilis, lotus bendy, bark ; Hibiscus rosa-sinensis, china rose bendy, bark ; Hibiscus sabdariffa, red hemp bendy, bark ; Hibiscus tiliaceus, cork wood bendy, bark ; Hibiscus vitifolius, vine-leafed bendy, bark ; Linum usitatissimum, flax, bark ; Maranta dichotoma, seetalpaty, stem ; Melia azadirachta, margosa, bark ; Moringa pterygosperma, indian horse radish, bark ; Musa paradisiaca, plantain, sheathing foot-stalk ; Musa superba, wild plantain, sheathing foot-stalk ; Musa textilis, demon plantain, sheathing foot-stalk ; Nelumbium speciosum, sacred lotus, stalk ; Odina wodier, wodier, bark ; Opuntia dillenii, prickly pear, stem ; Pæderia fœtida, stinking opal berry, stalk ; Pandanus odoratissimus, screw pine, leaf ; Parkinsonia aculeata, jerusalem thorn ; Pavonia odorata, peramootty, stem ; Pavonia zeylanica, shittamootty, stem ; Phœnix farinifera, small date ; Phœnix sylvestris, wild date, leaflet and petiole ; Phragmites roxburghii, large naunal, stalk ; Pongamia glabra, indian beech ; Saccharum munja, moonj, leaf ; Saccharum sara, moonshee grass, leaf ; Saccharum spontaneum, naunal, leaf ; Salix tetrasperma, indian willow ; Sanseviera roxburghiana, bowstring hemp, leaf ; Sesbania aculeata, prickly sesban, bark ; Sesbania ægyptiaca, common sesban, bark ; Sesbania grandiflora, west-indian sesban, inner bark ; Shorea robusta, common saul ; Sida carpinifolia, lance-leaved balah, stem ; Sida rhombifolia, common balah, bark ; Sponia wightii, indian nettle, bark ; Sterculia colorata, wild papaw, bark ; Sterculia guttata, dung tree, bark ; Sterculia urens, false tragacanth, liber ; Sterculia villosa, odul, bark ; Thespesia populnea, portia, bark ; Tylophora asthmatica, indian ipecacuanha ; Ventilago madraspatana, pappily, bark ; Vernonia anthelmintica, wild cumin ; Vitis quadrangularis, piranday, stem ; Yucca aloifolia, adam's needle, leaf ; Zea mays, maize, stalk.—"*b*" Adam's needle, yucca ; Aloe, agave, fourcroya ; Babool, acacia ; Balah, sida ; Bamboo, bambusa ; Banyan, ficus ; Baobab, adansonia ; Beech, pongamia ; Bendy, hibiscus ; Blue gum, eucalyptus ; Bread fruit, artocarpus ; Bullock's heart, anona ; Chinese laurel, antidesma ; Cocoanut, cocos ; Coral tree, erythrina ; Cotton, dæmia, gossypium ; Cumin, vernonia ; Cuscus, andropogon ; Darbhay, eragrostis ; Date, phœnix ; Dung tree, sterculia ; Ebony, bauhinia ; Falsah, grewia ; Flax, linum ; Gasambilla, antidesma ; Giligitcha, crotalaria ; Hemp, cannabis, sanseviera ; Hollyhock, althæa ; Horse radish, moringa ; Ipecacuanha, tylophora ; Jack, epicarpurus ; Jerusalem thorn, parkinsonia ; Jute, corchorus ; Kino, butea ; Lemon grass, andropogon ; Lotus, nelumbium ; Maize, zea ; Mallow, abutilon ; Margosa, melia ; Moonj, saccharum ; Moonshee grass, saccharum ; Mudar, calotropis ; Naunal, phragmites, saccharum ; Nettle, girardina, sponia ; Odallam, cerbera ; Odul, sterculia ; Opal berry, pæderia ; Palmyra, borassus ; Papaw, sterculia ; Pappily, ventilago ; Peepul, ficus ; Peramootty, pavonia ; Pine-apple, ananas ; Piranday, vitis ; Plantain, musa ; Portia, thespesia ; Prickly pear, opuntia ; Rattan, calamus ; Red cotton, bombax ; Roodrauck, guazuma ; Sack tree, antiaris ; Sago palm, arenga, caryota ; Saul, shorea ; Screw pine, pandanus ; Screw tree, helicteres ; Sebesten, cordia ; Sedge, cyperus ; Seetalpaty, maranta ; Sesban, sesbania ; Shittamootty, pavonia ; Silk cotton, cryptostegia, dregea, eriodendron ; Slow match, careya ; Solah, æschynomene ; Spear grass, andropogon ; Sunn, crotalaria ; Tadda, grewia ; Talipot, corypha ; Talura, corypha ; Thorn, acacia ; Tragacanth, sterculia ; Tsiela, ficus ; Turmeric, bixa ; Willow, salix ; Wodier, odina ; Wody, dolichandrone ; Yaipy, hardwickia.——*Nauroo* (نارو - nárú, Hind. ; ನಾರಿಹುಣ್ಣು - nárihunnu, Can. ; నారిపుండు - náripundu, Tel. ; നാഡീവ്രണം - nádívranam, Mal. ; நரம்புச்சிலந்தி - narambuççilandi, Tam.). All mean fibre + sore. Guinea-worm. Average length 25 inches. Incubation after embryo has entered system about twelve months. The germ becomes deposited beneath the skin working its way into some sudoriparous duct ; disease caught while standing or bathing in water [veidyan].

NAUS (नस्य - nasya, *San.* ; ناس - nás, *Hind.* ; ನಶಿಪುಡಿ - nashipudi, *Can.* ; ముక్కుపొడి - mukkupodi, *Tel.* ; മൂക്കുപ്പൊടി - múkkuppoti, *Mal.* ; மூக்குத்தூள் - múkkuttúl, *Tam.*). Title from sanscrit through hindostany. San. means belonging to the nose. Tel., Mal., Tam. mean nose-powder. Tam. also (podi) meaning powder. Snuff. The pulverised leaves of tobacco [pogauk] ground down with ghee [q.v.] and prepared lime [choonam]. A famous snuff used to be made at Masulipatam. The native snuff-taker usually keeps his supply in a folded leaf. An ornamental snuff-box is made out of the shell of the fruit of Ægle marmelos, corr. [bael], with a hole in one end furnished with a stopper.

NAUSHTA (ناشته - náshtah, *Hind.* ; నాస్త - násta, *Tel.*). From (noshídan, pers. to drink). Morning breakfast [khanah].

NAUSIR (ناصر - násir, *Ar.*). From (nasara, ar. to succour). Defender. Prefixed to an alam forms a lacab ; as Nausir ood dowlah, defender of the empire [ism, noosrat].——*Naseer* (نصير - nasír, Ar.). From (nasara, ar. to succour). Defender. Part of lacab ; as Naseer ood deen, defender of religion [ism, noosrat]. ——*Nauzir jung* (ناصر جنگ - násirjang, Hind.). Descriptive + khitaub alaumat. Nizam of Hyderabad, 1748–50. Killed by Nawaub of Cuddapah. Vol. I (107), (122), 4, 9 ; II, 253.

NAUTAN (नाथ - nát'ha, *San.* ; நாதன் - náthan, *Tam.*). From (nát'h, san. to have power). Lord [nayagan]. Epithet of the Supreme being, Shiva [q.v.] and Arghan [aroogan] ; also applied to a sage or any worthy person. Suffix to names of god and men, as Raghoonautan, Sawminautan [peyar].

NAUTT (నాటు - nátu, *Tel.* ; நாற்று - náttu, *Tam.*). Title and Tam. from (náru, tam. to shoot up). Tel. from (nátu, tel. to transplant). Plants thickly sown in a prepared seed-bed for the purpose of being transplanted.——*Nautmoody* (நாற்றுமுடி - náttumudi, Tam.). From (above + mudi, tam. to tie). A handful of plants tied in a bundle for transplanting. Otherwise moody [q.v.].——*Nauttangaul* (நாற்றங்கால் - náttangál, Tam.). From (above + kál, tam. place). Otherwise Nautt pathy or seedling bed. Plant nursery.——*Nautt nadavoo* (நாற்றுநடவு - náttunadavu, Tam.). From (above + natu, tam. to plant) ; to plant seedlings. Transplanting [paddy].

NAUZIM (ناظم - názim, *Hind.*). From (nazm, ar. order). A governor [nizam]. Part of lacab ; as Nauzim jung, arranger in war [ism].

NAUZIR (ناظر - názir, *Hind.*). From (nazr, ar. sight). An inspector. Commonly the officer of a civil court, who is charged with the serving of process and the execution of decrees.

NAVAM (नव - nava, *San.*). Nine.——*Nava chola charitram* (నవచోళచరిత్రము - navachólacharitramu, Tel.). From (above + chóla, san. the king + charitra, san. story). Tale of the nine Cholas ; translation from Canarese, into dwipada Teloogoo by Leela manoopa chetty, a Jangam [q.v.]. The names of the nine Cholas :—Caricaulan, Vicraman, Oottoongan, Ahivaran, Varan, Dharman, Satyendran, Veeran and Oottaman. The three first, and two last often occur in books and inscriptions.——*Nava dhaunyam* (నవధాన్యము - navadhányamu, Tel.). From (above + dhánya, san. grain). Nine grains proper to be presented with burnt offerings, oblations to gods or to nine planets [graham], one to each are :—wheat [geung], to sun [sooryan] ; paddy [q.v.], to moon [chundran] ; tovray [common dholl], to Mars [coojan, mungalan] ; payar [green gram], to Mercury [boodhan] ; cadalay [bengal gram], to Jupiter [brihaspaty] ; avaray [country bean], to Venus [shoocran] ; sesamum [gingelly], to Saturn [shany] ; oolandoo [black gram], to Rahoo [q.v.] ; horse-gram [gram] to Kait [q.v.].——*Nava graham* (नवग्रह - navagraha, San.). Nine planets. See Graham. Compare Najm.——*Nava khandam* (नवखण्ड - navakhanda, San.). From (above + khanda, san. portion). Nine-fold division of India. First actually described by astronomers Parausharan and Varanha mihiran [q.v.], but far older in reality. Nava khandam of Mahabhaurat [q.v.] will be found at vol. I (1), foot-note, para. 3. This was repeated by Bhascaracharry [q.v.], who was later than Varauha mihiran, also by several Pooraunams [q.v.]. Nava khandam of Varauha mihiran was different, and will be found at vol. I (2), foot-note, para. 7. Only the Braumhaundam and Marcandeya pooraunams state the names of the districts in each of the nine divisions. The Vishnoo, Vayoo, and Matsya pooraunams agree with the Mahabhaurat [q.v.] in describing in detail only five divisions, namely the middle province and those of the four cardinal points [punchakhandam]. According to Hwen thsang's account, peninsular India was divided into nine separate kingdoms, exclusive of Ceylon, which was not considered as belonging to India [q.v.]. These kingdoms were Andhram, Calingam, Choolyam, Concanam, Cosalam, Dhanacataca, Dravidam, Maharashtram, and Malacoota. See those heads.——*Navamy* (नवमी - navamí, San.). The ninth lunar day [tity] of the Pacsham [q.v.]. Lunar festival [pundigay, 5e] [doorganavamy, mahanavamy, shreeram navamy].——*Nava narsimhan* (నవనరసింహుడు - navanarasimhudu, Tel.). From (above + narasimha, san. man-lion form of vishnu). Nine pagodas [q.v.] at Ahobalam.——*Nava naugam* (नवनाग - navanága, San.). From (above + nága, san. serpent). Nine serpents. See vol. I (82).——*Nava nauta siddhar* (நவநாதசித்தர் - navanáthasittar, Tam.). From (above + nát'ha, san. lord + siddha, san. saint). The nine lords [siddhan].——*Nava nidhy* (नवनिधि - navanidhi, San.). From (above + nidhi, san. treasure). Nine jewels held by Coobairan [q.v.], god of wealth. According to the tauntric system [tantram] these divine treasures are worshipped as demi-gods attendant either on coobairan the lord of Nidhies, or Lutchmy [q.v.] the goddess of prosperity. They are:—Pudmam or lotus-like, Maha pudmam or great lotus-like, Chunk or conch-like, Macaram or sword-fish-like, Cutchapam or tortoise-like, Moocoondam or quicksilver-like, Nundam or gem of felicity, Neelam or blue lotus-like, and Kharvam. Pudmam is gold in the form of lotus, and Chunk is gold in the form of conch. These two species of divine gold are held to possess life and yield whatever is desired. Compare the Nibelungs of the Teutons.——*Nava ratnam* (नवरत्न - navaratna, San.; نورتن - nauratan, Hind.). From (above + ratna, san. gem). The nine gems [ratnam]; coral [moongah], diamond [vajram], emerald [zamarrood], gomaidam [cinnamon stone], lapislazuli [veidooryam], pearl [moty], ruby [laul], sapphire [neelam] and topaz [pookhrauj]. An ancient ornament; compare Urim and Thummim of Jews. The churning of the ocean [samoodram] produced nine gems according to shastrams [coormam]. The nine gems were also nine distinguished poets at the court of Vicramadityan [q.v.]. Their names are by tradition as follows:—Amarasimhan, Calidass, Cshapanacan, Dhanvantary, Ghatacarparan, Shankoo, Vararoochy, Varauha mihiran, Vetaula bhattan.——*Navarautry* (నవరాత్రి - navarátri, Tel.; நவராத்திரி - navaráttiri, Tam.). Means nine nights. Same as Dusserah.——*Nava shacty* (नवशक्ति - navashakti, San.). From (above + shakti, san. power). Nine faculties personified; epithet of Shiva [q.v.] or Vishnoo [q.v.]. The nine personified female energies are:—Bramhauny, of Bramha; Caurtiky, of Soobramanyan; Indrauny, of Indran; Mauheshwary, of Shiva, the great lord; Naurasimhy, of Vishnoo in man-lion form; Pradhaunay, of the first originant; Rowdry, of Roodran; Varauhy, of Vishnoo in the form of a boar; Veishnavy, of Vishnoo. Compare Sapta mautah.——*Navaunicam* (నవానికము - navánikamu, Tel.). Means nine + daily observance. Any nine days' feast [pundigay, 6d]. Examples are Navarautry, Shreeramnavamy.——*Nawara* (നവര - navara, Mal.). From (navati, san. ninety); ninety-days paddy. A Malabar paddy [q.v.]. Sown in the month of Yedavam [mausam], May-June, and reaped in Carcatacam July-August. Rice light. Possesses medicinal properties. Carootta nawara is black; Nawara mookkouy is three-cornered; Velootta nawara is white. Distinguish from Nivvary [q.v.].——*Nowtauk* (నవటాకు - navatáku, Tel.). From (nava, san. nine + táku, tel. notch); one of a nine-notched tally or $\frac{1}{8}$th.—"*a*" Measure of weight. 2 chittacks = 1 nowtauk; 8 nowtauks = 1 pucka seer [niray, 2e]. Approximate actual value, 1 nowtauk = 4 oz. $1\frac{3}{5}$ drs. avoirdupois. Ganjam and Vizagapatam.—"*b*" Measure of capacity. 2 chittacks = 1 nowtauk; 2 nowtanks = 1 pow [alavay, 3e]. Approximate actual value, 1 nowtauk = $8\frac{3}{4}$ cubic inches. Used where pucka seer is used. Compare olluck. See vol. I, 609.

NAVAUR (نوار - navár, *Hind.*). Strong office tape.

NAVEES (نویس - navís, *Hind.*). From (navishtan, pers. to write) [nasindah, nauma]. A writer, secretary.——*Badar naveesy* (بدر نویسی - badarnavísí, Hind.). From (badar, pers. outside + navísí, pers. writing). Writing off items of an account [hisaub, lekka].——*Hoolis navees* (هولس نویس - húlisnavís, Hind.). Official in Canara analogous to modern Revenue inspector.——*Jawaub navees* (جواب نویس - jawábnavís, Hind.). From (jawáb, ar. answer + above). A clerk [goomasta] who reads reports and petitions [arzee] and drafts replies.——*Nasindah* (نویسنده - navísindah, Hind.). From (navishtan, pers. to write) [nauma, navees]. An accountant.

NAVITEY (నవితె - navite, *Tel.*).—"*a*" Measure of weight. 4 tooms = 1 navitey [niray, 2b]. Approximate actual value 1 navitey = 25 lbs. avoirdupois. Ganjam. Equal to 12 pucka seers of 80 tolahs each. Same as maund. Compare Toolaum.—"*b*" Measure of capacity. 4 tooms = 1 navitey; 5 naviteys = 1 pootty [alavay, 3b]. Approximate actual value, 1 navitey = 910 cubic inches. Ganjam. Compare Can. kulsy, Tel. cooncham of nellore, marcam of godavery, Mal. parrah.—"*c*" Superficial measure. Land requiring a navitey of seed. 20 naviteys = 1 bharnam [alavay, 2b]. Ganjam. As there are two bharnams wet and dry, so there are two naviteys. Compare puddy or nauzhy. See vol. I, 609; II, 510.

NAWAUZ (نواز - nawáz, *Hind.*). From (nawázidan, pers. to caress). Alam from the title of a saint; as Nawauz khan, alam + alaumat [ism].

NAYA (നായ - náya, *Mal.*). Dog [nye].——*Nayaudy* (നായാടി - náyáti, Mal.). From (above + ati, mal. to beat); hunters with dogs. The most degraded of Dravidian tribes, found scattered in jungles of Malabar. They are small in stature, of deep black color, and with hair bushy and curled. Not allowed to approach within 96 feet of Hindoos. They have neither homes nor implements; bushes afford them shelter and roots and proceeds of begging give food. There is a tradition that they are descendants of sons of Vasishtan [q.v.] cursed by Vishwamitran [q.v.] and this accounts for the Bramin [q.v.] names they bear. Numbers have become converts to Mahomedan faith [jauty].——*Nayautt* (നായാട്ട് - náyáttu, Mal.). From (above + áttam, mal. play). Hunting with dogs.

NAZARETH (நாசரத்து - násarattu, *Tam.*). After the town in Palestine. Village; Tinnevelly dist., Tencaray tal.; pop. 3,849; acres 2,947; lat. 8° 34′; long. 78° 01′; from Shreeveicoontam S.E. 6 miles; from Tinnevelly E.S.E. 23 miles; from the sea W. 11 miles. Mission station.——*Nasrauny* (نصرانی - nasrání, Hind.; നസ്രാണി - nasráni, Mal.). From the word nazarene. Malabar syrian christians [syrian].

NEDOO (നെടു - nedu, *Mal.*). Long.——*Nediyiroopp* (നെടിയിരിപ്പ് - netiyirippu, Mal.). From (above + iru, mal. to be). Prolonged existence. A place in Yernaud where the Zamorin's family once resided. The title of the Calicut or Zamorin [q.v.] dynasty [raj].——*Nediyone* (நெடியோன் - nediyón, Tam.). The tall one. Vishnoo [q.v.].——*Nedoom* (നെടും - netum, Mal.; நெடும் - nedum, Tam.). Long. Prefix in place names; as Nedoompalam, meaning long bridge.——*Nedoomaul* (நெடுமால் - nedumál, Tam.). From (mál, tam. vishnu). Same as Nediyone.——*Nedoomullay* (ನಿಡುಮಲೆ - nídumale, Can.). From (nídu, can. long + male, can. a hill). Can. also (himagala), meaning cold rock. Range of hills; Neilgherry district, Coondah and Todanaud divisions. One of three ranges into which the Neilgherries are popularly divided. A division of the Western ghauts which, after touching the coast line of Malabar, runs north and culminates in Neilgherry and Macoorty peaks. The Coondahs, another division, run south; and the central or principal range rises to the summit of Dodabetta.——*Nedootralpaud* (നെടുതറാൽപാട് ? - netutrálpátu, Mal.). From (above + tara, mal. village + pátu, mal. chief, title). The fifth prince of the Zamorin's family.——*Nidadvole* (నిడదవోలు - nidadavólu, Tel. nidadavólu *). From (niduda, tel. long + prólu, tel. town). Zemindarry, Village; Godavery dist., Tanookoo tal.; pop. of village 3,561; acres 6,761; lat. of village 16° 54′; long. 81° 43′; from Cocanada W.S.W. 37 miles; from Tanookoo N. 11 miles. For description of Zemindarry, see vol. I, 59. On the Ellore canal. Once the capital of the Puncha maha pautacas. Fort in the village constructed by Ibrahim shah of Golcondah as a protection to the Godavery frontier. Two old temples [coil]. Peshcush Rs. 1,15,050.

NEE (नी - ní, *San.*). To lead.——*Naick* (नायक - náyaka, San.; نایک - náyak, Hind.; నాయకుడు - náyakudu, Tel.; നായക്കൻ - náyakkan, Mal.; நாயக்கன் - náyakkan, Tam.). San. means a leader [naidoo]. In the army naick is a rank below havildar [q.v.] and equivalent to corporal. Naick is also another name for the Beydar caste. In poetry naick is the term for hero. In Southern india, the hereditary title of certain Teloogoo castes. In the early part of the sixteenth century, A.D. 1532, the great Hindoo state of Vijianugger established a Naick dynasty [raj], in the person of Vishwanauta naick, under its protection, at Madura. When the Vijianugger sovereignty fell, the Naick dynasty of Madura continued to be dominant. The founder of this dynasty, Vishwanautan, was the son of an officer of the king of Vijianugger. He established himself as king of Madura in 1559, and subjugated Trichinopoly soon afterwards. The greater portion of the fort of Trichinopoly and most of the city itself were built in his reign. The Naicks ruled Trichinopoly and Madura from 1559 to 1740. The greatest of them was the famous Trimal naick, who died in 1659. His grandson, Chokka naick, removed the capital of the kingdom from Madura to Trichinopoly, where he raised the building known as the Nawaub's palace. Its last ruler, a queen, was first aided and then betrayed by Chundah sahib of Tanjore. The ordinary name by which the Naick rulers of Madura are styled in the Tamul country is the Curtaukkal. See vol. I (122), (154); II, 250. Naickan in the Tamul country is a Hindoo third name; common among Vunniyar and

Pullies [peyar]. But more properly applied to Teloogoo shoodras, who have immigrated from the north; these are mostly clerks and farmers, but are also tradesmen, brokers, shopkeepers, and hawkers. In Malabar, Nayaka is the head of the village watch. ——*Naicknairy* (நாயக்கனேரி - náyakkanéri, Tam.). From (náyakkan, tam. title + éri, tam. tank). Village, Pass; North arcot dist., Pulmanair tal.; lat. 12° 57′; long. 78° 38′; from Chittore W.S.W. 39 miles; from Pulmanair S.S.W. 21 miles. Village at summit of pass, almost deserted. The trunk road to Bangalore used to pass up ghaut [q.v.] and on to Vencatagherry-cottah, 10 miles to W. Chuttram [q.v.] in ruins. Upon N. hill stands old fort, Peddanayeny droog, stronghold of Poligar [q.v.] of Chauragal, a village to the south. He rebelled in 1794 but was taken prisoner and his fort dismantled. He escaped from prison, and joining the Chittore poligars in rebellion was seized and hanged. Upon a hill to the south are kistvaens [paundi-coozhy].——*Naickvaudy* (నాయకవాడి - náyakavádi, Tel.). From (náyaka, san. leader + váda, tel. village). A peon attached to a village, a village watcher. The Taliyaur [q.v.] of Southern districts.——*Naidoo* (నాయుడు - náyadu, Tel.). Contracted from (náyakudu, tel.). Tel. form of Naick.——*Naidoopett* (నాయుడిపేట - náyadipéta, Tel. náyudupet*). From (náyadu, tel. naick + péta, tel. suburb); called after the naick or rajah of vencatagherry. Village, Head-quarters of Deputy collector; Nellore dist., Polore division of Vencatagherry zemindarry; pop. 2,621; lat. 13° 55′; long. 79° 56′; from Madras N.N.W. 64 miles; from Nellore S. 38 miles; from Ongle S. 111 miles; from Polore N.W. 16 miles; from Raupore S.E. 32 miles. On the right bank of the Swarna-mookhy. A hamlet of Vinnamaula. Junction of roads from Madras, Nellore, Calastry, Vencatagherry and Kota. Travellers' bungalow [q.v.]. Well supplied with trees and topes [q.v.]. A spring channel [q.v.] flows through it from the river. Lac [q.v.] bangles [gauzoo] made here and exported to Madras. Also the Cooncoomam powder worn by native females on the forehead. Old temple, not of any importance. Head-quarters of the ameel [q.v.] of the Zemindar [q.v.] of Vencatagherry.——*Naraca chatoordashy* (నరకచతుర్దశి - narakachaturdashi, Tel.). Means the asooran, so called + fourteenth lunar day; because in commemoration of the defeat and death of Naracausooran by Krishnau [q.v.]. Same as Deepauvaly.——*Naracam* (नरक - naraka, San.). From (nara, san. man + kai, san. to cry); place of punishment for man. Hell [pautaulam].——*Naracan* (नरक - naraka, San.). A demon, better known as Naracausooran.——*Narahary* (ನರಹರಿ - narahari, Can.). From (nara, san. man + hari, san. lion); epithet of vishnoo, the man-lion god. Hindoo 2nd or pers. name [narsimhan, peyar]. Confined to Madhwas. ——*Naran* (नर - nara, San.). From (ní, san. to lead); leader or controller. Man, individually or generally. The divine imperishable spirit pervading the universe [poorsham]. Water as the first product of Naran. Narayanan is he who moves on the water, Vishnoo [q.v.].——*Nara narayanan* (नरनारायण - naraná-ráyana, San.). Incarnate Vishnoo, krishnan. Also a compound name meaning arjoonan [q.v.] and krishnan [q.v.], naran referring to arjoonan as the best of men.——*Naranayyan* (நாராணய்யன் - náranayyan, Tam.). From (náráyana, san. vishnu, the water wanderer + aiyyan, tam. master). Familiarly Naunoo, Nauny. Hindoo 2nd or pers. name [peyar].——*Narapaty* (నరపతి - narapati, Tel.). From (nara, san. man + pati, san. ruler). Ruler of men. Andhra kings of Telingana [q.v.] whose capital was Warangal. Said to have been subjugated by Krishna deva royel of Vijianugger.——*Nurasa* (నరస - narasa, Tel.). Short for Narsimhan.——*Narayanan* (नारायण - náráyana, San.). From (nára, san. water + ayana, san. habitation). The divine spirit moving on the water. In the pure monotheistic system, the idea has a coincidence with Parabramh [q.v.] of the Oopanishads [q.v.]. In the pooranical statement Narayanan is represented as having been once reposing on the waters after the great deluge [pralayam], when a lotus [nelumbo] sprang from his navel, in which Bramha [q.v.] was born, and the latter proceeded to restore the creation [srishty]. Compare the expression in the Hebrew Genesis, that the spirit of god moved on the face of the waters. This title like Eeshwaran [q.v.] is claimed by the followers of the three principal deities. Vishnoo [q.v.] is however principally called Narayanan, in which character he is fabled to be sleeping on the serpent Sheshan [q.v.], or Anantan [q.v.], on the waters of eternity, and causing the creation of the world [srishty].——*Narayany* (नारायणी - náráyaní, San.). Lutchmy [q.v.], the wife of Vishnoo——*Narrain* (நாராயணன் - náráyanan, Tam.). Familiarly Naunoo, Nauny. Hindoo 2nd or pers. name [peyar]. Also as Narrainsawmy. ——*Narrainavaram* (నారాయణవరము - náráyanavaramu, Tel. náráyanavaram*). From (náráyana, san. vishnu, the mover on the waters + vana, san. forest). Sanscrit name (náráyanavana), means vishnoo forest.—"*a*" Sub-magistracy, Carvetnugger zemindarry, North arcot district. Pay Rs. 100.—"*b*" Village, Place of pilgrimage, River; Carvetnugger zemindarry; pop. 4,410; lat. 13° 26′; long. 79° 38′; from Arcot N.N.E. 40 miles; from Arnee N.N.E. 56 miles; from Carvetnugger E. 9 miles; from Chittore E.N.E. 37 miles; from Madras W.N.W. 52 miles; from Poottore E. 3 miles; from Ranipett N.N.E. 38 miles; from Tripatty S.E. 19 miles; from Vellore N.E. 46 miles. On the Arnauuddy, at base of Nagary hills, in the gap through which the river flows to Naugalaupooram. Coorumbar [q.v.] strongholds. Inscriptions found of Chalookya [q.v.], Pullava [q.v.], and Chola [q.v.] dynasties [raj]. Three miles S. is site of ancient town Acasarauzpooram, in village of Kempoolapolliem. The length of the idol's foot in this village is the standard measurement of length in the zemindarry [q.v.]. Bramhotsavam [pundigay, 6a] in May. Fair every Wednesday. Cloths are woven.——*Narsammah* (నరసమ్మ - narasamma, Tel.). From (narasa, tel. man-lion vishnoo, proper name + amma, tel. mother). Hindoo female proper name. Familiarly shortened into Narsa and Narasoo and Nasy [peyar].——*Narsannapett* (నరసన్నపేట - narasannapéta, Tel. narsannapet*). From (narasanna, tel. proper name + péta, tel. suburb).—"*a*" Deputy tahsildarry, Ganjam district. Pay Rs. 70.—"*b*" Town, Deputy tahsildar's station; Ganjam dist., Chicacole tal.; pop. 5,821; acres 1,023; lat. 18° 24′; long. 84° 05′; from Balligooda S.S.E. 122 miles; from Berhampore S.W. 78 miles; from Chetterpore S.W. 90 miles; from Chicacole N.E. 12 miles; from Madras N.E. 440 miles; from Russellcondah S.S.W. 111 miles; from the sea W. 9 miles.——*Narsapatam* (నరసపట్టణము - narasapattanamu, Tel. narsapatnam*). From (narasimha, san. proper name + pattana, san. town), called after the founder. Town, Head-quarters of Principal assistant collector, Assistant superintendent of Police and Tahsildar; Vizagapatam dist., Golcondah tal.; pop. 5,279; acres 1,686; lat. 17° 40′; long. 82° 39′; from Coraputt S. 77 miles; from Madras N. 349 miles; from Parvatipore S.S.W. 91 miles; from Vizagapatam W. 44 miles; from Vizianagram W. 60 miles. Ruined mud fort, built by Narsimha gajapaty of Vizianagram.——*Narsapore* (నరసాపురము - narasá-puramu, Tel.). See sep. title.——*Narsarowpett* (నరసారావుపేట - narasárávupéta, Tel.). See sep. title.——*Narsimha* (నరసింహ - narsimha, Tel.). From (nara, san. man + simha, san. lion). Second of the three Vijiaungger dynasties. See vol. I (148); II, 251.——*Narsimha avatar* (नरसिंहावतार - narasimhávatára, San.). From (narasimha, san. man-lion + avatára, san. incarnation). The fifth or man-lion avatar [q.v.] of Vishnoo [q.v.]. A king called Hiranya cashipoo had a son named Prahlaudan, one who was a devoted servant of Vishnoo, and much celebrated for his virtues. On these accounts, and especially as being a votary of Vishnoo, his father persecuted him. At a time when Prahlaudan's life was in danger, Vishnoo burst from one of the pillars of the palace in the shape of a man-lion, killed the king, and drank his blood. With this legend may be compared the remains at Nineveh, where the pillars of palaces were made in the shape of a winged lion with a human face. See vol. I (79). ——*Narsimhacondah* (నరసింహకొండ - narasimhakonda, Tel.). From (narasimha, san. man-lion god + konda, tel. hill). Sanscrit name (védagiri), meaning sacred writing + hill. Hill; Nellore dist., Nellore tal.; lat. 14° 27′; long. 79° 56′; from Nellore W. 7 miles; from the sea W. 20 miles. On the opposite side of the large tank near Nellore, in village of Moolmoody. Important temple dedicated to Narsimhasawmy. Forms triad with Runganaicksawmy at Nellore and Zonnavauda. Europeans visit spot for picnics. Trig. station in lat. 14° 27′ 29·80″; long. 79° 55′ 12·53″; from Nellore W. 7 miles; from Zonnavauda S.S.W. 1¾ miles; from the sea W. 20 miles.——*Narsimha jayanty* (నరసింహజయంతి - narasimhajayanti, Tel.). Means man-lion god + birthday. Lunar [chaundramaunam] festival [pundigay, 6c], subject to intercalation [adhicam]. Fourteenth day of the waxing moon [shooclapacsham] of second lunar month Veishaukham [mausam] between 28th April and 27th May. Anniversary of Vishnoo's Narsimha avatar [q.v.]; devout Bramins fast; observed in temples; it lasts nine days and processions are made provided any person will be at the expense [maryauday].——*Narsimha moorty* (नरसिंहमूर्ति - narasimhamúrti, San.). From (narasimha, san. man-lion vishnoo + múrti, san. embodiment). Vishnoo.——*Narsimhan* (नरसिंह - narasimha, San.; நரசிங்கம் - narasingam, Tam.). From (nara, san. man + simha, san. lion). Epithet of Vishnoo, the man-lion god. Hindoo 2nd or pers. name. Familiarly shortened into Narsa and Narsoo [peyar]. ——*Narsimhooloo* (నరసింహులు - narsimhulu, Tel.). Plural of Narsimhan. Hindoo 2nd or pers. name [peyar].——*Narsingam* (ನರಸಿಂಗ - narasinga, Can.; நரசிங்கன் - narasingan, Tam.). From (nara, san. man + simha, san. lion). Dravidian form of narsimhan [q.v.] above. Old european name for Vijianugger dynasty [raj]. The original dynasty became extinct about 1487, and was replaced by one Narsimhan, who reigned at the time of first arrival of Portuguese. See vol. I (150); II, 251. Narsinga deo again was Gajapaty king of Orissa, surnamed Langoolya, 1237 to 1282, who extended his conquests to Nellore and founded about 185 temples in Oodayagherry talook; he built the great sun temple at Canaurac called the Black pagoda. ——*Narsing row* (نرسنگ راو - narsingráú, Hind.; నరసింగరావు - narasingarávu, Tel.). Proper name [peyar].——*Nauchy* (நாச்சி - náççi, Tam.). Feminine of Nayan. Mistress. Also as Nauchiyaur.——*Nauradan* (नारद - nárada, San.; நாரதன் - nárathan, Tam.). From (nara, san. man + dá, san. to give); giving counsel to man or mankind. ἑρμῆς of Greeks; Mercury of Romans; Apis of Egyptians. Son of Bramha [q.v.]; god of music [sangeetam]. There was a sage of this name. Hindoo third name [peyar].——*Nauram* (नार - nára, San.). From (ní, san. to lead); as leading to usefulness. Water.——*Nayágan* (நாயகன் - náyagan, Tam.). A leader [naick]; master [nautan]. Epithet of the Supreme being, especially of Shiva [q.v.]. Suffix in Tamul proper names among non-bramins; as Devanayagam, Tillainayagam [peyar].——*Nayan* (நாயன் - náyan, Tam.). From (ní, san. to lead). Master.——*Nayanaur* (நாயனார் - náyanár, Tam.). Honorific form of above. Shiva. Epithet of any of the sixty-three devotees of shiva [aroopatt moover]. A Jeina [q.v.] title. Hindoo third name [peyar].——*Nayar* (നായർ - náyar, Mal.). From (náyaka, san. leader). Hon. plural is Nayammaur.—"*a*" Name allied to Teloogoo Naidoo, Tamul and Canarese Naicken and Hindostany Naick. All these are titles of respect, applied in the manner that Sahib [q.v.] is at the end of a name.—"*b*" So specifically the Shoodras of Malabar. The Greek *νάουρα* as a tract stood for the country of the Nayars. Cf. *ἀριακή* for the part of the Malabar coast principally occupied by the Aryan [q.v.] or Mahratta [q.v.] bramins [q.v.]. The highest class among malabar nayars is that of the Kiriyatt nayars. For the undivided family life of the Nayars see Avibhactam and Tarwaud. For their marriage customs and their Maroomakkatoyem [q.v.] system of succession to rights or property, see vol. I (111), foot-note. There are traces of resemblance between the customs of the Nayar and those of the Maravar [q.v.] of Ramnaud. The sub-divisions of Nayars are too numerous to specify [jauty]. See vol. I (16), (17), (67), (111), foot-note and vol. II, 100.——*Nayar brigade* (മലയാംഗാട് - malayámgát, Mal.). From (malayálam, mal. malabar + gát, corruption of guard). A force of about 1,400 men, chiefly Nayars, maintained by the Travancore state. It is commanded by European officers of the Madras army appointed by the British government.——*Nayar naud* (நாயருநாடு - náyarunádu, Tam.). Part of Pozhal [q.v.] cottam [q.v.] in the ancient Tondaimundalam [q.v.]. In the present Ponnairy talook, Chinglepnt district.——*Neem* (نیم - ním, Hind.). See sep. title.——*Neetinery vilacum* (நீதிநெறிவிளக்கம் - níthinerivilakkam, Tam.). From (níti, san. justice + neri, tam. path + vilakkam, tam. illustration). A rather modern Tamul moral treatise. By Coomaragooroopara desican, born at Shreeveicoontam, became Tumbiraun [q.v.] of mutt at Dharmapooram, ended his life as head of a mutt [q.v.] at Benares. The work treats of four great objects of human desire; virtue, riches, enjoyment, and final beatitude [aram]. Arranged more or less after the fashion of the Cooral [q.v.] and the Nauladiyaur [q.v.].——*Neety* (नीति - níti, San.). Conduct in all the relations of domestic, social and political life. Justice, morality, obligation. The aim of Neety shastram is to serve as guide to correct conduct in the relations of domestic, social, and political life. Such are either collections of choice maxims, striking thoughts, and wise sentiments in the form of metrical stanzas; or else books of fables in prose which string together stories about animals and amusing apologues for the sake of the moral they contain [punchatantram]. The regular collections of moral maxims, sentiments, &c., are generally in metrical stanzas. The Dravidian writings which would be considered part of Neety shastram are such works as Cooral, Nauladiyaur, &c. They form the principal and characteristic part of Dravidian literature. The collections of fables and apologues are analogous to the works of the greek Æsop and the arabian Locmaun [q.v.]. There are no indigenous works of this sort among the Dravidians, though there are various translations from the Sanscrit.——*Nein* (نین - nain, Hind.). From (nayana, san. eye). Eye.——*Neinsook* (نین سکھ - nainsukh, Hind.). Title from (nain, hind. eye + sukh, hind. comfort). A kind of muslin [mull].——*Nemiyone* (நேமியோன் - némiyón, Tam.). Means discus one. Vishnoo [q.v.].——*Nemmy* (नेमि - némí, San.; काळापलस - kálápalasa, Mahr.; ನೇಹಿಮರ - néhimara, Can.; నెమ్మి - nemmi, Tel.; ବାନ୍ଧୋନ - bándhona, Oor.). Title from teloogoo. San. means wheel, from wood being used in making wheels of chariots. Mahr. from (kálá, mahr. black + palásha, san. butea frondosa, roxb.). Tel. from sanscrit. San. also (syandaná), meaning chariot, the tree was used in constructing chariot-wheels; (atimukta), meaning surpassing pearls in whiteness [madablota, musk jasmine]; (rat'hadru), meaning chariot tree; (vañjula), meaning desired [bengal ashocam]; (chitrakrit), meaning causing wonder; (tinisha), meaning lasting for nights, long-standing. Can. also (karimutal). Tel. also (mandamotuku); (tellamotuku); (dargu). Title otherwise Chariot tree, Syandanam, Tinisham. Botanically Ougenia dalbergioides, benth., leguminosæ [vricsham, 48]. Alias Dalbergia oojeinensis. Tree, 30 feet; leaves pinnately trifoliolate; leaflets ovate, roundish, rather villous, with undulated curved margins; pedicels one-flowered, rising in fascicles, and as well as the calyx villous; flowers smallish, pale rose, fragrant; flowering in hot season; leaves appear after blossoms; of slow growth, and attains full size in about thirty years. Kino [q.v.] from bark, useful in bowel-complaints. In hot weather branches given as fodder to cattle. Gives astringent red gum [gond]. Wood hard, strong and very tough, heavy and close-grained, not unlike sissoo [q.v.], but handsome; much used; a crystalline substance like magnesia is sometimes found in the wood. No other common species here.——*Nemy* (நேமி - némi, Tam.). From (ní, san. to lead). Wheel. Discus [chuckram].——*Netram* (नेत्र - nétram, San.). From (ní, san. to lead). Eye.——*Netrauvaty* (ನೇತ್ರಾವತಿ - nétrávati, Can. netrávati*). From (nétra, can. eye + vat, can. suffix of possession). River; South canara dist., Mangalore and Ooppinangady tals. Formed at Ooppinangady by the junction of the Netrauvaty proper and the Comauradhaury. The Netrauvaty proper rises in Mysore on the Western ghauts [q.v.] in lat. 13° 10′ and long. 75° 26′ and the Comauradhaury in Coorg. From Ooppinangady the united stream flows to Mangalore, and forms the southern and partly the western boundary of that place. It is affected by the tide to a distance of ten miles, and boats carrying about four tons can at all seasons ascend up to Buntwaul. In the rainy season they can go forty miles up or a few miles above Ooppinangady.——*Nossam* (నొసం - nósam,* Tel.). Corruption of (narasimham, tel. vishnu, the man-lion god). Town; Kurnool dist., Coilcoontla tal.; pop. 2,706; acres 9,261; lat. 14° 59′; long. 78° 26′; from Coilcoontla S. 18 miles; from Kurnool S. 62 miles. Former residence of a powerful Poligar [q.v.], who gave much trouble to the Cuddapah nawaubs [q.v.]. The Reddy ancestors of this family were, under the Vijianugger government, principal Potails [q.v.] of Chenchely mullay, and Deshmookhs [q.v.] of Cumbum, and kept up a body of peons [q.v.], for part of whose substance they had an assignment of fifty-four villages. On the decline of the Vijianugger power they seized the assigned villages. They were reduced by the Cootb shahy princes of Hyderabad, two years later, and permitted to hold their possession [cottacote, moondlapaud, velgode]. The family is extinct. Lacquered ware is manufactured. Weekly market on Wednesdays. Annual festival in Boogga venkateshwarasawmy's temple on fourteenth Jyeshtam [mausam] in June.——*Nowshaudar* (नवसागर - navaságara, San.; ارمینا - arminá, Ar.; نوسادر - nausádar, Hind.; نوساگر - nauságar, Dec.; سدار - sadár, Malay; ನವಸಾಗರ - navaságara, Can.; నవాసారము - navásáramu, Tel.; നവസാരം - navasáram, Mal.; නවසාර - navasára, Singh.; நவாசாரம் - navásáram, Tam.). San. corruption of (narasára, san. essence of man). Tam. also (sháram), meaning essence. Otherwise Nowsaugar. Sal ammoniac. Ammoniæ hydrochloras, Murias ammoniæ, Ammonii chloridum, of chemists. A compound formed by acids [tezaub] in union with alkalies [cauram], earth and metallic oxides. Not sal ammoniac of the ancients, which was impure common salt [ooppoo], perhaps rock salt [sondah namak]. Occurs in colorless, inodorous, translucent tough, fibrous masses, difficult to pulverise, but soluble in water, and of salt cold taste; that met with in bazaar is from unburnt residue of brick kilns [shoolay], in which manure of animals is used as fuel; this is chemically impure. May be formed by neutralizing hydrochloric acid with ammonia and evaporating to dryness. A mineral drug; used sometimes in solution with nitre as a lotion, and also internally as a resolvent; its nauseous taste, which is a great objection to its use, is covered by the addition of liquorice [indian liquorice]; its chief use however is to prepare a rough carbonate of ammonia [soongnah], by rubbing it in palm of hand with a little lime [choonam], this is smelt to relieve headache; in pharm. this substance is alterative in small and continued doses, in larger doses stimulant; the pharm. has also benzoate, carbonate, phosphate, bromide, acetate, citrate, &c., of ammonia. With nitre [shorah] in large quantities nowshaudar is a freezing mixture; it is used by solderers [pattoo] and tinmen to clean surface of metals [loham] and facilitate union between tin [tagaram] and iron [auhan] or copper [taumram]; also by dyers to brighten colors [shanyam]. For Sal volatile see Soongnah.

NEEL (नील - níla, *San.*; نیل - níl, *Hind.*). Means blue-black.—"*a*" Mammal first term. Ex., where transl. is of second term:—Macacus silenus (nílamanti), monkey, macacus genus, and (nílan), blue-black one; Portax pictus (nílgái), cow, bos indicus, and (nílgáú), cow, bos indicus. See gloss. paragraphs.—"*b*" Plant first term often joining two genera. Ex., where transl. is of second term:—Ægle marmelos (nílamalliká), jasminum sambac; Cuscuta reflexa (nílátár), thread; Dædalacanthus nervosus (nílámbramu), sky, (nílamulli), thorny plant; Evolvulus alsinoides (nílapushpí), flower; Ipomæa hederacea (nílkalmí), quill, from stem; Justicia gendarussa (nílanirgundí), vitex negundo; Mangifera indica (nílakapitt'ha), feronia elephantum; Monochoria vaginalis (nílattámarai), nelumbium speciosum; Oryza sativa (nílamañjari), flower-cluster; Phyllanthus maderaspatensis (nílakkadambai), anthocephalus cadamba; Plumbago capensis (nílachitramúla), plumbago zeylanicum, (nílashikhá), crest; Portulaca quadrifida (nílaccíra), greens; Wrightia tomentosa (nílampála), milk plant. See gloss. paragraphs.——*Neelacuntan* (नीलकण्ठ - nílakant'ha, San.). From (above + kant'ha, san. throat). A name of Shiva [q.v.], from his having a blue throat, caused by drinking the poison produced at the churning of the ocean [coormam]. Hindoo 2nd or pers. name [peyar].——*Neelacunty* (نیل کنٹھی - nílkanthí, Hind.; حسینی پدا - husaínípiddá, Dec.). Hind. from (níl, hind. blue + kanthí, hind. throat); cf. indian jay. Dec. from (husn, ar. beautiful + piddá, hind. black robin). Title otherwise Indian bluethroat. Cyaneula suecica, ruticillinæ, sylviadæ [calacuntam], dentirostres, insessores [pacshy, 23], of naturalists [jantoo]. Alias Cyaneula indica, suecicoides; Motacilla cœrulecula. Throat and breast bright shining azure-blue. No other common species here.——*Neelak* (नीलक - nílaka, San.). Unknown quantity in algebra [caulak, roopam].——*Neelam* (इन्द्रनील - indraníla, San.; ياقوت ازرق - yákútiazrak, Ar.; ياقوت كبود - yákútikabúd, Pers.; نيلم - nílam, Hind.; ನೀಲ - níla, Can.; నీలము - nílamu, Tel.; നീലക്കല്ലു - nílakkallu, Mal.; நீலம் - nílam, Tam.). Title from hindostany. San. from (indra, san. best + níla, san. blue). Ar. from (yákút, ar. garnet + azrak, ar. blue). Pers. from (yákút, ar. garnet + kabúd, pers. blue). Can., Tel. and Tam. from (níla, san. blue). Mal. means blue stone. Sapphire. After the diamond [vajram], the most valuable of gems [ratnam]. The colors are blue, red, grey, white, green, and yellow; the most prized are crimson and carmine red. The best are brought from Burmah; those found in Ceylon, though genuine, are much less beautiful. In that island the green sapphire is common.——*Neelan* (நீலன் - nílan, Tam.). The black man. Feminine Neely. Pariah proper name [peyar]. ——*Neelapully* (నీలపల్లి - nílapalli, Tel.). From (níli, tel. indigo, indigofera tinctoria, linn. + palli, tel. village). Zemindarry, Town, Port; Godavery dist., Cocanada division; pop. 3,700; lat. of town 16° 44′; long. 82° 16′; from Cocanada S. 15 miles; from Coringa S. 5 miles; from Injaram E. 3 miles; from Madras N.N.E. 278 miles; from Yanam E. 1 mile. Peshcush Rs. 479. On the Godavery. English factory established 1751, captured by Bussy in 1757. Once a place of commercial importance [bendamoorlunka]. Rice [q.v.] factory. ——*Neelaumbram* (اودجتی - udujati, Hind.; ಕಪ್ಪುಬೊಬ್ಬುಳಿ - kappu-bobbuli, Can.; నక్కతోక - nakkatóka, Tel.; കരിങ്കുറിഞ്ഞി - karinkuriñũi, Mal.; நீலாம்பரம் - nílámbaram, Tam.). Title from tamul [blue nail dye]; cf. dædalacanthus. Can. from (kappu, can. black + bobbuli. can. thorn tree, acacia). Tel. from (nakka, tel. fox + tóka, tel. tail). Mal. from (karu, mal. black + kuriñũi, mal. the plant, barleria). Tam. from (níla, san. blue + ambara, san. sky); from pale blue flowers. Can. also (kappu-kurni), meaning black + the plant, barleria. Mal. also (kuranta), meaning earth + delightening. Tam. also (nílámbari), meaning sky blue, from flowers. Title otherwise Black nail dye, Fox tail. Botanically Ecbolium linneanum, kurz., acanthaceæ [vricsham, 101]. Alias Justicia ecbolium. Shrubby; spikes terminal, four-sided; bracteas oval, entire, ciliate, mucronate, equalling the fruit; leaves elliptic-oblong, attenuated at both ends, pubescent; upper lip of the corolla linear, reflexed; flowers large, greenish livid; tube very long and slender; there are varieties dentata and rotundifolia; no other species here. Neelaumbram is also same as Blue nail dye. Compare also:—Barleria cristata (tellanílámbari), white ditto; Dædalacanthus nervosus (nallanílámbram), black ditto; see gloss. paragraphs. ——*Neeleshwar* (ನೀಲೇಶ್ವರ - níléshvara, Can.). From (níla, san. blue + íshvara, san. lord).—"*a*" Deputy tahsildarry, South canara district. Pay Rs. 70.—"*b*" Town; South canara dist., Cassergode tal.; pop. 9,842; lat. 12° 15′; long. 75° 10′; from Cassergode S.S.E. 19 miles; from Mangalore S.S.E. 46 miles; from the sea E. 2 miles. Southernmost town of Canara and old limit of Keralam [q.v.]. Residence of a rajah descended from the house of the zamorin [q.v.], whose ancestors ruled the northern portion of the Malayalam country.—"*c*" River; South canara district, Cassergode talook; rises in Coorg; flows in a south-westerly direction and falls into the Arabian sea. Length about forty-seven miles. Lies for the most part in South canara. Country craft of small burthen can enter its mouth for a short distance.——*Neely* (नीली - nílí, San.). From (níla, san. dark-blue); from the dye.—"*a*" Botanically the Indigofera genus, leguminosæ [vricsham, 48]. Annual or perennial herbaceous plants or shrubs; leaves pinnate; flowers rose-purplish, bluish or white; fruit a cylindrical or four-sided, straight or curved pod, with many seeds. The species best known to the natives are:—anil [west-indian indigo], argentea [arabian indigo], argentea, var. cærulea [wild indigo], aspalathoides [shiva's neem], echinata [black nerinjy], enneaphylla [red nerinjy], hirsuta [large zanzibar indigo], pentaphylla [dog green gram], tinctoria [common indigo], viscosa [dog neem]. Other s. indian species indigenous or naturalized are:—atropurpurea, cordifolia, glandulosa, linifolia, marginulata, mysorensis, parviflora, pauci-folia, pedicellata, pulchella, subulata, tenuifolia, trifoliata, trita, uniflora, wightii.—"*b*" The dark one. Parvaty [q.v.].——*Neilgherry* (நீலகிரி - nílagiri, Tam.). See sep. title.——*Nilghye* (ऋश्य - rishya, San.; रूही - ruhí, Mahr.; نيل گاو - nílgáú, Hind.; نيل گائی - nílgáí, Dec.; ಮರವಿ - maravi, Can.; మనుపోతు - manu-pótu, Tel.; ଘୋଡ଼ଙ୍ଗ - ghodango, Oor.; വെൺപെരുമാൻ - venperumán, Mal.; கடமை - kadamai, Tam.). Title from hindostany. San. from (ri, san. to go). Mahr. from (róhita, san. nilghye). Hind. from (níl, hind. blue + gáú, hind. cow). Tel. from (mannu, tel. earth + pótu, tel. male buffalo). Oor. means horse-bodied. Mal. from (ven, mal. white + peru, mal. large + mán, mal. deer). Tam. from (kadam, tam. forest + má, tam. animal). San. also (róhita). Hind. also (roz). Title otherwise White-footed antelope. Portax pictus, antilopinæ, bovidæ, ruminantia, mammalia [sastanam, 23], of naturalists [jantoo]. Alias Antilope trago-camelus; Damalis risia; risia from sanscrit. Male of an iron-gray color; lips, chin, lower surface of the tail, stripes inside the ears, rings on the fetlocks, and abdomen, white; head and limbs tinged with sepia-brown; mane, throat tuft, and tip of tail, black. The female is smaller than the male, and tawny or light brown. Length of a male about 6½ to 7 feet; height at the shoulder 4 feet 4 inches to 4½ feet; horns 8 to 9 inches, rarely 10; ear 7, very broad; tail 18 to 21 inches. Rare in the extreme south. It does not occur in Ceylon. Frequents thin forests, and low jungles. It does not affect a hilly country. Not much sought after by sportsmen, nor is its flesh highly esteemed. Is in appearance a mixture of antelope [jinka], bull [maud], and horse [ghorah]. Held peculiarly sacred by Hindoos, from its fancied kinship to the cow [pashoo].

NEEM (निम्ब - nimba, *San.* and *Mahr.*; बेवा - bévá, *Conc.*; آزاد درخت هندی - ázáddarakhtihindí, *Pers.*; نيمب - nínb, *Hind.*; نيم - ním, *Dec.*; ಬೇವು - bévu, *Can.* and *Too.*; వేప - vépa, *Tel.*; വേപ്പ് - véppu, *Mal.*; කොහොඹ - kohomba, *Singh.*; வேம்பு - vémbu, *Tam.*). Title from sanscrit through deccany. San. from (ní, san. to lead) [nee]; leading to health. Pers. from (ázáddarakht, pers. lilac, melia azedarach, linn. + hindí, pers. indian). Hind. and dec. from sanscrit. Mal. from (vévu, mal. to burn); the tree is proverbial for heat. Tam. from (vé, tam. to heat). San. also (ravipriyá), meaning sun favorite; (vrana-shódhakari), meaning sore cleaner; (arishta), meaning unhurt [black datura, soapnut]; (sarvatóbhadra), meaning good in every way; (hinguniryása), meaning having gum like that of ferula narthex, boiss.; (pichumarda), meaning destroying cooshtam. Mahr. also (bálantanimba), meaning woman after delivery + neem tree, chips used in feeding fire on the occasion; (limba), by corruption. Hind. also (arishtu), from sanscrit. Can. also (hebbévu), meaning big + the tree; (ollebévu), meaning good neem tree. Mal. also (áryavéppu), meaning the aryan neem tree; (rájavéppu), meaning royal neem tree; (áryatikta), meaning aryan bitter, to distinguish from (anáryatikta), the bitter plant of non-aryans [chiretta]. Singh. also (kosamba). Tam. also (arulurithi), meaning favor + strength; (shangu-maru). Title otherwise Ash-leaved bead tree, Margosa being portuguese for bitter, Neemb, Vaimboo, Vaipa. Botanically Melia azadirachta, linn., meliaceæ [vricsham, 36]. Specific name from persian meaning free tree. Alias Aria bepon; Azadirachta indica; Azedarach deletaria, fraxinifolia. Aria bepon is malayalam. Tree, 20 feet; calyx five-partite; petals five; anthers ten on the throat of the stamen tube; leaves pinnated; leaflets ovate-lanceolate, unequal-sided, acuminated, serrated; panicles axillary; flowers small, white, honey scented; fruit, when ripe, purple, size of a small olive [zeitoon], one-celled, one-seeded. A common, quick-growing, and handsome tree, putting forth leaves in hot season; every part especially the bark is bitter; bark varies much in appearance, according to the size and age of the tree; within the fleshy portion of the fruit is a thin hard woody shell, which encloses an oily bitter kernel like a small filbert [findak], greenish white, with a brown testa; the dried fruit resembles a small raisin, the inner portion of the pulp is adherent to the stone, and fibrous from the presence of very large liber cells; the oil expressed from fruit is of a pale yellow color and bitter taste; it has a powerful garlic-like [lussoon] odour; a true gum [gond] exudes like wood-apple [q.v.] gum, occurring in lumps and tears varying from a light yellow to a dark-brown color with slightly bitter taste; stem, &c., yield a sap or toddy. The bark from trunk is covered with a thick scaly epidermis, and varies in thickness from one-fourth to half an inch; that from the small branches is smooth, of a dullish purple color, marked by longitudinal lines of ash-colored epidermis, from one-eighth to one-twelfth of an inch apart; the inner layer of the bark, of a whitish color in the freshy state, is powerfully bitter, far more so than the outer dark-colored layer, which however possesses a greater amount of astringency; there is no difference between bark and root-bark. From the dried bark is obtained an amorphous resin [raul], which is the bitter principle; this resin is soluble in the usual solvents and in boiling solutions of fixed alkalies [cauram], and from the latter it is precipitated by acids [poolipp, tezaub], but in an altered form. The gum is yellowish, like inferior gum-arabic [q.v.], generally in longish vermiform pieces, not bitter, and freely soluble in cold water; it is unaffected by neutral acetate of lead [eeya carcaud], gives a curdy white precipitate with basic acetate, a reddish gelatinous precipitate with ferric chloride, is unaffected by borax [vengauram], which it turns of a dull red color; iodine does not affect it, but it precipitates with oxalate of ammonia; it makes a weak mucilage, and is of little value. The margosa toddy [q.v.] is yielded either spontaneously or extracted artificially. In the former case, a clear and colorless liquid begins to flow in a very thin stream or continuous drops from two or three parts of the plant, and continues to do so from three to seven weeks; the trunk and large branches and roots are the parts from which the flow takes place through very small and recent cracks or fissures, and the quantity of the liquid discharged in the 24 hours from the whole tree varies from two to eight bottles according to its size; before the sap begins to flow, a rushing or pumping noise of a liquid is heard within the trunk. The trees which yield the sap artificially are more rare; a root being exposed by removing the earth, it is cut through or only half through and a vessel placed beneath; the sap thus collected is comparatively small in quantity. The neem tree is dedicated to Mauriyamman [q.v.]; for this reason in small-pox epidemics, the leaves are spread on bed of the patient, fans made of them are used for fanning him, and a bunch of them is fixed above the door as a sign of the presence of the goddess in the house; on the decline of the disease, the whole body is covered with the leaves. In some parts of the country the neem will not grow on its own roots, but only when budded on its larger congener, the melia azedarach, linn. [large neem]. Every part except the wood, that is to say the bark, root-bark, young fruit, nuts or seeds, oil, flowers, leaves, gum and toddy, are medicinal; the root-bark, bark and young fruit are tonic and antiperiodic; the oil, nuts, and leaves are local stimulant, insecticide, and antiseptic; the flowers are stimulant-tonic and stomachic; the gum is demulcent-tonic; the toddy is refrigerant, nutrient and alterative tonic. Preparations of the root-bark, bark and young fruit are decoction, tincture and powder. Decoction; take of the inner layer of the root-bark, cut into small pieces, four ounces, water two pints, boil on a slow fire till the liquid is reduced to one pint, and strain while hot; decoction of bark precisely in same manner; in both cases fresh bark preferable to dry and old; in decoction of fruit, they should be selected before attaining half natural size, cut into small slices and dried in the sun, and then their proportion to the water and the method of boiling and straining are the same as in the decoction of the root-bark. Tincture; take of the inner layer of the root-bark or bark, in coarse powder, four ounces, alcohol or proof spirit one pint, macerate for seven days in a closed vessel with occasional agitation, press, filter and add more spirit, if necessary, to make one pint. Powder; the inner layer of the root-bark or bark, or the dry young fruit; may be reduced to powder, passed through a fine sieve and kept in a closed vessel. Preparations of the leaves, nuts and oil are decoction, paste or poultice, and solution. Decoction; take of the fresh leaves, four ounces; water, two pints; boil till the liquid is reduced to half of its quantity, and strain when cool. Paste or poultice; bruise and rub the fresh leaves with hot or cold water in a stone mortar till they are reduced to a soft and pulpy mass. Solution; bruise and rub the kernel of the nuts with cocoanut [q.v.] oil, water or some other liquid, in a mortar till it becomes well mixed and thin. The oil is either applied by itself or in combination with other drugs, as chaulmoogra [q.v.] oil, &c. Preparation of the flowers is the infusion; take of the flowers, three ounces, hot water, one pint or just sufficient to cover the flowers, infuse in a covered vessel for an hour and strain. Preparation of the gum is mucilage, prepared same as indian gum-arabic. There is no preparation of the sap or margosa toddy, it being always used alone. Doses; of the decoction of the root-bark, bark or young fruit, from one and-a-half to three fluid ounces; of the tincture of the root-bark or stem bark, from one to three fluid drachms; of the powder of any of the above drugs, from one to two drachms; of the infusion of flowers, from one and-a-half to three fluid ounces; of the mucilage of gum, from one to two fluid ounces; of toddy, from two to four fluid ounces. Substituted; the root-bark, bark and young fruit, for cinchona-bark [koinah] and gentian [chiretta]; the oil, nuts and leaves, for carbolic acid; the flowers, for elder flowers, and coriander [cassibor], aniseed [anise] and dill [sowa] oils; the gum, for acacia [babool] and feronia [wood apple] gums; the toddy, for elm bark, diluted phosphoric acid, jamaica sarsaparilla [sarsaparilla china root] and chaulmoogra [q.v.] and cod-liver oils. Bark in decoction and powder is a remedy in ague or intermittent fever, convalescence after fevers, general debility, and loss of appetite; leaves beaten into pulp are externally applied in pustular eruptions, rheumatism, bruises and sprains; a watery or vinous infusion of the leaves is applied to bruises after the application of leeches [attay], and effect is heightened when spirit of camphor is sprinkled over the cloth, steeped in the infusion; dried leaves added to common poultices to prevent glandular tumours from coming to maturity; acrid bitter deep yellow oil, from pericarp of seeds has valuable antispasmodic properties anthelmintic and stimulant, used in leprosy [cooshtam] and as liniment for rheumatic affections; bark gum is stimulant; fruit antiseptic, purgative, emollient and anthelmintic; air passing through neem trees is thought to be highly beneficial to health, and hence the practice among the natives of planting neem trees near their dwelling houses; when carefully prepared the toddy [q.v.], is an excellent stomachic, being taken in doses of about one ounce; gives to pharm. the bark, azadirachtæ cortex: and the fresh leaves, azadirachtæ folia; bark, astringent tonic, and antiperiodic; leaves stimulant; bark used like cinchona; officinal; the air waved with a neem branch is supposed to be a cure for syphilis; the insane are passed through a cleft of the tree, or a stem which having parted and re-united forms a circular opening. Flower is edible; leaves being slightly bitter are put into curry [q.v.]; the leaves are chewed at funeral ceremonies; also simply parched and eaten; pulp between the skin and the seed of the fruit is used as famine food. Margosa cake [ponnauk] is used as a manure in planting districts; the powdered cake, like linseed [alsee] meal, makes a very useful luting in chemical and physical laboratories, and is not liable to the attack of insects [poochy]; leaves also useful in keeping away the boring worm from books; the kernels powdered and mixed with water used for washing the hair; the oil used for imparting colors [shauyam] to cotton [q.v.] cloths; small branches used as tooth brushes; oil sometimes burned in lamps, but emits a heavy and disagreeable smoke; oil makes a good, useful hard soap [sauboon]; trunk yields gum included among gum ghautty [q.v.] of commerce; bark yields a fibre [naur]; tree much used for planting road-sides [shaulay], but the foliage is deciduous. Wood very like mahogany, mottled, hard and heavy, used for cart wheels and ordinary building purposes; old trees yield excellent furniture; wood well adapted for ship-building; so bitter that no insect will attack it. Of this species there are two varieties; one which has a black appearance is called black neem in vernaculars; the other with green prickly leaves, which have an exceedingly bitter taste, is known as arya black neem. There is a Tamul proverb:—வீட்டில் அழகு வேம்பு அடியாகும்—"The shade of a neem tree is good for a house." There is another:—வேப்பெண்ணெய் விருந்து எண்ணெய் அல்ல, மருந்து எண்ணெய்—"Neem oil is not used in entertain-"ments; it is medicinal." The following is a Hindostany proverb:—ایک نیم سب گھر سیتل—"One neem tree cools the "whole house." The following is from Vemana:—[illegible]—"By talking and conversing, affection "increases; as you continue to eat even the bitter neem leaf, "it becomes sweet; so by practice may we succeed in any art "whatever."——(1) *Neemgherry* (నింగిరి - nímgiri, Tel.). From (nim, hind. neem tree, melia azadirachta, linn. + giri, san. hill). Range of hills; Vizagapatam dist., Bissemcuttack tal.; Parvatipore division; between lat. 19° 27′, and 19° 41′, and between long. 83° 22′ and 83° 32′; height 4,972; from Bissemcuttack W. 3 miles; from Coraput N.E. 57 miles; from Madras N.N.E. 475 miles; from Narsapatam N.N.E. 126 miles; from Parvatipore N. 40 miles; from Vizianagram N. 86 miles; from Goonapore N.W. 29 miles; from Jeypore N.E. 64 miles; from Vizagapatam N. 115 miles. In the extreme north of district. A lofty range, grass covered, at right angles to Eastern ghauts [q.v.], constructing the Royagada valley. A pass 1,200 feet in height leads along its eastern face from Parvatipore to Central provinces. It divides Bissemcuttack and Singapore estates. The Vamshadhaura rises in the range, and the foot-path from Bissemcuttack to Singapore crosses it by the Paupicanama gorge.——(2) *Bitter neem* (کڑوی نیم - karvínim, Dec.). Same as Curry-leaf tree.——*Black neem* (కరివేప - karivépa, Tel.; கருவேம்பு - karuvémbu, Tam.). Same as Curry-leaf tree, and Garooga.——*Dog neem* (நாய்வேம்பு - náyyémbu, Tam.). Title from being wild. The pinnate leaf gives the connection. Tam. from (náy, tam. dog + vémbu, tam. neem tree, melia azadirachta, linn.). Title otherwise Viscid wild indigo plant. Botanically Indigofera [neely] viscosa, lamk., leguminosæ [vricsham, 48]. Suffruticose, erect, much branched; branches, petioles, peduncles and legumes glutinous and rigidly hairy; leaves petioled, pinnated; leaflets four to eight pair, elliptic-oblong, pubescent, particularly beneath; racemes about the length of the leaves; legumes cylindrical, horizontal, straight; seeds six to twelve, cylindrical, truncated at both ends; flowers distant, small, greenish-red; flowering nearly all the year.——*Foreign neem* (विलायतीनिंब - viláyatínimba, Mahr.). Same as Large neem.——*Fragrant neem* (सुरभिनिम्ब - surabbinimba, San.). Same as Curry-leaf tree.——*Ground neem* (भूनिम्ब - bhúnimba, San.). Title from bitter taste and lowly habit. Same as French chiretta.——*Hill neem* (निंबर - nimbara, Mahr.; ಬೆಟ್ಟಬೇವು - bettabévu, Can.; ලුණුමිදෙල්ල - lunumidella, Singh.; மலைவேம்பு - malaivémbu, Tam.). Can. from (betta, can. hill + bévu, can. the tree, melia azadirachta, linn.). Singh. from (lúnu, singh. saline taste + midella, singh. the tree, barringtonia). Tam. from (malai, tam. mountain + vémbu, tam. neem tree). Can. also (hebbévu), meaning large + the tree; (kádabévu), meaning wild + the tree. Botanically Melia dubia, cav., meliaceæ [vricsham, 36]. Alias Melia composita, robusta, superba. Large tree; young shoots, petioles and panicles very mealy; leaves bi-pinnate, alternate; pinnæ about three pair; leaflets three to seven pair to each pinnæ, ovate, acuminate, crenulated, glabrous, 2–3 inches long; panicles axillary, scarcely half the length of the leaves; flowers numerous, small, whitish, inodorous; flowering in hot season; calyx and petals mealy; stigma large with a five-pointed apex; drupe ovate, size of a large olive [zeitoon], smooth, and yellowish green when ripe. The dried fruit is in size, shape, and color very much like a date [kharjooram], but upon closer examination the pulp is found to adhere firmly to a large and very hard stone; when soaked in water the fruit becomes like an oval yellowish-green plum [aulcoochah]; the pulp of the fruit has a bitter nauseous taste. Fruit is a remedy for colic, half a fruit being the dose for an adult. Sap-wood grey; heart-wood reddish-white, soft; timber used for building.——*Large neem* (महानिम्ब - mahánimba, San.; विलायतीनिंब - viláyatínimba, Mahr.; بان - bán, Ar.; آزاددرخت - ázáddarrakht, Pers.; مہانینب - mahánínb, Hind.; گولی نیم - gaulíním, Dec.; ಹುಚ್ಚುಬೇವು - huççubévu, Can.; తురకవేప - turakavépa, Tel.; മലവേമ്പ് - malavémbu, Mal.; මහනිඹ - mahanimba, Singh.; மலைவேம்பு - malaivémbu, Tam.). San. from (mahá, san. large + nimba, san. neem tree, melia azadirachta, linn.). Mahr. from (viláyatí, mahr. european + nimba, san. neem tree). Pers. from (ázád, pers. free + darakht, pers. tree). Hind. from sanscrit. Dec. from (gaulí, dec. goddess + ním, hind. the tree). Can. from (huççu, can. mad + bévu, can. the tree). Tel. from (turaka, tel. mahomedan + vépa, tel. the neem tree). Mal. from tamul. Singh. from sanscrit. Tam. from (malai, tam. mountain + vémbu, tam. neem tree). San. also (parvatanimba), meaning mountain neem tree; (himadruma), meaning snow tree, applies better to melia dubia, cav., from grey-wood. Ar. also (hábbulbán), meaning seed of melia azedarach, linn. Hind. also (bakáyan). Dec. also (gaurinim), meaning parvaty's neem. Can. also (turukabévu), meaning turk + the tree; (chikkabévu), meaning small + the tree. Tel. also (kondavépa), meaning hill + the neem tree. Singh. also (lunumidella), meaning saline barringtonia is melia dubia. Tam. also (shigarinimbam), meaning mountain + neem tree. Title otherwise Bastard bead tree, Bastard cedar [chikrassy, soymida], Evergreen bead tree, False sycamore, Holy tree, Hook tree, Indian lilac, Margosa, Persian lilac, Pride of china, Pride of india, Syrian bead tree, Tauk, White cedar. Botanically Melia azedarach, linn., meliaceæ [vricsham, 36]. Specific name from persian. Alias Azedarach commeline, deleteria; Melia bukaim, commelini, sempervirens. Bukaim is hindostany. Tree, 40 feet; foliage like ash; petals five, nearly glabrous; calyx small, five-cleft; stamen tube ten-cleft; leaves alternate, bipinnate, deciduous; leaflets about five together, obliquely ovate-lanceolate, serrated, finely acuminated, glabrous; peduncles axillary, simple below, above panicled, branched, and many-flowered; flowers smallish, white externally, lilac at the top, fragrant; flowering in march; fruit size of a cherry [q.v.], pale yellow when ripe; nut five-celled; cells one-seeded. The bi-pinnate and occasionally tri-pinnate leaves distinguish it from melia azadirachta, linn. [neem]. The root-bark is very thin and light, rough and dark-brown externally, pale-white internally, and bitterish in taste; the seeds are generally about the size and shape of thick and long grains of rice, but dark-brown and shining; kernel albuminous, pale or yellowish-white, and slightly bitterish and oily in taste; the nut or shell of the berries in which the seeds are contained is oval, hard, rough and five-celled with one seed in each cell. Hard brown nut; gum [gond] looks like mocharas [q.v.], similar to ordinary neem gum; the root is nauseous and bitter. Introduced into southern india by mahomedans. The root-bark and seeds are medicinally tonic and anthelmintic. Preparations, powder and decoction; for latter take four ounces of the fresh root-bark, water two pints, boil to one pint. Doses; of powder of root-bark, from forty to eighty grains; of decoction of root-bark, from four fluid drachms to a fluid ounce, of powder of seeds, from one to two drachms. Substituted for gentian [chiretta] and calumba [q.v.]. The pulp surrounding the seeds is in large doses poisonous, and mixed with grease is given to kill dogs [nye]; a decoction of the leaves is astringent, anthelmintic, and stomachic, and injurious to insects; seeds emetic, laxative, and anthelmintic; bark bitter and anthelmintic, substituted for british santonin [absinth]; gives to pharm. root-bark, non-officinal. Fruit is greedily eaten by goats and sheep [aud]. Seeds are often strung as beads [munkah], especially by roman catholics; leaf contains green coloring matter. Sap-wood yellowish-white; heart-wood soft, red; wood used for furniture, but it warps and splits; it polishes well. Large neem is also another name for the Toon [q.v.].——*Lowly neem* (भूनिम्ब - bhúnimba, San.). From the bitterness of the plant. Same as French chiretta, Coromandel gendarussa, and Himalayan chiretta.——*Madagherry neem* (மதகிரிவேம்பு - mathagirivémbu, Tam.). From place so called. Same as Chickrassy and Javanese cedar.——*Parvaty's neem* (گوری نیم - gaurinim, Dec.). Same as Large neem.——*Sandal neem* (சந்தனவேம்பு - shandanavémbu, Tam.). Title from neem-like leaf, and fragrant wood. Same as Toon.——*Shiva's neem* (शिवनिम्ब - shivanimba, San. and Mahr.; ಶಿವಮಲ್ಲಿ - shivamalli, Can.; മണലി - manali, Mal.; சிவனார்வேம்பு - shivanárvémbu, Tam.). San. from (shiva, san. the deity + nimba, san. melia azadirachta, linn.). Mahr. from sanscrit. Can. from (shiva, san. deity + mallika, san. jasminum sambac, ait.). Mal. from (manal, mal. sand) [manaly]. Tam. from (shiva, tam. the deity + vémbu, tam. neem tree, melia azadirachta, linn.); from red flowers. Title otherwise Manelly, Small-flowered aspalathus. Botanically Indigofera [neely] aspalathoides, vahl., leguminosæ [vricsham, 48]. Alias Aspalathus indicus; Indigofera aspalathifolia. Shrubby, erect, young parts whitish, with adpressed hairs; branches slender, spreading in every direction; leaves sessile, digitately three or five-foliolate; leaflets narrow cuneate, small, under side with a few scattered hairs; peduncles solitary, one-flowered, about the length of the leaves; legumes cylindrical, pointed, straight, four to six-seeded; flowers very small, purplish-red; flowering nearly all the year. Leaves, flowers and tender shoots considered by veidyans [q.v.] cooling, demulcent, and alterative; prescribed in decoction in leprous and cancerous affections; root has virtues in easing toothache, and in aphthæ; preparation made from ashes of the burnt plant used to clean dandriff from the hair; oil is got from the root, used to anoint the head in erysipelas.——*Stunted neem* (మొక్కవేప - mokkavépa, Tel.). Title from pinnate leaves like neem. Tel. from (mokka, tel. stump + vépa, tel. margosa tree, melia azadirachta, linn.). Tel. also (mushkamu); (mukkapukokkisa); (kokkisa); (nélakaligottu), meaning ground + stereospermum chelonoides, dec. Title otherwise Ground trumpet flower tree. Botanically Bignonia genus, bignoniaceæ [vricsham, 99]. A similar title for the Pauthiry.——*Turk's neem* (ತುರುಕಬೇವು - turukabévu, Can.). Title from being introduced into India by mahomedans. Same as Large neem.——*Water neem* (جل نیم - jalnim, Hind.). Same as Water zoofah.

NEEM (نیم - ním, *Hind.*). From persian. Half.——*Meetaun* (میتان - mítán, Hind.). Corruption of (ním, pers. half + tan, hind. body). A waistcoat with sleeves [sadry, sheelay].——*Neemah* (نیمہ - nímah, Hind.). From (ním, pers. half). Coat made of muslin [q.v.], has sleeves, and is tied across the breast. It descends to below the calf of the leg, and is worn by male Mahomedans in hot weather [sheelay].——*Neem tunkam* (نیم تنکا - nímtanká, Hind.). From (above + tankamu, tel. coin). A half rupee [tunkam].

NEER (जल - jala, *San.*; पाणी - páni, *Mahr.*; ماء - má, *Ar.*; آب - áb, *Pers.*; پانی - páni, *Hind.* and *Dec.*; ايار - ayár, *Malay.*; ನೀರು - níru, *Can.* and *Too.*; నీళ్లు - níllu, *Tel.*; വെള്ളം - vellam, *Mal.*; වතුර - vatura, *Singh.*; நீர் - nír, *Tam.*). Title from tamul. San. from (jal, san. to be cold). Mahr. from (pána, san. drink). Pers. from (ap, san. water). Hind. from (pána, san. drink). Mal. from (vel, mal. white). Tam. from (nira, tam. to spread). Water. The water available in this country is of three kinds, viz., well water from springs [oott], river [aur], water, and tank [q.v.] water collected during rain [mazhay].—"*a*" Springs issuing from the surface of the ground are scarce, they occur however on the tops of high mountains. If the soil is dug almost anywhere veins of water may be found under the surface proceeding from the high land and the ghauts [q.v.]. The depth at which these veins occur is various. In valleys near mountains they are more superficial than elsewhere. Mineral springs do not occur on the coast, but there are several in Jeypore. There is a hot spring in the middle of the Godavery, near Bhadrachellam. The goodness of spring water depends, in a great measure, on the nature of the strata through which it runs. If these strata be impregnated with common salt [ooppoo], or any other similar substance, the water is brackish. A calcareous or gypseous soil [choonam] will produce hard water, because a portion of the calcareous salts will be dissolved by the liquid. In clayey soil [calimunn] the water will be muddy, but generally soft and good, unless the clay happen to contain a mixture of iron or matrial pyrites [auhan]. In primitive tracts of country spring water is always transparent and good. The Padaurta chintaumany says that the water of wells, or natural springs in the sandy beds of rivers, is the most wholesome of all. Well water is often contaminated by the infiltration of sewage, but it is on the whole that most preferred. Varauha mihiran says:—"Just in the same way as "there are arteries for the circulation of blood in human bodies, "there are water courses running in all directions above and "below within the earth; there are eight currents bearing the "same names as those of the eight dicpaties [ashtadicpaulacan], "and there is a large current in the centre known as mahasiray; "besides these there are hundreds of well-known minor currents "bearing distinct names."—"*b*" River water requires no special mention. It ranks in Padaurta chintaumany next after river-bed springs for purity. The water of mountain streams is considered heating.—"*c*" Tank water is generally muddy contains organic and inorganic impurities, the kind, and amount of which depend on the sanitary state and nature of the gathering grounds; it is often rendered impure by people bathing in it, and from the washing in it of clothing and even cattle. Tank water is according to Padaurta chintaumany the worst of all; nevertheless it is sweet.—"*d*" The distinction of water into hard and soft has reference to its less or greater purity. Hard waters are unfit for washing in consequence of containing sulphate of lime, and curdling in place of dissolving soap [sauboon]. 100 parts of water consist of 88·24 oxygen, and 11·76 hydrogen. Sea water contains muriate of soda, muriate of magnesia, muriate of lime, sulphate of soda.—"*e*" At certain season, especially during the monsoon [q.v.], the best water is apt to be muddy. Under these circumstances, recourse is had to the practice of rubbing the inside of a vessel or chatty [q.v.] with clearing nut [q.v.] previous to the water being poured into it.—"*f*" For the value of water to the natives, see Mazhay. There is a Tamul proverb;—தண்ணீரையும் தாயையும் பழிக்கலாமா?—"May one abuse water, or one's mother?"—"*g*" Plant first term often joining two genera. Ex., where transl. is of second term:—Ammannia baccifera (nírmélneruppu), upper + fire, cool to touch but causing blister; Calamus rotang (nírvañji), reed; Canthium didymum (níralli), nymphæa lotus; Canthium parviflorum (nírúri), creeper; Clerodendron inerme (nírnocci), vitex negundo; Colocasia esculenta (nírchémpu), colocasia antiquorum; Commelyna communis (nírukasuvu), grass; Desmanthus virgatus (nírçcundi), to shrink, flowers during rains and is sensitive to touch; Dolichandrone falcata (nirponnalyam), ailanthus malabarica; Hydnocarpus venenata (níruduchettu), to drop out + tree, from usefulness in skin diseases; Hygrophila salicifolia, var. dimidiata (nírçculli), thorny plant; Jussiæa repens (nírubattsali), basella cordifolia; Jussiæa suffruticosa (nírkkirámbu), eugenia caryophyllata, and (nírugnirendramu), ammannia baccifera; Leersia hexandra (níryvallippullu), creeper + grass, as

MANUAL OF THE ADMINISTRATION
OF THE
MADRAS PRESIDENCY,
IN ILLUSTRATION OF THE
RECORDS OF GOVERNMENT & THE YEARLY ADMINISTRATION REPORTS

MANUAL OF THE ADMINISTRATION
OF THE
MADRAS PRESIDENCY,
IN ILLUSTRATION OF THE
RECORDS OF GOVERNMENT & THE YEARLY ADMINISTRATION REPORTS.

IN THREE VOLUMES

VOL. III—GLOSSARY,

Containing a Classification of terminology, a Gazetteer and Economic dictionary of the province, and other information, the whole arranged alphabetically and indexed.

GYAN

Published by

GYAN

Gyan Publishing House
5, Ansari Road
Daryaganj, New Delhi-110002
Phone: 011-47034999, 9811692060
E-mail: books@gyanbooks.com

Distribution Network
gyanbooks.com
India, USA, Canada, UK, Australia, France

ISBN : 978-81-212-4379-7 (PB)
First Published, 1893

2nd Impression 2020

Printed at: Gyan Press, Delhi.

The book at your disposal is the edition of an old book originally published long back. The Text quality of this book may not be at par as compared to our other books but many readers approached us to reprint this important book so that it could satiate their hunger. We request all the readers of this book to help us to improve its quality by providing the necessary text of those pages which are not properly visible. Your valuable support in this case will be highly appreciated and acknowledged and our future readers will be benefitted immensely.

growing in wet ground; Monochoria hastæfolia (nírutámara), nelumbium speciosum; Neptunia oleracea (nírutalavápu), to touch from floating on water; Pistia stratiotes (níráku), leaf; Polygonum barbatum (níralari), nerium odorum; Revenalia madagascariensis (nírvágai), albizzia lebbek; Rivea hypocrateriformis (níruboddi), macaranga peltata; Sagittaria obtusifolia (níroçembu), colocasia nymphæifolia; Stephegyne parvifolia (nírkkadambu), anthocephalus cadamba; Vernonia anthelmintica (nírnoççi), vitex negundo. See gloss. paragraphs.—"*h*" Mammal first term. Ex., where transl. is of second term:—Delphinus perniger (nírupandi), pig; Halicore dugong (nírmanithan), man; Lutra vulgaris (nírnáy), dog. See gloss. paragraphs.—"*i*" Abruck neer, from (abhraka, san. talc) is spring water, having a mineral solution of abruck [q.v.]. Choonam neer is mineral water impregnated with choonam [q.v.]. Mazhay neer is rain water. Ooppoo neer is brackish water. Oottoo neer is spring water. Teeneer, from (tí, tam. fire) is distilled water. Tunneer, from (tan, tam. cool) is cold water. Venneer, from (vem, tam. hot) is hot water.——*Neerady mootl* (நீரடிமுத்து - níradimuttu, Tam.). From (above + adi, tam. to strike + muttu, tam. pearl); useful in cooshtam [q.v.] in removing bad secretions. Plant name common to:—Baliospermum montanum; Hydnocarpus venenata. See gloss. paragraphs.——*Neerah* (نیرا - nírá, Hind.; ఎలెకల్లు - elekallu, Can.; ഇളങ്കള്ള - ilankallu, Mal.; பதனி - pathani, Tam.). Hind. from (nira, san. water). Mal. from (ila, mal. fresh + kallu, mal. toddy). Tam. from (pathani, tam. proper quality + nír, tam. water). Toddy [q.v.] which is fresh + drawn and not yet begun to ferment, in which condition it is always found early in the morning before sunrise [verry].——*Neerattipair* (നീരട്ടിപ്പേറു - nírattippéru, Mal.). From (above + atti, mal. to come in contact + péru, mal. birth-right). Birth-right obtained by coming in contact with water. Final sale of jenm [q.v.], succeeding Otty [q.v.] when the jenmy [q.v.] after previous transactions can no longer avoid an absolute transfer. In this the jenmy for some further and final consideration gives up all connection with the land, even the remaining right of pre-emption. At the time of executing and delivering the deed, the following persons must be present:—Swajauty, a person of the same caste; Bandhoo, a relative; Pootran, literally the son, but in malabar construed to mean the heir, whether a nephew or son; Narapaty, the rajah; the writer of the deed; Tatra sambandhy, a resident round the spot. In practice the attendance of the Rajah, or the execution of the deed before the Rajah, is dispensed with. It is only necessary that he should be apprized of the transaction. The mortgagee gives two fanams [q.v.], which is placed in a small vessel of water, supposed to come off the estate. The mortgagor, holding the deed in his hand, pours the water over it, which the mortgagor receives as it falls, and either swallows it, or puts it upon his head, or upon his feet, or upon the ground, according to the relative caste of the two parties. The deed is then delivered to the mortgagee. This deed mentions generally that the full value of the property disposed of has been received, and states the boundaries of it, but it does not specify any amount received. The purchaser, in coming into possession, is bound by all the obligations which attached to the proprietor. He cannot disturb those who may be holding the property or any portion of it on Caunom [q.v.] mortgage, but merely receives the surplus rent produce in place of the former landlord. On the other hand, he comes into all the rights and privileges of the former landlord, and may pay off Otty [q.v.] mortgages and sell or transfer the property as he pleases. The deed is Caranam attipair. See vol. II, 104.——*Neeraunican* (நீராணிக்கன் - nìránikkan, Tam.). From (above + ánai, tam. command). A village peon [q.v.] superintending the water-courses [neergunty].——*Neer caul* (நீர்க்கால் - nírkkál, Tam.). From (above + kál, tam. channel). A water-course [caul].——*Neer choondy* (நீர்ச்சுண்டி - nírçundi, Tam.). Tam. from (above + shundu, tam. to shrink); flowers during rains and is sensitive to touch. Title otherwise Water mimosa. Botanically Desmanthus virgatus, willd., leguminosæ [vricsham, 48]. Alias Mimosa virgata. Suffruticose; stem erect, angled; leaves bipinnated; pinnæ three to four pair, with a large concave gland between the lowest pair; leaflets fifteen to twenty pair; peduncles axillary, about as long as the leaves, naked, bearing a globose, few-flowered head; legume narrow-linear, many-seeded; flowers small, white; flowering in the rainy season. No other species here.——*Neer cooly* (நீர்க்கூலி - nírkkúli, Tam.). From (above + kúli, tam. wages). Water-rate; includes either Teervay jausty [q.v.] or Fusl jausty [q.v.].——*Neercorattay* (پانی کا سانپ - pánikásámp, Dec.; నీరుహావు - níruhávu, Can.; నిల్లకొయ్య - nillakoyya, Tel.; നീർമണ്ഡലി - nírmandali, Mal.; நீர்க்கொறட்டை - nírkkorattai, Tam.). Title from tamul. Dec. from (páni, hind. water + sámp, hind. snake). Can. from (níru, can. water + hávu, can. snake). Tel. from (nillu, tel. water + koyya, tel. stick). Mal. from (nír, tam. water + mandali, mal. the snake). Tam. from (nír, mal. water + kuradu, tam. pincers); means water-hold-fast; from the fact that when it bites it will not let go till the flesh is torn out. Title otherwise Checkered snake. Tropidonotus quincunciatus, schleg., colubridæ [paumb], ophidii colubriformes, ophidia [sarpam] reptilia [sarpy, 17], of naturalists [jantoo]. From its frequenting wet paddy fields is commonly reckoned a water snake, but it is not venomous.——*Neercutty* (நீர்க்கட்டி - nírkkatti, Tam.). From (above + kattu, tam. to confine). Same as Neergunty.——*Neergunty* (నీరుగంటి - níruganti, Tel.). From (above + kattu, tel. to confine). Water distributor of a village. The Neergunty's province is to take care of the reservoirs, frequently to inspect the toom [q.v.] or outlet from the tank [q.v.] to the fields, to see that it be not choked with sand or dirt, to prevent every unnecessary and unusual expense of the water, which it is his duty to distribute to each field under the orders of the village headman impartially in quantities proportioned to the extent of the field and stage of the crop [inam].——*Neermootty* (कोकिलाक्ष - kókiláksha, San.; कोलिस्ता - kólistá, Mahr.; कोम्बुलेझाड - komlbulójháda, Conc.; تال مکهانے کاپر - tálmakhánekáper, Hind.; کولسی کا جهاڑ - kolsekájhár, Dec.; ಕೊಳವಂಕೆಗಿಡ - kolavankegida, Can.; ಕೋವೆಮುಳ್ಳುದೈ - kóvemulludai, Too.; నీరుగొబ్బి - nírugobbi, Tel.; വയൽചുള്ളി - vayalchulli, Mal.; ඉකිරි - ikiri, Singh.; நீர்முள்ளி - nírmulli, Tam.). Title from tamul. San. from (kókila, san. cuckoo + aksha, san. eye); from flowers. Hind. from sanscrit. Dec. from (kolsá, hind. charcoal + jhár, hind. tree) [indian nettle, indian nightshade]. Can. from (kola, can. pond + vanka, can. crooked + gida, can. plant). Tel. from (níru, tel. water + gobbi, tel. the plant). Mal. from (vayal, mal. field + chulli, mal. thorny plant). Tam. from (nír, tam. water + mulli, tam. thorny plant). San. also (gókshura), meaning cow + razor; (kulika), meaning cluster; (ikshura); meaning like sugar-cane; (ikshugandha), meaning sugar-cane, saccharum officinarum, linn. + smell [naunal, nerinjy]; (ékakantaka), meaning having one thorn; (súryabhíra), meaning sun-fearing plant; (gókantaka), meaning cow + thorn [nerinjy]; (kándékshu), meaning knot + sugar-cane, by reason of knots. Mahr. also (tálimakháná), meaning seed of hygrophila spinosa, t. and. Hind. also (Gochru); (ikshuganda); (gokshura), from sanscrit meaning cow + razor. Can. also (kolavalike); (mullankóle); (górimidi); (níruppi). Tel. also (gobbi); (korimidi) [coratty pausy]. Title otherwise Cow-thorn, Cuckoo's eye, Long-leaved barleria, Water thorn. Botanically Hygrophila spinosa, t. ander, acanthaceæ [vricsham, 101]. Alias Asteracantha longifolia; Barleria hexacantha, longiflora, longifolia; Ruellia longifolia. Annual; stem erect, bluntly quadrangular, hispid; leaves opposite, ensiform, very long; calyx four-cleft; corolla funnel-shaped; five-cleft, one division deeper than the rest; flowers in whorls, axillary, blue or bright violet; flowering in rainy season; spines, three on each side of the stem, equal in length to the whorls; swampy places, very common; native of west coast. The seeds are one of the Punchabeejam or five seeds, the others being those of Celastrus [malkangany], Fenugreek [maitee], Ajwaun [q.v.] and Cumin [jeerah]. Roots often biennial, tapering, with numerous rootlets; the seeds are small and flattish, of irregular form and brown color, the largest $\frac{1}{16}$ of an inch long and $\frac{1}{16}$ broad; when placed in the mouth they immediately become coated with a large quantity of extremely tenacious mucilage, which adheres to the tongue and palate and is of rather agreeable flavor. The roots are employed in dropsical affections and gravel; the leaves boiled in vinegar [caudy] are diuretic. Other common species are:—phlomoides, salicifolia, serphyllum.——*Neer moozhoogy* (நீர்முழுகி - nírmuzhugi, Tam.). From (above + muzhugi, tam. diver). Men who, when the tanks are full and the sluices are out of order, dive down into the sluice and remove the obstruction, &c., a perilous occupation [inam].——*Neermothal* (നീർമുതൽ - nírmutal, Mal.). From (above + mutal, mal. principal. The property in water; as a mode of transfer, is the same as Coodimaneer [otty]. See vol. II, 104.——*Neer nilay* (நீர்நிலை - nírnilai, Tam.). From (above + nil, tam. to stand). Marshy ground.——*Neeroory* (भूम्यामलक - bhúmyámalaka, San.; भुईआवळा - bhuíávalá, Mahr.; भूम्यावळि - bhúmyáváli, Conc.; بهوئین انولہ - bhuínáunlah, Hind. and Dec.; ಕಿರುನೆಲ್ಲಿ - kirunelli, Can.; ನೆಲನೆಲ್ಲಿ - nelanelli, Too.; నేలఉసిరిక - nélausirika, Tel.; നീരുരി - níruri, Mal.; පිටවක්කා - pitavakká, Singh.; கீழாநெல்லி - kízhánelli, Tam.). Title from malayalam. San. from (bhúmi, san. ground + ámalaka, san. phyllanthus emblica, linn.). Hind. from sanscrit. Mahr., &c., from sanscrit. Can. from (kirn, can. small + nelli, can. phyllanthus emblica, linn.). Too. from (nela, too. ground + nelli, too. phyllanthus emblica, linn.). Tel. from (néla, tel. ground + usirika, tel. phyllanthus emblica, linn.). Mal. from (nír, mal. water + úri, mal. creeper). Tam. from (kízh, tam. below + nelli, tam. phyllanthus emblica, linn.); from lowly habit and resemblance. San. also (bhútadhátrí), meaning earth nelly; (putrashrení), meaning multitude of sons; (pitabahup'hala), meaning yellow + many + fruit. Mal. also (kízhánelli); (cherunírúri), meaning small water creeper; (kízhkáynelli), meaning nelly with fruits below. Singh. also (sadáp'hala), meaning always + fruit [cocoanut]. Tam. also (kízhkkáynelli), meaning below + fruit + phyllanthus emblica, linn.; (shimutti). Title otherwise Chimooty, Indian annual phyllanthus, Kizhánelly. Botanically Phyllanthus [aumlacam] niruri, müll., var. genuinus, euphorbiaceæ [vricsham, 118]. Specific name from malayalam. Alias Nymphanthus niruri; Urinaria erecta. Annual, erect, ramous; branches herbaceous, ascending; floriferous branchlets filiform; leaves small, elliptic, mucronate, entire, glabrous; flowers axillary; male flowers minute, two or three with one longer pedicelled; female in each axil, terminating in three transverse anthers; capsule globose, glabrous, three-angled, with two seeds in each cell; seed triangular; flowers minute, greenish; white root; leaves bitter; a common weed. Root, leaves, and young shoots used medicinally as deobstruent and diuretic; root and leaves, either in powder or decoction, used in jaundice or bilious complaints; young shoots in infusion given in dysentery; substituted for british copaiba and sweet nitre; quoted in pharm., non-officinal. An undershrub species urinaria called Red neeroory from color of stems has similar diuretic properties. The poolah [q.v.] shrub is called Wild neeroory. Large neeroory is melanthesopsis patens, muller, euphorbiaceæ [vricsham, 118]; alias melanthesa obliqua, turbinata; phyllanthus turbinatus; leaves membranaceous; female flowers solitary, males proceeding from minute about six to nine-bracteolated racemules; calyx obconical, sharply lengthened out, and crenately twelve-lobed round the base of the segments; large shrub; fruit size of a pea [calauyam]; varieties are genuina, oblongifolia, turbinata, vulgaris.——*Neerpayir* (நீர்ப் பயிர் - nírppayir, Tam.). From (above + payir, tam. crop). Wet cultivation [nunjah].——*Nirvala* (वरुण - varuna, San.; वायवरण - váyavarana, Mahr.; برنا - barná, Hind.; بيل پهل كا جهاڑ - belphalkájhár, Dec.; ಬಿಲಪತ್ರಿ - bilapatri, Can.; ನಿರುಜನಿ - nirujani, Coorg; ತುದೆಮಧಿರೆಂಗಿ - tudemadirengi, Too.; ఉలిమిడి - ulimidi, Tel.; നീർവ്വാൽ - nírvvál, Mal.; වරණ - varana, Singh.; மாவி லங்கை - mávilangai, Tam.). Title from malayalam. San. from (vri, san. to envelope). Hind. from sanscrit. Dec. from (belphal, hind. fruit of ægle marmelos, corr. + jhár, hind. tree) [bael]. Can. from (bilva, san. the tree, ægle marmelos, corr. + patar, san. leaf). Mal. from (nír, mal. water + vilá, mal. feronia elephantum, corr.). Tam. means great bael [ashy babool, weaver's beam]. San. also (tiktasháka), meaning bitter herb; (ashmaríghna), meaning gravel, the disease + destroyer; (pashugandhá), meaning cow + smell; (ajápá); (vasaha); (varana). Hind. also (belpatrí), meaning bael-leafed. Dec. also (barmíkájhár). Can. also (nirvála); (holenekkimara), meaning river + to lick + tree; (nárumbóle); (mavalanga). Tel. also (usiki); (urumitti); (tellaulimidi), meaning white + the tree; (bilvamu); (márédu), meaning tree + king [bael]; (peddaulimidi), meaning large + cratæva religiosa, forst.; (chinnaulimidi), meaning small + the tree. Mal. also (nírmátalam), meaning water + punica granatum, linn. Singh. also (lunuvarana), meaning salt + the plant. Tam. also (vilvam) [bael]; (periyamávilingai), meaning large + the tree; (shinnamávilangai), meaning small + the tree; (athisáranam). Title otherwise Garlic pear, Holy garlic pear, Mauvilingam, Three-leaved caper tree, Water wood-apple. Botanically Cratæva religiosa, forst., capparideæ [vricsham, 11]. Alias Capparis nurvala, roxburghii, trifoliata; Cratæva inermis, nurvala, tapia. Shrub or small tree; flowers whitish, or cream-colored; Malabar. Gives to pharm. leaves, non-officinal; somewhat aromatic, slightly bitter, stomachic; root has sub-aromatic and bitterish taste, with alterative quality. Wood yellowish-white, when old turning light-brown, moderately hard, even-grained; used for drums, models, writing-boards, combs and in turnery. There are two well-known varieties:—"*a*" Large nirvala is Cratæva religiosa, forst., var. nurvala, ham. Tree, 15–20 feet; leaves trifoliolate; leaflets ovate-lanceolate, acuminated, lateral ones unequal at the base; limb of the petals ovate-roundish; torus hemispherical, very ovoid; calyx four-sepalled; petals four, unguiculate; berry stipitate, pulpy inside; flowers greenish white, with red stamens; racemes terminal. Leaves aromatic, slightly bitter, and stomachic; root having alterative qualities; juice of bark given in convulsions and flatulency, and boiled in oil externally applied in rheumatism.—"*b*" Small nirvala or three-leaved caper, is Cratæva religiosa, forst., var. roxburghii. Tree; flowers large, white, becoming cream-colored with purple filaments; common on banks of rivers, much planted by natives; fruit hard, globose and woody, something like wood-apple [q.v.]; wood soft and easily cut, but tolerably tough, and used for carving models, making writing-boards, and combs, &c.

NEEROO (भस्म - bhasma, *San.*; راكه - rákh, *Hind.* and *Dec.*; abu, *Malay*; బూడిద - búdide, *Tel.*; നീറു - níru, *Mal.*; අළු - alu, *Singh.*; நீறு - níru, *Tam.*). San. from (bhas, san. to consume). Hind. and Dec. from (raksha, san. protector). Tel. from (bhúti, san. ashes). Mal. from tamul. Tam. also (shámbal). Ashes. Earthy part of any substance after it has been burnt. Distinguish from Neer, water.——*Pooneer* (பூநீறு - púníru, Tam.). Means flower ashes. Saline efflorescence. See sep. title.——*Tirneer* (திருநீறு - tiruníru, Tam.). Tam. from (tiru, tam. holy). Ashes of burnt cow-dung [shauny] with which Shiva [q.v.] is said to smear his body and hence in imitation of him his followers. Also ashes taken from fire of an agnihotry [q.v.] Bramin [q.v.] or any sacrificial fire. The three transverse lines made with the sacred ashes on the forehead of Sheivites are called Tripoondram [q.v.]. Consecrated by muntram [q.v.], it is worn on forehead or rubbed on whole body as a charm or for soul's benefit. Balls of cow-dung ashes are sold in bazaar [q.v.]. Used in Hindoo houses in scouring brass plates and glassware, also used in cleaning military accoutrements and brass mountings of harness, &c. [vibhooty].

NEEYATT (نيت - níyat, *Hind.*). From (navá, ar. intend). Will. Royal decree.

NEGAPATAM* (ناگپٹن - nágpatan, *Hind.*; நாகப்பட்டணம் - nágappattanam, *Tam.*). From (nága, san. snake + pattana, san. town) [naug]. Tam. also (nágai), meaning snake + place; also (tirunágai), meaning holy + snake place. Sanscrit name (nágapuri), meaning snake town; also (cháritrapura), meaning historic fame + town [cauveryputnam]. Greek νίγαμος.——**(1)** Talook; Tanjore dist., Tahsildar's pay Rs. 250; area 240 square miles; pop. 220,348; language Tamul. Central coast talook. Boundaries; North Nunnilam talook and Caricaul territory, east the sea, south Tritrapoondy talook, west Nunnilam and Munnargoody talooks. Flat level sloping towards the east and south-east. Soil, sandy along the sea coast and black clayey in the interior. Export of rice [q.v.]. Import of timber, betel-nuts [q.v.] and spices, dyeing cloth, and railway workshop materials. Oodambadikay, Pandaviyaur, Seetaur, Velliyaur, Vettaur and Yedaiyaur, give irrigation. Camping ground at Caudambaudy. Places of archæological interest:—Ayyinaurcovilputt, Coottamporetaunirooppoo, Eivacoody, Keevalore, Keezhaiyore, Kidarangandaun, Nágore, Negapatam, Poyyore, Shivanandaurcoil, Sikkil, Taivore, Tappanam pooliyore, Tircarvausal, Tircoovalay, Tirpoondy, Tirvoymore, Trivarore, Tyaugarajapooram, Vadacoody, Vadakk poyyore, Vazhivalam, Yettoocoody. Principal trig. stations:—Nirdhanamungalam, Shilagoory. The leading places &c., in the talook are the following.——*Andanapett* (அந்தணப்பேட்டை - andanappéttai, Tam.). From (andanan, tam. bramin + péttai, tam. village). Town; pop. 4,519; acres 716; lat. 10° 46′; long. 79° 52′; from Negapatam W.S.W. 1¾ miles; from Tanjore E. 44 miles; from the sea W. 2 miles. Shiva temple. Copper [taumram] and brass [pittalay] vessels manufactured.——*Devoor* (தேவூர் - tévúr, Tam.). From (té, tam. deity + úr, tam. village). Sanscrit name (dévapura), meaning god + town. Village; pop. 1,313; acres 1,162; lat. 10° 44′; long. 79° 46′; from Negapatam W.S.W. 8 miles; from Tanjore E. 40 miles; from the sea W. 8 miles. On the Cadoovaiyaur. Old Shiva temple with inscriptions, one dated A.D. 1425.——*Keevalore* (கீழ்வளூர் - kízhvalúr, kívalúr, Tam.). From (kízh, tam. east + val, tam. a hillock + úr, tam. village). Village, Railway station; pop. 2,108; acres 1,387; lat. 10° 46′; long. 79° 47′; height 28 feet; from Negapatam W. 7 miles; from Tanjore E. 40 miles; from the sea W. 7 miles. In 1758 ransacked by Lally in the hopes of finding treasure. Old Shiva temple with inscriptions.——*Nagore* (நாகூர் - nágúr, Tam.). See sep. title.——*Negapatam* (நாகப்பட்டணம் - nágappattanam, Tam.). See below.——*Nirdhanamungalam* (நிர்த்தனமங்கலம் - nirttanamangalam, Tam.). From (nis, san. without + dhana, san. riches + mangala, san. prosperity). Trig. station; lat. 10° 42′ 24·76″; long. 79° 51′ 6·13″; from Negapatam S.S.W. 5 miles; from Vadavore W. ½ mile; from the sea W. 3 miles.——*Pooravacherry* (புறவச்சேரி - puravaççéri, Tam.). From (puravam, tam. forest + shéri, tam. village). Village; pop. 2,661; acres 657; lat. 10° 45′; long. 79° 51′; from Negapatam W. 3 miles; from Tanjore E. 45 miles; from the sea W. 3 miles. Weaving centre.——*Seetaur* (சித்தாறு - shittáru, Tam.). See sep. title.——*Shilagoory* (சிலகுரி - shilaguri, Tam.). Trig. station; lat. 10° 39′ 32·67″; long. 79° 53′ 40·85″; from Negapatam S. 7 miles; from Tirpoondy N.E. 4 miles; from Velangauny S. 1½ miles. On the seashore.——*Sikkil** சிக்கில் - shikkil, Tam.). From (shikkil, tam. temple + il, tam. place). Sanscrit name (mallikáranya), meaning the plant, jasminum sambac, ait. + forest. Town, Railway station; pop. 2,648; acres 1,288; lat. 10° 45′; long. 79° 51′; height 17 feet; from Negapatam W. 3 miles; from Tanjore E. 44 miles; from the sea W. 3 miles Old Shiva temple with inscriptions.——*Tirvarore* (திருவாரூர் - tiruvárúr, Tam.). See sep. title.——*Vadoogacherry* (வடுகச்சேரி - vadugaççéri, Tam.). From (vadugan, tam. member of the váduga caste + shéri, tam. village). Village; pop. 726; acres 998; lat. 10° 43′; long. 79° 49′; from Negapatam W. 7 miles; from Tanjore E. 42 miles; from the sea W. 6 miles. On the Cadoovaiyaur.——*Velangauny* (வேளாங்காணி - vélángáni, Tam.). From (vélán, tam. member of the vellála caste + káni, tam. land). Village, Port; pop. 2,682; acres 1,020; lat. 10° 41′; long. 79° 53′; from Madras S.S.W. 166 miles; from Negapatam S. 6 miles; from Tanjore E.S.E. 47 miles; from Topetoray N. 19 miles. The Cadoovaiyaur flows past. Open road-stead. Church of some importance resorted to during annual festival by R.C. christians.——*Vettacauraniroopp* (வேட்டக்காரனிருப்பு - véttakkáraniruppu, Tam.). From (véttaikkáran, tam. hunter + iruppu, tam. dwelling). Village; pop. 2,098; acres 3,224; lat. 10° 34′; long. 79° 53′; from Negapatam S. 14 miles; from Tanjore E.S.E. 48 miles; from the sea W. 1½ miles.——**(2)** Deputy tahsildarry, Tanjore district. Pay Rs. 100.——**(3)** Town, Municipality, Port, Railway station, Head-quarters of Head assistant collector, Talook, Executive engineer, Assistant commissioner of salt and abkary revenue, Telegraph office, Subordinate judge, District moonsif, and Deputy tahsildar, Place of pilgrimage; Tanjore dist., Negapatam tal.; pop. 59,221; acres 2,059; lat. 10° 46′; long. 79° 53′; height 13 feet ; from Combaconam S.E. 34 miles ; from Madras S.S.W. 160 miles ; from Mayavaram S.S.E. 26 miles ; from Munnargoody E.N.E. 27 miles ; from Nagore S. 4 miles ; from Tanjore E. 48 miles ; from Velangauny N. 6 miles. At the mouth of the Cadoovaiyaur on an open level, sandy expanse, having a gentle slope to the sea. Chief port of Tanjore and terminus of the South indian railway. Its harbour has a fixed white dioptric light, 82 feet above high water-mark. Light on the jetty near the river mouth ; lat. 10° 45′ 30″ ; long. 79° 50′·20.″ White ; fixed ; 14 miles range ; visible from all directions seaward, masonry column painted white guide to anchorage. The estuary is capable of receiving small coasting-vessels. With Nagore, which forms part of the municipality, it contains a large Lubbay [q.v.] population. One of the earliest Portuguese settlements on the Coromandel coast [q.v.]. Taken from the Portuguese by the Dutch in 1660 and become the head-quarters of the Dutch trade on the Coromandel coast. Taken from the Dutch by the English in 1781. After the cession of Tanjore territory by treaty in 1799, Negapatam became the head-quarters of the Collector and continued to be so until 1845, when the Collector's head-quarters were removed to Tranquebar. Fourteen temples, all old, twelve Shiva and two Vishnoo. In a Shiva temple is a stone, bearing an epitaph in Dutch to the memory of a European who died in A.D. 1777. Ancient brick tower, 70 feet high, supposed of Booddhist [booddha] or Jeina [q.v.] origin and known as the China tower. The ruins of the old Dutch fort are surrounded by a ditch filled up in many places. Government salt depôt, Wesleyan mission establishment. Ships and coasters maintain a considerable trade, principally in rice, with Ceylon, Burmah and Straits settlements. The following are the travelling distances by road from Negapatam to different places :—

To	Via	Miles and Furlongs.	
Adiramputnam ...	Munnargoody and Puttoocottah ...	61	1
Arantaungy ...	Munnargoody and Puttoocottah ...	84	1
Caricaul ...	Nagore	12	6
Chidambaram ...	Tranquebar and Shiyally	55	0
Chingleput ...	Chidambaram, Cuddalore and Pondicherry.	159	5
Coimbatore ...	Trichinopoly, Caroor and Pulladam ...	221	1
Cuddalore ...	Shiyally and Chidambaram	80	4
Madras	Cuddalore and Chingleput	194	4
Madura	Munnargoody. Puttoocottah, Arantaungy and Tripatore.	155	5
Munnargoody ...	Tirvarore	33	6
Palamcottah ...	Munnargoody, Tondy and Ramnaud...	234	1
Palamcottah ...	Puttoocottah, Tripatore and Madura..	251	3
Paumben ...	Puttoocottah, Tondy and Ramnaud...	171	3
Point calimere ...	Vedaranyam	37	5
Pondicherry ...	Tranquebar, Shiyally, Chidambaram and Cuddalore.	92	3
Poodoocottah ...	Tanjore	93	0
Puttoocottah ...	Tirvarore and Munnargoody	53	4
Rameshwaram ...	Puttoocottah, Tondy and Ramnaud ...	179	0
Ramnaud ...	Puttoocottah and Tondy	142	0
Salem	Tanjore, Trichinopoly and Namcull ...	180	1
Shiyally	Tranquebar	42	3
Tanjore	Tirvarore	56	0
Tondy	Munnargoody and Puttoocottah ...	111	4
Tranquebar ...	Caricaul	22	2
Trichinopoly ...	Tanjore	93	2
Tripatore	Munnargoody and Arantaungy ...	117	1

NEILGHERRY (நீலகிரி - nílagiri, *Tam.*). From (níla, san. blue + giri, san. mountain) [neel]. Sanscrit name (astagiri), meaning mountain behind which the sun sets. Old Tamul name, Malainaud, or hill country. One of the ranges of the Hindoo pooraunic cosmography has the same name ; but the title is not uncommon. Revenue district ; situated inland, containing the hill plateau and a portion of Wynaud ; between 11° 11′ and 11° 42′ N. lat., and between 76° 17′ and 77° 01′ E. long. ; bounded N. by Mysore, E. by Coimbatore district, S. by Coimbatore and Malabar districts, W. by Malabar district ; square miles 957 ; pop. 91,034 ; language Canarese, Tamul and Malayalam. Contains rivers Moyaur, Pycarrah, and Beypore. The whole area of the district is represented by the following sub-areas :—Coondah division, Merkoonaud division, Paranginaud division, Todanaud division, Wynaud division being the south-east portion of Wynaud. For general administrative purposes the district is distributed between the following revenue and magisterial officers, who have their head-quarters at the places shown. The pay set opposite the subordinate officers gives the grade of the corresponding charge :—Collector, Ootacamund. Head assistant collector, Pundalore, in charge of South-east Wynaud division. Deputy tahsildars ; Coonoor, Rs. 100, range situated in the south of Paranginaud division and embracing Paranginaud and Merkoonaud divisions ; Goodalore, Rs. 100, range situated in the Numbalagode amshom, South-east Wynaud division ; Ootacamund, Rs. 100, range situated in the Todanaud division and embracing Todanaud and Coondah divisions. Similarly judicial officers :—Additional sessions judge, Ootacamund ; Subordinate judge, Ootacamund, with civil jurisdiction over the whole district ; District moonsif, Goodalore with jurisdiction extending over Wynaud south-east division. Similarly Public works officers :—District engineer, Ootacamund ; Sub-divisional officers, Nos. 1 and 2. Contains Registration sub-districts Coonoor, Goodalore and Ootacamund. Contains Forest ranges Coonoor, Kotagherry, Kullaur, Mailore, Moothoomullay, Nediwuttam, Ootacamund and Seegore. Contains Municipalities Coonoor and Ootacamund. The following general references should be made to the preceding volumes :—general geography, I (1) to (29) ; general ethnology, I (29) to (109) ; general history, I (110) to (188) ; physical geography, II, 1 ; meteorology, II, 3 ; geology, II, 8 ; fauna, II, 21 ; flora, II, 26 ; mineralogy, II, 29. The following references in the preceding volumes will furnish details special to the district :—particulars about towns, II, 48 ; comparative population, II, 172 ; location of revenue officers, II, 389 ; registrars' and sub-registrars' stations, II, 421 ; rain-guage stations, II, 428 ; maps published, II, 436 ; survey topographical lists, II, 443 ; hospitals and dispensaries, II, 447 ; missionary stations, II, 455 ; head-quarter stations of gazetted officers, II, 461 ; incidence of taxation, II, 463 ; weights and measures of the district, II, 516. A special gazetteer account of the whole district is given at II, 107. For Neilgherry sholahs see Sholah. The following are the principal elevations :—Bevoybetta, 8,488 feet ; Coondabetta, 6,555 ; Coondamoogy, 7,816 ; Coondah peak, 8,353 ; Coonoor, 5,886 ; Devarbetta, 6,571 ; Devasholahbetta, 8,380 ; Dimhutty, 6,330 ; Dodabetta, 8,760 ; Hokkabetta, 7,267 ; Kodanaud, 6,815 ; Kotagherry, 6,571 ; Macoorty peak, 8,402 ; Oorbetta, 6,915 ; Ootacamund, 7,361 ; Tamrabetta, 7,292. The following table gives various travelling distances in miles on the plateau. These are by new carriage roads, but by old roads the distances are often shorter :—

Avalanchey to Banghy tappaul	9	Nediwuttam to Goodalore ...	9
Banghy tappaul to Sisparra ...	9	Ootacamund to Avalanchey ...	13
Berliaur to Kullaur ...	4	Ootacamund to Bilicull ...	7
Coonoor to Berliaur ...	12	Ootacamund to Calicut ...	103
Coonoor to Hoolicull ...	5	Ootacamund to Coonoor ...	11
Coonoor to Lamb's rock ...	3	Ootacamund to Croremund ...	10
Croremund to Macoorty ...	6	Ootacamund to Cullhutty ...	8
Cullhutty to Seegore	4	Ootacamund to Devasholah ...	9½
Devasholah to Kartairy ...	9	Ootacamund to Kartairy ...	7
Devasholah to Mailore ...	3	Ootacamund to McIvor's bund.	12
Devasholah to Tyemullay ...	6½	Ootacamund to Pycarrah ...	12
Goodalore to Calicut by Carcoor	69	Ootacamund to Pycarrah falls by Pycarrah road	14
Goodalore to Cannanore ...	126	Ootacamund to Wellington ...	10
Kartairy to Colacumbey ...	6	Ootacamund to Yellanhully chuttram	6
Kartairy to Coonoor	6	Pycarrah to Nediwuttam ...	9
Kartairy to Hoolicull	7	Seegore to Teppacadav ...	10½
Kotagherry to Kodanaud ...	8	Sisparra to Sholacull	10½
Kotagherry to Mettupolliem ...	20	Teppacadav to Mysore ...	45
Kullaur to Mettupolliem ...	6	Wellington to Kotagherry ...	13
Lamb's rock to the Dolphin's nose	3	Yellanhully to Kartairy ...	5
McIvor's bund to Mailcoondah.	9		

——(1) The principal places, &c., in the district are the following.——*Adderley estate* (ಗೂಬೆತೋಟ - gúbetóta, Can.). Can. from (gúbe, can. owl + tóta, can. garden). Coffee estate, Berliaur village, Paranginaud ; acres 407 ; lat. 11° 21′ ; long. 76° 54′ ; from Coonoor E. 4 miles. In Berliaur village.——*Annappa sholah* (അണ്ണപ്പഷോല - annappashóla, Mal.). From (annappa, can. proper name + shólai, tam. plantation). Coffee estate, Moonnanaud amshom, S.E. Wynaud ; from Nelacottah W.N.W. 2 miles. 16·45 acres.——*Arattapauray* (അറ്റപ്പാറ - arattappára, Mal.). From (aratti, tam. fear + párai, tam. rock). Tea estate, Ouchterlony valley ; from Goodalore S.S.W. 3 miles. 295 acres. ——*Arvencaud* (அரவங்காடு - aravangádu, Tam.). See sep. title.——*Atticull* (ಅತ್ತಿಕಲ್ಲು - attikallu, Can.). From (atti, can. fig tree, ficus glomerata, willd. + kallu, can. stone). Cinchona estate, Todanaud ; from Ootacamund N.N.W. 5 miles. 90 acres. ——*Avalanchey* (ಅವಲಾಂಚೆ - avalánche, Can.). See sep. title. ——*Bairhutty* (ಬೇರಹಟ್ಟಿ - bérahatti, Can.). From (béra, can. trade + hatti, can. shepherd village). Hamlet, Paranginaud ; lat. 11° 23′ ; long. 76° 50′. Hamlet of Jackatalla [q.v.] village. Also Tea [q.v.] and Blue gum [q.v.] estate, Paranginaud ; from Wellington barracks N.E. 1 mile. 49 acres.——*Baitmund* (ಬೆಟ್ಟಮಂದು - bettamandu, Can.). From (betta, can. mountain + mandu, can. todah hut). Village, Hill, Paranginaud division ; lat. 11° 24′ ; long. 76° 50′ ; from Coonoor N.N.W. 4 miles ; from Ootacamund E. 6 miles.——*Barahuddy* (ಬರೆಅಡಿ - bareadi, Can.). From (bare, can. bare + adi, can. bottom). Tea and cinchona estates, Paranginaud ; from Kotagherry E. 3 miles. 166 acres. ——*Bear hill* (ಡೇರಬೆಟ್ಟ - dérbetta, Can.). See sep. title.——*Bellatty* (ಬೆಳ್ಳಟ್ಟಿ - bellatti, Can.). From (bel, can. white + hatti, can. shepherd village). Coffee estate, Coondah division, 58 acres.——*Belliky* (ಬೆಳ್ಳಿಕಿ - belliki, Can.). See sep. title. ——*Benhope* (மரப்பாலம் - marappálam, Tam.). Tam. from (maram, tam. wood + pálam, tam. bridge). Coffee estate, Paranginaud ; lat. 11° 20′ ; long. 76° 52′. On Coonoor ghaut. About 179 acres.——*Benhutty* (ಬನಹಟ್ಟಿ - banahatti, Can.). From (bana, can. temple + hatti, can. village). Coffee estate, Merkoonaud ; from Coonoor S.W. 4 miles. 155 acres. ——*Berliaur* (ಬರಲಿಯಾರು - baraliyáru, Can.). See sep. title.——*Bigooly* (ಬಿಗುಳಿ - biguli, Can.). From (bigu, can. to swell). Name of the Coondah river.——*Bilicull* (ಬಿಳಿಕಲ್ಲು - bilikallu, Can.). See sep. title.——*Billimullay* (ಬಿಳ್ಳಿಮಲೆ - billimale, Can.). From (bili, can. tree, rhododendron arboreum, smith + male, can. hill). Cinchona ; in Hoolicull village. 3 miles from Coonoor S.W. ; 3 acres.——*Brooklands* (புரூக்லாண்ட்சு - purúglándsu, Tam.). Tea estate ; acres 149 ; lat. 11° 21′ ; long. 76° 51′. A tea estate ; within Coonoor town.——*Burnside* (ಗೊಟ್ಟೆಯಟ್ಟು - gotteyattu, Can.). Can. from (gotte, can. fissure

+ attu, can. to burn). Coffee estate; acres 92; 3 miles east of Kotagherry in Conacary village.——*Canavatty* (ಕಣವಟ್ಟಿ - kanavatti, Can.; கணவட்டி - kannavatti, Tam.). From (kanive, can. pass + hatti, can. shepherd village). Coffee and cinchona estates, Paranginaud; from Kotagherry S.E. 3 miles. 101 acres. ——*Canning seat* (கானிங்சீட்டு - kaningsittu, Tam.). See sep. title.——*Carabill sholah* (ಕರಬಿಲ್ಲುಶೋಲೆ - karabillushóle, Can.). From (kara, san. hand + billu, can. bow + shóle, can. cluster of trees). Coffee estate, Todanaud; from Ootacamund N. 7 miles. 51 acres.——*Catherine fall* (கொட்டக்கிரியருவி - kóttakkiriyaruvi, Tam.). See sep. title.——*Caulairy* (ಕಾಳೇರಿ - káléri, Can.). From (kálu, can. quarter + éri, can. tank-bund). Hill, Coondah division; lat. 11° 18′; long. 76° 36′; height 8,622 feet; from Ootacamund S.W. 13 miles; from Macoorty S.S.E. 6 miles.——*Caundal* (காந்தல் - kándal, Tam.). See sep. title. ——*Cauval combey* (ಕಾವಲಕೊಂಬೆ - kávalakombe, Can.). From (kával, tam. guard + kombé, can. kurumbar village). Coffee estate, Merkoonaud. E. of Hoolicull droog. 51 acres.—— *Chappatody* (ചപ്പത്തോടി - chappattódi, Mal.). From (chappu, mal. leaf + todi, mal. garden). Coffee and cinchona estates, Cherangode amshom, S.E. Wynaud; from Cherambaudy N. ¾ mile. 471 acres.——*Cherambaudy* (ചേരമ്പാടി - chérampáti, Mal.). See sep. title.——*Cherangode* (ചേരങ്കോട - chérankótu, Mal.). See sep. title.——*Chinna coonoor* (ಚಿನ್ನಕುನ್ನೂರು - chinnakunnúru, Can.). From (chinna, can. small + kunnúru, can. village so called). Hill, Todanaud division; lat. 11° 29′; long. 76° 47′; from Ootacamund N.N.E. 6 miles. Overhangs the Moyaur valley.——*Chinna dodabetta* (ಚಿನ್ನದೊಡ್ಡಬೆಟ್ಟ - chinnadoddabetta, Can.). From (chinna, can. small + doddabetta, can. the great hill). So called in contradistinction to Dodabetta proper. Hill, Merkoonaud division; lat. 11° 22′; long. 76° 45′; height 7,349 feet; from Coonoor W.N.W. 7 miles; from Ootacamund S. 3 miles. Behind the Lawrence Asylum.——*Cholaudy* (ചോലാടി - choláti, Mal.). From (chóla, mal. grove + nátu, mal. country). Coffee and cinchona estates, Cherangode amshom, S.E. Wynaud; from Cherambaudy W.N.W. 2 miles. 739·74 acres.——*Chowgatcully* (ಚೌಗತಕಳ್ಳಿ - chaugatakalli, Can.). From (chauka, can. square + kalli, can. milk-hedge, euphorbia genus). Village, Government plantation, Todanaud division; from Ootacamund W. 4 miles.——*Clifton* (கிளிப்டன் - kilibdan, Tam.). Estate, Moonnanaud amshom, S.E. Wynaud; from Nelacottah N. 1¾ miles. 350 acres.——*Codamoolay* (ಕೋಡಮೂಲೆ - kódamúle, Can.). From (kóda, can. monkey + múle, can. corner). Hamlet of Berliaur village, Paranginaud; acres 423; lat. 11° 22′; long. 76° 53′; from Coonoor E.N.E. 3 miles.——*Codamund* (ಕೋಡಮಂದೆ - kódamande, Can.). From (kóda, can. monkey + mandu, can. cattle-fold). Estate, Merkoonaud; from Coonoor S.W. 6 miles. 38 acres.——*Colacumbey* (ಕೊಲಕಂಬೆ - kolakambe, Can.). See sep. title.——*Colcaray* (ಕೊಳಿಕರೆ - kolikare, Can.). Coffee estate, Paranginaud; from Kotagherry S.E. 5 miles. 82 acres.—— *Conabetta* (ಕೋಣಬೆಟ್ಟ - kónabetta, Can.). From (kóné, can. crooked + betta, can. hill). Hill, Todanaud division; lat. 11° 30′; long. 76° 46′; height 6,777 feet; from Ootacamund N.N.E. 7 miles. Also called Seegore peak.——*Conavacoray* (ಕೊಣವಕೊರೈ - konavakorai, Can.). From (konava, can. a badaga name + korai, can. a small shola). Hamlet of Jackanairy village, Paranginaud; lat. 11° 25′; long. 76° 56′; from Kotagherry S.E. 2 miles.—— *Coocalbetta* (ಕೂಕಲ್‌ಬೆಟ್ಟ - kúkalbetta, Can.). From (kú, tam. the sound + kal, can. stone + betta, can. hill); echoing rocks. Hill, Todanaud division; lat. 11° 28′; long. 76° 50′; height 7,161 feet; from Ootacamund N.E. 8 miles; from Kotagherry N.W. 6 miles. At almost an equal distance from it and Ootacamund. ——*Coolyaud* (കുള്ളിയാട - kulliyátu, Mal.). From (kulli, mal. female dwarf + nátu, mal. country). Coffee estate, Numbalagode amshom, S.E. Wynaud; from Goodalore N.E. ½ a mile. Also a Chetty [q.v.] village. 426·50 acres.——*Coomal* (ಕೂಮಲ್ - kúmal, Can.). From (kúmal, tam. proper name); after a coorumban [q.v.] of that name. Coffee estate, Merkoonaud; on S. slopes of Neilgherries overlooking Bhawauny valley. 89 acres.——*Coondabetta* (ಕುಂದಬೆಟ್ಟ - kundabetta, Can.). From (kunru, tam. hill + betta, can. hill). Hill, Coondah division; lat. 11° 17′; long. 76° 43′; height 6,555 feet; from Ootacamund S.S.W. 9 miles.——*Coondah* (ಕುಂದ - kunda, Can.). See sep. title. ——*Coondamoogy* (ಕುಂದಮೂಗೆ - kundamúge, Can.). From (kunru, tam. hill + múge, can. dumb woman). Hill, Paranginaud division; lat. 11° 24′; long. 76° 51′; height 7,690 feet; from Coonoor N. 4 miles; from Ootacamund E. 7 miles. Kotagherry road passes round the eastern face and there is a Government Australian tree [australian gum tree] plantation known as Rallia [q.v.].——*Coonoor* (ಕುನ್ನೂರು - kunnúru, Can.). See sep. title.——*Coorumbaudy* (ಕುರುಂಬಾಡಿ - kurumbádi, Can.). From (kurumba, can. shepherd + pádi, tam. village). Coffee estates, Paranginaud. Above Coonoor ghaut road. From Coonoor E.S.E. 3 miles. 76 acres.——*Coottacaud* (குட்டக்காடு - kuttakkádu, Tam.). From (kuttam, tam. smallness + kádu, tam. jungle). Hill, Todanaud division; lat. 11° 25′; long. 76° 40′; height 7,933·4 feet; from Ootacamund W.N.W. 5 miles; from Dodabetta W N.W. 7 miles.——*Cotacull* (ಕೋಟಕಲ್ಲು - kótakallu, Can.). From (kóta, can. tribe so called + kallu, can. stone). Coffee estate, Merkoonaud; from Mailoor S. 3 miles. 100 acres.——

Craigmore (ಬರಲನೆ - baralane, Can.). Can. from (baralu, can. dry + ane, can. bund). Coffee and Cinchona estate, Merkoonaud; acres 300; lat. 11° 18′; long. 76° 47′; from Kartairy S. 3 miles.——*Croremund* (ಕ್ರೂರಮಂದು - krúramandu, Can.). See sep. title.——*Culcoodiyore* (ಕಲ್ಕುಡಿಯೂರು - kalkudiyúru, Can.). From (kal, tam. stone + kudi, tam. house + úr, tam. village). Hill, Wynaud S.E. division; lat. 11° 25′; long. 76° 40′; height 8,002·4 feet; from Goodalore S.E. 10 miles; from Ootacamund W.N.W. 5 miles.——*Cullhutty* (ಕಲ್ಹಟ್ಟಿ - kalhatti, Can.). See sep. title.——*Cullicoodal* (ಕಳ್ಳಿಕುಡಲು - kallikudalu, Can.). From (kalli, can. milk-hedge plant, euphorbia genus + kúdu, can. junction). Coffee estate, Paranginaud; from Kotagherry S.E. 6 miles. 131 acres.——*Cullore* (ಕಲ್ಲೂರು - kallúru, Can.). Means stone + village. Coffee estate, Paranginaud; from Kotagherry S. 3 miles. 60 acres.——*Culramode* (ಕಲ್ರಮೇಡು - kalramédu, Can.). From (kalla, can. robber + médu, can. rising ground). Coffee estate, Paranginaud; from Coonoor S.E. 1¼ miles. 57 acres.——*Cunnairimookk* (கன்னேரிமுக்கு - kannérimúkku, Tam.). Hamlet of Kotagherry village, Paranginaud; lat. 11° 26′; long. 76° 54′; from Kotagherry N.N.W. 1¼ miles.—— *Cutchambaura* (കച്ചമ്പാറ - kaççampára, Mal.). Village, Wynaud S.E. division. Gold mining station on the Coothirapoya.—— *Dairbetta* (ದೇರ್‌ಬೆಟ್ಟ - dérbetta, Can.). See Bear hill.——*Devamullay* (ದೇವಮಲೆ - dévamale, Can.). From (déva, san. god + + male, can. mountain). Coffee estate, Todanaud and Numbalagode amshoms; from Goodalore E. 1¾ miles. 441 acres.—— *Devancoonn* (ദേവങ്കുന്നു - dévankunnu, Mal.). From (déva, san. god + kunnu, mal. hill). Coffee estate, Moonnanaud, S.E. Wynaud; from Nelacottah W. 3 miles. 113·95 acres.——*Devarbetta* (ದೇವರಬೆಟ್ಟ - dévarabetta, Can.). See sep. title.——*Devasholah* (ದೇವರಶೋಲೆ - dévarashóle, Can.). See sep. title.—— *Devaulah* (ദേവാല - dévála, Mal.). See sep. title.——*Dimhutty* (ದಿಮ್ಹಟ್ಟಿ - dimhatti, Can.). See sep. title.——*Dodabetta* (ದೊಡ್ಡಬೆಟ್ಟ - doddabetta, Can.). See sep. title.——*Dolphin's nose* (மூக்கு மலை - múkkumalai, Tam.). See sep. title.—— *Droog* (ದುರ್ಗ - durga, Can.). Means inaccessible. Coffee estate, Merkoonaud; from Coonoor S.E. 3 miles. 1,089 acres.—— *Eechoray* (ಈಚೊರೆ - íchóre, Can.). Coffee estate, Paranginaud; from Kotagherry S.E. 5 miles. 68 acres.——*Glenburnie* (கிளென்பார்னி - kilenbarni, Tam.). Coffee estate, Paranginaud; acres 387; lat. 11° 22′; long. 76° 54′; from Coonoor E.N.E. 4 miles.——*Glencairnie* (ಹಾಲುಹಾಡಾ - háluhádá, Can.). From (hálu, can. milk + háda, can. flat land). Coffee estate, Merkoonaud; acres 188; lat. 11° 18′; long. 76° 46′; from Kartairy S. 3 miles. Lies on both sides of the Alaudeer river. It lies partly in Mailore and partly in Adhicauratty villages.—— *Glendale* (ಬೆಲ್ಲನ್ನಿ - bellanni, Can.). Can. from (bella, can. white + anni, can. swamp). Tea estate, Merkoonaud; acres 219; lat. 11° 20′; long. 76° 50′; from Coonoor S.S.W. 1½ miles.——*Goodalore* (ഗൂടലൂർ - gútalúr, Mal.). See sep. title.——*Goodalore mullay* (ഗൂടലൂർമ്മല - gútalúrmmala, Mal.). Coffee estate, Ouchterlony valley; from Goodalore S.S.E. 1½ miles. 144 acres.—— *Goodicaud* (ಗುಡಿಕಾಡು - gudikádu, Can.). From (gudi, can. temple + kádu, can. jungle). Hill, Coondah division; lat. 11° 18′; long. 76° 37′; height 8,492 feet; from Ootacamund S.W. 11 miles. At the head of the Avalanchey valley.——*Goolicullmullay* (ഗുളിക്കൽമല - gulikkalmala, Mal.). From (gulikan, mal. the demon + mala, mal. mountain). Hill, Coondah division; lat. 11° 15′; long. 76° 30′; from Ootacamund W.S.W. 20 miles.——*Halashana* (ಹಲಶನ - halashana, Can.). From (halasa, can. jack tree, artocarpus integrifolia, willd. + hane, can. grassy meadow). Coffee estate, Merkoonaud; from Coonoor S.W. 5 miles. 119 acres.——*Haudatoray* (ಹಡತೊರೆ - hadatore, Can.). From (háda, can. flat land + tore, can. ford). Coffee and tea estates, Paranginaud; from Kotagherry S.W. 2 miles. 176 acres.——*Haurcull* (ಹಾವುಕಲ್ಲು - hávukallu, Can.). From (hávu, can. snake + kal, tam. rock). Coffee estate, Paranginaud; from Kotagherry E. 3 miles. 159 acres.——*Hill grove* (இல்குரோவ் - ilgurów, Tam.). Tea and coffee estate, Paranginaud; acres 464; lat. 11° 21′; long. 76° 52′; from Coonoor E. 3 miles.——*Hokkabetta* (ಹೊಕ್ಕಬೆಟ್ಟ - hokkabetta, Can.). From (hokka, can. entering + betta, can. hill). Peak; height 7,267 feet.——*Hookoor* (ಹುಕೂರು - hukúru, Can.). Tea and coffee estates, Merkoonaud; from Coonoor S.W. 3 miles. 54 acres.—— *Hoolicull droog* (ಹುಲಿಕಲ್ಲುದುರ್ಗ - hulikalludurga, Can.). See sep. title.——*Ibex hill* (ಮುಟ್ಟುಬೆಟ್ಟ - muttubetta, Can.). See sep. title.——*Ilitoray* (ಇಲ್ಲಿತೊರೆ - illitore, Can.). From (illi, mal. bamboo branch + tore, can. river). Village, Paranginaud; from Wellington N.N.E. 3 miles. 963 acres.——*Jackanairy* (சக்கலாரை - shakkalarai, Tam.). See sep. title.——*Jackatalla* (ಜಗತಾಳ - jagatála, Can.). See sep. title.——*Kaity* (ಕೇತಿ - kéti, Can.). See sep. title.——*Kartairy* (ಕಾಟೇರಿ - kártéri, Can.). See sep. title.——*Keel kotagherry* (ಕೀಳ್‌ಕೋಟಗಿರಿ - kílakótagiri, Can.; கீழ்க்கோத்தகிரி - kízhkkóttagiri, Tam.). From (kízh, tam. east + kóttagiri, tam. the mountain). Village, Paranginaud division; acres 687; lat. 11° 27′; long. 76° 58′; from Coonoor N.E. 12 miles; from Ootacamund E.N.E. 15 miles. Special residence of Kotars [q.v.]——*Keelnaud* (கீழ்நாடு - kízhnádu, Tam.). From (kízh, east + nádu, tam. country). Division, Todanaud division. One of the two divisions of

Todanaud, occupying the country lying east and north of Dodabetta hill range and north of the Marlemund hill line, as far as Cullhutty and Sholore.——*Kengaray* (ಕೆಂಗರೆ - kengare, Can.). From (kem, can. red + kare, can. bank). Coffee and cinchona estates, and village, Paranginaud; from Kotagherry E. 5 miles. 7,259 acres.——*Kerehauda* (ಕೆರೆಹಾಡಾ - kerehádá, Can.). From (kere, can. tank + háda, can. flat land). Village, Merkoonaud; lat. 11° 23′; long. 76° 46′. Is a hamlet of Kittoo village.——*Kinnacoray* (ಕಿನ್ನಕೊರೈ - kinnakorai, Can.). Coffee and cinchona estates; Coondah division; from Ootacamund S. 12 miles. 241 acres.——*Kodanaud* (ಕೋಡನಾಡು - kódanádu, Can.). See sep. title.——*Koktoray* (ಕೊಕ್ಕುತೊರೆ - kokkutore, Can.). From (kokku, can. bandicoot + tore, can. bank). Estate, Coondah division; from Ootacamund S.W. 14 miles. No part yet cultivated. 271 acres.——*Koliputty* (ಕೋಳಿಪಟ್ಟಿ - kólipatti, Can.). From (kóli, can. cock + patti, can. place). Coffee estate, Todanaud; from Cullhutty waterfalls N. ½ mile. 292 acres.——*Kotagherry* (ಕೋತಗಿರಿ - kótagiri, Can.). See sep. title.——*Kullaur* (கல்லாறு - kallâru, Tam.). See sep. title.——*Lousiana* (லூசியானா - lúsiyáná, Tam.). Coffee and cinchona estate, Merkoonaud; acres 223; lat. 11° 18′; long. 76° 48′; from Kartairy S.S.E. 4 miles.——*Lovedale* (மஞ்சனக்கோரை - mañjanakkórai, Tam.). See sep. title.——*Lower deva mullay* (കീഴ്ദേവന്മല - kízhdévanmala, Mal.). From (kízh, mal. lower + déva, san. god + mala, mal. mountain). Coffee estate, Numbalagode amshom, S.E. Wynaud and Todanaud; from Goodalore S.E. 1 mile. 117 acres.——*Macoorty* (ಮೂಕುರ್ತಿ - múkurti, Can.). See sep. title.——*Madanaud* (ಮದನಾಡು - madanádu, Can.). From (madai, tam. cave + nádu, can. country). Coffee and cinchona estates. Paranginaud; from Curzon estate N.N.E. 3 miles; from Kotagherry N.E. 8 miles. 216 acres.——*Mailcoondah* (ಮೇಲ್ಕುಂದ - mélkunda, Can.). See sep. title.——*Mailcottah* (மேலக்கோட்டை - mélakkóttai, Tam.). See sep. title.——*Mailnaud* (மேல்நாடு - mélnádu, Tam.). From (mél, tam. west + nádu, tam. country). Division, Todanaud division. One of the two divisions of Todanaud comprising the tract lying between the western slopes of Dodabetta and the Nedoo mullay and Coondah ranges.——*Mailore* (ಮೇಲೂರು - mélúru, Can.). See sep. title.——*Manjore* (ಮಂಜೂರು - manjúru, Can.). From (manju, can. dew + úru, can. village). Coffee and cinchona estates, Coondah division. Situated on right bank of Coondah river. 139 acres.——*Maramoottoo* (മരമുട്ടു - maramuttu, Mal.). From (maram, mal. tree + muttu, mal. support). Coffee estate, Moonnanaud amshom, S.E. Wynaud; from Nelacottah W. 1 mile. 357 acres.——*Marlemund* (ಮಾಲೇಮಂದು - málémandu, Can.). See sep. title.——*Marpanmoody* (மொறப்பிமுடி - morappimudi, Tam.). Village, Wynaud S.E. division; lat. 11° 31′; long. 76° 27′; height 5,014 feet; from Goodalore W.N.W. 6 miles; from Ootacamund W.N.W. 21 miles.——*Marvoohulla* (ಮಾರ್ವುಹಳ್ಳ - márvuhalla, Can.). From (máru, can. fathom + halla, can. pit). Coffee and cinchona estates, Todanaud; from Ootacamund N.E. 12 miles. 340 acres.——*Merkoonaud* (மேற்குநாடு - mérgunádu, Tam.). See sep. title.——*Mettoocherry* (மேட்டுச்சேரி - méttuççéri, Tam.). See sep. title.——*Moodcaud* (ಮೂಡುಕ್ಕಾಡು - múdukkádu, Can.). From (múdu, can. east + kádu, can. jungle). River, Paranginaud and Todanaud divisions; forms the boundary between Todanaud and Paranginaud divisions.——*Moonanaud* (മുന്നാട് - múnnanátu, Mal.). See sep. title.——*Moothoomullay* (മുതുമല - mutumala, Mal.). See sep. title.——*Mootnaud* (ಮುತ್ತನಾಡು - muttanádu, Can.). From (muttu, tam. high ground + nádu, can. country). Coffee estate, Merkoonaud; from Coonoor S.W. 4 miles. 302 acres.——*Moottinaudbetta* (ಮುತ್ತಿನಾಡುಬೆಟ್ಟ - muttinádubetta, Can.). From (muttu, tam. high ground + nádu, can. country + betta, can. hill). Hill, Todanaud division; lat. 11° 27′; long. 76° 43′; height 7,620 feet; from Ootacamund N.N.W. 3 miles. At the head of the Seegore pass.——*Mount gordon* (ಗಾರ್ಡನ್‌ಬೆಟ್ಟ - gárdanbetta, Can.). Tea and cinchona estates, Todanaud; from Pycarrah N. 2 miles. 150 acres.——*Moyaur* (ಮೊಯಾರು - moyáru, Can.). See sep. title.——*Muddanah sholah* (ಮದ್ದಣ್ಣಶೋಲೆ - maddannashóle, Can.). From (maddanna, can. proper name + shóla, can. plantation). Tea, cinchona and gum estates, Todanaud; from Ootacamund W. 3 miles outside settlement boundary. 52 acres. Another from Ootacamund W. 3 miles within settlement boundary. 62 acres.——*Mullanore* (ಮಲ್ಲನೂರು - mallanúru, Can.). From (malla, san. wrestler + úru, can. village). Coffee, tea, and fruit estates, Paranginaud; from Coonoor E. 1½ miles. 67 acres.——*Munja combey* (ಮಂಜಕೊಂಬೆ - manjakombe, Can.). From (manju, can. dew + kombe, can. village). Coffee estate, Merkoonaud; from Coonoor W. 8 miles. 25 acres.——*Mushnigoody* (ಮಶಿನಿಗುಡಿ - mashinigudi, Can.). See sep. title.——*Naicken sholah* (നായക്കൻശോല - náyakkanshóla, Mal.). Means naicken's plantation. Coffee and cinchona estates, Numbalagode amshom, S.E. Wynaud. Close to Cherambaudy. 626 acres.——*Naudgauny* (നാട്ടുകാണി - nátukáni, Mal.). From (nátu, mal. country + káni, mal. landmark); free height overlooking the low country. Village, Hill, Wynaud S.E. division; acres 384; lat. 11° 28′; long. 76° 28′; from Goodalore W.S.W. 6 miles; from Ootacamund W.N.W. 20 miles. Gold mining locality. The hill is the highest in the west of the Neilgherries. Also coffee [q.v.] and gum [blue gum] estates, Numbalagode amshom, S.E. Wynaud; from Devaulah S.S.E. 2 miles. 184 acres.——*Nediwuttam* (നാടുവട്ടം - nátuvattam, Mal.). See sep. title.——*Nedoomullay* (ನೀಡುಮಲೆ - nídumale, Can.). See sep. title.——*Nedooncoolam* (நெடுங்குளம் - nedungulam, Tam.). From (nedu, tam. long + kulam, tam. tank). Village; Paranginaud Division; acres 8,552; lat. 11° 29′; long. 76° 56′; from Coonoor N.E. 11 miles; from Ootacamund E.N.E. 13 miles. Once every year, the Badagas [q.v.] tread upon fire during a religious ceremony.——*Neilgherry peak* (நீலகிரிமலை - nílagirimalai, Tam.). See sep. title.——*Nelacottah* (നല്ലക്കോട്ട - nallekótta, Mal.). See sep. title.——*Nelliyaulam* (നെല്ലിയാളം - nelliyálam, Mal.). From (nelli, tam. emblic tree, phyllanthus emblica, linn. + ázham, tam. depth). Village, Wynaud S.E. division; acres 22,134; lat. 11° 31′; long. 76° 24′; from Goodalore W. 10 miles; from Ootacamund W.N.W. 25 miles. Gold mining locality. Residence of Nelliyaulam arasoo, a jenmy. Also Coffee estate, Moonanaud amshom, S.E. Wynaud; from Devaulah N. 4 miles. 102 acres.——*Nircumbey* (ನೀರಕಂಬೆ - nírakambe, Can.). From (níru, can. water + kambe, can. cave). Village, Merkoonaud division; lat. 11° 21′; long. 76° 47′; from Coonoor W. 3 miles; from Ootacamund S.E. 5 miles. Outstation of the Basel mission.——*Numbalagode* (നമ്പലക്കോട് - nambalakótu, Mal.). See sep. title.——*Nundhutty* (ನಂದ್ಹಟ್ಟಿ - nandhatti, Can.). From (nane, can. to moisten + hatti, can. village). Coffee estate, Numbalagode amshom, S.E. Wynaud; from Goodalore W. 1¼ miles. 244·39 acres.——*Nunjenaud* (நஞ்சநாடு - nañjanádu, Tam.). See sep. title.——*Ooliyat* (ಉಳಿಯತ್ತು - uliyattu, Can.). From (ulu, can. to plough + ettu, can. bullock). Coffee and cinchona estates, Coondah division; from Mailcoondah N.E. 2 miles. 331 acres.——*Oombely mullay* (ഉമ്പിളിമല - umbalimala, Mal.). Coffee and cinchona estates, Ouchterlony valley; from Goodalore S.W. 6 miles. 289 acres.——*Oorbetta* (ಊರ್‌ಬೆಟ್ಟ - úrbetta, Can.). From (úru, can. country + betta, can. hill). Can. also (dimhattibetta), meaning inferior + village + hill. Other name for Dimhutty hill.——*Ootacamund* (ஒத்தகைமந்து - ottagaimandu, Tam.). See sep. title.——*Orange valley* (ನಾರಂಗಹಳ್ಳ - nárangahalla, Can.). See sep. title.——*Ouchterlony valley* (ಆಕ್ಟರಲೋನಿಹಳ್ಳ - áktaralónihalla, Can.). See sep. title.——*Paranginaud* (ಪರಂಗಿನಾಡು - paranginádu, Can.). See sep. title.——*Paundy* (പാണ്ടി - pánti, Mal.). River, Wynaud S.E. division. Rises in the hills north of Macoorty, and with the Nelambore river forms the Beypore river. It forms the boundary on the North between Ouchterlony valley and the Numbalagode amshom proper.——*Peechulbetta* (ಪೀಚಲ್‌ಬೆಟ್ಟ - píchalbetta, Can.). From (píchu, can. coir + betta, can. hill). Hill, Todanaud division; lat. 11° 22′; long. 76° 36′; height 8,348 feet; from Ootacamund W.S.W. 10 miles. E. of Macoorty, northern extremity of the Coondahs. Between these two peaks the Pycarrah river takes its rise.——*Peermund* (ಪೇರಮಂದು - péramandu, Can.). See sep. title.——*Periya sholah* (പെരിയശോല - periyashóla, Mal.). Means large plantation. Coffee and cinchona estates, Ouchterlony valley; from Goodalore S.W. 6 miles. 188 acres.——*Pilloor* (ಪಿಲ್ಲೂರು - pillúru, Can.). Coffee estate, Merkoonaud; from Coonoor S. 4 miles. 715 acres.——*Poortey* (ಪೂರ್ತೆ - púrte, Can.). Village, stream, Merkoonaud division; lat. 11° 21′; long. 76° 41′; from Coonoor W. 12 miles; from Ootacamund S.W. 7 miles. The bungalow [q.v.] here was erected at the site of a bund [q.v.] across the stream made on a certain silting process in 1868-69, but the project failed. The stream is often known as the Coondah.——*Pundalore* (പന്തല്ലൂർ - pantalúr, Mal.). See sep. title.——*Pycarrah* (ಪಾಯಕರೆ - páyakare, Can.). See sep. title.——*Rallia* (ಕುಂದಮೂಗೆ - kundamúge, Can.). Vern. from (kunru, tam. hill + múge, can. dumb woman). Village; lat. 11° 25′; long. 76° 52′; height 7,375 feet. Plantation [coondamoogy].——*Rungasawmy's peak* (ರಂಗಸಾಮಿಮಲೆ - rangasámimale, Can.). See sep. title.——*Salada* (ಸೇಲಾಡಾ - séládá, Can.). Coffee and cinchona estates, Paranginaud; from Kotagherry S. 1¼ miles. 283 acres.——*Seegore* (ಸೀಗೂರು - sigúru, Can.). See sep. title.——*Seeputty* (சிப்பட்டி - shippatti, Tam.). From (shígu, tam. thatch grass, aristida setacea, retz. + patti, tam. shepherd village). Village; Wynaud S.E. division; lat. 11° 29′; long. 76° 42′; from Goodalore 4 miles; from Ootacamund 34 miles. Auriferous beds.——*Sholore* (ಶೋಲೂರು - shólúru, Can.). From (shóle, can. grove + úru, can. village). Village, Todanaud division; pop. 1,564; acres 22,541; lat. 11° 29′; long. 76° 42′; from Ootacamund N.N.W. 6 miles. Groups of cromlechs [paundoocull] with sculptures of the nundy [q.v.] and lingam [q.v.] and male and female figures. A cairn [paundicoozhy] opened here was found to contain an iron sickle and some pottery. Several cairns and barrows in the neighbouring hills. Also a tea [q.v.] and cinchona [koinah] estate, Todanaud; from Ootacamund N.W. 5 miles. 251 acres.——*Sisparra* (ചിച്ചിപ്പാറ - chiççippára, Mal.). See sep. title.——*Snowdon* (ದೇವಶೋಲಬೆಟ್ಟ - dévashólabetta, Can.). See sep. title.——*Soondabetta* (ಸೂಂದಬೆಟ್ಟ - súndabetta, Can.). From (súda, can. mud + betta, can. hill). Hill, Merkoonaud division; lat. 11° 16′; long. 76° 46′; from Coonoor S.W. 8 miles; from Ootacamund S.S.E. 11 miles. Summit of the Mailore pass.——*Tainaud* (ತೇನಾಡು - ténádu, Can.). From (tén, tam. honey + nádu, tam. country). Village;

Paranginaud division; pop. 1,144; acres 7,224; lat. 11° 27′; long. 77° 00′; from Coonoor E. 6 miles; from Ootacamund E. 18 miles. Immediately to south of Kodanaud village.——*Tamrabetta* (ತಾಮ್ರಬೆಟ್ಟ - támrabetta, Can.). From (támra, san. coppery color + betta, can. mountain). Peak; lat. 11° 22′; long. 76° 48′; height 6,957 feet; from Ootacamund S.E. 5 miles.——*Tattapullam* (தட்டப்பள்ளம் - tattappallam, Tam.). From (tattai, tam. level + pallam, tam. valley). Coffee estate, Paranginaud; from Kotagherry S.E. 4 miles. Lies on both sides of the new ghaut road from Kotagherry to Mettapolliem. 363 acres.——*Teppacadav* (ತೆಪ್ಪಕಡವು - teppakadavu, Can.). From (teppa, can. raft + kadavu, can. passage). Village; S.E. Wynaud division; lat. 11° 35′; long. 76° 38′; from Goodalore N.E. 8 miles; from Ootacamund N.N.W. 14 miles. Halting station on the Seegore road. Travellers' bungalow [q.v.]. The road from the Neilgherries to Mysore here crosses the Moyaur, whence the name. ——*Todanaud* (ತೋಡನಾಡು - tódanádu, Can.). See sep. title.——*Tondanoray* (ತೊಂಡನೊರೆ - tondanore, Can.). Coffee estate, Merkoonaud; from Coonoor W. 6 miles. 70 acres.——*Torapully* (തൊറപ്പള്ളി - torappalli, Mal.). From (tora, mal. ford + palli, mal. village). Coffee estate, Numbalagode amshom, Wynaud S.E.; from Goodalore N.E. 2 miles. 904 acres.——*Tudor valley* (ತುದರಹಳ್ಳ - tudaraballa, Can.). Coffee and cinchona estates, Merkoonaud; from Coonoor S.W. 7 miles. 94 acres.——*Tullapoya* (തല്ലപ്പൊഴ - tallappozha, Mal.). From (tala, mal. head + puzha, mal. river). Ghaut, Merkoonaud division; west of the Mailore pass. Leaving the lowland at a point on the Bhawauny some distance above Shoondaputty, it reaches the plateau near Mailcoondah. Used solely by hill people.——*Tyemullay* (ತಾಯಿಮಲೆ - táyimale, Can.). From (táyi, tam. mother, epithet of a deity + malai, tam. hill). Coffee and cinchona estates, Merkoonaud; from Coonoor S.S.W. 7 miles. 379 acres.——*Velliyangherry* (வெள்ளியங்கிரி - velliyangiri, Tam.). From (velli, tam. silver + am, tam. beauty + giri, san. mountain). Hill, Todanaud division; lat. 11° 26′; long. 76° 36′; height 8,247 feet; from Ootacamund W.N.W. 10 miles; from Macoorty N.N.E. 5 miles.——*Wellington* (ಜಗತಾಳ - jagatálá, Can.). See sep. title.——*Wodayaroyacottah* (ಉದಯರಾಯಕೋಟೆ - udayaráyakóte, Can.). See sep. title.——*Woodlands* (உட்லாண்ட்ச் - udlánds, Tam.). Coffee estate, Merkoonaud; acres 718; lat. 11° 17′; long. 76° 47′; from Kartairy S.S.E. 5 miles.——*Wottputray* (ஓட்டுப்பட்டறை - óttuppattarai, Tam.). From (ódu, tam. tile + pattarai, tam. mechanic's workshop). Village, Paranginaud; from Coonoor W. 1 mile. Is a hamlet in Coonoor village, situated on the old road about 1 mile from Coonoor.——*Wynaud, S. E.* (വയനാട് - vayanátu, Mal.). See sep. title.——*Yedapully* (ಎಡಪಳ್ಳಿ - edapalli, Can.). From (ede, can. middle + palli, can. village). Village, Paranginaud; acres 3,000; lat. 11° 23′; long. 76° 51′. Midway between Coonoor and Kotagherry.——*Yellanhully* (ಎಲ್ಲನಹಳ್ಳಿ - ellanhalli, Can.). From (ellana, can. proper name + halli, can. village). Village, Merkoonaud division; lat. 11° 23′; long. 76° 47′; from Coonoor W.N.W. 4½ miles; from Ootacamund S.E. 4 miles.——*Yellay mullay* (எல்லைமலை - ellaimalai, Tam.). See sep. title.——**(2)** *Neilgherry blue flower* (انتمول - 'antamúl, Hind.). Same as Indian ipecacuanha.——*Neilgherry nettle* (बिछुआ - bichhuá, Hind.; ತುರಿಸಿಕೆಗಿಡ - turisikegida, Can.; ಅರಿಕೆಗಿಡ - árikegida, Too.; ആനച്ചൊറിയണം - ánaççoriyanam, Mal.; ගස්කහඹිලියා - gaskahambiliyá, Singh.). Hind. means scorpion; touch of plant painful. Can. from (turisu, can. to scratch + gida, can. plant). Mal. from (ána, mal. elephant + choriyanam, mal. tragia involucrata, mueller). Singh. from (gas, singh. tree + kahambiliyá, singh. nettle). Can. also (turikegida), meaning cutaneous eruption + plant. Title otherwise Itching plant. Botanically Girardina heterophylla, dalz., urticaceæ [vricsham, 119]. Alias Girardinia leschenaultiana; Urtica heterophylla. Annual, erect; leaves broad-cordate, seven-lobed, lobes oblong, acute, coarsely serrated, clothed on both sides with fine whitish down, armed above with thin scattered prickles, thickly clothed beneath with the same; male and female flowers in distinct glomerate peduncled spikes; flowers small, green; flowering in rainy season; the least touch of any part produces intense pain. Bark abounds in fine, white, glossy, silk-like, strong fibres [naur]; todahs [q.v.] separate the fibres by boiling the plant, and spin it into thin coarse thread. Cf. Indian nettle.——*Neilgherry peak* (നീലഗിരിശിഖരം - nílagirishikharam, Mal.; நீலகிரிமலை - nílagirimalai, Tam.). Means blue-mountain peak. Peak; lat. 11° 23′ N.; long. 76° 32′ E.; height 8,118 feet; from Calicut E. 46 miles; from Munjery N.E. 30 miles; from the sea E. 48 miles; from Goodalore S. 8 miles; from Ootacamund W. 15 miles. N.W. of Culcoodiyore; on Malabar and Neilgherry boundary.——*Neilgherry rhododendron* (ಬಿಲಿಮರ - bilimara, Can.; මාරත්මල් - máratmal, Singh.). Can. from (bili, can. white + mara, can. tree). Singh. from (má, singh. large + ratmal, singh. the plant, ixora coccinea, linn.). Can. also (billimara); (púmara), meaning flower + tree, used on neilgherries; (bilipúmara), meaning white-flowered tree. Title otherwise Dwarf rosebay, Large ixora. Botanically Rhododendron arboreum, smith, ericaceæ [vricsham, 78]. Alias Rhododendron puniceum. Tree, 25 feet, leaves very coriaceous, lanceolate, acute, cordate at the base, or attenuated into the thick petiole, shining green above, glabrous below, silvery or rusty-pubescent; flowers densely capitate; calyx none; corolla campanulate, white, rose, or blood-colored; ovary seven to ten-celled; neilgherries and other lofty mountain ranges; in flower all year round, but most profusely in february. Young leaves poisonous to cattle; flowers medicinal, applied to the forehead for headache. Flowers make a sub-acid jelly; flowers eaten by hill tribes. Wood close in the grain, but wanting in fibre and shrinks and twists in seasoning; used for fuel charcoal [adoopp kary]. Varieties are very numerous. No other common species here.

NEIM (نعيم - naím, *Ar.*). From (nama, ar. to bestow in abundance) [nimat]. Grace, favor. Part of lacab; as Neim ood deen, the grace of religion [ism].

NEL (നെൽ - nel, *Mal.*; நெல் - nel, *Tam.*). Grain, especially paddy grain. Common still in french and portuguese.—"*a*" Linear measure. 8 yels = 1 nel; 8 nels = 1 ungoolam [alavay, 1a]. Approximate actual value, 1 nel = ·09375 inch. Same as San. yavam, Hind. jow, Mal. tora.—"*b*" Used as goldsmith's weight. 4 nel manies = 1 coondrimany or goomchy seed [niray, 3d]. Approximate actual value, 1 nelmany = $\frac{1}{8}$ grain. Same as Hind. dhaun, Can. and Tam. veesha tookkam. See vol. I, 609.——*Nellilakkam* (நெல்லிலக்கம் - nellilakkam, Tam.). Paddy numbers. Reckoning by grains instead of abstract figures [ponnilakkam].——*Nellore* (నెల్లూరు - nellúru, Tel.). See sep. title.——*Nelly* (നെല്ലി - nelli, Mal.). See sep. title.——*Nel many* (நென்மணி - nenmani, Tam.). From (above + mani, tam. grain). Goldsmith's weight; see above. ——*Nelpoora* (നെല്പുര - nelpura, Mal.). From (above + pura, mal. shed). Granary [ganj].

NELLORE * (నెల్లూరు - nellúru, *Tel.*). From (nellu, tam. paddy + úru, tel. village) [uel]. There is also a legend that one Mookkanty reddy found a Moola staunam lingam under a Nelly [q.v.] tree and built a temple on the spot. Sanscrit name (lingapurí), meaning phallic emblem of shiva + town; also (simhapuri), meaning lion + town; also (dhányapura), meaning grain + town. Greek name μάλαγγα. Revenue district; situated on the Coromandel coast [q.v.]; between 13° 29′ and 16° 00′ N. lat., and between 79° 07′ and 80° 19′ E. long.; bounded N. by Kistna district, E. by Bay of Bengal, S. by North arcot and Chingleput, W. by Veligonda hills; square miles 8,760; pop. 1,463,736; language Teloogoo. Rivers:—Goondlacumma, Pennair, Swarnamookhy. Ports:—Canoopurty, Chennayapollem, Cottapatam, Doogaranzpatam, Eetamookkala, Iskapully, Kistnapatam, Meipaud, Paucala, Paumanjy, Ponnapoody, Poody, Ramapatam, Toommalapenta, Toopily, Zoovvaldinney. Mountains:—Cheeemacoorty hill, Oodayagherry droog, Veligonda hills. Sanitarium, Oodayagherry droog. The whole area of the district is represented by the following sub-areas, where talook [q.v.] means an ordinary tract administered by a Tahsildar [q.v.], and division means a zemindarry [q.v.] tract administered by a superior Deputy tahsildar:—Atmacore talook, Canigherry talook, Cauvaly talook, Cundoocore talook, Darshy division, Goodoor talook, Nellore talook, Ongole talook, Oodayagherry talook, Podily division, Polore division, Raupore talook, Vencatagherry division. For general administrative purposes the district is distributed between the following revenue and magisterial officers, who have their head-quarters at the places shown. The pay set opposite the subordinate officers gives the grade of the corresponding charge:—Collector, Nellore; Subcollector, Ongole, in charge of Ongole, Cundoocore and Canigherry talooks and Darshy and Podily zemindarry divisions; Head assistant collector Nellore, in charge of Atmacore, Cauvaly, and Oodayagherry talooks; General deputy collector, Naidoopett, in charge of Raupore talook, Polore and Vencatagherry divisions. Tahsildars; Atmacore, Rs. 175, Canigherry, Rs. 150, Cauvaly, Rs. 175, Cundoocore, Rs. 175, Goodoor, Rs. 200, Nellore, Rs. 225, Ongole, Rs. 200, Oodayagherry, Rs. 150, Raupore, Rs. 150. Deputy tahsildars; Addanky, Rs. 100, range situated in the north of Ongole talook; Alloor, Rs. 100, range situated in the north of Nellore talook, north of the Pennair; Darshy, Rs. 120, division situated to the north-west of Ongole talook bordering on Kistna district; Kotah, Rs. 100, range situated in the south-east of Goodoor talook; Podily, Rs. 120, division situated to the south-west of Ongole and north of Canigherry talook; Polore, Rs. 120, division situated to the south-west of Goodoor talook; Vencatagherry, Rs. 120, division situated to the west of Goodoor and to the south of Raupore talooks; Submagistrate, Nellore, Rs. 120, jurisdiction extending over Nellore town and 64 villages in the Nellore talook, south of the Pennair. Similarly judicial officers:—Judge, Nellore. District Moonsifs; Nellore, with jurisdiction extending over Goodoor and Raupore talooks and portions of Nellore and Atmacore south of Pennair, and Polore and Vencatagherry divisions; Cauvaly with jurisdiction extending over Cauvaly, Oodayagherry, and portions of Nellore and Atmacore north of Pennair; Canigherry with jurisdiction extending over Canigherry, Cundoocore, Darshy and Podily; Ongole over Ongole talook. Similarly Public Works officers:—District engineer, Nellore. Sub-divisional officers; Codavalore with range extending over Sangam delta, Atmacore talook north of the Pennair and Oodayagherry talook; Ongole with range extending over Ongole, Cundoocore, Cauvaly and Canigherry and Podily division and Darshy divisions; Goodoor with range extending over Atmacore talook south of the Pennair, Goodoor and Raupore talooks and Sooloorpett division and Vencatagherry divisions. Supervisors; Nellore, in charge of Nellore talook south of the Pennair; Bootchireddipollem, in charge of the southern central and a portion of the Eastern channel and Canigherry tank; Pudmanaubha chuttram, in charge of the Eastern channel works and its distribution. Contains registration sub-districts, Addanky, Alloor, Atmacore, Canigherry, Cauvaly, Cottapatám, Cundoocore, Darshy, Goodoor, Nellore, Ongole, Oodayagherry, Podily, Raupore, Sooloorpett, Vencatagherry. Contains Forest ranges, Canigherry, Nellore, Ongole, Oodayagherry, Ramapatam, Raupore, Shreeharicote. Contains Municipalities, Nellore, Ongole. Contains District board; and Talook boards; Nellore embracing Goodoor and Nellore talooks; Atmacore embracing Atmacore, Oodayagherry and Cauvaly talooks; Naidoopett embracing Raupore, Vencatagherry division and Polore division; Ongole embracing Ongole, Cundoocore and Canigherry talooks and Darshy and Podily divisions. The following are the zemindarries in the District:—Calastry a portion, Choondy, Moottiaulpaud, Vencatagherry. The following general references should be made to the preceding volumes:—general geography, I (1) to (29); general ethnology, I (29) to (109); general history, I (110) to (188); physical geography, II, 1; meteorology, II, 3; geology, II, 8; fauna, II, 21; flora, II, 26; mineralogy, II, 29. The following references in the preceding volumes will furnish details special to the district:—latitudes and longitudes, II, 47; particulars about towns, II, 48; coast survey, II, 163; light-house, II, 169; comparative population, II, 172; location of revenue officers, II, 388; revenue settlement of the district, II, 415; registrars' and sub-registrars' stations, II, 421; ports, II, 423; salt factories, II, 426; rain-guage stations, II, 428; police divisions, II, 431; maps published, II, 436; survey topographical lists, II, 443; hospitals and dispensaries, II, 447; head-quarter stations of gazetted officers, II, 461; incidence of taxation, II, 463; weights and measures of the district, II, 505; zemindarries contained, I, 56, and II, 299; special public works, I, 398. A special gazetteer account of the whole district is given at II, 112. For the detailed topography of the district, reference should be made to the talook notices in the present volume, viz.:—Atmacore, Canigherry, Cauvaly, Cundoocore, Darshy, Goodoor, Nellore, Ongole, Oodayagherry, Podily, Polore, Raupore, Vencatagherry.——**(2)** Talook, Nellore district. Tahsildar's pay Rs. 225. Area 638 square miles. Centre coast part of district. Bounded by Cauvaly to the north, Atmacore to the west, Goodoor to the south, and the sea east. There is comparatively little jungle. Towards the south the ground is high and covered with brushwood. Laterite [q.v.] is quarried near Nellore town. Soil rocky and gravelly in the western parts and sandy and loamy in the eastern. Large exports of cattle [maud], paddy [q.v.] and indigo [q.v.]. The Pennair separates the talook into two portions. Channels are the Maldaivy and the Peidair; local drainages for the northern portion. Two supplying channels [q.v.] from the south side of the Nellore anicut [q.v.], with numerous feeders to the different tanks [q.v.], bring a large area of rice [q.v.] land under cultivation. All land that can be irrigated is being rapidly taken up and the prosperity of the cultivators is yearly increasing. Camping grounds:—Alloor, Aumancherla, Bodwauripollem, Caukpulley, Códavalore, Codoor, Comarapoody, Comarica, Condlapoody, Cortore, Covoor, Daumaramadoogoo, Devarpollem, Dontauly, Doorvoor, Gundavaram, Gungaputnam, Indoocoorpett, Indoopore, Iskapully, Laibore, Meipaud, Moolmoody, North aumoolore, North mopore, Ootcore, Padamatipollem, Pedoor, Penoobully, Ponnapoody, Siddipooram, Talamunchy, Varigonda, Varny, Vavvair, Yeedore. Places of archæological interest:—Alloor, Bootchireddipollem, Codavalore, Cortore, Covoor, Daumaramadoogoo, Dontauly, Doovvoor, Gowndlapollem, Gundavaram, Maudrauz goodoor, Moolapett, Nellore, Ootcore, Pedapoottaid, Ponnapoody, Pooriny, Rama teertam, Runganaickoolapett, Sangam, Vellanty, Vidavalore. Principal trig. stations:—Narsimhacondah, Nishanbote, Pennair beacon, Sangam. The leading places, &c., in the talook are the following.——*Alloor* (అల్లూరు - allúru, Tel.). See sep. title.——*Beerapair* (బీరపేరు - bírapéru, Tel.). See sep. title.——*Bootchireddipollem* (బుచ్చిరెడ్డిపాలెము - buççireddipálemu, Tel.). See sep. title.——*Canigherry reservoir* (కనిగిరిచెరువు - kanigiricheruvu, Tel.). See sep. title.——*Codoor* (కోడూరు - kódúru, Tel.). From (kóde, tel. bull + úru, tel. village). Village; pop. 3,443; acres 6,874; lat. 14° 25′; long. 80° 10′; from Nellore E.S.E. 13 miles; from the sea W. 1 mile. On the Buckingham canal [q.v.]. Exports a large quantity of pishaunam [q.v.] paddy [q.v.]. Shell lime [kilinjal choonam] is made.——*Comarica* (కొమరిక - komarika, Tel.). From (komaru, tel. beauty). Village; pop. 1,814; acres 1,864; lat. 14° 31′; long. 80° 10′; from Nellore E.N.E. 11 miles; from the sea W. 4 miles. Toonga [q.v.] mats [boriyah] are made.——*Condayapollem* (కొండయపాలెము - kondayapálemu, Tel.). From (kondayya, tel. proper name + pálemu, tel. fortified village). Village; pop. 445; acres 1,588; lat. 14° 25′; long. 80° 01′; from Nellore S. 3 miles; from the sea W. 13 miles.——*Condlapoody* (కొండ్లపూడి - kondlapúdi, Tel.). From (konda, tel. hill + púdi, tel. village). Village; pop. 1,087; lat. 14° 28′; long. 79° 58′; from Nellore W. 4 miles; from the sea W. 18 miles. In face of Narsimhacondah.——*Cortore* (కొరుటూరు - korutúru, Tel.). From (koriti, tel. tree, plecospermum spinosum, trec. + úru, tel. village). Village; pop. 1,194; acres 2,678; lat. 14° 29′; long. 80° 12′; from Nellore E. 12 miles; from the sea W. 1¼ miles. Large tank and ancient Shiva temple dedicated to Pullanautasawmy.——*Covoor* (కోవూరు - kóvúru, Tel.). See sep. title.——*Daumaramadoogoo* (దామరమడుగు - dámaramadugu, Tel.). From (támara, tel. lotus flower, nelumbium speciosum, willd. + madugu, tel. pool). Village; pop. 1,935; acres 2,831; lat. 14° 30′; long. 79° 59′; from Nellore N.W. 5 miles; from the sea W. 17 miles. West of the village was once pool full of lotus [nelumbo] flowers. A low-lying village with Pennair on south, and fed by Canigherry reservoir. Shiva temple with inam [q.v.].——*Doorvoor* (దువ్వూరు - duvvúru, Tel.). From (tuvva, tel. sandy soil + úru, tel. village). Sanscrit name (dúrvásapura), meaning doorvausan, the ill-clad sage + town. Pop. 2,369; lat. 14° 33′; long. 79° 53′; from Nellore N.W. 12 miles; from the sea W. 24 miles. Remains of Mahomedan fort. Once the head-quarters of a Pergunnah [q.v.]. Protected from Pennair by a large flood-bank.——*Durgamittah* (దర్గామిట్ట - dargametta, Tel.). See sep. title.——*Gogoolpully* (గోగులపల్లి - gógulapalli, Tel.). From (gógu, tel. hibiscus cannabinus, linn. + palli, tel. village). Village; pop. 1,403; acres 5,427; lat. 14° 40′; long. 80° 10′; from Nellore N.N.E. 17 miles; from the sea W. 3 miles. Formerly a salt station.——*Gundavaram* (గండవరము - gandavaramu, Tel.). From (gandu, tel. great + pura, san. town). Hind. name (alinagar), meaning proper name + city. Sanscrit name (grant'hapura), means book + town. Village; pop. 3,094; acres 6,418; lat. 14° 34′; long. 80° 01′; from Nellore N. 8 miles; from the sea W. 15 miles. Fine curtain cloths [purdah] are made. An ancient seat of learning. Two ancient temples of Shiva and Vishnoo built by Chola kings. The Shiva god is known by the very unusual name of Oodayacauleshwara sawmy, meaning rise + time + lord; because, at certain seasons of year, rays of rising sun fall upon lingam [q.v.].——*Inamadoogoo* (ఇనమడుగు - inamadugu, Tel.). From (inumu, tel. iron + madugu, tel. pool). Village; pop. 2,071; acres 2,805; lat. 14° 31′; long. 81° 04′; from Nellore N.N.E. 5 miles; from the sea W. 11 miles. A low-lying village with extensive cloth weaving.——*Indoocoorpett* (ఇందుకూరుపేట - indukúrupéta, Tel.). From (indu, tel. date tree, phœnix farinifera, roxb. + úru, tel. village + péta, tel. suburb). Village; pop. 4,514; acres 5,542; lat. 14° 28′; long. 80° 09′; from Nellore E. 9 miles; from the sea W. 5 miles. Rattan [q.v.] baskets [tokrah] are made.——*Iskapully* (ఇస్కపల్లె - iskapalle, Tel.). See sep. title.——*Kedamanair* (కేతామన్నేరు - kétámannéru, Tel.). See sep. title.——*Laigoontapaud* (లేగుంటపాడు - léguntapádu, Tel.). From (léga, tel. calf + gunta, tel. pond + pádu, tel. village). Tel. also (lágalakonda), meaning calf + hill. Village; pop. 767; acres 1,204; lat. 14° 31′; long. 80° 04′; from Nellore N.E. 6 miles; from the sea W. 10 miles. A low-lying village inaccessible in the rainy season, with the Pennair running close to it. A feeder from the Canigherry reservoir irrigates the lands of the village.——*Maldaivy* (మాల్దేవి - maldévi, Tel.). See sep. title.——*Meipaud* (మైపాడు - maipádu, Tel.). See sep. title.——*Modeygoonta* (మోదేగుంట - módégunta, Tel.). From (móda, tel. salt-pan + gunta, tel. pond). Village; pop. 862; acres 782; lat. 14° 33′; long. 80° 05′; from Nellore N.E. 8 miles; from the sea W. 9 miles. The Teloogoo poet [cavy] Pooshpagiry timmappa lived here.——*Moodivarty* (ముదివర్తి - mudivarti, Tel.). From (mudi, tel. old + parti, tel. village). Village; pop. 1,805; acres 4,793; lat. 14° 33′; long. 80° 09′; from Nellore N.E. 11 miles.——*Moolapett* (మూలపేట - múlapéta, Tel.). See sep. title.——*Moolmoody* (ములుమూడి - mulumúdi, Tel.). From (mulumu, tel. stubble field + púdi, tel. village). Tel. also (munulapúdi), meaning sage + village. Sanscrit name (munipura), meaning sage + town. Village; pop. 1,637; acres 5,561; lat. 14° 28′; long. 79° 54′; from Nellore W. 9 miles; from the sea W. 22 miles. Said by Stala pooraunam [q.v.] to have been a residence of Ashwattauman who fought on the side of Cowravas during the Mahabhaurat [q.v.] war. Contains Narsimhacondah.——*Moonoolapoody* (మునులపూడి - munulapúdi, Tel.). From (muni, san. hermit + púdi, tel. village). So called because hermits are said to have made penance here in times of old. Village; pop. 187; acres 2,432; lat. 14° 36′; long. 79° 55′; from Nellore N.W. 12 miles; from the sea W. 19 miles.——*Murripaud* (మర్రిపాడు - marripádu, Tel.). From (marri, tel. banyan tree, ficus bengalensis, linn. + pádu, tel. village). Village; pop. 1,232; acres 5,740; lat. 14° 39′; long. 79° 52′; from Nellore N.W. 17 miles; from the sea W. 21 miles. Ancient temple to Chennakeshwarasawmy. Extensive paddy [q.v.] cultivation.——*Narsimhacondah* (నరసింహకొండ - narasimhakonda, Tel.). See sep. title.——*Naugamambaupooram* (నాగమాంబాపురము - nágamámbápuramu, Tel.). From (nágamámba, tel. proper name + pura, san. town). Village; pop. 471; acres 1,062; lat. 14° 32′; long. 79° 57′; from Nellore N.W. 8 miles; from the sea W. 18 miles. Deshye [q.v.] reddies [q.v.] of Codavalore built the temple. Cultivation is carried on by a feeder from the Canigherry reservoir.——*Navaubpett* (నవాబుపేట - navábupéta, Tel.). See sep. title.——*Nellore* (నెల్లూరు - nellúru, Tel.). See below.

——*Nidimooshily* (నిడిముశిలి - nidimushili, Tel.). From (nidi, tel. very + mushili, tel. old). Village; pop. 683; acres 1,242; lat. 14° 32′; long. 80° 08′; from Nellore N.E. 9 miles; from the sea W. 6 miles. Curtain cloths [purdah] are made.——*Nishanbote* (నిశాన్‌బోటు - nishanbótu, Tel.). From (nishání, hind. signal + bótu, tel. high ground). Trig. station; lat. 14° 41′ 47·90″; long. 79° 58′ 24·01″; height 234 feet; from Chennore N.E. 4 miles; from Nellore N. 17 miles; from the sea W. 14 miles.——*Padoogoopaud* (పడుగుపాడు - padugupádu, Tel.). From (padugu, tel. woof + pádu, tel. village). Village; pop. 817; acres 1,299; lat. 14° 29′; long. 80° 02′; from Nellore N.N.E. 3 miles; from the sea W. 12 miles. The poetess Molla [q.v.] lived here [cavy].——*Pautore* (పాటూరు - pátúru, Tel.). From (páti, tel. high level + úru, tel. village). Village; pop. 1,849; acres 2,783; lat. 14° 31′; long. 79° 59′; from Nellore N.N.W. 5 miles; from the sea W. 16 miles. The village was originally built over a mound near the temple of Yaumaulamma [q.v.]. A small stream from the Canigherry reservoir irrigates the lands. Tikkana somayaujooloo [cavy], the translator of Mahabhaurat [q.v.], lived here. Cloths are woven to a large extent by the jendravar [q.v.].——*Pedoor* (పేడూరు - pédúru, Tel.). From (pédu, tel. wood + úru, tel. village); from trees in tank. Village; pop. 1,271; acres 2,442; lat. 14° 26; long. 80° 07′; from Nellore E. 7 miles; from the sea W. 7 miles. Produces large quantities of pishaunam [q.v.] paddy [q.v.].——*Peidair* (పైడేరు - paidéru, Tel.). From (paidi, tel. gold + éru, tel. river). Channel. This is a feeder to the Alloor tank.——*Pennair* (పెన్నేరు - pennéru, Tel.). See sep. title.——*Penoobully* (పెనుబల్లి - penuballi, Tel.). From (penu, tel. great + bali, tel. sacrifice). Village; pop. 1,060; acres 2,365; lat. 14° 30′; long. 79° 56′; from Nellore W.N.W. 7 miles; from the sea W. 19 miles. Stala pooraunam [q.v.] says that Cashyapa prajaupaty [q.v.], while performing a great fire offering in Zonnavauda, made a sacrifice here. Ruined Shiva temple. Small hill near. Cultivation from the Canigherry reservoir.——*Pinaukiny* (పినాకిని - pinákiní, Tel.). See sep. title. ——*Ponnapoody* (పొన్నపూడి - ponnapúdi, Tel.). From (ponna, tel. tree, calophyllum inophyllum, linn. + púdi, tel. village). Village, Port; lat. 14° 40′ N.; long. 80° 11′; from Iskapully S.E. 5 miles; from Madras N. 107 miles; from Nellore N.E. 18 miles; from Varny N.E. 3 miles. A port 3 miles north of the Pennair, carrying on a large coasting trade, principally in grain. Resorted to by native craft. Granaries on the beach.——*Raibaula* (రేబాల - rébála, Tel.). From (régu, tel. jujube tree, zizyphus jujuba, lamk. + palle, tel. village). Village; pop. 1,280; acres 2,987; lat. 14° 32′; long. 79° 57′; from Nellore N.W. 8 miles; from the sea W. 19 miles. A low-lying village with extensive cultivation by feeder from Canigherry reservoir. Surrounded with thick jungle.——*Rama teertam* (రామతీర్థము - rámatírt'hamu, Tel.). From (ráma, san. the god + tírt'ha, san. place of sacred waters). Tel. also (gaundhapálemu), meaning toddy-drawer + fortified village. Village; pop. 1,586; lat. 14° 40′; long. 80° 12′; from Nellore N.E. 18 miles; from the sea W. 1¼ miles. On the western bank of the Buckingham canal [q.v.] at the mouth of the Peidair. On the north bank of the channel on the beach is the Rama teertam. Temple, with annual festival. Good choultry [q.v.]. ——*Sangam* (సంగం - sangam, Tel.). See sep. title.——*Somrauzpully* (సోమరాజుపల్లె - sómarádzupalle, Tel.). From (sómarádzu, tel. proper name + palle, tel. village). Village; pop. 687; acres 2,209; lat. 14° 29′; long. 80° 12′; from Nellore E. 11 miles; from the sea W. 2 miles.——*Talamunchy* (తలమంచి - talamanchi, Tel.). From (st'halam, san. site + manchi, tel. goodness). Village; pop. 1,880; acres 5,919; lat. 14° 37′; long. 80° 01′; from Nellore N. 11 miles; from the sea W. 10 miles. Large quantities of laterite [q.v.] stone quarried.—— *Toorimerla* (తురిమెర్ల - turimerla, Tel.). From (turru, tel. village + mirru, tel. highland). Village; pop. 694; acres 2,570; lat. 14° 38′; long. 79° 57′; from Nellore N.N.W. 13 miles; from the sea W. 17 miles. Curtain cloths [purdah] manufactured.—— *Vangull* (వంగల్లు - vangallu, Tel.). From (vanga, tel. brinjal, solanum melongena, linn. + kallu, tel. stone). Tel. also (dzangálavangólu), meaning jangam, member of the caste + place so called. Sanscrit name (ónkálípattana), means omcauly, the deity + town. Village; pop. 1,585; acres 5,278; lat. 14° 36′; long. 79° 52′; from Nellore N.W. 15 miles; from the sea W. 25 miles. Ancient Shiva temple on hill. The Teloogoo poet [cavy] Condoory seetaramiah lived here.——*Varny* (వరిణి - variní, Tel.). From (varanamu, tel. enclosure). Village, Port; pop. 1,586; acres 8,100; lat. 14° 38′ N.; long. 80° 10′; from Madras N. 104 miles; from Meipaud N.N.W. 10 miles; from Nellore N.E. 16 miles; from Ponnapoody S.W. 3 miles. Near mouth of Pennair. ——*Viloocaunipulley* (విలుకానిపల్లె - vilukánipalle, Tel.). From (vilukádu, tel. archer + palle, tel. village). Village; pop. 431; acres 740; lat. 14° 27′; long. 80° 10′; from Nellore E. 10 miles; from the sea W. 4 miles. Gold coins [naunyam] formerly found after heavy showers.——*Yellayapollem* (యెల్లాయపాలెము - yellayapáiemu, Tel.). From (ella, tel. border + pálemu, tel. fortified village); border settlement. Village; pop. 2.570; acres 3,975; lat. 14° 33′; long. 80° 00′; from Nellore N.N.W. 7 miles; from the sea W. 16 miles. People from Gundavaram emigrated and settled themselves on the borders of Pautore. Hence the name. To the north is a ruined fort, once flourishing in the time of Raja raja naraindran. Unendowed temple to Mullicarjoona sawmy with annual Bramhotsavam [pundigay, 6a]. Cloths are manufactured.——*Zonnavauda* (జొన్నవాడ - dzonnaváda, Tel.). See sep. title.——**(3)** Town, Sub-magistracy, Nellore district. Pay Rs. 120.——**(4)** Town, Municipality, Head-quarters of Collector, Tahsildar, Police superintendent, District registrar, District judge, Executive engineer, Superintendent of Post and Telegraph offices, District moonsif, Deputy tahsildar, Railway station; Nellore dist., Nellore tal.; pop. 29,336; acres 15,752; lat. 14° 27′; long. 80° 02′; height 57 feet; from Madras N.N.W. 96 miles; from Naidoopett N. 38 miles; from Ongole S. 73 miles; from the sea W. 13 miles. On right bank of Pennair, 12 miles from its mouth. Of great antiquity. Traditionally in the wilderness Dandacauranyam [q.v.]. Climate is dry and salubrious, being subject to no sudden changes of temperature. The prevailing winds during January and February are north-easterly; during March and April, north-easterly and south-easterly; in May and June, south-easterly and south-westerly; in July and August, south-easterly and north-westerly; in September and October, the direction is varying; in November and December it blows steadily from the north-east. The fall of rain [mazhay] during the year is from thirty to forty inches, and it takes place partly during the south-west monsoon [q.v.] in August and September, but chiefly in October, November, and December, under the north-east monsoon. It is connected with Madras by railway, by the Northern trunk road, and also by Buckingham canal. Held by the Vencatagherry zemindars till the Mussalman period, and in 1750 formed fowjdurry [q.v.] of Arcot. In 1752, seized by one Mahomed camaul, who was captured and executed twelve months later. Najeeb oollah the governor rebelled in 1757, and the English forces under Forde assisted in the unsuccessful siege of the town. The Mahrattas and the French visited the town in 1758. The latter were received as friends; but on the raising of the siege of Fort st. george in the same year, Najeeb oollah murdered all the French soldiers in the town save one, and gave in his submission to the English. The houses of the European residents are on the south of the town, along the bank of a large tank, on the farther side of which rises the temple crowned hill of Narsimhacondah. The offices of the Collector are in the old fort now in ruins; opposite stands the police office, formerly a range of barracks. The old cemetery has about 160 tombs, the oldest of which dates back to 1785. American baptist mission, Roman catholic mission, and a mission of the Hermansburg lutherans. The rampart which formerly defended the place has fallen into ruins. In 1787, a peasant ploughing near the town, struck upon the remains of a Hindoo temple, beneath which was found a pot containing gold Roman coins of the second century A.D., mostly bearing the names of Trajan, Hadrian, and Faustina. Some were fresh, but others were worn and perforated, as if they had been used as personal ornaments. When the anicut [q.v.] across the Pennair was being constructed, the workmen found several coffins, apparently of burnt clay, embedded in quartz [vencull]. Some contained more than one body each; which when first seen, were in a perfect state of preservation. There were also found with them spear heads and other implements. Annual festival of Moolastauneshwarasawmy held about February. Festival of Shree ruuganaicksawmy held about March. The festival visitors camp in the open bed of the river. To the east are extensive rice [q.v.] fields. Large quantities of laterite [q.v.] are quarried in the neighbourhood and used for building purposes and the repair of roads. The following are the travelling distances by read from Nellore to different places:—

To	Viâ	Miles and Furlongs.	
Bangalore ...	Calastry, Chittore and Colaur	238	7
Bellary ...	Cuddapah and Gooty	260	0
Berhampore ...	Guntoor, Rajahmundry and Chicacole ...	537	7
Bezwada ...	Ongole and Guntoor	164	6½
Budwail ...	Ooppalapaud	72	7
Calastry ...	Wojelly	57	7
Caligherry ...	Sangam	39	7
Canigherry ...	Caligherry	85	4
Canigherry ...	Shingaroyacondah	96	0
Chetterpore ...	Rajahmundry, Chicacole and Berhampore.	552	2
Chicacole ...	Guntoor and Rajahmundry	438	6½
Chingleput ...	Sooloorpett and Madras	142	5
Chittore ...	Calastry and Chundragherry	125	5
Chundragherry ...	Calastry and Tripatty	91	6
Cocanada ...	Ongole and Masulipatam	271	3
Cuddalore ...	Madras, Chingleput and Pondicherry ...	221	6
Cuddapah ...	Budwail	107	7
Cumbum ...	Caligherry and Canigherry	118	0
Cumbum ...	Shingaroyacondah and Canigherry ...	128	4
Cuttack ...	Rajahmundry, Chicacole and Khoordhah.	654	4
Ellore ...	Ongole, Guntoor and Bezwada	203	7½
Guntoor ...	Ongole and Maurtore	144	6
Guntoor ...	Ongole and Incolloo	142	1
Haitipamla ...	Ongole and Pondakholl	217	2
Kurnool ...	Cumbum and Nundiaul	219	3½
Madras ...	Wojelly and Sooloorpett	107	6
Masulipatam ...	Ongole and Baupatla	161	5
Masulipatam ...	Ongole and Guntoor	192	6½
Nagary ...	Wojelly and Calastry	94	1
Ongole ...	Shingaroyacondah	76	3
Pondakholl ...	Ongole and Nekaricull	270	4
Rajahmundry ...	Ongole, Bezwada and Ellore	259	0½

To		Vià	Miles and Furlongs.	
Ranipett	...	Calastry and Nagary	129	0
Samulcottah	...	Ongole, Masulipatam and Cocanada	279	3
Secunderabad	...	Ongole, Pondakholl, Haitipamla and Malacaupore.	282	2
Sooloorpett	...	Wojelly	57	4
Tripatty	...	Wojelly and Calastry	80	7
Vellore	...	Calastry and Chittore	147	5
Vellore	...	Nagary and Ranipett	142	6
Vizagapatam	...	Bezwada, Rajahmundry and Cassimcote.	382	0½
Vizianagram	...	Bezwada, Rajahmundry and Soobaraum.	405	3½

NELLY (నెల్లి - nelli, *Tel.*; நெல்லி - nelli, *Tam.*). Rice-like [nel], from small leaflets, rice being emblem of smallness. The premna genus [moonnay]. Also the emblic myrobalan [tripalam].——**(1)** *Neliampathy* (നെല്ല്യാമ്പതി - nelyámpati, Mal.). From (nelliyán, mal. the deity of the phyllanthus emblica, linn. + pati, mal. place). Range of mountains; Cochin state, Chittoor tal.; from Chittoor S. 10 miles; from Ernacolum N. 34 miles; from the sea E. 20 miles. Forms portion of the south side of the gap in the Western ghauts [q.v.] through which the Ponnany flows, the north side of the gap being bounded by the Palghaut hills. Extreme elevation, about 5,000 feet. At an elevation of from 1,500 to 4,000 feet the hills are covered with forests yielding valuable timber, cardamoms [q.v.], ginger [q.v.], pepper [q.v], &c. Large quantities of honey [shahad] are collected by the Kadar [q.v.], a jungle tribe inhabiting these hills not unlike the Wynaud coorumbar [q.v.]. Coffee [q.v.] has been grown since 1860. Thermometer ranges from 45° to 90°. In June, July and August the monsoon [q.v.] is heavy and high winds blow. Rainfall, annual average 150 to 160 inches.——*Nelliyappan* (நெல்லியப்பன் - nelliyappan, Tam.). From (above + appan, tam. father); meaning deity presiding over nelly tree, shiva [q.v.] or ganesh [q.v.]. Hindoo 2nd or pers. name. Common among non-bramins [peyar].——**(2)** *Coora nelly* (కూరనెల్లి - kúranelli, Tel.). From (kúra, tel. curry + nelli, tel. premna latifolia, roxb.). Same as Curry moonnay.——*Creeper nelly* (നെല്ലിത്താളി - nellittáli, Mal.). Same as Solah and Common sesban.——*Foreign nelly* (சீமைநெல்லி - shímainelli, Tam.). Same as Barbadoes cherry.——*Forest nelly* (കാട്ടുനെല്ലി - káttunelli, Mal.; கீழாநெல்லி - kízhánelli, Tam.). Mal. from (kátu, mal. forest + nelli, mal. phyllanthus emblica, linn.). Tam. from (kízh, tam. below + nelli, tam. phyllanthus emblica, linn.). Title otherwise Many-leaved phyllanthus. Botanically Phyllanthus [aumlacam] polyphyllus, willd., euphorbiaceæ [vricsham, 118]. Alias Phyllanthus emblicoides, lawii, taxifolius. Shrub; leaves narrow or linear-oblongate-elliptic, obtuse at both ends, mucronulate at the apex, densely approximated, recurved at the margin, glabrous, equally broad for some distance; stipules triangular, ovate or lanceolate, denticulate, acuminated; flowers fascicled, very shortly pedicelled, rising from the very small densely bracteated branchlets, all very shortly pedicelled; glands of the male flowers distinct; disc hypogynous, dwarf, annular-crenulate; anthers shortly apiculated; ovary globose; styline column slender; styles thin, elongated, two-cleft; capsules three-furrowed; seeds pale, deeply pitted.——*Kizhanelly* (கீழா நெல்லி - kízhánnelli, Tam.). From (kízh, tam. low + nelli, tam. phyllanthus emblica, linn.). Same as Neeroory.——*Lowly nelly* (भूम्यावळि - búmyávali, Conc.; ನೆಲನೆಲ್ಲಿ - nelanelli, Can. and Too.; నేలఉసిరికె - nélausirike, Tel.; കീഴാനെല്ലി - kízhánelli, Mal.; நிலநெல்லி - nilanelli, Tam.). Title from habit. Conc. from (bhúmi, san. earth + áválo, conc. phyllanthus emblica, linn.). Can. and Too. from (nela, can. ground + nelli, can. phyllanthus emblica, linn.). Tel. from (néla, tel. ground + usiriko, tel. phyllanthus emblica, linn.). Mal. from (kízhu, mal. below + nelli, mal. phyllanthus emblica, linn.). Tam. from (nilam, tam. ground + nelli, tam. phyllanthus emblica, linn.). Can. also (kirunelli), meaning small + phyllanthus emblica, linn. Tam. also (nílakkadambai), meaning blue + anthocephalus cadamba, miq.; (mélanelli), meaning surface + phyllanthus emblica, linn. Title otherwise Madras phyllanthus. Botanically Phyllanthus [aumlacam] maderaspatensis, linn., euphorbiaceæ [vricsham, 118]. Very variable in habit, erect or decumbent below; stems low and herbaceous, or erect, slender, woody with spreading branches; leaves from ⅓ inch and cuneate or almost obcordate to 1½ inch, and narrowly oblong-cuneate; nerves few slanting; petiole minute, stipules lanceolate membranous; male flower $\frac{1}{20}$ inch diameter usually fascicled with one much larger female; female $\frac{1}{16}$ inch diameter in fruit; sepals rounded or obcuneate; disk of glands in both sexes; anthers almost sessile on the column, erect, apiculate; fruit dry, ⅛ inch diameter, globose. The seeds are polished, triangular, of a grey color, finely marked with delicate dark-brown lines like basket-work; length $\frac{1}{16}$ of an inch; breadth somewhat less; one side is arched, the other presents two sloping surfaces united to form a longitudinal ridge, at the pointed end is a small scar marking the attachment to the ovary; the testa is hard and brittle; when soaked in water they immediately become thickly coated with a semi-opaque mucilage; the kernel is oily and has a sweet nutty taste. The seeds are used medicinally on account of the mucilage which they afford.——*Mail nelly* (மேலநெல்லி - mélanelli, Tam.). From (mél, tam. high + nelli, tam. phyllanthus emblica, linn.); tall shrub. Same as Poolah.——*Netted nelly* (ఎఱ్ఱపురుగుడు - errapurugudu, Tel.; වල්කයිල - valkayila, Singh.). Title from reticulated appearance of leaf. Tel. from (erra, tel. red + purugudu, tel. phyllanthus multiflorus, willd.). Singh. from (vel, singh. creeper + kayila, singh. the plant, phyllanthus reticulatus, mull.). Tel. also (nallapurugudu), meaning black + phyllanthus multiflorus, willd. Singh. also (kayilavela), meaning same. Title otherwise Netted phyllanthus. Botanically Phyllanthus [aumlacam] reticulatus, mull., euphorbiaceæ [vricsham, 118]. Flowers fascicled; ovary twelve to six-celled, globose, glabrous; styles short, erect, two-lobed; capsules sub-globose, depresso-truncated at the apex. The bark is dark-brown externally, and thickly studded with little elliptic warty rings; beneath the suber is a deposit of chlorophyll, but the substance of the bark is of a dull-red color; taste sweet and astringent. Bark, as it appears in the bazaars, is commonly in pieces about a foot long, and as thick as the wrist, of a dark color outside, and of a faint sweetish taste. Leaves and bark are diuretic alterative and cooling medicine.——*Root nelly* (గద్దనెల్లి - gaddanelli, Tel.). Same as Indian nettle.——*Small nelly* (அருநெல்லி - arunelli, Tam.). Same as Brazil cherry.——*Sour nelly* (നെല്ലിപ്പുളി - nellippuli, Mal.). From sour fruit. Same as Brazil cherry.——*Stinking nelly* (గబ్బునెల్లి - gabbunelli, Tel.). From stinking leaves. Same as Moonnay.——*White nelly* (తెల్లఉసిరిక - tellausirika, Tel.). Title from color of fruit. Tel. from (tella, tel. white + usirika, tel. phyllanthus emblica, linn.). Title otherwise White phyllanthus. Botanically Phyllanthus [aumlacam] pendulus, roxb., euphorbiaceæ [vricsham, 118]. Shrub, glabrous; branches flexuose, often somewhat pendulous; leaves lanceolate-elliptic, sub-acute, colored at the margin, upper ones smaller; flowers monœcious; racemules situated in the lower part of the branchlets at length half-equalling the leaves, densely bracteated in four rows, pendulous; female flowers solitary in the upper axils; calycine segments orbicular-ovate, acute; disc of either sex urceolar; ovary globose; styles spreading divergingly, two-cleft; flowering in the rainy season.——*Wild kizhanelly* (காட்டுக்கீழாநெல்லி - káttukkízhánelli, Tam.). Same as Poolah.

NELUMBO (पद्म - padma, *San.*; कमळ - kamala, *Mahr.*; सालक - sálaka, *Conc.*; نیلو فر - nílofar, *Ar.* and *Pers.*; کنول - kanwal, *Hind.* and *Dec.*; تارتي - tárate, *Malay*; ಕಮಲ - kamala, *Can.*; ತಾವರೆ - távare, *Too.*; తామర - támara, *Tel.*; ପଦ୍ମ - padam, *Oor.*; താമര - támara, *Mal.*; නෙළුම් - nelum, *Singh.*; தாமரை - támarai, *Tam.*). Title from singhalese [nal]. San. from (pat, san. to go + ma, san. water), water-going plant. Mahr. from (kam, san. water + ala, san. to adorn). Ar. from (níla, san. blue + utpala, san. water-lily). Hind. from like mahratta [red indian water-lily, white indian water-lily]. Malay from (tárang, malay, bright). Can. from sanscrit. Too. from tamul. Tel. from tamul [oval-leaved china root]. Oor. from sanscrit. Mal. from (tázh, mal. to sink + maram, mal. plant). Singh. from (nalina, san. lotus). Tam. from (támarasa, san. the plant). San. also (kamala), meaning supported by water or adorning water [red indian water-lily]; (kókanada), meaning praised by ruddy goose, the red variety; (pundaríka), meaning white lotus; (támarasa), meaning red-colored lotus; (jalaja), meaning water born; (aravinda), meaning having filament; (padmachári), meaning lotus + moving; (shatapatra), meaning hundred petalled [cabbage rose]; (sahasrapatra), meaning thousand petalled; (ambuja), meaning water born; (nálika), meaning having reed-like stalk; (kushéshaya), meaning water resting; (pankéruha), meaning mire growing; (sárasa), meaning pertaining to tank; (sarasíruha), meaning tank growing; (rájíva), meaning shining; (pushkara), meaning nourishing [arabian costum]; (nalina), meaning tied or closed by the moon. Pers. also (báklaikabtí), meaning coptic potherb. Hind. also (lálkanwal), meaning red lotus; (ambuj); (padam). Malay also (sároja), meaning tank-born. Can. also (támare). Too. also (allige). Tel. also (saugandhikamu), meaning sweet smelling; (tellatámara), meaning white + the plant; (tellanipadmamu), meaning white + the plant; (verratámara), meaning red + the plant; (erratámarapadmamu), meaning red + lotus. Mal. also (tandár), meaning water flower; (ventámara), meaning white lotus. Singh. also (nelumbu); (kamal). Tam. also (tirumálundi), meaning vishnoo's navel, from mythological place of origin [pralayam]; (shivapputtámarai), meaning red lotus. κρίνεα ῥόδοις ἐμφέρεα of herodotus, κύαμος αἰγύπτιος of theophrastes. Title otherwise Chinese water-lily, Coptic bean, Egyptian bean, Egyptian lotus, Hundred-petalled flower, Moonfoe, Mystic lotus, Nutty lotus, Peltated water-lily, Pudmam, Pythagorean bean, Sacred lotus, Spiral thread, Taumaray, Thousand-petalled flower, Vishnoo's navel, Water bean. Botanically Nelumbium speciosum, willd., nymphæaceæ [vricsham, 7]. Generic name from singhalese. Alias Cyamus mysticus, nelumbo; Nelumbium asiaticum, tamara; Nelumbo indica, nucifera; Nymphæa nelumbo; Tamara alba, rubra. Tamara is tamul. Aquatic; leaves orbicular, attached by their centre, glabrous, under surface pale, margins somewhat waved; peduncles longer than the petioles, erect; root-stock horizontal, fleshy, sending out many fibres from the under-surface; petioles long, rising above the surface of the water, scabrous with acute tubercles; corolla polypetalous; connectivum produced beyond the cells of the anthers into a clavate appendage; nuts loose in the hollows of the torus, one to two-seeded; flowers large, white or rose-colored; flowering nearly all year. Large, broad-leaved herb of the water-lily family; found in tanks; flowers during hot season; new blown flowers of rose-colored [gool] variety have agreeable fragrance, those of white and yellow have less odour; produces seed in drooping, cone-shaped seed-vessels; ripens seed about close of rains [mazhay]; the seed receptacle has been compared to a pomegranate [anaur] cut in half, and by herodotus to a wasp's nest; seeds consist of oblong nuts, twice the size of peas [calauyam], when perfectly ripe so hard as to require a hammer to break them; when ripe, the seeds are loose each in their separate cell, and if shaken make a noise like a rattle; stems, petioles, and flower-stems are raised above the water; leaf from its structure growing entirely round the stalk defends both flowers and fruit arising from its centre from contact with water. The seeds or nuts are hard and dark brown, round, oval or oblong, about the size of the seeds of soap-nut [q.v.] tree, with a white, albuminous and slightly sweetish kernel; the root occurs in the bazaar in small and circular pieces, varying in diameter from 3 or 4 lines to 1 inch, with several holes arranged in a circular form with a solitary and generally smaller one in the centre; odourless and slightly mucilaginous in taste; the holes are the result of the cut ends of the spiral tubes; long, fine filaments are found within the cells of the stalks. This is the sacred egyptian lotus, which originally found its way from india where it was indigenous; as a device the flower enters into all the ornaments of brass [pittalay] vessels used in hindoo temples [coil, pagoda]; it is the immediate attribute of vishnoo [q.v.] from being the first of aquatic plants and a personification of water; it is also sacred to lutchmy [q.v.] who is called camalay [q.v.]; it is generally an emblem of female beauty. In cultivation, the mode of sowing the seeds is by enclosing them in balls of clay [calimunn] and throwing them into the water. The flowers, seeds and roots are medicinally similar to indian water-lily [q.v.]; filaments are astringent and cooling; seeds are diuretic and refrigerant; large leaves form a cool bed in fever; the milky viscid juice of the leaf and flower-stalks is a remedy in diarrhœa; petals are slightly astringent; sherbet [q.v.] of the plant is used as refrigerant; root is used as a paste in cutaneous affections. Seeds eaten by the natives either raw, roasted, or boiled; roots after being cut into slices, dried and fried in oil, are eaten; stalk and leaf eaten as vegetables [keeray]; unripe nuts have flavor of filberts [findak]; on ripening, they become hard and are then roasted. Fibres [naur] used as wicks to burn in the temple worship, and leaves used as plates on which offerings are placed. The Tamul Cooral has the following:—வெள்ளத் தனைய மலர்நீட்ட மாந்தர்தம் முள்ளத் தனைய துயர்வு—"the stalks of "water-flowers are proportionate to the depth of water; so is "men's greatness proportionate to their minds." There are several varieties with white or rose-colored flowers, and with or without a prickly stem; a blue variety is native of cashmere and persia. No other common species here. This lotus [q.v.] must be distinguished from two other plants of the same name known to the ancients; viz., the herb Melilotus officinalis, willd.; and the lotus of the lotophagi, Zizyphus jujuba [bair]. Distinguish also from the Indian water-lily.——*Black nelumbo* (కృష్ణతామర - krishnatámara, Tel.). Same as Indian shot.——*Blue nelumbo* (నీరుతామర - nírutámara, Tel.; കരിങ്കുവലയം - karinkuvalayam, Mal.; நீலத்தாமரை - nílattámarai, Tam.). Title from color of flowers. Tel. from (níru, tel. water + támara, tel. nelumbo). Mal. from (kari, mal. black + kuvalaya, san. water-lily, nymphæa). Tam. from (níla, san. blue + támarai, tam. lotus, nelumbium speciosum, willd.). Tel. also (nírukátsa), meaning water + plant so called. Mal. also (karinkúvalam) by corruption. Tam. also (karunguvalai), meaning black + monochoria, from blue flowers. Title otherwise Blue lotus. Botanically Monochoria vaginalis, presl., pontederaceæ [vricsham, 135]. Alias Pontederia vaginalis. Root perennial, creeping; leaves radical, narrow-cordate, pointed, entire, smooth, glossy; from 2–4 inches long, 1–2 inch broad; petioles sub-erect, tapering, fistulous, smooth, from 6–12 inches long; those that bear a raceme are swelled a little about the middle, and there open like a spathe lengthways near the base, those that do not bear flowers are enlarged into a sheath, which embraces the exterior leaves; raceme short peduncled, after flowering time, drooping, from six to twelve-flowered; pedicels about $\frac{3}{4}$ inch long; flowers blue and pretty; calyx no other than the common spathe of the raceme; petals six, three exterior are the smallest and oblong, three interior obovate; filaments ascending, inserted round the base of the germ, the lowermost one is generally broad, and two-cleft, its lower division bears a blue anther, the other nothing; the rest are yellow, germ superior; style single; stigma glandular. Aquatic herb on margins of tanks. Root used in diseases of liver and stomach; pulverized and mixed with sugar [q.v.], administered for asthma; leaves, bruised and mixed with milk [paul], administered in cholera; root chewed for toothache; young shoots are edible. Another species is hastæfolia.——*Floating nelumbo* (कालानुशारिवा - kálánushárivá, San.; कातरी - kátarí, Mahr.; چولی - chulí, Hind.; بڑا انتر گنگا - baráantargangá, Dec.; ಅಂತರಗಂಗೆ - antaragange, Can.; అంతరతామర - antaratámara, Tel.; ചെറുചിറ്റാമ്പൽ - cheruchittámbal, Mal.; நெய்தலாம்பல் - neydalámbal, Tam.). Title from resemblance and floating roots. San. from (kála, san. time + anusri, san. to follow); follows seasons. Hind. from (shítalí, san. the plant). Dec. from (bará, dec. large + antargangá, dec. the plant). Can. from (antara, san. atmosphere + gangá, san. ganges); from roots floating on water. Tel. from (antara, san. atmosphere + támara, tel. lotus, nelumbium speciosum, willd.); from roots floating on water, without grounding. Mal. from (cheru, mal. small + chittámbal, mal. the lily, nymphæa stellata, willd.). Tam. from (ney, tam. to become fleshy + ámbal, tam. water-lily, nymphæa lotus, linn.); from fleshy leaves. San. also (kumuda), meaning earth + delight [red indian water-lily]; (kumudiní), meaning assemblage of lily; (kumudvatí), meaning abounding in lilies; (shítalí), meaning cooling, from roots used as sarsaparilla, hemidesmus indicus, r. br.; (shítalíjatá), meaning cooling tuft of hair. Hind. also (baráchulí), meaning large variety; (kamúdní); (guljafarí), meaning the marigold, tagetes patula, linn.; (khairposh), meaning wood cover. Tel. also (chirialli), meaning small + nymphæa lotus, linn.; (peddaákáshatámara), meaning large + sky + nelumbium speciosum, wild.; (peddaantaratámara), meaning large + the plant; (tórelaga). Mal. also (neytalámbal), meaning water-lily of maritime tracts; (nírámbal), meaning water + nymphæa lotus, linn. Tam. also (ágásattámarai), meaning same; (ágásavalli), meaning sky creeper; (andarattámarai), meaning atmosphere + lotus; from roots floating in water without adhering to soil; (periyavágásathámarai), meaning large + the plant. Title otherwise Buck-bean, Camoodee, Floating heart, Fringed water-lily, Indian buck bean, Marsh buck bean, Marsh flower, Marsh trefoil, Water fringe. Botanically Limnanthemum cristatum, griseb., gentianaceæ [vricsham, 90]. Alias Menyanthes cristata; Villarsia cristata. Aquatic; leaves cordate-orbicular, roughish above, glandular beneath; calyx segments ovate-lanceolate; segments of the corolla waved, ciliated, with a longitudinal crest within; flowers white, cymose, inserted on the petiole; capsule one to two-seeded; seeds muricated. Found floating in lakes and tanks; middle-sized flowers with a yellow tube and a white-bearded limb; tuberous roots are used medicinally. Another and similar species is Indicum.——*High ground nelumbo* (మెట్టతామర - mettatámara, Tel.). From habitat and resemblance. Same as Foreign agatty and Malabar arrowroot.——*Hill nelumbo* (மலைத்தாமரை - malaittámarai, Tam.). Same as Oval-leaved china root.——*One-leaf nelumbo* (चारटी - chárati, San.; रतान्पुरस् - ratánpurus, Mahr.; पुरुषरत्न - purusharatna, Conc.; رتن پرس - ratanpurs, Hind.; رتن پرس - ratanpurus, Dec.; ಓರೆಲೆದಾವರೆಗಿಡ - óreledávaregida, Can.; పురుషరత్నము - purusharatnamu, Tel.; ഒറിലത്താമര - orilattámara, Mal.; මහයොතුවන්න - mahayotuvanna, Singh.; ஓரிலைத்தாமரை - órilaittámarai, Tam.). Title from single petal of flower. San. from (char, san. to spread). Mahr. from (ratna, san. gem + purusha, san. man); as a tonic. Conc. from (purusha, san. man + ratna, san. gem). Hind. from (ratna, san. gem + purusha, san. man). Can. from (ór, can. one + ele, can. leaf + dávare, can. lotus, nelumbium speciosum, willd. + gida, can. plant). Tel. from (purusha, san. man + ratna, san. precious stone). Mal. from (oru, mal. one + ila, mal. leaf + támara, mal. lotus). Singh. from (maha, singh. large + yotuvanna, singh. the plant so named). Tam. from (ór, tam. one + ilai, tam. leaf + támarai, tam. nelumbium speciosum, willd.); from monopetalous flower. San. also (purusharatna), meaning man + gem; (ékapatri), meaning single + leaf; (padmachárini), meaning lotus + spreading; (atichará), meaning greatly spreading. Can. also (purusharatna), meaning man + gem. Tel. also (nélakobbari), meaning ground + cocoanut, cocos nucifera, linn.; (súryakánti), meaning sun + lover [soorya caunty]; (magalingamu), meaning male + emblem of shiva, reputed aphrodisiac [weaver's beam]. Mal. also (nilampiranda), meaning ground + spreading plant. Tam. also (shúryagándi), meaning sun + lustre; (purusarattinam), meaning man + gem; (órithazhttámarai), meaning one + petal + lotus; from monopetalous flower. Title otherwise Cape green violet, Madder-leaved violet, One-leaf lotus, Shrubby ionidium, Suffruticose violet. Botanically Ionidium suffruticosum, ging., violaceæ [vricsham, 13]. Alias Ionidium capense, enneaspermum, frutescens, heterophyllum; Solea enneasperma, erecta; Viola enneasperma, frutescens, suffruticosa. Perennial; stem scarcely any; leaves alternate, subsessile, lanceolate, slightly serrate, smoothish; peduncles axillary, solitary, one-flowered, shorter than the leaves, jointed above the middle, with two bracts at the joints; calyx five-cleft; petals five, two upper ones smallest, linear-oblong, two lateral ones sub-ovate, with long recurved apices, lower one largest, broad-cordate, supported on a claw; capsules round, one-celled, three-valved; seeds several; flowers small, rose-colored, flowering nearly all year; common weed; grows abundantly in low and damp places. The drug as sold in the shops consists of the root and some of the leafy portion of the plant attached to it; the roots are yellowish-white, 3–4 inches in length, about $\frac{1}{12}$th of inch in diameter at the upper part, gradually tapering downwards, woody and tough, and covered with a corky bark. Whole plant is medicinally demulcent, refrigerant, tonic and diuretic; juice of fresh leaves is pressed out by bruising them with water, and administered alone or in combination with fenugreek [maitee] seeds; dose of the leaves is one drachm, twice or three times a day; substituted for oleum copaibæ and spiritus ætheris nitrosi; leaves and tender stalks demulcent, used by natives in decoction [kwautam] and electuary; also employed, in conjunction with mild oil, in preparing cooling liniment for head; root in infusion is diuretic. ——*Pit nelumbo* (గుఱ్ఱపుడెక్క - gurrapudekka, Tel.; കുഴിത്താമര - kuzhittámara, Mal.; நீர்ச்சேம்பு - nírççémbu, Tam.). Title from usual habitat. Tel. from (gurramu, tel. horse + dekka tel. hoof). Mal. from (kuzhi, mal. pit + támara, mal. nelumbium speciosum, willd.). Tam. from (nír, tam. water + shémbu, tam. colocasia nymphæifolia, kunth.). Tam. also (kuliri), meaning cold. Title otherwise Adder's tongue, Arrowhead, Arrowleaf, Water archer, Water kachvee. Botanically Sagittaria obtusifolia, l., alismaceæ [vricsham, 133]. Root fibrous, annual; leaves radical, erect, long-petioled ovate-sagittate; apex circular, lobes or barbs divaricate, tapering to long, narrow, fine points, smooth many-nerved; 6–12 inches long, 4–8 inches broad; petioles 2–3 feet long, thick, one side flat, the other angular; scapes including flower bearing part 2–4 feet high, erect, five to six-angled, striated, the lower verticle, and sometimes the second, bear branches mixed with one-flowered pedicels; involucre at each verticle three-fold, sessile, conical; flowers numerous, small, white; male flowers for the most part terminal, peduncled; peduncles slender; calyx three-leaved; corol three-petalled; filaments six, below they are enlarged, so as to occupy the whole of the centre of the flowers; anthers two-lobed; hermaphrodite flowers, for there are no female flowers, more numerous below, robust, peduncled; calyx and corol as in the male; filaments six, with their enlarged bases surrounding the germs; germs about thirty, sessile; stigma-lobed, bearded, or downy; drupes numerous, collected on a globular receptacle, turbinate, dry, wrinkled; nut one-seeded, but there are also two empty cavities, one on each side of the seed; seed bent double, with the two extremities pointing to the base, by one of which it is affixed to the bottom of the drupe. Handsome aquatic plant. Other common species are:—cordifolia, sagittifolia.——*Rootless nelumbo* (कुंभिका - kumbhiká, San.; انترگنگا - antargangá, Hind. and Dec.; ಅಂತರಗಂಗೆಗಿಡ - antaragangegida, Can.; ನೀರಟ - nírata, Too.; అంతరతామర - antaratámara, Tel.; കുടപ്പായൽ - kutappáyal, Mal.; ஆகாசத்தாமரை - ágásattámarai, Tam.). Title from floating roots. San. from (kumbha, san water pot); cf. coomby. Hind. from (antar, hind. inside + gangá, hind. ganges). Can. from (antara, san. inside + gange, can. water + gida, can. plant). Tel. from (antara, san. inside + támara, tel. lotus, nelumbium speciosum, willd.), from roots floating in water and not grounding in the earth. Mal. from (kuta, mal. pitcher + páyal, mal. duck-weed, lemna). Tam. from (ákásha, san. sky + támarasa, san. lotus flower, nelumbium speciosum, willd.); floating lotus. San. also (váriparní), meaning having water-colored leaves. Too. also (antaragange). Tel. also (ákáshatámara), meaning sky + lotus; (nírubadiki), meaning water + bathing; (níráku), meaning water + leaf; (túdikúra). Mal. also (nírççíra), meaning water greens; (annillápponnu), meaning shapeless floating plant. Tam. also (andarattámarai), meaning sky + the lotus plant, nelumbium speciosum, willd. Title otherwise Antargunga, Aucausha taumaray, Sky lotus, Tropical duck-weed, Water soldier, Water spogel, West indian water lettuce. Botanically Pistia stratiotes, linn., pistiaceæ [vricsham, 151]. Alias Plantago aquatica; Tala indica. Stemless, floating; roots numerous, fibrous; leaves subsessile, wedge-shaped at the base, elliptic or obovate, alternated at the base, glaucous on the upper surface, radiate-veined, about twenty, spreading out, central leaves smaller than the outer ones, inner ones erect, tomentose; fibres long, terminated by other plants; flowers axillary, solitary, erect, on short peduncles, white or pale yellow; flowering in april; tanks and ditches, everywhere. Decoction or infusion cooling and demulcent; leaves made into poultice for piles; mixed with rice and cocoanut [q.v.] milk are given in dysentery, and with rosewater [goolaub] and sugar in cough and asthma; root is laxative and emollient. In moderate quantity the living plant in wells, &c., helps to purify the water. Other species are:—ægyptiaca, crispita.——*Round-leaved nelumbo* (चांदा - chándá, Mahr.; चंदडे - chandadé, Conc.; ಬೆಟ್ಟದಾವರೆ - bettadávare, Can.; ಉಪ್ಪಾಲ - uppála, Too.; పుట్టతామర - puttatámara, Tel.; ഉപ്പില - uppila, Mal.; வட்டத்தாமரை - vattattámarai, Tam.). Can. from (betta, can. hill + dávare, can. lotus). Too. from (uppu, too. salt). Tel. from (putta, tel. ant hill + támara, tel. nelumbinm speciosum, willd.). Mal. from (uppu, mal. salt + ila, mal. leaf), from leaves preserving salt from damp. Tam. from (vattam, tam. circle + támarai, tam. lotus). Can. also (uppalige); (chendakanni); (upligi); (upalkai); (kanchupranthi). Mal. also (vattattámara), meaning round lotus. Tam. also (kandubárangi) [knotted bhraungy]; (vattikkanni). Title otherwise Round-leaved lotus, Salt lotus, Varee tree. Botanically Macaranga indica, wight, euphorbiaceæ [vricsham, 118]. Tree; leaves stipuled, peltate; stipules paired, broad-ovate, cuspidate; male flowers panicled, glomerate; bracts petioled, glandulose; calyx three-parted, pubescent; stamens six to eight; female panicles axillary; flowers solitary or paired, pedicelled, bracteate; style one; ovary one-celled; calyx four-parted; capsule covered with resinous points, flowers greenish; flowering in december and january; very common in western forests. Coffee [q.v.] trees thrive under the shade, as the fallen leaves are good manure; gummy substance of tragacanth [kateerah] kind exudes from cut branches and base of the petioles, of light crimson color, and has been used for taking impressions of leaves, coins, and medallions; wood greyish-red, moderately hard. A species peltata is called hill-lotus. Other species are:—digyna, flexuosa, tomentosa.——*Shrinking nelumbo* (మునుగుతామర - munugutámara, Tel.). See under Shoondy.

NERAID (నేరేడు - nérédu, *Tel.*). Same as Common jaumoon. Compare:—Flacourtia ramontchi, var. sapida (nakkanérédu), fox jaumoon; Premna herbaceæ (nélanérédu), lowly jaumoon.

NERIJA (నెరిజ - neridza, *Tel.*; නෙරළු - neralu, *Singh.*; செலுப்பை - sheluppai, *Tam.*). Title from teloogoo. Tel. also (bíra); (nerasi); (nirasi); (niradza); (niridza); (botanskam); (kanemis). Tam. also (karkavá); (irkuli); (siri). Title otherwise Chelooppay, Olive-wood. Botanically Elæodendron glaucum, pers., celastrineæ [vricsham, 40]. Alias Elæodendron paniculatum, roxburghii; Nerija dichotoma; Rhamnus nerija. Nerija from teloogoo. Tree; leaves opposite, elliptical or ovate, crenate-serrated, young ones glaucous; calyx five-partite; petals five, linear-oblong; peduncles axillary; cymes lax, dichotomous, divaricated, about half the length of the leaves, usually with a solitary flower in the forks; drupe one-celled, obovoid; but somewhat crustaceous and soft; flowers small, yellow; found everywhere, most variable as to size. The root bark is compact and brittle, and has a granular fracture; it occurs in small irregular fragments, is of a dull reddish color, and is covered by a scabrous brittle suber, the external surface of which is brown or sometimes yellowish, and the substance and internal surface of a bright brick red; some pieces of the bark show small warty prominences which are usually fissured exposing the brick red color of the suber. Both leaves and bark are astringent to the taste and slightly bitter. Gum [gond] occurs in roundish tears about half inch in diameter, rough or cracked on the surface, tasteless, forming a sherry-colored solution; root is called specific in snake bites; fresh bark of roots rubbed with water applied externally to remove almost any swelling, a very strong astringent; bark also used for dyeing [shauyam]. Wood not very strong or stiff, but tough, close and even grained, the surface curled and flowered and of a reddish brown, suited for cabinet work; used by natives for the manufacture of combs, suited for picture frames, &c. No other common species here.

NERINJY (गोक्षुरक - gókshuraka, *San.*; गोखरू - gókharú, *Mahr.*; नेगल्मुळ्ळु - négalmullu, *Conc.*; حسك - hasak, *Ar.*; خسك - khasak, *Pers.*; گوکھرو - gokhrú, *Hind.* and *Dec.*; ಸಣ್ಣನೆಗ್ಗಿಲು - sannaneggilu, *Can.*; ನೆಗಿಲುಮುಳ್ಳು - négilumullu, *Too.*; పల్లేరు - palléru, *Tel.*; ഞെരുഞ്ഞിൽ - ñeruññil, *Mal.*; සෙම්බුනෙරෙඤ්චි - sembunereñchi, *Singh.*; நெருஞ்சில் - neruñjil, *Tam.*). Title from tamul. San. from (gó, san. cow + kshura, san. hoof); from the resemblance of the cocci when adhering together in pairs to a cloven hoof. Mahr. from sanscrit. Ar. from (hasaka, ar. to bear rancour). Pers. from arabic. Hind. and dec. from sanscrit. Can. from (sanna, can. small + neggilu, can. small caltrops). Too. from (négilu, too. caltrops + mullu, too. thorn). Mal. from tamul. Tam. from (neri, tam. to press). San. also (vanashringáta), meaning wild trapa bispinosa, roxb.; (shvadamshtrá), meaning dog's tooth, as having thorn resembling dog's tooth; (trikantakavallí), meaning triple thorned creeper; (ikshugandhá), meaning sugar-cane smelling, in allusion to the aroma of the plant [naunal, neermoolly]; (palamkashá), meaning flesh injuring; (svádukantaka), meaning sweet-thorned [swaudoocantacam]; (gókantaka), meaning cow's thorn [neermolly]; (sudamshtra), meaning well-toothed; (raktasudamshtra), meaning red + the plant. Ar. also (bastítaj). Can. also (negalu); (neggilumullu), meaning caltrops + thorn; (nerigilu). Tel. also (chiripalléru), meaning small + the plant; (errapalléru), meaning red + the plant. Singh. also (nereñchi). Tam. also (açççuram); (tirigandagam), meaning three-thorned. Greek τρίβολος. Title otherwise Cow's thorn, Dog tooth, Gokhoor, Gokroo, Land caltrops, Small caltrops. The thistles of St. Mathew. Botanically Tribulus terrestris, linn., zygophylleæ [vricsham, 30]. Alias Tribulus lanuginosus. Trailing; leaves opposite, abruptly pinnated, pleasant smelling and sweet tasted; leaflets about five to six pair, nearly equal, with a close-pressed villous pubescence; peduncles shorter than the leaf; flowers axillary; calyx deeply five-partite; petals five, broad, obtuse; fruit five-coccous, cocci each with two prickles; flowers solitary, bright yellow, sweet-scented; fibrous root; fruits, small and spiny. The fruit is roundish, five-cornered, five-celled, about the size of bengal-gram [q.v.], and armed with prickles, source of annoyance to foot travellers; each of cells contains one or two four-horned seeds; the fruit possesses no particular taste or smell, but the seeds are slightly bitterish, due to the presence of an alkaloid. Fruit, leaves and root diuretic, in decoction; seeds powdered in infusion used in dropsy and gonorrhœa; fruits one of the ten dashamoolam [q.v.]; all parts in pharm. non-officinal. Decoction; take of the dry fruit, bruised, three ounces; water, one pint and-a-half; boil on slow fire till the liquid is reduced to one pint, strain when cool. Juice of the fresh leaves pressed out by bruising without water and passing through cloth. Doses; of the decoction, from one to three fluid ounces; of the juice, from one to two fluid ounces; four or five times a day. A weak substitute for spirit. æther. nit., tragacanth, buchu and uva ursi. There is a variety with red flowers whose leaves have smell of cloves [lavangam]. No other common species here.——*Black nerinjy* (ಕಾರ್ನೆಗ್ಗಿಲು - kárneggilu, Can.; నల్లపల్లేరు - nallapalléru, Tel.; கருநெருஞ்சில் - karuneruñjil, Tam.). Title from yielding indigo; the legumés are bristly on the convex side; hence native association with the thistles. Can. from (káru, can. black + neggilu, can. tribulus terrestris, linn.). Tel. from (nalla, tel. black + palléru, tel. tribulus terrestris). Tam. from (karumai, tam. blackness + neruñjil, tam. tribulus terrestris, linn.). Tel. also (nílipalléru), meaning indigo + nerinjy. Title otherwise Black pallair, Round-leaved camel's thorn. Botanically Indigofera [neely] echinata, willd., leguminosæ [vricsham, 48]. Alias Hedysarum erinaceum, rotundifolium; Onobrychis rotundifolia. Herbaceous, prostrate; branches angular; leaves simple, obovate, dotted with glands; racemes peduncled, shorter than the leaves, six to eight-flowered; keel pointed; legumes crescent-shaped, bristly on the convex side; seed solitary, reniform; moist sandy soils near the coast; very common.——*Elephant nerinjy* (गजदंष्ट्री - gajadamshtrí, San.; गोखरू - gókharú, Mahr.; حسك كبير - hasakikabír, Ar.; خسك كلان - khaskikalán, Pers.; بڑا گوکھرو - barágokhrú, Hind.; هتی گهوکرو - hattíghokrú, Dec.; ಆನೆನೆಗ್ಗಿಲು - áneneggilu, Can.; ಆನೆನೆಗಿಲ್ - ánenégil, Too.; ఏనుగపల్లేరు - énugapalléru, Tel.; കാക്കമുള്ള - kákkamullu, Mal.; අතනෙරංචි - atnerañchi, Singh.; ஆனைநெருஞ்சில் - ánaineruñjil, Tam.). Title from size of leaf and drupe. San. from (gaja, san. elephant + damshtra, san. tusk). Mahr. from (gókshura, san. cow's hoof, tribulus terrestris, linn.). Ar. from (hasak, ar. tribulus terrestris, linn. + kabír, ar. large). Pers. from (khask, ar. tribulus terrestris, linn. + kalán, pers. large). Hind. from (bará, hind. large + gokhrú, hind. tribulus terrestris, linn.). Dec. from (hattí, dec. elephant + ghokrú, dec. tribulus terrestris, linn.). Can from (áne, can. elephant + neggilu, can. tribulus terrestris, linn.). Too. from canarese. Tel. from (énuga, tel. elephant + palléru, tel. tribulus terrestris, linn.). Mal. from (kákka, mal. crow + mullu, mal. thorn). Singh. from (at, singh. elephant + nereñchi, singh. tribulus terrestris, linn.). Tam. from (ánai, tam. elephant + neruñjil, tam. tribulus terrestris, linn.). Hind. also (farídbútí), meaning fareed's plant; from a saint so called having lived on the water rendered mucilaginous with the leaves [jamtee]. Can. also (ánnegilu), meaning elephant + tribulus terrestris, linn.; (doddaneggilu), meaning large + the plant. Tel. also (peddapalléru), meaning large + tribulus terrestris, linn. Mal. also (káttuñeriññil), meaning wild, tribulus terrestris, linn.; (ánañeriññil), meaning elephant or large caltrop. Tam. also (peruneruñjil), meaning large + small caltrop, tribulus terrestris, linn.; from large leaf. Title otherwise Crow thorn, Fareedbootee, Fareed's plant, Large nerinjy, Prickly pedalium. Botanically Pedalium murex, linn., pedalineæ [vricsham, 100]. Small plant, one to two feet; calyx five-parted, upper segments shortest; corolla with a three-cornered tube and five-lobed limb, sub-labiate; stamens four; leaves opposite, obovate, obtuse, regularly toothed, truncate, smooth; flowers yellow on short pedicels; drupe armed with sharp spines, and containing a two-celled, four-winged nut; cells two-seeded; seeds arillate; flowers axillary, solitary, yellow; found particularly at cape comorin on seashore; flowers in the rainy and cold seasons. Whole plant has odour of musk [custoory]; root of deep orange color; the young branches, petioles, under-surface of leaves and immature capsules have a frosted appearance, which is due to the presence of numerous small, sessile, brilliant, crystalline, four to five-partite glands; the substance of the fruit consists in great part of dense fibro-vascular tissue, forming a kind of four-winged nut, the corky part consists of delicate cellular tissue, when fresh it is green and succulent; simple agitation of the young branches in water, without any crushing, produces a viscid mucilage like white of egg. Juice is a good gargle; the fresh plant as above said renders water or milk very mucilaginous without altering the taste, color, or smell of the liquid; the thickening disappears in a few hours; this beverage given in gonorrhœa, being diuretic; quoted in pharm. non-officinal. The leafy stems are used in the same way in thickening butter-milk [mor], to which they give a rich appearance; plant acts as sand-binder [manal]. No other common species here.——*Red nerinjy* (वसुका - vasuká, San.; भुईगुली - bhuígulí, Mahr.; ಕೆನ್ನೆಗ್ಗಿಲು - kenneggilu, Can.; ఎఱ్ఱపల్లేరు - errapalléru, Tel.; ചെറുപുള്ളടി - cherupullati, Mal.; செப்புநெருஞ்சில் - sheppuneruñjil, Tam.). Title from color of flowers; the trailing character makes the native association with the trailing thistles; see also black nerinjy. San. from (vas, san. to dwell), possessing virtue; medicinal. Mahr. from (bhuí, mahr. ground + gulí, mahr. indigo plant, indigofera tinctoria, linn.). Can. from (kem, can. red + neggilu, can. tribulus terrestris, linn.). Tel. from (érra, tel. red + palléru, tel. tribulus terrestris, linn). Mal. from (cheru, mal. small + pullati, mal. desmodium gangeticum, dec.). Tam. from (shem, tam. red + neruñjil, tam. tribulus terrestris, linn.). San. also (suvarççala), meaning shining; (gópála), meaning cow-protector; cattle fodder. Can. also (chenneggilu), meaning red + caltrops. Tel. also (chiragadamu) [sweet potato]; (chalapaççi). Title otherwise Red pallair, Trailing camel's thorn, Trailing indigo plant. Botanically Indigofera [neely] enneaphylla, linn., leguminosæ [vricsham, 48]. Alias Hedysarum prostratum; Indigofera cæspitosa. Perennial, procumbent; young parts and leaves pubescent with white hairs; branches prostrate and edged; leaves pinnate, sessile, leaflets three to five pairs, obovate-oblong racemes sessile, short, dense, many-flowered; legumes oval, pubescent, not winged; seeds two, ovate and truncated at one end; flowers small, bright red; flowering nearly all the year. Infusion of the whole plant diuretic and given by veidyans [q.v.] in fevers and coughs; expressed juice is given as an alterative in old syphilitic diseases; it is sub-acid and pleasant tasted. The plant is eaten by cattle.——*Small nerinjy* (چهوٹا گوکهرو - chhotágokhrú, Hind.). From small bristly germs. Same as Burdock datura.——*Vegetable nerinjy* (కూరపల్లేరు - kúrapalléru, Tel.). Title from use. Tel. from (kúra, tel. vegetable + palléru, tel. tribulus terristris, linn.). Botanically Vitis [draucshay] auriculata, roxb., ampelideæ [vricsham, 42]. Alias Cissus auriculata. Young shoots succulent; petioles and inflorescence softly pubescent; stipules large, linear-oblong, recurved; leaves long-petioled, with five pedate or digitate leaflets; leaflets oblong-obovate or rhomboid, shortly acuminated, serrulated, under side softly pubescent; peduncles as long as the petioles, axillary or terminal; cyme much branched; petals distinct; fruit red, size of a cherry [q.v.], one-seeded; flowers small, green; flowering throughout the year.

NERRUCK (نرخ - nirkh, *Hind.*). From persian. A tariff, especially established by authority. Nerruck nauma is a list of market prices [bazaar].

NESAVOO (वाय - váya, *San.*; باف - báf, *Pers.*; بنا - bunná, *Hind.*; నేత - néta, *Tel.*; നെയ്ത്തു - neyttu, *Mal.*; நெசவு - nesavu, *Tam.*). San. from (vé, san. to weave). Tam. from (ney, tam. to weave). Weaving. Carried on in most villages, where men of the proper caste are found [keikkila]. Indian loom [tarry] is probably oldest machine in the world. Cloths are woven either with the fine foreign thread [nool] sold in the bazaar, or oftener with the rough thread spun by the native agriculturalists. The thread is first steeped in water for three days, and then dried. It is then wound round large spindle-like bamboo [q.v.] frames [taur], which are on a small scale what the warping-mill is to the English warper. A small hollow piece of smooth bamboo [ausmaur] 2 inches long, held in the hand, answers to the English mechanical heck-box. To get the length of warp [pauv] and make the leash [pinay], the thread is then passed in and out round pegs fixed in a certain order on a wooden frame [ausmaun]. It is taken off this in skeins made by going 30, 60 or 120 times round the pegs. Each skein is a poonjam [q.v.]; and as the higher number of threads is given to the finest yarn, 120 poonjam or 120 times round the pegs indicates a fine cloth. The thread thus skeined is then attached to the warp-beam [mady cumboo] by the beamer the same as in England, and flat thin bits of bamboo are inserted between the threads and the various warp threads [pauv] are separated from one another. After this the warp is elevated off the ground on trestles [muttay coothiray] and the thread is softened by soaking it with conjee [q v.], by means of a long brush [cootchoo]. This process is to be seen under every tree in a weaving village. The warp threads are then rolled round the warp-beam [mady cumboo] and so left till the loom [tarry] is ready to receive them. The heddles [viloothoo] for shedding the warp threads, the batten [atchoo] for laying the woof, the treadles [mithy], and the shuttles [naudah], do not differ materially from the portions of an old English hand-loom. The weaver sits with his feet in a pit below the loom. The most primitive looms are sometimes erected in the open air under trees.

NEW (نو - nau, *Hind.*). Prefix [now].——*New year* (نوروز - nauroz, Hind.; సంవత్సరాది - samvatsarádi, Tel.; வருடப்பிறப்பு - varudappirappu, Tam.). First day of the year; universally a day of consecration and feasting. Falls on different dates among hindoos according as they follow the lunar [chaundramaunam] or luni-solar [chaundramaunam] or solar [madhyamasowramaunam] calendar [punchaungam]. The tamuls follow sowramaunam reckoning and their year is sidereal; begins 12th April, gregorian reckoning; see Tamul new year. The teloogoos and the canarese follow the chaundramaunam reckoning and their year is luni-solar; begins some days earlier than 12th April; see Teloogoo new year. The malayalam year like the tamul is sidereal; begins 15th September; see Collam. For the Mahomedans who follow the purely lunar reckoning the first day of the year in the first of moharram [q.v.]; begins any day in the year. Chittray or cheitram is the name of first month of the year in the south, Veishaukh in the north of India; for reasons see Maunam and Mausam.

NEY (நெய் - ney, *Tam.*). Ghee [q.v.].——*Neyoonny* (कार्टे - kárta, Conc.; گرگونرو - gargunaru, Hind.; ಲಿಂಗತೊಂಡೆ - lingatonde, Can.; లింగదొండ - lingadonda, Tel.; നെയ്യുണ്ണി - neyyunni, Mal.; ஐவிரலி - aivirali, Tam.). Title from malayalam. Can. from (linga, san. emblem of shiva + tonde, can. the plant), from seeds. Tel. from (linga, san. emblem of shiva + donda, tel. cephalandra indica, naud.), from seeds. Mal. from (ney, mal.

ghee + unni, mal. eater), from medicinal use. Tam. from (aindu, tam. five + viral, tam. finger); from palmate leaf. Mal. also (neyyómakam), meaning ghee + bishop's weed, carum copticum, benth. Tam. also (aivéli), perhaps by corruption. Greek βριωνία. Title otherwise Bryony, Ghee ajwaun. Botanically Bryonia laciniosa, linn., cucurbitaceæ [vricsham, 62]. Creeper; stems glabrous; tendrils bifid; leaves slightly scabrous, palmately five-lobed; segments oblong-lanceolate; acuminated, serrated; petioles shorter than the leaves, muricated; male flowers fascicled; female solitary in the same axil; berries the size of a cherry [q.v.], spherical, glabrous, three-celled; seeds few in each cell, with a pulpy aril; margins tuberose; sides gibbous and suberose; flowers small, yellowish-green; flowering all the year; the fruit is pale-red with white streaks; whole plant is bitter. Juice of leaves mixed with milk taken internally in bilious complaints. Leaves boiled and eaten as greens [keeray]. No other common species here.

NEYZA (نیزہ - nezah, *Hind.*). Spear. On the seventh khun of Moharram [q.v.] Mahomedans take out a spear in procession. A lime [q.v.] is fixed on the top of it, emblematic of Hoossain's [q.v.] head, which was thus carried by Yazeed's order through different cities.

NI (नि - ni, *San.*). Prefix of intensity; also means in, down. ——*Neecha* (नीच - nícha, San.). From (ni, san. prefix meaning down + anch, san. to bend). Low. The Neecha or polluted castes [jauty] are of the plains four:—Pariahs, Poolayar, Nayaudies, Oollaudar. And of the hills, four:—Veydan, Caniyaur, Coorooba, Malaiyarasar. See each head.——*Neidatham* (नैषध - naishadha, San.; நைடதம் - naidatham, Tam.). From (nishadha, san. country so called). The history of Nalan [q.v.], king of Nishadham [neishadam]. It comprises 1,171 stanzas arranged in 29 cantos. The Tamulians call it the nectar of poets. The following stanza celebrates the beauty of Damayanty's face:—ஒழுகொளிவிரிந்த கதிர்மதிவண்ண னுந்தியந் தாமரையுறை வோன்—முழுமதிக்கலையு ணிறைந்தபோழுகை மொண்டுகொண் டரிபாந்தகன்ற —மழைமதர் நெடுங்கட் டமயந்தி வதனம் வகுத்தனன் காத்திறு லெடுத்த—புழைழித் தோன்றும் விசும்பி னையன்றே களங்கமென் றின்னமும் புகல்வார்—"He "Bramha [q.v.], who dwells in the lotus-flower [nelumbo], "blooming from the navel of the bright sapphire-colored Vishnoo "[q.v.], formed the face of the long-eyed Damayanty [q.v.] by "taking his materials from the great beauty which is concen- "trated in the full moon [chundran]; and it is the blue sky, "which is seen through the cleft thus made in the moon "that people still call the moon-spot."——*Neimishauranyam* (नैमिषारण्य - naimisháranya, San.). From (nimisha, san. moment + aranya, san. forest); so called because in it the sage gowramookhan destroyed an army of asoorans [q.v.] in a nimisham [q.v.]. A paradisiacal wilderness; sometimes styled Shadauranyam [q.v.] or six wildernesses. It is probable that the original site was the valley of Cashmere.——*Nelambore* (നിലമ്പൂർ - nilampúr, Mal. nilambúr*). From (nilimpa, san. god + úr, mal. village). Sanscrit name (nilimpapura), meaning god + village.—"*a*" Village, Head-quarters of Assistant conservator of Forests, Government forest; Malabar dist., Yernaud tal.; pop. 13,699; lat. 11° 17'; long. 76° 16'; from Calicut E. 30 miles; from Munjery N.N.E. 14 miles; from the sea E. 31 miles. Extensive teak [q.v.] plantations belonging to Government, begun about 1853. Numerous dolmens [coday cull] and menhirs [paundoocull] and rock-cut caves. Gold-washing.—"*b*" Valley; Malabar dist., Yernaud tal. Shape of a horse shoe, elevation about 400 feet. A great part is an alluvial deposit of enormous depth. The river which drains valley empties into sea at Beypore, and 4 miles from mouth of the river a navigable canal communicates with another river, which traverses heart of Calicut bazaar. The river is connected with Calicut roadstead by a bar always open. A good cart road is carried from Calicut through Nelambore up the Carcoor ghaut [q.v.] to S.E. Wynaud, whence main line is carried on to Mysore, with branches on north to Devaulah goldfields and South wynaud and on south to Ouchterlony valley and to Ootacamund. Besides the teak [q.v.] plantations, Government now possess a wide tract of forest purchased in 1818 at a court sale, and formerly belonging to the family of the Amarambalatt trimalpaud.——*Nepaul* (नेपाल - népála, San.). From (niyamapála, san. protector of vows, a sage the reputed founder of the first of ruling race). An independent native state at the foot of the Himalayas. Compare:—Aconitum ferox, nepaul aconite plant; Berberis aristata, nepaul barberry plant; Capsicum frutescens, nepaul chilly; Cinnamomum glanduliferum, nepaul camphor wood, nepaul sassafras; Osyris nepalensis, nepaul tea; Rumex nepalensis, nepaul sorrel. The name Nepaulam is given by natives to the plants:—Baliospermum montanum; Croton tiglium; Jatropha curcas. See gloss. paragraphs. ——*Nibandhanay* (निबन्धन - nibandhana, San.). From (above + bandh, san. to tie). An agreement [oodambadikay].—— *Nicoombham* (निकुम्भ - nikumbha, San.). From (ni, san. prefix of certainty + kumbha, san. pot); from oil-bearing seeds. Botanically the Jatropha genus, euphorbiaceæ [vricsham, 118]. Woody plants, with alternate stipulate leaves and flowers in cymes. The species best known to the natives are:—curcas [wild aumanac] glandulifera [rat aumanac], multifida [small wild aumanac].—— *Nidhy* (निधि - nidhi, San.). From (above + dhá, san. to put). A fund. One of the nine divine treasures [nava nidhy] of Coobairan [q.v.] who is styled lord of nidhies. Nidhy shastram is a system of metallurgy embracing rules for discovering buried treasure.

——*Nigamam* (निगम - nigama, San.). From (above + gam, san. to go). Entrance; quotation. Collective name for the four Vedas [q.v.], while Augamam [q.v.] is Sheiva religion and ritual. ——*Nigantoo* (निघण्टु - nighantu, San.). San. from (above + han, san. to destroy); as explaining doubts. Vocabulary or dictionary from a language with itself; same as Abhidhaunam, Acarauthy. There is no Dravidian word. There is no separate word for dictionaries in the European sense, from one language into another. The Sanscrit vocabularies are numerous; best known is Amara cosham [q.v.]. The three old Tamul vocabularies are Divaucauram, Pingalam, and Choodaumany in that order. From these Beschi [veera maumoony] made the Chatooracarauthy [q.v.]. In the other languages there is nothing ancient; but in Teloogoo the modern Andhra deepacam and Shabdaurta calpataroo may be mentioned.——*Nimisham* (निमिष - nimisha, San.). From (above + mish, san. to look). Winking. Measure of solar time. 15 nimishams or eye-winks = 1 caushtay [caulam, 2]. Approximate actual value, 1 nimisham = ·213 of an English second. Also $\frac{1}{3600}$th of an alipalam according to solar calendar [caulam, 6]. Generally roughly used for an English minute. See vol. I, 609.——*Nishaudam* (निषाद - nisháda, San.). From (nishad, san. to sink down). Last note of gamut [swaram].——*Nishaudan* (निषाद - nisháda, San.). From (above + sad, san. to go). Name applied in the Ramayanam [q.v.] to the wild forest tribes, by Menoo [q.v.] to the son of a Bramin by a Shoodra woman [mlecha].——*Nishaun* (نشان - nishán, Hind.). From (nishándan, pers. to fix in the ground); by way of signal. Standard [dhwajam, jenda].——*Nishauny* (نشانی - nisháni, Hind.). From (nishándan, pers. to place). Signature [keiyoppam], a mark.——*Nisheen* (نشین - nishín, Hind.). From (nishastan, pers. to sit). Seated.——*Nishkam* (निष्क - nishka, San.). Ancient gold coin. 16 dharanams = 1 nishkam [naunyam, 2f]. Approximate actual value, 1 nishkam = 56 rupees or 4 gold mohurs [q.v.].——*Nisinda* (نسندہ - nisinda, Hind.). From (ni, san. prefix meaning out + syand, san. to shed); from juice. Same as Notchy.——*Nityam* (नित्य - nitya, San.). Ever; perennial. ——*Nityan* (नित्य - nitya, San.). The eternal. Shiva [q.v.].—— *Nitya poojah* (नित्यपूजा - nityapújá, San.). From (nitya, san. daily + pújá, san. worship). Daily worship [poojah].——*Nityaunandam* (நித்தியானந்தம் - nittiyánandam, Tam.). From (nitya, san. eternal + ánanda, san. happiness). Hindoo 2nd for pers. name [peyar, sadaunandan].——*Nivritty* (निवृत्ति - nivritti, San.). From (above + vrit, san. to turn), turning back, returning. Release from transmigrations [samsauram].——*Nivvary* (नीवार - nívára, San.; నివ్వరి - nivvari, Tel.). San. from (nivri, san. to ward off). Title otherwise Mountain paddy, Mountain rice, Upland rice, Wild rice. Botanically Oryza mutica, roxb., graminaceæ [vricsham, 156]. See Paddy.——*Niyamam* (नियम - niyama, San.). Literally restraint. Religious observances; the second stage of yogam [q.v.].——*Niyogy* (नियोगी - niyógí, San.). From (niyóga, san. appointment); holder of government appointment under native rule. A class of secular andhra Bramins [q.v.], as opposed to the Veidica or priestly class.——*Nyausam* (न्यास - nyása, San.). From (nyas, san. to lay down). The lowering of voice. Tonic at conclusion [swaram].——*Nyauyam* (न्याय - nyáya, San.). See sep. title.

NICKA (نکاح - nikáh, *Hind.*). From (nukh, ar. to marry). The religious ceremony of marriage, among Mahomedans. The wedding festivities are shaudy [q.v.]. In Arabia, Egypt, and Persia the nicka is the principal part of the marriage ceremony. In India, a marriage confined to the nicka is deemed wanting in respectability. The term is also here applied to a second or less honorable marriage, the shaudy [q.v.] wife being alive. Nickanauma is a marriage certificate.

NICOBAR (نیکوبار - nikobár, *Hind.*; நக்கவாரம் - nakkaváram, *Tam.*). Otherwise Sambalang, or Nine islands. A group of islands in the Bay of Bengal to the south of the Andamans. Nicobar traffic is ready money transaction where one party does not trust another; Nicobar talk is a mistrustful speech; Nicobary is a dwarf cocoanut tree.——*Nicobar bread fruit* (کیورا - keurá, Hind.). Same as Screw-pine.

NIEPA (نیپا کی چھال - nípákíchhál, *Hind.*). Samadarah.

NIFT (نفت - nift, *Hind.*). Naphtha [q.v.].——*Naphtha* (نفت - nift, Ar.). Title from arabic from (nafata, ar. to boil); earth ebullition. Petroleum [niftroomy, munnteilam] rectified by distillation, and this in turn refined gives kerosene. Also in Europe the product of destructive distillation of coal [nilakary]. Naphtha does not congeal at zero; it ignites readily and burns with voluminous sooty flame; not soluble in water but is so in alcohol, ether and oils [nift]. In veterinary practice used externally with other oils [yennay] for mange.——*Niftroomy*

(نفترومی - niftrúmí, Hind.). Hind. from (nift, ar. naphta + rúm, hind. turkish empire). Petroleum [munnteilam]. Liquid form of bitumen [shilajit].

NIL (நில் - nil, *Tam.*). To stand.——*Naula* (నాల - nála, Tel.). Common form of (néla, tel. ground). Suffix in place names; as Goontanaula, meaning low land.——*Nilacottah* (நிலக்கோட்டை - nilakkóttai, Tam.). From (nilam, tam. ground + kóttai, tam. fort); the situation being low.—"*a*" Deputy tahsildarry, Madura district. Pay Rs. 70.—"*b*" Village, Head-quarters of Deputy tahsildar and Sub-registrar; Madura dist., Dindigul tal.; pop. 4,893; acres 2,423; lat. 10° 10′; long. 77° 54′; from Dindigul S.S.W. 15 miles; from Kodaykarnal E.S.E. 24 miles; from Madras S.W. 258 miles; from Madura N.W. 24 miles; from Rameshwaram W.N.W. 112 miles; from Ramnaud N.W. 84 miles. One of the twenty-four polliems [q.v.] of the former Dindigul district, resumed in 1773.——*Nilam* (ನೆಲ - nela, Can.; నేల - néla, Tel.; നിലം - nilam, Mal. நிலம் - nilam, Tam.). From (nil, tam. to stand).—"*a*" Ground, land. For the five kinds see Desham.—"*b*" Plant first term, meaning of lowly habit, often joining two genera. Ex., where transl. is of second term:—Andrographis paniculata (nélabévalagida), (nélabévu), and (nélavému), melia azadirachta; Arachis hypogæa (nélagadlé), (nélkadale), and (nélashanaga), cicer arietinum; Baliospermum montanum (nélajídi), semecarpus anacardium; Calamus erectus (nélapóka), areca catechu; Cassia species (nélaponna), calophyllum inophyllum; Cleome viscosa (nélaváminta), gynandropsis pentaphylla; Curculigo orchioides (nélatádi), borassus flabelliformis; Enicostema littorale (nélaguli), capparis grandis, (nélagurugudu), casteria tomentosa; Geniospermum prostratum (nilatulasi), ocimum sanctum; Ipomæa digitata (nélakumbala), cucurbita maxima; Jatropha glandulifera (néiaámudapuchettu), ricinus communis; Justicia gendarussa (nélavávili), vitex trifolia; Justicia procumbens (nélabévinagida), melia azadirachta; Kœmpferia rotunda (nelasampige), michelia champaca; Lippia nodiflora (nélapippali), piper longum; Naregamia alata (nelanáranga), citrus; Polianthes tuberosa (nélasampenga), michelia champaca; Premna herbacea (nélanérédu), eugenia jambolana; Sida cordifolia (nilattutti), abutilon indicum; Sida humilis (nélabenda), hibiscus esculentus, (nélatutti), abutilon indicum; Swertia chirata (nélvému), melia azadirachta; Vernonia anthelmintica (nélavávili), vitex trifolia. See gloss. paragraphs.——*Nila maunyam* (நிலமானியம் - nilamániyam, Tam.). From (nilam, tam. land + mánya, san. privilege). Emolument given in land, not cash [inam].——*Nilanashtam* (நிலநட்டம் - nilanattam, Tam.). From (nilam, tam. land + nashta, san. loss). Loss on land by its being left uncultivated or thrown up. In the communal village system the loss had to be made good by contributions from the remaining ryots [q.v.]——*Nilapanay* (நிலப்பனை - nilappanai, Tam.). From palm like leaf. Same as Black moosly.——*Nilaveeram* (நிலவீரம் - nilavíram, Tam.). From (nilam, tam. land + víra, san. strength). Medicinal earth; also soda earth [pooneer].——*Niloovoo* (నిలువు - niluvu, Tel.). From (nilutsu, tel. to stand). The height of a man standing. Fathom. Linear measure. 4 mooras = 1 niloovoo; 2,000 niloovoos = 1 pargoo [alavay, 1b.]. Approximate actual value, 1 niloovoo = 6 feet. Same as San. vyaumam, dandum, Hind. baum, Can. bauroo, Tam. maur, bauham. See vol. I, 609; II, 505. Compare Poorsham.——*Nirttal* (നിറുത്തൽ - niruttal, Mal.). Cessation. Land abandoned on account of becoming unfit for cultivation.

NIMAT (نعمت - nimat, *Ar.*). From (nama, ar. to bestow in abundance) [neim]. Grace. Prefixed to an alam forms a lacab; as Nimat ally, grace of ally [isni].

NIOTA (കരിന്നൊട്ട - karinnotta, *Mal.*). Samadarah.

NIR (निर् - nir, *San.*). Prefixed to verbs and verbal derivatives expresses out, forth, out of, away from; before substantives, away from; also forms negative adjectives with other nouns.——*Negundo* (निर्गुण्डी - nirgundí, San.; निगंडु - nigundu, Conc.). From (nir, san. out + gam, san. to go); from shedding juice. Specific title. Same as Notchy. White negundo is the same as Coral jasmine.——*Neirritan* (नैरृत - nairrita, San.; நிருதி - niruthi, Tam.). From (nirriti, san. the deity). The regent of the south-west quarter [ashtadic paulacan].——*Niracsham* (निरक्ष - niraksha, San.). From (nir, san. negative prefix + aksha, san. latitude). The terrestrial equator [naudy mundalam]. Niracsha desham are the equatorial parts of the earth [bhoomy]. Niracsha pooram are the four cities supposed to lie under the equator, 90° apart [lunka].——*Nirayanam* (निरयण - nirayana, San.). From (nir, san. negative prefix + ayana, san. motion); in astronomy [jyotisham], without precession [ayanam, craunty pautagaty].——*Nirgrantan* (निर्ग्रन्थ - nirgrant'ha, San.). From (above + grant'ha, san. tie); free from ties. Mendicant [jeina].——*Nirmalan* (निर्मल - nirmala, San.). From (above + mala, san. dirt), free from dirt; pure. Shiva [q.v.].——*Nirooctam* (निरुक्त - nirukta, San.). From (above + vach, san. to speak). The fourth Vedaungam [q.v.]. Its object is etymological explanation of difficult Vedic words.——*Nirrity* (निर्ऋति - nirriti, San.; நிருதி - niruthi, Tam.). From (nirri, san. to die). Means destruction. God of death. Regent of the asterism [nacshatram] Moolam [q.v.]. Regent of the south-west [ashtadic paulacan]. See vol. I (78).——*Nirvamshyam* (निर्वंश्य - nirvamshya, San.). From (nir, san. negative prefix + vamsha, san. spine). Invertebrate. Animals [jantoo] that have no back-bone or vertebral column, and which have a body consisting of a single cavity enclosing all their vital organs. This sub-kingdom [oopaganam] includes the lower forms of animal life. Such as in ascending scale. Sponges [mooabaudal], Corals [moongah], Starfishes [taurah matsyam], Worms [keerah, poochy], Centipedes [kankhajoor], Spiders [makree], Crustaceans [kavachiny], Insects [poochy], Molluscs [chippy]. For vertebrate see Vamshyam.——*Nirvaunam* (निर्वाण - nirvána, San.). From (nirvá, san. to be liberated). Term used by Booddhists [booddha] for final emancipation from matter and reunion with the deity [samsauram].

NIRAY (நிறை - nirai, *Tam.*). From (niru, tam. to weigh). Weight. That is to say the natural property of matter, proportioned to its bulk and the density of its parts, determined by being balanced in a scale against some known or acknowledged weights placed in the opposite scale. A standard for length [alavay] being determined, a standard for weight is thence deduced; as a vessel of any certain dimensions filled with distilled water, or other homogeneous liquid, weighs the same in the same latitude.——**(1)** For the native standards of weight see vol. 616, and II, 505. The fifth book of the Malayalam kanak sauram treats of the weights of gems [ratnam], gold [pon], pearls [moty], &c., for ascertaining which it gives the following formula:—1 nel = 1 veesha tookkam, 4 nels = 1 coonny or retty, 2 coonnies or retties = 1 munjaudy, 2 munjaudies = 1 pana tookkam, 10 pana tookkams = 1 calanjy. All of these, except the punnum [q.v.], are the names of well-known vegetable products, the first being the staple cereal [dhaunyam] of the province, like grain in english, the other three are the seeds of common trees or shrubs. At the present day the employment of seeds for the purposes of weighing is confined to village goldsmiths [tattaun] and petty jewellers. The larger merchants dealing in precious stones [ratnam] employ standard artificial weights, neatly made of brass [pittalay], like the European apothecary and troy weights, following the testaceous assumed standards. They are called emerald weights, but are used for all kinds of gems except the diamond [vajram]. The native heavy weights are shown at vol. I, 617.——**(2)** The following is an attempt to reduce to an average table and a standard value the bazaar weights of the Presidency, taking them under five divisions according to nationality of the populations using, and adding Sanscrit:—"*a*" Average table of bazaar weights in Tamul districts:—9 panatookkams or fanam weights = 1 varauhaniday or pagoda weight, 10 varauhanidays = 1 pollum, 40 pollums = 1 viss, 8 viss = 1 maund, 20 maunds = 1 candy. Extras:—1¼ viss = 1 took, 2 tooks = 1 yeday; 100 pollums = 1 toolaum, 12 toolaums = 1 pothy or bullock-load. Approximate actual value:—1 pollum = 540 grs. 1 maund = 25 lbs. avoir.—"*b*" Average table of bazaar weights in Teloogoo districts:—10 varahahyettoos or pagodas weight = 1 pollum, 40 pollums = 1 viss, 8 viss = 1 maund, 20 maunds = 1 bauroo. Extras:—10 pollums = 1 yebalam; 2 viss = 1 dhaday = 1 yettoo; 8 maunds = 1 nagoo; 15 maunds = 1 cuntum or bullock-load. Approximate actual value:—1 pollum = 540 grs.—"*c*" Average table of Canarese bazaar weights:—24 rupees = 1 cutcha seer, 1¾ cutcha seers = 1 rattel, 6 rattels = 1 dhaday, 4 dhadays = 1 maund, 20 maunds = 1 bauroo. Approximate actual value:—1 rattel = 1 lb.—"*d*" Average table of bazaar weights of Malabar:—10 rupee weights = 1 pollum, 100 pollums = 1 toolaum, 20 toolaums = 1 bhauram or cart-load. Extras:—4 pollums = 1 rattel. Approximate actual value:—1 rattel = 1 lb.—"*e*" Average table of Mahomedan bazaar weights:—3 tolahs = 1 pollum, 8 pollums = 1 cutcha seer, 5 cutcha seers = 1 punch seer, 2 punch seers = 1 dhurrah, 4 dhurrahs = 1 maund, 20 maunds = 1 candy. Extras:—5 tolahs = 1 chittack; 3⅛ cutcha seers = 1 pucka seer, 40 pucka seers = 1 Indian maund. Approximate actual value:—1 Indian maund = 82⅔ lbs. avoir.—"*f*" Average table of Sanscrit commercial weights:—16 maushams or black gram seeds = 1 carsham, 4 carshams = 1 palam, 100 palams = 1 toolaum, 20 toolaums = 1 bhauram or cart load, 10 bhaurams = 1 auchitam. Approximate actual value:—1 palam = 1,440 grs.——**(3)** The following is an attempt to reduce to an average table and a standard value the goldsmith's weights of the Presidency, taking them under five divisions according to nationality of the populations using, and adding Sanscrit:—"*a*" Average table of goldsmith's weights in Tamul districts:—2 coondrimanies or abrus seeds = 1 munjaudy or adenanthera seed, 2 munjaudies = 1 pana tookkam or fanam weight, 9 pana tookkams = 1 varauhaniday or pagoda weight. Extras:—12 munjaudies = 1 tunkam; 12 pana tookkams = 1 calanjy; 20 munjaudies = 1 calanjy; 44 munjaudies = 1 rupee weight. Approximate actual value:—1 pagoda weight = 54 grains Troy.—"*b*" Average table of goldsmith's weights in Teloogoo districts:—4 gooriginjas or abrus seeds = 1 chinnam, 9 chinnams = 1 varahahyettoo or pagoda weight, 4 varahah yettoos = 1 dub, 16 dubs = 1 tunkam. Extras:—1 gooriginja = 1 baida, 2 baidas = 1 doogoola, 2 doogoolas = 1 chowlam, 4 chowlas = 1 mauda, 2 maudas = 1 varahahyettoo. Approximate actual value:—1 pagoda weight = 54 grains troy.—"*c*" Average table of Canarese goldsmith's weights:—4 veesam or rice grains = 1 gooriginja or hauga or abrus seed, 2 haugas =

1 manjoty or addá, or adenanthera seed, 2 manjoties = 1 hana or fanam weight, 9 hanas = 1 varaubaniday or pagoda weight. Approximate actual value:—1 pagoda weight = 54 grains troy.—"d" Average table of goldsmith's weights of Malabar:—2 coonny cooroo or abrus seeds = 1 munjaudy or adenanthera seed, 2 munjaudies = pana tookkam or fanam weight, 30½ pana tookkams = 1 rupee weight. Approximate actual value:—1 rupee weight = 180 grains troy.—"e" Average table of Mahomedan goldsmith's weights:—6 zarrahs or mustard seeds = 1 jow or barley corn, 2 jows = 1 dhaun or rice in husk, 4 dhauns = 1 retty or goomchy or abrus seed, 8 goomchies = 1 mausha seed or black gram, 4 maushas = 1 miscal, 3 miscals = 1 tolah. Approximate actual value:—1 tolah = 180 grains troy.—"f" Average table of Sanscrit goldsmith's weights:—6 sarshapams or mustard seeds = 1 yavam or barley corn, 3 yavams = 1 goonjam seed or abrus seed, 6 goonjams = 1 aunah, 2 aunahs = 1 mausham or black gram seed, 8 maushams = 1 tolah, 8 tolahs = 1 palam, 8 palams = 1 sharauvam. Extras:—24 racticams or retties or abrus seeds = 1 tunkam, 16 maushams = 1 carsham, 4 carshams = 1 palam.—(4) The following is an attempt to reduce to an average table and a standard value the old testaceous weights of the Presidency:—3 likhyams or poppy seeds = 1 rajasarshapam or black mustard, 3 rajasarshapams = 1 gowrasarshapam or white mustard, 6 gowrasarshapams = 1 yavam or barley corn, 3 yavams = 1 retty or krishnalah or coondrimany or abrus seed, 2 retties = 1 maushacam or munjaudy, 20 munjaudies = 1 calanjy or bonduc seed. Extras:—5 retties = 1 mausham of gold; 4 veesam or rice grain = 1 coondrimany; 6 zarrahs or mustard = 1 jow or barley, 2 jows = 1 dhaun or rice in husk, 4 dhauns = 1 goomchy or abrus seed, 8 goomchies = 1 maush or phaseolus grain. Approximate actual value:—1 coondrimany = 1·5 grains, 1 goomchy = 1·875 grains, 1 retty = 1·75 grains.—(5) The beads of this glossary can be consulted for the different terms for weights.

NISAUR (نثار - nisár, *Ar.*). From (nasara, ar. to scatter). Offering. Prefixed to an alam forms a lacab; as Nisaur ally, offering of ally. Mostly Shiah name [ism]. Cf. Nuzzer.

NISBAT (نسبت - nisbat, *Hind.*). From (nasabá, ar. to refer). Relationship [ism].

NISHASTAH (श्यानद्रव्य - shyánadravya, *San.*; نشسته - nishastah, *Hind.*; ಜಿಗಟು - jigatu, *Can.*; అటకలి - atakali, *Tel.*; പശ - pasha, *Mal.*; பசை - pasai, *Tam.*). San. from (shyána, san. adhesive + dravya, san. substance). Starch. Amylum of chemists. Starch may be divided into starch used for food and starch used for industrial purposes. The best kind for the latter purpose is white, soft, friable, and easily reduced to powder; insoluble in cold water, alcohol, and in ether, but readily affording a gelatinous solution in warm water [gum, vajram]. The following are two key-lists in the briefest possible terms of the principal starch products of s. india; further information must be traced in the glossary paragraphs through the small type cross-references at end of this volume; see also vricsham, 7, for the method of expressing the products, &c., of the plants in the dravidian languages.—"a" Arenga saccharifera, sago palm, heart of stem; Caryota urens, bastard sago palm, pith of trunk; Corypha umbraculifera, talipot, pith of trunk; Curcuma angustifolia, malabar arrowroot, root; Curcuma leucorrhiza, red malabar arrowroot, root; Cycas circinalis, indian sago palm, nut; Cyperus rotundus, common sedge, tuber; Eulophia, sp., salep, tuber; Gracilaria lichenoides, ceylon moss; Ipomæa batatas, sweet potato, tuber; Manihot utilissima, tapioca, tuber; Musa paradisiaca, plantain, fruit; Nymphæa lotus, red indian water-lily, underground stem and root; Phœnix farinifera, small date, pith of stem; Phœnix sylvestris, wild date, pith of stem; Saccharum munja, moonj, pith of culm; Tacca pinnatifida, otaheite salep, root; Trapa bispinosa, water caltrops, kernel; Triticum vulgare, wheat, grain.—"b" Arrowroot, curcuma; Caltrops, trapa; Ceylon moss, gracilaria; Date, phœnix; Moonj, saccharum; Plantain, musa; Potato, ipomæa; Sago palm, arenga, caryota, cycas; Salep, eulophia, tacca; Sedge, cyperus; Talipot, corypha; Tapioca, manihot; Water-lily, nymphæa; Wheat, triticum.

NISSA (نساء - nisá, *Hind.*). From arabic. A female suffix usually found with the names of Syeds [q.v.], but it has now become the termination of the generality of female names of respectable classes.

NITTA (نتا - nitta, *Hind.*; ಶಿವಲಿಂಗಮರ - sivalingamara, *Can.*; సాంబ్రాణిమాను - sámbránimánu, *Tel.*; சாம்பிராணி மரம் - shámbiránimaram, *Tam.*). Title from african. Can. from (shiva, san. god + linga, san. phallic emblem + mara, can. tree). Tel. from (sámbráni, tel. frankincense + mánu, tel. tree). Tam. from (shámbiráni, tam. frankincense + maram, tam. tree). Title otherwise Meenso tree. Botanically Parkia biglandulosa, W. et A., leguminosæ [vricsham, 48]. Alias Mimosa pedunculata. Rachis of leaf downy, 1 foot or more long; pinnæ 40–60, 3–4 inches long; leaflets one-nerved, rigid, ¼ inch by $\frac{1}{24}$ inch; peduncle under a foot long; calyx ⅓ inch; tube glabrous; teeth pilose; immature pod downy, narrowed gradually into a long stalk. Large tree; white bark, feathery foliage; flowers in balls, pendulous from a long stalk; flower buds resemble balls of red velvet; came from africa. The legumes are filled with a farinaceous pulp; this is made into sweetments; good avenue [shaulay] tree, requires care and regular watering; wood hard, surrounded by an astringent bark. Another species is roxburghii.

NIVAYAT (نائطی - náití, *Pers.*). From (náit, ar. name of clan in arabia). A sect of Mahomedans. Most of them are Sheikhs [q.v.]. Early emigrants from Arabia which they left on being persecuted by a local governor. Settled in Concan [q.v.], and thence spread. Divided into several clans. Very enterprizing.

NIYAUZ (نياز - niyáz, *Pers.*). Humility. Offering. Cf. Nuzzer. Prefixed to an alam forms a lacab; as Niyauz hoossain, the offering of hoossain. Mostly taken by Shiahs [ism].

NIZAM (نظام - nizám, *Ar.*). From (nazama, ar. to arrange) [nauzim]. Regulator. Part of lacab; as Nizam ood deen, regulator of religion [ism].——*Nizam ally asaf jah i sauny* (نظام على آصف جاه ثانى - nizámaliásafjáhisáni, Hind.). Alam + khitaub. One of the best known Nizams of Hyderabad, 1761 to 1800; the first to become English feudatory and to maintain what is known as the Hyderabad subsidiary force, for which he ceded the territories acquired after the Mysore conquests in 1792 and 1799. See vol. I (180), 9; II, 253.——*Nizam ool moolk* (نظام الملك - nizámulmulk, Hind.). From (above + mulk, ar. kingdom). Title conferred by Emperor Farrookh siyar, on the first ruler of Hyderabad; afterwards assumed by his successors when the kingdom became independent of the Moghul dynasty. See vol. I (145), (150), 9; II, 252.——*Nizampatam* (నిజాముపట్టణము - nijámupattanamu, Tel.). From (nizám, ar. nizám + pattana, san. town). Tel. also (peddapalli), meaning great + village; changed by english to Pettipoly. Native name Arjamputnam. Town, Port, Salt factory, Sea custom assistant superintendent's head-quarters, Kistna dist., Repully tal.; pop. 4,598; acres 11,576; lat. 15° 54′; long. 80° 42′; from Eepoorpollem E. 17 miles; from Madras N. 193 miles; from Masulipatam W.S.W. 36 miles; from Repully S.W. 14 miles. In bay to west of Kistna delta. Considerable coasting trade in small country craft. Mentioned by Ferishta. In the time of Rama royel, when the Mahomedan confederation against him had ended in his defeat and death, Ibrahim padshah gave to Pooligaddapaupa narsimhan and to his three sons, Mullappan, Nundy, and Veeran the districts of Oodayagherry, Nizampatam and Sarwapully. The subordinates of the descendants of Mullappan and Veeran rebelled and the three districts were subsequently united under the descendants of Nundy rajah. English commenced to trade here for the first time on the Eastern coast, 1611. In 1679 the name was changed to Nizampatam. Factory established 1621; dissolved, 1653; resettled, 1697; ceded to the French by the Nizam as part of the Northern circars [q.v.], 1753; part of the Nizampatam circar bestowed on the English by Nizam salaubut jung, 1759; grant confirmed by the Moghul's firmaun [q.v.], 1765; plundered by Hyder's cavalry during the second Mysore war 1780 to 1784. Now the site of an extensive salt manufactory. The Assistant superintendent of Sea customs takes charge of the extensive swamps covered with mangrove [q.v.] which provide Masulipatam with firewood. Nizampatam beacon trig. station in lat. 15° 52′ 49·85″; long. 80° 42′ 22·61″; from Nizampatam S. 2 miles; from Repully S. 16 miles; on the seashore.——*Nizam shahy* (نظام شاهى - nizámsháhí, Hind.). The name of the branch of the Bahmany [q.v.] dynasty [raj] which, on the dismemberment of the latter in 1489 A.D., established itself at Ahmednugger in the Deccan [q.v.]. The founder was Malik ahmed nizam ool moolk bahry, meaning in charge of falcons, from whom it is sometimes called the Bheiry dynasty. The dynasty lasted till 1637, when its territories were divided between the Moghuls and Beejapore. See vol. I (149); II, 252.——*Nizaumat* (نظامت - nizámat, Hind.). Administration of police and criminal law [adawlut].——*Nizaumat adawlut* (نظامت عدالت - nizámatadálat, Hind.). The court of criminal justice. Under the Mahomedan government, the highest criminal court was so called, while the district criminal court was called the Fowjdarry adawlut [q.v.].

NIZHAL (നിഴൽ - nizhal, *Mal.*). Shadow, shade [chauyay].——*Nizhalcoot* (നിഴൽക്കൂട്ടം - nizhalkkúttam, Mal.). From (above + kúttam, mal. assembly). Meeting of corporate bodies in temples [coil, pagoda], and graumams [q.v.] under a tree [coot].

NO (நோ - nó, *Tam.*). To afflict.——*Nómboo* (நோன்பு - nónbu, Tam.). From (nól, tam. to do penance). Penance [tapas], fasting [vratam].——*Notchy* (நொச்சி - noççi, Tam.). See sep. title.

NODY (நொடி - nodi, *Tam.*). A snap; time of a snap of the finger. The following is the scale:—60 nodies or finger-snaps = 1 vinaudy or indian minute [caulam, 1]. Approximate actual value, 1 nody or indian second = ·4 english seconds. Same as san. param [caulam, 4, 5], caushta calay [caulam, 6], vipalam [caulam, 6].

NOKE (നോക്കു - nókku, *Mal.*). To see.——*Nokichartt* (നോക്കിച്ചാർത്ത - nókkiççártta, Mal.). From (nókku, mal. to see + chárttu, mal. assessment). Statement of survey from inspection of the quantity of seed required for sowing a field [viraippaud].——*Notagar* (నోటగాడు - nótagádu, Tel.; நோட்டக்காரன் -

nóttakkáran, Tam.). Tel. from (nóta, tel. inspection + kádu, tel. person). Tam. from (nóttam, tam. inspection + káran, tam. doer). The village shroff [q.v.] who examines the coins [naunyam] handed to him by the tandalcauran [q.v.], and accounts for the same to the nauttaunmeicauran [nautamcar]. He acts under the orders of the latter, and accompanies remittances [irsaul] to the talook [q.v.] cutcherry [q.v.]. In Malabar, a money-changer [balootah].——*Nottam* (ನೋಟ - nóta, Can.; നോട്ടം - nóttam, Mal.; நோட்டம் - nóttam, Tam.). From (nókku, tam. to see). Inspection, especially of coin [inam, naunyam].——*Nottan* (நோட்டன் - nóttan, Tam.). Same as Notagar.

NOLLA (నొల్ల - nolla, *Tel.*). From (nollu, tel. to level land). Otherwise Nollamaun. Leveller. Plank of wood slightly hollowed, with handle like a plough [calappay] attached, drawn over the ground by bullocks [maud, paramboo].

NONDY (நொண்டி - nondi, *Tam.*). Means a lame person. A comic poem in which a rogue is represented as losing his foot in attempting to steal a horse [ghorah].

NOOGA (නුග - nuga, *Singh.*). Botanically Ficus [atty] laccifera, roxb., moraceæ [vricsham, 121]. Arboreous; leaves long-petioled, from cordate to oval, obtuse, pointed, shining, three-nerved; fruit-receptacles axillary, sessile, oval, smooth, size of a gooseberry, appearing in the hot season and ripening in the rains; malabar, &c.

NOOH (نوح - núh, *Ar.*). Noah. Used to form sait [q.v.] names; as Nooh sait [ism].

NOOJOOM (نجوم - nujúm, *Hind.*). Plural of (najm), meaning star. Also (ilminujúm) or science of stars. Astrology [heiyat, ilm, jyotisham]. Noojoomy is an astrologer [joshy]. The following are some of the commonest terms.——*Arz* (عرض - arz, Hind.). From (araza, ar. to become broad). Latitude [acsham, vicshaipam].——*Aseer* (اثير - asír, Hind.). From (asara, ar. to affect); from its affecting all other spheres. Also (arsh). The ninth or highest sphere.——*Astrolabe* (اصطرلاب - usturláb, Hind.). Instrument for measuring the altitude [avanataumsham, irtifah] of the sun [sooryan] and stars [nacshatram].——*Azimuth* (السمت - assamt, Hind.). From (al, ar. the + samt, ar. the region towards which aim is directed). See Agracoty [zenith].——*Badr* (بدر - badr, Hind.). From (badara, ar. to become full). Moon [chundran] in her fourteenth night [hilaul].——*Bood i shams* (بعد شمس - budishams, Hind.). From (bud, ar. distance + shams, ar. sun). Apogee.——*Boorj* (برج - burj, Hind.). From (baraja, ar. to build a tower). Constellation [nacshatram]; sign [raushy] of the zodiac [raushy chuckram].——*Coorb i doonyah* (قرب دنيا - kurbidunyá, Hind.). From (kurb, ar. near + dunyá, ar. earth). Perigee.——*Coorb i shams* (قرب شمس - kurbishams, Hind.). From (kurb, ar. near + shams, ar. sun). Perihelion [chalotcham, sheeghrotcham].——*Coorra* (كرة - kurrah, Hind.). Globe [golam].——*Coorra i arz* (كرة ارض - kurrahiarz, Hind.). From (above + arz, ar. earth). Terrestrial globe [bhoogolam].——*Coorra i falak* (كرة فلك - kurrahifalak, Hind.). From (above + falak, ar. firmament). Celestial globe [bhagolam, khagolam].——*Coors* (قرص - kurs, Hind.). Means round. Sun's disc.——*Cowkab i mootahayira* (كوكب متحيرة - kaukabimutahayirah, Ar.). Erratic star which at one time appears to retrograde and at another time to pursue a direct and forward course. Such are the planets [graham, najm]:—Mars [coojan, mirreek, mungalan], Jupiter [brihaspaty, mooshtary], Mercury [boodhan, ootaurid], Venus [shoocran, zohra], Saturn [shany, zoohal].——*Dayirah* (دائرة - dáirah, Hind.). Means circle. Orbit [cacsham].——*Doomdaur sitaura* (دم دار ستارة - dumdársitárah, Hind.). From (dum, pers. tail + dár, pers. having + sitárah, pers. star). Also (jhárútárah), meaning broom + star. Comet [dhoomkait, kait, oolcay].——*Dowr* (دور - daur, Hind.). Cycle. Dowr i cumr is lunar cycle, at the commencement of which Adam was created.——*Falak* (فلك - falaka, Hind.). From (falaka, ar. to become round). Celestial sphere; seven in number each containing a planet.——*Halo* (هالة - hálah, Hind.). Luminous circle [paridhy].——*Hazeez* (حضيض - hazíz, Hind.). From arabic, low. The lower apsis [ootcham] of a planet [owj].——*Hilaul* (هلال - hilál, Hind.). From (halla, ar. to agree). *i.e.*, from month to month. New moon [amavausyay, arcaindoo, sangamam, badr].——*Ijtimah i cumr* (اجتماع قمر - ijtimáikamar, Hind.). Moon [chundran] in conjunction [moocaubilah i cumr].——*Ikhtilauf manzar* (اختلاف منظر - ikhtiláfmanzar, Hind.). From (ikhtiláf, ar. difference + manzar, ar. position of an object). Parallax [acshavalanam, sheeghram].——*Inhirauf* (انحراف - inhiráf, Hind.). From (harufa, ar. to incline). Declination [craunty].——*Inkilaub* (انقلاب - inkiláb, Hind.). From (kalaba, ar. to change). Precession [ayanaumsham, craunty pautagaty, maunam].——*Inkilaub i noocta i itidaul* (انقلاب نقطة اعتدال - inkilábinuktahiitidál, Hind.). Precession of equinoxes [maishauyanam].——*Irtifah* (ارتفاع - irtifá, Hind.). From (rafa, ar. to rise). Altitude [avanataumsham].——*Ittisaul* (اتصال - ittisál, Hind.). From (vasala, ar. to unite). Contact [lagnam].——*Khatt i istiwah* (خط استواء - khattiistiwá, Hind.). From (khatt, ar. line + istiwá, ar. equal). Equator [niracsham].——*Khatt i itidaul* (خط اعتدال - khattiitidál, Hind.). From (khatt, ar. line + itidál, ar. even); from days and nights being equal. Equinoctial line [naudy mundalam].——*Kiraun* (قران - kirán, Hind.). From (karana, ar. to live together). Conjunction [crauntam, sangamam, yogam, yoog].——*Kiraun ool nahsein* (قران النحسين - kiránulnahsain, Hind.). From (kirán, hind. conjunction + nahas, ar. inauspicious). Conjunction of two malignant planets, Jupiter [mooshtary] and Venus [zohrá].——*Kiraun ool sadein* (قران السعدين - kiránulsadain, Hind.). From (kirán, hind. conjunction + saad, ar. auspicious). Conjunction of two beneficent planets [graham, najm], Saturn [shany, zoohal] and Mars [coojan, mirreek, mungalan].——*Mintakat ool boorooj* (منطقة البروج - mintakatulburúj, Hind.). From (mintakah, ar. belt + burúj, ar. signs of zodiac). Zodiac [raushy chuckram].——*Mooaddil ool nahaur* (معدل النهار - muaddilunnahár, Hind.). From (muaddil, ar. equalizer + nahár, ar. days). Celestial equator [naudy mundalam].——*Moocaubilah i cumr* (مقابلة قمر - mukábilahikamar, Hind.). Moon [chundran] in opposition [ijtimahicumr].——*Nadir* (نظير - nazír, Hind.). From (nazara, ar. to see), looking towards or opposite of zenith. Ar. also (simtulkadam), meaning towards the feet. Hind. also (patál). Point of the heavens [bhagolam] directly beneath observer's feet. Opposed to zenith [q.v.]. See sep. title.——*Nisf oon nahaur* (نصف النهار - nisfunnahár, Hind.). From (nisf, ar. half + nahár, ar. days). Meridian [raikhay].——*Noocta i itidaul i khareefy* (نقطة اعتدال خريفي - nuktahiitidálikharífí, Hind.). From (nuktah, ar. point + itidál, ar. even + kharíf, ar. autumn). Autumnal equinox [toolauyanam].——*Noocta i itidaul i rabee* (نقطة اعتدال ربيعي - nuktahiitidálrabíyí, Hind.). Vernal equinox [maishauyanam, rishy].——*Oofook* (افق - ufak, Hind.). Horizon [cshitijam].——*Oorooj* (عروج - urúj, Hind.). From (araja, ar. to ascend). Culmination [oordhwa sancramanam].——*Owj* (اوج - auj, Hind.). Higher apsis [ootcham] of a planet [graham, hazeez].——*Raus* (راس - rás, Hind.). Ascending node [craunty pautam, rahoo, zanab].——*Raus ool hamel* (راس الحمل - rásulhaml, Hind.). From (rás, ar. head + haml, ar. aries). First point of Aries [maisham].——*Russud* (رصد - rasad, Hind.). From (rasuda, ar. to watch). Observatory.——*Samt ool inkilaub* (سمت الانقلاب - samtulinkiláb, Hind.). From (samt, ar. path + inkiláb, ar. changing). Solstitial colure.——*Samt ool itidaul* (سمت الاعتدال - samtulitidál, Hind.). From (samt, ar. path + itidál, ar. equinox). Equinoctial colure [maishauyana mundalam].——*Sawaubit* (ثوابت - sawábit, Hind.). From (sabata, ar. to fix). Fixed star [nacshatram].——*Seiyaurah* (سيارة - saiyárah, Hind.). From (sair, ar. to wander). Planet [graham].——*Shafak* (شفق - shafak, Hind.). Twilight [sundhyay].——*Shihaub* (شهاب - shiháb, Hind.). From (shahaba, ar. to gleam). Meteor [kait, oolcay].——*Tareek ool shums* (طريق الشمس - taríkulshams, Hind.). From (tarík, ar. way + shams, ar. sun). Also (samtulshams), meaning path of the sun. Ecliptic [craunty mundalam].——*Tool* (طول - túl, Hind.). From (tála, ar. to elongate). Longitude [deshauntaram, sauyanam].——*Zanab* (ذنب - zanab, Hind.). From (zanaba, ar. to follow closely). Descending node [craunty pautam, kait, raus].——*Zaut ool halk* (ذات الحلق - zátulhalk, Hind.). From (zát, ar. possessed of + halk, ar. circle). Armillary sphere [golayantram].——*Zenith* (سمت الراس - samturrás, Hind.). From (samt, ar. direction + rás, ar. head). The point of the heavens [bhagolam] directly or vertically over head [oordhwam, ootcham]. Opposed to Nadir [q.v.].

NOOL (तन्तु - tantu, *San.*; تاگا - tágá, *Hind.*; நூல் - núl, *Tam.*). Spun thread, especially cotton [q.v.]. As soon as cotton berries ripen and open, the cotton is gathered and dried, and put through the seeding machine [rautnam]. The cotton free of seed is then given to the cotton cleaner [doodeycoolam], who bows it clean of husk and other dirt, the result being that the cotton becomes clean and soft. It is then formed into flocks [cottay], and thread is spun from these flocks by means of either the spindle [cathir] or the spinning wheel [rautnam]. These two are the well known articles. In either case as soon as the front of the spindle is covered by yarn sufficiently twisted, the yarn is wound back on to the body of the spindle by guiding its direction. The flocks of cotton are generally held in the left hand. Cotton is spun into thread generally in the hot season, being damp in the cold season. The spinning is done by the women inside their houses [nesavoo]. Nool also means any literary composition [grantam].——*Nolatauly* (നൂലിത്താലി - núlittáli, Mal.; කරවැල කැබෙල්ල - karavalakabella, Singh.; நொலைதாளி - nolaithåli, Tam.). Title from tamul. Mal. from (núl, mal. thread + táli, mal. creeper, convolvulus); bark used for rope. Tam. from malayalam. Title otherwise Chinese laurel. Botanically Antidesma [amla shaucam] bunias, müller, euphorbiaceæ [vricsham, 118]. Alias Antidesma alexiteriæ; Stilago bunias. Middle-sized tree; leaves alternate, entire, lanceolate-oblong; spikes axillary and terminal; male flowers triandrous, with an abortive column in the centre; flowers green; fruit red. Whole plant a remedy against bites of snakes; leaves are acid and diaphoretic, and when young are boiled with pot-herbs for syphilitic affections. The fruit is eatable, sub-acid. Bark used for making ropes [naur]. The timber is greatly affected by immersion in water, becoming heavy and black as iron [auhan].

NOONAH (நுணா - nuná, *Tam.*). Same as Dyeing mulberry.

NOONGH (நுங்கு - nungu, *Tam.*). Means to swallow. The pulpy kernel of the young palmyra [q.v.] fruit.

NOOR (نور - núr, *Hind.*). From (nára, ar. to shine). Light. Attribute of god [allah]. Title of prophet. Common alam. Also part of lacab; as Noor ahmed, light of the prophet; Noor bee, alam + female alaumat; Noor ood deen, light of the faith [ism]. The following were Jehaungeer's gold coins:—Noorauny, means full of light, weight ½ tolah; Noor i jehauny, means light of the world, weight 1 tolah; Noor i mihr, means light of love, weight 5 tolahs; Noor i carm, means light of grace, weight 10 tolahs; Noor i dowlat, means light of the empire, weight 20 tolahs; Noor i sultauny, means sultan's light, weight 50 tolahs; Noor i shahy, means royal light, weight 100 tolahs.

NOOSRAT (نصرت - nusrat, *Ar.*). From (nasara, ar. to succour) [nausir]. Victory. Prefixed to an alam forms a lacab; as Noosrat ally, victory of ally. Noosrat jung, victorious in war [ism].

NOOTLA (నూతల - nútala, *Tel.*). From (núyi, tel. well). Plural locative form. Wells. Suffix in place names.

NOOZVEED (నూజివీడు - nújivídu, *Tel.* núzvíd *). From (núvu, tel. oil-seed plant, sesamum indicum, dec. + vídu, tel. town).—(1) Zemindarry, Kistna district. Area 694 square miles. Population 153,628. Language Teloogoo. N.E. inland part of district. Boundaries; north Nizam's dominions and Ellore talook of Godavery district, east Ellore talook of Godavery district and Goodivauda talook, south Bezwada talook, west Bezwada talook and Vissanapett division. Plain interspersed by hills. Soil regar [q.v.]. Irrigation by anicut [q.v.] canals. See vol. I, 59, foot-note. Places of archæological interest:—Augiripully, Auvatapulley, Ayilore, Condanainavaram, Gollanapulley, Medore, Moostabauda, Mullavilly, Noozveed, Ooyoor, Pedda maddauly, Poorshottapatam, Rauvoolapaud, Shoorsainacote, Sooravaram, Yeedara, Yeedore. Trig. station:—Doodgut. The leading places, &c., in the zemindarry are the following.—*Augiripully* (ఆగిరిపల్లి - ágiripalle, Tel.). From (ávu, tel. cow + giri, san. hill + palle, tel. village). Village, Hill, Place of pilgrimage; pop. 3,078; lat. 16° 41′; long. 80° 49′; from Gunnavaram N. 10 miles; from Masulipatam N.W. 41 miles; from Noozveed S. 9 miles. Sacred temple on high rock with stone steps. And a number of shrines along the ascent. Temple below hill. Cave temples close to temple on the hill.—*Boodamair* (బుడమేరు - budaméru, Tel.). See sep. title.—*Capileshwarapooram* (కపిలేశ్వరపురము - kapiléshvarapuramu, Tel.). From (kapila, san. sage so called + íshvara, san. lord + pura, san. town). Zemindarry, Village; pop. 3,042; lat. 16° 20′; long. 80° 54′; from Gunnavaram S.S.E. 15 miles; from Masulipatam W.N.W. 20 miles; from Noozveed S. 31 miles. Head-quarters of a zemindar of the Noozveed family. Peshcush Rs. 15,838.—*Doodgut* (దుద్దుగట్టు - duddugagattu, Tel.). From (duddekku, tel. to surpass + gattu, tel. hill); high hill. Trig. station; lat. 16° 46′ 10·34″; long. 80° 59′ 01·90″; height 488 feet; from Cautrenipaud S. 2 miles; from Noozveed E. 6 miles.—*Gollapully* (గొల్లపల్లె - gollapalle, Tel.). See sep. title.—*Gunnavaram* (గన్నవరము - gannavaramu, Tel.). See sep. title.—*Medore* (మేడూరు - médúru, Tel.). From (médi, tel. fig tree, ficus glomerata, miq. + úru, tel. village). Zemindarry, Village; pop. 1,885; acres 3,250; lat. 16° 18′; long. 80° 53′; from Gunnavaram S. 18 miles; from Masulipatam W.N.W. 19 miles; from Noozveed S. 35 miles. Zemindar of the pergunnah [q.v.] of that name has a tannah [q.v.] here. Inscription [shausanam] records a battle fought by Krishna deva royel of Vijianugger. Peshcush Rs. 16,292.—*Noozveed* (నూజివీడు - nújivídu, Tel.). See below.—*Ooyoor* (ఉయ్యూరు - uyyúru, Tel.). Zemindarry, Village; pop. 4,044; lat. 16° 22′; long. 80° 53′; from Gunnavaram S. 12 miles; from Masulipatam W.N.W. 22 miles; from Noozveed S. 29 miles. Someshwaran temple with inscriptions. Peshcush Rs. 15,656.—*Tailaprole* (తేలప్రోలు - télaprólu, Tel.). From (télu, tel. scorpion + prólu, tel. town). Zemindarry, Village; pop. 2,253; lat. of village 16° 35′; long. 80° 55′; from Gunnavaram E.N.E. 6 miles; from Masulipatam N. 32 miles; from Noozveed S. 15 miles. Peshcush Rs. 15,728.—*Vedoorpauvoolore* (వెదురుపావులూరు - vedurupávulúru, Tel.). From (veduru, tel. bamboo, bambusa arundinacea, willd. + pávulúru, tel. village so called). Village; pop. 2,048; lat. 16° 34′; long. 80° 46′; from Gunnavaram W.N.W. 4 miles; from Masulipatam N.W. 37 miles; from Noozveed S.S.W. 17 miles. Good water wells.—*Ventrapragada* (వెంట్రప్రగడ - ventrapragada, Tel.). After a person of that name. Zemindarry, Village; pop. 1,803; lat. of village 16° 27′; long. 80° 57′; from Gunnavaram S.E. 10 miles; from Masulipatam N.W. 23 miles; from Noozveed S. 23 miles. Peshcush Rs. 15,429.—(2) Deputy tahsildarry, Kistna district. Pay Rs. 100.—(3) Town; Kistna dist., Noozveed zemindarry; pop. 7,637; acres 921; lat. 16° 47′; long. 80° 53′; from Bezwada N.E. 26 miles; from Guntoor N.E. 43 miles; from Gunnavaram N.N.E. 17 miles; from Madras N. 258 miles; from Masulipatam N.N.W. 45 miles; from Vinoocondah N.E. 90 miles. On rising ground, surrounded by jungle. Head-quarters of zemindarry. Captured by English twice in 1783, and once in 1788. Large cocoanut [q.v.] and mango [q.v.] topes [q.v.]. Modern fort. Temple of Vencateshwarasawmy built 400 years ago and a mosque [musjid] of the same age.

NORTH ARCOT (ఉత్తరఆర్కాడు - uttaraárkádu, *Tel.*; வடார்க்காடு - vadavárgádu, *Tam.*). Always called by natives Chittore zillah [q.v.]. Revenue district; situated inland, between 12° 20′ and 13° 55′ N. lat., and between 78° 17′ and 80° 09′ E. long.; bounded N. by Cuddapah and Nellore districts, E. by Chingleput district, S. by South arcot and Salem districts, W. by Mysore; square miles 7,620; pop. 2,180,487; lang. Teloogoo and Tamul. Contains rivers Cheyaur, Palaur, Poyney; mountains Eastern ghauts, Jawaudy hills, Nagary hills; sanitarium Pulmanair. The whole area of the district is represented by the following sub-areas:—Arcot talook, Arnee jagheer, Calastry zemindarry, Carvetnugger zemindarry, Chittore talook, Chundragherry talook, Cungoondy zemindarry, Goodiyattam talook, Polore talook, Poonganore zemindarry, Pulmanair talook, Vellore talook, Wallajahpett talook, and Wandiwash talook. For general administrative purposes the district is distributed between the following revenue and magisterial officers, who have their head-quarters at the places shown. The pay set opposite the subordinate officers gives the grade of the corresponding charge:—Collector, Chittore; Sub-collector, Vellore, in charge of Arcot, Goodiyattam and Vellore talooks and Cungoondy zemindarry; Head assistant collector, Ranipett, in charge of Wallajahpett and Chundragherry talooks and Calastry and Carvetnugger zemindarries; General deputy collector, Arnee, in charge of Wandiwash and Polore talooks and Arnee jagheer. Assistant collector or Special deputy collector, Chittore, in charge of Chittore and Pulmanair talooks and Poonganore Zemindarry. Tahsildars; Arcot, Rs. 225; Chittore, Rs. 175, this talook includes the polliems of Naraganty, Bungaur, Toomba, and Goodiputty; Chundragherry, Rs. 150, this talook includes the polliems of Cullore and Poolicherla; Goodiyattam, Rs. 175; Polore, Rs. 150; Pulmanair, Rs. 150; Vellore, Rs. 175; Wallajahpett, Rs. 250, this talook includes the mittah of Argilavaudy; Wandiwash, Rs. 200. Deputy tahsildars; Arconum, Rs. 70, range situated in the east of Wallajahpett talook; Tripatty, Rs. 70, range situated in the east of Chundragherry talook; Vencatagherrycottah, Rs. 70, range situated in the south-west of Pulmanair talook. Sub-magistrates; Arnee, Rs. 70, jurisdiction extending over whole of the Arnee jagheer, square miles 183; Calastry, Rs. 100, jurisdiction extending over one-half of the western portion of Calastry zemindarry, square miles 471; Cungoondy, Rs. 100, jurisdiction extending over whole of the Cungoondy zemindarry, square miles 346; Maderpauk, Rs. 70, jurisdiction extending over one-half of the eastern portion of Calastry zemindarry, square miles 403; Poottore, Rs. 100, jurisdiction extending over one-half of the northern portion of Carvetnugger zemindarry, square miles 510; Poonganore, Rs. 100, jurisdiction extending over whole of the Poonganore zemindarry, square miles 674; Trittany, Rs. 100, jurisdiction extending over one-half of the southern portion of Carvetnugger zemindarry, square miles 433; Vellore town, Rs. 70, range situated in the east of Vellore talook. Similarly judicial officers:—Judge, Chittore. District moonsifs; Arnee, with jurisdiction extending over Arcot, Wandiwash and Polore talooks and Arnee jagheer; Chittore with jurisdiction extending over Chittore and Pulmanair talooks and Poonganore zemindarry; Sholinghur with jurisdiction extending over Wallajahpett talook and Trittany division; Tripatty with jurisdiction extending over Chundragherry talook and Calastry zemindarry, and Poottore division; Vellore with jurisdiction extending over Vellore and Goodiyattam talooks and Cungoondy zemindarry. Similarly Public works officers:—District engineer, Vellore. Sub divisional officers; Assistant engineer, Vellore; Sub-engineer, Ranipett. Contains Registration sub-districts, Amboor, Arconum, Arcot, Arnee, Calastry, Chittore, Cungoondy, Goodiyattam, Maderpauk, Polore, Poonganore, Poottore, Pulmanair, Tripatty, Trittany, Trivettore, Vellore, Wallajahpett, Wandiwash. Contains Forest ranges Chundragherry, Pulmanair, Vellore. Contains Municipalities Goodiyattam, Tripatty, Vellore, Wallajahpett. Contains District board. And Talook boards; Chittore embracing Chittore, Pulmanair and Chundragherry talooks and Poonganore zemindarry; Vellore embracing Vellore, Arcot and Goodiyattam talooks and Cungoondy zemindarry; Ranipett embracing Wallajahpett talook and Calastry and Carvetnugger zemindarries; and Arnee embracing Arnee jagheer and Polore and Wandiwash talooks. Government have recently sanctioned the transfer of Chundragherry talook to Ranipett talook board from 1890-91. The following general references should be made to the preceding volumes:—general geography, I (1) to (29); general ethnology, I (29) to (109); general history, I (110) to (188); physical geography, II, 1; meteorology, II, 3; geology, II, 8; fauna, II, 21; flora, II, 26; mineralogy, II, 29. The following references in the preceding volumes will furnish details special to the district:—latitudes and longitudes, II, 47; particulars about towns, II, 48; comparative population, II, 172; location of revenue officers, II, 378; revenue settlement of the district, II, 406; registrars' and sub-registrars' stations, II, 420; rain-gauge stations, II, 428; police divisions, II, 431; maps published, II, 436; survey topographical lists, II, 443; hospitals and dispensaries, II, 447; head-quarter stations of gazetted officers, II, 461; incidence of taxation, II, 463; weights and measures of the district, II, 506; zemindarries contained, I, 58 and II, 294. Special public works, I, 403. A special gazetteer account of the whole district is given at II, 53. For the detailed topography of the district, reference should be made to the talook notices in the present volume, viz.:—Arcot, Arnee, Calastry, Carvetnugger, Chittore, Chundragherry, Cungoondy, Goodiyattam, Polore, Poonganore, Pulmanair, Vellore, Wallajahpett, Wandiwash.

NOTCHY (निर्गुंडी - nirgundí, *San.*; निर्गुंड - nirgunda, *Mahr.*; निगुंडु - nigundu, *Conc.*; اثلق - aslak, *Ar.*; پنجنگشت - panjangusht, *Pers.*; نرگندی - nirgandí, *Hind.*; شمبالی - shambálí, *Dec.*; ಲಕ್ಕಿ - lakki, *Can.*; ನೆಕ್ಕಿ - nekki, *Too.*; నల్లావావిలి - nallavávili, *Tel.*; ବେଇଗୁଣ - beygúna, *Oor.*; നൊച്ചി - noççi, *Mal.*; සුදුනික - sudunika, *Singh.*; நொச்சி - noççi, *Tam.*). Title from tamul [no]. San. from (nirga, san. to go out); to shed, from juice. Pers. from (panj, pers. five + angusht, pers. finger); five-foliolate leaf. Hind. from sanscrit. Tel. from (nalla, tel. black + vávili, tel. vitex trifolia, linn.). Mal. from tamul. Singh. from (sudu, singh. white + nika, singh. vitex). Tam. from (nosi, tam. to pain); leaves are pungent and stimulating and used in fomentations. San. also (sinduvára), meaning preventing flow; the plant being used to prevent flow of humours and laxity; (indrásurasa), meaning indran + the plant; (shvétasurasa), meaning white + the plant; (indrání), meaning beloved of indran; (surasa), meaning good + juice [common toolsy]. Ar. also (fanjangusht), meaning five + finger; (zúkhamsatulaurák), meaning lord of five leaves; (zúkhamsatulasábi), meaning lord of five fingers. Pers. also (sísbán). Hind. also (sambhálú); (nisinda). Dec. also (shamálú). Can. also (karinekkilu), meaning black + vitex; (bilenekki), meaning white + the plant; (karlekki), black + the plant. Tel. also (tellavávili), meaning white + vitex trifolia, linn.; (vávili). Mal. also (velnoççi), meaning white + the plant. Singh. also (nilnika), meaning black + vitex. Tam. also (vellainoççi), meaning white + the plant, from color of leaf. Title otherwise Five-leaved chaste tree, Nisinda, Quadrangular chaste tree. Botanically Vitex [sindoocam] negundo, linn., verbenaceæ [vricsham, 102]. Specific name from sanscrit. Alias Vitex bicolor, incisa, paniculata. Tree; branchlets, petioles and rachis of the panicle pubescently tomentose; leaves long-petioled, three to five-foliolate, leaflets oblong, attenuate-acuminate, acute at the base and with the middle ones petioled, quite entire or coarsely serrated, puberulous above, canescent below, or afterwards glabrous; panicle terminal, compound, spreading; cymes very shortly peduncled, divaricately-dichotomous, bracteolate, white with velvety tomentum; calyx shortly five-toothed; lower lip of the corolla somewhat downy at the base, flowers smallish, blue; flowering nearly all the year. Root tonic, febrifuge and expectorant; the leaves when heated and applied externally are discutient, and are applied to swellings of joints, &c.; internally they are anodyne, diuretic and emmenagogue; the dried leaves are smoked to relieve headache and catarrh; pillow stuffed with the leaves is placed under the head for relief of headache; mahomedans smoke the dried leaves for headache and catarrh; decoction of leaves used as warm bath for women after delivery; in pharm. non-officinal; the dried fruit acts as vermifuge. Branches are used for wattle-work; ashes used as mordant [cauram]; tree used for hedges. Wood greyish-white, hard.——*Black notchy* (கருநொச்சி - karunoççi, Tam.). Same as Common gendarussa.——*Field notchy* (ಹೊಲನೆಕ್ಕಿ - holanekki, Can.; నెవలేడి - nevalédi, Tel.; കാറിൽ - káril, Mal.). Can. from (hola, can. field + nekki, can. vitex). Mal. from (kár, mal. black + il, mal. spot). Can. also (sengenitkarril); (karril). Tel. also (luki). Title otherwise Cotton-leaved notchy. Botanically Vitex [sindoocam] leucoxylon, linn. f., verbenaceæ [vricsham, 102]. Alias Rothia leucoxylon; Vitex bombacifolia, saligna. Small tree; leaves long-petioled, three to five-foliolate; leaflets elliptic or ovate-oblong, shortly and obtusely acuminated; attenuated into the petiole, entire, sub-coriaceous, shining and glabrous above; cymes axillary, long peduncled, corymbose, many-flowered; lower lip of corolla densely woolly; drupe large, obovate, black when ripe; flowers whitish-yellow; flowering from february to april; small, black fruit containing very soft pulp; bark and root astringent; wood whitish and compact.——*Tall notchy* (నెవలియడుగు - nevaliadugu, Tel.; ମୁରିଆ - muriya, Oor.; மயிலடி - mayiladi, Tam.). Tel. from (nevali, tel. peacock + adugu, tel. foot). Tam. from (mayil, tam. peacock + adi, tam. foot); probably from appearance of leaf. Tel. also (búsi), meaning frightful looking. Title otherwise Peacook's foot notchy. Botanically Vitex [sindoocam] pubescens, vahl., verbenaceæ [vricsham, 102]. Alias Vitex arborea; Wallrothia articulata. Large tree; branchlets four-sided, channelled, and with the petioles and young leaves pubescent or slightly tomentose; leaves long-petioled, three to five-foliolate; leaflets elliptic or ovate-oblong, attenuate-acuminate, rounded at the base, subsessile, coriaceous, penni-nerved, glabrous, shining above, pale and finely puberulous beneath; panicles whitish, powdery tomentose, terminal, compound, ovato-pyramidal, compact; cymes interspersed with foliaceous bracts longer than the calyx; forests in malabar. Drupe globose, size of a pea [calauyam]; bears flowers in hot season. Wood smooth, grey, with an olive-brown tinge, very hard, close-grained; wood becomes chocolate colored on exposure.——*Water notchy* (सुरस - surasa, San.; राननिर्गुंडी - rànanirgundí, Mahr.; काळीनिर्गुंड - kálónigundu, Conc.; اثلق آبی - aslakiábí, Ar.; پنجنگشت آبی - panjangushtiábí, Pers.; سفید سنبهالو - sufédsambhálú, Hind.; اجلی شمبالی - ujlíshambálí, Dec.; لگوندی - lagundí, Malay; ನೀರುಲಕ್ಕಿ - nírulakki, Can.; ಕರಿನೆಕ್ಕಿ - karinekki, Too.; వావిలి - vávili, Tel.; കരുനൊച്ചി - karunoççi, Mal.; මියම්ජිල - míammjila, Singh.; நீர்நொச்சி - nírnoççi, Tam.). Title from habitat. San. from (su, san. good + rasa, san. juice); from usefulness. Mahr. from (rána, mahr. wild + nirgundí, san. vitex negundo, linn.). Ar. from (aslak, ar. vitex negundo, linn. + áb, pers. water). Pers. from (panjangusht, pers. vitex negundo, linn. + áb, pers. water). Hind. from (sufed, hind. white + sambhálú, hind. vitex negundo, linn.). Dec. from (ujlí, hind. white + shambálí, hind. vitex negundo, linn.). Can. from (níru, can. water + lakki, can. vitex negundo, linn.). Too. from (kari, too. black + nekki, too. vitex negundo, linn.). Mal. from (karu, mal. black + noççi, mal. vitex negundo, linn.). Tam. from (nír, tam. water + noççi, tam. vitex negundo, linn.). San. also (nílanirgundí), meaning black vitex negundo, linn.; (jalanirgundí), meaning water notchy; (krishnanirgundí), meaning black notchy; (shéphálíká) is blue-flowered variety [coral jasmine]; (suvahá), meaning well-enduring tree, blue-flowered variety; (nílika), meaning blue variety; (shvétasurasa) is white-flowered variety. Hind. also (páníkísambhálú), meaning water chaste tree; (nísindha); (seduari); (somalu); (sinbálú). Dec. also (páníkíshambálí), meaning water chaste tree. Malay also (samálusanbálú). Can. also (karnuççi), meaning black + the plant. Tel. also (tellavávili), meaning white + the plant; (níruvávili), meaning water + the tree; (chiruvávili), meaning small + the plant; (nílavávili), meaning blue + the plant; (nélavávili), meaning ground + the plant. Mal. also (nírnoççi), meaning water notchy. Tam. also (shirunoççi), meaning small + the plant; (karunoççi), meaning black + the plant; from color of stem and leaf. Greek ἄγνος, Latin castus, derived from use at sacred rites of Ceres by Athenian women. Title otherwise Common chaste tree, Hemp tree, Indian privet, Indian wild pepper, Monk's pepper, Three-leaved chaste tree, Tree of chastity, Vauvily, White-leaved panicled chaste tree. Botanically Vitex [sindoocam] trifolia, linn., verbenaceæ [vricsham, 102]. Alias Vitex integerrima. Shrub, 10 feet; leaves ternate and quinate; leaflets ovate, acute, entire, hoary beneath; panicle with a straight rachis; pedicels dichotomous; flowers terminal, racemose, violet; flowering in april and may; leaves lightly bitter but of aromatic taste and smell. A clear sweet oil of greenish color is extracted from root. Medicinal properties like notchy, but stronger; this generally used in medicine in preference; leaves and young shoots are powerfully discutient; leaves powdered and taken with water are a cure for intermittent fevers; the fruit is said by veidyans [q.v.] to be nervine, cephalic, and emmenagogue, and is prescribed in powder in electuary and decoction [kwautam]; leaves in pharm. non-officinal; useful in baths and fomentations, in treatment of beribery [q.v.] and in the allied and obscure affection called burning of the feet. Fruit sometimes used for pepper [q.v.].

NOW (نو - nau, *Hind.*). From (nava, san. new). New [hosa, poothoo].——*Nowgàum* (నగాము - naugámu, Tel.). From (nau, hind. new + gráma, san. village). Proprietary estate, Village; Ganjam dist.; pop. 754; lat. of village 18° 41′; long. 84° 20′; from Chetterpore S.W. 65 miles; from Chicacole N.E. 36 miles; from the sea W. 11 miles. Sub-division of Temboor. Peshcush Rs. 2,257.——*Nowpada* (నపాడ - naupadá, Tel. naupada*). From (nau, hind. new + pádu, tel. village). Village, Port; Ganjam dist., Chicacole tal., Tekkaly estate; pop. 1,835; lat. 18° 33′; long. 84° 21′; from Bhauvanpaud W. 4 miles; from Chetterpore S.W. 70 miles; from Chicacole N.E. 32 miles; from Madras N.E. 456 miles; from Poondy S.W. 12 miles. On Orissa coast [q.v.]. Chief place of salt manufacture in district. Open roadstead.——*Nowroz* (نوروز - nauroz, Pers.). Persian new year's day, 21st March, when the sun [sooryan] enters Aries [maisham] of the tropical zodiac [maunam, raushy chuckram]; is celebrated by feasts. Mahomedan proper name [ism].——*Nowrungapore* (నవరంగపురము - navarangapuramu, Tel.). See sep. title.

NOWBUT (نوبت - naubat, *Hind.*). From (naub, ar. to take turn); as beaten by turns. A large kettle drum [paray, sangeetam].

NOWCAR (نوکر - naukar, *Hind.*). From persian. A servant, an official.

NOWRUNGAPORE (نورنگاپور - naurangápur, *Hind.*; నవరంగపురము - navarangapuramu, *Tel.*). From (nava, san. nine + ranga, san. vishnu + pura, san. town) [now].——(1) Division, Vizagapatam district; population 116,399; language Ooriya. Boundaries:—E. Calahundy, S. Coraputt and Jeypore divisions, W. Bustar, N. Central provinces. An undulating plain mostly covered with saul [q.v.]. The greater part forms a sub-division of the Jeypore estate, allotted to the support of the family of Cheitanya deo [goodaury]. Places of archæological interest:—

Coorsy, Dodrah, Hoody, Nowrungapore, Oommarcote, Palsagaum, Podagauda, Pooppgaum, Puppadahundy, Royagada. Principal trig. stations :—Bor dougry, Deo pahar, Hattibena, Heerapore, Shirasy. The leading places, &c., in the division are the following.——*Bor dongry* (బొరడొంగిరి - bóradongiri, Tel.). From (bora, mahr. jujube tree, zizyphus jujuba, lam. + dongari, mahr. little hill). Trig. station ; lat. 19° 53′ 47·53″ ; long. 82° 15′ 31·56″ ; height 2,158 feet ; from Nowrungapore N.N.W. 50 miles.——*Deo pahaur* (دیوپہار - deupahár, Hind. ; దేవుపహార - dévupahará, Tel.). From (deu, pers. giant + pahár, hind. mountain). Trig. station ; lat. 19° 40′ 19·40″ ; long. 82° 29′ 08·58″ ; height 2,704 feet ; from Chotchah N.N.E. 1¼ miles ; from Nowrungapore N. 31 miles.——*Hattibena* (హత్తిబెణ - hattibená, Tel.). From (hattí, hind. elephant + bennu, can. back). Trig. station ; lat. 19° 51′ 42·34″ ; long. 82° 03′ 53·14″ ; height 2,013 feet ; from Cotagaum W.S.W. 2 miles ; from Nowrungapore N.N.W. 53 miles.——*Heerapore* (హీరాపురము - hírápuramu, Tel.). From (híra, san. diamond + pura, san. town). Trig. station ; lat. 19° 36′ 14·99″ ; long. 82° 09′ 34·42″ ; height 3,063 feet ; from Heerapore S.S.E. 2½ miles ; from Nowrungapore N.W. 38 miles.——*Jugganautpore* (జగన్నాథపురం - jagannát'hapuram, Tel.). From (jagannát'ha, san. lord of world, a king + pura, san. town) ; from burial place of jagganath rauz. Village ; pop. 926 ; lat. 19° 12′ ; long. 82° 47′ ; from Jeypore N.E. 25 miles ; from Nowrungapore E.S.E. 12 miles ; from Vizagapatam N.N.W. 106 miles. One old temple and one new temple.——*Nowrungapore* (నవరంగపురము - navarangapuramu, Tel.). See below.——*Oommarcote* (ఉమ్మరకోట - ummarakóta, Tel.). From (umr, ar. proper name + kóta, tel. fort). Old fort, Village, Head-quarters of a Revenue ameen ; pop. 526 ; lat. 19° 40′ ; long. 82° 15′ ; from Jeypore N.N.W. 59 miles ; from Nowrungapore N.W. 37 miles ; from Vizagapatam N. 148 miles.——*Puppadahundy* (పప్పడహండి - papadáhandi, Tel.). From (pappada, tel. a cake + handi, tel. pot). Village ; pop. 428 ; lat. 19° 20′ ; long. 82° 34′ ; from Jeypore N. 33 miles ; from Nowrungapore N. 8 miles ; from Vizagapatam N. 123 miles. Two old temples.——*Shirasy* (శిరసి - shirasi, Tel.). From (shira, san. head). Trig. station ; lat. 19° 19′ 39·21″ ; long. 82° 30′ 43·75″ ; height 2,311 feet ; from Nowrungapore N.W. 8 miles ; from Puppadahundy W.S.W. 4 miles.——*Tentoolicoonty* (తెంతులికుంటి - tentulikunti, Tel.). From (tintulí, san. tamarind tree, tamarindus indica, linn. + kunta, tel. pond). Village ; lat. 19° 18′ ; long. 82° 46′ ; from Jeypore N.N.E. 31 miles ; from Nowrungapore E.N.E. 12 miles ; from Vizagapatam N.N.W. 115 miles. Manufacture of match-locks and battle axes. Large weekly market on Monday.——**(2)** Deputy tahsildarry ; Vizagapatam district ; pay Rs. 150.——**(3)** Village, Head-quarters of Deputy tahsildar ; Vizagapatam dist., Jeypore zemindarry, Nowrungapore magisterial division ; pop. 2,976 ; lat. 19° 14′ ; long. 82° 36′ ; from Coraputt N.N.W. 35 miles ; from Jeypore N. 26 miles ; from Madras N.N.E. 440 miles ; from Narsapatam N. 104 miles ; from Parvatipore W.N.W. 63 miles ; from Vizagapatam N.N.W. 112 miles ; from Vizianagram N.W. 92 miles. Old town, but temples are modern.

NOY (நொய் - noy, *Tam.*). Small.——*Noyil* (நொய்யல் - noyyal, Tam. nóyil *). From (noymai, tam. smallness + al, tam. darkness) ; from its small moss-covered dark stream. River ; Coimbatore dist., Coimbatore, Pulladam and Dharaupooram tals. Rises in the Velliyangherry hills in lat. 10° 55′ 45″ ; long. 76° 45′ 40″ immediately W. of Coimbatore town and above Bolamputty valley. It runs through valley and directly across district from W. to E., traversing Coimbatore talook in the south and Pulladam, and forming the N. boundary of Dharaupooram talook and S. boundary of Erode talook. Joins Cauvery at Neycooppam at junction of Erode and Caroor talooks in lat. 11° 4′ N., long. 77° 59′ 30″ E. Length 108 miles. Little more than a jungle stream, being dry for many months together, and then in high and rapid flood for several days. There are twenty-six old anicuts [q.v.]. The denudation of the hills surrounding the Bolamputty valley and the cultivation of the valley itself have tended to diminish the continual supply of water. At present only anicuts in first 30 miles are efficient.

NRITYAM (नृत्य - nritya, *San.*). From (nrit, san. to dance) [nat]. Dance, including all theatrical representation. One of the three parts of books on Indian music [gaunam, vaudyam].

NUKKEE (نکھی - nakkhí, *Hind.*). Means nailed. Gold and silver lace [kinaury] used for bodices [cholee] and for edgings.

NUL (நல் - nal, *Tam.*). Good.——*Nakkeeran* (நற்கீரன் - nargíran, Tam.). From (above + gír, san. speech). One of the literati of the Madura college [q.v.] and author of the Antaudy panayam, a poem in honor of Shiva [q.v.]. Chunk-cutter by caste [jauty].——*Nalvazhy* (நல்வழி - nalvazhi, Tam.). From (above + vazhi, tam. method). A good method. One of Avvay's five aphoristic works taught in schools [avvay].——*Nelacottah* (നല്ലകോട്ട - nallakótta, Mal. nellakóta *). From (nalla, mal. good + kótta, mal. fort). Tract of country, Village ; Neilgherry dist., Wynaud S.E. division ; acres 10,770 ; lat. of village 11° 33′ ; long. 76° 27′ ; from Goodalore N.W. 7 miles ; from Ootacamund W.N.W. 21 miles. In Moonanaud amshom. Fort built during Mysore wars, but now in ruins, resisted repeated attacks of Tippoo sultan. Held by Pychee [q.v.] rebel during early years of century.——*Nulla* (நல்ல - nalla, Tam.). Good.——*Nullamoottoo* (நல்லமுத்து - nallamuttu, Tam.). From (nalla, tam. good + muttu, tam. pearl). Hindoo 2nd or pers. name. Common among non-bramins [peyar].——*Nullannan* (நல்லண்ணன் - nallannan, Tam.). From (nalla, tam. good + aunan, tam. elder brother). Hindoo 2nd or pers. name. Common among non-bramins [peyar].——*Nullasheragan* (நல்லசேவகன் - nallasévagan, Tam.). From (nalla, tam. good + sévaka, san. servant). The good warrior ; Ayenaur [ayen].——*Nullatumby* (நல்லதம்பி - nallattambi, Tam.). From (nalla, tam. good + tambi, tam. younger brother). Hindoo 2nd or pers. name. Common among non-bramins [peyar].——*Nullatunneer* (நல்லதண்ணீர் - nallathannír, Tam.). From (nalla, tam. good + tannír, tam. water). Fresh water. Name of one of the seven oceans [bhoogolashastram, samoodram].——*Nullauthan* (நல்லாதன் - nalláthan, Tam.). From (above + áthan, tam. teacher). Ancient poet [pauvalan]. Made hundred epigrams called Tricatoocam. Each epigram contains a comparison of three things and their result as :—கொல்யானைக்கோடுங் குனைமியியு மெல்லிற் பிறன்கடைநின் றொழுகுவானு—மறந்தெரியா தாடும் பாம்பாட்டுமறிவிலியும்மூவர் நாடுங்காற்றூங்குபவர், —"He who runs against the killing elephant [q.v.], he who "stands outside his neighbour's door in the night time, he who "makes the snake [sarpam] dance ; these three do so at their "peril."——*Nunjah* (நஞ்செய் - nañjey, Tam.). Tam. from (nal, tam. good + shey, tam. cultivation). Soil fit for the cultivation of rice [paddy] and admitting of artificial irrigation. Generally called wet land [poonjah, wet crop]. Nunjah baughayet is cultivation of garden crop on Nunjah land. Nunjah mail poonjah is dry grain raised on Nunjah. Nunjah taram poonjah is land classed as wet, but used as dry. There is a Tamul proverb :—மதகினடி நஞ்செயும் மலையடிப் புஞ்செயும்—"Nunjah at the foot of a sluice [mathagoo] and poonjah at the "foot of a hill are alike ;" both are best.——*Nunjenaud* (நஞ்சநாடு - nañjanádu, Tam.). From (nañjai, tam. wet land + nádu, tam. country). Village, Valley ; Neilgherry dist., Todanaud division ; acres 33,218 ; lat. 11° 22′ ; long. 76° 41′ ; from Ootacamund S.W. 5 miles. Village is on W. slope of the valley. The head of the latter is a ravine formed by two spurs of Dodabetta and known as Lovedale. It gradually opens out, and stretches for some miles in the direction of the Avalanchey valley. It is watered by a tributary of the Pycarrah and consists mainly of undulating stretches of grazing land. There is a low hill with excavations round its base, resembling an entrenched camp.——*Nunnaury* (நன்னாரி - nannári, Tam.). Means sweet smelling. Same as Indian sarsaparilla. Foreign nunnaury is Sarsaparilla china root.——*Nunnery* (நன்னெறி - nanneri, Tam.). From (nal, tam. good + neri, tam. way). Ethical treatise by Shiva pracausa desican, at Conjeeveram, seventeenth century.——*Nunnilam* (நன்னிலம் - nannilam, Tam.). See sep. title.——*Nunnool* (நன்னூல் - nannúl, Tam.). See sep. title.

NULLA (నల్ల - nalla, *Tel.*). Black.——*Nullamada* (నల్లమడ - nallamada, Tel.). Same as Ooppata mangrove.——*Nullamullay* (నల్లమల - nallamala, Tel.). From (above + mala, tel. hill). Range of mountains ; Kurnool and Cuddapah districts. From Budwail W. 11 miles ; from Cuddapah N. 16 miles ; from Kurnool E. 41 miles ; from Nundicotcore E. 28 miles. For description, see vol. II, 115.——*Nulla vaulagily* (دریا کا سانپ - daryákásámp, Hind. ; నల్లవాలగిలి - nallaválagili, Tel.). Title from teloogoo. Hind. from (daryá, hind. sea + sámp, hind. snake). Tel. from (nalla, tel. black + válaga, tel. a sea fish). The genus Pelamis, hydrophidæ [tuttapaumb], ophidii colubriformes venenosi, ophidia [sarpam], reptilia [sarpy, 28], of naturalists [jantoo]. One of the most common of sea-snakes. The best known species is Pelamis bicolor. Alias Hydrus bicolor ; Hydrophis pelamis, variegata ; Pelamis ornata, platurus. The following four varieties of this species are known :—"*a*" Color black above ; sides and belly uniform brownish-olive ; tail with black spots.—"*b*" Back black ; belly and sides brown, separated by a black and a yellow band. Large spots posteriorly.—"*c*" Black of back narrow, become sinuous behind middle of the body ; posteriorly a dorsal series of rhombic confluent spots. Sides and belly with an irregular series of rounded, black or brown spots. This variety has been named sinuata.—"*d*" Yellow, with about fifty brown, black-edged cross bands, extending nearly to the belly, which is crossed by narrow vertical brownish-black streaks, alternating with the dorsal bands. Some of the dorsal bands are confluent, forming a zigzag band. Head yellow, variegated with black.

NULLAH (نالا - nálá, *Hind.*). A water-course [caulvye], a ravine.

NUM (நம் - nam, *Tam.*). Our. Prefixed to Veishnavite proper names [peyar].——*Nannayya bhatt* (నన్నయ్యభట్టు - nannayyabhattu, Tel.). From (nánnayya, tel. familiar form of address for father + bhatta, san. title). First of the three Teloogoo Andy cavies [cavy] [ticcana, yerra pragada]. Under Raja raja naraindran in Rajahmundry. Translated first three parvams [q.v.] of Bhauratam [q.v.]. Also Andhrashabda chintaumany, Teloogoo grammar in Sanscrit metre ; otherwise

Nannayya bhatteeyam.——*Numbermaul* (நம்பெருமாள் - namberumál, Tam.). From (above + perumál, tam. vishnu, the great god). Hindoo 2nd or pers. name. Common among non-bramins [peyar].——*Nummalwar* (நம்மாழ்வார் - nammázhvár, Tam.). From (above + ázhvár, tam. a disciple of vishnu). Hindoo 2nd or pers. name. Common among non-bramins [peyar].——*Nummayya* (ನಮ್ಮಯ್ಯ - nammayya, Can.). From (above + ayya, can. master). Hindoo 2nd or pers. name [peyar].——*Nyna* (నాయన - náyana, Tel.). From (ná, tel. my + anna, tel. father). Hindoo 2nd or pers. name. More commonly term of address to father; also term of address by elders towards young men [peyar].

NUMB (நம்பு - nambu, *Tam.*). Belief. Vedam [q.v.], the hindoo sacred writings.——*Numbalagode* (നമ്പലക്കോട് - nambalakótu, Mal.). From (nampólan, mal. a ruler of that name + kódu, mal. fort). Amshom; Neilgherry dist., Wynaud S.E. division; pop. 14,868; acres 88,842; lat. 11° 26′ to 11° 42′; long. 76° 24′ to 76° 38′; from Ootacamund W. 14 miles. Tract consists of five deshoms [q.v.], Chermalittara, Devaulah, Goodalore, Paudantara, and Shreemadhoora. Five temples of repute are situated in this amshom [q.v.], viz., Ayira villy, Calingara, Moothoomullay, Numbalagode, and Shree madhoora. Belongs to the Nelambore tirmalpaud. A temple of Baidagan [q.v.], the hunting god of the Todahs [q.v.].——*Numban* (நம்பன் - namban, Tam.). From (nambu, tam. to desire). Shiva [q.v.].——*Numbeeshan* (നമ്പീശൻ - nampíshan, Mal.). From (above + accan, mal. father). Honorific form of Numby.——*Numberoya* (ನಂಬೇರಾಯ - numbéráya, Can.). From (above + ráya, can. king). Hindoo 2nd or pers. name [peyar].——*Numbidy* (നമ്പിടി - nampiti, Mal.). From (above + ati, mal. foot). A trustworthy dependent. Another form of Numby.——*Numbiyaur* (നമ്പിയാർ - nampiyár, Mal.). From (above + ár, mal. honorific plural termination). A temple priest. A title among petty chiefs of North malabar. Hindoo third name [peyar].——*Numbiyauttiry* (നമ്പിയാതിരി - nampiyátiri, Mal.). From (above + tiri, mal. prosperity, title). Originally the head of fighting Bramins [keraloputty], now a title among the junior rajahs of Calicut [zamorin].——*Numboodripaud* (നമ്പൂതിരിപ്പാട് - nampútirippátu, Mal.). From (nampu, mal. veda + tiri, mal. holy + pátu, mal. chief, a title). A head Numboory.——*Numboory* (നമ്പൂരി - nampúri, Mal.). See sep. title.——*Numbootiry* (നമ്പൂതിരി - nampútiri, Mal.). From (nampu, mal. veda + tiri, mal. blessed). The original form of Numboory.——*Numby* (നമ്പി - nampi, Mal.). Means trustworthy. Priest. To be distinguished from Numboories. Inferior Bramins in Malabar; others being Elliads and Moottads. They perform ceremonies for Shoodras. Follow Maroomakkatoyem [jauty, maroomakkatoyem, numbidy].

NUMBOORY (നമ്പൂരി - nampúri, *Mal.*). From (nambu, mal. veda + óthu, mal. to teach + tiri, mal. holy, title) [numb]. Caste, title. The Bramins [q.v.] peculiar to the west coast; as opposed to the modern stranger bramins from the east coast or Puttar [q.v.].——**(1)** The portion of the Malabar coast immediately to the north of Dymirice is called by Ptolemy and the author of the Periplus ἀριακὴ or Aryan land; this latter probably refers in part to the Numboories. Compare ναούρα or the country of the Nayars. Numboory bramins belong neither to Gowda [q.v.] nor Dravida [q.v.]; nevertheless they are said to have been invited into Malabar by Parshooraman [keraloputty]. Evidently they are a very early immigration of Bramin colonists. See vol. I (66); II, 100, 135. In the early history of the Numboory caste in Malabar there was a division into two factions, the Punniyore [q.v.] graumam adopting the Veishnavite faith with the Veishnavite emblem of the pig or boar, and the Chovoor [q.v.] graumam that of Shiva with the emblem of a bird. These are not to be understood as single villages merely. The Chovoor graumams finally prevailed. The whole caste however has since adopted the Vedantist sheiva doctrines of Shuncaracharry, himself believed to have been a Numboory [talee]. Their organization is by graumams [q.v.] or villages, as the Nayar [q.v.] are organized by taras [q.v.] and nauds [q.v.], and Teeyar [q.v.] and other foreigners by cherries. The principal pure Numboory graumams now extant are:—Aulatore, Caricaud, Irinyaulacode, Punniyore, Perinchelloor, Peroovanam, Chovoor, Trishivaperoor, Venganaud, Yedacaud, but see below. The graumams are presided over by six Smartas [q.v.], who are presidents of the assemblies at which caste offences are tried. The Numboory caste divides at the present day into two larger classes; Numboodripauds and Numboories. The former, as their name implies, or of superior rank. Those Numboories who have performed a public sacrifice or yaugam [q.v.] are called Chomaudripauds, or persons who have sacrificed with Somam [q.v.] juice. As a rule the Numboories lead very simple lives. The women are styled antarjanam [q.v.] or agattamaur [q.v.], that is to say indoors people. Numboories wear the chooday [q.v.] or sacred tuft of hair not on the crown of the head but on the forehead. They seldom go abroad without holding a chuttram or large umbrella. They are extensive landowners, often possessed of much wealth. The family property is owned and enjoyed in common by all the members of the family; and to preserve this intact for the general welfare and protection, in order that is to say that the family property may descend undivided, the eldest son alone is permitted to marry, the younger sons being only provided with subsistence and obliged to form temporary connections with Shoodra and other females of inferior caste. The mistresses of the younger sons remain in their own homes, for the Bramins cannot on account of caste eat food with them, and the children being by Hindoo law of necessity illegitimate can only be supported by and inherit property from their mothers' brothers. If the eldest son be without issue, he may marry one or two additional wives. If the eldest brother still have no children, or die without issue, the next in succession may marry, and so on. Division of family property is forbidden among these, and is not practised. Those who can claim support from the common fund are:—all the males of the family, their wives, their virgin daughters, and sisters, widows; and this for the last two classes only while residing in the house. The law of inheritance followed is Makkatoyem [q.v.], as opposed to the Maroomakkatoyem [q.v.] of the shoodras [nayar]. The Numboory's hospitality and charity are proverbial. Besides Numboories there are in Malabar several classes of inferior Bramins styled Numbidies, Elliads, Yembrauntries, &c.——**(2)** The following are the principal Numboory houses in North malabar, all Chiracal talook.——*Anakye* (ആനക്കഴി - ánakkazhi, Mal.).——*Caricherry parappore* (കരിശ്ശേരിപറപ്പൂർ - karishshériparappúr, Mal.).——*Carmaurat* (കരുമാരത്ത് - karumárattu, Mal.).——*Cartiyairy parappore* (കാർത്തിയേരിപറപ്പൂർ - kárttiyériparappúr, Mal.).——*Chembocoonnat* (ചെമ്പോകുന്നത്ത് - chempokunnattu, Mal.).——*Chiracote mallicherry* (ചിറക്കോട്ട് മല്ലിശ്ശേരി - chirakkóttumallishshéri, Mal.).——*Codal cokkoonnam* (കൊടൽ കൊക്കുന്നം - kotalkokkunnam, Mal.).——*Codallore peroor* (കൊടല്ലൂർപേരൂർ - kotallúrpérúr, Mal.).——*Cooditala* (കുടിത്തല - kutittala, Mal.).——*Coormattore* (കുറുമാത്തൂർ - kurumáttúr, Mal.).——*Irraishy podavar* (ഇരുവേശ്ശിപ്പുടവർ - iruvéshshiputavar, Mal.).——*Keeyatral* (കീഴത്രിൽ - kízhatril, Mal.).——*Madattil mallicherry* (മാടത്തിൽമല്ലിശ്ശേരി - mátattilmallishshéri, Mal.).——*Maniyal cokkoonnam* (മണിയാൽകൊക്കുന്നം - maniyálkokkunnam, Mal.).——*Mannore* (മണ്ണൂർ - mannúr, Mal.).——*Marcaunattil peroor* (മാർക്കാണത്തിൽപേരൂർ - márkkánattilpérúr, Mal.).——*Meppully* (മേപ്പള്ളി - méppali, Mal.).——*Moolloor poothoocoody* (മുള്ളൂർപുതുക്കുടി - mulúrputukkuti, Mal.).——*Moondrote poolipada* (മുന്ത്രോത്ത് പുളിപ്പട - muntróttupulippata, Mal.).——*Moottedat mallicherry* (മുത്തേടത്ത് മല്ലിശ്ശേരി - muttétattumallishshéri, Mal.).——*Mothachira mallicherry* (മൊതച്ചിറമല്ലിശ്ശേരി - motaççiramallishshéri, Mal.).——*Nadoovat podavar* (നടുവത്ത് പൊടവർ - natuvattupotavar, Mal.).——*Naricode* (നരിക്കോട് - narikkótu, Mal.).——*Ottoopooracal* (ഓട്ടുപുരക്കൽ - óttupurakkal, Mal.).——*Padinyaurat colacherry* (പടിഞ്ഞാറത്ത് കുളശ്ശേരി - patiññárattukulashshéri, Mal.).——*Padinyauttat* (പടിഞ്ഞാറ്റത്ത് - patiññáttattu, Mal.).——*Palamrita parappore* (പാലമൃതപറപ്പൂർ - pálamritaparappúr, Mal.).——*Panyote* (പന്ന്യോട്ട് - pannyóttu, Mal.).——*Pappinyote* (പാപ്പിനിയോട്ട് - pápinyóttu, Mal.).——*Poondotattilpodavar* (പൂന്തോട്ടത്തിൽപൊടവർ - púntóttattilpotavar, Mal.).——*Poothoocoody cokkoonnam* (പുതുക്കുടി കൊക്കുന്നം - putukkutikokkunnam, Mal.).——*Poothoocoody colacherry* (പുതുക്കുടികൊളശ്ശേരി - putukkutikolashshéri, Mal.).——*Poovva coonnoonmal* (പുവ്വക്കുന്നുമ്മൽ - puvvakkunnunmal, Mal.).——*Shekhara pooliyapada* (ശേഖരപുളിയപ്പട - shékharapuliyappata, Mal.).——*Tertala mallicherry* (തേരത്തലമല്ലിശ്ശേരി - térattalamallishshéri, Mal.).——*Vadakote pooliyapadamba* (വടക്കോട്ട് പുളിയപടമ്പ - vatakkóttupuliyapatampa, Mal.).——*Varnacode* (വാരണക്കോട് - váranakkótu, Mal.).——*Vauricote mallicherry* (വാരിക്കോട്ടുമല്ലിശ്ശേരി - várikkóttumallishshéri, Mal.).——*Vengaprat bhattatiry* (വെങ്ങപ്രത്ത് ഭട്ടതിരി - vénnaprattubhattatri, Mal.).——*Vycaulcokkoonnam* (വായക്കാൽ കൊക്കുന്ന് - váyakkalkókkunn, Mal.).——*Yedattat* (എടത്തട്ട് - etattattu, Mal.).——*Yedavalat podavar* (എടവലത്ത് പൊടവർ - etavalattupotavar, Mal.).——*Yeledat colacherry* (എളേടത്ത് കുളശ്ശേരി - elétattukulashshéri, Mal.).——*Yeledat mallicherry* (എളേടത്ത് മല്ലിശ്ശേരി - elétattumallishshéri, Mal.).——**(3)** The following are the principal Numboory houses in South malabar, with the talook indicated.——*Aghoram* (അഘോരം - aghóram, Mal.), Cochin.——*Alacat* (അളകത്ത് - alakattu, Mal.), Valavanand.——*Alwancherry tumbraukkal* (ആഴ്വാഞ്ചേരിതമ്പ്രാക്കൾ - ázhuvánchéritamprákkal, Mal.), Ponnany.——*Andalaud* (അണ്ടലാട് - antalátu, Mal.), Valavanaud.——*Auttpooratt bhattatiripaud* (ആറ്റുപുറത്ത് ഭട്ടതിരിപ്പാട് - áttupurattubhattatiripátu, Mal.), Valavanaud.——*Avanyicautt bhattatiripaud*

(അവഞ്ഞിക്കാട്ട് ഭട്ടതിരിപ്പാട് - avaññikkáttubhattatirippátu, Mal.), Ponnany.——*Caccaud* (കക്കാട - kakkátu, Mal.), Valavanaud.——*Callore* (കല്ലൂർ - kallúr, Mal.), Ponnany.——*Caravatt edatt* (കരവത്തേടത്ത് - karavattétattu, Mal.), Valavanaud.——*Carvanambatt* (കരിവനമ്പൊററ - karivanampotta, Mal.), Yernaud.——*Caudambatt* (കാടമ്പൊററ - kátampotta, Mal.), Valavanaud.——*Caulady* (കാലടി - kálati, Mal.), Ponnany.——*Caunipayyore* (കാണിപ്പയ്യൂർ - kánippayyúr, Mal.), Ponnany.——*Caunyore* (കാഞ്ഞൂർ - káññúr, Mal.), Valavanaud.——*Caunyore bhattatiripaud* (കാഞ്ഞൂർഭട്ടതിരിപ്പാട് - kaññúrbhattatirippátu, Mal.), Valavanaud.——*Cautmaudat* (കാട്ടുമാടത്ത് - káttumátattu, Mal.), Ponnany.——*Chembauly* (ചെമ്പാഴി - chempázhi, Mal.), Yernaud.——*Chennamungalat* (ചേന്നമംഗലത്ത് - chénnamangalattu Mal.), Ponnany.——*Chermungalat* (ചെറുമംഗലത്ത് - cherumangalattu, Mal.), Valavanaud.——*Chermook veideecan* (ചെറുമുക്കു വൈദികൻ - cherumukkuvaidíkan, Mal.), Valavanaud.——*Chittore* (ചിററൂർ - chittúr, Mal.), Cochin.——*Chovoor* (ചോവൂർ - chóvúr, Mal.), Cochin.——*Chovoor bhattatiripaud* (ചോവൂർ ഭട്ടതിരിപ്പാട് - chovúrbhattatirippátu, Mal.), Cochin.——*Colicherry* (കോഴിശ്ശേരി - kózhishshéri, Mal.), Valavanaud.——*Coodallore* (കൂടല്ലൂർ - kútalúr, Mal.), Ponnany.——*Coorvatt avanaumana* (കുറുവത്തു് അവണാമന - kuruvattuavanámana, Mal.), Ponnany.——*Cowoongal* (കാവുങ്ങൽ - kávunnal, Mal.), Yernaud.——*Deshmungalat* (ദേശമംഗലത്ത് - déshamangalattu, Mal.), Valavanaud.——*Gooroovayore* (കുരുവയൂർ - kuruvayúr, Mal.), Cochin.——*Keerangautt* (കിരങ്ങാട്ട് - kírannáttu, Mal.), Valavanaud.——*Killoorchy* (കില്ലൂശ്ശി - killúrshshi, Mal.), Valavanaud.——*Kiyakedat* (കിഴക്കേടത്ത് - kizhakkétattu, Mal.), Valavanaud.——*Kiyakiny yedat* (കിഴക്കിനിയെടത്ത് - kizhakkiniyetattu, Mal.), Ponnany.——*Kyedakkal* (കയ്തക്കൽ - kaytakkal, Mal), Yernaud.——*Mantredat* (മന്ത്രേടത്ത് - mantrétattu, Mal.), Valavanaud.——*Manyapat bhattatiripaud* (മഞ്ഞപ്പററഭട്ടതിരിപ്പാട് - maññappattabhattatirippátu, Mal.), Ponnany.——*Mapaut* (മപ്പാട്ട് - mappáttu, Mal.), Valavanaud.——*Maraut* (മരാട്ട് - maráttu, Mal.), Yernaud.——*Maravancherry tekkedatt* (മറവഞ്ചേരിതെക്കേടത്ത് - maravañchéritekkétattu, Mal.), Ponnany.——*Maravancherry vadakedat* (മറവഞ്ചേരിവടക്കേടത്ത് - maravañchérivatakkótattu, Mal.), Ponnany.——*Mauttore* (മാത്തൂർ - máttúr, Mal.), Valavanaud.——*Mauttore bhattatiripaud* (മാത്തൂർ ഭട്ടതിരിപ്പാട് - máttúrbhattatirippátu, Mal.), Valavanaud.——*Melapaut bhattatiry* (മേലപ്പാട്ട് ഭട്ടതിരി - méléppáttubhattatiri, Mal.), Valavanaud.——*Moodcoorchy* (മുതുകുറിശ്ശി - mutukurishshi, Mal.), Valavanaud.——*Mootringote bhattatiripaud* (മൂത്രിങ്ങോട്ട ഭട്ടതിരിപ്പാട് - mútrinnóttubhattatirippátu, Mal.), Valavanaud.——*Nadoovat* (നടുവത്ത് - natuvattu, Mal.), Yernaud.——*Nadoovattedat kiyekoombaut* (നടുവത്തെടത്തു കിഴക്കുമ്പാട്ട് - natuvattétatatukizhakkumpáttu, Mal.), Yernaud.——*Narrainmungalatt* (നാരായണമംഗലത്ത് - náráyanamangalattu, Mal.), Ponnany.——*Olapamana* (ഒളപ്പമന - olappumana, Mal.), Valavanaud.——*Oloovil* (ഒഴുവിൽ - ozhuvil, Mal.), Valavanaud.——*Oodiyanore* (ഉദിയന്നൂർ - udiyannúr, Mal.), Ponnany.——*Orlacherry* (ഒരളാശ്ശേരി - oraláshshéri, Mal.), Valavanaud.——*Padaucara* (പാതാക്കര - pátákkara, Mal.), Valavanaud.——*Padinyautt edat* (പടിഞ്ഞാറെടത്ത് - patiññáttetattu, Mal.), Valavanaud.——*Paledat* (പഴേടത്ത് - pazhétattu, Mal.), Valavanaud.——*Paryaurambat* (പരിയാരമ്പൊററ - pariyárampotta, Mal.), Valavanaud.——*Paukkat bhattatiripaud* (പാക്കത്തു് ഭട്ടതിരിപ്പാട് - pákkattubhattatirippátu, Mal.), Ponnany.——*Paundamparambatt bhatttatiripaud* (പാണ്ടമ്പറമ്പത്തു് ഭട്ടതിരിപ്പാട് - pándamparampattubhattatirippátu, Mal.), Ponnany.——*Poolome mana* (പൂലോമന - púlómana, Mal.), Valavanaud.——*Poolyanore* (പുലിയന്നൂർ - puliyanúr, Mal.), Cochin.——*Poovoolly* (പൂവുള്ളി - púvulli, Mal.), Ponnany.——*Porayanore* (പുറയന്നൂർ - purayannúr, Mal.), Valavanaud.——*Shreeharichedat* (ശ്രീഹരിച്ചേടത്ത് - shríhariççétattu, Mal.), Valavanaud.——*Tarnanullore* (തരണനല്ലൂർ - taranamallúr, Mal.), Cochin.——*Tirnavoya vaudhyaun* (തിരുന്നാവായി വാദ്ധ്യാൻ - tirunnáváyiváddhyán, Mal.), Ponnany.——*Tycaut veideecan* (തയ്ക്കാട്ട് വൈദികൻ - taykkáttuvaidikan, Mal.), Ponnany.——*Vadakedat* (വടക്കേടത്ത് - vatakkétattu, Mal.), Valavanaud.——*Vadakinyedat* (വടക്കിനിയേടത്ത് - vatakkiniyétattu, Mal.), Ponnany.——*Vadakkancherry* (വടക്കാഞ്ചേരി - vatakkáñchéri, Mal.), Cochin.——*Vadakoongara* (വടക്കുങ്കര - vatakkunkara, Mal.), Valavanaud.——*Varikacherry* (വരിക്കാശ്ശേരി - varikkáshshéri, Mal.), Valavanaud.——*Vaulpully* (വാഴപ്പള്ളി - vázhappalli, Mal.), Ponnany.——*Veishravanat* (വൈശ്രവണത്ത് - vaishravanattu, Mal.), Valavanaud.——*Vemancherry* (വേമഞ്ചേരി - vémañchéri, Mal.), Valavanaud.——*Vettat moottedat* (വെട്ടത്തുമുറ്റേടത്ത് - vettattumúttétattu, Mal.), Ponnany.——*Vettat orlacherry* (വെട്ടത്തുഒരലാശ്ശേരി - vettattnoraláshshéri, Mal.), Ponnany.——*Yedamana* (എടമന - etamana, Mal.), Ponnany.——*Yelangolat* (എളങ്കുളത്ത് - élankulattu, Mal.), Valavanaud.

NUMDAH (نمدا - namdá, *Hind.*). From (namad, pers. a rag). A saddle cloth. Properly made of felt.

NUND (नन्द् - nand, *San.*). To be happy.——*Nundam* (नन्द - nanda, San.). From (nand, san. to be glad). Happiness.——*Nundan* (नन्द - nanda, San.; நந்தன் - nandan, Tam.). Name of a cowherd, otherwise Nundagopan, the foster father of Krishnan [q.v.]. Also that of a chuckler [q.v.] who is reputed to have reigned as a king for three hours, and to have issued leather coin. There is a Tamul proverb :—என் காரியம் எல்லாம் நந்தன் படைவீடாய்ப் போயிற்று—"My affairs are gone "like Nundan's ruined capital." Nundan is a common Hindoo 2nd or pers. name [peyar].——*Nundavanam* (नन्दवन - nandavana, San.; నందనము - nandavanamu, Tel.). From (nanda, san. pleasure + vana, san. garden). Elysium. Name given to flower pot containing Toolsy [q.v.] worshipped in honor of Vishnoo. Land held for growing flowers for use of a temple [inam].——*Nundiaul* (నంద్యాల - nandyála, Tel.). See sep. title.——*Nundicanama* (నందికనమ - nandikanama, Tel.). From (nandi, san. the bull of shiva + kanama, tel. ravine). From the temple of mahanundy or bull-god in its neighbourhood. Pass; Kurnool dist., Nundiaul and Cumbum tals.; lat. 15° 25′ N.; long. 78° 49′ E.; from Cumbum S.W. 25 miles; from Kurnool E.S.E. 53 miles; from Madras N.W. 195 miles; from Nundiaul E.S.E. 19 miles; from Pyaupaly E.N.E. 69 miles. Most southerly pass in the Nullamullays. First opened in 1852. Chiefly used for transport of salt from coast districts. Carries main road from Kurnool to Cumbum and the east coast at Ongole over the Nullamullay hills. The distance from Gauzoolapully, at the western foot of the hills to Krishnamshettipully on the eastern side is 22 miles. The highest point of the road is about 2,000 feet. Traversed by railway. Formerly lead [eeyam] and diamond [vajram] mines were worked near entrance.——*Nundicotcore* (నందికోటకూరు - nandikótukúru, Tel.). See sep. title.——*Nundidroog* (ನಂದಿದುರ್ಗ - nandidurga, Can.; nundydroog, Mys. gov.). From (nandi, san. shiva's bull + durga, san. mountain fortress). Fortified hill and place of pilgrimage in the Chikbullapore talook, Colaur district, 31 miles north of Bangalore.——*Nundigauma* (నందిగామ - nandigáma, Tel.). See sep. title.——*Nundikeshwaran* (नन्दिकेश्वर - nandikéshvara, San.). From (nandi, san. the bull god + íshvara, san. lord). Shiva.——*Nundinagry* (नन्दीनागरी - nandínágarí, San.). From being specially sacred. Southern kind of Devanagry. See vol. I (49).——*Nundrauz* (نندراج - nandráj, Hind.; నందరాజు - nandarádzu, Tel.). The joyful king. Proper name [peyar].——*Nundy* (नन्दि - nandi, San.). Means the happy one. μινώταυρος of Greeks; Apis of Egyptians. Otherwise Shaulancauvanan, meaning hall + resident; Taundava taulicau, meaning dance + beater, or who beats time to the dance of shiva; Basava and Rishabham. The snow white bull, the attendant and favorite vehicle [vauhan] of Shiva [q.v.]. It is always represented on a pedestal, crouching in front of Sheiva fanes; the head turned towards the small door of the shrine, as if waiting to receive its rider, the deity. Evidently a relic of bull-worship. Compare the calves at Dan and Bethel; the molten calf at Sinai; the Apis and Mnevis of Egypt; Mithra's bull in Persia; in all these cases, worshipped as the symbol of the presence of a power higher than itself. The importance of cattle [maud] to primitive life probably gave rise first to bull-worship. In the Institutes of Menoo [q.v.], chapter 8, vol. 16, the divine form of justice is represented as vrisham or a bull. The bull itself is worshipped among the Lingadhauries [lingayet] of Mysore under the name of Basava [q.v.]. Nundy has had avatars. When Nundy, by assuming a likeness to Shiva, caused a blush on the cheeks of Parvaty [q.v.], Shiva sent his vehicle down to earth to do penance; hence the mountain Nundidroog. Another mission to earth was in the person of the elder Basava. Though the cow [pashoo] is a sacred animal, she does not share the special worship paid to the bull. See vol. I (72), (86). Nundy also means the first, sixth or eleventh day [tity] of a fortnight [pacsham] considered as three auspicious days. Cf. Jayay.

NUNDIAUL (నంద్యాల - nandyála, *Tel.* nandyál *). From (nandí, san. the bull of shiva + álaya, san. abode) [nund].——**(1)** Talook, Kurnool district. Tahsildar's pay Rs. 200. Area 854 square miles. Population 96,292. Language Teloogoo and Hindostany. Centre of district. Bounded N. by Nundicotcore talook; E. by Nullamullays, which separate it from Cumbum talook; W. by Yerramalas; S. by Coilcoontla and Sirwail talooks. Formed a portion of the old Gundicote province. Is the N. part of Coondair valley. Being shut in by hills and jungles, is unhealthy. The Coondair valley is extensive flat open country, covered with black-cotton soil [regar], deposited on a stratum of slaty limestones [choonam cull] and shales. The rest of talook is mountainous tract forming a plateau on Yerramalas. Chief products are arikeloo [varagoo], paddy [q.v.], great millet [cholum], Italian millet [tinay], horse-gram [madras horse-gram]; orchard and garden produce, tobacco [pogauk], linseed [alsee], castor-oil [aumanac] seeds, indigo [q.v.] and cotton [q.v.]. Grain exported by rail to Bellary, &c. Piece-goods, dried cocoanuts [q.v.], jaggery [q.v.], and betel [q.v.] nuts imported from Bellary. Trade in grain and tobacco with Bestavaurpettah in Cumbum talook and Vinoocondah in Kistna district. Jaggery [q.v.] and coarse sugar [q.v.] are manufactured at Cadamalcaulwa, Caulwa and Nundiaul; the greatest portion of it is consumed locally while a portion finds its way to Kurnool. China ware, European goods and European liquors are brought down by rail either from Bellary or Madras. Gingelly [q.v.] oil and lamp oil [q.v.] are manufactured by indigenous oil-mill owners. Cotton tape [navaur] for cots made in the talook. Mats [boriyah] at Goracull out of Toonga [coray] reed, by side of Tummarpully channel. Merchants from Proddootore in Cuddapah district, &c., have established indigo manufactories. Steatite [sowcauracull] grey and green is quarried in Mooddavaram and Balapalapully, hamlet of Coolmoolapully and exported to Madras and Hyderabad. Close-grained grits quarried out in plateau of Gany and worked into grinding stones by Woddars. Formerly diamond [vajram] mines at Mooddavaram and Baswapore. Timber exported by rail to Bellary, and Putticondah talook. Salt imported from Nellore district. Lubbays from south and Cuddapah mussalman merchants buy hides [chamrah] from local butchers and chucklers [q.v.] and export to Madras and Cuddapah. Ghee [q.v.] to Bellary. In 1843 Mauritius sugar-cane [q.v.] was introduced and has nearly supplanted the native cane, now confined to Cadamalcaulwa at foot of hills. Chief river is Coondair fed by Cauly and Palaur from Nullamullays and Munnair from Yerramalas. Largest tank is Nundiaul fed by Palaur, and by Mahanundy. Kurnool-Cuddapah irrigation canal, runs through talook. Camping grounds:—Caulwa boogga, Chindoocore, Ganzoolapully, Tammirauzpully. Places of archæological interest:—Ayalore, Ayyavaury codore, Baitamcheroo, Bandy atmacore, Baswapore, Bilcala goodoor, Boojanore, Bramhanapully, Cadamalcaulwa, Carimaddoola, Caulwa, Caunaula, Channakkapully, Chindoocore, Chintalapulley, Conatalapaud, Condazootoor, Cowlore, Gadigeyraivla, Gadivaimla, Galchenpollem, Gany, Gonavaram, Goontanaul, Goracull, Mahanundy, Mittanaula, Narayanapooram, Nundiaul, Parmatore, Paunem, Paurnapully, Peddacaunala, Pesaravye, Polore, Poolimuddy, Santa zootoor, Shekoonaula, Togarchaid, Worvacoll, Yerragoontla. Principal Trig. stations:—Goommanacondah, Goondlabramheshwar. The leading places, &c., in the talook are the following.——*Ayulore* (అయ్యలూరు - áyalúru, Tel.). From (ayyalu, tel. proper name + úru, tel. village). Sanscrit name (shat'hakópapura), meaning vishnoo, the foe of rogues + town. Village; pop. 1,340; acres 4,048; lat. 15° 27′; long. 78° 34′; from Kurnool S.E. 41 miles; from Nundiaul S. 4 miles. Shiva temple. Chola inscription. In A.D. 1493 the village was granted as Sarwa maunyam [q.v.] by Narsimha deva of Vijianugger.——*Baitamcheroo* (బెత్తంచెరువు - bétamcheruvu, Tel.). From (bettamu, tel. cane, calamus rotang, linn. + cheruvu, tel. tank). Village, B.K.S. railway station; pop. 1,776; acres 6,353; lat. 15° 27′; long. 78° 11′; from Kurnool S.S.E. 27 miles; from Nundiaul W. 23 miles. Vijianugger inscriptions. Caves in neighbourhood. Situated on a pleateau. Ruined fort. Fair on Sunday.——*Bandy atmacore* (బండిఆత్మకూరు - bandiátmakúru, Tel.). From (bandi, tel. cart + átmakúru, tel. place so called). Village, Railway station; lat. 15° 35′; long. 78° 34′; pop. 2,416; from Kurnool E. 35 miles; from Nundiaul N.E. 7 miles. Three miles east of route from Cuddapah to Kurnool.——*Baswapore* (బసవపురము - basavapuramu, Tel.). From (basava, can. the bull-god + pura, san. town). Sanscrit name (mahánandí), meaning the great nundy, the bull-god. Village; pop. 273; acres 869; lat. 15° 25′; long. 78° 41′; from Kurnool S.E. 48 miles; from Nundiaul E. 10 miles. Once famous for lead [eeyam] and diamond [vajram] mines. Former residence of a Poligar [q.v.]. Baupoo naidoo, the ancestor of the Poligars of Baswapore, Poollalcheroo and Bolloopully, served under the Vijianugger royel and obtained district of Dornaul in jagheer [q.v.]. About 1,712 pollem was divided among the three branches of family and in 1709 Baswapore and Bolloopully were annexed to Kurnool, while Poollalcheroo remained under Cuddapah. Baswapore division resumed by Munro. At foot of Nullamullay hills and principal timber mart.——*Bilcala goodoor* (బిలకలగూడూరు - bilakalagúdúru, Tel.). From (bilakamu, tel. bamboo work + gúdúru, tel. place so called). Village; pop. 1,022; acres 4,052; lat. 15° 41′; long. 78° 29′; from Kurnool E.S.E. 28 miles; from Nundiaul N. 14 miles. Inscription of Warangal dynasty, dated A.D. 1307.——*Caulwa* (కాలవ - kálava, Tel.). See sep. title.——*Coondair* (కుందేరు - kundéru, Tel.). See sep. title.——*Galchenpollem* (గాలిచెన్నయపాలెము - gálichennayapálemu, Tel.). From (gálichennaya, tel. proper name + pálemu, tel. fortified village). Village; pop. 1,078; acres 4,768 lat. 15° 37′; long. 78° 37′; from Kurnool E.S.E. 38 miles; from Nundiaul N. 11 miles. South-east are three old temples. Irrigated by four tanks.——*Gany* (గని - gani, Tel.). Means a mine. Village; pop. 1,790; acres 10,163; lat. 15° 40′; long. 78° 22′; from Kurnool E.S.E. 21 miles; from Nundiaul N.W. 17 miles. Near Goommanacondah hill. Good tobacco [pogauk].——*Gaulicondah* (గాలికొండ - gálikonda, Tel.). See sep. title.——*Gauzoolapully* (గాజులపల్లి - gádzulapalli, Tel.). From (gádzu, tel. glass bracelet + palli, tel. village). Village; pop. 943; acres 3,743; lat. 15° 25′; long. 78° 40′; from Kurnool S.E. 47 miles; from Nundiaul E. 10 miles. Irrigated by spring channel on the road to Cumbum. Tamarind [q.v.] tope [q.v.] is best camping ground in talook.——*Goommunacondah* (గుమ్మనకొండ - gummanakonda, Tel.). From (gummana, tel. proper name + konda, tel. hill). Trig. station; lat. 15° 38′ 18·94″; long. 78° 20′ 05·61″; height 1,567 feet; from Gany S.W. 2 miles; from Nundiaul N.W. 17 miles.——*Goondlabramheshwar* (గుండ్లబ్రహ్మేశ్వరం - gundlabrahméshvaram, Tel.). From (gundu, tel. rock + brahma, san. the god + íshvara, san. lord). Hill; lat. 15° 37′; long. 78° 46′; height 2,964 feet; from Kurnool E.S.E. 47 miles; from Nundiaul E.N.E. 18 miles. One of highest peaks of Nullamullays. The plateau is reached from Nundiaul and Velgode. Trig. station in lat. 15° 36′ 58·94″; long. 78° 45′ 53·61″; height 2.964 feet; from Narayanapooram E.S.E. 9 miles; from Nundiaul E.N.E. 18 miles.——*Mahanundy* (మహానంది - mahánandi, Tel.). From (mahá, san. great + nandi, san. the bull of shiva). Place of pilgrimage; lat. 15° 28′; long. 78° 40′; from Kurnool E.S.E. 45 miles; from Nundiaul E. 9¾ miles. Uninhabited in Nullamullay forests, with tepid spring. The formation is altered sandstone [manal cull] and limestone [choonam cull]. Once famous diamond and lead mines of Baswapore are in vicinity. Annual festival on Shivarantry [pundigay, 6a]. Temple to Mahanundeshwara sawmy with five inscriptions. The temperature of spring is about 89°. The water reddens litmus paper; oxalate of ammonia renders it slightly milky. The channel [q.v.] from the spring irrigates a large area.——*Munnair* (మన్నేరు - mannéru, Tel.). From (mannu, tel. sand + éru, tel. river). River. Tributary of the Coondair. Rises in the Yerramalas.——*Nullamullay* (నల్లమల - nallamala, Tel.). See sep. title.——*Nundiaul* (నంద్యాల - nandyála, Tel.). See below.——*Nundicanama* (నందికనమ - nandikanama, Tel.). See sep. title.——*Omcauram* (ఓంకారం - ómkáram, Tel.). From (ómkára, san. the symbol of the trinity). Place of pilgrimage. Tepid spring in Nullamullay forest like Mahanundy. Bathing makes barren women bear.——*Paunem* (పానెము - pánemu, Tel. pánem *). From (páni, san. hand); after its tutelar deity, paunikeshwaran or hand-god, shiva. Village, B.K.S. railway station, Hills; pop. 3,706; acres 11,756; lat. 15° 31′; long. 78° 24′; from Kurnool S.E. 29 miles; from Nundiaul W.N.W. 9 miles. Village at foot of Yerramalas, on Cuddapah-Kurnool road. Residence of a Beydar [veddah] poligar [q.v.]. Temple of Paunikeshwarasawmy. Old fort. Irrigated by two tanks.——*Peddacaunala* (పెద్దకానల - peddakánala, Tel.). From (pedda, tel. great + kána, tel. forest). Sanscrit name (krishnarájasamudra), meaning krishnaroya + ocean. Village; pop. 1,329; acres 5,991; lat. 15° 25′; long. 78° 30′; from Kurnool S.E. 39 miles; from Nundiaul S.S.W. 5 miles. Inscriptions. Tank. On road from Nundiaul to Coilcoontla.——*Polore* (పోలూరు - pólúru, Tel.). From (póli, tel. proper name + úru, tel. village). Village; pop. 1,879; acres 3,841; lat. 15° 32′; long. 78° 29′; from Kurnool S.E. 32 miles; from Nundiaul N.W. 5 miles. Residence of surviving representative of Handey poligar family, who, as zemindars of Nundiaul and Anantapore, played an important part in the local history of seventeenth century. Roman catholic mission station.——*Poolimuddy* (పులిమద్ది - pulimaddi, Tel.). From (puli, tel. sour + maddi, tel. terminalia arjuna, bedd.). Village; pop. 1,018; acres 3,061; lat. 15° 32′; long. 78° 30′; from Kurnool S.E. 34 miles; from Nundiaul N.N.W. 4 miles. Has good stone quarries.——*Rungapooram* (రంగాపురము - rangápuram, Tel.). From (rangadu, tel. proper name + pura, san. town). Village, Railway station; pop. 2,080; acres 9,464; lat. 15° 25′; long. 78° 07′; from Kurnool S. 29 miles; from Nundiaul W.S.W. 29 miles.——*Vandootla* (వందుట్ల - vandutla, Tel.). From (vandi, san. panegyrist + unta, tel. residence). Village, Plateau; lat. 15° 36′; long. 78° 23′; from Kurnool S.E. 24 miles; from Nundiaul N.W. 13 miles. On Paunem hills. Long narrow wall of quartz [vencull] joins its northern end with the plateau of Chintalapulley.——*Worvacoll* (వోరవకొల్లు - vóravakollu, Tel.). From (varava, tel. channel + kollu, tel. pool). Village; pop. 1,358; acres 6,871; lat. 15° 41′; long. 78° 13′; from Kurnool S.E. 13 miles; from Nundiaul W. 24 miles. Old fort. Ancient temple of Keshavasawmy. Two temples built by Goozeratty diamond merchants. On high road from Kurnool to Nundiaul.——*Yerramala* (ఎర్రమల - erramala, Tel.). See sep. title.——

(2) Village, Head-quarters of Tahsildar, Divisional officer, District moonsif and Deputy conservator of Forests, Railway station; Kurnool dist., Nundiaul tal.; pop. 10,737; acres 11,912; lat. 15° 29′; long. 78° 32′; from Cumbum W.S.W. 41 miles; from Kurnool S.E. 38 miles; from Madras N.W. 203 miles; from Pyanpaly E.N.E. 52 miles. On E. bank of Coondair, rising in importance. The houses are built of soft purple shales, which crumble to pieces during the rains. Nine Sheivite pagodas [q.v.]. Temples of Vencateshwarasawmy, Bramhaunandeshwara sawmy, and Mullicarjoonan. Noted for lacquer-work. Largest fair in district on Saturday. Tank built in twelfth century by Chola prince.

NUNDICOTCORE (నందికోటుకూరు - nandikótukúru, Tel. nandikótkur *). From (nandi, san. the bull of shiva + kóta, tel. fort + úru, tel. village) [nund].——(1) Talook, Kurnool district. Tahsildar's pay Rs. 175. Area 1,322 square miles. Population 88,560. Language Teloogoo. Largest talook. N. of district. Bounded N. by Kistna, E. by Nullamullays, S. by Nundiaul talook, and W. by Ramalcottah talook and Toongabudra. Nearly half covered with hills and jungles, near which extensive pasture lands. Climate unhealthy. Through middle runs great water shed between Kistna and Pennair, and it was by a heavy cutting across it at Mittacoondala through purple shale rocks that the waters of the Toongabudra were turned into the valley of the Coondair. Soil is black 50 per cent., loamy 37 per cent. and red 13 per cent. chiefly in the north and near the hills. Principal crops are arikeloo [varagoo], paddy [q.v.], great millet [cholum], Italian millet [tinay], horse-gram [q.v.], green gram [q.v.], tobacco [pogauk], chillies [q.v.], omam [ajwaun], castor-oil [aumanac] seeds, indigo [q.v.], cotton [q.v.] and mustard [rayaun]. The principal article of industry is cumblies [q.v.] of wool, very thick in texture and durable. Commerce is confined to export of Omam [ajwaun] and timber and import of lamp-oil [q.v.] from Nizam's dominions. Toongabudra and Kistna drain almost the whole talook. Bhavanausy is principal hill stream. Kurnool-Cuddapah irrigation canal runs through talook. In only eleven villages Boyaraivla, Cooroocoonta, Cottapully, Daumgatla, Goovvalcoonta, Indreshwaram, Modecoor, Moosalimadoogoo, Rampore, Shivapooram, and Velgode, there are tanks. Camping grounds :—Atmacore, Gaudideymadoogoo, Mandlem, Nundicotcore, Velgode, Zootoor. In Joopaud, Pagidyaula and Velpoonore there are Canal bungalows available for Europeans. Places of archæological interest :—Alaganore, Allotta, Anantapooram, Atmacore, Bhaunmookkala, Bijnivaimla, Bollavaram, Boyaraivla, Bramhana cotacore, Cadoomore, Cherookcherla, Chintapully, Collamnullah, Conidyaula, Cooroocoonta, Cunnamadacala, Daumgatla, Doorgam, Ganapooram, Gaudideymadoogoo, Indreshwaram, Iscala, Jalacanore, Kaidavaram, Maddigootta, Mandlem, Midootore, Mittacoondala, Moosalimadoogoo, Moravacondah, Naugalooty, Naugatore, Nootanapulley, Nundicoonta, Nundicotcore, Pagidyaula, Pasoopoola, Pauroomantsala, Pautacote, Peddachervoo, Sangameshwaram, Shikharam, Shivapooram, Shuncaraneinipulley, Siddapore, Siddepully, Siddeshwaram, Srisheilam, Talamoodipy, Tarigoppoola, Tartoor, Vaddeymaun, Vaimpenta, Veerabhadra droog, Yellagode, Yellaula, Yerramatam, Zootoor. Principal trig. stations :—Peddacoodwa, Siddapore. The leading places, &c., in the talook are the following.——*Atmacore* (ఆత్మకూరు - átmakúru, Tel.). See sep. title.——*Beilooty* (బైలూటి - bailúti, Tel.). From (bailu, tel. open plain + úru, tel. village). Village; lat. 15° 52′; long. 78° 45′; from Kurnool E. 43 miles; from Nundicotore E. 30 miles. Cluster of Chentsoo huts at W. entrance of Muntraula canama [ghaut]. Halting stage.——*Bhavanausy* (భవనాశి - bhavanáshi, Tel.). From (bhava, san. birth + násha, san. destruction). River; Tributary of Kistna. Rises in Nullamullays near ruined village of Siddapore and running by Atmacore, Pautacote and Zootoor empties itself into Kistna at Sangameshwaram.——*Chundragoortypatnam* (చంద్రగూర్తిపట్నము - chandragúrtipatnamu, Tel.). From (chandra, san. moon + gúrti, san. praise + pattana, san. town). Lat. 16° 10′; long. 78° 56′; from Kurnool E.N.E. 59 miles; from Nundicotcore E.N.E. 46 miles. Site of ruined city on north of Kistna which separates it from the Srisheilam. A legend is related about this place of a king who wished to commit incest and hence its ruin. The Chentsoos [q.v.] who live near Srisheilam say that at nights sounds like the bustle of a town are heard.——*Gaudideymadoogoo* (గాడిదెమడుగు - gádidemadugu, Tel.). From (gádide, tel. ass + madugu, tel. pond). Village; pop. 2,125; acres 5,352; lat. 15° 47′; long. 78° 11′; from Kurnool E.S.E. 7 miles; from Nundicotcore W.S.W. 10 miles. Vijianugger inscription dated A.D. 1547. Shiva temple with inscription dated A.D. 1551.——*Iscala* (ఇసుక - iskala, Tel.). From (isuka, tel. sand). Village; pop. 1,219; acres 2,401; lat. 15° 51′; long. 78° 34′; from Kurnool E. 31 miles; from Nundicotcore E. 17 miles. Temple of Naugeshwaran very old. Ruined temple of Anjaneyan. Mosque 200 years old. Vijianugger inscription dated A.D. 1562.——*Joty canama* (జోటికనము - jótikanama, Tel.). See sep. title.——*Kistna* (కృష్ణ - krishna, Tel.). See sep. title.——*Midootore* (మిడుతూరు - midutúru, Tel.). From (midata, tel. locust + úru, tel. village). Village; pop. 2,610; acres 9,148; lat. 15° 46′; long. 78° 20′; from Kurnool E.S.E. 16 miles; from Nundicotcore S. 6 miles. Vijianugger inscriptions dated A.D. 1547, 1553, 1561 and 1581.——*Moosalimadoogoo* (ముసలిమడుగు - musalimadugu, Tel.). From (mosali, tel. crocodile + madugu, tel. pond). Village; pop. 983; acres 4,205; lat. 15° 58′; long. 78° 29′; from Kurnool N.E. 28 miles; from Nundicotcore N.E. 13 miles. Strong fort, attacked in seventeenth century by Cootb shahy prince of Golcondah, on account of diamond [vajram] mines then worked. For a time residence of several Pataun [q.v.] families. Inscriptions. Trig. survey station near.——*Moravacondah* (మొరవకొండ - moravakonda, Tel.). From (morapa, tel. gravel + konda, tel. hill). Village, Hill; pop. 911; acres 6,549; lat. 16° 01′; long. 78° 19′; from Kurnool N.E. 19 miles; Nundicotcore N. 10 miles. Three deserted temples and an old mosque [musjid]. Ruins of old fort dismantled in 1839 when Kurnool was annexed.——*Muntraula canama* (మంత్రాలకనము - mantrálakanama, Tel.). See sep. title.——*Nullamullay* (నల్లమల - nallamala, Tel.). See sep. title.——*Nundicotcore* (నందికోటుకూరు - nandikótukúru, Tel.). See below.——*Pautacote* (పాతకోట - pátakóta, Tel.). From (páta, tel. old + kóta, tel. fort). Village; pop. 1,755; acres 6,484; lat. 15° 57′; long. 78° 26′; from Kurnool E.N.E. 23 miles; from Nundicotcore N.E. 10 miles. Three deserted temples. Old fort originally built by colonists from Telingana about same time as Moosalimadoogoo, during Andhra [q.v.] period. Town once very large. Brass [pittalay] utensils and bells [ghantay] are made.——*Pedda coodwa* (పెద్దకుడువ - peddakuduva, Tel.). From (pedda, tel. great + kuduva, tel. mountain foot path). Trig. station; lat. 16° 01′ 01·94″; long. 78° 30′ 43·61″; height 2,070 feet; from Moosalimadoogoo N.E. 4 miles; from Nundicotcore N.E. 17 miles.——*Sangameshwaram* (సంగమేశ్వరం - sangaméshvaram, Tel.). See sep. title.——*Siddapore* (సిద్ధాపురం - siddhápuram, Tel.). From (siddha, san. saint + pura, san. town). Village; pop. 1,274; lat. 15° 54′; long. 78° 45′; from Kurnool E. 43 miles; from Nundicotcore E. 30 miles. In Nullamullay forests. Remains of bund of an immense tank which reaches S. to Velgode, 16 miles off. Naugalooty temple, 2½ miles N.E., is connected with Srisheilam, 15 miles away, by a stone-paved roadway, passing through Collam nullah. Several small shrines stand by roadside on way to Srisheilam. Trig. survey station in lat. 15° 55′ 46·94″; long. 78° 43′ 53·61″; height 2,064 feet; from Nundicotcore E.N.E. 29 miles; from Siddapore N.N.W. 3 miles.——*Srisheilam* (శ్రీశైలం - shríshailam, Tel.). See sep. title.——*Tartoor* (తర్తూరు - tartúru, Tel.). From (tariti, tel. sack cloth + úru, tel. village). Village; pop. 1,002; acres 5,470; lat. 15° 51′; long. 78° 22′; from Kurnool E. 18 miles; from Nundicotcore S.S.E. 4 miles. Old temple of Keshavasawmy. Another temple 400 years old. Annual festival to Rungasawmy. No proper temple for this god. The image is 6 inches high and made of wood covered with gold armour. It is in a Caupoo's house which is frequented by worshippers.——*Toongabudra* (తుంగభద్ర - tungabhadra, Tel.). See sep. title.——*Vaddeymaun* (వడ్డెమాను - vaddemánu, Tel.). From (vadde, tel. member of the caste of earth-diggers + mánu, tel. tree). Village; pop. 1,459; acres 5,831; lat. 15° 51′; long. 78° 15′; from Kurnool E. 11 miles; from Nundicotcore W. 4 miles. Vijianugger inscriptions of A.D. 1563 and 1544.——*Veerabhadra droog* (వీరభద్రదుర్గము - vírabhadradurgamu, Tel.). From (vírabhadra, san. distinguished hero, epithet of shiva + durga, san. fort). Village, Hill; lat. 16° 04′; long. 78° 29′; from Kurnool N.E. 30 miles; from Nundicotcore N.E. 18 miles.——*Velgode* (వెలుగోడు - velugódu, Tel.). See sep. title.——*Velgoty canama* (వెలుగోటికనము - velugótikanama, Tel.). See sep. title.——*Velpoonore* (వేల్పునూరు - vélpunúru, Tel.). From (vélpu, tel. angel + úru, tel. village). Village; pop. 1,966; acres 7,171; lat. 15° 42′; long. 78° 33′; from Kurnool E.S.E. 32 miles; from Nundicotcore S.E. 20 miles. Ceremonies annually performed at temple of Cauly [q.v.] ammah, when children are thrown over bushes of thorn.——*Yerramala* (ఎర్రమల - erramala, Tel.). See sep. title.——(2) Village, Tahsildar's head-quarters; Kurnool dist., Nundicotcore tal.; pop. 2,753; acres 5,714; lat. 15° 52′; long. 78° 19′; from Cumbum W. 59 miles; from Kurnool E. 14 miles; from Madras N.W. 232 miles; from Nundiaul N.N.W. 30 miles; from Pyaupaly N.N.E. 55 miles. Eight deserted Shiva temples. Idol of Hanooman [q.v.] 11½ feet high which was left untouched by the Nawaubs of Kurnool.

NUNDIGAUMA (నందిగామ - nandigáma, * *Tel.*). From (nandi, san, shiva's bull + gráma, san. village) [nund]. Sanscrit name (nandigráma), meaning same.——(1) Talook, Kistna district. Tahsildar's pay Rs. 150. Area 531 square miles; pop. 126,701. Language Teloogoo. Lies west of the Condapully range between the Kistna and the Nizam's dominions. N. of district. Bounded north Nizam's dominions, east Bezwada talook, south Suttenapully talook, west Suttenapully talook and Nizam's dominions. Includes the two detached zemindarries of Lingagherry and Moongaula. The road from Bezwada to Hyderabad traverses the talook from east to west. The diamond [vajram] producing villages of Partiaul, Codavettycull, and Oostepully, on the left bank of the Kistna, were reserved by the Nizam when the Condapully circar was ceded to the East india company in 1766. In this talook there are very many stone circles [azhauram] and various spots supposed to contain remains of Booddhist monuments. Physical aspect is plain interspersed by hills. Regar [q.v.] soil predominates. Agriculture and silk-weaving industries. Commerce in silk cloths, cotton [q.v.] and lamp-oil [q.v.] seeds. The Moonair with its tributary the Varair and also the Palair flow from the north through this talook and enter the Kistna. Irrigation from rainfed tanks [q.v.] and a few channels [q.v.] from the Moonair. Camping grounds :—Comarabanda, Cunchacacherla, Maudhavaram, Moongaula, Nawaubpett, Nundigauma, Shermahomedpett. Places of archæological interest :—Adivy rowlapaud,

Anoomanchipully, Rabbellapaud, Bheemavaram, Boodavanda, Conacanchy, Cowtavaury agrahauram, Cunchacacherla, Cunchala, Goodimetla, Jayantipooram, Joojjoor, Juggayapett, Malacaupooram, Mooctyaula, Moonagaulapully, Mooppaula, Nawaubpett, Partiaul, Peddavaram, Penooganchiprole, Pokkoonore, Polampulley, Ramreddipully hill, Rauvairila, Rauvoolapaud, Sowtapully, Vedaudry. Trig. stations :—Chintalpaud, Joojjoor droog, Rungapooram, Zonnalagudda. The leading places, &c., in the talook are the following.——*Boodavauda* (బూదవాడ - búdaváda, Tel.). From (búda, tel. milk-vessel + váda, tel. village). Village; pop. 291; acres 5,035; lat. 16° 53′; long. 80° 04′; from Masulipatam W.N.W. 84 miles; from Nundigauma W. 18 miles. Ruins of an ancient village inhabited by Booddhists. Stone circle and dolmens [coday cull]. East is a temple of Mootyaulamman.——*Chintalpaud* (చింతలపాడు - chintalapádu, Tel. chintalapád *). From (chinta, tel. tamarind, tamarindus indica, linn. + pádu, tel. village). Trig. station; lat. 16° 39′ 53·07″; long. 80° 17′ 24·55″; height 194 feet; from Nundigauma S.S.W. 8 miles; from Yaitore N.W. 4 miles.——*Conacanchy* (కోనకంచి - kónakanchi, Tel.). From (kóna, tel. hill valley + kanchi, tel. place so called). Village; pop. 1,692; acres 4,664; lat. 16° 49′; long. 80° 15′; from Masulipatam N.W. 73 miles; from Nundigauma N.W. 7 miles. Inscriptions.——*Cunchacacherla* (కంచకచర్ల - kanchakacherla, Tel.). See sep. title.——*Joojjoor droog* (జుజ్జూరుదుర్గము - dzuddzúrudurgamu, Tel.). From (dzudzuru, tel. cluster + durga, san. hill). Trig. station; lat. 16° 42′ 25·54″; long. 80° 30′ 35·09″; height 1,791 feet; from Joojjoor S.E. 4 miles; from Nundigauma E. 13 miles.——*Juggayapett* (జగ్గయ్యపేట - jaggayyapéta, Tel.). See sep. title.——*Kistna* (కృష్ణ - krishna, Tel.). See sep. title.——*Lingagherry* (లింగగిరి - lingagiri, Tel.). See sep. title.——*Mooctyaula* (ముక్త్యాల - muktyála, Tel.). From (mukti, san. absolution + álaya, san. abode). Village; pop. 696; acres 3,700; lat. 16° 49′; long. 80° 07′; from Masulipatam W.N.W. 82 miles; from Nundigauma W. 14 miles. On the Kistna. Residence of the zemindar of Chintapully. Ancient village site with remains of foundation of temple. Close by are dolmens [coday cull] and stone circles [azhauram]. Five inscriptions, two in the Vishnoo and three in the Shiva temple.——*Moonair* (మునియేరు - muniyéru, Tel.). See sep. title.——*Moongaula* (మునగాల - munagála, Tel.). See sep. title.——*Nundigauma* (నందిగామ - nandigáma, Tel.). See below.——*Palair* (పాలేరు - páléru, Tel.). See sep. title.——*Partiaul* (పర్తియాల - partiyála, Tel.). See sep. title.——*Penooganchiprole* (పెనుగంచిప్రోలు - penuganchipr6lu, Tel.). From (penu, tel. great + kancha, tel. hedge + prólu, tel. town). Village; pop. 3,959; acres 9,588; lat. 16° 54′; long. 80° 17′; from Masulipatam N.W. 77 miles; from Nundigauma N.N.W. 9 miles. Inscription dated 1620.——*Raghavapooram* (రాఘవపురము - rághavapuramu, Tel.). From (rághava, san. ráma the hero + pura, san. town). Village; pop. 1,504; acres 3,291; lat. 16° 46′; long. 80° 21′; from Masulipatam N.W. 66 miles; from Nundigauma E. 2 miles. Remains of a fort built in 1686 by Vasireddy chowdaury ramayya. Church mission society station with about eight hundred Christians. Ramreddipully hill lies north.——*Rungapooram* (రంగాపురము - rangápuramu, Tel.). From (ranga, san. the god + pura, san. town). Trig. station; lat. 16° 46′ 16·92″; long. 80° 21′ 22·04″; height 574 feet.——*Zonnalagudda* (జొన్నలగడ్డ - dzonnalagadda, Tel.). From (dzonna, tel. millet, sorghum vulgare, pers. + gadda, tel. mound). Trig. station; lat. 16° 51′ 38·52″; long. 80° 21′ 22·73″; height 564 feet; from Zonnalagudda W. 1¼ miles; from Nundigauma N.N.E. 6 miles.——(2) Village, Talook head-quarters, Sub-registry office; Kistna dist., Nundigauma tal.; pop. 3,064; acres 6,987; lat. 16° 46′; long. 80° 20′; from Bezwada N.W. 28 miles; from Guntoor N.N.W. 35 miles; from Madras N. 254 miles; from Masulipatam N.W. 66 miles; from Vinoocondah N.E. 60 miles. Formerly zemindarry [q.v.] village.

NUNDOO (कर्कटक - karkataka, *San.*; سرطان - sartán, *Ar.*; خرچنگ - kharchang, *Pers.*; کیکڑا - kekrá, *Hind.*; ನಳ್ಳಿ - nalli, *Can.*; ఎండ్రకాయ - endrakáya, *Tel.*; ഞണ്ട് - ñantu, *Mal.*; நண்டு - nandu, *Tam.*). Title from tamul. San. from (karka, san. beauty). Ar. from (surata, ar. to swallow). Pers. from (khar, pers. rough + chang, pers. claw). Hind. from (karkata, san. crab). Can. from (nali, can. smooth). Tel. from (endu, tel. to dry + káya, tel. fruit); from the dry appearance. Crab. Cancer pagurus of naturalists [jautoo, kavachiny]. The one commonly met with here differs from the English black-clawed crab; being smaller, and the claws not so dark-colored. Good and edible at proper season on Coromandel coast [q.v.]. Not used by veidyans [q.v.]. The following are the chief kinds.——*Cadal nundoo* (கடல்நண்டு - kadalnandu, Tam.). From (kadal, tam. sea). Sea-crab.——*Cadookye nundoo* (கடுக்காய்நண்டு - kadukkáynandu, Tam.). From (kadukkáy, tam. indian gallnut). Small crabs size of gallnuts [chebulic myrobalan], used in broth, medicinally.——*Coola nundoo* (குளநண்டு - kulanandu, Tam.). From (kulam, tam. tank). Small tank crab.——*Neelacauly nundoo* (நீலக்காலிநண்டு - nílakkálinandu, Tam.). From (nílam, tam. blue + kál, tam. leg). Blue legged.——*Orcaul nundoo* (ஒருகால்நண்டு - orugálnandu, Tam.). From (oru, tam. one + kál, tam. leg). With one claw only.——*Pee nundoo* (பீநண்டு - pínandu, Tam.). From (pí, tam. dung). Common, found in holes in moist ground.——*Shembauray nundoo* (செம்பாறைநண்டு - shembárainandu, Tam.). From (shem, tam. red + párai, tam. rock). Large and red.——*Tillay nundoo* (தில்லைநண்டு - tillainandu, Tam.). From (tillai, tam. the tree, excæcaria agallocha, müller). Black, found under the Tillay [tiger's milk] tree on the seashore.——*Vayal nundoo* (വയൽഞണ്ട് - vayalñantu, Mal.; வயல்நண்டு - vayalnandu, Tam.). From (vayal, tam. field). Fresh water, found in the fields. Also called Cazhany nundoo.——*Vellay nundoo* (வெள்ளைநண்டு - vellainandu, Tam.). From (vellai, tam. white). Whitish. Also called Paul nundoo or Milk-crab, from its color.

NUNJOO (நஞ்சு - nanju, *Tam.*). Poison. Frequently appears in proper names as a contraction for Nunjoondan or shiva, the poison-eater.——*Nunjammah* (ನಂಜಮ್ಮ - nanjamma, Can.). From (nanju, can. short for nanjundappa, can. shiva, the poison lord + amma, can. mother, feminine suffix, titular affix). Familiarly Nunja, Nunjoo. Hill-tribe female proper name [peyar].——*Nunjappan* (ನಂಜಪ್ಪ - nanjappa, Can.). From (nañju, can. poison + appa, can. father, masculine suffix). Shiva, the poison lord, as having drunk poison [neelacuntan]. Familiarly Nunja, Nunjoo. Hindoo 2nd or pers. name [peyar].——*Nunjoondam* (खरपेंढरी - kharapéndharí, Mahr.; ಬೊಂಗೆರಿ - bongeri, Can.; ఉడిమంజ - udimanja, Tel.; ବମେନିୟା - bameniyá, Oor.; நஞ்சுண்டமரம் - nañjundamaram, Tam.). Title from tamul. Mahr. from (khara, mahr. dirt + péndharí, mahr. the shrub). Can. from (bonge, can. hole). Tam. from (nañju, tam. poison + un, tam. to eat + maram, tam. tree). Botanically Gardenia [gandharajah] turgida, roxb., rubiaceæ [vricsham, 71]. Deciduous; branches rigid, robust; bark pale; leaves 1–4 inches; narrowed into a short petiole, pale when dry; stipules triangular, caducous; calyx of male flower small ⅛ inch; mouth wide truncate; of female flower ⅓–⅔ inch, limb shortly campanulate; teeth oblong, or sub-spathulate, foliaceous; corolla white, fragrant; tube slightly dilated upwards, ⅓–½ inch long; limb 1 inch diameter; fruit 1–3 inches, ovoid, or globose, smooth, pericarp thick; endocarp woody, shining within; placentas five or six. Small armed tree or large shrub, flowers large white fragrant; wood close-grained, hard white with a purplish tinge, no heart-wood; annual rings indistinct; good but splits and cracks in seasoning; there is a variety montana.——*Nunjoondan* (ನಂಜುಂಡ - nanjunda, Can.). From (nañju, can. poison + unnu, can. to eat). Shiva, the poison-eater [neelacuntan], who is worshipped in this character as Nunjoondeshwaran in Nanjangode in mysore. Familiarly Nunjoo, Nunja. Hindoo 2nd or pers. name [peyar].——*Nunjooraikandan* (நஞ்சுறைக்கண்டன் - nañjuraikkandan, Tam.). From (above + urai, tam. abode + kant'ha, san. neck). Shiva [neelacuntan].

NUNNILAM (நன்னிலம் - nannilam, * *Tam.*). From (nal, tam. good + nilam, tam. soil) [nul].——(1) Talook, Tanjore district. Tahsildar's pay Rs. 250. Area 293 square miles. Population 215,907. Language Tamul. Inland centre part of district. Boundaries; north Mayavaram talook, east Caricaul territory, south Negapatam and Munnargoody talooks, west Combaconam talook. Flat level. Soil, black clayey. Agriculture and cloth weaving. Irrigation by Arasilaur, Moodicondanaur, Prauvidayanaur, Trimalrajanaur, Valappaur, Vettaur. Places of archæological interest :—Covilputt, Nunnilam, Shreevaunjyam, Teevangoody, Tirvilimooyalay, Tricalavore, Trichengauttangoody, Tricunnamangay, Tricunnapooram, Tripoogalore. The leading places, &c., in the talook are the following.——*Autalaiyore* (ஆத்தலையூர் - áttalaiyúr, Tam.). From (á, tam. cow + talai, tam. field + úr, tam. village). Village; pop. 1,621; acres 760; lat. 10° 53′; long. 79° 43′; from Nunnilam E. 4 miles; from Tanjore E.N.E. 43 miles.——*Codavausal* (குடவாசல் - kudavásal, Tam.). See sep. title.——*Coolicaray* (குளிக்கரை - kulikkarai, Tam. kulikarai *). From (kuzhi, tam. hollow + karai, tam. boundary). Village, Railway station; pop. 587; acres 867; lat. 10° 46′; long. 79° 38′; height 47 feet; from Nunnilam S.S.W. 8 miles; from Tanjore E. 29 miles.——*Coondalore* (கூந்தலூர் - kúndalúr, Tam.). From (kúndal, tam. palmyra leaf + úr, tam. village). Village; pop. 1,016; acres 994; lat. 10° 56′; long. 79° 35′; from Nunnilam W.N.W. 7 miles; from Tanjore E.N.E. 28 miles.——*Cundramaunicem* (கண்டராமாணிக்கம் - kandaramánikkam, Tam.). From (kandu, tam. found + edutta, tam. taken + mánikkam, tam. gem). Village; pop. 1,435; acres 1,241; lat. 10° 55′; long. 79° 34′; from Nunnilam W.N.W. 7 miles; from Tanjore E.N.E. 27 miles. An old Vishnoo temple.——*Moodicondaun* (முடிகொண்டான் - mudigondán, Tam.). From (mudi, tam. crown + kondán, tam. wearer). Sanscrit name (makutapura), meaning crown + town; also (makutéshvara), meaning crown + lord or shiva, the peak lord. Village; pop. 2,344; acres 1,912; lat. 10° 54′; long. 79° 41′; from Nunnilam N.E. 3 miles; from Tanjore E.N.E. 35 miles. A Shiva temple.——*Nunnilam* (நன்னிலம் - nannilam, Tam.). See below.——*Prauvidayanaur* (பிறவிடையாறு - pirávidaiyanáru, Tam.). See sep. title.——*Sectaur* (சித்தாறு - shittáru, Tam.). See sep. title.——*Shreevaunjyam* (ஸ்ரீவாஞ்சியம் - shirívánjiyam, Tam.). From (shrí, san. holy + váñchhya, san.

desirable). Village, Place of pilgrimage; pop. 1,571; acres 1,065; lat 10° 52′; long. 79° 37′; from Nunnilam W. 3 miles; from Tanjore E.N.E. 29 miles. Old Shiva temple. Sacred tank resorted to for bathing on Sundays in Caurtigay [mausam] or November.——*Trichengauttangoody* (திருச்செங்காட்டாங் குடி - tiruççengáttángudi, Tam.). From (tiru, tam. beautiful + shem, tam. red + kádu, tam. jungle + kudi, tam. place); called after shiva consecrated in shengaud or red forest. Tam. also (shengádu), (shengáttángudi), meaning shiva of the red forest + village. Village; pop. 974; acres 828; lat. 10° 52′; long. 79° 46′; from Nunnilam E. 8 miles; from Tanjore E.N.E. 40 miles. Old Shiva temple.——*Tricunnapooram* (திருக்கண்ணப்புரம் - tirukkannappuram, Tam.). From (tiru, tam. beautiful + kannan, tam. god krishna + pura, san. city). Village; pop. 1,381; acres 1,557; lat. 10° 52′; long. 79° 45′; from Nunnilam E. 6 miles; from Tanjore E.N.E. 39 miles. Old Vishnoo temple.——*Tripoogalore* (திருப்புகளூர் - tirappugalúr, Tam.). From (tiru, tam. holy + pugazh, tam. praise + úr, tam. village). Tam. also (pugalúr), praise + town. Village; pop. 1,416; acres 1,072; lat. 10° 53′; long. 79° 45′; from Nunnilam E. 6 miles; from Tanjore E.N.E. 39 miles. Old Shiva temple. ——**(2)** Village; talook head-quarters; Tanjore dist., Nunnilam tal.; pop. 2,758; acres 1,158; lat. 10° 53′; long. 79° 40′; from Combaconam E.S.E. 16 miles; from Madras S.S.W. 156 miles; from Mayavaram S.S.W. 16 miles; from Munnargoody N.E. 18 miles; from Negapatam W.N.W. 18 miles; from Tanjore E.N.E. 32 miles. Old Shiva temple.

NUNNOOL (நன்னூல் - nannúl, *Tam.*). From (nal, tam. good + núl, tam. treatise) [nul]. Cf. French belles lettres and Latin literæ humaniores. Work on tamul grammar [lacshanam, vyaucaranam] by Pavanandy [q.v.] independent of Paniny [q.v.]. The most learned tamul work. Cf. Cooral for ethics, and tamul Ramayanam and Chintaumany for epic style. Follows the plan of Tolgauppyam [q.v.], which in turn is based on Agastyan's [q.v.] lost sootrams. Dedicated to Gungan, a petty chieftain of Madura country.——**(1)** The Nunnool consists theoretically of the six following portions.—"*a*" *Pauyiram* (பாயிரம் - páyiram, Tam.). Preface sub-divided into Pothoo pauyiram or general preface and Shirapp pauyiram or special preface. The writer of a preface to any work and the author of the work itself are not identical in Indian writings. The person from whom the preface to Nunnool proceeded was a pupil of Pavanandy. It is much the most generally interesting part. "i" In the general preface, the writer treats on the five following subjects:—the nature of a classical work, the character and qualifications of a teacher, the method of teaching, the character and qualifications of the scholar, and the conduct of scholars during the time of instruction. He writes largely on the first subject. All works, he says, are of three kinds; primary, supplemental, and deducive. The primary work originates from the deity, who is of perfect and infinite understanding. There is no wisdom without revelation. Supplemental and deducive works are human, but must be in accordance with the divine. Original communications should be quoted in all their purity and integrity. He enumerates seven principles or characteristics of authorship, viz., consent, dissent, neutrality, originality, selection, criticism, and dogmatism. He specifies ten defects and ten beauties of language. The defects are:—brevity, redundancy, tautology, contradiction, vulgarisms, ambiguity, weakness, irrelevancy, inappropriate transitions, and unintelligibleness. The ten beauties are:—conciseness, clearness or comprehensiveness, agreeableness, use of appropriate words, harmony, profundity, method, respect for standard authorities, choice of proper subjects, and illustrations. He enumerates thirty-two canons of criticism. True criticism, he says among other things, consists first in showing the consistency of the subject of a work with generally received opinions as well as with those of approved authors, and secondly in a nicety of judgment by the exercise of which fit places are awarded to appropriate topics. His definition of a sootram is to the effect that it contains as much matter in as few words as possible, and still the force and minuteness of the same is so unaffected thereby that they appear as clear as the reflexion of an object in a mirror. In his estimation a commentary should contain fourteen particulars:—the text, its purport, its several bearings, definition, divisions, examples, objections, answers, explanatory notes, analysis, paraphrase, dogma, advantage, and proof. "ii" In the particular preface, the writer treats on various subjects regarding authorship and the art of book-making. A work is to be named from the nature of its contents, the name of the author, the character of the metre or style in which it is written, or according to the author's option or fancy. There are four ways in which a book may be produced; by abridgment, by enlargement, by a union of both, and by translation. A preface should not be written by the author himself, at least that part of the preface which must be necessarily egotistic, but by the author's tutor, or a fellow student, or a pupil, or by a fit commentator or editor. There are circumstances however when a man may praise himself. They are, when appeal is made to a superior for support; when it is necessary to make known one's own worth; and when railed at for ignorance by opponents.—"*b*" *Yezhoot adhicauram* (எழுத்ததிகாரம் - ezhuttathigáram, Tam.). From (ezhuttu, tam. letter + adhikára, san. subject). Orthography, comprising:—Yezhoottiyal and Pathaviyal, denominated caroovy or theoretic orthography; Ooyireett poonariyal; Meyyeett poonariyal; Ooroopp poonariyal, designated sheygay or practical orthography. Written by Pavanandy.—"*c*" *Shol adhicauram* (சொல்லதிகாரம் - shollathigáram, Tam.). From (shol, tam. word + adhikára, san. subject). Consisting of:—Peyariyal, of nouns; Vinayiyal, of verbs; Pothooviyal, of parts of speech in general; Ideitcholliyal, of affixes, prefixes, and unmeaning particles; Ooritcholliyal, of adjectives and adverbs. Written by Pavanandy.—"*d*" *Porool* (பொருள் - porul, Tam.). From (poru, tam. to unite with). Matter; or the mode in which, by uniting words, a discourse is formed. This head treats on amplification, the affections of the mind, &c. It is sub-divided into agaporool, and pooraporool; that is to say, into matter interior and exterior. The former relates to the passions and affections of the mind, which act on man internally; the latter, to things external to man. This portion was since written by Naurcaviraja numby.—"*e*" *Yaup* (யாப்பு - yáppu, Tam.). From (yá, tam. to bind). Versification. The Tamul writers confine their remarks on this head to the subject of prosody, and say nothing of the art of poetry. This portion was since written by Amrita saugaran.—"*f*" *Any* (அணி - ani, Tam.). Embellishment. This head treats on tropes and figures. Written by Dandy.——**(2)** The five heads beyond the preface are called in sanscrit Puncha lutchanam. The writer lays down rules, and then gives the exceptions in minute detail. The five parts are comprised in the following line:—எழுத்துச்சொற்பொருளி யாப்பணி.——**(3)** There have been various commentators on the Nunnool; the most popular one is that by Shuncara namashivauyan, a native of Tinnevelly.

NURM (نرم - narm, *Hind.*). From (narma, san. sport). Mild. ——*Nerbudda* (नर्मदा - narmadá, San.). From (narma, san. happiness + dá, san. to give). Called by Ptolemy ναμαδός. This river has from time immemorial marked the boundary between Upper and Southern india. It takes its source near the Vindhyam mountain in the province of Malwah and flows into the sea near Surat.——*Nurm gurm* (نرم گرم - narmgarm, Hind.). Literally mild and hot. Threats and persuasions alternating.

NUT OIL (پهلی کا تیل - phallíkátel, *Hind.*). Generally means oil from the Ground-nut.

NUTT (నట్టు - nattu, *Tel.*). Title otherwise Bent grass. Botanically Andropogon [beard grass] pilosus, wight., graminaceæ [vricsham, 156]. Alias Ischæmum pilosum. Diœcious; culms 4–5 feet, smooth; leaves glaucous, smooth; spikes terminal, fascicled, three to four together, white and hairy; sessile spikelet with the lower flower male, the upper female, pedicelled floret female, all bearded with long white hairs, upper valve of the female floret awned; glumes all minutely two-cleft; common in black soil.

NUTTAM (నత్తము - nattamu, *Tel.*; நத்தம் - nattam, *Tam.*). —"*a*" Land reserved for building ground and gardens, &c., above irrigation level. Inhabited by Shoodras, in opposition to an Agrahauram [q.v.]. Nuttamaur are a sub-division of Vellaula [q.v.]. Nuttapaul is a deserted village.—"*b*" Name of a village and Range of hills, Pass; Madura dist., Mailore tal.; pop. 4,017; acres 1,372; lat. 10° 13′; long. 78° 16′; from Madura N.N.E. 23 miles; from Mailore N.N.W. 15 miles. Formerly a road from Madura to Trichinopoly passed through, but was abandoned on account of fever.

NUTTAY (शम्बूक - shambúka, *San.*; گھونگا - ghungá, *Hind.*; ಬಸವನಹುಳ - basavanahula, *Can.*; నత్తగుల్ల - nattagulla, *Tel.*; അച്ചു - açça, *Mal.*; நத்தை - nattai, *Tam.*). Can. from (basava, can. bull + hula, can. worm); from its slow gait. Whelk. Buccinum, sp. of naturalists. The same tamul name is given to the eating snail or Helix pomatia [chippy].

NUTTER (نظہر - nathar, *Ar.*). From arabic. Purified. Name of a saint [walee] buried at Trichinopoly. Taken as alam; as Nutter beg, alam + alaumat [ism].——*Nutternagar* (نظہر نگر - natharnagar, Hind.). From (above + nagar, pers. city). Same as Trichinopoly.

NUZZER (نذر - nazr, *Ar.*). From (nazara, ar. to vow). Gift or offering. Prefixed to an alam makes a lacab; as Nuzzer ally, ally's gift; most taken by shiahs [ism]. Nuzzer is a ceremonial present from inferior to superior, converse of inam [q.v.].——*Nuzrauna* (نذرانہ - nazránah, Hind.). Sums exacted by the State on various occasions.——*Nuzzer o niyauz* (نذر و نیاز - nazrwaniyáz, Hind.). From (above + niyáz, ar. oblation). Vows and oblations:—"*a*" in the name of god [allah],—"*b*" in the name of the prophet [mahomed],—"*c*" in the name of companions,—"*d*" in the name of the saints [walee]. These are not observed on any fixed day, but each performs them according to the vow he has made.

NYAUNAM (ज्ञान - ñána, *San.*; ஞானம் - ñánam, *Tam.*). From (ñá, san. to know) [naumam]. Knowledge in general; knowledge of a specific and religious kind, that which is derived from meditation [dhauranay], and the study of philosophy [darshanam], which teaches man the divine nature and origin of his immaterial part [autmam], with unreality [mauyay] of corporeal enjoyments or worldly forms, and which separating him during life from terrestrial objects, secures him after death a final emancipation [mocsham] from existence and re-union [sauyoojyam] with the universal spirit [samsauram]. Nyaunam is also male and female proper name; taken by native christians by itself and in combination [peyar]. Suffix in proper names as Shivanyaunam.——*Nyauna caundam* (ज्ञानकाण्ड - ñánakánda, San.). From (above + kánda, san. section). Knowledge section. The esoteric portion of the Vedam [q.v.], as distinguished from exoteric portion Carma caundam or the section on ceremonies and works.——*Nyaunacunn* (ஞானக்கண் - ñánakkan, Tam.). From (above + kan, tam. eye). Proper name. Common among non-bramins and native christians [peyar].——*Nyaunamany* (ஞானமணி - ñánamani, Tam.). From (above + nani, san. gem). Hindoo 2nd or pers. name. Common among non-bramins. Epithet of Bramha [peyar].——*Nyauna moorty* (ज्ञानमूर्ति - ñánamúrti, San.). From (above + múrti, san. embodiment). Saraswaty [q.v.].——*Nyannapracausham* (ஞானப்பிரகாசம் - ñánappiragásam, Tam.). From (above + prakásha, san. shining). Hindoo 2nd or pers. name. Common among non-bramins [peyar].——*Nyauna prasoonaumba* (జ్ఞానప్రసూనాంబ - ñánaprasúnámba, Tel.). From (above + prasúna, san. flower + ambá, san. mother). Parvaty at Calastry.——*Nyauna sambandhan* (ஞானசம்பந்தன் - ñánasambandan, Tam.). From (above + sambandha, san. union). A Sheiveite bramin who visited Madura in the reign of the Paundya king Coon [soondra paundy tevar], and gained him over from the Jeina to the Sheiva sect. The Jeina [q.v.] or Shamanar [q.v.] followers, to the number of eight thousand, were then persecuted and hanged or banished. He instituted several monasteries. Some remain to this day, whose spiritual head has the title of Nyauna shiva acharry.——*Ngaunashikhaumany* (ஞானசிகாமணி - ñánasigámani, Tam.). From (above + shikhámani, san. crest jewel). Hindoo 2nd or pers. name. Common among non-bramins [peyar].——*Nyaunaubharanam* (ஞானாபரணம் - ñánábaranam, Tam.). From (above + ábharana, san. jewel). Hindoo 2nd or pers. name. Common among non-bramins [peyar].——*Nyaunaudhicam* (ஞானாதிகம் - ñánáthigam, Tam.). From (above + adhika, san. additional, superior), meaning having spiritual knowledge. Hindoo 2nd or pers. name. Common among non-bramins [peyar].——*Nyaunopadesham* (ज्ञानोपदेश - ñánópadésha, San.; ஞானோபதேசம் - ñánóbathésam, Tam.). From (above + upadésha, san. instruction). Spiritual instruction.——*Nyauny* (ज्ञानी - ñání, San.). From (ñána, san. wisdom). Bramha, the wise. Wise authors; as of Shiva vaucyam, Cooral, Neetisauram, &c.

NYAUYAM (न्याय - nyáya, *San.*). From (ni, san. prefix + i, san. to go); signifies going into a subject, that is to say investigating it analytically [ni].——**(1)** Justice, reason, propriety right, equity, rule, precept of morality, peculiar class of doctrine. Nyauya stalam is a Court of judicature. Nyauyaudhipaty is a Judge.——**(2)** One of the six schools of philosophy [darshanam]. Ascribed to Gowtaman [q.v.]. The Nyauyam is, as generally accepted, chiefly concerned with logic, but this is actually merely one part of a single topic. The Nyauyam proper differs from its later development, the Veishaishicam, by propounding sixteen topics in its first sootram.—"*a*" The first topic of these sixteen is Pramaunam, this is, the means or instruments by which pramay or the right measure of any subject is to be obtained. Under this head are enunciated the different processes by which the mind arrives at true and accurate knowledge. These processes are declared in the third sootram of the first book to be four, viz.:—Pratyacsham, perception by the senses, Anoomaunam, inference; Oopamaunam, comparison; Shabdam, verbal authority or trustworthy testimony, including vedic revelation. The treatment of the second of these, viz., inference, possesses special interest as indicating that the Hindoos have not, like other nations, borrowed their logic and metaphysics from the Greeks. Inference is divided into five Avayavams or members:—Pratinyay or proposition, stated hypothetically; Haitoo or the reason; Oodauharanam sometimes called Nidarshanam or example, equivalent to the minor premise; Nigamanam or conclusion, i.e., the pratinyay or proposition restated as proved. This method of splitting an inference or argument into five divisions is familiarly illustrated by native commentators thus. The hill is fiery; for it smokes; whatever smokes is fiery, as a kitchen-hearth; this hill smokes; therefore this hill is fiery. Here there is a combination of enthymeme and syllogism.—"*b*" The second topic of the Nyauyam is Prameyam, by which is meant all the objects or subjects of Pramay; those points, in short, about which correct knowledge is to be obtained. This topic includes all the most important subjects investigated by native philosophy. The Prameyam are twelve thus. Soul (átman); Body (sharíram); Senses (indriyam); Objects of sense (art'ham); Understanding or intellection (buddhi); Mind (manas); Activity (pravritti); Faults (dósham); Transmigration (prétyabhávam); Consequences or fruits (p'halam); Pain (duhkham); Emancipation (apavargam).—"*c*" With regard to the fourteen other topics, they are not so much philosophical categories as an enumeration of the regular stages through which a controversy is likely to pass. There is first the state of Samshayam or doubt about the point to be discussed. Next there must be a Prayojanam or motive for discussing it. Next a Drishtauntam or familiar example must be adduced in order that a siddhauntam or established conclusion may be arrived at. Then enters an objector with Avayavam or argument split up into five members. Next follows the Tarcam or refutation and reductio ad absurdum of such objection, and the Nirnayam or ascertainment of the true state of the case. But even a further vaudam or controversy takes place, which leads to Jalpam, wrangling, followed by; Vitanday, cavilling; Haitoo aubhausam, fallacious reasoning; Chalam, quibbling artifices; Jauty, futile replies; and Nigraha staunam, the putting an end to all discussion by a demonstration of the objector's incapacity for argument.—"*d*" The above are the sixteen topics. After enumerating them the system proceeds to state how deliverance from the misery of repeated birth is to be attained. Thus:—misery, birth, activity, fault, false notions; on the removal of these in turn, beginning with the last, there is the removal also of that which precedes it; then ensues final emancipation. That is to say, from false notions comes the fault of liking, disliking, or being indifferent to anything; from that fault proceeds activity; from this mistaken activity proceed actions involving either merit or demerit, which merit or demerit forces a man nolens volens to pass through repeated births for the sake of its reward or punishment. From these births proceed misery, and it is the aim of philosophy to correct the false notions at the root of this misery [samsauram]. See vol. I (74).

NYAYIR (ஞாயிறு - náyiru, *Tam.*). From (ñálu, tam. to drop + éru, tam. to rise); that which ascends and descends. Sun [sooryan].——*Nairam* (நேரம் - néram, Tam.). From (ñáyir, tam. sun). Time. Moonnairam is forenoon and Pinnairam is afternoon. The following is the scale:—2 jaumams or watches = 1 nairam or half day light, 2 nairams = 1 pagal or day light [caulam, 1]. Approximate actual value, 1 nairam = 6 European hours.——*Nyayit kizhamay vratam* (ஞாயிற்றுக்கிழமைவிரதம் - ñáyittukkizhamaivirathan, Tam.). From (ñáyiru, tam. sun + kizhamai, tam. day of the week + vrata, san. vow). Solar observance [pundigay, 6d]; a fast on sundays in honor of sun, for prevention and cure of diseases especially of eyes. This in the fifth solar month Auvany [mausam], i.e., between 15th August and 14th September, is specially meritorious [maryauday].

NYE (श्वान - shvána, *San.*; कुत्रा - kutrá, *Mahr.*; كلب - kalb, *Ar.*; سگ - sag, *Pers.*; كتا - kuttá, *Hind.*; انجنگ - anjing, *Malay*; ನಾಯಿ - náyi, *Can.* and *Too.*; కుక్క - kukka, *Tel.*; କୁକ୍କୁର - kukkura, *Oor.*; നായ - náya, *Mal.*; බල්ලා - ballá, *Singh.*; நாய் - náy, *Tam.*). Title from tamul. San. from (shvi, san. to go); as going to and fro. Hind. from (kukkura, san. dog). Tel. from (kukkura, san. dog). Ar. also (abúkhálid), meaning father of rats. Dog. Canis [shwaunam] familiaris, canidæ [cookooram], digitigrada, carnivora, mammalia [sastanam, 12], of naturalists [jantoo]. Plant first term, meaning wild or inferior. Ex., where transl. is of second term:—Achyranthes aspera (náyuruvi), piercing plant, from pricks; Atalantia monophylla (náyibéladamara), feronia elephantum, wood-apple; Carissa spinarum (náyikalamegida), carissa; Cleome viscosa (náyvélai), gynandropsis pentaphylla; Dillenia pentagyna (náyttékku), tectona grandis; Gynandropsis pentaphylla (náykkadugu), brassica juncea, mustard; Indigofera pentaphylla (náyppayaru), phaseolus mungo; Indigofera viscosa (náyvémbu), melia azadirachta; Ocimum canum (náyttulasi), ocimum sanctum; Tylophora asthmatica (náyppálai), milky plant; Urginia indica (náyulli), allium sativum. See gloss. paragraphs.——*Konye* (वृक - vrika, San.; लांडगा - lándagá, Mahr.; ذيب - zíb, Ar.; گرگ - gurg, Pers.; بھیڑیا - bheriyá, Hind.; لانڈگا - lándgá, Dec.; ತೋಳ - tóla, Can.; ಚೆಂನನಾಯಿ - chennanáyí, Too.; తోడేలు - tódélu, Tel.; ଢେଙ୍କ୍ୟ - dhenkya, Oor.; ചെന്നായ - chenáya, Mal.; கோநாய் - kónáy, Tam.). Title from tamul. San. from (vrik, san. to seize); the seizer. Mahr. from (landa, san. excrement); depreciatory. Too. from (channa, too. red + náyi, too. dog). Mal. from (chem, mal. red + náya, mal. dog). Tam. from (kó, tam. great + náy, tam. dog). Ar. also (abújadah), meaning father of curly hair. Hind. also (hundár); (nekra); (bighána). Title otherwise Indian wolf. Canis [shwaunam] pallipes, canidæ [cookooram], digitigrada, carnivora, mammalia [sastanam, 12], of naturalists [jantoo]. Alias Canis lupus. The Indian wolf is hoary fulvous or dirty reddish white, some of the hairs tipped black, which gives it a grizzled appearance; somewhat reddish on the face and limbs, the latter paler than the body; lower parts dingy white; tail thinly bushy, slightly black tipped. Ears rather small. Rare in wooded districts, abundant in open country. Wolves breed in holes in the ground, or caves, having only three or four young, it is said. Usually silent, but sometimes bark like a pariah dog [pye]. The howling after their prey, recorded of the European wolf, is seldom heard in India. The Indian wolf is somewhat inferior in size to the European one, and is probably less ferocious. Stories have been related of Indian wolves suckling young infants carried off. Wolves hunt in packs in the open plains, where there is no cover or concealment; they scrape a hole in the earth, in which one of the pack lies down and remains hid, while the others drive a herd of antelope [jinka] over him. Their chief prey however is sheep [aud]. Sometimes a large wolf is seen to seek his prey singly. These are reckoned particularly fierce. Wolves are not killed by native shikárries [q.v.], who consider that the gun which shoots a wolf will miss other animals. Indian species not here found are:—Laniger or thibetan wolf, Lupus or european wolf.——*Neernye* (उद्र - udra, San.; पाणिमांजर - pánimáñjara, Mahr.; سگ دریا - sagidaryá, Pers.; اود - úd, Hind.; پانی کاکتا - pánikákuttá, Dec.; مامبرنگ - mámbrang, Malay; ನೀರುನಾಯಿ - nírúnáyi, Can. and Too.; నీటికుక్క - nítikukka, Tel.; ଓଧ - lodna, Oor.; നീർനായ - nírnáya, Mal.; நீர்நாய் - nírnáy, Tam.). Title from tamul. San. from (ud, san. to wet). Mahr. from (páni, mahr. water + máñjara, mahr. cat). Pers. from (sag, pers. dog + daryá, pers. sea). Hind. from sanscrit. Dec. from (páni, hind. water + kuttá, hind. dog). Tam. from (nír, tam. water + náy, tam. dog). Mahr. also (jalamáñjara), meaning water + cat. Pers. also (gurbahiábí), meaning water cat; (sagiáb), meaning water dog. Hind. also (údbilás), meaning wet cat. Malay also (anjinglaut), meaning dog + sea. Tam. also (mínáy), meaning fish + dog. Title otherwise Otter. Lutra vulgaris, lutrinæ, mustelidæ, semi-plantigrada, carnivora, mammalia [sastanam, 8], of naturalists [jantoo]. Alias Lutra indica. Otters are a well marked group of animals, distinguished by their elongated and somewhat flattened form, short and stout limbs, with the toes well webbed and spreading, and with naked soles. The fur is close, fine and short, consisting of a woolly fur beneath, and a layer of smooth glossy hairs above. The eyes are provided with a nyctitating membrane, or additional half-transparent eyelid like that of birds, as a defence to them under water. The teeth are strong and sharp, and the tubercles of the molars very pointed, to secure their prey, which is almost entirely fish, which they hunt for and capture under water with wonderful activity and skill. The skull is said to have something in common with seals. Frequents alike rivers, and salt water inlets. It has its lair under large rocks, and, in alluvial countries, excavates extensive burrows; partly nocturnal in habits. On the Malabar coast it hunts in the sea. Indian species not here found are:—Aurobrunnea, Leptonyx or clawless otter, Ellioti.

O (ओ - ó, *San.*; و - wáu, *Hind.*; ஒ - o, ஓ - ó, *Tam.*). San. long for Bramha [q.v.]. Hind. numerically symbol for 6; Friday the sixth day of the week [vauram], sign [raushy] Libra [toolaum].

OART (ഓട - ótu, *Mal.*). Portuguese horta. Old Anglo-indian for garden [tote].

ODALAY (ஓதலை - óthalai, *Tam.*). From (ótham, tam. moisture + ali, tam. to preserve); as growing in dry land. Same as Catechu [q.v.] acacia [cantalam].

ODÉ (ஓடு - ódu, *Tam.*). To run.——*Oday* (ஓடை - ódai, Tam.). From (ódu, tam. to run). A water-course [caulvye, channel].——*Oodata* (ఉడత - udata, Tel.). From (ódu, tel. to run). Squirrel [anil].——*Oodatavaur* (ఉడతవారు - udataváru, Tel.). From (udata, tel. a squirrel). Poligar family. For skill in shooting a squirrel [anil], Lingam naidoo founder of family, was made poligar [q.v.] by rajah of Golcondah and gained this name. His jurisdiction was over 147 villages of Nellore, Goodoor, Atmacore and Raupore. Present poligar, tenth in descent.——*Ottapidauram* (ஓட்டப்பிடாரம் - óttappidáram, Tam.). See sep. title.

ODHRAM (ओड्र - ódra, *San.*). The northern part of Orissa [ootcalam, ooriya]. See vol. I (2).

ODUL (اودل - udar, *Hind.*; ಬಿಳಿದಾಳೆ - bilidále, *Can.*; ஓடல் - ódal, *Tam.*). Title from tamul. Hind. from tamul. Can. from (bili, can. white + táli, can. borassus flabelliformis, linn.); from white grey spongy wood. Tam. also (tanakku) [golden silk cotton, tanakk]; (ánainármaram), meaning elephant + fibre + tree; (vakkunármaram), meaning bark + rope + tree [sunu]. Title otherwise Aunay naur, Elephant rope tree, Wuck naur tree. Botanically Sterculia [cauvalam] villosa, roxb., sterculiaceæ [vricsham, 26]. Small tree; leaves deeply and palmately five to seven-lobed, under side soft, velvety, lobes acuminated, deeply toothed; calyx five-partite, patent; carpels coriaceous, rough, with stellate pubescence; flowers small, pale yellow, scarlet; flowering in march. Gives a white pellucid gum [gond]; only slightly soluble and has no adhesive properties. Bark yields a valuable fibre [naur], made into very strong ropes used by elephants [q.v.] to drag timber with; bags [gunny] also made from it. Wood grey, very soft and spongy. Distinguish from Odallam.

OHDAH (عہدہ - ohdah, *Hind.*). From (ahd, ar. agreement). An office [amal], civil or military.

OIL (تل - til, *Hind.*). Prefix.——*Oil-cake tree* (அரப்புமரம் - arappumaram, Tam.). Title from leaves being used to wash with, like mohwah [q.v.] oil cake [ponnauk]. Same as Dark sirissa.——*Oil plant* (تل کا جہاڑ - tilkájhár, Hind.). Same as Gingelly.

OKKALIGA (ಒಕ್ಕಲಿಗ - okkaliga, *Can.*). From (okkalu, can. tenancy). Low-caste laborers of Canara. Numbers about 50,000 [janty].

OKRO (اوکرو - okro, *Hind.*). W. indian word. Common bendy.

OLAY (تارکا پتا - tárkápattá, *Hind.*; తాటాకు - tátáku, *Tel.*; ഓല - óla, *Mal.*; ஓலை - ólai, *Tam.*). Tam. also (narukku), meaning a piece cut off, of olay; applied to an olay document or note of hand [chit]. Leaf of any palm [taur], especially for writing upon [cadjan]. Also worn by lower orders on lower lobe of ear [nagay]. For Olay paumb see Cadjan snake.

OLE (ఓలు - ólu, *Tel.*). Congregation. Suffix in place names as Madgole, meaning chuckler's association.

OLIBANUM (कुन्दुरुकी - kundurukí, *San.*; لبان - lubán, *Ar.*; பறங்கிச்சாம்பிராணி - parangiççámbiráni, *Tam.*). Title from hebrew lebonah, signifying milk. San. from (kundu, san. olibanum). Ar. from (laban, ar. juice). Tam. from (parangi, tam. european + shámbiráni, tam. frankincense). Greek λίβανος, Latin olibanum. Title otherwise Frankincense. A gum resin [googal]. Product of the Boswellia genus, burseraceæ [vricsham, 35]; balsamiferous trees; leaves compound; flowers white, in clusters; fruit triangular and three-celled; seeds compressed and winged. The species best known to the natives are:—carterii [true olibanum], serrata [indian olibanum], serrata, var. glabra [yellow dammer]. The product is gummi-resina olibanum, thus masculum, of chemists. Occurs in semi-transparent tears of light yellow color; brittle and adhesive when warm; in taste bitterish and somewhat pungent and aromatic; when burnt very fragrant, and as such used as an incense [ood]; in medicine stimulant, astringent and diaphoretic. Cf. and distinguish the Bdellium [q.v.] trees, which are Balsamodendrons.——*Indian olibanum* (सल्लकी - sallakí, San.; सालई - sálaí, Mahr.; विशेषधूप - vishéshadhúmpu, Conc.; لبان - lubán, Ar.; کندر - kundur, Pers. and Hind.; کندر کا جہاڑ - kundurkájhár, Dec.; ವಿಶೇಷಧೂಪದಮರ - vishéshadhúpadamara, Can.; అందుగు - andugu, Tel.; വെള്ളക്കുന്തുരുക്കം - vellakkunturukkam, Mal.; හල් - hal, Singh.; குந்துருக்கம் - kundurukkam, Tam.). San. from (shall, san. to go); as yielding gum. Mahr. from sanscrit. Conc. from (vishésha, san. distinction + dhúpa, san. incense); as yielding good incense. Ar. from (laban, ar. juice). Dec. from (kundur, ar. olibanum + jhár, hind. tree). Can. from (vishésha, san. distinction + dhúpa, san. incense + mara, can. tree). Tel. from (andukonu, tel. to take fire); incense. Mal. from (vella, mal. white + kunduruka, san. frankincense). Tam. from (kunduruka, san. olibanum) [piney, piney dammer, yellow dammer]. San. also (surabhi), meaning fragrant; (gajabhakshyá), meaning eaten by elephants; cf. peepul; (kundurukí), meaning producing coondoor; (hládiní), meaning delightening; (kunduru); (sálashi). Ar. also (kundur); (kundurizakr), meaning male olibanum; (bastaj). Hind. also (avalkundur), meaning olibanum of first sort; (sálgá); (sálhe); (gandaberoza), meaning turpentine from similarity of consistence when fresh from tree [ganda firoza]. Can. also (chittu). Mal. also (kuntirukkam); (chiténti). Singh. also (hadumula). Tam. also (kungiliyam) [yellow dammer]; (parangisámbiráni), meaning european + frankincense. Title otherwise Indian frankincense, Lobaun, Male olibanum, Ood, Salye. Botanically Boswellia [olibanum] serrata, roxb., burseraceæ [vricsham, 35]. Alias Boswellia thurifera; Libanus thurifera. Large tree; leaves unequally pinnated; leaflets oblong, obtuse, serrated, pubescent; racemes axillary, single, shorter than the leaves; calyx five-toothed; petals five; flowers small, white; flowering in march and april; seeds solitary, with a winged membrane; capsule three-angled. The gum-resin [googal] is distributed through the leaves and bark, and even exudes as a milky juice from the flowers; it occurs as a transparent golden yellow, semi-fluid substance, which slowly hardens with time; it is pungent, having a slightly aromatic taste and balsamic resinous odour; it becomes opaque when immersed in alcohol or in water; the opaque, soft, whitish mass produced by water when rubbed in a mortar forms an emulsion. The gum-resin is medicinally internal and external stimulant, expectorant, stimulant-diuretic and stomachic; also a slight hepatic stimulant; substituted for benzoate of soda, gummi-rubrum [australian gum tree], gum-ammoniacum [ooshak] and abietis resina. Used as incense in roman catholic and greek churches. Wood rough, white when fresh cut, darkening on exposure, moderately hard; used for fuel and for making charcoal [adooppkary].——*Male olibanum* (کندر ذکر - kundurizakr, Ar.). Same as Indian olibanum.——*True olibanum* (कुन्दुरुकी - kundurukí, San.; साळी - sálí, Mahr.; سلائی - salái, Hind.; لبان کا جہاڑ - lubánkájhár, Dec.; பறங்கிச்சாம்பிராணிமரம் - parangiççámbiránimaram, Tam.). San. from (kundu, san. olibanum). Mahr. from (sallakí, san. boswellia serrata, roxb.). Hind. like mahratta. Dec. from (lubán, ar. olibanum + jhár, hind. tree). Tam. from (parangi, tam. european + shámbiráni, tam. frankincense, boswellia serrata, roxb. +

maram, tam. tree). San. also (pálankí), meaning brought up by protection [paulak]; (kunda); (mukunda); (sallakí), meaning gum-yielding tree. Hind. also (gandaberoza), meaning turpentine. Title otherwise Coondoor tree, Foreign sambrauny, Ganda firoza, Lobaun, Male frankincense, Ood, True frankincense. The best or medicinal product is called Male frankincense. Resin [raul] in tears is known as Coondoor, but in soft masses is called Ganda firoza [q.v.]. Botanically Boswellia [olibanum] carterii, bird., burseraceæ [vricsham, 35]. Middling-sized tree of the northern somauly country in africa and of southern arabia; cape guardafui used to be called promontorium aromatum. The stem gives the gum-resin [googal], true olibanum; as this flows from the tree, it is of the consistence of turpentine [carpoora teilam], a clear greenish color; when dry it consists of tears often an inch in length and of an ovate or oblong, clavate or stalactitic form, and mixed with impurities; the pieces are light yellow to brown or pale green or colorless; the odour is balsamic and resinous, especially while being burned; taste is bitter and terebinthinous, and the resin softens in the mouth; adhesive when warm; when burnt it flames with steady clear light but dense smoke, not easily extinguished, burns for a long time leaving behind a black ash not whitish; it is not perfectly soluble in water or alcohol; the powder is citron yellow; frequently adulterated by dammer [q.v.], sandrach [q.v.], and other cheaper resins [raul]. Very ancient commercial commodity. In pharm. a terebinthinate stimulant, action directed on the mucous membrane, especially of the lungs; preparation, unguentum olibani; officinal; substituted for british ammoniacum. Continues, unless when its place is supplied by the javanese product benzoin [q.v.], to perfume the churches, mosques [q.v.], and temples of europe and asia. Several other species yield true olibanum.——*Turkish olibanum* (كندرورومى - kundurirúmí, Pers.). Same as Mastic.

OLIVE WOOD (زيتون كى لكڑى - zaitúnkílakrí, *Hind.*). From similar wood. Same as Nerija.

OLLUCK (ஆழாக்கு - ázhákku, *Tam.*). From (arai, tam. half + ozhakku, tam. the measure) [oyak]. Tamul form of Ayak [q.v.]. Measure of capacity. 8 ollucks = 1 puddy [alavay, 3a, d]. Approximate actual value, 1 olluck = 12½ cubic inches. Used in Madras. Equal to $\frac{1}{20}$th of a gallon. Compare Nowtauk. See vol. I, 609; II, 514.

OLOOGOO (ഒഴുക - ozhuku, *Mal.*; ஒழுங்கு - ozhungu, *Tam.*). From (ozhugu, tam. to act according to rule). Boundary; and so register of the measurement and extent of fields and holdings [adungal]. Standard; and so a standard rate for assessment [teervay], for price of grain [agavilay], &c. As a method for making the demand in ryotwarry [q.v.] see vol. I, 124, 136.

OM (ओम् - óm, *San.*). An antiquated form of ayam, That one or He. Later taken to represent the vedic trinity of Adity [q.v.], Varoonan [q.v.], and Mitran [q.v.]. Later again taken to be from (a, san. vishnu + u, san. shiva + ma, san. brahma). Compare the greek ὀμφή, and the arabic and hebrew Amen. A mystic ejaculation uttered in place of naming the supreme being [bramh] or the supreme spirit poorsham [q.v.]. The hand is placed before the mouth while saying it, or it is pronounced inaudibly. A Bramin beginning or ending any holy exposition must always pronounce the syllable. It is also placed at the beginning of books. A whole chapter of the Vayoo pooraunam [q.v.] is devoted to this term. It is said to typify the three spheres of the world [trilocam], the three holy fires, the three Vedams [q.v.], the three steps of Vishnoo [q.v.], &c. In the Devanagry [q.v.] and Grantam [q.v.] alphabets, it is expressed by a triple sound in one character [pranavam]. It is common to all classes of Hindoos, and so was historically antecedent to the five letters of the Sheivas [punchaucsharam], or eight of the Veishnavas [muntram]. The Booddhists [booddha] also use it [matam]. See vol. I (92).——*Omcauram* (ओंकार - ómkára, San.). From (above + kára, san. sound). The syllable om.——*Omnamo narayanauya* (ओंनमोनारायणाय - ómnamónáráyanáya, San.). From (above + namas, san. salutation + náráyana, san. vishnu). Salutation to Vishnoo [q.v.].——*Omramauya nama* (ओंरामायनमः - ómrámáyanamah, San.). From (above + ráma, san. the god + namas, san. salutation). Salutation to Rama [q.v.].——*Ómtatsat* (ओंतत्सत् - ómtatsat, San.). From (above + tat, san. that + sat, san. reality). A muntram [q.v.].——*Oncauly* (ఓంకాళి - ómkáli, Tel.). From (above + káli, san. the deity). Deity [cauly].

OMALORE (ஓமலூர் - ómalúr, *Tam.* omalúr *). From (váma, san. shiva + úr, tam. village). Otherwise Walmere. Village, Deputy tahsildar's station; Salem dist., Salem tal.; pop. 1,158; acres 1,907; lat. 11° 45′; long. 78° 05′; from Madras S.W. 175 miles; from Namcull N.W. 37 miles; from Oossoor S.E. 70 miles; from Salem N.W. 10 miles; from Tripatore S. 63 miles; from Yercaud S.W. 12 miles. On bank of Sharabhunganuddy. Formerly a petty chieftainship. Old Shiva temple with inscriptions [shausanam]. Fort.

OMAM (ಓಮ - óma, *Can.*; ஓமம் - ómam, *Tam.*). From (yamáni, san. the plant). Bishop weed seed [ajwaun].——*Omam-water* (ஓமத்திராவகம் - ómattirávagam, Tam.). From (above + drávaka, san. essence). Distilled from seeds.

ONGIL (ஓங்கில் - óngil, *Tam.*). From (óngu, tam. to rise to the surface + il, tam. not). Otherwise Tunny fish. There is a Tamul proverb:—ஆழமறியும் ஓங்கில் மேளம் அறியும் அரவம்—"the ongil fish is acquainted with depth, and the "snake knows the sound of a drum." And another:—ஓங்கில் அறியும் உயர் கடலின் ஆழம், பாங்கி அறிவாள் தன் பத்தாவின் வலிமை—"an ongil fish knows the depth of the "ocean, a wife knows her husband's strength."

ONGOLE * (వంగోలు - vangólu, *Tel.*). From (vangala, tel. proper name + prólu, tel. town); from house name of astrologer of an addanky rajah. Greek κόττις [cottapatam].——(1) Talook, Nellore district. Tahsildar's pay Rs. 200. N. coast part of district. Area 797 square miles. Bounded N. by Baupatla and Narsarowpett talooks in Kistna district, E. by Bay of Bengal, S. by Cundoocore. Zemindarry divisions of Darshy and Podily form the western limit. Little jungle. The extensive plains are devoted to unirrigated cultivation, and in consequence of the superior quality of the soil very fine crops are raised. Small hills at and near Ongole and in the Addanky division and a high group of hills at Cheemacoorty. The hills in Ongole contain good iron [auhan] stone. In Addanky division the soil consists of the best black-cotton soil [regar]. Most villages have good topes [q.v.]. The Great northern trunk road runs north to south through the talook and a branch takes off near Medaramittah to Hyderabad. A trunk road connecting Cottapatam with Cumbum runs through the talook from east to west. The cattle [maud] are finer than those in any other part of the district, and are famed throughout the presidency. Pulses [dholl] and oil-seeds [yennay] are largely exported. Intersected by Goondlacumma and Mooshy, and minor streams, viz., Coniky vaugoo, Inagalair and Moodigondy. Garden lands [totacaul] extend along the banks of the rivers, and the water is obtained from wells sunk in the beds. Streams are not made use of for irrigation. Gonasapoody and some adjoining villages are partly irrigated by water from Kistna canals. But few wells. Camping grounds:—Addanky, Alloor cottapatam, Ammanabrole, Canoopurty, Caurmanchy, Cheemacoorty, Dooddoocore, Eetamookkala, Inamanamelloor, Maddoolore, Ongole, Ramateertam, Rauvinootla, Santanootalapaud, Tangootore, Valaparla, Velampulley, Yendlore. Places of archæological interest:—Addanky, Canoopurty, Ongole, Pelloor. Principal trig. stations:—Cheemacoorty, Condalore, Conijaid, Medaramittah, Nishaunicondah, Ongole, Pashoomoodra beacon, Pautapaud beacon. The leading places, &c., in the talook are the following.——*Addanky* (అద్దంకి - addanki, Tel.). See sep. title.——*Ammanabrole* (అమ్మనబ్రోలు - ammanabrólu, Tel.). From (amma, tel. mother + prólu, tel. town); because water is sweet as mothers' milk. Village; pop. 3,250; acres 7,747; lat. 15° 35′; long. 80° 11′; from Nellore N.N.E. 78 miles; from Ongole N.E. 8 miles; from the sea W. 6 miles.——*Beeramgoonta* (బీరంగుంట - bíramgunta, Tel.). From (bíra, tel. luffa acutangula, roxb. + gunta, tel. pond). Village; pop. 188; lat. 15° 30′; long. 80° 13′; from Nellore N. 72 miles; from Ongole E. 8 miles; from the sea W. 3 miles. Formerly a salt [ooppoo] factory [cotaur]. Now a hamlet of Paudarty.——*Canoopurty* (కనుపర్తి - kanuparti, Tel.). See sep. title.——*Caravady* (కరవది - karavadi, Tel.). From (khara, san. a giant + vadha, san. destruction). Familiarly Carody. Sanscrit name (kharavadha), meaning kharan, the giant + killing. Village; lat. 15° 33′; long. 80° 10′; from Nellore N.N.E. 75 miles; from Ongole E.N.E. 5 miles; from the sea W. 7 miles. This village and Dasarauzpully are clubbed. It is said that the giant called Kharausooran the cousin of Ravanan was killed by Rama here [caramana].——*Caurmanchy* (కారుమంచి - kárumanchi, Tel.). From (káru, tel. season + manchi, tel. good). Village; pop. 2,414; acres 2,618; lat. 15° 23′; long. 80° 02′; from Nellore N. 64 miles; from Ongole S.S.W. 10 miles; from the sea W. 9 miles. On Mooshy. Remarkable for its breed of cattle [maud].——*Chedalvauda* (చెదలవాడ - chedalaváda, Tel.). From (chedalu, tel. white-ants + váda, tel. village). Village; pop. 1,198; acres 4,049; lat. 15° 37′; long. 80° 08′; from Nellore N. 80 miles; from Ongole N.N.E. 7 miles; from the sea W. 10 miles. On Goondlacumma. Temple of Vishnoo as Runganaick sawmy. Festival for ten days during Cheitram [mausam] or april. Dyeing [shauyam] of cloths is carried on.——*Cheemacoorty* (చీమకుర్తి - chímakurti, Tel.). See sep. title.——*Condalore* (కొండలూరు - kondalúru, Tel.). From (konda, tel. hill + úru, tel. village). Tel. also (konijédu), meaning corner + marsh. Trig. station; lat. 15° 26′ 16·93″; long. 80° 01′ 25·76″; height 383 feet; from Ongole S.W. 7 miles; from Tammavaram S. 19 miles; from the sea W. 12 miles.——*Conijaid* (కొనిజేడు - konijédu, Tel.). From (kona, tel. corner + jédu, tel. marsh). Village; pop. 2,506; acres 6,892; lat. 15° 27′; long. 80° 00′; from Nellore N. 68 miles; from Ongole W.S.W. 8 miles; from the sea W. 16 miles. Indigo [q.v.] manufacture. Trig. station in lat. 15° 27′ 9·48″; long. 80° 0′ 50·66″; from Conijaid E.N.E. 1¾ miles; from Ongole S.W. 6 miles.——*Cottapatam* (కొత్తపట్నం - kottapatnam, Tel.). See sep. title.——*Dasarauzpully* (దసరాజుపల్లి - dasarádzupalli, Tel.). From (dasarádzu, tel. proper name + palli, tel. village). Village; pop. 3,240; lat. 15° 32′; long. 80° 08′; from Nellore N. 75 miles; from Ongole E.N.E. 3 miles; from the sea W. 9 miles. A hamlet of Caravady.——*Eedoomoody* (ఈదుమూడి - ídumúdi, Tel.). From (íta, tel. date palm, phœnix farinifera, roxb. + púdi, tel. village). Village; pop. 1,142; acres 1,514; lat. 15° 43′; long. 80° 14′; from Nellore N. 88 miles; from Ongole N.E. 17 miles; from the sea W. 6 miles. Manufacture of white blankets [cumbly].——*Eetamookkala* (ఈతముక్కల - ítamukkala, Tel.). From (íta, tel. date palm, phœnix farinifera, roxb. + mukka, tel. portion). Village, Port; pop. 3,223; lat. 15° 23′; long. 80° 09′; from Cottapatam S.W. 6 miles; from Madras N. 155 miles; from Nellore N. 64 miles; from Ongole S.S.E. 10 miles; from Paucala N.N.E. 7 miles. Between Paucala and Paudarty. Resorted to chiefly by native craft. Anchorage good. Formerly a salt [ooppoo] factory [cotaur]. Village goddess is Jwaulamookhy. Festival for five days in Shraunvanam [mausam] or august.——*Goondamorla* (గుండమొర్ల - gundamorla, Tel.). From (gundu, tel. round + móra, tel. face). Village, Bay; lat. 15° 30′ N.; long. 80° 15′ E.; from Nellore N.N.E. 73 miles; from Ongole E. 10 miles. The bay is north of the village, about 2 miles south of the Goondlacumma river. Bar open throughout the year. Vessels formerly resorted to it as an anchorage during N.E. monsoon [q.v.]. A hamlet of Paudarty.——*Goondlacumma* (గుండ్లకమ్మ - gundlakamma, Tel.). See sep. title. ——*Inamanamelloor* (ఇనమనమెల్లూరు - inamanamellúru, Tel.). From (inumu, tel. iron + meda, tel. neck + úru, tel. village). Village; pop. 2,562; acres 5,041; lat. 15° 36′; long. 80° 07′; from Nellore N. 79 miles; from Ongole N.N.E. 7 miles; from the sea W. 11 miles. On right bank of Goondlacumma. Formerly head-quarters of a Tahsildar [q.v.]. Ruins of fort. Cloth dyeing [shauyam].——*Medaramittah* (మేదరమిట్ట - médaramitta, Tel.). From (médari, tel. basket-weaver + mitta, tel. mound). Village; pop. 2,717, the village is clubbed with Bodwauripollem; acres 8,130; lat. 15° 43′; long. 80° 04′; from Nellore N. 87 miles; from Ongole N. 15 miles; from the sea W. 17 miles. Trig. station in lat. 15° 43′ 54·04″; long. 80° 02′ 53·59″; height 568 feet; from Ongole N.N.W. 15 miles; from Tammavaram E.N.E. 3 miles; from the sea W. 19 miles.——*Meilavaram* (మైలవరము - mailavaramu, Tel.). From (máila, tel. dirt + pura, san. town). Village; pop. 308; acres 2,011; lat. 15° 39′; long. 80° 02′; from Nellore N. 82 miles; from Ongole N.N.W. 11 miles; from the sea W. 18 miles. Brass [pittalay] vessels manufactured.——*Mooshy* (ముశి - mushi, Tel.). See sep. title.——*Nidamanore* (నిడమనూరు - nidamanúru, Tel.). From (nidama, tel. long + úru, tel. village). Village; pop. 2,841; acres 3,541; lat. 15° 39′; long. 80° 07′; from Nellore N. 83 miles; from Ongole N. 10 miles; from the sea W. 13 miles. On Mooshy. Remarkable for breed of cattle [maud].——*Nishaunicondah* (నిశానికొండ - nisháníkonda, Tel.). From (nisháni, hind. signal + konda, tel. hill). Trig. station; lat. 15° 31′ 01·96″; long. 79° 37′ 12·62″; height 2,185 feet; from Irsaulagoondam E.S.E. 5 miles; from Ongole W. 31 miles; from the sea W. 42 miles.——*Ongole* (వంగోలు - vangólu, Tel.). See below.——*Pashoomoodra beacon* (పసుముద్ర - pasumudra, Tel.). From (pasulu, tel. cattle + mudra, tel. stamp). Trig. station; lat. 15° 18′ 30·73″; long. 80° 8′ 13·96″; from Anantavaram S.S.E. 3 miles; from Ongole S.S.E. 14 miles.——*Paudarty* (పాదర్తి - pádarti,* Tel.). From (pádu, tel. ruin + parti, tel. village). Village, Port; pop. 2,186; acres 8,276; lat. 15° 28′; long. 80° 14′; from Canooparty S.S.W. 9 miles; from Cottapatam N.N.E. 1¾ miles; from Madras N. 161 miles; from Nellore N. 71 miles; from Ongole E.S.E. 9 miles.——*Pautapaud beacon* (పాతపాడు - pátapádu, Tel.). From (páta, tel. old + pádu, tel. village). Trig. station; lat. 15° 30′ 24·03″; long. 80° 14′ 29·66″; from Devarâmpaud S. 3 miles; from Ongole E. 10 miles.——*Pelloor* (పెల్లూరు - pellúru, Tel.). From (pella, tel. ruin + úru, tel. village). Village; pop. 1,376; lat. 15° 28′; long. 80° 06′; from Nellore N. 69 miles; from Ongole S. 4 miles; from the sea W. 10 miles. On the great northern road. Fort in ruins. Head-quarters of the Vencatagherry rajah's tahsildar [q.v.] of Pelloor talook [q.v.].——*Pondore* (పొందూరు - pondúru, Tel.). From (ponnu, tel. gold + úru, tel. village). Village; pop. 2,678; acres 3,272; lat. 15° 25′; long. 79° 58′; from Nellore N. 66 miles; from Ongole S.W. 11 miles; from the sea W. 15 miles. Trade in indigo [q.v.]. On the Mooshy.——*Santanootalapaud* (సంతనూతలపాడు - santanútalapádu, Tel.). From (santa, tel. fair + núyi, tel. well + pádu, tel. village). Village; pop. 1,246; acres 9,272; lat. 15° 33′; long. 79° 59′; from Nellore N. 75 miles; from Ongole W.N.W. 8 miles; from the sea W. 19 miles. Indigo trade.——*Shingaricondah* (శింగరికొండ - shingarikonda, Tel.). From (singamu, tel. lion + konda, tel. hill). Hill; lat. 15° 52′; long. 80° 01′; from Nellore N. 96 miles; from Ongole N.N.W. 25 miles; from the sea W. 38 miles. A small hill 3 miles north-west of Addanky. Temple to Vishnoo [q.v.] as Narsimhasawmy.——*Tangootore* (తంగుటూరు - tangutúru, Tel.). Town; pop. 8,096; acres 9,290; lat. 15° 21′; long. 80° 05′; from Nellore N. 61 miles; from Ongole S. 12 miles; from the sea W. 5 miles. On the trunk road from Madras to Ganjam. Traveller's bungalow [q.v.]. Two temples one of Shiva as Naugeshwarasawmy, the other of Vishnoo as Chennakeshwarasawmy. Festivals to Shiva in Maugham [mausam] or february and to Vishnoo in Veishaukham or may. Car ceremonies [ratotsavam] are celebrated. Coloopoo [q.v.] or festival of village goddess performed to Ledotamma once in two years in June.——*Valaparla* (వలపర్ల - valaparla, Tel.). From (vala, tel. right + pari, tel. side). Village; pop. 2,705; acres 3,453; lat. 15° 56′; long. 80° 05′; from Nellore N. 101 miles; from Ongole N. 29 miles; from the sea W. 67 miles. Handkerchiefs [roomaul] woven.——**(2)** Town, Head-quarters of Sub-collector, Assistant superintendent of Police, District moonsif, Tahsildar and Sub-registrar. Hospital, Telegraph station. A municipal town; Nellore dist., Ongole tal.; pop. 10,860; acres 2,838; lat. 15° 31′; long. 80° 06′; from Madras N. 168 miles; from Naidoopett N. 111 miles; from Nellore N. 72 miles; from the sea W. 11 miles. In northern extremity of district; 11 miles north-east of left bank of Mooshy. In 1794 seat of a collectorate distinct from Nellore. Before British rule, this part of the country was ruled over by a dynasty of Shoodra rajahs, one of whom, about 150 years ago, built the fort. His seat of government however was at Addanky. The fort is now in ruins. The scenery in the neighbourhood is picturesque. The town is subject to occasional shocks of earthquake [mahy campam]. The hill near the fort is impregnated with iron [auhan]. American baptist mission has a large station. Travellers' bungalow [q.v.]. The rajah's descendants built a Vishnoo [q.v.] temple on one hill and his diwaun [q.v.] Vencauyalapauty veeranna built a Shiva [q.v.] temple on another. Trade in dry grain [q.v.] and pulses [dholl]. The great Northern trunk road and a branch road through Addanky connects it with Santamauglore 50 miles distant in the Kistna district on the Bellary-Kistna railway. Trig. station in lat. 15° 29′ 56·85″; long. 80° 04′ 53·90″; height 249 feet; from Coppole W.N.W. 3 miles; from Ongole S.W. 1 mile; from the sea W. 12 miles.

OOBBEY (ಉಬ್ಬೆ - ubbe, *Can.*). From (ubbu, can. to swell). Steam, worshipped as god by washermen [dhoby].

OOBHAYA (उभय - ubhaya, *San.*). From (ubh, san. to break). Both.——*Oobhaya cavy* (उभयकवि - ubhayakavi, San.). From (above + kavi, san. poet). A poet who writes in two languages, as Sanscrit and Tamil.——*Oobhayam* (ഉഭയം - ubhayam, Mal.; உபயம் - ubayam, Tam.). Anything offered or devoted to religious purposes; ceremonies performed in temples [coil, pagoda]. In malabar applied to the fruit-bearing trees; cocoanut [q.v.], betel nut [q.v.], jack [q.v.] and pepper [q.v.] vine [keracalpam].——*Oobhaya raushy* (ಉಭಯರಾಶಿ - ubhayaráshi, Can.). From (above + ráshi, san. heap). Heap of corn gathered and stacked, but not yet apportioned between the two sharers.

OOD (عود - úd, *Ar.*). From (áda, ar. to restore). Benzoin. ——*Oodbutty* (عود بتی - údbattí, Hind.). From (above + battí, hind. stick). Incense stick.

OOD (ال - ud, *Ar.*). Al before d in Arabic compounds, as Mohee ood deen [al].

OODAH (اودا - úda, *Hind.*; ஊதா - úthá, *Tam.*). Purple or blue. Plant first term, often joining two genera. Ex., where transl. is of second term:—Barleria cristata (úthámulli), thorny shrub; Exacum bicolor (údácharáitah), swertia chirata; Hibiscus syriacus (údágudhel), hibiscus rosa-sinensis; Justicia gendarussa (údísambhálú), vitex negundo. See gloss. paragraphs.

OODAMALPETT (உடுமலைப்பேட்டை - udumalaippéttai, *Tam.* udamalpet*). From (udu, tam. sheep + malai, tam. mountain + péttai, tam. suburb). Sanscrit name (chakragiri), meaning circle + mountain.——**(1)** Talook, Coimbatore district. Tahsildar's pay Rs. 175. Area 583 square miles. Population 143,056. Language Tamul. S. of district. Bounded N. by Pulladam talook; E. by Dharaupooram talook and Pulney talook of Madura district; S. by Travancore territory, the Anamullays being the great S. barrier; W. by Pollachy talook. Amaravatty flows nearly due north on the eastern edge. An open, gently undulating plain, flat in black cotton [regar] tract on W. and N., but undulating in the S. and E. The climate is fairly good, but the winds of the south-west monsoon are severely felt. Western portions share in the moisture brought by the south-west monsoon [q.v.]. The proximity of the hills gives a fair rainfall and abundant water to villages on the south. Forests are a notable feature. The open, sandy, and treeless wastes south-east of Oodamalpett near the foot of the hills were once rich jungles like those of Anamullay, but are now treeless and exhausted. Pasture, except in forests and proximity of hills, is scanty; especially in black cotton and stony tracts. Soils comprise 15 per cent. of red loam, 62 per cent. of red sand, 12 per cent. of black clay, and 11 per cent. of black loam. Red soil is chiefly on the N., S. and E.; black on the S. and W.; hardly any of the latter is found E. of the road running N. and S. between Dhully and Periyaputty. The so-called red sand is in some parts very stony and gravelly, and in the N. and E. there is a good deal of hard calcareous tufa [munn]. Wet crops are paddy [q.v.] and sugar-cane [q.v.]. Dry crops are cholum [q.v.], cumboo [bajrah], raggy [q.v.], tinay [q.v.], shaumay [q.v.], varagoo [q.v.], horse-gram [q.v.], pulses [dholl], Bengal gram [q.v.], gingelly [q.v.] seed, castor-seed [aumanac], cotton [q.v.]. Garden crops are cholum, cumboo, raggy, tinay, shaumay, varagoo, tobacco [pogauk], and cummin [jeerah]. The fine yield of cholum and cotton seed provides a vast amount of dry and rich cattle food and the cumboo, dholl and cotton stalks yield fuel. Firewood is largely supplied from the forests. Fruit trees grow well, the tamarinds [q.v.] and pomegranates [anaur] being very good, the latter the finest of their species. Trade is considerable; chiefly in cotton, grain and cloths. The only important ferry is that over the Amravatty on the Pulney road. The talook is chiefly irrigated by the Amravatty and partly by the Coothiraiyaur and Palaur, and tanks supplied by them, and also a few rain-fed tanks [q.v.]. The river irrigation is good and continues from June to April. Projects for a new anicut [q.v.] below Cullaupooram. Zemindarries :—Jotamputty, Meivaudy, Metrautty, Toongauvy, Vedaputty. Places of archæological interest :—Cadatore, Caniyore, Cholamaudevy, Comauralingam, Cooroomullay, Cozhmam, Cunnaudipoottore, Dhully, Goodimungalam, Madattoocalam, Poondy, Shuncararamanullore, Trimoortycoil. Principal Trig. station :—Colloopolliem. The leading places, &c., in the talook are the following.——*Amravatty* (ஆமராவதி - ámarávathi, Tam.). See sep. title.——*Anamullay* (ஆனைமலை - ánaimalai, Tam.). See sep. title.——*Bhootinuttam* (பூதிநத்தம் - púthinattam, Tam.). From (bhúti, san. prosperity + nattam, tam. village). Village; pop. 1,459; acres 3,857; lat. 10° 34′; long. 77° 15′; from Coimbatore S.S.E. 34 miles; from Oodamalpett S.W. 3 miles. Well irrigated by Amravatty. Sugar-cane [q.v.]. Gives name to a chain of tanks extending from Dhully to Oodamalpett.——*Cadatore* (கடத்தூர் - kadattúr; Tam.). From (kadam, tam. jungle + úr, tam. village). Village; pop. 2,661; acres 1,534; lat. 10° 37′; long. 77° 27′; from Coimbatore S.E. 40 miles; from Oodamalpett E. 10 miles. Old Shiva temple built by Chola king.——*Caniyore* (கணியூர் - kaniyúr, Tam.). From (kani, tam. cultivated land + úr, tam. village). Village; pop. 2,987; acres 765; lat. 10° 36′; long. 77° 26′; from Coimbatore S.E. 39 miles; from Oodamalpett E. 9 miles. Small temple in ruins. Small ruined fort which belonged to Coomaran, a ruler celebrated in country ballads. 4 miles W. are ruined Mahomedan buildings.——*Cauratoloo* (காரத்தொழுவு - kárattozhuvu, Tam.). From (kárai, tam. tree, canthium parviflorum, lamk. + tozhuvam, tam. cattle stall). Village; pop. 2,293; acres 3,046; lat. 10° 37′; long. 77° 26′; from Coimbatore S.E. 38 miles; from Oodamalpett E.N.E. 9 miles.——*Colloopolliem* (கொள்ளுப் பாளையம் - kolluppálaiyam, Tam.). From (kollu, tam. horse-gram, dolichos biflorus, linn. + pálaiyam, tam. camp). Trig. station; lat. 10° 41′ 43·96″; long. 77° 21′ 38·76″; height 1,208 feet; from Goodimungalam E. 3 miles; from Oodamalpett N.E. 9 miles.——*Comauralingam* (குமாரலிங்கம் - kumáralingam, Tam.). From (kumára, san. the son god + linga, san. phallic emblem of shiva). Village; pop. 4,320; acres 6,653; lat. 10° 29′; long. 77° 24′; from Coimbatore S.E. 44 miles; from Oodamalpett S.E. 10 miles. Ancient Shiva temple built by a Chola king. Irrigated by Amravatty.——*Cullaupooram* (கல்லாபுரம் - kallápuram, Tam.). From (kal, tam. stone + pura, san. town). Village; pop. 250; acres 2,603; lat. 10° 26′; long. 77° 20′; from Coimbatore S.S.E. 45 miles; from Oodamalpett S.S.E. 11 miles. Enclosed by hills and jungle. Irrigated by Amravatty.——*Dhully* (தளி - tali, Tam.). Means a temple. Village; pop. 2,085; acres 7,982; lat. 10° 31′; long. 77° 14′; from Coimbatore S.S.E. 37 miles; from Oodamalpett S.W. 7 miles. Close to Anamullay and Trimoortycoil. Former head-quarters of poligar [q.v.]. Village resumed after rising of poligar in 1800.——*Jelliputty* (செல்லிப்பட்டி - shellippatti, Tam.). From (jalli, can. road metal + patti, tam. cattle-fold). Village; pop. 3,063; acres 3,317; lat. 10° 30′; long. 77° 15′; from Coimbatore S.S.E. 38 miles; from Oodamalpett S.S.W. 7 miles.——*Jotamputty* (சோத்தம்பட்டி - shóttambatti, Tam. jotampati *). From (jótanu, can. proper name + patti, tam. cattle-fold). Village; pop. 646; acres 2,086; lat. 10° 36′; long. 77° 24′; from Coimbatore S.E. 38 miles; from Oodamalpett E. 7 miles. Poliput [q.v.]. Peshcush Rs. 143.——*Meivaudy* (மைவாடி - maivádi,* Tam.). From (mai, tam. black + vádi, tam. enclosure). Village; pop. 1,670; acres 6,025; lat. 10° 36′; long. 77° 22′; from Coimbatore S.E. 36 miles; from Oodamalpett E. 5 miles. Poliput [q.v.]. Peshcush Rs. 561.——*Metrautty* (மெட்ராத்தி - medrátti, Tam. metráthi *). From (metta, tel. mound + ráyi, tel. stone). Village; pop. 3,031; acres 7,208; lat. 10° 39′; long. 77° 23′; from Coimbatore S.E. 35 miles; from Oodamalpett E.N.E. 8 miles. Poliput [q.v.]. Peshcush Rs. 1,965.——*Oodamalpett* (உடுமலைப்பேட்டை - udumalaippéttai, Tam.). See below. ——*Palaur* (பாலாறு - pálāru, Tam.). See sep. title.——*Toongauvy* (துங்காவி - tungávi,* Tam.). From (tunga, san. height + ávi, tam. tank). Village; pop. 2,701; acres 6,309; lat. 10° 38′; long. 77° 23′; from Coimbatore S.E. 36 miles; from Oodamalpett E.N.E. 6 miles. Poliput [q.v.]. Peshcush Rs. 848.——*Trimoortycoil* (திருமூர்த்திக்கோவில் - tirumúrttikkóvil, Tam.). From (trimúrti, san. the trinity + kóvil, tam. temple). Village; lat. 10° 28′; long. 77° 12′; from Coimbatore S.S.E. 39 miles; from Oodamalpett S.W. 10 miles. Venerated shrine of Hindoo triad [trimoorty], consisting of old mantapam [q.v.] with rock sculptures. Near a stone-built chuttram [q.v.] close by eight stone images surround a stone pillar. Pilgrims on Sundays all year round. Annual festival. The temple is built exactly on the water-shed; that part of the stream on which it is situated flows into the Arabian sea, and the other part, diverted by a dam, flows into a feeder of the Cauvery and thence into the Bay of Bengal.——*Vedaputty* (வேடப்பட்டி - védappatti, Tam. vedapati *). From (védan, tam. a hunter + patti, tam. cattle-fold). Village; pop. 440; acres 1,371; lat. 10° 35′; long. 77° 24′; from Coimbatore S.E. 39 miles; from Oodamalpett E. 8 miles. Poliput [q.v.]. Peshcush Rs. 146.——**(2)** Town, Talook head-quarters; Coimbatore dist., Oodamalpett tal.; pop. 5,308; acres 1,942; lat. 10° 35′; long. 77° 18′; height 1,192 feet; from Coimbatore S.E. 34 miles; from Erode S.S.W. 62 miles; from Madras S.W. 268 miles; from Ootacamund S.S.E. 66 miles; from Pollachy E.S.E. 17 miles; from Suttimungalam S. 63 miles. Staging bungalow [q.v.]. Weekly market on Monday.

OODAN (உடன் - udan, *Tam.*). With.——*Oodumbadikay* (உடம்படிக்கை - udambadikkai, Tam.). From (above + padi, tam. to unite). A covenant [caraur nauma, dastavaiz].

OODAYAGHERRY (اودگیر - udgír, *Hind.*; ఉదయగిరి - udayagiri,* *Tel.*). From (udaya, san. rising + giri, san. mountain) [oot]; hill of sunrise or the east.——**(1)** Talook, Nellore district. Tahsildar's pay Rs. 150. Area 871 square miles. Centre inland part of district. Bounded :—On north by Ganigherry, on west by Eastern ghauts, on south by Atmacore, on east by Cauvaly. The extreme north-west is occupied entirely by the Calastry zemindarry. Other villages belonging to the Zemindarry are scattered throughout the talook. The west of the talook is very hilly. In the north-west there is a detached range of hills, and the country between them and the Veligondas is very unhealthy. The south of the talook is drained by the Boggair and the north by the Munnair and its tributary the Pillapair. Soil fertile in the east, rocky and covered with jungle in the west. A large indigo [q.v.] factory at Garimenpenta. Copper [taumram], formerly found in same neighbourhood. Rivers are Munnair and Boggair. Principal tanks [q.v.] :—Choontsoolore, Mondaulla nauyoonipulley tanks, Nundavaram, Oodayagherry, Totala chervoopulley and Vencatrowpulley. A large reservoir once existed in the zemindarry villages near Gundypollem. No other means of irrigation except wells on the banks of the Boggair, from which water is raised. Many garden lands are watered by private wells. Camping grounds :—Doottalore, Nundipaud, Oodayagherry, Yaipalgoonta. Places of archæological interest :—Alamail mungaupcoram, Dausaripully, Devammacheroo, Masahibpett, Maseedpulley, Nullagonda, Nundipaud, Oodayagherry. Principal trig. stations :—Chaucolloo, Oodayagherry droog, Yerracondah. The leading places, &c., in the talook are the following.——*Chaucolloo* (చాకొల్లు - tsákollu, Tel.). From (tsáki, tel. washerman + kolanu, tel. tank). Trig. station; lat. 14° 56′ 47·83″; long. 79° 33′ 25·68″; height 610 feet; from Bolinivauripollem W.S.W. ¾ mile; from Oodayagherry E.N.E. 15 miles.——*Corisa condah* (కొరిసకొండ - korisakonda, Tel.). From (gorise, tel. hoof + konda, tel. hill). Hill.——*Cumpasamoodram* (కంపసముద్రము - kampasamudramu, Tel.). From (kampa, tel. brushwood + samudra, san. ocean). Village; pop. 1,027; acres 4,513; lat. 14° 47′; long. 79° 17′; from Nellore N.W. 54 miles; from Oodayagherry S.S.W. 7 miles. The Boggair takes its rise in the Veligondas near Vencatapooram village, 4 miles from village.——*Dausaripully* (దాసరిపల్లె - dásaripalle, Tel.). From (dásari, tel. member of the caste + palle, tel. village). Village; pop. 328; lat. 14° 52′; long. 79° 23′; from Nellore W.N.W. 51 miles; from Oodayagherry E. 3 miles. Cave with an inscription [shausanam].——*Doottalore* (దుత్తలూరు - duttalúru, Tel.). See sep. title.——*Dornaul* (దోరనాల - dóranála, Tel.). See sep. title.——*Garimenpenta* (గరిమెనపెంట - garimenapenta, Tel.). From (garima, tel. great + penta, tel. heap). Village; pop. 2,323; lat. 15° 00′; long. 79° 36′; from Nellore N.W. 47 miles; from Oodayagherry N.E. 20 miles. Large indigo [q.v.] factory. Copper [taumram] formerly found.——*Gundy pollem* (గండిపాలెము - gandipálemu, Tel.). See sep. title. ——*Khancheroo* (ఖానచెరువు - khāncheruvu, Tel.). From (khán, hind. mahomedan title + cheruvu, tel. tank). Shrotriem [q.v.] village; pop. 662; acres 1,799; lat. 15° 01′; long. 79° 24′; from Nellore N.W. 56 miles; from Oodayagherry N.N.E. 10 miles. Ancient temple to Varadarajan and Anjaneyan. Endowed by the Shrotriemdar [q.v.]. On a small hill in the village a Shivaulyam founded by a Cumsaula [q.v.] about fifty years ago, still living. Festivals are celebrated on Shivarautry [pundigay, 6a] and Caurtigay [mausam] or November soma vauram [q.v.] or monday. Part of the village belongs to Calastry zemindarry. Dry and garden crops [vellaumay] are raised.——*Munnair* (మన్నేరు - mannéru, Tel.). See sep. title.——*Oodayagherry* (ఉదయగిరి - udayagiri, Tam.). See below.——*Saucalacondah* (చాకలకొండ - tsákalakonda, Tel.). From (tsákali, tel. washerman + konda, tel. hill). Shrotriem village; pop. 2,568; acres 16,471; lat. 41° 57′; long. 79° 34′; from Nellore N.W. 46 miles; from Oodayagherry E.N.E. 16 miles. Belongs to Bootchireddipollem reddy.——*Seetaramapooram* (సీతారామపురము - sítárāmapuramu, Tel.). From (sítáráma, san. ráma with síta + pura, san. town). Village; pop. 3,233; lat. 15° 01′; long. 79° 11′; from Nellore N.W. 68 miles; from Oodayagherry N.W. 15 miles. Belongs to Calastry. Near the Veligondas. Remains of an old fort, built of stone in mud, which enclosed 1 gorroo [q.v.] or 3½ acres of land. The walls are eight cubits high.——*Singanapulley* (సింగనపల్లె - singanapalle, Tel.). From (singanna, tel. proper name + palle, tel. village). Village; pop. 806; lat. 14° 42′; long. 79° 16′; from Nellore N.W. about 53 miles; from Oodayagherry S.S.W. 13 miles. At the foot of the Veligondas.——*Varigoontapaud* (వరిగుంటపాడు - variguntapádu, Tel.). From (vari, tel. paddy + gunta, tel. pond + pádu, tel. village). Village;

pop. 1,220; lat. 15° 00′; long. 79° 28′; from Nellore N.W. 52 miles; from Oodayagherry N.E. 12 miles. Many Balijes [q.v.] here who trade in pearls [moty].——*Veligonda* (వెలిగొండ - veligonda, Tel.). See sep. title.——*Venganapollem* (వెంగనపాలెము - venganapálemu, Tel.). From (vengauna, tel. proper name + pálemu, tel. fortified village). Village; pop. 3,902; lat. 14° 57′; long. 79° 31′; from Nellore N.W. 48 miles; from Oodayagherry N.E. 13 miles.——*Vinjamore* (వింజమూరు - vinjamúru, Tel.). From (vinjamma, tel. proper name + úru, tel. village). Village; pop. 5,256; lat. 14° 50′; long. 79° 38′; from Nellore N.W. 37 miles; from Oodayagherry E. 19 miles. Belongs to Calastry. Many betel [q.v.] leaf gardens.——*Yaipalgoonta* (ఏపలగుంట - épelagunta, Tel.). From (épe, tel. tree, hardwickia binata, roxb. + gunta, tel. pond). Village; pop. 1,160; acres 6,053; lat. 14° 47′; long. 79° 21′; from Nellore N.W. 50 miles; from Oodayagherry S. 7 miles. Exceedingly fine muslins [q.v.] once made.——*Yerracondah* (ఎర్రకొండ - errakonda, Tel.). See sep. title.——**(2)** Town, Hill, Head-quarters of Tahsildar and Sub-registrar; Nellore dist., Oodayagherry tal.; pop. 3,885; acres 10,651; lat. 14° 53′; long. 79° 20′; height of hill 2,954 feet; from Madras N.W. 141 miles; from Naidoopett N.W. 77 miles; from Nellore N.W. 54 miles; from Ongole S.W. 66 miles. A channel [q.v.] called Conacaulwa brings water from the hill. Very numerous Mahomedan population, descendants of the courts of former nawaubs [q.v.], now in a state of poverty. Formerly a wall round this town, which has entirely disappeared. There are said to have been 360 pagodas [q.v.], demolished by the Mahomedans. There were three more important than the rest, two in the village and one at the foot of the droog [q.v.]. Formerly a place of importance, and the capital of a small kingdom founded by Langoolya gajapaty [q.v.] in the fourteenth century, one of whose descendants was defeated by Krishnaroyel in 1509. From that date it was held by semi-independent chiefs, who repeatedly rebelled against the central authority at Golcondah. Four generations ago the Jagheer [q.v.] of Oodayagherry was granted by the Court of Hyderabad to a certain family, who remained undisturbed till 1839, when the holder Abbaus ally khan was deprived of it for treasonable conduct. He died a state prisoner in 1841. The next representative of the family Ghouse ally khan resided at Nellore as quasi state prisoner with a monthly pension of Rs. 250. He died in 1873. His son Davood ally now enjoys the pension. The hill once strongly fortified is quite isolated, being 8 miles from main chain of Eastern ghauts [q.v.]. The position was a very strong and commanding one. It consisted of thirteen fortresses, eight on hill and five below. About nine-tenths of hill is rendered inaccessible, except by three or four paths communicating with the low country, by precipices varying from 400 to nearly 1,000 feet in height; and every path is defended by several lines of fortification, aided by horse-shoe towers, which, built upon every rock commanding the roads or rather steps render it a very formidable place to attack. The northern part of the hill is lowest, and on this side is the principal approach, which consists of a flight of steps, running along the face of a deep ravine, and commanded by several towers and many lines of rampart and bastion. Within the fortifications is a small village, inhabited by Mootraucha [q.v.] people, descendants of former servants of the Hindoo rajahs, and the remains of temples, palaces and tombs. The southern or highest part of the hill is connected with the northern by a narrow way flanked on either side by precipices, with very precipitous paths to the low country on the east and west sides, and here again the fortifications are very numerous though not in such good repair as on the north. The southern hill is the highest, and from within the fortifications which enclose it there is only one path to the low country, constructed almost entirely in masonry steps along the face of the precipices on the west side. This staircase is a most extraordinary work, taking advantage of every mass of rock which could give it some support and zigzagging along and under overhanging cliffs many hundred feet high, while the sheer drop from the edge of the steps is in many places 100 to 150 feet. These stairs lead to a lower line of ramparts on the west side, within which the principal supplies of water are found. The climate on the top of the hills is about 15 degrees cooler than Oodayagherry itself. The water is most excellent, though difficult of access from the higher levels, while the hills are entirely free from fever at all times of the year. On the top of the Droog is a mosque [musjid] on which are two Persian inscriptions [shausanam] relating the establishment of a garden on the hill in Hijra [q.v.] 1070 or A.D. 1659, and of the mosque in question in Hijra 1071 or A.D. 1660 by Sheikh hoossain in the reign of Abdoollah shah of the Golcondah Cootb shahy dynasty [raj]. There are other inscriptions dated A.D. 1543 and 1546. Trig. station in lat. 14° 51′ 54·14″; long. 79° 19′ 03·91″; height 2,954 feet; from Gungireddipollem S.W. 4 miles; from Oodayagherry W.S.W. 2 miles. For Oodayagherry in Ganjam and Travancore see under Oot.

OODAYARPOLLIEM (உடையார்ப்பாளையம் - udaiyárppálaiyam, *Tam.* udayarpalaiyam *). From (udaiyán, tam. member of the caste + pálaiyam, tam. fortified village); no connection with oodaya, east [wodeya]. Sanscrit name (brahmapurí), meaning bramha, the god + town; also (mudgapurí), meaning kidney bean, phaseolus mungo, linn. + town.——**(1)** Talook, Trichinopoly district. Tahsildar's pay Rs. 200. Area 753 square miles. Greatest length from N. to S. 29 miles, breadth from S.W. to N.E. 45 miles. 222 square miles are included in Oodayarpolliem and Ariyalore zemindarries. The former is entirely in this talook, and the latter divided between it and Perambalore. Population 290,563. Language Tamul. N.E. of district. Bounded N. by the Vellaur and Vriddachellam talook of South arcot, S. by the Coleroon, E. by Chidambaram talook of South arcot, and W. by Perambalore and Trichinopoly talooks. The general aspect is flat, and there are no mountains or hills of importance. About 63,750 acres are covered with low brushwood jungle. Soil is for the most part a mixture of red sand [manal] and clay [calimunn]. Stripes of black soil run along the banks of the Vellaur and Coleroon. To the west and throughout the greater part of Ariyalore zemindarry the soil is black cotton [regar] thinly spread over a substratum of limestone [choonam cull]. Varagoo [q.v.], cumboo [bajrah], raggy [q.v.], dholl [q.v.], horse-gram [q.v.], gingelly [q.v.], oil [yennay] seed, groundnut [q.v.] and indigo [q.v.], are grown. Large quantities of firewood are carried for sale from different parts to Tanjore district. Weaving [nesavoo] and auvauram [tungaid] bark industry. There is little wet cultivation. The Ponnairy channel from the Coleroon irrigates seventeen villages. Candaraudityam channel, taken off at the Nandaiyaur anicut [q.v.] in Trichinopoly talook, irrigates seven villages. The most important tanks [q.v.] are the Candarauditvam tank, the tank in Shreepoorandaun village, and Shoocra tank. Places of archæological interest:—Ambaupooram, Ariyalore, Candárauditvam, Carookkeicauvalapparcoil, Caumarasavully, Gungaycondapooram, Jayancondacholapooram, Keelaiyore, Keelpaloovore, Oodayarpolliem, Tirmalvaudy, Tirmanore, Vicramam, Vunnam. Principal Trig. stations:—Colattore, Cutchipermaul, Moottoovancherry, Neinapiriyaun, Shalooppay. The leading places, &c., in the talook are the following.——*Ariyalore* (அரியலூர் - ariyalúr, Tam.). See sep. title.——*Colattore* (குளத்தூர் - kulattúr, Tam.). From (kulam, tam. tank + úr, tam. village). Trig. station; lat. 11° 17′ 01·33″; long. 79° 22′ 40·55″; height 214 feet; from Oodayarpolliem N.N.E. 8 miles.——*Coleroon* (கொள்ளிடம் - kolladam, Tam.). See sep. title.——*Cutchipermaul* (கச்சிப்பெருமாள் - kaççipperumál, Tam.). From a person of that name. Trig. station; lat. 11° 12′ 06·50″; long. 79° 21′ 07·37″; height 258 feet; from Oodayarpolliem N. 1 mile.——*Gungaycondapooram* (கங்கைகொண்டபுரம் - kangaikkandappuram, Tam.). See sep. title.——*Jayancondacholapooram* (செயங்கொண்டசோளப்புரம் - sheyangondasólappuram, Tam.). See sep. title.——*Keelpaloovore* (கிழப்பழுவூர் - kízhappaluvúr, Tam.). See sep. title.——*Maroothiyaur* (மருதையார் - maruthaiyár, Tam.). See sep. title.——*Moottoovancherry* (முத்துவாஞ்சேரி - muttuváñjéri, Tam.). From (muttuván, tam. proper name + shéri, tam. village). Trig. station; lat. 11° 02′ 12·90″; long. 79° 18′ 32·01″; height 183 feet; from Oodayarpolliem S. 10 miles.——*Neinapiriyaun* (நயினப்பிரியான் - nayinappiriyán, Tam.). From (nayinan, tam. aiyyanár + pirán, tam. lord). Trig. station; lat. 11° 07′ 51·83″; long. 79° 23′ 19·11″; height 133 feet; from Oodayarpolliem S.E. 5 miles.——*Oodayarpolliem* (உடையார்ப்பாளையம் - udaiyárppálaiyam, Tam.). See below.——*Shalooppay* (சலுப்பை - shaluppai, Tam.). From (shaluppu, tam. top of branches). Trig. station; lat. 11° 14′ 54·83″; long. 79° 28′ 59·76″; height 111 feet; from Oodayarpolliem E.N.E. 11 miles.——*Tirmalvaudy* (திருமழவாடி - tirumalaivádi, Tam.). From (tiru, tam. beautiful + mazhu, tam. the battle axe of shiva + pádi, tam. village). Sanscrit name (parashunrityapura), meaning battle axe + dance + town. Village; pop. 1,567; acres 1,287; lat. 10° 53′; long. 79° 07′; from Ariyalore S. 16 miles; from Oodayarpolliem S.W. 26 miles; from Trichinopoly E. 25 miles. Highly sculptured Shiva temple with Chola inscriptions.——*Valanday* (வளந்தை - valandai, Tam.). From (valam, tam. fertility + ai, tam. place). Village; pop. 4,761; acres 4,015; lat. 11° 20′; long. 79° 27′; from Ariyalore E.N.E. 25 miles; from Oodayarpolliem N.E. 12 miles; from Trichinopoly N.E. 59 miles. Weaving and bangle [gauzoo] making.——*Vellaur* (வெள்ளாறு - vellâru, Tam.). See sep. title.——**(2)** Zemindarry; Trichinopoly dist., Oodayarpolliem tal.; pop. 290,563. About 1,696 a peshcush [q.v.] of Rs. 40,000, was fixed upon this zemindarry by Nawaub [q.v.] of Carnatic [q.v.]. In 1757 the poligar [q.v.] was invaded by the French and forced to pay a tribute of same amount. In 1765 Nawaub assisted by English drove him from his polliem for refusal to contribute men and money for reduction of Madura. The expelled poligar took refuge first in Tanjore and then in Mysore until 1780, when with the assistance of Hyder he regained possession and was in possession till 1783, when he became renter of his district. The entire management of the estate was in 1798 handed over to an agent of the Nawaub; a monthly allowance of Rs. 1,000 being paid to poligar. This continued till Trichinopoly was made over to Company in 1801. On the 23rd December 1817 a Sunnud-i-milkyat-i-istimrar [q.v.] was issued to the poligar, he receiving merely the village in which he lived together with villages surrounding head-quarters. Present peshcush, Rs. 642.——**(3)** Town, General deputy collector's division; Trichinopoly dist., Oodayarpolliem tal.; pop. 7,739; lat.

11° 11′; long. 79° 21′; from Ariyalore E.N.E 15 miles; from Madras S.S.W. 144 miles; from Moosiry E.N.E. 59 miles; from Shreerungam N.E. 46 miles; from Trichinopoly E.N.E. 47 miles. Agricultural and market town, built in 1314 by poligar [q.v.] Chinna nullapoodeiyaur as directed in a dream. Head-quarters of the zemindarry. Formerly considerable but now much decayed. The zemindar's palace is in a ruinous state, but contains a fine durbar [q.v.] hall with some good wooden carving, and an inscription [shausanam]. It is in an old fort built by Mahrattas. Old Shiva temple with semi-circular tank.

OODID (उडिद - udída, *Mahr.*). Same as Black gram.

OODIPY (ಉಡಿಪಿ - udipi, * *Can.*). From (udu, san. star + pati, san. chief). The chief of the stars, i.e., the moon [chundran].——(1) Talook, South canara district. Tahsildar's pay Rs. 225. Area 787 square miles; N. central coast of district. Boundaries:—North, Coondapore talook; south, Mangalore talook; east, Mysore territory; west, Arabian sea. Western part is fairly level. East and north-east are hilly and include the lower spurs of the Western ghauts [q.v.]. Soil ferruginous and generally fertile. Agriculture is chief industry. Hand looms [tarry], exist. Inferior cloths manufactured at Oodipy. A tile [wode] factory at Malpey. Rice [q.v.], coir [q.v.], areca-nuts [q.v.], turmeric [country saffron], sandal-wood [sandal], sandal-wood oil and paddy [q.v.] are exported. Imports are kerosine oil, cloth, salt [ooppoo], glass-ware [cunnaudy] and china-ware. Irrigation is chiefly dependant upon rain, average fall 150 inches. During the dry season a supply of water is derived from rivers, streams, tanks and private wells. Camping grounds on the coast:—Oodipy, Bramhahwar, Caup, Kotey. Inland:—Hiriyadka, Caurcal, Ajekaur, Moodraudy, Hebry, Someshwaram and Halady. Places of archæological interest:—Bailore, Bramhahwar, Caurcal, Honnholey, Irvettore, Keravaushey, Maraney, Miyaura, Moollore, Nullore, Varanga, Yermaul, Yellarey, Yellore. The leading places, &c., in the talook are the following.——*Agoomby* (ಆಗುಂಬಿ - águmbi, Can.). See sep. title.——*Alevore* (ಅಲೆವೂರು - alevúru, Can.). Village; pop. 1,283. One of the sixteen nagarams mentioned in Bhootanla pandya's aliya santauna [q.v.] law.——*Andaur* (ಅಂಡಾರ - andára, Can.). From (anda, san. egg), from egg-shaped peak of ghaut.—"*a*" Village; pop. 751; lat. 13° 20′; long. 75° 4′.—"*b*" Pass [ghaut]. South canara dist., Oodipy tal.; lat. 13° 20′ 15″ N.; long. 75° 4′ E. Leads into Mysore; impracticable for vehicles.——*Balisauvira* (ಬಳಿಸಾವಿರ - balisávira, Can.). From (bali, can. family + sávira, can. thousand). A Maugaunam [q.v.] or Sub-division of the talook comprising a large area of forty-six villages; pop. 37,650. According to tradition one thousand balies [q.v.] or families of Naudavar [q.v.] following the Aliya santauna [q.v.] law of inheritance once lived in this area.——*Barcore* (ಬಾರ್ಕೂರು - bárkúru, Can.). See sep. title.——*Bramhahwar* (ಬ್ರಹ್ಮಾವರ - brahmávara, Can.). From (brahmá, san. the creator + pura, san. town). Sanscrit name (brahmapura), meaning same. Village; pop. 1,084; lat. 13° 26′; long. 74° 47′; from Mangalore N. 40 miles; from Oodipy N. 7 miles; from the sea E. 4 miles. On the route from Mangalore to Bednore. Former residence of Tahsildar of Barcore talook. Camping station.——*Calyaunapooram* (ಕಲ್ಯಾಣಪುರ - kalyánapura, Can.). See sep. title.——*Caup* (ಕಾಪ್ - káp, Can.). From (kápu, can. protection). Maugaunam [q.v.] or Sub-division of talook [q.v.] comprising five villages, Sub-port; pop. 6,100; lat. 13° 13′; long. 74° 47′; from Bombay S.S.E. 406 miles; from Mangalore N.N.W. 25 miles; from Oodiyauvar S. 6 miles; from Oodipy S. 8 miles; from Ootchil N. 3 miles; from the sea E. 1½ miles. A camping station in Moollore village.——*Caurcal* (ಕಾರ್ಕಳ - kárkala, Can.). See sep. title.——*Chitpaudy* (ಚಿಟ್‌ಪಾಡಿ - chitpádi, Can.). From (chitta, can. small + pádi, can. a jungle); so called probably from scrub jungle surrounding the village. Village; pop. 421. Gives its name to a family of Ballaulas [q.v.] in Canara.——*Coonjaur* (ಕುಂಜಾರು - kunjáru, Can.). From (kunja, too. hill + úru, can. country). Can. also (durgabetta), meaning doorga, the goddess + hill. Sanscrit name (durgáchala), meaning doorga, the goddess + hill. Part of Caurcal, village.——*Daryah bahaudur ghur* (دریا بہادر گڑھ - daryábahádurgarh, Hind.). See sep. title.——*Hangarcutta* (ಹಂಗಾರಕಟ್ಟೆ - hangárakatte, Can.). See sep. title.——*Krishnapooram* (ಕೃಷ್ಣಾಪುರ - krishnápura, Can.). From (krishna, san. deity + pura, san. town). Mutt [q.v.]. One of the eight mutts [q.v.] in the town of Oodipy.——*Malpey* (ಮಲ್ಪೆ - malpe, Can.). See sep. title.——*Moodraudy* (ಮುದ್ರಾಡಿ - mudrádi, Can.). From (mudra, san. seal + adi, can. dependent). Village; pop. 1,897; from Mangalore N. 51 miles. Seat of a Ballaula chief under the Jeina [q.v.] chowtar rajah.——*Munnarghur* (ಮನ್ನಾರಘಡ - mannáraghada, Can.). From (mannéyaru, can. king + garh, hind. fort). Site of a fort; lat. 13° 13′; long. 74° 46′, from Mangalore N.W. 25 miles; from Oodipy S.S.W. 8 miles; from the sea E. ½ mile.——*Nellicaur* (ನೆಲ್ಲಿಕಾರು - nellikáru, Can.). From (nellu, can. paddy, oryza sativa, linn. + káru, can. wet season). Village; pop. 939. Good granite [caroom cull] quarries.——*Nidambore* (ನಿಡಂಬೂರು - nidambúru, Can.). From (nidamba, can. the surname of a ballala who owned extensive estates in the mágani + úru, can. country). Village; pop. 1,645. Gives its name to a Ballaula [q.v.] family in Canara.——*Oodipy* (ಉಡಿಪಿ - udipi, Can.). See below.——*Ootchil* (ಉಚ್ಚಿಲ - uççila, Can.). From (uçça, san. high + achala, san. mountain). A Sub-port; lat. 13° 11′; long. 74° 47′; from Bombay S.S.E. 408 miles; from Caup S. 3 miles; from Mangalore N.N.W. 23 miles; from Yermaul N. 1½ miles; from the sea E. ¼ mile. On a creek north of Mangalore.——*Padbidry* (ಪಡುಬಿದ್ರಿ - padubidri, Can.). From (paduva, can. west + bidu, can. vishnu + adri, can. mountain). Village, Sub-port; pop. 2,183; lat. 13° 07′; long. 74° 49′; from Bombay S.S.E. 412 miles; from Mangalore N.N.W. 19 miles; from Moolky N. 3 miles; from Oodipy S. 14 miles; from Yermaul S.S.E. 3 miles; from the sea E. ½ mile. On a creek north of Moolky. Seat of a Ballaula family still extant.——*Palamar* (ಫಲಮಾರ - p'halamára, Can.). From (p'hala, san. fruit + ára, can. country). Village; pop. 1,290. Contains a mutt [q.v.] of one of the Oodipy sawmies.——*Poottigey* (ಪುತ್ತಿಗೆ - puttige, Can.). From (puttu, can. ant-hill + ga, can. suffix of possession). Village; pop. 3,241. A mutt [q.v.] belonging to one of the Oodipy sawmies.——*Saint Mary's isles* (ತೋನಸೆಪಾರ - tónasepára, Can.). See sep. title.——*Seetanuddy* (ಸೀತಾನದಿ - sítánadi, Can.). See sep. title.——*Someshwaram* (ಸೋಮೇಶ್ವರ - sóméshvara, Can.). From (sóma, san. epithet of shiva + íshvara, san. lord). Village; pop. 1,345; lat. 13° 29′; long. 75° 06′; from Mangalore N.N.E. 45 miles; from Oodipy E.N.E. 23 miles; from the sea E. 25 miles.——*Sooda* (ಸೂಡ - súda, Can.). From (chúdá, san. head). Village; lat. 13° 12′; long. 74° 54′; from Mangalore N. 23 miles; from Oodipy S.E. 12 miles; from the sea E. 8 miles. Temple of Soobramanyan [q.v.]. Car festival [ratotsavam].——*Sooraul* (ಸುರಾಲು - surálu, Can.). Village; pop. 355; lat. 13° 27′; long. 74° 53′; from Mangalore N. 39 miles; from Oodipy N.E. 10 miles; from the sea E. 10 miles. Seat of a Jeina [q.v.] rajah.——*Swarnanuddy* (ಸುವರ್ಣನದಿ - suvarnanadi, Can.). See sep. title.——*Varanga* (ವರಂಗಾ - varangá, Can.). Village; pop. 959; Jeina temple. Seat of a Jeina rajah of the Heggadey [q.v.] family. *Yermaul* (ಯಮಾರ್ಳ - yarmála, Can.). Village, Sub-port; pop. 1,750; lat. 13° 10′; long. 74° 48′; from Bombay S.S.E. 410 miles; from Mangalore N.N.W. 21 miles; from Oodipy S. 12 miles; from Ootchil S.S.E. 1½ miles; from Padbidry N.N.W. 3 miles. On a creek between Padbidry and Moolky.——(2) Town, Talook head-quarters, Place of pilgrimage; South canara dist., Oodipy tal.; pop. 7,272; lat. 13° 21′; long. 74° 47′; from Bombay S.S.E. 398 miles; from Coondapore S.S.E. 20 miles; from Malpey E. 3 miles; from Madras W. 374 miles; from Mangalore N. 33 miles; from Oodiyauvar N.N.E. 3 miles; from Poottore N.W. 50 miles; from Soobramanya N.W. 74 miles; from the sea E. 3 miles. Near the mouth of the Oodipy river. Formed of parts of Badagabett, Moodanidambore, Poollore and Shivully villages. Malpey is the recognized port. A road proceeds across the Agoomby ghaut [q.v.] into Mysore. Some islands form a harbour. Considered the most sacred spot in the Canarese country, and its shrines of Krishnan [q.v.] is much frequented by pilgrims from Mysore. There are three temples and eight mutts [q.v.]. Important festival once in two years. The temples are rude buildings, roofed with copper [taumram].

OODOO (உடு - udu, *Tam.*). Arrow.——*Oodoomoo* (गोधा - gódhá, San.; ضب - zabb, Ar.; سوسمار - súsmár, Pers.; گوہ - goh, Hind.; گھورپھور - ghorphor, Dec.; ಗೊದ್ದ - godda, Can.; ఉడుము - udumu, Tel.; ഉടുമ്പ - utumpu, Mal.; உடும்பு - udumbu, Tam.). Title from teloogoo. San. from (gudh, san. to envelop). Ar. from (zabba, ar. to attack); from the habit of striking with its tail. Hind. and Can. from sanscrit. Tel., Mal. and Tam. from (udu, tam. arrow). West indian title is Guana or Iguana. The terms may be considered co-extensive with the family Varanidæ, sauria [godhicay], reptilia [sarpy, 6], of naturalists [jantoo]. Water lizards. Belly protuberant; tail long and round, thick at commencement, tapering gradually towards sharp point; back, tail, and throat are serrated, whole surface covered with numerous shining scales, reflecting various colors in sunshine. This family contains the largest species of lizards [chipkalee]; most of them live in the neighbourhood of large rivers, excellent swimmers; carnivorous, feeding on all the different water-animals and on the eggs of birds, and likewise on those of other large reptiles. Movements on land are not much less rapid than in the water. Several species climb trees; active during a part of the night; able to remain under water for a prolonged period without the necessity of rising to the surface in order to breathe. Body of dried guana, made into electuary with ghee [q.v.] given in consumptive complaints, head, tail and feet, being removed. Flesh relished by Mahomedans, supposed to be strengthening. There is a Tamul proverb:—உடும்புக்கு இரண்டு நாக்கு மனிதனுக்கு ஒரு நாக்கு—"the iguana has two tongues, "man only one;" referring to its forked tongue. The representative species in southern india is Varanus lunatus. Banded water lizard. Neck, trunk, and tail marked with cross-bands, sides and legs dotted with white.

OOGAH (உகா - ugá, *Tam.*). From (uga, tam. to please); from shining leaves. Same as Tooth-brush tree.

OOGRA (उग्र - ugra, *San.*). Means pungency; in allusion to the pepper [q.v.]. The Malabar country.

OOKH (اوکھ - úkh, *Hind.*). From (ikshu, san. sugar-cane). Same as Sugar-cane.

OOL (ഉൾ - ul, *Mal.*; உள் - ul, *Tam.*). Within.——*Oolcoody* (உள்குடி - ulkkudi, Tam.). From (above + kudi, tam. an inhabitant). Khoodkasht of N. india. A permanent resident tenant with hereditary rights, as distinguished from the paracoody [q.v.]. He stands between the mirassidar [q.v.] and the paracoody. See vol. I, 114.——*Ool cundauyam* (உடகந்தாயம் - udgandáyam, Tam.). From (above + kandáyam, tam. period of three months for the payment of taxes). Assessment not paid to Government, but to some other person.——*Oollauda* (ഉള്ളാട - ulláta, obl.; ഉള്ളാടൻ - ullátan, pers. sing.; ഉള്ളാടർ - ullátar, pers. pl., Mal.). From (above + álu, mal. to rule); interior proprietors. A hunter tribe [veddah] at the base of the Cochin ghauts [q.v.].——*Oolmanay* (உள்மனை - ulmanai, Tam.). From (above + manai, tam. house). House within site of the village, opposed to Paramanay beyond.——*Oolsharat bhoomy* (உள்சரத்துப்பூமி - ulsarattuppúmi, Tam.). From (above + shart, hind. condition + bhúmi, san. earth). Sub-tenure.——*Ootchamayam* (உட்சமயம் - udchamayam, Tam.). From (ul, tam. within + samaya, san. religion). The six systems of religion considered orthodox by the Sheivas:—Veiravam making bheirava supreme; Vaumam regarding the female principle in nature as the primæval form of deity; Caulamookham. similar to vaumam; Mauvratam teaching that the deity is a pure spirit; Paushoopatam similar to mauvratam; Sheivam which teaches that the deity is both spirit and matter, assuming form for accomplishing his purposes [augamam, matam, moorty].

OOLAH (உலா - ulá, *Tam.*). Abbreviation from (ulávu, tam. to walk). Procession. A species of poem in which the praises of a hero are sung.

OOLAMAH (علما - ulamá, *Ar.*). Plural of (álim, ar. learned). Part of lacab; as Shums ool oolamah, sun of the learned.

OOLANDOO (உளுந்து - ulundu, *Tam.*). From (uzha, tam. to exert energy)? toffic. Same as Black gram.——*Oolandoorpett* (உளுந்தூர்ப்பேட்டை - ulundúrppéttai, Tam. ulundurpet *). From (ulundu, tam. black-gram, phaseolus mungo, linn., var. radiatus, linn. + úr, tam. village + péttai, tam. suburb).—"*a*" Deputy tahsildarry, South arcot district. Pay Rs. 70.—"*b*" South arcot dist., Tricalore tal.; pop. 1,221; acres 1,874; lat. 11° 42′; long. 79° 20′; from Chidambaram N.W. 34 miles; from Cuddalore W. 32 miles; from Madras S.W. 118 miles; from Tindivanam S.S.W. 43 miles; from Tricalore S.S.E. 19 miles; from Vriddhauchellam N. 14 miles. Halting station for travellers on the Salem, Trichinopoly, Madras, and Cuddalore trunk roads. Weekly fair on Wednesday. Trig. station in lat. 11° 40′ 30·99″; long. 79° 19′ 25·24″; height 250 feet; from Oolandoorpett S.S.W. 1½ miles; from Tricalore S.S.E. 21 miles.

OOLINJA (ज्योतिष्मती - jyótishmatí, *San.*; कानफुटी - kánapʼhutí, *Mahr.*; طفطف - taftaf, *Ar.*; حب الخلخال - habbulkhalkhál, *Pers.* and *Hind.*; ಎರುವಬಳ್ಳಿ - éruvaballi, *Can.*; ଉରୁଣ୍ଡେବୁରା - urundebúra, *Too.*; బుడ్డకాకర - buddakákara, *Tel.*; ഉഴിഞ്ഞ - uzhiñña, *Mal.*; පෙනෙලවැල - penelavala, *Singh.*; முடக்கொத்தான் - mudakkottán, *Tam.*). Title from malayalam. San. from (jyótis, san. light + mat, san. suffix of possession); as shining in the dark [malkangany]. Mahr. from (karnaspʼhótá, san. the plant). Can. from (éru, can. climbing + balli, can. creeper). Tel. from (budda, tel. bladder + kákara, tel. momordica charantia, linn.). Singh. from (penella, singh. fire brand + vala, singh. creeper). Tam. from (mudakkam, tam. contraction by paralysis + kottam, tam. victory), as curing palsy and gout. San. also (nagná), meaning naked; (jyótirvriksha), meaning bright tree; (káravi), meaning stimulant [black jeerah]; (párávatánghri), meaning pigeon + knee, from red stalk; (karnaspʼhóta), meaning ear + boil, from juice used to cure earache. Can. also (agniballi), meaning fire + creeper; (kákaralata), meaning momordica charantia, linn. + creeper; (buddakákaratíge); (érumballi), meaning climbing creeper. Tel. also (nallagulivinda), meaning black + abrus precatorius, linn.; (apparinta), meaning blistering; (ullena), meaning insignificant; (ekkudutíga), meaning climbing + creeper; (pátalitivva); (vekkudutíga), meaning hiccup + creeper; (nallagulisinda). Tam. also (periyayilaimudakkottán), meaning large + leaf + the plant; (tiragamúlagam), meaning to be wrinkled + root; (samuttirathóyam), meaning ocean + water; from similarity of use; (kottavan), meaning victorious one; cf. cottaun. Title otherwise Balloon vine from capsules, Black liquorice, Bladder fruit, Blister creeper, Fire-brand creeper, Heart-pea, Heart-seed, Joty, Palsy-curer from root, Pigeon's knee, Shining tree. Botanically Cardiospermum halicacabum, linn., sapindaceæ [vricsham, 43]. Alias Corindum halicacabum. Annual, climbing; stem, petioles, and leaves nearly glabrous; leaves biternate; leaflets stalked, oblong, much acuminated, coarsely cut and serrated; petals four, each with an emarginate scale above the base, the two lower ones with their scales furnished with a glandular crest at their extremity, and ending in a yellow inflexed appendage beneath the apex; fruit a membranous bladdery capsule, three-celled, three-valved; seeds globose, with a two-lobed aril at the base; flowers racemose; common peduncles with two opposite tendrils under the racemes; flowers small, white or pink, on long axillary peduncles; flowering all year. Climbing herb with wiry stems, small flowers producing large inflated membranous capsules enclosing seeds; when ripe, black, with a distinct heart-shaped white mark; a tree which appears to shine in the dark; roots white and fibrous with a rather disagreeable odour, and an acrid nauseous and somewhat bitter taste; the plant owes its medicinal properties to the presence of saponin. The root, which is diaphoretic and diuretic, is given in decoction as an aperient; it is mucilaginous and slightly nauseous to the taste; on the malabar coast the leaves are administered in pulmonic complaints, and, mixed with castor-oil [aumanac], are internally employed in rheumatism and lumbago; the whole plant, rubbed up with water, is applied to rheumatism and stiffness of the limbs; the leaves, mixed with jaggery [q.v.] and boiled in oil, are a good specific in sore eyes; the whole plant, steeped in milk [paul], is successfully applied to reduce swellings and hardened tumours. In moluccas, leaves cooked as vegetables [keeray]; not here except in famine.

OOLLAUN (پنکوا - pankawwá, *Hind.* and *Dec.*; ఉల్లంగిపిట్ట - ullangipitta, *Tel.*; உள்ளான் - ullán, *Tam.*). Title from tamul. Hind. from (páni, hind. water + kavvá, hind. crow). Tel. from (ullangi, tel. lapwing + pitta, tel. bird). Tam. from (ulai, tam. mire) [ooloovay], so called from its frequenting marshes, &c. Tam. also (ullal). Snipe. Scolopacinæ family, scolopacidæ [vanacookkootam], longirostres, grallatores, aves [pacshy, 41], of naturalists [jantoo]. Those to be scientifically distinguished are shown in the sub-heads below. The following are varieties recognised in tamul:—Coray oollaun as frequenting sedges; Keery oollaun as resembling an ichneumon; Shoottautty oollaun or water wag-tail, as shaking its tail continually while walking; Tadimook oollaun, whose bill resembles a stick; Toodoop oollaun, whose bill resembles a paddle.——*Common snipe* (जलकुक्कुट - jalakukkuta, San.; اسناف - isnáf, Hind. and Dec.; ముక్కుపురిడి - mukkupuridi, Tel.; നീർക്കോഴി - nírkkózhi, Mal.; மாரியுள்ளான் - máriyullán, Tam.). San. from (jala, san. water + kukkuta, san. fowl). Tel. from (mukku, tel. bill + puridi, tel. quail). Mal. from (nír, mal. water + kózhi, mal. fowl). Tam. from (mári, tam. rain + ullán, tam. snipe). Hind. also (surkháb), meaning sucker of water. Tam. also (pathukkáy), meaning one that hides. Gallinago scolopacinus, scolopacinæ, scolopacidæ [vana cookkootam], longirostres, grallatores [pacshy, 41], of naturalists [jantoo]. Alias Scolopax burka, gallinago, uniclavus. Crown black divided longitudinally by yellowish white line; dusky brown eye-streak, yellowish supercilliary one; back and scapulars velvet black, crossed with chestnut brown bars, and with longitudinal streaks of ochre yellow; wing-coverts dusky brown, edged reddish white; quills blackish; chin and throat white; cheeks, neck and breast above mottled black and ferruginous; flanks barred white and dusky; lower part of breast and abdomen pure white; tail black, with terminal third red-brown, barred black and tipped whitish; lower wing-coverts white, very faintly barred; bill reddish brown, paler at base; irides deep brown; legs greyish green; length 11–12 inches; very abundant during cold weather; frequent marshes, inundated paddy [q.v.] fields, rice [q.v.] stubble fields; rise with a piping call, and fly against the wind.——*Jack snipe* (கோழியுள்ளான் - kózhiyullán, Tam.). Tam. from (kózhi, tam. fowl + ullán, tam. snipe). Title otherwise Judcock, Juddock. Gallinago gallinula. scolopacinæ, scolopacidæ [vana cookkootam], longirostres, grallatores [pacshy, 41], of naturalists [jantoo]. A smaller bird; difficult to flush; makes its appearance later than the common snipe, and departs earlier.——*Painted snipe* (కసువుకోడి - kasuvukódi, Tel.; ଚେକୁଚୋଡ଼ - chekkuchodai, Oor.; மயிலுள்ளான் - mayilullán, Tam.). Title from variegated plumage. Tel. from (kasuvu, tel. grass + kódi, tel. fowl). Tam. from (mayil, tam. peacock + ullán, tam. snipe); from variegated plumage. Tam. also (shivappumúkkullán), meaning redness + bill + snipe. Rhynchæa bengalensis, scolopacinæ, scolopacidæ [vana cookkootam], longirostres, grallatores [pacshy, 41], of naturalists [jantoo]. Variegated plumage; larger bird than either species just mentioned, flight more resembles that of woodcock [indian woodcock] than snipe; it has the cry of the snipe on rising, but of a deeper tone.——*Wood snipe* (காட்டுள்ளான் - káttullán, Tam.). Gallinago nemoricola, scolopacinæ, scolopacidæ [vana cookkootam], longirostres, grallatores [pacshy, 41], of naturalists [jantoo]. Alias Nemoricola nipalensis. Solitary snipe found in elevated regions; not common.

OOLOOCAM (उलूक - ulúka, *San.*). From (ul, san. to burn); from dazzling eyes at night. Owls. Strigidæ family, raptores, aves [pacshy, 3], of naturalists [jantoo]. Divide into:—Striginæ, screech owls; Syrniinæ, hooting owls; Asioninæ, large-eared owls; Buboninæ, great horned owls, eagle owls, and small scops owls; Surniinæ, owlets. There is a Tamul proverb:—அத்திப்பூவைக் கண்டவர்கள் உண்டா ஆந்தைக்குஞ்சைப் பார்த்தவர்கள் உண்டா—"are there any who have seen the blossom of the fig [atty]? are there any who have seen the young of an owl?" And another:—ஆந்தைசிறிது இச்சப்பெரிது—"the owl is small, its screech is loud." The species best known to the natives are shown below.——*Booríchoory* (ضوع - zuva, Ar.; چغد - chughd, Pers. and Hind.; بری چڑی - burichuri, Dec.; ಹಂಡಿಕಿರ - handikíra, Can.; చావుపిట్ట - tsávupitta, Tel.; നത്ത് - nattu, Mal.; சாக்குருவி - shákkuruvi, Tam.). Title from deccany. Ar. from (zuva, ar. to be timid). Dec. from (burí, hind. bad + churí, hind. bird). Can. from (handi, can. pig + kíra, can. parrot). Tel. from (tsávu, tel. death + pitta, tel. bird). Mar. means to limp. Tam. from (shá, tam. death + kuruvi, tam. small bird); bird of ill omen. Title otherwise Indian screech-owl. Strix javanica, striginæ, strigidæ [ooloocam], raptores [pacshy, 3], of naturalists. Alias Strix delicatula, flammea. Lives in deserted buildings; hunts by night. The Grass owl is strix candida; lives in long grass; rises heavily and flies only a short distance, when it drops suddenly into the grass.——*Chinna goodlagooba* (چھوٹا گگھو - chhotághuggú, Hind. and Dec.; చిన్నగుడ్లగూబ - chinnagudlagúba, Tel.). Hind. from (chhotá, hind. little + ghuggú, hind. owl). Tel. from (chinna, tel. small + gudlagúba, tel. owl). Title otherwise Short-eared owl. Otus brachyotus, asioninæ, strigidæ [ooloocam], raptores [pacshy, 3], of naturalists. Alias Brachyotus palustris. Hunts by night, though it flies by day; its voice is a double or treble hoot, not unlike the call of the hoopoe [hoodhood].——*Chittagooba* (ಚಿಟ್ಟಗೂಬೆ - chittagúbe, Can.; చిట్టగూబ - chittagúba, Tel.). Can. and Tel. from (chitti, tel. small + gúba, tel. owl). Title otherwise Indian scops owl. Ephialtes pennatus, buboninæ, strigidæ [ooloocam], raptores [pacshy, 3], of naturalists. Alias Ephialtes spilocephalus; Scops aldrovandi, malayanus, sunia, zorca. A larger kind is Ephialtes lempigi.——*Choghadbesrah* (چغد بیسرا - choghadbesrá, Hind.; పైడికంటివేసదము - paidikantivésadamu, Tel.). Hind. from (choghad, pers. owl + besrá, hind. hawk). Tel. from (paidikanti, tel. owlet + vésadamu, tel. hawk). Hind. also (kalpechak), meaning death owl. Title otherwise Brown hawk owl. Ninox scutellatus, surniinæ, strigidæ [ooloocam], raptores [pacshy, 3] of naturalists. Alias Athene malayensis; Ninox nipalensis; Strix hirsuta, lugubris. Peculiar call, resembling the cry of a strangling cat [poonay], or a hare [mosal] when caught by hounds. Natives consider this bird very unfortunate, and when one of them cries near a house the inhabitants go out with lights, to which it has a great aversion, and drive it away.——*Hoohoo cheel* (بوم - búm, Ar. and Pers.; هوهو چیل - húhúchíl, Hind.; ഊമൻ - úman, Mal.). Hind. from (húhú, hind. the call + chíl, hind. kite). Mal. from (úma, mal. dumb). Title otherwise Forest eagle owl. Huhua nipalensis, buboninæ, strigidæ [ooloocam], raptores [pacshy, 3], of naturalists. Generic name from hindostany. Alias Bubo orientalis; Huhua pectoralis. It has a low deep and far-sounding, moaning hoot.——*Nulla goodlagooba* (جنگلی گگھو - janglíghuggú, Hind. and Dec.; నల్లగుడ్లగూబ - nallagudlagúba, Tel.). Hind. from (janglí, hind. wild + ghuggú, hind. owl). Tel. from (nalla, tel. black + gudlagúba, tel. owl). Title otherwise Dusky horned owl. Urrua coromanda, buboninæ, strigidæ [ooloocam], raptores [pacshy, 3], of naturalists. Alias Urrua umbrata.——*Peidicunty* (पिङ्गल - pingala, San.; पिंगला - pingalá, Mahr.; بوم - búm, Pers.; چغد - choghad, Hind. and Dec.; ಹಾಲಹಕ್ಕಿ - hálahakki, Can.; పైడికంటి - paidikanti, Tel.; നത്ത - natta, Mal.; ஆந்தை - ándai, Tam.). San. means yellow. Can. from (hálu, can. milk, means white + hakki, can. bird). Tel. from (paidi, tel. gold + kannu, tel. eye). Mal. from (nattu, mal. to limp). Hind. also (katoriapechak), meaning harsh owl. Title otherwise Spotted owlet. Athene brama, surniinæ, strigidæ [ooloocam], raptores [pacshy, 3], of naturalists. Alias Noctula indica, tarayensis. Extremely common; noisy; call is double note; is regarded with aversion; used by shikarries [q.v.] for catching small birds. The forest species is Athene radiata. The malabar species is Athene malabarica.——*Yerra goodlagooba* (घुबड - ghubada, Mahr.; هامه - hámah, Ar.; كوربوم - korbúm, Pers.; گگھو - ghuggú, Hind. and Dec.; ఎర్రగుడ్లగూబ - erragudlagúba, Tel.; கோட்டான் - kóttán, Tam.). Pers. from (kor, pers. blind + búm, pers. owl). Hind. from (ghúka, san. owl). Tel. from (erra, tel. red + gudlagúba, tel. owl). Tam. from (kódu, tam. branch); from its horn. Title otherwise Rock horned owl. Urrua bengalensis, buboninæ, strigidæ [ooloocam], raptores [pacshy, 3], of naturalists. Alias Urrua cavearia. The cry is a loud hoot, like durgoon, durgoon.

OOLOOVAY (உளுவை - uluvai, *Tam.*). From (ulai, tam. mud) [oollaun]; mudfish. Title otherwise Goby, White caboose. The genus Gobius, gobiidæ, acanthopterygii, teleostei, pisces [matsyam, 23], of naturalists [jantoo]. The species best known to the native are shown below. Cf. also Ground goby.——*Ground goby* (పొట్టేలుసొర్ర - pottélusorra, Tel.; மண்ணுளுவை - mannuluvai, Tam.). Title from frequenting sea bottom. Tel. from (pottélu, tel. ram + sorra, tel. shark, carcharias genus). Tam. from (man, tam. ground + uluvai, tam. white caboose, gobius genus). Tel. also (nalladindi), meaning black + stump. Title otherwise Mudskate. Rhynchobatus ancylostomus, rhinobatidæ, batoidei, plagiostomata, chondropterygii [matsyam, 49], of naturalists [jantoo]. Alias Rhamphobatis ancylostomus; Rhina ancylostomus, cyclostomus. Snout very broad with a semi-circular outline; has longitudinal rows of tubercles; dull brown, lighter beneath; the body and sometimes the fins covered with whitish spots; occasionally some tortuous black lines; swims slowly just above the bottom of the sea not far from the shore, picking up what it finds. Another common species is Djeddensis.——*Ringed goby* (మాతురి - máturi, Tel.; குண்டலவுளுவை - kundalavuluvai, Tam.). Title from markings. Tam. from (kundala, san. ring + uluvai, tam. white caboose, gobius genus). Gobius [ooloovay] striatus, gobiidæ, acanthopterygii, teleostei [matsyam, 23], of naturalists. Alias Euctenogobius striatus. Body elongated; sides compressed. Snout elongated, cheeks inflated. Jaws of equal length, or the lower slightly longer. Cleft of mouth nearly horizontal. Scales ctenoid, those anterior to dorsal fin smaller than rest on body; none on cheeks and head; thirty rows between occiput and dorsal fin; fourteen rows between origin of second dorsal and anal fins. Colors generally light fulvous, with bluish tinge along sides, becoming dirty-white beneath; irregular bands from back towards middle of body, also some thin black lines proceed upwards on abdomen opposite to anal fin; cheeks glossed silver; pectoral, ventral and anal whitish-yellow; both dorsals diaphanous, with five or six rows of brown dots; caudal with eight or nine vertical rows of spots in upper half or two-thirds. Fresh waters and backwaters of Madras and Canara.——*River goby* (खर्पे - kharpa, Mahr.; میٹھے پانی کا شیخرا - míthepáníkáshekhrá, Hind.; ಅಬ್ರೋಣಿ - abróni, Can.; చికిడొందు - chíkidondu, Tel.; കതിരാൻ - katirán, Mal.; நல்லதண்ணுளுவை - nallathannuluvai, Tam.). Title from habitat. Hind. from (míthá, hind. fresh + páni, hind. water + shekhrá, hind. gobius genus). Can. from (abra, san. cloud + oni, can. line); from marking on head; cf. abrony. Tel. from (chíku, tel. blind + dondu, tel. eel, anguilla genus). Mal. from (katiram, mal. beauty). Tam. from (nalla, tam. good + tan, tam. water + uluvai, tam. white caboose, gobius genus). Mahr. also (kóka); (ballikóka,), meaning lizard koka. Hind. also (naddíkáshekhrá), meaning river + gobius genus. Tel. also (isukadondu), meaning sand + eel, anguilla, genus; (kóramutte), meaning fang + fish, clupea longiceps; (ballimutte), meaning lizard + clupea longiceps. Mal. also (ottippúzhán), meaning retiring + the fish, eleotris fusca; (púvan), meaning flowery, from reddish color. Title otherwise Koke. Gobius [ooloovay] giuris, gobiidæ, acanthopterygii, teleostei [matsyam, 23], of naturalists. Specific name from (gaura, san. reddish). Alias Gobius bulleekokah, catebus, kokius, koku, kora, korah mottah, kurpah, platycephalus, spectabilis. Bullee kokah from mahratta; koku from mahratta; koramottah from teloogoo; kurpah from mahratta. Lower jaw longer; scales extend superiorly to nearly as far as hind edge of eyes, and twenty-five to thirty rows before base of dorsal fin, where they are smaller than those on body which are angular and ctenoid; colors vary both with localities and also with color of water, generally fawn-color, with cloudy markings on head, and irregular bands, spots, or blotches, on back and sides of body; vertical fins spotted; much esteemed by natives as being very light and wholesome, unless elaborately cooked is not relished by europeans, because of deficiency in or earthy taste; very voracious and takes a bait freely; all pieces of freshwater throughout plains; an edible fish 8 inches long.——*Scorpion goby* (بچھو مچھی - bicçhúmaççhí, Hind.; నూనెముట్టె - núnemutte, Tel.; தேள்கெண்டை - télgendai, Tam.). Title from tail. Hind. from (biççhú, hind. scorpion + maççhí, hind. fish); from its dreaded wounds. Tel. from (núne, tel. oil + mutte, tel. fish, clupea longiceps), from gloss of body; cf. caranx ire. Tam. from (tél, tam. scorpion + kendai, tam. carp, barbus genus). Gobius [ooloovay] viridipunctatus, gobiidæ, acanthopterygii, teleostei [matsyam, 23], of naturalists. Alias Gobius nuna mottah, venenatus. Nunamottah from teloogoo. Cheeks swollen, having many rows of warts; lower jaw longer, cleft of mouth oblique; scales about thirty-two rows between dorsal fin and hind edge of orbit, a few on upper portion of opercle; colors olive, with series of four or five large badly defined blotches along sides; many scales with light centre, which in life is emerald green; dorsals dark at bases, usually having light edges with dark basal band; ventral, anal, and caudal gray, last with light upper edge; sea; common at madras; 5 inches in length.

OOLY (ಉಳಿ - uli, *Can.*). From (ul, can. live). Survivorship [aliyasantauna].

OOLY (ఉలి - uli, *Tel.*). Small.——*Oollangy* (तुणतुणें - túnatunem, Mahr.; تمتما - timtimá, Hind.; ఉల్లంగి - ullangi, Tel.). Mahr. from imitation of call. Tel. from (uli, tel. small + anga, san. body). Hind. also (chobaha); (tuntuna); (pankukrí), meaning water hen. Sandpipers. Totaninæ, scolopacidæ [vanacookkootam], longirostres, grallatores, aves [pacshy, 41], of naturalists [jantoo]. Bill moderate, tip hard and pointed; outer toe joined by web to middle one; change of plumage in summer to black or dusky beneath, and not rufous; migratory birds; winter visitants to india; they pick up small crustacea [kavachiny] and molluscs [chippy] from the surface, and do not insert their bills deeply like snipes [oollaun] and stints; solitary in habit. The species best known to the natives are:—Spotted sandpiper, actitis glareola; a marsh sandpiper; Green sandpiper, actitis ochropus; Common sandpiper, actitis hypoleucos; Green shanks, totanus glottis; rises with loud shrill cry: excellent eating; reaches this country towards the middle or end of september, and leaves for the north in april; Small green shanks, totanus stagnatilis; Spotted red shanks, totanus fuscus; Red shanks, totanus calidris; the μάρτυρος or tell-tale of greeks.——*Oollauk* (ఉల్లాకు - ulláku, Tel.). From (uli, tel. small + áku, tel. palmyra leaf). Memorandum left with goods specifying the quantity and the owner [olay].

OOLYAM (ஊழியம் - úzhiyam, *Tam.*). From (úzh, tam. custom). Service from an inferior to a superior; so wages for such service. Circar oolyam are personal gratuitous services and forced labor for Government and temples [amaujy, maraumut].

OOM (أم - umm, *Ar.*). Mother. Coonyat [ism].

OOMAY (उमा - umá, *San*). From (av, san. to protect). Parvaty [q.v.].——*Oomamaheshwaran* (உமாமகேசுவரன் - umámagésuvaran, Tam.). From (above + mahéshvara, san. shiva, the great lord). Shiva [q.v.] with Parvaty [ardhanaury]. Hindoo 2nd or pers. name [peyar].——*Oomanautan* (உமாநாதன் - umánáthan, Tam.). From (above + nat'ha, san. lord). Shiva, the lord of Parvaty. Hindoo 2nd or pers. name [peyar].

OOMDA (عمده - umdah, *Ar.*). From (amada, ar. to support). Pillar. Part of lacab; as Oomdat ool moolk, pillar of state [ism].——*Oomdat ool oomrah* (عمدةالامرا - umdatulumará, Hind.). From (above + umará, ar. ameers). Pillar of nobles. Name of eldest son of Wallajah [q.v.] and nawaub [q.v.] of Carnatic [q.v.], 1795 to 1801. See vol. I (186), 44; II, 252.

OOMED (امید - umíd, *Hind.*). From arabic. Hope. Oomedwar is a candidate for employment, a volunteer. Oomedwar pattaulam is volunteer corps.

OOMR (عمر - umr, *Ar.*). From (amara, ar. to preserve). Life, existence. Name of prophet's companion. Common alam; as Syed oomr, alaumat + alam [ism].

OOMRAH (امرا - umará, *Ar.*). Pl. of (amír, ar. commander; lord). The nobles of a native mahomedan court collectively. Lacab suffix; as Ameer ool oomrah, lord of lords [ameer, ism].

OON (ان - un, *Ar.*). Al before n in Arabic compounds; as Abd oon nabee, slave of the prophet [al].

OON (உண் - un, *Tam.*). To eat.——*Oombaly* (ಉಂಬಳಿ - umbali, Can.). From (unnu, can. eating). Subsistence. Inam [q.v.] land.——*Oonny* (உண்ணி - unni, Tam.). From (un, tam. to eat). Means a wart on the body. Also an infant. Hindoo 2nd or pers. name [peyar]. Also hindoo third name in Malabar assumed by members of some families and showing royal descent.——*Oo'pera* (ഊട്ടുപുര - úttupura, Mal.). From (úttu, mal. feeding + pura, mal. house). Free inn for bramins, a peculiar religious institution of Travancore. They are about forty-two in number, situated at convenient stages throughout the country, mostly in connection with the principal temples [coil, pagoda]. In them bramins are fed at the expense of the circar [q.v.] with curry [q.v.] and rice [q.v.], rice boiled in water, chutney [q.v.], curd [tyre], milk [paul], fruits [pazham], &c. Neither travelling nor resident bramins however are allowed to remain in the same Ootpera longer than two days, unless sickness or other unavoidable cause prevents their leaving the place. In some of these houses only one meal a day is allowed, while in others meals are provided both morning and evening. A small quantity of boiled rice is distributed to poor shoodras [q.v.] daily at noon, and in two or three instances this is given to all castes [jauty] indiscriminately [chuttram]. The principal Ootpera is at the temple of Pudmanaubhan at Trivandrum. See vol. II, 135, 291.

OONDEE (اُنڈی - undí, *Hind.*). Same as Common poon.

OONJAL (ஊஞ்சல் - úñjal, *Tam.*). Swing.——*Oonjal tirnaul* (ஊஞ்சற்றிருநாள் - úñjattirunál, Tam.). Swinging the images [shilay, vigraham] of gods and goddesses in an ornamental swing at the close of the annual festival [pundigay, 6d]. Dolotsavam of the north.

OOPA (उप - upa, *San.*). Prefix denoting subordination or inferiority. Also means near.——*Oohary* (ഓഹരി - óhari, Mal.). From (upa, san. together + hri, san. to take). A share [bhaugam].——*Oopadaunam* (उपदान - upadána, San.). From (above + dá, san. to give). Offering; alms, charity [kheirauty].——*Oopadesham* (उपदेश - upadésha, San.). From (above + dish, san. teach). Doctrine, teaching [oopanishad].——*Oopugraumam* (उपग्राम - upagráma, San.). From (above + gráma, san. village). A hamlet.——*Oopamaunam* (उपमान - upamána, San.). From (above + má, san. to measure). Measuring one thing near another; comparison; one of the four processes, according to Nyauya [q.v.] philosophy, by which the mind arrives at true and accurate knowledge. The other three are pratyacsham or sense perception, anoomaunam or inference, and shabdam or verbal testimony.——*Oopanayanam* (उपनयन - upanayana, San.). From (above + ní, san. to lead); approaching a gooroo [q.v.] to receive auricular instruction in the gayatry [q.v.], which is the essential part of the ceremony. The ceremony of investiture with the sacred thread [poonool] or cord worn over the left shoulder and under the right, for the twice-born castes [dwijan], or Bramins [q.v.], Cshatriyas [q.v.], and Veisyas [q.v.]. Cotton [q.v.] for Bramin, flax [sunn] for Cshatriya, wool [pushm] for Veisya. See vol. II, 235.——*Oopanishad* (उपनिषद् - upanishad, San.). From (above + ni, san. down + sad, san. to sit). Sitting at the feet of a teacher [gooroo]. Certain mystical writings attached to the Bramhanam [q.v.] portion of the old Vedams, the aim being ascertainment of secret sense of Vedam [q.v.]. Also called Rahasyam or mystical doctrine [oopadesham]. The Greeks and Romans had their so-called mysteries reserved only for the initiated. Even the Koran [q.v.] is held to possess an exoteric meaning called Zauhir [q.v.] and an esoteric called Bautin; and in latter times a mystical system of pantheistic philosophy called Soofeeism [soofee] was developed in Persia out of this esoteric teaching. Similarly Vedam or sacred knowledge is said to possess two distinct branches. The first is called Carma caundam [q.v.], which, embracing both Muntram [q.v.] and Bramhanam is for that large majority of persons who are unable to conceive of religion except as a process of laying up merit by external rites [carmam]. The second is called Nyauna caundam [q.v.], and is reserved for that select few who are capable of the true knowledge. The one, it may be added, implies action, the other cessation from all action. The Oopanishads are for the most part short, mystical and obscure. The ordinary enumeration of them is said to be 51; but there are others bearing that name, considered to be spurious. The following are some of the most important :—the Eitareya oopanishad and Cowsheetaky bramhana oopanishad of the Rig vedam; the Teittireeyam belonging to the Teittireeya samhitay of the Yajoor vedam, the Brihad auranyacam attached to the Shatapata bramhanam of the Vaujasaneyee samhitay of that Vedam and the Eesham or Eeshauvausyam forming an actual part the fortieth chapter of this latter Samhitay, this being the only instance of an Oopanishad attached to a Samhitay rather than a Bramhanam; the Chandogyam and Kena oopanishad belonging to the Sauma vedam; the Prashnam, Moondacam, Maundoocyam, and Katam belonging to the Atarva vedam [matam].——*Oopapooraunam* (उपपुराण - upapuráña, San.). From (above + puráña, san. history). Secondary pooraunams [q.v.]. This name is given to eighteen works subordinate, one to each, to the eighteen Maha pooraunams or principal pooraunams. The general character of these works is very similar to that of the principal pooraunams. The Oopapooraunams, as reckoned in the south, are :—Aungiram, Bhaurgavam, Capilam, Canly, Doorvausam, Maunavam, Maureecham, Naurasimham, Nauradeeyam, Nundy, Ooshanam, Parausharam, Sanatcoomauram, Shaumbhavam, Shivatanmam, Sowram, Vasishta lingam, Vauroonam.——*Oopaucarmam* (ఉపాకర్మం - upákarmam, Tel.). From (above + á, san. prefix meaning near + kri, san. to do). Preparation to read the vedam. Same as Auvany avittam.——*Oopaudhy* (उपाधि - upádhi, San.). From (above + ádhá, san. to place). Condition. In vedauntam [q.v.] specially applied to certain forms or properties considered conditions or disguises of spirit; attributive. In luni-solar [chaundramaunam] calendar [punchaungam], an expunged day [adhicam, tity].——*Oopaudhyaujan* (उपाध्याय - upádhyáya, San.). From (above + adhí, san. to study). Priest [acharry], teacher [gooroo, peyar].——*Oopaungam* (उपाङ्ग - upánga, San.). From (above + anga, san. limb). Additional limbs of the Vedam [q.v.]. To be distinguished from Vedaungam and Oopavedam. They are six :—Dharma shastram, on jurisprudence; Itihausam, or epic poems; Mimaumsam, on philosophy; Pooraunam, or legendary histories; Tuntram, on ritual; Yogam, on logic.——*Oopauntyam* (उपान्त्य - upántya, San.). From (above + antya, san. last). Corner of the eye. Last but one, in mathematics [ganitam].——*Ooparausam* (उपवास - upavása, San.; நோம்பு - nómbu, Tam.). From (upa, san. at + vas, san. to dwell); dwelling in a state of abstinence. Fast [pundigay, 6d]. As a religious act comprises abstinence not merely from food and drink but from all sensual gratification, from perfumes, flowers, unguents, ornaments, betel, music, dancing, &c., the use of a mattress when sleeping, and even sleep itself. The fasts observed for each deity are mentioned under the heads of those deities. Some are observed in behalf of deceased parents, brothers, sisters, children, &c. For a deceased child a partial fast is observed for eight days, and for a deceased grown-up person the same for sixteen days with carmauntram [q.v.] at the end. The fasts and the various rites are repeated on every thirtieth day from day of decease for the first year, and this is called mausicam [mausam]; and then again at every anniversary of the deceased, which is called tity [q.v.]. The eleventh day [yecaudashy] of every fortnight [pacsham] is kept as a rigid fast; and on the days of the new [amavausyay] and full moon [powrnimay] and those in which an eclipse [grahanam] of either the sun [sooryan] or moon [chundran] takes place, and on several other occasions, a half fast is observed [maryauday].——*Oopavedam* (उपवेद - upavéda, San.). From (above + véda, san. sacred writing, so called). Secondary vedams [q.v.], which however have really little or no connection with either the Vedam or Smrity [q.v.]. To be distinguished from Vedaungam, Oopaungam. They are :—Ayoor vedam, or science of medicine [veidyan], derived from the rig vedam; Dhanoor vedam, or military science, derived from the yajoor vedam; Gaundharva vedam, or science of music [sangeetam], derived from the sauma vedam; Shilpam [q.v.], or staupatya vedam [staupatyam], on the mechanical arts and architecture, derived from the atarva vedam [shastram].

OOPPINANGADY (ಉಪ್ಪಿನಂಗಡಿ - uppinangadi, * *Can.*). From (uppu, can. salt + angadi, can. shop) [ooppoo]; salt store.——(1) Talook, South canara district. Tahsildar's pay Rs. 175. Area 951 square miles; S. inland of district. Boundaries:—on the north, the Mysore territory; on the south the Cassergode talook and Coorg; on the east, Mysore territory and Coorg; and on the west, Mangalore and Cassergode talooks. For the most part a hilly country well-clothed with forest. Rice [q.v.], pepper [q.v.], cardamoms [q.v.], areca-nuts [q.v.], timber and other forest produce are exported. Imports chiefly cotton [q.v.] goods and articles of european manufacture. Irrigation dependent chiefly on the rains, but after close of the monsoon [q.v.], the streams, natural pools and private tanks [q.v.] and wells are resorted to. Camping grounds on the Mangalore and Mercara road:—Sumpanjey, Soolya, Cauv poottore. On the Codicull-Charmaudy ghaut road:—Charmaudy, Beltangady. On the Mangalore and Manjarabad road:—Sirady, Golitutt, Ooppinangady, Mauny. Places of archæological interest:—Alancauram, Bantra, Beltangady, Byle, Cadaba, Goorvauyankerey, Indoobett, Jemalabad, Mauchina, Mullarmaudy, Oojrey, Ooppinangady, Panja, Poottore, Soobramanya. Principal trig. stations:—Ammedicull, Bullanaudgoodda, Coothiraymookh. The leading places, &c., in the talook are the following.——*Ambatamoory* (ಅಂಬಟಮುರಿ - ambatamuri, Can.). From (ambata, can. wild mango, spondias mangifera, willd. + muri, mal. village). Pass [ghaut]; lat. between 13° 01′ and 13° 4′ N.; long. between 75° 31′ and 75° 33′ E. Leads into Mysore, but is little used.——*Ammedicull* (ಅಮ್ಮೆಡಿಕಲ್ಲು - ammedikallu, Can.). Trig. station; lat. 12° 58′ 38·82″; long. 75° 33′ 13·38″; height 4,267 feet; from Poottore N.E. 26 miles.——*Beilangady* (ಬೈಲಂಗಡಿ - bailangadi, Can.). From (bailu, can. a plain + angadi, can. shop). A Sub-division of talook [q.v.] or Maugaunam [q.v.] comprising six villages; pop. 1,979.——*Beltangady* (ಬೆಳ್ತಂಗಡಿ - beltangadi, Can.). See sep. title.——*Bisley* (ಬಿಸಲೆ - bisale, Can.). See sep. title.——*Bullanaudgoodda* (ಬಲ್ಲನಾಡುಗುಡ್ಡ - ballanádugudda, Can.). Trig. station; lat. 12° 41′ 00·40″; long. 75° 12′ 23·20″.——*Cadaba* (ಕಡಬ - kadaba, Can.). Village; pop. 1,025; lat. 12° 45′; long. 75°31′; from Mangalore E. 43 miles; from Poottore E. 18 miles. In ancient days one of the four centres, when the country along the coast was divided into 64 sections [graumam] under Bramin governors by Mayoora varman [keraloputty]. Temple [coil, pagoda] of Ganesh [q.v.].——*Charmaudy* (ಚಾರ್ಮಾಡಿ - chármádi, Can.). See sep. title.——*Comauradhaury* (ಕುಮಾರಧಾರಿ - kumáradhári, Can.). See. sep. title.——*Coothiraymookh* (ಕುದುರೆಮುಖ - kuduremukha, Can.). See sep. title.——*Coottiyaur* (ಕುತ್ತಿಯಾರ - kuttiyára, Can.). Village; pop. 1,182; lat. 12° 59′; long. 75° 19′; from Mangalore E.N.E. 30 miles; from Poottore N.N.E. 17 miles. Jeina [q.v.] temple [basty] and mantapam [q.v.]. The town of Beltangady lies in this village.——*Dharmastala* (ಧರ್ಮಸ್ಥಳ - dharmast'hala, Can.). From (dharma, san. charity + st'hala, san. place). Place of Hindoo pilgrimage in the village of Mullarmaudy; pop. 1,325; lat. 12° 57′; long. 75° 26′; from Beltangady E.S.E. 8 miles; from Mangalore E. 38 miles; from Poottore N.E. 18 miles. Well endowed temple of Munjoonautan. The Dharmastala jautrey [q.v.] or illumination festival for four days in November or December. Nadauvaly festival once in 12 years for 13 days.——*Jemalabad* (جمال آباد - jamálábád, Hind.). See sep. title.——*Manjarabad* (ಮಂಜರಾಬಾದ್ - manjarábád, Can.). See sep. title.——*Mardala* (ಮರ್ದಾಲ - mardala, Can.). A maugaunam [q.v.] or sub-division of talook comprising seven villages; pop. 1,638.——*Neranky* (ನೆರಂಕಿ - neranki, Can.). A sub-division of talook comprising 24 villages; pop. 7,640.——*Neriya* (ನೆರಿಯ - neriya, Can.). Village; pop. 659; contains cardamom [q.v.] jungles.——*Netrauvaty* (ನೇತ್ರಾವತಿ - nétrávati, Can.). See sep. title.——*Ooppinangady* (ಉಪ್ಪಿನಂಗಡಿ - uppinangadi, Can.). See below.——*Pooshpagherry* (ಪುಷ್ಪಗಿರಿ - pushpagiri, Can.). See sep. title.——*Poottore* (ಪುತ್ತೂರು - puttúru, Can.). See sep. title.——*Sissal* (ಶಿಸಲ - shisala, Can.). Village; pop. 255; lat. 12° 54′; long. 75° 32′; from Mangalore E. 45 miles; from Poottore E.N.E. 23 miles.——*Soobramanya* (ಸುಬ್ರಹ್ಮಣ್ಯ - subrahmanya, Can.). See sep. title.——*Soolya* (ಸುಳ್ಯ - sulya, Can.). A small town in the village of Canattil cayartody; pop. 618; lat. 12° 33′; long. 75° 26′; from Mangalore E. 42 miles; from Poottore S.E. 18 miles.——*Sumpaujey* (ಸಂಪಾಜೆ - sampáje, Can.). See sep. title. ——**(2)** Village; South canara dist., Ooppinangady tal.; pop. 1,612; lat. 12° 50′; long. 75° 17′; from Mangalore E. 27 miles; from Poottore N.N.E. 6 miles. On the Netrauvaty. Until recently head-quarters of the talook. An old temple at the confluence of the Netrauvaty and Comauradhaury is held very sacred.

OOPPOO (लवण - lavana, *San.*; मीठ - mít'ha, *Mahr.*; ملح - milh, *Ar.*; نمك - nimak, *Pers.*; لون - lon, *Hind.*; نمك - namak, *Dec.*; گرام - garám, *Malay*; ಉಪ್ಪು - uppu, *Can.* and *Too.*; ఉప్పు - uppu, *Tel.*; ഉപ്പ് - uppu, *Mal.*; ලුණු - lunu, *Singh.*; உப்பு - uppu, *Tam.*). San. from (lú, san. to cut); as a digestive. Mahr. from (mishta, san. savoury). Hind. and Singh. from sanscrit. Tam. from (uva, tam. to expand); native salt is an efflorescence. Hind. also (namak) [namak]. Any chemical salt, whether acid [poolipp, tezaub] or alkaline [cauram].——**(1)** Usually stands for common salt; sodii chloridum of chemists, alias sodæ murias. This when obtained by the evaporation of sea-water with more or less artificial processes for its purification, &c., is common salt or sea-salt; see vol. I, 440. When found native in large masses, which only requires to be dug and reduced to powder it is rock-salt [sondah namak]. When it is obtained naturally and without artificial processes as the result of a single evaporation of sea-water lying in hollows or on marshes it is called swamp salt [parra ooppoo]. When found in a state of efflorescence on the surface of the soil after rains in the inland districts and subsequently purified it is called effloresced salt. When educed from earth containing saline properties [sowdoo] by filtration, and evaporation or boiling of the liquid, it is called educed salt [att ooppoo]. In small and repeated doses common salt promotes appetite and assists the processes of digestion and assimilation; in large doses in solution it acts as an emetic, purgative and anthelmintic; locally applied rubefacient; a chemical antidote in poisoning by nitrate of silver [caudy cauram]. Used in dyeing [shauyam]. There is a Tamul proverb:—உப்புக்கட்டிஞல் லோகம் கட்டும்—"if there be a "supply of salt the world will be sustained." See vol. I, 436; II, 40.——**(2)** For medicinal salts see Sarakk.——**(3)** The following are the different terms for salt or alkaline earth [sowdoo].——*Calar* (களர் - kalar, Tam.). From (kalam, tam. dark). Same as Ooppalar.——*Ooppalar* (చవటనేల - tsavatinéla, Tel.; உப்பளறு - uppalaru, Tam.). From (alaru, tam. mud). Tel. means saline earth + soil. Also called Calar. A soil which is a mixture of clay [calimunn] and sand [manal] largely impregnated with alkaline matters; it is generally met with in hollows or swamps on the coasts, and occurs also in particular localities inland; it is absolutely unproductive except when large volumes of fresh water are available, in which case the salts are washed away by repeated flooding.——*Ooshar bhoomy* (ऊषरभूमि - úsharabhúmi, San.; చవటనేల - tsavatinéla, Tel.). Same as Ooppalar.——*Oovar munn* (సున్నపుచవుడు - sunnaputsavudu, Tel.; உவர்மண் - uvarman, Tam.). Tel. means lime + saline earth. Dhoby's earth [q.v.].——*Oozhamunn* (உழமண் - uzhaman, Tam.). Corruption of Oovar munn.——*Pooneer* (பூநீறு - púníru, Tam.). Means flowering ashes. Otherwise Nilaveeram. A kind of bangle earth [gauzoo sowdoo]. See separate head.——*Poo vazhalay* (பூவழலை - púvazhalai, Tam.). Means earth soap. Same as Pooneer.——*Shavatt munn* (చవటనేల - tsavatinéla, Tel.; சவட்டுமண் - shavattuman, Tam.). Any earth containing sowdoo [q.v.]——*Valaiyal munn* (గాజుచవుడు - gádzutsavudu, Tel.; வளையல்மண் - valaiyalman, Tam.). Means glass bangles + earth. Otherwise Gauzoola ooppoo bhoomy. Mineral sand [manal] of which glass bangles [gauzoo] are made [gauzoo sowdoo].——**(4)** *Ooppalam* (ఉప్పళము - uppalamu, Tel.; உப்பளம் - uppalam, Tam.). A salt pan.——*Ooppalapaud* (ఉప్పలపాడు - uppalapádu, Tel.). From (uppalamu, tel. salt marsh + pádu, tel. village). Village, Hill; Kurnool dist., Coilcoontla tal.; lat. 15° 11′; long. 78° 05′; from Coilcoontla W.S.W. 18 miles; from Kurnool S. 45 miles. Largest hill plateau in the district. East lies Coondair valley and beyond are Nullamullays. On E. is a sudden descent to the low country and on other sides to a narrow flat terrace. It is difficult of ascent. The only way of getting to it is from the south-west by the denuded bay north-east of Goodipaud. Even here the cart traffic is only from Ooppalapaud to this bay, there being a terrace of flat beds of limestone [choonam cull] beyond it. Drained by the Tirmalair.——*Ooppanaur* (ఉప్పుకయ్య - uppukayya, Tel.; உப்பனூர் - uppanár, Tam.). Means salt river. A channel communicating with the sea [ooppatair].——*Ooppary* (ఉప్పరి - uppari, Tel.). From (above + ari, tel. personal suffix). Tel. form of Ooppaura.——*Ooppatair* (ఉప్పుటేరు - upputéru, Tel.). From (uppu, tel. salt + éru, tel. river). A tidal or salt-water river [ooppanaur].——*Ooppaura* (ಉಪ್ಪಾರ - uppára, Can.). A caste in Canara and Mysore, including bricklayers, laborers, gardeners, &c.; originally salt-makers. The Ooppaurar were originally of teloogoo origin. They have hereditary chiefs called Yejmaun [q.v.]. They may eat meat, but may not drink spirituous liquors [arrack]. They are allowed a plurality of wives. The girls continue to be marriageable after the age of puberty, but a widow cannot marry again. They bury the dead [shavacaud]. The god of the caste is Vishnoo [q.v.], but they pray to Dharma rajan [q.v.], and offer sacrifices to the Shacties [q.v.]. They have no knowledge of a future life. To be distinguished from the Woddar [q.v.]. Numbers about 100,000, chiefly in Bellary and Godavery [jauty]. See vol. II, 230.——*Ooppellore* (ఉప్పేలూరు - uppuélúru, Tel.). From (uppu, tel. salt + élúru, tel. place so called). Native name of Ellore, Godavery district, to distinguish it from Vellore or Rye ellore.——*Ooppinangady* (ಉಪ್ಪಿನಂಗಡಿ - uppinangadi, Can.). See sep. title.——*Ooppoo cottauram* (ఉప్పుకోఠారము - uppukot'háramu, Tel. உப்புக்கொட்டாரம் - uppukkottáram, Tam.). Salt depôt [cotaur]. ——*Ooppoo nilam* (చవటనేల - tsavatinéla, Tel.; உப்புநிலம் - uppunilam, Tam.). Brackish ground [calar, ooppalar, sowdoo]. ——*Ooppoovaudy* (నట్టు - nattu, Tel.; உப்புவாடி - uppuvádi, Tam.). From (vádi, tam. enclosure). Tel. means platform. A platform for piling salt upon.——**(5)** *Attooppoo* (ಅಟ್ಟುಪ್ಪು - attuppu, Can.; కాచుడుప్పు - kátsuduppu, Tel.; அடுப்பு - attuppu, Tam.). From (adu, tam. to boil + uppu, tam. salt). Tel. means boiled + salt [cautch ooppoo]. Common salt educed from soils containing it simple or in combination with other salts, by the process of filtration and then evaporating or boiling. ——*Bhaidy ooppoo* (భేదిఉప్పు - bhédiuppu, Tel.; பேதியுப்பு - péthiyuppu, Tam.). From (bhédí, san. purgative + uppu, tam.

salt). Epsom salts or sulphate of magnesia [caunta munn].——*Caroopp ooppoo* (నల్లఉప్పు - nallauppu, Tel.; கறுப்புப்பு - karuppuppu, Tam.). From (karuppu, tam. black + uppu, tam. salt). Same as Bitloban [q.v.].——*Caur ooppoo* (పర్రఉప్పు - parrauppu, Tel.; കാരുപ്പ് - káruppu, Mal.; காருப்பு - káruppu, Tam.). Means black + salt. Wild salt that appears spontaneously; otherwise swamp salt [parra ooppoo].——*Cautch ooppoo* (కాచుడుప్పు - kátsuduppu, Tel.; காய்ச்சுப்பு - káyççuppu, Tam.). Means boiled + salt. Same as Att ooppoo.——*Cull ooppoo* (రాతిఉప్పు - rátiuppu, Tel.; கல்லுப்பு - kalluppu, Tam.). Means stone + salt. Same as Indooppoo.——*Curry ooppoo* (వంటఉప్పు - vantauppu, Tel.; கறிபுப்பு - kariyuppu, Tam.). Means curry stuff + salt. Tel. means cooking + salt. Name for common salt.——*Draucsha ooppoo* (द्राक्षालवण - drákshálavana, San.; द्राक्षीमीठ - drákshímít'ha, Mahr.; نمك انگور - namakiangúr, Pers., Hind. and Dec.; ದ್ರಾಕ್ಷಿಉಪ್ಪು - drákshiuppu, Can.; ద్రాక్షఉప్పు - drákshauppu, Tel.; திராக்கவுப்பு - tirákkavuppu, Tam.). San. from (drákshá, san. grape + lavana, san. salt). Mahr. from (drákshá, san. grape + mít'ha, mahr. salt). Pers from (nimak, pers. salt + angúr, pers. grape). Tel. from (drákshá, san. grape + uppu, tel. salt). Tartar. Also called Tartrate of potash, Cream of tartar. Potassæ tartras acida, or Potassæ bitartras of chemists. With veidyans [q.v.], refrigerant, diuretic and laxative; in large doses, hydragogue, cathartic [namak, ospitry].——*Gandhac ooppoo* (గంధకఉప్పు - gandhakauppu, Tel.; கந்தகவுப்பு - kandagavuppu, Tam.). Means sulphur + salt. That kind of bitloban [q.v.] which has the smell of sulphur [gandhac].——*Indooppoo* (सैन्धव - saindhava, San.; سوندا نمك - sondánamak, Hind.; لاهوری نمك - láhorínamak, Dec.; ఇందుప్పు - induppu, Tel.; ഇന്തുപ്പ് - induppu, Mal.; இந்துப்பு - induppu, Tam.). Title and Drav. from (sindhu, san. country so called + uppu, tam. salt). San. means produced in sind. Hind. means sind salt; Dec. means lahore salt. Rock salt; same as Sondah namak.——*Mara ooppoo* (दारुलवण - dárulavana, San.; మానుప్పు - mánuppu, Tel.; மரவுப்பு - maravuppu, Tam.). Means tree + salt. Potash [jharka namak]; used as mineral dye [shauyam].——*Moongil-ooppoo* (వెదురుప్పు - veduruppu, Tel.; மூங்கிலுப்பு - múngiluppu, Tam.). Bamboo [q.v.] salt. Same as Tabasheer.——*Parra ooppoo* (పర్రఉప్పు - parrauppu, Tel.; கழியுப்பு - kazhiyuppu, Tam.). Tel. from (parra, tel. salt marsh + uppu, tel. salt). Swamp or spontaneous salt [caur ooppoo].——*Pottle ooppoo* (ಪೆಟ್ಲುಪ್ಪು - petluppu, Can.; పెట్లుప్పు - petluppu, Tel.; பொட்டிலுப்பு - pottiluppu, Tam.). From (pottil, tam. firelock + uppu, tam. salt). Can. from (pettalu, can. to burst). Tel. from (petlu, tel. to explode + uppu, tel. salt). Saltpetre [shorah].——*Savity ooppoo* (చవిటిఉప్పు - tsavitiuppu, Tel.; சவட்டுப்பு - shavattuppu, Tam.). Title and Tel. from (tsavudu, tel. fuller's earth + uppu, tel. salt). Same as Attooppoo.——*Shaumbel ooppoo* (బూడిదెఉప్పు - búdideuppu, Tel.; சாம்பலுப்பு - shámbaluppu, Tam.). Means ashes + salt. Potash from vegetable ashes; same as Sujjee khaur [q.v.]——*Valaiyal ooppoo* (ಗಾಜುಪ್ಪು - gájuppu, Can.; గాజుప్పు - gádzuppu, Tel.; വളയുപ്പ് - valayuppu, Mal.; வளையலுப்பு - valaiyaluppu, Tam.). Can. from (gáju, can. glass + uppu, can. salt). Mal. from (vala, mal. bangle + uppu, mal. salt). Tam. means glass bangles + salt. A very white medicinal salt from Pooneer [q.v.] earth. Fel vitri or glass gall. Carminative in medicine. Same as Poongauram [q.v.].——*Vediyooppoo* (పెట్లుప్పు - petluppu, Tel.; വെടിയുപ്പ് - vetiyuppu, Mal.; வெடியுப்பு - vediyuppu, Tam.). From (vedi, tam. explosion + uppu, tam. salt). Saltpetre; same as Pottle ooppoo.

OOR (ار - ur, *Ar.*). Al before r in Arabic compounds; as Abd oor raheem, slave of the merciful [al].

OOR (ಊರು - úru, *Can.*; ఊరు - úru, *Tel.*; ഊര് - úr, *Mal.*; ஊர் - úr, *Tam.*). From (uru, tam. to dwell). Agricultural village [graumam]; as opposed to Caud [q.v.], or wild untilled tract. Suffix in place names; as Ahtoor, meaning river village. In Anglo-indian termination changed always, except in an iambus, to ore [q.v.]; as Coimbatore, Nellore, Tanjore, Vellore. There are 23 places in Southern india mentioned by Ptolemy which end in *ουρ* or *ουρα*. The following are examples :—*σαλούρ*, *κορέουρα*, *ποδοπέρουρα*, *παλούρα*, *ἀρεμβούρ*, *μαγούρ*, *μαντιττούρ*, *κορινδιούρ*. *ποδοπέρουρα* evidently means new great town, and *παλούρα* milk town. A south indian village consists not only of the residences of the inhabitants, but of a tract of land around them within determinate boundaries, including arable [sheygaul] and pasture lands [cuncha], wood [caud], waste [beed], and water [neer]. For village tenures see vol. I, 112, foot-note. Every village has an establishment of officers and servants, more or less complete according as its original organization has been less or more interfered with [balootah, graumam].——**(1)** The following translations from original Teloogoo papers show the way in which villages have been formed.—"*a*" Account of the village of Mahimalore in Nellore district. Thirteen hundred years ago this neighbourhood was an entire forest; that is to say in Shal. Sac. 424. A person named Mahimaloo in consequence of the oppression of Vencata bhauscara row, a petty ruler, emigrated from the Pauk naud, and Mahimaloo is alluded to in the account, as Our ancestor. He came to the neighbourhood of Pondore, and remained there six months, protected by the Boy [q.v.] and Mootraucha [q.v.] tribes. But the emigrating family [valsa] being large, they built another village, consisting at first only of four or five mud huts. It was called Mahimalore, after the name of the head of the family. Acquiring wealth, Mahimaloo called hither other families; and, the village being enlarged, he attended to its regulation. A Bramin named Vencannah, who had accompanied him from the first in his emigration, was made village accountant [curnum]. The younger brother of Mahimaloo from some disagreement left him, and built another village to the north-east, which he called Nundivaram. This person called Nundy reddy had two sons named Ramayya and Bheemayya, one of whom was a cowherd, and the other a shepherd. Both of these formed distinct hamlets, called Bheemavaram and Ramaya pully. The former becoming spiritually enlightened resolved not to eat without having a god, and accordingly built a Shiva [q.v.] fane [coil, goody], the image [shilay, vigraham] of which received the name Bheemalingeshwaran. After his death the building went to ruin, but vestiges of it remain. The aforesaid Nundy reddy appointed Vencannah, the Bramin as accountant both of his own villages and his son's villages. The descendants of that Bramin have continued to be hereditary accountants. In Shal. Sac. 1,139, the chief of the Velgotiwaur, named Vencatapaty naidoo, built a fane to Shree vengopaulsawmy. Subsequently people from other places came hither and built eight villages around. In a Shooclam [brihaspaty chuckram] year a famine occurred, and these villages became entirely desolate. When Krishnaroya [q.v.] conquered the Gajapaty [q.v.] prince, he placed three persons, named Lakky rauz, Chittam rauz and Narrain rauz in possession of the fort [cottay] of Mahimalore, each of which persons formed a district called after his own name. After their death the management was in the hands of people appointed by the Circar [q.v.] under the Oodayagherry jagheer [q.v.], and so it continues to the present time. The names of the subsequent headmen are all Mahomedan; down to the English rule, wherein the name of Mr. Travers as Collector appears. There follow very minute details of villages, fanes, reservoirs, groves, classes, and numbers of trees.—"*b*" Account of the village of Raupore in Nellore district. About 524 years ago, this place was wild and uninhabited; the diwaun [q.v.] of the Gajapaty [q.v.] had the jungle cleared, and, by permission of the Circar, established a village which he called Raupore. Some villages were built by other persons. A Bramin was named as accountant [curnum] and his descendants held the office. When the Chola rajah came hither the office was sold to a person under the Chola [q.v.] ruler. The fort was built by Pedda comaura yautsama naidoo of the Velgotiwaur race, who excavated three water reservoirs; he also built some fanes [coil, pagoda]. The accountants built a shrine to the tutelary goddess, which alone now continues. One named Krishnappa naick came from the west and plundered, when one Vijnam khan fought with him and took him prisoner. The names of two or three Mahomedan rulers follow, down to the assumption of the district by the Honorable Company.—"*c*" Account of the village of Kota in Nellore district. The formation of the village is dated in Shal. Sac. 513, and ascribed to the accountants of Tondiman [q.v.] chuckravurty [q.v.]. Some Jeinas [q.v.] from the neighbourhood engaged in cultivation. The Bramins were accountants. One named Mookkanteshwaran governed. His son was Ranadheeran. His younger brother was Manodheeran. Then Nundan chuckravurty. Next the Jeinas from the Conjeeveram country. Then the Chola rajah. Next Ambhojam rajah. Then Siddhy rauz. Then Vaimareddy. At the request of the people, owing to the dread of robbers, the latter appointed one named Chittait bodhanalingama naidoo as a guardian of the town and neighbourhood. Subsequently when Narsimha deva royer ruled a dispute arose between the Bramins and the Jeinas and many of the Jeinas were killed. The remains of their class emigrated towards the south. In the time of Krishnaroya some one excavated a water reservoir [cheroo]. Fanes were built by different people. The government came into the hands of the Royel [q.v.] by whom the population was increased. Timma naidoo built a village called by his own name, and brought some merchants to the place. Others built villages, and, after a few transitions of power, the rule came into possession of the Nellore chieftain.——**(2)** The ninth chapter of the Maunasauram [q.v.] treats of villages and towns. It regards the formation of streets [veety] and the allotment of suitable sites for the building of temples [coil, pagoda], piazzas, &c. The extent of villages or towns is declared to admit of forty varieties, consisting of from five hundred to twenty thousand dandams [q.v.] square, each sort exceeding the one immediately below it by five hundred dandams. The whole area of a village, with the lands thereunto belonging, being divided into twenty equal parts, one is assigned for the occupation of Bramins, six or more for that of the three other classes, and the remainder for agriculture. A street that goes round the village or town is called mungala veety [q.v.], which should be from one to five dandams in width. That which runs from east to west is called raja patam; that which has gates on both sides raja veety; that which has sundhies or angles, sundhy veety; and that which is in a southerly direction, maha caulam or vimaunam [q.v.].

There are eight sorts of villages or towns, namely :—dandacam or that which resembles a staff; sarwatobhadram, or in every respect happy; nundyauvartam or the abode of happiness; pudmacam or that which has the form of a lotus [nelumbo] flower; swasticam [q.v.] or that which resembles the mystical figure so named; prastaram or that which has the shape of a couch; caurmookam or that which resembles a bow; chatoor mookham or that which has four faces. The height of the buildings should correspond in every street as far as practicable, and in all structures of the same number of storeys. The outer door should be placed not exactly in the middle of the façade, but a little more to one side than to the other. In the front of the houses should be erected a vaidicay [pyall], or raised seat or pedestal on each side of the door. An edifice is called shooddham which is composed of but one kind of material, as stone [cull], brick [shengal], &c., and this is considered the best of all. Mishram is that which is composed of two kinds of materials, as brick and stone, or stone and metal [loham]. Sankeernam is that composed of three or more kinds of materials, as timber, stone, brick, metal, &c. [maunasauram, staupatyam, veed].——*Ooran* (ஊரான் - úran, Tam.). From (above + an, tam. personal termination). Chief of agricultural tract [maroothara].——*Ooraulan* (ഊരാളൻ - úrálan, Mal.). From (above + álu, mal. to own). Formerly the representatives of villages, part of whose duty it was to manage the village temples. Now the founders or present managers of temples [coil, pagoda]. Their office is Ooroyma.——*Oorauly* (ഊരാളി - úráli, obl.; ഊരാളൻ - úrálan, pers. sing.; ഊരാളർ - úrálar, pers. pl., Mal.). A forest tribe on the West coast. Inhabit the Todoopoya hills. They build their huts on trees, like the Arayar [malayarasar]. They entertain a singular aversion to buffaloes [khoolgah], whose approach they anxiously avoid; and are expert in the use of the bow. Ooraulies and Oollaudar intermarry. From the practice of polyandry, they are, like the Todahs [q.v.] on the Neilgherries, fast diminishing in numbers. They consider themselves superior to the Poolayar [q.v.] and Pariahs [jauty]. See vol. II, 104.——*Oorautchy* (ஊராட்சி - úrádchi, Tam.). From (above + ál, tam. to rule). Management of a village [maniyam].——*Oorcheroo* (ఊరుచెరువు - úrucheruvu, Tel.). From (above + cheruvu, tel. tank). Tank [q.v.] for common use of villagers.——*Oorcuttey* (ಊರುಕಟ್ಟೆ - úrukatte, Can.). From (above + katte, can. raised ground). Raised seat round a tree in front of a village where villagers assemble.——*Oor gownden* (ஊர்க்கௌண்டன் - úrkkaundan, Tam.). Head of a village [gownden].——*Oor maniyam* (ஊர்மணியம் - úrmaniyam, Tam.). From (above + maniyam, tam. superintendence). Revenue head of a village [maniyam, monigar].——*Oor maunyam* (ஊர்மானியம் - úrmániyam, Tam.). From (above + mánya, san. privilege). Village free lands, exempted from revenue for the performance of village duties [inam].——*Oorote* (ഊരോത്ത - úrótta, Mal.). Oblique form of Ooragam. From (úr, mal. village + akam, mal. inside). Village; Malabar dist., Yernaud tal.; lat. 11° 5′; long. 76° 01′; from Calicut S.E. 20 miles; from Munjery W. 8 miles. Oorotemala hill and trig. station is in the same amshom [q.v.].——*Ooroyma* (ഊരായ്മ - úráyma, Mal.). The office of an Ooraulan. Proprietorship of a temple [coil, pagoda].——*Ooroymacauran* (ഊരായ്മക്കാരൻ - úráymakkáran, Mal.). Same as Ooraulan.——*Oor valam* (ஊர்வலம் - úrvalam, Tam.). From (above + valam, tam. right side). A procession, through a town, &c., when the party begins to move to the right [pradacshinam].——*Ore* (ಊರು - úru, Can.; ఊరు - úru, Tel.; ഊർ - úr, Mal.; ஊர் - úr, Tam.). Suffix in place names.

OOR (ஊறு - úru, *Tam.*). To ooze.——*Oorny* (ஊறணி - úrani, Tam.). From (úru, tam. to ooze). Tank [q.v.]. Suffix in place names.——*Ootancaray* (ஊத்தங்கரை - úttangarai, Tam.). See sep. title.——*Ootatoor* (ஊட்டத்தூர் - úttattúr, Tam.). From (úttu, tam. fountain + úr, tam. village). Village; Trichinopoly dist., Perambalore tal.; acres 2,910; lat. 11° 5′; long. 78° 55′; from Perambalore S. 11 miles; from Trichinopoly N.N.E. 21 miles. Gave its name to a talook abolished in 1817. Taken by French in 1750. Old and well-sculptured Shiva temple [coil] with inscriptions [shausanam].——*Ootcore* (ఊటకూరు - útukúru, Tel.). From (úta, tel. spring + úru tel. village). Village; Nellore dist., Raupore tal.; pop. 465; acres 2,982; lat. 14° 15′; long. 79° 47′; from Nellore S.W. 22 miles; from Raupore E. 14 miles. Inscriptions. Small tank and much wet cultivation. Abruck [q.v.] found mixed with sand [manal]. Trig. station in lat. 14° 14′ 26·38″; long. 79° 44′ 56·59″; height 524 feet; from Raupore E.N.E. 12 miles; from Toorimerla S.S.W. 4 miles.——*Oott* (ఊట - úta, Tel.; ஊற்று - úttu, Tam.). From (úru, tam. to ooze). Spring. Suffix in place names; as Nariyoott, meaning jackal spring. Oottcaul, from (kál, tam. channel), is a water-course leading from a spring [casham, caul, spring channel].

OORAFAH (عرفا - urafá, *Ar.*). Plural of (árif, ar. the intelligent). Part of lacab of the religious; as Ayeen ool oorafah, the eye of the contemplative.

OORAY (உரை - urai, *Tam.*). Means speech. Commentary. This should, according to the Nunnool, contain the following fourteen particulars :—"*a*" the text;—"*b*" the general scope or purport of the text;—"*c*". grammatical connection or parsing;—"*d*" literal meaning or giving equivalent words;—"*e*" free rendering of the text or paraphrase;—"*f*" illustration by examples;—"*g*" anticipating objections;—"*h*" answering objections;—"*i*" explanatory notes or special remarks;—"*j*" supplying ellipses;—"*k*" determining the meaning of doubtful terms, or giving the opinion of different commentators;—"*l*" determining the meaning between a diversity of opinions;—"*m*" practical application;—and "*n*" textuary proofs. There are two sorts of commentaries, viz., Caundigay or brief, and Vriddhy or diffuse [nunnool].

OORDHWAM (ऊर्ध्व - úrdhva, *San.*). From (vridh, san. to increase); raised upwards. Elevation [oonnatam], zenith [jyotisham, ootcham, zenith].——*Oordhwa avanataumsham* (ऊर्ध्वावनतांश - úrdhvávanatámsha, San.). From (above + ava vanatámsha, san. altitude). Meridian altitude [jyotisham].——*Oordhwa bauhoo* (ऊर्ध्वबाहु - úrdhvabáhu, San.). From (above + báhu, san. arm). A devotee who holds his arms above his head till they are fixed in that position.——*Oordhwa nataumsham* (ऊर्ध्वनतांश - úrdhwanatámsha, San.). From (above + natámsha, san. zenith distance). Meridian zenith [q.v.] distance [jyotisham].——*Oordhwa poondram* (ऊर्ध्वपुण्ड्र - úrdhvapundra, San.). From (above + pundra, san. a mark on the forehead). The perpendicular line on the forehead worn by the Veishnavas [naumam]. Cf. Tripoondram.——*Oordhwa sancramanam* (ऊर्ध्वसंक्रमण - úrdhvasankramana, San.). From (above + sankramana, san. transit). Culmination of a celestial object, time of transit [sancramanam] or of passing the meridian [jyotisham, raikhay].

OORDOO (اردو - urdú, *Hind.*). From turkish; means camp. Hindostany language as formerly spoken at courts of Delhi and Lucknow; formed by Arabic, Persian, and Turkish words upon a grammatical basis of the pracritic Hindee and original Sanscrit [bhaushay]. Took its rise with the first invasions of the mahomedans in the twelfth century, in the mahomedan court at Delhi; as the invaders were a mixed multitude consisting of Arabs, Persians, Afghans, Turks, &c., this half court and half camp dialect consisted of a great number of Arabic and Persian words and a sprinkling of the Turkish, while nevertheless based on the grammar of the Hindee dialect as spoken round Agra and Delhi. Under Acbar and his successors Jehaungeer and Shah jehaun, it became the speech of the cultivated classes and attained the status of a new language from its extensive Arabic and Persian vocabulary, its readiness to adapt itself to new words and new ideas, and its elegant idioms. It has now a literature of its own and is fast replacing, if it has not already done so, the lingua franca of the south, the Deccany [q.v.] dialect. Oordoo poesy may be said to be the fashionable accomplishment of every educated Mahomedan in his leisure hours. Oordoo writers are innumerable and Oordoo prose and poetical works are text books at the Madras university. See vol. I (60).

OORF (عرف - urf, *Hind.*). From (arafa, ar. to know). Known as, alias. Also a pet-name, formed generally with the addition of Laul, Sahib, Miyaun, and Jaun to an alam [ism].

OORIYA (ఓఢ్ర - ódhra, obl.; ఓఢ్రుడు - ódhrudu, pers. sing.; ఓఢ్రులు - ódhrulu, pers. pl., *Tel.*). Inhabitants of Orissa [q.v.]. The bramins of this name are a branch of the Gowda [q.v.] division of bramins [q.v.]; called also odhra desham or ootcala bramins; they are chiefly employed in government and priestly offices. The Ooriya language is an aryan pracritic language [bhaushay, jauty].

OOROO (उरु - uru, *San.*). From (vri, san. to cover). Great.——*Oorlaum* (ఉర్లాము - urlámu, Tel. urlám *). From (uru, san. great + lámu, tel. cave). Proprietary estate, Village; Ganjam dist., pop. 11,536; sq. miles 2½; lat. of village 18° 25′; long. 84° 02′; from Chetterpore S.W. 91 miles; from Chicacole N.E. 10 miles; from the sea W. 12 miles. Zemindarry [q.v.] was formerly in possession of Cunnepully ramavadhaunooloo, but sold by Government for arrears about 1812. Booddhirauz basavarauz, who purchased it, died in 1814, and his widow afterwards managed the estate. One of her three daughters, Viyyamma, married Cundoocoory perayya lingam, and had a son Basavarauz puntooloo, on whom the estate devolved in 1855. On his death in 1878 his only son, Vishwananta row, was a minor, and the estate came under the Court of Wards. The boy died in 1880 from an accident. His widow, Maha lutchmamma, is the present proprietrix without any issue. The estate still continues under Court of Wards. Jiroyaty [q.v.] villages in the estate are Chodavaram, Cobagaum, Devaudy, Gopaulapenta, Killaum, Mabagaum and Oorlaum. Inam [q.v.] villages are :—Jonnaum, Loocoolaum, Mankivalsa, Pervataulapett, subsequently acquired by purchase, Pattanja valsa, Vantamundalam and Vencatroya pooram. Besides these there is a family property in Godavery district consisting of a share in Cunchanapully, paying a yearly rent of Rs. 443. The proportion of dry lands [poonjah] to wet [nunjah] is about one to ten. The estate is devoid of hills or forests and no cultivable land is waste. Peshcush Rs. 12,467.——*Oorvashy* (उर्वशी - urvashí, San.). From (above + vashí, san. having will). Hot desire. An apsaras of Indran's [q.v.] heaven [swargam]. Also identified with Gungay [q.v.]. How she was rescued from a demon by Pooroorayan whom she married afterwards has been dramatized by Calidass [q.v.] in his Vicramorvashy [q.v.].——*Oorvauroo* (उर्वारु - urváru, San.). See sep. title.

OOROO (உரு - uru, *Tam.*). From (rúpa, san. shape). Shape.——*Oorav* (ఉరవు - uravu, Tel.). Beauty.——*Ooravacondah* (ఉరవకొండ - uravakonda,* Tel.). From (uravu, tel. beauty + konda, tel. hill).—"*a*" Deputy tahsildarry, Anantapore district. Pay Rs. 70;—"*b*" Village, Deputy tahsildar's station; Anantapore dist., Gooty tal.; pop. 8,557; acres 7,477; lat. 14° 57'; long. 77° 18'; from Anantapore N.W. 29 miles; from Bellary S.E. 26 miles; from Gooty W.S.W. 29 miles; from Madras N.W. 240 miles; from Penoocondah N.N.W. 62 miles. Fine tope [q.v] outside the town. Built at the foot of a triangular-shaped hill, height 1,922 feet.——*Oorvilly* (உருவில்லி - uruvilli, Tam.). From (above + villi, tam. bowman). Manmatan [q.v.], the beautiful bowman.——*Oorvily* (உருவிலி - uruvili, Tam.). From (above + ili, tam. one who has not); formless. Manmatan.

OOROOL (ഉരുള - urula, *Mal.*). Circular.——*Oondavully* (ఉండవల్లి - undavalli, Tel.). From (unda, tel. round + palli, tel. village). Sanscrit name (anantashayana), meaning vishnoo, the eternal + seat. Village, Hill; Kistna dist., Guntoor tal.; pop. 1,194; acres 1,690; lat. 16° 30'; long. 80° 37'; from Guntoor N.N.E. 16 miles; from Masulipatam W.N.W. 41 miles. On the Kistna. The celebrated four-storeyed rock-cut cave temple is a specimen of the hindoo religious art of the seventh or eighth century. Probably excavated by veishnavite Chalookyas [q.v.] who came from Calyaun, after they had conquered the Shaulancauyana [q.v.] dynasty [raj] of this or the Vengy [q.v.] country. Dedicated to Vishnoo as Narayanan [q.v.] or Ananta shayanan, a colossal sculpture of whom recumbent is seen in the third storey. Many other rock-cut shrines and mantapams [q.v.] about the hill.——*Oorool kiyang* (ഉരുളക്കിഴങ്ങ് - urulakkizhannu, Mal.). From (above + kizhannu, mal. root). A potato [q.v.].

OORS (عرس - urs, *Hind.*). From (arasa, ar. to unite); union of soul. Religious ceremony celebrating the union of the soul of deceased saint [walee] with the deity. Generally applied to the anniversary of a saint's death; as Cawder wally ka oors, the festival dayof Cawder wally [q.v.].

OORVAUROO (उर्वारु - urváru, *San.*). From (uru, san. much + ár, san. to cause to flow) [ooroo]; diuretic. San. also (gavákshí), meaning cow + eye. Botanically the Cucumis genus, cucurbitaceæ [vricsham, 62]. Melons and cucumbers. Climbing herbs, hispid or scabrous; leaves stalked, palmately lobed or five-angled or entire, dentate or serrate; flowers yellow, shortly peduncled; fruit fleshy, indehiscent, large or small, spherical or elongate, smooth or tuberculate; seeds very many, oblong, compressed, mostly smooth. The species best known to the natives are shown below. For water-melons see Indravally; for pumpkin see Carcauroo; for white pumpkin see Wax-gourd and Fakeer's bottle; for snake cucumber see Snake gourd; for spiked bitter cucumber see Carolah.——*Common cucumber* (त्रपुषा - trapushá, San.; कांकडी - kámkadí, Mahr.; तौसे - tausé, Conc.; قثاء - kisá, Ar.; خيارزه - khiyárzah, Pers.; كهيرا - khírá, Hind. and Dec.; تيمون - timun, Malay; ಮುಳ್ಳುಸವುತೆ - mullusavute, Can.; ತೆಕ್ಕರೆ - tekkare, Too.; ముల్లుదోస - mulludósa, Tel.; - kaknai, Oor.; മുള്ളൻവെള്ളരി - mullanvellari, Mal.; රට කැකිරි - ratakékiri, Singh.; முள்வெள்ளரி - mulvellari, Tam.). San. from (trapa, san. bashfulness + ush, san. to burn), from soft flesh and being easily cooked; cf. tagaram. Ar. from (kassa, ar. to collect); from abundant growth. Pers. from (khiyár, pers. cucumber + zah, pers. born); referring to smallness of fruit. Can. from (mullu, can. thorn + savute, can. cucumber). Tel. from (mullu, tel. thorn + dósa, tel. cucumber). Mal. from tamul. Singh. from (rata, singh. foreign + kakira, singh. cucumis). Tam. from (mul, tam. thorn + vellari, tam. the plant). San. also (urváru), meaning much + discharging, applied to urine, a diuretic; (hastiparní), meaning elephant + leaf; (mútrap'hala), meaning urine fruit; (sukhásha), meaning eaten with pleasure. Hind. also (bislombí); (indráwan), meaning colocynth; (khírákankarí), meaning short cucumber; (kankarí), meaning cucumber; (pahárííndráyan), meaning mountain colocynth. Malay also (antimun); (katimun). Can. also (kakkarikáyi); (savuteballi), meaning cucumber + creeper. Tel. also (dósa); (kondabudama), meaning hill + the plant, cucumis trigonus, roxb. Mal. also (kakkari); (vellari), meaning having white grains, from the white rice-like seeds. Tam. also (malaittummatti), meaning mountain + the plant, cucumis trigonus, roxb.; (kakkari), from (kakrí, hind.) [country melon]; (vellari), meaning white + stripe; (kíraikkáy), meaning vegetable + fruit. Greek κολοκύνθη; compare bitter water-melon [q.v.]. Title otherwise Foreign cucumber, Hill colocynth, Wine fruit. Botanically Cucumis [oorvauroo] sativus, linn., cucurbitaceæ [vricsham, 62]. Alias Cucumis hardwickii, muricatus. Leaves ovate five-angular or slightly lobed, lobes acute hispidulous on both surfaces and also often with soft hairs, petals ⅜ inch, fruit glabrous sometimes tuberculated commonly elongate; flower largish, yellow. The juice mixed with alcohol is used in rheumatic affections; seeds possess cooling properties, also diuretic; pulp of fruit is purgative like colocynth [bitter water melon]; mentioned in pharm. Curried or pickled [chutney]; young ones known as gherkins. A fixed fat oil [yennay] from the seeds, used in cookery and for lamps. Compare:—Citrullus colocynthis, bitter cucumber; Cucumis trigonus, fowl's cucumber, and pubescent cucumber; Luffa acutangula, acute-angled cucumber; Momordica charantia, spiked bitter cucumber; Trichosanthes anguina, snake cucumber. See gloss paragraphs.——*Common melon* (खर्बूजा - kharvújá, San. and Mahr.; بطيخ هندى - bittíkhihindí, Ar.; خربوزه - kharbuzah, Pers., Hind. and Dec.; سامڠک - sámangka, Malay; ಮಿನಿಕೆಗಿಡ - minikegida, Can.; కరుబూజదోస - karubúdzudósa, Tel.; വത്തക്ക - vattakka, Mal.; மொலாம்பழம் - molámbazham, Tam.). San. from persian. Ar. from (bittíkh, ar. melon + hindí, ar. indian). Pers. from (khar, pers. large + buzah, pers. sweet fruit). Can. from (minuku, can. to shine). Tel. from (kharbuzah, hind. melon + dósa, tel. cucumber, cucumis sativus, linn.). Mal. from (pateca, port. melon). Tam. from (melon + pazham, tam. fruit). Malay also (bakaka); (páteka); (manaiki); (tamiki). Can. also (ibbudlu). Tel. also (mulámpandu), meaning melon fruit. Tam. also (vellari), meaning white + streak. The cucumber of the Bible, Numb. xi. 14. Greek σίκυς. Title otherwise Common melon, Indian melon, Kharboja, Melon cucumber, Musk melon of old writers, Sweet melon [true musk melon]. Botanically Cucumis [oorvauroo] melo, linn., cucurbitaceæ [vricsham, 62]. Alias Cucumis maltensis; Melo vulgaris. Trailing; stems scabrous; leaves broad cordate, more or less five-lobed; lobes rounded and toothed; male flowers crowded, females solitary; fruit short, oval, when young pubescent, when old glabrous, variegated; flowers largish yellow; native of n.w. india; extensively cultivated. Seeds a cooling medicine; used in suppression of urine. Flesh of the fruit sweetish.——*Country cucumber* (पिण्डारक - pindáraka, San.; कारी - kárí, Mahr.; पेंडारे - péndárí, Conc.; جنگلى ککڑى - janglíkakrí, Hind.; جنگلی کنکڑی - janglíkankarí, Dec.; ಕಾಡುಮಿನಿಕೆಬಳ್ಳಿ - káduminikeballi, Can.; ಅಡಕಬಾರೆ - adakabáre, Too.; బుడమ - budama, Tel.; കരുമത്തൻ - karumattan, Mal.; කැකිරි - kakira, Singh.; தும்மட்டி - tummatti, Tam.). Hind. from (janglí, hind. wild + kakrí, hind. cucumber, cucumis melo, linn.). Dec. from hindostany. Can. from (kádu, can. wild + minikeballi, can. + cucumis melo, linn.). Tel. compare indian winter cherry. Mal. from (karu, mal. black + mattan, mal. pumpkin, cucurbita maxima, duch.). San. also (vishálá), meaning wide. Hind. also (kachari); (indráwan), meaning colocynth [bitter water melon]; (janglíindráyan), meaning wild colocynth; (bislombhí); (baramkáíkájhár). Can. also (budumékayi); (mekke); (haimekkeballi); (hirimekke); (doddamekke); (adikabálí); (paççekáyigida). Too. also (pendáre). Tel. also (nakkadósa), meaning fox + cucumber, cucumis sativus, linn.; (nélabudama), meaning ground + the plant; (adavibudama), meaning forest + the plant; (adaviputtsa), meaning forest + the plant; (nallabudama), meaning black + the plant; (puttsa); (kódibudama), meaning fowl + the plant. Mal. also (valiyamukkálpíra), meaning large bryonia. Tam. also (péyttummatti), meaning wild + the plant; (káttuttummatti), meaning forest + the plant; (kommatti); (shukkam). Title otherwise Callous-leaved bryonia, Dark pumpkin, Fowl's cucumber, Pubescent cucumber. Botanically Cucumis [oorvauroo] trigonus, roxb., cucurbitaceæ [vricsham, 62]. Alias Bryonia callosa, punctata; Cucumis madraspatanus, pseudocolocynthis, pubescens, turbinatus. Climbing shrub, spreading; stem filiform, furrowed, rough with bristly hairs; leaves on long petioles, cordate, three to five-lobed, roundish, toothed, scabrous, and hispid on the veins below; berries globose, largish, smooth; flowers yellow; flowering nearly all the year. Small bitter seeds are mixed with oil and employed as vermifuge; also in veterinary practice; pulp of fruit, purgative like colocynth; mentioned in pharm. Fruit used as pickle [chutney]. Fixed fat oil [yennay] from seeds by boiling used for lamps. There is a variety called in all the languages Wild.——*Country melon* (कर्कटी - karkatí, San.; कांकडी - kámkadí, Mahr.; قثاء - kisá, Ar.; خيار - khiyár, Pers.; ککڑى - kakrí, Hind.; کنکڑی - kankarí, Dec.; ಕರ್ಗುಂಬಳ - kargumbala, Can.; ಕರುಕುಂಬಡ - karukumbada, Too.; దోస - dósa, Tel.; കക്കരി - kakkari, Mal.; கக்கரி - kakkari, Tam.). San. from (karka, san. thorn + at, san. to go); from the prickly nature of fruit. Mahr. from sanscrit. Ar. from (kassa, ar. collect); from growing in abundance. Hind. from sanscrit. Dec. from sanscrit. Can. from (karu, can. black + kumbala, can. gourd). Mal. from sanscrit. Pers. also (khiyáridaráz), meaning long cucumber; (khiyárzah), meaning small cucumber. Malay also (smangha). Can. also (mullusavute). Tel. also (mulludósa), meaning thorn + cucumber; (vellagummadi), meaning white + pumpkin, cucurbita maxima, duch.; (nakkadósa), meaning fox + cucumber; (pandilidósa), meaning pandaul + cucumber. Mal. also (narayankumbalam), meaning grey + white gourd. Tam. also (narivellari), meaning fox + cucumis sativus, linn.; (mulvellari), meaning thorn + the plant, cucumis sativus, linn. Title otherwise Field cucumber, Fox cucumber, Grey cucumber, Kakree, Pandaul cucumber, Prickly cucumber, Prickly melon. Botanically Cucumis [oorvauroo] melo, linn., var. utilissimus, roxb., cucurbitaceæ [vricsham, 62]. Alias Cucumis utilissimus. Stems exactly as in cucumis sativus [common cucumber], but not quite so extensive; tendrils simple; leaves broad-cordate, generally more or less five lobed; lobes rounded, tooth letted; above pretty smooth, below scabrous, the largest about 6 inches each way; floral leaves of the female flowers sessile, and very small; male flowers axillary, peduncled, crowded, but opening in succession; female flowers axillary, peduncled, solitary; both sorts yellow about 1–1½ inches diameter; flowering nearly all year; fruit fleshy, generally a very perfect oval; when young downy and clouded with lighter and darker green; when ripe perfectly smooth, variegated with deeper and lighter yellow; 4–6 inches long, and 3–4 inches diameter. Fruit varies in color from dark green to nearly white, usually changing to a bright orange color when ripe; when little more than one-half grown, is oblong, and somewhat downy, in this state pickled; when ripe about as large as an ostrich's egg, and same shape. Seeds, like those of the other cucurbitaceous fruits, contain much farinaceous matter, blended with a large portion of mild oil; for applying the seeds to different purposes, the usual mode of cleaning them from the pulpy mass in which they are contained is to mix them up with wood ashes, rub them therein, and spread them out to dry. In cultivating, the seeds are mixed with those of sorghum vulgare, pers. [cholum], or some others of the large culmiferous tribe and sown together with them; latter shade the former. The powder of the toasted seeds mixed with sugar is a powerful diuretic; promotes the passage of sand or gravel; substituted for british spiritus ætheri nitrosi, and pareira brava [indian pareira]. When cut these gourds have much the flavor of the melon, and they will keep good for several months if carefully gathered without being bruised and hung up; they are also in this stage eaten raw, and much used in curries [q.v.] by the natives; the natives dry and grind the seeds into a meal, which they employ as an article of diet; they also express a mild oil [yennay] from them, which they use in food for lamps and in arts and manufactures.——*Mottled melon* (उर्वारु - urváru, San.; پھونٹ - phúnt, Hind.; پھوٹ - phút, Dec.; పెద్దదోస - peddadósa, Tel.; പുട്ടുവെള്ളരി - puttuvellari, Mal.; வெள்ளரி - vellari, Tam.). Hind. means cracked or burst, from its bursting spontaneously when ripe. Tel. from (pedda, tel. large + dósa, tel. the cucumber plant). Mal. from (pishta, san. flour + vellari, mal. cucumis sativus, linn.); from flour-like pulp of ripe fruit. Tam. from (vel, tam. white + ari, tam. streak). Hind. also (túti); (kachrá) when unripe. Tel. also (dósa); (peddakáya), meaning large + fruit. Tam also (kakkari). Title otherwise Flour cucumber, Phoont. Botanically Cucumis [oorvauroo] melo, linn., var. momordica, roxb., cucurbitaceæ [vricsham, 62]. Alias Cucumis momordica. Leaves round-cordate, sometimes five-angled, scollop-toothed; male flowers fascicled axillary, peduncled, crowded; female flowers solitary peduncled; fruit very smooth, oblong, generally tapering a little towards the end, with elevation or depression; 20–24 inches long, 3–6 inches diameter; when ripe bursting slowly into various portions. Flower largish, yellow; fruit pale yellow when ripe, quite smooth, 1–2 feet long, 3–6 inches diameter; seeds rather smaller than those of the common melon [q.v.]. Seeds are a cooling medicine. Fruits much eaten; when young they are a substitute for common cucumber [q.v.]; when ripe, with the addition of sugar [q.v.] they are little inferior to the melon.

OORY (ഉറി - uri, *Mal.*; உறி - uri, *Tam.*). From (uru, tam. to unite with).—"*a*" A net or swinging tray for suspending articles in a house, out of reach of ants, &c.—"*b*" Measure of capacity, chiefly grain. 2 oyaks = 1 oory; 2 oories = 1 nauzhy [alavay, 3d]. Approximate actual value, 1 oory = 8 cubic inches. Variable. Compare olluck. See vol. I, 609; II, 516. ——*Oory ady* (உறியடி - uriyadi, Tam.). From (above + adi, tam. to beat); from ceremony of breaking pots. Lunar [chaundramaunam] festival [pundigay, 6d]. A ceremony in honor of Krishnan [q.v.], between 9th August and 8th September, commemorating his juvenile exploits in stealing ghee, butter, etc., from the houses of the gopies [q.v.]. Observed specially by the Yaudavas [q.v.] or shepherds. On the evening of the day after Krishna jayanty [q.v.], the idol is borne through the streets in procession and shepherds climb greased poles for money at the top [maryauday].

OORY (உரி - uri, *Tam.*). Quality [goonam].——*Ooritchol* (உரிச்சொல் - uriççol, Tam.). Adjectives and adverbs. Thus defined in the Nunnool:—*பல்வகைப் பண்பும் பகர்பெயராகி, ஒருகுணம் பலகுணம் தழுவிப் பெயர்வினை. ஒருவா செய்யுட் குரியன உரிச்சொல்*—"qualifying words are "words that stand immediately before a noun or verb to denote "some one or more properties or qualities that are seen in things "and actions."—"*a*" The Nunnool [q.v.] divides all qualities or attributes into four classes. The qualities of organized bodies [indriyam], i.e., of spirit in connection with body are thirty-two:—knowledge, kindness, desire, fear, modesty, fortitude, patience, determination, retention, confusion, thought, aversion, lust, mercy, shame, anger, boldness, envy, love, want, langour, weariness, affliction, pleasure, youth, old age, hatred, superiority, evil, perseverance, cruelty, haughtiness, and forgetfulness. The qualities of action of embodied living principle are five:—eating, sleeping, adoring, adorning, and walking. The qualities common to all bodies [bhootam] are six:—form, as square, length, circle, angle, &c.; measure, as one, two, three; color, as white, red, gold, black, green, &c.; smell, as good smell, bad smell; taste, as bitter, sour, astringent, saltness, sweetness, acridness; sensation, as heat, cold, softness, hardness, heaviness, lightness, smoothness, and roughness. Qualities which spirits have with or without bodies are nine, viz.:—visibility, concealment, increase, decrease, removal or motion, reception, trembling, connection, and giving.—"*b*" Adjectives and adverbs may be formed of all the above terms, by adding *ஆன*, *உள்ள*, or *ஆகிய*. They are indeclinables. Adjectives have no comparative and superlative degrees as in English and Sanscrit, but they are formed by the use of the fourth or fifth case, as, *இதற்கு அது பெரிது*, *இதிலும் அது பெரிது*, that is greater than this, and by addition of *எல்லாம்*, as *எல்லாவற்றிலும் அது பெரிது*, that is greatest of all.

OOS (أص - أس - أث - us, *Ar.*). Al before s in Arabic compounds; as Abd oos samad, slave of the eternal [al].

OOSH (أش - ush, *Ar.*). Al before sh in Arabic compounds; as Abd oosh shakoor, slave of the grateful [al].

OOSHAK (اشق - ushshak, *Ar.*; اشه - ushshah, *Pers.*; اشق - ushshak, *Hind.* and *Dec.*; గమనాయకచెట్టు - gamanáyaka-chettu, *Tel.*; கமநாயகச்செடி - kamanáyagaççedi, *Tam.*). Title from arabic. Tel. corruption of gum ammoniacum. Tam. corruption of gum ammoniacum. Title otherwise Eastern giant fennel, Gum ammoniac tree. Botanically Dorema Ammoniacum, don., umbelliferæ [vricsham, 67]. Stem of plant abounds in a milky juice; agent for extracting it a beetle [zeerangy], multitudes of which pierce the stem; gum [gond] is then gathered and hardens into gum ammoniac. The article occurs in bazaars [q.v.] in two forms; first in voluminous masses of yellowish color, enclosing white almond-like [baudam] tears, the whole being of plastic consistence, and very impure; secondly, in tears of irregular form, white or yellowish, opaque, rather solid, agglutinated or distinct, compact, brittle, of glassy fracture, and free from impurities. Medicinally similar to, but less powerful than, asafœtida [q.v.]; officinal in pharm.; activity resides in a volatile oil [yennay] and a resin [raul]. Aureum is similar.

OOSHAS (उषस् - ushas, *San.*). From (vas, san. to shine). Aurora. The dawn, in the Aryan system [aroonan].

OOSHBAH (عشبہ - ushbah, *Hind.*). From arabic meaning green. Sarsaparilla.——*Country ooshbah* (ناٹ کا عشبہ - nátkáushbah, Dec.). Same as Indian sarsaparilla.——*Wild ooshbah* (جنگلی عشبہ - janglíushbah, Hind.). Same as Oval-leaved china root.

OOSHTRAM (उष्ट्र - ushtra, *San.*). From (ush, san. to burn); as bearing heat. Camel [ottagam].——*Ooshtarkhaur* (दुष्पर्शा - dushparshá, San.; धमासा - dhamásá, Mahr.; شوكة البيضا - shaukatulbaizá, Ar.; اشترخار - ushturkhár, Pers., Hind. and Dec.). Title from persian. San. from (dus, san. preposition showing difficulty + sprish, san. to touch); from prickly nature. Ar. from (shaukat, ar. thorn + baizá, ar. egg). Pers. from (ushtur, pers. camel + khár, pers. thorn). Ar. also (ákúl); (háj). Pers. also (bádáwurd), meaning wind breaker. Title otherwise Camel thorn. Botanically Fagonia arabica, linn., salvadoraceæ [vricsham, 86]. Alias Fagonia mysorensis. Shrub; leaves opposite, bistipulate; stipules thorny, subulate, very sharp, longer than the leaf; leaflets linear, cuspidate; peduncles from between the stipules of the opposite leaves, solitary, one-flowered; capsule pubescent; flowers white; on high lands. Leaves and twigs possess cooling properties. No other common species here. Same title given to Arabian manna [q.v.].

OOSSOOR (ಹೊಸೂರು - hosúru, Can. hosúr *). From (hosa, can. new + úru, can. village) [hosa].——(1) Talook, Salem district. Tahsildar's pay Rs. 200. Area 1,169 square miles. Population 155,768. Language chiefly Teloogoo and Canarese and partly Tamul. Between N. lat. 12° 09′ and 12° 53′ and E. long. 77° 31′ and 78° 18′. Extreme length from north to south 50 miles, and breadth from east to west 43 miles; average breadth being about 30 miles. Is a Balaghaut [q.v.] talook, or talook above the ghauts [q.v.], W. of district. Bounded north and west by Mysore territory; east by Krishnagherry and Dharmapoory talooks; and south by Dharmapoory talook and Collegaul talook of Coimbatore, between which and Oossoor frontier the Cauvery runs. Comprises the ancient talooks of Dencanicottah and Oossoor, which were merged into one in 1860, and is the most recently acquired portion of the district, having come into the hands of the British after the death of Tippoo in 1799. The northern portion is almost level. On the east is a series of rocky hills. On the south-east for about twenty miles, the Melagherries form an unbroken chain, separating the talook from Dharmapoory. The whole north and western part as far as Dencanicottah and Jowlikerey, is on the Mysore plateau. Beyond this the talook drops in excessive plateaus. To one of the lower access is gained by the Anchatty ghaut. After that there are eight or nine descents before the level of Pennagaram and the Cauvery is attained viâ Nautroypolliem. The talook profits more from the south-west than from the north-east monsoon [q.v.]. Soil is chiefly red and sandy loam. There is a great absence of black soil; the only parts of the talook sufficiently level to admit of marshes and vast water-spreads being too well drained by nature for water to stand there. Red soils form 80 per cent. of the whole; regar [q.v.] 19 per cent., and there is only 1 per cent. of exceptional soil. Iron [auban] is obtained at Vepanahully. The presence of gold [pon] is possible. It was found in Mysore territory in olden times not far from the Oossoor boundary, and a remarkably fine quartz [ven cull] reef exist near Camalaupooram to the north-west of Tully. There is some trade in grain and oil-seeds [yennay]. Weaving [nesavoo] is also carried on. Crops are cumboo [bajrah], raggy [q.v.], black cholum [q.v.], motchay [country bean], mustard [rayaun] and castor-oil seeds [aumanac], horse-gram [q.v.], and dholl [q.v.]. The talook is noted for the large number of areca [q.v.] gardens, mostly growing under tanks [q.v.]. The culture of black cholum for fodder is notable, as no crop is grown specially for that purpose below the ghauts. Large quantities of jack [q.v.] fruit, limes [lemon], and oranges [q.v.] of particularly good quality, and of a peculiar but excellent kind of plantain [q.v.] are grown in the neighbourhood of Tully. Sugar-cane [q.v.] is much grown in Dencanicottah division. Tobacco [pogauk] of a fair quality is also grown for local consumption. Exports are raggy [q.v.], beans [country bean], gram [q.v.], gingelly-oil, gingelly [q.v.] seeds and cattle [maud] chiefly to North arcot, Bangalore, and other parts of this district. Imports are rice [q.v.], green gram [q.v.], wheat [geung], cloths, salt [ooppoo], iron [auban], ploughshares [calappay], &c., principally from Bangalore, Madras and Arnee and other parts of this district. The cattle of the talook are very fine and large herds of them graze in the forests of the Dencanicottah division. The breed is that known as the Mysore breed, the animals being of larger frame than the Aulambaudy cattle, but shorter in the leg. Both as milkers and for draught they are in much demand, large numbers being sent to the annual fairs at Trinomallee, Shreerungam. The Ponniaur, Chennaur, and other minor streams traverse the talook. The most important irrigation works are the Auliyaulam anicut [q.v.] across the Ponniaur about 9 miles east of Oossoor, Sauraundahully tank, and Tully tank. As the talook is influenced by both monsoons [q.v.], the supply of water for wet cultivation is more certain and regular than in the other parts of the sub-division. Camping ground :—Jakkairy. Zemindarries :—Ancooshagherry poliput, Baugalore, Shoolagherry. Places of archæological interest :—Bailore, Baugalore, Berikay, Birjapully, Dencanicottah, Devarcoondany, Goomalaupooram, Kelamungalam, Mullicaurjoona droog, Oodenapully, Oossoor, Ratnagherry, Shoolagherry, Tully. Principal trig. stations :—Anchatty droog, Ancooshagherry droog, Devarbetta, Gootroyenmullay, Mariyaulam, Oossoor. The leading places, &c., in the talook are the following.——*Anchatty* (அஞ்சட்டி - añjatti, Tam.). See sep. title.——*Anchatty droog* (அஞ்சட்டித்துருக்கம் - añjattitturukkam, Tam.). Trig. station; lat. 12° 35′ 20·69″; long. 77° 55′ 54·42″; height 3,195 feet; from Anchatty droog S. ¼ mile; from Oossoor S.S.E. 11 miles.——*Ancooshagherry* (ಅಂಕುಶಗಿರಿ - ankushagiri, Can. ankusagiri *). From (ankusha, san. elephant goad + giri, san. mountain); from its resemblance to an elephant goad. Tam. also (périgaippálaiyam), meaning kettle-drum + fortified village. Zemindarry, Village, Hill; pop. 1,527; lat. of village 12° 41′; long. 78° 07′; from Oossoor E.S.E. 18 miles; from Salem N. 70 miles. Polliem also known as Berikay. Peshcush Rs. 7,190. Ancooshagherry droog is Trig. station in lat. 12° 40′ 25·56″; long. 78° 07′ 34·32″; from Ancooshagherry E. ¾ mile; from Oossoor E.S.E. 18 miles.——*Bailore* (ಬೇಲೂರು - bélúru, Can.). From (bélu, can. to sacrifice + úru, can. village); supposed site of vasishtan's sacrifice. Can. also (doddabélúru), meaning great bailore. Village; pop. 375; acres 485; lat. 12° 34′; long. 77° 48′; from Oossoor S.S.W. 12 miles; from Salem N.N.W. 68 miles. Inscription [shausanam] of Mysore dynasty [raj], dated A.D. 1673.——*Balaghaut* (بالا گهات - bálághát, Hind.). See sep. title——*Baugalore* (ಬಾಗಲೂರು - bágalúru, Can.). See sep. title.——*Chennaur* (சென்னாறு - shennáru, Tam.). See sep. title.——*Dencanicottah* (ಡೆಂಕಣಿಕೋಟೆ - denkanikóte, Can.). See sep. title.——*Devarbetta* (ದೇವರಬೆಟ್ಟ - dévarabetta, Can.). From (déva, san. god + betta, can. hill). Hill; pop. 73; lat. 12° 38′; long. 77° 40′; height 3,368 feet; from Oossoor W.S.W. 16 miles; from Salem N.N.W. 75 miles. Trig. station in lat. 12° 37′ 29·93″; long. 77° 40′ 05·22″; height 3,368 feet; from Devarbetta W. ¼ mile; from Oossoor W.S.W. 16 miles.——*Gootroyen hills* (ಗುತ್ತಿರಾಯನಮಲೆ - guttiráyanamale, Can.; குத்திராயன்மலை - kuttiráyanmalai, Tam.); means gootroyen's hill, from a chieftain who ruled the surrounding country. Hills; lat. 12° 16′; long. 77° 54′; height 4,580 feet; from Oossoor S. 32 miles; from Salem N.N.W. 46 miles. Trig. station in lat. 12° 15′ 47·25″; long. 77° 53′ 48·67″; height 4,580 feet; from Gootroyen N.N.E. ½ mile; from Oossoor S. 32 miles. ——*Hoscote* (ಹೊಸಕೋಟೆ - hosakóte, Can.). From (hosa, can. new + kóta, san. fort). Village; pop. uninhabited; acres 149; lat. 12° 38′; long. 77° 57′; from Oossoor S.S.E. 9 miles; from Salem N.N.W. 68 miles.——*Jakeery* (ಜಕ್ಕೇರಿ - jakkéri, Can.). See sep. title.——*Jowlikerey* (ಜವಳಿಕೆರೆ - javalikere, Can.). From (javali, can. proportionate + kere, can. tank). Village; pop. 461; acres 759; lat. 12° 31′; long. 77° 41′; from Oossoor S.W. 19 miles; from Salem N.N.W. 68 miles.——*Kelamungalam* (ಕೆಲಮಂಗಲ - kelamangala, Can.). See sep. title.——*Mariyaulam* (மரியாளம் - mariyálam, Tam.). Trig. station; lat. 12° 22′ 43·02″; long. 77° 44′ 48·97″; height 3,448 feet; from Mariyaulam W.S.W. 1 mile; from Oossoor S.S.W. 26 miles.——*Matagherry* (ಮತ್ತಗಿರಿ - mattagiri, Can.). See sep. title.——*Melagherry* (ಮೇಲಗಿರಿ - mélagiri, Can.). See sep. title.——*Oodenapully* (ಉದ್ದನಹಳ್ಳಿ - uddanahalli, Can.). From (uddanu, can. proper name + halli, can. village). Village; pop. 289; lat. 12° 36′; long. 77° 59′; from Oossoor S.E. 12 miles; from Salem N.N.W. 67 miles. At the foot a large bare rock of numerous gneissic out-crops. Public bungalow [q.v.]. The approach from Oossoor is picturesque. Dolmen [codaycull] with sculptured figures of warriors in the neighbourhood. One and-a-half miles west are sculptured cromlechs [paundoo coozhy] and holed dolmens.——*Oossoor* (ಹೊಸೂರು - hósúru, Can.). See below.——*Ponniaur* (பெண்ணையாறு - pennaiyáru, Tam.). See sep. title.——*Shoolagherry* (ಶೂಲಗಿರಿ - shúlagiri, Can.). From (shúla, san. trident + giri, san. mountain); the three lumps of the hills suggesting a resemblence to the sacred trident [shoolam]. Zemindarry, Village, Hill; pop. 1,104; acres 57,729; lat. of village 12° 40′; long. 78° 04′; from Oossoor E.S.E. 13 miles; from Salem N. 70 miles. The Poligar [q.v.] is related by marriage to the zemindar [q.v.] of Poonganore. Peshcush Rs. 5,499.——*Tully* (ತಳಿ - tali, Can.). See sep. title.——*Vepanahully* (ಬೇವನಹಳ್ಳಿ - vépanahalli, Can.). From (vépa, tel. margosa, melia azadirachta, linn. + halli, can. village). Village; pop. 1,171; lat. 12° 42′; long. 78° 14′; from Oossoor E. 25 miles; from Salem N. 72 miles. Iron is smelted.——**(2)** Town, Divisional and Talook head-quarters; Salem dist., Oossoor tal.; pop. 5,756; acres 2,111; lat. 12° 44′; long. 77° 52′; from Madras W. 165 miles; from Namcull N. 106 miles; from Salem N.N.W. 77 miles; from Tripatore W.N.W. 53 miles; from Yercaud N.N.W. 71 miles. On the side of a slight elevation. It is feverish and the water-supply has fallen off. Large community of weavers. Trade is almost entirely in grains and seeds. About half a mile from the town is a rocky hill, 300 feet above the plain and 3,120 feet about the sea, crowned by a pagoda [q.v.] of some size, visible for a considerable distance. In the side of the hill is a cave with a lingam [q.v.]. West of the town is an old fort [cottay], though useless now, from the commanding position which the pagoda hill occupies. It was taken by the British in 1791. Trig. station in lat. 12° 43′ 34·90″; long. 77° 52′ 51·49″; height 3,120 feet; from Choodavaudy W. ¼ mile; from Oossoor E. ⅜ mile.

OOSTAUD (استاد - ustád, *Pers.*). From persian. Preceptor.

OOSY (ஊசி - úsi, *Tam.*). From (súchi, san. needle). Needle, slender or fine. Plant first term from small pointed fruit or flower. Ex., where transl. is of second term:—Asclepias prolifera (úsippálai), milk plant; Capsicum minimum (úsimilagáy), capsicum; Jasminum auriculatum (úsimalligai), jasminum sambac; Oxystelma esculentum (úsippálai), milk plant; Phaseolus semi-erectus (úsittagarai), cassia tora. See gloss. paragraphs.——*Oosilam* (உசிலம் - usilam, Tam.). From (usi, tam. sharpness); from thorns. Same as Biswool.——*Oosilamputty* (உசிலம்பட்டி - usilambatti, Tam.). From (usilam, tam. a tree, acacia pennata, willd. + patti, tam. village).—"*a*" Deputy tahsildarry, Madura district. Pay Rs. 70.—"*b*" Village, Head-quarters of Deputy tahsildar and Sub-registrar, Madura dist., Tirmungalam tal.; pop. 6,183; acres 3,646; lat. 9° 58′; long. 77° 50′; from Dindigul S.S.W. 30 miles; from Kodaykarnal S.E. 27 miles; from Madras S.S.W. 272 miles; from Madura W. 22 miles; from Rameshwaram W.N.W. 112 miles; from Ramnaud W.N.W. 79 miles; from Tirumungalam N.W. 15 miles. Weekly market every Wednesday.

OOT (उत् - ut, *San.*). Up, forth [ood].——*Ood* (उद् - ud, San.). Prefix meaning up.——*Oodaunam* (उदान - udána, San.). From (above + an, san. to breathe). One of the five vital airs [vayoo], that which rises up the throat and passes into the head.——*Oodaya* (ഉദയ - udaya, Mal.). From (above + i, san. to go). Rising. Epithet of sun [sooryan]. Prefixed to names of Travancore rulers, as Oodayamaurtandan. Not the same word as Wodeyar [q.v.] of Mysore and Coorg.——*Oodayagherry* (ఉదయగిరి - udayagiri, Tel.; ഉദയഗിരി - udayagiri, Mal.). From (udaya, san. sunrise + giri, san. mountain).—"*a*" Deputy tahsildarry, Ganjam district. Pay Rs. 200.—"*b*" Village, Head-quarters of Deputy tahsildar, Sub-magistrate and District moonsif; Ganjam dist., Goomsoor maliah division; pop. 501; lat. 20° 08′; long. 84° 25′; from Balligooda E.S.E. 29 miles; from Berhampore N.N.W. 61 miles; from Chotterpore N.W. 65 miles; from Chicacole N.N.E. 128 miles; from Madras N.N.E. 545 miles; from Russellcondah N.W. 20 miles.—"*c*" Deputy tahsildar's station, pay Rs. 200. Ganjam dist., Pedda kimedy maliahs, Senior assistant agent's division; lat. 19° 09′; long. 84° 12′; from Balligooda S.S.E. 72 miles; from Berhampore W.S.W. 42 miles; from Chetterpore W.S W. 56 miles; from Chicacole N.N.E. 61 miles; from Russellcondah S.S.W 60 miles. A Sowrah [q.v.] village situated in the centre of Pedda kimedy maliahs of which it is the head-quarters. Is called Ramagherry-oodayagherry to distinguish it from Goomsoor-oodayagherry. Is on the maliah [q.v.] military road.—"*d*" Hill, Fort and town; Travancore state, Pudmanaubhapooram division, Cullcoolam tal.; lat. 8° 15′; long. 77° 23′; from Trivandram S.E. 31 miles; from the sea N. 8 miles. Also called Pooliyacoorchy, meaning pooliyar jungle. Formerly one of the principal military stations of the province. The fort is built of strong granite [caroom cull] blocks round a lofty isolated hill by the southern main road to Trivandrum and lies a little to the south-east of the ancient town of Pudmanaubhapooram. Built for the Maharajah by a Dutch general named D'Lanoy. There is a cloth manufactory here. A detachment of the Company's troops was formerly stationed there. Inside the fort are the ruins of a church now overgrown with jungle. The Dutch general's tombstone still exists in the chapel. At the foot of the hill outside the fort there is a Bramin village.—"*e*" Talook of Nellore district; see sep. title.—"*f*" General sanscrit name for eastern ghauts [q.v.].——*Oodayam* (उदय - udaya, San.). From (above + ay, san. to go). Rising, ascending, creation. Prefix in place names. For hours of sunrise and sunset see Sooryan. For the astrological effects of rising of a planet [graham] or zodiacal sign see Raushy.——*Ooddesham* (उद्देश - uddésha, San.). From (above + dish, san. o show). Estimate.——*Oodgautry* (उद्गातृ - udgátri, San.). From (above + gai, san. to sing). One of the four chief priests [hotry]. The one who chants the hymns of the Sauma vedam [q.v.].——*Oodgeetam* (उद्गीथ - udgít'ha, San.). From (above + gá, san. to sing). The office of the oodgautry; also the syllable Om [q.v.].——*Oodyogam* (उद्योग - udyóga, San.). From (above + yuj, san. to join). Office [amal].——*Oojaula* (اجالا - ujálah, Hind.). From (above + jval, san. to blaze). Bright. Oojaula bee, bright lady [ism].——*Oojjein* (उज्जयिनी - ujjayiní, San.). From (ut, san. intensive prefix + jí, san. to conquer). Greek ὀζήνη. Capital of Vicramadityan [q.v.], and one of the seven sacred cities [caushy, nagaram]. Sanscrit geographers calculate their longitude [deshauntaram] from it, making it their first meridian [jyotisham, luuka, raikhay].——*Oonmattan* (उन्मत्त - unmatta, San.). From (above + matta, san. mad). Mad; a form of Shiva [q.v.].——*Oonnatam* (उन्नत - unnata, San.). From (above + nata, san. bent, inclination). Elevation.——*Ootcalam* (उत्कल - utkala, San.). From (utkala, san. to unbind); open or coast country. The modern Orissa, or the Ooriya country. Bounded on south by Telingana [q.v.], and on east by sea. On west and north a line drawn from Sonapore to Midnapore in Bengal is the boundary. See vol. I (2). Ootcalam is one of the main sub-divisions of Gowda [q.v.] or Northern bramins [odhram, ooriya].——*Ootcham* (उच्च - uçça, San.). Means apex.—"*a*" Apsis of a planet's [graham, noojoom] orbit [cacsham]. Maudotcham [q.v.] is the higher apsis or aphelion, and Sheeghrotcham [q.v.] or chalotcham is the lower apsis or perihelion.—"*b*" Also zenith [q.v.], that point of the heavens [bhagolam] which is directly over or vertical to an observer, and is the prolongation of the earth's radius to meet the celestial sphere. The nadir [q.v.] is the point directly beneath, or vertical below, the observer; the natives have no name for this. The zenith and nadir are the poles of the horizon [cshitijam, jyotisham, oordhwam].——*Ootchangy droog* (ಉಚ್ಚಂಗಿದುರ್ಗ - uççangidurga, Can.). From (huççangi, can. durgá, the terrific deity + durga, san. fort). Sanscrit name (utsavámbádurga), meaning festival + goddess + fort. Village, Hill; Bellary dist., Hurpanhully tal.; pop. 2,875; acres 9,852; lat. 14° 33′; long. 76° 06′; from Bellary S.W. 69 miles; from Hurpanhully S.S.E. 16 miles. The village is at the foot of the droog [q.v.]. The hill fort, built by one of the Hurpanhully poligars [q.v.], is now in ruins. The droog has a natural position of great strength, being almost perpendicular on the north and west sides.——*Ootchasamayam* (ഉച്ചസമയം - uççasamayam, Mal.). From (uçça san. high + samaya, san. time). Midday [ooroomam].——*Ootchicamullay* (உச்சிகமலை - uççigamalai, Tam.). From (uchhikha, san. high-crested + malai, tam. hill). Hill; North arcot dist.; Vellore tal.; lat. 12° 54′; long. 79° 01′; from Chittore S.S.W. 24 miles; from Vellore W. 12 miles. A chief peak of the jawaudies.——*Ootpatty* (उत्पत्ति - utpatti, San.). From (above + pad, san. to fall). Birth [jenmam], production.——*Ootramallore* (உத்திரமேரூர் - uttiranmérúr, Tam.). From (uttara, san. name of a viráta king + mél, tam. west + úr, tam. village). Sanscrit name (rájéndrachólachaturvédamangala), meaning rajendra cholan, the chola king + four sacred writings + village, or sacred place of bramins versed in the four vedams built by rajendra cholan.—"*a*" Deputy tahsildarry, Chingleput district. Pay Rs. 70.—"*b*" Town, Deputy tahsildar's head-quarters; Chingleput dist., Madrantacam tal.; pop. 2,733; acres 10,931; lat. 12° 37′; long. 79° 48′; from Chingleput S.W. 16 miles; from Conjeeveram S. 16 miles; from Madrantacam N.W. 12 miles; from Madras S.W. 47 miles; from St. Thomas' mount S.W. 39 miles, from Sydapett S.W. 41 miles; from the sea W. 30 miles. Important under Hindoo and Mahomedan rule. Came into British possession when Carnatic [q.v.] was cleared of French by Clive in 1752 after battle of Cauverypauk. Captured by French in 1754 and in same year recaptured by English with assistance of Maufooz khan. Again occupied by French in June, and retaken in July 1757 by British. In August French again took it, and, during next six or eight months, made forays in surrounding villages, from which they collected money in return for sparing standing crops. In beginning of 1758 it was again in possession of English. In October 1759 it had again fallen into hands of French. Finally recovered in December after Coote's reduction of Wandiwash and Carangooly. The old fort, now dismantled, was built by a rajah, Oottara comauran, son of a North india ruler; and restored by Rajendra cholan. Principal antiquities are temple of Soondra varadarajahsawmy, temple of Veicoonta permaul and historical inscription [shausanam] of Chola [q.v.] dynasty [raj], inscriptions of Chola dynasty on walls of temple of Kedaureshwaran, and on temple of Keilausa nautan. The architecture of the Shiva [q.v.] temple [coil] is curious and imposing. Roman catholics are numerous in the neighbourhood.——*Ootsarpiny* (उत्सर्पिणी - utsarpiní, San.). Age of increase, according to Jeinas [avasarpiny, caulam, jeina].——*Ootsavam* (उत्सव - utsava, San.). From (above + su, san. to produce); that which produces joy. Fustival [pundigay, 6d]. Is a Sheivite term and corresponds to Veishnavite tirnaul [q.v.]. The principal festival in temple is called Bramhotsavam [q.v.], or Mahotsavam. Every year the return of spring [vasantam] is celebrated in temples by a festival called Vasanta ootsavam which is held in the month of Chittray [mausam], i.e., between 12th April and 12th May [maryauday].——*Oottamam* (उत्तम - uttama, San.). From (above + tama, san. superlative suffix). Perfection, excellence, virtue.——*Oottamapolliem* (உத்தமபாளையம் - uttamappálaiyam, Tam.). From (uttama, san. best, epithet of a pándiyan + pálaiyam, tam. fortified village). Village, Deputy tahsildarry, pay Rs. 70. Head-quarters of the Deputy tahsildar and Sub-registrar; Madura dist., Periyacoolam tal.; pop. 7,475; acres 4,624; lat. 9° 49′; long. 77° 23′; from Madura W. 54 miles; from Periyacoolam S.S.W. 25 miles. Former head-quarters of a polliem [q.v.]. Large stone statue represents a servant of a king of Madura. Old Shiva temple with copper [taumram] plate shausanam [q.v.]. Inscription dated A.D. 1493.——*Oottarajyay* (उत्तरज्या - uttarajyá, San.). From (above + jyá, san. sine). The versed sine [jyah] of an arc [chaupam, jyotisham].——*Oottaram* (उत्तर - uttara, San.). From (above + tara, san. comparative suffix). Posterior, later. The poems denominated thus are secondary or apocryphal. Thus Oottara ramayanam is founded on history of Rama [q.v.], and Oottara harichendra oopaukhyaunam relates that hero's adventures in a formerb irth. These are grounded on a Sanscrit poem, as Ovid's tales are founded on Greek legends. Oottara mimaumsam is another name for Vedauntam [q.v.]. Oottaram is also the north, from that direction having been at back of aryans [q.v.] after entering india. For the lunar mansion of this name see Nacshatram. Also means a written statement or answer given back. Pungoony ottaram or Oottara phalgoony is a Luni-solar [chaundramaunam] festival [pundigay, 5c] on the day when the moon [chundran] falls in the asterism [nacshatram] Phalgoony, in the twelfth solar month of Pungoony [mausam], i.e., between 12th March and 11th April, and a feast is kept in honor of the marriage of Shiva [q.v.], Vishnoo [q.v.] and other gods. Season for private weddings [maryauday]. See vol. I (92).——*Oottarauyanam* (उत्तरायण - uttaráyana, San.). From (above + ayana, san. going). The sun's course northwards; also southern solstice [ayanam, jyotisham].——*Oottarauyana poonya caulam* (உத்தராயணபுண்ணியக்காலம் - uttaráyanap-punniyakkálam, Tam.). Means northward motion of sun + auspicious time. Otherwise Macara sancraunty [q.v.]. Same as Pongal. Cf. Dacshinaunyana poonyacaulam.——*Oottaunaicaudashy* (ఉత్థానైకాదశి - utt'hánaikádashi, Tel.). From (utt'hána, san. rising + ékádashi, san. eleventh). Otherwise Bodhana yecaudashy or waking eleventh day. Lunar [chaundramaunam] festival [pundigay, 3e], subject to intercalation [adhicam]. The eleventh tity [q.v.] of the waxing moon [shooclapacsham] of the eighth lunar month Caurteecam [mausam] between 28th October and 26th November, the anniversary of that on which Vishnoo [q.v.] awoke from his slumber of four months. A day for contemplation [maryauday].

OOT (ات - اُت - ut, *Ar.*). Al before in Arabic compounds; as Abd oot tauhir, slave of the pure [al].

OOTACAMUND * (ஒத்தகைமந்து - ottagaimandu, *Tam.*). From (ottai, canarese, dwarf bamboo + káy, tam. fruit + mandu, tam. todah village). Sanscrit name by corruption (udakamandala), meaning water + region.—"*a*" Deputy tahsildarry, Neilgherry district. Pay Rs. 100.—"*b*" Town, Municipality, Sanitarium, Collector's head-quarters, Deputy tahsildar's station, Seat of subordinate civil court; Neilgherry dist., Todanaud div.; pop. 15,053; acres 14,842; lat. 11° 25′; long. 76° 44′; height 7,228 feet; from Coimbatore N.N.W. 34 miles; from Coonoor N.W. 8 miles; from Devaulah E.S.E. 21 miles; from Kotagherry W. 12 miles; from Madras W.S.W. 266 miles; from Pundalore E.S.E. 25 miles. Includes a tract of country lying within a circle three miles in radius. For description see vol. II, 116. The following are the travelling distances by road from Ootacamund to different places:—

To		Viâ	Miles and Furlongs.	
Avanashy	...	Coonoor ghaut and Mettapolliem ...	57	4¾
Bangalore	...	Seegore ghaut and Mysore	167	2
Calicut	...	Sisparra ghaut, Vandoor and Arriyacode.	99	7
Cannanore	...	Goodalore ghaut, Manantoddy and Periya ghaut.	141	1
Cannanore	...	Goodalore ghaut, Manantoddy and the Coottiyaudy ghaut.	139	7¾
Coimbatore	...	Coonoor ghaut and Mettapolliem ...	55	0¾
Coimbatore	...	Kotagherry and Mettapolliem	58	3½
Coottiyaudy	...	Goodalore, Manantoddy and Coottiyaudy ghaut.	105	3¾
Dindigul ...	...	Coonoor and Avanashy	152	4¾
French Rocks	...	Seegore ghaut and Seringapatam ...	94	4
Goodalore	...	Goodalore ghaut	30	0
Goondloopett	...	Seegore ghaut	42	0
Harihar ...	...	Mysore, Cadoor and Shimoga	274	4
Kotagherry	...	......	14	6
Manantoddy	...	Goodalore ghaut	82	0
Mercara	...	Seegore ghaut, Mysore and Fraserpett.	152	7
Mettapolliem	...	Coonoor ghaut	32	2¾
Mettapolliem	...	Kotagherry ghaut	35	5¾
Mysore ...	...	Seegore ghaut and Goondloopett ...	78	4
Palghaut	...	Coonoor and Coimbatore	85	7¾
Salem ...	...	Coonoor, Avanashy and Erode	129	1¼
Seringapatam	...	Seegore ghaut and Mysore	88	0
Sisparra ...	...	Avalanchey	34	2
Trichinopoly	...	Coonoor, Avanashy, Caungyam and Caroor.	170	1¾

—"*c*" Lake; Neilgherry district, Todanaud division. Formed by a dam thrown across the openings between two hills. At the upper or south end it is constantly fed by a small stream, which escapes by an overflow under a bridge at its lower or northern extremity, but the great bulk of the water is derived from the heavy rains during the S.W. monsoon [q.v.]. Divided into two portions by a bund [q.v.], under the centre of which is a bridge. Its form is sinuous, the bends being caused by projecting spurs of the hills on either side. A road follows the windings of its banks. Nearly one and-a-half miles in length. In some parts of considerable breadth and depth. The temperature of the water is almost invariably higher than that of the air.

OOTANCARAY (ஊத்தங்கரை - úttangarai, *Tam.* uttankarai *). From (úttu, tam. spring + karai, tam. bank) [oor] from a spring near the town.——(1) Talook, Salem district. Tahsildar's pay Rs. 150. Area 910 square miles. Population 138,113. Language Tamul. East of district. Between N. lat. 11° 47′ and 12° 25′ and E. long. 78° 15′ and 78° 47′. Extreme length from north to south is about 36 and from east to west 34 miles, the average being about 24 and 30 miles respectively. Bounded north by Tripatore talook; west by Krishnagherry and Dharmapoory talooks; south by Salem and Ahtoor talooks; and east by Cullacoorchy and Trinomallee talooks in South arcot district. Lies in a basin surrounded on the south east, and partially on the west by hill ranges, and on the north merges in the Tripatore valley. The uncultivated portions are more or less covered with scrub, which, in the southern and eastern portions becomes denser; while in the south-west, where the railway traverses Cadatore mittah, a large area of black soil lies waste. The principal basin [nadee] of the talook is the valley of the Ponniaur, which is recruited from north and south by the Paumbaur and Vauniyaur. Though apparently hill-girt the talook has free communication by the ghauts [q.v.] at Chengamam, Cottaputty, Moocanore, Mullapooram, Munjavaudy, while on the north and north-west the way is open to Tripatore and Krishnagherry. The railway runs through the centre of the talook. The gneissic system prevails, traversed by numerous trap-dykes. Magnetic iron [anhan] beds of unusual richness exist at Teertamullay. There is but little granite [caroom cull]. Tillage, weaving [nesavoo], grain and hide [chamrah] trades, the collection of bark for dyeing [shauyam] and tanning [chamrah], and trade in other jungle produce, from the chief industries of the talook. An indigo [q.v.], factory at Pullyputty is in ruins. The trade with South arcot and Pondicherry through the Singaurapett pass used to be considerable; but since the construction of the coast railway, it has decreased. Chief products are raggy [q.v.], cumboo [bajrah], varagoo [q.v.], horse-gram [q.v.], gingelly [q.v.], tovray [dholl], oolandoo [blackgram], tinay [q.v.], and shanmay [q.v.], toovalauriyam [raggy], motchay [country bean], &c., in dry lands; and paddy [q.v.] of various kinds, tobacco [pogauk], chillies [q.v.], betel [q.v.], cocoanut [q.v.], arecanut [q.v.], plantains [q.v.], groundnut [q.v.], &c., in wet lands and gardens. An interesting fact is the successful cultivation of coffee [q.v.], in the plains, near Bheiranuttam. The numerous palmyras [q.v.] which grow in the Government waste lands supply building materials. The cattle [maud] are inferior. The best are generally to be found in or about Cadatore mittah. The chief article of export is Auvauramputtay [tungaid], which, with raw hides [chamrah], is sent to Vaniyambaudy. Tamarind [q.v.] goes to Pondicherry in exchange for salt [ooppoo], and is also exported to Vaniyambaudy and through the Cottapputty valley to Salem and Ahtoor. Horse-gram [q.v.], dholl [q.v.], gingelly [q.v.], and castor-oil seeds [aumanac], and, in small quantities, ghee [q.v.] are exported to Bangalore, Tripatore, Coimbatore and Salem. Salt [ooppoo] is also imported from Madras. The Jalacanteshwaram aur, Meenaur, Paumbaur, Ponniaur, Varattaur, Vauniyaur, and many other streams are almost wholly unutilized, or flow away to enrich fields in South arcot. The Ponniaur, the only river of the first rank, the Jalacanteshwaram nuddy, Paumbaur, and Vauniyaur are perennial, though their supply is scanty in the dry season. On the Ponniaur, during the freshes, ferries ply at Hanoomateertam and Irmattore. The principal tanks are those of Aulapooram, Haroor, Moottootaungal, Naicknairy, Teertagirivalsay, and Vencatasamoodram. There is an agreeable camping ground at Periya munjavaudy. The camping grounds at Haroor and Ootancaray are deficient in shade. Those at Shingaurapett and other places are indifferent. Zemindarries:—Anandore, Cadatore, Cammeynullore, Taulanuttam, Tirvanaputty, Vaunyaputty. Places of archæological interest:—Adhicauraputty, Agrahauram, Ajjamputty, Anandore, Andiyore, Atchalavaudy, Aulambaudy, Bheiranuttam, Bodipauray forest, Bommady, Bommamputty, Cadatore, Cammeynullore, Caragambutty, Chettipolliem, Chintalpaudy, Comauraputty, Conambutty, Congavaimb, Coodoomiyamputty, Cottauraputty, Cullauvy, Govindapooram, Gowndaputty, Hanoomateertam, Haroor, Irmattore, Jangalvaudy, Keelchengambaudy, Keelpauray, Keeraiputty, Keezhanore, Krishnapody, Mahavanoreputty, Mattiyamputty, Mauramputty, Mettooputty, Molayanore, Mondacooly, Mookanoreputty, Mookareddiputty, Moppiriputty, Mottancoorchy, Mullapooram, Nadooputt, Pauppaputty, Payyamputty, Periyadalavoypaudy, Periyaputty, Polliem, Ponnairy, Poongany, Poyyaputty, Puttooconaumbutty, Samalputty, Shekkamputty, Shellaputty, Shengapaudy, Shoolacaray, Taulanuttam, Taumarcoliyamputty, Taumbal, Tauthamputty, Teertamullay, Tencaraycottah, Vauthaputty, Vedacuttamadoogoo, Vencataupooram, Veppamputty, Veppanuttam, Wodasalputty, Woddaputty, Yeechambaudy, Yeedalputty, Yehoor, Yelavaday, Yettiputty. The leading places, &c., in the talook are the following.——*Anandore* (ஆனந்தூர் - ánandúr, Tam.). From (ánanda, san. shiva, the joyful + úr, tam. village). Zemindarry, Village; pop. 1,029; sq. miles $6\frac{7}{16}$; lat. of village 12° 16′; long. 78° 25′; from Ootancaray W. 11 miles; from Salem N.N.E. 44 miles. Ruined Shiva temple in the village. Considerable trade. Peshcush Rs. 1,526.——*Beiranaickenputty* (பைரநாயக்கம்பட்டி - pairanáyakkambatti, Tam.). From (bhairanáyaka, can. name of a person + patti, tam. cattle-fold). Village; pop. 1,250; acres 6,834; lat. 12° 02′; long. 78° 41′; from Ootancaray S.S.E. 17 miles; from Salem N.E. 42 miles.——*Bodipauramullay* (போடிப்பாறைமலை - pódippáraimalai, Tam.). From (bódi, tel. bare + párai, tam. rock + malai, tam. mountain). Hill; lat. 12° 03′; long. 78° 39′; from Ootancaray S.S.E. 17 miles; from Salem N.E. 40 miles. Several dolmens [codaycull] in the jungle.——*Bommady* (பொம்மடி - pommadi, Tam.). From (bomma, tel. proper name). Zemindarry, Village; pop. 1,418; lat. of village 11° 59′; long. 78° 19; from Ootancaray S.W. 26 miles; from Salem N. 24 miles. Ten dolmens [codaycull]. Now an amauny [q.v.] village. Weekly fair on Thursdays.——*Booddireddiputty* (புட்டிரெட்டிப்பட்டி - puttirettippatti, Tel.). From (buddireddi, tel. name of a person + patti, tam. cattle-fold). Village, Railway station; pop. 845; lat. 12° 03′; long. 78° 21′; height 1,432 feet; from Ootancaray S.W. 22 miles; from Salem N.N.E. 28 miles.——*Cadatore* (கடத்தூர் - kadattúr, Tam, kadatúr *). From (kadaru, tam. a jungle + úr, tam. village). Zemindarry, Village; pop. 1,279; acres 59,820; lat. of village 12° 05′; long. 78° 20′; from Ootancaray S.W. 20 miles; from Salem N. 30 miles. West is a ruined Shiva temple, said to have been built by Cholas [q.v.]; with which are three inscriptions [shausanam], and near it a Vishnoo temple. Peshcush Rs. 4,295.——*Cammeynullore* (கம்மெநல்லூர் - kammenallúr, Tam. kambainellúr *). From (kammai, tam. a plant, amarantus campestris, willd. + nal, tam. good + úr, tam. village). Zemindarry [q.v.], Village; pop. 1,194; lat. of village 12° 13′; long. 78° 22′; from Ootancaray W.S.W. 15 miles; from Salem N.N.E. 39 miles. Healthy and connected by road with Morapore. The residence of Baulajee row. Ruined fort. Ancient Shiva temples with inscriptions. Peshcush Rs. 8,575.——*Caurapaudy mullay* (காரைப்பாடிமலை - káraippádimalai, Tam.). From (kárai, tam. plant, thorny webera, canthium parviflorum, lamk. + pádi, tam. village + malai, tam. mountain). Mountain; lat. 11° 59′; long. 78° 38′; from Ootancaray S.S.E. 20 miles; from Salem N.E. 36 miles.——*Cheppauny mullay* (செப்பாணிமலை - sheppánimalai, Tam.). From (cheppuvádu, tel. chuckler + malai, tam. mountain). Mountain; lat. 12° 02′; long. 78° 39′; from Ootancaray S.S.E. 14 miles; from Salem N.E. 41 miles.——*Chintalpaudy* (சிந்தலப்பாடி - shindalappádi, Tam.). From (chinta, tel. tamarind, tamarindus indica, linn. + pádi, tam. village). Village; pop. 141; lat. 12° 05′; long. 78° 24′; from Ootancaray S.W. 18 miles; from Salem N.N.E. 32 miles. Has a weekly market on Tuesdays and a large tank.——*Chittairimullay* (சித்தேரிமலை - shittérimalai, Tam.). From (shiru, tam. small + éri, tam. tank + malai, tam. mountain). Hill; lat. 11° 53′; long. 78° 33′; from Ootancaray S. 26 miles; from Salem N.E. 28 miles. There are a few habitations on the hill.——*Coonnatore* (குன்னத்தூர் - kunnattúr, Tam.). From (kunru, tam. hill + úr, tam. village). Village; pop. 1,035; acres 1,586; lat. 12° 21′; long. 78° 33′; from Ootancaray N.N.W. 6 miles; from Salem N. 53 miles. Three miles north-east from Samalputty railway station, with which it is connected by a road, as also with the road from Tripatore to Ootancaray.

Formerly a cusbah [q.v.].——*Cottapputty* (கோட்டப்பட்டி - kóttappatti, Tam.). From (kóttam, tam. cattle-pen + patti, tam. village). Village, Pass; pop. 924; acres 261; lat. 11° 59′; long. 78° 43′; from Ootancaray S.S.E. 22 miles; from Salem N.E. 41 miles. The ghaut [q.v.] passes to Vaulapaudy viâ Ballore and thence east and west to Ahtoor and Salem.——*Cullauvy* (கல்லாவி - kallávi, Tam.). From (kal, tam. stone + ávi, tam. tank). Village, Railway station; pop. 1,081; lat. 12° 15′; long. 78° 29′; height 1,321 feet; from Ootancaray W. 6 miles; from Salem N.N.E. 45 miles. Ruined fort.——*Hanoomateertam* (ಹನುಮತ್ತೀರ್ಥ - hanumattírt'ha, Can.). See sep. title.——*Haroor* (ಹರೂರು - harúru, Can.). See sep. title.——*Irmattore* (இரமத்தூர் - iramattúr, Tam.). From (iravu, tam. descent + maddi, tel. tree, terminalia tomentosa, bedd., var. typica + úr, tam. village). Village; pop. 732; lat. 12° 16′; long. 78° 21′; from Ootancaray W. 16 miles; from Salem N.N.E. 43 miles. On bank of Ponniaur.——*Iroolaputty* (இருளப்பட்டி - irulappatti, Tam.). From (irulan, tam. member of a tribe of foresters, so called + patti, tam. cattle-pen). Village; pop. 578; acres 1,517; lat. 11° 56′; long. 78° 27′; from Ootancaray S.S.W. 23 miles; from Salem N.E. 26 miles. Yearly festival in August.——*Jendamode* (செண்டாமேடு - shendámédu, Tam.). See sep. title.——*Maukkal* (மாக்கல் - mákkal, Tam.). From (má, tam. blackness + kal, tam. stone); slate stone. Mountain; lat. 11° 58′; long. 78° 41′; from Ootancaray S.S.E. 22 miles; from Salem N.E. 37 miles.——*Menisy* (ಮೆಣಸಿ - menisi, Can.). From (menasu, can. black pepper, piper nigrum, linn.). Village, Peak; pop. 1,629; acres 3,817; lat. 11° 58′; long. 78° 24′; from Ootancaray S.S.W. 23 miles; from Salem N.N.E. 26 miles.——*Morapore* (மொரப்பூர் - morappúr,* Tam.). From (morapa, tel. gravel + úr, tam. village). Village, Railway station; pop. 374; acres 407; lat. 12° 08′; long. 78° 26′; height 1,307 feet; from Ootancaray S.W. 14 miles; from Salem N.N.E. 36 miles.——*Mullapooram* (மல்லாப்புரம் - mallappuram, Tam. mallápuram *). From (malla, san. a wrestler + pura, san. town). Village, Railway station; pop. uninhabited; acres 868; lat. 11° 59′; long. 78° 17′; height 1,389 feet; from Ootancaray S.W. 27 miles; from Salem N.N.E. 23 miles. Old Shiva temple [coil] with inscriptions [shausanam].——*Mullay cull* (மலைக்கல் - malaikkal, Tam.). Means mountain rock. Mountain; lat. 11° 59′; long. 78° 42′; from Ootancaray S.S.E. 22 miles; from Salem N.E. 40 miles.——*Ootancaray* (ஊத்தங்கரை - úttangarai, Tam.). See below.——*Paumbaur* (பாம்பாறு - pámbáru, Tam.). See sep. title.——*Paupy reddy putty* (பாப்பிரெட்டிப்பட்டி - páppirettippatti, Tam.). From (pápireddi, tel. proper name + patti, tam. cattle-fold). Village; pop. 2,175; acres 1,510; lat. 11° 55′; long. 78° 25′; from Ootancaray S.S.W. 27 miles; from Salem N.E. 22 miles. At foot of Shevaroy hills.——*Pedaur* (பெடார் - pedár, Tam.). From (bidáru, tel. halting place). Village; pop. 124; acres 788; lat. 12° 17′; long. 78° 28′; from Ootancaray W. 7 miles; from Salem N.N.E. 45 miles. Near is a temple to Chendroyasawmy. Annual festival in March. A place of pilgrimage.——*Ponniaur* (பெண்ணையாறு - pennaiyáru, Tam.). See sep. title.——*Pulliputty* (பள்ளிப்பட்டி - pallippatti, Tam.). From (palli, tam. member of the caste + patti, tam. cattle-fold). Village; pop. 577; acres 2,222; lat. 11° 56′; long. 78° 27′; from Ootancaray S.S.W. 24 miles; from Salem N.E. 25 miles. Weekly market on Thursdays. Has a camping ground, and an Orr's chuttram [q.v.].——*Samalputty* (சாமல்பட்டி - shámalbatti, Tam. sámalpati*). From (tsámalu, tel. grain, panicum miliaceum, linn. + patti, tam. cattle-fold). Village, Railway station; pop. 240; acres 921; lat. 12° 19′; long. 78° 32′; height 1,265 feet; from Ootancaray N.W. 5 miles; from Salem N.N.E. 50 miles. Near the 157th mile from Madras is a rock with the figures of a lingam [q.v.], two bulls, and two men; and an inscription.——*Shingaurapett* (சிங்காரப்பேட்டை-shingárappéttai, Tam.). From (shringára, san. beauty + péttai, tam. suburb). Tam. also (shingárakkóttai), meaning beauty + fort. Village; acres 196; lat. 12° 15′; long. 78° 40′; from Ootancaray E.S.E. 6 miles; from Salem N.E. 51 miles. Lies under the lee of the Jawaudy hills near the frontier of the talook where the road to Cuddalore enters Chengam pass [ghaut].——*Tarsal mullay* (தரசல்மலை - tarasalmalai, Tam.). From (darusu, tel. boundary + malai, tam. mountain). Mountain; lat. 11° 58′; long. 78° 40′; from Ootancaray S.S.E. 22 miles; from Salem E.N.E. 36 miles.——*Taulanuttam* (தாளநத்தம் - tálanattam, Tam.). From (tála, san. palmyra tree, borassus flabelliformis, linn. + nattam, tam. village). Zemindarry, Village; pop. 660; lat. of village 12° 03′; long. 78° 22′; from Ootancaray S.W. 21 miles; from Salem N.N.E. 28 miles. North-west is a ruined temple said to have been built by Cholas [q.v.]. Peshcush Rs. 755.——*Teertamullay* (தீர்த்தமலை - tírttamalai, Tam.). From (tírt'ha, san. sacred water + malai, tam. mountain); from the sacred springs it contains. Village, Mountain, Place of pilgrimage, Hill; pop. 570; acres 496; lat. 12° 06′; long. 78° 38′; from Ootancaray S.S.E. 12¾ miles; from Salem N.E. 42 miles. Old Shiva temple on a steep and lofty hill with inscriptions and copper-plate grant. Annual festival in February or March. Forms northern extremity of Tennaunday mullay pass [ghaut]. The Valasamullay and Teertamullay were, at the time of the cession of this district, the seats of forts built and held by two poligars [q.v.] of Dharmapoory.——*Tencaraycottah* (தென்கரைக்கோட்டை - tengaraikkóttai, Tam.). From (ten, tam. south + karai, tam. boundary + kóta, san. fort). Village; pop. 504; acres 3,871; lat. 12° 01′; long 78° 26′; from Ootancaray S.S.W. 20 miles; from Salem N.N.E. 29 miles. Now deserted but once the cusbah [q.v.] of the talook [q.v.]. A mud fort, commanding one of the entrances to the Baramahaul [q.v.], gave it some importance in Mysore wars. In 1768, it changed hands two or three times. The fort is dismantled and the tank in disrepair. The fort contains a ruined Shiva [q.v.] temple and a Rama [q.v.] temple. Tradition attributes building of temple to Chennappa naick, Poligar [q.v.] of Salem. The tank [q.v.] and anicut [q.v.] over Jalacanteshwaram river are attributed to his brother.——*Tennaunday mullay* (தென்னாண்டைமலை - tennándaimalai, Tam.). See sep. title.——*Tirvanaputty* (திருவணம்பட்டி - tiruvanambatti, Tam.). From (tiru, tam. holy + vana, san. forest + patti, tam. cattlefold). Mittah; pop. 815; acres 1,865; lat. 12° 15′; long. 78° 25′; from Ootancaray W. 11 miles; from Salem N.N.E. 43 miles. Peshcush Rs. 777.——*Valasamullay* (வலசைமலை - valasaimalai, Tam.). From (valasa, tel. migration + malai, tam. mountain). Hill; lat. 12° 01′; long. 78° 45′; from Ootancaray S.S.E. 22 miles; from Salem E.N.E. 43 miles. On the borders of Ootancaray.——*Vauniyaur* (வாணியாறு - vániyáru, Tam.). From (vání, san. the goddess of speech + áru, tam. river). River. Has its rise in the northern slopes of the Shevaroy hills, and flowing in a northerly direction joins the Ponniaur river.——*Vellay cull* (வெள்ளைக்கல் - vellaikkal, Tam.). Means white stone, referring to quartz [ven cull]. Mountain; lat. 12° 01′; long. 78° 40′; from Ootancaray S.S.E. 18 miles; from Salem N.E. 40 miles.——*Vencatasamoodram* (வெங்கடசமுத்திரம் - vengadasamuttiram, Tam.). From (vénkata, san. vishnu + samudra, san. ocean). Village; acres 1,058; lat. 11° 56′; long. 78° 23′; from Ootancaray S.S.W. 26 miles; from Salem N.N.E. 22 miles. Between the Munjavaudy road and the northern slopes of the Shevaroys.——*Yeralvauny* (ஏரல்வாணி - éralváni, Tam.). From (éral, tam. bivalve shell + váni, tam. water). Hill; lat. 11° 58′; long. 78° 45′; from Ootancaray S.S.E. 23 miles; from Salem E.N.E. 43 miles.——**(2)** Town, Talook head-quarters, Salem dist., Ootancaray tal.; pop. 1,380; acres 293; lat. 12° 16′; long. 78° 35′; from Madras W.S.W. 129 miles; from Namcull N.N.E. 76 miles; from Oossoor E.S.E. 57 miles; from Salem N.N.E. 49 miles; from Tripatore S.S.W. 16 miles; from Yercaud N.N.E. 40 miles. Inhabitants are chiefly Chetties [q.v.] and deal in grains. An Orr's chuttram north of the town is fitted up as a public bungalow [q.v.]. The Arbuthnott tope [q.v.] contains 40 acres. The town is intersected by two roads, one of which leads from Salem to Tripatore and the other from the Samalputty railway station, which is only 5 miles off, viâ Ootancaray, Shingaurapett, and the Chengam pass to Mercaunum in South arcot. From the latter road, about 3 miles west of Ootancaray, branches off another road which, near Poothore, taps the Cullauvy and Anandore markets, and joins the trunk road from Madras near Irmattore.

OOTAURID (عطارد - utárid, *Ar.*). The planet [graham, najm] Mercury [boodhan]. Called also the Celestial moonshee [q.v.]. Its orbit [cacsham] is in the second heaven [asmaun], and is considered to be a propitious star [nacshatram], for those born under its reign will be men of wisdom and learning and of admirable memory. So part of lacab; as Ootaurid jung, propitious in war [ism].

OOTHOO (ஊது - úthu, *Tam.*). To swell.——*Odallam* (होंड्यारूकु - hóndyárúku, Conc.; بنتن باسر - bintanbásar, Malay; ಮೊಂಡೇಮರ - mondémara, Can.; ತೆಂಡೇಮರ - tendémara, Too.; ഉതളം - utalam, Mal.; ගොන්කඩුරු - gonkaduru, Singh.; காட்டரளி - káttarali, Tam.). Title from malayalam. Can. from (mondu, can. lopped + mara, can. tree). Singh. from (gon, singh. oxen + kaduru, singh. poisonous tree); from property. Mal. from (útu, mal. to swell); bladder, hence round fruit floating in water. Tam. from (kádu, tam. forest + arali, tam. nerium); from appearance of leaf and flower. Can. also (chendémara); (hondémara). Mal. also (ponna), meaning rising up, from the round fruits. Tam. also (káttumá), meaning forest + mangifera indica, linn.; from fruit like mango [chironjee, wild mango]; (uthalai). Title otherwise Jungle mango, Oothalay, Wild nerium. Botanically Cerbera odollam, gærtn., apocynaceæ [vricsham, 87]. Specific from malayalam. Alias Cerbera lactaria, manghas, quaternifolia; Manghas lactescens; Tanghinia lactaria, laurifolia, manghas, odollam. Manghas on account of mango-like fruits. Bushy tree, 20 feet, native of salt swamps [ooppalar]; leaves alternate, lanceolate, approximate, shining; calyx five-cleft, segments revolute; corymbs terminal; segments of corolla sub-falcate; stigma large and conical, two-cleft at the apex, resting on a saucer-shaped receptacle, the circumference fluted with ten grooves; large cymes of pure white with yellowish throat, fragrant, flowers; flowering nearly all the year; the ripe carpel is ovoid, 2–4 inches long, somewhat resembling a green mango [q.v.], fibrous and woody within, and contains a single broad, compressed, white seed, consisting of two irregularly attached oily cotyledons. The fleshy drupe is medicinally inert, the nut is narcotic and even poisonous, and the bark is purgative; milky sap and leaves, emetic and purgative; in pharm. non-officinal. Natives in travancore employ the fruit to kill dogs [nye]. Oil [yennay] is extracted from the seed, burnt in lamps; fibre [naur] from bark. Wood grey, very soft, spongy; annual rings marked by a sharp line; ouly occasionally used for firewood. There is a Malayalam saying :—സുഖദുഃഖങ്ങൾ വെള്ളത്തിൽ ഇട്ട ഉഗ്ഗളെപോലെ—"pleasure and pain are "like odallam fruits dropped in water," i.e., ever turning and never vanishing. No other common species here. Distinguish from Odul.——*Oothalay* (உதளை - uthalai, Tam.). From (úthu, tam. swell). Same as Odallam.

OOTRAJ (اترج - utraj, *Ar.*). Same as Citron.

OOTTA (ఉత్త - utta, *Tel.*). False.——*Oottrainy* (ఉత్తరేణు - uttarénu, Tel.). Means false jujube. Same as Indian burr.

OOVA (உவ - uva, *Tam.*). To expand, delight.——*Oovah* (ఉవ్వ - uvva, Tel.; உவா - uvá, Tam.). From (uva, tam. to please). Means pleasing tree. Same as Chaltah.——*Oovar* (உவர் - uvar, Tam.). From (uva, tam. to expand); natural salt being an efflorescence. Saltish [ooppoo]. Oovarneer is one of the seven oceans; the brackish ocean [samoodram].

OOYIR (உயிர் - uyir, *Tam.*). From (uy, tam. to subsist). Life [jeevam]. A vowel. There are 12 vowels in Tamul, of which அ, இ, உ, எ, ஒ are the five short vowels, and ஆ, ஈ, ஊ, ஏ, ஐ, ஓ, ஔ are the seven long vowels. See vol. II, 205.——*Ooyirmey* (உயிர்மெய் - uyirmey, Tam.). Combined vowel-consonant sign. There are 216 in Tamul.——*Ooyirtoondilcauran* (உயிர்த்தூண்டிற்க்காரன் - uyirttúndirkkáran, Tam.). From (above + túndil, tam. fish-rod + káran, tam. suffix denoting doer). He who fishes life. A minor deity in the temple of Ancaulamman [q.v.], whose business is to bring to the latter the souls of those who die by their own hands [yaman].

OOZ (اط - اض - از - اذ - az, *Ar.*). Al before z in Arabic compounds; as Ahl ooz zikr, meaning men of prayers [al].

OPIUM (افيم - afím, *Hind.*). See Aphainam.

OR (ஒரு - oru, *Tam.*). One [yecam].——*Orila* (पृश्निपर्णि - prishniparni, San.; ഓരില - órila, Mal.). Title from malayalam. San. means spotted leaf. Mal. means single leaf. San. also (atiguha), meaning great mystery; (nágabalá), meaning serpent + sida. Title otherwise Sweet-smelling hare-foot. Botanically Uraria lagopoides, dec., leguminosæ [vricsham, 48]. Alias Doodia lagopoides; Hedysarum alopecuroides, lagopoides. Suffruticose, procumbent, rooting at the joints; stems pubescent; leaves simple and ternate, terminal leaf-let much the larger, roundish-ovate, mucronate, sprinkled with scabrous pubescence; racemes dense, very hairy; pedicels incurved at the apex and with the calyx densely bearded; upper lip of calyx short, segments ovate-acuminated, lower reflexed, the segments elongated and subulate-setaceous; legume two-jointed; joints orbicular-ovate, polished; flowers rose colored; flowering nearly all year. Veidyans [q.v.] consider it alterative, tonic and anticatarrhal; given to pregnant women with milk to prevent abortion; an ingredient in dashamoolam [q.v.]. Tendrils used for dyeing [shauyam]. Another species is picta.——*Orsaul* (ஒருசால் - orusál, Tam.). From (above + shál, tam. furrow). Once ploughed.

ORANGE (कमलाफल - kamaláp'hala, *San.*; نارنج - náranj, *Ar.*; نارنگ - nárang, *Pers.*; కిచ్చిలి - kiççili, *Tel.*; നാരകം - nárakam, *Mal.*; நாரத்தை - nárattai, *Tam.*). Title from (náranj, ar.); 'a norange' being corrupted into 'an orange.' San. from (kamala, san. lovely + p'hala, san. fruit). Mal from (nága, san. red lead + ranga, san. color). Tam. from (náru, tam. to smell). San. also (náranga), meaning not displeasing; (nágaranga), meaning red oxide of lead + color. Tel. also (dabba); (kittali). Tam. also (kozhuñji), meaning plumpness [sweet orange, zanzibar indigo]; (tambaikkáy), from teloogoo. Botanically Citrus [jambeeram] aurantium, linn., rutaceæ [vricsham, 32]. Tree, 20–25 feet; spines axillary, solitary; young shoots glabrous; leaves oval, elongated, acute, sometimes slightly toothed; petioles more or less dilated and winged; flowers white, large; fruit orange-colored, roundish or ovoid, usually depressed, rarely terminated by a small knob; rind with convex vesicles of oil; pulp sweet. The above is the typical plant, found in india and china; several varieties are wild in forests, particularly on mountains. For the citrus decumana see Pummelow; for the citrus japonica see Cumquot; for the different citrus medicas see Lime.——

(1) *Orange grass* (نارنگی کے باس کا گھاس - nárangíkebáskághás, Dec.). Title from smell. Same as Indian grass.——*Orange root* (కిచ్చిలిగడ్డ - kiççiligadda, Tel.). Same as Europe zedoary and Long zedoary.——*Orange valley* (ನಾರಂಗಹಳ್ಳ - nárangahalla, Can.). From (náranga, san. orange + halla, can. valley); wild oranges [q.v.] and limes [lemon] abound. Valley; Neilgherry district. Todanaud and Paranginaud divisions; height 4,500 feet; from Ootacamund N.E. 14 miles. Starts from N.E. angle of Dodabetta, and skirting Kotagherry tableland, breaks through edge of plateau, and descends to low country exactly opposite Guzzelhutty pass [ghaut]. It is a deep indentation, and being shut in by lofty hills, the temperature is very high. Owing to this feature and richness of soil, vegetation is tropical.——

(2) *Bergamot orange* (जम्बीर - jambira, San.; निंबू - nimbú, Mahr.; निंबुवों - nimbuvó, Conc.; ليمو - límú, Ar., Pers. and Hind.; نيمبو - nimbú, Dec.; ನಿಂಬೆ - nimbe, Can.; ಲಿಂಬೆಮರ - limbemara, Too.; నిమ్మ - nimma, Tel.; ചെറുനാരകം - cherunárakam, Mal.; දෙහි - dehi, Singh.; எலுமிச்சை - elumiççai, Tam.). Title from turkish; the name bergamotta was originally applied to a large kind of pear [amrood], called in turkish prince's pear; the name has no reference to the town of bergamo. San. from (jam, san. to eat). Mahr. from (nimbúka, san. the plant). Can. from (nimbe, can. lime). Mal. from (cheru, mal. small + nárakam, mal. lime, citrus). San. also (jambha), meaning attractive; (nimbúka), from arabic. Ar. also (límúihámiz), meaning sour lime. Pers. also (límúitursh), meaning sour lime; (burtukalánah), meaning portugal orange. Can. also (limbe). Tel. also (gajanimma), meaning elephant + lime. Mal. also (jónakanárakam), meaning mahomedan lime. Tam. also (ambu); (shambíram); (shadábalam), meaning always + fruit. Title otherwise Lemon bergamot, Lime tree, Mahomedan's lime Giving Bergamot lime, Bergamot oil, Oleum bergamii, Oleum bergamottæ of chemists. Botanically Citrus [jambeeram] aurantium, linn., var. bergamia, brandis, rutaceæ [vricsham, 32]. Alias Citrus bergamia. Small tree; leaves oblong, acute or obtuse, under side somewhat pale; petiole more or less winged; flowers small, white; fruit pale-yellow, pear-shaped or depressed; closely resembling in flowers and foliage the bitter orange [q.v.]; taste of fruit acidulous with pleasant aroma. Used as condiment [chutney]; possesses all virtues attributed to lemon [q.v.]; an essence much used by perfumers is prepared from flowers and fruit——*Bile orange* (پتماری - pitmárí, Hind.). Same as Shrub orange.——*Bitter orange* (नागरङ्ग - nágaranga, San.; نارنج - náranj, Ar.; نارنگ - nárang, Pers.; نارنگی - nárangí, Hind.; جاروك پوش - járukpos, Malay; కిచ్చిలి - kiççili, Tel.; கடாரை - kadárai, Tam.). Title from taste of all parts. San. from (nága, san. red lead + ranga, san. color). Tam. from (kadu, tam. pungency + ár, tam. sharpness). Tel. also (kittali). Tam. also (kadáranárttai). Title otherwise Bigarade orange, Box-leaved orange, Seville orange. Botanically Citrus [jambeeram] aurantium, linn., var. bigaradia, brand., rutaceæ [vricsham, 32]. Alias Citrus aurantium, var. amara, bigaradia, vulgaris. Shrub or small tree; leaves oblong, more or less elongated, acute or obtuse, under side somewhat pale; petioles more or less winged or margined; flowers usually small, white; fruit pale yellow, pyriform or depressed; rind with vesicles of fragrant oil. The leaves differ from those of the sweet orange [q.v.] by the petiole only; the flowers are alike in both species; the rind of the fruit is bitter, acrid, and hot to the taste, the pulp acid and bitter, the seeds excessively bitter. Hardly known here; but this was the first cultivated in europe.——*China orange* (چینی نارنگی - chíninárangí, Dec.). Same as Musk lime and Sweet orange.——*Shrub orange* (तिपानी - tipání, Mahr.; भुयिनारिंगी - bhuyinárıngí, Conc.; پتماری - pitmárí, Hind.; ನೆಲನಾರಂಗ - nelanáranga, Can.; ನೆಲಕಂಚಿ - nelakanchi, Too.; നിലനാരകം - nilanárakam, Mal.). Title from lowly habit and resemblance. Mahr. means three-leaved; from trifoliate leaves. Conc. from (bhúmi, san. earth + náranga, san. orange, citrus aurantium, linn.). Hind. from (pit, hind bile + márí, hind. killer); from use of leaves against biliousness. Can. from (nela, can. earth + náranga, can. orange). Too. from (nela, too. ground + kanchi, too. orange). Mal. from (nila, mal. ground + nárakam, mal. orange). Mahr. also (pittavéla), meaning bile + creeper; (pittamárí), meaning heat killer. Can. also (nelakanchi), meaning earth + orange; (nalakanugida). Title otherwise Bile orange. Botanically Naregamia alata, w. & a., meliaceæ [vricsham, 36]. Generic name from (nárakam, mal. citrus aurantium, linn.). Alias Turrea alata. Small shrub, glabrous; calyx small, cup-shaped, five-cleft; petals five, very long, strap-shaped, distinct, free; filaments united into a long slender tube that is inflated and globular at the apex, the mouth with ten very slight antherbearing crenatures; leaves trifoliolate; leaflets cuneate-obovate, quite entire, sessile; petiole margined; flowers on long axillary solitary peduncles, white; capsule slightly membranaceous, three-cornered, three-valved; seeds two; flowering in april and may. Root and leaves used in rheumatism; juice mixed with cocoanut [q.v.] oil used in psora.——*Sweet orange* (नागरङ्ग - nágaranga, San.; नारिंगी - náringí, Mahr.; सोन्नारिंग - sónnáringa, Conc.; شجر نارنج - shajarináranj, Ar.; درخت نارنگ - darakhtinárang, Pers.; نارنگی کا پیڑ - nárangíkáper, Hind.; نارنگی کا جہاڑ - nárangíkájhár, Dec.; جاروك منس - járúkmanis, Malay; ಕಿತ್ತಳೆಮರ - kittalemara, Can.; ಕಿತ್ತ್ಲಿ - kitli, Too.; కిచ్చిలి - kiççili, Tel.; മധുരനാരകം - madhuranárakam, Mal.; දොඩම - dodama, Singh.; கொழுஞ்சி - kozhuñji, Tam.). Title from taste of fruit. San. from (nága, san. red lead + ranga, san. color). Mahr. from sanscrit. Conc. means gold orange. Ar. from (shajar, ar. tree + náranj, ar. orange, citrus aurantium, linn.). Pers. from arabic. Hind. from (nárangí, hind. orange + per. hind. tree). Dec. from hindostany. Malay from (járuk, malay, citron + manis, malay, sweet). Mal.

from (madhura, san. sweet + nárakam, mal. lime, citrus). Tam. from (kozhumai, tam. plumpness) [orange, zanzibar indigo]. San. also (svádunáranga), meaning sweet orange; (náranga), by corruption. Hind. also (nímbú), meaning lime; (sangtrá); (kaunlánímbú), meaning thin-skinned orange. Malay also (járuk-jápun), meaning japan orange. Tel. also (nárinja); (gajanimma), meaning elephant + lime, citrus medica, linn. var. acida, brandis; (dabba); (kittali); (nárijamu). Mal. also (kolañchiná-rakam). Singh. also (náranga). Tam. also (kiççili), from teloogoo. Title otherwise China orange, Common country orange, Portugal orange. Botanically Citrus [jambeeram] aurantium linn., var. aurantium proper, brandis, rutaceæ [vricsham, 32]. Alias Aurantium acre, orientale; Citrus bigaradia, nobilis. Tree, 20–25 feet; flowers white, large; differs little in appearance from the lime [q.v.] tree, citrus medica, linn.; fruit globose, cortex thin, pulp sweet; tree attains great age, upwards of 600 years; superior kinds come from sumatra and ceylon; originally introduced into europe from india by portuguese. The juice is used in lieu of british lemon-juice and citric acid; gives to pharm. dried outer portion of the rind of the fruit, auranti cortex, stomachic and tonic, for british lemon peel. For eating, the native orange has a poor flavor; sherbet [q.v.], made with juice of ripe fruit, a favorite beverage in hot whether, safer than lime juice; the flowers distilled produce orange water, used in cooking, medicine, and as a perfume, ingredient in oil of neroli. Wood yellowish-white, like box moderately hard, close and even-grained; but not available of any size; good for engraving. The following sub-varieties are cultivated:—Cownlanimboo, meaning large loose skinned orange; the hill orange of northern circars [q.v.]; sometimes called mandarin orange; Burrachin, or large china, fine smooth-skinned, cloved, large, very sweet, resembling china-orange, citrus sinensis; Hyderabaudy, smaller than last, but like it, cloved and smooth-skinned, very sweet; Chotachin, small china, small cloved orange; makes marmalade; Coffrie, large, skin very rough; a sweet, well-flavored fruit; Common orange of the country, austere and coarse.

ORIENTAL (هرقی - sharkí, *Hind.*). From (sharaka, ar. to shine as when the sun rises). Prefix.——*Oriental liquidamber* (اصطرك هرقی - ustarakisharkí, Hind.). Same as Indian storax. ——*Oriental nettle* (گزنۂ هرقی - gaznahisharkí, Hind.). Same as Indian nettle.——*Oriental sesamum* (سمسم'هرقی - simsimisharkí, Hind.). Same as Gingelly.

ORISSA (ओड्र - ódhra, *San.*). Province of Bengal forming the northern boundary of Ganjam [odhram; ootacalam].——*Orissa flower* (ओड्रपुष्प - ódhrapushpa, San.). Same as China rose bendy.

OSARY (ஓசரி - ósari, *Tam.*). Misfortune.——*Osoorammah* (ஓசூரம்மா - ósúrammá, Tam.). From (ósari, tam. misfortune + ammá, tam. mother). One of the village ammans [q.v.]

OSHADHY (ओषधि - óshadhi, *San.*). From (avasa, san. food + dhá, san. to hold). Herb [vricsham].——*Oshadhipaty* (ओषधिपति - óshadhipati, San.). From (above + pati, san. master). The moon [chundran].

OSHTAM (ओष्ठ - ósht'ha, *San.*). From (ava, san. down + st'ha, san. stand). Lip.——*Oshtacarnaca* (ओष्ठकर्णक - ósht'hakarnaka, San.). From (above + karna, san. ear). Having lips extending to their ears. A term of derision applied by early aryans to aborigines of India [kirantan, mlecha, nishaudan].

OSMAN (عثمان - usmán, *Ar.*). Means literally a young serpent or dragon. The name of the third caliph [q.v.] and prophet's companion and son-in-law, who, in consequence of his having married two of the daughters of the prophet, was called Zin noorain, master of two lights. Common alam; as Osman khan, alam + alaumat [ism]. Osmauny was a copper coin of Tippoo's equivalent to double peisa [q.v.].

OSPITRY (آسپتری - áspatrí, *Hind.*; ಆಸ್ಪತ್ರಿ - áspatri, *Can.*; ఆస్పత్రి - áspatri, *Tel.*; ആസ്പത്രി - áspatri, *Mal.*; ஆசுபத்திரி - ásubattiri, *Tam.*). Title is a native term in use in all the languages for hospital, corrupted from the english.——**(1)** The following are two key-lists in the briefest possible terms of the products of the vegetable kingdom utilised in the prescribed indian pharmacopœia, for which vernacular equivalents are with certainty known; further information must be traced in the glossary paragraphs through the small type cross-references at end of this volume; see also vricsham, 7, for the method of expressing the products, &c., of the plants in the dravidian languages.—"*a*" Abrus precatorius, indian liquorice, root; Acacia arabica, babool, bark, gum; Acacia catechu, catechu, cutch; Acacia farnesiana, cassie oil plant, bark, gum; Acacia ferruginea, anasandra, bark; Acacia leucophlæa, white babool, bark; Acalypha indica, cooppamainy, juice; Achyranthes aspera, indian burr, all parts; Aconitum ferox, indian aconite, root; Aconitum heterophyllum, atees, root; Aconitum napellus, european aconite, root, leaf; Acorus calamus, sweet flag, root; Adansonia digitata, baobab, pulp, bark; Adhatoda vasica, malabar nut, whole plant, inspissated juice of leaves and root; Ægle marmelos, bael, fruit; Agave americana, american aloe, root; Ailanthus excelsa, coromandel ailanto, bark; Ailanthus malabarica, malabar ailanto, bark, gum resin; Albizzia amara, dark sirissa, bark; Albizzia lebbek, common sirissa, gum; Aleurites triloba, lumbang nut, oil; Alhagi maurorum, arabian manna, saccharine exudation from stem; Aloe indica, common indian aloe, aloes, fresh juice; Aloe socotrina, bombay aloe, aloes; Aloe vulgaris, barbadoes aloe, aloes; Alpinia galanga, greater galangal, root, seed; Alpinia nutans, nodding galangal, rhizome; Alpinia officinarum, lesser galangal, root; Alstonia scholaris, dita, bark; Altingia excelsa, java storax, balsamic fluid; Anacardium occidentale, cashew, gum, oil from shell, oil from nut, spirit from fruit; Anacyclus pyrethrum, pellitory, root; Anamirta cocculus, indian berry, berry; Andrographis paniculata, french chiretta, dried stalk, root; Andropogon muricatus, cuscus, root; Andropogon nardus, citronella, oil; Andropogon schœnanthus, lemon grass, oil; Anisochilus carnosus, country lavender, juice; Anisomeles malabarica, malabar catmint, leaf; Anthemis nobilis, chamomile, flowers; Antiaris saccidora, sack tree, bark, seed; Arachis hypogæa, ground-nut, oil; Areca catechu, areca, nut, cutch; Argemone mexicana, mexican poppy, oil; Argyreia speciosa, broad-leaved bind-weed, leaf; Aristolochia bracteata, indian worm-killer, juice; Aristolochia indica, isharmool, root, leaf; Artemisia vulgaris, indian absinth, dried plant; Astragalus verus, tragacanth, gummy exudation from stem; Atropa belladonna, belladonna, leaf, root; Baliospermum montanum, wild croton, seed; Balsamodendron mukul, mookul bdellium, resin; Balsamodendron myrrha, myrrh, resin; Bambusa arundinacea, common bamboo, tabasheer, splints; Bassia butyracea, butter mohwah, oil; Bassia latifolia, wild mohwah, oil, spirit from flower; Bassia longifolia, common mohwah, oil, spirit from flower; Berberis aristata, berberry, root bark; Bœrhaavia repens, var. diffusa, spreading hog-weed, root; Bombax malabaricum, red-cotton tree, mocharas gum; Borassus flabelliformis, palmyra, toddy, downy substance from base of frond; Brassica alba, white mustard, seed; Brassica juncea, indian mustard, seed; Brassica nigra, black mustard, seed; Butea frondosa, bengal kino, kino, seed; Cæsalpinia bonducella, bonduc, seeds; Cæsalpinia coriaria, divy-divy, legume; Cæsalpinia sappan, sappan, wood; Calophyllum inophyllum, common poon, oil; Calotropis gigantea, mudar, root-bark; Canarium commune, elemi, resin; Canarium strictum, black dammer, resin; Cannabis sativa, indian hemp, whole plant; Capsicum minimum, bird's eye chilly, fruit; Carapa moluccensis, crab oil plant, bark; Carica papaya, papaw, juice; Carum carui, caraway, fruit; Carum copticum, ajwaun, seed; Carum roxburghianum, ajmood ajwaun, fruit; Caryota urens, bastard sago palm, toddy; Cassia absus, black horse gram, seeds; Cassia acutifolia, nubian senna, leaf; Cassia alata, ringworm shrub, leaf; Cassia angustifolia, tinnevelly senna, leaf; Cassia auriculata, tungaid, seed, bark; Cassia fistula, indian laburnum pulp; Cassia obovata, aleppo senna, leaf; Cassia occidentalis, stinking-weed, leaf; Cassia sophera, stinking casondy, leaf; Cassia tora, chakondah, leaf; Casuarina equisetifolia, whip tree, bark; Cedrela toona, toon, bark; Cedrus deodara, deodar, oil; Celastrus paniculatus, malkangany, seed, oil; Cerbera odollam, odallam, bark, milky sap, leaf; Chrysanthemum coronarium, indian chamomile, flower, root; Cicer arietinum, bengal gram, acid juice; Cinchona calisaya, calisaya bark; Cinchona officinalis, crown bark; Cinchona succirubra, red bark; Cinnamomum camphora, camphor cinnamon, camphor; Cinnamomum iners, country cinnamon, inner bark; Cinnamomum tamala, cassia cinnamon, buds, bark; Cinnamomum zeylanicum, ceylon cinnamon, bark; Cissampelos pareira, indian pareira, root, bark; Citrullus colocynthis colocynth, pulp; Citrus aurantium, var. aurantium, proper, sweet orange, rind; Citrus aurantium, var. bergamia, bergamot orange, fruit; Citrus aurantium, var. bigaradia, bitter orange, rind; Citrus medica, var. limonum, lemon, rind, oil of rind, juice; Clerodendron infortunatum, saraswaty's leaf, leaf, juice; Clerodendron serratum, knotted bhraungy, root; Clitoria ternatea, crow creeper, seed, root bark; Cocculus palmatus, calumba, root; Cocculus villosus, jamtee, stem; Cochlospermum gossypium, golden silk cotton, gum; Cocos nucifera, cocoanut, oil, toddy, downy substance from base of fronds; Colchicum autumnale, wild colchichum, fresh corm, seed; Coleus aromaticus, country borage, juice; Colocasia antiquorum, indian kale, juice; Convolvulus scammonia, scammony, root, gum resin; Coptis teeta, mishmee bitter, root; Corallocarpus epigæa, snake caper, root; Cordia myxa, small sebesten, fruit, bark; Cordia obliqua, large sebesten, fruit, bark; Cordia rothii, narrow-leaved sebesten, bark; Coriandrum sativum, coriander, fruit; Coscinium fenestratum, false calumba, stem; Cratæva religiosa, garlic pear, leaf; Crinum asiaticum var. toxicarium, root; Crocus sativus, saffron, stigmas; Croton oblongifolius, devil's goad, oil; Croton tiglium, purging croton, seed; Cucumis sativus, common cucumber, juice, seed, pulp; Cucumis trigonus, country cucumber, seed, pulp; Cucurbita maxima, great pumpkin, seed; Cucurbita pepo, common pumpkin, seed; Cuminum cyminum, cummin, seed; Curculigo orchioides, weevil root, root; Curcuma amada, mango-ginger, root; Curcuma angustifolia, malabar arrowroot, starch; Curcuma aromatica, round zedoary, root; Curcuma longa, turmeric, root; Curcuma zedoaria, long zedoary, root; Cydonia vulgaris, quince, seed; Cyperus pertenuis, straight sedge, root; Cyperus rotundus, common sedge, root; Dæmia extensa, hedge cotton, leaf; Datura fastuosa, purple datura, leaf, seed; Datura fastuosa, var. alba, white datura, leaf, seed; Datura stramonium, europe datura, leaf, seed; Diospyros embryopteris, gaub, fruit; Diospyros melanoxylon, coromandel ebony, bark; Dipterocarpus turbinatus, gurjan, balsam; Dorema ammoniacum, gum ammoniac; Dracontium polyphyllum, wild telinga potato, root; Dregea volubilis, nakchiknee silk cotton, leaf; Echium sp., gajwaun, leaf, stem, flower; Eclipta alba, bhangrah, root; Ehretia buxifolia, rough coorvitchy, root; Elettaria cardamomum, cardamom, capsule; Enicostema littorale, small chiretta, whole plant; Erythræa roxburghii, roxburgh's chiretta, whole plant; Eugenia caryophyllata, clove tree, flower bud; Eugenia jambolana, common jaumoon, bark; Eupatorium ayapana, agrimony hemp, leaf; Euphorbia antiquorum, square milk-hedge, juice; Euphorbia nereifolia, leafy milk-hedge, root; Euphorbia tirucalli, round milk-hedge, juice; Exacum bicolor, country gentian, whole plant; Exacum pedunculatum, whole plant; Exacum tetragonum, whole plant; Exogonium purga, jalap, dried root; Feronia elephantum, wood-apple, gum; Ferula galbaniflua, galbanum, gum-resin; Ferula narthex, asafœtida, gum; Ficus bengalensis, banyan, juice; Ficus carica, european fig tree, fruit; Ficus oppositifolia, devil fig, fruit, seed, bark; Flacourtia cataphracta, indian plum, leaf and tender shoots; Fœniculum vulgare, indian fennel, fruit; Fraxinus ornus, sicilian manna, saccharine exudation; Garcinia indica, mate mangosteen, oil from seed; Garcinia mangostana, mangosteen, fruit; Garcinia morella, ceylon gamboge, gum-resin; Garcinia morella var. pedicellata, siam gamboge, gum-resin; Gardenia gummifera, decamallee, resin; Gardenia lucida, decamallee, gum-resin; Gisekia pharnaceoides, sand greens, whole plant; Glycirrhiza glabra, liquorice, root; Gmelina asiatica, small cashmere tree, leaf; Gossypium arboreum, tree cotton, cotton-wool; Gossypium barbadense, peruvian cotton, cotton-wool; Gossypium herbaceum, indian cotton, wool; Gracilaria lichenoides, ceylon moss, whole plant; Gymnema sylvestre, small indian ipecacuanha, leaf; Gynandropsis pentaphylla, dog mustard, leaf; Gynocardia odorata, chaulmoogra, seed; Hedychium spicatum, european zedoary, root; Heliotropium indicum, indian heliotrope, leaf; Hemidesmus indicus, indian sarsaparilla, root; Herpestis monniera, water hyssop, juice of leaf; Hibiscus esculentus, common bendy, capsule; Hibiscus rosa-sinensis, china-rose bendy, juice of flowers; Holarrhena antidysenterica, tellicherry bark, seed, bark; Hordeum vulgare, barley; Hydnocarpus venenata, fish-poison tree, oil from seed; Hydrocotyle asiatica, indian pennywort, leaf; Hygrophila spinosa, neermoolly, leaf, root; Hyoscyamus niger, henbane, leaf; Illicium anisatum, star anise, seed; Ipomæa cymosa, frog creeper; Ipomæa hederacea, kaladanah, seed; Ipomæa sepiaria, laldanah, seed; Ipomæa turpethum, indian jalap, root; Jasminum sambac, arabian jasmine, flower; Jatropha curcas, physic nut, oil from seed; Jatropha glandulifera, adul oil, oil from seed; Jatropha multifida, small french physic nut, oil from seed; Juniperus communis, juniper, berry; Justicia gendarussa, common gendarussa, leaf; Kœmpferia galanga, indian galangal, root; Kœmpferia rotunda, false zedoary, root; Lathyrus sativus, vetch, seed; Lawsonia alba, henna plant, leaf; Leucas aspera, rough toombay, dried plant; Linum usitatissimum, flax, seed; Liquidambar orientale, indian storax, prepared storax; Lobelia nicotianæfolia, wild tobacco, seed; Luffa acutangula, var. amara, bitter luffa, whole plant; Mallotus philippensis, kamela, kamela powder; Mangifera indica, mango, kernel; Melaleuca leucodendron, cajeput, oil; Melia azadirachta, margosa, bark, leaf; Melia azedarach, large neem, root-bark; Mentha piperita, peppermint, oil from fresh plant; Mentha viridis, spearmint, oil from fresh plant; Meriandra bengalensis, bengal sage, leaf; Mesua ferrea, nauga champak, flower, bark, root; Methonica superba, wild bachnaug, root; Michelia champaca, champak, bark; Mimusops elengi, ilanjy, bark; Mirabilis jalapa, false jalap, root; Moringa pterygosperma, indian horse-radish, root; Mucuna pruriens, common cowitch, hair of pod; Murraya kœnigii, curry-leaf tree, bark, root, leaf; Musa paradisiaca, plantain, leaf; Myrica sapida, box myrtle, bark; Myristica fragrans, common nutmeg, nut; Myristica malabarica, malabar nutmeg, oil; Nardostachys jatamansi, indian spikenard, root; Nerium odorum, oleander, flower; Nicotiana tabacum, tobacco, leaf; Nigella sativa, small fennel, seed; Ochrocarpus longifolius, soora poon, flower; Ocimum basilicum, sweet basil, leaf, seed; Ocimum gratissimum, shrubby basil, seed; Ocimum sanctum, holy basil, leaf; Odina wodier, wodier, bark, gum; Olea europæa, olive, oil; Ophiorrhiza mungos, mongoose snake-root, root; Oryza sativa, paddy, rice, rice flour; Papaver rhœas, red poppy, petals; Papaver somniferum, opium poppy, capsule, and opium; Pedalium murex, elephant nerinjy, fresh plant; Peganum harmala, syrian rue, seed; Peucedanum graveolens, dill, fruit; Phyllanthus emblica, emblic myrobalan, fruit; Phyllanthus niruri var. genuinus, neeroory, root, leaf, young shoot; Picrorhiza kurrooa, bitter root, root; Pimenta acris, pimento, dried unripe berry; Pimpinella anisum, anise seed, oil; Piper betel, betel pepper, leaf; Piper chaba, chaab pepper, fruit; Piper cubeba, cubeb pepper, dried berries; Piper longum, long pepper, root, fruit; Piper nigrum, black pepper, dried berries; Pistacia lentiscus, mastic, resin; Plantago ovata, spogel, seed; Plumbago rosea, officinal leadwort, root, root-bark; Plumbago zeylanica, ceylon leadwort, root-bark; Pogostemon patchouli, patchouli; Polygala senega, senegal naugay, dried root; Polygala telephioides, large naugay, root; Pongamia glabra, indian beech, seed; Prunus amygdalus, almond, nut; Prunus domestica, plum, dried drupe; Psidium guyava var. pomiferum, red guava, bark; Psidium guyava var. pyriferum, white guava, bark; Pterocarpus marsupium, malabar kino, inspissated juice obtained from incisions in the trunk; Pterocarpus santalinus, red sanders, wood; Punica granatum, pomegranate, root-bark; Quercus infectoria, dyer's oak, galls; Quercus robur, british oak, bark; Quisqualis indica, rangoon creeper, seed; Randia dumetorum, common emetic nut, fruit; Rauwolfia serpentina, snake root, root; Rheum emodi, indian rhubarb, root; Rheum moorcroftianum, indian rhubarb, root; Rheum webbianum, indian rhubarb, root; Rhinacanthus communis, snake jasmine, fresh root, seed; Rhus succedanea, red lac sumach, galls; Ricinus communis, castor oil, seed; Rosa centifolia, cabbage rose, petals, and volatile oil from petals; Rosa gallica, french rose, petals, dried petals, petals of unexpanded flowers; Rubia cordifolia, munjeet, root; Ruta graveolens, rue, whole plant, oil; Saccharum officinarum, sugarcane, sugar; Salicornia brachiata, glosswort, ashes; Salix caprea, hedge willow, flower; Salix tetrasperma, indian willow, bark; Salvadora oleoides, large tooth-brush tree, oil, root-bark; Salvadora persica, tooth-brush tree, leaf, bark, fruit; Santalum album, sandal-wood, wood-oil; Scindapsus officinalis, elephant long pepper, fruit; Semecarpus anacardium, marking nut, juice between laminæ of shell; Sesamum indicum, gingelly, oil, seed, leaf; Sesbania grandiflora, west-indian sesban, bark, leaf; Shorea robusta, common saul, resin; Sida carpinifolia, lance-leaved balah, root; Smilax glabra, large china root, root; Smilax lanceæfolia, indian china root, root; Smilax officinalis, sarsaparilla china root, root; Smilax ovalifolia, oval-leaved china root, root; Solanum ferox, hairy nightshade, leaf; Solanum indicum, indian night shade, root; Solanum nigrum, indian hound's berry, juice of leaf; Solanum trilobatum, prickly shoonday, root, leaf; Solanum verbascifolium, shoonday, leaf; Solanum xanthocarpum, prickly brinjaul, stem, flower and fruit; Soymida febrifuga, rohan tree, bark; Strychnos colubrina, snake-wood tree, wood; Strychnos nux-vomica, poison nut, seed; Strychnos potatorum, clearing nut, seed; Styrax benzoin, gum benjamin, resin; Suæda indica, indian saltwort, ashes; Suæda nudiflora, sea-side indian saltwort, ashes; Swertia affinis, blue-flowered chiretta, stem; Swertia angustifolia, stem; Swertia chirata, himalayan chiretta, dried stalk and root; Swertia decussata, mahableshwar chiretta, stem; Tamarindus indica, tamarind, pulp; Tamarix articulata, red tamarisk, galls, bark; Tamarix gallica, indian tamarisk, galls, manna; Tectona grandis, teak, flower; Terminalia belerica, belleric myrobalan, fruit; Terminalia catappa, country almond, kernel, oil; Terminalia chebula, chebulic myrobalan, fruit, gallnut, flower; Terminalia tomentosa var. typica, black murdah, bark; Thalictrum foliolosum, momiree, root; Thespesia populnea, portia, gamboge from fruit; Thevetia nereifolia, exile tree, bark; Tinospora cordifolia, goolancha, root; Toddalia aculeata, lopez root, root; Tribulus terrestris, land caltrops, fruit, leaf, root; Trichodesma indicum, donkey toombay, leaf; Trichosanthes palmata, bitter snake gourd, rind; Triticum vulgare, wheat, flour, starch; Tylophora asthmatica, indian ipecacuanha, leaf; Typhonium orixense, elephant yam, root; Uncaria gambier, gambier, catechu; Urginia indica, squill, bulb; Vateria indica, piney, resin; Vernonia anthelmintica, wild cumin, seed; Viscum monoicum, misseltoe, leaf; Vitex negundo, notchy, root, leaf; Vitex trifolia, water notchy, leaf; Vitis vinifera, grape vine, raisins; Withania coagulans, country asgand, fruit; Withania somnifera, asgand, root; Zanthoxylum alatum, tejbul, fruit, seed, bark; Zingiber cassumunar, bengal root, rhizome; Zingiber officinale, ginger, rhizome; Zingiber zerumbet, false ginger, rhizome.—"*b*" Absinth, artemisia; Adul oil, jatropha; Ailanto, ailanthus; Ajwaun, carum; Almond, prunus, terminalia; Aloe, agave; Anasandra, acacia; Anise, illicium, pimpinella; Asafœtida, ferula; Asgand, withania; Atees, aconitum; Babool, acacia; Bachnaug, methonica; Bael, ægle; Balah, sida; Bamboo, bambusa; Banyan, ficus; Baobab, adansonia; Barley, hordeum; Basil, ocimum; Bdellium, balsamodendron; Beech, pongamia; Belladonna, atropa; Bendy, hibiscus; Bengal root, zingiber; Benjamin, styrax; Berberry, berberis; Betel, piper; Bhangrah, eclipta; Bhraungy, clerodendron; Bitter root, picrorhiza; Bonduc, cæsalpinia; Borage, coleus; Box myrtle, myrica; Brinjaul, solanum; Burr, achyranthes; Cajeput, melaleuca; Calisaya bark, cinchona; Caltrops, tribulus; Calumba, cocculus; Caraway, carum; Cardamom, elettaria; Cashew, anacardium; Cashmere tree, gmelina; Cassie oil, acacia; Castor, ricinus; Catechu, acacia; Catmint, amisomeles; Ceylon moss, gracilaria; Chakondah, cassia; Chamomile, anthemis, chrysanthemum; Champak, mesua, michelia; Chaulmoogra, gynocardia; Chilly, capsicum; China root, smilax; Chiretta, andrographis, enicostema, erythræa, swertia; Citronella, andropogon; Clearing nut, strychnos; Clove, eugenia; Cocoanut, cocos; Colocynth, citrullus; Cooppamainy, acalypha; Coorvitchy, ehretia; Coriander, coriandrum; Cotton, gossypium; Cowitch, mucuna; Crab oil, carapa; Croton, baliospermum; Crow creeper, clitorea; Crown bark, cinchona; Cubeb, piper; Cucumber, cucumis; Cumin, cuminum, vernonia; Curry leaf, murraya; Cuscus, andropogon; Dammer, canarium; Decamallee, gardenia; Deodar, cedrus; Devil's goad, croton; Dill, peucedanum; Dita, alstonia; Divy divy cæsalpinia; Ebony, diospyros; Elemi, canarium; Emetic nut, randia; Exile tree, thevetia; False calumba, coscinium; Fennel, fœniculum, nigella; Fig, ficus; Fish poison, hydnocarpus; Flax, linum; Frog creeper, ipomæa; Gajwaun, echium; Galangal, alpinia, kœmpferia; Gal-

157

banum, ferula; Gambier, uncaria; Gamboge, garcinia; Garlic pear, cratæva; Gaub, diospyros; Gendarussa, justicia; Gentian, exacum; Gingelly, sesamum; Ginger, zingiber; Glosswort, salicornia; Golden silk cotton, cochlospermum; Goolancha, tinospora; Gram, cassia, cicer; Groundnut, arachis; Guava, psidium; Gum ammoniac, dorema; Gurjan, dipterocarpus; Hart's ear, cacalia; Hedge cotton, dæmia; Hemp, cannabis, eupatorium; Henbane, hyoscyamus; Henna, lawsonia; Hog weed, bœrhaavia; Horse radish, moringa; Hound's berry, solanum; Hyssop, herpestes; Ilanjy, mimusops; Indian berry, anamirta; Indian plum, flacourtia; Ipecacuanha, gymnema, tylophora; Isharmool, aristolochia; Jalap, exogonium, ipomæa, mirabilis; Jamtee, cocculus; Jasmine, jasminum, rhinacanthus; Jaumoon, eugenia; Kaladanah, ipomæa; Kale, colocasia; Kameta, mallotus; Kino, butea, pterocarpus; Laburnum, cassia; Laldanah, ipomæa; Lavender, anisochilus; Leadwort, plumbago; Lemon, citrus; Lemon grass, andropogon; Liquorice, abrus, glycirrhiza; Lopez root, toddalia; Lumbang, aleurites; Malabar arrowroot, curcuma; Malabar nut, adhatoda; Malkangany, celastrus; Mango, mangifera; Mango ginger, curcuma; Mangosteen, garcinia; Manna, alhagi, fraxinus; Margosa, melia; Marking nut, semecarpus; Mastic, pistacia; Mexican poppy, argemone; Milk-hedge, euphorbia; Mishmee bitter, coptis; Misseltoe, viscum; Mohwah, bassia; Momiree, thalictrum; Mudar, calotropis; Munjeet, rubia; Murdah, terminalia; Mustard, brassica, gynandropsis; Myrobalan, phyllanthus, terminalia; Myrrh, balsamodendron; Nangay, polygala; Neem, melia; Neermoolly, hygrophila; Neeroory, phyllanthus; Nerinjy, pedalium; Night shade, solanum; Notchy, vitex; Nutmeg, myristica; Oak, quercus; Odallam, cerbera; Oleander, nerium; Olive, olea; Orange, citrus; Paddy, oryza; Palmyra, borassus; Papaw, carica; Pareira, cissampelos; Patchouli, pogostemon; Pellitory, anacyclus; Pennywort, hydrocotyle; Pepper, piper, scindapsus; Peppermint, mentha; Physic nut, jatropha; Piney, vateria; Plantain, musa; Plum, prunus; Poison nut, strychnos; Pomegranate, punica; Poon, calophyllum, ochrocarpus; Poppy, papaver; Portia, thespesia; Potato, dracontium; Pumpkin, cucurbita; Quince, cydonia; Rangoon creeper, quisqualis; Red bark, cinchona; Red cotton, bombax; Red sanders, pterocarpus; Rhubarb, rheum; Ringworm shrub, cassia; Rohan, soymida; Rose, rosa; Rue, peganum, ruta; Sack tree, antiaris; Saffron, crocus; Sage, meriandra; Sago palm, caryota; Saltwort, suæda; Sandal, santalum; Sand greens, gisekia; Sappan, cæsalpinia; Saraswaty's leaf, clerodendron; Sarsaparilla, hemidesmus; Saul, shorea; Scammony, convolvulus; Sebesten, cordia; Sedge, cyperus; Senna, cassia; Sesban, sesbania; Shoonday, solanum; Silk cotton, dregia; Sirissa, albizzia; Snake caper, corallocarpus; Snake gourd, trichosanthes; Snake root, ophiorrhiza, rauwolfia; Snake wood, strychnos; Spearmint, mentha; Spikenard, nardostachys; Spogel, plantago; Squill, urginia; Stinking weed, cassia; Storax, altingia, liquidambar; Sugar cane, saccharum; Sumach, rhus; Sweet flag, acorus; Tamarind, tamarindus; Tamarisk, tamarix; Teak, tectona; Tejbul, zanthoxylum; Tellicherry bark, holarrhena; Tobacco, lobelia, nicotiana; Toombay, leucas, trichodesma; Toon, cedrela; Tooth-brush tree, salvadora; Tragacanth, astragalus; Tungaid, cassia; Turmeric, curcuma; Vetch, lathyrus; Vine, vitis; Weevil root, curculigo; Wheat, triticum; Whip tree, casuarina; Willow, salix; Wodier, odina; Wood apple, feronia; Worm-killer, aristolochia; Yam, typhonium; Zedoary, curcuma, hedychium, kœmpferia.——**(2)** The following is a list of the principal products of the animal kingdom utilised in the indian pharmacopœia:—Acipenser huso, sturgeon, isinglass [meen vajram]. Apis mellifica, honey bee, honey [shahad], wax [mom]. Coccus cacti, cochineal [kirmiz]. Cybium commersonii, liver oil [seer]. Euphesetes macrocephalus, spermaceti [hoot]. Mylabris cichorii, telini fly [q.v.]. Sanguisuga, leech [attay]. Squalus carcharias, sharkliver oil [soorah]. Viverra zibetha, civet [custoory].——**(3)** The following is a list of the principal products of the mineral kingdom utilised in the indian pharmacopœia:—Acidum arseniosum, arsenic [paushaunam]. Acidum hydrochloricum [namak tezaub]. Acidum nitricum, nitric acid [shoreyka tezaub]. Acidum sulphuricum, sulphuric acid [gandhac tezaub]. Alumen, alum [fatakree, padicauram]. Ammonia [nowshaudar]. Ammonii chloridum, nowsaugar [nowshaudar]. Antimonium, antimony [soorma]. Antimonium sulphuratum [soorma]. Aqua, water [neer]. Argenti nitras, nitrate of silver [caudy cauram]. Argenti oxidum, oxide of silver [velly paspam]. Argentum, silver [velly]. Argentum purificatum, refined silver [chokka velly]. Arsenicum, arsenic [paushaunam]. Calx, quicklime [choonam]. Carbon, charcoal [kary]. Creta præparata, prepared chalk [sheemay choonam]. Cupri sulphas, mor toottam [mayil toottam]. Cuprum or copper [taumram]. Ferri oxidum magneticum [cauntam]. Ferri peroxidum hydratum [iroomboo tooroo]. Ferri sulphas [annabhaidy]. Ferrum [auhan]. Hydrargyri oxidum rubrum, red oxide of mercury [rasa sindooram]. Hydrargyri perchloridum, perchloride of mercury [shavveeram]. Hydrargyri subchloridum, subchloride of mercury [rascapoor]. Hydrargyri sulphas, sulphate of mercury [rasa paspam]. Hydrargyrum, mercury [rasam]. Magnesia [caunta munn]. Plumbi acetas, acetate of lead [eeya carcand]. Plumbi carbonas, carbonate of lead [eeyam, moottoovelly]. Plumbi nitras, nitrate of lead [vediyoopp eeyam]. Plumbi oxidum [moordarsing]. Plumbum, lead [eeyam]. Potassæ nitras, saltpetre [shorah]. Potassæ tartras, tartrate of potash [draucsha ooppoo]. Potassæ tartras acida, acid tartrate of potash [draucsha ooppoo]. Sodæ biboras, biborate of soda, borax [vengauram]. Sodæ carbonas, carbonate of soda [sujjee khaur]. Sodæ sulphas, glauber's salt [namak]. Sodii chloridum, common salt [ooppoo]. Sulphur [gandhac]. Sulphur sublimatum, sublimed sulphur. Zinci carbonas, carbonate of zinc [madal toottam]. Zinci sulphas, sulphate of zinc [vellay toottam]. Zincum, zinc [tootnaug].——**(4)** The following list shows the pharmacopœia terms for medicinal powers arranged alphabetically, with the sanscrit equivalents; compare Veidyan:—Alteratives, rasauyanam; Anthelmintics, krimignam; Antidotes to bites of snakes and other animals, vishagnam; Antiscorbutics, cooshtagnam; Antispasmodics, aucshepagnam; Astringents, stambhanam; Carminatives, vautagnam; Counter-irritants, praty copanam; Demulcents, shamacam; Diuretics, mootralam; Emetics, vamanam; Emmenagogues, ritoo janacam; Expectorants, chedanam; Febrifuges, jvaragnam; Gums, niryausam; Insecticides, keetagnam; Lactagogues, stanya jananam; Lactifuges, stanya shoshanam; Mydriatics, taurah vivauranam; Nutritives, vrimhanam; Oils, teilam; Parturifacients, prasava saudhanam; Purgatives, viraichanam; Refrigerants, nirvaupanam; Sedatives, shamanam; Silagogues, laulah srauvy; Stimulant applications in affections of the eye, netra roga deepanam; Stimulant applications in skin diseases, tvak roga deepanam; Stimulants, general, deepanam; Stimulant to ulcers, abscesses, &c., vrana vidradhy deepanam; Styptics, shonita staupanam; Sudorifics, svedanam; Terebinthinate stimulants, tilaparneeya deepanam; Tonics, astringent, toovara balyam; Tonics, bitter and aromatic, tikta soogandhy balyam; Vesicants, spotacapralepanam.

OTAHEITE (تہیتی - tahítí, *Hind.*). Otherwise Tahiti; the largest of the Society islands.——*Otaheite apple* (ولایتی امرا - viláitíamrá, Hind.; மரிமா - marimá, Tam.). Hind. from (viláítí, hind. foreign + amrá, hind. spondias mangifera, willd.). Tam. from (marul, tam. devil + má, tam. mango, mangifera indica, linn.). Title otherwise Hog plum, Vi tree. Botanically Spondias [amrautam] dulcis, willd., anacardiaceæ [vricsham, 45]. Tree of south sea islands; graceful foliage of alternate odd-pinnate leaves, small yellow flowers, producing an oval fruit; this has a large fibre-covered stone in the centre, the size and form of a large hen's egg, of a deep amber [karbah] color, blotched for the most part with rusty russet like the color of tarnished gold; fragrance resembles that of the quince [bedauna]; to taste, very acid, flavor like that of bad mango [q.v.]. No other species here.——*Otaheite cashew* (تہیتی کاکاجو - tahítíkákájú, Hind.). Same as Malacca jaumoon.——*Otaheite gooseberry* (تہیتی کی حرفالیوڑی - tahítíkiharfáleurí, Hind.). Same as Brazil cherry.——*Otaheite salep* (सूरण - súrana, San.; کندہ - kandah, Hind.; بڑا کندا - barákandá, Dec.; تکا - takka, Malay; పెద్దకంద - peddakanda, Tel.; ചേന - chéna, Mal.; காருக்கருணை - kárákkarunai, Tam.). San. from (súr, san. to hurt) [telinga potato]. Hind. means bulbous root. Dec. from (bará, hind. large + kandá, hind. bulbous root). Tel. from (pedda, tel. large + kanda, tel. amorphophallus campanulatus, blume). Tam. from (káru, tam. to taste bitter + á, tam. negative particle + karunai, tam. dracontium polyphyllum, linn.). Malay also (takkaliker). Tel. also (kanda) [elephant yam, telinga potato]; (chunda). Tam. also (periyagarunai), meaning big + dracontium polyphyllum, linn.; (kárácçénai). Title otherwise Chaina, Elephant yam [telinga potato], Mergui arrowroot, Pi plant, Salep tacca, South sea arrowroot, Tacca starch, Tahiti arrowroot. Botanically Tacca pinnatifida, forsk., taccaceæ [vricsham, 147]. Generic name from malay. Root tuberous, perennial, very large, round and smoothish, with a few fibres issuing from the surface; leaves radical, three-parted, divisions two to three partite, and alternately pinnatifid, margins waved; petioles slightly grooved, 1 to 3 feet long; scapes radical, round, smooth, slightly grooved, and striped with darker and paler green; umbels consisting of ten to forty long-pedicelled, drooping, greenish flowers, intermixed with as many long drooping bracts; involucel six to twelve leaved; leaflets lanceolate, recurved, beautifully marked with pale-purple veins; calyx globose, fleshy, six-cleft, segments incurved, green, with purplish margins; corolla none. Root yields large quantity of white nutritious fecula, resembling arrowroot; root intensely bitter when raw; however much eaten by natives, specially in travancore. The Tahitians prepare from the floral scapes a white straw, with which they make hats. No other common species here.——*Otaheite walnut* (تہیتی اکروٹ - tahítíakrot, Hind.). Same as Lumbang nut.

OTCHAN (ഓച്ചൻ - óççan, *Mal.*; ஒச்சன் - óççan, *Tam.*). From (óççu, tam. to drive away); as expelling devils. A class of Shoodras in Malabar. Employed amongst fishermen as priests and servants of temples [coil, pagoda] dedicated to village deities [jauty]. Beat drums [paray] like pariahs [q.v.]. See vol. I (68).——*Ochira* (ഓച്ചറ - óççara, Mal.). From (óççan, mal. drum-beater + kara, mal. village). Village; Travancore state, Quilon division, Carounaugapully tal.; from Cauyancollam S. 6 miles. At present noted for a mock fight exhibited on the occasion of the annual festival, in commemoration of battles fought on the spot between Cauyancollam and Champakacherry rajahs. Festival about the 15th June of each year lasting for two days when a cattle [maud] market is held.——*Osy* (ஓசி -

ósi, Tam.). Priestess at a Pidanry [q.v.] temple [coil, pagoda]. Pariah female proper name [peyar].

OTE (ഓട്ട് - óttu, *Mal.*). Corr. of (akattu), from (akam, mal. inside). Suffix in place names as Cangote, Corote, Cotiote, Oorote, Tannote, Terriote.

OTTAGAM (उष्ट्र - ushtra, *San.*; ऊट - úta, *Mahr.*; جمل - jamal, *Ar.*; شتر - shutr, *Pers.*; اونٹ - únt, *Hind.*; اونتا - unta, *Malay*; ಒಂಟೆ - onte, *Can.* and *Too.*; ఒంటె - onte, *Tel.*; ଓଟ - ota, *Oor.*; ഒട്ടകം - ottakam, *Mal.*; ඔටුවා - otuvá, *Singh.*; ஒட்டகம் - ottagam, *Tam.*). San. from (ush, san. to burn); as bearing heat [ooshtram]. Rest from sanscrit. San. also (kraméla). Ar. also (hijíd); (bakhtí), meaning bactrian. Title otherwise Dromedary camel. Camelus dromedarius, camelidæ, ruminantia, mammalia [sastanam, 26], of naturalists [jantoo]. Camels are sometimes classed as Tylopoda. Their feet are composed of toes protected by cushion-like soles, and not by a horny covering like those of the Artiodactyli generally. Two species of camelidæ are known, Camelus dromedarius, the one-humped camel or domedary; and Camelus bactrianus, or the two-humped. They are now completely domesticated. The former spread from Arabia into North africa, India, &c.; the latter spread from Central asia. The Dromedary camel is used in southern india as a beast of burden, and is also kept by zemindars [q.v.] for display [ooshtram].

OTTAPIDAURAM (ஒட்டப்பிடாரம் - óttappidáram, *Tam.* otapidáram *). From (ódai, tam. tank + pidári, tam. the village goddess so called + agam, tam. place) [ode].——(1) Talook, Tinnevelly district. Tahsildar's pay Rs. 150. Area 1,061 square miles, including Yettiyaupooram zemindarry. Population 342,145. Languages, Tamul and Teloogoo. N.E. of district. Bounded E. by sea, W. by Tinnevelly and Shuncaraneinarcoil talooks, S. by Tinnevelly and Tencaray talooks, and N. by Ramnaud zemindarry and Shauttore talook. A few detached masses of gneiss rocks rising abruptly from the plains form conspicuous objects, but generally the country is level, rising and falling very slightly in long and broad slopes, which follow the drainage lines from north-west to south-east. The soil is almost wholly of a uniform character, the talook being a wide black cotton [regar] plain relieved by scanty and poor topes [q.v.] of tamarind [q.v.] here and there, and by thickets of babool [q.v.] in every tank bed. To the west and south however there is a considerable area of red sands and loams, amounting to nearly one-tenth of the area of the talook. There are extensive areas of rich black loamy soil producing fine crops of cotton [q.v.], cumboo [bajrah], cholum [q.v.] fodder and bengal-gram [q.v.], and also a large area of poor gravelly soil impregnated with soda [munn canram]. Near the coast the white sea sands [manal] prevail, producing chiefly palmyras [q.v.] and babool [q.v.] thorns. The latter are valued for making agricultural implements, being extremely hard, and for firewood; also for their seeds, which are excellent food for sheep [aud]. Trade is chiefly in cotton, for which there are several steam cotton presses. The annual export is estimated at about 51,000 bales of 500 lbs. each and 33,000 bales of 400 lbs. each, nearly the whole being sent to Tuticorin. Coffee [q.v.] from the ghaut [q.v.] estates, salt [ooppoo], cotton-goods, and palmyra [q.v.] jaggery [q.v.] are other exports. Imports are chiefly english piece-goods and yarn, paddy [q.v.], rice [q.v.], metals [loham] and betelnuts [q.v.]. The only important manufactures are native cloths and palmyra jaggery. There are numerous irrigation tanks [q.v.], chiefly rainfed, and almost every village has an oorny [q.v.], for the storage of drinking water, collected during the north-east monsoon [q.v.] and subsequent showers for use during the hot weather. Wells frequently dry up or are very generally impregnated with salt. Well cultivation by means of bullocks is much followed in parts and good crops of tobacco [pogauk], cholum [q.v.], chillies [q.v.], vegetables, and betel [q.v.] leaf are obtained. The largest part of the talook [q.v.] is zemindarry [q.v.], Government lands being less than one-third of the whole. Besides Yettiyaupooram zemindarry, the talook contains the following estates:—Auttangaray, Cadambore, Caudalgoody, Cauraycoorchy mittah, Coolatore, Mailmaunday, Maniyauchy, Mulleeswarapooram, Naugalaupooram, Peroorany mittah, Poothoor mittah, Ramasawmypooram, Soondraputchaiyaupooram, Tattanairy. Places of archæological interest:—Atchangoolam, Audanore, Carishalcoolam, Caumayyanaickenputty, Cayataur, Cazhoogoomullay, Coolatore, Coomarettiyaupooram, Culcoomy, Gownagherry, Mandicoolam, Meenautchipooram, Moodookkmindaunputty, Mooramban, Mungalam, Naugalaupooram, Naulvausancottah, Pashoovandanay, Punchaulamcoorchy, Tuticorin, Vaunarmootty, Veippaur, Vellaram, Vilauticoolam, Yelavalangaul, Yettiyaupooram, Yilamboonam. Principal trig. stations:—Coolayanullore, Meenautchy, Melaculloorny, Mottoorny, Shooplaupooram, Soorangoody. The leading places, &c., in the talook are the following.——*Auttangaray* (ஆத்தங்கரை - áttangarai, Tam.). From (árn, tam. river + karai, tam. bank). Zemindarry, Village; pop. 1,631; acres 9,227; lat. of village 9° 11′; long. 78° 10′; from Ottapidauram N. 20 miles; from Tinnevelly N.E. 43 miles; from the sea W. 16 miles. Peshcush Rs. 3,372.——*Cadambore* (கடம்பூர் - kadambúr, * Tam.). From (kadambu, tam. a tree, barringtonia racemosa, blume + úr, tam. village). Zemindarry, Village, Railway station; pop. 2,421; Cadambore village 17,282 acres; lat. of village 9° 00′; long. 77° 54′; height 292 feet; from Ottapidauram W.N.W. 12 miles; from Tinnevelly N.E. 22 miles; from the sea W. 27 miles. Weekly fair on Wednesdays. Peshcush Rs. 3,742.——*Caudalgoody* (காடற்குடி - kádargudi, Tam.). From (kádu, tam. forest + al, tam. without + kudi, tam. village). Zemindarry, Village; pop. 853; Zemindarry 24,473 acres; lat. of village 9° 12′; long. 78° 17′; from Ottapidauram N.E. 25 miles; from Tinnevelly N.E. 50 miles; from the sea W. 15 miles. Peshcush Rs. 880.——*Caumayyanaickenputty* (காமயநாயக்கன்பட்டி - kámayanáyakkanbatti, Tam.). From (kámayanáyakkan, tam. proper name + patti, tam. village). Village; pop. 1,269; lat. 9° 05′; long. 77° 59′; from Ottapidauram N. 12 miles; from Tinnevelly N.E. 29 miles; from the sea W. 29 miles. In Yettiyaupooram zemindarry. Mission established in 1660. Roman catholic church.——*Cayataur* (கைத்தார் - kaittár, Tam. kayatár *). From (kaittá, tam. wild croton, jatropha curcas, linn. + áru, tam. river). Village; pop. 3,233; acres 2,050; lat. 8° 57′; long. 77° 49′; from Ottapidauram W. 17 miles; from Tinnevelly N.E. 16 miles; from the sea W. 29 miles. On the Madura road. Deserted Vishnoo [q.v.] temple with four inscriptions. The copper [taumram] images [vigraham] of the temple were carried away to Yettiyaupooram and are now worshipped there. Ancient and well-sculptured Shiva [q.v.] temple. Ruined fort. Large market on Thursdays. Dawk [q.v.] bungalow [q.v.].——*Cazhoogoomullay* (கழுகுமலை - kazhugumalai, Tam.). See sep. title.——*Coolatore* (குளத்தூர் - kulattúr, Tam.). From (kulam, tam. tank + úr, tam. village). Zemindarry, Village; pop. 4,195; village 11,558 acres; lat. of village 9° 00′; long. 78° 14′; from Ottapidauram E.N.E. 13 miles; from Tinnevelly E.N.E. 39 miles; from the sea W. 4 miles. Jeina [q.v.] statue [gomataroya], worshipped by ordinary Sheivites. Market on Tuesdays. S.P.G. mission station. Peshcush Rs. 1,897.——*Coolayanullore* (குலயநல்லூர் - kulayanallúr, Tam.). From (kolaiñan, tam. a hunter who lives by killing + nal, tam. good + úr, tam. village). Trig. station; lat. 8° 55′ 33·71″; long. 78° 01′ 24·93″; height 346 feet; from Ottapidauram W.N.W. 3 miles; from the sea W. 14 miles.——*Cooroomullay* (குருமலை - kurumalai, Tam.). See sep. title.——*Crownchateev* (கிரௌஞ்சத்தீவு - kirauñjattívu, Tam.). See sep. title.——*Eeraul* (ஈரால் - írál, Tam.). From (ír, tam. two + ál, tam. banyan tree, ficus bengalensis, linn.). Village; pop. 3,355; lat. 9° 06′; long. 78° 03′; from Ottapidauram N. 13 miles; from Tinnevelly N.E. 34 miles; from the sea W. 25 miles.——*Mailmaunday* (மேல்மாந்தை - mélmándai, Tam.). From (mél, tam. west + mándai, tam. cattle stand). Zemindarry, Village; pop. 5,161; acres 20,032; lat. of village 9° 04′; long. 78° 20′; from Ottapidauram E.N.E. 21 miles; from Tinnevelly E.N.E. 47 miles; from the sea N. 4 miles. Weekly market on Mondays. Peshcush Rs. 1,412.——*Maniyauchy* (மணியாச்சி - maniyáççi, Tam.). See sep. title.——*Meenautchy* (மீனாச்சி - mínáççi, Tam.). From a person of that name. Trig. station; lat. 9° 12′ 34·00″; long. 78° 01′ 17·06″; height 322 feet; from Malaputty W.N.W. ½ mile; from Ottapidauram N. 20 miles; from the sea W. 29 miles. *Melaculloorny* (மேலக்கல்லூரணி - mélakkallúrani, Tam.). From (mél, tam. west + kal, tam. stone + úrani, tam. spring). Trig. station; lat. 9° 14′ 14·99″; long. 78° 12′ 55·76″; height 141 feet; from Ottapidauram N.N.E. 24 miles; from the sea N. 23 miles.——*Mottoorny* (மொட்டூரணி - mótturani, Tam.). From (módu, tam. high ground + úrani, tam. spring). Trig. station; lat. 9° 17′ 25·76″; long. 78° 19′ 02·72″; height 133 feet; from Ottapidauram N.N.E 31 miles; from the sea N. 19 miles.——*Naugalaupooram* (நாகலாப்புரம் - nágaláppuram, Tam. nágalápuram *). From (nágal, tam. the nauval wood tree, eugenia jambolana, lamk., var. caryophyllifolia + pura, san. town). Zemindarry, Village; pop. 2,490; estate 15,812 acres; lat. of village 9° 14′; long. 78° 11′; from Ottapidauram N.E. 22 miles; from Tinnevelly N.E. 46 miles; from the sea N.W. 18 miles. Jeina statue [gomataroya] formerly here taken to Madras museum. Chief S.P.G. mission station. Peshcush Rs. 6,445.——*Ottapidauram* (ஒட்டப்பிடாரம் - óttappidáram, Tam.). See below.——*Poothoor* (புதூர் - puthúr, Tam. pudúr). From (puthu, tam. new + úr, tam. village). Zemindarry, Village; pop. 1,255; mittah 13,088 acres; lat. of village 9° 17′; long. 78° 11′; from Ottapidauram N.N.E. 27 miles; from Tinnevelly N.E. 49 miles; from the sea N.W. 22 miles. S.P.G. mission station. Peshcush Rs. 6,414.——*Punchaulamcoorchy* (பாஞ்சாலக்குறிச்சி - páñjálakkuriççi, Tam.). See sep. title.——*Shoolliteev* (சுள்ளித்தீவு - shullittívu, Tam.). See sep. title.——*Shooplaupooram* (சுப்பலாப்புரம் - shuppaláppuram, Tam.). From (subbulu, tel. proper name + pura, san. town). Sanscrit name (subrahmanyapura), meaning soobramanyan, the pious god + town. Trig. station; lat. 9° 04′ 20·93″; long. 78° 07′ 23·11″; height 149 feet; from Coomarettiyaupooram S.E. ½ mile; from Ottapidauram N.N.E. 11 miles; from the sea W. 18 miles.——*Soorangoody* (சுரங்குடி - shurangudi, Tam.). From (shuram, tam. desert + kudi, tam. village). Trig. station; lat. 9° 06′ 02·71″; long. 78° 21′ 59·22″; height 67 feet; from Ottapidauram E.N.E. 23 miles; from the sea N. 4 miles.——*Tattanairy* (தத்த

டேனேரி - tattanéri, Tam.). From (tattan, tam. proper name + éri, tam. tank). Zemindarry, Village; pop. 2,644; lat. of village 9° 05′; long. 78° 18′; from Ottapidauram N.E. 20 miles; from Tinnevelly E.N.E. 46 miles; from the sea N. 6 miles. Peshcush Rs. 237.——*Tattapauray* (தட்டப்பாறை - tattappárai, Tam. tatapárai *). From (tattai, tam. flat + párai, tam. rock). Village; pop. 1,368; acres 3,838; lat. 8° 49′; long. 78° 03′; height 98 feet; from Ottapidauram S. 6 miles; from Tinnevelly E.N.E. 24 miles; from the sea W. 9 miles.——*Tuticorin* (தூத்துக்குடி - túttukkudi, Tam.). See sep. title.——*Veippaur* (வைப்பாறு - vaippáru, Tam.). See sep. title.—*Vembaur* (வேம்பார் - vémbár, Tam.). From (vémbu, tam. margosa tree, melia azadirachta, linn. + pár, tam. bank). Village, Port; lat. 9° 5′ N.; long. 78° 24′ E; from Madras S.S.W. 302 miles; from Ottapidauram E.N.E. 25 miles; from Tinnevelly E.N.E. 52 miles; from Veippaur E.N.E. 8 miles. In Mailmaunday zemindarry. On Gulf of Manaar, at mouth of the Ooppaur creek and on boundary between Tinnevelly and Madura.——*Vilauticoolam* (விளாத்திக்குளம் - viláttikkulam, Tam.). See sep. title.——*Yettiyaupooram* (எட்டையாப்புரம் - ettaiyáppuram, Tam.). See sep. title.——**(2)** Town, Talook head-quarters, Tinnevelly dist., Ottapidauram tal.; pop. 3,631; acres 9;205; lat. 8° 55′; long. 78° 04′; from Madras S.S.W. 318 miles; from Palamcottah E.N.E. 24 miles; from Shermadevy E.N.E. 35 miles; from Shreevillipoottore S.E. 48 miles; from Tinnevelly E.N.E. 27 miles; from Tuticorin N.W. 12 miles; from the sea W. 11 miles. Weekly fair on Tuesdays.

OTTOO (ಒಟ್ಟು - ottu, *Can.*). Whole. Ottoogoottagay is the entire assessment or rent.

OTTY (ഒററി - otti, *Mal.*). From (ottuka, mal. to step aside). The stepping aside or making way for another. Veppoo in Palghaut talook, meaning deposit; Palishamadak in Nedooonganaud and Valavanaud talooks, meaning return of interest [palisha]. The tenure of land where a Malabar caunom, in the progressive scale of tenancies which is always regarded as an essential characteristic of land tenure there, commences to give the tenant a right of pre-emption, with other incidents strengthening his dominion, and making it still less like lease and still more like mortgage [panayam]. The tenure gives the tenant or mortgagee possession and the entire produce of the land, not merely possession with an interest as in Caunom [q.v.]. The landlord here retains nothing but the proprietary title, a nominal rent, and the power to redeem. Where no period has been stipulated, the landlord may redeem at any time. The twelve years' term does not appear to have been applied to the Otty tenure until some time after it was recognized as an ordinary incident of a caunom. The principal alone is repayable at redemption, the mortgagee recovering the interest of his money currently from the produce of the land. The mortgage that is to say is usufructuary, the usufruct extinguishing the interest. If the landlord be desirous of raising a further sum and the Otty mortgagee refuse to advance it, the money may be received from a third party and the mortgage transferred to him. But the original mortgagee has a right to be first consulted. In fact the same incidents are attached to an Otty tenure as to a Caunom, and in addition the mortgagee has the right of pre-emption if the mortagagor wishes to dispose of the property. Between an Otty deed and a final sale-deed or Neer attipair [q.v.] caranam, [q.v.], some one or more of three deeds may according to circumstances be interposed, termed respectively:—Keividotty, Otticoompooram, Coodimaneer. These are deeds [caranam] of sale with reservation of certain detailed seigniorial rights to original proprietor, a mode of disposing of land highly feudal and still practised in some parts of Europe. In all of them however the power of redemption is gone for the landlord, and in that respect pre-emption merely has been transferred from the mortgagee to him. For conspectus of Malabar tenures, see vol. II, 104. The following are the three intermediate transactions mentioned above. See vol. I, 128.——"*a*" *Keividotty* (കൈവിടൊററി - kaivitotti, Mal.). From (kai, mal. hand + vitá, mal. without leaving + otti, mal. mortgage). The first stage between Otty and Neer attipair. The landlord demands a further loan and gives this deed in exchange. The landlord relinquishes the power of transferring the property to a third party, and binds himself to borrow any further sum he may require only from the mortgagee. The mortgagee is precluded from disposing of the land to a third party for more than he paid or on any other terms than those on which he acquired the occupation. Also if he wish to dispose of it, he is bound to give the proprietor the option of redeeming it. The deed is Caranamkeividotty.——"*b*" *Otticoompooram* (ഒററിക്കുമ്പുറം - ottikkumpuram, Mal.). From (above + puram, mal. beyond). The Caunom which is in addition to the Otty. A tenure differing scarcely appreciably from Keividotty. The deed is Caranamotticoompooram.——"*c*" *Coodimaneer* (കുടിമനീർ - kutimanír, Mal.). From (kutima, mal. tenantry + nír, mal. water). Otherwise Neermoothal, Jenmpanayam. When the landlord requires to borrow a still further sum on the security of land assigned to an Otty mortgagee to whom he has already executed a Keividotty or Otticoompooram deed, he gives him a Neermoothal or Coodimaneer document, by which he makes over to him all excepting the right got by water. The further advance is recoverable with the amount of the original mortgage, the Otty claim being in fact merged in the Coodimaneer deed. A payment not exceeding two fanams [q.v.] is now annually made to the possessor of the title. In executing the deed under this mode of transfer the landlord goes through the form of casting a few drops of water from his hand. This tenure prevails only in the neighbourhood of Calicut. The deed is Caranamcoodimaneer [maryauday].

OTY (ഓടി - oti, *Mal.*). A piece of rice-ground.

OUCHTERLONY VALLEY (ಆಕ್ಟರಲೋನಿಹಳ್ಳ - áktaralónihalla, *Can.*). After Colonel James Ouchterlony. Valley; Neilgherry dist., Wynaud S.E. div.; area 40 square miles; lat. 11° 23′ to 11° 29′ N.; long. 76° 27′ to 76° 35′ E.; from Goodalore S. 3 miles; from Ootacamund W. 13 miles. A beautiful valley, at an average elevation of 3,000 feet above sea-level; situated below S.W. wall of Neilgherries. First explored by Colonel Ouchterlony, in 1844–45, and at that time covered with virgin forest. Coffee cultivation was introduced, and there are now very numerous coffee [q.v.] estates, occupying about 5,200 acres. Cinchona [koinah] and tea [q.v.] also flourish. The whole valley has been converted into a busy English settlement, employing over 5,000 native hands. The expenditure in the valley is about Rs. 9,00,000 annually.

OWK * (ఔక - auka, *Tel.*). Means bog.—"*a*" Deputy tahsildarry, Kurnool district. Pay Rs. 70.—"*b*" Village, Deputy tahsildar's station; Kurnool dist., Coilcoontla tal.; pop. 2,862; acres 8,584; lat. 15° 13′; long. 78° 10′; from Coilcoontla W. 13 miles; from Cumbum S.W. 70 miles; from Kurnool S. 43 miles; from Madras N.W. 207 miles; from Nundiaul S.W. 30 miles; from Pyaupaly E. 25 miles. Built or improved by Timmaraja in 1463 A.D. Former seat of a powerful line of local chiefs. The ancestors were servants under Bookka roya of Vijianugger, from whom in 1450 they obtained a jagheer [q.v.] in Yaudiky district, which was continued by the Hyderabad kings, together with an assignment of 33 additional villages for the service of 1,800 men. Under Aurangzeeb the jagheer [q.v.] was resumed, but Owk assigned for the service of 1,000 peons [q.v.]. The last holder was pensioned by Munro. A scion of the family is the present Reddy of Owk who lives in the dilapidated fort. Vishnoo temple. Annual festival on 14th Veishaukham [mausam] in May. A fine tank [q.v.] between two hillocks. The Tirmalair escapes from the hills west of the town. Opposite the town are two waterfalls [aroovy] Gollalair and Palair. Weekly market on Wednesdays.

OWVAL (اول - awwal, *Hind.*). From (awala, ar. to precede). Principal.

OY (ఓయి - óyi, *Tel.*; ஓய் - óy, *Tam.*). Appellative masculine termination and vocative; used towards equals and inferiors [peyar]. The feminine term corresponding is Osy [ra].

OYAK (ഉഴക്ക് - uzhakku, *Mal.*; ஒழக்கு - ozhakku, *Tam.*). Measure of capacity, chiefly grain. Also liquid measure. Twice the ayak [q.v.] or olluck [q.v.].—"*a*" 2 ayaks = 1 oyak; 2 oyaks = 1 oory [alavay, 3d]. Approximate actual value, 1 oyak = 4 cubic inches. Malabar. Varies with yidangazhy.—"*b*" 2 ollucks = 1 oyak; 4 oyaks = 1 puddy [alavay, 3a]. Approximate actual value, 1 oyak = 25 cubic inches. Madras. Compare the Pow. See vol. I, 609; II, 514, 516.

P (प - pa, पा - pá, *San.*; پ - pe, *Hind.*; ப - pa, பா - pá, *Tam.*). Hind. symbol for two. Tam. the fraction $\frac{1}{20}$ [mah].

PACH (पच् - pach, *San.*). To cook.——*Pachwye* (پچوی - pachwí, Hind.). An intoxicating drink prepared in Ganjam from fermented grain. It is made either from maize [mecca cholum] or rice [q.v.] or sorghum [cholum]. The grain is boiled and spread out on a mat to cool. It is then mixed with a ferment of vegetables and kept in a large earthen vessel for some days. Warm water may at any time be mixed with it. In a few hours it ferments, and is ready for use [joogady, mooskiraut].——*Pauchanam* (पाचन - páchana, San.). A decoction [kwautam], infusion. Also a dissolvent.——*Paungah* (پانگا - pángá, *Hind.*). Culinary salt obtained from sea-sand. Subsequently purified by boiling [curry ooppoo].

PACSHAM (पक्ष - paksha, *San.*). From (paksh, san. to take). Side, half wing.—"*a*" One of two halves of a lunar month [mausam]; the half called Shoocla pacsham or the Bright half extending from new moon [amavausyay] to full moon [powrnimay], and the half called Krishna pacsham or the Dark half extending from full moon to new moon. These sanscrit and anglo-indian terms are tolerably descriptive of the facts as appearing immediately after sunset or say from 6 to 8 p.m., which is their origin; but they are very misleading in respect of the phenomena of the entire night or the distinctive quantity of the fortnight. The following table shows actual figures for a sample period of thirty days, and they are nearly the same for every lunar month [chaundramausam] throughout the year:—

Date of lunar month [chaundramausam].	Date of solar month [sowramausam].	Sun [sooryan]. Rises.	Sun [sooryan]. Sets.	Moon [chundran]. Rises.	Moon [chundran]. Sets.	Number of hours of moonlight [chundricay].	Period of moonlight [chundricay]. From	Period of moonlight [chundricay]. To	Age of moon [calay, piray].	Remarks.
1	2	3	4	5	6	7	8	9	10	11
		A. M.	P. M.	A. M.	P. M.					
1	Sept. 17	5 50	5 58	5 22	5 59	.. ...	......	......	New moon [amavausyay].	
							P. M.	P. M.		
2	,, 18	5 50	5 58	6 23	6 50	52 mins.	5 58	6 50		
3	,, 19	5 50	5 57	7 24	7 40	1 hr. 43 ,,	5 57	7 40		
4	,, 20	5 50	5 56	8 24	8 31	2 hrs. 35 ,,	5 56	8 31	Crescent moon, horns to the east [ardhachundran].	
5	,, 21	5 50	5 55	9 24	9 22	3 ,, 27 ,,	5 55	9 22		
6	,, 22	5 50	5 55	10 23	10 14	4 ,, 19 ,,	5 55	10 14		
7	,, 23	5 50	5 54	11 21	11 8	5 ,, 14 ,,	5 54	11 8		Bright fortnight so called [shoocla pacsham].
8	,, 24	5 50	5 53	Afternoon.	Morning.	6 ,, 7 ,,	5 53	Midnight	Moon's 1st quarter, otherwise half-moon [chundraurdham].	
				P. M.	A. M.			A. M.		
9	,, 25	5 50	5 52	1 11	0 1	6 ,, 9 ,,	5 52	0 1		
10	,, 26	5 51	5 52	2 2	0 55	7 ,, 3 ,,	5 52	0 55		
11	,, 27	5 51	5 51	2 49	1 47	7 ,, 56 ,,	5 51	1 47		
12	,, 28	5 51	5 50	3 34	2 38	8 ,, 48 ,,	5 50	2 38		
13	,, 29	5 51	5 50	4 15	3 27	9 ,, 37 ,,	5 50	3 27		
14	,, 30	5 51	5 49	4 55	4 15	10 ,, 26 ,,	5 49	4 15	Full moon [powrnimay].	Real bright fortnight.
15	October 1	5 51	5 48	5 34	5 2	11 ,, 14 ,,	5 48	5 2		
16	,, 2	5 51	5 47	6 11	5 48	11 ,, 37 ,	6 11	5 48		
17	,, 3	5 51	5 47	6 50	6 34	11 ,, 1 ,,	6 50	5 51		
18	,, 4	5 51	5 46	7 28	7 20	10 ,, 23 ,,	7 28	5 51		
19	,, 5	5 51	5 45	8 9	8 7	9 ,, 42 ,,	8 9	5 51		
20	,, 6	5 51	5 45	8 51	8 55	9 ,, 0 ,,	8 51	5 51		
21	,, 7	5 51	5 44	9 36	9 44	8 ,, 15 ,,	9 36	5 51	Moon's 3rd quarter, otherwise half-moon [chundraurdham].	Dark fortnight so called [krishna pacsham].
22	,, 8	5 51	5 44	10 25	10 34	7 ,, 26 ,,	10 25	5 51		
23	,, 9	5 51	5 43	11 16	11 26	6 ,, 35 ,,	11 16	5 51		
24	,, 10	5 51	5 42	Morning.	Afternoon.	5 ,, 51 ,,	Midnight	5 51		
				A. M.	P. M.		A. M.			
25	,, 11	5 51	5 42	0 10	1 11	5 ,, 41 ,.	0 10	5 51		
26	,, 12	5 52	5 41	1 6	2 3	4 ,, 46 ,,	1 6	5 52	Crescent-moon, horns to the west [ardhachundran].	
27	,, 13	5 52	5 41	2 4	2 54	3 ,, 48 ,,	2 4	5 52		
28	,, 14	5 52	5 40	3 2	3 45	2 ,, 50 ,,	3 2	5 52		
29	,, 15	5 52	5 39	4 2	4 35	1 ,, 50 ,,	4 2	5 52		
30	,, 16	5 52	5 39	5 3	5 25	0 ,, 49 ,,	5 3	5 52		
31	,, 17	5 52	5 38	6 4	6 16	......	......	......	New moon [amavausyay].	

The three periods, bright fortnight so called, dark fortnight so called, and fortnight made up of posterior week of first and prior week of second, can be compared thus:—Bright fortnight, so called; there is moonlight immediately after sunset with its period gradually lengthening from an hour or so to the whole night, and simultaneously with the lengthening of period the moon itself gradually grows from new to full; the nights altogether get brighter and brighter. Dark fortnight so called; there is an interval of an hour or so of darkness after sunset before the moon appears, the interval gradually increasing to the whole night, and the moon simultaneously proceeds from full to new; the nights altogether get darker and darker. Period from 8th to 21st of lunar month; in first week the evenings have moonlight and in second week they lose it more and more; but throughout the whole fortnight the moon is never less than half-moon, and the period of moonlight during the night is a minimum of 6 hours rising to 12. It is evident that the third of these periods is the real bright fortnight, wherein moonlight generally prevails; the remainder of the month is the real dark fortnight, as well known both to agriculturalists and criminal classes. The moon-waxing fortnight is also called Poorva pacsham or first half, and Apooryamauna pacsham or waxing half. The moon-waning fortnight is also called Apara pacsham or latter half and Apacsheeyamauna pacsham or waning half. The moon-waxing fortnight is known in tamul as Valar piray and the other as Tey piray [q.v.]. The following is the scale of lunar time measure:—30 moohoortams = 1 tity or lunar day, 15 tities = 1 pacsham or lunar fortnight, 2 pacshams = 1 chaundra mausam or lunar month or lunation [caulam, 4]. See vol. I, 611.—"*b*" Each tity [q.v.] is called numerically, closing with new moon or full moon; so that there are two tities of the same name or number in each month. The bright fortnight commences with the new moon, of which the tity or lunar day is called Paudyamy or the first, and continues until Poonnama [q.v.] or the full moon; the dark fortnight then begins in the same manner with a tity or lunar day named Paudyamy or the first, and ends with Amavausyay [q.v.] or the change, when the moon, by its conjunction with the sun [arcaindoo sangamam], concludes the lunar month [mookhyam, shooclaudy]. Sometimes, as in N. india, the lunar month is made to begin with paudyamy of Krishna pacsham and ends with powrnimay [gownam, krishnaudy].—"*c*" The dark pacsham of the month of Bhaudrapadam or Poorataushy [mausam] or september called Mahaulya pacsham [q.v.] is consecrated to the worship of deceased parents.—"*d*" Parties to a quarrel sometimes call themselves the Shoocla pacsham, and their opponents the Krishna pacsham.—"*e*" Pacsham is also a premise in logic [nyauyam, tarcam]. Major premise is poorva pacsham and minor premise is, aparapacsham.——*Bahoola pacsham* (बहुलपक्ष - bahulapaksha, San.). From (bahula, san. black). Same as Krishna pacsham [bahoolam].——*Krishna pacsham* (कृष्णपक्ष - krishnapaksha, San.). From (krishna, san. black). Moon-waning fortnight. Otherwise Bahoolam [q.v.]. For the method of reckoning [maunam] the month by beginning of krishna pacsham see Krishnaudy.——*Pacshy* (पक्षी - pakshí, San.). See sep. title.——*Paucala* (పాకల - pákala,* Tel.). From (páka, tel. village). Village; Nellore dist., Cundoocore tal.; pop. 3,404; acres 5,565; lat. 15° 17′; long. 80° 07′; from Cundoocore E.N.E. 12 miles; from Eetamookkala S.S.W. 7 miles; from Nellore N. 57 miles; from Ramapatam N. 16 miles. Temple of Vengopaulsawmy, and Ramalingasawmy. Three small tanks. Salt factory at Oorlapolliem close by. Formerly a port. Connected with interior by a good metalled road. Anchorage good. About four miles to north is the outlet of an estuary which receives the Palair and Mooshy and forms the boundary between what navigators consider the Coromandel and Golcondah coasts [q.v.]——*Paukam* (పాకం - pákam, Tel.; பாக்கம் - pákkam, Tam.). From (pakkam, tam. side); seaside. A maritime tract [waukam].——*Poyacarry* (پایکاری - páikárí, Hind.). From (pákhí, hind. side + kárí, hind. workman). A cultivator without hereditary rights [paracoody, pykasht]. Similar to Metayer in old France.——*Punkah* (پنکها - pankhá, Hind.). From (paksha, san. wing). A portable fan made from the leaf of the palmyra [taur]. So a large, fixed, and swinging fan, formed of cloth stretched on a rectangular frame, and suspended from the ceiling; or similarly a bar with a weighted curtain attached; kept in motion by the pulling of a cord.——*Pykasht* (پائی کاشت - páikásht, Hind.). From (paksha, san. side + kásht, pers. cultivation). Non-resident cultivator, who cultivates lands in a village to which he does not belong by birth or hereditary claim, and holds his lands either for a stipulated term, or at pleasure of some member or members of the proprietary body [khoodkasht, paracoody, poyacarry].——*Shoocla pacsham* (शुक्लपक्ष - shuklapaksha, San.). From (shukla, san. white). Moon-waxing fortnight. Otherwise Shooddham. For the method of reckoning [maunam] the month by beginning of shoocla pacham see Shooclaudy.——*Shooddha pacsham* (शुद्धपक्ष - shuddhapaksha, San.). From (shuddha, san. clear). Same as Shooclam [jyotisham].

PACSHY (पक्षी - pakshí, *San.*). From (paksha, san. wing). [pacsham].——**(1)** Term equivalent to class Aves, sub-kingdom vertebrata [vamshyam] of animal kingdom [jantoo]. Animals which are covered with feathers and are oviparous. The european orders are founded partly on form of bill, and more especially on form of feet. Families are characterized by more minute distinctions of the bill and feet, together with the characters drawn from the wings, tail, and certain habits more or less common to all. A genus comprises one or many species closely resembling one another in the structure of bill, feet, wings and tail, and in habits; yet differing in color, size, or some minute differences of structure.——**(2)** The following is a key-synopsis for the birds of s. india carried down to species, connecting the european and native terminology; the small capitals indicate orders, the small capitals in inverted commas indicate sub-orders or tribes, the italic indicates families, the italic in inverted commas indicates sub-families, and the genera and species stand in ordinary roman type.—RAPTORES.—1 *Vulturidæ* [*gridhram*]. "*Vulturinæ.*"—Otogyps calvus [rangidh]; Gyps indicus [burragidh], bengalensis [gidh].—"*Neo-*

phroninæ."—Neophron percnopterus [dung kite].—2 *Falconidæ* [*bheroondam*]. "*Falconinæ* [*pattry*]."—Falco peregrinus [bheiry], peregrinator [shahin], jugger [laggar]; Hypotriorchis chicquera [toormty]; Tinnunculus alaudarius [narzee]; Erythropus cenchris.—"*Accipitrinæ* [*shyainam*]."—Astur palumbarius [bauz], trivirgatus [gorbesrah]; Micronisus badius [shikrah]; Accipiter nisus [baushah], virgatus [besrah].—"*Aquilinæ* [*cooralam*]."—Aquila imperialis [jammash], nævia [cauly cheel], fulvescens [wokhaub], hastata [gootimar], pennata [gilherimar]; Neopus malaiensis; Nisaetus bonelli [mhorangy]; Limnaetus cristatellus [shahbauz], nipalensis; Circaetus gallicus [saumpmar]; Spilornis cheela [sabcheer]; Pandion haliætus [machrangah]; Polioætus ichthyœtus; Haliætus leucogaster [kohassa].—"*Buteoninæ* [*shyainacam*]."—Buteo vulgaris; Poliornis teesa [tisah]; Circus swainsonii [dastmal], cineraceus, melanoleucos, æruginosus.—"*Milvinæ* [*chillam*]."—Haliastur indus [braminy kite]; Milvus govinda [pariah kite]; Pernis cristata [honey kite]; Baza lophotes; Elanus melanopterus.—3 *Strigidæ* [*ooloocam*]. "*Striginæ*."—Strix javanica [boorichoory], candida.—"*Syrniinæ*."—Syrnium indranee, sinense.—"*Asioninæ*."—Otus brachyotus [chinnagoodlagooba].—"*Buboninæ*."—Urrua bengalensis [yerragoodlagooba], coromanda [nullagoodlagooba]; Huhua nipalensis [hoohoo cheel]; Ketupa ceylonensis; Ephialtes pennatus [chittagooba] lempigi.—"*Surniinæ*."—Athene brama [peidicunty], radiata, malabarica; Ninox scutellatus [choghad besrah].—INSESSORES. "FISSIROSTRES."—4 *Hirundinidæ* [*abaubil*]. "*Hirundininæ*."—Hirundo rustica, domicola, filifera, daurica [musjid abaubil]; Cotyle sinensis, concolor, rupestris; Chelidon urbica.—"*Cypselinæ*."—Acanthylis sylvatica, gigantea; Cypselus melba, affinis, leuconyx, batassiensis [taur abaubil]; Collocalia nidifica; Dendrochelidon coronatus.—5 *Caprimulgidæ* [*ajapye*]. "*Steatorninæ*."—Batrachostomus moniliger.—"*Caprimulginæ*."—Caprimulgus indicus, kelaarti, atripennis, asiaticus, mahrattensis, monticolus.—6 *Trogonidæ* [*cufnee choory*].—Harpactes fasciatus.—7 *Meropidæ* [*patringah*].—Merops viridis, philippensis, quinticolor; Nyctiornis athertoni.—8 *Coraciadæ* [*indian jay*].—Coracias indica.—9 *Halcyonidæ* [*kilkilah*]. "*Halcyoninæ*."—Halcyon leucocephalus, fuscus, atricapillus, coromandelianus; Todiramphus collaris; Ceyx tridactyla.—"*Alcedininæ*."—Alcedo bengalensis; Ceryle rudis.—10 *Eurylaimidæ*.—Serilophus rubropygia.—11 *Bucerotidæ* [*sooliman moorghy*].—Homraius bicornis; Hydrocissa coronata; Meniceros bicornis; Tockus gingalensis.—"SCANSORES."—12 *Psittacidæ* [*keeram*]. "*Palæorninæ* [*totah*]."—Palæornis alexandri [roytotah], torquatus [lahbar totah], rosa [tooria totah], columboides [madangowr totah].—"*Loriinæ*"—Loriculus vernalis [lorikeet].—13 *Picidæ* [*marangotty*]. "*Picinæ*."—Picus mahrattensis; Hypopicus hyperythrus; Yungipicus hardwickii.—"*Campephilinæ*."—Hemicircus canente; Chrysocolaptes sultaneus, goensis; Mulleripicus hodgsoni.—"*Gecininæ*."—Gecinus striolatus; Chrysophlegma flavinucha, chlorophanes; Micropternus gularis; Brachypternus aurantius, chrysonotus; Chrysonotus shorei, intermedius, rubropygialis.—"*Yunginæ*."—Yunx torquilla [gardan eyengtha].—14 *Megalaimidæ*.—Megalaima caniceps, viridis; Xantholæma indica, malabarica.—15 *Cuculidæ* [*cokam*]. "*Cuculinæ* [*koel*]."—Cuculus canorus, poliocephalus, sonneratii [banded koel], micropterus; Hierococcyx varius [hawk koel], sparverioides; Polyphasia nigra [small hawk koel]; Surniculus dicruroides; Coccystes melanoleucos [shepherd koel], coromandus; Eudynamys orientalis [common koel].—"*Phœnicophainæ*."—Zanclostomus tristis, viridirostris.—"*Centropodinæ*."—Centropus rufipennis [crow pheasant], viridis; Taccocua leschenaultii [jungle parrot].—"TENUIROSTRES."—16 *Nectarinidæ*. "*Nectarininæ*."—Arachnothera pusilla; Leptocoma zeylonica, minima; Arachnechthra asiatica, lotenia.—"*Dicœnæ*."—Dicœum minimum, concolor; Piprisoma agile.—17 *Certhiadæ*. "*Sittinæ*"—Sitta castaneoventris; Dendrophila frontalis.—18 *Upupidæ* [*hood hood*]. "*Upupinæ*."—Upupa epops, nigripennis.—"DENTIROSTRES."—19 *Laniadæ* [*pingalam*]. "*Lanianæ* [*latorah*]."—Lanius lahtora, erythronotus, nigriceps, hardwickii, cristatus.—"*Malaconotinæ* [*hili latorah*]."—Tephrodornis sylvicola, pondiceriana; Hemipus picatus.—"*Campephaginæ* [*aukroy*]."—Volvocivora sykesii, melaschistos; Graucalus macei; Pericrocotus [sahely], flammeus, roseus, peregrinus, erythropygius—"*Dicrurinæ* [*king crow*]."—Dicrurus macrocercus, longicaudatus, cærulescens; Chaptia ænea; Edolius paradiseus, malabaricus; Chibia hottentota.—"*Artaminæ*."—Artamus fuscus [palmyra swallow].—20 *Muscicapidæ* [*macsha grauhy*]. "*Myiagrinæ*."—Tchitrea paradisi [shah boolbool]; Myiagra azurea; Leucocerca albofrontata [mynautty], pectoralis; Cryptolopha cinereocapilla.—"*Muscicapinæ* [*dhoby boolbool*]."—Alseonax latirostris, ferrugineus; Ochromela nigrorufa; Eumyias melanops, albicaudata; Cyornis rubeculoides, banyumas, pallipes; Muscicapula superciliaris; Erythrosterna leucura.—21 *Merulidæ* [*shauricay*]. "*Myiotherinæ*."—Myiophonus horsfieldii; Pitta bengalensis [golden thrush].—"*Merulinæ*."—Petrocossyphus cyaneus [blue rock thrush]; Orocetes cinclorhynchus; Geocichla cyanotus [red-headed thrush]; Turdulus wardii; Merula nigropileus, simillima [neilgherry black bird]; Oreocincla dauma, nilgiriensis.—"*Timalinæ*."—Pyctorhis sinensis; Alcippe poiocephala, atriceps; Dumetia albogularis; Pellorneum ruficeps; Pomatorhinus horsfieldii [dausary bird]; Garrulax delesserti; Trochalopteron cachinnans, jerdoni; Acanthoptila nipalensis; Malacocircus griseus [dung bird], malabaricus, malcolmi; Layardia subrufa; Chatarrhæa caudata; Chætornis striatus [grass bird]; Schœnicola platyura.—22 *Brachypodidæ* [*boolbool*]. "*Pycnonotinæ*."—Hypsipetes neilgherriensis, ganeesa; Criniger ictericus; Ixos luteolus [turmeric boolbool], xantholæmus; Kelaartia penicillata; Rubigula gularis; Brachypodius poiocephalus; Otocompsa jocosa [hill boolbool]; Pycnonotus hæmorhous [madras boolbool].—"*Phyllornithinæ*."—Phyllornis jerdoni [green boolbool], malabaricus; Iora zeylonica [shoubiga boolbool].—"*Ireninæ*."—Irena puella.—"*Oriolinæ* [*mango bird*]."—Oriolus kundoo, indicus, ceylonensis.—23 *Sylviadæ* [*calacuntam*]. "*Saxicolinæ* [*shyaumay*]."—Copsychus saularis [dayar]; Kittacincla macroura [malabar robin]; Thamnobia fulicata [washerwoman robin]; Pratincola caprata, atrata, indica.—"*Ruticillinæ*."—Ruticilla rufiventris [tirtira]; Larvivora cyana; Cyanecula suecica [neelcunty].—"*Calamoherpinæ* [*cumpajitta*]."—Acrocephalus brunnescens [large cumpajitta], dumetorum [small cumpajitta], agricolus [red cumpajitta]; Arundinax olivaceus; Locustella certhiola.—"*Drymoicinæ* [*indian tailor bird*]."—Orthotomus longicauda; Prinia socialis, hodgsoni; Cisticola schœnicola, erythrocephala; Drymoipus inornatus, longicaudatus, sylvaticus, neglectus; Franklinia buchanani.—"*Phylloscopinæ*."—Phyllopneuste rama; Phylloscopus tristis, magnirostris, lugubris, nitidus, viridanus, affinis; Reguloides occipitalis, proregulus.—"*Sylviinæ*."—Sylvia orphea, affinis, curruca.—"*Motacillinæ* [*pilkya*]."—Motacilla maderaspatana [khanjan], dukhunensis; Calobates sulphurea; Budytes viridis, citreola; Nemoricola indica; Pipastes agilis [khorassan sparrow], montanus; Corydalla richardi, rufula [indian titlark]; Agrodroma campestris, cinnamomea.—24 *Ampelidæ*. "*Leiotrichinæ*."—Zosterops palpebrosus.—"*Parinæ*."—Parus cinereus, nuchalis; Machlolophus jerdoni.—"CONIROSTRES."—25 *Corvidæ* [*caurvam*]. "*Corvinæ*."—Corvus culminatus [carrion crow], splendens [common crow].—"*Dendrocittinæ*."—Dendrocitta rufa [beggar's crow], sinensis, leucogastra.—26 *Sturnidæ* [*myna*]. "*Sturninæ*."—Sturnopastor contra [pied myna]; Acridotheres tristis [common myna], fuscus [bush myna]; Temenuchus pagodarum [braminy myna], malabaricus, blythii; Pastor roseus [cholum bird].—"*Lamprotorninæ*."—Eulabes religiosa [hill myna].—27 *Fringillidæ* [*boosa priyam*]. "*Ploceinæ*."—Ploceus baya [weaver bird].—"*Estreldinæ* [*avaduvat*]."—Munia malacca, pectoralis, striata, malabarica; Estrelda amandava—"*Passerinæ* [*chiriyah*]."—Passer indicus, falvicollis.—"*Emberizinæ*."—Euspiza luteola; Melophus melanicterus.—"*Fringillinæ*."—Carpodacus erythrinus.—"*Alaudinæ* [*aghiyah*]."—Mirafra affinis [charcharah], erythroptera, cantillans [bharatapitta]; Ammomanes phœnicura; Pyrrhulauda grisea [dabakchoory]; Calandrella brachydactyla [bageyra]; Otocoris penicillata; Spizalauda deva; Alauda gulgula [vaunambaudy], malabarica; Galerida cristata [chandool].—GEMITORES.—28 *Treronidæ* [*haritaulam*]. "*Treroninæ*."—Crocopus chlorigaster [green pigeon]; Osmotreron bicincta, malabarica, flavogularis—"*Carpophaginæ*."—Carpophaga sylvatica [imperial pigeon], insignis.—29 *Columbidæ* [*capotam*]. "*Palumbinæ*."—Palumbus elphinstonei.—"*Columbinæ*."—Palumbaena eversmanni; Columba intermedia [blue-rock pigeon].—"*Turturinæ* [*tootroo*]."—Turtur meena, cambayensis [common dove], suratensis [spotted dove], risoria [ring dove], humilis.—30 *Gouridæ*. "*Phapinæ*."—Chalcophaps indicus [imperial dove].—RASORES.—31 *Pteroclidæ*.—Pterocles fasciatus, exustus [rock pigeon].—32 *Phasianidæ* [*jeevanjeevam*]. "*Pavoninæ*."—Pavo cristatus [mayil].—"*Gallinæ* [*jungle fowl*]."—Gallus ferrugineus [red jungle fowl], sonneratii [grey jungle fowl]; Galloperdix spadiceus [red spur fowl], lunulosus [painted spur fowl].—33 *Tetraonidæ* [*tittiram*]. "*Perdicinæ* [*teetar*]."—Francolinus pictus [black partridge]; Ortygornis ponticeriana [indian partridge]; Perdicula cambayensis [girzah partridge], asiatica [lowah partridge], erythrorhyncha [small lowah partridge].—"*Coturnicinæ* [*batair*]."—Coturnix communis [common quail], coromandelica [rain quail].—34 *Tinamidæ*. "*Turnicinæ*."—Turnix taigoor [black quail], dussumierii, sykesii [dabky].—GRALLATORES. "PRESSIROSTRES."—35 *Otididæ*.—Eupodotis edwardsii [toghdar]; Sypheotides auritus [florican].—36 *Cursoridæ*.—Cursorius coromandelicus; Rhinoptilus bitorquatus.—37 *Glareolidæ*.—Glareola orientalis, lactea.—38 *Charadridæ* [*battan*]. "*Charadrinæ*."—Squatarola helvetica; Charadrius longipes [chota battan]; Ægialitis geoffroyi, pyrrhothorax, cantianus, philippensis [raiva], minutus.—"*Vanellinæ*."—Lobivanellus goensis [titibham]; Sarciophorus bilobus; Hoplopterus ventralis. "*Esacinæ*."—Esacus recurvirostris; œdicnemus crepitans [jungle hare].—39 *Hæmatopodidæ*. "*Strepsilinæ*."—Strepsilas interpres.—"*Dromadinæ*."—Dromas ardeola.—"*Hæmatopodinæ*."—Hæmatopus ostralegus.—40 *Gruidæ* [*saurasam*].—Grus antigone [cyrus crane], cinerea [common crane]; Anthropoides virgo [demoiselle crane].—"LONGIROSTRES."—41 *Scolopacidæ* [*vana cookkootam*]. "*Scolopacinæ* [*oollaun*]."—Scolopax rusticola [indian wood cock]; Gallinago nemoricola [wood snipe], scolopacinus [common snipe], gallinula [jack snipe]; Rhynchæa bengalensis [painted snipe].—"*Limosinæ*."—Limosa ægocephala; Terekia cinerea.—"*Numeninæ*."—Numenius arquata, phæopus.—"*Tringinæ*."—Tringa canutus, subarquata, minuta, temminckii, platyrhyncha; Calidris arenaria.—"*Totaninæ* [*oollangy*]."—Actitis glareola, ochropus, hypoleucos; Totanus glottis, stagnatilis, fuscus, calidris.—42 *Himantopidæ*.—Himantopus candidus; Recurvirostra avocetta.—"LATITORES."—43 *Parridæ*. "*Parrinæ*."—Metopidius indicus; Hydrophasianus chirurgus.—44 *Rallidæ* [*krishaungy*]. "*Gallinulinæ*."—Porphyrio poliocephalus; Fulica atra; Gallicrex cristatus [water cock]; Gallinula chloropus [water hen], phœnicura.—"*Rallinæ*."

—Porzana maruetta, pygmæa, fusca, ceylonica; Rallus striatus, indicus.—" CULTIROSTRES."—45 *Ciconidæ* [*adjutant bird*].—Leptoptilos argala [common adjutant], javanica [small adjutant]; Mycteria australis; Ciconia alba [laklak], leucocephala [beafsteak bird].—46 *Ardeidæ* [*paddy bird*].—Ardea cinerea [blue heron], purpurea [snake heron]; Herodias alba [pariah heron], egrettoides, garzetta [black bill heron]; Buphus coromandus [cattle heron]; Ardeola leucoptera [blind heron]; Butorides javanica [green heron]; Ardetta flavicollis [black heron], cinnamomea [red heron], sinensis [yellow heron]; Botaurus stellaris; Nycticorax griseus [night heron].—47 *Tantalidæ* [*deerghachanchoocam*].—" *Tantalinæ*."—Tantalus leucocephalus [pelican ibis].—" *Plataleinæ*."—Platalea leucorodia [spoon bill ibis].—" *Anastomatinæ*."—Anastomus oscitans [shell ibis].—" *Ibisinæ*."—Threskiornis melanocephalus [white ibis]; Geronticus papillosus [black ibis]; Falcinellus igneus [glossy ibis].—NATATORES. " LAMELLIROSTRES."—48 *Phœnicopteridæ* [*rajahamsam*].—Phœnicopterus roseus.—49 *Anseridæ* [*hamsam*].—" *Plectropterinæ*."—Sarkidiornis melanonotus [comb duck].—" *Nettapodinæ*."—Nettapus coromandelianus [cotton teal].—" *Tadorninæ*."—Dendrocygna awsuree [whistling teal], major; Casarca rutila [braminy duck]. 50 *Anatidæ* [*varatam*].—" *Anatinæ*."—Spatula clypeata; Anas pœcilorhyncha, caryophyllacea; Chaulelasmus streperus; Mareca penelope; Querquedula crecca [common teal], circia,—" *Fuligulinæ*."—Branta rufina; Aythya nyroca; Fuligula cristata [golden eye duck].—" MERGITOERS."—51 *Podicipidæ*.—Podiceps philippensis [paun doob].—" VAGATORES."—52 *Procellaridæ*. " *Halodrominæ*."—Pelicanoides urinatrix.—53 *Laridæ* [*samoodra caukkay*]. " *Larinæ*."—Kroikocephalus ichthyætus; Xema brunnicephala, ridibunda.—" *Sterninæ*."—Sylochelidon caspius; Gelochelidon anglicus; Hydrochelidon indica; Seena aurantia; Sterna nirundo, javanica; Sternula minuta; Thalasseus cristatus, bengalensis; Rhynchops albicollis.—" PISCATORES."—54 *Phætonidæ*.—Phæton rubricauda.—55 *Sulidæ*.—Sula fiber.—56 *Attagenidæ*.—Attagen aquilus.—57 *Pelecanidæ*.—Pelecanus onocrotalus, mitratus, javanicus, philippensis [goodroo pacshy].—58 *Graculidæ* [*jala caukkay*]. Graculus carbo [large cormorant], sinensis, javanicus [small cormorant].—" *Plotinæ*."—Plotus melanogaster [snake cormorant].——**(3)** The following are the orders arranged alphabetically, with the Sanscrit equivalents, references to the key-synopsis, and brief notes as to classification.——*Gemitores* (कपोतसन्तान - kapótasantána, San.). From (kopóta, san. pigeon). Pigeons and doves. Intermediate to Rasores and Insessores. Divided into the following families:—Treronidæ [haritaulam], fruit-eating or tree pigeons; Columbidæ [blue rock pigeon, capotam, tootroo], ordinary pigeons and doves, feeding partly on the ground and partly on trees; Gouridæ, or ground pigeons [imperial dove].——*Grallatores* (जलचारिसन्तान - jalachárisantána, San.). From (jala, san. water + char, san. to move). Waders; shorebirds. Divided into two large groups, one in which the young run at once when hatched, the other in which the young are helpless at birth and remain in the nest till near maturity. " i " Young when hatched able to run at once. Pressirostres, containing the bustard [toghdar], plovers [battan], and cranes [saurasam]. Longirostres containing snipes [oollaun] and sandpipers [oollangy]. Latitores containing rails [krishaungy] and waterhens [krishaungy]. " ii " With young helpless at birth. Cultirostres containing storks [adjutant bird], herons [paddy bird] and ibises [deerghachanchoocam].—" *a* " Pressirostres. Alias Cursores. Comprise bustards [toghdar], plovers [battan], and cranes [saurasam]. May be distinguished from longirostres, by usually shorter and thicker bill, more robust make, average greater size; and in habits frequent open dry plains more habitually than banks of rivers, shores or marshes. Distributed among the following families:—Otididæ or bustards [toghdar], and floricans [q.v.], Cursoridæ or courser-plovers, Glareolidæ or swallow-plovers, Charadridæ or plovers [battan], Hæmatopodidæ or shore-plovers, Gruidæ or cranes [saurasam].—" *b* " Longirostres. Small wading birds. Very closely related to the plovers [battan] in structure and internal anatomy, but differ in their more lengthened bill, slender form, more aquatic habits, and mode of coloration [indian wood-cock, oollangy, oollaun, vanacookkootam].—" *c* " Latitores [krishaungy]. Alias Macrodactyli, Alectorides. Include Rails, Waterhens, Coots [krishaungy] and Jacanas. Moderate sized birds, stout legs and long feet, walk on soft and marshy ground, even on aquatic plants, fly badly. Body much compressed. Divided into two families, Parridæ and Rallidæ.—" *d* " Cultirostres. Alias Gradatores. Differs from all preceding tribes of Grallatores in young being born naked or nearly so, helpless, requiring to be fed by their parents in the nest till nearly full grown. Nestle on trees and among reeds. Comprise storks [adjutant bird], herons [paddy bird], and ibises [deerghachanchoocam]. All stalk slowly along the ground, or in water, looking for their food; flight powerful and easy.——*Insessores* (निषादीसन्तान - nishádísantána, San.). From (nishad, san. to sit down). Alias Passeres and Picæ, Passerinæ and Zygodactyli, Passores and Scansores, Oscines and Volucres, Oscines and Clamatores, Cantores and Strepitores. Perching birds; comprise all birds not included among swimming or wading birds, gallinaceous or game birds, and the birds of prey; form nearly three-quarters of all known birds. Insessores differ from all birds, except Raptores, the Ardeidæ [paddy bird], Columbidæ [capotam], Cracidæ, and Megapodidæ, by having the toes all on one plane. All singing birds belong to this order. The following are the tribes:—" *a* " Fissirostres. Gape of mouth wide. Divided into the following families:—Hirundinidæ or swallows and swifts [abaubil]; Caprimulgidæ or goatsuckers [ajapye]; Trogonidæ, or trogons [cuffnee choory]; Meropidæ or bee-eaters [patringah]; Coraciadæ or rollers [indian jay]; Halcyonidæ or kingfishers [kilkilah]; Bucerotidæ or hornbills [sooliman moorghy]; and Eurylaimidæ or broad bills.—" *b* " Scansores. Alias Zygodactyli. Toes in pairs. They do not all of them climb, some hop about branches of trees in search of fruit and insects. Divided into the following families:—Psittacidæ or parrots [keeram, lory]; Picidæ or woodpeckers [gardan eyengtha, marangotty]; Megalaimidæ or barbets; Cuculidæ or cuckoos [cokam, crow pheasant, jungle parrot, koel].—" *c* " Tenuirostres. Bill, most slender and long, often curved; in a few, short and thick. Comprise the following groups, which may be divided into:—" i " Richly colored. Troidæ or humming birds; Nectariuidæ or honey suckers; Paradiseidæ or birds of Paradise. " ii " Plain plumage. Meliphagidæ or honeyeaters; Certhiadæ or creepers; Upupidæ or hoopoes [hood-hood].—" *d* " Dentirostres. Bill usually with tooth or notch in upper mandible near tip. The families are:—Laniadæ or shrikes [pingalam]; Muscicapidæ or flycatchers [macshagrauhy]; Merulidæ or thrushes [shauricay]; Brachypodidæ or short-legged thrushes [boolbool]; Sylviadæ or warblers [calacuntam].—" *e* " Conirostres. Bill usually entire at tip, thick, more or less conic. Divided into the following families:—Corvidæ, comprising crows and magpies [caurvam]; Sturnidæ, mynas and starlings [myna]; Fringillidæ [boosapriyam], the most numerous of all, comprising sparrows, weaver-birds [q.v.], amaduvads [avadavat], buntings, and rose linnets; Alaudidæ or larks [aghiyah].——*Natatores* (प्लवसन्तान - plavasantána, San.). From (plu, san. to swim). Alias Palmipedes. Feet webbed, legs placed far backwards on body. Like grallatores, some are capable of running at once from the shell, and soon feed themselves, autophagi; while others form rude nests on trees, or rocks, or among the herbage of the shore, and feed their young till they are able to fly, heterophagi.—" *a* " Lamellirostres. Bill furnished at the edges with thin horny lamellæ, which serve as a sieve. Geese [hamsam] and ducks [varatam]. Chiefly frequent fresh waters, marshes, lakes, and rivers; a few preferring salt water [rajahamsam].—" *b* " Mergitores. Alias Colymbides. Comprise two families of the Divers or loons, colymbidæ, and the Grebes, podicipidæ [paundoob].—" *c* " Vagatores. Alias Longipennes, Laridæ. Wings long; divided into two families:—Procellaridæ, comprising the albatrosses and petrels; Laridæ, the gulls and terns [samoodra caukkay].—" *d* " Piscatores. Alias Pelicanidæ. Divided into:—Flying fishers or Phaetonidæ; Plunging fishers or Sulidæ; Pouncing fishers or Attagenidæ; Swimming fishers or Pelecanidæ; Diving fishers [jalacaukkay] or Graculidæ.——*Raptores* (चौरसन्तान - chaurasantána, San.). From (chaura, san. robber). Alias Accipitres, Rapaces, Raptatores. Birds of prey. Agree with insessores in having all their toes upon one plane, but differ in their strong bill and strong feet, with curved claws; upper mandible is always longer than the lower one, hooked at tip and pointed. Large wings, often very long; sight very acute. Analogous to the feræ among the mammalia [sastanam]. Divided into:—Vulturidæ or true vultures [gridhram]; Falconidæ or hawks and eagles [bheroondam]; and Strigidæ [ooloocam] or owls [chillam, cooralam, dung kite, gidh, pattry, shyainacam, shyainam].——*Rasores* (क्षुरीसन्तान - kshurísantána, San.). From (kshur, san. to scratch). Alias Gallinæ, Gallinacei, Pulveratrices. Game birds. Capable of domestication. Evince analogies with ruminating animals among mammals [sastanam]. Crop represents paunch, have both a low degree of intelligence, easily domesticated, head too is in many of both orders adorned with appendages, horns, and crests; afford more wholesome food to man than any other orders. Divided into the following families:—Pteroclidæ or sand-grouse [rock pigeon], Phasianidæ [jeevanjeevam, jungle fowl, mayil, moorghy], Tetraonidæ or grouse and partridges [batair, teetar, tittiram], Tinamidæ [black quail, dabky].——**(4)** The following are the families and sub-families in alphabetical order with references:—Accipitrinæ, falconidæ, raptores, 2; Alaudinæ, fringillidæ, insessores, 27; Alcedininæ, halcyonidæ, insessores, 9; Ampelidæ, insessores, 24; Anastomatinæ, tantalidæ, grallatores, 47; Anatidæ, natatores, 50; Anatinæ, anatidæ, natatores, 50; Anseridæ, natatores, 49; Aquilinæ, falconidæ, raptores, 2; Ardeidæ, grallatores, 46; Artaminæ, laniadæ, insessores, 19; Asioninæ, strigidæ, raptores, 3; Attagenidæ, natatores, 56; Brachypodidæ, insessores, 22; Buboninæ, strigidæ, raptores, 3; Bucerotidæ, insessores, 11; Buteoninæ, falconidæ, raptores, 2; Calamoherpinæ, sylviadæ, insessores, 23; Campephaginæ, laniadæ, insessores, 19; Campephilinæ, picidæ, insessores, 13; Caprimulgidæ, insessores, 5; Caprimulginæ, caprimulgidæ, insessores, 5; Carpophaginæ, treronidæ, gemitores, 28; Centropodinæ, cuculidæ, insessores, 15; Certhiadæ, insessores, 17; Charadridæ, grallatores, 38; Charadrinæ, charadridæ, grallatores, 38; Ciconidæ, grallatores, 45; Columbidæ, gemitores, 29; Columbinæ, columbidæ, gemitores, 29; Coraciadæ, insessores, 8; Corvidæ, insessores, 25; Corvinæ, corvidæ, insessores, 25; Coturnicinæ, tetraonidæ, rasores, 33; Cuculidæ, insessores, 15; Cuculinæ, cuculidæ, insessores, 15; Cursoridæ, grallatores, 36; Cypselinæ, hirundinidæ, insessores, 4; Dendrocittinæ, corvidæ, insessores, 25; Dicæinæ, nectarinidæ, insessores,

16; Dicrurinæ, laniadæ, insessores, 19; Drymoicinæ, sylviadæ, insessores, 23; Emberizinæ, fringillidæ, insessores, 27; Esacinæ, charadridæ, grallatores, 38; Estreldinæ, fringillidæ, insessores, 27; Eurylaimidæ, insessores, 10; Falconidæ, raptores, 2; Falconinæ, falconidæ, raptores, 2; Fringillidæ, insessores, 27; Fringillinæ, fringillidæ, insessores, 27; Fuligulinæ, anatidæ, natatores, 50; Gallinæ, phasianidæ, rasores, 32; Gallinulinæ, rallidæ, grallatores, 44; Geciuinæ, picidæ, insessores, 13; Glareolidæ, grallatores, 37; Gouridæ, gemitores, 30; Graculidæ, natatores, 58; Gruidæ, grallatores, 40; Hæmatopodidæ, grallatores, 39; Halcyonidæ, insessores, 9; Halcyoninæ, halcyonidæ, insessores, 9; Halodrominæ, procellaridæ, natatores, 52; Himantopidæ, grallatores, 42; Hirundinidæ, insessores, 4; Hirundininæ, hirundinidæ, insessores, 4; Ibisinæ, tantalidæ, grallatores, 47; Ireninæ, brachypodidæ, insessores, 22; Lamprotorninæ, sturnidæ, insessores 26; Laniadæ, insessores, 19; Laniauæ, laniadæ, insessores, 19; Laridæ, natatores, 53; Larinæ, laridæ, natatores, 53; Leiotrichinæ, ampelidæ, insessores, 24; Limosinæ, scolopacidæ, grallatores, 41; Loriinæ, psittacidæ, insessores, 12; Malaconotinæ, laniadæ, insessores, 19; Megalaimidæ, insessores, 14; Meropidæ, insessores, 7; Merulidæ, insessores, 21; Merulinæ, merulidæ, insessores, 21; Milvinæ, falconidæ, raptores, 2; Motacillinæ, sylviadæ, insessores, 23; Muscicapidæ, insessores, 20; Muscicapinæ, muscicapidæ, insessores, 20; Myiagrinæ, muscicapidæ, insessores, 20; Myiotherinæ, merulidæ, insessores, 21; Nectarinidæ, insessores, 16; Nectarininæ, nectarinidæ, insessores, 16; Neophroninæ, vulturidæ, raptores, 1; Nettapodinæ, anseridæ, natatores, 49; Numeninæ, scolopacidæ, grallatores, 41; Oriolinæ, brachypodidæ, insessores, 22; Otididæ, grallatores, 35; Palæorninæ, psittacidæ, insessores, 12; Palumbinæ, columbidæ, gemitores, 29; Parinæ, ampelidæ, insessores, 24; Parridæ, grallatores, 43; Parrinæ, parridæ, grallatores, 43; Passerinæ, fringillidæ, insessores, 27; Pavoninæ, phasianidæ, rasores, 32; Pelecanidæ, natatores, 57; Perdicinæ, tetraonidæ, rasores, 33; Phœnicophainæ, cuculidæ, insessores, 15; Phætonidæ, natatores, 54; Phapinæ, gouridæ, gemitores, 30; Phasianidæ, rasores, 32; Phœnicopteridæ, natatores, 48; Phyllornithinæ, brachypodidæ, insessores, 22; Phylloscopinæ, sylviadæ, insessores, 23; Picidæ, insessores, 13; Picinæ, picidæ, insessores, 13; Plataleinæ, tantalidæ, grallatores, 47; Plectropterinæ, anseridæ, natatores, 49; Ploceinæ, fringillidæ, insessores, 27; Plotinæ, graculidæ, natatores, 58; Podicipidæ, natatores, 51; Procellaridæ, natatores, 52; Psittacidæ, insessores, 12; Pteroclidæ, rasores, 31; Pycnonotinæ, brachypodidæ, insessores, 22; Rallidæ, grallatores, 44; Rallinæ, rallidæ, grallatores, 44; Ruticillinæ, sylviadæ, insessores, 23; Saxicollinæ, sylviadæ, insessores, 23; Scolopacidæ, grallatores, 41; Scolopacinæ, scolopacidæ, grallatores, 41; Sittinæ, certhiadæ, insessores, 17; Steatorninæ, caprimulgidæ, insessores, 5; Sterninæ, laridæ, natatores, 53; Strepsilinæ, hæmatopodidæ, grallatores, 39; Strigidæ, raptores, 3; Striginæ, strigidæ, raptores, 3; Sturnidæ, insessores, 26; Sturninæ, sturnidæ, insessores, 26; Sulidæ, natatores, 55; Surniinæ, strigidæ, raptores, 3; Sylviadæ, insessores, 23; Sylviinæ, sylviadæ, insessores, 23; Syrniinæ, strigidæ, raptores, 3; Tadorninæ, anseridæ, natatores, 49; Tantalidæ, grallatores, 47; Tantalinæ, tantalidæ, grallatores, 47; Tetraonidæ, rasores, 33; Timalinæ, merulidæ, insessores, 21; Tinamidæ, rasores, 34; Totaninæ, scolopacidæ, grallatores, 41; Treronidæ, gemitores, 28; Treroninæ, treronidæ, gemetores, 28; Tringinæ, scolopacidæ, grallatores, 41; Trogonidæ, insessores, 6; Turnicinæ, tinamidæ, rasores, 34; Turturinæ, columbidæ, gemitores, 29; Upupidæ, insessores, 18; Upupinæ, upupidæ, insessores, 18; Vanellinæ, charadridæ, grallatores, 38; Vulturidæ, raptores, 1; Vulturinæ, vulturidæ, raptores, 1; Yunginæ, picidæ, insessores, 13.——

(5) The following are the genera in alphabetical order, with references :—Acanthoptila, merulidæ, 21; Acanthylis, hirundinidæ, 4; Accipiter, falconidæ, 2; Acridotheres, sturnidæ, 26; Acrocephalus, sylviadæ, 23; Actitis, scolopacidæ, 41; Ægialitis, charadridæ, 38; Agrodroma, sylviadæ, 23; Alauda, fringillidæ, 27; Alcedo, halcyonidæ, 9; Alcippe, merulidæ, 21; Alseonax, muscicapidæ, 20; Ammomanes, fringillidæ, 27; Anas, anatidæ, 50; Anastomus, tantalidæ, 47; Anthropoides, gruidæ, 40; Aquila, falconidæ, 2; Arachnechthra, nectarinidæ, 16; Arachnothera, nectarinidæ, 16; Ardea, ardeidæ, 46; Ardeola, ardeidæ, 46; Ardetta, ardeidæ, 46; Artamus, laniadæ, 19; Arundinax, sylviadæ, 23; Astur, falconidæ, 2; Athene, strigidæ, 3; Attagen, attagenidæ, 56; Aythya, anatidæ, 50; Batrachostomus, caprimulgidæ, 5; Baza, falconidæ, 2; Botaurus, ardeidæ, 46; Brachypodius, brachypodidæ, 22; Brachypternus, picidæ, 13; Branta, anatidæ, 50; Budytes, sylviadæ, 23; Buphus, ardeidæ, 46; Buteo, falconidæ, 2; Butorides, ardeidæ, 46; Calandrella, fringillidæ, 27; Calidris, scolopacidæ, 41; Calobates, sylviadæ, 23; Caprimulgus, caprimulgidæ, 5; Carpodacus, fringillidæ, 27; Carpophaga, treronidæ, 28; Casarca, anseridæ, 49; Centropus, cuculidæ, 15; Ceryle, halcyonidæ, 9; Ceyx, halcyonidæ, 9; Chætornis, merulidæ, 21; Chalcophaps, gouridæ, 30; Chaptia, laniadæ, 19; Charadrius, charadridæ, 38; Chatarrhœa, merulidæ, 21; Chauleasmus, anatidæ, 50; Chelidon, hirundinidæ, 4; Chibia, laniadæ, 19; Chrysocolaptes, picidæ, 13; Chrysonotus, picidæ, 13; Chrysophlegma, picidæ, 13; Ciconia, ciconidæ, 45; Circætus, falconidæ, 2; Circus, falconidæ, 2; Cisticola, sylviadæ, 23; Coccystes, cuculidæ, 15; Columba, columbidæ, 29; Collocalia, hirundinidæ, 4; Copsychus, sylviadæ, 23; Coracias, coraciadæ, 8; Corvus, corvidæ, 25; Corydalla, sylviadæ, 23; Coturnix, tetraonidæ, 33; Cotyle, hirundinidæ, 4; Criniger, brachypodidæ, 22; Crocopus, treronidæ, 28; Cryptolopha, muscicapidæ, 20; Cuculus, cuculidæ, 15; Cursorius, cursoridæ, 36; Cyanecula, sylviadæ, 23; Cyornis, muscicapidæ, 20; Cypselus, hirundinidæ, 4; Dendrochelidon, hirundinidæ, 4; Dendrocitta, corvidæ, 25; Dendrocygna, anseridæ, 49; Dendrophila, certhiade, 17; Dicæum, nectarinidæ, 16; Dicrurus, laniadæ, 19; Dromas, homatopodidæ, 39; Drymoipus, sylviadæ, 23; Dumetia, merulidæ, 21; Edolius, laniadæ, 19; Elanus, falconidæ, 2; Ephialtes, strigidæ, 3; Erythropus, falconidæ, 2; Erythrosterna, muscicapidæ, 20; Esacus, charadridæ, 38; Estrella, fringillidæ, 27; Eudynamys, cuculidæ, 15; Eulabes, sturnidæ, 26; Eumyias, muscicapidæ, 20; Eupodotis, otididæ, 35; Euspiza, fringillidæ, 27; Falcinellus, tantalidæ, 47; Falco, falconidæ, 2; Francolinus, tetraonidæ, 33; Franklinia, sylviadæ, 23; Fulica, rallidæ, 44; Fuligula, anatidæ, 50; Galerida, fringillidæ, 27; Gallicrex, rallidæ, 44; Gallinago, scolopacidæ, 41; Gallinula, rallidæ, 44; Galloperdix, phasianidæ, 32; Gallus, phasianidæ, 32; Garrulax, merulidæ, 21; Gecinus, picidæ, 13; Gelochelidon, laridæ, 53; Geocichla, merulidæ, 21; Geronticus, tantalidæ, 47; Glareola, glareolidæ, 37; Graculus, graculidæ, 58; Graucalus, laniadæ, 19; Grus, gruidæ, 40; Gyps, vulturidæ, 1; Hæmatopus, hæmatopodidæ, 39; Halcyon, halcyonidæ, 9; Haliastur, falconidæ, 2; Haliætus, falconidæ, 2; Harpactes, trogonidæ, 6; Hemicircus, picidæ, 13; Hemipus, laniadæ, 19; Herodias, ardeidæ, 46; Hierococcyx, cuculidæ, 15; Himantopus, himantopidæ, 42; Hirundo, hirundinidæ, 4; Homraius, bucerotidæ, 11; Hoplopterus, charadridæ, 38; Huhua, strigidæ, 3; Hydrochelidon, laridæ, 53; Hydrocissa, bucerotidæ, 11; Hydrophasianus, parridæ, 43; Hypopicus, picidæ, 13; Hypotriorchis, falconidæ, 2; Hypsipetes, brachypodidæ, 22; Iora, brachypodidæ, 22; Irena, brachypodidæ, 22; Ixos, brachypodidæ, 22; Kelaartia, brachypodidæ, 22; Ketupa, strigidæ, 3; Kittacincla, sylviadæ, 23; Kroikocephalus, laridæ, 53; Lanius, laniadæ, 19; Larvivora sylviadæ, 23; Layardia, merulidæ, 21; Leptocoma, nectaranidæ, 16; Leptoptilos, ciconidæ, 45; Leucocerca, muscicapidæ, 20; Limnætus, falconidæ, 2; Limosa, scolopacidæ, 41; Lobivanellus, charadridæ, 38; Locustella, sylviadæ, 23; Loriculus, psittacidæ, 12; Machlolophus, ampelidæ, 24; Malacocircus, merulidæ, 21; Mareca, anatidæ, 50; Megalaima, megalaimidæ, 14; Melophus, fringillidæ, 27; Meniceros, bucerotidæ, 11; Merops, Meropidæ, 7; Merula, merulidæ, 21; Metopidius, parridæ, 43; Micronisus, falconidæ, 2; Micropternus, picidæ, 13; Milvus, falconidæ, 2; Mirafra, fringillidæ, 27; Motacilla, sylviadæ, 23; Mulleripicus, picidæ, 13; Munia, fringillidæ, 27; Muscicapula, muscicapidæ, 20; Mycteria, ciconidæ, 45; Myiagra, muscicapidæ, 20; Myiophonus, merulidæ, 21; Nemoricola, sylviadæ, 23; Neophron, vulturidæ, 1; Neopus, falconidæ, 2; Nettapus, anseridæ, 49; Ninox, strigidæ, 3; Nisaetus, falconidæ, 2; Numenius, scolopacidæ; 41; Nyciornis, meropidæ, 7; Nycticorax, ardeidæ, 46; Ochromela, muscicapidæ, 20; Œdicnemus, charadridæ, 38; Oreocincla, merulidæ, 21, Oriolus, brachypodidæ, 22; Orocetes, merulidæ, 21; Orthotomus, sylviadæ, 23; Ortygornis, tetraonidæ, 33; Osmotreron, treronidæ, 28; Otocompsa, brachypodidæ, 22; Otocoris, fringillidæ, 27; Otogyps, vulturidæ, 1; Otus, strigidæ, 3; Palæornis, psittacidæ, 12; Palumbæna, columbidæ, 29; Palumbus, columbidæ, 29; Pandion, falconidæ, 2; Parus, ampelidæ, 24; Passer, fringillidæ, 27; Pastor, sturnidæ, 26; Pavo, phasianidæ, 32; Pelecanus, pelecanidæ, 57; Pelicanoides, procellaridæ, 52; Pellorneum, merulidæ, 21; Perdicula, tetraonidæ, 33; Pericrocotus, laniadæ, 19; Pernis, falconidæ, 2; Petrocossyphus, merulidæ, 21; Phæton, phætonidæ, 54; Phœnicopterus, phœnicopteridæ, 48; Phyllopneuste, sylviadæ, 23; Phyllornis, brachypodidæ, 22; Phylloscopus, sylviadæ, 23; Picus, picidæ, 13; Pipastes, sylviadæ, 23; Piprisoma, nectarinidæ 16; Pitta, merulidæ, 21; Platalea, tantalidæ, 47; Ploceus, fringillidæ, 27; Plotus, graculidæ, 58; Podiceps, podicipidæ, 51; Poliœtus, falconidæ, 2; Poliornis, falconidæ, 2; Polyphasia, cuculidæ, 15; Pomatorhinus, merulidæ, 21; Porphyrio, rallidæ, 44; Porzana, rallidæ, 44; Pratincola, sylviadæ, 23; Prinia, sylviadæ, 23; Pterocles, pteroclidæ, 31; Pycnonotus, brachypodidæ, 22; Pyctorhis, merulidæ, 21; Pyrrhulauda, fringillidæ, 27; Querquedula, anatidæ, 50; Rallus, rallidæ, 44; Recurvirostra, himantopidæ, 42; Reguloides, sylviadæ, 23; Rhinoptilus, cursoridæ, 36; Rhynchæa, scolopacidæ, 41; Rhynchops, laridæ, 53; Rubigula, brachypodidæ, 22; Ruticella, sylviadæ, 23; Sarciophorus, charadridæ, 38; Sarkidiornis, anseridæ, 49; Schœnicola, merulidæ, 21; Scolopax, scolopacidæ, 41; Seena, laridæ, 53; serilophus, eurylaimidæ, 10; Sitta, certhiadæ, 17; Spatula, anatidæ 50; Spilornis, falconidæ, 2; Spizalauda, fringillidæ, 27; Squatarola, charadridæ, 38; Sterna, laridæ, 53; Sternula, laridæ, 53; Strepsilas, hæmatopodidæ, 39; Strix, strigidæ, 3; Sturnopaster, sturnidæ, 26; Sula, sulidæ, 55; Surniculus, cuculidæ, 15; Sylochelidon, laridæ, 53; Sylvia, sylviadæ, 23; Sypheotides, otididæ, 35; Syrnium, strigidæ, 3; Taccocua, cuculidæ, 15; Tantalus, tantalidæ, 47; Tchitrea, muscicapidæ, 20; Temenuchus, sturnidæ, 26; Tephrodornis, laniadæ, 19; Terekia, scolopacidæ, 41; Thalasseus, laridæ, 53; Thamnobia, sylviadæ, 23; Threskiornis, tantalidæ, 47; Tinnunculus, falconidæ, 2; Tockus, bucerotidæ, 11; Todiramphus, halcyonidæ, 9; Totanus, scolopacidæ, 41; Tringa, scolopacidæ, 41; Trochalopteron, merulidæ, 21; Turdulus, merulidæ, 21; Turnix, tinamidæ, 34; Turtur, treronidæ, 28; Urrua, strigidæ, 3; Upupa, upupidæ, 18; Volvocivora, laniadæ, 19; Xantholæma, megalaimidæ, 14; Xema, laridæ, 53; Yungipicus, picidæ, 13; Yunx picidæ, 13; Zanclostomus, cuculidæ, 15; Zosterods, ampelidæ, 24.——

(6) Title heads in this glossary cover each family and

contained sub-family, genus and species, clearly known to be distinguished by the natives. The bird nomenclature of the natives being as yet not very well ascertained, the number of such items in volume may be found comparatively inconsiderable. ——(7) For insects see Poochy; for fishes see Matsyam; for batrachians see Bhaicam; for reptiles see Sarpy; for mammals see Sastanam. A general conspectus of the fauna [jantoo] of s. india was given in vol. II, appendix IV.

PADAM (पद् - pada, *San.*). From (pad, san. to fall). Step; foot-mark; footing or station; abode; position, place or office of dignity; foot-measure; fourth part; line of a verse; a quarter or quadrant [paudam]; word [mozhy]. Plant second term, as meaning foot; ex., where transl. is of first term:—Bauhinia malabarica (basavanapáda), ox; Clitoria ternatea (vrishapádi), bull; Coldenia procumbens (gódápadí), iguana, (hamsapádi), swan, (tripádí), three; Ficus bengalensis (bahupád), many; Jasminum sambac (bhúpadi), earth, fixed in the earth; Leea hirta (parvatapádi), mountain, (sumpádi), divine; Vitis pedata (gódhápadi), iguana; see gloss. paragraphs. Compare Payeen, Pye.——*Padaurtam* (पदार्थ - padárt'ha, San.). From (pada, san. thing + art'ha, san. meaning). Lit. meaning of a word or thing. General property or attribute that may be predicated or affirmed of existing things. Otherwise category. Aristotle made ten categories, viz., substance, quantity, quality, relation, action, passion, time, place, situation and habit. The tamulians specify seven, viz.:—Dravyam, substance; Goonam, quality; Carmam, action; Saumaunyam, identity; Vishaisham, variety; Samavauyam, relation; and Abhauvam, annihilation [veishaishicam]. See this expanded at vol. I (74), foot-note. For elementary substance, see Dravyam; for matter, see Bhootam; for organic and inorganic, see Indriyam and Anindriyam, and Punchendriyam; for organic kingdom, see Ganam [jantoo, vriesham]; for organic class, see Vargam; for organic order, see Santaunam; for organic family, see Coolam; for organic genus, see Jauty; for organic species, see Bhaidam. Oopa prefixed to either of the above means a sub-head. For inorganic minerals, see Dhautoo.——*Padya* (ಪದ್ಯ - padya, Can.). From (pad, san. foot). A stanza of four lines.——*Pauda caunicay* (பாதக்காணிக்கை - páthakkánikkai, Tam.). Offering to the feet, contribution to gooroo [q.v.]. Compare Wolfa. ——*Pauda chauram* (पादचार - pádachára, San.). From (páda, san. a quadrant + chára, san. motion); progress of planets reckoned by quartering the signs [rausby]. The position of the planets [graham] on a particular day, being one of the five articles of Punchaungam [jyotisham, punchaungam].——*Paudam* (पाद - páda, San.; பாதம் - pátham, Tam.). From (pad, san. to go). The foot; foot-print. The foot-measure of 12 ungoolams [q.v.]. Also fourth part, from foot of a quadruped being one out of four [pautica]. The fourth part of a stanza of four lines or any verse [padya]. The quadrant of a circle [chuckram, mundalam]. The paudams of the ayanaumsham [q.v.] are the four quadrants of the epicycle [paridhy, prauk chuckram], or parts of the arc [chaupam] described by the first point [craunty pautam, maishauyanam] of the tropical zodiac [raushy chuckram] in consequence of the precessional variation [craunty pauta gaty]. Title of respect added to proper names; term of address. Also suffix in proper names as Gooroopaudam, Shivapaudam [padam, peyar]. Compare Payeen, Pye.——*Paudamoodray* (पादमुद्रा - pádamudrá, San.). From (páda, san. foot + mudrá, san. stamp). The tradition of an impressed footstep in ascending to heaven is very common among the tamulians [q.v.]. The mark on Adam's peak [q.v.] in Ceylon, although it has from the Portuguese been called Adam's footstep, is a Booddhist [booddha] tamul relic [dharmaraja cull, kadam]. ——*Pauda poornacam* (పాదపూర్ణకం - pádapúrnakam, Tel.). From (páda, san. fourth part of stanza, verse + púrna, san. full). A phrase inserted in verse merely to fill the metre.——*Paujy* (پاجی - pájí, Hind.). From (pái, pers. foot). A scoundrel; term of abuse.——*Pautica* (పాతిక - pátika, Tel.). From (páda, san. foot), that being fourth part in quadrupeds. A fourth part [paudam]. Goldsmith's weight. 2 pauticas = 1 baida [niray, 3b]. Approximate actual value, 1 pautica = $\frac{3}{4}$ grain. $\frac{1}{2}$ of one goonj [goomchy] seed.——*Payeen* (پائین - páin, Hind.). Foot [padam, paudam, pye].——*Payeen ghaut* (پائین گھاٹ - páinghát, Hind.). From (páin, hind. foot + ghát, hind. hill-pass). The country below table-land. The term used to be applied principally on the west coast; but the expression Carnatic payeen ghaut is also frequent as applied to the low country of Madras on the east side of the peninsula [carnatic]. Talaghaut [q.v.] is the low country not so near the foot of the ghauts [q.v.] as Payeen ghaut. See vol. I (25) [balaghaut].——*Peik* (پیک - paik, Hind.; పైక - paika, Tel.). From (pái, pers. foot). A foot messenger [peon] having arms [sillah]. In Cuttack irregular foot soldiers [inam]. Military tribe of Vizagapatam [jauty]. See vol. I (66); II, 141.——*Peikam* (పైకము - paikamu, Tel.). From (paiká, mahr.). Money. Peikam bunt is a zemindarry [q.v.] peon [q.v.] paid in cash [q.v.] instead of in grain.——*Peisa* (پیسا - paisá, Hind.). From (pai, hind. foot). The original form of Pice [q.v.]. Corresponds to the hindoo Doody [q.v.] or Dub [q.v.].——*Peon* (پیادہ - piyádah, Hind.). From persian through portuguese peáo. A foot messenger. A servant waiting in offices. A police officer [buntrote, jawaun, peik].——*Pice* (پیسا - paisá, Hind.; ಪೈಸಾ - paisá, Can.; పైసా - paisá, Tel.; பைசா - paisá, Tam.). From (pái, mahr. from páda, san. foot). Copper coin. 3 pies = 1 pice; 4 pice = 1 anna [naunyam, 2e]. $\frac{1}{64}$th of a rupee. Also called quarter anna. Approximate actual value, 1 pice = $1\frac{1}{2}$ farthings. Almost same as hindostany Adhelah. Anjengo pice is $\frac{1}{48}$th of a rupee [q.v.]. The pice, though not used in accounts, is in popular bazaar use. The coin was at one time precisely an inch in diameter, weighing 100 grains troy. The aunay pice, or elephant pice, was a mysore coin having a figure of an elephant [q.v.] with the sun [sooryan] or moon [chundran] or both above. Pice is sometimes used as a name for money generally; cf. Cash. The name pice is also applied to a weight; a variable division of the seer [q.v.] ranging in different localities from $156\frac{1}{4}$ grains up to $276\frac{1}{2}$ grains. See vol. I, 609.——*Pie* (پائی - pái, Hind.). Through mahratta. From (páda, san. quarter). The plural is pies. Cf. the singular Pice.—"*a*" Small copper coin. 12 pies = 1 anna [naunyam, 2e]. Approximate actual value, 1 pie = $\frac{1}{2}$ a farthing. Same as Hind. damree, Tel. roowa, Tam. cash.—"*b*" Superficial measure. 12 pies = 1 anna [alavay, 2e]. Approximate actual value, 1 pie = 200 square feet. Used in N. arcot, S. arcot, Chingleput and the Neilgherries. $\frac{1}{192}$th of a cawny [q.v.].—"*c*" The title is also Anglo-indian for pariah [q.v.] or unowned village dogs [nye]; corruption of pariah. Also spelt Pye. See vol. I, 609. ——*Pow* (پاؤ - páu, Hind.; పావు - pávu, Tel.). From (páda, san. one-fourth). Through mahratta.—"*a*" Measure of capacity. 2 nowtauks = 1 pow; 4 pows = 1 pucka seer [alavay, 3e]. Approximate actual value, 1 pow = $17\frac{1}{2}$ cubic inches. Compare Oyak.—"*b*" Bazaar weight. 2 pollums = 1 pow; 4 pows = 1 cutcha seer [niray, 2e]. Approximate actual value, 1 pow = $2\frac{1}{2}$ oz. avoir.—"*c*" Goldsmith's weight. 2 chowlams = 1 pow; 2 pows = 1 mauda [niray, 3b]. Approximate actual value, 1 pow = $13\frac{1}{2}$ grains. $\frac{1}{4}$ of a pagoda weight [q.v.]. Compare Mausham. See vol. I, 609.——*Powlah* (پاولا - páulá, Hind.). From (pán, hind. one-fourth). Coin. 4 annas = 1 powlah; 4 powlahs = 1 rupee [naunyam, 2e]. Approximate actual value, 1 powlah = 4 annas. Commonly used. Same as Hind. chowanny, Can. caul, Tel. doogoolam, Tam. caul. Compare Mal. velly. ——*Pownah* (پاؤنا - páuná, Hind.). From (páda, san. one-fourth + úna, san. deficient). Through Mahratta. A quarter less than unity. Three-fourths. Pownah cowle is a cowle [q.v.] on three-fourths of original assessment [teervay].——*Poyel* (پایل - páyal, Hind.). From (pái, pers. foot). Anklet. Of gold [pon] or silver [velly], hollow or solid, knocking together as the wearer walks and making a ringing noise. Generally worn by dancing girls among Hindoos [poyzeb].——*Poyzeb* (پائی زیب - páezeb, Hind.). From (pá, pers. foot, + zeb, pers. adorner). Ornament [zewar] worn round ankles resembling a horse's curb chain, set with a fringe of small spherical bells, which tinkle at motion of limbs [poyel].——*Pye* (پای - páe, Hind.). From sanscrit. A foot [padam, paudam, payeen].——*Pyejan* (پینجن - painjan, Hind.). From (pada, san. foot + rañjana, san. pleasing). Small bells fastened round the feet of children [zewar].——*Pyekhana* (پاخانا - páikháná, Hind.). From (pái, hind. foot + khánah, pers. house). A latrine.——*Pyemauly* (پائی مالی - páimálí, Hind.). From (pái, hind. foot + málí, pers. trampled). Damage done by foot-trampling, as by troops or cattle passing.——*Pyjauma* (پائی جامہ - páijámah, Hind.). From (pái, hind. foot + jámah, pers. clothing). Trousers tied with string at waist, such as are worn by mussalman [q.v.] men and women [jauma]. Among europeans, sleeping drawers. Trousers of natives in the Central provinces are generally tight [sharayee]; here loose [izaur]. The English took the habit of sleeping drawers from the Portuguese [sheelay].——*Pyly* (పావలి - páyali, Tel.). From (pávu, tel. quarter). Measure of capacity. 2 pows = 1 pyly; 2 pylies = 1 seer [alavay, 3c]. Approximate actual value, 1 pyly = 35 cubic inches. Mysore. Compare Tavva of godavery, Sola of kistna.——*Pyrahan* (پیرہن - pairahan, Hind.). From (pái, hind. foot + rahan, hind. keeper). A gown with flaps in the skirt, having buttons in three places [sheelay].

PADDY (धान्य - dhánya, *San.*; तांदूळ - tándúla, *Mahr.*; तांदुल - tándula, *Conc.*; ارز - arruz, *Ar.*; برنج - birinj, *Pers.*; دھان - dhán, *Hind.* and *Dec.*; پدی - padi, *Malay*; ಭತ್ತ - bhatta, *Can.*; ಅರಿ - ari, *Too.*; వడ్లు - vadlu, *Tel.*; ଧାନ - dháno, *Oor.*; നെല്ല - nellu, *Mal.*; හාල් - hál, *Singh.*; நெல் - nel, *Tam.*). Title from malay. San. from (dhá, san. to support) [dhaunyam]. Mahr. and conc. from (tandula, san. rice). Hind. from sanscrit. Can. from (bhakta, san. boiled rice; food) [bhatta]. Tel. from (vari, tel. corruption of nívára, san. paddy). San. also (nívára), meaning warding off, applies to a wild variety; (tandula), meaning beaten rice; (nílamañjarí), meaning blue cluster of flowers; (abdhiká), meaning relating to sea; (vríhi), meaning covering; eight sorts are enumerated; the word is not mentioned in the rig vedam [q.v.], but first appears in atarva vedam [q.v.], together with mausham [black gram], tilam [gingelly] and yavam [jow]; specially applied to variety ripening in the rains; (aranya), meaning forest; (áshuvríhi), meaning rice ripening quickly in the rainy season; (sháli), meaning produced in an enclosed space; said to be of ten varieties, and two are specially distinguished, one white growing in deep water and the other red requiring only a moist soil. Hind. also (chával), meaning rice threshed. Dec. also (chánwal), meaning rice not in husk. Malay also (gabah). Can. also (nellu); (navare-bhatta); (akki) is rice. Tel. also (biyyamu); (úrivadlu), meaning village + paddy; (chénivadlu), meaning dry land + paddy; (errajilamavadlu), meaning red + kind of rice so called; (mattakárulu), meaning inferior + kind of rice so called; (vari). Mal. also (ari), meaning rice. Tam. also (arisi), meaning husked paddy. Greek ὄρυζον, ὄρυζα. Latin oryza. Title is applied only when plant is growing, or when at any rate the grain has not been husked. Title otherwise Rice [q.v.] plant. Botanically Oryza sativa, linn., graminaceæ [vricsham, 156]. Generic is from tamul through arabic.——**(1)**—"*a*" Cultivated throughout the country, but met with also in a truly wild condition in some swampy expanses. The majority of the wild states of this grass are annuals growing in dense tufts and producing coarse much branched radical stems, the erect portions of which root at the deflected nodes. They form spongy sheaths, through the presence of air-chambers in their texture, which sheaths are intended to support the ascending stems, as these in their growth have to keep pace with the rise of the level of water, rice being killed when completely submerged. The lower sheaths are often devoid of lamina; ligule large, membranous, bifurcated into sickle-shaped arms on either side of the stem, each arm having seven pairs of erect rigid hairs. Inflorescence a panicle of spikes on short peduncles which have an ochreate-like hairy scale at the point of origin of the spikes; pedicels short with the receptacular apex large and often greatly distorted, the upper and lower facets sometimes fully one-eighth of an inch apart; the scale-like ears of these facets are sometimes very large, and in exceptional cases one or both are even produced into what might be called additional outer glumes. Outer glumes large, very often tri-dentate, midrib prominent; inner glumes considerably elongated, being as a rule 0·325 inches in length, curved, pointed at both extremities, and in the great majority the larger one is produced into a long awn frequently distinctly articulated and possessed at its base of two glandular processes which correspond to the extremities of the lateral nerves; surface more or less hairy, especially on the keel and nerves, structure manifesting regular rows of shining granulations. There are endless cultivated forms; the progression from the wild to the cultivated forms is in the reduction of the size and alteration of the shape of the receptacle, in the loss of the awn, and in the shortening but widening of the combined outline of the inner glumes, a character consequent doubtless on the formation of a shorter, though thicker and more compact, grain; in cultivated rices again the progression in value is from the awned to the awnless forms, and from the colored to the colorless. The following is the description of an average cultivated type:—grass; culms numerous, jointed, round and smooth; leaves sheathing, long, scabrous outside; panicles terminal; rachis common and partial, angular, hispid; flowers simple, pedicelled; calyx glume two-valved, one-flowered, the larger valve ending in a long, hispid, colored awn; corolla two-valved, growing to the seed. Seeds when barked are white, nearly transparent, cylindrical, linear, furrowed, obtuse at both ends, brittle; flour very white, friable, insipid, dry, inodorous and tasteless, very soft, and swelling much when cooked; gluten none. Paddy seed was originally taken from this country to north america, and its cultivation has been so successful in carolina as to have led to its being reimported here as seed [viray].—"*b*" The most fertile soil for rice-sowing is land periodically inundated in the neighbourhood of large rivers [aur], where the plant can receive much fertilising matter [adaimunn, vandalmunn] from the overflow of the streams; the crop needs a temperature of at least 73°, humidity and heat being indispensable conditions of its growth; the outturn per acre varies according to natural climatic conditions and method of cultivation [vellaumay]. For the ordinary process of cultivation, the ground is squared off into plots varying in size, generally averaging from 30 to 40 yards in length and breadth marked off by ridges [varapp] or small bunds [q.v.] about two feet high and one broad; this plot, after being freely saturated with water from some irrigation source, is thoroughly ploughed up and manured [yeroo]; frequently green herbs and shrubs are ploughed into the soil, the favorite shrub for this purpose being the mudar or calotropis gigantea [yercum]; the ground thus prepared is covered over with water and allowed to stand from two to four inches over the soil to favor putrefaction and create a puddle; in a few days it is again ploughed up into a deep muddy mixture [sher]; a piece of board tied on to the yoke of a pair of bullocks [yair] is then drawn over the puddle to equalize it; it is now ready to receive the seed [viray]; the rice is prepared for sowing by being first steeped in water until it begins to germinate, which generally occurs in from two to three days, when it is conveyed to the field ready for sowing; the seedsman takes as much seed as he can conveniently carry in the cloth around his waist and enters the field; as he passes from one end to the other he scatters the seed broadcast, whilst an assistant carries a supply in a basket and walks along the bund [q.v.] to replenish the seedsman as the quantity becomes exhausted; the soil is then allowed to dry for some three or four days, by which time the seedlings [nautt] will have sprung up and have attained about two inches in height, when the field is irrigated and the water is allowed to stand a couple of inches above the soil and so maintained till the harvest is gathered; during the first and second months the fields are handweeded by women and boys, when, should the plants be found crowded together at any place, they are removed so as to leave from four to six inches of space between each; plants are also put in, so as to complete the stand; should at any time the plants grow lanky, from eight to ten inches of the tops are cut away by the sickle, which by arresting their rapid growth renders the plants much more fruitful. The above is the ordinary and wet sowing system of cultivation [coodapa, shettcaul]. In some circumstances or with some varieties of rice the field is ploughed up after a shower of rain [mazhay, monsoon] merely and without regard to the irrigation source, and the seeds are thereupon sown in their natural condition and unsoaked; when the sprouts [nautt] are between four and six weeks old, the field is artificially irrigated for the first time, and the water-supply maintained till the grain ripens and the stalks are ready for the sickle; this is the so called dry sowing system of cultivation [gaddavary, pooldy caul, veligada], but note that the land is still nunjah [q.v.] land and the artificial irrigation is only postponed; this system is adopted when the early irrigation fails, and where the soil is loamy [pasalay munn] or light sandy [manal]; weeding is much heavier under this. By a third method nurseries [nauttangaul] are prepared and the seeds sown therein; when the plantlings [nautt] have attained the age of six or eight weeks, they are transplanted into the fields prepared in the first of the two methods mentioned above to receive them; this is the nursery system of cultivation [nautt nadavoo]; the system gives trouble, but is highly remunerative; there is a Tamul proverb:— நடவுக்குத்தெளி நாலத்தொன்று—"paddy sown yields but "a fourth of that planted." As a fourth system dry paddy even occurs amongst dry cultivation [modan, pulliyaul]; for this the land is specially well manured [yeroo]. Whichever of the above systems of cultivation is adopted, irrigation is unnecessary for the last twenty or thirty days before a paddy crop is harvested; should an unfavorable wind prevail, and the plant be attacked by any grub, the usual course is to cut off the water altogether for a time and let the soil dry; rice suffers often from a yellowish green fly. The manure used in rice cultivation, briefly mentioned above, consists of every kind of refuse procurable excepting human excrement; the dung [shauny] and urine of cattle [maud], goats [vellaud], horses [ghorah], asses [gadhah], sheep [aud], and bats [vavvaul], ashes [neeroo], lime [choonam], sweepings of houses, husks [boosam] of paddy and other grains [dhaunyam], skins of fruits, decayed leaves of various kinds, bark, muck from the taupit, milk hedge [q.v.], varagoo [q.v.] and other straw, are some of the many substances commonly used, and many are applied only in particular circumstances and on highly scientific principles; the practice of diluting manure [yeroo] with large quantities of water is known to the ryot [q.v.], and various modes of making, altering, and correcting soils are well understood; the fluviatile deposits [adaimunn, vandal munn] found in the beds of channels [q.v.] and tanks [q.v.] are largely made use of; sheep [aud], goats [vellaud] and cattle [maud] are frequently enfolded on the land for purposes of manure [yeroo]. The principle of raising different crops in rotation is understood and to a limited extent acted upon, but the peculiarity of the mode of agriculture necessarily followed in a country where deep ploughing generally ruins the soil precludes the ryot from doing exactly the same as the english farmer. The number of crops of paddy that may be obtained from the same ground in the course of twelve months will depend much on the nature of the country. The districts through which large rivers [aur] run have a great advantage in this respect, such for instance as those of trichinopoly and tanjore, which have an almost continual succession of rice crops throughout the year owing to the cauvery being filled by both the south-west and north-east monsoons [q.v.]. In the northern and eastern parts of the carnatic [q.v.] which are in a great measure dependent on the natural rains [mazhay] and the water that is preserved in tanks [q.v.] or reservoirs, the different seasons for sowing and reaping rice are as follows; the shumbah [q.v.] or winter crop, which is reckoned the best, is sown towards the end of september, and is cut in february and march, the water by which it is nourished is that which falls during the north-east monsoon [q.v.] and what has been left by the monsoon in low grounds and tanks; this being reaped, on the same ground where it grew provided that water can be had is sown the madangal [q.v.] or summer catch crop, which is commonly got in june and july, but is in general the least productive and the most uncertain of the whole year's cultivation, as from the extreme heat of the weather during the time that it is growing the ears frequently fail to fill well; the caur [q.v.] or autumn crop, which is considered the second best, is put into the ground when the first rains begin to fall and after the excessive heat is a little abated, in other words in july and august, and is brought to maturity by the monsoon rains and reaped in december and january about a month or six weeks before that of the shumbah; upon the ground whence the caur crop is taken, in december and january, is sown the nawara or spring catch crop, provided there is water enough remaining, and this is got in a month or six weeks before that of the madangal; shumbah [q.v.], madangal [q.v.], caur [q.v.] and nawara [q.v.] are described by the natives as the four sorts of crop yielded by nadee mautricam [q.v.] or lands irrigated by rivers and first class devamautricam or lands dependant on rain. After rice-stalks have been cut they are carried off the fields, when they are stacked and left for two or three days or more; the sheaves are then spread on a prepared ground [calam] and are beaten with long bamboo [q.v.] sticks, or buffaloes and cattle [khoolgah, maud] are made to tread on the stalks so spread until seeds separate from them; to separate the grain from dust and chaff [boosam] baskets filled with paddy are held up above the head and the paddy allowed to drop, when the breeze blows the dust and chaff away; if there be no breeze a cooly [q.v.] winnows the grain with a fan; the mode of separating the husk from the grain is by beating it with the rice-stamper, this work being usually performed by women, see later.—"*c*" The above are general particulars of cultivation; the following are special for different localities.—"*d*" In the Nellore district rice cultivation is carried on under both coodapa [q.v.] and veligada [q.v.], wet sowing and dry sowing. The latter system is adopted only where the supply of irrigation will not suffice early in the season for the land, or where the soil is loamy or light sandy and so favors that mode of cultivation. Under coodapa, paddy can be sown at any time that water may be available, for one of the several crops is sure to suit the season of the year. As a rule however coodapa cultivation may be considered to commence late in june or during july, and continue till february; and after that it is rarely resorted to, save in second crop land or in submerged land that could not have been sown before. The early coodapa [q.v.] cultivation towards the end of june or during july is generally under the river channels [q.v.] or river-supplied tanks [q.v.]. The crops most extensively put down under these sources are pishaunam [q.v.] or tawny husked paddy and sannavary [q.v.] or fine paddy, which take six months to mature and yield the white or superior description of rice. These two kinds are only cultivable till about the end of august, after which the common descriptions which mature in a less period are sown. The mode of cultivating each description of paddy under Coodapa is the same, irrespective of the season at which put down. The land is first ploughed, with the water on it, from five to eight different times, either each time separately or twice at the same time, with an interval of a few days between each operation according to local usage. The number of times it is ploughed will depend on the soil in some measure, as the loamy soils work up far more speedily than the heavy. The interval between the ploughings is requisite to allow time for the grass and weeds to rot and be killed in some measure by being ploughed into and worked up with the slush. Upon the completion of the requisite ploughing, the banks are made up, the water is partly let off, and the beam-leveller is used to level the surface of the field and make it as smooth as practicable. The field is next flooded, and the seed, which will invariably have been previously steeped and closely packed in leaves, is sown broadcast over the field. The quantity of seed expended varies somewhat, but is generally about 2½ tooms [q.v.] or 80 maunicas [q.v.] per gorroo [q.v.]; equivalent to about 30 Madras measures or 40 seers [q.v.] per acre. The water is left on the whole field the first night, but is completely drawn off in the morning. Subsequent irrigation is regulated with reference to the position of the soil whether high or low-lying, and the nature of the soil whether porous or retentive of moisture. In either of the former cases the field will be flooded on the third, fourth, or fifth day, and again let off; in the latter cases from the sixth to the ninth day, and at varying intervals afterwards, depending very much on the same conditions up to about the fifteenth or twenty-fifth day, where the crop is regularly irrigated. After thirty or forty days, the latter most frequently, the crop is weeded, and any thin parts are transplanted with plants taken from where the paddy may be overthick. Again after another month it is weeded a second time if requisite. In some villages it is usual for the teethed leveller or bushes heavily weighted to be drawn over the young crop to submerge the weeds; this is done when the plant is a month old, and with a view of reducing the labour of weeding. After this treatment the paddy rises again, but the weeds and grasses are in some measure killed; what weeds may afterwards remain are removed by the hand at the close of the second month. Water is afterwards let on and off regularly according to the soil and season. A large series of forms of rice are cultivated under coodapa [q.v.]. Under Veligada the loamy and light sandy soils are ploughed with the first early rains and the operation is repeated at intervals until the land may have been ploughed some five or six times. The seed is then either sown broadcast and ploughed in twice, or else is drilled in with the gorroo [q.v.] and covered up and levelled with the goontaca [q.v.]. Should rain not fall within the second or third day, the goontaca is used once more. The seed is only drilled as a rule in villages where the gorroo happens to be kept for dry cultivation. The seed sown under veligada [q.v.] is usually 2 tooms or 64 maunicas per gorroo, equivalent to about 23·87 Madras measures per acre. For nearly two months paddy thus planted is dependent on rain. After one month the gorroo [q.v.] or teethed leveller is used to loosen the soil, and about the end of the second month, but sometimes earlier if the weeds are very thick, water is let on, and the whole is once well weeded, or this is done if heavy rain sets in. Whilst the crop is being weeded, the plants are thinned in parts and transplanted in places where the crop may have partially failed. After weeding, the crop is regularly irrigated as far as may be practicable, and a second weeding, if necessary, takes place during the third month. Weeding is a very much heavier business under veligada [q.v.] than coodapa [q.v.]. The period during which paddy can be put down under veligada is limited to the period of the early rains, say august and september. Only pedda sannavary, vauda sannavary, and calinga shumbah are regularly put down under veligada; sometimes, but very seldom, pishaunam and mosanam are thus cultivated as well. From the foregoing details it will be observed that the system of cultivation throughout the district is that of sowing the paddy broadcast under one or other method. The method of transplanting the seed [nautt nadavoo] prevails only in the extreme northern part of the district bordering on the kistna, and in the shreeharicote villages formerly appertaining to the chingleput district. The advantage which the transplanting system may be considered to have over the broadcast system is that the former admits of well-grown and vigorous young plants raised in highly manured beds being transplanted, which readily take root, and having the start are able to vanquish the weeds which at once spring up besides them. Under the broadcast system, the weeds sprout with the young paddy, and as the latter grows it has to contend for existence against the weeds, and the growth of the paddy is consequently more or less checked. The transplanting system may be regarded as particularly advantageous for the poorer descriptions of soil, inasmuch as a strong and healthy plant once transplanted in poor land is able to thrive better than seed sown in land deficient in strength, which affords the plant but slight chance of growing vigorously at first. As to the length of period for which irrigation water has to be taken the transplanting method stands midway between coodapa [q.v.] and veligada [q.v.]. Where pursued, it is the better class of paddies which are treated by the nursery process.—"*e*" In Kistna district there are three classes of rice:—poonausa [q.v.] or early crop, sown in may or june, and reaped in september; pedda, or great crop, sown intermediately from july to september, and cut between november and february; peira [q.v.] or late crop, sown in november and december, and gathered in february and march.—"*f*" In Chingleput district wet sowing is called shettcaul [q.v.], dry sowing is called pooldycaul [q.v.], and transplantation is called nautt nadavoo [q.v.]. In shettcaul and pooldycaul 3 mercauls [q.v.] of seed of 8 measures each are sown on an acre of land, and will generally produce 100 mercauls of paddy in return if the growth flourishes. The transplanting method requires 4 mercauls of seed per acre; this kind of cultivation is very common in the district. The chief descriptions of paddy are shumbah [q.v.], caur [q.v.] and manacuttay [q.v.]; of these shumbah is the best its rice being white in color, caur ranks next, the third and last is manacuttay; the rice of the two latter is somewhat red; there are different sub-heads under each. Of the shumbah kinds, Codan shumbah or hot weather shumbah is cultivated in the beginning of the cultivation year, viz., about may or june. In many places a second crop is raised about the month of december or january on lands on which a first crop of codan shumbah has been already raised. All the other kinds of shumbah are cultivated as a rule from the month of july onwards. Shirmany meaning small grain or Calavan meaning mixed shumbah and Chinna shumbah, are six and four month crops respectively, raised abundantly. Vauda shumbah and Shaday shumbah are raised in pooldy caul in great quantities; not being so readily liable to wither, their period is long. In places where there is not a large supply of water, three months' shumbah and two months' shumbah, are cultivated; these rarely yield a good crop. The raising of the first Caur crop generally commences about the month of may and june, and the second in december. The second crop is raised on the same fields on which the first crop has been already raised. Mutta or palm stem caur and Peroom or large caur are raised in large quantities. The various kinds of Mosanam are cultivated to a considerable extent from the month of july, the season for shumbah. Poombaulay is cultivated in the foreshores of tanks and pools just previous to the rainy season; and even if water after rainfall stands to a height of a half or three-fourths of a yard, it shoots up higher than the level of the water and yields a good outturn. Some of the species of caur are raised to a slight degree in certain villages in dry seed cultivation. Manacuttay, the third class, is cultivated on a small scale in april or may, in lands irrigated by wells, &c.; among these Pishiny is raised in pooldycaul on high level nunjah [q.v.] lands; this grain is even cultivated in dry lands when they are fairly moist.—"*g*" In the Madura district the times of ploughing [yair], sowing [viray], transplanting [nautt nadavoo], &c., vary very considerably in different seasons according as the rains are early or late, plentiful or the reverse, and also according as lands lie near to or far from sources of irrigation and are rapidly or slowly supplied with water. But as a rule the ploughing is done in june or july after the early rains have thoroughly softened the ground and the seed is sown in the nurseries [nauttangaul] at the end of july or beginning of august. After about thirty days the seedlings [nautt] are fit for transplanting, and in january the crop is ready for the sickle. The best farmers in Madura like light falls of rain [mazhay, monsoon] at intervals of about thirty days. In lands well supplied with water as soon as the january crop is got in, preparations are made for a second catch crop called Maushy coday, meaning summer crop of february month, which is raised in the same mode as the first and comes to maturity about may. Or, if the season be unpropitious during january and february, the second sowing will be in march or april or may, and the second reaping in july or august. The catch crop will then be called the Audy coday. Sometimes there will be three crops of rice raised in succession in a period of 13 or 14 months. Rapidly-growing and therefore inferior kinds of rice are always set down for the second and third crops. Where the irrigational supplies are sufficient, the second crop may be of plantains [q.v.], sugar-cane [q.v.], betel [q.v.] vines, &c., or where the supplies are insufficient for the highest kind of crops, raggy [q.v.], cumboo [bajrah], cholum [q.v.], varagoo [q.v.], or rape-seed [rara sarsoon] may be cultivated immediately after the caulam [q.v.] or seasonal rice crop. The paddy is grown on almost every description of soil indifferently, the only essential being a constant supply of water; but the richer soils yield much larger crops than the poorer. The seed is sometimes sown broadcast, but as a rule it is sown in nurseries [nauttangaul] specially prepared. In the former case the expense of cultivation is light, but the produce is not very remunerative; in the latter, the crops are generally good. Sometimes the young plants raised in a nursery are transplanted into a second nursery and afterwards retransplanted into the field, and where this is done the yield is much larger than is ordinarily obtained. In this district the finest kinds of paddy are Shumbah and Milagy; these forms germinate in five days, are transplanted in 25 days, form the ear in 105 days, and are harvested in 45 days more, thus taking in all six months. It is observable that pishaunam rice is not now grown in the madura district, but at the beginning of the last century was extensively cultivated; pishaunam is however grown in both tanjore and tinnevelly.—"*h*" In the Tanjore district the coarser sorts of paddy are sown broadcast, but this mode of cultivation is very limited, being carried on only in a few places beyond the delta [conamoogam], and there on rain-fed land; in all cases of irrigated cultivation, young plants are raised in seed-beds [nattangaul] and transplanted [nautt nadavoo]. Caur [q.v.] is the inferior, and Pishaunam [q.v.] is the superior, paddy of the district; caur is referred to two kinds, Cadapoo [q.v.] or black paddy and Caur proper, and pishaunam is similarly spoken of as of two kinds, Shumbah or red paddy and Pishaunam proper. The dates of actual commencement and termination of agricultural operations vary in the different parts of the district. This is due to the first supply of freshes reaching the eastern portion of the delta later; not that a flood takes any number of days in travelling within the district, but because the early flood is almost wholly utilised westward, and the cultivators at the eastern end have to wait until the more copious and therefore uninterrupted series of freshes reach them. Thus in the further west of the delta the caur planting begins in may and the crop is harvested in september; the pishaunam cultivation there begins in september and the crop is harvested in january; then a few days before a third crop, a pulse [dholl] called vayalpayar or low land pulse [field gram], is sown and this is picked two months after or in march; this pulse requires no ploughing and grows chiefly with the aid of the moisture that remains in the fields and succeeds even if there be no rain afterwards. In the extreme east of the delta, on the other hand, where more than one crop is hardly ever cultivated, the cultivation generally begins in august and sometimes, as when freshes are later than usual, in september and the crop is harvested in march. Where only one crop is grown in the year it is usually one of seven months' duration from planting to reaping. The general mean may be taken broadly as four months, from july to october, for the caur species; and as six months, from september to february, for the pishaunam. Wherever two crops are raised, the second is usually one of the quicker-growing varieties of shumbah [q.v.]. Taking the delta as a whole, the proportion of cadapoo or black caur species to the entire paddy crop may be taken to be one-sixth. In some villages in the central part of the delta, one of the varieties of pishaunam [q.v.] called Ottadan [q.v.] is planted along with cadapoo [q.v.] proper; when the latter which grows quicker is reaped, the ends of the ottadan plant then only about half-grown are cut along with it, and the latter then shoots up all the more luxuriantly and comes to maturity at the usual season of the pishaunam harvest; in this case the seeds of the two varieties are mixed together, in the proportion of $\frac{3}{4}$ cadapoo and $\frac{1}{4}$ ottadan, before they are put down in the nursery, and the young plants of both which are hardly distinguishable are planted promiscuously. The caur species draws more water than the pishaunam; it will bear almost any amount of moisture without being injured. Allusion has been made to the pulse [dholl] or vayalpayar [field gram] grown as a third crop on paddy lands; more generally however a dry crop forms an auxiliary to only a single crop of paddy, being adopted as an alternative where, as often happens, the available supply of water is not sufficient for two paddy crops, or the mirassidars [q.v.] cannot afford the requisite labor; the dry crop is either the pulse above mentioned, gingelly [q.v.] or raggy [q.v.], and the latter two require ploughing but it is only raggy that is planted; this additional crop is raised either before or after the paddy season; in the first case it is sown or planted, as the case may be, with the aid of the summer shower or the first fresh when it happens to come earlier than usual, but cannot be relied on for beginning operations for the cultivation of a regular wet crop; in the second case, if the dry crop is gingelly [q.v.] or raggy [q.v.], the field is ploughed when there is yet moisture in it; the crop is then sown or planted in february and reaped in may, being matured entirely by the summer showers.—"*i*" In the Coimbatore district paddy may be roughly divided into three months Caur and five months Shumbah; the former is grown both as a first and second crop, the latter, save very occasionally, only as a second or single crop and in the cold weather. The best known varieties of these two sorts are tabulated below. Dry land paddy is also added, but is rare :—

Three months; Caur [q.v.].	Four to six months; Shumbah [q.v.].	Dry land [poonjah].
Cooroovay	Shumbah	Shoornay vellay.
Annadaunam	Calingaroyan shumbah.	
Aroovathaum coday ...	Caurtigay shumbah.	
	Milagy or Shemmilagy.	

Either variety succeeds raggy or other so-called dry crop, or paddy. The treatment, season, and yield are different in each talook owing to the variety of water-supply and soil. Common features are as follows. First crop; caur; the ground is prepared in june and july in the usual way by swamping, cross-ploughing several times, green-manuring and smoothing with the beam; seed is generally sown broadcast at the rate of from 24 to 30 madras measures, or from 1 to $1\frac{1}{2}$ bushels per acre; in the fourth week the land is weeded and the plants thinned out if necessary, and bare places planted up; there is no subsequent weeding; water is let on as often as possible, and harvest takes place in september, october; the quantity of seed sown varies greatly; the estimates of seed are high, viz., 30 to 36 measures per acre transplanted, and from 24 to 60 measures for broadcast sowing; if the soil is rich and the plants good, four or five seedlings will form a bunch and be planted at from 6 to 8 inches apart. Second crop; by which is understood a crop following a first crop either of raggy or other dry grain or of paddy; this may be either cooroovay [q.v.] or shumbah [q.v.]; with good irrigation, shumbah is the rule as a second crop; this is usually transplanted from nurseries prepared in october, after the first crop is reaped in october, the land is again prepared by ploughing, green-manuring, treading and levelling, and the seedlings [nautt] rapidly transplanted in november-december; there is little difference between the second crop and the single crop paddy either in yield, kind or season; the quantity of seed required somewhat exceeds that for the first crop. The chief pest here for paddy is an insect called navay pootchy, whitish, and from half to one inch long; it bores into and feeds on the tender plant, which then produces only empty husks.—"*j*" In the South canara district land is thus classified according to its capacity for irrigation; byle [q.v.] or rich wet land, majal [q.v.] or middling wet land, bettoo [q.v.] or land watered only by the rainfall. On byle land of the best quality, three rice crops can be raised in the year; on the best majal land, two crops; bettoo land produces only a single crop. The zeneloo or carty is the earliest rice crop of the season, on whatever description of land it may be grown. The seed is usually first sown in nurseries, which are highly manured, and the plants are afterwards transplanted. In about two months after transplantation, the crop comes into ear, and about twenty-one days more is ready for reaping.—"*k*" In the Malabar district rice is sometimes sown broadcast, but is usually transplanted from nursery beds. The first or Cunny crop is sown in april and may, and cut in august and september. The second or Macaram or january reaped crop is sown in september and october, and reaped in january and february. These are the principal rice harvests, but there are intermediate crops in some places; and a third, known as poonjah [colpoonjah], is sown in february and reaped in april or may. The greater portion of land however bears only one crop. For detailed information see the heads Cunny, Colpoonjah, Macaram, Modan and Pulliyaul.—"*l*" A large part of the rice sold in the shops, and which is exported to europe has been husked by being first half-boiled, then dried in the sun, and finally husked by the ordinary pestle and mortar; this Par-boiled rice, as it is called in the trade, is an important article, but one which the higher caste hindoos are forbidden to eat since it may have been boiled by low caste persons. Husking without boiling is a tedious process, the more so since it is done entirely by hand labor; this is however facilitated by exposing the grain to the sun before treatment in the mortar. The mortar may be made of stone, but it is commonly an hour-glass-shaped log of wood about two feet in height with a central cavity excavated for half its depth and only very slightly greater in diameter than the pestle which is usually about 3 to 4 feet long and about 3 inches in thickness; the mortar is as a rule firmly fixed in the ground; the operation of husking, which may be almost daily witnessed, requires not only considerable agility but great exertion. Over by far the larger part of the country the rice for the family use is husked by the females of the family as it is wanted, the stock of unhusked grain being kept in granaries adjoining the house. The grain is sometimes first milled by hand. The mortar is then partly filled with grain and is beaten with the pounder until the chaff [boosam] is separated. The rice is then winnowed by throwing it up into the air.—"*m*" Internally riceflour and water is used as a chemical antidote in poisoning by preparations of mercury [rasam], copper [taumram], zinc [tootnaug], silver [velly] and tin [tagaram], and by iodine; the conjee [q.v.] is a good demulcent and refrigerant drink in febrile and inflammatory diseases; it is rendered more palatable by being acidulated with lime-juice [lime] and sweetened with sugar [q.v.]; rice is of a less aperient quality than any other grain, and is therefore generally ordered as the safest and best food in bowel complaints; externally the rice-flour is used most commonly for poultices, and to protect burnt or excoriated surfaces; substituted for british linseed [alsee] meal. arrow-root [malabar arrowroot], and sago [q.v.]; gives to pharm. oryzæ farina, properties analogous to those of wheat [geung], officinal. Veidyans [q.v.] are particular as to the kind of rice they prescribe, supposing the rices of different crops to have very different effects. Composition of rice is in 100 parts:—water 12·8, albuminoids 7·3, starch 78·3, oil ·6, fibre ·4, ash ·6.—"*n*" Wild rice [nivvary] is gathered and eaten by the richer classes in the northern circar [q.v.] districts, who boil it in steam; it is white, palatable, and wholesome; coarse kind of confection made from it is sold in most bazaars. Ordinary rice forms the staple food of a very large proportion of the population; it is a valuable food abounding in starch, not destitute of albuminates and salts, easily grown, easily cooked and easily digested; it is deficient as above shown in nitrogenous aliment, being in this respect the lowest of the cereals [dhaunyam], hence it demands the addition of meat or fish or leguminous seeds [dholl], of milk or buttermilk [paul]; it is deficient in fat, and therefore requires butter, ghee [q.v.] or other fat to be added; salt is also ill-provided and must be supplied by other foods, hence a dietary consisting mainly of rice requires a more generous salt ration than one of wheat [geung] or millet [q.v.]; it is in fact generally insipid and needs the aid of condiments [chutney]. Madrassees say that the rice of n. india is dry and insipid, and causes them to be constipated; early sown rice is much more wholesome than late sown; rice should have been kept at least six months before it is used as food, otherwise indigestion and diarrhœa are likely to follow, nor does it boil well, the grains adhering together in lumps; the grains should be of average size, free from epiphytic spots and from holes made by insects; they should not break readily on pressure; there is some reason to suspect that the obscure disease called beribery [q.v] is attributable to diseased rice. Paddy is as above said partially boiled and then dried before it comes into the grain-market, except in the case of what is called table rice, used by bramins and europeans, which has not undergone this process. After purchase rice is prepared in the house for actual eating by slow boiling or steaming till the grain becomes soft, when the superfluous water is strained away and the rice allowed to cool; it should not be over-boiled into a pulpy mass, but the grains should be soft and not adhere to each other. Rice-flour is also in use for the preparation of cakes, &c.; for this purpose the rice is either steeped in water and then pounded in a mortar and the flour subsequently dried in the sun, or the grain itself is dried in the sun and then ground in a mill. Rice-cakes under the name of hoppers [q.v.] are in general use among most of the lower orders of europeans, east indians, and native christians; the rice-flour is mixed with water and allowed to ferment overnight; this process is frequently assisted by the use of toddy [q.v.] or the cocoanut [q.v.] tree sap; the next morning it is baked into cakes; frequently cocoanut milk is added to improve the flavor of the cakes; different kinds of sweet cakes are prepared from riceflour. Two pounds of cleaned rice weigh five pounds after boiling; the liquor [conjee] is either thrown away or is drunk as a beverage after the addition of a little common salt [ooppoo], or is given to stall-fed milch cows [pashoo]; throwing away of the water involves loss of some mineral matter, no more water should be used in cooking this grain than can be absorbed by it. The absence of gluten prevents the conversion of rice into bread, but it may be employed for preparing a kind of beer and a form of arrack [q.v.]. The stalk is the chief dry fodder [ghaus] of cattle [maud] throughout the year; the plant before it seeds is capable of conversion into hay, but it contains very little nutritious matter.—"*o*" Rice husk [boosam] contains a small amount of a pale yellowish-brown coloring matter, and when boiled in water the infusion may, by the use of various processes, be made to dye light shades [shauyam]. Rice straw, and more especially the lower portion of the stems and roots, left generally to enrich the soil; may be used as a paper material. Rice glue is made by mixing rice flour with cold water and then boiling the mixture; this conjee [q.v.] is used in the process of paper making, and also by weavers [nesavoo] in dressing and preparing thread [nool] for the loom [tarry], and generally used by mechanics whenever strong adhesion [pattoo] may be required.

——**(2)** As indicated at head there are several hundred varieties and sub-varieties of paddy or oryza sativa; but they do not possess any very marked peculiarities, except such as are due to difference in climate, soil, and mode of cultivation [vellaumay]; some forms possess two and others three grains within the pericarp, thus showing a tendency to revert to an ancestral type; the best known wild variety is known as nivvary [q.v.], found about the lakes in the northern circars [q.v.]; hill-rice again is that which is raised in upland, arable lands, in malabar called modan [q.v.], smaller and less valuable than common rice. The following are some of the kinds known to the natives, with their derivations and a few particulars.——*Aroovathaum cottay* (அறுவதாங்கொட்டை - aruvathángottai, Tam.). From (aruvathu, tam. sixty + kottai, tam. seed). Two months growth to harvest, very quick. Coimbatore.——*Aryan* (ആര്യൻ - áryyan, Mal.). From (áryam, mal. the mahrátta country). Four months. Malabar, named after the Mahratta country. For the varieties see sep. title.——*Aunacauyan* (ആനക്കായൻ - ánakkáyan, Mal.). From (ána, mal. elephant + káya, mal. fruit); that is, large grain. Six months. Malabar.——*Aunacodam* (ആനക്കുടം - ánakkutam, Mal.). From (ána, mal. elephant + kutam, mal. anything round); large grain. Six months. Malabar.——*Aunucomban* (ആനക്കൊമ്പൻ - ánakkompan, Mal.; ஆனைக்கொம்பன் - ánaikkomban, Tam.). From (ána, mal. elephant + kompu, mal. tusk); from color. Five months; sown in Malabar in Cunny [mausam] or September-October, and reaped in Macaram or January-February; rice is white. Also in southern districts, cultivated in sandy or red soil [shevval munn]; ground prepared at end of pooratanshy [mausam] or september, by ploughing and manuring [yeroo]; seedlings [nautt] transplanted in arpisy or october; regular watering and weeding once a month for the first three months; the crop attains a height of 3 feet and is of a brown color; cut six months after sowing.——*Bhogaul* (భోగాలు - bhógálu, Tel.). Means enjoyable. Indicating superiority. Paddy of N. circars. There are several varieties named after Balaraman, Dasharatan, Seetay, &c.——*Boodama* (బుడమబియ్యము - budamabiyyamu, Tel.). From (budama, tel. the plant, solanum verbascifolium, linn. + biyyamu, tel. rice); from small size. Four months. Kistna.——*Cadapoo* (கடப்பு - kadappu, Tam.). Means black. A species of Caur paddy.——*Calama* (കഴമ - kazhama, Mal.). From (kalama, san. rice growing in deep water). Five months. Malabar.——*Calinga shumbah* (కళింగశంబా - kalingashambá, Tel.; கலிங்கசம்பா - kalingasambá, Tam.). Introduced from calingam [q.v.], teloogoo country. Four to five months. Coromandel coast. Same as Vauda shumbah.——*Carim coora* (കരിങ്കൂര - karinkúra, Mal.). From (kari, mal. black + kúra, mal. a sharp-pointed grain). Six months. Malabar.——*Carippauly* (കരിപ്പാലി - karippáli, Mal.). Means black paula or milky paddy. Four months. Malabar.——*Carootta caudan* (കറുത്തകാടൻ - karuttakátan, Mal.). From (karutta, mal. black + kátan, mal. wild paddy). Six months. Malabar.——*Carootta chaura* (കറുത്തചാര - karuttachára, Mal.). From (karutta, mal. black + chára, mal. striped paddy). Four months. Malabar.——*Carroottainy* (കറുത്തേനി - karutténi, Mal.). From (karutta, mal. black + chíni, mal. foreign rice). Four months. Malabar.——*Cauday caloottan* (കാടക്കഴുത്തൻ - kátakkazhuttan, Mal.). From (káta, mal. quail + kazhuttu, mal. neck); from long and slender grain. Five to six months. Malabar. Cf. Quail-necked paddy.——*Caur* (கார் - kár, Tam.). Any paddy set down in the rainy season, but especially in S.W. monsoon [q.v.]. For different kinds see sep. title.——*Caurany* (കാരണി - kárani, Mal.). From (kár, mal. black + ani, mal. row); from appearance of ears. Five months. Malabar.——*Chambaun* (ചമ്പാൻ - champán, Mal.). Four to six months. Same as Shumbah.——*Cheera* (ചീര - chira, Mal.). Means cumin seed, from similar grain. Six months. Malabar. See sep. title.——*Chembily piriyan* (ചെമ്പിലിപിരിയൻ - chempilipiriyan, Mal.). From (chempu, mal. copper + piriyan, mal. twisted), from appearance of ears. Five to six months. Malabar. Rice white.——*Chempaula* (ചെമ്പാല - chempála, Mal.). From (chem, mal. red + pála, mal. the milky grained paddy). Five months. Malabar. Rice white.——*Chendaula* (ചെന്താഴ - chentázha, Mal.). From (chem mal. red + tázha, mal. screw-pine, pandanus odoratissimus, linn. f.); from color of grain. Four months. Malabar.——*Chendaur many* (ചെന്താർമണി - chentármani, Mal.). From (chentár, mal. red flower, lotus, nelumbium speciosum, willd. + mani, mal. grain); from red grain. Four months. Malabar.——*Chennell* (ചെന്നെല്ലു - chennellu, Mal.). From (chem, mal. red + nellu, mal. paddy). Four months. Malabar.——*Chittainy* (ചിറ്റേനി - chitténi, Mal.). From (chiru, mal. small + chíni, mal. chinese). Five months. Said to come from China. Malabar.——*Chornauly* (ചുരണാലി - churanáli, Mal.). Four months. Malabar. See sep. title.——*Codavilootala* (കൊടവിഴുതല - kotavizhutala, Mal.). From (kuta, mal. umbrella + vizhu, mal. to fall + tala, mal. head); from stalks in ears drooping like an umbrella. Nine months. Malabar.——*Cokkan* (കൊക്കൻ - kokkan, Mal.). From (kokku, mal. crane), white paddy. Four months. Malabar.——*Colpoonjah* (കോൽപുഞ്ച - kólpuñcha, Mal.). From (kol, mal. to hold + puñcha, mal. land); land holding water. Paddy in lowlying lands bordering malabar backwater [cauyal]. The land reclaimed is protected by fences of wattle and mud. Seedlings [nautt] planted in Marcaram [mausam] or January or in Coombham or February. Crop cut in Maidom or April.——*Coly* (കോലി - kóli, Mal.). From (kól, mal. stick); from size of grain, long and slender. Five months. Malabar.——*Coodivitt* (കുടിവിത്തു - kutivittu, Mal.). From (kuti, mal. house + vittu, mal. seed). Six months. Malabar rice for lower classes.——*Cooroovay* (குருவை - kuruvai, Tam.). From (kuru, tam. short). Short crop of 2 or 3 months. Tanjore and Tinnevelly. See sep. title. ——*Coottaudan* (കുട്ടാടൻ - kuttátan, Mal.). From (kuttanátu, mal. the low land near ambalappuzha). Ten months. Malabar. Black and white varieties as usual. See sep. title.——*Culloonday* (கல்லுண்டை - kallundai, Tam.). From (kal, tam. stone + undai, tam. ball); from hard round rice. Six and half months. South arcot.——*Cunny* (കന്നികൃഷി - kannikrishi, Mal.). From time of harvest. A principal paddy of W. coast. Soil most suitable, soft clayey soil [calimunn]; ground prepared, in macaram [mausam] or january, coombham or february and meenam or march; the land is ploughed three or four times in macaram or january and one or more times in coombham or february, so that the soil is broken and turned up into clods; in meenam or march dried cowdung, straw, &c., is deposited in heaps and burnt; at the time of sowing, the land is ploughed six or seven times and the earth pulverised; seed is sown either in the latter part of meenam or march, i.e., in raivaty nautt vaila [caurtey], or in the early part of maidom or april, i.e., in ashwaty nautt vaila [caurtey], seed may be sown in nursery or otherwise; if in nursery, sowing must be made in the latter part of meenam or march, so that the seedlings may be transplanted in yedavam or may; if the seed is sown broadcast, the weeds should be removed during the latter part of yedavam or may and early in mitoonam or june; cowdung [shauny] should be mixed with water in the openings on the embankments; a full grown plant attains the height of 3–4½ feet; if a plant thrives well, it will have three or four shoots from the stem; cut three to five months after sowing; average price, 38 to 45 imperial seers for 1 rupee——*Cuttaulay* (கற்றாழை - kattázhai, Tam.). From (kal, tam. stone + tázhai, tam. screw-pine, pandanus odoratissimus, linn.) Five months. Is the only variety of paddy sown broad-cast in Tanjore, and is grown chiefly in the upland parts. Tanjore. ——*Eeshwara cora* (ఈశ్వరకోర - íshvarakóra, Tel.). Meaning shiva's tinay. A principal paddy of coromandel coast; soil most suitable, sandy and clay; ground prepared in aushweejam [mausam] or october and caurteecam or november; soil is moistened and then ploughed four or five times; the field is then levelled by a harrow [goontaca]; seed sown broadcast or by transplantation in aushweejam or october and caurteecam or november; after two months' growth, it is weeded and transplanted if necessary; full grown crop is 4 feet high; cut after five months; average price, 30 imperial seers for 1 rupee.—— *Gaddavary* (గడ్డవరి - gaddavari, Tel.). From (gadda, tel. clod + vari, tel. paddy). Any paddy sown in wet-land, but without waiting for direct flow from irrigation source.——*Gandool* (గండులు - gandulu, Tel.). Means large. Four months. Kurnool. ——*Jeeracattary* (ചീരകത്തരി - chírakattari, Mal.). From (chírakam, mal. cumin seed, cuminum cyminum, linn. + ari, mal. rice); from fineness. Four months. Malabar.——*Kesary* (కేసరి - késari, Tel.). From (késara, san. gold); from color of paddy. A principal paddy of Coromandel coast. Cultivated in sandy and clay soil; ground prepared in pooshyam [mausam] or january and maugham or february; ploughed four or five times and levelled by a harrow [goontaca]; seed sown in pooshyam or january and maugham or february; no nursery; sown broadcast; usual watering and weeding; full grown crop 2 feet high; cut after four months; average price 28 imperial seers for 1 rupee.——*Krishna leelay* (കൃഷ്ണലീല - krishnalíla, Mal.). From (krishna, san. black + lílá, san. sport, semblance); from color of grain. Five months. Malabar.——*Macaram* (മകരകൃഷി - makarakrishi, Mal.). From time of harvest. A principal paddy of W. coast. Soil most suitable, soft clayey; ground prepared soon after the first crop is gathered early in toolaum [mausam] or october; seed must be sown in nursery; should be transplanted before the 25th toolaum or october; until the seedlings strike root after transplantation, care must be taken to adjust water-supply, after this stage water may be allowed to stagnate as much as is required; full grown crop attains 4 to 4½ feet; cut three to five months after sowing, according to quality of seed; average price, 32 to 45 imperial seers for 1 rupee.——*Madangal* (மடங்கல் - madangal, Tam.). From (madangu, tam. to turn). A summer catch crop got in June and July; sown on the ground after shumbah [q.v.] has been reaped.——*Manacuttay* (மணக்கத்தை - manakkattai, Tam.). From (manam, tam. fragrance). Four months. The third sort of paddy cultivated in nunjah [q.v.] in Chingleput; has varieties white and black.——*Maunavaury* (மானவாரி - mánavári, Tam.). Means sky rain. Three to five months. Any paddy grown without irrigation [pooldycaul, veligada]; these are rare. In southern districts, sown in maurgaly [mausam] or december, reaped in pungoony or march. Paddy white and rice red.——*Mayil caloottan* (മയിൽകഴുത്തൻ - mayilkazhuttan, Mal.). From (mayil, mal. peacock + kazhuttu, mal. neck); from color of grain. Five months. Malabar.—— *Meshattary* (മേശത്തരി - méshattari, Mal.). From (mésha, mal. table + ari, mal. rice). Six months. Paddy small and white. Malabar.——*Milagy* (மிளகி - milagi, Tam.). From (milagu, tam. black pepper, piper nigrum, linn.). Six to seven months. Same as Milagoo shumbah.——*Modan* (മോടൻ - mótan, Mal.). From (métu, mal. high land). Four months. A hill paddy in Malabar. Caroottary modan is a black, and Veloottary modan is a white variety. Land is ploughed twice in carcatacam [mausam] or july, then once a month from chingom or august to coombham or february; ploughed again in maidom or april when seed is sown with ten times the quantity of manure [yeroo] in the shape of ashes [neeroo] and cattle-dung [shauny]; over sown bed plough is plied once more; weeded in yedavam or may; crop cut in chingom or august.——*Molagoliky* (మొలకొలికి - molagoliki, Tel.). From (mola, tel. sprout + kuluku, tel. beauty). A principal paddy of Coromandel coast. Soil most suitable, black clay [calimunn]; ground prepared in july and august; by ploughing both in water and dry; seeds sown in august and september; first sown in nursery where there is good supply of water; transplanted after thirty or forty days' growth in nursery; must be watered well until it is ripe; grown to the height of 5 feet and appears white; cut after six months in the same way as pishaunam [q.v.]; average price, 28 imperial seers for 1 rupee.—— *Moondagampaula* (മുണ്ടകമ്പാല - muntakampála, Mal.). From (muntam, mal. dwarf + pála, mal. milky paddy). Five months. A Malabar paddy. Carotta moondagampaula is black; Chonna moondagampaula from (chukanna, mal. red) is red; Velootta moondagampaula is white.——*Moondagan* (മുണ്ടകൻ - muntakan, Mal.). From (muntam, mal. dwarfish); from absence of tail to ear. Five months. A Malabar paddy. Of slow growth, yields best straw. Caroo moondagam is black; Chompan moondagam, from (chempu, mal. copper) is red; Cheroo moondagam, is small; Chonna moondagam from (chukanna, mal. red) is red.——*Mosanam* (மோசனம் - mósanam, Tam.). From (mó, tam. to smell). A principal paddy of southern districts. Soil most suitable, regar [q.v.] sand [manal]; ground prepared in september and october; ploughing dry [gaddavary, pooldy caul, veligada]; seed sown in october and november broadcast; the crop must be cleared of weeds when it is tender; it does not require much water; full grown crop appears somewhat red and yellow; grows to 3 feet; cut after three months; average price, 34 imperial seers for 1 rupee; consumed by the poor.——*Nariyan* (நரியன் - nariyan, Tam.). From (nari, tam. jackal); wild paddy. Five months. Madura.——*Nawara* (നവര - navara, Mal.; நவரை - navarai, Tam.). From (navati, san. ninety); ninety days' paddy. Three months. A Malabar paddy; sown in the month of yedavam [mausam], may-june, and reaped in carcatacam [mausam], july-august; rice light; possesses medical properties. Carootta nawara is black; Nawara mookkony is three-cornered; Velootta nawara is white. Distinguish from Nivvary [q.v.].——*Neela shumbah* (நீலச்சம்பா - nílaççambá, Tam.). Means black shumbah, from color of paddy. A principal paddy of southern districts. Soil most suitable, regar [q.v.] sand [manal]; ground prepared in august and september, by ploughing dry [pooldycaul]; seed sown in august and september; sometimes by nursery [nauttangaul], generally by gorroo [q.v.]; no irrigation necessary for two months, but during that time weeds must be removed, afterwards the crop must be watered well till ripe; full grown crop is 5 feet high and appears somewhat black; cut after six months; average price, 30 imperial seers for 1 rupee.——*Neervellay* (நீர்வெள்ளை - nírvellai, Tam.). From (nír, tam. water + vellai, tam. white). Eight months. Chingleput.——*Nivvary* (नीवार - nívára, San.). Wild rice. See sep. title.——*Noova* (നൂവ - núva, Mal.). Five months. Malabar. Usual black and white varieties.——*Nullavary* (నల్లవరి - nallavari, Tel.). Means black paddy; from color of grain. A principal paddy of Coromandel coast. Soil most suitable is red clay or black loam; ground prepared at all times of the year, by ploughing wet [coodapa] four or five times, and manuring [yeroo]; seed sown broadcast at all times of the year; watering and weeding necessary; plant green up to 2 or 2½ feet; cut after three months; average price from 32 to 40 imperial seers for 1 rupee; generally eaten by the poor.——*Orpooval* (ഒരുപൂവൽ - orupúval, Mal.). Means single crop. A principal paddy of W. coast. Soil most suitable is that where silt has accumulated [adaimunn, vandalmunn]; ground prepared for the first crop in maidom [mausam] or april and yedavam or may; for the second in chingom or august and cunny or september; prepared by ploughing the land four or five times to the depth of 3 or 4 inches; rarely green manuring [yeroo] and mixing the ashes of dried leaves and cowdung [shauny] with the soil; first crop is sown in maidom or april and yedavam or may; second crop in chingom or august and cunny or september; generally the seeds are sown in nursery [nauttangaul] and transplanted; occasional weeding and thinning out are the only treatments while under growth; full grown crop has a yellow appearance; cut after five months.——*Ottadan* (ஒட்டடன் - ottadan, Tam.). From (ottu, tam. to stick); from the rough hairy grain sticking to hands and clothes. One of the varieties of pishaunam [q.v.]. Six and half months. Tanjore.——*Paundy* (പാണ്ടി - pánti, Mal.). Means paundyan land, as introduced from tinnevelly. Five months. Malabar. Choora paundy means bad smell; Ora paundy means border; Tekkan paundy means south.——*Pedda kesary* (పెద్దకేసరి - peddakésari, Tel.). Means large kesary [q.v.] A principal paddy of Coromandel coast. Soil most suitable, red loam; ground prepared in december and january; ploughed in water; seed sown in december and january; treatment like pishaunam [q.v.]; full grown crop appears somewhat white, grows to 3½ or 4 feet; cut after four months; average price, 52 imperial seers for 1 rupee.——*Pishaunam* (పిషానము - pishánamu, Tel.; பிசானம் - pisánam, Tam.). From (pishanga, san. tawny); from color of husk. A principal paddy of Coromandel coast. Soil most suitable, black clay [calimunn]; ground prepared in august and september being ploughed in water; seed sown in july, august and september; sown broadcast; the crop requires careful watering while tender and has to be cleared of weeds; when the plant grows to a height of a foot free supply of water is required until the crop bears fruit; full grown crop looks white and bows down level to the ground when the ears are long and full; cut after six months; average price, 28 imperial seers for 1 rupee; generally consumed by well-to-do people. Pishaunam is generally a later crop, as caur [q.v.] is an earlier one; all varieties of pishaunam are finer, and all varieties of caur are coarser; pishaunam rice is white; it is principally grown in the deltaic tracts [conamoogam] of the pennair and the cauvery.——*Pishiny* (பிசினி - pisini, Tam.). From (pisin, tam. gum). This is raised with dry seed sowing [pooldy caul] on high level nunjah [q.v.] lands, and also in poonjah [q.v.] lands which have some moisture. No irrigation is required; like poonjah crops, moisture alone contributes to the growth. The out-turn is not great. Four months. Chingleput.——*Ponnauran* (പൊന്നാരൻ - ponnáran, Mal.). From (pon, mal. gold + ñáru, mal. seedling). Four months. Malabar. ——*Poombaulay* (பூம்பாளை - púmbálai, Tam.). From (pú, tam. flower + pálai, tam. spathe); from color of grain. Eight months. Chingleput. This is cultivated in the fore shores of tanks and pools just previous to the rainy season; and even if water after rainfall stands to a height of a half or three fourths of yard, it shoots up higher than the level of the water and yields a good outturn.——*Potta* (പൊട്ട - potta, Mal.). Means high ground. So rice grown there. Four months. Malabar. Paddy dark.——*Potty kesary* (పొట్టికేసరి - pottikésari, Tel.). A short kesary. A principal paddy of Coromandel coast. Soil most suitable, red loam; ground prepared in january and february by ploughing in water; seed sown in january and february broadcast; treatment same as pishaunam [q.v.]; full grown crop appears somewhat white; grows to 3 feet; cut after three and half months; average price, 32 imperial seers for 1 rupee. ——*Potty nullavary* (పొట్టినల్లవరి - pottinallavari, Tel.). A short nullavary [q.v.]. A principal paddy of Coromandel coast. Soil most suitable, red loam; ground prepared in december, january, february and march by ploughing in water; seed sown in december, january, february and march, broadcast; treatment like pishaunam [q.v.], but weeding is not particularly observed; grows to 2½ feet and appears somewhat black; cut after three months; average price, 36 imperial seers for 1 rupee; consumed by poor.——*Pulliyaul* (പള്ളിയാൽ - palliyál, Mal.). From (pallam, mal. low land + ñáru, mal. seedling). Three months. A Malabar rice. Quick growing; needs no water; land is ploughed two rounds in yedavam [mausam] or may and soil pulverized; in mitoonam or june again ploughed and harrowed; in carcatacam or july the process is repeated and manure applied; seedlings [nautt] are then planted; crop cut in cunny or september. Cheroo pulliyaul is a small variety.——*Quail-necked paddy* (காடைக்கழுத்தன் - kádaikkazhuttan, Tam.). Southern districts; cultivation wet; ground prepared in pooratausby [mausam] or september by ploughing five or six times and richly manuring [yeroo]; seedlings [nautt] transplanted in arpisy or october; requires regular watering for the first three months; cut after five months; average price 20 measures per rupee [canday calootan].——*Rama baunam* (രാമബാണം - rámabánam, Mal.). From (ráma, san. the hero + bána, san. arrow); arrow-headed grain. Five months. Malabar.——*Sanna biyyam* (సన్నబియ్యము - sannabiyyamu, Tel.). From (sanna, tel. fine + biyyamu, tel. rice). Anantapore, Bellary and N. arcot. Capila sannabiyyam means brown; Garica sannabiyyam means bent grass, cynodon dactylon, pers., from stalks; Poolla sannabiyyam means whitish or reddish; Tella sannabiyyam means white. ——*Sanna raushy* (సన్నరాశి - sannaráshi, Tel.). From (sanna, tel. fine + ráshi, tel. kind). Four months. Kurnool.—— *Sannauloo* (సన్నాలు - sannálu, Tel.). Means fine grains. A Vizagapatam paddy. Caushy sannauloo means benares; Eetey sannauloo means lance, as fine as lance point; Gutty sannauloo means solid, from hard rice; Jaltaur sannauloo means gold lace, from color and fineness; Vanka sannauloo means curved, from grain; Yerra sannauloo means red, from color of grain.—— *Sannavary* (సన్నవరి - sannavari, Tel.). From (sanna, tel. fine + vari, tel. paddy). A principal paddy of Coromandel coast. Cultivated in clay soil [calimunn]; ground prepared in shrauvanam [mausam] or august and bhaudrapadam or september; ploughing the soil and levelling by harrow [goontaca]; seed sown in shrauvanam or august and bhaudrapadam or september; no nursery; sown broadcast; usual watering and weeding; full-grown crop 2 feet high; cut after six months; average price, 28 imperial seers for one rupee.——*Sarooloo* (సరులు - sarulu, Tel.). Means garland. A Vizagapatam paddy. Auk sarooloo means seedling; Canaka sarooloo means gold, from appearance of ears; Mootakauk sarooloo means coarse; Mootya sarooloo means pearl, from roundness of rice; Raja sarooloo means king, coarse; Ratna sarooloo means precious stone, fine; Sannauk sarooloo means fine; Vankauk sarooloo means curved. ——*Shirmany* (சிறுமணி - shirumani, Tam.). Means small grain. Six months.——*Shiva's neclace* (ஈசுரக்கோவை - ísurakkóvai, Tam.). From brown rice. Five to eight months. ——*Shoornay vellay* (சுருணைவெள்ளை - shurunaivellai, Tam.). From (shurul, tam. to curl + vellai, tam. white). A rare paddy on dry land. Coimbatore.——*Shumbah* (సంబావు - sambávu, Tel.; ചമ്പാൻ - champán, Mal.; சம்பா - shambá, Tam.). From (chempu, mal. copper); from color of grain. Four to six months. Superior kind of rice sown about July. Especially in Nellore, two Arcots, Chingleput, Tinnevelly, Madura, Coimbatore, and Malabar. Paddy white and rice red. The following are some of the different kinds:—Annadauna means cooked rice + gift, three to five months; Anna means food, good for food, five months; Aroopathaum means sixty days; Aunacomban means elephant tusk, from white and long rice, five months; Avaurampoo means cassia auriculata, linn. + flower, otherwise called gowry shumbah or red shumbah, five months; Bengal is imported seed; Calavan means mixed, six months; Calinga named from the country, four to six months; Camoogamboo means areca catechu, linn. + flower; from grains smelling like areca flowers; Caroom means dark; Cauday means quail; Caulaun means fungus, from smell; Caur means dark; Chinna means small, four months; Chinna bhogam means small and good; Choppoo, from (chukappu, mal. red), means red, eight months; Codan from (kódai, tam. hot season), means summer shumbah, cultivated in beginning of cultivation year, five months; Cooncooma means saffron, crocus sativus, linn., from color of grains; Coondrimany means retty seeds, abrus precatorius, linn.; Cooroom means short; Coothiray vauly means horse-tail, from appearance of ears; Coray means rush; Custoory means musk, two months; Cutty means lump, four months; Devaroyan from the ruler; Eerk from the rib of palm-leaf, grain long and slender, five months; Garica means bent grass, cynodon dactylon, pers., from stalks; Garoodan means braminy-kite, from color of braminy kite, red and yellow and rice white, five months; Goondoo means round, six months; Irpapoo means bassia longifolia, linn. + flower, from smell, five months; Jeeraca means seed of cuminum cyminum, linn., from size and fragrance, five to six months; Madhoora means sweet, seven months; Many means jewel; Milagoo means pepper, piper nigrum, linn., from appearance, six to seven months; Moottoo means pearl, paddy and rice grey, five months; Moplah meaning son-in-law, as being superior; Mullicay means jasmine, jasminum sambac, ait.; Mye means jet-black; Neela means black, six months; Oonda means ball, five months; Oosy means needle, from slender grain; Panamaram means palmyra, borassus flabelliformis, linn., three months; Paul meaning milky; Pedda means large; Periya means large, seven months; Poola means flowery; Poombaulay meaning flower spathe, from color of grain; Poonoogoo means civet, from smell; Sanna means small; Shaday means bushy, from appearance of ears, devaroyen first introduced it, four to seven months; Shem means red; Shem paulay means red palm flower spathe, from color of grain, four to five months; Shem pavala means red coral, from color of grain; Shirmany means small grain; Shiroo cooroombay means small + tender cocoanut or palmyra fruit, from fineness and color of grain; Tady means thick, eight months; Tirvarungam from (tiru, tam. sacred + arangam, tam. island), after shreerungam, six and a half to seven months; Totta means garden; Valiya means large, five months; Vauda means ship or originally imported; five months [paddy]; see below, separate title.——*Sookhdas* (سکھداس - sukhdás, Hind.). From (sukha, san. comfort + dá, san. to give). Also known as Irpa poo shumbah, from fragrance; used by Mahomedans in pilows [q.v.]. Five months. Superior.—— *Tavala cunnan* (തവളക്കണ്ണൻ - tavalakkannan, Mal.). From (tavala, mal. frog + kannu, mal. eye). Four months. Malabar. ——*Tekkan* (തെക്കൻ - tekkan, Mal.). Means southern. Four months. Malabar.——*Tillay* (தில்லை - tillai, Tam.). Means chidambaram. Six and half months. Tanjore.——*Tirvarungam* (திருவரங்கம் - tiruvarangam, Tam.). From Shreerungam originally. A principal paddy of southern districts. Soil most suitable, red loam; ground prepared in july and august; by ploughing the ground in water; seed sown in july and august; sown broadcast; carefully watered while plant is tender and weeds removed; after the plant grows to the height of a foot and a half, free supply of water is necessary until the crop is about to be reaped; full-grown crop has reddish appearance and grows to about 5 feet; cut after six and a half or seven months; average price, 30 imperial seers for 1 rupee.——*Tooyamully* (தூய்யமல்லி - tuyyamalli, Tam.). From (tuyya, tam. pure + malli, tam. jasmine, jasminum sambac, ait.); from clear white grain. Four to six months. Coimbatore and Salem.——*Vankey biyyam* (వంకెబియ్యము - vankebiyyamu, Tel.). From (vanke, tel. hook + biyyamu, tel. rice). Four months. Kurnool.——*Vary shumbah* (வரிசம்பா - varisambá, Tam.). From stripes or spots on paddy. A principal crop of southern districts. Cultivated in red or black loam; ground prepared at end of pungoony [mausam] or march and beginning of chittray or april; ploughed seven times and manured richly; seed sown at end of chittray or april; nursery sometimes used, sometimes not; no water is used till end of veiyaushy or may then fields are watered regularly and weeded once a month for three months from auny or june; full-grown crop about 3 feet high and of dim white color; cut after five months; average price, 20 measures per rupee.——*Vauda sannavary* (వాడసన్నవరి - vádasannavari, Tel.). From (váda, tel. ship + sannavari, tel. kind of paddy). Five to six months.——*Vauda shumbah* (வாடைசம்பா - vádaisambá, Tam.). Means ship shumbah. Otherwise calinga shumbah, from place whence introduced. A principal paddy of southern districts. Soil most suitable, regar [q.v.] sand [manal]; ground prepared in august and september by ploughing dry [gaddavary, pooldycaul, veligada]; seed sown in august and september; sown broad-cast; the same treatment as sannavary [q.v.]; full grown crop is 1 foot high and looks white; cut after five months; average price, 30 imperial seers for 1 rupee.——*Vaulaun* (வாலான் - válán, Tam.). From (vál, tam. tail); long-tailed grain.——*Velivary* (వెలివరి - velivari, Tel.). From (veli, contraction for veligada, tel. dry cultivation + vari, tel. paddy). Four months. Dry paddy cultivated to a very slight extent along different parts of the coast in low-lying land of the Nellore district. The land is manured [yeroo] and ploughed up two or three times, then twice more with the gorroo [q.v.], and a third time drilling the seed, and all is covered in. The seed is sown in August or early in September, and the crop harvested during December.——*Vellary* (വെള്ളരി - vellari, Mal.). From (vella, mal. white + ari, mal. rice). Four months. Malabar.——*Vellay* (வெள்ளை - vellai, Tam.). Meaning whiteness. Six months. Tinnevelly.——*Vellayauttan* (വെള്ളയാത്തൻ - vellayáttan, Mal.). From (vella, mal. white + akam, mal. inside). Five months. Malabar.——*Vellay milagy* (வெள்ளைமிளகி - vellaimilagi, Tam.). From (vellai, tam. white + milagu, tam. pepper, piper nigrum, linn.). White round grain.——*Yauradam* (యారదాలు - yáradálu, Tel.). From (eru, tel. to pick). Choice paddy.——*Yerra bakka* (ఎఱ్ఱబక్క - errabakka, Tel.). From (erra, tel. red + bakka, tel. lean). Four months. Kurnool.——(3) *Paddy bird* (बक - baka, san.). See sep. title.——*Paddy-field grass* (ಗದ್ದೆಮಡುವಿನಹುಲ್ಲು - gaddemaduvinahullu, Can.; దూస - dúsa, Tel.; தினை - tinai, Tam.). Can. from (gadde, can. paddy field + maduvu, can. hollow in a river + hullu, can. grass). Tam. from (tin, tam. to eat). Botanically Panicum [priyangoo] fluitans, retz., graminaceæ [vricsham, 156]. Clums 2–3 feet, creeping at the base; leaves long and smooth; mouths of the sheaths bearded and sub-ciliate; spike compound, partial ones alternate, adpressed; spikelets bifarious, elliptic; lower glume very short and truncated, upper obovate, rounded, a little shorter than the paleæ; lower flower neuter, one-valved; seed elliptic, acute, minutely wrinkled; moist rich soil; especially along banks of streams, ditches and edges of paddy fields.

PADDY BIRD (बक - baka, *San.*). Title from frequenting rice fields [paddy]. San. from (vak, san. to go crookedly). Ardeidæ family, cultirostres, grallatores, aves [pacshy, 46], of naturalists [jantoo]. Herons. Bill typically more slender than in storks [adjutant bird], very sharp, deeply cleft; legs long, scutellated; toes long, slender; outer toe only joined by web to middle one; hind toe long, on same plane as others; middle toe with inner edge of the claw dilated and pectinated; nostrils narrow, at basal extremity of a long furrow. Vary in size from that of stork [adjutant bird] to a rail [krishaungy]; most typical have long legs, long neck, and a considerable portion of tibia bare. For the most part solitary when feeding, but many roost together; habitually breed in society, majority on trees, a few among thick reeds. Eggs are from four to six in number, very pale blue or greenish. Young are helpless, and are fed by their parents till nearly full-grown. Sexes are alike or nearly so, the female being generally smaller, and with shorter crests or plumes. Usually watch for their prey, moving slowly about; and when unsuccessful, flying off to a fresh bit of water. They feed chiefly on fish [matsyam], crabs [nundoo], frogs [bhaicam]; a few on insects [poochy], which they seek for on land, among cattle [maud]. They rarely run; fly with ease, though not very fast. All have remarkable patches of dense down on breast and groins; these abound in a greasy powder which is secreted by the down, or rather consists of the abortive quill-shafts broken up; latter is used to render the feathers impervious to water, supplying the place partly of the oil-glands of other birds. The species best known to the natives are shown below.——*Black bill heron* (کلچیا - kilchiyá, Hind.; నల్లముక్కుకొంగ - nallamukkukonga, Tel.). Tel. from (nalla, tel. black + mukku, tel. bill + konga, tel. crane). Hind. also (kirchiyabaglá). Title otherwise Little egret. Herodias garzetta, ardeidæ [paddy bird], cultirostres, grallatores [pacshy, 46] of naturalists. Alias Ardea orientalis; Herodias immaculata.——*Black heron* (کالا بگلا - kálábaglá, Hind. and Dec.). Hind. from (kálá, hind. black + baglá, hind. heron). Hind. also (nolbaglá). Title otherwise Black bittern. Ardetta flavicollis, ardeidæ [paddy bird], cultirostres, grallatores [pacshy, 46], of naturalists. Alias Ardetta nigra, picta. Comes out to feed about sunset, and has low deep booming call, like the sound of a small drum [paray].——*Blind heron* (اندھا بگلا - andhábaglá, Hind. and Dec.; గుడ్డికొంగ - guddikonga, Tel.; കൊക്ക - kokka, Mal.; நொள்ளைமடையன் - nollaimadaiyan, Tam.). Title from oblique vision. Hind. from (andhá, hind. blind + baglá, hind. heron). Tel. from (guddi, tel. blind + konga, tel. crane). Mal. from (kottu, mal. to peck). Tam. from (nollai, tam. blindness + madaiyan, tam. fool). Hind. also (kánábaglá), meaning squint-eyed heron; (konchbaglá), meaning curlew heron. Tel. also (ralpuchake) from gond. Mal. also (koçça); (kuriyan). Tam. also (nárai), meaning grey. Title otherwise Madras paddy-bird, Pond heron. Ardeola leucoptera, ardeidæ [paddy bird], cultirostres, grallatores [pacshy, 46], of naturalists. Alias Ardea leucoptera, malaccensis. Adult in full breeding plumage has head crested, with long occipital white plumes; head and neck greyish yellow; back with feathers decomposed, dark maroon; wings, rump and upper tail-coverts, tail, and all beneath white; bill blue at base, yellowish in middle and edges, black at tip; orbits greenish yellow; irides bright yellow; legs and feet dull green; length 18½ inches; non-breeding dress, head, neck and breast fulvous with brown stripes, darkest on head; upper plumage pale ashy brown, wings except uppermost tertials white, and lower parts from the breast white; thigh-coverts fulvous. Common in rice-fields, close in the wake of grazing cattle [maud].——*Blue heron* (کبود - kabúd, Hind.; నారాయణపక్షి - náráyanapakshi, Tel.; നാരായണപക്ഷി - náráyanapakshi, Mal.; நாராயணன் - náráyanan, Tam.). Title from color of wings. Hind. from persian meaning blue. Tel. from (nára, san. water + ayana, san. abode + pakshi, san. bird); from being an aquatic bird and of blue color. Mal. like teloogoo. Tam. similar. Hind. also (sádákanka), meaning white + heron. Beng. also (aujan). Ardea cinerea, ardeidæ [paddy bird], cultirostres, grallatores [pacshy, 46], of naturalists. Alias Ardea brag. Back and wings fine bluish-grey. A favourite quarry for the Bheiry [q.v.].——*Cattle heron* (گائی بگلا - gáibaglá, Hind.; స్వాతికొంగ - svátikonga, Tel.). Title from following cattle. Hind. from (gái, hind. cow + baglá, hind. heron). Tel. from (sváti, contraction for svátikárte, tel. a part of the rainy season + konga, tel. crane), from its appearance at that time. Hind. also (surkhiyábaglá), meaning red heron; (doriyábaglá), meaning striped heron. Title otherwise Cattle egret. Buphus coromandus, ardeidæ [paddy bird], cultirostres, grallatores [pacshy, 46], of naturalists. Alias Ardea affinis, bubulcus, caboga, russata. In summer dress, whole head crested, neck and breast, rich golden buff, except chin and narrow median line on neck; dorsal plumes of the same hue, filamentose and decomposed, 8 or 9 inches long; elongated feathers of breast white at base, yellow at tip; rest of plumage pure white. Bill deep orange yellow; orbitar region yellowish pink; irides pale yellow; legs whitish green on tibia and below knee; rest of tarsus blackish green, with a reddish tinge on toes, which are greenish beneath. Length 21 inches. In non-breeding dress plumage is entirely white. Attends cattle [maud] whilst grazing, picks up grasshoppers [tattoo kily] and larvæ disturbed by them.——*Green heron* (کانچ بگلا - kánchbaglá, Hind.; ہرا بگلا - harábaglá, Dec.; దోసికొంగ - dósikonga, Tel.; தோசிக்கொக்கு - tósikkokku, Tam.). Title from color of wings. Hind. from (kánch, hind. glass + baglá, hind. heron). Dec. from (hará, hind. green + baglá, hind. heron). Tel. from (dóshí, san. wicked person + konga, tel. crane) [red heron]. Tam. from (dóshí, san. wicked + kokku, tam. stork). Hind. also (kánábaglá), meaning blind heron. Butorides javanica, ardeidæ [paddy bird], cultirostres, grallatores [pacshy, 46], of naturalists. Feathers of back dull green, upper tail-coverts greenish; wing-coverts glossy green; legs pale yellow green, soles dark yellow; affects nullahs [q.v.] perching on boughs overhanging water.——*Night heron* (واق - wák, Ar., Pers., Hind. and Dec.; చింతొక్కు - chintokku, Tel.). Title from appearing after sunset. Ar. from its cry. Nycticorax griseus, ardeidæ [paddy bird], cultirostres, grallatores [pacshy, 46], of naturalists. During day it roosts in groves, issuing forth after sunset; cry wak-wak.——*Pariah heron* (دھیربگلا - dherbaglá, Hind.; ಬಕ - bagala, Can.; మాలకొంగ - málakonga, Tel.). Hind. from (dher, hind. pariah + baglá, hind. heron). Tel. from (mála, tel. pariah + konga, tel. crane). Hind. also (turrabaglá), meaning tufted heron; (malangbaglá), meaning mendicant heron. Tel. also (peddatellakonga), meaning large + white + crane. Title otherwise Bengal paddy bird, Large egret. Herodias alba, ardeidæ [paddy bird], cultirostres, grallatores [pacshy, 46], of naturalists. Alias Ardea flavirostris, egretta, modesta, syrmatophorus, torra. Plumage pure white; roosting on trees.——*Red heron* (لال بگلا - lálbaglá, Hind. and Dec.; ಬಕ - baka, Can.; దోసికొంగ - dósikonga, Tel.). Title from color. Hind. from (lál, hind. red + baglá, hind. heron). Tel. from (dóshí, san. wicked person + konga, tel. crane) [green heron]. Beng. also (khyribogla.) Title otherwise Chestnut bittern. Ardetta cinnamomea, ardeidæ [paddy bird], cultirostres, grallatores [pacshy, 46], of naturalists.——*Snake heron* (ناری - nárí, Hind.; పాములనారిగాడు - pámulanárigádu, Tel.). Title from habit of protruding its head and long neck above grass. Tel. from (pámu, tel. snake + nárigádu, tel. proper name). Hind. also (lálkanka), meaning red heron. Ardea purpurea, ardcidæ [paddy bird], cultirostres, grallatores [pacshy, 46], of naturalists. Frequenting marshes. Rises with loud harsh cry, which it repeats as it flies along.——*Yellow heron* (جن بگلا - jinnbaglá, Hind.). Title from color. Hind. from (jinn, ar. a spirit + baglá, hind. heron). Hind. also (katbaglá), meaning wood heron. Ardetta sinensis, ardcidæ [paddy bird], cultirostres, grallatores [pacshy, 46], of naturalists. Alias Ardetta lepida, nebulosa.

PADOO (படு - padu, *Tam.*). To make, form; to fall, sink, die; to lie; to strike.——*Pada* (പട - pata, Mal.). From (padu, tam. to strike). War [paday].——*Padacootam* (പടക്കൂട്ടം - patakkúttam, Mal.). From (pata, mal. war + kúttam, mal. assembly). An assembly for war.——*Padaiyautchy* (படையாட்சி - padaiyáççi, tam.). From (padai, tam. ploughshare + ádchi, tam. rule). One of the higher divisions of the Pully [q.v.] caste. Employed in former times as soldiers. Some of them style themselves Naicks [q.v.]. They are now mostly cultivators. Numbers about 400,000; mostly in Tanjore and Trichinopoly [jauty].——*Padamara* (పడమర - padamara, Tel.). From (padu, tel. to fall, sink). Means west [padinyaur]. Prefix in place names; as Padamaty cumbum, meaning west cumbum.——*Padappam* (படப்பம் - padappam, Tam.). A populous centre, town surrounded by villages.——*Padavaid* (படவேடு - padavédu, Tam.). From (padai, tam. army + vídu, tel. town). Tam. also (nandapadavédu), meaning nundan, local ruler + place of that name. Village; North arcot dist.; Polore tal.; pop. 654; acres 11,899; lat. 12° 40′; long. 79° 09′; from Chittore S. 39 miles; from Polore N. 11 miles. Now almost deserted. Traditional capital of the Coorumba [q.v.] dynasty. Old city 16 miles in circumference. Shandavausal where fair was held and Pooshpagherry site of the flower market are 4 miles apart. Believed to have been entombed by a shower of dust and stones. Jungle has overgrown the whole ancient area. Two extensive ruined forts upon the plain built by Coorumbar. Another fort upon peak of Jawandies overlooks city. Two temples, one to Renoocaumbaul, other to Ramasawmy. The destruction of this great city is ascribed to the curse of Hanooman [q.v.] when Ravanan [q.v.] was protected by the goddess of the place. A pool of water is called Rama teertam. The place is called Nunda padavaid after the Chola nundan [q.v.], son of Oottoonga rajah, who after the conquest of the Coorumbar [q.v.] by the Cholans [q.v.] was placed in Padavaid as ruler.——*Padaveed* (പടവീട് - patavítu, Mal.; படைவீடு - padaivídu, Tam.). From (pada, tam. army + vídu, tam. house). Soldiers' quarters; arsenal [magazine].——*Paday* (படை - padai, Tam.). From (padu, tam. to strike). Army [pada]. Also plough-share [caur].——*Padinyaur* (പടിഞ്ഞാറ - patiññáru, Mal.). From (patu, mal. to sink + ñáyar, mal. sun). West [padamara]. Prefix in place names; as Padinyaurattara, meaning western village.——*Padinyaura corilagam* (പടിഞ്ഞാറ കോവിലകം - patiññárakóvilakam, Mal.). From (patiññár, mal. west + kóvilakam, mal. palace). Residence of the last junior rajah of Calicut [covilagam, zamorin]. See vol. I, 53.——*Padiyalandone* (படியளந்தோன் - padiyalandón, Tam.). From (padi, tam. step + alandón, tam. one who measured); from vishnoo as vaumanan having measured the three worlds [locam] by three steps. Vishnoo [trivicraman, vaumanan].——*Padoogay* (படுகை - padugai, Tam.). Land in the bed or on the banks of a river [aur] especially fit for rice [q.v.] cultivation. Ward of a town.——*Pady* (படி - padi, Tam.). From (padu, tam. to form). Step [padam].——*Paliport* (പള്ളിപ്പുറം - pallippuram, Mal.). From (palli, mal. church + puram, mal. outside); the village beyond the church. Mal. also (munambam), meaning point. Village, Port; Cochin state, Cochin tal.; pop. 1,283; lat. 10° 9′ N.; long. 76° 14′ E.; from Bombay S.E. 637 miles; from Cranganore S.S.W. 3 miles; from Ernacolum N.W. 12 miles; from Naracal N. 8 miles; from Cochin N.N.W. 13 miles. On Malabar coast. The seaport of Cranganore. Off this place is a mud-bank similar to those of Naracal and Alleppey. Chief place of a tract of country held in 1863 by an Englishman from the Travancore government. At one time property of Dutch. On a large island in the lake.——*Patla* (పట్ల - patla, Tel.). From (pattu, tel. to hold); holding. Place. Plural locative form. Suffix in place names; as Baupatla, meaning bramin's place.——*Patnaick* (പടനായക്കൻ - patanáyakkan, Mal.). From (pata, mal. army + náyakkan, mal. leader). Military officer in ancient Keralam [q.v.].——*Paud* (പാട് - pátu, Mal). From (petu, mal. to fall, lie). Situation. Rank of princes [padam].——*Paud* (పాడు - pádu, Tel.; പാട് - pátu, Mal.; பாடு - pádu, Tam.). From (padu, tam. to kill). Literally waste [haul, paul]. Village. Suffix in place names; as Calasapaud, meaning village of the waterpots.——*Paudair* (పాడేరు - páderu, Tel.). From (pádu, tel. waste + éru, tel. river).—"*a*" Division; Vizagapatam district; language partly Teloogoo and partly Khond; Boundaries:—E. Pottinghy division, S. Veeravilly and Golcondah division, W. Golcondah division, N. Mulkangherry division; physical aspect mountainous and rugged; soil fertile to some extent; agriculture is the chief industry; commerce, hill products, saffron [country saffron], tamarind [q.v.], piplee [long pepper], soap-nut [q.v.], myrobalans [q.v.], wax [mom], honey [shahad]. No irrigation.—"*b*" Deputy tahsildarry; Vizagapatam district. Pay Rs. 120.—"*c*" Village, Deputy tahsildar's station; Vizagapatam dist., Madgole zemindarry, Paudair magisterial division; lat. 18° 05′; long. 82° 42′; from Coraputt S. 48 miles; from Jeypore S.S.E. 52 miles; from Madras N.N.E. 370 miles; from Narsapatam N. 28 miles; from Parvatipore S.W. 68 miles; from Vizagapatam N.W. 48 miles; from Vizianagram W. 48 miles.——*Pauly* (പാടി - páti, Mal.; பாடி - pádi, Tam.). Village in a jungle tract [baudy, paud].——*Pauttom* (പാട്ടം - páttam, Mal.). See sep. title.——*Pulla* (பள்ள - palla, obl., Tam.). From (pallam, tam. low land). The corresponding terms are:—Tel. pully, Can. holeya, Mal. poolayan. A low caste employed in the cultivation of wet lands [nunjah], most commonly under the Vellaular [q.v.]. They are much upon the same footing as the Pariah [q.v.], but hold themselves superior to him, as they abstain from eating the flesh of the cow [pashoo]. They are the lowest of the right-hand caste [valangay]. They bury their dead [shavacaud] and have poojarries [q.v.] of their own castes. Their widows freely remarry. Divorces are common. They profess to be worshippers of Shiva [q.v.] or of Vishnoo [q.v.], but demon-worship is their real religion. Pullar are peculiar to the districts on the east coast south of the Coleroon. There is a Tamul proverb:—நெல்லு வகை எண்ணினாலும் பள்ளவகை எண்ணக் கூடாது—" though one may enumerate the various kinds of "rice [paddy], he cannot enumerate the varieties of the pulla "caste [jauty, pully]." See vol. I (35), (68); II, 226.——*Pullacherry* (பள்ளச்சேரி - pallaççéri, Tam.). Pully village [parcherry].——*Pulladam* (பல்லடம் - palladam, Tam.). See sep. title.——*Pullam* (పల్లము - pallamu, Tel.; പള്ളം - pallam, Mal.; பள்ளம் - pallam, Tam.). From (padu, tel. to fall). Low-lying ground.——*Pullava* (पल्लव - pallava, San.). From (pallam, tam. low land); people of the low-lying rice fields. The dynasty [raj] ruled at Conjeeveram from the 5th to 9th century. They are said to be the constructors of the monolithic raths [q.v.] at the Seven pagodas [q.v.] and the Booddhist [booddha] tope [q.v.] at Amravatty. Device a tiger [pooly]. Overthrown by Athonday [q.v.], the Chola [q.v.] king, who annexed the whole of their territories [charitram]. See vol. I (129).——*Pullaramulla* (पल्लवमल्ल - pallavamalla, San.). From (pallava, san. proper name + malla, san. wrestler). A Pullava king. See vol. I (130).——*Pullava rajah* (பல்லவராசா - pallavarásá, Tam.). One of the thirty-two gotrams [q.v.] of the true tamul-speaking Vellaular [q.v.] of Madura, Tanjore and Arcot. The name is borne as a title by the Chola vellaular inhabiting the valley of the Cauvery in Tanjore, who lay claim to the first rank; they found their claim to the title on the assertion that all their women are of royal race. The Tondiman [q.v.] of Poodoocottah, chief of the Culla [q.v.] tribe, has the title.——*Pullavaram* (பல்லாவரம் - pallávaram * Tam.). From (pallava, san. the dynasty + pura, san. city). Sanscrit name (pallavapura), meaning pullava city.—"*a*" Zemindarry; Chingleput dist., Sydapett tal.; pop. 1,597; acres 2,322; lat. 12° 58′; long. 80° 14′. Peshcush Rs. 1,430.—"*b*" Town, Cantonment, Railway station; Chingleput dist., Sydapett tal.; pop. 3,956; acres 902; lat 12° 59′; long. 80° 13′; height 74 R.S.; from Sydapett S.W. 5 miles; from St. Thomas' mount S. 3 miles; from the sea W. 8 miles. Formerly known as Presidency cantonment, native troops being stationed for garrisoning Presidency town. The lines were constructed for four regiments. Now a European pensioners' depôt. As a range of hills stand between the sea and the station, the temperature is high. The place is however healthy and the water is good and abundant. There is a bungalow [q.v.] on each of the two peaks of the range, the height of which is between 400 and 500 feet. In the neighbourhood is the Puncha pandava mullay which contains ancient remains. The foot of the hill contains mud pots and troughs being sarchophaguses of Pullavas [q.v.] or other ancient native tribes.——*Pullicondah* (பள்ளிக்கொண்டை - pallikkondai, Tam.). From (palli, tam. member of the caste + konda, tel. hill). Sanscrit name (ádiranga), means the first rungasawmy. Town; North arcot dist., Vellore tal.; pop. 2,814; acres 525; lat. 12° 55′; long. 78° 59′; height 2,187 feet; from Chittore S.S.W. 24 miles; from Vellore W. 13 miles. On southern bank of Palaur, opposite confluence with Goodiyattam river. Upon southern side rises a granite [caroomcull] hill Beejauchellam. Head-quarters of the old Vellore talook. Temple of Runganaicksawmy. The idol is Runganautan, a name applied also to deities of Tirpaucadal or Madhyarungam and Shreerungam or Antyarungam. Of the three Pullicondah the most ancient, Shreerungam the most modern. Bramhotsavam [pundigay, 6a] festival about May. In January the god circumambulates the hill. Two birds are fed with rice [q.v.] and ghee [q.v.]. If both eat greedily famine comes. If both eat moderately year flourishing. If only one eats, bad days. A free-standing dolmen [coday cull] with no subterranean or kistvaen [paundicoozhy] character, surrounded by a double ring of stones. Trade in hands of Lubbays [q.v.]. Manufacture of gunny [q.v.] and coray [q.v.] mats [boriyah]. Keikkilar [q.v.] weave rough cloths.——*Pullicootam* (പള്ളിക്കൂടം - pallikkútam, Mal.). From (palli, mal. village + kúttam, mal. assembly). A village school [pyall].——*Pulliyaul* (പള്ളിയാൽ - palliyál, Mal.). From (pallam, mal. lowland + ñáru, mal. seedling). A Malabar rice. Quick growing; needs no water; sown in April; two crops annually. Cheroopulliyaul is a small variety [paddy].——*Pully* (پلی - pallí, Hind.; పల్లి - palli, Tel.; പള്ളി - palli, Mal.; பள்ளி - palli, Tam.). From (pallam, tam. low land).—"*a*" Agricultural village. Suffix in place names [hully, milly, villy]. Also public building, palace.—"*b*" A tribe synonymous with Vunniyan [q.v.]; similar to the Pullar [q.v.], but more especially occupying the country districts. They are properly called Vanapully, and to be distinguished from the Meenpully who are fishermen. They eat animal food and drink spirituous liquors. Their women continue marriageable after the age of puberty. They cannot be divorced for any cause except adultery. The men are allowed a plurality of wives. They bury their dead [shavacaud]. They have no gooroo [q.v.], but the Punchaungy [q.v.] acts as their poorohit [q.v.] at births, marriages, and other celebrations. They wear the mark of Vishnoo's sect [naumam], and sometimes pray to Vencatramanan, but the proper god of the caste is Dharma rajah, who is worshipped by offerings of fruit, flowers, &c. They have temples of this god attended by poojarries [q.v.] of their own caste. They also worship the Shacties [q.v.] or destructive powers, and endeavour to avert their wrath by bloody sacrifices [baly, yanyam]. Deities of this sort worshipped by them are Mootyaulamman, Mauriyamman, and Poolauriyamman. They have hereditary chiefs called Yejmauns, who settle disputes with the assistance of an assembly of the people, when such matters are referred to them by the persons interested. The Pullies have many sub-divisions, none of which intermarry with each other, but all can eat in common. Numbers about a million and a quarter, mostly in southern Tamul districts. See vol. I (129); II, 230.——*Pulmanair* (பல்லமனேரி - pallamanéri, Tam.). See sep. title.——*Putcut* (పట్టుకట్టు - pattukattu, Tel.; பத்துக்கட்டு - pattukkattu, Tam.). From (pattu, tam. to hold + kattu, tam. to bind). A ryot's [q.v.] usual holding.——*Putnool* (பட்டுநூற்காரன் - pattunúrgáran, Tam.). From (pattu, tam. silk + núl, tam. thread + kára, san. doer). Tel. is Puttsauley. People that work in silk [puttoo], supposed to have come from places adjoining Surat near Bombay. They speak a Goozeratty [q.v.] dialect, often called here the Putnool language. They have settled in Tripatty, Arnee, Vellore, Trichinopoly, Combaconum, Tanjore, Madura, and other large towns. They are called Chetties [q.v.] or merchants by tamuls, presumably because they themselves retail the cloths which they weave without the intervention of middlemen. They have a fair skin and expressive features, and their women are beautiful but do not bear a very reputable character. They wear thread [poonool]. They never intermarry except in their own community. They profess to abstain from animal food. They rank among the higher castes. They acknowledge priests from among themselves as well as from among bramins. In religion they are divided into Smartas [q.v.], Veishnavites [q.v.], and Vyaupauries [q.v.], some among the Smartas being Lingayets [q.v.]. Those who can write employ the teloogoo characters in writing their language. The Putnoolcaurar were induced to settle in Madura by one of the earlier Naick [q.v.] kings. The Putnoolcaurar make cloth of a very rich, strong fabric, also turbans [q.v.] of a thin fabric of cotton [q.v.], and silk [puttoo]; also thin white muslins [q.v.] with silk borders; also plain green and colored striped muslins with silk borders. Numbers about 80,000 [janty]. See vol. I (66); II, 230.——*Putt* (పట్టు - pattu, Tel.; പട്ടു - pattu, Mal.; பட்டு - pattu, Tam.). Tel. from (pattu, tel. to hold). Village. Suffix in places names [putty].——*Puttaday* (பட்டடை - pattadai, Tam.). From (padu, tam. to lie + adai, tam. resort). A mechanic's shop [caurgah, panipoora].——*Puttay* (பட்டை - pattai, Tam.). From (padu, tam. to lie); layer. Anything flat and broad. Bark; one of the Dravidian terms for plant products added to the word-root [vricsham.].——*Putticaud* (பட்டிக்காடு - pattikkádu, Tam.). From (patti, tam. cattle-fold + kádu, tam. forest). Scattered hamlet.——*Puttimaud* (பட்டிமாடு - pattimádu, Tam.). From (patti, tam. cattle-pen + mádu, tam. bull or cow). Stray cattle [bandela, inam, putty].——*Puttoo* (कीटज - kítaja, San.; ریشم - resham, Hind.; ಪಟ್ಟೆ - patte, Can.; పట్టు - pattu, Tel.; പട്ടു - pattu, Mal; பட்டு - pattu, Tam.). San. from (kíta, san. worm + jan, san. to be born). Hind. from persian. Dravid. from (padu, to form a layer). Silk. Produced by two families of Lepidopterous caterpillars, Bombycidæ and Saturnidæ. The family Bombycidæ comprises four genera; Bombyx, Ocinera, Theoahila, Trilocha. The genus Bombyx includes six species, forming the domesticated silk-worm or the mulberry silk-worm. The only south indian species of this genus is the Bombyx mori, linn., or the common silk-worm. The other south indian representative of the Bombycidæ is the Trilocha varians, walker. The family of Saturnidæ comprises two south indian genera, the Actias and the Antheræa. The genus Actias contains the south indian species Actias selene, mcleay; the genus Antheræa contains the south indian species Antheræa perrottei, guer men., and Antheræa mylitta, drury, the tusser silk moth. Of all these silkworms the best known are Bombyx mori, linn., and Antheræa mylitta, drury. The worms pass through four different stages, a period of five days intervening between each. These stages are called by the natives the first, second, third and fourth fevers, each one lasting for a day. At the first fever the worm turns red, and ten days after the last attack it turns white; after this second change it again turns red on the following day, upon which it begins to spin. When the cocoons [peelah] are gathered they are boiled for some time; they are then dried in the sun and again soaked in boiling water, after which they are reeled. The principal plants upon which the indigenous silkworms feed are as follows:—Anogeissus latifolia, vekkauly; Bombax malabaricum, red cotton tree; Careya arborea, hindostany slow match; Carissa carandas, carondah; Eugenia jambolana, common jaumoon; Ficus religiosa, peepul; Ficus retusa, chinese banyan; Lagerstrœmia indica, china privet; Lagerstrœmia parviflora, loose strife; Odina wodier, wodier; Ricinus communis, castor oil; Shorea robusta, common saul; Tectona grandis, teak; Terminalia arjuna, arjoon; Terminalia catappa, country almond; Terminalia tomentosa, var., typica, black murdah; Zizyphus jujuba, bair. The manufacture of colored silk stuffs was originally introduced into India from China. They are mentioned in the Ramayanam [q.v.]. νῆμα σηρικόν or silk thread was imported from China into Barugaza and the marts of the Tamul country according to the Periplus. Raw silk in the Tamul country comes now chiefly from Bombay, Bangalore, and Collegaul in the Coimbatore district. That imported from Bombay is China produce and the best; the others are indigenous. In reeling or winding, silk is classified according to fineness of the thread, the several descriptions being fine, thin, thick, rough. Silk not classified is called mottapiry. The refuse or rubbish called boochkah [q.v.] is used for carpet-making [jamkhana]. The first three are largely used. The rough is in requisition for use in the manufacture of female silk cloths. In dyeing, the colors in use are white, red, yellow, amber color, black, blue, green, crimson. The dyeing materials used are mostly vegetable, but metal dyes are used for black. All the colors may be called fast colors. The following are the articles used for each dye:—white, fuller's earth [dhoby's earth]; red, fuller's earth, saffron [country saffron], alum [padicauram] powder, stick-lac [q.v.]; yellow, milk hedge [q.v.] ashes, choonam [q.v.], capilapody [kamela] dye powder, alum [padicauram], fuller's earth [dhoby's earth], sesamum [gingelly] oil; amber color or nimilay, the same articles as for yellow; black, iron [anhun] dross or oxide of iron, gallnut [mauchicoy] powder, sulphate of iron [annabhaidy], castor [aumanac] oil; blue, the same as for red silk, and in addition indigo [q.v.] and gallnut [mauchicoy]; green, the same as for yellow, and in addition saffron, peels of pomegranate [anaur], and gallnut; crimson, alum, seeds called vishtoo, crimson seeds [shauyam]. Coloring requires much practical skill. It consists chiefly in boiling water to a certain degree and mixing the powder or solution of the articles and steeping the silk. Dyers combine with dyeing a trade either in dyed silk or in articles used for dyeing or weaving [nesavoo]. It is not lawful for Mussalmans [q.v.] to wear pure silk, but they can wear silk mixed with cotton [q.v.]. Silk-worm's nests are said to be medicinally tonic, used with electuaries. The cocoon is Peelah. Reeled silk is Putnool, which gives its name to a caste. The silkworm is Puttoopoochy. For jungle silk see Tusser.——*Puttoocottah* (பட்டுக்கோட்டை - pattukkóttai, Tam.). See sep. title.——*Putty* (பட்டி - patti, Tam.). From (padu, tam. to lie). Cattle or sheep fold; land sufficient for cattle [maud] or sheep [aud] fold; small area; small corn-field; share; salt-pan; small village. Common suffix to village names. Towards the west pully or pulley, and in Canarese tracts hully or hutty.

PADOUK (महाकुटज - mahákutaja, *San.*; ಹನಿ - hani, *Can.*; ఎఱ్ఱవేగిస - erravégisa, *Tel.*). Title from burmese. San. from (mahá, san. great + kutaja, san. holarrhena antidysenterica, wall). Tel. from (erra, tel. red + végisa, tel. pterocarpus marsupium, rox.); from color of wood. Can. also (hane). Title otherwise Andaman redwood, Burmese kino, Burmese rosewood, Rangoon kino. Botanically Pterocarpus [vengay] indicus, willd., leguminosæ [vricsham, 48]. Alias Pterocarpus dalbergioides, wallichii. Tree; leaflets about nine, alternate, ovate or oval with a sudden bluntish acumination; panicles axillary; bracts subulate, caducous; petals long-clawed, curled and waved on the margins; stamens united into a sheath, split down on the upper side only, flowers yellow. A large timber tree [maram]; long waving branches and clusters of yellow flowers, fragrant; yields a kino [q.v.]. The wood is not unlike mahogany, but is more heavy, red and coarse grained; that of the root is highly variegated, closer-grained and darker-colored; used for furniture, and by the burmese to make their musical instruments; also employed for light field beams, cheeks, axle cases, poles, waggon perches, and framing, &c.

PADRE (பாதிரி - páthiri, *Tam.*). Portuguese for father. A missionary or clergyman [mishammah]. Distinguish from pauthiry [q.v.] tree.

PAGODA (بتکده - butkadah, *Hind.*). Title from (bhagavatí, san. durgá, the auspicious deity). Hind. from (but, pers. idol + kadah, pers. place).—"*a*" Anglo-indian for a native temple [coil], the first noticed by Portuguese having been on the W.

coast to that goddess. An old saying is that a village [oor] without a temple is unfit for human habitation, and so every considerable village has them dedicated either to Vishnoo [q.v.] or Shiva [q.v.]. There is a Tamul proverb :—கோயிலே யும் குளத்தையும் அடுத்து இருக்கவேண்டும்—" one "should reside near a temple [coil] and a tank [q.v.]." There is another:—கோயில் இல்லா ஊரிலே குடியிருக்கலாமா— "may one dwell in a village in which there is no temple ?" In many temples no service [poojah] is performed except on festival occasions [puudigay]. In the more wealthy temples daily service is kept up, a regular establishment being entertained as follows :—Acharries [q.v.] or local preceptors ; Poojarries [q.v.] or officiating priests ; Musicians [mailam], generally of the barber [mungala] caste ; Dancing girls [devadausy] ; Condicaud or sweeper and peon, who also supplies flowers for service. In a larger number of cases, especially in pagodas situated upon hills, weekly service is performed on Saturdays or Mondays, according as the deity is Vishnoo or Shiva. Idols [shilay, vigraham] as a rule face the east or towards the rising sun. In a few temples, said to have been built by Janamejayan, they face towards the west. Cf. the temples of Isis and Osiris in Egypt Hanooman [q.v.] as a rule faces to the south in commemoration of his expeditious journey to Lunka or Ceylon. There are besides, village goddesses [graumadevatay], who are generally worshipped at the outskirts of the villages under various names, Sooncoolamma, Yellamma, Gungammah, Ramoolamma. Tuesday and Friday are their favourite days, on which vows are performed and sheep [aud] or fowls [moorghy] sacrificed. All classes of people worship the goddesses, but the Bramins [q.v.] and others who do not eat flesh make the animal offerings through Shoodras [q.v.]. Almost all temples are endowed with lands [devadauyam], grants [inam] of former rulers. They are registered in the name of the deity or the officiating priest or the attendant servant. Vishnoo [q.v.] is worshipped under a variety of names, and the idol is generally an image formed according to the particular legend [mahautmyam, stala pooraunam] applicable. Thus Chennakeshwarasawmy, besides the chuckram [q.v.] and chunk [q.v.] in his two upper hands, holds the gadah or club in his left hand and exhibits the palm of the right hand uplifted to the worshipper as a symbol of encouragement and hope. Shree vencataishan stretches his right hand downwards , a symbol of his adoring shiva [q.v.]. Vengopaul is represented as playing upon a flute like a shepherd boy [krishnan], with his left leg carried over the lower part of the right leg. In a few places sacred shalagrams [q.v.] are worshipped, while in others a simple stone with perpendicular marks representing Vishnoo's feet is worshipped by the name of Ramasawmy. Shiva [q.v.] is generally worshipped in the form of a lingam [q.v.] or stone, generally rounded at the top but in some cases unworked. In Shiva temples the service is performed by Jangams [q.v.] and Tambalas, but abhishaicam [q.v.] or ablutions [snaunam] with vedic muntrams [q.v.] are performed by bramins [q.v.] alone [matam]. Friar jordanus, the quilon bishop of the fourteenth century, has the following :—" in this greater india [q.v.] many " sacrifice themselves to idols in this way ; when they are sick, " or involved in any grave mischance, they vow themselves to " the idol if they should happen to be delivered ; then when they " have recovered, they fatten themselves for one or two years " continually eating and drinking fat things, &c. ; and when " another festival comes round, they cover themselves with " flowers and perfumes, and crown themselves with white " garlands, and go singing and playing before the idol when it " is carried through the land, like the image of the virgin mary " [maryam] here among us at the rogation tides, and those men " who are sacrificing themselves to the idol carry a sword with " two handles, like those knives which are used in currying " leather [chamrah] ; and after they have shown off a great deal, " they put the sword to the back of the neck, cutting strongly " with a vigorous exertion of both hands, and so cut off their " own heads before the idol." Barbosa says that the king of quilacare or coliacaud [calicut], a city near cape comorin [q.v.], after reigning twelve years, always sacrificed himself to an idol in this way [mahamagham]. See vol. I (78).—" *b* " Ancient gold coin not now current. So called on account of impression of temple thereon. 22½ double fanams = 1 pagoda [naunyam, 2 a.e.f]. Approximate actual value, 1 pagoda = 3½ rupees. In the tamul countries called star pagoda, the value being 3½ rupees ; in teloogoo countries called kurruck pagoda, the value being 4 rupees. Same as San. dharanam ; Hind. hoon. Pagodas differ in shape from all european coins ; they have a convex side with prominent dots, and a flat side, which generally bears a figure, and in some three figures, of native deities ; pagodas of masulipatam and pondicherry have nothing on the convex side but the dots ; tippoo's pagodas have no figures on the flat side, but a legend. As to the figures, three principal types are conspicuous ; the standing figure of vishnoo [q.v.], with or without his two wives ; the seated figure of doorga [q.v.] ; the effigies of shiva [q.v.] and parvaty [q.v.] seated. Of the first type are :—the Star pagoda of the East india company so called from the star impressed on the granulated reverse ; Porto novo pagoda, believed to have been first coined by the Portuguese at Porto novo or Farangipett, and at Arcot under the Nivayat [q.v.] nawaubs [q.v.] of the Carnatic [q.v.] ; Kurruck [q.v.] pagoda of Wallajah, having the three standing figures strongly marked and a plain granulated reverse. As to the second type ; Doorga pagodas constituted the bulk of those current in the Ceded districts [q.v.] at the time they were brought under British administration ; they are known by the names of Doorga, Goorramcondah, Hurpanhully old and new, Chitaldroog, &c. The third class having the figure of Shiva and Parvaty, someties called Oomamaheshwara pagodas, were coined at Ikkairy and afterwards at Bednore ; they were current chiefly in Mysore. Accounts at madras down to 1818 were kept in pagodas, fanams [q.v.], and cash [q.v.] ; viz., 80 cash = 1 single fanam, 42 single fanams = 1 pagoda ; in the year named the rupee [q.v.] was made the standard coin ; the pagoda was then reckoned as equivalent to 3½ rupees. The following are different kinds of pagoda coins :—Ahmedy from ahmed, one of prophet's alams [q.v.] ; coimbatore coin, $23\frac{151}{1024}$ to 100 star pagodas ; canara coin, $21\frac{7}{8}$ to 100 star pagodas ; cuddapah coin, 23 and 15 fanams to 100 star pagodas. Anandrye ; gold, issued by anandrye [q.v.] of travancore ; 100 equal to 21·708 madras mohurs [q.v.] of 15 rupees each, or 92·857 star pagodas. Bahaudry, called after hyder ally, gold struck at mysore being a substitute for the ikkairy ; ordinarily 97 to 100 star pagodas ; madura coin 92 and 11¼ cash to 100 star pagodas ; malabar coin $84\frac{28}{33}$ or $92\frac{1}{3}$ to 100 star pagodas ; canara coin, 87½ to 100 star pagodas ; coimbatore coin $92\frac{151}{256}$ to 100 star pagodas ; bellary coin 92 and 36 fanams and 45 cash to 100 star pagodas ; arcot coin $92\frac{16}{27}$ to 100 star pagodas ; salem coin $91\frac{77}{103}$ to 100 star pagodas. Bangalore ; gold ; bellary coin 92 and 27 fanams and 52 cash to 100 star pagodas ; cuddapah coin 94 and 5 fanams 50 cash to 100 star pagodas ; salem coin $94\frac{2}{17}$ to 100 star pagodas. Canteroy, from king canteroy narsa ; bellary and cuddapah, rs. 2-14-8 sub-divided into 10 fanams of $4\frac{2}{3}$ annas each [canteroy]. Cully, from one kaliyoog [q.v.] rajah of w. coast ; rs. 2-12-0 ; contains 10 fanams, each of ·212 rupees or 3 annas 4¾ pies, and = 80 cash. Ferokhee, from (farrukhí, hind. auspicious) ; coimbatore coin, $92\frac{151}{256}$ to 100 star pagodas ; salem coin, $91\frac{29}{32}$ to 100 star pagodas. Gajapaty, having impression of elephant [q.v.], struck by prataupa roodran [q.v.], of cuttack. Ganda perandam, impression of the fabulous bird [gandaperandam]. Ghutty, from (ghatti, can. solid), same value as bahaudry ; s. canara. Haley ikkairy, old ikkairy, struck by shivaroya of ikkairy ; as distinguished from hosa ikkairy by poorniah in 1800. Hurpanhully, bellary coin, old, 102 and 29 fanams and 43 cash to 100 star pagodas ; new, 109 and 3 fanams and 60 cash to 100 star pagodas. Ikkairy, from the place near seringapatam ; coimbatore coin, 93 to 100 star pagodas ; salem coin, $92\frac{8}{11}$ to 100 star pagodas ; about 4 rupees contained 13 gold fanams ; no gold pagodas were before hyder struck by the mysore rulers themselves, they were issued by the local rajah of ikkairy ; these were adopted by hyder ally under the name of the bahaudry pagoda ; the latter was followed by the sultauny hoon [q.v.] of tippoo. Jemsherry, canara coin, 93½ to 100 star pagodas ; bellary, coin ,98 and 21 fanams and 7 cash to 100 star pagodas. Kurruck, from (karukku, tam. bas-relief) ; arcot coin $90\frac{10}{11}$ to 100 star pagodas. Lutchmy narrain, from the impression of the god vishnoo and his wife. Mitta, from (mitta, tel.) means high relief ; nellore, guntoor and other former nawaub's districts = rs. 3-15-7⅕ or 100 to 385 arcot rupees ; it was divided into 52 fanams and each fanam into 80 cash. Mysore, struck by hyder ; figure on one side of lutchmy [q.v.] and narsimhan [q.v.]. New veeroye, malabar = 2-13-8½ ; divided into 10 fanams of 4·57 annas each, or 3½ fanam = 1 rupee ; the fanam divided into 40 cash. Oomamaheshwara, from (umámahéshvara, san. shiva and párvatí) ; struck by krishna deva royel of vijianugger. Porto novo, about 17¼ carats [q.v.], or ·720 fine ; the exchange used to be 120 porto novo pagodas for 100 star, or 1 porto novo pagoda = 36 fanams in government accounts, and 37½ in the bazaar ; malabar coin, 116½ to 100 star pagodas ; seringapatam, 120 and 13 fanam and 68 cash to 100 star pagodas ; salem, tanjore, coimbatore, and madura coins 120 to 100 star pagodas ; arcot coins, 123½ to 100 star pagodas. Pulliputt, from place so called, in north arcot = rs. 2-10-0. Sawmy ; otherwise three sawmy-pagoda ; gold coin, bearing on one side the figure of the god chennakeshwarasawmy and on the other side, oobhaya nauchiyaur, his two wives bhoodevy and shreedevy ; 10 per cent. better than star pagoda. Scott, from name of some european officer or adventurer ; tanjore ; 121½ to 100 star pagodas. Shooly, from (shuzhi, tam. curve) ; otherwise chuckram [q.v.] of the south carnatic [q.v.] ; = 1·165 rupees or 3 to a star pagoda ; divided into 10 fanams, each = 1 anna 10·4 pies. Sowdaury, bellary, 108 and 19 fanams and 55 cash to 100 star pagodas. Star pagoda from star impression on the reverse coined at tirvaumore near madras [naunyam, varauhan] ; see vol. I, 617, foot note. St. thomas' ; canara coin ; $63\frac{7}{11}$ to 100 star pagodas. Sultauny, tippoo's coin, malabar coin, $84\frac{28}{33}$ to 100 star pagodas ; arcot coin $92\frac{16}{27}$ to 100 star pagodas ; coimbatore coin, $92\frac{151}{256}$ to 100 star pagodas ; salem coin, $91\frac{77}{103}$ to 100 star pagodas. Vencatramana, from tripatty god ; a chundragherry coinage.—" *c* " Goldsmith's weight 9 fanams = 1 pagoda ; 10 pagodas = 1 pollum [niray, 3a.b.c.] Approximate actual value 1 pagoda = 54 grains. In seed weight equal to 36 goonj [goomchy] seeds. As a jewel weight = 19 carats [q.v.]. Same as Varauhaniday. See vol. I, 609 ; II, 518.——*Pagoda tree* (खैराचांपा - khairáchámpá, Mahr. ; काडचंपे - kádachampé, Conc. ; گل آچین - guláchín, Hind., ದೇವಗಣಗಲು - dévaganagalu, Can. ; ಗೋಸಂಪಗೆ - gósampige, Too. ; వాడగన్నేరు - vádagannéru, Tel. ; വെളുത്തരളി - veluttarali, Mal. ; அலரிய-

alariya, Singh.; ஈழத்தலரி - ízhattalari, Tam.). Title from being found about pagodas [q.v.]. Mahr. from (khairá, mahr. white sprinkled with red + champaka, san. michelia champaca, linn.). Conc. means wild champak. Can. from (déva, san. god + ganagalu, can. nerium odorum, sol.); from being found ab ut temples. Too. from (gó, too. cow + champaka, san. michelia champaca, linn.). Tel. from (váda, tel. fragrance + gannéru, tel. nerium odorum, sol.). Mal. from (velutta, mal. white + arali, mal. nerium odorum, soland). Tam. from (ízham, tam. gold + alari, tam. nerium odorum, soland); flower like gannair [q.v.] and yellow within. Can. also (kádusampige). meaning forest + michelia champaca, linn.; from similar odour of flowers. Tel. also (adavigannéru), meaning forest + nerium odorum, sol. Mal. also (arali). Singh. also (kanéru). Tam. also (perungalli), meaning large + euphorbia tirucalli, linn., from leafless branches resembling milk hedge [q.v.]; (kallimandárai), meaning euphorbia tirucalli, linn. + bauhinia, from milky stem and flowers like ebony [q.v.]; (návillávalari), meaning tongue + having not + nerium odorum, soland, without filaments in flower. Title otherwise Gool-i-cheen, Milky bauhinia, Red jasmine, Spanish jasmine. Botanically Plumeria acutifolia, poir., apocynaceæ [vricsham, 87]. Alias Plumeria acuminata, obtusifolia. Flos convolutus of rumphius. Small size with crooked trunk and rough bark; branches swollen and leafy at the tips; leaves 8–12 inches; petiole 1–1½ inches, one-glandular at the top; flowers many, fragrant, pink externally, white within; follicles about 5 inches long, cylindric. Hardy tree; large, lanceolate, smooth leaves; corymbs of large, pure-white flowers, with interior of cup yellow; flowers during hot and rainy seasons; introduced into india by the portuguese from brazil; planted in churchyards of native christians, that it may deck the graves with its white deciduous flowers. Leaves made into poultice used medicinally to dispel swellings; milky sap rubefacient in rheumatic pains; root violent cathartic. No other common species here. Same title is also sometimes given to the Banyan [q.v.].

PAGOO (பகு - pagu, *Tam.*). To divide.——*Pagal* (பகல் - Tam.). From (pagu, tam. to separate). Break of dawn. So day light [ahas], as measure of time; 2 nairams or half daylights = 1 pagal [caulam, 1].——*Pagoothy* (പകുതി - pakuti, Mal.; பகுதி - paguthi, Tam.). From (pagu, tam. to divide). Portion [bhangam]. Suffix in place names; as Keel pagoothy, meaning eastern portion. Pagoothy olay, from (óla, mal. palm leaf), is a deed of division of hereditary property [cawny] among relations [amshapatram]. ——*Pauthy* (പാതി - páti, Mal.; பாதி - páthi, Tam.). From (pagu, tam. to divide). Half. Portion. Suffix in place names; as Vadapauthy, meaning northern portion.——*Puggum* (పగ్గము - paggamu, Tel.). From (pagu, tam. to divide); a composite twisted cord. Rope. Linear measure. Used in measuring land. 16 veesams = 1 puggam [alavay, 1b]. Approximate actual value, 1 puggam = 132 feet. Godavery. There are other puggams. Compare jareeb. See vol. 1 609; II. 511.——*Pungoo* (பங்கு - pangu, Tam.). From (pagu, tam. to divide). Share. Pungauly is a shareholder, especially of village lands. Pungoocauran is a co-sharer. Pungoo maulay is a list of shares. Pungoovaly, from (vazhi, tam. succession), is a village held by coparceners; the lands are distributed at various times according to the votes of the majority of the sharers, and are held in severalty for a given time under such distribution [caraiyeed].

PAGOOTHY (பகுதி - paguthi, *Tam.*). From (prakriti, san. root) [pra]. Root in grammar [lacshanam], thus defined in Nunnool:—"Indivisible words, or either nouns, verbs, particles, "or qualifying words, as adjectives and adverbs, which have "been arbitrarily set apart from time immemorial, and cannot "be divided or analysed, except into unmeaning sounds or "syllables." Regarding the connection of Dravidian roots among themselves the following twenty-four examples consist of the words which are cited by Maumidy vencayya in the Andhra deepacam [q.v.] as an example of pure Teloogoo words. They are taken without addition or rejection, and against them are set the roots which mean the same thing in Canarese and Tamul. It will be seen that with very few failures there are identical words with identical senses in each language.——*Child* (కొడుకు - koduku, Tel.; குழந்தை - kuzhandai, Tam.; Can. fails).——*Cold* (ಛಳಿ - chhali, Can.; చలి - tsali, Tel.; சளி - shali, tam.)——*Curd* (పెరుగు - perugu, Tel.; பெருகு - perugu, Tam.; Can. fails). ——*Displeasure* (అలుక - aluka, Tel.; அலுப்பு - aluppu, Tam.; Can. fails).——*Earth* (ಪೊಡವಿ - podavi, Can.; పుడమి - pudami, Tel.; புடவி - pudavi, Tam.).——*Field* (ಮಡಿ - madi, Can.; మడి - madi, Tel.; மடி - madi, Tam.).——*Ghee* (ಬೆಣ್ಣೆ - benne, Can.; నెయ్యి - neyyi, Tel.; நெய் - ney, Tam.). The Canarese here means butter, which is almost the same thing.——*Gold color* (ಪಸುರು - pasuru, Can.; పసిడి - pasidi, Tel.; பசுப்பு - pasuppu, Tam.).——*Head* (ತಲೆ - tale, Can.; తల - tala, Tel.; தலை - talai, Tam.).——*Hot weather* (ಬೇಸಿಗೆ - bésige, Can.; వేసవి - vésavi, Tel.; வெசவி - vesavi, Tam.).——*Man* (ಮಗ - maga, Can.; మగవాడు - magavádu, Tel.; மகன் - magan, Tam.).——*Milk* (ಹಾಲು - hálu, Can.; పాలు - pálu, Tel.; பால் - pál, Tam.).——*Month* (నెల - nela, Tel.; நிலவு - nilavu, Tam.; Can. fails).——*Mortar* (ಒರಳು - oralu, Can.; రోలు - rólu, Tel.; உரல் - ural, Tam.).——*Net* (ಉಟ್ಟಿ - utti, Can.; ఉట్టి - utti, Tel.; உறி - uri, Tam.). This is the long net in households for holding pots or other utensils [oory]. Regarding the genitive case of the Tamul word see the letter R.——*Pestle* (ಒನಕೆ - onake, Can.; రోకలి - rókali, Tel.; உரோங்கல் - uróngal, Tam.).——*Pool* (ಮಡು - madu, Can.; మడుగు - madugu, Tel.; மடு - madu, Tam.).——*Temple* (ಗುಡಿ - gudi, Can.; గుడి - gudi, Tel.; குடி - kudi, Tam.). The Tamul word signifies any habitation; so did the others originally.——*Tiger* (ಹುಲಿ - huli, Can.; పులి - puli, Tel.; புலி - puli, Tam.).——*Village* (ಊರು - úru, Can.; ఊరు - úru, Tel.; ஊர் - úr, Tam.).——*Woman* (ఆడది - ádadi, Tel.; ஆடவள் - ádaval, Tam.; Can. fails).

PAH (பா - pá, *Tam.*). From (pávu, tam. to spread, to extend) [pauv]. Web or warp; so poetry. The character of Dravidian poetry may be seen especially from the Tamul. With the exception of commentaries and some modern works, the entire Tamul literature is in poetry. Alliteration is its essence as in the case of Welsh. The chief peculiarity of Tamul rhyme consists in fact in its seat being not at the end of the line but at the beginning, a natural result of alliteration. The rule in Tamul as in all the other Dravidian dialects is that the consonant which intervenes between the first two vowels in a line is the seat of rhyme. The agreement of these two consonants constitutes the minimum of rhyme which is admissible, but often the entire first foot of one line rhymes with the same foot in the second; sometimes the second feet in each line also rhyme; and the rhyme is sometimes taken up again further on in the verse according to fixed laws in each variety of metre. There are thirty kinds of feet, divisible into five classes, in Tamul poetry. In Latin a verse would be considered lame and devoid of harmony, if each word in it were a distinct foot; the feet of a verse therefore are so disposed that in scanning the words are run into each other and concatenated like the links of a chain. The cadence of the Tamul verse on the contrary requires that not only in singing, but even in reading, the close of each foot should be marked by a slight pause; so that to read a verse and to scan are one and the same thing. Hence although a Tamul foot may consist of several whole words yet no word can be divided as among the Romans so as to belong partly to one foot and partly to another. As a rule, every Tamul poem however secular its aim begins with an invocation. There are three treatises on this single point. Numerous rules are laid down. There are twenty-three fortunate words with which or their synonyms the poem and invocation should commence; certain letters are allotted to the twenty-seven constellations [nacshatram]; each caste [jauty, varnam] has its appropriate letters [varnamaulay]; certain feet are fortunate, others the reverse. When a poet wishes to injure an enemy, he begins with inauspicious letters; Cumban [q.v.] is reported to have caused the death of a king by combinations of this character. The difficulty in understanding Tamul poetry is much increased by the very complicated rules for enphonic changes. These changes are made not only in syllables of words, but in the beginnings and endings of words themselves; so that a whole line may be considered as forming a polysyllabic word of great length. Dravidian grammarians have bestowed more attention and care on euphonic permutations than on any other subject, and the permutations which the grammar [lacshanam] of Tamul requires or allows are at least twice as numerous, and more than twice as perplexing to beginners, as those of Sanscrit [q.v.]. In native manuscripts, words are not in any way divided. The difficulty is increased again by the use of peculiar or obsolete words. A Tamulian of average intelligence, who can read and write with ease the language as spoken, cannot understand classic poetry unless he has made it a special study; he cannot even divide the lines into their component words. Hence the Tamul classics have most elaborate commentaries. Each word presenting any difficulty is explained separately, and the general sense is given, with any grammatical remarks which may be required. Vailayya desican says as follows:—"Born as I am second of three brothers, "whose poetry even the god [bramha] enthroned on the "lotus-flower [nelumbo] could not easily understand." The principal versifying styles in Tamul are Ammaunay, Antaudy, Ausryappah or agaval, Calambagam, Coommy, Covay, Oolah or maulah, Parany, Pillay tamul, Shind or keertanay, Taulautt, Tooray, Venbah, Vroottam, Vunnam. Of these the Venbah or pure and Vroottam or expanded are the most used [bhaushay]. ——*Paun* (பாண் - pán, Tam.). Melody.——*Paunan* (പാണൻ - pánan, Mal.). From (pána, mal. melody). Pariah proper name [peyar]. Musicians actors and players on the west coast [jauty]. ——*Pautt* (பாட்டு - páttu, Tam.). Compare poem from ποιεῖν. Song. See sep. title.——*Pauvalan* (பாவலன் - pávalan, Tam.). From (above + val, tam. powerful). Poet. The following is a list of the chief Tamul poets, ancient and modern:—Agastyan, Alvandar, Ativeeraramapandiyan, Avvay, Bhogan, Capilan, Caukkaypaudinyan, Conganan, Corakkan, Cullaudan, Cumban, Irattaiyar, Maunica vauchacan, Nakkeeran, Pavanandy, Poogazhendy, Sambandhan, Shattaimoony, Shekkilaun, Shendan, Shiva pracausha desican, Shiva vaucyan, Soondran, Tatwa bodhacar, Tirvulloovan, Tirtevar, Tolgauppyan, Veera maumoony. Each of these may be seen in the present volume under the corresponding heading. For other names see under Alwar, Aroopatt moover and Madura college. For Teloogoo poets, see Cavy.

PAHAUR (پہاڑ - pahár, *Hind.*). Hill [q.v.].——*Pahaury* (پہاڑی - pahárí, Hind.). Hill. Plant first term, often joining two genera. Ex., where transl. is of second term :—Cycas circinalis (pahárimadanmastkájhár), artabotrys odoratissimus, madmaunty; Jatropha curcas (pahárìarand), ricinus communis, castor-oil; Thespesia populnea (pahárípípal), ficus religiosa, peepul. See gloss. paragraphs.

PAHLAVA (पह्लव - pahlava, *San.*). From (balkhavi), meaning pertaining to balkh. A northern or north-western nation often mentioned in Hindoo writings. πάκτυες of Herodotus. See vol. I (129).

PAID (پیٹھ - peth, *Hind.*; పేట - pédu, *Tel.*; பேடு - pédu, *Tam.*). Village. Suffix in place names; as Vitpaid, meaning bow-shaped village [baid, paud].

PAL (पल - pal, *San.*). To move.——*Palabhay* (पलभा - palabhá, San.). From (above + bhá, san. shadow). The midday shadow [chauyay] of a gnomon [shunk], when the sun [sooryan] is in the equinoctial points [ayanam, craunty pautam, vishoo].——*Palum* (पल - pala, San.; പലം - palam, Mal.). From (pal, san. to move).—"*a*" A weight of gold or silver, the hundredth part of a toolaum [q.v.].—"*b*" Measure of solar time. 60 vipalums or indian seconds = 1 palam or indian minute; 60 palams = 1 dandam or indian hour [caulam, 6]. Approximate actual value, 1 palam or indian minute = 24 english seconds. Same as San. vighaticay [caulam, 4, 5], vinaudy [caulam, 1], vicalay [caulam, 6], Tel. vighadiya [caulam, 4, 5], Tam. vinaudy [caulam, 1].——*Palaus* (पलाश - palásha, San.). See sep. title.——*Palingoo* (స్ఫటికము - sp'hatikamu, Tel.; පළිඟු - palingu, Singh.; பளிங்கு - palingu, Tam.). Title and Tam. from (paligha, san. glass vessel). A common term for mineral crystals [cull].——*Pollum* (पल - pala, San.; பலம் - palam, Tam.). From (pal, san. to move), as judged by motion on balance. Bazaar weight. 10 pagoda weight = 1 pollum; 8 pollums = 1 cutcha seer [niray, 2]. Approximate actual value, 1 pollum = 3 tolahs or rupee weights or $1\frac{1}{4}$ oz. avoir. Used throughout Presidency. In Coimbatore, 3 oz. $4\frac{1}{2}$ drs.; in Madura 3 oz. $1\frac{3}{4}$ drs.; Tinnevelly, 2 oz. 4 drs.; in Malabar 4 oz. $1\frac{1}{2}$ drs. and same as Nowtauk. Compare Arapow for the smaller values. See vol. I, 609; II, 506.

PAL (పల్లు - pallu, *Tel.*). Tooth.——*Palgorroo* (పలుగొర్రు - palugorru, Tel.). From (above + gorru, tel. harrow). A harrow [goontaca] used as a leveller [gorroo].

PALA (பல - pala, *Tam.*). Many.——*Pala bhogam* (பலபோகம் - palabógam, Tam.). From (above + bhóga, san. enjoyment). Tenure by which inhabitants hold lands in severalty, each responsible for revenue [teervay] of his own holding [aroothy caray, caray, samoodauyam, yecabhogam].——*Palavaisham* (பலவேசம் - palavésam, Tam.). From (above + vésha, san. disguise). A Maravan [q.v.] who made himself celebrated for his robberies during the latter part of the Mahomedan government of Seringapatam. Since his death he has been worshipped as one of the demons [moony] of the Shaunaur [q.v.] of Tinnevelly. Thousands of persons are called after his name.——*Palgoondram* (பல்குன்றம் - palgunram, Tam.). From (pala, tam. many + kunram, tam. hill). Ancient division of Tondaimundalam [q.v.]. The Calastry neighbourhood.——*Pulnaud* (పల్నాడు - palnádu, Tel.). See sep. title.

PALAM (फल - p'hala, *San.*). From (p'hal, san. to split). Fruit [pazham]. Consequence, one of the twelve Prameyams [q.v.] of the Nyauyam [q.v.] philosophy, or points about which correct knowledge is to be obtained. An equation. When applied to the sun [sooryan] or planets [graham], their anomalistic equation [mandapalam].——*Phal* (फल - p'hala, San.; پھل - phal, Hind.). Fruit.—"*a*" Plant first term. Ex., where transl. is of second term :—Artabotrys odoratissimus (p'halasampenga), michelia champaca; Citrus medica, var. medica proper, (p'halapúra), full; Feronia elephantum (p'halasugandhi), fragrant; Stereospermum suaveolens (p'haléruhá), born; fruit appearing with flower buds on the top; Zizyphus jujuba (p'halashaishira), dewy season. See gloss. paragraphs.—"*b*" Plant second term. Ex., where transl. is of first term :—Barringtonia acutangula, (samandarphal), sea; Corallocarpus epigæa (garajphal), thunder; Helecteris isora (jonkphallí), leech; Lagenaria vulgaris (káshíphal), benares; Myrica sapida (káíphal), pungent; Randia dumetorum (mendphal), intoxication; Rubus indicus (gauríphal), gowry, the goddess; Rubus lasiocarpus (gauríphal), gowry, the goddess; Trapa bispinosa (pániphal), water. See gloss. paragraphs.——*Palanashtam* (फलनष्ट - p'halanashta, San.). From (above + nashta, san. loss). Loss of produce by unsuccessful cultivation [vellaumay].

PALAUS (पलाश - palásha, *San.*; ककरा - kakrá, *Mahr.*; फलसा - p'halasá, *Conc.*; درخت پلاہ - darakhtipaláh, *Pers.*; پلاس - palás, *Hind.*; پلاس کاجھار - paláskájhár, *Dec.*; ಮುತ್ತುಗ - muttaga, *Can.*; మోదుగ - móduga, *Tel.*; ପୋରାସୁ - porásu, *Oor.*; പലാശം - palásham, *Mal.*; කෑල - kála, *Singh.*; புரசு - purasu, *Tam.*). Title from hindostany [pal]. San. from (pal, san. to go), useful. Mahr. from (kankara, mahr. gravel), useful in gravel. Conc. from sanscrit. Pers. from (darakht, pers. tree + palásha, san. the tree). Hind. from sanscrit. Dec. from (palásha, san. the tree + jhár, hind. tree). Can. from (muttu, can. pearl + mara, can. tree). Oor., Mal. and Tam. from sanscrit. San. also (kimshuka), meaning beautiful tree; (kamalásana), meaning seat of lutchmy; (tripatriká), meaning three petalled; (lákshataru), meaning lac-tree; from branches yielding lac [q.v.]. Hind. also (dhák). Tel. also (tellamóduga), meaning white + the tree; (togarumóduga), meaning red color + the tree. Mal. also (murukku); (chamata), meaning sacrificial fuel [samit], from twigs used to feed sacred fire; Singh. also (gaskála), meaning tree + butea frondosa, roxb.; (etkan); (kálukála), meaning black + the butea tree. Tam. also (murukku), meaning beautiful tree [common coral tree]. Gave its name to the battle-field of Plassey in bengal. Title otherwise Bastard teak [common coral tree], Bengal kino, Butea gum, Dhak tree, Gum lac tree, Lac tree, Modooga, Pismire tree, Porasam, Tisso flower. Botanically Butea frondosa, roxb., leguminosæ [vricsham, 48]. Alias Erythrina monosperma; Rudolphia frondosa. Middle-sized tree; leaves pinnately trifoliolate; leaflets large, roundish ovate, rather velvety beneath; corolla papilionaceous; racemes simple many flowered, lax; calyx segments short, slightly acute, several times shorter than the tube; corolla densely pubescent; vexillum ovate, acute, recurved; keel and alæ incurved; legume chestnut-colored, flat, thin, with a large solitary seed at the apex; seed is thin, flat, oval, or kidney-shaped, of a mahogany brown color, $1\frac{1}{4}$–$1\frac{3}{4}$ inches in length, almost devoid of taste and smell. Flowers bright scarlet, in clusters, are produced before the leaves; in full flower in march and april; lac [q.v.] insects are frequently found on the small branches and petioles of the leaves; widely dispersed and common in dry forests. From fissures and wounds in the bark issues during the hot season a red juice, soon hardening into a ruby-colored, brittle, astringent gum [q.v.]; which however soon loses its color by exposure to the air; this is butea kino or bengal kino, gummi rubrum astringens of old druggists, otherwise butea gum; it is inodorous, soluble in water, the solution being of a deep red color, partially soluble in alcohol, giving a pale tincture; the salts of iron blacken all the solutions; it contains 73 per cent. of tannin and is sometimes substituted for true kino [common vengay] though not so efficient; occurs in the form of irregular shining fragments, seldom as large as a pea [calauyam], more or less mixed with adherent pieces of greyish bark, of an intense ruby color and astringent taste; its astringency is due to the presence of tannic and gallic acids; more common in bazear than officinal kino [q.v.]. Leaves medicinally astringent, tonic and aphrodisiac; flowers astringent, depurative, diuretic, aphrodisiac; seeds, pounded with lemon [q.v.] applied to the skin act as a rubefacient; seeds act also as a vermifuge, and when made into a paste used for ringworm [dadroo]; decoction of seeds, to which a little nitre [shorah] added, prescribed in gravelly complaints; bark given in conjunction with ginger [q.v.] in snake-bites; gives to pharm. buteæ gummi, officinal; seeds, non-officinal. In veterinary practice two drachms of seed in powder given in gram [q.v.] daily, for horses [ghorah] with worms. Leaves used as fodder for buffaloes [khoolgah] and elephants [q.v.]. Flowers are offered in temples, and women intertwine them in their hair; expressed juice of fresh flowers and infusion of dried flowers yield a water color brighter than gamboge [q.v.]; also yield a lake [q.v.]; strong ropes made from fibre [naar] of roots, used immediately after bark has been stripped; the kino is one of the most useful kinds of gum for all purposes; the leaves form a substitute for platters. Wood somewhat resembles teak [q.v.] in appearance, and is used for gunpowder charcoal [adoopp kary]; also for building purposes and well curbs. Creeping palaus, so called in the vernaculars is Butea superba, roxb.; twining shrub with pinnated three foliolate leaves; leaflets roundish, velvety beneath; racemes simple, lax; pedicels about twice the length of the calyx; corolla papilionaceous; legumes flat, compressed, thin, clothed with rusty tomentum, with one solitary seed at the apex; calyx segments shortish, acuminate; vexillum ovate, acute; flowers large, bright scarlet; flowering in march; flowers and legumes larger than frondosa; scarcely differing from frondosa except in habit; sensible properties same as in frondosa.——*Black palaus* (कालापलाश - kálápalásha, Mahr.). Same as Nemmy,——*Thorny palaus* (ముళ్లుమోదుగ - mullumóduga, Tel.; முள்முருக்கம் - mulmurukkam, Tam.). Same as Thorny coral tree.

PALCONDAH (పాలకొండ - pálakonda, *Tel.* pálkonda *). From (pálu, tel. milk + konda, tel. hill); on account of pasture [paul].——**(1)** Talook, Vizagapatam district; area 502 square miles including agency tracts; population non-agency 208,821, agency 11,824; language Teloogoo. E. inland of district. Boundaries :—east, Chicacole talook; south, Cheepoorpully talook; west, Bobbily and Parvatipore talooks; north, Meranghy, Cooroopaum and Parlakimedy estates. Palcondah is on the eastern border of the district and adjoins the south-western portion of Ganjam. The northern portion forming Palcondah agency consists of a range of hills from which flow several streamlets. Excluding the hilly tract, it is plain and fertile and well watered by the Langoolya. The soils belong to regar [q.v.] and red ferruginous [sevval munn], the former 44 per cent. and latter 56 per cent. of arable area. The regar soil contains regar clay, regar loam, and regar sand, in the proportion of 41, 52 and 7 per cent. respectively. The red series contain red loam and red sand [manal] in the proportion of 67 and 33 per cent. respectively. Agriculture [vellaumay] is chief industry. Indigo [q.v.] and sugar-cane [q.v.] are grown. Messrs Arbuthnot & Co. have rented the talook for many years. Exports are paddy [q.v.], jaggery [q.v.], indigo [q.v.] and oil-seeds [yennay]. Chief imports are piece-goods and salt [ooppoo]. The Naugauvaly which in its lower course is known as the Langoolya or Chicacole river of Ganjam, with its tributary the Swarnamookhy, is chief source of irrigation. The best irrigation is from the river channels [q.v.]. Places of archæological interest:—Audoorpett, Galavully, Siripooram. Principal trig. stations:—Naulcondah, Yerra cuntsaram. The leading places, &c., in the talook are the following.——*Honzaram* (హొంజరాము - hondzarámu, Tel.). See sep. title.——*Langoolya* (లాంగూలియా - lángúliyá, Tel.). See sep. title.——*Muntena* (మంటెన - mantena, Tel.). From (mantanamu, tel. solitary abode). Proprietary estate, Village; pop. 1,017. Is a small fertile estate. Peshcush Rs. 7,220.——*Naulcondah* (నాలుకొండ - nálukonda, Tel.). From (nál, hind. horse-shoe + konda, tel. hill). Trig. station; lat. 18° 35′ 15·00″; long. 83° 51′ 58·39″; height 2,143 feet; from Palcondah E.S.E. 4 miles.——*Oongarauda* (ఉంగరాడ - ungaráda, Tel.). From (ungaramu, tel. ring + váda, tel. village). Proprietary estate, Village; pop. 1,589; lat. of village 18° 31′; long. 83° 47′; from Palcondah S. 6 miles; from Vizagapatam N.N.E. 63 miles. Peshcush Rs. 3,080.——*Palcondah* (పాలకొండ - pálakonda, Tel.). See below.——*Poolleta* (పుల్లెట - pulleta, Tel.). From (pullu, tel. grass + eda, tel. place). Proprietary estate, Village; pop. 637; from Palcondah S. 10 miles; from Vizagapatam N. 58 miles. Peshcush Rs. 1,818.——*Rajaum* (రాజాము - rádzámu, Tel.). From (rájá, san. king + gám, hind. village). Village, District moonsif's station; pop. 4,687; lat. 18° 27′; long. 83° 42′; from Palcondah S.S.W. 12 miles; from Vizagapatam N.N.E. 56 miles. Famous for silver [velly] work and palankeens [q.v.]. Belongs to Bobbily rajah.——*Seetampett* (శీతంపేట - shítampéta, Tel.). See sep. title.——*Seetarampooram* (సీతారాంపురము - sítárámpuramu, Tel.). From (sítáráma, san. síta and ráma + pura, san. town). Village; pop. 1,429; lat. 18° 29′; long. 83° 46′; from Palcondah S. 9 miles; from Vizagapatam N.N.E. 60 miles. Fine temple built by Bobbily rajah. Good water-supply.——*Siripooram* (సిరిపురము - siripuramu, Tel.). From (siri, tel. wealth + pura, tan. town). Proprietary estate, Villago; pop. 2,885; lat. of village 18° 23′; long. 83° 50′; from Palcondah S. 15 miles; from Vizagapatam N. 56 miles. Inscription of Orissa dynasty [raj] dated A.D. 1153. Large tank [q v.] on the bund [q.v.] of which are old stone images. Peshcush Rs. 8,800.——*Veeraghattam* (వీరఘట్టము - víraghattamu, Tel.). From (víra, san. warrior + ghatta, san. ford). Village; pop. 5,546; acres 2,088; lat. 18° 41′; long. 83° 39′; from Palcondah W. 12 miles; from Vizagapatam N.N.E. 72 miles. Trading place.——*Yerra cuntsaram* (యర్రకంచరాం - yarrakantsarám, Tel.). From (erra, tel. red + kantsara, tel. brazier + gám, hind. village). Trig. station; lat. 18° 43′ 45·89″; long. 83° 40′ 48·83″; height 1,766 feet; from Palcondah N.W. 12 miles; from Veeraghattam N. 3 miles.——**(2)** Deputy tahsildarry; Vizagapatam district. Pay Rs. 100.——**(3)** Zemindarry; now forfeited to Government; Vizagapatam dist., Palcondah tal.; pop. 203,833. Ancient zemindarry granted by the rajah of Jeypore early in the sixteenth century. The founder was a Khond [q.v.]. When the East india company came into possession, the family was tributary to Vizianagram. In 1796 the estate was taken from the zemindar for rebellion and given to his son. Each succeeding zemindar gave the Company trouble, till in 1828 the Collector was obliged to take charge for a time. The new zemindar in 1832 broke out into open rebellion, which led to the forfeiture of the estate and the prolonged imprisonment of the male members of the family. For some years after this, the estate was managed by the Collector, but from 1846 till the present time it has been rented to Messrs. Arbuthnot & Co. of Madras, who now pay Rs. 126,500 per annum as rent.——**(4)** Town, Deputy tahsildar's head-quarters; Vizagapatam dist., Palcondah tal.; pop. 10,367; acres 1,519; lat. 18° 36′ 05″; long. 83° 48′; from; Coraputt E.S.E. 68 miles; from Madras N.N.E. 440 miles; from Narsapatam N.E 98 miles; from Parvatipore E. 24 miles; from Vizagapatam N.N.E. 68 miles; from Vizianagram N. 40 miles. 2½ miles from Langoolya. Connected by road with Parvatipore and the coast viâ Chicacole.——**(5)** Sanscrit name (shésháchala), meaning sheshan, the serpent + hill. Range of hills; Cuddapah dist., Poollampett, Sidhout, Royachoty, Cuddapah, Poolivendla, Cadiry tals.; lat. 13° 44′ to 14° 14′ N.; long. 78° 55′ to 79° 27′ E. The most extensive of the Cuddapah hill ranges. Average elevation 2,000 feet, highest point Booditaid 3,060 feet. A few miles to the north of Tripatty, the Sheshachellam hills take a sharp turn to the west, after about five miles they again turn almost at right angles to the north, and from this point are known as the Palcondahs. After taking the turn the hills enter Cuddapah district and run in one unbroken range of almost unvarying height in a north-westerly direction to the neighbourhood of Goolcheroo. Here they turn suddenly off to the west and continuing in that direction for about 60 miles, and forming the boundary between Poolivendla and Cadiry talooks, finish in the latter talook near the Bellary frontier in a number of rocky hills. They constitute a well-defined boundary between the main division and the sub-division, shutting in a table-land, the lowest point of which is 1,500 feet above the sea, to the west and south, and form low valleys on the north and east averaging, about 50 feet above the sea level. The western side of the hills is precipitous and overlooks the Mysore plateau. The passes are few. The Naugapootla pass [ghaut], carrying the road from Mysore to Tripatty, passes over a portion of the hills about 20 miles from the pagoda [q.v.]. It stops short at the hills, and the pass is merely jungle pass. About 20 miles further to the north, the Cheyair finds a passage through the hills, and at Saunipoya, about 10 miles further on, there is a fine ghaut [q.v.] road which forms a feeder to the railway, joining it at the Rajampett station and crossing Cheyair near Baularauzpully. At Goolcheroo is the Soorya comauroola canama through which runs the road from Chittore to Cuddapah. This road has been recently built, but the pass has been used for traffic for centuries. There are the vestiges of an old road. About 20 miles west of Goolcheroo and near Vompully in Poolivendla talook the range affords a passage to the Paupughny. In Cadiry talook is the Coorly ghaut named after a village near its foot, and near this road a small river also finds a way through the hills and eventually joints the Chitrauvaty. There are two water-falls 10 miles from Cuddapah. Trig. station in lat. 14° 29′ 14·23″; long. 78° 02′ 37·77″; height 2,156 feet; from Boodanampully E. 3 miles; from Cadiry N.N.W. 28 miles.

PALGHAUT (പാലക്കാട് - pálakkátu, *Mal.* pálghat *). From (pála, mal. milk plant, alstonia scholaris, r. br. + kátu, mal. jungle) [paul]. Sanscrit name (shāradápattana), meaning saraswaty's city.——**(1)** Talook, Malabar district. Tahsildar's pay Rs. 200. Easternmost inland talook of the district; lies between 10° 25′ and 10° 56′ N. lat., 76° 27′ and 76° 54′ E. long. Area 613 square miles. Boundaries:—north, Valavanaud talook; east, Coimbatore and Pollachy talooks in Coimbatore district and Cochin state; south, native state of Cochin; west, Cochin state and Valavanaud talook. Formerly comprised talooks of Palghaut and Temmalapooram, amalgamated in 1861. Most striking feature is the Palghaut gap in which it lies, and for which see below. The extensive forests of the numerous projecting off-shoots of the main chain of the Western ghauts [q.v.] separating the talook from the Coimbatore district, are all private property, except the two Government forests Chenat nayar and Walayaur. Soil in general is black loam. Chief exports are various kinds of food grains [dhaunyam], timber [maram], tobacco [pogauk], Palghaut mats [boriyah] and coarse cloths manufactured in Vadacancherry, &c. Chief imports are tobacco, various kinds of cloth, spices, and cattle [maud]. Of the rivers, the most important are the Cullpauty locally called the Nelanuddy, the Cunnaudy, and the Collangode locally called the Gayatry nuddy. The first two uniting near Parly take the name of Ponnany or Bhaurata poya; and the last, the Collangode river, joins the Ponnany river a little farther on. The Cullpauty has its source at Chentaumaracoolam in the hills north of Walayaur, where the stream forms boundary between Malabar and Coimbatore districts. The other two rise in the north-western extremities of the Anamullays. Places of archæological interest:—Agattettara, Candattaur, Cautchancoorchy, Cauvacherry, Cauvalpaud, Chengalore, Chittalancherry, Choolanore, Codoomtirapully, Congaud, Coodallore, Coonicherry, Coottanore, Cooyalmannam, Cunnanorepauttola, Cunnaudy, Kilakoompooram, Madapully, Manyalore, Mauttore, Moondore, Mungalam, Munnalore, Palghaut, Panangauttiry, Poothoocherry, Poottore, Pullachaina, Pullattairy, Pullavore, Tadookkacherry, Taroor, Tenaury, Tirvaulattore, Tripauvalore, Tripoolamand, Vadacancherry, Vilayanore, Vuttacaud, Yedattara, Yerimayore. Principal trig. stations:—Aulatore, Carimala, Coorchimala. The leading places, &c., in the talook are the following.——*Aulatore* (ആലത്തൂർ - álattúr, Mal.). See sep. title.——*Canyicode* (കഞ്ഞിക്കോട് - kaññikkótu, Mal. kanyikód *). From (kaññi, mal. rice gruel + kótu, mal. place); a charity place. Village, Railway station; pop. 7,213; lat. 10° 48′; long. 76° 48′; height 376 feet; from Calicut E.S.E. 72 miles; from Palghaut E.N.E. 7 miles. Chuttram [q.v.] founded by a family residing in Tellicherry in Palghaut.——*Carimala* (കരിമല - karimala, Mal.). From (kari, mal. black + mala, mal. hill). Mal. also (udayagiri), sun-rise mountain. Hill. Trig. station in lat. 10° 55′ 45·89″; long. 76° 42′ 05·30″; height 6,556 feet; from Palghaut N. 12 miles.——*Chenat nayar* (ചേനാട്ടുനായർ - chénáttunáyar, Mal.). See sep. title.——*Coderauyore* (കൊടുവായൂർ - kotuváyúr, Mal.). From (kotu, mal. severe + váyu, san. wind + úr, mal. village). Sanscrit name (kéralapura), meaning keralan's town. Village, Sub-registrar's office; pop. 15,402; acres 4,886; lat. 10° 41′; long. 76° 42′; from Calicut S.E. 70 miles; from Palghaut S. 5 miles. Weekly market.——*Collangode* (കൊല്ലങ്കോട് - kollankótu, Mal.). See sep. title.——*Congaud* (കോന്നാട് - kónnátu, Mal.). From (kón, mal. king + kátu, mal. forest). Village; pop. 8,113; acres 3,558; lat. 10° 51′; long. 76° 34′; from Calicut E.S.E. 57 miles; from Palghaut N.W. 10 miles. Weekly cattle market held on Mondays. Ancient temple at present in use. Many dolmens [codaycull] and menhirs [paundoo cull]. Pooram [pundigay, 50] festival celebrated for eight days in March-April, and fairs held on the occasion.——*Coorchimala* (കുറിച്ചിമല - kuriççimala, Mal.). From (kuriççi, mal. hill village + mala, mal. mountain). Hill, Trig. station; lat. 10° 47′ 10·15″; long. 76° 39′ 29·61″; height 479 feet; from Palghaut N.W. 2½ miles; from Yedattara E. 4¼ miles.——*Cootchimala* (കുച്ചിമല - kuççimala, Mal.). From (kuççi, mal. brush-wood + mala, mal. mountain). Hill; lat. 10° 32′ long. 76° 53′; height 3,919 feet; from Calicut S.E. 86 miles; from Palghaut S.E. 20 miles. Well-defined pinnacle-shaped peak terminating the Collangode range.——*Cullpauty* (കല്പാത്തി - kalpátti, Mal.). See sep. title.——*Moothalamada* (മുതലമട - mutalamata, Mal.). From (mutala, mal. crocodile + mata, mal. cave). Village, Amshom, Cutcherry situated on the site of a ruined fort; pop. 5,924; lat. 10° 37′; long. 76° 49′; from Calicut S.E. 79 miles; from Palghaut S.E. 13 miles.——*Mungara* (മങ്കര - mankara, Mal.). From (man, mal. earth + kara, mal. village). Village; lat. 10° 46′; long. 76° 32′; from Calicut S.E. 57 miles; from Palghaut W. 10 miles. Railway station.——*Olavacode* (ഒലവക്കോട് - olavakkótu, Mal. olavakód *). From (ulavu, mal. custom + kótu, mal. corner); place where timber toll is collected. Village, Railway station opened in 1862, whence branch line to Palghaut; from Palghaut N. 3 miles. Timber depôts.——*Palghaut* (പാലക്കാട് - pálakkátu, Mal.). See below.——*Parly* (പറളി - parali, Mal. parli *). Village, Railway station; pop. 7,432; lat. 10° 48′; long. 76° 35′; height 203 feet; from Calicut E.S.E. 60 miles; from Palghaut W.N.W. 7 miles. Large distillery.——*Paultoolly* (പാലത്തുള്ളി - pálattulli, Mal.). From (pála, mal. milk plant, alstonia scholaris, r. br. + tulli, mal. drop). Village; pop. 5,863; acres 943; lat. 10° 42′; long. 76° 45′; from Calicut S.E. 72 miles; from Palghaut S.S.E. 5 miles. Weekly cattle [maud] market held on Sundays. Chiefly inhabited by Chetties [q.v.]. Centre of cattle trade.——*Ponnany* (പൊന്നാനി - ponnáni, Mal.). See sep. title.——*Poothoonagaram* (പുതുനഗരം - putunagaram, Mal.). From (putu, mal. new + nagara, san. town); recent settlement formed by hyder's followers. Village in Codevauyore amshom; pop. 15,402; lat. 10° 41′; long. 76° 41′; from Calicut S.E. 72 miles; from Palghaut S.S.E. 6 miles. Weekly market. Most important Rowtan [q.v.] village in the talook. The Rowtar are descended from Mysore mussalman [q.v.] emigrants. Jumma musjid [q.v.].——*Temmalapooram* (തെമ്മലപ്പുറം - temmalappuram, Mal.). From (tenmala, mal. southern mountain + puram, mal. side). Village; lat. 10° 39′; long. 76° 32′; from Calicut S.E. 63 miles; from Palghaut S.W. 13 miles. Formerly gave its name to a talook.——*Tenmullay* (തെമ്മല - temmala, Mal.). See sep. title.——*Vadacancherry* (വടക്കഞ്ചേരി - vatakkañchéri, Mal. vadakanchéri *). From (vatakkan, mal. northern + chéri, mal. village). Village; pop. 12,750; acres 1,727; lat. 10° 36′; long. 76° 32′; from Calicut S.E. 65 miles; from Palghaut S.W. 16 miles. A mile distant is very ancient shiva temple of Trivara. Tank called Bramhacoondam, where Bramha [q.v.] performed yaugams [q.v.]. On northern side of hill ranges separating the talook from the adjoining Cochin state; hill-bound on south and west. Chiefly inhabited by Mahomedans. Also Roman catholic church. Manufacture of coarse cloths. Trade in hill produce and timber. Travellers' bungalow [q.v.]. The hills near contain many cromlechs [paundoo cull].——*Vadamullay* (വടമല - vatamala, Mal.). See sep. title.——*Walayaur* (വാളയാർ - válayár, Mal.). See sep. title.——*Yelapully* (എലപ്പുള്ളി - elappalli, Mal.). From (ela, mal. small + palli, mal. village). Village; pop. 11,138; acres 5,966; lat. 10° 45′; long. 76° 47′; from Calicut E.S.E. 73 miles; from Palghaut E. 6 miles. Weekly market. Natural spring called Tenaury teertam. Frequented for Amavausyay [q.v.] in Carcataoam [mausam] or July and Toolaum or October.——**(2)** Town, Municipality, Railway station, Head-quarters of Head assistant collector, Sub-judge, Tahsildar and Moonsif, Telegraph office, Sub-registrar's office and Head-quarters of Assistant superintendent of Police; Malabar dist., Palghaut tal.; pop. 39,418; lat. 10° 46′; long. 76° 42′; height 259 feet; from Calicut S.E. 67 miles; from Cannanore S.E. 113 miles; from Madras W.S.W. 291 miles; from Malapooram E.S.E. 44 miles; from Manantoddy S.S.E. 81 miles; from Ponnany E. 48 miles; from Tellicherry S.E. 102 miles. In the Palghaut gap and on the north or right side of the Palaur. Being the key to Travancore and Malabar from the east, it was formerly of considerable strategic importance. In 1768, captured for the first time by the British, but retaken by Hyder a few months later; retaken by the British in 1783; restored to Tippoo sultan in 1784; September 21, 1790, taken by Colonel Stuart. From that time it was a basis of operations against Tippoo, which terminated in the storming of Seringapatam. The fort still stands, built by Hyder ally. Now used as the office of the Tahsildar. Sub-jail and Sub-registrar's offices are also located here. Palghaut is a busy entrepôt for exchange of produce between Malabar and the Eastern districts. The Bramin puttar [q.v.] exist in large numbers. Cullpauty shiva temple. A car festival celebrated in November. Special trade in Palghaut grass mats [boriyah], and centre of tobacco [pogauk] trade. The following are the travelling distances by road from Palghaut to different places :—

To		Viâ	Miles and Furlongs.	
Angaudipooram	...	Wottapollem	41	0
Angaudipooram	...	Manaar	43	0
Arriyacode ...	...	Wottapollem and Angaudipooram ...	65	5
Avanashy ...	...	Coimbatore	57	1
Calicut ...	...	Angaudipooram, Munjery and Condotty.	83	6
Calicut ...	...	Angaudipooram and Malapooram ...	84	4
Calicut ...	...	Manaar and Malapooram...	86	4
Calicut ...	...	Trittaula and Taunore	86	0
Calicut ...	...	Angaudipooram and Arriyacode ...	93	1
Cannanore ...	...	Angaudipooram, Malapooram and Calicut.	143	5
Caroor ...	...	Coimbatore and Pulladam	110	2
Caroor ...	...	Dharaupooram	112	6
Caungyam ...	...	Coimbatore	72	5
Chowghaut ...	...	Trittaula and Ponnany	68	1
Cochin ...	...	Trichore and Cottaparamba	86	0
Coimbatore ...	...	Walayaur	30	7
Cottaparamba	...	Trichore	62	4
Dharaupooram	...	Oodamalpett	67	6
Dindigul ...	...	Pollachy, Oodamalpett and Pulney ...	102	7
Erode ...	...	Coimbatore and Avanashy	91	7
Madras ...	...	Coimbatore, Erode, Salem, Munjavaudy ghaut and Ranipett.	338	0
Madura ...	...	Dindigul	143	0½
Malapooram	...	Wottapollem and Angaudipooram ...	53	0
Malapooram	...	Manaar and Angaudipooram	55	0
Ootacamund	...	Coimbatore and Coonoor	85	4¾
Palamcottah	...	Pulney, Dindigul and Madura	238	6½
Pollachy ...	...	......	27	5
Pulney ...	...	Pollachy and Oodamalpett	68	3
Quilon ...	...	Trichore and Cochin	174	1
Salem ...	...	Coimbatore and Erode	129	4
Taunore ...	...	Trittaula	67	0
Trichinopoly	...	Coimbatore and Caroor	159	6
Trichinopoly	...	Dharaupooram and Caroor...	162	2
Trichore ...	...	Aulatore	42	1
Trittaula ...	...	Vaunyamcoolam	37	0

——**(3)** Hills; Malabar district, Palghaut talook.——**(4)** Valley; Malabar district, Palghaut talook. Also known as Palghautcherry valley and Palghaut gap. This valley breaks the line of western ghauts [q.v.], otherwise unbroken from the valley of the Tapty to Cape comorin, and joins by a comparatively low level the plains of the south and east side of the peninsula with the low and habitable country of the west coast. A good road has always been maintained between Ponnany on the coast and Coimbatore and Pulney inland. This road passes through Palghaut, where it bifurcates, one branch going to Coimbatore the other to Pulney. The highest point in the centre of the valley does not exceed 500 feet above the sea, and the ascent is very gradual. The gap is 25 miles broad at the narrowest part, nearly abreast of the town of Palghaut, and the length between the parallel walls of hills is about 35 to 40 miles. Bounded on the north by the Vadamullay range which separates it from the Noyil valley of Coimbatore, and on the south by the Tenmullay range. It contains the talooks of Palghaut of Malabar district and Chittoor of Cochin state. The valley comes within the influence of both monsoons [q.v.]. The population of the Tamul and Malayalam districts imperceptibly blends about Palghaut. There is a Mussalman [q.v.] population but chiefly Pataun [q.v.] and Rowtan [q.v.]. There are but very few resident Moplahs [q.v.]. The soil is generally light and sandy. The crops depend on the south-west monsoon [q.v.]; there is no general irrigation. The staple production is rice [q.v.]. The palmyra [q.v.] takes the place of the cocoanut [q.v.] of the coast. Jaggery [q.v.] is cheap, and exported largely. The valley is drained by the Ponnany river and its tributaries. The valley has belonged to Malabar from time immemorial. Its rajah was one of those who, with the zamorin [q.v.] and the Chiracal and Cochin rajahs, ruled the Malabar country from early times. The Malayalam descent by the female line prevails in the family [maroomakkatoyem], and the routine of succession to the rank of rajah, is similar to that existing in the zamorin's family. The aggressions of the zamorin [q.v.] were felt by the Palghaut rajah from early times. To the Cochin rajah he was obliged to cede the four deshoms [q.v.] of Chittoor, Nullapully, Tattamungalam and Nemmaura, in the valley. In 1764 he invited Hyder ally to support him against these rivals. A fort was built and garrisoned at Palghautcherry, the key of South malabar, and tribute paid by the Palghaut rajah; and gradually the whole country was reduced under mahomedan influence. A land assessment, till then supposed to have been unknown in Malabar, was introduced under the Mahomedan rule.

PALGOO (फल्गु - p'halgu, *San.*). Spring.——*Palgootsavam* (फल्गुत्सव - p'halgutsava, San.). From (p'halgu san. spring + utsava, san. festival). Same as Cauman pundigay.——*Pungoony* (பங்குனி - panguni, Tam.). From (p'halguni, san. eleventh and twelfth nakshatram); from full moon then. The month [mausam].——*Pungoony oottaram* (பங்குனியுத்திரம் - panguniyuttiram, Tam.). Same as Oottara phalgoony. See Oottaram.

PALISHA (പലിശ - palisha, *Mal.*). From (poli, mal. to increase). Interest. See below.——**(1)** *Palishamadak* (പലിശമടക്കം - palishamatakkam, Mal.). From (above + matakkam, mal. return). Equivalent to Otty [q.v.] in Nedoonganaud and Valavanaud talooks. See vol. II, 104.——**(2)** *Aracaulpalisha* (അരക്കാൽപലിശ - arakkálpalisha, Mal.). From (ara, mal. half +

kál, mal. quarter). ⅛ fanam for every ten or 1¼ per cent.——*Arapalisha* (അരപ്പലിശ - arappalisha, Mal.). From (ara, mal. half). ½ fanam for every ten or 5 per cent.——*Caulpalisha* (കാല്പ്പലിശ - kálpalisha, Mal.). From (kál, mal. quarter). ¼ fanam for every ten or 2½ per cent.——*Maugauny palisha* (മാകാണിപ്പലിശ - mákánippalisha, Mal.). From (mákáni, mal. one-sixteenth). $\frac{1}{16}$ fanam for every ten or ⅝ per cent. [vriddhy].

PALK'S BAY (பாக்குக்குடாக்கடல் - pákkukkudákkadal, *Tam.*). Named by the Dutch after governor Palk. Greek *κόλπος ἀργαρικός*. Bay and straits; Tanjore dist.; lat. from 9° 17′ to 10° 10′; long. from 78° 56′ to 80° 12′. Between Ceylon and the peninsula, separating the northern part of Ceylon from the mainland. The strait [jalsand] is formed between Point calimere and Point pedro. It is 35 miles wide at its entrance. The gulf is bounded by Calimere point and the coast of Tanjore and Madura to the northward and westward; by Adam's bridge and its contiguous islands to the south; and by the north part of Ceylon with its islands to the east.

PALMYRA (ताल - tála, *San.*; ताटी - tátí, *Mahr.*; درخت تاڑی - darakhtitárí, *Pers.*; تاڑ - tár, *Hind.*; تاڑ کا جھاڑ - tárká-jhár, *Dec.*; لونتر - lontar, *Malay*; ತಾಳೆ - tále, *Can.*; తాడి - tádi, *Tel.*; ତାଳ - talo, *Oor.*; പന - pana, *Mal.*; තල් - tal, *Singh.*; பனை - panai, *Tam.*). Title from portuguese palmeira, generic term for palms. San. from (tal, san. to fix) [talipot]. Mahr. from sanscrit. Pers. from (darakht, pers. tree + tárí, pers. toddy). Hind. from sanscrit. Dec. from (tála, san. borassus flabelliformis, linn. + jhár, hind. tree). Can., &c., from sanscrit. Mal. from tamul. Singh. from sanscrit. Tam. from (pani, tam. to be agitated); from the rustle of leaves when blown upon by the wind. Can. also (pané), from tamul. Tel. also (pótutádi), meaning male + palmyra; (pentitádi), meaning female + palmyra; (karatálamu), meaning hand + palmyra; from resembling hand with fingers extended. Mal. also (ámpana), meaning male palm; **(karimpana),** meaning black palm. Title otherwise Brab, Char palm, Fan palm, Great fan palm, Indian wine palm, Noongh palm, Taul palm. Botanically Borassus flabelliformis, linn., palmaceæ [vricsham, 149]. Alias Lontarus domestica. Trunk, 30–100 feet, everywhere marked with old cicatrices of fallen leaves; fronds composed of several folded linear-lanceolate divisions united as far as the centre; flowers male and female on different trees; drupe sub-globular, flattened at the apex, filled with soft yellow pulp; nut three, perforated at the apex. A tall, branchless palm, with a stiff radiating head of fan-shaped leaves; it is straight like the date [kharjooram] and areca [q.v.], and unlike the cocoanut [q.v.] which always inclines; may have on a girth of 5½ feet at bottom and 2½ at top; next to caryota urens, linn. [bastard sago palm], the largest palm on the coast of the peninsula; enjoys, next to the date [kharjooram] palm, the widest geographical distribution; it is however nowhere wild in southern india, and, like the tamarind [q.v.], was originally introduced from africa; very abundant, especially in sandy tracts near sea; it begins to produce when twenty-five or, in favorable soil and circumstances, fifteen or sixteen years old; it is always diœcious, that is to say bearing male and female flowers on separate plants, one tree producing only barren or staminiferous flowers, another bearing the pistil and fruits; it flowers generally in the hot season or in the mouths of pungoony and chittray [mausam] or march and april; some trees flower also in cold season; the male flowers are minute, and are produced between scales closely set on a branched flower-stalk, each stalk is estimated to bear 90,000, and as there are usually seven of these on each tree, the male flowers on a single tree are probably 630,000 in number, but not one of these produces a fruit; the fruiting or female palms bear on each flowering stalk from ten to twenty fruits, about ten of these bunches are produced in a year, so that over 200 fruits are sometimes obtained from a single tree; the fruit is round, black, about the size of a large orange [q.v.], the interior consists of an insipid, gelatinous, pellucid kind of pulp, generally contains three good-sized nuts or seeds; the sap or juice is abundant and obtained by wounding the spathe; when collected before sunrise it is known as neerah [q.v.] in hindostany, and is drunk as a mild saccharine refreshing beverage [pathaneer], but soon after sunrise it undergoes a vinous fermentation and becomes converted into the intoxicating drink toddy [q.v.]; stem gives a gum [gond], black and has a shining fracture. The palmyra flourishes best as above indicated in inferior and especially sandy and arid ground, where scarcely anything else will grow, and where its long roots, penetrating to an immense depth, draw perennial supplies from hidden sources of nourishment; for cultivation the soil is ploughed in furrows and pits half foot deep are dug; seed sown in south in auvany [mausam] or august, on coromandel in caurteecam or november, on w. coast in mitoonam or june and carcatacam or july; while under growth weeds are cleared and adjacent ground is ploughed; the plant is dependent on rain [mazhay]; leaves are cut after eight or ten years according to nature of soil; fruits are cut and toddy [q.v.] is drawn in favorable circumstances after fifteen years; the leaves are dried and otherwise prepared before they are brought to store; price of the commodities vary with locality. For writing purposes the leaves are taken while tender, and the flat portions being cut into strips, and freed from the ribs and woody tendons are boiled and dried first in the shade and afterwards in the sun; the leaves are made smooth by being damped and then repeatedly drawn between two blocks of wood; see below. Fresh juice is medicinally useful in inflammatory affections and dropsy; juice fermented used in diabetes; ash of spadix given in bilious affections; a poultice prepared with toddy [q.v.] is a good substitute for yeast poultice; the neerah [q.v.] is refrigerant, nutritive, diuretic, stomachic, and alterative tonic; in a large dose, as a tumbler-full, it is laxative; patients laboring under phthisis pulmonalis, chronic dyspepsia, secondary syphilis, sopriosis, and some other skin diseases, undergo a course of neerah [q.v.] every year in the hot weather; substituted for british wine, beer, and yeast; in pharm. non-officinal; a fine downy substance is found at the base of the leaves used for stopping bleeding wounds. The germ of the nut pushed to the first stage of growth, when dried in the sun constitutes a palatable vegetable; the same sun-dried and reduced to powder forms a delicate flour; the fusiform roots of the young trees are an article of food by the poorer classes; the fruit, when young and green, is cut open, and the immature seeds are cut out of the fleshy part; each seed then forms a thin, soft, pulpy [noongh] shell filled with juice; these are sold by street hawkers; they are cool and refreshing, sometimes cut into small pieces, sugared and flavored with rose water [goolaub, panneer]; a certain proportion of the fruits ripen on the trees; their seeds then become hard and are of no use except for reproduction; the pulp inside the hard shell is the part in that case eaten. The sap or toddy of the palm has been above mentioned; arrack [q.v.], jaggery [q.v.], and vinegar [caudy] are made from it; arrack is usually distilled from the jaggery; the sugar [q.v.] is first broken up and put in water for four days to ferment; it is then boiled in an earthen pot, the vapour being caught in a bamboo tube which falls into another vessel, in which the liquor is cooled and condensed; this operation is repeated a second time when necessary; arrack is occasionally made from the toddy; see vol. I, 450 [arrack]. Leaves are used for thatching houses and making baskets [tokrah] and mats [boriyah]; they are also used for writing on with a style pointed with steel [cadjan, olay]; during the operation of writing the leaf is supported by the left-hand and the letters are cut or scratched upon its surface with the style, which is kept always in the same position, and the leaf is moved to the left-hand side by means of the thumb; to render the characters more legible, the engraved lines are occasionally filled by smearing the leaves with fresh cow-dung [shauny], which is tinged black by rubbing the lines over with cocoanut [q.v.] oil, or a mixture of oil and charcoal [adoopp kary] powder; all the sacred books of the hindoos, burmese, singhalese, &c., are still made of these olays [q.v.], some of them being highly ornamented; all old accounts [kanakk] in the village revenue department, and the majority of all grants of lands, leases, and accounts in shops, are still kept on these leaves; they used likewise to be sent as letters; palm-leaf books [grantam] are never much beyond 2 feet in length and 2 inches in breadth; they are said to last from one to four or five hundred years; small specimens of the leaves are also smoothed and flattened, the ends of the rays being cut off, then ornamented with mica [abruck], tinsel [caukkay pon], and peacock's [mayil] feathers, and made into ornamental fans; the leaves are also folded up so as to make light buckets for carrying water, or small temporary drinking vessels; they take a dye well; the fibres of the petioles of the leaves, palmyra naur [q.v.], are employed for making twine and small rope, they are about two feet in length. The centre of the stem is soft, but not often hollow; fibro-vascular bundles black, crowded in the outer portion of the stem; outer wood hard, heavy, and durable; the hollowed-out stems are used as water pipes [caurem]; and, split in half, for gutters and open water channels; the hard outer wood is used for posts, rafters, picottahs [q.v.], and other purposes; when of good age, the timber is very valuable for these purposes; the trunk is split into four for rafters, into eight for laths, these are dressed with an adze; from the structure of the fibres, the tree splits easily in the direction of its length, but supports a greater cross strain than any other wood; on the other hand iron nails rust rapidly in it; for house-building and various domestic purposes, the timber is the most generally used of the palm tribe; the trees have to attain a considerable age before they become fit for timber, as their wood becomes harder and blacker by age, and the harder and blacker it is the better; the wood near the circumference of old trees is very heavy and durable, the tree being endogenous; a cubic foot weighs 65 lb., and it is calculated to last eighty years. Small canoes are formed of this tree; two of the stems lashed to a couple of spars form the usual mode of crossing lakes and rivers in the circars [q.v.]; the root forms the head of the canoe, the smaller end is either elevated out of water by the form, or some six inches of the pith is left at that end; as this decays, a lump of olay supplies its place; formerly sea-going vessels were planked with this wood, but the iron fastenings were soon destroyed; boats planked with it were, till the middle of the nineteenth century, common on the godavery; the wood, known as porcupine wood [q.v.], is used in England for veneers and inlaying; in ceylon, it is used for rafters, pillars, and posts of native houses; in the sandy parts of Jaffna a hollow palmyra is inserted to form a well; the dark outside wood of very old trees is used to some extent in Europe for umbrella handles, walking canes, paper rulers, fancy boxes, wafer stamps, and other articles; the whole stem of a tree is occasionally polished and used as a pillar in building; the timber of the female tree is the hardest and best, and that of the male tree is never used unless the tree be very old; the large carpenter beetle [zeerangy], xylocopa, delights in boring the wood, hard though it is. A special variety of this palm is particularly hard, close-grained, and dark-colored; it is generally brought from jaffna. The tamulians say that the palmyra will live and bear for 1,000 years; a tamul poem, the taula vilausam, enumerates 801 purposes to which it may be applied; the tamulians indeed regard it as only inferior in usefulness to the bamboo [q.v.] and the cocoanut [q.v.] palm [taur]. There is a Tamul proverb:—பனையின் நிழலும் நிழலோ பகைவர் உறவும் உறவோ?—"is the shadow of a palmyra tree a shade; is the acquaintance "of an enemy friendship?" There is another:—பனை விதை பெரிதாய் இருந்தும் நிழல் கொடுக்கமாட்டாது—"the "palmyra though from a large seed casts no shade." Nauladiyaur [q.v.] has a stanza:—கடையாயார் நட்பிற் கமுகனைய ரேனை இடையாயார் தெங்கினனையர்—தலையாயார் எண்ணரும் பெண்ணைபோன் றிட்டஞான் றிட்டதே தொன்மையுடையார் தொடர்பு—"in friendship those who are low "are like the areca palm; while those who are mediocre are like "the cocoanut palm; and the great who are at the top are like "the palmyra palm whose uses are difficult to reckon; the friend-"ship of those who have experience of the past when once made is "made for ever." The areca [q.v.] palm requires daily care; the cocoanut [q.v.] occasional care; and the palmyra no care after planting but its uses are countless.——(1) The vernacular identifications of the principal products of the palmyra palm are for convenience shown separately as follows.——*Arrack* (تاڑ کے گڑکی شراب - tárkegurkísharáb, Hind.; പനഞ്ചാരായം - panañcháráyam, Mal.; பனங்கள்ளுச்சாராயம் - panangalluççáráyam, Tam.).——*Cabbage* (تاڑ کا کرد - tárkákrud, Hind.; പനഞ്ചോറു - panañchóru, Mal.; பனங்குருத்து - panangaruttu, Tam.). Tam. also (panangizhangu), meaning palmyra root, applied to young edible root.——*Fibre* (تاڑ کا نار - tárkánár, Hind.; പനനാർ - pananár, Mal.; பனநார் - pananár, Tam.).——*Fruit* (تاڑ پھل - tárphal, Hind.; പനമ്പഴം - panampazham, Mal.; பனங்காய் - panangáy, Tam.).——*Gum* (பனம்பிசின் - panambisin, Tam.).——*Jaggery* (تاڑ کا گڑ - tárkágur, Hind.; പനവെല്ലം - panavellam, Mal.; பனங்கட்டி - panangatti, Tam.). Also called Panay vattoo, meaning palmyra + ball.——*Leaf* (تاڑ کا پتا - tárkápattá, Hind.; తాటాకు - tátiáku, Tel.; ഓല - óla, Mal.; பனையோலை - panaiyólai, Tam.).——*Matting* (பனம்பன்னாடை - panambannádai, Tam.). Fibrous web covering leaf rib. ——*Nut* (تاڑ کی گٹلی - tárkígntlí, Hind.; പനങ്കുരണ്ടി - panankuranti, Mal.; பனங்கொட்டை - panangottai, Tam.).——*Porcupine wood* (பனஞ்சேகுமரம் - panañjégumaram, Tam.). Outer portion of the trunk, from the resemblance of black and white fibres to the porcupine's quills [kharpoosht].——*Root* (گینگل - gengul, Hind.; പനങ്കൂമ്പു - panankúmpu, Mal.; பனங்கிழங்கு - panangizhangu, Tam.).——*Sago* (இளம்பனங்கிழங்குமாவு - ilambanangizhangumávu, Tam.). Tam. means tender palmyra root flour.——*Spathe* (பனம்பாளை - panambálai, Tam.). The fibrous covering of the inflorescence.——*Stem* (பனமரம் - panamaram, Tam.).——*Toddy* (تاڑی - tárí, Hind.; പനങ്കള്ള് - panankallu, Mal.; பனங்கள் - panangal, Tam.).——*Vinegar* (கள்ளுக்காடி - kallukkádi, Tam.).——(2) *Palmyra fish* (कवयी - kavayí, San.; تاڑکھول - tárkhaval, Hind.; గొరక - goraka, Tel.; କୋୟି - kóyi, Oor.; അന്തികള്ളി - antikalli, Mal.; කැවයියා - kávaiyá, Singh.; பனையேறி - panaiyéri, Tam.). Title from being sometimes found on the stem of palmyra trees near water's edge. San. from (kavi, san. intelligent) [cavy]. Hind. from (tár, hind. palmyra + khaval, hind. the fish, barbus ticto). Tel. means a missile. Oor. from sanscrit. Mal. from (anti, mal. nut + kalli, mal. thief). Singh. from sanscrit. Tam. from (panai, tam. palmyra, borassus flabelliformis, linn. + éru, tam. to ascend) [palmyra snake]. Oor. also (korvu). Tam. also (shennal), meaning red one. Title otherwise Climbing fish, Climbing perch, Kavay, Kay, Tree climber, Tree fish. Anabas scandens, labyrinthici, acanthopterygii, teleostei [matsyam, 30], of naturalists [jantoo]. Alias Amphiprion testudineus, scansor; Anabas spinosus, testudineus, trifoliatus; Anthias testudineus; Cojus cobojius; Lutjanus testudo, scandens; Perca scandens; Sparus testudineus, scandens. Cobojius from sanscrit. Freshwater; lower jaw slightly longer; scales between lateral-line and the commencement of base of dorsal fin, over soft dorsal, caudal, anal, and base of pectoral; rifle-green, lightest on abdomen; during life there are usually four wide vertical body-bands, and a dark stripe from angle of mouth to preopercle; young have black blotch on side of base of tail, surrounded by light, sometimes yellow, ring; usually they have a black spot at end of opercle, and sometimes another at base of pectoral; extensively employed for stocking ponds, estuaries and freshwaters; 8½ inches in length; breeding season about june and july. The peculiar apparatus with which their gills are provided enables these fish to breathe as well out of the water as in it; the fishermen keep them for five or six days in an earthen pot or covered basket; if in a basket, it is necessary to keep it securely covered, as they can climb up the sides and escape with the greatest ease; they can travel a long distance on land, on occasions when the water they are living in becomes stagnant or dried up, and they can also, in common with several other indian fishes, remain in a semi-torpid condition under the mud for months together; hence they are often found after a heavy storm in places where they would the least be expected, and have frequently been supposed to fall from the clouds.——*Palmyra point* (பனைமரமுனை - panaimaramunai, Tam.). Otherwise called Point pedro. The north-east point of Ceylon, the high palmyra [q.v.] trees on which are conspicuous.——*Palmyra snake* (تاڑ کا سانپ - tárkásámp, Hind.; తాటికట్టెడ - tátikatteda, Tel.; പനയൻ - panayan, Mal.; பனையேறி - panaiyéri, Tam.). Title from the haunt. Hind. from (tár, hind. palmyra tree + sámp, hind. snake). Tel. from (tádi, tel. palmyra + katteda, tel. snake so called). Tam. from (panai, tam. palmyra + éru, tam. to ascend) [palmyra fish]. The term may be considered co-extensive with the family Dipsadidæ, ophidii colubriformes, ophidia [sarpam], reptilia [sarpy, 22], of naturalists [jantoo]. Not venomous. These are nocturnal tree snakes, attain length of 6 or 7 feet, live on warm-blooded animals; some prey on birds [pacshy] only, others attack nothing but mammals [sastanam]. Coloration varied; green rarely forms the ground-color, brown and black prevail. The two species in Southern india are:—"*a*" Dipsas forsteni. Alias Triglyphodon forsteni. Brownish olive; lower parts yellow, with blackish spots along each side; a longitudinal median black band along the occiput and nape of neck; short black band along each side of the neck; another from eye to angle of mouth.—"*b*" Dipsas trigonata. Alias Coluber trigonalis; Dipsadomorphus trigonatus. Yellowish olive, with irregular white or yellow zigzag band along back, edged with black; crown of head with two dark bands edged with black, indistinct crown band from eye towards angle of mouth; belly white, with irregular series of brown dots along each side. Feeds on mice [shoondely].——*Palmyra swallow* (تاڑ ابابیل - tárabábíl, Hind. and Dec.; తాటిపిట్ట - tátipitta, Tel.). Title from resort and swallow-like flight. Hind. from (tár, hind. palmyra + abábíl, ar. swallow). Tel. from (tádu, tel. palmyra + pitta, tel. bird). Hind. also (tálchatak), meaning palm + sparrow. Title otherwise Ashy swallow shrike. Artamus fuscus, artaminæ, laniadæ [pingalam], dentirostres, insessores [pacshy, 19], of naturalists [jantoo]. Alias Ocypterus leucohynchos, rufiventer. General hue cinereous, or ashy-grey, purest on head, with tinge of rufous on back and scapulars; breast, abdomen, under wing-coverts, and under tailcoverts ashy-white, tinge of rufous on belly; quills and tail blackish ashy-grey, latter tipped narrowly with pale ashy; upper tail-coverts white beneath, showing white border next dark tail. Bill pale bluish, darker at the tip; legs slaty; irides dark brown. Length about 7 inches. Common in wooded districts, especially near the palmyra [q.v.] palm; small party may occasionally be seen; live entirely on insects [poochy]; flight is swallow-like [ababil]. No other common species here.

PALO (پلو - palo, *Hind.*). Preparation of Goolancha [q.v.].

PAMIDY (పమిడి - pamidi, *Tel.*). A form of (paidi, tel. gold from pasi, tel. yellow). Gold. Plant first term. Ex.:— Cæsalpinia pulcherrima (pamiditangédu), golden cassia auriculata.

PAN (पण् - pan, *San.*). To barter, to stake.——*Panayam* (പണയം - panayam, Mal.). See sep. title.——*Paniny* (पाणिनि - pánini, San.). From (panin, san. proper name). Son of Panin. The celebrated ancient Sanscrit grammarian. The Paunineeyam grammar [lacshanam] is in eight books; it is, except to the initiated, in great confusion; yet it originally made an epoch in Indian literature. Paniny lived in the fourth century B. C.; born in the extreme north-west of India. See vol. I (57). Nunnool [q.v.] is quite independent.——*Pauny* (पाणि - páni, San.). From (pan, san. to deal in). Hand; also suffix in proper names, as Chuckrapauny or discus-handed vishnoo, Shoolapauny or the trident-handed shiva [peyar].——*Pundam* (പണ്ടം - pantam, Mal.). From (panya, san. article of trade). Articles. ——*Pundaula* (പണ്ടശാല - pantála, Mal.). From (pantam, mal. articles + shálá, san. hall); once store-keeper in temples. Tribe in Malabar, of which the Rajah of Calicut is a member.——*Pundauram* (പണ്ടാരം - pantáram, Mal.). Treasury, government. ——*Punnum* (பணம் - panam, Tam.). From (pan, san. to barter). Money. General term for coin, or other representative of property that passes current from hand to hand as a circulating medium [naunyam]. Same as Fanam.——*Punsawry* (پنساری - pansárí, Hind.). From (panya, san. ware + shálá, san. house). A druggist; a dealer in groceries, spices, herbs, &c.

PAN (பன் - pan, *Tam.*). Rush.——*Panrooty* (பன்ரொட்டி - panrotti, Tam. panruti*). From (pan, tam. rush grass used in mat-making + urattu, tam. uneven ground of dried mud).—"*a*" Deputy tahsildarry, South arcot district. Pay Rs. 70.—"*b*" Town, Deputy tahsildar's station, Railway station; South arcot dist., Cuddalore tal.; pop. 8,956; acres 725; lat. 11° 47'; long.

79° 36′; height 82 feet; from Chidambaram N.N.W. 27 miles; from Cuddalore W.N.W. 16 miles; from Madras S.S.W. 100 miles; from Tindivanam S.S.W. 31 miles; from Tricalore E.S.E. 26 miles; from Vriddhauchellam N.E. 23 miles; from the sea W. 16 miles. Large market town at junction of several roads. Centre for ground-nut [q.v.] trade of district. Old Shiva temple with fine gopooram [q.v.], and an old mosque [musjid].

PAN (பண் - pan, *Tam.*). To make, produce.——*Panikkan* (പണിക്കർ - panikkar, Mal.). From (pani, mal. work + káran, mal. doer). Teacher of the use of arms in a family.——*Panipoora* (പണിപ്പുര - panippura, Mal.). From (pani, mal. work + pura, mal. house). A manufactory [caurgah, puttaday].——*Paniseyra* (பணிசெய்வ - paniseyva, Tam.). From (pani, tam. service + shey, tam. to do). Caste of conch-blowers to the tamul shoodras, corresponding to the teloogoo Dausaries [q.v.].——*Paniyan* (പണിയൻ - paniyan, obl.; പണിയൻ - paniyan, personal sing.; പണിയർ - paniyar, pers. pl., Mal.). From (pani, mal. work + an, mal. personal suffix). A rude tribe in Malabar. They dwell in small villages, each consisting of four or five huts, which are called Maudam [q.v.]. They are attached to Tumboorauns [q.v] or lords who give them daily subsistence, and exact daily labor. Disputes among them are settled by their masters, who must also furnish money to procure wives for their Paniyar. They take only one wife, but the marriage may be dissolved at either party's pleasure; all the children belong to the husband's master. This caste eat all kinds of animal food and carrion except beef, and may lawfully drink spiritnous liquors [arrack]. They bury the dead without any particular ceremony [shavacaud]. The deity is called Cootty shauttan [q.v.], a juggler. They have no kind of priest. In Wynaud they wash river-lands and surface soils for gold [pon] See vol. II, 99.——*Punnay* (பண்ணை - pannai, Tam.). From (pan, tam. to produce). Lit. a farm establishment of laborers. A paddy field [vayal]. Punnaicaur is a watcher employed by the farmer; often used as general term for a pariah [q.v.] tribe man. Punnay choomay is a bundle of corn in the straw given to laborers in the time of harvest. Punnaiyaul is a laboring cultivator.

PANAY (பனை - panai, *Tam.*). From (pani, tam. to be agitated); from the rustle of leaves when blown upon by the wind. Same as Palmyra.——*Panayairy* (பனையேறி - panaiyéri, Tam.). Means palmyra + climber. The naturalists' fish family Percidæ [matsyam, 1].——*Pennay* (பெண்ணை - pennai, Tam.). Means palmyra. Old Tamul name for either the Pennair [q.v.] or the Ponniaur [q.v.].——*Punnauday* (பன்னாடை - pannádai, Tam.). From (panai, tam. palm + ádai, tam. texture). Fibrous netlike covering about the base of palmyra [q.v.] and cocoanut [q.v.] leaf stalks. Sometimes used for straining ghee [q.v.] and toddy [q.v.]; hence called neyyary or ghee-strainer.

PANAYAM (പണയം - panayam, *Mal.*). From (pan, san. to stake) [pan]. A simple mortgage of land, not necessarily with possession [adavoo]. If usufructuary, it is generally called Caripanayam or Coy panayam; if hypothecatory, Todpanayam or Choondy panayam. See vol. I, 128 and II, 104.——**(1)** *Panayam ola* (പണയഓല - panayamóla, Mal.). From (above + óla, mal. cadjan). Otherwise Panayachaurtt. Mortgage-deed [adavoochit].——*Panayapaud* (പണയപ്പാട് - panayappátu, Mal.). From (above + pátu, mal. state). Article pledged or mortgaged.——**(2)** *Caripanayam* (കരിപണയം - karipanayam, Mal.). From (kari, mal. plough). Otherwise Coypanayam. Usufructuary form of mortgage, where the excess of the usufruct over the interest on the sum borrowed, if any, is to be returned to the mortgagor. No such return is made in Otty [q.v.].——*Choondy panayam* (ചൂണ്ടിപ്പണയം - chúntippanayam, Mal.). From (chúntu, mal. to point out). Hypothecatory form of simple mortgage. Same as Todpanayam.——*Oondarty panayam* (ഉണ്ടരുതി - untaruti, Mal.). From (un, mal. to eat + aruti, mal. end). A form of panayam, or simple mortgage, where the mortgagee has possession [caripanayam] and holds the estate till the usufruct or rents and profits repay the sum borrowed. The pauttom [q.v.] or rent is previously determined, and it is therefore known beforehand in how many years the debt will be liquidated, and the mortgagee is under no necessity of rendering to the proprietor an account of the produce of the estate. See vol. I, 128 and II, 104.——*Todpanayam* (തൊട്ടുപണയം - totupanayam, Mal.). From (totu, mal. to touch). Mortgage of grounds without handing them over; same as Choondy panayam.

PANDAM (பந்தம் - pandam, *Tam.*). From (bandh, san. to bind) [bandah, bandhoo, bund]. Tie; torch [masaul].——*Pandacaural* (പന്തക്കാവൽ - pantakkával, Mal.). From (pantal, mal. shed + kával, mal. guard). A fee consisting of portion of crop given to a hired servant.——*Panda sairvay* (பந்தச் சேர்வை - pandaççérvai, Tam.). Means torch + worship. Solar [madhyamasowramaunam] festival [pundigay, 6d]. Celebrated in villages in honor of Vishnoo [q.v.] on a Saturday in Pooratanshy [mausam], i.e., between 15th September and 15th October. Performance consists in affecting to be possessed by the spirit of a deity, and beating the body with a flaming torch [maryanday]——*Pandaul* (పందిలి - pandili, Tel.; പന്തൽ - pantal, Mal.; பந்தல் - pandal, Tam.). From (bandh, san. to bind). A shed [cotaur, cottye]. A temporary structure erected for a marriage ceremony [calyaunam]. A water pandaul is a place where water is given gratis to passers by [salivendla, tanneer pandaul], for which inams [q.v.] were assigned in former days. Plant first term. Ex., where transl. is of second term:—Cucumis melo, var. utilissimus (pandilidósa), cucumis sativus; Ipomæa bonanox (panditivankáya), solanum melongena. See gloss. paragraphs.——*Pandaul cucumber* (పందిలిదోస - pandilidósa, Tel.). Same as Country melon.——*Pundalore* (പന്തല്ലൂർ - pantalúr, Mal.). From (pandal, mal. shed + úr, mal. village).—"*a*" Hill; Malabar dist., Valavanaud tal.; lat. 11° 4′ N., long. 76° 13′ E; height 2,000 feet; from Calicut E.S.E. 30 miles; from Perindalaman N.N.W. 8 miles. Overlooking Malapooram. Covered for the most part with dense scrub jungle, but one or two semi-abandoned coffee [q.v.] gardens on its northern slopes. Race-course here for Europeans.—"*b*" village; Neilgherry dist., S.E. Wynaud tal.; lat. 11° 29′; long. 76° 23′. Was made headquarter of the Head assistant collector, Neilgherries, in March 1889. Was of importance during early part of Wynaud gold mining speculations.

PANDANG (پندن - pandan, *Malay*). The screw-pine palm. Origin of generic name Pandanus.

PANDOO (पाण्डु - pándu, *San.*). From (pand, san. to move); mind-moving, attracting; applied to white color as being attractive; pale as of some northern race. The north-country king of Cooroos, reputed father of the five Pandavas, viz., Yoodhishtiran, Bheemau, Arjoonan, Nacoolau and Sahadevan. These in poetical language are said to have been the sons of gods; Yoodhishtiran being the son of dharman [q.v.] or justice; Bheeman of vayoo [q.v.] or the wind; Arjoonan of indran [q.v.] or the firmament; and the other two, who were twins, of the ashwiny [q.v.] comaurar, the twin physicians of the gods [deva]. These five brethren were famous for valour, but particularly Arjoonan [q.v.] who was the friend of Krishnan [q.v.]. Yoodhishtiran [q.v.] was also remarkable for truth and equity, and Bheeman [q.v.] for strength. The battle between them and Dooryodhanan [q.v.], and their conquest and possession of Cooroo cshetram, are circumstantially related in the Mahabhaurat [charitram, mahabhaurat]. See vol. I (1), (117).——*Pandava* (पाण्डव - pándava, San.). Son or descendant of king Pandoo. Has become confused with the Tamul word Paundy [q.v.] meaning a tamulian. See vol. I (79).——*Paundarungan* (पाण्डुरङ्ग - pánduranga, San.). From (above + ranga, san. color). Shiva [pundauram].——*Pundauram* (பண்டாரம் - pandáram, Tam.). See sep. title.

PANEER (پنیر - panír, *Hind.*). Cheese. Plant first term. Ex:—Guettarda speciosa (panírkáphúl), cheese flower. See gloss. paragraphs. Distinguish from Panneer.

PANTHY (پنتھی - panthí, *Hind.*). From (pant'há, san. a road) [pauthay]. The follower of any particular sect.

PANY (شبنم - shabnam, *Pers.*; اوس - os, *Hind.*; ಮಂಜು - manju, *Can.*; మంచు - mantsu, *Tel.*; മഞ്ഞു - maññu, *Mal.*; பனி - pani, *Tam.*). Pers. from (shab, pers. night + nam, pers. wet). Hind. from (avashyá, san. fog). Dew. There is a Tamul proverb:—தையும் மாசியும் வையகத்து உறங்கு—"in tye" or january and maushy [mausam] or february sleep under "thatch;" because dew is then excessive [caulam]. And another:—பனிக்கண் திறந்தால் மழைக்கண் திறக்கும்—"if there be dew fall, there will be rain fall;" heavy fall of dew in dewy season is held to prognosticate good rainfall [mazhay] in the rainy season [caurtey, ritoo]. In agricultural economy dew serves to bring to perfection some of the dry grains [q.v.] and pulses [dholl]. Pany cutty is ice; also applied to frost or snow.——*Panipayar* (பனிப்பயறு - panippayaru, Tam.). From (above + payaru, tam. the pulse). A wild kind of pulse [dholl, vellaumay].——*Panneer* (పన్నీరు - panníru, Tel.). Rose water. Plant first term. Ex., where transl. is of second term:—Guettarda speciosa (pannírupuvvuchettu), flower tree; Rosa damascena (pannírucbettu), tree. See gloss. paragraphs. Distinguish from Paneer.

PAPARKHAR (پپڑکھار - paparkhár, *Hind*). From (pappar, hind. cake so called + khár, hind. alkali). Country potash used in poppadams [q.v.]. See under Khar.

PAPAW (पोपया - pópayá, *Mahr.*; पोप्पायि - póppáyi, *Conc.*; عنبة هندى - anabahihindí, *Ar.* and *Pers.*; پپیہ - papaíyah, *Hind.*; پپائی کا جہاڑ - popáikájhár, *Dec.*; پپیا - papaya, *Malay*; ಪರಂಗಿಮರ - parangimara, *Can.*; ಬಪ್ಪಂಗಾಯಿ - bappangáyi, *Too.*; బొప్పాయి - boppáyi, *Tel.*; പപ്പായം - pappáyam, *Mal.*; පැපොල් - papol, *Singh.*; பப்பாளி - pappáli, *Tam.*). Title from malay. Mahr. and conc. from hindostany. Ar. from (anabah, ar. grape, vitis vinifera, linn. + hindí, ar. indian). Can. from (parangi, can. european + mara, can. tree). Mal. from hayti; Malay also (kálíki). Can. also (pappangáyimara); (pangimara);

(goppenmara); (pappáyimara). Tel. also (madanaánapa), meaning pleasing + lagenaria vulgaris, ser.; (madhurnakamu). Mal. also (karmmós), meaning melon; (kappalam), meaning foreign fruit; (pappáyampázham), meaning papaw tree + spondias mangifera, willd. Tam. also (parangiyámanakku), foreign + castor-oil plant, ricinus communis, linn., from similar leaves; (pasalai), meaning green, from greenish fruit [indian spinach, small indian purslane]; (pappáyi). Title otherwise Foreign castor, Melon tree, Papaw mango, Papaya. Botanically Carica papaya, linn., passifloreæ [vricsham, 61]. Alias Papaya carica, communis, vulgaris. Tree, 20–30 feet, without branches; leaves alternate, palmate, seven-partite; segments oblong, acute, sinuated, the middle one trifid; fruit succulent, oblong, furrowed; calyx small, five-toothed; corolla tubular in the male and five-lobed in the female, divided nearly to the base into five segments; male flowers axillary in slightly-compound racemes or panicles, white female ones in short simple racemes, sometimes on a different tree; corolla longer than in the male, yellowish. Fast-growing, soft-wooded tree; native of tropical america; introduced; fruit formed by a large oblong pepo suspended like the jack [q.v.] fruit; form of a pear [amrood], much larger than a cocoanut [q.v.]; ripens of a pale greenish yellow, resembling that of a fine orange-flesh melon [oorvauroo]; interior of fruit filled with small, olive-colored [zeitoon], shot-like seeds. The seeds contain an oil, papaya oil; caricin, an oil-like substance with a disagreeable taste and smell, soluble in ether and alcohol; an acid similar to palmitic acid, carica fat acid; a crystalline acid, papayic acid, insoluble in cold water, but soluble in hot water and alcohol; a resin acid, having an irritating and bitter taste, insoluble in water and ether, soluble in alcohol and alkalies; and a soft resin similar to that found in the fruit flesh of the female plant. The fruit secretes a milky viscid juice, which has the property of hastening the decay of muscular fibre, when the latter is exposed to its influence; the younger the fruit, the more milk it yields; when nitric acid [shorey ka tezaub], diluted with four parts of water, is added drop by drop to the milk expressed from very young fruit, at the centre of each drop a gelatinous pellicle is formed, divided by greyish streaks; at the same time the centre of the pellicles becomes opaque and of the color of the yolk of an egg, they enlarge as if by the prolongation of divergent fibres; the whole liquid assumes at first the appearance of an agate [akeek] with milky clouds and it seems as if organic membranes were forming under the eye of the observer; when the coagulum extends to the whole mass, the yellow spots again disappear; by agitation it becomes granular like soft cheese; the yellow color reappears on adding a few more drops of nitric acid [shorey ka tezaub]; after a few hours the yellow color turns to brown. Milky juice is medicinally anthelmintic; chiefly in round worms; substituted for british santonin [absinth]; seeds same as juice; gives to pharm. juice non-officinal. The fruit is best for eating during the summer; when ripe the interior is soft, yellow and sweetish, eaten by all classes and esteemed innocent and wholesome; when green it is used by natives in curry [q.v.], also pickled; the green fruit, when peeled, boiled, cut into small pieces, and served with sweet oil [zeitoon], vinegar [caudy], salt [ooppoo], and pepper [q.v.], serves as a palatable vegetable and is similar to squash [carcauroo] in taste; also made into tarts, when not easily distinguished from those made of apples [seb]; seeds have a water cress-like flavor [haleem]. Water impregnated with the juice makes meat washed in it tender; or another operation is to hang the flesh under the tree for two or three hours; another way is to wrap the meat in the leaves and then roast it; or a small portion may be boiled with the meat. Leaves employed by negroes in west indies to wash linen instead of soap [sauboon]. Tree is used for avenue-planting [shaulay]. No other common species here.——*Wild papaw* (కారుబొప్పాయి - káruboppáyi, Tel.). Tel. from (káru, tel. wild + boppáyi, tel. carica papaya, linn.). Tel. also (kódidzuttumánu), meaning cock + crest + tree; (karaka) [chebulic myrobalan]. Title otherwise Scarlet-flowered sterculia. Botanically Sterculia [cauvalam] colorata, roxb., sterculiaceæ [vricsham, 26]. Alias Erythropsis roxburghiana; Firmiana colorata. Leaves palmately five-lobed; segments acuminated; calyx cylindrical, clavate; carpels oblong, glabrous, long-stalked; calyx and carpels reddish-orange-colored; flowers large, red; flowering in the cold season. Large tree; forests of the plains, about foot of mountains throughout presidency; sheds its leaves in the cold weather, shortly afterwards covered with flowers, appearing as covered with numerous ramifications of red coral [moongah]. Bark used in rope-making; wood grey, very soft.

PAPEETA (پپیتہ - papítah, *Hind.*; கைப்பங்கொட்டைச் செடி - kaippangottaiççedi, *Tam.*). Title from spanish through hindostany. Tam. from (kaippu, tam. bitterness + kottai, tam. seed + shedi, tam. tree). Title otherwise St. ignatius' bean, Strychnine tree. Botanically Strychnos [mooshty] ignatii, bergius, loganiaceæ [vricsham, 89]. Alias Ignaziana philippinica. A branching tree, native of philippine islands; flowers white, smelling like jasmine [q.v.]; fruit large, pear-shaped [amrood]. Seeds are about an inch in length, their form is ovoid, but by mutual pressure it is rendered very irregular, and they are three to four or five-sided, bluntly angular or flattish, with a conspicuous hilum at one end; in the fresh state they are covered with silvery adpressed hairs; portions of a shaggy brown epidermis are here and there perceptible on those found in commerce; but in the majority the seed shows the dull grey granular surface of the albumen itself; notwithstanding the different outward appearance, the structure of papeeta beans accords with that of nux-vomica [poison nut]; only the radicle is longer, thicker, and frequently somewhat bent, and the cotyledons are more pointed; the horny brownish albumen is translucent, very hard, and difficult to split; the whole seed swells considerably by prolonged digestion in warm water, and has then a heavy, earthy smell; the beans are intensely bitter, and highly poisonous. Strychine is present in three times the quantity of that in nux-vomica nuts, but there is no brucine; medical uses same as nux-vomica [poison nut].

PAPPAH (பாப்பா - páppá, *Tam.*). From (pápa, tel. child). Non-bramin female proper name [peyar].

PAPPARAM (பப்பரம் - papparam, *Tam.*). From (babhru, san. a country, so called). Tamul name for the Goozerat country [bhoogolashastram, goorjaram].——*Pappara pooly* (பப்பரப் புளி - papparappuli, Tam.). Same as Baobab.

PAPPILY (रक्तवल्ली - raktavallí, *San.*; खांडवेल - khándavéla, *Mahr.*; ಪಾಪುಲಿಗಿಡ - pápuligida, *Can.*; సురుగుడు - surugudu, *Tel.*; பப்பிளி - pappili, *Tam.*). Title from tamul. San. from (rakta, san. red + vallí, san. creeper); from red dye. Mahr. also (lókhandí), meaning hard [large jungle geranium]. Can. also (papli); (pampli); (paplichakke). Tel. also (suralatíga); (errachiratali); (yerrachicatti); (suratipattatíga). Tam. also (shurulbattaikkodi), meaning rolled + bark + creeper, from appearance of bark in the market; (vémbádai), meaning margosa + covering. Title otherwise Red creeper, Vembaudam bark creeper. Botanically Ventilago madraspatana, gærtn., rhamneæ [vricsham, 41]. Alias Ventilago denticulata. Large scandent shrub, reaches to top of highest trees in forests; the leaves are ovate, acuminate, coriaceous and shining flowers in slender spikes; fruit is samaroid, from 1½ to 2 inches long, and ⅜ inch broad; nut is about size of a pea [calauyam], girt at the base by remains of the calyx forming a disc; roots are from ½ to 1 inch in diameter, and rough with reddish loose scales. The bark occurs in very thin and light pieces, varying generally in length from ½ to 2¼ inches, and in breadth from 1 to 6 lines; it is of a brown or reddish-brown color, odoriferous but almost tasteless; as sold in the bazaar, it contains a large quantity of small scaly pieces of its epidermis, which are still thinner, lighter and darker in color; the bark is collected extensively on northern slopes of neilgherries. Medicinal drug consists of the root-bark in scales made up of numerous papyraceous layers of a deep reddish-brown color, and in some of the older pieces, with a metallic lustre; this root-bark is medicinally carminative, stomachic, tonic and stimulant-diuretic; preparation is simple powder; doses, from thirty to ninety grains three or four times in the twenty-four hours; substituted for cascarilla, pimento [china pepper], calumba [q.v.] and cinchona [koinah]. Stem gives a gum [q.v.]; bark used for cordage; the root bark yields a red dye [shauyam], orange and chocolate with oldenlandia umbellata, linn. [chayroot], and black with galls [mauchicoy]; chocolate often seen on borders of native cloths. Wood greyish-yellow, porous, soft. No other common species here.

PARA (पर - para, *San.*) [pra]. Distant, supreme, best, high, after, foreign, other. Enemy.——*Parabramh* (परब्रह्म - parabrahma, San.). From (above + brahma, san. the absolute). The supreme being [autmam, bramh]; a post-vedic term of the oopanishads [q.v.]. Since the time of Shuncaracharry [shuncaran], the term has been specially used by the sheivas for Shiva [q.v.]. Sometimes this appears shorter as Paran [q.v.]. In modern books there is the assertion that Rama [q.v.], even Hanooman [q.v.], is Parabramh. The term Parashacty [q.v.] in the same works is applied to Seetay [q.v.]. Earlier books ascribe no shacty [q.v.] or feminine energy of any sort to Parabramh; but now the Parashacties are numerous [matam, paraupara vast, paty]. See vol. I (76).——*Paradesham* (परदेश - paradésha, San.). From (para, san. foreign + désha, san. region). Foreign land. Paradeshy is a foreigner or stranger, in common usage applied to a pilgrim or beggar.——*Paralocam* (परलोक - paralóka, San.). Means other world. Heaven. Going to paralocam is a euphemism common for dying [shivalocam, veicoontam].——*Param* (पर - para, San.). The east point of the compass. The duration of Bramha's [q.v.] life, consisting of a hundred of his years [calpam]. As measure of astronomical sidereal or star time, indian second; 60 soorams = 1 param; 60 params = 1 vighaticay or indian minute [caulam, 4, 5]; approximate actual value, 1 param = ·4 european second, or 24‴; same as vipalam [caulam, 6], caushta calay [caulam, 6]. See vol. I, 609.——*Parama hamsan* (परमहंस - paramahamsa, San.). From (parama, san. best + hamsa, san. an ascetic order so called). A religious man who has subdued all his senses [indriyam] by abstract meditation [yogam].——*Paramam* (परम - parama, San.). Extreme.——*Paraman* (परम - parama, San.). Shiva [q.v.] the supreme [paran]. Parama shivan or shiva the supreme is a common hindoo 2nd or pers. name [peyar].——*Paramatty* (பரமதி - paramathi, Tam.). From (paraman, tam. shiva + pathi, tam. place). Sanscrit name (paraméshtʼhípura), meaning shiva, the supreme god + town.—" *b* " " *a* " Deputy; tahsildarry, Salem district. Pay Rs. 70.— Namcull Town, Deputy tahsildar's head-quarters; Salem dist., Namcull tal.; pop. 3,003; acres 2,623; lat. 11° 09′; long. 78° 04′; from Madras S.W. 199 miles; from Namcull S.W. 11 miles; from Oossoor S.S.E. 109 miles; from Salem S.S.W. 36 miles; from Tripatore S.S.W. 99 miles; from Yercaud S.S.W. 45 miles. Old Shiva temple with inscriptions and old Vishnoo temple. In the hamlet of Manrootty is an old Shiva temple with inscriptions. The Yidoomban coolam tank, really a dam across the Tirmany moottaur, is close.——*Paramaunoo* (परमाणु - paramánu, San.). Smallest atom. Thirty such atoms are supposed to form a mote in a sunbeam. The invisible base of aggregate bodies [bhootam]. The atomic bases of the puncha bhootam are as follows:—of earth, water; of water, fire; of fire, air; of air, ether; of ether, mauyay.——*Paramaupamam* (परमापम - paramápama, San.). From (parama, san. extreme + apama, san. declination); the greatest declination. The inclination [natam] of a planet's [graham] orbit [cacsham] to the ecliptic [craunty mundalam]. Paramaupamacramam is the obliquity of the ecliptic which is constantly 24° by Hindoo siddhauntams [q.v.]. Paramaupama cramajyay is sine of a planet's greatest declination [cramam, craunty, jyotisham].——*Paramaurtam* (परमार्थ - paramártʼha, San.). From (parama, san. great + artʼha, san. object). The great object or end of life [aram, samsauram], true wisdom or truth, knowledge of the real and universal nature of soul [autmam, nyaunam]. Paramaurtan is epithet of the Supreme being. Also a simpleton not experienced in worldly wisdom. Paramaurta gooroo katay is a story of gooroo noodle by Beschi [veeramaumoony].——*Paramautman* (परमात्मन् - paramátman, San.; பரமாத்துமா - paramáttumá, Tam.). From (parama. san. best + átma, san. soul). The soul of the world in opposition to Jeevautman [jeevam] the human soul [autmam]. For the discussion whether these are two or one, see Adweitam and Dweitam.——*Parameshty* (परमेष्ठी - paraméshtʼhí, San.). From (parama, san. supreme + stʼha, san. to stand). The supreme deity.——*Parameshwaran* (परमेश्वर - paraméshvara, San.; பரமேசுரன் - paramésuran, Tam.). From (parama, san. supreme + íshvara, san. lord). The heavenly lord, an epithet of the divine being. Also hindoo 2nd or pers. name [peyar].——*Paramparam* (परम्परा- parampará, San.). From (para, san. after + para, san. other). In succession, hereditary.——*Paran* (பரன் - paran, Tam.). Means distant with regard to time and space. He that is best. It corresponds with Bramh [q.v.], or Parabramh [q.v.] of the Oopanishad [q.v.]. In S. india the controversy is whether Vishnoo [q.v.] or Shiva [q.v.] is paran [paraman].——*Parasamayam* (பரசமயம் - parasamayam, Tam.). From (para, san. foreign + shamayam, tam. faith). Any religious system [samayam] except the six divisions of the Sheiva religion.——*Parashacty* (पराशक्ति - paráshakti, San.). From (para, san. supreme + shakti, san. power). Shacty, as the feminine power of the Paraupara vast [q.v.]. This shacty is represented as a woman in natural form with two hands, one of which she lets hang down, and in the other she holds a red water-lily [indian water lily]; while on another flower, called taumaray or lotus [nelumbo], she stands, and two of the same kind she has behind her ears; this flower is regarded as sacred. The color of her body is green. On her head she has a crown and on her brow three white streaks with a round spot [tilacam], the mark of all Sheivas. Her ears, with large holes in them, hang full of jewels. Round her neck she wears a string of pearls [moty], and another long one with various jewels hangs down to her breast. On her arms she has bracelets and rings after the fashion of the tamul women. Her garment is red. Round her waist she wears a golden belt with various jewels, and on her feet, silver rings; while a long garland hangs down from her shoulders. From this shacty [q.v.] Tamulians derive nine other shacties called Nava shacty; Ancaulamman, Bhadra cauly, Chamoondy, Doorga, Mauriyamman, Pidaury, Poodcalay, Poornay, Yellamma. Of these Poornay and Poodcalay are Ayenaur's [ayen] wives. Others say that the Parashacty has produced many thousands of other shacties. These shacties are evidently the village goddesses assimilated. The shacty is dignified with the name of Parvaty [q.v.] by orthodox followers of shiva [q.v.]; Lutchmy [q.v.] by those of Vishnoo [q.v.]. Some practise also a special shacty worship; see Vaumacharry [matam, paty]. See vol. I (77).——*Paraucrama tevan* (பராக்கிரமத்தேவன் - parákkiramattévan, Tam.). From (parákrama, san. valour + tévan, tam. title). Last of the second line of the Paundyan [q.v.] dynasty [raj]. Driven out in 1324 by Malik caufoor [q.v.]. See vol. I (123).——*Paraupara vast* (परापरवस्तु - paráparavastu, San.). From (para, san. distant + apara, san. near + vastu, san. thing). The being or existence which is itself the first and the last [parabramh]. The Tamulians in rare cases represent this as a material visible being. They then represent it with four arms. In two of its hands, which are lifted up, it holds weapons, viz., in the one the chunk [q.v.], and in the other the chuckram [q.v.], weapons of Vishnoo [q.v.]. With these however it is represented only by the Veishnavas. The Sheivas on the other hand represent the figure with a weapon and a device of Shiva [q.v.]. On its head it has a crown with the sun [sooryan] and the moon [chundran]. The color of its body is green. In its ears, and round its neck, hands and feet, it wears manifold decorations of pearls [moty], precious stones [ratnam], gold [pon] and silver [velly], like the gods. From its shoulder a cloth hangs down, and also a garland of various flowers; while both sides are covered with a cloth representing twelve worlds with various paintings in them. The remaining two of the fourteen worlds [locam] are on the breast, in the upper one of which is Bramha [q.v.], with four heads and four arms, having on his left hand his consort Saraswaty [q.v.], and on his right Devendran [q.v.], the king of the subordinate gods, standing as though he had something to report; while in the lower one, the world of the gods, there is Devendran, in a sitting posture, with four arms, and some gods standing before him, as though they were informing him of something. Further down on the body is the mountain Veicoontam [q.v.], where Vishnoo, having four arms, is sitting with his two wives, viz., Lutchmy [q.v.] on his right hand and Bhoomidevy [q.v.] on his left, and serpents [sheshan] are bending over his head. Then comes the mountain Keilausam [q.v.] on which Shiva likewise with four arms resides in a sitting posture, having on his right hand Nundikeshwaran [q.v.] with the head of an ox, standing, and on his left Parvaty [q.v.] his consort sitting; besides them, there are on both sides two Dwaura paulacans [q.v.] or door-keepers, while over Shiva to the right is Soobramanyan [q.v.], with a peacock [mayil] on which he rides, and to the left Vigneshwaran [q.v.] with an elephant's [q.v.] head. Through all these worlds and places passes the great mountain Mahameroo [q.v.], whose summit projects over the crown of the whole figure. At the bottom it is supported by eight elephants [ashtadic gajam] and eight serpents [ashta dicpaulacan], which rest on a tortoise [coormam], which is Vishnoo himself in his second incarnation [avatar]. But below the tortoise, there are still to be seen the feet of the figure representing the supreme being, to indicate that it is this which must support all in all. Round about the figure in the outer circle, there is a painting representing the seven great oceans [samoodram] and the seven great islands [dweepam]. This figure is only a painting found in some of the large pagodas [q.v.], nor does it receive adoration, [poojah] or offerings. See vol. I (79) [matam].——*Parauparay* (परापरा - parápará, San.) From (pará, san. distant + apará, san. near). Parvaty [q.v.] ——*Parausharan* (பராசரன் - parásaran, Tam.). From (pará san. away + shrí, san. to kill). Destroyer. The sage so called. Hindoo 2nd or pers. name [peyar].——*Paropacaury* (പരോപകാരി - parópakári, Mal.). From (para, san. other + upakára, san. help). Vernacular newspaper.——*Parshoo* (परशु - parashu, San.). From (para, san. another, enemy + shri, san. to hurt). A battle-axe, the weapon of Parshooraman [q.v.] Mazhoo [q.v.] is battle-axe of shiva [q.v.]——*Parshoorama mahautmyam* (परशुराममाहात्म्य - parashurámamáhátmya, San.). From (parashuráma, san. the hero, so called + máhátmya, san. greatness). Sanscrit work taken from the Bramhaunda pooraunam [q.v.]. This contains the early life of Parshooraman [q.v.], the quarrel of his father with the Cshatriyas [q.v.], the slaughter of the Cshatriyas, his proceeding to the west and there obtaining from the sea king and goddess of the sea as much land as he could cover by the flight of an arrow discharged from his bow. Having settled the country, he called in Bramins [q.v.] from the Aryavartam and located them there. As disputes arose among them he advised asking for a king from the Cholam [q.v.] country. The document omits any mention of the fishermen made Bramins, or of his displeasure against them. In some histories, the calling in of the Bramins from Hindostan is ascribed, not to Parshooraman, but to Mayoora vurman [keraloputty].——*Parshooraman* (परशुराम - parashuráma, San.). From (parashu, san. axe + ráma, san. name). Sixth avatar [q.v.] of Vishnoo [q.v.]. There are four legends, which may have historic bearings. Jamadagny was a rishy [q.v.], who with his wife Renoocay and his son Raman, lived in a hermitage in some place north of India. The wives of such sages were patyvratay [q.v.], preeminently chaste; and so cold that ice did not melt when held by their fingers. One day Jamadagny sent his wife to a river to fetch a block of ice, and, on her bringing it, it was found to be partly dissolved in her hands. In wrath he commanded his son to strike off her head, which he did with an axe or parshoo [q.v.]. Some pariah [q.v.] women interposed, and Raman struck off their heads likewise. Jamadagny repenting his rashness, meant to restore his dead wife; but in the hurry of the moment he joined her head to a Pariah's body, and the head of the Pariah to her body. Hence the Pariahs worship Renoocay as a goddess. Jamadagny again had with him the cow Caumadhain [q.v.], or cow of plenty, which a neighbouring chief with 100 arms coveted and on its being denied took by force. The rishy sent his son Raman, who in combat lopped off the arms one by one with his battle axe; whence the name Parshooraman. After this, making a third legend, Parshooraman exterminated all the Cshatriyas or soldier tribe, and gave their lands to Bramins. The Keraloputty [q.v.] and the Kerala mahautmyam [q.v.] add a fourth that Parshooraman demanded from the sea on their coast a further domain, which was granted to the extent that he could throw his battle axe. Standing north at Gocurnam near Goa he threw his axe forty yojanams [q.v] or four hundred miles; and, to that extent on a parallel with Gocurnam the sea retreated. He placed fishermen on the recovered land and made them semi-Bramins. He returned to

Ahichatray on the Kistna; but thence afterwards brought a colony of pure Bramins, disgracing and displacing the former colony. The high land of the West coast presents unmistakeable traces of a plateau or terraced character, which is best displayed about Trivandrum and northwards past Cochin into the Malabar country. This terrace must be of late tertiary or postpliocene period, and it marks, like the long stretches of laterite [q.v.] and sandstones [manal cull] on the eastern side of the country, the last great elevation of Southern india, prior to which the Indian land rose almost directly from the sea by its Western ghauts [q.v.] and had an eastern shore line which is now indicated very well by the inner edge of the Tanjore, South arcot, Madras, Nellore, and Godavery belts of laterite [q.v.] and sand-stone [manal cull]. In S. india Renoocay has become Yellamma. Parshoorainan is one of the ever-living saints or chiranjeevies [q.v.]. The present Malabar era [saca] is called after him; it is reckoned in cycles [chuckram] of a thousand years. According to many accounts Ramchendran [q.v.] and Parshooramian were contemporaries [matam]. See vol. I (74), (115).——*Parshooramasrishty* (परशुरामसृष्टि - parashurámasrishti, San.). From (srishti, san. creation). The creation of Parshooraman [q.v.], or the Malabar coast from Gocurnam to Cape comorin.——*Paurpatya* (పారపత్యము - párapatyamu, Tel.). From (para, san. other + pati, san. lord); lordship over others. Management. Paurpatyagar is under manager of a chuttram [q.v.] or temple. [coil, pagoda]. A clerk under a village accountant [curnum].

PARA (పర - para, *Tel.*; പറ - para, *Mal.*; பற - para, *Tam.*). From (para, tam. to be extended). Plain.——*Par* (பார் - pár, Tam.). Bank; pearl [chunk, moty] bank. There are numerous off the Tuticorin coast, all known by different names, as for instance:—Devy par, queen-bank; Mosal teev par, hare-island bank; Nullatunniteev par, fresh-water island bank; Odacaray par, ferry bank; Ooppootunniteey par, salt-water island bank; Pausy par, moss bank; Poondotta par, flower-garden bank; Poothoo par, new bank; Tolauyiram par, nine-hundred bank.——*Paramacoody* (பரமக்குடி - paramakkudi, Tam. paramakudi *). From (parambu, tam. embankment + kudi, tam. village); on the veigay. Town, Telegraph office, seat of District moonsif; Madura dist., Ramnaud zemindarry; pop. 9,287; lat. 9° 33′; long. 78° 38′; from Madura S.E. 40 miles; from Ramnaud N.W. 20 miles; from the sea W. 22 miles. On southern bank of Veigay and on Ramnaud-Madura road. Large and spacious stone pavilion and chuttram [q.v.], where alms are daily distributed. Inhabitants mostly weavers. The ironsmiths are Mussalmans. Cloths, silks [puttoo], muslins [q.v.], silk carpets, vestures, turbans [puggry], women's silk and colored cloths are manufactured. Annual festival. Yams [auloo] thrive in great abundance. Weekly market on Thursday.——*Paramba* (പറമ്പ് - parampu, Mal.). High ground unsuited for rice [q.v.] cultivation. Also a garden of cocoanut [q.v.] and other trees which may contain a dwelling-house. The low slopes bordering ravines in Travancore. Suffix in place names; as Goottooparamba; meaning dancing ground.——*Parambil chaundy* (പറമ്പിൽചാണ്ടി - parambilchándi, Mal.): From (paramba, mal. garden + chándi, mal. alexander). A native cattanar, called Alexander de campo. First Native bishop of the Roman catholic faith, consecrated at Cadootoortty, north-east of cottayam, which was then one of the chief strongholds of the Romo-syrian party [syrian].——*Paramboo* (பரம்பு - parambu, Tam.). Roller for consolidating soil [nolla].——*Parava* (பரவ - parava, obl., Tam.). From (paravai, tam. expanse, sea); seaman. A dark-skinned almost black race in the extreme south of the peninsula, living in villages along the sea coast and earning their bread as fishermen with nets, lines, and hooks. In 1532, Michael Vaz, afterwards Archbishop of Goa, assisted the Paravar fishermen against the Mahomedans, since which time they have been Roman catholics. Ten years after, Xavier lived among them. Then the Jesuit fathers of the Madura mission worked there, notably Beschi [veeramaumoony]. To be distinguished from Pariahs. See vol. I (68); II, 131.——*Paraval* (பரவல் - paraval, Tam.). From (paravu, tam. to spread). Overspreading. Paravalcaud is brushwood.——*Paravanaur* (பரவனாறு - paravanáru, Tam.). From (paravan, tam. fisherman + áru, tam. river). River; South arcot dist., Chidambaram and Cuddalore tals. Rises in lat. 11° 36′ N., and long. 79° 33′ E. and after a course of about 32 miles, generally north and parallel to the coast, enters the sea at Cuddalore in lat. 11° 43′ N., long. 79° 49′ E. Navigable for short distance by boats of 4 tons burthern throughout year. Connected with Vellaur by a canal, which, begun in 1856–57 and stopped at the time of the mutiny, was reopened as a famine work in 1878.——*Paravay* (பரவை - paravai, Tam.). From (paravu, tam. to spread). Expanse.——*Paravore* (പറവൂർ - paravúr, Mal.). From (pára, mal. plain + úr, mal. village). Title otherwise Paroor.—"*a*". Talook, Travancore state, Cottayam division. Area 47 square miles. The most densely populated portion of the state. Population 61,966. Its extreme north and south points are 17 miles apart, and its extreme east and west points are 12 miles apart. Sub-divided into six praverties [q.v.] and containing eighty-nine caras [q.v.] or villages. At one time belonged to Cochin but in 1762 made over to Travancore. Bounded N., S. and W. by the Cochin state. E. by the Aulangaud talook. Soil is sandy. There are some backwaters. Cocoanut [q.v.] trees largely cultivated. Paddy [q.v.] cultivation. Periyaur waters a portion.—"*b*" Village, Port; Travancore state, Cottayam division, Parávore tal.; pop. 11,024; lat. 10° 9′; long. 76° 16′; from Alleppey N. 46 miles; from Cottayam N.N.W. 43 miles; from Madras W.S.W. 340 miles; from Nagarcoil N.N.W. 156 miles; from Quilon N.N.W. 88 miles; from Trivandrum N.N.W. 123 miles; from Bombay S.S.E. 640 miles; from Calicut S.S.E. 82 miles; from the sea E. 4 miles. Chief place of talook. Zillah [q.v.] and Moonsif's court. Formerly a large military station. Its decay dates from Tippoo's invasion. Most of its churches and pagodas [q.v.] were destroyed by him. Still a large mart. Large temple.——*Parla* (పర్ల - parla, Tel.). From (parra, tel. open plain). Locative plural. Suffix in place names; as Valaparla, meaning right-hand plain.——*Parony* (പറോണ്ണ - parónna, Mal.). From (paravan, mal. fisherman + úr, mal. village). Village, Sub-port attached to Taunore; Malabar dist., Ponnany tal.; pop. 4,243; lat. 10° 54′; long. 75° 56′; from Bettatt poothiyangaudy W.N.W. 3 miles; from Bombay S.S.E. 578 miles; from Calicut S.S.E. 25 miles; from Cootye N.N.W. 4 miles; from Ponnany N.N.W. 8 miles; from Taunore S.S.E. 5¼ miles. Contiguous to Taunore. Residence in former days of Paravannore Panikkar, a deshavauly [q.v.]. Small Moplah [q.v.] village lying by side of sea in Patchattiry amshom [q.v.].——*Parpunangaudy* (പരപ്പനങ്ങാടി - parappanannáti, Mal. parpanangádi *). Means bazaar in parapnaud. Town, Moonsif's court, Railway station, Port; Malabar dist., Yernaud tal.; pop. 5,219; lat. 11° 03′; long. 75° 54′; height 38 feet; from Bombay S.S.E. 564 miles; from Cadaloondy S.S.E. 4 miles; from Calicut S.S.E. 14 miles; from Munjery W. 18 miles; from Taunore N.N.W. 6 miles; from the sea E. ½ mile. Small port on open coast, between Taunore and Beypore, with trade in salt-fish and country produce. Palace of Cshatriya [q.v.] family of Parapnaud rajah at a short distance. In event of failure of heirs in Travancore family a girl may be adopted from this family to continue that line.——*Parroo* (పర్రు - parru, Tel.). From (parava, tel. flood). Swamp.——*Paumb* (பாம்பு - pámbu, Tam.). See sep. title.——*Paura* (పార - pára, Tel.). From (paratsu, tel. to spread). Spade; iron with a wooden handle.——*Paura* (പാറ - pára, Mal.). Rock. Suffix in place names; as Aunipaura, meaning nail-like rock.——*Pauray* (शिला - shilá, San.; کرنگ - karang, Malay; ಬಂಡೆ - bande, Can.; ಪಾಡೆ - páde, Too.; చట్టు - tsattu, Tel.; പാറ - pára, Mal.; பாறை - párai, Tam.). Title from tamul. San. from (shí, san. to sharpen). Tam. from (para, tam. to spread); layer or bed [par]. Rock. In geological writings this word is understood to mean any mineral substance occurring in large masses. Sand [manal] and clay [calimunn] in large quantities form rocks, as well as limestone [choonam cull] or granite [caroom cull]. Suffix in place names; as Manapauray, meaning sand rock. For fishes of this name see sep. title.

PARACA (పరక - paraka, *Tel.*). Corruption of (ara, tel. half + kálu, tel. quarter). An eighth part [ganitam].

PARADISE (فردوس - firdaus, *Ar.*). Greek παράδεισος. Prefix.——*Paradise apple* (سیب فردوس - sebifirdaus, Hind.). Same as Pummelow.——*Paradise fish* (ماهی فردوس - máhiifirdaus, Hind.). Title from shining colors. Same as Robaul.

PARANGHY (പറങ്കി - paranki, *Mal.*; பறங்கி - parangi, *Tam.*). From the mediæval term Franky. European [europe, faranghee, firangy, foreign, seema, vilauyaty]. Plant first term, often joining two genera. Ex., where transl. is of second term:—Anacardium occidentale (párankimávu), mangifera indica; Ananas sativus (parangihalasu), and (parangipelakáyi), artocarpus integrifolia, (parangittázhai), pandanus odoratissimus; Anona reticulata (parangiççakka), artocarpus integrifolia; Benincasa cerifera (parangikkáy), fruit; Boswellia serrata (p'harangisámbránichettu), incense + tree; Capsicum annuum (parangimunchi), (p'harangimenasinakáyi), and (parankimulaku); piper nigrum; Carica papaya (parangimara), tree, (parangiyámanakku), ricinus communis; Cucurbita maxima (parangikkáy), fruit; Jatropha curcas (parangiharalu), ricinus communis; Parkinsonia aculeata (parangivél), acacia. See gloss. paragraphs.

PARAY (பறை - parai, *Tam.*). Drum. The drums used vary as to their size, construction, material, and manner of being carried. A damaroo [q.v.] is carried by a bull, a dunkah [q.v.] on a horse [ghorah], a nakkaura [q.v.] by an elephant [q.v.] or camel [ottagam], and a bhairy on a cart [bandy]. Other kinds of drums are carried by men, as the tappattay [q.v.], a small drum which hangs from the left shoulder and is beaten under the left arm from below with a stick in the right hand and from above with a small stick in the left hand. The tausha, a small semi-globular shaped drum, is worn in front round the neck below the chest and beaten with two small sticks. The dole [q.v.] is a big drum, which is also carried over the neck, but is beaten with the hand one side and a stick the other. The paray proper, which has the complimentary name of alancauram, is not carried when beaten, but lies on the ground between the feet of the drummer and is used at festivals, weddings, and funerals. It is beaten only by Vettiyauns who burn corpses and dig graves. The tappattay and tausha are in fashion among the

Pariahs [q.v.] and other low classes, though Mahomedans and Shoodras use them occasionally. The beaters of the other drums are mostly Shoodras. The Kotar [q.v.] and the Todahs [q.v.] on the Neilgherries also have the tappattay and tausha [sangeetam]. ——*Pariah* (मातङ्ग - mátanga, San.; ڈھیر - dher, Hind.; ಹೊಲೆಯ - holeya, Can.; మాల - mála, Tel.; പുലയൻ - pulayan, Mal.; *பறையன்* - paraiyan, Tam.). Title and Tam. from (parai, tam. drum); cf. maula. San. from (mata, san. will + ga, san. to go), self-willed; as being beyond caste pale [maudiga]. One of the great aboriginal tribes. Most of such tribes have general titles; that of the tamul Pariah is Shaumbaun [q.v.], which also means drummer. Poolaya [q.v.] is the term by which they are known in Shen tamul [q.v.].—"*a*" Pariahs are regarded by the mixed Dravidian population who have adopted the creed and thoughts of Hindooism as of very low grade, but they are anything but out-castes or men who have been expelled from other castes. In the Capardagiry inscription of Asoca [q.v.], which is engraved also on the rocks at Girnar in Cattywar and of Dhowlee in Cuttack, are the words:—"In all "the subjugated territories of king Priyadarshy and also in the "bordering countries, as Choda palaya or paraya, Satyapootra "Keralapootran, Tambapunny, &c." Here the Pariahs are named in the centre of the Dravidian group, with the Cholans, Keralans of malabar, and Singhalese. The Pariahs of the Tamul countries believe that they were once the most important race. Those of Tondaimundalam [q.v.] in South arcot consider themselves the real proprietors of the soil. The head Vettiyaur pariah at Trivalore in Tanjore carries the chowry [q.v.] or fan of the god Tyaugarajan [q.v.] or Shiva [q.v.]; and in Madras, at the festival of Yegauttaul, [q.v.] the sole mother, it is a Pariah who puts the talee [q.v.] or marriage cord around the neck of the goddess. The Comaty [q.v.] shopkeepers of Madras before contracting marriage, send an offering of betel [q.v.] to the Chucklers or shoemakers; and in Vizagapatam Bramins go through the ceremony of asking the consent of the Maulas [q.v.] to their marriage. At Mailcote, the chief seat of the followers of Ramaunoojacharry, the Holeyar [q.v.] have the right of entering the temple on three days in the year, specially set apart for them. At the bull games at Dindigul the Cullar [q.v.], or robber caste, can alone officiate as priests. There is a proverb:—*பறையர் இடங்கை அல்ல அவர்கள் தமிழர்.*—"the pariahs "are not left-hand [yidangay] they are tamulians." Compare the following from Athenæus:—"Berossus, in the first book of "his Babylonian history, says, that in the eleventh month, called "Loos, is celebrated in Babylon the feast of Sacea for five days, "in which it is the custom that the masters should obey their "domestics, one of whom is led round the house, clothed in a "royal garment, and him they call Zoganes."—"*b*" The Pariahs are not even the lowest of the aboriginal races. In the Tamul country there are ten castes who are lower in the social scale than the Pariah, and from these are excluded the Pullar [q.v.], who dispute precedence with the Pariah. As regards the question whether the Pariahs are Dravidian, see vol. I (32) (36), and (69). The view taken in these pages is that they are distinctly Dravidian without fusion, as the Hindooized castes are Dravidian with fusion. They comprise a tenth of the population and are probably a race of almost unmixed blood. No other race in immediate contact with civilization is known which presents the characteristic to the same extent. They constitute indeed a well-defined distinct ancient race, independent of all others, and which has its own sub-divisions, its own peculiar usages, its own traditions, and its own jealousy of the encroachments of the castes which are above it and below it. Political revolutions have been the cause of their subversion by other kindred Dravidian tribes. The Pariahs call themselves the elder brothers of the Bramin [q.v.]. They have according to the Nyauna vettiyaun eighteen titles like the Vellaular [q.v.] and possess also the same insignia.—"*c*" Pariahs are wholly different in appearance from the leather-working race, the Chuckler or Maudiga [q.v.].—"*d*" Pariahs have their own spiritual pastors, called in tamul Vulloovar, Tauthar, Pundauram, Sanjeevy. Pariahs nominally worship Shiva, but really are devil-worshippers or else worship the female deities called Mauriyauttaul, Cauly, Ponniyammah and Maudiammaul, in whose small temples they offer rice, flowers, turmeric [country saffron], &c. About 1 in 150 of the Pariahs have become Christians and these only marry among themselves. From the peculiar stand-point of Tamul literature, the Pariahs have often excelled in education. Avvaiyaur [avvay], a Pariah woman, is famed throughout the Tamul nation for her poetry. The Cooral [q.v.], the most popular poem ever produced in the Tamul country, was written by Tirvulloovar, the divine Vulloovar a Pariah. It is read and admired by Tamul hindoos of every class and creed. Another Pariah poet, Capilan, author of the Agaval, was supposed to have been a brother of the author of the Cooral, and his works still hold a high place in public esteem.—"*e*" The Pariahs are by occupation usually the servants of the Shoodra agriculturists paid in kind. Those in the large towns in the employ of the Europeans in Southern india, are quick, intelligent, and active. The race is emigrating with great rapidity to the West indies, Mauritius, Cape colony, and the Burmese provinces, &c., where all sectarian or social distinctions are unknown. The Pariah clans are found in every village and town in the peninsula. They are settled in houses, their quarter being usually apart from other residents and outside the walls of fortified places, and called parcherry [q.v.] in the Tamul country. The mark for their signature is a staff, while that of the chuckler [q.v.] is a knife. Their original most distinctive occupation was beating the paray [q.v.] or tom-tom at funerals, but, as they multiplied, they were obliged to do indiscriminately all kinds of work. The Vetty, the village servant of the Tamul people, is a Pariah. They are still theoretically despised by all but a few of the lowest classes of natives. They are obliged to live apart from their employers in their parcherry [q.v.], and must never come near a Bramin [q.v.] or a Vellaular [q.v.] or indeed, any respectable man; but they are so numerous and so useful that they are gradually pushing their way into a better position. They are the principal supporters of the right-hand caste [valangay] in the periodical disputes between the two hands [yidangay], in which they always range themselves against the Pullar [q.v.]. Pariahs have their own washermen and their own barbers. They have also their own musicians of the Periya mailam [q.v.] class to perform on occasions of marriages among them. They eat carrion and even beef and may drink spirituous liquors. They will not eat with others. They bury their dead [shavacaud]. At their marriages no religious service takes place, but guests assemble, the priest sings songs to an accompaniment upon a drum, and some of the guests dance. When the auspicious moment arrives, the bridegroom ties the talee [q.v.] to the bride's neck, all his friends clap their hands loudly. With the exception of the minor section called Aroott cattantha, all Pariahs allow their widows to remarry, and all guard the chastity of their married women as jealously as do caste people. Indeed among the higher sections as they are called of the Pariahs, a married woman guilty of a proved act of adultery is doomed to perpetual concubinage or single life, so is also an unmarried woman, whose virginity has been violated or who has been guilty of a single act of incontinence. They are a most patient and industrious class and generally faithful to their masters; they rarely commit open robberies, and their thefts are restricted generally to their immediate wants.—"*f*" The Tamul literature of later days speaks of Pariahs with a kind of good-natured contempt. The following are Tamul proverbs:—எழுபதுசென்ருலும் பறை ஏவிஞற்ருன் செய்யும்—"though seventy years old, a pariah "will do nothing unless he is prompted."—பறைப்பாட்டுக்கும் பறைப்பேச்சுக்கும் சுரைப்பூவிற்கும் மணம் இல்லை—"a pariah's song, his dialect, and a shooray [fakeer's bottle] "flower have no fragrance in them."—பனைமரத்திற்கு நிழல் இல்லை பறையனுக்குமுறை இல்லை—"a palinyra [q.v.] "tree casts no shade, a pariah has no rules."—பார்ப்பான் கறுப்பும் பறையன் சிவப்பும் ஆகாது—"a black bramin and "a fair pariah are not trustworthy."—"*g*" The numbers for the presidency, including those of all languages are some $3\frac{1}{2}$ millions: —"*h*" There are very many sub-divisions of the Pariahs. Thus taking the pariahs of the southernmost districts alone:—Aliya pariah; from (ála, tam. term of address); from form of address to parents; address their fathers by title of aléi and their mothers by that of ala, meaning father, mother; compare ayya-ammay pariah below; many of them are employed in dressing skins [chamrah] for exportation, &c. Amboo pariah; from (ambu, tam. arrow); proper profession is hunting with the bow and arrow; they act as shikarries [q.v.] and beaters to zemindars [q.v.] and others. Arippoocaura; from (arippu, tam. sifting + kára, san. doer); wash sand for gold [pon], where gold is procurable; they find very minute particles of the precious metal in the veigay in madura, but not in sufficient abundance to repay their exertions. Aroott cattautha pariah; from (aru, tam. to cut + kattu, tam. to tie + á, tam. negative particle); talee when once cut, not tied again by re-marriage; so called because their widows are not allowed to remarry; the observance of this high caste custom causes them to be somewhat respected. Ayya-ammay pariah; from (aiyan, tam. father + ammai, tam. mother); from form of address to parents; are in the habit of addressing their fathers and mothers respectively by those two titles; cf. aliya pariah. Chunk pariah; from (shankha, san. shell); wear shells on the left arm and are thereby readily distinguished; they blow conches [chunk] at ceremonies and do various kinds of work. Coliya pariah; from (kóliya, tam. caste of weavers so called); weave cloths of a coarse description. Coody pariah; from (kudi, short for kudimagan, tam. barber); the barbers who shave pariahs. Cottagacaur pariah; from (kottagai, tam. shed); stable man; mostly rough riders and grooms. Doorchauly pariah; from (dur, san. prefix implying inferiority + játi, san. caste); eaters of frogs [bhaicam], mussels [chippy], jackals [q.v.], &c. Mooraja pariah; from (muraja, san. drum so called); play on a kind of tom-tom [q.v.]. Ooppa-raiya pariah; scavengers, remove night-soil, &c. Ottagacaur pariah; spinners of cotton [q.v.] thread [nool]; when work is slack, they till the soil and do other kinds of work. Peroom pariah; from (perum, tam. great); a better sort of pariahs, employed principally as gentlemen's servants, &c. Pola pariah; from (polam, tam. badness); make mats [boriyah], baskets [tokrah], &c., of bamboo [q.v.], rushes, osiers, and similar materials. Shoolagoo catty pariah; from (shulagu, tam. winnowing sieve + kattu, tam. to bind); live chiefly by winnowing paddy [q.v.] and other kinds of grain [dhaunyam]. Shozhiya pariah; from (shozham, tam. country so called); are generally hawkers of cheap wares. Tamul pariah; from (tamizh, tam.

tamul) ; are usually merchants and are regarded as men of some substance and respectability ; these have three divisions, tungalaun, vella, and congoo, of which the first is the highest and the last not largely represented ; the vella pariahs are those who do scavengering work, which the tungalauns refuse to do ; both vella and congoo pariahs eat cows [pashoo] that have died a natural death, while tungalauns only eat such as have been slaughtered ; the tungalauns profess to have once been a very respectable class and still wear the thread at weddings and funerals, while the other divisions never assume it ; the tungalauns are sometime called marialis. Tautha pariah ; from (táthan, tam. vaishnava mendicant) ; often wander about as religious beggars of the veishnava sect and subsist entirely on alms given to them by all classes of people. Tavalay tinnoom pariah ; from (tavalai, tam. frog + tin, tam. to eat) ; eat frogs [bhaicam], the local name of the doorchauly [q.v.] tribe. Tee pariah ; from (tíyan, mal. toddy drawer) ; belong properly to malabar. Tonda pariah ; from (tondu, tam. slavery) ; usually employed as cultivators and predial slaves ; but some are petty traders, some artisans, some domestic servants, some horse-keepers [q.v], and the like. Toty pariah ; from (tótti, tam. village servant so called) ; are to be found in every southern village ; they are the village scavengers and messengers, and a certain number of them are paid for their services by government [inam]. Tungalaun pariah ; from (tangalán, tam. honorary title of pariah) ; see tamul pariah above ; the most numerous group, and, with the exception of the vulloovans [q.v.], the most respectable ; they are usually employed as cultivators and predial slaves, but some of them are petty traders, some artisans, some domestic servants, some horsekeepers, and the like. Vadooga pariah ; from (vadugu, tam. telugu language) ; belong properly to the teloogoo country and veishnava sect and are hippophagists ; they are often employed as palankeen bearers [boy]. Valay pariah ; from (valai, tam. net) ; live properly by netting birds and work of a similar nature. Vettiyaur pariah ; from (vettimai, tam. work of a town servant) ; properly beat tom-toms and act as undertakers at funerals ; they also attend as tom-tom beaters when other ceremonies are performed, and eke out a living by hawking goods and doing odd jobs of various kinds ; some of them are to be found in every village, their services being indispensably necessary wherever hindoos live in numbers. Vulloovar pariah ; from (valluvan, tam. pariah priest) ; are the most respectable, inasmuch as they act as gooroos [q.v.] or spiritual pastors to the others ; tiruvalloovar [q.v.], the celebrated tamul poet, belonged to this family. Yecauly pariah ; from (égáli, tam. washerman) ; are washermen [dhoby, vunnaun] by profession.—"*i*" See vol. i (85) ; ii, 232, 236.—"*j*" As the term pariah has come to mean one rejected and condemned by society, it has been applied by anglo-indians to the ownerless village dogs [nye] of the villages [pie, pye].

PARGOO (పరుగు - parugu, *Tel.*). Means a run. As far as a man can run without stopping. Linear measure. 2,000 niloovoes = 1 pargoo ; 4 pargoos = 1 aumada [alavay, 1b]. Approximate actual value; 1 pargoo = 2½ miles. Varies. Same as San. crosham, Hind. coss, Can. hardaury. See vol. I, 609 ; II, 505.

PARI (परि - pari, *San.*) [pra]. Prefix meaning about, over. ——*Palampore* (پلنگپوش - palangposh, Hind.). Hind. from (palang, hind. bed + púsh, pers. cover). Title corrupted through the analogy of Salampore ; which see. Counterpane. Often erroneously applied to all varieties of printed cottons [chintz], including canopies, prayer cloths or mats [boriyah], handkerchiefs [roomaul], and cloths for male and female wear. These are manufactured in the district of Cuddalore, at Pounairy, also at Sydapett in the outskirts of Madras, but especially in the town of Masulipatam ; the last always of a superior kind, and in various sizes, 5½ to 6 cubits in breadth, and 7 to 8 long, and are sold from 6 to 51 rupees, according to size. The Cuddalore, Pounairy, and Sydapett fabrics are of ordinary quality and are sold at from 2 to 7 rupees each.——*Palang* (پلنگ - palang, Hind.). From (paryanka, san. bed). Bed.——*Palankeen* (پالکی - pálkí, Hind. ; పల్లకి - pallakí, Tel. ; பல்லக்கு - pallakku, Tam.). Title corr. from teloogoo. Tel. from (paryanka, san. bed) [palang]. Otherwise Palky. A long, low, closed carriage in which the occupant reclines at full length, and which is borne, by means of two projecting poles one at each end, on the shoulders of 4 or 6 men. Palankeens used to form one of the articles which Eastern rulers presented to their subjects, or gave them permission to use. Grants were sometimes made for their use. Double or treble sets of bearers generally attend it to render the burden as light as possible, and those who carry are relieved every five or ten minutes by fresh relays [anchey]. Good bearers are distinguished from bad by not stopping to change shoulders or for relay. When changes are avoided, they do 5 miles an hour without discomfort.——*Palky* (پالکی - pálkí, Mal.). Same as palankeen.——*Parichauracam* (परिचारक - paricháraka, San.). From (above + char, san. to move). Serving in a temple [coil, pagoda].——*Paridhy* (परिधि - paridhi, San.). From (pari, san. on all sides + dhá, san. to place). Properly the circumference of a circle [chuckram], but more generally an epicycle [cacsham, prauk chuckram]. Also applies to halos round sun [sooryan] and moon [chundran], much regarded in astrology [jyotisham].——*Paripoornam* (பரிபூரணம் - parippúranam, Tam.). From (above + púrna, san. full). Hindoo 2nd or pers. name. Common to both sexes [peyar]. Generally given to the last born when no more children are desired.——*Parishishtam* (परिशिष्ट - parishishta, San.). From (above + shish, san. to leave). Treatises supplementary to the sootrams [q.v.]. They are intended to convey to the multitude, in a popular form, general information regarding religion. They mark the transition from the Vedic [vedam] to the Pooraunic literature [pooraunam].——*Parivauram* (பரிவாரம் - parivárám, Tam.). From (above + vára, san. cover). Retinue.——*Parivraujacan* (परिव्राजक - parivrájaka, San.). From (above + vraj, san. to go). Mendicant, or one at the fourth stage [aushramam] of a Bramin's life.

PARNAM (पर्ण - parna, *San.*). From (pri, san. to fill, to protect) ; foliage a vesture and protection. Leaf. Plant second term, often joining two genera. Ex., where transl. is of first term :—Alpinia officinarum (éláparní), elettaria cardamomum ; Desmodium gangeticum (shálaparní), shorea robusta ; Flacourtia cataphracta (khadiraparní) ; acacia ; Pterocarpus santalinus (tilaparní), sesamum indicum ; Sanseviera roxburghiana (piluparní), salvadora persica ; Teramnus labialis (máshaparní), phaseolus mungo, var. radiatus. See gloss. paragraphs.——*Parny* (पर्णी - parní, San. ; بناس پتی - banáspattí, Hind. ; ಪರ್ಣಿ - parni, Can. ; పర్ణ - parna, Tel ; പന്ന - panna, Mal. ; நீர்வேம்பு - nírvémbu, Tam.). Title, &c., from sanscrit. Hind. from (ban, hind. forest + pattí, hind. leaf). Tam. from (nír, tam. water + vémbu, tam. margosa tree, melia azadirachta, linn.). Fern. Botanically the order of Filices [vricsham, 157]. That is to say the first branch of acotyledons, or acrogens, or cryptogamic plants, or plants with disguised flowering organs ; the other branches being the Club-mosses or lycopodiaceæ [shookaram], the Horse-tails or equisetaceæ [ashwa vauly], the Mosses or musci [pausy], the Mushrooms and moulds or fungi [caulaun], the Lichens [cullpausy], and the Seaweeds or algæ [cadalpausy].——*Paun* (پان - pán, Hind.). From (parna, san. a leaf). Same as betel [q.v.]; given to guests after entertainment.——*Paundaun* (پاندان - pándán, Hind.). From (pán, hind. leaf + dán, pers. holder). Betel leaf box.——*Paun kah beerah* (پان کا بیڑا - pánkábírá, Hind.). The parcel of betel [q.v.] leaf, nut and quicklime [choonam], &c. [putty].——*Paunmalah* (पानमळा - pánamalá, Mahr.). From (pán, hind. betel + malá, mahr. plantation). Betel-vine garden.——*Paunsoopyaury* (پان سپیاری - pánsupiyárí, Hind.). From (pán, hind. betel + supiyárí, hind. areca nut). The total ingredients chewed in combination with the betel [q.v.]. Include betel-leaves [q.v.], areca nut [q.v.], catechu [q.v.], quicklime [choonam], aniseed [anise], bishop's weed seed [ajwaun], coriander seed [cassibor], cardamoms [q.v.] and cloves [lavangam]. These are folded up in a leaf. The compound offered along with otto of roses [attar] to visitors, intimates the termination of the visit. It is sometimes sent abroad to friends at festival time [charvanam, eed, putty].

PARPATAM (पर्पट - parpata, *San.*). So called from sound of bursting. Botanically the Mollugo genus, ficoideæ [vricsham, 66]. Inconspicuous annuals having dichotomously branched stems with verticillate leaves, rarely opposite and small inconspicuous flowers. The species best known to the natives are :—cerviana [hazaurdanah], spergula [tirye], stricta [wild tirye]. ——*Field parpatam* (क्षेत्रपर्पटी - kshétraparpatí, San. ; کهیت پاپڑ - khetpápar, Hind.). San. from (kshétra, san. field + parpatí, san. oldenlandia). San. also (gandhabhadra), meaning fragrant bhadray. Botanically the Oldenlandia genus, rubiaceæ [vricsham, 71]. Slender erect or diffuse branched herbs ; leaves small and narrow ; flowers small, white or pink ; capsule small, many-seeded ; seeds angled or globose. The species best known to the natives are :—corymbosa [wild chay root], dichotoma [counterfeit chayroot], umbellata [chayroot]. Other s. indian species indigenous or naturalized are :—aspera, biflora, crystallina, heynii, nudicaulis, paniculata, shuteri, trinervia.

PARRAH (పర - para, *Tel.* ; പറ - para, *Mal.* ; பறை - parai, *Tam.*). From (paru, tam. to become bulky, to swell). See vol. I, 609 ; vol. II, 514, 516, 519.—"*a*" Measure of capacity on W. coast. 10 yidangazhies = 1 parrah ; 2½ parrahs = 1 mooda [alavay, 3d]. Approximate actual value, 1 parrah = 1,140 cubic inches, or say half a bushel. Pauttaparrah is a large measure used by jenmies [q.v.] in measuring pauttom [q.v.]. Compare Marcam.—"*b*" Measure of capacity of choonam [q.v.]. 5 mercauls = 1 parrah ; 80 parrahs = 1 garce [alavay, 3a]. Approximate actual value, 1 parrah = 2 cubic feet 144 cubic inches. Compare Pootty of ganjam, Toom of nellore.—"*c*" A superficial measure on W. coast implying land requiring a parrah of seed. 10 yidangazhies = 1 parrah [alavay, 2d]. Approximate actual value, 1 parrah = ⅛ acre.—"*d*" Superficial measure of N. circars [q.v.]. 16 parrahs = 1 veesam [alavay, 2b]. Approximate actual value, 1 parrah = 3,315 square feet. Compare Aana, Puddy or Nauzhy.

PARROT TREE (توت - tút, *Pers.*). From (tútí, hind. parrot). Same as Indian mulberry.

PARS (پارس - párs, *Pers.*). Persia.——*Parsee* (پارسی - pársí, Hind.). Community settled chiefly in Western india, and especially in Surat and Bombay, the descendants of refugees from Persia. They have in a measure adopted Hindoo customs. They observe the Zoroastrian or fireworshipping religion. They have adopted Goozeratty [q.v.] as a language. They have a special aptitude for trade. Distinguishable by their hats which have a square front but towards the back of the head form a hollow.——*Pauraseecam* (पारसीक. - párasíka, San.). Persian race. See vol. I (3).——*Persia* (پارس - párs, Pers.). The country. Compare :—Alhági maurorum, persian mahna ; Carum carui, persian carraway ; Melia azedarach, persian lilac ; Prunus amygdalus, persian almond ; Rosa centifolia, persian rose ; Rosa damascena, persian-rose ; Sálvadora persica, persian salvadora. See gloss. paragraphs.

PARTY (పర్తి - parti, *Tel.*). Village.——*Partiaul* (పర్తియాల - partiyála, Tel.). From (above + ella, tel. frontier). Village ; Kistna dist., Nundigauma tal. This and a few other villages are those whence the celebrated Golcondah diamonds [vajram] were derived. The old workings are to be seen in every direction. Belongs to Nizam.

PARVAM (पर्व - parva, *San.* ; பருவம் - paruvam, *Tam.*). From (prí, san. to fill). Knot or joint ; joint of body, limb ; a break or pause, division ; a division of time ; the days of conjunction [amavausyay] and opposition [powrnimay] of sun [sooryan] and moon [chundran]. Section of a book, especially in mahabhaurat [q.v.] ; the latter goes by some descriptive name, as vana parvam, forest section ; compare the third book of the iliad called by the greeks the bravery of diomede ; or the volumes of herodotus called clio, euterpe, &c. ; the bhaugavatam uses no titles but numerals ; thus dashamam means the life of krishnan [q.v.] in 10th book of bhaugavatam [q.v.] ; in many sanscrit works the chapter or books are denoted by fanciful names, oollausam, samoodram, dweepam, stabacam, meaning delight, sea, isle, nosegay and so forth. Means season specifically in tamul districts, the rains [mazhay] proper of the N.E. monsoon [peira]. In Madura in this sense called Caulam [caulam, caur, caurtey]. ——*Parvatam* (पर्वत - parvata, San.). From (parva, san. knot or joint); means having elevations. Mountain. In ceded districts [q.v.] commonly understood of Srisheilam. Female proper name among the lower castes [peyar]. Plant first term often joining two genera. Ex., where transl. is of second term :—Jatropha curcas (parvateranda), ricinus communis ; Leea hirta (parvatapadi), foot ; Melia azedarach (parvatanimba), melia azadirachta. See gloss. paragraphs.——*Parvateeshan* (பார்வதீசன் - párvathísan, Tam.). From (párvatí, san. the mountain goddess, so called + ísha, san. lord). Epithet of Shiva, lord of Parvaty [q.v.]. Hindoo 2nd or pes. name [peyar].——*Parvateeya* (पार्वतीय - párvatíya, San.). Dwellers in mountains. A Sanscrit designation of the aborigines.——*Parvatipore* (పార్వతీపురము - párvatípuramu, Tel.). See sep. title.——*Parvaty* (पार्वती - párvatí, San.). From (parvata, san. mountain) ; as born of the Himalaya. Ἥρα of Greeks ; Juno of Romans, Isis of Egyptians. The mountain goddess, daughter of Dacshan [q.v.], wife of Shiva [q.v]. Parvaty is represented in S. india by the form of a woman with four arms and hands, two of which she lifts up, holding in one a damarcam [q.v.] or small drum, and in the other a paushain [q.v.] or cord ; and the remaining two she bends and keeps empty. On her head she wears a crown, and on her forehead Shiva's sign of sacred ashes [tirneer, vibhooty]. The color of her body is green. Her ears, neck, breast, arms, hands, and feet are adorned with jewels and ornaments ; from her shoulders a garland hangs down ; and a flower is her standing place. Of this description an image of her, cast of metal, may be seen in the pagodas [q.v.] by the side of Shiva ; but she is also represented by other forms. Parvaty has no pagodas of her own, but she is always worshipped together with her husband in the Shiva pagodas ; she has also separate small shrines within the Vishnoo pagodas, where she is adored under the form of an image of stone. In the former pagodas she is moreover daily worshipped together with her husband under the form of the lingam [q.v.] ; and the offerings which she receives are of the same kind as those made to Shiva, only the forms of prayer are different. Her principal names are the following :—Abhiraumy or the beautiful one, Aghora shaoty or the wife of aghoran, Akhilaunda naicky or the mistress of the universe, Ambicay, Ammah or mother, Caumacotatty, Caumautchy or with fascinating eyes, Chamoondy, Chitravully or the choice one, Cunniyammaul or the virgin, Devy or goddess, Doorga, Eeshwary or the mistress, Gowry or red one, Haranidattaval or she who is haran's left side, Cauly, Malaimadanay or the mountain lady, Mautah or mother, Meenautchy or the fish-ruler, Oomah the protector, Parameshwary or the heavenly mistress, Parauparay or the most high, Saty or the virtuous wife, Shacty or energy, Shaumbhavy, Shivacaumy or shiva's beloved one, Soondary or the beautiful one. There are many books containing stories concerning Parvaty. Among those written more especially in her honor the following may be mentioned :—Abhiraumyantandy, a poem in which she is extolled as abhiraumy or the beautiful ; Ambica maulay, a book containing 30 songs ; Shivacauma sowndary, a collection of songs ; Sowndarya lahary, a poem in which her beauty is extolled. All these books the children at school learn by heart. It will be seen that Parvaty, like her husband, has two characters, a pleasing and a terrible one. In the latter form she is identified in Southern india with Graunmadevatays [q.v.] or village deities. The history of the development of the idea of feminine energy [shacty] deified may be clearly traced through the names given to this goddess. Ambicay, who at a later period is identified with the wife of Roodran [q.v.], is in the Vedas [q.v.] declared to be his sister. Oomah, the daughter of Himavat or the Himalaya, is the next form. Parvaty, the mountain-goddess, also the daughter of Himalaya, is now the common title. In her girlhood she had the epithet of Girijay, mountain-born ; when older, she was termed Gowry, the bronze-colored one ; and as married she became Parvaty. She appeared latest as Cauly [q.v.], the black goddess, and in this capacity was once propitiated by human sacrifices and invoked when the destruction of an enemy was sought. There is a legend at Conjeevaram that Parvaty once put her hands over Shiva's two eyes, and the consequence was universal darkness ; she was sent down to Conjeeveram to do penance for this fault. The legend seems to show that the Bramins have a record of a total and preternatural darkness once on the earth. By the shactibhactens Parvaty is worshipped as Lalitay, Shyaumay, Tripoora soondary. See vol. I (78) [cauly, doorga, matam]. Parvaty is also a Hindoo proper name ; applied to males and females ; as a female name it is familiarly shortened into Pye, Pauty, Pautchy, Paurvo, Pauroo [peyar].——*Parvaty cozhnan* (பார்வதிக்கொழுநன் - párvathikkozhunan, Tam.). From (párvatí, san. the goddess + kozhunan, tam. husband). Shiva, as husband of parvaty.

PARVATIPORE (పార్వతీపురము - párvatípuramu, *Tel.* ; parvatipur *) ; called after parvatamma of the belgaum zemindar's family [parvam]. Sanscrit name (párvatípura).——(1) Division ; Vizagapatam district ; area 799 square miles ; population non-Agency 109,185, Agency 40,259 ; language Teloogoo in the plains ; Ooriya and Khond in the Narrainpatam agency. N. inland talook of district. Boundaries :—north, Royagada, Coraputt and Goonapore divisions ; west, Bobbily and Saulore divisions ; south, Palcondah division ; east, Goonapore division. Physical aspect undulating with small rocky hills in the south. The north is occupied by lofty portions of the Eastern ghauts [q.v.]. Soil regar [q.v.], red ferruginous [sevval munn], white and gray calcareous [sookkaun munn] and arenaceous [manal] series. Brass [pittalay], bellmetal [cunts] and copper [taumram] vessels are made. Iron [auban] is manufactured. Cloths of ordinary description are made. Gold [pon] and silver [velly] ornaments also manufactured. There is much trade in hill produce such as lac [q.v.], horns [sing], skins [chamrah], wax [mom], turmeric [country saffron], drugs and dyes [shauyam], &c. Irrigated by numerous tanks [q.v.]. Places of archæological interest :—Belgaum, Cooroopaum, Parvatipore. The leading places, &c., in the division are the following. ——*Belgaum* (బెలగాము - belagámu, Tel.). See sep. title.——*Cooroopaum* (కురుపాము - kurupámu, Tel.). See sep. title.——*Langoolya* (లాంగూలియా - lángúliyá, Tel.). See sep. title.——*Lutchmipore* (లక్ష్మీపురము - lakshmípuramu, Tel.). See sep. title.——*Merangy* (మెరంగి - merangi, Tel.). See sep. title.——*Mrityoonjayanugaram* (మృత్యుంజయనగరము - mrityunjayanagaramu, Tel.). Called after the zemindar of that name. Zemindarry village ; pop. 1,541 ; lat. of village 18° 47′ ; long. 83° 25′ ; from Parvatipore W. 4 miles ; from Vizagapatam N. 74 miles. The village was built by Mrityoonjayan, the present zemindar of Sangamvalsa. The founder of the family was a retainer of Ramchendra deo, successor of Vishwambhara deo of Jeypore, who made him zemindar of Sangamvalsa with the title of Nishanka bahaudur. These chiefs were dispossessed with the other hill zemindars by Vizianagram in 1769, and admitted to a towjee. In 1796 the estate was restored to the representative of the eldest branch, Nishanka vencannah. With Nishanka vencannah the permanent settlement was made, the assessment being Rs. 6,700. Vencannah was succeeded by his son Peddanna, owing to whose mental incapacity the estate was placed under the Court of Wards in 1820. He died in 1829 and shortly after his posthumous son Mrityoonjayan was recognised as his heir. The latter, on coming of age in May 1847, was put into possession of the estate. He left the old fort at Sangamvalsa, built a good tiled house about 2 miles to the east and called it with the surrounding houses Mrityoonjayanagaram after his own name. The chiefs belong to the Condaraus [q.v.] tribe.——*Narrainpatam* (నారాయణపట్టణము - náráyanapattanamu, Tel.). From (náráyanudu, tel. proper name + pattana, san. town). Village, Hill, Place of pilgrimage of Juggernautsawmy ; pop. 1,804 ; lat. 18° 52′ ; long. 83° 13′ ; from Parvatipore W. 18 miles ; from Vizagapatam N. 80 miles. One of the original seats of the Jeypore maharajah. Had a guddee [q.v.] with 32 steps called after Vioramarcan under ground.——*Parvatipore* (పార్వతీపురము - párvatípuramu, Tel.). See below.——(2) Deputy tahsildarry ; Vizagapatam district. Pay Rs. 100.——(3) Town, Head-quarters of Belgaum zemindar ; Vizagapatam dist., Parvatipore division ; pop. 10,053 ; lat. 18° 47′ ; long. 83° 28′ ; from Coraputt E. 45 miles ; from Madras N. 438 miles ; from Narsapatam N.E. 91 miles ; from Vizagapatam N. 74 miles ; from Vizianagram N.

45 miles. Named after the founder Parvatamma, of the Belgaum zemindar's family. The Belgaum zemindar, whose capital is at this place, belongs to the Condaranz caste. Veeravara toder mull taut rauz, Jugganath patro, paternal great grandfather of the present zemindar [q.v.], was Diwaun [q.v.] to Ramchendra deo of Jeypore. He was influential in keeping the Jeyporeans from joining the insurgents in 1794, and was afterwards confidentially employed in settling that part of the country which was apportioned amongst the representatives of the ancient families dispossessed by the Poosapauties [q.v.]. He had accumulated a good deal of money; the zemindars restored by the company had little or no capital, and the Patro [q.v.] took advantage of his position by making his own terms for the accommodation of these feudatories towards the payment of the public demands. In 1796, fourteen villages in the neighbourhood of the town of Parvatipore, taken from the contiguous hill zemindarries, were granted for life to the son, Soondra narayana patro, as an acknowledgment of his father's services; and at the permanent settlement, the lease was converted into zemindarry [q.v.] tenure at a peshcush [q.v.] of Rs. 10,500. In 1856, the zemindar borrowed Rs. 75,000, principal and interest, of the Merangy zemindar, and put him in possession of the estate for a term of twelve years. He died in July 1865 and was succeeded by his eldest son, Narayana ramchendra. This zemindar was in his turn succeeded by Dhananjayataut rauz who died in October 1888, leaving a widow empowered to adopt a son. The estate has been lately taken under the Court of Wards. Peshcush Rs. 10,332. A very important centre of trade between the hills and Central provinces on the one side and the plains on the other, being at the junction of the three roads from Palcondah, Central provinces, and Vizianagram.

PASANCARAY (பசங்கரை - pasangarai, *Tam.*). From (pasu, can. to divide + karai, tam. field); holding by shares. Equitable distribution, joint proprietary of lands of a village by coparceners. Cf. Aroothy caray, Samoodauyam. See vol. I, 112.

PASCHIMAM (पश्चिम - pashchima, *San.*). Means behind. The west point of the compass [ashta dic, tisay]. Paschimakhandam is coast of Malabar. Paschimaumboodhy is Arabian sea.

PASH (पश् - pash, *San.*). To bind.——*Pashoo* (गो - gó, San.; गाय - gáya, Mahr.; بقر - bakr, Ar.; گاو - gáú, Pers.; گائی - gáí, Hind.; لامبو باتنہ - lámbubátina, Malay; ಆಕಲು - ákalu, Can.; ಪೆತ್ತ - petta, Too.; ఆవు - ávu, Tel.; ଗାଈ - gáyi, Oor.; പൈ - pai, Mal.; ගෝ - gó, Singh.; பசு - pasu, Tam.). San. from (gam, san. to go) [go]. Malay from (lámbu, malay, kine + bátina, malay, female of animals). Tam. from (pash, san. to bind); as bound to a stake in sacrifice. Cow. There is a Tamul proverb:—அசைந்து தின்கிறது மாடு அசையாமல் தின்கிறது வீடு—"a cow eats moving; a house eats standing "still." For cattle generally see Maud. Pashoo also means an animal in general; also soul [autmam, paty].——*Pashoopaty* (पशुपति - pashupati, San.). From (pashu, san. soul + pati, san. a lord). Shiva. There is a special treatise on the Paushoopatam worship, which is one of the six orthodox forms of Sheivism [ootchamayam]. Distinguish from Poosapauty [q.v.].——*Pashoopaty pausham* (पशुपतिपाश - pashupatipásha, San.). From (pashu, san. soul + pati, san. lord + pásha, san. bondage). A technical expression among the Sheivas to indicate life [jeevam], the deity [eeshwaran], and illusive power [mauyay, paty].——*Pashoorogam* (पशुरोग - pashuróga, San.). See sep. title.——*Pausham* (पाश - pásha, San.). From (pash, san. to bind). The cord of Shiva [paty, shiva].——*Paushandy* (पाषण्डी - páshandí, San.). From (pásha, san. fetter + an, san. to sound); one who teaches false doctrines which lead to fetters of wordly existence. Heterodox hindoo; a jeina [q.v.] or boodhist [booddha]. A heretic also among the Jeinas.——*Paushaunam* (بارنگن - bárangan, Malay; పాషాణము - páshánamu, Tel.; പാഷാണം - páshánam, Mal.; පාෂාණ - pásánam, Singh.; பாடாணம் - pádánam, Tam.). Title from tamul. Tel., &c., from (pash, san. to bind). Malay also (wárangan). Mineral poison. Especially arsenic. Arsenic is a steel-grey metal with brilliant lustre, very brittle and tarnishes on exposure to the air; sublimes at a temperature below fusing point, and gives off colorless fumes with a garlic-like [lussoon] odour. Hakeems [q.v.] do not give arsenic internally, but veidyans [q.v.] have for many centuries given white oxide in very minute doses with aromatics to check obstinate intermittent fevers [jwaram]; also in glandular complaints, tendency to apoplexy, and leprous affections [cooshtam]. To render arsenic inert solutions of alkaline sulphurets, or of soap [sauboon], or vinegar [caudy] are used. Arsenic in small doses is a medicine in elephantiasis [cochin leg]. For realgar see Manoshilay. For yellow orpiment see Hartaul. According to natives paushaunam is either native or prepared, and thirty-two kinds are recognised in each. The following are some of the different kinds:—Gowry paushaunam, from (gauri, san. yellowish) is golden colored arsenic; Parangy paushaunam, from (parangi, tam. portuguese) is sublimate of mercury [sowveeram]; Vellay paushaunam, from (vellai, tam. white) is arsenious acid [soofaid soombal]; Yely paushaunam, from (eli, tam. rat) is white arsenic or rat's bane.——*Paushoopatastram* (पाशुपतास्त्र - páshupatástra, San.). From (pashu, san. soul + pati, san. lord + astra, san. missile weapon). The bow of Shiva given to Arjoonan [q.v.].

PASHAPA (పచ్చెపువాడు - paççepuvádu, *Tel.*). From (paççemu, tel. swindling + vádu, tel. doer). A swindler [cuttiry].

PASHOO ROGAM (पशुरोग - pashuróga, *San.*) [pash]. Cattle disease. To rinderpest [vishajooram] and anthrax [pilavay] most of the mortality here is due. Pleuro-pneumonia is rare. As also foot-and-mouth disease [caulvyecomaury]. Among the Tamuls the best known cattle [maud] maladies are the following.——*Alary* (அலரி - alari, Tam.). From (alar, tam. to spread). Rinderpest [vishajooram].——*Ammay* (मसूरिका - masúriká, San.; سیتلا - sítlá, Hind.; అమ్మవారు - ammaváru, Tel.; വസൂരി - vasúri, Mal.; அம்மை - ammai, Tam.). Title and Tam. from (ammá, tam. mother). San. from (masúra, san. lentil, vicia hirsuta, koch.); hence lentil-shaped eruption. Hind. from (shítala, san. coldness), from cool treatment or offerings; goddess of small-pox. Tel. from (amma, tel mother + váru, tel. title of respect). Mal. from sanscrit. A kind of small-pox.——*Ashay podaumay* (அசைபோடாமை - asaibódámai, Tam.). From (asaibódu, tam. to chew the cud). Loss of cud.——*Cadoopp noppy* (शूल - shúla, San.; کرکری - kurkurí, Hind.; కడుపునొప్పి - kadupunoppi, Tel.; வயிற்றுவலி - vayittuvali, Tam.). San. from (shúl, san. to be ill). Hind. from (kurakura, mahr. grumbling sound). Tel. from (kadupu, tel. belly + noppi, tel. pain). Tam. from (vayiru, tam. belly + vali, tam. pain). Gripes.——*Calitchal* (ग्रहणी - grahaní, San.; اسہال - ishál, Hind.; கழிச்சல் - kazhiççal, Tam.). San. from (grah, san. to seize); epithet of the small intestines, as retaining food and assisting digestion by discharge of bile. Hence affection of small intestines. Hind. from arabic, meaning loosening of the bowels. Tam. from (kazhi, tam. to pass out). Diarrhœa.——*Capaula shoolay* (कपालशूल - kapálashúla San.; دماغکا ورم - damághkávaram, Hind.; கபாலசூலை - kabálasúlai, Tam.). San. from (kapála, san. skull + shúla, san. pain). Tam. means skull + pain. Inflammation of the brain.——*Caul canay* (காற்கணை - kárganai, Tam.). From (kál, tam. leg + kanai, tam. plumpness). Soreness of the hoofs.——*Caul noy* (கால்நோய் - kálnóy, Tam.). Tam. means foot + disease. Various diseases of the feet.——*Caulvye comaury* (کوماری - komárí, Hind.; கால்வாய்க்கோமாரி - kálváykkómári, Tam.). Tam. means leg + mouth + cow + epidemic. Foot-and-mouth disease. See sep. title.——*Caura calitchal* (காரக்கழிச்சல் - kárakkazhiççal, Tam.). Means pungent + diarrhœa. A sort of diarrhœa.——*Causam* (कास - kása, San.; نزلہ - nazlah, Hind.; காசம் - kásam, Tam.). San. from (kás, san. to cough). Hind. from (nazala, ar. defluxion). Bronchitis.——*Cautchal* (ज्वर - jvara, San.; تپ - tap, Hind.; காய்ச்சல் - káyççal, Tam.). Fever.——*Cautt novoo* (காற்றுநோவு - káttunóvu, Tam.). Means wind + pain. Rinderpest. Same as Alary [vishajooram].——*Cautt rogam* (پیچش - pechish, Hind.; காட்டுரோகம் - kátturógam, Tam.). Title from tamul from (kádu, tam. forest + róga, san. disease); caused by eating the first growth of grass after rains. Hind. from (pechídan, pers. to twist). Dysentery.——*Codiroo janny* (हनुस्तम्भ - hanustambha, San.; دانت کیلی - dántkilí, Hind.; கொடிறுசன்னி - kodirusanni, Tam.). Title and Tam. means jaw + convulsion. San. from (hanu san. jaw + stambha, san. obstruction). Hind. from (dánt, hind. tooth + kílí, hind. key). Lock-jaw or tetanus.——*Colly veengoo* (مونگا - múngá, Hind.; கொள்ளிவீங்கு - kollivíngu, Tam.). Means fire brand + swelling. Malignant sore-throat, generally fatal.——*Comaury* (கோமாரி - kómári, Tam.). From (gó, san. cow + mári, tam. epidemic). Same as Caulvyecomaury.——*Coodal vautam* (अन्त्रवृद्धि - antravriddhi, San.; روده - rodah, Hind.; குடல்வாதம் - kudalvátham, Tam.). Title from tamul means bowels + wind. San. from (antra, san. bowels + vriddhi, san. expansion). Hind. means a gut. Hernia.——*Coodal yeritchal* (رودونکی جلن - rodonkíjalan. Hind.; குடலெரிச்சல் - kudaleriççal, Tam.). Means bowels + burning. Inflammation of the bowels.——*Coolay mootty* (குலைமுட்டி - kulaimutti, Tam.). Means liver + obstruction. Congestion of lungs and swelling of belly.——*Coondikye yeritchal* (گردےکی جلن - gurdekíjalan, Hind.; குண்டிக்காயெரிச்சல் - kundikkáyeriççal, Tam.). From (kundikkáy, tam. kidneys + eriççal, tam. burning). Inflammation of kidneys.——*Coraury* (கோவாரி - kóvári, Tam.). From (gó, san. cow + váru, tam. to kill in numbers). Rinderpest. Same as Alary.——*Cull adeippoo* (मूत्रकृच्छ्र - mútrakrichhra, San.; سنگ مثانہ - sangimasánah, Hind.; கல்லடைப்பு - kalladaippu, Tam.). Title from tamul means stone + obstruction. San. from (mútra, san. urine + krichhra, san. difficulty). Hind. from (sang, pers. stone + masánah, ar. bladder). Calculus.——*Cunnoy* (नेत्ररोग - nétraróga, San.; آشوب - áshúb, Hind.; కన్నునొప్పి - kannunoppi, Tel.; கண்ணோய் - kannóy, Tam.). Means eye + disease. Ophthalmia.——*Jala bhaya rogam* (अलर्करोग - alarkaróga, San.; دیوانے کتے کا مرض -

divánekuttekámarz, Hind.; சலபயரோகம் - shalabayarógam, Tam.). Title from tamul from (jala, san. water + bhaya, san. fear + róga, san. disease). San. from (alarka, san. mad dog + róga, san. disease). Hydrophobia.——*Jalaga rogam* (گیندوے - gendwe, Hind.; జలగరోగము - jalagarógamu, Tel.). From (jalaga, tel. leech + róga, san. disease). Disease in which leeches are bred in the stomach.——*Mahoduram* (महोदर - mahódara, San.; استسقا - istiská, Hind.; மகோதிரம் - magóthiram, Tam.). Title from sanscrit means great + belly. Hind. from (saká, ar. to drink). Dropsy.——*Mala bandham* (मलावरोध - malávaródha, San.; قبض - kabz, Hind.; மலபந்தம் - malabandam, Tam.). Title from tamul means excrement + binding. San. from (mala, san. excrement + avaródha, san. obstruction). Hind. from (kabaza, ar. to grasp). Constipation.——*Manday adappaun* (अङ्गविकृति - angavikriti, San.; سکتہ - saktah, Hind.; மண்டையடைப்பான் - mandaiyadaippán, Tam.). Title from tamul means head + obstruction. San. from (anga, san. limb + vikriti, san. change), from the collapse. Hind. from (sakata, ar. to become still). Apoplexy.——*Manjal caumalay* (कामला - kámalá, San.; یرقان - yarkán, Hind.; పచ్చకామాల - pattsakámála, Tel.; மஞ்சட்காமாலை - manjadgámálai, Tam.). Title from tamul from (mañjal, tam. yellow + kámálai, tam. jaundice). San. from (káma, san. brightness + lú, san. to cut). Tel. from (pattsa, tel. yellow + kámála, tel. jaundice). Jaundice.——*Mooch adappoo* (மூச்சடைப்பு - múççadaippu, Tam.). Means breath + obstruction. Choking.——*Mookk adappaun* (पीनस - pínasa, San.; زکام - zukám, Hind.; மூக்கடைப்பான் - múkkadaippán, Tam.). Title from tamul means nose + obstruction. San. from (apí, san. to pour out + nása, san. nose). Hind. from (zakama, ar. to fill). Catarrh.——*Moolay vedippoo* (மூலைவெடிப்பு - mulaivedippu, Tam.). Means udder + crack. Sore teats.——*Mooit adappaun* (استسقاء طبلی - istiskáitabalí, Hind.; முட்டடைப்பான் - muttadaippán, Tam.). Title from tamul from (muttu, tam. extremity + adaippán, tam. obstruction). Hind. from (istiská, ar. dropsy + tabalí, ar. skin). Tympanitis.——*Nenj adappaun* (நெஞ்சடைப்பான் - neñjadaippán, Tam.). Means chest + obstruction. Inflammation of the lungs.——*Oodainda comboo* (உடைந்தகொம்பு - udaindagombu, Tam.). Broken horn.——*Odoo vayoo* (वात - váta, San.; وجع مفاصل - vajimafásil, Hind.; ஓடுவாயு - óduváyu, Tam.). Title from tamul means running + wind. San. from (vá, san. to blow). Hind. from (vaja, ar. pain + mafásil, ar. joints). Rheumatism.——*Paursavayoo* (पक्षाघात - pakshágháta, San.; فالج - fálij, Hind.; పార్శ్వవాయువు - párshvaváyuvu, Tel.; பாரிசவாயு - párisaváyu, Tam.). Title from tamul means side + wind. San. from (paksha, san. side + ágháta, san. blow). Hind. from (falija, ar. to divide). Paralysis.——*Pilavay cautchal* (பிளவைக்காய்ச்சல் - pilavaikkáyççal, Tam.). Means cleft + fever Anthrax fever.——*Racta calasha yeritchal* (کلیجے کی جلن - kalí jekijalan, Hind.; இரத்தக்கலச வெரிச்சல் - irattakkalasa vériççal, Tam.). Hind. means heart + burning. Tam. from (rakta, san. blood + kalasha, san. vessel + eriççal, tam. burning). Inflammation of the heart.——*Racta calitchal* (अतिसार - atisára, San.; இரத்தக்கழிச்சல் - irattakkazhiççal, Tam.). Title from tamul means blood + flux. San. from (ati, san. intensive prefix + sri, san. to move). Dysentery.——*Racta mootram* (रक्तमेह - raktaméha, San.; لہوکا پیشاب - lahúkápísháb, Hind.; இரத்தமூத்திரம் - irattamúttiram, Tam.). Title from tamul. San. from (rakta, san. blood + méha, san. urine). Hind. and Tam. means blood + urine. Hæmaturia.——*Shithamay coodal mandacutt* (சிதமைக்குடல் மந்தக்கட்டு - shithamaikkudalmandakkattu, Tam.). Tam. from (shithamai, tam. mucus + kudal, tam. bowels + mandam, tam. torpidity + kattu, tam. constriction). Fardel bound.——*Shoolookk* (موچ - moch, Hind.; சுளுக்கு - shulukku, Tam.). Sprains.——*Shory* (कण्डु - kandu, San.; گر - gar, Hind.; சொறி - shori, Tam.). Means itching. Mange.——*Tonday adappaun* (தொண்டையடைப்பான் - tondaiyadaippán, Tam.). Means throat + obstruction. Malignant sore-throat.——*Vayir ooppoosam* (अलसक - alasaka, San.; வயிறுப்புசம் - vayiruppusam, Tam.). Title from tamul means stomach + distension. San. from (alasa, san. inactivity + kri, san. to do). Tympanitis.——*Vayitt valy* (शूल - shúla, San.; پیٹ کا درد - petkádard, Hind.; வயிற்றுவலி - vayittuvali, Tam.). Means stomach + pain. Colic.——*Visha jooram* (விடசுரம் - vidasuram, Tam.). Means poison + fever. Rinderpest. See sep. title.——*Yeeral yeritchal* (معدے کی جلن - medekíjalan, Hind.; ஈரலெரிச்சல் - íraleriççal, Tam.). Hind. and Tam. means liver + burning. Inflammation of the liver.——*Yery cautchal* (எரிகாய்ச்சல் - erigáyççal, Tam.). Means burning fever. Inflammatory fever.——*Yirappay veekkam* (இரைப்பைவீக்கம் - iraippaivíkkam, Tam.). Tam. from (irai, tam. food + pai, tam. bag. + víkkam, tam. swelling). Distension of the rumen.

PASPAM (भस्म - bhasma, *San.*; భస్మము - bhasmamu, *Tel.*; ഭസ്മം - bhasmam, *Mal.*; பற்பம் - parbam, *Tam.*). From (bhas, san. to consume). Metallic ashes, any metallic oxide. The following are some principal Paspams.——*Caunta paspam* (कान्तभस्म - kántabhasma, San.; காந்தப்பற்பம் - kándapparbam, Tam.). From (kánta, san. loadstone). Medicinal powder made of loadstone [cauntam] by chemical process.——*Eeya paspam* (सीसभस्म - sísabhasma, San.; ஈயப்பற்பம் - íyapparbam, Tam.). From (íyam, tam. lead). Calcined lead [eeyam].——*Krishna paspam* (कृष्णभस्म - krishnabhasma, San.). From (krishna, san. black). Black sulphate of mercury [cajjaly, rasam], made by rubbing together and dissolving over the fire three parts of mercury with one of sulphur [gandhac]. Also called Rasaparparty, meaning mercury + incrustation. For the ordinary sulphate, which has 6 mercury to 1 sulphur, see Rasa paspam.——*Linga paspam* (இலிங்கப்பற்பம் - ilingapparbam, Tam.). From (ilingam, tam. cinnabar). Ashes of cinnabar [rasam, shangarf] used medicinally.——*Peeta paspam* (पीतभस्म - pítabhasma, San.). From (píta, san. yellow). Yellow preparation of mercury [rasam], prepared thus. Take of mercury and sulphur [gandhac] equal parts rub them together for seven days with the juice of Phyllanthus niruri [neeroory] and Heliotropium indicum [indian heliotrope]. Place the mixture in a covered crucible, and heat it in a sand bath for twelve hours. The result will be the yellow compound. Cf. the proportions in Rasa paspam.——*Racta paspam* (रक्तभस्म - raktabhasma, San.). From (rakta, san. red). Another name of Rasa sindooram [q.v.].——*Rasa paspam* (रसभस्म - rasabhasma, San.). Sulphate of mercury. See sep. title.——*Shweta paspam* (श्वेतभस्म - shvétabhasma, San.). From (shvéta san. white). Another name of Rascapoor.——*Swarna paspam* (स्वर्णभस्म - svarnabhasma, San.). Title and San. from (svarna, san. gold). Medicinal powder of gold, called ashes of gold [pon].——*Taulaca paspam* (तालकभस्म - tálakabhasma, San.). From (tálaka, san. orpiment). Roasted orpiment [hartaul].——*Taumra paspam* (ताम्रभस्म - támrabhasma, San.). From (támra, san. copper). Sulphide of copper [taumram.]——*Tootnaug paspam* (துத்தநாகப்பற்பம் - tuttanágapparbam, Tam.). Flowers of zinc [tootnaug].——*Vanga paspam* (वङ्गभस्म - vangabhasma, San.). From (vanga, san. tin). A greyish white powder consisting chemically of oxide of tin [tagaram] with some impurities.——*Velly paspam* (रौप्यभस्म - raupyabhasma, San.; வெள்ளிப்பற்பம் - vellipparbam, Tam.). Title and Tam. from (velli, tam. silver). San. from (rúpya, san. silver). San. also (rajatabhasma), meaning silver + ashes. Black oxide of silver. Argento oxidum of chemists. Prepared thus:—Purified silver leaves are mixed with twice their weight of cinnabar [shangarf] and heated in a subliming apparatus. This process is repeated fourteen times. The resulting compound is a fine greyish black powder with minute shining white particles intermixed. Medicinal properties analogous to those of the nitrate; milder, anthelmintic.

PAT (पत् - pat, *San.*). To fall, go; to fly.——*Patacam* (पतक - pataka, San.). From (pat, san. to fall). Arrangement, classification. An astronomical table.——*Patam* (पत्तन - pattana, San.; پٹن - patan, Hind.; ಪಟ್ಟಣ - pattana, Can.; పట్టణము - pattanamu, Tel.; പട്ടണം - pattanam, Mal.; பட்டணம் - pattanam, Tam.). From (pat, san. to go); trade resort. Town. Suffix in place names; as Bimlipatam, meaning bheema's town [putnam].——*Patanam* (पतन - patana, San.). Latitude, when referred to the stars [nacshatram, vicshaipam]. Patanacaindram is argument of the latitude [caindram].——*Patanjaly* (पतञ्जलि - patañjali, San.). From (pat, san. to go + añjali, san. the joined hands); habitually clasping hands, pious. A saint; the teacher of the Yoga philosophy [yogam]. See vol. I (74).——*Patingah* (शलभ - shalabha, San.; पतंग - patanga, Mahr.; فراشہ - faráshah, Ar.; پروانہ - parwánah, Pers.; پتنگا - patingá, Hind. and Dec.; ನುಸಿ - nusi, Can.; ପୁରି - puri, Too.; പാറ്റ - pátta, Mal.; பொட்டு - pottu, Tam.). Title from hindostany. San. from (shal, san. to cover). Ar. from (farasha, ar. to expand). Pers. from (par, pers. wing + wánah, pers. possessive particle). Hind. from (patanga, san. moth). Mal. from (páru, mal. to fly). Mal. also (urappuzhu), meaning sheath worm. Moth. Co-extensive with the order lepidoptera, holometabola, insecta [poochy], of naturalists [jantoo]. For silkworms see Puttoo.——*Patita* (पतित - patita, San.). From (pat, san. to fall). Fallen. Any caste arisen from the unlawful intercourse of persons of differing castes [jauty] in Malayalam country. They are:—Caniyaun, astrologer; Coorpoo; Ilavan, cocoanut [q.v.] tree cultivator and distiller; Paravan, lime [choonam] burner; Paunan, tailor; Shaunaun, cultivator of the palmyra [q.v].; Tolcoorooppan, makes shields and other articles of leather [chamrah]; Vaulan, boatman; Vailan, sorcerer, removes rubbish from Bramin houses; Vilcoorooppan, bowmaker and painter.——*Patram* (पत्र - pattra, San.). From (pat, san. to fly), what enables to fly; wing of a bird [pacshy]. Feather. Leaf of a tree regarded as its plumage; leaf of a flower or petal. Leaf prepared for writing on; paper, letter, written document [dastavaiz, nauma, putricay] in law. Bandhacapatram is a mortgage deed. Cadan patram is a bond of debt. Vennilay cadam patram is a bond of debt without security. Jaumeen patram is a bail or security bond. Adhicaura patram is a written authority or permission, power of attorney [adhicaura putricay, iktiaurnauma, mooctiaurnauma].——*Patringah* (हरियळ - hariyala, Mahr.; ورور - varvar, Ar.; پترنگا - patrangá, Hind.; చిన్నపసరిక - chinnapasarika, Tel.; കോലിക്കിളി - kólikkili, Mal.). Title from hindostany. Mahr. means green. Hind. from (pat, hind. leaf + rang, hind. color). Tel. from (chinna, tel. small + pasarika, tel. bee-eater). Mal. from (kólu, mal. stick + kili, mal. bird). Hind. also (hariyál), meaning green colored; (banspattí), meaning bamboo leaf; (barápatrangá), meaning large + bee-eater. Tel. also (kommupasarika), meaning branch + bee-eater. Meropidæ family, fissirostres, insessores, aves [pacshy, 7], of naturalists [jantoo]; bee-eaters or flycatchers; green is predominant color of plumage, varied with blue, yellow, and chestnut; feed on insects [poochy], often on wasps and bees [tainee], they always capture them in the air; usually crush their insect prey when they seize it, killing it at once, and thus do not get stung; their skin also is remarkably thick. The common indian bee-eater is merops viridis; alias merops ferrugiceps, indicus, orientalis, torquatus; very common bird; has a loud rather pleasant rolling whistling note. The blue-tailed bee-eater is merops philippensis; alias merops javanicus, typicus. The chestnut-headed bee-eater is merops quinticolor; alias merops erythrocephalus, urica; found in malabar forests. The blue-necked bee-eater is nyctiornis athertoni; alias bucia nipalensis; merops cyanogularis; napophila meropina; nyctiornis amherstiana, cæruleus.——*Patsunn* (پاتسن - pátsan, Hind.). From (pát, hind. leaf + san, hind. crotalaria juncea, linn.). Same as hemp bendy.——*Pattry* (पत्री - pattrí, San.). See sep. title.——*Patwarry* (پٹواری - patwárí, Hind.). From (patra, san. writing + kára, san. doer). A village accountant [curnum].——*Pautam* (पात - páta, San.). From (pat, san. to fall). Falling. The node of a planet's orbit [ayanaumsham, cacsham, craunty pautam, dhroovam, graham, vishoo].——*Pautarny* (चित्राङ्ग - chitránga, San.; پاترنی - pátarní, Dec.; رامارما - ramaramá, Malay; ಪ್ರಾತ್ತಿಹುಳ - práttihula, Can.; ಪಾಂತೆ - pánte, Too.; సీతాకోకచిలుక - sítákókachiluka, Tel.; வண்ணாத்திப்பூச்சி - vannáttippúççi, Tam.). Title from deccany. San. from (chitra, san. variegated + anga, san. body). Malay from (rama, malay, the hero). Tel. from (sítá, san. ráma's wife + kóka, tel. female garment + chiluka, tel. parrot); from variegated color. Tam. from (vannátti, tam. washerwoman + púççi, tam. insect); from the shaking of the tail as a washerwoman moves her back when washing clothes. Tam. also (tattárappúççi), meaning goldsmith insect; (tattán), meaning the dragon fly. Butterfly. Synonymous with the order lepidoptera, holometabola, insecta [poochy], of naturalists [jantoo].——*Pautaula garoodan* (ಪಾತಾಳ ಗರುಡ - pátálagaruda, Too.). From (pátála, san. nether regions + garuda, san. braminy kite); useful in snake-bites. Pautaulam is the region of snakes and garoodan [q.v.] is their enemy. Same as Mongoose snake root.——*Pautaulam* (पाताल - pátála, San.). From (páta, san. descent + tala, san. ground). One of the seven lower worlds [locam] and the best known; called also Yamalocam. Identical with the Greek Tartarus, as the abode of Titans or Raucshasans [q.v.]; Naracam [q.v.] is the proper term for hell as the abode of wicked men.——*Pudmam* (पद्म - padma, San.). From (pat, san. to go + ma, san. water); water-going plant. Lotus [nelumbo]. Pudma simhausanam is a lion-seat or throne supported by sculptured lotuses. Pudminy is a woman of the first or most excellent of the four classes into which the sex is distinguished; the others being:—chitriny wonderful, one endowed with various talents and excellencies; shankiny, resembling conch [chunk], middling class; hastiny, resembling elephant [q.v.], lowest class.——*Pudmanaubhan* (पद्मनाभ - padmanábha, San.). From (padma, san. lotus + nábhi, san. navel). Lotus-navelled. With the addition of sawmy, a name of Vishnoo in the Malayalam country. One of the titles of the Travancore rajah is the slave of Pudmanaubhan. Hindoo 2nd or pers. name [peyar].——*Pudmanaubhapooram* (പത്മനാഭപുരം - patmanábhapuram, Mal.). From (padmanábha, san. vishnu, the lotus navelled + pura, san. town). Mal. also (kalkulam), meaning stone + tank. Title otherwise Pulpanavaram.—"*a*" The southern division of Travancore, divided into five talooks. Population some 400,000.—"*b*" Town, Divisional head-quarters, Tahsildar's station; Travancore state, Pudmanaubhapooram division, Cullcoolam tal.; pop. 13,602. Former capital of province before removed to Trivandrum. Almost in ruins. Surrounded by strong fort of granite [caroom cull], and lies at foot of hills a mile east from main road. Old palace built after native style. Tradition says there is underground passage from palace to Tamrapurny river. Celebrated pagoda [q.v.] to Neelacunta sawmy.——*Pudmaraugam* (पद्मराग - padmarága, San.; حجریمانی - hajariyamání, Ar.; یاقوت زرد - yákútizard, Pers.; ಪದ್ಮರಾಗ - padmarága, Can.; పద్మరాగము - padmarágamu, Tel.; പത്മരാഗം - patmarágam, Mal.; பதுமராகம் - pathumarágam, Tam.). San. from (padma, san. lotus + rága, san. color). Ar. mean stone of yemen. Pers. from (yákút, ar. garnet + zard, pers. yellow). Tel. also (támarakempu), meaning lotus + ruby. Jacinth. ὑάκινθος was according to the Periplus exported from Mouziris [cranganore] and Nelkunda [cullada]. According to Salmasius this was the Ruby [laul]. In Selinus it would seem to be meant for the Amethyst [martees].——*Pudmauvaty* (पद्मावती - padmávatí, San.). From (padma, san. lotus + vat, san. suffix of possession). Lutchmy [q.v.], as seated on a lotus-flower [alamail, nelumbo].——*Putnam* (पट्टण - pattana, San.; پٹن - patan, Hind.; పట్నము - patnamu, Tel.; പട്ടണം - pattanam, Mal.; பட்டணம் - pattanam, Tam.). Town. Suffix in place names [patam].——*Putnasawmy* (பட்டணச்சுவாமி - pattanaççuvámi, Tam.). From (pattana, san. town + svámí, san. master). Headman among some of the castes [jauty].——*Putricay* (पत्रिका - patriká, San.). From (patra, san. leaf). Document [caranam, dastavaiz]. Also a letter [tappaul] or newspaper [acbaur]. Adhicaura putricay is a written authority or permission; power of attorney [iktiaurnauma, mooctiaurnauma]. For jenmaputtricay or horoscope see sep. title.——*Puttah* (पट्ट - patta, San.; پٹا - pattá, Hind.; ಪಟ್ಟ - patta, Can.; పట్టా - pattá, Tel.; பட்டா - pattá, Tam.). From (patra, san. leaf). Originally a band of silk [puttoo], mark of royalty. So a title deed of lease, now written on paper [caugaz], but formerly engraved with a style on cadjan [q.v.] leaves [olay], given to a ryot [q.v.] by government, or zemindar [q.v.]. It specifies the particulars of his holding, the rent payable for it, the kists [q.v.] according to which the rent should be paid, the road cess, village cess, and other particulars such as restrictions as to mining rights, &c. Zemindars sometimes include Coody maraumut [amanjy]. Puttah means also title to office. Puttah monigar is the recognized and appointed monigar [q.v.]. See vol. I, 112.——*Puttam* (पट्ट - patta, San.; பட்டம் - pattam, Tam.). From (patra, san. leaf). Same origin as Puttah. A head ornament symbolical of authority. In S. canara office of dignity in a family governed by the Aliya santauna [q.v.] law. It is indivisible, and whether the family be divided or not, the Puttam, no special arrangement having been made about it, descends to the eldest male of the surviving members of the family. Varauha mihiran [q.v.] has the following:—"That it may do "good, the king's puttam shall be 8 inches broad in the middle, "the queen's shall be 7 inches broad, and the prince's shall be "6 inches broad; the general's shall be 4 inches broad in the "middle; the prasaudaputtam worn by a person as a token of "royal favor shall be 2 inches broad; thus puttams are five in "number; if the puttam were made of pure gold, and twice "as long, with its sides half as broad as the dimension at the "middle, it would make the wearer happy; the king's puttam "shall have five points or crests; the queen's and the prince's "shall have three crests; the general's shall have a single crest "and the prasaudaputtam shall have no crest."——*Puttaubhiraman* (பட்டாபிராமன் - pattábiráman, Tam.). From (patta, san. plate of gold worn on forehead as an ornament and symbol of office + abhiráma, san. delightful). Rama at the coronation. Hindoo 2nd or pers. name [peyar].——*Puttimar* (പത്തേമാരി - pattamári, Mal.; பாட்டிமார் - páttimár, Tam.). From (patár, hind. tidings + márí, mahr. carrier). Sailing vessel common in coasting trade of W. coast. These vessels have a prow stem, the same length as the keel. The dimensions of the larger class are 76 feet in length, 21 feet in breadth, 11 feet 9 inches in depth, and about 200 tons burden. They are planked with teak [q.v.], upon jungle-wood frames, their bottoms are sheathed with inch-board, and a layer of choonam [q.v.] mixed with cocoanut [q.v.] oil and a portion of dammer [q.v.]. Some of the smaller class of about 60 tons burden, are sewed together with coir [q.v.]. The smaller class has one, and the larger class two masts, with the lateen sail, the foremast raking forward for the purpose of keeping the yard clear when it is raised or lowered. These vessels are navigated by Moplahs [q.v.] and other Mahomedans, and have a crew of ten or twelve men, and a tindal [q.v.].——*Puttolay* (பட்டோலை - pattólai, Tam.). From (patta, san. tablet + ólai, tam. palm leaf). An edict, a balance sheet [olay].——*Puttuck* (ಪತಾಕ - pataka, Can.). From (patáka, san. banner); body of men under one flag [dhwajam]. A body of horse.——*Putty* (پٹی - pattí, Hind.). From (patra, san. leaf). A bandage. Tribute, such as nuzzer [q.v.], &c. A number of betel [q.v.] leaves folded up with areca-nuts [q.v.] in one of them [paunkabeerah, paun soopyaury].

PATAULAM (پٹالم - patálam, *Hind.*). Corruption of battalion [dandoo].

PATAUN (پٹھان - pathán, *Hind.*). From (fathán, ar. victor). Founder of the sect so called by the prophet. Same here as Afghaun. They have come to Madras principally from the Mahratta country. All are Soonnees [q.v.]. Numbers about 15,000. See vol. II, 233.

PATCHAC (پچک - pachak, *Hind.*). Malay word. Same as Costum.

PATHAKK (பதக்கு - pathakku, *Tam.*). Measure of capacity. 2 cooroonies = 1 pathakk; 2 pathakks = 1 toony [alavay, 3a]. Varies with the mercaul or cooroony.

PATHAM (பதம் - patham, *Tam.*). From (pathi, tam. to fix); properly fixed or disposed. Fit state.——*Padoonoo* (పదును - padunu, Tel.). From (patham, tam. fitness). A wetting, used for rain [mazhay]; about an inch [q.v.] and a half [dookky]. ——*Pathaneer* (பதநீர் - pathanír, Tam.). From (above + nír, tam. water). Sweet toddy [q.v.] drawn in a pot lined with choonam [q.v.] to prevent fermentation [neerah].

PATHY (பதி - pathi, *Tam.*). Ten.——*Pathigam* (பதிகம் - pathigam, Tam.). From (pattu, tam. ten). Poem of praises to a deity, &c., commonly of ten verses.——*Pathin* (பதின் - pathin, Tam.). Change of (pattu, tam. ten) in combination.——*Pathinettaum perook* (பதினெட்டாம்பெருக்கு - pathinettám-berukku, Tam.). From (pathinettu, tam. eighteen + perukku, tam. rise). Solar [madhyama sowra maunam] festival [pundigay, 6d]. Festival in Cauvery delta to celebrate rising of river, on the eighteenth of the fourth solar month Audy [mausam] or about 1st August. Otherwise Audy perook or July freshes. Also Audy pathinett [maryauday].

PATNAVA (பட்டினவன் - pattinavan, *Tam.*). From (pattinam, tam. maritime village). A fishing caste on the Tanjore coast. Numbers about 22,000 [jauty]. See vol. I (69).

PATTOO (लेप - lépa, *San.*; గట్టు - gattsu, *Tel.*; பற்று - pattu, *Tam.*). Title from tamul, means catching. San. from (lip, san. to smear, to adhere to). Cement. Limes, concretes, septariæ, dolomites, magnesite, gypsum, &c., are used in manufacturing cements, and there is an abundant supply of these all over Southern india. The pure carbonates of lime cannot be used for out-door plastering [cauray] near the sea. The kankars [q.v.] or nodular limes are more durable though not so white. The septariæ are very common though the beds are not extensive; they accompany the strata of blue and white potters' clay and kaolin [q.v.]. The best hydraulic septariæ occur at Avady, Bangalore and Chingleput. A very fine natural hydraulic cement occurs on the banks of the Godavery and was extensively used in the construction of the Godavery and Kistna anicuts. A hydraulic limestone [choonam cull] occurs along with the blue slate [cull palagay] of Cuddapah, and the dolomites of the Ceded districts [q.v.] and the Northern circars [q.v.] make good cement. The following are native recipés:— Put into a dronam [q.v.] of water the raw leaves of the tindoocam [gaub] and of the capittam [wood apple], the flowers of the shaulmaly [silk cotton], the seeds of the sullaky [indian olibanum], the bark of the dhanvanam [arabian manna], and a small quantity of vacha [vashamboo]; heat the water on fire till it is reduced to one-eighth of its original quantity; remove the jar from fire; put into the calcam thus prepared goolgooloo [bdellium] and the juice of the shreevausacam [gandafiroza], and of sarjam [saul] and bhallautam [marking nut], coondoorcam [olibanum] and the fruit of the atasy [alsee] and of bilvam [bæl]; the cement thus formed is known as vajralaipam or adamant cement. In the construction of temples [coil, pagoda] and of the palaces of kings, of turrets, and in fixing the lingam [q.v.] or the image [shilay, vigraham] in the temple, in the construction of walls and wells, if the vegetable cement above referred to be melted and used, the structures will last for a crore [q.v.] of years. Form a mixture of shel-lac [lac], the resin [raul] of the plant, boswellia serrata, roxb. [indian olibanum], bdellium [q.v.], soot in the ceilings of houses, the fleshy part of the fruit of capittam [wood apple] and of bilvam [bael], the fruit of the naugabalah [orila], madhoocam [mohwah] and munjishtay [munjeet], the juice of the sarjam [saul] as well as vinegar [caudy] made from fruit [pazham], and put it in a jar of water, heat it till it is reduced to an eighth of its bulk; the resulting calcam is also known as vajralaipam and is an excellent one and can be used for the several purposes already mentioned. Form a mixture of the horns [sing] of the cow [maud], the buffalo [khoolgah], and the goat [aud] reduced to powder, the hair of the ass [gadhah], the skin of the buffalo [khoolgah], the milk of the cow [pashoo] and the juice of the nimbam [neem] and the capittam [wood apple] trees; throw the mixture in a jar of water and heat it, the resulting calcam is also an excellent animal cement. Melt together eight parts of lead [eeyam], two parts of bronze, and one part of brass [pittalay]; the result will be a strong metallic cement.

PATTRY (पत्त्री - pattri, *San.*). From (pattra, san. knife) [pat]; from curved bill. Falcons. Falconinæ, falconidæ [bheroondam], raptores, aves [pacshy, 2], of naturalists [jantoo]. Bill short and curved throughout, toothed on tip; cere long and rounded; wings long and pointed; tail long and rounded; black eyed birds of prey. The species best known to the natives are shown below.——*Bheiry* (पत्त्री - pattrí, San.; بحری - bahrí, Ar., Pers. and Hind.; بھیری - bhairí, Dec.; ಭೈರ - bhaira, Can.; భైరిడేగ - bhéridéga, Tel.). Title from deccany. San. from (pattra, san. knife); knife-beaked bird. Ar. from (bahr, ar. sea); from resort. Pers., &c., from arabic. Tel. from (bhairi, hind. falcon + déga, tel. hawk). Male bird is hind. (bhairbaçça), meaning bheiry + young one. Title otherwise Peregrine falcon. Falco peregrinus, falconinæ [pattry], falconidæ [bheroondam], raptores [pacshy, 2], of naturalists. Alias Falco calidus, communis, micrurus. Adult, above deep bluish grey, feathers with dark markings; wings blackish brown, more or less spotted or barred with white on the inner web; tail grey, with some dark bands, and a pale tip; beneath chin pure white; bill bluish, black at tip, cere yellow; legs and feet yellow; length 16, wings 12½, tail 5¾; at each moult the feathers become more grey; abundant along the east coast; prefers the sea coast, strikes down teal, duck [varatam], &c.; does not breed in this country, but migrates to the north; still trained for falconry, trained to strike herons [paddy bird], storks [adjutant bird], cranes [saurasam], &c.; strikes only with talons, and chiefly with the hind claw.——*Laggar* (لگر - lagar, Hind.; ಗಿಡಗ - gidaga, Can.; లగుడు - lagudu, Tel.). Male bird is hind. (jaggar). Title otherwise Jugger. Falco jugger, falconinæ [pattry], falconidæ [bheroondam], raptores [pacshy, 2], of naturalists. Alias Falco luggur, themophilus; Adult, plumage above dusky ashy or slate color; head in some rufous, with faint brown streaks; male measures 16–17 inches; abundant in open cultivated districts; generally one standing alone among grain-fields; preys on small birds, even in the midst of a cantonment; trained to hunt crows [caurvam], paddy birds [q.v.], night herons [q.v.], partridges [teetar], and florikin [florican].——*Narzee* (نارزی - nárzí, Hind.; తొండలముత్సుగద్ద - tondalamuttsugadda, Tel.). Tel. from (tonda, tel. bloodsucker + muttsu, tel. thief + gadda, tel. kite); lizard-killing kite. Male bird is hind. (narzank). Tel. also (tondalamuttsugádu), meaning bloodsucker + thief + fellow; (tondaladótsugádu), meaning bloodsucker + rob + fellow. Title otherwise Kestril. Tinnunculus alaudarius, falconinæ [pattry], falconidæ [bheroondam], raptores [pacshy, 2], of naturalists. Alias Falco interstinctus, tinnunculus. Female and young male, above reddish, long dark stripes on head and neck, tail with numerous dark bars and a broader one at the end, white tipped; plumage beneath reddish ochraceous with numerous and close brown spots; adult male has fore-head yellowish; head, nape and tail fine ashy grey, latter with broad black band, former sometimes tinged black; beneath creamy or rusty with spots of brown; 13–14 inches; cold weather visitant; one of the earliest and does not leave till april; chief food lizards [chipkalee]. The lesser kestril is erythropus cenchris; alias falco tinnunculoides; on neilgherries, breeding on cliffs in may and june; seizes insects on the wing, and pulls off the elytra of beetles [zeerangy].——*Shahin* (شاهین - sháhín, Ar., Pers., Hind. and Dec.; ಡೇಗೆ - dége, Can.; డేగడము - dzávadamu, Tel.; രാജാളി - rájáli, Mal.; வல்லூறு - vallúru, Tam.). Pers. from (sháh, pers. king). Tel. from (java, san. speed). Mal. from (rájá, san. king + kili, mal. bird). Tam. from (val, tam. powerful + úru, tam. killing). Male bird is hind. (kohí). Tam. also (irásáli), meaning king hawk. Title otherwise Royal falcon, Shaheen. Falco peregrinator, falconinæ [pattry], falconidæ [bheroondam], raptores [pacshy, 2], of naturalists. Alias Falco shaheen, sultaneus. Adult, head, nape, and cheek stripe almost black, almost without any markings; changes of plumage from the young bird consist in the head gradually becoming darker, the back becoming lighter; length 15, wing 10¾, tail 5¼; not common; destroys game, partridges [teetar], quails [batair], &c.; very partial to parroquets [totah]; breeds on steep and inaccessible cliffs; prized by the natives for hawking; taken for sale to hyderabad, where falconry is yet carried on; caught with bird-lime; varieties red, white, blue and black.——*Toormty* (ترمتی - turumtí, Hind.; చెట్వ - chetva, Tel.). Hind. from calmuc name of the hobby, falco subbuteo. Tel. is properly the female. Male bird is tel. (dzalakatte), (jelákante). Title otherwise Red-headed merlin. Hypotriorchis chicquera, falconinæ [pattry], falconidæ [bheroondam], raptores [pacshy, 2], of naturalists. Chicquera from Hindostany name for sparrow-hawk [baushah]. Adult, head, nape and cheek stripe, bright rufous; rest of plumage above fine pale grey; length of male 11–12 inches; affects chiefly open country over cultivation; often hunts in pairs; preys on small birds; four eggs of a yellowish brown color, mottled with brown spots; has a shrill angry scream; occasionally reclaimed, and flown at quail [batair], partridges [teetar], mynas [q.v.] but especially at the indian jay [q.v.].

PAU (पा - pá, *San.*). Protect.——*Palamcottah* * (பாளையங்கோட்டை - pálaiyangóttai, Tam.). From (pálaiyam, tam. fortified village + kóttai, tam. fort). Tam. also (mangainagaram), meaning maiden + city.—"*a*" Deputy tahsildarry, Tinnevelly district. Pay Rs. 70.—"*b*" Town, Head-quarters of Deputy tahsildar, Municipality; Tinnevelly dist., Tinnevelly tal.; pop. 18,686; acres 2,080; lat. 8° 43′; long. 77° 46′; from Madras S. 443 miles by rail; from Shermadevy E.N.E. 12 miles; from Shreevillipoottore S. 54 miles; from Tinnevelly E. 4 miles; from Tuticorin by rail 36 miles. One mile from the Tamraporny in an extensive plain. At one time a strongly fortified town, but hardly any trace now remains of the fortifications. The fort was 3 furlongs square with 40 bastions, 4 gates, and 8 slopes for ascending the ramparts. In 1780 Schwartz baptized at Palamcottah the Bramin woman Clarinda, who erected there the first English church south of Trichinopoly, which in 1784 was put under Satyanautan, the first Hindoo-born minister of the Church of England. Church missionary society's institutions; where Rev. J. Hough, chaplain in 1816, and historian of Christianity in India, revived the Protestant mission. The following are the travelling distances by road from Palamcottah to different places:—

To	Viâ	Miles	Furlongs
Aryancauv ...	Tencaushy	48	2
Bangalore ...	Dindigul, Coochilanbauray and Salem.	355	3½
Bangalore ...	Dindigul, Aravacoorchy and Salem ...	354	4½
Bellary ...	Dindigul, Coochilanbauray, Salem and Bangalore.	542	6½
Bellary ...	Dindigul, Aravacoorchy, Salem and Bangalore.	541	7½
Calicut ...	Madura, Dindigul and Palghaut ...	323	2½
Cannanore ...	Madura, Dindigul, Palghaut and Calicut.	382	3½
Caroor ...	Madura and Coochilanbauray	184	7½
Caroor ...	Madura and Aravacoorchy	184	0½
Dindigul ...	Tirmungalam and Madura	135	7½
French rocks ...	Dindigul and Suttimungalam	354	7½
Madras ...	Madura, Dindigul, Trichinopoly and Chingleput.	407	3
Madras ...	Madura, Trichinopoly and Chingleput.	377	1
Madura ...	Viroothooputty and Tirmungalam ...	95	6
Mercara ...	Dindigul, Suttimungalam and Mysore..	413	2½
Mysore ...	Dindigul and Suttimungalam	338	7½
Nagarcoil ...	Aramboly and Nangoonairy	47	5
Namcull ...	Madura and Coochilanbauray	205	7½
Namcull ...	Madura and Aravacoorchy	205	0½
Negapatam ...	Ramnaud, Tondy and Munnargoody ...	236	1
Negapatam ...	Madura, Tripatore and Puttoocottah ...	251	5
Palghaut ...	Madura, Dindigul and Pulney	238	6½
Panagoody ...	Nangoonairy	32	4
Paupanausam ...	Culladacoorchy	32	4
Quilon ...	Aramboly, Nagarcoil and Trivandrum.	131	4
Quilon ...	Aulangoolam, Tencaushy and Aryancauv.	98	2
Quilon ...	Cadayam, Tencaushy and Aryancauv...	102	1
Ramnaud ...	Ottapidauram and Veippaur	94	1
Salem ...	Madura and Coochilanbauray	234	3½
Salem ...	Madura and Aravacoorchy	233	4½
Tencaushy ...	Aulangoolam	34	4
Tencaushy ...	Cadayam	38	3
Tondy ...	Veippaur and Ramnaud	124	5
Trichinopoly ...	Madura	176	6
Trichinopoly ...	Madura and Dindigul	196	7
Trivandrum ...	Tencaushy and Cotacara	128	7
Trivandrum ...	Aramboly and Nagarcoil	89	3
Trivandrum ...	Tencaushy and Quilon	140	1
Tuticorin ...	Vulnaud	32	0
Vellore ...	Madura, Trichinopoly, Jinjee and Arnee.	258	6

—"*c*" Palamcottah base, east end is a trig. station in lat. 8° 43′ 24·07″, long. 77° 45′ 39·72″; from Palamcottah N.N.W. 3 miles; from Tinnevelly N.E. 4 miles. Palamcottah base, west end is a trig. station in lat. 8° 43′ 32·71″, long. 77° 46′ 10·11″; from Palamcottah N.W. 8 miles; from Tinnevelly N.W. 5 miles.——*Pali* (பாலி - páli, Tam.). Means a line, on account of the written character. Called Maugady in Ceylon. An Arya [q.v.] pracritic language. Sacred language of Booddhists [booddha], extinct in India; still extant in Burmah and Ceylon [bhaushay].——*Patniyammay* (பத்தினியம்மை - pattiniyammai, Tam.). From (patní, san. chaste wife + ammá, tam. mother). The faithful woman; Lutchmy [q.v.].——*Patny* (पत्नी - patní, San.). Faithful wife [paty vratay, suttee].——*Paty* (पति - pati, San.). From (pá, san. to protect). Master. Epithet of the supreme being; a superior or elder. Affix to proper names as Ganapaty, Sabhaupaty. Also applied to tutelary deities or regents [peyar]. In tamul sheiva siddhauntam one of the three unoriginated, eternal principles in the universe, the other two being pashoo [q.v.] or soul and pausham [q.v.] or cord, the natural or moral evil. The male energy, shacty [q.v.] being the female; these two the cause of all the endless modifications [mauyay] appearing in the evolution of nature. Often used in composition, as Senaupaty, a commander-in-chief.——*Paty vratay* (पतिव्रता - pativratá, San.). From (pati, san. husband + vrata, san. devotion). Chaste wife [patny, suttee].——*Paul* (پال - pál, Hind.). From (pá, san. to protect). A place of shelter from the sun made by extending a piece of cloth across a transverse pole [dandam]. Also a tent on same principle [derah].——*Paulak* (पालङ्की - pálankí, San.; سلق - silk, Ar.; چغندر - chughandar, Pers.; پالك - pálak, Hind.; چقندر - chukandar, Dec.). Title from hindostany. San. from (pála, san. nourisher + ank, san. to mark); requiring great care and attention for growth [true olibanum]. Ar. from greek. Hind. from sanscrit. Hind. also (pálang). Greek σεῦτλον, τεῦτλον, τεῦτλις. Title otherwise Bengal beet, Common beet, Country spinach, Indian beet, Red beet. Botanically Beta vulgaris, linn., salsolaceæ [vricsham, 108]. Alias Beta benghalensis. Stem 1–3 feet, erect, furrowed; lower leaves 1–10 inches, often trowel-shaped, base decurrent on the petiole, margin waved, upper short incurved; spikes 6–18 inches, slender; clusters remote; sepals with membranous margins. Cultivated; used as pot-herb [keeray]; several varieties vary more in form and in color than in flavor; for the table that of the deepest blood-color is used. No other common species here.——*Paulam* (പാലം - pálam, Mal.). From (páli, san. bridge). Bridge.——*Paulan* (पाल - pála, San.). From (pá, san. to protect). Protector. Suffix in proper names, as Gopaulan, Rajagopaulan [peyar].——*Pauleiyacaura* (பாளையக்காரன் - pálaiyakkáran, Tam.). From (pálaiyam, tam. camp + kára, san. doer). Tamul for Moottrauz [q.v.].——*Paupum* (पाप - pápa, San.). From (pá, san. to protect), what requires to be guarded against. Sin.——*Paupanausam* (பாவநாசம் - pávanásam, Tam.). From (pápa, san. sin + násha, san. destruction). Sanscrit name (pápanáshatírt'ha), meaning sin + destruction + sacred place. Village; Tinnevelly dist., Ambasamoodram tal.; lat. 8° 43′; long. 77° 25′; from Ambasamoodram W. 6 miles; from Tinnevelly W. 22 miles. At junction of Serviaur and Tamrapurny. Fall of 80 feet, known as Calyauny teertam, and a shrine. The fish are fed by Bramins. There is a water power spinning mill [aroovy].——*Paupicanama* (పాపికనమ - pápikanama, Tel.). From (pápí, san. sinner + kanama, tel. pass). Pass; Vizagapatam dist., Royagada tal., Parvatipore division. Goes through Neemgherry hills, between Bissemcuttack and Singapore [ghaut].——*Paupicondah* (పాపికొండ - pápikonda, Tel.). From (pápí, san. sinner + konda, tel. hill). Also called Bison range. Range of hills; Godavery dist., Bhadrachellam tal.; height 4,200 feet. Extends along the whole northern frontier of the district. Remarkable for scenery, abundance of large game and teak [q.v.] forests. The highest point is situated to the west of the gorge through which the Godavery passes.——*Paupughny* (పాపఘ్ని - pápaghni,* Tel.). From (pápa, san. sin + han, san. to destroy). Tel. also (gundéru), meaning rock + river. River; Cuddapah dist., Madanapully, Cadiry, Royachoty, Cuddapah, and Poolivendla tals. Rises in Mysore. After entering Madanapully talook in lat. 13° 39′ N., long. 78° 08′ E., flows through the Vyausasamoodram tank at Cundocore, and thence north through the Palcondah hills at Vempully, where it is known as the Coondair. Thence it flows along a broad and sandy bed through Cuddapah talook into the Pennair at Camalaupooram in lat. 14° 36′ N. and long. 78° 44′ E. The river is sacred. The gorge is noted for its temple of Anjaneshwarasawmy. A girder bridge on the north-west line of the Madras railway, with 22 spans of 72 feet, crosses the river near Camalaupooram.——*Peepul* (पिप्पल - pippala, San.). See sep. title.——*Pinaucam* (पिनाक - pináka, San.). From (pá, san. to protect). Shiva's bow.——*Pinaucapauny* (पिनाकपाणि - pinákapáni, San.). From (pináka, san. bow + páni, san. hand). Shiva.——*Pinaugay* (பிநாகை - pinágai, Tam.). From (pináka, san. shiva's bow). Tamul way of writing the Southern pinaukiny or Ponniaur.——*Pinaukiny* (पिनाकिनी - pinákiní, San.). From (pináka, san. shiva's bow). Braminical name for the Pennair, both north and south [pennair, ponniaur].——*Pitah* (पिता - pitá, San.). From (pá, san. to protect). Father [pitry].——*Pitaumahan* (पितामह - pitámaha, San.). From (pitá, san. father + mahá, san. great). The grandfather [bandhoo]; name of Bramha [q.v.].——*Pitry* (पितृ - pitri, San.). From (pá, san. to protect). Father [pitah]. In plural are the manes of ancestors to whom Shrauddham [q.v.] is paid. Feralia of the Romans. Supposed to reside in a region above the moon [chundran] or in it. Pitraurjitam, from (arj, san. to acquire), is hereditary right. Pitrya dinam is a day of the pitries, or a lunation [chaundra mausam]. Pitrya maunam is the mode of calculating by pitrya dinams [maunam].——*Poligar* (ಪಾಳೆಗಾರ - pálegára, Can.; పాళెగాడు - pálegádu, Tel.; பாளையக்காரன் - pálaiyakkáran, Tam.). Means holder of a camp.—"*a*" Title given by the Vijianugger kings to the chiefs of the Teloogoo colonies planted in the neighbouring provinces for the purpose of controlling the original inhabitants. In Canarese country called Wodeyar [q.v.] or proprietors, and this title is borrowed by some Tamul zemindars [q.v.]. Poligars were known formerly as Main cauvalgars [q.v.] or superior guardians in contradistinction to the village watchmen or Stala cauvalgar [q.v.] or local guardians. These persons established many small principalities in secluded places, and by siding with the larger powers they retained their petty sovereignties. Towards the close of the eighteenth and beginning of the ninteenth century, the British government found it necessary to reduce several of the Poligar chiefs. In 1802–3 Cataboma naick, the dumb chief of Punchaulamcoorchy in Tinnevelly, thrice beat back British detachments, and was at last subdued by a small army with Europeans and guns.—"*b*" Also the name of a country breed of dogs [nye]. See vol. I (19).——*Poliput* (பாளையப்பட்டு - pálaiyappattu, Tam.). From (pálegádu, tel. poligar + pattu, tam. village). The tract held by a poligar.——*Pollem* (పాళెము - pálemu, Tel.). From (páli, san. row); military lines. North country usage. Camp, fortified village. Also the country of a Poligar [q.v.].——*Polliem* (പാളയം - pálayam, Mal.; பாளையம் - pálaiyam, Tam.). From (páli, san. row); military lines. Southern usage. Camp, fortified village. Also the country of a Poligar [inam]. Proper name, common to both sexes [peyar], where short for poligar.——*Polliett atchan* (പാല്യത്തച്ചൻ - pályattaççan, Mal.). From (pálayam, mal. camp + aççan, mal. father). The hereditary minister [muntry] of Cochin.——*Poomaun* (पुमान् - pumán, San.). From (pá, san. to protect). A man, a male [poorsham].

PAU (पा - pá, *San.*). Drink.——*Patro* (ପାତ୍ରୋ - patró, Oor.). From (pátra, san. a worthy person) [pautram]. The chief of a collection of Khond [q.v.] mittahs [paut].——*Paunay* (பானை - pánai, Tam.). From (pána, san. drinking). Pot. Oil measure. 4 chemboos = 1 paunay; 8 paunays = 1 pothy [alavay, 4a]. Approximate actual value, 1 paunay = 864 cubic inches, Trichinopoly. Same as Marcam. See vol. I, 609; II, 519.——*Paun doob* (پاندوب - pándúb, Hind.; ನೀರ್ಕೋಗಿಲೆ - nírkógile, Can.;

మునుగుడుకోడి - munugudukódi, Tel.). Hind. from (pání, hind. water + dúb, hind. dive). Can. from (níru, can. water + kókila, san. cuckoo). Tel. from (munugu, tel. to dive + kódi, tel. fowl). Hind. also (pántirrí), meaning swimmer in water; (churaká). Can. also (plava). Beng. also (dubari). Title otherwise Indian diver, Indian grebe. Podiceps philippensis, podicipidæ, mergitores, natatores [pacshy, 51], of naturalists [jantoo]. Alias Podiceps minor.——*Pauny* (پانی - pání, Hind.). From (pána, san. drink). Water [ab, neer]. Plant 1st term. Ex., where transl. is of second term:—Flacourtia cataphracta (pániáunla), phyllanthus emblica; Polygonum flaccidum (pánímirch), piper nigrum; Salix tetrasperma (pánijama), close to; Trapa bispinosa (pániphal), fruit; Vitex trifolia (pánikishambálí), vitex negundo. See gloss. paragraphs.——*Paut* (పాత - páta, Tel.). From (pátra, san. worthy person). Title of a chief [patro].——*Pautram* (पात्र - pátra, San.). From (pá, san. to drink). Vessel. Also worthy person [patro, paut].——*Pautra saumaun* (పాత్రసామాను - pátrasámánu, Tel.). From (pátra, san. vessel + sámánu, tel. things). Plate, metal ware.——*Payashwany* (ಪಯಸ್ವಿನಿ - payasvini, Can.). From (payas, san. water + vin, san. suffix of possession). Mal. name (perumpuzha), meaning large + river. Known also at Chundragherry village as the Chundragherry, and elsewhere as the Noojicull. River; South canara dist., Cassergode and Ooppinangady tal. Rises in the Western ghauts near Sumpaujey in lat. 12° 26′; long. 75° 43′; and, after a westerly course of 65 miles, enters the sea two miles south of Cassergode in lat. 12° 29′ N., long. 75° 1′ E. When in flood, timber is floated from the ghauts [q.v.]. Except for about 15 miles above its mouth, not at other seasons navigable. A fort, situated on its left bank, commands the river. Forms northern boundary between the Malayalam and Tooloovam countries. No Nayar woman may cross it, it being unlucky for women to cross boundaries.——*Puckally* (پکھالی - pakhálí, Hind.). A waterman, one who carries water by means of a double bag borne by a bullock [maud] or buffalo [bheesty, khoolgah].——*Puckaul* (پکھال - pakhál, Hind.). From (payas, san. water + khalla, san. leather). Large leather bag for carrying water in, usually double, thrown over a bullock; also a leather bag used for raising water from wells, being attached to a rope passing through a pulley and drawn up by oxen passing up and down an inclined plane [capilay, mhote].——*Puneeala* (پانی آنولہ - pániáunlá, Hind.). Means water + phyllanthus emblica, linn. Same as Indian plum.

PAUD (پاد - pád, *Hind.*). Means protecting. Throne [takht].——*Padshah* (پادشاہ - pádshah, Pers.). From (above + sháh, pers. lord). King. Equivalent to Arabic sultan [q.v.]. In composition forms a lacab; as Padshah begum, royal lady [ism]. Padshahy is royal. Padshah zaudah is a prince. Also written Pachah, Pashah, Bashaw.

PAUK (पूग - púga, *San.*; فوفل - faufal, *Ar.* and *Pers.*; سپاری - supárí, *Hind.*; ಅಡಿಕೆ - adike, *Can.*; వక్క - vakka, *Tel.*; അടക്ക - atakka, *Mal.*; பாக்கு - pákku, *Tam.*). San. from (pú, san. to purify). Tel. from (valka, san. areca palm). Mal. from (ata, mal. to be closed + káya, mal. fruit); from the kernel being covered up by husk. Tam. from sanscrit. San. also (udvéga), meaning going swiftly. Areca-nut; product of Areca catechu, linn. [areca] boiled and dried for market; commonly called betel-nut [q.v.].——(1) *Paukmuttay* (பாக்குமட்டை - pákkumattai, Tam.). The lower part of leaf stalk which wraps round the areca tree.——*Pauk paulay* (سپاری کا پالا - supárikápálá, Hind.; പാള - pála, Mal.; பாக்குப்பாளை - pákkuppálai, Tam.). The flower sheath or spathe of the areca tree.——*Pauk vettilay* (பாக்குவெற்றிலை - pákkuvettilai, Tam.). Areca nut and betel [paun soopyaury].——*Pauk vetty* (பாக்குவெட்டி - pákkuvetti, Tam.). A pair of scissors for cutting or paring areca nuts in slices.——(2) *Alagoo pauk* (அலகுப்பாக்கு - alaguppákku, Tam.). From (alagu, tam. weapon blade). Areca nut sliced thin and boiled in the water in which its husk has been boiled, giving it reddish hue.——*Aurang pauk* (ஆரங்கம்பாக்கு - árangambákku, Tam.). From (árang, hind. factory). Areca nut sliced and boiled and rendered superior by being kept in godowns [q.v.].——*Coor sheevina pauk* (கூர்சீவினப்பாக்கு - kúrsívinappákku, Tam.). From (kúr, tam. apex + shívu, tam. to scrape). Scraped areca nut.——*Cottay pauk* (गुवाक - guváka, San.; گھوٹی سپاری - ghotísupárí, Hind.; ಅಡಿಕೆ - adike, Can.; పోకవక్క - pókavakka, Tel.; കൊട്ടടക്ക - kottatakka, Mal.; கொட்டைப்பாக்கு - kottaippákku, Tam.). Entire nut dried without boiling. Areca nut raw.——*Deshauwar pauk* (ದೇಶಾವಾರಡಿಕೆ - déshávára-dadike, Can.; தேசாவரம்பாக்கு - tésávarambákku, Tam.). From (déshávara, mahr. foreign country). Imported areca nut.——*Kali pauk* (കളിയടക്ക - kaliyatakka, Mal.; களிப்பாக்கு - kalippákku, Tam.). Mal. from (kali, mal. glutinous paste + atakka, mal. areca nut). Areca nut boiled and dried.——*Lavangachoor pauk* (ಲವಂಗಚೂರಡಿಕೆ - lavangachúradike, Can.; இலவங்கச்சூர்ப்பாக்கு - ilavangaccúrppákku, Tam.). Title and Tam. from (lavanga, san. clove + chúrú, can. piece). Areca nut broken into pieces the size of cloves [lavangam].——*Shaulyam pauk* (சாலியம்பாக்கு - sháliyambákku, Tam.). From (cháli, mal. to mix ingredients in fluid). Same as Alagoo pauk. Also called Shauya pauk or colored betel nut [charvanam].

PAUKYAM (பாக்கியம் - pákkiyam, *Tam.*). From (bhágya, san. good luck). Non-bramin proper name. Also taken by native Christians [peyar].——*Paukyanautan* (பாக்கியநாதன் - pákkiyanáthan, Tam.). From (above + nát'ha, san. lord). Hindoo 2nd or pers. name. Common among non-bramins. Also taken by native Christians [peyar].

PAUL (क्षीर - kshíra, *San.*; لبن - laban, *Ar.*; شیر - shír, *Pers.*; دودھ - dúdh, *Hind.*; ಹಾಲು - hálu, *Can.*; పాలు - pálu, *Tel.*; പാൽ - pál, *Mal.*; பால் - pál, *Tam.*). San. from (kshar, san. to flow) [cauram, khar]. Pers. from sanscrit. Milk [sheer]. Ass's, buffalo's, cow's, and goat's, are those used in native dietary. Ass's milk has a strong resemblance to human milk in color and consistence; used by veidyans [q.v.] in maniacal cases, leprous affections [cooshtam], and in black carpang [q.v.] or milk-rash of children; differs from cow's milk in cream being less abundant and more insipid, in containing less curd [tyre] but greater proportion of sugar [q.v.]. Buffalo [khoolgah] milk is inferior to cow's [pashoo] but abundant; has peculiar taste and smell, affords a great deal of coarse kind of butter, of which the natives make ghee [q.v.] and curd [tyre]; plentiful and cheap; veidyans consider it predisposing to catarrh, and tending to cloud the intellect; cow's milk is fully treated of by agastyan [q.v.] in his veidya einnoor; he considers it the most aperient of all milk, and tending to clear the intellect; milk of a white cow [pashoo] is of use in hypochondriacal cases; that of red one, for such as suffer from biliary derangements; that of a black one, particularly if it has also a dark colored udder, for those who are troubled with phlegm [sheetam]; that a cow which is of the color of gold, for all manner of disorders; if drunk in the morning it alleviates rheumatism; at noon it gives appetite, but if taken at bed-time it is good for every ailment of the body. Whey is a common drink in the hot weather; as also butter-milk or mor [q.v.]. Tyre [q.v.], a preparation of milk, from its slight acidity is gently aperient; made by adding to warm fresh milk a little butter-milk, and the whole allowed to stand all night; usually eaten with rice [q.v.]. Ghee is butter that has been clarified by boiling, and afterwards having some tyre, salt [ooppoo], or betel [q.v.] leaf added; constantly employed in making curries [q.v.]. What is called sugar of milk, is obtained from milk by evaporation and crystallization. Veidyans [q.v.] consider goat's [vellaud] milk as a powerful restorative, and order it in consumptive complaints; in padaurta chintaumany it is said that goat's milk ought to be administered in such cases as are accompanied with a deficiency of bile [pittam], and in certain bowel-complaints; that it is useful when the bowels are inclined to be over loose, and the appetite delicate; it resembles cow's milk, except in its greater consistence; it throws up abundance of cream, which can be converted into butter. Paul is a common plant first term, meaning either white or milky plant, and often joining two genera. Ex., where transl. is of second term:—Alstonia scholaris (pálagaruda), braminy kite; Argyreia speciosa (pálasamudra), ocean; Curcuma angustifolia (pálagunda), pot; Dregea volubilis (pálakúra), vegetable; Ehretia lævis (páladantamu), ivory; Ficus bengalensis (pálumaram), tree; Hemidesmus indicus (pálasugandhi), and (pálatsukkandéru), good smelling; Holostemma rheedii (pálagurugu), celosia argentia; Ichnocarpus frutescens (pálvalli), creeper; Ipomæa digitata (pálnódikka), and (pálmutakku), modecca palmata; Ipomæa pentaphylla (pálanélagummudu), ipomæa digitata; Leptadenia reticulata (pálatíga), creeper; Maranta ramosissima (pálagunda), pot; Oxystelma esculentum (pálakúra), vegetable; Vallaris heynei (pálamalle), jasminum sambac; Wrightia tinctoria (pálanîli), indigofera tinctoria. See gloss. paragraphs. Paul is also a prefix in place names; as Paulore, meaning milk village.——(1) *Palair* (పాలేరు - páléru, Tel. pálér*). From (pálu, tel. milk + éru, tel. river).—"*a*" River; Kistna dist., Nundigauma tal. Tributary of Kistna. Nearly coincides with the boundary line between Nizam's and British dominions. Rises in the Nizam's territories, and passing west of Juggayapett, empties itself into the Kistna near Rauvairila, after a course of 15 miles in the talook S.E. Not navigable. Irrigates Takkellapaud village.—"*b*" River; Kurnool dist., Coilcoontla tal. Tributary of the Coondair; takes its rise on Moonimadoogoo hill and flowing over Ooppalapaud plateau descends into plains by a waterfall 50 feet high, 2 miles west of Owk and joins Coondair [aroovy].—"*c*" River; Nellore district, Canigherry and Cundoocore talooks. Rises in Canigherry talook near Pandava naugoolavaram in the Veligondas, flows first southerly then south-easterly through Canigherry and Cundoocore talooks and Choondy zemindarry, and empties itself into the sea near Paucala in the last talook. Runs during October, November and December. Not at all navigable. A causeway near Bitragoonta.——*Palaur* (பாலாறு - páláru, Tam. pálár*). From (pál, tam. milk + áru, tam. river). Sanscrit name (kshíranadí), means the same.—"*a*" River; Salem, N. arcot and Chingleput dists. Rises in Mysore in lat. 13° 21′ N., long. 78° 00′ E. Flows south-east for 55 miles through Mysore, when it crosses the frontier into the North arcot district, cutting off a small portion of Salem district and passing through the gorges of the Eastern ghauts [q.v.] in lat. 12° 40′, long. 78°

35′, about 85 miles from its source. Quitting the hills, it holds a course generally east for 87 miles, and passes by Vellore and Arcot to lat. 12° 48′, long. 79° 41′, where it crosses into Chingleput district, through which it continues its direction south-eastwards for 48 miles, to its fall into the Bay of Bengal, a few miles south at Sadras in lat. 12° 28′, long. 80° 12′. Total length about 230 miles. The chief tributaries are the Poyney and Cheyaur, the latter joining it at Tirppacoodal about 8 miles east of Conjeeveram. On its banks are the towns of Krishnapooram, Vaniyambaudy, Amboor, Goodiyattam, Vellore, Arcot, Wallajahbad and Chingleput. Sometimes it is not in flood for several years together. Owing to this together with the rapid fall the current is very strong. The entrance is contracted by a bar of sand, inside of which the river becomes of considerable width. Crossed by railway bridges at Mailputty in North arcot, 2,376 feet long, 18 spans, and between Chingleput and Madrantacam, 2,160 feet long, 18 spans. The waters are largely used for irrigation. Palaur anicut [q.v.] is thrown across near Arcot; for description see vol. I, 403. This river once flowed in present Corteliaur valley. The two alluvial valleys diverge, about 10 miles east of Arcot. A stream is even now connected with the Palaur, just at the fork, by which water is carried down the Corteliaur valley for many miles and eventually falls into that river; called the old Palaur. There is a Tamul proverb :— நாலு ஆறு கூடி ஒரு பாலாறு ஆயிற்று—"if four rivers "unite, the stream will be equal to the Palaur." Palaur beacon is a trig. station; Madrantacam talook; lat. 12° 26′ 48·83″; long. 80° 11′ 15·26″; from Madrantacam E.S.E. 18 miles; from Veppancherry S.E. 3 miles.—"*b*" River; Coimbatore dist., Pollachy tal. Descends from hills in frontiers of Dhully in Oodamalpett talook, and after passing through that talook enters the frontiers of Pollachy talook, and empties itself into the Anliyaur, a few miles below Anamullay village. It runs from May to February. Nowhere navigable. Not bridged.——*Palcole* (పాలకొల్లు - pálakollu, Tel. pálakol *). From (pálu, tel. milk + kollu, tel. pond). Sanscrit name (kshírráma), milk garden. Town; Godavery dist., Narsapore tal.; pop. 8,657; acres 2,877; lat. 16° 31′; long. 81° 46′; from Cocanada S.W. 44 miles; from Narsapore N.N.E. 6 miles; from the sea N. 13 miles. On the Narsapore canal. First settlement of Dutch on this part of coast who opened factory in 1652. They founded indigo [q.v.] factories, iron-works, and extensive weaving [nesavoo] industries, and planted large orange [q.v.] and shaddock [pummelow] gardens. Ceded to English by treaty of Versailles in 1783, but Dutch remained in possession, paying a small quit-rent till 1804; formally restored to Holland in accordance with the Convention of the Allied Powers, 1814, on 31st March 1818; ceded to Great Britain under treaty of March 1824 on 1st June 1825. Seat of a Protestant mission. The oranges still retain the name of the Batavia orange [q.v.]. In the churchyard Dutch inscriptions, as old as 1662, are still legible. Very old temple of Rameshwarasawmy noted for a high tower over front gate.——*Palcondah* (పాలకొండ - pálakonda, Tel.). See sep. title.——*Palghaut* (പാലക്കാട് - pálakkátu, Mal.). See sep. title.——*Pauchamma* (పాచమ్మ - páchamma, Tel.). From (páchi, tel. milk + amma, tel. mother). Feeding mother or own mother. The village goddess worshipped by the Pullies [q.v.].——*Pauchonty* (പാച്ചോറ്റി - páççótti, Mal.; பாலை - pálai, Tam.). Title from malayalam. Mal. from (pál, mal. milk + chori, mal. to shed) [lodh]. Tam. from (pál, tam. milk) [dita, edible paulay, eve's apple, ground paulay, monkey face paulay, nakchiknee silk cotton, nauga champak, paula indigo, paulay silk cotton, tellicherry bark]. Tam. also (páççottippálai), meaning milk + to shed + the plant. Title otherwise Indian gutta-percha, Malabar caoutchouc, Malabar paulay, Milk tree, Oval mohwah. Botanically Dichopsis elliptica, benth., sapotaceæ [vricsham, 82]. Alias Bassia elliptica; Isonandra acuminata. Large tree, 80–90 feet; the bark rusty, often whitish from the presence of numerous lichens [cull pausy]; tree runs to such a height without giving off branches that naked eye is unable to distinguish forms of leaves, and it is generally recognised by the fruit and flowers found fallen at the base; leaves fascicled at the extremities of the branches, somewhat coriaceous, dark green above, paler beneath, entire, long-petioled, oblong-obovate, tapering at the base, terminating in a sudden blunt acumination; flowers axillary, generally solitary, occasionally two to three together; calyx biserial, outer deeply three-cleft, segments broad, acute at the apex, leathery, valvate, inner of three distinct sepals attached to the base of the outer calyx, alternate with its divisions, smaller, longer, equal, acuminated at the apex, of dirty white color, imbricated in estivation; corolla deeply six-cleft, occasionally five-cleft, deciduous, tomentose at point of insertion at the stamens, color darkish red; stamens twelve to eighteen, usually sixteen, inserted into the throat of the corolla, shorter than the corolla, sessile, extrorse, two-celled, all perfect, alternate in two rows; ovary tomentose, superior six-celled, each cell with one ovule; style nearly three times the length of the ovary; stigma simple; fruit chartaceous, size of an almond [baudam]; seed exalbuminous, erect; flowers dullish red; flowering in february; anamullays and w. coast. When incisions are made in the bark, a substance exudes somewhat similar to caoutchouc [indian caoutchouc] and guttapercha [q.v.], but hitherto of no practical value; resembles bird-lime; when fresh, milky white [gond]. Has a hardish, ornamentally veined wood, which takes a good polish; not unlike saul [q.v.] in the grain, but takes after the character of some of the harder kinds of cedar [deodar]; employed by planters for building. No other common species here. The following are other elastic giving plants of the presidency :—Achras sapota, sapodilla [foreign mohwah]; Alstonia scholaris [dita]; Calotropis gigantea, mudar [yercum]; Cryptostegia grandiflora, paulay silk cotton [q.v.]; Euphorbia antiquorum, square milk hedge [q.v.]; Euphorbia cattimandoo, cement plant [cuttimandoo]; Euphorbia nereifolia, leafy milk hedge [q.v.]; Euphorbia tirucalli, round milk hedge [q.v.]; Euphorbia tortilis, twisting milk hedge [q.v.]; Ficus bengalensis, banyan [q.v.].——*Pauladay* (பாலாடை - páladai, Tam.). Milk ladle for feeding infants. Plant second term. Ex., where transl. is of first term :—Euphorbia thymifolia (shittirappáladai), bright-colored; Indigofera pedicellata (shírubáladai), small. See gloss. paragraphs.——*Paulaul* (பாலாள் - pálál, Tam.). From (above + ál, tam. a person). The highest kind of priest among the Todahs [q.v.].——*Paulay* (பாலை - pálai, Tam.). From (pál, tam. white). Arid tract [desham]. For plants of this name see sep. title.——*Paultchy* (ಪಾಲ್ಚಿ - pálçi, Can.). Milk house of Todahs. There is one paultchy in each mund [q.v.]. Besides the ordinary dairy, there is in some villages a larger paultchy, in which relics are kept and which is looked on as a shrine.——(2) *Vedroo paul* (వెదురుపాలు - vedurupálu, Tel.). Bamboo milk [q.v.]. Same as Tabasheer [q.v.].——(3) The following are the different forms of milk.——*Ghee* (گهی - ghí, Hind.). Clarified butter, made by boiling butter for a few minutes when the watery part is dissipated. See sep. title.——*Mor* (तक्र - takra, San.; چھاچھ - chhách, Hind.; ಮಜ್ಜಿಗೆ - majjige, Can.; మజ్జిగ - majjiga, Tel.; മോര് - mór, Mal.; மோர் - mór, Tam.). Tel. also (tsalla), meaning cooling. Butter-milk. Sour milk produced while converting cream into butter. In conjunction with quick-lime [choonam], is used in preparing a stringy mixture, which native painters employ to give adhesion to colors [rangh]. As a drink, allays irritability of stomach in dyspeptic affections. In cases of incipient phthisis of great advantage.——*Paneermayeh* (پنیرمایه - panírmáyah, Hind.; ಹೆಪ್ಪು - heppu, Can.; చెమిరి - chémiri, Tel.). Hind. from (panír, hind. cheese + máyah, pers. leaven). Rennet. An aqueous infusion of dried stomach of calf used to coagulate the casein of milk, preparatory to manufacture of cheese [paneer, paulcutty]. Contains a soluble ferment which acts directly on the milk. Here the stomach of the calf is not used, but that of kid substituted. In Arabian works on medicine rennet is described as deobstruent, attenuant and aphrodisiac. Preparing cheese by rennet is entirely confined to higher classes of mahomedans. Among Hindoos cheese-making is unknown, since the use of ordinary rennet is altogether contrary to their religion. Cheese to be saleable among them would have to be made with some vegetable rennet. The best known vegetable substitute for rennet is Paneerbund [asgand] or cheese-maker, withania coagulans, dun. This has been used from very early times. An ounce of the pounded capsules in a quart of water is a suitable strength for use; a table-spoonful of this decoction coagulates a gallon of warm milk in about half an hour. Other plants substituted for rennet are, Epicarpurus orientalis, bl. [stunted jack] and Leucas cephalotes, spr. [large toombay].——*Paulauday* (பாலாடை - páládai, Tam.). From (ádai, tam. scum). Cream, the butyraceous part of milk, which rises to surface on milk standing.——*Paulcutty* (किलाट - kiláta, San.; پنیر - panír, Hind.; ಗಿಣ್ಣ - ginna, Can.; జున్ను - dzunnu, Tel.; പാലട - pálata, Mal.; பாற்கட்டி - párgatti, Tam.). Tel. from (tsundu, tel. to evaporate). Tam. from (pál, milk + katti, tam. clot). Tam. also (páládaikkatti), meaning milk + cream + clot. Cheese. Generally prepared by boiling milk [paul] till reduced to a thick mass, and sugar [q.v.] added. See Paneermayeh above.——*Tyre* (दधि - dadhi, San.; دهی dahí, Hind.; ಮೊಸರು - mosaru, Can.; పెరుగు - perugu, Tel.; തയിര് - tayir, Mal.; தயிர் - tayir, Tam.). Tel. from (péru, tel. to harden); Tam. corr. from sanscrit. Curdled milk. Generally prepared by adding a little butter-milk [mor] to boiled milk, and allowing the whole to stand a whole night. Other acids are used, such as dried mango [q.v.], tamarind [q.v.], lime-juice [lime], and even a piece of tarnished silver [velly], but none of these are so effective. The acid is in some places put into raw cold milk; by this process however a longer time is necessary to curdle the milk.——*Vennay* (வெண்ணெய் - venney, Tam.). From (vel, tam. white + ney, tam. ghee). Butter. Made by churning cream, and then kneading the product. The butter of this country is thin and poor, except on the hill ranges.

PAUL (పాలు - pálu, *Tel.*). From (pantsu, tel. to divide). Share.——*Paulcoonda* (పాలకుండ - pálakunda, Tel.). From (above + kunda, tel. an earthen pot). A grain fee allowed to ryots [q.v.] before the grain is measured.

PAULAY (పాల - pála, *Tel.*; പാല - pála, *Mal.*; பாலை - pálai, *Tam.*). Milky plant, from (pál, tam. milk) [paul]. Very common plant second term. See the cases below, and there are others.——*Coorg paulay* (കുടകപ്പാല - kutakappála, Mal.). Same as Tellicherry bark.——*Cotton paulay* (దూదిపాల - dúdipála,

Tel.). From milky plant + cotton-like fibres. Same as Nakchicknee silk cotton.——*Crow paulay* (కాకిపాల - kákipála, Tel.). Same as Carook vauly.——*Dog paulay* (కుక్కపాల - kukkapála, Tel.). From milky plant useful in dog cure. Same as Indian ipecacuanha.——*Edible paulay* (तालवृन्त - tálavrinta, San.; खिरणी - khiraní, Mahr.; کھیرنی - khírní, Hind.; بواسا - buásá, Malay; ಹಾದರಿ - hádari, Can.; ପାଟଳି - pátali, Too.; പഴമുണ്ണിപ്പാല - pazhamúnippálai, Mal.; பாலை - pálai, Tam.). Title from fruit being edible, especially in malabar. San. from (tála, san. palmyra, borassus flabelliformis, linn. + vrinta, san. leaf). Mahr. from (kshíra, san. milk). Hind. like mahratta. Mal. from (pazham, mal. fruit + unnu, mal. to eat + pála, mal. milk plant). Tam. from (pál, tam. milk) [dita, eve's apple, ground paulay, monkey-face paulay, nakchiknee silk cotton, nauga champak, pauchonty, paula indigo, paulay silk cotton, tellicherry bark]. San. also (vasantadútí), meaning messenger of spring; cf. mango. Hind. also (khírí), like mahratta, above. Can. also (pátali) [common bendy, jungle geranium, pauthiry, weaver's beam]; (némi). Mal. also (manilakkára), meaning manilla canthium. Title otherwise Khirny, Manilla caunay, Obtuse-leaved mimusops, Obtuse-leaved molsaree. Botanically Mimusops [csheericay] kauki, linn., sapotaceæ [vricsham, 82]. Alias Mimusops binectaria, obtusifolia. Tree; leaves alternate, obovate, very blunt, silvery or hoary beneath, crowded at the ends of the branches; flowers fascicled, hexandrous; fruit oval, drooping; flowers yellowish-white, tinged with rose; cultivated in malabar on account of fruit. Bark medicinally astringent; leaves ground and mixed with root of curcuma [country saffron] and ginger [q.v.] used as cataplasm for tumours; leaves boiled in gingelly [q.v.] oil and added to the pulverised barks are remedy in beribery [q.v.]; seeds yield an oil applied to the eyes in ophthalmia, and also internally as an anthelmintic. Fruit eaten; bark yields gum [gond].——*Fire-brand paulay* (కొరవిపాల - koravipála, Tel.). From boughs being used as torches. Same as Large jungle geranium.——*Fragrant paulay* (సుగంధిపాల - sugandhipála, Tel.). From milky plant and fragrant root. Same as Indian sarsaparilla.——*Golden paulay* (കനകപ്പാല - kanakappála, Mal.). Same as Country radish.——*Ground paulay* (कालाइन्द्रजव - káláindrajava, Mahr.; دودھی - dúdhí, Hind.; ಕಾಡುಗಣಗಲು - káduganagalu, Can.; పుట్టజిల్లేడు - puttajillédu, Tel.; ପାଲ୍‌କୁର୍ବନ - pálkurvan, Oor.; നിലമ്പാല - nilampála, Mal.; வெட்பாலை - vedbálai, Tam.). Title from small size. Mahr. from (kálá, mahr. black + indrajava, mahr. seed of holarrhena antidysenterica, wall.). Hind. from (dúdh, hind. milk). Can. from (kádu, can. wild + ganagalu, can. the plant, nerium odorum, sol.). Tel. from (putta, tel. ant hill + jillédu, tel. calotropis gigantea, r. br.). Mal. from (nilam, mal. ground + pála, mal. milk plant). Tam. from (vel, tam. white + pálai, tam. milky plant). Tel. also (koyilamokiri); (peddapála), meaning large + milky plant; (tellapála), meaning white + milky plant. Oor. also (harido). Mal. also (nílampála), meaning blue milk plant. Tam. also (pálai), meaning milky plant [dita, edible paulay, eve's apple, monkey-face paulay, nakchiknee silk cotton, nauga champak, pauchonty, paula indigo, paulay silk cotton, tellicherry bark]. Title otherwise Downy oleander. Botanically Wrightia [veppaulay] tomentosa, rœm. & schult., apocynaceæ [vricsham, 87]. Alias Nerium tomentosum; Wrightia mollissima, pubescens, wallichii. Small tree; leaves oblong, acuminated, downy; corymbs terminal, small; tube of corolla longer than the calyx; corona fleshy, lacerated into obtuse segments; follicles distinct; branches downy; flowers with a white corolla and orange-colored corona. Milky juice from stem used to stop bleeding; bark of stem and root used in snake bites and stings of scorpions [tail]. Juice mixed with water forms a good yellow dye [shauyam]; gives a thick, scarlet-colored oil. Wood yellowish-white, moderately hard, close-grained.——*Ground paulay* (നിലപ്പാല - nilappála, Mal.). Same as Garrar and Madras absinth.——*High ground paulay* (మెట్టపాల - mettapála, Tel.). Same as Giant sweet potato.——*Hill paulay* (కొండపాల - kondapála, Tel.). Same as Somam.——*Jointed paulay* (ರೆಂಗ - renga, Can.; கணுப்பாலை - kanuppálai, Tam.). Title from knotty timber. Tam. from (kanu, tam. joint + pálai, tam. mimusops hexandra, roxb.). Botanically Mimusops [csheericay] roxburghiana, wight, sapotaceæ [vricsham, 82]. Tree; leaves obovate, oval, obtuse at both ends; fascicles two to three-flowered; pedicels about thrice the length of the petioles; lobes of the calyx ovate-acute, about the length of the corolla, rusty-velvety; sterile stamens about the length of the filaments, broad-obovate, fimbriated on the margin; fruit globose, depressed above, about six-seeded; flowering in march and april. Timber coarse-grained, but strong, fibrous and durable.——*Kite paulay* (கருடப்பாலை - karudappálai, Tam.). From antidote to snake bite. Same as Paulay silk cotton.——*Monkey-face paulay* (राजादनी - rájádaní, San.; खिरणी - khiraní, Mahr.; کھیرنی - khírní, Hind.; పాలచెట్టు - pálachettu, Tel.; ଚର୍କୁଳି - charkuli, Oor.; පලු - palu, Singh.; பாலை - pálai, Tam.). Title from appearance of flowers. San. from (rájá, san. king + ad, san. to eat); superior fruit [chironjee]. Mahr. from (kshíra, san. milk). Hind. from mahrattta. Tel. from (pálu, tel. milk + chettu, tel. tree). Tam. from (pál, tam. milk) [dita, edible paulay, eve's apple, ground paulay, nakchiknee silk cotton, nauga champak, pauchonty, paula indigo, paulay silk cotton, tellicherry bark]. Mahr. also (ráyaní), from sanscrit. Tel. also (nunni). Tam. also (kanuppálai), meaning joint + the tree. Title otherwise Indian ape-face flower, Indian mimusops. Botanically Mimusops [csheericay] hexandra, roxb., sapotaceæ [vricsham, 82]. Alias Mimusops indica. Large tree; leaves alternate, cunei-form or obcordate, deeply emarginate, glabrous and shining on both surfaces; calyx six-cleft, with three-interior and three-exterior segments; corolla tube very short, interior segments six, the exterior twelve; pedicels one to six together, nearly as long as the smooth petioles, one-flowering; berry size and shape of an olive [zeitoon], yellow when ripe; flowers small, whitish. Handsome tree, with rigid branches and broad wedge-shaped leaves, often found planted in groves near mahomedan buildings. Bark which much resembles that of mimusops elengi [ilanjy] is used medicinally on account of its astringent properties; seeds yield an oil which is used as a demulcent, emollient, tonic and alterative. Fruit edible both fresh and dried. Oil from seeds; stem gives a gum [gond]. Wood very heavy, close, even-grained, hard, compact, durable, purplish color when fresh, turning to reddish-brown, susceptible of high polish; used for oil presses, building, and a variety of other purposes; excellent for rulers, handles of instruments, and all articles of turnery, and for cabinet purposes.——*Needle paulay* (दुग्धिका - dugdhiká, San.; दुधाणी - dudhání, Mahr.; دودھلتا - dúdhlatá, Hind.; పాలకూర - pálakúra, Tel.; ଦୁଧିୟାଲତା - dudhiyalata, Oor.; ஊசிப்பாலை - úsippálai, Tam.). Title from narrow linear leaves. San. from (dugdha, san. milk), from milky sap. Mahr. from (dugdha, san. milk). Hind. from (dúdh, hind. milk + latá, hind. creeper). Tel. from (pála, tel. white + kúra, tel. pot herb). Oor. from hindostany. Tam. from (úsi, tam. needle + pálai, tam. milk plant), from narrow linear leaves; cf. ammayaur coondal. Tel. also (chirupála), meaning small + the plant; (nélapála), meaning ground + the plant; (pinnapála), meaning small + the plant; (dúdipála), meaning cotton + the plant [nakchikne silk cotton]; (sépachettu). Title otherwise Doodipaula, Rosy milk-wort. Botanically Oxystelma esculentum, r. br., asclepiadeæ [vricsham, 88]. Alias Asclepias rosea; Oxystelma wallichii; Periploca esculenta. Twining under-shrub; leaves opposite linear-lanceolate; corolla ciliated at the margin; racemes inter-petiolar; follicles oblong, acuminated. Slender-stemmed, herbaceous, creeping plant; narrow linear leaves, about 5 inches long; saucer-formed flowers of size of eight-anna piece, white without and rose-colored and purple-veined within. Decoction of plant used medicinally as gargle; the milky sap in combination with turpentine [ganda firoza] prescribed for itch. Fruit eaten; cattle [maud] eat the plant. No other common species here.——*Night paulay* (मेरशिंगी - mérashingí, Mahr.; இராப்பாலை - iráppálai, Tam.). Title from flowering at night. Mahr. from (méra, mahr. hill-border + shingi, mahr. horned). Tam. from (irá, tam. night + pálai, tam. milky plant); from evening flower. Tam. also (pesalatti), meaning sallowness + fig tree. Title otherwise Arcuate trumpet flower. Botanically Dolichandrone [water ailanto] arcuata, clarke, bignoniaceæ [vricsham, 99]. Alias Spathodea arcuata. Arboreous; leaves unequally pinnate, four to five pairs, leaflets from ovate subacute to orbicular, unequal at the base; entire, softly pubescent when young, afterwards glabrous, racemes terminal, elongated, many-flowered; calyx cylindrical-oblique, pubescent externally; tube of the corolla slender, limb funnel-shaped, five-lobed, fimbriated on the margin; capsule acute, compressed, eight to twelve inches long by about one broad; flowering in september; flowers expand in evening and drop in morning. Gives strong wood, used by the turner.——*Pauchonty paulay* (പാച്ചോന്തിപ്പാല - páççóntippála, Mal.). Same as Pauchonty.——*River paulay* (ஆற்றுப்பாலை - áttuppálai, Tam.). As growing near rivers. Same as Indian willow.——*Scented paulay* (సుగంధపాల - sugandhapála, Tel.). From milky plant and fragrant root. Same as Indian sarsaparilla.——*Sea-shore paulay* (वृद्धदारक - vriddhadáraka, San.; समुद्रपान - samudrapána, Mahr.; سمندر پات - samandarpát, Hind.; سمندر پتا - samandarpattá, Dec.; ಸಮುದ್ರಹಾಲಬಳ್ಳಿ - samudrahálaballi, Can.; సముద్రపాల - samudrapála, Tel.; സമുദ്രപ്പച്ച - samudrappaçça, Mal.; මහදුමුදු - mahadumudu, Singh.; கடற்பாலை - kadarbálai, Tam.). Title from place where found. San. from (vriddha, san. old age + drí, san. to split). Mahr. from (samudra, san. ocean + parna, san. leaf). Hind. from (samandar, hind. ocean + pát, hind. leaf). Dec. from (samandar, hind. ocean + pattá, hind. leaf). Can. from (samudra, san. ocean + hálu, can. milk + balli, can. creeper). Tel. from (samudra, san. ocean + pála, tel. milky plant). Mal. from (samudra, san. ocean + paçça, san. green). Tam. from (kadal, tam. sea + pálai, tam. milky plant). San. also (chhagalántrí), meaning sheep + bowels; (chhagaládí), meaning sheep + testicles; (dírghaváluká), meaning long sand creeper; (rikshagandha), meaning bear + smell [giant sweet potato]; (ajántrí), meaning goat + bowels; (samudrashósha), meaning ocean + drying; (samudrapatra), meaning ocean + leaf; (chhagalá), meaning she-goat; (chhagalánghrí), meaning she-goat + knee. Mahr.

also (guggulf), meaning bdellium gum, from its fragrance; (samudrasókha), meaning ocean + drying up. Hind. also (samandar), meaning ocean; (samandarsokh), meaning ocean + dry; (samandarsof); (brishtarak); (chhotábishtarak). Can. also (samudrasóge), meaning ocean + dyer. Tel. also (chandrapoda), (kokkita) [hill emetic nut]; (kokkiti) [indian medicago]; (kakkita); (pálasamudra), meaning paulay tree ocean; (samudrapattsa), meaning ocean + green. Mal. also (samudrappála), meaning ocean + paulay; (samudrayógam); meaning ocean + mixture; (samudrastókam), ocean creeper. Tam. also (shamuttirappaççai), meaning ocean + green leaf; (shamuttirappálai), meaning ocean + milky plant; (péymusuttai), meaning devil + ipomæa candicans; (shamuttirasógi), meaning ocean + drying. Title otherwise Broad-leaved bindweed, Elephant creeper, Goat's entrails, Goat's knee, Large sand binder, Ocean-dryer, Samandar, Sea green. Botanically Argyreia [ajauntry] speciosa, swt., convolvulaceæ [vricsham, 93]. Alias Convolvulus nervosus, speciosus; Ipomæa speciosa; Lettsomia nervosa. Large climber, tomentose; leaves cordate, acute, glabrous above, thickly nerved and like white velvet beneath, and silky silvery; sepals five; corolla campanulate; peduncles equal in length to the petioles, umbellately capitate; corolla nearly 2 inches long, deep rose-colored, hairy in the plicæ outside. The roots are long, woody and tough, covered with a dark brown bark; on transverse section they present a central porous woody column, and several concentric rings of woody fibre, between which are situated portions of parenchyma; in the woody portions of the root there are large laticiferous vessels which contain a yellowish latex; the vascular system consists of very large dotted vessels; in the parenchyme are numerous conglomerate raphides. Root medicinally alterative, tonic; mixed with vinegar [caudy] sap is rubbed over the body to reduce obesity; the upper side of leaves is used as a discutient; the under, or white side, as a maturant; leaf in pharm. non-officinal. Gives an oil.——*Seven-leaf paulay* (ఏడాకులపాల - édákulapála, Tel.). From leaves appearing in whorls of seven. Same as Dita.——*Small paulay* (குறுப்பாலை - kuruppálai, Tam.). Same as Pootranjeeva.——*Thorny paulay* (కంటపాల - kuntapála, Tel.). Same as Adjutant's hedge.——*White paulay* (తెల్లపాల - tellapála, Tel.). From milky plant and white wood. Same as Paula indigo.

PAUMB (పాము - pámu, *Tel.*; പാമ്പു - pámbu, *Mal.*; பாம்பு - pámbu, *Tam.*). Title from tamul. Tam. from (para, tam. to spread) [para]; from its diffusive motion. The terms may be considered co-extensive with the family Colubridæ, ophidii colubriformes, ophidia [sarpam], reptilia [sarpy, 17], of naturalists [jantoo]. The Paumb family proper comprises the greater part of the non-venomous snakes, namely all those which do not present any striking character either in their general habit, in the shields of the head, in the dentition, or in any other part of their organization; the body is of moderate length compared with its circumference, flexible in every single part; the head well-proportioned in every dimension, and distinct from neck; the eye of moderate size, the nostril lateral; the cleft of the mouth in accordance with the length of the head; they have numerous teeth in the jaws and on the palate, but no fangs in front or in the middle of the maxillary; the sub-caudals are two-rowed, and the chin-shields symmetrically arranged, separated by a longitudinal mental groove. They are divided into four groups, thus:—Ground Colubrides or group Coronellina; containing genera Ablabes, Coronella, Cyclophis, Nymphophidium, Odontomus. True Colubrides or group Colubrina; containing genera Coluber, Compsosoma, Cynophis, Elaphis, Ptyas, Xenelaphis, Zamensis. Bush Colubrides or group Dryadina; containing genera Herpetoreas, Zaocys. Fresh-water Colubrides or group Natricina; containing genera Atretium, Prymmeniodon, Tropidonotus, Xenochrophis. The following are the species in Southern india, arranged alphabetically:—"*a*" Ablabes humberti. Alias Calamaria sagittaria; Enicognathus humberti. Small, living on the ground. Reddish olive, darker on the sides, the lighter back separated from the dark-colored side by indistinct punctated line; black dots edged with yellow along the vertebral line; upper part of head brown; broad black or dark-brown collar, edged with yellow; belly white, each ventral shield with black dot on each side.—"*b*" Ablabes olivaceus. Dark greenish olive, paler below; small black dots along each side of the back, less distinct, along the middle of the side.—"*c*" Atretium schistosum [chitty paumb]. Alias Coluber schistosus; Tropidonotus mœstus et surgens, schistosus. Forms the transition from Tropidonotus or rain-snake [vaunapaumb] to the true fresh-water snakes [tunny paumb]; very fierce, prepares to attack by raising the head 3 or 4 inches. Upper parts uniform blackish olive; outer series of scales and lower parts uniform yellowish; young with purple stripe from the orbit, along anterior part of body.—"*d*" Compsosoma radiatum. Alias Coluber quadrifasciatus, radiatus; Compsosoma radiatum; Tropidonotus quinque. Narrow head with a long, anteriorly truncated snout. Light yellowish-bay above and behind, paler on the sides; black streak across extremity of the occipitals, extending downwards to throat; three black lines radiate from the eye; on each side of back broad longitudinal black band; lower parts uniform yellow; black longitudinal streaks along the abdomen; attains a length of 6 feet; it inhabits bushes, marshes and paddy-fields; equally nocturnal and diurnal, preying on rats [ely], birds [pacshy], lizards [chipkalee] and frogs [bhaicam].—"*e*" Coronella orientalis. Above greyish brown, neck with a very narrow white collar; belly white, with subquadrangular blackish spots.—"*f*" Cyclophis calamaria. Ground snakes, frequenting grassy plains rather than dry places. Greyish or brownish grey above; each scale on the sides with two indistinct, very small brown streaks on the base; scales on each side of the back are edged with black, black edges forming small irregular spots; lower parts entirely white.—"*g*" Cynophis helena [maigha recoola poda]. Alias Coluber helena; Cynophis bistrigatus; Heretodryas helena; Plagiodon helena. Reddish olive, with numerous black transverse bands across anterior of back; neck with pair of parallel longitudinal black bands above, and oblique black band on side; lower parts uniform white; feeds on field mice [varappoo shoondely] and rats [ely].—"*h*" Cynophis malabaricus. Alias Herpetodryas malabaricus. Light brownish olive, with black cross-bands; the first band is modified into a white, black-edged collar; broad brown band along the side of the tail and of the posterior part of the trunk; short black vertical streak below the eye; another oblique streak from behind the eye.—"*i*" Nymphophidium maculatum. Light brownish, with two dorsal series of rounded dark-brown spots; sides with very small brown spots; lower parts uniform whitish.—"*j*" Odontomus gracilis. White, with about thirty-eight broad, round, dark-brown cross-bands; first occupies the head, second the neck, both separated by a white collar; lower parts uniform white.—"*k*" Odontomus nympha [cutla paumb]. Alias Coluber nympha; Lycodon nympha; Odontomus nympha. Like Gracilis.—"*l*" Odontomus semifasciatus. Alias Hydrophobus semifasciatus. White, with fifty rounded, dark-brown bands, each about twice as broad as the intervals of the ground color.—"*m*" Ptyas mucosus. Alias Coluber blumenbachii, dhumna, mucosus; Leptophis trifrenatus. The rat-snake [q.v.].—"*n*" Tropidonotus beddomii. Alias Spilotes vittatus. Brown above; transverse streaks of orange-color along each side of the back; narrow yellow cross bar behind occipitals; labials edged with black; yellowish, black-edged band from eye to angle of mouth; belly whitish, its sides and the sub-caudals dotted with brown.—"*o*" Tropidonotus monticola. Green above, with black bands across the trunk; lower parts are white; common in the Wynaud.—"*p*" Tropidonotus plumbi-color. Alias Xenodon viridis. Called by the Tamuls the Water-snake [tunny paumb]. Dirty greenish trunk; with ten or eleven narrow black cross bars; sides of throat dotted with black; belly more or less blackish; all these markings generally disappear with age, with exception of an oblique, more or less distinct blackish band on each side of the neck, upper parts being uniform dirty green, the lower whitish; frequently enters houses.—"*q*" Tropidonotus quincunciatus. Alias Coluber anastomosatus, braminus et umbratus, hippus, rectangulus; Hydrus piscator et palustris; Tropidonotus umbratus. Generally two oblique black streaks behind the eye; belly white; ground-color of upper parts generally greyish or brownish olive; one of the most widely spread species. Frequents the neighbourhood of fresh-waters, feeds on frogs [bhaicam], toads [bhaicam], and fishes [matsyam]; they do not overpower or kill their prey by throwing a coil of the body round it, but having seized it, they at once commence to swallow it; excellent swimmers; more frequently live near water than in it. See Neercorattay.—"*r*" Tropidonotus stolatus. Alias Amphiesma stolatum; Coluber stolatus. Greenish or brownish olive, two yellow or white longitudinal bands; lower parts white; anterior ventral shields have frequently a black dot on each side; head brown above; one of the most common of all snakes; of gentle habits, feeding on small frogs; readily recognized by the peculiar pattern of its coloration [vaunapaumb].—"*s*" Tropidonotus subminiatus. Alias Amphiesma subminiatum. Greenish above, uniform or with small indistinct black and reddish-white spots; round the eye whitish, with oblique triangular black spot below; belly white, with black dots on each side; young specimens with broad black collar edged with yellow behind.—"*t*" Zamenis fasciolatus. Alias Coluber fasciolatus, hebe, curvirostres; Coryphodon fasciolatus; Tyria fasciolata. Yellowish or brownish olive above, with white, brown and black variegated cross-bands; in old ones they may entirely disappear; lower parts uniform yellowish.—"*u*" Zemenis gracilis. Yellowish olive, with round brown spots edged with black, along anterior half of trunk; blackish streak across snout; crown of head with two brown, black-edged cross-bands; black spots on each side of the belly, which is uniform yellow.—"*v*" Zamenis ventrimaculatus. Alias Coluber diadema, ventrimaculatus. Yellowish olive, with narrow black cross bars on back; small black spots along each side; belly yellowish, irregular series of black dots along each side; black cross-band between eyes, oblique black streak below them, another oblique streak on temple, blackish spot in loreal region, black streak along median line of the neck.——*Pambah* (പമ്പാനദി - pampánadi, Mal.). From (pámbu, mal. snake); from winding course. River; Travancore state, Quilon division, Chenganore, Tiroovalla and Ambalapoya talooks. One of finest rivers of Travancore. Formed by junction of Cullaur, Cakkadaur and Pambah proper, which rise in the Rauny mountains and unite short distance above Rauny. The course above this is south-westerly. The united stream then runs a devious course west for 25 miles; the latter part of the course being north-westerly. It flows into the Vembanaud lake by two distinct mouths. It unites with the Coolacudda river about 20 miles above its mouth. Length, 90 miles. Navigable by boats for 52 miles from its mouth. Below the hills the banks lose their wildness and are capable of cultivation; sugarcane [q.v.], areca-nut [q.v.] and cocoanut [q.v.] plantations being extensively formed. Principal tributary is Manimala.——*Pamoor* (పామూరు - pámúru, Tel.). From (pámu, tel. snake + úru, tel. village). Sanscrit name (sarpapurí), meaning snake village.—"*a*" Talook of Calastry zemindarry lying within Nellore district. Included in Government talooks of Cundoocore and Canigherry. Cundoocore talook contains seven villages which are bounded:—on the north by Shameerapollem and Pokore and the Choondy zemindarry; on the south by Choondy zemindarry; on the east by Choondy zemindarry; on the west by Choondy zemindarry and Cauvaly talook. Canigherry talook contains seventy-two villages which are bounded:—north by Canigherry talook, east Cundoocore and Cauvaly talooks, south Oodayagherry talook, and west Budwail talook in Cuddapah district and Cumbum talook in Kurnool district. Pamoor talook was given to Calastry about 150 years ago by the Nawaab. The talook is interspersed with hills denuded of verdure. Most part is rocky and on high ground. The Munnair passes through. Vegetation very sparse. Flanked on western side by Veligondas [q.v.]. Soil, regar [q.v.], clay [calimunu] and sand [manal]. In the portion belonging to Canigherry charcoal [adoopp kary] is manufactured and sold to blacksmiths. Tape called Navaur [q.v.] and curtains called purdahs [q.v.] are made. Country cloths and blankets also made. Three tanks in Cundoocore. In Canigherry fourteen. The talook is managed for the zemindar by a Tahsildar on Rs. 150 a month.—"*b*" Village; Nellore dist., Canigherry tal.; pop. 2,629; lat. 15° 06'; long. 79° 28'; from Canigherry S.S.W. 22 miles; from Nellore N.W. 58¼ miles. Chief village of the above. A decayed fort in the midst of which is Tahsildar's cutcherry [q.v.]. Two temples of Gopaulsawmy and Shiva. Fine tank. Festivals about February and May of each year. Sack cloth woven [gunny].——*Paumbaur* (பாம்பாறு - páumbáru, Tam.). From (pámbu, tam snake + áru, tam. river); from winding course.—"*a*" River; Trichinopoly dist., Poodoocottah territory; general direction W. to E.; length about 20 miles. Rises in Peroondoray cummye, Poodoocottah territory; flows into Bay of Bengal, after passing through Tanjore district.—"*b*" River; Madura dist., Periyacoolam tal. Rises in Upper pulneys near Kodaykarnal, and passing through Vadacaray and Taumaray coolam, joins Varauhanuddy near Periyacoolam at five miles from foot of ghauts. Has four small anicuts [q.v.].—"*c*" River; Salem dist., Tripatore tal. Perennial stream having rise in Jawaudy hills. Joined by streams from Yelagherry hills and from Krishnagherry talook, and flows south joining Ponniaur river in Ootancaray talook.——*Paumben* (பாம்பன் - pámban, * Tam.). From (pámbu, tam. snake); from tortuous course of the channel. Sanscrit name (sarpanadí), meaning same.—"*a*" Town, Port, Sub-registrar's office, Government telegraph office, Deputy tahsildars station, Light-house, Place of pilgrimage; Madura dist., Ramnaud zemindarry; pop. 4,494; lat. 9° 17'; long. 79° 16'; from Dindigul E.S.E. 112 miles; from Kodaykarnal E.S.E. 135 miles; from Madras S.S.W. 270 miles; from Madura E.S.E. 87 miles; from Pillaymadam E. 10 miles; from Rameshwaram W. 7 miles; from Ramnaud E. 27 miles. On the W. extremity of Rameshwaram island; which is called Paumben island by the Tamuls. In the town is a fort built by the Dutch. The population, chiefly Lubbays [q.v.], are employed as pilots, divers, and in other sea-faring pursuits. The Ceylon government immigration depot is fixed here for half the year; and this, with the constant influx of pilgrims and the grain trade, gives the port an appearance of great activity. The place was formerly noted for pearl fishery [chunk, moty], and at an early period it was used as a refuge for the Ramnaud chiefs.—"*b*" Artificial channel known as the Pass, affording means of communication between India and Ceylon. It lies between the mainland of Madura district and Rameshwaram island, the first link in the chain of islets and rocks forming Adam's bridge [q.v.]. The formation is sandstone [manal cull]. Records in the temple of Rameshwaram relate that in the year 1480 a violent storm breached the isthmus, and that subsequent storms rendered the breach permanent. The passage was formerly impracticable for ships, being obstructed by two parallel ridges of rock about 140 yards apart. The more northerly of these ridges was the higher of the two and used to appear above water at high tide. The space between was occupied by a confused mass of rocks, lying for the most part parallel to the ridges and in horizontal strata. A survey of the passage was begun in 1822, and experiments in blasting and removing the rocks were undertaken in 1828. The first scientific marine survey was conducted in 1837. The charts made on this occasion still remain the standard authority. Operations for deepening and widening the channel were commenced in 1838. By 1844 the channel had been deepened to 8 feet of water at low spring tides, and two men of war were able to pass through. In 1854 the uniform depth was 10½ feet, and the passage was navigable for keeled vessels of 200 tons; the extension of the channel so as to be practicable for ocean steamers is forbidden by the shallow character of the neighbouring coast. Blasting and dredging operations have since been carried on regularly and the main channel through the larger reefs of rocks has been carried down to a minimum depth of 14 feet. Its length is 4,232 feet and its width 80 feet. A second channel to the south of the main channel, called Keelakaray passage, 2,100 feet long and 150 feet wide, has been dredged through a sandbank to the depth of 12 feet. The traffic is mostly of a coasting nature between Ceylon and the mainland, though there is some emigration by this route to British burmah and the Straits.—"*c*" Light on a sand hill about one mile east of northern Paumben channel. Lat. 9° 17'; long. 79° 16'. White, fixed. 14 miles range. Visible from all directions seaward. Circular masonry column. Guide to vessels making for the Paumben channel.——*Paumidy* (పామిడి - pámidi, Tel.). From (pámu, tel. serpent + eda, tel. place). The local god is bhogeshwaran or shiva; lord of serpents. Town and travellers' bungalow; Anantapore dist., Gooty tal.; pop. 6,120; acres 7,788; lat. 14° 57'; long. 77° 38'; from Anantapore N. 18 miles; from Gooty S.S.W. 12 miles. Occupied chiefly by weavers. Large dyeing [shauyam] works. Chintzes [q.v.], coarse cloths, and palampores [q.v.], manufactured. Trig station is in lat. 14° 57' 49·86"; long. 77° 37' 24·61"; height 1,680 feet; from Anantapore N. 20 miles; from Cottapully N. 5 miles; from Gooty S.S.W. 11 miles.——*Paupanna* (పాపన్న - pápanna, Tel.). From (pámu, tel. serpent + anna, tel. elder brother, titular affix). Hindoo 2nd or pers. name [peyar].——*Pauparauz* (పాపరాజు - páparádzu, Tel.). From (pámu, tel. serpent + rádzu, tel. king). Hindoo 2nd or pers. name [peyar].

PAUNDY (பாண்டி - pándi, *Tam.*). From (pandu, tam. antiquity); but (pán, tam. toddy) is also connected. πανδαίη of Megasthenes. Some very ancient Dravidian population of the Tamul country. The similarity of name with the Aryan pandavas [q.v.] is only accidental, but hence the introduction into S. india of an extraordinary number of Pooranic legends. Sandar bandi of Marco Polo is a corruption of Soondra paundyan of Madura; see vol. I (13), (116); II, 250. Paundy is suffix in place names [vaundy]. Also title of certain Christian fishermen and palankeen [q.v.] bearers at Cannanore, who came from Tinnevelly. Also name of a Malabar paddy [q.v.]; choora paundy means bad smell; ora paundy means border; tekkan paundy means south.——*Paundara beed* (పాండవబీడు - pándavabídu, Tel.). From (pandu, tam. antiquity + bídu, tel. waste land); connected with the most ancient times. Waste land from time immemorial [anandi beed].——*Paundicoozhy* (பாண்டிக்குழி - pándikkuzhi, Tam.). From (pandu, tam. antiquity + kuzhi, tam. pit). Kistvaen or ancient grave, especially when sunk in the ground. Found both in lands that have been irrigated for hundreds of years and in now untrodden unhealthy jungles. The present population cannot be said to have any veneration for these remains. By the traditionary accounts of the people they are ascribed variously as follows. To a desire of obtaining shelter from a predicted shower of fire, about the beginning of the era [saca] of Shalivahanan [q.v.]; to certain pigmies that lived towards the end of the Dwauparyoog [q.v.], who constructed for themselves these dwellings underground; to the five Pandavas [mahabhaurat] as a refuge from the persecution of Dooryodhanan, which is evidently an imported tradition; to the votaries of the goddess named Neela mookary, who had offered to her monthly sacrifices therein; to the Veddahs [q.v.] and Coorumbar [q.v.], or hunters and savages, of former days, as places of protection for their wives and children from wild beasts; to certain men in the time of Rama [q.v.], who had monkey's tails, whence these pits are by some called Vauly coody [vauly]; to Raucshasans [q.v.], or evil beings, who constructed these places of safety for their wives and children; to a custom of very early times after the deluge, when men lived so long as to be a burden to themselves and their relatives, so that the latter put them in certain earthen shells with a supply of provisions and left them to die. Tradition states that great wealth has from time to time been carried away from some of these excavations. The Paundicoozhies were evidently intended for the reception either of cinerary remains or of bodies in a sitting posture, a mode of burial still observed by Lingadhauries [q.v.] and others. All are placed east and west. They vary in size, some of those buried in tumuli having a floor area of 8½ × 5½ feet and being as much as 6½ feet in depth. In some cases a rectangular stone slab like a couch or bed, and supported at the corners by pieces of stone like legs, has been found resting on the floor of the dolmen [coday cull]. The articles lodged in Paundicoozhies along with human bones are personal ornaments in the shape of beads, rings, &c., small pots for holding food or water, and various implements and weapons. Some of the beads are cornelian [akeek i soorkh] and have some show of patterns on them worked into the stone by grinding, and containing a hard white enamel which renders the patterns more distinct. The Paundicoozhy pottery, except the very large sepulchral vessels, has evidently been moulded on a wheel. In some cases the small articles of pottery have a fine polish of the kind at the present day communicated by rubbing the surface with Tanakk [q.v.] seeds of Gyrocarpus jacquini, roxb. Some articles are ornamented by stripes, alternately brown and red, of colored pigments and transparent varnish. No inscription has ever been found. Everywhere in Southern india a great resemblance may be observed in shape and size of the vessels found in these prehistoric graves, a fact indicative of a primitive state of civilization.

Paundicoozhies contain no implements belonging to the stone age. On the other hand articles made of iron are very common in them, and consist of bill-hooks or grass knives, swords, arrow-heads, &c. They contain in many cases human bones. No complete human skull has ever been found; but the fragments of skulls indicate that the people were dolichocephalic and had low, narrow, retreating foreheads. The Coorumbar [q.v.] of North arcot still construct Paundicoozhies upon a small scale when a Gowda [gownden] or head of a sect dies. It is clear that the tumulus, with its Paundicoozhy in the interior, and often with its enclosing concentric circles of stones [azhauram], was the prototype of the Booddhist [booddha] tope or dagoba with its rails, mound and relic casket [aursham, booddha, dagoba, mady moottaur tauzhy, maundavar coozhy, tope, vaulicoody].——*Paundoo cull* (பாண்டுக்கல் - pándukkal, Tam.). From (pandu, tam. antiquity + kal, tam. stone). General term for megalithic structures, standing free above ground. European menhir. Three or more stones placed upright, and over them a large flat stone placed so as to form a small rude chamber, is the usual dolmen [codaycull] form. To be distinguished from small buildings, formed with dressed stones and generally having one or two figures of Hindoo deities carved upon them. Paundoo-culls are of a much ruder description, formed with unhewn stone and without any carving or inscriptions. The purposes of the ortholithic structures were sepulchral and sacrificial in connection with the worship of deceased ancestors or chiefs. Pillar stones marking boundaries are found everywhere. Most are dressed stones; some inscribed. Many have carvings of Hindoo figures. Occasionally pillar stones commemorate some exploit in the destruction of tigers [pooly], as they are carved with representations of the fight. These appear to be of somewhat modern date. Paundooculls seem mostly later than Paundicoozhies [aursham, codaycull, mausticull, paundicoozhy, rauchsa-sagoondloo, topicull, veeracull].——*Paundyam* (பாண்டியம் - pándiyam, Tam.). Greek χώρα πανδιόνων. The people are called Pandæ in Pliny. Ancient tamul kingdom. Well-known to the Romans as the kingdom of king Paundyan, who sent ambassadors on two different occasions to Augustus cæsar. Nothing can be added to what is said at vol. I (116) to (121) [charitram].——*Paundyan* (பாண்டியன் - pándiyan, Tam,). Hindoo third name [peyar]. Any Pandyan king.——*Paundya rajaukkal* (பாண்டிய ராசாக்கள் - pándiyarásákkal, Tam.). From (pándiyam, tam. the kingdom + rájá, san. king). Tamul prose work sometimes attributed to the three most eminent of the professors of the Madura college [q.v.], Nakkeeran, Paranan, and Capilan. Agrees closely with Madura pooraunam [q.v.], and is therefore probably, as well as it, a branch from the sanscrit Halausya mahautmyam [q.v.]. Purports to be a history of Paundyan kings in thirteen books, chiefly of a legendary and sectarial character. It begins with Coolottoongan, in the year of kaly [q.v.] one thousand, and records anecdotes of the following princes, Anantagoonan, Caulabhooshanan, Rajendra paundyan, Rajeshwaran, Gambheeran, Vamshapradeepacan, Poorhootajit, Paundya vamsha pataucan, Soondreshwaran. Paudashekharan, Varagoonan, Rajendran, Soogoonan, Chitraratan, Chitrabhooshanan, Chitradhwajan, Chitravurman, Chitrasenan, Chitravicraman, Oodantan, Rajachoodaumany, Rajashaurdoolan, Coolottoongan, Yodhanapraveeran, Rajacoonjaran, Rajabhayancaran, Oograsenan, Mahasenan, Shatroonjayan, Bheemaratan, Bheemaparaucraman, Prataupamartaundan, Vicramacoonjaran, Yooddhacootoohalan, Atoolavicraman, Atoolakeerty, Keerty vibhooshanan, Vamshashekharan, Vamshachoodaumany, or thirty-nine of the seventy-four princes, which tradition usually ascribes to Paundya dynasty [raj]. With the exception of the first three, of Varagoonan, and the last two, the notice of these princes is restricted to simple enumeration of their names, and the stories found in the accounts of the others are commonly miraculous legends, illustrating the power of the tutelary deities of the Paundyan kingdom, Parvaty [q.v.] and Shiva [q.v.], combined as Meenautchisoondreshwaran. The last five chapters are devoted to marvellous anecdotes of the college of Madura [madura college] founded by Vamshashekharan, for the cultivation of Tamul [q.v.]; the first professors of which forty-eight in number, it is said, were incarnations of the forty-eight letters of the Sanscrit alphabet [varnamaulay] and Soondreshwaran himself was the forty-ninth. The latter presented the college with a diamond [vajram] bench or desk [sangapalagay], which would give place to no heterodox or inferior productions. The professors becoming arrogant, Shiva appeared as Tripoorauntaca caveeshwaran, or according to some accounts, Tirvulloovan [q.v.], the celebrated moral poet, and produced a work [cooral] which being laid on the desk with the books of the forty-eight professors thrust every one of them off and occupied the whole in solitary dignity.

PAUNO (పాణో - pánó, *Tel.*); Ooriya word. From (pánasi, tel. pariah). Also written Panoh. Hill Pariahs in the Parla-kimedy and Goomsoor maliahs [q.v.]. Each Khond [q.v.] village has a Pariah [q.v.] low-caste hamlet attached to it [jauty]. Numbers about 35,000.

PAUR (பார் - pár, *Tam.*). To see.——*Pauppautty* (பாப்பாத்தி - páppátti, Tam.). From (pár, tam. to see). A Bramin woman. Pauppautty myna is braminy myna, which see.——*Paurppaur* (பார்ப்பான் - párppán, pers. sing.; பார்ப்பார் - párppár, pers. pl., Tam.). From (pár, tam. to see). Overseer. Honorific name for bramin [q.v.] caste [jauty]. Compare Adansonia digitata (páppárappuli), bramin's tamarind.

PAURAY (बांगड - bángada, *Mahr.*; పర - parra, *Tel.*; பாறை - párai, *Tam.*). Title from tamul [para]. Mahr. from (bága, mahr. curvature). Tam. means flat. Horse-mackerel, Scad. The genus Caranx, carangidæ, acanthopterygii, teleostei, pisces [matsyam, 16], of naturalists [jantoo]. The species best known to the natives are shown below. Cf. also Barber pauray, Thick skin pauray.——*Barber pauray* (அம்பட்டன்கத்தி - ambattan-gatti, Tam.). Title from being long and narrow like handle of the razor. Tam. from (ambattan, tam. barber + katti, tam. knife). Title otherwise Razor-fish of Tamuls. Cf. Notopterus kapirat [barber vaulay]. Mene maculata, coryphænidæ, acanthopterygii, teleostei [matsyam, 18], of naturalists [jantoo]. Alias Mene anna-carolina; Zeus ambata kuttee, maculatus. Ambata kuttee from tamul. Body ovoid, highest anteriorly; mouth oblique; lateral line sometimes ceases below end of dorsal fin, or on reaching upper caudal lobe may divide into two branches, the lower of which descends; deep blue along back, becoming silvery white on sides and abdomen; two to three rows of large spots along superior half of body above level of pectoral fin; sea; 8½ inches in length. No other common species here.——*Black-headed pauray* (నూనెపర - núneparra, Tel.; ഉളിമ്പാറ - ulimpara, Mal.; கருமூஞ்சிப்பாறை - karumúñjippárai, Tam.). Tel. from (núne, tel. oil + parra, tel. caranx genus); from gloss of body [scorpion goby]. Mal. from (uli, mal. chisel + pára, mal. caranx genus). Tam. from (karumai, tam. blackness + múñji, tam. face + párai, tam. caranx genus). Tam. also (iruppárai), meaning dark + caranx genus. Caranx [pauray] ire, carangidæ, acanthopterygii, teleostei [matsyam, 16], of naturalists. Specific name perhaps from (irul, tam. darkness). Alias Carangoides præustus; Caranx melanostethos, præustus; Citula præusta; Selar ire. Dorsal and anal profiles about equally convex; snout slightly elevated; jaws of about equal length anteriorly, or lower slightly the longer; scales cover body except just in front of ventral fins; extend forwards on head to above eyes, cheeks and upper portion of opercle, none on the snout, preorbital, nor occipital crest; soft dorsal and anal fins have high scaly sheath; lateral line consists of about 102 scales, at first it is moderately curved, becoming straight below eighth dorsal ray, keeled scales do not commence until underneath the fifteenth ray, they are well developed but not strong; free portion of the tail rather longer than high; colors gray along back, becoming lighter on abdomen, whole glossed with purple and gold; head and chest occasionally brownish-black; no opercular spot; fins yellow, with black points, anterior portion of second dorsal black with white tip, rest of fin and of anal more or less dark; caudal sometimes with black tips and white edge; sea; upwards of a foot in length; in malabar mostly captured during cold months.——*Golden pauray* (कतलिकावलि - katalikávali, Mahr.; تنگپارا - tangpárá, Hind.; చెవులపర - chevulaparra, Tel.; தங்கப்பாறை - tangappárai, Tam.). Title from sides of head and body. Hindostany from tamul. Tel. from (chevi, tel. ear + parra, tel. caranx genus). Tam. from (tangam, tam. gold + párai, tam. caranx genus) [gray pauray]. Title otherwise Cobbler fish, Cordonnier. Caranx [pauray] armatus, carangidæ, acanthopterygii, teleostei [matsyam, 16], of naturalists. Alias Carangoides armatus, citula; Caranx ciliaris, citula; Citula armata, ciliaria, plumbea; Olistus malabaricus, rüppellii; Sciæna armata. Body oval, dorsal and anal profiles about equally convex; lower jaw the longer, cleft of mouth commences opposite middle of eyes; scales a few on hind portion of head, round eyes, and on cheeks, also over body except chest and portion anterior to bases of pectoral and ventral fins; also form a groove for soft dorsal and anal fins; lateral-line consists of 104 scales, makes a long low curve becoming straight beneath middle of second dorsal, keeled plates developed in last half of horizontal portion of lateral-line, but are not large; free portion of tail hardly so high at its base as it is long; upper surface of head and back bluish-green, sides of head and body golden, with purple reflections; opercular spot moderately distinct; first dorsal blackish, second and anal yellowish, with darker edges; pectoral dark behind base; the young vertically banded; sea; 20 inches in length.——*Gray pauray* (தங்கப்பாறை - tangappárai, Tam.). Tam. from (tangam, tam. gold + párai, tam. caranx genus) [golden pauray]. Caranx [pauray] nigrescens, carangidæ, acanthopterygii, teleostei [matsyam, 16], of naturalists. Sea; dorsal profile slightly more convex than that of the abdomen; lower jaw very slightly longer, cleft of mouth commences anteriorly below level of eye, very slightly oblique; scales on cheeks, round eyes, upper portion of opercle and body, none on chest as high as base of pectoral fin; lateral-line contains 140 scales, at first forms very low long curve to below thirteenth dorsal ray, from whence it gradually becomes straight, length of base of arch equalling that of straight portion of fin; keeled scales, slightly developed, being only distinct in last eight scales; free portion of tail at its base nearly equals its length; colors dusky-grayish, innumerable fine black points, and generally glossed purple; well marked black opercular spot; fins nearly black, especially dorsal; madras fishermen assert that it annually arrives from deep sea about march.——*Rama pauray* (இராமப்பாறை - irámappárai, Tam.). Tam. from (ráma, san. pleasing + párai, tam. caranx genus); from color. Tam. also (námappárai), meaning the caste mark of the white clay [naumam, tirmunn] streak on forehead + caranx genus; from stripe. Caranx [pauray] leptolepis, carangidæ, acanthopterygii, teleostei [matsyam, 16], of naturalists. Alias Caranx bidii, mertensii; Letaspis leptolepis; Sclaroides leptolepis. Jaws about the same length, or lower slightly longer; scales over body, chest, cheeks, and superiorly on head to above middle of eye; lateral-line ninety-five scales, makes gentle curve, becoming straight from below first third of second dorsal fin; keeled scales begin gradually under last portion of second dorsal, longest are below commencement of free portion of tail; free portion of tail one-fourth higher at base than it is long; colors silvery, broad golden stripe from above eye to upper edge of tail, lower two-third of dorsal fin yellow, upper third dark; anal having outer third white, rest yellow; large deep black spot on shoulder, said to be sometimes absent; sea; 6¾ inches in length.——*Shark pauray* (करटाबांगडा - karatábángadá, Mahr.; సొరపర్ర - soraparra, Tel.; கொமரப்பாறை - komarappárai, Tam.). Title from appearance. Mahr. from (karatá, mahr. wretched + bángada, mahr. caranx genus). Tel. from (sora, tel. shark, carcharias genus + parra, tel. caranx genus). Tam. from (komari, tam. unchanging youthfulness + párai, tam. caranx genus). Mahr. also (gaura), meaning reddish white. Tel. also (varaga). Caranx [pauray] rottleri, carangidæ, acanthopterygii, teleostei [matsyam. 16], of naturalists. Alias Megalaspis rottleri; Scomber guara, rottleri, woragoo. Guara from mahratta; woragoo from teloogoo. Very gradual ascent from snout to first dorsal fin; cleft of mouth slightly oblique, lower jaw slightly longer; scales about seventy-eight rows, fifty-five of which are large plates; on the cheeks, upper edge of opercle, and top of head, only a narrow band in central line in front ventral fin, otherwise the chest in front is scaleless; also form low sheath over bases of soft dorsal and anal fins; lateral-line at first makes strong curve, becomes straight below middle of first dorsal fin where wide plates commence, most strongly keeled over free portion of tail which is strongly depressed; colors back glossy-green, abdomen silvery tinged with yellow; large black spot on upper and posterior portion of opercle; fins yellow, dorsal and anal tipped black; upper half of pectoral darker than lower; sea; 5 feet in length. ——*Striped pauray* (మీసపర్ర - mísaparra, Tel.; கன்னிப்பாறை - kannippárai, Tam.). Tel. from (mísamu, tel. whiskers + parra, tel. caranx genus). Tam. from (kanni, tam. rope + párai, tam. caranx genus). Caranx [pauray] atropus, carangidæ, acanthopterygii, teleostei [matsyam, 16], of naturalists. Alias Brama atropus; Carangoides atropus; Caranx nigripes; Olistus atropus; Scomber mais-parah. Mais-parah from teloogoo. Body oval, strongly compressed, with crest on summit of head well developed; cleft of mouth commences anteriorly opposite centre of front edge of eye, and maxilla reaches to below middle of orbit; lower jaw longer; scales a few on checks and below eye, none on remainder of head; body scaled except on chest and from between bases of pectoral and ventral fins to head; they form rather high scaly sheath to second dorsal and anal fins; lateral-line consists of about seventy-five rows, curves to below fifth ray of dorsal fin, subsequent to which keeled scales commence; colors bluish-green along back, becoming silvery shot with purple on sides and beneath; well marked black opercular spot; ventrals deep black; the young are vertically banded and opercular spot indistinct or absent; sea; a foot in length.——*Thick skin pauray* (پارا - pára, Hind.; தோற்பாறை - tórbárai, Tam.). Hind. from tamul. Tam. from (tól, tam. skin + párai, tam. caranx genus); from thick skin. Chorinemus lysan, carangidæ, acanthopterygii, teleostei [matsyam, 16], of naturalists [jantoo]. Alias Chorinemus aculeatus, commersonianus, farkharii; Scomber akenparah, forsteri, lysan, madagascariensis; Scomberoides commersonianus. Body rather strongly compressed, profile over nape slightly concave; cleft of mouth deep; scales distinct and lanceolate; lateral-line has slight angular elevation soon after commencement; colors six to eight large, round, gray spots like finger marks on side, lateral-line sometimes going through two first, while others are all above it; summit of soft dorsal black; sea; attains a considerable size; no other common species here.——*Thief pauray* (கள்ளப்பாறை - kallappárai, Tam.). Title from cunning habits. Tam. from (kallam, tam. guile + párai, tam. caranx genus). Caranx [pauray] kalla, carangidæ, acanthopterygii, teleostei [matsyam, 16], of naturalists. Specific name from tamul meaning guile. Alias Caranx brevis, calla; Selar brevis, kalla. Abdominal profile more convex than that of back; lower jaw longer; scales over body, chest, and some on cheeks; well developed sheath to dorsal and anal fins; lateral-line having 80 scales, rather strongly curved anteriorly, but not ending abruptly; keeled plates begin at commencement of straight portion; free portion of tail longer than high; colors bluish-green above, shot with silver, sides and abdomen silvery, with nacreous reflections; distinct black spot on opercle; tail and caudal fin brilliant yellow, upper lobe tinged green; other fins white, excepting dorsal which has black upon it; sea; 8 inches in length.

PAURITHAM (பாரிதம் - páritham, *Tam.*). Barytes [cull].

PAURY (पारी - párí, *San.*). From (pára, san. shore). Sea [samoodram].——*Paurijautam* (पारिजात - párijáta, San.). From (above + já, san. to be born); produced at churning of ocean [coormam, samoodram]. Tree of paradise [calpacam]; tree of plenty. Cf. Common coral tree, Coral jasmine.

PAUSY (शैवल - shaivala, *San.*; शेवाळ - shévála, *Mahr.*; کنجال - kanjál, *Hind.*; ಪಾಚಿ - páchi, *Can.*; పాచి - páchi, *Tel.*; പായൽ - páyal, *Mal.*; பாசி - pási, *Tam.*). San. from (shí, san. to rest); from cooling property. Drav. from (pasumai, tam. greenness) [pye]. Otherwise Poolloory, as being parasitic on plants. Mosses, order Musci [vricsham, 160]. Or else green and mouldy formations on objects. Pausy uncompounded generally means moss [pauchy]. Also variegated glass beads or green earthen beads making necklace for children of lower orders.——**(1)** *Pauchimaun* (फसि - p'hasi, Mahr.; ತಿರಪು - tirapu, Can.; పాచిమాను - páchimánu, Tel.; ପଞ୍ଚି - panchi, Oor.; நமை - namai, Tam.). Title from teloogoo. Tel. from (páchi, tel. moss + mánu, tel. tree); perhaps from moss green color of wood. Tam. means itching; or probably connected with (nemi, san. wheel); from use of wood for cart wheel [nemmy]. Tel. also (bhúchakramu), meaning earth + wheel. Oor. also (pasi). Botanically Anogeissus [dhavam] acuminata, wall., combretaceæ [vricsham, 55]. Alias Conocarpus acuminata. Large tree; limb of calyx five-cleft; petals none; leaves without glands, nearly opposite, oval or oblong-lanceolate, entire, acute; when young, pubescent, adult ones glabrous; peduncles simple, with one head of flowers; flowers small, pale-greenish; abundant in circars [q.v.]; flowering in cold season. Leaf used in tanning [chamrah]. Wood grey, sometimes yellowish-grey with a greenish tinge, shining, in structure moderately hard; like vekkauly [q.v.], but not so good.——*Pauchipenta* (పాచిపెంట - pachipenta, Tel.). From (páchi, tel. moss + penta, tel. heap). Sanscrit name (práchínapura), meaning ancient city.—"*a*" Zemindarry; Vizagapatam dist., Saulore division; pop. 18,436. Feudatory of Jeypore. The founder of the family was a Naick [q.v.] under Jeypore, who was appointed to guard the ghaut [q.v.] and received the title of Dacshina cavauta yoovarauz, and some villages both above and below the pass. He built a fort at Taida, but his descendants moved down to Pauchipenta. The estate is sometimes called Taida or Taida pauchipenta. The family belong to the Condarauz [q.v.] caste. The Mahratta horse of Jaffer ally descended into the Chicacole circar [q.v.] in 1754, by the treachery of the Pauchipenta zemindar, who was consequently imprisoned. At his death in 1789 a small Towjee [q.v.] was allowed to his son Mullappa rauz, who after battle of Padmanaubham received a cowle [q.v.] for his patrimonial villages. He died in 1797, and the permanent settlement was made with Annama rauz, his only son. The zemindar is greatly in debt and the estate is being disintegrated. Peshcush Rs. 2,584.—"*b*" Village, Head-quarters of zemindar, Pass; Vizagapatam dist., Saulore division; pop. 4,962; lat. 18° 29'; long. 83° 09'; from Coraputt S.E. 33 miles; from Madras N. 411 miles; from Narsapatam N.N.E. 64 miles; from Parvatipore S.W. 29 miles; from Saulore W.S.W. 6 miles; from Vizagapatam N.N.W. 54 miles; from Vizianagram N.N.W. 31 miles. Old fort. A large weekly market of hill products. The pass [ghaut] carries the road from Saulore to Jeypore.——**(2)** *Autt pausy* (ஆற்றுப்பாசி - áttuppási, Tam.). From (áru, tam. river). River-weeds; especially Najas indica, cham., fluviales.——*Cadal pausy* (समुद्रशाक - samudrasháka, San.; دریاکاکنجال - daryákákanjál, Hind.; సముద్రపుపాచి - samudrapupáchi, Tel.; കടല്പായൽ - kata'páyal, Mal.; கடற்பாசி - kadarbási, Tam.). Sea-weed, order Algæ [vricsham, 163] of naturalists. Especially species of Gracilaria [agar-agar] and Laminaria. Almost all the plants of this class yield soda [sujjee khaur] and iodine on incineration. Gracilaria lichenoides, greville, is Ceylon moss or edible sea-weed. Gracilaria tenax is Malay Agar-agar.——*Cody pausy* (கொடிப்பாசி - kodippási, Tam.). From (kodi, tam. creeper). Moss creeping upon water; especially Hydrilla verticillata, rich., hydrocharidaceæ.——*Coondal pausy* (கூந்தற்பாசி - kúndarbási, Tam.). From (kúndal, tam. anything radiating like woman's hair). Trailing moss; especially Zannichellia indica.——*Coratty pausy* (गवेधु - gavédhu, San.; रानजोंधला - ránajóndhalá, Mahr.; వడ్లపూస - vadlapúsa, Tel.; കുരത്തിക്കൊണ്ട - kurattikkonda, Mal.; කිරින්දිමානා - kirindimáná, Singh.; குறத்திப்பாசி - kurattippási, Tam.). Title from tamul. San. from (gó, san. water + édh, san. to grow). Mahr. from (rána, mahr. wild + jóndhalá, mahr. sorghum valgare, pers.). Tel. from (vadlu, tel. paddy + púsa, tel. grain); from rice-like seeds. Mal. from (kuratti, mal. corava woman + konda, mal. tuft of hair). Tam. from (kuratti, tam. corava woman + pási, tam. greenish, variegated beads); from use as ornament by corava [q.v.] women. San. also (jargadi); (gavédhuka), meaning water-grower. Tel. also (goliye); (kókiláksbamu), meaning cuckoo + eye; (korimidi) [neermoolly]; (gilagaddi); (golimidi) [small chiretta]; (adavigódhuma), meaning forest wheat, triticum vulgare, vill. Mal. also (káppirikkonda), meaning negro + tuft of hair. Tam. also (nerbul), meaning paddy + grass; (nenmani), meaning paddy, oryza sativa, linn. + grain, from rice-like seeds; (púnáççippul), meaning earth + goddess + grass. Title otherwise Coix millet,

Coratty's hair, Cuckoo's eye, Job's tears, Negro's hair, Paddy grass, Wild millet, Wild wheat. Botanically Coix lachryma, linn., gramineæ [vricsham, 156]. Alias Coix arundinacea; Lithagrostis lachryma. Annual grass, foot or more in height, native of india; culm branched, full of pith, half-terete above, obtuse; spikelets axillary, peduncled, not involucrate; fruit ovate; root annual; flowering in the rainy season; the hardened involucres are known as job's tears. Seeds oblong, globose, size of peas [calauyam]; coarse cereal [dhaunyam] with hill tribes taking the place of millets [q.v.]. Seeds used as beads [munkah]. Other species are:—barbata, gigantea.——*Cullpausy* (शिलावल्कल - shilávalkala, San.; بهق الحجر - bahakulhajar, Ar.; گل سنگ - gulisang, Pers.; پتھر کا پھول - pattharkáphúl, Hind. and Dec.; రాతిపాచి - rátipáchi, Tel.; കല്പായൽ - kalpáyal, Mal.; கர்பாசி - karbási, Tam.). San. from (shilá, san. rock + valkala, san. bark). Ar. from (bahak, ar. ringworm + hajar, ar. stone); from supposed curing properties. Pers. from (gul, pers. flower + sang, pers. stone). Hind. from (patthar, hind. stone + phúl, hind. flower). Tel. from (ráyi, tel. stone + páchi, tel. moss). Mal. from (kal, mal. stone). Tam. from (kal, tam. stone). Tam. also (marappási), meaning tree moss. Any lichen, order Lichenes [vricsham, 162], of naturalists. Order of flowerless or cryptogamic plants, occurring either as crust-like or leafy expansions or in small branching shrub like tufts, usually colored grey, yellow, or greenish-yellow; over stones, brick-walls, the bark of trees, &c. On the Coondah hills in the Neilgherries all the rocks are covered with lichens. In this country the relative proportion of lichens growing upon the leaves of trees or epiphyllous lichens is large, and gives a special character to tropical lichenology. One or two species of lichen growing upon rocks in S. india are used in medicine; especially Lichen rotundatus, rottl., used as a liniment. Parmelia perlata, ach., a yellow dye lichen, is found on Neilgherries. As a food such as Iceland moss, lichens not known here.——*Ilay pausy* (இலைப்பாசி - ilaippási, Tam.). From (ilai, tam. leaf). Large-leafed moss; especially Lemna obcordata.——*Moottay pausy* (முட்டைப்பாசி - muttaippási, Tam.). From (muttai, tam. egg). Aquatic plants with inflated appendages to root; especially Utricularia stellaris, linn. f., lentibularieæ.——*Neer pausy* (शैवल - shévala, San.; நீர்ப்பாசி - nírppási, Tam.). From (nír, tam. water). San. from (shí, san. to rest); from the cooling property. Duck-weed. Lemnaceæ family.——*Pazham pausy* (பழம்பாசி - pazhambási, Tam.). From (pazham, tam. fruit). Otherwise called Cottay pausy meaning seed + moss, Coray pausy meaning reed + moss, and Tott pausy meaning palm leaf + moss. Especially Sida humilis, willd., malvaceæ [vricsham, 25].——*Vailam pausy* (வேலம் பாசி - vélambási, Tam.). From (vél, tam. acacia). Also called Veppam pausy, meaning margosa + moss. Especially Chara corallina.——*Vazhookk pausy* (വഴുക്കുപ്പായൽ - vazhukkuppáyal, Mal.; வழுக்குப்பாசி - vazhukkuppási, Tam.). From (vazhukku, tam. slimy). Genus Vallisneria, order Hydrocharaceæ or floating water plants. Grow at the bottom generally of running waters. Possess cooling powers.

PAUTA (పాత - páta, *Tel.*). Old [haley, pazha]. Prefix in place names; as Pautapaud, old village.

PAUTALAM (पाटल - pátala, *San.*). Means pale-red rose color. Botanically the Stereospermum genus, bignoniaceæ [vricsham, 99]. Trees; leaves pinnate, terminated by a single leaflet; flowers white, often fragrant, and in terminal panicles; capsule cylindrical or almost square; seeds bony, scarcely winged. The species best known to the natives are:—chelonoides [pauthiry], xylocarpum [valencoorny].——*Paudalam* (பாடலம் - pádalam, Tam.). From (pátala, san. pale red); from the color. Name of Cheran's chestnut horse. See vol. I (126).——*Paudel* (पाडल - pádala, Mahr.). Same as Pauthiry.——*Pautalagandhy* (పాటలగంధి - pátalagandhi, Tel.). From (pátala, san. pale-red + gandha, san. smell). Same as Snake root.——*Pauthiry* (பாதிரி - páthiri, Tam.). See sep. title.

PAUTAM (पाठ - pát'ha, *San.*). From (pat'h, san. to read aloud). Lesson. Pautashaulay is a school [madrissa].

PAUTHAY (பாதை - páthai, *Tam.*). From (pat'ha, san. path) [panthy]. Road-path. Irooppoo pauthay is rail-road.

PAUTHIRY (पाटलि - pátali, *San.*; पाडल - pádala, *Mahr.*; پارل - páral, *Hind.*; ಪಾದರಿ - pádari, *Can.*; ನಜುಡಿ - najudi, *Coorg*; తగడ - tagada, *Tel.*; ପଂଫୁନିୟ - pamp'húniya, *Oor.*; പാതിരി - pátiri, *Mal.*; ලුණුමඩලා - lunumadalá, *Singh.*; பாதிரி - páthiri, *Tam.*). Title from tamul; no connection with paudry or padre [pautalam]. San. from (pátala, san. red), from flower [common bendy, edible paulay, jungle geranium, weaver's beam]. Mahr. from sanscrit. Mal. from sanscrit. Can. also (kalladi). Coorg also (mallali). Tel. also (kaligottu); (mokkavépa), meaning stump + margosa tree, melia azadirachta, linn.; (pádiri); (kaligóru); (pisúl); (pulakail). Tam. also (ponbáthiri), meaning gold + the tree; (vellaippáthiri), meaning white + the tree; (appu); (kánavirukkam), meaning forest tree. Title otherwise Paudel, Paural, Trumpet flower. Botanically Stereospermum [pautalam] chelonoides, dc., bignoniaceæ [vricsham, 99]. Alias Bignonia chelonoides; Heterophragma chelonoides. Trunk straight, of a great height and thickness; bark thick, scabrous, brown; branches very numerous, the inferior horizontal above, gradually becoming more and more erect to the top; leaves opposite, pinnate, with an odd one, about 20 inches long; leaflets opposite, short petioled, generally four pair, the interior smallest, obliquely oval, pointed, sometimes slightly notched about the margins, when young downy, afterwards smooth, about 4 inches long by two broad; petioles about 9 inches long, channelled, smooth; stipules none; panicles terminal, the larger ramifications decussate, the smaller or terminal two-forked, with a sessile flower in the cleft; peduncles and pedicels round, covered with oblong grey scabrous specks; bracts small, caducous; flowers pretty large, yellow, very fragrant; calyx five-notched; nectary, a yellow fleshy ring surrounding the base of the germ; filaments four, a fifth sterile one between the lower pair; anthers double, stigma two-cleft; silique very long, slender, twisted; receptacle of the seeds spongy, white, with alternate notches on the sides for the seeds to lodge in. A pagoda [q.v.] flower. Infusion of root and flowers, a cooling drink in fevers. Flowers make a scented water. Wood orange yellow; close, even-grained, elastic, durable, easily worked, gives smooth glossy surface; sapwood rather coarse-grained, brownish white color, not durable. There is a Tamul proverb:—பலா உத்தமம், மா மத்திமம், பாதிரி அதமம்—"the jack "[q.v.] tree, is the best, the mango [q.v.] is middling, the "pauthiry tree is indifferent." A similar species is suaveolens; a middle-sized tree with pinnate leaves and panicled inflorescence; flower dark, dull crimson, very fragrant, common; planted about gardens and temples; gum [gond] from the bark; root-bark is an ingredient in dashamoolam [q.v.]; ashes used as mordant [cauram]; has a wood similar to chelonoides, but rather redder.——*Flowering pauthiry* (பூம்பாதிரி - púmbáthiri, Tam.). Title from resemblance. Tam. from (pú, tam. flower + páthiri, tam. trumpet-flower tree, stereospermum chelonoides, dec.). Title otherwise Crispate trumpet flower. Botanically Dolichandrone [water ailanto] crispa, seem., bignoniaceæ [vricsham, 99]. Alias Bignonia crispa; Spathodea crispa. Arboreous; leaves unequally pinnate; leaflets one to three pair; branchlets and racemes pubescent and velvety; leaflets oval-oblong, acuminated at both ends, quite entire; raceme terminal, few-flowered; corolla tube slender, elongated; lobes much curled and crisped; flowers pure white, fragrant; capsule pod-like, elongated, obtusely-acuminated, pendulous; flowering in may and june. Tree of subalpine forests; white flowers open towards evening, fall off early next morning; timber good.

PAUTT (പാട്ട് - páttu, *Mal.*). From (pan, mal. melody) [pah]. Poetical dialect, song.——*Coratty pautt* (കുറത്തിപ്പാട്ട് - kurattippáttu, Mal.; குறத்திப்பாட்டு - kurattippáttu, Tam.). Coravar woman's song. Malayalam and Tamul poem.——*Oonjal pautt* (ഊഞ്ഞാൽപ്പാട്ട് - úñchalppáttu, Mal.). From (úñchal, mal. swing). Swing song.——*Taurautt pautt* (താരാട്ടുപാട്ട് - tárāttupáttu, Mal.). From (tárāttu, mal. caressing). Lullaby song.——*Toolla pautt* (തുള്ളപ്പാട്ട് - tullappáttu, Mal.). From (tullu, mal. to leap). Song with dance.

PAUTTOM (പാട്ടം - páttam, *Mal.*). From (pád, mal. chief) [padoo]. The chief's share. Not to be confounded with puttah [q.v.], or title deed. Rent. The fixed proportion agreed between Jenmy [q.v.] and cultivator [coodiyaun] on lease of any sort to be given to the Jenmy as his share or rent; this proportion is usually paid in kind for rice cultivation and in money for plantations. The amount is now very variable, though originally the whole of the net produce was paid to the proprietor deducting only estimated quantity of seed and an equal quantity for cultivation expenses. This last form remains as Veroompauttom, or the simplest form of Malabar leasehold, where the tenant has least rights or advantages [veroompauttom]. For a conspectus of Malabar tenures, see vol. II, 104; I, 112.——**(1)** *Pauttacauran* (പാട്ടക്കാരൻ - páttakkáran, Mal.). From (above + káran, mal. doer, personal suffix). Tenant but generally one on a simple lease without giving any Otty [q.v.] loan.——*Pauttachit* (പാട്ടച്ചീട്ട് - páttaççíttu, Mal.). From (above + chíttu, mal. receipt). Rent receipt.——*Pauttanell* (പാട്ടനെല്ല് - páttanellu, Mal.). From (above + nel, mal. paddy). The rent when paid in kind.——*Pauttaparamba* (പാട്ടപ്പറമ്പ് - páttapparampu, Mal.). From (above + parambu, mal. garden). A garden let on lease.——*Pauttaparrah* (പാട്ടപ്പറ - páttappara, Mal.). From (above + para, mal. measure). A large measure [parrah] used in measuring rent or mitchauram [q.v.] to jenmy [q.v.].——*Pauttauly* (പാട്ടാളി - páttáli, Mal.). From (above + álu, mal. to own). One who collects rents, especially of a temple [coil, pagoda].——*Pauttavauram* (പാട്ടവാരം - páttavāram, Mal.). From (above + váram, mal. rent). The rent of trees is generally called pauttom; the rent of fields is called vauram [q.v.]; this is a combination of both.——**(2)** *Cauna pauttom* (കാണപ്പാട്ടം - kánappáttam, Mal.). See under Caunom.——*Chetpauttom* (ചെത്തുപാട്ടം - chettupáttam,

Mal.). From (chettu, mal. to tap). Rent of cocoanuts [q.v.] or other palms [taur] for extracting toddy [q.v.].——*Cundupauttom* (കണ്ടപ്പാട്ടം - kandappáttam, Mal.). From (kán, mal. to see). Rent on fields after inspection. Used in south for Veroompauttom.——*Maroopauttom* (മറുപാട്ടം - marupáttam, Mal.). From (maru, mal. next). Counter-agreement, or covenant of lease by the tenant to the proprietor.——*Moonpauttom* (മുമ്പാട്ടം - munpáttam, Mal.). From (mun, mal. before). One year's rent paid in advance of a lease being effected, but no interest thereby claimable. The first step from Veroompauttom to Caunom [q.v.]. See vol. II, 104 [cuttacaunom].——*Nairppauttom* (നേർപ്പാട്ടം - nérppáttam, Mal.). From (nér, mal. just). A customary fixed rent on land. Is more generic than Cauna pauttom.——*Oobhayapauttom* (ഉഭയപ്പാട്ടം - ubhayappáttam, Mal.). From (ubhayam, mal. rice-field). Rent for rice fields, in South malabar only.——*Payitt pauttom* (പയറ്റുപാട്ടം - payattupáttam, Mal.). Pulse [dholl] rent. Rent levied on dry lands [poonjah] or gardens [tottam].——*Talapauttom* (തലപ്പാട്ടം - talappáttam, Mal.). The yearly rent due under Caunom tenure.——*Veroompauttom* (വെറുമ്പാട്ടം - verumpáttam, Mal.). From (verum, mal. empty). Plain rent. Simple rent which the renter gives without any further arrangement of paying money down to the jenmy. Veroompauttom lease is the simplest lease in Malabar, and on the other hand has least advantages for the tenant. It is generally so arranged as to leave only a bare subsistence to the tenant. The lease runs only for a single year, unless otherwise specified. At the end of the year the landlord is at liberty either to renew the lease or to let the land to another tenant; but he cannot under any circumstances disturb the tenant in his enjoyment until the year has expired. Where the lease is for a specified period, the tenant cannot be ejected during that period unless he endeavours to defraud the landlord or allows the rent to fall into arrears. In either of these cases however an action of ejectment will lie against the tenant. The tenant cannot transfer his tenancy without the consent of the landlord. No compensation [chamayam] is allowed for improvements, unless they were effected with the knowledge of the landlord. Next higher in the interests of the tenant in the scale of tenures above Veroompauttom is Caunom [q.v.].

PAUV (प्रोत - próta, *San.*; تانا - táná, *Hind.*; పడుగు - padugu, *Tel.*; പാവു - pávu, *Mal.*; பாவு - pávu, *Tam.*). Title from tamul. San. from (pra, san. forth + ve, san. to sew); as woven lengthwise. Tel. from (podugu, tel. length). Tam. from (pávu, tam. to spread). Warp thread [nesavoo].——*Paugal* (பாகல் - págal, Tam.). From (pávu, tam. to spread); creeper. Same as Carolah.——*Pauvauday* (பாவாடை - pávádai, Tam.). Means cloth carpet. Proper name. Common among the lower orders [pauvauday veeran, peyar].——*Pauvauday veeran* (பாவாடைவீரன் - pávádaivíran, Tam.). From (pávádai, tam. proper name + víra san. hero); probably from the cloth being spread before him when going out as mark of distinction. A deity whose image is placed in the temples [coil, pagoda] of Ancaulamman [q.v.].

PAUY (பாய் - páy, *Tam.*). To run, leap, flow.——*Pauchal* (பாய்ச்சல் - páyçcal, Tam.). From (páy, tam. to flow). Irrigation; applied to the natural flow from an irrigation source as distinguished from Yiraipp, irrigation by baling and Yaittam or irrigation by picottah.——*Pautchay* (झिल्लिका - jhilliká, San.; झिल्लि - jhilli, Mahr.; صرصر - sarsar, Ar.; چرواشك - charwáshak, Pers.; جهينگر - jhíngur, Hind. and Dec.; چنگرك - chingarak, Malay; ಝಿಲ್ಲಿಕೆ - jhillike, Can.; చిమట - chimata, Tel.; മണ്ണട്ട - mannatta, Mal.; රැහියා - ráhiyá, Singh.; பாச்சை - páççai, Tam.). Title from tamul. San. from (jhil, san. the sound made by the insect). Ar. means noisy. Hind. from sanscrit. Tel. from (chimmu, tel. to spring); from its motion. Mal. from (man, mal. ground + atta, mal. leech). Tam. from (páy, tam. to leap). Ar. also (sarrárullail), meaning night crier; (saddá), meaning noisy. Tam. also (shuvargózhi), meaning wall + fowl; (shilvandu), meaning beetle making shrill noise. Cricket. Term co-extensive with family gryllidæ, orthoptera, hemimetabola, insecta [poochy], of naturalists [jantoo].

PAVANANDY (பவணந்தி - pavanandi, *Tam.*). From (bhava, san. existence + nanda, san. joy). Author of Nunnool [q.v.], the son of Sanmaty of Shanagapooram, Jeina [q.v.] by religion. Wrote under patronage of one Gungan.

PAVETTA (काकछेदी - kákachhédí, *San.*; کنکرا - kankrá, *Hind.*; ಸೂಳೆಬೊಟ್ಟುಗಿಡ - súlebottugida, *Can.*; ಪಾವಟೆ - pávate, *Too.*; పాపట - pápata, *Tel.*; പാവട്ട - pávatta, *Mal.*; පාවට්ට - pávattá, *Singh.*; பாவட்டை - pávattai, *Tam.*). Title from malayalam. San. from (káka, san. crow + chhid, san. to cut). Can. from (súle, can. strumpet + bottu, can. forehead mark + gida, can. plant); from glossy leaves. Tam. from (pávu, tam. to leap + vattu, tam. ball); from bead-like fruits being used for shooting pellets by children in their pop-guns. San. also (tiryakp'bala), meaning going across + fruit; refers to shooting across by children. Can. also (pávate). Tel. also (tellapápata), meaning white + the tree; (núuepápata), meaning oil + the tree; from oily gloss of leaves. Mal. also (mallikamuti), meaning jasmine + head, alluding to white corymbs of flowers. Tam. also (karanaiççedi). Title otherwise Indian pavetta. Botanically Pavetta indica, linn., rubiaceæ [vriesham, 71]. Alias Ixora paniculata, pavetta; Pavetta alba. Generic name from malayalam. Shrub, 3-4 feet; calyx-tube ovate, limb four-toothed, teeth minute, acute; corolla hypocrateriform, lobes four or occasionally five, two to three times shorter than the tube, oval obtuse; leaves opposite, oval-oblong, acuminated, tapering at the base, petioled; corymbs terminal and from the upper axils, their primary ramifications opposite; stamens four or occasionally five; style twice the length of the corolla, glabrous; flowers white; drupe globose, crowned with the calyx, two-celled, cell one-seeded. Large, laurel-form, dark, glossy-green leaves, with white midrib; the leaves on the underside and the young shoots are either pubescent or glabrous; grows in dry jungles and about hedges; trusses of dirty-white fragrant flowers appearing in february; foliage is its principal point of beauty; the root is crooked, from 1 inch to ½ inch in diameter; the bark is grey, with a light brown papery epidermis, and seems to be the most active part; it has a sweetish aromatic taste followed by a bitterness. The root is medicinally aperient, pulverized and mixed with ginger [q.v.] and rice-water [conjee] is given in dropsy; boiled in water, a fomentation is made from the leaves for hæmorrhoid pains. The fruit is made into pickles; the leaves are used for manuring fields; handles for knives are made from the roots. Wood light-brown, hard, close-grained; timber very small. There is a Tamul proverb:—பாவட்டம் பூப்போல நரைத்தும் புத்தி இல்லை—"though as grey as a pavetta flower, he has no sense." A variety tomentosa is called Hill pavetta.——*Bramha's pavetta* (బొమ్మపాపట - bommapápata, Tel.). Same as Tirauna.

PAZHA (பழ - pazha, *Tam.*). Old [haley, pauta]. Pazhamullay is Vriddhauchellam, the old mountain; Pazhavailcaud is Poolicat, the old acacia forest.——*Palaya* (பழைய - pazhaiya, Tam.). Old [haley, pauta].——*Palayaur* (പഴയാർ - pazhayár, Mal.). From (pazhaya, mal. old + áru, mal. river). Sanscrit name (dantanadí), meaning tusk + river. When the Shiva [q.v.] temple at Sooshindram was built by Indran [q.v.], he directed his elephant [q.v.] Eirauvatam [q.v.] to cut with his tusk [dant] a river for its use. River; Travancore state, Pudmanaubhapooram division, Tovaula and Agasteeshwaram talook. Most southern river of Travancore. Rises in the secondary range of Sahyadry and derives much water from Tamrapurny, being united to it by canal. It flows south-east and south-south-east for 23 miles, passing Bhootapaundy, Cottaur and Sooshindram, and falls into sea through Manacoody estuary. Much used for cultivation. Irrigation by means of dams. Banks are low and the bed is sandy, and from twelve to thirty paces in breadth. It is shallow and unnavigable. One of its canals, the Poottanaur waters a space of seventeen miles along its borders. Length of the river is about 23 miles.——*Paul* (ಪಾಳು - pálu, Can.; പാഴ് - pázh, Mal.; பாழ் - pázh, Tam.). Waste land [beed, haul, paud].——*Payyangaudy* (പഴയങ്ങാടി - pazhayannáti, Mal.). From (pazhaya, mal. ancient + annáti, mal. bazaar). Moplah [q.v.] name of Maudye.——*Pazham* (பழம் - pazham, Tam.). See sep. title.——*Pazhamozhy* (ضرب الامثال - zarbulamsál, Hind.; பழமொழி - pazhamozhi, Tam.). From (above + mozhi, tam. word). Hind. from (zarb, ar. striking + masal, ar. expression). Proverb. The following are specimens of Tamul proverbs:—அழுகிற ஆணையும் சிரிக்கிற பெண்ணையும் நம்பக்கூடாது—"a weeping man and a "smiling woman are not to be trusted."—வேலை இல்லா ஊருக்கு ராஜா ஏன், பாம்பு இல்லா ஊருக்குக் கீரிப்பிள்ளை ஏன்—"what need is there of a king in a country "where there is no work, or of a mongoose [q.v.] where there "are no snakes [sarpam]?"—பொறுத்தார் அரசாள்வார் பொங்கினார் காடாள்வார்—"they who endure will reign as "kings, the irascible will wander through the jungles."—சொல்லிச் செய்வார்நல்லோர், சொல்லாமற் செய்வார் பெரியோர் சொல்லியும்செய்யார் சடர்—"those who say "and do, are good; those who say not and do, are great; but "those who say and do not, are bad." The following are specimens of Hindostany proverbs:—زر زمین زن جھگڑے کی جڑ ھین—"wealth, land, woman, are the roots of quarrel."—سچ اور جھوٹ مین چار انگل کا فرق ھی—"between truth and falsehood, the "distance is four fingers;" truth is seen, falsehood heard, and the distance between the eye and ear is four fingers.——*Pazhayacoor* (പഴയകൂറ് - pazhayakúru, Mal.). From (above + kúr, mal. division). The section of Malabar syrian [q.v.] christians that remained faithful to Rome in the schism of 1657 [poottancoor].——*Pazhayanore* (പഴയന്നൂർ - pazhayannúr, Mal.). From (pazhaya, mal. ancient + úr, mal. village).—"*a*" River; Cochin state, Talapully tal. A small stream 9 miles long. Falls into Ponnany river.—"*b*" Village; Cochin state, Talapully tal.; pop. 4,529; lat. 10° 41′; long. 76° 27′; from Ernacolum N.N.E. 48 miles; from Trichore N.E. 16 miles; from Vadacancherry E.N.E. 11 miles. Has a famous temple dedicated to

Bhagavaiy [q.v.], festival March-April.——*Poolicat* (پلیاگھات - paliyághát, Hind.; பழவேர்க்காடு - pazhavérkkádu, Tam. pulicat*). From (pazha, tam. old + vél, tam. babool, acacia arabica, willd. + kádu, tam. forest). Sanscrit name (pralaya-kávéri), meaning flood + the cauvery river. Greek name ποδούκη. Town, Port; Chingleput dist., Ponnairy tal.; pop. 5,392; acres 2,923; lat 13° 25′; long. 80° 23′; from Arcot N.E. 76 miles; from Ennore N. 12 miles; from Madras N. 24 miles; from Nellore S. 75 miles; from Ponnairy N.E. 10 miles; from Poody S. 29 miles; from Sydapett N.E. 28 miles. Mentioned in the Devauram [q.v.]. On Coromandel coast at southern extremity of an island in the inlet between the sea and lake of same name. The latter or backwater is connected with Madras by Cochrane's canal now Buckingham canal [q.v.]. Off the coast are the Poolicat shoals. From 1 to 2 miles off shore is the Poolicat anchorage, with 6 or 7 fathoms water. There is a lighthouse near the beach; lat. 13° 25′ 12·39″; long. 80° 22′ 06·86″; white; fixed; 14 miles range; visible from all directions seaward; masonry column, with black bands; to guide vessels clear of the Poolicat shoal; when the light bears W. ½ N., a vessel is to the northward of all dangers. The Dutch erected a factory here in 1609. This was their earliest settlement in Southern india. They built a fort and called it Geldria. In 1619 they gave the English a share in the pepper [q.v.] trade with Java and a British factory was established in 1621 by permission of the Dutch under the operation of the treaty concluded between King James I and the States-General, dated 7th July 1619. Factory withdrawn in consequence of the oppressions of the Dutch in 1622. Fort, factory and dependencies, viz., the Island of Iroocam and the villages of Avirivaukam, Canavandoray, and Vanjivaukam taken from the Dutch, 2nd July 1781. The Island of Iroocam is now attached to Nellore district. Restored to Holland in July 1785 under treaty with the States-General of 20th May 1784. Surrendered to the English on 16th July 1795. Restored to Holland on 31st March 1818 agreeably to the Convention of the allied powers in 1814. Restored to Great britain on 1st June 1825 under the treaty of March 1824. There is an old Dutch cemetery. Trade between this port and the Straits settlements, formerly considerable, has declined. Poolicat lake is about 37 miles in length by from 3 to 11 in breadth. It is under the influence of the tide. The water is constantly changed, yet brackish. The lake contains some large islands besides that on which the town is situate. The lake, throughout its whole length, forms the south-eastern limit of Nellore district. The Buckingham canal [q.v.] utilizes this lake nearly as far as Doogarauzpatam.——*Pulney* (பழனி - pazhani, Tam.). See sep. title.——*Pychee* (പഴശ്ശി - pazhashshi, Mal.). From (pazham, mal. fruit + shrí, san. prosperity). Amshom; Malabar dist., Cottayam tal.; pop. 5,724; lat. 11° 54′; long. 75° 38′; from Calicut N.N.W. 46 miles; from Tellicherry N.E. 12 miles; from the sea E. 17 miles. Seat of the Pychee rajah of Cottayam, who carried on warfare against the East india company for a long time and was finally killed in 1805, his whole estate being confiscated; small fort in ruins. See vol. I, 176; II, 143, 144.

PAZHAM (फल - p'haln, *San.*; میوہ - mewah, *Hind.*; ಹಣ್ಣು - hannu, *Can.*; పండు - pandu, *Tel.*; പഴം - pazham, *Mal.*; பழம் - pazham, *Tam.*). From (pazhu, tam. to ripen) [pazha]. Fruit in the popular, not scientific sense; and generally ripe fruit, raw fruit being coy [q.v.]. Vegetables of a superior nature are often unprocurable; under such circumstances advantage is taken of the infinite variety of fruits which Southern india supplies. Fresh or boiled fruits are often substituted for a vegetable ration; very many common fruits contain citric, tartaric, oxalic, malic or other organic acid in combination with alkalies or alkaline earths and are powerfully antiscorbutic in properties. Some are useful in the raw state, others require the addition of sugar and boiling or stewing to make them palatable. Some, as the plantain [q.v.], which contains about 27 per cent. of solid matter of equal nutritive value with rice [q.v.], are useful as proper foods. On the western coast plantains enter very largely into the dietary of the people. The green plantain is usually sliced and fried in ghee [q.v.] and salt [ooppoo] added and in this condition the plantain occupies the place of the potato [q.v.] in European dietaries. The freedom of the poorer classes of the native population of the country, under ordinary conditions, from scorbutic affections may be attributed to their constant use of acid and subacid fruits.——**(1)** The following are two key-lists of the principal edible fruits of southern india whether indigenous or introduced, taking the term as defined above; further information must be traced in the glossary paragraphs through the small type cross-references at end of this volume; see also vricsham, 7, for the method of expressing the products, &c., of the plants in the dravidian languages.—"*a*" Achras sapota, sapodilla; Adansonia digitata, baobab; Ægle marmelos, bael; Alangium lamarckii, ancola; Anacardium occidentale, cashew; Ananas sativus, pine apple; Anona muricata, sour sop; Anona reticulata, bullock's heart; Anona squamosa, sweet sop; Artocarpus incisa, ratadel; Artocarpus integrifolia, bread-fruit; Artocarpus lakoocha, lakoocha; Averrhoa bilimbi, blimbing; Averrhoa carambola, coromandel gooseberry; Bauhinia vahlii, large mountain ebony; Borassus flabelliformis, palmyra; Canthium parviflorum, thorny webera; Capparis aphylla, common caper; Capparis zeylanica, ceylon caper; Carica papaya, papaw; Carissa carandas, carondah; Cephalandra indica, indian caper; Citrullus vulgaris, sweet water melon; Citrus aurantium, var. aurantium proper, sweet orange; Citrus aurantium, var. bergamia, bergamot orange; Citrus decumana, pummelow; Citrus japonica, cumquot; Citrus medica, var. acida, sour lime; Citrus medica, var. limetta, sweet lime; Citrus medica, var. limonum, lemon; Citrus medica, var. medica proper, citron; Cordia obliqua, large sebesten; Cucumis melo, common melon; Cucumis melo, var. momordica, mottled melon; Cucumis sativus, common cucumber; Cucumis trigonus, country cucumber; Cucurbita ovifera, vegetable marrow; Cucurbita pepo, common pumpkin; Cydonia vulgaris, quince; Dillenia indica, chaltah; Diospyros kaki, chinese date plum; Diospyros melanoxylon, coromandel ebony; Diospyros tomentosa, sweet gaub; Durio zibethinus, durian; Ehretia buxifolia, rough coorvitchy; Eriobotrya japonica, loquat; Eugenia aquea, red jaumoon; Eugenia jambolana, common jaumoon; Eugenia jambos, rose apple; Eugenia javanica, java jaumoon; Eugenia malaccensis, malacca jaumoon; Eugenia uniflora, barbadoes cherry; Feronia elephantum, wood apple; Ficus bengalensis, banyan; Ficus carica, european fig; Ficus racemosa, country fig; Ficus religiosa, peepul; Ficus repens, creeper fig; Flacourtia cataphracta, indian plum; Flacourtia inermis, tomi-tomi; Flacourtia montana, attack; Flacourtia ramontchi, var. sapida, ceylon plum; Flacourtia sepiaria, forest bair; Garcinia cambogia, malabar gamboge; Garcinia mangostana, mangosteen; Garcinia pedunculata, tickor; Garcinia xanthochymus, yellow mangosteen; Gardenia gummifera, decamallee; Garuga pinnata, garooga; Glycosmis pentaphylla, conjy; Grewia asiatica, falsah; Hibiscus esculentus, common bendy; Hibiscus sabdariffa, red-hemp bendy; Lagenaria vulgaris, bottle gourd; Loranthus longiflorus, gooloom; Luffa acutangula, common luffa; Luffa ægyptiaca, oil giving luffa; Lycopersicum esculentum, tomato; Maba buxifolia, neilgherry satinwood; Malpighia glabra, barbadoes cherry; Mangifera indica, mango; Memecylon edule, cassa; Mesua ferrea, nauga champak; Michelia champaca, champak; Mimusops elengi, ilanjy; Mimusops hexandra, monkey-face paulay; Mimusops kauki, edible paulay; Momordica charantia, balsam apple; Momordica dioica, balsam apple; Morus indica, indian mulberry; Musa paradisiaca, plantain; Nephelium lappaceum, rambutan; Nephelium litchi, litchy; Nephelium longana, longan; Ochrocarpus longifolius, soora poon; Olea dioica, indian olive; Olea europæa, olive; Pavetta indica, pavetta; Persea gratissima, alligator pear; Phœnix dactylifera, arabian date; Phœnix farinifera, small date; Phœnix sylvestris, wild date; Phyllanthus distichus, brazil cherry; Phyllanthus emblica, emblic myrobalan; Physalis peruviana, indian winter cherry; Pithecolobium dulce, corcapilly; Prosopis spicigera, shamee; Prunus amygdalus, almond; Prunus armeniaca, apricot; Prunus communis, bokhara plum; Prunus domestica, plum; Prunus persica, peach; Psidium guyava, guava; Psidium guyava, var. pomiferum, red guava; Psidium guyava, var. pyriferum, white guava; Punica granatum, pomegranate; Pyrus communis, pear; Pyrus malus, apple; Rhodomyrtus tomentosa, hill guava; Salvadora persica, large tooth-brush tree; Sandoricum indicum, malay red wood; Schleichera trijuga, ceylon oak; Shorea robusta, common saul; Solanum melongena, brinjaul; Solanum nigrum, indian hound's berry; Sonneratia acida, blatty; Spondias dulcis, otaheite apple; Spondias mangifera, hog plum; Sterculia balanghas, edible sterculia; Strychnos nux-vomica, poison nut; Tamarindus indica, tamarind; Terminalia citrina, citrine myrobalan; Trichosanthes anguina, common snake gourd; Trichosanthes dioica, palwal; Triphasia trifoliata, musk lime; Vitis vinifera, grape vine; Webera corymbosa, tirauna; Zizyphus jujuba, bair; Zizyphus vulgaris, sinjid.—"*b*" Alligator pear, persea; Almond, prunus; Ancola, alangium; Apple, pyrus; Apricot, prunus; Attack, flacourtia; Bael, ægle; Bair, flacourtia, zizyphus; Balsam apple, momordica; Banyan, ficus; Baobab, adansonia; Barbadoes cherry, eugenia, malpighia; Bendy, hibiscus; Blatty, sonneratia; Blimbing, averrhoa; Brazil cherry, phyllanthus; Bread fruit, artocarpus; Brinjaul, solanum; Bullock's heart, anona; Caper, capparis, cephalandra; Carondah, carissa; Cashew, anacardium; Cassa, memecylon; Chaltah, dillenia; Champak, mesua, michelia; Citron, citrus; Conjy, glycosmis; Coorvitchy, ehretia; Corcapilly, pithecolobium; Cucumber, cucumis; Cumquot, citrus; Date, phœnix; Date plum, diospyros; Decamallee, gardenia; Durian, durio; Ebony, diospyros; Falsah, grewia; Fig, ficus; Gamboge, garcinia; Garooga, garuga; Gaub, diospyros; Gooloom, loranthus; Gooseberry, averrhoa; Gourd, lagenaria; Guava, psidium, rhodomyrtus; Hog plum, spondias; Hounds' berry solanum; Ilanjy, mimusops; Jaumoon, eugenia; Lakoocha, artocarpus; Lemon, citrus; Lime, citrus; Litchy, nephelium; Longan, nephelium; Loquot, eriobotrya; Mango, mangifera; Mangosteen, garcinia; Melon, cucumis; Mountain ebony, bauhinia; Mulberry, morus; Musk lime, triphasia; Myrobalan, phyllanthus, terminalia; Oak, schleichera; Olive, olea; Orange, citrus; Otaheite apple, spondias; Palmyra, borassus; Palwal, trichosanthes; Papaw, carica; Paulay, mimusops; Peach, prunus; Pear, pyrus; Peepul, ficus; Pine apple, ananas; Plantain, musa; Plum, flacourtia, prunus; Poison nut, strychnos; Pomegranate, punica; Pummelow, citrus; Pumpkin, cucurbita; Quince, cydonia; Rambutan, nephelium; Ratadel, artocarpus; Red-wood, sandoricum; Rose

apple, eugenia ; Sapodilla, achras ; Satin-wood, maba ; Saul, shorea ; Sebesten, cordia ; Shamee, prosopis ; Sinjid, zizyphus ; Snake gourd, trichosanthes ; Soora poon, ochrocarpus ; Sour sop, anona ; Sweet sop, anona ; Tamarind, tamarindus ; Tickor, garcinia ; Tirauna, webera ; Tomato, lycopersicum ; Tomi-tomi, flacourtia ; Tooth-brush tree, salvadora ; Vegetable marrow, cucurbita ; Vine, vitis ; Water melon, citrullus ; Webera, canthium ; Winter cherry, physalis ; Wood apple, feronia.——
(2) The following are the different kinds of fruit, scientifically distinguished, with examples.—"*a*" *Aspootam* (अस्फुट - asp'huta, San.). From (a, san. negative prefix + sp'hut, san. to burst). Achene, apocarpous, dry, indehiscent, usually one-seeded ; clematis, ranunculus, rose [gool].—"*b*" *Pootam* (पुट - puta, San.). San. from (put, san. to fold). Follicle, apocarpous, dry, dehiscing by the ventral suture ; star anise [q.v.].—"*c*" *Shimby* (शिम्बी - shimbí, San. ; پهلی - phallí, Hind.). San. from (shi, san. to attenuate) ; thin cover. Legume, apocarpous, dry, dehiscing by both sutures ; pea [calauyam], indigo [q.v.].—"*d*" *Ashty* (अस्थि - asht'hi, San. ; جوز - jauz, Ar. ; تخم - tukhm, Pers. ; گٹهلی - guthlí, Hind.). Nut, properly syncarpous, dry and indehiscent, the pericarp usually hard and bony ; oak [belote].—"*e*" *Ashty palam* (अस्थिफल - asht'hip'hala, San.). San. means nut fruit. Drupe, usually apocarpus, succulent, indehiscent, and one-seeded, with the inner layer of the pericarp stony ; mango [q.v.], almond [baudam], jujube [bair].—"*f*" *Beeja palam* (बीजफल - bíjap'hala, San. ; حب - habb, Ar. ; دانه - dánah, Hind.). Berry, syncarpous, succulent, indehiscent, few or many-seeded ; coffee [q.v.], cape gooseberry [indian winter cherry], physalis [takkauly], grape [angoor].—"*g*" *Beeja coshy* (बीजकोशी - bíjakóshí, San. ; خريطه - kharítah, Ar. ; بونڈا - bondá, Hind.). Capsule, syncarpous, dry, dehiscent ; cotton [q.v.], lily [indian water-lily], camellia [tea], rhododendron [neilgherry rhododendron], trumpet flower [pauthiry].

PEACOCK (मयूर - mayúra, *San.*) [mayil]. Prefix for variegated color. Compare :—Actiniopteris dichotoma, peacock fan ; Adenanthera pavonina, peacock flower fence ; Adiantum caudatum, peacock-tailed adiantum ; Cæsalpinia pulcherrima, peacock flower ; Chloris barbata, peacock crest grass ; Michrochloa setacea, peacock grass ; Poinciana regia, peacock's pride. See gloss. paragraphs.——*Peacock fish* (मयूरमत्स्य - mayúramatsya, San. ; तदमास - tadamása, Mahr. ; مهر مچهی - mohrmaçç̧hí, Hind. ; மயில்மீன் - mayilmín, Tam.). Title from purple color of body and fins. San. from (mayúra, san. peacock + matsya, san. fish) ; beautiful fish. Mahr. means rainbow fish. Hind. from sanscrit. Tam. from (mayil, tam. peacock + mín, tam. fish). Tam. also (iyamangólá), meaning god of death + flying fish, exocætus pœcilopterus. The genus Histiophorus, xiphiidæ [macaram], acanthopterygii, teleostei, pisces [matsyam, 13], of naturalists [jantoo]. This fish is a beautiful sight in water. In calm weather, it lies sunning itself on the surface. Caught in deep water with hook and line, and when near the surface, is spread. The species best known to the natives are as follows :—"*a*" Histiophorus gladius, xiphiidæ [macaram], acanthopterygii, teleostei [matsyam, 13], of naturalists. Title otherwise Purple-finned sailor fish. Snout produced and longer than remainder of head ; stomach elongated, intestines very short not exceeding length of fish ; air-vessel in last third of abdominal cavity, consisting of two distinct lateral portions, each of which are sub-divided internally into numerous cavities ; colors body bluish-gray, dull white underneath ; dorsal fin-bright ; prussian-blue with darker spots ; other fins dusky ; common in cold season off madras, arriving about october and continuing until march.—"*b*" Histiophorus immaculatus, xiphiidæ [macaram], acanthopterygii, teleostei [matsyam, 13], of naturalists. Lateral-line at first makes very strong curve, but becomes straight above hind extremity of pectoral fin ; colors gray, dorsal and ventral blackish ; sea ; 5 feet 9 inches in length.

PEDDA (పెద్ద - pedda, *Tel.*). Great ; elder [hey, pen, per].——*Peddacaulwa* (పెద్దకాలువ - peddakálava, Tel.). Any large channel [q.v.].——*Peddacawp* (పెద్దకాపు - peddakápu, Tel.). From (above + kápu, tel. person of that caste). Headman of a village [inam]. Sanscrit, graumadhipaty, pradhaunan ; Tamul, ambalacauran, graumattaun, monigar, yejmaun ; Canarese, gowda ; Malayalam, adhicaury, praverticauran ; Teloogoo, naidoo, pedda reddy, reddy. See vol. I, 112.——*Pedda kimedy* (పెద్దకిమిడి - peddakimedi, Tel. peddakimedi *). From (pedda, tel. large + kimedi, tel. place so called). Sanscrit name (vijayanagara), meaning victory + city. Also called Vizianagram ; which distinguish from that in Vizagapatam. Zemindarry, Village ; Ganjam dist., Berhampore tahsildar's range ; pop. 31,853 ; sq. miles 592 ; lat. of village 19° 18′ ; long. 84° 30′ ; from Berhampore W. 22 miles ; from Chetterpore W.S.W. 36 miles. The southern part of the estate is well-watered and fertile. The western portion is jungly and thinly populated. North of Parlakimedy, Soorangy and Cheekaty and south of Chinna kimedy. The rajah claims descent from the ancient kings of Orissa, being a younger branch of Parlakimedy family. For origin of estate see Kimedy. He holds the Government sunnud [q.v.], for the Pedda kimedy maliahs [q.v.] a strip of country lying between the Parlakimedy and Goomsoor maliahs, which are attached to the zemindarry [q.v.], and cover an area of 377 square miles. A fort was formerly at Vijianugger. The present residence is at Digoopoody. Contains one hundred and ninety-four villages, divided into the five Mittahs [q.v.] of Kara, Adoopauda, Gopalpore, Kara khaury and Nowpada. Peshcush Rs. 23,307. Annual revenue Rs. 1,72,000. Contains trig. stations, Bodagherry [q.v.], Dhobahdhobny [q.v.], Ryegodo [q.v.].——*Peddammavauroo* (పెద్దమ్మవారు - peddammaváru, Tel.). From (above + ammaváru, tel. small-pox goddess). Small-pox. Same as Ammay [veidyan].——*Peddanna* (పెద్దన్న - peddanna, Tel.). From (above + anna, tel. brother). Hindoo 2nd or pers. name [peyar].——*Peddapoory* (పెద్దాపురం - peddápuri, Tel.). From (above + puri, san. town). A superior sort of soft sugar [q.v.], made originally at Peddapore, near Rajahmundry.——*Peddapore* (పెద్దాపురము - peddápuramu, Tel.). See sep. title.——*Peddatally* (పెద్దతల్లి - peddatalli, Tel.). From (above + talli, tel. mother). A mother's elder sister ; or the wife of a father's elder brother [bandhoo].——*Peddatandry* (పెద్దతండ్రి - peddatandri, Tel.). From (above + tandri, tel. father). A father's elder brother ; or the husband of a mother's elder sister [bandhoo].——*Pettipoly* (పెట్టపోలి - pettapóli, Tel.). From (pedda, tel. great + palli, tel. village). Native name of Nizampatam adopted by British.

PEDDAPORE (పెద్దాపురము - peddápuramu, *Tel.* peddápuram *). From (pedda, tel. great + pura, san. town) [pedda].——
(1) Talook, Godavery district. Tahsildar's pay Rs. 150. Area 993 square miles. Population 137,688. Language Teloogoo. E. centre of district. Bounded :—north by Vizagapatam district ; south by Rajahmundry and Ramchendrapooram talooks ; east by Cocanada, Pittapore, and Toony divisions ; west by Rajahmundry talook. Physical aspect rocky except under the Yelair where it is alluvial. Greater part hilly and jungly. Trade consists chiefly in jaggery [q.v.], chillies [q.v.], turmeric [country saffron], tamarinds [q.v.], cotton [q.v.], gingelly [q.v.], oil seed [yennay], and soap-nuts [q.v.] of which large quantities are produced. These are carried to Cocanada both for consumption and exportation. A kind of fine silk [puttoo] cloth and turbans [puggry] are made here. Irrigated by the Yelair and channels [q.v.] branching from it, and various tanks [q.v.]. Camping ground at Juggampett. Zemindarries :—Borrampollem, Dontamore, Juggampett, Kirlampoody, Royavaram, Veeravaram. Places of archæological interest :—Gungapollem, Jaddangy, Peddapore, Tallore, Tripatty. Principal trig. station :—Yailangye. The leading places, &c., in the talook are the following.——*Gungapollem* (గంగపాలెం - gangapálem, Tel.). From (ganga, tel. ganges + pálemu, tel. fortified village). Village ; lat. 17° 25′ ; long. 82° 05′ ; from Cocanada N.N.W. 35 miles ; from Peddapore N.N.W. 24 miles. In the hills. Cave temple with image of Veerabhadran [q.v.]. Near it is a mantapam [q.v.] and a well. Uninhabited.——*Jaddangy* (జడ్డంగి - dzaddangi, Tel.). From (dzaddu, tel. sickness + angu, tel. beauty). Zemindarry, Village ; pop. 508 ; lat. of village 17° 29′ ; long. 82° 12′ ; from Cocanada N.N.W. 37 miles ; from Peddapore N. 28 miles. Estate, like that of Totapully, formerly held on feudal tenure from the Zemindar of Peddapore, on whose behalf it was bound to provide an armed force to assist the zemindar to repel incursions from the hills. It was not brought under the Permanent settlement like other parts of the district. In a hill west of the village is a cave containing a lingam [q.v.].——*Juggampett* (జగ్గమ్మపేట - jaggammapéta, Tel. jaggammapet *). From (jaggamma, tel. proper name + péta, tel. suburb). Zemindarry town ; pop. 3,632 ; lat. 17° 10′ ; long. 82° 06′ ; from Cocanada N.W. 19 miles ; from Peddapore N.W. 8 miles. Peshcush Rs. 33,062.——*Kilrampoody* (కిర్లంపూడి - kirlampúdi, Tel. kirlampúdi *). From (kirli, tel. wrestling + púdi, tel. village). Zemindarry, Village ; pop. 3,992 ; lat. of village 17° 12′ ; long. 82° 13′ ; from Cocanada N.N.W. 18 miles ; from Peddapore N.N.E. 9 miles. Peshcush Rs. 23,282.——*Lingampurty* (లింగంపర్తి - lingamparti, Tel.). From (linga, san. symbol of shiva + parti, tel. place). Village ; pop. 2,888 ; acres 3,251 ; lat. 17° 17′ ; long. 82° 09′ ; from Cocanada N.N.W. 24 miles ; from Peddapore N. 14 miles. Has got Timmarajan tank of about a square mile in extent. This irrigates seven villages. Double crop assessment.——*Peddapore* (పెద్దాపురము - peddápuramu, Tel.). See below.——*Royavaram* (రాయవరం - ráyavaram, Tel.). From (ráya, tel. king + pura, san. town). Zemindarry village ; lat. 17° 10′ ; long. 82° 16′ ; from Cocanada N. 16 miles ; from Peddapore N.N.E. 9 miles. Peshcush Rs. 1,998.——*Tripatty* (తిరుపతి - tirupati, Tel.). From (tiru, tam. holy + pathi, tam. village). Village ; pop. 1,414 ; lat. 17° 09′ ; long. 82° 11′ ; from Cocanada N. 15 miles ; from Peddapore N. 5 miles. Twenty inscriptions, dating from A.D. 1400 to 1644. The temple belongs to the proprietor of the Veeravaram estate.——*Veeravaram* (వీరవరము - víravaramu, Tel. viravaram *). From (víra, san. hero + pura, san. town). Sanscrit name (vírapura), meaning hero + town. Zemindarry, Village ; pop. 3,095 ; lat. of village 17° 10′ ; long. 82° 11′ ; from Cocanada N.N.W. 16 miles ; from Peddapore N. 6 miles. Peshcush Rs. 26,876.——*Yailangye* (ఏలంగాయి - élangáyi, Tel.). Trig. station ; lat. 17° 03′ 23·09″ ; long. 82° 06′ 23·09″ ; height 345 feet ; from Condapully N.E. 1½ miles.——*Yelair* (ఏలేరు - éléru, Tel.). See

sep. title.——*Yeleshwaram* (ఏలేశ్వరము - éléshvaramu, Tel.). See sep. title.——**(2)** Town, Talook and District moonsif's head-quarters; Godavery dist., Peddapore tal.; pop. 13,658; acres 9,595; lat. 17° 04′; long. 82° 10′; from Cocanada N.N.W. 11 miles; from Coonavaram E.S.E. 66 miles; from Ellore E.N.E. 72 miles; from Madras N.N.E. 299 miles; from Narsapore N.N.E. 53 miles; from Rajahmundry E.N.E. 25 miles. Former head-quarters of a zemindarry now dismembered. Part of the family now hold Cotaum estate. Fort of eighteen towers in a dilapidated condition. Growing in commercial importance for jaggery [q.v.] trade.

PEELA (పీల - píla, *Tel.*). Thin or narrow.——*Peelair* (పీలేరు - píléru, Tel. pílér*). From (píla, tel. thin + éru, tel. river). Sanscrit name (piñchhánadí), meaning tail + river.—"*a*" Deputy tahsildarry, Cuddapah district. Pay Rs. 70.—"*b*" Village, Deputy tahsildar's station; Cuddapah dist., Voilpaud tal.; pop. 1,781; acres 1,437; lat. 13° 40′; long. 78° 59′; from Cuddapah S. 57 miles; from Madanapully E.N.E. 30 miles; from Madras W.N.W. 96 miles; from Sidhout S. 56 miles; from Voilpaud E. 21 miles.

PEEPUL (अश्वत्थ - ashvatt'ha, *San.*; पिंपळ - pimpala, *Mahr.*; پیپل -pípal, *Hind.*; دم پپل - dumpippal, *Dec.*; ಅರಳಿ - arali, *Can.*; ಅತ್ತಸ - attasa, *Too.*; రావిచెట్టు - rágichettu, *Tel.*; ଜରି - jari, *Oor.*; അരയാൽ - arayál, *Mal.*; බෝ - bó, *Singh.*; அரசு - arsu, *Tam.*). Title from hindostany [pan]. San. from (ashva, san. horse + st'ha, san. to stand); from the legend that badavaugny in the form of a mare resides in this tree [ashwattam]. Mahr. and Hind. from (pippala, san. the tree). Dec. from (dum, hind. tail + pippala, san. the tree). Can. from (aralu, can. to expand). Tel. from (rága, san. redness + chettu, tel. tree); from light red of tender leaves. Mal. from (arayan, mal. king + ál, mal. the banyan tree, ficus bengalensis, linn.). Tam. from (arasan, tam. king). San. also (bódhidruma), meaning knowledge tree; (chaladala), meaning having leaves in perpetual motion; (pippala), meaning protecting; (kuñjarásbana), meaning elephant's food; cf. indian olibanum; (vriksharája), meaning king of trees; (vishála), meaning broad; (shrívriksha), meaning holy tree; (gajapatra), meaning elephant's leaf; (guru), meaning heavy or adorable. Hind. also (anípípal), meaning pointed peepul, from tapering leaf. Can. also (arase), meaning king; (rangimara), meaning dyeing + tree; (rágimara); (basari). Tel. also (rávi), meaning red; (kallarávi), meaning eye + ficus religiosa, linn. Singh. also (bódhi), meaning tree of knowledge. Tam. also (náráyanam), from vishnoo's abode in it. Title otherwise Arasoo, Ashwattam, Bo tree, Holy fig, Indian aspen, Indian poplar, Poplar-leaved fig, Rauvy, Sacred fig, Vishnoo's tree, Wisdom tree. Botanically Ficus [atty] religiosa, linn., moraceæ [vricsham, 121]. Alias Urostigma religiosum. Large tree; leaves long-petioled, ovate, cordate, narrow acuminate, acumen one-third the length of the leaf, entire, or repandly undulated towards the apex; fruit-receptacles axillary, paired, sessile, depressed, size of a small cherry [q.v.], appearing in the hot season and ripening in the rainy season. Has strong resemblance in wood and foliage to poplar, especially aspen, and its leaves with their long footstalks quiver similarly; this trembling is attributed to spirits agitating each leaf. Held very sacred [poonyoshadhy]; frequently met with near pagodas [q.v.], houses and other buildings; vishnoo [q.v.] was born among the branches; siddhaurtan [q.v.] became booddha [q.v.] while seated under this tree at gayay in behar, and the identical tree is believed still to exist; the bo-tree now growing at anooraudhapoora in ceylon is said to be a branch of that at gayay. The seeds medicinally cooling and alterative; prescribed in electuary and in powder; leaves and young shoots purgative; an infusion of the bark internally in scabies; ripe fruit is laxative; a paste of powdered bark is absorbent in inflammatory swellings. Leaves and branches are good elephant [q.v.] fodder; young leaf buds and fruit eaten by men in famine times. Birds are fond of fruit, and drop the seeds in cracks of buildings, where they vegetate, occasioning great damage if not removed in time; silk-worms eat the leaves [puttoo]. Commonly planted along road-sides [shaulay]; birdlime is made from the glutinous juice from the stem, fibre [naur] from bark; leaf forms one of the ingredients in certain dyes [shauyam]. Wood white, light and very perishable, rather coarse-grained and brittle and not durable; only fit for fuel, and bad even for that; one however of the nine kinds of wood [samit] used in burnt offerings [homam].——*Flowering peepul* (பூவரசு - púvarasu, Tam.). Same as Portia.——*Hill peepul* (لتا دومر - latádumr, Hind.; కొండరావి - kondarávi, Tel.). Title from habitat. Hind. from (latá, san. creeper + udumbara, san. fig tree, ficus glomerata, miq.). Tel. from (konda, tel. hill + rávi, tel. ficus religiosa, linn.). Botanically Ficus [atty] vagans, r., moraceæ [vricsham, 121]. Shrubby, scandent, rooting to other trees; leaves long-petioled, cordate, villous beneath; fruit-receptacles axillary, paired or solitary, long peduncled, nearly globular, size of a nutmeg [jautikye].——*Wild peepul* (प्लक्ष - plaksha, San.; काडपिंपळु - kádapimpalu, Conc.; جنگلی پیپل - janglípípal, Hind. and Dec.; ಕಾಡುಅಶ್ವತ್ಥ - káduashvatt'ha, Can.; ಕಾಡುಅತ್ತಸ - kádu-attasa, Too.; കല്ലരയാൽ - kallarayál, Mal.). Title from habitat. San. from (plush, san. to burn). Conc. from (káda, conc. forest + pimpala, conc. the peepul tree). Hind. from (janglí, hind. wild + pippala, san. ficus religiosa, linn.). Can. from (kádu, can. wild + ashvatt'ha, san. the peepul tree). Too. from (kátu, too. wild + attasa, too. the peepul tree). Mal. from (kal, mal. stone + arayál, mal. peepul tree, ficus religiosa, linn.). Conc. also (kádaashvatt'hu), meaning wild peepul tree. Botanically Ficus [atty] arnottiana, miq., moraceæ [vricsham, 121]. Alias Urostigma arnottianum. Tree or shrub; leaves 3–8 inches; nerves ten to fifteen pairs, reticulations lucid, minute; petiole 2–6 inches; stipules ovate-lanceolate, ½–1 inch, caducous, reddish-brown when dried; male flowers few, near the mouth of the receptacles, sessile; sepals three, loose, inflated, broadly acuminate, much larger than the single small ovate-rotund subsessile anther; gall and female flower undistinguishable except by contents of ovary, sessile or pedicelled; perianth lax, toothed, completely investing the ovary; style elongate; stigma flat.

PEER (پیر - pír, *Pers.*). Old. A respectful address amongst Mahomedans. Taken as alam; as Peer khan, alam + alaumat [ism]. Common title for those who by miracles and an ascetic life have established a reputation for sanctity. After the death of such saints and divines, it is usual for their followers to erect a shrine over their graves [durgah] and to light them up on Thursdays [shamba]. All fakeers [q.v.] have originated from Chaurpeer or four spiritual guides, and Chowda khanwaudey or fourteen households, the following being the connection. The first peer was Hazrat moortezah ally [ally]; he invested with the caliphate or deputyship the second peer Cauja hassan basry; the latter constituted as his deputies the third peer Cauja habeeb e ajmy and the fourth peer Abd ool wauhid bin zaeede coofy. See vol. 1 (96). From the third peer have descended nine households. From the fourth peer have sprung five households.——**(1)** Descendants of the Chaurpeer met with in this country are as follows.—"*a*" Cawdiriya, alias Baunwah, sprung from Syed abdool cawder jeelauny [q.v.], surnamed Peer e dastgheer [q.v.]; his disciples [mooreed] assuming his name call themselves Cawdiriya; their dress is white, green, or colored with red ochre [cauvy].—"*b*" Chishtiya, followers of Cauja banda nawauz [q.v.], the long-ringletted. These fakeers [q.v.] specially cultivate vocal music; they dress as they please.—"*c*" Shoottauriya, descendants of Shah abdoollah shoottar e nauk; their dress is similar to Cawdiriya.—"*d*" Tabacautiya or Madauriya. These are followers of Zinda shah madaur [q.v.]. They generally wear a puggry [q.v.], jauma [q.v.], doputta [q.v.], all black; also a loonghee [q.v.] and a black neck-cloth.—"*e*" Malang fakeers are descendants of Jamman juttee, a follower of Zinda shah madaur. They resemble the gosain [q.v.], and wander in deserts or on mountains and visit the shrines of reputed saints. Wherever they sit down they burn dhoony or smoke fire and sometimes rub its ashes over their bodies.—"*f*" Rafayee or Goorzmaur originated from Syed ahmed cabeer; they strike the point of an iron club or goorz against their breasts or into their eyes, and strike blows at their backs with a sword.—"*g*" Jalaulya or followers of Syed jalaul ood deen bokhaury; their dress generally consists of a cloth of wool or thread of various colors on the head, a goloobund, loonghee [q.v.], or lungooty [q.v.]; in the hand they carry a sontah or club.—"*h*" Soohaugiya, descended from Moosa soohaug whose name they bear, are generally musicians.—"*i*" Nakshbundiya are followers of Cauja baha ood deen nakshbund. They carry a lighted lamp [chiraugh] in their hands, and go about at night singing religious verses; bystanders drop pice [q.v.] into their lamps; they are exorcists.——**(2)** *Peeraun* (پیران - pírán, Hind.). An assignment of land for the support of tomb of a saint [durgah].——*Peeraun e peer* (پیران پیر - piránipír, Hind.). Saint of saints; epithet of Sheikh abdool cawder [q.v.] jeelauny [q.v.].——*Peer e dastgheer* (پیر دستگیر - píridastgír, Hind.). Otherwise Abdool cawder [q.v.] jeelauny; esteemed the chief among walees and was a great performer of miracles. The disciples [mooreed] and followers of his household are very numerous. The tomb is at Bagdad. He was born 1078, died 1175. Fautihas [q.v.] are offered in his name every Mahomedan month [maheena], especially the fourth [dastgheer].——*Peermaid* (പീരുമേട് - pírumétu, Mal.). From (pír, hind. saint + métu, mal. plateau), once residence of a mahomedan saint. Plateau, Hill station; Travancore state, Cottayam division; Chungacherry tal.; lat. 9° 33′; long. 77° 01′; height 3,000 feet. Europeans resort here for health. Centre of coffee [q.v.] planting industry. Connected with low countries on Travancore and British sides by good roads [hill-station].——*Peer o moorshid* (پیرومرشد - pírwamurshid, Pers.). Saint and teacher. A respectful salutation.

PEERK (பீர்க்கு - pírkku, *Tam.*). From (pír, tam. pale green). Same as Luffa.

PEETAM (पीत - píta, *San.*). Yellow.——*Peelah* (پیلا - pílá, Hind.). Yellow. Plant first term, often joining two genera. Ex., where transl. is of second term:—Argemone mexicana (píládhatúrá), datura; Celosia cristata (pílámurghá), cock; Cochlospermum gossypium (pílikapás), gossypium herbaceum; Euphorbia tortilis (pílisendh), euphorbia tirucalli; Michelia nilagirica (pílácbampá), michelia champaca; Thalictrum foliolosum (pílíjarí), root; Thevetia nereifolia (píláganer), nerium odorum, (pílephúlkáganer), flower + nerium odorum; Wedelia calendulacea (pílábhangrá), eclipta alba. See gloss. paragraphs. ——*Peetaumbaran* (पीताम्बर - pítámbara, San.). From (above + ambara, san. cloth). Vishnoo [q.v.].——*Peet saul* (پیتسال - pítasála, Hind.). Means yellow shorea. Same as Common vengay.

PEHIMBIA (පෙහෙඹිය - pehembiya, *Singh.*; காட்டுப்பூவரசு - káttuppúvarasu, *Tam.*). Title from singhalese. Tam. from (kádu, tam. forest + púvarasu, tam. thespesia populnea, linn.). Title otherwise Fern-leaved thespesia, Wild thespesia. Botanically Filicium decipiens, thw., burseraceæ [vricsham, 35]. Alias Pteridophyllum decipiens; Rhus decipiens. Leaves unequally pinnated; rachis interruptedly winged; wings tapering at the base, truncated at the apex; leaflets narrow-oblong, tapering at the base quite entire; panicles axillary, shorter than the leaves; branches angled, spreading horizontally; ovary ovate; styles shortly three-cleft at the apex; flowers greenish white. Very elegant fern-leaved tree, bright green compound leaves. Timber is strong and valuable. No other common species here.

PEI (ಪೈ - pai, *Can.*). Means excellence. A Concany title. Hindoo third name [peyar].

PEIDASH (پیدایش - paidáish, *Hind.*). From persian, meaning to become public. Produce.

PEIDY (పైడి - paidi, *Tel.*). Gold. Plant first term. Ex., where transl. is of second term:—Cassia sophera (paiditangédu), cassia auriculata; Ficus glomerata (paidichettu), tree; Gossypium barbadense, var. acuminatum (paidipatti), gossypium herbaceum. See gloss. paragraphs.

PEIMASH (پیمایش - paimáish, *Hind.*). From (paímúdan, pers. to measure). The survey of lands; generally applied to the old native surveys.——*Kole peimash* (കോൽപൈമാശി - kól-paimáshi, Mal.). From (kól, mal. measuring rod). Old survey in Malabar at beginning of century by actual measurement in cawnies [q.v.] and goolies [q.v.]. All other Peimashes in that district had been merely inspections without measurement. The result of the Kole peimash was embodied in what are known in the district as the Hindoovy or Mahratta accounts. It refers to wet lands alone.——*Nokpeimash* (നോക്കിപ്പൈമാശി - nókkip-paimáshi, Mal.). From (nókku, mal. to see). Measurement by inspection, usual under native governments.——*Peimashy compass* (پیمایشی کمپاس - paimáyashikampás, Hind.). Native term for Trigonometrical survey. See vol. I, 112.

PEIRA (పయర - payara, *Tel.*). Means soft. Cool zephyr wind. The crops cultivated on Coromandel coast [q.v.] under the north-east monsoon [q.v.]; same as Parvam [q.v.] in Tamul districts; sown in November and reaped in March or April.

PEN (పెను - penu, *Tel.*). Large [hey, pedda, per].——*Penjera* (పెంజెర - penjera, Tel.). From (penu, tel. large + jerri, tel. a centipede). The Daboia snake [chain viper]. The natives recognize the following; they cannot be scientifically distinguished:—Pedda penjera, large daboia; Pooly penjera, tiger daboia; Potta penjera, big-belly daboia; Racta penjera, red daboia; Tootch penjera, small daboia.——*Pennagaram* (பென்னாகரம் - pennágaram, Tam.). From (penu, tel. large + nagara, san. town).—"*a*" Deputy tahsildarry, Salem district. Pay Rs. 70.—"*b*" Village, Deputy tahsildar's station, Sub-divisional head-quarters; Salem dist., Dharmapoory tal.; pop. 2,230; acres 192; lat. 12° 08′; long. 77° 56′; from Dharmapoory S.W. 18 miles; from Madras W.S.W. 172 miles; from Namcull N.N.W. 66 miles; from Oossoor S. 42 miles; from Salem N.N.W. 37 miles; from Tripatore S.W. 52 miles; from Yercaud N.W. 33 miles. To the south-west is Ponautchy bett and on the west and north-west are Gootroyen hills and the Melagherries, while Pikkily mullay lies to the north-east. Owing to its situation in a hollow and to its proximity to the jungles, it is unhealthy; and has been for many years in a declining state. Old Shiva [q.v.] temple. The fort, now in ruins, was a border fortress a hundred years ago, and, like Palcode, is often mentioned in the history of the wars with Mysore. On the glacis is the tomb of Captain Turing, who died in 1793. Two miles south is a Vishnoo [q.v.] temple with inscription. Trade chiefly in timber, jungle produce, and grain.——*Pennair* (ಪೆಂನೊಳೆಯು - pennoleyu, Can.; పెన్నేరు - pennéru, Tel.; பெண்ணையாறு - pennaiyáru, Tam. pennér*). From (penu, tel. great + éru, tel. river). Tam. also (pennai), meaning palmyra river; name common to northern and southern rivers; this may be the real indigenous derivation of title. Compare pauny or toddy as originating paundy the kingdom and porny the river. Greek name τύνδις ποταμός. TYNNA in capitals taken as an error for ΠΥΝΝΑ. But it must be mentioned that τύνδις was formerly identified with the Kistna [q.v.]. Sanscrit name (pinákiní), meaning shiva with his bow called pinaucam; from a tradition that water was raised by a shaft from shiva's bow at the site of its source; title always Pinaukiny in Mysore. Sanscrit name also (uttarapinákiní), meaning northern pinaukiny, as distinguished from (dakshinapinákiní), the southern pennair [ponniaur]. The northern pennair rises, in lat. 13° 38′; long. 77° 43′ in the Chenna keshava hill N.W. of Nundidroog. It derives its earliest supply from a square stone tank in the centre of the ruined fort of Chundradroog. The tank overflows in the rainy season, and the redundant water, falling into a deep cleft in the rock, issues in a stream from the side of the mountain about 200 yards lower down. This source fails during the dry season. The stream flowing to the north-west for 30 miles through Colaur district then crosses the northern boundary of the territory of Mysore, and takes a northerly course for 95 miles to Ooderpidroog in Anantapore district, where it makes an abrupt turn to the east. Passing by the town of Tadpatry, it is joined by the Chitrauvaty and the two pass through the narrow gorge of Gundicote into Cuddapah district. It there passes through the talooks Jummalmadoogoo, Proddootore, Cuddapah and Sidhout. It receives at Camalaupooram the Coondair, which has its source in the mountains on the north-east; about one mile from this village, and close to Appayyapully, it is also joined by the Paupughny coming from the southward. At Audinimmoypully, 10 miles from Cuddapah, the Kurnool-Cuddapah canal is conveyed across the river by an aqueduct. The river enters Nellore district through a gorge in the Eastern ghauts [q.v.] at Somashila or Someshwaram in Atmacore talook 285 miles from its source. It flows in an irregular easterly direction through Atmacore and Nellore talooks for 70 miles, dividing the district into two unequal portions, being joined by the Boggair on its left bank at Colagotla and by the Beerapair at Sangam. It falls into the sea by several mouths at Ootcore, in lat. 14° 36′, long. 80° 13′, 15 miles, below Nellore town. Total length 355 miles. Area of drainage basin [nadee] 20,500 square miles. Principal tributaries are the Paupughny, Chitrauvaty and Cheyair on the right and Coondaur on the left. Receives its first supply during July, August and September when the south-west monsoon [q.v.] falls in the western districts. Runs mostly in October and November. In flood for about sixty days in the year. For nine months annually the bed is in most places nearly dry. During the north-east monsoon [q.v.] however the volume of water at Nellore town is 800 yards wide and 30 feet deep. The bed is sandy in the lower part of the course. Higher up it is rocky with deep pools well stocked with fish, which are swept down by the inundations to the tanks fed by the river. The stream is useless for navigation, being liable to sudden freshes, one of which carried away an important railway bridge in 1874. There is a Tamul proverb:—வெண்ணெய் உருக்கிறதற்குள்ளே பெண்ணை ஆற்றிலே தண்ணீர் வருகிறது—"ere butter can melt, freshes appear in the pennair." The water however is largely utilized for purposes of irrigation. In Colaur district in Mysore it is estimated that about 85 per cent. of the total drainage is intercepted by means of tanks [q.v.] and minor channels [q.v.]. The Kurnool canal has been constructed to connect the North pennair with the Kistna river. An anicut at Nellore erected in 1855 and repaired in 1866 has two main artificial channels to Kistnapatam and to Sarwapully in Goodoor talook. There is another and more recent irrigation anicut at Sangam, 20 miles to the west of Nellore, to irrigate lands on the northern bank of the river [aur]. Another anicut [q.v.] designed at Somashila. For accounts of Irrigation works see vol. I, 398 and 402. An arc of slightly raised ground may be observed to extend from Iskapully, having Nellore for its centre and touching the old coast line again near Goodoor; the Pennair has gradually reclaimed from the sea the whole area included within this semi-circle. Pennair beacon is a Trig. station in lat. 14° 34′ 58·24″; long. 80° 14′ 0·90″; from Moodivartypoliem N.E. 6 miles; from Nellore N.E. 17 miles; from the sea W. ¼ mile.——*Pennamurry* (పెన్నమర్రి - pennamarri, Tel.). From (penu, tel. great + marri, tel. banyan tree, ficus bengalensis, linn.). One of the old talooks of North arcot district.——*Penoo* (పెను - penu, Tel.). Great [pedda, per]. Prefix in place names; as Penoocondah, meaning great hill.——*Penoocondah* (పెనుకొండ - penukonda, Tel.). See sep. title.——*Ponniaur* (ಪೆಂನೊಳೆಯು - pennoleyu, Can.; పెన్నేరు - pennéru, Tel.; பெண்ணையாறு - pennaiyáru, Tam. ponniár*). Title meaning gold river by corruption [pon]. Can. and tel. mean large river. Tam. really from (pennai, tam. a palmyra tree + áru, tam. river). In old tamul the river is simply pennay. Sanscrit name (dakshinapinákiní), means south + pinaukiny, river of that name; also (pápaghni), meaning sin-destroyer [pennair]. Otherwise Cheyyaur or Yenautt cheyyaur meaning from yenaud or trichinopoly and tanjore. Also called Southern pennair. River; Salem and South arcot districts. Rises in Chenna keshava hill, east of Nundidroog, in lat. 13° 24′; long. 77° 44′; close to where the Northern pennair rises. Receiving the redundant water of series of tanks [q.v.] at that place, it flows circuitously, but generally south, for 55 miles, through Bangalore district to Mootanhully, where it crosses the south-eastern frontier of Mysore into the Carnatic [q.v.], through which it holds a south-easterly course of 190 miles, and falls into the Bay of Bengal, in lat. 11° 45′, long. 79° 51′ a mile north of Fort St. David. For some distance it forms the boundary between Cuddalore and Villoopooram talooks. It is sacred and its banks are studded with Shiva temples. Total length, 245 miles; area of drainage basin [nadee], 6,200 square miles. Gold [pon] is found in its sands, in its passage through the Carnatic [q.v.].

PEN (പെൺ - pen, *Mal.*; பெண் - pen, *Tam.*). Female.——*Pennaul* (பெண்ணாள் - pennál, Tam.). From (above + ál, tam. person). Laboring women of a village employed in transplanting, cutting, gathering, sifting, winnowing the crops, &c. Pennaul ary is the sheaf distributed to them as perquisite.——*Penvazhy* (പെൺവഴി - penvazhi, Mal.). From (above + vazhi, mal. way). The female line in questions of descent of rights or property [maroomakkatoyem]. Cf. Aunvazhy and Makkatoyem.

PENANG (پيناڠ - pinang, *Malay*). Means areca palm. Title otherwise Prince of wales island, Pulo-penang. Island in lat. 5° 25′ N.; long. 100° 19′ E. Granted by king of Qedah to Captain Light in 1785 as marriage portion of king's daughter whom he married; but subsequently sold to the British in 1800. See vol. I, 31.——*Penang lawyer* (پيناڠ ليار - pinángliyar, Malay). Malay means wild areca catechu, linn. Botanically Licnala acutifida, mart., palmaceæ [vriesham, 149]. A small fan-leaved palm [taur], native of penang; stems dressed and polished give walking-sticks.——*Penang palm* (پيناڠ - pinang, Malay). Areca. Varieties in malay are:—(pinángbulan), moon areca; (pinángrándah), lowly areca; and (pinángwangi), fragrant areca.

PENCHALCONDAH (పెంచెలుకొండ - penchelukonda, *Tel.*). From (penutsu, tel. intertwined + konda, tel. hill); from the idol represented by two pieces of stone worked as twining round each other. Hill; Nellore dist., Raupore tal.; lat. 14° 17′; long. 79° 28′; height 3,635 feet; from Nellore W.S.W. 39 miles; from Raupore N.W. 9 miles. Over the village of Calavoy on the south bank of the Pennair. Marked by ripple marks or indentations denoting the line of an ancient sea beach. The loftiest hill in the district forming part of the Veligondas. Vishnoo [q.v.] temple in Penchalcona or the valley at the foot of the hill a little elevated. Worship celebrated every Saturday, and at the annual festival in May and June. Pilgrims come from Nellore, Cuddapah, and Kurnool. Umbrellas of paper and pith are presented at the shrine. The Candlair takes its rise here as a waterfall [aroovy]. The summit of the hill commands a view of much of the Cuddapah district. During the festival people ascend and cross over the hill to the other side as an act of devotion. Sanitarium [hill-station] for Nellore might be made here.

PENOOCONDAH (పెనుకొండ - penukonda,* *Tel.*). From (penu. tel. great + konda, tel. hill) [pen].——**(1)** Talook. Anantapore district. Tahsildar's pay Rs. 150. Area 647 square miles. Population 80,272. Language Teloogoo. S. centre of district. Boundaries:—north Dharmavaram talook, east Cadiry talook of Cuddapah, west Pauvoogada talook of Mysore, south Hindoopore talook. A hilly talook, and part quite unfit for cultivation. The principal ranges of hills are those near Penoocondah and those on the eastern frontier of the district near Bookkapatam and Vengalamcheroo. There is no black soil in the talook; mixed and gravelly soils predominate. The principal crops raised are cholum [q.v.], and horse-gram [q.v.], and on the irrigated land rice [q.v.], sugar-cane [q.v.], and to a limited extent, raggy [q.v.]. The produce is sent for sale to the markets at Hindoopore and Madaksira. Agricultural tract traversed by Hindoopore extension railway. The river Pennair flows along the western frontier of the talook, past the town of Roddam, and the Chitrauvaty goes through the east of the talook and passes close to Bookkapatam, where it is dammed up by a strong bund [q.v.] connecting two low ranges of hills so as to form the Bookkapatam tank. There are in the talook 173 tanks [q.v.], 70 river channels [q.v.], 115 spring channels [q.v.], and 2,703 wells. Seven tanks [q.v.] irrigate an area of more than 300 acres. The largest are those at Bookkapatam, Calipy, Cholmary and Roddam. Camping grounds are at Goottoor, Penoocondah. Places of archæological interest:—Bookkapatam, Calipy, Cuppalabunda, Dooddebunda, Goottoor, Moonimadoogoo, Nelacottah, Nulloor, Paumdoorty, Pedapully, Penoocondah, Roddam, Yerramunchy. Principal trig. stations:—Bommasamoodram, Mullapacondah. The leading places, &c., in the talook are the following.——*Bommasamoodram* (బొమ్మసముద్రము - bommasamudramu, Tel.). From (bommayya, tel. proper name + samudra, san. ocean). Trig. station: lat. 14° 00′ 00·00″; long. 77° 33′ 00·00″; from Anantapore S. 46 miles; from Nangalore W.S.W. 1½ miles; from Penoocondah S.W. 8 miles.——*Bookkapatam* (బుక్కపట్నము - bukkapatnamu, Tel.). See sep. title.——*Calipy* (కలిపి - kalipi, Tel.). Village; pop. 1,461; acres 5,812; lat. 13° 59; long. 77° 29′; from Anantapore S.S.W. 48 miles; from Penoocondah W.S.W. 12 miles. Contains a tank, and three temples. Two of these in ruins. On the Pennair.——*Chitrauvaty* (చిత్రావతి - chitrávati, Tel.). See sep. title.——*Cholmary* (చోళమర్రి - chólémarri, Tel.). From (chóla, tel. the chola ruler + madi, tel. field). Village; pop. 817; acres 4,313; lat. 14° 03′; long. 77° 30′; from Anantapore S.S.W. 44 miles; from Penoocondah W.S.W. 9 miles. Contains a tank.——*Cottacheroo* (కొత్తచెరువు - kottacheruvu, Tel.). From (kotta, tel. new + cheruvu, tel. tank). Sanscrit name (anantaságara), meaning boundless ocean. Village; pop. 3,794; acres 3,754; lat. 14° 11′; long. 77° 49′; from Anantapore S.S.E. 35 miles; from Penoocondah E.N.E. 14 miles. Situated at the western end of Bookkapatam tank. Has a car festival [bookkapatam].——*Cottacote* (కొత్తకోట - kottakóta, Tel.). From (kotta, tel. new + kóta, tel. fort). Village; pop. 1,787; acres 26,739; lat. 14° 14′; long. 77° 59′; from Anantapore S.E. 37 miles; from Penoocondah E.N.E. 25 miles. Surrounded by wooded hills.——*Goottoor* (గుట్టూరు - guttúru, Tel.). From (gutta, tel. hill + úru, tel. village). Village; pop. 1,885; acres 4,877; lat. 14° 11′; long. 77° 41′; from Anantapore S. 34 miles; from Penoocondah N.N.E. 8 miles. On Hindoopore extension railway line and on Bangalore high road. Glass bangles [gauzoo] are made.——*Moonimadoogoo* (మునిమడుగు - munimadugu, Tel.). From (muni, san. sage + madugu, tel. pool). Village; pop. 1,373; acres 9,731; lat. 14° 11′; long. 77° 42′; from Anantapore S. 34 miles; from Dharmavaram S.S.W. 17 miles; from Penoocondah N. 8 miles. Has a diamond [vajram] mine not now worked.——*Mullapacondah* (మల్లప్పకొండ - mallappakonda, Tel.). From (mallappa, tel. proper name + konda, tel. hill). Trig. station; lat. 14° 15′ 05·57″; long. 77° 51′ 38·65″; height 3,092 feet; from Anantapore S.S.E. 33 miles; from Mylasamoodram E. 3 miles; from Penoocondah N.E. 20 miles.——*Nulloor* (నల్లూరు - nallúru, Tel.). From (nalla, can. good + úru, can. village). Village; pop. 669; acres 3,802; lat. 14° 03′; long. 77° 29′; from Anantapore S.S.W. 45 miles; from Penoocondah W.S.W. 10 miles. Contains a tank and a channel dug from Pennair.——*Paumdoorty* (పాముదుర్తి - pámudurti, Tel.). From (pámu, tel. snake + durti, tel. village). Village; pop. 3,396; acres 8,839; lat. 14° 16′; long. 78° 01′; from Anantapore S.E. 37 miles; from Penoocondah E.N.E. 28 miles. Fine breed of cattle [maud] in this town and some of the neighbouring villages. Ruined poligar [q.v.] fort. The poligar was deprived of office by Sir Thomas Munro. His descendant is the village headman [peddacaup].——*Pedapully* (పెదపల్లె - pedapalle, Tel.). From (peda, tel. hinder + palle, tel. village). Village; pop. 1,040; acres 8,902; lat. 14° 04′; long. 77° 49′; from Anantapore S.S.E. 43 miles; from Penoocondah E. 13 miles. Chitrauvaty enters Penoocondah talook at this place.——*Pennair* (పెన్నేరు - pennéru, Tel.). See sep. title.——*Penoocondah* (పెనుకొండ - penukonda, Tel.). See below.——*Roddam* (రొద్దము - roddamu, Tel.). See sep. title.——*Sidrampore* (సిద్ధారాంపురము - siddárámpuramu, Tel.). From (siddharáma, san. proper name + pura, san. town). Village; pop. 1,892; acres 9,598; lat. 14° 17′; long. 77° 56′; from Anantapore S.E. 33 miles; from Penoocondah N.E. 24 miles. Among wooded hills.——*Talamarla* (తలమర్ల - talamarla, Tel.). From (tala, tel. head + mára, san. killing); murder village; pop. 2,043; acres 11,146; lat. 14° 12′; long. 77° 46′; from Anantapore S.S.E. 33 miles; from Penoocondah N.E. 12 miles. Tradition ascribes the name of the village to a sanyausy [q.v.], who having been officially tortured expired with a curse against the life of any official who halted there. No Hindoo official will stay in the village.——*Vengalamcheroo* (వెంగళమ్మచెరువు - vengalammacheruvu, Tel.). From (vengalamma, tel. proper name + cheruvu, tel. tank). Village; pop. 1,407; acres 11,225; lat. 14° 09′; long. 77° 54′; from Anantapore S.S.E. 39 miles; from Penoocondah E.N.E. 18 miles. Among wooded hills.——**(2)** Town, fort, mountain, divisional and talook head-quarters; Anantapore dist., Penoocondah tal.; pop. 6,363; acres 16,209; lat. 14° 05′; long. 77° 38′; from Anantapore S. 41 miles; from Bellary S.S.E. 86 miles; from Gooty S. 71 miles; from Madras W.N.W. 195 miles. On the Hindoopore extension railway. Formerly the capital of a powerful Hindoo dynasty. Numerous large wells, temples, and ruins attest its former greatness. After the defeat of the Hindoos in 1564 at Talicote [q.v.], they fled to this place from Vijianugger [q.v.], but were afterwards dispossessed by Hyder ally's dependents, who converted some of the finest temples into mosques [musjid]. The town is strongly fortified and commands the passes up to the Mysore plateau. The hill has a bungalow [q.v.] on the summit. The old palace, formerly known as the Gunga mahaul [q.v.], is used for the District moonsif's court. Outside the fort are a Mahomedan suburb and some new public cutcherries [q.v.]. A Mahomedan festival called Baba oors [q.v.] is held in March or April, at which Mahomedans from long distances attend. Good grapes [angoor] are grown in the fort. There are two Jeina [q.v.] temples in the town, in one of which worship is still performed. In a recess at the north gateway of the fort is a colossal figure of Hanooman [q.v.].

PENTA (పెంట - penta, *Tel.*). Mound. Rubbish. Suffix in place names; as Wonipenta, meaning mound in the forest.——*Pentacote* (పెంటకోట - pentakóta, Tel.). From (penta, tel. heap + kóta, san. fort). Village, Port; Vizagapatam dist., Sarwasiddhy tal.; pop. 1,737; lat. 17° 17′; long. 82° 39′; from Madras N.E. 320 miles; from Ooppauda N.E. 23 miles; from Vizagapatam S.W. 52 miles; from Wattauda S.W. 19 miles; from Yellamanchily S.S.W. 24 miles. At the mouth of a considerable stream, and at the extremity of a road to the interior. A bar closes the mouth of the river during fine season and a wide stretch of marsh and sand impedes the landing of goods. Temple built 600 years ago and an old fort. The manufacture of salt [ooppoo] has been discontinued.——*Pentapaud* (పెంటపాడు - pentapádu, Tel.). From (penta, tel. rubbish + pádu, tel. village).—"*a*" Deputy tahsildarry, Godavery district. Pay Rs. 70.—"*b*" Government agrahauram, Village, Deputy tahsildar's head-quarters; Godavery dist., Tanookoo tal.; pop. 985;

acres 1,567; lat. 16° 46′; long. 81° 33′; from Cocanada W.S.W. 48 miles; from Coonavaram S.S.E. 57 miles; from Ellore E.N.E. 27 miles; from Madras N.N.E. 264 miles; from Narsapore N.N.W. 25 miles; from Rajahmundry S.W. 23 miles; from Tanookoo W. 12 miles. Ruined temple. Large weekly fair.

PEPPER (पिप्पली - pippalí, *San.*). Title from sanscrit through arabic. San. from (prí, san. to nourish). Greek πέπερι. Botanically the Piper genus, piperaceæ [vricsham, 125]. Climbing shrubs with alternate stalked leaves. The species best known to the natives are :—betel [betel pepper], chaba [chaab pepper], cubeba [cubeb pepper], longum [long pepper], nigrum [black pepper]. Other s. indian species indigenous or naturalized are :—arborescens, argyrophyllum, attenuatum, sylvestre, trioicum, wightii.——**(1)** *Pepper nangay* (மிளகுநங்கை - milagunangai, Tam.). Same as Common nangay.——*Pepper rat* (मरीचमूषिक - maríchamúsnika, San.; ಮೆಣಸಿಲಿ - menaseli, Can.; മുളകെലി - mulakeli, Mal.; மிளகெலி - milageli, Tam.). Title from its attacks on pepper vine. San. from (marícha, san. pepper, piper nigrum, linn. + múshika san. rat). Can. from (menasu, can. pepper + ili, can. rat). Mal. from (mulaku, mal. pepper + eli, mal. rat). Tam. from (milagu, tam. pepper + eli, tam. rat). Title otherwise Long-tailed spiny mouse. Platacanthomys lasiurus, muridæ, rodentia, mammalia [sastanam, 17], of naturalists [jantoo]. Is a genus distinct from ordinary rats [ely] and mice [shoondely]. These at first sight resemble dormice. General color a somewhat light rufescent brown; under fur paler. On the forehead and crown, where the hair is very full, the color is more rufescent; whiskers chiefly black; lower parts dull or subdued white. The hairs on the tail darker than the body color, infuscated, except at the tip of the tail, where they are dull white, forming a conspicuous pale tail tip. Found in the hill ranges of Western ghauts, of South malabar, and also in Cochin and Travancore. The hill-people call them the pepper-rat, from their destroying large quantities of ripe pepper. Anjely [wild jack] and jack fruit [common jack] are also subject to their ravages. Large numbers of the Caryota palm [bastard sago palm] are found in the hills, and toddy [q.v.] is collected from them; these rats or dormice often eat through the covering of the pot as suspended and get in.——**(2)** *Betel pepper* (नागवल्ली - nágavallí, San.; पानवेल - pánavéla, Mahr.; पान - pána, Conc.; تنبول - tambol, Ar. and Pers.; پان - pán, Hind. and Dec.; سرح - sirih, Malay; ವಿಳ್ಳೆದೆಲೆ - villedele, Can.; ಬಚ್ಚಿರೆ - baççire, Too.; తమలపాకు - tamalapáku, Tel.; ପାନ୍ନ - pánno, Oor.; വെറ്റില - vettila, Mal.; බුලත් - bulat, Singh.; வெற்றிலை - vettilai, Tam.). Title from malayalam through portuguese. San. from (náka, san. heaven + vallí, san. creeper); heavenly creeper, supposed to be introduced into earth by arjoonan [snake-like mountain ebony]. Mahr. from (pána, mahr. betel + véla, mahr. creeper). Conc. from (parna, san. leaf). Ar. from (támbúlí, san. the plant). Hind. like mahratta. Can. from (ville, can. betel + ele, can. leaf). Tel. from (tamalamu, tel. chewing betel nuts + áku, tel. leaf). Mal. from (verum, mal. mere + ila, mal. leaf). Tam. from (vettu, tam. bare + ilai, tam. leaf). San. also (támbúlí), meaning causing exhaustion; (bhujangavallí), meaning serpent creeper; (parna), meaning leaf; (támbúlavallí), meaning betel vine. Conc. also (p'hodipána). Hind. also (nágbel), meaning serpent creeper. Can. also (vílyadaballi), meaning betel + creeper; (eleballi), meaning leaf creeper; (vílya). Tel. also (kammérákn), meaning burning + leaf, from the taste of leaf. Greek φύλλον μαλάβαθρον [malabathrum]. Title otherwise Betel-leaf vine, Betel vine, Malabar leaf, Paun vine, Tambool, Vettilay. Botanically Piper [pepper] betel, linn., piperaceæ [vricsham, 125]. Alias Chavica betel. Chavica is properly sanscrit for chaab pepper. Shrubby, scandent, rooting, branches striated; leaves membranaceous, or the adult ones coriaceous, shining above, glabrous on both sides; the inferior ones ovate, broadly cordate, equal-sided; slightly unequally cordate, or rounded at the base, five to six-nerved; catkins peduncled; male ones long, slender, patulous or deflexed; female deflexed, shorter, long-peduncled. Similar in habit of growth to the piper nigrum, linn. [black pepper]; stems shrubby, much branched running along the ground, or climbing to a great height, throwing out roots from the joints; leaves 4 to 7 inches long, glabrous; bears no nut; cultivated. Ludovicodi varthema says :—"this betel resembles the leaves of the sour "orange [q.v.], and they are constantly eating it; when they "eat the said leaves, they eat with them a certain fruit which "is called coffolo, and the tree of the said coffolo is called arecha "[areca], and is formed like the stem of the date [kharjooram] "tree, and produces its fruit in the same manner; and they "also eat with the said leaves a certain lime made from oyster "shells [chippy], which they call cionama [choonam]." The betel vine is planted in rows, requires a moist situation and a rather rich soil; hilly places not favorable; ground prepared in south in auny [mausam] or june, on coromandel in cheitram or april and veishaukham or may, on w. coast in toolaum or october, coombham or february, maidom or april and carcatacam or july; trenches are cut and the part between two trenches is levelled and worked up; seed sown in south in auvany or august, on coromandel in cheitram or april and veishaukham or may; on w. coast the cuttings are planted in toolaum or october; coombham or february and carcatacam or july; cuttings are transplanted on the ridge prepared, in which agatty seeds have been previously sown to raise agatty [west-indian sesban] trees for the vine to creep upon; while under growth the vine spreads over the agatty plant and is irrigated with water from the trenches, weeding also proceeds; the leaves are nipped when tender, say after one year; average price in south 14 lbs. per rupee, on coromandel and w. coast 1 bundle per 6 pies, in the winter can be had at half or less; the leaves should not be plucked indiscriminately at all seasons, as this is apt to destroy the plant. Warm juice of leaves is a valuable stomachic; given with musk [castoory] in hysteria; in catarrhal and pulmonary affections, leaves warmed and smeared with oil are applied over chest, acting as rubefacient; similar for liver; in pharm., non-officinal. Betel leaf wrapped round areca nut [q.v.] and lime [choonam] constitutes the narcotic [mookhadiraut] masticatory [charvanam] of this country; for brevity usually called betel [q.v.], consumed as largely as tobacco [pogauk]; sometimes camphor [q.v.] and other drugs are added; it acts as a carminative and antacid tonic; chewed by natives, especially after meals; presented to guests and visitors, and sometimes sent to friends and relations, especially at family festivals, inclosed in gold or silver paper or leaf. The hindostany term paun [q.v.] is familiar; and the mixed package is called paunsoopyaury [charvanam, paunsoopyaury]. The greater and lesser galangals [q.v.] are often erroneously considered to be the roots of this plant.——*Black pepper* (मरीच - marícha, San.; मिरि - miri, Mahr.; فلفل اسود - filfiliaswad, Ar.; پلپل گرد - pilpiligird, Pers.; کالی مرچ - kálímirch, Hind.; کالی مرچی - kálímirchí, Dec.; لدا - lada, Malay; ಒಳ್ಳೆಮೆಣಸು - ollemenasu, Can.; ಎಡ್ಡೆಮುಂಚಿ - eddemunchi, Too.; మిరియాలు - miriyálu, Tel.; കുരുമുളക - kurumulaku, Mal.; කළුමිරිස් - kalumiris, Singh.; மிளகு - milagu, Tam.). San. from (mri, san. to die); causing immense pain to the tip of the tongue. Mahr. from sanscrit. Ar. from (filfil, ar. pepper + aswad, ar. black). Pers. from (pilpil, pers. pepper + gird, ar. round). Hind. from (kálí, hind. black + mirch, hind. pepper). Dec. from hindostany. Can. from (olle, can. good + menasu, can. pepper). Too. from (edde, too. superior + munchi, too. pepper). Tel. from sanscrit. Mal. from (kuru, mal. seed + mulaku, mal. pepper); properly berry. Singh. from (kalu, singh. black + miris, singh. pepper). San. also (tíkshna), meaning pungent; (úshana), meaning pungent; (réksha), meaning very pungent; (vélaja), meaning produced on the sea coast; (kólaka), meaning occurring in clusters; (krishna), meaning black; (dhármavartana), meaning produced in dharmavartanam perhaps malabar dharmapatam; (maliná), meaning black; (shyámá), meaning black [shaumay]. Pers. also (pilpilisiyáh), meaning black pepper. Hind. also (golmirch), meaning round pepper; (choka); (chokamirch); (mirch) [shrubby chilly]. Malay also (chabe); (chabai); (ladaitam); (máricha). Can. also (menasu), means pepper; (menasinakálu), meaning pepper + black. Too. also (munchi). Tel. also (savyamu); (paluk). Mal. also (mulaku). Singh. also (gammiris), meaning village + pepper. Tam. also (shevviyam), meaning the root; (milaguvalli), meaning pepper creeper; (kalinai), meaning strong. Greek πέπερι στρόγγυλον and πέπερι μέλαν. Latin piper. The greek, latin and english name is from the sanscrit for Long pepper; transferred by foreign traders to present article. Title otherwise Aromatic pepper, Miriyaul, Pepper vine, Pungent pepper, Round pepper, White pepper. Botanically Piper [pepper] nigrum, linn., piperaceæ [vricsham, 125]. Alias Piper aromaticum. Stem shrubby, climbing, rooting, round; leaves coriaceous, glabrous, pale glaucous beneath, adult ones revolute on the margins, the lower ones roundish-ovate, about equal-sided, slightly cordate or truncated at the base, seven to nine-nerved, upper ones ovate-elliptic or elliptic, usually unequal-sided, acutely acuminate, seven to five-nerved; catkins hermaphrodite or female, filiform, pendulous, shortly peduncled, shorter than the leaves; berries globose, red when ripe; floriferous calycule in the hermaphrodite, four-lobed. An epiphytal plant, climbing and clinging to rough bark trees, having heart-shaped leaves about the size of ivy leaves, very green and glossy, paler beneath; and producing flowers in spikes, followed from third to seventh year by berries like currants; they are at first green, then red, but after being gathered and dried become black; indigenous to travancore and malabar; cultivated all along malabar coast; wild among the northern circar [q.v.] hills; in malabar flowers in may and june, and the fruits become fit for gathering at the commencement of the following year. The immature fruit is globular, about ⅕ of an inch in diameter, much wrinkled, and of a brown-black color, on one side are the remains of the peduncle, and on the other of the style and stigmas; the pericarp is closely adherent to the seed; the latter consists of a thin reddish-brown testa and a copious albumen, the exterior portion of which is horny and the interior farinaceous; the embryo is undeveloped. The mature seed, known as white pepper, is less acrid than black, as the pericarp has been removed, it is also rather smaller and of a grey color, striated from base to apex by about a dozen light stripes; the transverse section of a grain of black pepper exhibits a soft, yellowish epidermis covering the outer pericarp; this is formed of a closely-packed yellow layer of large, mostly radially arranged, thick-walled cells, each containing in its small cavity a mass of dark-brown resin [raul]; the middle layer of the pericarp consists of soft, tangentially-extended parenchyme, containing an abundance of extremely small starch granules and drops of oil; the shrinking of this loose middle layer is the chief cause of the deep wrinkles on the surface of the berry; the next inner layer of the pericarp exhibits towards its circumference, tangentially arranged soft parenchyme, the cells of which possess either spiral striation or spiral fibres, but towards the interior, loose parenchyme free from starch and containing very large oil cells; the testa is formed in the first place of a row of small yellow thick-walled cells; next to them follows the true testa, as a dense, dark-brown layer of lignified cells, the individual outlines of which are undistinguishable; the albumen of the seed consists of angular, radially arranged, large celled parenchyme; most of its cells are colorless and loaded with starch; others contain a soft, yellow, amorphous mass; if thin slices are kept under glycerine for some time, these masses are lowly transformed into needle-shaped crystals of piperin. Black pepper is the berry dried on mats in the sun, with the pulp; the ash of black pepper should not exceed 5·5 per cent.; white pepper is prepared from the black by removing the dark outer layer of pericarp, by rubbing and washing, thereby making it smoother and depriving it of a part of its pungency, made whiter by chlorine; pepper contains an acrid resin [raul], volatile oil [yennay], piperin, gum [gond], malic and tartaric acids, &c.; the color being due to the volatile oil, and the pungent taste to the resin; berries of embelia ribes, burm. [byebarang], are used in adulteration; root also has a peculiar and slightly warm taste. The trees commonly planted for support are:—Areca palm, areca catechu, linn. [areca]; Moochee wood tree, erythrina indica, lam. [common coral tree]; Mango tree, mangifera indica, linn. [mango]; Jack tree, artocarpus integrifolia, willd. [common jack]; Moringa tree, moringa pterygosperma, gærtn. [moringa]. The vines which cling round the two last thrive best. Pepper was for ages the staple article of export to europe from india, and it was with it that vasco de gama loaded his ships on his first voyage; now of little importance compared to others, such as sugar [q.v.], coffee [q.v.], cotton [q.v.], and indigo [q.v.]; still it is largely exported. The pepper vine grows best on sides of narrow valleys where the soil is rich and moist, producing lofty trees by which a constant favorable coolness is maintained; the vine first runs along the ground and propagates itself by striking out root into the soil; cultivators then tie up the end of the vine lying on the ground to the nearest tree, on the bark of which the stems put out roots so far as they have been tied, the shoots above that hanging down; the plant is capable of growing to 20 feet, but for convenience is usually kept low; in places where no vines occur naturally, the plant is propagated by planting slips near the roots of the trees on which it is to climb; after it has been planted, it requires no great trouble or attention, the cultivator having little more to do than to collect the produce in the proper season; when the fruit is intended for black pepper, it is not allowed to ripen, but is collected green; that which is intended for white pepper is left to ripen thoroughly. The longer it remains after being plucked, the more valuable it becomes for medicinal purposes; an infusion of the seeds is an antidote to arsenic [paushaunam]; the juice of the leaves boiled in oil applied externally in scabies; the distilled oil has very little acrimony; a tincture made in rectified spirit is extremely hot and fiery; gives to pharm. piper nigrum, crystalline principle, piperine; stimulant, carminative, antiperiodic, externally applied rubefacient; officinal; also in british pharm.; root also is stimulant, tonic and cordial; in veterinary practice 2 drachms of pepper with 4 of common salt [ooppoo] mixed in the evening gram [q.v.], is given for horses exposed to the open air in rain or cold season. Both black and white pepper are used as well-known condiments [chutney].——*Chaab pepper* (चविका - chaviká, San.; चवक - chavaka, Mahr.; چاب - cháb, Hind.). Title from sanscrit through hindostany. San. from (chav, san. to eat). Mahr. and hind. from sanscrit. San. also (chavya), meaning fit to be eaten. Hind. also (gajphal), meaning the fruit of piper chaba. Title otherwise Chavica, Gajpal. Botanically Piper [pepper] chaba, hunter, piperaceæ [vricsham, 125]. Specific from hindostany. Alias Chavica officinarum; Piper officinarum. Chavica from sanscrit. Branches flexuous, terete, hard, finely striate when dry, pale; leaves 5–7 by $2\frac{1}{2}$–$3\frac{1}{2}$ inches, rather shining above, pale when dry, base very variable, nerves three to six pair above the three to five basal; nervules arching; petiole $\frac{1}{4}$–$\frac{1}{2}$ inch; fruiting spikes 1–2 inches long, $\frac{1}{2}$ inch diameter, broadest at the base, obtuse, forming a fleshy cone of innumerable fruits $\frac{1}{8}$ inch diameter. Native of moluccas, cultivated here. Fruit is medicinally stimulant, anticatarrhal, carminative, expectorant; in pharm. non-officinal.——*Cool pepper* (చలవమిరియాలు - tsalavamiriyálu, Tel.). Same as Cubeb pepper.——*Cubeb pepper* (सुगन्धमरीच - sugandhamarícha, San.; कबाबचिनी - kabábachiní, Mahr.; गंधमेणसु - gandhamenasu, Conc.; كبابه - kabábah, Ar.; كباب چينى - kabábchíní, Pers., Hind. and Dec.; كامو كوس - kámukus, Malay; ಬಾಲಮೆಣಸು - bálamenasu, Can.; ഗന്ധമുഞ്ചി - gandhamunchi, Too.; చలవమిరియాలు - tsalavamiriyálu, Tel.; വാൽമുളക - válmulaku, Mal.; වල්ගම්මිරිස් - valgámiris, Singh.; வால்மிளகு - válmilagu, Tam.). Title from arabic. San. from (sugandha, san. fragrant + marícha, san. pepper, piper nigrum, linn.). Mahr. from persian. Conc. from (gandha, san. fragrant + menasu, can. pepper). Pers. from (kabába, pers. cubeb + chíní, pers. chinese) [china pepper]. Hind. from persian. Malay means like vapour. Can. from (bála, can. tail + menasu, can. pepper). Too. from (gandha, san. smelling + munchi, too. pepper). Tel. from (tsalava, tel. coolness + miriyálu, tel. pepper); from cool sensation in the mouth after eating them. Mal. from (vál, mal. tail + mulaku, mal. pepper). Singh. means creeping pepper. Tam. from (vál, tam. tail + milagu, tam. pepper). San. also (kankóla); (katukóla), meaning pungent pepper. Ar. also (habbularús), meaning bridegroom's berry. Hind. also (dumkímirchí), meaning tail pepper. Malay also (ladabárekor), meaning tailed pepper; (timukus). Can. also (gandhamenasu), meaning scented + pepper. Too. also (chinamunchi), meaning chinese pepper. Tel. also (tókamiriyálu), meaning tail + pepper, piper nigrum, linn. Mal. also (chínimulaku), meaning foreign pepper. Singh. also (válmolavú). from tamul. Tam. also (takkólam), meaning useful pepper. Greek μυρτίδανον. Title otherwise Cabob cheeny of bengal, Cabob pepper, Chinese pepper, Cool pepper, Fragrant pepper, Java pepper, Seetal cheeny of madras, Tailed pepper. Botanically Piper [pepper] cubeba, linn., piperaceæ [vricsham, 125]. Specific from arabic. Alias Cubeba officinalis. Shrubby, creeping; leaves petioled, ovate-lanceolate, scarcely triple-nerved; aments leaf-opposed, on peduncles longer than the petioles; berries pedicelled. The fruits are elevated on a kind of stalk, formed from the contraction of the base of the fruit itself, so that they are not really but only apparently stalked; the dry berries are spherical, wrinkled, of a brown color, and are easily distinguished from black pepper [q.v.] by the pedicel at their base, beneath the pericarp is a nut which contains the seed; the albumen is white and oily; as the fruit is gathered when immature, the drug usually consists of little else than the pericarp. Shrub is native of the eastern archipelago. The cubebs of the shops contain:—a volatile oil [yennay], nearly solid; resin [raul], resembling balsam copaiba; a quantity of another colored resin [raul]; a colored gummy matter. An essential oil [attar] is obtained by distillation with water. Cubebs are medicinally stimulant to the mucous membranes, particularly to that of the genito-urinary system; substituted for british copaiba, gives to pharm. cubeba, crystalline principle, cubebin, stimulant; preparation, oleum cubebæ, tinctura cubebæ; officinal; used in veterinary practice. Cubebs used as masticatory [charvanam] with betel [q.v.] leaf; a gum resin [googal] is prepared.——*Curry pepper* (ഉപ്പേരിമുളക - uppérimulaku, Mal.). Title from use. Same as Caffree chilly.——*Elephant long pepper* (गजपिप्पली - gajapippalí, San.; थारोंपिपळी - t'hórápimpalí, Mahr.; گج پپلی - gajpipli, Hind.; هتی پپلی - hattípiplí, Dec.; ದೊಡ್ಡಹಿಪ್ಪಲಿ - doddahippali, Can.; ఏనుగపిప్పలి - énugapippali, Tel.; അത്തിത്തിപ്പലി - attittippali, Mal.; ගජතිප්පිලි - gajatippili, Singh.; ஆனைத்திப்பிலி - ánaittippili, Tam.). Title from size; cf. elephant creeper. San. from (gaja, san. elephant + pippalí, san. long pepper, piper longum, linn.). Mahr. from (t'hóra, mahr. large + pimpalí, mahr. long pepper, piper longum, linn.). Hind. from sanscrit. Dec. from (hattí, hind. elephant + piplí, hind. long pepper, piper longum, linn.). Can. from (dodda, can. large + hippali, can. long pepper). Tel. from (énuga, tel. elephant + pippali, tel. long pepper). Mal. from (atti, mal. elephant + tippali, mal. long pepper). Singh. from (gaja, san. elephant + tippili, singh. long pepper, piper longum, linn.). Tam. from (ánai, tam. elephant + tippili, tam. long pepper). San. also (vashira), meaning powerful, from pungent seeds; (karipippalí), meaning elephant long pepper; (kapivallí), meaning monkey creeper, from the hairy appearance; (kólavallí), meaning hog creeper, perhaps from bristles with which the germ is replete; (shréyasí), meaning excellent. Hind. also (barípiplí), meaning large piplee. Mal. also (ánattippali), meaning elephant or large long pepper. Singh. also (gajakaná), meaning elephant + long pepper, piper longum, linn. Tam. also (attittippili), meaning elephant + long pepper. Title otherwise Aunay tiplee, Hog creeper, Monkey creeper. Botanically Scindapsus officinalis, schott., araceæ [vricsham, 152]. Alias Pothos officinalis. Pothos from singhalese, see pothos scandens, linn. [elephant creeper]. Perennial, epiphytic, stems rooting; leaves alternate, sub-bifarious, oblong-cordate, entire, smooth on both sides; petioles sheathing, channelled; peduncles terminal, solitary, smooth, erect when in flower; spathe sub-cylindric, greenish without, pale yellow within; apex filiform; spadix sub-cylindric, equalling the spathes, pale greenish, dotted with the dark-colored stigmas; berries seeded, arillate at the base; flowering in july-august; grows in moist forests. Dried fruit is stimulant, diaphoretic and anthelmintic; in pharm. non-officinal. Other common species are:—peepla, specific from hindostany; pertusus, or indian ivy.——*Europe pepper* (പറങ്കിമുളക - parankimulaku, Mal.). Same as Common chilly.——*Foreign pepper* (കപ്പൽമുളക - kappalmulaku, Mal.). Same as Shrubby chilly.——*Forest pepper* (ಕಾಡುಮೆಣಸು - kádumenasu, Can.). Same as Toddaly.——*Ground pepper* (నేలపిప్పలి - nélapippali, Tel.). Same as Wild long pepper.——*Jamaica pepper* (كباب چينى - kabábchíní, Hind.). Same as China pepper.——*Long pepper* (पिप्पली - pippalí, San.; पिंपळी - pimpalí, Mahr.; हिप्लि - hipli, Conc.; دارفلفل - dárfilfil, Ar.;

فلفلدراز - filfilidaráz, Pers.; پپلی - piplí, Hind. and Dec.; چبئی جوز - chabaijawá, Malay; ಹಿಪ್ಪಲಿಬಳ್ಳಿ - hippaliballi, Can.; ఇప్పలి - ippali, Too.; పిప్పలి - pippali, Tel.; തിപ്പലി - tippali, Mal.; තිප්පිලි - tippili, Singh.; திப்பிலி - tippili, Tam.). Title from form of seed. San. from (prí, san. to nourish). Mahr. and conc. from sanscrit. Ar. from (dár, ar. wood + filfil, ar. pepper, piper nigrum, linn.). Pers. from (filfil, ar. pepper + daráz, pers. long). Hind. from sanscrit. Malay meaning pepper of java. Can. from (hippili, can. long pepper + balli, can. creeper). Tel. from sanscrit. Mal. from sanscrit. Singh. from sanscrit. Tam. from sanscrit. San. also (trikaná), meaning three-grained; (krishná), meaning black; (mágadhí), meaning produced in magadham [needle jasmine]; (upakulyá), meaning growing near river; (shaundí), meaning effective; (kólá), meaning occurring in groups; (grant'hika), meaning having knot, is the root; (krishnapippalí), meaning black long pepper; (chapalá), meaning hot [cow gram]; (vaidéhí), meaning produced in videham; (kaná), meaning small; (úshaná), meaning sickening or heating. Pers. also (pipal). Hind. also (pipluján). Dec. also (piplámol), referring to root; (gajpipal), meaning elephant long pepper. Malay also (chabaichanggek). Can. also (tippili); (kuna); (yippali). Tel. also (módi). Mal. also (káttutippali), meaning wild long pepper. Tam. also (kalini), meaning strong; (shamilági), meaning digestive pepper. Greek πέπερι μακρὸν, Latin piper longum. Title otherwise Elephant pepper, Hiplee, Piplee, Tiplee. Botanically Piper [pepper] longum, linn., piporaceæ [vricsham, 125]. Alias Chavica roxburghii. Stem somewhat shrubby, the sterile ones decumbent, the floriferous ones ascending, dichotomously branched, at first slightly downy, afterwards glabrous; inferior leaves long-petioled, ovate, roundish, broadly cordate, acute or obtuse, seven-nerved; upper ones short-petioled; top ones sessile, embracing the stems, oblong, unequally cordate, five-nerved, all thick, membranaceous; petioles and nerves beneath, especially near the base, finely downy, afterwards glabrous; male catkins filiform, cylindrical, with the peduncle as long as the leaves; female ones thicker, less than half that length, about the length of the peduncle. Plant cultivated and wild in moist forests; the root is woody and perennial, stems numerous creeping, branches bearing the fruit erect; the berries are lodged in a pulpy matter; they are at first green, becoming red when ripe; dried in the sun, they change to a dark-grey color; the taste of the berries is pungent, though rather faint; contain a volatile oil [yennay] an acrid resin [raul] and piperine; met with in entire spikes about an inch long, possessing a darkish brown or gray color; the female spikes dried form the long pepper of the shops. The plant is readily propagated by cuttings; the stems are annual, but the roots live several years, and when cultivated usually yield three or four crops, after which they become exhausted and require to be renewed by fresh planting; the fruit is hottest in its immature state, and is therefore gathered whilst green and dried in the sun. The medicinal effects of long pepper are analogous to those of black pepper [q.v.] but weaker; in pharm. non-officinal; veidyans [q.v.] use it in infusion, mixed with honey [shahad]; substituted for british peppermint [poodeenah] and clove [lavangam] oils; the root and thickest part of the stems cut into small slices and dried are much consumed for medical purposes; the root possesses the virtues of the berry, but in a weaker degree. Chiefly used as a condiment [chutney].——*Monkey pepper* (मर्कटपिप्पली - markatapippalí, San.). Title from hairy leaf and spikes like long pepper. Same as Indian burr. ——*Monk's pepper* (سفید سنبھالو - sufiedsambhálú, Hind.). From (sufed, hind. white + sambhálú, hind. notchy). Same as Water notchy.——*Red pepper* (ಕೆಂಪುಮೆಣಸು - kempumenasu, Can.). Title from red fruit and hot, biting taste like pepper. Same as Common chilly.——*Round pepper* (सूर्य्यावर्त्ता - súryávarttá, San.; سوبلی - súballí, Hind.; లింగమిరియము - lingamiriyamu, Tel.). Title from round small fruit. San. from (súrya, san. sun + ávrit, san. to turn to). Tel. from (linga, tel. round + miriyamu, tel. pepper, piper nigrum, linn.). Title otherwise Dyers' litmus, Dyers' turnsole, Folded croton. Botanically Crozophora plicata, müller, euphorbiaceæ [vricsham, 118]. Alias Croton plicatum, tinctorium. Small annual, hoary; stems and branches round, dichotomous; leaves alternate, waved, toothed, broadly cordate, tapering to a stalk; flowers small, greenish white; male ones above the females; capsules scabrous. A cloth moistened with the juice of the green capsules become blue on exposure to the open air; useful in leprosy [cooshtam], dry plant being made into a decoction [kwautam] to which is added a little mustard [rayaun]; gives a dye [shauyam]. No other common species here.——*Scented pepper* (ಗಂಧಮೆಣಸು - gandhamenasu, Can.). Title from fragrance of pepper Same as Cubeb pepper.——*Tailed pepper* (తోకమిరియాలు - tókamiriyálu, Tel.). Same as Cubeb pepper. ——*Tree pepper* (ಮರಮೆಣಸು - maramenasu, Can.). Same as China pepper.——*Water long pepper* (నీరుపిప్పలి - nírupippali, Tel.; പൊന്നത്തു - ponnattu, Mal.). Title from habitat. Tel. from (níru, tel. water + pippali, tel. long pepper, piper longum, linn.). Mal. from (ponnu, mal. to float). Title otherwise Neer piplee, Pongaty. Botanically Sphenoclea zeylanica, gærtn., campanulaceæ [vricsham, 76]. Alias Gærtnera pongati; Pongatium indicum; Rapania herbacea; Sphenoclea pongatium; Pongati, pongatium from malayalam. Annual, herbaceous, erect, branched, glabrous; leaves alternate, exstipulate, lanceolate, entire, smooth; terminal or leaf-opposed, peduncled, cylindric; bracts three or three-partite, under the flowers very small, white; common in rice [q.v.] fields, flowering nearly all the year. No other common species here.——*Water pepper* (پانی مرچ - pánímirch, Hind.). Title from habitat. Hind. from (páni, hind. water + mirch, hind. piper nigrum, linn.). Title otherwise Ciderage, Culrage, Lake-weed, Red-knees, Smartweed. Botanically Polygonum [water gannair] flaccidum, roxb., polygonaceæ [vricsham, 110]. Everywhere scattered more or less with brown, sessile, pellucid glands; ochreæ narrow, bristly-ciliate; leaves lanceolate, acuminate, ciliolate, glabrous; spikes one to three, erect, interrupted at the base; bracts somewhat contiguous, narrow, horizontally truncated, ciliated; pedicels at length exserted, organs enclosed; achenium granular, striated, somewhat shining; in moist places; flowering in the rains.——*White pepper* (வெள்ளைமிளகு - vellaimilagu, Tam.). Special preparation of black pepper [q.v.] berries.——*Wild long pepper* (वाशिर - vashira, San.; بھوئی آکرا - bhuíákrá, Hind.; تان - tán, Dec.; ಕರೆಹಿಪ್ಪಲಿ - karehippali, Can.; బొక్కెన - bokkena, Tel.; കാട്ടുതിപ്പലി - káttutippali, Mal.; பொடுதலை - poduthalai, Tam.). Title from habitat and resemblance of fruit. San. from (vash, san. to subdue), powerful. Hind. from (bhuí, hind. ground + ákrá, hind. a kind of grass, vicia hirsuta, koch.). Can. from (kare, can. bank + hippali, can. long pepper); creeping plant and fruits resemble long pepper. Mal. from (kátu, mal. forest + tippali, mal. long pepper, piper longum, linn.). Tam. from (podugu, tam. small + talai, tam. head); from small fruits. San. also (ankóta), meaning sharp and useful plant [alanjy]. Can. also (nelahippali), meaning ground + long pepper. Tel. also (nélapippali), meaning ground + long pepper, piper longum, linn. Mal. also (ánakkozhuppu), meaning elephant's fat; (valiyaittikkanni), meaning large parasitical plant. Tam. also (talaibódam), by inversion. Title otherwise Creeping vervain. Botanically Lippia nodiflora, rich., verbenaceæ [vricsham, 102]. Alias Blairia nodiflora; Verbena capitata, nodiflora; Zapania nodiflora. Annual, creeping; stem roughish, with adpressed biacuminate hairs, herbaceous, filiform, ramous, procumbent, rooting at the joints; leaves cuneate-spathulate, entire at the base, above rounded, obtuse or sub-acute, equally and sharply serrated, obsoletely veined, flat; peduncles axillary, solitary, filiform, exserted; capitula ovoid and at length cylindrical; calyx two-parted, slightly bicarinate; carinæ puberulous; flowers small, white. Is a native of southern italy and sicily, as well as india. Tender stalks and leaves toasted, are in infusion a bitter tonic. No other common species here.

PER (పెద్ద - pedda, *Tel.*; പെരു - peru, *Mal.*; பெரு - peru, *Tam.*). Great [hey, pedda, pen]. Prefix in place names; as Perungger meaning great town. In each of the languages, plant first term, often joining two genera. Ex., where transl. is of second term:—Agave vivipara (peddakalabanda), aloe indica; Ailanthus excelsa (peyyápa), hardwickia binata; Albizzia procera (peddapaççeru), dalbergia paniculata; Amomum subulatum (peddaélaki), elettaria cardamomum; Andrographis affinis (péddavému), melia azadirachta; Barleria cristata (peddagóranta), lawsonia alba; Celastrus paniculatus (peddachinta), tamarindus indica; Cleome viscosa (peddavávminta), gynandropsis pentaphylla; Cordia obliqua (periyamari), indigofera tinctoria; Fœniculum vulgare (peddajílakarra), cuminum cyminum; Fourcroya gigantea (perundázhai), pandanus odoratissimus; Gomphrena globosa (peddagóranta), lawsonia alba; Lawsonia alba (peddapattsagóranta), barleria prionitis; Leucæna glauca (periyatagarai), cassia tora; Limnanthemum indicum (peddaákáshatámara), pistia stratiotes; Melanthesopsis patens (perunnírúri), phyllanthus niruri, var. genuinus; Miliusa velutina (peddachilakaduddnga), polyalthia suberosa; Pedalium murex (peddapalléru), tribulus terrestris; Puecedanum graveolens (peddasadápa), ruta graveolens, var. angustifolia; Phragmites roxburghii (peddarellu), saccharum spontaneum; Pimpinella anisum (peruñjíragam), cuminum cyminum; Plumeria acutifolia (perungalli), euphorbia tirucalli; Saccopetalum tomentosum (peddachilakaduddnga), polyalthia suberosa; Salvadora oleoides (peddavaragógu), toddalia aculeata; Salvadora persica (peddavaragógu), toddalia aculeata; Securinega leucopyrus (perinklávu), memecylon edule, var. typica; Tacca pinnatifida (peddakanda), amorphophallus campanulatus; (periyagarunai), dracontium polyphyllum; Tragia involucrata (peddadúlagondi), mucuna pruriens; Zizyphus jujuba (perintutali), scutia indica. See gloss. paragraphs.——*Paranginaud* (ಪರಂಗಿನಾಡು - paranginádu, Can.). From (pér, can. great + ranga, can. vishnu + nádu, can. tract); from the god rungasawmy worshipped by the badagas [q.v.], and his temple located on the peak of that name within the arrondissement. Division, Neilgherries; area 138 square miles; pop. 18,116, exclusive of Coonoor and Wellington. Eastern division of the plateau. Contains settlement of Coonoor and Kotagherry and military depôt of Wellington. Separated from Todanaud on the west by the Moodcaud stream and Orange valley and the north-east spur of Dodabetta range. On the west and south it is divided from Merkoonaud by the southern spur of the same range and the Kartairy river.——*Peermund* (ಪೇರಮಂದು - péramandu, Can.). From (per, can. large + mandu, can. a fold). Village; Neilgherry dist., Coondah division; acres 4; lat. 11° 13′; long. 76° 37′; from Ootacamund S.S.W. 15 miles. A private bungalow [q.v.] here.——*Perambalore* (பெரம்பலூர் - perambalúr, Tam.). See sep. title.——*Peraroolaulan* (பேரருளாளன் - pérarulálan, Tam.). From (above + arul, tam. mercy + álan, tam. one who commands). The most gracious god; Vigneshwaran [q.v.].——*Peraul* (പേരാൽ - perál, Mal.). From (above + ál, mal. the banyan). A banyan [q.v.] tree.——*Pergadey* (ಪೆರ್ಗಡೆ - pergade, Can.). Means chief [heggadey]. Title to Bunts. Hindoo third name [peyar].——*Perimpadapp* (പെരിമ്പടപ്പ് - perimpatappu, Mal.). From (peru, mal. large + patappu, mal. population). Ancient name of Cochin province. A title of the Zamorin [q.v.], Cochin dynasty [raj].——*Perincaura* (പെരിങ്കാര - perinkára, Mal.). Means large cauray [q.v.]. Same as Roodrauck.——*Perindalman* (പെരിന്തൽമണ്ണ - perintalmannu, Mal.). From (peru, mal. large + talam, mal. flat + man, mal. earth). Town, Talook head-quarters, Moonsif's station, Sub-jail, Sub-registrar's office; Malabar dist., Valavanaud tal.; pop. 6,502; acres 1,253; lat. 10° 58′; long. 76° 17′; from Calicut E.S.E. 37 miles; from Cannanore S.E. 84 miles; from Madras W.S.W. 312 miles; from Malapooram E.S.E. 14 miles; from Manantoddy S.S.E. 59 miles; from Palghaut W.N.W. 31 miles; from Ponnany E.N.E. 24 miles; from Tellicherry S.E. 73 miles. Chiefly Moplah [q.v.]. Six miles off is Mungada, seat of Valavanaud rajah [q.v.], who enjoys a Malikhana [q.v.] of Rs. 13,400 from Government. Weekly market; moosaufer khana [q.v.]; travellers' bungalow [q.v.].——*Peringollan* (പെരിങ്കൊല്ലൻ - perinkollan, obl.; പെരിങ്കൊല്ലൻ - perinkollan, pers. sing.; പെരിങ്കൊല്ലർ - perinkollar, pers. pl., Mal.). From (above + kollan, mal. blacksmith). Caste-title. Blacksmith [jauty].——*Periya* (പെരിയ - periya, Mal.; பெரிய - periya, Tam.). Great.——*Periyacoolam* (பெரியகுளம் - periyakulam, Tam.). See sep. title.——*Periyammah* (பெரியம்மா - periyammá, Tam.). Means great goddess.——*Periyasaumy* (பெரியசாமி - periyasámi, Tam.). From (above + svámí, san. lord). Hindoo 2nd or pers. name [peyar].——*Periya tirvady* (பெரியதிருவடி - periyathiruvadi, Tam.). From (above + tiru, tam. sacred + adi, tam. foot). Hanooman [q.v.].——*Periyaun* (பெரியான் - periyán, Tam.). Pariah proper name. Feminine form is Periyaul [peyar].——*Periyaur* (പെരിയാറ് - periyáru, Mal.). From (periya, mal. large + áru, mal. river). Sanscrit name (brihannada), meaning same. Greek ψευδόστομος ποταμός. River; Travancore state, Cottayam division, Todoopoya, Mooatpoya, Coonnat naud, Aulangaud and Paravoro talooks. Largest river in Travancore. Rises in the highest parts of Sahyaparvatam or the Western ghauts [q.v.] in lat. 9° 24′ N. and long. 77° 22′ E. in Todoopoya talook. Flows through Todoopoya, Coonnatnaud and through some parts of Paravore. It forms many small cascades in its earlier course, and when it has descended from the higher hills also it hurls itself over several falls of some size. Many large and beautiful islands are also formed in its winding course. After it has reached the plain country, it is called the Alwye. On reaching Alwye, it separates into two branches. The northern proceeds to Paliport. The southern branch after leaving Veerapoly again separates into two streams; one of these is speedily lost in the estuary to which it flows through numerous channels; the other continuing in a southerly direction, falls into the lake south of Tripoontora in lat. 9° 55′; long. 76° 24′. At Alwye the river passes over a bed of mica [abruck] which makes the waters peculiarly healthy. Its mouth, called by seamen Cranganore or Ayicottah river, flows between the south-west boundary of the territory of Cochin and north-west boundary of Travancore. Length 142 miles, only 60 of which are navigable. The principal tributaries are the Minla, Sherdhonay, Peringacootay, Moodrapully, Candanapara, Yedamulla. With the exception of the last 35 miles of its course the river passes through a complete wild, the populated tracts not extending beyond the town of Mullyattore. Sugar-cane [q.v.] plantations on both banks. It is not materially beneficial in irrigating the country on its borders. Much teak wood [teak], floated down to the coast. A work known as the Periyaur project is in hand for diverting the course of this stream from west to east, viz., across the water-shed of the ghauts [q.v.] into the Veigay river, in Madura district. See vol. I, 408.——*Permacoil* (பெருமுக்கல் - perumukkal, Tam.). Meaning great triad of rocks. Also taken from (peru, tam. great + mukkal, tam. travail); great travail, where seetay bore twins. Sanscrit name (válmíkyáshrama), means valmeeky the sage + hermitage. Hill, Place of pilgrimage; South arcot dist., Tindivanam tal.; pop. 2,117; acres 1639; lat. 12° 12′; long. 79° 47′; from Cuddalore N.N.W. 32 miles; from Tindivanam E.S.E. 6 miles; from the sea W. 15 miles. Small fort on a rocky hill. The summit is 400 by 200 yards in extent, and the ascent on all sides is difficult. Strongly fortified during eighteenth century. In 1761, captured by Sir Eyre Coote; in 1780 besieged unsuccessfully by Hyder ally; captured by Hyder in 1782; regained by the British in 1783. It was then dismantled, but remained a post of observation till 1790, when it was taken by Tippoo sultan. A few ruins indicate the position of the fortifications. There are two other villages ending with Mookkal very near to this village, viz., Palamookkal and Nalmookkal. It is said that Seetay, wife of Rama, travailed in all these three villages and finally bore twins in this village. Trig. station in. lat. 12° 11′ 54·14″; long. 79° 46′ 40·50″; height 437 feet; from Permacoil S. ¼ mile; from Tindivanam E.S.E. 6 miles; from the sea W. 15 miles.——*Permaul* (പെരുമാൾ - perumál, Mal.; பெருமாள் - perumál, Tam.). From (above + ál, mal. man), great man. Chief, especially of the old Dravidian dynasties [raj]. Used on W. coast for a viceroy from Cheram [q.v.]. But it is mentioned in the Keraloputty [q.v.] that there were two other Permauls besides the Chera permaul; viz., Chola permaul of Chola mundalam, and Paundy or Coolashekhara permaul of Paundy mundalam [q.v.]. Veishnava title. Hindoo proper name. Suffix in proper names, as Numbermaul, Teppermaul, Varauhapermaul [peyar].——*Permaul tirnaul* (பெருமாள் திருநாள் - perumáldirunál, Tam.). Means vishnoo's sacred day. Same as Vishnoo deepam.——*Perook* (பெருக்கு - perukku, Tam.). From (perugu, tam. to everflow). Flood [vellam]. Also multiplication in arithmetic [ganitam]. Perkkaulan, ruler of flood is a man of the vellaula [q.v.] caste [jauty]. For Audy perook or Pathinettaum perook see Fathinettaum perook.——*Peroom* (പെരും - perum, Mal.; பெரும் - perum, Tam.). Great. Prefix in place names; as Peroombaid, meaning great village. Peroongaut tariss is land left waste for upwards of fifteen years.——*Peroomay* (பெருமை - perumai, Tam.). Greatness. A favorite theme with the tamul moralists. See the following specimens from the Cooral:—பணியுமா மென்றும் பெருமை சிறுமையணியுமாந் தன்னை வியந்து—"the great will always "humble himself; but the mean will exalt himself in self-"admiration." பெருமை பெருமித மின்மை சிறுமை பெருமித மூர்ந்து விடல்—"freedom from conceit is great-"ness, obstinacy therein is meanness."—அற்ற மறைக்கும் பெருமை சிறுமைதான் குற்றமே கூறி விடும்—"the "great hide the faults of others; the base only divulge them."—பெருமைக்கு மேனைச் சிறுமைக்குந் தத்தங் கருமமே கட்டளைக் கல்—"a man's deeds are the touch-stone of his "greatness and littleness."—ஒழுக்கத்தி னெய்துவர் மேன்மை யிழுக்கத்தி னெய்துவ ரெய்தாப் பழி—"from "propriety of conduct men obtain greatness; from impropriety "comes insufferable disgrace."—திறையுடைமை நீங்காமை வேண்டிற் பொறையுடைமை போற்றி யொழுகப்படும்—"if you desire that greatness should never leave you preserve "in your conduct the exercise of patience."—அழுக்கற் றகன்றாரு மில்லை யஃதிலார் பெருக்கத்திற் றீர்ந்தாரு மில்—"never have the envious become great; never have those "who are free from it been without greatness."—வெள்ளத் தனைய மலர்நீட்ட மாந்தர்தம் முள்ளத் தனைய துயர்வு—"the stalks of water-flowers are proportionate to the depth of "water; so is men's greatness proportionate to their minds."—இலக்க முடம்பிடும்பைக் கென்று கலக்கத்தைக் கையாறாக் கொள்ளாதா மேல்—"the great will not regard trouble "as trouble, knowing that the body is but the butt of trouble."——*Peroondoray* (பெருந்துறை - perundurai,* Tam.). From (perum, tam. large + turai, tam. ford).—"*a*" Deputy tahsildarry, Coimbatore district. Pay Rs. 70.—"*b*" Village, Deputy tahsildar's and Sub-registrar's station, Railway station; Coimbatore dist., Erode tal.; pop. 6,404; acres 10,878; lat. 11° 17′; long. 77° 38′; height 853 feet; from Coimbatore E.N.E. 46 miles; from Erode W.S.W. 11 miles; from Madras S.W. 224 miles; from Ootacamund E. 59 miles; from Pollachy N.E. 58 miles; from Suttimungalam S.E. 28 miles. Railway station is 4 miles distant. Originally talook head-quarters. Old Vishnoo temple. Market.——*Peroor* (பேரூர் - pérúr, Tam. perúr*). From (pér, tam. large + úr, tam. village). Tam. also (mérççithambaram), meaning west chidambaram. Sanscrit name (ádipurí), meaning ancient + town. Village, Place of pilgrimage; Coimbatore dist., Coimbatore tal.; pop. 484; acres 1,602; lat. 10° 59′; long. 76° 57′; from Coimbatore W.S.W. 3 miles. On the Noyil. One of the seven Congoo [q.v.] shivaulyams. Richly carved temple about 200 years old, built round a small but far older shrine dating from days of Cholas [q.v.]. Dhwaja stambham [q.v.] outside temple is a fine monolith [laut]. The temple is one of the few that Tippoo respected both in its buildings and lands. In the vicinity of the temple, and in the streets, and by the roadsides are stone figures, &c., some evidently of great age. There are several veeraculls [q.v.], the sculpture of which resembles that on sculptured dolmens [coday cull] on the Neilgherries. Salt [ooppoo] and saltpetre [shorah] are produced by lixiviation.——*Peroovazhy* (பெருவழி - peruvazhi, Tam.). From (peru, tam. great + vazhi, tam. way). Tam. also (vazhuthikkál), meaning paundyan king + way. Ancient name for Atchancoil pass from Tinnevelly to Travancore, western boundary of Paundies [q.v.] at one time. In later times less frequented, and the principal pass now is at Aryancauv [ghaut]. See vol. I (119).——*Peroovely* (பெருவெளி - peruveli, Tam.). Means the great open plain. In philosophy applied to the ethereal expanse as the abode of the supreme deity. The sphere of pure intelligence in adweitam [q.v.]; also the all-pervading spirit or intelligence itself [bramh, parabramh].——*Perrauz*

(ౘ్రాడు - perrádzu, Tel.). From (above + rádzu, tel. king). Hindoo 2nd or pers. name [peyar].——*Perr neer* (பெருநீர் - perunír, Tam.). From (perugu, tam. to overflow + nír, tam. water). Water allowed to flow without limitation during the rainy season [caur].——*Pragada* (ప్రగడ - pragada, Tel.). From (peru, tel. chief + kada, tel. person). Prime minister [muntry, pradhauny, peshwah, vizier].

PERAMBALORE (பெரம்பலூர் - perambalúr, * *Tam.*). From (peru, tam. great + puli, tam. tiger + úr, tam. village) [per]. Sanscrit name (brihadvyághrapura), meaning great + tiger + town; cf. cooroombalore below.——**(1)** Talook, Trichinopoly district. Tahsildar's pay Rs. 175. Area 674 square miles. Greatest length from N. to S. 42 miles; greatest breadth W. to E. 21 miles. Centre of district. Bounded N. by Vellaur which separates it from Salem and South arcot districts; E. by Oodayarpolliem talook; S. by Trichinopoly talook; and W. by Moosiry talook. Twenty-two villages of Ariyalore zemindarry are in the talook. Population 195,006. Language Tamul. The general aspect is flat, the north-western portion being more rugged and hilly than the rest. The only important hills are the Putchamullays, which separate it from Moosiry and run for a short distance into the talook. From the Putchamullays along the banks of the Vellaur and stretching up as far as the Oodayarpolliem talook, there is a continued plain of black cotton [regar] soil, in which there are large tracts of stiff black clay [calimunn]. In the southern portion bordering on Trichinopoly, the country is rocky and the soil generally poor. Perambalore is one of the Caudaurambam [q.v.], or upland talooks, and possesses little irrigated land. Varagoo [q.v.], raggy [q.v.], cumboo [bajrah], and cotton [q.v.] are cultivated. Indigo [q.v.], carpets [cumbly, jamkhana] and cotton [q.v.], are the only industries. Two affluents of the Vellaur irrigate a small portion. The most important tanks [q.v.] are Aroombavore, Attiyore and Ogalore. There is a camping ground at Tooramungalam on the trunk road to Madras. Places of archæological interest:—Aroombavore, Audootoray, Calookkanuttom, Ootatoor, Perambalore, Periyammapolliem, Ranjengoody, Venganore, Vengoolam, Volcondapooram. The leading places, &c., in the talook are the following.——*Aroombavore* (அரும்பாவூர் - arumbávúr, Tam.). From (arumai, tam. excellence + pávu, tam. yarn + úr, tam. village). Greek ἀρεμβοὐρ. Village; pop. 3,869; acres 4,318; lat. 11° 23′; long. 78° 48′; from Perambalore N.W. 14 miles; from Trichinopoly N. 39 miles. Temple and inscriptions of the Vijianugger and Madura naick [q.v.] dynasties [raj].——*Audootoray* (ஆடுதுறை - áduthurai, Tam.). From (ádu, tam. sheep + turai, tam. ford). Village; pop 1,226; acres 155; lat. 11° 24′; long. 79° 07′; from Perambalore N.E. 17 miles; from Trichinopoly N.N.E. 47 miles. Old Shiva temple with inscriptions of Chola [q.v.] and Vijianugger [q.v.] dynasties [raj].——*Cooroombalore* (குரும்பலூர் - kurumbalúr, Tam.). From (kuru, tam. small + puli, tam. tiger + úr, tam. village). Sanscrit name (kharavavyághrapura), meaning small + tiger + town; cf. perambalore at head. Village; pop. 5,767; acres 7,406; lat. 11° 14′; long. 78° 52′; from Perambalore W. 4 miles; from Trichinopoly N.N.E. 30 miles. Gave its name to a talook abolished in 1817-18. Brass [pittalay] and zinc [tootnaug] ware made in adjacent village of Polliem.——*Maroothiyaur* (மருதையாறு - maruthaiyár, Tam.). See sep. title.——*Ootatoor* (ஊட்டத்தூர் - úttattúr, Tam.). See sep. title.——*Perambalore* (பெரம்பலூர் - perambalúr, Tam.). See below.——*Putchamullay* (பச்சைமலை - paççaimalai, Tam.). See sep. title.——*Ranjengoody* (இரஞ்சன்குடி - irañjangudi, Tam.). From (irañjan, tam. proper name + kudi, tam. agricultural village). Village, Hill; pop. 1,331; lat. 11° 21′; long. 79° 00′; from Perambalore N.E. 10 miles; from Trichinopoly N.N.E. 40 miles. Ruins of a fort on a low rocky hill. Belonged to the Carnatic [q.v.] family. Shiva temple once existed. Centre of cattle [maud] breeding.——*Vellaur* (வெள்ளாறு - vellâru, Tam.). See sep. title.——*Volcondapooram* (வாலிகண்டபுரம் - váligandappuram, Tam.). See sep. title.——**(2)** Town, Talook head-quarters; Trichinopoly dist., Perambalore tal.; pop. 3,714; acres 3,584; lat. 11° 14′; long. 78° 56′; from Ariyalore W.N.W. 16 miles; from Madras S.W. 160 miles; from Moosiry N.E. 35 miles; from Shreerungam N.N.E. 28 miles; from Trichinopoly N.N.E. 31 miles. Almost in centre of talook, on trunk road to Madras. Old Shiva temple.

PERGUNNAH (پرگنہ - parganah, *Hind.*). From persian. N. indian sub-division of a zillah [q.v.] answering to the S. indian talook [q.v.].

PERIYACOOLAM (பெரியகுளம் - periyagulam, *Tam.* periyakulam *). From (periya, tam. large + kulam, tam. tank) [per]. Sanscrit name (champakavana), meaning champak tree, michelia champaca, linn. + forest. Known as Pundry naud, one of the thirteen Codoon tamul nauds of Paundyan [q.v.] kingdom in the Madura stala pooraunam [q.v.], and Chatoor acaranthy [q.v.], &c.——**(1)** Talook, Madura district, Tahsildar's pay Rs. 150. Area 1,628 square miles. Population 263,253. Language Tamul. W. of district. Bounded on the north Pulney hills, east Dindigul and Tirmungalam talooks, south Travancore hills, west Travancore and Pulney hills. A valley surrounded by hills. Soil mostly red loam. Rough cumblies [q.v.] are woven in five or six villages. Chiefly agriculture. Tanks [q.v.] and channels [q.v.] are fed by Munjalaur, Shoorooly, Tainiyaur, Varauhanuddy, and Veigay rivers, and a very few rain-fed tanks. Camping grounds on road side near Periyacoolam, Allinagaram, Veerpaundy, Oottamapolliem, and Cumbum villages. Places of archæological interest:—Chinnammanore, Coollapooram, Cumbum, Devadaunaputty, Goodalore, Hanoomantaputty, Marcayancottay, Oottamapolliem, Tencaray, Vadacaray, Veerpaundy. The leading places, &c., in the talook are the following.——*Allinagaram* (அல்லிநகரம் - allinagaram, Tam.). From (alli, tam. the lily, nymphæa lotus, linn. + nagara, san. city). Village; pop. 4,926; acres 9,960; lat. 10° 02′; long. 77° 31′; from Madura W. 44 miles; from Periyacoolam S.S.W. 8 miles. Anicut [q.v.] across the Tainy river [tainiyaur].——*Andiputty* (ஆண்டிப்பட்டி - ándippatti, Tam.). See sep. title.——*Bodinaickanore* (போடிநாயக்கனூர் - pódináyakkanúr. Tam.). See sep. title.——*Chinnammanore* (சின்னமனூர் - shinnammanúr, Tam. chinnammanúr *). From (shinna, tam. small + amman, tam. goddess + úr, tam. village). Village; pop. 6,107; acres 4,179; lat. 9° 51′; long. 77° 26′; from Dindigul S.W. 53 miles; from Kodaykarnal S.S.W. 28 miles; from Madras S.W. 294 miles; from Madura W. 50 miles; from Periyacoolam S.S.W. 22 miles; from Rameshwaram W.N.W. 134 miles; from Ramnaud W.N.W. 102 miles. Ruined Vishnoo temple and ancient Shiva temple with inscriptions. Anicut [q.v.] across the Shoorooly.——*Combau* (கொம்பை - kómbai, Tam.). Means tender cocoanut [q.v.] in shell. Village; pop. 5,692; acres 10,962; lat. 9° 51′; long. 77° 21′; from Madura W.S.W. 57 miles; from Periyacoolam S.W. 25 miles. Residence of an ex-zemindar receiving Malikhana [q.v.] allowance. Originally one of the seventy-two polliems of Madura. Noted for its breed of dogs [nye, poligar].——*Cottay peak* (கோட்டை - kóttai, Tam.). See sep. title.——*Cumbum* (கம்பம் - kambam, Tam.). Means pillar. Village, Valley; pop. 3,941; acres 6,091; lat. 9° 45′; long. 77° 20′; from Madura W. 59 miles; from Periyacoolam S.S.W. 31 miles. Old Shiva temple with Malayalam inscriptions. Ancient Vishnoo temple. Fort was stormed by Vishwanauta naick, first of the Naick [q.v.] dynasty [raj], in sixteenth century. The valley is a fertile tract between the Travancore hills and the Pulneys, watered by a feeder of the Veigay. The pleasantest part of the district next to the Pulneys. Cool winds sweep down it from the direction of the Malabar coast and it is well wooded and watered [hill-station].——*Devadaunaputty* (தேவதானப்பட்டி - tévathánappatti, Tam.). From (déva, san. deity + dána, san. gift + patti, tam. village). Village; pop. 6,389; acres 8,579; lat. 10° 09′; long. 77° 41′; from Madura N.W. 35 miles; from Periyacoolam E.N.E. 7 miles. Polliem [q.v.] resumed by Hyder ally in eighteenth century. Now a Government village. Ruined fort. A temple called Caumautchy amman coil [q.v.]; inner door never opened. Festival in March.——*Goodalore* (கூடலூர் - kúdalúr, Tam.). From (kúdal, tam. junction + úr, tam. village); on the travancore frontier. Village; Mail goodalore, pop. 3,432; Keel goodalore, 2,966; total 6,398; acres total 20,807; lat. 9° 41′; long. 77° 17′; from Madura W.S.W. 62 miles; from Periyacoolam S.S.W. 36 miles. At the extreme south-western corner of the district, near Travancore territory. Old Shiva temple with several inscriptions.——*Guntamanaickanore* (கண்டமநாயக்கனூர் - kandamanáyakkanúr, Tam.). See sep. title.——*Munjalaur* (மஞ்சளாறு - mañjaláru, Tam.). See sep. title.——*Ooppaurputty* (உப்பாரப்பட்டி - uppárappatti, Tam.). From (uppára, can. salt maker + patti, tam. village). Village; pop. 1,206; acres 2,283; lat. 9° 57′; long. 77° 28′; from Madura W. 48 miles; from Periyacoolam S.S.W. 15 miles. Anicut [q.v.] across the Shoorooly.——*Oottamapolliem* (உத்தமபாளையம் - uttamapâlaiyam, Tam.). See sep. title.——*Oottamapooram* (உத்தமபுரம் - uttamappuram, Tam.). From (uttama, san. best, epithet of a pándiyan + pura, san. town). Town; pop. 4,486; acres 6,766; lat. 9° 44′; long 77° 20′; from Madura W.S.W. 58 miles; from Periyacoolam S.W. 32 miles.——*Palliyamparavay* (பள்ளியம்பரவை - palliyambaravai, Tam.). From (palliyan, tam. one of that caste + paravai, tam. a flat field). Lat. 9° 45′; long. 77° 22′; from Madura W.S.W. 55 miles; from Periyacoolam S.S.W. 29 miles. Anicut across the Shoorooly by name Palliyamparavay.——*Paumbaur* (பாம்பாறு - pámbáru, Tam.). See sep. title.——*Periyacoolam* (பெரியகுளம் - periyagulam, Tam.). See below.——*Periyaur* (பெரியாறு - periyáru, Tam.). See sep. title.——*Seeliyamputty* (சீலையம்பட்டி - shílaiyambatti, Tam.). From (shílaiyan, tam. proper name + patti, tam. village). Village; pop. 1,757; acres 2,796; lat. 9° 52′; long. 77° 26′; from Madura W. 50 miles; from Periyacoolam S.S.W. 19 miles. Anicut across the Shoorooly.——*Shooroolliyaur* (சுருளியாறு - shuruliyáru, Tam.). See sep. title.——*Tainiyaur* (தேனியாறு - téniyáru, Tam.). See sep. title.——*Tevauram* (தேவாரம் - tévâram, Tam.). From (té, tam. god + váram, tam. doorway). Sanscrit name (dévárha), meaning god deserving. Zemindarry, Village; pop. 10,041; acres 13,161; lat. 9° 54′; long. 77° 19′; from Madura W. 57 miles; from Periyacoolam S.W. 23 miles. Zemindarry [q.v.] pays peshcush [q.v.]

of Rs. 1,101. One of the twenty-four polliems resumed by Tippoo sultan in 1788.——*Varauhanuddy* (வராகநதி - varáganathi, Tam.). See sep. title.——*Varshanaud mullay* (வரிசைநாட்டுமலை - varisainátumalai, Tam.). See sep. title.——*Veerpaundy* (வீரப்பாண்டி - virappándi, Tam.). Called after veera paundyan. Village; pop. 3,148; acres 6,467; lat. 9° 58′; long. 77° 29′; from Madura W.N.W. 44 miles; from Periyacoolam S. 13 miles. Anicuts across the Shoorooly. West is a Shiva temple with inscriptions.——*Veigay* (வைகை - vaigai, Tam.). See sep. title.——*Yerachakkanaickanore* (எரசக்கநாயக்கனூர் - erasakkanáyakkanúr, Tam.). From a man of that name. Zemindarry, Village; pop. 6,058; acres 28,217; lat. 9° 48′; long. 77° 26′; from Madura W.S.W. 49 miles; from Periyacoolam S.S.W. 24 miles. Zemindarry [q.v.] pays a peshcush [q.v.] of Rs. 2,061. One of the twenty-four polliems resumed by Tippoo sultan in 1788.——**(2)** Town, Municipal town, Head-quarters of talook and Sub-registrar; Madura dist., Periyacoolam tal.; pop. 16,363; acres 7,685; lat. 10° 07′; long. 77° 35′; from Dindigul S.W. 33 miles; from Kodaykarnal S.S.E. 8 miles; from Madras S.S.W. 278 miles; from Madura W. 40 miles; from Rameshwaram W.N.W. 132 miles; from Ramnaud W.N.W. 102 miles. Consists of three hamlets, Keicoolancoolam, Tencaray and Vadacaray; on both banks of the Varauhanuddy. Ancient Shiva temple with a tasdik [q.v.] allowance of Rs. 3,182 annually; inscriptions around the Garbhagriham [q.v.]. Vishnoo temple in the middle of the town with a tasdik allowance of Rs. 582. A mile west there is a perpetual spring called Chidambara teertam. Near Shiva temple a large tank called Periyacoolam from which the town derives the name.

PESH (پیش - pesh, *Hind.*). From persian. Respected, foremost, front.——*Peshcar* (پیشکار - peshkár, Hind.; పేష్కారు - péshkáru, Tel.). From (above + kár, pers. business). A revenue officer placed in charge of a division of a zemindarry [q.v.] talook [q.v.] and invested with the same authority as a Tahsildar [q.v.].——*Peshcubz* (پیش قبض - peshkabz, Hind.). From (above + kabz, pers. grip). Dagger, the blade of which has a straight thick back, whilst the edge curves inwardly from a broad base to a very sharp point.——*Peshcush* (پیشکش - peshkash, Hind.). From (above + kash, pers. drawn). Literally first fruits. Rent to the Government paid by the proprietor of a permanently-settled estate.——*Peshgy* (پیشگی - peshgí, Hind.). From persian. Advance of money.——*Peshwah* (پیشوا - peshwá, Hind.; பேசுவாய் - pésuváy, Tam.). From (above + affix denoting agent). Title of prime minister of the old Mahratta [q.v.] kingdom. See vol. I (166) [muntry, pradhauny, pragada, vizier].——*Pishwauz* (پشواز - pishwáz, Hind.). From (pesh, pers. front + váz, pers. opening). Mahomedan dress reaching to the ankle, usually of colored muslin [q.v.]. The upper portion to the waist is similar to the full dress jauma [q.v.], the lower portion being as much frilled as the waistband will carry. The lower part of the skirt is trimmed with bands and flounces of gold lace [kinaury], and silver and gold tissue; the upper portion being also richly ornamented. Worn by Mahomedan brides, and by Mahomedan ladies on occasions of household festivals. The invariable costume of Mahomedan dancing women [cunchany].

PETT (پیٹھ - peth, *Hind.*; ಪೇಟೆ - péte, *Can.*; పేట - péta, *Tel.*; പേട്ട - pétta, *Mal.*; பேட்டை - péttai, *Tam.*). Originally bazaar [q.v.] or trading town contiguous to a fortress [cottay, kila], sometimes separately fortified. Some have since themselves become towns, as Ranipett, Laulapett.

PEY (పెయ్య - peyya, *Tel.*). Female. Plant first term. Ex.:— Grewia orientalis (peyyarégu), female jujube [female bair].

PEY (பேய் - péy, *Tam.*). Devil. The subject of devil-worship is fully treated at vol. I (71) and (80). Devil-worship is the foundation of the Tamulian religion. Compare Statius Theb. iii, 661; primos in orbe deos fecit timor. When a person is believed to be possessed of a devil, he is brought to the pagoda [q.v.] of a Graumadevatay [q.v.], where the devil is cast out with ceremonies. Among the books that treat of devils, those best known are Vetaula katay containing stories about familiar spirits, and Neelinautacam the play of the demoness Neely. There is a Tamul proverb :—பேய்க்கூத்தும் ஆமணக்கும் ஆள்போனால் ஆள்தெரியாது—"a devil dance is a garden "of castor-oil plants [aumanac]; if one gets in he is not seen "again;" in each case he is lost. And another :—பேய்க்கு வேப்பிலைபோல—"as repugnant as neem leaves are to "devils;" margosa leaves are used by exorcists. See vol. I (81). Plant first term often joining two genera, showing inferiority or wild growth. Ex., where transl. is of second term :—Lycopersicum esculentum (péyttakkáli), physalis; Rhamnus wightii (péyppúlá), phyllanthus multiflorus; Sponia wightii (péymunnai), premna; Wedelia calendulacea (péykkayyanni), eclipta alba. See gloss. paragraphs.——*Peyalwar* (பேயாழ்வார் - péyázhvár, Tam.). Means mad sage. For more information see under Alwar.——*Peycoil* (பேய்க்கோயில் - péykkóyil, Tam.). Devil temple. Some are small mean tomb-like buildings with an image at the further end. The majority are simply pyramidal heaps of earth adorned with streaks of choonam and red ochre; this is both the temple and the image; a smaller heap in front is the altar; these are generally built under trees.——*Peyodaudy* (பேயோடாடி - péyódádi, Tam.). The dancer with the devil; a name applied to Shiva [q.v.] who once danced with Bhadracauly [q.v.].——*Peytair* (பேய்த்தேர் - péyttér, Tam.). Means devil chariot. The mirage or vapour of the noonday sun [sooryan], said to be the chariot of devils.

PEYAR (பெயர் - peyar, *Tam.*). Name [naumam].——*Augoopeyar* (ஆகுபெயர் - águbeyar, Tam.). Means made + name. Trope. Such words in Tamul are formed from words connected with the six common-places :—measurement or numbering, the container for the thing contained, cause for the effect, effect for cause, the work for the author, the author for the work. The name of one thing is put for another on account of a supposed resemblance between the two things. Thus :—Caul for leg, measure for the thing; Agam for mind, container for the thing contained; Tirvauchacam, for the book so called, cause for the effect; Alancauram for the chapter on rhetoric, effect for the cause; Tolgauppyan, work for the author; Tirvulloovan for cooral, author for the work; Togay, plumage for woman, from the resemblance of the hair on the head; and Woly, light for knowledge.——*Shirappoo peyar* (சிறப்புப்பெயர் - shirappuppeyar, Tam.). Proper name. The method of forming these among the Dravidians will be seen from page (104) of vol. I and appendix XXXIV of vol. II. A difficulty in ascertaining the exact form of such names arises from the doubt whether they should appear with a neuter termination, or a masculine or feminine termination. The following rules may be taken as holding good for ordinary conversational purposes. Pure dravidian names will follow the sex of the person; as Carooppan, Carooppy. The same will be the case in names derived from the sanscrit, if the name or the last part of it when compound is the name of a person in the sanscrit; as Abhirauman, Abhiraumy. In names from the sanscrit, if the name or the last part of it when compound is the name of a thing in the sanscrit, the dravidian name will appear in the neuter; as Camalam. As a rule, the names of individuals among hill tribes are not hindoo; they severally signify some peculiarity; as :—Cunnan the eyed one, Pottan the blind one, Tadiyan the fat one, for men; Madhooram the sweet one, Ponnan the fair one, Chakra the sugar one, for females. A special language of a highly artificial and conventional character is used of the royal person, property and actions; ordinary terms being forbidden. The palace occupied by the prince is called bhajanapooram, worship building; the royal food, nectar; a birth, an incarnation; and a birthday, a holy day; a death, leaving the country or going to the heaven of vishnoo namely veicoontam; travelling, yeroonelly or procession; and the word pully, church, or tiroo, sacred, is applied to almost everything connected with the king. For Mahomedan proper names see Alam and Ism [maryauday].

PHAUNSY (پھانسی - phánsi, *Hind.*). A noose. Phaunsigar is a strangler, thug [q.v.].

PHIN (ಫಿನ್ - phin, *Can.*). Todah [q.v.] name for the stone circles on the Neilgherries [aursham, azhauram].

PHOOL (पुष्प - pushpa, *San.*; پھول - phúl, *Hind.*; ಹೂವು - húvu, *Can.*; పువ్వు - puvvu, *Tel.*; പൂവ് - púvu, *Mal.*; பூ - pú, *Tam.*). Title from hindostany. San. from (push, san. to increase). Hind. from (p'hul, san. to unfold). Flower [poo, pooshpam]. Of edible flowers, some are eaten by themselves plain or mixed with sugar [q.v.], others are added to vegetables of a different nature and made into curries [q.v.] and stews; they are chiefly used during festivals [pundigay], when a deviation from the usual mode of living is observed.——**(1)** The following are two key-lists of the principal flowers of s. india edible or used as offerings to gods; further information must be traced in the glossary paragraphs through the small type cross-references at end of this volume; see also vricsham, 7, for the method of expressing the products, &c., of the plants in the dravidian languages.—"*a*" Acacia arabica, babool; Acacia concinna, soap-pod wattle; Ægle marmelos, bael; Bassia longifolia, common mohwah; Bauhinia acuminata, white mountain ebony; Cæsalpinia pulcherrima, gold mohur tree; Calophyllum inophyllum, common poon; Chrysanthemum indicum, indian chamomile; Eragrostis cynosuroides, darbhay; Graptophyllum hortense, face plant; Guettarda speciosa, indian zebra wood; Hibiscus rosa-sinensis, china rose bendy; Ixora coccinea, flame of the woods; Jasminum angustifolium, wild jasmine; Jasminum auriculatum, needle jasmine; Jasminum grandiflorum, common jasmine; Jasminum sambac, arabian jasmine; Lagerstrœmia flos-reginæ, adambo; Lagerstrœmia indica, china privet; Lawsonia alba, henna plant; Mangifera indica, mango; Melia azadirachta, margosa; Mesua ferrea, nauga champak; Methonica superba, wild bachnaug; Michelia champaca, champak; Millingtonia hortensis, indian cork; Mimusops elengi, ilanjy; Morinda umbellata, small ach root; Moringa pterygosperma, indian horse radish; Murraya exotica, andaman satin wood; Musa paradisiaca, plantain; Nelumbium speciosum, sacred lotus; Nerium odorum, oleander; Nyctanthes arbor-tristis, coral jasmine;

Nymphæa odorata, purple indian water-lily; Ocimum sanctum, holy basil; Origanum marjorana, marjoram; Pandanus odoratissimus, screw-pine; Pavonia odorata, peramootty; Rosa centifolia, cabbage rose; Saraca indica, bengal ashocam; Stereospermum chelonoides, pauthiry; Strychnos potatorum, clearing nut; Tabernæmontana coronaria, adam's apple; Vitis quadrangularis, piranday.—"*b*" Achroot, morinda; Adambo, lagerstrœmia; Ashocam, saraca; Babool, acacia; Bachnaug, metbonica; Bael, ægle; Basil, ocimum; Bendy, hibiscus; Chamomile, chrysanthemum; Champak, mesua, michelia; Clearing nut, strychnos; Cork, millingtonia; Darbhay, eragrostis; Face plant, graptophyllum; Flame of the woods, ixora; Gold mohur, cæsalpinia; Henna, lawsonia; Horse radish, moringa; Ilanjy, mimusops; Jasmine, jasminum, nyctanthes; Lotus, nelumbium; Mango, mangifera; Margosa, melia; Marjoram, origanum; Mohwah, bassia; Mountain ebony, bauhinia; Oleander, nerium; Pauthiry, stereospermum; Peramootty, pavonia; Piranday, vitis; Plantain, musa; Poon, calophyllum; Privet, lagerstrœmia; Rose, rosa; Satin-wood, murraya; Screw-pine, pandanus; Water-lily, nymphæa; Wattle, acacia; Zebra wood, guettarda.——**(2)** The following are Varauha mihiran's remarks on omens [shacoonam] of fruits and flowers:—"judging from "the growth of the fruits and flowers of trees and plants "we may determine beforehand what articles can be had "cheap and in abundance and what crops [veilaumay] will "thrive; if the saulam [saul] tree should bear fruits and "flowers, kalama [q.v.] or white rice [q.v.] will grow in "abundance; if the red ashocam [bengal ashocam] should bear "fruits and flowers red paddy [q.v.] will grow; if the csheericay "[q.v.] should bear fruits and flowers white paddy [q.v.] will "grow, and if the black ashocam [q.v.] should bear fruits and "flowers black rice will grow; the growth of the nyagrodham or "banyan [q.v.] tree indicates the growth of barley [jow]; the "growth of tindoocam [gaub] indicates the growth of the shashtyacam [nawara] rice; and the growth of the ashwattam "[peepul] indicates the growth of all crops [dhaunyam, vellaumay]; the growth of the jamboo or rose-apple tree [rose-"apple] indicates the growth of the gingelly [q.v.] and black "gram [q.v.]; the growth of shireesham [sirissa] indicates the "growth of the cangoo [tinay]; the growth of madhoocam "[mohwah] indicates the growth of wheat [geung] and the "growth of the saptaparnam [dita] indicates the growth of the "barley [jow]; the growth of atimooctacam or mountain "ebony [q.v.] and that of coondam or cassia [soovarnacam] "indicate the growth of carpausam or cotton [q.v.]; the growth "of asanam [black murdah] indicates the growth of sarshapam "or mustard [rayaun]; the growth of badary or jujube tree "[bair] indicates the growth of cooloottam [madras horse-"gram], and the growth of chirabilvam [karanj] indicates the "growth of the moodgam [green gram]; if the atasy or flax "[alsee], vaitasam or rattan [q.v.] and palaus [q.v.] trees "should bear blossoms, kodravam [khoda] will thrive; if "tilacam [peacock gingelly] should bear blossoms, conch-shells "[chunk], pearls [moty] and silver [velly] can be had in "abundance and if ingoodam [chironjee] should bear blossoms, "shanam [sunn] or hemp will thrive; the growth of hasticarnam or castor-oil tree [aumanac] shows that elephants "[q.v.] will thrive; that of ashwa carnam [saul] shows that "horses [ghorah] will thrive; that of trumpet flower [pauthiry] "shows that cows [pashoo] will thrive and the growth of "plantains [q.v.] shows that goats [vellaud] and sheep [aud] "will thrive; if the champak [q.v.] should bear blossoms, gold "[pon] can be had in abundance; if the bandhoojeevacam [jungle "geranium] should bear blossoms corals [moongah] can be had "in abundance, if cooravacam [nail dye] should bear blossoms, "diamonds [vajram] can be had in abundance and if nundicauvartam [adam's apple] should bear blossoms, cat's eye gem "[lahsanyah] can be had in abundance; the growth of the "sindhoovauram [notchy] indicates that pearls [moty] can be "had in abundance; that of coosambah or safflower [bastard "saffron] indicates that cooncoomam [saffron] can be had in "abundance, that of the red lotus [nelumbo] indicates that "rulers will prosper and that of the blue lotus indicates "that ministers will prosper; if soovarnapooshpam or globe "amaranth [jaffer goondy] should blossom, merchants will "prosper; if the lotus should blossom, the bramins will prosper, "if the white water-lily [indian waterlily] should blossom, "priests will prosper and if sowgandhicam or blue lotus should "blossom the commanders of armies will prosper and if the "arcam [yercum] plant should blossom, gold [pon] will become "cheap; if the mango [q.v.] should thrive well, there will be "prosperity in the land; if bhallautam or marking-nut [q.v.] "should thrive, there will be fear in the land; if the peeloo "[coomby] tree should thrive there will be health in the land; "if khadiram [catechu] and shamee [q.v.] should thrive, there "will be famine in the land; and if the arjoonam [white "murdah] tree should thrive there will be good rain [mazhay]; "if pichoomandam or neem [q.v.] tree and naugam [nauga "champak] should bear blossoms, there will be prosperity in the "land; if capittam [wood apple] should bear blossoms, there "will be storm; if nichoolam or hijjal [indian oak] should bear "blossoms there will be drought and if cootajam [tellicherry "bark] should bear blossoms there will be disease in the land; "if doorvay or bent grass [hurrially] or the coosham [q.v.] grass "should blossom, sugar-cane [q.v.] will thrive; if kovidauram "[variegated mountain ebony] should blossom there will be fear "from destructive fires; and if shyaumalatay [indian sarsaparilla] "should blossom, dancing-girls will prosper; there will be good "rain in those countries where trees, shrubs and creepers grow "luxuriantly with glossy leaves uninjured by worms, but if the "leaves are otherwise there will be little rain [mazhay]."——**(3)** *Phoolcaury* (پھولکاری - phúlkárí, Hind.). From (phúl, hind. flower + kárí, hind. workmanship). Means a tissued flower. Punjauby word. A peasant woman's Chudder [q.v.] or outer garment worked with sprigs of embroidery [casheeda].

PHOONT (پھونٹ - phúnt, *Hind.*). Means bursting. Same as Mottled melon.

PICOTTAH (उत्तोलन - uttólana, *San.*; ایتم - etam, *Hind.*; ಯಾತ - yáta, *Can.*; ఏతము - étamu, *Tel.*; ഏത്തം - éttam, *Mal.*; ஏற்றம் - éttam, *Tam.*). Title from portuguese. San. from (ut, san. prefix, meaning up + tul, san. to weigh). Hind. from dravidian from (éttu, to raise). The Shadoof of the nile and the old english Swape or swaypole. Contrivance for drawing water from well or low level. A fixed piece of wood generally the trunk of a large tree is forked at the top. In the cleft a palmyra [q.v.] tree is fixed with a pin to form a swipe, and steps are cut on the palmyra [q.v.], by which the person working the machine may mount and descend. To the upper part is fixed a bamboo [yaitcole], at the end of which hangs a bucket [yaittachaul] made of iron plates rivetted together or formed of a hollow stump of a palmyra. A man ascends the ladder to the top of the swipe, supporting himself by a bamboo [q.v.] screen erected by the side of the swipe, while another man below plunges the bucket into the water, after which the one above descends and by his weight draws up the water raised by the bucket. By prepared furrows the water is distributed where wanted [mhote, yaittam]. They are not without danger. There is a Tamul proverb:—இயமன் ஒருவனைக் கொல்வான், ஏற்றம் மூவரைக் கொல்லும்—"yaman kills one, a picottah kills "three;" as there are often three, one to raise bucket, and two on sway-pole.

PIDAUGA (പിടാക - pidáka, *Mal.*). District. Division of a talook [q.v.] in Travancore, like Amshom [q.v.] in Malabar.

PIDAURY (பிடாரி - pidári, *Tam.*). Corruption of (vishahárí, san. poison-remover). A common form of the village goddess. She is represented in a sitting posture, fire issuing from her whole body, to indicate her great wrath. On her head she wears a crown; in her erect locks, various ornaments; on her forehead, the mark of Shiva [q.v.]; in the large holes of her ears, bulky jewels; and behind her ears, two flowers. She has four arms and hands, holding in them, respectively, a drum [damaroo] with a snake [paumb], a trident [shoolam], the skull of Bramha [q.v.], and a goad [ancoosham]. Her throne is an altar. Her pagodas are numerous and of different sizes, containing besides the image of Pidaury one of Vigneshwaran [q.v.]; and the entrance is guarded by two door-keepers of terrible appearance called Moonnadiyaar. In the larger pagodas many more images of stone, representing her eighteen generals with their soldiers, as well as images of metal, are found. The image of stone is never removed, and to it drink offerings and meat offerings with incense are made once a week by the priest [poojarry]; whilst on the altar before the pagoda [q.v.], common people lay various other offerings, which the priest receives. The festival celebrated in her honor lasts seven or nine days, and is, on the whole, like those of the other Graumadevatays [q.v.]. See vol. I (78). There is a Tamul proverb:—அண்டாத பிடாரி ஆருக்கு அடங்குவாள்—"whom will the unapproachable demoness "obey" [matam].——*Pidauran* (പിടാരൻ - pitáran, Mal.). A very small class of Bramins in the north of Malabar. They drink liquor and sometimes exorcise devils [janty].——*Pishauram* (പിഷാരം - pishåram, Mal.). From (pisháran, mal. the caste so called). Ambalavausy's house [mana].

PIG PLANT (கடம்பு - kadambu, *Tam.*). Title from strong smell. Tam. commonly applied to anthocephalus cadamba [common cadamba]. Botanically Siegesbéckia orientalis, linn., compositæ [vricsham, 74]. A much branched, erect herb, 1–3 feet high, with opposite, broadly triangular or ovate, coarsely toothed, more or less scabrous leaves; flowers yellow, the ray-florets are strap-shaped and pistil bearing, those of the disk tubular and perfect; the exterior scales of the involucre are twice the length of the inner; the achenes are without pappus, and are half inclosed by the chaffy scales of the receptacle. Known in china as a remedy for ague, rheumatism, and renal colic.

PILA (பிள - pila, *Tam.*). To crack.——*Pilavay* (பிளவை - pilavai, Tam.). From (pila, tam. to crack). Anthrax in cattle [pashoo rogam]. Otherwise splenic apoplexy, black-quarter, congestive fever, malignant sore-throat, inflammatory fever, &c. It is communicable in this country not only to healthy cattle [maud] but to man. The characteristic symptom, which frequently appears first at night, is the formation of puffy, crackling swellings under the skin, generally of the loins or extremities; or mucous membrane of the tongue or fauces, the disease when occupying the last position being often termed, malignant sore-throat. Temperature is raised, respiration and circulation are hurried. Death supervenes in from two to nine hours.

PILAH (பிலா - pilá, *Tam.*). Same as Jack.——*Cootty pilah* (குட்டிப்பிலா - kuttippilá, Tam.). Same as Stunted jack.——*Pelandoray* (பெலாந்துரை - pelándurai, Tam.). From (pilá, tam. jack tree, artocarpus integrifolia, willd. + turai, tam. ford). South arcot dist., Vriddhauchellam tal.; pop. 1,437; acres 2,178; lat. 11° 25′; long. 79° 19′; from Vriddhauchellam S.S.W. 8 miles. A river-fed system of tanks [q.v.]. See vol. I, 404.

PILKYA (खञ्जन - khañjana, *San.*; پلکیا - pilkiyá, *Hind.*). San. from (khanj, san. to limp). Wagtails and pipits. Motacillinæ, sylviadæ [calacuntam], dentirostres, insessores, aves [pacshy, 23], of naturalists [jantoo]. The species best known to the natives are shown below.——*Indian titlark* (روجل - rújal, Hind.; గుర్రపుమారిజిట్ట - gurrapumárijitta, Tel.). Tel. from (gurramu, tel. horse + mári, tel. personal suffix + jitta, tel. bird). Hind. also (chacharí). Corydalla rufula, motacillinæ [pilkya], sylviadæ [calacuntam], dentirostres, insessores [pacshy, 23], of naturalists. Alias Anthus agilis, malaiensis; Cichlops ubiquitarius. Runs rapidly on the ground, and when raised does not fly far. Song mere repetition of one note.——*Khanjan* (खञ्जन - khañjana, San.; ذعرة - zuarah Ar.; دم جنبانك - dumjumbának, Pers.; کھنجن - khanjan, Hind.; ممولا - mamolá, Dec.; చాకలచారలగాడు - tsákalatsáralagádu, Tel.; വാലാട്ടി - válátti, Mal.; சூத்தாட்டியுள்ளான் - shúttáttiyullán, Tam.). San. from (khañja, san. lame). Ar. from (zuara, ar. to frighten); for it is never seen unless scared. Pers. from (dum, pers. tail + jumbának, pers. one who wags). Hind. from sanscrit. Tel. from (tsákala, tel. the caste + tsára, tel. stripe + gádu, tel. personal suffix). Mal. from (vál, mal. tail + áttu, mal. to shake). Tam. means rump + shake + snipe [oollaun]. Ar. also (hazzázuzzanab), meaning wagger of tail; (savah). Pers. also (dumícha). Hind. also (bhúinmamolá), meaning earth wagtail. Title otherwise Pied wagtail. Motacilla maderaspatana, motacillinæ [pilkya], sylviadæ [calacuntam], dentirostres, insessores [pacshy, 23], of naturalists. Alias Motacilla picata, variegata. A water wagtail; found on banks of rivers. Male is occasionally caged for its song.——*Khorassan sparrow* (خراسانی چڑی - khurásáníchurí, Hind.; లిక్కుజిట్ట - likkujitta, Tel.). Tel. from (likki, tel. small sickle + jitta, tel. bird). Hind. also (masarichi), meaning mosquito-killer. Title otherwise Blind bird, Indian tree-pipit. Pipastes agilis, motacillinæ [pilkya], sylviadæ [calacuntam], dentirostres, insessores [pacshy, 23], of naturalists. Alias Anthus arboreus, maculatus. Very similar to its European congener. Said to kill mosquitoes [q.v.].

PILL (புல்லு - pullu, *Tam.*). Grass; one of the five Dravidian terms for generic terms for plants [vricsham].——*Pillangrovy* (ಪಿಳ್ಳಂಗೋವಿ - pillangóvi, Can.; పిల్లనగ్రోవి - pillanagróvi, Tel.; பில்லாங்குழல் - pillánguzhal, Tam.). Tel. from (pillu, tel. reed + króvi, tel. tube). Tam. from (pul, tam. grass + kuzhal, tam. pipe). Flageolet. Same as Algoja [sangeetam].——*Pilloory* (کچلے کا ملنگ - kuchlekámalang, Hind.; کچلے کی سوکن - kuchlekísaukan, Dec.; పుల్లురివి - pullurivi, Tel.; புல்லுருவி - pulluruvi, Tam.). Title from tamul. Hind. from (kuchlá, hind. nux vomica, strychnos nux vomica, linn. + malang, hind. companion); from being a parasite on nux vomica. Dec. from (kuchlá, hind. nux vomica + saukan, hind. rival wife); probably from growing on that plant. Tel. from tamul. Tam. from (pul, tam. grass + uruvu, tam. to pierce through); a parasite. Title otherwise Misseltoe. Botanically Viscum monoicum, roxb., loranthaceæ [vricsham]. Monoicous, branches opposite and dichotomous, jointed, round and smooth; leaves opposite, subsessile, lanceolar, three to five-nerved; flowers axillary and at the divisions of the branchlets, sessile, usually three together, the centre one of which is generally male and the lateral ones female; berry long; flowering about the beginning of the hot season. Other common species are:—angulatum, attenuatum, capitellatum, grossum, moniliforme, orbiculatum, orientale, ramosissimum, wallichianum.——*Poollary* (புல்வரி - pulvari, Tam.). See sep. title.

PILLY (పిల్లి - pilli, *Tel.*). Cat. Plant first term, from hairy growth of plant or fruit. Ex., where transl. is of second term:—Asparagopsis floribunda (pillitíga), creeper; Crotalaria biflora (pillivattachettu), testicle + plant; Mucuna pruriens (pilliadugu), foot; Phaseolus trilobus (pillipesara), phaseolus mungo; Pistacia lentiscus (pillikandlaguggilamu), eye + dammer. See gloss. paragraphs.

PILOW (پلاؤ - puláu, *Hind.*). Persian. A dish, in origin purely Mahomedan, consisting of meat, or fowl [moorghy], boiled along with rice [q.v.] and highly seasoned with cinnamon [q.v.], cardamoms [q.v.], mace [jauty patry] and ghee [q.v.].

PILPAY (پیلپائی - pilpái, *Hind.*). From (védapriya, san. knowledge-lover). Author of Punchatantram [bidpay].

PIN (பின் - pin, *Tam.*). After.——*Pillaiyaur* (பிள்ளையார் - pillaiyár, Tam.). Honorific plural form. Literally the noble child. The most common name of Vigneshwaran [q.v.] in the Tamul country [ganapaty, ganesh].——*Pillaiyaur chatoorty* (ಪಿಳ್ಳರಿಚೌತಿ - pillárichauti, Can.; பிள்ளையார்ச்சதுர்த்தி - pillaiyárççathurtti, Tam.). Means ganesh, the son-god + fourth. Otherwise Pillaiyaur nomboo. Sanscrit is Vinauyaca chatoorty; Teloogoo Vinauya a chowty. Lunar [chaundramaunam] festival [pundigay, 3a], subject to intercalation [adhicam]. On the fourth day of the increasing moon [shooclapacsham] of the sixth lunar month Bhaudrapadam [mausam] between 20th August and 19th September. Celebrated in houses and in Shiva [q.v.] pagodas [q.v.] in honor of Ganesh [q.v.] for the purpose of getting understanding. Hindoos observe a demi-fast [oopavausam]. Clay images of the deity, riding upon the back of a rat [ely] are made, duly consecrated and worshipped in houses and families; they are afterwards thrown into a river or tank [maryauday]. See vol. I (93).——*Pillamaur* (പിള്ളമാർ - pillamár, Mal.). Title for accountants [curnum, kanakkan].——*Pillay* (പിള്ള - pilla, Mal.; பிள்ளை - pillai, Tam.). Means child. Title added to the names of persons engaged in agriculture [vellaumay] and to tamul shoodra curnums [q.v.]. It belongs properly to the Yiday [q.v.] or great pastoral race of the Tamul country. The Vulloova [q.v.] priests of the Pariah [q.v.] also call themselves Pillay. Also largely assumed by Native christians [peyar]. Pillay is also affix to names of small animals and birds; compare Pitta. Ex., where transl. is of first term:—Halicore dugong (nírupille), water; Herpestes mungo (kírippillai), mongoose, herpestes genus; Sciurus palmarum (anirbillai), squirrel, sciurus genus. See gloss. paragraphs.——*Pillay tamul* (பிள்ளைத்தமிழ் - pillaittamizh, Tam.). From (pillai, tam. child + tamizh, tam. the language). Poem celebrating different stages in the infancy and childhood of a hero, in ten parts. There are two celebrated compositions bearing this title, one in praise of Meenautchy [q.v.] the goddess at Madura by Comaragooroopara deshican, and the other reciting the childhood of Scandan [soobramanyan] by Maurgasahauya devan. The ten prescribed points are:—putting on the arm-rings, with magical rites; first voluntary movement of the child compared to the motion of herbs by the breeze; lulling the child in the cradle with songs [pautt]; the first clapping of its hands; kissing; extending its hands and calling to be taken; showing the moon to the infant; amusement of a small drum; making in play small houses; drawing small carriages.——*Pillaytyaugar* (பிள்ளைத்தியாகர் - pillaittiyágar, Tam.). From (pillai, tam. child + tyaj, san. to give). Shiva, the child giver. There is a legend connected with Shirtondan, one of the sixty-three devotees [aroopatt moover] of shiva [q.v.]. To try his piety and hospitality, Shiva appeared to him in the form of a mendicant guest and when invited to food insisted on having the flesh of his son cooked for him; on this being done Shiva gave him back his child restored to life.——*Pinj* (பிஞ்சு - piñju, Tam.). Newly-formed fruit; one of the Dravidian terms for plant products added to the word-root [vricsham].——*Pinna* (పిన్న - pinna, Tel). Small. Plant first term, often joining two genera. Ex., where transl. is of second term:—Hydrocotyle asiatica (pinnaélaki), elettaria cardamomum; Salvadora persica (pinnavaragógu), toddalia aculeata. See gloss. paragraphs.

PINAH (پینانار - pinánár, *Hind.*). Fabric made in Philippines from fibres of the pine-apple leaf [ananas]; very soft, and transparent, and generally has a slight tinge of pale yellow.

PINAR (പിണർ - pinar, *Mal.*). Stiff.——*Penarvully* (दीर्घपत्रा - dírghapatrá, San.; പിണർവള്ളി - pinarvalli, Mal.). San. from (dírgha, san. long + patra, san. leaf) [plantain, poison nut]. Mal. from (pinar, mal. stiff + valli, mal. creeper). San. also (kuntalí), meaning produced in coontalam; (tiktaka), meaning bitter; (pindavalli), meaning ball creeper. Title otherwise Bandolier fruit tree. Portuguese name given to fruit from resemblance to leather cases called bandoleers, each containing a charge of powder, of which every musketeer anciently wore twelve suspended by a shoulder belt. Botanically Zanonia indica, linn., cucurbitaceæ [vricsham, 62]. Leaves 6 to 8 by 3 to 4 inches, usually acute; petiole one inch; male flowers very small, pedicels $\frac{1}{6}$ to $\frac{1}{4}$ inch; female flowers, including the ovary, $\frac{1}{2}$ inch; ovary early becoming one-celled by the separation of the three fleshy placentas; seeds much compressed, hardly $\frac{1}{10}$th inch thick; capsule large, like a candle extinguisher. In malabar a bath by boiling leaves for boils, and an antispasmodic liniment by pounding leaves with milk and butter; in ceylon the plant is used as a febrifuge.

PINDAM (पिण्ड - pinda, *San.*). From (pind, san. to accumulate).—"*a*" Sum total in arithmetic [ganitam]. The $\frac{1}{24}$th part of the quadrant [paudam] of a circle [chuckram]; equal to 3° 45′, the constant ratio of the Hindoo trigonometrical tables.—"*b*" Plant first term, meaning round. Ex., where transl. is of second term:—Daucus carota (pindamúlam), root; Dioscorea globosa (pindálu), esculent root; Ipomæa batatas (pindálú), esculent root; Lagenaria vulgaris (pindap'hala), fruit; Manihot utilissima (pindálú), esculent root. See gloss. paragraphs.—"*c*" A ball of rice [q.v.] or meat, especially that which is offered at obsequial ceremonies or Shrauddhams [q.v.] to deceased parents and progenitors [pitry].——*Poondy oil* (പിണ്ടിഎണ്ണ - pindienna, Mal.). Product of Malabar nutmeg.

PINDARRY (پنڈارا - pindárá, *Hind.*; పిండారి - pindári, *Can.*). From (pendhú, mahr. a drink from millet). See vol. I (158); II, 59. Originally freebooters attached to Mahratta [q.v.] armies, who took to plunder when the latter ceased to spread. They fought no pitched battles, and always retreated before a regular army [dandoo]. They were put down by Marquis of Hastings [jauty].

PINDY (పిండి - pindi, *Tel.*). From (pishta, san. flour from pish, san. to grind). Flour. Plant first term, from being covered with powdery dust or from reducing rocks to powder. Ex., where transl. is of second term:—Ærua lanata (pindidonda), cephalandra indica; Ficus asperrima (pindichettu), plant. See gloss. paragraphs.

PINEY (धूप - dhúpa, *San.*; धुंपारूकु - dhumpárúku, *Conc.*; شجر سندروس - shajarisandrús, *Ar.*; درخت چندرس - darakhtichandras, *Pers.*; چندرس کا پیڑ - chandraskáper, *Hind*; چندرس کا جھاڑ - chandraskájhár, *Dec.*; ಧೂಪದಮರ - dhúpadamara, *Can.*; ತಂಡೋಳಿಗೆದಮರ - tandóligedamara, *Too.*; తెల్లదమ్మరుమాను - telladammarumánu, *Tel.*; പയൻമരം - payanmaram, *Mal.*; හල් - hal, *Singh.*; வெள்ளைக்குந்துருக்கம் - vellaikkundurukkam, *Tam.*). Title from malayalam. San. means incense. Ar. from (shajar, ar. tree + sandrús, ar. sandarach). Pers., &c., from arabic. Can. from (dhúpa, can. incense + mara, can. tree). Tel. from (tella, tel. white + dammaru, tel. dammer + mánu, tel. tree). Mal. from (paya, mal. resin + maram, mal. tree); from copious resin exuding from the tree. Tam. from (vellai, tam. white + kundurukkam, tam. olibanum tree, boswellia serrata, roxb.). Hind. also (sufeddámarkáper), meaning white dammer tree; (kahrubá), meaning amber, from resemblance [karbah]. Dec. also (rál), meaning resin [raul]. Can. also (ráladamara); (paini); (mandadhúpa), meaning slow incense; (pene). Tel. also (tellaguggilapuchettu), meaning white + dammer + tree; (dhúpadammaruchettu), meaning incense + dammer + tree. Mal. also (vellakkunturukkam), meaning white clibanum. Tam. also (kundurukkam) [indian olibanum, white dammer]; (vellaikkungiliyam), meaning white googal; (túbamaram), meaning incense tree; (shadakula). Title otherwise Doopada tree, Gum piney, Indian copal, Indian gum anime, Piney dammer, Piney tallow, Piney varnish tree, Vateria copal, White dammer. Botanically Vateria indica, linn., dipterocarpeæ [vricsham, 24]. Alias Elæocarpus copalliferus; Vateria malabarica. Large handsome tree; bark whitish; foliage dense; young shoots and all tender parts, except the leaves, covered with fine stellate pubescence; leaves alternate, petioled, oblong, entire, slightly cordate at the base, shortly pointed or obtuse at the apex, coriaceous and smooth, petioles 1 inch in length; stipules oblong; flowers rather remote, on large terminal panicles; bracts ovate, pointed; filaments forty to fifty, very short; anthers not auricled at the base, terminating in a single long bristle at the apex; style a little longer than the stamens; stigmas acute; capsule oblong, obtuse, coriaceous fleshy; seed solitary; native of malabar. The resin [raul], when recent and soft, is called piney varnish; when hardened, piney dammer [q.v.], otherwise white dammer [q.v.], indian copal or indian gum anime [q.v.]. The resin is found from pale green to a deeper amber color with all the intermediate shades; it is a true resin and occurs in large lumps emitting an agreeable balsamic odour when fresh; it is easily distinguished from all other indian resins by its superior hardness, its color, and amber-like [karbah] appearance; piney resin resembles the american copal [q.v.] but differs most advantageously from it by being at once soluble in turpentine [carpoora teilam] and drying oils [yennay], without the necessity of the preliminary destructive fusion required by that resin, a process which tends greatly to impair its color when used as a varnish [rangh]; the solution of the piney resin in turpentine is turbid and milky, but by the addition of powdered charcoal [adoopp kary] and subsequently filtering, it yields a solution transparent and colorless as water, and gives a varnish which dries with a purity and whiteness not to be surpassed; piney resin yields, on destructive distillation, a pluresent oil, of agreeable odour but not differing essentially from that obtained from cheaper resins; piney resin burns with a clear steady light, giving off a pleasant smell and but little smoke. The resin is procured by cutting a notch in the tree, sloping inwards and downwards; this is soon filled with the juice which hardens by exposure to the air. An oil [yennay] again is prepared by cleaning the seeds, then roasting and grinding them into a mass; to five seers of seed twelve seers of water are added, and the whole is boiled until the oil rises to the surface; on removing the oil, stirring the contents of the vessel and allowing it to stand until the following day, a further portion of oil will be found on the surface; this is known as piney tallow, or vegetable butter of canara; it has the properties of tallow, and is of a nature betwixt wax [mom] and oil [yennay], a concrete inflammable substance; on cooling this forms a solid cake, generally white, sometimes yellow; greasy to touch, with a degree of waxiness, has rather an agreeable odour. Plant gives to pharm. the white dammer [q.v.]; non-officinal, like pine resin; under the influence of gentle heat this resin [raul] combines with wax [mom] and oil [yennay] and forms an excellent resinous ointment; substituted for british burgundy pitch; piney tallow also is highly valued as a local application in chronic rheumatism and some other painful affections. The bark, bitter and astringent, retards fermentation; beads are made of the resin, which resemble amber beads [karbah], even to being electrical when excited by rubbing; the resin is on the malabar coast also made into candles, while burning these diffuse an agreeable fragrance, give a fine clear light with little smoke, and consume the wick so as not to require snuffing; a spirit varnish is prepared by reducing to powder about six parts of piney dammer and one of camphor [q.v.], and then adding hot alcohol sufficient to dissolve the mixed powder; the varnish thus prepared is good for varnishing pictures, but before being used requires to be gently heated to evaporate the camphor, which otherwise would produce a roughness on the picture in consequence of its subsequent evaporations; the oil or tallow is suitable for lubrication of wheels and axles of railway carriages, equally applicable to manufacture of soap [sauboon] and candles, also used in lamps. Sap-wood white with a tinge of red; heart-wood grey, rough; wood used in ship-building, being proof against attacks of teredo navalis. Observe that the Pinnay tree, which is quite another thing, is the Calophyllum angustifolium, roxb. For other varnishes compare:—Ailanthus glandulosa, false varnish, japan varnish; Holigarna longifolia, malabar black varnish; Melanorrhæa usitata, black varnish, burmese varnish, martaban varnish; Rhus succedanea, japanese varnish; Semecarpus anacardium, singhalese varnish, indian varnish, sylhet varnish. See gloss. paragraphs. For Dammers generally see that head.

PINJ (पिञ्ज - piñj, *San.*). To shine.——*Pingalam* (पिंगल - pingala, San.). Title from shining color of some species. Laniadæ family, dentirostres, insessores, aves [pacshy, 19], of naturalists [jantoo]. Shrikes. Bill strong, short, moderate length, notched or toothed at tip; gape rather wide; tarsus short, strong, usually with large scutæ in front and on the toes. Divided into several sub-families:—Lanianæ, true shrikes; many kill small birds and mammals, as mice [shoondely] and shrews [musk rat]; some impale their victims on thorns; flight is direct, moderately rapid, with repeated strokes of the wings [latorah]. Malaconotinæ, wood shrikes; feeding on insects which they pick off leaves and branches; usually have a rather pleasing song whilst thus employed [hill latorah]. Campephaginæ, cuckoo shrikes [aukroy, sahely]. Dicrurinæ, drongo shrikes [king crow]. Artaminæ, swallow shrikes [palmyra swallow].——*Pingalan* (पिङ्गल - pingala, San.). Coobairan [q.v.].——*Pingam* (पिङ्ग - pinga, San.). From (piñj, san. to shine). Reddish brown.——*Pinjem* (पिञ्ज - piñja, San.). Cotton [q.v.].——*Pinjarry* (پنجارا - pinjárá, Hind.; பிஞ்சாரி - piñjári, Tam.). From (piñja, san. cotton). Lubbays [q.v.]. Cotton-cleaners [doodeycoolam, jauty]. Distinguish from Brinjarry.——*Punj* (कर्पास - kárpasa, San.; روئی - rúí, Hind.; ಹತ್ತಿ - hatti, Can.; ప్రత్తి - patti, Tel.: പരുത്തി - parutti, Mal.; பஞ்சு - pañju, Tam.). From (piñj, san. to shine); from shining wool. Cotton [indian cotton].——*Punjy* (ಪಂಜಿ - panji, Can.). From (piñj, san. to shine). Means cotton. Pariah proper name [peyar].

PINNAY (பின்னை - pinnai, *Tam.*). Same as Common poon. Distinguish from Piney.——*Shiroopinnay* (சிறுபின்னை - shirubinnai, Tam.). Same as Small poon.

PINTADO (پنٹیڈو - pintado, *Port.*). Title from portuguese means spotted cloth. A painted cloth, chintz [q.v.].

PIPLEE (پپلی - piplí, *Hind.*). Means nourishing. Same as Long pepper, and origin of term Pepper [q.v.].——*Piplee mor* (پپلاموڑ - piplámor, Hind.). From (above + múla, san. root). Otherwise Papriemor. Root of piper longum, linn. [long pepper].

PIRA (பிற - pira, *Tam.*). To be born.——*Pair* (പേറു - péru, Mal.). From (peru, tam. to beget). The vernacular for the sanscrit Jenm [q.v.].——*Piraisoody* (பிறைசூடி - piraisúdi, Tam.). From (pirai, tam. moon + shúdu, tam. to wear). Shiva [q.v.]. Cf. Chundrashekharan.——*Pirapp* (പിറപ്പ - pirappu, Mal.). Birth [jenmam, samsauram]. Tye pirapp or birth of Tye, the tenth tamul solar month [mausam]; see Pongal. For Varshapirapp or birth of the year see New year.——*Piray* (பிறை - pirai, Tam.). From (pira, tam. to be born). Properly the new moon [amavausyay]. Valar piray is the crescent moon [shoocla pacsham]; and Tey piray is the decrescent moon [krishna pacsham]. For more information see Pacshan.

PIRANDAY (अस्थिसंहार - ast'hisamhára, *San.*; चौधारीखांडवेल - chaudhárikhándavéla, *Mahr.*; संदबाळ्ळि - sandaballi, *Conc.*; هڈجوڑا - hadjorá, *Hind.*; نلیر - naller, *Dec.*; ಮಂಗರವಳ್ಳಿ - mangaravalli, *Can.*; ಸಂದುಬೂರು - sandubúru, *Too.*; నల్లేరు - nalléru, *Tel.*; ചങ്ങലംപിരണ്ട - channalampiranta, *Mal.*; වල්හිරැස්ස - valhírassa, *Singh.*; பிரண்டை - pirandai, *Tam.*). Title from tamul. San. from (ast'hi, san. bone + sambára, san. drawing together); bone-maker. Mahr. from (chaudhárí, mahr.

quadrangularis + khándavéla, mahr. the creeper. ventilago madraspatana, gærtn.). Hind. from (had, hind. bone + jorá, hind. one who sets); from use of beds of stems in spine affections. Can. from (mangu, can. blackness + balli, can. creeper). Too. from (sandu, too. joint + báru, too. creeper). Mal. from (channala, mal. chain + piranta, mal. the creeper). Singh. from (val, singh. creeper + hírassa, singh. the plant). Tam. from (pural, tam. to roll); low rolling creeper. San. also (vajravallí), meaning adamantine creeper; (kandalatá), meaning bulbous root + creeper; (ast'hishrinkhalá), meaning bone + chain; (ast'hisandhána), meaning bone joining. Hind. also (hárjorá), meaning flesh-joiner; (harsankar), meaning bone + joiner. Can. also (mangaruli); (sanduballi), meaning joint + creeper. Mal. also (piranta), meaning rolling. Singh. also (hírassa). Title otherwise Adamant creeper, Bone-setter, Square-stalked wild grape. Botanically Vitis [draucshay] quadrangularis, wall., ampelideæ [vricsham, 42]. Alias Cissus bifida, quadrangularis. Climbing; glabrous; stem four-angled, winged; stipules lunate, entire; leaves alternate, cordate-ovate, serrulated, short-petioled; umbels shortly peduncled; stamens four; petals four, distinct; fruit globose, size of a large pea [calauyam], very acrid, one-celled, one-seeded; flowers small, white; cultivated; berries very acrid. The fresh stem is deep or pale green in color, four-angled, winged and jointed, each joint varying in length from 2–4 inches; very acrid in taste. Leaves and young shoots dried and powdered are given in bowel-affections. Same when young and tender are eaten. Gives fibre [naur].——*Bristly pirandaу* (هرمل - harmal, Hind.; బఱ్ఱెబచ్చలి - barre-battsali, Tel.; புளிப்பிரண்டை - pulippirandai, Tam.). Title from character of stems. Hind. from syriac [harmal]. Tel. from (barre, tel. buffalo + battsali, tel. basella cordifolia, lam.). Tam. from (puli, tam. sour + pirandai, tam. vitis quadrangularis, wall.). Tel. also (pullabattsali), meaning sour + basella cordifolia, lam. Tam. also (puliyárilaikkizhangu), meaning oxalis corniculata, linn. + leaf + thick root. Title otherwise Hairy wild vine. Botanically Vitis [draucshay] setosa, wall., ampelideæ [vricsham, 42]. Cissus acida, setosa. Climbing; clothed with scattered glandular bristly hairs, but otherwise glabrous; stem herbaceous; leaves succulent, trifoliate, without a common petiole; leaflets stalked, roundish-ovate or obovate, obtuse with numerous sharp serratures, cymes peduncled with divaricating branches; petals four, distinct; stamens four; style conspicuous; berries red, ovoid, hairy, one-seeded; flowers in the rainy season. Acrid in all its parts, leaves toasted and oiled are applied to indolent tumours to bring them to suppuration.

PISANG (پسنگ - pisang, *Malay*). Same as Plantain.

PISHAUCH (पिशाच - pisháсha, *San.*). From (pishita, san. flesh + ash, san. to eat).—"*a*" An evil spirit haunting the places where dead bodies are buried or burnt [shavacaud, shoodcaud], and occasionally animating them; or even possessing living bodies [bhootam, pey].—"*b*" Also a sandstorm. These are common at the end of March and beginning of April. They show themselves between eleven and twelve at noon, increasing daily both in strength and number, and moving from west to east in varying directions all over the country. They carry dust and light articles along with them [munnmaury mazhay]. See vol. II, 5.

PISH-PASH (پاش پاش - páshpásh, *Hind.*). Hind. means broken to bits. Indian dish for invalids; fresh meat cooked amongst rice.

PISIN (பிசின் - pisin, *Tam.*). From (pasai, tam. moisture). Gum [gond]; one of the Dravidian terms for plant products added to the word-root [vricsham].

PISTAH (پسته - pistah, *Pers.*). Title otherwise Turpentine trees. Botanically the Pistacia genus, anacardiaceæ [vricsham, 45]. Small trees with pinnate leaves; the fruits are dry egg-shaped drupes, containing a one-seeded stone. The species best known to the natives are:—integerrima [kakrasinghy], lentiscus [mastic], terebinthus [turpentine pistah], vera [edible pistah].——*Edible pistah* (شجرفستق - shajarifustuk, Ar.; درخت پسته - darakhtipistah, Pers.; پستے کا پیڑ - pistekáper, Hind.; پستے کا جھاڑ - pistekájhár, Dec.). Title from nuts which are eaten. Ar. from persian. Pers. from (darakht, ar. tree + pistah, pers. pistachio). Hind. from (pistah, pers. pistachio + per, hind. tree). Dec. from hindostany. Ar. also (shajaribuzghanj). Pers. also (darakhtibuzghand). Title otherwise Jacob's nut tree, Pistachio nut tree. Botanically Pistacia [pistah] vera, linn., anacardiaceæ [vricsham, 45]. Pistacia from (fustuk, arabic). The fruit, a drupe, is dry, oval, oblong, oblique, wrinkled, of ashy green color, the nut bony, glabrous, white, with a spongy stain at the base; the almond pale green, covered with white or brownish perisperm; the odour of the pericarp is resinous, and slightly balsamic, its taste bitter and resinous. The so-called galls [mauchicoy] from margins of leaves are when fresh bright pink on one side and yellowish white on the other; they vary much in shape and size, some being perfectly fig-shaped [atty] and others almost spherical, the majority are ovoid; the largest are an inch in length; some are no larger than a pea [calauyam]; the taste acidulous, very astringent and slightly terebinthinous; caused by presence of an aphis; these were the nuts sent by jacob into egypt. Nuts are medicinally warm, and used in general debility; oil from the kernels is demulcent and restorative; the bark is tonic. Nuts fried in butter are eaten; sometimes simply dried like almonds [bandam]; sometimes made into articles of confectionery.——*Turpentine pistah* (بطم - batm, Ar.; سقز - sukkar, Pers.). Ar. also (katingirámí). Pers. also (khinjak); (zangbárí). Hebrew alah. Greek τέρμινθος, τερέβινθος. Title otherwise Cabool mastic, Chian turpentine, Cyprian turpentine, Scio turpentine, Terebinth tree. Botanically Pistacia [pistah] terebinthus, linn., anacardiaceæ [vricsham, 45]. Deciduous tree, 20 feet high; leaves pinnate, with an odd one; leaflets about seven, ovate-lanceolate, rounded at the base, acute mucronate; flowers apetalous, flowering in june and july. The galls [mauchicoy] from margins of leaves are very small sacs, three or four of which communicate together; they are of a pink color, and have a terebinthinate and astringent taste. By pressing kernels is got the original oil of turpentine, τερεβίνθινον ἔλαιον, a mixture of essential and fat oils; of thick consistence; yellowish white color, pellucid and tenacious; its odour is strong, peculiar, and agreeable, its flavor slightly bitter; by keeping it loses its essential oil [attar] and becomes hard; much the same as true mastic [q.v.], but the color is rather deeper, and it wants the fine perfume of the latter article. This turpentine is employed as a masticatory [charvanam] to sweeten the breath, and preserve the teeth. For common pine turpentine see Carpoora teilam.

PITACAM (पिटक - pitaka, *San.*). From (pit, san. to heap together). Basket, granary, collection. A division of the sacred books of the Booddhists [booddha]; in which there are three pitacams, Sootram, Vinayam, and Abhidharmam; compiled many years after the death of Booddha who himself left no writings.

PITAH (پتا نار - pitánár, *Hind.*). Title from portuguese. Fibre of the American aloe.

PITCHAY (பிச்சை - piççai, *Tam.*). From (bhiksh, san. to beg). Alms. Hindoo 2nd or pers. name [peyar]. Applied to males and females among the lower orders. Cala pitchay are alms given at the threshing-floor [calam]. The tamuls are in favor of alms-giving, but do not class alms-taking as a virtue, as the bramins do. See the following from Cooral:—*வறியார்க்கொன் றீவதே யீகைமற் றெல்லாங் குறியெதிர்ப் பை நீர துடைத்து*—"to give to the destitute is true charity; "all other gifts have the nature of what is done for a measured "return."—*ஈத லிசைபட வாழ்த லதுவல்ல தூதிய மில்லை யுயிர்க்கு*—"give to the poor and live with praise; there is "no greater profit to man than that."—*இகழ்ந் தெள்ளா தீவாரைக் காணின் மகிழ்ந்துள்ள முள்ளு ளுவப்ப துடைத்து*—"beggars rejoice exceedingly when they behold "those who bestow with kindness and courtesy."—*இரவென்னு மேமாப்பி றோணி கரவென்னும் பார்தாக்கப் பக்கு விடும்*—"the unsafe raft of begging will split when it "strikes on the rock of refusal."—*தெண்ணீ ரடுபுற்கை யாயினுந் தாடந்த துண்ணலி னூங்கினிய தில்*—"even thin "gruel is ambrosia to him who has obtained it by labor."——*Pitchayyan* (பிச்சையன் - piççaiyyan, Tam.). From (above + aiyyan, tam. master). Familiarly Pitchoo. Hindoo 2nd or pers. name [peyar].——*Pitchoogoonty* (బిచ్చుగుంటి - pittsugunti, Tel.). From (bittsamu, tel. alms + konu, tel. to take). A class of vagrants in Kurnool and Nellore. Numbers about 7,000 [jauty].——*Pitchoomany* (பிச்சுமணி - piççumani, Tam.). From (above + mani, tam. gem.). Familiarly Pitchoo. Hindoo 2nd or pers. name. Common to both sexes [peyar].

PITTA (పిట్ట - pitta, *Tel.*). Any small bird [cooroovy]. Compare Pillay.—"*a*" Very common bird second term. Ex., where transl. is of first term:—Alauda gulgula (bharatapitta), singer; Ammomanes phœnicura (dóvapitta), road; Artamus fuscus, (tátipitta), palmyra; Caprimulgus indicus (kappapitta), frog; Chætornis striatus (gaddipitta), grass; Coracias indica (pálapitta), milk-producing; Galerida cristata (dzuttupitta), crest; Hierococcyx varius (kátipitta), wild; Iora zeylonica (pattsapitta), green; Leucocerca albofrontata (dásaripitta), veishnava mendicant, from stripes; Mirafra cantillans (agnipitta), fire, and (bharatapitta), singer; Otocompsa jocosa (turakapikilipitta), mussalman + pycnonotus hæmorhous; Pericrocotus peregrinus (kunkumapitta), red powder worn by women on the forehead; Petrocossyphus cyaneus (podakaççipipitta), spot + quarrel; Ploceus baya (pasupupitta), yellow; Polyphasia nigra (chinnakátipitta), small + forest, hierococcyx varius; Pomatorrhinus horsfieldii (dásaripitta), veishnava mendicant, from stripes, and (námálapitta), stripe; Pratincola indica (adavikampapitta), jungle + bush; Scolopax gallinago (ullangipitta) lapwing, actitis genus; Strix javanica (tsávupitta), death; Tchitrea paradisi (tókapikilipitta), tail + pycnonotus hæmorhous; Tephrodornis pondiceriana (úlapitta), whistle; Turnix dussumierii (peddadábapitta), large + turnix genus; Upupa nigripennis (kondapitta), crest. See gloss. paragraphs.—"*b*" Plant first term, meaning small. Ex.:—Ehretia buxifolia (pittapisinika), bird satin wood; Ficus tomentosa (pittamarri), bird banyan. See gloss. paragraphs.

PITTAM (पित्त - pitta, *San.*). Gall or bile. The bile of the buffalo [khoolgah], wild boar [jungly soor], goat [vellaud] peacock [mayil], and rohitacam [rohitam] fish are used in medicine, single or mixed, as laxatives, and chiefly in place of water to soak powders intended to be made into pills. Pittam is one of the three vital humours of the body [veidyan], and from it are derived forty human diseases. Such as the following:—drowsiness, constant singing and dancing, biting with the teeth like a dog, crying out and calling out as if in a great fury, pain over the whole body, constant drinking without being able to quench the thirst, decoloration of the face and body, an inclination to put everything into the mouth, constant chattering of nonsense, constant singing, red urine, constant sleepiness, &c. [veidyan]. Pittam is not infrequently a plant first term. Ex., where transl. is of second term:—Naregamia alata (pittamári), killer; Tinospora cordifolia (pittaghní), killer. See gloss. paragraphs.——*Pitpapra* (شاهترج - sháhtraj, Ar.; شاهتره - sháhtrah, Pers.; پت پاپڑا - pitpáprá, Hind.; شاترا - shátrá, Dec.; ಕಾಡುಸಬ್ಬಸಿಗೆ - kádusabbasige, Can.; చాతరాశి - chátaráshi, Tel.; துரா - turá, Tam.). Title from hindostany. Ar. from persian. Pers. from (sháh, pers. king + tara, pers. garden herb). Hind. from (pit, hind. bile + páprá, hind. plant, gardenia latifolia, linn.). Dec. from persian. Can. from (kádu, can. jungle + sabbasige, can. peucedanum graveolens, benth.). Tam. from (tura, tam. to expel), medicinal. Ar. also (bakalatulmalik), meaning king of pot-herbs. Greek καπνὸς. Title otherwise Earth smoke, Fumiterre, Fumitory, King of herbs. Botanically Fumaria parviflora, lamk., fumariaceæ [vricsham, 9]. Alias Fumaria vaillantii. Annual; smooth; leaves linear, channelled; bracteas at first as long as the flower, afterwards as short as the fructiferous pedicel; petals four, the lower one distinct, linear, the three upper united, the middle one spurred downwards; sepals minute; fruit globose, slightly pointed; flowers very small, pale rose-colored, tipped with dark purple; generally found in paddy-fields. The whole plant except the root is medicinally alterative tonic, diaphoretic and febrifuge; the plant contains fumaric acid and fumarine; its physiological action is due to the latter. Decoction; take of the leaves and thin branches, three ounces; water one pint and-a-half; boil on a very slow fire till the liquid is reduced to one pint, and strain when cool. Dose, from two to three ounces, three times a day. Substituted for sassafras, jamaica sarsaparilla [sarsaparilla china root], guaiacum wood, mezereon root and pulv. jacobi vera. No other common species here.——*Pittalay* (पित्तल - pittala, San.; برنج - biranj, Pers.; پیتل - pítal, Hind.; پتل - pittal, Dec.; کنڠن - kuníngan, Malay; ಹಿತ್ತಾಳೆ - hittále, Can.; ಪಿತ್ತಳೆ - pittale, Too.; ఇత్తడి - ittadi, Tel.; പിച്ചള - piççala, Mal.; பித்தளை - pittalai, Tam.). Title from tamul. San. from (pitta, san. bile); from increasing bile. Hind. and dec. from sanscrit. Malay from (kuning, malay, yellow). Tam. from sanscrit. Malay also (támbagakuning), meaning yellow copper; (loyang). Brass. Aurichalcum of chemists. Factitious metal, made of copper [taumram] and zinc [tootnaug]. Is in greater request than copper among the natives. Pittalay cumby is brass wire. Pittalay raikk is brass leaf. Pittalay saumaun is brass ware.

PITTAPORE (పిఠాపురము - pit'hápuramu, *Tel.*). From (pít'ha, san. throne seat + pura, san. town); as rajah's capital.——**(1)** Division, Godavery. Area 192 square miles. Zemindarry tract. Population 83,824. Language Teloogoo. E. coast of district. Bounded by:—N. Toony division and Peddapore talook, S. Cocanada division, E. Bay of Bengal, W. Peddapore talook. No mountains, traversed by Yelair. Black-cotton soil [regar]. Manufacture of bell metal [cunts] vessels. No commerce. Irrigation by Yelair and a few tanks. Camping grounds; Gollaprole, Dharmavaram. Zemindarries:—Gollaprole, Mullavaram, Pittapore. Principal trig. stations:—Gorasa, Iskapully, Vizianagram, Wontimauvidy beacon. The leading places, &c., in the division are the following.——*Ameenbaudah* (అమీనాబాదా - amínbádá, Tel.). From (amín, hind. proper name + bárá, hind. locality). Zemindarry village; pop. 798; lat. of village 17° 05′; long. 82° 22′; from Cocanada N.N.E. 12 miles; from Pittapore E.S.E. 6 miles; from the sea W. 1½ miles. Peshcush Rs. 673.——*Condavaram* (కొండవరము - kondavaramu, Tel.). From (konda, tel. mountain + pura, san. town). Village; pop. 1,539; lat. 17° 06′; long. 82° 19′; from Cocanada N.N.E. 11 miles; from Coonavaram E.S.E. 74 miles; from Ellore E.N.E. 81 miles; from Madras N.N.E. 300 miles; from Narsapore N.E. 60 miles; from Pittapore E.S.E. 2 miles; from Rajahmundry E.N.E. 35 miles; from the sea W. 6 miles. Scene of a battle in December 1758 between English and French.——*Dharmavaram* (ధర్మవరము - dharmavaramu, Tel.). From (dharma, san. piety + pura, san. town). Zemindarry village; lat. of village 17° 14′; long. 82° 16′; from Cocanada N. 20 miles; from Pittapore N.N.W. 8 miles; from the sea W. 19 miles. Peshcush Rs. 2,402.——*Gollaprole* (గొల్లప్రోలు - gollaprólu, Tel.). From (golla, tel. shepherd caste + prólu, tel. town). Zemindarry village; pop. 5,381; lat. of village 17° 10′; long. 82° 20′; from Cocanada N.N.E. 15 miles; from Pittapore N.E. 4 miles; from the sea W. 8 miles. Peshcush Rs. 11,567. Encamping ground.——*Gorasa* (గొరస - gorasa, Tel.). Means hoof. Trig. station; lat. 17° 04′ 55·01″; long. 82° 19′ 32·71″; from Comauragherry N. 1⅔ miles.——*Iskapully* (ఇసుకపల్లె - isukapalle, Tel.). From (isuka, tel. sand + palle, tel. village). Trig. station; lat. 17° 07′ 36·15″; long. 82° 21′ 27·69″; from Naugoolapully W. 1½ miles.——*Mullavaram* (మల్లవరము - mallavaramu, Tel.). From (mallaya, tel. proper name + pura, san. town). Zemindarry village; pop. 1,320; lat. of village 17° 10′; long. 82° 23′; from Cocanada N.N.E. 18 miles from Pittapore N.E. 7 miles; from the sea W. 6 miles. Peshcush Rs. 947.——*Naugoolapully* (నాగులపల్లి - nágulapalli, Tel.). From (nága, san. snake + palli, tel. village). Village; pop. 2,613; lat. 17° 07′; long. 82° 22′; from Cocanada N.N.E. 14 miles; from Pittapore E.N.E. 6 miles; from the sea W. 4 miles.——*Ooppauda* (ఉప్పాడ - uppáda, Tel.). From (uppu, tel. salt + váda, tel. village). Zemindarry village, Port; pop. 3,611; lat. of village 17° 04′; long. 82° 23′; from Cocanada N.N.E. 11 miles; from Madras N.N.E. 300 miles; from Pentacote S.W. 24 miles; from Pittapore E.S.E. 7 miles. Fine muslins [q.v.] are manufactured. Peshcush Rs. 673.——*Pittapore* (పిఠాపురము - pit'hápuramu, Tel.). See below.——*Vizianagram* (విజయనగరము - vijayanagaramu, Tel.). From (vijaya, san. victory + nagara, san. city). Trig. station; lat. 17° 11′ 53·64″; long. 82° 24′ 18·45″; from Mullavaram N. 3 miles.——*Wontimauvidy beacon* (ఒంటిమావిడి ontimávidi, Tel.). From (onti, tel. single + mávidi, tel. mango, mangifera indica, linn.). Trig. station; lat. 17° 12′ 00·00″; long. 82° 32′ 00·00″; from Tondangy S. 2 miles.——**(2)** Deputy tahsildarry, Godavery district. Pay Rs. 100.——**(3)** Zemindarry; Town, Head-quarters of Deputy tahsildar, and of the Pittapore zemindarry, Place of pilgrimage; Godavery dist., Pittapore division; pop. 13,731; lat. of town 17° 07′; long. 82° 17′; from Cocanada N. 12 miles; from Coonavaram E.S.E. 72 miles; from Ellore E.N.E. 78 miles; from Madras N.N.E. 312 miles; from Narsapore N.E. 59 miles; from Rajahmundry E.N.E. 32 miles; from the sea W. 8 miles. Peshcush Rs. 2,48,937. For an account of the zemindarry, see vol. I, 57. The town is the residence of the Rajah. Possesses sculptured buildings and other objects of interest. Inscription of A.D. 584. Booddhist [booddha] remains have been found.

PIT VIPER (رنگاری سانپ - rangárísámp, *Hind.*; هرا سانپ - harásámp, *Dec.*; ನೇತ್ರಕನ್ನಡಿ - nétrakannáde, *Can.*; బొద్రుపాము - bodrupámu, *Tel.*; கண்குத்திப்பாம்பு - kanguttippámbu, *Tam.*). Title from the depression between eye and nostrils. Hind. from (rang, hind. color + árí, pers. bringing + sámp, hind. snake). Dec. from (hará, hind. green + sámp, hind. snake). Can. from (nétra, san. eye + kannádi, can. glass). Tel. from (boddu, tel. ledge + pámu, tel. snake). Tam. from (kan, tam. eye + kuttu, tam. to strike at + pámbu, tam. snake) [whip snake]. Terms co-extensive with family Crotalidæ, ophidii viperiformes, ophidia [sarpam], reptilia [sarpy, 29], of naturalists [jantoo]. The family of Crotalidæ or Pit vipers as represented in Southern india are not so dangerous as their American congeners, though all are venomous. They are distinguished by the pit or depression between the eye and the nostrils in the loreal region; the triangular broad head and the short thick body. The Halys is the only genus that has any vestige of the caudal appendage which has given to some of the American crotalidæ the name rattle-snake; and in this species it is reduced to a simple horny spine at the end of the tail. Many of the Pit vipers are arboreal snakes, and in color resemble the foliage or branches of the trees in which they live. There are four South indian genera:—Halys, Hypnale, Peltopelor, Trimeresurus. The following are the species, alphabetically arranged:—"*a*" Halys elliotti. Alias Trigonocephalus elliotti.—"*b*" Hypnale nepa. The Carawilla. Alias Coluber nepa; Cophias hypnale; Hypnale carawala; Trigonocephalus hypnale, zara [carawilla].—"*c*" Peltopelor macrolepis. Alias Trimeresurus macrolepis. Recognized by the very large scales with which the head and body are covered; uniform green; dark olive-green in adults; bright grass-green in young ones; yellow line along the outer series of scales; lower parts pale green.—"*d*" Trimeresurus anamallensis. Upper side of the head marbled with black in adults, uniform greenish in young; black or brown band from back edge of eye to angle of the mouth. Belly yellowish green, with numerous yellow and black spots along its side; tail black, with yellow and green spots. Tree snake; in general sluggish, not attempting to move out of the way, as they very closely resemble the branch on which they rest, frequently not perceived until they prepare to dart. The bite of large specimens is dangerous and has occasionally proved fatal. When roused these snakes are extremely fierce, striking at everything within their reach. Frogs [bhaicam], mammals [sastanam], and birds [pacshy] form their food.—"*e*" Trimeresurus gramineus. Alias Coluber gramineus; Trimeresurus elegans, viridis; Vipera gramineus, viridis. Grass-green above, lighter on the sides; tail sometimes cinnamon-red; yellow or brick-red line runs from behind the eye along the outer series of scales. Lower parts pale greenish. Common, hanging from branches of trees, or concealed under the dense foliage. It feeds on small birds and frogs.—"*f*" Trimeresurus strigatus. Alias Trigonocephalus neelgherriensis. Brown, with series of large irregular darker spots; horse shoe-like white marking on the neck, sometimes rather indistinct; lips yellowish; indistinct brown band from eye to side of neck; lower jaw with black spots; belly marbled with black; extremity of the tail white in young [viriyan].

PIY (పియ్యి - piyyi, *Tel.*; பீ - pí, *Tam.*). Dung. Plant first term often joining two genera; from smell. Ex., where transl. is of second term: — Acacia farnesiana (piyyitumma), acacia; Clerodendron inerme (pínárisangu), smelling + azima tetracantha; Daucus carota (pítikanda), amorphophallus campanulatus; Physalis minima (pinottánotiyan), physalis; Sterculia fœtida (pínárimaram), smelling + tree. See gloss. paragraphs.——*Piy maram* (गोलदडा - góladadá, Mahr.; گلدار - guldár, Dec.; ಕಾವಿಲಿಮರ - kávilimara, Can.; രമണപ്പൂ - ramanappú, Mal.; பீமரம் - pímaram, Tam.). Title from tamul. Mahr. from hindostany. Dec. from (gul, pers. flower + dár, pers. holder), meaning spotted; on the bombay ghauts. Mal. from (ramana, san. delighting + pú, mal. flower). Tam. from (pí, tam. dung + maram, tam. tree). Tam. also (kamille); (kávilli), from canarese; used by kadar [q.v.] on the anamullays. Title otherwise Dung tree. Botanically Sterculia [cauvalam] guttata, roxb., sterculiaceæ [vricsham, 26]. Tree, 70 feet; leaves between broadly and oblong ovate, entire, obtuse, or with sudden acumination, prominently nerved and veined beneath; young leaves densely pubescent; racemes somewhat fascicled; pedicels short; calyx deeply five-cleft, tomentose; segments lanceolate, distinct; flowers yellow; flowering in december. Bright red capsules, very common; root is aromatic. Bark yields cordage [naur]; that of the young parts made into a kind of clothing on w. coast; for which purpose taken off in strips, beaten, washed, and dried in the sun. Timber not used.

PIYAUZ (पलाण्डु - palándu, *San.*; कांदा - kárdá, *Mahr.*; पियावु - piyávu, *Conc.*; بصل - basl, *Ar.*; پیاز - piyáz, *Pers.*, *Hind.* and *Dec.*; بونكميرا - buvangmerah, *Malay*; ಈರುಳ್ಳಿ - írulli, *Can.*; ನೀರುಳ್ಳಿ - nírulli, *Too.*; ఎర్రగడ్డ - erragadda, *Tel.*; ପିୟାଜ - piyájó, *Oor.*; ചുവന്നുള്ളി - chuvannulli, *Mal.*; ලූනු - lúnu, *Singh.*; வெங்காயம் - vengáyam, *Tam.*). Title from hindostany. San. from (pala, san. flesh + anda, san. ball). Mahr. from (kanda, san. bulbous root). Malay from (bavang, malay, an onion + merah, malay, red). Can. from tamul. Too. from (níru, too. water + ulli, too. garlic). Tel. from (erra, tel. red + gadda, tel. root). Mal. from (chuvanna, mal. red + ulli, mal. onion). Tam. from (ven, tam. white + káyam, tam. pungency). San. also (ugragandha), meaning strong smelling [vashamboo]; (ugranámá), meaning named oogra; (latárka), meaning creeper + shining, is green onion; (sukandaka), meaning having good root. Dec. also (piyáj). Malay also (bavang); (brambang). Can. also (nírulli); (ulligadde). Tel. also (ulli), meaning mean; (nírulli), meaning water + onion; (tellaulli), meaning white + onion; (erraulli), meaning red + onion. Mal. also (venkáyam); (írulli), moist onion. Tam. also (írulli), meaning moisture + garlic, allium sativum, linn.; (íravengáyam), meaning moisture + onion. Greek κρόμμυον. Latin cepa. Title otherwise Onion, Water garlic. Botanically Allium cepa, linn., liliaceæ [vricsham, 136]. Alias Allium esculentum; Cepa vulgaris; Porrum cepa. Biennial, bulbous-rooted plant, with a swelling stem, leafy at the base, tapering fistular leaves, a reflex spathe, a large globose umbel, usually not bulbiferous; lobes of the perianth obtuse and hooded, not half as long as the stamens; bulb simple, not made of cloves as in garlic [lussoon], and in common variety solitary; flowers, small, white or greenish, purplish-white with a green keel. Cultivated in black loam, or sandy soil, dry; in south in chittray [mausam] or april for caur [q.v.] crop and in arpisy or october for pishaunam [q.v.] crop; on coromandel in caurteecam or november and margashiram or december; ground divided into small squares with banks; bulbs of the previous year preserved as seed have sprouts at this season and are dibbled in in rows and hand watered, manure [yeroo] is used; from each bulb a tuft of grass-like blades grows to nearly a foot; when crop is full grown upper part is dry while lower part still green; dug up after three months; the plant is stripped from the bulbs and the latter aired on ground; ready at once for market; average price 48 imperial seers for one rupee. As medicine, stimulant, diuretic and expectorant; in veterinary practice is a good cooling diet with tyre [q.v.] and boiled rice [q.v.]. As food, produce flatulency and occasion thirst; mussalmans [q.v.] never cook curry [q.v.] without onions; bramins [q.v.] do not eat them regarding as similar to mutton. Bombay onions are large and mild. The leek is Allium porrum, linn.; very scarcely cultivated here. Garlic is Allium sativum, linn. [lussoon]. Compare also: —Urginia indica (káttulli), jungle onion; Crinum revolutum (narivengáyam), fox onion; see gloss. paragraphs.

PLANTAIN (कदली - kadalí, *San.*; केळ - kéla, *Mahr.*; केळि - kéli, *Conc.*; شجرةالموز - shajaratulmauz, *Ar.*; درخت موز - darakhtimauz, *Pers.*; کیلے کا پیڑ - kelekáper, *Hind.*; موز کا جہاڑ - mauzkájhár, *Dec.*; پسنک - pisang, *Malay*; ಬಾಳೆ - bále, *Can.*; ಬಾರೆ - báre, *Too.*; అరటి - arati, *Tel.*; କଦଳୀ - kodilo, *Oor.*; വാഴ - vázha, *Mal.*; කෙසෙල් - kehel, *Singh.*; வாழை - vázhai, *Tam.*). Title from the latin plantago through portuguese. San. from (ka, san. water + dala, san. leaf); from watery sheaths of the stem. Mahr. and conc. from sanscrit. Ar. from (shajar, ar. tree + mauz, ar. plantain). Pers. from (darakht, pers. tree + mauz, pers. plantain). Hind. from (kadalí, san. the plant + per, hind. tree). Dec. from (mauz, ar. plantain + jhár, hind. tree). Oor. from sanscrit. Mal. from tamul. Tam. from (vázh, tam. to prosper); regarded as an emblem of fertility and prosperity. San. also (rambhá), meaning delighting; (vanalakshmí), meaning forest lutchmy; (dírghapatrá), meaning long-leaved [penarvully, poison nut]; (vrishapushpá), meaning sprinkling flower, perhaps from flowers shedding water; (bálakapriyá), meaning child favorite [bair]; (bhánup'halá), meaning having fruits radiating from stem like sun-rays; (guchhadantiká), meaning cluster of flowers + tooth; (guchhap'halá), meaning bunch of fruits; (hastivisháni), meaning elephant's tusk, fruits likened to it; (sukumárá), meaning beautiful; (sup'halá), meaning good fruit; (sakritp'halá), meaning bearing fruit once; (kásht'hílá), meaning having small seed; (alabú); (móchá), meaning abandoning, from the falling off of sheaths; (úrustambhá), meaning thigh + pillar; (rájéshta), meaning king beloved; (amshumatp'halá), meaning sun fruit; (vanabhúshá), meaning forest ornament. Ar. also (talh), meaning plantain tree. Hind. also (rámkelá), meaning rama's plantain. Malay also (banana). Tel. also (tatachhadamu); (anati); (ananti); (anti); (bontarati), meaning large + the tree; (kommarati), meaning horn + the tree; (chakrakéliarati), meaning sugar or sweet plantain; (nallaarati), meaning black + plantain tree. Singh. also (kesel); (ánaválu); (ratukehal), meaning red plantain. Tam. also (arambai); (arésigam), meaning not purgative; (púvanvázhai), meaning flower + plantain; (námavázhai), meaning striped plantain. Title otherwise Adam's fig, Banana, Fig of india, Fig of paradise, Forbidden fruit, Pisang, Vauzbay. Has been thought by some to be the tree of life of the garden of eden; and by others, who distinguish between the two, the tree of knowledge of good and evil. The grape [angoor], shaddock [pummelow], cherry [q.v.], apple [seb], and many other fruits [pazham], have also been thought to be the forbidden fruit [q.v.]. Some say it was this tree from whose leaves adam and eve made themselves aprons. Botanically Musa paradisiaca, linn., musaceæ [vricsham, 142]. Alias Musa cliffortiana, mensaria, sapientum. Musa from arabic, meaning taste. Herbaceous; stem simple, thickly clothed with the sheathing petioles of the leaves; leaves forming a tuft on the apex of the stem; spike of flowers compound, rising from the apex of the stem, each division enclosed in a large spathe with male flowers at the base, female or hermaphrodite ones at the upper end; perianth with six superior divisions, five of which are grown together into a tube, slit at the back, the sixth is small and concave; style short; fruit oblong, fleshy, obscurely three to five-cornered, with numerous seeds buried in pulp; flowers yellowish whitish. The long, vertical, sheathing leaf-stalks overlap one another, forming soft stems, 4–15 or more feet high; from the top of the sheath broad leaves expand 6–10 feet in length; fruit is produced in a large bunch from the top of the sheathing stem; a bunch of plantains may contain as many as a hundred fruits, each bunch from 4–9 inches long and 3–5 inches in circumference; fruit itself is about six inches long, ripens of a pale straw color, and is not fit to be eaten till it can be removed from the bunch without the slightest effort; the fruit gives 37 per cent. of dry matter; the composition of the ash of the plantain bears a close resemblance to that of potato [q.v.]; both contain much alkaline matter [cauram], potash [jharka namak] and soda [munn cauram] salts; and there is nearly the same percentage of phosphoric acid and magnesia [caunta munn]. Original habitat probably the valley of the euphrates; more easily cultivated and more prolific than even the potato [q.v.]; cultivated nearer coast than inland, in garden soil rich in decayed vegetable matter; ground prepared in south in chittray [mausam] or april, on coromandel in cheitram or april and veishaukham or may, on w. coast in toolaum or october, vrishchicam or november and dhanoo or december; first the ground is ploughed four or five times, then hand-hoed two or three times; manure [yeroo] then applied; tubers put down in south in audy or july, on coromandel in veishaukham or may, on w. coast in vrishchicam or november, dhanoo or december, and macaram or january; tubers are deposited in pits exposing only about 3–4 inches above ground; while under growth land is watered once in ten days, and plants pruned; heaps of mud are raised against stem to serve as a prop; green leaves, ashes, and dried cowdung applied as manure [yeroo]; in full-grown crop, leaves become yellow; ripe fruits in a bunch bend downwards from the top; ten months after sowing the leaves and fruits are cut with knives close to the stem; the fruits are placed in pots filled with margosa [neem] or other leaves and allowed to remain so for three or four days; then they become ripe; brought to market as soon as ripe. Tender leaves used medicinally for dressing blistered surfaces; fresh plantain leaf forms shade for eyes in ophthalmia; unripe fruit cooling and astringent, useful in diabetes; juice of unripe fruit and lymph of stamens are slightly astringent; powdered and dried leaf stop bleeding in nose; root is anthelmintic; sap of fresh stem allays thirst in cholera; leaves quoted in pharm. non-officinal. The fruit contains every element of animal food mixed with fragrant principles; almost the only tropical fruit without stone or core of any sort, and which can be eaten unaided by any instrument without inconvenience; it may well have been the primæval food of man; in green state, sliced and made into curry [q.v.], when it eats not unlike potatoes [q.v.]; the ripe fruit is served either raw, stewed or fried; sometimes roasted in ashes and used as bread; vinegar [caudy] is manufactured from it; the preserved fruit, which resembles dried figs [atty], is a nourishing and antiscorbutic article of diet for long voyages; in this state it will keep for a long time; a meal is prepared from the fruit by stripping off the skins, slicing the core, and, when thoroughly dried in the sun, powdering and sifting it; plantain meal is more digestive and strengthening than arrowroot [malabar arrowroot], and thus more suitable for children and invalids; its flavor is also preferable; mahomedans eat it with milk [q.v.] and sugar [q.v.]; the natives also use the extremities of the flower shoots, the heart of the stem, and that portion of it from which the roots proceed in their curries. The stems laden with branches of fruit are invariably placed at the entrance of houses during marriage or other festivals as emblematic of plenty and fruitfulness; stem yields a fine white silky fibre [naur] of considerable length, lighter than hemp [kinnab], flax [alsee] and aloe [q.v.] fibre, by one-fourth or one-fifth and possessing considerable strength; the outer layers of the sheathing foot-stalks yield the thickest and strongest fibres; some tough kinds of paper [caugaz] have been made from the fibres; the leaves form a substitute for platters; skins are used by chucklers [q.v.] in dyeing [shauyam] leather [chamrah] black; ashes used as mordant [caurom]. Many varieties of fruit, differing in size and shape. The kind popularly known as the guindy plantain, poovauzhay in tamul, is considered the best, and is round, small sized, with a very thin rind, luscious, sweet, and of a most delicate flavor; a good bunch may contain over a thousand fruits; this kind is used entirely as a table fruit, being considered too valuable for cooking purposes. The rustauly is the sort generally sold as table plantains, though not of such good quality as the former. A large plantain, known in tamul as mondan is one of the commonest cooking fruits of the presidency. The cadaly, cultivated in the Tinnevelly and Malabar districts, is considered sacred and used chiefly as offerings to the gods. East indian plantains and West indian bananas are mere varieties of the same plant; the banana tree is marked with purple spots, fruit shorter and rounder, softer pulp, more delicate taste. There is a Tamul proverb:—வாழ்கிற வீட்டுக்கு வாழைவைத்துப் பார்—"ascertain the future of a family by putting down "plantain trees;" it is said that plantains naturally put forth their bunches to the north; should the fruit appear otherwise, it is considered ominous to the homestead. And another:— வாழைக்குக்கொத்து வழுதலைக்குத்தண்ணீர்—"the hoe "for plantain and water for brinjaul." There is a Teloogoo proverb:—వంకాయరుచి తోటవానికెరుకను, అరటిపండురుచి రాజుకెరుకను—"the gardener knows the taste of brinjaul, the king "knows the taste of plantain;" brinjauls [q.v.] should be cooked and eaten fresh from the garden; plantains when used in an unripe state as vegetable, should be kept a few days. And another:—జ్ఞాతులపోరు అరటికఱ వదలవు—"the stain of plantain, "the grumbling of cousins, never cease."——*Demon plantain* (रानकेळी - ránakelí, Mahr.; پسنگوتن - pisangutan, Malay; பேயன்வாழை - péyanvázhai, Tam.). Title from tamul. Mahr. from (rána, mahr. wild + kélí, mahr. plantain, musa paradisiaca, linn.). Malay means wild plantain. Tam. from (péy, tam. wild + vázhai, tam. plantain), from habitat and resemblance. Malay also (koffo). Title otherwise Manilla hemp. Botanically Musa textilis, nees., musaceæ [vricsham, 142]. Introduced; fibre [naur] lately much employed for cordage of various kinds.——*Liquorice plantain* (குன்றிமணிச்செடி - kunrimaniççedi, Tam.). Title from seed. Same as Indian shot. ——*Stone plantain* (கல்வாழை - kalvázhai, Tam.). Same as Wild plantain.——*Wild plantain* (राणकेळ - ránakéla, Mahr.; रानकेलि - ránakéli, Conc.; ಕಾಡುಬಾಳೆ - kádubále, Can.; ಕಲ್ಲುಬಾರೆ - kallubáre, Too.; అడవిఅరటి - adaviarati, Tel.; കല്ലുവാഴ - kalluvázha, Mal.; கல்வாழை - kalvázhai, Tam.). Title from habitat. Mahr. from (rána, mahr. wild + kéla, mahr. plantain tree, musa paradisiaca, linn.). Conc. from mahratta. Can. from (kádu, can. wild + bále, can. plantain). Too. from (kallu, too. stone + báre, can. plantain). Tel. from (adavi, tel. forest + arati, tel. plantain tree). Mal. from (kal, mal. stone + vázha, mal. plantain), from small stone-like seeds imbedded in pulp. Tam. from (kal, tam. stone + vázhai, tam. plantain). Mal. also (káttuvázha), meaning wild plantain. Tam. also (káttuvázhai), meaning forest + plantain. Title otherwise Stone plantain. Botanically Musa superba, roxb., musaceæ [vricsham, 142]. Stem short, conical, thickly covered with the spongy petioles of decayed not sheathing leaves; leaves petioled, linear, rounded at both ends, cuspidate; spadix drooping; spathes broad, oblong, obtuse, sub-cordate at the base, many-flowered, hermaphrodite ones persistent; gives fibre [naur].

PLAUTCHY (பிலாச்சை - piláççai, *Tam.*). From (plava, san. frog + matsya, san. fish), frog fish; from ugly appearance. Title otherwise Coffer fish, Trunk fish. The genus Ostracion, sclerodermi, plectognathi, teleostei, pisces [matsyam, 44], of naturalists [jantoo]. The species best known to the natives are Bony plautchy, Bull plautchy. Cf. also Prickly plautchy, which is another genus.——*Bony plautchy* (கற்பிலாச்சை - karbiláççai, Tam.). Title from bony plates on back. Tam. from (kal, tam. stone + piláççai, tam. sea frog, ostracion genus). Ostracion [plautchy] turritus, sclerodermi, plectognathi, teleostei [matsyam, 44], of naturalists. Alias Chameau marin; Lactophrys camelinus; Ostracion dromadaire, gibbosus; Tetrosomus turritus. Body about as wide as high, being of a triangular shape, the apex being above. Olive brown, with three badly marked dark bands in the lower one-third of the body, and a fourth just behind the base of the dorsal fin. A light blue spot in the centre of each scute. Fins straw-colored, the caudal with two dark vertical bands, one at its base, the other at its outer extremity. The young have several dark blotches and bands over various parts of the body, and a ridge extends from the orbit to the upper part of the bridge over the tail. Sea; at least 9 inches.——*Bull plautchy* (மாட்டுப்பிலாச்சை - máttuppiláççai, Tam.). Title from appearance of head. Tam. from (mádu, tam. bull or cow + piláççai, tam. ostracion genus). Title otherwise Coffer fish, Thorned trunk fish. Ostracion [plautchy] cornutus, sclerodermi, plectognathi, teleostei [matsyam, 44], of naturalists. Alias Lactophris cornutus; Ostracion arcus, valentini; Ostracium cornutum. Colors carapace of a light brown, with round blue spots all over it in moderate numbers, about one on each scute, some, however, being destitute of any. Caudal blue spotted. Sea.——*Prickly plautchy* (முள்ளம்பிலாச்சை - mullambiláççai, Tam.). Title from erectile spines. Tam. from (mul, tam. thorn + piláççai, tam. sea frog, ostracion genus). Title otherwise Globe fish, Prickly globe fish, Sea-hedge hog, Urchin fish. Diodon hystrix, gymnodontes, plectognathi, teleostei [matsyam, 45], of naturalists [jantoo]. Alias Diodon atringa, brachiatus, plumieri, punctatus; Holocanthus hystrix; Hystrix piscis; Paradiodon hystrix; Reversus indiens. Body covered with coarse spines, which are longest on the sides of the body behind the pectoral fin; they are dilated at their bases. The whole of the fish except the ventral surface of a light brown covered with round blue or brown spots, rarely above one to the base of a single spine. The fins similarly spotted. Sea; attains a large size. Diodon pilosus is hairy urchin fish.

PO (போ - pó, *Tam.*). To go.——*Poke* (പോക്കു - pókku, Mal.; போக்கு - pókku, Tam.). From (pó, mal. to go). Going; way [caday poke, poramboke].——*Pokevaravoo* (പോക്കുവരവു - pókkuvaravu, Mal.). From (pókku, tam. going + varavu, mal. coming). Transfer of registry of lands.——*Pokkachit* (പുക്കശ്ശീട്ടു - pukkashíttu, Mal.). From (pukku, mal. to receive + shíttu, mal. note). A receipt.

PODE (పోడు - pódu, *Tel.*). Bushy land.——*Podalacore* (పొదలకూరు - podalakúru, Tel.). From (poda, tel. bush + úru, tel. village). Village; Nellore dist., Raupore tal.; pop. 1,795; acres 9,089; lat. 14° 24′; long. 79° 36′; from Nellore W.S.W. 17 miles; from Raupore N.E. 18 miles. Here five roads from Raupore, Manoobole, Nellore, Somashila, and Sangam meet. Ancient temple dedicated to Ganesh [q.v.]. Annual festival in February. Walls of the old fort may be traced by mounds of earth. Has large tank. Paddy [q.v.] cultivation. The greater part of the population are weavers who manufacture roomauls [q.v.] and cloths.——*Pode caud* (போடுகாடு - pódugádu, Tam.). Nomadic cultivation [cautcaud, coomry, ponacaud].——*Podily* (పొదిలి - podile, Tel.). See sep. title.

PODILY (పొదిలి - podile, *Tel.* podili *). From (poda, tel. bush) [pode]. Sanscrit name (prit'hulápurí), meaning pritoola, the village goddess + town.——(1) Zemindarry, Deputy tahsildar's division, Nellore; pay Rs. 120. The Podily division consists of hundred and twenty-three villages, all Vencatagherry zemindarry, of which eighty-six village belong to Podily zemindarry talook, and thirty-seven to Cotcherlacote zemindarry talook. N. inland part of district. It is bounded on north by Darshy division, on south by Canigherry talook, on west by Cumbum and Marcapore talooks of Kurnool district, and on east by Ongole talook. The country is generally hilly and dry. In some villages pots [chatty] are made and rough cloths are woven. Trade in grain, ghee [q.v.] and rough cloths to a limited extent. Money is laid out on interest. The people are generally uneducated. Bellary-Kistna railway passes through north of the division. There are stations at Royavaram and Toorlapaud. Places of archæological interest:—Badgoolair, Boodamacauyalpaud, Caljoovvalpaud, Coonchepulley, Dondlair, Eegalpaud, Gaurladinney, Goorraulmadoogoo, Kellampully, Mungalacoontla, Paumoolpaud, Pauta gaurlapett, Pedda auricutla, Podily, Ramlaveed, Tarloopaud, Vaugimadoogoo, Vedraulpaud. The leading places, &c., in the division are the following. ——*Coochipoody* (కూచిపూడి - kúchipúdi, Tel.). From (kúchi, tel. long + púdi, tel. village). Village; pop. 916; lat. 15° 28′; long. 79° 42′; from Nellore N.N.W. 73 miles; from Ongole W.S.W. 26 miles; from Podily S.S.E. 10 miles. To the west, at about 1½ miles, is a hill called Andhracondah, on which is a small temple of Andhra rameshwara sawmy. The stone from the hill is made into wheels, mortars and pillars and sold in neighbouring villages.——*Eegalpaud* (ఈగలపాడు - ígalapádu, Tel.). From (íga, tel. fly + pádu, tel. village). Village; lat. 15° 44′; long. 79° 38′;

from Nellore N.N.W. 91 miles; from Ongole W.N.W. 39 miles; from Podily N.N.W. 9 miles. Inscription of A.D. 1523. ——*Gaurladinney* (గారెలదిన్నె - gáreladinne, Tel.). From (gáre, tel. bramble + dinne, tel. a mound). Zemindarry, Village; pop. 736; lat. 15° 39′; long. 79° 26′; from Nellore N.W. 91 miles; from Ongole W.N.W. 45 miles; from Podily W. 16 miles. On the Veligonda hill in this village is a temple of Shree veligonda roya sawmy, where an annual festival in the month of Phaulgoonam [mausam] or march takes place. On bank of Mooshy.——*Mooshy* (ముశి - mushi, Tel.). See sep. title. ——*Nimmavaram* (నిమ్మవరము - nimmavarmu, Tel.). From (nimma, tel. lime tree, citrus medica, linn., var. limonum, brandis + pura, san. town). Village; pop. 375; lat. 15° 37′; long. 79° 42′; from Nellore N.N.W. 83 miles; from Ongole W.N.W. 27 miles; from Podily E.N.E. 3 miles. Mats [boriyah] made by people called Pitchoogoonties [q.v.].——*Paumoolpaud* (పాములపాడు - pámulapádu, Tel.). From (pámu, tel. snake + pádu, tel. village). Village; lat. 15° 43′; long. 79° 41′; from Nellore N.N.W. 90 miles; from Ongole W.N.W. 31 miles; from Podily N. 8 miles. Inscription of A.D. 1551. ——*Pedda auricutla* (పెద్దఅరికట్ల - peddaárikatla, Tel.). From (pedda, tel. large + árikatlu, tel. obstacle). Village; pop. 2,070; lat. 15° 31′; long. 79° 34′; from Nellore N.N.W. 79 miles; from Ongole W. 34 miles; from Podily S.S.W. 8 miles. Old temple built by Janamejayan.——*Podily* (పొదిలె - podile, Tel.). See below.——**(2)** Village, Head-quarters of Deputy tahsildar and Ex-officio Sub-registrar; Nellore dist., Podily division; pop. 4,412; lat. 15° 36′; long. 79° 39′; from Madras N.N.W. 176 miles; from Naidoopett N. 116 miles; from Nellore N.N.W. 81 miles; from Ongole W.N.W. 29 miles. Chief village of one of the northern divisions of Vencatagherry zemindarry. Festival of Nirmaleshwarasawmy celebrated on Shivarautry [pundigay, 6a] in Maugham [mausam] or February. Lies on trunk road from Ongole to Cumbum. Connected by road with Darshy and Canigherry. At 6 miles to the south is Podily hill, on which is a temple of Lutchmy narsimhasawmy. The idol [shilay, vigraham] is worshipped every Saturday, and an annual marriage festival takes place there in Phaulgoonam [mausam] or March. Podily is head-quarters of a zemindarry [q.v.] tahsildar [q.v.]. Two tanks [q.v.]. Principal crops are paddy [q.v.], sadza [bajrah], zonna [cholum], oil seeds [yennay], cotton [q.v.], corra [tinay], aroogoo [varagoo], and green gram [q.v.]. The soil is stony, here and there brackish [calar, sowdoò]. There are modas [q.v.] on which saltpetre [shorah] is annually manufactured in the dry season. The climate is good.

PODWAUL (പൊതുവാൾ - potuvál, sing.; പൊതുവാന്മാർ - potuvánmár, pl., *Mal.*). From (potu, mal. common + ál, mal. man). Half bramins [ambalavausy] in Malabar [jauty]. For Agapodwaul, the sub-division, see sep. title.

POGADA (పొగడ - pogada, *Tel.*). From (pravála, san. coral); applied to tree from coral-like fruit. Gum of mimusops elengi, linn. [ilanjy].

POGAUK (ताम्रकूट - támrakúta, *San.*; तंबाखू - tambákhú, *Mahr.*; धुरापान - dhurápána, *Conc.*; تنباك - tambák, *Ar.*; تنباكو - tambákú, *Pers.* and *Hind.*; تماقو - tamákú, *Dec.*; تمبكو - tambaku, *Malay*; ಹೊಗೇಸೊಪ್ಪು - hogésoppu, *Can.*; ಪುಗೆರೆ - pugere, *Too.*; పొగాకు - pogáku, *Tel.*; ଧୂମ - dhúma, *Oor.*; പുകയില - pukayila, *Mal.*; දුංකොළ - dunkola, *Singh.*; புகையிலை - pugaiyilai, *Tam.*). Title from teloogoo, means smoke leaf [pogay]. San. from (támra, san. copper color + kúta, san. head), appears to be sanscritized form of tobacco. Mahr. from hindostany. Ar., Pers., Hind., Dec. from sanscrit. Can. from (hoge, can. smoke + soppu, can. leaf). Too. from tamul. Tel. from (poga, tel. smoke + áku, tel. leaf). Mal. from tamul. Tam. from (pugai, tam. smoke + ilai, tam. leaf); from use of leaf. San. also (dhúmrapatra), meaning having black-red leaves; (dhúmapatra), meaning smoke-leaf. Hind. also (bajjarbhang), meaning slow + bhang. Can. also (hogetoppalu), meaning smoke + leaf. Mal. also (pukala), by corruption; (kalañjam). Title otherwise Slow bhang, Smoke-leaf, Tobacco. The native american name for the herb is Cohiba; for the burning brand, Tabaco. The older writers, when alluding to the plant, generally used the word Petun, the indian name in common use in brazil, mexico, and florida; from this word is derived the name of a plant of the same order as tobacco, the Petunia. Nicot, ambassador at the portuguese court to catherine de'medici and the grand prior of france, caused the plant to be scientifically examined and described, and nicotiana is the scientific name now universally applied. Botanically Nicotiana tabacum, linn., solanaceæ [vricsham, 94]. Herbaceous, pubescent, glutinous, stem erect, tapering, branched above; leaves oblong-lanceolate, acuminate, sessile, lower ones decurrent, half stem-clasping; flowers pedicelled, bracteate; segments of the oblong calyx lanceolate, acute, unequal; corolla outwardly downy, throat somewhat inflated, segments of the much-spreading limb acute; capsule the length of the calyx, or slightly longer. Native of america, cultivated; root long and fibrous, stem 4–6 feet high, erect; leaves very large, pale green; flowers panicled; delicately pink flowers; recent leaves possess very little odour or taste; when well cured, they are of a yellowish green color; the dried leaves are narcotic; the active principle is nicotine, which is present in quantity varying from 1·5 to 8 per cent. Attempts have been made of late years to introduce foreign species, but defects do not lie in the plant, so much as in the curing of the leaf; the plant was originally introduced into india about the end of the sixteenth century in the reign of jehaungeer or his predecessor; it is possible that it may have been introduced from the new world by the portuguese. The soils most suitable for cultivation, generally speaking, are alluvial lands [adaimunn, vandalmunn], black loam, deserted village sites and backyards of houses; in the south for the first cultivation which begins in arpisy [mausam] or october and caurtigay on november, the ground is prepared during the months of auvany or august and poorataushy or september, and for the second cultivation which commences in the month of tye or january, the ground is prepared in the month of caurtigay or november and the early part of maurgaly or december; on coromandel the ground is prepared in aushweejam or october and caurteecam or november; on w. coast in chingom or august; the ground is well ploughed up and richly manured; seed sown in south for the first cultivation in latter part of auvany or august and in poorataushy or september and for the second cultivation in arpisy or october and in the beginning of caurtigay or november, on coromandel first sown in nursery in aushweejam or october and caurteecam or november and transplantation takes place two months after sowing, on w. coast sown in the end of mitoonam or june; sown in nursery in all cases; the seed germinates on the seventh or eighth day after sowing; till transplanted, watered on every alternate day; every exertion is made to remove the weeds; in sixty days transplanted out; then watered once in every third or fourth day till cut; when plants are 2 feet high they are topped and trimmed; flowers are nipped except of those left for seed; maturity indicated by golden color on stems and by ends of leaves becoming red and dried up; when the plants become ripe, the average size of the leaf is 25–30 inches in length and 5–7 inches in breadth; cut three or four months after transplantation; the whole plant is cut with a knife just a little above the root then gathered and stacked; the next day the ground is spread over with palmyra [q.v.] leaves and straw of varagoo [q.v.] or panicum miliaceum, linn.; on this the plants are stacked and covered with straw and palm leaves [olay], and pressed with stones for five or six days, when the weights, straw, &c., are removed, and the tobacco plants are taken up and hung in the shade by their stalks till the stalks become dry when they are placed in a small close room and covered as before with palm-leaves and straw, and pressed down by weights; the leaves are stripped off the stalks and tied into bundles; these are again stacked in bundles, and have weights placed over them, after being covered with straw, &c.; the bundles are re-arranged once in three or four days for some two or three weeks, when the tobacco is considered cured and fit for use, and is removed. When the tobacco stalks have been cut down, the stumps left in the soil soon throw out fresh shoots; the tobacco from the second crop is greatly inferior to the first in quantity and quality. The plants throughout their growth are subject to attacks from insects of the caterpillar [cumbly poochy] kind. Tobacco is chiefly grown now in the alluvial soils of the godavery, trichinopoly and madura districts; the trichinopoly and madura or dindigul tobaccos are very much alike both in appearance and quality, but the lunka [q.v.] tobacco grown in delta [conamoogam] of the godavery differs materially from both; as a rule, the trichinopoly and dindigul leaf has a stronger taste and flavor than the lanka, but the latter, although tasting milder, have a more marked effect on the nervous system and contain more nicotine. A cigar is the roll pointed at the extremities; a cheroot [q.v.] is the roll truncated; snuffs [naus] are preparations of the leaf powdered and fermented dry or moist. Plant gives to pharm. dried leaves, tabaci folia, powerful sedative and antispasmodic, in over-doses an acronarcotic poison; preparation, enema tabaci, officinal; veidyans [q.v.] use tobacco to excite vomiting; in veterinary practice tobacco smoke injected for flatulent colic. Tobacco smoked, acts as a sedative, soothing nervous irritability and allaying appetite for food [mookhadiraut]; in excess it weakens the heart's action, produces nervous tremors and impairs vision; by the multitude of the working and poorer classes it is chewed in the form of leaf, or smoked in the shape of a small coarsely made cheroot; many of the better classes also smoke or chew tobacco, while men of sedentary habits, engaged in office work, consume brown snuff, of which the best quality is made from godavery tobacco in masulipatam. From seed is expressed a clear, limpid, colorless oil, used in painting [rangh]. Canda tobacco, from (káda, tel. stalk), or (kámbu, tam. stalk) is tobacco with a part of its stem. Oorvay tobacco, from (kórva, tel. series), or (kovai, tam. anything strung), is tobacco strung on a line.——*Wild pogauk* (देवनळ - dévanala, Mahr.; काडधुरापान - kádadhurápána, Conc.; ಕಾಡಹೊಗೆಸೊಪ್ಪುಗಿಡ - kádahogesoppugida, Can.; ಕಾಟುಪುಗೆರಿ - kátupugeri, Too.; అడవిపొగాకు - adavipogáku, Tel.; കാട്ടുപുകയില - káttupukayila, Mal.; රස්නි - rasni, Singh.; காட்டுப்புகையிலை - káttuppugaiyilai, Tam.). Mahr. from (déva, san. god + nala, mahr. reed). The rest mean wild tobacco, nicotiana tabacum, linn. Title otherwise Wild tobacco. Botanically Lobelia nicotianæfolia, heyn., campanulaceæ [vriosham, 76]. Alias Rapuntium nicotianæfolium. Stem erect; leaves subsessile, oblong, lanceolate, denticulate, narrowed at the base, acuminated; racemes many-flowered; bracts leafy; pedicels slightly longer than the bract, bi-bracteolate in the middle; sepals lanceolate serrated; corolla pubescent, lateral lobes long-linear, centre ones lanceolate; two lower anthers penicillate at the apex; flowers purple. The leaves resemble those of the tobacco; they are finally serrated and covered with simple hairs; the lower part of the stem is woody, an inch and-a-half or more in diameter, and almost solid; the upper portion is a hollow tube ending in a crowded head of flower spikes; the latter are about a foot in length, and when the plant is in fruit, are thickly set with globular capsules about the size of a pea [calauyam], to which a portion of the dry flower is often adherent; the capsules are two-celled, each cell containing a fleshy placenta; the seeds are numerous and very small, one-fiftieth of an inch in length, oval, flattened, of a light brown color, and marked with delicate lines; several small tubercles surround the site of the placental attachment; the whole plant when dry is studded with small spots of resinous exudation, and is hot and acrid to the taste; the leaves and aërial parts of the fresh plant exude a white latex when broken. Dry herb, when handled extremely acrid, dust irritating the throat and nostrils like tobacco; infusion of leaves is antispasmodic; quoted in pharm., but not officinal. There is also the species Inflata. Laggera aurita, schultz., is sometimes also called Wild tobacco.

POGAY (புகை - pugai, *Tam.*). From (pugu, tam. to penetrate). Smoke, the sign of Agny the regent of the south [ashtadic]. Pogay chooroot is a cigar roll, see Cheroot. Pogay coodoo is a chimney or a balloon [dhoomam, dhoopam].——*Pogaivary* (புகைவரி - pugavari, Tam.). From (above + vari, tam. tax). Tax on houses.——*Pogauk* (పొగాకు - pogáku, Tel.). See sep. title.

POINT GODAVERY (గోదావరిమొన - gódávarimona, *Tel.*). Greek καλλιγικὸν ἄκρον. Point; Godavery dist., Amalaupooram tal.; lat. 16° 46′; long. 82° 23′; from Amalaupooram N.E. 26 miles; from Cocanada S.S.E. 15 miles. Low narrow sand bank extending several miles north and south, and west of which is the estuary of the great northern branch of the Godavery. Opposite are shoals and low islands, caused by the accumulation of silt [adaimunn].

POISON (विष - visha, *San.*). Prefix.——*Poison ball* (நஞ்சுண்டான் - nañjundán, Tam.). Same as Fire-work plant.——*Poison berry* (गरलफल् - garalap'hala, San.). Title from taste. Same as Indian berry.——*Poison fruit* (കരളിക്കായ - karalikkáya, Mal.). Same as Common emetic nut.——*Poison nut* (विषमुष्टि - vishamushti, San.; कुचला - kuchalá, Mahr.; कार्यारूकु - káryárúku, Conc.; خانق الكلب - khánikulkalb, Ar.; قاتل الكلب - kátilulkalb, Pers.; کچلہ - kuchlah, Hind.; کچلا - kuchlá, Dec.; ನಂಜನಕೊರಡು - nanjinakoradu, Can.; కాయెరు - káyeru, Too.; ముష్టి - mushti, Tel.; കാഞ്ഞിരം - káññiram, Mal.; ගොඩකදුරු - godakaduru, Singh.; எட்டி - etti, Tam.). Title from character of nut. San. from (visha, san. poison + mushti, san. handful). Ar. from (khánik, ar. bane + kalb, ar. dog). Pers. from (kátil, pers. killer + kalb, ar. dog). Can. from (nanju, can. poison + koradu, can. pollard). Tel. from sanscrit. Mal. from (káraskara, san. the plant). Singh. from (goda, singh. land + kaduru, singh. poisonous tree). Tam. from (edu, tam. to vomit). San. also (kupílu), meaning inferior + salvadora persica, linn.; (kulaka), meaning chief of a family; (káraskara), meaning killing + doing; (kákasp'húrja), meaning crow's diospyros; (markatatinduka), meaning monkey's diospyros embryopteris, pers.; (vishatinduka), meaning poisonous diospyros; (dírghapatra), meaning long-leaved [penarvully, plantain]; (kákánda), meaning crow's ball; (kákapílu), meaning crow's salvadora persica, linn.; (kákatinduka), meaning crow's diospyros. Ar. also (izáráki). Pers. also (fulúsmáhí), meaning fish scales. Can. also (kásarkanamara). Tel. also (musidi). Tam. also (kákodi); (káñjirai), meaning fruit + killer; (kiruttinabánam), meaning krishna's arrow. Greek στρύχνος. Title otherwise Caunjiray, Coochlah, Dog bane, False angostura bark tree, Krishna's arrow, Mechel, Methel, Mooshty, Nuxmechil, Nux vomica, Strychnine tree, Vomit nut, Yetty. Botanically Strychnos [mooshty], nux vomica, linn., loganiaceæ [vricsham, 89]. Alias Caniram vomiquier. Caniram from malayalam. Tree, middling-sized; leaves short-petioled, opposite, smooth, shining, three to five-nerved, oval; calyx five-parted, permanent; corolla tubular, funnel-shaped; flowers small, greenish white; filaments, scarcely any, inserted over the bottom of the divisions of the corolla; style the length of the tube of the corolla; fruit round, smooth, very variable in size, orange-colored when ripe, many-seeded; pulpy. Trunk short, often crooked, but thick; branches covered with smooth ash-colored bark; native of coromandel; common in dry forests. Fruit when ripe is about the size of an apple [seb], is covered with a shell of an orange color, and contains a pulp in which from three to five seeds are immersed; these seeds are round, flattish, about three-quarters of an inch in diameter, have a weak, nauseous, balsamic smell, an intense bitter taste, and contain a virulent poison; nux vomica is the seed removed from the pulp and shell; it contains a peculiar principle, strychnine, which, like morphia, possesses alkaline properties; strychnine is not restricted to the fruit but also occurs in the wood and bark; an empyreumatic oil is prepared from the fresh nut. The wood occurs in the shops in pieces of variable length, and from ½ to 1 inch or more in diameter; it is covered by a thin light brown bark, which on one side of the stem is rougher than on the other, and is marked by numerous small light-colored elliptic corky warts; a transverse section shows numerous very fine medullary rays; touched with nitric acid [shorey ka tezaub] the section is stained a dull orange red. The seeds were first introduced into medicine by the arabs; they have not been described by sanscrit writers; the nut, when finely pounded and mixed with margosa [neem] oil, is medicinally tonic and astringent, given in minute doses; a decoction of the leaves is employed in paralysis and rheumatic swelling; the bark forms the principal ingredient in the chief of the medicated oils commonly in use among the natives as local applications to leprous, syphilitic, and other obstinate eruptions; officinal in pharm.; the nux vomica seed is in overdoses a virulent poison, death taking place by tetanus; in veterinary practice the nut when burnt but not to ashes and powdered, is used to cover long standing ulcers. The seeds are exported for the manufacture of strychnine, as also of the tincture and extract; seeds produce a sort of intoxication, for which they are habitually taken by some natives as an aphrodisiac; those who do so gradually become so far accustomed to the poison that they often come to one seed daily, which is cut into small pieces and chewed with a packet of betel [q.v.] leaf; pulp of the fruit is quite harmless and the favorite fruit of many birds; seeds employed in the distillation of country spirits to render them more intoxicating. Wood very bitter, light-brown color streaked with white, impervious to the attack of white-ants [q.v.]; hard, durable and stiff. Parasitic plants of the loranthaceæ growing on the plant acquire its poisonous properties. There is a Tamul proverb :—கடல்நீர் நிறைந்து ஆவது என்ன, காஞ்சிரை பழுத்து ஆவது என்ன?—"what benefit arises from the water of the ocean, what good comes "from the ripening of the caunjiray fruit?" And another :—எட்டிமரமானாலும் வைத்த மரத்தை வெட்டாதே—"cut not down the tree you planted though it is the yetty." And another :—எட்டி பழுத்து என்ன, ஈயாதார் வாழ்ந்து என்ன—"what if the fruit of the yetty tree ripens; of what "use is the prosperity of the niggardly?" And another :—எட்டிமரமானாலும் பச்சென்று இருக்கவேண்டும்—"though a poisonous tree, it should be green." Compare :—Diospyros sylvatica (nallakákamushti), black crow poison nut; Olax scandens (bápanamushti), bramin poison nut; Strychnos colubrina (tígamushtí), creeper poison nut; Tiliacora racemosa (tígamushti), creeper poison nut. See gloss. paragraphs.——*Poison root* (विष - visha, San.). Same as Bachnaug.

POKRY (پوکری - pokrí, *Hind.*). A villain. Term of abuse.

POLAM (పొలము - polamu, *Tel.*; புலம் - pulam, *Tam.*). From (poli, tam. to thrive), as arable land. A field [hola]; especially for growing dry grain [q.v.].——*Poolaya* (പുലയ - pulaya, Mal.). From (above + an, mal. personal term). Low class in Malabar connected with rice cultivation. The Holeyar [q.v.] of Coorg and Canara, Pariahs [q.v.] and Pullar [q.v.] of Tinnevelly. But the Poolayar are in a far lower condition than the Pariahs. Of this tribe the most debased are now found on the strip of land between Alleppey and Cochin, where they are entirely isolated between the sea and the backwater. In the neighbourhood of Trivandrum, Poolayar are accustomed to boast of having once had a chieftain or rajah of their own, who resided in a fort not far off. The two great divisions of this caste, are the Eastern and Western poolayar. The former are found principally about Chungacherry and at Mullpully and other hilly parts. The Western poolayar prevail near Cottayam. The whole caste is divided into illams [q.v.]. Men and women belonging to the same illam cannot intermarry; they are considered to be the descendants of one family, therefore brethren, and such marriages are regarded as incestuous. Their dwellings are huts formed of sticks cut out of the woods, with walls of reed or mud, and thatched with grass or cocoanut [q.v] leaf, situated by the sides of the rice [q.v.] swamps, or on mounds in their centre. The work of the Poolayar lies almost exclusively in the rice fields. Their food is chiefly rice [q.v.]. The worship practised by the Poolayar is that of demons and evil spirits [pey], or of deceased ancestors [jauty]. See vol. I (35), (110); II, 99. The ancient historical capital of Ceylon went by the name of Poolastinagaram, and the Periplus Maris Erythræi calls Ceylon παλαισίμουνδου. A small division of Pariahs are called Poolaya pariah [q.v.].

POLE (پول - pol, *Hind.*; పోలు - pólu, *Tel.*). Corruption of (prólu, *Tel.*). Town. Suffix in place names; as Pallapole [prole, vole, wail].

POLLACHY (பொள்ளாச்சி - pollâççi, *Tam.* pollâchi *). From (porul, tam. wealth + ádchi, tam. possession) [porool].——(1) Talook, Coimbatore district. Tahsildar's pay Rs. 175. Area 710 square miles. Population 183,669. Language Tamul. S.W. of district under shadow of Anamullays. Bounded

N. by Coimbatore and Pulladam talooks; E. by Oodamalpett and Pulladam talooks; W. by Anamullays, Cochin state and Palghaut talook, Malabar district; S. by Travancore state, from which it is separated by Anamullays. Diversified by undulations. The hills are in several ranges; as Cootchimullay on west, Toonacadav on south-west, and the Ponautchy on south. From these flow streams, the chief Auliyaur. Climate healthy. Forests abundant. Teak [q.v.] from Toonacadav by way of Beypore. At end of last century a vast teak forest extended between Pollachy and Palghaut, and troops traversing it had actually to cut their way through. Soils good, near hills. Red loam forms 39 per cent. and red sand 54 per cent. of the surveyed area, while black-cotton soil [regar] of a superior description, chiefly on the extreme east of the talooks, occupies 7 per cent. Red soils near Anamullay are extremely fertile, and produce very fine cholum crops. Dry crops are cholum [q.v.], shaumay [q.v.], cumboo [bajrah], raggy [q.v.], horse-gram [q.v.], tinay [q.v.], castor [aumanac], gingelly [q.v.], chillies [q.v.], tobacco [pogauk], tovray [dholl]. Garden crops are cholum, raggy, chillies, and tobacco. Wet crops are paddy [q.v.], gingelly [q.v.] seed and sugar-cane [q.v.]. Tobacco is fairly good. Chillies are among the best in the district and noted for pungency. Coffee [q.v.] is grown to a small extent at Ponautchy on the Anamullays, and cardamoms [q.v.] are procured to some extent by the Kadar [q.v.]. Forest products are honey [shahad], wax [mom], shellac [q.v.], paula indigo [q.v.], wild ginger [caurallam], turmeric [country saffron], cardamoms [q.v.], horns [sing] and ivory [dant]. Cloth is woven to some extent. The talook is irrigated chiefly by jungle streams and by tanks fed by them. The chief jungle streams are the Auliyaur, Ooppaur and Palaur. Camping grounds:—Anamullays, Cotaumputty, Gomungalam, Kinatcadavoo, Pollachy. Zemindarries:—Avalappamputty, Cotaumputty, Negamam, Ootcooly, Poravipolliem, Ramaputnam, Shamattore. Places of archæological interest:—Anamullay, Autchiputty, Cotore, Garoodancottay, Kinatcadavoo, Marchanaickenpolliem, Nautcullpolliem, Ootcooly, Periyacazhattay, Pollachy. Principal trig. station:—Kinatcadavoo. The leading places, &c., in the talook are the following.——*Anamoody* (ஆனைமுடி - ánaimudi, Tam.). See sep. title.——*Anamullay* (ஆனைமலை - ánaimalai, Tam.). See sep. title.——*Auliyaur* (ஆளியாறு - áliyáru, Tam.). See sep. title.——*Avalappamputty* (ஆவலப்பம்பட்டி - ávalappambatti, Tam. avalappampati *). Means avalappan's village. Village; pop. 897; acres 8,916; lat. 10° 42′; long. 77° 10′; from Coimbatore S.S.E. 22 miles; from Pollachy E.N.E. 8 miles. Poliput. Peshcush Rs. 4,200.——*Cotaumputty* (கோட்டாம்பட்டி - kóttámbatti; Tam. kótámpati *). From (kóttán, tam. screech owl + patti, tam. hamlet). Village; pop. 1,118; acres 1,681; lat. 10° 37′; long. 77° 03′; from Coimbatore S. 27 miles, from Pollachy S.S.W. 3 miles. Poliput. Peshcush Rs. 1,860.——*Cotore* (கோட்டூர் - kóttúr, Tam. kótúr *). From (kódu, tam. ridge + úr, tam. village). Village; pop. 8,226; acres 10,697; lat. 10° 33′; long. 77° 02′ from Coimbatore S. 31 miles; from Pollachy S.S.W. 8 miles. At foot of a pass in Anamullays.——*Kinatcadavoo* (கிணத்துக்கடவு - kinattukkadavu, Tam.). From (kinaru, tam. well + kadavu, tam. a tree, gyrocarpus jacquini, roxb.). Village; pop. 3,681; acres 6,687; lat. 10° 49′; long. 77° 04′; from Coimbatore S.S.E. 13 miles; from Pollachy N. 11 miles. Temple with copper-plate grants. Weekly-market. Trig. station; lat. 10° 49′ 17·13″; long. 77° 03′ 35·85″; height 1,212 feet; from Kinatcadavoo N.W. ¼ mile; from Pollachy N. 12 miles.——*Negamam* * (நெகமம் - negamam, Tam.). From (nigama, san. city). Village; pop. 3,230; acres 3,976; lat. 10° 45′; long. 77° 09′; from Coimbatore S.S.E. 20 miles; from Pollachay N.E. 9 miles. Poliput. Peshcush Rs. 2,480.——*Palaur* (பாலாறு - páláru, Tam.). See sep. title.——*Pollachy* (பொள்ளாச்சி - polláçci, Tam.). See below.——*Poravipolliem* (பொராவிப்பாளையம் - poravippálaiyam, Tam. poravipálaiyam *). From (puravu, tam. hill tract + pálaiyam, tam. fortified village). Village; pop. 3,526; acres 12,375; lat. 10° 44′; long. 77° 01′; from Coimbatore S. 18 miles; from Pollachy N. 6 miles. Poliput. Peshcush Rs. 2,804.——*Ramaputnam* (இராமப்பட்டணம் - irámappattanam, Tam. rámapatnam *). From (ráma, san. the god + pattana, san. town). Village; pop. 3,265; acres 7,750; lat. 10° 42′; long. 76° 58′; from Coimbatore S. 20 miles; from Pollachy N.W. 7 miles. Poliput. Peshcush Rs. 1,436.——*Shamattore* (சமத்தூர் - shamattúr, Tam. samatúr *). From (shamattu, tam. power + úr, tam. village). Village; pop. 2,202; acres 5,337; lat. 10° 36′; long. 77° 04′; from Coimbatore S. 27 miles; from Pollachy S. 3 miles. Poliput. Peshcush Rs. 1,683.——*Vettacauranpoothore* (வேட்டக்காரன்புதூர் - véttakkáranbuthúr, Tam. vétakáranpudur *). From (véttaikkáran, tam. hunter + puthu, tam. new + úr, tam. village). Village; pop. 7,725; acres 12,787; lat. 10° 34′; long. 76° 58′; from Coimbatore S. 30 miles; from Pollachy S.W. 9 miles. Formerly a hamlet of Anamullay, but now distinct.——*Wodayacolam* (ஒடையக்குளம் - odaiyakkulam, Tam. odayákulam *). From (udaiyán, tam. one of the udaiya caste + kulam, tam. tank). Village; pop. 3,996; acres 8,166; lat. 10° 34′; long. 76° 57′; from Coimbatore S. 30 miles; from Pollachy S.W. 9 miles.——**(2)** Town, Divisional and talook head-quarters; Coimbatore dist., Pollachy tal.; pop. 5,805; acres 2,612; lat. 10° 39′; long. 77° 03′; from Coimbatore S. 24 miles; from Erode S.W. 68 miles; from Madras S.W. 275 miles; from Ootacamund S.S.E. 55 miles; from Suttimungalam S.S.W. 61 miles. Dolmens [codaycull], rude stone circles [azhauram]; &c., are found. One and-a-half miles east-south-east is a circle of very large boulders. Roman coins found of Augustus and Tiberius. Large weekly fair on Thursday. Has been always a place of trade.

POLORE (போளூர் - pólúr, *Tam.* pólúr *). From (póli, tel. proper name + úru, tel. village) [poly].——**(1)** Talook, North arcot district. Tahsildar's pay Rs. 150. Area 596 square miles. In the south-west corner of the district. Population 131,380. Language Tamul. S. of district. Triangular in shape. Length of each side about 30 miles. N. apex touches Vellore talook; N.E. side borders on Arnee jagheer and a portion of Wandiwash; southern on Trinomallee talook, South arcot; northwestern on Tripatore talook, Salem district. The N. and W. parts are hilly, being occupied by the Jawaudies. The chief eminences are Carnautighur and Padavaid droog. There are isolated hills near Polore in the centre, and Chetput in the extreme south-east corner. The rest of the talook is tolerably flat, and here the climate is salubrious; in the hilly portions fever is very prevalent. The forests are considerable in hilly tracts. Soils are black and red clay mixed with sand or gravel, and near the hills a rich loam is found. The talook is fertile and good crops of rice [q.v.], cumboo [bajrah], raggy [q.v.] and varagoo [q.v.] are raised. Besides the ordinary minerals of the district, magnetic iron [cauntam] ore occurs in small nodules near Pottaray. At Caundapolliem garnets [tamrah] are found of little value. Manufactures are weaving and shoe-making. The chief weaving centres are Mansoorabad and Maumbut, where superior cloth is turned out and exported mostly to Baugalore. Coarse cloth are made at Alliyabad, Mahadevamungalam, Palancoil, and Shingauravaudy. Cumblies [q.v.] are woven at Autvaumbaudy and Cauraputt, the latter village producing the fine kind. Shoe-making is in the hands of the Lubbays [q.v.] of Chetput, their shoes are sold all over this district as well as South arcot. This industry is however failing. Jungle produce is collected by the Iroolar [q.v.] and Malayaulies [q.v.]. The principal rivers are Cheyaur and affluents, Bheemanuddy, Camandalanuddy or Padavaid, Mricandanuddy and Munjalaur; all rising in Jawaudies. The number of spring and river channels [q.v.] is small. Chief tanks [q.v.] Alliyabad and Polore. Places of archæological interest:—Cadalaudy, Carnautighur, Cauppalore, Chetput, Mahadevamungalam, Mailauttvambaudy, Modaiyore, Padavaid, Paudagam, Polore, Pulliputt, Tirmaley, Tutchambaudy, Yelattore. Principal trig. stations:—Carnautighur, Narsingapooram. The leading places, &c., in the talook are the following.——*Alliyabad* (علی آباد - aliábád, Hind.; அலியாபாத் - aliyábád, Tam.). From (alí, hind. proper name + ábád, pers. city). Tam. also (kalambúr), meaning threshing floor + water + village. Village; pop. 5,096; acres 3,284; lat. 12° 38′; long. 79° 16′; from Chittore S.S.E. 41 miles; from Polore N.E. 11 miles. Tank [q.v.], fed by channel [q.v.] from the Padavaid. Built by Chola [q.v.] rajah.——*Carnautighur* (கருநாடகக்கிரி - karunádagakkiri, Tam.). See sep. title.——*Cauraputt* (காரப்பட்டு - kárappattu, Tam.). From (kárai, tam. thorny werbera, canthium parviflorum, lam. + pattu, tam. village). Village; pop. 3,652; acres 3,562; lat. 12° 23′; long. 78° 59′; from Chittore S. 59 miles; from Polore S.W. 16 miles.——*Chengam* (செங்கமம் - shengamam, Tam.). See sep. title.——*Chetput* (சேத்துப்பட்டு - shéttuppattu, Tam.). See sep. title.——*Cheyaur* (செய்யாறு - sheyyáru, Tam.). See sep. title.——*Mansoorabad droog* (மன்சுராபாத்துருக்கம் - mansurábáttyrukkam, Tam.). From (mansúr, hind. mahomedan proper name + ábád, hind. city + durga, san. fort). Village, Hill; pop. 1,179; acres 1,187; lat. 12° 24′; long. 79° 16′; from Chittore S. 57 miles; from Polore S.E. 10 miles. A hill fort in ruins.——*Maumbut* (மாம்பட்டு - mámbattu, Tam.). From (má, tam. mango tree, mangifera indica, linn. + pattu, tam. village). Village; pop. 1,387; acres 1,275; lat. 12° 31′; long. 79° 08′; from Chittore S. 49 miles; from Polore W. 2 miles. Weaving centre.——*Mricanda nuddy* (மிருக்கண்டநதி - mirukkandanathi, Tam.). From (mrikanda, san. the sage + nadí, san. river). River. Affluent of Cheyaur. Rises in Jawaudy hills and joins the Cheyaur near Yelattore.——*Mundacolattore* (மண்டக்கொளத்தூர் - mandakkolattúr, Tam.). From (manda, tam. large + kolam, tam. tank + úr, tam. village). Village; pop. 1,579; acres 2,273; lat. 12° 32′; long. 79° 15′; from Chittore S. 48 miles; from Polore E. 5 miles. Large Bramin population.——*Munjalaur* (மஞ்சளாறு - mañjaláru, Tam.). From (mañjal, tam. country saffron, curcuma longa, roxb. + áru, tam. river). Sanscrit name (haridránadí), meaning the same. River. Streamlet rising in Jawaudy hills, empties into Polore tank.——*Nacshatra coil* (நக்ஷத்திரக்கோவில் - naççattirakkóvil, Tam.). From (nakshatra, san. star + kóvil tam. temple); from kritticay [q.v.] star [nacshatram]. Hill; lat. 12° 28′; long. 79° 06′; from Chittore S. 51 miles; from Polore S.W. 5 miles. Temple of Soobramanya sawmy, only second in importance to Padavaid. Penances performed consist in going round the hill several times.——*Narsingapooram* (நரசிங்கப்புரம் - narasingappuram, Tam.). From (narasimha, san. vishnu, the man-lion god + pura, san. town). Trig. station; lat. 12° 31′ 09·57″; long. 79° 18′ 43·07″; height 967 feet.——*Padavaid* (படவீடு - padavédu, Tam.). See sep. title.——*Paudagam* (பாடகம் - pádagam, Tam.). From (pádu, tam. waste + agam, tam. place). Village; pop. 1,253; acres 3,300; lat. 12° 26′; long. 79° 14′; from Chittore S. 55 miles; from Polore S.E. 8 miles. Remains of a palace.——*Polore* (போளூர் - pólúr, Tam.). See below.——*Sampatgherry* (சம்பத்துக்கிரி - shambattukkiri, Tam.). From (sampat, san. wealth + giri, san. hill). Hill.——*Tirmaley* (திருமலை - tirumalai, Tam.). From (tiru, tam. holy + malai, tam. hill). Village, Hill; pop. 633; acres 2,045; lat. 12° 34′; long. 79° 15′; from Chittore S. 46 miles; from Polore E.N.E. 6 miles. Granite [caroomcull] hill with Jeina [q.v.] relics. Jeina families in village. The temples on and below the hill still belong to them. On the hill is a rude Jeina figure, 16½ feet high, cut on the face of a cliff near the summit. It is not surrounded with the usual spiral branches of leaves. Upon its left is a long inscription in archaic characters. Close to the lower temple are rock chambers. Jeina figures stood in these, but were destroyed during Hyder's invasion. Upon the walls are frescoes, of naugams [q.v.], monks, white-hooded nuns and others. Close to village are two large stone circles [azhauram].——**(2)** Town, Talook head-quarters; North arcot dist., Polore tal.; pop. 7,743; acres 2,997; lat. 12° 31′; long. 79° 10′; from Arnee S.W. 16 miles; from Chittore S. 49 miles; from Madras W.S.W. 89 miles; from Ranipett S.S.W. 32 miles; from Tripatty S.S.W. 80 miles; from Vellore S. 29 miles. Two miles from north bank of Cheyaur and east of Sampatgherry and Vasoor hills. Between these is built the bund of the tank, which receives the Munjalaur. The Sampatgherry is topped by a temple. The road to Trinomallee passes through main bazaar. Small ruined fort. Five miles from town magnetic [cauntam] ore occurs in small nodules.

POLORE (పోలూరు - pólúru, *Tel.*). From (póru, tel. combat + úru, tel. village). Tel. also (mannárupólúru), meaning battle place of enemies. Sanscrit (malláripura), meaning krishnan, the wrestler-foe + town.——**(1)** Zemindarry, Deputy tahsildar's division, Nellore; pay Rs. 120. Area 355 square miles. Territory of the zemindar of Vencatagherry. S. inland part of district. Bounded north and west by Vencatagherry division, east by Kotah division of Goodoor talook, and south by the North arcot district. Extends from Ramapore on the extreme east to the Swarnamookhy, a distance of 32 miles, and from Goodoor village on the north to Calastry zemindarry in south. The history of the talook can be traced as far back as the year 1596, when Bungauroo yautsama naidoo, the twenty-second Zemindar of Vencatagherry, who had obtained the title of Rajah bahaudur from the court of Hyderabad, having suddenly died, his three young sons and an adopted Bramin boy Rama row were summoned to Hyderabad, and the ancestral property was equally divided among them, the eldest taking the talook of Vencatagherry, the second the talook of Sagatore, and the adopted son the talook of Polore. But the adoptive son Rama row leaving no issue at his death Polore returned to the eldest branch of the family. The division is a plain country intersected by the Caulingy and the Swarnamookhy. The soil is good and fertile. The special industry is in indigo [q.v.]. Almost every five villages has a vat. Handkerchiefs [roomaul] and ordinary cloths manufactured in several large villages. In some parts Appalacauram [q.v.] is dug and sent to Madras. In Naidoopett cooncoomam, a red powder from turmeric [country saffron] and limes [q.v.], is largely manufactured and sent to Madras. Lac [q.v.] bangles with ornamental work. The natural products are paddy [q.v.] and dry grains [q.v.]. Much paddy exported to Madras. Water is plentiful and salubrious. Principal trig. station:—Auneypoody. The leading places, &c., in the division are the following.——*Aunepoody* (ఆనెపూడి - ánepúdi, Tel.). From (áne, can. elephant + púdi, tel. village). Village; pop. 211; lat. 13° 50′; long. 80° 03′; from Nellore S. 43 miles; from Polore N 8 miles; from Raupore S.E. 44 miles. Trig. station in lat. 13° 48′ 24·40″; long. 80° 02′ 04·56″; height 135 feet; from Aunepoody S.W. 2 miles; from Polore N. 7 miles.——*Aurore* (ఆరూరు - árúru, Tel.). From (áru, tel. six + úru, tel. village). Village; pop. 686; lat. 13° 55′; long. 80° 06′; from Nellore S. 37 miles; from Polore N.N.E. 15 miles; from Raupore E.S.E. 40 miles. Four tanks.——*Body lingampaud* (బోడిలింగంపాడు - bódilingampádu, Tel.). From (bódi, tel. bare + lingampádu, tel. lingam town). Village, Head-quarters of Salt inspector; pop. 349; lat. 13° 44′; long. 80° 02′; from Nellore S. 49 miles; from Polore N. 2 miles; from Raupore S.E. 44 miles. On backwater. Salt manufactured. Port half a mile distant. Fuel and grain largely exported to Madras. Zemindar [q.v.] collects tolls on the channel [q.v.] leading to the port [toray].——*Caulingy* (కాళింగనది - kálinganadi, Tel.). See sep. title.——*Cotta polore* (కొత్తపోలూరు - kottapólúru, Tel.). From (kotta, tel. new + pólúru, tel. place so called). Village; pop. 2,648; lat. 13° 44′; long. 80° 4′; from Nellore S. 50 miles; from Polore N.N.E. 2 miles; from Raupore S.E. 46 miles. Ruins of a fort. Rich paddy [q.v.] lands.——*Mullam* (మల్లం - mallam, Tel.). Means oil vessel. Village; pop. 1,757; lat. 13° 58′; long. 80° 09′; from Nellore S.S.E. 35 miles; from Polore N.N.E. 19 miles; from Raupore E.S.E. 42 miles. Once in possession of Chola kings. Temple dedicated to Sawminautasawmy, highly soulptured and with gopooram [q.v.] built entirely of black granite [caroom cull]. Also an old temple of Marcandeyan. Festival in August and September. Rich paddy lands.——*Naidoopett* (నాయుడుపేట - náyudipéta, Tel.). See sep. title.——*Polore* (పోలూరు - pólúru, Tel.). See below.——*Poody* (పూడి - púdi, Tel.). See sep. title.——*Sooloorpett* (సూళూరుపేట - sulúrupéta, Tel.). See sep. title.——*Swarnamookhy* (స్వర్ణముఖి - svarnamukhi, Tel.). See sep. title.——*Tadda* (తడ - tada, Tel.). See sep. title.——**(2)** Village; Nellore dist., Polore division; lat. 13° 43′; long. 80° 02′; from Madras N.N.W. 48 miles; from Naidoopett S.S.E. 15 miles; from Nellore S. 52 miles; from Ongole S. 124 miles; from Raupore S.E. 47 miles. The same as Munnaurpolore. The division goes by this name; but the head-quarter of the division is Sooloorpett 1 mile distant. Famous temple. Remains of ancient fort. For the Shree codanda ramasawmy festival held in Cheitram [mausam] or April, and which lasts nine days, many people collect. Another festival of nine days, in Jyeshtam [mausam] or June in honor of Mullary krishna sawmy. The Caulingy nuddy flows to the left.

POLY (பொலி - poli, *Tam.*). Field bank.——*Polairamma* (పోలేరమ్మ - póléramma, Tel.). From (poliméra, tel. boundary + amma, tel. goddess). Village deity. Said to produce small-pox [ammay] and cholera [vaunty bhaidy], and as such worshipped when these epidemics prevail.——*Polavaram* (పోలవరము - pólavaramu, Tel.). From (pólayya, tel. proper name + pura, san. town).—"*a*" Deputy tahsildarry, Godavery district. Pay Rs. 100.—"*b*" Zemindarry, Village, Deputy tahsildar's head-quarters; Godavery dist., Yernagoodem tal.; pop. 3,552; lat. of village 17° 15′; long. 81° 41′; from Cocanada W.N.W. 44 miles; from Coonavaram S.E. 33 miles; from Ellore N.E. 51 miles; from Madras N.N.E 298 miles; from Narsapore N. 55 miles; from Rajahmundry N.N.W. 19 miles; from Tullapoody N.N.W. 9 miles. Peshcush Rs. 6,710. The Zemindarry was one of the most ancient in the Northern circars [q.v.], and belonged together with those of Gootaula and Cottapully to a family of Reddies [q.v.]. Between 1785 and 1790 there were serious disturbances. In 1800 Polavaram fort was captured and destroyed by a British force. Two old temples. Temple of Mahanundeshwarasawmy said to have been built by Booddha [q.v.]. Remains of a ruined fort north of the village.——*Polore* (போளூர் - pólúr, Tam.). See sep. title.

POMFRET (حلوا ماهی - halwámáhí, *Hind.*; చందువాయి - tsanduváyi, *Tel.*; ആവോലി - ávóli, *Mal.*; வவ்வால்மீன் - vavválmín, *Tam.*). Title from portuguese meaning vine-leaf; from broad compressed shape. Hind. from (halwá, hind. sweet electuary + máhí, hind. fish); from its softness. Tel. from (chennu, tel. beautiful + váyi, tel. face). Tam. from (vavvál, tam. bat + mín, tam. fish). Tel. also (tsandanapuchépa), meaning sandal + fish. Mal. also (assalmín), meaning best fish. Title otherwise Pamphlet. Stromateus genus, stromateidæ, acanthopterygii, teleostei, pisces [matsyam, 17], of naturalists [jantoo]. Common on coromandel coast; light nourishing diet; after whiting [indian whiting] and sole [indian sole], the safest for sick persons; greatly compressed and oval, 8–10 inches long, not much less in breadth. The species best known to the natives are shown below.——*Bat-faced pomfret* (चान्दवा - chándavá, Mahr.; سفيد حلوا ماهی - sufedhalwámáhí, Hind.; అటుకోయ - atukoyá, Tel.; വെള്ളാവോലി - vellávóli, Mal.; முகம்வவ்வால் - mugamvavvál, Tam.). Hind. from (sufed, hind. white + halwámáhí, hind. pomfret, stromateus genus). Mal. from (vella, mal. white + ávóli, mal. pomfret, stromateus genus). Tam. from (mukha, san. face + vavvál, tam. bat). Title otherwise White pomfret. Stromateus [pomfret] sinensis, stromateidæ, acanthopterygii, teleostei [matsyam, 17], of naturalists. Alias Stromateus albus, atoo koia, atous, candidus. Atoo koia from teloogoo. Lower jaw longer, especially in young; scales small and very deciduous, especially in immature, in adult they cover the vertical fins; colors upper surface of head and body as far as the lateral-line of a deep neutral-tint, rest of body with mixture of brownish-grey, having metallic reflections, becoming lighter and silvery towards abdomen; dotted all over with brown, larger spots having silvery point in centre; fins silvery-gray, marginal half blackish; cavity of mouth and tongue pale bluish-gray with brown dots, silvery in centre; iris reddish-silver or copper colored, minutely dotted brown; young are gray, the head covered with irregularly star-shaped spots, and fins nearly black, especially at edges; sea; most esteemed for eating; in malabar common during the south-west monsoon [q.v.]; should be cooked when quite fresh; young are common round coasts and ascend estuaries.——*Black pomfret* (सरगा - saragá, Mahr.; నల్లచందువాయి - nallatsanduváyi, Tel.; ବାଲ - bál, Oor.; കാരാവോലി - káráválí, Mal.; கருப்புவவ்வால் - karuppuvavvál, Tam.). Tel. from (nalla, tel. black + tsanduváyi, tel. pomfret, stromateus genus). Mal. from (kár, mal. black + ávóli, mal. pomfret, stromateus genus). Tam. from (karuppu, tam. blackness + vavvál, tam. bat). Stromateus [pomfret] niger, stromateidæ, acanthopterygii, teleostei [matsyam, 17], of naturalists. Alias Apolectus stromateus; Stromateus nalasundawah, paru. Nalasundawah from teloogoo. Lower jaw longer; scales small, and extended over vertical fins; lateral-line gently curves downwards, and in last fourth passes straight to centre of caudal, in form of raised keeled line with lateral shields as perceived in genus caranx [pauray] colors deep brown or grayish-brown with blue reflections; cheeks, opercles, and abdomen pale-neutral or brownish-neutral: dorsal and anal greyish-brown, stained black towards margins; pectoral and caudal brownish, edged with black; iris brownish-blue; in the young it is gray; dorsal and anal fins black, and tail yellow, with three brown cross bands; sea; two feet in length, excellent eating; the people of tranquebar dislike it, because a species of parasite similar to a wood-louse is often found in its mouth; appears in malabar about the same time as the sinensis; it comes in shoals, and disappears as suddenly as it arrives.——*White pomfret* (सरगा - saragá, Mahr.; سفيدحلوا ماهى - sufedhalwámáhí, Hind.; తెల్లచందువాయి - tellatsanduváyi, Tel.; വെള്ളാവോലി - vellávóli, Mal.; வெள்ளைவவ்வால் - vellaivavvál, Tam.). Hind. from (sufed, hind. white + halwámáhí, hind. pomfret, stromateus genus). Tel. from (tella, tel. white + tsanduváyi, tel. pomfret, stromateus genus). Mal. from (vella, mal. white + ávóli, mal. pomfret, stromateus genus). Tam. from (vellai, tam. white + vavvál, tam. bat). Tel. also (súditsanduváyi), meaning needle + pomfret, stromateus genus. Title otherwise Silver pomfret, when immature; Grey pomfret, when adult. Stromateus [pomfret] cinereus, stromateidæ, acanthopterygii, teleostei [matsyam, 17], of naturalists. Alias Stromateoides cinereus; Stromateus argenteus, candidus, griseus, securifer, sudisandawah, tellasandawah. Sudisandawah and Tellasandawah from teloogoo. Snout projecting over mouth; scales small and deciduous; colors upper surface of head and back as low as lateral-line of grayish neutral-tint with purplish reflections, sides of head and body silvery-gray, fading to white on abdomen, and everywhere covered with minute black dots; dark spot on upper portion of opercle; dorsal and anal gray minutely dotted with black, outer half being darker; caudal and pectoral yellowish white, also minutely dotted black, outer half being darker; iris silvery; young are much darker, vertical fins being nearly black; the occiput in the adult is striated almost horizontally, but the commencement of these furrows is apparent in the immature; the larger specimens, gray pomfrets, are considered superior to the immature silver pomfrets for eating; sea; a foot in length.

PON (सुवर्ण - suvarana, *San.*; सोनें - sóném, *Mahr.*; ذهب - zahab, *Ar.*; زر - zar, *Pers.*; سونا - soná, *Hind.* and *Dec.*; آمس - ámas, *Malay*; ಚಿನ್ನ - chinna, *Can.*; బంగారు - bangára, *Too.*; బంగారు - bangáru, *Tel.*; പൊൻ - pon, *Mal.*; රන් - ran, *Singh.*; பொன் - pon, *Tam.*). Title from tamul. San. from (su, san. good + varna, san. color). Mahr. from sanscrit. Hind. from sanscrit. Mal. from (pol, mal. to shine). Tam. conventionally restricted to alloyed pagoda [q.v.], gold, pure, malleable gold being called tungam [q.v.]; pon meant originally any metal [loham].—"*a*" Gold. Aurum of chemists. More generally found native than any other metal. It is the most tough and ductile, as well as the most malleable of all metals [loham], more elastic than lead [eeyam] or tin [tagaram], but less so than iron [auhan] or even copper [taumram]; hammering renders it brittle, but it resumes its ductility on being slowly heated; it is not sonorous, and is the heaviest of all bodies, platina [goorootwam] excepted; for its fusion it requires a low degree of white-heat, somewhat greater than that in which silver [velly] melts. Gold mingles in fusion with all metals; it amalgamates very readily with mercury [rasam], and is remarkably disposed to unite with iron; every metal except copper débases the color of gold; that gives it a red hue, and a greater degree of firmness than when very pure; hence the combination is employed in making coins [naunyam], and different articles of plate, &c. The alloy with silver is made with difficulty, and forms the green gold [pashoom pon] of jewellers. Proper quantities of copper [taumram] filings, nitre [shorah], prepared tootty [q.v.], borax [vengauram], and hepatic aloes [q.v.], fused together by a skilful artist give a compound which much resembles gold. While gold is indestructible by the common operations of fire, it is altogether exempted from rusting. The solution in aqua regia [swarna drauvacam] is a strong poison. For distribution and mining, see vol. I, 309; II, 33. Gold is the national metal of S. india, in spite of its present scarcity there. In jewelry the beaten gold of S. india is celebrated. The workmen elaborate an extensive surface of ornament out of a trifling quantity of metal, beating it almost to the thinness of tissue paper, without weakening the effect of solidity. Gold ornaments are made at Vizianagram, Vizagapatam and Tanjore, in mythological designs; in these the ornamentation consists of figures of the Pooraunic gods in high relief [jalee], either beaten out from the surface, or affixed to it, whether by soldering, or wedging, or screwing them on. The gold jewelry of Trichinopoly contains, among other things, rose chains, ear pattern necklaces and bracelets. The jewelry of Trichinopoly is very similar to that of the Punjaub. Gold or silver thread [sarigay] is made by twisting the flattened wire, called Badlah, around silk thread [calaubat]. In gold or silver tissues the flattened wire instead of being twisted round silk thread, is itself used; the warp or the weft, as the case may be, being of very fine silk thread. For tinsel see Caukkay pon.—"*b*" The Pon is specifically an ancient small gold coin, equal to 9 or 10 fanams [q.v.], the origin of the mahomedan Hoon [q.v.] through the canarese, and the english Pagoda [q.v.]. Whenever a sum of money is mentioned in ancient Tamul records, the denomination is Pon. In the Harichendrapooraunam when the minister sells his prince to a Poolayan [q.v.] or outcaste, the price set upon him is 10,000 pons. In Tanjore the revenue accounts were kept up to a comparatively recent period in pons, panams [fanam], and cashes [q.v.]. The normal coin was a piece equal to the modern half pagoda, the pagoda itself being the double pon. The following was the table:—2 goonj = 1 doogoolam; 2 doogoolams = 1 chavalam; 2 chavalams = 1 dharnam; 2 dharnams = 1 honn; 2 honns = 1 varauhan.—"*c*" Pon is also a plant first term, often joining two genera. Ex., where transl. is of second term:—Argemone mexicana (ponnummattam), datura; Cassia occidentalis (ponnáviram), cassia auriculata; Mallotus philippensis (ponnakam), holding; Putranjiva roxburghii (ponkólam), body; Sapindus trifoliatus (ponnángottaimaram), seed + tree; Wedelia calendulacea (ponnirakkayyanni), color + eclipta alba. See gloss. paragraphs.——(1) *Pon arippoo* (பொன்னரிப்பு - ponnarippu, Tam.). From (above + ari, tam. to sift). Sifting gold out of other substances.——*Ponmalay* (பொன்மலை - ponmalai, Tam.). Means the gold mountain. Tamul name for Meroo [q.v.].——*Pon moolaum* (பொன்முலாம் - ponmulám, Tam.). From (above + mulamma, ar. plating). Gilt.——*Ponnair* (பொன்னேர் - ponnér, Tam.). From (above + ér, tam. plough). Golden plough. Ploughing for the first time in the season on an auspicious day with appropriate ceremonies [yair].——*Ponnairy* (பொன்னேரி - ponnéri, Tam.). See sep. title.——*Ponnam* (பொன்னம் - ponnam, Tam.). Lutchmy [q.v.], as of gold color.——*Ponnambalam* (பொன்னம்பலம் - ponnambalam, Tam.). Means golden hall. Proper name. Common among non-bramins. Compare Canacasabhay [peyar].——*Ponnamber* (பொன்னம்பர் - ponnambar, Tam.). Means gold or yellow amber; see Karbah.——*Ponnan* (பொன்னன் - ponnan, Tam.). Means golden man. Epithet of Arghan, the deity. Non-bramin proper name. Feminine form is Ponny [peyar].——*Ponnany* (പൊന്നാനി - ponnáni, Mal.). See sep. title.——*Ponnappan* (பொன்னப்பன் - ponnappan, Tam.). From (above + appan, tam. father). Hindoo 2nd or pers. name. Common among non-bramins [peyar].——*Ponnilakkam* (பொன்னிலக்கம் - ponnilakkam, Tam.). From (ilakkam, tam. number). Money numbers [nellilakkam].——*Ponnoo* (பொன்னு - ponnu, Tam.). Applied to males and females. Hindoo 2nd or pers. name. Compare Bungaur, Canacam, Tungam [peyar].——*Ponnoosawmy* (பொன்னுசாமி - ponnusámi, Tam.). From (above + svámi, san. master, titular affix). Hindoo 2nd or pers. name. Common among non-bramins. Familiarly Ponnoo [peyar].——*Ponnore* (పొన్నూరు - ponnúru, Tel.). From (ponnu, tel. gold + úru, tel. village). Sanscrit name (svarnapuri), meaning gold + city.—"*a*" Deputy tahsildarry, Kistna district. Pay Rs. 70.—"*b*" Village, Deputy tahsildar's station; Kistna dist., Baupatla tal.; pop. 2,604; acres 2,439; lat. 16° 04′; long. 80° 35′; from Baupatla N.N.E. 13 miles; from Bezwada S. 30 miles; from Guntoor S.S.E. 15 miles; from Masulipatam W. 38 miles; from Vinoocondah E. 52 miles; from the sea N. 15 miles. Large Vishnoo [q.v.] temple with inscriptions. Important festival at full moon [powrnimay] about beginning of May.——*Pon paulam* (బంగారుకడ్డి - bangárukhaddi, Tel.; பொற்பாளம் - porbálam, Tam.). Title and Tam. from (pon, tam. gold + pálam, tam. bar). Tel. from (bangáru, tel. gold + khaddi, tel. bar). Bars of gold, bullion.——*Ponpoya* (പൊൻപുഴ - punpuzha, Mal.). From (pon, mal. gold + puzha, mal. river). River; Malabar dist., Yernaud tal. One of main branches of Beypore river. Rises in Coondahs and joins Beypore river west of Nelambore, where it is spanned by an iron bridge. Gold [pon] dust from bed by washing.——*Pon raikk* (सुवर्णपत्र - suvarnapatra, San.; ورق الذهب - varakuzzahab, Ar.; ورق طلا - varakitilá, Pers.; سنهرى ورق - sunehrívarak, Hind.; سنهرى تگت - sunehrítagat, Dec.; ಬಂಗಾರದರೇಕು - bangáradaréku, Can.; కుందనపురేకు - kundanapuréku, Tel.; തങ്കരേഖ - tankarékha, Mal.; தங்கரேக்கு - tangarékku, Tam.). Ar. from (varak, ar. leaf + zahab, ar. gold). Pers. from (varak, ar. leaf + tilá, ar. gold). Hind. from (soná, hind. gold + varak, ar. leaf). Dec. from (soná, hind. gold + tagat, hind. leaf.). Tel. from (kundanamu, tel. pure gold + réku, tel. plate). Mal. from (taukam, mal. gold + réka, tel. plate). Gold leaf. Prescribed by native practitioners in consumptive complaints and in cases of general debility, as tonic, cordial and restorative. The metal is first beaten into leaf free from any amalgam. It is then heated and rubbed with mercury [rasam] some thirteen or fourteen times, when it is said to lose its metallic character, and becomes reduced to a reddish powder. In this condition it is prescribed. Used by moochees [q.v.] for ornamenting fans, umbrellas, images, &c.——*Ponrungan* (பொன்ரங்கன் - ponrangan, Tam.). From (above + ranga, san. vishnu). Hindoo

2nd or pers. name. Common among non-bramins [peyar].——*Pon sarigay* (سنہری کناری - sunehríkinárí, Hind.; బంగారుజరి - bangárudzari, Tel.; பொற்சரிகை - porcharigai, Tam.). Hind. from (soná, hind. gold + kinárí, hind. lace). Tel. from (bangáru, tel. gold + zar, hind. lace). Tam. from (above + sarit, san. thread). Gold lace [kinaury, sarigay].——*Poongam* (புங்கம் - pungam, Tam.). From (pon, tam. gold + agam, tam. inside); from yellow wood. Same as Karanj. Gives generic term Pongamia thereto. The oil is known as Poongam oil. Bead poongam, in tamul (manippungam), from use of tough nuts as beads [munkah] and necklaces [maulay], is same as Soapnut.——*Poongoo* (പുന്നു - punnu, Mal.; புங்கு - pungu, Tam.). Means gold-holding, from yellow color of wood. Plant name common to:—Calophyllum bracteatum, Calophyllum tomentosum, Dalbergia lanceolaria, Pongamia glabra. See gloss. paragraphs. ——*Pottaumaray* (பொற்றாமரை - pottámarai, Tam.). From (above + támarai, tam. lotus). A sacred tank at the temple in Madura.——(2) *Caroom pon* (கரும்பொன் - karumbon, Tam.). From (karum, tam. black). Iron [auhan].——*Pashoom pon* (பசும்பொன் - pasumbon, Tam.). From (pasum, tam. green). Gold of a greenish yellow color.——*Shem pon* (செம்பொன் - shembon, Tam.). From (shem, tam. red). A kind of gold red in color.——*Ven pon* (வெண்பொன் - venbon, Tam.). From (ven, tam. white). Silver [velly].

PONAM (പുനം - punam, *Mal.*; புனம் - punam, *Tam.*). From (pun, tam. inferior). Jungle; high ground not fit for rice [q.v.].——*Perambaudy* (പെരമ്പാടി - perampáti, Mal.). From (perambu, mal. cane, calamus rotang, linn. + átu, mal. country). Village, Pass; Malabar district, Wynaud talook. The ghaut [q.v.] leads from Tellicherry and Cannanore, through Coorg, to Seringapatam and Mysore.——*Peramboo* (பிரம்பு - pirambu, Tam.). From (punam, tam. hilly tract). Same as Rattan.——*Ponacaud* (പുനക്കാട് - punakkátu, Mal.). From (above + kátu, mal. forest). A jungle, chiefly highland, overrun with underwood, &c. So jungle cultivation [cautcaud, podecaud]. This is made after long intervals with particular kinds of grain sown in holes dug with a spade. The Coomry [q.v.] of Canara.——*Ponamvauram* (പുനംവാരം - punamváram, Mal.). From (above + váram, mal. rent). Landlord's share of the produce of jungle cultivation.

PONDICHERRY (پلچری - pulcharí, *Hind.*; புதுச்சேரி - puthuççéri, *Tam.*). From (puthu, tam. new + shéri, tam. village) [poothoo]. Tam. also (puthuvai), meaning new place; also (páudi), from the french corruption pondy. French territory, Town. Lies embraced by Cuddalore talook of South arcot district; lat. 11° 56′ N.; long. 79° 52′ E.; from Chidambaram N.N.E. 38 miles; from Cuddalore N.N.E. 15 miles; from Madras S.S.W. 84 miles; from Mercaunum S.S.W. 20 miles; from Tindivanam S.S.E. 23 miles; from Tricalore E. 42 miles; from Vriddhauchellam N.E. 44 miles. Chief settlement of the French possessions in the East indies [india] and the residence of the Governor. Situated at the mouth of a small river, south-east of a long flat hill. The settlement forms part of the delta [conamoogam] of the Ponniaur, and a great portion of its surface is alluvial. Many artesian wells have been sunk, and excellent drinking water is obtainable. The hills known as the Montagnes Rouges form a natural girdle to the country about Pondicherry. The coast board of the settlement is about five miles, and its breadth from three to four miles. The climate is healthy. The territory is divided into three districts:—the district of Pondicherry, properly so called, containing besides the town eleven villages; the district of Villenoor containing forty-five villages; the district of Bahoor containing thirty-six villages. These ninety-two villages are not all contiguous to each other, several being separated by English villages. The total superficies of the three districts is estimated at 69,000 acres which, in consequence of the parcelment, is scattered over a space of about 173,000 acres. The first French settlement was made here in 1674, under Francois Martin. In 1693, captured by the Dutch; restored at the peace of Ryswick in 1699; besieged by the English unsuccessfully in 1748; captured by Sir Eyre Coote in 1761; restored, 1763; captured by Sir Hector Munro in 1778; restored, 1785; captured by Colonel Braithwaite in 1793; finally restored, 1816. Down to the middle of last century Pondicherry was the finest city in India. It now extends along the sea coast about a mile and a quarter, and is about three quarters of a mile in breadth. The town is regularly built and is divided into two parts, the White town and the Black town, separated by a canal. Compare Madras city. The White town is by the seaside. Its streets, lined with trees, are regularly laid out and cut each other at right angles, and the houses are well built. The town has no port, but an open roadstead; which being to windward for nine months of the year, having less surf and possessing a river, is superior to that at Madras. In consequence of the small depth of water on the bar and the violence of the surf, landing can be effected only by a sort of rafts or flat-bottomed boats, constructed for the purpose. Light in square near the beach; lat. 11° 56′; long. 79° 53′; white, fixed, 14 miles; visible from all directions seaward; masonry column, painted light yellow; a guide to the anchorage. In the fair-weather season, from January to October, the common anchorage in the road is abreast the town, in seven or eight fathoms, about three-quarters of a mile from it. Small ships moor in about six fathoms, but during stormy weather anchor well out in twelve or fourteen fathoms. The coast is flat and sandy. In 1879 railway communication was opened with the South indian system. The soil in the territory is composed in part of argillaceous earth, more or less mixed with sand; and in part of very light sandy earth. Principal crops are rice [q.v.], indigo [q.v.], and cocoanuts [q.v.]. Betel [q.v.], tobacco [pogauk], sugar-cane [q.v.], cotton [q.v.], and oil-seeds [yennay] are grown to a small extent. There are spinning, weaving [nesavoo], dyeing [shauyam], and tanning [chamrah] industries. Weaving has of late years languished in consequence of European competition. Pondicherry is a free port. Customs duties are, however, levied on imported arrack [q.v.] and rum manufactured to the east of the Cape of Good Hope or in the Antilles. Tobacco [pogauk] and snuff [naus] are also liable to import duty. For particulars regarding the convention regarding the sale, &c., of salt between the British and French government, see vol. I, 7. The importation of salt [ooppoo], ganjah [q.v.] and bhang [q.v.] are strictly prohibited. Betel [q.v.] and tobacco [pogauk] are monopolies. The revenue from them is raised by leasing plantations to farmers. The chief public buildings are Government house, two pagodas, the new bazaar, clock-tower, light-house, barracks, military hospital, and town hall. There is also an exceedingly neat iron screw pile pier. The supply of drinking water is unrivalled for purity in any other town in Southern india. A colonial college and 172 other schools, attended by nearly 5,000 children, provide for the educational wants of the territory; and a public library of 12,000 volumes, a Catholic mission, two orphanages, and two refuges are among its institutions. The principal places of worship are Church of the Jesuits and the larger but less showy Church of the Capuchins. The buildings of the former Jesuit's college are now occupied as dwelling-houses by the bishop and clergy. The Jinjee or Ariancooppam is the only river. It is navigable during four months in the year for small flat bottom boats. A canal from the Jinjee traverses nearly the whole of the territory of Villenoor. The Coodooveiyaur is, after Ariancooppam, the only water-course in the territory deserving notice. There are sixty artificial tanks [q.v.]. The two most considerable are in the districts of Villenoor and Bahoor. The first covers 1,852 acres, of which one-third is in the English territory, and the second 1,730 acres. There are eleven principal springs. The French monetary system is in force for official purposes, though the real monetary unit is the rupee [q.v.], which is worth 2·40 francs. It is sub-divided into 8 fanams, each fanam [q.v.] being equal to 2 annas [q.v.]. The following are the travelling distances by road from Pondicherry to different places:—

To	Viâ	Miles and Furlongs.	
Arnee	Tindivanam and Wandiwash	70	0
Arnee	Meilam and Wandiwash	74	1
Bangalore ...	Tindivanam, Trinomallee and Oossoor ...	191	3
Chidambaram ...	Cuddalore and Poothoochuttram ...	37	3
Chingleput ...	Tindivanam and Carangooly	67	2
Combaconam ...	Cuddalore, Shiyally and Mayavaram ...	85	1
Cuddalore ...	......	11	7
Jinjee	Meilam and Devanore	39	2
Madras	Tindivanam and Chingleput	102	1
Madras	Meilam, Tindivanam and Chingleput ..	105	6
Mayavaram ...	Cuddalore and Shiyally	63	1
Negapatam ...	Cuddalore and Shiyally	92	3
Palamcottah ..	Tanjore and Madúra	306	5
Palamcottah ...	Negapatam and Ramnaud	327	4
Point calimere ...	Cuddalore, Shiyally and Negapatam ...	130	0
Point calimere ...	Cuddalore, Mayavaram and Tritrapoondy.	131	4
Ramnaud... ...	Negapatam and Tondy	234	2
Ranipett	Tindivanam and Wandiwash	83	1
Ranipett	Meilam, Tindivanam and Wandiwash ...	86	6
Salem	Vriddhauchellam and Talavausal ...	131	0
Salem	Oolandoorpett and Talavausal ...	131	7
Tanjore	Chidambaram and Combaconam ...	108	5
Tindivanam ...	Kilyanore	26	1
Tindivanam ...	Meilam	29	6
Tranquebar ...	Cuddalore and Shiyally	70	1
Trichinopoly ...	Cuddalore, Vriddhauchellam and Volcondapooram.	123	2½
Trichinopoly ...	Cuddalore, Shiyally and Combaconam ...	137	5
Trinomallee ...	Tindivanam and Jinjee	67	1
Trinomallee ...	Meilam, Devanore and Jinjee	64	2
Vellore	Tindivanam, Wandiwash and Arnee ...	93	1
Vellore	Meilam, Devanore and Arnee	97	5
Vriddhauchellam.	Cuddalore	49	7
Wandiwash ...	Tindivanam	44	5
Wandiwash ...	Meilam and Devanore	48	6

The following are the villages within the territory with their direction and distance from the light-house.——*Arautchicooppam* (ஆராச்சிக்குப்பம் - áráççikkuppam, Tam.). From (áráyççi, tam. examination + kuppam, tam. village). Lat. 11° 47′; long. 79° 48′; from Pond. S.S.W. 13 miles:——*Ariancooppam* (அரியாங்குப்பம் - ariyánguppam, Tam.). From (ariñan, tam. sage, epithet of shiva or vishnu + kuppam, tam. village). Lat. 11° 54′; long. 79° 51′; from Pond. S.S.W. 4 miles.——*Bahoor* (பாகூர் - págúr, Tam). See sep. title.——*Caltramputt* (கல்த்திராம்பட்டு - kalttirámbattu, Tam.). Acres 389; lat. 11° 58′; long. 79° 45′; from Pond. W. 9 miles.——*Camalam*

(கமலம் - kamalam, Tam.). Means lotus. Acres 430; lat. 11° 57′; long. 79° 41′; from Pond. W. 14 miles.——*Candiancooppam* (கண்டியாங்குப்பம் - kandiyánguppam, Tam.). From (kandiyan, tam. lyrist + kuppam, tam. village). Lat. 11° 56′; long. 79° 46′; from Pond. W. 8 miles.——*Caradicooppam* (காடிக்குப்பம் - karadikkuppam, Tam.). From (karadi, tam. bear + kuppam, tam. village). Lat. 11° 59′; long. 79° 51′; from Pond. N.W. 4 miles.——*Caulaputt* (காலாப்பட்டு - kálápattu, Tam.). From (kálá, tam. sturgeon fish + pattu, tam. village). Lat. 12° 02′; long. 79° 54′; from Pond. N.N.E. 7 miles.——*Cautpolliem* (காட்டுப்பாளையம் - káttuppálaiyam, Tam.). From (kádu, tam. forest + pálaiyam, tam. fortified village). Lat. 11° 51′; long. 79° 51′; from Pond. S.S.W. 6 miles.——*Condalancooppam* (கொண்டலாங்குப்பம் - kondalánguppam, Tam.). From (kondalán, tam. vishnu, the cloud-colored deity + kuppam, tam. village). Acres 1,083; lat. 12° 02′; long. 79° 44′; from Pond. N.W. 13 miles.——*Cooppam* (குப்பம் - kuppam, Tam.). Means hamlet. Lat. 12° 00′; long. 79° 45′; from Pond. W.N.W. 9 miles.——*Cooppanchauvady* (குப்பன் சாவடி - kuppansávadi, Tam.). From (kuppan, tam. proper name + shávadi, tam. choultry). Lat. 11° 46′; long. 79° 49′; from Pond. S.S.W. 12 miles.——*Corcaday* (கோர்க்கடை - kórkkadai, Tam.). From (kól, tam. beauty + kadai, tam. place). Lat. 11° 52′; long. 79° 48′; from Pond. S.W. 7 miles.——*Cottacooppam* (கோட்டக்குப்பம் - kóttakkuppum, Tam.). From (kóttam, tam. rice field + kuppam, tam. village). Acres 2,361; lat. 11° 58′; long. 79° 53′; from Pond. N. 2 miles.——*Cundamungalam* (கண்டமங்கலம் - kandamangalam, Tam.). From (kandan, tam. a chola king + mangala, san. prosperity). Acres 720; lat. 11° 55′; long. 79° 44′; from Pond. W. 10 miles.——*Cunganauncooppam* (கங்கனாங்குப்பம் - kanganánguppam, Tam.). Acres 218; lat. 11° 47′; long. 79° 49′; from Pond. S.S.W. 12 miles.——*Cungaraumpolliem* (கங்கராம்பாளையம் - kangarámbálaiyam, Tam.). From (kangaráman, tam. proper name + pálaiyam, tam. fortified village). Acres 1,674; lat. 11° 54′; long. 79° 39′; from Pond. W. 15 miles.——*Ghory* (கோரி - kóri, Tam.). Means a tombstone. Lat. 11° 58′; long. 79° 50′; from Pond. W.N.W. 4 miles.——*Mailalanjiputt polliem* (மேலழிஞ்சிப்பட்டுப்பாளையம் - mélazhiñjippattuppálaiyam, Tam.). From (mél, tam. west + azhiñjippattu, tam. village so called + pálaiyam, tam. fortified village). Acres 347; lat. 11° 56′; long. 79° 49′; from Pond. S.W. 8 miles.——*Mandagaputt* (மண்டகப்பட்டு - mandagappattu, Tam.). From (mandabam, tam. a public resting place + pattu, tam. village). Acres 1,453; lat. 11° 52′; long. 79° 43′; from Pond. W.S.W. 11 miles.——*Maroothaud* (மருதாடு - maruthádu, Tam.). From (marutham, tam. cultivated land + ádu, tam. sheep). Acres 395; lat. 11° 47′; long. 79° 46′; from Pond. S.W. 13 miles.——*Matharapaukum* (மதுரைப்பாக்கம் - mathuraippákkam, Tam.). From (mathurai, tam. sweet liquor + pákkam, tam. village). Lat. 12° 00′; long. 79° 39′; from Pond. W.N.W. 16 miles.——*Mauncooppam* (மாங்குப்பம் - mánguppam, Tam.). From (má, tam. mango tree, mangifera indica, linn. + kuppam, tam. hamlet). Acres 146; lat. 11° 55′; long. 79° 40′; from Pond. W. 15 miles.——*Moongilputt* (மூங்கிற்பட்டு - múngirbattu, Tam.). From (múngil, tam. bamboo, bambusa arundinacea, willd. + pattu, tam. village). Acres 955; lat. 11° 58′; long. 79° 39′; from Pond. W. 15 miles.——*Moottiaulpett* (முத்தியால்ப்பேட்டை - muttiyálppéttai, Tam.). From (mutyálu, tel. proper name + péttai, tam. suburb). Lat. 11° 57′; long. 79° 53′; from Pond. N. 2 miles.——*Mortaundichauvady* (மொரட்டாண்டிச்சாவடி - morattándiççávadi, Tam.). From (muradu, tam. rudeness + ándi, tam. religious mendicant + shávadi, tam. choultry). Lat. 11° 59′; long. 79° 50′; from Pond. N.W. 4 miles.——*Nernayaputt* (நெர்நயப்பட்டு - nernayappattu, Tam.). Lat. 11° 50′; long. 79° 48′; from Pond. S.W. 9 miles.——*Nullatore* (நல்லாத்தூர் - nalláttúr, Tam.). From (nalla, tam. good + áru, tam. river + úr, tam. village). Acres 1,147; lat. 11° 52′; long. 79° 46′; from Pond. S.W. 9 miles.——*Oolgaray* (உழவக்கரை - uzhavakkarai, Tam.). From (uzhavan, tam. ploughman + karai, tam. bank). Lat. 11° 56′; long. 79° 50′; from Pond. W. 3 miles.——*Oonnaumalay chetty chauvady* (உண்ணாமலைச் செட்டிச்சாவடி - unnámalaiççettiççávadi, Tam.). From (unnámalaiççetti, tam. proper name + shávadi, tam. choultry). Lat. 11° 46′; long. 79° 48′; from Pond. S.S.W. 13 miles.——*Ootchimode* (உச்சிமேடு - uççimédu, Tam.). From (uççi, tam. top of a mountain + médu, tam. rising ground). Acres 217; lat. 11° 47′; long. 79° 50′; from Pond. S.S.W. 12 miles.——*Parangany* (பரங்கணி - parangani, Tam.). From (paran, tam. god + kani, tam. agricultural district). Acres 2,235; lat. 12° 03′; long. 79° 45′; from Pond. N.W. 12 miles.——*Parausy reddipolliem* (பராசிரெட்டிப்பாளையம் - parásirettippálaiyam, Tam.). From (parásiretti, tam. proper name + pálaiyam, tam. fortified village). Acres 713; lat. 11° 51′; long. 79° 39′; from Pond. W.S.W. 17 miles.——*Paukkam* (பாக்கம் - pákkam, Tam.). Means maritime village. Acres 1,678; lat. 11° 51′; long. 79° 44′; from Pond. S.W. 12 miles.——*Pavpanchauvady* (பாப்பான்சாவடி - páppánsávadi, Tam.). From (párppán, tam. bramin + shávadi, tam. choultry). Lat. 12° 00′; long. 79° 49′; from Pond. N.W. 6 miles.——*Perambay* (பெரம்பை - perambai, Tam.). From (pirambu, tam. cane). Acres 756; lat. 11° 56′; long. 79° 48′; from Pond. W. 5 miles.——*Pillaychauvady* (பிள்ளைச்சாவடி - pillaiççávadi, Tam.). From (pillai, tam. one of the caste + shávadi, tam. choultry). Lat. 12° 00′; long. 79° 55′; from Pond. N.N.E. 5 miles.——*Pootoray* (பூத்துறை - pútturai, Tam.). From (pú, tam. flower + turai, tam. ford). Acres 3,804; lat. 11° 58′; long. 79° 49′; from Pond. W.N.W. 5 miles.——*Poottooputt* (புத்துப்பட்டு - puttuppattu, Tam.). From (puttu, tam. hole of snakes, ants, rats, &c. + pattu, tam. village). Acres 1,451; lat. 11° 52′; long. 79° 42′; from Pond. W.S.W. 13 miles.——*Rambaukam* (இராம்பாக்கம் - irámbákkam, Tam.). From (ráma, san. the hero + pákkam, tam. village). Acres 1,020; lat. 11° 50′; long. 79° 39′; from Pond. W.S.W. 17 miles.——*Reddichauvady* (இரெட்டிச்சாவடி - irettiççávadi, Tam.). From (reddi, tel. one of that caste + shávadi, tam. choultry). Lat. 11° 50′; long. 79° 50′; from Pond. S.S.W. 7 miles.——*Shirvandaud* (சிருவந்தாடு - shiruvandádu, Tam.). Acres 928; lat. 11° 52′; long. 79° 39′; from Pond. W.S.W. 16 miles.——*Shorapore* (சொரப்பூர் - shorappúr, Tam.). From (shurappu, tam. abundance + úr, tam. village). Acres 906; lat. 11° 51′; long. 79° 42′; from Pond. W.S.W. 15 miles.——*Shornavore* (சொர்ணவூர் - shornávúr, Tam.). From (shornam, tam. proper name + úr, tam. village). Acres 2,307; lat. 11° 49′; long. 79° 41′; from Pond. W.S.W. 16 miles.——*Tennal* (தென்னல் - tennal, Tam.). From (tennal, tam. south wind). Acres 1,451; lat. 11° 54′; long. 79° 46′; from Pond. W.S.W. 8 miles.——*Tircanore* (திருக்கனூர் - tirkkanúr, Tam.). Lat. 11° 59′; long. 79° 41′; from Pond. W.N.W. 14 miles.——*Valdavore* (வழுதாவூர் - vazhuthávúr, Tam.). From (vazhuthi, tam. epithet of a pándyan king + úr, tam. village). Acres 1,373; lat. 11° 59′; long. 79° 45′; from Pond. W.N.W. 9 miles.——*Vattacaray* (வட்டக்கரை - vattakkarai, Tam.). From (vattam, tam. circle + karai, tam. bank). Lat. 11° 58′; long. 79° 53′; from Pond. N. 2 miles.——*Vaunore* (வானூர் - vánúr, Tam.). From (ván, tam. rain + úr, tam. village). Acres 3,231; lat. 12° 01′; long. 79° 47′; from Pond. N.W. 8 miles.——*Villenoor* (வில்லியனூர் - villiyanúr, Tam.). From (villiyan, tam. a bowman + úr, tam. village). Lat. 11° 54′; long. 79° 48′; from Pond. W.S.W. 5 miles.——*Yembalam* (ஏம்பலம் - émbalam, Tam.). Lat. 11° 52′; long. 79° 46′; from Pond. S.W. 9 miles.

PONDRAUCA (పొండ్రాక - pondráka, *Tel.*). Village, Port; Kistna dist., in the former Krittivenn zemindarry, Bunder tal.; lat. 16° 21′; long. 81° 18′; from Guntoor E. 54 miles; from Masulipatam N.E. 15 miles; from Vinoocondah E.N.E 102 miles. On Golcondah coast [q.v.]. Salt [ooppoo] manufactured.

PONGAL (పొంగలి - pongali, *Tel.*; பொங்கல் - pongal, *Tam.*). From (pongu, tam. to boil). Because new rice is boiled in milk [paul] and sugar [q.v.] and distributed. Cf. Harvest home. Otherwise Macarasancraunty, Maha sancraunty, Mautt pongal, Peroom pongal, Sancraunty, Tye pirapp, Tye pongal. The greatest of the unsectarian festivals of the Tamulians, probably for past harvest. Solar [madhyama sowra maunam] festival [pundigay, 6d]. It is celebrated when the sun [sooryan] enters Capricorn [macaram] to take northward course [oottarauyanam] on the first day of the tenth solar month Tye [mausam] about the 11th of January, and lasts three days. Sufficiently described at vol. 1 (93) [maryauday].

PONNAIRY (پونیر - ponner, *Hind.*; பொன்னேரி - ponnéri, *Tam.*). From (pon, tam. beauty + éri, tam. tank) [pon].——**(1)** Talook, Chingleput district. Tahsildar's pay Rs. 150. Area 347 square miles. Population 122,418. Language Tamul and Teloogoo. N. of district. Bounded E. by Bay of Bengal, N. by Polore division of Nellore district, W. by Vencatagherry and Calastry zemindarries and Trivellore talook, and S. by Sydapett talook. Consists of an almost unbroken flat of paddy [q.v.] fields and desert plain, while its eastern and northern borders are covered with salt swamps and low-lying sandy tracts. The high road from Madras to Calcutta traverses the talook. Average rainfall 35 inches. The soil is much less fertile than that of Trivellore and Sydapett and in the majority of villages it falls under the lowest classification. Casuarina [chowkmaram] planting is carried on, although not so extensively as in Sydapett talook. Red handkerchiefs [roomaul] and Mussalman [q.v.] cloths are woven at Poolicat. The fame of the Arnee muslins [q.v.] has departed. The Corteliaur flows through the southern portion and the Aranyanuddy through the centre. The largest tank is that at Cholavaram. About 23,084 acres of dry land are cultivated, 4,491 being entered as topes, and 32,067 acres as wet. In the former are 10,767 acres, or 46·64 per cent., under paddy [q.v.], representing the old Maunavaury [q.v.] lands of the talook, and ordinary dry land irrigated at the cost of the cultivator. Petty Zemindarries:—Agaram, Alinjivaukam, Arivadoray, Aroovaukam, Aumore, Canacambaukam, Caroongooly, Caunjivauyal, Chinnacauvanam, Codoor, Colattore, Coloor, Coommungalam, Covantaungal, Devaranjery, Giridhanapooram,

Iroolaputt, Juggannautapooram, Keelmathalambaid, Keerapaukam, Krishnaupooram, Lingasamoodram, Lutchmeepooram, Madimey, Mathiravaid, Nedoovarambaukam, Ooppalam, Oracaud, Panapaukam, Paricaputt, Paudyanullore, Peroovoyil, Ponnairy, Poolicoolam, Poottaharam, Pullambaukam, Shellapillaiyaurcooppam, Shembiyamanaly, Shennivaukam, Shittarasore, Shivapooram, Tatchoor, Tautharasore, Tirvencatapooram, Tirvyepaudy, Vembaukam, Yelimbaid. Places of archæological interest:—Arnee, Arvattoray, Aundaurcooppam, Cholavaram, Mailore, Minjoor, Nauyar, Panjutty, Ponnairy, Poolicat, Tirpaulaivanam, Tirvellavauyal, Yermaivettipolliem. Principal trig. stations:—Rettambaid, Yerauncherry. The leading places, &c., in the talook are the following.——*Arnee* (ஆரணி - árani, Tam.). See sep. title.——*Attiputt* (அத்திப்பட்டு - attippattu, Tam.). From (atti, tam. fig tree, ficus racemosa, linn. + pattu, tam. village). Village; pop. 1,293; acres 2,260; lat. 13° 16′; long. 80° 21′; from Ponnairy S.E. 8 miles; from Sydapett N. 17 miles; from the sea W. 3 miles. Salt-producing centre.——*Aumore* (ஆமூர் - ámúr, Tam.). From (ámá, tam. wild ox + úr, tam. village). Zemindarry, Village; pop. 628; acres 1,091; lat. of village 13° 18′; long. 80° 15′; from Ponnairy S. 3 miles; from Sydapett N. 19 miles; from the sea W. 11 miles. Peshcush Rs. 2,618.——*Cholavaram* (சோழவரம் - shózhavaram, Tam.). See sep. title.——*Cochrane canal* (கொக்கரேன் வாய்க்கால் - kokkarénváykkál, Tam.). See sep. title.——*Coromandel* (கருமணல் - karumanal, Tam.). See sep. title.——*Corteliaur* (கொர்த்தலையாறு - korttalaiyáru, Tam.). See sep. title.——*Goommidipoondy* (கும்மிடிப்பூண்டி - kummidippúndi, Tam.). From (gummadi, tel. cucurbita maxima, duch. + púndi, tam. village). Village; pop. 1,145; acres 915; lat. 13° 24′; long. 80° 11′; from Ponnairy N.W. 7 miles; from Sydapett N.W. 27 miles; from the sea W. 14 miles. A road side village at 30th mile of great northern trunk road from Madras to Nellore. Spacious choultry [q.v.] and tank [q.v.] built and endowed by a wealthy native of Madras. Travellers' bungalow [q.v.]. Frequented for snipe [oollaun].——*Keelmathalambaid* (கீழ்மதலம்பேடு - kízhmathalambédu, Tam.). From (kízh, tam. east + mathalambédu, tam. place so called). Zemindarry, Village; pop. 1,232; acres 1,103; lat. of village 13° 21′; long. 80° 12′; from Ponnairy N.W. 4 miles; from Sydapett N.W. 23 miles; from the sea W. 14 miles. Peshcush Rs. 1,468.——*Panapaukam* (பனப்பாக்கம் - panappákkam, Tam.). From (panai, tam. a palmyra, borassus flabelliformis, linn. + pákkam, tam. village). Zemindarry, Village; pop. 671; acres 1,419; lat. of village 13° 23′; long. 80° 12′; from Ponnairy N.W. 5 miles; from Sydapett N. 25 miles; from the sea W. 13 miles. Peshcush Rs. 1,336.——*Peroovoyil* (பெருவாயல் - peruváyal, Tam.). From (peru, tam. big + váyil, tam. entrance). Zemindarry, Village; pop. 753; acres 1,160; lat. of village 13° 21′; long. 80° 13′; from Ponnairy W. 4 miles; from Sydapett N.W. 23 miles; from the sea W. 13 miles. Peshcush Rs. 1,655.——*Ponnairy* (பொன்னேரி - ponnéri, Tam.). See below.——*Poolicat* (பழவேர்க்காடு - pazhavérkkádu, Tam.). See sep. title.——*Poothoovoyil* (புதுவாயில் - puthuváyil, Tam. puduváyil *). From (puthu, tam. new + váyil, tam. gate). Shrotriem [q.v.] village; pop. 814; acres 1,233; lat. of village 13° 20′; long. 80° 13′; from Ponnairy W. 3 miles; from Sydapett N. 22 miles; from the sea W. 13 miles.——*Rettambaid* (இரெட்டம்பேடு - irettambédu, Tam.). From (irattai, tam. double + pédu, tam. village). Trig. station; lat. 13° 26′ 05·04″; long. 80° 12′ 39·30″; height 63 feet; from Ponnairy N. 7 miles; from Sheganiem S.W. 1 mile; from the sea W. 11 miles.——*Tirvyepaudy* (திருவாய்ப்பாடி - tiruváyppádi, Tam.). From (tiru, tam. holy + váy, tam. word + pádi, tam. village). Zemindarry, Village; pop. 576; acres 66; lat. of village 13° 21′; long. 80° 15′; from Ponnairy N. ¼ mile; from Sydapett N. 22 miles; from the sea W. 10 miles. Peshcush Rs. 63. Hamlet of Ponnairy. Shiva temple with inscriptions.——*Vulloor* (வல்லூர் - vallúr, Tam.). From (val, tam. hillock + úr, tam. village). Village; pop. 3,643; acres 4,927; lat. 13° 16′; long. 80° 21′; from Ponnairy S.E. 8 miles; from Sydapett N. 17 miles; from the sea W. 4 miles. Centre of large salt-producing tract. Tank is fed by the Corteliaur.——*Yerauncherry* (எராஞ்சேரி - eráñjéri, Tam.). From (éra, tam. high + shéri, tam. village). Trig. station; lat. 13° 12′ 45·54″; long. 80° 19′ 43·67″; from Ponnairy S.E. 10 miles; from Vellivauyal S. 1 mile; from the sea W. 4 miles.——*Yermaivettipolliem* (எருமைவெட்டிப்பாளையம் - erumaivettippálaiyam, Tam.). From (erumai, tam. a buffalo + vetti, tam. way + pálaiyam, tam. fortified village). Village; pop. 423; acres 1,291; lat. 13° 15′; long. 80° 11′; from Ponnairy S.W. 8 miles; from Sydapett N.W. 16 miles; from the sea W. 14 miles. Two old Shiva and Vishnoo temples; the latter with an inscription of the Vijianugger dynasty dated A.D. 1517. On the cliffs to the north-east rude stone implements have been found.——**(2)** Zemindarry; Chingleput district, Ponnairy talook. Peshcush Rs. 262.——**(3)** Village, Talook head-quarters; Chingleput dist., Ponnairy tal.; pop. 717; acres 337; lat. 13° 20′; long. 80° 15′; from Chingleput N. 45 miles; from Conjeeveram N.E. 47 miles; from Madras N. 19 miles; from St. Thomas' mount N. 23 miles; from Sydapett N. 21 miles; from the sea W. 10 miles. On the right or S. bank of Narrainuvaram river. Comprises Coommungalam, Ponnairy and Tirvyepandy all zameen [q.v.] villages. Shiva and Vishnoo temples. Dyeing [shauyam] of cloths and manufacture of palampores [q.v.].

PONNANY (പൊന്നാനി - ponnáni, *Mal.* ponáni *). From (pon, mal. gold + nánayam, mal. coin) [pon]. The Araby cash [q.v.] was first circulated here by Arab and Persian merchants. ——**(1)** Talook, Malabar district. Tahsildar's pay Rs. 225. Area 482 square miles. Southernmost talook of the district. Extreme length from north to south along the coast 64 miles, width from 3 to 20 miles. S. coast of district. Boundaries:—north, Yernaud talook; east, Valavauad talook and native state of Cochin; south, native state of Cochin; west, Arabian sea. Formerly comprised three talooks of Bettatnaud, Cootnaud, and Chowghaut, which were amalgamated in 1861. Soil along the coast poor and sandy; open sea-board fringed with cocoanut [q.v.] trees. No granite on coast, but in the interior the formation is gneissic, traversed by granite [caroom cull] veins. The most striking feature is the series of backwaters [canyal] lying zigzag along coast and affording with the connecting artificial canals inland water communication. They extend southwards from Tiroor to Ponnany, Chowghaut and Cochin and thence into Cochin and Travancore states. Total length from Tiroor to Cochin is 93 miles, of which 77 lie in the talook. The talook is also intersected by the Ponnany and minor streams. Timber from the Anamullays and Munnarcaud forests is floated down river during rainy season to the timber depôts at Ponnany. Has two large shallow lakes; the Viyyattil lake three miles east of Ponnany and Trichore lake, about the same distance east of Chetwye, and eight miles from Chowghaut. They respectively connected with the backwaters communicating with the sea at Velliangode and Chetwye. Protected by strong artificial dams from tidal influence, the beds of both are to a considerable extent cultivated with paddy [q.v.] after the monsoon [q.v.]. The Viyyattil lake lies entirely in this talook, while the greater portion of Trichore lake belongs to Cochin state. Staple produce cocoanuts [q.v.]. Paddy [q.v.] is largely cultivated. Places of archæological interest:—Alangode, Anantavore, Annakara, Atchipooram, Autavanaud, Cauttiparootty, Chamravuttam, Chekkode, Chetwye, Chowghaut, Claury, Codacull, Comauranullore, Cummaunam, Cuppore, Gooroovayore, Keralaudheeshwarapooram, Mailmoory, Moollacherry, Nauglacherry, Nirmaroottore, Olore, Paroothore, Pullipooram, Punniyore, Soocapooram, Tanalore, Taunore, Tirnavoya, Tirvanjicoolam, Toliyore, Tricaniyore, Triprangode, Trittaula, Vadakoombram, Vairore. Principal trig. station:—Coornaud. The leading places, &c., in the talook are the following.——*Andattode* (അണ്ടത്തോട് - antattótu, Mal.). Means a frequented canal. Village; pop. 6,028; lat. 10° 41′; long. 76° 01′; from Calicut S.S.E. 41 miles; from Ponnany S.S.E. 8 miles; from the sea E. ¾ mile. Amshom [q.v.] cutcherry [q.v.], market on Tuesdays. Ponnany-Cochin canal is half-a-furlong east. Temple called Vettakkormagan cshetram.——*Anjoor* (അഞ്ചൂർ - añchúr, Mal.). From (añchu, mal. five + úr, mal. village). Village; pop. 7,620. Syrian christian village.——*Attacooy* (അട്ടക്കുഴി - attakkuzhi, Mal.). From (atta, mal. leech + kuzhi, mal. hollow). Village, Port; pop. 4,563.——*Autavanaud* (ആതവനാട് - átavanátu, Mal.). From (átapa, san. heat + nátu, san. country). Village; pop. 9,884; lat. 10° 54′; long. 76° 5′; from Calicut S.E. 30 miles; from Ponnany N.E. 11 miles; from the sea E. 10 miles. Residence of Alwancherry tumbraukkal [q.v.], or chief of Numboories [q.v.].——*Bettatnaud* (വെട്ടത്തുനാട - vettattunátu, Mal.). See sep. title.——*Bettatt poothiyangaudy* (വെട്ടത്തുപുതിയങ്ങാടി - vettattuputiyannáti, Mal.). See sep. title.——*Chaulicherry* (ചാലിശ്ശേരി - chálishshéri, Mal.). From (cháli, mal. rice + shéri, mal. village). Pop. 891. Small village and bazaar [q.v.] on the borders of Cuppore and Cottatchira amshoms [q.v.], about 6 miles south of Trittaula. Syrian [q.v.] christians have a small church. Trade in areca-nuts [q.v.]. Weekly market on Thursdays.——*Chetwye* (ചേററുവായ - chéttaváya, Mal.). See sep. title.——*Chowghaut* (ചാവക്കാട - chávakkátu, Mal.). See sep. title.——*Codacull* (കൊടക്കൽ - kotakkal, Mal.). Means umbrella stone; from the archæological relics. Village; pop. 5,393; lat. 10° 59′; long. 76° 04′; from Calicut S.E. 24 miles; from Ponnany N.E. 14 miles; from the sea E. 10 miles. Rock-cut burying places half a mile distant. Small village of native Christians, and German mission church. Weaving establishment under the mission.——*Coornaud* (കുറനാട് - kurnátu, Mal.). From (kuru, mal. small + nátu, mal. country). Trig. station; lat. 10° 47′ 32·64″; long. 76° 08′ 36·50″; height 354 feet; from Mailattore W. 2 miles; from Ponnany E. 12 miles; from the sea E. 13 miles.——*Cootnaud* (കുറ്റനാട് - kúttanátu, Mal.). From (kúttan, mal. large + nátu, mal. country). Village; lat. 10° 45′; long. 76° 09′; from Calicut S.S.E. 40 miles; from Ponnany E.S.E. 12 miles; from the sea E. 11 miles. Formerly gave its name to a talook, now comprised in Ponnany talook.——*Coottingal* (കുട്ടിങ്ങൽ - kúttinnal, Mal.). Means junction place;

from the market on Wednesdays. Pop. 2,646; lat. 10° 35′; long. 76° 04′; from Calicut S.S.E. 48 miles; from Ponnany S.S.E. 14 miles; from the sea E. 1¼ miles. In Paulayore amshom by the side of the canal from Ponnany to Cochin, about 17 miles south of the former. District moonsif's court. Syro-Roman catholic church, called Paulayore church, one of the seven original churches of Malabar. St. Thomas the Apostle preached here.——*Coottipooram* (കുററിപ്പുറം - kuttippuram. Mal. kuttipuram *). From (kutti, mal. boundary + puram, mal. beyond). Village, Railway station, a market every Sunday; pop. 2,646; lat. 10° 51′; long. 76° 05′; height 47 feet; from Calicut S.S.E. 33 miles; from Ponnany E.N.E. 9 miles; from the sea E. 9 miles.——*Cootye* (കൂട്ടഴി - kúttazhi, Mal.). From (kúttu, mal. junction + azhi, mal. river mouth). Here the backwaters from Tiroor and Ponnany unite and communicate with sea, or have done so. Village, Sub-port attached to the Ponnany port; pop. 5,069; lat. 10° 51′; long. 75° 57′; from Bettatt poothiyangaudy S.W. 3 miles; from Bombay S.S.E. 580 miles; from Calicut S.S.E. 29 miles; from Ponnany N.N.W. 4 miles. Large Mahomedan village, by the side of the sea.——*Cottapady* (കോട്ടപ്പടി - kóttappati, Mal.). From (kótta, mal. fort + pati, mal. gate). Deshom [q.v.] partly lying in Vayilattore and partly in Gooroovayore amshom [q.v.]. Close to seat of the old Poonnattore rajah, whose family still remain. Syrian [q.v.] christians. Trade in cocoanut [q.v.] oil and rearing of country pigs [soor] by Christians. These animals are transported to Neilgherries, &c.——*Gooroovayore* (ഗുരുവായൂർ - guruváyúr, Mal.). From tradition that temple was founded by brihaspaty [q.v.] and the god of wind [vayoo]. Sanscrit name (gurupavanapura), meaning brihaspaty + vayoo + town; also (vátálaya), meaning wind + abode. Village, Place of pilgrimage and renowned Hindoo temple; pop. 7,423; lat. 10° 35′; long. 76° 05′; from Calicut S.S.E. 46 miles; from Ponnany S.S.E. 14 miles; from the sea E. 3 miles. Inhabitants chiefly Numboory bramins [q.v.] and Nayars [q.v.]. Large temples, destroyed by Tippoo in 1784, and restored by the Zamorin [q.v.] in 1794.——*Parony* (പരൂണ - parúna, Mal.). See sep. title.——*Ponnany* (പൊന്നാനി - ponnáni, Mal.). See below.——*Taunore* (താനൂർ - tánúr, * Mal.). From (tánni, mal. tree, terminalia belerica, roxb. + úr, mal. village). Village, Railway station, Port, a Moplah town, Sub-registrar's office, Moosaufer khana and Travellers' bungalow; lat. 10° 58′; long. 75° 55′; height 26 feet; from Bombay S.S.E. 570 miles; from Calicut S.S.E. 20 miles; from Mangalore S.S.E. 146 miles; from Parony N.N.W. 5 miles; from Parpanangaudy S.S.E. 7 miles; from Ponnany N.N.W. 14 miles. At the mouth of a small river, 2 miles west of the railway station. It was a small kingdom at the arrival of the Portuguese, in partial subjection to the Zamorin [q.v.]. In 1782, the British army, acting against the forces of Hyder ally, took refuge here from a storm of five days' continuance, which dispersed the boats, spoiled the provisions, and damaged the ammunition of the expedition. Formerly prosperous, but now much decayed.——*Tirnavoya* (തിരുനാവായ - tirunáváya, Mal.). See sep. title.——*Tiroor* (തിരൂർ - tirúr, Mal.). See sep. title.——*Tripriaur* (തൃപ്രയാർ - tripraýár, Mal.). From (tri, mal. holy + pura, san. town + áru, mal. river). Village, Place of pilgrimage; pop. 1,965. Is on the western side of the canal from Tiroor to Cochin. Temple belonging to Cochin state.——*Trittaula* (തൃത്താല - trittála, Mal.). From (tri, mal. holy + tála, san. palm tree, borassus flabelliformis, linn.); lat. 10° 48′; long. 76° 11′; from Calicut S.S.E. 39 miles; from Ponnany E. 14 miles; from the sea E. 15 miles. Small village in Cootnaud amshom by the side of Ponnany river on the road from Ponnany to Palghaut. Travellers' bungalow [q.v.]. Weekly market. About four miles south are the ruins of Cootnaud fort.——*Valappaud* (വലപ്പാട് - valappátu, Mal.). From (vala, mal. net + pátu, mal. village). Pop. 4,563; lat. 10° 24′; long. 76° 10′; from Coottingal S.S.E. 14 miles; from Calicut S.S.E. 62 miles; from Ponnany S.S.E. 29 miles; from the sea E. 2 miles. Syrian christians. In Pullipooram amshom. Market on Thursdays.——*Velliangode* (വെളിയങ്കോട് - veliyankótu, Mal.). From (veliyan, mal. open + kótu, mal. place). Village, Port; lat. 10° 44′; long. 75° 59′; from Bombay S.S.E. 590 miles; from Calicut S.S.E. 36 miles; from Chowghaut N.N.W. 12 miles; from Ponnany S. 4 miles. At the mouth of the river of the same name. A small port of call for coasting craft loading with cocoanuts [q.v.] and other country produce. Chiefly Moplahs [q.v.].——*Yedappaul* (എടപ്പാൾ - etappál, Mal.). From (eta, mal. middle + pázh, mal. empty space). Large trading village; pop. 7,538; lat. 10° 48′; long. 76° 02′; from Calicut S.S.E. 34 miles; from Ponnany E. 5 miles; from the sea E. 5 miles. Chiefly Moplahs [q.v.]. The ancient Chovoor [q.v.] is close to this. Ancient Shoocapooram temple to Dacshinamoorty [q.v.] or Shiva. No yaugams [q.v.] by Numboories are recognized as such until they are registered at this pagoda [q.v.]. This registration takes place once in twelve years. The Shreecovil, Garbhagriham [q.v.] or shrine of the temple [coil, pagoda] is a massive laterite [q.v.] structure. About 6 miles north-east is an ancient temple attached to the Numboory [q.v.] bramin colony of Punniyore [q.v.], of Chiracal talook; presiding deity Varauha moorty, the third incarnation [avatar] of Vishnoo [q.v.].——*Yedatirootty* (എടത്തുരുത്തി - etatturutti, Mal.). From (eta, mal. middle + turutti, mal. island). Pop. 10,409; lat. 10° 23′; long. 76° 12′; from Valappaud S.E. 3 miles; from Calicut S.S.E. 64 miles; from Ponnany S.S.E. 32 miles; from the sea E. 4 miles. Syrian christians.——*Yenamacull* (ഏനാമാക്കൽ - énámákkal, Mal.). See sep. title.——**(2)** Town, Port, Divisional and talook headquarters, Moonsif's court, Telegraph office, Sub-registrar's office; Malabar dist., Ponnany tal.; pop. 13,143; lat. 10° 47′; long. 75° 58′; from Bangalore S.W. 186 miles; from Bombay S.E. 586 miles; from Cootye S.S.E. 4 miles; from Calicut S.S.E. 33 miles; from Mangalore S.S.E. 160 miles; from Madras W.S.W. 330 miles; from Cannanore S.S.E. 82 miles; from Malapooram S.W. 20 miles; from Manantoddy S.S.W. 68 miles; from Tellicherry S.S.E. 71 miles; from Velliangode N. 4 miles. At the mouth of Ponnany river. Here Moplah seaport, most important between Cochin and Calicut, possessing water communication with railway station at Tiroor and with Cochin and Travancore. Nearest port to Palghaut gap. Once proposed as terminus of Madras railway. Moplah [q.v.] tangal [q.v.] or Makhdoom [q.v.] or high priest has head-quarters here. Also centre of Mussalman education on the west coast, possessing a religious college which confers degrees. The proficients are called Moosaliyaurs [q.v.]; the Makhdoom [q.v.] gives the degrees. Here the English retired from Cochin in 1662, and Colonels Macleod and Humberstone repulsed Tippoo and Lally in 1782. When Colonel Hartley in 1790 made his celebrated descent upon the west coast, the inhabitants of Ponnany gave in their adhesion readily. The population is supported by fishing and by trade; having numerous puttimars [q.v.] which ply to Surat. Arabia, Bombay, Madras, and even as far as Bengal, exporting principally pepper [q.v.], betel [q.v.], rice [q.v.], cocoanuts [q.v.], iron [auhan], and very fine timber sent down the river from the ghauts [q.v.]. The trade in salt [ooppoo] was once extensive. The imports are wheat [geung], sugar-cane [q.v.], molasses [jaggery], oil-seeds [yennay], groceries and spices. Contains Cootnaud district moonsif's court, Travellers' bungalow. About half mile south-east at Tricauv, an ancient Hindoo temple to Doorga bhagavaty [q.v.]. Tippoo plundered the temple, broke the idol [shilay, vigraham] into pieces, and used the Shreecovil as his powder magazine [q.v.].——**(3)** River; Malabar dist., Palghaut, Ponnany, Valavanaud tals. Otherwise Bhauratapoya or river where the pandavas bathed. Named from the town situate on the south side of its estuary. Rises in the Anamullays in Coimbatore district in the vicinity of some tanks in lat. 10° 19′; long. 77° 6′. Flowing north-west, through the Palghaut gap, it crosses the east boundary of Malabar about 55 miles from its source in lat. 10° 42′, long. 76° 45′. Then turning west, it flows by Palghaut, and continuing to hold the same direction for 25 miles in lat. 10° 45′, long. 76° 31′ it becomes the boundary between Cochin and Malabar and continues so for 23 miles to lat. 10° 47′, long. 76° 14′, where it enters the district, and flows westward through it for 25 miles, to its fall into the Arabian sea at Ponnany town in lat. 10° 47′, long. 75° 58′. During its course it flows for about 70 miles parallel to the south-west line of the Madras railway. The Walayaur and Varattaur join the Cauriyaur, 5 miles east of Palghaut. The stream so formed is again joined by the Palaur, about 2 miles north of Palghaut, and the united river then falls into the Ponnany at Yedattara. About 15 miles lower down at Wottapollem, the Ponnany receives with other less significant tributaries the Meengara, Collangode, and the Aulatore river with its tributaries. From December to May these rivers are dry. During six months of the monsoon [q.v.] they have water and are subject to heavy freshes. The river is navigable for canoes as high as Palghaut 63 miles from the sea. It can be navigated only by small craft, on account of a bar with small depth of water at the mouth as shoal water inside, but is useful during the monsoons, when it floats down to the coast great quantities of fine timber. It is the longest river which discharges into the Arabian ocean in Malabar proper. The main stream is about 156 miles long, and the lengths of its three chief tributaries before they join the main stream are respectively about 60, 50 and 46 miles. But the volume of water discharged from the large area drained by this river and its tributaries is probably not so great and is certainly not so constant as that discharged either by the Belliapatam or by the Beypore river.

PONNAUK (पिण्याक - pinyáka, *San.*; کهل - khal, *Hind.*; గానుగపిండి - gánugapindi, *Tel.*; പിണ്ണാക്ക് - pinnákku, *Mal.*; பிண்ணாக்கு - pinnákku, *Tam.*). San. from (pish, san. to grind). Tel. from (gánuga, tel. oil mill + pindi, tel. flour). Mal. and Tam. from sanscrit. Oil cake. Otherwise Oil-seed cake. The solid compressed mass remaining after the expression of oil [yennay] from the many oil-yielding seeds, nuts, &c. It retains after the most perfect treatment by pressure, a considerable portion of oil with practically the whole of the albuminous matter, sugar, mucilage and starchy components of the seed, thus forming a concentrated nutritious food for cattle [maud] and sheep [aud].—"*a*" The following is a key-list of the chief oil cakes of S. india:—Arachis hypogæa, ground-nut; Bassia longifolia, common mohwah; Brassica campestris, subsp. nupus, rape; Carthamus tinctorius, safflower, seed cake; Cocos nucifera, cocoanut; Gossypium herbaceum, indian cotton; Guizotia abyssinica, ramtil; Linum usitatissimum, flax; Papaver somniferum, opium poppy; Sesamum indicum, gingelly.—"*b*" Compare:—Corchorus olitorius (pinnákkuççedi); Melochia corchorifolia (pinnákkupúndu); each meaning oil-cake plant from greens being cooked as vegetable with sesamum [gingelly] oil cake.

POO (പൂ - pú, *Mal*; பூ - pú, *Tam.*). Flower [phool].—"*a*" Plant first term, in sense of conspicuous bright flowers or soft wood, often joining two genera. Ex., where transl. is of second term:—Canna indica (púvázhai), musa paradisiaca; Dolichandrone crispa (púmbáthiri), stereospermum chelonoides; Givotia rottleriformis (púttarali), nerium odorum; Nephelium longana (púvatti), ficus glomerata; Randia dumetorum (púngárai), canthium parviflorum; Schleichera trijuga (púvatti), ficus glomerata; Thespesia populnea (púpparutti), gossypium herbaceum, (púvarasu), ficus religiosa. See gloss. paragraphs.—"*b*" Plant second term. Ex., where transl. is of first term:—Barringtonia racemosa (samudrapú), ocean; Eugenia caryophyllata (karayámbú), black + to become; Heliotropium indicum (nakkipú), to lick; Lagerstrœmia flos-reginæ (katalpú), sea; Lagerstrœmia indica (shínappú), china; Lantana indica (arippú), small, (nátapú), fragrance; Passiflora leschenaultii (shimikkippú), ear ornament; Pergularia minor (tongippú), to hang; Sterculia guttata (ramanappú), delighting; Vinca rosea (shudugáttuppú), place of cremation; Webera corymbosa (kuppippú), bottle. See gloss. paragraphs.—"*c*" Fish first term.; showing bright colors. Ex., where transl. is of second term:—Barbus chrysopoma (púgálá), sturgeon, polynemus genus; Barbus sarana (púngálá), sturgeon, polynemus genus; Barbus tor (púmíngendai), fish + carp, barbus genus; Chanos salmoneus (púmínu), fish; Gobius giuris (púván), flowery; Ophiocephalu smarulius (púchépa), fish and (púvirál), ophiocephalus genus; Ophiocephalus striatus (púchépa), fish; Silundia sykesii (púnattai), snail. See gloss. paragraphs.——*Poogil* (പൂകിൽ - pukil, Mal.). From (pú, mal. to flower). Harvest. Poogil vivaram is crop-account.——*Poolah* (பூலா - púlá, Tam.). See sep. title.——*Poolay* (பூளை - púlai, Tam.). See sep. title.——*Poonamallee* *(پھولمری - phúlmarí, Hind.; பூந்தமல்லி - púndamalli, Tam.). From (pú, tam. flower + iru, tam. to be + malli, tam. the jasmine creeper, jasminum sambac, ait.); from large cultivation of jasmine [q.v.] flowers with which the madras market is supplied. Sanscrit name (pushpakavallí), meaning flower + vully, the goddess.—"*a*" Deputy tahsildarry, Sydapett talook, Chingleput. Pay Rs. 70.—"*b*" Town, Cantonment, Head-quarters of Cantonment joint magistrate, District moonsif, Deputy tahsildar and Sub-registrar; Chingleput dist., Sydapett tal.; pop. 7,468; acres 1,250; lat. 13° 03′; long. 80° 10′; from Chingleput N. 26 miles; from Conjeeveram E. 31 miles; from Madras W. 13 miles; from St. Thomas' Mount W. 6 miles; from Sydapett W.N.W. 7 miles; from the sea W. 11 miles. On high western trunk road. Salubrious and well drained. Granted in jagheer [q.v.] to the Company on 26th September 1750 by Anwar ood deen khan, revenue with customs 34,840 pagodas [q.v.]. Confirmed by way of inam [q.v.] or free gift by a sunnud [q.v.] from the Moghul [q.v.] on 12th August 1765. Now cantonment for European recruits and invalids. Contains barracks for 500 men. 400 yards east of cantonment is old fort now used principally for godowns [q.v.] for stores and for a hospital. It is a Mahomedan work, 175 yards long, 142 broad, surrounded by a rampart 18 feet high, and was of considerable use during the wars of the Carnatic [q.v.]. Old Shiva temple with three modern Tamul inscriptions, two dated A.D. 1770 and 1778. Rude stone implements were found four miles south-west by west of the town at Palanjore river.——*Pooncadal varnan* (பூங்கடல்வண்ணன் - púngadalvannan, Tam.). From (above + kadal, tam. sea + varna, san. color). The sea-colored Ayenaur [ayen].——*Pooneer* (பூநீறு - púníru, Tam.). Tam. means flowering ashes. Very light white-colored, saline efflorescence on ground [sujjeekhaur, sowdoo] containing a great proportion of carbonate of soda; from this as well as from oovar munn [q.v.] or dhoby's earth [q.v.], soda is prepared; it is employed in making glass [gauzoo], in dyeing [shauyam] blue and scarlet, and also by the chucklers [q.v.] in dyeing leather [chamrah] red and in tanning [chamrah]. Cf. Paulasowdoo, which is something similar.——*Poongaud* (பூங்காடு - púngádu, Tam.). From (above + kádu, tam. forest). Tender forest. Poongant tariss is land left waste for upwards of five years.——*Poosany* (பூசனி - púsani, Tam.). From (above + shanai, tam. to grow luxuriantly); grows luxuriantly and puts forth many flowers which do not fruit. Cucurbita maxima. Plant second term. Ex., where transl. is of first term:—Cucumis melo, var. utilissimus (kaliyánappúsani), marriage; Cucurbita ovifera (shímaippúsani), foreign; Ipomæa digitata (nilappúsani), ground. See gloss. paragraphs.——*Pooval* (പൂവൽ - púval, Mal.). A crop.——*Poovana* (பூவெண்ணெய்ச்செடி - púvenneyççedi, Tam.). Tam. from (pú, tam. flower + enney, tam. oil + shedi, tam. plant); from fragrant oil. Botanically Sarcostigma kleinii, w. & a., olacineæ [vricsham, 38]. Climbing shrub, branched; leaves alternate, short-petioled, oblong-oval, acuminate, coriaceous, glabrous; racemes usually paired axillary, very long, interrupted; flowers forming numerous sessile fascicles, without pedicels; fruit an oval somewhat flattened nut, about an inch long and half an inch broad; malabar coast. Oil has a very peculiar but not disagreeable odour; medicinal also burnt in lamps. No other species here.——*Poovauly* (பூவாளி - púváli, Tam.). From (above + váli, tam. arrow). Manmatan [q.v.].

POO (पू - pú, *San.*). Purify.——*Pavanan* (पवन - pavana, San.). From (pú, san. to purify). Wind [vayoo] personified.——*Paritram* (पवित्र - pavitra, San.). From (pú, san. to purify). Sacred thread [jandiram, jaunwah, poonool].——*Poonya bhoomy* (पुण्यभूमि - punyabhúmi, San.). From (punya, san. holy + bhúmi, san. earth). The holy land of Aryavartam in N. india.——*Poonyacaulam* (पुण्यकाल - punyakála, San.). Auspicious time. Any day held sacred on account of the conjunction [sangamam] of certain stars [nacshatram, dacshinauyana poonya caulam, oottarauyana poonya caulam, pundigay 6d, vishoo poonya caulam].——*Poonyagherry* (పుణ్యగిరి - punyagiri, Tel.). From (punya, san. holy + giri, san. hill). Sanscrit name (kótilingatírt'ha), meaning crore + phallic emblem + place of sacred waters. Hill; Vizagapatam dist., Srungavarapoocote division. Cascades on hill, with petrifactive properties, into which bones of dead are thrown. On Shivarautry [pundigay, 6a] a festival. In valley a goddess Dhaura gungamma.——*Poonyam* (पुण्य - punya, San.). From (pú, san. to purify). Sacred religious merit.——*Poonya prauny* (पुण्यप्राणी - punyapráni, San.). From (purya, san. sacred + práni, san. animal). Title otherwise Poonya jantoo. Sacred animal. Various animals are regarded as the vauhans [q.v.] or vehicles upon which the gods and goddesses travel. Thus Indran [q.v.] rides upon the elephant [q.v.] eirauvatam [q.v.], Shiva [q.v.] on the bull nundy [q.v.], Yaman [q.v.] on a buffalo [khoolgah], Doorga [q.v.] on a lion [simham] or tiger [pooly], Agny [q.v.] on a ram [aud], Vayoo [q.v.] on an antelope [jinka], Cauma devan [manmatan] on a parrot [totah], Ganesh [q.v.] on a rat [ely], and Shashty [q.v.] on a cat [poonay]. Veerabhadran [q.v.], the emanation of Shiva which destroyed Daeshan's [q.v.] sacrifice rode on a dog [nye]. The jackal [q.v.] is regarded as a representative of Doorga [q.v.], who in this form assisted in preserving Krishnan [q.v.], on the night of his birth, from Cumsan's anger. Monkeys [bandar], as representatives of Hanooman [q.v.], are very commonly worshipped. The dog, though worshipped by some, is regarded as unclean by others. Amongst birds, the goose [hamsam] is a vehicle of Bramha [q.v.], the peacock [mayil] that of Caurtikeyan [q.v.], and the vulture [gidh] that of Shany [q.v.]. The Braminy kite [q.v.] is said to be a form of Doorga [q.v.]. The Khanjanam, or wag-tail [pilkya], represents Vishnoo [q.v.], because the mark on its throat resembles the shalagram [q.v.]. The owl [ooloocam] is worshipped at the festivals of Caurtikeyan [q.v.], Bramha [q.v.], and Lutchmy [q.v.]. Garoodan [q.v.], the vehicle of Vishnoo [q.v.], and Jatauyoo [q.v.] and Sampauty [q.v.], the vultures who assisted Rama [q.v.], are note-worthy. The cow [pashoo], though not regarded as the vehicle of any deity, is the object of particular worship. Bramha is said to have created cows and Bramins at the same time; the Bramin to officiate at worship [poojah], and the cow to provide milk [paul], ghee [q.v.], &c., as offerings. Cow-dung [shauny] also is necessary for various purifying ceremonies. Regular worship of the cow takes place yearly, at which similar ceremonies are performed to those which are employed at the worship of images of the deities; the horns and bodies of the cows are at these times painted, and they are bathed in rivers. By some the cow is worshipped daily. The sacrifice of animals as being the most valuable offering has always attended their worship. A chapter of the Eitareyabramhanam [q.v.] on the sacrifice of animals shows how, next to man, the horse [ghorah] was the supreme sacrifice offered to the gods; how the cow afterwards took the place of the horse, the sheep [shemmariyaud] of the cow, the goat [vellaud] of the sheep; and at last vegetable products were substituted for animals. The historical aspect of animal worship has been discussed in the foot-note on the History of Hindoo religion at volume I (72) [matam, yanyam].——*Poonya stalam* (पुण्यस्थल - punyast'hala, San.). From (punya, san. sacred + st'hala, san. place). Sacred place [cshetram, stalam]. The seven sacred Indian cities, a visit to which confers eternal happiness, are:—Ayodhyay or oudh, the city of rama; Matooray or muttra, the city of krishnan; Maya or booddhagayay, the city of illusion; Caushy or benares, the city of shiva as vishweshwaran; Canjy or conjeeveram; Avanticay or oojjein; Dwarca or dwaurauvaty. But Gocurnam near mangalore, Rameshwaram, and Somnaut putnam, all having celebrated temples [coil, pagoda] of shiva, are also sacred cities. All rivers [aur] are sacred [teertam]. The place of junction of two rivers is sacred and is called Sangam [q.v.].——*Poonyoshadhy* (पुण्योषधि - punyóshadhi, San.). From (punya, san. sacred + óshadhi, san. plant). Sacred plant. Various trees are held sacred as being representative of, or under the special care of, the different deities. It is a meritorious act to plant and water them, and their withered branches are not allowed to be burnt. The same ceremonies are observed at the planting of these trees, or, when they have been taken care of for some time, at their consecration, as are observed at the setting up of an image [shilay, vigraham] of a deity. The following are the names of the sacred trees in Southern india:—Ashwattam or peepul [q.v.], ficus religiosa, sacred to vishnoo; Vatam or banyan [q.v.], ficus bengalensis, also sacred to vishnoo; Vilvam or bael [q.v.], ægle marmelos, sacred to shiva; Vacoolam or ilanjy [q.v.], mimusops elengi; Hareetakee or chebulic myrobalan [q.v.], terminalia chebula; Aumalaky or emblic myrobalan [q.v.], phyllanthus emblica; Nimbam or neem [q.v.], melia azadirachta; Toolsy [q.v.], ocimum gratissimum or sanctum. The last-named is very commonly worshipped by the followers of vishnoo; and the plant is carefully tended as his representative; every morning the ground near it is cleaned with cow-dong [shauny] and water, and at night a lamp is hung near it; during the two hottest months of the year, a vessel of water is hung over it so that it can constantly receive moisture; when the plant dies, it is cast into the river, as an idol which has been worshipped would be when the worship is concluded; when a person is dying, it is a common custom to plant a spring of toolsy [q.v.] near his head. In addition to these trees should be mentioned the Doorvay grass or Hurrially [q.v.], cynodon dactylon, pers. and Coosham [q.v.] grass or eragrostis cynosuroides, retz., which form part of the offerings made to the gods; as do all the leaves or flowers [phool] of most of the trees previously mentioned. The historical aspect of tree-worship has been discussed at vol. I (71).

POOCHY (कीट - kíta, *San.*; کیڑا - kírá, *Hind.*; ಹುಳ - hula, *Can.*; పురుగు - purugu, *Tel.*; പുഴു - puzhu, *Mal.*; பூச்சி - púççi, *Tam.*). San. from (kít, san. to color). Hind. from sanscrit. Mal. from (puru, mal. small). Any insect.——**(1)** Insects, invertebrate articulated animals, the Arthropoda of european naturalists, are divided into four divisions. Thus:—"*a*" Crustacea; respiration by means of gills, or by the general surface of the body; two pairs of antennæ; locomotive appendages more than eight, borne by the segments of the thorax, and usually of the abdomen also; examples are crabs [nundoo], lobsters, shrimps [iraul], wood-lice, etc.—"*b*" Arachnida; respiration by pulmonary vesicles, by tracheæ, or by the general surface of the body; head and thorax united; antennæ absent; legs eight; abdomen without locomotive appendages; examples are spiders [makree] and scorpions [tail].—"*c*" Myriopoda; respiration by tracheæ; head distinct; the remainder of the body composed of nearly similar segments; one pair of antennæ; legs numerous; examples are centipedes [kankhajoor] and millepedes.—"*d*" Insecta proper; respiration by tracheæ; head, thorax, and abdomen distinct; one pair of antennæ; three pairs of legs borne by the thorax; abdomen without limbs; the adult form with a few exceptions winged; examples are beetles [zeerangy], bees [tainee], wasps, flies [makkhee], butterflies [pautarny], locusts [tiddah], cockroaches [jhingoor], earwigs, dragon-flies [pautarny], ant-lions, may-flies, bugs [moott poochy]. Insecta proper divide again into the following three sub-classes:—"i" Ametabola; young not passing through a metamorphosis, and differing from the adult in size only; imago destitute of wings; eyes simple, sometimes wanting. "ii" Hemimetabola; metamorphosis incomplete; the larva differing from the imago chiefly in the absence of wings, and in size; pupa usually active, or, if quiescent, capable of movement. "iii" Holometabola; metamorphosis complete; the larva, pupa, and imago differing greatly from one another in external appearance; the larva vermiform, and the pupa quiescent.——**(2)** The word poochy, which would include a wood-louse, comprises examples at any rate from each of these divisions. The following are some of the commonest so-called poochies.——*Cumbly poochy* (کملی کیڑا - kamlíkírá, Dec.; ریڠ - riyang, Malay; ಕಂಬಳಿಹುಳ - kambalihula, Can.; కంబొళిపురి - kambolipuri, Too.; కంబళిపురుగు - kambalipurugu, Tel.; കമ്പിളിപ്പുഴു - kampilippuzhu, Mal.; கம்பளிப்பூச்சி - kambalippúççi, Tam.). Means blanket worm from being hairy. Tam. also (musukkattaippúççi), meaning mulberry worm [puttoo]. Caterpillar.——*Minminy poochy* (खद्योत - khadyóta, San.; काजवा - kájavá, Mahr.; حباحب - hubáhib, Ar.; کرم شب تاب - kirmishabtáb, Pers.; جگنو - jugnú, Hind.; جگنہ - jignah, Dec.; اڤي اڤي - apiapi, Malay; ಮಿಣಿಚೇಹುಳ - minichéhula, Can.; ಮಿಂಚುಪುರಿ - minchupuri, Too.; మినుగురుపురుగు - minugurupurugu, Tel.; മിന്നാമിനുങ്ങ് - minnáminunnu, Mal.; කණමැදිරියා - kanamadiriya, Singh.; மின்மினிப்பூச்சி - minminippúççi, Tam.). Title from tamul. San. from (kha, san. sky + dyóta, san. light). Pers. from (kirm, pers. worm + shab, pers. night + táb pers. shining). Malay from (api, malay, fire). Can. from (minuku, can. glitter + hula, can. insect). Too. from (minchu, too. lightning + puri, too. insect). Tel. from (minuguru, tel. spark + purugu, tel. insect). Mal. from (minnu, mal. to gleam). Tam. from (minmin, tam. to glitter + púççi, tam. insect). Malay also (kálibkálib). Tam. also (minnambúççi), by corruption. Fire-fly, small luminous beetle. Belongs to the families elateridæ and lampyriedæ, coleoptera, holometabola, insecta, of naturalists. The lower part of the body has an apparatus for emitting phosphorescent light. Usually emitted in flashes at intervals of a second. The female is the glow-worm. The fire-flies assemble around particular trees.——*Moottpoochy* (मत्कुण - matkuna, San.; فسافس - fusáfus, Ar.; سرخک - surkhak, Pers.; کھٹمل - khatmal, Hind.; مکھون - makhún, Dec.; کڤيندڠ - kapinding, Malay; ತಗಣಿ - tagani, Can.; ತಗುಳೆ - tagule, Too.; నల్లి - nalli, Tel.; മൂട്ട - mútta, Mal.; மூட்டுப்பூச்சி - múttuppúççi, Tam.). Title from tamul. Pers. from (surkh, pers. red). Dec. from sanscrit. Tel. from (nalla, tel. blood); from its feeding on the blood of man. Tam. from (múttu, tam. joint + púççi, tam. insect). Malay also (pijad); (pinding). Tam. also (mugattuppúççi), meaning ridge insect; (múttai), short form. Bug. Belongs to family cimicidæ, hemiptera hemimetabola, insecta of naturalists. Coffee [q.v.] bugs are brown, white, and black. The brown or scaly bug, Lecanium coffeæ, is the most injurious; male of a light pinkish brown and slightly hairy; the females when young yellow, marked with grey or light brown, when old light brown with dark margin; they affect cold and damp localities, 3,000 feet in height. The white or mealy bug is Pseudococcus adonidum; male of a dirty brown, slightly hairy and minute, being much smaller than the female; female oval, brownish purple and covered with a white mealy powder. The black bug is Lecanium nigrum, of which the female only is known; in color from yellowish grey deep brown, almost black in age and of a shield-like shape; it gives rise to a glutinous saccharine substance called honey dew. The green bug is seen on leaves; it is inoffensive if unmolested but if irritated exhales an offensive odour. Of the aquatic species, Belostoma indicum attains a size of nearly three inches.——*Shilandy poochy* (लूता - lútá, San.; कोष्टी - kóshtí, Mahr.; عنكبوت - ankabút, Ar.; کارتنہ - kártanah, Pers.; مکڑی - makrí, Hind. and Dec.; لابالابا - labalaba, Malay; ಜೇಡಹುಳ - jédahula, Can.; ಜಾಡಪುರಿ - jádapuri, Too.; సాలెపురుగు - sálepurugu, Tel.; എട്ടുകാലി - ettukáli, Mal.; මකුළුවා - makuluvá, Singh.; சிலந்திப்பூச்சி - shilandippúççi, Tam.). Title from tamul. San. from (lú, san. to cut). Mahr. applied to a caste whose occupation is spinning and weaving. Hind. from (markata, san. spider). Can. from (jéda, can. weaver + hula, can. insect). Tel. from (sále, tel. weaver + purugu, tel. insect). Mal. from (ettu, mal. eight + kálu, mal. leg). Singh. from (markata, san. spider). Tam. from (shilambu, tam. to rush + púççi, tam. insect). Malay also (lálaba). Spider. Belongs to class arachnida, sub-kingdom articulata. Breathe atmospheric air, have no antennæ, have four pairs of legs attached to fore parts of the body, and undergo no metamorphosis like that of insects. Mandibles furnished with a curved claw perforated at the extremity, like a poison fang. A gland furnishes a certain colorless fluid which is injected into the object wounded by the claw. The fluid is poisonous. All spin nets.——*Telloopoochy* (पिसू - pisú, Mahr.; برغوث - burghús, Ar.; پشہ - pashshah, Pers.; پسو - pissú, Hind. and Dec.; کتوانجيڠ - kutuanjing, Malay; ಚಿಕ್ಕಾಡಿ - chikkádi, Can.; ನಲ್ಲು - nallu, Too.; మిన్నల్లి - minnalli, Tel.; ചെള്ള് - chellu, Mal.; தெள்ளுப்பூச்சி - telluppúççi, Tam.). Title from tamul. Ar. from ethiopic meaning to spring. Hind. from persian. Malay from (kutu, malay, louse + anjing, malay, dog). Can. from (chikku, can. to scratch + adi, can. foot). Tel. from (midiyu, tel. to hop + nalli, tel. bug). Mal. from (chel, mal. sharp). Tam. from (telgu, tam. to spring up + púççi, tam. insect). Pers. also (shabgaz), meaning night-bitter. Flea. Co-extensive with family pulicidæ, aphaniptera, holometabola, insecta, of naturalists. Breed in rocky ground. Branches of Euphorbia tirucalli [round milk-hedge] in a room disperse them. Pastilles containing sulphate of copper [toottam] when burned have same effect.——**(3)** For fishes see Matsyam; for batrachians see Bhaicam; for reptiles see Sarpy; for birds see Pacshy; for mammals see Sastanam; a general conspectus of the fauna [jantoo] of s. india was given in vol. II, appendix IV.

POODEENAH (पुदिना - pudiná, *Mahr.*; نعنع الهند - nanaulhind, *Ar.*; پودینہ - púdínah, *Pers.*; پودینا - pudíná, *Hind.* and Dec.; పుదీనా - pudíná, *Tel.*; പുതിയിനാ - putiyiná, *Mal.*; ඔඩුතලන් - odutalan, *Singh.*; புதினா - puthíná, *Tam.*). Mahr. from hindostany. Ar. from (nana, ar. mint + hind, ar. india). Hind., &c., from persian. Ar. also (fútanjihind), meaning indian mint; (habakulhind), meaning indian mint; (nanaihindí), meaning indian mint. Tel. also (ígaengilikúra), meaning fly + spittle + potherb. Tam. also (íyeççirgírai), meaning fly + saliva + vegetable; said to spring from deposits of flies; (oduthalám). Title otherwise Mint. Botanically the Mentha genus, labiatæ [vricsham, 103]. Herbaceous plants with flowers in dense whorls, arranged in terminal or axillary heads or spikes. Arvensis is common mint, corn mint, field mint; stem 1–2 feet; leaves 1–2 inches, obtusely or acutely serrate; bracts acute, shorter than the flowers; calyx hoary; corolla hairy without and within; leaves carminative, stomachic, antispasmodic and emmenagogue; substituted for british oleum menthæ piperitæ; leaves used in food; gives oil [yennay]. Piperita is peppermint or brandy mint; greek μίνθη; perennial, deciduous herbaceous plant, 2 feet high; spikes oblique, blunt, interrupted at base; leaves ovate-oblong, acute, serrate, stalked, smooth; calyx quite smooth at base; flowers purple, flowering in august and september; herbaceous plant; much resembles common mint; oil is colorless or faint greenish-yellow; has a peculiar odour and a pleasant, cooling flavor; gives to pharm. the oil, oleum menthæ piperitæ; valuable carminative, stomachic, and antispasmodic; preparations; aqua menthæ piperitæ; spiritus menthæ piperitæ, officinal; used for culinary and confectionery purposes. Pulegium is pennyroyal; greek γλήχων; expectorant. Sativa is marsh mint, indian peppermint, in use by hakeems [q.v.].

Viridis is garden mint, spear mint or mackerel mint; perennial, deciduous, herbaceous plant, 2 feet high; spikes cylindrical interrupted; leaves lanceolate, sub-sessile, cuneate at the base, finely serrated, smooth on each side; teeth of calyx somewhat hairy; flowers purple, flowering in august; different variety from the english; stimulant in cholera; gives to pharm. the oil, oleum menthæ viridis; properties similar to peppermint, but less powerful; preparation; aqua menthæ viridis, officinal; more largely used for culinary purposes under the name of mint than peppermint, as its flavor is preferable; gives a volatile oil [yennay]. Compare also:—Anisomeles malabarica, cat mint; Ocimum basilicum, wild mint; see gloss. paragraphs.

POODEIYAN (పొడలపాము - podalapámu, *Tel.*; புடையன் - pudaiyan, *Tam.*). Tel. from (poda, tel. wart + pámu, tel. snake). Tam. from (pudai, tam. to swell). Wart snake. The terms may be considered co-extensive with the family Acrochordidæ, ophidii colubriformes, ophidia [sarpam], reptilia [sarpy, 26] of naturalists [jantoo]. See Paumb. The only representative here is Chersydrus granulatus. Alias Acrochordus fasciatus, granulatus; Chersydrus annulatus, fasciatus; Hydrus granulatus. Brownish black, with whitish cross-bands on sides and abdomen; head with some small yellowish spots. In the young the bands are more clearly defined, and extend on to the back where they are generally interrupted. Aquatic species. Found in the rivers and on the eastern coast sometimes three or four miles distant from the shore. Not venomous. The following varieties are recognized by the Tamulians.——*Black wart snake* (నల్లపొడ - nallapoda, Tel.; கரும்புடையன் - karumbudaiyan, Tam.).——*Red wart snake* (ఎర్రపొడ - errapoda, Tel.; செம்புடையன் - shembudaiyan, Tam.).——*Small wart snake* (చిన్నపొడ - chinnapoda, Tel.; சிறுபுடையன் - shirubudaiyan, Tam.).

POODOOCOTTAH (புதுக்கோட்டை - puthukkóttai, *Tam.* pudukóta *). From (puthu, tam. new + kóttai, tam. fort), means new fort [poothoo].——**(1)** Native state, Trichinopoly district. For general and historical accounts, see vol. I, 40; II, 118. Divided into three talooks; Alangoody, Coolatore and Trimayam. Places of archæological interest:—Coodoomiyamullay, Nauradamullay, Peraiyore, Tirgocurnam, Tirvarangoolam and Trimayam. The leading places, &c., in the territory are the following.——*Agnyaur* (அக்கினியாறு - akkiniyáru Tam.). See sep. title.——*Alangoody* (ஆலங்குடி - álangudi,' Tam.). From (álam, tam. banyan tree, ficus bengalensis, linn. + kudi, tam. village). Sanscrit name (rudrapura), means town of roodran. Village, Head-quarters of a Tahsildar; pop. 588; lat. 10° 21′; long. 79° 01′; from Poodoocottah E. 12 miles; from Trichinopoly S.E. 36 miles. Gives its name to a talook. On road to Puttoocottah. Natural springs which irrigate rice [paddy]. Weekly market on Thursday.——*Annavausal* (அன்னவாசல் - annavásal, Tam.). From (anna, san. food + vásal, tam. entrance); a place where charity is dispensed. Town; pop. 2,598; lat. 10° 28′; long. 78° 44′; from Coolatore S.W. 8 miles; from Ilooppore S.E. 6 miles; from Poodoocottah W. 10 miles; from Trichinopoly S. 25 miles. On declivity on road to Viraulimullay. Chiefly Mussalmans [q.v.]. Weekly market on Thursday.——*Arimbalam* (அரிம்பலம் - arimbalam, Tam.). From (arumai, tam. rareness + p'hala, san. fruit); place of rare merit as a holy place. Town; pop. 3,907; lat. 10° 15′; long. 78° 56′; from Poothooputty S.E. 41 miles; from Poodoocottah S.S.E. 10 miles; from Trichinopoly S.S.E. 41 miles. On the road to Arantaungy. Nautcottay chetty [q.v.] town. Shiva temple. Feeding chuttram [q.v.] maintained by Chetties [q.v.]. Mutt [q.v.] for caste travellers with a fine tank in front.——*Auvore* (ஆவூர் - ávúr Tam.). From (á, tam. cattle + úr, tam. village). Village; lat. 10° 39′; long. 78° 43′; from Poodoocottah N.N.W. 21 miles; from Trichinopoly S. 12 miles. On Trichinopoly-Poodoocottah road. Station of Jesuits of Madura mission.——*Carambacoody* (கரம்பக்குடி - karambakkudi, Tam.). See sep. title.——*Cavinaud* (கவிநாடு - kavinádu, Tam.). From (kavi, san. poet + nádu, tam. country). Also called (kapilanádu), country of capilan [q.v.]. Village; pop. 8,226 Tank called Cavinaud cummye, bund 5 miles long. Surplus discharges into Goondair to S. of Poodoocottah.——*Coodoomiya mullay* (குடுமியாமலை - kudumiyámalai, Tam.). From (kudimiyán, tam. possessor of hair tuft + malai, tam. mountain). Sanscrit name (shikhánát'ha), means hair-tuft + lord; epithet of a jeina deity. Hill; lat 10° 25′; long. 78° 42′; from Poodoocottah W.N.W. 11 miles; from Trichinopoly S. 27 miles; from Annavausal W. 4 miles. Bare of vegetation. At foot temple to Shiva. Coronations of rajahs formerly here. Treasure buried in vaults. Monkeys [bandar] abound.——*Coolatore* (குளத்தூர் - kulattúr, Tam.). From (kulam, tam. tank + úr, tam. village). Village; pop. 1,930; lat. 10° 33′; long. 78° 49′; height 375 feet; from Poodoocottah N. 12 miles; from Trichinopoly S. 18 miles. Gives name to a talook. On road to Trichinopoly. Originally seat of branch of Tondiman [q.v.] family. Tank, surplus of which forms Agniyaur.——*Keeranore* (கீரனூர் - kíranúr, Tam.). From (kíra, san. parrot + úr, tam. village). Sanscrit name (shukapurí), means shoocan, name of a sage, also parrot + town. Village, Head-quarters of the Tahsildar of Coolatore talook; pop. 1,953; lat. 10° 34′; long. 78° 49′; from Ariyalore S.S.W. 44 miles; from Coolatore N. 1 mile; from Madras S.S.W. 198 miles; from Moosiry S.E. 35 miles; from Poodoocottah N. 14 miles; from Shreerungam S.S.E. 20 miles; from Trichinopoly S. 18 miles. On road from Trichinopoly to Poodoocottah. Shiva temple. Largely inhabited by Cullar [q.v.]. Weekly fair on Mondays.——*Kilanelly* (கீழநிலை - kízhánilai, Tam.). See sep. title.——*Nauradamullay* (நாரதமலை - nárathamalai, Tam.). From (nárada, san. the sage + malai, tam. mountain). Sanscrit name (náradaparvata), means same. Village, Hill; lat. 10° 30′; long. 78° 49′; from Coolitalay S.E. 38 miles; from Poodoocottah N. 10 miles; from Trichinopoly S.S.E. 22 miles. A little to west of road to Trichinopoly. Rock-cut Booddhist [booddha] temples and carvings. Near is a Mauriyamman [q.v.] temple called Telinga mahamye [q.v.]. Large concourse of people during annual feast. Spring on the hill in which a small temple cut on the rock is submerged. Near the Mauriyamman temple is a never-failing spring called Aucausha oorny [q.v.].——*Faumbaur* (பாம்பாறு - pámbáru, Tam.). See sep. title.——*Peraiyore* (பேரையூர் - péraiyúr, Tam.). From (pér, tam. great + ai, tam. beauty + úr, tam. village). Sanscrit name (bhúchandakshétra), meaning earth + shiva, the fierce + sacred place. Village; pop. 843; lat. 10° 21′; long. 78° 48′; from Poodoocottah west 5 miles; from Trichinopoly S. 32 miles; from Trimayam N. 8 miles. On S. bank of Vellaur. Fine pagoda [q.v.] on low flat rock, with spring. Scene of battle between Tanjore rajah and Tondiman [q.v.] in early part of eighteenth century.——*Ponnamarauvathy* (பொன்னமராவதி - ponnamarávathi, Tam.). From (ponnan, tam. the name of a chief + amaran, tam. the name of another chief + pathi, tam. place). Town; pop. 6,298; lat. 10° 17′; long. 78° 34′; from Poodoocottah W.S.W. 20 miles; from Trichinopoly S.S.W. 38 miles. Near S.W. frontier. Principally occupied by Nautcottay chetties [q.v.]. Shiva temple. Colored mats [boriyah] of palmyra [q.v.] leaf form chief home industry of Chetty [q.v.] women. Large tank.——*Poodoocottah* (புதுக்கோட்டை - puthukkóttai, Tam.). See below.——*Poothooputty* (புதுப்பட்டி - puthuppatti, Tam.). From (puthu, tam. new + patti, tam. village). Village, Head-quarters of the Deputy tahsildar of Kilanelly; lat. 10° 11′; long. 78° 57′; from Poodoocottah S. 15 miles; from Trichinopoly S.S.E. 45 miles. On road to Arantaungy. Plantains [q.v.] luxuriant. Shiva temple. Market on Wednesdays.——*Royapooram* (இராயப்புரம் - iráyappuram, Tam.). From (ráyadu, tel. king + pura, san. town). Town; from Trimayam S.E. 10 miles. A large Nautcottay chetty [q.v.] town. Shiva temple. Chetties have built palatial houses.——*Tercolumbore* (தெருக்கொளம்பூர் - terukkolambúr, Tam.). From (teru, tam. street + kulam, tam. tank + úr, tam. village). Village; lat. 10° 12′; long. 78° 33′; from Poodoocottah W. 24 miles; from Trichinopoly S. 44 miles. Near confines of Shivagunga. Inhabited mostly by Cullar [q.v.] and Chetties [q.v.]. The general boundary runs adjacent to this.——*Tirgocurnam* (திருக்கோகரணம் - tirukkógaranam, Tam.). From (tiru, tam. holy + gókarna, san. cow's ear, the local name of shiva). Sanscrit name (gókarnakshétra), means gocurnan, the local shiva + sacred place. Town; lat. 10° 23′; long. 78° 51′; from Alangoody 11 miles west; from Poodoocottah north-west 1¼ miles; from Trichinopoly S. 30 miles. Suburb of Poodoocottah on road to Trichinopoly. Pagoda [q.v.] where Tondiman occasionally resorts for public worship; to Shiva as Gocurna sawmy, but more generally known after goddess Shree brihannayaky from whom rajah takes title of Shree brihadambah doss, servant of shree brihadambah. Annual feasts.——*Tirvappore* (திருவப்பூர் - tiruvappúr, Tam.). From (tiru, tam. holy + váyppu, tam. success + úr, tam. village). Town; lat. 14° 23′; long. 78° 50′; from Alangoody W. 13 miles; from Poodoocottah west 1½ miles; from Trichinopoly S.S.E. 32 miles. Suburb of Poodoocottah; chiefly inhabited by weavers. Cotton [q.v.] and silk [puttoo] fabrics of superior texture manufactured. Scene of battle between Saitoopaties [q.v.] of Ramnaud and Tondiman [q.v.] in middle of eighteenth century.——*Tirvarangoolam* (திருவரங்குளம் - tiruvarangulam, Tam.). From (tiru, tam. holy + aran, tam. shiva + kulam, tam. tank). Sanscrit name (ranganát'hapura), means vishnoo + town. Village; pop. 625; lat. 10° 21′; long. 78° 55′; from Alangoody W. 7 miles; from Poodoocottah S.E. 4 miles; from Trichinopoly S.S.E. 35 miles. On confines of a wood on road to Alangoody. Remarkably high Shiva temple built by chola king, whose figure is sculptured on the stone pillars. At annual car festival, Pariahs [q.v.] claim priority of breaking cocoanuts [q.v.] on the wheels of the car [rath].——*Trimayam* (திருமயம் - tirumayam. Tam.). From (tiru, tam, holy + maiyyam, tam. centre). Sanscrit name (ádirangam), means first + place of vishnoo. Village, Head-quarters of Tahsildar; lat. 10° 15′; long. 78° 48′; from Ariyalore S.S.W. 65 miles; from Madras S.S.W. 218 miles; from Moosiry S. 53 miles; from Poodoocottah S.S.W. 10 miles; from Shreerungam S. 43 miles; from Trichinopoly S. 40 miles. On road to Madura. Rich well conducted chuttram [q.v.] founded by Nautcottay chetties. Well preserved fort. Curious old chain armour, &c., was discovered here. Ancient Vishnoo [q.v.] temple built by a Paundyan [q.v.] king; described as Audy rungam, that is to say, the original rungam existing prior to Shreerungam on the Cauvery at Trichinopoly. In ancient times fort was one of strongholds of Saitoopaties of Ramnaud. It was a gift to Tondiman from Ramnaud.——*Vellaur* (வெள்ளாறு -

vellâru, Tam.). See sep. title.——Viraulimullay (விராலிமலை - virálimalai, Tam.). From (viráli, tam. a plant, dodonæa viscosa, linn. + malai, tam. mountain). Town; pop. 1,860; lat. 10° 36′; long. 78° 35′; from Coolatore W.N.W. 17 miles; from Poodoocottah N.W. 23 miles, from Trichinopoly S.W. 19 miles. Headquarters of a Deputy tahsildar. On the trunk road from Trichinopoly to Madura. Formerly part of polliem [q.v.] of Lakky naick. Temple to Soobramanyasawmy. Camping station for troops. A spacious chuttram [q.v.] supported by Tondiman [q.v.]. Travellers' bungalow [q.v.].——(2) Town; Trichinopoly district, Poodoocottah territory; pop. 16,885; lat. 10° 23′; long. 78° 52′; from Ariyalore S.S.W. 53 miles; from Madras S.S.W. 208 miles; from Moosiry S.S.E. 45 miles; from Shreerungam S.S.E. 32 miles; from Trichinopoly S.S.E. 30 miles. Seat of Poodoocottah rajahs. Palace occupies a large square in centre of town. E. of palace a tank called Pullavancoolam, or Shivagunga, with mantapam [q.v.] in centre. Residency bungalow [q.v.]. Travellers' bungalow. Lutheran mission. In the valley of the Vellaur. A thick belt of almost impenetrable jungle formed the natural defence of the town in bygone days. Fair on Fridays.

POOGAZH (புகழ் - pugazh, Tam.). Praise. Ancient name of Warriors [q.v.]. See vol. I (125).——Poogazhendy (புகழேந்தி - pugazhéndi, Tam.). From (above + éndu, tam. to support). Tamul poet contemporary with Cumban and Ottacoottan, but at court of king Varagoona paundyan at Madura. Called the tiger of poets [pauvalan]. Wrote Nalavenbah [q.v.].

POOJ (पूज् - púj, San.). To adore.——Poojah (पूजा - pújá, San.; பூசை - púsai, Tam.). From (púj, san. to worship). Adoration of the deity; also the respect paid to superiors [matam]. In the Shiva pagodas [coil, pagoda] poojah is performed by bramins throughout the year every day thrice, viz., in the morning, at noon, and in the evening; and this is called Nitya poojah, the continual or daily offering. Among the thirty-two mistakes that may occur in worship is the visiting of the temple at the improper time. The daily offering consists in three things:—Abbishaicam [q.v.], holy anointing; Dhoopam [q.v.], incense; Neivedyam, food offering, oblation. These are done together as forming the three acts of every poojah. For the first, the Abhishaicam, the priest takes honey, sugar, cocoanut-water, milk, &c. [punchaumritam], with which he anoints the lingam. The second, Dhoopam, is made of odorous wood and sambrauny [q.v.], or frankincense [q.v.], which he kindles in a censer and so offers to the lingam [q.v.]. The third, Neivedyam, is an oblation of various articles of food, which are afterwards divided among the bramins and servants of the pagodas [q.v.].——Poojarry (پوجاری - pújárí, Hind.; பூசாரி - púsári, Tam.). From (púja, san. worship + áchárí, san. instructor). A priest among the Shoodras in small temples [gooroocal, numby]. See vol. I (82). Hindoo third name [peyar].——Poojaurambham (पूजारम्भ - pújárambha, San.). From (pújá, san. worship + árabh, san. to begin). Beginning of ceremonial worship [saraswaty poojaurambham].

POOL (पुल् - pul, San.). To be high.——Poolastyan (पुलस्त्य - pulastya, San.). From (pul, san. to be lofty). One of the seven great rishies [q.v.] who escaped from the deluge [pralayam]. In the Tamul version of the Oottara ramayanam, he is stated to have been the progenitor of the Yacshans [q.v.]. Otherwise one of the nine Bramhaudicans, the father of Coobairan [q.v.] and Ravanan [q.v.]. Also one of the stars in the constellation [nacshatram] of the maharisham [q.v.]. For Poolastinagaram see under Poolayan.——Poolikeshy (ಪುಲಿಕೇಶಿ - pulikéshi, Can.). From (pula, san. extensive + késha, san. hair of head). There were two kings of this name in the Chalookya [q.v.] dynasty [raj]. Poolikeshy the first was the most powerful of the early kingdom before it was divided into eastern and western by his grandsons. Established a dynasty [raj] in western india, making Vautaupy capital. It was owing to this fact that early grants trace the genealogy of the chalookya kings from his name. About Poolikeshy the second see Satyaushrayan [charitram]. See vol. I (139).——Poolinda (पुलिंद - pulinda, San.). From (pul, san. to be high); as frequenting hill jungles. A barbarian.

POOL (புள் - pul, Tam.). Palmyra.——Poollalore (புள்ளலூர் - pullalúr, Tam.). From (above + úr, tam. village). Title in old books always Polilore. Village; Chingleput dist., Conjeeveram tal.; pop. 1,271; acres 2,132; lat. 12° 59′; long. 79° 46′; from Conjeeveram N. 9 miles; from Sydapett W. 35 miles. Remarkable as the scene of the most grievous disaster which has as yet befallen the British arms in India. On the 10th September 1780, Colonel Baillie, who was marching from Madras to effect a junction with Sir Hector Munro at Conjeeveram, was here totally routed and his whole force either cut to pieces or captured by the united armies of Hyder ally and Tippoo sultan. The palmyra [q.v.] trees still bear evidence of the fierceness of the cannonade. Another battle took place on the same ground between Sir Eyre Coote and Hyder in the following year, in which the former was so far victorious that he occupied the posts taken up by the enemy; Hyder however claimed it as a drawn battle.

POOLA (പുല - pula, Mal.). From (pul, tam. low). Pollution.——Poolasambandham (പുലസംബന്ധം - pulasambandham, Mal.). From (above + sambandha, san. relationship). Community of pollution or separation, as opposed to community of property [moothal sambundham].

POOLAH (कृष्णकाम्बोजी - krishnakámbójí, San.; काकेसप्पु - kákkésappu, Conc.; کالی مدھ کا پیڑ - kálemadhkáper, Hind.; کالی مدھ کا جھاڑ - kálemadhkájhár, Dec.; ಸಣ್ಣಕಾಗೆಸೊಪ್ಪು - saṇnakágesoppu, Can.; ಕಾಕೆಸೊಪ್ಪು - kákesoppu, Too.; పురుగుడు - purugudu, Tel.; കാട്ടുനീരൂരി - káttunírúri, Mal.; වල්කයිල - valkayila, Singh.; பூலா - púlá, Tam.). Title from tamul [poo]. San. from (krishna, san. black + kámbójí, san. abrus precatorius, linn.). Hind. from (kálá, hind. black + madhú, san. honey + per, hind. tree); from sweet juice. Dec. from hindostany. Can. from (sanna, can. small + káge, can. crow + soppu, can. leaf). Mal. from (kátu, mal. wild + nírúri, mal. phyllanthus niruri, mull., var. genuinus). Tam. from (pú, tam. flower, hence redness); from red dye of bark [poolah coral tree, red-cotton tree, silk cotton, white poolah]. Hind. also (kámuní), meaning solanum nigrum, linn. Tel. also (nallapagadapuchettu), meaning black + breynia rhamnoides, muller, var. genuina; (nallapurugudu), meaning black + the plant; (pulugudu); (nallapulugudu), meaning black + the plant; (núgubenda), meaning downiness + hibiscus esculentus, linn. Tam. also (karuppuppilláñji), meaning black + the plant; (pilláñji), corruption of (púláñjedi); (nírppúlá), meaning water + the plant; (mélanelli), meaning upward + phyllanthus emblica, linn.; from climbing habit. Title otherwise Black honey shrub, Downy bendy, Many-flowered kizhanelly, Wild neeroory. Botanically Phyllanthus [aumlacam] multiflorus, willd., euphorbiaceæ [vricsham, 118]. Alias Anisonema multiflora; Kirganelia multiflora. Kirganelia, from (kízhánelli, tam. phyllanthus niruri, müller var. genuinus). Shrubby; primary branches virgate, young shoots pubescent; floriferous branchlets angular; leaves nearly oval, obtuse, bifarious; flowers axillary, aggregated, several males and usually one-female; male flowers purplish; berries eight to twelve-seeded, dark, purple, or black, soft and pulpy, sweet-tasted. Flowering nearly all year; common near water; climbing if it has the support of bushes; berries give a syrup called black honey [q.v.]. The root is sweetish-tasted; medicinally alterative and attenuant and given in decoction. Bark used for dyeing [shauyam] a reddish brown; the thin branches form a tooth-brush, the ends being beaten so as to make them soft. No other common species here.——(1) Poolah root (பூலாக்கிழங்கு - púlákkizhangu, Tam.). Plant name common to:—Curcuma zedoaria; Manihot utilissima. See gloss. paragraphs.——(2) Demon poolah (பேய்ப்பூலா - péyppúlá, Tam.). Same as Red robitacam.——Red poolah (சிகப்புப்பூலா - shigappuppúlá, Tam.). Same as Poolah coral tree.——White poolah (कृष्णपाक - krishnapáka, San.; سفید مدھ کا پیڑ - sufedmadhkáper, Hind.; سفید مدھ کا جھاڑ - sufedmadhkájhár, Dec.; ಕರಿಯಹೂಲಿ - kariyahúli, Can.; తెల్లపురుగుడు - tellapurugudu, Tel.; പെരിങ്ക്ലാവ് - perinklávu, Mal.; வெள்ளைப்பூலாஞ்சி - vellaippúláñji, Tam.). Title from color of fruit and similarity to poolah. San. from (krishna, san. black + páka, san. syrup) [carondah]. Hind. from (sufed, hind. white + madhu, san. honey + per, hind. tree); from syrup of fruit. Dec. from hindostany. Can. from (kariya, can. black + húli, can. the plant, eugeinia dalbergioides, benth.). Tel. from (tella, tel. white + purugudu, tel. phyllanthus multiflorus, willd.). Mal. from (peru, mal. large + kalávu, mal. the plant, memecylon edule, roxb., var. typica). Tam. from (vellai, tam. white + pilláñji, tam, phyllanthus multiflorus, willd.). San. also (apriyadruma), meaning not liked tree; (shvétakámbóji), meaning white abrus precatorius, linn., perhaps from whitish-colored small round fruit. Hind. also (sufedmahmúdah), meaning white scammony. Can. also (karehúla), meaning black + the plant, phyllanthus multiflorus, willd.; (karesúla), meaning black + the plant, phyllanthus multiflorus, willd.; (gudapála), meaning jaggery + protector; (helamágalichéra), meaning earth + the plant. Tel. also (sálemunta), meaning weaver + pot; (tsallamunta), meaning cool + pot; (mékaráyi), meaning goat + rubbing. Tam. also (varadbúlá), meaning to grow dry + the plant; (púlá) [poolah, poolah coral tree, red-cotton tree, silk cotton]; (irubúlai), meaning dark poolah. Title otherwise Cool pot, White goomchy, White honey shrub. Botanically Securinega leucopyrus, müll., euphorbiaceæ [vricsham, 118]. Alias Cicca leucopyrus; Fluggea leucopyrus; Phyllanthus leucopyrus. Tree; branchlets spinescent at the apex, glabrous; leaves obovate, obtuse or retuse, acute or cuneate, narrowed at the base, paler below; calycine segments broadish hyaline at the margin, and usually deeply lacinulate; male flowers very numerous; capsule depresso-globose; branches of the styles narrow, entire. Common; small round whitish-colored fruit, bitter to taste; root medicinally mild astringent; fruit, eaten; syrup prepared from the fruit is considered equal to honey [shahad]; wood pink, hard, close-grained. Another species is Obovata.

POOLAMBAN (புலம்பன் - pulamban, Tam.). From (pulambu, tam. to roar); as lord of a roaring tract near the sea. Chief of a maritime tract [neydal].

POOLAY (புலை - púlai, *Tam.*). From (pú, tam. flower), from soft downy leaves and flowers [poo]. Botanically the Ærua genus, amarantaceæ [vricsham, 106]. Woolly herbs or undershrubs; leaves alternate or opposite; flowers minute, in dense terminal or axillary spikes; have a more or less white tomentose appearance. The species best known to the natives are shown below. Other s. indian species indigenous or naturalized are:—monsonia, scandens.——*Large poolay* (کل کا جہاڑ - kulkájhár, Hind.; పెద్దపిండికొండ - peddapindikonda, Tel.; பெரிய புலை - periyabúlai, Tam.). Tel. from (pedda, tel. large + pindikonda, tel. ærua lanata, juss.). Tam. from (periya, tam. big + púlai, tam. ærua). Tel. also (pindikonda), meaning flour + hill; hill plant with downy leaves. Title otherwise Javanese ærua. Botanically Ærua [poolay] javanica, juss., amarantaceæ [vricsham, 106]. Ærua from arabic. Alias Illecebrum javanicum. Herbaceous; stem rigid, one cubit, erect or ascending, tomontose, hoary; leaves short-petioled, obovate-lanceolate, tomentose; spikes alternate, very flexuose, solitary, sessile, woolly, upper ones fifteen to twenty, arranged as a large lax panicle; flowers white; bracts glabrous, whitish; utricle oblong, green; flowering all the year. Flowers have refreshing smell, and placed under pillow relieve nervous irritation and headache, inducing sleep; root is diuretic.——*Small poolay* (कापूरमधुरा - kápúramadhurá, Mahr.; चिरंपुटल - chiraputla, Conc.; کل کا جہاڑ - kulkájhár, Hind.; ಬಿಳೇಸೂಲಿ - bilésúlí, Can.; పిండిదొండ - pindidonda, Tel.; ചെറുപൂള - cherupúla, Mal.; சிறுபுலை - shirubúlai, Tam.). Mahr. from (kápúra, mahr. camphor + madhura, san. sweet); from silvery-looking leaves and white sweet-scented flowers. Can. from (bili, can. white + súle, can. pain); ash-colored plant and root used in headache. Tel. from (pindi, tel. flour + donda, tel. cephalandra indica, naud.). Mal. from tamul. Tam. from (shiru, tam. small + púlai, tam. ærua). Can. also (bilihindisoppu), meaning white + to wring + leaf; (biléhuligida), meaning white + sour + plant. Tel. also (pindikonda), meaning flour + hill; (chinnapindikonda), meaning small + the plant. Tam. also (kaubúlai), meaning eye + ærua, small plant; (uzhiñai), meaning strength giving; a garland of this plant was to be worn by soldiers in storming a fort. Title otherwise Woolly ærua, Woolly caper. Botanically Ærua [poolay] lanata, juss., amarantaceæ [vricsham, 106]. Alias Achyranthes lanata, villosa; Ærua floribunda, tondalo; Illecebrum lanatum, linn. Ærua from arabic. Stem herbaceous, suffruticose below, ascending, much branched, somewhat tomentose; leaves alternate, short petioled, obovate, mucronulate, pubescent on both sides; spikes solitary or biternate, sessile, ovate, woolly; flowers hoary white; calyx twice as long as the apiculated bracts; sepals keeled, two outer ones lanceolate with whitish nerves, inner ones sub-spathulate, greenish-nerved; utricles roundish, compressed, green; seed reniform, shining, black. Common weed; has woolly silvery looking leaves and oval heads of white flowers. Flowering tops are medicinally officinal, roots used in headache. Leaves mixed with others used as greens [keeray]; famine-food.——*Thornless poolay* (മുള്ളില്ലാപ്പൂള - mullilláppúla, Mal.). Same as Silk-cotton tree.——*Thorny poolay* (മുള്ളൻപൂള - mullanpúla, Mal.). Same as Red-cotton tree.

POOLDY (புழுதி - puzhuthi, *Tam.*). Soil of fields prepared for seed [viray]. Pooldycaul is cultivation by dry ploughing and sowing; pooldycaud is a dry-ploughed field; pooldynautt is seedling [nautt] standing on dry ground; pooldy viray is sowing a dry field just before rains for the seed to remain in dust till rain [mazhay, monsoon] comes. For wet ploughing and sowing see Shettcaul.——*Chikat pooldy* (சிகத்துப்புழுதி - shigattuppuzhuthi, Tam.). Wet lands ploughed, but not sown. See sep. title.

POOLIVENDLA (పులివెందల - pulivendala, *Tel.* pulivendla*). From (puli, tel. tiger + mandala, san. region) [pooly]. Sanscrit name (vyághrapurí), meaning tiger + town.——**(1)** Talook, Cuddapah district. Tahsildar's pay Rs. 175. Area 701 square miles, length from east to west 40 miles, breadth from north to south about 24 miles. Population 105,842. Language Teloogoo. Lies along W. boundary of district, and abuts upon Tadpatry talook, Anantapore district. Bounded N. by Jummalmadoogoo talook from which it is separated by the Bhauncote and Pedda gungamma mala hills; E. by Cuddapah and Royachoty talooks from which it is partly separated by the Paupughny; S. by Cadiry talook from which it is separated by the Sheshachellam range; W. by Tadpatry talook of Anantapore. The talook includes a small tract lying along right bank of the Paupughny, and south of the gorge through which the stream cleaves the Sheshachellam range. This is naturally a portion of Royachoty talook, but has been artificially annexed to Poolivendla. Apart from this detached section, the talook presents a compact area, almost a parallelogram in form. Before the subjugation of the Ceded districts [q.v.] in 1800, the talook was given up to the rule of several small poligars [q.v.]. Apart from the two ranges of hills above mentioned, the country is dotted and intersected by isolated hills, and low ranges striking at various angles from the main hill ranges. Soils may be classified under black, red and grey. The first includes about 75 per cent. of the whole arable lands [sheygaul], although the quality of the cotton soil [regar] varies greatly over different parts, from a rich loam [pasalay munn] of great depth to a mixed and stony soil [desham, munn]. The better qualities of the black lands, near the villages of Balpanore, Cassanore, and Lomada, and generally over the westernmost division, are very productive. The second and third kinds are found mostly in the vicinity of the hills. Crops of cotton [q.v.] and seeds and grain are however raised constantly on such soil. The sole industry is agriculture. Along the eastern limits the waters of the Paupughny are carried by an elaborate system of irrigating channels [q.v.], renewed after every fresh, over large areas on either bank. The Chitrauvaty just touches the extreme north-west boundary of the talook. Artificial works for the storage of water are of little service, and there are no large tanks [q.v.]; those that were formerly available are rapidly becoming useless by the process of silting up, while in others the looseness and porousness of the soil defeat all efforts to make them efficient reservoirs. Cultivation under wells is general, and in favored situations, such as the eastern portion of the talook where water lies at no great depth, the soils so cultivated become most productive; but westwards wells become deeper, and therefore scarcer. Places of archæological interest:—Chinna coodaula, Commanootla, Lopatnootla, Maddoolapaud, Maurellamadaka, Mopore, Nullacheroopully, Paurnapully, Poolivendla, Vaimla, Vempully, Yerrabulla. The leading places, &c., in the talook are the following.——*Balpanore* (బలపనూరు - balapanúru, Tel.). From (balapamu, tel. soap-stone + úru, tel. village). Village; pop. 4,054; acres 9,168; lat. 14° 32′; long. 78° 14′; from Cuddapah W. 42 miles; from Poolivendla N.N.W. 8 miles.——*Bauhoodah nuddy* (బాహుదనది - báhudanadi, Tel.). See sep. title.——*Bhauncote* (భానుకోట - bhánukóta, Tel.). See sep. title.——*Casanore* (కసనూరు - kasanúru, Tel.). From (kashamu, tel. fountain + úru, tel. village). Village; pop. 3,782; acres 7,770; lat. 14° 37′; long. 78° 12′; from Cuddapah W.N.W. 45 miles; from Poolivendla N.N.W. 14 miles. Richest village in talook; has endowed choultry [q.v.].——*Chitrauvaty* (చిత్రావతి - chitrávati, Tel.). See sep. title.——*Comauracaulwa* (కొమారకాలవ - komárakálava, Tel.). From (komaru, tel. pleasant + kálava, tel. stream). Village; pop. 1,137; acres 4,772; lat. 14° 17′; long. 78° 31′; from Cuddapah W.S.W. 27 miles; from Poolivendla E.S.E. 19 miles. On a peak of the Palcondahs.——*Commanootla* (కొమ్మనూతల - kommanútala, Tel.). From (komma, tel. branch + núyi, tel. well). Village; pop. 1,652; acres 11,178, lat. 14° 31′; long. 78° 03′; from Cuddapah W. 54 miles; from Poolivendla W.N.W. 16 miles. Former seat of a petty poligar [q.v.], a cauvalgar [q.v.] under Vijianugger government. Family extinct. Ruins of fort. Old temple of Tirvencatanauta sawmy.——*Lomada* (లోమద - lómada, Tel.). From (ló, tel. inside + mada, tel. channel). Village; pop. 1,352; acres 6,379; lat. 14° 36′; long. 78° 16′; from Cuddapah W. 41 miles; from Poolivendla N. 12 miles.——*Lopatnootla* (లోపటనూతల - lópatanútala, Tel.). From (lópata, tel. inside + núyi, tel. well) Village; pop. 627; acres 6,120; lat. 14° 30′; long. 78° 08′; from Cuddapah W. 49 miles; from Poolivendla W.N.W. 10 miles. Seat of a petty poligar [q.v.], a cauvalgar [q.v.] under Vijianugger government. Family extinct. Old fort.——*Nullacheroopully* (నల్లచెరువుపల్లి - nallacheruvupalli, Tel.). From (nalla, tel. black + cheruvu, tel. tank + palli, tel. village). Village; pop. 1,721; acres 8,192; lat. 14° 29′ 00″; long. 78° 24′; from Cuddapah W. 31 miles; from Poolivendla E.N.E. 10 miles. Temple of Bheiraveshwarasawmy situated near hamlet of Mopore, enlarged and beautified by a Vijianugger sovereign in A.D. 1544. Monastery of ascetic jogies [q.v.].——*Palcondah* (పాలకొండ - pálakonda, Tel.). See sep. title.——*Paupughny* (పాపఘ్ని - pápaghni, Tel.). See sep. title.——*Paurnapully* (పార్నపల్లి - párnapalli, Tel.). From (párna, san. leafy + palli, tel. village); from its foliage. Village; pop. 1,476; acres 2,719; lat. 14° 34′; long. 78° 01′; from Cuddapah W. 57 miles; from Poolivendla W.N.W. 20 miles. Vijianugger inscription of A.D. 1476. Old Poligar [q.v.] fort partly in ruins. Two miles south-east is the hermitage of Canwa in hills, where are two old Shiva and Vishnoo temples.——*Poolivendla* (పులివెందల - pulivendala, Tel.). See below.——*Vaimla* (వేముల - vémula, Tel.). From (vému, tel. margosa tree, melia azadirachta, linn.). Village; pop. 1,577; acres 5,686; lat. 14° 22′; long. 78° 22′; from Cuddapah W.S.W. 34 miles; from Poolivendla E.S.E. 8 miles. Head-quarters of the Vaimla poligar, who acquired a brief notoriety by resistance to Col. Munro in 1800. He was soon subjugated, and his family is now almost extinct. The fort is about five miles from the village close to Meedipentla, a position commanding one of the more passable roads leading southwards across the hills into Cadiry and Mysore.——*Vempully* (వేంపల్లి - vémpalli, Tel.). From (vému, tel. margosa tree, melia azadirachta, linn. + palli, tel. village). Village; pop. 5,638; acres 11,292; lat. 14° 22′; long. 78° 30′; from Cuddapah S.W. 25 miles; from Poolivendla E.S.E. 16 miles. On the Paupughny. Large and wealthy village. Centre of trade. On a hill opposite the village is a temple of Vrishabhauchaleshwara sawmy. Opposite the hill there is a cave containing a Lingam [q.v.] and an image of Parvaty [q.v.].——**(2)** Village, Talook head-quarters; Cuddapah dist., Poolivendla tal.; pop. 1,784; acres 1,644; lat. 14° 26′; long. 78° 16′; from Cuddapah W. 40 miles; from Madanapully N.N.W. 63 miles; from Madras W.N.W. 166 miles; from Sidhout W. 50 miles. Considered unhealthy. Poligar hill-fort in ruins. 1¼ miles west is an old temple of Runganauta sawmy. The image of the deity is declared to have been self-created in another yoog [q.v.].

POOLLAMPETT (పుల్లంపేట - pullampéta, *Tel.* pullampet *). From (pullamma, tel. proper name + péta, tel. suburb); said to have been founded by poollamma, a female relative of the chitwail rajah.——(1) Talook, Cuddapah district. Tahsildar's pay Rs. 200. Area 979 square miles. Greatest length from north to south 46 miles, breadth from east to west 30 miles. Population 149,109. Language Teloogoo. S.E of district. Bounded north by Sidhout talook, east by Raupore and Vencatagherry in Nellore district, south by Chundragherry talook of North arcot district, west by Voilpaud and Royachoty talooks. To the east and west intersected by hill ranges. Cultivation is principally carried on in two valleys. Of these, the Cheyair valley, which formerly constituted the petty kingdom of Chitwail, is most fertile and productive. There are two forests, the Sheshachellaparvatam on the hills of the same name and the Cundacharloo connected with the ghauts [q.v.] of Raupore. The former comprises about 5,000 and the latter 2,000 acres. Red soil is predominant. Principal manufactures are indigo [q.v.] and fine cloth in Naugayapett and Poollampett. At Hoblampett a considerable trade is carried on in dyeing [shauyam] cotton thread [nool] red. At Poollampett fine mats [boriyah] of colored grass are manufactured. The greater number of the channels [q.v.] are led from the Cheyair, which brings down the drainage waters of the high table-lands of Royachoty and Voilpaud. Camping grounds, Chitwail, Codoor and Poollampett. Places of archæological interest:—Attiraula, Gandlore, Lepauka, Mundapully, Nundalore, Penagalore, Tungatore, Wobaly. Principal trig. stations:—Cunclacondah, Yecoolasaury. The leading places, &c., in the talook are the following.——*Attiraula* (అత్తిరాల - attirála, Tel.). From (atti, tel. fig, ficus racemosa, linn. + ráyi, tel. stone). Village, Place of pilgrimage; pop. 83; acres 88; lat. 14° 14′; long. 79° 13′; from Cuddapah S.E. 29 miles; from Poollampett N. 8 miles. On the route from Cuddapah to Madras, 2 miles north-north-east of Rajampett railway station, and on the right bank of the Cheyair. Of great sanctity. Deserted temple of Parshooramau [q.v.]. Car festival [ratotsavam] three days before and after Shivarautry [pundigay, 6a].——*Bullipully* (బల్లిపల్లె - ballipalle, Tel.). From (balli, tel. lizard + palli, tel. village). Village, Hamlet of Shetticoonta; pop. 5,668; lat. 13° 47′; long. 79° 28′; from Cuddapah S.E. 63 miles; from Poollampett S.S.E. 28 miles. Forest timber depôt:——*Cheyair* (చెయ్యేరు - cheyyéru, Tel.). See sep. title.——*Chinna orampaud* (చిన్నఓరంపాడు - chinnaórampádu, Tel.). From (chinna, tel. small + óra, tel. border + pádu, tel. village). Village, Railway station; pop. 4,943; acres 7,900; lat. 14° 04′; long. 79° 19′; height 618 feet; from Cuddapah S.E. 42 miles; from Poollampett S.E. 6 miles. On the route from Cuddapah to Madras.——*Chitwail* (చిట్టివేలు - chittivélu, Tel.). See sep. title.——*Codoor* (కోడూరు - kódúru, Tel. kódúr *). From (kódi, tel. a fowl + úru, tel. village). Village, Railway station; pop. 6,557; acres 18,895; lat. 13° 58′; long. 79° 24′; height 643 feet; from Cuddapah S.E. 51 miles; from Poollampett S.E. 15 miles. Former Forest head-quarters.——*Condore* (కొండూరు - kondúru, Tel.). From (konda, tel. hill + úru, tel. village). Village; pop. 1,281; acres 15,068; lat. 14° 19′; long. 79° 20′; from Cuddapah S.E. 34 miles; from Poollampett N.E. 14 miles.——*Cunclacondah* (కనికలకొండ - kanikalakonda, Tel.). From (kanika, tel. quartz stone + konda, tel. hill). Hill; Trig. station; lat. 14° 17′ 43·05″; long. 79° 11′ 19·44″; height 2,040; from Cuddapah S.E. 26 miles; from Poollampett N.N.W. 12 miles.——*Eegalsaricondah* (ఈగలసరి కొండ - ígalasarikonda, Tel.). From (íga, tel. fly + tsari, tel. a precipice + konda, tel. hill). Hill; lat. 14° 01′ 25·75″; long. 79° 28′ 50·09″; from Cuddapah S.E. 52 miles; from Poollampett E.S.E. 17 miles.——*Goonjana* (గుంజన - gunjana, Tel.). See sep. title.——*Hoblampett* (ఓబులంపేట - óbulampéta, Tel.). From (óbulamma, tel. proper name + péta, tel. suburb). Village, Hamlet of Rungayapully; pop. 698; lat. 14° 23′; long. 79° 15′; from Cuddapah S.E. 27 miles; from Poollampett N.N.E. 18 miles. Considerable trade in dyeing [shauyam] cotton [q.v.] thread [nool] red. At confluence of Cheyair and Pennair.——*Naugavaram* (నాగవరము - nágavaramu, Tel.). From (nága, san. snake + pura, san. town). Village; pop. 2,412; acres 8,185; lat. 14° 03′; long. 79° 24′; from Cuddapah S.E. 47 miles; from Poollampett S.E. 12 miles.——*Nundalore* (నందలూరు - nandalúru, Tel. nandalúr *). From (nandi, san. bull + úru, tel. village). Village, Railway station, Head-quarters of District moonsif; pop. 2,588; acres 3,975; lat. 14° 16′; long. 79° 10′; height 475 feet; from Cuddapah S.E. 25 miles; from Poollampett N.W. 11 miles. Old temple.——*Ootcore* (ఊటుకూరు - útukúru, Tel.). From (úta, tel. spring + úru, tel. village). Village; pop. 2,838; acres 4,044; lat. 14° 11′; long. 79° 14′; from Cuddapah S.E. 32 miles; from Poollampett N.N.W. 4 miles. Agricultural village with large tank.——*Palcondah* (పాలకొండ - pálakonda, Tel.). See sep. title.——*Pedda orampaud* (పెద్దఓరంపాడు - peddaórampádu,* Tel.). From (pedda, tel. great + órampádu, tel. the village). Village; pop. 3,363; acres 14,412; lat. 14° 06′; long. 79° 19′; from Cuddapah S.E. 41 miles; from Poollampett E.S.E. 5 miles.——*Poly* (పోలి - póli, Tel). From (poli, tel. sacrifice). Village; pop. 7,786 including Rajampett; acres 13,446, including Rajampett; lat. 14° 13′; long. 79° 13′; from Cuddapah S.E. 30 miles; from Poollampett N.N.W. 6 miles. Hill in the neighbourhood produces good building stone [cull].——*Poollampett* (పుల్లంపేట - pullampéta, Tel.). See below.——*Rajampett* (రాజంపేట - rájampéta, Tel. rájampet *). From (rájamma, tel. proper name + péta, tel. suburb). Village, Railway station; pop. see Poly above; acres 4,890; lat. 14° 12′; long. 79° 13′; height 462 feet; from Cuddapah S.E. 30 miles; from Poollampet N.N.W. 6 miles. Important centre of trade.——*Raullamadoogoo canama* (రాళ్లమడుగుకనమ - rállamadugukanama, Tel.). See sep. title.——*Raupore canama* (రాపూరుకనమ - rápúrukanama, Tel.). See sep. title.——*Reddipully* (రెడ్డిపల్లె - reddipalli, Tel. reddipalle *). From (reddi, tel. headman of a village + palli, tel. village). Village, Railway station; pop. 2,014; acres 4,834; lat. 14° 06′; long. 79° 16′; height 561 feet; from Cuddapah S.E. 39 miles; from Poollampett S.S.E. 3 miles.——*Sheshachellam* (శేషాచలము - shésháchalamu, Tel.). See sep. title.——*Shetticoonta* (శెట్టికుంట - shettikunta, Tel.). From (shetti, tel. merchant + kunta, tel. pond). Village; pop. 5,668; acres 68,837; lat. 13° 52′; long. 79° 26′; from Cuddapah S.E. 58 miles; from Poollampett S.S.E. 22 miles. Peddapaud, a hamlet, is a Railway station.——*Veligonda* (వెలిగొండ - veligonda, Tel.). See sep. title.——*Yecoolasaury* (ఏకులసారి - ékulasári, Tel.). From (éku, tel. cleaned cotton + siri, tel. wealth). Trig. station; lat. 14° 01′ 25·75″; long. 79° 28′ 50·09″; from Bommavaram E.S.E. 7 miles.——*Yerragoontlacota* (ఎర్రగుంట్లకోట - erraguntlakóta, Tel.). From (erra, tel. red + gunta, tel. tank + kóta, san. fort). Village; pop. 2,812; acres 41,583; lat. 13° 58′; long. 79° 19′; from Cuddapah S.E. 47 miles; from Poollampett S. 11 miles.——(2) Village, Talook head-quarters; Cuddapah dist., Poollampett tal.; pop. 2,207; acres 2,822; lat. 14° 08′; long 79° 15′; from Cuddapah S.E. 36 miles; from Madanapully N.E. 62 miles; from Madras N.W. 101 miles; from Sidhout S.E. 29 miles. Indigo [q.v.] and cloth of fine texture are manufactures.

POOLLARY (పుల్లరి - pullari, *Tel.*; புல்வரி - pulvari, *Tam.*). Tel. from (pullu, tel. grass + ari, tel. tax). Tam. from (pul, tam. grass + vari, tam. a tax) [pill]. Tax on grazing [maita]. There have been many kinds all over the country.——*Alaga poollary* (అలగాపుల్లరి - alagápullari, Tel.). From (alag, hind. separate + above). The proportion of the muctah poollary charged on cattle-owners not being occupiers of land on puttah [q.v.].——*Chowty poollary* (சௌதாய்ப்புல்வரி - shautháyppulvari, Tam.). From (chauthá, hind. one-fourth + above). Tax levied for grazing equal to one-fourth full assessment [teervay] of the land when used for cultivation. Trijye was one-third.——*Feisal poollary* (பைசல்புல்வரி - paisalbulvari, Tam.). From (faisal, ar. settlement + above). Fixed grazing assessment. Same as Muctah poollary.——*Muctah pooliary* (మక్తాపుల్లరి - maktápullari, Tel.). From (makta, ar. assessment + above). A money assessment levied on the total common pasturage [maita] of a village and modified with reference to occupation out of the waste land for cultivation.——*Paravay poollary* (பரவைப்புல்வரி - paravaippulvari, Tam.). From (paravai, tam. expanse + above). A tax paid to graze cattle [maud] on large tract.——*Yennika poollary* (ఎన్నికపుల్లరి - ennikapullari, Tel.). From (ennu, tel. to count + above). Pasture tax by capitation on the cattle [maud] of a village.

POOLLY (புள்ளி - pulli, *Tam.*). Means spot. Mammal first term. Ex.:—Axis maculatus (pullimán), spotted deer; Felis rubiginosa (pullippúnai), spotted cat. See gloss. paragraphs.

POOLY (व्याघ्र - vyághra, *San.*; वाघ - vágha, *Mahr.*; ببر - babar, *Pers.*; باگھ - bágh, *Hind.*; باگ - bág, *Dec.*; اريماوتڠڬل - árimautunggal, *Malay*; ಹುಲಿ - huli, *Can.*; బలిపే - balipe, *Too.*; పెద్దపులి - peddapuli, *Tel.*; ବାଘ - bágho, *Oor.*; കടുവാ - katuvá, *Mal.*; ව‍ග් - vag, *Singh.*; புலி - puli, *Tam.*). Title from tamul. San. from (vi, san. intensive prefix + ághrá, san. to smell). Mahr. and Hind. from sanscrit. Malay from (árimau, malay, tiger + tunggal, malay, one); solitary tiger. Tel. from (pedda, tel. large + puli, tel. tiger). Mal. from (katu, mal. fierce + váya, mal. mouth). Singh. from sanscrit. Tam. from (pul, tam. low); from its crouching habit. Pers. also (sher). Hind. also (pátáyatbágh), meaning striped tiger. Can. also (hebbuli), meaning great + tiger. Mal. also (variyanpuli), meaning striped tiger; (perimpuli), meaning large tiger. Title otherwise Tiger, Royal tiger. Felis [marjauram] tigris, felidæ [deeptaucsham] digitigrada, carnivora, mammalia [sastanam, 9], of naturalists [jantoo]. The tiger is a large heavy bodied cat [poonay], much developed in the fore-quarters, with short, close hair of a bright rufous ground tint from every shade of pale yellow ochre to burnt sienna, with black stripes arranged irregularly and seldom in two individuals alike the stripes being also irregular in form, from single streaks to loops and broad bands. The males have prolonged hairs extending from the ears round the cheeks, forming a ruff. The pupil of the tiger's eye is round, and not vertical. The plan of measuring is to measure the animal as it lies on the ground, taking the tape from the tip of the nose to the end of the tail. One that is ten feet by this measurement is large. 12 feet is maximum. The tiger breeds in the forest and mountain tracts, and comes into the open country when the grain is on the ground. Naturally a cowardly animal, and always retreats from opposition, until wounded or provoked. When a tiger takes to killing man, it always perseveres. In general, very old tigers, whose teeth are blunted or gone, are man-eaters [q.v.]. The tiger is often successfully killed on foot; occasionally it is shot by night from a platform on a tree. There is a Tamul proverb :—ஆனைக்கும்புலிக்கும் நெருப்பைக்கண்டால் பயம்—"the elephant [q.v.] and "tiger are afraid of fire;" which is a fact. The tiger's favorite food is deer [mrigam], antelope [jinka], and wild hog [jungle soor]. When these abound, it does not attack domestic cattle [maud]. Tiger's fat is made into oil [yennay], and being mixed with gorochanay [q.v.] or ox gall and custoory [q.v.] or musk is used as an application in cases of rheumatic pain. Tiger skins are considered sacred and used as seats by bramin [q.v.] ascetics [yogy], when they are engaged in prayer. The tiger is the emblem of power. The natives say that an additional lobe is added to a tiger's liver every year; that his flesh possesses many medicinal qualities; that his claws arranged together so as to form a circle, and hung round a child's neck, preserves it from the effect of the evil eye [cunnoor]; that the whiskers constitute a deadly poison, which for this reason are carefully burnt off the instant the animal is killed. Several of the lower castes [jauty] eat his flesh. The tiger is not found in Ceylon. Pooly is a not uncommon plant first term, from thorns or leaves resembling tiger's foot-print. Ex., where transl. is of second term :—Cæsalpinia sepiaria (pulittadukki), and (pulittodakki), to prevent; Helmia dæmona (pulidumpa), root; Ipomæa pestigridis (puliççóvadi), foot mark; Pterolobium indicum (pulitodugu), jacket. See gloss. paragraphs.——*Cazhoothay pooly* (तरक्ष - taraksha, San.; तरस - tarasa, Mahr.; ضبع - zaba, Ar.; كفتار - kaftár, Pers.; ترس - taras, Hind.; ಕಿರಬ - kiraba, Can.; ಕತ್ತೆಕಿರುಬ - kattekiruba, Coorg; ನಾಯಿಪಿಲಿ - náyipili, *Too.*; కొర్నగండు - kornagandu, Tel.; ଗଦ୍ଧଭବାଘ - goddnabágho, Oor.; കഴുതപ്പുലി - kazhutappuli, Mal.; கழுதைப்புலி - kazhuthaippuli, Tam.). Title from tamul. San. from (tara, san. crossing + kshí, san. to kill); as annoying on the road. Mahr. from sanscrit. Ar. from (zabaa, ar. to stretch the arms). Hind. from sanscrit. Too. from (náyi, too. dog + pili, too. tiger). Oor. means like tiger. Mal. from (kazhuta, mal. ass + puli, mal. tiger). Tam. from (kazhuthai, tam. ass + puli, tam. tiger); from the resemblance to the ass [gadhah] in head, ears and tail. Ar. also (ummirimál), meaning mother of sandy tracts. Hind. also (hundár), meaning wolf; (lakarbágh), meaning tree + tiger. Tel. also (dummalagondi); corrupted into dummergundy [q.v.] as a term of abuse. Tam. also (kazhuthaikkudatti), meaning ass + hyæna. Title otherwise Hyæna, Strand wolf. Hyæna striata, hyænidæ, digitigrada, carnivora, mammália [sastanam, 10], of naturalists [jantoo]. Alias Canis hyæna, Hyæna vulgaris. The hyæna, though somewhat resembling the dog [nye] in outward appearance, connects the cat [poonay] with the civet [poonoogoopoonay]. The differences between the Felidæ and the Hyænidæ, setting aside minor details, are in the teeth, and the possession by the latter of a caudal pouch. The tongue is rough, with a circular collection of retroflected spines. The hind legs are much shorter than the front, and the feet have only four toes with blunt worn claws, not retractile, but like those of the dog. The hair is coarse and bristly, and usually prolonged into a sort of crest or mane along the neck and shoulders, and to a slighter degree down the back; the tail is bushy. Of a pale yellowish gray color, with transverse tawny stripes; neck and back maned. Rare in forest districts, and abundant in open country, especially where ravines offer holes and caverns. Nocturnal. The call of hyæna is a disagreeable cry. Destructive to dogs [nye] and constantly carries off pariah dogs [q.v.] from the outskirts of villages. The hyæna is found wherever the wolf [konye] is absent. The bone of this animal rubbed into a paste and mixed with gorochanay [q.v.] and custoory [q.v.] is used to alleviate rheumatic pains. The head is sometimes buried in cattle-sheds to prevent cattle-disease [pashoo rogam]. Its incisors are tied round the loins of a woman in labor to lessen her pains. Its nasal bone is believed to possess the power of digesting food; for this purpose however it must be removed before the animal is dead.——*Poolivendla* (పులివెందల - pulivendala, Tel.). See sep. title.

POOLY (புளி - puli, *Tam.*). Sour. Plant first term often joining two genera. Ex., where transl. is of second term :—Anona muricata (pulippalá), artocarpus integrifolia; Averrhoa bilimbi (puliççakkáy), fruit; Bauhinia malabarica (pulichinta), tamarindus indica; Buchanania angustifolia (pulimá), mangifera indica; Cinnamomum iners (pulippilá), artocarpus integrifolia; Crotalaria juncea (pulivaññi), reed; Garcinia morella (puliñchakka), artocarpus integrifolia; Hibiscus cannabinus (pulimañji), fibre of sanseviera roxburghiana; Oxalis corniculata (pulichinta), tamarindus indica; Pterolobium indicum (puliyindu), mimosa rubicaulis; Vitis carnosa (pulinaralai), vitis lanata; Vitis setosa (pulippirandai), vitis quadrangularis; Webera corymbosa (puliyáyini), artocarpus hirsuta. See gloss. paragraphs. Compare also Tamarind.——*Karipoolipp* (अङ्गाराम्ल - angárámla, San.; బొగ్గుపులుసు - boggupulusu, Tel.; கரிப்புளிப்பு - karippulippu, Tam.). San. from (angára, san. charcoal + ámla, san. sour). Tel. from (boggu, tel. charcoal + pulusu, tel. acid). Tam. from (kari, tam. carbon + pulippu, tam. sour). Carbonic acid. Composed of 1 of carbon and 2 of oxygen [vayoo].——*Poolipp* (புளிப்பு - pulippu, Tam.). Acid [tezaub].——*Poolitchay* (புளிச்சை - puliççai, Tam.). Same as Hemp bendy.

POON (पुन्नाग - punnága, *San.*; പുന്ന - punna, *Mal.*). Title from sanscrit through malayalam. San. from (pums, san. male + nága, san. tree so called, mesua ferrea, linn.). Title otherwise American calaba, Pinnay; the last not connected with piney dammer [q.v.]. Botanically the Calophyllum genus, guttiferæ [vricsham, 22]. Large trees with shining leaves marked by numerous parallel transverse veins, and having racemes of flowers; fruit contains one seed. The species best known to the natives are shown below. Includes also species from the following genera:—cassia, desmodium, ochrocarpus, pseudarthria, rhizophora, sterculia.——*Bastard poon* (فرنگی بادام - farangíbádám, Hind.; جنگلی بادم - janglíbádam, Dec.; ಭಾತಾಳ - bhátála, Can.; ಪಿನಾರಿ - pínári, Too.; గుర్రపుబాదంచెట్టు - gurrapubádamchettu, Tel.; പൊട്ടക്കാവലം - pottakkávalam, Mal.; තෙලඹු - telambu, Singh.; பீநாறி - pínári, Tam.). Title from use and likeness. Hind. from (farangí, hind. foreign + bádam, hind. almond, prunus amygdalus, baill.). Dec. from (janglí, hind. wild + bádam, hind. almond). Too. means disagreeable odour. Tel. from (gurramu, tel. horse + bádamchettu, tel. almond). Mal. from (potta, mal. worthless + kávalam, mal. sterculia balanghas, linn.). Singh. means poon oil. Tam. from (pí, tam. ordure + náru, tam. to smell); from fetid flowers. Can. also (pénári). Mal. also (pínári), meaning dirty + smelling. Tam. also (kuthiraippidukkan), meaning horse + testicle, from fruit like horse testicle; (púthagarappánbattaimaram), meaning devil + skin disease so called + bark + tree; from use. Title otherwise Deodar of Western india, Devil carpang tree, Fœtid sterculia, Fœtid tree, Horse-almond, Horse testicle. Giving Sterculia oil, Sterculia seeds. Botanically Sterculia [cauvalam] fœtida, l., sterculiaceæ [vricsham, 26]. Tree; leaves compound, peltate; leaflets seven to nine, oblong-lanceolate, acuminated, young ones slightly pubescent; flowers panicled; calyx deeply divided, segments lanceolate, slightly velvety within; carpels oblong, many-seeded; flowers brownish; tinged with red at the base, very fetid. Stately tree with a smooth stem rising to a considerable height without branches; every part has disagreeable smell when bruised; capsules size of man's fist, containing ten to fifteen seeds, black and oblong, about one inch in length, and about the same in circumference; the kernel is generally grey and sweetish in taste; the oil obtained by boiling seeds in water is of a pale yellow color, inodorous, with a faintly sweetish taste; the seeds afford as much as 40 per cent. of fixed oil [yennay] which contains a large quantity of stearic acid. Leaves and bark are medicinally aperient, repellent, diuretic, and diaphoretic; seeds are oily, and if swallowed incautiously bring on nausea and vertigo; decoction of the capsule is mucilaginous and astringent, the seeds and oil are medicinally similar to catapang [q.v.]. Seeds roasted and eaten like chestnuts. Used as avenue tree [shaulay], only objectionable from the fetor of the flowers and the falling of the leaves. Wood light, tough, open grained, yellowish white, easily worked, not liable to split or warp; harder and firmer than sterculia villosa, roxb. [odul], which it resembles in structure and appearance; furnishes some of the smaller poon spars for masts of ships.——*Bracteate poon* (کوچك چمپا - kochakchampá, Hind.). Botanically Calophyllum [poon] bracteatum, thw., guttiferæ [vricsham, 22]. Large tree, closely resembling tomentosum [malabar poon]; leaves dimorphic, the fully developed 3–8 inches long, tapering to the obtuse base, highly polished, golden brown when dry; petiole $\frac{1}{4}$—$\frac{1}{2}$ inch; abnormal or undeveloped leaves 1–2 by $\frac{1}{6}$—$\frac{1}{3}$ inch, sub-sessile, linear-lanceolate or linear, pubescent, resembling bracts; racemes in the axils of and shorter than the normal leaves, few flowered; flowers $\frac{1}{3}$ inch diameter; pedicels with an oblong bract $\frac{1}{4}$ inch long at the base; sepals four; petals four; fruit $\frac{3}{4}$ inch long, oblong. Found on west coast. Wood coarse-grained, ornamental.——*Common poon.* (पुन्नाग - punnága, San.; नागचांपा - nágachámpá, Mahr.; उंडी - undí, Conc.; سلطان چمپا - sultán-champá, Hind.; سرفن - surfan, Dec.; بنتنگور - bintanggur, Malay; ಸುರಹೊನ್ನೆ - surahonne, Can.; ಪೊನ್ನೆ - ponne, Too.; పొన్న - ponna, Tel.; ପୁନଙ୍ଗ - punang, Oor.; പുന്ന - punna, Mal.; දොඹ - domba, Singh.; பின்னை - pinnai, Tam.). San. from (pums, san. male + nága, san. the tree so called, mesua ferrea, linn.) [kamela, soora poon]; distinguished or beautiful mesua. Mahr. from (nága, san. snake + chámpá, mahr. champak tree). Hind. from (sultán, ar. royal + champaka, san. michelia champaca, linn.). Can. from (sura, san. celestial + honne, can. poon tree). Tel. from sanscrit. Mal. from (pon, mal. gold + akam, mal. within) [kamela, malabar poon, wild mohwah], by corruption. Tam. from (pon, tam. gold), beautiful tree with reddish brown wood [small chaltah], by corruption,

San. also (naméru), meaning worship tree; (pañchakésara), meaning five + filament; (tungakásara), meaning tall + mesua ferrea, linn. Mahr. also (surangí), meaning good + color [soora poon]. Hind. also (undí); (surpan). Malay also (bítangur). Can. also (vúma); (pinekai); (ponné) [kamela, soora poon]. Tel. also (púna); (púnás). Mal. also (ponnakam), meaning gold holding. Singh. also (teldomba), meaning oil + calophyllum. Title otherwise Alexandrian laurel, Balsam poon, Bintagor, Dilo oil plant, Domba nut, Laurel nut, Mest wood tree, Oondee, Pinnay-oil plant, St. mary's wood, Sultan champak, Sweet-scented calophyllum, Tamana-oil plant. Botanically Calophyllum [poon] inophyllum, linn., guttiferæ [vricsham, 22]. Alias Balsamaria inophyllum; Calophyllum bintagor. Bintagor from malay. Tree, 50 feet, of rather crooked growth, branches terete; leaves dark-green elliptical or oboval, obtuse or retuse, furnished with numerous parallel slender nerves; racemes longer than the leaves, from the upper axils, or disposed in a terminal panicle; sepals four; drooping racemes of flowers white, very fragrant; followed by globular smooth yellow one-seeded fruit one inch in diameter; kernels of nuts bitterish when ripe, unctuous taste; flowers twice a year, and attains a great age; common in malabar, but largely planted elsewhere, particularly near the coast; one of the most beautiful trees in the world; found in many gardens. The fruit is ovoid or round, and greenish-yellow when ripe; it varies in size; on old trees it is often as large as a bantam's egg; the pulp surrounding the nut dries up when the seed is mature, and the previously smooth skin covering it becomes brown or black and much wrinkled; endocarp is hard, woody, white, as thick as shell of a filbert [findak]; within it is an inner endocarp, soft, and corky, of a red color, thicker than the woody shell towards the apex of the fruit, but gradually becoming very thin towards the base, the inner surface of this layer is highly polished; the seed is of the same shape as the nut, it is very oily and has a rancid taste, it consists of two hemispherical cotyledons very closely united. Fresh seeds, when shelled and subjected to pressure, yield a dark green oil [yennay] of a peculiar fragrant odour; the oil has an odour of tonquin beans if the seeds are small and young; but smells like old and rancid ghee [q.v.], if they are large and well matured; the oil is bitter in both cases. Leaves used by ancient romans for laurel wreaths of monarchs and heroes; flower here offered to shiva [q.v.] and vishnoo [q.v.]. The seeds and oil are medicinally stimulant to the mucous membrane and skin; used externally only; the watery paste of the kernel of the seeds may be resorted to in the absence of the oil; the best way of using the oil is floating on water, or as an emulsion with mucilage. Doses; if the oil is greenish brown, from fifteen to twenty minims; and if pale and greenish-yellow, from twenty to thirty minims; three or four times in the twenty-four hours. The oil substituted for copaiba and cubebs [cubeb pepper]. From bark exudes a black resin [raul], powdering to green, which resembles myrrh [q.v.], and is useful application to indolent ulcers; resembles the bourbon tacamahaca; the gum [gond] from the wounded branches, being mixed with strips of the bark and leaves, is steeped in water, and the oil which rises to the surface is used as an application to sore eyes; the oil is in pharm. nonofficinal. Oil is also a lamp oil [q.v.] in travancore; oil used for caulking vessels. Wood reddish-brown, moderately hard, close-grained; used for masts, spars, railway sleepers, machinery, also for cabinet-work.——*Lowly poon* (నేలపొన్న - nélaponna, Tel.). Same as Nubian senna.——*Malabar poon* (नागणि - nágani, Mahr.; ತಿರುಪೊನ್ನೆಮರ - shiruponnemara, Can.; പുന്ന - punna, Mal.; කීන - kína, Singh.; புன்கு - pungu, Tam.). Title from habitat. Can. means small poon. Mal. from (pon, mal. old + akam, mal. within) [common poon, kamela, wild mohwah]. Tam. like malayalam [caunooga, karanj]. Can. also (bobbi). Botanically Calophyllum [poon] tomentosum, wight, guttiferæ [vricsham, 22]. Alias Calophyllum elatum. Large straight tree with numerous longitudinal cracks down the bark; young shoots, panicles, and outer sepals ferruginous; leaves elliptic, acuminate, attenuated at the base, very shining; panicles terminal and from the upper axils, large, many-flowered; sepals four, two outer ones sub-rotund, small, two inner ones petaloid; petals four; fruit ovoid, pointed, about the size of a thrush's [shauricay] egg; flowers in january and february; grows abundantly in most moist ghaut [q.v.] forests or sholahs [q.v.] on western coast from canara down to cape comorin, and in similar forests on the lower pulneys, anamullays; never found in dry deciduous forests; never been planted. Gives a black, opaque gum [gond], feebly astringent, and very soluble in cold water; the solution is brownish-yellow, exhibiting a strong blue florescence. Oil [yennay] from seeds. Yields the poon spars of commerce; in the ghaut forests of south canara they are floated down rivers to the coast; wood is scarcely known except as a spar, being only occasionally used for building and bridge work by planters, reddish, coarse-grained but ornamental.——*Narrow-leaved poon* (باریك پتے كا چنپا - báríkpattekáchampá, Hind.). Botanically Calophyllum [poon] angustifolium, roxb., guttiferæ [vricsham, 22]. A splendid tree from 100 to 150 feet high, with fine straight stem; leaves short-petioled, lanceolate, somewhat obtusely pointed; flowers in axillary fascicles; pedicels with a cup-shaped apex. In demand for ship spars, &c., and has become very scarce and costly; it may be procured from 100 feet to 130 feet long, squaring 3 feet at the butt; it is very tough and elastic, but easy to saw and work up; it is used for all building purposes, but is not capable of enduring exposure or moisture long.——*Salt poon* (ఉప్పుపొన్న - uppuponna, Tel.). Title from habitat and resemblance. Same as White candel mangrove.——*Seven-leafed poon* (ఏడాకులపొన్న - édákulaponna, Tel.). Same as Dita.——*Small poon* (ಕಿರಿಹೊನ್ನೆಮರ - kirihonnemara, Can.; ತಿರಿಪೊನ್ನೆ - shiriponne, Too.; ചെറുപുന്ന - cherupunna, Mal.; ගුරුකීන - gurukína, Singh.; சிறுபின்னை - shirubinnai, Tam.). Title from general size. Can. from (kiri, can. small + honnemara, can. the poon tree). Too. from (shiru, too. small + ponne, too. calophyllum inophyllum, l.). Mal. from (cheru, mal. small + punna, mal. calophyllum inophyllum, linn.). Singh. from (guru, san. heavy + kína, singh. calophyllum tomentosum, wight). Tam. from (shiru, tam. small + pinnai, tam. calophyllum inophyllum, linn.). Can. also (bubbimara); (kalponne); (kaiponne). Title otherwise Calaba tree, False poon, Keena-nut tree, Santamaria tree, Shiroopinnay, True east india tacamahaca resin tree. Botanically Calophyllum [poon] wightianum, wall., guttiferæ [vricsham, 22]. Alias Calophyllum apetalum, calaba, calabioides, decipiens, inophyllum, var. wall., spurium. Tree; leaves cuneate-obovate, obtuse, or emarginate; young branches square; racemes lax, as long as the leaves, axillary near the ends of the branches; sepals two; petals two; drupe oblong, one-celled; petals white; western coast mountains; common near banks of rivers. Resin [raul] is yellow, translucent, adhesive, of acrid taste, and pleasant aromatic smell. The gum [gond] occurs in large translucent irregular lumps of a yellowish color; it is of horny texture, somewhat brittle, without odour; the taste is soapy; when placed in water it gradually softens, and finally disintegrates into a fine granular matter which floats in the form of flaky particles of a dirty white color, and numerous oil globules which gradually collect upon the surface; the water dissolves a small portion and becomes slightly viscid. Oil used as medicine in leprosy [cooshtam] and cutaneous affections, and in infusion mixed with honey [shahad] in scabies and rheumatism. Fruit when ripe is red and sweet; eaten by natives. Oil [yennay] is used in lamps. Timber red, very hard and heavy, valuable for engineering purposes.——*Soora poon* (सुरंगी - surangí, Mahr.; ناگیسر - nágesar, Hind.; ಪೊನ್ನೆ - ponne, Can.; సురపొన్న - suraponna, Tel.; சுரபுன்னை - shurabunnai, Tam.). Title from teloogoo. Mahr. from (su, san. good + ranga, san. color) [common poon]; properly pterocarpus santalinus, linn. [red sanders]. Hind. from (nágakésara, san. mesua ferrea, linn.) [nauga champak]. Can. from (ponnu, can. gold) [common poon, kamela]. Tel. from (sura, san. divine + ponna, tel. calophyllum inophyllum, linn.). Tam. from (sura, san. divine + punnai, tam. calophyllum inophyllum, linn.). Hind. also (nágchampá). Can. also (wandi); (taringi); (punnága), meaning male + mesua ferrea, linn. [common poon, kamela]; (wúndi); (suringi); (gardúndi). Title otherwise Fragrant poon, Long-leaved poon, Red naugaisar, Woondy. Botanically Ochrocarpus longifolius, benth. and hook. f., guttiferæ [vricsham, 22]. Alias Calophyllum longifolium; Calysaccion longifolium; Mammea longifolia. Small tree, straight stem with opposite branches at nearly right angles, leaves bright copper-colored while young, and when mature dark green and leathery; flowers are white, followed by an obliquely ovoid fruit tipped by hard-pointed style; fruit size of an acorn and resembles one; encloses a large stone, between which and the rind is a soft pulpy juice; flower-buds are about the size of cloves [lavangam], and of a red color. Habitat, malabar and western ghauts. Medicinal properties very similar to mesua ferrea [nauga champak]; the flowers are medicinally stimulant and carminative; a very weak substitute for spirit. ammon. arom., lavender and peppermint. Pulpy juice, of rose water-like [goolaub] flavor, is not accounted edible; globular flower buds are used for dyeing [shauyam] silk [puttoo]; emit fragrance like violets [banafshah], used as perfume; wood used in house-building. No other common species here.——*Straight-leafed poon* (కోలాకుపొన్న - kólákuponna, Tel.). Same as Indian medicago.——*Three-leaf poon* (ముయ్యాకుపొన్న - muyyákuponna, Tel.). Title from trifoliate leaf. Tel. from (múdu, tel. three + áku, tel. leaf + ponna, tel. calophyllum inophyllum, linn.). Tel. also (náyákuponna), meaning four + leaf + calophyllum inophyllum, linn. Botanically Pseudarthria viscida, w. & a., leguminosæ [vricsham, 48]. Alias Desmodium viscidum; Glycine viscida; Hedysarum viscidum; Rhynchosia viscida. Diffuse, prostrate; leaves pinnately trifoliolate; lateral leaflets obliquely ovate, terminal one, rhomboid-ovate, pubescent above, when old villous underneath; racemes filiform, elongated; legumes three to four-seeded; flowers purple, in threes from each bract, on longish pedicels, jointed close under the calyx; flowering nearly all the year. No other species here.

POON (பூண் - pún, *Tam.*). To wear.——*Poonarchy* (புணர்ச்சி - punarçç̧i, Tam.). From (punar, tam. to join). Syntax. The mode of collocating words in Dravidian languages follows the logical order, more so than even in Latin or Greek. The leading principles are the following:—the cause precedes the effect; that which qualifies precedes that which is qualified; the similitude precedes that which is similar and the comparative that which is compared; the secondary clause precedes the primary one; the noun precedes the preposition; the verb ends the sentence. See vol. I (52); II, 205, 209. Neither the

Nunnool nor the other Tamul grammars treat of syntax as a separate subject, but connect it with etymology [bhaushay, lacshanam].——*Poonool* (பூணூல் - púnúl, Tam.). From (above + núl, tam. thread). Three-fold cotton [q.v.] string, suspended from the left shoulder to the right side, and put on for the first time, with ceremony [oopanayanam], when a young Brawin [q.v.] or other twice-born person is seven or nine years old [dwijau, jandiram, jaunwah]. See vol. I (99).

POONAR (पुनर् - punar, *San.*). Again.——*Poonarjenmam* (पुनर्जन्म - punarjanma, San.). From (above + janma, san. birth). Transmigration [samsauram].——*Poonausa* (పునాస - punása, Tel.). From (punarvasu, san. the seventh asterism). The season of the south-west monsoon [q.v.] on Golcondah coast [q.v.], which comes late, about June-July; otherwise Moodroo [q.v.]. For N.E. monsoon on Golcondah coast, see Peira. For tamul seasons see Caur and Mausam.

POONAY (मार्जार - márjára, *San.*; मांजर - mañjara, *Mahr.*; سنور - sinnaur, *Ar.*; گربه - gurbah, *Pers.*; بلی - billí, *Hind.*; كوچيڠ - kuching, *Malay*; ಬೆಕ್ಕು - bekku, *Can.*; ಪುಚ್ಚೆ - puççe, *Too.*; పిల్లి - pilli, *Tel.*; ବିରାଡି - birádi, *Oor.*; പൂച്ച - púçça, *Mal.*; බළලා - balalá, *Singh.*; பூனை - púnai, *Tam.*). San. from (márj, san. to cleanse); from constantly cleaning itself. Mahr. from sanscrit. Tel. and Singh. from (bidála, san. cat). Tam. from (púsu, tam. to wash); from constantly cleaning itself. Ar. also (abúkharásh), meaning father of scratches. Title otherwise Cat. Felis [marjauram] domestica, felidæ [deeptaucsham], digitigrada, carnivora, mammalia [sastanam, 9], of naturalists [jantoo]. Natives do not keep cats to any great extent in their houses. The cat is considered the devil's helpmate and an animal of ill omen. A penitent cat means a sanctimonious hypocrite. It is believed that when the cat cleans itself behind its ears with its wet paw, it presages rain [mazhay]. Flying lemurs [devaunga] are often called Flying cats. There is a Tamul proverb:—ஆனைக்கவடும் பூனைத்திருடும்—"the deceit of an elephant [q.v.] and the thievishness "of a cat." And another:—மார்ச் சாலநியாயத்தீர்ப்பு—"cat's judgment;" i.e., a partial judgment. And another:—பித்திகாமார்ச்சால நியாயத் தீர்ப்பு—"cat-upon-a-wall "judgment;" i.e., a dubious judgment. There is a Teloogoo proverb:—మార్జాలాభ్యంజనం—"anointing a cat;" i.e., injuring by indirect means, as a cat is said to scratch itself to death when oil is put over its head.——*Meencolly poonay* (خفيه باگه - khufyahbágh, Hind.; باگهداسا - bághdásá, Dec.; ಮೀನುಗುಲಿಬೆಕ್ಕು - mínugulibekku, Can.; മീൻകൊല്ലിപ്പൂച്ച - mínkollippúçça, Mal.; හාඩුන්දිව - hándúndiva, Singh.; மீன்கொல்லிப்பூனை - míngollippúnai, Tam.). Hind. from (khufyah, ar. concealed + bágh, hind. tiger), tiger-like. Dec. from (bágh, hind. tiger + dásá, hind. like). Can. from (mínu, san. fish + guli, can. an affix of nouns from kollu, tam. to kill + bekku, can. cat). Mal. from (mín, mal. fish + kol, mal. to kill + púçça, mal. cat). Tam. from (mín, tam. fish + kollu, tam. to kill + púnai, tam. cat). Title otherwise Fishing tiger cat. Felis [marjauram] viverrina, felidæ [deeptaucsham], digitigrada, carnivora, mammalia [sastanam, 9], of naturalists [jantoo]. Alias Felis celidogaster, himalayanus, viverriceps; Viverrina bennettii. Of a mouse gray color, more or less deep, and sometimes tinged with tawny, with large dark spots more or less numerous, oblong on the back and neck, and in lines, more or less rounded elsewhere, and broken or coalescing; cheeks white; a black face stripe; beneath dull white; chest with five or six dark bands; belly spotted; tail with six or seven dark bands and a black tip; feet unspotted; whiskers either entirely white, or with a white tip. The nasal bones are somewhat attenuated, causing a narrowness of visage which has suggested the names viverrina and viverriceps. In old animals the bony orbital rings are complete. Common in Travancore extending up the Malabar coast as far as Mangalore. An Indian species not here found is Felis marmorata or marbled tiger-cat.——*Poolly poonay* (चित्रमार्जार - chitramárjára, San.; ابلق بلا - ablakbillá, Hind.; ಚುಕ್ಕೆಬೆಕ್ಕು - chukkebekku, Can.; నామాలపిల్లి - námálapilli, Tel.; പുള്ളിപ്പൂച്ച - pullippúçça, Mal.; කලදියා - kuladiya, Singh.; வரிப்பூனை - varippúnai, Tam.). San. from (chitra, san. variegated + márjára, san. cat). Hind. from (ablak, hind. piebald + billá, hind. cat). Can. from (chukke, can. spot + bekku, can. cat). Tel. from (námamu, tel. stripe + pilli, tel. cat). Mal. from (pulli, mal. spot + púçça, mal. cat). Tam. from (vari, tam. stripe + púnai, tam. cat). Title otherwise Rusty-spotted cat. Felis [marjauram] rubiginosa, felidæ [deeptaucsham], digitigrada, carnivora, mammalia [sastanam, 9], of naturalists [jantoo]. Alias Felis jerdoni; Leopardus sumatrensis; Viverriceps rubiginosa.—"*a*" Greenish gray, with a faint rufous tinge; beneath and inside of limbs white; a white superciliary streak, extending on the side of the nose; two dark face streaks; top of head and nape with four narrow dark brown stripes, becoming interrupted posteriorly, and passing into a series of rusty-colored spots on the back and sides, somewhat longitudinal on the back, but roundish on the sides; tail short, more rufous than the body, and uniform in color, or very indistinctly spotted, the tip not dark; the lower surface, and inside of the limbs with large dark brown spots; feet rufous-gray above, black on the soles; ears small; whiskers long, white; fur short and very soft. This cat varies somewhat both in the ground-color of the fur and the character of the spots. Procured in the vicinity of Nellore and Madras. This cat frequents grass in the dry beds of tanks, brush-wood, and occasionally drains in the open country and near villages, and is not a denizen of the jungles.—"*b*" Akin is the Spotted wild cat. Felis torquata of naturalists. Ground-color of the fur cat-gray, more or less fulvescent, or pale grayish fulvous; with numerous small black roundish spots; on the head, nape and shoulders, the spots are smaller, and tend to form longitudinal lines on the occiput and nape; some distinct cross bands on the limbs, with one or two black streaks within the arm; cheek striped as usual; the breast spotted, but the belly almost free from spots, tail short, with a well defined series of dark rings and a black tip, ears externally dull rufous, with a very small dusky pencil-tuft; cheek stripes as usual; paws blackish underneath.——*Poonoogoo poonay* (गन्धमार्जार - gandhamárjára, San.; سنور الزباد - sinnauruzzabád, Ar.; گربهٔ زباد - gurbahizabád, Pers.; مشك بلی - mushkbillí, Hind.; رسه - rase, Malay; ಪುನುಗಿನಬೆಕ್ಕು - punuginabekku, Can.; ಪುನುಂಗುಪುಚ್ಚೆ - punungupuççe, Too.; పునుగుపిల్లి - punugupilli, Tel.; ଶାଳିୟାପୋତି - sáliyápotni, Oor.; മെരുക് - meruku, Mal.; ගන්ධමෘග - gandhamriga, Singh.; புனுகுப்பூனை - punuguppúnai, Tam.). San. from (gandha, san. fragrance + márjára, san. cat). Ar. from (sinnaur, ar. cat + zabád, ar. musk). Pers. from (gurbah, pers. cat + zabád, pers. musk). Hind. from (mushk, pers. musk + billí, hind. cat). Can. from (punugu, can. civet + bekku, can. cat). Tel. from (punugu, tel. civet + pilli, tel. cat). Mal. from (mriga, san. animal). Singh. means fragrant animal. Tam. from (punugu, tam. civet + púnai, tam. cat). Title otherwise Civet cat. Viverra civettina, viverrinæ, viverridæ, digitigrada, carnivora, mammalia [sastanam, 11], of naturalists [jantoo]. The civets proper are animals of more or less elongated form, with the muzzle produced, and a long and generally tapering tail. The tongue is rough from rigid papillæ directed backwards; and most of them have a large glandular pouch between the anus and the genital organs, secreting an odorous substance called civet. The pupils contract circularly. They are nocturnal in their habits; and, according to their genus, are more or less carnivorous in their habits.—"*a*" The species above-mentioned is specially called the Malabar civet cat, being found on the Malabar coast, from the latitude of Honore to Cape comorin, and very possibly it extends further north. Its hair is long, coarse, and of a dusky or brownish grey, and marked with interrupted transverse bands or spots in rows, two obliquely transverse black lines on the neck; the snout, throat, and neck are white; the tail tinged with black. From the shoulders along the back a mane or crest of lengthened hair. This species closely resembles the African civet; only that in the latter the mane begins on the occiput.—"*b*" Allied is the Lesser civet cat. Viverricula malaccensis of naturalists. Alias Genetta rasse; Viverra bengalensis, gunda, indica, malaccensis, pallida, rasse. Tawny gray or grayish brown, with several longitudinal lines or streaks on the back and croup; the side spotted more or less in rows; some transverse bands on the sides of the neck, and also a few indistinct lines; abdomen without spots; head darker, with a black stripe from the ear to the shoulder; tail long, with eight or nine complete dark rings. The native civet of commerce is extracted from this species kept in confinement.—"*c*" Indian allied species not here found are:—Prionodon gracilis or malayan linsang, Prionodon maculosus or spotted linsang, Prionodon pardicolor or tiger-civet or linsang, Viverra megaspila, Viverra zibetha or large civet cat.——*Shiringy poonay* (शार्दूलबिडाल - shárdúlabidála, San.; वाघट - vághata, Mahr.; چیتا بلا - chítábillá, Hind.; اريمو اكر - árimauakar, Malay; ಹುಲಿಬೆಕ್ಕು - hulibekku, Can.; ఆకుచిరుత - ákuchiruta, Tel.; കാട്ടൻപൂച്ച - kátanpúçça, Mal.; சிவிங்கிப்பூனை - shivingippúnai, Tam.). San. from (shárdúla, san. leopard + bidála, san. cat). Mahr. from (vyághra, san. tiger). Hind. from (chítá, hind. cheetah + billá, hind cat). Malay from (árimau, malay, tiger + ákar, malay, climbing plant). Can. from (huli, can. tiger + bekku, can. cat). Tel. from (áku, tel. leaf + chiruta, tel. leopard), meaning thin. Mal. from (kátan, mal. wild + púçça, mal. cat). Tam. from (shivingi, tam. pard + púnai, tam. cat). Title otherwise Leopard cat. Felis [marjauram], bengalensis, felidæ [deeptaucsham], digitigrada carnivora, mammalia [sastanam, 9], of naturalists [jantoo]. Alias Felis ogilbii, chinensis, herschellii, javanensis, jerdoni, minuta, nepalensis, pardochrous, sumatrensis, tenasserimensis, undata, wagati; Leopardus ellioti, Wagati from mahratta. Ground hue varying from fulvous gray to bright tawny yellow, occasionally pale yellowish gray or yellowish, rarely greenish-ashy, or brownish gray; lower parts pure white; four longitudinal spots on the forehead, and in a line with these four lines run from the vertex to the shoulders, the outer one broader, the centre ones narrower, and these two last are continued almost uninterruptedly to the tail; the others pass into larger bold, irregular, unequal, longitudinal spots on the shoulders, back, and sides, generally arranged in five or six distinct rows, decreasing and becoming round on the belly; two narrow lines run from the eye along the upper lip to a dark transverse throat band; and two similar transverse bands run across the breast, with a row of spots between; tail spotted above, indistinctly ringed towards the tip; the inside of the arm has two broad bands, and the soles of all the feet are dark brown; there is generally a small white superciliary line. A variable species. Most abundant in Wynaud, and the forest tract along the Western ghauts; rare on the east coast.

POOND (பூண்டு - púndu, *Tam.*). Plant, applied generally to medicinal plants.——*Poodimadaca* (పూడిమడక - púdimadaka, Tel.). From (púdi, tel. village + madaka, tel. plough). Village, Port; Vizagapatam dist., Sarwasiddhy tal.; pop. 1,589; lat. 17° 30′; long. 83° 02′; from Vizagapatam S.W. 23 miles; from Yellamanchily E. 9 miles. Was a port for exportation till 1884 when it was abolished. Has a conspicuous land mark called the pillar rock.——*Poody* (పూడి - púdi, Tel.). Means village. Village, Port; Nellore dist., Polore division; pop. 758; lat. 13° 51′; long. 80° 16′; from Armegam S.S.E. 3 miles; from Madras N. 51 miles; from Nellore S.S.E. 44 miles; from Polore N.E. 18 miles; from Poolicat N. 29 miles; from Raupore E.S.E. 52 miles. Near point Poody, the southernmost port of Nellore district. Boats are made and repaired.——*Poondy* (పూండి - púndí,* Tel.; பூண்டி - púndi, Tam.). From (púndu, tam. shrub).—"*a*" Shrubbery or garden; village. Pariah proper name [peyar].—"*b*" Village, Port; Tekkaly zemindarry; pop. 980; lat. 18° 40′; long. 84° 29′; from Barwah S.W. 17 miles; from Chetterpore S.W. 59 miles; from Chicacole N.E. 43 miles; from Madras N.E. 467 miles; from Nowpada N.E. 11 miles. Small port on Orissa coast at mouth of Mahendratanaya, having several rocks projecting seaward from north-east ¾ east. Port is marked by a white obelisk [laut], 50 feet high on a hillock, 19 feet above the sea. A few yards east is flagstaff, 75 feet high, and north at same distance is travellers' bungalow [q.v.]. Anchorage is with the obelisk bearing north-west by west. Under Sea customs superintendent of Calingapatam. Road to Kimedy and Central provinces.

POONGANORE (పుంగనూరు - punganúru, *Tel.* punganúr *). From (pungamma, tel. a woman who constructed the tank + úru, tel. village).——(1) Zemindarry, North arcot. Area 648 square miles. Population 92,023. Language Teloogoo. Above ghauts, north-west of district. Bounded west by Mysore; north by Madanapully talook of Cuddapah; east by Chundragherry and Chittore talooks; and south by Pulmanair talook. One of the Cuddapah polliems [q.v.]. The family settled in the country in thirteenth century. The founder, Seetappa gownivaur, orginally settled at Varigapully in Chittore talook. In A.D. 1249 he founded Sangattore and built the fort there. In 1479 the head of the family, Timmayya gownivaur, founded the present town of Colaur and built its fort. His son Immady timmayya gownivaur drove away Adil shah when he attacked Penoocondah. Krishna deva royel for this act granted him the district of Auneeull near Oossoor without tribute, and gave title of Royel. He built Jangamcottah and Hoscote 25 miles west of Colaur and later fortified Auneeull. His sway extended over Auneeull, Colaur, Jangamcottah, Hoscote and Soogatore, which at his death were divided by his two sons. The elder, Chikkayya timmayya, from whom the present Zemindar is descended, took Colaur and Soogatore. He later built the fort of Poonganore. In 1642 the country was taken by the Mahrattas, in 1713 by the Cuddapah nawaub and, afterwards by Hyder. The family was restored by the British in 1799. In 1841, the present zemindar, then eleven years old, succeeded. He was installed in 1847 and received a permanent sunnud [q.v.] in 1861. The present peshcush [q.v.] is Rs. 66,821. Natural features are those of Mysore plateau. The south-eastern portion is drained by Cowndinyanuddy, which passes through Pulmanair into Goodiyattam; the waters of the north-west flow northwards, uniting eventually, with the Bauhoodah river of Cuddapah. The finest jungle is in the east. Paricondah jungles on the west and Basavapooram on the south afford extensive pasture grounds leased out by zemindar. The soil is light loam [pasalay munn]. Granite [caroomcull] is obtained throughout, and lime [choonam] at Paulamanda, Poonganore, Suddam. Iron sand [irooppoo manal] is collected in most hill streams, but chiefly near Auvoolapully, Cundore, and Chembacore. The metal is sold in Sowdapully fair. Excellent breed of cows [maud, pasboo]. Weaving of coarse cloths and cumblies [q.v.]. The former by Pariahs, and the latter by Coorumbar [q.v.]. There are also a few braziers. Exports are chiefly tamarinds [q.v.], sugar [q.v.], jaggery [q.v.], gram [q.v.], and jungle produce in the shape of tanning barks [chamrah]. Imports are almost confined to salt [ooppoo] and fine cloths. Places of archæological interest:—Auvoolapully, Baulasamoodram, Bheemagaunipulley, Chadalla, Chintamaucoolapully, Cottacote, Cundore, Goottapulley, Modgalapully, Peddacoorapully, Poojagaunipulley, Poonganore, Ramasamoodram, Somala, Sowdapully, Yedapaujoney. Principal trig. stations:—Auvoolapully-droog, Chintamaucoolapully. The leading places, &c., in the zemindarry are the following.——*Auvoolapully droog* (ఆవులపల్లి దుర్గము - ávulapallidurgamu, Tel.). From (ávu, tel. cow + palli, tel. village + durga, san. fort). Trig. station; lat. 13° 23′ 23·90″; long. 78° 55′ 06·08″; height 3,829 feet; from Auvoolapully E.S.E. 4 miles; from Poonganore E. 21 miles.——*Chintamaucoolapully* (చింతమాకులపల్లి - chintamákulapalli, Tel.). From (chintamánu, tel. tamarind tree, tamarindus indica, linn. + palli, tel. village). Trig. station; lat. 13° 35′ 38·90″; long. 78° 51′ 24·08″; from Chintamaucoolapully S. ¾ mile; from Poonganore N.E. 23 miles.——*Cowndinyanuddy* (కౌండిన్యనది - kaundinyanadi, Tel.). See sep. title.——*Peddacoorapully* (పెద్దకురప్పల్లి - peddakurappalli, Tel.). From (peddakurappa, tel. proper name + palli, tel. village). Chinnacoorappa his brother founded another village. Village; pop. 108; lat. 13° 23′; long. 78° 28′; from Chittore W.N.W. 47 miles; from Poonganore N.N.W. 10 miles. Inscriptions of Vijianugger dynasty. Temple on hill to Vauleeshwarasawmy. Annual festival in November or December.——*Poonganore* (పుంగనూరు - punganúru, Tel.). See below.——*Royelpett* (రాయల్పేట - ráyalpéta, Tel.). From (ráyalu, tel. king + péta, tel. suburb). Village; pop. 975; lat. 13° 20′; long. 78° 46′; from Chittore W.N.W. 26 miles; from Poonganore E.S.E. 11 miles. Weekly market. Trade in tamarind [q.v.] fruit. Jaggery [q.v.] manufactured.——*Sowdapully* (చౌడపల్లి - chaudépalli, Tel.). From (chaudéshvari, tel. durgá, the goddess of barren salt marsh + palli, tel. village). Village; pop. 1,546; lat. 13° 26′; long. 78° 44′; from Chittore W. 31 miles; from Poonganore E.N.E. 10 miles. On elevated ground. Ancient temple with fine carvings. Annual festival in April or May. Weekly fair. Commerce by Comaties [q.v.]. Iron ore [auhan]. Coarse cumblies [q.v.] manufactured. ——(2) Sub-Magistracy, North arcot district. Pay Rs. 100. ——(3) Town, Head-quarters of Zemindarry and Deputy tahsildar; North arcot dist., Poonganore zemindarry; pop. 5,565; lat. 13° 22′; long. 78° 37′; from Arnee N.W. 68 miles; from Chittore W.N.W. 37 miles; from Madras W. 117 miles; from Ranipett W.N.W. 59 miles; from Tripatty W.S.W. 60 miles; from Vellore N.W. 49 miles. Zemindar's palace, ancient building, in which accommodation for European travellers is set apart. In front is courtyard, containing dens in which wild beasts are confined, and a museum with a collection of curiosities, the most remarkable being life-sized models representing various native castes. Old fort. Ruins of a large Roman catholic chapel bearing date 1780. Climate suited to cultivation of roses [gool]. In April, after local festival to Maunica royasawmy, a large cattle fair. Poonganore samstaunam or Poonganore government has given rise to a proverb in native usage for nominal government but real anarchy.

POONJAH (ಬೆಟ್ಟ - betta, *Can.*; మెట్ట - metta, *Tel.*; புன்செய் - punsey, *Tam.*). From (pul, tam. inferior + shey, tam. cultivation). Otherwise Poonjey. Land which cannot be irrigated and is therefore unfit for the growth of rice [q.v.], but fit for dry grain [q.v.] cultivation [nunjah]. Poonjah baughayet is dry land rated as garden cultivation. Poonjah mail nunjah are wet crops on fields classed as dry. Poonjah varavoo nunjah, meaning dry land coming under wet, is poonjah converted into nunjah [q.v.]. Tidal poonjah, from (tidal, tam. high ground), are high lands dependant entirely on rainfall [mauLavaury, mazhay, vellaumay]. See vol. I, 112.——*Poonyicara* (പുഞ്ചിക്കര - púññikkara, Mal.). From (puñcha, mal. wet land + kara, mal. village). Island; Cochin state, Cochin tal.; lat. 9° 59′; long. 76° 18′; from Ernacolum N.W. 2 miles; from Cochin N. 1¼ miles. In the Cochin backwater. Bungalow [q.v.] used by the Resident. The residency is known as Balgotty. Population mostly Christians, but Jews [jonaca] and Concanies [q.v.] are also found. Two Roman catholic churches.

POONJAM (పుంజము - punjamu, *Tel.*; புஞ்சம் - puñjam, *Tam.*). Literally a collection. In Teloogoo a collection of 60 threads and in Tamul of 120 threads skeined [nesavoo], ready for the formation of a warp [pauv] for weaving. A cloth is denominated 10, 12, 14, up to 40 poonjam, according to the number of times 60, or else 120, is contained in the total number of threads [nool] in the warp. Poonjam thus also came to mean a cloth of the length of one poonjam as usually skeined; this usual length is 36 cubits, or 18 yards, and the width from 38 to 44 inches, 14 lbs. being the common weight; pieces of half length were formerly exported as Salampores [q.v.].

POONOOGOO (गन्धमार्जारबीज - gandhamárjárabíja, *San.*; جند بیدستر - jundíbedastar, *Ar.*; آش بچگان - áshibachagán, *Pers.*; جند - jund, *Hind.*; جن - jun, *Dec.*; ಪುನುಗು - punugu, *Can.*; పునుగు - punugu, *Tel*; പുഴുക - puzhuku, *Mal.*; புனுகு - punugu, *Tam.*). Title from tamul. San. from (gandha, san. fragrance + márjára, san. cat + víja, san. seed). Ar. from (jund, ar. medicine + bedastar, ar. beaver). Pers. from (ásh, pers. gruel + bachagán, pers. children). Hind. from arabic. Ar. also (kasiyatikalbulbahr), meaning testicles of sea dog. Pers. also (kháyahisagiábí), meaning testicle of water dog. Tel. also (nírukukkabíjam), meaning water + dog + seed. Tam. also (shunnu), from deccany; (nírnáyvirai), meaning water + dog + seed; (punuguççattam), meaning civet + ventricle of the civet cat. Title otherwise Civet, Zibet perfume. Product of Viverra civettina [poonoogoo poonay]. Chiefly used, diluted, as perfume; also considered anodyne and antispasmodic, resembling castor;

when good, is clear yellowish white, soft, unctuous, of about consistence of honey [shahad]; like musk [custoory], its smell is unpleasant till diluted; sometimes adulterated with ox-gall [gorochanay], storax [q.v.], or honey [shahad]; antispasmodic to a certain degree, used as perfume to augment smell of odoriferous substances, chiefly waters and spirits, such as the lily of the valley, roses [gool], rhodium, orange [q.v.] flowers, yellow saunders, &c. Cf. castor, concrete substance obtained from two small bags in the preputial follicles of the beaver, castor fiber; not found here.

POONYET (پونیت - punyat, *Burm.*). A honey-comb black resin [raul], met with in burmah, formed by a hymenopterous insect, which obtains the resinous matter from hopea odorata, roxb. [caung], dipterocarpus turbinatus [gurjan], and canarium strictum, roxb. [black dammer]; it constructs its hive in the hollows or bifurcations of trees, the crevices of rocks and on ground; a trumpet-shaped entrance is constructed of the resinous matter, protruding for about a foot in length, and widening to about the same extent; to obtain the hive, the trees have in majority of cases to be hewn down, each yielding about 20 lbs. The principal use of Poonyet is for caulking boats, for which purpose it is mixed with earth-oil or petroleum [naphtha, munn teilam].

POOR (पुर - púr, *San.*). To fill.——*Poonnama* (పున్నమ - punnama, Tel.). From (paurnamí, san. full moon). Full-moon day [powrnimay].——*Poorah* (پورا - púrá, Hind.). Complete. ——*Pooram* (पुर - pura, San.; پور - púr, Hind.; ಪುರ - pura, Can.; పురము - puramu, Tel.; പുരം - puram, Mal.; புரம் - puram, Tam.). From (pri, san. to fill). A populous centre [coody]. A place containing large buildings surrounded by a ditch and extending not less than one coss [q.v.] in length. If it extends for half that distance it is called a khaitam. If less than that, a carvatam or small market town. Any smaller cluster of houses is called a graumam [poory, pore, poro].——*Pooruntacan* (पुरान्तक - purántaka, San.). From (pura, san. town + antaka, san. destroyer). A contracted form of Tripoorauntacan, a name of Shiva [q.v.].——*Poorna chundran* (పూర్ణచంద్రుడు - púrnachandrudu, Tel.). Full moon [poonnama, powrnimay]. Ardha chundran is literally half moon, but applied to crescent moon also. Baula chundran is young or waxing moon or moon of the first quarter.——*Poornam* (पूर्ण - púrna, San.). Full.——*Poornaubhishaicam* (पूर्णाभिषेक - púrnábhishéka, San.). From (púrna, san. full + abhishéka, san. ablution). An ablution [snaunam] ceremony in Shacty [q.v.] worship. See vol. I (83).——*Poornaudy* (పూర్ణాది - púrnádi, Tel.). From (púrna, san. full). Intoxicating electuary composed of all kinds of narcotics [mookhadiraut].——*Poornay* (पूर्णा - púrná, San.; பூரணை - púranai, Tam.). Means full. Name of the fifth, tenth, and fifteenth days [tity] in a lunar fortnight [pacsham]. As a proper name means like the full moon [poonnama, powrnimay]; the wife of Ayenaur [ayen, poodcalay]. Poornaykizhavan, from (kélvan, tam. husband), is conversely the husband of Poornay, Ayenaur.——*Poornayya* (ಪೂರ್ಣಯ್ಯ - púrnayya, Can.). From (púrna, san. short for púrnapraña, san. having perfect knowledge, epithet of madhwa, the reformer + ayya, can. father, titular affix). Hindoo 2nd or pers. name [peyar].——*Poorniinay* (पूर्णिमा - púrnimá, San.). Same as Powrnimay.——*Poory* (पुरि - puri, San.; پوری - púrí, Hind.; ಪುರಿ - puri, Can.; పురి - puri, Tel.). From (pri, san. to fill). Populous centre [coody]. A small city [pooram, pore, poro].——*Pore* (पुर - pura, San.; پور - púr, Hind.; ಪುರ - pura, Can.; పురము - puramu, Tel.; പുരം - puram, Mal.; புரம் - puram, Tam.). Town. Suffix in place names [pooram, poory, poro]. ——*Poro* (ପୁର - poro, Tel.). Ooriya corruption of (pura, san. town). Town. Suffix in place names [pooram, poory, pore].——*Powrnamausy* (पौर्णमासी - paurnamási, San.). Day of full moon. ——*Powrnimay* (पौर्णिमा - paurnimá, San.; పౌర్ణమి - paurnami, Tel.). From (púrna, san. full). Day of full moon. Lunar [chaundramaunam] festival [pundigay, 3e]. The fifteenth day [tity] of the waxing moon [shoocla pacsham] of any lunar month [chaundra mausam]. The following are the full-moon days for the year which are especially observed:—Caurtigay, Chittray, Hootaushanam, Maula, Shrauvanam, and Vyausan.

POORA (പുര - pura, *Mal.*). A house, chiefly thatched house of a Teeyan [mana, teeyan]. For Ootpera or feeding houses see sep. title.

POORAH (पुरा - purá, *San.*). Of old.——*Pooram* (പൂരം - púram, Mal.). From (púrva, san. former). Short for Audy pooram. Also the eleventh constellation [nacshatram] in the moon's path. Same as Poobbam.——*Pooraunam* (पुराण - purána, San.). See sep title.——*Pooraunican* (పౌరాణికుడు - pauránikudu, Tel.). From (purána, san. legend so called). Hindoo third name. Generally applied to bramins versed in pooraunams [q.v.] and able to expound them to others [peyar].——*Poorohit* (पुरोहित - puróhita, San.). From (puras, san. before + hita, san. placed). Family or village priest [acharry]. The office of a poorohit is to prognosticate what are good and what are evil days for beginning any affair, or for putting it off; to avert by muntrams [q.v.] or prayers the pernicious effects of maledictions or the influence of malign constellations [nacshatram, raushy]; to assign names to new born children and calculate nativity [jautacam]; to bless new houses, wells, or tanks; to purify temples and consecrate them; and to imbue idols [shilay, vigraham] with the divine essence [matam].——*Poorvam* (पूर्व - púrva, San.). From (puras, san. before). Prior [poorva mimaumsam].

POORAM (പുറം - puram, *Mal.*; புறம் - puram, *Tam.*). Side, outside, back. Distinguish from Pooram, a town [poor]. Suffix in place names; as Malapooram, meaning hill side. Prefix in place names; as Pooramala, meaning outer mountain [poram]. ——*Paracoody* (பறக்குடி - parakkudi, Tam.). From (puram, tam. outside + kudi, tam. inhabitant). An outsider, a cultivator without hereditary rights. Pykasht of N. india [oolcoody]. See vol. I, 112.——*Pooranaud* (പുറനാട് - puranátu, Mal.). From (above + nátu, mal. country). Foreign land; title of the Cotiote rajahs.——*Poorangcadom* (പുറങ്കടം - purankatam, Mal.). From (above + katan, mal. debt). An additional loan taken from a caunacaur; same as Caunom poorangcadom. See vol. II, 104. ——*Poorapaud* (പുറപ്പാട് - purappátu, Mal.). From (above + petu, mal. to fall). Going forth. The net produce or net rent payable to a Jenmy [q.v.] after deducting interest [palisha] or advances made by the tenant and the Government tax or Nigoody [caunom, otty].——*Poorattavan* (புறத்தவன் - purattavan, Tam.). From (above + avan, tam. suffix of third person sing.). Ayenaur [ayen] who is always by the side as watchman. ——*Pooravoo* (புறவு - puravu, Tam.). From (puram, tam. outside). Hilly forest tract.——*Poracoody* (புறக்குடி - purakkudi, Tam.). Same as Paracoody.——*Poram* (പുറം - puram, Mal.). Outside. Prefix in place names, as Poracaud, meaning outer forest.——*Poramboke* (புறம்போக்கு - purambókku, Tam.). From (puram, tam. excluded + pókku, tam. a way). Lands reserved as being required for purposes other than those of cultivation; such as the sites of villages, beds of tanks, banks of channels, &c. [cadaypoke].——*Poravaday* (புறவடை - puravadai, Tam.). From (puram, tam. foreign + adai, tam. resort). A field given to other people to till.——*Porca* (പുറക്കാട് - purakkátu, Mal.). From (pura, mal. outside + kátu, mal. jungle). Title otherwise Piracada. Village; Travancore state, Quilon division, Ambalapoya tal.; pop. 6,036; lat. 9° 21′; long. 76° 25′; from Ambalapoya S. 2 miles; from Alleppey S. 10 miles; from Bombay S.S.E. 690 miles; from Cochin S. 42 miles; from Trivandrum N.W. 71 miles. Large Concany town on the coast. Formerly a separate principality, known as Champakacherry, and the principal port of the country. It passed to Cochin in 1678, and to Travancore in 1746. Both the Dutch and Portuguese had a settlement here, and the remains of the Portuguese fort still stand. Extensive mud bank here. When Alleppey is closed in the monsoon [q.v.] weather steamers call at Porca. Ships may anchor 2 miles from the shore in 6 fathoms water. Of late the mud bank [mud bay] has been shifting south towards Tottapully. A portion of the village was formerly submerged in the sea, and the eastern gate of a pagoda [q.v.] which then escaped the ruin can be still seen standing. Considerable fishing industry. Exports timber [maram], coir [q.v.], and pepper [q.v.].

POORAUNAM (पुराण - purána, *San.*; புராணம் - puránam, *Tam.*). From (purá, san. ancient) [poorah]. Literally an ancient matter. In usage it is applied to large treatises on theogony, cosmogony, history, genealogy, and connected matters. These treatises formed a comparatively modern and very important modification of vedic pantheism and oopanishad [q.v.] monotheism. The popular credence is based mainly on the Pooraunams, and the Itihausams [q.v.] or bhauratam [q.v.] and ramayanam [q.v.]. The pooranic period of hindooism is the period of its decline. In these the legends of the epic poems relating to the gods became distorted according to sectarian tendencies. Of the ideas implied by the vedic rites, scarcely a trace is visible in the pooraunams. Each pooraunam is supposed to treat of the following five [punchalutchanam] subjects:—the creation of the universe, its destruction and recreation, the genealogy of gods and heroes, the reigns of the menoos [q.v.], and the history of the solar and lunar races of kings [vamsham]. The pooraunams claim to be the inspired revealers of scientific as well as theological truth: They treat of physical science, geography [bhoogola shastram], the form of the earth [bhoomy], astronomy [jyótisham], chronology; and even in the case of one or two pooraunams, anatomy, medicine, grammar, and the use of military weapons. All this is conveyed in the form of leading dialogues, connecting numerous subordinate dialogues, in some of which a sage like Parausharan is the principal speaker and answers the inquiries put to him by his disciples. The recounting of royal genealogies consists of a dry chronicle of names. Similar chronicles were those of the early λογογράφοι, but those developed into real histories which the Indian never did. The main object of most of the pooraunams is a sectarian one. They aim at exalting one of the three members of the Trimoorty [q.v.], Bramha [q.v.], Vishnoo [q.v.], or Shiva [q.v.]. Pooraunams are composed chiefly in the simple shlocam [q.v.] metre, with occasional passages in prose. Those recognized in the south of India are the eighteen:—Agneyam, Bhaugavatam,

Bowddhicam, Bramham, Bramhaundam, Bramha veivartam, Coormam, Cundam, Gauroodam, Lingam, Marcandoyam, Matsyam, Nauradeeyam, Pndmam, Sheivam, Vaurauham, Vaumanam, Veinavam. The Veinavam means the Vishnoo pooraunam. The most comprehensive and complete is the Vishnoo pooraunam, and the most popular the Bhagavat pooraunam. The rest are very little known except to Bramins. They are usually distinguished as either Veishnava or Sheiva. The Matsyam, Coormam, Lingam, Shivam, Cundam are considered to be Sheiva, the Agny medium, and the remainder Veishnava or leaning in that direction [matam, oopapooraunam, stalapooraunam]. See vol. I (75), (87).——*Agny pooraunam* (अग्निपुराण - agnipurána, San.). Called also Agneyam. The fire pooraunam. The contents are miscellaneous and unconnected, and include chapters on law, grammar, prosody, &c. An ancient pooraunam called Vayoo, which is probably one of the oldest of the eighteen, is often substituted for Agny.——*Audy pooraunam* (आदिपुराण - ádipurána, San.). From (ádi, san. first). Another name of Bramha pooraunam.——*Basava pooraunam* (ಬಸವಪುರಾಣ - basavapurána, Can.). From (basava, san. bull, proper name). Lingayet [q.v.] work on first founder of that religion. Five different versions; two Canarese, two Sanscrit, one Teloogoo. The Canarese are by Bheema cavy and Yellendra shadaucsharappa. The former best. The two Sanscrit are by Shuncara aradhya and Basalingappa. The Teloogoo is by Somaradhya.——*Bhagavatpooraunam* (भागवतपुराण - bhágavatapurána, San.). From (bhagaván, san. the fortunate vishnu). Title otherwise Bhaugavatam. One of the latest. Teaches Veishnava doctrines. So named from its being dedicated to the glorification of Bhagavat [q.v.] or Vishnoo [q.v.]. It consists of 18,000 shlocams [q.v.], distributed amongst 332 chapters, divided into twelve scandhams [q.v.] or books. It exercises a more direct and powerful influence upon the opinions and feelings of the people of India than perhaps any other pooraunam. Its tenth book narrates in detail the history of Krishnan [q.v.], and has been translated into all the languages of India. It is understood to have been written by the grammarian Vopadeva who lived about the twelfth or thirteenth century at the court of Hemaudry, Rajah of Devagiry, i.e., Deogarh or Dowlatabad. The Teloogoo version of the Bhaugavatam was written by Potrauz and is in the highest esteem with all the Teloogoos. It is not very faithful; much is omitted and much is inserted. The Roocminy calyaunam, the Gajendra mocsham, and other episodes selected from it, are excessively popular.——*Bhavishya pooraunam* (भविष्यपुराण - bhavishyapurána, San.). From (bhú, san. to be). Literally future. One of the six Raujasa pooraunams or those which relate to Bramha [q.v.].——*Bramha pooraunam* (ब्रह्मपुराण - brahmapurána, San.). From (brahma, san. creator). Revealed by Bramha [q.v.] to Dacshan [q.v.]. Also called Audy pooraunam.——*Bramhaunda pooraunam* (ब्रह्माण्डपुराण - brahmándapurána, San.). From (brahma, san. creator + anda, san. egg); bramha's universe. Sets out in 12,000 verses the magnificence of the egg of Bramha [q.v.], and an account of the future calpams [q.v.]. No longer procurable in a collective body. Adhyautma ramayanam [q.v.] a popular work considered a part.——*Linga pooraunam* (लिङ्गपुराण - lingapurána, San.). From (linga, san. phallic emblem of shiva). The pooraunam in which Shiva has explained the objects of life [aram, poorshaurtam], viz., virtue, wealth, pleasure, and final liberation at the end of the agny calpam [q.v.]. It is mystical and spiritual.——*Madura pooraunam* (மதுரைப்புராணம் - mathuraippuránam, Tam.). From (mathurai, tam. the town, so called). Same as Tirvilaiyaudal.——*Marcandeya pooraunam* (मार्कण्डेयपुराण - márkandéyapurána, San.). From (mrikandu, san. proper name). Is quite unsectarian in character.——*Matsya pooraunam* (मत्स्यपुराण - matsyapurána, San.). Communicated by Vishnoo [q.v.] as a fish to the seventh Menoo [avatar, satyavratan].——*Pudma pooraunam* (पद्मपुराण - padmapurána, San.). From (padma, san. lotus). The latest.——*Raujasa pooraunam* (राजसपुराण - rájasapurána, San.). From (rajas, san. passion). Any pooraunam which relates to Bramha [q.v.]; from his own peculiar goonam [q.v.] Rajas [q.v.].——*Sheiva pooraunam* (शैवपुराण - shaivapurána, San.). From (shiva, san. the deity). Contains the genealogies of the patriarchs [rishy], a description of the universe, and the incidents of the first six Manwantarams [q.v.], intermixed with legends and praises of Shiva [q.v.]. A long account of the Pitries [q.v.] or progenitors is peculiar to this pooraunam; as are stories of some of the most celebrated rishies [q.v.], who were engaged in the distribution of the vedams [q.v.].——*Stala pooraunam* (स्थलपुराण - st'halapurána, San.). From (st'hala, san. place). Otherwise called Mahautmyam [q.v.]. Histories of temples [coil, pagoda], enumerated in connection with the local gods. They generally begin with the creation of the universe, and relate the appearances of Shiva or Vishnoo at the particular spot which led to the erection of the temple. Though consisting of legendary notices, examination elicits historical facts. They usually purport to be taken from some of the larger Pooraunams; but such is not the case. They always contain much self-assertion. For example in that of Madura there is the statement that the Vedams are old and obsolete books, and that the substance of the Vedam [q.v.] and of true wisdom consists in worshipping the lingam [q.v.] in the great pagoda [q.v.] at that place. The Shreerunga mahautmyam states that the goddess manifested in the Cauvery river obtained the boon of being equal to the Ganges. There is a Sheiva legend at Conjeeveram, that Soobramanyan [q.v.] took Bramha [q.v.] to task, and confined him in prison, himself undertaking the work of creation. At Tripatty there is a legend that the hill is a peak of Mahameroo [q.v.]. In a variety of instances it is asserted that the stain of the most malignant of sins or the murder of a Bramin can be washed away by bathing in the local pool. All these documents are intended to show that celebrated events in Hindoo mythology took place at particular localities, the names of which have been transferred from Northern india or trans-northern india to Southern india. The following is abstract of a specimen stalapooraunam from Conjeeveram. After the customary invocations, the eulogy of the Tondainaud [tonday] is begun. This is introduced by the poetical description of a mass of clouds, raised from the sea, appearing like the body of Vishnoo, between which clouds personified and Badavaugny or great heat personified, a dispute arises; the clouds threaten to make use of the rainbow in combat, and they teach a muntram [q.v.] to the vajrangam or lightning. A profusion of rain [mazhay] falls from a body of clouds, like the assemblage of the four clouds, which once according to the Tirvilaiyaudal [q.v.] rained on Madura. The hills were refreshed and honey streamed down from them; the channel of the Palaur river was filled; and a great number of other rivers or streams, like good and evil in their results centering in one deity, mingled at length altogether in the sea. The course of the Palaur especially gives occasion to poetical description of the country through which it flows. With these subjects, inclusive of the descriptive matters, one hundred and forty-five stanzas are occupied. The varalaur or fountain head of the pooraunam is then entered on by a reference to a great assemblage of rishies [q.v.] in the Neimishauranyam [q.v.] wilderness. These, all of fame in Hindoo books, are represented as discoursing together concerning the chief good. One declares in favor of penance; another in favor of equity; another in praise of alms; another is for truth or integrity; another prefers sacrifice; another domestic virtue; another utter renunciation of family cares and all worldly concerns [aram, poorshaurtam, yanyam]. As they are thus occupied without agreeing, Soota rishy, expert in the Sheiva system and learned in the eighteen pooraunams which were delivered through him, comes among them; is saluted by them; and with general consent is appointed to decide their difference of opinion. He refers to a section of the Scaunda pooraunam, delivered by Sanatcomauran to Vyausan, by Vyausan to Shoocan, and by the latter to himself. Sootan then proceeds to explain his meaning. The Sanatcomaura patalam or chapter follows. Sanatcomauran, the son of Bramha [q.v.], was occupied in meditation when Oomay [q.v.], wife of Shiva [q.v.], passed, so that he did not rise to pay her homage, on which account Nundikeshwaran [q.v.], the vehicle [vauhan] of Shiva, spoke of him contemptuously as having no more sense than a camel, and denounced on him the doom of becoming a camel [ottagam]. Under this metamorphosis the sage came to Canjy or Conjeeveram and is made to declare that after comparing the Neimishauranyam, the Cooroo cshetram, and other places famous in Hindoo story, upon the whole, Conjeeveram wilderness deserved preference. Bramha interceded with Shiva in order to get the metamorphosis of his son removed; but Shiva declared that what had been done by one of his servants he did not choose to reverse, referring the case to Nundikeshwaran. Application being accordingly made, one favorable look from Nundy [q.v.] immediately removed the evil, and restored the sage to his proper form. He then received instructions respecting the different modes of life [aushramam], domestic, ascetic, and the like, with the respect due to each. Sanatcomauran says that there are many Sheiva fanes and asks which of them is chief. Nundy after reflection tells him that he recollects what Shiva told to Oomay, which it will be proper for Sanatcomauran to hear. Chapter on the speciality of the fane. After introductory matter, an enumeration is given of several distinguished Sheiva fanes, beginning from the extreme south and ending at the extreme north. Beyond Himalaya one is mentioned, and then Keilausam the last. Among these Shiva declares the chief to be Conjeeveram. Immediately afterwards an exception is made in favor of Caushy, or Benares; and then Shiva informs Oomay that he always reigns, together with herself, rejoicing at Conjeeveram, and so great is the merit of that place that if any one reside there only for a cshanam or moment, his beatification [mocsham] is certain. At the close of the chapter, Sootan says that Shiva told this to Oomay, and Nundy to Sanatcomauran, who told it to Vyausan, and the latter to himself, who repeated it to the sages assembled in the Neimishauranyam, as aforesaid. Whosoever hears or reads this chapter will be healed of all sickness, will receive prosperity, and long dwell with children on earth, and afterwards receive beatification in a future world. The animus of this pooraunam is throughout ultra Sheiva, and pours contempt on Bramha and Vishnoo, the latter especially, his being the rival fane at the present day in highest estimation, owing to the number of Veishnavas at and near Madras [charitram].——*Tirtondar pooraunam* (திருத்தொண்டர்ப்புராணம் - tiruttondarppuránam, Tam.). From (tiru, tam. holy + tondan, tam. servant of god). Pooraunam of sixty-three devotees of Shiva. Also Periya pooraunam. This contains special memoirs of Sambandhan, Soondran and Appar, the three most celebrated of the sixty-three devotees [aroopatt moover]. ——*Vishnoo pooraunam* (विष्णुपुराण - vishnupurána, San.). From (vishnu, san. the deity). The most celebrated of the eighteen pooraunams. It is in six books, and is dedicated to the exaltation of Vishnoo, whom it identifies with the supreme being. Book I treats of the creation of the universe; the peopling of the world and the descent of mankind from seven or nine patriarchs [rishy], sons of Bramha [q.v.]; the destruction of the universe at the end of a Calpam [q.v.] and its recreation or pratisargam; and the reigns of kings during the first Manwantaram [q.v.]. Book II describes the various worlds [locam], heavens [swargam], hells [naracam], and planetary spheres [graham]; and gives the formation of the seven circular continents [dweepam] and concentric oceans [samoodram]. Book III describes the arrangement of the Vedams [q.v.], Itihausams [q.v.], and Pooraunams [q.v.] by Vyausan [q.v.], and the institution and rules of caste, in which it follows and resembles Menoo [q.v.]. Book IV gives list of kings and dynasties. Book V corresponds to Book X of the Bhagavat pooraunam and is devoted to the life of Krishnan [q.v.]. Book VI describes the deterioration of mankind during the four ages [yoog], the destruction of the world by fire and water [pralayam], and its dissolution at the end of a Calpam [q.v.]. The above is a bare outline of the contents of this pooraunam. It is encyclopædical, like the others, and is rich in philosophical speculations and curious legends. The Teloogoo version in eight books is by Vennelacunty soorayya. This contains only the Poorva caundam, first half of the Sanscrit original. For secondary pooraunams see Oopapooraunam.

POORSHAM (पुरुष - purusha, *San.*). From (pur, san. body + shi, san. to rest). A man, a male, the soul [matam]. Supreme spirit or soul of the universe, unaffected by works, affliction, &c., and having the appellation Pranavam [q.v.] or Om [q.v.]. Also measure of a man's height [niloovoo]; strictly measure of a man with his hands raised over his head; approximate actual value is 8 english feet; applied to measure depth of water.——*Poorshamedham* (पुरुषमेध - purushamédha, San.). From (above + médha, san. sacrifice). A human sacrifice [yanyam].——*Poorshauntaram* (पुरुषान्तर - purushántara, San.). From (above + antara, san. different). Succession duty.——*Poorshaurtam* (पुरुषार्थ - purushárt'a, San.). From (above + art'ha, san. object). Object of human pursuit in this world. There are four chief objects of human existence [aram]:—dharmam, virtue; artam, wealth; caumam, pleasure; and mocshams, final emancipation.——*Poorsha vauhanan* (पुरुषवाहन - purushaváhana, San.). From (above + váhana, san. vehicle). Coobairan [q.v.] whose vehicle [vauhan] is a man.——*Poorshottama deo* (పురుషోత్తమదేవ - purushóttamadéva, Tel.). The greatest of Gajapaty [q.v.] rulers of Orissa. Invaded Conjeeveram because the king refused to marry his daughter to the sweeper of Juggernaut; defeated him and took prisoner his daughter whom he married [charitram]. See vol. I (151).——*Poorshottaman* (पुरुषोत्तम - purushóttama, San.). From (above + uttama, san. best). The supreme being. Hindoo 2nd or pers. name [peyar].——*Poorshottapore* (పురుషోత్తపురము - purushóttapuramu, Tel. purushottapur *). From (purushóttama, san. vishnu, the best of men + pura, san. town).—"*a*" Deputy tahsildarry; Ganjam district. Pay Rs. 100.—"*b*" Town, Deputy tahsildar's head-quarters, Sub-registrar's station; Ganjam dist., Berhampore tal.; pop. 3,541; acres 1,591; lat. 19° 31′; long. 84° 56′; from Balligooda S.E. 77 miles; from Berhampore N.N.E. 16 miles; from Chetterpore N.W. 13 miles; from Chicacole N.E. 104 miles; from Madras N.E. 530 miles; from Russellcondah S.E. 33 miles; from the sea W. 24 miles. On Rooshcoolya, but being gradually driven back by river encroachment. During last quarter century four streets have disappeared.

POORVA (పురవ - purava, *Tel.*; മണങ്ങു - manannu, *Mal.*; நெத்தலி - nettali, *Tam.*). Tam. from (ney, tam. ghee + tól, tam. skin). Tel. also (nattu). Tam. also (púzhalam). Anchovy. The genus Engraulis, clupeidæ, physostomi, teleostei, pisces [matsyam, 40], of naturalists [jantoo]. Mouth very wide, upper jaw projecting; body oblong or elongated, compressed, and serrated along the abdominal edge; teeth small. The species best known to the natives are:—indicus, malabaricus, purava.

POOSA (పూస - púsa, *Tél.*). Bead.——*Poosapauty* (పూసపాటి - púsapáti, Tel.). From (púsa, tel. a bead + pádu, tél. village). Family name of the Vizianagram chiefs. See vol. I, 54. Distinguish from Pashoopaty [q.v.].

POOSH (पुष् - push, *San.*). To increase, unfold.——*Poodcalay* (पुष्कला - pushkalá, San.; புட்கலை - pudgalai, Tam.). From (pushkalá, san. splendid). Wife of Ayenaur [ayen, poornay].——*Poodcalay manaulan* (புட்கலைமணாளன் - pudgalaimanálan, Tam.). From (pushkalá, san. wife of aiyyanár + manálan, tam. husband). Husband of Poodcalay; Ayenaur.——*Pookhrauj* (पुष्पराग - pushparága, San.; ياقوت اصفر - yákútiasfar, Ar.; پکھراج - pukhráj, Hind.; పుష్యరాగము - pushyarágamu, Tel.; പുഷ്പരാഗം - pushparágam, Mal.; புட்பராகம் - pudbarágam, Tam.). Title from hindostany. San. from (pushpa, san. flower + rága, san. color). Ar. from (yákút, ar. garnet + asfar, ar. saffron colored). Hind. corrupted from sanscrit. Tel., &c., from sanscrit. A topaz. χρυσόλιθος was exported from Egypt to Barbaricon in Indo Scythia and to Barugaza, Mouziris [cranganore] and Nelkunda [cullada] according to the Periplus; some take this to be the topaz. Found in Burmah and Ceylon. In the latter country a genuine, greenish yellow-colored topaz is improperly called the yellow tourmaline [q.v.]; a light-colored smoky topaz is improperly called a yellow crystal; and a dark-colored smoky topaz is called a brown crystal [palingoo, spaticam]. The occidental topaz, or that which comes from Saxony and Siberia, contains a greater proportion of silex [ratnam].——*Pooshcaram* (पुष्कर - pushkara, San.). Lotus [nelumbo]. Feast [pundigay, 6d] held once in twelve years at sacred rivers [cotipully, kistna].——*Pooshcarny* (पुष्करिणी - pushkariní, San.). Tank with lotus growing. Any sacred pool.——*Pooshpacam* (पुष्पक - pushpaka, San.). From (pushpa, san. flower). The self-moving aerial chariot of Coobairan [q.v.] carried off by the demon Ravanan [q.v.] and used by him till he was slain by Rama [q.v.], who then employed the car [rath] to transport himself and Seetay [q.v.] along with Lutchmanan [q.v.] to Ayodhyay.——*Pooshpagherry* (ಪುಷ್ಪಗಿರಿ - pushpagiri, Can.). From (pushpa, san. flowers + giri, san. hill). Sanscrit name (subrahmanyagiri), meaning soobramanyan's hill. Hill; South canara dist., Ooppinangady tal.; lat. 12° 40′ N.; long. 75° 44′ E.; height 5,626 feet; from Mangalore E.S.E. 60 miles; from Poottore E.S.E. 33 miles. Prominent bullock-hump-shaped peak of the Soobramanya range of mountains, a spur of the Western ghauts [q.v.] at the north-western boundary of Coorg, and on the border of Hassan district of Mysore. The ascent is difficult. On the lower slopes there is dense jungle, haunted by wild elephants [q.v.]; on the summit are many ancient stone cairns [paundicoozhy].——*Pooshpam* (पुष्प - pushpa, San.). Flower [phool, poo]. Plant second term. Ex., where transl. is of first term:—Bassia latifolia (lódhrapushpa), symplocos racemosa; Bombax malabaricum (raktapushpa), red; Cordia obliqua (gandhapushpa), fragrant; Evolvulus emarginatus (añjanapushpa), black; Guettarda speciosa (himapushpa), dew, (pannírpushpam), rose-water; Hibiscus rosa-sinensis (ódhrapushpá), orissa; Mesua ferrea (nágapushpá), serpent, (gajapushpamu), elephant; Michelia champaca (dípapushpa), lamp; Morinda umbellata (klíbapushpá), neuter; Musa paradisiaca (vrishapushpa), sprinkling; Ocimum basilicum (paççapushpam), green; Peucedanum graveolens (shatapushpá), hundred; Pimpinella anisum (shatapushpá), hundred; Rauwolfia serpentina (vasupushpá), beautiful; Rosa centifolia (pannírpushpam), rose-water; Saraca indica (gandhapushpá), fragrant; Solanum ferox (chandrapushpá), moon. See gloss. paragraphs.——*Pooshpicam* (पुष्पिका - pushpiká, San.). Having flower [phool]. Plant second term. Ex., where transl. is of first term: Gynandropsis pentaphylla (arkapushpiká), sun; Jasminum humile (hémapushpiká), gold; Peucedanum graveolens (chámarapushpika), fan; Woodfordia floribunda (dhátripushpika), (dhátupushpiká), mineral, from red flower. See gloss. paragraphs.——*Pooshpy* (पुष्पी - pushpí, San.). Having flower. Plant second term. Ex., where transl. is of first term:—Andropogon aciculatus (chórapushpí), thief; Bauhinia variegata (támrapushpí), copper; Clitorea ternatea (shankhapushpí), conch; Crotalaria verrucosa (shanapushpí), crotalaria juncea; Evolvulus alsinoides (nílapushpí), blue, (sankpushpi), conch; Leucas linifolia (drónapushpí), cup; Pimpinella anisum (avákpushpí), turned down. See gloss. paragraphs.

POOTCOOLY (ಪುಟ್ಕುಳಿ - putkuli, *Can.*). Todah waist cloth.

POOTERAH (پوتیرا - puterá, *Hind.*). Elephant grass.

POOTHOO (പുതു - putu, *Mal.*; புது - puthu, *Tam.*). New.——*Pondicherry* (புதுச்சேரி - puthuççéri, Tam.). See sep. title.——*Poodameny* (പുതുമേനി - putuméni, Mal.). From (putu, mal. new + méni, mal. shape). New or Veeroye [q.v.] coinage; so called in contradistinction to the Palayameny or ancient coinage [naunyam].——*Poodoocottah* (புதுக்கோட்டை - puthukkóttai, Tam.). See sep. title.——*Poothiya* (പുതിയ - putiya, Mal.; புதிய - puthiya, Tam.). New.——*Poothiyacovilagam* (പുതിയകോവിലകം - putiyakóvilakam, Mal.). From (putiya, mal. new + kóvilakam, mal. palace). Residence of the junior; rajah of Calicut [covilagam]. See vol. I, 53.——*Poothooval* (പുതുവൽ - putuval, Mal.). Reclaimed or newly cultivated land.——*Poothooveppoo* (പുതുവെപ്പു - putuveppu, Mal.). New deposit. Vypeen near Cochin, a deposit formed in 1341. The special Cochin era is also called by this name [saca].——*Poottan* (പുത്തൻ - puttan, Mal.). Means new. A silver Cochin coin, first struck during the Dutch occupation. 10 cash = 1 poottan; 5½ poottans = 1 fanam [naunyam, 2d]. Approximate actual value, 1 poottan = 10 pies. The coin is made of impure metal and weighs $\frac{1}{32}$ of a tolah [q.v.], while at present 19¼ poottans are exchanged for a rupee [q.v.]; a double poottan has shiva [q.v.] on one side wearing a crown, and a snake emerging from either side of his chair and meeting over his head; round his neck is a string of skulls [capaulam], in his left hand wheel of fate, round each shoulder two circlets, on each wrist two bracelets; on the obverse a palankeen [q.v.]; formerly instead of shiva there was a chunk [q.v.] shell. See vol. I, 609.——*Poottancoor* (പുത്തൻകൂറ - puttankúru, Mal.). From (puttan, mal. new + kúr, mal. division). The Malabar syrian [q.v.] christians who separated from Rome [pazhayacoor].——*Poottore* (புத்தூர் - puttúr, Tam.*). From (puthu, tam. new + úr, tam. village). Village, Head-quarters of Deputy tahsildar, Narrainavaram division, Railway station; North arcot dist., Carvetnugger zemindarry, Narrainavaram division; pop. 2,686; lat. 13° 26′; long. 79° 36′; height 493 feet; from Arnee N.N.E. 56 miles; from Curvetnugger E. 7 miles; from Chittore E.N.E. 35 miles; from Madras W.N.W. 57 miles; from Narrainavaram W.N.W. 3 miles; from Ranipett N.N.E. 38 miles; from Tripatty S.E. 15 miles; from Vellore N.E. 46 miles. Railway station serves Carvetnugger and Narrainavaram. Mostly weavers. Fair Thursday.

POOTRAN (पुत्र - putra, *San.*). From (put, san. hell + trá, san. to protect). Son [comauran]. The tamulian appreciation of children is rather domestic than religious, as among the bramins. See the following from Cooral:—பெறுமவற்றுள் யாமறிவ தில்லை யறிவறிந்த மக்கட் பேறல்ல பிற—"among all the benefits that may be acquired, we know no "greater benefit than the acquisition of intelligent children."—எழுபிறப்புந் தீயவை தீண்டா பழிபிறங்காப் பண்புடை மக்கட் பெறின்—"the evils of the seven births will not "touch those who obtain children of a good disposition, free from "vice."—தம்பொருள் என்பதம் மக்க ளவர்பொருள் தந் தம் வினையான் வரும்—"men will call their sons their "wealth, because it flows to them through the deeds which the "sons perform on their behalf."—அமிழ்தினு மாற்ற வினி தேதம் மக்கள் சிறுகை யளாவிய கூழ்—"the rice in "which the little hand of their children has dabbled will be "far sweeter to the parent than ambrosia."—மக்கண்மெய் தீண்ட லுடற்கின்ப மற்றவர் சொற்கேட்டல் இன்பஞ் செவிக்கு—"the touch of children gives pleasure to the body "and the hearing of their words, pleasure to the ear."—குழலி னிதி யாழினி தென்பதம் மக்கண் மழலைச்சொற் கேளா தவர்—"the pipe is sweet, the lute is sweet, say "those who have not heard the prattle of their own children."—தந்தை மகற்காற்று நன்றி யவையத்து முந்தி யிருப்பச் செயல்—"the benefit which a father should confer on his son "is to give him precedence in the assembly of the learned."—தம்மிற்றம் மக்க ளறிவுடைமை மாநிலத்து மன்னு யிர்க் கெல்லா மினிது—"that their children should possess "knowledge is more pleasing to all men of this great earth than "to themselves."—ஈன்ற பொழுதிற் பெரிதுவக்குந் தன் மகனைச் சான்றோ னெனக்கேட்ட தாய்—"the mother "who hears her son called a wise man will rejoice more than "she did at his birth."—மகன்றந்தைக் காற்று முதவி யிவன்றந்தை யென்னோற்றான் கொல்லெனுஞ் சொல்—"so to act that it may be said by what great penance did "his father beget him, is the benefit which a son should render "to his father."——*Pootra joovvy* (పుత్రజువ్వి - putradzuvvi, Tel.). Title from small size. Same as Small tsiela.——*Pootranjeeva* (पुत्रञ्जीव - putrañjíva, San.; जीवनपुत्र - jívanaputra, Mahr.; पुत्रजिब्बेमणि - putrajibbémani, Conc.; ಪುತ್ರಜೀವ - putrajíva, Can.; కుదురుజువ్వి - kudurudzuvvi, Tel.; പൊങ്കോലം - ponkólam, Mal.; බුත්සරණ - butsarana, Singh.; குறுப்பாலை - kuruppálai, Tam.). Title from sanscrit. San. from (putra, san. son + jíva, san. life); the fruits used to make necklaces [maulay], and are reputed to be of prolific efficacy, when worn by children to keep them in good health. Mahr. means enlivening son. Can. from (putra, san. son + jíva, san. life). Tel. from (kuduru, tel. firm + dzuvvi, tel. ficus tsiela, roxb.). Mal. from (pon, mal. gold + kólam, mal. body). Singh. means booddha's foot. Tam. from (kurumai, tam. shortness + pálai, tam. milky plant). San. also (sutajíva), meaning giving life to children. Tel. also (yárála), meaning giving life to children; (máháputrajívi), meaning great + the tree. Tam. also (pongólam), meaning gold + body. Title otherwise Grey barked nageia, Pongolam, Wild olive. Botanically Putranjiva roxburghii, wall., euphorbiaceæ [vricsham, 118]. Putranjiva from sanscrit. Alias Nageia putranjiva; Putranjiva sphærocarpa. Tree; branchlets and petioles pubescent; leaves elliptic, unequal-sided at the base, serrately denticulate; glomerules of male flowers numerous; segments of male calyx densely ciliate-pubescent, sparingly puberulous at the back; ovary tawny-silky; fruit oblong-ellipsoid, clothed with thick, pale, rusty hairs; flowers small, yellowish white. A large timber tree with an erect straight trunk and a large spreading shady head composed of innumerable expanding branches; fruit always one-seeded; mountains; flowering in hot weather. Leaves and stones of the fruit given in decoction for colds and fevers. Leaves lopped for fodder. The nuts are threaded and worn as necklaces [maulay, munkah] for children, and are supposed to keep them in good health; olive brown oil from seeds used for burning. Wood grey, shining, moderately hard, close-grained; sometimes used for tools and turning. No other common species here. The same title is given to Polyalthia longifolia, benth. [ashocam].——*Pootra pradam* (पुत्रप्रद - putraprada, San.). Means child-giving. Same as Prickly brinjaul.——*Pootra shrainy* (पुत्रश्रेणी - putrashréní, San.). Means multitude of children, from fruits. Same as Neeroory.

POOTTA (పుట్ట - putta, *Tel.*). Ant hill. Plant first term, as growing near one. Ex., where transl. is of second term:—Agaricus campestris (puttagodugu), umbrella; Gymnema sylvestre (puttapodara), bush; Macaranga indica (puttatámara), nelumbium speciosum; Mærua arenaria, var. glabra (puttatíga), creeper; Wrightia tomentosa (puttajillédu), calotropis gigantea. See gloss. paragraphs.——*Pootla* (పుట్ల - putla, Tel.). From (putta, tel.). Ant hill. Plural locative form. Suffix in place names.——*Pootlore* (ಪುತ್ತೂರು - puttúru, Can.). From (puttu, can. ant hill + úru, can. town). Town, Divisional and talook head-quarters; South canara dist., Ooppinangady tal.; pop. 3,745; lat. 12° 46′; long. 75° 15′; from Coondapore S.S.E. 70 miles; from Madras W. 344 miles; from Mangalore S.E. 25 miles; from Oodipy S.E. 50 miles; from Soobramanya W. 28 miles. Owing to the Coorg insurrection which first broke out at Bellarey, 16 miles south-east, troops were stationed here from 1837 till the introduction of the mofussil [q.v.] police in 1860.

POOTTOO (పుట్టు - puttu, *Tel.*). To be born.——*Poottooga* (పుట్టుక - puttuga, Tel.). From (puttu, tel. to be born). Birth. Suffix in place names; as Bhauvanapoottooga, meaning bhauvanan's birth place.

POOTTY (పుట్టి - putti, *Tel.*; புட்டி - putti, *Tam.*). A basket; also a wicker-boat.—"*a*" Measure of capacity. 20 tooms = 1 pootty; 30 pootties = 1 garce [alavay, 3b]. Teloogoo districts. Varies with toom. Same as candy.—"*b*" Superficial measure. 20 coonchams = 1 pootty [alavay, 2b]. Vizagapatam and Godavery. In former land which will yield a pootty of grain, equal to 1,768 square feet. In latter land requiring a pootty of seed; pootty varying from 8 to $11\frac{1}{2}$ acres. Compare Vithaicottay.—"*c*" Bazaar weight. 20 maunds = 1 pootty [niray, 2b]. Approximate actual value, 1 pootty = 500 lbs. avoir. Ganjam, Vizagapatam and Kistna. Same as Candy and Bhauram. See vol. I, 609; II, 510, 511, 512, 516, 519, 520.

POOZHY (பூழி - púzhi, *Tam.*). Means dust. One of the twenty-one nauds [q.v.] around Paundyam [q.v.] where corrupt Tamul was spoken. So the sandy tract to the west of the ghauts [q.v.] ruled by Cheran [q.v.].——*Poozhiyan* (பூழியன் - púzhiyan, Tam.). Ruler of Poozhy country. Title of the Chera king. See vol. I (142).

POPPADAM (पर्पट - parpata, *San.*; پاپڑ - pappar, *Hind.*; ಹಪ್ಪಳ - happala, *Can.*; అప్పడం - appadam, *Tel.*; പപ്പടം - pappatam, *Mal.*; அப்பளம் - appalam, *Tam.*). Mal. from (parippu, mal. dholl + ata, mal. cake). Tam. from (appu, tam. to clap on with the hand). Called also Hopper [q.v.]. A light thin cake of the flour of Phaseolus mungo, linn., var. radiatus [black gram], and other flours, and flavored with salt [ooppoo] and asafœtida [q.v.]. When required for use it is fried in ghee [q.v.] and eaten with rice [q.v.]. Used by Europeans with curry [q.v.] and rice. For Appalacauram see under Cauram.

POR (போர் - pór, *Tam.*). Corn-stack. Por cooripp is an account of stacks cut.

PORA (പൊറ - pora, *Mal.*). Mountain.——*Pooraly* (പുരളി - purali, Mal.). From (pora, mal. hill). A fort belonging to the old kings of Cottayam in the interior of Travancore state. Hence Pooraleeshan, lord of Pooraly, was one of the titles of those kings. This title is now poetically applied to the kings of Travancore. Confounded probably by the Greeks with παραλία, coast [q.v.].——*Porlattiry* (പോറളാതിരി - póralátiri, Mal.). From (above + álu, mal. own + tiri, mal. holy, title). The title of Cadatnaud rajah. See vol. I, 52.——*Potta* (പൊറ്റ - potta, Mal.). Means high ground. So rice [q.v.] grown there; paddy [q.v.] dark; Malabar.——*Pottay* (പൊറ്റ - potta, Mal.; பொற்றை - pottai, Tam.). Small hills [coonn].

PORAH (پھوڑا - phorá, *Hind.*). Canker in horses [ashwarogam].

PORNY (பொருணி - poruni, *Tam.*). Means toddy. Native name of the Tamrapurny. See vol. I (1).

POROO (பொறு - poru, *Tam.*). To bear.——*Poroopp* (பொறுப்பு - poruppu, Tam.). Duty. A quit-rent [jody] levied from lands originally granted in inam [q.v.] or rent-free.——*Porooppan* (பொருப்பன் - poruppan, Tam.). From (poruppu, tam. hill). Chief of a hilly tract [coorinjy, desham].

POROOL (பொருள் - porul, *Tam.*). From (poru, tam. to join). Subject-matter. One of the five parts of lacshanam [q.v.]. It is divided into two parts:—Agaporool, treating of rules for amatory poems, and Pooraporool, treating of public or state affairs. Porool also means wealth [sott]. The following are from the Cooral on the subject of wealth:—உறுபொருளு

முல்கு பொருளுந்தன் ஒன்னார்த் தெறுபொருளும் வேந்தன் பொருள்—"unclaimed wealth, wealth acquired "by taxes, and wealth got by conquest of foes are all the wealth "of the king."—குன்றேறி யானைப்போர் கண்டற்றாற் றன்கைத்தொன் றுண்டாகச் செய்வான் வினை—"an undertaking of one who has wealth in his hands is like "viewing an elephant-fight from a hill-top."—செய்க பொருளைச் செறுநர் செருக்கறுக்கு மெஃகதனிற் கூரிய தில்—"accumulate wealth; it will destroy the arrogance of your foes; "there is no weapon sharper than it."—ஒண்பொருள் காழ்ப்ப வியற்றியார்க் கெண்பொரு ளேனை யிரண்டு மொருங்கு—"to those who have honestly acquired an abundance of "riches, the other two virtue and pleasure are things easy of "acquisition."—உள்ள முடைமை யுடைமை பொருளுடைமை நில்லாது நீங்கி விடும்—"the possession of energy "of mind is true property; the possession of wealth passes away "and abides not."—ஆக்க மிழந்தேமென் றல்லாவா ரூக்க மொருவந்தங் கைத்துடை யார்—"they who are possessed "of enduring energy will not trouble themselves saying we have "lost our property."—ஆக்க மதர்வினாய்ச் செல்லு மசைவிலா வூக்க முடையா னுழை—"wealth will find its own "way to the man of unfailing energy."—அறனறிந்து வெஃகா வறிவுடையார்ச் சேருந் திறனறிந் தாங்கே திரு—"lutchmy knowing the manner in which she may approach "will immediately come to those wise men who, knowing that "it is virtue, covet not the property of others."—தாளாற்றித் தந்த பொருளெல்லாந் தக்கார்க்கு வேளாண்மை செய்தற் பொருட்டு—"all the wealth acquired with perseverance "by the worthy is for the exercise of benevolence."—பொருளற்றார் பூப்ப ரொருகா லருளற்றா ரற்றார்மற் றாத லரிது—"those who are without wealth may, at some future "time, become prosperous; those who are destitute of kindness "are utterly destitute; for them there is no change."—அருட்செல்வஞ் செல்வத்துட் செல்வம் பொருட்செல்வம் பூரியார் கண்ணு முள—"the wealth of kindness is wealth "of wealth, in as much as the wealth of property is possessed "even by the basest of men."——*Aseiya porbol* (அசையாப் பொருள் - asaiyápporul, Tam.). Immovable property [stanvaram].——*Aseiyoom porool* (அசையும்பொருள் - asaiyum·borul, Tam.). Movable property [jangamam].——*Pollachy* (பொள்ளாச்சி - polláççi, Tam.). See sep title.——*Porool shelvy* (பொருள்செல்வி - porulselvi, Tam.). The rich woman; Lutchmy [q.v.].

PORTIA (गर्दभाण्ड - gardabhánda, *San.*; भेंडी - bhéndí, *Mahr.*; پارس پیپل - páraspípal, *Hind.*; پارس پپل - páraspippal, *Dec.*; ಹೂವರಸಿ - húvarasi, *Can.*; ಜೋಗಿಮರ - jógimara, *Too.*; గంగరావి - gangarávi, *Tel.*; പൂവരച്ചു - púvarachu, *Mal.*; සූර්ය - súrya, *Singh.*; பூவரசு - púvarasu, *Tam.*). Title from tamul. San. from (gardabha, san. ass + anda, san. testicle); from roots [stone banyan]. Mahr. from (bhánda, san. the portia tree). Hind. from (páras, hind. portia + pípal, hind. ficus religiosa, linn.). Dec. from hindostany. Can. from (húvu, can. flower + arase, can. peepul tree). Tel. from (ganga, tel. excellent + rávi, tel. ficus religiosa, linn.). Mal. from tamul. Tam. from (pú, tam. flower + arasu, tam. peepul tree, ficus religiosa, linn.). San. also (párisha), sanscritized from tamul; (kubéráksha), meaning coobairan's eye [bonduc]; (supárshvaka), meaning having good sides; (nandivriksha), meaning happiness + tree. Mahr. also (lákhípimparí), meaning lac-colored portia tree; (párósápimpala), meaning side + ficus religiosa, linn.; (pimparí). Hind. also (pahárípípal), meaning hilly ficus religiosa, linn.; (imlíkhurásání), meaning khorassan, tamarindus indica, linn. Dec. also (páraskájhár), meaning portia tree. Can. also (arasha), meaning king; (jógiyarale), meaning mendicant + ficus religiosa, linn.; (kandarola); (bangáli). Too. also (jógiattasa). Tel. also (gangarénu), meaning excellent + jujube tree, zizyphus jujuba, lamk.; (munigangarávi), meaning sage + portia tree; (gárachettu) [firework plant]. Mal. also (púpparutti), meaning flower + gossypium herbaceum, linn.; (kallál), meaning stone + banyan, ficus bengalensis, linn.; cf. stone banyan. Singh. also (gansurí), meaning fragrant portia. Tam. also (púpparutti), meaning flower + cotton tree, gossypium herbaceum, linn., from similar flowers. Title otherwise Bendy tree, Demarara mahoe, Flowering cotton, Flowering peepul, Khorassan tamarind, Pauras, Poplar-leaved hibiscus, Poplar mallow, Soorya, Tulip tree, Umbrella tree. Botanically Thespesia populnea, corr., malvaceæ [vricsham, 25]. Alias Hibiscus populneoides, populneus; Malvaviscus populneus; Thespesia populneoides. Tree; leaves roundish-cordate, acuminated, quite entire, five to seven-nerved, sprinkled beneath with small rusty scales; calyx truncated; involucel three-leaved; capsule five-celled, coriaceous; cells about four-seeded; flowers yellow, with a dark blood-colored eye. A favorite ornamental tree, thriving best near the sea; never wild; easily reared from cuttings, of quick growth, and yielding good shade; abounds in old gardens and about all european stations; flowers succeeded by turban-shaped black seed-pods, which hang on the tree a long time; capsule is filled with a yellow pigment [rangh] like liquid gamboge [q.v.]. The bark of the trunk and large branches is reddish brown, very rough and scaly externally, and of reddish-grey color internally; it is odourless and possesses no distinct taste; it contains a garnet-colored resin [raul] and a small quantity of tannin. The fresh and half-ripe capsule is green, roundish and obtusely five-angled, with a cup-shaped and persistent calyx; it abounds in yellow, viscid and somewhat acrid juice, consisting of a gum-resin [googal] forming a yellow emulsion with water. The bark is medicinally a mild astringent tonic, but neither alterative nor insecticide, as is supposed by natives; the fresh fruit or capsule is insecticide. Decoction of the bark; take of the bark, cut into small pieces, six ounces; water, three pints; boil until the liquid is reduced to one pint, and strain. Decoction of the capsules; take of the fresh and half-ripe capsules, cut into small pieces, ten ounces; water, three pints; boil until the liquid is reduced to one pint, and strain when cool. The yellow juice is best obtained by wounding or making small incisions on the fresh and half-ripe capsules, but the juice is generally so scanty that it cannot be collected in a vessel. Dose; of the decoction of the bark, from two to four fluid ounces, three or four times a day; the decoction of the fresh capsules is not intended for internal use, but is employed externally as a wash for the parts affected with scabies. Substituted; the fresh capsules, for ung. hydrarg. nitratis and ung. sulph. co.; and the bark, for calumba [q.v.]. The gamboge is a good external application in scabies and other cutaneous diseases. Frequently used for roadside avenues [shaulay], and is valuable from its easy growth and from the large amount of annual cuttings; it prefers the sea air and saline soil; the singhalese dye yellow [shanyam] with the capsules, sepals, and calyx; a good fibre [naur] from the bark. Timber is strong, straight, even-grained and durable, pale reddish fading to reddish brown, easily worked. There is another species Lampas, called by natives hill cotton; otherwise three-pointed hibiscus; largish tree with heart-shaped leaves; deep primrose flowers with a dark purple eye; young twigs yield a fibre [naur]; fit for rope and paper.——*Jungle portia* (காட்டுப்பூவரசு - káttuppúvarasu, Tam.). Same as Pehimbia.——*River portia* (ஆற்றுப்பூவரசு - áttuppúvarasu, Tam.). Same as Caunchy.

PORTO NOVO* (பறங்கிப்பேட்டை - parangippéttai, *Tam.*). Title from portuguese, meaning new harbour. Vern. from (farangí, bind. european + péttai, tam. town). Mahomedan name (mahmúdbandar), meaning excellent + port. Town, Port, Sea customs superintendent's head-quarters, Railway station; South arcot dist., Chidambaram tal.; pop. 8,869; acres 1,142; lat. 11° 30′; long. 79° 48′; from Chidambaram N.E. 8 miles; from Codiyampolliem N.N.E. 6 miles; from Cuddalore S. 15 miles; from Madras S.S.W. 115 miles; from Pondicherry S. 32 miles. On Coromandel coast situated north of the mouth of Vellaur. The river mouth is small and admits only coasting craft. Larger vessels anchor 2 miles off shore in six or seven fathoms of water with good holding-ground in mud. Formerly of considerable prosperity, but suffered much in Mysore wars. Cowle [q.v.] for making a settlement obtained by the English from Harjoe rajah, soobahdar [q.v.] of Jinjee, in 1681. When English commenced trading in 1682, the Danes and Portuguese were already established. In 1748 the factory being in a ruinous condition, a good house was purchased for 500 pagodas [q.v.] and a Resident appointed. In 1749 the Madras army marching against Tanjore halted here. In 1758 captured by the French with Fort St. David and Cuddalore; French driven out in 1760 by Coote after his defeat of Lally at Wandiwash; burned by Hyder ally in July 1780. In 1781 Sir Eyre Coote marched out of Porto novo with 8,000 men to meet the whole army of Mysore, some 60,000 strong, under Hyder; in the battle which ensued at Mettapolliem, the English won the most signal victory of the war. The French landed a large force here in 1782 and marched thence with Tippoo and captured Cuddalore. Restored to England under the treaty of Versailles, on the 1st February 1785. In 1824 efforts were made to establish iron [anhan] works. The Porto novo iron company established a large factory to work ore brought from Salem, but the enterprise was abandoned. The Iron company cut a short canal of their own from the Vellaur into the backwater adjoining the embouchure of the Coleroon before the Khan sahib's canal was rendered navigable. The canal, which is only about 2 miles long, is now much silted up. The excavation of the East coast canal at Porto novo was commenced in 1853, and considerable progress was made up to 1857, when the mutiny put a stop to it. In an old Dutch cemetery here, one of the tombstones bears date 1717. The only special manufacture is a species of mat [boriyah], made from the leaves of the wild pineapple [ananas], in imitation of those imported from Acheen [q.v.]. Trade is considerable. Weekly fair. Trig. station in lat. 11° 29′ 9·14″; long. 79° 48′ 8·58″; from Ariyagoshty E. 2 miles; from Chidambaram N.E. 7 miles; from the sea W. ½ mile.

PORTUGUESE (پرتگیس - purtagís, *Hind.*). Here means community of mixed Portuguese and Indian descent.

POTAIL (پتیل - patel, *Hind.*; ಪಟೇಲ - patéla, *Can.*). From (pata, san. a register). A Mahratta title for headman of village [balootah]. In bengal Mokaddam [q.v.]. Corresponding terms are :—Tel. peddacaup, Mal. adhicaury, Tam. monigar.

POTATO (आलु - álu, *San.* and *Mahr.*; बट्टटो - battató, *Conc.*; بطاطة - batátah, *Ar.*; آلو - álú, *Hind.* and *Dec.*; اوبی - úbí, *Malay*; ಉರುಳೆಗಡ್ಡೆ - urulegadde, *Can.*; ಬಟಾಟೆ - batáte, *Too.*; ఉరలగడ్డ - urlagadda, *Tel.*; ഉരുളക്കിഴങ്ങ - urulakkizhannu, *Mal.*; රට ඉන්නල - ratainnala, *Singh.*; உருளைக்கிழங்கு - urulaikkizhangu, *Tam.*). Title from spanish. San. from (ri, san. to go), moving and hence round. Can. from (urulu, can. round + gădde, can. root). Tel. from (urulaĭ, tam. round + gadda, tel. root). Mal. from (urula, mal. round + kizhannu, mal. esculent root). Singh. from (rata, singh. foreign + innaló, singh. plectranthus rugosus, wall.). Tam. from (urulai, tam. round thing + kizhangu, tam. esculent root). Malay also (kantang). Tel. also (álugadda). Title otherwise Common potato plant, Round root. Botanically Solanum [cooly] tuberosum, linn., solanaceæ [vricsham, 94]. Alias Lycopersicum tuberosum; Solanum esculentum, parmenteru. Perennial herbaceous plant; stem 1–3 feet high, without thorns or prickles; leaves pinnate; leaflets two or more with an odd one, entire at the margin; flowers 1–1½ inches, diameter, the wheel-shaped corolla white or purple, more or less veined; fruit globular, purplish; of the size of an ordinary gooseberry; roots produce tubers. Herbage has a slightly narcotic smell; native of peru, introduced into spain, whence into india; in wild state bitter and acrid; for many years natives would not eat them. A pure starch, obtainable from tubercles by washing with cold water; convertible into sugar [q.v.] and alcohol by fermentation. For various potatoes so called in other genera, see below. For the yams see Auloo.——*Bitter potato* (காற்கருணை - kárgarunai, Tam.). Same as Elephant yam.——*Caustic potato* (सूरण - súrana, San.). Title from roots. San. from (súr, san. to hurt). Same as Telinga potato.——*Giant potato* (विदारी - vidárí, San.; भुईकोहळी - bhuíkóhalí, Mahr.; भुइंकुवाले - bhuinkuválé, Conc.; لال شکر کندا - lálshakarkandá, Hind.; ನೆಲಕುಂಬಳ - nelakumbala, Can.; ನೆಲಕುಂಬುಡು - nelakumbudu, Too.; భూచక్రగడ్డ - bhúchakragadda, Tel.; പാൽമുതക്ക - pálmutakku, Mal.; ක්ෂීරවිදාරි - kshíravidárí, Singh.; நிலப்பூசணி - nilappúsani, Tam.). Title from size of root. San. from (vidrí, san. to split) [cashmere tree, shoonday]. Mahr. from (bhui, mahr. ground + kóhalí, mahr. benincasa cerifera, savi.). Conc. from mahratta. Hind. from (lál, hind. red + shakarkandá, hind. ipomæa batatas, lamk.). Can. from (nela, can. ground + kumbala, can. pumpkin). Tel. from (bhú, san. earth + chakra, san. wheel + gadda, tel. root). Mal. from (pál, mal. milk + mutakku, mal. the plant, modecca tuberosa, roxb.). Singh. from (kshíra, san. milk + vidárí, san. the plant). Tam. from (nilam, tam. ground + púsani, tam. cucurbita maxima, duch.). San. also (bhúmikúshmánda), meaning ground + pumpkin, benincasa cerifera, sav.; (kshírakandá), meaning milk + bulbous root; (shréshťhakandá), meaning superior + root; (vrishyavallí), meaning aphrodisiac + creeper; (ikshugandhá), meaning sugar-cane, saccharum officinarum, linn. + smell [naunal, necrmoolly, nerinjy]; (rikshagandhá), meaning bear + smell, applies to black variety; (kshírashuklá), meaning milk white; (kshíravidári), meaning milk + the plant; (mahásvétá), meaning very white. Hind. also (bhuínkumrá), meaning earth gourd. Can. also (guddagenasu), meaning hill + potato, ipomæa batatas, lam. Tel. also (dévakánchanamu), meaning god + gold; (nélagummudu), meaning ground + the plant; (mettapálatíga), meaning dry ground + milk + creeper; (chirigummudu), meaning small + the plant; (gummudu) [false zedoary, small cashmere tree]; (nallanélagummudu), meaning black + the plant. Mal. also (mutalakkanta), meaning alligator + bulbous root; (kappalkizhannu), meaning foreign root. Singh. also (kshíravallí), meaning milk + creeper. Tam. also (pálmódikká), meaning milk + the plant, modecca tuberosa, roxb.; (valli); (púçcakkirakkizhangu), meaning earth + ipomæa batatas, lam. Beng. also (bhúmikumra). Title otherwise Alligator yam, Aphrodisiac creeper, Cotton-leaved bind-weed, Earth pumpkin, Milky yam, Naila goommoodoo, Panicled bind-weed, Paulmodecca, Red sweet potato, White yam. Botanically Ipomæa [calamby] digitata, linn., convolvulaceæ [vriçsham, 93]. Alias Batatas paniculata; Convolvulus gossipifolius, insignis, paniculatus, roseus; Ipomæa eriosperma, gossipyfolia, insignis, mauritiana, paniculata, pentaloba, quinqueloba. Batatas from malay [sweet potato]. Stem twining, glabrous, thick; leaves large, palmate, five to seven-cleft, glabrous, petioled, lobes ovate-lanceolate, seldom acuminate; peduncles much exceeding the petioles, many-flowered, dichotomous; sepals ovate-rounded, concave, very obtuse, equal; corolla purple, narrowed at the base, showy; seeds long, hairy; flowering in the rainy season. A tuberous-rooted, extensive climber with large ornamental finger-formed leaves; flower large, rose-colored, with a dark purple eye. The root is a simple or branched tuber, sometimes as much as 40 to 50 lbs. in weight; externally it is of a brown color, and somewhat warty and scabrous; when a transverse section is made the cut surface is of a dirty white color, and marked by concentric rings, which are formed by the vascular and laticiferous vessels; from the latter a viscid milky fluid exudes; the taste is astringent and somewhat acrid, not unlike raw potato; the bulk of the tuber consists of a starchy parenchyme; the vascular system is scalariform; the laticiferous vessels are most numerous towards the cortical part; raphides abound. Root, dried in sun, reduced to powder, boiled with sugar and butter, is medicinally tonic, alterative, aphrodisiac, demulcent, and lactagogue. The young tapering roots of a small variety are known in the herbalist's shops as Asgand [q.v.]. The Hill giant potato is Ipomæa [calamby] pentaphylla, convolvulaceæ [vricsham, 93]; alias batatas pentaphylla; convolvulus hirsutus, munitus, nemorosus, pentaphyllus; ipomæa pilosa; twining, hirsute; leaves digitate, leaflets five, elliptic-lanceolate, entire; peduncles as long as the petioles, hirsute, one to three-flowered; sepals very hairy, lanceolate, acute, corolla a little longer than the calyx, white; capsule and seeds smooth; flowering in the rainy season; flower largish, white.——*Goa potato* (ഗോവക്കിഴങ്ങ - góvakkizhannu, Mal.). Same as Goa yam.——*Pondicherry potato* (புதுச்சேரிக்கிழங்கு - puthuççérikkizhangu, Tam.). Same as Pondicherry yam.——*Spanish potato* (بطاطة اسبانيه - batátahiisbániyah, Hind.). Same as Sweet potato.——*Striped potato* (చారకంద - tsárakanda, Tel.). See Kachvee.——*Sweet potato* (शर्करावल्ली - sharkarávallí, San.; रताळी - ratálí, Mahr.; चीनिकनंग - chínikananga, Conc.; شکر قند - shakarkand, Pers.; شکر کندا - shakarkandá, Hind.; نترالو - natrálú, Dec.; کاتیلا - kátela, Malay; ಗೆಣಸು - genasu, Can.; ಮರಕೆರೆಂಗು - marakerengu, Too.; గెనుసు - genusu, Tel.; କନ୍ଦମୂଳ - kondamúlo, Oor.; ചക്കരവള്ളി - chakkaravalli, Mal.; சர்க்கரைவள்ளி - sharkkaraivalli, Tam.). Title from taste of root. San. from (sharkará, san. sugar + vallí, san. creeper). Mahr. from (raktálu, san. the plant). Conc. from (chiní, mahr. china + kóna, mahr. yam + kanda, mahr. root). Pers. from hindostany. Hind. from (shakar, hind. sugar + kandá, hind. tuber). Too. from (mara, too. tree + kerengu, too. potato). Mal. from sanscrit. Tam. from sanscrit. San. also (raktálu), meaning red esculent root; (sharkarákanda), meaning sugar + esculent root; (lóhita), meaning reddish; (lóhitálu), meaning red esculent root; (raktakanda), meaning red esculent root; (raktapindálu), meaning red + ball + esculent root; (raktapindaka), meaning red ball. Pers. also (zardakiláhorí), meaning lahore carrot. Hind. also (rattálú), from sanscrit; (míthaálú), meaning sweet potato. Dec. also (pindálú), meaning sweet esculent root. Malay also (batatas). Can. also (maragenasu), meaning tree + sweet potato; (shígenasu), meaning sweet potato. Tel. also (chilagadamu); (chiragadamu) [red nerinjy]; (shilagadamu); (móhanamu), meaning pleasing. Mal. also (kappalkizhannu), meaning foreign esculent root; (marakkizhannu), meaning wood + esculent root; (chínikkizhannu), meaning china esculent root; (madhurakkizhannu), meaning sweet esculent root; (vallikkizhannu), meaning creeper + esculent root. Tam. also (valli), meaning beautiful, useful plant; (sharkkaraikkizhangu), meaning sugar + esculent root; (shínikkizhangu), meaning china + esculent root; (vellaivalli), meaning white + esculent root. Title otherwise China yam, Lahore carrot, Spanish potato, Sweet yam, Tuberous bind-weed. The potato of Shakespeare and old english writers. The Kissing comfits of Falstaff were conserved Sweet potatoes and Eryngo root or sea holly. Botanically Ipomæa [calamby] batatas, lam., convolvulaceæ [vricsham, 93]; specific from malay. Alias Batatas edulis; Convolvulus batatas, edulis, esculentus; Ipomæa catesbæi. Tuberous rooted plant; stem creeping, rarely twining; glossy verdant leaves variable, usually angular, also lobed, cordate; sepals five; corolla campanulate; peduncles equal in length to the petioles, three to four-flowered; flowers white outside, purple inside; native of both indies. The root is about 4 or 5 inches long, and about 2 or more round; resembling the potato, but seldom so dry. Cultivated like potato [q.v.]; will grow on any soil; ground prepared in south in pungoony [mausam] or march, on coromandel in margashiram or december and pooshyam or january, on w. coast in vrishchicam or november; land is ploughed five times; sheep-folded; sown in south in veiyaushy or may, on coromandel in margashiram or december and pooshyam or january, on w. coast the cuttings are planted generally in the month of yedavam or may; previous year's creeper is cut and buried in furrows and watered; once in eight days it is watered, and the tendrils occasionally pruned; as the tubers ripen the leaves and stems become yellow and leaves fall off; dug up after six months; brought to market at once; average price 10 imperial seers for 1 rupee. Nutritious and palatable, though slightly laxative; in taste sweet and palatable, possessing saccharine matter; natives eat the tubers, leaves, and tender shoots; herbage is employed for feeding cattle [ghaus, maud]; roasted under hot ashes or boiled in water. Two kinds, one with red tubers, the other with white; the red better.——*Tacca potato* (تکا - takka, Malay). Same as Otaheite salep.——*Telinga potato* (सूरण - súrana, San. and Mahr.; زمین کندا - zamínkandá, Hind.; کندا - kandá, Dec.; ಸೂರಣಗಡ್ಡೆ - súranagadde, Can.; ಪರಿಂಕಿಗಡ್ಡೆ - parinkigadde, Too.; మంచికంద - manchikanda, Tel.; ചീനപ്പാവ - chínappávu, Mal.; கருணை - karunai, Tam.). Title from habitat where first known. San. from (súr, san. to hurt); from caustic root. Hind. from (zamín, hind. ground + kandá, hind. tuber) [malacca yam]. Can. from sanscrit. Tel. from (manchi, tel. good + kanda, tel. yam). Mal. from (chína, mal. china + pávu, mal. root). Tam. from (karakara, tam. to feel itching in the throat) [elephant yam, wild telinga potato]. San. also (dílla); (kanda), meaning root; (arshóghna), meaning piles + killing. Hind. also (ol), meaning the root; (súran), from sanscrit; (álú), meaning potato. Can.

also (gandíra). Tel. also (kanda), meaning root; (dúlakanda), meaning itching + yam; (pátikanda), meaning waste land + yam; (úrakanda), meaning village + yam; (álukamu); (genusukanda); (tiyyakanda), meaning sweet root. Mal. also (chéna) [elephant yam, otaheite salep]; (malaíchéna), meaning hill + typhonium orixense, schott. Tam. also (karanaippalá), meaning the plant + jack tree, artocarpus integrifolia, willd.; (shénaikkizhangu). Title otherwise Caroonay root, Caustic potato, Itching yam, Piles-killer, Sooran. Botanically Amorphophallus campanulatus, blume, araceæ [vriesham, 152]. Alias Arum campanulatum, rumphii, zeylanicum; Candarum roxburghii. Stemless; leaves decompound; flowers small, mahogany-colored, sessile with respect to the surface of the ground, and appearing when the plant is destitute of leaves; spathe the length of the spadix, campanulate; margins curled; nectary none; club broad-ovate, lobate, anthers two-celled; flowers have a disagreeable odour; flowering in june. Roots resemble yam [auloo]; the small tuberosities in the roots are planted in the manner of potatoes. Roots are very caustic and abound in starch, and are employed medicinally as external stimulants. Roots are boiled like potatoes [q.v.] and eaten with mustard [rayaun]; cooked in curries [q.v.]; cut into slices, boiled with tamarind [q.v.] leaves, and made into pickles; also cooked in syrup and made into preserves. A jungle species is Lyratus, chiefly in circar [q.v.] mountains; this requires two or three boilings to render inoffensive. A species Sylvaticus is called jungle shaimay [kachvee] in vernaculars. Other species are dubius, giganteus. Compare Colocasia antiquorum, schott. [kachvee]. *Wild telinga potato* (काननकन्द - kánanakanda, San.; काडसूर्ण - kádasúrna, Conc.; جنگلی کندا - janglíkandá, Hind. and Dec.; ಕಾಡುಸೂರಣ - kádusúrana, Can.; ಕಾಟುಕೇನೆ - kátukéne, Too.; అడవికంద - adavikanda, Tel.; കാട്ടുചേന - káttuchéna, Mal.; காட்டுக்கருணை - káttukkarunai, Tam.). Title from habitat and resemblance. San. from (kánana, san. forest + kanda, san. esculent root). **Conc.** from canarese. Hind. from (janglí, hind. wild + kandá, hind. colocasia esculenta, schott.). Can. from (kádu, can. jungle + súrana, san. esculent root). Too. from (kátu, too. forest + kéne, too. amorphophallus campanulatus, blume). Tel. from (adavi, tel. forest + kanda, tel. yam, amorphophallus campanulatus, blume). Mal. from (kátu, mal. forest + chéna, mal. yam, typhonium orixense, schott.). Tam. from (kádu, tam. forest + karunai, tam. amorphophallus campanulatus, blume). Hind. also (janglíkandekágaddá), meaning wild yam root. Can. also (kandagida), the plant. Tel. also (kanda). Tam. also (karunai), meaning itching root [elephant yam, telinga potato]. Title otherwise Many-leaved dragon, Purple-stalked dragon, Wild kachvee. Botanically Dracontium polyphyllum, linn., araceæ [vriesham, 152]. Alias Arum lyratum. Stalk 1 foot, smooth, purple-colored, full of sharp variegated protuberances, with a tuft of leaves at the top; scape very short; petiole rooted; leaflets three-parted; divisions pinnatifid; root irregular, knobbed, covered with a rugged skin; flower-stalk, rising from the root, about 3 inches high; spathe oblong, opening lengthwise; flowers closely arranged on a short thick style. Roots medicinally antispasmodic and a powerful stimulant; quoted, non-officinal, in pharm. No other common species here.

POTEE (پوتی - potí, *Hind.*; పత్తి - patti, *Tel.*). Red cotton wool [cotton].

POTHAN (போதன் - póthan, *Tam.*). From (budh, san. to know). Means Bramha [q.v.], the wise. Hindoo 2nd or pers. name [peyar].

POTHY (പൊതി - pothi, *Mal.*; பொதி - pothi, *Tam.*). From (pothi, tam. to roll up, tie). A pack, bullock-load. Also close elephant [q.v.] forest.—"*a*" Grain measure. 20 yidangazhies = 1 pothy [alavay, 3d]. Approximate actual value, 1 pothy = 65 lbs. or 1 cubic foot and 547 cubic inches. Wynaud. Same as Colagam.—"*b*" Bazaar weight. 10 maunds = 1 pothy; 2 pothies = 1 candy [niray, 2a]. Approximate actual value, 1 pothy = 250 lbs. avoir. Salem, Coimbatore and Madura. In the first two pothy is 10 maunds or 250 lbs.; in Madura, is 12 toolaums or 231 lbs. Compare Tel. cuntlam, Tam. cundaga.—"*c*" Liquid measure. 8 paunays = 1 pothy [alavay, 4a]. Approximate actual value, 1 pothy = 3 cubic feet 1,536 cubic inches. Coimbatore and Trichinopoly. In Coimbatore pothy is 8 coodams of $6\frac{2}{3}$ pucka puddies or 3 cubic feet, 1,501 cubic inches. In Trichinopoly, a pothy of ghee is 105 seers of 75 tolahs or 3 cubic feet, 1,676 cubic inches, and a pothy of oil is 120 seers of 75 tolahs, 4 cubic feet, 963 cubic inches.—"*d*" Superficial measure [alavay, 2d]. Approximate actual value, 1 pothy = 2,640 square yards. Wynaud. Same as Colagam. Compare garce or veesam of Vizagapatam. See vol. I, 609; II, 509, 515, 516, 519.——*Pothigay* (பொதிகை - pothigai, Tam.). From (pothi, tam. elephant forest + kai, tam. place). Tam. also (pothiyam), meaning elephant [q.v.] forest place; also (pothimunai), meaning elephant forest peak; also (tenmalai), meaning southern mountain. Sanscrit name (agastyagiri), meaning agastyan's hill; also (chandanagiri), meaning sandal [q.v.] mountain. Greek βηττιγώ. Native name of Agastya mullay [agastyan]. Also called Periya pothigay, the great pothigay, to distinguish it from a smaller mountain adjoining it called Eindootalay pothigay or pothigay with five peaks. Mountain; Tinnevelly dist., Ambasamoodram tal.; lat. 8° 36′ 54·80″; long. 77° 17′ 16·40″; height 6,125 feet; from Ambasamoodram W.S.W. 15 miles; from Tinnevelly W.S.W. 31 miles. Here the Tamrapurny takes its rise. This mountain is the highest in the Tinnevelly range of ghauts [q.v.], and is regarded by native poets as the distinguishing mountain of the Tamul paundy country, one of the titles of the Paundy [q.v.] king being Lord of Pothiyam. It stands back nearly ten miles from the rest of the range, so that the Tamrapurny drains a considerable extent of mountain country before it emerges into the plains. Agastya mullay is visible from Palamcottah and Trivandrum. In 1852 a meteorological observatory was erected near the summit. The rainfall on the top amounts to about 300 inches in the year. The rainfall at Palamcottah, half way between the mountains and the east coast, is less than 27 inches, whilst 25 inches is the general average in the Tinnevelly plains. From the summit the whole south of Indian peninsula is seen, from Cape comorin to Cochin on one side and to Adam's bridge on the other.

POTOO (పోతు - pótu, *Tel.*). Male, as of cattle [maud]. Plant first term, often joining two genera. Ex., where transl. is of second term:—Grewia abutilifolia (pótushálmali), bombax malabaricum; Zehneria umbellata (pótudonda), cephalandra indica. See gloss. paragraphs.——*Pothanore* (போத்தனூர் - póttanúr, Tam. pódanúr *). From (póttu, tam. male buffalo + úr, tam. village). Tam. also (kallambálaiyam), meaning cullar fortified village. Village, Railway station; Coimbatore dist., Coimbatore tal. Hamlet of Cooritchy, which contains population of 5,747; lat. 10° 58′; long. 77° 02′; height 1,308 feet; from Coimbatore S.E. 3 miles. Junction of Neilgherry branch and south-west main line of Madras railway.——*Potrauz* (పోతురాజు - póturádzu, Tel.). From (pótu, tel. ox + rádzu, tel. king). Rustic god worshipped with his wife Ancaulamman [q.v.] in Teloogoo countries; goats [vellaud], pigs [soor], fowls [moorghy] and buffaloes [khoolgah] being beheaded before them.

POTTA (പൊട്ട - potta, *Mal.*). From (pottu, mal. to break). Worthless. Plant first term. Ex., where transl. is of second term:—Cyperus puncticulatus (pottappullu), grass; Sterculia fœtida (pottakkávalam), sterculia balanghas. See gloss. paragraphs.——*Pottal* (பொட்டல் - pottal, Tam.). Arid tract [desham, paulay].

POTTINGHY (పొట్టంగి - pottingi, *Tel.*). From (potti, tel. short + angu, tel. beauty) [potty].——**(1)** Division; Vizagapatam district; language Ooriya. Boundaries:—E. Saulore and Parvatipore divisions, S. Saulore and Srungavarapoocote divisions, W. Padair and Mulkangherry divisions, N. Jeypore and Coraputt divisions. A net work of steeply undulating valleys and ranges with deep nullahs [q.v.] between and occasional lofty hills. Soil red. The leading places, &c., in the division are the following.——*Nundapore* (నందపురము - nandápuramu, Tel.). From (nanda, san. felicity + pura, san. city). Village, zemindarry; lat. 18° 33′; long. 82° 47′; from Pottinghy W. 13 miles; from Vizagapatam N.W. 68 miles. Former capital of Jeypore rajahs. Old mud fort with a simhausanam [q.v.], reached by a flight of thirty-two steps. This was the place of installation. Six old temples. Temple of Sarweshwaran with inscriptions. Head-quarters of an ameen [q.v.] of Jeypore maharajah.——*Owrada* (ఔరద - aurada, Tel.). From (auru, tel. bulrush, andropogon muricatus, retz. + eda, tel. place). Zemindarry village, formerly Sub-magistrate's station. Subdivision of Jeypore agency.——*Pottinghy* (పొట్టంగి - pottingi, Tel.). See below.——**(2)** Deputy tahsildarry; Vizagapatam district. Pay Rs. 120.——**(3)** Village, Head-quarters of Deputy tahsildar and Assistant engineer, D.P.W.; Vizagapatam dist., Pauchipenta zemindarry, Pottinghy magisterial division; lat. 18° 32′; long. 82° 59′; height 3,000 feet; from Coraputt S.S.E. 23 miles; from Madras N.N.E. 410 miles; from Narsapatam N.N.E. 63 miles; from Parvatipore S.W. 36 miles; from Vizagapatam N.N.W. 61 miles; from Vizianagram N.W. 42 miles. A hill village important only as occupying head of the fine ghauts [q.v.] from Saulore.

POTTOO (బొట్టు - bottu, *Tel.*; பொட்டு - pottu, *Tam.*). From (pódu, tam. to put on). Sandal [q.v.] spot on the forehead as a sectarial mark [naumam, tilacam]. The dot is the mark of the sun [sooryan], the supreme being, or the world. Has the lines of Vishnoo [q.v.] or Shiva [q.v.] added, as the case may be [matam]. See vol. I (85).

POTTY (పొట్టి - potti, *Tel.*). Short. Plant first term, often joining two genera. Ex., where transl. is of second term:—Cucurbita pepo (pottigummadi), cucurbita maxima; Methonica superba (pottidumpa), root; Mukia scabrella (pottibudama), solanum verbascifolium. See gloss. paragraphs.——*Pottapy* (పొట్టప్పి - pottappi, Tel.). From (potti, tel. short + appi, tam. corr. of abbi, tel. titular affix). Title of the Chola [q.v.] king.——*Pottinghy* (పొట్టంగి - pottingi, Tel.). See sep. title.——*Pottivaudoo* (పొట్టివాడు - pottivádu, Tel.). From (above + vádu, tel. person). Pariah proper name [peyar].

POY (పోయు - póyu, *Tel.*). To pour.——*Poyney* (పోయిని - póyini, Tel.; பொன்னெ - ponné, Tam.). From (poy, tel. to pour). Sanscrit name (níranadí), meaning water river; also (nílanadí), meaning black river. River; North arcot dist., Chittore, Chundragherry tals. Tributary of Palaur. Rises in the rocky hills in W. of Chundragherry. Known first as Daumalcheroo. After leaving Chundragherry talook it flows through Chittore, where called Poyney. Its course is almost due south, and after receiving the Arangonda, Chittore, Eiraula and Vencatagherry flowing from Eastern ghauts [q.v.], it joins Palaur not far from Arcot. Length 45 miles, though smaller than Palaur, more frequently in flood and more useful for irrigation.

POY (பொய் - poy, *Tam.*). False.——*Poy maun* (பொய் மான் - poymán, Tam.). From (poy, tam. false + mán, tam. deer). Rock; Salem dist., Salem tal.; from Salem S.E. 6 miles. Rock between Salem and Mullore; when viewed in a particular direction, the figure of a deer [mrigam] is seen through a crevice.——*Poyyauthameyyoodaiyore* (பொய்யாதமெய்யுடையோர் - poyyáthaméyyudaiyór, Tam.). From (above + á, tam. neg. neuter termination + mey, tam. truth + udai, tam. possession). The possessor of truth that is not false; Vigneshwaran [q.v.].

POYA (పాయ - páya, *Tel.*). From (páyu, tel. to separate). Ford. Suffix in place names; as Saunipoya, meaning dancing girl's ford.

POYA (പുഴ - puzha, *Mal.*). River. Suffix in place names; as Ambalapoya, meaning sky river. Prefix in place names; as Poyavye meaning river mouth.——*Pycarrah* (ಪಾಯಕರೆ - páyakáre, Can.). From (puzha, mal. river + kara, mal. bank).—"*a*" Village; Neilgherry dist., Todanaud div.; acres 3; lat. 11° 28′; long. 76° 39′; height 6,767 feet; from Ootacamund W.N.W. 7 miles. First stage between Ootacamund and Goodalore, a few miles north of Culcoodiyore. Public bungalow [q.v.]. Near the Tiriyairy todah mund, close to this place, is an isolated ancient stone circle [azhauram, phin].—"*b*" River; Neilgherry dist., Todanaud div. Above ghaut name for the Moyaur. Rises at Macoorty peak. It takes a winding northerly course diverging both to the east and west and passing between granitic [caroom cull] hills. On reaching the edge of the plateau it turns to the west, and passing through the Government cinchona [koinah] plantations, falls in a succession of cascades to the tableland beneath. These form the Pycarrah waterfall, but they are far from the bungalow. After reaching the plains of Wynaud, it is known as the Moyaur [q.v.]. Length about 10 miles from Macoorty to the falls [aroovy].—"*c*" Valley; Neilgherry dist., Todanaud div. Follows the line of the lower slopes of the Nedoo mullay range. Its most remarkable features are the broad reaches of the river which are found here and there in the wider openings, and are supposed to be the beds of ancient lakes. This and the Coondah valley are favorite grazing grounds of the Todahs [q.v.].—"*d*" Hill; Neilgherry dist., Todanaud div.; lat. 11° 27′; long. 76° 40′; height 7,511 feet; from Ootacamund W. 6 miles.—"*e*" Tea [q.v.] and cinchona [koinah] estates, Todanaud, Neilgherries. At the falls. From Pycarrah bungalow N.W. 3 miles. 368 acres.

POZHAL (புழல் - puzhal, *Tam.*). Means a hollow. Village; Chingleput dist., Sydapett tal.; pop. 2,823; acres 4,104; lat. 13° 10′; long. 80° 15′; from Sydapett N. 10 miles; from the sea W. 7 miles. Formerly a division of Tondaimundalam [q.v.], but now known as Red hills [q.v.]. An extensive necropolis of cistvaens [paundicoozhy] and circles [azhauram]. Old Shiva [q.v.] temple and a new temple to Booddha [q.v.]. Coorumbar [q.v.] had a fortress here before subjugation by Cholas [q.v.]. Athonday [q.v.] transported the bronze gates found in Pozhal to ornament the great temple at Tanjore. Contains the Red hills tank.

PRA (प - pra, *San.*). Before; intensive prefix [para, pari].——*Pagger* (ಪಾಗಾರ - págára, Can.). From (prákára, san. enclosure). A small fortified village.——*Pagoothy* (பகுதி - paguthi, Tam.). See sep. title.——*Pahrah* (پہرا - pahrá, Hind.). From (prahara, san. watch). One who strikes the gong [q.v.] to announce time. A guard.——*Paleetah* (پلیتا - palítá, Hind.). From (pradípta, san. kindled from pra, san. intensive prefix + díp, san. to kindle). A lamp charm. Anglo-Indian application is to a cotton [q.v.] slow match to light cigars, often furnished with a decorated silver tube; otherwise a Ramasawmy.——*Parbutty* (పారుపత్తి - párupatti, Tel.). From (pravritti, san. employment). A subordinate village officer, under the potail [q.v.], sometimes the village crier, &c. [praverticauran].——*Parlakimedy* (పర్లాకిమెడి - parlákimedi,* Tel.). From (pravála, san. coral + akshi, san. eye + munda, san. head); from pravaulakhimoondo, the coral-eyed and coral-headed man, the last of the aboriginal rulers of the tract.—"*a*" Deputy tahsildarry; Ganjam district. Pay Rs. 100.—"*b*" Zemindarry, Talook and town, Residence of the zemindar, Deputy tahsildar's office, Police assistant superintendent's office, Telegraph office; Ganjam dist., pop. of zemindarry 240,980; pop. of the town 15,365; area 972 square miles. The largest zemindarry in the district. The original of the three estates forming Kimedy [q.v.] tract; the two others are Pedda kimedy and Chinna kimedy. For history, see vol. I, 60, foot-note. Full of hills, between which are numerous extensive and fertile valleys. The highest mountain is Deodangar. The rainfall amounts to between 80 and 90 inches yearly. Teak [q.v.] plantations at Wollaudy and Kimedy and saul [q.v.] wood forests near Serangy. The mango [q.v.] and jack [q.v.] topes [q.v.] are celebrated. The principal produce is paddy [q.v.]; sugar-cane [q.v.] and dry grain [q.v.] are also grown, indigo [q.v.] also recently. Manufactures of cloth and muslin [q.v.]. Well supplied with rivers [aur], channels [q.v.] and tanks [q.v.]. Principal tanks are Rama saugaram and Seeta saugaram near Kimedy, Brindauvana saugaram near Ooppalauda, Krishna saugaram near Goppily, and Cheitanya saugaram north-west of Parlakimedy. Other sources are Raudha saugaram, Seeta saugaram and Asarla cheroo.—"*c*" Maliah tract; Ganjam dist., pop. 39,152. Attached to Parlakimedy zemindarry, and inhabited by Sowrahs [q.v.], its centre is in lat. 19° 20′, long. 84° 10′.—"*d*" Village, Head-quarters of Assistant superintendent of Police and Deputy tahsildar; Ganjam dist., Parlakimedy zemindarry; pop. 10,812; lat. 18° 47′; long. 84° 08′; height 1,093 feet; from Balligooda S.S.E. 96 miles; from Berhampore S.W. 58 miles; from Chetterpore S.W. 70 miles; from Chicacole N.N.E. 36 miles; from Madras N.E. 460 miles; from Russelcondah S.S.W. 86 miles. Residence of the zemindar [q.v.] for whom a large palace has lately been built. Baskets [tokrah], mats [boriyah] and other articles of a fine texture are woven from the bark of a species of weed. Fine tanks. Contains Chinnamallipooram, Deodangar and Poolsara trig. stations.——*Paseenah* (پسینا - pasíná, Hind.). Hind. from (prasvéda, san. perspiration). Thrush in horses [ashwarogam, ghorah].——*Paudyamy* (పాడ్యమి - pádyami, Tel.; பாட்டியமி - páttiyami, Tam.). From (prat'hama, san. first). The first day of the lunar Pacsham [q.v.], or demi-month. The day [tity] after new moon [amavausyay] or full moon [powrnimay].——*Pavalum* (பவளம் - pavalam, Tam.). Corruption of (pravála, san. coral). Coral [moongah].——*Pavalamullay* (பவளமலை - pavalamalai, Tam.). Coral mountains. The eastern ghauts [q.v.]. See vol. I (141).——*Poorutaushy* (புரட்டாசி - purattási, Tam.). From (prósht'hapáda, san. twenty-fifth constellation); from full moon in or near it. The sixth tamul solar month [mausam].——*Pooratanshy shanikizhamay* (புரட்டாசி சனிக்கிழமை - purattásisanikkizhamai, Tam.). From (purattási, tam. the solar month + shani, tam. saturn + kizhamai, tam. day of the week). Solar [madhyama sowra maunam] festival [pundigay, 2d]. Any Saturday in sixth solar month Poorataushy [mausam], i.e., between 15th September and 15th October is specially sacred. A fast to avert evil influences of saturn [shany]. Before eating, crows [caurvam] are fed [maryauday].——*Prabandham* (प्रबन्ध - prabandha, San.). From (above + bandh, san. to tie). A composition. General term for various kinds of poems, as juvenile poem, war poem, love poem, epic poem, &c.; and ninety-six such varieties are recognized in tamul. For naulauyira prabandham see Tirvyemozhy.——*Prabhoo* (प्रभु - prabhu, San.). From (above + bhú, san. to be). Lord. A military leader. Nayar [q.v.] chief. Hindoo third name [peyar].——*Pracaranam* (प्रकरण - prakarana, San.). From (above + karana, san. doing). Chapter.——*Pracausham* (பிரகாசம் - piragásam, Tam.). From (above + kásh, san to shine). Hindoo 2nd or pers. name; also suffix in names as Nyaunapracausham, Shivapracausham [peyar]. Pracausham wodeyar was a Mysore ruler of Paundyam [q.v.], A.D. 1372–1404. See vol. II, 250.——*Pracrit* (प्राकृत - prákrita, San.). From (prakriti, san. origin). That which is derived. Old provincial dialects of the Sanscrit [q.v.], exhibiting more or less deterioration from the original language. They occupied an intermediate position between that language and the modern vernaculars of India, very similar to that of the historical Romance languages between the Latin and the modern languages of Europe. The most completely preserved of old Pracrits is that which was used in Magadham and which has come down in the Booddhist [booddha] books of Ceylon under the name of Pali [q.v.]. In Sanscrit plays Pracrit is spoken by the female characters and the inferior personages. See vol. I (39).——*Pracrity* (प्रकृति - prakriti, San.). From (above + kri, san. to do). The original source of the material world in the Saunkhyam [q.v.] philosophy. See Pradhaunam, Poorsham and Vicrity. Pracrity means also principal. Also a in the algebraic form $ax^2 + b = y^2$.——*Pradacshinam* (प्रदक्षिण - pradakshina, San.). From (above + dakshina, san. the right). Reverential salutation [namascauram] by circumambulation, with the right side towards the person saluted. Turning to the right in conformity with the sun's shadow [chauyay]. The Swasticam [q.v.] symbolizes this idea; it is the cross + with the crampons 卐 at the end of its arms; it is the sign of good luck. The Tamulians also apply the term to the circumambulation of their temples [coil, pagoda]; to be seen daily everywhere, the worshipper keeping the right hand towards the temple. The six years' pilgrimage from the source to the mouth of the Ganges and back again is also a Pradacshinam. The term also is applied to the circumambulatory passage [praucauram] itself surrounding the inner wall of temples [matam].——*Pradesham* (प्रादेश - prádésha, San.). From (pradish, san. to point out). The span of the thumb and the forefinger or the short span. Linear measure. 10 ungoolams = 1 pradesham [alavay, 1f]. Approximate actual value, 1 pradesham = 7½ inches. Same as Tam. wettay. Compare Jaun.——*Pradhaun* (پردهان - pardhán, Hind.). From (above + dhá, san. to place). Headman of a village; minister [muntry, peshwah, vizier]. Corresponding terms are:—Mahr. potail, Tel. peddacaup, Mal. adhicaury, Tam. monigar.——*Pradhaunam* (प्रधान - pradhána, San.). From (above + dhá, san. place). Prominent, chief. The supreme spirit, epithet of Pracrity. See Pracrity and Poorsham [matam].——*Pradhauny* (प्रधान - pradhána, San.; *பிரதானி* - pirathâni, Tam.). From (above + dhá, san. to place). Literally prime minister [muntry, peshwah, pragada, vizier]. But in usage the treasurer, the third officer of the king after muntry the minister, and senaupaty the commander-in-chief.——*Pradosham* (प्रदोष - pradósha, San.). From (above + dósha, san. dark). Properly speaking the evening-tide, comprising three and three-quarters of a Nauzhigay [q.v.] or Indian hour of 24 minutes, before sunset and the same after; which time is considered as auspicious for the performance of sacred rites, and in particular the Pradosham on the thirteenth day [tity] from the new [amavausyay] and full moon [powrnimay], for the following reason. When Shiva [q.v.] had swallowed the poison [neelacuntan] arising from the sea of milk when churned by the gods [deva] for nectar [amritam], he lay motionless on the ground from the eleventh day [yecaudashy] of the lunar half month [pacsham] till the Pradosham of the thirteenth day, when he sprung up, swung his trident [shoolam], and danced the divine dances [coormam].——*Praharam* (प्रहर - prahara, San.). From (prahri, san. to strike at). Measure of time. $7\frac{1}{2}$ ghaticams = 1 praharam; 8 praharams = 1 dinam [caulam, 7f]. Approximate actual value, 1 praharam = 3 hours. Same as San. yaumam, Tel. jaumoo, Tam. jaumam.——*Prahlaudan* (प्रह्लाद - prahláda, San.). From (above + hláda, san. joy). Son of Hiranyacashipoo; see Narsimhan.——*Prajaupaty* (प्रजापति - prajápati, San.). From (prajá, san. mankind + pati, san. lord). A name of Bramha [q.v.]. An epithet common to ten divine personages who were first created by Bramha [q.v.]; Angiras, Atry, Bhrigoo, Dacshan, Mareechy, Nauradan, Poolahan, Cratoo, Poolastyan, Vasishtan [maharicsham, sapta rishy].——*Prajaupatya maunam* (प्रजापतिमान - prajápatiména, San.). Reckoning by Menoos or Prajaupaties [manwantaram, maunam, monoo].——*Pralayam* (प्रलय - pralaya, San.). From (above + laya, san. dissolution). Dissolution. The end of a Calpam [q.v.] or destruction of the world. The absorption of all things into Bramha [matam].—"*a*" In the reign of the sun-born monarch Veivaswatan [q.v.], the Sanscrit writers state that the earth was submerged entire, and the human race destroyed by a flood; except the monarch himself, the seven rishies [sapta rishy], and their several wives. This general pralayam or destruction is told in one version of the eighth book of the Bhaugavatam [q.v.] thus abridged. The account is evidently an Aryan [q.v.] tradition transplanted to Southern india. "The demon Hayagreevan having purloined the Vedams [q.v.] "from the custody of Bramha [q.v.], while he was reposing at "the close of the sixth Manwantaram [q.v.], the whole race of "men became corrupt, except the seven rishies and Satyavratan "[q.v.] who then reigned in Dravira [q.v.], a maritime region "to the south of Carnautam [q.v.]. This prince was performing "his ablution in the river Kritamaulay, when Vishnoo [q.v.] "appeared to him in the shape of a small fish, and after several "augmentations of bulk in different waters, was placed by "Satyavratan in the ocean, where he thus addressed his amazed "votary. In seven days all creatures who have offended me "shall be destroyed by a deluge, but thou shalt be secured "in a capacious vessel miraculously formed; take therefore all "kinds of medicinal herbs and esculent grain for food, and "together with the seven holy men, your respective wives, and "pairs of all animals, enter the ark without fear; then shalt "thou know God face to face, and all thy questions shall be "answered. Saying this, he disappeared; and after seven days, "the ocean began to overflow the coasts, and the earth to be "flooded by constant showers, when Satyavratan, meditating "on the deity, saw a large vessel moving on the waters: he "entered it, having in all respects conformed to the instructions "of Vishnoo [q.v.]; who in the form of a vast fish [matsyam], "suffered the vessel to be tied with a great sea-serpent, as with "a cable, to his measureless horn. When the deluge had "ceased, Vishnoo slew the demon, and recovered the Vedams "[q.v.], instructed Satyavratan [q.v.] in divine knowledge, "and appointed him the seventh Menoo by the name of Veivaswatan [q.v.]."—"*b*" Here follow two statements of the same leading event from the Bhauratam [q.v.], or tamul version of the Mahabhaurat [q.v.]; one much abridged being in prose and indeed in inferior language, the other poetical and in shen tamul [q.v.] or polished language.—"*c*" The following is the prose version:—மாறகணடெயன சொலலககேடடு தறமராசசநதோஷபபடடு பினனையுமசெல்லுகிறான ஓ்சுவாமி நீமகா னுபாவனபிறமமாணடஙகளெலலா மநாசமான போது மஅநேகமபிறமமாககளபபடடமிற நதுபோயுமபதினாறுவயசு பாலகுமாரனைபபோலயிருக கிறீர் யிநதபபிறப ஞசம பிறநதுவளாநதலயமாகிறது கேடக வேணடியி ருககுதசொலலுமையா வெனறார் மாறகணடேயன சொலலுகிறான ஓ்ராசாவே உஙகளு ககுததோழனுமஉறவிலே நலலமைததுனனும் பிறதா னியாயிருககிற யிந தகிஷணதேவன பாததததைததலே மேலவைசசுக கொணடுயிவருடைய அனுமதியினாலே நீகேடடகதை செல லுகிறேன கேளும கிறேதாயுகம திறேதாயுகம துவா பரியுகம கலியுகம யிநதநாலுயுக முமபனனீராயிரமதேவ வருஷம யிநத நாலுயுகமும ஒருககாலதிருமபினால அதுவொருமகா யுகமெனறு சொல்லபபடும. அபபடி கொததமகாயுகம ஆயிரமதி ரமதிருமபினால பிறமாவுககு ஒருநாள் அநதநாள் முடி கிறபோது பூமியிலேநூறுவ ருஷம மழையிலலாமல கருபபாம அபபோ சூரியன்யேழுசரீநதரிதது ஆறுகள குளங கள கிணறுகள சமுதகிரஙகளையெலலாம வறற டிபபான அநத கிறணங கள அககினிஸ்வரூபமாயமக ாவாயுவினாலேபெருகி மலைகள காடுகளையுமமூனறு லோ கஙகளையும சுடடுபபோடும அபபோகறுபபும வெளு பபும செகபபும மஞசளு மயிநதவறணங்களான கால மேகஙகள மலைபோலே வளாநது ஆகாசமெலலாம நிறைஞசு யிடிகளுடனேகூட ஆனைததுமபிககைகளபோ லே பெரியதானமழைகள பேயும அதினாலே லோகங களெலலாமயேக சமுததிரம ாயிருககும். யிநதபூமி மெததவுமமுழுகி செலலுபமாம. அபபோதிககுகள விதி ககுகளெனறு அறியபபோகாம லமெத்தயிருளகபபிக கொளளும. அபபோ பிறமா வினாலே அனுபபபபட்ட காதது வநது அநதகால்மேக ஙகளைதாததும அநதகா றறை பொசிசசுக கொணடுபிற மாதேவன பொறருமை யாயின பேரிலபளளிககொணடுநி ததிரைபோவான. தறமராசா வைவசுவதமனுவுககு யெதினாலேபிறபா வமுணடாசசெனறு கேடடார். மாறகணடயன சொ லலுகிறான முனனேசாஷசிராஷ மனுவநதாததிலே வைவசுவதன பதினாயிரம வருஷம விஷணுவை நோ ககி தவசு பணணசசே அவன முழுகுகிற ஆறறிலே ஒரு மீனகுடடி வெளியேவநது அயயா நான சினன மீ னன்படியினாலே பெரியமீனகள முழுஙகிபோடப போ குதெனகிற பயததினாலே வெளியே வநதேன யெனனை ககாதது இரட்சிசசு வேறெயொரு யிடததிலே வை சசால உமககு நான பிறிதியுபகாரம பணணுகிறேனெ னறுசொனனது கேட்டு ஆசசரியபபடடுஅநத இராசா தனகமணடததிலே விடடான. அந்திககுததானே அந தகமணடலம நிறைஞசு அநத மீன தனககு இடமபோ ாதாதெனறது பெரியபானையிலே விடடான. அதுவும நிறைஞசுது பிறகதொரு கிணறறிலே விடடான. அதி லேயுமஇடம போதாதெனறதறகு ஒரு யேரியிலெ விட டான. அதுவுமநிறைஞச பிறகு சமுததிரததிலேவிட டான. அநத மீன லஷஷம யோசனை தூரமவளாநது ஓய ராசாவே யினனையிலே நாளையிலேபிரளயகாலம வரு குது. அபபோ சமுததிரங களெலலாம ஒனறாயப போம. ஆனபடியினாலேயெனனிட மாயையினாலே ஒரு கபபல நிற்மிசசுஉனனணடைககு அனுபபுகிறேன. சததரிஷகளுடனே அநதக கபபலிலேநீ யேறிக கொ ணடு அநதபபிரளய காலதது இராததிரியிலே யெனனை நினையும நான வநது கொமபினாலே கபபலைததாஙகி ககொணடு உனனையும் முனியீசுபரரை யுமஇரட்சிக கிறேன யெனறுசொலலி காணபியாமலபோசசுது. அதின பிறகுபிரளயகாலமாய சமுததிரஙகளெலலா ம ஒனறாசசுது. அபபடியே கபபல வநதுதுஇராசா சத தரிஷிகளுடனே கபபலின மேலேறிககொணடு அநத மீனை நினைததான. அது வநதுதனகொமபுகளிலே கபபலைத தாஙகிககொணடியிருககசசே அநேகமாயிரம வருஷம அநதபபிரளய சமுததிரததிலே கபபல மே லே டயபபடாமல யிருநத பிறகு அநத மீன பிரளய ராததிரிவநதது. இதோ யிமவத் பறுவம இதின சிகரத திலேகபபலைககடடி வைசசுககொணடிருஙகளெனறு சொலலி வேதஙகளை திருடிககொண்டுபோன இராஷத னைககொனறுபோடடு வேதங்களையெடுததுவநதுபிறமா வுககுககொடுத்தது. வைவசுவதனுக்கும்சததரிஷிகளுக் கும ஞான உபதேசம பண்ணினபடியினாலேவைவசுத ன மகானுபாவனானான. இந்தககதைகேடடவர்களுககு நி னைததகாரியமெலலாம்கைககூடும்—"Dharmarajan [q.v.] "on hearing the narration of Marcandeyan [q.v.] was glad. He "again said, O my lord, most learnedly illustrious, you are in "appearance like a youth of sixteen, notwithstanding that in "your time all the worlds have perished, and many Bramhas "have died. I am desirous to hear of the birth, growth, and "destruction of this world. Be pleased to tell me. Marcandeyan replied, O king! placing on my head the foot of this "chief, the god Krishnau [q.v.], who is your friend, and in "relationship your brother-in-law, by his assistance I will tell "you the narrative which you desire. Be pleased to listen. "The Kritam [q.v.], Tretay [q.v.], Dwauparam [q.v.], Kaliyoogs "[q.v.] comprise twelve thousand years of the gods. The revolution of these four ages [yoog] makes a Maha yoog [caulam]. "The lapse of a thousand such great ages is a day of Bramha "[calpam]; when that day is about being accomplished, the "earth will be parched by a reason of a want of rain during one "hundred years. The sun, then increasing seven times in size, "will dry up all rivers, lakes, wells, and seas. The rays of the "sun, like flame, being acted on by a strong wind, will burn up "mountains, forests, and the three worlds. Afterwards heavy "rain, clouds of various colors, black, white, red, and yellow, "rolling together and increasing like mountains, will fill the "visible heavens; attended with thunder and torrents of rain, "with the streams comparable to the trunks of elephants. "Thus all the worlds will become one vast sea; this earth, being "submerged will present the form of water. The cardinal and "subordinate points [ashtadic] of the heavens being undiscernible, "a thick darkness will cover all things. Then a wind, sent by "Bramha, having come and driven away the clouds, the god "Bramha will swallow up that wind and reposing on the "golden lotus [nelumbo] will go to sleep. Dharmarajan in-"quired, how was it that Veivaswata menoo became renowned? "Marcandeyan answered. In the Manwantaram of Swarochi-"shan, when Veivaswatan was performing a penance of a thou-"sand years in devotion to Vishnoo, he was on one occasion "bathing in a river, when a young fish leaped out and said:— "Respectable man, because I am small, the large fishes are "seeking to devour me for which cause I am come out of the "water; if you protect and deliver me, and put me in another "safe place, I will render you an adequate return. Being "astonished at this request, the said king put the fish into a "small pitcher. At evening of the same day the pitcher was "filled by the fish, which, on its applying for more room, he put "into a large earthen water-pot. The fish having also filled "this vessel, he put it into a well. This even not affording room "enough, he put it into a lake; and on that becoming filled, he "placed it in the sea. Thereupon the fish grew to the bulk of a "hundred thousand yojanams [q.v.] or one million of miles. "It then said. Oh king! to-day and to-morrow a time of deluge "comes on; then all the seas will become one. But having "formed by my divine power a floating vessel, I will send it to "you; whereupon, in company with the seven rishies, ascend "thou the ship, and in the night of that flood time think on me, "when I will come and bear up the vessel with my horn; and "will save both you and the holy men who accompany you. "So saying, the fish disappeared. Afterwards the seas became "all one in the flood time. Accordingly the floating vessel came. "The king, together with the seven rishies, went on board the "vessel, and thought on the fish. That having come, bore up "the vessel with its horn; and after they had continued many "thousand years in that vessel on the deluge sea without fear, "the fish said:—The night of the deluge has come; see here "the mountain imaut; fasten the vessel to its peak and remain. "Saying thus, it proceeded to kill the giant that had stolen the "Vedams; and having taken the Vedams, it restored them "to Bramha. And because it gave spiritual instructions to "Veivaswatan and to the seven rishies, Veivaswatan became "learned and illustrious. Whoever hears this narrative, "the thought of his mind will be accomplished."—" *d* " The following is the poetical version:—என்ன முனனர் மிருகண்டா் தந்த வனியம் பவெனறி புனேகினற வே ன மனனர் மனனன றனமைநதனின புறமகிறநது பினனிது மொழிநதன ன பனனு நின சொன மறை யனறி புனனு மொருபணபு வெறு முள தோ வே ன வினனு மொனனொனது சிநதை தங்குமிதை யினறுதநதருள வழுங்கு வாய ஈசனேபபாவி வநதவனு சதம னெஞச வெனறல கடஙக லு நாசமுறறிடினு முறறுணாநதுயிர்நவிததிடா வர மியங்குவொய நேச முறறனனம டஙகலகறபமது நெருஙினறபொ ழுதெவ வண ங காசினிபபலு யிர்மாளுமஙகனிதுகடடுரைததி யெனவொதுவா ன நாலுகஙகளு மொருஙகு கூடினது நாமமெயத றமகாயு கமெனு மவவுகமுமாயிரஙகளோ ரிாணடயனறின மிதெனபாான மெனுறு மபகலிலவான வா்கசாசா மெவுமீரொழுவர் தீர்வாா ன மூலமொனறு மலர் வெதனுகஙாவுமுடு மாயிரமுகததி னே பலவுயிர தடுதாகைபாபபனிஙகி யொருபஙகயத தனிமலா்ககு ளே யலவினிறறுயில பொருநதமூவுலகழிநது வான வா்வ ரமபுதா் ந தொலவெனககடலொலிதத மெவை ருயுறச சிததளவிறுககி மே லெலேலமுறறுமுற மூடி ருடபுனலின யாஞெருத தனுமிருநது ளே ன அண பிததிகையினனவு நீாலதறிநது கூறவொ ருபொருளி லே கணடு புததிமிகநொந்திஙேபபினிரகணகவறசியுறு போதினி ற் கொணடலொததிரு மேனியோ டொரு குருநது பசசையிலேபீதுவ ந தணடிநிறகவது கணடெ னெககு மனமாதரததின மகிழவான தே மாதவததினு ருவான நியுடல் வநதத மாறிடவிரு ததியெ ன காதலு றறவுதாததினெனறு கனிவாயதிறககவதி னெயுதினே ன பூதலததினுடேனகளுால மவர்புநதியோடுெ விருத தலக ண டாதாததினுடு சிநதைசெயதவன கட்டி லெண ணில பகலவைகக்னே ன மீளவாயவழி திறககவ நது புனலவேலேயிற குதி கொளகரலேயி ற ருள தாமனா மலர்சசெவவாயுடை தனிககுருந தின முகநோககி யே யாளுமெநதையென வநதினேதத பொழுதாதரி தது தவியாபினுய க காளவேனியுடையா யுனவாறு புகலெ

னறு காத லில்வினுவினே ன கருணேயஙகுழவி நகைபுரி நதுலகுகாககு நீலமணி வணணன யா னிருணெருஙகு முடஙகலம் புனலிசைநதுனேதது யாவினேககுமெ ன றருகணேநதன் திரைபபாறறினனயற சியினறியி னியெ னறுமி வ வருணவாாந்த டாாதெனசசொலி வாஙகொ தெதிது விளம்பிஞ ன காலமேற சிலசழிதத பினன ரொழுகடலுமாதிாமு மேருவு ம ஞாலமுறறு மூனதாகி நான முகனலஙகொள கணயில தறகுமி க கொல முறறுபுனலவறறு மருசலென்வ ககுருநதி னுருவானவ ன சாலவெற கருளபுரிநதிசைசகுமொழி தனனிலெ னறுயர் தவிர்நத தே நிரை படிகருணேசெர் நீலமே னியெ ன றுரைபபுகுழவியை யுகநது நோககி யே மீனபடி நினனுதாததின மாயகைபொ ற் கனாபடவரி யன கணடு னொனியா ன ஏழ்கடலெழ் முகிலெழுமாத வ ரொழ்கிரி யெழுதல மெழுமாதா ஞ ளொழ்நதி யெழுல கெழுமா மருந் தெழ வரையாருயிர் யாவுஙகணடு ளே ன பாதவ மாயிரம பணமுடிதத லே யொதுயர் மாசுண முயர் தவததி ஞே ர் காதல விண மீனுடன கனகமெரு வு மாதவா நினறிருவயறறிற கணடு ளே ன சுருதியிணே ஜையுந தொகையின நாதி ா வொருதனி யோசையு முனைககு மாகம ந தருதிற லொசையுந தாம்விலேனே னூ ற பெருமி தவொசையும பிறழதல கேடடுளே ன கணவிபபரி சினே ககருததிற றொ்நதில ன தொணட னேய மென குறைகள வே யணடமுனனுப்படு மாய் வாறெ லா முணடக வாயினுய மொழிய வெணடுமா லி எனறியான வினவவாவிலேயின மீது றி மனறிலம மைநதூழாயமாலேவான வ னனறனககுள தெலாந விலவன கெட்டியென் றுனறிய கருணே யாலுனாத தன மெயினு ன பூரண நாததிற பொருநதிககாதத லா ரைணனெனப் பெயர கொளவனுடொ று மாரண னுயுல காககி மூன்றுக ட காாணஞகி யெகழிபபன காணமி ஞே மணடலம் பாதமாயவானமேனியா ய புணடசன முதலினே ரொழியுறுபபதா ய பணடந லவ தனமாயபருதிமாம தி விணடிருவிழிகளாயவிளங குவெளியா ன வனறிறனமருபபிஞல வயஙகரும பெரு ம பனறியாயிபபெரும பாவைகுமபு வி நினறிடா்நத தல பாதலஙகணிஙகி மீ ண டனறு வநதெயதிய மமல னை ொா உடுகணுளகொள கடேனுறலஙக லா யடு தத மாருதஙகளெ சுவாசமாக வே கடுததி கழனநதன மெற கடவினுபபணி ற டுதெதறிது யிலமா் பாமனயான ாோ அகிலமு மெருவுஙகடல களான வு மிகவுறுவனா களு மெநதியோர் பெரு ம புகலரும பாநதளாயப்பொ றபினுயி ா மிகவொளிர் சிததெரடுமெவிளஙகு வென ரொ பணடொரு மநதாமபடுததுவாருதித் தணடயிர் மதிததெதிர் தானவா்குல ம விணடிட நீககிவிணண வா்ககுவெணச் தெ யுணடிதநததுதவிய வொருவனுன ாோ இயஙகுமிபபெருமபுனவிாவு தீர்நது ழி தயஙகன வுருவமாயககவா்நத தாா னி மூயஙகுமெமூல கிறு மு டிவினீககுவ ன வயுஙகுமிவவுல கினேவைபபன் மீளவு ம முக்ததினுமம புயததினுமுதற கவானப த யுகததினுமீ ளவு மூயய நலகுவ ன மிகுததநலவேதியாா திமெயத ரு மகததுவமுடைய நாலவருணத தொனா யெ அகந தையுஙகாமமு மருஙகொாத மு மிகுநதமாறசரியமுய விடததமெலவ ரிகமபாமிாணடினு மெனதுதாள்கனெ சுகநதரு மெனறெமைதடுதொழுது போறறுவா ர் என லே விடடொரு பிாபஞசமிலலேயி ங சனனநறபிாபஞச மன றியானி ரா ஹுனனுமெனன கததினும்புறதது முணட டொ் சொனனமனநதா சுவரகமாகிக ள அறநதலே ஙேகாலேயினும மாாத்மமு மை மறநதலே கொலேயிஜ மறு விலாருயி ர் சிறநதவேபடுகினுந தோற்றிதீர்கருவு ன பறநதலே யெதிர்நதசூர் பாமபடுதெதி யே முநதுநாலு கஙகளின மெ!ழிநதசிற மபநதநீஙகாவகை பரிககும பானமைய்ா யிநதுவெணமையுஞ சிவப்பீசைதத நீலமும ம் விநதைசேர்பீதமுமேனி கொளவனு ல் இநதநலவி ாணிய கருபபனெனனு டை யுநதியிஜதித்தவனுறஙகு கஙகுலவாய் சநதமீவவணந திகிரிதாஙகி யே பைந திறலுத கததிறபயில வனபணடுளா ய ஞானமாமுனி வருமம பிறருமந மபெருந கானமாயகையை ககனாகா ணவலல ரா மொனசிறசுருவரன முனிவநினவ யி ஞனநறகரு ணேயாலறிய வோதினே ம—"Thus spake "the descendant of the rishy [q.v.], Marcandeyan [q.v.]; and "the son of Dharmarajan [q.v.] being himself the ruler of kings, "possessing the conquest giving arrow, was rejoiced. Again "he said, what you have spoken has equal authority with the "Vedam [q.v.], and must be not otherwise regarded. But there "is a further inquiry arising in my mind, can you graciously "satisfy it? O benevolent sage; who, by worshipping the su-"preme being, didst conquer death, by his losing his power when "he came to destroy thee; thou that knowest all the circum-"stances which occurred while the world was being destroyed; "I have a desire to learn how all living things were annihilated "when the night of Bramha's day [calpam] was advancing; "tell me this. So freely spoke the king. The sage replied:—"The four lesser ages [yoog] joined into one become a Maha "yoog [q.v.]. And further, it is considered that two thousand "of these great ages make a day of Bramha. One thousand of "these ages were his night, during which time the first born "Bramha dwelt in the lotus [nélumbo] flower; at which time "fourteen Indrans [q.v.] of the celestials had died. The night "of Bramha being come, he, having discontinued the production "of many generations of living beings, was sleeping in the "lotus flower. Then the three worlds upper, middle, and lower, "were destroyed; the celestial inhabitants expired; the sea, "roaring with a great noise, flowed over the highest peak of the "mountain Meroo [q.v.], reaching even to the heavenly "expanse; and all places were shrouded and veiled with its dark "gloom. I alone survived. Water only excepted, no inanimate "things had existence, even unto the walls of heaven; seeing "this state of things, with deep anguish of mind my eyes "became weary, and while sinking into half torpid insensibility, "a handsome child, on an Aul [banyan] leaf, resembling a cloud, "came near, and seeing it, my soul was rejoiced. Thou, of the "penance-making form, to remove thy distress enter into my "body. Thus spake the child, opening its rosy-colored lips; "and I entered by its mouth, I therein saw the earth, with the "forms of many other worlds; and, contemplating these with "satisfaction, while reflecting also on what I saw, I remained "thus enclosed during unnumbered days. On its again opening "its mouth, I came forth again into the flood; and regarding "the being who had saved me, having the red mouth like the "lotus flower, with the countenance of a child incomparable, I "inquired, with eagerness, Oh my father! who didst succour "me when weary; tell me, Oh thou, possessing the dark-colored "form; what are thy character and circumstances? The "gracious child, smiling replied:—When the darkness had "increased, I, Vishnoo narayanan, who preserve the world and "have the color of the sapphire [neelam], approaching to thee, "delivered thee from the trouble occasioned by the deluge; but "in future, even for ever, this distress caused by the overflowing "waters cannot occur again. Thus it gave me assurance and "further added:—Fear not; for when a short time more has "gone by, Bramha, the author of good, again opening his eyes, "will reproduce the seven seas [samoodram], the eight points "[ashtadic] of the heavens, and the earth [bhoomy]; when this "azure-tinted deep will become dried up. Thus greatly favoring "me spoke the being having the form of a child; and by these "words which he had spoken my grief was removed. Regarding "with gladness the child possessor of the blue form, exercising "dignified favor, I said:—I have seen within your lotus-like "form illusory types of innumerable things. I have seen the "seven seas, the seven clouds, the seven rishies, the seven "mountains, the seven dweepams, the seven celestial females, "the seven rivers, the seven worlds, the seven physicians of the "gods, the seven genera of things; all these. O divinity; within "thy splendid form, I have seen the inferior world, the lofty "Audy sheshan [q.v.], styled the thousand-crested crown; I "have seen the elevated, the penance-making men, the stars "desirable to look on, and the golden mountain Meroo [q.v.]. I "have heard the sonorous-sounding voice of the Vedams, the echo "of innumerable modes of prayer, the voice of the Angamams "[q.v.], and the resonance of other sacred books innumerable. "Attending to these without full comprehension, I am in doubt. "O thou, having the lotus-colored mouth; supply my deficiency, "and explain to me, I implore thee, the import of all the various "and illusory forms of things in the universe within thee. Thus "I besought him. He, the divine being, possessing the odour "of the green toolsy garland, who was reposing on the aul "leaf, said:—It is well. I will tell you these various things. "Listen. Thus preparing me, he alone replenished with favor "proceeded:—Understand, my name is Narayanan [q.v.], "because I preserve the world, thus enclosed within me, and "am surrounded everywhere by water. At the same time, I am "always Bramha [q.v.], producing the world; and, as the three-"eyed Shiva [q.v.] I shall destroy. The earth is the place of "my feet; the heavens are my form; Bramha and the gods are "my members; my countenance is the primæval light; the sun "and moon are my two kinds of eyes; with this splendour I "shine forth. As an immense boar possessing power, by my "club, I divided the earth, surrounded by this large sea; and "passing below to the inferior regions, thence returning, "possessing beauty, I am he. I am Paraman [q.v.], whose "ornamental garland is formed by the stars [nacshatram], the "zodiacal mansions [rausby], and the nine planets [graham]; "the winds are as my breath; I repose on the venom-bearing "Audy sheshan, in the midst of the sea; sleeping, yet not "unconsciously, but knowing all things. With the brightness of "the splendid thousand-headed snake, which is vast beyond "expression, supporting the earth, the mountain Meroo, the "seas, and the mountains, having strength, I shine forth. I "alone am he who placed the mountain Mandaram [q.v.] in the "midst of the seas; churned them like cold curdled milk; "destroyed the Raucsbasans [q.v.], adversaries of the gods "[deva]; and helping these, gave to them the white ambrosia "[amritam] adapted for food. And after the night of this "great flood, now covering all things, I will replace the "shining universe by removing the waters; and by taking "it out of them, I will reproduce the earth and the seven "worlds; together with my splendid fiery form. I will "again establish four divisions of caste [jauty], the eximious "Bramins, and the others, truly possessing glory in the face, in "the shoulders, in the thighs, and in feet. Those ancient men "who forsake pride, desire, and anger, adore me; worshipping "my feet, that give health, both for the present time and for "futurity. Without me there is no world; nor do I exist apart "from this goodly world. Within me resides thought; and "exterior to me are the before mentioned earth, and paradise, "and connected things. If justice be perverted, and the moral "force of the gods be diminished, and if their life, being with-"out guilt, be troubled by means of austerities of evil beings, "then I become incarnate on earth, oppose the adversaries of "the celestials in the scene of contest, and remove the distress "of these by destroying the former. Preserving by my nature "the attributes of the before stated four ages [yoog] in due "order, without failure, my form possesses the whiteness of the "moon, with its red and its azure light, together with its beauti-"ful color of gold. O thou of the good disposition; thus shall I "always be holding the chuckram [q.v.], abiding in the green "water, the god Bramha dwelling in the lotus springing out of "my navel always during the night of his sleep. O good Moony "[q.v.]; we have spoken these things, seeing there is benignant "favor towards thee, for thy information concerning our inex-"pressible immaterial form; but can even the great and wise "rishies perceive the boundary of my immeasurable, illusive "immensity [peroovely]?"—"*e*" The legend of Xisuthrus as ascribed to Sanconiathon is substantially one and the same with the statements in the Bhaugavatam [q.v.] and Bhauratam [q.v.] concerning Vishnoo's appearance to Veivaswatan [q.v.] or Satyavratan [q.v.], and then piloting the vessel in the shape of a fish, a rope being attached to his horn.—"*f*" With the Jeina [q.v.] people there is a period of great heat of fire, rain, previous to the deluge; then other kinds of showers, among them of sugar-cane [q.v.] juice, of poison, quintessence of poison, by which means the earth sinks down depressed; then come showers of milk [paul], nectar [amritam], water [neer]; and afterwards the earth becomes restored; grass, plants, shrubs, &c., reappear; men also again inhabit the earth, who dwell on it, and increase. After forty thousand years the Menoos and Chuckravurties are born and continue to rule. Then comes a period of twenty crores of years, at the close of which the seven kinds of showers as before introduce the yoog pralayam or periodical deluge.——

Pramaunam (प्रमाण - pramána, San.). From (above + má, san. to measure). Dimension, quantity, standard, limit. Authority, proof by oath, an oath. On w. coast is same as Caranam [q.v.].—"*a*" The Tamulians enumerate eight kinds of testimonies, viz.:—Proof given by the senses, especially by the sight or by experiments; Proof by inference, or supposition; as where smoke is, there is fire; Proof by testimony, the assertion of great men or the vedams; Proof by conclusion, as the inference that he who eats nothing during the night, and fasts during the day, cannot be stout; Proof by comparison; as one having heard that the gayal [gowr] is like an ox [maud], afterwards sees this animal, and the recollection of that which he has heard of it makes him conclude that it is the same; Proof by non-existence, known by the non-appearance of a present object; Proof by traditional testimony, as a devil is dwelling in this tree; Proof by co-existence, as where a thousand is there is a hundred [maryauday].—"*b*" Pramaunam is also the first topic of Nyauyam [q.v.] philosophy which exhibits the means or instruments by which Pramay or the right measure of any subject is to be obtained. Under this head are enunciated four different processes by which the mind arrives at true and accurate knowledge, viz.:—Pratyacsham or perception by the senses, Anoomaunam or inference, Oopamaunam or comparison, and Shabdam or verbal testimony or authority.—"*c*" Pramaunam means in astronomy diurnal revolution [bhaganam]. Aha pramaunam, from (ahas, san. day), the sun's revolution from the horizon [cshitijam] to the same again. Dina pramaunam, from (dina, san. day), the time of any star from rising to setting. Rautry pramaunam, from (rátri, san. night), the time of any star from setting to rising [jyotisham].——*Pramauny* (പ്രമാണി - pramáni, Mal.). An umpire [madhyastan].——*Pramay* (प्रमा - pramá, San.). Measure; true and certain perception in philosophy.——*Prameyam* (प्रमेय - praméya, San.). From (above + méya, san. measurable). Measurable or ascertainable. An object of certain knowledge. A topic of the Nyauyam [q.v.] philosophy, by which is meant all the objects or subjects of pramay or right measure, those about which correct knowledge is to be obtained. These, are twelve in number, viz., soul, body, objects of sense, understanding or intellection, mind, activity, faults, transmigration, consequences, pain, and emancipation.——*Pranaumam* (प्रणाम - pranáma, San.). From (above + nam, san. to bow down). Prostration or respectful salutation before an idol or a superior. Compare Namascauram.——*Pranavam* (प्रणव - pranava, San.). From (pranu, san. to utter). The mystical syllable om [gayatry, om].——*Prenyay* (प्रज्ञा - prañá, San.). From (above + ñá, san. to know). Intelligent soul. That by which the properties of things are known. There is a Tamul saying:—பிரக்ஞையே ஞானம், ஞானமே பிரமம்—"intellect is wisdom [nyaunam], and wisdom is bramh [q.v.]."——*Prapuncham* (प्रपञ्च - prapañcha, San.). From (prapach, san. spread). Extent, expanse, the world; so error, illusion [mauyay].——*Prasaud* (پرشاد - prashád, Hind.). From (above + sad, san. to sit). Favor. Hindoo third name; also suffix in proper names as Balaprasaud, Shrivaprasaud [peyar].——*Prasaudam* (प्रसाद - prasáda, San.). From (above + sad, san. to settle); soothing. Propitiatory offering. Boiled rice or anything which, having been offered to an idol [poojah, shilay, vigraham], is given to the people, all castes and strangers may eat prasaudam. See vol. I (80). Hindoo 2nd or pers. name, common among non-bramins [peyar].——*Prasiddham* (प्रसिद्ध - prasiddha, San.). From (above + sidh, san. to go). Advertisement.——*Prasritam* (प्रसृत - prasrita, San.). From (prasri, san. to flow onwards). Contents of two palms [anjaly] joined. Liquid measure. 2 pollums = 1 prasritam; 2 prasritams = 1 coodavam [alavay, 4f]. Approximate actual value, 1 prasritam = 14 cubic inches. Compare Mal. oory, Tam. olluck.——*Prastam* (प्रस्थ - prast'ha, San.). From (prast'ha, san. to place before). Measure of capacity. 4 coodavams = 1 prastam; 4 prastams = 1 audhacam [alavay, 3f]. Approximate actual value, 1 prastam = 105 cubic inches. Compare Puddy, Yedangaly.——*Pratamah yecaudashy* (ప్రథమైకాదశి - pradhamaikádashi, Tel.). Means first + eleventh. Lunar [chaundramaunam] festival [pundigay, 3e], subject to intercalation [adhicam]. The eleventh day [tity] of the waxing moon [shooclapacshain] of the third lunar month Jyeshtam [mausam] between 26th May and 24th June. First Yecaudashy of Vishnoo's slumber. Otherwise Toly yecaudashy, Shayana yecaudashy. From Vishnoo's sleep on that day for four mouths, till he rises at Ottaunaicaudashy in Caurteecam. Strict fast [maryauday, oopavausam].——*Pratamay* (प्रथमा - prat'hamá, San.). The first. The first day [tity] in a lunar fortnight [pacsham]. Pratama chauram, from (chára, san. motion), is the ascensional difference of the first sign [raushy] of the hindoo tropical zodiac [raushy chuckram]; the same for the sun's declination [craunty] and amplitude [agram]. Pratama tity, from (tit'hi, san. lunar day), is the first tity or lunar day in the half month; that which always follows the day of last conjunction [sangamam] or opposition [amavausyay, jyotisham, powrnimay].——*Prataupam* (प्रताप - pratápa, San.). From (tap, san. to burn). Power. There were two rulers called Prataupa roodra deva in the Ganapaty [q.v.] line of Warrangal. The first extended his kingdom towards the south as far as Nellore; conquered the Rajah of Devagherry, whose daughter he married; patronized learning; built cities and pagodas [q.v.]. The second, his grandson, known to Mahomedan historians as Ludder deo, who succeeded the interregnum of Roodramma, in 1295, was virtually the last of the line. Taken prisoner and sent captive to Delhi in 1323, subsequently released and returned to Warrangal where he died. Vol. I (132), (151). Another of this name was king of Orissa, 1504 to 1562. Extended his conquests as far as Cape Comorin; captured Vizianagram on the way. His reign was marked by theological discussions as to Booddhist [booddha] and Braminical religions; and he was finally converted to Veishnavite faith by the reformer Cheitanyan. Hence the fane of Srisheilam [charitram].——*Prataup sing* (پرتاپ سنگھ - partápsingh, Hind.). Name + third name. Rajah of Tanjore 1749–1765. Wrested the kingdom from his brother Sahojee with the aid of the English to whom he ceded Devicottah. By the treaty of 1762, acknowledged the sovereignty of the Nawaub of Arcot, and agreed to pay an annual tribute of four lakhs [charitram]. See vol. I, 50.——*Praucauram* (प्राकार - prákára, San.). From (above + krí, san. to disperse). Enclosure; rampart; corridor [pradacshinam] of a temple [coil].——*Prauchy* (प्राची - práchí, San.). From (pra, san. before + añch, san. to bend). Turned before. East [poorvam].——*Prauchya* (प्राच्य - práchya, San.). Eastern people. Greek πράσιοι.——*Prauk* (प्राक् - prák, San.). From (above + añch, san. to bend). Front, prior. Prauk chuckram is the epicycle on which ancient astronomers corrected the precessional variation [ayanaumsham, craunty pauta gaty, paridhy].——*Prauna calay* (प्राणकला - pránakalá, San.). From (prána, san. breath + kalá, san. part), measure of time by respiration [praunam]. A measure of solar time in which a word of two letters as 'ta' can be uttered ten times neither very quickly nor very slowly. 10 caushta calays or indian second = 1 prauna calay; 6 prauna calays = 1 vicalay or indian minute [caulam, 6]. Approximate actual value, 1 prauna calay = 4 english seconds. The 'ta' itself will then be ·4 or ⅖ths of a second; with which compare calculation of the beats of a chronometer by five beats in 2 seconds. The 'ta' is sometimes divided into eye-twinklings.——*Prauna lingam* (प्राणलिङ्ग - pránalinga, San.). Life lingam, or lingam [q.v.] worn on the person by a lingayet [q.v.].——*Praunam* (प्राण - prána, San.). From (pra, san. prefix + an, san. to breathe). Life, Breath, inspiration, vital actions. Also vital air or principle, The Vedantists [vedauntam] allege that Praunam is Bramh [q.v.], and that it is absorbed into Bramh during profound sleep while a man sleeps without dreaming that his soul is with Bramh. For the five vital airs or principles see Puncha praunam. Praunavaty is colloquial for praunahooty an indispensable ceremony among bramins in daily life; for more information see Puncha praunahooty.——*Praunauchauram* (प्राणाचार - pránáchára, San.). From (prána, san breath + áchára, san. observance). A mode of invoking the blessings of the deity. Women who have no offspring, go after their bath to the temple and lie on the ground with their head turned towards the idol [shilay, vigraham].——*Praunayaumam* (प्राणयाम - pránáyáma, San.). Breathing in a peculiar way through the nostrils during the mental recitation of the names or attributes of some deity.——*Praurtanay* (प्रार्थना - prárt'haná, San.). From (above + art'h, san. to request). Request, prayer, an offering, a vow.——*Prauvidayanaur* (பிறவிடையனாறு - pirávidaiyanáru, Tam. právidayanár*). From (pirávidaiyan, tam. proper name + áru, tam. river). River; Tanjore dist. Takes its source in eastern part of Nunnilam talook and passing through Caricaul territory empties itself into the sea.——*Prauyaschittam* (प्रायश्चित्त - práyashchitta, San.). From (práya, san. sitting down and fasting + chitta, san. mind). Expiation for forbidden and evil acts. A man who for any forbidden act is put out of caste can re-enter only by prauyaschittam.——*Pravachanam* (प्रवचन - pravachana, San.). From (above + vach, san. to speak). The Vedaungams [q.v.] are so called.——*Pravartacan* (प्रवर्तक - pravartaka, San.; பிரவர்த்தகன் - piravarttagan, Tam.). From (above + vrit, san. live). A trader.——*Pravauham* (प्रवाह - praváha, San.; பிரவாகம் - pirávágam, Tam.). From (above + vah, san. to carry). A flood.——*Praverty* (പ്രവൃത്തി - pravritti, Mal.). From sanscrit. Means employment. Hence village. Praverticauran is a subordinate revenue officer having charge of the collections of one or more villages [chundracaur, parbutty].——*Prayogam* (प्रयोग - prayóga, San.). From (above + yuj, san. to unite). Instructions for particular rites. Manuals of modern date.——*Prowdham* (प्रौढ - praudha, San.). From (above + vah, san. to proceed); advanced. Bold. Prowdhadeva was a Rajah of Vijianugger of the Harihar dynasty. A.D. 1476. See vol. I (58).

PRATI (प्रति -prati, *San.*). Prefix meaning again, against.——*Pratibimbam* (प्रतिबिम्ब - pratibimba, San.). From (prati, san. against + bimba, san. picture). Reflection.——*Pratiloma* (प्रतिलोम - pratilóma, San.). From (above + lóma, san. hair on the body). Against the hair. That is, read or repeated backwards [anooloma]. Irregular or unusual, as a marriage wherein the husband is inferior to the wife. Pratilomaja is born in the inverse order of the classes from men of inferior castes carrying on commerce with women of superior caste; these are:—"*a*" born of a Cshatriya father and Bramin mother and known as Sootan;—"*b*" born of a Veisya father and Bramin mother and known as Veidyan;—"*c*" born of a Shoodra father and Bramin mother and known as Chandaulan;—"*d*" born of a Veisya father and Cshatriya mother and known as Maugadhan;—"*e*" born of a Shoodra father and Cshatriya mother and known as Cshautry;—"*f*" born of a Shoodra father and Veisya woman and known as Ayogavan. See vol. I (64).——*Pratinyay* (प्रतिज्ञा - pratiñá, San.). From (prati, san. against + ñá, san. to know). Promise, resolution.——*Pratisargam* (प्रतिसर्ग - pratisarga, San.). From (above + srij, san. to create). Recreation; one of the five topics which every pooraunam [q.v.] is supposed to treat of. The other four are sargam, vamsham, manwantaram, and vamshaunoocharitam.——*Prativaudy* (प्रतिवादी - prativádí, San.). From (above + vad, san. to speak). Defendant, opponent or replicant [yethiry].——*Pratyacsham* (प्रत्यक्ष - pratyaksha, San.). From (above + akshi, san. eye). Present before the eyes; perception by the senses; one of the four processes, according to Nyauyam [q.v.] philosophy, by which the mind arrives at true and accurate knowledge. The other three are anoomaunam or inference, oopamaunam or comparison, and shabdam or verbal testimony or authority.——*Pratyauhauram* (प्रत्याहार - pratyáhára, San.). From (above + áhára, san. drawing). Drawing back or restraining. Restraint of the organs of senses [indriyam]. The fifth stage of the yogam [q.v.] practice.——*Pratyoottaram* (प्रत्युत्तर - pratyuttara, San.). From (above + uttara, san. reply). Rejoinder [oottaram].

PREMEIRA (ಮೂಲ್ಕಿಬಂಡೆ - múlkibande, *Can.*). Can. means moolky rocks. Rocks; South canara dist., Mangalore tal.; lat. 13° 05′; long. 74° 50′; from Mangalore N. 16 miles [moolky]. See vol. II, 146.

PRICKLY (கூரு - kúru, *Tam.*). Prefix.——*Prickly-heat* (دھو پیلیاں - dhúpeliyán, Hind.; ಬೆವರುಸಾಲೆ - bevarusále, Can.; చెమటకాయ - chematakáya, Tel.; വേർക്കുരു - vérkkuru, Mal.; வேர்க்குரு - vérkkuru, Tam.). Hind. from (dhúp, hind. sunshine). Can. from (bevaru, can. perspiration + sálu, can. a line). Tel. from (chemata, tel. perspiration + káya, tel. eruption). Mal. and tam. from (vér, Tam. sweat + kuru, tam. pricking). Lichen tropicus of physicians. A cutaneous rash. Natives use a paste of sandal-wood [q.v.] to alleviate it.——*Prickly-pear* (नागफणी - nágap'haní, San. and Mahr.; काट्यानिवलि - kántyánivali, Conc.; ناگ پھنا - nágphaná, Hind.; چپل سینڈھ - chappalsend, Dec.; ಮುಳ್ಳುಕಳ್ಳಿ - mullukalli, Can.; ಕಳ್ಳಿ-

kalli, Tod.; నాగజెముడు - nágajemudu, Tel.; നാഗമുള്ള - nága-mullu, Mal.; කටුපතුක් - katupatuk, Singh.; நாகதாளி - nága-tháli, Tam.). Title from leaves and fruit like pear [amrood]. San. from (nága, san. cobra + p'hana, san. hood); from leaves like snake hood. Conc. means prickly cactus. Hind. from sanscrit. Dec. from (chappal, hind. slipper + send, hind. euphorbia); from its appearance. Can. from (mullu, can. thorn + kalli, can. milk-hedge). Tel. from (nága, san. cobra + jemudu, tel. euphorbia tirucalli, linn.). Mal. from (nága, san. cobra + mullu, mal. thorn). Singh. from (katu, singh. thorny + patuk, singh. euphorbia nereifolia, linn.). Tam. from (nága, san. cobra + táli, tam. convolvulus); leaves like cobra hood. San. also (vidára), meaning tearing asunder; (vishvasáraka), meaning having all essence. Can. also (dabbagalli), meaning big + milk-hedge; (sivarámakalli); (pápásukattále), meaning shoe + aloe indica, royle. Mal. also (nágatáli), meaning cobra creeper; (palakakkalli), meaning plate + the plant, euphorbia. Singh. also (kodugaha). Tam. also (shappáttumul), meaning european shoe + thorn; (palagaikkalli), meaning plate + euphorbia tirucalli, linn.; (shappáttuççedi), meaning european shoe + plant; from shape of leaves. Title otherwise Cochineal fig, Hedge prickly pear, Indian fig, Nopul, Oblong indian fig, Plate-leaf milk hedge, Slipper milk hedge, Slipper thorn, Snake-hood fig. Called by the portuguese Palmatoria d' inferno, from the resemblance of its flat branches to a palmatoria, or flat piece of wood used in schools to beat children upon the hand. Botanically Opuntia dillenii, haw., cacteæ [vricsham, 65]. Alias Cactus dillenii, indicus; Opuntia tuna. A plant of south america naturalized; bears large, bright, yellow flowers, two inches in diameter; stems when young fleshy and nearly flat, but in age become cylindrical, hard, and branched. Fruits are pear-shaped [amrood], 2–3 inches, green, yellow, or red; stand erect on the margins of the thick fleshy leaf-like joints of the stem; contain a somewhat refrigerant and highly refreshing pulp. The plant is very apt to spread from the fact that birds which eat the fruits cannot digest the hard seeds; in its growth however it has a distinct preference for waste arid soils that will grow nothing else, and it does not flourish freely on rich well-cultivated land; owing to the immense tracts of country now covered with prickly-pear various attempts have been made to get rid of it or to utilise it for industrial purposes; under the former head tree seeds have been sown among the prickly-pear, so that in the first place the cactus may act as nursery to the seedlings, protecting them from the sun and browsing animals, and afterwards the trees growing up may shade the cactus itself so as to destroy it; in dry rainless regions this experiment has failed, elsewhere it has had some success; from the severe pain its prickles occasion, its vitality, and the rapidity of its growth it is a very troublesome plant to actually eradicate; when this is attempted, it is cut with long spuds or with knives attached to sticks; if left on the ground it very soon begins to grow again, and must therefore be destroyed by water or fire; for destroying by water put it into a rather shallow pool and sink it to the bottom with stones, in 24 hours the water will begin to get thick and muddy, in two days it smells sour, on the third day a scum rises and the whole substance of the prickly-pear is decomposed, it then makes good manure and will not grow or vegetate; for destroying by fire, cut a number of the shrubby plants that usually accompany it, spread these over the ground to the height of a foot or two, lay the prickly-pear on the top, and leave the pile to dry for some days, then set fire to the heap; if too much of the prickly-pear be piled up, it will require a second firing; potash may be prepared from the ashes. Natives esteem the fruit as a remedy in whooping cough and asthma; its action is due to the soluble malate of manganese contained. On cutting open the thick succulent rind of fruit, a jelly-like pulp is found, which, though of little flavor, is cool and refreshing; village children are adepts at extracting it; it contains a large hard flat black thorn, which has to be rejected before putting in mouth; fruit and tender shoots eaten during famines; the cochineal [kirmiz] insect of south america thrives on this. Fibre gives a paper material; as hedge plant prickly-pear is both impenetrable and uninflammable; the unrestrained growth of the plant around villages which generally arises from its employment is however very inimical to sanitation, the close growth of the flat jointed stems which branch out in every direction making it difficult to keep the ground underneath free from decaying vegetation; these hedges moreover harbour reptiles. No other common species here.

PRITIVY (पृथिवी - prit'hiví, *San.*). From (prithú, san. wide). The earth; Cybele. The earth, the first of the elementary substances [bhootam], is of two kinds; eternal and non-eternal. Eternal in the form of Paramaunoo [q.v.] roopam or atoms, non-eternal in the form of Caurya roopam or products. The non-eternal character of aggregated earth is shown by the want of permanence in a chatty [q.v.] when crushed to powder. Hindoo 2nd or pers. name [peyar].——*Partasauraty* (पार्थसारथि - párt'hasárat'hi, San.). From (párt'ha, san. arjúna, son of prit'há + sárat'hi, san. a charioteer). Krishnan [q.v.], because he acted as the charioteer of Arjoonan [q.v.] at the chief battle of the Mahabhaurat [q.v.], between the Cowrava and Pandava princes. This is the name of a deity at the Vishnoo temple in Triplicane, Madras. Hindoo 2nd or pers. name, chiefly among the Veishnavites [peyar].——*Parteshwaran* (பார்த்தேசுவரன் - párttésuvaran, Tam.). From (párt'ha, san. arjuna, son of prit'há + íshvara, san. lord); arjoonan, the lord. Hindoo 2nd or pers. name [peyar].——*Paurtan* (पार्थ - párt'ha, San.). From (prit'há, san. kuntí, the extender); born of coonty, one of the wives of pandoo [q.v.]. Arjoonan.

PRIYAM (प्रिय - priya, *San.*). From (prí, san. to please). Love.—"*a*" Plant first term. Loveable or good. Ex., where transl. is of second term:—Panicum italicum (priyangu), parts; Prosopis spicigera (priyadarshiní), looking. See gloss. paragraphs.—"*b*" Plant second term. Dear to or liked by. Ex., where transl. is of first term:—Albizzia lebbek (munipriya), sage; Andropogon muricatus (ranapriya), battle; Commelyna communis (vatsapriya), calf; Curcuma longa (yóshitpriya), woman; Mangifera indica (nripapriya), king; Melia azadirachta (ravipriya), sun; Musa paradisiaca (bálakapriya), boy; Tinospora cordifolia (bhishakpriyá), physician; Zizyphus napeca (shikhipriya), peacock. See gloss. paragraphs.——*Piyah* (پیا - piyá, Hind.). From (prí, san. to love). Lover.——*Piyal* (प्रियाल - priyála, San.; پیال - piyál, Hind.). Means desired. Same as Wild mohwah.——*Piyauree* (پیاری - piyárí, Hind.). Dear. In composition makes a lacab; as Piyauree begum, dear lady [ism].——*Priyadarshy* (प्रियदर्शी - priyadarshí, San.). From (above + drish, san. to see). Means kindly looking. An epithet of Asoca [jowgada].——*Priyangoo* (प्रियंगु - priyangu, San.). From (priya, san. pleasing). Panic grass, Panic millet. Botanically the Panicum genus, graminaceæ [vricsham, 156]. Grasses found in tropical and sub-tropical regions, distinguished by having spikelets of two flowers, one perfect and the other imperfect; constitute the principal fodder-grasses. The species best known to the natives are:—antipodum [wild small shaumay], burmanni [wild hurrially], ciliare [trembling tinay], colonum [matted purple grass], crusgalli [wild darbhay], egyptiacum [red shaumay], erucæforme [small raggy], flavidum [purple grass], fluitans [paddy field grass], frumentaceum [large shaumay], glaucum [white tinay], grossarum [cumboo grass], helopus [quilled purple grass], helvolum [jackal tinay], indicum [black tinay], italicum [tinay], javanicum [surprise grass], jumentorum [guinea grass], miliaceum [varagoo], miliare [shaumay], paludosum [soda grass], prostratum [wild white shaumay], remotum [wild varagoo], repens [ginger grass], stagninum [large purple grass], uliginosum [goondra grass], verticillatum [sticky grass]. Other s. indian species indigenous or naturalized are:—acuminatissimum, æquatum, asperum, brachyglume, canaliculatum, canaræ, cimicinum, conjugatum, corymbosum, courtallense, curvatum, dilatatum, dubium, elatius, interruptum, kunthianum, lanceolatum, leptochloa, mangaloricum, megalanthum, metzii, montanum, multibrachiatum, nepalense, nilagiricum, nodibarbatum, oxyphyllum, peninsulanum, roxburghii, serrulatum, tenue, tomentosum, trigonum, wallichianum.

PRODDOOTORE (ప్రొద్దుటూరు - proddutúru, *Tel.* proddutur*). From (proddu, tel. sun + úru, tel. village), town of the sun, from a legend concerning its foundation.——(1) Talook, Cuddapah district. Tahsildar's pay Rs. 175. Area 478 square miles. Population 98,418. Language Teloogoo. N. of district. Bounded north by Sirwail talook of Kurnool district; east by the Nullamullays and Budwail talook; west by Jummalmadoogoo talook; south by the Pennair and Cuddapah talook. Physical aspect flat, treeless and uninteresting, on the east however the talook is bounded by the Nullamullay hills. The Nullamullays are nearly bare. The principal soil is black cotton [regar]. Cotton [q.v.] is the principal product. In the valley of the Pennair dry grains [q.v.] and rice [q.v.] are raised by means of channels [q.v.]. Indigo [q.v.] is largely grown, frequently adulterated with mud. The Kurnool-cuddapah irrigation and navigation canal runs through the talook. There are 25 tanks, 19 channels, and 900 wells, private and dasbandam [q.v.]. Camping grounds are at Chilmacore, Chintalaconda, Doovvoor and Meidcore. Places of archæological interest:—Allaudpulley, Arcativaimla, Bollavaram, Caumanore, Chilmacore, Chiyyapaud, Cootsoopaupa, Corrapaud, Cottapully, Doovvoor, Gopavaram, Jillella, Mauchenapulley, Maulepaud, Neelapooram, Nidzoovvy, Payidela, Peddashettipully, Proddootore, Pullavole, Rameshwaram, Sowdore, Taullamaurepooram, Tendaldinney, Tungatore. The leading places, &c., in the talook are the following.——*Bollavaram* (బొల్లవరం - bollavaram, Tel.). From (bollu, tel. chaff + pura, san. town). Village; pop. 1,632; acres 2,876; lat. 14° 46′; long. 78° 34′; from Cuddapah N.W. 27 miles; from Proddootore W.N.W. 1½ miles. Inscription of Vijianugger dynasty in Vengopaulsawmy temple.——*Chilmacore* (చిలమకూరు - chilamakúru, Tel.). From (chelama, tel. a spring in a river bed + úru, tel. village). Village; acres 9,420; lat. 14° 39′; long. 78° 31′; from Cuddapah W.N.W. 26 miles; from Proddootore S.W. 9 miles. Lies in a plain bounded on each side by low ridges of hills, and surrounded by ruined walls said to have been built by Shuncary yogeysheshappa, a Bramin. Ancient temples to Eeshwaran [q.v.] and Hanooman [q.v.]. Inscription of Vijianugger. Inhabitants principally Coonbies [q.v.], pursuing agriculture. Mounds of old salt manufactures, used during the Pataun government, still to be seen on the banks of the rivulet crossing the plain.——

Coondair (కుందేరు - kundéru, Tel.). See sep. title.——*Doovvoor* (దువ్వూరు - duvvúru, Tel.). From (duvvu, tel. a leopard + úru, tel. village). Village; pop. 3,003; acres 6,779; lat. 14° 51′; long. 78° 42′; from Cuddapah N.N.W. 29 miles; from Proddootore N.E. 10 miles. Former talook head-quarters, and seat of a Moonsif's court. Deserted on account of its unhealthiness. Battle fought here in 1779 between Hyder ally and the Nawaub of Cuddapah. Old temples and a mosque [musjid]. Dismantled fort with a ditch. West is a temple of Ramasawmy, with inscription dated A.D. 1619. Here is a standard "peimash chain" marked by two stones that distance apart, one of which bears an inscription.——*Meidcoro* (మైదుకూరు - maidukúru, Tel.). From (médi, tel. fig tree, ficus racemosa, linn. + úru, tel. village). Village; pop. 3,264; acres 6,710; lat. 14° 44′; long. 78° 47′; from Cuddapah N.N.W. 18 miles; from Proddootore E. 12 miles. Small temple to Shiva.——*Nidzoovvy* (నిడుజువ్వి - nidudzuvvi, Tel.). From (nidu, tel. long + dzuvvi, tel. shining leaved fig tree, ficus tsiela, roxb.). Village; pop. 1,893; acres 4,435; lat. 14° 39′; long. 78° 33′; from Cuddapah W.N.W. 24 miles; from Proddootore S.S.W. 8 miles. 2½ miles S.W. of Yerragoontla railway station. Noted for block limestone [choonam cull] quarries, largely worked for export to Madras for use and in the district. Inscriptions in the temples of Bheiraveshwarasawmy, Chandikeshwarasawmy, and Vigneshwarasawmy. The first, dated A.D. 1545, records a grant by Rama rajah chinna timmayyadeva maharajah, in the reign of Sadaushivan of Vijianugger. The second is dated A.D. 1206. The third, dated A.D. 1548, records a grant by Chinna timmayyadeva maharajah, son of Rama rajah, in the reign of Sadaushivan.——*Nullamullay* (నల్లమల - nallamala, Tel.). See sep. title.——*Nundyailampetı* (నంద్యాలంపేట - nandyálampéta, Tel.). From (nandi, san. the bull god + álaya, san. temple + péta, tel. suburb). Village; pop. 3,533; acres 12,532; lat. 14° 44′; long. 78° 51′; from Cuddapah N. 17 miles; from Proddootore E. 17 miles. Former head-quarters of a District moonsif, whose office is now used as a police station. Near are some topes [q.v.]. Indigo [q.v.] formerly manufactured. High hills all round; on top of one group called Mookkondaloo is a little temple, near it is an unfinished well.——*Peddashettipully* (పెద్దశెట్టిపల్లె - peddashettipalli, Tel.). From (pedda, tel. head + shetti, tel. merchant + palli, tel. village). Village; pop. 2,952; acres 5,675; lat. 14° 46′; long. 78° 33′; from Cuddapah N.W. 29 miles; from Proddootore W.N.W. 3 miles. Noted for limestone quarries, largely worked. Two old temples of Keshava sawmy and Eeshwaran.——*Pennair* (పెన్నేరు - pennéru, Tel.). See sep. title.——*Proddootore* (ప్రొద్దుటూరు - proddutúru, Tel.). See below.——*Rameshwaram* (రామేశ్వరము - rámésh-varamu, Tel.). From (ráma, san. the god + íshvara, san. lord). Village; pop. 3,443; acres 3,420; lat. 14° 45′; long. 78° 35′; from Cuddapah N.W. 26 miles; from Proddootore W. 1 mile. Bramin suburb of Proddootore. Large Shiva temple.——*Tippareddipully* (తిప్పారెడ్డిపల్లె - tippáreddipalli, Tel.). From (tippáreddi, tel. proper name + palli, tel. village). Village; pop. 1,065; acres 24,456; lat. 14° 52′; long. 78° 50′; from Cuddapah N. 26 miles; from Proddootore E.N.E. 17 miles. Former residence of a poligar.——*Tungatore* (తంగటూరు - tangatúru, Tel.). From (tangu, can. to halt + úru, tel. village). Village; pop. 2,539; acres 5,871; lat. 14° 53′; long. 78° 39′; from Cuddapah N.N.W. 31 miles; from Proddootore N.N.E. 11 miles. On the Coondair.——*Wonipenta* (వనిపెంట - vanipenta, Tel.). From (vaní, san. forest + penta, tel. heap). Village; pop. 4,185; acres 5,361; lat. 14° 48′; long. 78° 50′; from Cuddapah N. 22 miles; from Proddootore E.N.E. 16 miles. Trade in brass vessels manufactured locally.——*Yerramala* (ఎర్రమల - yerramala, Tel.). See sep. title.——**(2)** Town, Talook and District moonsif's head-quarters; Cuddapah dist., Proddootore tal.; pop. 6,841; acres 3,848; lat. 14° 45′; long. 78° 36′; from Cuddapah N.W. 26 miles; from Madanapully N. 83 miles; from Madras N.W. 163 miles; from Sidhout W.N.W. 34 miles. Large and wealthy town with considerable commerce in indigo and cotton, rice, cloths and precious metals. European cotton press. Old fort.

PROLE (ప్రోలు - prólu, *Tel.*). Town. Suffix in place names [pole, vole, wail].

PROW (ڤراو - práú, *Malay*; പാറു - páru, *Mal.*). Title from (prau, jav. a boat). Malay word. A term for all vessels between a canoe and a square-rigged vessel.

PUCKA (پکا - pakká, *Hind.*). Through mahr. from (pakva, san. mature). Mature, complete, contrast in all respects of Cutcha [q.v.]. For instance planting seed thickly, betel-nut [q.v.] in a raw state, permanent building, &c., &c. Pucka puddy is opposed to chinna puddy, pucka seer to cutcha seer.

PUDDY (پڑی - parí, *Hind.*; படி - padi, *Tam.*). From (padi, tam. to settle). Means a regulated measure; also allowance.—"*a*" Measure of capacity. 4 oyaks = 1 puddy; 8 puddies = 1 mercaul [alavay, 3a]. Approximate actual value, 1 puddy = 100 cubic inches and holds 120 tolah's weight or 3 lbs. $1\frac{2}{3}\frac{3}{5}$ oz. of rice. Varies in different places. The ratio of imperial quart to puddy is 34,659 to 50,000. The puddy is the same for grains as for liquids. Compare Yedangaly, Seer of cuddapah.—"*b*" Superficial measure. Land requiring a puddy of seed. 8 puddies = 1 mercaul [alavay, 2a]. Approximate actual value, 1 puddy = 420¼ square feet. Tinnevelly. Same as Nauzhy. Compare Yedangaly. See vol. I, 609; II, 506, 507, 509, 514, 515, 518, 519.——*Paudam* (പാദം - pátam, Mal.). An oil vessel. Liquid measure. 16 cootties = 1 paudam [alavay, 4d]. Approximate actual value, 1 paudam = 1 cubic foot and 1,002 cubic inches. Malabar. Compare Calam of Tanjore. See vol. I, 609.

PUGGRY (پگڑی - pagrí, *Hind.*; ಪಗಡಿ - pagadi, *Can.*; పాగా - págá, *Tel.*; பாகை - págai, *Tam.*). A turban [q.v.]. A narrow scarf folded round the head to form a head-dress. Usually of a fine muslin-like [muslin] texture which, when folded, is at once light, bulky, and porous. Of materials, cotton [q.v.] occupies the first place, being a non-conductor and permitting escape of perspiration. Silk [puttoo] used to some extent by the higher classes. Wool [pushm] not often used, but sometimes in the form of small shawls [q.v.]. The caste frequently determines the size and shape of the turban [q.v.]. White is the commonest color. Red next, then yellow, and after these green, blue, purple, and occasionally even black; the darker colors being relieved by embroidery. Among turbans made of silk, there are buffs, shots, and greys. The turban unfolded consists of a strip of cloth varying in breadth from 9 to 12 inches, and in length from 15 to 25 yards. In the process of making up, the outer end is usually left free to hang down a little, or is turned up over the folds at the back when the tying is finished. In the simpler forms, colored thread is introduced into this free end as an ornament, in others gold in stripes [sarigay], varying in breadth from one-eighth of an inch to several inches. Sometimes the gold [pon], or other decorative medium, in addition to running across the end is made to extend longitudinally a little way up from the end, so as to be seen on the side of one or two of the last folds of the turban. In some instances again the embellishment is carried so far up that all the outer folds of the turban present it to view. Turban-pieces are undressed; size interfering with the lightness and openness of the article, and with the feel of the fabric. The following are Hindostany proverbs:—چراغ گل پگڑی غیب—"light put out, turban gone;" said of maladministration.—پگڑی رکھ گھی چکھ—"turban [q.v.] or honor keep, taste ghee [q.v.];" that is to say, honesty is the best policy. The Dravidian has really no national head costume, the head being naturally worn bare; a skull-cap with ear-flaps for children and old people is the only exception. The puggry or turban was borrowed from the mahomedans. The natives have an almost infinite variety of ways of tying the turban; thereby exhibiting some individuality as well as showing their caste. The following are different kinds of puggry distinguished by name.——*Amauma*(عمامہ - amámah, Hind.). Means winding round the head. Worn by judges and doctors.——*Araby* (عربی - arabí, Hind.). Worn by Arabs.——*Baunky* (بانکی - bánkí, Hind.). Means curved. A turban [q.v.] adopted by the gay.——*Casauwah* (کساوا - kasává, Hind.). From (kasná, hind. to tie). Simple scarf tied round the head.——*Chuckridar* (چکریدار - chakrídár, Hind.). From (chakrí, hind. circular + dár, pers. holder). Circular, used by Hajees [q.v.].——*Coolah* (کلاہ - kuláh, Hind.; ಕುಲಾವಿ - kulávi, Can.; குல்லாய் - kulláy, Tam.). Means a crown. A cap worn by dervishes [q.v.].——*Goondidar* (گنڈی دار - gundídár, Hind.). From (gundí, hind. a stud + dár, pers. holder). Globular.——*Jodidar* (جوڑیدار - júrídár, Hind.). From (júrá, hind. top knot + dár, pers. holder). The hinder part resembles a hair knot [conday] of women tied behind.——*Khidkeedar* (کھڑکیدار - khirkídár, Hind.). From (khirkí, hind. opening + dár, pers. having). Chobdar's turban.——*Latpaty* (لٹپٹی - latpatí, Hind.). Means hanging loose. An irregular loose turban.——*Lattoodar* (لٹودار - lattúdár, Hind.). Top-shaped.——*Mandeel* (مندیل - mandíl, Hind.). From (mandá, hind. head). A silk or gold woven band applied over the turban.——*Mansabee* (منصبی - mansabí, Hind.). Worn by Mansabdars [q.v.] in Hyderabad.——*Masheikhy* (مشایخی - masháikhí, Hind.). Worn by Masheikhs [q.v.].——*Moorassa* (مرصع - murassa, Hind.). From (rasa, ar. adhere). A short turban closely tied.——*Nastalik* (نستعلیق - nastalík, Hind.). A small round turban and closely fits the head. Durbar [q.v.] turban.——*Pethah* (پیٹھا - pethá, Hind.). Means a gourd. Worn by Mowlvies [q.v.].——*Saitee* (سیٹھی - sethí, Hind.). Used by bankers.——*Shamla* (شملہ - shamlah, Hind.). Turban made up of square shawl pieces; also end of a turban left hanging behind by ecclesiastics.——*Sipar e ally* (سپر علی - sipariali, Hind.). From (sipar, pers. shield + alí, ar. name of the companion of the prophet).——Broad like shield worn by the Shiahs [q.v.].——*Tauj* (تاج - táj, Hind.). Means a crown. A conical cap.——*Teencony* (تین کونی - tínkoní, Hind.). Three-cornered, which Tippoo sultan used to wear.——*Topee* (ٹوپی - topí, Hind.; தொப்பி - toppi, Tam.). From (topná, hind. to cover). Cap worn underneath a turban.

PULLADAM (பல்லடம் - palladam,* *Tam.*). From (palli, tam. a member of the caste + idam, tam. place) [padoo].——**(1)** Talook, Coimbatore district. Tahsildar's pay Rs. 225,

Area 741 square miles. Population 270,390. Language Tamul. Centre of district. Bounded N. by Suttimungalam talook, E. by Erode and Dharaupooram talooks, S. by Oodamalpett, Pollachy and Dharaupooram talooks, and W. by Coimbatore talook. A flat plain, having neither hills nor forests. The Noyil bisects it, and, with the exception of the Nullaur a jungle stream, is its only river. The climate is hot and rainless. The wind is furious, but fairly cool in the south-west monsoon [q.v.], as the talook lies opposite to the Palghaut gap. Soils are black cotton [regar], chiefly in the south and south-west, with conglomerated calcareous tufa in parts bordering on Dharaupooram. About Pulladam and northwards to Avanashy and Shaivore the soil is chiefly reddish gravel. Near the railway from Mungalam to Shoolore are rich tracts of red loam [sevval] and red sand [manal], with occasionally black and reddish-black tracts. A peculiar kind of sheep [aud] known as cooroombaud [q.v.] are reared. Characterized by having white bodies and black heads, and a true wool [pushm] instead of hair; these are always tended by Cocrumba [q.v.] shepherds, whose females weave the wool into coarse blankets [cumbly]. The yield of wool is very small. Industries other than those of blanket [cumbly, jamkhana] weaving and cotton [q.v.] pressing are unimportant. Good spectacles of pebble are made by lapidaries at Moottampolliem; those also work the crystals [palingoo cull] into lingams [q.v.] and other vigraham [q.v.]. Products are wholly rural produce. Dry crops [dry grain] are cholum [q.v.], cotton [q.v.], horse-gram [q.v.], bullock-gram, and cumboo [bajrah], and pulses [dholl]. Garden crops [tottacaul] are cholum [q.v.], raggy [q.v.], chillies [q.v.], onions [piyauz] and tobacco [pogauk]. Wet crops [q.v.] are paddy [q.v.], sugar-cane [q.v.] and turmeric [country saffron]. Only 1·06 per cent. of the occupied area falls under the head of irrigated. There are thirteen dams across the Noyil, but the supply is generally scanty. Anicut channels [q.v.] lead directly from the river. The Nullaur, a tributary of the Noyil, rising in the uplands in the neighbourhood of Annoor in Coimbatore talook, is utilised to some extent, but is a precarious source. The petty tanks are dependent on rainfall [mazhay, monsoon] and surface drainage. Spring channels [q.v.] used to be dug in the Noyil bed. Camping grounds :—Avanashy, Caroomuttamputty, Chinnayampolliem, Covilpolliem, Pulladam, Shoolore, Tirpore. Places of archæological interest :—Aulatore, Avanashipolliem, Avanashy, Candyancovil, Caniyampoondy, Canjipully, Moottanampolliem, Mungalam, Nadoovacherry, Peroongarnaipolliem, Poodarsal, Shaivore, Shanvadipolliem, Shoolore, Tirmoorganpoondy, Vailampolliem. Principal trig. stations :—Alagoomullay, Vediyapolliem. The leading places, &c., in the talook are the following.——*Alagoomullay* (அலகுமலை - alagumalai, Tam.). From (alagu, tam. blade of a weapon + malai, tam. mountain). Village; pop. 2,995; acres 4,576; lat. 11° 01′; long. 77° 29′; from Coimbatore E. 32 miles; from Pulladam E. 11 miles. Small temple to Soobramanyasawmy on the Alagoomullay hills and a camping ground in Covilpolliem, a hamlet of the village. Trig. station; lat. 11° 00′ 48·03″; long. 77° 28′ 48·08″; height 1,353 feet; from Alagoomullay N. ½ mile; from Pulladam E.N.E. 11 miles.——*Avanashipolliem* (அவனாசிப்பாளையம் - avanásippálaiyam, Tam.). From (avanási, tam. village of that name + pálaiyam, tam. fortified village). Village; pop. 3,151; acres 6,378; lat. 10° 58′; long. 77° 29′; from Coimbatore E.S.E. 32 miles; from Pulladam E.S.E. 10 miles. Old Shiva temple. Vishnoo temple both in the hamlet of Codoovye. In the hamlet of Poothoopolliem another old Shiva temple.——*Avanashy* (அவனாசி - avanási, Tam.). See sep. title.——*Caradibauvy* (ಕರಡಿಬಾವಿ - karadibávi, Can.; கரடிப்பாவி - karadippávi, Tam.). From (karadi, can. bear + bávi, can. well). Village; pop. 1,813; acres 3,112; lat. 10° 58′; long. 77° 14′; from Coimbatore E.S.E. 16 miles; from Pulladam W.S.W. 6 miles.——*Caravalore* (கறவைஊர் - karavalúr, Tam.). From (karavai, tam. a milch cow + úr, tam. village). Village; pop. 1,845; acres 2,956; lat. 11° 13′; long. 77° 14′; from Coimbatore N.E. 22 miles; from Pulladam N.N.W. 16 miles. Famous Mauriyamman [q.v.] temple. Car festival [ratotsavam] in February or March, during which large cattle [maud] fair. Large weekly fair.——*Caroomuttamputty* (கருமத்தம்பட்டி - karumattambatti, Tam.). From (karu, tam. black + úmattai, tam. thorn apple, datura fastuosa, linn. + patti, tam. cattle-fold). Village; pop. 3,640; acres 6,619; lat. 11° 07′; long. 77° 14′; from Coimbatore E.N.E. 17 miles; from Pulladam N.W. 11 miles. On trunk road to Madras. Ancient Roman catholic settlement, with Roman catholic chapel built in 1660.——*Mondipolliem* (மொண்டிப்பாளையம் - mondippálaiyam, Tam.). From (mundi, tam. to shave the head + pálaiyam, tam. fortified village); place where people shave their heads and perform vows. Village, Place of pilgrimage; pop. 708; acres 1,097; lat. 11° 17′; long. 77° 12′; from Coimbatore N.N.E. 24 miles; from Pulladam N.N.W. 22 miles. Famous Vishnoo temple. Twenty dolmens [codaycull] in a field. Devotees frequent on Saturdays in Poorataushy [mausam] or September and October.——*Mungalam* (மங்கலம் - mangalam,* Tam.). Means prosperity. Village, Railway station; pop. 1,726; acres 1,676; lat. 11° 07′; long. 77° 19′; height 1,052 feet; from Coimbatore E.N.E. 22 miles; from Pulladam N. 9 miles. Inhabited by Lubbays [q.v.], chiefly traders. Dolmens [coday cull], &c., a mile east.——*Neelambore* (நீலம்பூர் - nílambúr, Tam.). From (níla, san. black + ambu, san. water + úr, tam. village). Village; pop. 4,481; acres 5,965; lat. 11° 04′; long. 77° 08′; from Coimbatore E.N.E. 10 miles; from Pulladam W.N.W. 14 miles. Large ruined tank.——*Noyil* (நொய்யல் - noyyal, Tam.). See sep. title.——*Pulladam* (பல்லடம் - palladam, Tam.). See below.——*Shaivore* (சேவூர் - shévúr, Tam.). From (shé, tam. redness + úr, tam. village). Village; pop. 2,101; acres 1,483; lat. 11° 15′; long. 77° 17′; from Coimbatore N.E. 26 miles; from Pulladam N. 18 miles. Two old Shiva temples.——*Shomanore* (சோமனூர் - shómanúr, Tam. sómanúr *). Means soman's village. Village, Railway station, Hamlet of Caroomuttamputty; lat. 11° 06′; long. 77° 14′; height 1,121 feet; from Coimbatore E. 16 miles; from Pulladam N.W. 9 miles. Inhabitants Roman catholics.——*Shoolore* (சூலூர் - shúlúr, Tam. súlúr *). From (súle, can. dancing girl + úr, tam. village). Village, Railway station; pop. 4,713; acres 2,708; lat. 11° 03′; long. 77° 10′; height 1,182 feet; from Coimbatore E.N.E. 12 miles; from Pulladam W. 11 miles. Large chuttram [q.v.] by Maudayya rauz of Coimbatore during reign of Krishna rajah wodeyar of Mysore. Good tanks fed by the Noyil. Weekly market.——*Tirpore* (திருப்பூர் - tiruppúr, tam. tirupúr *). From (tiru, tam. holy + úr, tam. village). Village, Railway station; pop. 5,235; acres 2,137; lat. 11° 07′; long. 77° 23′; height 989 feet; from Coimbatore N.E. 28 miles; from Pulladam N.N.E. 9 miles. Car festival and large cattle fair in June. Good market. Bridge over Noyil. Cotton press. Good private chuttram [q.v.].——*Vediyapolliem* (வெடியப்பாளையம் - vediyappálaiyam, Tam.). From (vediyal, tam. explosion of gunpowder + pálaiyam, tam. fortified village). Trig. station; lat. 10° 55′ 18·26″; long. 77° 09′ 30·38″; height 1,467 feet; from Pulladam W.S.W. 13 miles; from Shelacaratchal W.S.W. 4 miles.——**(2)** Village, Talook head-quarters; Coimbatore dist., Pulladam tal.; pop. 1,190; acres 1,372; lat. 11° 00′; long. 77° 20′; from Coimbatore E. 22 miles; from Erode S.W. 38 miles; from Madras S.W. 248 miles; from Ootacamund S.E. 50 miles; from Pollachy N.E. 31 miles; from Suttimungalam S. 35 miles. Ruined fort. Two cotton [q.v.] presses. Weekly market.

PULMANAIR (పలమనేరు - palamanéru, *Tel.*; பல்லமனேரி - pallamanéri, *Tam.* palmanér *). From (pallaman, tam. proper name + éri, tam. tank) [padoo].——**(1)** Talook; North arcot district. Tahsildar's pay Rs. 150. Area 439 square miles. Population 48,135. Language Teloogoo. W. of district. Bounded west by Mysore; north by Poonganore; east by Chittore and Goodiyattam; south-west by Cungoondy zemindarry and Krishnagherry talook of Salem district. Upon Mysore plateau. General level nearly 2,500 feet. Some hills 3,000 feet. Chief are Beirapullycondah, Devarcondah, and Putticondah. Sparsely populated. Large extent of jungle land, but large trees confined to eastern portions, where plateau descends to plains. Elsewhere large numbers of tamarinds [q.v.]. The commonest tree is the Caunooga or Pongamia glabra, vent. [karanj], which affords oil [yennay] from seeds, and manure [yeroo] from loppings and faded flowers. Soil more fertile than that of two zemindarries [q.v.] above ghauts [q.v.], and being heavily manured produces fine crops. Chief crops, paddy [q.v.], raggy [q.v.], sugar-cane [q.v.], and horse-gram [q.v.]. Iron found near Chintamaucoolapully, Gonamaucoolapully, Moodaramdoddy, and Nakkanapully, was made into agricultural instruments. Weaving of coarse female cloths. Cumblies [q.v.] woven by Cooroobar [q.v.], who tend flocks of long-fleeced sheep [aud]. Jaggery [q.v.] extensively manufactured. Rivers are Cowndinyanuddy and Goddaur. Tanks are Beireddipully, Culloopully, Dundapully, Jeedimaucoolapully, Keelery cadapa nuttam, and Maumadoogoo agrahauram. Places of archæological interest :—Baupanuttam, Beireddipully, Cadapanuttam, Dundapully, Nellipatta, Padigelacooppam, Peddanayeny droog, Pulmanair, Veeracull, Vencatagherrycottah, Vencatasamoodram, Vibhootiyantanagaram. Principal trig. stations :- Carvauda, Devarcondah, Krishnamacondah, Putticondah. The leading places, &c., are the following.——*Baupanuttam* (బాపనత్తం - bápanattam, Tel.). From (bápana, tel. bramin + nattam, tam. village). Tel. also (irulabandabápanattam), meaning dark + rock + village so called. Village; pop. 91; acres 322; lat. 13° 05′; long. 78° 44′; from Chittore W.S.W. 30 miles; from Pulmanair S.S.W. 9 miles. A group of dolmens [coday cull], called Pandava's temples. Usual sepulchral relics, but iron weapons scarce.——*Beireddipully* (బైరెడ్డిపల్లె - baireddipalle, * Tel.). From (baireddi, tel. short for bhairavareddi, tel. proper name + palle, tel. village). Village; pop. 1,256; acres 2,504; lat. 13° 06′; long. 78° 39′; from Chittore W.S.W. 34 miles; from Pulmanair S.W. 11 miles. Large tank. Trade in gram [q.v.], tamarind [q.v.], jaggery [q.v.], and sugar [q.v.]. Vishnoo temple. Festival five days in Maugham [mausam] or February. Chuttram [q.v.].——*Cadapanuttam* (కడపనత్తము - kadapanattamu, Tel.). From (kadapa, tel. threshold + nattam, tam. village). Village; acres 554; lat. 13° 04′; long. 78° 40′; from Chittore W.S.W. 35 miles; from Pulmanair S.W. 13 miles. At head of Talapoolla ghaut [q.v.]. Once head-quarters of talook. Fine tank. Two forts, several times besieged by invaders of Carnatic [q.v.]. Vishnoo temple; a festival for seven days in Veishaukham [mausam] or May. Weekly market on Wednesday.——*Carvauda*

(కారువాడ - kárváda, Tel.). From (káru, tel. forest + váda, tel. village). Trig. station; lat. 13° 07′ 20·41″; long. 78° 34′ 12·57″; height 2,592 feet; from Pulmanair W.S.W. 16 miles.——*Cowndinyanuddy* (కౌండిన్యనది - kaundinyanadi, Tel.). See sep. title.——*Devarcondah* (దేవరకొండ - dévarakonda, Tel.). From (dévaru, tel. title of marava rulers + konda, tel. hill). Hill; lat. 13° 05′; long. 78° 43′; height 2,732 feet; from Chittore W.S.W. 30 miles; from Pulmanair S.W. 2 miles. Trig. station in lat. 13° 04′ 46·19″; long. 78° 42′ 40·21″; height 2,732 feet; from Nellipatta N.N.W. 1 mile; from Pulmanair S.S.W. 10 miles.——*Goddaur* (గొడ్డారు - goddáru, Tel.). From (goddu, tel. barron + áru, tam. river). River. Also called Amboor. Rises in the west of Pulmanair, and discharges down the gorges in the neighbourhood of Naicknairy pass [ghaut].——*Krishnamacondah* (కృష్ణమ్మకొండ - krishnammakonda, Tel.). From (krishnamma, tel. proper name + konda, tel. hill). Trig. station; lat. 12° 57′ 07·10″; long. 78° 33′ 24·55″; height 2,768 feet; from Beirapulley S.S.E. 1 mile; from Pulmanair S.S.W. 24 miles.——*Krishnapooram* (కృష్ణపురము - krishnápuramu, Tel.). From (krishna, san. the god + pura, san. town). Village; pop. 312; lat. 12° 54′; long. 78° 27′; from Chittore W.S.W. 51 miles; from Pulmanair S.W. 30 miles. Polliem [q.v.] resumed 1848. Weekly market on Sunday.——*Naicknairy* (நாயக்கனேரி - náyakkanéri, Tam.). See sep. title.——*Peddanayeny droog* (పెద్దనాయనిదుర్గము - peddanáyanidurgamu, Tel.). From (peddanáyadu, tel. proper name + durga, san. fort). Hill; lat. 12° 58′; long. 78° 40′; height 2,425 feet; from Chittore W.S.W. 37 miles; from Pulmanair S.S.W. 19 miles. Old fort, stronghold of Poligar [q.v.] of Chauragal. See Naicknairy.——*Pulmanair* (పలమనేరు - palamanéru, Tel.). See below.——*Putticondah* (పత్తికొండ - pattikonda, Tel.). From (patti, tel. cotton + konda, tel. hill). Hill; lat. 13° 11′; long. 78° 41′; height 2,908 feet; from Chittore W. 31 miles; from Pulmanair W. 7 miles. A Shiva pagoda [q.v.] on the hill. Trig. station in lat. 13° 10′ 22·82″; long. 78° 41′ 11·74″; height 2,908 feet; from Pulmanair W.S.W. 7 miles; from Putticondah S.S.E. ¾ mile.——*Synigoonta* (శ్యానిగుంట - shyánigunta, Tel.). See sep. title.——*Vencatagherrycottah* (వెంకటగిరికోట - venkatagirikóta, Tel.). See sep. title.——**(2)** Town, Sanitarium, Head-quarters of Tahsildar; North arcot dist., Pulmanair tal.; pop. 5,040; acres 6,254; lat. 13° 12′; long. 78° 47′; height 2,247 feet; from Arnee N.W. 51 miles; from Chittore W. 24 miles; from Madras W. 104 miles; from Ranipett W.N.W. 44 miles; from Tripatty W.S.W. 54 miles; from Vellore N.W. 33 miles. At N.E. end of talook, near summit of Mogily pass [ghaut]. 10° Fahr. cooler than rest of district. Formerly frequented before use of Neilgherries. The fort, levelled thirty-five years ago, was constructed by a poligar [q.v.], Sowram vencatapaty naidoo. Family extinct. The town is clean and well-built; the houses being flat terraced. Trade in grain [dhaunyam, rice], jaggery [q.v.], tamarind [q.v.], cloths, cumblies [q.v.], &c., at weekly fair. Tannery [chamrah]. Arrack [q.v.] and rum distillery. Travellers' bungalow [q.v.], excellent chuttram [q.v.], American mission and Roman catholic chapels. Weekly market Friday. Vishnoo temple. Festival for five days in Cheitram [mausam] or April. A favorite excursion is to Gungamma chittsoo or Gungammah's valley. By Goodiyattam road, and three miles to north of town, are enormous banyan [q.v.] trees covering ground upon which a large camp [derah] may be pitched [hill-station].

PULNAUD (పల్నాడు - palnádu, *Tel.* palnád*). From (palu, tel. several + nádu, tel. country) [pala]. The Amravatty country was Cronnaud new land, and the Sundavole country was Velnaud or outer land.——**(1)** Talook, Kistna district. Tahsildar's pay Rs. 200; stationed at Dauchepully. Area 1,066 square miles. Population 142,011. In extreme west of district. Bounded north and west by the Kistna, which separates it from the Nizam's dominions; south and east by hills and jungles dividing it from Vinoocondah, Narsarowpett, and Suttenapully talooks. Inaccessible geographical position. The exploits of local chiefs known as the Pulnautyveerooloo [q.v.] have lived in popular story. During the last century when the empire built up by Aurungzeeb was parcelled out among his lieutenants, the Pulnaud was not portion of the Northern circars [q.v.]; but, like Ongole and Nellore, was included in the jurisdiction of the Nawaub of Arcot. The hereditary deshmookhs [q.v.] were a family named Ramrauz, and the deshpandyas [q.v.] a family named Comaura. At the close of the last century, when the Condaveed district was annexed by the Kings of Golcondah, the Pulnaud became an asylum into which defeated armies retreated. On the 24th February 1787 the Pulnaud, with other districts, was mortgaged by the Nawaub to the Company, and in July 1790 the Company assumed the direct management. On the 31st July 1801 the Pulnaud was ceded by treaty to the company. The stone circles [azhauram] and tombs of early races are very numerous. Mostly hilly. Regar [q.v.] soils predominate. Cotton [q.v.] trade. Rainfed tanks [q.v.] generally. Camping grounds at Dauchepully, Pidoogooraula, Pondoogala. Places of archæological interest:—Algoorauzpulley, Atmacore, Aukrauzpulley, Bodanapaud, Bodiliveed, Boodavauda, Boogga, Cancharcoontla, Candlagoonta, Caraulapaud, Caumepully, Caurampoody, Cauvelapulley, Chinnacodamagoolla, Chinnagarlapaud, Chintapully, Colagotla, Cottapully, Cumbampaud, Darvaimla, Dauchepully, Doorgy, Gogoolapaud, Goly, Goollapaud, Goorzaula, Gootticondah, Gottimookkala, Gottipaula, Gungavaram, Inooprauzcottapully, Jettipollem, Madgolo, Mandaudy, Maucherla, Mautsavaram, Miryaula, Mootcore, Morjampaud, Mullavaram, Munchicull, Nadicode, Narmalpaud, Naugavaram, Obaleshwarapully, Ooppalapaud, Pasharlapaud, Pashvaimla, Patlaveed, Paulvye, Peddagarlapaud, Pettahsannigalla, Pidoogooraula, Poleypully, Pondoogala, Pulleygoonta, Rauchamullapaud, Rentachintala, Rentaula, Royavaram, Shingarootla, Shreegherrypaud, Taudootla, Taullapulley, Teraula, Toommalcheroo, Toomaracote, Tungeda, Vappicherla, Veldoorty. Trig. station:—Saurangpully. The leading places, &c., in the talook are the following.——*Caurempoody* (కారెంపూడి - kárempúdi, Tel.). See sep. title.——*Chintapully* (చింతపల్లి - chintapalli, Tel.). From (chinta, tel. tamarind tree, tamarindus indica, linn. + palli, tel. village). Village; pop. 1,485; acres 4,444; lat. 16° 27′; long. 79° 47′; from Dauchepully S. 10 miles; from Masulipatam W. 91 miles. Old Vishnoo and Shiva temples. Inscription dated A.D. 1302 recording erection of a temple. Other inscriptions dated A.D. 1304 and 1752.——*Dauchepully* (దాచేపల్లె - dáchépalle, Tel.). See sep. title.——*Doorgy* (దుర్గి - durgi, Tel.). Means goddess parvaty. Village; pop. 2,877; acres 5,057; lat. 16° 26′; long. 79° 35′; from Dauchepully S.W. 17 miles; from Masulipatam W. 103 miles. Block of ruined temples in the middle of the town. East is Obaleshwarapully with good tope [q.v.] and ruined temple where Chentsoos [q.v.] worship.——*Goorzaula* (గురజాల - guradzála, Tel.). From (kuraja, tel. a class of shepherds so called). Village; pop. 2,841; acres 16,721; lat. 16° 34′; long. 79° 40′; from Dauchepully W.S.W. 8 miles; from Masulipatam W. 99 miles. A capital of the Pulnautyveerooloo [goojjerla, pulnautyveerooloo]. Two Portuguese epitaphs, dated 1767 and 1769. Many old temples with inscriptions.——*Gootticondah* (గుత్తికొండ - guttikonda, Tel.). From (gutti, tel. cluster + konda, tel. hill). Village, Hill, Place of pilgrimage; pop. 1,798; acres 6,369; lat. 16° 26′; long. 79° 53′; from Dauchepully S.S.E. 13 miles; from Masulipatam W. 87 miles. Old Shiva temple. Cave with tank much frequented by pilgrims.——*Kistna* (కృష్ణ - krishna, Tel.). See sep. title.——*Maucherla* (మాచర్ల - mácherla, Tel.). From (mávi, tel. mango tree, mangifera indica, linn. + cherla, tel. village). Village, Place of pilgrimage; pop. 2,907; acres 8,738; lat. 16° 29′; long. 79° 28′; from Dauchepully W.S.W. 22 miles; from Masulipatam W. 111 miles. A capital of the Pulnaud heroes [pulnautiveerooloo]. Vishnoo temple built by Bramha naidoo, hero of the story of the Pulnaud, with fine monolithic Dhwaja stambham [q.v.] and numerous inscriptions.——*Mootcore* (ముటకూరు - mutakúru, Tel.). From (mutamu, tel. cow-dung fuel + úru, tel. village). Village; pop. 3,178; acres 7,034; lat. 16° 23′; long. 79° 31′; from Dauchepully S.W. 23 miles; from Masulipatam W. 107 miles. Vishnoo temple 400 years old. Inscriptions dated A.D. 1268 and 1654.——*Nadicode* (నడికూడె - nadikúde, Tel.). From (nadi, tel. middle + kúdu, tel. to meet). Village; pop. 1,636; acres 4,932; lat. 16° 36′; long. 79° 46′; from Dauchepully W. 1½ miles; from Masulipatam W.N.W. 94 miles. Four ruined temples. Inscription of A.D. 1212.——*Naugilair* (నాగిలేరు - nágiléru, Tel.). See sep. title.——*Patlaveed* (పట్లవీడు - patlavídu, Tel.). From (pattu, tel. silk + vídu, tel. town). Village; pop. 1,611; acres 6,698; lat. 16° 23′; long. 79° 29′; from Dauchepully S.W. 24 miles. Inscription of Krishna deva royel, dated A.D. 1518.——*Pidoogooraula* (పిడుగురాళ్ళ - pidugurálla, Tel.). From (pidugu, tel. thunderbolt + ráyi, tel. stone). Village; pop. 1,550; acres 7,781; lat. 16° 29′; long. 79° 56′; from Dauchepully S.E. 12 miles; from Masulipatam W.N.W. 82 miles. On the Hyderabad road. Many broken carvings and other remnants of old temples. Travellers' bungalow [q.v.].——*Pondoogala* (పొందుగల - pondugula, Tel.). From (bondu, tel. a flower garland). Also Pondakholl. Village; pop. 945; acres 5,827; lat. 16° 41′; long. 79° 42′; from Dauchepully N.W. 8 miles; from Masulipatam W.N.W. 99 miles. On trunk road from Madras to Hyderabad and on right bank of Kistna. Ferry to opposite bank, where in the Nizam's territory, stands the ancient town of Vaudapully and modern town of Vazeerabad. Jeina [q.v.] remains. West, deserted temple. Travellers' bungalow [q.v.].——*Pulnaud* (పల్నాడు - palnádu, Tel.). See below.——*Renta chintala* (రెంటచింతల - rentachintala, Tel.). From (rendu, tel. two + chinta, tel. tamarind tree, tamarindus indica, linn.). Village; pop. 3,244; acres 5,362; lat. 16° 33′; long. 79° 35′; from Dauchepully W. 12 miles; from Masulipatam W.N.W. 104 miles. Two old temples. Christian ryots [q.v.] have built a stone church and a house for priests.——*Saurangpully* (సారంగపల్లె - sárangapalle, Tel.). From (sáranga, san. deer + palli, tel. village). Trig. station; lat. 16° 40′ 41·92″; long. 79° 47′ 48·04″; height 522 feet; from Saurangpully W.N.W. 1¼ miles.——*Shreegherrypaud* (శ్రీగిరిపాడు - shrígiripádu, Tel.). From (shrí, san. holy + giri, san. mountain + pádu, tel. village). Village; pop. 3,187; acres 7,204; lat. 16° 19′; long. 79° 22′; from Dauchepully S.W. 34 miles; from Masulipatam W. 118 miles. Group of abandoned temples. Shiva temple built by Cholas. Roman catholic station.——*Toomaracote* (తుమ్మరకోట - tummarakóta, Tel.). See sep. title.——*Tungeda* (తంగెడ - tangeda, Tel.). From (tangédu, tel. plant, cassia auriculata, linn.). Village; pop. 1,552; acres 10,082; lat. 16° 40′; long. 79° 51′; from Dauchepully N.E. 7 miles; from Masulipatam W.N.W. 91 miles. Old fort containing sixteen deserted temples. Ancient mosque [musjid]. Inscriptions of A.D. 1372 and 1552.——*Vappicherla* (వప్పిచర్ల - vappicherla, Tel.). Village; pop. 2,250; acres 5,078; lat. 16° 27′; long. 79° 44′; from Dauchepully S. 12 miles; from Masulipatam W. 96 miles. Inscriptions of A.D. 1299 and 1311.——*Veldoorty* (వెలుదుర్తి - veludurti, Tel.). From (velugu, tel. hedge + turti, tel. village). Village; pop. 2,735; acres 7,747; lat. 16° 21′; long. 79° 25′; from Dauchepully S.W. 30 miles; from Masulipatam W. 116 miles. The police here watch the mountain passes. Inscription dated A.D. 1165. Sculpture of a battle scene on a slab near a well and inscription dated A.D. 1130 at the temple of Doorgam. Veeraculls [q.v.] and Naugaculls [q.v.] in the neighbourhood.——**(2)** *Pulnautyveerooloo* (పల్నాటివీరులు - palnátivírulu, Tel.). From (víra, san. hero). Pulnaud heroes who carried on a seven years' war against the Goojjerla [goorzaula] and Maucherla [q.v.] towns, originating in a dispute at a cock-fight. Many popular stories about them.——*Pulnauty veera charitra dwipada* (పల్నాటివీరచరిత్రద్విపద - palnátivíracharitradvipada, Tel.). From (above + víra, san. hero + charita, san. story + dvipada, san. couplet). Wars of the Pulnautiveerooloo. The occurrences described took place about the year A.D. 1160. The poem gives a picture of the Teloogoos [q.v.] as they lived before the Mussalman [q.v.] invasion.

PULNEY (பழனி - pazhani, *Tam.* palni *). From (pazhamai, tam. antiquity + ani, tam. greatness) [pazha]. Tam. also (tiruvávinangudi), meaning holy + tank born + village or village of soobramanyan [q.v.] born of the sacred lake sharvanam, the reed tank; also (ávinangudi), meaning same; also (vaiyáppuri), meaning earth + interior + town.——**(1)** Talook, Madura district. Tahsildar's pay Rs. 150. Area 599 square miles. Population 195,050. Language Tamul. N.W. inland part of district. Bounded on the east by Dindigul talook, south by Periyacoolam talook, west by Oodamalpett and north by Caroor and Dharapooram talooks of Coimbatore district. Western portion of the talook is elevated sloping down towards the east. In the vicinity of the river and channels soil is generally fertile. It is sandy towards the north-east, loamy towards the east and red towards the west. A large number of the population are employed in agriculture. Coffee and cardamom plantation and coffee-curing are carried on in the Lower pulney hills. Cotton [q.v.], coffee [q.v.], cardamom [q.v.] are the important articles of commerce. Rivers, tanks. Shunmooganuddy river and Nangaunjy river. Veiyaupoory tank, Idoombancoolam tank, Poothoocolam tank of Cothamungalam and Shadayacolam of Cauppiliyaputty and Permaulcolam of Viroopautchy. District officers pitch their tents [derah] in the following places:—Woddar chuttram of Ayacoody, Chuttraputty, Cullimandayam, Keeranore, Ooppilyaputty, Vayalore, Viroopautchy. Places of archæological interest:—Ambilikkay, Baulasamoodram, Calyampoottore, Condaurankeeranore, Coottampoondy, Coricadavoo, Cottayam, Cullimandayam, Dausariputty, Eivarmullay, Keeranore, Maudavaudy, Maunore, Munnavanore, Naickerputty, Periyacottay, Permaul mullay, Peroor, Podoovaurputty, Pooliyore nuttam, Pombauray, Pulney, Shaittraiv, Tauvattore, Viriyappore, Viroopautchy. Principal trig. stations:—Chucklitchy mullay, Partimullay, Permaul mullay. The leading places, &c., in the talook are the following.——*Amravatty* (அமராவதி - ámarávathi, Tam.). See sep. title.——*Auttcaul* (ஆற்றுக்கால் - áttukkál, Tam.). See sep. title.——*Ayacoody* (ஆயக்குடி - áyakkudi, Tam. ayakudi *). From (áyan, tam. a shepherd + kudi, tam. village). Zemindarry, Village; pop. 10,617; acres 51,350; lat. 10° 27′; long. 77° 33′; from Madura N.N.W. 52 miles; from Pulney E.S.E. 4 miles. Peshcush Rs. 16,785. One of the twenty-four polliems of the late Dindigul district. Very valuable estate and the best portion of the Pulney polliem when attached thereto.——*Baulasamoodram* (பாலசமுத்திரம் - bálasamuttiram, Tam.). From (bála, san. young + samudra, san. ocean). Village; lat. 10° 25′; long. 77° 34′; from Madura N.W. 53 miles; from Pulney S.S.W. 3 miles. Former capital of the Poligar [q.v.] chiefs of the Pulney tract. The ruins of their fort remains. Old Vishnoo temple.——*Chucklitchy mullay* (சக்கிலிச்சிமலை - shakkiliççimalai, Tam.). From (shakkiliççi, tam. a female of the leather-working caste + malai, tam. mountain). Trig. station; lat. 10° 26′ 59·33″; long. 77° 22′ 37·44″; height 2,372 feet; from Andiputty W.N.W. 1 mile; from Pulney W. 12 miles.——*Codyartanaur* (கொடியார்த்தனூறு - kodiyarttanáru, Tam.). See sep. title.——*Coottampoondy* (குட்டம்பூண்டி - kuttambúndi, Tam.). From (kuttam, tam. tank + púndi, tam. village). Village; pop. 3,698; acres 9,422; lat. 10° 41′; long. 77° 43′; from Madura N.N.W. 60 miles; from Pulney N.E. 20 miles. In the Pulneys. Very old Shiva temple with inscription containing name of a Paundy sovereign.——*Eivarmullay* (ஐவர்மலை - aivarmalai, Tam.). From (aivar, tam. the five pándavas + malai, tam. mountain). Sanscrit name (panchapándavagiri), meaning five + pandava + hill. Hill; lat. 10° 29′; long. 77° 27′; height 1,402; from Madura N.W. 62 miles from Pulney W.N.W. 7 miles. Old and sacred temple with a cave and inscriptions. The cave is 160 feet long and 13 feet high and has numerous sculptured figures. A subterranean passage leads into the hill.——*Keeranore* (கீரனூர் - kíranúr, Tam.). From (kíran, tam. nakkíran, the poet + úr, tam. village). Sanscrit name (gírapurí), meaning geeran, the eloquent author + town. Village; pop. 2,965; acres 2,344; lat. 10° 36′; long. 77° 33′; from Madura N.N.W. 62 miles; from Pulney N. 9 miles. Three ancient and well-sculptured Shiva temples with numerous inscriptions, mostly Chola.——*Kodaykarnal* (கொடைக்கானல் - kodikkánal, Tam.). See sep. title.——*Maumbauray* (மாம்பாறை - mámbárai, Tam.). From (má, tam. mango tree, mangifera indica, linn. + párai, tam. rock). Zemindarry; square miles 12; lat. of village 10° 40′; long. 77° 50′; from Madura N.N.W. 56 miles; from Pulney E.N.E. 25 miles. Comprises three villages; Athappanputty, Markamputty, Yellaputty, population 2,456.——*Maunore* (மானூர் - mánúr, Tam.). From (mán, tam. deer + úr, tam. village). Village; pop. 2,553; acres 3,347; lat. 10° 31′; long. 77° 31′; from Madura N.N.W. 60 miles; from Pulney N.N.W. 4 miles. Very old and well-sculptured Shiva temple containing inscription of Soondra paundy [q.v.].——*Partimullay* (பருத்திமலை - paruttimalai, Tam.). Means cotton mountain. Trig. station; lat. 10° 39′ 57·81″; long. 77° 37′ 06·83″; height 1,254 feet; from Pulney N.N.E. 15 miles.——*Periyacottay* (பெரியகோட்டை - periyagóttai, Tam.). From (periya, tam. great + kóttai, tam. fort). Village; pop. 1,299; acres 2,413; lat. 10° 31′; long. 77° 44′; from Madura N.N.W. 49 miles; from Pulney E.N.E. 12 miles. South are two old Shiva and Vishnoo temples, the former well sculptured and covered with inscriptions of the Chola [q.v.] dynasty [raj].——*Permaul mullay* (பெருமாள்மலை - perumálmalai, Tam.). Means vishnoo's mountain. Sanscrit name (varáhagiri), meaning boar + hill. Hill; lat. 10° 18′; long. 77° 38′; from Madura N.N.W. 46 miles; from Pulney S.S.E. 11 miles. Peak of the Pulneys. The west slope is covered with dolmens [codaycull]. Trig. station in lat. 10° 17′ 55·92″; long. 77° 36′ 22·54″; height 7,326 feet; from Kodaykarnal N.N.E. 8 miles.——*Pombauray* (பூம்பாறை - púmbárai, Tam.). From (pú, tam. flower + párai, tam. rock). Sanscrit name (pushpagiri), meaning flower + mountain. Village, Hill; pop. 1,735; acres 11,979; lat. 10° 16′; long. 77° 27′; from Madura W.N.W. 54 miles; from Pulney S.S.W. 15 miles. Soobramanyan [q.v.] temple, much neglected.——*Pulney* (பழனி - pazhani, Tam.). See below.——*Pulney hills* (பன்றிமலை - panrimalai, Tam.). See vol. II, 118.——*Rettayambaudy* (இரெட்டையம்பாடி - irettaiyambádi, Tam.). From (irattaiyan, tam. proper name + pádi, tam. village). Zemindarry; acres 54,877; lat. 10° 26′; long. 77° 28′; from Madura N.W. 60 miles; from Pulney E. 8 miles. Peshcush [q.v.] Rs. 11,930.——*Taundigoody* (தாண்டிக்குடி - tándikkudi, Tam.). From (tánri, tam. a tree, terminalia belerica, roxb. + kudi, tam. village). Village, Hill; pop. 2,127; acres 5,612; lat. 10° 19′; long. 77° 41′; from Madura N.W. 41 miles; from Pulney S.E. 14 miles. Principal hill village in the Lower pulneys. Coffee [q.v.] and cardamom [q.v.] cultivation largely carried on.——*Veloor* (வேலூர் - vélúr, Tam. velúr *). From (vél, tam. acacia arabica, willd. + úr, tam. village). Zemindarry, Village; pop. 3,620; acres 21,855; lat. of village 10° 29′; long. 77° 42′; from Madura N.N.W. 48 miles; from Pulney E. 10 miles. Peshcush Rs. 10,568.——*Viroopautchy* (விருப்பாச்சி - viruppáççi, Tam.). From (virúpa, san. deformed + akshi, san. eye); an epithet of shiva. Village; pop. 2,001; acres 3,317; lat. 10° 28′; long. 77° 45′; from Madura N.N.W. 47 miles; from Pulney E. 13 miles. One of the twenty-four polliems of the former Dindigul district. Attached with Pulney to Dharaupooram district by Hyder ally. Ancient Shiva temple with inscriptions. Old Vishnoo temple.——*Yettoor* (எட்டூர் - ettúr, Tam.). From (ettu, tam. eight + úr, tam. village). Village; pop. 2,672; acres 44,730; from Pulney S.W. 20 miles. In the Pulneys. Inscription on a rock.——*Yidayancottah* (இடையன்கோட்டை - idaiyangóttai, Tam. idaiyankóta *). From (idaiyan, tam. a shepherd + kóttai, tam. fort). Village, Zemindarry; pop. 3,157; acres 33,249; lat. of village 10° 37′; long. 77° 53′; from Madura N.N.W. 50 miles; from Pulney E.N.E. 25 miles Peshcush Rs. 7,000. One of the twenty-four polliems. With Maumbauray, belonged to Aravacoorchy in Coimbatore district, but was added to Dindigul province by Hyder ally.——**(2)** Town, Place of pilgrimage, Head-quarters of talook and Sub-registrar; Madura dist., Pulney tal.; pop. 16,940; acres 4,252; lat. 10° 28′; long. 77° 33′; height 1,519 feet; from Dindigul W. 31 miles; from Kodaykarnal N. 17 miles; from Madras S.W. 264 miles; from Madura N.W. 54 miles; from Rameshwaram N.W. 143 miles; from Ramnaud about N.W. 114 miles. One of the twenty-four polliems of the former Dindigul district and once annexed by Mysore, when it was attached to Dharaupooram district. Old fort. Old and well-sculptured Shiva temple on a hill, with inscriptions of the Paundy [q.v.] Vijianugger [q.v.] and Wodeya [q.v.] dynasties [raj] and Sanscrit stala pooraunam [q.v.]. Large Vishnoo temple below the hills with many inscriptions round its garbhagriham [q.v.]. Old Shiva temple at the foot of the hill, and a number of bathing tanks with sculptured work. Sculptured and painted temple called Tirvarnangoody at Adivauram, a mile and a half north. Here there is a temple dedicated to Shany [q.v.] or Saturn, within the walls of the great pagoda [q.v.], which is seldom seen anywhere in the peninsula. The image [shilay, vigraham] has on a sable garment, and the vehicle [vauhan] is a crow [caurvam].——

(3) *Pulney aundy* (பழனியாண்டி - pazhaniyándi, Tam.). From (above + ándi, tam. shaiva mendicant). Scandan. Hindoo 2nd or pers. name. Common among non-bramins and native christians [peyar].——*Pulneyvailan* (பழனிவேலன் - pazhanivélan, Tam.). From (above + vélan, tam. he who holds lance). Soobramanyan [q.v.].

PUMMELOW (मधुराम्लफल - madhurámlap'hala, *San.*; पपनस - papanasa, *Mahr.*; तोरंज - tóranja, *Conc.*; چکوترہ - chakotrah, *Hind.*; چکوترا - chakotrá, *Dec.*; پمپولمس - pumpulmas, *Malay*; ಚಕೋರಮರ - chakóramara, *Can.*; ಚಕ್ಕುಲ್ಲಿಮರ - chakkullimara, *Too.*; పంపరమాస - pamparamása, *Tel.*; ബംബിളിനാരകം - bambilinárakam, *Mal.*; මහනාරං - mahanáram, *Singh.*; பம்பளிமாசு - pambalimásu, *Tam.*). Title from malay. San. from (madhura, san. sweet + ámla, san. sour + p'hala, san. fruit). Can. from (chakóra, san. greek partridge + mara, can. tree). Mal. from (bambili, mal. pumplemose + nárakam, mal. lime, citrus). Singh. from (maha, singh. large + náram, singh. citrus). Tam from malay. Hind. also (batávilimú), meaning batavian lime; (mahánimbú), meaning large lime. Malay also (járukbali), meaning baly orange; (jarukgádang); (járukmachan), meaning tiger orange; (kádangsa). Can. also (tórangi); (chakkottimara). Tel. also (pullapamparapanasa), meaning sour + the tree; (edapandu); (pamparapanasa); (pamplimása). Title otherwise Batavian lemon, Batavian orange, Forbidden fruit [plantain], Jamboa, Paradise apple, Pompoleon, Pumplemose, Pumplenose, Shaddock. Different names by size are:—Pummelow, when of the largest size; Shaddock, of intermediate size, after captain shaddock, who first introduced them into w. indies from batavia; Forbidden fruit, about size of an orange [q.v.]. Amoy pummelow is a variety; Canton pummelow is another variety. Botanically Citrus [jambeeram] decumana, linn., rutaceæ [vriesham, 32]. Alias Aurantium decumanum. Evergreen tree, 15 feet high; petioles winged; leaves blunt emarginate; large white fragrant rich waxy flowers; massive fruit attains 4 lbs. in weight and 7 inches in diameter, in form globular, skin smooth in comparison with others of its tribe, but roughened by the oil glands, pulp varying in color from that of a common orange to a deep carmine. Largest of orange [q.v.] tribe and in taste somewhat resembles sweet orange; tree introduced from java. The fruit eaten. Gives a gum [gond]. Two botanical varieties:—Maliformis, fruit globose, with the pulp of a pale pink color, approaching to a very light yellow. Pyriformis; fruit more or less pear-shaped [amrood], pulp of a crimson color more or less intense; variety most esteemed, being sweet and juicy.

PUNCHAM (पञ्चन् - pañchan, *San.*). From (pach, san. to spread); the opened hand and fingers. Greek πέντε. Five. A very sacred number. Plant first term. Ex., where transl. is of second term:—Calophyllum inophyllum (pañchakésara), filament; Ricinus communis (pañchángula), finger; Santalum album (pañchasugandha), good scent; Terminalia chebula (pañcharasa), taste. See gloss. paragraphs.——*Pacheesy* (پچیسی - pachísí, Hind.). From (pachís, pers. twenty-five); the highest throw being twenty-five. Game played with cowries [q.v.] for dice on a kind of cloth chess board, consisting of four rectangles, each divided into twenty-four small squares of three rows of eight squares each. Not played for money [chatrangam, chowsar shatranj].——*Paunch* (پانچ - pánch, Hind.). From (panj, pers. five). The number 5 [punch, punj].——*Pauncharautram* (पाञ्चरात्र - páñcharátra, San.). From (above + rátri, san. night) [puncharautram]. Sacred book of the Veishnavites promulgated by Shaundilyan. In this Vausoodevan is made the supreme being and the one omniscient first principle, which is both efficient and material cause of the universe, evolving jeevan [q.v.] or soul, manas [q.v.] or mind and ahancauram [q.v.] or consciousness. And Mocsham [q.v.] consists in deliverance from these worldly shackles by knowledge, contemplation and worship of him. The whole system rests upon the aphorism, faith in Eshwaran, here Krishnan [q.v.]. Followers of this system are styled Pauncharautries, otherwise Bhaugavatas or worshippers of Bhagavat krishnan. See vol. I (89), (90).——*Punch* (پنچ - panch, Hind.). Originally in Anglo-indian a drink of five ingredients; water, tea [q.v.], lemon-juice [lemon], sugar [q.v.], and arrack [q.v.]. Also in N. india abbreviation of punchayet [q.v.].——*Puncha bandham* (पञ्चबन्ध - panchabandha, San.). From (above + bandha, san. tie). The fifth caste [punchama]; a very early name for the Pariahs [q.v.].——*Puncha baunam* (पञ्चबाण - pañchabána, San.). From (above + bána, san. arrow). Five arrows of Manmatan [q.v.]. The following five kinds of flowers:—lotus [nelumbo], mango [q.v.], asbocam [q.v.], jasmine [q.v.], blue water-lily [blue indian water-lily, cauma baunam].——*Puncha baunauvastay* (पञ्चबाणावस्था - pañchabánávast'há, San.). From (above + bána, san. arrow + avast'há, san. state). Five effects of the five arrows [puncha baunam] of Manmatan [q.v.]. Thinking and talking of the person loved; sighing and lamenting; heat or feverishness; nausea and languishing; weeping and bewilderment of the faculties; death or suspension of the natural powers [cauma baunam].——*Puncha bhootam* (पञ्चभूत - pañchabhúta, San.). From (bhúta, san. element). The five elements [bhootam] of nature, including ether.——*Punchacam* (पञ्चक - pañchaka, San.). An aggregate of five, a pentad. Measure of capacity. 5 colagams = 1 punchacam; 4 punchacams = 1 cundaga [alavay, 3c]. Approximate actual value, 1 punchacam = 54 cubic feet 768 cubic inches. Bellary. See vol. I, 609; II, 508.——*Punchacatcham* (पञ्चकच्छ - pañchakachha, San.). From (above + kachha, san. hem of lower garment tucked into the girdle). Five folds of lower garment tucked into waistband [katchay]. See vol. I (98).——*Puncha cosham* (पञ्चकोश - pañchakósha, San.). From (above + kósha, san. sheath). Five sheaths to the soul in philosophy [vedauntam]. Anna mayam cosham, that supported by food, the gross form; Praunamayam cosham, the organs of action; Manomayam cosham, the organs of perception, with the manas or mind; Vinyaunamayam, the same with booddhy or intellect; Ananda mayam consisting of the elements of identity and wisdom. These coshams represented in terms of shareerams [q.v.] or the triple investitures of the soul are as follows:—Annamayam agrees with stoola shareeram; the three next praunamayam, manomayam and vinyaunamayam correspond to soocshmam or linga shareeram and anandamayam agrees with caurana shareeram. And moocty or mocsham [q.v.] consists in freedom from these shackles and liberation from these vestitures or material obstructions.——*Puncha dravidam* (पञ्चद्राविड - pañchadrávida, San.). From (above + drávida, san. the people). The five ancient countries south of Vindhyas:—Carnautam, Dravida, Goozerat, Maharashtram, Telinga [puncha gowdam]. Same classification applied to Bramin [q.v.] tribes.——*Puncha gandham* (पञ्चगन्ध - pañchagandha, San.). From (above + gandha, san. smell). Five perfumes:—Cinnamon [q.v.], Cardamom [q.v.], Camphor [q.v.], Nutmeg [jautikye], Takkolam, a perfume prepared from either eugenia jambolana [common jamoon], pimenta atris [china pepper], or illicium anisatum [star anise].——*Puncha gavyam* (पञ्चगव्य - pañchagavya, San.). From (above + gavya, san. cow-product). Five articles from the cow [pashoo], milk [paul], curds [tyre], ghee [q.v.], urine and dung [shauny]. These are mixed together and drunk by Bramins, as means of purification either from sin, or caste trespasses, or at death.——*Puncha gowdam* (पञ्चगौड - pañchagauda, San.). From (above + gauda, san. the people). The five ancient countries north of the Vindhyas:—Canyahcoobjam, Gowda proper, Mitilay, Ootcalam, Sauraswatam [puncha dravidam]. Same classification applied to Bramin [q.v.] tribes.——*Punchair* (ಪಂಚೇರು - panchéru, Tel.). Means five + seer [punchseer]. Bazaar weight. 5 seers = 1 punchair; 8 punchairs = 1 maund [niray, 2e]. Approximate actual value, 1 punchair = 3 lbs. 3 oz. 13⅜ drs. avoir. Used in Bellary. Though it means 5 seers it really consists of 6 seers as the seer there is 21 tolahs [q.v.] and not 24 like the ordinary seer [q.v.]. Also used in Kurnool, where it is the same as Viss [q.v.].——*Punchakhandam* (पञ्चखण्ड - pañchakhanda, San.). From (above + khanda, san. division). Five Indies [india]. A division later than Nava khandam [q.v.].—"*a*" According to Vishnoo pooraunam, the centre was occupied by Cooroos and Paunchaulas; east was Caumaroopam or Assam; south were Poondras, Calingas, and Maugadham; west were Sourashtras, Sooras, Abheeras, Arboodas, Caurooshas, Maulavar, Sowveeras, and Seindhavas; north were Hoonas, Shaulwas, Shaucalas, Ramas, Ambashtas, and Pauraseecas.—"*b*" The Chinese had a Punchkhandam, thus:—First, Northern india comprised the Punjaub proper, including Cashmere and the adjoining hill states, with the whole of Eastern afghanistaun beyond the Indus and the present Cissutlej states to the west of the Saraswaty river. Secondly, Western india comprised Scinde and Western rajpootana, with Cutch and Goozerat, and a portion of the adjoining coast on the lower course of the Nerbudda river. Thirdly, Central india comprised the whole of the Gangetic provinces from Thaneswar to the head of the delta and from the Himalaya mountains to the banks of the Nerbudda. Fourthly, Eastern india comprised Assam and Bengal proper, including the whole of the delta of the Ganges, together with Sumbulpore, Orissa, and Ganjam. Fifthly, Southern india comprised the whole of the peninsula from Nassick on the west and Ganjam on the east to Cape comorin on the south, including the modern district of Berar and the Mahomedan Telingana [q.v.], Maharashtram [q.v.], and the Concanam [q.v.], with the separate states of Hyderabad, Mysore, and Travancore, or very nearly the whole of the peninsula to the south of the Nurbudda and Mahanuddy rivers.——*Puncha lingam* (पञ्चलिङ्ग - pañchalinga, San.). From (above + linga, san. emblem of shiva). He who has five lingams, a name of Shiva [q.v.], from the five places celebrated for his symbol [lingam], viz.—"*a*" Conjeeveram, where there is the Pritivy lingam, or lingam made of earth;—"*b*" Jambookeshwaram, where the Aplingam exudes water perpetually;—"*c*" Trinomallee, where the Tejolingam sparkles with light;—"*d*" Calastry, where there is the Vayoolingam, the lamp of which is in constant vibration with the wind; and—"*e*" Chidambaram, where there is the Aucaushalingam or ethereal lingam, worshipped without any material form of it being kept in the temple [coil, pagoda].——*Punchalingeshwar* (पञ्चलिङ्गेश्वर - pañchalingéshvara, San.). From (above + linga, san. phallus + íshvara, san. lord), shiva who is worshipped in the form of the five elements [bhootam], as the supporter and regenerator of the universe. An epithet of Eeshwaran.——*Puncha lutchanam*

(पञ्चलक्षण - pañchalakshana, San.). From (above + lakshana, san. characteristic). The five characteristics of a Pooraunam [q.v.]; Sargam, Pratisargam, Vamsham, Manwantaram and Vamshaunoocharitam.——*Punchama* (पञ्चम - pañchama, San.). Fifth. A Pariah [q.v.], as being fifth caste [jauty] man [puncha bandham]. A very early term.——*Puncha maha pautacam* (पञ्चमहापातक - pañchamahápátaka, San.). From (above + mahá, san. great + pátaka, san. vice). The five capital vices; viz., murder, theft, intoxicating drinks, lust, and falsehood.——*Puncha maha yanyam* (पञ्चमहायज्ञ - pañchamaháyaña, San.). From (above + mahá, san. great + yaña, san. sacrifice). The five special sacrifices or oblations:—Reciting the vedams [q.v.], Homam [q.v.], or oblation by fire, Sacrifices to cauly [q.v.] and other demons, Oblation of darbhay [q.v.] grass to ancestors, Hospitality or feeding the poor [maha yanyam, yanyam]. These are daily sacrifices of obligation. For occasional or periodical sacrifices see Yanyam. Compare on the other hand Cooral:— தென்புலத்தார் தெய்வம் விருந்தொக்க லொன்றாங் கைம்புலத்தா றோம்ப றலை—"the chief duty of the house-"holder is to preserve the five-fold rule of conduct towards the "manes, the gods, his guests, his relations, and himself."——*Punchamam* (पञ्चम - pañchama, San.). The fifth note in musical scale [sangeetam, swaragraumam].——*Punchamookha maurooty* (पञ्चमुखमारुति - pañchamnkhamáruti, San.). From (above + mukha, san. face + máruti, san. son of wind). Five-headed Shiva [q.v.].——*Punchamoolam* (पञ्चमूल - pañchamúla, San.). Five medicinal roots:—Gmelina arborea, linn. [cashmere tree], Oroxylum indicum, vent. [pajanely], Premna integrifolia, linn. [moonnay], Stereospermum suaveolens, dec. [pauthiry], Ægle marmelos, corr. [bael].——*Punchamy* (పంచమి - panchami, Tel.). From (pañcha, san. five). The fifth day [tity] of the waxing [shoocla pacsham] and waning [krishnapacsham] moon of any lunar month [chaundra mausam, pacsham]. Lunar [chaundra maunam] festival [pundigay, 3e]. Held particularly sacred in the fifth and sixth lunar months of Shrauvanam [mausam] between 15th August and 14th September, and Bhaudrapadam [mausam] between 15th September and 15th October [garooda-punchamy, nauga punchamy, rishy punchamy].——*Punchanadam* (பஞ்சநதம் - pañjanatham, Tam.). From (above + nadi, san. river). Punjaub, the country of the five sacred rivers. In this presidency applied to Trivaudy near Tanjore town. Hindoo 2nd or pers. name. Familiarly shortened into Punjoo [peyar].——*Punchanimbam* (पञ्चनिम्ब - pañchanimba, San.). A medicine which contains the flowers, fruit, leaves, bark, and root of the neem [q.v.] tree, of each fifteen parts, and one part each of a number of other drugs.——*Punchanuddy* (పంచనది - panchanadi, Tam.). From (pañcha, san. five + nadí, san. river). River; Cuddapah dist., Voilpaud tal. Rises in the Poonganore zemindarry and flows in a northerly direction past Peelair in Voilpaud talook, then joins the Bauhoodah.——*Puncha-pacshy shastram* (पञ्चपक्षिशास्त्र - pañchapakshishástra, San.). From (above + pakshin, san. bird + shástra, san. science). A system of divination [shacoonam] by five different species of birds; hawk [shyainam], crow pheasant [q.v.], cock [moorghy], crow [caurvam], peacock [mayil].——*Punchapallavam* (पञ्चपल्लव - panchapallava, San.). Aggregate of five sprigs used in Hindoo ceremonial:—Mangifera indica [mango]; Eugenia jambolana [common jaumoon]; Feronia elephantum [wood apple]; Citrus medica [lime]; Ægle marmelos [bael].——*Puncha pandava mullay* (பஞ்சப்பாண்டவமலை - pañjappándavamalai, Tam.). From (pañcha, san. five + pándava, san. the brothers of that name + malai, tam. mountain). A Braminical name. Village, Hill; North arcot dist., Arcot tal.; lat. 12° 52′; long. 79° 19′; from Arcot W.S.W. 5 miles; from Chittore S.S.E. 27 miles. Hamlet of Velapaukam. Hill remarkable for rock-cut sculptures and caves, connected by Braminical legend with the five Pandavas of N. india. The principal cave is the Yelvausapady, or seven thresholds; where six rough pillars stand at entrance and form seven doorways. Inner line of similar pillars supports the roof and corresponds with the outer line. A short distance above, upon face of rock, a figure two feet square, representing a Joina [q.v.] teertancaran [q.v.]. On southern side of hill is a cave with figures cut in relief [jalee]. One group of five here represents the five Pandavas, said to have wandered here. Place taken possession of by Mussalmans [q.v.].——*Puncha parvam* (पञ्चपर्व - pañchaparva, San.). From (above + parvan, san. feast). Five religious ceremonial days in each fortnight, viz.:—pratamay, ashtamy, navamy, pradosham, and amavausyay or powrnimay; which see under separate titles.——*Puncha praunam* (पञ्चप्राण - pañchapráṇa, San.). Five vital airs constituting animal life in man. They are:—Praunam, the air in the lungs, pre-eminently identified with life; Apaunam, the air in the lower intestine; Samaunam, the air essential to digestion; Oodaunam, the air supposed to move upwards from the throat to the head; and Vyaunam, the air pervading the whole body. Puncha praunahooty is the offering or addressing the first five mouthfuls of every meal to the five vital airs respectively; an act of obligation among bramins every day before meals. There are also five other oopapraunams or minor vital airs recognised among hindoos [praunam, vayoo].——*Puncharautram* (పంచరాత్రము - pancharátramu, Tel.). Means five nights [pundigay, 6d]. The Sheivas were the first to develop the popular festivals of several days' continuance. Subsequently the Veishnavas devised the Puncharautram on the same method. The legend is that during Menoo's flood [pralayam], Vishnoo [q.v.], as Narayanan [q.v.], floated on the waters; and then during five nights of that dark period he delivered to Satyavratan [q.v.] and the seven rishies [q.v.] the dogmas of the Puncharautram. Many Veishnavas separated from the rest on this account. On the other hand there is a modern book published at Conjeeveram, entitled, 'a book to take out the thorn from such as deny the Puncharautram.' The modern dispute at Conjeeveram between the Vadagalays [q.v.] and Tengalays [q.v.] has to a great extent obliterated the remains of this controversy [matam]. Compare Paunchcharautram.——*Puncha shooddhy* (पञ्चशुद्धि - pañchashuddhi, San.). From (above + shuddhi, san. purification). The five kinds of purification, practised among the sheivas; viz., purification of the body by washing [snaunam], purification of the soul by prayer [muntram], ceremonial purification of sacred vessels, purification [abhishaicam] and adorning of the lingam [q.v.], final purification by mentally repeating [japam] the mystic om [q.v.] and the five-lettered [punchaucsharam] salutation to shiva [q.v.].——*Puncha siddhaunticay* (पञ्चसिद्धान्तिका - pañchasiddhántiká, San.). From (above + siddhánta, san. dogma). Summary of the five original astronomical Siddhauntams [q.v.]; by Varauha mihiran [q.v.].——*Punchatantram* (पञ्चतन्त्र - pañchatantra, San.; பஞ்சதந்திரம் - pañjathandiram, Tam.). From (above + tantra, san. device). The five devices. Originally a collection of Sanscrit tales and fables in five books, compiled by a bramin, Vishnoo sharman, at early part of Christian era or before. Original of the better-known and smaller Hitopadesh [q.v.], or salutary instruction; also of Brihat katay [q.v.], or original of Arabian nights' entertainments. A Pehlvi or old Persian version of Punchatantram was the first real translation of the work; it was made in the time of Nowsheerwan about A.D. 570, and perished with much of the Pehlvi literature when the Arabs invaded Persia; before its destruction it had been translated into Arabic about A.D. 760, and was called Kaleela damna [q.v.], equivalent of sanscrit Caratacan and Damanacan, the name of two jackals [q.v.], or fables of the bramin Pilpay [q.v.]. The well-known persian Anwar oos sooheily, or lights of Canopus [nacshatram, sooheil], of Hoossain vaeez written about the beginning of the fifteenth century, was an amplification of the Punchatantram; Abool fazl, Acbar's celebrated minister, translated it into simpler persian and called it Iyaur e daunish [q.v.], or criterion of knowledge; a turkish version is Hoomayoon nauma [q.v.]; an oordoo version, called Khirad afroz or illuminator of the understanding, was made in 1803 by Hafeez ood deen ahmed. The hebrew version of the punchatantram is attributed to one Rabbi joel; this was translated into Latin by John of Capua at the end of the fifteenth century; and from this various Italian, Spanish, and German translations were made. The english Pilpay's fables were taken from a french translation. The tamul version of the punchatantram was translated in 1862 by Taundava roya moodelly, a teacher in the College of Fort St. George, from the Mahratta version. With the exception of the Bible and the Pilgrim's progress, there is no work that has been translated into so many languages as the Punchatantram. These stories are not aggregated promiscuously and without method, but are strung together upon some one connected thread, and arranged in the framework of a continuous narrative, out of which they successively spring. The complicated scheme of story-telling, tale within tale, like the Arabian nights, seems to be of Hindoo invention. Compare the twenty-five stories of a demon [vetaulapuncha vimshaty], thirty-two tales of the animated images supporting the throne of Vicramadityan [vicramarca charitram], twenty tales of a swan [hamsavimshaty], &c. The scheme of the punchatantram is that a king in Mahilauropyam, treated as Mylapore in S. indian versions, had three sons who were deficient in ability and application. He made this known to his counsellors and sought their advice. A learned bramin composed in their benefit these five chapters:—Mitra bhedam, dissension of friends; Mitra praupty, acquisition of friends; Caucolookeeyam, inveterate enmity; Labdha nausham, loss of advantage; Asampraicshya cauritwam, inconsiderateness. Through reading these the princes became in six months highly accomplished. Sanscrit versions make the site Pautalipootram on the Ganges. The following is a specimen from Tamul version:—தண்டகாரணியத்திற் சஞ்சரிப்போனாகிய சண்டகருமனென்னும் ஓர் இராக்கதத்தலைவன் அவன் நேரிட்ட ஓரந்தணன் தோண்மேலேறி நடத்திக்கொண்டு போவுழி, அவ் வேதியன் அவ்வரக்க னடிகள் மிக மெல்லியவா யிருப்பனவற்றைப் பார்த்த, ஐய! அரக்கத்தலைவ? உன்கா லடிகள்எப்படிமெல்லியவாயினவென, அரக்கன்நான் நீராடி யீரம்புலராவும் நிலன்மீது செல்லேனெனக் கேட்டுச் சிறிதாறு முன்னே தாங்கிப்போய் பிறகு இராக்கதன் ஓர் குளனில் மூழ்கப்புக்குழிப் பார்ப்பானைப்பார்த்து, யான் நிந்த கருமஞ் செய்துவருகாறும் நீ அடிபெயற்க, இங்குத்தானே நிற்றியெனச்சொல்லி, பின்னர் ஸ்நானஞ்செய்தனன். அந்தணன் இதைப்பார்த்து இவன் மூழ்கிப்புறம்போந்தானானால் நாம் இவன் வயிற்றழலின் மூழ்காதிரோம். ஆதலான் ஓடி உய்ய இதுவே

நல்ல சமயம். நீராடிக் கால் புலருமுன் இவன் நடவா னல்லோ என்று தனக்குள் தெரிந்துகொண்டு விரைந் தோடினன் அதுகண்ட அவுணன் யான் வாய்பதறிக் கைக்கெட்டினது வாய்க்கெட்டாமலிழிப்புற்றேன், கடிதில் பின்சென்று கவர்வேன் எனினும் கொண்ட நோன்பு குறையுறுகின்றதென்று மறுக்கமுற்று ஆங்கே நெட்டுயிர்த்து வாளாநின்றனன். ஆதலான் யாதும் உய்த்துணராது இயற்றலாகாதெனச் சொல்லி—"In the forest "of Dandacauranyam [dandacam], a chief Raucshasan [q.v.] "named Chundacarman met one day a Bramin, upon whose "shoulders he climbed and directed him. The Bramin observing "that the feet of the goblin were slender, asked him, O chief of "the goblins, how is it your feet are slender? The goblin "replied, I do not walk on the ground after bathing till the "water is dried. After going a short distance, the goblin went "to bathe in a tank and ordered the Bramin to remain there "without stirring till his return. In the meantime, the Bramin "reflected, if the goblin return after bathing, he will not fail "to devour me. Therefore, this is the only chance of escaping "with life. Moreover, he will not walk after bathing before "the water is dried. Having thus considered, he ran away as "quickly as possible. On seeing this, the goblin said to himself; "by speaking rashly I have let go what was within my "power; I cannot even follow him, because of a vow which I "have made. So saying, he stood there on the spot, heaving a "deep sigh. Therefore no work should be done without due "consideration." The following is a specimen from Canarese version:—ಒಂದು ಊರಿನಲ್ಲಿ ಒಬ್ಬ ಮನುಷ್ಯನೂ ಒಂದು ಹುಲಿಯೂ ಸ್ನೇಹಿತರಾಗಿದ್ದು ಒಂದು ಮಠೀತಿಗೆ ಹೋದರು - ಆ ಮಠೀತಿಯಲ್ಲಿ ಒಂದು ಹುಲಿಯನ್ನು ಒಬ್ಬ ಮನುಷ್ಯನು ಏರಿಕೊಂಡು ಕಠಾರಿಯಿಂದ ತಿವಿಯುತ್ತಾ ಇರುವಹಾಗಿ ಚಿತ್ರದಲ್ಲಿ ಬರೆದಿತ್ತು - ಅದನ್ನು ಈ ಮನುಷ್ಯನು ನೋಡಿ ಐಯ್ಯಾ ಹುಲಿ ರಾಯನೇ ನೋಡು ಈ ಮನುಷ್ಯನು ಎಷ್ಟು ಘಟ್ಟಿಗನು ಇಂಥಾ ಕ್ರೂರವಾದ ಹುಲಿಯನು ತಾನು ಹತ್ತಿಕೊಂಡು ಕಠಾರಿಯಿಂದ ಇರಿಯುತ್ತಾನೆ ಎಂದು ಹೇಳಲು ಅದಕ್ಕೆ ಆ ಹುಲಿಯು—ಈ ಚಿತ್ರವನ್ನು ಮನುಷ್ಯ ಬರೆದು ಇದ್ದಾನೆ ಹುಲಿಯು ಎಂದಿಗೂ ಹೀಗೆ ಬರೆಯಲಾರದು ಎಂದು ಹೇಳಿದ್ದರಿಂದ ಮನುಷ್ಯನು ನಾಚಿ ಕೊಂಡು ಸುಮ್ಮನಾದನು—"In a certain village, a tiger and a man were "friends. They went to a temple. In that temple there was "a drawing, representing a man as mounted on a tiger and "stabbing him with a spear. The man seeing it exclaimed:—"O Sir, O king of tigers? See what a clever man that "is? He has mounted on this fierce tiger and is stabbing "him with a spear. On his saying this the tiger observed:—"The picture was painted by a man and would not have been "thus painted by a tiger [pooly]. Hearing this the man "was ashamed and kept silent." See vol. I (57), (58).——*Punchatiktam* (पञ्चतिक्त - pañchatikta, San.). Five bitters. Justicia gendarussa [common gendarussa]; Melia azadirachta [neem]; Solanum xanthocarpum [prickly brinjaul]; Tinospora cordifolia [goolancha]; Trichosanthes cucumerina [wild snake gourd].——*Punchaucsharam* (पञ्चाक्षर - pañchákshara, San.). The five mysterious letters, a Sheiva formula, viz., namashivauya ந, ம, சி, வா, ய [moolamuntram]. See Om. Punchaucsharan is a Hindoo 2nd or pers. name [peyar]; meaning he who has it for his chief muntram [q.v.].——*Punchaula* (पाञ्चाल - páñchála, San.). From (pañchan, san. five); association of five guilds. Sanscrit for Cummaular [q.v.]. Five castes of artizans:—goldsmith, carpenter, blacksmith, brazier, and mason. See vol. I (61) to (70), and the following foot-notes:—history of caste I (61), abbé dubois opinion I (64), punchaular I (67); groups of castes II, 225, hindoo proper names II, 239. The punchaular wear the Janivaura [q.v.] and consider themselves as equal to Bramins [q.v.]. The goldsmiths are admitted to be the head of the confederation and have a caste jurisdiction over the rest. The Punchaular bury their dead [shavacaud] and strictly abstain from meat and intoxicating liquors. They regard themselves as descendants of the divine artificer Vishwacarman and call themselves Vishwa bramins. They assume the title of Acharry [q.v.], wear the holy thread [poonool], and claim the right to perform religious ceremonies among themselves, especially at marriages. They declare that there were originally five Vedams [q.v.], but that Veda vyausan, in order to curtail their privileges, suppressed the fifth [jauty]. See Acharry for the possible origin of this assumption.——*Punchaulamcoorchy* (பாஞ்சாலக் குறிச்சி - páñjálakkuriççi, Tam.). From (páñchála, san. the five artisan caste + kuriççi, tam. village). Site of old village; Tinnevelly dist., Ottapidauram tal.; from Ottapidauram N.E. 1½ miles. Former residence of a poligar [q.v.], a naick [q.v.] of the Cumblattaur caste of the Cataboma naick family. An expedition led against the place in 1755 was recalled. It was besieged in 1767. The next poligars succeeded in 1760, 1791 and 1799. On the place being attacked in 1799, the poligar escaped and fled first to Shivagunga and then to the Tondiman rajah. He was however captured and hanged. The two brothers of this poligar were confined in the Palamcottah jail, whence they made their escape to Punchaulamcoorchy in 1801. After several assaults, the fort was taken by the English and the poligar force routed. The events of the last siege form the subject of a native poem, called the Paunchaulacoorchy sindoo by Namashivauyam.——*Punchaumritam* (पञ्चामृत - panchámrita, San.). From (above + amrita, san. nectar). The mixture of five kinds of food; the divine offering. Generally milk [paul], curds [tyre], ghee [q.v.], sugar [q.v.], and honey [shahad]. In a mixture of these, idols are bathed on special days, and then it is distributed to worshippers.——*Punchaungam* (पञ्चाङ्ग - pañchánga, San. பஞ்சாங்கம் - pañjángam, Tam.). From (above + anga, san. limb). Means five members; calendar as containing five principal heads. These are not always the same, but the following may be taken as specimen, and note that this is the same whether for Ravy punchaungam or Chaundra punchaungam:—Nacshatram [q.v.] in which the moon happens to be on any particular day; with the time of her passing to the next. Yogam [q.v.], or the space of time during which the sum of the sun and moon's motion amounts to one nacshatram, or 13° 20′, with the time when that is completed. Caranam [q.v.], or space of time during which the moon's motion from the sun amounts to 6°, there being two caranams in a tity [q.v.], and the calendar registering the time of its ending. Tyaujyam [q.v.], of the varjyam [q.v.], being the unlucky period of the day, the mean duration of which is about 4 ghadiyas or 1 hour 36 minutes european time, and pending which all voluntary business of importance ought to be suspended, marking the time of its beginning; when the varjyam occurs at day time, it is called divah, and when at night rautry. Chauram [q.v.]; being an account of the position of the planets [graham], including rahoo [q.v.] ☊ and kait [q.v.] ☋, on any day in the year; and the time when either of them enters any of the four quarters, or paudams [q.v.], of a nacshatram; marking thus the time of their position at every 3° 20′ of the lunar zodiac [raushy chuckram]. Such a punchaungam exhibits also the solar and lunar eclipses [grahanam]; the time when the sun is in the equinoxes [maishauyanam, toolauyanam, vishoo] or the solstices [oottarauyanam, dacshinauyanam], and the time of his entering [sancramanam] a new sign [raushy]. Also birthdays, accessions, and anniversaries of memorable event and feasts of certain gods, goddesses, spirits, patriarchs and other worthies; including the anniversaries of the beginning of the Calpam [q.v.], Manwantarams [q.v.], Mahayoogs [q.v.], and of the four lesser Yoogs [q.v.] of the present Manwantaram. Also local holy days [pundigay], and the feasts of the most considerable pagodas [q.v.], situated about hundred miles around the place for which the calendar is computed. Lastly will be found in the margin certain articles of a civil description, such as the length of the artificial solar days [dinam], and nights, indicated at least once in the course of the month; the sun's entrance [sancramanam] into the different signs [raushy] of the tropical zodiac [raushy chuckram], and predictions of abundance or Vriddhyaurgham, of middle state of prosperity or Samaurgham, and of scarcity or Shoonyaurgham, &c. The punchaungam is sold and read in every village. The system on which it rests rules all the astronomical computations [maunam] of the natives, governs their religious festivals [pundigay] and sacrifices [yanyam], the expiatory ceremonies for the dead, the agricultural dispositions [vellaumay] depend on the contingencies of the seasons [ritoo], and lastly the endless train of observances the epochs of which are determined by the science of astrology. The doctrines on which these humble calendars are calculated have from time immemorial ruled the chronology of many civilized and wealthy nations. The calculation of the measures of time [caulam] is made by a class of astronomers who have received the knowledge from tradition, called Joshies [joshy, jyotisham]. See vol. I, 611.——*Punchaungy* (पञ्चांगी - pañchángí, San.). Village astronomer or astrologer; usually a Bramin and holds his office by descent [inam]. He informs the farmer of the day and hour most favorable for commencing ploughing, and for performing the ceremonies in honor of his deceased relations; so the day and hour most propitious for the celebration of marriage, at which he always attends. He consults his calendar and gives notice of the approach of the principal feasts. He calculates and foretells eclipses, dearths, plenty, the approach of rain, &c. The benediction of the Punchaungy is required by the cultivator on commencing and finishing a dwelling [jauty].——*Punchaupakeshan* (பஞ்சாபகேசன் - pañjábagésan, San.). From (above + ápagá, san. river + ísha, san. lord); epithet of shiva as lord of the country of five rivers, as at Trivaudy near Tanjore. Trivaudy is near five rivers; Coleroon, Cauvery proper, Coodamoorty, Vellaur and Vennaur. Hindoo 2nd or pers. name. Compare Punchanadam [peyar].——*Punchauyoodham* (पञ्चायुध - pañcháyudha, San.). The five weapons or insignia of Vishnoo:—Chuckram [q.v.], a round missile; Dhanoos [q.v.], a bow; Vaul [q.v.], a sword; Dandoo [q.v.], a club; and Chunk [q.v.], a conch.——*Punchayet* (पंचायित - pancháyita, San.). San. from (above + aya, san. to go). A native court of arbitration consisting generally of five persons, but may be more or less. पञ्चमेंपरमेश्वर—"in the punchayet is god," is a common saying. A punchayet may be chosen by parties themselves, or appointed by officers of government. Generally for determination of petty disputes, and especially in matters affecting the usages of castes or occupation. The punchayet is identical with the Hebrew and Roman custom of elders sitting at the gate, the γερουσία of the Greeks. Punchayetdar is a member of the arbitration committee. Punchayet nauma is the written decision or verdict of the committee. See vol. I, 112.——*Punchbaub* (پنچ باب - panchbáb, Hind.). From (above + báb, ar. door). Five items of excise; toddy [q.v.], liquor [sharaub], tobacco [pogauk], ganjah [q.v.] and betel [q.v.].——*Puncheecaranam* (पञ्चीकरण - pañchíkarana, San.). From (above + kri, san. to do). The operation of the five elements [bhootam] in the human body [shareeram]; by the varied union of which, according to the Tatwam [q.v.] system, different operations or acts, of mental faculties or corporeal powers, are considered to be effected. In cosmogony the reduction into union and order of chaos or the discordant principles of matter, by harmoniously blending together of the five elementary substances.——*Punchendriyam* (पञ्चेन्द्रिय - pañchéndriya, San.). From (above + indriya, san. sense). The five senses. According to the Saunkhyam [q.v.] philosophy the five senses [indriyam] are at one stage of creation the causes of all that exists. He therefore who possesses a knowledge of all that relates to the five senses is supposed to know all that is in the world. The Tamul Cooral has the following:—சுவையொளியூறோசைநாற்ற மென்றைந்தின் வகைதெரிவான் கட்டேயுலகு—"the "world is within him who knows the properties of taste, sight, "touch, hearing and smell." Pavanandy [q.v.] in his nunnool [q.v.] classifies all living existences or organized life into five classes according as they are efficiently endowed with one or more of the five senses as follows:—one sense being, having body or sense of touch or feeling, as the vegetable kingdom [vricsham]; two sense being, having body and tongue or sense of touch and taste, as molluscs [chippy], &c.; three sense being, having body, tongue and nose or touch, taste and smell, as white-ants [q.v.], ants [choomtee], &c.; four sense being, having body, tongue, nose and eyes or touch, taste, smell and sight, as beetles [zeerangy], &c.; five sense being, having all the five sense-organs and sense-perceptions, as celestials, men, infernals, beasts, birds, &c.——*Punchseer* (పంచేరు - panchéru, Tel.). Same as Punchair.——*Punj* (پنج - panj, Hind.). Persian five [paunch, puncham]. Punjshamba is Thursday.——*Punja* (پنجہ - panjah, Hind.). From (panj, pers. five). The hand with the fingers extended. A representation of the same mounted on a staff and carried in procession at the Moharram [q.v.], supposed to represent the hand of Ally [q.v.], Hoossain's [q.v.] father. Also emblematic of the creator.——*Punjam* (پنجم - panjum, Hind.). Fifth. Punjam hissa, from (hissah, ar. share) is the fifth portion of the revenue collection.

PUNDAURAM (பண்டாரம் - pandáram, *Tam.*). From (pándu, san. white + ranga, san. color) [pandoo]. A Sheiva devotee; officiating priest at temples [coil, pagoda] of Shiva [q.v.]. The name comes from their smearing themselves with ashes [tirneer, vibhooty]. Many are professed mendicants, but some are learned men. The Lingayets [q.v.] have no Pundaurams. Hindoo third name. See vol. I (68).——*Hill pundauram* (മലമ്പണ്ടാരം - malampantáram, Mal.). A tribe without clothing, implements, or huts of any kind, living in holes, rocks, or trees in Travancore. They bring wax [mom], ivory [dant], and other produce to the Arayans, and get salt [ooppoo] from them. They dig roots [gadda], snare the ibex [saddleback] of the hills and jungle-fowls [q.v.], and eat rats [ely] and snakes [sarpam] and even crocodiles [mugger]. They speak Malayalam [q.v.] in a curious accent.

PUNDIGAY (उत्सव - utsava, *San.*; عید - íd, *Hind.*; ಹಬ್ಬ - habba, *Can.*; పండుగ - panduga, *Tel.*; അടിയന്തരം - atiyantaram, *Mal.*; பண்டிகை - pandigai, *Tam.*). San. from (ud, san. up + su, san. to possess power), meaning a moment of elevation. Hind. from (aud; ar. returning). Can. from (habbu, can. to spread). Tel. from (pandu, tel. ripen). Mal. from (ati, mal. fixed + antara, san. interval). Festival. See vol. I (92). Hindoo festivals may be classified, in respect of mode in which the dates are regulated, into:—"*a*" local and regulated by both calendars [punchaungam];—"*b*" general and regulated by solar-sidereal calendar [madhyamasowramaunam, ravy punchaungam] only;—"*c*" general and regulated by lunar [chaundramaunam] considerations only;—"*d*" common to both the above systems;—"*e*" general and regulated by the composite luni-solar calendar [chaundramaunam, chundrapunchaungam] only. The nomenclature of the festivals is extremely various and complicated. It is based for the most part on astronomical facts, as for instance on the mutual position of the sun [sooryan] and moon [chundran], the occurrence of which situation marks the time for the festival; but it also introduces the names of the hindoo pantheon. The following details give further information.——(1) The local festivals are:—Cottye ootsavam, Garoodotsavam, Gungah yautray, Lacshadeepam, Magizhady saivay, Maha magham, Magham, Oonjal tirnaul. Their nomenclature is generally descriptive.——(2) The general festivals regulated wholly by the solar-sidereal calendar [madhyamasowra maunam] are:—Audy pathinett, Audy pundigay, Bhadradeepam, Bhogy pundigay, Cheitrotsavam, Dacshinauyana poonyacaulam, Lacshadeepam, Macarasancramanam, Mahasancraunty, Nyauyit kizhamay vratam, Oottarauyana poonyacaulam, Pandasairvay, Pathinettaum perook, Pongal, Pooratausby shani kizhamay, Sancraunty, Tamul new year, Vishoo, Vishoo poonya caulam. The nomenclature here may be analysed as falling under four heads; the plus sign showing compound words:—"*a*" sign [raushy] of solar zodiac [raushy chuckram] + term showing sun's entry [sancramanam] therein [macara sancramanam];—"*b*" other astronomical solar facts [dacshinauyana poonyacaulam, maha sancraunty, oottarauyana poonyacaulam, sancraunty, vishoo, vishoo poonyacaulam];—"*c*" solar month + number of the day in that month, as in European system, this being rare [audy pathinett];—"*d*" solar month + name of ceremony belonging thereto [audy pundigay, cheitrotsavam, poorataushy shani kizhamay].——(3) The general festivals regulated wholly by lunar [chaundramaunam] considerations are:—Acsha tadiya, Amavausyay, Anantachatoordashy, Aparapacsham, Ashtamy, Aushwinashooddham, Ayoodha poojay, Balarama jayanty, Bhaunoovidiya, Bhascara saptamy, Bheeshma yecaudashy, Bhootachatoordashy, Cauman pundigay, Chatoorty, Chatoordashy, Dashamy, Deepauvaly, Doorganavamy, Dusserah, Dwaupar yoogaudy, Garooda punchamy, Gocoolaushtamy, Gowry, Haritaulica, Hootaushana powrnamy, Jayanty, Kaliyoogaudy, Kedaura gowryvratam, Krishna ashtamy, Krishna jananam, Krishna jayanty, Krishna pacsham, Krita yoogaudy, Madhyaushtamy, Maha navamy, Maha shivarautry, Mahaulyam, Mahaulya amavausyay, Mahaulya pacsham, Mahaulyaurambham, Mooccoty yecaudashy, Naraca chatoordashy, Narsimhajayanty, Navamy, Nauga punchamy, Naugoolachavity, Navarautry, Oopaucarmam, Oottaunaicaudashy, Pillayaurchatoorty, Poornimay, Powrnimay, Pratamah yecaudashy, Punchamy, Ratasaptamy, Rig oopaucarmam, Rishypunchamy, Samvatsaraudy, Saptamy, Saraswaty poojaurambham, Saraswatypoojay, Scandashasty, Shashty, Shivarautry, Shooclapacsham, Shrauvana powrnimay, Shreerama navamy, Soobbaroya shashty, Teloogoo new year, Trayodashy, Triteeyay, Varalutchmy vratam, Veicoonta yecaudashy, Vijayadashamy, Vinauyacachatoorty, Vyausapoornama, Yamatarpanam, Yecaudashy, Yoogaudy. The terms of the nomenclature may be thus analysed:—"*a*" name or epithet of a deity + tity [q.v.] sacred to him or her; very common; it is understood that this happens on a certain one of the lunar months [chaundra mausam] which is not mentioned as being supposed to be understood [ananta chatoordashy, bhaunoovidiya, bheeshma yecaudashy, bhoota chatoordashy, bhascara saptamy, doorganavamy, garooda punchamy, hootaushana powrnamy, krishna ashtamy, madana trayodashy, naugapunchamy, naugoolachavity, pillayaurchatoorty, rishypunchamy, scandashashty, shreeramanavamy, soobbaroyashashty, veicoonta yecaudashy, vinauyaca chatoorty, vyausa poornama];—"*b*" lunar month + tity; means the same thing, but the name of the month is here given, and that of the deity omitted [aushwina shooddham, shrauvana powrnimay];—"*c*" lunar month by itself [shrauvanam];—"*d*" nacshatram by itself [moolam];—"*e*" tity by itself [acsha tadiya, amavausyay, aparapacsham, ashtamy, chatoordashy, chatoorty, dashamy, gocoolaushtamy, madhyaushtamy, mahaulya amavausyay, mahanavamy, maulapoornama, mooccoty yecaudashy, naraca chatoordashy, navamy, oottaunaicaudashy, poornimay, powrnimay, pratamah yecaudashy, punchamy, ratasaptamy, saptamy, shashty, trayodashy, triteeyay, vijayadashamy, yecaudashy].——(4) The general festivals regulated by both calendars [punchaungam], that is to say occurring on one date for the Tamuls and under the same or an analogous term on another date for the Teloogoos, are Tamul new year, and Teloogoo new year.——(5) The general festivals regulated by the composite luni-solar calendar [chaundramaunam] are very numerous:—Ardrah darshanam, Ashtamy, Audy amavausyay, Audy pooram, Auny amavausyay, Auny tirmanjanam, Auvany avittam, Auvany moolam, Bharany, Bharany deepam, Caurtigay, Chittraypowrnimay, Garoodotsavam, Hastodayam, Magham, Maghatirnaul, Mahamagham, Maurgalytirmanjanam, Maushimagham, Oottaram, Pooram, Poosham, Pungoonyoottaram, Shany trayodashy, Tengayair, Tircaurtigay, Tirvauthiray, Tye amavausyay, Tyepoosham, Vanabhojanam, Vishnoodeepam, Wonam. The terms of the nomenclature may be thus analysed:—"*a*" solar month + tity, meaning the point of time when the moon is in such a stage of growth in that solar month [audy amavausyay, auny amavausyay, chittraypowrnimay, tye amavausyay];—"*b*" solar month + nacshatram, meaning the point of time when the moon stands in that nacshatram in that solar month [audypooram, auvanyavittam, auvany moolam, maushimagham, pungoonyoottaram, tye poosham];—"*c*" nacshatram alone, being short for the latter [bharany, caurtigay, magham, mahamagham, oottaram, pooram, poosham, tircaurtigay, tirvauthiray, wonam];—"*d*" week day + tity, meaning whenever these two coincide [shany trayodashy];—"*e*" some astronomical luni-solar fact [ardrah darshanam, hastodayam].——(6) There are various nomenclature terms for festivals which are indeterminate as regards the astronomical facts. These may be analysed thus:—"*a*" deity + festival name [bheemarautry, bhogy pundigay, bramhasauvitry, bramhotsavam, doorga poojay, garoodotsavam, gowry, gungahyautray, mahashivarautry, shivarautry, vishnoodeepam, yamatarpanam];—"*b*" deity + vow [kedaura gowryvratam, saraswaty poojaurambham, saraswaty poojay, varalutchmy vratam];—"*c*" deity + birthday [ayenaurtirnaul, balaramajayanty, krishna jananam, krishna jayanty, narsimha jayanty, permaultirnaul, shreejayanty];—"*d*" a ceremony, general descriptive term [aunytirmanjanam, ayoodhapoojay, bhadradeepam, bharanydeepam, calyaunam, cauman pundigay, cottye ootsavam, darshanam, deepam, deepauvaly, dwauparyoogaudy, dusserah, graumadevatay, haritaulica, holy, jautrey, jayanty, kaliyoogaudy, kritayoogaudy, lacshadeepam, lingapoojay, magizhadysaivay, mahaulyaurambham, mahaulyam, mahaulya pacsham, maurgaly tirmanjanam, navarautry, navaunieam, nyauyitkizhamay vratam, oonjaltirnaul, oopaucarmam, oopavausam, ootsavam, pandasairvay, patbinettuumperook, pongal, poonyacaulam, pooshcaram, pradosham, puncharautram, ratotsavam, rig oopaucarmam, sairvay, samvatsaraudy, saumavaidy oopaucarmam, sevay, swarga dwauram, tairottam, tarpanam, tengayair, tircalyaunam, tirnacshatram, tirnaul, vanabhojanam, varshaurambham, vratam, yajoor oopaucarmam, yoogaudy].——(4) For Mahom. festivals see Eed.

PUNDIT (पण्डित - pandita, *San.*). From (pandá, san. wisdom). A Bramin [q.v.] who makes some branch of Sanscrit [q.v.] learning his special study, and teaches it. There is a Tamul proverb :—சொல்லாமல் இருக்கிறவனே பண்டிதன்—" he who is of few words is a pundit." Also the law officer formerly appointed in the Company's courts for the interpretation of braminical law. Hindoo third name [peyar, punt].——*Pandah* (پنڈا - pandá, Hind.). Head priest [mahant, maryauday].——*Punt* (पण्डित - pandita, San. ; पंत - panta, Mahr.). Abbreviation of Pundit. Mahratta term. In the Circars [q.v.] a Bramin [q.v.] employed as a writer by the Government. Also used as third name [peyar].——*Puntooloo* (పంతులు - pantulu, Tel.). Plural of Punt. In the north of presidency a caste title among Niyogy [q.v.] bramins [q.v.] ; an official title among other bramins [peyar] ; is also the title of the village schoolmaster.

PUNDRY (பன்றி - panri, *Tam.*). From (pari, tam. to dig). Hog [soor]. For common pundry or domestic hog and cautt pundry or wild hog see Soor. For moollampundry or hedge hog see Moollely. For cadal pundry see below. Pundry is a not uncommon plant first term indicating coarse, large or wild. Ex., where transl. is of second term :—Andropogon contortus (panrippul), grass ; Dioscorea pentaphylla (pandimukkudumpa), snout + esculent root ; Momordica charantia (panrippudal), trichosanthes anguina ; Trapa bispinosa (panrimondángizhangu), to smell + root ; (panrimottai), lump. See gloss. paragraphs. ——(1) *Pundry meen* (शंकु - shanku, San. ; دلفین - dulfín, Ar. ; خوک ماهی - khokmáhí, Pers. ; سوس مار - súsmár, Hind. ; ಹಂದಿಮೀನು - handimínu, Can. ; ಪಂಜಮೀನು - panjimínu, Too. ; గండుమీను - gandumínu, Tel. ; പന്നിമീൻ - pannimín, Mal. ; பன்றிமீன் - panrimín, Tam.). San. from (shank, san. to fear). Pers. from (khok, pers. hog + máhí, pers. fish). Hind. from (shishu, san. child + mára, san. killer). Can. from (handi, can. hog + mínu, can. fish). Tel. from (gandu, tel. large + mínu, tel. fish). Tam. from (panri, tam. hog + mín, tam. fish). Ar. also (bintulbahr), meaning daughter of the sea. Title otherwise Goose beak, Sea goose. Equivalent of the family delphinidæ, cetacea, mammalia [sastanam, 29], of naturalists [jantoo]. Popularly the word dolphin is, for a reason not yet ascertained, applied to the fish Coryphæna [dolphin fish], celebrated for its changeable tints when dying. By naturalists however the term is a family as above, including in these seas the Porpoise and the Caaing whale [cadalpundry].——(2) *Cadalpundry* (जलशूकर - jalashúkara, San. ; دلفین - dulfín, Ar. ; خنز برالبحر - khinzirulbahr, Pers. ; سوسمار - súsmár, Hind. ; لالومبا - lálomba, Malay ; ನೀರುಬಂಡಿ - nírubandi, Can. ; ಕಡಲ್‌ಪಂಜಿ - kadalpanji, Too. ; నీరుపంది - nírupandi, Tel. ; കടല്പന്നി - katalpanni, Mal. ; கடற்பன்றி - kadarbanri, Tam.). San. from (jala, san. water + shúkara, san. hog) ; from roundness of back as it appears in water. Pers. from (khinzír, ar. hog + bahr, ar. sea). Hind. from (shishu, san. child + mára, san. killer). Can. from (níru, can. water + handi, can. hog). Too. from (kadal, too. sea + panji, too. pig). Tel. from (níru, tel. water + pandi, tel. pig). Tam. from (kadal, tam. sea + panri, tam. hog). Title otherwise Black dolphin, Hog fish, Porpoise, Sea hog. Delphinus perniger, delphinidæ cetacea, mammalia [sastanam, 29], of naturalists [jantoo]. Twenty-six teeth on each side, above and below, obtuse, slightly curved inwards. Of an uniform shining black above ; beneath blackish. Porpoises or Marine dolphins generally are characterised by a convex forehead, with a protruding muzzle which forms a sort of beak ; they have teeth in both jaws, numerous and conical, broad and high cranium, nasal passage vertical, no cæcum. They are gregarious in habit, carnivorous and extremely swift. They must not be confounded with the dolphin of sailors, which is a true fish, Coryphæna hippurus [dolphin fish], of a great velocity and brilliant colors, changing like rainbow tints when the fish is dying. The modern porpoise is the dolphin of the ancients, the ἱερὸς ἰχθὺς represented in all the old pictures and sculptures. The porpoises are distinguished from all their allies by their great strength and ferocity, being the only cetaceans which habitually prey on warm-blooded animals, for, though fish form part of their food, they also attack and devour seals and various species of their own order.—"*a*" Allied to the species mentioned at head is the Plumbeous dolphin. Delphinus plumbeus of naturalists. Thirty-six teeth on each side in the upper jaw and thirty-two in the lower jaw. Of an uniform leaden color, with the lower jaw white. Has been taken on the Malabar coast.—"*b*" There are several others on the Madras coast generally ; as Delphinus gadamu ; Delphinus lentiginosus ; Delphinus maculiventer or Spot-bellied dolphin ; Delphinus fusiformis or Spindle-shaped dolphin ; Delphinus pomeegra.—"*c*" Allied is the Caaing whale, an Orkney name, Globicephalus indicus, delphinidæ, cetacea, mammalia [sastanam, 29], of naturalists. Called also Black whale, Grindval, Pilot fish, &c. Of an uniform leaden black color, slightly paler beneath ; similar in form and size to Globicephalus deductor of European seas, but the teeth fewer and larger than in that species, being six or seven above, seven or eight beneath. Head globular in front ; the dorsal fin is high, situated nearer to the head than to the tail ; the flippers very long and narrow ; the fingers possessing an unusually large number of bones. This is much more a porpoise than a whale [timingilam].——*Punniyan* (പന്നിയൂർക്കാർ - panniyúrkkár, obl. ; പന്നിയൂർക്കാരൻ - panniyúrkkáran, pers. sing. ; പന്നിയൂർക്കാരർ - panniyúrkkárar, pers. pl., Mal.). Punniyore numboory bramins as opposed to Chovoor. To be distinguished from Paniyan.——*Punniyore* (പന്നിയൂർ - panniyúr, Mal.). Means boar village. Sanscrit name (varáhagráma), meaning same. Vishnoo [q.v.] in his boar [varauham] incarnation [avatar] is worshipped here. Village or villages'; Malabar dist., Chiracal tal. ; not exactly identified. Here Numboory [q.v.] bramins [q.v.] first settled, being Veishnavite by religion. Compare Chovoor.

PURDAH (పర్దా - pardah, *Hind.*). From persian. A curtain, especially one which hides the women of a family.——*Purda nisheen* (پردہ نشین - pardahnishín, Hind.). From (above + nishín, pers. seated). One who lives within the curtain [gosha nisheen].

PURPLE GRASS (برتی - birtí, *Hind.* ; ఊదగడ్డి - údagaddi, *Tel.*). Title from color throughout. Tel. from (úda, tel. purple + gaddi, tel. grass). Botanically Panicum [priyangoo] flavidum, retz., graminaceæ [vricsham, 156]. Alias Panicum brizoides, colonum, flaccidum. Culm slender, erect, simple ; leaves linear, glabrous ; racemes six to twelve, alternate, much shorter than the interstices, by degrees shorter ; spikelets solitary, in two rows, somewhat roundish-oblong, acutish, glabrous ; lower glume rounded, upper ones a little shorter than the florets, hermaphrodite ones hooked at the apex, a little wrinkled ; both in wet and dry situations ; parts of the plant are often tinged with purple. ——*Large purple grass* (పెద్దఊద - peddaúda, Tel. ; மருக்குருப்புல் - marukkuráppul, Tam.). Title from size and color. Tel. from (pedda, tel. large + úda, tel. panicum flavidum, retz.). Tam. from (maru, tam. fragrance + kurá, tam. webera corymbosa, willd. + pul, tam. grass). Title otherwise Hedge-hog grass, Twisted grass. Botanically Panicum [priyangoo] stagninum, retz., graminaceæ [vricsham, 156]. Culms 1–4 feet, ascending ; leaves soft and smooth ; mouth of the sheaths ciliated ; spike compound, erect ; partial ones alternate ; spikelets ovate-oblong, tubercled, bristly and ciliated ; lower glume ovate-elliptic, acute, a half shorter than the flower, upper one awned ; in wet cultivated ground, flowering in the rainy season.——*Matted purple grass* (श्यामक - shyámaka, San. ; ಜಡೆಶಂಕರಹುಲ್ಲು - jadeshankarahullu, Can. ; ఊదగడ్డి - údagaddi, Tel.). Title from appearance. San. from (shyáma, san. dark-brown). Can. from (jade, can. matted + shankara, san. happy making + hullu, can. grass). Tel. means purple grass. Botanically Panicum [priyangoo], colonum, linn., graminaceæ [vricsham, 156]. Alias Echinochloa colonna ; Oplismenus colonus. Culms below resting on the ground and rooting, above sub-erect, branched, a little compressed, smooth ; leaves short, smooth, tapering from the base to a sharp point ; spikes compound, secund, seven to nine, alternate, distant, spikelets in four series ; glumes scabrous, mucronate, unequal, three-nerved ; common in cultivated fields ; one of the best grasses for forage [ghaus].——*Quilled purple grass* (శల్లఊద - shallaúda, Tel.). Title from appearance. Tel. from (shalamu, tel. porcupine quill + úda, tel. panicum flavidum, retz.). Botanically Panicum [priyangoo] helopus, trin., graminaceæ [vricsham, 156]. Alias Panicum hirsutum. Culm 1–2 feet, decumbent, rooting, ascending, knots bearded ; sheaths hairy ; racemes alternate, much longer than the interstices ; spikelets somewhat solitary, loosely imbricated, ovate, acute, densely pubescent hairy ; lower glume four times shorter than the florets, hermaphrodite one acuminate, wrinkled ; pastures and borders of cultivated ground.

PURTY (పర్తి - parti, *Tel.*). Uncultivated land ; village. Suffix in place names, as Peddapurty, meaning large waste.

PURWANNA (پروانہ - parwánah, *Hind.*). From the persian. A license or pass [rawauna].

PUSHM (ऊर्णा - úrna, *San.* ; پشم - pashm, *Pers.* ; ಹಣ್ಣೆ - hanne, *Can.* ; బొచ్చు - bottsu, *Tel.* ; ആട്ടുരോമം - átturómam, *Mal.* ; ஆட்டுரோமம் - átturómam, *Tam.*). San. from (vri, san. to cover). Mal. and Tam. means sheep + hair [lomam, romam]. Wool. The different kinds generally employed in trade are of two sorts, black, and mixed grey. Real wool-bearing sheep [aud] are met with only in Mysore and Coimbatore. In other parts of the country, the sheep are covered with a shaggy hair, resembling that of goats [velland]. An imported article is shawl [q.v.] wool, a downy substance, found next the skin and below the thick hair of the Thibetan goat. Pushmee is woollen. Pushmeenah is a woollen cloth especially from Cashmere. For wool of plants see Cotton.

PUTTAN (പട്ട - patta, *Mal.*; பட்டன் - pattan, *Tam.*). Generally appears as Puttar, honorific plural. From (bhatta, san. lord).—"*a*" Title among Tamul bramins of Malabar; also borne by Shoodras who are astrologers [joshy] and serve as carriers. The chief puttar settlements in malabar lie in the palghaut talook; the puttar are mostly worshippers of shiva; their occupation is trading and the conveyance of commodities into the interior [jauty]; see vol. II, 100.—"*b*" In tamul country title applied to a goldsmith [tattaun]; also applied to members of the Punchaula [q.v.] caste in districts about Madras [peyar].——*Pattairy* (പട്ടേരി - pattéri, Mal.). Corruption of Bhattatiry.

PUTTICONDAH (పత్తికొండ - pattikonda,* *Tel.*). From (patti, tel. cotton + konda, tel. hill); from a shepherd who first cleared the jungle and cultivated cotton [q.v.].——**(1)** Talook, Kurnool district. Tahsildar's pay Rs. 175. Area 1,134 square miles. Population 138,703. Language mainly Teloogoo and Canarese to a small extent. On W. of district. Bounded N. by Toongabudra, S. by Gooty and Tadpatry talooks of Anantapore, E. by Ramalcottah and Coilcoontla talook, and W. by Aulore and Adony talooks of Bellary district. Till 1858 it belonged to Bellary district, when it was called Punchapollem being under the sway of five poligars. Their capitals were at Chennampully, Cuppatraula, Devanacondah, Maddikera, and Pyaupaly. At all these places are the remains of fine hill forts but those at the first two are greatly demolished. The first and last families are extinct, the others being pensioners. Being on high road between Hyderabad and Southern provinces, it suffered very much in latter part of eighteenth century from invasion by Hyder and Tippoo, as well as the Mahrattas, and from internal disturbances between Poligars [q.v.] and Jagheerdar [q.v.] of Adony, so that when the country came under British rule in 1800, a very large portion of the land had been left uncultivated. In 1802, the survey and assessment of the lands was commenced by Lieutenant-Colonel Munro and brought to close about the end of 1806. The triennial and decennial leases of villages were then given. But this having failed, the ryotwarry [q.v.] system was introduced in 1822, modified by Chowtye [q.v.] and Trijye [q.v.] reductions. These schemes lasted till A.D. 1858 when Mr. Pelly's scheme was introduced. In the centre and towards the east and south the country is hilly, gradually rising till it terminates in the flat-topped Yerramala. Lying between the Carnautacam [q.v.] country and Telingana [q.v.], the Lingayets [q.v.] or Canarese-speaking people are to be found in larger number than in any other talook. In the northern and western portions which form the valley of the Hindry, the soil is generally regady [regar] or black. Formerly noted for rich diamond [vajram] fields. Weaving of cotton [q.v.] clothes and cumblies [q.v.] is the chief industry in the talook and cotton and castor [aumanac] oil seeds and grams [q.v.] the principal exports. The talook is chiefly dependent on S.W. monsoon [q.v.]. The Hindry is the chief river. In the hilly parts the spring level is high and shallow wells are dug for irrigation purposes at little cost. There are seventy-seven tanks [q.v.] and sixty-three spring channels [q.v.] under which wet cultivation is carried on, but the tanks are not large except at Kereybelagull. Pyaupalay and Yainoogamurry are military camping grounds. Places of archæological interest:—Candanauty, Chennampully, Cotacondah, Cuppatraula, Devanacondah, Goondaula, Keirpully, Maddikera, Moonimadoogoo, Peravaly, Putticondah, Pyaupaly, Yerragoody. Principal Trig. stations:—Kereybelagull, Poolicondah, Shiddannaghatt. The leading places, &c., in the talook are the following.——*Caurlacondah* (కార్లకొండ - kárlakonda, Tel.). From (káru, tel. black + konda, tel. hill). Hill; lat. 15° 19′; long. 77° 39′; from Kurnool S.W. 46 miles; from Putticondah S.E. 9 miles. Near Coilcoontla.——*Codoomoor* (కోడుమూరు - kódumúru, Tel.). From (kodumu, tel. pot + úru, tel. village). Village; pop. 5,525; acres 7,245; lat. 15° 41′; long. 76° 49′; from Kurnool W.S.W. 22 miles; from Putticondah N.E. 27 miles. Important weaving place noted for cotton [q.v.] and silk [puttoo] cloths, chiefly exported to Mysore. Weekly market on Saturday.——*Cotacondah* (కోటకొండ - kótakonda, Tel.). From (kóta, san. fort + konda, tel. hill). Village; pop. 1,990; acres 8,766; lat. 15° 35′; long. 77° 45′; from Kurnool S.W. 28 miles; from Putticondah N.E. 20 miles. Former seat of a poligar [q.v.]. Permappa naidoo, the ancestor, was taliyaur [q.v.] of the village of Gonegandla in Kurnool. On the fall of Vijianugger he obtained the cauvaly [q.v.] of the districts of Adony, Gadwal, Kurnool, Moodgull, and Ryechore and served with 500 men. One of his descendants, Madappa naidoo, served under Aurungzeeb and procured from him a confirmation of the cauvaly [q.v.] and the districts of Cotacondah and Cuppatraula. Asaf jah continued the districts on the same terms. A partition then took place between two branches of the family, one getting Cotacondah and the other Cuppatraula. In 1770 Basaulut jung, being unable to enforce payment of peshcush [q.v.], called in Hyder, who reduced the forts. The poligars [q.v.] had various fortunes. Munro resumed this place and granted the family a pension. Old hill-fort and ancient temple.——*Cumbagherry* (కంబగిరి - kambagiri, Tel.). From (kambamu, tel. pillar + giri, tel. hill). Hill, Place of pilgrimage. Rock and temple. Fine brick [shengal] built gopooram [q.v.] 4 miles from Raucherla. In seasons of drought, oblations of Paramannam are made on a rock.——*Cuppatraula* (కప్పట్రాళ్ల - kappatrálla, Tel.). See sep. title.——*Devanacondah* (దేవనకొండ - dévanakonda, Tel.). From (dévanna, tel. proper name + konda, tel. hill). Village; pop. 2,347; acres 4,341; lat. 15° 32′; long. 77° 36′; from Kurnool S.W. 39 miles; from Putticondah N. 10 miles. Former residence of a Poligar [q.v.]. The ancestor served under the Beejapore government with 100 peons [q.v.] and held Devanacondah for a peshcush [q.v.] of Canteroy pagodas [q.v.] 812·5. His son having been engaged in some disturbances under Nausir jung was taken and circumcised. Family now extinct. Fort. Copper and silver idols and dolls and curtain cloths made here. Weekly market on Wednesday.——*Doodcondah* (దూదేకొండ - dúdékonda, Tel.). From (dúdi, tel. cotton + konda, tel. hill). Village; pop. 1,028; acres 9,657; lat. 15° 27′; long. 77° 34′; from Kurnool S.W. 44 miles; from Putticondah N. 4 miles. Former seat of a Poligar. Family now receive small pension.——*Goondaula* (గుండాల - gundála, Tel.). From (gundu, tel. rock + ila, tel. ground). A place of pilgrimage; pop. 60; acres 1,593; lat. 15° 21′; long. 77° 46′; from Kurnool S.S.W. 40 miles; from Putticondah E.S.E. 14 miles. Ancient Vishnoo temple. By shutting the doors and letting light through a hole in the door made for the purpose, the gopooram [q.v.] is seen reflected on the floor in a position which is the reverse of a reflected object. Annual festival from fourteen to twenty-five Cheitram [mausam] or in march or april.——*Hindry* (హింద్రి - hindri,* Tel.). See sep. title.——*Keirpully* (ఖైరుపల్లి - khairupalli, Tel.). From (khair, hind. alms + palli, tel. village). Village; pop. 1,656; acres 7,396; lat. 15° 33′; long. 77° 31′; from Kurnool W.S.W. 42 miles; from Putticondah N. 11 miles. Vishnoo temple. Annual festival, Teloogoo new year's day [pandigay, 4]. On the second day of the festival, right [valangay] and left hand [yidangay] castes [jauty] carry on mimic warfare with cow-dung cakes [bratty].——*Kereybelagull* (ಕೆರೆಬೆಳಗಲ್ಲು - kerébelagallu, Can.). From (keré, can. tank + bella, can. white + kallu, can. rock). Village; pop. 2,025; acres 10,380; lat. 15° 49′; long. 77° 43′; height of hill 1,422 feet; from Kurnool W. 25 miles; from Putticondah N.N.E. 31 miles. Trig. station in lat. 15° 48′ 45·61″; long. 77° 43′ 26·83″; height 1,423 feet; from Kereybelagull S.E. 1 mile; from Putticondah N.N.E. 31 miles.——*Maddikera* (మద్దికెర - maddikera, Tel.). See sep. title.——*Peravaly* (పెరవలి - peravali, Tel.). From (pera, tel. awe-inspiring + vali, tel. god of the winds). After Hanooman. Village; pop. 2,664; acres 7,441; lat. 15° 17′; long. 77° 33′; from Kurnool S.W. 52 miles; from Putticondah S. 7 miles. Former site of a settlement of Goozeratties [q.v.]. Old temple of Rungasawmy. Annual festival in February from 17th to 25th Phaulgoonam [mausam] or march.——*Poolicondah* (పులికొండ - pulikonda, Tel.). From (puli, tel. tiger + konda, tel. hill). Hill; lat. 15° 28′; long. 77° 37′; height 1,802 feet; from Kurnool S.W. 39 miles; from Putticondah N.E. 7 miles. Trig. station in lat. 15° 28′ 11·30″; long. 77° 38′ 24·13″; height 1,802 feet; from Pundicona N.E. 3 miles; from Putticondah N.E. 8 miles.——*Pundicona* (పందికోన - pandikóna, Tel.). From (pandi, tel. hog + kóna, tel. ravine). Village; pop. 2,108; acres 12,917; lat. 15° 27′; long. 77° 37′; from Kurnool S.W. 42 miles; from Putticondah N.E. 5 miles. Poligar same family as Doodcondah. Now small pension.——*Putticondah* (పత్తికొండ - pattikonda, Tel.). See below.——*Pyaupaly* (ప్యాపలి - pyápali, Tel.). See sep. title.——*Rampore* (రామపురం - rámapuram, Tel.). See sep. title.——*Shiddannaghatt* (సిద్దన్నఘట్టు - siddannaghattu, Tel.). From (siddana, tel. proper name + gattu, tel. border). Trig. station; lat. 15° 14′ 02·94″; long. 77° 54′ 44·61″; height 2,121 feet; from Caloogotla S.S.W. 29 miles; from Kurnool S.S.W. 43 miles; from Putticondah S.E. 26 miles; from Pyaupaly E. 9 miles.——*Tooggaly* (తుగ్గలి - tuggali, Can.). Village, Railway station; pop. 1,867; acres 11,398; lat. 15° 19′ 06″; long. 77° 36′; from Kurnool S.W. 49 miles; from Putticondah S.S.E. 6 miles.——*Varacoor* (వరకూరు - varakúru, Tel.). From (varakamu, tel. grain, panicum miliaceum, linn. + úru, tel. village). Village; pop. 1,012; acres 3,817; lat. 15° 42′; long. 77° 47′; from Kurnool W.S.W. 23 miles; from Putticondah N.N.E. 26 miles. Former residence of a Poligar. The family now reside in Cuddapah district.——*Yerramala* (ఎఱ్ఱమల - erramala, Tel.). See sep. title.——**(2)** Village, Talook head-quarters; Kurnool dist., Putticondah tal.; pop. 4,383; acres 11,319; lat. 15° 24′; long. 77° 33′; from Cumbum W.S.W. 106 miles; from Kurnool S.W. 46 miles; from Madras W.N.W. 244 miles; from Nundiaul W. 65 miles; from Pyaupaly W.N.W. 19 miles. On the road between Gooty and Adony, about 12 miles from Aspry railway station. Three miles west runs the Hindry. Built in the time of Harihara roya in fourteenth century. A shepherd first cleared the jungle and cultivated cotton [q.v.]. Vencata rajah, the descendant of Conairy royan, a Vijianugger prince to whom the village was given in jagheer [q.v.], removed the village to near the hill. After Vencata rajah's family became extinct, Bojjappa naidoo, Poligar of Devanacondah, an ancestor of the present Poligar of Maddikera, took possession of the town, but was soon ousted by the Mahomedans, who annexed it to the Adony district. A Mahomedan named Shere ally baba sahib obtained the village in jagheer [q.v.] and held it for twenty years, residing in the hill fort. In A.D. 1756 Basaulut jung obtained the jagheer of Adony, and in 1761 he gave Putticondah in jagheer to Oottaman. Meer buksh subjar jung, Tahsildar [q.v.] of Sanoogondla, with the assistance of Lally soon afterwards seized and plundered the place. The town passed to the British with the Ceded districts [q.v.] in 1800. Sir Thomas Munro, Governor of Madras, died here on the 6th June 1827 of cholera. Government constructed a fine cut-stone well with a mantapam [q.v.], and grove of tamarind [q.v.] trees around it to his memory. Munro-pettah was also built on this occasion. Weaving industry. Weekly market on Monday. Annual festival in Keshava sawmy temple from 22nd to 30th Cheitram [mausam] or in March-April.

PUTTOOCOTTAH (பட்டுக்கோட்டை - pattukkóttai, *Tam.* patukóta *). From (patti, tam. robbery + kóttai, tam. fort) [padoo]. Vuttamullay narrain, a robber chieftain, built the town.——(1) Talook, Tanjore district. Tahsildar's pay Rs. 175. Area 904 square miles. Population 271,374. Language Tamul. South coast of district. Boundaries :—N. Tanjore and Munnargoody talooks, S. sea, E. Tritrapoondy talook and sea, W. Poodoocottah state and Madura district. An open flat, sloping towards the east. Soil, generally sandy and in some parts red. Agricultural and export of rice [q.v.] and cocoanuts [q.v.]. Import of betel-nuts [q.v.] from Ceylon. Irrigation by rain-fed tanks [q.v.]. Zemindarries :—Ativetty, Mathoocore, Nedoovausal, Palayavanam, Paupanaud, Pautharancottah, Sheudangoody, Shillattore, Shingavanam. Places of archæological interest :—Adiramputnam, Arantaungy, Arasarcoolam, Aundacottay, Auvidayaurcoil, Carsaivayal, Chinnaauvidayaurcoil, Colloocaud, Maraimadaky, Mungalam, Nedoovausal, Neyvaily, Neyvuttaly, Okkadar, Parcullcottah, Parmandore, Periyauloodaiyarcoil, Pillaivayal, Puttoocottah, Saitbauvachuttram, Shauttacoody, Shevalavayal, Shillattore, Tirvainam, Vadacherry, Vellaula vidoothy, Vigneshwarapooram, Vishwanautapooram, Yetyattaly. Principal trig. stations :—Caunaud, Coolamungalam, Culloornicaud, Mailpanacaud, Maunore, Pautharancottah, Pullattivayal, Puttoocottah, Rajahmadam beacon, Rettavayal, Wokkoor. The leading places, &c., in the talook are the following.——*Adiramputnam* (அதிராம்பட்டணம் - athirámbattanam, Tam.). See sep. title.——*Agnyaur* (அக்கினியாறு - akkiniyáru, Tam.). See sep. title.——*Ammaputnam* (அம்மாப்பட்டணம் - ammáppattanam, Tam.). From (ammá, tam. title of a woman + pattana, san. town). Village, Port ; pop. 3,559 ; lat. 10° 1′ ; long. 79° 17′ ; from Cottapatam N.E. 4 miles ; from Krishnaujiputnam S. 5 miles ; from Madras S.S.W. 220 miles ; from Puttoocottah S.S.W. 29 miles ; from Tanjore S. 53 miles. The sea trade consists in the export of rice [q.v.] to Ceylon and import of timber from Ceylon. This village forms part of Manamailcoody.——*Arantaungy* (அறந்தாங்கி - arandángi, Tam.). See sep. title.——*Ativetty* (அத்திவெட்டி - attivetti, Tam.). From (atti, tam. a tree, ficus racemosa, linn. + vetti, tam. way). Zemindarry, Village ; pop. 1,719 ; lat. of village 10° 26′ ; long. 79° 29′ ; from Puttoocottah E. 8 miles ; from Tanjore S.E. 31 miles ; from the sea N. 7 miles and W. 30 miles. Peshcush Rs. 913.——*Auvidayaurcoil* (ஆவுடையார்கோவில் - ávudaiyárgóvil, Tam.). From (ávudaiyár, tam. phallic emblem of shiva + kóvil, tam. temple). Village, Place of pilgrimage ; pop. 2,480 ; acres 11,526 ; lat. 10° 05′ ; long. 79° 05′ ; from Puttoocottah S.S.W. 30 miles ; from Tanjore S.S.W. 49 miles ; from the sea W. 14 miles. Old Shiva temple with elaborate sculptures and covered with inscriptions of the Chola [q.v.] dynasty [raj]. Its erection by the minister of a Paundyan [q.v.] king is related in the Madura stala pooraunam [q.v.]. In the hamlet of Tirpoonnavausal is another well-sculptured Shiva [q.v.] temple [coil, pagoda] with inscriptions. There are two important festivals at Auvidayaurcoil in the months of Auny [mausam] or June and Maurgaly [mausam] or December.——*Caunaud* (கானாடு - kánádu, Tam.). From (ká, tam. grove + nádu, tam. country). Trig. station ; lat. 9° 58′ 40·64″ ; long. 79° 09′ 44·22″ ; height 30 feet ; from Puttoocottah S.S.W. 34 miles ; from Tauzhanore E. 1 mile ; from the sea W. 6 miles.——*Cautmauvady* (காட்டுமாவடி - káttumávadi, Tam.). From (káttumá, tam. wild mango tree, spondias mangifera, willd. + adi, tam. foot). Village, Port ; pop. 756 ; lat. 10° 08′ ; long. 79° 17′ ; from Krishnaujiputnam N. 8 miles ; from Puttoocottah S.S.W. 22 miles ; from Shalwanaickenputnam S.S.W. 11 miles ; from Tanjore S. 45 miles. On Palk's bay. A salt manufactory. Fairs on Mondays.——*Coolamungalam* (குலமங்கலம் - kulamangalam, Tam.). From (kulam, tam. tank + mangala, san. prosperity). Trig. station ; lat. 10° 16′ 46·78″ ; long. 79° 04′ 36·26″ ; height 158 feet ; from Puttoocottah W.S.W. 23 miles ; from Yercalacottah N.N.W. 4 miles ; from the sea W. 19 miles.——*Culloornicaud* (கல்லூறணிக்காடு - kallúranikkádu, Tam.). From (kal, tam. stone + úrani, tam. fountain + kádu, tam. forest). Trig. station ; lat. 10° 20′ 27·03″ ; long. 79° 15′ 28·03″ ; height 81 feet ; from Puttoocottah S.W. 9 miles ; from Tennangoody N. 2 miles ; from the sea W. 12 miles.——*Gopaulputnam* (கோப்பாலப்பட்டணம் - kóppálappattanam, Tam.). From (gópála, san. krishna, the cowherd + pattana, san. town). Village, Port ; pop. 1,318 ; lat. 10° 18′ ; long. 79° 24′ ; from Adiramputnam S.W. 3 miles ; from Madras S.S.W. 199 miles ; from Shalwanaickenputnam E. 5 miles ; from Puttoocottah S.S.E. 9 miles ; from Tanjore S.S.E. 37 miles. On Palk's bay.——*Mailpanacaud* (மேற்பனைக்காடு - mérbanaikkádu, Tam.). From (mél, tam. west + panai, tam. palmyra tree, borassus flabelliformis, linn. + kádu, tam. forest). Trig. station ; lat. 10° 15′ 06·66″ ; long. 79° 09′ 00·57″ ; height 89 feet ; from Maroondangoody N. 4 miles ; from Puttoocottah S.W. 19 miles ; from the sea W. 13 miles.——*Manamailcoody* (மணமேற்குடி - manamérgudi, Tam.). From (manal, tam. sand + mél, tam. over + kudi, tam. village). Sanscrit name (draupadámbápura), meaning drowpady + goddess + town. Village, Port ; pop. 3,559 ; lat. 10° 02′ ; long. 79° 17′ ; from Puttoocottah S.S.W. 27 miles ; from Tanjore S. 51 miles. Chuttram [q.v.] built by the Rajah for travellers to Rameshwaram.——*Mathoocore* (மதுக்கூர் - mathukkúr, Tam.). From (mathagu, tam. sluice + úr, tam. village). Zemindarry, Village ; pop. 4,093 ; lat. of village 10° 30′ ; long. 79° 26′ ; from Puttoocottah N.E. 7 miles ; from Tanjore S.E. 27 miles ; from the sea N. 10 miles. Peshcush Rs. 2,491. Fairs on Tuesdays. A commercial town.——*Maunore* (மானூர் - mánúr, Tam.). From (mán, tam. deer + úr, tam. village). Trig. station ; lat. 10° 07′ 13·70″ ; long. 79° 09′ 19·61″ ; height 70 feet ; from Amaunjy S. 1 mile ; from Puttoocottah S.W. 26 miles ; from the sea W. 8 miles.——*Mimisal* * (மீம்பெசல் - mímbesal, Tam.). From (mín, tam. fish + pisal, tam. storm). Tam. also (kóvirbattanam), meaning temple + town. Sanscrit name (rájakumárámbápura), meaning king + son + woman + town. Village, Port ; pop. 187 ; acres 284 ; lat. 9° 55′ ; long. 79° 11′ ; from Cottapatam S.W. 5 miles ; from Madras S.S.W. 229 miles ; from Puttoocottah S.S.W. 37 miles ; from Soondrapaundyaputnam N.N.E. 7 miles ; from Tanjore S. 59 miles. On Palk's bay, between Point calimere and Paumben. A few country vessels resort in N.E. monsoon [q.v.]. Choultry [q.v.] established by rajah for pilgrims to Rameshwaram. Fairs on Wednesdays. A Vishnoo [q.v.] temple [coil, pagoda].——*Nedoovausal* (நெடுவாசல் - neduvásal, Tam.). From (nedu, tam. long + vásal tam. entrance). Zemindarry, Village ; pop. 2,412 ; square miles 2 ; lat. of village 10° 22′ ; long. 79° 10′ ; from Puttoocottah W. 13 miles ; from Tanjore S. 30 miles ; from the sea W. 16 miles. Peshcush Rs. 2,087. Old Shiva temple in ruins with inscriptions. This is now a Government village. But the Zemindarry passes by that name. The village is divided into Mailpauthy and Keelpauthy.——*Paumbaur* (பாம்பாறு - pámbáru, Tam.). See sep. title.——*Pautharancottah* (பாதரங்கோட்டை - pátharangóttai, Tam.). From (páthu, tam. protection + aran, tam. beauty + kóttai, tam. fort). Zemindarry, Village ; pop. 868 ; lat. of village 10° 28′ ; long. 79° 16′ ; from Puttoocottah W. 7 miles ; from Tanjore S.S E. 24 miles ; from the sea N.W. 15 miles. Peshcush Rs. 1,369. Trig. station in lat. 10° 28′ 05·08″ ; long. 79° 15′ 11·60″ ; height 106 feet ; from Puttoocottah W.N.W. 8 miles ; from Vettoovacottah E.S.E. 1½ miles ; from the sea N.N.W. 16 miles.——*Pullattivayal* (பள்ளத்திவயல் - pallattivayal, Tam.). From (pallatti, tam. female of the palla caste + vayal, tam. field). Trig. station ; lat. 10° 09′ 13·99″ ; long. 79° 03′ 29·16″ ; height 133 feet ; from Puttoocottah S.W. 28 miles ; from the sea W. 14 miles.——*Puttoocottah* (பட்டுக்கோட்டை - pattukkóttai, Tam.). See below.——*Rajahmadam* (இராசாமடம் - irásámadam, Tam.). From (rájá, san. king + madam, tam. choultry). Sanscrit name (móhanámbápura), meaning mohanaumba, the fascinating wife of the tanjore king + town. Head-quarters of the Chuttram superintendent ; pop. 1,252 ; lat. 10° 18′ ; long. 79° 24′ ; from Puttoocottah S.S.E. 9 miles ; from Tanjore S.S.E. 36 miles ; from the sea W. 1½ miles. Travellers are fed gratuitously. Trig. station in lat. 10° 17′ 26·54″ ; long. 79° 24′ 6·03″ ; from Puttoocottah S.S.E. 10 miles. On the seashore.——*Rettavayal* (இரெட்டவயல் - irettavayal, Tam.). From (iraitai, tam. two + vayal, tam. field). Trig. station ; lat. 10° 12′ 46·10″ ; long. 79° 14′ 36·61″ ; height 34 feet ; from Permagalore vadapauthy N. 1½ miles ; from Puttoocottah S.S.W. 18 miles ; from the sea W. 5 miles.——*Saitbauva chuttram* (சேதுபாவாச்சத்திரம் - shéthubáváççattiram, Tam.). From (sétubáva, can. proper name + satra, san. choultry), from sait bauva sawmy who endowed the choultry. Village, Sanitarium ; pop. 500 ; lat. 10° 15′ ; long. 79° 19′ ; from Puttoocottah S.S.W. 13 miles ; from Tanjore S.S.E. 37 miles ; from the sea W. ½ mile. Bungalow [q.v.] built by a Tanjore rajah. A column here like that at Puttoocottah.——*Shalwanaickenputnam* (சாளுவநாயக்கன்பட்டணம் - shāluvanáyakkanbattanam, Tam.), means shaulwanaicken's town. Village, Sanitarium, Port ; pop. 486 ; lat. 10° 16′ ; long. 79° 21′ ; from Cautmauvady N. 10 miles ; from Gopaulputnam S.W. 5 miles ; from Madras S.S.W. 202 miles ; from Puttoocottah S. 11 miles ; from Tanjore S. 37 miles. On Palk's bay, west of Point calimere. Sarbhojee of Tanjore in 1814 erected a miniature fort with a column at this place to commemorate the downfall of Bonaparte, like that at Puttoocottah. The town is in ruins.——*Shillattore* (சிலத்தூர் - shilattúr, Tam.). From (shílam, tam. a creeper, tinospora cordifolia, miers + úr, tam. village). Sanscrit name (shíladharípura), meaning shiva, the virtue-holder + town. Zemindarry, Village ; pop. 1,364 ; square miles 7 ; lat. of village 10° 33′ ; long. 79° 15′ ; from Puttoocottah N.W. 11 miles ; from Tanjore S. 17 miles ; from the sea N.W. 20 miles. Peshcush Rs. 2,165. Old Shiva temple with inscriptions.——*Tumbikky nullavancottah* (தம்பிக்குநல்லவன்கோட்டை - tambikkunallavangóttai, Tam.). From (tambi, tam younger brother + nallavan, tam. friend + kóttai, tam. fort). Salt factory; pop. 5,756; lat. 10° 22′; long. 79° 28′; from Puttoocottah E.S.E. 9 miles; from Tanjore S.S.E. 35 miles; from the sea N. 1¾ miles.——*Velluur* (வெள்ளாறு - velláru, Tam.). See sep. title.——*Wokkoor* (ஒக்கூர் - okkúr, Tam.). From (okka, tam. plentiful + ór, tam. village). Trig. station; lat. 10° 01′ 20·63″; long. 79° 03′ 02·06″; height 78 feet; from Puttoocottah S.W. 35 miles; from Toonjanore N.W. 1½ miles; from the sea W. 17 miles.——**(2)** Town, Talook head-quarters; Tanjore dist., Puttoocottah tal.; pop. 5,028; acres 7,121; lat. 10° 26′; long. 79° 22′; height 88 feet; from Combaconam S. 36 miles; from Madras S.S.W. 191 miles; from Mayavaram S.S.W. 51 miles; from Munnargoody S.S.W. 19 miles; from Negapatam W.S.W. 42 miles; from Tanjore S.S.E. 27 miles; from the sea N. 11 miles. In 1815 the Mahratta rajah of Tanjore erected a miniature fort and column here in honor of the English victories over the French. In the western portion is an old and large Shiva temple elaborately sculptured and containing inscriptions of the Chola [q.v.] dynasty [raj]. Old fort in ruins with inscription dated A.D. 1684. In Maharaja samoodram, a suburb, is another Vishnoo temple. S.P.G. mission station. Trig. station in lat. 10° 26′ 17·09″; long. 79° 20′ 31·03″; height 88 feet; from the sea N.W. 10 miles.

PYALL (திண்ணை - tinnai, *Tam.*). From portuguese poyal. A bench, made of brick [shengal] and mortar [cauray], extending along the whole front of the house against the main wall. Almost every house in S. india possesses such a pyall. It is usually about 2½ feet high and three feet broad. A stranger must halt here until his business and caste [jauty] are known. In the hot weather the male members of the family sleep on the pyall. The pyall is often used as a school-room [pullicootam]; in these the schoolmaster is taught from father to son, and imparts the rudiments in turn to the village children.

PYE (పై - pai, *Tel.*). Up, high.——*Pyaupaly* (పైపల్లి - pyápali,* Tel.). From (pai, tel. high + palli, tel. village).—"*a*" Deputy tahsildarry, Kurnool district. Pay Rs. 70.—"*b*" Village, Head-quarters of Deputy collector and Deputy tahsildar; Kurnool dist., Putticondah tal.; pop. 3,719; acres 9,202; lat. 15° 14′; long. 77° 47′; from Cumbum W.S.W. 94 miles; from Kurnool S.S.W. 46 miles; from Madras N.W. 224 miles; from Nundiaul W.S.W. 52 miles; from Putticondah S.E. 19 miles. One of coolest places in district. One of the polliems [q.v.] resumed by Munro in 1800. An early poligar [q.v.] obtained the favor of the Vijianugger rajahs by reducing the chieftain of Chingleput who had rebelled. In later times another poligar [q.v.] assisted the Cuddapah nawaubs [q.v.] in capturing Gundicote. Traveller's bungalow [q.v.]. Weekly market on Saturday.——*Pyekeely* (పైకిలి - paikili, Tel.; கல்கொறுக்கை - kalgorukkai, Tam.). Tel. from (pai, tel. above + gíra, tel. line); from stripes. Tam. from (kal, tam. stone + korukkai, tam. pristipoma hasta). Pristipoma [caripey] furcatum, percidæ [panayairy], acanthopterygii, teleostei [matsyam,1], of naturalists [jantoo]. Alias Grammistes furcatus; Perca paikeeli; Pristipoma paikeeli; Paikeeli from teloogoo. Colors silvery with six horizontal brownish-black bands, darkest externally, three above lateral-line; spinous portion of dorsal fin with three rows of brown spots and dark edge; upper half of soft dorsal dark; dark band along the anal. Sea; Madras.

PYE (பை - pai, *Tam.*). Green, tender, fresh. Beauty.——*Pajanely* (अरलु - aralu, San.; टेंटू - témtú, Mahr.; चाम्मुयि - chámmuyi, Conc.; ಆನೆಮುಂಗು - ánemungu, Can. and Too.; పంపెన - pampena, Tel.; ପମ୍ପୋନିୟା - pomponiya, Oor.; പയ്യാഞ്ഞലി - payyáññali, Mal.; තොටිල - totila, Singh.; பாலையுடைச்சி - pálaiyudaiççi, Tam.). Title means soft anjely [wild jack]; from malayalam. San. means spreading. Can. from (áne, san. elephant + mungu, can. to sprout). Mal. from (pai, mal. soft + áññali, mal. artocarpus hirsuta, lamk.). Tam. from (pálai, tam. spathe + udai, tam. burst), opening out like spathe; from efflorescence; cf. spathodea. San. also (shónáka), meaning spreading; (mandúkaparna), meaning frog + leaf [indian pennywort, munjeet]; (patrórna), meaning hairy leaved; (shukanása), meaning parrot + beak, alluding to flower-bud; (dírghavrinta), meaning having long leaves; (bhallakapriya), meaning dear to bears; (prit'hushimbí), meaning having broad pod. Can. also (dundukara); (bági); (mokkada); (alangi). Tel. also (dundilamu). Oor. also (p'hunp'hunia). Mal. also (veluttapátiri), meaning white + the tree, stereospermum; (árantal); (palakappayyána), meaning plank + the tree. Tam. also (vangamaram), meaning trumpet tree; (púthabudbam), meaning demon + flower; (açqi); (pana). Title otherwise Indian calosanthes, Indian oroxylum, Indian trumpet flower. Botanically Oroxylum indicum, vent., bignoniaceæ [vricsham, 99]. Alias Bignonia indica; Calosanthes indica; Spathodea indica, pentandra. Tree; leaves opposite, pinnate, leaflets on the branches of the petioles two to three pair, petioletted, subcordate, ovate-acuminated; panicle terminal, erect; flowers fleshy, of a dark, lurid appearance, fœtid; pod 2 feet long, 3 inches broad, straight and flat; flowering in rainy season; smaller on w. coast. Bark and capsule used medicinally [dashamoolam]. Also astringent, used in tanning [chamrah]; fruit gives a dye [shauyam]. Timber soft and useless. The Tender wild jack, botanically Pájanelia rheedii, dec., bignoniaceæ [vricsham, 99], has the same vernaculars, and derives its generic name from the malayalam; arboreous; leaves unequally pinnate, leaflets unequal sided, acuminate; calyx campanulate, five-lobed, lobes emarginate at the points; corolla campanulate, sub-bilabiate, five-lobed, lobes dilated and crisp on the outer margin, furnished on the edges with a line of dense woolly tomentum externally, tube glabrous, limb pubescent; longer stamens connivent; capsule 12–15 inches long, winged, cuspidate; seed orbicular, compressed, winged; flowering in july and august.——*Patchonty* (कृकलास - krikalása, San.; بوقلمون - búkalamún, Hind.; ಊಸರವಲ್ಲಿ - úsaravalli, Can.; ఊసరవల్లి - tsáraballi Tel.; പച്ചോന്ത - paççóntu, Mal.; කටුස්සා - katussá, Singh.; பச்சோந்தி - paççóndi, Tam.). Title from malayalam. San. from (krika, san. throat + lás, san. to cause to shine). Hind. means changing color. Tel. from (tsára, tel. stripe + balli, tel. lizard). Mal. from tamul. Singh. from (katu, san. fierce); from its furious habit. Tam. from (paççai, tam. greenness + óndi, tam. a lizard). Tam. also (kómbi), the angry lizard; from its furious habit. The terms may be taken as co-extensive with the family Chamælionidæ, sauria [godhicay], reptilia [sarpy, 11], of naturalists [jantoo]; and to be distinguished from Bloodsucker [q.v.]. The Chameleons have a head large, angular, covered with numerous very small, flattish or convex shields; body compressed, covered with granular scales above and below; tail long and prehensile; tongue exceedingly long, worm-like, club-shaped and viscous in front, very extensile; eye globular, very mobile, covered with a circular lid which is pierced with a small central hole; tympanum hidden; legs thin, each with five toes, formed into two grasping opposable groups; live on trees; strong prehensile tail, on the ground and in water they are nearly helpless; although extremely slow in locomotion, they feed on insects [poochy]. Inflexibility of the neck, wonderful structure of the eyes, faculty of changing color much developed; oviparous, depositing, under leaves, from ten to twelve oval eggs with calcareous shells. The representative species of S. india is Chamæleo vulgaris, the common Chameleon, alias Chamæleo ceylanicus; Lacerta chamæleo. Most specimens are of a green color, uniform or irregularly spotted and banded with dark green or brown. The faculty of changing color possessed by the chameleons, although common to numerous other lizards, has became proverbial in this species, and is here so much developed that one side may assume a color different from that of the other. The inflexibility of the neck is compensated by the structure of the eyes, which are so prominent that more than one-half of the ball stands out of the head; and not only can they be moved in any direction, but each has an action independent of the other.——*Patchouli* (پچولی - pacholí, Hind.; ಪಚ್ಚೆತೆನೆಗಿಡ paççetenegida, Can.; కొట్టము - kottamu, Tel.; കൊട്ടം - kottam, Mal.; பச்சிலை - paççilai, Tam.). Title from tamul. Can. from (paççe, can. green + tene, can. panicum italicum, linn. + gida, can. plant); similar flower stalk. Mal. from (kósht'ha, san. costus speciosa, smith), from similarity. Tam. from (paççai, tam. green + ilai, tam. leaf). Tam. also (kottam). Title otherwise Acheen leaf, Atchy patchy, Indian marjoram, Patch leaf. Botanically Pogostemon patchouli, pellet, labiatæ [vricsham, 103]. Specific from tamul. Alias Origanum indicum; Pogostemon heyneanus. Suffruticose, 2–3 feet, pubescent; stems ascending; leaves petioled, rhombo-ovate, slightly obtuse, crenato-dentate; spikes terminal and axillary, densely crowded with flowers interrupted at the base; calyx hirsute; segments lanceolate; filaments bearded; flowers white, with red stamens and yellow anthers; flowering from june to november. The dried tops imported into england are a foot or more in length; they have a peculiar perfume and are used for many purposes; scent of patchouli at one time was considered the test of real indian shawls [q.v.], but now it cannot be depended on as home-spun shawls scented with it are sold as real indian; leaves an ingredient in tobacco [pogauk], used by arabs for stuffing pillows; by distillation yield an oil [attar] which is used as a toilet perfume and in india for imparting fragrance to clothes. Other species are:—atropurpureus, hirsutus, mollis, paludosus, paniculatus, parviflorus, plectranthoides, rotundatus, speciosus, vestitus, wightii.——*Pausy* (பாசி - pási, Tam.). See sep. title.——*Payar* (பயறு - payaru, Tam.). From (pasumai, tam. greenness); from color of the common kind. Pulse [dholl] generally and especially green gram [q.v.], phaseolus mungo. Plant second term. Ex., where transl. is of first term:—Dolichos lablab (tattaippayaru), flat; Indigofera pentaphylla (náyppayaru), dog; Phaseolus aconitifolius (tulukkappayaru), turk; Phaseolus adenanthus (káttuppayaru), forest; Phaseolus mungo, var. radiatus (narippayaru), fox; Phaseolus trilobus (elippayaru), rat, (kollaippayaru), field, (narippayaru), fox, (panippayaru), dew, (vayappayaru), field; Phaseolus trinervius (shadaippayaru), matted hair; Rothia trifoliata (narippayaru), fox; Vigna catiang (kantampayar), field, (kóttappayar), stick for creepers to climb, (kármanippayaru), vigna catiang, (karkatakappayaru), carcatacam, the month, (mampayaru), earth, (tattaippayaru), flat. See gloss. paragraphs. Distinguish from Payir, though same root.——*Payarammavaur* (పైరమ్మవారు - pairammavaru, Tel.). From (payarammai, tam. pox with pustules of the size of green gram + váru, tel. suffix of respect). Village goddess.——

Payir (ಪೈರು - pairu, Can.; పైరు - pairu, Tel.; பயிர் - payir, Tam.). From (pasumai, tam. greenness). Growing corn. Applies to cultivation in general [vellaumay]. Payir coody is a cultivator. Payir tozhil is husbandry. Payir vazhy are cultivated fields. Cathir payir is corn just earing. Moothoo payir is ripe grain. Nadavoo payir is corn transplanted. For Nunjah payir and Poonjah payir see Nunjah and Poonjah. Distinguish from Payar, though same root.——*Payyan* (பையன் - paiyan, Tam.). From (pai, tam. tender). Boy.——*Payyanore* (പയ്യന്നൂർ - payyannúr, Mal.). From (payyan, mal. child, epithet of skanda + úr, mal. village). Village, Amshom; Malabar dist., Chiracal tal.; pop. 6,488; lat. 12° 06′; long. 75° 15′; from Calicut N.N.W. 68 miles; from Cannanore N.N.W. 19 miles; from Cavvye E. 2 miles; from sea E. 4 miles. The northernmost amshom [q.v.] of talook [q.v.] contains the deshoms of Cavvye and Payyannore; the former on an island contains the bungalow [q.v.] of that name at frontier of district. Large mosque [musjid], and old redoubt built by the French. Ancient temple to Soobramanyan [q.v.]. Mantapam [q.v.] elaborately sculptured. Seat of Payyannore graumacaur bramins, whose descendants follow Maroomakkatoyem [q.v.] law of inheritance, unlike other Bramins of district. They were Malayaulies converted to Braminism. A poem, the Payyannore puttolay, is oldest specimen of Malayalam composition existing.——*Pesaloo* (పెసలు - pesalu, Tel.). From (pasumai, tam. greenness). Same as Green gram.——*Putchaippan* (பச்சையப்பன் - paççaiyappan, Tam.). From (paççai, tam. green + appan, tam. father). Vishnoo, the green lord. Hindoo 2nd or pers. name. Common among non-bramins [peyar].——*Putchamullay* (பச்சமலை - paççamalai, Tam. pachaimalai *). From (paççai, tam. green + malai, tam. hill). Hills; Salem and Trichinopoly dists., Ahtoor tal.; pop. 2,202; lat. 11° 19′ to 11° 29′; long. 78° 30′ to 78° 45′ E.; from Ahtoor S.E. 14 miles; from Salem S.E. 34 miles. Greatest length from north to south, about 20 miles. Average height, 2,000 feet. In shape the range resembles an hour-glass, being nearly cut in two by two large ravines opening to the north-east and south-west. Of the two parts thus formed, the north-western is the larger and has generally a higher level than the south-eastern. The western slopes are very steep compared with those on the east, which are rarely precipitous, and are broken by sundry long buttress-like spurs projecting far into the low country. The hills are unhealthy. The forests are poor, having been injured by wasteful nomad cultivation [ponacaud]. The western slopes are covered chiefly with oosilay [biswool]. Towards the summits the jungle is dense and intermixed with bamboo [q.v.] and thorny bushes. On the summits are large forests of vengay [q.v.], teak [q.v.], black-wood [q.v.], and sandal-wood [sandal]. The eastern slopes are covered with dense bamboo jungle, vengay and small teak trees. Principal products are gall-nuts [mauchicoy]. vembaudamputtay bark [pappily], hill-gooseberries, and honey [shahad]. There are three villages Combay, Tembaranaud, and Vunnaud. To be distinguished from the Green hills of the shevaroys.——*Putchay* (പച്ച - paçça, Mal.; பச்சை - paççai, Tam.). From (pasu, tam. green). Green.—"*a*" Epithet of Vishnoo [q.v.] the green god. Proper name; applied to males and females among the lower orders [peyar].—"*b*" Plant first term. Ex., where transl. is of second term:—Allium tuberosum (paççaúrulli), allium cepa; Cucumis trigonus (paççekáyigida), meaning fruit + plant; Dalbergia paniculata (paççelaimaram), leaf + tree; (paççárimara), meaning bauhinia racemosa, linn.; Ocimum basilicum (paççapushpam), flower; Parkinsonia aculeata (paççaivél), acacia; Phaseolus mungo (paççaippayaru), pulse; Phaseolus mungo, var. radiatus (paççaippayaru), pulse; Pogostemon patchouli (paççilai), leaf; Thevetia nereifolia (paççaiyalari), and (paççayarali), nerium odorum. See gloss. paragraphs.—"*c*" Plant second term. Ex., where transl. is of first term:—Argyreia speciosa (samudrappaçça), ocean; Artemisia vulgaris (tiruníttippaçça), holy + ashes; Garcinia xanthochymus (samudrappaçça), ocean, (malaippaççai), hill; Guazuma tomentosa (ténbaççai), honey; Heliotropium indicum (vénappaçça), summer; Hoya pendula (naññarappaçça), poison + cutting. See gloss. paragraphs.——*Pytore mullay* (பைத்தூர்மலை - paittúrmalai, Tam.). From (paittu, tam. green + úr, tam. village + malai, tam. mountain). Range of hills; Salem dist., Ahtoor tal.; pop. 1,522; lat. 12° 32′; long. 78° 34′; from Ahtoor S. 6 miles; from Salem S.E. 26 miles. Running across Ahtoor talook and dividing the Vasishtanuddy and Shwetanuddy watersheds [nadee].

Q (ق - káf, *Hind.*). Symbol for 100.

QUAIL EYE (காடைக்கண்ணி - kádaikkanni, *Tam.*). Title from color. Same as Varagoo. Cf. Quail-necked paddy.

QUAMOCLIT (कामलता - kámalatá, *San.*; كو مقليط - komklit, *Hind.*). Title from sanscrit, through greek. San. from (káma, san. lovo + latá, san. creeper), beautiful creeper. Same as Indian pink.

QUIHYE (كوئى هے - koíhaí, *Hind.*). From (koí, hind. any + haí, hind. is). Is anyone there? Word used in Bengal for calling a servant [nowcar].

QUILON (കൊല്ലം - kollam, *Mal.*). From (kóvilakam, mal. palace) [co]. Greek ἐλάγκων ἐμπόριον [collam].—"*a*" Revenue division; Travancore state; population about 900,000. Divided into eleven talooks. Was formerly ruled by rajahs of Cottaura cara, Cauyancollam and Pundalam. These were subdued by the Bramin warrior, Ramayyan dalavoy [q.v.], and annexed to Travancore.—"*b*" Talook, Travancore state, Quilon division. Hundred and sixty caras [q.v.] or parishes. Population 108,469. Extreme length, N. to S., 20 miles; extreme breadth, E. to W., 10 miles. Sub-divided into seven praverties [q.v.]. Bounded N. by Caroonaugapully and Coonnatore talooks, E. by Cottaura cara talook, S. by Cheraukeel talook and W. by the Indian ocean. Traversed by lakes, ground undulating. Soil productive. Fishing industry on coast and much trade in coppray [q.v.], timber [maram], &c. Watered by the Culluda river.—"*c*" Town, Port, Divisional and Zillah judges head-quarters, Tahsildar's station, Cantonment, Travancore dist., Quilon division, Quilon tal.; pop. 23,380; lat. 8° 54′; long. 76° 38′; from Alleppey S.S.E. 44 miles; from Cottayam S. 47 miles; from Madras S.W. 380 miles; from Nagarcoil N.W. 76 miles; from Paravore S.S.E. 88 miles; from Bombay S.S.E. 730 miles; from Poovaur N.W. 52 miles; from Shertala S.S.E. 56 miles; from Trivandrum N.W. 37 miles; from Tungacherry E. 1½ miles. Port next in importance to Alleppey. There is shelter for shipping from winds under Tungacherry point and reef about 3 miles from the fort, and navigable communication through the canals and lagoons [cauyal] and the shore, both to north and south. Ships, puttimars [q.v.] and steamers call. With Trivandrum communication is carried on almost entirely by canals. There is also a military road, northwards, towards Alleppey and Cochin. A road leads over the Aryancauv pass [ghaut] to Tinnevelly. It was formerly the head-quarters of the state; is still military head-quarters. During the early centuries of the Christian era Quilon was the great port of trade in Malabar with China and Arabia. It is the Coilum of Marco Polo, and Columbum of ecclesiastical writers of that age; one of whom, Friar Jordanus, was consecrated Bishop of Columbum, circ. 1330. The best kind of ginger [q.v.] was known till the middle ages as Columbine ginger. Throughout the middle ages it was one of the chief seats of the Saint Thomas christians; and it formed with Cauyal one of the seven churches [cranganore] ascribed by Indo-Syrian tradition to Saint Thomas himself. In 1503 the Portuguese established a factory [aurang] and fort, captured by the Dutch 150 years later. The town was at different times subject to Cochin and Travancore. In 1741 Travancore unsuccessfully besieged it, but in 1745 the Quilon rajah submitted. From 1803 to 1830 a British garrison was stationed here. Till 1829 principal town of the province where the Diwaun [q.v.] and the British resident held their head-quarters. There are two palaces [covilagam], a Residency, and other public buildings. The subsidiary force is now reduced to one native regiment, whose cantonments lie to the east of the town. Has still considerable inland and foreign trade. Of late a cotton-spinning mill has been set up. Chief entrepôt of pepper and ginger on the Malabar coast. Vegetable productions are timber [maram], cocoanuts [q.v.], coir [q.v.] or cocoanut fibre, pepper [q.v.], cardamoms [q.v.], ginger [q.v.], betel-nuts [q.v.] and coffee [q.v.]. For the Collam era see Collam and Saca. For Cully quilon see Cauyancollam. The following are the travelling distances by road from Quilon to different places:—

To	Via	Miles and Furlongs.	
Alleppey	Cauyancollam	55	2
Aramboly ...	Trivandrum	92	0
Aryancauv ...	Cottaura cara	50	0
Bangalore ...	Goodalore ghaut, Dindigul, Namcull and Salem.	434	2
Bangalore ...	Cochin, Palghaut, Coimbatore, Hassanore and Seringapatam.	419	5
Bellary	Goodalore ghaut, Dindigul, Salem and Bangalore.	621	5
Bellary	Cochin, Palghaut, Coimbatore, Hassanore ghaut, Seringapatam and Hiriyore.	572	4
Calicut	Cochin and Chowghaut	185	7
Cannanore ...	Cochin and Calicut	245	0
Cochin	Alleppey	88	1
Coimbatore ...	Cochin and Palghaut	205	0
Dindigul	Goodalore ghaut	214	6
Dindigul	Aryancauv pass, Shreevillipoottore and Madura.	193	6½
French rocks ...	Cochin, Palghaut, Coimbatore and Hassanore.	342	0
Goodalore ...	Pundalam and Peermaid	130	3
Madras	Cochin, Palghaut, Coimbatore and Ranipett.	517	2
Madras	Palamcottah, Madura, Trichinopoly and Chingleput.	508	5
Madras	Goodalore ghaut, Dindigul, Trichinopoly and Chingleput.	476	0½
Madras	Aryancauv ghaut, Madura, Trichinopoly and Chingleput.	435	0
Madura	Aryancauv ghaut and Shreevillipoottore.	153	5
Madura	Peermaid, Goodalore ghaut and Allinagaram.	216	4½
Madura	Trivandrum and Palamcottah	227	2
Mercara	Cochin, Calicut and Cannanore	316	3
Nagarcoil ...	Trivandrum	83	7
Palamcottah ...	Trivandrum and Nagarcoil	131	4
Palamcottah ...	Aryancauv, Tencaushy and Aulangoolam.	98	2
Palamcottah ...	Aryancauv, Tencaushy and Cadayam ...	102	1
Palghaut	Cochin and Trichore	174	1

To	Viâ	Miles and Furlongs.	
Panagoody ...	Trivandrum and Ramboly	90	5
Panagoody ...	Aryancauv and Tencaushy	117	6
Peermaid ...	Cotacara and Tungacherry	108	3½
Salem	Goodalore ghaut and Dindigul	316	2
Salem	Aryancauv ghaut, Shreevillipoottore and Madura.	292	2½
Shreevillipoottore	Aryancauv and Shivagherry	107	2
Tencaushy ...	Aryancauv ghaut	63	6
Trichinopoly ...	Aryancauv ghaut, Shreevillipoottore and Madura.	234	5
Trichinopoly ...	Goodalore ghaut and Dindigul	275	5½
Trivandrum ...	Attingal	41	7
Trivandrum ...	Cotacara and Vellaumai!	62	3
Tuticorin	Aryancauv ghaut and Palamcottah ...	133	1
Vellore	Madura, Trichinopoly, Villoopooram and Arnee.	412	3

——*Quilandy* (കൊയിലാണ്ടി - koyilánti, Mal. quilandi*). From (kóyil, mal. palace + kanti, mal. a gap) [co].—"*a*" Deputy tahsildarry, Malabar district. Pay Rs. 70.—"*b*" Town, Port, Deputy tahsildar's station, District moonsif's station, Sub-registrar's station, Customs house; Malabar dist., Cooroombranaud tal.; lat. 11° 26'; long. 75° 44'; from Badagara S.S.E. 13 miles; from Bombay S S.E. 540 miles; from Calicut N.N.W. 14 miles; from Cannanore S.S.E. 36 miles; from Caupautt N.W. 5 miles; from Collam S.E. 1½ miles; from Madras W.S.W. 329 miles; from Malapooram N.W. 36 miles; from Manantoddy S.W. 32 miles; from Palghaut W.N.W. 79 miles; from Ponnany N.N.W. 47 miles; from Tellicherry S.S.E. 25 miles. Moplah [q.v.] seaport between Calicut and Mahé, with considerable trade. Gives name to a backwater [canyal]. The roadstead, which is protected by a mud bank [mud bay], is more secure than most anchorages on the coast; and it was here in 1498 that Vasco da Gama's fleet rode out the south-west monsoon [q.v.]. One of the E.I. company's ships was lost here in 1793. Towards close of the last century the port was suddenly destroyed by a cyclone. Close to seaport on north is one of the nine original Mahomedan mosques [musjid] established on the Malabar coast by Malik ibn e deenaur. It was built in imitation of one at Mecca, and is saluted from the sea by all Mahomedan craft. Government in 1846 made over to the Quilandy mosque as Sarwa maunyam [q.v.] certain escheated farms producing a net revenue of Rs. 1,800 per annum. These lands lie in the amshoms [q.v.] of Cauracoonn, Munjery and Tricalangode in Yernaud talook.

QUINDAH (کوندہ - kuindah, *Hind.*). Same as Wild mohwah.

QUIRPELE (கிரிப்பிள்ளை - kírippillai, *Tam.*). Old Anglo-Indian for the Mongoose, which see.

R (र - ra, रा - rá, *San.*; ر - re, *Hind.*; ர - ra, ரா - rá, *Tam.*). Hind. for the numeral 200; in almanacs [punchaungam] stands for moon [chundran] and the third mahomedan month [maheena]. Tamul contraction for Rajah [q.v.] or Rupee [q.v.]. Sanscrit means Agny [q.v.], fire; hence deemed an unpropitious letter. No Tamul poem of good import should begin with the letter. The letter ற and its corresponding nasal ன are additional letters peculiar to Tamul. Nunnool [q.v.] says:—"ற and "ன will come forth if the tip of the tongue is brought into close "contact with the roof of the mouth." ற is really a cerebro-dental 't' [moordhanyam]. Thus:—பொன் தீது becomes பொன்றீது; or still further பொன் தீமை becomes பொற்றீமை. The letters த, ட, and ற, with their corresponding nasals, are the usual sign-letters of the past tense of verbs. In the numeral words from one up to ten there is for termination in almost every instance, some modification of the syllable 'tu;' as பத்து, ஐந்து, ஒன்பது, எட்டு, இரண்டு, மூன்று, ஆறு. Uneducated persons pronounce போதும் as போரும் and விதை as விரை. See vol. II, 186, 206.

RA (ரா - rá, *Tam.*). Colloquial corruption of (adá, tam. from édá, tam. voc. of yédan, tam. companion). Appellative termination added to verb roots, expressing familiarity, contempt, anger, reproof, surprise. Of universal usage among lower classes. One of the numerous grammatical forms found neither in the native grammars [lacshanam] of the classical style, nor in the missionary grammars of the assumed modern style. Examples are:—(párrá), look; (padirá), read; (sholrá), speak.

RABAUB (رباب - rabáb, *Hind.*). From arabic. A rebeck, kind of violin [sangeetam].

RABEE (ربیع - rabí, *Hind.*). From arabic. Spring. Also spring crop. First rabee is the third mahomedan month, and second rabee is the fourth [fusly, maheena].

RACSH (रक्ष् - raksh, *San.*). To injure.——*Racshas* (रक्षस् - rakshas, San.). A malignant being or evil divinity [bhootam, pey, raucshasan].——*Raucshasagoondloo* (రాక్షసగుండ్లు - rákshasagundlu, Tel.). From (rákshasa, san. giant + gundu, tel. rock). General term for natural megalithic objects, especially what would be called in English tors and loggan stones [aursham, paundoocull].——*Raucshasam* (राक्षस - rákshasa, San.). From (raksh, san. to hurt). A giant marriage [calyaunam], that is to say carrying off the woman by violence. See vol. I (62). Also one of the three ganams [q.v.] or classes into which asterisms in the moon's [chundran] path are divided for astrological purposes; they are maunoosham [q.v.] or human, raucshasam or infernal, and devam [q.v.] or divine; indicating the character of influence on persons born under them. See detail in the table of hindoo lunar mansions under Nacshatram.——*Raucshasan* (राक्षस - rákshasa, San.). From (raksh, san. to injure). A giant, an evil spirit hostile to man [racshas]. Compare the hebrew Khelabim. In their earliest conception, the Raucshasans were unknown creatures of darkness, to which were attributed the evils that attend life. In the Aryan [q.v.] epic period they were personifications of the aborigines of India. In this character they play a prominent part in the Ramayanam [q.v.]. In the Pooraunic [pooraunam] period they are infernal giants, the children of the rishy [q.v.] Poolastyan [q.v.], and enemies of the gods [deva]. They are then divided into three classes:—the slaves of coobairan [q.v.] the god of wealth, and guardians of his treasures [navanidhy, nidhy]; malevolent imps [bhootam, pey] whose chief delight is to disturb the pious in their devotions; giants of enormous proportions, inhabiting naracam [q.v.] or hell, and hostile to the gods. Ravanan [q.v.], the demon king of Lunka [q.v.], is the most celebrated Raucshasan in S. india, and belongs to the class last named. See vol. I (78). Distinguish from the Asoorans [q.v.] and Deityans [q.v.], who are enemies of the gods only.

RAEES (رئیس - raís, *Ar.*). From (rása, ar. to rule). Chief. Part of lacab; as Raees ool islam, the head of islam [ism].

RAFEE (رفیع - rafí, *Ar.*). From (rafa, ar. to raise). Exalted. Part of lacab; as Rafee ood deen, exalted of the faith [ism].

RAFT (رفت - raft, *Hind.*). From (raftan, pers. to go) [rah]. Export.——*Rafzee* (رافضی - ráfzí, Hind.). From (rafazu, ar. to abandon). Heretic. Also called Zaidiyahs from holding that imaumat descended to Zaid upon the death of fourth imaum and not to Imaum baukir as held by all others. They hold that the people have the right of choosing their imaum [q.v.] but restricting the choice to the family of Mahomed [q.v.]; and that among the other qualities required for the pontifical office, the imaum should possess the capacity to assert his right by force of arms [ismailiyah]. Used in S. india for shiahs [q.v.] in general.——*Rawauna* (روانہ - rawánah, Hind.). From (raftan, pers. to go). A permit [raudaury].

RAGGY (रागी - rágí, *San.*; नाचणी - náchaní, *Mahr.*; नांचनो - nánchanó, *Conc.*; راگی - rágí, *Hind.* and *Dec.*; ರಾಗಿ - rági, *Can.* and *Too.*; రాగి - rági, *Tel.*; ମଣ୍ଡିଆ - mandiya, *Oor.*; മുത്താറി - muttári, *Mal.*; කුරක්කන් - kurakkan, *Singh.*; கேழ்வரகு - kézhvaragu, *Tam.*). Title from hindostany [ranj]. San. from (rága, san. red); from color. Mahr. from (náchana, mahr. gay woman, from nácha, mahr. nautch), from shining grain. Conc. from mahratta. Hind., &c., from sanscrit. Mal. from (muttu, mal. pearl + ari, mal. rice) [bajrah]. Tam. from (kézh, tam. color + varagu, tam. panicum miliaceum, linn.). San. also (krishná), meaning black [black pepper, long pepper]; (chikkana), meaning smooth and glossy, from seeds; (rájiká), meaning shining; (lala), meaning desirous; (guchhakanisha), thick-spiked grass; (kshutábhijanana), hunger creator, and (rájiká), which are applicable to black mustard, brassica nigra, koch. [cauly rayaun]. Hind. also (marua); (manraví). Dec. also (nágla). Can. also (kurukkan), from singhalese; (sodehullu), meaning raggy grass. Tel. also (tsódi); (udatatótagaddi), meaning squirrel + garden + grass; (tumide); (tavide). Mal. also (kóra) [coray]; (chettippullu), meaning chetty + grass. Tam. also (kévuru), by corruption; (kávaragu), meaning gruel + plant, panicum miliaceum, linn.; (áriyam), meaning bright grain; (muttári), meaning pearl + rice; (képpai), meaning bright grain. Title; otherwise Chetty grass, Corakkan, Dog-tail grass, Great millet, Marua millet, Natcheny, Pearl rice, Pudding paspalum, Red paspalum, Tocussa. Botanically Eleusine coracana, gærtn., graminaceæ [vricsham, 156]. Specific name from singhalese. Alias Cynosurus coracanus, tristachyos. Cereal; culms erect, 2–4 feet, a little compressed, smooth; leaves bifarious, large, smooth; mouths of sheaths bearded; calyx three to six-flowered, glumes keeled, obtuse, with membranaceous margins; spikes four to six digitate, incurved, secund, 1–3 inches long, composed of two rows of sessile three to four-flowered spikelets; rachis slightly waved; valves of corolla nearly equal; seeds globular, size of mustard [rayaun] seed, brown, a little wrinkled, covered with a thin aril. The most prolific of cultivated grasses; the staple grain of the mysore country, where it is stored in pits keeping sound for many years; is grown under both wet [coodapa, maugauny] and dry cultivation [gaddavary, veligada]; in black or red loam [pasalay munn], sandy [manal] soils not being favorable; ground prepared in south in chittray [mausam] or april, on coromandel in caurteecam or november and margashiram or december, on w. coast in vrishchicam or november; ground is ploughed four or five times and manured [yeroo]; seed sown in south in auny or june, on coromandel in margashiram or december and pooshyam or january, on w. coast in yedavam or may; generally first sown in nursery [nauttangaul]; when 6 inches in height transplanted; while under growth weeds are removed thrice or four times; watered once in ten days; full-grown crop attains 2½ feet; leaves then become yellow, seeds become black; cut in four months by sickles at 6 inches from ground and tied in sheaves; on fifth day taken out and exposed to the sun and beaten with sticks; straw separated; residue winnowed; produce brought to market a month after cutting; average price 20 imperial seers for 1 rupee; cotton [q.v.] is very often drilled with this crop, it then outtops the raggy and grows up vigorously after the latter crop is harvested. Raggy is a wholesome and nutritious grain, with which ordinary poor people make choopatties [q.v.], puddings, &c.; excellent for doing out-door work upon; straw is good fodder [ghaus] for cattle [maud]; a kind of paste made of the grain is used in preparing and tanning leather [chamrah]. Cf. Bojah. The only other species here is Indica [wild raggy].——*Dry raggy* (వెలగాడి - velirági, Tel.). From (veli, contraction for veligada, tel. dry cultivation). Any raggy raised on dry land [meit, metta], not wells.——*Small raggy* (ಅಂಟುಗರಿಕೆಹುಲ್ಲು - antugarikéhullu, Can.; சின்னரியம் - shinnáriyam, Tam.). Can. from (antu, can. gum + garikéhullu, can. cynodon dactylon, pers.). Tam. from (shinna, tam. small + áriyam, tam. raggy, eleusine coracana, gærtn.). Botanically Panicum [priyangoo] erucæforme, sibth., graminaceæ [vricsham, 156].——*Wild raggy* (కారుత్సోడి - kárutsódi, Tel.; වල්කුරක්කන් - valkurakkan, Singh.; குஞ்சப்புல் - kunjappul, Tam.). Tel. from (káru, tel. forest + tsódi, tel. eleusine coracana, gærtn.). Singh. from (val, singh. jungle + kurakkan, singh. eleusine coracana, gærtn.). Tam. from (kuñjam, tam. cluster + pul, tam. grass); from dense inflorescence. Singh. also (belatana), meaning dog grass; from being eaten by dogs [nye] to induce vomiting. Tam. also (kévuru), corruption from (kézhvaragu), meaning color + varagoo. Title otherwise Cluster grass, Crab grass. Dog grass, Winding grass, Wire grass [hoonrauj]. Botanically Eleusine indica, gærtn., graminaceæ [vricsham, 156]. Root fibrous, cæspitiferous; culm compressed, leafy, ½–2 feet; sheaths hairy at the mouth; leaves flat, linear, somewhat obtuse, here and there scattered with hairs, or altogether glabrous; ligula short, hairy; spikes straight, linear, somewhat in whorls of four, one usually remote from the rest, rachis narrow; spikelets about six-flowered, valves oblong, entire at the apex. Grain not usually eaten.

RAGHOO (रघु - raghu, *San.*). From (rangh, san. to go) [rath]; fleet. Ancestor of Rama [q.v.]. Hindoo 2nd or pers. name [peyar].——*Raghavan* (రాఘవుడు - rághavudu, Tel.). From (raghu, san. the myth. king). Rama of raghoo family [raghooraman]. Hindoo 2nd or pers. name [peyar].——*Raghavendran* (ರಾಘವೇಂದ್ರ - rághavéndra, Can.). From (rághava, san. rama + indra, san. the chief of gods); the best of the raghoo race [raghottaman]; epithet specially of rama. Hindoo 2nd or pers. name [peyar].——*Raghojee bhonslay* (रघुजीभोंसला - raghujíbhónsalá, Mahr.). From (above + jí, hind. title). Mahratta [q.v.] chief who invaded Carnatic [q.v.] in 1740, attacked Dost ally near Daumalcheroo pass [ghaut], and defeated and killed him, taking his diwaun [q.v.] Meer asad prisoner. Bought off by Sufder ally the son and heir of the late Nawaub [q.v.] with whom he entered into a secret compact against Chundab sahib [q.v.]; the latter was then besieged at Trichinopoly and carried off prisoner to Sattaura [charitram]. See vol. I (176).——*Raghoodevapooram* (రఘుదేవపురము - raghudévapuramu, Tel.). From (raghudéva, san. proper name + pura, san. town). Sanscrit name (rahitapura), meaning solitary + town.—"*a*" Deputy tahsildarry, Godavery district. Pay Rs. 100. Otherwise called Cottapully.—"*b*" Village; Godavery dist., Rajahmundry tal.; pop. 2,717; acres 4,197; lat. 17° 10′; long. 81° 45′; from Cocanada W.N.W. 38 miles; from Rajahmundry N.N.W. 12½ miles. Former head-quarters of Deputy tahsildar. Old ruined fort.——*Raghoonautan* (இரகுநாதன் - iragunáthan, Tam.). From (above + nát'ha, san. lord). Rama, lord of the raghoo race [raghoopaty]. Hindoo 2nd or pers. name [peyar].——*Raghoonauttevar* (இரகுநாதத்தேவர் - iragunáthattévar, Tam.). Name + title. See Kizhavan saitoopaty.——*Raghoopaty* (இரகுப்பதி - iraguppathi, Tam.). From (above + pati, san. lord). Rama, lord of the raghoo race [raghoonautan]. Hindoo 2nd or pers. name [peyar].——*Raghooraman* (இரகுராமன் - iragurámau, Tam.). From (above + ráma, san. rama); rama of the raghoo family as distinguished from parshooraman [q.v.] of the bhaurgavam family [raghavan]. Hindoo 2nd or pers. name [peyar].——*Raghooveeran* (இரகுவீரன் - iraguvíran, Tam.). From (above + víra, san. hero). Rama, hero of the raghoo family. Hindoo 2nd or pers. name [peyar].——*Raghottaman* (இரகோத்தமன் - iragóttaman, Tam.). From (above + uttama, san. the best). Rama, best of raghoos [raghavendran]. Hindoo 2nd or pers. name [peyar].

RAH (راه - ráh, *Hind.*). Way [raft].——*Rahbardaur* (راهبردار - ráhbardár, Hind.). From (above + bardár, pers. carrier). Guide.——*Raudaury* (راهداری - ráhdárí, Hind.). From (above + dárí, pers. keeping). A pass [rawauna]. Raudaury boat is a boat for passengers.——*Rustah* (راسته - rástah, Hind.). From persian. Road [pauthay].

RAHASYAM (रहस्य - rahasya, *San.*). From (rah, san. to abandon), lonely, solitary, hidden. Literally mystery. Oopanishad [q.v.] or mystical doctrine which forms the third division of the vedam [q.v.], the other two being samhitay [q.v.] and brambanam [q.v.].

RAHM (رحم - rahm, *Hind.*). Pity.——*Raheem* (رحیم - rahím, Hind.). From (rahima, ar. to pity). Merciful. Attribute of God [allah]. Common alam; as Raheem khan, alam + pataun alaumat. Also part of lacab; as Raheem ood deen, merciful in religion [ism].——*Rahman* (رحمان - rahmán, Hind.). From (rahima, ar. to pity). The benevolent. Attribute of God [allah]. Common alam, as Rahman khan, alam + pataun alaumat [ism].——*Rahman ghur* (رحمان گڑھ - rahmángarh, Hind.; ರಹಿಮಾನ್‌ಘಡ - rahimánghadi, Can.). Means rahman, proper name + fort. Hill, Colaur district, Mysore, to the south of Ambanjidroog, 4,227 feet above the level of the sea. To be distinguished from Ramandroog in Bellary district.——*Rahmat* (رحمت - rahmat, Ar.). From (rahima, ar. to pity). Divine mercy, grace. Prefixed to an alam forms a lacab; as Rahmat ool lah, grace of god [ism].——*Raoof* (رؤف - raúf, Hind.). From (ráfa, ar. to pity). Very merciful. Epithet of God [allah]. Common alam, as:—Raoof ahmed, double alam [ism].

RAHOO (राहु - ráhu, *San.*). From (rabh, san. to seize). The moon's ascending node [pautam], or point when in her northward course she cuts the ecliptic [craunty mundalam]; ☊ In Hindoo astronomy [jyotisham] one of the two obscure planets [graham] which occasion eclipses [grahanam], these being in fact the personifications of the umbra. According to mythology, Rahoo is the head of a monster, of which Kait [q.v.] is the trunk. Cf. the Typhæus of Hesiod. A deityan [q.v.], disguising himself, obtained some of the amritam [q.v.] when the gods churned the ocean [coormam]; but the sun [sooryan] and moon [chundran] detected him, and told Vishnoo [q.v.], who cut him in two, his head and arms forming Rahoo and the rest of him Kait; in revenge he sometimes seizes the sun [sooryan] or moon [chundran] and so causes eclipses. Varauha mihiran [q.v.] however in the sixth century A.D. states as follows:—"Now, if "he has a body or be simply a head with a regular motion in the "ecliptic [craunty mundalam], how comes it that he eclipses "[grahanam] the sun and moon when they are 180° from him? "The truth is that in his own eclipse, the moon [chundran] "enters the shadow of the earth, and in that of the sun [sooryan], "the solar disc; hence the lunar eclipse does not commence at "the western limb nor the solar at the eastern limb; when the "moon, whose course is always from west to east, is due opposite "to the sun swerving neither much to the north nor to the south, "he enters the shadow of the earth; the moon, moving from "the west, hides the solar disc from below just like a cloud; "and the solar eclipse varies differently in different countries "according to the different degrees of visibility of the eclipsed "disc; what eclipses the moon is bigger than the moon; what "eclipses the sun is smaller than the sun; hence in semi-lunar "and semi-solar eclipses the luminous horns are respectively "blunt and sharp." The current ideas on this subject evidently date from far behind that period. Rahoo is variously represented on a lion [simham], a flying dragon, an owl [ooloocam], and a tortoise [aumay], with a spear in his hand. He is worshipped in misfortune and to avert the approach of evil spirits, malignant diseases, earthquakes [mahy campam], comets [dhoomkait, nacshatram], &c., and especially during an eclipse [grahanam]. The astrological works rule thus:—if a person be born when Rahoo is rising above the horizon [cshitijam], his wisdom, riches, and children will be destroyed, he will be exposed to many afflictions, and he will be subject to his enomies.——*Rahoo caulam* (राहुकाल - ráhukála, San.). The time when the planet Rahoo is above the horizon [cshitijam]. This time varies according as the planet is moving in this or that direction during each particular day of the week; and such a time is unfortunate for any enterprise [goolica caulam, jyotisham, vauram]. Found in all calendars [punchaungam]. Cf. Rijaul ool gheib.——*Rahoo seed* (ರಾಹುಬೀಜ - ráhubíja, Can.). Means paralysis + seed, from shrunken appearance. Same as Roodrauck.

RAHTY (رهتی - rahtí, *Hind.*). From (rahta, hind. wheel). Water wheel [chuckram].——*Rautnam* (چرخه - charkhah, Hind.; రాట్నము - rátnamu, Tel.; റാട്ട - ráttu, Mal.; இராட்டினம் - iráttinam, Tam.). From (rahta, hind. a spinning wheel). A machine to remove seed from cotton [q.v.] consisting of two rollers revolving in grooves against each other. Cotton is inserted between the rollers; the seeds fall on one side and cotton comes out on the other [punj]. Compare the Doodey coolar who clean cotton with a large bow suspended to the roof and having a gut string. Also a spinning wheel [nool].

RAIKHAY (रेखा - rékhá, *San.*). From (likh, san. to scratch). Means a line. Meridian. Also the first or prime hindoo meridian, considered to be a line drawn from Lunka [q.v.] to Meroo [q.v.], that is to say from ceylon supposed to lie on the equator [niracsham] to the north pole [oottaradhroovam, soomeroo]. Raikhauntaram is terrestrial longitude [deshauntaram, jyotisham]. For the two kinds of hindoo celestial longitude see Sauyanam and Dhroovacam. For the Rishy raikhay or line of the rishies in hindoo shastrams, that is to say for the great circle drawn from the pole of the ecliptic to the equinoctial colure, see Rishy, Maunam, and Mausam.

RAIN TREE (زمنگ - zamang, *Jav.*). From the dew falling from its extensive foliage. Same as Zamang.

RAIV (ريو - reu, *Hind.*; రేవు - révu, *Tel.*; இரேவு - irévu, *Tam.*). Ford [toray]. Also applied to the Custom house.——*Raila* (రేల - réla, Tel.). From (révu, tel. ford). Locative plural. Suffix in place names; as Saukiraila, meaning washermens' ford.

RAIWAND (ريوند - revand, *Pers.*). Rhubarb.

RAJ (राज् - ráj, *San.*). To shine, rule.——*Rai* (رائی - rái, Hind.). A hindee title equivalent to rajah [q.v.] or roya [q.v.] of the south, and in bengal usually corrupted into Roy [rao, row, roya]. Does not belong to this presidency.——*Raj* (राज्य - rájya, San.; راج - ráj, Hind.). From (ráj, san. to rule). A kingdom [rashtram].—"*a*" The following is an alphabetical list of the ancient native dynasties of southern india. Each can be seen under its own heading:—Audhras of calingam; Cadambas of banavausy; Calachooryas of calyaun; Caucateeyas of hanoomacondah or warangal; Chalookyas of coontalam; Chalookyas of rajahmundry and vengy; Cheras of dravida desham; Chola-chalookyas; Cholas of dravida desham; Congoo or gunga cheran; Pullavas of badaumy, vengy and canjy; Paundya-cholas; Paundyas of dravida desham; Rattas of maunyakhetam; Vaimareddies of condaveed; Yaudava hoysala ballaulas of dwaura samoodram or halabeed; Yaudavas of devagiry or dowlatabad; Yaudavas of vijianugger or anagoondy.—"*b*" The following is an alphabetical list of the Mahomedan dynasties of Southern india. Each can be seen under its own heading:—Adil shahies of beejapore, 1489–1672; Ahmed shahies of Berar, 1489–1574; Bahmanies of goolburga, 1347–1525; Bareed shahies of beedar, 1492–1609; Cootb shahies of golcondah, 1512–1671; Nizam shahies of ahmednugger, 1490–1607 [charitram]. Compare also the Carnatic nawaub family, 1692–1801.—"*c*" The following is the idea of a kingdom in Cooral:—தள்ளா விளையுளுந் தக்காருந் தாழ்விலாச் செல்வருஞ் சேர்வது நாடு—"a kingdom is that in which "those who carry on a complete cultivation, virtuous persons, "and merchants with inexhaustible wealth, dwell together."—பெரும்பொருளாற் பெட்டக்க தாகி யருங்கேட்டா லாற்ற விளைவது நாடு—"a kingdom is that which is desired "for its immense wealth, and which grows greatly in prosperity, "being free from destructive causes."—பொறையொருங்கு மேல்வருங்காற் றாங்கி யிறைவற் கிறையொருங்கு நேர்வது நாடு—"a kingdom is that which can bear any burden "that may be pressed on it from adjoining kingdoms and yet pay "the full tribute to its sovereign."—உறுபசியு மோவாப் பிணியுஞ் செறுபகையுஞ் சேரா தியல்வது நாடு—"a kingdom is that which continues to be free from excessive "starvation, irremediable epidemics, and destructive foes."—பல்குழுவும் பாழ்செய்யு முட்பகையும் வேந்தலைக்குங் கொல்குறும்பு மில்லது நாடு—"a kingdom is that which is "without various irregular associations, destructive internal "enemies, and murderous savages who sometimes harass "the sovereign."—இருபுனலும் வாய்ந்த மலையும் வருபுனலும் வல்லரணு நாட்டிற் குறுப்பு—"the constituents of a kingdom are the two waters from above and "below, well situated hills and an indestructible fort."——*Rajacoonjaran* (राजकुञ्जर - rájakuñjara, San.). From (rájá, san. king + kuñjara, san. elephant); best of kings. Name of a Paundyan [q.v.] king.——*Rajadhauny* (राजधानी - rájadhání, San.; راجدھانی - rájdhání, Hind.). From (rájá, san. king + dhána, san. seat). A capital city.——*Rajagopaul* (இராசகோப்பாலன் - irásagóppálan, Tam.). From (rájá, san. king + gópála, san. cowherd). Krishnan [q.v.], the cowherd king. Familiarly raujiga, rajoo. Hindoo 2nd or pers. name [peyar].——*Rajah* (राजा - rájá, San.; راجہ - rájah, Hind.; இராசா - irásá, Tam.). King.—"*a*" A common title for any Hindoo ruler, and bestowed sometimes on private persons of high rank. Hindoo second or third name, common to both sexes; familiarly Rajoo, Rajy, Rajam.—"*b*" Plant first term either from shining leaves, fruits or flowers; or from the fruits and flowers being used by kings; sometimes also large. Ex., where transl. is of second term:—Cassia fistula (rájavriksha), tree; Datura fastuosa (rájadhúrta), cheat; Eugenia jambos (rájajambú), eugenia jambolana; Mimusops hexandra (rájádana), to eat; Momordica charantia (rájavallí), creeper; Musa paradisiaca (rájéshta), beloved; Pæderia fœtida (rájabalá), tonic; Vigna catiang (rájamásha), phaseolus mungo, var. radiatus; Webera corymbosa (rájataru), tree; Zizyphus jujuba (rájavallabhá), beloved. See gloss. paragraphs.—"*c*" Plant second term. Ex., where transl. is of first term:—Bauhinia racemosa (vanarája), forest; Cocos nucifera (trinarája), grass; Ficus religiosa (vriksharája), tree; Gardenia florida (gandharája), fragrance. See gloss. paragraphs.—"*d*" The Dravidian literature teems with reflections on regality. Compare the following from Cooral:—படைகுடி கூழமைச்சு நட்பரணா றுடையா னரசரு ளேறு—"he who possesses these six things, an army, a people, wealth, "ministers, friends, and a fortress, is a lion among kings."—அஞ்சாமை யீகை யறிவூக்க மிந்நான்கு மெஞ்சாமை வேந்தற் கியல்பு—"never to fail in these four things, fearlessness, liberality, wisdom, and energy, is the kingly character.—அறனிழுக்கா தல்லவை நீக்கி மறனிழுக்கா மான முடைய தரசு—"he is a king who, with manly modesty, "swerves not from virtue, and refrains from vice."—இவறலு மாண்பிறந்த மானமு மாணா வுவகையு மேத மிறைக்கு—"avarice, undignified pride, and low pleasures, are faults in a "king."—இயற்றலு மீட்டலுங் காத்தலுங் காத்த வகுத்தலும் வல்ல தரசு—"he is a king who is able to acquire "wealth, to lay it up, to guard it, and to distribute it."—காட்சிக் கெளியன் கடுஞ்சொல்ல னல்லனேன் மீக்கூறு மன்ன னிலம்—"the whole world will exalt the country of "the king who is easy of access, and who is free from harsh "language."—இன்சொலா லீத்தளிக்க வல்லாற்குத் தன்சொலாற் றான்கண் டனைத்திவ் வுலகு—"the world will "praise and submit itself to the mind of the king who is able "to give with affability, and to protect all who come to him."—முறைசெய்து காப்பாற்று மன்னவன் மக்கட் கிறையென்று வைக்கப் படும்—"that king will be esteemed a god "among men, who performs his own duties and protects his "subjects."—செவிகைப்பச் சொற்பொறுக்கும் பண்புடைவேந்தன் கவிகைக்கீழ்த் தங்கு முலகு—"the whole "world will dwell under the umbrella of the king, who can "bear words that embitter the ear."—உற்றநோய் நீக்கி யுறாஅமை முற்காக்கும் பெற்றியார்ப் பேணிக் கொளல்—"let a king procure and kindly care for men who can overcome "difficulties when they occur and guard against them before they "happen."—அரியவற்று ளெல்லா மரிதே பெரியாரைப் பேணித் தமராக் கொளல்—"to cherish great men and make "them his own, is the most difficult of all difficult things."—தம்மிற் பெரியார் தமரா வொழுகுதல் வன்மையு ளெல்லாந் தலை—"so to act as to make those men his own, who "are greater than himself, is of all powers the highest."—சூழ்வார் கண்ணாக வொழுகலான் மன்னவன் சூழ்வாரைச் சூழ்ந்து கொளல்—"as a king must use his ministers as eyes, "let him well examine their character and qualifications before "he engages them."—தக்கா ரினத்தனாய்த் தானொழுக வல்லானைச் செற்றார் செயக்கிடந்த தில்—"there will be "nothing left for enemies to do, against him who has the power "of acting so as to secure the fellowship of worthy men."—இடிக்குந் துணையாரை யாள்வாரை யாரே கெடுக்குந் தகைமை யவர்—"who are great enough to destroy him who "has servants that have power to rebuke him?"—இடிப்பாரை யில்லாத வேமரா மன்னன் கெடுப்பா ரிலானுங் கெடும்—"the king, who is without the guard of men who can rebuke "him, will perish, even though there be no one to destroy him."—முதலிலார்க் கூதிய மில்லை மதலையாஞ் சார்பிலார்க் கில்லை நிலை—"there can be no gain to those who have no "capital; and in like manner there can be no permanence to "those who are without the support of adherents."—ஒற்று முறைசான்ற நூலு மிவையிரண்டுந் தெற்றென்க மன்னவன் கண்—"let a king consider as his eyes these two "things, a spy and a book of laws universally esteemed."—வானோக்கி வாழு முலகெல்லா மன்னவன் கோனோக்கி வாழுங் குடி—"when there is rain, the living creation thrives; "and so when the king rules justly, his subjects thrive."—அந்தணர் நூற்கு மறத்திற்கு மாதியாய் நின்றது மன்னவன் கோல்—"the sceptre of the king is the firm support of the "vedams of the Bramin, and of all virtues therein described."—குடிதழீஇக் கோலோச்சு மாநில மன்ன னடிதழீஇ நிற்கு முலகு—"the world will constantly embrace the feet of "the great king who rules over his subjects with love."—இயல்புளிக் கோலோச்சு மன்னவ னாட்ட பெயலும் விளையுளுந் தொக்கு—"rain and plentiful crops will ever dwell "together in the country of the king who sways his sceptre with "justice."—வேலன்று வென்றி தருவது மன்னவன் கோலதூஉங் கோடா தெனின்—"it is not the javelin that "gives victory, but the king's sceptre, if it do no injustice."—இறைகாக்கும் வையக மெல்லா மவனை முறைகாக்கு முட்டாச் செயின்—"the king defends the whole world; and "justice, when administered without defect, defends the king."—எண்பதத்தா னோரா முறைசெய்யா மன்னவன் றண்பதத்தாற் றானே கெடும்—"the king who gives not facile "audience, and who does not examine and pass judgment, will perish in disgrace."—நாடொறு நாடி முறைசெய்யா மன்னவ னாடொறு நாடு கெடும்—"the country of the king "who does not daily examine into the wrongs done and distribute justice, will daily fall to ruin."—கடிதோச்சி மெல்ல வெறிக நெடிதாக்க நீங்காமை வேண்டு பவர்—"let the "king, who desires that his prosperity may long remain, "commence his preliminary enquiries with strictness, and then "punish with mildness."—கொலையிற் கொடியாரை வேந்

தொறுத்தல் பைங்கூழ் களைகட் டதனொடு நேர்—"for a king to punish criminals with death, is like pulling up "the weeds in the green corn."—துளியின்மை ஞாலத்திற் றற்றே வேந்த னளியின்மை வாழு முயிர்க்கு—"as is the world without rain, so live a people whose king is "without kindness."—இனத்தாற்றி யெண்ணாத வேந்தன் சினத்தாற்றிச் சீறிற் சிறுகுந் திரு—"the prosperity of "that king will waste away, who without reflecting on his affairs "himself, commits them to his ministers, and when a failure "occurs gives way to anger, and rages against them."—கண்ணோட்ட மென்னுங் கழிபெருங் காரிகை யுண்மையா னுண்டிவ் வுலகு—"the world exists through that greatest "ornament of princes, a gracious demeanour."——*Rajahamsam* (राजहंस - rájahamsa, San.; اوز - iwaz, Ar.; قاز - káz, Pers.; راج هنس - rájhans, Hind.; قاز - káz, Dec.; ರಾಜಹಂಸ - rájahamsa, Can.; పూగొంగ - púgonga, Tel.; ରାଜହଂସ - rájohomso, Oor.; രാജഹംസം - rájahamsam, Mal.; பூநாரை - púnárai, Tam.). Title from sanscrit. San. from (rájá, san. king + hamsa, san. swan). Dec. from persian. Tel. from (puvvu, tel. flower + konga, tel. crane). Tam. from (pú, tam. flower + nárai, tam. crane); from red color. Ar. also (nuhámah). Pers. also (murghábí), meaning water fowl. Hind. also (bághans), meaning heron goose. Tel. also (samudrapuchiluka), meaning sea + parrot. Beng. also (kanthunti). Title otherwise Flamingo. Phœnicopteridæ family, lamellirostres, natatores, aves [pacshy, 48], of naturalists [jantoo]. Neck and legs of enormous length; bill suddenly bent down. There is only one genus, Phœnicopterus roseus. Alias Phœnicopterus antiquus, minor. Throughout rosy white, rose color more marked on head, back and tail; wing-coverts, except primary coverts, which are white, and tertiaries fine rosy red; quills black, last of secondaries white; lower wing-coverts black; bill rosy, black at tip; irides pale golden-yellow; legs and feet pale rosy red; length 4 feet 4 inches; female smaller; very abundant in the poolicat lake; sleep on one leg, with the neck bent back, and the head under the wing; swim well with the port of swans [hamsam].——*Rajah boil* (راج پھوڑا - rájphorá, Hind.; రాచపుండు - rátsapundu, Tel.; பக்கப்பிளவை - pakkappilavai, Tam.). A carbuncle. Natives are very subject to these [veidyan].——*Rajahmundry* (రాజమహేంద్రవరము - rájamahéndravaramu, Tel.). See sep. title.——*Rajah's drug* (خسرو دارویٔ کلان - khusravidárúikalán, Pers.). Same as Greater galangal.——*Rajah's tree* (राजवृक्ष - rájavriksha, San.). Same as Common condray.——*Rajah vycaul* (இராசவாய்க்கால் - irásavâykkál, Tam.). Means king's canal. Any main channel [q.v.]. So Rajah rustah is a high-road.——*Rajalingam* (இராசலிங்கம் - irásalingam, Tam.). From (rájá, san. king + linga, san. phallic emblem of shiva), having royal ensigns or tokens. Hindoo 2nd or pers. name [peyar].——*Rajaparny* (राजपर्णी - rájaparní, San.). Means shining leaved. Same as Gandhaulee.——*Rajarajan* (राजराज - rájarája, San.). From (above + rájá, san. king), king of kings. Chola king 1023–1064. So called from having defeated the Paundyan [q.v.] king. United the Vengy [q.v.] and Calingam [q.v.] kings, by intermarriage, to Chola [q.v.] territories [charitram]. See vol. I (126).——*Rajaram* (ರಾಜಾರಾಮ - rájáráma, Can.). From (rájá, san. king + ráma, can. the god), rama, the king. Hindoo 2nd or pers. name [peyar].——*Rajaratnam* (இராசரத்தினம் - irásarattinam, Tam.). From (rájá, san. king + ratna, san. gem). The best king. Familiarly Rajam. Hindoo 2nd or pers. name [peyar].——*Rajaratnaucary* (राजरत्नाकर - rájaratnákara, San.). From (rájá, san. king + ratna, san. gem + ákara, san. mine). Ceylon work. Written by a priest, Abejaraja pirivanan. Extracts from ancient books. Contains history of Booddha [q.v.] abridged from Mahavanso [q.v.]. It records the history of the N. indian ceylon rulers from the date of Vijaya rajah, who was the first king in 540 B.C. to the settlement of the Portuguese in the island.——*Rajashekharan* (இராசசேகரன் - irásaségaran, Tam.). From (rájá, san. king + shékhara, san. head). The chief of kings. Hindoo 2nd or pers. name [peyar]. Name of a Paundyan [q.v.] king. See vol. I (124).——*Rajashree* (राजश्री - rájashrí, San.). From (rájá, san. king + shrí, san. prosperity). The fortune of a king, majesty; a term of address used in writing [peyar]. For the full form Maharajah raja shree, see M.R.Ry.——*Rajasooyam* (राजसूय - rájasúya, San.). From (rájá, san. king + su, san. to perform sacrifice). A religious sacrifice [yanyam] performed at the coronation of a great king.——*Rajatty* (இராசாத்தி - irásátti, Tam.). Queen [ranee].——*Rajauvaly* (राजावली - rájávalí, San.). From (rájá, san. king + ávali, san. row). Ceylon work. Compiled from local histories. A corollary to Mahavanso [q.v.] and Rajaratnaucary [q.v.], continuing the narration through the struggles between the Portuguese and their rivals, the Dutch; until the latter power, having succeeded expelling their opponents, gained possession of Colombo, and ultimately subjugated the whole of the maritime districts of the island. See vol. I (4), (82).——*Rajaveety* (राजवीथी - rájavít'hí, San.). From (rájá, san. king + vít'hí, san. street). Principal street [maunasauram, oor, veety]. So Rajah rustah, a high road.——*Rajcoomar* (राजकुमार - rájakumára, San.). From (rájá, san. king + kumára, san. son). A prince [shahzauda].——*Rajendra* (राजेन्द्र - rájéndra, San.). From (rájá, san. king + indra, can. lord), best king. See vol. I (126), (130). Also called Bookka [q.v.]. Rajah of Vijianugger of Harihar [q.v.] dynasty A.D. 1350—1379. See vol. II, 251. Rajendra is another name of the Cholan [q.v.] Coolotoongan [charitram, coolotoongan].——*Rajpindey* (ರಾಜಪಿಂಡ - rájapinde, Can.). From (rájá, san. king + pinda, san. ball offering of rice); means sapinda [q.v.] or relation of the king. Title of ruling family in Mysore [jauty, urs].——*Rajpoot* (راجپوت - rájpút, Hind.). From (rájá, san. king + putra, san. son). A son. A prince. The general designation of the races in the north and west of India, said to be sprung from the ancient dynasties of the sun and moon [vamsham] forming the Soorya vamsham [q.v.] and Chundra vamsham [q.v.] tribes, or else from a sacred fire kindled on Mount aboo by the saint Agastyan [q.v.] and who are thence termed Agnicoolam [q.v.] or of the family of fire. From these sources thirty-six primary royal races have originated. The solar dynasties are the Grahilote, Rahtore, Kachwaha. There is but one race sprung from the moon, through Krishnan [q.v.], that of Yadoo [q.v.]. The Agnicoolam races are originally four, the Pramaura, Pariharah, Chalookya, and Chauhan [jauty]. Modern rajpoots speak hindostany [q.v.]; take the title of singh [q.v.]; keep their wives gosha [q.v.]; very jealous in caste rules; many of them sepoys [q.v.] and police men. Probably recent immigrants from the north. Numbers in Presidency about 15,000; mostly in Bellary and Salem, see vol. I (66); II, 227.——*Rajya lutchmy* (राज्यलक्ष्मी - rájyalakshmí, San.). From (rájya, san. kingdom + lakshmí, san. the goddess). The goddess of royalty [ashtalutchmy].——*Ranee* (రాణి - ráni, Tel.). The wife of a rajah, a queen or princes [peyar, rajatty].——*Ranipett* (رانی پیٹھ - ránípeth, Hind.; இராணிப்பேட்டை - iránippéttai, Tam.). From (iráni, tam. queen + péttai, tam. suburb); after the wife of deshinga rajah. Village, Head assistant collector's head-quarters; North arcot dist., Wallajahpett tal.; pop. 3,697; acres 2,697; lat. 12° 56′; long. 79° 23′; from Arnee N. 18 miles; from Chittore S.E. 25 miles; from Madras W. 65 miles; from Tripatty S. 49 miles; from Vellore E. 13 miles; from Wallajahpett W. 2 miles. On left bank of Palaur opposite Arcot. The country round is flat. Built, about 1771, by Saudat oollah khan in honor of youthful widow of Deshinga rajah of Jinjee, who committed suttee [q.v.]. The Rajah revolted and was killed. Until 1850 belonged to Arcot talook. Till 1855 military station. In 1861 41st Regiment stationed here for a time. Most buildings dismantled. Owing to cheapness of house-rent European pensioners used to live here. Large native christian community. Cattle fair Friday on parade ground. A mile east is tope [q.v.] known as Nowlakbaugh extending along Palaur for three miles; means nine-lakh garden from many fruit trees especially mangoes of sorts. Contain mango [q.v.], orange [q.v.], cocoanut [q.v.] and other fruit trees. The following are the travelling distances by road from Ranipett to different places:—

To		Viâ	Miles	Furlongs
Amboor ...	...	Vellore and Pullicondah	44	3
Bargalore	...	Vellore and Shoolagherry and Oossoor ...	143	3
Bangalore	...	Pulmanair and Colaur	135	2½
Bangalore	...	Goodiyattam, Naicknairy ghaut and Colaur.	132	7
Bellary	...	Pulmanair, Poonganore, Cadiry and Anantapore.	253	5
Calastry ...	...	Sholinghur and Nagary	71	1
Chingleput	...	Conjeeveram and Wallajahbad	50	3
Chittore ...	...	Shercaud	30	1½
Colaur ...	...	Pulmanair	93	4½
Colaur ...	...	Naicknairy ghaut	91	1
Combaconam	...	Tindivanam, Vicravaundy and Shauttatope.	152	2
Conjeeveram	...	Wocherry	29	7
Cuddalore	...	Wandiwash, Tindivanam, Kilyanore and Pondicherry.	95	0
Cuddalore	...	Wandiwash, Meilam and Pondicherry ...	98	5
Cuddapah	...	Chittore and Royachoty	131	4½
Goodiyattam	...	Vellore	34	4
Madras ...	...	Rajah chuttram and Poonamallee ...	70	5
Nellore ...	...	Sholinghur, Calastry and Wojelly ...	129	0
Oossoor ...	...	Vaniyambaudy and Krishnagherry ...	117	6
Pondicherry	...	Tindivanam and Kilyanore	83	1
Pondicherry	...	Tindivanam and Meilam	86	6
Poonamallee	...	Rajah chuttram and Shreepermatore ...	58	1
Poonganore	...	Shercaud and Pulmanair	69	6
Pulmanair	...	Shercaud	51	0½
Sadras ...	...	Chingleput	69	7
Salem ...	...	Vellore, Amboor and Munjavaudy ghaut.	138	7
Salem ...	...	Vellore, Amboor and Toppoor ghaut ...	150	1
Tanjore ...	...	Tindivanam, Shauttatope and Combaconam.	175	6
Tindivanam	...	Wandiwash	57	0
Trichinopoly	...	Tindivanam, Oolandoorpett and Volcondapooram.	179	7
Tripatore	...	Vellore and Amboor	68	7
Vaniyambaudy	...	Vellore and Amboor	54	7
Vellore ...	...	......	13	6
Vencatagherry	...	Shercaud	39	5½
Wallajahbad	...	Conjeeveram	36	3

——*Rao* (راو - ráu, Hind.). Oordoo form of Row [q.v.]. Does not belong to this presidency. Cf. Rai, Roya.——*Rashtracootam* (राष्ट्रकूट - ráshtrakúta, San.). From (ráshtra, san. kingdom +

kúta, san. eminence). Ancient tribe. Flourished between about the fifth and eighth centuries. Subverted the Chalookyas [q.v.] of Bombay. Did not come much in contact with dynasties [raj] of the south [charitram]. Vol. I (138).——*Rashtram* (राष्ट्र - ráshtra, San.). From (ráj, san. to rule). Kingdom [rajyam].——*Raucha* (రాచ - rátsa, obl.; రాచవారు - rátsavádu, pers. sing.; రాచవారు - rátsaváru, pers. pl., Tel.). From (rájá, san. king). Tel. oblique form for Rauz [q.v.]. The plural Rauchavaur often appears.——*Raupore* (రాపూరు - rápúru, Tel.). See sep. title.——*Rauz* (రాజు - rádzu, Tel.). See sep. title.——*Rayaun* (رایان - ráyán, Dec.). See sep. title.——*Reddy* (రెడ్డి - reddi, Tel.). From (rédu, tel. king). The corresponding terms are:—Tam. vellaula, Can. okkaliga, Mal. nayar.—" *a* " The general caste-title of the agricultural class in the Teloogoo country. Also called Caupoo [q.v.] or cultivator and Naidoo [q.v.] or master. They are the cultivators of Nellore and the Ceded districts [q.v.], and throughout a large portion of the Teloogoo country, in some places in which they form a preponderating element among the Hindoo population. Most are engaged in agriculture [vellaumay] either as farmers or cultivators [ryots], but some of them are traders. They have a character for energy and thrift. In physique these agriculturists are a finer race than Tamul cultivators. They appear to have spread out from Rajahmundry. They have penetrated as far as the Mahratta country, being met with up to Poona where they are considered the most thriving cultivators. They are often found also in the Tamul country. In their customs they resemble other ordinary Shoodra [q.v.] castes [jauty]. There are several divisions among them, the chief being the Pauknauty, Pocanauty, Dessore, Panta, Peddacunty, Pullam, Morasoo, Pully, Tota, and Yerlam caupoos. The caste-title of all these is Reddy, and the names of their sub-divisions are derived from their original country or their particular occupations. Thus the Pauknauty caupoos are those who came from the east country. The Pocanauties are from the areca [q.v.] palm-growing land. The Dessore reddies were residents originally of some place called Dessore. The Pantas are so called from panta, a crop. The Peddacunties from some place called Peddagull. The Pullams are low-country people. The Morasoos were so called because they used to weave mats [boriyah] and baskets [tokrah], though now they only cultivate. Yerlam caupoos are partly of braminical descent. These northern agriculturists think themselves superior to the Tamul cultivating castes. In the Madura district, soon after the establishment of the Naick [q.v.] dynasty [raj], the Telinga immigrants became so numerous and so influential that the Jesuit priests of Madura regarded them with the Bramins [q.v.] as constituting the chief part of the people. The reddies are divided into clans, who marry in their own clans. They eat all flesh but cow's flesh. Property descends through the issue of a son and grand-daughter, uncle and niece. They refuse to eat with any other caste whatever, or even to take choonam [q.v.] from any but their own people. Numbers about 500,000 throughout telinga country; but found also considerably in S. arcot, Madura, Salem, Tinnevelly and Trichinopoly. See vol. I (67); II, 237.—" *b* " Reddy is the title of the head of the village authorities in the Telinga country; but more properly designated as pedda reddy, senior reddy or villager [jauty].—" *c* " Sometimes this is a mere Hindoo third name [peyar].——*Renigoonta* (రేణిగుంట - réniguinta,* Tel.). From (rédu, tel. king + gunta, tel. tank). Village, Railway station; North arcot dist., Chundragherry tal.; pop. 781; lat. 13° 38′; long. 79° 33′; height 368 feet; from Chittore N.E. 41 miles; from Chundragherry E.N.E. 13 miles. Junction of N.W. line of Madras railway and Nellore-tripatty section of the S. indian railway.——*Row* (राव ráva - Mahr.; راو - ráu, Hind.; రావు - rávu, Tel.). From (rájá, san. king). Title originally taken by Cshatriyas [q.v.]; but extended by Mahomedan rulers to Hindoo civil officers of high rank. Now common among madhwas [q.v.] who are not priests, the priests being styled Acharries [q.v.], answering to Shastries [q.v.] among the smartas [q.v.]. Hindoo third name [peyar]; as Balajee row. The title is now being taken even by naidoos [q.v.] and others [peyar].——*Row bahaudur* (راوبهادر - ráubahádur, Hind.). A high title of honor bestowed on very distinguished Hindoos [khitaub, peyar].——*Row sahib* (راو صاحب - ráusáhib, Hind.). A title of a honor bestowed on distinguished Hindoos. The equivalent among Mahomedans is Khan sahib [khitaub, peyar].——*Rowtan* (राउत - ráúta, Mahr.; இராவுத்தன் - irávuttan, Tam.). From (ráva, mahr. king + dúta, san. messenger). A cavalier. Title of Lubbays [q.v.].——*Roya* (رای - rái, Hind.; ರಾಯ - ráya, Can.; రాయడు - ráyadu, Tel.) [rai, rajah, rao, row, rye]. Provincialism for Rajah; under Mahomedan governments title given to Hindoo civil officers of high rank [khitaub, peyar]. Also a usual name amongst the Teloogoo races. Suffix in Tamul and Teloogoo proper names as Soobbaroya. The plural Royel [q.v.] is a title taken by the Velamas [q.v.] of the Northern circars [q.v.], who claim to be Rajpoots [peyar].——*Royachoty* (రాయచోటి - ráyatsóti, Tel.). See sep. title.——*Royacottah* (ರಾಯಕೋಟೆ - ráyakóte, Can.). Means king's fort.—" *a* " Zemindarry; Salem dist., Krishnagherry tal.; pop. 1,347; square miles 14. Peshcush Rs. 1,266.—" *b* " Village, Hill; Salem dist., Krishnagherry tal.; pop. 1,347; acres 9,117; lat. 12° 31′; long. 78° 05′; height 2,364; from Krishnagherry W. 12 miles; from Salem N.N.W. 60 miles. One of the Baramahaul [q.v.] fortresses, British frontier garrison on the Mysore borders and until recently occupied by troops. Commanded one of the most important passes [ghaut]. Captured in 1791 by Lord Cornwallis. Ceded to the English by the treaty of 1792. Under its walls the British army encamped in 1799 on the way to Seringapatam. A place of residence for military pensioners, who abandoned it after the famine of 1876–78. Near the town is a large square well hewn from the solid rock. Public bungalow [q.v.]. Between this place and Krishnagherry is a winding ghaut [q.v.] remarkable for its beautiful scenery. North stands the Droog. It is ascended by an easy gradient passable to a considerable distance on horseback. From the summit there is a view of the Dharmapoory, Krishnagherry and Oossoor talooks, while to the east the Jawaudies and Yelagherry are visible. There is a European cemetery at the base. The fortifications are in comparatively good order, and one almost entirely of European construction.——*Royadoo* (రాయడు - ráyadu, Tel.). From (rádzu, tel. king). A title adopted as a surname by the Velama [q.v.] caste in the Northern circars [q.v.]. Plural is Royel [q.v.]. Hindoo second or third name [peyar].——*Royadroog* (ರಾಯದುರ್ಗ - ráyadurga, Can.). See sep. title.——*Royagada* (రాయఘడ - ráyaghada, Tel.). See sep. title.——*Royalcheroo* (రాయల్‌చెరువు - ráyalcheruvu, Tel. ráyalcheru *). From (ráyalu, tel. king + cheruvu, tel. tank). Called after Krishna deva royel of Vijianugger. Village, Railway station; Anantapore dist., Tadpatry tal.; pop. 1,855; acres 3,502; lat. 15° 03′; long. 77° 52′; height 942; from Anantapore N.N.E. 29 miles; from Tadpatry N.W. 16 miles. On trunk road midway between Gooty and Tadpatry. Travellers' bungalow [q.v.]. From a hill in the neighbourhood Tippoo obtained flints [teettatty cull] for matchlocks. A soft limestone [choonam cull] is found close by, from which cups and vases are made.——*Royanandam* (రాయానందము - ráyánandamu, Tel.). From (rádzu, tel. king + ánanda, san. pleasure), means king pleaser. Hindoo 2nd or pers. name [peyar].——*Royappan* (இராயப்பன் - iráyappan, Tam.). From (iráyan, tam. king + appan, tam. father, titular affix). Means king, the father. Hindoo 2nd or pers. name [peyar]. Applied to St. Peter by native Christians; gives name to Royapettah, the suburb of madras [q.v.].——*Royavalsa* (రాయవలస - ráyavalasa, Tel.). From (ráyadu, tel. king + valasa, tel. colony). Ghaut; Vizagapatam dist., Srungavarapoocote division; lat. 18° 14′; long. 83° 04′; from Srungavarapoocote N.W. 11 miles. On route from Caushiputnam to Jeypore by Gaulicondah. The crest is 2,850 feet above sea. Maharajah of Vizianagram has a coffee [q.v.] estate.——*Royel* (రాయలు - ráyalu, Tel.). Plural of Roya [q.v.]. Hindoo third name. Title taken by the Velamas [q.v.] of the Northern circars [q.v.]. The title of the Hindoo sovereigns of Vijianugger [q.v.], the last Hindoo principality of importance in the South of India [peyar].——*Royer* (ರಾಯರು - ráyaru, Can.). Plural of Roya. Same as Royel.——*Rye* (రాయ - ráya, Tel.). King [roya]. Distinguish from Rye, meaning stone.——*Rye ellore* (రాయవేలూరు - ráyavélúru, Tel.). From (ráya, tel. king + vélúr, tam. vellore). Another name for Vellore to distinguish it from Ooppellore or Ellore [q.v.].——*Ryroo* (രൈരു - rairu, Mal.). From (ráyan, mal. king). Hindoo 2nd or pers. name [peyar].

RAJAB (رجب - rajjab, *Hind.*). From (rajiba, ar. to honor). Honored, as it was in the time of ignorance prior to Mahomet held unlawful to make war during this month. Name of the seventh month [maheena] of the Mahomedans. In this Mahomet's nocturnal journey [leilat ool mirauj] to heaven took place.

RAJAHMUNDRY * (రాజమహేంద్రవరము - rájamahéndravaramu, *Tel.*) [raj]. From mahendradeva of the orissa dynasty. Sanscrit name (rájanaréndrapura), meaning rajanarendran's town.——**(1)** Former district named from its principal town. One of the five Northern circars [q.v.]. It lay between lat. 16° 18′ to 17° 38′; long. 81° 7′ to 82° 40′. Area 6,050 square miles. Bounded north by Nagpore territory; north-east by the district of Vizagapatam; south-east by the Bay of Bengal; west by the district of Masulipatam; and north-west by the territory of the Nizam. Coringa, Rajahmundry, and Samulcottah are the towns of importance. For history see under head of the town. ——**(2)** Talook, Godavery district. Tahsildar's pay Rs. 175. Area 2,058 square miles. Centre of district. Bounded:—North by Bustar country; south by Ramchendrapooram talook; east by Peddapore talook; and west by the Godavery. Partly hilly and partly flat. In some places very rocky. Special industry is the manufacture of cotton [q.v.] carpets [jamkhana]. Considerable trade is also carried on in tobacco [pogauk] and dry grains [q.v.]. Many large tanks [q.v.] in the talook, of which the Cottapully, Gokavaram and Goommulladoddy are the principal. Booradacaulwa channel [q.v.] rises in the hills and falls into the river Godavery. Zemindarries:—Bommoor, Bootchampett, Cautavaram, Dandangy, Hookumpett, Hoondeshwarapooram, Moormunda, Pettah, Vangalpoody, Zaulimoody. Places of archæological interest:—Coroocondah, Dowlaishweram, Gaudaranda, Koty, Mirtipaud, Raghoodevapooram, Rajahmundry. Principal trig. stations:—Calimaumidy, Nullacondah, Potoocondah. The leading places, &c., in the talook are the following. ——*Bommoor* (బొమ్మూరు - bommúru, Tel.). From (bomma, tel. doll + úru, tel. village). Zemindarry, Village; square miles 4; lat. of village 16° 58′; long. 81° 51′; from Cocanada W. 28 miles; from Rajahmundry S.E. 4 miles. Peshcush Rs. 833.——*Booradacaulwa* (బురదకాలవ - buradakálava, Tel.). From (burada, tel. mud + kálava, tel. channel). Channel. Rises in the Rumpa country and irrigates a large number of villages above Rajahmundry. Is not navigable.——*Bootchampett* (బుచ్చంపేట - buççampéta, Tel.). From (buççamma, tel. proper name, meaning little mother + péta, tel. suburb). Zemindarry, Village; lat. of village 17° 07′; long. 81° 50′; from Cocanada W.N.W. 31 miles; from Rajahmundry N.N.E. 8 miles. Peshcush Rs. 738.——*Calimaumidy* (కలిమామిడి - kalimámidi, Tel.). From (kali, tel. gruel + mámidi, tel. mango, mangifera indica, linn.). Trig. station; lat. 17° 34′ 43·59″; long. 82° 09′ 23·25″; height 2,822 feet.——*Cautavaram* (కాటవరము - kátavaramu, Tel.). From (kádu, tel. forest + pura, san. town). Zemindarry, Village; square miles 26; lat. of village 17° 06′; long. 81° 47′; from Cocanada W.N.W. 34 miles; from Rajahmundry N.N.W. 8 miles. Peshcush Rs. 2,121.——*Coroocondah* (కోరుకొండ - kórukonda, Tel.). From (kóru, tel. steep + konda, tel. hill). Village, Place of pilgrimage; pop. 2,329; acres 1,611; lat. 17° 10′; long. 81° 51′; from Cocanada W.N.W. 30 miles; from Rajahmundry N.N.E. 12 miles. Temple of Narsimhasawmy built about A.D. 1443. West of the village is an old fort. On the same side is the Panndavoola condah, which contains five rock-cut caves, one with sculptured figures. A weekly fair every Sunday.——*Dandangy* (దండంగి - dandangi, Tel.). From (dandu, tel. army + angu, tel. beauty). Zemindarry, Village; lat. of village 17° 19′; long. 81° 45′; from Cocanada W.N.W. 42 miles; from Rajahmundry N.N.W. 22 miles. Peshcush Rs. 564. ——*Dootsarty* (దూట్సర్తి - dútsarti, Tel.). From (dúchi, tel. a game + parti, tel. a village). Zemindarry, Village; lat. of village 17° 35′; long. 82° 06′; from Cocanada N.N.W. 45 miles; from Rajahmundry N.N.E. 44 miles. Belonged to the Vizagapatam district up to time of late Rumpa fitoory [fitoor] when it was transferred to this district.——*Dowlaishweram* (ధవళేశ్వరము - dhavaléshvaramu, Tel.). See sep. title.——*Godavery* (గోదావరి - gódávari, Tel.). See sep. title.——*Gokavaram* (గోకవరము - gókavaramu, Tel.). See sep. title.——*Goommulladoddy* (గుమ్మళ్లదొడ్డి - gummalladoddi, Tel.). From (gummadi, tel. pumpkin, cucurbita maxima, duch. + doddi, tel. enclosure). Village; lat. 17° 12′; long. 81° 53′; from Cocanada N.W. 31 miles; from Rajahmundry N.N.E. 4 miles. Tank.——*Hookumpett* (హుకుంపేట - hukampéta, Tel.). From (hukm, hind. order + péta, tel. suburb). Hind. name (zuhúrullábád), meaning zoohooroollah, proper name, meaning manifestation of god + city. Zemindarry, Village; lat. of village 16° 59′; long. 81° 50′; from Cocanada W. 28 miles; from Rajahmundry S.E. 2 miles. Peshcush Rs. 1,401.——*Hoondeshwarapooram* (హుండేశ్వరపురము - hundéshvarapuramu, Tel.). From (hundéshvarudu, tel. shiva, the tiger-lord + pura, san. town). Zemindarry, Village; lat. of village 17° 06′; long. 81° 48′; from Cocanada W.N.W. 32 miles; from Rajahmundry N. 7 miles. Peshcush Rs. 630.——*Moormunda* (మురుమండ - murumanda, Tel.). From (muruvu, tel. beautiful + manda, tel. a cattle herd). Zemindarry, Village; lat. of village 16° 53′; long. 81° 54′; from Cocanada W.S.W. 25 miles; from Rajahmundry S.S.E. 10 miles. Peshcush Rs. 1,850.——*Nullacondah* (నల్లకొండ - nallakonda, Tel.). From (nalla, tel. black + konda, tel. hill). Trig. station; lat. 17° 18′ 15·85″; long. 81° 59′ 35·44″; height 1,267 feet; from Lodaipollem N. ¾ mile.——*Paumoolair* (పాములేరు - pámuléru, Tel.). From (pámu, tel. snake + éru, tel. river). A hill stream; Perennial tributary of Godavery; flows through Paumoolair valley.——*Potoocondah* (పోతుకొండ - pótukonda, Tel.). From (pótu, tel. ox + konda, tel. hill). Trig. station; lat. 17° 15′ 45·60″; long. 81° 46′ 58·23″; height 1,520 feet; from Ramannapollem N.W. 2 miles.——*Raghoodevapooram* (రఘుదేవపురము - raghudévapuramu, Tel.). See sep. title.——*Rajahmundry* (రాజమహేంద్రవరము - rájamahéndravaramu, Tel.). See below.——*Soodicondah* (సూదికొండ - súdikonda, Tel.). From (súdi, tel. needle + konda, tel. hill). Village; lat. 17° 17′; long. 81° 58′; from Cocanada N.W. 30 miles; from Rajahmundry N.E. 22 miles.——*Vangalpoody* (వంగలపూడి - vangalapúdi, Tel.). From (vanga, tel. brinjal, solanum molongena, linn. + púdi, tel. village). Zemindarry, Village; lat. of village 17° 12′; long. 81° 43′; from Cocanada W.N.W. 41 miles; from Rajahmundry N.N.W. 16 miles. Peshcush Rs. 3,788.——*Zaulimoody* (దాలిమూడి - dzálimúdi, Tel.). From (dzále, tel. a hawk + múdi, tel. collection). Zemindarry, Village; lat. of village 17° 06′; long. 81° 47′; from Cocanada W.N.W. 33 miles; from Rajahmundry N.N.W. 7 miles. Peshcush Rs. 254.——

(3) Town, Port, Head-quarters of Judge, Sub-collector and Superintendent of police; Godavery dist., Rajahmundry tal.; pop. 28,397; acres 8,842; lat. 17° 00′; long. 81° 48′; from Cocanada W.N.W. 30 miles; from Coonavaram S.E. 51 miles; from Ellore N.E. 48 miles; from Madras N.N.E. 287 miles; from Narsapore N. 39 miles. On elevated ground on left bank of Godavery, here a mile broad. Connected by canal with Cocanada, Coringa and Kistna district. Origin attributed by some to Mahendradeva of the Orissa dynasty [gajapaty], and by others to a Chalookya [q.v.] ruler. In the preface to a Teloogoo translation of the Mahabhaurat [q.v.] it is called the central gem of the Vengy [q.v.] desham and the capital of Rajanarendran. Rajahmundry was comprised in the ancient kingdom of Golcondah. In 1471 taken by the Mahomedans and given to Nizam ool moolk as a jagheer [q.v.]. In 1512 retaken by Krishna deva roya and restored to Orissa. For over sixty years Hindoo rule continued, and Rajahmundry withstood two protracted sieges till in 1571-72 it yielded to the Mussalmans of the Deccan [q.v.] under Rifat khan. For the next century and a half it was the scene of perpetual fighting, and at last fell to Golcondah and became one of the four nawaubships of that Government. Granted to the French in 1753, and Bussy's head-quarters from 1754 to 1757. Hither, retreating before Forde, came the remains of Conflan's army after the battle of Condore in 1758 only to be driven out by the Company's sepoys [q.v.]. Shortly afterwards Forde proceeded against Masulipatam, and during his absence the French recaptured Rajahmundry; but finding nothing of value, the treasure having been sent to a Dutch settlement, evacuated it almost immediately. Transferred to the British in 1759 and ceded to them by treaty in 1765. There was a slight disturbance in 1765. The country in the neighbourhood is low and chiefly composed of black-cotton soil [regar]. The town consists of one principal street. Innespett is the southern suburb. The houses of the European residents are to the north and north-east of the town. A Protestant mission of the American evangelical lutheran church carries on work in Rajahmundry, Moormunda, and outlying villages. Old fort north of the town with walls originally of great size and height, made of earth faced with stone. Ancient temple. Mosque [musjid] of Mahomed toghlak of Delhi with inscription of A.D. 1325, probably the earliest royal Mahomedan inscription in S. india. Mussalmans [q.v.] form now a small and indigent class. The following are the travelling distances by road from Rajahmundry to different places :-

To	Viâ	Miles and Furlongs.	
Bangalore ...	Ongole, Nellore, Chittore and Colaur ...	494	7½
Bellary	Guntoor, Cumbum and Gooty	402	2
Berhampore ...	Toony, Chicacole and Ichapore	278	6½
Bezwada	Ellore	94	2
Chetterpore ...	Toony, Chicacole and Berhampore ...	293	1½
Chicacole	Toony	179	6
Cocanada	Samulcottah	38	0
Cuddapah ...	Ellore, Guntoor and Cumbum	323	5½
Cuttack	Chicacole, Berhampore and Khoordhah ...	395	3½
Ellore	Nullacherla	55	1
Guntoor	Ellore and Bezwada	114	2½
Madras	Ellore, Guntoor and Nellore	366	6½
Masulipatam ...	Mogultoor	90	3
Masulipatam ...	Ellore	99	7½
Mogultoor ...	Penoocondah	52	2
Nellore	Bezwada, Guntoor and Ongole	259	½
Ongole	Bezwada and Guntoor	182	5½
Raghavapooram.	Lakkavaram	66	5
Samulcottah ...	Nullacheroo	30	0
Secunderabad ...	Bezwada and Sooryapett	231	½
Sironchah ...	Dammapett, Mungapatnam and Chinnore	234	1
Vizagapatam ...	Toony and Cassimcote	123	0
Vizianagram ...	Toony and Soobaraum	146	3

RAM (रम् - ram, *San.*). To please.——*Rama* (राम - ráma, San.; இராமன் - iráman, Tam.). From (ram, san. to please). Proper name common to both sexes, used in composition with distinctive feminine suffixes [peyar]. In composition it sometimes intimates excellence. This name belongs to the Aryan [q.v.] epic period, and is given to three persons of historical importance, all incarnations [avatar] of Vishnoo [q.v.]—"*a*" The first is Parshooraman [q.v.] or rama of the axe. He is considered sixth avatar [q.v.] of Vishnoo, and belongs to the period of the first struggle between the Bramins [q.v.] and the Cshatriyas [q.v.], the hierarchy and the government.—"*b*" The second is Rama with the affix of Chundran [q.v.] in the North and prefix of Codandam [q.v.] in South india. The seventh special manifestation of Vishnoo as a warrior king and conqueror. He was held to be the son of Dasharatan, king of Ayodhyay [cosalam], of the solar race. As a previous progenitor was named Raghoo [q.v.], he is often named Raghavan [q.v.]; and is worshipped under that name at Trivellore. His birth, adventures, and exploits form the subject of the Ramayanam [q.v.], the most popular of books in the south. In his pupilage he was placed under the care of Vishwamitran [q.v.] and received supernatural arms. At a swayamvaram by Janacan [q.v.], king of Mitilay, he succeeded in bending the prescribed bow and hitting the mark, carrying off as his prize Jannaky [q.v.], better known as Seetay [q.v.], his future consort. Owing to the intrigues of Keikeyee, youngest wife of Dasharatan, who favored her son Bharatan's accession to the throne, Rama and Seetay were banished to a wilderness; Lutchmanan [q.v.], Rama's brother, going with them. By the device of Mareechan, Rama was led away in pursuit of a deceptive deer [mrigam]; and Ravanan [q.v.], a raucshasa [q.v.] king, passing by, took up Seetay and carried her off through the air. Two fabulous birds fought with Ravanan, but were killed, and their bodies falling to the ground gave intimation to Rama of what had occurred. Rama had made acquaintance in the wilderness [dandacam] with two forester princes, Vauly [q.v.] and Soogreevan [q.v.], and also with Hanooman [q.v.], whom he now employed, and sent on an embassy to discover where Seetay was concealed. After inquiries, he discovered that she was captive at Lunka [q.v.], the capital of Ravanan. Hanooman was then sent to Lunka as an ambassador to demand the release of Seetay, and met with refusal. The two brothers Vauly and Soogreevan quarrelling, Rama had taken part with the younger; and killing Vauly, had placed Soogreevan on the vacant throne. Soogreevan placed an army of Vaunarams or monkeys [bandar] at the disposal of Rama under Hanooman as general. By their aid he constructed an isthmus or bridge [saitoo]; and passing over it, slew Ravanan, took Lunka, rescued Seetay, and placing Vibheeshanan on the throne of Lunka, returned with his wife to Ayodhyay, and was there crowned. In jealousy, he repudiated Seetay, and sent her to a wilderness, attended by Lutchmanan. She took refuge in the hermitage of Valmeeky [q.v.], and was there delivered of twins, Lavan and Cooshan. Bhavabooty [q.v.], in a play, makes Rama and Seetay meet in their old age and be reconciled. In one interpretation Codandaraman [q.v.] belongs to the age when the Aryan [q.v.] race, already settled in the north, pushed their conquests towards the southern part of the peninsula, and introduced into those wild districts civilization and agriculture, which are typified as Seetay, who is represented in the Vishnoo pooraunam [q.v.] as having been found in the earth. He gives his name to Ramasait, 'rama's bridge,' the line of rocks between India and Ceylon; and to Rameshwaram, where he set up one of the twelve great lingams [q.v.] to Shiva [q.v.]. The zemindar [q.v.] of Ramnaud still bears the title of Saitoopaty [q.v.], or 'keeper of the bridge,' that is to say of Rama's bridge. See vol. I (79). Ramachendran and all the personages of the Sanscrit poem which takes its name from him, are nearly as familiar to the Malays, and more especially to the Javanese, as they are to the inhabitants of this country. The Javanese have poems, both in the ancient and modern tongue, narrating the adventures of Rama, and from these have been formed romances in prose by the Malays. Rama rajyam has become proverbial for a government of equity and goodness.—"*c*" The third Rama is Balaraman, the strong rama, born at the end of the Dwauparam [q.v.], or third age [yoog], as the seventh son of Vasoodevan and Devaky, but mystically transferred from the womb of the latter to that of Vasôo devan's other wife Rohiny, and thus saved from the hands of Cumsan. He was the brother and play-fellow of Krishnan [q.v.]. He is sometimes regarded as an incarnation [avatar] of the serpent Anantan [q.v.] or Sheshan [q.v.]; sometimes called the eighth incarnation of Vishnoo. He is the Hercules of this mythology. See vol. I (79) [matam].—"*d*" Plant first term meaning tall, straight, graceful; of large size; of shining dark; wild. Ex., where translation is of second term:—Guizotia abyssinica (rámtil), sesamum indicum; Hibiscus esculentus (rámturaí), luffa acutangula; Melissa officinalis (rámtulsí), ocimum sanctum; Solanum xanthocarpum (rámagulla), solanum ferox; Typha elephantina (rámabána), arrow. See gloss. paragraphs.——*Ramabramhan* (இராமப்பிரம்மன் - irámappiramman, Tam.). From (ráma, san. the hero + brahma, san. the supreme spirit); one who meditates on rama as on the supreme spirit [bramh]. Hindoo 2nd or pers. name [peyar].——*Rama charitram* (രാമചരിതം - rámacharitam, Mal.). From (ráma, san. the hero + charita, san. story). The history of the second Rama. Oldest malayalam work.——*Ramadevan* (रामदेव - rámadéva, San.). From (ráma, san. the hero + déva, san. lord), rama, the lord. Also called Ramachendran. Yaudava king of Devagiry. A.D. 1271–1309. Attacked by Malik caufoor [q.v.] for irregular payment of tribute, and sent captive to Delhi. Restored subsequently [charitram]. See vol. I (140). Ramadevan is common Hindoo 2nd or pers. name [peyar].——*Ramah* (రామ - ráma, Tel.). See sep. title.——*Ramakka* (రామక్క - rámakka, Tel.). From (ráma, san. the hero + akka, tel. sister, titular affix of affection). Woman's name [peyar].——*Ramakrishnan* (இராமக்கிருட்டிணன் - irámakkiruttinan, Tam.). From (ráma, san. balaráma + krishna, san. krishna), balaraman and krishnan who were together as play-fellows; see Rama above. Two titles to form one name. Hindoo 2nd or pers. name [peyar].——*Ramalingam* (இராமலிங்கம் - irámalingam, Tam.). From (ráma, san. the hero + linga, san. phallic emblem of shiva). Rama's lingam or shiva as worshipped by rama at rameshwaram [ramanaickar]. Hindoo 2nd or pers. name [peyar].——*Ramalingasawmy* (இராமலிங்கசாமி - irámalingasámi, Tam.). From (ráma, san. the hero + linga, san. phallic emblem of shiva + svámí, san. lord), lord shiva as worshipped by rama. Hindoo 2nd or pers. name [peyar].——*Ramamoorty* (இராமமூர்த்தி - irámamúrtti, Tam.). From (ráma, san. the hero + múrti, san. form), rama, the incarnate vishnoo. Hindoo 2nd or pers. name [peyar].——*Ramamritam* (இராமாமிருதம் - irámámirutham, Tam.). From (ráma, san. the hero + amríta, san. ambrosia), rama the pleasing god. Hindoo 2nd or pers. name [peyar].——*Raman* (இராமன் - iráman, Tam.). Tam. form of Rama. Feminine Ramy. Hindoo 2nd or pers. name [peyar].——*Ramanaickar* (இராமநாயக்கர் - irámanáyakkar, Tam.). From (ráma, san. the hero + náyaka, san. lord), shiva, the lord of rama. Otherwise Ramalingam [q.v.], the god at Rameshwaram.——*Ramanautan* (இராமநாதன் - irámanáthan, Tam.). From (ráma, san. the hero + nát'ha, san lord). Epithet of Shiva, as worshipped by Rama. Hindoo 2nd or pers. name [peyar].——*Ramandroog* (ರಾಮನದುರ್ಗ - rámanadurga, Can.; rámandrug *). From (ráma, san. the god + durga, san. fort). Village, Hill, Sanitarium; Bellary district, Sundoor territory; pop. 256; lat. 15° 08′; long. 76° 31′; from Bellary W. 30 miles; from Sundoor W.N.W. 6 miles. Trig. station; lat 15° 07′ 34·57″; long. 76° 30′ 26·65″; height 3,256 feet; from Sundoor W. 7 miles. See vol. II, appendix XII.——*Ramannan* (ರಾಮಣ್ಣ - rámanna, Can.). From (ráma, san. the hero + anna, can. elder brother, titular affix of affection). Hindoo 2nd or pers. name [peyar].——*Ramapatam* (రామయ్యపట్నం - rámayyapatnam, Tel.). From (ráma, san. the god + pattana, san. town). Village; Nellore dist., Cundoocore tal.; pop. 1,151; acres 1,784; lat. 15° 03′; long. 80° 05′; from Chennayapollem N. 4 miles; from Cundoocore S.E. 15 miles; from Madras N. 133 miles; from Nellore N. 41 miles; from Paucala S. 16 miles. Formerly head-quarters of the Sub-collector. Small fishing village. In former years a coasting trade in grain and firewood, since diverted to Buckingham canal [q.v.] which runs through village. Ruined granaries on beach. Only frequented by native craft. Old temple of Ramalingeshwaran. American baptist mission station with a hospital supported by the mission. Beiraugy [q.v.] mutt [q.v.] supported by a russoom [q.v.]. Small tank. Noted for dyeing [shauyam] cloths. Ramapatam beacon trig. station in lat. 15° 3′ 51·21″; long. 80° 5′ 25·49″; from Cundoocore S.E. 14 miles; from Mocherla E.N.E. 3 miles; on the sea coast.——*Rama rajah* (రామరాజ - rámarája, Tel.). From (ráma, san. the hero + rájá, san. king). Vijianugger ruler. Son of Timmarajah, the Bramin minister of the previous ruler Krishna deva roya [q.v.]. Became guardian to the son of the latter. In a rebellion which followed he contrived to assume supreme power and became one of the most powerful of the line. In 1564 engaged the united army of Mahomedans at Talicote [q.v.] and was defeated and killed. With him the power of Vijianugger fell [charitram]. See vol. I (148); II, 251.——*Ramasait* (रामसेतु - rámasétu, San.). Means rama's bund. Adam's bridge [saitoo]. Distinct from Rameshwaram which is only one end of it.——*Rama's areca* (ರಾಮನಡಿಕೆ - rámanadike, Can.). Same as Travancore nutmeg.——*Ramasawmy* (இராமசாமி - irámasámi, Tam.). From (ráma, san. the hero + svámí, san. lord), rama, the lord. The second name or Codandaraman [q.v.]. The commonest proper name among hindooized dravidians, even extending down to pariahs.——*Ramasheshan* (இராமசேசன் - irámasésan, Tam.). From (ráma, san. balaráma + shésha, san. the serpent). Balaraman, the third rama [q.v.] who is said to be Audisheshan [q.v.] incarnate. Compound name. Familiarly Ramasheshoo. Hindoo 2nd or pers. name [peyar].——*Ramasimhum* (இராமசிம்மம் - irámasimmam, Tam.). From (ráma, san. the hero + simha, san. lion). The heroic rama. Hindoo 2nd or pers. name [peyar].——*Ramasomayauj* (రామసోమయాజి - rámasómayáji, Tel.). From (ráma, san. the hero + sómayáji, san. soma sacrificer, personal title). Hindoo 2nd or pers. name [peyar].——*Ramasoobboo* (இராமசுப்பு - irámasuppu, Tam.). From (ráma, san. the hero + shuppu, tam. familiar contraction of subba, can. serpent). Compound name. Balaraman, the third rama [q.v.] who is said to be incarnation of Audisheshan [q.v.]. Hindoo 2nd or pers. name [peyar].——*Ramasoobramanyan* (இராமசுப்பிரமணியன் - irámasuppiramaniyan, Tam.). From (ráma, san. the hero + subrahmanya, san. skanda the very pious god). Composite name. Hindoo 2nd or pers. name [peyar].——*Ramaunoojacharry* (रामानुजाचार्य - rámánujáchárya, San.). From (ráma, san. the hero + anuja, san. younger brother + âchárya, san. teacher). Otherwise Ramaunoojan. Veishnavite reformer near the end of the eleventh century. Ramaunoojan was born in Shreepermatore near Madras, and studied at Conjeeveram, where he taught his system of the Veishnava faith. His Tamul name was Yembramaunaur [q.v.]. He followed out the vishishtaudweitam development of philosophy, propounded and partially promulgated by the twelve alwars [q.v.] before his time, and engaging in public disputations in different places established and popularized this form of vedauntam [q.v.] more than any of his predecessors in the same school. Besides some original works on religion he wrote commentaries on Vyausa sootram or oottara mimaumsam [q.v.] and Bhagavat geeta [q.v.]; hence he is called Bhaushyacaur or commentary-maker, which in its short form of Bhaushyam, makes a common hindoo proper name [peyar]. As an ascetic he is known as Yatiraaz or king of Yaties [q.v.]. He is supposed to be an avatar [q.v.] of Sheshan or audisheshan [q.v.] and it is to be noted that Lutchmanan, rama's brother is also supposed to be sheshan [q.v.] incarnate. Cf, the title Ramaunoojan. The reformer's life is sketched in the foot-note on the History of Hindoo Religion at vol. I (76). His followers are called either Ramaunoojeeyans or Shreeveishnavas. For Ramanoojan's philosophy see Vishishtaudweitam; for the sect see Shreeveishnava [matam].——*Ramaunoojan* (రామానుజుడు - rámánujudu, Tel.; இராமாநுசன் - irámánusan, Tam.). From (ráma, san. the hero + anuja, san. younger brother). Lutchmanan, Rama's younger brother, Hindoo 2nd or pers. name [peyar].——*Ramaunoojeeyan* (రామా

జీయు - rámánujíya, obl., Tel.). Also called Shree veishnava. Followers of Ramaunoojacharry. See vol. I (74), (89).——*Ramauramy* (రామారామి - ramárami, Tel.). From (rámaráma, san. the word of salutation). Strictly means equality, implying that the two sides can meet on terms of salutation. An average [sarausaree].——*Ramavurma* (രാമവർമ്മ - rámavarmma, Mal.). From (ráma, san. the hero + varma, san. coat of mail); Rama who bears armour as king. Hindoo 2nd or pers. name [peyar].——*Ramayanam* (रामायण - rámáyana, San.). See sep. title.——*Ramayya* (రామయ్య - rámayya, Tel.). From (ráma, san. the hero + ayya, tel. master, titular affix). Hindoo 2nd or pers. name [peyar].——*Ramchendran* (रामचन्द्र - rámachandra, San.). From (ráma, san. the hero + chandra, san. moon). Moon-like Rama. Common in northern india. The second Rama [q.v.]. See vol. I (74), (79). Hindoo 2nd or pers. name [peyar].——*Ramchendrapooram* (రామచంద్రపురము - rámachandrapuramu, Tel.). See sep. title.——*Ramchendrayya* (இராமசந்திரய்யன் - irámasandirayyan, Tam.). Hindoo 2nd or pers. name.——*Ramdoss* (இராமதாசன் - irámathásan, Tam.). From (ráma, san. the hero + dása, san. servant), slave of rama. Hindoo 2nd or pers. name [peyar].——*Rameshwaram* (रामेश्वर - ráméshvara, San. rámesvarum *). From (ráma, san. the hero + íshvara, san. shiva, the lord); eeshvaran worshipped by second rama [q.v.], the older deity. Sanscrit name (dévanagara), meaning god + city. Tamul name (pámbandívu), meaning paumben island. Greek name for the promontory was κῶρυ, for the island ἀργάλος νῆσος. The bay between Point calimere and the island of Rameshwaram is called Rama's bow, and is the Sinus colchicus of the ancients. Each end is called Dhanooshcoty, the tip of the bow, or simply Coty. The most celebrated of the two was that at Rameshwaram, and this word became Greek κῶρυ. Cf. (kóti) and crore. Island, Town, Place of pilgrimage, Promontory; Madura dist., Ramnaud zemindarry; pop. 5,930; lat. 9° 18′; long. 79° 22′; from Dindigul E.S.E. 117 miles; from Kodaykarnal E.S.E. 141 miles; from Madras S.S.W. 270 miles; from Madura E.S.E. 92 miles; from Mantapam E.N.E. 12 miles; from Paumben E. 7 miles; from Ramnaud E. 33 miles. Rameshwaram is a low sandy island at the extremity of Adam's bridge extending east and west between Ceylon and the south-eastern coast of the peninsula at the entrance of Palk's passage, and forming the northern boundary of the Gulf of Manaar. The eastern half is merely a narrow strip of sand. About 14 miles length from south-east to north-west, and five in breadth. It is in a line with Manaar island with which it is united by a bank of sand and was probably once connected with the mainland. It is to their control of the passage from the mainland that the chiefs of Ramnaud owe their hereditary title of Saitoopaty [q.v.], or lord of the causeway. The island is to a great extent covered with babool [q.v.] trees. Cocoanut [q.v.] palms and a few gardens make up all the cultivation. The inhabitants are principally Bramins and their followers, who are supported by the profits derived from the temples. The great temple of Ramalingasawmy stands on rising ground in the northern part of the island. It is near the sacred Dhanooshcoty teertam on a spit of sand that runs out south-east of the island, and great wealth has been lavished on it by the Saitoopaty. Originally founded by Rama after invasion of Ceylon. Has two lingams [q.v.], one which Seetay made, and one which Hanooman [q.v.] brought from Mount keilausam [q.v.]. The temple buildings are surrounded by a high wall covering an area about 865 feet from east to west by 657 feet from north to south, height about 120 feet. There are unfinished gopoorams [q.v.], built wholly of stone from the base to the summit, on the north, south and east, and a single complete one on the west. The best and oldest portion is built of a dark and hard limestone [choonam cull], to which there is nothing similar in the rest of the building. The gateway on the west is 78 feet high and is elaborately carved with mythological figures, its form being trapezoid. The workmanship is massive and regular, and the architecture resembles the Egyptian style. The other three gopoorams are 19 feet high, composed of single upright stones, with others laid across at the top. The largest of these three is that on the east. It is not on the wall of the present outer enclosure, but on that of an inner one surrounding the second praucauram [q.v.]. Outside the main wall on the same side are two large porticos, one opposite this gopooram and leading up towards it, and the other to the south, leading into a subordinate gopooram [q.v.] in line with the last and surmounting the gateway in front of the goddess Amman [q.v.]. Inside the gateway is a colonnade, having a passage between a triple row of pillars to a square of about 600 feet, into which the sacred temples open. The colonnade runs along the four sides of the quadrangle. It measures from north to south 353 feet, and east to west 671 feet, by 17 feet in breadth. The ceiling is composed of large slabs of granite, supported by numerous carved granite [caroom cull] pillars, each 12 feet high, raised on each side on a platform 5 feet high. Most of the pillars are single blocks of stone, all brought from a distance of 40 miles. The corridors are the most celebrated feature of the temple. These extend to nearly 4,000 feet in length from 20 to 38 feet broad, and from the floor to the centre of the roof about 30 feet in height. Each pillar is compound, and highly elaborate in design. The impression produced by such a display of labor when extended to an immense length is unique. None of the European cathedrals are more than 500 feet, and even the nave of St. Peter's is only 600 feet from the door to the apse. Here the side corridors are 700 feet long and open into transverse galleries as rich in detail as themselves. These, with the varied devices and modes of lighting, produce an effect that is not equalled certainly anywhere in India. Unfortunately the whole has been so extensively whitewashed and painted that the general effect is altered, and much of the intrinsic sharpness of detail is destroyed. The art displayed is perhaps not so good as in some other temples. Much of the effect produced on the mind of the observer is due to the immensity of the labour employed, combined with a certain picturesqueness and mystery. Inside the great enclosure is third praucauram [q.v.], abutting on the east wall and measuring about 690 feet by 435. Like the entrance passage it has a corridor on a raised platform on each side of it and runs round the four sides of the rectangle, which it encloses. This praucauram alone is open to all castes. Within it, and nearer the east face than the west, is an area 386 feet from east to west by about 314 feet from north to south, also surrounded by a high wall enclosing the second praucauram. This praucauram is by no means so imposing as, though somewhat older than, the third. Within this again is the first praucauram, or inner enclosure, round the shrines of the god Ramalingasawmy and of his consort Parvatavardhiny amman, of Vishwanauta sawmy and Vishaulautchy amman, besides a number of smaller chapels and rooms. It is difficult to judge of the age of the temple because it is so injured by sea air, but it is probably older than the Seven pagodas [q.v.]. The principal shrines were built by Oodeiyaun saitoopaty, with the aid of a Ceylon prince styled Pararaja shekharan in A.D. 1414, the latter having had the stones hewn at Trincomalee and numbered on the spot ready to be put together. The north and south gopoorams were built by Keerana royer of the Deccan [q.v.] about 1420 A.D. The western gopooram and the outer surrounding walls are the work of Oodeyaun saitoopaty and a Comaty of Nagore, in 1434 A.D.; and statues of the merchant and his wife surmount the eastern wall. In 1450 additions were made to the inner buildings by a wealthy Hindoo from Madura, and others in 1560 by Chinna wodeyan saitoopaty cautta tevar, then a feudatory of Vishwanauta naickar of Madura, whose statue and that of his son Krishnappa were set up in front of the nundy [q.v.]. The southern half of the second praucauram was erected about 1650 by Tirmullay saitoopaty, whose statue and that of his son, Raghoonautan, stand by the side of the south entrance into the Amman temple, and are honored with garlands and an offering of betel-nut [q.v.] and flowers every Friday night when the image of the sawmy is brought to this place on its way to pulliyaray or bed in the Amman temple. Ragboonauta tirmullay saitoopaty also built the rest of the second praucauram. The great unfinished eastern gopooram is the work of Dalavoy saitoopaty, about 1640, who also built the Sabhanpaty [q.v.] shrine in the north-east corner of the third praucauram. Half a century later Hiranya garbhayaujee ravicoola vijaya raghoonauta saitoopaty, besides other buildings, erected the pulliyaray or bed room of the Amman temple, and the mantapam [q.v.] in front, in which are statues of himself and his brother Cadamba tevar. About 1740 the Saitoopaty began the third praucauram, setting up the entrances into it from the gopoorams on all four sides, and it was completed by Moottoo ramalinga saitoopaty, in 1769. The statues of the latter and of his two muntries [q.v.] Moottiroolappa pillay, son of Sowndra paundya pillay and Krishna iyengar, with members of his family, are conspicuous in the western entrance corridor. The temple is therefore not the work of one age, but extends over a period of 350 years, and has been erected and endowed almost exclusively by one family, the Saitoopaty chiefs of Ramnaud. It is one of the last great works of the Hindoos, and the latest addition to it is the finest of all. On a small hillock near Rameshwaram stands a peculiarly constructed mantapam [q.v.] of two storeys. It is here that Hanooman [q.v.] ascended in order to get a view of Lunka [q.v.]. South of the great temple is a fresh-water tank about three miles in circumference. The great pagoda [q.v.] is under the guardianship and management of a chief, styled Pundauram [q.v.], who must observe celibacy through life, and on his death is succeeded by his sister's son, or, should there not be any such, by the next eldest collateral male relative. The image of the deity is every morning drenched with water brought on the shoulders of fakeers [q.v.] from the Ganges, and poured over it, and which, having received additional sanctity by this rite, is sold to devotees at a high price. The temple, its ceremonies, and its attendant Bramins are maintained from the revenue of fifty-seven villages, yielding an annual income of about Rs. 40,000, granted by former Rajahs of the Ramnaud zemindarry. It is still visited daily by scores of pilgrims from all parts of India, who come through Ramnaud to the crossing, and at seasons by hundreds and thousands. More come from Nepaul and north of the Ganges than from the Tamul districts in the immediate vicinity, while the Deccan and Mysore contribute the majority. Veishnavites as well as Sheiveites congregate, but Sheiveites predominate. Many Teloogoo and Tamul astronomers, as Baulaudityacan and Mullicarjoonan, refer their computations to the meridian [raikhay] of Rameshwaram. See vol. I (7). There is a Tamul proverb :—
இராமேசுரத்துக்குப் போயும் சனீசுரன் தொலையவில்லை

—"though he went on a pilgrimage to rameshwaram, saturn "[shany] has not left him;" he is still unlucky.——*Rameshwaran* (रामेश्वर - ráméshvara, San.). From (ráma, san. the hero + íshvara, san. lord); shiva, the lord of rama. Name of the lingam [q.v.] at Rameshwaram.——*Ramnaud* (இராமநாதப்புரம் - irámanáthappuram, Tam.). See sep. title.——*Ramoolamma* (రాములమ్మ - rámulamma, Tel.). From (ráma, san. the hero + amma, tel. mother, titular affix). A village goddess [graumadevatay].——*Ramoonny* (രാമുണ്ണി - rámunni, Mal.). From (ráma, san. the hero + unni, mal. infant); rama, the darling. Hindoo 2nd or pers. name [peyar].——*Rampore* (రామపురం - rámapuram, Tel.). From (ráma, san. the hero + pura, san. town). Pass; Kurnool dist., Putticondah tal.; lat. 15° 19′; long. 78° 02′; from Kurnool S.S.W. 36 miles; from Putticondah E.S.E. 32 miles. Southernmost pass [ghaut] in Yerramalas between Putticondah talook and Bunganapully state. Used by carts carrying the produce of Coondair valley to Gooty railway station.——*Ramrauz* (రామరాజు - rámarádzu, Tel.). From (ráma, san. the hero + rájá, san. king).—"*a*" Family of hereditary Deshmookhs [q.v.] of Pulnaud.—"*b*" Same as Rama rajah above.—"*c*" One Ramrauz was local governor of the Jinjee country. Sold to the East india company the fort at Tegnapatam, since known as Fort saint david, in 1690. Fled to Sattaura on the capture of Jinjee by Zoolfacar khan [charitram]. See vol. I (169).——*Ramtil* (काळातीळ - kálátíla, Mahr.; رام تل - rámtil, Hind.; کالی تل - kálítil, Dec.; ಹುಚ್ಚೆಳ್ಳುಗಿಡ - huççellugida, Can.; వెర్రినూగు - verrinúgu, Tel.; கானெள் - kánel, Tam.). Title from hindostany. Mahr. from deccany. Hind. from (rám, hind. rama + til, hind. sesamum indicum, dec.). Dec. from (kálí, hind. black + til, hind. sesamum indicum, dec.). Can. from (huççu, can. madness + yellu, can. sesamum + gida, can. plant). Tel. from (verri, tel. wild + núgu, tel. gingelly plant, sesamum indicum, dec.). Tam. from (kán, tam. forest + el, tam. sesamum). Can. also (kádellu), meaning wild + sesamum; (kutrellu). Tel. also (gúréllu); (tilalu), meaning gingelly seed; (adavinuvvu), meaning jungle + gingelly plant; (kondanuvvu), meaning hill + gingelly plant; (valise); (ulisi). Tam. also (káttel), meaning forest + sesamum. Title otherwise Hill gingelly, Niger seed, Nook, Oil seed, Wild gingelly, Wild sesamum. Botanically Guizotia abyssinica, cass, compositæ [vricsham, 74]. Alias Anthemis mysorensis; Bidens ramtilla; Buphthalmum ramtilla; Guizotia oleifera; Helianthus oleifera; Heliopis platyglossa, werinnua; Jægeria abyssinica; Parthenium luteum; Polymnia abyssinica, frondosa; Ramtilla oleifera; Tetragonotheca abyssinica; Verbesina sativa. Ramtilla from hindostany. Werinnua from teloogoo. Annual, herbaceous, erect; leaves opposite, long lanceolate, coarsely serrated; peduncles elongated, sub-corymbose; flowers large, bright yellow. The achenes are of a greyish-black color, about $\frac{2}{10}$ of an inch long, somewhat angular from lateral compression, tapering towards the base, quite smooth, taste oily and nutty. Ramtil oil expressed from the large seeds is the common lamp-oil [q.v.] of upper india and is very cheap; it is sweet tasted, and used like gingelly-oil [gingelly] for culinary purposes, &c.; the cake [ponnauk] given to milk-cows; the oil mixes with colors as well as linseed [alsee] and dries without litharge [moordarsing]. No other common species here.——*Ramyajamautry* (रम्यजामातृ - ramyajámátri, San.). From (ramya, san. beautiful + jámátri, san. son-in-law). Another name of Manavaula maumoony [q.v.], the founder of the Tengalay [q.v.] sect. See vol. I (85).——*Raticauthalan* (இரதிகாதலன் - irathigáthalan, Tam.). From (rati, san. wife of cupid + káthalan, tam. husband). Manmatan [q.v.].——*Ratnagandhy* (रत्नगन्धि - ratnagandhi, San.). Means gem + fragrance; from showy flowers. Botanically the Poinciana genus, leguminosæ [vricsham, 48]. Trees; leaves twice-pinnate; flowers showy orange or yellowish. The species best known to the natives are:—elata [soonkeshwaram], regia [foreign tungaid].——*Ratnagherry* (இரத்தினகிரி - irattinagiri, Tam.). From (ratna, san. precious stone + giri, san. mountain); from the varied landscape. Hill; Trichinopoly dist., Coolitalay tal.; lat. 10° 53′; long. 78° 26′; height 1,179 feet; from Coolitalay S.S.W. 5 miles; from Trichinopoly W. 22 miles. A boss of gneiss, pear-shaped [amrood] and resting on small end. Within limits of Shivauyam village and close to road from Coolitalay to Manapauray. A flight of 952 steps leads to summit, which commands magnificent view. On summit is small Shiva temple.——*Ratnam* (रत्न - ratna, San.; جوهر - jauhar, Ar. and Dec.; گوهر - gauhar, Pers.; رتن - ratan, Hind.; ರತ್ನ - ratna, Can.; రత్నము - ratnamu, Tel.; രത്നം - ratnam, Mal.; மணி - mani, Tam.). San. from (ram, san. to please). Ar. from (jahr, ar. to become plain). Hind. from sanscrit. Tam. from (man, tam. excellence). Gem.—"*a*" The following is a key-list of the commonest gems of S. india:—Agate [akeek], Amber [karbah], Amethyst [martees], Ammonite [shalagram], Beryl [zabarjad], Bloodstone [hajrdam], Cambay pebble [q.v.], Carbuncle [shabcharaugh], Cat's eye [lahsanyah], Chalcedony [akeek i soofeed], Cinnamon stone [q.v.], Coral [moongah], Cornelian [akeek i soorkh], Corundum [q.v.], Crystal [spaticam], Diamond [vajram], Emerald [zamarrood], Garnet [tamrah], Gold stone [sang i sitaura], Jacinth [pudmaraugam], Jasper [yashab], Lapis lazuli [veidooryam], Mocha stone [akeek i bahree], Onyx [sang i soolimauny], Opal [csheera spaticam], Pearl [moty], Porphyry [sang i samauk], Ruby [laul], Sapphire [neelam], Sardonyx [akeek i siyah], Tamarind stone [q.v.], Topaz [pookhrauj], Turquoise [firozah].—"*b*" The following is the list reversed:—Akeek, agate; Akeek i bahree, mocha stone; Akeek i siyah, sardonyx; Akeek i soofeed, chalcedony; Akeek i soorkh, cornelian; Csheera spaticam, opal; Firozah, turquoise; Hajrdam, blood-stone; Karbah, amber; Lahsanyah, cat's eye; Laul, ruby; Martees, amethyst; Moongah, coral; Moty, pearl; Neelam, sapphire; Pookhrauj, topaz; Pudmaraugam, jacinth; Sang i samauk, porphyry; Sang i sitaura, gold stone; Sang i soolimauny, onyx; Shabcharaugh, carbuncle; Shalagram, ammonite; Spaticam, crystal; Tamrah, garnet; Vajram, diamond; Veidooryam, lapis lazuli; Yashab, jasper; Zabarjad, beryl; Zamarrood, emerald.—"*c*" Hindoo 2nd or pers. name. Suffix in names as Naugaratnam, Ramaratnam [peyar].——*Ratnamaulay* (रत्नमाला - ratnamálá, San.). From (ratna, san. gem + málá, san. necklace). Gem-necklace. Term of praise appended to titles of works.——*Ratnasabhaupaty* (இரத்தினசபாபதி - irattinasabáppathi, Tam.). From (ratna, san. gem + sabhá, san. assembly + pati, san. lord). Epithet of Shiva, as lord of ratnasabhay a sacred decorated hall in the temple of chidambaram. Hindoo 2nd or pers. name [canacasabhaupaty, peyar, sabhay].——*Ratnaucaram* (रत्नाकर - ratnákara, San.). From (ratna, san. gem + ákara, san. mine). Jewel mine. Title of various works, especially dictionaries [nigantoo].——*Ratnavailoo* (రత్నవేలు - ratnavélu, Tel.). From (ratna, san. gem + vélu, tam. familiar contraction of vélan, tam. skanda, the lance-bearer). Means scandan with the beautiful decorated spear. Hindoo 2nd or pers. name. Common among non-bramins [peyar].——*Raty* (रति - rati, San.; இரதி - irathi, Tam.). From (ram, san. to make happy). The shacty [q.v.] or wife of Manmatan [q.v.]. When Manmatan attacked Shiva [q.v.] doing penance [tapas], by shooting an arrow [cauma baunam], Shiva opened his frontlet eye and burnt the assailant to ashes [cauman pundigay]. Raty went to Shiva, who agreed to restore her husband to life with the proviso that he should be visible to her eyes alone. Compare the legend of Cupid and Psyche. Raticauthalan is manmatan, raty's husband; see sep. title.

RAMAH (రామ - ráma, *Tel.*). From (ram, san. to please) [ram]; from appearance. The genus Gobioides, gobiidæ, acanthopterygii, teleostei, pisces [matsyam, 23], of naturalists [jantoo]. Coasts, estuaries, and tidal rivers; frequent muddy localities and use their teeth as organs of attack or defence. The species best known to the natives are Crooked ramah, Eating ramah. Cf. also Black ramah which is another genus.——*Black ramah* (चांगल - chángala, Mahr.; నల్లరామ - nallaráma, Tel.; ପିତଲୁ - pitallu, Oor.). Title from dark dorsal bands. Mahr. from (changa, san. handsome). Tel. from (nalla, tel. black + ráma, tel. gobioides genus). Oor. from (pittala, san. brass); from brown spots. Apocryptes lanceolatus, gobiidæ, acanthopterygii, teleostei [matsyam, 23], of naturalists [jantoo]. Alias Apocryptes changua; Eleotris lanceolata; Gobius changua; Pseudapocryptes lanceolatus; Scartelaos calliurus. Changua from mahratta. Jaws of nearly equal length anteriorly; scales minute, becoming most distinct in posterior portion of body; colors dull greenish superiorly, with numerous fine brown spots and usually many dark bands descend from back towards abdomen; dorsals with several rows of fine spots; caudal barred in a few or many rows; sea; 8 inches in length. No other common species here.——*Crooked ramah* (గొగ్గిరామ - goggiráma, Tel.). Title from wavy motion of body. Tel. from (goggi, tel. irregular shaped + ráma, tel. fish, gobioides genus). Gobioides [ramah] cœculus, gobiidæ, acanthopterygii, teleostei [matsyam, 23], of naturalists. Alias Amblyopus cæculus; Cæpola cæcula. Body rounded, lower jaw the longer, with some small barbels on it; cleft of mouth oblique; scales absent; colors are mostly of leaden hue, becoming light on abdomen; vertical fins gray, central caudal rays black; pectorals and ventrals reddish, or they may be coppery color along back, shot with blue along sides, fins reddish except caudal which is deep brown with reddish outer edges; some are of general reddish brown color; exceedingly vicious, and when captured snaps at everything near it; should its tail be touched it springs round and anything it seizes it holds on to; sea, estuaries, tidal rivers and tanks along the coasts.——*Eating ramah* (ఆహారరామ - áhárarāma, Tel.). Title from use. Tel. from (áhára, san. food + ráma, tel. gobioides genus). Gobioides [ramah] anguillaris, gobiidæ, acanthopterygii, teleostei [matsyam, 23], of naturalists. Alias Amblyopus hermannianus; Gobioides anguliformis; Gobius anguillaris; Tænioides hermannii. Lower jaw the longer and anterior, with its cleft nearly vertical; scales absent; colors pinkish, caudal darkest in its centre; sea; nearly 15 inches long.

RAMALCOTTAH (راملکوٹ - rámalkot, *Hind.*; రామల్లకోట - rámallakóta, *Tel.* rámallakot *). From (ráyi, tel stone, here precious stone + mala, tel. hill + kóta, tel. fort) [ryo]. Otherwise Rolaconda of Tavernier.——**(1)** Talook, Kurnool district. Tahsildar's pay Rs. 200. Area 846 square miles. Population 100,595. Teloogoo is the vernacular but Hindostany is spoken by all Mahomedans and about $\frac{1}{4}$ Hindoos. W. centre of district. Bounded N. by Toongabudra, excepting near Kurnool, where five villages on the north side of the river; E. by Nundicotcore and Nundiaul talooks; and S. and W. by Putticondah talook. Includes Yerramala hills. In N.W soil is black. Towards S. from Taicore to Pyaupaly, soil is blended with reddish alluvial sandy soil, while in E. parts, which comprise a great portion of the flat-topped hills of the Yerramalas, the soil is generally red. The soil is generally not deep, and rocks are sometimes so near the surface that the land is hardly cultivable. The chief industry is weaving [nesavoo]. Cotton [q.v.] carpets [jamkhana], turbans [puggry] and woollen blankets [cumbly] are manufactured at Kurnool and silk [puttoo] cloths at Goodoor. Agriculture is chief occupation. Cotton [q.v.], indigo [q.v.], hides [chamrah], melons [oorvauroo], tobacco [pogauk], betel [q.v.] leaves, blankets [cumbly, jamkhana], mahomedan women's clothes called soosies [q.v.], turbans [q.v.], wheat [geung], gram [q.v.], pulses [dholl] and ghee [q.v.] are the chief articles of export. Talook is watered by Hindry and Toongabudra. Kurnool-Cuddapah irrigation canal irrigates eleven villages. Several streams of which Donnavaugoo is chief run from south and fall into Hindry. Some have been dammed. Camping grounds:—Kurnool, Taicore, Veldoorty, and Dhone on the Kurnool-Gooty road; Narnoor on the Nundiaul road; and Naugalaupooram on the Bellary road. Places of archæological interest:—Anoogonda, Bollavaram, Caloogotla, Culloor, Gorintla, Johaurapooram, Kurnool, Lanja polore, Narnoor, Nauyacull, Poollagoommy, Pooslore, Punchalingaula, Ramalcottah, Taducanapulley, Veldoorty. Principal trig. stations:—Cautamrauz, Coilacondah, Donacondah, Juggernautghaut. The leading places, &c., in the talook are the following.——*Auiadoddicondah* (ఆలదొడ్డికొండ - áládoddikonda, Tel.). From (ávu, tel. cow + doddi, tel. pound + konda, tel. hill). Hill; lat. 15° 27′; long. 78° 00′; from Kurnool S.S.W. 27 miles.——*Candenarole* (కందనవోలు - kandenavólu, Tel.). See Kurnool.——*Cautamrauz* (కాటమరాజు - kátamarádzu, Tel.). Means proper name. Trig. station; lat. 15° 25′ 23·13″; long. 78° 01′ 01·92″; height 2,053 feet; from Caumagaunicoontla E. 4 miles; from Kurnool S.S.W. 28 miles.——*Coilacondah* (కోయిలకొండ - kóyilakonda, Tel.). From (kóyila, tel. temple + konda, tel. hill). Trig. station; lat. 15° 19′ 16·25″; long. 77° 39′ 03·85″; height 1,947 feet; from Chityaula S.W. 15 miles; from Kurnool S.W. 46 miles.——*Donacondah* (దోనకొండ - dónakonda, Tel.). From (dóne, tel. boat + konda, tel. hill). Trig. station; lat. 15° 22′ 51·50″; long. 77° 53′ 40·60″; height 2,035 feet; from Dhone S.W. 2 miles; from Kurnool S.S.W. 34 miles.——*Dronauchellam* (ద్రోణాచలం - drónáchalam, Tel.). From (dróna, san. a wooden trough + achala, san. mountain). Means situated in hollow formed by surrounding hills. Village, Railway station; pop. 1,917; acres 13,071; lat. 15° 24′; long. 77° 55′; height 2,035 feet; from Kurnool S.S.W. 32 miles. On the Kurnool-Gooty road. Travellers' bungalow [q.v.]. A spring channel [q.v.] runs through village.——*Ganighaut* (గనిగట్టు - ganigattu, Tel.). From (gani, tel. a mine + gattu, tel. hill). Hill; lat. 15° 34′; long. 78° 04′; from Kurnool S. 18 miles. Diamond [vajram] mines worked in old days.——*Goodoor* (గూడూరు - gúdóru, Tel.). From (gúdu, tel. hovel + úru, tel. village). Village; pop. 5,063; acres 13,413; lat. 15° 46′; long. 77° 51′; from Kurnool W.S.W. 16¾ miles. Former head-quarters of talook. Cotton cloths and silk-weaving. Cloths exported to Mysore and S. districts.——*Gorintla* (గోరింట్ల - górintla, Tel.). From (górinta, tel. the nail dye plant, lawsonia alba, lamk.). Village; pop. 1,454; acres 7,768; lat. 15° 38′; long. 77° 53′; from Kurnool S.W. 20 miles. Temple of Maudhavasawmy with inscription of Vijianugger dynasty [raj], recording grant by Runga roya. Shiva temple with inscription.——*Hindry* (హింద్రి - hindri, * Tel.). See sep. title.——*Juggernautghaut* (జగన్నాథగట్టు - jagannát'haghattu, Tel.). From (jagannát'ha, san. lord of the universe + gattu, tel. hill). Hill; lat. 15° 46′; long. 78° 04′; height 1,452 feet; from Kurnool S.S.W. 5 miles. Spur of the Yerramalas. Vishnoo temple with annual festival. Trig. station in lat. 15° 45′ 51·97″; long. 78° 04′ 30·01″; height 1,452 feet; from Dinney devarapaud S. 1 mile; from Kurnool S.S.W. 5 miles.——*Kurnool* (కర్నూలు - karnúlu, Tel.). See sep. title.——*Ladagherry* (లద్దగిరి - laddagiri, Tel.). From (laddi, tel. dung of elephants and horses + giri, tel. hill). Village; pop. 2,068; acres 8,294; lat. 15° 38′; long. 77° 56′; from Kurnool S.W. 17 miles. On the Hindry.——*Malacaupore* (మలకాపురం - malakápuram, Tel.). From (mala, tel. mountain + kápuramu, tel. residence). Village, Railway station; pop. 1,665; acres 7,089; lat. 15° 81′; long. 78° 02′; from Kurnool S. 33 miles.——*Narnoor* (నర్నూరు - narnúru, Tel.). From (nari, can fox + úru, can. village). Village; pop. 2,518; acres 10,575; lat. 15 43′; long. 78° 08′; from Kurnool S.S.E. 8 miles. On a rock, on the Cuddapah road. Temple of Veerabhadran [q.v.]. Large ancient temple of Maudhavasawmy, well sculptured. Good limestone [choonam cull] as well as nodular kankar [q.v.]; also yellow ohundoo or magnesia [caunta munn] used for plastering walls.——*Polecull* (పోలేకల్లు - pólékallu, Tel.). From (póli, tel. martin + kallu, tel. rock). Village; pop. 2,394; acres 7,459; lat. 15° 50′; long. 77° 47′; from Kurnool W. 21 miles. Black abruck [q.v.].——*Pyaulacoorty* (ప్యాలకుర్తి - pyálakurti, Tel.). From (peyya, tel. calf + kurti, tel. place). Village; pop. 1,216; acres 7,151; lat. 15° 44′; long. 77° 51′; from Kurnool W.S.W. 18 miles. Quarry of black abruck [q.v.]. Old temple to Chennakeshwarasawmy. Inhabited by Gollas [q.v.] only. They say if Boya [q.v.] settle here they would die.——*Ramalcottah* (రామల్లకోట - rámallukóta, Tel.). See below.——*Sanoogondla* (చన్నుగొండ్ల - tsanugondla, Tel.). From (tsannu, tel. breast + konda, tel. hill). Village; pop. 1,334; acres 5,536; lat. 15° 44′; long. 77° 49′; from Kurnool W.S.W. 19 miles. Inscriptions.——*Soonkesala* (సుంకేసల - sunkésala, Tel.). See sep. title.——*Taicore* (టేకూరు - tékúru, Tel.). From (téku, tel. teak wood, tectona grandis, linn. + úru, tel. village). Village; pop. 747; acres 3,135; lat. 15° 48′; long. 78° 02′; from Kurnool S.SW. 9 miles. On the Gooty road. Travellers' bungalow [q.v.].——*Toongabudra* (తుంగభద్ర - tungabhadra, Tel.). See sep. title.——*Veeranna ghaut* (వీరన్నగట్టు - vírannaghattu, Tel.). From (víranna, tel. the god virabhadra + gattu, tel. hill). Sanscrit name (víra-bhadráchala), meaning same. Village, Hill; Temple of Veerabhadra sawmy.——*Veldoorty* (వెలుదుర్తి - veludurti, Tel. veldurti *). From (velugu, tel. hedge + durti, tel. village). Village; pop. 2,587; acres 12,109; lat. 15° 33′; long. 77° 59′; from Kurnool S.S.W. 21 miles. On Kurnool-Gooty road. Temple of Ramasawmy. Shiva temple on hill. Travellers' bungalow [q.v.]. Tepid spring.——*Yerramala* (ఎర్రమల - erramala, Tel.). See sep. title.——(2) Village; pop. 1,424; acres 3,005; lat. 15° 35′; long. 78° 02′; from Cumbum W. 73 miles; from Kurnool S. 18 miles; from Madras N.W. 228 miles; from Nundiaul W.N.W. 33 miles; from Pyaupaly N.E. 29 miles. Former head-quarters of talook. Vencateshwarasawmy temple with elaborately carved pillars built by Goozeratty [q.v.] diamond [vajram] merchants. Diamond-field near the town.

RAMAYANAM (रामायण - rámáyana, *San.*). From (ráma, san. the god + ayana, san. going) [ram]. Many poems bearing this name all relating to same hero; but most famous is that of Valmeeky [q.v.]. First and greatest epic of the Hindoos. Prior to Mahabhaurat [q.v.]. Not committed to writing till long after original composition. In the 4th chapter of the 1st book there is special reference to the reciters [cooshan, lavan], the Greek ῥαψῳδοί. Ramayanam is the legend of the solar race [aryan, vamsham] and Rama may be regarded as the first real Cshatriya [q.v.] hero of the post-vedic age. Dasharatan, king of Ayodhyay [cosalam], had four sons, Rama [q.v.] now worshipped as an incarnation [avatar] of Vishnoo [q.v.], Lutchmanan [q.v.], Bharatan [q.v.] and Shatroognan [q.v.]. The mother of Bharatan was Keikeyee. Soomitray was mother of Lutchmanan and Shatroognan. Cowsalyay was mother of Rama. Rama was married to Seetay, daughter of Janacan [q.v.], king of Mitilay or Tirhoot; and by the voice of the people was designated his father's coadjutor [yoova rajah]. Keikeyee, to whom the king had promised whatever she should ask, demanded the banishment of Rama and the appointment of her son Bharatan. Rama accordingly departed into exile, attended by Seetay and Lutchmanan. The wanderers, after traversing the districts around the Jumna and the Ganges, at length reached the great forest of Dandacam [q.v.] to the south. Dasharatan now died, worn out with grief, and Bharatan refusing to supplant Rama, the shoe of the latter was placed on the vacant throne. The exiles visited Agastyan [q.v.], the mighty rishy [q.v.], and Rama received from him the bow and arrows of magical power. Proceeding southward, they met with raucshasans [q.v.], incarnate demons of huge size. One of this race, called Ravanan [q.v.], was king of Ceylon at the time, and he carried off Seetay to his palace in that island. Rama, after destroying an army of fourteen thousand raucshasans, hastened to Ceylon to recover his wife. His allies were the monkeys [bandar], of whom an innumerable host accompanied him. Soogreevan [q.v.], was the monkey-king, whose capital [kishkindyay] was on the site where Vijianugger [humpy, vijianugger] afterwards stood; and the famous Hanooman [q.v.] was the monkey general. This latter passed over to Ceylon in search of Seetay and set the island on fire. In extinguishing the flames he blackened his face; but Seetay promised that on his return he should not be singular on that account, as he should find all his race with black faces; hence the dark color of the Dravidians. A bridge [saitoo] was then constructed from the mainland to Ceylon. This was at Ramnaud, the zemindar of which claims the title of Saitoopaty [q.v.], or guardian of the bridge. Ravanan was slain, Seetay was freed, her purity was ascertained by an ordeal of fire, the whole party returned in triumph to Ayodhyay the fourteen appointed years of exile being accomplished, and Rama ascended his ancestral throne. The Ceylon portion of the Ramayanam is almost certainly a north asian or european legend transposed. The two vulture [gidh] kings, Sampauty [q.v.] and Jatauyoo [q.v.], recall to mind the winged sons of Oreithyia in the Argonautic expedition; they watch over Seetay, and, when she is carried off by the demon king Ravanan, Jatauyoo throws himself in the path of the ravisher, and endeavours to defeat his purpose, but is slain in the struggle. As Laomedon drew a curse upon Ilium when he oppressed the gods and used threats to Apollo and Poseidon, so the behaviour of Ravanan the demon-king, who had enslaved gods and men and was ever boasting of his power, brought on his city Lunka [q.v.] the wrath of the deities. The oldest commentary on the Ramayanam known is the Catacateecay; so called after the clearing-nut [q.v.], for reasons given by the author that 'the ambrosia of 'the holy pool of the ramayanam had been made muddy 'by the dust of unsuitable commentaries.' The Tamul version of Ramayanam, reduced to half the size of the original by the poet Cumban [q.v.], is a work of great poetic merit, and without doubt the most popular book in S. india, notwithstanding that Sheivism predominates here. It is an imitation rather than a translation. The Chintanmany [q.v.] alone can rival it. It is written in a metre called the Vroottam [q.v.]. It is sung in every Tamul village, in bazaars and houses, on festive occasions, by wandering Cavy royans [q.v.], native minstrels. It is the folk-song of Southern india, but it is not intelligible to ordinary people, and a running comment is kept up by the singer or an assistant. The following is a specimen :— *தள்ளரும்பரந்தாங்கிய வொட்டகந் தெள்ளுதண் கரும்பி யாவையுந்தின்கில உள்ளமென்னத்தம் வாயுமுலர்ந்தன கள்ளுண்பார் கனிற்கைப்பனதேடிய*—"the camels [ottagam] that carried burdens difficult to move, refused to eat "the pure and cool sugar-cane [q.v.]; but their mouths and "stomachs being parched up, sought for bitter things like men "who drink intoxicating liquors." There is a Tamul proverb :— *இராமுழுதும் ராமாயணம் கேட்டுச் சீதைக்கு ராமன் என்ன என்ற கதை*—"the story of one who having listened "to the reading of the ramayanam a whole night, asked what "relationship existed between seetay and rama." There is a Teloogoo translation, the Dwipada ramayanam, usually called the Runganauta ramayanam by Cona boodharauz, son of Cona vittala bhoopaty. The Molla ramayanam again is an imitation of Valmeeky, written by Molla [q.v.], the daughter of a Nellore potter. It is called the Niroshtam or non-labial Ramayanam, a feat of ingenuity, without using (p, p'h, b, bh, m) a single labial letter [varnamaulay]. Besides the ancient Ramayanam, there is another popular work of comparative modern times called the Adhyautma ramayanam. The authorship of it is ascribed to Vyausan [q.v.], but it is generally considered to be a part of the Bramhaunda pooraunam [q.v.]. It is a sort of spiritualised version of the poem, in which Rama is depicted as a saviour and deliverer, as a god rather than a man. It is divided into seven books, which bear the same names as those of the original poem, but it is not so long. There is also an Oottara ramayanam, relating a previous transmigration [samsauram]. Valmeeky's ramayanam is divided into seven Caundams [q.v.] and contains about 24,000 shlocams [q.v.] thus.—"*a*" *Baula caundam* (बालकाण्ड - bálakánda, San.). From (bála, san. boy + kánda, san. section). The boyhood of Rama.—"*b*" *Ayodhya caundam* (अयोध्याकाण्ड - ayódhyákánda, San.). From (ayódhyá, san. the country, so called). The scenes at Ayodhyay and the banishment of Rama by his father, King Dasharatan.—"*c*" *Aranya caundam* (अरण्यकाण्ड - aranyakánda, San.). From (aranya, san. forest). Forest section. Rama's life in the forest and the kidnapping of Seetay by Ravanan.—"*d*" *Kishkindya caundam* (किष्किन्ध्याकाण्ड - kishkindhyákánda, San.). From (kishkindhyá, san. place, so called). Rama's residence at Kishkindyay [humpy], the capital of his monkey ally, King Soogreevan.—"*e*" *Soondra caundam* (सुन्दरकाण्ड - sundarakánda, San.). From (sundara, san. beautiful). Beautiful section. The marvellous passage of the straits by Rama and his allies and their arrival in Ceylon.—"*f*" *Yooddha caundam* (युद्धकाण्ड - yuddhakánda, San.). From (yuddha, san. war). War section. The war with Ravanan, his defeat and death, the recovery of Seetay, the return to Ayodhyay, and the coronation of Rama. This is sometimes called the Lunka or Ceylon caundam.—"*g*" *Oottara caundam* (उत्तरकाण्ड - uttarakánda, San.). From (uttara, san. later). Later section. Rama's life in Ayodhyay, his banishment of Seetay, the birth of his two sons [cooshan, lavan], his recognition of them and of the innocence of his wife, their reunion, her death, and his translation to heaven.

RAMBHAY (रम्भा - rambhá, *San.*). From (rabh, san. to embrace). A damsel in Indran's paradise [swargam]; the Venus of this mythology. Also a plantain [q.v.]; also a bamboo [q.v.]. ——*Rambha** (రంభ - rambha, Tel.). Village; Ganjam dist., Biridy zemindarry; pop. 3,508; lat. 19° 31′; long. 85° 08′; from Chetterpore N.N.E. 13 miles; from Russellcondah E.S.E. 44 miles. Picturesquely situated at southern extremity of Chilka lake, of which it is principal port. The scenery is Italian in character. On border of lake is a large house built by a former Collector in 1792. Since purchased by Aska sugar factory. Trig. station, Biridy zemindarry; lat. 19° 30′ 59·98″; long. 85° 09′ 35·02″; height 514 feet; from Berhampore E.N.E. 26 miles; from Chetterpore N.N.E. 13 miles; on a point in the Chilka lake.——*Rumpa* (రంప - rampa, Tel.). From (rambha, san. bamboo, bambusa arundinacea, willd.).—"*a*" Division, Godavery. Area 821 square miles. Hill division on north bank of Godavery, constituting a portion of the Agency tract of the district. Lat. 17° 18′ to 17° 52′ N., long. 81° 34′ to 82° 05′ E. Extends from about 20 miles north of Rajahmundry almost to the Sillair river, which forms the southern boundary of Jeypore. Bounded :—west by Rekapully talook; east and north by Golcondah talook, Vizagapatam; south by Rajahmundry talook. Very thinly populated. Yields no revenue to Government. Originally granted to the mansabdar [q.v.] as a jagheer [q.v.] for the maintenance of a force of peons [q.v.]. When these were disbanded he was ordered to pay their annual cost to government. Disturbances broke out in 1858, and lasted until 1862. A police force was in consequence recruited from the hillmen. In 1879 another rising again involved the employment of troops. It lasted until December 1880, when Chundrayya the rebel leader was killed, the rebels dispersed, and the mansabdar deported to Gopalpore as a State prisoner, his mansabdarry tenure being cancelled. A fresh settlement has been made with the mittahdars [q.v.], who held groups of villages on condition of paying a quit-rent [jody] to government, and of assisting to preserve peace. The Deputy tahsildar of Chotapully has charge of Rumpa under the Sub-collector, and is also invested with a limited civil jurisdiction. Police forces are maintained at Chodavaram and Kotah. Both stations are stockaded. The country presents a succession of hills from two to four thousand feet high, covered with dense jungle, and separated by valleys. The highest peak is Daumcondah, 4,478 feet above sea-level. There is a good road from Rajahmundry to Chodavaram, 33 miles; a rough road, made by the Madras sappers during the Rumpa revolt, from Chodavaram to Kotah, 14 miles; and a third from Chodavaram to Mauraidpully, 14 miles. The rest are jungle tracts. A passable road, two miles long, connects Chodavaram with the village of Rumpa. The hills are infested with tigers [pooly], leopards [kerkal], bears [ricsham], bison [gowr], and wolves [konye]. The climate is very cold in the winter months. Fever is common, and malaria is prevalent throughout the year. The inhabitants are chiefly Khonds [q.v.] and Reddies [q.v.]. Their bamboo [q.v.] huts are stockaded to keep out wild beasts. Products are bamboos [q.v.] and tamarinds [q.v.], which grow to an enormous size. Cultivation is principally of the nomadic kind locally termed Paidoo, in which the forest is burned down and the seed sown among the ashes [coomry]. A little tobacco [pogauk] is grown to satisfy local wants.—"*b*" Village; Godavery dist., Rumpa division; lat. 17° 27′; long. 81° 49′; from Cocanada N.W. 45 miles; from Coonavaram E.S.E. 35 miles; from Ellore N.E. 68 miles; from Madras N.N.E. 316 miles; from Narsapore N.N.E. 70 miles; from Rajahmundry N. 32 miles.

RAMBIYA (رمبيا - rámbiya, *Malay*). Same as Sago.

RAMBOOTAN (رمبوتن - rambutan, *Malay*). Title from (rambut, malay, hair), from shaggy covering of fruit. Title otherwise Rampostan. Botanically Nephelium lappaceum, linn., sapindaceæ [vricsham, 43]. Lofty tree; leaves 3–18 inches; leaflets 2–9 by 1–4 inches, shining and dark green above, paler and marked with sub-parallel lateral veins beneath; petioles $\frac{1}{12}$–$\frac{3}{8}$ inches; branches of the panicle spreading; flowers fascicled, pubescent, $\frac{1}{12}$–$\frac{1}{10}$ inches diameter; calyx campanulate, at length patent; stamens five to eight, exserted; filaments pubescent, especially towards base; style deeply two to three-lobed; lobes recurving; fruit lobes $\frac{1}{2}$–2 inches long, red yellowish orange or nearly black, setæ subulate; aril transparent, milky, fleshy, edible. The fruit is oval, red, covered with long, soft, fleshy spines; introduced into gardens from china and straits; nearly allied to the Litchy [q.v.] and Longan [q.v.].

RAMCHENDRAPOORAM (రామచంద్రపురము - rámachandrapuramu, *Tel.* rámachandrapuram *). From (rámachandra, san. proper name + pura, san. town) [ram].——**(1)** Talook, Godavery district. Tahsildar's pay Rs. 250. Area 400 square miles. Population 261,194. Language Teloogoo. Centre of inland district. Bounded :—south and east by the Gowtamy branch of the Godavery, north by Peddapore talook and Cocanada division, and west by Rajahmundry talook. It is a plain talook, mostly intersected by canals. Is productive and healthy, but in the cold season feverish, being almost entirely under water. The Gowtamy branch of the Godavery flows to the south and east. In it there are several islands or Lunkas [q.v.], formed by the accumulation of sand [manal] and alluvium [adaimunn, vandalmunn] brought down by the freshes. These Lunkas are continually changing, some years being fertilized anew by the Godavery freshes, but sometimes completely washed away, covered with sand, and thus rendered unfit for cultivation. Soil alluvial. Trade is chiefly in paddy [q.v.] grain, oil-seeds [yennay], jaggery [q.v.] and tobacco [pogauk], and in cloths manufactured in the talook. Nearly half of the products is consumed in the talook, and the rest is exported. Six anicut [q.v.] main canals run through in various directions; Cocanada, Coringa bank, Inzaram, Mundapett and Samulcottah. These are used both for irrigation and navigation. Numerous minor irrigation channels [q.v.], branches of the main. Zemindarries :—Capileshwarapooram, Goodigalla bhaugam, Paunangipully Veeravallipollem, Vegayammapett, Vella. Places of archæological interest :—Bickavole, Cotipully, Cowzalore, Draucsharaumam, Mautsavaram, Someshwaram, Vegayammapett. The leading places, &c., in the talook are the following.——*Alamore* (ఆలమూరు - álamúru, Tel.). See sep. title.——*Anaparty* (అనపర్తి - anaparti, Tel.). From (ana, tel. bank + parti, tel. village). Village; pop. 4,088; acres 4,477; lat. 16° 55′; long. 82° 00′; from Cocanada W. 8 miles; from Ramchendrapooram N.N.W. 18 miles. Between Cocanada and Samulcottah canals. Jaggery [q.v.] and grain [paddy].——*Artamore* (అర్తమూరు - artamúru, Tel.). From (art'ha, san. wealth + úru, tel. village). Village; pop. 3,110; acres 1,641; lat. 16° 53′; long. 81° 58′; from Cocanada W.S.W. 20 miles; from Ramchendrapooram N.W. 7 miles. The Vautaupy and Ilvalan [kankar] legend is found here [ippanapaud, taupeshwaram]. ——*Bickavole* (బిక్కవోలు - bikkavólu, Tel.). From (bikki, tel. walnut, gardenia latifolia, ait. + prólu, tel. town). Tel. also (birudánkaráyapuramu), meaning birdaunca roya, a king + town. Village; pop. 3,699; acres 4,841; lat. 16° 57′; long. 82° 05′; from Cocanada W. 12 miles; from Ramchendrapooram N. 9 miles. The earlier Chalookya [q.v.] kings resided here. Extensive ruins. Temple of Golingeshwaran and deserted Shiva temple.——*Capileshwarapooram* (కపిలేశ్వరపురము - kapiléshvarapuramu, Tel.). From (kapiléshvara, san. shiva, the lord of kapila + pura, san. town). Zemindarry, Village; pop. 5,590; acres 6,311; lat. 16° 44′ N.; long. 81° 57′ E.; from Cocanada S.W. 26 miles; from Ramchendrapooram S.W. 10 miles. Peshcush Rs. 8,742. On the Godavery. Originally the monastery of Capilamahamoony [capilau], who built a temple for Shiva.——*Chennore* (చెన్నూరు - chennúru, Tel.). From (chennu, tel. beauty + úru, tel. village). Zemindarry, Village; pop. 2,540; acres 3,594; lat. of village 16° 49′; long. 82° 2′; from Cocanada W.S.W. 18 miles; from Ramchendrapooram W.S.W. 3 miles. On the route from Rajahmundry to Coringa.——*Cotipully* (కోటిపల్లి - kótipalli, Tel.). See sep. title.——*Cowzalore* (కౌజులూరు - kádzulúru, Tel.). From (kauzu, tel. partridge + úru, tel. village). Village; pop. 2,948; acres 3,372; lat. 16° 47′; long. 82° 13′; from Cocanada S.S.W. 12 miles; from Ramchendrapooram E.S.E. 10 miles. Two Jeina [q.v.] statues.——*Draucsharaumam* (ద్రాక్షారామము - drúksharámamu, Tel. drákshárámam*). From (daksha, san. a proper name + aráma, san. garden). Sanscrit name (daksharáma), meaning same. Otherwise Dracharam by corruption. Dacsha prajaupaty [dacshan], one of the nine Bramhas [q.v.], performed a yanyam [q.v.] here. Town; pop. 3,103; acres 1,166; lat. 16° 47′; long. 82° 06′; from Cocanada S.W. 17 miles; from Ramchendrapooram S.E. 4 miles. Former head-quarters of the talook. Sacred place with large temple of Bheemeshwaran [lingam]. Two carved Dutch tombs, at a place which still goes by the name of Olandoo dibba or Holland mound. Large market on Monday.——*Godavery* (గోదావరి - gódávari, Tel.). See sep. title.——*Gollalamaumidauda* (గొల్లలమామిడాడ - gollalamámidáda, Tel.). From (golla, tel. shepherd + mámidi, tel. mango tree, mangifera indica, linn. + váda, tel. village). Village; pop. 4,719; acres 1,927; lat. 16° 56′; long. 82° 07′; from Cocanada W. 11 miles; from Ramchendrapooram N.N.E. 8 miles. Delta [conamoogam] village; jaggery [q.v.], tobacco [pogauk] and rice [q.v.]; market on Saturday.——*Gollapollem* (గొల్లపాలెము - gollapálemu, Tel.). From (golla, tel. shepherd + pálemu, tel. fortified village). Village; pop. 1,505; acres 985; lat. 16° 51′; long. 82° 13′; from Cocanada S.S.W. 8 miles; from Ramchendrapooram E. 10 miles. In 1787 in possession of the Dutch. Noted for dyeing [shauyam] of cloths.——*Goodiyalla bhaugam* (గుడిగడ్డభాగము - gudigadlabhágamu, Tel.). From (gudi, tel. temple + gadda, tel. mound + bhága, san. portion). Zemindarry, Village; pop. 155; lat. of village 16° 45′; long. 82° 08′; from Cocanada S.S.W. 16 miles; from Ramchendrapooram S.E. 8 miles. Peshcush Rs. 57.——*Ippanapaud* (ఇప్పనపాడు - ippanapádu, Tel.). From (ippa, tel. tree, bassia longifolia, linn. + pádu, tel. village). Sanscrit name (ilvalapura), meaning ilvalan, the giant + town [artamore, kankar, taupeshwaram]. Village; pop. 1,190; acres 594; lat. 16° 54′; long. 81° 58′; from Cocanada W.S.W. 21 miles; from Ramchendrapooram N.W. 8 miles. Delta village.——*Masakapully* (మసకపల్లి - masakapalli, Tel.). From (maskara, san. hollow bamboo + palli, tel. village). Sanscrit name (maskaríkshétra), meaning bramin mendicant + place. Village; pop. 2,066; acres 1,506; lat. 16° 42′; long. 82° 08′; from Cocanada S.S.W. 18 miles; from Ramchendrapooram S.S.E. 10 miles. Northern side of the bank canal.——*Mautsavaram* (మాచవరం - mátsavaram, Tel.). From (mátsanna, tel. proper name + pura, san. town). Village; pop. 2,349; acres 1,756; lat. 16° 50′; long. 82° 01′; from Cocanada W.S.W. 19 miles; from Ramchendrapooram W.N.W. 4 miles. Two Jeina [q.v.] statues in a tank west of the village. ——*Mundapett* (మండపేట - mandapéta, Tel.). See sep. title. ——*Poottacondah* (పుట్టకొండ - puttakonda, Tel.). From (putta, tel. ant-hill + konda, tel. hill). Sanscrit name (valmíkyáshrama), meaning valmeeky, the sage + hermitage. An agrahauram [q.v.]; pop. 1,074; acres 383; lat. 16° 55′; long. 82° 08′; from Cocanada W.S.W. 9 miles; from Ramchendrapooram N.E. 8 miles. A great ant-hill here grew up on Valmeeky [q.v.], author of Ramayanam [q.v.], when he was in deep meditation for ages. ——*Ramchendrapooram* (రామచంద్రపురము - rámachandrapuramu, Tel.). See below.——*Someshwaram* (సోమేశ్వరము - sóméshvaramu, Tel.). From (sóma, san. the moon + íshvara, san. lord), from temple of shiva, the moon-lord. Village; pop. 2,497; acres 1,963; lat. 16° 51′; long. 82° 01′; from Cocanada W.S.W. 18 miles; from Ramchendrapooram N.W. 4 miles. Two old temples. ——*Taupeshwaram* (తాపేశ్వరము - tápéshvaramu, Tel.). From (tápa, san. torment + íshvara, san. lord). Sanscrit name (vátápéshvara), meaning vautaupy, the giant + shiva, the lord; place of Shiva as worshipped by Vautaupy [artamore, kankar, ippanapaud]. Village; pop. 2,852; acres 1,569; lat. 16° 53′; long. 81° 58′; from Cocanada W.S.W. 21 miles; from Ramchendrapooram N.W. 8 miles. Delta village; jaggery [q.v.] and grain [dhaunyam, paddy].——*Tekky* (తేకి - téki, Tel.). From (tenki, tel. abode), meaning hermit abode. Village; pop. 2,496; acres 2,557; lat. 16° 45′; long. 81° 59′; from Cocanada S.W. 23 miles; from Ramchendrapooram S.W. 7 miles. Delta village. ——*Veeravallipollem* (వీరవల్లిపాలెము - víravallipálemu, Tel.). From (víravalli, tel. the heroic goddess + pálemu, tel. fortified village). Zemindarry, Village; pop. 2,091; acres 3,229; lat. of village 16° 42′; long. 82° 02′; from Cocanada S.W. 23 miles; from Ramchendrapooram S.S.W. 9 miles. Peshcush Rs. 3,534. ——*Vegayammapett* (వేగాయమ్మపేట - végáyammapéta, Tel. végayammapet*). From (végáyamma, tel. proper name + péta, tel. suburb). Tel. also (doddammapéta), meaning the great queen + suburb. Zemindarry, Village; pop. 1,702; acres 1,456; lat. of village 16° 46′; long. 82° 08′; from Cocanada S.W. 16 miles; from Ramchendrapooram S.E. 6 miles. Peshcush Rs. 8,234. Named after Vegayammah, relative of a former zemindar. West near a shrine of a village goddess, is a Jeina [q.v.] statue.——*Vella* (వెల్ల - vella, Tel.). Means white. Zemindarry, Village; pop. 3,431; acres 1,712; lat. of village 16° 49′; long. 82° 06′; from Cocanada S.W. 14 miles; from Ramchendrapooram E.S.E. 3 miles. Peshcush Rs. 1,240.——*Yedida* (ఏడిద - yédida, Tel.). From (édu, tel. seven). Literally seven villages. Sanscrit name (sangaméshvara), meaning junction + lord. Village; pop. 3,676; acres 5,391; lat. 16° 51′; long. 81° 55′; from Cocanada W.S.W. 24 miles; from Ramchendrapooram W.N.W. 9 miles. Composed of the seven villages:—Bademiyapaud, Canoopurtipaud, Juggernautpore, Narsimharajpore, Pencoolapaud, Savaram, Seetanagaram. Delta village. A mile distant are three temples to Shiva and Vishnoo. Festival at Shivarautry pundigay, 6a]. People bathe in the drainage channel, originally old Toolyabhauga, a branch of the Godavery.——(2) Village, Talook head-quarters; Godavery dist., Ramchendrapooram tal.; pop. 3,622; acres 2,226; lat. 16° 50′; long. 82° 04′; from Cocanada W. 16 miles; from Coonavaram S.E. 17 miles; from Ellore E.N.E. 60 miles; from Madras N.N.E. 280 miles; from Narsapore N.E. 34 miles; from Rajahmundry E. 20 miles. Ancient zemindarry bought in by Government for arrears of revenue. Old fort.

RAMEE (اُتنگن - utangan, *Hind.*). Malay archipelago name for China grass.

RAMNAUD (இராமநாதப்புரம் - irámanáthappuram, *Tam.*). From (ráma, san. the hero + nát'ha, san. lord + pura, san. town); lord rama's town [ram]. Tam. also (mugavai), meaning chief + place.——(1) Zemindarry, Madura district. Area 2,104 square miles. Population 128,452. Language Tamul. E. coast of district. Bounded on the north by Shivagunga, Poodoocottah and Tanjore, on the east by Palk's strait, on the south by the Gulf of Manaar and Ottapidauram and Shauttore talooks in Tinnevelly district, and on the west by Shivagunga, Tirmungalam talook of the Madura district and also by the Shreevillipoottore talook of Tinnevelly district. Peshcush Rs. 3,13,997. For history see vol. I, 55. There are no mountains or hills and very little jungle. Near the coast palmyras [q.v.] and cocoanut [q.v.] flourish especially towards the east. The waters from the high lands form a wide stream, discharging itself into the sea at Vaulimookham bay. There are three large salt water lakes; one near Vaulimookham, the second near Tirpoollauny, and the third east of the first and communicating with a salt water basin east of Poothoomadam. The principal manufactures are cotton [q.v.] cloths and carpets [jamkhana]; the chief manufacturing towns being Abhiraumam, Arooppoocottah, Cadalady, Camoothy, Chittracottah, Cottapatam, Keelakaray, Numboodalay, Paramacoody, Polliemputty, Poonnacoolam, and Tondy. Salt [ooppoo] is manufactured in the neighbourhood of the sea coast, and saltpetre [shorah] at Poonalcoody. Country arrack [q.v.] is distilled in several places. The chunk-fishery [chunk] lasts from April to September on the eastern coast and from October to March on the southern coast. It is usually rented by the zemindar for about 3,000 rupees per annum. About one million chunks [q.v.] are collected annually. Those fished on the eastern coast are reckoned better than those of the southern. The commercial transactions were formerly extensive. A commercial resident and assistant were for many years established at Ramnaud by the Company, for the purpose of procuring cloth for the English market; and the Mahomedans carried on an extensive trade in piece goods with the Eastern island and Persian gulf, &c. Exports are chayroot [q.v.], chunks [q.v.], salt [ooppoo], salt-fish, tobacco [pogauk], cotton [q.v.], skins [chamrah], paddy [q.v.], coarse cloth, &c. Imports are shawls [q.v.], woollen cloths, wheat [geung], sugar [q.v.], sugar-candy [candy], pepper [q.v.], nuts [areca], nutmegs [jautikye], cinnamons [q.v.], cloves [lavangam], cardamoms [q.v.], mace [jautipatry], brimstone [gandhac], quicksilver [rasam], iron [auhan], pearls [moty], corals [moongah], and a variety of precious stones [ratnam], teakwood [teak], blackwood [q.v.], and Ceylon wood, red and yellow ochre [cauvy]; and, in times of scarcity, grain [paddy] from the west and from Tanjore. The zemindarry is well stocked with cattle [maud], but of small size. Antelope [jinka] and hog [soor] are found in small numbers in the plains and jungles. The streams, of which there are many, are not navigable, and are as a rule nothing more than broad rivulets, and all are everywhere fordable. They supply several lakes. Freshes occur in October and November, and occasionally water comes down in April. A small supply of water is procurable even in the hottest months by digging in the beds of the rivers, and picottahs [q.v.] are erected on the banks for the purposes of irrigation. At some seasons of the year a dam is thrown across Toravoo lake, and portion of the bed cultivated with rice [q.v.]. Places of archæological interest :— Armoogam cottay, Arooppoocottah, Audy sait teertam, Aukkalore, Cadoogoosanday, Camoothy, Chokkalingapooram, Codoomalore, Coolashekharanullore, Covilaungoolam, Cunnagoody, Deviputnam, Hanoomantagoody, Kedauram, Keelakaray, Lutchmeepooram, Manjiyore, Mauriyore, Moodookkancoolam, Mookkore, Moothoocoolatore, Moottoonaud, Neinaurcoil, Nullcoorchy, Ooppooteroo, Oottara coshamungay, Pandalgoody, Parlatchay, Paulvanuttam, Paumben, Periyaputnam, Peroongarnay, Pidauranendal, Pillcoody, Poolaungal, Poottore, Pullimadam, Puttamungalam, Rajasingamungalam, Rameshwaram, Ramnaud, Shaukkivayal, Shaulagraumam, Shayalgoody, Sheloovnore, Shooranore, Taraicoody, Teetaundadaunam, Tirmaul cauttauncottay, Tirpaulacoody, Tirpoollauny, Tirshooly, Tirtervalay, Tirvadaunay, Veeracholan, Velimootty, Vengadangoorchy, Vidauttacoolam. Principal trig. stations:—Annappanaickenputt, Appateev, Arapothoo, Cadalady, Caunjirangoody, Codicoolam, Coottipauray, Gandhamaudanam, Kidatirkkay, Manigundy, Marcauyaputnam, Maunicancottah, Moothooputnam, Moottoorny, Mosal teev, Neinarcoil, Numboodalay, Ooraunancoody, Oottaracoshamungay, Oppilaun, Pandalgoody, Periyaputnam, Pishauchmundalam, Poolaputty, Pooliyamputty, Poomooritchan, Poragoody, Ramasawmy mutt, Ramnaud bastion, Shendatty yendal, Shiroaumbore, Shoolacaray, Tanichanday, Taraicoody, Vaulay teev, Venniyore, Yervaudy. The leading places, &c., in the talook are the following.——*Abhiraumam* (அபிராமம் - abirámam, Tam.). Means delightful. Village; pop. 6,278; lat. 9° 27′; long. 78° 29′; from Madura S.E. 40 miles; from Ramnaud W. 27 miles; from the sea N. 20 miles. On the Madura road below a large lake named from it. Inhabited principally by Mussalmans [q.v.], Chetties [q.v.], Maravar [q.v.] and Vellaular [q.v.]. Trade considerable in grain [dhaunyam], cotton [q.v.] and cloths. Popular belief is that within an area of 2 miles of the village, the bite of a snake is harmless. Weekly market on Wednesday.——*Adam's bridge* (சேது - shéthu, Tam.). See sep. title.——*Annappanaickenputt* (அன்னப்பநாயக்கன்பட்டு - annappanáyakkanbattu, Tam.). From (annappanáyakkan, tam. proper name + pattu, tam. village). Trig. station; lat. 9° 11′ 45·91″; long. 78° 20′ 13·42″; from Moothoocoolatore W.S.W. 19 miles; from Pernauzhy S.W. 3 miles; from Ramnaud W.S.W. 38 miles.——*Appa teev* (அப்பத்தீவு - appattívu, Tam.). From (appam, tam. plant, cissampelos pareira, linn. + dvípa, san. island). Trig. station in island; lat. 9° 09′ 52·86″; long. 78° 52′ 14·02″; height 10 feet; from Ramnaud S. 13 miles. ——*Arapothoo* (அறப்போது - arappóthu, Tam.) From (aral, tam. low jungle + póthi, tam. hill). Trig. station; lat. 9° 18′ 55·05″; long. 78° 38′ 48·18″; height 54 feet; from Moothoocoolatore E.S.E. 7 miles; from Ramnaud W.S.W. 17 miles.—— *Arooppoocottah* (அருப்புக்கோட்டை - aruppukkóttai, Tam. aruppukóta *). From (aruppu, tam. harvest + kóttai, tam. fort). Town, Zemindarry; pop. 12,673; lat. 9° 31′; long. 78° 08′; from Madura S. 28 miles; from Ramnaud W. 51 miles; from the sea N.N.W. 34 miles. Small ancient Shiva temple said to have been built by Soondra paundyan [soondra paundy tevar]. Sub-registrar's office. Weekly market on Monday. Inhabited by weavers, who make long cloths.——*Attangaray* (ஆத்தங்கரை - áttangarai, Tam.). From (áru, tam. river + karai, tam. bank); at the mouth of the veigay. Village, Port, Zemindarry; pop. 1,393; lat. 9° 21′; long. 79° 02′; from Madras S.S.W. 270 miles; from Madura E.S.E. 71 miles; from Moodiapatam S.S.E. 8 miles; from Pillaymadam N.W. 7 miles; from Ramnaud E. 11 miles. On the coast of Palk strait at the place where the surplus waters of the Veigay enter the sea. Noted for chunk [q.v.] fishery in the south-west monsoon [q.v.]; these shells, with rice [q.v.] and excellent tobacco [pogauk], are the principal exports and maintain an active coasting trade.——*Audy sait teertam* (ஆதிசேதுத்தீர்த்தம் - áthiséthuttírttam, Tam.). From (ádi, san. first + sétu, san. causeway + tír'tha, san. place of sacred water). Sacred bathing place on the coast frequented by pilgrims on their return from Rameshwaram. Rama [q.v.] bathed here on his expedition to Lunka [q.v.].——*Cadalady* (கடலடி - kadaladi, Tam.). From (kadal, tam. sea + adi, tam. vicinity). Trig. station, Ramnaud talook; lat. 9° 13′ 25·17″; long. 78° 32′ 20·46″; from Auppanore S. 3 miles; from Moothoocoolatore S.S.W. 9 miles; from Ramnaud W.S.W. 25 miles.—— *Camoothy* (கமுதி - kamuthi, Tam. kamuti *). Town, Headquarters of a Zemindarry; pop. 6,483; lat. 9° 25′; long. 78° 25′; from Madura S.S.E. 38 miles; from Ramnaud W. 31 miles; from the sea N. 21 miles. On south bank of Coondair. Old fort about 150 years old and Shiva temple said to have been built by Soondra paundyan [soondra paundy tevar]. The fort, on high ground above the Goondaur, built by a French engineer. Captured and dismantled by British after capture of Punchaulamcoorchy fort. Considerable trade in cotton [q.v.]. Weekly market on Tuesday.——*Caumancottay* (காமன்கோட்டை - kámangóttai, Tam.). From (káman, tam. god of love + kóttai, tam. fort). Village; pop. 1,267; lat. 9° 28′; long. 78° 45′; from Madura S.E. 51 miles; from Ramnaud W.N.W. 11 miles; from the sea W. 14 miles. North of the Madura-Ramnaud road. Opposite is a pavilion on south bank of a large reservoir from Veigay. Neighbourhood is richly cultivated.——*Caunjirangoody* (காஞ்சிரங்குடி - káñjirangudi, Tam.). From (káñjiram, tam. nux vomica tree, strychnos nux vomica, linn. + kudi, tam. village). Trig. station, Ramnaud talook; lat. 9° 14′ 48·17″; long. 78° 51′ 11·25″; height 55 feet; from Keelakaray N.E. 2 miles; from Ramnaud S.S.E. 9 miles.——*Chuckracottay* (சக்கரைக்கோட்டை - shakkaraikkóttai, Tam.). From (shakkarai, tam. man's name + kóttai, tam. fort); founded by mussalman of that name. Village; pop. 3,769; lat. 9° 21′; long. 78° 53′; from Madura S.E. 61 miles; from Ramnaud S.E. 1¼ miles; from the sea N. 7 miles.——*Codicoolam* (கோடிக்குளம் - kódikkulam, Tam.). From (kódi, tam. corner + kulam, tam. tank). Trig. station; lat. 9° 30′ 06·68″; long. 78° 50′ 50·90″; height 30 feet; from Poothoovayal W. 2 miles; from Ramnaud N. 9 miles. ——*Coottipauray* (குட்டிப்பாறை - kuttippárai, Tam). From (kuttai, tam. short + párai, tam. rock). Trig. station; lat. 9° 28′ 47·55″; long. 78° 03′ 05·90″; height 345 feet; from Ramnaud W.N.W. 56 miles; from Tirshooly W.S.W. 13 miles. ——*Cottacaraiyaur* (கொட்டக்கரையாறு - kottakkaraiyáru, Tam.). See sep. title.——*Cottaputam* (கோட்டப்பட்டணம் - kóttappattanam, Tam.). From (kóttai, tam. fort + pattana, san. town). Village, Port; lat. 9° 58′; long. 79° 15′; from Ammaputnam S.S.W. 4 miles; from Madras S.S.W. 228 miles; from Mimisal N.E. 5 miles; from Poodoocottah S.E. 38 miles; from Tanjore S.S.E. 55 miles. On Palk's bay. Salt factory. ——*Damodaraputnam* (தாமோதரப்பட்டணம் - támótharappattanam, Tam.). See sep. title.——*Devacottah* (தேவக்கோட்டை - tévakkóttai, Tam. devakóta *). From (déva, san. proper name + kóttai, tam. fort). Town, Sub-registrar's office; pop. 9,929; lat. 9° 57′; long. 78° 52′; from Madura E. 48 miles; from Ramnaud N. 39 miles; from the sea W. 21 miles. Principal residence of Nautcottay chetties [q.v.]. Weekly market on Wednesday and Saturday.——*Deviputnam* (தேவிப்பட்டணம் - tévippattanam, Tam.) See sep. title. ——*Gandhamaudanam* (கெந்தமாதன் - kendamáthan, Tam.). From (gandha, san. fragrance + mad, san. to intoxicate); place of high fragrance. Trig. station; lat. 9° 18′ 07·21″; long. 79° 20′ 51·60″; height 100 feet; from Paumben E. 7 miles; from Rameshwaram N.W. 1¼ miles; from Ramnaud E. 32 miles.——*Goondaur* (குண்டாறு - kundáru, Tam.). See sep. title.——*Gungaycondaun* (கங்கைக்கொண்டான் - kangaikkondán, Tam.). From (gangá, san. river + kondán, tam. one who brought); cf. caumeshwaram. Epithet of a Paundyan king. Village; pop. 1,020; lat. 9° 28′; long. 78° 46′; from Madura S.E. 52 miles; from Ramnaud N.W. 11 miles; from the sea W. 12 miles. Mosque [musjid] and Roman catholic church. Considerable trade in paddy [q.v.].——*Hanoomantagoody* (அனுமந்தக்குடி - anumandakkudi, Tam.). From (hanumanta, can. monkey-god + gudi, can. temple). Village; lat. 9° 56′; long. 78° 55′; from Madura E. 52 miles; from Ramnaud N. 38 miles; from the sea W. 15 miles. Formerly gave its name to a tract in Madura country. The Zameen [q.v.] talook of Hanoomantagoody is called after this place; the headquarters of which is at Cunnangoody. Old Shiva temple and old musjid [q.v.] with inscriptions.——*Keelacaray* (கீழக்கரை - kízhakkarai, Tam.). See sep. title.——*Kidatirkkay* (கிடாத்திருக்கை - kidáttirukkai, Tam.). From (kidá, tam. male of cattle + irukkai, tam. village) Trig. station; lat. 9° 18′ 02·14″; long. 78° 30′ 04·71″; from Auppanore N.W. 3 miles; from Moothoocoolatore S.W. 5 miles; from Ramnaud W.S.W. 26 miles.——*Munuar gulf* (மன்னார்குடாக்கடல் - mannárkkudákkadal, Tam.). See sep. title.——*Manaar island* (மன்னார்த்தீவு - mannárttívu, Tam). See sep. title.——*Manigundy* (மணிகண்டி - manigandi, Tam.). From (mani, tam. beauty + gandi, tel. pass). Trig. station; lat. 9° 46′ 17·88″; long. 78° 57′ 48·95″; height 48 feet; from Ramnaud N.N.E. 28 miles; from Tirvadaunay S. 1 mile.——*Mantapam* (மண்டபம் - mandabam, Tam.). Means hall. Village, Port; pop. 2,925; lat. 9° 17′; long. 79° 12′; from Madras S.S.W. 272 miles; from Madura E.S.E. 82 miles; from Rameshwaram W.S.W. 12 miles; from Ramnaud E.S.E. 21 miles; from Vedaulay E.N.E. 3 miles. Fishing village on Gulf of Manaar, four miles west of Paumben channel.—— *Mantapa shaulay* (மண்டபசாலை - mandabasálai, Tam.). From (mandapa, san. consecrated hall + shálá, san. room). Village; pop. 2,975; lat. 9° 13′; long. 79° 24′; from Madura E.S.E. 95 miles; from Ramnaud E.S.E. 36 miles; from the sea W. ½ mile. Mission station.——*Marcauyaputnam* (மரக்காயப்பட்டணம் - marakkáyappattanam, Tam.). From (maraikkáyan, tam. member of so called mahomedan class + pattana, san. city). Village, Port; pop. 130; lat. 9° 17′; long. 79° 11′; from Madras S.S.W. 276 miles; from Madura E.S.E. 82 miles; from Moottoopett E. 14 miles; from Ramnaud E.S.E. 20 miles; from Vedaulay E. 1¾ miles. On the Gulf of Manaar. Trig. station in lat. 9° 16′ 32·33″; long. 79° 10′ 18·84″; height 46 feet; from Mantapam S.W. 1½ miles; from Paumben W.S.W. 6 miles; from Ramnaud E.S.E. 21 miles.——*Maunicancottah* (மாணிக்கங்கோட்டை - mánikkangóttai, Tam.). From (mánikkam, tam. proper name + kóttai, tam. fort). Trig. station; lat. 9° 54′ 35·02″; long. 78° 57′ 31·56″; height 86 feet; from Devacottah E.S.E. 7 miles; from Ramnaud N.N.E. 36 miles; from Tirvadaunay N. 9

miles.——*Moothoocoolatore* (முதுகுளத்தூர் - muthugulattúr, Tam.). See sep. title.——*Moothooputnam* (முதுப்பட்டணம் - muthuppattanam, Tam.). Means old town. Trig. station; lat. 9° 40′ 16·03″; long. 78° 50′ 53·37; height 36 feet; from Rajasingamungalam N.W. 4 miles; from Ramnaud N. 21 miles; from Tirvadaunay S.W. 10 miles.——*Moottoopett* (முத்துப்பேட்டை - muttuppéttai, Tam.). From (muttu, tam. pearl + pétttai, tam. suburb); from the fishery. Village, Port; pop. 1,336; lat. 9° 16′; long. 78° 58′; from Keelakaray E.N.E. 10 miles; from Madras S.S.W. 275 miles; from Marcauyaputnam E. 15 miles; from Madura S.E. 66 miles; from Ramnaud S.S.E. 8 miles. Hamlet of Periyaputnam. Fishing village on Gulf of Manaar, chiefly inhabited by Roman catholics. Large Roman catholic church, Goanese priest. Mahomedan inhabitants are chunk-fishers [chunk].——*Moottoorny* (முட்டூறணி - muttúrani, Tam.). From (muttu, tam. rising ground + úrani, tam. fountain). Trig. station; lat. 9° 17′ 25·76″; long. 78° 19′ 02·72″; from Ramnaud W.S.W. 39 miles; from Tirshooly S.S.E. 17 miles.——*Mosal teev* (முசத்தீவு - musattívu, Tam.). Means hare island. Trig. station; lat. 9° 12′ 26·61″; long. 79° 06′ 41·90″; height 1 foot; from Ramnaud S.E. 19 miles.——*Neinaurcoil* (நயினார்கோவில் - nayinárkkóvil, Tam.). From (nayinár, tam. aiyyanár, the god + kóyil, tam. temple). Tam. also (maruthúr), meaning maroo-tham tree, terminalia tomentosa, bedd., var. typica + village. Village; pop. 1,085; lat. 9° 33′; long. 78° 44′; from Madura E.S.E. 46 miles; from Ramnaud N.W. 16 miles; from the sea W. 16 miles. Old Shiva temple in the centre of the village well sculptured. Two annual festivals in April and July. Trig. station in lat. 9° 32′ 26·64″; long. 78° 44′ 26·67″; height 69 feet; from Maroothoor S. ½ mile; from Ramnaud N.W. 16 miles.——*Nullatunniteev* (நல்லதண்ணீர்த்தீவு - nallathannittívu, Tam.). From (nalla, tam. fresh + tannír, tam. water + tívu, tam. island). Sanscrit name (shuddhódakadvípa), meaning the same. Island uninhabited; lat. 9° 06′; long. 78° 37′; from Madura S.S.E. 62 miles; from Ramnaud W.S.W. 24 miles. The island is by the Zemindar planted with trees of all sorts.——*Numboodalay* (நம்புதலை - nambuthalai, Tam.). From (namban, tam. shiva + talai, tam. place). Village, Port; pop. 1,947; lat. 9° 44′; long. 79° 03′; from Madras S.S.W. 245 miles; from Madura E.S.E. 62 miles; from Poothooputnam N.N.E. 4 miles; from Ramnaud N.N.E. 27 miles; from Tondy S.W. 1½ miles. On Palk's bay. A fishing village. Trig. station in lat. 9° 44′ 02·67″; long. 79° 02′ 49·73″; height 3 feet; from Ramnaud N.N.E. 28 miles; from Tirvadaunay S.E. 6 miles; from Tondy S.W. 1¼ miles.——*Ooppootunniteev* (உப்புத்தண்ணீர்த்தீவு - upputtannittívu, Tam.). From (uppu, tam. salt + tannír, tam. water + tívu, tam. island). Sanscrit name (lavanódakadvípa), meaning the same. Island uninhabited; lat. 9° 05′; long. 78° 32′; from Madura S.S.E. 60 miles; from Ramnaud W.S.W. 30 miles. Close to Nullatunniteev covered with low shrubs.——*Oorannancoody* (ஊரண்ணன்குடி - úrannangudi, Tam.). From (úrannan, tam. proper name + kudi, tam. village). Trig. station; lat. 9° 37′ 21·73″; long. 78° 57′ 33·53″; height 13 feet; from Ooppoor N. ¾ mile; from Ramnaud N.N.E. 18 miles; from Tirvadaunay S. 11 miles.——*Oottaracoshamungay* (உத்தரகோசமங்கை - uttarakkósamangai, Tam.). From (uttara, san. north + kósha, san. véda + mangai, tam. goddess). Trig. station; lat. 9° 18′ 52·33″; long. 78° 46′ 52·41″; height 65 feet; from Ramnaud W.S.W. 8 miles.——*Oppilaun* (ஒப்பிலான் - oppilán, Tam.).——From a person of that name. Trig. station; lat. 9° 08′ 13·40″; long. 78° 33′ 36·17″; from Moothoocoolatore S. 13 miles; from Periyacoolam S. 1¾ miles; from Ramnaud W.S.W. 26 miles.——*Palamanaar* (பழமன்னார் - palamannar, Tam.). From (pazha, tam. old + mannár, tam. place so called). Village. In Manaar island.——*Pandalgoody* (பந்தற்குடி - pandargudi, Tam.). From (pandal, tam. booth + kudi, tam. village). Sub-division, Zemindarry, Village; pop. 5,114; lat. 9° 23′; long. 78° 09′; from Madura S. 36 miles; from Ramnaud W.N.W. 50 miles; from the sea N.W. 28 miles. Peshcush Rs. 8,140. Best stone choonam [q.v.] in this province. Salt-petre [shorah] manufactured. Weekly market on Saturday. Trig. station in lat. 9° 23′ 30·36″; long. 78° 08′ 22·24″; from Andiputty S.S.E. 51 miles; from Ramnaud W. 50 miles; from Tirshooly S.S.W. 12 miles.——*Paramacoody* (பரமக்குடி - paramakkudi, Tam.). See sep. title.——*Paulvanuttam* (பாலவனத்தம் - pálavanattam, Tam.). From (pálavan, tam. proper name + nattam, tam. habitation). Sub-division, Zemindarry, Village; pop. 2,430; lat. of village 9° 34′; long. 78° 03′; from Madura S.S.W. 25 miles; from Ramnaud W.N.W. 58 miles; from the sea N.N.W. 40 miles. Peshcush Rs. 8,204. Old Shiva temple built by Soondra paundyan [soondra paundy tevar].——*Paumben* (பாம்பன் - pámban, Tam.). See sep. title.——*Pausiputnam* (பாசிப்பட்டணம் - pásippattanam, Tam.). From (pási, tam. seaweed + pattana, san. city). Village, Port; lat. 9° 49′; long. 79° 07′; from Damodaraputnam N.N.E. 1½ miles; from Madras S.S.W. 240 miles; from Madura E.S.E. 64 miles; from Ramnaud N.N.E. 34 miles; from Soondrapaundyaputnam S.S.W. 2 miles. On Palk's bay. Northernmost coast village of Madura.——*Pausiyaur* (பாசியாறு - pásiyáru, Tam.). From (pási, tam. moss + áru, tam. river). River. Lower branch of the Varshalaiyaur.——*Periyaputnam* (பெரியப்பட்டணம் - periyappattanam, Tam.). Means large town. Trig. station; lat. 9° 15′ 05·62″; long. 78° 57′ 03·26″; height 16 feet; from Ramnaud S.S.E. 9 miles; from Vunnaungoondoo S.S.E. 3 miles.——*Pishauch mundalam* (பிசாசுமண்டலம் - pisásumandalam, Tam.). Means spirit region. Trig. station; lat. 9° 19′ 38·12″; long. 79° 21′ 11·49″; height 5 feet; from Paumben E.N.E. 7 miles; from Ramnaud E. 32 miles.——*Pogalore* (போகலூர் - pógalúr, Tam.). From (pugazh, tam. praise + úr, tam. village). Village; pop. 1,395; lat. 9° 24′; long. 78° 45′; from Madura S.E. 52 miles; from Ramnaud W.N.W. 9 miles; from the sea W. 15 miles. Ancient capital of Ramnaud. Below a large lake. Ceremony performed here on installation of the zemindar as Saitoopaty.——*Poolaputty* (புலப்பட்டி - pulappatti, Tam.). From (pulam, tam. field + patti, tam. village). Trig. station; lat. 9° 14′ 13·70″; long. 78° 25′ 07·95″; from Moothoocoolatore S.W. 12 miles; from Ramnaud W.S.W. 33 miles.——*Pooliyamputty* (புளியம்பட்டி - puliyambatti, Tam.). From (puli, tam. tamarind tree, tamarindus indica, linn. + patti, tam. village). Otherwise Black station. Trig. station; lat. 9° 31′ 04·00″; long. 78° 05′ 26·98″; from Aroopoocottah W.N.W. 4 miles; from Ramnaud W.N.W. 55 miles; from Tirshooly W. 11 miles.——*Poomooritchan* (பூமுரிச்சான் - púmuriççán, Tam.). Trig. station; lat. 9° 14′ 30·51″; long. 79° 13′ 18·16″; height 29 feet; from Paumben S.W. 4 miles; from Ramnaud E.S.E. 25 miles.——*Poragoody* (பொராகுடி - poragudi, Tam.). From (porai, tam. mountain + kudi, tam. village). Trig. station; lat. 9° 29′ 45·66″; long. 78° 55′ 52·11″; from Deviputnam N.N.W. 1¼ miles; from Ramnaud N.N.E. 9 miles.——*Rajasingamungalam* (இராசசிங்கமங்கலம் - irásasingamangalam, Tam.). From (rájá, san. king + singam, tam. lion + mangala, san. prosperity). Talook head-quarters; pop. 4,519; lat. 9° 38′; long. 78° 53′; from Madura E.S.E. 53 miles; from Ramnaud N. 18 miles; from the sea W. 8 miles. An ancient Shiva temple.——*Ramappayyan's causeway* (இராமப்பையனணை - irámappaiyananai, Tam.). From (irámappaiyyan, tam. proper name + anai, tam. causeway). Between Mantapam and Paumben. Erected by Ramappayya, general of Trimal naick [q.v.], in order to capture Dalavoy saitoopaty, who had taken refuge in Paumben and defied the authority of the Naick [q.v.] ruler of Madura. Now in ruins; only a few detached rocks being visible.——*Ramasawmy mutt* (இராமசுவாமிமடம் - irámasuvámimadam, Tam.). From (irámasuvámi, tam. proper name + mat'ha, san. convent). Trig. station; lat. 9° 16′ 04·40″; long. 79° 06′ 11·21″; height 36 feet; from Paulcoolam S. ¾ mile; from Ramnaud E.S.E. 16 miles.——*Rameshwaram* (இராமேசுவரம் - irámésuvaram, Tam.). See sep. title.——*Ramnaud* (இராமநாதப்புரம் - irámanáthappuram, Tam.). See below.——*Shaulagraumam* (சாளக்கிராமம் - shálakkirámam, Tam.). Means the sacred ammonite stone [shalagram]. Village; pop. 2,459; lat. 9° 37′; long. 78° 46′; from Madura E.S.E. 46 miles; from Ramnaud N.N.W. 18 miles; from the sea W. 15 miles. Inhabited by Vellaular [q.v.]. Old Shiva temple. Manufacture of brown sugar [q.v.]. Weekly market on Tuesday.——*Shayalgoody* (சாயல்குடி - sháyalgudi, Tam.). From (sháyal, tam. beauty + kudi, tam. village). Village; pop. 942; lat. 9° 10′; long. 78° 29′; from Madura S.S.E. 56 miles; from Ramnaud W.S.W. 30 miles; from the sea N. 3 miles. Ancient Shiva temple. The jungles abound with deer [mrigam].——*Shendatty yendal* (செந்தட்டியேந்தல் - shendattiyéndal, Tam.). From (shendatti, tam. nettle plant, tragia involucrata, mueller, var. cannabina + éndal, tam. height). Trig. station; lat. 9° 23′ 18·06″; long. 78° 44′ 34·10″; height 45 feet; from Ariyacoody S.S.E. 2 miles; from Ramnaud W.N.W. 10 miles.——*Shircaumbore* (சிறுகாம்பூர் - shirugámbúr, Tam.). From (shiru, tam. small + kámbu, tam. bamboo, bambusa arundinacea, willd. + úr, tam. village). Trig. station; lat. 9° 52′ 29·23″; long. 79° 03′ 29·75″; height 31 feet; from Pathanacoody S. 6 miles; from Ramnaud N.N.E. 37 miles; from Tirvadaunay N.E. 10 miles.——*Shoolacaray* (சூலக்கரை - shúlakkarai, Tam.). From (shúla, san. trident + karai, tam. field). Trig. station; lat. 9° 32′ 15·95″; long. 77° 59′ 19·38″.——*Tanichanday* (தனிச்சந்தை - taniççandai, Tam.). From (tani, tam. solitary + shandai, tam. market). Trig. station; lat. 9° 13′ 06·92″; long. 78° 40′ 14·21″; height 37 feet; from Cottangoolam E.S.E. ¾ mile; from Moothoocoolatore S.E. 12 miles; from Ramnaud S.W. 17 miles.——*Taraicoody* (தரைக்குடி - taraikkudi, Tam.). From (tarai, tam. surface + kudi, tam. village). Trig. station; lat. 9° 09′ 20·11″; long. 78° 26′ 00·63″; from Cokkady S. 1¾ miles; from Moothoocoolatore S.W. 15 miles; from Ramnaud W.S.W. 34 miles.——*Tirpoollauny* (திருப்புல்லாணி - tiruppulláni, Tam.). From (tiru, tam. holy + pul, tam. grass + ani, tam. excellence). Sanscrit name (darbhashayana), meaning darbhay grass, eragrostis cynosuroides, retz. + bed; also (p'hullapura), meaning poollan, the sage + town; also (p'hulláranya), meaning poollan, the sage + forest. Village, Place of pilgrimage; pop. 2,300; lat. 9° 17′; long. 78° 52′; from Madura E.S.E. 66 miles; from Ramnaud S. 6 miles; from the sea N. 3 miles. On a commanding plain. Held sacred. Rama laid himself on a bed of darbhay [q.v.] grass here and invoked Varoonan's [q.v.] aid in crossing the straits to Lunka. Temple to Shiva [q.v.] as Juggernaut [q.v.] highly sculptured, very sacred with inscriptions of Chola [q.v.] and Wodeyar [q.v.] dynasties [raj], dated A.D. 1374. Annual festivals in April and July.——*Tirshooly* (திருச்சுழி - tiruççuzhi, Tam.). See sep. title.——*Tirvadaunay* (திருவாடானை - tiruvádánai, Tam.). See sep. title.——*Tondy* (தொண்டி - tondi, Tam.). See sep. title.——*Tonitory* (தோணித்துறை - tónitturai, Tam.). From (tóni, tam. boat + turai, tam. ford). Village, Hamlet of Mantapam; pop. 2,925. A large choultry [q.v.] for pilgrims. ——*Varshalaiyaur* (வரிசலையாறு - varisalaiyáru, Tam.). See sep. title.——*Vaulay teev* (வாளைத்தீவு - válaittívu, Tam.). From (válai, tam. fish so called, wallago attu + tívu, tam. island). Trig. station in island; lat. 9° 11′ 11·63″; long. 78° 59′ 07·01″; height 5 feet; from Ramnaud S.S.E. 15 miles.——*Vaulimookham* (வாலிமுகம் - válimugam, Tam.). From (váli, san. myth. person + mukha, san. face). Hamlet, Port; lat. 9° 10′; long. 78° 41′; from Madras S.S.W. 294 miles; from Madura S.S.E. 64 miles; from Mookkore E. 11 miles; from Ramnaud S.W. 19 miles; from Yemanangoondoo W.S.W. 27 miles. On the west of a small bay on the Madura side of the Gulf of Manaar. This bay is the western entrance of the Paumben navigation. Good harbour for coasting vessels during land winds [q.v.] and monsoon [q.v.]. Contiguous to the bay is a large salt water lake extending 7 miles west, greatest breadth 1½ miles.——*Vedaulay* (வேடாலை - vedálai, Tam.). See sep. title.——*Veera-cholan* (வீரசோழன் - vírasózhan, Tam.). After a chola ruler of that name. Village; lat. 9° 33′; long. 78° 25′; from Madura S.E. 31 miles; from Ramnaud W.N.W. 34 miles; from the sea N. 32 miles. On the south bank of the Credama nuddy. Former residence of Rajahs and of great importance. Traditional residence of Chola [q.v.] king. Old Shiva temple attributed to Vicramarca paundyan. Abounds with remains of antiquity. Present population consists of Cullar [q.v.], Marwarries [q.v.], and Mussalmans [q.v.]. Weekly market on Monday.——*Veigay* (வைகை - vaigai, Tam.). See sep. title.——*Venniyore* (வெண்ணியூர் - venniyúr, Tam.). From (vanni, tam. the suma tree, prosopis spicigera, linn. + úr, tam. village). Trig. station; lat. 9° 48′ 57·57″; long. 78° 51′ 20·79″; height 87 feet; from Ramnaud N. 31 miles; from Tirvadaunay W.N.W. 8 miles.——*Yerraudy* (எருவாடி - eruvádi, Tam.). From (eru, tam. manure + vádi, enclosure). Village, Port; lat. 9° 14′; long. 78° 45′; from Keelakaray W.S.W. 5 miles; from Madras S.S.W. 286 miles; from Madura S.E. 62 miles; from Ramnaud S.W. 13 miles; from Yemanangoondoo W.S.W. 22 miles. On the Gulf of Manaar. Attached to Keelakaray. Trig. station in lat. 9° 13′ 30·83″; long. 78° 46′ 20·24″; height 65 feet; from Mayaucoolam S.W. 6 miles; from Moothoocoolatore S.E. 17 miles; from Ramnaud S.W. 13 miles.——**(2)** Deputy tahsildarry. Madura district. Pay Rs. 100.——**(3)** Town, Deputy tahsildar's station. Sub-registrar's office, Head-quarters of the Head assistant collector of Madura and Assistant superintendent of Police, S.P.G. high school; Madura dist., Ramnaud zemindarry; pop. 13,619; lat. 9° 22′; long. 78° 53′; from Dindigul S.S.E. 90 miles; from Kodaykarnal E.S.E. 110 miles; from Madras S.S.W. 271 miles; from Madura S.E. 62 miles; from Rameshwaram W.N.W. 33 miles; from the sea N. 9 miles. About three miles from where the Veigay empties itself into Ramnaud large tank. Surrounded by a wall and a ditch and defended by numerous small bastions, now ruined. Stormed by Trimal naick in 1638-39 and the Saitoopaty captured and taken to Madura; captured by General Smith in 1772; occupied by the British in 1792; zemindar deposed for rebellion in 1795. The place was formerly garrisoned by a company of native infantry. A mile west are the remains of the fort and palace of the Saitoopaties, called the Shoorancottay; built by Raghoonaut or khizhavan saitoopaty, 1673–1708 A.D. Near the palace is a handsome residence built by Colonel Martinez, who commanded here previous to 1804. Within the fort the majority of the inhabitants are Vellaular [q.v.] and Maravar [q.v.], depending for their livelihood upon the palace. Outside live Chetties [q.v.] and Lubbays [q.v.], in whose hands is the whole coast trade. West is an old Amman [q.v.] temple and north is an old musjid [q.v.]. A neat Protestant church belongs to the Society for the Propagation of the Gospel, who have a mission here. Two Roman catholic churches. Several large rest-houses, the resort of pilgrims passing through Ramnaud on their way to Rameshwaram. The only manufacturing industry is that of coarse cloths for native wear. Artizans [cummaulan, punchaula] are gold and silversmiths, braziers, and ironsmiths; the latter are Mussalmans and reside in the town. The east part is inhabited by manufacturers of chintzes [q.v.] and printed cloths. A market is held every Wednesday, when cotton, grain, and other provisions are brought in for sale. Ramnaud bastion trig. station in lat. 9° 21′ 54·71″; long. 78° 51′ 45·81″; height 34 feet; from Ramnaud W. 1½ miles; from Shoorancottay S. 1 mile.

RAMZAUN (رمضان - ramazán, *Hind.*). From (ramaza, ar. to scorch); it was the hot season when the name was given. Mahomedan fasting month. Ninth month of Mussalman [q.v.] year [hijra, saul], following Shabaun [maheena]. The year being lunar [maunam], each month occurs at all periods of the solar year [madhyama sowra maunam]. Ramzaun is observed as a fast [roza] because the revelation of the Koran [q.v.] began in it [leilat ool kadr]. Ramzaun ends with the Eed ool fitr [q.v.]. Both sufficiently described at vol. I (97). Sometimes alam; as Ramzaun ally, double alam [ism].——*Ramzaunkah roza* (رمضان کا روزه - ramazánkározah, Hind.). From (above + rozah, ar. fast). The fast of Ramzaun.——*Ramzaunkee eed* (رمضان کی عید - ramazánkíid, Hind.). From (above + íd, ar. festival). The festival following the fast of Ramzaun [eed ool fitr].

RANAM (रण - rana, *San.*). From (ran, san. to sound). War.——*Ranabhadracauly* (இரணபத்திரக்காளி - iranabat-tirakkáli, Tam.). From (above + bhadrakálí, san. the goddess). Goddess of war.——*Ranaveeran* (रणवीर - ranavíra, San.). From (above + víra, san. hero). The hero in war. A deity whose image stands in Ancaulamman's [q.v.] temple. Hindoo 2nd or pers. name [peyar].——*Ranavicraman* (இரணவிக்கிரமன் - iranavikkiraman, Tam.). From (above + vikrama, san. valour). The valorous in war. Hindoo 2nd or pers. name [peyar].

RAND (രണ്ടു - randu, *Mal.*). Two [ir].——*Randatarra* (രണ്ടുതറ - randutara, Mal.). From (randu, mal. two + tara, mal. village). Mal. also (póyanátu), meaning gone + country, because cherma permaul [q.v.] took his final departure to mecca from this place [colachel]. Village; Malabar dist., Chiracal tal.; lat. 11° 52′; long. 75° 33′; from Calicut N.N.W. 46 miles; from Cannanore E. 9 miles; from the sea E. 11 miles. Same as Anjarcundy.——*Ruttera* (രട്ടറ - rattara, Mal.). From (randu, mal. two + tara, mal. village). Same as Covalam in Travancore.

RANDOM SHOT (குண்டுக்கிராமம் - kundukkirámam, *Tam.*). Tam. from (gundu, tel. ball + gráma, san. village). Villages included within range of cannon fired from Fort st. david, South arcot dist., Cuddalore tal. This comprises about eleven villages round the fort purchased by the Company from the Mahrattas [q.v.] in 1690 for 32,000 pagodas [q.v.].

RANGH (वर्ण - varna, *San.*; رنگ - rang, *Hind.*; ಬಣ್ಣ - banna, *Can.*; రంగు - rangu, *Tel.*; വർണ്ണം - varnam, *Mal.*; வண்ணம் - vannam, *Tam.*). San. from (varn, san. to paint). Hind. from (rañj, san. to dye) [ranj]. Pigment. Various kinds of mineral pigments are sold in bazaars [q.v.], but only two of these are indigenous, viz., yellow ochre or gopy [q.v.], and red ochre or poon cauvy [q.v.]. A reddish-brown pigment is also obtained by roasting the yellow ochre [cauvy]. From the animal kingdom the well-known shell-lime [kilinjal choonam] is obtained and used for whitewashing houses. In the vegetable kingdom there is indigo [q.v.], used sometimes with oil and water for paints; and a black pigment is produced by the burning of empty shells of the cocoanut [q.v.]. A yellow wash is obtained from yellow mixed with lime [choonam] according to the shade desired; a red wash from red ochre [cauvy] used as above; a blue or grey wash from indigo [q.v.] and lime [choonam] for internal work, and lime [choonam] and burnt cocoanut [q.v.] shell for external work; a pink wash from lime and red ochre mixed in due proportions; a whitewash from lime alone. In some parts the natives also use a whitish kind of earth, vellay munn [jaidy munn], for whitewashing their houses. Other colored washes can be obtained by admixture of these in varying proportions. The following are the principal pigments.——*Caroopoo* (कृष्ण - krishna, San.; کالا - kálá, Hind.; ಕಪ್ಪು - kappu, Can.; నలుపు - nalupu, Tel.; കറുപ്പ് - karuppu, Mal.; கறுப்பு - karuppu, Tam.). Dark wash. This consists of burnt cocoanut [q.v.] shells reduced to powder, used in color-washing or plastering [cauray] mixed with lime [choonam]; it forms various shades of grey. A small portion mixed with yellow or red tones down those colors.——*Gopy* (गोपीचन्दन - gópíchandana, San.; گوپی - gopí, Hind.; ಗೋಪಿಚಂದನ - gópi-chandana, Can.; పసుపుకావి - pasupukávi, Tel.; ഗോപി - gópi, Mal.; கோபிச்சந்தனம் - kóbiççandanam, Tam.). San. from (gópí, san. a cowherd's wife + chandana, san. sandal). Tel. from (pasupu, tel. yellow + kávi, tel. ochre). Title otherwise Manjalcauvy, Yellow ochre. May be used with water or oil. Is the pigment commonly used in color-washing buildings. If burnt it passes into red ochre [cauvy], and various shades of warm tints can be obtained by mixing these together. It is well adapted for distemper work and does not lose its color when mixed with lime [choonam].——*Poon cauvy* (रक्तोपल - raktópala, San.; گيرو - gerú, Hind.; ಕಾವಿಕಲ್ಲು - kávikallu, Can.; ఎర్రకావి - errakávi, Tel.; കാവി - kávi, Mal.; பூங்காவி - púngávi, Tam.). Title from (pú, tam. flower + kávi, tam. ochre). San. from (rakta, san. red + upala, san. stone). Can. from (kávi, can. red + kallu, can. stone). Tel. from (erupu, tel. red + kávi, tel. ochre). Red ochre. Used with water or oil.——*Sookkaun cull* (मृत्स्ना - mritsná, San.; کھری - kharí, Hind.; ಸುದ್ದಿಮಣ್ಣು - suddimannu, Can.; సుద్ద - sudda, Tel.; ചേടി - chéti, Mal.; சுக்கான்கல் - shukkángal, Tam.). Title from (shukkán, tam. lime + kal, tam. stone). San. from (mrit, san. earth). Can. from (shuddhi, can. pure + mannu, can. earth). Tel. from (shuddha, san. purity). Pipe clay. Used as a primary coat. When purified, is used for sectarial marks [naumam] on foreheads.——*Vellay* (श्वेत - shvéta, San.; سفیده - sufedah,

Hind.; ಬಿಳುಪು - bilupu, Can.; తెలుపు - telupu, Tel.; വെള്ള - vella, Mal.; வெள்ளை - vellai, Tam.). Whitewash from calcined chalk [sheemay choonam] shells almost equal to paint. Now much superseded by white lead [moottoo velly], which is imported at cheaper rates [shauyam].

RANGOON (இரங்கூன் - irangún, *Tam.*). Means war-end. Chief town in Lower Burmah.——*Rangoon creeper* (विलायतीचमेली - viláyatíchamélí, Mahr.; رنگون کی بیل - rangúnkíbel, Dec.; రంగూనుమల్లె - rangúnumalle, Tel.; இரங்கூன்மல்லி - irangún-malli, Tam.). Mahr. from (viláyatí, mahr. foreign + chamélí, mahr. jasminum grandiflorum, linn.). Dec. from (rangún, hind. rangoon + bel, hind. creeper). Tel. means rangoon jasmine. Tam. from (irangún, tam. rangoon + malli, tam. jasmine, jasminum sambac, ait.). Title otherwise Chinese honeysuckle, Rangoon jasmine. Botanically Quisqualis indica, linn., combretaceæ [vricsham, 55]. Shrub, with scandent branches; young branches densely pubescent; leaves opposite, ovate, quite entire, rounded or slightly cordate at the base, when young more or less villous or pubescent, afterwards almost glabrous; bracts ovate-rhomboid, acuminated, slightly hairy, particularly on the margin; spikes axillary and terminal; flowers lax, red; calycine tube slender; stamens ten, protruded, inserted into the throat of the calyx, alternately shorter; style filiform, exserted; drupe dry, five-furrowed, acutely five-angled; seed solitary, pendulous, five-angled. Extensively growing; bears during hot and rainy seasons in constant succession profuse clusters of flowers of middling size, at first white, but turning on the following day to a blood color; the fruits are about an inch in length, oval or oblong, pointed at either extremity, and sharply pentagonal; they dehisce from the apex; the woody pericarp is thin, fragile and of a deep mahogany color; it encloses a pentagonal seed nearly black when dry, yellowish and oily internally; the seeds afford 7 per cent. of an alkaline deliquescent ash; cultivated in gardens; a native of burmah and the malayan archipelago. Seeds are anthelmintic; given with honey [shahad] in electuary for expulsion of entozoa in children; in pharm. non-officinal. No other common species here.——*Rangoon kino* (رنگون کا کنیا گوند - rangúnkákinyágond, Hind.). Same as Padouk.

RANJ (रञ्ज - rañj, *San.*). To redden, dye; to be affected, please. ——*Racta chamoondy* (இரத்தசாமுண்டி - irattasámundi, Tam.). From (rakta, san. blood + chámundi, san. the goddess). One of the seven matrons [mautah] in the temple of Ayenaur [ayeu].——*Ractam* (रक्त - rakta, San.). From (rañj, san. to redden). Red. So also blood.—"*a*" Plant first term, in the sense of red. Ex., where transl. is of second term:—Adhatoda vasica (raktapittaghní), meaning plethora + killing; Bombax malabaricum (raktapushpá), flower; Dioscorea purpurea (raktálu), esculent root; Ipomæa batatas (raktapindaka), ball; Mangifera sylvatica (raktámra), mango; Plumbago rosea (raktashikhá), crest; Pterocarpus santalinus (raktachandana), santalum album; Ventilago maderaspatana (raktavallí), creeper. See gloss. paragraphs.—"*b*" Plant second term. Ex.:—Crocus sativus (bhavaraktá), meaning shiva's blood; Hibiscus hirtus (pushparaktá), meaning flower blood. See gloss. paragraphs. ——*Ractaumram* (रक्ताम्र - raktámra, San.). From (rakta, san. red + ámra, san. mango tree, mangifera indica, linn.). Title otherwise Gamboge tree, Mangosteen, Red mango. Botanically the Garcinia genus, guttiferæ [vricsham, 22]. Evergreen trees or shrubs, mostly natives of tropical india; yield a viscid, yellow, acrid and purgative resinous juice or gamboge [q.v.], which is obtained by removing the bark, or by breaking the leaves or young shoot; fruits of many species eaten; leaves glossy, laurel-like, leathery; flowers white or yellow, arranged in clusters or in panicles; wood close-grained, hard. The species best known to the natives are:—cambogia [malabar gamboge], indica [mate mangosteen], mangostana [mangosteen], morella [ceylon gamboge], morella, var. pedicellata [siam gamboge], pedunculata [tickor], xanthochymus [yellow mangosteen]. Other s. indian species indigenous or naturalized are:—cowa, eugeniæfolia, travancorica, wightii.——*Racteshwary* (रक्तेश्वरी - raktéshvarí, San.). From (rakta, san. red + íshvarí, san. goddess). Doorga [q.v.].——*Raggy* (रागी - rágí, San.). See sep. title.——*Rajas* (रजस् - rajas, San.). From (ranj, san. to dye). Passion. One of the three cosmic qualities; the other two being Satwam [q.v.] and Tamas [goonam, tamas].——*Rajogoonam* (रजोगुण - rajóguna, San.). The second property of humanity, the quality of passion [goonam].——*Rangh* (رنگ - rang, Hind.). See sep. title.——*Raugam* (राग - rága, San.; راگ -rág, Hind. and Dec.). From (rañj, san. to be affected). Properly signifies an affection of the mind; thence a mode of music, each mode being intended to move one of such. The six primary modes, in the system ascribed to Pavana, were ranged according to the six ritoos [q.v.] or seasons, each consisting of two months [mausam]. In mythology, the raugams are modes, or melodies personified, six or more in number; the Rauginies are their consorts, and the Raugapootras are their sons. Both the latter are secondary and derived raugams [sangeetam, swaram].——*Raugola* (రాగోల - rágóla, Tel.). From (rága, san. mode of music + kóla, tel. stick). A pitch-fork.——*Raujasam* (राजस - rájasa, San.). Relating to rajas or passion. Raujasam, taumasam and sautwicam are choler, depravity, and purity [goonam].——*Rauvy* (రావి - rávi, Tel.). Means red. Same as Peepul. Cf.:—Ficus vagans (kondarávi), hill peepul; Michelia champaca (gangarávi), large peepul; Thespesia populnea (gangarávi), excellent peepul. See gloss. paragraphs.——*Retty* (रत्ती - ratí, Mahr.; رتی - rattí, Hind.; రతి - rati, Tel.). From (rakta, san. red). Seed of the abrus precatorius, linn. [indian liquorice], used as a goldsmith's weight. 4 dhauns or paddy grains = 1 retty; 8 retties = 1 mausham [niray, 3e]. Used as the basis of weights for gold, silver and drugs; the seed varies, but from various trials appears to average about $1\frac{9}{16}$ths of a grain; the artificial weight has been found to average nearly $2\frac{1}{4}$ grains. Same as sanscrit Goonjam, hindostany Gocmchy or goonj, canarese and teloogoo Gooriginja, malayalam Coonnycooroo, and tamul Coondrimany. See vol. I, 609; II, 518. In arabic and persian called Cock's eyes. Also called Prayer bead; compare specific name of plant.——*Rungabhashyam* (இரங்கப்பாசியம் - irangappásiyam, Tam.). From (ranga, san. vishnu + bháshya, san. short for bháshyakára, san. the commentary maker); meaning ramaunoojan who is supposed to be a form of vishnoo or sheshan incarnate. Hindoo 2nd or pers. name. Common among Veishnavas [peyar].——*Rungam* (रङ्ग - ranga, San.). From (ranj, san. to please); place of pleasure. River-island, raised platform or stage of theatre, so any place of public amusement or assembly. Vishnoo [q.v.] worshipped in the river island at Shreerungam. Compare Sabhay and Ambalam. Applied to females. Also suffix in proper names as Vencatrungam, Vijiarungam [peyar].——*Rungammah* (రంగమ్మ - rangamma, Tel.). From (ranga, san. vishnu + amma, tel. mother, titular affix). Familiarly Rungoo, Rungy. Proper name [peyar].——*Rungamunnaur* (இரங்கமன்னார் - irangamannár, Tam.). From (ranga, san. vishnu + mannan, tam. king); epithet of vishnoo at Shreerungam. Hindoo 2nd or pers. name [peyar].——*Rungan* (இரங்கன் - irangan, Tam.). Feminine Rungy, familiarly Rungoo. Hindoo 2nd or pers. name [peyar].——*Rungunautan* (रङ्गनाथ - ranganát'ha, San.). From (ranga, san. vishnu, island god + nát'ha, san. lord). Vishnoo, as lord of Shreerungam.——*Rungappah* (ರಂಗಪ್ಪ - rangappá, Can.). From (ranga, san. vishnu + appa, can. father, titular affix). Hindoo 2nd or pers. name [peyar].——*Rungappan* (இரங்கப்பன் - irangappan, Tam.). From (ranga, san. vishnu + appan, tam. father, titular affix), vishnoo, the father. Hindoo 2nd or pers. name [peyar].——*Runga row* (రంగారావు - rangarávu, Tel.). Name + third name. Title given by the fowjdar [q.v.] of Chicacole to one Peddaroyadoo for rescuing his son out of the hands of certain rebels, for which he was rewarded with Rajam estate since known as Bobbily. The title has been borne by all his successors [charitram]. See vol. I, 60.——*Rungasawmy* (இரங்கசாமி - irangasámi, Tam.). From (ranga, san. vishnu + svámí, san. master); epithet of vishnoo, lord of the island, Shreerungam. Hindoo 2nd or pers. name [peyar]. Nearly as common as Ramasawmy.——*Rungasawmy's peak* (ರಂಗಸ್ವಾಮಿಮಲೆ - rangasámimale, Can.). From (rangasvámí, san. the deity + male, can. hill). Hill; Neilgherry dist., Paranginaud div.; lat. 11° 27′; long. 77° 01′; height 5,865; from Coonoor E.N.E. 14 miles; from Ootacamund E.N.E. 18 miles. At extreme E. of Neilgherries, at top of Guzzelhutty pass [ghaut]. Conical shape. The god of this place is worshipped by all the hill tribes.——*Rungasheshan* (இரங்கசேசன் - irangasésan, Tam.). From (ranga, san. vishnu + shésha, san. the serpent god), sheshan, the serpent god with vishnoo. Hindoo 2nd or pers. name [peyar]. ——*Rungiah* (రంగయ్య - rangayya, Tel.). From (ranga, san. vishnu + ayya, tel. master, titular affix). Hindoo 2nd or pers. name [peyar].

RASAM (रस - rasa, *San.*; पार - pára, *Mahr.*; زیبق - zíbak, *Ar.*; سیماب - símáb, *Pers.*; پارا - pará, *Hind.* and *Dec*; رسا - rasa, *Malay*; ಪಾದರಸ - pádarasa, *Can.*; ಪಾರದ - párada, *Too.*; పాదరసము - pádarasamu, *Tel.*; രസം - rasam, *Mal.*; රසදිය - rasadiya, *Singh.*; இரசம் - irasam, *Tam.*). Title means juice, essence. Ar. from persian. Pers. from (sím, pers. silver + áb, pers. water). Hind. from (párada, san. mercury). Malay from sanscrit. Can. from (páda, san. foot + rasa, san. essence); by corruption from (páradarasa), meaning quicksilver. Tel. from (páda, san. foot + rasa, san. essence), but really like canarese. Singh. meaning mercury + water. Tam. from sanscrit. San. also (súta), meaning producing, supposed to produce gold from base metals, cf. rasauyanam; (párada), meaning expeller of diseases. Pers. also (jíva), from sanscrit meaning life. Title otherwise Mercury, Quicksilver. A brilliant silver-white metal, fluid at a natural temperature. Boils at 670°, and becomes solid at 40° below zero. Easily divisible into spherical globules. Hydrargyrum of chemists. Not indigenous; see vol. II, 33. Greater part is brought from Japan, both in its native state and combined with sulphur [gandhac] as cinnabar [shangarf]. No medicine so often adulterated. Impurity seen by its dull aspect; by its tarnishing, and becoming covered with a grey film; by its diminished mobility. It is commonly adulterated by lead [eeyam], bismuth, zinc [tootnaug], and tin [tagaram]. For native preparations of mercury see Raseshwaram, Rasapaspam, Rascapoor, Shangarf, Shavveeram, Rasa sindooram. Diseases in which it is used by veidyans [q.v.] are anasarca or neercovay, ascites or mahodaram, apoplexy or asathijanny, venereal disease or maiha vyaudhy, and leprosy or cooshtam [q.v.]. Pharm. articles are numerous and well known. The tamul shastram, Congana neinaur nool is a work on preparations of mercury, and other powerful minerals. Similarly Bhoga neinaur tirmuntram. In sanscrit, the most celebrated works are Rasa ratna samootchayam, Rasa sauram and Rasa ratnaucaram. The following are the different kinds of Rasam. For cinnabar see Shangarf, for corrosive sublimate see Shavveeram, for black sulphide of mercury see Cajjaly.——*Rasa choornam* (रसचूर्ण - rasachúrna, San.; இரசச்சுண்ணம் - irasaççunnam, Tam.). From (rasa, san. mercury + chúrna, san. powder). Peroxide of mercury.——*Rasa goondoo* (രസമണി - rasamani, Mal.; இரசக்குண்டு - irasakkundu, Tam.). Mal. from (rasa, san. mercury + mani, san. bead). Tam. from (rasa, san. mercury + kundu, tam. ball). A globular glass filled with mercury as a decoration at weddings. Also called Rasa coodookkay, meaning mercury bottle.——*Rasa paspam* (रसभस्म - rasabhasma, San.; کشته‌سیماب - kushtahisímáb, Pers.; پارے کی خاک - párekíkhák, Hind.; రసభస్మము - rasabhasmamu, Tel.; രസഭസ്മം - rasabhasmam, Mal.; இரசப்பற்பம் - irasapparbam, Tam.). From (rasa, san. mercury + bhasma, san. ashes). Pers. from (kushtah, pers. calcined + símáb, pers. mercury). Hind. from (pára, hind. mercury + khák, hind. ashes). Calcinated mercury. Sulphate of mercury. Hydrargyri sulphas of chemists. The following recipe for preparation is taken from Agastya veidya einnoor:—Twelve pagodas [q.v.] weight of sulphur [gandhac] is to be put into an earthen pot, and fused over a slow, but strong fire; when in a state of fusion, eighty pagodas weight of quicksilver must be added to it, and kept gently stirred till the whole is reduced to a black powder; another pot is then to be taken, and filled half full of small pieces of brick [shengal], over which is to be laid one measure of common salt [ooppoo]; on the top of this salt is to be put the black powder just mentioned, covering the whole with another earthen vessel; the part where the mouth of the two vessels meet is to be well coated over with soft clay, and afterwards bound round with five piles of coarse cloth; the pots thus joined are then to be placed on a strong fire, and there to be kept for twelve hours; after which time they are to be taken off and left to cool, when the rasa paspam will be found collected in the uppermost. According to the same the mode of administering is as follows:—Four pagodas weight of omam [ajwaun] seed must be roasted, and reduced to a powder; four pagodas weight of palmyra [q.v.] jaggery [q.v.] is to be added to this, and the whole to be well ground; eight fanams [q.v.], weight of the rasa paspam is then to be mixed with the other two ingredients, when all are to be rubbed together for a considerable time, and afterwards made into sixteen boluses; one of which is to be taken morning and evening for eight days, at the end of which period the mouth will generally be found to be much affected. The Einnoor says that rasa paspam is a most useful and efficacious remedy in eighteen different kinds of contractions of the sinews, the same number of granty or venereal affections, twenty sorts of scurvy eruptions, the dangerous ulcer which makes its appearance over or near the back-bone [rajah boil], the boil which assumes the appearance of an ant-hill, in spreading or corroding sores, swellings on the neck or scrofulous affections and leprosies [cooshtam].——*Rasa sindooram* (रससिन्दूर - rasasindúra, San.; రససింధూరము - rasasindúramu, Tel.; இரசசெந்தூரம் - irasasendúram, Tam.). From (rasa, san. mercury + sindúra, san. vermilion). Red precipitate of mercury. Hydrargyri oxidum rubrum of chemists. Used by native practitioners as an escharotic, and for cleaning foul ulcers. Veidyans [q.v.] prepare it in the following manner:—Ten pagodas [q.v.] weight of tootnaug [q.v.] or zinc is first melted in an earthen pot, in a sand-bath, after which ten pagodas weight of rasam or quicksilver is added to it. Two and-a-half pagodas weight of blue vitriol [mayil toottam] and twenty pagodas weight of nitre [shorah] are then reduced to fine powder, which fine powder is sprinkled over the metals, at the same time stirring the whole with the root of the plant, Amarantus campestris, willd. [field spinach]; this having been done, the heat of the sand-bath is increased, and the process continued till such time as the Rasa sindooram is found.——*Rasauyanam* (रसायन - rasáyana, San.). From (rasa, san. mercury + ayana, san. manner). Originally alchemy, the art of converting base metals [loham] into gold [pon]; later chemistry [ilm, shastram].——*Rascapoor* (रसकर्पूर - rasakarpúra, San.; رسکپور - raskapúr, Hind. and Dec.; రసకర్పూరము - rasakarpúramu, Tel.; രസകർപ്പൂരം - rasakarppúram, Mal.; රසකපුර - rasakarpúra, Singh.; இரசக்கருப்பூரம் - irasakkaruppúram, Tam.). From (rasa, san. mercury + karpúra, san. camphor), being white like camphor. Calomel. Otherwise Bichloride of Mercury. Hydrargyri sub-chloridum of chemists. Impure as procured in the bazaar [q.v.] and there contains some perchloride or corrosive sublimate [shavveeram]. The article should properly be white, with an acrid metallic and persistent taste, without smell; in small crystals or in semi-transparent masses. It has been long known to natives. The following method of preparing it is taken from the Poorna sootram:—Sixteen pagodas [q.v.] weight of sulphur [gandhac] is to be fused in an earthen pot; after which eighty pagodas weight of quicksilver is to be added to it, and the whole to be kept stirred until reduced to a black powder; another earthen vessel is then to be taken and filled half full of small pieces of brick [shengal], over which is to be laid half a measure of common salt [ooppoo]; upon the top of this salt is to be put the black powder, and the whole to be covered with another empty earthen pot; the part where the mouths of the two pots meet is now to be well coated with soft clay and bound round with seven piles of coarse cloth. The two vessels, thus joined with their contents, are to be kept on a strong fire for twelve hours, and then the pots are to be taken off and left to cool. When perfectly cool, the uppermost is to be carefully removed from the other; when in the uppermost will be found a whitish saline substance in a lump. A sort of phial called cooppy [q.v.] is then to be well coated over in every part with clay, which phial is to be half filled with the white saline substance just mentioned. An open hollow earthen vessel is now to be taken, and, after being filled quarter full of river sand [manal], is to be placed upon a strong fire; into this sand thus heated is to be set the bottom of the cooppy, at the same time heaping up fresh sand to near its mouth. In this situation the white saline substance is to be kept purifying or subliming from six in the morning until twelve in the middle of the day, at which time the fire is to be extinguished and the whole left to cool until six in the evening; then again the fire is to be lighted and kept burning until twelve o'clock at night; and in this manner is the process to be continued for three days successively; after which period the rascapoor will be found in the upper part of the cooppy. Veidyans [q.v.] employ it for external and internal use more frequently than any other preparation of mercury. When given in a large dose, or its use continued for some time, it is apt to produce salivation, purging, palsy and erethism. Is purgative in moderate doses, and alterative in small. It is also used as an ointment, gargle, lotion, &c., in various complaints. According to Poorna sootram the mode of administering is thus;—One copper cash [q.v.] weight of palmyra [q.v.] jaggery [q.v.] and a quarter of a silver fanam [q.v.] weight of the rascapoor are to be well mixed together and made into a bolus; one half of which is to be taken in the morning and the other half in the evening, till the mouth is properly affected. In stronger habits double this dose may be given. When the rascapoor is administered in nervous or convulsive habits, or when the stomach is weak, five grains of long pepper [q.v.] must be added to the bolus. Rascapoor is according to the Poorna sootram a medicine of great efficacy in all the the eighteen kinds of leprosy [cooshtam], in twenty sorts of scurvy eruptions, in contractions of the sinews, in the venereal disease, in the dangerous ulcer which comes over the back-bone [rajah boil], in spreading ulcers, in deep-seated sores, in fistulas, in infectious itches, and in a certain species of hypochondriasis.——*Raseshwaram* (रसेश्वर - raséshvara, San.; రసము - rasamu, Tel.). From (rasa, san. fluid + íshvara, san. lord); as being the most valuable and useful of fluids. Same as Rasam. For the philosophical sect so called see Sarwa darshana sangraham.——*Rasnah* (रास्ना - rásná, San.; راسنا - rasná, Hind.; కనపబదనిక - kanapabadanika, Tel.). Title from hindostany. San. from (rasa, san. juice) [galangal]. Hind. from sanscrit meaning tasty. Tel. from (kanapa, tel. barringtonia acutangula, gærtn. + badanika, tel. parasitic plant). San. also (vandáka), meaning praising, parasitical; (gandhanákuli), meaning fragrant ichneumon plant; (vriksharuha), meaning growing on tree. Tel. also (chitteduru), meaning small + bamboo, bambusa arundinacea, willd.; (mardáru); (vadanika). Title otherwise Ichneumon plant, Vanda. Botanically Vanda roxburghii, r. br., orchidaceæ [vricsham, 141]. Generic from sanscrit. Alias Cymbidium tessaloides. Stem short, thick; leaves obliquely three-toothed at the apex; racemes erect, longer than the leaves; sepals and petals oblong-obovate, wavy, tessellated, obtuse; middle lobe of the lip convex, ovate, emarginate, very obtuse, channelled, obtusely callous before the spur, auricles acuminate, nearly equalling the column. Flowers above checkered with yellow and dusky ferruginous purple, beneath white; flowering nearly all the year. Root fragrant, bitter and useful in rheumatism. No other common species here.——*Rasoot* (رسوت - raswat, Hind.). From (rasa, san. juice + vat, san. suffix of possession). Watery extract from sliced root of berberry [q.v.].——*Rastauly* (రస్తాళి - rastáli, Tel.; இரசதாளி - irasatháli, Tam.). From (rasa, san. juice + dálu, tel. color). Having good color and taste. Same as Plantain.

RASHEED (رشید - rashíd, *Hind.*). From (rushada, ar. to lead aright). Prosperous, rightly directed. Also director. Attribute of God [allah]. Forms an alam; as Abdoor rasheed, slave of god. Also part of lacab; as Rasheed ood dowlah, director of the kingdom [ism].

RASOOL (رسول - rasúl, *Ar.*). From (rasala, ar. to send message). Messenger. Lacab of the prophet. Common alam; as Ghoolaum rasool, slave of the prophet [ism].

RATA (රට - rata, *Singh.*). From (ráshtra, san. country). Foreign [europe, faranghee, firangy, foreign, seema, vilauyaty].——*Ratadel* (රටදෙල් - ratadel, Singh.). Same as Foreign jack.

RATANHIA (कुकुरजिह्वा - kukurajihvá, *San.*; कर्कनि - karkani, *Mahr.*; ಅಂಕಡೋಸ - ankadósa, *Tel.*). Title from portuguese. San. from (kukura, san. dog + jihvá, san. tongue). Tel. from (anka, tel. side + dósa, tel. country melon). Title otherwise Ankados, Bois de sureau, Dino. Botanically Leea sambucina, willd., ampelideæ [vricsham, 42]. Alias Leea gigantea, ottilis, staphylea. Stems shrubby, with straight branches, leaves pinnate or tripinnate, often 3½ by 4 feet, leaflets stalked, very variable in size and shape, nerves arcuate; flowers greenish-white, anthers connate; fruit the size of a small cherry [q.v.], dry; grows in patches in thick jungle, looking something like elder; the root is woody, porous and tough, and covered with a striated, dark brown slightly scabrous bark, the internal surface of which is of a deep red color; the bark has an astringent and rather agreeable flavor. A decoction of the root is given in colic, cooling and relieves thirst; the roasted leaves are applied to the head in vertigo; the juice of the young leaves is digestive; much used in diarrhœa and chronic dysentery; a sudorific.

RATH (रथ - rat'ha, *San.*; رتھ - rath, *Hind.*). From (ramh, san. to go) [raghoo]. Chariot. The sun [sooryan], moon [chundran], and planets [graham] are all represented in the pooraunams [q.v.] as having chariots or vehicles [vauhan]. That of the sun is stated in Vishnoo pooraunam [q.v.] to be nine thousand leagues [yojanam] in length, and the pole of twice that length; that of the moon has three wheels and is drawn by ten white horses [ghorah]; the chariot of Mercury [boodhan] is composed of air and fire and is drawn by eight bay horses; the chariots of Mars [coojan, mungalan] and Jupiter [brihaspaty] are of gold [pon]. So an idol car [tair]. To every South indian temple [coil, pagoda] of any celebrity a large wooden car is attached, in which once a year an image of the divinity to whom the temple is dedicated is placed with ceremonies, and paraded in triumph, accompanied by Bramins, who are seated beside it. The car is decorated by a profusion of flags and banners, garlands of flowers, pictures, &c., and is frequently painted for the occasion. A long open space before the temple is kept level for the purpose of the procession; and ropes having been attached to the rings and axles of the large vehicle, it is dragged by as many as can lay hold of them amidst the din of drums, trumpets, and clarionets. In other cases the car is taken by a prescribed route through the streets of the town, the streets being constructed and preserved specially with a view to this occurrence. The image is afterwards removed, bathed, and put to rest, and for the year the festival is over [ratotsavam]. The tamul Cooral has the following:—உருவுகண் டெள்ளாமை வேண்டு முருள் பெருந்தேர்க் கச்சாணி யன்னா ருடைத்து—"let none be despised for size; the world has those who "resemble the linch-pin of the big rolling car." The Seven pagoda [q.v.] temples are called Raths.——*Rata saptamy* (రథసప్తమి - rat'hasaptami, Tel.). Car + seventh; so called as anniversary of a manwantaram [q.v.] when a new sun ascended his car. Lunar [chaundramaunam] festival [pundigay, 3e], subject to intercalation [adhicam]. The seventh tity [q.v.] of the waxing moon [shooclapacsham] in the eleventh lunar month Maugham [mausam] between 21st January and 19th February. On this day the present Manwantaram [q.v.] began [veiwaswatan]. The sun [sooryan] is worshipped after bathing in water mixed with the green leaves of the gigantic swallow-wort [yercum], and ancestral rites [tarpanam] are performed [maryauday].——*Ratotsavam* (రథోత్సవం - rat'hótsavam, Tel.). From (above + utsava, san. festival). Temple festival when the car [tair] with the idol [shilay, vigraham] is drawn round the streets. See Rath above [pundigay, 6d].

RAT'S EAR (शम्बरी - shambarí, *San.*; उंदीरकानी - undírakání, *Mahr.*; ఎలుకచెవ్వి - elukachevvi, *Tel.*; എലിച്ചെവി - eliççevi, *Mal.*; எலிக்காது - elikkáthu, *Tam.*). Title from leaves. San. from (sham, san. happiness + vri, san. to cover); from usefulness. Mahr. from (undura, san. rat + karna, san. ear). Tel. from (eluka, tel. rat + chevvi, tel. ear). Mal. from (eli, mal. rat + chevi, mal. ear). Tam. from (eli, tam. rat + káthu, tam. ear). Tam. also (perattai); (eliççevi), meaning rat + ear. Botanically Ipomæa [calamby] reniformis, chois., convolvulaceæ [vricsham, 93]. Alias Convolvulus reniformis; Evolvulus emarginatus. Stem creeping and rooting; leaves kidney-shaped, waved and dentate on the margin, obtuse; petioles hairy; peduncles very short, one to two-flowered; corolla small, yellow; common in places where water has lodged, flowering in the cold weather. Medicinally deobstruent and diuretic; leaves used as greens [keeray] mixed with tamarind [q.v.].

RAT SNAKE (دھامن - dhámin, *Hind.*; دھامن - dhámin, *Dec.*; జెర్రిపోతు - jerripótu, *Tel.*; ଧମନ - dhamana, *Oor.*; ചേര - chéra, *Mal.*; சாரைப்பாம்பு - sháraippámbu, *Tam.*). Title from its habit of feeding on rats. Hind. from (dháv, san. to run quickly). Tel. from (jerri, tel. centipede + pótu, tel. male); centepede's husband. Mal. from (chéru, mal. to join). Tam. from (shárai, tam. stripes + pámbu, tam. snake). Tel. also (tsárapótu), meaning stripe + male. Title otherwise Dhauman, Male cobra, Whip snake [q.v.]. Ptyas mucosus, colubridæ [paumb], ophidii colubriformes, ophidia [sarpam], reptilia [sarpy, 17], of naturalists [jantoo]. Not dangerous. Natives assert that its bite occasions blindness in persons aged above forty. Often found in company with the Cobra de Capello. It is believed by natives to breed with it. Brownish or yellowish olive with interstitial skin coloring of yellow and black scales with black tips forming a fasciolation posteriorly and often a reticulated pattern on the tail; belly greenish or yellowish white. When young this snake often has delicate green color unlike the adult. Its food consists of mammals [sastanam], birds [pacshy], and frogs [bhaicam]; it frequently enters the dwellings of man in search of mice [shoondely], rats [ely], and young fowls [moorghy]; it is of fierce habits, always ready to bite, and never becomes tame; utters when irritated a peculiar sound, not unlike that produced by a gently struck tuning fork. The natives hold that the rat snake does not bite. And there is a Malayalam proverb:—അടച്ചുകിടന്നാൽ ചേരയും കടിക്കും—"stop its hole, even a rat snake will bite;" meaning the same as tread on a worm and it will turn. The Tamulians recognize the following different kinds.——*Black rat snake* (నల్లచార - nallatsára, Tel.; കരിഞ്ചേര - kariñchéra, Mal.; கருஞ்சாரை - karuñjárai, Tam.).——*Hill rat snake* (மலைஞ்சாரை - malañjárai, Tam.).——*Large rat snake* (పెద్దచార - peddatsára, Tel.; பெருஞ்சாரை - peruñjárai, Tam.).——*Long rat snake* (పొడుగుచార - podugutsára, Tel.; நெடுஞ்சாரை - nedunjárai, Tam.).——*White rat snake* (తెల్లచార - tellatsára, Tel.; வெண்சாரை - vensárai, Tam.).——*Yellow rat snake* (పసిచార - pasitsára, Tel.; മഞ്ഞച്ചേര - maññaççéra, Mal.; மஞ்சட்சாரை - mañjadchárai, Tam.).

RATTA (ರಟ್ಟ - ratta, *Can.*). From (ratte, can. arm). Dynasty [raj]. By some considered to be of the same stock as Rashtracootas [q.v.] whom they succeeded. Flourished for about 3½ centuries either as feudatories of Rashtracootas or Western chalookyas [q.v.], or independent. They were of Jeina [q.v.] religion. Finally conquered by Yaudavas [q.v.] of Devagiry. Did not come much in contact with southern chiefs. See vol. I (138) [charitram].

RATTAN (روتن - rotan, *Malay*); meaning pared or trimmed. The long stem of various species of climbing palms [taur], belonging to the genus calamus [vaitasam] and its allies, of which canes are made.——*Country rattan* (वेतस - vétasa, San.; वेत - véta, Mahr.; बेत - béta, Conc.; خيزران - khaizurán, Ar.; خزران - khuzrán, Pers. بيت - bet, Hind. and Dec.; روتن - rotan, Malay; ಬೆತ್ತ - betta, Can.; ಸುರಲ್ಬೆತ್ತ - suralbetta, Too.; పేము - pému, Tel.; ചൂരൽ - chúral, Mal.; වේවැල - vévala, Singh.; மெல்லிசுப்பிரம்பு - mellisnppirambu, Tam.). San. from (vé, san. to plait); from stems being split into strips which are plaited into baskets, mats, &c. Mahr. from sanscrit. Conc. from sanscrit. Ar. from (khuzara, ar. slender). Pers. from arabic. Hind. from sanscrit. Can. from sanscrit. Too. from (surali, too. coil + betta, too. rattan). Tel. from (vétra, san.). Mal. from (churul, mal. coil). Singh. from (vé, singh. rattan + val, singh. creeper). Tam. from (meli, tam. thinness + pirambu, tam. rattan). San. also (vétra), meaning plaiting plant; (dírghavallí), meaning long creeper; (latávamsha), meaning creeper bamboo, bambusa arundinacea, willd. Pers. also (bed). Tel. also (prabba), meaning spreading; (prabbali), meaning spreading; (níruprabba), meaning water + the plant; (sannabettamu), meaning slender + rattan; (bettamu), from (vétra, san.). Mal. also (níravaññi), meaning water + reed; (punambu), meaning hill plant. Tam. also (pirambu), meaning hill plant; (vaníram), meaning water-rattan. Title otherwise Chair-bottom cane, Creeper bamboo, Slender rattan, Water rattan. Botanically Calamus [vaitasam] rotang, linn., palmaceæ [vricsham, 149]. Specific name from malay. Alias Calamus roxburghii. Stem scandent; fronds without tendrils, pinnæ somewhat equidistant, linear-lanceolate, acuminate; prickles of the sheaths frequent, compressed, straight, of the rachis straight and recurved, of the spathes and tendrils bent; spadix compound; male calyx three-cleft, campanulate, a half shorter than the broad triangular segments of the corolla; berries ovate, sub-globose, size of a small cherry [q.v.]; moist jungles, flowering in the rains; a very graceful small palm [taur]. Seeds are surrounded by fleshy kind of substance, which is eaten, as well as young tender shoots. Yields the best rattan cane of commerce; split into strips and plaited or woven into baskets [tokrah], chairs, sofas, and carriages; twisted into ropes, or stretched entire across rivers, as the main supports of indigenous suspension bridges; burnt makes a black paint [rangh]. The actual article chiefly used here for making the mats [boriyah] with which the floors of rooms are covered is imported from singapore.——*Walking-stick rattan* (अम्बुवेतस - ambuvétasa, San.; بري بيت - baríbet, Hind.; బెత్తము - bettamu, Tel.; ചൂരൽ - chúral, Mal.; பிரம்பு - pirambu, Tam.). San. from (ambu, san. water + vétasa, san. calamus rotang, linn.). Hind. from (barí, hind. large + bet, hind. calamus rotang, linn.). Tel. from (vétra, san. cane). Mal. from (churul, mal. coil). Tam. from (punam, tam. hill tract). San. also (sahasravédhí), meaning thousand + piercer, from confluent prickles. Tel. also (ámlavétasamu), meaning sour cane. Title otherwise Rattan-cane, Sour cane, Water cane. Botanically Calamus [vaitasam] fasciculatus, roxb., palmaceæ [vricsham,

149]. Stem scandent, elongated; fronds without tendrils; pinnæ aggregated into many distant fascicles, ensiform; prickles of the fronds straight, scattered, and confluent; spadix decompound, abortive ones whip-shaped; berries ovate. Stems when divested of their sheaths are about as thick as the forefinger; used as walking-sticks. Cf. Penang lawyer.——*Water rattan* (నీరుప్రబ్బ - níruprabba, Tel.). Title from habitat. Same as Country rattan.——*Wild rattan* (هرچرل - harcharal, Hind.; పనంబువళ్ళి - panambuvalli, Can.; వనచంద్ర - vanachandra, Tel.; പനമ്പുവള്ളി - panambuvalli, Mal.). Tel. from (vana, tam. forest + chandra, san. moon); probably from white flowers. Mal. from (panambu, mal. rattan, calamus rotang, linn. + valli, mal. creeper). Hind. also (banchandar), meaning forest moon; (ranchandar), meaning forest moon. Title otherwise Forest moon, Rattan creeper. Botanically Flagellaria indica, l., commelynaceæ [vricsham, 139]. Perennial, scandent; leaves narrow, ending in long slender spiral tendrils, contracted and sheathing at the base; flowers terminal, panicled, bracteolate, white, inconspicuous; berries globose, red, smooth, pulpy, one-seeded, with two abortive ovules; flowering in the rains. Leaves are astringent and vulnerary. No other species here.

RATTEL (رطل - ratl, *Ar.*; ರಾತ್ಲು - rátlu, *Can.*; റാത്തൽ - ráttal, *Mal.*; இறாத்தல் - iráttal, *Tam.*). Ar. from (ratala, ar. to weigh in the hand). A weight equal to the english avoirdupois pound. Scale in Malabar:—4 west coast pollums = 1 rattel; 25 rattels = 1 toolaum [niray, 2d]. Scale in S. canara:—40 rupee weights = 1 rattel; 28 rattels = 1 canara maund [niray, 2c]. Used in Tamul districts by Lubbays [q.v.] for weighing leather [chamrah]. See vol. I, 609; II, 508, 515.

RAUBIA (رابعه - rábiah, *Ar.*). A female devotee who promoted soofeeism [soofee]. Taken as alam, as:—Raubia bee, alam + alaumat [ism].

RAUDHAY (राधा - rádhá, *San.*). From (rádh, san. to be favorable). Wife of Krishnan [q.v.]. Proper name among the Madhwas. Hindoo 2nd or pers. name [peyar]. The following is a Hindostany proverb:—اپنی رادھا کو یاد کرو—"attend to your own raudhay;" mind your own business.——*Raudha krishnan* (राधाकृष्ण - rádhákrishna, San.). From (above + krishna, san. the god). Compound name, meaning krishnan with his mistress. Vishnoo [q.v.].——*Raudhaupooram* (இராதாப்புரம் - iráthápparam, Tam. rádhápuram *). From (above + pura, san. city).—"*a*" Deputy tahsildarry, Tinnevelly district. Pay Rs. 70.—"*b*" Town, Deputy tahsildar's station; Tinnevelly dist., Nangoonairy tal.; pop. 2,235; acres 9,436; lat. 8° 16′; long. 77° 44′; from Madras S.S.W. 372 miles; from Nangoonairy S. 15 miles; from Palamcottah S. 32 miles; from Shermadevy S.S.E. 30 miles; from Shreevillipoottore S. 84 miles; from Tinnevelly S. 32 miles; from Tuticorin S.W. 49 miles; from the sea W. 7 miles. Large temple. Festival in Chittray [mausam] April-May. Weekly fair on Monday. S.P.G. mission station. The Cape comorin base line of the Great trigonometrical survey is measured from Codangoolam in the extreme south to this village. Trig. station here in lat. 8° 17′ 02·07″; long. 77° 44′ 35·95″; height 163 feet; from Nangoonairy S.S.E. 15 miles; from Vijayapathy N.N.W. 7 miles; from the sea N. 8 miles.

RAUHAT (راحت - ráhat, *Ar.*). From (rauha, ar. to be pleasant). Comfort. Prefixed to an alam forms a lacab; as Rauhat ally, comfort of ally [ism].

RAUL (सर्जरस - sarjarasa, *San.*; رال - rál, *Hind.*; گاته - gátah, *Malay*; సజ్జరసము - sajjarasamu, *Tel.*; കുങ്കില്യം - kunkilyam, *Mal.*; குங்கிலியம் - kungiliyam, *Tam.*). Title from hindostany. San. from (sarja, san. the tree, shorea robusta, gærtn. + rasa, san. juice). Hind. from (rála, san. shorea resin). Tam. from (guggulu, san. the fragrant gum resin) [googal]. Resin. Inflammable substance of vegetable origin. Obtained either by spontaneous exudation from plants, or by extraction by heat and alcohol. Resins are solid, brittle, of a certain degree of transparency, and of a color commonly inclining to yellow. Under friction electric. When pure, they are soluble in alcohol and in oils [yennay] but not in water, in which respect they differ from gums [gond]. They are more or less acted upon by the alkalies [alkali, cauram]. The acid resins comprise rosin, dammer [q.v.], gamboge [q.v.], sandrach [q.v.], benzoin [q.v.], lac [q.v.], &c.; the neutral resins elemi [q.v.], guaiacum, dragon's-blood [q.v.], and storax [q.v.]. Europe resin from the pine [cheer] is prized by tinmen, who employ it with borax [swauga, vengauram] in soldering [pattoo]; for which purpose country resin or dammer [q.v.] does not answer so well. There are also so-called mineral resins; as amber [karbah], asphalt [shilajit], bitumen [shilajit], petroleum [naphtha, niftroomy, munnteilam] and other mineral hydrocarbons.

RAUNA (रान - rána, *Mahr.*). From (aranya, san. forest). Wild. Plant first term, often joining two genera. Ex., where transl. is of second term:—Jatropha curcas (ránaérandí), ricinus communis; Lagenaria vulgaris (ránabhómpalí), benincasa cerifera; Spondias mangifera (ránaámba), mangifera indica; Urginia indica (ránakándá), allium cepa; Vernonia anthelmintica (ránajírem), cuminum cyminum. See gloss. paragraphs.——*Ramoosy* (रामोसी - rámósí, San.). From (rána, mahr. forest + vásí, san. inhabitant). The Thugs' [q.v.] slang dialect.

RAUPORE (రాపూరు - rápúru, *Tel.* rápúr *). From (rádzu, tel. king + pura, san. town). The town of krishna deva royel [raj]. Sanscrit name (ráhupura), meaning rahoo, the giant + town.——(1) Talook; Nellore district. Tahsildar's pay Rs. 150. Area 596 square miles. Most southerly of the inlying Government talooks. Bounded north by Atmacore talook, south by Vencatagherry division, east by Nellore and Goodoor talooks, west by Poollampett and Sidhout talooks of Cuddapah district. The Candlair, which rises from the Veligondas, and the Vencatagherry river, run through it. These receive the drainage from the Eastern ghauts [q.v.], and uniting in the Manoobole valley flow into the Kistnapatam backwater. The Veligondas run by the west of the talook, of which Penchalcondah is a prominent peak. Penchalcondah might be made a sanitarium for Nellore, and a road is now under construction towards it. There are also some scattered hills here and there. Valuable jungle, especially at foot of Veligondas. The country is generally of black loamy soil. The sub-soil is rocky, and wells are in consequence deep and costly. Abruck [q.v.], or native talc [q.v.] is found mixed with the sand in the villages of Griddalore and Ootcore and elsewhere. Fuel exports give occupation to many. Except weaving to a limited extent in a few villages there is no industry worth mention. Tobacco [pogauk] and chillies [q.v.] and dyeing [shauyam] barks are exported to Madras. The irrigation is mostly from rain-fed tanks [q.v.]. A large number of private wells irrigate the garden lands. The largest tanks are those of Podalacore, Raupore, Sydapore and Vadlapoody. There are also large tanks irrigating more than 200 acres of their ayacut [q.v.] in the villages of Joreypully, Marpore, Rama saugaram, Siddhavaram, and Todair. Camping grounds:—Marlapoody, Podalacore, Raupore, Sydapore. Places of archæological interest:—Aultoorty, Calichaid, Chauganam, Cheecavole, Commipaud, Dausore, Dooggoonta, Gilacapaud, Gonoopulley, Goondavole, Griddalore, Marpore, Mogullore, Nairnore, Ootcore, Palicherlapaud, Pautagoonta, Penoobarty, Permaulpaud, Podalacore, Raupore, Sydapore, Taunamcherla, Toorimerla, Vadlapoody, Wooyyaulpulley, Yaipore, Yettoor, Yinoocoorty. Principal Trig. stations:—Allicondah, Ootcore, Paulcherla, Pullacondah. The leading places, &c., in the talook are the following.——*Allicondah* (అల్లికొండ - allikonda, Tel.). From (allu, tel. to spread + konda, tel hill). Trig. station; lat. 14° 22′ 41·93″; long. 79° 43′ 50·76″; height 639 feet; from Nellore W. 20 miles; from Raupore N.E. 16 miles.——*Biradavole* (బిరదవోలు - biradavólu, Tel.). From (birudu, tel. badge + prólu, tel. town). Village; pop. 1,052; acres 7,174; lat. 14° 21′; long. 79° 49′; from Nellore S.W. 16 miles; from Raupore E.N.E. 19 miles. A high bald hill, is seen for miles around as a land mark. Much reserved jungle and considerable pasture. There is a Rauzoopollem here, the Rauzooloo [rauz] having come down from the north and settled. Is on the road from Manoobole to Podalacore, 6 miles from the latter place.——*Caukoolacondah* (కాకులకొండ - kákulakonda, Tel.). From (káki, tel. crow + konda, tel. hill). Hill; lat. 14° 14′; long. 79° 32′; height 500 feet; from Nellore W.S.W. 36 miles; from Raupore N.W. 3 miles.——*Chauganam* (చాగనం - cháganam, Tel.). From (chágamu, tel. charity). Village; pop. 1,440; acres 7,473; lat. 14° 13′; long. 79° 44′; from Nellore S.W. 26 miles; from Raupore E. 10 miles. Half a mile from the right side of the road from Goodoor to Raupore, half way between Sydapore and Marlapoody which is 6 miles from Raupore. Has a large tank. The people of Rauz [q.v.] caste live in a separate pollem [q.v.]. Their houses are surrounded by high walls to protect females from public view.——*Goondavole* (గుండవోలు - gundavólu, Tel.). From (gundamu, tel. deep gorge + prólu, tel. town). Village; pop. 1,206; acres 7,532; lat. 14° 17′; long. 79° 34′; from Nellore W.S.W. 32 miles; from Raupore N. 6 miles. On the road from Raupore to Penchalcondah. Has a large tank.——*Gooticondah* (గూటికొండ - gútikonda, Tel.). From (gúdu, tel. recess + konda, tel. hill). Hill; lat. 14° 17′; long. 79° 41′; height 3,635 feet; from Nellore W.S.W. 26 miles; from Raupore N.E. 9 miles.——*Marla condah* (మర్లకొండ - marlakonda, Tel.). From (marri, tel. ficus bengalensis, linn. + konda, tel. hill). Title also Mullemcondah, hill of mountain goddess. Hill; lat. 14° 19′; long. 79° 40′; height 2,000 feet; from Nellore W.S.W. 26 miles; from Raupore N.E. 10 miles.——*Ootcore* (ఊటుకూరు - útukúru, Tel.). See sep. title.——*Paulcherla* (పాలచెర్ల - pálacherla, Tel.). From (pálu, tel. milk + cherla, tel. village). Trig. station; lat. 14° 10′ 19·11″; long. 79° 30′ 41·29″; height 2,156 feet; from Raupore S.W. 5 miles; from Yaipore S.S.W. 7 miles.——*Penchalcondah* (పెంచలకొండ - penchalakonda, Tel.). See sep. title.——*Podalacore* (పొదలకూరు - podalakúru, Tel.). See sep. title.——*Potecondah* (పోతుకొండ - pótukonda, Tel.). From (pótu, tel. ox + konda, tel. hill). Hill; lat. 14° 15′; long. 79° 37′; height 800 feet; from Nellore W.S.W. 31 miles; from Raupore N.E. 4 miles.——*Pullacondah* (పల్లెకొండ - pallekonda, Tel.). From (palle, tel. village + konda, tel. hill). Village; pop. 365; acres 4,810; lat. 14° 26′; long. 79° 33′;

from Nellore W. 32 miles; from Raupore N. 16 miles. Trig. station in lat. 14° 24′ 19·03″; long. 79° 30′ 28·95″; height 1,178 feet; from Raupore N.N.W. 14 miles; from Tirmalpaud W.S.W. 3 miles.——*Raupore* (రాపూరు - rápúru, Tel.). See below.——*Siddhoolacondah* (సిద్ధులకొండ - siddhulakonda, Tel.). From (siddulu, tel. proper name + konda, tel. hill). Sanscrit name (siddhagiri), meaning sage + hill. Hill; lat. 14° 19′; long. 79° 47′; height 200 feet; from Nellore W.S.W. 18 miles; from Raupore E.N.E. 16 miles. Soapstone [sowcaura cull] quarries. ——*Sydapore* (సైదాపురము - saidápuramu, Tel.). See sep. title. ——*Toommalatalpore* (తుమ్మలతలుపూరు - tummalatalupúru, Tel.). From (tumma, tel. babul tree, acacia arabica, willd. + talupúru, tel. place so called). Village; pop. 1,202; acres 9,139; lat. 14° 18′; long. 79° 44′; from Nellore W.S.W. 22 miles; from Raupore E. 13 miles. Formerly head-quarters of a Tahsildar. ——*Vadlapoody* (వడ్లపూడి - vadlapúdi, Tel.). From (vadlu, tel. paddy + púdi, tel. village). Village; pop. 2,221; acres 9,608; lat. 14° 19′; long. 79° 51′; from Nellore S.W. 15 miles; from Raupore E.N.E. 20 miles. A large village with a revenue next to Raupore. Has a large tank. Is on the road from Manoobole to Podalacore. The Candlair passes by. It is dammed and its waters are taken for irrigation to zemindarry [q.v.] villages by a canal excavated by the Zemindar [q.v.] of Vencatagherry.——*Veligonda* (వెలిగొండ - veligonda, Tel.). See sep. title.——*Yerracondah* (ఎర్రకొండ - errakonda, Tel.). See sep. title.——**(2)** Village, Head-quarters of Tahsildar; Nellore dist., Raupore tal.; pop. 3,217; acres 10,190; lat. 14° 12′; long. 79° 35′; from Madras N.W. 93 miles; from Naidoopett N.W. 32 miles; from Nellore W.S.W. 34 miles; from Ongole S.S.W. 96 miles. Remains of a fort built by Velgoty yautsama naidoo, Zemindar of Vencatagherry, and held by Krishna deva royel, subsequently by rulers of the Gajapaty [q.v.] dynasty [raj] of Vizianagram, then by the Mahomedan rulers of the Golcondah dynasty, and lastly by the Nawaub [q.v.] of the Carnatic [q.v.]. At the beginning of the present century there was a jagheerdar [q.v.] in the fort named Abd ool mabood shumsheer jung related to Nawaub wallajah [q.v.]. The fort walls are massive, and there is a fine ditch. Inside are the remains of the old palace and other buildings. Raupore has a large tank which is supplied by a hill stream. With a hill on one side and three tanks on different sides it presents picturesque scenery. A ghaut [q.v.] over the hills goes into Chitwail. A German mission. A newly built mosque [musjid].——**(3)** *Rauporecanama* (రాపూరుకనుమ - rápúrukanama, Tel.). From (rápúru, tel. the town + kanama, tel. pass). Ghaut; Cuddapah dist., Poollampett tal.; lat. 14° 11′; long. 79° 26′; from Cuddapah S.E. 54 miles; from Poollampett E.N.E. 13 miles. Over the Veligondas between Cuddapah and Nellore districts [ghaut].

RAUSHY (राशि - ráshi, *San.*; راس - rás, *Hind.*; రాశి - ráshi, *Tel.*; രാശി - ráshi, *Mal.*; இராசி - irási, *Tam.*). From (ash, san. to heap). Literally a heap. Sum total in arithmetic [ganitam]. Oobhaya raushy is a heap of grain comprising both the government share [mailvauram] and the cultivator's share [coodivauram].——**(1)** A sign of the zodiac [raushy chuckram] as being a certain sum of degrees [bhaugam].—"*a*" One-twelfth part of the ecliptic [craunty mundalam] containing 30 degrees; equal to 2¼ Nacshatrams [q.v.] or lunar mansions.—"*b*" The signs are called by specific names when reckoned on the sidereal zodiac, when counted on the tropical sphere they are only called numerically. Raushy chuckram [q.v.] or Raushy mundalam [q.v.] is the zodiacal circle or zodiac. The twelve raushies are also called twelve Lagnams [q.v.].—"*c*" The terms Kriyam [maisham] *κριός*, Tauvoory [vrishabham] *ταῦρος*, Jitoomam [mitoonam] *δίδυμος*, Cooleeram [carcatacam] *κόλουρος*, Leyam [simham] *λέων*, Pauthonam [canyay], *παρθένος*, Joocam [toolaum] *ζυγόν*, Cowrpyam [vrishchicam] *σκορπίος*, Towcshicam [dhanoos] *τοξότης*, Aukokeram [macaram] *αἰγοκέρως*, Hridrogam [coombham] *ὑδροχόος*, and Antyabham [meenam], are other names for the signs of the Zodiac; all these excepting Antyabham Greek, as shown.—"*d*" In astrology the signs have the following terrestrial and applied significations:— Maisham represents cotton [q.v.] and woollen fabric [pushmeenah], leathern oil jars, beans [shimbicam], wheat [geung], raggy [q.v.], barley [jow], dry crops [dry grain] in general, and gold [pon]. Vrishabham represents cloths in general, flowers [phool], wheat [geung], rice [q.v.], barley [jow], buffalo [khoolgah] and cows [pashoo]. Mitoonam represents the autumnal crops, creepers, the root of the lily [indian water-lily] and cotton [q.v.]. Carcatacam represents kodravam [khoda], plantains [q.v.], bent grass [hurrially], fruits [pazham], roots, leaves and bark. Simham represents food grains [dhaunyam], juice, the skin of the lion and the like animals, and jaggery [q.v.]. Canyay represents common flax [alsee], barley [jow], horse-gram [q.v.], wheat [geung], kidney-beans [moodgam] and nishpauvam [cow gram]. Toolaum represents black gram [q.v.], wheat [geung], and mustard seed [rayaun]. Vrishchicam represents sugar-canes [q.v.], wet crops [q.v.], metals [loham], and woollen fabric [pushmeenah]. Dhanoos represents horses [ghorah], salt [ooppoo], cloth, weapons, gingelly [q.v.] seeds, and roots. Macaram represents trees, bushes, wet crops [q.v.], sugar-canes [q.v.], gold [pon], and black-lead [eeyam]. Coombham represents water-fruits and flowers [phool], gems [ratnam] and articles of various shapes. Meenam represents pearls [moty] and other shell gems, diamonds [vajram], various oils [yennay] and fishes [matsyam].—"*e*" Signs that rise by their feet are known as Prishtodaya raushies, viz., Maisham, Vrishabham, Carcatacam, Dhanoos, and Macaram; powerful astrologically by night. Signs that rise by their heads are known as Shirodaya raushies, viz., Mitoonam, Simham, Canyay, Toolaum, Vrishchicam, and Coombham; powerful by day. The two fish [hoot] rise by both head and foot; powerful by day and night.—"*f*" The odd numbered signs are all astrologically malefic and masculine; the even numbered signs are all benefic and feminine.— "*g*" Maisham, Carcatacam, Toolaum, and Macaram are called movable signs; Vrishabham, Simham, Vrishchicam, and Coombham are fixed signs; Mitoonam, Canyay, Dhanoos, and Meenam are both movable and fixed.—"*h*" Maisham, Simham and Dhanoos are called eastern signs; Vrishabham, Canyay and Macaram are southern signs; Mitoonam, Toolaum and Coombham are western signs; Carcatacam, Vrishchicam and Meenam are northern signs.—"*i*" The signs Maisham, Vrishabham, Macaram, Canyay, Carcatacam, Meenam, and Toolaum are respectively the ootcham or exaltation or astrologically highest signs of the sun and the six other planets [graham]; the sun and moon being here treated as planets, and the five others as per the days of the week [vauram]. Each sign is divided into 30 degrees [bhaugam]; the 10th, 3rd, 28th, 15th, 5th, 27th, and 20th degrees are the degrees of main exaltation of the several planets. The seventh sign from ootcham of a planet, is its neecham, e.g., sun is ootcham in maisham and seventh from maisham is toolaum, and the sun is neecham in that sign. The degrees of main depression are the same as given above. A planet in his exaltation sign is considered as exceedingly powerful and one in his depression sign as exceedingly weak. The following table shows the above:—

Planets.	Ootcham or exaltation signs.	Neecham or depression signs.	Degree of main exaltation or main depression.
Sooryan.	Maisham.	Toolaum.	10
Chundran.	Vrishabham.	Vrishchicam.	3
Coojan.	Macaram.	Carcatacam.	28
Boodhan.	Canyay.	Meenam.	15
Brihaspaty.	Carcatacam.	Macaram.	5
Shoocran.	Meenam.	Canyay.	27
Shany.	Toolaum.	Maisham.	20

—"*j*" The twelve signs beginning from the ascendant [lagnam] or sign which happens to be rising at time of a birth, &c., are known technically as the signs of:—1, Calpam or power, 2, Swam or wealth, 3, Vicramam or prowess, 4, Graham or dwelling place, 5, Pratibhay or intelligence, 6, Cshatam or wound, 7, Manmatam or desire, 8, Randhram, or aperture, 9, Gooroo or preceptor, 10, Maunam or respectability, 11, Bhavam or acquisition, 12, Vyayam or loss.—"*k*" The following diagram, a common mode of constructing the astrological figure of the heavens, exhibits the signs in their order as shown by numerals, and the places among them of sun moon and five planets who are considered to occupy particular signs as their houses or fixed residences. The planets are the lords of the houses thus constituted. Thus coojan, shoocran, boodhan, chundran, sooryan, boodhan, shoocran, coojan, brihaspaty, shany, shany and brihaspaty are respectively the lords of the signs or raushies in their order; or coojan is the lord of maisham and vrishchicam; shoocran, of vrishabham and toolaum; boodhan, of mitoonam and canyay; brihaspaty, of dhanoos and meenam; shany, of macaram and coombham; chundran, of carcatacam and sooryan, of simham. It will be seen that the sun and moon have each a house while the other planets have each two houses. The houses are known as swacshetrams. Compare Dashavargam under Vargam:—

<table>
<tr><td>12
Meenam, pisces. Brihaspaty, jupiter.</td><td>1
Maisham, aries. Coojan, mars.</td><td>2
Vrishabham, taurus. Shoocran, venus.</td><td>3
Mitoonam, gemini. Boodhan, mercury.</td></tr>
<tr><td>11
Coombham, aquarius. Shany, saturn.</td><td colspan="2" rowspan="2">Raushy chuckram showing planetary houses in the fixed sidereal zodiac.</td><td>4
Carcatacam, cancer. Chundran, Moon.</td></tr>
<tr><td>10
Macaram, capricornus. Shany, saturn.</td><td>5
Simham, leo. Sooryan, sun.</td></tr>
<tr><td>9
Dhanoos, sagittarius. Brihaspaty, jupiter.</td><td>8
Vrishchicam, scorpio. Coojan, mars.</td><td>7
Toolaum, libra. Shoocran, venus.</td><td>6
Canyay, virgo. Boodhan, mercury.</td></tr>
</table>

The fourth and eighth houses are known as Chatoorashram or quadrangular signs; the seventh house is known as Dyoonam; the tenth house is known as Anyam.——(2) The following table shows the signs of the fixed sidereal zodiac displayed against lunar mansions [nacshatram]. 10, 11, 12, 1, 2 and 3 are Oottarauyanam [q.v.], and 4—9 are Dacshinauyanam [q.v.]. Sign Maisham consists of the asterisms of Ashwiny [q.v.], and Bharany and the first quarter of Kritticay [q.v.]. Sign Vrishabham consists of the last three quarters of Kritticay [q.v.], the asterism of Rohiny [q.v.] and the first two quarters of Mrigashiras [q.v.]. Sign Mitoonam consists of the last two quarters of Mrigashiras, the asterism of Ardray [q.v.] and the first three quarters of Poonarvas [q.v.]. Sign Carcatacam consists of the last quarter of Poonarvas [q.v.] and the asterisms of Pooshyam [q.v.] and Aushlaisham [q.v.]. Sign Simham consists of the asterisms of Magham [q.v.] and Poorva phalgoony [poobbam], and the first quarter of Oottara phalgoony [oottaram]. Sign Canyay consists of the last three quarters of Oottara phalgoony [oottram], the asterism of Hastam [q.v.], and the first two quarters of Chitta [q.v.]. Sign Toolaum consists of the last two quarters of Chitta [q.v.], the asterism of Swauty [q.v.], and the first three quarters of Vishaukham [q.v.]. Sign Vrishchicam consists of the last quarter of Vishaukham [q.v.] and the asterisms of Anooraudhay [q.v.] and Jyeshtay [q.v.]. Sign Dhanoos consists of the asterisms of Moolam [q.v.] and Poorvashaudham [q.v.] and the first quarter Oottarashaudham [q.v.]. Sign Macaram consists of the last three quarters of Oottarashaudham [q.v.], the asterism of Shravanam [q.v.] and the first two quarters of Shravishtay [q.v.]. Sign Coombham consists of the last two quarters of Shravishtay [q.v.] the asterism of Shatabhishay [q.v.], and the first three quarters of Poorvabhaudram [q.v.]. Sign Meenam consists of the last quarter of Poorvabhaudram [q.v.] and the asterisms of Oottarabhaudram [q.v.] and Raivaty [q.v.]. Signs Maisham, Simham and Dhanoos begin respectively with the asterisms of Ashwiny, Magham and Moolam and the several signs end with the first, second, third or fourth quarters of the odd asterisms succeeding the said three asterisms:—

No.	Hindoo name.	European name.	Arabic name.	Sign.	Corresponding nacshatrams [q.v.] of the fixed lunar zodiac [bhamundalam].	Dravidian solar months [madhyamasowra maunam], solilunar nomenclature [mausam], during which the sun is supposed to be in these signs.	Beginning of month mentioned in Column 7 in terms of Gregorian calendar.	No.
1	2	3	4	5	6	7	8	9
1	Maisham, ram ...	Aries, ram ...	Hamel, lamb.	♈	Ashwiny, 1 ... Bharany, 2 ... Kritticay, 3 ...	Chittray ...	April 12 ...	1
2	Vrishabham, bull...	Taurus, bull ...	Sowr, bull.	♉	Rohiny, 4 ... Mrigashiras, 5 ...	Veiyaushy	May 13 ...	2
3	Mitoonam, twins ...	Gemini, twins ...	Jowzah, middle.	♊	Ardray, 6 ... Poonarvas, 7 ...	Auny ...	June 13 ...	3
4	Carcatacam, crab ...	Cancer, crab ...	Sartaun, crab.	♋	Pooshyam, 8 ... Aushlaisham, 9 ...	Audy ...	July 15 ...	4
5	Simham, lion ...	Leo, lion	Asad, lion.	♌	Magham, 10 ... Poobbam, 11 ... Ottaram, 12 ...	Auvany ...	August 15 ...	5
6	Canyay, virgin ...	Virgo, virgin ...	Soomboola, virgin.	♍	Hastam, 13 ... Chitta, 14 ...	Poorataushy	September 15...	6
7	Toolaum, balance...	Libra, balance ...	Meezaun, balance.	♎	Swauty, 15 ... Vishaukham, 16 ...	Arpisy ...	October 16 ...	7
8	Vrishchicam, scorpion.	Scorpio, scorpion.	Akrab, scorpion.	♏	Anooraudhay, 17 ... Jyeshtay, 18 ...	Caurtigay	November 15...	8
9	Dhanoos, bow ...	Sagittarius, archer.	Kows, archer.	♐	Moolam, 19 ... Poorvashaudham, 20.	Maurgaly	December 14...	9
10	Macaram, alligator.	Capricornus, goat.	Jaddy, goat.	♑	Oottarashaudham, 21. Shravanam, 22 ...	Tye ...	January 12 ...	10
11	Coombham, pot ...	Aquarius, waterman.	Dalo, water-bucket.	♒	Dhanishtay, 23 ... Shatabhishay, 24 ... Poorva Bhaudram, 25.	Maushy ...	February 12 ...	11
12	Meenam, fish ...	Pisces, fishes ...	Hoot, fish.	♓	Oott Bhaud, 26 ... Raivaty, 27 ...	Pungoony	March 12 ...	12

——(3) The following is a diagram of the same as used in the native calendars [punchaungam, vaunashastram, zyecha]:—

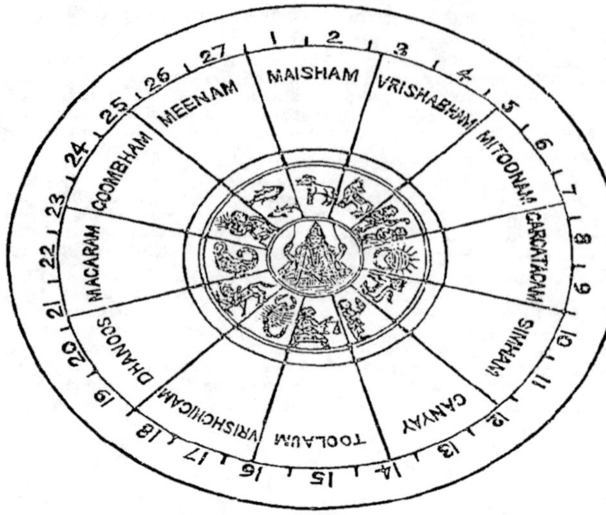

——(4) The following are the names of the signs in alphabetical order.——*Canyay* (కన్య - kanya, Tel.; கன்னி - kanni, Tam.). Sixth. The Virgin. Virgo [soomboola].——*Carcatacam* (కర్కాటకము - karkátakamu, Tel.; கடகம் - kadagam, Tam.). Fourth. The Crab. Cancer [sartaun].——*Coombham* (కుంభము - kumbhamu, Tel.; கும்பம் - kumbam, Tam.). Eleventh. The Pot. Aquarius [dalo].——*Dhanoos* (ధనస్సు - dhanussu, Tel.; தனுசு - tanusu, Tam.). Ninth. The Bow. Sagittarius [kows]. ——*Macaram* (మకరము - makaramu, Tel.; மகரம் - magaram, Tam.). Tenth. The Alligator. Capricornus [jaddy].——*Maisham* (మేషము - méshamu, Tel.; மேடம் - médam, Tam.). First. The Ram. Aries [hamel].——*Meenam* (మీనము - mínamu, Tel.; மீனம் - mínam, Tam.). Twelfth. The Fishes. Pisces [hoot].——*Mitoonam* (మిథునము - mit'hunamu, Tel.; மிதுனம் - mithunam, Tam.). Third. The Twins. Gemini [jowzah].——*Simham* (సింహము - simhamu, Tel.; சிங்கம் - shingam, Tam.). Fifth. The Lion. Leo [asad].——*Toolaum* (తుల - tula, Tel.; துலாம் - tulám, Tam.). Seventh. The Balance. Libra [meezaun].——*Vrishabham* (వృషభము - vrishabhamu, Tel.; இடபம் - idabam, Tam.). Second. The Bull. Taurus [sowr]. ——*Vrishchicam* (వృశ్చికము - vrishchikamu, Tel.; விருச்சிகம் - viruççigam, Tam.). Eighth. The Scorpion [akrab]. Scorpio [jyotisham, nacshatram].——(5) Raushy also stands for a gold coin with fourteen dots, twelve representing the signs of the zodiac and the remaining two the sun and the moon, called raushy fanam [q.v.]. 10 chuckrams = 1 raushy fanam; 3 raushy fanams = 1 rupee [naunyam, 2d]. Approximate actual value, 1 raushy fanam = 5 annas 4 pies. The most ancient of the indigenous fanams. Still found in large numbers in Coimbatore, both buried in the ground and picked up after heavy rains in the approach to fords of the principal rivers. Tradition says that Parshooraman [q.v.] sowed them broadcast over Keralam [q.v.], depositing what remained in the kistvaens [paundicoozhy] on the eastern slope of the hills some of which are called by his name to this day and held sacred by the hill Arayans or Malaiyarasar [q.v.]. Though seldom seen in circulation, it is still the denomination used in Northern malabar for recording the value of lands and the ancient revenue assessed on them. The Raushy fanam has been superseded by the Kaliyoog fanam, the Veeroye fanam, and others.——(6) *Raushicoor* (രാശിക്കൂറ - ráshikkúru, Mal.). From (above + kúr, mal. part). Class of soil [desham, munn] in which particles appear as if heaped up or placed one above the other without pashima or cohesion. Poor light soil, consisting of loose sand [manal] chiefly; it will not fill again the hole from which dug. ——*Raushipashimacoor* (രാശിപ്പശിമക്കൂറ - ráshippashimakkúru, Mal.). From (above + pashima, mal. moisture + kúr, mal. part). Class of soil in which the particles firmly cohere to each other. Soil of an equal or middling sort, a quantity of which exactly fills up a pit or hole from which it is dug on being placed in it again.——*Razipore* (இராசிபுரம் - irásippuram, Tam.). From (ráshi, san. a heap + pura, san. town), meaning thereby that the soil is very productive. Hind. name (gházípúr), meaning warrior + town.—"*a*" Deputy tahsildarry, Salem district. Pay Rs. 70.—"*b*" Deputy tahsildar's head-quarters, Mittah village; Salem dist., Salem tal.; pop. 10,539; acres 1,996; lat. 11° 27′; long. 78° 14′; from Madras S.W. 179 miles; from Namcull N. 16 miles; from Oossoor S.E. 91 miles; from Salem S. 14 miles;

from Tripatore S. 76 miles; from Yercaud S. 22 miles. On the Salem-Namcull road in the valley between the Collimullay and the Bodhamullay. Inhabitants chiefly Putnoolcaurar [putnool], Comaties [q.v.] and Jeydar [q.v.]. Sugar-cane [q.v.] is grown abundantly in the neighbourhood. Large iron boilers for the manufacture of jaggery [q.v.] and sugar [q.v.], and iron [auhan] and brass [pittalay] vessels of different kinds are manufactured. Turmeric [country saffron] and rice [q.v.] of superior kind are exported largely. Principal industries are silk-weaving, iron-smelting, and sugar-boiling. Peshcush Rs. 2,914.

RAUTIB (راتب - rátib, *Hind.*). From (rataba, ar. to remain constant). Daily allowance of food to laborers; or to animals, as elephants [q.v.], camels [ottagam], &c.

RAUTRY (रात्रि - rátri, *San.*). From (ram, san. to stop). Time of rest and stillness. Night. One of the forms of Bramha [caulam]. All the ancient Sanscrit authorities placed night before day, and the Asoorans [q.v.] or Titans before the gods, in the order of appearance. Compare Hesiod. Cf. Ahorautram and Irauppagal. For Paunchrautram, the work so called see sep. title.——*Raut* (رات - rát, Hind.). From (rátri, san. night). Night. Raut kah khanah is supper [knanah, teeny].

RAUZ (రాజు - rádzu, *Tel.*). From (rájá, san. king) [raj]. General term for certain Teloogoo-speaking castes who profess a Cshatriya [q.v.] origin. They are certainly slightly different in race to the ordinary Dravidians. They do not enlist in native army, being now quite agricultural. They are mostly Veishnavites [q.v.], though a few follow Shiva [q.v.], and the worship of village deities [grauma devatay] forms a part of the belief of all. Their peculiar goddess is called Nimishaumbah. They generally assume sacred thread [poonool]. In all the more well-to-do families the women are gosha [q.v.]. Also merely a Hindoo third name [jauty, peyar].——*Bhatrauz* (భట్రాజు - bhatrádzu, Tel.). From (bhatta, san. learned man). Branch of the Rauz class. Originally the bards who sung the praises of the various petty rajahs [q.v.] and poligars [q.v.] of the country; but their employment in this way has almost disappeared, and they now live by cultivation and by singing traditions current regarding Shoodra castes at marriages and other ceremonies. Some are Mussalmans [q.v.] or members of other castes, who, possessing an aptitude for extempore versification, were taken by rajahs to sing their praises and so called themselves Bhatrauzool. They bury their dead [jauty, shavacaud].——*Mootrauz* (ముత్రాచ - muttarátsa, Tel.). From (mutta, tel old). Also called Yecary. Teloogoo caste; take the title of naidoo [q.v.]; most of them poor; serve as village watchmen; probably immigrants during the time of the Vijianugger kings [jauty]. The Oodayagherry droog is occupied by a remnant of this race, formerly in all probability superior servants of the fortress.——*Rauzooloo* (రాజులు - rádzulu, Tel.). Plural of Rauz. Hindoo third name [peyar].

RAUZEE (راضی - rází, *Hind.*). Consent, compromise. Rauzee-nauma is a written assent or deed of compromise, e.g., resignation of office, or deed of relinquishment executed by the cultivator [ryot] when he wishes to give up land in his puttah [q.v.] or enjoyment.——*Razah* (رضا - razá, Ar.). From (razú, ar. to be pleased). Title of eighth Imaum. Common alam; as Razah ally, double alam; Razah khan, alam + alaumat [ism].——*Razah sahib* (رضا صاحب - razásáhib, Hind.). Alam + alaumat. Son of Chundah sahib [q.v.], who when engaged in besieging Mahomed ally [q.v.] at Trichinopoly, was sent to relieve Arcot which Clive had attacked to create a diversion. Defeated there Razah sahib fell back upon Arnee, and then retreated to Cauverypauk where he suffered another defeat.

RAVAM (रव - rava, *San.*). From (ru, san. to cry). Cry, shriek.——*Rauvanauttam* (இராவணத்தம் - irávanáttam, Tam.). From (rávana, san. the giant + hasta, san. hand). A small old-fashioned lute formed with a hollow cocoanut [q.v.] shell. ——*Ravanan* (रावण - rávana, San.). From (ráva, san. shriek). Mythological king of Lunka [q.v.], a state supposed to comprise Ceylon and the whole of southern India. He was the son of Vishravan moony by his wife Nicashah. He had a brother Coombhacarnan and a sister Shoorpanakhay. Ravanan carried off Seetay [q.v.], wife of Rama [q.v.], and brought on an invasion of his island by Rama, in which Rama was assisted by the uncivilised races of the southern part of the peninsula. The story of the Ramayanam [q.v.] purports to recount this war. There may have been some large national convulsion in the south, to which the Hindoo legend was fitted. A festival is celebrated in honor of Ravanan by the Shaunaur [q.v.] race. Ravanan is also called Dashagreevan, the ten-necked, and Powlastyan, and also Veishravanan as son of Vishravan, the father also of Coobairan [q.v.]. His numerous heads and his hundred hands, sometimes reduced to twenty, are the usual symbols of dominion. Compare Briareus. See vol. I (63), (115).——*Ravanan's whiskers* (రావణాసురునిమీసము - rávanásurunimísamu, Tel.; എലിമുള്ളു - elimullu, Mal.; இராவணன்மீசை - irávanan-mísai, Tam.). Title from stiff, pointed leaves. Tel. from (rávanásura, san. the giant + mísamu, tel. whiskers). Mal. from (eli, mal. rat + mullu, mal. thorn). Tam. from (rávana, san. the giant + mísai, tam. whiskers). Tam. also (elikkuççippul), meaning rat + stalk + grass; (irávananbul), meaning ravana grass. Title otherwise Ground rattan, Rat thorn, Sea pink, Water pink. Botanically Spinifex squarrosus, linn., graminaceæ [vricsham, 156]. Frutescent; culms large, glaucous, fasciculate-leafy at the knots; leaves convolute, recurved, spreading, stiff, pointed; sheaths woolly at the mouth, the rest striated, and with the spikelets and leaves glabrous; male axils flower-bearing; bracts of the capitules fascicled, very large, involucres mucronate. Sand-binding [manal] diœcious grass; grows abundantly on the coromandel coast; it comes nearest to the sand carex of england in its habit of growth, creeping along horizontally, sometimes above, sometimes below, the surface of the earth emitting roots and shoots at short intervals of a few inches; extremely tenacious of life, the shoot at every node capable of renewing the existence of the individual as fast as destroyed, and the whole plant offering a resistance to the storm which is rarely overcome; seeds are contained in a circular head, composed of a series of spine-like divisions, which radiate from the stalk in all directions; when the seeds are mature, these heads become detached and are carried with great velocity along the sands; the globular heads float lightly on water, and the uppermost spines acting as sails, they are carried across narrow estuaries to continue the process of embanking on newly-formed sand bars. The fishermen collect it for fuel and thus destroy their greatest protection; they do so as the spiny leaves injure their naked feet, and the turf does not answer for spreading nets [valay] upon. No other common species here.——*Ravy* (रवि - ravi, San.). From (ru, san. to sound), the praised one. Sun. Identical with Sooryan [q.v.] and Audityan [q.v.].——*Ravy madhya graham* (रविमध्यग्रह - ravimadhyagraha, San.). From (ravi, san. sun + madhya, san. middle + graha, san. the place of a planet). Sun's mean place in sidereal ecliptic [craunty mundalam].——*Ravy mandotcham* (रविमन्दोच्च - ravimandóçça, San.). From (ravi, san. sun + mandóçça, san. upper apsis). Sun's apogee [mandam].——*Ravy palam* (रविफल - ravip'hala, San.). From (ravi, san. sun + p'hala, san. equation). Sun's anomalistic equation [palam].——*Ravy punchaungam* (रविपञ्चाङ्ग - ravipañchánga, San.). The solar calendar [punchaungam].——*Ravy vauram* (रविवार - ravivára, San.). From (ravi, san. sun + vára, san. day). Sunday [jyotisham, shoolam, tisay, vauram].

RAVINE DEER (हरिण - harina, *San.*; काळासिपि - kálasipi, *Mahr.*; کالپونچھ - kálpúnchh, *Hind.*; ಬುದರಿ - budari, *Can.*; బూరదుజింక - búradujinka, *Tel.*; കലമാൻ - kalamán, *Mal.*; வெளிமான் - velimán, *Tam.*). Title from its habitat. San. means reddish white. Mahr. means black tail. Hind. from (kálá, hind. black + puchha, san. tail). Tel. from (búradu, tel. a haughty person + jinka, tel. deer). Mal. from (kala, mal. stag + mán, mal. deer). Tam. from (velil, tam. whiteness + mán, tam. deer). Hind. also (chikárá); (bárásinghí), meaning twelve-horned. Can. also (tiska), from its hiss; (mudari). Tel. also (irri), meaning butting. Title otherwise Goat antelope, Indian gazelle. Roe and Roebuck of the Bible. Cf. Jinka. Gazella bennettii, antilopinæ, bovidæ, ruminantia, mammalia [sastanam, 23], of naturalists [jantoo]. Color above deep fawn brown, darker where it joins the white on the sides and buttocks, chin, breast, lower parts and buttocks behind white; tail, knee tufts and fetlocks behind black; a dark brown spot on the nose, and a dark line from the eyes to the mouth, bordered by a light one above. Length of a buck 3½ feet; tail 8½ inches; height 26 at shoulder, 28 at the croup; horns 12–13. The horns [sing] of the female are small, rarely longer than 6 inches, usually 4–5, slender, slightly wrinkled at the base, inclining backwards with the tip bent forwards. Found very generally, but not on the Malabar coast. Never found in forest country, nor in districts having a damp climate. When alarmed it utters a sort of hiss by blowing through the nose and stamps with the fore feet. Indian species not here found are:—Fuscifrons or beloochistaun gazelle, Picticaudata or thibetan gazelle, Sub-gutterosa or persian gazelle.

RAVY (రవిక - ravika, *Tel.*). A bodice or close fitting jacket [cholee]. Now sometimes used by Hindoo women; generally however no special needle-made covering for this purpose is worn [sheelay]. See vol. I (98).

RAYAUN (राजसर्षप - rájasarshapa, *San.*; मोहरी - móharí, *Mahr.*; सासम - sásama, *Conc.*; خردل - khardal, *Ar.*; سپندان - sipandán, *Pers.*; رائی - ráí, *Hind.*; رایان - ráyán, *Dec.*; ಸಾಸಿವೆ - sásive, *Can.*; దాసెమి - dásemi, *Too.*; ఆవాలు - áválu, *Tel.*; ସୋରିଷ - soriso, *Oor.*; കടുക - katuku, *Mal.*; අබ - aba, *Singh.*; கடுகு - kadugu, *Tam.*). Title from deccany [raj]. San. from (rájá, san. king + sarshapa, san. mustard), from its strength. Conc. from (sarshapa, san. mustard). Hind. from (rájí, san. black mustard). Dec. from (rájí, san. black mustard). Can. from (sarshapa, san. mustard). Mal. from tamul. Tam. from (kadumai, tam. sharpness). San. also (sarshapa), meaning pervading, medicinally influential; (raktaráji), meaning red + shining; (rájiká), meaning shining [raggy]; (tívraka), meaning pungent; (kshutábhijanana), meaning hunger producing [raggy]; (ásuri), meaning sorceress, because witches are discovered by means of mustard oil. Hind. also (sarsún); (barírái), meaning large mustard; (bádsháhírái), meaning royal mustard; (sháhzádahrái), meaning princely mustard. Can. also (sásimegida). Tel. also (chinnaáválu), meaning small + mustard; (sarsáválu), meaning mustard; (sásuvulu), meaning mustard. Tam. also (shirugadugu), meaning small + mustard. Title otherwise Brown mustard, Country mustard, Indian mustard, Royal mustard, Small mustard, Sorceress mustard. Botanically Brassica [sarshapam] juncea, h. f. & t., cruciferæ [vricsham, 10]. Alias Sinapis brassicata, juncea, nigra, ramosa. Herbaceous; lower leaves ovate-lanceolate, deeply serrated, upper ones lanceolate, attenuated at the base, quite entire; branches fascicled; siliqua somewhat erect, upper joint valveless, awl-shaped; flowers yellow; seeds of a brown color; cultivated. The seeds are hotter and more active than the imported articles; they are ground and the husks sifted from the flour, the residue yielding to expression a useful fixed oil [yennay]; this is bright yellow, and has a strong smell and a slight taste of mustard. Cultivated in black and red loam dry fields, often along with raggy [q.v.]; ground prepared in south in pungoony [mausam] or march and subsequently, on coromandel in aushweejam or october and caurteecam or november, on w. coast from maidom or april to yedavam or may; seed sown broadcast in south in chittray or april, on coromandel in margashiram or december and pooshyam or january, on w. coast in yedavam or may; manuring and weeding where necessary; if there be no drizzle it must be watered after a fortnight; full-grown crop shows green, 4 or 5 feet high; cut three or four months after with sickles; plant is dried and beaten with sticks; seed is then winnowed from the chaff; produce brought to market any time after; average price 12 imperial seers for 1 rupee. Chemically, mustard seeds consist of a bland fixed oil and a peculiar inodorous substance called myroxoic acid, together with a third substance which has been called myrosyne; essential oil known as pyrosyne. Seeds medicinal substitute for black and white mustard, especially in poultices; fixed fat oil is superior to all other oils for anointing and invigorating the body; in medicine given internally as a remedy for colic, but not very safe; more frequently applied as a rubefacient and as a cure for burns and wounds; used in pharm.; in veterinary practice a counter irritant for rheumatism. Seeds, whole or broken, used to flavor curries [q.v.]; a small quantity of mustard seed is put into boiling cocoanut oil and the whole poured into the curry [q.v.]; ground into flour used to adulterate european mustard flour. The two mustards shown below are foreign articles. For dog mustard see Cleome viscosa, linn. [dog vailay], and jungle mustard see Gynandropsis pentaphylla, dec. [vailay].——*Cauly rayaun* (सर्षप - sarshapa, San.; خردل اسود - khardaliaswad, Ar.; سپندان سیاہ - sipandánsiyáh, Pers.; کالی رائی - kálírái, Hind.; کالی رایان - kálíráyán, Dec.; ಸಾಸಿವೆ - sásive, Can.; ఆవాలు - áválu, Tel.; കടുക - katuku, Mal.; கடுகு - kadugu, Tam.). Title from color of seed. San. from (sri, san. to go), pervading; medicinally influential. Ar. from (khardal, ar. mustard + aswad, ar. black). Pers. from (sipandán, pers. mustard + siyáh, pers. black). Hind. from (kálí, hind. black + rái, hind. mustard) brassica juncea, h. f. & t.). Dec. from (kálí, hind. black + ráyán, hind. mustard). Mal. from tamul. Tam. from (kadumai, tam. sharpness). San. also (rájiká), meaning shining, from reddish color. Hind. also (rái); (aslrái), meaning true mustard seed. Can. also (karisásivegida), meaning black + mustard + plant. Title otherwise Black mustard, European mustard, True mustard. Greek νᾶπυ, σίνηπι. Botanically Brassica [sarshapam] nigra, koch., cruciferæ [vricsham, 10]. Alias Sinapis erysimoides, nigra. Semen sinapis nigræ of chemists. Annual, 2–3 feet high, rigid, branched, more or less hispid; leaves 4–8 inches; flowers $\frac{1}{3}$–$\frac{1}{2}$ inch in diameter, bright yellow; pod $\frac{1}{4}$–$\frac{1}{2}$ inch, subulate; valves keeled, torulose; cells three to five-seeded; seeds small and roundish; externally of a reddish or blackish brown color, internally yellow; inodorous, but have an acrid oleaginous taste. Uses just like country mustard, but a less powerful article.——*Soofaid rayaun* (सिद्धार्थक - siddhártt'haka, San.; पांढरा मोहरी - pándharámóhari, Mahr.; خردل ابیض - khardaliabyaz, Ar.; سپندان سپید - sipandánisupíd, Pers.; سفید رائی - sufedrái, Hind.; سفید رایان - sufedráyán, Dec.; ಬಿಳಿಸಾಸಿವೆ - bilisásive, Can.; తెల్లఆవాలు - tellaáválu, Tel.; വെള്ളക്കടുക - vellakkatuku, Mal.; සුදුඅබ - suduaba, Singh.; வெள்ளைக்கடுகு - vellaikkadugu, Tam.). Title from color of seed. San. from (siddha, san. accomplished + art'ha, san. object); from medicinal value. Mahr. from (pándhari, mahr. white + móhari, mahr. mustard, brassica juncea, h. f. & t.). Ar. from (khardal, ar. mustard + abyaz, ar. white). Pers. from (sipandán, pers. mustard + sufíd, pers. white). Hind. from (sufed, hind. white + rái, hind. mustard). Dec. from hindostany. Can. from (bili, can. white + sásive, can. mustard). Tel. from (tella, tel. white + áválu, tel. mustard). Singh. from (sudu, singh. white + aba, singh. mustard. Tam. from (vellai, tam. white + kadugu, tam. mustard). Title otherwise Charlock mustard, Salad mustard, White mustard. Botanically Brassica [sarshapam] alba, h. f. & t., cruciferæ [vricsham, 10]. Alias Sinapis alba. Seed is Semen sinapis albæ of chemists. Erect, annual, 2 feet high, with a hispid, or rarely glabrous stem; leaves all petioled, usually hispid; segments ovate, toothed or lobulate; pods about 1 inch, stalked, spreading, cylindric, beak half as long, flattened, sometimes two-seeded, valves and base of beak white with hispid hairs. Cultivated; smallish bright yellow flowers, seeds white or yellowish and much larger than those of black mustard. Flour used in pharm. mixed with black mustard flour [cauly rayaun]; similarly for table when young, leaves are eaten as salad; seeds yield by expression a bright yellow edible oil [yennay] having a strong smell and slight taste of mustard.

REAPER (रीप - rípa, *Mahr.*). Lath work of a roof.

RED (रक्त - rakta, *San.*; لعل - lál, *Hind.*). Prefix.——*Red cedar* (மலைக்கோன் - malaikkón, Tam.). Title from resemblance to toon [q.v.] timber. Tam. means mountain king. Same as Shingle tree.——*Red cliffs* (വർക്കലക്കുന്നു - varkkalakkunnu, Mal.). Means Warkully hills. πυῤῥὸν ὄρος of the Periplus. Hill; Travancore state, Trivandrum division, Cherankeel tal. Nautical name of steep coast below Quilon. This presents the only bluffs on the shore from Mount delly to Cape comorin. Is near Warkully and formed by the Warkully bar.——*Red cotton* (پوتی - potí, Hind.; ಕೆಂಬತ್ತಿ - kembatti, Can.; ఎఱ్ఱపత్తి - errapatti, Tel.; ചെമ്പഞ്ഞി - chempaññi, Mal.; செம்பஞ்சு - shembañju, Tam.). Can. from (kempu, can. red + hatti, can. cotton). Tel. from (erra, tel. red + patti, tel. cotton). Otherwise Shempunjy, Potee. For this product see Red-cotton wool under Cotton.——*Red dog* (வேர்க்குரு - vérkkuru, Tam.). Tam. means sweat + pricking. An old name for Prickly-heat [q.v.].——*Red gum* (لالگوند - lálgond, Hind.). Same as Eucalyptus resinifera [australian gum tree].——*Red hills* (புழல் - puzhal, Tam.). Vern. means a hollow. Chingleput dist., Sydapett tal.; lat. 13° 10′; long. 80° 14′; from Sydapett N.W. 10 miles; from the sea W. 10 miles. Trig. station in lat. 13° 9′ 32·07″; long. 80° 14′ 27·99″; from Mauthavaram W. 4 miles; from Sydapett N. 10 miles; from the sea W. 9 miles. For description of tank, see vol. I, 404 [pozhal].——*Red sanders* (لال چندن - lálchandan, Hind.). See sep. title.——*Red wood* (رکت چندن - rakatchandan, Hind.). ചെമ്മരം - chemmaram, Mal.; செம்மரம் - shemmaram, Tam.). Hind. means red sandal. Same as False red sanders, Rohitacam, and Deccany deodar. Cf. also:—Gluta tavoyana, mergui red wood; Pterocarpus indicus, andaman red wood; Soymida febrifuga, coromandel red wood, indian red wood. See gloss paragraphs.

RED SANDERS (रक्तचन्दन - raktachandana, *San.* and *Mahr.*; रचंदन - rachandana, *Conc.*; صندل احمر - sandaliahmar, *Ar.*; صندل سرخ - sandalisurkh, *Pers.*; رگت چندن - ragatchandan, *Hind.*; لال چندن - lálchandan, *Dec.*; ರಕ್ತಚಂದನ - raktachandana, *Can.*; ಬೆಂಞ - béñña, *Tuo.*; ఎఱ్ఱగంధపుచెక్క - erragandhapuchettu, *Tel.*; രക്തചന്ദനം - raktachandanam, *Mal.*; රත්සඳුන් - ratsandun, *Singh.*; சிவப்புச்சந்தனம் - shivappuççandaram, *Tam.*). Title from color of wood [red]. San. from (rakta, san. red + chandana, san. sandalwood, santalum album, linn.); from use similar to that of sandal. Ar. from (sandal, ar. sandalwood, santalum album, linn. + ahmar, ar. red). Pers. from (sandal, ar. sandalwood + surkh, pers. red). Hind. from (rakta, san. red + chandan, pers. red wood). Dec. from (lál, hind. red + chandan, hind. red wood). Can. from (rakta, san. red + chandana, san. sandal). Tel. from (erra, tel. red + gandhapuchettu, tel. santalum album, linn.). Singh. from (rata, singh. redness + chandana, san. sandalwood). Tam. from (shivappu, tam. redness + chandana, san. sandalwood). San. also (kuchandana), meaning bad sandal [false red sanders]; (harichandana), meaning tawny sandal; (agarugandhá), meaning smelling like agaroo; (tilaparní), meaning sesamum-leaved; (rañjana), meaning red; cf. indigo. Mahr. also (támbadáchandana), meaning red sandal. Can. also (honne), meaning gold colored; (kempugandha), meaning red + sandal. Tel. also (agarugandhamu); (errachandanamu), meaning red + sandalwood; (tsandam); (raktagandhamu), meaning red + sandal. Mal. also (cheñchandanam), meaning red sandal. Tam. also (sheñjandanam), meaning red sandal; (shivappuççendúram), meaning red + red powder. Title otherwise Indian red-wood, Red chandanam, Red sandalwood, Ruby wood, Three-leaved pterocarpus, Whonnay. Botanically Pterocarpus [vengay] santalinus, linn. f., leguminosæ [vricsham, 48]. Tree, 60 feet or more; leaves unequally pinnated; calyx five-cleft; corolla papilionaceous; leaflets three, roundish, retuse; racemes axillary, simple or branched; petals long-clawed, waved or curled on the margins; stamens triadelphous, five, four, and one; legume one-seeded, slightly membranaceous, waved; flowers yellow, streaked with red; closely related to common vengay [q.v.]; plentiful in kurnool and cuddapah districts. The dye-wood is usually seen in billets of 2 to 3 feet in length, of a deep red color, the concentric circles being divided by dark lines; the coloring principle is called santalin; it communicates a deep-red to alcohol, but gives no tinge to cold water. The wood given internally in hæmorrhages in powder ground up with milk [paul], and externally mixed with honey [shahad] in case of scabies; in certain cases of ophthalmia and sore eyes, beaten up into a paste and applied to the eyes; gives to pharm. lignum santalinum rubrum, coloring principle santalin ; officinal only as a coloring agent. Cattle during dry season are fed on leaves and young saplings. Bark contains much coloring juice ; roots and stumps yield the red sandalwood of commerce, much used by dyers and color makers [shauyam] ; this sold by weight and forms a regular article of export ; with different mordants [cauram], it yields various shades of red ; the powdered wood mixed with oil is used for bathing and purifying the skin much as the true sandalwood powder also is used. The timber is compact, heavy, red internally, becoming brown by exposure to the air, sonorous, in squared pieces, of fibrous texture, when polished numerous cells filled with resin are exposed ; it sinks in water ; the odour is weak, taste slightly astringent, it reddens the saliva, is unalterable by time ; water has but little action on this wood ; used for carved work in houses and temples.——*False red sanders* (ताम्रक - támraka, San. ; थोरलागुंज - t'hóra-lágunja, Mahr. ; मंजटिरूकु - manjutirúku, Conc. ; رکت چندن - rakatchandan, Hind. ; هاتهی گمچی - háthígumchí, Dec. ; ಮಂಜೆಟ್ಟಿ - manjetti, Can. ; బందిగురివెంద - bandigurivenda, Tel. ; മഞ്ചാടി - mañcháti, Mal. ; මදටිය - madatiya, Singh. ; ஆனைக்குன்றி - ánaikkunri, Tam.). Title from timber which resembles red sanders when fresh cut. San. from (támra, san. copper) ; from bright red berries. Mahr. from (t'horalá, mahr. great + gunjá, san. abrus precatorius, linn.). Hind. from (rakta, san. blood + chandana, san. sandalwood, santalum album, linn.) ; from structure of wood. Dec. from (háthí, hind. elephant + gumchí, hind. abrus precatorius, linn.) ; from similarity of seeds. Tel. from (bandi, tel. round + gurivenda, tel. abrus precatorius, linn.). Mal. from (mañju, san. beautiful), from seeds. Tam. from (ánai, tam. elephant + kunri, tam. abrus precatorius, linn.). San. also (kuchandana), meaning inferior sandalwood, properly pterocarpus santalinus, linn. f. [red sanders]. Hind. also (kuchandana), meaning inferior sandal. Can. also (mandatíya). Tel. also (bandigurigindza), meaning round + abrus precatorius, linn. ; (peddagurigindza), meaning large + abrus precatorius, linn. Tam. also (manjádi), meaning beautiful and variegated, from seed ; (tilam), meaning spot, originally of the size of sesamum, from paste used to mark foreheads. Title otherwise Barbadoes pride, Barricary seed plant, Bastard flower fence, Coral pea tree, Elephant goomchy, False red sandal, Large goomchy, Munjaudy tree, Peacock flower fence, Wheel goomchy. Botanically Adenanthera pavonina, linn., leguminosæ [vricsham, 48]. Large tree, unarmed : leaves bipinnated ; pinnæ four to six pair ; leaflets oval, obtuse, glabrous, ten to twelve pair, on short petioles ; calyx five-toothed ; petals five ; racemes terminal or from the upper axils, spike-like ; legumes somewhat falcate, twisted, ten to twelve-seeded ; flowers numerous, small, yellow and white mixed, fragrant, producing pods, early opening and displaying seeds of a shining, scarlet color with a circular streak in centre. The seeds are poisonous if taken internally, especially when in a powdered state ; large leaves given in decoction for chronic rheumatism. Seeds are strung as beads [munkah] ; seeds are used as weights by jewellers, each of them weighing four grains [goomchy, munjaudy, retty] ; a cement [pattoo] is made by beating the seeds up with borax [q.v.] and water ; heart-wood yields a dye which bramins use after bathing for marking their foreheads [pottoo], merely rubbing the wood on a wet stone [shaunay cull] ; stem gives a gum [gond] ; oil from seeds ; tree well suited for avenues [shaulay]. Timber, when fresh cut, resembles red sanders ; has a pleasant smell ; strong, but not stiff, hard, durable, tolerably close and even-grained, takes a good polish ; when fresh of a red color, streaks of a darker shade, afterwards turns purple ; used for house-building and cabinet making purposes. No other common species here.

REETAH (रिठा - rit'há, *Mahr.*). From (arishta, san. soap-nut). Same as Soapnut.——*Rintah* (रिंथ्या - rint'hyá, Conc.). Same as above.

REG (ریگ - reg, *Hind.*). Sand [manal].——*Regar* (ریگر - regar, Hind. ; لیگر - legar, Dec. ; రేగడ - régada, Tel. ; கரிசல் - karisal, Tam.). Tam. means darkness. Otherwise Regady by corruption from the Tel. genitive. Rich black loam ; a soil in which cotton [q.v.] is usually planted, and thence commonly termed black-cotton soil. Met with in great tracts of country in this presidency, especially in the ceded districts [q.v.] ; it is not found near the coast ; similar to the soil which forms the plains of surat and broach in goozerat. When uncultivated usually support but few trees, and those, as a rule, of no great size, but the principal product is grass, commonly growing to a height of 3 to 4 feet ; when cultivated the fertility is so great that it has produced crops for two thousand years without manure, without having been left fallow, and without irrigation. It is a true alluvium [adaimunn], deposited from still water ; it consists chemically of silica [manal] in a minute state of division, with portions of lime [choonam], alumina [calimunn], and oxide of iron [auhan] ; it fuses readily before the blow-pipe into a dry, black slag ; in composition it nearly resembles that of basalt [caroom palingoo cull]. The purest regar is of a deep bluish-black color, or greenish or dark-greenish black, shining ; when placed in water, it crumbles slowly, with emission of air bubbles, and forms a tenacious paste ; when moistened, it gives out an argillaceous odour. The muriate and carbonate of soda [sowdoo] are frequently accidental ingredients in the composition of the regar ; they render it sterile when in large quantities. During the dry season, it rends into gaping cracks ; contracting under the powerful heat of the sun, it is divided, like the surface of dried starch, by countless and deep fissures, into figures usually affecting the pentagon, hexagon, and rhomboid ; while the upper part for a few inches in depth is dried to an impalpable powder, raised in clouds by the wind and darkening the air, the under portions, of the depth of 8 or 10 feet, retain their character of a hard black clay [calimunn], approaching a rock, usually moist and cold, when the surface dust has a temperature of 130°. On the other hand regar is absorbent of moisture and very retentive ; and during the rainy season it presents a uniform glazed surface of black tenacious clay.——*Regmahee* (اسقنقور - iskinkúr, Ar. ; ریگ ماهی - regmáhí, Pers. and Hind.). Ar. from greek. Hind. from (above + máhí, pers. fish). The terms may be considered co-extensive with the family Scincidæ, sauria [godhicay], reptilia [sarpy, 8], of naturalists [jantoo]. The Skinks or Scincidæ have generally four limbs, moderately developed, sometimes feeble or hidden below the skin. Species exceedingly numerous ; land lizards [chipkalee] preferring dry ground and hiding themselves in the sand, under stones, &c. ; none of them enter the water ; do not attain any considerable size ; deposit from eight to twelve globular eggs. The following are the representative species in Southern india :—"*a*" Anguis melanosticta. Small blind worm-like reptile ; coast of Coromandel ; reddish brown ; part of tail is cineritious, or of a pale blue ; abdominal and subcaudal squamæ glossy white, without dots ; quickly buries itself in the sand when pursued.—"*b*" Chiamela lineata. Brownish, with black lines corresponding to the series of scales ; slow-worm-like lizard.—"*c*" Eumeces albopunctatus. The White-dotted skink. Alias Eumeces punctata ; Riopa albo-punctata. Back uniform olive-colored, or with line of small dots along each series of scales ; anterior part of sides blackish brown, with numerous small white spots ; uniform whitish below.—"*d*" Eumeces bilineatus. The Black-striped skink. Alias Mocoa bilineata. Limbs rather feeble ; brownish olive above, greenish below ; broad brown or black band from shoulder along upper half of the side, enclosing below whitish longitudinal line ; pair of black lines along the back.—"*e*" Eumeces hardwickii. The White-streaked skink. Alias Mabouya elegans ; Riopa hardwickii. Back brownish, with four series of black dots and with yellowish-white band arising from the nose and from the superciliaries ; series of black dots along each edge of bands ; each scale on the sides with a black dot, the upper dots being largest and confluent ; lower parts uniform white.—"*f*" Eumeces punctatus. The dotted skink. Alias Lacerta interpunctata, punctata ; Riopa punctata ; Seps scincoides. Each scale with a black dot, the dots forming longitudinal series ; largest on the back of tail, sometimes entirely absent on belly ; outer series of scales on each side of back has very small dots rather large.—"*g*" Euprepes rufescens. The common Indian skink. Alias Lacerta rufescens ; Plestiodon sikkimensis ; Scincus multifasciatus ; Tiliqua affinis, carinata, rubriventris, rufescens. Limbs of moderate strength ; the coloration varies ; specimens have a distinct yellowish band along the upper part of the side of the neck ; sides below yellow band are dark brown ; upper parts brown, with blackish streak ; lower parts whitish ; may be seen basking in the sun, in bamboo [q.v.] hedges, or on trees ; fearlessly enter houses in pursuit of insects [poochy], in which this displays great agility. The largest of the family.—"*h*" Euprepes trilineatus. Alias Euprepes trilineata. Yellowish olive, with three yellowish-white longitudinal bands ; first from crown of head to the middle of the back ; from upper lip to the loin ; edged with black superiorly and with red inferiorly ; hinder part of back dotted with yellow ; limbs and tail rose-colored ; found in sandy ground near the sea concealing itself in holes and fissures, and under shrubs.——*Renaud* (రేనాడు - rénádu, Tel.). From (régada, tel. black-cotton soil + nádu, tel. country). Name of the black cotton land [regar] along the valley of the Coondair, Cuddapah.

REGULATION (ஒழுங்கு - ozhungu, *Tam.*). From (ozhungu, tam. to act). Legislative enactment under the Company as distinguished from the Acts of the later legislative councils.

REH (ریہ - reh, *Hind.*). Same as Sujjee matty.

REIS (രേസ്സ് - réss, *Mal.*). From the portuguese. A small copper coin. 2 reis = 1 cash or pie [nannyam, 1d]. Approximate actual value, 1 reis = $\frac{1}{400}$ of a rupee. This imaginary coin was introduced into the public accounts of Malabar, when the company became possessed of it, from Bombay. Eighty of these were equivalent to one Tellicherry fanam [q.v.]. Not in current use unless to mean a very small sum of money. Similar to Cochin cash [q.v.].

REKAPULLY (రేకపల్లి - rékapalli, *Tel.*). From (rekka, tel. wing + palli, tel. village), meaning side village.——(1) Talook, Godavery district. Area with Bhadrachellam 911 square miles. Language Teloogoo. N.W. of district. Bounded :—N. Bustar and Vizagapatam, E. Rumpa, S. Godavery, W. Bhadrachellam talook. Transferred from the Central provinces in 1874. Now forms part of the Agency tract. Western portion is flat, Eastern portion mountainous, except a strip of land on the banks of the Godavery, and Severy, which is covered with dense forest. Soil good black cotton [regar] on the banks of Godavery and Severy rivers. The rest is sandy and rocky. Trade in timber and forest produce. No irrigation at all. Camping grounds :—Abbicherla, Bendiraiv, Caudoolore, Chintore, Cottapully, Gandicottagoodem, Jeedigooppa, Lakkavaram, Maroomore, Nauracondah, Peddacondah, Posaram, Soppoomaumidy, Vaddigoodem, Vankagoodem, Yedoogooraullapully. Places of archæological interest:—Comaursawmygoodem, Rekapully, Shreeramagherry, Vaddigoodem. Trig. stations :—Cullair, Nauracondah, Peddacondah and Raupauk. The leading places, &c., in the talook are the following.——*Chintore* (చింతూరు - chintúra, Tel.). From (chinta, tel. tamarind tree, tamarindus indica, linn. + úru, tel. village). Zemindarry, Village ; pop. 268 ; lat. 17° 45′ ; long. 81° 26′ ; from Rekapully N.N.E. 14 miles ; from Cocanada N.W. 77 miles. Weekly market; timber trade.——*Coonavaram* (కూనవరము - kúnavaramu, Tel.). From (kúna, tel. young + pura, san. town). Zemindarry, Village, Division head-quarters, Post office ; pop. 958 ; lat. 17° 34′ ; long. 81° 18′ ; from Bhadrachellam E.S.E. 25 miles ; from Cocanada W.N.W. 76 miles ; from Rekapully W.N.W. 3 miles. At junction of Godavery and Severy.——*Cullair* (కల్లేరు - kalléru, Tel.). From (kallu, tel. stone + éru, tel. river). Trig. station ; lat. 17° 48′ 15·78″ ; long. 81° 28′ 10·86″ ; height 833 feet ; from Rekapully N.N.E. 18 miles ; from Cullair E. 2 miles.——*Godavery* (గోదావరి - gódávari, Tel.). See sep. title.——*Marrigoodem* (మర్రిగూడెము - marrigúdemu, Tel.). From (marri, tel. banyan tree, ficus bengalensis, linn. + gúdemu, tel. village). Zemindarry, Village, Head-quarters of forest ranger ; village, pop 336. On Godavery. Formerly head-quarter station of Soory reddy vencatrama narsiah, Mittahdar [q.v.]. Weekly market. ——*Nauracondah* (నారకొండ - nárakonda, Tel.). From (náráyadu, tel. proper name + konda, tel. hill). Trig. station ; lat. 17° 50′ 37·88″ ; long. 81° 13′ 31·30″ ; height 1,688 feet ; from Rekapully N.N.W. 20 miles ; from Nauracondah N. 1¼ miles.——*Peddacondah* (పెద్దకొండ - peddakonda, Tel.). From (pedda, tel. great + konda, tel. hill). Hill ; height 4,476 feet. Highest point in talook, situated in Eastern ghauts [q.v.]. Temple of goddess worshipped by Reddies [q.v.] and Gonds [q.v.]. Trig. station ; lat. 17° 50′ 23·27″ ; long. 81° 48′ 56·46″ ; height 4,476 feet ; from Rekapully N.E. 36 miles.——*Raupauk* (రాపాక - rápáka, Tel.). From (ráyi, tel. rock + páka, tel. village). Trig. station ; lat. 17° 39′ 17·75″ ; long. 81° 17′ 10·03″ ; height 2,002 feet ; from Rekapully N.W. 7 miles ; from Raupauk W.S.W. 3 miles.——*Rekapully* (రేకపల్లి - rékapalli, Tel.). See below.——*Severy* (శబరి - shabari, Tel.). See sep. title.——*Shreeramagherry* (శ్రీరామగిరి - shrírámagiri, Tel.). From (shrírâma, san. holy ráma + giri, san. hill). Zemindarry, Village ; pop. 103 ; lat. 17° 32′ ; long. 81° 20′ ; from Cocanada W.N.W. 72 miles ; from Rekapully S. 3 miles. Temple of Rama [q.v.] on hill close by. ——*Sillair* (సిలేరు - siléru, Tel.). See sep. title.——*Socoolair* (సోకులేరు - sókuléru, Tel.). See sep. title.——*Vaddigoodem* (వడ్డిగూడెము - vaddigúdemu, Tel.). From (vadde, tel. a caste name + gúdemu, tel. village). Zemindarry, Village ; pop. 1,289 ; lat. 17° 33′ ; long. 81° 19′ ; from Bhadrachellam E.S.E. 26 miles ; from Cocanada W.N.W. 75 miles ; from Rekapully W.S.W. 1¾ miles. Largest village in talook. Remains of an earthwork fort dating from time of Reddy [q.v.] chiefs.——**(2)** Zemindarry, Village ; Godavery dist., Bhadrachellam tal. ; pop. 535 ; lat. of village 17° 34′ ; long. 81° 20′ ; from Bhadrachellam E.S.E. 28 miles ; from Cocanada W.N W. 73 miles ; from Coonavaram E.S.E. 3 miles ; from Ellore N.N.E. 60 miles ; from Madras N.N.E. 312 miles ; from Narsapore N.N.W. 81 miles ; from Rajahmundry N.W. 48 miles. Formerly head-quarters station of Soory reddy vencayya, proprietor of the talook. Weekly market much frequented by hill people. Peshcush Rs. 16,709.

REKLA (ریکلا - reklah, *Hind.*). Small kind of bullock car [bandy], generally for one bullock between shafts.

RENOOCAY (रेणुका - rénuká, *San.*). From (rénu, san. proper name). A matronymic from renoo, her mother. Wife of jamadagny [q.v.] and mother of parshooraman [q.v.] ; same as Yellamma. See vol. I (77).

REPULLY (రేపల్లె - répalle,* *Tel.*). From (vrédu, tel. shepherd + palle, tel. village).——**(1)** Talook, Kistna district. Tahsildar's pay Rs. 250. Area 644 square miles. Population 222,757. Language Teloogoo. On right bank of Kistna extending from sea to within few miles of Seetanagaram and Mungalagherry hills. S. coast of district. Bounded north by the Kistna, south Bay of Bengal, west Baupatla and Guntoor talooks, east the Kistna. With the exception of a slight sandstone [manal cull] ridge at Colacalore, the talook is wholly river alluvium [adaimunn] and in fact it lies below flood level, protected by embankments, like Holland. Many villages are situated on mounds, a few feet above surrounding fields. Irrigation by Kistna aniout [q.v.]. Places of archæological interest :—Anantavaram, Bhattiprole, Booddaum, Casooparroo, Chauvaly, Chiloomore, Chiloovore, Chinna parimy agrahauram, Colacalore, Collipara, Collore, Cootchellapaud, Dauvoolore, Dooggiraula, Goodavully, Intoor, Jampany, Modecoor, Moolcoodore, Moparroo, Nadimipully, Nandiveloogoo, Nidbrole, Nizampatam, Pedda condore, Peddapoody, Peddapully, Pedda rauvore, Peravaly, Pinnapaud, Ponnapulley, Poolivarroo, Sundavole, Tenally, Vaimore, Vallabhapooram, Vellatore, Vettapollem, Wolair, Yedlapulley, Yeevany. Principal trig. stations :—Adavooladivy, Cottapollem beacon, Pesarlunka, Potoomeraca, Repully fort, Shingoopollem. The leading places, &c., in the talook are the following.——*Adavooladivy* (అడవులదీవి - adavuladívi, Tel.). From (adavi, tel. forest + dívi, tel. island). Trig. station ; lat. 15° 54′ 42·27″ ; long. 80° 50′ 10·82″ ; from Adavooladivy E. 2 miles ; from Repully S.S.W. 8 miles ; from the sea N. 4 miles.——*Bhattiprole* (భట్టిప్రోలు - bhattiprólu, Tel.). From (bhatti, tel. proper name + prólu, tel. town). Village ; pop. 2,880 ; acres 2,461 ; lat. 16° 06′ ; long. 80° 49′ ; from Masulipatam W.S.W. 24 miles ; from Repully N.W. 7 miles ; from the sea N. 16 miles. High mound called Lanja dibba, belonging to time of Jeinas [q.v.]. Demolished Booddhist [booddha] stoopam [q.v.]. Inscriptions at temples of Vittaleshwaran and Mulleshwaran dated A.D. 1144, 1252, 1260, 1528, and 1542.——*Colacalore* (కొలకలూరు - kolakalúru, Tel.). From (kolanu, tel. tank + úru, tel. village). Village ; pop. 3,333 ; acres 6,295 ; lat. 16° 19′ ; long. 80° 39′ ; from Masulipatam W.N.W. 35 miles ; from Repully N.W. 24 miles ; from the sea N. 30 miles. Several old inscriptions and hidden treasure [nidhy] have been discovered. Agasteeshwaran temple with inscriptions of Chola [q.v.] kings, dated A.D. 1202 and 1241 ; and on a slab south of the eastern gateway an inscription, dated A.D. 1318, recording a grant by a son of the General of Prataupa roodran. Two other inscriptions at the south gateway of the Keshavasawmy temple record grants by the same authority.——*Collipara* (కొల్లిపర - kollipara, Tel.). From (kolli, tel. tree, ipomœa hederacea, jacq. + parra, tel. a swamp). Village ; pop. 4,025 ; acres 4,292 ; lat. 16° 18′ ; long. 80° 47′ ; from Masulipatam W.N.W. 26 miles ; from Repully N.N.W. 19 miles. Inscription near the Mooceteshwaran temple. Gives its name to a channel.——*Collore* (కొల్లూరు - kollúru, Tel.). From (kollu, tel. pond + úru, tel. village). Village ; pop. 3,989 ; acres 4,589 ; lat. 16° 11′ ; long. 80° 50′ ; from Masulipatam W. 22 miles ; from Repully N.N.W. 11 miles ; from the sea N. 21 miles. Temples with inscriptions dated A.D. 1172, 1173, 1177 and 1533. Lock.——*Cottapollem beacon* (కొత్తపాలెము - kottapálemu, Tel.). From (kotta, tel. new + pálemu, tel. fortified village). Trig. station ; lat. 15° 52′ 18·53″ ; long. 80° 49′ 6·77″ ; from Cottapollem W. 2 miles ; from Repully S.S.W. 12 miles. On seashore.——*Dindey* (దిండె - dinde, Tel.). Means a sheaf of corn. Village ; pop. 2,014 ; acres 11,882 ; lat. 15° 54′ ; long. 80° 44′ ; from Masulipatam W.S.W. 35 miles ; from Repully S.W. 13 miles ; from the sea N. ½ mile. Bungalow [q.v.] on beach built by Mr. Rhode, former judge of Guntoor. ——*Dooggiraula* (దుగ్గిరాల - duggirála, Tel.). From (dugga, tel. goddess párvatí + ráyi, tel. stone). Village, Head-quarters of Executive engineer in charge of Kistna western delta ; pop. 1,991 ; acres 1,990 ; lat. 16° 20′ ; long. 80° 40′ ; from Masulipatam W.N.W. 34 miles ; from Repully N.N.W. 25 miles ; from the sea N. 30 miles. On main canal. Temple of Keshavasawmy repaired by Reddies [q.v.] of Condaveed, built by Chola kings.——*Gungavole* (గంగవోలు - gangavólu, Tel.). See sep. title.——*Intoor* (ఇంటూరు - intúru, Tel.). From (illu, tel. house + úru, tel. village). Village ; pop. 2,483 ; acres 5,374 ; lat. 16° 04′ ; long. 80° 40′ ; from Masulipatam W.S.W. 34 miles ; from Repully W. 14 miles ; from the sea N. 13 miles. Ancient temple of Veerabhadran [q.v.]. Public bungalow [q.v.]. Choultry [q.v.].——*Keitpully* (కైతేపల్లి - kaitepalli, Tel.). From (kaitamu, tel. poetic talent + palli, tel. village). Village ; pop. 1,051 ; acres 2,299 ; lat. 15° 56′ ; long. 80° 54′ ; from Masulipatam S.W. 25 miles ; from Repully S.S.E. 7 miles ; from the sea N.E. 6 miles. On the Kistna. Formerly important but much deteriorated by inundation of 1864. It formed part of the old Nellore Oodayagherry circar [q.v.], of which the Zoopully [q.v.] family were joint deshmookhs [q.v.] in past centuries and so did not come under the jurisdiction of the Guntoor zemindars [q.v.]. Basaulut jung gave it as a jagheer [q.v.] to his Diwaun [q.v.] futteh ally khan. In 1801 it was formally restored to him and considered part of Nellore district. In 1811 Futteh ally khan died. In 1813 Keitpully was tranferred to Masulipatam and in 1823 to Guntoor.——*Kistna* (కృష్ణ - krishna, Tel.). See sep. title. ——*Lunkevaunidibba* (లంకెవానిదిబ్బ - lankevánidibba, Tel.). From (lankevádu, tel. proper name + dibba, tel. mound). Trig. station ; lat. 15° 49′ 27·99″ ; long. 80° 54′ 5·52″ ; from Lunkevaunidibba N.N.E. 3 miles ; from Repully S. 14 miles ; from the sea N. 7 miles.——*Modecoor* (మోదుకూరు - módukúru, Tel.). From (módugu, tel. palásha tree, butea frondosa, r. + úru, tel. village). Village ; pop. 2,538 ; acres 4,199 ; lat. 16° 08′ ; long. 80° 37′ ; from Masulipatam W. 37 miles ; from Repully W.N.W. 19 miles ; from the sea N. 17 miles. Temples founded by Cholans [q.v.].——*Mortota* (మోర్తోట - mortóta, Tel.). Village, Port ; pop. 1,517 ; lat. 15° 59′ N. ; long. 80° 56′ E. Ancient temple.——*Nandiveloogoo* (నందివెలుగు - nandivelugu, Tel.). From (nandi, san. sacred bull + velugu, tel. hedge). Village ; pop. 1,891 ; acres 1,158 ; lat. 16° 18′ ; long 80° 41′ ; from Masulipatam W. 33 miles ; from Repully N.W. 22 miles ; from the sea N. 28 miles. Agasteshwara sawmy temple, with inscription, dated A.D. 1132. Seetaramasawmy temple built by Cholans [q.v.].——*Nidbrole* (నిడుబ్రోలు - nidubrólu, Tel.). From (nidu, tel. long. + prólu, tel. town). Village ; pop. 2,127 ; acres 3,990 ; lat. 16° 04′ ; long. 80° 36′ ; from Masulipatam W. 39 miles ; from Repully

W. 19 miles; from the sea N. 14 miles. Temple with inscription recording its erection in A.D. 1132.——*Nizampatam* (నిజాముపట్నము - nijámupattanamu, Tel.). See sep. title.——*Oollipollem* (ఉల్లిపాలెము - ullipálemu, Tel.). From (ulli, tel. onion, allium cepa, linn. + pálemu, tel. fortified village). Village; pop. 2,235; lat. 16° 00′; long. 80° 50′; from Repully W.S.W. 3 miles. Nizampatum ex-zemindar's fort.——*Penoomoody* (పెనుమూడి - penumúdi, Tel.). From (penu, tel. great + múdi, tel. village). Village, Port; pop. 1,374; acres 1,059; lat. 16° 02′; long. 80° 55′; from Madras N. 206 miles; from Masulipatam W.S.W. 20 miles; from Repully E.N.E. 2 miles; from the sea W. 20 miles. Bungalow [q.v.]. Ferry.——*Peravaly* (పెరవలి - peravali, Tel.). From (pera, tel. great + vali, tel. god of the winds, father of hanumán). Village; pop. 2,653; acres 4,575; lat. 16° 09′; long. 80° 45′; from Masulipatam W. 28 miles; from Repully N.W. 12 miles; from the sea N. 17 miles. Two temples built by Chola [q.v.] kings. Inscription dated A.D. 1439. Lake called Gungavole.——*Pesarlunka* (పెసర్లంక - pesarlanka, Tel.). From (pesara, tel. green gram, phaseolus mungo, linn. + lanka, tel. island). Trig. station; lat. 16° 4′ 43·59″; long. 80° 53′ 52·35; from Pesarlunka S.S.E. 8 miles; from Repully N.N.E. 4 miles; from the sea W. 21 miles.——*Potoomeraca* (పోటుమెరక - pótumeraka, Tel.). From (pótu, tel. high water + meraka, tel. high ground). Trig. station; lat. 15° 55′ 32·45″; long. 80° 53′ 5·16″; from Potoomeraca S. ⅜ mile; from Repully S. 7 miles; from the sea N. 14 miles.——*Repully* (రేపల్లె - répalle, Tel.). See below. ——*Repully fort* (రేపల్లెకోట - répallekóta, Tel.). Trig. station; lat. 16° 1′ 25·30″; long. 80° 53′ 6·90″; from Repully S.E. ⅜ mile; from the sea N.N.E. 20 miles.——*Singoopollem* (శింగుపాలెము - shingupálemu, Tel.). From (shingu, tel. proper name + pálemu, tel. fortified village). Trig. station; lat. 15° 57′ 53·77″; long. 80° 54′ 20·06″; from Repully S.S.E. 5 miles; from Singoopollem N.W. ¼ mile; from the sea N. 16 miles.——*Sundavole* (చండవోలు - tsandavólu, Tel.). See sep. title.——*Tenally* (తెనాలి - tenáli, Tel.). See sep. title.——*Vellatore* (వెల్లటూరు - vellatúru, Tel.). From (vella, tel. white + úru, tel. village). Village; pop. 1,738; acres 1,581; lat. 16° 07′; long. 80° 51′; from Masulipatam W. 21 miles; from Repully N.N.W. 7 miles; from the sea N. 24 miles. Ancient temple of Agasteeshwarasawmy. Vishnoo [q.v.] temple with inscription.——*Wolair* (వోలేరు - vóléru, Tel.). From (óli, tel. line + éru, tel. river). Village; pop. 2,319; acres 2,820; lat. 16° 04′; long. 80° 54′; from Masulipatam W.S.W. 20 miles; from Repully N. 3 miles; from the sea N. 22 miles. Last century the village was almost wholly Christian and part of the large church then built is still standing. About 50 families of Cumma [q.v.] cultivators migrated in 1787 under Father Manenti and settled at Keelcherry [q.v.] in Chingleput district, where they still form a Teloogoo christian colony. Near the church is an epitaph in French and Teloogoo on the grave of Ignatius, a native of Pondicherry, who died in 1792. Old villagers recollect that the festival of St. francis xavier was kept with some splendour. The only Christians in the village are seven or eight Pariah [q.v.] families. The chancel of the church fell in during the cyclone of 1864. Madana gopalsawmy temple, with inscription, of A.D. 1538 in the reign of Atchoota deva roya of Vijianugger.——**(2)** Town, Talook head-quarters, Sub-registrar's office; Kistna dist., Repully tal.; pop. 3,248; acres 2,039; lat. 16° 02′; long. 80° 53′; from Bezwada S.S.E. 36 miles; from Guntoor E.S.E. 31 miles; from Madras N. 208 miles; from Masulipatam W.S.W. 22 miles; from Vinoocondah E. 72 miles; from the sea N. 19 miles. Ruined fort.

RHEEA (اتنگن - utangan, *Hind.*). Title from assamese. Same as China grass.

RHETSA (चिरफळ - chirap'hala, *Mahr.*; तेपळिरुकु - tépalirúku, *Conc.*; ಜಿಮ್ಮಿಮರ - jimmimara, *Can.*; కావటె - kávate, *Too.*; రత్సమాను - rattsamánu, *Tel.*; മുള്ളില - mullila, *Mal.*; කටුකීන - katukína, *Singh.*; இரச்சைமரம் - iraççaimaram, *Tam.*). Title from teloogoo. Mahr. from (chira, san. long time + p'hala, san. fruit). Tel. from (rattsa, tel. assembly + mánu, tel. tree), from hill people assembling under the tree to determine public affairs. Mal. from (mul, mal. sharp-pointed + ila, mal. leaf). Singh. from (katu, singh. thorny + kína, singh. calophyllum tomentosum, wight.). Tam. from teloogoo. Mahr. also (tirap'hala); (tisala), by corruption. Mal. also (karimurikku), meaning black erythrina indica, Tamk.; (mulakila), meaning pepper leaf. Title otherwise Black palaus, Pepper leaf, Thorn leaf, Toothache tree. Botanically Zanthoxylum [toomroo] rhetsa, dec., rutaceæ [vricsham, 32]. Specific name from teloogoo. Alias Fagara rhetsa; Lacuris illicioides; Tipalia limonella; Xanthoxylon rhetsa. Tipalia from concany. Tree, 50 feet, everywhere armed with prickles; bark corky; leaves alternate, equally pinnated; leaflets eight to sixteen pair, lanceolate, unequal-sided, entire, glabrous; panicles terminal; petals and stamens four; capsule sessile, solitary, globose; seeds solitary, round, glossy black; flowers small, yellow; capsule one-celled. Unripe capsules aromatic, tasting like fresh orange-peel; inner lamina of the bark bitter and acrid; seeds like that of black pepper [q.v.] and used as a stimulant.

RHOODA (رده - rúdah, *Hind.*). From (rúd, pers. a bow string). Catgut, made of the twisted intestines of sheep [aud].

RICE (तण्डुल - tandula, *San.*; ارز - aruz, *Ar.*; برنج - biranj, *Pers.*; چاول - chával, *Hind.*; బియ్యము - biyyamu, *Tel.*; അരി - rai, *Mal.*; அரிசி - arisi, *Tam.*). Title through arabic, and perhaps others, from tamul. San. from (tad, san. to beat). Tam. from (ari, tam. to beat). Greek ὀρύζα from tamul. Husked paddy [paddy, wet crop]. Raw rice is rice husked after sun-drying. Prepared rice is parboiled.——*Millet rice* (باجرا چاول - bájráchával,|Hind.). Same as Matted purple grass.——*Mountain rice* (پہاڑی چاول - pahárichával, Hind.). Oryza mutica, roxb; otherwise upland rice, wild rice [nivvary].——*Pearl rice* (മുത്താരി - muttári, Mal.). Title from round seeds. Mal. means same. Same as Raggy.

RICSHAM (ऋक्ष - riksha, *San.*; असवल - asavala, *Mahr.*; دب - dubb, *Ar.*; خرس - khirs, *Pers.*; ریچھ - ríchh, *Hind.*; ریچ - rích, *Dec.*; برونگ - bruvang, *Malay*; ಕರಡಿ - karadi, *Can.* and *Too.*; ఎలుగు - elugu, *Tel.*; ଭଲ୍ଲୁ - bhallu, *Oor.*; പന്നിക്കരടി - pannikkarati, *Mal.*; ඌසා - usa, *Singh.*; கரடி - karadi, *Tam.*). San. from (riksh, san. to hurt). Tam. from (karadu, tam. rough). San. also (bhalluka), injuring animal. Hind. also (bhál); (ádamzád), meaning son of man. Can. also (kaddi). Mal. also (karati). Tam. also (aiváymirugam), meaning five-mouthed animal; from prehensile power of its four feet and mouth.—"*a*" Title otherwise Bear, Indian black bear Sloth bear. Melursus ursinus, ursidæ, plantigrada, carnivora, mammalia [sastanam, 7], of naturalists [jantoo]. Alias Bradypus ursinus; Melursus lybicus; Ursus inornatus, labiatus. The brown bear of Europe, Ursus arctos is the type of the family, and has been known from the earliest ages. An extinct species of bear, Ursus spelæus, commonly called the cave bear, seems again to have been the ancestor of the brown bear. The present species are large, heavy animals, strictly plantigrade. Black, hair very long and shaggy; muzzle and tip of feet dirty white or yellowish; a white crescentic, or V-shaped mark on the breast. Soles of the feet usually devoid of hair; ears small; snout lengthened; tail usually very short. Their claws are adapted for digging, being long and stout, and they are mostly expert climbers. The sole of the hind foot leaves a mark not unlike that of a human print. Found chiefly in hilly districts; especially where there are decomposed masses of granite [caroomcull] with natural caverns. They ascend the top of the Neilgherries and other high ranges in spring to feed. Their food is black ants [choomtee], termites, beetles [zeerangy], fruit [pazham], particularly the seeds of Cassia fistula [common condray], of the date tree [kharjooram], honey [shahad], &c. The power of suction in the bear as well as of propelling wind from its mouth is great. They are commonly led about to perform various antics. Among the Poligars [q.v.] of the south bears used to be hunted by dogs [nye]. When pursued, they carry their cubs on their back. They are long-lived, living in a state of captivity for forty years. They do not rise to hug their adversary; they use their claws however with great effect. Bear's hair is enclosed in amulets and tied around the neck of children. Its skin is cut into straps and tied round the necks of bulls as a safeguard against disease. Sometimes its blood is preserved on cloths and used in rheumatic pains. Bear's grease is also used as an emollient in rheumatism. Indian species not here found are:—Ailuropus melanoleucos, Ursus isabellinus or himalayan brown bear, Ursus malayanus or bruang or malayan sun bear, Ursus torquatus or himalyan black bear.—"*b*" Ricsham is in very ancient sanscrit astronomy the general term for a constellation [nacshatram]; in this sense probably originally from (ruch, san. to shine), but corrupted to present meaning [rooch]. Maha ricsham is then not only the Great bear [doobhe acbar] but any other large constellation. Very ancient hindoo astronomers ascribe to the stars in the great bear [doobhe acbar] a particular motion or variation of longitude, different from other stars, and unconnected with the precession [ayanaumasham] of the equinoxes [maunam]; but this appears to be an error of confusion arising out of the line of the rishies [rishy raikhay]. The line of the rishies or rishy raikhay [ayanaumsham, craunty pautam, maunam, rishy raikhay] so called in bengal appears by corruption as the line of the ricshams in teloogoo [jyotisham, nacshatram].—"*c*" Plant first term meaning shaggy. Ex., where transl. is of second term:—Hemigyrosa canescens (karadippungam), pongamia glabra; Methonica superba (karadikanninagadde), eye + root. See gloss, paragraphs.

RIDY (റിടി - riti, *Mal.*). From (ridí, singh. silver). Coin consisting of two silver wires hooked, &c. Fish-hook coin [larin].

RIFAT (رفعة - rifat, *Ar.*). From (rafa, ar. to raise). Exalted. Part of lacab; as Rifat ool moolk, exalted in the state [ism].

RIG (ऋक् - rik, *San.*). From (rich, san. to praise). The first Vedam [q.v.].

RIJAUL (رجال - rijál, *Hind.*). Plural of (rajul). Men.——*Rijaul ool gheib* (رجال الغيب - rijálulghaib, Hind.). From (above + ghaib, ar. concealed). An invisible spiritual being who moves in a circular orbit round the world. On different days his station is in different places. His influence on each day [roz] is especially exerted during nine ghurries [q.v.] or three hours and thirty-six minutes at the close of that lunar day [tity], and in this interval it is unfortunate to begin a journey. Amongst the Mahomedans when a man starts on a journey his friends and relations often tie on his left upper arm a band of silk riband containing silver or gold coin, which they call Imaum zaumin or imaum's protection. When the journey is accomplished in safety, these deposits are distributed amongst the poor. Rijaul ool gheib should not be in front of the traveller nor on his right, but either behind or to his left. The following table shows his position on different days of the month; always noted in the calendar. Compare Rahoo caulam and Goolica caulam of the hindoos :—

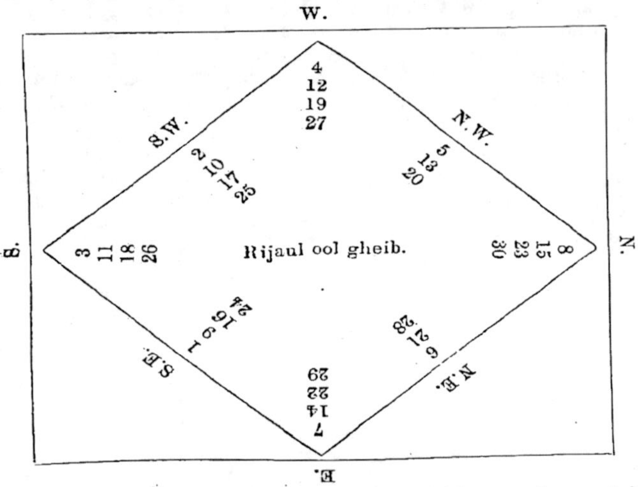

RIKTAM (रिक्त - rikta, *San.*). From (rich, san. to empty). Empty. Riktatity is the name of the fourth, ninth and fourteenth days in a lunar fortnight [jayay, pacsham].

RINAM (ऋण - rina, *San.*). Literally decrease. Minus in mathematics [ganitam]. Also debt. Funeral rites, anniversary rites [shrauddham], and tarpanam [q.v.], &c., are termed Pitry rinam or debt of obligation to deceased ancestors.

RISAULAH (رساله - risálah, *Hind.*). From (rasula, ar. to go or send a message). Detachment of native irregular cavalry. Now current in Mysore. Rissaldar is the native officer commanding the same. Next come in order the Jemadar, Havildar, Duffedar, and Sillahdar; which see in their places.

RISHABHAM (ऋषभ - rishabha, *San.*; بیل - bail, *Hind.*; ಗೂಳಿ - gúli, *Can.*; ఎద్దు - eddu, *Tel.*; കാള - kála, *Mal.*; எருது - eruthu, *Tam.*). San. from (rish, to sprinkle, the idea of impregnating being involved). Mal. from (kálu, mal. to bellow). Bull [raushy]. Second note of gamut, represented by abbreviation Ri [sangeetam, swaram]. Also applied to Nundy [nundy, poonya prauny, vauhan].——*Rishabha devan* (ऋषभदेव - rishabhadéva, San.). From (above + déva, san. god). Basava [q.v.], the founder of Lingayet [q.v.] sect [jauty].

RISHY (ऋषि - rishi, *San.*; இருடி - irudi, *Tam.*). From (drish, san. to see). One who has seen the words of revelation. A holy sage. Distinguish from Moonies who are a minor class and much more numerous [matam].—"*a*" The vishnoo pooraunam [q.v.] says there are three kinds of rishies :—royal rishies or princes, who have adopted a life of devotion, as Vishwamitran [q.v.]; divine rishies or sages, who are demi-gods also, as Nauradan [q.v.]; and bramharishies, or sages who are the sons of bramha [q.v.] or bramins, as Vasishtan [q.v.] and others. In the epic period rishy is merely a name for historical personages, distinguished for their piety and wisdom, either by their acts or their writings. In the pooraunic period the chief rishies are seven primeval personages, born of Bramha's mind, and presiding under different forms over each Manwantaram [caulam, menoo]. The seven great rishies [saptarishy] usually named are:—Angiran, Atry, Bharadwaujan, Gowtaman, Jamadagny, Vasishtan, Vishwamitran. Another list is :—Agastyan, Angiran, Caushyapan, Gowtaman, Marcandeyan, Poolastyan, Vasishtan. These with Satyavratan escaped the waters of the deluge [pralayam] by the favor of Vishnoo [q.v.].—"*b*" The names of these seven rishies have been given to the seven stars [nacshatram] of Ursa major [doobhe acbar]; their festival is the fifth of waxing fortnight [pacsham] of bhaudrapadam [mausam] or September. The following are the great bear rishies usually enumerated:—Mareechy, Atry, Angiran, Poolastyan, Poolahan, Cratoo and Vasishtan. The seven rishies have wives, but probably by a later poetical invention; these are then in astronomy the Pleiades [kritticay, sooreiyah]. There is also a list of thirty-one astronomical rishies, probably connected with the stars in the Fishes [hoot, meenam]. See vol. I (78), (115).——*Rishicondah* (ఋషికొండ - rishikonda, Tel.). From (above + konda, tel. hill). Village, Hill; Vizagapatam dist., Vizagapatam division; pop. 307. Otherwise Sugar-loaf hill. On seashore between Vizagapatam and Bimlipatam. Formerly abode of Rishies. At foot is a Shiva temple. Rishicondah beacon trig. station is in lat. 17° 46′ 40·38″; long. 83° 25′ 30·62″; from Rajpollem N.E. 5 miles; from Vizagapatam N.E. 8 miles; from the sea W. ¾ mile.——*Rishy punchamy* (ఋషిపంచమి - rishipanchami, Tel.). Means sage + fifth. Lunar [chaundramaunam] festival [pundigay, 3a], subject to intercalation [adhicam]. On the fifth lunar day [tity] in the waxing moon [shooclapacsham] of sixth lunar month Bhaudrapadam [mausam] between 19th August and 20th September. Sacred to the seven sages [saptarishy]. Follows after Pillaiyaur chatoorty [q.v.]. Women of advanced age are in general charged with performance of ceremony, which consists in ornamenting and worshipping seven stones intended to represent the sages. They are obliged to fast [oopavausam] the whole day and night on the occasion.——*Rishy raikkay* (ऋषिरेखा - rishirékhá, San.). From (above + rékhá, san. line). The line of the Rishies. A great circle passing through the pole of the ecliptic [craunty mundalam], and according to some shastrams cutting a certain star in the constellation [nacshatram] of the great bear or Maha ricsham [doobhe acbar, maha ricsham], supposed by some to β [alanak] by others to be γ or δ Ursæ majoris, and meeting the yogam [q.v.] star Veidhrity [q.v.], the same as either η or ζ Piscium [hoot] or some neighbouring star; although no great circle [mundalam] passing through the pole of the ecliptic [craunty mundalam] could now be made to intersect these points [madhyama sowra maunam, ricsham]. The line of the Rishies is really only a great circle drawn through the pole of the ecliptic and the equinoctial colure [maishauyana mundalam, vishoo mundalam] of the time being. This passed through the great bear some 5,000 years B.C., whence may have come the tradition mentioned above. See Madhyama sowra maunam.——*Rooshcoolya* (ఋషికుల్య - rishikulyá, Tel. rushkulya*). From (above + kulyá, san. channel). River; Ganjam dist., Berhampore and Goomsoor tals., Dhauracote zemindarry, Aska estate, and Chinna kimedy maliahs. Largest river in district. Rises in Chinna kimedy maliahs in lat. 19° 51′ and long. 84° 04′ and runs south-east to Aska, where it is joined by Mahanuddy; thence south-east and east till it enters the sea at Ganjam in lat. 19° 22′ north and long. 85° 7′ east. Length about 115 miles. Principal towns on its banks; Sooradah, Aska, Poorshottapore and Ganjam. Spanned at Aska by a masonry bridge of 19 arches. For account of Rooshcoolya project, see vol. I, 407.——*Sapta rishy* (सप्तर्षि - saptarshi, San.). From (sapta, san. seven + above). Ursa major [doobhe acbar, maha ricsham]. See under Saptam.

RISHYAM (ऋश्य - rishya, *San.*). From (rish, san. to go). White-footed antelope [jinka].——*Rishyamoocam* (ऋश्यमूक - rishyamúka, San.). From (above + múka, san. mute); with silent antelopes. A mountain in the Deccan [q.v.], the temporary abode of Rama [q.v.] with the monkey chief Soogreevan [q.v.]; somewhere in north of Mysore, near source of Pumpah river. See vol. I (1), (3).

RITOO (ऋतु - ritu, *San.*). From (rí, san. to go). A fixed time epoch [caulam, 2]. A season, a period of two months, dividing the year according to the sanscrit into the six seasons of:—Vasantam, spring; Greeshmam, hot weather; Varsham, rains; Sharad, autumn; Hemantam, cold; Shishiram, dewy or foggy. The following is given by a Bramin to a rajah as a blessing:—"May you enjoy in Hemantam the congenial warmth of your "wife, in Shishiram, the gentle heat of the sun; the pleasures "of a shady garden in Vasantam, and of cool bathing in Greesh-"mam; comfortable high room in Varsham, and a copious "draught of fresh milk in Sharad." The dravidians reckon their first season from August after the establishment of the S.W. monsoon, thus Caur, Coothir, Moon pany, Pin pany, Yila venil, Moothir venil; but they have terms which correspond to the weather [caulam, caur, caurtey, mausam]. See vol. I, 610.——*Caur* (கார் - kár, Tam.). Means blackness. First Tamul season. Corresponding to August and September, Auvany-Poorataushy [mausam].——*Coothir* (கூதிர் - kúthir, Tam.). Cold. Second Tamul season. Corresponding to October-November or Arpisy Caurtigay [mausam].——*Greeshmam* (ग्रीष्म - gríshma, San.). From (gras, san. to consume). Hot season. Second Sanscrit. Comprehending Teloogoo months Jyeshtam and Ashaudham, when the sun [sooryan] is in the signs [raushy] Mitoonam ♊ and Carcatacam ♋, answering to the Tamul months Auny or june and Audy [mausam] or july.——*Hemantam* (हेमन्त - hémanta, San.). From (hima, san. dew). Fifth Sanscrit. The cold season. Comprehending Teloogoo months Margashiram and Pooshyam, when the sun [sooryan] is in the signs [raushy] Dhanoos ♐ and Macaram ♑, answering to the Tamul months Maurgaly or december and Tye [mausam] or january.——*Moon pany* (முன்பனி - munbani, Tam.). From (mun, tam. fore + pani, tam. dew). Early dewy season. Third Tamul. Corresponding to December-January or Maurgaly-Tye [mausam].——*Moothir venil* (முதிர்வேனில் - muthirvénil, Tam.). From (muthir, tam. mature + vénil, tam. heat). Very hot season. Sixth Tamul. Corresponding to June-July or Auny-Audy [mausam].——*Pin pany* (பின்பனி - pinbani, Tam.). From (pin, tam. after + pani, tam. dew). Later dewy season. Fourth Tamul. February-March or Maushy-Pungoony [mausam].——*Sharad* (शरद् - sharad, San.). From (shri, san. to wither). Autumn. Fourth Sanscrit. Comprehending Teloogoo months Aushweejam and Caurteecam, when the sun [sooryan] is in the signs [raushy] Toolaum ♎ and Vricshicam ♏, answering to the Tamul months Arpisy or october and Caurtigay [mausam] or november.——*Shishiram* (शिशिर - shishira, San.). Cold or dewy season. Sixth Sanscrit. Comprehending the Teloogoo months Maugham and Phaulgoonam, when the sun [sooryan] is in the signs [raushy] Coombham ♒ and Meenam ♓, answering to the Tamul months Maushy or february and Pungoony [mausam] or march.——*Varsham* (वर्षा - varshá, San.; வருடம் - varudam, Tam.). From (vrish, san. to rain). Rainy season. Third Sanscrit. Comprehending the Teloogoo months Shrauvanam and Bhaudrapadam, when the sun [sooryan] is in the signs [raushy] Simham ♌ and Cauyay ♍, answering to the Tamul months Auvany or august and Pooratanshy [mausam] or september.——*Vasantam* (वसन्त - vasanta, San.). From (vas, san. to shine). Spring. First Sanscrit. Comprehending the Teloogoo months Cheitram and Veishaukham, when the sun [sooryan] is in the signs [raushy] Maisham ♈ and Vrishabham ♉, answering to the Tamul months Chittray or april and Veiyaushy [mausam] or may.——*Yila venil* (இளவேனில் - ilavénil, Tam.). From (ilam, tam tender + vénil, tam. heat). Milder hot season. Fifth Tamul. Corresponding to April-May or Chittray-Veiyaushy [jyotisham, mausam].

RIWAUJY (رواجی - riwájí, *Hind.*). Means current. A gold coin of Jehaungeer [q.v.]. Weight ¼ tolah [q.v.].

RIYAUZY (ریاضی - riyází, *Hind.*). From (rowza, ar. to train). Mathematics [ganitam] or exact sciences [ilm, shastram].

RIYOYATY (رعایت - riáyat, *Hind.*). From (rau, ar. to abstain). Otherwise Royaty. Favor, especially a remission of the government claim.

RIZYE (رضائی - razái, *Hind.*). From (razú, ar. to please). A coverlet quilted with cotton [sheelay].

ROBAUL (காலா - kálá, *Tam.*). Title otherwise Indian sturgeon. The genus Polynemus, polynemidæ, acanthopterygii, teleostei, pisces [matsyam, 11], of naturalists [jantoo]. The species best known to the natives here are Golden robaul, Screw-pine robaul. Cf. also Streaked robaul in another genus. The Pilgrim fish of bengal, from going up the ganges to benares, or from long fibres resembling unshaven hairs of penitent [tupsee]; otherwise Mango fish [q.v.], because it fills the ganges in the mango [q.v.] season; is Polynemus, paradisea.——*Golden robaul* (रावस - rávasa, Mahr.; మాగజెల్ల - mágajella, Tel.; വാഴിമീൻ - vázhimín, Mal.; பொலன்காலா - polangálá, Tam.). Title from color. Tel. from (mága, tel. robaul, polynemus indicus + jella, tel. sphyræna jello). Mal. from (vázhu, mal. to rule + mín, mal. fish). Tam. from (polam, tam. gold + kálá, tam. sturgeon, polynemus genus). Mahr. also (chéláchi). Tel. also (errakála), meaning red robaul. Polynemus [robaul] tetradactylus, polynemidæ, acanthopterygii, teleostei [matsyam, 11], of naturalists. Alias Eleutheronema tetradactylus; Polynemus magajellee, salliah et quadrifilis, teria. Magajellee from teloogoo. Silvery-green, becoming yellowish-white on sides and abdomen, dorsal and caudal grayish with minute black points and nearly black at edges; ventral and anal pale orange in outer halves, pectoral filaments white; dark mark on upper portion of opercle; sea; 6 feet and upwards in length; excellent eating; well-known to sportsmen; the best fish to be caught in estuaries on the west coast.——*Screw-pine robaul* (भात - bhát, Mahr.; کالا مچھی - kálámaçqhí, Hind.; మాగబొచ్చె - mágaboççe, Tel.; എട്ട - étta, Mal.; தாழங்காலா - tázhangálá, Tam.). Title from color like the yellow screw-pine flower. Hind. from tamul. Tel. from (mága, tel. robaul + boççe, tel. robaul, polynemus indicus). Mal. from (chétta, mal. elder), mischievous. Tam. from (tázhai, tam. screw-pine + kálá, tam. sturgeon, polynemus genus). Mahr. also (dára). Tel. also (mága); (máva). Polynemus [robaul] indicus, polynemidæ, acanthopterygii, teleostei [matsyam, 11], of naturalists. Alias Polynemus magabooshee, sele, uronemus; magabooshee from teloogoo. Air-vessel oval and thick, occupying entire length of abdomen; lateral-line continued along lower caudal lobe almost to its end; vertical fins rather densely scaled; back purplish-black, abdomen silvery-white, dashed with gold; first and second dorsals also anal stained with black, as is the lower half of the opercle; caudal with many black points; sea; 4 feet in length; rarely above 20 lbs. weight; yields about two ounces of rough isinglass [meen vajram].——*Streaked robaul* (माल - mála, Mahr.; తాళ్లమేవ - tállaméva, Tel.; ମୋରର - morara, Oor.). Title from markings. Mahr. means streaked. Tel. from (tádu, tel. rope + méva, tel. polynemus indicus). Mahr. also (chitala), meaning spotted antelope, from markings on back. Amblypharyngodon mola, cyprininæ, cyprinidæ, physostomi, teleostei [matsyam, 39], of naturalists [jantoo]. Specific name from mahratta. Alias Cyprinus mola; Leuciscus chitul, mola; Mola buchanani; Rhodeus macrocephalus. Chitul from mahratta. Silvery lateral band, and usually dark markings on the dorsal, caudal, and anal fins. No other common species here.

ROBIN (اربعین - arbaín, *Hind.*). From (ruba, ar. fourth). Canara measure of capacity, one-fourth of candy [alavay, 3c]. Same as Mooda.

ROCK (چٹان - chatán, *Hind.*). Prefix indicating habitat and resort, or hardness and mass [cull].——*Black rock cod* (खार्वा - khárvá, Mahr.; کالا مدوان - kálámadwán, Hind.; కలమరి - kalamari, Tel.; അരി - ari, Mal.; மட்டிவாயன் - mattiváyan, Tam.). Hind. from (kálá, hind. black + madwán, hind. chrysophrys genus). Tel. corrupted from hindostany. Mal. from (aru, mal. small). Tam. means clumsy mouth. Title otherwise Calamara. Chrysophrys berda, sparidæ, acanthopterygii, teleostei [matsyam, 5], of naturalists [jantoo]. Alias Chrysophrys calamara; Sparus berda, calamara, hasta; Calamara from teloogoo. Snout compressed and pointed; scales four entire and two half rows between lateral-line and base of spinous dorsal; nine rows between base of ventral and lateral-line; air-vessel notched posteriorly; colors silvery-grey; scales darkest at bases and usually a black spot behind opercle on shoulder; black edge to dorsal interspinous membrane, soft dorsal, caudal, and anal with black edges; dark band along anal fin; sea; very common at madras; excellent eating. Chrysophrys sarba, is a lighter colored species; as food it is inferior to the berda.——*Red rock cod* (ताम्ब - támba, Mahr.; రంగు - rangu, Tel.). Mahr. from (támbadá, mahr. red). Tel. means color. Lutjanus [taumbam] argentimaculatus, percidæ [panayairy], acanthopterygii, teleostei [matsyam, 1], of naturalists [jantoo]. Alias Alphestes gembra et sambra; Diacope argentimaculata; Labrus argentatus; Lutjanus sambra; Mesoprion argentimaculatus, gembra, immaculatus, rangus, sambra, tœniops; Perca argentata; Sparus rangoo; Sciæna argentata, argentimaculata; Rangoo from teloogoo. Scales in horizontal rows above lateral-line, in some specimens a little sinuous; below lateral-line they are horizontal; cherry-red, darkest at bases of scales; front edge of anal fin pinkish-white as is also the first ventral ray; upper margin of spinous dorsal orange; in some specimens dark spots on dorsal, caudal and anal fins; very young have six to nine narrow, vertical, silvery-white bands, which become more or less lost as age increases; sea; attains upwards of two feet in length, and is good eating.——*Rock dammer* (உரப்புப்பிசின் - urappuppisin, Tam.). Title from being found in rock-like masses. See under Dammer.——*Rock oil* (மண்ணெண்ணெய் - mandailam, Tam.). Petroleum. Same as Munn teilam.——*Rock pigeon* (بن تیتر - bantítar, Hind.; జాముపోలంక - dzámupólanka, Tel.; ବଟେଲ - battel, Oor.; മലമ്പ്രാവ് - malamprávu, Mal.; கற்கவுதாரி - kargavuthári, Tam.). Title from haunt and from fancied resemblance in flight to pigeon; is a misnomer; distinguish from blue rock pigeon [q.v.]. Hind. from (ban, hind. forest + títar, hind. partridge). Tel. from (dzámu, tel. time equal to three hours + pólanka, tel. sand grouse), from being seen only in the morning; the first jaumam [q.v.] of the day. Mal. from (mala, mal. mountain + právu, mal. pigeon). Tam. from (kal, tam. stone + kavuthári, tam. partridge). Hind. also (kumartíl); (bakhttítar); (kuhar). Tam. also (káttukkózhi), meaning forest + fowl. Title otherwise Common sand-grouse. Pterocles exustus, pteroclidæ, rasores [pacshy, 31], of naturalists [jantoo]. Male general color fulvous isabelline, brighter and more yellow about lores, face, and chin, mixed with dusky greenish on back, wings and upper tail-coverts; primaries black, tips of all, except first three, white, broader on inner web; longitudinal median line on wing, formed by some coverts and secondaries being brighter buff; tail with central pair of feathers elongated and highly attenuated, isabelline yellow; lateral feathers deep brown, edged and tipped pale; fulvous; narrow black band in breast; abdomen deep chocolate brown burnt or singed color, hence exustus, paling on a vent, under tail-coverts creamy white, as are tarsal plumes; bill leaden; orbits lemon yellow; irides dark brown; feet plumbeous; length 13 inches; female has whole upper plumage, including tail-feathers, except plain bar on wing formed by greater coverts, fulvous, closely barred deep brown; also the space between pectoral band and abdomen; neck and breast unspotted dingy isabelline, abdomen as in male; central rectrices not elongated; commonest species of sand-grouse, never occurring in forest districts; unknown in malabar; frequents open plains, ploughed lands and bare fallow fields; feeds chiefly in the morning; when seated on ground, difficult to observe, from similarity of color to ground; flesh with high game flavor. No other common species here. The painted sand-grouse called in tel. (sandapólanka), or evening sand-grouse is Pterocles fasciatus.——*Rock salt* (கல்லுப்பு - kalluppu, Tam.). From hard mass. Same as Indooppoo, Sondah namak.——*Rock snake* (अजगर - ajagara, San.; اژدہا - azhdahá, Pers.; اژدہا - azhdahá, Hind. and Dec.; ಹೆಬ್ಬಾವು - hebbhávu, Can.; కొండచిలువ - kondachiluva, Tel.; പെരിമ്പാമ്പ് - perimpámbu, Mal.; வெண்ணந்தை - vennándai, Tam.). Title from their size and strength. San. from (aja, san. goat + gri, san. to devour). Pers., &c., from sanscrit. Can. from (hedda, can. large + hávu, can. snake). Tel. from (konda tel. hill + chiluva, tel. snake). Mal. from (peru, mal. large + pámbu, mal. snake). Tam. from (vans, san. wilderness + ándai, tam. lord). Tel. also (peddapoda), meaning large + stripe; (kondashila), by corruption. Tam. also (malaippámbu), meaning hill-snake; (másunam). Title otherwise Indian boa, Python. Terms co-extensive with family Pythonidæ ophidii colubriformes, ophidia [sarpam], reptilia [sarpy, 24], of naturalists [jantoo]. The Rock-snakes have the body and tail of moderate length or rather slender, rounded; tail prehensile; head with the snout rather long, depressed, truncated or rounded in front. Adult individuals with a spur-like prominence on each side of the vent; it is the extremity of a rudimentary hind limb hidden between the muscles. Individuals which measured 30 feet are on record. Rock-snakes from 15–20 feet long have the thickness of a man's thigh and will easily overpower a small deer [mrigam], a sheep [aud], or a good-sized dog [nye]. But although able to kill these animals, the width of their mouth is not so large that they can swallow one larger than a half-grown sheep. After having seized the victim, they smother it by throwing several coils of the body over and round it. In swallowing they always commence with the head; they live entirely on mammals [sastanam] and birds [pacshy]. During the time of digestion they move but slowly when disturbed, or defend themselves with little vigour when attacked; at any other time they will fiercely defend themselves. Rock-snakes must attain to a considerable age. The males remain smaller than the females. Rock-snakes will propagate in captivity. They are found in the hottest parts; climb as well as they swim; most prefer the neighbourhood of water. This family contains the largest snakes. The only South indian species is Python molurus. Alias Coluber molurus; Python bivittatus, tigris. The ground-color is light greyish brown; brown spot, shaped like the head of a lance, occupies the crown of the head and nape. Dark-brown streak runs from the nostril through the eye to behind the angle of the mouth, another band running along the lower jaw; sub-triangular brown spot below the eye; back of the body and tail with large quadrangular spots; sides of the body with irregular brown spots; lower parts yellowish, brownish or blackish on the sides. Prefers swampy ground, or at least the neighbourhood of water. Feeds on birds [pacshy], rodentia [moosham], young or small deer [mrigam], sheep [aud], &c. There is a Tamul stanza in Neetinery vilacam :—கண்கூடாப்பட்டது கெடெனினுங் கீழ்மக்கட் குண்டோரவுணர்ச்சிமற் றில்லாகுர்—மண் டெரி தான்வாய்மடுப்பினு மாசுணங்கண்டுயில்வ பேரி பெருமூச்செறிந்து—"though ruin be before their eyes, will "fools perceive it? no, they will not; though conflagration "rages near it, the sleeping rock-snake will not awake from its "loud-breathing slumbers."

RODA (రొడ - roda, *Tel.*). Marsh.——*Roddacumma* (రొడ్డకమ్మ - roddakamma, Tel.). From (above + amma, tel. goddess). Deity of the marsh and other sterile tracts. Compare Chowdamma. ——*Roddam* (రొడ్డము - roddamu, Tel.). From (roda, tel. marsh); village goddess is roddacumma. Sanscrit name by corruption (rudrapáda), meaning shiva + footstep. Village; Anantapore dist., Penoocondah tal.; pop. 2,901; acres 13,542; lat. 14° 06′; long. 77° 28′; from Anantapore S.S.W. 42 miles; from Penoocondah W. 11 miles. On the Pennair. There is an irrigation project here to supply the Roddam large tank [q.v.] by a channel [q.v.] which, it is proposed to lead from an anicut [q.v.] to be built across the Pennair river about two miles below where it is joined by the Jayamungaly. The length of the channel will be 6 miles by 15 yards broad with an average depth of from 4 feet of water. It will pass above the tanks of Calipy, Cottapully and Nulloor, and Cholmary, and greatly improve their supply. When the Cholmary tank is filled, its surplus water will be discharged into the Roddam large tank. 1,344 acres will be brought under cultivation. Two large tanks [q.v.] and a river channel [q.v.] irrigate a large extent. On the southern bank of Pennair is a small ancient temple supposed to contain Shiva's footstep [dharmaraja cull].

ROGAM (रोग - róga, *San.*). From (ruj, san. to injure). Disease. For Ashwarogam or horse diseases and Pashoorogam or cattle diseases see those heads. For fevers see Jwaram. For information on hindoo pathology generally see Veidyan and Ospitry. For hindoo astrology on rogam see Nacshatram.

ROGUE (ಕಳ್ಳಾನೆ - kalláne, *Can.*; దొంగఏనుగు - dongaénugu, *Tel.*; திருட்டுயானை - tiruttuyánai, *Tam.*). Tel. from (donga, tel. rogue + énugu, tel. elephant). Tam. from (tirudu, tam. to steal + yánai, tam. elephant). An elephant [q.v.], generally if not always a male, living in isolation from a herd and usually predacious.

ROHITACAM (रोहितक - róhitaka, *San.*; रोहिडा - róhidá, *Mahr.*; ہرن ہرا - harinhará, *Hind.*; రోహితక - róhitaka, *Tel.*; ചെമ്മരം - chemmaram, *Mal.*; රොහින් - róhin, *Singh.*; செம்மரம் - shemmaram, *Tam.*). San. from (róhita, san. red) [rohy, soymida]. Mahr. from sanscrit. Tel. from sanscrit. Mal. from (chem, mal. red + maram, mal. tree) [alanjy]. Singh. from sanscrit. Tam. from (shem, tam. red + maram, tam. tree). San. also (plíhaghna), meaning spleen destroying; (plíhashatru), meaning spleen + enemy, from being useful in enlargement of spleen. Hind. also (harinkhána). Can. also (shina); (mulen). Tel. also (chévamánu), meaning strong wood. Title otherwise Amoora bark tree, Red wood, Rohira, Rohiny, Spleen tree. Botanically Amoora rohituka, w. and a., meliaceæ [vricsham, 36]. Specific name from sanscrit. Alias Andersonia rohituka. Small tree; leaves unequally pinnated; leaflets six pair, opposite, obliquely-oblong, glabrous; young petioles slightly hairy on their lower part; male flowers in panicles shorter than the leaves, subsessile; calyx three-leaved; female flowers numerous, sessile, solitary, erect on spikes, which are rather more than half the length of the leaves; petals three; capsule pale yellow, three-celled, three-valved; seeds solitary, enclosed in a fleshy scarlet aril; flowers small, white, or cream-colored. Rohitacam bark is of a blackish-brown color externally, and rough from the presence of numerous small, elliptic, warty projections, arranged longitudinally, and from minute fissures; its substance is of a deep reddish-brown, and shows a striated internal surface; fracture short; when fresh it is soft and easily cut; the bulk of the bark is composed of parenchyme cells, containing starch and coloring matter; there are numerous yellow stone cells arranged in broken concentric layers, and very little woody fibre; the bark has a very astringent taste and turns of a greenish black when touched with a solution of ferric chloride; it has no particular odour. Bark is used as a medicinal astringent; oil [yennay] from seeds is stimulant in rheumatism. Wood reddish, close and even-grained, hard. Other species are :—cucullata, lawii, spectabilis. ——*Fever rohitacam* (சுரக்கள்ளி - shurakkalli, Tam.). Tam. means fever milk-hedge. Same as Soymida.——*Red rohitacam* (रक्तरोहिता - raktaróhitá, San.; रक्तरोहिडा - raktaróhidá, Mahr.; பேய்ப்பூலா - péyppúlá, Tam.). Title from flower and fruit. San. from (rakta, san. red + róhitá, san. red, amoora rohituka w. and a.). Mahr. from (rakta, san. red + róhidá, mahr. the plant so called, amoora rohituka, w. and a.). Tam. from (péy, tam. devil + púlá, tam. many-flowered phyllanthus, phyllanthus multiflorus, willd.). Mahr. also (raktaródá), by corruption. Title otherwise Demon poolah, Indian buck-thorn. Botanically Rhamnus wightii, w. & a., rhamneæ [vricsham, 41]. Alias Ceanothus wightiana. Common shrub upon the highest hills of the western ghauts, and extends to the neilgherries and ceylon; the leaves are glabrous, sub-opposite, elliptic, shortly acuminate, sharply serrate, and sub-coriaceous; pedicels axillary, fascicled, much shorter than the petiole; calyx five-cleft; petals cuneate-obovate; flowers greenish-yellow; styles three to four, diverging; ovary three to four-celled. The dried bark occurs as single quills or in curved pieces from two to three millimetres in thickness; the outer surface is dull brown; the younger bark is ashy-grey; the fracture is short externally, and tough and fibrous internally; the taste is astringent and bitter, but not unpleasant, a sweetish after-taste being left on the palate; the odour of the bark recalls that of tan. Bark is medicinally tonic, astringent and deobstruent. Common buck-thorn, otherwise purging buck-thorn, rain-berry thorn, rhine-berry thorn, way-thorn, is botanically Rhamnus catharticus, linn.; gives to pharm. buck-thorn juice the recently expressed juice of the ripe berries, rhamni succus, hydragogue cathartic; official; the pigment [rangh] sap green is made from the juice. Dahurian buck-thorn, chanto in hindostany, otherwise siberian buck-thorn, slender-branched buck-thorn, is botanically rhamnus dahuricus, pall., rhamneæ, a large erect shrub, flowers small, greenish yellow; sap-wood whitish, heart-wood brown, very hard and close-grained; used as firewood; there is a variety of this, hirsutus.

ROHITAM (रोहित - róhita, *San.*). Means red [rohy]. The genus Labeo, cyprininæ, cyprinidæ, physostomi, teleostei, pisces [matsyam, 39], of naturalists [jantoo]. Large tropical genus, of importance as food. Mouth situated below the snout, lips thickened, and sometimes fringed, with a horny inner fold on one or both. The genus can be divided into species having a pair of barbels on the snout, and species without barbels on the snout. The species best known to the natives are shown below. Other S. indian species are :—bata, boga, gonius, nigrescens.——*Black labeo* (रोहित - róhita, San.; कानोषि - kánóshi, Mahr.; کالا بہینس - kálábhains, Hind.; ಕರಿಮೀನು - karimínu, Can.; నల్లగండుమీను - nallagandumínu, Tel.; କାଳାବିୟେନ୍ସେ - kálábiyense, Oor.). San. means red. Hind. from (kálá, hind. black + bhains, hind. buffalo); from size. Can. from (kari, can. black + mínu, can. fish). Tel. from (nalla, tel. black + gandumínu, tel. fish, labeo fimbriatus). Oor. from hindostany. Labeo [rohitam] calbasu, cyprininæ, cyprinidæ, physostomi, teleostei [matsyam, 39], of naturalists. Specific name from hindostany. Alias Cirrhina micropogon; Cirrhinus affinis, belangeri, calbasu; Cyprinus calbasu; Labeo velatus; Rohita belangeri, calbasu, reynauldi. Rohita from sanscrit. Mouth narrow; snout depressed; lips thick, fringed, more especially the lower one, and each having a distinct inner fold; caudal deeply forked; colors blackish; sometimes, especially in examples from clear streams, many scales have scarlet centre; fins black, occasionally end of upper lobe of the caudal white; in some districts adults have very elongated fins; southern india and malabar, from kistna through orissa; grows to 3 feet in length; were it not for its numerous bones, it would be excellent eating.——*Fringed labeo* (रोहित - róhita, San.; तांब्र - támbra, Mahr.; గండుమీను - gandumínu, Tel.; ବାହ୍ରୁମ - bahrum, Oor.; சாலை - shálai, Tam.).

San. means red. Mahr. means copper colored. **Tel.** from (gandu, tel. male + mínu, tel. fish). Tam. also (vengendai), meaning white + carp, barbus genus. Labeo [rohitam] fimbriatus, cyprininæ, cyprinidæ, physostomi, teleostei [matsyam, 39], of naturalists. Alias Cirrhinus fimbriatus, leschenaultii, nancar; Cyprinus fimbriatus, nancar; Labeo leschenaultii; Leuciscus bobree; Rohita fimbriata, leschenaultii; Varicorhinus bobree. Rohita from sanscrit; bobree from mahratta. Colors silvery along back, lighter on sides and beneath; fins, more especially the ventral, anal, and lower caudal lobe, stained with black; sometimes a diffused dark blotch at the base of the caudal, and which is almost invariably present in the young; southern india to orissa, recorded from malabar or canara; attains a foot and a half in length, and is good eating, but bony.——*Red labeo* (ಕೆಮ್ಮೀನು - kemmínu, Can.; கருமணிக்கெண்டை - karumanik-kendai, Tam.). Title from fleshy tinge. Can. from (kempu, can. red + mínu, can. fish). Tam. from (karumai, tam. blackness + mani, tam. apple of the eye + kendai, tam. carp, barbus genus). Tam. also (karumuzhikkendai), meaning blackness + eyeball + carp, barbus genus. Labeo [rohitam] kontius, cyprininæ, cyprinidæ, physostomi, teleostei [matsyam, 39], of naturalists. Alias Cirrhinus rubropunctatus; Cyprinus kontius. Muzzle blunt, truncated, covered with pores, and having a short fleshy lateral prolongation; colors general reddish or fleshy tinge, darkest along back; rivers along the base of the neilgherries, and cauvery and coleroon in all their branches down to the coast; it grows to two feet in length.——*Scaled labeo* (रोहित - róhita, San.; തുളി - túli, Mal.). Title from reddish scales. San. from (róhita, san. red). Mal. means scales of fish. Labeo [rohitam] dussumieri, cyprininæ, cyprinidæ, physostomi, teleostei [matsyam, 39], of naturalists. Alias Cirrhinus dussumieri, rouxii; Labeo rouxii; Rohita dussumieri, rouxii. Grayish, lightest beneath, scales with reddish centre, edged with darker shade; usually a dull diffused dark spot on either side of the tail; fins dusky; rivers of south malabar; attains at least 13 inches in length.

ROHY (रोही - róhí, *San.*). Means red. Fourth lunar mansion [nacshatram, rohiny], personified as the favorite wife of Chundran [q.v.].——*Rohan* (روهن - rohan, Hind.). Same as Soymida.——*Rohicaunta* (రోహికాంతుడు - róhikántudu, Tel.). From (above + kánta, san. lover). Moon. Hindoo 2nd or pers. name [peyar].——*Rohidoss* (ರೋಹಿದಾಸ - róhidása, Can.). From (above + dása, san. slave). Hindoo 2nd or pers. name [peyar].——*Rohiny* (रोहिणी - róhiní, San.; உரோகிணி - urógini, Tam.). Literally red. One of the daughters of Dacshan [q.v.], and the favorite wife of Soman or Chundran [q.v.]. The mother of Balaraman [q.v.]. For the lunar mansion so called see under Nacshatram.——*Rohitacam* (रोहितक - róhitaka, San.). See sep. title.——*Rohitam* (रोहित - róhita, San.). See sep. title.

ROLONG (سوجی - sújí, *Hind.*; இரவை - iravai, *Tam.*). Corruption of portuguese Ralão. The hard central part of wheat grains [geung]. Cf. Soojee.

ROO (رو - rú, *Hind.*). Face.——*Roobcaury* (روبکاری - rúbakárí, Hind.). From (above + ba, pers. to + kár, pers. face). Proceedings on record of a case. Letter from an equal.——*Roobroob* (روبرو - rúbarú, Hind.). From (above + ba, pers. with + rú, pers. face). Face to face [mookhautib].——*Roomaul* (رومال - rúmál, Hind.). From (above + mál, pers. to wipe). A handkerchief. Also a square shawl [q.v.]. A roomaul is used in the place of a turban [puggry] by the poorer natives. Although the end of the saury [q.v.] is made to act as a covering for the head, in many instances roomauls are specially used by women also. In trade it is applied to thin silk piece-goods with handkerchief patterns. The strangling cloth of the Thug [q.v.]. Khauny roomaul are loom-manufactured, and Amlee roomaul are needle embroidered [sheelay] handkerchiefs.——*Roshan* (روشن - roshan, Hind.). From (above + shan, pers. suffix of similarity). Same as Rowshan. Conspicuous.——*Roshanbaugh* (روشن باغ - roshan-bágh, Hind.). From (roshan, hind. bright + bágh, pers. garden). One of the Nawaub's gardens at Sydapett. Now occupied by the Government farms.——*Roshan chowky* (روشن چوکی - roshan-chaukí, Hind.). From (roshan, hind. bright + chaukí, pers. guard). A band of musical instruments playing at the residence of the chief Mahomedan authority.——*Rowshan* (روشن - raushan, Ar.). Bright. Same as Roshan. In composition makes a lacab; as Rowshan banno, enlightened lady [ism].

ROOBAH (روباه - rúbah, *Pers.*). Fox. Plant second term, meaning wild and inferior. Ex., where transl. is of first term:—Citrullus colocynthis (kharbúzahirúbah), melon; Solanum nigrum (angúrrúbáh), grape. See gloss. paragraphs.

ROOCH (रुच् - ruch, *San.*). To shine.——*Ricsham* (ऋक्ष - ricsha, San.). Constellation. See under Ricsham, bear.——*Rokkadauyam* (உரொக்காதாயம் - urokkáthâyam, Tam.). From (rókam, san. cash + ádáya, san. taking). Ready money collections from sources other than land.——*Rokkam* (रोक - róka, San.). From (ruch, san. to shine). Cash [q.v.], in contradistinction to goods. Rokka jaumeen is money security [nagad jaumeen].——*Roocmam* (रुक्म - rukma, San.). Means gold [bangaur, pon, tungam]. Hindoo 2nd or pers. name [peyar].——*Roocminy* (रुक्मिणी - rukminí, San.; உருக்குமணி - urukkumani, Tam.). The wife of Krishnan [q.v.], an incarnation [avatar] of Lutchmy [q.v.].

ROODRAN (रुद्र - rudra, *San.*; உருத்திரன் - uruttiran *Tam.*). From (rud, san. to roar). In the Rig vedam the god of tempests. In the pooraunams [q.v.] a name of Shiva [q.v.] denoting the destroying power of deity. There are eleven forms or manifestations of Roodran according to South indian books; Bhavotbhavan, Bheemadevan, Capauly, Eeshaunan, Haran, Mahadevan, Neela lohitan, Roodran, Shuncaran, Sowmyan, Vijayan. There is some similarity with Apollo. Both gods bear the bow. Roodran knows a thousand medicines [veidyanautan]; so Apollo is called ἀκέσιος, and is father of Asklepios. Roodran goes through storm and clouds, and has his hair therefore made up in a great knot, whence he is called Capardy he who has his hair wound into the form of a shell [chunk]; so Homer Il, 20, 39 calls Apollo ἀκερσεκόμης. Roodran is called vankan, going athwart, as god of the storm; so Apollo is λοξίας from λοξός, oblique. Roodran had a sister Ambicay [q.v.]; so Apollo had a sister Artemis. The mouse [shoondely] is sacred to Roodran, while Apollo was called Smintheus from σμίνθος a mouse, and was represented by the sculptor Skopas with a mouse at his feet. See vol. I (73) [matam].——*Roodramma deva* (రుద్రమదేవ - rudrammadéva, Tel.). From (above + ammá, tam. mother, title). Queen of Ganapaty deva of Warangal. Assumed government on her husband's death and reigned for 38 years when she abdicated in favor of her grandson Prataupa roodran [charitram]. See vol. I (132), (142); II, 83.——*Roodra's flower* (रुद्रपुष्प - rudrapushpa, San.). Same as China rose bendy.——*Roodra's hair* (రుద్రజడ - rudrajada, Tel.). Same as Fragrant toolsy.——*Roodrauck* (رداک - rudrák, Hind.). See sep. title.——*Roodraucsham* (रुद्राक्ष - rudráksha, San.). From (above + akshi, san. eye). Roodran's eye and so his tear. When Shiva, once in a war with the Asooran [q.v.], had burned three cities [tripooram], he wept at the loss of lives, and his tears falling to the ground sprung up as shrubs, producing berries. Roodraucsham is the fruit of the Elæocarpus, and resembles as to form, size, and color the nutmeg [jautikye].——*Roodrauny* (रुद्राणी - rudrání, San.). The shacty [q.v.] of Roodran; a name sometimes applied to Parvaty [q v.].

ROODRAUCK (रुद्राक्ष - rudráksha, *San.*; वावलि - vávali, *Conc.*; رداکش - rudrákash, *Hind.*; رداک - rudrák, *Dec.*; ಬಿಕ್ಕೆ - bikki, *Can.*; ರಾಹುಬೀಜ - ráhubíja, *Too.*; రుద్రాక్ష - rudráksha, *Tel.*; അവിൽ - ávil, *Mal.*; වෙරළු - weralu, *Singh.*; உருத்திராட்சம் - uruttirádcham, *Tam.*). San. from (rudra, san. shiva + aksha, san. bead) [roodran, roodraucsham]. Hind. from sanscrit. Dec. from sanscrit. Too. from (ráhu, san. sudden fit of apoplexy or paralysis + bíja, san. seed). Tam. from sanscrit. San. also (aksha), meaning to accumulate, from ball-like seed; (chiribilva), meaning long + bael tree, ægle marmelos, corr. [karanj]. Hind. also (kassau). Can. also (guddanérale), meaning hill + eugenia jambolana, lamk.; (kuntanérale), meaning crippled + eugenia jambolana, lamk.; (kalbikki), meaning stone + the plant; (bigadamara); meaning distention + tree, removes, distention; (guddarenji), meaning hill + the tree, mimusops elengi, linn. Mal. also (perinkára), meaning large + thorny plant, canthium. Title otherwise Bracelet tree, Linden bloom, Perincara, Saw-leaved elæocarpus. Botanically the Elæocarpus genus, tiliaceæ [vricsham, 27]. Trees or large shrubs with simple leaves and racemes of small flowers; natives of india, java and other tropical parts; fruit contains a very hard rough-shelled nut, with edible pulp surrounding the stone used in curries [q.v.] or pickled [chutney]; the hard, dry, deeply-grooved and elegantly-sculptured seeds are frequently worn as beads [munkah] by bramins [q.v.] and fakeers [q.v.], and set in gold are sometimes sold as ornaments. Different species are:—Cuneatus, middling-sized tree, quilon. Ferrugineous, leaves boat-shaped, timber used for building. Ganitrus; flower middle-sized, white; sacred tree; found on the higher ghauts of the western coast; the common roodrauck. Lanceæfolia; flowers small, white; called hill neraly. Munroii; large tree throughout western forests; timber valuable; whitish, with a brown heart; called stone bikky. Oblongus; wood white, strong and tough, and adapted for the lathe; called bikky. Serratus; tree; western coast; numerous small, white flowers; fruit called rahoo seed [q.v.], very hard, oblong-shaped and smooth; dried and used in curries [q.v.] by the natives, and also pickled [chutney]; fleshy exterior of fruit eaten; has a strong wood. Tuberculatus; very fine tree; flowers largish, white; western forests. Distinguish from the next item.——*Roodrauck tree* (بندوق کا جہاڑ - bandúkkájhár, Hind.; ರುದ್ರಾಕ್ಷಿಮರ - rudrákshimara, Can. and Too.; రుద్రాక్షపుచెట్టు - rudrákshapuchettu, Tel.; உருத்திராட்சமரம் - urutti-rádchamaram, Tam.). Title from resemblance. Hind. from (bandúk, ar. musket + jhár, hind. tree), from seeds resembling shot. Can. from (rudráksha, san. the berry of the elæocarpus ganitrus, roxb. + mara, can. tree). Tel. from (rudráksha, san. braminy bead, berry of the elæocarpus genus + chettu, tel. tree). Tam. from (rudráksha, san. braminy bead, berry of the elæocarpus genus + maram, tam. tree). Tam. also (téngáymaram), meaning honey + fruit + tree; (tubákkimaram), meaning musket + tree; (ténbaççai), meaning honey + greenness; (valamburi), meaning turned to the right [screw-tree]. Title otherwise Bastard cedar [chickrassy, large neem, soymida, wild anaur], Cedar, Honey-fruit tree, Musket tree, West-indian elm. Botanically Guazuma tomentosa, kunth., sterculiaceæ [vricsham, 26]. Alias Boubroma tomentosa; Guazuma ulmifolia. Tree, 40–60 feet, not unlike english elm; leaves alternate, ovate or oblong, unequal at the base, toothed, acuminate at the apex, stellately puberulous on the upper side, tomentose beneath; petals five, yellow, with two purple awns at the apex; capsules five-celled, many-seeded; seeds angular; peduncles axillary and terminal; flowers scented; introduced from w. indies. The bark is very scaly, but the scales are separated easily when dry; the bark underneath the scales is reddish-brown, without any particular taste or smell; the fruit is tubercled, about the size of a cherry [q.v.]. A decoction of inner bark is of medicinal use in elephantiasis [cochin leg]; the older bark is used as a sudorific and is given in diseases of the chest and cutaneous complaints. Decoction; take of the inner bark, cut into small pieces or in coarse powder, four ounces; water, one pint and half; boil till the liquid is reduced to one pint, and strain when cool. Substituted for calumba [q.v.] and gentian [chiretta]. Fruit filled with mucilage, gives good fodder; leaves used as famine food; the bark is very mucilaginous and is used by arrack [q.v.] manufacturers in clarifying their liquors; grows quickly and is suited for avenues [shaulay]; bark yields fibre [naur]; but slightly woody, only fit for rope. Wood, light and loose-grained, light brown, used for furniture, by coach-makers for pannels, and for packing cases, pannelling, &c.——*Roodrauck yam* (రుద్రాక్ష పెండలము - rudrákshapendalamu, Tel.). See under Auloo.

ROOH (روح - rúh, *Hind.*). From arabic. Spirit, the Koran [q.v.], Jesus Christ. Forms an alam; as Rooh ool lah, spirit of god, lacab of Jesus. Is now itself an alam [ism].——*Roohauda coodisha* (روح القدس - rúhulkuds, Hind.; റൂഹാദകുദിശ - ruhádakudisha, Mal.). The Holy Ghost with the Malabar syrian christians [syrian].——*Rooh i haiwauny* (روح حیوانی - rúhihaiwání, Hind.). Animal spirit, or the life the seat of which is in the heart and moves in the veins with the pulsations of the body.——*Rooh i insauny* (روح انسانی - rúhiinsání, Hind.). Also (aklulawwal), meaning first intelligence. Human spirit. Mind or spiritual faculty of man of the true essence of which nothing is known.——*Rooh i jaury* (روح جاری - rúhijárí, Hind.). Means travelling spirit. That which leaves the body in sleep and gives rise to dreams.——*Rooh i nabauty* (روح نباتی - rúhinabátí, Hind.). Vegetable spirit.——*Rooh i siflee* (روح سفلی - rúhisiflí, Hind.). Means the lower spirit, that which belongs merely to animal life.

ROOKH (رخ - rukh, *Hind.*). Castle in chess [chatrangam, chowsar, shatranj].

ROOKHSAT (رخصت - rukhsat, *Hind.*). From (rakhusa, ar. to relax). Leave, the dismissal of a guest. It is usual here for the host, not at all the visitor, to close an interview. This act may be signalized by the host putting a garland of flowers round the guest's neck, and sometimes also bracelets of flowers on his wrists, and presenting him with bouquets and attar [q.v.] and paunsoopyaury [q.v.], and sprinkling rose water [goolaub, pauneer] on his handkerchief [roomaul, shelavoo, tambool].

ROOKIA (رقیه - rukiyah, *Ar.*). From (rakí, ar. to enchant). Name of the prophet's daughter. Common female alam; as Rookia bee, alam + alaumat [ism].

ROOKN (رکن - rukn, *Ar.*). From (rakana, ar. to rely on). Pillar. Part of lacab; Rookn ood deen, pillar of religion [ism].

ROOM (روم - rúm, *Hind.*). Constantinople.——*Roomy* (رومی - rúmí, Hind.). Turkey.——*Roomy mustakee* (रुमामस्तकी - rumámastakí, Mahr.; مصطکی - mastakí, Ar.; کندر رومی - kundurirúmí, Pers.; مصطکی - mastakí, Hind.; رومی مصطکی - rúmímastakí, Dec.; పిల్లికండ్లగుగ్గిలము - pillikandlaguggilamu, Tel.; பூனைக்கண் குங்கிலியம் - púnaikkangungiliyam, Tam.). Title from deccany. Pers. from (kundur, ar. olibanum + rúm, ar. turkish empire). Hind, from arabic. Dec. from (rúmí, hind. turkish empire + mastakí, ar. mastich), as chewed by the turks to preserve the gums and teeth and to sweeten breath. Tel. from (pilli, tel. cat + kannu, tel. eye + guggilamu, tel. dammer). Tam. from (púnai, tam. cat + kan, tam. eye + kungiliyam, tam. resinous gum); from the yellow white and semi-transparent color. Ar. also (ilakirúmí), meaning turkish gum. Title otherwise Mastich. A resin [gond, raul] from Pistacia lentiscus, linn., anacardiaceæ [vricsham, 45]. An astringent in diarrhœa, and phlegm diseases. Dissolved in turpentine [carpoora teilam], spirits of wine [sharaub] or oil [yennay] makes a pale brilliant varnish [rangh]; transparent, tough and tenacious.

ROOPAM (रूप - rúpa, *San.*). From (rúp, san. to form). Outward appearance; object of vision, as color, &c.; one of the seventeen qualities of the Neiyauyican [nyauyam]. An entire number. Known quantity in algebra [beejaganitam]; the unknown quantity being caulak [q.v.].——*Roopa vilutchanan* (రూపవిలక్షణుడు - rúpavilakshanudu, Tel.). From (above + vilakshana, san. strange). Referring to shiva [q.v.] with his three eyes [viroopaucshan]. Hindoo 2nd or pers. name [peyar].——*Roopyam* (रूप्य - rúpya, San.). Silver [velly], especially a piece of such, bearing a stamp or figure.——*Rupee* (روپیه - rúpiyah, Hind.; உருப்பாய் - urúppáy, Tam.). From (rúpa, hind. silver). Silver coin, the unit of the standard of value in India since commencement of Mahomedan rule. The Government rupee in make and size resembles the English florin; weighs 180 grains, of which 165 are pure silver [velly]. It used to exchange at the rate of ten to a sovereign, but its exchange value is now greatly reduced. Rupees of many older coinages are still current. The rupee is divided for purposes of account into annas [q.v.] and pies [q.v.], twelve pies making one anna and sixteen annas one rupee. The divisions coined are:—in silver, the half, quarter, eighth; in copper, the thirty-second, sixty-fourth, one hundred and ninety-second part or pie [q.v.]. The following are different kinds of old rupee:—Adony; from place so called; 376 and 5 fanams 50 cash to 100 star pagodas. Arcot; the rupee at madras was originally that of the nawaub [q.v.] of the carnatic [q.v.] otherwise called the nawaub of arcot from his residence and was known usually as the arcot rupee; its issues varied from 171 to 177 grains in weight, and from 160 to 170 of pure silver. Chalawany; the current rupee of account, in which the company's accounts were kept, of which 116 were with them equal to 100 sicca rupees; the following have been varieties; bellary old, 426 and 7 fanams and 2 cash to 100 star pagodas; bellary new, 492 and 2 fanams and 65 cash to 100 star pagodas; old salauk, 436 and 3 fanams and 60 cash to 100 star pagodas; new salauk, 518 and 7 fanams and 78 cash to 100 star pagodas. Char goshah; means four-cornered; rupee of acbar; value about 40 daums. Char yauree, from (chár, hind. four + yár, hind. friend); rupee having the names of the first four caliphs on the margin. Chinnamaila, from (mélam, tam. a drum); tinnevelly coin, equal to 11 fanams 60 $\frac{29}{32}$ cash. Furruckabad rupee; weighed 180 grains, containing 165·215 of pure silver. Goa; canara coin, $437\frac{1}{2}$ to 100 star pagodas. Gold; madras coin, of 15 silver rupees, weighing 180 grains troy. Goozerat; coined at ahmedabad. Haley vijianugger; rajaram's stamp in nagry. Isfahaun; persian rupee coined at isfahaun. Lucknow; also called furruckabad rupee; struck at fategarh. Mahratta; issued from mints of mahratta states on disruption of moghul empire; emperor's name was however retained. Mekhy, from (mekhí, hind. nailed); a rupee that is plugged, hollowed and filled with lead. Mooba urak shahy; coin of moobaurak shah of the syed dynasty. Mullars, from (mallarasu, can. king so called); canara coin 388 $\frac{5}{8}$ to 100 star pagodas. Poonhacutt; poona band rupee; ganjam coin, 350 to 100 star pagodas. Rajah; seringapatam coin, 343 and 11 fanams and $76\frac{1}{4}$ cash to 100 star pagodas. Sicca; weighed 192 grains, and contained 176 grains of pure silver; the exceptional sicca was abolished as a coin in 1836; and the universal rupee of british territory has since been the company's rupee, as it was long called, of 180 grains weight and 165 pure silver, representing therefore in fact the furruckabad rupee; see sep. title. Sultauny; coin of tippoo sultan; bore hindostany letter "h" for hyder. Zodiacal; pieces of twelve different impressions, representing the twelve signs of the zodiac [raushy]; they were coined between the years 1616 and 1624 of the christian era by jehaungeer; these rupees are exceptions to the mahomedan law which forbids the representations or embossment of figures.

ROOSTAM (رستم - rustam, *Hind.*). The Hercules of Persia. One of the twelve champions. Hero in general. Heroic alam; as Roostam beg, alam + alaumat. Also part of lacab; as Roostam jung, hero of war [ism].

ROOWA (రువ్వ - ruvva, *Tel.*). A pie. 2 roowas=1 dooggauny [naunyam, 2b]. Same as Hind. pie, damree, Tam cash.

ROSE (گلاب - guláb, *Hind.*). Prefix [goolaub].——*Rose apple* (जम्बुराज - jamburája, San.; जांब - jámba, Conc.; گلابی جامن - gulábíjáman, Hind.; گلابی جام - gulábíjám, Dec.; ಜಂಬುನೇರಳು - jambunéralu, Can.; ಪನ್ನೇರಳೆ - pennérale, Coorg; ಜಂಬುನೇರೊಳು - jambunérolu, Too.; జంబునేరేడు - jambunérédu, Tel.; ଗୋଲାପଜାମ - golápjám, Oor.; ജംബു - jambu, Mal. and Singh.; சம்புநாவல் - shambunával, Tam.). Title from appearance and perfume of fruit. San. from (jambu, san. jaumoon tree, eugenia jambolana, lamk. + rájá, san. king); the large jaumoon fruit. Conc. from sanscrit [common jaumoon, dark vail, malacca jaumoon]. Hind. from (gulábí, hind. rose-colored + jám, hind. eugenia jambolana, lamk.). Dec. from hindostany. Coorg from canarese. Tel. from (jambu, san. the tree + nérédu, tel. eugenia jambolana, lamk.). San. also (jambu), meaning edible; (rájajambú), meaning king + jaumoon tree. Hind. also (jamrúl), meaning eugenia malaccensis, linn. Can. also (pannéralemara), meaning rose water + jaumoon tree; from delicate rose water perfume. Coorg also (mallenérale), meaning hill + jaumoon tree. Tel. also (allanérédu), meaning famous + eugenia jambolana, lamk. Tam. also (perunával), meaning large + the jaumoon tree. Title otherwise Large-fruited jaumoon, Malabar plum, Smaller jaumoon. Botanically Eugenia [jamboo] jambos, linn., myrtaceæ [vricsham, 56]. Specific name from sanscrit. Alias Eugenia vulgaris; Jambosa vulgaris; Myrtus jambos. Moderate-sized tree; branchlets compressed or sub-tetragonous; leaves variable in length, $1\frac{1}{2}$–2 inches broad; nerves reticulate beneath; midrib stout; petiole short and stout, $\frac{1}{4}$ inch or less; calyx-tube produced above the ovary; lobes round; berries 1–2 inches diameter. Has opposite, lanceolate, oleander-formed [gannair] short-stalked leaves and large flowers, greenish white followed by a sub-globular berry of rich pink and white colors, but of an indifferent flavor; flowers in february and bears fruit during cold season. Fruit is of the size and somewhat of the form of a small apple [seb], of a fine opaque apricot color with a blush of red upon it, and with a fine delicate rose water [goolaub] perfume; hardly eatable, being of a poor flavor and of a dry, pithy consistency; sometimes made into preserve [chutney]; differs from the smaller jaumoon [q.v.] fruit. Rose water can be distilled from the fruit, taking the seed out first. The tree grows rapidly, yielding much firewood.——*Roselle* (لال انبارًا - lálambárá, Hind.). From (lál, hind. red + ambárá, hind. hemp plant). Same as Red hemp bendy.

ROSE MALLOES (دخان الضرو - dukhánuddarrú, *Ar.*; است لبان - astlubán, *Hind.*; رسمل - rasamala, *Malay*). Title from malay. Ar. from (dukhán, ar. smoke + darrú, ar. liquidamber orientale, miller). Latin Rasimilius. Same as Java storax.

ROTEE (روٹی - rotí, *Hind.*). Bread. For coarse wheaten bread see Choopatty. For cakes of rice see Hopper.

ROUSSA (भूस्तृण - bhústrina, *San.*; (रोशें - róshém, *Mahr.*; اذخرهندی - izkhirihindí, *Ar.*; کاه مکه - káhimakkah, *Pers.*; روسا - rúsá, *Hind.*; گنجنی کا گھاس - ganjníkághás, *Dec.*; ಬೋದಹುಲ್ಲು - bódehullu, *Can.*; కామంచిగడ్డి - kámanchigaddi, *Tel.*; ചോരപ്പുല്ല - chórappulla, *Mal.*; சுன்னாரிப்புல் - shunnárippul, *Tam.*). Title from hindostany. San. from (bhú, san. earth + trina, san. grass). Mahr. from (rúksha, san. rough). Ar. from (izkhir, ar. andropogon iwarancusa, roxb. + hindí, ar. indian). Pers. from (káh, pers. hay + makkah, ar. mecca). Hind. like mahratta [ibharancoosha, stunted jack]. Dec. from (gandha, san. aromatic + ghás, hind. grass). Tel. from (káru, tel. forest + manchi, tel. good + gaddi, tel. grass). Mal. from (chóra, san. perfume + pullu, mal. grass). Tam. from (shukku, tam. dried ginger + náru, tam. to smell + pul, tam. grass). Pers. also (gaznahidashtí), meaning desert nettle. Hind. also (gandbel), meaning fragrant grass; (akhiyághás), meaning bird, alanda aggia + grass. Can. also (sambárahullu); (cháhullu), meaning tea + grass; (shunt'hihullu), meaning ginger, zingiber officinale, roscoe + grass; (doddabilikáchihullu), meaning large + white + andropogon schœnanthus, roxb. Tel. also (kámákshigaddi), by corruption; (allapugaddi), meaning ginger, zingiber officinale, roscoe + grass. Mal. also (kámákshippullu), meaning beautiful grass, corruption from teloogoo. Tam. also (shukkunárippul), meaning dried ginger + to smell + grass [ginger grass, indian grass]; (kasattambul), meaning bitter + grass; (kámátchíppul), by corruption from teloogoo; (mándappul), meaning indigestion + grass. Sometimes confounded with Cuscus [q.v.] grass or Andropogon muricatus, retz. Title otherwise Bitter grass, False spikenard, Geranium grass, Ginger grass, Indigestion grass, Juncus odoratus, Mecca hay, Nemaur oil plant, Palmarosa oil plant, Roussa oil grass, Roussa paper grass, Tea grass. Botanically Andropogon [beard grass] martini, roxb., graminaceæ [vriesham, 156]. Alias Andropogon calamus, aromaticus, nardoides; Cymbopogon martinianus, pachnodes. Root long, fibrous; culm erect, branched, 5–6 feet, glabrous; leaves elongated, very delicate, soft, glabrous, acuminate; ligula membranaceous; panicles linear, sub-secund; spikelets twin; rachis jointed, woolly; corolla of the hermaphrodite floret one-valved, awned, male muticous. A coarse-looking grass; grows wild; the roots, &c., have a peculiar smell, between lemon [q.v.] and turpentine [ganda firoza]. Oil [yennay] by distillation from fresh plant assimilates in characters, properties, and uses with that of andropogon schœnanthus, roxb. [lemon grass]; the color varies from pale greenish-yellow to yellowish brown. Oil is valuable as a rubefacient, substitute for cajeput [q.v.] oil, externally in rheumatism, also stimulant and diaphoretic; prevents the hair of the head from falling off after acute diseases. Fresh leaves used as substitute for tea [q.v.]; white succulent centre of the leaf-bearing culms put into curries [q.v.] to give them flavor; cattle are fond of it, notwithstanding its strong aromatic and pungent taste, but not only the flesh of the animals, but also the milk and butter, get a strong scent of it. Oil much used in perfumery; after oil [yennay] extracted fibres [naur] used for paper [caugaz].

ROWGHAN (روغن - raughan, *Hind.*). Oil [tel, yennay].——*Rowghany cupdah* (روغنی کپڑا - raughaníkaprá, Hind.). Oil cloth; used for packages in monsoon [q.v.].

ROYACHOTY (రాయచోటి - ráyatsóti, *Tel.* ráyachóti *). From (rádzu, tel. king + tsótu, tel. place) [raj].——**(1)** Talook, Cuddapah district. Tahsildar's pay Rs. 175. Area 997 square miles; lat. 13° 50′ to 14° 20′ N.; long. 78° 27′ to 79° 13′ E. Population 113,236. Language Teloogoo. S. centre of district. Bounded north by Cuddapah talook from which it is separated by the Sheshachellam hills and Poolivendla talook; south by Voilpaud talook; west by Cadiry and Madanapully talooks; and east by Poollampett talook, from which it is divided by the Sheshachellam hills running north-west to south-east. The general appearance is level, with here and there scattered granite [caroom cull] rocks, and with a horizontal line of unbroken hills to the north and east. The talook is well provided with roads. There are good pasture lands, and there is generally no lack of grazing ground [shekadah]. A very large portion lies waste. Some of this land is saline [oovar] and unproductive, but a great deal is of the same quality as that cultivated. Soils are of different kinds, red soil [sevval munn] being predominant. There is no black-cotton soil [regar], and none of the rich loam [pasalay munn] found in the main division. Timber generally is scarce, with the exception of tamarind [q.v.] trees, of which there are a large number of thick topes [q.v.], teak [q.v.], sandal-wood [sandal], rose and black-wood [q.v.] are found in the hill jungles. Principal products paddy [q.v.] and sadza [bajrah]. Manufactures are confined to indigo [q.v.], common cloths, coarse cumblies [q.v.], and gunny [q.v.] bags. There is some trade in skins [chamrah], which are exported, and also in tamarind fruits. Travelling merchants bring round pearls [moty] and corals [moongah] for sale. The horned cattle [maud] are small, but hardy. The Paupughny flows into Poolivendla and Cuddapah talooks and joins Pennair at Camalaupooram. Bauhooodah and Pinchah nuddy join at Royavaram in this talook thence run into Poollampett talook; after running through Palcondah hills they join Maundavair in Poollampett talook and there they are known by name Cheyair. Places of archæological interest:—Gadicote, Hasanpore, Royachoty, Vangimulla. Principal trig. stations:—Booditaid, Nelacoorty, Rajanmala, Saunipoya. The leading places, &c., in the talook are the following.——*Anantapooram* (అనంతపురము - anantapuramu, Tel.). From (ananta, san. vishnu; the eternal + pura, san. town). Village, Place of pilgrimage; pop. 572; acres 2,536; lat. 14° 11′; long. 78° 47′; from Cuddapah S. 22 miles; from Royachoty N. 9 miles. At Gunga jautra festival [pundigay, 6d] held here, the Shoodra community of surrounding talooks assemble and buffaloes [khoolgah] and goats [vellaud] are sacrificed.——*Arvaid* (అరవేడు - aravédu, Tel.). From (arava, tel. tamul + vídu, tel. town). Village; pop. 2,412; acres 6,906; lat. 14° 00′; long. 78° 34′; from Cuddapah S.W. 39 miles; from Royachoty W.S.W. 16 miles. Former residence of a poligar [q.v.].——*Bauhoodah nuddy* (బాహుదనది - báhudanadi, Tel.). See sep. title.——*Bonamulla* (బోనమల - bónamala, Tel.). From (bónamu, tel. sacrificial meal + mala, tel. hill). Village; acres 2,988; lat. 13° 54′; long. 78° 44′; from Cuddapah S.S.W. 40 miles; from Royachoty S.S.W. 12 miles. Once the seat of a poligar.——*Booditaid* (బుడితేడు - buditédu, Tel.). From (búdide, tel. ashes + vídu, tel. town). Trig. station; lat. 13° 55′ 05·05″; long. 79° 09′ 00·44″; height 3,063 feet; from Moodcompaud E. 7 miles; from Royachoty E.S.E. 26 miles.——*Calibunda* (కలిబండ - kalibanda, Tel.). From (kali, san. battle + banda, tel. rock). Village; pop. 350; acres 4,434; lat. 13° 57′; long. 78° 38′; from Cuddapah S.S.W. 40 miles; from Royachoty S.W. 12 miles. Once the seat of a poligar.——*Cheyair* (చెయ్యేరు - cheyyéru, Tel.). See sep. title.——*Chinnamundem* (చిన్నమండెము - chinnamandemu, Tel.). From (chinna, tel. small + mandemu, tel. factory). Town; pop. 2,793; acres 9,167; lat. 13° 57′; long. 78° 43′; from Cuddapah S.W. 39 miles; from Royachoty S.S.W. 10 miles.——*Gopagoodipully* (గోపగుడిపల్లి - gópagudipalli, Tel.). From (gópa, san. vishnu, the cowherd + gudi, tel. temple + palli, tel. village). Village; pop. 2,169; acres 13,534; lat. 14° 17′; long. 78° 46′; from Cuddapah S.W. 16 miles; from Royachoty N. 16 miles. Once residence of a poligar.——*Hasanpore* (హసనాపురము - hasanápuramu, Tel.). From (hasan, hind. proper name + pura, san. town). Sanscrit name (ayódhyápura), meaning ayodhyay, the city + town. Village; pop. 3,400; acres 29,102; lat. 14° 10′; long. 78° 50′; from Cuddapah S. 22 miles; from Royachoty N.N.E. 8 miles.——*Lakkireddipully* (లక్కిరెడ్డిపల్లి - lakkireddipalli, Tel.). From (lakkireddi, tel. proper name + palli, tel. village). Village; pop. 1,210; acres 5,954; lat. 14° 11′; long. 78° 45′; from Cuddapah S.W. 22 miles; from Royachoty N.N.W. 10 miles. Battle fought in vicinity in 1751 between Cuddapah nawaub and Moozuffer jung, in which latter was killed.——*Matly* (మట్లి - matli, Tel.). From (mattu, tel. limit). Village; pop. 2,311; acres 10,144; lat. 14° 06′; long. 78° 52′; from Cuddapah S.E. 27 miles; from Royachoty E.N.E. 5 miles. The source of the family of the Chitwail rajahs, who ruled over Chitwail, Sidhout, and Budwail.——*Maundavair* (మాండవేరు - mándavéru, Tel.). See sep. title.——*Moodoompaud* (ముదుంపాడు - mudumpádu, Tel.). From (mudi, tel. cluster + pádu, tel. village). Village; pop. 1,031; acres 34,266; lat. 13° 56′; long. 79° 03′; from Cuddapah S.E. 40 miles; from Royachoty E.S.E. 19 miles. Seat of the old poligar family of Boodavauda.——*Motacutla* (మోటకట్ల - mótakatla, Tel.). From (móta, tel. load + katla, tel. place). Village; pop. 1,000; acres 6,803; lat. 14° 00′; long. 78° 49′; from Cuddapah S.E. 34 miles; from Royachoty S.E. 5 miles. Once residence of a poligar family, being a branch of the Saunipoya.——*Nelacoorty* (నెలకుర్తి - nelakurti, Tel.). From (nela, tel. moon + gurtu, tel. mark). Trig. station; lat. 14° 17′ 48·40″; long. 78° 40′ 23·40″; height 2,966 feet; from Bramhana yerragoody N. 5 miles; from Royachoty N.N.W. 18 miles.——*Palcondah* (పాలకొండ - pálakonda, Tel.). See sep. title.——*Paupughny* (పాపఘ్ని - pápaghni,

Tel.). See sep. title.——*Rajanmala* (రాజనమల - rájanamala, Tel.). From (rájanna, tel. proper name + mala, tel. hill). Trig. station; lat. 13° 58′ 01·05″; long. 78° 39′ 46·44″; height 3,580 feet; from Royachoty S.W. 11 miles; from Saukibunda S.W. 3 miles.——*Raullamadoogoo canama* (రాళ్లమడుగుకనమ - rállamadugukanama, Tel.). See sep. title.——*Royachoty* (రాయచోటి - ráyatsóti, Tel.). See below.——*Saunipoya* (సానిపాయ - sánipáya, Tel.). From (sáni, tel. dancing girl + páya, tel. portion). Village; pop. 1,883; acres 9,571; lat. 14° 07′; long. 79° 00′; from Cuddapah S.E. 26 miles; from Royachoty E.N.E. 14 miles. A fine ghaut [q.v.] road forms a feeder to the railway. Trig. station in lat. 14° 08′ 09·05″; long. 78° 59′ 53·44″; height 2,392 feet; from Saunipoya N.E. 1 mile.——*Sheshachellam* (శేషాచలము - shéshâchalamu, Tel.). See sep. title.——*Soondoopully* (సుండుపల్లె - tsundupalle, Tel.). From (tsundu, tel. to dry up + palle, tel. village). Village; pop. 3,580; acres 17,861; lat. 13° 59′; long. 78° 58′; from Cuddapah S. 35 miles; from Royachoty E.S.E. 12 miles. On the Bauhoodah. Weekly market.——*Timma samoodram* (తిమ్మసముద్రము - timmasamudramu, Tel.). From (timma, tel. monkey + samudra, san. ocean). Village; pop. 1,734; acres 5,921; lat. 13° 58′; long. 78° 58′; from Cuddapah S. 36 miles; from Royachoty E.S.E. 13 miles.——*Toommalgoondy* (తుమ్మలగుండి - tummalagundi, Tel.). From (tumma, tel. babul tree, acacia arabica, willd. + gandi, tel. gorge). Village; pop. 1,458. On E. bank of Bauhoodah. Once residence of a poligar.——*Yegoova goottivaid* (ఎగువ గొట్టివీడు - eguvagottivédu, Tel.). From (eguva, tel. up + gotti, tel. a thorny tree, zizyphus xylopyrus, willd. + vídu, tel. town). Village; pop. 890; acres 4,758; lat. 14° 01′; long. 78° 38′; from Cuddapah S.S.W. 36 miles; from Royachoty W.S.W. 12 miles. Very wealthy merchants.——*Yerramnainipollem* (ఎర్రంనేనిపాళెం - erramnénipálem, Tel.). From (erramanáyadu, tel. proper name + pálemu, tel. fortified village). Village; pop. 607; acres 6,795; lat. 13° 56′; long. 78° 56′; from Cuddapah S. 38 miles; from Royachoty S.E. 13 miles. Once seat of a poligar, a branch of the Saunipoya family.——**(2)** Town, Talook head-quarters; Cuddapah dist., Royachoty tal.; pop. 4,383; acres 4,514; lat. 14° 04′; long. 78° 48′; height 1,600 feet; from Cuddapah S. 30 miles; from Madanapully N.N.E. 39 miles; from Madras W.N.W. 124 miles; from Sidhout S.S.W. 32 miles. On the Maundavair, with seven roads converging on it. Old pagoda [q.v.] to Veerabhadra sawmy. Car festival [ratotsavam] in middle of February for seven days. Weekly market.

ROYADROOG (ರಾಯದುರ್ಗ - ráyadurga, *Can.* ráyadrug *). From (ráya, can. king + durga, san. fort) [raj].——**(1)** Talook, Bellary district. Tahsildar's pay Rs. 175. Area 815 square miles. Population 97,801. Language Teloogoo and Canarese. S.E. of district. Bounded N. by Bellary talook, E. by Gooty and Anantapore talooks, S. by Dharmavaram and W. by Mysore territory. There are a few hills in the extreme west, the highest point being the droog [q.v.], at the foot of which Royadroog is built. The soil in the north and west round Honnore and Bellagooppa is regar [q.v.]; in the rest a poor kind of red stony soil. The chief crops are paddy [q.v.], cholum [q.v.], raggy [q.v.], gram [q.v.], cotton [q.v.], and corra [tinay]. Coarse country cloths are woven at Royadroog. Rice [q.v.] from Canacull and fried rice from Royadroog are largely exported in to Bellary. The Pennair and Hagary flow through the talook, but, with the exception of a few, small channels which are made afresh every year through the sand [manal], are not utilized for irrigational purposes. The most important tanks [q.v.] are Canacull, Codihully, Talikerey and Yerradikerey. Places of archæological interest:—Ancampulley, Audagooppa, Auvooladotla, Bandore, Bauginaickenhully, Belagooppa, Bheirasamoodram, Bheirownitippa, Bhoopasamoodram, Bidaracoonta, Boodigoomma, Bramhasamoodram, Caloogode, Canacull, Caudoolore, Codihully, Coodlore, Coontanahully, Coorlagoonda, Cowcoontla, Dharmapoory, Doodagootta, Doorgacondaupooram, Eigarhully, Eitanahully, Ganigera, Garoodacheroo, Garoodaudry vencatanahully, Gollapully, Goommagutty, Govindavauda, Hadgully, Hanacanhully, Hanoomaupooram, Harisamoodram, Hoolikerey, Keidevanhully, Keriyauganahully, Maulyam, Metchaury, Mooradv, Mullakaity, Mullapooram, Naugalaupooram, Naugenhully, Naugireddipulley, Nemacull, Oopparhully, Pedda cowcoontla, Pillahully, Poolacoonta, Poolacoorty, Rampooram, Rancutla, Rautsamurry, Royadroog, Rungasamoodram, Shaittore, Shreedharaghatt, Shreerungapooram, Singanahully, Sirpy, Taggoopurty, Taullakera, Teetecull, Toombiganore, Vaiparaulla, Vaiplapurty, Veerapore Vyansapooram, Woodegolam, Yailanjy, Yautacull, Yerradikerey, Yerragoody, Yerragoonta. Principal trig. stations:—Bandore, Honnore, Royadroog, Yerragoonta. The leading places, &c., in the talook are the following.——*Bandore* (బండూరు - bandúru, Tel.). From (bandu, tel. vulture + úru, tel. village). Trig. station; lat. 14° 57′ 43·11″; long. 77° 02′ 33·91″; height 1,659 feet; from Bandore village N. 2 miles; from Bellary S.S.E. 14 miles; from Royadroog N.N.E. 21 miles.——*Bidaracoonta* (బిదరకుంట - bidarakunta, Tel.). From (biduru, can. bamboo, bambusa arundinacea, willd. + kunta, tel. pond). Village; pop. 417; acres 2,930; lat. 14° 53′; long. 77° 08′; from Bellary S.S.E. 21 miles; from Royadroog N.E. 20 miles. On bank of Hagary.——*Canacull* (ಕಣಕಲ್ಲು - kanakallu, Can.). From (kana, can. threshing floor + kallu, can. stone). Village; pop. 5,602; acres 15,703; lat. 14° 48′; long. 77° 07′; from Bellary S. 25 miles; from Royadroog N.E. 17 miles. Tank. Market Friday.——*Codihully* (ಕೋಡಿಹಳ್ಳಿ - kódihalli, Can.). From (kódi, can. a weir + halli, can. village). Village; pop. 928; acres 6,727; lat. 14° 31′; long. 76° 57′; from Bellary S. 42 miles; from Royadroog S. 14 miles. Tank.——*Hagary* (ಹಗರಿ - hagari, Can.). See sep. title.——*Honnore* (ಹೊನ್ನೂರು - honnúru, Can.). From (honnu, can. gold + úru, can. village). Village; pop. 1,782; acres 6,771; lat. 14° 55; long. 77° 08′; from Bellary S.S.E. 18 miles; from Royadroog N.E. 20 miles. On the military road from Bellary to Bangalore on the right bank of the Hagary. Near this place are some singular dunes, formed by the sand [manal] raised from the wide bed of the Hagary by the strong westerly winds. Their progress like that of similar drifting sands on the southern coast of France renders barren the country immediately to the leeward of them. Boodoorty, a village about 3 coss [q.v.] hence, was totally overwhelmed some years ago by one of these moving hills. Trig. station in lat. 14° 55′ 21·61″; long. 77° 08′ 30·29″; height 1,583 feet; from Bellary S.E. 20 miles; from Honnore village N.E. 1½ miles; from Royadroog N.E. 22 miles.——*Royadroog* (ರಾಯದುರ್ಗ - ráyadurga, Can.). See below.——*Talikerey* (ತಲೆಕೆರೆ - talekere, Can.). From (tale, san. head + kere, can. tank). Village; pop. 1,515; acres 10,733; lat. 14° 35′; long. 76° 52′; from Bellary S. 39 miles; from Royadroog S. 9 miles. Contains a tank. There are eight inscriptions on stone in this village, two being dated A.D. 1329 and 1727.——*Yerradikerey* (ಯರ್ರಡಿಕೆರೆ - yerradikere, Can.). From (eradu, can. two + kere, can. tank). Village, Hill; pop. 920; acres 5,021; lat. 14° 31′; long. 76° 58′; from Bellary S. 43 miles; from Royadroog S. 15 miles. Contains two tanks.——*Yerragoonta* (ఎర్రగుంట - erragunta, Tel.). From (erra, tel. red + gunta, tel. pond). Trig. station; lat. 14° 48′ 25·89″; long. 77° 00′ 45·26″; height 1,703 feet; from Bellary S.S.E. 22 miles; from Royadroog N.E. 15 miles.——**(2)** Town, Talook head-quarters; Bellary dist., Royadroog tal.; pop. 10,382; acres 12,290; lat. 14° 42′; long. 76° 54′; from Adony S.S.W. 71 miles; from Bellary S. 30 miles; from Hospett S.E. 48 miles; from Hurpanhully E. 57 miles; from Madras W.N.W. 258 miles; from Tadpatry W. 76 miles. Consists of a citadel and lower fort, the latter containing the town, which is regularly laid out. The citadel occupies the summit of a mass of granite [caroom cull] rocks, rising to the height of 1,200 feet, and connected by a lower ridge with a group of hills which from the north-eastern boundary of the plain of Chitaldroog. The south face of the rock is abrupt and inaccessible. The lower fort is guarded by a triple line of works, and a narrow path-way hewn in the rock leads from it to the citadel. At intervals along this path are gateways of solid masonry and fresh lines of fortification. About half-way up the hill is the old palace of the poligar [q.v.], said to have been built about the beginning of the sixteenth century, and close by are two handsome temples [coil, pagoda] dedicated to Rama [q.v.] and Krishnan [q.v.]. There are also the ruins of houses and gardens on the rock. This fortress was founded about A.D. 1371 by Bhoopaty row, who was entrusted with the management of this part of the country by Harichendra row of Vijianugger. It was originally of mud. About A.D. 1517 it was given to the Beydar [boya] chief Junga naick, who built the present fort and palace on the top of the hills. It remained under the Beydar poligars, tributary to Vijianugger, till the fall of the latter place in 1564, when it became tributary to the Mahomedan sovereigns of Beejapore, paying at first an annual peshcush [q.v.] of 12,000 rupees to the Beejapore leader Dowlat khan ameer-ool-oomrah. It subsequently was governed by a Telinga rajah of the Balije [q.v.] caste. The town below the hill was founded by Timmappa naidoo. The Diwaun vencatapaty succeeded Timmappa. He died leaving three sons, Cably naidoo, Gopaul rajah, and Timmappa naidoo, and two daughters, Nicajamma and Roodramma. Cably succeeded, but was assassinated by his brother Gopaul, who died through remorse and was shortly afterwards succeeded by the youngest brother Timmappa naidoo. This chief having convicted his Paurpatyagar [q.v.] or secretary of embezzlement, threw him into prison. On this the Paurpatyagar wrote secretly to Hyder ally, inviting him to come and take the place. Hyder accordingly sent a large army for this purpose under Jehaun khan and Makhdoom sahib, who took the chief and his family prisoners to Seringapatam, but afterwards reinstated him. About the end of the sixteenth century the family of the poligars of Royadroog were deposed, and one of the descendants of the ex-commander-in-chief of Vijianugger made himself master of Royadroog and the adjacent fort of Coondarpy droog. In 1766 the poligar assisted Hyder ally in the reduction of Sheerah, as a reward for which his tribute was reduced as soon as Hyder became master of the country. Subsequently the poligar Vencatapaty naidoo gave offence to Tippoo by refusing to join him when about to attack Adony. Tippoo captured Royadroog and sent the poligar to Seringapatam, where he was assassinated in 1791, just before Royadroog was stormed by Lord Cornwallis. In 1799, his sister's son, Gopaul naidoo, was released from Seringapatam and made his way to Royadroog, where he attempted to collect a following. He was taken prisoner by Mahomed ameen khan, who had been sent by the Nizam [q.v.] to settle the district, and removed to Hyderabad. After the cession to the British, he was sent to Gooty where he resided as a quasi-State prisoner till his death. Pensions were granted to his family, which are now extinct. Trig. station; lat. 14° 42′ 19·30″; long. 76° 53′ 09·10″; height 2,727 feet; from Bellary S. 31 miles; from Royadroog village N.W. ½ mile.

ROYAGADA (رائگڑھ - ráigarh, *Hind.*; రాయఘడ - ráyaghada, *Tel.*). From (ráyadu, tel. king + ghada, oor. fort) [raj]. —**(1)** Division; Vizagapatam district; population 91,228; language Ooriya, Teloogoo and Khond in some parts. Boundaries:—North, Central provinces and Bissemcuttack division; south, Parvatipore division; east, Goonapore division; west, Coraputt division and Calahundy. A large dry plain surrounded with hills covered with jungle. Soil black and red. South of the division unfertile. In Calyauna singapooram very fertile. Brinjarry trade from Central provinces. Grain [dhaunyam], &c., imported and salt [ooppoo] from the Parvatipore market exported. The leading places, &c., in the division are the following.—*Bijauya* (బిజయ - bijáya, Tel.). See sep. title.—*Calyauna singapooram* (కల్యాణసింగుపురము - kalyánasingupuramu, Tel.). From (kalyánasingu, tel. proper name + pura, san. town). Distinguish from Bheirava singapooram in Jeypore. Village, Head-quarters of Mokhausa zemindarry; pop. 2,768; lat. 19° 30′; long. 83° 21′; from Jeypore N.E. 65 miles; from Royagada N. 24 miles; from Vizagapatam N. 122 miles. On route to Calahundy. Shiva temple on top of high mountain. Near it are caves and wells, also an inscription. The estate is a feudatory under Jeypore.—*Devagherry* (దేవగిరి - dévagiri, Tel.). See sep. title.—*Keilausacote* (కైలాసకోట - kailásakóta, Tel.). From (kailása, san. the sacred mountain in the himalayas + kóta, san. fort). Town; lat. 19° 14′; long. 83° 35′; from Jeypore E. 68 miles; from Royagada N.E. 10 miles; from Vizagapatam N. 104 miles.—*Langoolya* (లంగూలియా - lángúliyá, Tel.). See sep. title.—*Poycapaud* (పాయకపాడు - páyakapádu, Tel.). From (páik, hind. village watchman + pádu, tel. village). Village; pop. 544; lat. 19° 09′; long. 83° 34′; from Jeypore E.N.E. 64 miles; from Royagada E. 7 miles; from Vizagapatam N. 99 miles. Mokhausa [q.v.] given to a Bramin [q.v.] family by the Maharajah of Jeypore. Old temple with inscription, much resorted to at Shivarautry [pundigay, 6a]. At the foot of hill near is a temple of Pautaleshwaran, built by Balaraman [q.v.], elder brother of Krishnan [q.v.].—*Royagada* (రాయఘడ - ráyaghada, Tel.). See below.—**(2)** Deputy tahsildarry; Vizagapatam district. Pay Rs. 150.—**(3)** Village. Head-quarters of Deputy tahsildar, Ameen of Maharajah of Jeypore, Government hospital; Vizagapatam dist., Jeypore zemindarry, Royagada magisterial division; pop. 2,286; lat. 19° 09′; long. 83° 27′; from Coraputt N.E. 50 miles; from Joypore N.E. 56 miles; from Madras N.E. 460 miles; from Narsapatam N.N.E. 112 miles; from Parvatipore N. 26 miles; from Vizagapatam N. 98 miles; from Vizianagram N. 70 miles. Population almost entirely Khonds and Ooriya bramins. Former capital of the Jeypore rajah, Vishwanauta deo, who built a large mud fort the ruins of which are still visible. The site of the self-immolation of his 116 wives who ascended the funeral pyre in a body on the occurrence of his death, is still pointed out [suttee]. Emporium of trade between Central provinces and coast.

ROYASAM (రాయసము - ráyasamu, *Tel.*). Tel. from (ráyu, tel. colloquial form of vráyu, meaning to write). The business of a clerk. So a clerk [goomastah].

ROZ (روز - roz, *Hind.*). From persian. A day [dinam, naul]. The Mahomedans attach some importance to their luckiness or the reverse [rijaul ool gheib], but not so much as the Hindoos do. Daily wages. For Nowroz or new year's day see that heading.—*Roza* (روزہ - rozah, Hind.). From the persian. A daily fast, especially during Ramzaun [q.v.].—*Rozeenah* (روزینہ - rozínah, Hind.). From (above + distributive suffix). A daily allowance granted to Bramins [q.v.], fakeers [q.v.], poor persons, &c., to be enjoyed during their lifetime [yeomiah].—*Rozmurrah* (روز مرہ - rozmarrah, Hind.). From (above + marrah, ar. once). Same as Rozeenah.—*Roz nauma* (روز نامہ - roznámah, Hind.). From (above + námah, pers. writing). A journal.—*Rozwar* (روز وار - rozwár, Hind.). Daily.

RUBY WOOD (لال چندن - lálchandan, *Hind.*). Red sanders.

RUDD (رد - radd, *Hind.*). From (radda, ar. to send back). Rejection, repeal. In Mahomedan law applies especially to the return or surplus of an inheritance which remains after legal portions have been distributed among sharers, and which in default of a residuary heir returns or is to be divided amongst the original sharers [vaurs]. Rudd nauma is a deed abrogating a former one.

RUNJA (రంజ - ranja, *Tel.*). A brazen drum [paray].

RUSSELLCONDAH (రసూలుకొండ - rasúlukonda, *Tel.* russellkonda *). Town, Head-quarters of General deputy collector and talook, Telegraph office, Registrar's station; Ganjam dist., Goomsoor tal.; pop. 3,412; lat. 19° 56′; long. 84° 38′; from Balligooda E.S.E. 46 miles; from Berhampore N.N.W. 45 miles; from Chetterpore N.N.W. 47 miles; from Chicacole N.N.E. 123 miles; from Madras N.E. 544 miles. On the Loharacundy, here spanned by a bridge; at the foot of a small hill, on N.W. frontier towards Orissa. Made a cantonment in 1837 at end of second Goomsoor campaign, and named after Mr. Russell, Special Commissioner, deputed to Ganjam to suppress disturbances caused by Dhananjaya bhoonj. Cantonment abandoned in 1863. Two small rivers flow south-east through the cantonment. In the rains when the hills are very feverish the Special assistant agent and the Assistant superintendent of Police reside here. Chief mart for the product of the Goomsoor hills consisting chiefly of wheat [geung], turmeric [country saffron], wax [mom], honey [shahad], hides [chamrah] and horns [sing] which the Khonds [q.v.] exchange for saltfish, iron [auhan], brass [pittalay] vessels, beads [munkah], &c. Salt [ooppoo] is taken through Russellcondah by Brinjarries [q.v.] and others for the Boad zemindarry and the Central provinces.

RUSSOOM (رسوم - rusúm, *Hind.*). Plural of (رسم - rasm, ar. usage). Fees. Ready-money payments received by public officers, as perquisites attached to their situations. Russooms formerly often took the form of right to levy transit duties, e.g., the right to collect three pies on every basket of paddy [q.v.] entering a certain market, &c. [merah, swatantram, vartanay]. See vol. I, 112.

RUSSUM (رسم - rasm, *Hind.*). From (rasama, ar. to mark or sketch). Prescribed form, vestige.—*Russum col arz* (رسم العرض - rasmularz, Hind.). From (above + arz, ar. earth). Mathematical geography [ilm].—*Russum ool khatt* (رسم الخط - rasamulkhatt, Hind.). From (above + khatt, ar. writing). Orthography [ilm].

RUZZAUK (رزاق - razzák, *Hind.*). From (rizk, ar. food). Provider. Epithet of God [allah]. Common alam; as Abd oor ruzzauk, slave of god [ism].

RYE (रै - rai, *San.*; റൈ - rai, *Mal.*). From (rá, san. to bestow). Wealth. Prefix in place names, as Ryemungalam meaning wealthy prosperous town.—*Raivaty* (रेवती - révatí, San.). From (rai, san. wealth + vat, san. suffix of possession); having prosperity. The last of the twenty-seven lunar mansions [nacshatram] or asterisms, comprising thirty-two stars of the fishes [hoot, meenam], figured by a tabor. Yogam [q.v.] or leading star is Veidhrity [q.v.], and this star is the starting-point [maisham] whether exact or inexact of the present hindoo fixed solar zodiac [ayanaumsham, maunam, mausam, raushy chuckram, rishy]. Veidhrity is either η or ζ piscium.

RYE (రాయి - ráyi, *Tel.*). Stone. Suffix in place names. Distinguish from Rye meaning king.—*Ramalcottah* (రామల్లకోట - rámallakóta, Tel.). See sep. title.—*Raula* (రాల - rála, Tel.). From (ráyi, tel. stone). Stone. Plural locative form. Suffix in place names; as Dooggiraula, meaning the stones dedicated to doorga.—*Raullamadoogoo canama* (రాళ్లమడుగుకనమ - rállamadugukanama, Tel.). From (ráyi, tel. stone + madugu, tel. pool + kanama, tel. pass). Tel. also (sampájekanama), meaning sumpaujey, proper name + ghaut. Ghaut [q.v.]; Cuddapah district, Poollampett and Royachoty talooks; from Cuddapah S.S.E. 42 miles; from Poollampett S.W. 16 miles. In the Sheshachellam hills between Royachoty and Poollampett talooks.

RYOT (رعیت - raiyat, *Hind.*). From (rai, ar. to pasture). A peasant, a cultivator [coody].—*Ryotwarry* (رعیت واری - raiyatwárí, Hind.). From (above + wár, hind. distributive suffix). Relating to the cultivator; especially as ryotwarry settlement, a settlement with each individual cultivator without the intervention of a third party [graumam, zemindarry]. See vol. I, 112.

S (स - sa, श - sha, सा - sá, *San.*; ث - se, س - sín, ص - sád, *Hind.*; ஶா - shá, *Tam.*). San. श for shiva [q.v.]. San. स for Lutchmy [q.v.]. Hind. ث in enumeration, symbol for 500. Hind. س numerically symbol for 60; astronomically the sun [sooryan] in its sextile aspect. Hind. ص numerically symbol for 90; abbreviation for the second Mahomedan month [maheena]; for the word 'correct' as a mark of attestation, being the first letter of sahee [q.v.].

SA (स - sa, *San.*). With [sam]. Also intensive.—*Sabhaupaty* (சபாபதி - shabáppathi, Tam.). From (sabhá, san. asssembly + pati, san. lord). Shiva, as lord of the sacred hall at Chidambaram [q.v.]. Hindoo 2nd or pers. name [peyar.—*Sabhauratnam* (சபாரத்தினம் - shabárattinam, Tam.). From (sabhá, san. assembly + ratna, san. gem). Ornament of an assembly. Hindoo 2nd or pers. name [peyar].—*Sabhay* (सभा - sabhá, San.; சபை - shabai, Tam.). From (sa, san. together + bhá, san. to appear). A society [samauj, sangam, sangham]. Also a council chamber. There are five mantapams [q.v.] in Chidambaram wherein Shiva is said to manifest himself:—Cancasabhay, Chitrasabhay, Chitsabhay, Deva sabhay and Nritya sabhay. Either of these names is used as a proper name, especially the first. Suffix in proper names among the non-bramin classes. Compare Ambalam and Rungam [peyar].——*Sadah* (सदा - sadá, San.). Always.——*Sadauchauram* (सदाचार - sadáchára, San.). From (sadá, san always + áchára, san. practice). The perpetual obligations of a householder [grihastan], consisting of daily purifications [samscauram], ablutions [snaunam], libations [savam], oblations [baly, yanyam], hospitality, obsequial rites [tarpanam], ceremonies to be observed at meals, at morning and evening worship [sundhyauvandanam], and on going to rest [maryauday].——*Sadaunandan* (சதாநந்தன் - shathánandan, Tam.). From (sadá, san. always + ánanda, san. happiness). Epithet of Shiva. Hindoo 2nd or pers. name [peyar, sadaushivan].——*Sadaushivan* (சதாசிவன் - shathásivan, Tam.). From (sadá, san. always + shiva, san. happiness). Epithet of Shiva. Hindoo 2nd or pers. name [peyar, sadaunandan]. Name of a minor rajah of the Vijianugger of the Narsimha [q.v.] dynasty [raj], who was set up as nominal successor of Krishna deva roya [q.v.]. See vol. I (153); II, 251. ——*Saha* (सह - saha, San.). With.——*Sahely* (سہیلی - sahelí, Hind.; ಅರಸಿನಬುರಡಿ - arasinaburadi, Can.; కుంకుమపిట్ట - kunkumapitta, Tel.) [soohely]. Hindostany, from (sa, san. with + hélá, san. sport); playful, companion. Tel. from (kunkuma, tel. red saffron powder + pitta, tel. bird). Hind. also (paharíbalalchashm); (sátsahelí), meaning seven companions, from being seen in groups of seven; (bulalchashm); (sátbhái), meaning seven brothers or companions. Can. also (sulisang), male. Title otherwise Minivets. The Pericrocotus genus, campephaginæ [sukroy], laniadæ [pingalam], dentirostres, insessores [pacshy, 19], of naturalists [jantoo].—"*a*" The orange minivet is Pericrocotus flammeus, confined to jungles of South-west india; bright and showy colors; males keep up continuing whistling call, wheet-wheet-wheet.—"*b*" The rosy minivet is Pericrocotus roseus.—"*c*" The small minivet is Pericrocotus peregrinus. Always in flocks, at times six or seven females seen with only one male, hence the Hindostany name Saut sahely.—"*d*" The white-bellied minivet is Pericrocotus erythropygius.——*Sam* (सम् - sam, San.). Same as title.——*Samashrayanam* (समाश्रयण- samáshrayana, San.). From (sam, san. well + áshri, san. to adhere) Branding of the shoulders with chunk [q.v.] and chuckram [q.v.]; performed on Veishnavites [moodrah dhauranam]. See vol. I (85).——*Samasyam* (సమస్య - samasya, Tel.). From (sam, san. together + as, san. to throw). Part of a stanza proposed by one person to be completed by another as a trial of skill. ——*Samaudhy* (समाधि - samádhi, San.). From (sam, san. with + ádhá, san. to place), collecting the mind. Abstract meditation. The eighth or last stage in the practice of yogam [q.v.].——*Samaugamam* (समागम - samágama, San.). From (sam, san. together + ágama, san, coming). The occultation of star [jyotisham, nacshatram, sangamam].——*Samauj* (समाज - samája, San.). From (sam, san. together + aj, san. to go). Assembly [sabhay, sangam, sangham].——*Samausam* (समास - samása, San.). From (sam, san. together + ás, san, to sit); combination. Ellipsis in grammar [vyaucaranam].——*Samayam* (समय - samaya, San.). From (sam, san. together + i, san. to go); covenant. Any religious persuasion or system.—"*a*" There are twelve principal religious sheiva systems of which six are orthodox or approved and six heterodox or rejected. The oolsamayam [ootohamayam] or six orthodox systems are:—Veirávam [q.v.], making bheiravan [q.v.] supreme; Vaumam [q.v.], regarding the female principle [shacty] in nature as the primeval form of deity and teaching the worship of the female organ; Caulaumookham [q.v.], similar to vaumam; Mauvratam [q.v.], teaching that the deity is a pure spirit; Paushoopatam [q.v.], similar to mauvratam; Sheivam [q.v.], teaching that deity is both spirit and matter assuming forms [avatar, moorty] for accomplishing his purposes [augamam]. The poorasamayam or other heterodox systems are:—Locauyatam [q.v.], a species of atheism regarding sensual gratifications as the chief good, as taught by chaurvaucan [q.v.]; Bowddham [booddha], which rejects the notion of a supreme being, maintaining that all material existences proceed from a fortuitous combination of the four primitive elements [bhootam] earth, water, fire and air, and that mental phenomena are the mere results of organization; Shamanam [q.v.], the jeina [q.v.] system, being a modification of booddhism, and regarding arghan [arhat] as the deified preceptor and object of worship; Mimaumsam [q.v.], regarding bramh [q.v.] as the soul [autmam] of the universe; Pauncharautram [q.v.] or the system taught by vishnoo [q.v.] during five successive nights; Bhattauchauryam or the system of bhattaucharry who regard the vedams [q.v.] as god and consider that virtuous actions of themselves result in felicity. Other systems are Caupaulam, Sowtrauntícam, Yogachauram, Autmicam, Veibhaushicam, Nirgranta vaudam, Neiyauyicam, Veishaishicam, Patanjalyam, Saunkhyam, Siddhauntam, Vedauntam.—"*b*" The six orthodox veishnava systems are Yaudavam, that of yaudava mishran; Mauyah vaudam, that of shuncaracharry [shuncaran]; Hiranyagarbham, that of hiranyagarbhan; Ramaunoojeeyam, that of ramaunoojan [q.v.]; Bhauscaram, that of bhauscaran; Tatwa vaudam, that of madhwacharry [madhwa, matam]. The six heterodox veishnava systems are the same as the above six heterodox sheiva systems. For the various systems of Hindoo philosophy see Darshanam.——*Sambandham* (सम्बन्ध - sambandha, San.). Tie. Relationship by birth or marriage generally; but commonly understood of relationship by marriage. Sambandha calapp or mixing by marriage is intermarriage. Sambandhy is the parents of the married pair in their relation to one another. Coorangoo sambandham is the monkey grasp in philosophy; as the cub clings to its mother so the soul clings to the deity [samsauram, g]; the doctrine of Vadagalays [q.v.]. Poonay sambandham or cat's grasp is the hold of the deity on a soul; the stronger carrying the weaker; the doctrine of the Tengalays [q.v.]. Pausha sambandham is a cord-tie, applied to bondage of soul [autmam] in body [pashoo, paty, pausham, shareeram]. ——*Sambandhamoorty* (சம்பந்தமூர்த்தி - shambandamúrtti, Tam.). From (sam, san. well + bandha, san. tie + múrtti, san. image of deity, title to pious persons); means an attached soul, a pious devotee. Hindoo 2nd or pers. name [peyar]. ——*Sambandhan* (सम्बन्ध - sambandha, San.; சம்பந்தன் - shambandan, Tam.). From (sam, san. well + bandh, san. to tie); well tied or attached; devotee. One of the three champions of the Sheiva [q.v.] faith against the Jeinas [q.v.] in the reign of the Madura ruler Coon paundyan [soondra paundy tevar]; his life related at length in the Tirtondar pooraunam [aroopatt moover, periya pooraunam]. Born of the Bramin tribe of Cownya at Shiyally, while yet a child acquired distinction as a poet [pauvalan]. Coon paundyan embraced the Jeina religion, but Sambandhan having succeeded in curing the king of a fever, reconverted him to the Sheiva religion, and instigated him to impale alive on the bank of the Veigay river eight thousand Jeinas. In his sixteenth year married daughter of Numbiyandaur numby, a Bramin of Tirnellore; but both he and his wife died on their wedding day, whilst worshipping in the temple at Tirnellore. The number of Pathigams [q.v.] he composed was 16,000 [matam].——*Samber* (शांबर - shambara, San.; सांबर - sámbara, Mahr.; سانبر - sánbar, Hind.; سامبر - sámbar, Dec.; ಕಡವೆ - kadave, Can.; ಕಡಮ - kadama, Too.; కణితి - kaniti, Tel.; ସମ୍ବର - somboro, Oor.; കട്ടുമാൻ - katumán, Mal.; ගෝනාරුසා - gónárusa, Singh.; கடம்பை - kadambai, Tam.). Title from hindostany. San. from (sam, san. together + vri, san. to surround). Tel. means a hump, perhaps from its having one. Oor. from sanscrit. Mal. from (katu, mal. fierce + mán, mal. deer). Tam. from (kadam, tam. forest). Title otherwise Samber stag. Sometimes wrongly called Elk. The Jerrow of Himalayas. Greek ἱππέλαιος. Rusa aristotelis, rusinæ, cervidæ [mrigam], ruminantia, mammalia [sastanam, 24], of naturalists [jantoo]. Alias Cervus aristotelis, equinus, hippelaphus, leschenaultii. The largest of Indian stags. Horns with a basal antler springing directly from the burr or base of the horn, and pointing forwards, upwards and outwards, the beam bifurcating at the extremity, a snag separating posteriorly and pointing obliquely to the rear. Color dark brown, in summer somewhat slaty; the chin, limbs within, tail beneath, and irregularly marked patch on the buttocks pale yellowish, or orange yellow; neck and throat with long hair, forming a sort of mane; tail moderately long. Female and young dusky olive brown, lighter than the buck. Ordinary length, 6 to 7 feet; height, 13–14 hands at the shoulder. The horns vary much in thickness and length, and the divergence varies much, as well as the degree of curvature, and the relative size of the terminal snags. The horns are considered to attain their complete form in the fourth year, and after that go on increasing in size for several years more, without any normal alteration of form. The length of the horns rarely exceeds 40 inches, but some are recorded 4 feet along the curvature. The basal antler 10–12 inches or more. The color too varies, some being much darker than others. Found in the Western ghauts [q.v.] throughout their whole extent, the Wynaud, Coorg, the Neilgherries, many parts of Mysore, the Eastern ghauts [q.v.], where sufficient cover is afforded by the forests. They prefer hilly ground to flat land. They may be seen morning and evening outside a patch of jungle, grazing on the new grass that springs up after the old grass is burnt off. They still abound, but have become very wary. The stags drop their horns in April, sometimes earlier, and the new horns are not perfected till the end of September, about which time the rutting season commences, and their peculiar call may be heard, especially morning and evening. The eye-pit or suborbital sinus is very large in these deer [mrigam], and when the animal is excited it is distended. In hunting it, it is either stalked or else driven by a line of beaters. It has been killed by fox hounds on the Neilgherries. According to native shikarries [q.v.] the samber drinks only every third day, whereas the Nilghye [q.v.] drinks daily. Soft leather, somewhat resembling chamois leather, is prepared from the hide [chamrah].——*Samhauran* (संहार - samhára, San.). From (sam, san. completely + hri, san. to draw). A form of Shiva [q.v.], destroyer. Called also Samhaura bheiravan. Shoora samhauran is Soobramanyan [q.v.], the destroyer of Shooran, the giant, which is commemorated in Scanda shashty [q.v.]. ——*Samhitay* (संहिता - samhitá, San.; சங்கிதை - shangithai, Tam.). From (sam, san. together + dhá, san. to put). Collection of prayers, invocations, or hymns. The ancient Samhitays constitute the Shankhays or branches of each vedam [q.v.]. Every such collection belonging to one Vedam is entitled its Samhitay. The arrangement of the Samhitays is in a liturgical form, containing petitions addressed to the sun [sooryan], moon [chundran] and stars [nacshatram], to fire [agny], earth [bhoomy], and water [neer], to Indran [q.v.], Yaman [q.v.], Vishnoo [q.v.], Roodran [q.v.], and other deities. The prayers are partly homologatory, partly doxological, and partly supplicatory. They are the devotions for the most part of particular rishies [q.v.] expressed in particular metres, and addressed to particular deities, specified in the prayers themselves. The names of the rishy [q.v.], metre [chandas], and god [devatay], for every hymn, are inscribed at the head. In this respect, compare the Psalms of David. The tune or metre is also occasionally given. See vol. I (74). Samhitay means at present day a treatise on any branch of knowledge [vidyay].——*Samit* (सामित् - samit, San.). From (sam, san. well + indh, san. to kindle). Fuel for feeding sacred fire [agny, homam, yanyam]. The common sacrificial woods are:—Achyranthes aspera [indian burr], Butea frondosa [palans], Calotropis gigantea [yercum], Cynodon dactylon [hurrially], Eragrostis cynosuroides [darbhay], Ficus bengalensis [banyan], Ficus glomerata [cluster fig], Ficus religiosa [peepul], Prosopis spicigera [shamee].——*Sammaty* (सम्मति - sammati, San.). From (sam, san. together + mati, san. mind). Consent.——*Samoodauyam* (समुदाय - samudáya, San.). From (sam, san. together + ut, san. forwards + í, san. to go). Anything held in common. Especially by villagers, such as trees, fisheries, grazing land, firewood, irrigation, jungles, and the like [aroothycaray, graumam, palabhogam]. Underlying the government control there is a vast system of samoodauyam or communal organization, too often ignored.——*Samoodra devy* (समुद्रदेवी - samudradévi, San.). The sea-goddess; Lutchmy [q.v.].——*Samoodram* (समुद्र - samudra, San.). From (sam, san. with + udra, san. water).—"*a*" Ocean. The soorans [q.v.] and asoorans [q.v.] are said to have churned the ocean after the deluge [pralayam] with the mountain mandaram [q.v.] for the recovery or production of the fourteen sacred things [coormam], viz.:—Lutchmy, the goddess of prosperity; Cowstoobham, the jewel of krishnan; Paurijautam, the tree of paradise; Soorah, spirituous liquor personified as a nymph; Dhanwantary, the physician of the gods; Chundran, the moon; Caumadhain, the cow of plenty; Eirauvatam, elephant of indran; Ootcheishravas, horse of indran; Apsaras, nymph of indran's heaven; Caulacootam or halauhalam, the deadly poison; Amritam, ambrosia; Indra dhanoos, bow of indran; and the Conch [chunk]. The following are the 7 seas:—salt sea, sugar-cane juice sea, toddy sea, sea of ghee, sea of curds, sea of milk, sea of fresh water [bhoogolashastram].—"*b*" Any place with a large sheet of water [saugaram].—"*c*" Chapter of a book.——*Samoodricam* (सामुद्रिक - sámudrika, San.). From (sa, san. with + mudrá, san. mark). Palmistry. Very similar to the science introduced to Europe from Arabia. It dwells on the marks on the palms, on warts, moles, size, and shape of the different visible members, shape and height of person, length of arms and feet, and draws inferences from the whole. The Poorsha samoodrica lutchanam, is a treatise said to have been dictated by Soobramanyan [q.v.], son of Shiva [q.v.], to Agastyan [q.v.], the father of the Tamul language. The following are specimen mottoes of Samoodricam:—He will have wealth and long life whose lines in the palm of the hand are reddish and small; if they are thick, he will have sorrow; a person having lines in the palm of the hand like the chunk [q.v.] and the wheel [chuckram] will have ample income, and he will be charitable and liberal to everybody that may resort to him; if one has matsya raikhay, or the lines like the fish, he will be very liberal; if they are like the windpipe, he will win applause, if they are like the saw, he will be energetic and brave; one will be meek and humble whose lines in the palm are like the pitcher; and he will be a pundit [q.v.] if they are like the moon [chundran]; he will live in the company of several souls who has these lines like the white cowry [q.v.]; if they are like the lotus [nelumbo], he will always be a favorite of lutchmy [q.v.], the goddess of wealth; he will lead a happy life who has these lines in the form of a string of flowers; if they are like the spear or javelin, he will have success in his undertakings; if they are like the lingam [q.v.], he will be a devout worshipper of shiva [q.v.] and other gods [deva]; if they are like the ox [rishabham], he will have many conveyances; it is the sign of a wise man to have one line from the wrist to the foot of the middle finger; and if it runs as far below the middle finger, he will be a pundit or a proficient; if it runs as far below the little finger, he will be wealthy; if it is below the ring finger he will have ornaments but will have extreme sorrow; if it extends below the little finger, he will become a libertine; if it is in the palm of the hand, he will have riches and offsprings; a want of such a line in tho palm of a man is a sign of stupidity and dullness; if the line in the palm of the hand has the color of smoke, the person will become a great sinner. For indications of the curling mark see Shooly. For external omens see Shacoonam. Samoodrican is one versed in samoodricam, an interpreter of these marks, a chiromancer.——*Samoodry* (सामुद्रि - sámudri, San.). From (samudra, san. sea). Sea king. The Calicut zamorin [q.v.]. See vol. I (129), (139).——*Samoogam* (సముఖము - samukhamu, Tel.; சமுகம் - samugam, Tam.). From (above + mukha, san. face). Presence. Used in correspondence, as equivalent to your excellency [hazrat, huzoor].——*Sampauty* (सम्पाति - sampáti, San.). From (sam, san. well + pat, san. to fly). A fabulous bird. Eldest son of Garoodan [q.v.] and elder brother of Jatauyoo [q.v.]. Informed Hanooman [q.v.] that Ravanan [q.v.] had carried off Seetay [ramayanam, seetay].——*Sampradayee* (सम्प्रदायी - sampradáyí, San.). From (sam, san. well + pra, san. intensive prefix + dá, san. to give); traditionist. The Veishnava sect in Bengal; worshippers of Krishnan [q.v.] and Raudhay [q.v.] conjointly. To be distinguished from the Shree sampradayees or ramaunoojeeyans [ramaunoojan], and the Bramha sampradayees or madhwacharries [madhwa].——*Sampraty* (சம்பிரதி - shambirathi, Tam.). From (sam, san. together + prati, san. duplicate). Assistant to a village accountant [curnum].——*Samrajyam* (साम्राज्य - sámrájya, San.). From (sam, san. together + ráj, san. to shine, rule). Empire. Universal sovereignty. But applied to all prosperity and felicity. Samrajya lutchmy or lutchmy [q.v.] as conferring all felicity and prosperity is a common epistolary compliment. Compare Ashta lutchmy.——*Samsauram* (संसार - samsára, San.). From (sam, san. together + sar, san. to move). The world, the mundane state, secular condition, domestic life [illaram]. Transmigration; in which sense otherwise Jenmam [q.v.], Pirapp [q.v.] or Yaunam [q.v.]. Transmigration means transition of the soul into another body at death. Belief in a future life is first expressed positively in the Bramhanams [q.v.]. They assert that a recompense awaits all beings in the next world according to their conduct in this. The doctrine of transmigration in its present form, namely eternity of soul [autmam] backwards and forwards, is fully developed in the Oopanishads [q.v.], Darshanams [q.v.] and Menoo [q.v.].—"*a*" Expressed in its shortest terms the doctrine is this; Jenmam [q.v.] or birth is the result of Carmam [q.v.] or action; and action leads to continual existence, carried on through innumerable bodies [shareeram] till acts are adequately rewarded or punished.—"*b*" Philosophical hindooism, that is to say, looks upon soul as of two kinds, the Paramautman [q.v.] or supreme soul and the Jeevautman [q.v.] or the personal and individuated soul [autmam]. The union of the personal soul with the body is productive of bondage and misery, for when once so united the soul begins to apprehend objects through the senses [indriyam], receiving therefrom painful or pleasurable impressions. It also becomes conscious of personal existence and individuality [ahancauram]. Then it commences acting. But all action whether good or bad leads to bondage, because every act inevitably entails a consequence which must be rewarded or punished. An evil act follows a man through a hundred thousand transmigrations, says the Pauncharautram [q.v.]. This theory of actions is called shortly Carmam [q.v.].—"*c*" The conditions of existence just indicated are summed up in the theory of the Nidaunams, or twelve successive causes each of which is the consequence of the one which precedes. These are:—ignorance [anyaunam], the predispositions of mind which determine our acts or more simply the carmam or action, consciousness, individuality, sensibility, contact of the senses [indriyam] with objects, sensation, desire or thirst, clinging to existence, birth, old age, death or suffering. As regards the being which undergoes existence, it is viewed as a composite being resulting from the scandhams or aggregates; which in the case of the human being are reckoned as five, viz.:—Roopam, form or materiality; Vaidanay, sensation; Vinyaunam, perception; Sanyay, notion or abstract ideas; Samscauram, faculties and dispositions of mind or intellect. These scandhams or elements of being unite and arrange themselves so as to form a distinct being, undergo incessant modifications along with it, and dissolve at its death. The influence of its Carmam [q.v.] alone survives the being, and through this the formation of a new group of scandhams is immediately effected and a new individual rises into existence. —"*d*" In order to accomplish Carma vipaucam or the entire working out of these consequences, a life in conformity with the precepts of the sacred books is enjoined, and penances [tapas] and prauyaschittams [q.v.] or expiatory ceremonies are prescribed. The living personal soul [jeevautman] must shake off the fetters of action [carmam] and getting rid of body [shareeram], mind [manas] and all sense of separate personality return to the condition of simple soul [autmam]. This constitutes Pramay or Nyaunam [q.v.], the true measure of all existing difficulties, the right apprehension of truth, which if once acquired by the soul confers upon it final emancipation whether called Moocty, Mocsham, Nishreyasam, Apavargam or Nirvaunam.—"*e*" But to attain this the soul has to pass through innumerable bodies, migrating into higher, intermediate or lower forms, from a god to a demon, man, animal or plant or even a stone, according to its various shades of merit or demerit. The triple order of transmigrations through deities, men and beasts, and plants, is according to the dominance of one or other of the three goonams [q.v.] or cosmic qualities:—Satwam [q.v.], Rajas [q.v.] and Tamas [q.v.]. And each of these three degrees of transmigration has three sub-degrees. The grades of promotion are to Swargam [q.v.], the paradise of indran [q.v.], to Veicoontam [q.v.], the paradise of vishnoo [q.v.], and to Keilausam [q.v.], the paradise of shiva [q.v.]; and higher still to mocsham [q.v.], or liberation from a material body [cosham, shareeram] in the Satya locam [q.v.], or Bramha locam [q.v.], or highest heaven. The highest ascent is only for the mortified ascetic [beiraugy, sanyausy, yaty, yogy], who in the present life is considered to be Parama hamsan

[q.v.] a portion of the deity, or Jeevan mooctan a living divinity. Great crimes, on the other hand are punished by special forms of hell for a series of years, and then the guilty souls relapse into existence [jenmam, pirapp] and pass through various bodies. A bramin killer enters the body of a dog [nye], bear [ricsham], ass [gadhah], camel [ottagam], bull [maud], goat [vellaud], sheep [aud], stag [mrigam], birds [pacshy], &c. The violater of the bed of a gooroo [q.v.] migrates a hundred times into the forms of grasses, shrubs, plants, &c. It is implied under this theory that vegetables of all kinds have internal consciences and are susceptible of pleasure and pain.—"*f*" In connection with this system, a human being is regarded as a three-fold existence; the Stooladeham or visible body, the Soocshmadeham a minute or spiritual body, and Cauranadeham the causal or superior soul. The second is also called Yautanadeham, as capable of suffering, and therefore not wholly immaterial, but subtle and refined from grosser particles [cosham, shareeram].—"*g*" The belief in transmigration proceeds from the theory that human souls, being of divine essence, are originally pure, but during their earthly career lose more or less of their purity; being destined however to regain their original quality, they are reborn again and again, until they have become free from fault and thus worthy of returning to the place of their origin; the doctrine is obscurely taught, and among any but the philosophic is scarcely grasped at all; it is however common to all the hindoo systems, being a natural attempt to account for the existence of moral and physical evils, for all the inequalities of life, and for the dispensations of providence.—"*h*" The dravidians proper have no theory of transmigration; compare the following from the shivavaucyam [q.v.]:—*கறந்தபால் முலைபுகா கடைந்த வெண்ணெய் மோர்புகா உடைந்த சங்கினோசையும் உயிர்களு முடல் புகா வடிந்த வோரடையினி யுதிர்ந்த பூமரம்புகா இறந்துபோன மானிட ரினிப்பிறப்ப தில்லையே*—"as "milk once drawn cannot again enter the udder, nor butter "[vennay] churned be recombined with milk [paul]; as sound "cannot be produced from a broken conch [chunk], nor life be "restored to a corpse; as a decayed leaf and a fallen flower "cannot be reunited to the parent tree; so a man once dead "is subject to no future birth." However the idea has been largely imported by hindooism, even into purely tamul literature. The Cooral has the following: *அறத்தாறிதுவென வேண்டா சிவிகை பொறுத்தானோடூர்ந்தா னிடை*—"you need not describe the course of virtue [aram, dharmam]; "look at the bearer of a palankeen [q.v.] and him who rides in "it;" one, as the fruit of his virtues in a former birth, rides in a palankeen; while the other from former sin, is doomed to bearing it.—*வீழ்நாள்படாஅமை நன்றாற்றினஃ தொருவன் வாழ்நாள்வழியடைக்குங் கல்*—"he who acting well "permits no failing days; this will be a stone to stop the course "of births;" such a man delivered from the numerous births and deaths, to which other creatures are liable, will obtain absorption [matam, mocsham, pirapp, shivavaucyam].—*பிறவிப் பெருங்கட னீந்துவர் நீந்தா ரிறைவ னடிசேரா தார்*—"none can swim the great sea of births, but those who are "united to the feet of the deity."—*உறங்குவது போலுஞ் சாக்கா டுறங்கி விழிப்பது போலும் பிறப்பு*—"death is "like sleep; birth is like awaking from it."—*புக்கி லமைந்தின்று கொல்லோ வுடம்பினுட் டுச்சி லிருந்த வுயிர்க்கு*—"it seems as if the soul, which takes a temporary shelter in "a body, had not attained a home."—*பொருளல்ல வற்றைப் பொருளென் றுணரு மருளானா மாணாப் பிறப்பு*—"inglorious births are produced by the confusion of mind "which considers those things to be real which are not real."—*இருணீங்கி யின்பம் பயக்கு மருணீங்கி மாசறு காட்சி யவர்க்கு*—"a clear, undimmed vision of things will deliver its "possessors from the darkness of future births, and confer the "felicity of heaven."—*ஓர்த்துள்ள முள்ள துணரி னொருதலையாப் பேர்த்துள்ள வேண்டா பிறப்பு*—"let it not be "thought that there is another birth for him whose mind having "thoroughly considered all it has been taught, has known the "true being."—*அவாவென்ப வெல்லா வுயிர்க்குமெஞ் ஞான்றுந் தவாஅப் பிறப்பீனும் வித்து*—"the wise say "that the seed, which produces unceasing births, at all times, to "all creatures, is desire."—*அன்போ டியைந்த வழக்கென்ப வாருயிர்க் கென்போ டியைந்த தொடர்பு*—"they say "that the union of soul and body in man is the fruit of the union "of love and virtue in a former birth."—*இழத்தொறூஉங் காதலிக்குஞ் சூதேபோற் றுன்ப முழத்தொறூஉங் காதற் றுயிர்*—"as the gambler loves his vice the more he "loses by it, so does the soul love the body the more it suffers "through it."—*பொருளானா மெல்லாமென் றீயா திவறு மருளானா மாணாப் பிறப்பு*—"he who knows that wealth "yields every pleasure and yet is so blind as to lead a miserly "life will be born a demon."—*ஒருமையு ளாமைபோ லைந்தடக்க லாற்றி னெழுமையு மேமாப் புடைத்து*—"should "one throughout a single birth, like a tortoise keep in his five "senses, the fruit of it will prove a safeguard to him through"out the seven-fold births."—"*i*" See vol. I (70) to (94).——

Samscauram (संस्कार - samskára, San.). From (sam, san. well + kri, san. to do); well-doing.—"*a*" Purificatory rite. These purify a man from the taint of sin derived from his parents, and are enjoined with certain variations on all the three first classes [dwijan, jauty] of Hindoos alike. They are as follows:— Garbhadaunam, ceremony on conception. Poomsavanam, on the first indication of a living male's conception. Seemautonnayanam, arranging the parting of the mother's hair in the fourth, sixth, or eighth month of pregnancy. Jantacarmam, touching an infant's tongue with honey [shahad] and ghee [q.v.] out of a golden spoon thrice at birth before cutting the navel string. Nauma caranam [naumam, peyar], giving a name on the tenth or twelfth day after birth. Nishcramanam, taking out a child in the fourth month to see the sun [sooryan]. Annapraushanam, feeding an infant with rice between the fifth and eighth month or when he has cut teeth. Choodahcarmam, or chowlam, tonsure of the hair except one lock [coodoomy] on the crown of the head in the third year. Oopanayanam [q.v.], induction into the order of a twice-born [dwijan] man by investiture with the sacred cord [poonool]. Kaishauntam, cutting off the hair, performed on a bramin [q.v.] in his sixteenth year, on a cshatriya [q.v.] in his twenty-second, on a veisya [q.v.] in his twenty-fourth. Samauvartanam, solemn return home after completing a course of study with a preceptor. Vivauham, marriage [calyaunam], which completes the purification and regeneration of the twice-born [matam]. See vol. I (107).—"*b*" Samscauram is also faculty of memory, one of the twenty-four qualities of the Veishaishicam [q.v.] branch of Nyauyam [q.v.] philosophy.—"*c*" Also faculty and dispositions of mind or intellect influencing transmigration or samsauram [q.v.].——*Samstaunam* (संस्थान - samst'hána, San.). From (sam, san. well + st'há, san. to stand). Residence of a family of rank; zemindarry estate.——*Samvat* (संवत् - samvat, San.). From (sam, san. with + vas, san. to dwell); the seasons [ritoo] are supposed to abide in the year. A year [samvatsaram, saul, varsham]; especially of the era [saca] of Vicramadityan [q.v.].——*Samvatsaram* (संवत्सर - samvatsara, San.). From (sam, san. with + vas, san. to dwell). A year [samvat, saul, varsham]; mostly of the luni-solar reckoning [chaundramaunam]. The european calendar or common year contains 365 days. The european solar year, called also a tropical year [ayana caulam], is the period in which the sun [sooryan] moves from the vernal equinox [maishauyanam] to the vernal equinox again, and its average value, called a mean solar year [madhyama sowra maunam], is 365·24222 mean solar days, or 365^d 5^h 48^m 48^s; the odd time being nearly a quarter of a day it is allowed to accumulate till every fourth year, when february has 29 days; but the excess of the tropical year over 365 days is about 11¼ minutes less than a quarter of a day; hence the gregorian correction made by pope gregory xiii in 1582, and adopted in great britain in 1752, when the 3rd day of september was by act of parliament called the 14th. The european sidereal year is the time which elapses between the sun's leaving a fixed star [nacshatram] until his next return to it, and consists of 365^d 6^h 9^m 9·4^s. The european anomalistic year denotes the time between two successive passages of the earth through its aphelion or perihelion [ootcham] points, and consists of 365^d 6^h 13^m 45·7^s [maunam, mausam]. The teloogoo year consists of a certain number of lunar months [chaundramausam] reckoned from new moon to new moon [amavausyay, mookhyam, shooclaudy]; the luni-solar [chaundramaunam] years of the era [saca] of vicramadityan [q.v.] commencing with the year of the kaly [q.v.] age 3045 or 57 b.c. are those chiefly used in telingana [q.v.]; rare in the peninsula; fifteen days [tity] of thirty moohoortams [q.v.] each make a pacsham [q.v.] or lunar fortnight, two of these make a month [mausam], two months a solar season [ritoo], three seasons a northern or southern declination [ayanam], and these two compose a year; as to when the teloogoos begin their year, see Teloogoo new year. The tamul year consists of solar months [madhyama sowra maunam, mausam] containing as many days and parts of days [dinam] as the sun stays in each sign [raushy] of the zodiac [jyotisham, raushy chuckram]; for the commencement of the year among the tamuls, see Tamul new year. For Canarese, same as Teloogoo new year. For Malayalam see Collam and Vishoo. For Mahomedan see Hijra. For Persian see Nowroz. See vol. I, 612.——*Samvatsaraudy* (సంవత్సరాది - samvatsarádi, Tel.). From (samvatsara, sau. year + ádi, san. beginning). Same as Teloogoo new year. Otherwise Yoogaudy.——*San* (सम् - sam, San.). Same as Sam [q.v.] before gutturals, palatals, linguals, and dentals [varnamaulay].——*Sancalpam* (सङ्कल्प - sankalpa, San.). From (sam, san. well + klip, san. to resolve). Declaration of purpose; solemn vow. Solemn and formal enunciation of purpose preparatory to entrance upon any important religious rite [carmam] or work, as on the occasion of an ablution or snaunam [q.v.] at a place of sacred water [teertam], anniversary or shrauddham [q.v.], daunam [q.v.], or vratam [q.v.]. This utterance is made either by the subject [yejmaun] himself or by the poorohit [q.v.] or acharry [q.v.] for him.——*Sancramanam* (संक्रमण - sankramana, San.). From (sam, san. together + kram, san. to go). Means approach. In astronomy [jyotisham], passage of the sun [sooryan] or a planet [graham] into a sign [raushy] of the zodiac [raushy chuckram, sancraunty]. In algebra [ganitam] the working out of two unknown [caulak] quantities of which the sum and difference are given; also the rule for finding two such quantities.——*Sancraunty* (सङ्क्रान्ति - sankránti, San.). From (sam, san. together + kram, san. to go). Meeting. The passage of the sun [sooryan], &c., from any one sign [raushy] into another [sancramaunam]. The corresponding day is observed as a fast [oopavausam, pundigay, 2b]. In common usage specially applied to Macara sancraunty [q.v.], otherwise Mahasancraunty, the passage of the sun into the tenth sign macaram [q.v.] or capricorn, when he turns north or when dacshinauyanam [q.v.] ends and oottarauyanam [q.v.] begins. This is the season of Pongal [q.v.]. See vol. I (93).——*Sangam* (सङ्ग - sanga, San.). From (sam, san. with + gam, san. to go).—"*a*" Junction; a place of junction of two or more rivers [sangamam]. The debouche of a river [aur] into the sea. Assembly [sabhay, samauj, sangham].—"*b*" Village, Hill; Nellore dist., Nellore tal.; pop. 1,392; acres 5,357; lat. 14° 35′; long. 79° 47′; from Nellore N.W. 18 miles; from the sea W. 30 miles. Situated 3 miles from where Beerapair joins Pennair. On north bank of Pennair. Ancient Shiva and Vishnoo temples. In front of temple is a monolith pillar [laut] 30 yards in height and 2 yards in width. Annual festival in april in honor of Sangameshwara sawmy. An anicut [q.v.] across the Pennair and important irrigation works have been made. See the article on Irrigation in volume I. Trig. station on hill in lat. 14° 36′ 18·38″; long. 79° 47′ 24·35″; from Nellore N.W. 18 miles; from Shreecolan S.S.W. 5 miles; from the sea W. 29 miles.——*Sangamam* (संगम - sangama, San.; قران - kirán, Ar.). From (sam, san. together + gam, san. to go). Conjunction [crauntam]. When two celestial bodies have the same longitude [sauyanam], or right ascension [lagnam], they are in conjunction; when they have a difference of longitude of 180°, and are therefore in diametrically opposite parts of the heavens [bhagolam], they are in opposition; when the difference of longitude is 90°, they are in quadrature. The moon [chundran] is in conjunction with the sun [sooryan] at the time of new moon [amavausyay, pacsham], in opposition at the time of full moon [powrnimay]. With regard to mercury [boodhan] and venus [shoocran], they are said to be in inferior conjunction when passing between the sun [sooryan] and the earth [bhoomy]; and in superior conjunction when on the opposite of the sun to the earth [jyotisham]. For occultation see Samaugamam. Sangamam means also the confluence of two rivers [aur, sangam]. The junction of three rivers is called trivainy, meaning triple braid, or Trivainy sangamam; by pre-eminence applied to the place near Allahabad where Ganges and Jumna join Saraswaty.——*Sangameshwaram* (సంగమేశ్వరం - sangamésbvaram, Tel.). From (sangama, san. confluence + íshvara, san. shiva); so called from a temple of eeshwaran situated at the confluence of the rivers. Sanscrit name (nivrittisangama), meaning absolution + confluence. Village, Place of pilgrimage; Kurnool dist., Nundicotcore tal.; pop. 378; acres 941; lat. 16° 01′; long. 78° 22′; from Kurnool N.E. 23 miles; from Nundicotcore N.E. 12 miles. At the confluence of Toongabudra, Kistna and Bhavanausy. Double rock-cut cave with stone image. Important and sacred temple of Sangameshwaran with inscriptions. One of the temples has a gopooram [q.v.] in the form of a car [rath]. Several deserted temples. Annual festival on Shivarautry [pundigay, 6a].——*Sangapalagay* (சங்கப்பலகை - shangappalagai, Tam.). From (sanga, san. assembly + p'halaka, san. plank). The seat of the learned in former times at Madura on the tank of Pottaumaray [madura college, paundya rajaukkal].——*Sangaputnam* (సంగపట్నము - sangapatnamu, Tel.). From (sanganna, tel. proper name + pattana, san. town). Village; Kurnool dist., Coilcoontla tal.; pop. 1,144; acres 4,306; lat. 15° 09′; long. 78° 11′; from Coilcoontla W.S.W. 13 miles; from Kurnool S. 47 miles. The poligar [q.v.] family of this place is a branch of that of Nossam, from which it separated in 1644. Polliem [q.v.] now resumed.——*Sangattaur* (சங்கத்தார் - shangattár, Tam.). A collegiate body [madura college, paundya rajaukkal].——*Sangeetam* (सङ्गीत - sangíta, San.). From (sam, san. prefix meaning together + gá, san. to sing). Means symphony. Music in its largest sense, by the union of voices, instruments and action. Native books on this art consist of three parts, gaunam [pautt], vaudyam [q.v.], nrityam [q.v.]; or song, percussion, and dancing. The first comprises the measures of poetry [pah], the second instrumental music of all sorts, and the third theatrical representation [nautacam]. In all religious ceremonies and on the occasions of celebrating marriages [calyaunam], &c., music is an essential accompaniment. The tamul Cooral [q.v.] has the following:—பண்ணென்னாம் பாடற்கியைபின்றேற் கண்ணென்னாங் கண்ணோட்ட மில்லாத கண்—"of what "avail is a song if it be inconsistent with harmony? so what is "the use of eyes which possess no kindliness?" Stringed instruments played with the fingers with fixed frets are the veenay [q.v.] and kingry [q.v.]; with movable frets, the sitaur [q.v.]; without frets, the tambore [q.v.]. Played with bow are the saurangy [q.v.] or native fiddle and rabaub [q.v.]. Played with a plectrum of ivory [dant] or wood is the soorbut [q.v.]. Ancient stringed instruments out of use are the yauzh [q.v.] family. The rauvanauttam [q.v.] is also ancient. Reed instruments are the naugaswaram [q.v.], mailam [q.v.], mookha veenay [q.v.], jeenboorra [q.v.], magady [q.v.], toortty [q.v.] shahnaye [q.v.], tauray [q.v.], and bankah [q.v.]. Wind instruments without reed are algoja, chunk, comboo, pillangrovy, shree choornam, toortoory. Metal instruments of percussion are jaulry, jhaunj, taulam, jaugatey, morchang, ghuntay, and shalangay; secondly of wood and skin as jamadica, chitikey, daf, damaroo, dole, dunkah, mridangam, maddalam, kanjily, nowbut, tacorah, nakkaura, runja, paray, tappattay, tom-tom; thirdly of mud as ghatam and jala tarangam. The musical instruments chiefly in use in the Tamul districts are drums, the mookha veenay or clarionet, cymbals and toortty as bagpipe. The Teloogoos are less advanced than the Tamuls. A sketch account of the S. Indian musical system has been given at vol. I (103).——*Sangham* (संघ - sangha, San.). An assembly, especially of Booddhist [boodha] priests [sabhay, samauj, sangam].——*Sangharaumam* (सङ्घाराम - sanghárama, San.). From (sangha, san. assembly + áráma, san. garden). Same as Vihauram [q.v.].——*Sangraham* (सङ्ग्रह - sangraha, San.). From (sam, san. well + grah, san. to take). Epitome [sankshaipam].——*Sanjeevan* (சஞ்சீவன் - shañjívan, Tam.). From (sam, san. well + jíva, san. life); enlivening. Hindoo 2nd or pers. name [peyar]. Compare Sanjeevy.——*Sanjeevy* (సంజీవి - sanjívi, Tel.). From (sam, san. well + jíva, san. life); restorative. Applied to a revivifying medicament restoring from swooning or suspended animation, death, &c., and insuring long life; an elixir [amritam]. Proper name [peyar]. Long liver [chiranjeevy]. Priest of the Pariahs [q.v.].——*Sankhyay* (संख्या - sankhyá, San.). From (sam, san. well + khyá, san. to tell). Number; one of the seventeen qualities of the Neiyauyicans [nyauyam]. Sankhyah ganitam is algebra [beejaganitam].——*Sankshaipam* (सङ्क्षेप - sankshépa, San.). From (sam, san. well, together + kship, san. to throw). Abstract [sangraham].——*Sanscrit* (संस्कृत - samskrita, San.). From (sam, san. well + kri, san. to do), elaborated; language perfected by grammatical rules; also polished, elegant, embellished language. The classical language of the Bramins [q.v.]. See vol. I (52); II, 205, 209.—"*a*" The following declension of a noun and conjugation of two verbs show the similarity between Latin and Sanscrit and the dissimilarity between Latin and Tamul. "i" Noun "Father" (pater, Lat.; pitá, San.; appan, Tam.; patrem, Lat.; pitaram, San.; appanai, Tam.; patre, Lat.; pitrá, San.; appanál, Tam.; patri, Lat.; pitré, San.; appanukku, Tam.; patre, Lat.; pitus, San.; appanodu, Tam.; patris, Lat.; pitus, San.; appanudaiya, Tam.; patre, Lat.; pitari, San.; appanil, Tam.; patre, Lat.; pitah, San.; appané, Tam.; patres, Lat.; pitaras, San.; appanmár, Tam.; patres, Lat.; pitrín, San.; appanmárai, Tam.; patribus, Lat.; pitribhis, San.; appanmárál, Tam.; patribus, Lat.; pitribhyas, San.; appanmárukku, Tam.; patribus, Lat.; pitribhyas, San.; appanmárodu, Tam.; patrium, Lat.; pitrínám, San.; appanmárudaiya, Tam.; patribus, Lat.; pitrishu, San.; appanmáril, Tam.; patres, Lat.; pitaras, San.; appanmárgalé, Tam.). "ii" Verb "To be" (sum, Lat.; asmi, San.; irukkirén, Tam.; es, Lat.; asi, San.; irukkiráy, Tam.; est, Lat.; asti, San.; irukkirán, Tam.; sumus, Lat.; smas, San.; irukkiróm, Tam.; estis, Lat.; st'ha, San.; irukkirír, Tam.; sunt, Lat.; santi, San.; irukkirár, Tam.). "iii" Verb "To give" (do, Lat.; dadámi, San.; tarugirén, Tam.; das, Lat.; dadási, San.; tarugiráy, Tam.; dat, Lat.; dadáti, San.; tarugirán, Tam.; damus, Lat.; dadmas, San.; tarugiróm, Tam.; datis, Lat.; datt'ha, San.; tarugirírgal, Tam.; dant, Lat.; dadati, San.; tarugirárgal, Tam.).—"*b*" For the oldest Sanscrit literature see Vedam. The second large class of Sanscrit literature consists of the epic poems [mahabhaurat, ramayanam], pooraunams [q.v.], and tantrams [q.v.], which may be divided thus:—Epics. Pooraunic literature, containing first pooraunams, secondly stotrams and tracts connected with them, thirdly miscellaneous pooraunic works, abridgments, &c. Tantric literature, containing first tantrams, secondly digests and compilations. The third large class is modern Sanscrit literature, which may be divided thus:—"i" Technical literature, containing grammar [lacshanam], lexicography [nigantoo], prosody, rhetoric, music [sangeetam], dancing [nrityam], &c., architecture [stanpatyam], &c., medicine [veidyan], astronomy and astrology [jyotisham, vaunashastram]. "ii" Philosophy, containing Poorva mimaumsam [q.v.], Vedauntam [q.v.] or Oottara mimaumsam, which comprises the orthodox school [adweitam] of Shuncaracharry [shuncaran], the Vishishtaudweitam [q.v.] system of Ramaunoojan [q.v.], the Dweitam [q.v.] or school of Ananta teertan [madhwa], and the Sheiva [q.v.] system, Saunkhyam [q.v.] system, Yogam [q.v.] system, logical systems [tarcam], namely, the Nyauyam [q.v.] of Gowtaman [q.v.] and the Veishaishicam [q.v.] system, Booddhistic [booddha] and Jeina [q.v.] systems. "iii" Dharma shastram [q.v.], containing first original Smrities [q.v.], secondly digests, thirdly dissertations on special topics, such as Auchauram [q.v.], Caula nirnayam, Daunam [q.v.], Neety [q.v.], Prauyaschittam [q.v.], Vyavahauram [q.v.], Shrauddham [q.v.], &c. "iv" Cauvyam or artificial poetry and nautacams [q.v.] or drama, containing Maha cauvyams [q.v.], Cauvyams, including rhetorical compositions in prose, shatacams and anthologies, collections of popular tales [katay], and dramatic poems or nautacams [bhaushay].——*Santa* (సంత - santa, Tel.). From (sandhá, san. junction). Fair [chunda, melah, santey, shandy].——*Santapilly* (సంతపల్లె - santapalle, Tel.). From (santa, tel. fair + palle, tel. village). Otherwise Chantapully.

Village, Port; Vizagapatam dist., Bimlipatam tal., Magisterial division; pop. 907; lat. 18° 04′; long. 83° 42′; from Bimlipatam N.E. 18 miles; from Conauda N.E. 7 miles; from Madras N.E. 406 miles; from Vizagapatam N.E. 34 miles. Light on Santapilly hill, three-quarters of a mile inland; lat. 18° 04′ 11·03″; long. 83° 40′ 35·02″; white; fixed; 16 miles range; visible from all directions seaward; on a small basement on the top of a small hill with a small building by the side of the lantern on the west side; to warn off the Santapilly rocks, from which this light bears N.W. ⅝ W., distant 6½ miles.——*Santauna lutchmy* (सन्तानलक्ष्मी - santánalakshmí, San.). From (sam, san. well + tan, san. to stretch + lakshmí, san. the goddess). The goddess of lineage [ashta lutchmy].——*Santaunam* (सन्तान - santána, San.). From (sam, san. along + tan, san. to stretch).—"*a*" Meritorious act [dharmam] by which it is hoped to attain salvation [mocsham]. The seven are:—Construction of tanks, endowments of money for charitable purposes, performance of the sacred thread ceremonial to a Bramin [oopanayanam], construction of temple [coil, pagoda] dedicated to the supreme deity, plantation of topes [q.v.], writing of books, and digging wells.—"*b*" Also progeny, issue.—"*c*" In natural history an order. For category, see Padaurtam; for elementary substance, see Dravyam; for matter, see Bhootam; for organic and inorganic, see Indriyam and Anindriyam; for organic kingdom, see Ganam [jantoo,vricsham]; for organic class, see Vargam; for organic order, see present head; for organic family, see Coolam; for organic genus, see Jauty; for organic species, see Bhaidam. Oopa prefixed to either of the above means a sub-head. For inorganic minerals, see Dhautoo.——*Santey* (ಸಂತೆ - sante, Can. సంత - santa, Tel.; சந்தை - shandai, Tam.). From (sam, san. together + dhá, san. to hold). Market [chunda, melah, santa, shandy].——*Sanyausayyan* (சன்னியாசியய்யன் - shanniyásiyayyan, Tam.). From (sanyásí, san. ascetic + aiyyan, tam. master, titular affix). A composite Hindoo 2nd or pers. name [peyar].——*Sanyausy* (सन्यासी - sanyásí, San.). From (sam, san. completely + nyas, san. to throw up); abandoning world. Original meaning is one occupying the last of the four estates of a Bramin [aushramam]. An ascetic, who, renouncing all wordly affections and possessions, becomes legally dead. He is defined as one who performs no rite whatever, and appears sometimes in a state of nudity; who has renounced social life, with all its enjoyments and attachments, and subjected his passions; who lives on what is given him unasked, and remains in a village only one day, in a town not more than three days, and in a city only five; lest his mind become secularized. Menoo [q.v.] says:—"having performed "religious acts in a forest during the third portion of his life "[vaunaprastan], let a man become a sanyausy for the fourth "portion of it, abandoning all sensuous affections, and wholly "reposing in the supreme spirit [bramh]." In the present day the term is applied to various kinds of religious mendicants who wander about and subsist upon alms, generally devotees of Shiva [q.v.]. Asceticism is not at all a Dravidian idea. There is a Canarese proverb:—ಬೇಕು ಅಂದಾಕ್ಷಣ ನಾಕಾ ಸೇರುವನೇ—"can any one attain heaven by desiring it?" The tamul Cooral has the following:—அறத்தாற்றினில்வாழ்க்கையாற்றிற் புறத்தாற்றிற் போஒய்ப்பெறுவதெவன்—"what will he "who lives virtuously in the domestic state [illaram] gain by "going into the other state?" that is to say by becoming an ascetic [aram, matam]. Sanyausy is also Hindoo 2nd or pers. name; taken even by pariahs [peyar]. See vol. I (77).——*Sapindam* (सपिण्ड - sapinda, San.). From (above + pinda, san. sacrificial ball). An ancestor or descendant in the male line, and of the first, second, or third generation. These kinsmen are so called because they, and they only, are entitled to offer the pindam [q.v.] at a shrauddham [q.v.] to a deceased person. ——*Sastanam* (सस्तन - sastana, San.). See sep. title.——*Saugaram* (सागर - ságara, San.; ساگر - ságar, Hind.). From (sagara, san. the myth. king); from tradition that sagaran and his descendants dug the ocean. Ocean. So any large sheet of water [samoodram]. Suffix in place names, indicating existence of a tank or other large sheet of water.——*Saulokyam* (सालोक्य - sálókya, San.). From (sa, san. with + lóka, san world); within sight and in the same place or sphere. Saulokyam, Saumeepyam, Sauroopyam, Sauyoojyam are the four states of bliss. Saulokyam is obtaining the happiness of being in the place of God; Saumeepyam, that of being near to God; Sauroopyam, that of bearing the image of God; Sauyoojyam, that of being identified with God, being absorbed into his essence [mocsham]. See vol. I (88).——*Saumagree* (सामग्री - sámagrí, San.). From (sam, san. together + ang, san. to go round). Apparatus.——*Saumantan* (सामन्त - sámanta, San.). From (sam, san. with + anta, san. border); on all borders, neighbouring. West coast chief. Eight are specified:—Calicut, Colattiry, Cooroombranaud, Nedoonganaud, Travancore, Valavanaud, Vimbalanaud [vembanaud], Wonanaud.——*Saumaunyam* (सामान्य - sámánya, San.). From (samána, san. common). Community; one of the seven padaurtams [q.v.] or categories of the Neiyauyicans [nyauyam]. The other six are dravyam or substance, goonam or quality, carmam or act, vishaisham or particularity, samavauyam or co-inherence, and abhauvam or non-existence.——*Saumbamoorty* (சாம்பமூர்த்தி - shámbamúrtti, Tam.). From (sa, san. with + ambá, san. párvati + múrti, san. form); shiva with parvaty [ardhanaury]. Hindoo 2nd or pers. name [peyar, saumban, saumbashivan].——*Saumban* (साम्ब - sámba, San.). From (sa, san. with + ambá, san. párvatí). Shiva [saumbamoorty, saumbashivan].——*Saumbashivan* (சாம்பசிவன் - shámbasivan, Tam.). From (sa, san, with + ambá, san, párvatí + shiva, san. shiva) [ardhanaury]. Hindoo 2nd or pers. name [peyer, saumbamoorty, saumban].——*Saumbayyan* (சாம்பய்யன் - shámbayyan, Tam.). From (sámba, san. shiva with párvatí + aiyyan, tam. master), shiva, the master. Hindoo 2nd or pers. name [peyar].——*Saumeepyam* (सामीप्य - sámípya, San.). From (samípa, san. nearness). Proximity to the deity; state of beatitude [mocsham, saulokyam]. See vol. I (88).——*Saunkhyam* (सांख्य - sánkhya, San.). From (sankhyá, san. numbering). The name arises from its enumeration of entities [tatwam]. One of the six ancient Bramiuical systems of philosophy [darshanam]. The reputed author was Capilan, a bramin, of whose history nothing is known.—"*a*" It offers no explanation of the existence of the soul [autmam], but all other existences, including mind and intellect as well as the material world, it derives from a rootless germ called pracrity [q.v.]. Beginning with this original eternal germ or element, it reckons up synthetically various other Tatwams [q.v.] or entities, which are productions of the first.—"*b*" The root and substance of all things except soul is the Pracrity. It is no production. Seven things produced by it are also producers. Thence come sixteen productions. Soul, the twenty-fifth essence, is neither a production nor producer. That is to say from an original Pracrity, variously called Moolapracrity or root-principle, Amoola moolam or rootless root, Pradhaunam or chief one, Avyactam or unevolved evolver, Bramham or supreme, Mauyay or power of illusion, seven other producers are evolved, and as so evolved are regarded as Vicaurams or productions.—"*c*" The first production of the original producer is Booddhy, commonly called intellect or intellectual perception, or otherwise Mahat from its being the great source of the two other internal faculties, Ahancauram and Manas or self-consciousness and mind. Third in order comes this Ahancauram, the I-making faculty, that is, to say self-consciousness or the sense of individuality, which produces the next five principles, called Tanmautrams or subtle elementary particles, out of which the grosser elements Maha bhootam are evolved. These Tanmautrams nearly correspond to the πρῶτα στοιχεῖα of Plato.—"*d*" The above eight constitute the producers, then follow the sixteen that are productions only.—"*e*" First in order, as produced by the Tanmautrams, come the five grosser elements [bhootam]:—Aucausham, ether, with the distinguishing property of sound, or, in other words, the substratum of sound, which sound is the vishayam or object for a corresponding organ of sense, the ear. Vayoo, air, with the property of tangibility, which is the vishayam for the skin. Tejas or jyoty, fire or light, with the property of form or color, which is the vishayam for the eye. Aupas, water, with the property of savour or taste, which is the vishayam for the tongue. Pritivy or bhoomy, earth, with the property of odour or smell, which is the vishayam for the nose. Each of these elements after the first has also the property or properties of the preceding besides its own. Aucausham must not be exactly identified with the modern ether, though this word is usually taken as its nearest possible equivalent. In some of its properties and functions it more corresponds with the inane, vacant space, of Lucretius.—"*f*" Next follow the eleven organs [indriyam] produced, like the Tanmautrams, by the third producer Ahancauram, viz., the five organs of sense, the five organs of action, and an eleventh organ standing between these two sets, called manas the mind, which is an internal organ of perception, volition, and action.—"*g*" The eight producers then, with the five grosser elements, ether, air, fire, water, earth, and with the eleven organs, form the true elements and constituent substances of the phenomenal world. As however the most important of the producers after the mere unintelligent original germ is the third, called Ahancauram, self-consciousness or individuality, it may be held that according to the Saunkhyam view the whole world of sense is practically created by the individual Ego, who is nevertheless quite distinct from the soul, as this soul is supposed to possess in itself no real consciousness of separate individuality, though deluded by it. This idea of personal individual creation is what chiefly distinguishes the Saunkhyam from the pantheism of the Vedauntam [q.v.], which denies all real personal individuality.—"*h*" It should also be noted that, according to the Saunkhyam theory, Pracrity, though a subtle elementary essence, is yet to be regarded as consisting of three ingredients or constituent principles in equipoise, called Goonams [q.v.]. These are Satwam [q.v.], Rajas [q.v.] and Tamas [q.v.], goodness or purity, passion or activity, and darkness or ignorance.—"*i*" The Saunkhyam creed has never been known in South india except to the studious; mention of it or fragments of it is found in books, but no one professes it [matam]. See vol. I (74).——*Saunnidhyam* (सान्निध्य - sánnidhya, San.). From (sannidhi, san. proximity). Nearness, the divine presence.——*Saurangy* (سارنگی - sárangí, Hind.). From (sa, san. with + ranga, san. color); variegated, spotted. The native fiddle, with five wires, played with bow. European fiddles are largely superseding [sangeetam].——*Sauraty* (சாரதி - shárathi, Tam.). From (sárat'hi, san. charioteer). Hindoo 2nd or pers. name [peyar]. Paurtasauraty is Krishnan [q.v.] as the charioteer of Arjoonan [q.v.].——*Sauroopyam* (सारूप्य - sárúpya, San.). From (sa, san. same + rúpa, san. form). Assimilation to the deity; a state of beatitude [mocsham, saulokyam]. See vol. I (88).——*Saushtaungam* (साष्टाङ्ग - sáshtánga, San.). From (above + ashta, san. eight + anga, san. limb). Whole body. Saushtaunga namascauram is salutation so as to touch the ground with the eight parts of the body; the two hands, two feet, two knees, the breast, and the forehead [maryanday, namascauram].——*Sautchy* (साक्षी - sákshí, San.). From (above + aksh, san. to see). Evidence, so a witness [pramaunam, shahidy].——*Sauyanam* (सायन - sáyana, San.). From (sa, san. with + ay, san. to go). Tropical celestial longitude, with double meaning according as theoretical or practical.—"*a*" The longitude of a celestial body in the european system is the arc [chaupam] of the ecliptic [craunty mundalam] lying between the vernal equinoctial point [maishauyanam] and the point where a circle of celestial latitude so called passing through the object cuts the ecliptic; a circle of celestial latitude meaning a great circle drawn from the pole of the ecliptic to any point on the ecliptic; celestial longitude is reckoned in the order of the signs [raushy]; it is movable or tropical, that is to say subject to the increments of precession [ayanaumsham, craunty pauta gaty, madhyama sowra maunam].—"*b*" In theoretical hindoo astronomy Sauyanam is exactly the same as above, that is to say reckoned by taking great circles proceeding from the pole of the ecliptic as intercepting circles [rishy raikhay]. The recognition of this method is rare in the shastrams. However it is indicated in the following rough translation of a passage in the comparatively modern Siddhaunta saurwabhowmam of Mooneeshwaran, the commentator of Bhascara charry, where he quotes from a more ancient Siddhaunta soondaram:—"A tube, adapted to the summit of a gnomon, is "directed towards the star on the meridian; and the line of the "tube, pointed to the star, is prolonged by a thread to the "ground; the line from the summit of the gnomon to the base is "the hypothenuse, the height of the gnomon is the perpendicular, "and its distance from the extremity of the thread is the base of "the triangle; therefore, as the hypothenuse is to its base, so is "the radius to a base, from which the sine of the angle and "consequently the angle itself are known; if it exceed the "latitude the declination is south, or if the contrary it is north; "the right ascension of the star is ascertained by calculation from "the hour of the night, and from the right ascension of the sun "for that time; the declination of the corresponding point of the "ecliptic being found, the sum or difference of the declinations, "according as they are of the same or of different denominations, "is the distance of the star from the ecliptic; the longitude "of the same point is computed; and from these elements "with the actual precession of the equinox may be calculated "the true longitude of the star, as also its latitude on a "circle passing through the poles of the ecliptic."—"*c*" In practical hindoo astronomy however, while the ecliptic is still taken as the line of measurement, the intercepting circles are great circles from the pole of the equator, otherwise meridian circles, which fall upon the ecliptic thus at an angle and not perpendicularly [golayantram]. In the former case the longitude is called aspootam or invisible, in the latter case it is called spootam or visible. This is the same as european Right ascension, except that the distances are measured along the ecliptic instead of along the equator.—"*d*" The difference between the two sorts of longitude is large, being equal to the whole base of a right angled triangle, and it becomes larger the greater the distance from ecliptic. For terrestial longitude see Deshauntaram.—"*e*" Fixed celestial longitude or Dhroovacam [q.v.] is the same as Sauyanam in all respects in its two senses, except that it disregards precession and reckons from an assumed fixed sidereal point. All the recorded longitudes in hindoo astronomical books are Dhroovacams, or in other words they are sauyanams which once made have never been corrected for precession; add to this the fact above-mentioned that they are all from the pole of the earth which is constantly shifting and not from that of the ecliptic, and it will be understood how difficult it is to locate the stars indicated by the shastrams. It is generally assumed that the longitudes of extant shastrams were reckoned from the equinoctial point of the Hamel epoch [madhyama sowra maunam, g], when the pole was between 17 and 18 degrees from its present position and stood somewhat beyond the star near the ear of the Giraffe; and with these data some approximations are made to the facts. However among the hindoos themselves at any rate the stars pertaining to the different mansions, &c., are really identified by tradition only.—"*f*" For celestial latitude see Vicshaipam. There too there is a theoretical from the pole of the ecliptic and a practical from the pole of the earth. However the difference there is not so great, being only the difference between the hypothenuse and the perpendicular of a right-angled triangle.——*Sauyoojyam* (सायुज्य - sáyujya, San.). From (sa, san. with + yuj, san. to join). Absorption into the deity [mocsham, saulokyam]. See vol. I (88).——*Savah* (సవా - savá, Tel.). From (saha, san. along with + pávu, tel. a fourth). One and one-fourth. Liquid measure [alavay, 4b]. Approximate actual value, 1 savah = 15 oz. 10 $\frac{2}{3}$ drs. avoir. $\frac{4}{5}$ of a cutcha seer, though not used with that value. Bellary, for ghee [q.v.]. Compare Mal. nauzhy, Tam. oyak.——*Shakkalatty* (சக்களத்தி - shakkalatti, Tam.). From (saha, san. with + kalatra, san. wife), joint wife. Rival wife. Plant second term, meaning like but inferior. Ex., where transl. is of first term:—Hydrolea zeylanica (ponnánganniscakkalatti), alternanthera sessilis; Oldenlandia dichotoma (imbúrarchakkalatti), oldenlandia umbellata. See gloss. paragraphs.——*Shalagram* (शालग्राम - shálagráma, San.). From (sa, san. with + ala, san. ring + gráma, san. multitude). A fossil with the impression of ammonites having mystic virtues, found in certain rivers, especially connected with Veishnava [q.v.] doctrine. Akin to the eagle stone [q.v.] of the ancients. The principal sorts are the Lutchmy narayany, the Vaumanam, the Daumodaram, the Narsingam, &c. Their abundance in the beds of mountain torrents has been long known. They are used in propitiatory oblations to Vishnoo [q.v.], as well as in funeral [shoodcaud] and other ceremonies. They are black, mostly rounded, and are commonly perforated in one or more places by worms, or, as the Hindoos believe, by Vishnoo in the shape of a reptile. According to the number of perforations and of spiral curves in each, the stone is supposed to contain Vishnoo in various characters. The possessor of a shalagram preserves it wrapped in clean cloth. It is frequently perfumed and bathed [abhishaicam]; and the water thereby acquiring virtue is drunk, and prized for its sin-expelling property. It is always placed near persons when they are about to die. A garden or plantation is consecrated by the Hindoos by marrying the shalagram stone carried by one man to represent the bridegroom, to a branch of the toolsy [q.v.] tree carried by another to represent the bride. After this consecration, the fruit can be eaten. As Vishnoo [q.v.] is represented by this stone, so Shiva [q.v.] is represented by a small oval agate [akeek], and Vigneshwaran [q.v.] by a globular cornelian [akeek i soorkh]. There is a Tamul proverb:—கங்கையிலே பிறந்த நத்தை சாலக்கிராமம் ஆகாது—"a snail of the "ganges is not a shalagram." See vol. I (77).——*Shandy* (సంత - santa, Tel.; சந்தை - shandai, Tam.). From (sandhá, san. junction). A fair [chunda, melah, santa, santey].——*Shaurang* (शारङ्ग - sháranga, San.). From (saha, san. with + ranga, san. color). Means variegated in color. Spotted cloth. Term for chintz [q.v.], once employed in the Northern circar [q.v.] trade.——*Soohely* (സുഹേലി - suhéli, Mal.) [sahely]. Means companion. Island; Malabar district. One of the Laccadives, still uninhabited.——*Sundhy* (சந்தி - shandi, Tam.). From (sam, san. together + dhá, san. to put). Angle, juncture. Combination of words in grammar [lacshanam]. In Sanscrit all contiguous vowels are combined or changed, so that hiatus is unknown. In Tamul and Canarese, and generally in the Dravidian languages, hiatus between contiguous vowels is prevented by the use of v or y. Vowels are rarely combined or changed in the Dravidian languages, as in Sanscrit, except in the case of compounds which have been borrowed directly from Sanscrit itself; nor are final vowels elided in these languages before words commencing with a vowel, with exception of some short finals, which are considered as mere vocalisations. The rule of Tamul, which in most particulars is the rule of Canarese also, is that v is used after the vowels a, u, and o, with their long vowels, and au, and that y is used after i, e, with their long vowels and ei. Compare in Greek συν with γνώμη becoming συγγνώμη. εν with λάμπω becoming ἐλλάμπω. Compare in Latin with rogo becoming irrogo; rego making in the perfect not regsi but reksi contracted orthographically into rexi. See vol. I (52).——*Sundhyaumsham* (सन्ध्यांश - sandhyámsha, San.). From (sandhyá, san. twilight + amsha, san. part). The period which follows a yoog [q.v.].——*Sundhyauvandanam* (सन्ध्यावन्दन - sandhyávandana, San.). From (sandhyá, san. twilight + vand, san. to adore). Religious ceremonies performed at stated periods in the course of the day; as morning at sunrise, noon, and evening at sunset [sooryan, sundhyay]. There is a Tamul stanza from Shiva vaucyam [q.v.]:—நீரை யள்ளி நீரில்விட்டு நீர்நினைந்தகாரியமாவாயுன்னி நீரெல்லாமவத்திலேயி றைக்கிறீர்வேரையுன்னி வித்தையுன்னி வித்திலேமு ளைத்தெழுந்த சீரையுன்னவல்லிராய் சிவபதங்கள்சேரலாம்—"while taking up the water and throwing it again into "the water, what is the object on which you think? on whatever "you think you have thrown all the water vainly. Think on the "root, think on the seed and on the benefit arising from that "seed; when you are thus able to think, you may approach "the feet of God". For daily prayers of mahomedans see Namauz and Salaut.——*Sundhyay* (सन्ध्या - sandhyá, San.). From (sam, san. together + dhá, san. to place). Either sunrise, noon, or sunset [sooryan]. So twilight. So figuratively the name of the period preceding a yoog [q.v.]. This is equal to $\frac{1}{6}$th part of the same; the sundhyay of bramha [q.v.] consists of 1,728,000 solar sidereal years; the same duration as the krita [q.v.] or satya [q.v.] yoog, which quantity is used in its double capacity for constructing the calpam [q.v.]. Sundhyay or twilight is also personified as the daughter of Bramha [q.v.]. From the peculiar indications of twilight mundane effects are predicted in astrology [jyotisham, vaunashastram]. These indications are derived from animals, birds, the wind, the halo, the parhelion or mock-sun, the parigham or appearance in the sky of the shape of an iron bar, the abhravricsham or appearance resembling a tree in shape assumed by the clouds, the rainbow, the gandharvanagaram [q.v.], the solar rays, the dandam or appearance in the sky resembling a club, dust clouds as to their gloss and color, &c.——*Sundhy veety* (सन्धिवीथि - sandhivít'hi, San.). From (sandhi, san. junction + vít'hi, san. street). Street [veety].——*Sundoor* (ಸುಂದೂರು - sondúru, Tel.). See sep. title.

SABDARIFFA (سبدريفه - sabdarífah, *Hind.*). From turkish. Same as Red-hemp bendy.

SABZ (سبز - sabz, *Hind.*). From Persian. Green.——*Sabjah* (سبزه - sabzah, Hind.). Green leaves of cannabis sativa [kinnab], from which Bhang [q.v.] is made.——*Sabjee* (سبزی - sabzí, Hind.). Same as Bhang.

SACA (शक - shaka, *San.*). From (shak, san. to be able) [shac]. Dynasty [raj]. So era, epoch; especially that of shalivahanan [q.v.]. The following are the different South indian eras. See vol. I, 609.——*Brihaspaty chuckram* (बृहस्पतिचक्र - brihaspatichakra, San.). Means jupiter's cycle. Cycle of sixty years approximating to solar years. This cycle is constructed on the hypothesis that revolution [bhaganam] of the planet [graham] Jupiter [brihaspaty] is equal to twelve of the cycle years, and consequently five of his revolutions to sixty of the cycle years. These kind of years are no longer used as an immediate measure of time; but as each of them bears a specific name, they serve for giving a particular designation to every solar [varsham] and luni-solar year [samvatsaram] during its scope of sixty years, after which the series begins anew in the same order. In Northern india, when astronomers compute the succession of these years, they refer still to the revolutions of the planet; in consequence of which one year is expunged every eighty-sixth solar year. The Dravidian astronomers make no difference between the Brihaspaty and solar years, and consequently expunge nothing; so that their years correspond to a different point of the cycle, or Chuckram [q.v.], and bear a different name. For the planet and the years of the cycle see Brihaspaty.——*Collam* (കൊല്ലം - kollam, Mal.). From the town [collam, quilon]. Called also Aundoo. Modern form of the Parshooraman [q.v.] cycle. The collam era commenced originally on 25th August 825 A.D. when the second cycle of Parshooraman era ended; but local circumstances have introduced a change in the initial day of the year. As there are two Collam towns, so there are two different dates on which the malayalies begin the year under this era. In the north, the year begins on 1st of Cunny [mausam] or September 15 when the sun enters Virgo [canya, raushy, soomboola]; in the south on 1st of Chingom or August 15 when the sun enters Leo [asad, simham]. This change in the initial day is accounted for in many ways:—"*a*" As referring to the foundations of the two towns, north and south.—"*b*" As indicating the dates of acquiring independence by rulers of the Colattiry [q.v.] families of north and south.—"*c*" As indicating the dates on which Shuncaracharry [shuncaran] introduced Vedantism in the north and south.—"*d*" As being the date of Wonam [q.v.], taken in one case in one year, and in another case in another year; this and either of the three explanations preceding may be identical.——*Graha parivritty* (ग्रहपरिवृत्ति - grahaparivritti, San.). From (graha, san. planet + parivritti, san. revolution). Era of ninety solar years, used in Southern districts. Constructed of the sum of the products in days, of fifteen revolutions [bhaganam] of Mars [coojan, mungalan], twenty-two of Mercury [boodhan], eleven of Jupiter [brihaspaty], five of Venus [shoocran], twenty-nine of Saturn [shany], and one of the Sun [sooryan]. Its epoch is A.A.C. 24. Its years vary by a few hours.——*Hijra* (هجری - hijrí, Hind.). From (hijr, ar. separation); flight of mahomed from mecca to medina to escape persecution, from which the era dates. An era followed by the Mahomedans all over the world. Its years are lunar [chaundramaunam, cumree], and of 354 and 355 days according as they are common or intercalaries [nasee]. It has a cycle of 30 years, eleven of which are always of 355 days. Its epoch is here the 16th July 622, but according to most Arabian astronomers the 15th of the same month.——*Parshooraman* (परशुराम - parashuráma, San.). From (parashu, san. axe + ráma, san. the hero). Called also Aundoo. Reckoned in cycles of 1,000 years; each of which begins on the sun's entrance [sancramanam, sancraunty] in the sign [raushy] Canyay [q.v.] ♍, Indian Virgo. Began B.C. 1176. The first cycle ended 176 B.C.; the second 825 A.D.; and the third should have ended A.D. 1825. But the termination in the last case was neglected and the following year was reckoned 1,001 instead of one. For initial month date see Collam. To find the year subtract 824 from the year of Christ. Used from Mangalore to Cape comorin.——*Shalivahanan* (शालिवाहन - shálivåhana, San.). From (shåli, san. the saul tree + våhana, san. vehicle). A celebrated king, descendant of Vicramadityan [q.v.]. His capital was Pratishtaunam on the Godavery. The era, Shalivahana saca, dates from A.D. 78. It is still commonly used in the Deccan [q.v.]. Often called simply Saca. The Saca year is a solar year [madhyamasowramaunam, mausam]. The beginning of the era is possibly the date of the expulsion of the Bramins from the Magadha kingdoms; as their forefathers dated the beginning of the Kaliyoog [q.v.] from some previous historic event. The era still exists in Baly; and nominally in Java, but there, in consequence of the adoption of lunar [chaundramaunam] time in A.D. 1633, the years no longer correspond. To find the year of Shalivahanan subtract 78 from the Christian year.——*Vicramadityan* (विक्रमादित्य - vikramáditya, San.). From (vikrama, san. prowess + áditya, san. sun). Titular name of a king at Ojjein. An era was formed in his reign; sometimes termed the Samvat [q.v.] era. The era is more generally used with lunar [chaundramaunam] time. To find the year of Vicramadityan, add 56 years to the year of Christ. In the northern parts of India, instead of numbering the luni-solar [chaundramaunam] years from the beginning of the Kaliyoog [q.v.], the Hindoos count them from the accession of Vicramadityan. This denomination however makes no difference in the construction of the luni-solar year.——*Vypeen* (പുതുവെപ്പു - putuveppu, Mal.). Portuguese corruption of malayalam. Mal. from (putu, mal. new + veppu, mal. deposit). An era near Cochin. It dates from A.D. 1341, the year in which the new island Vypeen was formed by deposit of sand and silt between the mouths of the Cranganore and Cochin rivers, or in which perhaps this island was first inhabited.

SACALAUT (سقلات - sakilát, *Hind.*). From (sikiliya, ar. sicily); which during the arab domination had a large cotton [q.v.] and silk [puttoo] manufacture. Woollen stuff, particularly European broadcloth. Chaucer uses it, spelt Checklatoun.

SACK TREE (वल्कलवृक्ष - valkalavriksha, *San.*; चांदोड - chándóda, *Mahr.*; करवट - karavata, *Conc.*; چندال - chandál, *Hind.*; ಬೈರಿಮರ - bairimara, *Can.*; നെട്ടാവിൽ - nettávil, *Mal.*; රිටි - riti, *Singh.*; நெட்டாவில் - nettávil, *Tam.*). Title from use of bark as clothing. San. from (valkala, san. garment of bark + vriksha, san. tree); bark used by hill tribes for clothing. Mahr. from (chánda, mahr. moon + vada, mahr. ficus bengalensis, linn.), from white bark and fruit-like fig. Conc. means bitter. Mal. from (netu, mal. tall + ávil, mal. cæsalpinia bonducella, flem.). Tam. from malayalam. Can. also (sågguri), meaning the sack bark tree. Mal. also (arayáññali), meaning half + artocarpus hirsuta, lamk. Tam. also (alli), probably from shining dark gum; known on anamullays; (pattaimaram), meaning bark tree. Title otherwise Bark tree, Half wild jack, Malay arrow poison tree, Sacking tree, Tall bonduc, Upas tree. Botanically Antiaris saccidora, dalz., artocarpaceæ [vricsham, 122]. Alias Antiaris toxicaria; Lepurandra saccidora. Large tree found on west coast, but native of java; runs to 100 feet; bark pale and smooth; leaves alternate, ovate oblong, acuminate, entire, glabrous above, slightly villous beneath; capitule axillary, aggregated; drupe, shape and size of a small fig [atty], covered with purple down; flowers in rains and ripens fruit in january. On wounding fruit a milky viscid fluid exudes, which shortly hardens, becoming of a black and shining color and of the consistency of bees' wax [mom]; the inner bark is composed of very strong tenacious fibres. The nuts intensely bitter, contain an azotised principle; the upas poison is prepared with this juice, mixed with chilly [q.v.] seed and other aromatics; the poison acts first as a purgative and emetic, then as a narcotic causing death by violent fits of tetanic convulsions; plant gives to pharm. bark and seeds, non-officinal. The hill-tribes strip the bark into large pieces, soak it in water, and beat it well, when it becomes white and furry; in this state they use it as clothing and for sacks; a white resin [raul] used for poisoning arrows. Wood soft and of no value. No other species here.

SACRIFICE (बलि - bali, *San.*). Prefix.——*Sacrifice grass* (कुश - kusha, San.). Title from use in sacrifices of bramins. San. from (ku, san. earth + shi, san. to strew); strewn on ground to sit upon during religious ceremonies. Same as Darbhay.——*Sacrifice rock* (വെള്ളിയാങ്കല്ലു് - velliyánkallu, Mal.). Mal. from (velli, mal. white + kallu, mal. stone); from appearance. Can. name (bilikallúru), meaning white + stone + village. Greek λευκὴ νῆσος. Island; Malabar dist., Cooroombranaud tal.; lat. 11° 29′; long. 75° 34′; from Badagara S.S.W. 8 miles; from Calicut N.N.W. 23 miles; from Tellicherry S. 18 miles. Small steep rocky island opposite Cottacull, whitish in appearance, and 40 feet high, lying six miles off the coast. So called from having been the scene of sacrifice of crew of an English ship by pirates at beginning of seventeenth century. Has 12 and 13 fathoms close to it, 16 fathoms 2¾ miles outside, 10 fathoms within it, to 7 fathoms about midway between it and mainland in a very good channel. Ships passing through inside channel ought to give point a berth of 3 miles by borrowing towards the rock. Passing outside in the night, ships should not come under 16 or 17 fathoms water. Famous for edible birds' nests.

SADAF (मुक्तामाता - muktámátá, *San.*; صدف - sadaf, *Ar.*; سیپی - sípí, *Hind.*; ಮುತ್ತುಚಿಪ್ಪು - muttuchippu, *Can.*; ముత్యపుచిప్ప - mutyapuchippa, *Tel.*; മുത്തുചിപ്പി - muttuchippi, *Mal.*; முத்துச்சிப்பி - muttuççippi, *Tam.*). San. from (muktá, san. pearl + mátá, san. mother). Can. from (muttu, can. pearl +

chippu, can. shell). Tel. from (mutyamu, tel. pearl + chippa, tel. shell). Mal. from tamul. Tam. from (muktá, san. pearl + shippi, tam. shell). Mother-of-pearl [chippy, moty].

SADAUF (ब्राह्मी - bráhmí, *San.*; सदाब - sadába, *Mahr.*; فيجن - faijan, *Ar.*; سداب - sadáb, *Pers.* and *Hind.*; سداف - sadáf, *Dec.*; سدب - sadab, *Malay*; ಹಾವುನಂಜಿನಗಿಡ - hávunanjinagida, *Can.*; సదాపు - sadápu, *Too.*; సదాప - sadápa, *Tel.*; സോമരാജം - sómaráyam, *Mal.*; අරුඩ - arudá, *Singh.*; அர்வதா - arvathá, *Tam.*). Title from deccany. San. from (brahma, san. holy). Ar. connected with greek. Can. from (hávu, can. snake + nanju, can. poison + gida, can. plant). Too. and Tel. from hindostany. Mal. from (sóma, san. moon + rájá, san. king). Tam. corruption from botanic name. San. also (sómalatá), meaning moon creeper [somam]. Ar. also (sadáb). Can. also (sudábu). Tel. also (arudu). Mal. also (arúta). Greek πήγανον. Title otherwise Herb grace, Mooncreeper [gandhaulee, somam], Rue. Botanically Ruta graveolens, linn., rutaceæ [vricsham, 32]. Alias Ruta angustifolia, chalepensis. Small shrubby plant; cultivated in gardens; hoary-green foliage, greenish yellow flowers; leaves very small, have peculiar strong odour, bitter nauseous taste, possessing considerable acrimony in fresh state, dissipated on drying. The leaves are medicinally stimulant, carminative, stomachic, antispasmodic and emmenagogue. Infusion; take of the rue leaves, dried, ten drachms; boiling water, one pint; infuse in a covered vessel for two hours, and strain. Tincture; take of the leaves, in coarse powder, ten drachms; proof spirit, ten ounces; macerate the powder for seven days in seven ounces of the spirit in a closed vessel, agitating occasionally; then transfer to a percolator, and when the fluid ceases to pass, continue the percolation with the remaining three ounces of the spirit, and add more, if necessary, to make ten ounces. Fresh juice; press out the juice by bruising the fresh leaves without water. Doses; of the infusion, from an ounce and-a-half to three fluid ounces; of the tincture, from one to three fluid drachms; of the fresh juice a tea to a dessert spoonful. Substituted for sp. ammon. aromat., ol. anisi, tinct. cascarilæ, tinct. valerianæ, and pil. rhei. co.

SADDLE BACK (वनछाग - vanachhága, *San.*; جنگلی بکرا - janglíbakrá, *Hind.*; ಕಾಡುಆಡು - káduádu, *Can.*; కొండగొర్రె - kondagorre, *Tel.*; വരയാട് - varayátu, *Mal.*; வரையாடு - varaiyádu, *Tam.*). San. from (vana, san. wild + chhága, san. goat). Hind. from (janglí, hind. wild + bakrá, hind. sheep). Can. from (kádu, can. forest + ádu, can. goat). Tel. from (konda, tel. hill + gorre, tel. sheep). Tam. from (varai, tam. mountain + ádu, tam. sheep). Title otherwise Ibex, Neilgherry wild goat, Precipice goat, Steinbock. Hemitragus hylocrius, caprinæ, bovidæ, ruminantia, mammalia [sastanam, 23], of naturalists [jantoo]. Alias Kemas hylocrius, warrayato. Warrayato from malayalam. Adult male dark sepia-brown with a pale reddish-brown saddle, more or less marked, and paler brown on the sides and beneath; legs somewhat grizzled with white, dark brown in front, and paler posteriorly. The head is dark, grizzled with yellowish-brown, and the eye is surrounded by a pale-fawn colored spot. Horns short, much curved, nearly in contact at the base, gradually diverging; strongly kneeled internally, round externally, with numerous close rings, not so prominent as in himalaya species. There is a large callous spot on the knees surrounded by a fringe of hair, and the male has a short stiff mane on the neck and withers. The hair is short, thick and coarse. Length of adult to root of tail 4 feet 2 to 4 feet 8; tail 3 inches; height at shoulder about 32 to 34 inches; horns occasionally 15 inches, rarely more than 12. Found on the Neilgherry and neighbouring hills, extending south along the Western ghauts nearly to Cape comorin. It chiefly frequents the northern and western slopes, where the hills run down in a succession of steep stony slopes or rocky ridges to the high tableland of Mysore and the Wynaud. These animals have become very wary and it is difficult to shoot them.

SADER (صادر - sádir, *Hind.*). From (sadara, ar. to issue). Going.——*Saderwared* (صادروارد - sádirwárid, Hind.). From (above + wárid, ar. coming). Contingent charges for office stationery, oil, &c. There was a charge formerly levied on ryots [q.v.] for supplying the public cutcherry [q.v.] with these. ——*Sadrahee* (صدر - sadr, Hind.; సదరహీ - sadarahí, Tel.). From (sadara, ar. to go back). Abovesaid.

SADKA (صدقه - sadakah, *Hind.*). From (sadaka, ar. to bestow from religious motives). Charitable offerings; or propitiatory offerings in the name of God [allah], had recourse to in order to get rid of any distemper. This is supererogatory, as opposed to zakaut [q.v.] which is obligatory.——*Sadaucat* (صداقت - sadákat, Ar.). From (sadaka, ar. to utter truth). Sincerity. Prefixed to an alam forms a lacab; as Sadaucat hoossain, term of devotion + alam [ism].——*Saudic* (صادق - sádik, Ar.). From (sadaka, ar. to be true). The upright; just. Lacab of the sixth Imaum. Common alam; as Saudic hoossain, double alam [ism].——*Siddeek* (صدیق - siddík, Ar.). From (sadaka, ar. to be true). Just. Title of Aboo bakr, Mahomed's companion and father-in-law. Common Mahomedan alam; as Siddeek ally, double alam [ism].——*Siddeeky* (صدیقی - siddíkí, Hind.). A class of Mahomedan sheikhs [q.v.], named after the Caliph [ism].

SADRAS * (சதுரங்கப்பட்டணம் - shathurangappattanam, *Tam.*). From (chatur, san. four + anga, san. military arms, viz., infantry, cavalry, elephant and cars + pattana, san. town). Sanscrit name (chaturangapattana), meaning same; also town of chatoorangan, an asooran of the place [seven pagodas]. Greek σοβούρας ἐμπόριον. The Tamul name is Sadooray, being abbreviation of sanscrit, altered by the Teloogoos to Sadrauz. Compare Madras. Village, Port; Chingleput dist., Chingleput tal.; pop. 1,395; acres 640; lat. 12° 31′; long. 80° 12′; from Arcot S.E. 62 miles; from Chingleput S.E. 17 miles; from Covelong S. 20 miles; from Cuddalore N. 62 miles; from Madras S. 40 miles; from Mercaunum N.E. 24 miles; from Sydapett S. 35 miles. On Coromandel coast, north of mouth of Palaur. The river has silted up and its bar cannot be crossed by seagoing ships. The coast is low and wooded, though inland three or four miles is a range of rugged hills of no great height, called the Sadras hills. Dutch established a settlement in 1647. Captured by the English in 1765, temporarily restored to the Dutch in 1818, and an English possession since 1824. Ruins of the brick fort of considerable extent and strength still remain close to the shore. There are also the remains of the houses of the officials, one of which has long been used as a halting place for European travellers. The old Dutch cemetery within the fort is still maintained in order under treaty. The oldest tombstone is dated 1679. There is a German lutheran mission church on the esplanade opposite the fort. Wesleyan mission have also a small settlement. Once famous for the fine muslin [q.v.] produced. There are still a few looms [tarry], but the skill is lost.

SAF (صف - saf, *Hind.*). Rank.——*Safder* (صفدر - safdar, Hind.). From (above + dar, pers. breaker). Breaker of the ranks. Lacab of Ally. Common alam; as Safder hoossain, double alam [ism].

SAFAR (صفر - safar, *Hind.*). From (sifr, ar. empty). Second Mahomedan month [maheena], so called because it was in this that the arabs used to vacate their houses and go to war. In this month the mahomedan festivals [eed] Teyrah teyzee [q.v.] and Aukhiry chahaur shamba [q.v.] occur.

SAFEE (صفی - safí, *Ar.*). Sincere friend. In composition makes a lacab; as Safee oollah, sincere friend of god. Title of Adam, now an ordinary alam [ism].

SAFFRON (कुंकुम - kunkuma, *San.*; केशर - késhara, *Mahr.*; कुंकुम - kunkuma, *Conc.*; درخت زعفران - darakhtizafrán, *Ar.* and *Pers.*; کیسر کا پیڑ - kesarkáper, *Hind.*; کیسر کا جھاڑ - kesarkájhár, *Dec.*; کمکما - kumkuma, *Malay*; ಕುಂಕುಮ - kumkuma, *Can.*; కుంకుమపువ్వుచెట్టు - kunkumapuvvuchettu, *Tel.*; കുങ്കുമം - kunkumam, *Mal.*; කොකුම - kokum, *Singh.*; குங்குமம் - kungumam, *Tam.*). Title from arabic (zafrán), yellow. San. from sound of dried leaves. Mahr. means gold. Ar. from (darakht, ar. tree + zafrán, ar. saffron). Hind. from (késara, san. the plant + per, hind. tree). Dec. from (késara, san. the plant + jhár, hind. tree). Can. from sanscrit. Tel. from (kunkumapuvvu, tel. the drug + chettu, tel. plant). Tam. from sanscrit. San. also (agnishikha), meaning fire flame [bastard saffron, chitramoolam, wild bachnaug]; (bhavaraktá), meaning shiva's blood; (káshmírajanma), meaning produced in cashmere; cf. arabian costum; (késara), meaning gold [ilanjy, kamela, nauga champak, poison bamboo]. Hind. also (kumkumkájhár), meaning saffron + tree; (abír), meaning abeer powder. Malay also (zafron); (kungkuma). Can. also (kunkumakésari); (késari). Tam. also (turukkam), meaning red tree. Greek κρόκος. Title otherwise Common saffron, Crow saffron, Flame plant [flame tree], Gold plant, Saffron crocus, Shiva's blood. Botanically Crocus sativus, linn., irideæ [vricsham]. Alias Crocus autumnalis, hybernus, officinalis. Generic from Hebrew. Perennial bulbous plant, ½ a foot high; stigmas very long, reflexed, crenate at the end; flowers violet, flowering in september and october; much resembling the common spring crocus of gardens. Saffron prepared from the stigmas, with proportion of style, of flowers; when good has sweetish, penetrating, diffusive odour, taste little bitter, with warmth and pungency, color, deep-red; brought to india from seaports of red sea, persia, cashmere; very subject to adulteration. Ordinary article is called hay-saffron; if compressed into cakes it is called cake saffron, but all cake saffron is now practically from safflower [bastard saffron]. When taken internally in moderation, saffron as a medicine gives tone to stomach, strengthens circulation, favors functions of the skin, being stimulant and antispasmodic; taken in an over-dose, acts as narcotic poison and injures the brain and nerves; supposed to promote eruption of small-pox [ammay], keep off sea-sickness, relieve palpitation of the heart, induce sleep. Veidyans [q.v.] prescribe saffron in nervous affections, unattended with vertigo, and where there is no disposition to apoplexy; also in melancholia, hysteric depressions, and typhus fever; to women after child-birth, infusion administered to prevent fever, support spirits, and to assist in carrying off the lochia; external application in ophthalmia, mixed with small portion of pounded, chebulic myrobalan [q.v.] and lime-juice [lime], and applied round eye. Gives to pharm. saffron, at present chiefly as a coloring and flavoring agent; officinal. Saffron is used as a condiment [chutney]. The stigmas contain a strong-scented volatile oil [yennay] and a rich yellow dye [shauyam] and are largely used by dyers and liquor-manufacturers; moollahs [q.v.] make ink [mashy, shye] with the dye with which they write charms. No other common species here. Saffron is a common plant first term; ex., where transl. is of second term:—Mallotus philippensis (kunkumadamara), tree; (kunkumapuvvuchettu), flower + tree; Phaseolus aconitifolius (kunkumapesara), phaseolus mungo; Rhynchocarpa fœtida (kunkumadonda), cephalandra indica. See gloss. paragraphs.——*Bastard saffron* (कुसुम्भ - kusumbha, San.; कुसुंबा - kusumbá, Mahr.; قرطم - kurtum, Ar.; شجرخسکدانه - shajarikhaskdánah, Pers.; کرڑ کا پیڑ - kararkáper, Hind.; کسم کا جہاڑ - kusamkájhár, Dec.; ಕುಸುಂಬೆ - kusumbe, Can. and Too.; కుసుంబా - kusumbá, Tel.; കസുംഭ - kusumbha, Mal.; செந்துருக்கம் - shendurukkam, Tam.). Title from resemblance of dried flowers. San. from (kus, san. to embrace); from flower used to dye clothes red. Mahr. from sanscrit. Pers. means saffron tree. Dec., &c., from sanscrit. Tam. from (shem, tam. red + turukkam, tam. crocus sativus, linn.). San. also (kamalóttara), meaning lotus, nelumbium speciosum, willd. + superior; (vahnishikha), meaning fire + flame [flame tree]; (mahárajana), meaning great dye. Ar. also (asfar), meaning yellow. Pers. also (muasfir), meaning saffron dyed; (shajarikájirah). Hind. also (kusam), meaning safflower. Can. also (kushibigida). Tel. also (kusuma) [champak]; (agnishikha) [saffron, chitramoolam, wild bachnaug]. Mal. also (chentúrakam), meaning red saffron. Tam. also (muttirukkañjedi), meaning spiny saffron. Greek κνῆκος, κνίκος. Title otherwise Coosambah, Coosam, Curdy oil plant, False saffron, Flame tree, Officinal carthamus, Parrot seed, Safflower, Sendoorkum. Botanically Carthamus tinctorius, linn., compositæ [vricsham, 74]. Generic from arabic. Annual, 1–2 feet; stem erect, cylindrical, branching near the summit; leaves oval, sessile, much acuminated, somewhat spiny; heads of flowers enclosed in a roundish spiny involucre; flowers large, deep orange. The fruits are about the size of barley [jow] corns, somewhat four-sided, white and shining like small shells [chunk]. The flowers contain two colored principles, one yellow, soluble in water, and of no use in dyeing; the other red, soluble in alkalies, and precipitable by acids from its alkaline solutions, this is carthamin. To prepare carthamin, safflower is first washed repeatedly with water to free it from the yellow substance, then treated with solution of carbonate of sodium, the liquid is saturated with acetic acid [sirkey ka tezaub] and pieces of cotton [q.v.] are immersed in it, on which the carthamin is deposited; after twenty-four hours the cotton is removed and treated with solution of carbonate of sodium, which redissolves the coloring matter; the solution is mixed with citric acid, whereby the carthamin is precipitated in red flocks; and lastly these flocks are dissolved in alchol; the solution evaporated in vacuo yields the carthamin in the form of a powder, having a deep red color with greenish iridescence; it is sparingly soluble in water insoluble in ether, but easily soluble in alcohol, yielding a fine purple solution. The dried flowers, which are like saffron, often adulterate that drug; fixed oil [yennay] from seed used in rheumatism and paralysis; seeds laxative, employed in dropsy. Poultry fatten on seeds. The light-yellow oil from seeds is used for lamps and for culinary purposes; the coloring matter of safflower attaches itself without a mordant [cauram]; it is chiefly used along with chay [chay root], for coloring cotton [q.v.], and produces various shades of pink, rose, crimson, scarlet, &c.; an alkaline extract precipitated by an acid [poolipp, tezaub], as lime-juice, will give a fine rose [gool] color either to silk [puttoo] or cotton [q.v.], but the results are not permanent; the coloring matter is not suitable to wool [pushm̃]; this dye forms the basis of rouge, which is a mixture of the dry carthamic acid and finely powdered talc [abruck]. Chinese safflower is superior to present article. No other common species here.——*Country saffron* (हरिद्रा - haridrá, San.; हळद - halada, Mahr.; كركم - kurkum, Ar.; زرد چوبه - zardchobah, Pers.; هلد - halad, Hind.; هلدی - haldí, Dec.; کونتبا سر - kunitbásar, Malay; ಅರಸಿನ - arasina, Can.; ಮಂಜಳ್ - manjal, Too.; పసుపు - pasupu, Tel.; ହଳଦି - holodi, Oor.; മഞ്ഞൾ - maññal, Mal.; කහ - kaha, Singh.; மஞ்சள் - mañjal, Tam.). Title originally given by portuguese. San. from (hari, san. yellow + dru, san. tree). Mahr. from sanscrit. Ar. means saffron. Pers. from (zard, pers. yellow + chob, pers. stick). Hind. from sanscrit. Dec. from sanscrit [false calumba]. Mal. from (mañña, mal. yellow). San. also (káñchaní), meaning gold; (ranginí), meaning coloring; (varnavatí), meaning having color; (gauri), meaning yellowish; (pítá), meaning yellow; (nishá), meaning night; (yóshitpriyá), meaning women beloved, used by all women; (krimighná), meaning insect killer. Ar. also (zarsúd); (arúkuzzafrán), meaning saffron root; (hashíshatussafrá), meaning yellow leguminous plant; (arúkussifr), meaning yellow root; (arúkussabbághín), meaning dyer's yellow root; (bakalatulkhatátíf), meaning potherb of swallows. Pers. also (dárzard), meaning yellow wood. Can. also (haladigida), meaning yellow + plant. Tel. also (pampi). Mal. also (maññakkúva), meaning yellow + curcuma. Singh. also (ratakaha), meaning foreign turmeric. Tam. also (arisanam). Greek κύπειρος ἰνδικός; Latin Cypria herba indica. Title otherwise Crocus indicus, Gold root, Haridrah, Huldee, Indian saffron, Manjal, Turmeric, Woman root, Yellow root. Botanically Curcuma [haridrah] longa, roxb., zingiberaceæ [vricsham, 144]. Alias Amomum curcuma. Curcuma from arabic. Perennial herb; leaves broad lanceolate, long-petioled; bulbs small, and with the palmate tubers inwardly of a deep orange color; flowers large, whitish, with a faint tinge of yellow, tho tuft greenish white; flowering from july to september. The fresh root has an unpleasant smell, which goes off when it becomes dried; the dried roots or bulbs occur oblong, tough, externally yellowish gray, and internally of a deep yellow color, with an aromatic smell and a bitterish acrid taste; the coloring matter of the dried root is bright yellow, soluble in alcohol and water and changed to a deep red by alkalies [cauram]; the condiment and stem-powder turmeric is the old tuber boiled, dried in sun and rubbed to powder; the drug contains an essential oil [yennay] and a coloring matter called curcumin. Country saffron or turmeric is cultivated in black loam, or in red soil rich in decayed vegetable matter; ground prepared in south in maushy [mausam] or february; on coromandel in cheitram or april and veishaukham or may; on w. coast in vrishchicam or november; ground is ploughed four or five times then hand-hoed, furrows opened and tubers deposited; weeds cleared; water used once in ten days; manure [yeroo] applied; when matured, stems and leaves become yellow and decay; the tuber alone remain, below ground; ten months after sowing tubers are hoed out; the stem, &c., is then removed and the root is brought into store; produce brought to market generally a month or two after; average price before drying three pies and after drying one anna per lb. Turmeric root is medicinally a cordial and stomachic and is prescribed internally in diarrhœa; mixed with juice of the emblic myrobalan [q.v.] it is given in diabetes and jaundice; the juice of the fresh root is anthelmintic; the burnt root mixed with margosa [neem] oil applied to soreness in the nasal organs; powdered root a favorite application to recent wounds and bruises, leech-bites, &c.; also as a collyrium in ophthalmia; mixed with cow's urine an application in skin diseases; also for cleaning foul ulcers; gives to pharm. tubers, curcuma, officinal only as a chemical test for free alkalies. The starch of the young tubers forms one of the east indian arrowroots [coova]; old tubers one of the indispensable ingredient in curries [q.v.] Hindoo females who are not widows, grind turmeric and rub it over their bodies; similarly used by all at marriage ceremonies [calyaunam] and religious festivals [pundigay]; turmeric paper is unsized paper steeped in tincture of turmeric, and dried by exposure to the air, employed as a test for alkalies, which render it reddish or brownish. The rhizomes afford without a mordant [cauram] a yellow dye [shauyam] which is brilliant, but not permanent, with alkalies changes into a deep-red; this is used by the dyers in dyeing yellow and green; women dye the face with it; it makes in conjunction with lime-juice [lime], the veishnavites' yellow tirchoornam [q.v.], or perpendicular mark on foreheads [nammam]. Madras turmeric is considered the most showy of all kinds of turmeric. There is a Tamul proverb:—கையிலே மஞ்சள் ஆனல் காரியம் மஞ்சூர்தான்—"if the hands "are dipped in turmeric water, the undertaking will prove "successful." A wild turmeric grows in mysore. Turmeric is a common plant second term; ex., where transl. is of first term:—Berberis aristata (dárhald), wood; Berberis asiatica (maramaññal), tree; Berberis lycium (dárhald), wood; Bixa orellana (kurannumaññal), monkey; Coscinium fenestratum (jhárkíhaldí), tree; Costus speciosus (kúgaimañjal), meaning arrowroot; Curcuma zedoaria (ámbihaldí), spontaneous, (janglíhaldí), jungle, (kapúrhaldí), camphor; Morinda umbellata (maramañjal), tree; Rubia cordifolia (dárhald), wood. See gloss. paragraphs.——*Monkey country saffron* (केसरी - késarí, Mahr.; कुंकुमिफल - kumkumip'hala, Conc.; زعفرانجی - zafaránjí, Hind.; شال کے پنڈو کا جہاڑ - shálkepandúkájhár, Dec.; کسمبا کلنگ - kusumbakling, Malay; ಭಂಗಾರಕಾಯಿಮರ - bhangárakáyimara, Can.; జాఫరాచెట్టు - jáp'haráchettu, Tel.; ଗୁଲ୍ବାସ - gúlbas, Oor.; കുരങ്ങുമഞ്ഞൾ - kurannumaññal, Mal.; කහ - kaha, Singh.; குரகுமஞ்சள் - kuragumañjal, Tam.). Title from red seeds like monkey's cheek. Mahr. from (késara, san. gold); from color of pulp of fruit. Conc. from (kumkuma, san. saffron, crocus sativus, linn. + p'hala, san. fruit); from color of fruit. Dec. from (shál, hind. shawl + pandú, hind. fruit + jhár, hind. tree); from soft spines of capsules. Malay from (kusumbha, san. safflower, carthamus tinctorius, linn. + kling, malay, telinga country). Can. from (bhangára, can. gold + káyi, can. unripe fruit + mara, can. tree). Tel. from (záfarán, hind. a light red tint + chettu, tel. tree). Mal. from (kurannu, mal. monkey + maññal, mal. turmeric, curcuma longa, roxb.). Singh. means saffron. Tam. from (kudakku, tam. west + mañjal, tam. turmeric), west coast turmeric. Mahr. also (shéndarí), meaning having color of red lead. Mal. also (kuppamaññal), meaning heap + turmeric. Tam. also (vennayviraiççedi), meaning butter + seed + plant; from soft pulp of fruit; (sháppiráviraiççedi), meaning light red + seed + plant. Title otherwise Anatto,

Anotta, Arnatto, Arnotta, Arnotto, Butter seed tree, Cheese dye tree, Cooppa manjal, Gold fruit tree, Heart-leaved arnotto, Kling saffron, Monkey huldee, Monkey turmeric, Roucou, Saffron tree, Shawl fruit tree. Botanically Bixa orellana, linn., bixineæ [vricsham, 14]. Alias Bixa americana. Generic is S. american name. Tree, 30 feet; leaves cordate-ovate, acuminated, entire or angular, smooth on both surfaces; sepals five, orbicular; petals five, capsule two-valved, prickly on the outside; seeds eight to ten attached to each placenta, surrounded by a red pulp; corymbs terminal, panicled; peduncles two to four-flowered. Panicles of numerous white or rose flowers with very numerous stamens, resembling large peach-blossoms [shaft auloo]; followed by green or red capsules furnished with soft spines, and enclosing seeds which have a covering of a deep orange coloring matter. American origin; naturalized, particularly on western coast. The orange-colored pulp hardens when dry, and being separated forms arnatto used for coloring; that of the naturalized indian plant is inferior to the west indian; arnotto dye is soluble in alkalies [cauram], by which means it is fixed to silk [puttoo] or wool [pushm]; when properly made it should be of a bright yellow color; the dye [shauyam] may be extracted from the seeds direct, or the pulpy matter may by boiling be separated from the seeds and made into cakes like those of lac [q.v.] or indigo [q.v.]; sometimes the coloring matter is mixed with oil before drying. The root-bark is medicinally antiperiodic and antipyretic, and the seeds slightly astringent and remedy for gonorrhœa; seeds also antiperiodic and antipyretic, but to less extent. For decoction of the root-bark; take of root-bark, in coarse powder, six ounces; water two pints and-a-half; boil on a slow fire till the liquid is reduced to one pint, and strain when cool. For tincture of root-bark; take of root-bark, in coarse powder, six ounces; proof spirit one pint; macerate for seven days with occasional agitation; strain and add more proof spirit to make one pint. Dose of decoction of root-bark is from two or four fluid ounces; of tincture, from two or four fluid drachms; and of root-bark powder from one to two drachms; doses of seeds are similar. Substituted for warburg's tincture and james' powder as an antipyretic; for quinine [kpinah] and other alkaloids of cinchona [koinah] as an antiperiodic; for copaiba as remedy for gonorrhœa. Seeds are used in malabar as beads [munkah] in necklaces [maulay] by the moplah [q.v.] women and are called moollah [q.v.]; the dye imparts flesh or pale rose color to silk [puttoo] and cotton [q.v.], it is not very durable, and requires to be renewed from time to time; dye also used by milkmen to color butter and cheese, and by others for tinging oils [yennay], spirits and varnishes [rangh]; bark yields a good cordage [naur]. Wood good for producing fire by friction; pinkish-white, soft, even-grained. No other species here.——*Saffron wood* (బందారు - bandáru, Tel.). Title from color of wood. Same as Yellow cadamba.

SAG (سگ - sag, *Pers.*). Dog [nye]. Plant first term meaning wild or inferior. Compare:—Atropa belladonna (sagangúr), and Solanum nigrum (sagangúr); both meaning dog vine. See gloss. paragraphs.——*Sebesten* (سپستان - sapistán, Pers.). See sep. title.

SAGAPENUM (سکبینج - sakbínaj, *Ar.*; کندل - kandal, *Hind.*). Title from persian. Greek σαγάπηνον, Latin Sacopenium. Title otherwise Persian asafœtida. Botanically Ferula [haulhicam] persica, wight, umbelliferæ [vricsham, 67]. Perennial deciduous herbaceous plant, 2 feet high; leaves supra-decompound, many cut acute, decurrent; first umbel sessile; flowers yellow, flowering in july and august; native of persia. The gum [goud] is found in masses formed of soft, adhesive fragments, somewhat transparent, reddish-yellow externally, pale within, of waxy or brittle consistence; its odour resembles that of garlic [lussoon] and asafœtida [q.v.], its taste is hot, nauseous, and rather bitter; sometimes adulterated with bdellium [q.v.], gandafiroza [q.v.] and other similar gum resins [googal].

SAGLAIR (సగిలేరు - sagiléru, *Tel.* sagilér *). From (sagili, tel. richness + éru, tel. river). River; Kurnool and Cuddapah districts. Tributary of the Pennair. Rises among higher peaks of hills near Cumbum. Flows in a southerly course in a deep precipitous channel along a narrow valley under the Eastern ghauts [q.v.], draining the greater portion of Budwail and Sidhout talooks. Perennial. Not navigable in any portion.

SAGO (ساگو کا پیڑ - ságúkáper, *Hind.*; ساگو کا جھاڑ - ságúkájhár, *Dec.*; سگو - sagu, *Malay*; ಸಬ್ಬಕ್ಕಿ - sabbakki, *Can.*; జవ్వుబియ్యము - dzavvubiyyamu, *Tel.*; சவ்வரிசி - shavvarisi, *Tam.*). Title from malay. Hind. from (ságú, malay, sago + per, hind. tree). Dec. from (ságú, malay, sago + jhár, hind. tree). Can. and Tel. and Tam. mean sago rice. Hind. also (ságúdánah), meaning sago grain. Dec. also (ságúcháwal), meaning sago rice. Malay also (rámbiya). The farinaceous pith from stem of many plants, mostly palms [taur].——*Bastard sago palm* (सुरमाड - suramáda, Mahr.; बिर्लिमाद - birlimád, Conc.; ماڑی - márí, Hind.; ماڑی کا جھاڑ - máríkájhár, Dec.; نیبونگ - nibung, Malay; ಬೈನಿ - baini, Can.; ಈಂದ್ - índ, Too.; కొండజీలుగు - kondajílugu, Tel.; ସଲପ - salopa, Oor.; ഇരമ്പന - írampana, Mal.; කිතුල් - kitul, Singh.; கூந்தற்பனை - kúndarbanai, Tam.). Title from the pith of old trees producing a kind of sago. Mahr. from (surá, san. spirituous liquor + mádá, mahr. young tree). Tel. from (konda, tel. hill + jílugu, tel. the plant, æschynomene aspera, linn.). Mal. from (íram, mal. moist + pana, mal. palm). Tam. from (kúndal, tam. woman's hair + panai, tam. palmyra, borassus flabelliformis, linn.); from long pendulous spadix. Can. also (bagini); (painemara). Tel. also (máre); (jirugudu); (jirugu); (chirugu); (jiguru). Mal. also (chúntappana), meaning fishing hook + palm; its branches serve for fishing lines; (ánappana), meaning elephant + palm, from trunk being favorite food of elephant. Tam. also (írambanai), meaning moist + borassus flabelliformis, linn.; (udalimbana). Title otherwise Bynee, Goondalpanay, East indian wine palm, Elephant's palm, Fishing line palm, Four-leaved caryota, Ghaut palm, Jaggery palm, Kittal, Malabar sago, Stinging palm, Toddy palm, Torn-leaved caryota, Woman's hair palm. Botanically Caryota urens, linn., palmaceæ [vricsham, 149]. Trunk erect, 50–60 feet, slightly marked with the cicatrices of the fallen leaves; leaves pinnate; leaflets subalternate, sessile, obliquely præmorse, jagged with sharp points; spathe many-leaved; spadix pendulous, 6–10 feet long; branches covered with innumerable sessile flowers, regularly disposed in threes, one male on each side, and a single female between them; male calyx three-leaved; petals three, larger than the calyx, greenish outside; female flowers on the same spadix, with the calyx and corolla as in the male; flowering in december, march; fruit or berry roundish, one-celled, size of a nutmeg [jautikye], covered with thin yellow bark; seed or nut solitary, dark colored, oval. The rind of fruit is very acrid, and if applied to the tongue will produce a burning sensation, hence specific name. Yields more toddy than any other palm, as much as a hundred pints in twenty-four hours. Most easily cultivated and abundant. The toddy [q.v.] and arrack [q.v.] are well adapted for pharmaceutical purposes. The pith furnishes an inferior kind of sago, which is made into bread and boiled as a thick gruel; the trunks are favorite food of elephant [q.v.]; jaggery [q.v.] from the sap; fruit used as masticatory [charvanam]. Fibre from the sheathing petiole used for fishing-lines and bow-strings, the indian gut of english market; it is strong and durable, and will resist for a long time the action of water, but is liable to snap if suddenly bent or knotted; the fibre of the leaf stalks called kittal [q.v.] fibre is made into ropes and used for tying wild elephants [q.v.]; seeds used by mahomedans as beads [munkah]; the woolly substance found at bottom of leaves employed for caulking ships. Outer part of stem is hard and durable and the vascular bundles crowded, black, very large; wood used as rafters in building. No other species here [taur].——*Borneo sago palm* (رامبیا - rámbiya, Malay). Title otherwise Brown sago, Common sago, Pearl sago, Rambiya, True sago. Botanically Metroxylon sagu, rottl., palmaceæ [vricsham, 149]. Specific name from malay. Alias Sagus laevis. Unarmed; 20–25 feet high; trunk thick marked by the scars of fallen leaves, and usually invested towards the summit with the withered remains of leaf stalks; above these, the large, pinnate, smooth, stalked, rather erect leaves form a crown, from out of the centre of which the alternately branched, pyramidal flower spikes arise, their bases being enveloped by smooth sheaths. Native of moluccas, sumatra and borneo. Sago is farinaceous substance from the pith; occurs in partially rounded grains of ash-white color, smooth, hard, the size of mustard seed [rayaun]. First brought to europe by marco polo [taur].——*Common sago palm* (குமுதிப்பனை - kumuthippanai, Tam.). Same as Gomooty palm.——*Indian sago palm* (ساگو کے چاول کا پیڑ - ságúkecháwalkáper, Hind.; جنگلی مدن مست کا جھاڑ - janglímadanmastkájhár, Dec.; کبنگ - kabung, Malay; ಗೊಡ್ಡುಈಚಲು - godduíchalu, Can.; రణగువ్వ - ranaguvva, Tel.; ଉରସ୍ମରୋ - orasmaro, Oor.; തുടപ്പന - tutappana, Mal.; මඩු - madu, Singh.; காமமரம் - kámamaram, Tam.). Title from habitat and the produce of the nuts. Hind. from (ságú, hind. sago + cháwal, hind. rice, oryza sativa, linn. + per, hind. tree). Dec. from (janglí, hind. wild + madanmast, dec. artabotrys odoratissimus, r. br. + jhár, hind. tree) [madmaunty]. Can. from (goddu, can. barren + íchalu, can. wild date, phœnix sylvestris, roxb.); from appearance. Mal. from (tuda, mal. thigh + pana, mal. palm, borassus); as high as thigh. Tam. from (káma, san. desire + maram, tam. tree), from flower supposed to excite venery. Hind. also (ságúdáná), meaning sago grain. Dec. also (pahárímadanmastkájhár), meaning mountain variety. Can. also (mundíchalu), meaning stunted wild date. Tel. also (varaguna), meaning possessing excellent quality; (madanakámákshi), meaning intoxication + desire + eye; (madanamastu); (varagudu); (dzavvubiyyamu), meaning sago rice. Mal. also (úránpú); (íntu) [wild date]. Tam. also (shavvarisi), meaning sago rice [sago]; (táthappanai), corruption from malayalam meaning thigh + palmyra tree, borassus flabelliformis, linn.; (mathanagámamaram), meaning intoxicating + desire + tree; (mathanagámésuvaramaram), meaning same; (úrai), from malayalam. Title otherwise Barren wild date, Broad-leaved cycas, Love tree, Stunted palmyra, Taddappanay, Wild madmaunty. Botanically Cycas circinalis, linn., cycadaceæ [vricsham, 129]. Alias Cycas rumphii, sphærica; Olus calappoides. Small palm-like tree; trunk cylindrical, unbranched, surmounted with a terminal bud, consisting in the male of a cone composed of peltate scales; leaves pinnated, thorny, springing from the apex of the trunk; cultivated in gardens; very fertile and easily propagated from both nuts and branches. Sago prepared from nuts; these are dried in sun for a month, beaten in a mortar, and the kernel made into flour. Tree also yields a clear transparent gum [gond] something like tragacanth [kateerah], which, when dried in the air, coagulates into a gummy mass. The scales of the cone are useful narcotic medicine; gum [q.v.] applied to malignant ulcers. Sago much used by forest tribes; it however will not keep long. Nuts themselves are used for snuff-boxes; cf. Bael. No other species here.

SAHASRAM (सहस्र - sahasra, *San.*). Thousand [hazaur]. Also one of the twenty-eight sheiva augamams [q.v.]. Sahasra bhojanam or feeding a thousand bramins with appropriate ceremonies is considered a highly meritorious act among hindoos. Plant first term. Ex.:—Albizzia lebbek (sahasrakí), meaning lasting for a thousand years; Celosia cristata (sahasránghri), thousand roots; Cynondon dactylon (sahasravírá), thousand powers; Nelumbium speciosum (sahasrapatra), thousand leaves. See gloss. paragraphs.——*Sahasranaumam* (सहस्रनाम - sahasranáma, San.). From (above + náma, san. name). The thousand names of Vishnoo [q.v.], Shiva [q.v.], or any deity. Sahasranauma archanay is worshipping the deity with the leaves of toolsy [q.v.] or bael [q.v.] reciting the names of the deity.

SAHEE (صحیح - sahíh, *Hind.*). From (sahha, ar. to be sound). Correct, right. Often written, even by Hindoos, in lieu of signing their names.

SAHIB (صاحب - sahíb, *Hind.*). From (sahaba, ar. to keep company). A master. The usual designation of a respectable European. Also ordinary title like English "Mr." A lacab of the prophet; and so taken as alam, as Sahib ally, double alam [ism].——*Sahiba* (صاحبة - sáhibah, Hind.). Feminine of Sahib; mistress, lady.——*Sahibakhauna* (صاحبه خانه - sáhibahkhánah, Hind.). The lady of the house.——*Sahiblog* (صاحب لوگ - sáhiblog, Hind.). English gentlemen.——*Sahibzauda* (صاحبزاده - sáhibzádah, Hind.). From (above + zádah, pers. born). Noble.

SAHYAM (सह्य - sahya, *San.*). From (sah, san. to bear). One of the seven principal chains of mountains [parvatam] in Bhauratam [q.v.]; northern portion of Western ghauts [q.v.], or mountains of Concan [sukhein].——*Sahyadry* (सह्याद्रि - sahyádri, San.). Means sahyam mountain. Western ghauts [q.v.]. See vol. I (3), (4).——*Sukhein* (സഹ്യൻ - sahyan, Mal.). Corruption of Sahyam or Sahyachellam, the Western ghauts [q.v.].

SAINT (سینٹ - sent, *Eng.*). Prefix.——*Saint mary's isles* (ತೊನಸೆಪಾರ - tonasepára, Can.). Islands; South canara district, Oodipy talook; Vasco de Gama, on his return from the East indies in 1498, landed at one of these islands now known as Cocoanut island, and called it El Padron de sancta Maria. Small islands off Tonsey.——*Saint thomas* (പരിശുദ്ധതോമൻ - parishuddhatóman, Mal.; பரிசுத்ததோமாசு - parisuttatómásu, Tam.). From (parishuddha, san. pure + tómásu, tam. thomas). The foundation of a Christian church in the Malayalam country was effected by the apostle Thomas, who, after a residence in Arabia Felix and the island of Socotra, which lay in the direct line of trade at a little distance from the most eastern point of the coast of Africa, passed over to Cranganore. After a period of labor there, he delegated the care of the infant church to others, crossed the peninsula, and arrived at Mylapore, then a populous city under a Hindoo ruler. After that he proceeded to Pekin in China, whence returning he found himself exposed to the hostility of the Bramins [q.v.], who excited a tumult against him and caused his assassination. A crowd rushed upon him with stones, and one at last transfixed him with a lance. This was on the 21st December A.D. 68, as some say at the spot now known as St Thomas' mount, and as others say at the Little mount near the Marmelong bridge [q.v.], six miles from Fort St. George. At the latter place is shown a cave as the actual site of his death. There are writers who maintain that it was not the apostle, but Thomas the disciple of Manes A.D. 277, who first preached Christianity in India; but the tradition above given is supported by good evidence. It embodies the belief of all the Syrians, Arabs and Armenians, who have from time immemorial visited the shrine of St. Thomas on pilgrimage. Mylapore or St. Thomé was visited by the ambassador of Alfred the Great of England, as recorded in the Anglo-Saxon Chronicle:—"this year, A.D. 883, Sighelm and Athelstan "carried to Rome the alms which the king had vowed to send "thither and also to India to St. Thomas and to St. Bartho-"lomew." This fact is also mentioned by William of Malmesbury, Degestis Reg. Ang., vol. ii, c. 4, p. 44. In the "Ancient Accounts of India and China by two Mahomedan travellers," of the same period, the ninth century, mention is made of a place on the coast corresponding to Mylapore, which is named Betuma. This is evidently a corrupt form of Beit-Touma, meaning both in Arabic and Syriac, the house or church of St. Thomas. Ecclesiastical records confirm the facts at least as early as the third century, and perhaps in the first century. The Apocryphal history of the Apostles, by Abdias, was written at the end of the first century. The work has undoubtedly since been greatly interpolated, but the legend of St. Thomas contained in it bears no marks of interpolation. He names Gondaphorus as the Indian king at the time of St. Thomas' visit to India. In a Tamul manuscript translated from the Latin, which was found among the Mackenzie MSS., the ruler of Mylapore bears the Tamul name of Cundappa rajah. In the Paschal Chronicle is a fragment of a work by Bishop Dorotheus, born A.D. 254, in which he relates the acts and journeyings of the Apostles. He says of St. Thomas:—"the Apostle Thomas, "after having preached the Gospel to the Parthians, Medes, "Persians, Germanians, an agricultural people of Persia, men-"tioned by Herodotus, Bactrians and Magi, suffered martyrdom "at Calamina, a town of India." St. Hippolytus, Bishop of Portus, who flourished about A.D. 220, has a memorandum to the same effect. St. Gregory Nizianzen, A.D. 370, shows the belief of the Oriental church. Answering the remark that he himself was a stranger, he says:—"What had Paul in common with the "Gentiles, Luke with Achaia, Andrew with Epirus, John with "Ephesus, Thomas with India, or Mark with Italy?" St. Jerome, A.D. 390, shows the belief of the Western church. He speaks of the mission of St. Thomas to India as a fact universally believed in his time, and mentions Calamina as the town which was the place of his death. Calamina is supposed to be Mylapore. The statements of later European travellers to india indicate the undiminished strength of the traditionary belief and the existence of a Christian church and community on the spot keeping it alive. Marco Polo, A.D. 1220 says:—"the body of "St. Thomas the Apostle lies in this province of Malabar at a "certain little town having no great population; it is a place "where few traders go, because there is little merchandize to "be got there, and it is a place not very accessible. Both "Christians and Saracens however greatly frequent it in pilgri-"mage." See Syrian. See vol. I (161).——*Saint thomas' mount* (பறங்கிமலை - parangimalai, Tam.). Tam. from (farangi, pers. european + malai, tam. mountain). Sanscrit name (bhringigiri), meaning bhringy, the three-legged sage who worshipped shiva + mountain. Town, cantonment, Hill, Railway station; Chingleput dist., Sydapett tal.; pop. 13,137; acres 1,419; lat. 13° 01′; long. 80° 16′; height 34 feet miles; from Bangalore E. 178 miles; from Cuddalore N. 95 miles; from Fort St. George S.W. 8 miles; from Madura N.E. 252 miles; from Sydapett S.W. 2 miles; from Tanjore N. 170 miles; from the sea W. 5 miles. Cantonment is laid out at base of eastern and southern sides of hill and occupies 750 acres. The hill is the most northern and least elevated of a small range running parallel to the coast, and about 5 miles west of it. The barracks and most of the buildings have an eastern aspect and are open to the sea-breeze. The soil is gravelly, and the health of the station is exceptionally good. The mount itself is a granite [caroom cull] and syenite rock, about 220 feet above sea-level. In Anglo-indian history and notably in the wars of the Carnatic [q.v.], was of great importance. In battle fought here on the 7th February 1759 Colonel calliaud, who had been summoned from south to assist in raising siege of Madras with 2,200 horse, 2,500 foot and 6 cannon, of which only 1,500 natives, 80 Europeans, and 12 artillery men were disciplined, defeated Lally with 8 guns, and 2,600 men, half of whom were Europeans and all disciplined. The fight lasted from early morning till 5 P.M. On the 20th March 1769, the treaty of 2nd April was signed here between Hyder ally and Mr. Dupie. In 1774, the mount was established as the head-quarters of the artillery. The garrison of the mount formed the major part of the force under Sir Hector Munro that ought to have saved Baillie in 1780. During its absence, only five companies of sepoys [q.v.] and four guns had been left for the protection of the Mount, and a temporary earthwork was raised to strengthen the place against attack. This has long been levelled, but a slight depression crossing the plain midway between Pullavaram and the Mount indicates the position of what went by the name of the Mahratta ditch [q.v.]. Former head-quarters of the old Madras artillery, and still an important station of that arm. The town possesses numerous military buildings, including a handsome mess-house. The church, at south end of parade ground, is one of the best-looking edifices of its kind in the country. There are besides a Wesleyan chapel at foot of the Mount steps; and a Roman catholic church, 74 feet long by 25 wide, built in 1764 by the boatmen of Madras, and dedicated to the Presentation of the Blessed Virgin. On the summit of Mount stands the curious old Portuguese church of the Expectation of the Blessed Virgin. This is built over the spot where the Portuguese in 1547 discovered the celebrated Mount Cross, attributed to the legendary evangelism of St. Thomas. The Portuguese first visiting the Mount found the Christian church in ruins and occupied by a native fakeer [q.v.]. The cross is built into the wall behind the altar in the church. The date of the cross tablet and its Pehlvi [pahlava] inscription is probably about the eighth century. The church was plundered in 1752 by the troops of Chundah sahib, under his son Razab sahib, and the advanced force of Hyder ally later in the century again plundered it. There is a double ring of stones [azhauram] surrounding a mound near St. Thomas' mount, but the cromlech [paundoo cull] belonging to this, if it existed, has disappeared. An annual festival attracts a large assemblage of Native christians. Trig. station in lat. 13° 00′ 14·79″; long. 80° 14′ 08·56″; height 250 feet; from Nandambaukam S. ¾ mile; from Sydapett S.W. 2 miles; from the sea W. 5 miles.

SAIT (سیٹھ - set, *Hind.*; శేటు - shétu, *Tel.*). From (shrésht'ha, san. best), through hindee. Title assumed by certain merchants, both Hindoo and Mahomedan [peyar].——*Senth* (سینٹھ - senth, Hind.). Same as Sait.——*Senthee* (سینٹھی - senthí, Hind.). From (senth, hind. merchant), as being used by them for pens. Same as Moonshee grass.

SAJJAUD (سجاد - sajjád, *Ar.*). From (sajada, ar. to prostrate). Frequent adorer. Lacab of the fourth Imaum. Mahomedan alam; Sajjaud ally, double alam; mostly taken by shiahs [ism].

SAKEENA (سکینہ - sakínah, *Hind.*). From (sakana, ar. to rest). Tranquillity, repose. Name of the daughter of Hoossain. Common female alam; as Sakeena bee, alam + alaumat [ism]. ——*Saukin* (ساکن - sákin, Hind.). From (sakana, ar. to become steady). Inhabitant [coody].

SALAAM (سلام - salám, *Hind.*). From (salama, ar. safe). Peace. The common word of salutation among Mussalmans [q.v.] and now in general use by all classes of persons; sent as a message, as compliments. General name for a salutation; the usual form of this is by lifting the right hand to the forehead and bending the body [namascauram].——*Salaam oon aleik* (سلام علیك - salámunalaik, Hind.). Peace be on you. Salutation amongst Mahomedans. The reply is Aleikoom oos salaam, on you be peace. Among fakeers [q.v.] it is Ishk allah or love to God.

SALAKA (సలక - salaka, *Tel.*). Small bag. Measure of capacity. 80 maunicas = 1 salaka; 8 salakas = 1 pootty [alavay, 3b]. Approximate actual value, 1 salaka = 6 cubic feet 132 cubic inches. Kistna. Compare Calam of North arcot, South arcot, Chingleput and Madura.——*Shalagay* (சலகை - shalagai, Tam.). Measure of capacity, especially for grain. 32 bullahs = 1 shalagay; 3 shalagays = 1 pothy [alavay, 3a]. Approximate actual value, 1 shalagay = 4 cubic feet 1,152 cubic inches. Coimbatore. Compare Parrah of madras. See vol. I, 609; II, 509.

SALAR (سالار - sálár, *Pers.*). Chief. Mahomedan alam; as Salar beg, alam + alaumat. Also part of lacab; as Salar jung, chief in war [ism].

SALAUBUT (صلابت - salábat, *Ar.*). From (saluba, ar. to become hard). Terror. Part of lacab; as Salaubut jung, terror of war [ism].

SALAUK (సలాకు - saláku, *Tel.*). The dent or mark on coin that denotes its goodness. A Salauk rupee is a proved coin.

SALAUT (صلوٰة - salát, *Hind.*). From (salla, ar. to pray). Same as Namauz [q.v.]. Prayer, the repetition of which is directed five times a day [roz]. See five items below. For hindoo daily prayer see Sundhyauvandanam. For hours of sunrise and sunset see Sooryan.—"*a*" *Soobh* (صبح - subh, Hind.). Between day break and sunrise.—"*b*" *Zohar* (ظہر - zohr, Hind.). Immediately after noon.—"*c*" *Asr* (عصر - asr, Hind.). Shortly before sunset.—"*d*" *Magrib* (مغرب - maghrib, Hind.). Before dusk.—"*e*" *Yishah* (عشا - ishá, Hind.). On retiring to bed.

SALEM * (سیلم - sailam, *Hind.*; சேலம் - shélam, *Tam.*). From (shéram, tam. the ancient kingdom so called) [cheram, sheram]. Canarese name (shálya), corruption of (shálika, san. weaver), village of weavers, probably by confusion.——(1) Revenue district; situated inland; between 11° 01′ and 12° 54′ N. lat., and between 77° 31′ and 79° 04′ E. long.; bounded N. by Mysore and North arcot district, E. by North arcot, South arcot and Trichinopoly districts, S. by Trichinopoly and Coimbatore districts, W. by Coimbatore and Mysore; square miles 7,529; pop. 1,962,591; language Tamul, Canarese and Teloogoo. Contains rivers Cauvery, Palaur, Ponniaur, Sanatcomauranuddy, Sharabhunganuddy, Shwetanuddy, Tirmany moottaur, Toppoor, Vasishtanuddy, Vauniyaur; mountains Arnoottimullay, Bodhamullay, Collimullay, Cullroyen, Jawaudy, Melagherry, Putchamullay, Shevaroy, Talamullay, Tennaunday mullay, Toppoor hills, Valasamullay, Vattalamullay, Yelagherry, Yeralvauny; sanitarium Shevaroy hills. The whole area of the district is represented by the following sub-areas:—Ahtoor, Dharmapoory, Krishnagherry, Namcull, Oossoor, Ootancaray, Salem, Trichengode and Tripatore talooks. For general administrative purposes, the district is distributed between the following revenue and magisterial officers, who have their head-quarters at the places shown. The pay set opposite the subordinate officers gives the grade of the corresponding charge. Collector, Salem; Subcollector, Oossoor, in charge of Dharmapoory, Krishnagherry and Oossoor talooks; Head assistant collector, Tripatore, in charge of Tripatore and Ootancaray talooks; General deputy collector, Namcull, in charge of Namcull and Trichengode talooks. Personal assistant deputy collector, Salem, in charge of Salem and Ahtoor. Tahsildars; Ahtoor, Rs. 200; Dharmapoory, Rs. 175; Krishnagherry, Rs. 150; Namcull, Rs. 225; Oossoor, Rs. 200; Ootancaray, Rs. 150; Salem, Rs. 250; Trichengode, Rs. 225; Tripatore, Rs. 200. Deputy tahsildars; Dencanicottah, Rs. 70, range situated in the south of Oossoor talook; Haroor, Rs. 70, range situated in the south of Ootancaray talook; Paramatty, Rs. 70, range situated in the south of Namcull talook; Pennagaram, Rs. 70, range situated in the west of Dharmapoory talook; Razipore, Rs. 70, range situated in the south of the Salem talook; Salem, Rs. 100, range situated in the centre of the Salem talook; Shevaroy hills, Rs. 150, range situated in the north of the Salem talook; Shunkerrydroog, Rs. 70, range situated in the west of the Trichengode talook; Tauramungalam, Rs. 70, range situated in the north-west of the Salem talook; Vaniyambaudy, Rs. 70, range situated in the north of the Tripatore talook. Similarly judicial officers:—Judge, Salem. District moonsifs, Krishnagherry, Namcull, Salem, Tripatore. Contains Registration sub-districts:—Ahtoor, Dencanicottah, Dharmapoory, Krishnagherry, Namcull, Omalore, Oossoor, Ootancaray, Paramatty, Pennagaram, Razipore, Salem, Shevaroy hills, Shunkerrydroog, Trichengode, Tripatore, Vaniyambaudy. Contains Forest ranges:—Ahtoor, Dharmapoory, Krishnagherry, Namcull, Oossoor, Ootancaray, Salem, Trichengode, Tripatore. Contains Municipalities:—Salem, Tripatore, Vaniyambaudy. Contains District board and talook boards; Salem talook board embracing Salem and Ahtoor talooks, Oossoor talook board embracing Oossoor, Dharmapoory, and Krishnagherry talooks, Tripatore talook board embracing Tripatore and Ootancaray talooks, and Namcull talook board embracing Namcull and Trichengode talooks. The following general references should be made to the preceding volumes:—general geography, I (1) to (29); general ethnology, I (29) to (109); general history, I (110) to (188); physical geography, II, 1; meteorology, II, 3; geology, II, 8; fauna, II, 21; flora, II, 26; mineralogy, II, 29. The following references in the preceding volumes will furnish details special to the district:—latitudes and longitudes, II, 47; particulars about towns, II, 48; comparative population, II, 172; location of revenue officers, II, 389; revenue settlement of the district, II, 416; registrars' and sub-registrars' stations, II, 421; rain-guage stations, II, 428; police divisions, II, 431; maps published, II, 436; survey topographical lists, II, 443; hospitals and dispensaries, II, 447; head-quarter stations of gazetted officers, II, 461; incidence of taxation, II, 463; weights and measures of the district, II, 516; zemindarries, II, 299; special public works, I, 402. A special gazetteer account of the whole district is given at II, 120. For the detailed topography of the district, reference should be made to the talook notices in the present volume, viz.:—Ahtoor, Dharmapoory, Krishnagherry, Namcull, Oossoor, Ootancaray, Salem, Trichengode, Tripatore. ——(2) Talook, Salem district. Tahsildar's pay Rs. 250. Area 1,071 square miles. Population 349,669. Language Tamul prevailing. In the west centre of district, lying between 11° 24′ and 11° 55′ N. lat. and 77° 49′ and 78° 31′ E. long. Extreme breadth from north to south is about 41 and from east to west 47 miles, average breadth being about 35 and 30 miles respectively. Bounded north by Dharmapoory talook running along the Toppoor river from the Cauvery at Sholapaudy to Chikkannanputty, and by the Ootancaray talook from that village to Malapooram; north-east by Ootancaray talook from Malapooram, whence the boundary follows the Veppaudy river to the Shevaroys, and then follows their slopes to a point on the Arnoottimullay; east by Ahtoor talook from the Arnoottimullay to the northernmost spur of the Collimullay; south by Namcull talook as far as Moonchauvady, where the south-western boundary is formed by Trichengode talook up to Poolamputty on the Cauvery, which river, from Poolamputty to Sholapaudy, separates it on the west from Coimbatore district. Chief hill ranges are the Alavye mullay, Bodhamullay, Chera royan mullay, Coodmullay, Cunjoomullay, Jergoomullay, Keddamullay, Ramasawmy mullay and Vanavausy mullay. Besides these there are detached peaks or ranges of minor importance, such as the chalk hills, &c. The greater part is composed of valleys, from five to twelve miles wide, shut in by the hills. The talook consists of a gneissic formation with black cotton [regar] and red soils [sevval munn] at the surface. Of hornblende [shalavay cull] schist there is little trace, but trap [padicutt cull] dykes and beds of magnetic iron [cauntam] are common, especially in the east centre, where they cross each other at right angles. There is very little granite [caroom cull]. Weaving [nesavoo] is carried on to a great extent, and jewellers, cloth merchants and grain merchants generally drive a good trade. Iron [auhan] works at Naumagiripett. Brass [pittalay] works in Salem, Moottoonaickanputty, Razipore and Wodoovancoorchy and dyeing [shauyam] of silk [puttoo] and twist in Salem. Coffee [q.v.] on the Shevaroys is the chief speciality. Some tea [q.v.] plants also are to be found there. Indigo [q.v.] was formerly manufactured at Ponnammapett and is now to a small extent at Shooramungalam and Camalaupooram. Principal exports are rice [q.v.], lamp-oil seeds [aumanac], lamp-oil [q.v.], ghee [q.v.], cloths, coffee [q.v.], graft mangoes [q.v.], oranges [q.v.], tobacco [pogauk], saffron [country saffron], jaggery [q.v.], groundnuts [q.v.], horse-gram [q.v.], onions [piyauz], bamboos [q.v.], bamboo mats [boriyah] and pulses [dholl]. Imports are salts [ooppoo], wheat [geung], areca [q.v.] nuts, tobacco [pogauk], pulses [dholl], saffron [country saffron], garlic [lussoon], pepper [q.v.], gingelly [q.v.] seeds, coriander [cassibor] seeds, paddy [q.v.], jaggery [q.v.], plantain [q.v.] fruits, indigo [q.v.], sugar [q.v.] and spices. The chief sources of irrigation are the Sharabhunganuddy and Tirmany moottaur. There are only twelve tanks [q.v.] having an ayacut [q.v.] of over 200 acres, viz., Ammapolliem periyairy, Anaipolliemairy, Camalaupooram chinnaairy, Gownden anicut, Neycaurputty coottay, Noothanairy, Periyairy, Ponparappy, Putnam periyairy, Shaimore, Shirapuliyairy, Somashekhara gownden's tank and Vadaman.

Camping grounds are:—Cauriputty, Chinnappanputty, Mecherry, Mettore, Moon chauvady, Mullore, Poojarryputty, Salem chalk hills and Sholapaudy. Zemindarries:—Alagaupooram, Annadaunaputty, Arasampolliem, Canaka bommamputty, Carcalvaudy, Caucauvery, Chundrashekharapooram, Cunnancoorchy, Raukiputty, Razipore, Salem, Shingalauntapooram. Places of archæological interest:—Amaragoondy, Coilvellaur, Nangavelly, Omalore, Pottipooram, Salem, Sholapaudy, Tauramungalam, Yilavamputty. Principal trig. station:—Cunjoomullay. The leading places, &c., in the talook are the following.——*Alagaupooram* (அளகாப்புரம் - alagáppuram, Tam.). From (azhagan, tam. name of a person who founded the village + pura, san. town). Sanscrit name (alakápura), meaning alacay, capital of coobairan + town. Zemindarry, Village; pop. 1,376; square miles 9; lat. of village 11° 41′; long. 78° 11′; from Salem N.W. 2 miles. Principal village in the Mittah [q.v.] of the same name. Peshcush Rs. 2,817.——*Alavye mullay* (அலவாய்மலை - alaváymalai, Tam.). From (alaiváy, tam. furnace mouth + malai, tam. mountain). The tradition being that Congana siddhar [q.v.], who practised alchemy [rasauyanam], melted rock and made gold [pon] here. Village. The inhabited portion is Alavyeputty. Place of pilgrimage, Hill; pop. 1,091; acres 4,216; lat. 11° 28′; long. 78° 10′; from Salem S.S.W. 13 miles.——*Ammapett* (அம்மாப்பேட்டை - ammáppéttai, Tam.). See sep. title.——*Annadaunaputty* (அன்னதானப் பட்டி - annathánappatti, Tam.). See sep. title.——*Arnoottimullay* (அறுநூற்றிமலை - arunúttimalai, Tam.). See sep. title.——*Auttayamputty* (ஆட்டையாம்பட்டி - áttaiyámbatti, Tam.). From (áttayán, tam. name of the founder + patti, tam. cattle-fold). Village; pop. 3,094; acres 529; lat. 11° 32′; long. 78° 06′; from Salem S.W. 12 miles. A weekly market every Sunday. Cloth chiefly sold.——*Ayodhyapatam* (அயோத்தியாப்பட்டணம் - ayóttiyáppattanam, Tam.). From (ayódhyá, san. the city so called + pattana, san. town). Village; pop. 311; acres 1,548; lat. 11° 41′; long. 78° 17′; from Salem E. 5 miles. Formerly a place of pilgrimage named after Oudh on account of its fine temple dedicated to Rama [q.v.].——*Bodhamullay* (போதமலை - póthamalai, Tam.). See sep. title.——*Carcalvaudy* (கருக்கல்வாடி - karukkalvádi, Tam. karukalvádi *). From (karumai, tam. blackness + kal, tam. stone + vádi, tam. village); from the black granite stones found in the neighbourhood. Zemindarry, Village; pop. 1,019; area 9,376 acres; lat. of village 11° 41′; long. 78° 04′; from Salem W. 10 miles. Chief village in mittah [q.v.] of same name. Peshcush Rs. 7,642.——*Caucauvery* (காக்காவேரி - kákkávéri, Tam.). See sep. title.——*Cauvery* (காவேரி - kávéri, Tam.). See sep. title.——*Chundrashekharapooram* (சந்திரசேகரப்புரம் - shandiraségarappuram, Tam.). From (chandrashékhara, san. shiva, the moon-crested lord + pura, san. town). Called so having been dedicated to Shiva [q.v.] by the founder Toolookkanna gownden of the Agrahauram village. Zemindarry, Inam village; pop. 857; area 1,944 acres; lat. of village 11° 26′; long. 78° 14′; from Salem S. 17 miles. Peshcush Rs. 1,816.——*Cunjoomullay* (கஞ்சமலை - kañjumalai, Tam.). See sep. title.——*Cunnancoorchy* (கன்னன்குறிச்சி - kannánguriççi, Tam. kannánkurchi *). From (kannán, tam. blacksmith + kuriççi, tam. village). Zemindarry, Village; pop. 2,695; area 7,791 acres; lat. of village 11° 42′; long. 78° 13′; from Salem N.E. 3 miles. Extensive iron [auhan] works former times. Peshcush Rs. 9,597.——*Dinnamputty* (தின்னம்பட்டி - tinambatti, Tam.). From (dinne, tel. mound + patti, tam. cattle-fold). Village; pop. 1,299; lat. 11° 49′; long. 78° 09′; from Salem N N.W. 12 miles. Near foot of Shevaroy hills; railway station.——*Green hills* (பச்சமலை - paççamalai, Tam.). See sep. title.——*Hastamputty* (அத்தம்பட்டி - attambatti, Tam.). See sep. title.——*Mecherry* (மேச்சேரி - méççéri, Tam.). From (méyççal, tam. pasturage + éri, tam. tank), large grazing ground. Village, Place of pilgrimage; pop. 4,181; acres 4,770; lat. 11° 50′; long. 77° 59′; from Salem N.W. 19 miles. About half way between Omalore and Sholapaudy in an unhealthy tract. Annual festival and cattle [maud] fair. Potstone [sowcaura cull] utensils manufactured.——*Moottanaud* (முட்டநாடு - muttanádu, Tam.). See sep. title.——*Moottoonaickanputty* (முத்துநாயக்கன்பட்டி - muttunáyakkanbatti, Tam.). Means moottoonaicken village. Village; pop. 776; lat. 11° 45′; long. 78° 04′; from Salem N.W. 10 miles. Large weekly grain [dhaunyam] and cattle [maud] market.——*Nangavelly* (நங்கவெள்ளி - nangavelli, Tam.). From (nangai, tam. a woman of quality + palli, tam. village). Tam. also (narasingappázhi), meaning vishnoo, the man-lion god + fountain. Village; pop. 2,023; acres 2,023; lat. 11° 46′; long. 77° 56′; from Salem W. 20 miles. Two old temples with inscriptions; market every Sunday.——*Naumagiripett* (நாமகிரிப்பேட்டை - námagirippéttai, Tam.). From (námagiri, san. the name of the goddess at námakkal + péttai, tam. suburb). Village; pop. 3,345; acres 2,973; lat. 11° 27′; long. 78° 19′; from Salem S.S.E. 16 miles. On the Vadagamcoorchy, a small stream fed by mountain torrents from the Collimullay; chiefly inhabited by rich Comaties [q.v.] who live in hovels. The mound of ashes and cinders at corner of the town testifies to former iron-works. The denuded hills indicate cause of downfall of industry, viz., want of fuel. The ore still smelted on a small scale and is very superior.——*Omalore* (ஓமலூர் - ómalúr, Tam.). See sep. title.——*Poymaun* (பொய்மான் - poymán, Tam.). See sep. title.——*Pulliputty* (பள்ளிப்பட்டி - pallippatti, Tam.). From (palli, tam. member of the caste + patti, tam. cattle-fold). Village; pop. 939; acres 966; lat. of village 11° 23′; long. 78° 18′; from Salem S. 20 miles. Near Belcoorchy.——*Raukiputty* (இராக்கிப்பட்டி - irákkippatti, Tam.). From (irákki, tam. name of a person + patti, tam. cattle-fold). Zemindarry, Village; pop. 1,033; area 552 acres; lat. of village 11° 34′; long. 78° 05′; from Salem S.W. 11 miles. Peshcush Rs. 517.——*Razipore* (இராசிப்புரம் - irásippuram, Tam.). See sep. title.——*Salem* (சேலம் - shélam, Tam.). See below.——*Sharabhunganuddy* (ಶರಭಂಗನದಿ - sharabhanganadi, Can.). From (sharabhanga, san. a sage, so called + nadí, san. river). Otherwise the Omalore river. River. Drains the Omalore division and the western slopes of the Shevaroy hills.——*Sheraroy hills* (சேர்வராயன்மலை - shérvaráyanmalai, Tam.). See sep. title.——*Shevvapett* (செவ்வாய்ப்பேட்டை - shevváyppéttai, Tam.). See sep. title.——*Shingalauntapooram* (சிங்களாந்தப்புரம் - shingalándappuram, Tam. singalántapuram *). From (simhala, san. ceylon + andan, tam. enemy + pura, san. town). Zemindarry, Village; pop. 2,693; area 5,057 acres; lat. of village 11° 25′; long. 78° 16′; from Salem S.E. 18 miles. Chief village of mittah [q.v.] of same name. Peshcush Rs. 4,555.——*Sholapaudy* (சோலப்பாடி - shólappádi, Tam.). From (shólai, tam. grove + pádi, tam. village). Village; pop. 330; acres 4,694; lat. 11° 54′; long. 77° 54′; from Salem N.W. 27 miles. Old Vishnoo [q.v.] temple and a fort. Principal portion of the village is within the Dharmapoory talook.——*Shooramungalam* (சூரமங்கலம் - shúramangalam, Tam.). See sep. title.——*Shorgamullay* (ஜாக்கைமலை - shorkkaimalai, Tam.). From (dzarugu, tel. to slide + malai, tam. mountain). Hill; lat. 11° 37′; long. 78° 16′; from Salem W. 5 miles. Otherwise Jergoomullay.——*Siddheshwaram coil* (சித்தேசுவரன்கோவில் - shittésuvarangóvil, Tam.). See sep. title.——*Tauramungalam* (தாரமங்கலம் - táramangalám, Tam.). From (táran, tam. name of founder + mangala, san. prosperity). Village, Place of pilgrimage; pop. 4,933; acres 2,381; lat. 11° 42′; long. 78° 01′; from Madras S.W. 183 miles; from Namcull N.N.W. 35 miles; from Oossoor S.S.E. 72 miles; from Salem W. 12 miles; from Tripatore S.S.W. 68 miles; from Yercaud W.S.W. 18 miles. Former head-quarters of a Deputy tahsildar, but abandoned for unhealthiness. Temple of great architectural beauty. Inscriptions of Chola, Paundy and Vijianugger dynasties [raj]. Car festival in January.——*Tennaunday mullay* (தென்னண்டைமலை - tennándaimalai, Tam.). See sep. title.——*Tirmany moottaur* (திருமணிமுத்தாறு - tirumanimuttáru, Tam.). See sep. title.——*Yercaud* (ஏர்க்காடு - érkkádu, Tam.). See sep. title.——**(3)** Deputy tahsildarry, Salem district. Pay Rs. 100.——**(4)** Town, Head-quarters of Collector, Judge, Zillah surgeon, Superintendent of Police, Superintendent of Jail, Assistant collector, Treasury deputy collector, the District forest officer, the Local fund district engineer, Tahsildar and Town sub-magistrate, Zemindarry; Salem dist., Salem tal.; pop. 67,710; acres 21,543; lat. 11° 39′; long. 78° 12′; height 947 feet; from Madras S.W. 172 miles; from Namcull N. 30 miles; from Oossoor S.E. 77 miles; from Tripatore S. 64 miles; from Yercaud S. 9 miles. In a picturesque valley about 5 miles from the foot of the Shevaroy hills on the Tirmany moottaur, which is bunded just outside the town. The valley is formed by the Shevaroy hills to the northward and a smaller and undistinguished range to the southward. It is about 7 miles in width, and is prolonged about 5 miles from Salem in an easterly direction, when by the termination of the smaller hills the country again becomes open. The town is centrally situated as regards Madras, Bangalore, Calicut, Coimbatore, Madras, Trichinopoly, and other places on the line of rail. The climate is fluctuating, the thermometer ranging in December from 60° to 87°; in January from 58° to 82°; in February from 60° to 91°; in March from 66° to 95°; in April from 72° to 95° and in May from 75° to 96°. Early in June the south-west monsoon [q.v.] falls in short but heavy and frequent showers, attended with thunder and lightning, continuing till late in September; by the end of October the north-east monsoon sets and showers recur with a very clouded sky till the middle of December. Between June and December the extremes of the thermometer are 68° and 90°. A north-easterly wind prevails steadily from the beginning of November to about or middle of February, which is for the first two months rather moist, cool and agreeable, but becomes more and more arid as the season advances. In January the wind becomes disagreeably cold in the morning and unpleasantly warm at noon, being dry and parching at both periods. After the middle of February, the wind at times variable with frequent lulls, shifts round to the south and south-west and blows from that quarter in hot puffs and with much uncertainty during April and May. Cooled by the rains of the south-west monsoon, this wind blows freshly in June and July and more moderately in the two following months. In October the wind becomes again variable, till the setting in of the north-east monsoon [q.v.]. The town is straggling and extensive, being about three miles long and two broad. On the eastern side is Salem proper, where most of the merchants and officials live; on the south is Coogay, so named from a cave in which a hermit is supposed to have lived and died. The inhabitants are weavers. The western side comprises the fort, now no longer existing, and Shevvapett, the latter named from a fair held there on Tuesdays. Adjacent to the fort are most of the public buildings, but the Jail and District court are on the road to the Shevaroy hills beyond Hastamputty. The mahaul [q.v.] in the fort was originally the palace of Ismail khan, one of the tributary chiefs of Salem. Hastamputty is the European quarter, and Shooramungalam the railway station. A London mission church. Other public buildings are the Memorial hall, the Jail, and a pretty church. The chief industry is weaving [nesavoo] in silk [puttoo] and cotton [q.v.], the grain trade comes next and the remaining population are agricultural laborers, lace-makers, cloth printers, jewellers, braziers, manufacturers of all kinds of work in bamboo, carpenters, &c. Though never a place of any military strength, its position in a much contested district has made it the scene of frequent fighting. It was first captured by Captain Wood in 1768. The Tirmany is traversed by a substantial bridge of three arches. There is a zemindarry [q.v.] of same name. Peshcush Rs. 15,959. The following are the travelling distances by road from Salem to different places :—

To	Via	Miles and Furlongs.	
Adamancottah ...	Toppoor ghaut	36	7
Ahtoor	Olapaudy	31	0
Avanashy ...	Shunkerrydroog and Erode	71	5
Bangalore ...	Toppoor ghaut, Royacottah and Oossoor.	118	0
Bellary	Bangalore, Sheerah and Hiriyore ...	305	3
Bhawauny ...	Shunkerrydroog	36	7
Caroor	Namcull	52	7
Chingleput ...	Talavausal, Oolandoorpett	171	6
Coimbatore ...	Erode and Avanashy	98	5
Coimbatore ...	Bhawauny and Avanashy	100	4
Collegaul	Cauverypooram	91	4
Cuddalore ...	Ahtoor and Vriddhauchellam	119	1
Cuddalore ...	Ahtoor and Oolandoorpett	120	0
Dharmapoory ...	Toppoor ghaut	31	3
Dharaupooram ...	Namcull and Caroor	97	7
Dindigul	Namcull and Caroor	101	4
Erode	Shunkerrydroog	37	5
Madras	Toppoor ghaut, Tripatore and Vellore ...	220	6
Madras	Munjavaudy ghaut, Tripatore and Vellore.	209	4
Madura	Namcull and Dindigul	138	5½
Mysore	Cauverypooram and Collegaul	125	2
Namcull	......	31	4
Negapatam ...	Namcull, Trichinopoly and Tanjore ...	180	1
Palamcottah ...	Caroor, Coochilanbauray and Madura ...	234	3½
Palamcottah ...	Caroor, Aravacoorchy, Dindigul and Madura.	233	4½
Palghaut	Erode and Coimbatore	129	4
Pondicherry ...	Talavausal and Vriddhauchellam ...	131	0
Pondicherry ...	Talavausal and Oolandoorpett	131	7
Quilon	Dindigul and Goodalore ghaut	316	2
Quilon	Dindigul, Madura, Shreevillipoottore and Aryanoauv ghaut.	292	2½
Royacottah ...	Toppoor ghaut	70	6
Talavausal ...	Olapaudy and Ahtoor	41	4
Tanjore	Namcull and Trichinopoly	124	1
Trichinopoly ...	Namcull and Tottiyam	86	7
Tripatore ...	Munjavaudy ghaut	70	0
Tripatore... ...	Toppoor ghaut	81	
Vellore	Munjavaudy ghaut and Tripatore ...	125	2
Vellore	Toppoor ghaut and Tripatore	136	1
Vriddhauchellam	Ahtoor and Talavausal	81	3
			1

SALEP (خصى الثعلب - khusiyussalab, *Ar.*; ثعلب مصرى - salabmisrí, *Pers.*, *Hind.* and *Dec.*; సాలామిసిరి - sálámisiri, *Tel.*; സാലാമിസ്രി - sálámisri, *Mal.*; சாலாமிசிரி - shálámisiri, *Tam.*). Title abbreviated from arabic. Ar. from (khusiya, ar. testicle + salab, ar. fox); from form of tubers. Pers. from (salab, ar. fox + misrí, ar. egyptian). Tel. from hindostany. Mal. from hindostany. Tam. means egyptian salep. Tel. also (górutsúttugadda), meaning whitlow + root; (ráyedurudumpa), meaning king + bamboo, bambusa arundinacea, willd. + root; (vedurugadda), meaning bamboo + root. Mal. also (káttuttékkumaravázha), meaning wild + teak + parasite. Greek ὄρχις; Latin Satyrium; cf. english dogstone, foxstone, harestone and goatstone. Title otherwise Bamboo root, Egyptian salep, Fox's testicles, Oriental salep, Salep misry, Whitlow root. Distinguish from Jalap. Botanically Eulophia sp., orchidaceæ [vricsham, 141]; as Eulophia campestris, wall.; Eulophia herbacea, lindl., &c. Article is imported from the north. The bulb radix satyrii, or radix salep, used as a vegetable drug; natives ascribe great virtues as an aphrodisiac; it is simply nutritive, and idea of aphrodisiac properties is derived from the tubers having a resemblance in shape to the testes; the chief constituent of salep is a kind of mucilage. Most species of orchis are provided with tubers capable of furnishing salep.

SAL GEM (ملح الحجر - milhulhajar, *Hind.*). Title from salt like crystal [palingoocull]. From (milh, ar. salt + hajar, ar. stone). Commercial name for native rock-salt [sondah namak].

SALWA (సాల్వ - sálva, *Tel.*). From the country so called, near Narrainavaram in North arcot district. A family of Reddies [q.v.], who migrated from neighbourhood of Pittapore in delta [conamoogam] of Godavery, to country at base of Nagary hills about the eighth century.——*Saulvancooppam* (சாலுவங்குப்பம் - sháluvanguppam, Tam.). From (sháluvan, tam. petty ruler + kuppam, tam. village). Village; Chingleput dist., Chingleput tal.; pop. 363; acres 944; lat. 12° 40′; long. 80° 16′; from Chingleput E. 15 miles; from Sydapett S. 25 miles; from the sea W. ½ mile. Contains a tiger [pooly] cave two miles N. of Seven pagodas [q.v.]. Inscriptions.

SALYE (سلاكى - saláí, *Hind.*). From (sallakí, san. indian olibanum). Same as Indian olibanum.

SAM (صم - sam, *Hind.*). Sharp.——*Samsaum* (صمصام - samsám, Ar.). Sharp sword. Part of lacab; as Samsaum ood dowla, sword of the empire [ism].

SAMAD (صمد - samad, *Hind.*). From (samada, ar. to go to); from recourse being had to him in exigencies. Attribute of God [allah]. Common alam; as Abd oos samad, slave of god [ism].

SAMADARAH (കരിഞൊട്ട - karinnotta, *Mal.*; සමදරා - samadará, *Singh.*; நிபம் - níbam, *Tam.*). Title from singhalese. Mal. from (kari, mal. black + ñotta, mal. the tree), from dark brown outer bark. Tam. from (nípa, san. low ground), commonly applied to the common cadamba [q.v.] anthocephalus cadamba, miq. Mal. also (ñotta). Title otherwise Caringhote, Niepa bark tree, Niota. Botanically Samadera indica, gærtn., simarubeæ [vricsham, 33]. Generic name from singhalese. Alias Niota lamarckiana, tetrapetala; Vittmannia elliptica. Niota from malayalam. Tree, 30–35 feet; leaves alternate, oblong, elliptical, very long; calycine segments four to five each, marked with an external gland; petals five, longer than the calyx; flower-bearing peduncles longer than the leaves, pendulous, compressed, axillary or terminal, divided at the apex into a small umbel; drupe with a thick pericarp; flowers yellowish white. Fruit is oval, 1½ by 1 inch, and is one-seeded; its surface is coriaceous, smooth, or slightly reticulated, and of a brown color; the seed is brown and curved; the bark and the seeds are very bitter; the bark from the smaller branches occurs in quills from half an inch to one inch in diameter, its external surface is minutely fissured in every direction, of a dark brown color, with light-colored patches here and there caused by exfoliation of the suber; beneath the suber, which can be easily separated, the bark is yellowish-white, and this color extends through its substance to the inner surface; the bark has a short fibrous fracture and bitter taste like quassia. An infusion of the wood used medicinally as a general tonic, and is substitute for infusion of quassia; it is of a light lemon [q.v.] color and a good vehicle for the administration of iron [auhan], iodide of potash; bark febrifuge; oil [yennay] extracted from kernels of fruit is application in rheumatism; bruised leaves externally applied in erysipelas; seeds are worn round the neck as a preventive of asthma and chest affections. The wood is light but durable, and is used for shoes and other articles; it takes a good polish. No other species here.

SAMBRAUNY (देवधूप - dévadhúpa, *San.*; لوبانى عود - lobáníúd, *Hind.*; ಸಾಂಬ್ರಾಣಿ - sámbráni, *Can.*; సాంబ్రాణి - sámbráni, *Tel.*; സാംബ്രാണി - sámbráni, *Mal.*; சாம்பிராணி - shámbiráni, *Tam.*). Gum-resin [googal] of Styrax, Boswellia and Hardwickia species. See below. Natives call this female frankincense, and dammer [coongilyam, dammer] male frankincense.——**(1)** *Sambrauny poo* (अश्मपुष्प - ashmapushpa, San.; عودكاست - údkásat, Hind.; సాంబ్రాణిపువ్వు - sámbránipuvvu, Tel.; சாம்பிராணிப்பூ - shámbiránippú, Tam.). Title and Tam. from (above + pú, tam. flower). San. from (ashma, san. stone + pushpa, san. flower). Hind. from (úd, ar. benzoin + sat, hind. essence). Tel. from (sámbráni, tel. benzoin + puvvu, tel. flower). Benzoic acid. Acidum benzoicum of chemists.——**(2)** *Common sambrauny* (சாம்பிராணி - shámbiráni, Tam.). Same as Benzoin.——*Foreign sambrauny* (பரங்கிசாம்பிராணி - parangisámbiráni, Tam.). Same as True olibanum.——*Madeiyan sambrauny* (ചുരളി - churali, Mal.; மடையன்சாம்பிராணி - madaiyansámbiráni, Tam.). Title and Tam. from (madaiyan, tam. fool + shámbiráni, tam. frankincense). Mal. also (kolla). Tam. also (kolávu), used in tinnevelly. Gum-resin of Hardwickia binata and pinnata [yaipy].——*Malacca sambrauny* (மலாக்காச்சாம்பிராணி - malákkáççámbiráni, Tam.). Same as benzoin [q.v.].

SAMJHASH (سمجهايش - samjháish, *Hind.*). From (samjhána, pers. to make one understand). Satisfaction. Explaining. Reckoning.

SAMPUNGY (சம்பங்கி - shambangi, *Tam.*). Tamul corruption of (champaka, san. the tree, so called). Hindoo 2nd or pers. name. Common among non-bramins [peyar].

SAMT (سمت - samt, *Ar.*) [azimuth, zenith]. Direction [dic, tisay].——*Sammat* (سمت - samat, Hind.). Corruption of (samt, ar. direction). A sub-division of a talook [q.v.], corresponding to a hobly [q.v.]. Sammatdar is the manager thereof. Compare Taraf and Zillah.——*Samoot* (سمت - samt, Hind.). Means road or way. Quarter.

SAMULCOTTAH (చామర్లకోట - tsámarlakóta, *Tel.* sámalkót *). From (sámari, tel. gymnast + kóta, tel. fort). Town, Cantonment, Canal; Godavery dist., Cocanada div.; pop. 7,313; lat. 17° 03′; long. 82° 13′; from Cocanada N.N.W. 9 miles; from the sea W. 10 miles. On right side of a stream falling into Bay of Bengal. Connected with Cocanada, Dowlaishweram and Rajahmundry by a navigable canal. The cantonment, north-west of village, is about three-quarters of a mile in diameter. Former residence of rajah of Pittapore. Ceded by Nizam in 1766. Originally a sanitarium for troops in Godavery district. Barracks were built in 1786. Fort demolished in 1838. Abandoned as a military station in 1868, but owing to Rumpa disturbances of 1879, two companies under a British officer were stationed here. There are a few tanks in the neighbourhood, but there are good wells in the cantonment. The soil is alluvial and the surrounding country cultivated. Lutheran church mission station.

SAN (سن - san, *Hind.*). From (saná, ar. to turn round); so a single revolution of the sun. Year. The old arabic year prior to fusly. Consisted of four seasons each of three months. These months were lunar, and to adapt the year to solar the arabs added a month [nasee] at the end of every three years [hijra].——**(1)** The seasons [ritoo] were as follows:—"*a*" *Khareef* (خريف - kharíf, Ar.; خزان - khazán, Pers.; پتجهڑی - patjharí, Hind.). Ar. from (kharafa, ar. to pluck or gather). Pers. from (khazz, pers. woollen cloth); which people put on during the season. Hind. from (pat, hind. leaf + jharí, hind. falling). Autumn. Began when the sun entered Libra [meezaun]. September to November.—"*b*" *Shitah* (شتاء - shitá, Ar.; زمستان - zamistán, Pers.; جاڑا - járá, Hind.). Ar. means intensely cold. Pers. from (zam, pers. cold + sitán, pers. denoting excess). Hind. from (jada, san. chill). Hind. also (sarmá); (thandkálá). Winter. Began when the sun entered Capricornus [jaddy]. December to February.—"*c*" *Sayeef* (صيف - saif, Ar.; ربيع - rabí, Pers.; بہار - bahár, Hind.). Hind. also (basant). Means to stay. Also called Rabee. Spring. Began when the sun entered aries [hamel]. March to May.—"*d*" *Kyze* (قيظ - kaiz, Ar.; تابستان - tábistán, Pers.; گرما - garmá, Hind.; دھوپکالا - dhúpkálá, Dec.). Means the intense heat from the auroral rising of the pleiades [sooreiyah] to that of canopus [sooheil]. Summer. Began when the sun entered cancer [sartaun]. June to August.——**(2)** *Sanwar* (سنوار - sanvár, Hind.). From arabic. Yearly [saul].——*Saul* (سال - sál, Hind.). Year. 12 maheenas or lunar months = 1 saul [caulam]. Same as Samvatsaram [caulam, 4], Varsham [caulam, 2]. Saul e cumree is lunar year. Saul e einda is ensuing year. Saul e haul is current year. Saul e muzcoor is above-mentioned year. Saul e shumsee is solar year. Saulgoojasta is last year [hijra].——*Sonnut* (سنت - sanat, Hind.). Plural Sanwaut. Years.——*Sonnat rupee* (سنات روپیہ - sanátrúpiya, Hind.). An old rupee. Formerly rupees were distinguished by the years in which coined, and after four or five years suffered a depreciation and became Sonnat [rupee].

SANA (सन - sana, *San.*). Old.——*Sanatcomauran* (सनत्कुमार - sanatkumára, San.). From (sanat, san. bramha, the ancient + kumára, san. son). One of the four sons of Bramha [q.v.].——*Sanautanan* (सनातन - sanátana, San.). Means eternal. One of the secondary avatars [avatar] of Vishnoo [q.v.]. Distinguish from Sautauny.

SANAH (ثنا - saná, *Hind.*). Praise, congratulation. Prefixed to an alam forms a lacab; as Sanah ally, ally's praise [ism].

SANDAL (चन्दन - chandana, *San.*; गंध - gandha, *Mahr.*; श्रीगांद - shrígánda, *Conc.*; شجر صندل ابيض - shajarisandaliabyaz, *Ar.*; درخت صندل سپيد - darakhtisandalisupíd, *Pers.*; سفيد چندن - sufedchandan, *Hind.*; صندل کا جهاڑ - sandalkájhár, *Dec.*; ಶ್ರೀಗಂಧಮರ - shrígandhamara, *Can.*; గంధపుచెట్టు - gandhapuchettu, *Tel.*; ചന്ദനം - chandanam, *Mal.*; සඳුන් - sandun, *Singh.*; சந்தனம் - shandanam, *Tam.*). Title from arabic. San. from (chand, san. to gladden). Mahr. means fragrant. Conc. from means holy fragrance. Ar. from (shajar, ar. tree + sandal, ar. sandalwood + abyaz, ar. white). Pers. from (darakht, pers. tree + sandal, ar. sandal + supíd, pers. white). Hind. from (sufed, hind. white + chandana, san. sandalwood). Dec. from (sandal, ar. sandalwood + jhár, hind. tree). Can. from (shrí, san. holy + gandha, san. sandal + mara, can. tree). Tel. from (gandha, san. fragrance + chettu, tel. tree). Singh. from sanscrit. Tam. from sanscrit. San. also (pañchasugandha), meaning five good scented trees; (anindita), meaning not shunned; (shrígandha), meaning holy fragrance; (gandhasára), meaning essence of fragrance; (malayaja), meaning produced in malayam; (bhadrashrí), meaning auspicious + grace; (shríkhanda), meaning auspicious portion; (harichandana), meaning yellow sandal; (tailaparna), meaning produced in tilaparnam, is yellow sandal; (góshírsha), meaning produced in the cow head-like peak of malayam, is yellow sandal; (krishnachandana), meaning black sandal; (valgaka), meaning lovely. Hind. also (katchandan); (gandsárá), from sanscrit. Can. also (gandháchekke), meaning chip of sandalwood. Tel. also (chandanapuchettu), meaning sandal + tree; (malayamu); (raktakrishnachandanamu), meaning red + black + sandal; (krishnachandanamu), meaning black + sandal; (tellachandanamu), meaning white sandal. Singh. also (sudusandun), meaning white sandal. Tam. also (ulósitham), meaning red sandal; (kulavuri), meaning shining is red sandal. Greek σάνταλον, σάνδαν. Late greek ξύλα σαγάλινα. Lignum santalinum album vel citrinum, Lignum santali of chemists. Title otherwise Algum, Almug, Chandanam, Malayam tree, Sandalwood, Saunders, True sandalwood, White sandalwood. Botanically Santalum album, linn., santalaceæ [vricsham, 116]. Generic name from sanscrit through arabic. Alias Sirium myrtifolium. Tree, 20–25 feet; branches numerous, much dividing and spreading, and forming nearly spherical heads; leaves opposite on short petioles, oblong, smooth, entire, glaucous below; thyrsi axillary and terminal, shorter than the leaves; pedicels opposite, lower pair of each thyrsi usually three-flowered; flowers numerous, small, first straw-colored, afterwards deep ferruginous purple, inodorous; calyx campanulate, four-cleft; corolla none; berry round, smooth, black when ripe, succulent, crowned with the calyx, one-celled; nut solitary; flowering nearly all year; found up to 4,000 feet; the trees attain their prime in twenty to thirty years, and have then trunks as much as a foot in diameter; often cultivated in gardens. Essential volatile pale yellow oil [yennay] is obtained by distillation of the heart-wood and roots; its specific gravity is about 0·980. Sandal is one of the trees of the booddhistic [booddha] paradise. It is a somewhat delicate tree, is killed outright by fire, is very impatient of injuries to the roots and bark, and requires shade and protection while young; the value of the wood is dependent upon a volatile oil which is contained in the heart-wood only, and in order that this oil may be developed in the highest possible degree, it is necessary that the growth of the tree should be slow, consequently sandalwood grown in arid situations on poor stony soil is, though small, of far more value than is that produced by large well-grown trees growing in moist situations and in richer soil; sandalwood is not eaten by white-ants [q.v.], and its contained oil preserves it from decay in a remarkable degree, of which the present collection of old sandal roots left in the ground for many years past is a conclusive proof; in former times it was the custom not to uproot, but to fell, sandal trees, whereas for many years past the trees have been uprooted, and the roots, which contain a higher percentage of oil than the wood, are in great demand and command high prices. The method of preparation is as follows:—the trees having been uprooted are roughly deprived of bark and of some of the sap-wood; the trunks are then sawn off above the roots, cut into lengths, all the white wood removed, the billets adzed and subsequently planed and smoothed, the roots adzed and freed of all adhering bark, mud and white wood, and the various products, billets, chips, small pieces, hollow wood, saw powder, &c., collected and classified. Sandalwood oil is procured from the wood by distillation, the roots yielding the largest quantity and finest quality of oil; the body of the still is a large globular clay pot [chatty] with a circular mouth, and is about 2½ feet deep by 6½ in circumference at the bilge; no capital is used, but the mouth of the still, when charged, is closed with a clay lid having a small hole in its centre, through which a bent copper tube about 5½ feet long is passed for the escape of the vapour; the lower end of the tube is conveyed inside a copper receiver, placed in large porous vessel containing cold water; when preparing the sandal for distillation, the white or sap-wood is rejected, and the heart-wood is cut into small chips, and distillation is slowly carried on for ten days and nights, by which time the whole of the oil is extracted; as the water from time to time gets low in the still, fresh supplies are added from the heated contents of the refrigerator; the quantity of oil yielded by wood of good quality is at the rate of 10 oz. per maund, or 2·5 per. cent; it is transparent and of a pale yellow color, and has a resinous taste [raul] and sweet peculiar smell, which is best appreciated by rubbing a few drops of the oil on the warm hand; its specific gravity is about 0·980; the average price is about Rs. 8 per lb. The finest sandalwood is that which has grown slowly on rocky, dry and poor land; the trees found in a rich alluvial soil, though of very fine growth, produce no heart-wood and are consequently valueless; the wood is reduced, by rubbing on a stone, to a fine powder; the roots and chips go to the still for oil. The wood ground up with water to the consistence of paste is a common emulsion in cutaneous inflammations; the oil, a remedy in gonorrhœa, superior to copaiba and cubebs [cubeb pepper]; veidyans [q.v.] prescribe the wood in powder in ardent, remittent fever from its supposed sedative and cooling qualities; in cases of morbid thirst, the powder is taken in cocoanut [q.v.] water [yilaneer]; it is rubbed to the body after bathing in the hot weather, with a view to cool the system and check too copious a perspiration; the best remedy for prickly heat [q.v.]; gives to pharm. non-officinal sandalwood oil, like copaiba. Wealthy natives add sticks of sandalwood to the funeral pyre [shoodcaud]; the wood rubbed up into a paste, is used by bramins [q.v.] for caste-marks [naumam]; wood and saw-dust are burned as incense in temples; wood is a preservative against insects; large quantities of sandalwood oil are annually exported; the oil forms the basis of many scents. Two kinds of the wood known in commerce, white and yellow :—white sandalwood is coated with thick compact bark having a grey and brownish epidermis, the wood is very hard heavy susceptible of a fine polish, in billets of middling size, is nearly inodorous, its taste being slightly bitter; yellow or citron sandalwood is straight or twisted, lighter than water when taken from the trunk, heavier if from the roots in yellow, fawn-colored, or reddish billets, slightly shining, of middling hardness, taking a fine polish, and being very easily cleft; wood cannot be procured of a large size; the sap-wood and branches are worthless; heart-wood is used for carving, for incense and perfume. A variety with the wood almost scentless is found on eastern coast mountains; only differs slightly in the shape of the leaves which are more lanceolate, and in the scales or lobes of the disk being jagged. What is called agil cuttay [eagle wood] in tamul and agarkah khor in hindostany is reddish-colored resinous fragrant bitter wood, sometimes added in powder to powdered sandalwood to increase its fragrance. There is a Tamul proverb :—அரைக்கினும் சந்தனம் அதன் மணம் அருது—" though sandalwood be rubbed, its fragrance " will not be destroyed." There is another :—சத்துக்கள் ஓடு சத்துக்கள் சேர்வார், சந்தனத்தோடு கருப்பூரம் சேரும்—" the powerful associate with the powerful, sandal " paste mixes with camphor [q.v.]." Sandal with Mahomedans is a ceremony in honor of saints [walee] celebrated the day prior to Oors [q.v.], when pots containing sandal [q.v.] paste, &c., are carried in procession through town and placed at the tomb [durgah] for use of votaries [cawder wally].——*Bastard sandal* (காட்டுச்சந்தனம் - káttuççandanam, Tam.). Tam. means wild sandal. Same as Deccany deodar.——*False sandal* (నక్కెరు - nakkéru, Tel.). Title from yellow wood. Tel. also (kondanakkera), meaning hill + the tree; (úranakkera), meaning village + the plant. Title otherwise Hog plum [wild mango], Mountain plum, West indian sea-side plum. Botanically Ximenia americana, willd., olacineæ [vricsham, 38]. Straggling shrub, 15 feet; calyx small, four-cleft; petals four, very hairy inside; thorns axillary or terminating the branchlets, solitary, bearing occasionally leaves or flowers or even smaller thorns; leaves alternate, oval, emarginate; peduncles four to six-flowered; drupe oval, flesh thick; nut crustaceous; flowers small, dull white, fragrant; smelling of cloves [lavangam]. Small, oval, red or yellow pulpy fruit, an inch long, of an acid-sweet aromatic taste, with some degree of austerity; when ripe eaten by the natives; kernels also eaten taste much like filberts [findak]. Powder of wood used by bramins in religious ceremonies. Wood yellow, somewhat like sandalwood. No other common species here.——*Santoor* (سنتور - santur, Malay). Same as Malay red wood.

SANDRACH (चंद्रस - chandrasa, *Mahr.*; سندروس - sandrús, *Ar.* and *Pers.*; چندروس - chandrús, *Hind.*; چندرس - chandras, *Dec.*; சாந்திராசு - shándirásu, *Tam.*). Title from arabic. Mahr. from hindostany. Ar., &c., from persian. Title otherwise Citrus wood, Jointed arborvitæ, Pounce tree, Sandarach gum tree. Botanically Callitris quadrivalvis, vent., coniferæ [vricsham]. Evergreen ornamental tree 20 feet high; leaves flattened, articulated; female catkin tetragonal, with four oval valves each furnished with a point, and two of which bear seed only. Sandrach resin exudes naturally from the bark, but is commonly obtained from incisions. Formerly of wide renown as a medicine, now only an ingredient in varnishes [rangh]. Imported from Morocco.——*Sandroos* (سندروس - sandrús, Hind.). Same as Sandrach.

SANG (سنگ - sang, *Pers.*). Stone [cull].——*Sang i samauk* (سنگ سماق - sangisamák, Hind.; చలవరాయి - tsalavaráyi, Tel.). Hind. from (sang, pers. stone + samák, pers. sumach). Tel. from (tsalava, tel. coolness + ráyi, tel. stone). Tel. also (chandrakántamu), meaning moon + loving; from melting in moonlight. Porphyry. Granitic porphyry [dhoomra cull] is common in Mysore. It takes a fine polish, and is used in making ornaments of public buildings. It is chiefly composed of large masses of felspar [mauvayira cull] in a small grained mixture of grey quartz [vencull] and black mica [abruck, ratnam, shalavay cull].——*Sang i sitaura* (سنگ ستارہ - sangisitárah, Pers.). Pers. from (sang, pers. stone + sitárah, pers. star). Gold stone. A fossil. The ground is of a cinnamon [q.v.] color; it is opaque and completely marked and engrained in every part with small golden-colored speckles, which give it the appearance of glass filled with gold dust [ratnam].——*Sang i soolimauny* (गोमेद - góméda, San.; جزع - jaza, Ar.; سنگ سلیمانی - sangisulaimáni, Pers.; సులిమానురాయి - sulimániráyi, Tel.). San. from (gó, san. cow + méda, san. fat); of the color of cow's fat; being same as sardonyx and cinnamon stone. Pers. from (sang, pers. stone + sulaimán, ar. solomon). Tel. from (sulimánu, tel. solomon + ráyi, tel. stone). Onyx. A species of agate [akeek], in which the silicious particles are arranged in alternating horizontal layers of opaque, white and translucent, grey or brown. Found in the Godavery [ratnam].

SANGCOOPPY (कुण्डली - kundalí, *San.*; वनजाई - vanajái, *Mahr.*; سنگ کوپی - sangkúpí, *Hind.*; اسمدھاری - ismdhárí, *Dec.*; ವಿಷಮಧಾರಿ - vishamadhári, *Can.*; పిసినిక - pisinika, *Tel.*; ശങ്കുകുപ്പി - shankunkuppi, *Mal.*; වල්ගුරඳ - valguranda, *Singh.*; சங்கங்குப்பி - shanganguppi, *Tam.*). Title from tamul. San. means circular [hazaurdanah]. Mahr. from (vana, san. forest + jái, san. jasminum auriculatum, vahl.). Hind. from (sang, hind. companion + kúpí, hind. acalypha indica, linn.), by corruption. Dec. from canarese. Can. from (visha, san. poison + dhara, san. holder), from bitter root and leaves. Tel. from (pisini, tel. gum) [neilgherry satin wood]. Mal. from tamul [crow creeper]. Singh. from (val, singh. wild + gúranda, singh. celtis cinnamomea). Tam. from (shangu, tam. the plant, azima tetracantha, lamk. + kuppai, tam. heap of rubbish). Can. also (kundali). Tel. also (pisangi); (nallauppi), meaning black + capparis sepiaria, linn.; (érupittsa), meaning river + the plant; (ótipisinika), meaning river + the tree; (úti), meaning strong [neilgherry satin wood]; (takkólamu). Mal. also (nírnoççi), meaning water + vitex negundo, linn. [water notchy]. Tam. also (pínárisanganguppi), meaning excrement + to smell + the plant; (pínárisangu), meaning excrement + to smell + azima tetracantha, lamk. Title otherwise Smooth volkameria. Botanically Clerodendron [bhaurgam] inerme, gærtn., verbenaceæ [vricsham, 102]. Alias Clerodendron buxifolium; Volkameria inermis. Climbing branched shrub; leaves small, smooth, shining, oval or elliptic; cymes axillary, as long as the leaf, three-flowered, collected into a terminal corymbose panicle; flowers white; the tubes of the corolla long and slender, greenish-white; common along the coast, near the sea; flowering nearly all the year. Juice of root and leaves bitter, prescribed as alterative in scrophulous and venereal affections; given either pure, or in conjunction with castor-oil [lamp-oil]. The medicinal properties closely resemble those of chiretta [q.v.]. Often cultivated for hedges [vaily]. Another species is infortunatum [saraswaty's leaf].

SANNAM (సన్నము - sannamu, *Tel.*; சன்னம் - shannam, *Tam.*). Slender. Plant first term. Ex., where transl. is of second term :—Acacia farnesiana (sannajáli), acacia; Eragrostis plumosa (sannapurulehullu), parrot + grass. See gloss. paragraphs.——*Sanna biyyam* (సన్నబియ్యము - sannabiyyamu, Tel.). From (above + biyyamu, tel. rice). Paddy. Anantapore, Bellary and N. arcot. Capila sannabiyyam means brown; Garica sannabiyyam means bent grass, cynodon dactylon, pers., perhaps from stalks; Poolla sannabiyyam means whitish or reddish; Tella sannabiyyam means white [paddy].——*Sannauloo* (సన్నాలు - sannálu, Tel.). Means fine grain. A Vizagapatam paddy. Caushy sannauloo means benares; Eety sannauloo means lance, as fine as lance, point; Gutty sannauloo means solid, from hard rice; Jaltaur sannauloo means gold lace, from color and fineness; Vanka sannauloo means curved, from shape of grain; Yerra sannauloo means red, from color of grain [paddy].

SANOO (చను - tsanu, *Tel.*). Breast.——*Sanapaul* (చనుపాలు - tsanupálu, Tel.). Short for (tsanupáluvittulu), meaning breast-milk seeds, from paste of powdered seeds being applied in ophthalmia with breast milk. Same as Black horse-gram.——*Sanoobanda* (చనుబండ - tsanubanda, Tel.). From (tsanu, tel. breast + banda, tel. rock). Zemindarry, Village; Kistna dist., Vissanapett division; pop. 2,869; lat. of village 17° 02′; long. 80° 50′; from Masulipatam N.N.W. 61 miles; from Tirvore S.E. 14 miles. Built by the Zoopully [q.v.] zemindar about 100 years ago. Peshcush Rs. 1,357.

SAPPAN (पत्राङ्ग - pattránga, *San.*; पतंग - patanga, *Mahr.*; सप्पंगु - sappangu, *Conc.*; بقم - bakm, *Ar.* and *Pers.*; پتنگ کا پیڑ - patangkáper, *Hind.*; پتنگ کا جہار - patangkájhár, *Dec.*; ساپنگ - sápang, *Malay*; ಪತಂಗ - patanga, *Can.*; ಚಪ್ಪಂಗ - chappanga, *Too.*; బుక్కాపుచెట్టు - bukkápuchettu, *Tel.*; ବୋକ୍ମୋ - bokmo, *Oor.*; ചപ്പങ്ങം - chappannam, *Mal.*; පතංගි - patangi, *Singh.*; வத்தங்கி - vattangi, *Tam.*). Title from malayalam. San. from (patra, san. leaf + anga, san. body); from dye used in decorating body in fancy lines and figures. Mahr., &c., from sanscrit. Tel. from arabic. Mal. from (chappu, mal. leaf + anga, san. body), cf. sanscrit. Singh. from sanscrit. Tam. from sanscrit. San. also (raktamukta), meaning blood + liberator; from red dye. Pers. also (bakmikirmiz), meaning crimson sappan. Hind. also (tairí), referring to pods. Can. also (patangachekke); (chapengamara); (sappanga) [long zedoary]. Tel. also (bakánuchettu), by corruption from arabic; (patangachettu); (ókánuchettu). Tam. also (shappangam); (pattanam); (vattókku), meaning strong teak. Title otherwise Brasiletto, Brazil wood, Buckum, Narrow-leaved sappan, Red-wood tree, Vattangy. In mediæval commerce known as brazil wood, from color of the braise or hot coals of its wood; when on the discovery of brazil a similar dye wood was found there, the name of the indian wood was given to both country and dye; hence the term brazil; the present article is now generally called either sappan or buckum; botanically Cæsalpinia [coobairaucshy] sappan, linn., leguminosæ [vricsham, 48]; specific name from malayalam. Tree 40 feet, armed; pinnæ ten to twelve pair, leaflets ten to twelve, unequal-sided, obliquely oval-oblong, emarginate, pale on the under side; terminal panicles; legumes compressed, glabrous, elliptic-obovate, obliquely truncated, cuspidate at the apex, three to four-seeded; flowers yellow; flowering in hot season; common especially on w. coast. Wood contains much tannic and gallic acids, and is a good substitute medicinally for log-wood; decoction is astringent in diarrhœa; mentioned in pharm., but non-officinal. Cultivated on w. coast for sake of red dye [shauyam] yielded by chips of wood in decoction; the straw of palghaut mats [boriyah] is dyed with this; so also cheap cloths in many places; powder [goolaul] used at holy [q.v.] festival is extracted from it; a custom prevails among malabar moplahs [q.v.] to plant on the birth of a female child forty or fifty seeds of sappan, and the trees which reach maturity in ten or twelve years are her dowry when she is married; the wood is exported in timber, or with the dye in cakes; the dye is precipitated dark brown with iron [auhan] and red with alum [padicauram]; it is also employed along with chayroot [q.v.]; alcohol forms a deep red tincture. The wood takes a fine polish and does not warp or crack; it is solid, heavy, hard, compact, whitish while recent, but reddening on exposure to the air; it is tasteless and inodorous; communicates a fine red color to water.

SAPTAM (सप्त - sapta, *San.*). Seven [haft, saut]. Constant in combination, see below. For sapta locam or seven regions of the world see Locam. For sapta nagaram or seven sacred cities of the hindoos see Nagaram. For sapta naracam or seven hells see Locam, Pautaulam and Swargam. For sapta swaram or seven principal notes or tones in music [sangeetam] see Swaram. For saptauvastay or seven stages of soul in its progress from ignorance to pure knowledge see Avastay. For sapta vauram or seven days of the week see Vauram. For sapta padaurtam or seven categories in logic [nyauyam] see Padaurtam.——*Saptacam* (सप्तक - saptaka, San.). Collection of seven; the musical gamut [swaram]; also a religious ceremony performed on the twelfth day after death, which consists in giving seven kinds of things as rice, money, &c., to seven bramins.——*Sapta caranam* (सप्तकरण - saptakarana, San.). From (above + karana, san. action). The funeral rite of joining seven ingredients. Raw rice, milk, honey, curds, cow's urine, ghee and oil seeds are mixed into a mass, and then divided into three portions intended to represent three of the ancestors of the deceased. By this rite the deceased becomes assimilated with his ancestors [pitry], and is entitled to admission to the lowest station in the divine region [locam] up till this time occupied by his father, who now ascends higher. See vol. II, 237.——*Sapta dweepam* (सप्तद्वीप - saptadvípa, San.). The seven continents:—Coosham, Crowncham, Jamboo, Placsham, Pooshcaram, Shaucam, Shaulmaly [bhoogolashastram, dweepam]. See vol. I (2).——*Sapta jauty* (सप्तजाति - saptajáti, San.). More commonly Sapta jenmam. The 7 kinds of birth, or 7 genera, are:—gods, men, beasts, birds, reptiles, subaqueous creatures and inanimate things [jauty]. The idea of seven births is a common one among hindoos. There is a stanza from Cooral:—எழுபிறப்புந் தீயவை தீண்டாபழிபிறங்காப், பண்புடைமக் கட்பெறின்—"the evils of the seven births shall not touch those who "obtain children of a good disposition, free from vice." And another:—எழுமையெழுபிறப்பு முள்ளுவர்தங்கண், விழுமந்துடைத்தவர்நட்பு—"the wise will remember through-"out their seven-fold births the love of those who have wiped "away their affliction." And another:—ஒருமையுளாமை போலைந்தடக்கலாற்றி, னெழுமையுமேமாப்புடைத்து—"should one throughout a single birth, like a tortoise keep in, "his five senses, the fruit of it will prove a safeguard to him "throughout the seven-fold births." But compare the remarks under Samsauram.——*Sapta loham* (सप्तलोह - saptalóha, San.). Means seven metals [loham]. Applied by natives to:—five simple metals, of gold [pon], silver [velly], copper [taumram], iron [auhan] and lead [eeyam] or tin; and two mixed metals, of vengalam [cunts] a mixture of copper and tin making bell-metal, and tarah a compound of copper and zinc [tootnaug] making pinchbeck [tambauk].——*Sapta maigham* (सप्तमेघ - saptamégha, San.). The seven clouds; named from Sanscrit words respectively denoting:—gem, water, gold, flower, sand, stone, fire [maigham].——*Saptamautah* (सप्तमाता - saptamátá, San.). From (above + mátá, san. mother). Seven matrons; seven small figures of stone standing in the first enclosure of the temple [coil, pagoda] of Ayenaur [ayen, mautah].——*Saptamy* (సప్తమి - saptami, Tel.). Seventh lunar day. Lunar [chaundramaunam] festival [pundigay, 3e]. The seventh tity [q.v.] of the waxing [shooclapacsham] or waning [krishnapacsham] moon of any lunar month [bhauscara saptamy, rata saptamy].——*Sapta nuddy* (सप्तनदी - saptanadí, San.). Means seven rivers. The seven sacred rivers:—Gungay, Yamoonay, Saraswaty, Nerbudda, Cauvery, Coomary and Godavery. According to a later classification four more are added making the list eleven, as follows:—Sindhoo or indus, Tamrapurny, Toongabudra and Kistna.——*Saptapady* (सप्तपदी - saptapadí, San.). From (above + pada, san. foot). Pacing seven steps round the sacred fire, an essential part of a hindoo marriage [calyaunam]. They are taken towards the north-east quarter [ashtadic, tisay]; the first for bodily energy, the second for valour, the third for increase of wealth, the fourth for well-being, the fifth for offspring, the sixth for happy seasons [ritoo], and the seventh for devoted friendship.——*Saptaparnam* (सप्तपर्ण - saptaparna, San.). From (above + parna, san. leaf); from leaves appearing in whorls of seven. Botanically the Alstonia genus, apocynaceæ [vricsham, 87]. Trees or erect shrubs with milky juice; leaves entire, opposite, often whorled; flowers small, white and disposed in cymes at the ends of branches; fruits consist of two cylindrical pods; seeds have a tuft of silky hairs at each end. The species best known to the natives are:—scholaris [ditu], venenata [wild gannair].——*Sapta parvatam* (सप्तपर्वत - saptaparvata, San.). The seven mountains; Mahendram, Malayam, Pauripautram, Ricsham, Sahyam, Shooctimat, Vindhyam [coolaparvatam].——*Sapta rishy* (सप्तर्षि - saptarshi, San.). From (above + rishi, san. sage). Seven sages [moony, rishy]. The seven vedic sages or patriarchs, otherwise bramharishies or mind-born sons of bramha [q.v.], are:—Mareechy, Atry, Angiran, Poolastyan, Poolahan, Cratoo, Vasishtan. These form in astronomy [jyotisham], the constellation [nacshatram] of Ursa major or the Great bear [doobhe acbar, maharicsham]. Seven sages are also assumed for each manwantaram [q.v.], and the names of these differ with different series. The names for the present manwantram are:—Atry, Bharadwaujan, Cashyapan, Gowtaman, Jamadagny, Vasishtan, Vishwaumitran.——*Sapta samoodram* (सप्तसमुद्र - saptasamudra, San.). The seven seas; salt, sugar-cane, toddy, ghee, curd, milk and fresh-water [bhoogolashastram, samoodram].——*Sapta santaunam* (सप्तसन्तान - saptasantána, San.). From (above + santána, san. extension). The seven meritorious acts by the performance of which a hindoo hopes to attain salvation [mocsham, santaunam]. These acts are:—digging of tanks, digging of wells, endowments for charitable purposes, performance of the oopanayanam [q.v.] ceremony to a bramin, erecting a pagoda [q.v.] to the supreme deity, planting groves [tope], writing of books.——*Sapta saugara yautray* (सप्तसागरयात्रा - saptaságarayátrá, San.). From (above + ságara, san. ocean + yátrá, san. festival). A religious ceremony which consists in a gift of the seven seas, i.e., a quantity of each of the seven substances respectively composing the seven samoodrams [q.v.], milk, curd, ghee, honey, wine, salt water, and fresh water.——*Saptavaudy* (सप्तवादी - saptavádí, San.). From (above + váda, san. proposition). Jeinas; assertors of seven propositions or categories. The categories are:—a thing is; it is not; it is and it is not; it is not definable; it is but not definable; it is not neither is it definable; it is, and it is not, and it is not definable [jeina]. Compare Padaurtam.——*Saut* (سات - sát, Hind.). Seven [haft, saptam.]——*Sautghur* (ساتگڑھ - sátgarh, Hind.; సాత్ఘడి - sátghadi, Tel. satghur*). From (sát, hind. seven + garh, hind. hill). Sanscrit name (saptagiri), means seven hills. Tel. also (édukondaladurgamu), means seven-hill fort. Village; North arcot dist., Goodiyattam tal.; lat. 12° 57′; long. 78° 47′; from Chittore S.W. 31 miles; from Goodiyattam W. 10 miles. Small place. Seven hills with hill forts. The highest of the fortified peaks rises to 2,367 feet, the other six somewhat lower. They all form portions of one mass of hills, some of them with very precipitous sides. Narrow approaches exist which are easily defended, though the forts are scattered and must have required a large garrison. The works were improved by Mahrattas and Mahomedans. The Nawaubs [q.v.] of Carnatic [q.v.] had large gardens here of orange [q.v.] and mango [q.v.] trees, known as the Sautghur baughayets [q.v.]. Sautghur oranges still well known. Mango grafts originally taken from hence to Vellore and other places now produce noted fruits. The descendants of the people who used to tend the gardens are almost the sole inhabitants of the village. The jagheer [q.v.], worth three lakhs [q.v.], was originally granted by Mahomed shah to one Hirausat khan, who upon the assassination of Sufder ally at Vellore acted as Naib [q.v.] of the minor Mahomed Sayeed. When the latter was assassinated at Arcot, Anwarood deen sent Hirausat khan back to his jagheer. He was succeeded by his son and grandson, but Wallajah removed the latter on account of his relationship to Chundah Sahib, and gave him the small jagheer of Cauvanore worth Rs. 40,000. This was resumed after Hyder's war, and a small pension substituted. Trig. station in lat. 12° 57′ 24·94″; long. 78° 47′ 05·95″; height 2,317 feet; from Goodiyattam W. 9 miles; from Pernambutt N.E. 3 miles.

SAR (سر - sar, *Pers.*). Head. Prefix in compounds; as Sarhad, head + limit.——*Saranjaum* (سرانجام - saranjám, Hind.). From (above + anjám, pers. end). Baggage [saumaun].——*Sarausaree* (سراسری - sarásarí, Hind.). Means end to end. An average [ramaurámy].——*Sar carcoon* (سر کارکن - sarkárkun, Hind.). From (above + kárkun, pers. workman). Head vernacular clerk; also port officer.——*Sarfarah* (سربراهی - sarbaráhí, Hind.). From (above + ba, pers. for + ráh, pers. road). Furnishing supplies.——*Sarfrauz* (سرفراز - sarfaráz, Hind.). From (above + faráz, pers. one who raises). Exalted. Part of lacab; as Sarfrauz ood dowla, exalted of the empire [ism].——*Sarhad* (سرحد - sarhadd, Hind.). From (above + hadd, ar. boundary). Boundary [hudd].——*Sarpech* (سرپیچ - sarpech, Hind.). From (above + pech, pers. coil). A band consisting of square pieces of gold plates, threaded together, and 2 or $2\frac{1}{2}$ cubits long. Worn by the Mahomedan nobles [puggry].——*Sarwar* (سرور - sarvar, Ar.). Sovereign. Name of a Mahomedan saint. Alam; as Mahomed sarwar, double alam. Also part of lacab; as Sarwar ool moolk, chief of the empire [ism].——

Serang (سرهنگ - sarhang, Hind.; സ്രാങ്ക - sránku, Mal.). From (above + hang, pers. soldier). A head native boatman [tindal].——*Sherishta tahreer* (سرشته تحریر - sarishtahtahrír, Hind.). Fees paid for preparing accounts, &c.——*Sherista* (سرشته - sarishtah, Hind.). From (above + rishtah, pers. thread). Record; file.——*Sheristadar* (سرشته دار - sarishtahdár, Hind.). From (sarishtah, pers. a record + dár, pers. holder). Keeper of the records. The Recorder in a court of justice under the Company's government. The head manager in a revenue office or in a court. In the talook [q.v.] the Sheristadar ranks after the Tahsildar [q.v.] and has charge of the treasury work. The Huzoor [q.v.] sheristadar is the head of the Collector's office.——*Sirdar* (سردار - sardár, Hind.). From (above + dár, pers. holder). A chieftain. Prefixed to an alam forms a lacab; as Sirdar ally, ally the chief [ism].——*Sirkele* (سرخیل - sarkhail, Hind.; சர்க்கீல் - sharkkíl, Tam.). From (above + khail, pers. a body of men). A minister [muntry]. The head of a clan or sect. A title of rank amongst the Mahrattas [peyar].

SAR (सर् - sar, *San.*). To move, flow, extend, pervade; connected with roots (srij) to create and (srip) to creep.——*Sarakk* (சரக்கு - sarakku, Tam.). See sep. title.——*Saramay* (सरमा - saramá, San.). Means the runner. The dog of Indran [q.v.]. Compare Cerberus.——*Saras* (सरस् - saras, San.). From (sri, san. to go); originally applied to flowing water. Water.——*Saraswaty* (सरस्वती - sarasvatí, San.). From (saras, san. water + vat, san. suffix of possession); originally a river deity. Goddess of learning. The shacty [q.v.] or consort of Bramha [q.v.] as the author of the vedams [q.v.]. In the Rig vedam Bramha is a word, Saraswaty its utterance. Hence Saraswaty is the goddess of eloquence and poetry; as indicated by the name Vauny frequently applied to her. As such she is invoked by poets, but less frequently in modern times than Vigneshwaran [q.v.]. The local Sheiva legend at Madura states that Saraswaty became manifest in the letters of the Tamul alphabet [varnamaulay] in various localities. She is represented in the south by the image of a female in a standing posture, with four arms and hands; in one of the two right hands she holds a flower, which she offers to her husband by her side, and in the other right hand a book of palm-leaves [grantam], indicating that she is fond of learning and imparts knowledge to those who study; in one of her two left hands she holds a string of pearls [moty], called shiva maulay, which serves her as a rosary [maulay]; and in the other left hand a small drum; the color of her body is usually white; in her black hair she wears pearls and other ornaments, whilst her hair is so long as to reach to her feet. Her image is not worshipped in any pagoda, but, like that of her husband, only painted or carved as an ornament at pagodas [q.v.] and idol [shilay, vigraham] cars [rath]. Nor does she receive any of the usual offerings. But there are some books setting forth her praise, of which one called Saraswaty antaudy is best known. Also a great festival [navarautry], lasting nine days, is celebrated in her honor in the month of September, more especially by the teachers and their pupils, and by the poets and other writers [saraswaty poojay]; all of whom adore Saraswaty and ask her to grant them good understanding and knowledge. Compare Pillaiyaur chatoorty. The devout make also an image of the goddess, and carry it about in the streets with music; and on the ninth day, Saraswaty, together with Parvaty [q.v.] and Lutchmy [q.v.], is worshipped by teachers and pupils under the form of their iron styles and books, by soldiers under the form of their weapons, by artisans under that of their tools, &c. This is called Saraswatypoojay; also Ayoodha poojay, instrument worship. Of Saraswaty various stories are related in the Pooraunams [q.v.], and many names are given her, viz.:—Bhauraty, the goddess of speech; Devy; Gayatry, the most sacred verse of the vedams, being personified as saraswaty; Nyauna moorty, wisdom's form; Isaimadanday, music-girl; Calay magal, science daughter; Naumagal, tongue-lady; Oolagamautah, mother of the world; Panoovalautty, science dame; Vaukkaul, the same as bhauraty; Vauny, the same as bhauraty, &c. To Saraswaty poets are indebted for their skill and inspiration. The Jeinas [q.v.] have a female deity of this name peculiar to themselves [matam]. See vol. I (73), (79).——*Saraswaty bhandaura* (ಸರಸ್ವತಿಭಂಡಾರ - sarasvatibandára, Can.). From (sarasvati, san. goddess of wisdom + bhandára, san. treasury). Library.——*Saraswaty poojaurambham* (సరస్వతిపూజారంభం - sarasvatipújárambham, Tel.). Means saraswaty, the water goddess, the muse of science and art + worship + beginning. The fourth to ninth days of Dusserah [q.v.]. On these days natives collect their books and instruments of trade and profession for future adoration.——*Saraswaty poojay* (సరస్వతిపూజ - sarasvatipúja, Tel.). Means saraswaty, the water goddess, the muse of science and art + worship. The ninth day of Dusserah [q.v.] between 24th September and 23rd October. Same as Mahaunavamy. Adoration now takes place [maryanday]. See vol. I (93).——*Saraswaty pooroogoo* (حردون - hirdún, Ar. and Pers.; بامهنی - bámhaní, Hind.; సరస్వతిపురుగు - sarasvatipurugu, Tel.; அரணை - aranai, Tam.). Hind. from (báman, hind. bramin + female suffix). Tel. from (sarasvati, san. the goddess + purugu, tel. worm). Tam. from (aran, tam. beauty). House lizard [chipkalee] with red tail [aranay].——*Saraswaty's leaf* (भाण्डीर - bhándíra, San.; بهانٹ - bhánt, Hind.; సరస్వతిఆకు - sarasvatiáku, Tel.; പിറക - piraku, Mal.; පින්න - pinna, Singh.; கருக்கன்னி - karukkanni, Tam.). Title as mental tonic. San. from (bhand, san. to prosper), useful plant. Tel. from (sarasvatí, san. the goddess + áku, tel. leaf). Mal. from (peru, mal. large); from strengthening quality. Tam. from (karumai, tam. blackness + kanni, tam. the plant). Hind. also (bhat). Tel. also (mandúkabrahmi), meaning frog + the plant, clerodendron siphonanthus, r. br.; (gurrapugaddiáku), meaning horse + grass + leaf; (bokkada). Tam. also (vellaikkanni), meaning white + the plant. Title otherwise Bhaunt. Botanically Clerodendron [bhaurgam] infortunatum, gærtn., verbenaceæ [vricsham, 102]. Alias Clerodendron viscosum; Volkameria infortunata. Under shrub, 2–3 feet; branchlets quadrangular; leaves long-petioled, rounded or ovate-cordate, the upper ones ovate, entire or dentate, strigose and hairy on both sides; panicle terminal, large, spreading, naked; flowers white, tinged with rose inside, the calyx increasing and turning red after the flower withers; drupe black within the increased calyx. Cheap substitute for chiretta [q.v.] as medicinal tonic and antiperiodic; fresh juice of leaves employed as vermifuge and bitter tonic and febrifuge in malarious fevers especially of children; leaf-juice quoted in pharm. but non-officinal. Another species is Inerme [sangcooppy].——*Saraswaty vilausam* (सरस्वतीविलास - sarasvatívilása, San.). From (sarasvatí, san. goddess of wisdom + vilása, san. sport). Recreations of the goddess of learning. An extensive work embracing the entire range of the religious moral and civil laws of the Hindoos. The dauyabhaugam portion of it or the law of inheritance has been translated into English. A book of some authority to the northward of the Pennair, parallel to the commentary of Vinyauneshwaran, the prevailing authority in the south. Its authorship is ascribed to Prataupa roodra deva, who belonged to the Gajapaty [q.v.] dynasty [raj] of Orissa, and succeeded to that kingdom in A.D. 1503, on the extinction of the Gunga [q.v.] line of kings which had ruled over that country since A.D. 1131.——*Sargam* (सर्ग - sarga, San.). From (srij, san. to create). Creation of the universe [srishty]; one of the five topics which every pooraunam [q.v.] is supposed to treat of. The other four are pratisargam, vamsham, manwantaram and vamshaunoocharitam [punchalutchanam].——*Sarooloo* (సరులు - sarulu, Tel.). Means garland. A Vizagapatam paddy. Auk sarooloo means seedling + the paddy; Canaca sarooloo means gold, from appearance of ears; Mootakauk sarooloo means coarse; Mootya sarooloo means pearl from roundness of rice; Raja sarooloo means king, coarse; Ratna sarooloo means precious stone, fine; from appearance of corn in ears; Sannauk sarooloo means fine; Vankauk sarooloo means curved [paddy].——*Sarpam* (सर्प - sarpa, San.). Snake. See sep. title.——*Sarpy* (सर्पी - sarpí, San.). See sep. title.——*Sarshapam* (सर्षप - sarshapa, San.). From (sri, san. to go), from round and useful seeds.—"*a*" Title otherwise Cole, Colewort. Botanically the Brassica genus, cruciferæ [vricsham, 10]. Glabrous and herbaceous plants; native of the temperate regions of the old world; leaves large, rarely entire; flowers yellow; seeds compressed. The genus is wide yielding the majority of the vegetables used by the inhabitants of temperate countries, and many of these are being introduced into southern india. To it belong mustard [rayaun], cabbage [kobee], radish [country radish], and turnip [sarsoon, shalgham], with innumerable varieties of each. The species best known to the natives are:—alba [soofaid rayaun], campestris [sarsoon], campestris, sub. sp. campestris [cauly sarsoon], campestris, sub. sp. napus [rara sarsoon], campestris, sub. sp. napus, var. toria [toriya sarsoon], campestris, sub. sp. rapa [shalgham], juncea [rayaun], nigra [cauly rayaun], oleracea [kobee].—"*b*" Mustard seed. Goldsmiths' weight. 6 sarshapams = 1 yavam [niray, 3f]. Approximate actual value, 1 sarshapam = $\frac{1}{48}$th of a grain. Compare zarrah.——*Sarsoon* (سرسون - sarsón, Hind.). See sep. title.——*Sarwabhooman* (சார்வப்பூமன் - shárvappúman, Tam.). From (sarva, san. all + bhúmi, san. earth). Universal monarch. Hindoo 2nd or pers. name [peyar].——*Sarwa darshana sangraham* (सर्वदर्शनसंग्रह - sarvadarshanasangraha, San.). From (sarva, san. all + darshana, san. philosophy + sangraha, san. epitome). A concise description of various Hindoo systems and sects, religious and philosophical, orthodox and heterodox, even including the science of applying quicksilver or raseshwaram [rasam] regarded as a form of shiva [q.v.] or its preparations to various chemical and alchemical operations, and embracing also Paniny's theory of grammar [lacshanam]. Its author was Maudhavaucharry [maudhavan]. The Sarwa darshana sangraham treats of fifteen systems:—Chaurvaucam, Bowddham, Aurhatam or jeina system, Ramaunoojam or vishishtandweitam, Poornapranyam or dweitam, Nacooleesha paushoopatam, Sheivam, Pratyabhinyay or recognitive system, Raseshwaram or mercurial system, Owloocyam or veishaishicam, Acshapaudam or nyauyam, Jeimineeyam or poorva mimaumsam, Paunineeyam, Saunkhyam, Pautanjalam or yogam. The Vedauntam [q.v.] philosophy is not included in the list, as it is separately dealt with in a book called Punchadashy.——*Sarwa dayaubhary* (சருவதயாபரி - sharuvathayábari, Tam.). From (sarva, san.

all + dayá, san. clemency + bhri, san. to bear); bearing clemency towards all. Lover of all creatures, Parvaty [q.v.].——*Sarwa loca mautah* (சருவலோகமாதா - sharuvalógamáthá, Tam.). From (sarva, san. all + lóka, san. world + mátá, san. mother). Mother of the whole world; Parvaty [akhilaunda naicky].——*Sarwam* (सर्व - sarva, San.). From (sri, san. to pervade). All.——*Sarwa maunyam* (सर्वमान्य - sarvamánya, San.). From (sarva, san. all + mánya, san. privilege). Lands exempt from every kind of tax [inam].——*Sarwa medham* (सर्वमेध - sarvamédha, San.). From (sarva, san. all + médha, san. sacrifice). Sacrifice for universal success [yanyam].——*Sarwanyan* (सर्वज्ञ - sarvaña, San.). From (sarva, san. all + ñá, san. to know). Omniscient; epithet of the deity of the Jeinas [q.v.].——*Sarwarauz* (سروراج - sarvaráj, Hind.; సర్వరాజు - sarvarádzu, Tel.). From (sarva, san. all + rádzu, tel. king). Lord of all. Proper name [peyar].——*Sarwasautchy* (सर्वसाक्षी - sarvasákshí, San.). From (sarva, san. all + sákshí, san. witness). Epithet of the all-witnessing god.——*Sarwasiddhy* (సర్వసిద్ధి - sarvasiddhi, Tel.). See sep. title.——*Sarwauntaryaumy* (सर्वान्तर्यामी - sarvántaryámí, San.). From (sarva, san. all + antar, san. within + yá, san. to go). Epithet of god as the all-pervading spirit.——*Sarwautmam* (सर्वात्मा - sarvátmá, San.). From (sarva, san. all + átman, san. soul). The supreme spirit, as the universal soul [paramautman].——*Sarweshwaran* (சருவேசுவரன் - sharuvésuvaran, Tam.). From (sarva, san. all + íshvara, san. lord). Shiva, the lord of all [vishveshwaran]. Hindoo 2nd or pers. name [peyar].——*Sarwottaman* (சருவோத்தமன் - sharuvóttaman, Tam.). From (sarva, san. all + uttaman, san. the best). Vishnoo, the best of all [poorshottaman]. Hindoo 2nd or pers. name [peyar].——*Saump* (سانپ - sámp, Hind.). From (sarpa, san. serpent). Snake.——*Saumpmar* (سانپ مار - sámpmár, Hind.). Means serpent + killer. Bird name common to:—Circaetus gallicus; Haliætus leucogaster. See gloss. paragraphs.——*Saurasam* (सारस - sárasa, San.). See sep. title.——*Saury* (ساڑی - sárí, Hind.). From (shára, san. variegated). A long cotton scarf for women. As usually worn, one end is passed twice round the waist, the upper border tied in a strong knot, and allowed to fall in folds to the ankle, thus forming a sort of skirt. The other end is passed in front across the left arm and shoulder, one edge being brought over the top of the head. It is then allowed to fall behind and over the right shoulder and arm. When used by the women employed in out-door labor, the end which falls in front is passed between the legs, and tucked in behind, forming as it were drawers reaching to the knee [sheelay]. See vol. I (98).——*Shauranay* (पुनर्नव - punarnavá, San.; ناسورجنگی - násúrjangí, Hind.; ناسر جنگی - násarjangí, Dec.; ನೊಗಅಟಕುಮಾಮಿಡಿ - nogaatakumámidi, Can.; గలిజేరు - galijéru, Tel.; സാരണ - sárana, Mal.; சாரணை - sháranai, Tam.). Title from tamul. San. from (punar, san. again + nava, san. new); growing again if cut [tikry]. Hind. from (násúr, ar. ulcer + changá, hind. to heal). Dec. from hindostany. Can. from (noga, tel. yoke + atikemámidi, tel. bœrhaavia repens, linn., var. diffusa). Mal. and Tam. from (saraná, san. the plant). San. also (shvétapunarnavá) is the white variety. Hind. also (bishkoprá), meaning poisonous cocoanut kernel; (sufedsábuní), meaning white soap like; (lálsábúní), meaning red soap like. Tel. also (erragalijéru), meaning red + the plant; (ambatimádu), meaning porridge + burning; (tellagalijéru), meaning white + the plant; (nogaatikemámidi), meaning yoke, bœrhaavia repens, linn., var. diffusa; (boddupávili), meaning navel + portulaca quadrifida, linn. Tam. also (vellaiççáranai), meaning white + the plant. Title otherwise Nasar junghy, One-styled trianthema, Purslane-leaved trianthema. Botanically Trianthema monogyna, linn., ficoideæ [vricsham, 66]. Alias Trianthema obcordata, pentandra. Perennial; stems diffuse, prostrate, slightly pubescent on the upper side; leaves, one of each pair larger and obovate or obcordate, the other smaller and oblong; flowers solitary, sessile, nearly concealed within the broad sheath of the petioles; stamens fifteen to twenty; capsule six to eight-seeded, lid concave, with two spreading teeth, nearly enclosed at the bottom, including one seed; flowers small, greenish white. A diffuse, prostrate, branched, glabrous, fleshy plant, which springs up everywhere at the commencement of the rainy season; seeds black, scarcely shining, with concentric, broken, and undulating, raised lines; root pale color, much wrinkled, taste bitterish and somewhat nauseous. Root given medicinally in powder in combination with ginger [q.v.] as a cathartic. Leaves and tender tops used for food as spinach [maurisham]. Other common species are:—Crystallina, called in vernacular dog milk-greens, prostrate-branched herb; Decandra, called in vernacular white shauranay, or small shauranay; properties like monogyna; Pentandra. Red shauranay, so called in vernaculars from color of flowers, is botanically orygia decumbens, forsk., ficoideæ [vricsham, 66]; generic name from arabic; alias glinus trianthemoides; orygia trianthemoides; herbaceous, diffuse; leaves alternate, cuneate-obovate, rounded mucronate; panicles lax, axillary, leaf-opposed, dichotomously racemose; calyx-segments ovate, cuspidate, membranaceous on the margin, spreading; petals numerous, from spathulate to lanceolate, entire; style and stigma filiform; capsule smooth and shining externally, splitting from the apex; a procumbent herb with fleshy leaves of a brownish color; flower small, red; leaves used for food as spinach.——*Shauricay* (शारिका - sháriká, San.). See sep. title.——*Srishty* (सृष्टि - srishti, San.; சிருட்டி - shirutti, Tam.). From (srij, san. to create). Creation [sargam]. The Hindoo philosophers are disagreed in what manner the work of creation took place. Some say that Bramha [q.v.], the supreme being, first created nature from which the Hindoo triad [trimoorty] proceeded, as the Creator, Preserver and Destroyer of the world. Others say that the elements [bhootam] of the world were inclosed in an immense shell, called the mundane egg [bramhaundam], which burst and formed the fourteen upper and the fourteen lower worlds [locam]. Others again assert that as Vishnoo [q.v.] was sleeping on the serpent Anantan [q.v.] or eternity, on the face of the waters, after the annihilation of a former world, a lotus [nelumbo] sprung from his navel, from which issued Bramha who produced the elements [bhootam], and formed the world, Shiva [q.v.], and the human race [pralayam]. From his head he formed the Bramins, from his arm the Cshatriyas, from his thighs the Veisyas, and from his feet the Shoodras. In the Rig vedam [q.v.] is read as follows:—"Then there was neither non-existence nor existence; no world, "no air, nor anything above them; nothing anywhere in the "fortune of any one enveloping or enveloped. There was then "neither death nor immortality, nor difference between day and "night. But tat [q.v.], that, breathed without afflation, alone "with swadhay [q.v.], self-position, which is contained within it. "Besides it nothing sure existed. There was darkness, and "indistinguishable water; but the mass covered with the veil "was produced by the power of contemplation. Desire was "formed first in his mind, and this became the original "productive seed, which the wise, acknowledging it by compre-"hension in their hearts, distinguish as being in non-existence, "the bond of existence."——*Srishtyaudy dyooganam* (सृष्ट्यादिद्युगण - srishtyádidyugana, San.). From (above + ádi, san. beginning + dyu, san. day + gana, san. collection). The number of natural days [sauvana dinam] expired from the grand astronomical epoch when the planetary [graham] motions first commenced, to any other epoch for which their places are to be computed [aharganam]. Number of years to date is 1955,884,994.

SARAKK (சரக்கு - sharakku, *Tam.*). From (sarga, san. nature) [sar]. Production, goods, products. Minerals [dhautoo, loham] used for medicine; especially arsenic [paushaunam], of which natives reckon sixty-four kinds, half in native state, half prepared. Also alkalies [cauram] and salts [ooppoo] used in chemical preparation of medicines [ospitry, veidyan]. An alkaline or salifiable base is called Aunsarakk, masculine drug, and any acid [poolipp] which readily combines with the same is called Pensarakk, feminine drug. The following is a list of the principal alkaline bases and acids, in pairs:—Bitumen [shilajit], copper [taumram]; Camphor [q.v.], copperas [mayil toottam]; Corrosive sublimate [shavveeram], oxalis corniculata, linn. [sour auray]; Corrosive sublimate [shavveeram], zinc [tootnaug]; Crude camphor [camphor], rock salt [sondah namak]; Gold [pon], realgar [manoshilay]; Gold-colored arsenic [wurkee hartaul], averrhoa bilimbi, linn. [blimbing]; Magnet [cauntam], vinegar [caudy]; Mercury [rasam], sulphur [gandhac]; Mica [abruck], hibiscus cannabinus, linn. [hemp bendy]; Realgar [manoshilay], vitis setosa, wall. [bristly piranday], vitis carnosa, wall. [acid naralay]; Rock salt [sondah namak], vermilion [shangarf]; Salammoniac [nowshaudar], borax [vengauram]; Salt [ooppoo], tamarind pulp [tamarind]; Saltpetre [shorah], alum [padicauram]; White arsenic [soofaid soombal], palmyra toddy [q.v.].——*Ásal sarakk* (அசற்சரக்கு - asarcharakku, Tam.). From (asal, ar. original). Natural substance as distinguished from artificial compound.——*Audiyodoom sarakk* (ஆடியோடுஞ்சரக்கு - ádiyóduñjarakku, Tam.). From (ádu, tam. to move + ódu, tam. to run). Mineral [dhautoo], which on being exposed to the action of fire, disappears; said to be the case with fictitious cinnabar [shangarf], yellow sulphuret of arsenic [hartaul], &c. Sixty-four kinds of this are reckoned.——*Audoom sarakk* (ஆடுஞ்சரக்கு - áduñjarakku, Tam.). From (ádu, tam. to move). Mineral which evaporates on the fire; as mercury [rasam], sulphur [gandhac], &c.——*Caday sarckk* (கடைச்சரக்கு - kadaiççarakku, Tam.). From (kadai, tam. bazaar). Drugs, curry stuff, spices, &c., sold in bazaar.——*Culla sarakk* (கள்ளச்சரக்கு - kallaççarakku, Tam.). From (kallam, tam. stealing). Contraband goods.——*Cuppal sarakk* (கப்பற்சரக்கு - kapparcharakku, Tam.). From (kappal, tam. ship). Ship-goods. Cargo.——*Cuttoo sarakk* (கட்டுச்சரக்கு - kattuççarakku, Tam.). From (kattu, tam. to concrete). Mercury [rasam], &c., consolidated.——*Nautt sarakk* (நாட்டுச்சரக்கு - náttuççarakku, Tam.). Country goods.——*Oolloor sarakk* (உள்ளூர்ச்சரக்கு - ullúrççarakku, Tam.). From (ul, tam. inside + úr, tam. village). Production of the country.——*Oorgy audiyodoom sarakk* (உருகியாடியோடுஞ்சரக்கு - urugiyádiyóduñjarakku, Tam.). From (urugu, tam. to melt + ádu, tam. to move + ódu, tam. to run). Mineral which first melts in a crucible, and then is gradually sublimated; as sulphur [gandhac], mercury [rasam], &c.——*Pala sarakk* (பலசரக்கு - palasarakku, Tam.).

From (pala, tam. sundry). Grocery.——*Sheemay sarakk* (சீமைச் சரக்கு - shímaiççarakku, Tam.). From (shímai, tam. foreign). European goods.——*Veippoo sarakk* (வைப்புச்சரக்கு - vaippuççarakku, Tam.). From (vaippu, tam. deposit). Artificial drug.

SARBHOJEE (شرفوجی - sharfújí, *Hind.*). From (sharf, ar. saint's name meaning high or noble + jí, mahr. honorific title). Adopted son of Toolsajee. Placed on the throne of Tanjore in 1798 by the English on the deposition of his uncle Ameer sing. Transferred the country to the English in 1799, receiving a pension. Succeeded by his son Shivajee, the last of the Tanjore rulers. See vol. I, 50; II, 254.

SARF (صرف - sarf, *Hind.*). Expenditure [curts]. Exchange [shroff].——*Sarf i khas* (صرف خاص - sarfikhás, Hind.). From (above + khás, ar. own). Crown lands [havelly].——*Shroff* (صراف - sarráf, Hind.). From (sarf, ar. to exchange) [sarf]. To shroff is to sort coins, so as to discard refuse and to fix the various amounts of discount or agio upon the rest, establishing the value in standard coin. Hence to make selection generally. So as noun, a banker, cash-keeper.

SARO (सुराह्व - suráhva, *San.*; सरू - sarú, *Mahr.*; سرو - saro, *Pers.*, *Hind.* and *Dec.*). Title from deccany. San. from (sura, san. god + hvé, san. to call); called sooram or divine; from never-fading evergreen foliage. Mahr. from persian. Greek κυπάριττος εὐώδης. Title otherwise Cypress, Gopher-wood, of which the hebrew ark was built. Botanically Cupressus sempervirens, linn., coniferæ [vricsham]. Evergreen tree, 20 feet high; branches straight, quadrangular; leaves imbricate, in four rows, blunt approximate, convex; cones globose; scales unarmed; flowers apetalous, flowering in may. Habitat candia; cultivated widely; foliage dark green. The cone used medicinally. Cupressus torulosa, don., is bhootan cypress or himalayan cypress.

SARPAM (सर्प - sarpa, *San.*). From (srip, san. to creep) [sar].

——(1) Equivalent of the whole order Ophidia of the sub-class Reptile [sarpy]. The two halves of the lower jaw in snakes are not united by an osseous symphysis, but by an elastic ligament. This mobility of the jaw-bones enables most of them to extend the gape in an extraordinary degree and to work their prey down through the collapsed pharynx. Some snakes, as the Rock-snakes [q.v.] or pythonidæ and Irtalay maniyan [q.v.], or erycidæ, have rudiments of hind limbs. The organs of locomotion for the exceedingly elongate body of the snakes are the ribs, the number of which is very great, nearly corresponding to that of the vertebræ of the trunk. When a part of their body has found some projection of the ground which affords it a point of support, the ribs, alternately of one and the other side, are drawn more closely together, thereby producing alternate bends of the body on the corresponding side. The hinder portion of the body being drawn after, some part of it finds another support on the rough ground or a projection, and the anterior bends being stretched in a straight line, the front part of the body is propelled in consequence. Snakes are not able to move over a perfectly smooth surface. They are naked like all other reptiles. The epidermis is cast off in a single piece several times every year [coosam]. In non-venomous snakes [paumb], the teeth are either entirely smooth, or only the last of the maxillary series is provided with a faint longitudinal groove, which is not intended to convey a poisonous saliva into a wound. Poisonous snakes [naug], are armed with a long canaliculated tooth in front of the upper jaw; the channel terminates in a small slit at the extremity of the tooth, and is in connexion with a duct which carries the poisonous fluid from a large gland to the tooth. At the moment the snake opens its mouth to bite, these muscles compress the gland.**——(2)** The following are various popular errors about snakes:—"*a*" First that all snakes are more or less venomous. The possession of a poisonous salivary secretion is confined to a few kinds of snakes, and most of these are very rare. Of land snakes, about 10 per cent. are venomous. Of this 10 per cent., one-half are snakes fatal to human life. The half consists of two snakes only, the Cobra [q.v.], and the Chain viper [q.v.], in the proportion of about one of the former to about four or five of the latter.—"*b*" Secondly that they are slimy. This is the opposite of the truth. Most have their skin covered with smooth polished scales repellent of dirt and moisture.—"*c*" Thirdly that they have a forked sting which they dart at their victim. All snakes have a long bifid tongue, which, usually retracted in a sheath below the windpipe, is capable of rapid and vibrating protrusion through a chink in the rostral shield; it is moved by means of two long elastic bones extending along the greater part of its length in the form of a long V with the tongue rising perpendicularly from the angle of the V; muscles convert these bones into levers which jerk the tongue up and down with great celerity and freedom of play. This tongue is not peculiar to snakes; the large Water lizards, i.e., Guanas or Varanus [oodoomoo], for instance have this bifid organ still more developed. The tongue is probably used in early life for catching insects before the regular prey of the snake can be attacked; it is harmless and is never used for licking. It is said by natives that the tongue was cut in two by the blades of coosham [q.v.] or darbhay [q.v.] grass when the serpents of old licked the amritam [q.v.].—"*d*" Fourthly that the venomous kind have fangs of great length which are erected when required for use. Harmless snakes [paumb] have a row of about six to sixteen teeth in each upper jaw, besides generally two rows of palate teeth. In the venomous kinds the maxillary teeth are generally replaced by a single tubular tooth of variable length, but hardly exceeding a quarter of an inch in an adult cobra [q.v.] and half an inch in an adult Chain viper [q.v.] or Daboia. This length is from the origin of the fang to the tip, but not more than half the length can be seen by pulling up the fold of gum which envelopes the fang, and in the neutral state little or nothing can be seen of the fang, as it is entirely concealed, saving perhaps two or three hundredths of an inch of the point, in the gingival envelope. The often-mentioned erection of the fang takes place to a very slight extent in the cobra, which is unprovided with any special erective apparatus; the fang is always recurved backwards at an angle of about forty-five degrees and received into a depression in the lower lip. In some of the vipers [viriyan] there is a special erective muscle, but in every case the uncovering of the fang is a passive act as regards the snake, being effected by the gingival envelope being pushed up mechanically by the object bitten.—"*e*" Fifthly that the poison is contained in a bag at the base of the fang and is sent through the fang by the pressure of the object bitten. The fang is at the anterior extremity of the upper jaw-bone, while the poison gland is situated on the cheek behind the eye; the poison on being ejected either by direct muscular action or by a reflex nervous action similar to that excited in the human mouth by the idea of eating lemon, proceeds along a duct which passes below the eye over the jaw-bone, and terminates at the bottom of the gingival envelope of the fang, and just in front of the superior orifice of its canal. There is no continuity between the orifice of the poison duct and that of the poison fang. They are merely in apposition, and the poisonous salivary secretion is directed into the fang by the retraction of the gingival envelope round the fang in the act of biting.—"*f*" Sixthly that there are reserve fangs ready to replace those in use should they be broken off. There is no special arrangement of this kind for the poison fangs apart from the other teeth. Every tooth in the snake's mouth, whether simple tooth or poison fang, is enveloped more or less in a gingival envelope which contains at its base the matrix of a series of other teeth; these young teeth are constantly growing, and the eldest of them periodically replaces the fixed tooth and becomes fixed until it is shed in its return. This shedding is a gradual process compared to the shedding of the epidermis but the two operations coincide in time and take place about once in two months.—"*g*" Seventhly that a venomous snake [naug] may be known by a peculiar formation of the head, &c. A close inspection will alone tell whether the snake has poison fangs or not. A venomous snake has the upper maxillary row of teeth replaced by a single fang, sometimes followed by one or two short ordinary teeth rather difficult of detection. An inexperienced person is nevertheless liable to mistake the harmless long tooth that many snakes have in the front of the upper jaw for a poison fang, or else to overlook a short fang enveloped in its gingival fold. As to the external character of the head there is no single rule, but the following may be noted:—"i" A shielded head, that is to say with the crown occupied not by scales as on the rest of the body but by about seven large plates, is generally the sign of a harmless snake. Common exceptions are the Cobra [q.v.] and the Bungaur [q.v.] and the Sea-snakes [tuttapaumb], which have shielded heads. "ii" A scaly head, that is to say the crown covered with scales as on the rest of the body, is generally the sign of a poisonous snake. Common exceptions are the Irtalaymaniyans [q.v.] or erycidæ and Poodeiyans [q.v.] or acrochordidæ. The absence of a loreal shield is the only true external sign of a venomous snake; this is a small shield usually separating the antocular shield from the posterior nasal, so that there are but two shields instead of three between the eye and the nostril. On opening the mouth the presence of the poison fang of course reveals the venomous kind. Many different designations being given to the same species, this has led to the belief that there is in Southern india a very large number of poisonous snakes. A careful inquiry reduces the poisonous species to about eight. The four following, Naga tripudians or cobra [q.v.], Bungarus cæruleus or bungaur [q.v.], Daboia elegans or chain viper [q.v.], and Echis carinata or carpet snake [q.v.], are the most common in the different districts, and of these the first three are the most deadly and occasion the chief mortality. The other four poisonous snakes, Ophiophagus elaps [hill cobra] or hamadryad, Bungarus fasciatus or krait [q.v.], Trimeresurus or pit viper [q.v.], and Hypnale nepa or carawilla [q.v.], rarely cause deaths. They are never met with in the vicinity of inhabited villages, but restrict their movements to the jungles and hills or hilly districts. They are found chiefly in South canara and in the Northern provinces. Destruction of snakes is most effective during the pairing and breeding season in the months of May, June, July and August. Sea-snakes are very poisonous. Along the Eastern coast the Enhydrina bengalensis [vaulakidy] occasions the chief mortality among fishermen and boatmen. Others are the Pelamis bicolor [nulla vaulagily] and Hydrophis cyanocincta [chittal].—"*h*" Eighthly that there exist antidotes for snake poison generally. This is generally considered a popular error, but is not quite a settled question. It is stated that a snake-catcher tattooing with gradually increasing doses of cobra poison makes himself invulnerable.—" *i* " Ninthly that the male and female cobra are very different in appearance. There is no external difference in the appearance of the two sexes, except on close examination of the organs. The Rat-snake [q.v.] or Dhauman is generally supposed by natives to copulate with the cobra [q.v.], producing a very venomous hybrid offspring; hence it is frequently called the male cobra.——**(3)** There is a Tamul proverb:—கடித்த பாம்புக்கு பால் வார்த்தால் விஷத்தைத்தரும் அதுபோலப் பொல்லாத வர்க்குச் செய்யும் உபகாரம் இருக்கும்—" when milk is "placed before a biting snake in return it gives poison, and "such is the return for the favors done to the wicked." The following is a Hindostany proverb:—کالے کاکاٹا پانی نہیں مانگتا - " bitten by a black snake does not even ask for water;" because he dies before he can do so. There is a Teloogoo proverb:—పాము కాళ్లు పాముకెరుక—" the snake knows its own feet;" natives believe that the snake has feet, though they are invisible.——**(4)** The flesh and skin of certain snakes is held by veidyans [q.v.] to possess medicinal qualities. Dried flesh of a rock-snake [q.v.] is considered useful for leprosy [cooshtam]. According to the shastram [q.v.] Dhanwantary vaugadam, the snake slough [coosam] when reduced to powder, and mixed with fixed oil [yennay], obtained from seeds of Pongamia glabra, vent. [karanj], has virtues as an external application in epilepsy. The same is used as a ligature in intermittent fevers. For the mythology of the snake tribe see Audy sheshan. For serpent worship see Naugam.——**(5)** Popularly snakes are arranged under the following heads:—" *a* " Tree-snakes [q.v.]. Those that live for the most part in trees or bushes and are characterized by their brilliant colors, generally green, their slender and whip-like form, and great activity. Both non-venomous colubrine and viperine snakes are found in this section [combairy mookkan, whip snake].—" *b* " Water-snakes [mutty paumb]. These are salt-water and fresh-water, the first all venomous, the second all innocent. Salt-water snakes [tuttapaumb] have a peculiar form adapted to their mode of life, a compressed tail and nostrils above the snout; many, if not all, are viviparous [chittal, nullavaulagily, sea bungaur, vaulakidy]. Fresh-water snakes [mutty paumb] have the nostrils like those of the salt-water snakes. They live in fresh-water though they may be found in brackish water; they have not a compressed tail; they are viviparous, and all belong to the sub-order of non-venomous colubrines.—" *c* " Ground-snakes. Representatives are found in all the three sub-orders. They live generally above ground. They are more or less cylindrical in shape and very flexible in body. The greater number of snakes are found in this section.—" *d* " Burrowing snakes [coozhay vaulan]. These live much under ground; have a rigid cylindrical body, short tail, narrow mouth, and small teeth. No ventral shields; they are all innocuous. Snakes are divided by the natives into castes as Bramins, Rajahs, Chetties, Pariahs, &c.——**(6)** A key-synopsis connecting the european and native terminology will be found included under Sarpy. Title heads in this glossary cover each family, and contained genus and species, distinguished by the natives.——**(7)** For insects see Poochy; for fishes see Matsyam; for batrachians see Bhaicam; for reptiles see Sarpy; for birds see Pacshy; for mammals see Sastanam. A general conspectus of the fauna [jantoo] of s. india was given in vol. II, appendix IV.

SARPY (सर्पी - sarpí, *San.*). San. from (srip, san. to creep) [sar]. Reptile [jantoo]. Reptiles proper, excluding Batrachia, are cold-blooded vertebrata, which undergo no metamorphosis, and breathe air by lungs during their whole existence. They are divided into three orders:—Chelonia or tortoises [coormam], Sauria or lizards [godhicay], and Ophidia or snakes [sarpam].——**(1)** The following is a key-synopsis of the reptiles of southern india, ranged down to species, connecting the european and native terminology; the small capitals indicate the orders, the small capitals in inverted commas indicate the sub-orders, the italics indicate the families, and the ordinary type indicates the species:—CHELONIA.—1 *Testudinidæ* [*aumay*].—Testudo elegans.—2 *Emydidæ* [*aumay*].—Emys trijuga; Pangshura tentoria; Batagur ellioti.—3 *Trionycidæ* [*cadalaumay*].—Emyda vittata; Trionyx javanicus.—4 *Chelonidæ* [*cadalaumay*].—Caouana olivacea; Chelonia virgata; Caretta squamata; Dermatochelys coriacea.—SAURIA.—5 *Crocodilidæ* [*mugger*].—Crocodilus palustris, porosus, pondicerianus.—6 *Varanidæ* [*oodoomoo*].—Varanus dracæna, lunatus.—7 *Lacertidæ* [*aranay*].—Cabrita leschenaultii; Acanthodactylus nilgherrensis.—8 *Scincidæ* [*regmahee*].—Euprepes rufescens, trilineatus; Eumeces bilineatus, albopunctatus, hardwickii, punctatus; Chiamela lineata, anguis, melanosticta.—9 *Geckotidæ* [*chipkalee*].—Gecko guttatus; Hemidactylus triedrus, maculatus, sykesii, leschenaultii, punctatus; Gymnodactylus mysoriensis, indicus, malabaricus, littoralis, deccanensis; Eublepharis hardwickii.—10 *Agamidæ* [*bloodsucker*].—Draco dussumieri; Sitana pondiceriana, minor; Bronchocela jubata; Calotes versicolor, nemoricola, rouxii, ophiomachus; Salea horsfieldii; Charasia dorsalis.—11 *Chamæleonidæ* [*patchonty*].—Chamæleo vulgaris.—OPHIDIA.—" OPHIDII COLUBRIFORMES."—12 *Typhlopidæ* [*domoonh*].—Typhlops braminus, pammeces; Onychocephalus acutus.—13 *Tortricidæ*.—Cylindrophis rufus.—14 *Uropeltidæ* [*coozhay vaulan*].—Rhinophis sanguineus, pulneyensis; Silybura macrolepia, beddomii, ocellata, ellioti, bicatenata, shorttii, brevis; Plectrurus perrotetii, güntheri; Melanophidium punctatum, wynaudense.—15 *Calamaridæ* [*coozhay paumb*].—Calamaria leucocephala; Macrocalamus lateralis; Geophis microcephalus, platypteryx, perrotetii; Aspidura copii.—16 *Oligodontidæ* [*cuttachootta*].—Oligodon subgriseus, spilonotus, ellioti, subpunctatus, spinipunctatus, fasciatus, affinis, modestus, brevicauda; Simotes venustus, russellii, binotatus, trilineatus, bicatenatus.—17 *Colubridæ* [*paumb*].—Ablabes olivaceus, humberti; Cyclophis calamaria, nasalis; Odontomus nympha [cutlapaumb], semifasciatus, gracilis; Nymphophidium maculatum; Coronella orientalis; Compsosoma radiatum; Cynophis helena [maigharecoolapuda], malabaricus; Ptyas mucosus [rat snake]; Zamenis ventrimaculatus, gracilis, fasciolatus; Tropidonotus quincunciatus [neer corattay], subminiatus, stolatus, monticola, beddomii, plumbicolor [tunny paumb]; Atretium schistosum [chitty paumb].—18 *Homalopsidæ* [*mutty paumb*].—Cerberus rhynchops; Hypsirhina enhydris.—19 *Psammophidæ* [*condanaroos*].—Psammophis condanarus.—20 *Dendrophidæ* [*tree snake*].—Dendrophis picta [combairy mookkan]; Chrysopelea ornata, rubescens.—21 *Dryiophidæ* [*whip snake*].—Tragops dispar, fronticinctus; Passerita mycterizans.—22 *Dipsadidæ* [*palmyra snake*].—Dipsas forsteni, trigonata.—23—*Lycodontidæ* [*vazhalay*].—Lycodon aulicus, striatus, anamallensis; Leptorhytaon jara [saurapotoo]; Ophites albofuscus.—24 *Pythonidæ* [*rock snake*].—Python molurus.—25 *Erycidæ* [*irtalay maniyan*].—Gongylophis conicus; Eryx johnii.—26 *Acrochordidæ* [*poodeiyan*].—Chersydrus granulatus.—" OPHIDII COLUBRIFORMES VENENOSI."—27 *Elapidæ* [*naug*].—Naja tripudians [cobra]; Ophiophagus elaps [hill cobra]; Bungarus cæruleus [krait], fasciatus [bungaur]; Callophis annularis, nigrescens.—28 *Hydrophidæ* [*tuttapaumb*].—Platurus [sea bungaur] scutatus, fischeri; Disteira doliata; Hydrophis [chittal] jerdonii, major, robusta, cærulescens, spiralis, cyanocincta, melanosoma, subcincta, chloris, lindsayii, diadema, gracilis, fasciata, lapemoides, longiceps, stricticollis, ornata, ellioti, viperina, curta; Enhydrina bengalensis [vaulakidy]; Pelamis bicolor [nullavaulagily].—" OPHIDII VIPERIFORMES."—29 *Crotalidæ* [*pit viper*].—Trimeresurus gramineus, anamallensis, strigatus; Peltopelor macrolepis; Halys ellioti; Hypnale nepa [carawilla].—30 *Viperidæ* [*viriyan*].—Daboia russellii [chain viper]; Echis carinata [carpet snake].——**(2)** The following is an alphabetical list of the above orders with references to the key-synopsis.——*Chelonia* (कूर्म - kúrma, San.). Means slow in motion. 1–4. Tortoise [coormam].——*Ophidia* (सर्प - sarpa, San.). From (srip, san. to creep). 12–30. Snakes [sarpam].——*Sauria* (गोधिका - gódhiká, San.). From (gudh, san. to envelope). 5–11. Lizard [godhicay].——**(3)** The following is an alphabetical list of the above families, with references to the key-synopsis.——*Acrochordidæ* (अग्रवराटीयकुल - agravarátíyakula, San.). From (agra, san. top + varáta, san. rope). Ophidii colubriformes, ophidia, 26.——*Agamidæ* (स्त्रीजन्यकुल - stríjanyakula, San.). From (strí, san. woman + jan, san. to be born). Sauria, 10.——*Calamaridæ* (कलमधरीयकुल - kalamadharíyakula, San.). From (kalama, san. pen + dhri, san. to hold). Ophidii colubriformes, ophidia, 15.——*Chamæleonidæ* (कृकलासीयकुल - krikalásíyakula, San.). From (krikalása, san. chameleon), Sauria, 11.——*Chelonidæ* (समुद्रकूर्मीयकुल - samudrakúrmíyakula. San.). From (samudra, san. sea + kúrma, san. tortoise). Chelonia, 4.——*Colubridæ* (निर्विषकुल - nirvishakula, San.). From (nirvisha, san. not venomous). Ophidii colubriformes, ophidia, 17.——*Crocodilidæ* (नक्रीयकुल - nakríyakula, San.). From (nakra, san. crocodile). Sauria, 5.——*Crotalidæ* (कूपकमण्डलेयकुल - kúpakamandaléyakula, San.). From (kúpa, san. hole + mandala, san. viper). Ophidii viperiformes, ophidia, 29.——*Dendrophidæ* (द्रुमाहिकेयकुल - drumáhikéyakula, San.). From (druma, san. tree + ahi, san. serpent). Ophidii colubriformes, ophidia, 20.——*Dipsadidæ* (तृष्यदहिकेयकुल - trishyadahikéyakula, San.). From (trishyat, san. thirsty + ahi, san. serpent). Ophidii colubriformes, ophidia, 22.——*Dryiophidæ* (द्रुणसाहिकेयकुल - drunasáhikéyakula, San.). From (drunasa, san. larger-nosed + ahi, san. serpent). Ophidii colubriformes, ophidia, 21.——*Elapidæ* (भौमाहिककुल - bhaumáhikakula, San.). From (bhúma, san. earth + ahi, san. serpent). Ophidii colubriformes, venenosi, ophidia, 27.——*Emydidæ* (जलकूर्मीयकुल - jalakúrmíyakula, San.). From (jala, san. water + kúrma, san. tortoise). Chelonia, 2.——*Erycidæ* (इरिणाहिककुल - irináhikakula, San.). From (irina, san. desert + ahi, san. serpent). Ophidii colubriformes, ophidia, 25.——*Geckotidæ* (कृकवाकीयकुल - krikavákíyakula, San.). From (kríkaváku, san. gecko). Sauria, 9.——*Homalopsidæ* (नदीसर्पीयकुल - nadísarpíyakula, San.). From (nadí, san. river + sarpa, san. serpent). Ophidii colubriformes, ophidia, 18.——*Hydrophidæ* (समुद्राहिकेयकुल - samudráhikéyakula, San.). From (samudra, san. sea + ahi, san. serpent). Ophidii colubriformes, venenosi, ophidia, 28.——*Lacertidæ* (स्थलगोधेयकुल - st'halagódhéyakula, San.). From (st'hala, san. earth + gódhá, san. lizard). Sauria, 7.——*Lycodontidæ* (वृकदन्तीयकुल - vrikadantíyakula, San.). From (vrika, san. wolf + danta, san. tooth). Ophidii colubriformes, ophidia, 23.——*Oligodontidæ* (अल्पदन्तीयकुल - alpadantíyakula, San.). From (alpa, san. small + danta, san. tooth). Ophidii colubriformes, ophidia, 16.——*Psammophidæ* (सिकताहिकेयकुल - sikatáhikéyakula, San.). From (sikata, san. sand + ahi, san. serpent). Ophidii colubriformes, ophidia, 19.——*Pythonidæ* (शिलासर्पकुल - shilásarpakula, San.). From (shilá, san. rock + sarpa, san. serpent). Ophidii colubriformes, ophidia, 24.——*Scincidæ* (शल्कगोधेयकुल - shalkagódhéyakula, San.). From (shalka, san. scale + gódhá, san. lizard). Sauria, 8.——*Testudinidæ* (स्थलकूर्मीयकुल - st'halakúrmíyakula, San.). From (st'hala, san. earth + kúrma, san. tortoise). Chelonia, 1.——*Tortricidæ* (ह्रस्ववालेयकुल - hrasvaváléyakula, San.). From (hrasva, san. short + vála, san. tail). Ophidii colubriformes, ophidia, 13.——*Trionycidæ* (त्रिणखकूर्मीयकुल - trinakhakúrmíyakula, San.). From (tri, san. three + nakha, san. claw + kúrma, san. tortoise). Chelonia, 3.——*Typhlopidæ* (अन्धाहिकेयकुल - andháhikéyakula. San.). From (andha, san. blind + ahi, san. serpent). Ophidii colubriformes, ophidia, 12.——*Uropeltidæ* (रूक्षवालेयकुल - rúkshaváléyakula, San.). From (rúksha, san. rough + vála, san. tail). Ophidii colubriformes, ophidia, 14.——*Varanidæ* (वारुणगोधेयकुल - várunagódhéyakula, San.). From (váruna, san. water + gódhá, san. lizard). Sauria, 6.——*Viperidæ* (मण्डलीयकुल - mandalíyakula, San.). From (mandalí, san. viper). Ophidii viperiformes, ophidia, 30.——**(4)** The following is an alphabetical list of the above genera, showing the family to which they belong:—Ablabes, colubridæ, 17; Acanthodactylus, lacertidæ, 7; Aspidura, calamaridæ, 15; Atretium, colubridæ, 17; Batagur, emydidæ, 2; Bronchocela, agamidæ, 10; Bungarus, elapidæ, 27; Cabrita, lacertidæ, 7; Calamaria, calamaridæ, 15; Callophis, elapidæ, 27; Calotes, agamidæ, 10; Caouana, chelonidæ, 4; Caretta, chelonidæ, 4; Cerberus, homalopsidæ, 18; Chamæleo, chamæleonidæ, 11; Charasia, agamidæ, 10; Chelonia, chelonidæ, 4; Chersydrus, acrochordidæ, 26; Chiamela, scincidæ, 8; Chrysopelea, dendrophidæ, 20; Compsosoma, colubridæ, 17; Coronella, colubridæ, 17; Crocodilus, crocodilidæ, 5; Cyclophis, colubridæ, 17; Cylindrophis, tortricidæ, 13; Cynophis, colubridæ, 17; Daboia, viperidæ, 30; Dendrophis, dendrophidæ, 20; Dermatochelys, chelonidæ, 4; Dipsas, dipsadidæ, 22; Disteira, hydrophidæ, 28; Draco, agamidæ, 10; Echis, viperidæ, 30; Emyda, trionycidæ, 3; Emys, emydidæ, 2; Enhydrina, hydrophidæ, 28; Eryx, erycidæ, 25; Eublepharis, geckotidæ, 9; Eumeces, scincidæ, 8; Euprepes, scincidæ, 8; Gecko, geckotidæ, 9; Geophis, calamaridæ, 15; Gongylophis, erycidæ, 25; Gymnodactylus, geckotidæ, 9; Halys, crotalidæ, 29; Hemidactylus, geckotidæ, 9; Hydrophis, hydrophidæ, 28; Hypnale, crotalidæ, 29; Hypsirhina, homalopsidæ, 18; Leptorhytaon, lycodontidæ, 23; Lycodon, lycodontidæ, 23; Macrocalamus, calamaridæ, 15; Melanophidium, uropeltidæ, 14; Naja, elapidæ, 27; Nymphophidium, colubridæ, 17; Odontomus, colubridæ, 17; Oligodon, oligodontidæ, 16; Onychocephalus, typhlopidæ, 12; Ophiophagus, elapidæ, 27; Ophites, lycodontidæ, 23; Pangshura, emydidæ, 2; Passerita, dryiophidæ, 21; Pelamis, hydrophidæ, 28; Peltopelor, crotalidæ, 29; Platurus, hydrophidæ, 28; Plectrurus, uropeltidæ, 14; Psammophis, psammophidæ, 19; Ptyas, colubridæ, 17; Python, pythonidæ, 24; Rhinophis, uropeltidæ, 14; Salea, agamidæ, 10; Silybura, uropeltidæ, 14; Simotes, oligodontidæ, 16; Sitana, agamidæ, 10; Testudo, testudinidæ, 1; Tragops, dryiophidæ, 21; Trimeresurus, crotalidæ, 29; Trionyx, trionycidæ, 3; Tropidonotus, colubridæ, 17; Typhlops, typhlopidæ, 12; Varanus, varanidæ, 6; Zamenis, colubridæ, 17.——**(5)** Title heads in this glossary cover each family, and contained genus and species, distinguished by the natives.——**(6)** For insects see Poochy; for fishes see Matsyam; for batrachians see Bhaicam; for birds see Pacshy; for mammals see Sastanam. A general conspectus of the fauna of s. india was given in vol. II, appendix IV.

SARSOON (सर्षप - sarshapa, *San.*; درخت سرشف - darakhtisarshaf, *Pers.*; سرسون کا پیڑ - sarsúnkáper. *Hind.*; سرسون کا جھاڑ - sarsúnkájhár, *Dec.*). Title from hindostany [sar]. San. from (sri, san. to go), from round and useful seeds. Pers. from (darakht, pers. tree + sarshaf, pers. mustard). Hind. from (sarsún, hind. mustard, brassica + per, hind. tree). Dec. from (sarsún, hind. mustard + jhár, hind. tree). Botanically Brassica [sarshapam] campestris, linn., cruciferæ [vricsham, 10]. Erect, stout, simple or branched, glabrous or slightly hispid annual, 1–3 feet high; leaves large, petioled, more or less pinnatifid, upper oblong or lanceolate; flowers large, bright yellow; pedicels ¾ inch, ascending or spreading; pod 1½–3 inches, glabrous, sub-erect; valves with midrib and flexuous veins; seeds small, smooth, pale or dark. The turnip sub-division of Brassica. For the common turnip, which is here only acclimatized, see the sub-species rapa [shalgham]. The following are native articles.——*Cauly sarsoon* (कालसर्षप - kálasarshapa, San.; काळामोहरी - kálámóharí, Mahr.; خردل اسود - khardaliaswad, Ar.; درخت سرشف سیاہ - darakhtisarshafisiyáh, Pers.; کالی سرسون کا پیڑ - kálísarsúnkáper, Hind.; کالی سرسون کا جھاڑ - kálísarsúnkájhár, Dec.; ఆవాలు - áválu, Tel.; കടുക - katuku, Mal.; கடுகு - kadugu, Tam.). Title from hindostany. San. from (kála, san. black + sarshapa, san. mustard). Mahr. from (kálá, mahr. black + móharí, mahr. mustard, brassica juncea, h. f. and t.). Ar. from (khardal, ar. mustard + aswad, ar. black). Pers. from (darakht, pers. tree + sarshaf, pers. mustard + siyáh, pers. black). Hind. from (kálí, hind. black + sarsún, hind. mustard + pér, hind. tree). Dec. from hindostany. Mal. from tamul. Tam. from (kadumai, tam. intensity). Pers. also (sipandánisiyáh), meaning black mustard. Hind. also (kálírái), meaning black mustard; (bangasarsún). Title otherwise Cole seed, Colza, Navette, Sarson, Swedish turnip, Wild navew. Botanically Brassica [sarshapam] campestris, linn., sub-sp. campestris, linn., cruciferæ [vricsham, 10]. Alias Sinapis dichotoma. Root tuberous; leaves glaucous, radical hispid, upper glabrous; petals persistent till the corymb lengthens; bears smallish yellow flowers. Colza oil made from seeds; has very little smell; if properly prepared, is yellow and of rather a sweet taste; remains limpid at a much lower temperature, than most oils [yennay]. Oil medicinally less energetic than black mustard [cauly rayaun]. Oil largely used as an article of diet; leaves used for culinary purposes; oil cake [ponnauk] given to cattle. Oil used in manufacture of soap [sauboon]; also to anoint the body and for illuminating purposes.——*Rara sarsoon* (राजिका - rájiká, San.; رارسرسون - rárasarsún, Hind.; తెల్లావాలు - tellaáválu, Tel.). Title from hindostany. San. from (ráji, san. row), means striped. Tel. from (tella, tel. white + áválu, tel. mustard, brassica juncea, h. f. and t.). Hind. also (pílasarsún), meaning yellow mustard; (sarsúnizard), meaning yellow mustard; (bangsarsún). Title otherwise Cole seed, Navew, Rape, Shwet-rye. Brassica [sarshapam] campestris, linn., sub-sp. napus, linn., cruciferæ [vricsham, 10]. Alias Sinapis glauca. Root fusiform; leaves all glabrous and glaucous; petals deciduous before the corymb lengthens; cultivated extensively; seeds are exported. Leaves used for culinary purposes; the oil is superior to colza and much used in diet, also in anointing the body before daily ablutions [snaunam]. In spite of the commercial name for this, the sub-species rapa is different, viz., the common turnip [shalgham].——*Toriya sarsoon* (तीवक - tívraka, San.; توریا - toriyá, Hind. and Dec.). Title from deccany. San. from (tívra, san. sharp). Dec. from sanscrit. Botanically Brassica [sarshapam] campestris, linn., sub-sp. napus, linn., var. toria, cruciferæ [vricsham, 10]. Toria from hindostany. Alias Sinapis glauca. Whole plant quite smooth and glaucous, 2–3 feet in height; lower leaves lyrate or pinnatifid, upper amplexicaul, lanceolate, entire; flowers bright yellow, sepals spreading; pods rather slender, 1½–1¾ inches long, transversely compressed, more or less torulose; beak about ¼ inch long; seeds small roundish or semi-compressed, reddish brown or finely rugose. Leaves used for culinary purposes; oil not known.

SARWASIDDHY (సర్వసిద్ధి - sarvasiddhi, * *Tel.*). From (sarva, san. all + siddhi, san. success) [sar].——**(1)** Talook; Vizagapatam district. Tahsildar's pay Rs. 150; area 341 square miles; population 154,966; language Teloogoo. S. coast of district. Boundaries:—east, sea; west, Golcondah talook; north, Ankapully talook; south, Godavery district. The Maharajah of Vizianagram originally purchased this estate. In 1810 he sold it to Saugy ramchendra rauz, his maternal aunt's husband, whose son ran into arrears, when the Government purchased it in 1831. The talook is a plain country along the sea coast dotted with small hills and traversed by two rivers, Shaurada and Varauhanuddy. Red clay and red loam; generally fertile and especially in villages in Shaurada valley. Indigo [q.v.], gingelly [q.v.] and jaggery [q.v.] taken to Vizagapatam for exportation. Agriculture is chief industry. Shaurada and Varauhanuddy and Condakirla auva are main sources of irrigation. There are various anicuts [q.v.]. Camping grounds:—Naccapilly, Payacarowpett and Yellamanchily. Places of archæological interest:—Andalaupulley, Condakirla, Corcondah, Dimiley, Doopptoorroo, Gopaulputnam, Madootore, Mangavaram, Maumidivauda, Naccapilly, Oopamauca, Ooppalam, Payacarowpett, Pentacote, Punchadhaurla, Royavaram, Shreerampooram, Yellamanchily. Principal trig. stations:—Dongalcondah beacon, Goommalore, Locaurap, Mabraujy, Polavaram beacon, Punchadhaurla, Rambilly beacon, Soodicondah, Tantady beacon, Vemagherry. The leading places, &c., in the talook are the following.——*Condakiria auva* (కొండకిర్ల ఆవ - kondakirlaáva, Tel.). See sep. title.——*Corprole* (కొరుప్రోలు - koruprólu, Tel.). From (korru, tel. trident + prólu, tel. town). Proprietary estate, Village; pop. 3,455; lat. of village 17° 25′; long. 82° 48′; from Vizagapatam S.W. 38 miles; from Yellamanchily S.S.W. 10 miles; from the sea N. 4 miles. Peshcush Rs. 8,041.——*Dongalcondah beacon* (దొంగలకొండ - dongalakonda, Tel.). From (donga, tel. robber + konda, tel. hill). Trig. station; lat. 17° 20′ 00·00″; long. 82° 43′ 00·00″.——*Goodicherla* (గుడిచెర్ల - gudicherla, Tel.). From (gudi, tel. temple + cherla, tel. village). Proprietary estate, Village; pop. 1,544; lat. of village 17° 23′; long. 82° 40′; from Vizagapatam S.W. 48 miles; from Yellamanchily S.S.W. 19 miles; from the sea N. 6 miles. Peshcush Rs. 17,254.——*Goommalore* (గుమ్మలూరు - gummalúru, Tel.). From (gummamu, tel. entrance + úru, tel. village). Trig. station; lat. 17° 25′ 52·35″; long. 82° 46′ 08·18″; from Pedda goommalore S.W. ⅜ mile; from Sarwasiddhy S.W. 7 miles; from Yellamanchily S.W. 12 miles; from the sea N. 5 miles.——*Gopaulputnam* (గోపాలపట్నము - gópálapatnamu, Tel.). From (gópáludu, tel. proper name + pattana, san. town). Village;

pop. 798; lat. 17° 44′; long. 83° 16′; from Vizagapatam N.W. 5 miles; from Yellamanchily N.E. 27 miles; from the sea W. 8 miles. Old temple and eight rock-cut remains, six on Pandavool mittah hill and two on Boobcondah hill.——*Locaurap* (లోకారపు - lókárapu, Tel.). From (lóhakára, san. iron-smith). Trig. station; lat. 17° 20′ 11·48″; long. 82° 36′ 28·41″; from Pedda ramabhadrapooram N. 92 miles; from Sarwasiddhy S.W. 20 miles; from Yellamanchily S.W. 24 miles; from the sea N. 5 miles.——*Mabraujy* (మబ్రాజి - mabráji, Tel.). From (mabbu, tel. cloud + ráshi, san. heap). Trig. station; lat. 17° 24′ 00·83″; long. 82° 42′ 12·49″; from Chinna doddigull W. ½ mile; from Sarwasiddhy W.S.W. 12 miles; from Yellamanchily S.W. 17 miles; from the sea N. 6 miles.——*Madootore* (మదుటూరు - madutúru, Tel.). From (madati, tel. woman + úru, tel. village). Village; pop. 1,712; acres 2,438; lat. 17° 34′; long. 83° 03′; from Vizagapatam S.W. 21 miles; from Yellamanchily E. 10 miles; from the sea N. 4 miles. Old temple built by a Cholan [q.v.], with inscription.——*Maumidivauda* (మామిడివాడ - mámidiváda, Tel.). From (mámili, tel. mango, mangifera indica, linn. + váda, tel. village). Proprietary estate, Village; pop. 659; acres 1,021; lat. of village 17° 32′; long. 82° 56′; from Vizagapatam W.S.W. 27 miles; from Yellamanchily E. 3 miles; from the sea N. 7 miles. Two old temples built by Jeinas [q.v.]. Peshcush Rs. 1,793.——*Melpauca* (మేలుపాక - mélupáka, Tel.). From (mélu, tel. excellent + páka, tel. hamlet). Proprietary estate, Village; pop. 2,010; lat. of village 17° 35′; long. 82° 57′; from Vizagapatam S.W. 26 miles; from Yellamanchily N.E. 4 miles; from the sea N. 10 miles. Remains of an old mud fort. Peshcush Rs. 19,442.——*Naccapilly* (నక్కపిల్లి - nakkapilli, Tel.). From (nakka, tel. fox + palli, tel. village). Proprietary estate, Village, Travellers' bungalow and a native choultry; pop. 2,344; lat. of village 17° 25′; long. 82° 46′; from Vizagapatam S.W. 42 miles; from Yellamanchily S.S.W. 13 miles; from the sea N. 4 miles. Near summit of a hill; near is a grotto over which hang two enormous masses of gneiss, converted into a pagoda [q.v.]. There are 295 steps cut in the rock. Peshcush Rs. 5,393.——*Oopamauca* (ఉపమాక - upamáka, Tel.). From (úpa, tel. underwood + páka, tel. hamlet). Agrahauram, Place of pilgrimage; pop. 2,093; lat. 17° 24′; long. 82° 46′; from Vizagapatam S.W. 42 miles; from Yellamanchily S.W. 13 miles; from the sea N. 4 miles. Ancient pagoda [q.v.] built on a rock. There are no idols, but resemblances of the chunk [q.v.] or conch and chuckram [q.v.] or discus carried by Vishnoo [q.v.] are visible on a stone. Annual marriage festival of god [tircalyaunam] in March. Numerous marriage [calyaunam] and ceremonies of celibacy celebrated here. At foot of rock is another pagoda with image of Shree vencateshwaran.——*Pedda goommalore* (పెద్దగుమ్మలూరు - peddagummalúru, Tel.). From (pedda, tel. great + gummalúru, tel. the place). Proprietary estate, Village; pop. 2,983; square miles 6; lat. of village 17° 26′; long. 82° 47′; from Vizagapatam S.W. 40 miles; from Yellamanchily S.S.W. 12 miles; from the sea N. 5 miles. Peshcush Rs. 3,761.——*Pentacote* (పెంటకోట - pentakóta, Tel.). See sep. title.——*Polavarum beacon* (పోలవరము - pólavaramu, Tel.). From (póli, tel. proper name + pura, san. town). Trig. station; lat. 17° 23′ 40·39″; long. 82° 51′ 39·03″; from Polavaram S. ½ mile; from Sarwasiddhy S. 5 miles; from Yellamanchily S. 10 miles; from the sea N. ⅛ mile. Salt factory in a swamp close by.——*Poodimadaca* (పూడిమడక - púdimadaka, Tel.). See sep. title.——*Punchadhaurla* (పంచధారలు - panchadháralu, Tel.). From (pañcha, san. five + dhárá, san. stream), from the five fountains of the place. Village, Place of pilgrimage; pop. 2,289; acres 1,964; lat. 17° 32′; long. 82° 58′; from Vizagapatam S.W. 27 miles; from Yellamanchily E.S.E. 4 miles; from the sea N. 6 miles. On a small rock is an ancient pagoda to Shiva as Dharmeshwaran. Sixteen inscriptions on the temple of Shree dharma lingeshwaran, dating from A.D. 1394 to 1526. Trig. station in lat. 17° 35′ 05·12″; long. 83° 00′ 23·27″; height 935 feet; from Condakirla S.W. 1½ miles; from Sarwasiddhy N.E. 12 miles; from Yellamanchily N.E. 7 miles; from the sea N. 8 miles.——*Rambilly beacon* (రాంబిల్లి - rámbilli, Tel.). From (ráma, san. the god + palle, tel. village). Trig. station; lat. 17° 27′ 23·01″; long. 82° 59′ 21·34″; from Rambilly S.E. 1 mile; from Sarwasiddhy E. 8 miles; from Yellamanchily S.S.E. 9 miles; from the sea W. ⅛ mile.——*Royavaram* (రాయవరము - ráyavaramu, Tel.). From (ráyadu, tel. king + pura, san. town). Village; pop. 5,336; acres 1,232; lat. 17° 27′; long. 82° 51′; from Vizagapatam W.S.W. 36 miles; from Yellamanchily S.S.W. 7 miles; from the sea N. 4 miles. Inscription fixing date of conquest by Krishna deva royel of Vijianugger.——*Sarwasiddhy* (సర్వసిద్ధి - sarvasiddhi, Tel.). See below.——*Satyavaram* (సత్యవరము - satyavaramu, Tel.). From (satya, san. truth + pura, san. town). Village; pop. 1,604; lat. 17° 20′; long. 82° 38′; from Vizagapatam S.W. 52 miles; from Yellamanchily S.S.W. 22 miles; from the sea N. 4 miles. Betel [q.v.] gardens.——*Shaurada nuddy* (శారదానది - sháradánadi, Tel.). See sep. title.——*Shreerampooram* (శ్రీరామపురము - shrírámapuramu, Tel.). From (shrí, san. holy + ráma, san. the god + pura, san. city). Proprietary estate, Village; pop. 3,089; lat. of village 17° 19′; long. 82° 37′; from Vizagapatam S.W. 53 miles; from Yellamanchily S.S.W. 25 miles; from the sea N. 3 miles. Temple of Ramasawmy with inscription. Peshcush Rs. 17,907.——*Soodicondah* (సూదికొండ - súdikonda, Tel.). From (súdi, tel. needle + konda, tel. hill). Trig. station; lat. 17° 20′ 27·05″; long. 82° 39′ 04·60″; from Gopaulputnam N. 1 mile; from Sarwasiddhy S.W. 17 miles; from Yellamanchily S.W. 21 miles; from the sea N. 4 miles.——*Tantady beacon* (తంతడి - tantadi, Tel.). Trig. station; lat. 17° 31′ 51·64″; long. 83° 05′ 01·57″; from Sarwasiddhy N.E. 14 miles; from Yellamanchily E. 11 miles; from the sea N. 1 mile; from Tantady W. 1 mile.——*Varauhanuddy* (వరాహనది - varáhanadi, Tel.). See sep. title.——*Vemagherry* (వేమగిరి - vémagiri, Tel.). From (vému, tel. margosa tree, melia azadirachta, linn. + giri, tel. hill). Trig. station; lat. 17° 29′ 50·45″; long. 82° 51′ 49·83″; from Sarwasiddhy N. 2 miles; from Vemagherry N.N.W. ¼ mile; from Yellamanchily S.S.W. 4 miles; from the sea N. 7 miles.——*Wattauda* (వత్తాడ - vattáda, Tel.). See sep. title.——*Yellamanchily* (ఎల్లమంచిలి - ellamanchili, Tel.). See sep. title.——**(2)** Village; Vizagapatam dist., Sarwasiddhy tal.; pop. 1,096; acres 1,606; lat. 17° 28′; long. 82° 53′; from Vizagapatam S.W. 34 miles; from Yellamanchily S.S.W. 6 miles; from the sea N. 5 miles. Formerly headquarters of Tahsildar [q.v.] till 1861.

SARY (సరి - sari, *Tel.*). Straight.——*Sarwapully* (సర్వపల్లి - sarvapalle, Tel.). From (sari, tel. straight + palle, tel. village). Village; Nellore dist., Goodoor tal.; pop. 5,833; acres 22,388; lat. 14° 18′; long. 80° 01′; from Goodoor N.E. 13 miles; from Nellore S. 11 miles; from the sea W. 11 miles. Remains of old Rohilla fort. Stone tank in front of the fort gate and another within the fort. The chief tank [q.v.] under the Pennair anicut [q.v.] lies close by.

SARYE (سرای - sarái, *Hind.*). From (sará, pers. building). A rest-house for travellers [chuttram, dharmashaulay, moosaufer khana]. Compounded in the English caravansary.

SASTANAM (सस्तन - sastana, *San.*). From (sa, san. with + stana, san. breast of female) [sa]. Mammals. Vertebrate animals which suckle their young, and have some part of their skins protected by hair.——**(1)** The first step in their classification is the division into those in which the young are nourished in the maternal uterus by means of a placenta, placental mammals; and those in which the young fœtus is expelled at a very early period, and maintained in a pouch attached to a nipple, implacental or marsupial animals. None of these last occur in India; being chiefly developed in the Australian region, and a few in America; they have moreover very anomalous forms of dentition. After deducting the marsupial animals, the bulk of the mammals still remains. Taking the teeth as a guide, a large number of animals are found possessed of all four kinds of teeth, the incisors, the canines, the praemolars, and the molars; though in varying number and proportion; these are Typodontia, or animals with the typical forms of teeth developed, and include man, monkeys [bandar], bats [vavvaul], carnivorous animals and shrews, muskrat [q.v.], &c., in fact all the most perfect forms of mammals. There is next found a large and still more varied association of animals of inferior and more specialized organization, in which the teeth vary much from the typical formation, and have rarely more than two kinds of teeth developed; this group is Diplodontia, and includes rats [ely], and squirrels [anil], deer [mrigam], sheep [aud], and cattle [maud], the elephant [q.v.], pig [soor], and horse [ghorah], and the almost toothless ant-eaters [jungle carp]; they chiefly live on vegetable matter, as the majority of the Typodontia do on animal food. A third small division, comprising the whales [timingilam] and porpoises [cadal pundry], &c., are Isodontia, because the teeth when present are all of one kind. The three large groups are next divided into orders. And first the Typodontia. On examining the hairy covering of a monkey [bandar] and a bat [vavvaul], it is found that there is only one kind of hair, no under-hair or wool being present. As man belongs to this division, it goes under the general title of Primates. It is composed of two very distant orders, that of Quadrumana or the four-handed, comprising monkeys [bandar] and lemurs [devaunga], in most of which there is a thumb or opposable finger on the foot; and Cheiroptera, or hand-winged, the bats [vavvaul], which have the forearm and hand extended into an organ of flight. The remaining groups of perfect-toothed animals have two kinds of hair, in variable amount, and are called Secundates. They are likewise divided into two orders. The first is the Carnivora, or beasts of prey, the most typical of the two, and distinguished by powerful canines and trenchant molars, which are never studded with sharp points while the clavicle is generally imperfect. The other order is that of Insectivora, a group of small mammals, having their molar teeth studded with sharp points to bruise their insect prey, and these usually have a greater number of teeth than the Carnivora; they all possess clavicles. The Diplodontia present much greater differences of aspect and structure than the more perfect group, and it is only as a matter of convenience that they are grouped together. One order, which like the preceding orders has claws or is unguiculate, possesses two chisel-shaped teeth in front of each jaw, no apparent canines, and small number of flattened molars; this is the Rodentia, or gnawers, comprising rats [ely] and squirrels [anil], &c. Another order, likewise with claws, which are large and fossorial or capable of digging, but partially enclosing the toes and somewhat hoof-like, is distinguished by the total absence of incisors and canine teeth, and in some of all teeth whatsoever; these are called Edentata or toothless, and they include the ant-eaters [jungle carp] and armadillos. All the remaining animals of this group except one have the toes more or less joined together, and ending in a hoof, which is single and solid in the horse [ghorah], double or bisulcate in the deer [mrigam] and pig [soor], with three divisions as in the rhinoceros [gendah], with four unsymmetrical in the hippopotamus, and with five hoof-like nails terminating the pad of the elephant [q.v.]. These form the Ungulata of some writers, and are then divided into the Ruminantia, or ruminants, and the Pachydermata, or thick skinned mammals. Here they are divided into Proboscidea, Ungulata, and Ruminantia. The last-named is a very natural group and comprises all that chew the cud; deer [mrigam], cattle [maud], sheep [aud], &c. They have two hoofs and two upper supplemental ones, no upper incisors except in the camel and flattened molars. A canine is present in a few. The Ungulata and Proboscidea differ much in their dentition and only agree in the negative character of not ruminating. The herbivorous cetaceans, are separated as a distinct order called Sirenia, and are distinguished from the other Diplodonts by the absence of limbs. The Isodontia, comprising the whales [timingilam], dolphins and porpoises [cadal pundry], are as an order called Cetacea, and have no posterior extremities, whilst their anterior limbs are changed into fins.——**(2)** The following is a key-synopsis for the placental mammals of S. india, carried down to species, connecting the european and native terminology. The black letter indicates the dental divisions, the small capitals indicate orders, the small capitals in inverted commas indicate sub-orders or tribes. the italic indicates families, the italic in inverted commas indicates sub-families, and the genera and species stand in ordinary roman type. Note in abstract that the division Typodontia or teeth of all four kinds includes the orders Quadrumana or with thumb on the feet, Cheiroptera or winged, Carnivora or molars trenchant mixed with tubercular ones, and Insectivora or molars studded with cusps; that the division Diplodontia or teeth generally of two kinds only abnormal includes the orders Rodentia or front teeth long and chisel-like, Proboscidea or teeth varied with trunk and do not ruminate, Ungulata or teeth varied with hoofs, Ruminantia or upper incisors generally absent and chew the cud, Sirenia or want posterior extremities, and Edentata or incisors absent; and that the division Isodontia or teeth when present of one kind and often very numerous includes the order Cetacea with post-extremities wanting.——**Typodontia.**—QUADRUMANA.—1 *Cercopithecidæ.*—"*Semnopithecinæ* [*lungoor*]."—Semnopithecus priamus, hypoleucus, johnii.—"*Cercopithecinæ*" [*baboon*].—Macacus sinicus [bandar], silenus [siyah bandar].—2 *Lemuridæ.*—Loris gracilis [devaunga].—CHEIROPTERA.—3 *Pteropodidæ.*—Pteropus edwardsii [flying-fox], leschenaultii; Cynopterus marginatus.—4 *Vampyridæ* [*kaffaush*].—"*Megadermatinæ.*"—Megaderma lyra.—"*Rhinolophinæ.*"—Rhinolophus affinis, rouxi; Hipposideros speoris, murinus; Rhinopoma hardwickii.—5 *Noctilionidæ* [*chamgadal*].—Taphozous longimanus, melanopogon, saccolaimus; Nyctinomus plicatus.—6 *Vespertilionidæ* [*vavvaul*].—Scotophilus coromandelianus; Nycticejus heathii, temminckii, canus; Kerivoula picta.—CARNIVORA.—"PLANTIGRADA."—7 *Ursidæ.*—Melursus ursinus [ricsham].—"SEMI-PLANTIGRADA."—8 *Mustelidæ.*—"*Melinæ.*"—Mellivora indica [indian rattel].—"*Lutrinæ.*"—Lutra vulgaris [neernye].—"DIGITIGRADA."—9 *Felidæ.*—Felis tigris [pooly], pardus [honiga], viverrina [meencolly poonay], bengalensis [shivingy poonay], rubiginosa [poolly poonay], torquata, chaus [jungle cat], caracal [q.v.], domestica [poonay]; Cynælurus jubatus [cheetah].—10 *Hyænidæ.*—Hyæna striata [cazhoothay pooly].—11 *Viverridæ.*—"*Viverrinæ.*"—Viverra civettina [poonoogoo poonay]; Viverricula malaccensis; Paradoxurus niger [toddy cat].—"*Herpestinæ.*"—Horpestes mungo [mongoose], smithii, fuscus, vitticollis.—12 *Canidæ* [*cookooram*].—Canis [shwaunam] pallipes [konye], aureus [jackal], dukhunensis [dhole]. Vulpes bengalensis [lomree].—INSECTIVORA.—13 *Sorecidæ.*—Crocidura cærulea [musk-rat], murina, perroteti; Sorex niger.—14 *Erinaceidæ.*—Erinaceus micropus [moollely].—15 *Tupaiidæ.*—Tupaia ellioti [musk-rat].——**Diplodontia.**—RODENTIA.—16 *Sciuridæ* [*anil*].—Sciurus malabaricus [malabar squirrel], elphinstonei, macrourus, palmarum [anil pillay], tristriatus, layardi, sublineatus; Pteromys petaurista [paravay anil]; Sciuropterus fuscocapillus.—17 *Muridæ.*—Gerbillus indicus [shevvely]; Nesokia indica [kok]; Mus rattus, decumanus [ely], bandicota [bandicoot], infralineatus, brunneus [maravely], rufescens, oleraceus [mara shoondely], nilagiricus, urbanus [shoondely], crassipes, cervicolor [varappoo shoondely], terricolor; Leggada platythrix [moolloo shoondely], spinulosa, lepida; Platacanthomys lasiurus [pepper rat]; Golunda ellioti [golandy], meltada [varappely].—18 *Hystricidæ.*—Hystrix leucura [kharpoosht].—19 *Leporidæ.*—Lepus ruficaudatus, nigricollis [mosal].—PROBOSCIDEA.—20 *Elephantidæ.*—Elephas indicus [elephant].—UNGULATA.—"PERISSODACTYLA."—21 *Equidæ.*—Equus vulgaris [ghorah], asinus [gadhah].—"ARTIODACTYLA."—22 *Suidæ.*—Sus indicus [soor].—RUMINANTIA.—23 *Bovidæ.*—"*Caprinæ*" [*aud*].—Hircus œgagrus [velland]; Ovis aries [shemmariyaud]; Hemitragus bylocrius [saddle back].—"*Antilopinæ.*"—Gazella bennetti [ravine deer]; Antilope bezoartica [jinka]; Portax pictus [nilghye]; Tetraceros quadricornis [chowsingha].—"*Bovinæ.*"—Gavæus gaurus [gowr]; Bubalus arni [khoolgah]; Bos indicus [mand].—24 *Cervidæ* [*mrigam*].—Cervulus muntjac [jungle sheep]; Rusa aristotelis [samber]; Axis maculatus [cheetal].—25 *Moschidæ.*—Memimna indica [mouse deer].—26 *Camelidæ.*—Camelus dromedarius [ottagam].—SIRENIA.—27 *Sirenidæ.*—Halicore dugong [dugong].—EDENTATA.—28 *Manididæ.*—Manis pentadactyla [jungle carp].——**Isodontia.**—CETACEA.—29 *Delphinidæ* [*pundry meen*].—Delphinus perniger [cadal pundry], plumbeus, gadamu, lentiginosus, maculiventer, fusiformis, pomeegra; Globicephalus indicus.—30 *Physeteridæ.*—Euphysetes macrocephalus [hoot].—31 *Balænidæ.*—Balænoptera indica [timingilam].——**(3)** The following is a list of the eleven orders arranged alphabetically, with the Sanscrit equivalents for their titles, references to the key-synopsis, and brief description of each.——*Carnivora* (क्रव्यभुक्सन्तान - kravyabhuksantána, San.). From (kravya, san. flesh + bhuj, san. to eat). Typodontia, 7–12. Flesh-eating animals or beasts of prey. The teeth of the lower jaw pass inside those of the upper, and one of the molar teeth, which is of large size, and furnished with a sharp cutting edge like a scissor, is hence called the flesh tooth, or scissor tooth. Feet armed with strong curved claws, and clavicles either absent or merely rudimentary. Name of order not exclusively correct; some bears live on fruit [caracal, cheetah, dhole, honiga, jackal, jungle cat, lomree, marjauram, mongoose, nye, pooly, poonay, indian rattel, ricsham, shwaunam, toddy-cat].——*Cetacea* (तिमिसन्तान - timisantána, San.). From (timi, san. whale). Isodontia, 29–31. Otherwise the Whale tribes. Cetaceans are distinguished by the fish-like form of their members, and live in seas and large rivers. Bulky animals with very large heads, tapering bodies, terminated by a broad tail-fin, which is the principal agent in swimming; it is supported by cartilage only. The head is not separated from the body by a neck. The eye is of very small size, and from the great development of their facial bones, appears in some to be placed nearly in the middle of the body. Their skin is thick and intimately mixed with fat forming the blubber, which serves to preserve the warm temperature of the body in the cold seas they frequent, and at the same time renders them light. Their skin is usually devoid of hair. They have spiracles or external nostrils, sometimes on the fore part of the nose, but usually on the top of the head, which can be closed by a conical stopper or valve. They have large brains with many and deep convolutions. The organ of hearing is of great delicacy, but the ears are deficient externally. Their sense of smell is little developed. The spiracle, or blowhole, is single or double. This does not serve as an organ of smell, but is used as a respiratory aperture. The spouting of whales is the moisture of the lungs and air passages expelled along with the expired air [cadal pundry, hoot, pundry meen, timingilam].——*Cheiroptera* (करपत्रीसन्तान - karapatrísantána, San.). From (karapatra, san. bat). Typodontia, 3–6. Usually called generically bats. Of small size, with very small eyes and large ears capable of rapid and continuous flight for hours. All nocturnal. During day rest in secluded places hanging head downwards by hind claws. Most hybernate, all have acute hearing and sense of touch. The wings form an enormously expanded organ of touch, by means of which they direct flight. Most are insectivorous; a few frugivorous, such as the flying fox [q.v.]. The frugivorous differing much in their dentition from the insectivorous lead through the flying lemurs [devaunga] directly to the Quadrumana. The Harpy of the ancients was one of these large bats. Though an insignificant creature the bat ranks structurally high in the animal kingdom and is in this regard only a few removes from man [chamgadal, flying-fox, kaffaush, vavvaul].——*Edentata* (अदन्तसन्तान - adantasantána, San.). From (adanta, san. toothless). Diplodontia, 28. Incisor teeth wanting. The order is subdivided into two groups, Tardigrada or sloths and Effodientia or burrowers. The former peculiar to American continent [jungle-carp].——*Insectivora* (कीटभुक्सन्तान - kítabhuksantána, San.). From (kíta, san. insect + bhuj, san. to eat). Typodontia, 13–15. Resemble the Rodents, but differ in having clavicles and in wanting the remarkable incisors of that group. Mostly small animals of nocturnal habits. Their pointed dentition enable them to pierce and crush the hard-shelled insects [poochy] on which they feed. The skull is elongated, the bones of the face and jaw especially, and those of the latter are comparatively weak. The limbs are short, feet five-toed and plantigrade, with the entire sole placed on the ground in running [moollely, musk rat].——*Proboscidea* (शुण्डीसन्तान - shundísantána, San.). From (shundi, san. elephant). Diplodontia, 20 [elephant].——*Quadrumana* (चतुर्हस्तसन्तान - chaturhastasantána, San.). From (chatur, san. four + hasta, san. hand). Typodontia, 1, 2. Toes of forefeet usually five in number; inner toe of fore limb may be wanting, but when present opposable to other digits. Hind foot five-toed with opposable hullux, or great toe. The animal can thus use both front and hind extremities for seizing things, and is quadrumanous [bandar, devaunga, lungoor].——*Rodentia* (कर्तनकरसन्तान - kartanakarasantána, San.). From (kartana, san. cutting). Diplodontia, 16–19. Gnawing animals Glires of some. Distinguished by absence of canine teeth. Have further in each jaw only two incisors, which are curved and adapted for gnawing. The molar teeth are few in number. Are mostly animals of small size, the porcupines [kharpoosht], being unusually large specimens. Eyes are directed sideways. The opening of the mouth is small, and many have cheek-pouches. The ears are moderate or large. The limbs are usually short, the hind extremity in many much larger than the anterior. They are usually clad with hair, in a few with bristles or spines. The tail varies much in size, is sometimes hairy, at others naked or scaly. They live chiefly on vegetable substances, often on hard nuts, roots, the bark of trees, &c.; and many are nocturnal in habits. Many build artificial nests, and a few manifest a constructive instinct in association; whilst others are remarkable for migrations. They are very prolific, often producing several litters in the year, and the young quickly attaining maturity. Many hybernate like reptiles. In point of intelligence the rodents do not come up to other mammals, the brain is small and remarkably free from convolution. Rodents which have never more than two incisors, coated only in front with enamel, are sometimes termed Simplicidentata. The others which have rudimentary incisors, as in the case of hares [mosal], and in which the enamel is spread more or less over all the surface, are then termed Duplicidentata [anil, bandicoot, chamara pootcham, ely, golandy, kharpoosht, kok, malabar squirrel, moosham, mosal, pepper rat, shoondely].——*Ruminantia* (रोमन्थकरसन्तान - rómant'hakarasantána, San.). From (rómant'ha, san. ruminating). Diplodontia, 23–26. Differ greatly from families Equidæ or suidæ by construction of digestive organs. Instead of food being masticated and passed at once into the stomach, each mouthful is but slightly bruised and passed into the paunch, whence at leisure it is regurgitated into the mouth to be chewed. They comprise most of the animals useful to man, viz., camels [ottagam], deer [mrigam], cattle [maud], and sheep [aud]. They are exclusively vegetable feeders. They break or tear rather than cut their food, and this action is accompanied by a swinging motion of the head forwards. Their eyes are so placed laterally that they have a great range of vision. Their ears are large, placed well back, and very mobile. Their smell is very acute. The speed of most is great. Many are docile and can be easily tamed, but they show very little intelligence. Most of them possess horns [aud, cheetal, chowsingha, gowr, saddle back, jinka, jungle sheep, khoolgah, maud, mouse deer, nilghye, ottagam, ravine deer, samber].——*Sirenia* (जलनरसन्तान - jalanarasantána, San.). From (jala, san. water + nara, san. man). Dugong. Diplodontia, 27 [dugong].——*Ungulata* (खुरीसन्तान - khurísantána, San.). From (khura, san. hoof). Diplodontia, 21, 22. Characterised by having the foot furnished with a hoof instead of claws, an arrangement which enables them to bear without injury the concussion of vigorous leaps, and which especially fits them for carrying heavy burdens. Further distinguished by absence of clavicles and by never having more than four full-sized toes. They are vegetable feeders, and their molar teeth are furnished with broad crowns to enable them to grind and reduce their food to a pulp. The section Perissodactyla are Ungulates in which the toes are an uneven number, and in which the horns, if present, are not in pairs. They embrace the rhinoceros, the tapir, the horse [ghorah], the ass [gadhah], the zebra, and the quagga. The section Artiodactyla are Ungulates with an even number of toes, and with their horns, when present, in pairs [ashwam, gadhah, ghorah, soor].——**(4)** The following is a list of the thirty-one families arranged alphabetically, with the Sanscrit equivalents for their titles, references, and brief description of each.——*Balænidæ* (तिमिकुल - timikula, San.). From (timi, san. whale). Cetacea, 31. Whale-bone whales. Head enormous; no teeth, but transverse horny laminæ adhering to the upper jaw. The largest of all known animals; produce one young at a birth; often found in large shoals; most abundant in high latitudes; feed on small fish [matsyam], cuttle-fish, other mollusca [chippy], and small crustacea [kavachiny]. The whalebone or baleen, sometimes, in large whales, consisting of six hundred to eight hundred plates, 12–15 feet long, forms a regular sieve through which the animal strains his food from the vast gulps of water he takes in whilst feeding. The lower jaw has neither teeth nor baleen, but is furnished with fleshy lips; skull characterized by the great predominance of the facial over the cranial portions and the curvature of the right of the lower jaw [timingilam].——*Bovidæ* (गोकुल - gókula, San.). From (gó, san. cow). Ruminantia, 23. Hollow-horned ruminants. The family is often called the Cavicornia or hollow-horned, as their horns, unlike those of the deer [mrigam], consist of a conical bony process of the temporal bone covered with a horny sheath which is persistent and mostly present in both sexes. Their dentition is the same as that of deer [mrigam]. Canines rarely present; muffle generally present. Feet-pits usually in all four feet. Inguinal-pits in some; eye-pits usually present. Four mammæ in most. This family comprises three sub-families; Antilopinæ, Bovinæ, and Caprinæ.—"*a*" Antilopinæ are Antelopes [jinka]. Horns in both sexes or only in the males; eye-pits in all and feet-pits in most; bony nucleus of the horn is generally solid, often has a sinus at the base within; horns are seated below the crest of the frontals, and are usually considerably apart at the base; inguinal-pits in many, muffle is often wanting; resemble deer in the lightness of their make; are of still more slender form, with finer limbs; and possess greater speed, but physiologically they are far removed from them. Hair is generally finer and more smooth than in deer. Horns of antelopes are variously bent, usually ringed at the base, and round and smooth at the tip, is situated well forwards, almost over the edge of the orbits; never branched, except in one species of North america. One small group has four horns. Eye, usually very large, deep brown or almost black, contrasting with the light eye of the Caprinæ [aud], is situated at the upper margin of the forehead, remote from the nostrils; head is lengthened owing to the elongation of the nasal bones; the ears are seated well back and are long. Antelope mostly live in more or less numerous herds [chowsingha, jinka, nilghye, ravine deer].—"*b*" Bovinæ are Ox-like animals [maud]. Horns always in both sexes; muffle large and broad; tail moderately long; no eye-pits; of large size, heavy and massive body; limbs stout; a dewlap often present. The horns are inserted laterally on the apex of the frontal crest. The occipital plane of the skull forms a small angle with the frontal plane. This sub-family must be further sub-divided into three groups; the Bisontine, the Taurine and the Bubaline. "i" The Bisontine group comprise the true Bison [gowr] of Europe and North america, the Musk ox of Arctic america, and the Yak of Central asia. "ii" The next group is the Taurine, sub-divided into the Zebu [maud] or humped domestic cattle; Taurus, the humpless cattle with cylindrical horns; and Gavæus, the humpless cattle with flattened horns, peculiar to South-eastern asia. The common humped cattle of India belong to the Zebu [maud]. The genus Taurus contains the cattle of Europe with cylindrical horns. The genus gavæus called also flat-horned Taurines comprises Indian wild-bull or Indian bison. "iii" The Bubaline group gives the Buffaloes [khoolgah].—"*c*" Caprinæ are Goats and Sheep [aud]. Horns usually in both sexes, or in the males only, more or less compressed, usually angulated, rugose, and curving backwards, or spiral; bony cores of the horns thick, porous and cellular; no canines; muffle generally absent; feet-pits in all feet, or in the forefeet only, or none; eye-pits in all or in pits not usual; horns seated on the crest of the forehead, are closely approximate, covering the top of the head; eyes usually pale. This sub-family must again be sub-divided into the capricorns, the goats, and the sheep. Capricorns [saddle-back], or Antelope goat or Mountain antelope, have the horns somewhat rounded, conical, curving backwards, of small size, found in both sexes. Compared with real antelope [jinka] these animals have a heavy body, stronger limbs, large hoofs and false hoofs. Next come the true goats [vellaud], having the horns distinctly angulated. Domestic goats have feet-pits in the forefeet, but not in the hind, whilst sheep have them in all four feet, and by this means, a hind quarter of goat with the foot attached can be at once distinguished from one of sheep. Male goats emit a strong odour. The characteristics of the sheep compared with goats are as follows:—a feebler structure and more slender limbs, shorter hoofs, and small false hoofs; a larger and heavier head; an arched chaffron; longer and more pointed ears; croup higher than the withers; want of hircine odour; paler eyes; shorter and more equal hair, and straighter back. The sheep bears change of climate ill, is incurious, staid and timid; does not bark trees; and in fighting, runs a tilt, adding the force of impulse to that of weight [aud, chowsingha, gowr, jinka, khoolgah, maud, nilghye, ravine deer, saddle-back].——*Camelidæ* (क्रमेलकुल - kramélakula, San.). From (kraméla, san. camel). Ruminantia, 26. Camel-like animals [ottagam].——*Canidæ* (कुकुरकुल - kukurakula, San.). From (kukura, san. dog). Digitigrada, carnivora, 12. Dogs [cookooram]. Forefeet with five toes, the thumb raised; hind feet usually with four; head conical and pointed in front, jaws being produced; legs of nearly equal length; tongue smooth; some have a dermal gland above the base of the tail; others a sac or hollow gland on each side of the anus, opening by a pore, which secretes a pungent whey-like substance with the peculiar smell of the animal. In domestic dogs these pores exist, but are evanescent, and without a distinct sac or secretion. In these too there is often a fifth claw on the hind feet, but only connected by skin, and called the dew-claw [cookooram, dhole, jackal, konye, lomree, nye, shwaunam].——*Cercopithecidæ* (लांगूलीकुल - lángúlíkula, San.). From (lángúlí, san. tailed ape). Quadrumana, 1. Apes [lungoor]. Nails flat or somewhat rounded, blunt; forefeet usually with five toes; hind feet always pentadactylous; thumb remote; nostrils separated by a small and narrow septum, tail never prehensile, sometimes wanting; the region of the tuberosity of the ischium usually destitute of hair and callous. In their anatomical characters closely resemble man, differing in the relative proportions of parts. Some have cheek-pouches, others have none. Some have laryngeal pouches, or membranous expansions, sending prolongations into the muscles; these are receptacles of air and communicate with the cavity of the larynx by an aperture at the base of the epiglottis. Their probable use is to diminish the specific gravity of their body in the action of climbing. The cheek-pouches enable them to eat with rapidity; their callosities enable them to assume the sitting posture readily; and the long tails of some enable them to balance themselves in their surprising leaps. The points in which even the nearest allied species differ from man are the conspicuously longer forearms, the long flexible toes, and the thumb on the hind feet. The pelvis is narrow and does not assist the equilibrium in the erect position, and when they stand erect they cannot do so on the soles of their feet, but rest on the outer edge of the foot. The form of the skull approaches that of man, but with age it differs much, the jaws lengthening. The skeleton generally may be said to deviate from man towards some of the larger carnivora. The mass of the brain is smaller than in man. As a general rule herbivorous, but some live on a mixed diet. Most live in societies and they are chiefly arboreal in habit.—"*a*" Cercopithecinæ are Baboons [q.v.]. Comprise the true baboons of Africa and the monkey-like baboons of India. More compactly built than the next head. Less herbivorous in their diet, eating frogs [bhaicam], lizards [chipkalee], crabs [nundoo], and insects [poochy], as well as vegetables and fruit. Their callosities and cheek-pouches are large. Chief representatives in S. india are common monkey [bandar] and lion monkey [siyah bandar].—"*b*" Semnopithecinæ are Apes. They are described under the title-head Lungoor.——*Cervidæ* (मृगकुल - mrigakula, San.). From (mriga, san. deer). Ruminantia, 24. Deer [mrigam]. Remarkable for their fine horns or osseous prominences, shed and renewed annually, more or less contemporaneously with the renewal of the hair, and called antlers. In the reindeer alone the females possess horns normally, though very rarely old and barren females of other species have been known to assume them. Feet touch the ground only at the extremity of the two principal toes, usually two rudimentary toes with small hoofs at the back of the foot; end of the muzzle is bare in almost all deer, and is sometimes called the muffle; one or two glands covered with a small tuft of hair on the hind leg, the presence of which, in some cases at least, furnishes a good character to distinguish females of this family from hornless female antelope [jinka]; and there are feet-pits also, either in all four feet or only in the hind feet. When the horns first appear they are covered with a hairy skin, commonly called the velvet, which becomes dry and is thrown off; at each successive renewal of the horns, they become larger and more developed, getting additional branches in some till excessive age, when they diminish at each renewal. In their early condition the horns are soft and yielding. The rutting season immediately follows the development of the antlers.—"*a*" Cervinæ are True stags. Comprise the red deer of Europe and its affines, the reindeer and the fallow deer; possess a median tine or royal antler, found with very rare exceptions in no other deer; body longer, and with a somewhat different carriage.—"*b*" Rusinæ. With one basal tine and no median tine; summit more or less branched, generally with only one subterminal tine; muffle high. The group includes the samber [q.v.], the cheetal [q.v.], and the muntjac [jungle sheep]; cheetal is peculiar to the tropical and sub-tropical regions of Asia and its archipelago, or to the Indian kingdom taken in its widest sense [cheetal, jungle sheep, mrigam, samber].——*Delphinidæ* (शंकुकुल - shankukula, San.). From (shanku, san. nail, dolphin). Cetacea, 29. Dolphins [pundry meen]. Nostrils open by a single transverse aperture; head of moderate size; cranium broad and high; nasal passages nearly vertical. Dolphins, or porpoises [cadal pundry], are found all over the world, inhabiting seas and many ascending large rivers; generally associate in flocks or shoals; are very active, swimming and playing near the surface of the sea, and feeding on fishes [matsyam], crustacea [kavachiny], cuttle fish, &c.; often accompany ships for miles [cadal pundry, pundry meen].——*Elephantidæ* (गजकुल - gajakula, San.). From (gaja, san. elephant). Proboscidea, 20. Elephants [q.v.]. Two large incisive tusks [dant] in the upper jaw; feet with five toes, with nails surrounded by a thick callous skin; snout elongated into a long prehensile proboscis or trunk; cranium much elevated vertically, intermaxillary bones being much developed to support the tusks [dant] which are sometimes enormous and curved upwards, and to give origin to some of the numerous muscles which support the proboscis. This organ, flexible in every direction and endowed with great sensibility, enables the elephant to procure his food from the ground or high trees, sucks up the water he drinks, and conveys it to his throat. Brain occupies but a small space in the huge cranium; nasal bones shortened; the nostrils terminate in the end of the proboscis; stomach simple [elephant].——*Equidæ* (अश्वकुल - ashvakula, San.). From (ashva, san. horse). Ungulata, 21. Horse-like animals [ghorah]. Two anterior toes are soldered together, forming a single perfect toe, covered by a broad undivided hoof; tail moderately long with long hair; ears rather large and pointed; there is a mane; skull is elongated; lower jaw is of great size and strength; humerus and femur are short; the forearm and shank are long partially anchylosed; three phalanges complete the foot, the last of which bears the hoof; the stomach is simple. The animals of this family comprise horses [ghorah], asses [gadhah], and zebras, which are usually placed in one genus [ashwam, gadhah, ghorah, katcher].——*Erinaceidæ* (शलीकुल - shalíkula, San.). From (shalí, san. hedge-hog). Insectivora, 14. Hedge-hogs [moollely]. Back protected by spines, or rigid bristles; feet pentadactylous, not fossorial; tail very short or none; body short, thick, and stout; and the muzzle less pointed than in the other groups of this order. The cranium approaches the form of that of the smaller carnivora [moollely].——*Felidæ* (मार्जारकुल - márjárakula, San.). From (márjára, san. cat). Digitigrada, carnivora, 9. Cats [deeptaucsham, poonay]. Forefeet with five, hind feet with four or five, toes; jaws short and strong; head rounded; limbs powerful; teeth are particularly cutting; essentially carnivorous; foot-fall is noiseless, from the thick pads with which the under surface of their feet is furnished; claws habitually kept withdrawn between the toes by action of an elastic ligament which acts on the last joint of each toe, bending it upwards; fur usually dense and short; limbs of moderate length, very powerful, can take astonishing bounds; vision adapted for night as well as for day, all are nocturnal in habits, or nearly so; sense of hearing very acute; long whiskers, delicate organs of touch; tongue furnished with rough papillæ, directed backwards and somewhat recurved; usually take their prey by suddenly springing on it from a concealed spot; if they fail in seizing it rarely pursue; generally solitary, but occasionally hunt in families. Popularly divided into lions [simham], tigers [pooly], leopards [cheetah], cats [poonay], and lynxes [caracal, cheetah, deeptaucsham, boniga, jungle cat, marjauram, pooly, poonay].——*Hyænidæ* (तरक्षुकुल - tarakshukula, San.). From (tarakshu, san. hyæna). Digitigrada, carnivora, 10. Hyænas [cazhoothay pooly]. Trunk declining backwards from the shoulders; tail short; in general form hyænas resemble dogs [nye] more than cats [poonay]; in their dentition they more resemble felidæ [deeptaucsham]; hind legs are much bent, so that the hind quarters are always lower than the shoulders; feet have usually four strong claws, not retractile; tongue is rough with recurved spines [cazhoothay pooly].——*Hystricidæ* (शल्यकण्ठकुल - shalyakant'hakula, San.). From (shalya, san. thorn + kant'ha, san. neck), porcupine from sharp quills. Rodentia, 18. Porcupines [kharpoosht]. Body more or less clad with acuminate spines; hind feet with four or five toes; skull remarkable for the great size of the infra-orbital foramen; usually fourteen pairs of ribs; length of the tail very various; burrowing animals of strictly nocturnal habits, feeding on roots, fruit, bark, and young shoots [kharpoosht].——*Lemuridæ* (वनमानुषकुल - vanamánushakula, San.). From (vana, san. forest + mánusha, san. man). Lemur. Quadrumana, 2. Lemurs [devaunga]. Nostrils terminal; first finger of the hind feet with recurved claw; other nails flat; thumbs of both extremities opposable; molars with pointed and alternating tubercles. Classed by some under the name of Strepsirhini, separated into the sub-families Indrisinæ, Lemurinæ, Nycticebinæ, and Galaginæ. Distinguished from monkeys [bandar] by the two-horned uterus, by the lower jaw remaining permanently divided in the middle, and by the bony orbits being open behind, but with a bony ring separating them from the temporal fossæ. The Indian members belong to the sub-family Nycticebinæ [devaunga].——*Leporidæ* (शशकुल - shashakula, San.). From (shasha, san. hare). Rodentia, 19. Hares [mosal]. Forefeet with five toes, hind feet with four, all with hairy soles; nails long, compressed; tail short or none; distinguished from all other rodents by the possession of a small additional incisor placed behind each of the large incisive tusks of the upper jaw [mosal].——*Manididæ* (घुणकुल - ghunakula, San.). From (ghuna, san. ant-eater). Edentata, 28. Ant-eaters [jungle carp]. No teeth; body and tail covered with large, imbricate, horny scales; tail long; ears small, mostly indistinct; all feet with five toes; the scales are evidently, from their structure, a congeries of agglutinated hairs. They have the power of rolling themselves into a ball; the stomach is slightly divided in the middle [jungle carp].——*Moschidæ* (कस्तूरीमृगकुल - kastúrímrigakula, San.). From (kastúrí, san. musk + mriga, san. deer). Ruminantia, 25. Muskdeer-like animals. Without horns; feet very much cloven and large false hoofs; includes the musk-deer and the mouse-deer; mostly of small size with very slender limbs; stated to differ from other deer [mrigam] in possessing a gall-bladder [mouse-deer].——*Muridæ* (मूषिककुल - múshikakula, San.). From (múshika, san. rat). Rodentia, 17. Rat-like animals. The Jerboas [shevvely] have hind limbs much lengthened; tail long and tufted; they make most surprising jumps. Ordinary rats [ely] and mice [shoondely] have the forefeet with four wide-set toes and a hallucar unguiculate wart; hind feet with five toes; tail usually long and thinly clad or nude, short, and hairy in a few [bandicoot, ely, golandy, kok, moosham, pepper rat, shoondely].——*Mustelidæ* (नकुलकुल - nakulakula, San.). From (nakula, san. mongoose). Semi-plantigrada, carnivora, 8. Weasels and Martens, Badgers [indian rattel] and others. Claws sharp; snout short, rounded; restricted to the weasels and martens; animals of small size, elongated vermiform make, with very short limbs; head rounded in front like cats; skull has an elongated form posteriorly. They are very active and agile, highly carnivorous and blood-thirsty, destroying vast numbers of small animals and birds, which they seize by the back of the head; fur of many soft and fine, very highly prized; most abundant in cold climates.—"*a*" Lutrinæ are Otters [neernye]. Of large size; feet webbed; tail flattened.—"*b*" Melinæ are Badgers [indian rattel]. Ears small; anterior feet with large claws, fossorial in some; differ from weasels and martens by their heavy form, stout limbs and more inactive gait, by their decidedly fossorial claws and their harsh coarse hair; in this group are most animals that have the power of diffusing a fetid stench; entirely ground animals; ordinarily erect their tail, most more or less striped longitudinally [indian rattel, neernye].——*Noctilionidæ* (जतुकाकुल - jatukákula, San.). From (jatuká, san. bat). Cheiroptera, 5. Noctule bats [chamgadal]. No facial membrane; head, short and obtuse; lips, large; wings, long; tail usually free at the tip [chamgadal].——*Physeteridæ* (मेदस्तिमिकुल - médastimikula, San.). From (médastimi, san. sperm-whale). Cetacea, 30. Sperm whales [hoot].——*Pteropodidæ* (वातुलिकुल - vátulikula, San.). From (vátuli, san. large bat). Cheiroptera, 3. Flying foxes [q.v.]. Frugivorous bats. Ears small without a tragus; index with three phalanges, generally unguiculate; tail very short, or none; interfemoral membrane small, deeply excised posteriorly; face lengthened; gape moderate. The frugivorous bats, differing so much in their dentition from the insectivorous species, seem to lead through the flying lemurs directly to the quadrumana. They comprise the largest species in the order of bats [flying fox].——*Sciuridæ* (चमरपुच्छकुल - chamarapuchhakula, San.). From (chamarapuchha, san. squirrel). Rodentia, 16. Squirrels [anil, chamarapootcham]. Tail typically long, bushy; squirrels form a well-marked group of elegant animals, mostly with arboreal habits; one group only is quite terrestrial, the marmots. Most striking feature of the skull is the distinct post-orbital process; the palate is larger than in other rodents [anil, chamarapootcham, malabar squirrel].——*Sirenidæ* (जलनरकुल - jalanarakula, San.). From (jalanara, san. water-man, dugong). Ruminantia, 27. Dugong [q.v.].——*Sorecidæ* (गन्धमूषिककुल - gandhamúshikakula, San.). From (gandha, san. fragrance + múshika, san. mouse). Insectivora, 13. Shrews [musk rat]. Body, covered with soft hair; eyes, small but distinct; external ears in most, generally small; muzzle, elongated; forefeet, ordinary form; comprise a large number of small animals of nocturnal habits. The toes are well cloven; the tail of moderate length, more or less naked, or thinly clad with hairs; snout is lengthened, pointed and very mobile. On each side of the body in certain species there is a gland under the skin surrounded by a circlet of short hairs, which secretes a fluid of the odour of musk [custoory]. It exists in both sexes, and appears to be more developed at certain periods. During the day shrews remain concealed in drains or holes, dark out-houses, under boxes, mats, &c.; and those that dwell in forests, under stones, or in holes under trees. At nightfall they sally forth and hunt for their food, which is chiefly insects [musk rat].——*Suidæ* (शूकरकुल - shúkarakula, San.). From (shúkara, san. boar). Artiodactyla, ungulata, 22. Boars [jungly soor]. Feet with the hoofs insistent, with four toes usually on all feet, the hind feet sometimes with three; snout truncate, mobile, prominent; tail short. Pigs [pundry, soor] have a somewhat movable snout with a firm cartilaginous tip, which they employ in turning up the ground in search of roots; two middle toes are large, armed with strong hoofs, and the animal walks on them alone, the two upper lateral toes with their hoofs not touching the ground; eyes small; ears moderate and upright; skin clad with strong bristles; very prolific; found in warm and temperate portions [soor].——*Tupaindæ* (तरुगन्धमूषिककुल - tarugandhamúshikakula, San.). From (taru, san. tree + gandhamúshika, san. musk rat). Insectivora, 15. Tree shrews [musk rat]. Muzzle attenuated, lengthened; ears oval, rather large; feet pentadactylous; tail long, densely clothed with hairs, somewhat distichous; the hair of the body soft and glistening. Skull differs from that of other insectivora in having the bony orbit complete, and moreover they possess a small cœcum. Tree shrews are diurnal in their habits, live on trees, which they climb well, feed both on fruit and insects [poochy] which they hold in their paws like squirrels [anil]. Female only produces one young at a birth [musk-rat].——*Ursidæ* (ऋक्षकुल - rikshakula, San.). From (riksha, san. bear). Plantigrada, carnivora, 7. Bears [ricsham]. Soles of the feet usually devoid of hair; ears small; snout lengthened; tail usually very short; mostly large, heavy animals, strictly plantigrade in their walk; body covered with long and shaggy hair; claws adapted for digging, being long and stout; mostly expert climbers. Many live almost entirely on fruits and roots and other vegetable diet; others on insects [poochy], larvæ, honey [shahad], &c.; a few are more carnivorous in their habits. Conceal themselves in the day-time in caves, holes of trees, and thickets [ricsham].——*Vampyridæ* (काकपिशाचकुल - kákapisháchakula, San.). From (kákapishácha, san. crow-demon; vampires). Cheiroptera, 4. Vampires [kaffaush]. A nose leaf, either simple or complicated. Divided in the sub-families Magadermatinæ and Rhinolophinæ [kaffaush].——*Vespertilionidæ* (अजिनपत्रकुल - ajinapatrakula, San.). From (ajina, san. hairy skin + patra, san. wing); bat. Cheiroptera, 6. Common bats [vavvaul]. No facial leaf; ears usually separated; lips simple; tail long; wings wide; a single phalanx in the index fingers; comprises the ordinary bats [vavvaul] and is divided into two groups, differing in the number of teeth [vavvaul].——*Viverridæ* (गन्धमार्जारकुल - gandhamárjárakula, San.). From (gandha, san. fragrance + márjára, san. cat); civet cat. Digitigrada, carnivora, 11. Civets [poonoogoo poonay]. Civets comprise a varied assemblage of animals confined chiefly to warmer regions; most of them possess a pouch [mongoose, poonoogoo poonay, toddy-cat].——**(5)** The following is a list of the principal genera arranged alphabetically, with the Sanscrit equivalents for their titles, references, and brief descriptions.——*Antelope* (कुरङ्गजाति - kurangajáti, San.). From (kuranga, san. antelope). Antilopinæ, bovidæ, ruminantia, 23. The Antelope [jinka]. Horns in the males only, long, annulated with strong rings the tip smooth, spirally twisted, approximate at the base; no muffle; eye-pits, moderate, somewhat linear; no canines; large inguinal pits; feet-pits present; small knee brushes [jinka].——*Axis* (पृषतजाति - prishatajáti, San.). From (prishata, san. spotted deer). Cervidæ, ruminantia, 24. The Spotted deer [cheetal]. One basal and one sub-terminal snag; beam a good deal bent, pale and somewhat smooth; muffle large; eye-pits large; inguinal glands; feet-pits in the hind legs only; canine teeth in the upper jaw in the males only, or in both sexes; of small or moderate size; pelage more or less spotted; tail moderately long. Contains here Maculatus [cheetal].——*Balænoptera* (वाजतिमिजाति - vájatimijáti, San.). From (vájatimi, san. fin whale). Balænidæ, cetacea, 31. The Fin whale [timingilam]. An adipose fin on the back; belly marked by longitudinal grooves; head about one-fourth of total length; feed on small fishes; found in all seas. Largest animals of the family belong to this genus [timingilam].——*Bubalus* (गवलजाति - gavalajáti, San.). From (gavala, san. wild buffalo). Bovinæ, bovidæ, ruminantia, 23. The Wild buffalo [khoolgah]. Horns large, attached to the highest line of the frontals, inclining backwards and upwards; muffle large and square; no true dorsal ridge or hump; cranium elongated, narrow; thirteen pairs of ribs [khoolgah].——*Camelus* (क्रमेलजाति - kramélajáti, San.). From (kraméla, san. camel). Camelidæ, ruminantia, 26. The Dromedary [ottagam]. Cleft upper lip which is prehensile, two toes encased in skin with nail-like hoofs; the whole surface of the toes touches the ground; two upper incisors, and six in the lower jaw, and two canines in each jaw; eighteen to twenty molars; includes the camels of the old world and the alpacas of the new world; former have the two toes united below almost to the point by a common sole, and humps of fat on the back. Their humps are reservoirs of fat, which become absorbed during long fasts, and enable them to take long journeys on very little food. Their flat feet are admirably adapted for treading on loose sand [manal, ottagam].——*Canis* (श्वानजाति - shvánajáti, San.). From (shvána, san. dog). Canidæ, digitigrada, carnivora, 12. Tail moderately brushed. In this group are classed the wolf, the jackal and the dog. Wolves [konye] are of large size; muzzle obtuse, not much lengthened; tail short; no caudal gland. Jackals [q.v.] are of moderate size; gregarious; brush rather scanty. The Wild dog [dhole] has skull more uniformly arched than in domestic dogs [nye]; jaws shorter and stronger; has the odour and aspect of saccalius, but ears and tail larger, the latter more brushed, the brow and eye bolder, and the muzzle blunter. The shoulder and croup are about level [dhole, jackal, nye, shwaunam].——*Cervulus* (न्यंकुजाति - nyankujáti, San.). From (nyanku, san. jungle sheep). Cervidæ, ruminantia, 24. The Jungle sheep [q.v.]. Horns raised on high hairy pedicles with only one small basal snag; large canines in the upper jaw in both sexes; muffle large; two conspicuous longitudinal facial creases; tail rather short; eye-pits very large and mobile; large feet-pits in the hind feet; no inguinal pits; no calcic tuft Jungle sheep are deer [mrigam] of small size, inhabiting dense forest, and are peculiar to the Indian kingdom. By their long canines and small antlers they form a link to the moschidæ or musk-deer [jungle sheep].——*Crocidura* (गन्धमूषिकजाति - gandhamúshikajáti, San.). Sorecidæ, insectivora, 13. The Musk-rat [q.v.] or Shrew. Teeth generally wholly white; ear-conch very distinct; tail thick and tapering, and furnished with a few long scattered hairs, which certain species likewise exhibit upon the body. Some do not appear to be furnished with the musk gland [musk rat].——*Cynælurus* (चित्रकजाति - chitrakajáti, San.). From (chitraka, san. leopard). Felidæ, digitigrada, carnivora, 9. The hunting Leopard [cheetah].——*Cynopterus* (वातुलिजाति - vátulijáti, San.). From (vátuli, san. bat). Pteropodidæ, cheiroptera, 3. The Small fox bat. Snout, short; tail, very short, or none [flying fox].——*Delphinus* (शंकुजाति - shankujáti, San.). From (shanku, san. porpoise). Delphinidæ, cetacea, 29. The Porpoise [cadal pundry]. Teeth numerous, slightly recurved, vary from twenty-four to sixty on each side, both above and below; a median dorsal fin [cadal pundry].——*Elephas* (गजजाति - gajajáti, San.). From (gaja, san. elephant). Elephantidæ, proboscidea, 20. The Elephant [q.v.]. Huge tusks cylindrical with a conical tip formed of ivory and enamel only. It is said that the molars are renewed eight times in some elephants; the tusks [dant] are only renewed once, between the first and second years of age; the skin is very thick and nearly devoid of hairs; huge unwieldy animals with large ears, long and thick limbs, and a long tail [elephant].——*Equus* (अश्वजाति - ashvajáti, San.). From (ashva, san. horse). Equidæ, perissodactyla, ungulata, 21. The Horse [ashwam, gadhah, ghorah]. Sub-divides into horses [ghorah] properly so called, Equus vulgaris; asses [gadhah], Equus asinus; and zebras, Equus hippotigris. Asses are distinguished from horses by their longer head and ears, by the tail being covered with short hairs at the base and furnished with a tuft of long hairs towards the tip and on the sides only, not throughout as in horses; also want the peculiar hard horny excrescences found on the legs of horses; have almost invariably a dark, longitudinal, dorsal stripe [ashwam, gadhah, ghorah].——*Erina-*

ceus (शलीजाति - shalíjáti, San.). From (shalí, san. hedge-hog). Erinaceidæ, insectivora, 14. The Hedge-hog [moollely]. Snout lengthened; ears moderate; tail very short; body densely covered with spines on the back and sides, with hairs and bristles beneath; skin of the back furnished with muscles which enable the animal to roll itself into a ball, so as to present spines on every side. Hedge-hogs hybernate in cold countries, but do not burrow, concealing themselves under leaves, in hollow trees, ditches, and under thick bushes; feed chiefly on insects [poochy], also on slugs, frogs [bhaicam], mice [shoondely], snakes [paumb], and eggs; said at times to partake of vegetable food; nocturnal in their habits. Female produces as many as six or seven young sometimes at a birth [moollely].——*Euphysetes* (मेदस्तिमिजाति - médastimijáti, San.). From (médastimi, san. sperm whale). Physeteridæ, cetacea, 30. The Sperm whale [hoot]. Upper parts of heads cellular and filled with spermaceti [hoot].——*Felis* (मार्जारजाति - márjárajáti, San.). From (márjára, san. cat). Felidæ, digitigrada, carnivora, 9. Hind feet with four toes. Lions [simham], unspotted, of large size; pupil round distinguished by enormous head, maned neck, comparatively weak hind limbs, and a shortish tufted tail. Tigers [pooly], of large size, striped; pupil vertical. Leopards [cheetah], more or less spotted; of moderate or large size; tail long. Cats [poonay] smaller size, with shorter tails [caracal, honiga, jungle cat, marjauram, pooly, poonay].——*Gavæus* (गवयजाति - gavayajáti, San.). From (gavaya, san. bison). Bovinæ, bovidæ, ruminantia, 23. The Bison [gowr]. Head large, massive; horns slightly flattened on one side, thick, remote, spreading; tail short; muffle small; otherwise as in taurus [gowr].——*Gazella* (हरिणजाति - harinajáti, San.). From (harina, san. gazelle). Antilopinæ, bovidæ, ruminantia, 23. The Gazelle [ravine deer]. Horns rather short, lyrate, ringed, approximate at the base, diverging at the tip, present in the female but very small; ears long, acuminate; tail moderate; eye-pits small, obliquely transverse; groin-pits distinct; large feet-pits in all feet; knees tufted, and calcic tuft posteal. Comprises the gazelles, animals of rather small size, with large eyes and very active and graceful, inhabiting bare and desert countries [ravine deer].——*Gerbillus* (हरिणमूषिकजाति - harinamúshikajáti, San.). From (harinamúshika, san. mouse-deer). Murinæ, muridæ, rodentia, 17. The Jerboa rat. Ears oval; head lengthened and somewhat pointed; toes eloganted; tail long, hairy, with a tuft of hair at the tip. Field rats [varappely] have small fore limbs and well-developed hinder limbs; form somewhat slender; eyes large; extraordinarily agile; form extensive burrows in plains, especially in sandy districts, also in sand hills, but not generally in cultivated fields [shevvely].——*Globicephalus* (कायत्तिमिजाति - káyattimijáti, San.). From (kai, san. to sound + timi, san. whale). Delphinidæ, cetacea, 29. The Ca'ing whale [cadal pundry]. Head rounded in front; paddles long, narrow and pointed; teeth few in number, deciduous when old; dorsal fin distinct [cadal pundry].——*Golunda* (गुल्ममूषकजाति - gulmamúshakajáti, San.). From (gulmamúshaka, san. bush rat). Murinæ, muridæ, rodentia, 17. The Bush rat [golandy] or Field rat [varappely]. Molars when perfect low, with a broad flat crown; the cross ridges of the crown of the upper grinders divided into three distinct, slightly raised tubercles; upper incisors grooved. Two species are classed under this, which are apparently sufficiently distinct in general feature as well as in habits [golandy, varappely].——*Halicore* (जलनरजाति - jalanarajáti, San.). From (jalanara, san. dugong). Sirenidæ, sirenia, 27. The Dugong [q.v.]. Body elongated; pectoral fin without claws; caudal fin lunate, broad; the incisive teeth assume the form of pointed tusks, but are nearly covered by the thick fleshy lips which are bristled with moustaches; tongue, spiny in front, has a curious horny process on each side of its base; stomach is double; heart deeply cleft, separating the ventricles; superficial air-vessels of the lungs are large, turtle-like, and the lungs and bronchi generally are like those of the turtles [cadal aumay, dugong].——*Hemitragus* (वनच्छागजाति - vanachhágajáti, San.). From (vana, san. forest + chhága, san. sheep). Ibex. Caprinæ, bovidæ, ruminantia, 23. The Ibex [saddle-back]. Horns trigonal, compressed, knotted in front; a small muffle; no eye-pits nor feet-pits, nor inguinal pores [saddle back].——*Herpestes* (नकुलजाति - nakulajáti, San.). From (nakula, san. mongoose). Herpestinæ, viverridæ, digitigrada, carnivora, 11. The Mongoose [q.v.]. Ears small, short and rounded; feet all with five toes, with large compressed, incurved, somewhat retractile claws; tail long, thick at the base; hairs long, rigid, often ringed with distinct colors. Ichneumons or mongooses have a sharp muzzle, small eyes, short limbs, hinder ones semi-plantigrade, and toes connected by a membrane. Tongue is rough with horny papillæ; very active in their habits, bold and sanguinary in disposition; partly fossorial; in hot tropical countries of the old continent appear to take the place of the weasels of colder regions; numerously represented in India [mongoose].——*Hipposideros* (अश्वखुरत्रजाति - ashvakhuratrajáti, San.). From (ashvakhura, san. horse's hoof + trá, san. to protect). Rhinolophinæ, vampyridæ, cheiroptera, 4. The Horse-shoe bat [kaffaush]. Most species have a remarkable peculiarity, viz., a circular cavity or sac behind the nasal crest, which the animal can turn out at pleasure like the finger of a glove; it is lined by a pencil of stiff hairs, and is probably a glandular organ, as it contains a peculiar waxy matter; ears very tremulous [kaffaush].——*Hyæna* (तरक्षजाति - tarakshajáti, San.). From (taraksha, san. hyæna). Hyænidæ, digitigrada, carnivora, 10. The Hyæna [cazhoothay pooly]. Hyænas have a short solid skull; short muzzle; claws stout and blunt; beneath the tail is a deep pouch analogous to that in the civets [poonoogoo poonay] but not secreting an odorous substance; temporal muscles are very large and powerful, as are those of the neck; their jaws and teeth strong enough to crush large bones; quite nocturnal in habits, living in holes and caverns, feeding chiefly on the remains of carcases; not unfrequently carry off dogs [nye]. They are easily tamed, even susceptible of attachment [cazhoothay pooly].——*Hystrix* (शल्यकण्ठजाति - shalyakant'hajáti, San.). From (shalyakant'ha, san. porcupine). Hystricinæ, hystricidæ, rodentia, 18. The Porcupine [kharpoosht]. Hind feet with five unguiculate toes; all the claws stout; body armed with rigid spines, mixed with some longer flexible ones; tail very short, with a bundle of open tubes at the end; muzzle truncated. Take their popular name, signifying spiny pig, from their large size and grunting voice; found in the warmer regions of the old continent; peculiar open tubes of the tail are supported on slender stalks, and they make a rattling noise when shaken [kharpoosht].——*Kerivoula* (चित्राजिनपत्रजाति - chitrájinapatrajáti, San.). From (chitra, san. variegated + ajinapatra, san. bat). Vespertilioninæ, vespertilionidæ, cheiroptera, 6. The painted bat [vavvaul]. Face short, hairy; muzzle narrow; ears broad, not very acute at tip; feet hairy above, half attached; tail long [vavvaul].——*Leggada* (शल्यबालमूषिकजाति - shalyabálamúshikajáti, San.). From (shalya, san. spine + bálamúshika, san. mouse). Murinæ, muridæ, rodentia, 17. The Spiny mouse [moolloo shoondely]. Fur fine, mixed with numerous spines; somewhat flattened [shoondely].——*Lepus* (शशजाति - shashajáti, San.). From (shasha, san. hare). Leporidæ, rodentia, 19. The Hare [mosal]. Ears typically very long; tail short, recurved; hind legs much longer than the forelegs; well known for their timidity and watchfulness, increased by the situation of their eyes, which are so placed that they can see all round, and for their great speed. In some, as in hares, the young are born with their eyes open; in the rabbits with their eyes closed [mosal].——*Loris* (वनमानुषजाति - vanamánushajáti, San.). From (vanamánusha, san. forest man, loris). Lemuridæ, quadrumana, 2. The Lemur or Loris [devaunga]. Body and limbs slender; no tail; eyes very large, almost contiguous; nose, acute, slightly ascending [devaunga].——*Lutra* (उद्रजाति - udrajáti, San.). From (udra, san. otter). Lutrinæ, mustelidæ, carnivora, 8. The Otter [neernye]. Ears small; feet short; body lengthened; tail longish, stout at the base, round, depressed towards, the tip, flat beneath. Well marked group distinguished by their elongated and somewhat flattened form, short and stout limbs, with toes well webbed and spreading, and with naked soles. Fur is close, fine and short, woolly beneath, smooth glossy hairs above; eyes provided with nyctitating membrane, as a defence to them under water; teeth strong and sharp, tubercles of molars very pointed to secure their prey, which is almost entirely fish; skull said to have something in common with seals in the short muzzle, and wide and flat cranium; articulations of the extremities admit of great freedom of motion [neernye].——*Macacus* (केसरिवानरजाति - késarivánarajáti, San.). From (késarivánara, san. lion monkey). Cercopithecinæ, cercopithecidæ, quadrumana, 1. The Monkey [bandar]. Face, somewhat produced, but rounded; callosities, present; the last molar tooth of the lower jaw has five tubercles, the other two true molars with four tubercles; tail, short. The monkeys of this genus have a somewhat prominent muzzle, and protruded superciliary ridge; the nostrils open obliquely at some distance above the end of the muzzle; their canines are very strong, and the first molars are inclined backwards to make room for the large upper canine. The limbs are strong and compact, and they are as much terrestrial as arboreal. They eat frogs [bhaicam], crabs [nundoo], lizards [chipkalee] and insects [poochy] as readily as vegetable food. Their callosities are large, as are their cheek-pouches, and they have also laryngeal expansions. Their tails are short. They are quiet and intelligent in youth, but become ferocious and untameable in old age [bandar].——*Manis* (घुणजाति - ghunajáti, San.). From (ghuna, san. ant-eater). Manididæ, edentata, 28. The Pangolin or Scaly ant-eater [jungle carp]. Characteristics of the family, of which it is the only genus [jungle carp].——*Megaderma* (काकपिशाचजाति - kákapisháchajáti, San.). From (kákapishácha, san. crow demon; vampyre). Vampyridæ cheiroptera, 4. The Vampire bat [kaffaush]. Nose furnished with a complicated membranous apparatus; ears very large, connate at the base, with a small tragus; no tail [kaffaush].——*Mellivora* (भल्लशूकरजाति - bhallashúkarajáti, San.). From (bhalla, san. bear + shúkara, san. boar). Melinæ, mustelidæ, semi-plantigrada, carnivora, 8. The Badger [indian rattel]. No external ear, only a cutaneous border round the external auditory meatus; head rather short; feet short; tail very short; hair long, rigid; anterior claws very strong; very nearly allied to badgers in appearance; more ursine in its short tail and habit [indian rattel].——*Melursus* (ऋक्षजाति - rikshajáti, San.). From (riksha, san. bear). Ursidæ, plantigrada, carnivora, 7. The Indian bear [ricsham]. Snout produced; ears small, erect, rounded; tail very short; feet with very strong claws; their cylindrical bones are nearer those of man than those of most animals; the femur, especially, closely approximates the same bone in the human skeleton; hence the faculty possessed by bears of standing erect and of dancing; sole of the foot leaves a mark not unlike that of the human foot [ricsham].——*Memimna* (गिरिकामृगजाति - girikámrigajáti, San.). From (girikámriga, san. mouse deer). Moschidæ, ruminantia, 25. The Mouse deer [q.v.] Canines only in the males, small; false hoofs of ordinary make and size; tail very short; ears moderate; hinder edge of metatarsus covered with hair; no eye-pits nor groin-pits nor feet-pits; animals of very small size and with the hairs smooth. Limbs are exceedingly slender, and their hind quarters are high, causing their action to be very inelegant; frequent only in the thickest forests [mouse deer].——*Mus* (मूषिकजाति - múshikajáti, San.). From (múshika, san. rat). Murinæ, muridæ, rodentia, 17. The Rat [ely] or Bandicoot [q.v.]. Ears more or less rounded, somewhat naked; tail long, scaly, usually thinly haired. The genus comprises the house rats [ely] and mice [shoondely], and some field rats [varappely] of more or less allied form. The various species may be grouped together according to their size and habit:—"*a*" Rats more or less allied to the common brown rat;—"*b*" rats with the tail usually fully as long, or longer than, the head and body; some have quite arboreal habits, building nests among the branches of trees, among the rafters of houses, &c., and not burrowing in the ground;—"*c*" small, arboreal, long-tailed mice, diminutives of the last, ears hairy, hind feet very long, slender, claws small, tail long, with scattered hairs more crowded at the tip, the fur soft with long bristles interspersed;—"*d*" field mice, tail shorter than head and body, fur not spinous [bandicoot, ely, moosham, shoondely].——*Nesokia* (गर्ताश्रयजाति - gartáshrayajáti, San.). From (gartáshraya, san. mole rat). Murinæ, muridæ, rodentia, 17. The Mole rat [kok]. Claws small, compressed; ears moderate, nude; tail short, naked; this genus, easily known from mus by the large size of the cutting teeth and the comparative shortening of the tail, appears to be intermediate to the rats and rhizomys [kok].——*Nycticejus* (पीताजिनपत्रजाति - pítájinapatrajáti, San.). From (píta, san. yellow + ajinapatra, san. bat). Scotophilinæ, vespertilionidæ, cheiroptera, 6. The Yellow bat or Hoary bat [vavvaul]. Ears short and broad, distant, and stand out from the head; muzzle broad, brightly colored, being yellow beneath, of different shades; peculiar physiognomy caused by short muzzle and ears standing out laterally [vavvaul].——*Nyctinomus* (वलितोष्ठाजिनपत्रजाति - valitósht'hájinapatrajáti, San.). From (valita, san. wrinkled + ósht'ha, san. lip + ajinapatra, san. bat). Noctilioninæ, noctilionidæ, cheiroptera, 5. The Wrinkled-lipped bat [chamgadal]. Ears broad, short, approximate or connate, outer margin terminating in an erect lobe beyond the conch; wings narrow, folded as in Taphozous; tail free at the tip; feet short, thick, with strong toes; muzzle thick; lips tumid, lax; upper lip with coarse wrinkles [chamgadal].——*Ovis* (अविजाति - avijáti, San.). From (avi, san. sheep). Caprinæ, bovidæ, ruminantia, 23. The Sheep [shemmariyaud]. Horns in both sexes, large, angular, heavily wrinkled, turned downwards almost into a circle, with their flat points directed forwards and outwards; no muffle; no beard; chaffron convex; large but immobile eye-pits in some, wanting in others; small feet-pits in all feet; inguinal glands distinct. All wild races of sheep differ conspicuously from most of the domestic races by their short deer-like tail [aud].——*Paradoxurus* (ताडीमार्जारजाति - tádímárjárajáti, San.). From (tádímárjára, san. toddy cat). Viverrinæ, viverridæ, digitigrada, carnivora, 11. The Toddy-cat [q.v.]. All feet with five toes connected by a web, the thumb not raised; sole of the feet bald; claws semi-retractile; tail very long, cylindrical. Tree-cats are stouter in form than the genets, more uniform in their coloration; their gait is plantigrade; quite nocturnal in their habits; dentition very similar to that of dogs [nye]; cerebral cavity proportionally smaller; bony orbit not closed; glandular fold in some secreting a peculiar matter, without the odour of civet [poonoogoo] or musk [custoory]; but not a distinct pouch. They climb trees well; roost during the day either on trees or on the roofs of houses among the rafters. Diet is of a mixed character. The character of the tail from which the generic name was derived is the result of some deformity. It can be rolled up, but is not prehensile [toddy-cat].——*Platacanthomys* (मरीचमूषिकजाति - maríchamúshikajáti, San.). From (marícha, san. pepper, piper nigrum, linn. + múshaka, san. rat). Murinæ, muridæ, rodentia, 17. The Pepper rat [q.v.]. Muzzle acute; ears moderate, nude; tail hairy, the hairs arranged distichously; whiskers very long; upper parts densely covered with sharp flat spines, mixed with an exceedingly delicate, thin undercoat; few spines on the lower part but smaller and finer; rodential tusks are quite those of myoxus and its whole habit is myoxine. Resemblance of this genus to the dormouse is very striking, principally on account of the long-haired tail; in other respects, in its smaller eyes, very thin ears, and the well-developed, although very short, thumb of the forefoot, it more approaches several murine genera of Tropical India [pepper rat].——*Portax* (ऋश्यजाति - rishyajáti, San.). From (rishya, san. white-footed antelope). Antilopinæ, bovidæ, ruminantia, 23. The Nilghye [q.v.]. Horns only in males, short, recurved, distant, smooth; eye-pit rather small; upper lip broad, ample; nostrils approximate; tail long, tufted; a short erect mane, and a tuft of hairs on the throat of the male; of large size. Slight pit in front of the orbit; anterior to this a small longitudinal fold, in the middle of which there is a pore, through which exudes a yellow secretion from the gland beneath. The back is rather short, and slopes downwards from the high withers; neck is deep and compressed like that of a horse [ghorah, nilghye].——*Pteromys* (सपक्षवृक्षशायीजाति - sapakshavrikshasháyijáti, San.). From (sapaksha, san. winged + vrikshasháyí, san. tree-sleeper, squirrel). Sciuridæ, rodentia, 16. The Flying squirrel [paravay anil]. Feet as in sciurus [malabar squirrel]; skin of the flanks extended between the fore and hind feet, forming when expanded a wide parachute; tail rounded, hairy all round, as long as the body, or longer; long osseous or cartilaginous appendages to the feet, which serve to support the lateral membrane [anil].——*Pteropus* (वातुलिजाति - vátulijáti, San.). From (vátuli, san. large bat). Pteropodidæ, cheiroptera, 3. The Flying fox [q.v.]. Index finger unguiculate; snout lengthened; no tail in some; short one in others; tongue covered with large papillæ, pointing backwards, each terminating in a brush [flying fox].——*Rhinolophus* (पर्णनासाजाति - parnanásájáti, San.). From (parna, san. leaf + násá, san. nose). Rhinolophinæ, vampyridæ, cheiroptera, 4. The Leaf bat [kaffaush]. Nose furnished with a complicated apparatus, consisting of a cordate or semi-orbicular leaf, bilobed in front of the nostrils; longitudinal, crest along the nose; ears, large, not joined at the base, often with a lobe at the base of the outer margin; tail long, connate with the membrane; wings, long, ample; said to hang with their body rolled up in their wings as in a mantle [kaffaush].——*Rhinopoma* (दीर्घलांगूलपर्णनासाजाति - dírghalángúlaparnanásájáti, San.). From (dírgha, san. long + lángúla, san. tail + parnanásá, san. leaf bat). Rhinolophinæ, vampyridæ, cheiroptera, 4. The long-tailed Leaf bat [kaffaush]. Ears, moderate, connate; auricle, erect; forehead, excavated; nostrils, operculate by a small lamina; tail, connate by its base with the intercrural membrane, but produced beyond it. By its connate ears approaches Megaderma, near which it is classed by some [kaffaush].——*Rusa* (सम्बरजाति - sambarajáti, San.). From (sambara, san. samber). Rusinæ, cervidæ, ruminantia, 24. The Samber [q.v.]. Horns with one basal and one upper tine, thick, dark and rugose; muffle large; eye-pits large and reversile; no feet-pits; of large size; canines in the upper jaw in both sexes; the males heavily maned [samber].——*Sciuropterus* (सपक्षवृक्षशायिकाजाति - sapakshavrikshasháyikájáti, San.). Means winged small squirrel. Sciuridæ, rodentia, 16. The Small Travancore Flying squirrel [paravay anil]. Tail shorter than the body, flat, and the hairs more or less distichous; molar teeth tuberculated; usually of smaller size, otherwise as in Pteromys [anil].——*Sciurus* (चमरपुच्छजाति - chamarapuchhajáti, San.). From (chamarapuchha, san. squirrel). Sciuridæ, rodentia, 16. The Squirrel [anil, malabar squirrel]. Forefeet with only four toes, and a tubercle on the site of the thumb; tail very long, bushy, the hairs directed more or less laterally; large head; prominent eyes; large body; moderately long limbs; mostly quite arboreal in their habits, exceedingly active and lively, feeding on buds, fruit, nuts, and other vegetable substances; and building a large rude nest of leaves, grass, &c. Hold up their food to their mouth between the two thumb-tubercles. Three well-marked groups in India, distinguished by size, coloration, and habits. The first consists of squirrels of very large size, rich coloration, and more or less pencilled ears; second group consists of squirrels of medium size, with grizzled fur; they are confined to the south-east Himalayas and the provinces north-east of Bengal; third group, striped squirrels, named by some the Palmists, of small size affecting the ground more than any other squirrels, in this, as in general appearance, nearly approaching the group of ground squirrels called Tamias; fourth group flying-squirrels divided into two smaller groups, one of large size, with tail round and hairy throughout, Pteromys, other of smaller size with tail flat and the hairs distichous, Sciuropterus [anil, chamarapootcham, malabar squirrel].——*Scotophilus* (चोलमण्डलीयजाति - chólamandalíyajáti, San.). From (chólamandala, san. coromandel). Scotophilinæ, vespertilionidæ, cheiroptera, 6. The Coromandel bat [vavvaul]. Membranes attached to the foot close to the base of the toes; ears small, ovoid, rounded at the tip [vavvaul].——*Semnopithecus* (लांगूलीजाति - lángúlíjáti, San.). From (lángúlí, san. ape). Cercopithecidæ, quadrumana, 1. The Ape, Lungoor, Hanooman [lungoor]. Cheek-pouches rudimentary or wanting; head, round; the face but little produced, having a high facial angle; the last molar tooth of the lower jaw, with a fifth or accessory tubercle behind; canines much longer than the incisors; extremities and feet long; forefeet with the thumb short; and the third and fourth fingers long and subequal; tail very long, slender and straight; callosities present; peculiar to the Indian region. The body of these monkeys is comparatively slender, and the Germans call them slim-apes. Their long and slender limbs, long tail, and the black face with an eye-brow of long stiff black hairs, pointing forwards, distinguish the lungoors from all

other monkeys [bandar]. The tail of these monkeys is not prehensile [lungoor].——*Sus* (शूकरजाति - shúkarajáti, San.). From (shúkara, san. boar). Suidæ, artiodactyla, ungulata, 22. The Boar [jungly soor]. All the feet with four toes, which are enclosed in separate hoofs [soor].——*Taphozous* (जतुकाजाति - jatukájáti, San.). From (jatuká, san. bat). Taphozoinæ, noctilionidæ, cheiroptera, 5. The Noctule bat [chamgadal]. Snout, conical, with the nostrils approximate; forehead, with a rounded cavity; ears, moderate, apart; tail, short; face flat; nostrils can be closed at pleasure; large gular sac in males, which is glandular; a longitudinal fold on each side leads to this sac; fur is close, soft, and velvety; wing long and narrow, collapses with a double flexure outwards [chamgadal].——*Tetraceros* (रोहिषजाति - róhishajáti, San.). From (róhisha, san. a species of deer). Antilopinæ, bovidæ, ruminantia, 23. The Chowsingha [q.v.]. Horns in the males only, erect, slightly bent forwards at the tip, round, subulate, slightly ringed at the base, situated far back on the frontal bone; additional pair of small horns situated between the orbits, short, conical, sometimes replaced by a mere bony knob; eye-pit moderate, linear; muffle large; feet-pits in the hind feet only; no inguinal pits; canines in the males. Form of these animals is not so elegant as that of the true antelope and their hair is harsher; frequent jungles and thin forest, do not associate in herds, but are monogamous, and often found in pairs. Genus is strictly Indian [chowsingha].——*Tupaia* (तरुमूषिकजाति - tarumúshikajáti, San.). From (taru, san. tree + múshika, san. rat). Tupaiadæ, insectivora, 15. The Tree shrew [musk-rat].——*Viverra* (गन्धमार्जारजाति - gandhamárjárajáti, San.). From (gandhu, san. fragrance + márjára, san. cat). Viverrinæ, viverridæ, digitigrada, carnivora, 11. The Civet-cat [poonoogoo poonay]. Claws small; fur usually spotted; anal pouch large, divided into two sacs; secretes a strongly odorous sebaceous substance called civet; more or less erectile mane along the back; moderate-sized animals; most of them larger than a cat [poonay]. Diet partly carnivorous, but they will also feed on vegetable substances; divisible into two sections, which have been made types of genera. Size large, does not climb, thumb not remote. Size small, vermiform; nails more raptorial; thumb remote; of scansorial habits [poonay].——*Vulpes* (किखिजाति - kikhijáti, San.). From (kikhi, san. fox). Canidæ, digitigrada, carnivora, 12. The Fox [lomree]. Muzzle lengthened and very acute; head round; ears large, erect; body long; limbs short; tail thick, long and bushy, otherwise as in canis [shwaunam]. Foxes have a gland at the base of the tail above, which secretes a strongly odorous substance. Two types of foxes in India—the first the foxes of the desert or plains, not typical in their characters, having longer ears, longer and more slender limbs; inhabit bare open plains, in which they burrow; are less carnivorous in their habits than true foxes, feeding much on fruit, insects [poochy], crabs [nundoo], &c. [lomree].——**(6)** Title-heads in this glossary cover each species distinguished by the natives.——**(7)** For insects see Poochy; for fishes see Matsyam; for batrachians see Bhaicam; for reptiles see Sarpy; for birds see Pacshy. A general conspectus of the fauna [jantoo] of s. india was given in vol. II, appendix IV.

SAT (सत् - sat, *San.*). From (as, san. to be); being. Existence; truth. Good, proper, excellent.——*Sanmaurgam* (सन्मार्ग - sanmárga, San.). From (above + márga, san. way). Moral way [aram].——*Satchidaunandam* (सच्चिदानन्द - saççidánanda, San.). From (above + chit, san. thought + ánanda, san. joy). The Supreme spirit [parabramh].——*Satwam* (सत्त्व - sattva, San.). Purity. Satwagoonam is the quality of purity [goonam, samsauram].——*Saty* (सती - satí, San.; சதி - shathi, Tam.); truthful. The faithful [patny, patyvratay, suttee]. Parvaty [q.v.].——*Satyam* (सत्य - satya, San.). From (sat, san. truth). Truth, verity, an oath. The first Yoog [q.v.]. The first age of the world. The tamul Cooral has the following:—*அன்புநா ணொப்புரவு கண்ணோட்டம் வாய்மையொ டைந்துசால் பூன்றிய தூண்*—"affection, fear of sin, benevolence, favor "and truthfulness; these are the five pillars on which perfect "goodness rests."—*வாய்மை யெனப்படுவ தியாதெனின் யாதொன்றுந் தீமை யிலாத சொலல்*—"truth is the "speaking of such words as are free from the least degree of "evil to others."—*தன்னெஞ் சறிவது பொய்யற்க பொய்த்தபின் றன்னெஞ்சே தன்னைச் சுடும்*—"let not a man "knowingly tell a lie; for after he has told the lie, his mind will "burn him."—*மனத்தொடு வாய்மை மொழியிற் றவத்தொடு தானஞ்செய் வாரிற் றலை*—"he, who speaks truth "with all his heart, is superior to those who make gifts and "practise austerities."—*பொய்யாமை யன்ன புகழில்லை யெய்யாமை யெல்லா வறமுந் தரும்*—"there is no praise "like the praise of never uttering a falsehood; without causing "any suffering, it will lead to every virtue."—*புறந்தூய்மை நீரா னமையு மகந்தூய்மை வாய்மையாற் காணப் படும்*—"purity of body is produced by water and purity of "mind by truthfulness." Satyanautan, from (nát'ha, san. lord), proper name [peyar]. Satyaushrayan, meaning truth dependent; also called poolikeshy; name of a rajah who founded the western chalookya [q.v.] kingdom; conquered canouj; subdued the rashtracootas [q.v.] and pullavas [q.v.]; and acquired sovereignty of maharashtram [q.v.]; interchanged letters and presents with chosroes II of persia [charitram]; see vol. I (139); II, 250. Satyaushrayacoolam, from (áshraya, shelter + kula, san. family); name of a line of rulers in carvetnugger zemindarry [salwa]. Satya vaucya roya, from (vákya, san. word + rájá, san. king); name of a chera [q.v.] king in malabar; a.d. 875; see vol. II, 250. Satyavaudy, from (vádí, san. speaker); a common hindoo 2nd or pers. name [peyar]. Satyavratan, from (vrata, san. vow), otherwise known as veivaswatan [q.v.], is the hindoo noah [matsyam, pralayam]. Satya vurman, from (varman, san. coat, title), was a title of cadamba [q.v.] of banavausy and haungal.——*Satyavijayanagaram* (சத்தியவிசய நகரம் - shattiyavijayanagaram, Tam.). From (satyavijaya, san. proper name + nagara, san. city), called after the madhwa priest of that name. Jagheer village; North arcot dist., Arnee jagheer; pop. 3,767; lat. 12° 41′; long. 79° 22′; from Arnee E. 3 miles; from Chittore S.S.E. 40 miles. On the left bank of the cheyaur opposite to Arnee. Residence of the Jagheerdars of Arnee since 1762, when the fort, which till then had been their residence, was taken possession of by the Nawaub of Arcot. The Jagheerdar's palace is in Italian style. There is a mutt [q.v.] raised over the burial place of a Madhwa [q.v.] priest Satyavijayasawmy. Visited by votaries of the Madhwa sect from all parts of the country.——*Sautwatan* (सात्वत - sátvata, San.). From (sattva, san. truth); as being full of Satwagoonam [goonam]. Vishnoo [q.v.].——*Sautwicam* (सात्त्विक - sáttvika, San.). Proceeding from the Satwa goonam. One of the three Goonams, the quality of excellence or goodness; that which enlightens, constitutes knowledge [nyannam], and is the cause of truth; and the predominance of which renders the person, in whom it resides, virtuous, devout, &c. See Goonam. For its influence in transmigrations see Samsauram. See vol. I (91).——*Suttee* (सती - satí, San.). From (sat, san. true). A virtuous woman [patny, paty vratay, saty], a widow who burns herself on the funeral pile of her husband. Not an Aryan institution. See vol. I (71).——*Suttegaul* (சத்தேகாலம் - shattégálam, Tam.). From (satya, san. brahma, the god + hálu, can. waste land). Sanscrit name (brahmapurí), meaning bramha, the god + town; place where bramha [q.v.] is said to have performed penance. Jagheer village; Coimbatore dist., Collegaul tal.; pop. 2,404; acres 20,079; lat. 12° 15′; long. 77° 11′; from Coimbatore N. 86 miles; from Collegaul N.N.E. 6 miles. Granted to Triplicane ramasawmy moodelliar in recognition of his having repaired two bridges across the two branches of the Cauvery on the road from Collegaul to Mysore [shivasamoodram]. Old and well-sculptured Shiva temple, containing inscriptions, situated on Cauvery. Ruined fort. Peopled by a large number of Bramins [q.v.] at the time of Hyder [q.v.].——*Suttenapully* (సత్తెనపల్లి - sattenapalli, Tel.). See sep. title.——*Suttimungalam* (சத்தியமங்கலம் - shattiyamangalam, Tam.). See sep. title.——*Suttivaid* (சத்தியவேடு - shattiyavédu, Tam.). From (satya, san. truth + védu, tam. village).—"*a*" Deputy tahsildarry. Chingleput district. Pay Rs. 70. Also Village; Chingleput dist., Trivellore tal.; pop. 2,170; acres 3,835; lat. 13° 26′; long. 80° 01′; from Chingleput W. 51 miles; from Conjeeveram N.E. 44 miles; from Madras N.W. 33 miles; from St. Thomas' mount N.W. 34 miles; from Sydapett N.W. 34 miles; from Trivellore N. 20 miles. Old Shiva temple built by Matanga maharishy. Old rectangular fort, with bastions surrounded by a dry ditch. Rude stone implements.—"*b*" Also the name of an old district near Madras. Transferred in 1804-5 to the district of North arcot. At that time it consisted of eight talooks:—Chingleput, Tirporore, Carangooly, Ootramallore, Conjeeveram, Manimungalam, Peddapolliem and Nayar.

SATIN WOOD (बेहडा - béhadá, *Mahr.*; دهورا - dhaurá, *Hind.* and *Dec.*; ಹುರುಗಲುಮರ - hurugalumara, *Can.*; బిల్లుడు - billudu, *Tel.*; భేరు - bhéru, *Oor.*; බුරුත - buruta, *Singh.*; வம்மரம் - vammaram, *Tam.*). Title from color and appearance of wood; satin is from (zaitún) a port in china. Mahr. means terminalia belerica [belleric myrobalan]. Can. from (hurugu, can. itching sensation + mara, can. tree). Tam. from (val, tam. strong + maram, tam. tree). Hind. also (bhirra); (giryó). Can. also (vasemara). Tel. also (billu). Oor. also (bilugu). Singh. also (malburuta), meaning flower satin, from soft yellow wood. Tam. also (kodaváborasu), meaning crookedness + the tree; (mududa); (porasu); (vayimaram), meaning strong wood. Title otherwise Wood oil tree, Yellow wood, Zante wood. Botanically Chloroxylon swietenia, d.c., meliaceæ [vricsham, 36]. Alias Swietenia chloroxylon. Tree; leaves abruptly pinnate; leaflets pale-colored, small, numerous, alternate or nearly opposite, unequal-sided; calyx short, five-partite; petals five, shortly unguiculate; panicles terminal, branched; capsule oblong, three-celled, three-valved, dehiscing from the apex, septifragal; seeds about four in each cell, extending upwards into a wing; flowers small, greenish white; flowers in hot season; common at foot of hills, rarely ascends above a thousand feet; a native of n. circars. The suber of bark is dark brown, and very rough from the presence of numerous elliptic corky lenticels, it is very loosely attached, and when removed leaves a nearly smooth pale red surface; the tree also affords a soluble exudation allied to gum arabic [q.v.], which occurs in amber-colored tears, more or less cracked, it swells in water to a whitish and transparent jelly; the tree yields a wood oil [yennay]; flower satin, meaning a soft yellow wood, is obtained from the root in ceylon. Natives apply leaves to wounds. Wood close-grained yellow, very hard and durable, substitute for box, excellent for turning, much used for furniture and picture frames, takes good polish but loses beauty by age, unless well varnished; very liable to warp and split if not well seasoned in the shade; stands well under water; highly prized by natives for ploughs, axle trees, oil presses, &c., but especially the former; the richly-colored and feathery logs are used for cabinet-work, the more ordinary for building purposes; much used in england as a veneer for fancy work and is familiar on the back of brushes; for picture frames, it is nearly equal to american maple; occasionally planks of 10 to 15 inches in breadth may be procured. No other common species here.——*Andaman satin wood* (مورش کا دھورا - moraskádhaurá, Hind.). Same as Foreign conjy.——*Black satin wood* (నల్లఉతి - nallaúti, Tel.). Same as Ceylon ebony.——*Neilgherry satin wood* (ارمبلی کا جہاڑ - irambalíkájhár, Dec.; పిసినిక - pisinika, Tel.; ଗୁଆକୋଳି - guakoli, Oor.; කළුහබරලිය - kaluhabaraliya, Singh.; இரும்பிலி - irumbili, Tam.). Title from habitat. Dec. from tamul. Tel. from (pisini, tel. gum) [sangcooppy]. Singh. from (kalu, san. black + habaraliya, singh. the tree, so called). Tam. from (irumbu, tam. iron + ali, tam. tree, cordia); from dark wood; also from supposition that it was used by alchemists to turn iron into gold. Tel. also (úti), meaning strong wood [sangcooppy]; (pishańna); (alli); (nallamaddi), meaning black + the tree, terminalia arjuna, bedd. [black murdah]. Tam. also (kuruviñji), compare coorvitchy; (visaram). Title otherwise Cochin-china ebony, Coromandel ebony, Iroombily, Satin ebony. Botanically Maba buxifolia, pers., ebenaceæ [vricsham, 83]. Alias Ferriola buxifolia; Maba abenus, angustifolia, neilgherrense, nigrescens. Evergreen shrub or small tree; leaves alternate, oval, entire, smooth; male flowers axillary in the lower leaves, three-fold, sessile, white; calyx three-cleft; corolla three-cleft, hairy; stamens six, short, inserted round a semi-globose receptacle; female flowers axillary, sessile, white or yellowish, very small; style one; berry round, smooth, pulpy, size of a pea [calauyam]; seed two, flat on one side; berries universally eaten when ripe; wood small, very hard, dark-colored, heavy and durable, adapted for the lathe. Other species are micrantha and nigrescens, this last being called in bombay Rakta roda, meaning red + growing [soymida]. Compare also, where transl. is of first term:—Clerodendron inerme (étipisinika), river; Ehretia buxifolia (pittapisinika), bird; Salix tetrasperma (étipisinika), river; Woodfordia floribunda (gaddapisinika), root. See gloss. paragraphs.

SATRANJEE (आस्तर - ástara, *San.*; شطرنجی - shatranjí, *Hind.*; ತಿವಾಸಿ - tivási, *Can.*; తివాశి - tiváshi, *Tel.*; പരവതാനി - paravatáni, *Mal.*; கம்பளம் - kambalam, Tam.). Title from hind. from (chatr, hind. four + rang, pers. color). San. from (ástri, san. to spread). Tel. from (divya, san. excellent + ásana, san. seat). Mal. from (para, san. superior + vitána, san. canopy). Tam. from (kambala, san. woollen cloth). Carpet. Larger used to cover the floor of a room or tent [derah]; smaller to sleep or pray upon, or as door mat. Distinguish from Shatranj [q.v.].

SATTAUR (ستار - sattár, *Hind.*). From (satara, ar. to hide). Attribute of God. Concealer or thrower of a veil of mercy over men's sins [allah]. Common alam; as Sattaur khan, alam + pataun alaumat [ism].

SAUBIT (ثابت - sábit, *Hind.*). From (sabata, ar. to endure). Firm. Part of lacab; as Saubit jung, firm in war [ism].

SAUBOON (सर्वक्षार - sarvakshára, *San.*; صابون - sábún, *Ar.*, *Pers.* and *Hind.*; సబ్బు - sabbu, *Tel.*; சவுக்காரம் - shavukkáram, *Tam.*). San. and Tam. from (sarva, san. all + kshára, san. alkali); universal alkali. Soap. Product of the action of caustic alkali upon neutral fats. Potash [jharkanamak] forms soft soap, and soda [munncauram] hard soap; the latter most employed. Pure alkali [cauram] would injure hands or fabric; by combination with the fatty acids [tezaub] its action is rendered milder without destroying its property of combining with impurities. The articles employed in making country soap are oovar munn [q.v.], an impure carbonate of soda; pooneer [q.v.], a light-colored earth, containing a great proportion of carbonate of soda; puttleooppoo or saltpetre [shorah]; and choonam [q.v.] or quicklime. All these are bruised together, and fresh water is added. The mixture is then well agitated for several hours and allowed to stand for three days. The feculent matter having fallen to the bottom, the clear part is strained off and boiled to form the soap, a sufficient quantity of gingelly [q.v.] oil having been previously added when it began first to boil. Veidyans [q.v.] use this medicinally. Country soap on drying loses 50 per cent. in weight. The natives extensively employ as a substitute for soap for washing silk [puttoo], woollen [pushm] cloths, hair, wooden articles, &c., the fruits of Sapindus species [soapnut]; and the bark of Acacia intsia, willd. [corindah] These considered better than soap. A popular household article for promoting growth of hair is a decoction of pods of Acacia concinna, dec. [soap-pod].

SAUCALA (చాకల - tsákala, *Tel.*). Teloogoo washermen's caste. The corresponding terms are:—Can. agasa, Tam. vunnaun, Mal. veloottaidan [jauty]. See vol. II, 232.

SAUDAT (سعادت - saádat, *Ar.*). From (saada, ar. to be happy). Blessing. Prefixed to an alam forms a lacab; as Saadat ally, blessing of ally [ism].——*Saudat oollah khan* (سعادت الله خان - saádatulláhkhán, Hind.). From (above + alam + title of honor). A nawaub of arab extraction who first took the title of Nawaub [q.v.] of the Carnatic [q.v.]. A.D. 1710–1732 [charitram]. See vol. I (176) and 44; II, 252.

SAUDH (साधु - sádh, *San.*). To accomplish.——*Bramha siddhauntam* (ब्रह्मसिद्धान्त - brahmasiddhánta, San.). From (brahma, san. the person, so called + siddhánta, san. established truth). Astronomical [jyotisham] work by Bramha gooptan, 628 A.D. He set himself the task of correcting the earlier system which had ceased to agree with the phenomena, and of reconciling computation [maunam] with observation. This work, in twenty-one chapters, contains calculations of the mean motions and true places of the planets [graham], of lunar and solar eclipses [grahanam], of the rising and setting of planets, of the position of the moon's cusps, and of observations of altitudes [avanataumsham] by the gnomon [shunk]. The principles of Brahma gooptan's astronomical system are given in a compendious treatise on spherics. He frequently quotes from Aryabhatta [q.v.].——*Saudhanam* (साधन - sádhana, San.). Document [caranam, dastavaiz, nauma, patram].——*Saudhoo* (साधु - sádhu, San.). Religious mendicant. But more generally applied to one of subdued passions and contemplative habits; a sage [moony, sanyausy, yaty, yogy].——*Siddh* (सिधु - sidh, San.). To be established.——*Siddham* (सिद्धि - siddha, San.). Established. Common name among Linga balijes [q.v.] and Jangams [q.v.], in combination with Appa, Ayya and Amma [peyar].——*Siddhan* (सिद्ध - siddha, San.). Sage [corakkan]. The Siddhar were a Tamul sect, the adherents of which retained Shiva as the name of God, but rejected everything in the Sheiva system which was inconsistent with pure theism. They cultivated alchemy [rasauyanam] as sedulously as the Arabians. The poems of the Siddhar school are modern in style. The Siddhar took the names of rishies [q.v.]. The eighteen most celebrated were:—Agastyan, a bramin; Poolastyan, a bramin; Nundy, a bramin; Yidaicauttaun, a shepherd; Caroor siddhan, a barber; Conganan, a palinga, low tribe on west coast; Shattamoony, a weaver; Bhogan, a potter; Soondaraunandan, a reddy; Matsyan, a shemmaun, fisherman or shoemaker; Tirmoolan, a vulloovan; Pinnaukkeeran, a meravan; Calaunjy, a fisherman; Goracshacan, a cavaray yidaiyan or teloogoo shepherd; Roma rishy, a coravan; Bramha moony, a bramin; Aloogauny siddhan, a veydan; Chandikeshan, a vindan or shepherd [matam]. See vol. I (57).——*Siddharasam* (सिद्धरस - siddharasa, San.). From (siddha, san. sage + rasa, san. juice, mercury). From use by adepts. In its general acceptation mercury [rasam], but also refers to a liquid which converts into gold [pon] metals [loham] dipped into it.——*Siddhaunta augamam* (सिद्धान्तागम - siddhántágama, San.). From (siddhánta, san. established truth + ágama, san. a system of philosophy). Sheiva religious work [sheiva siddhauntam]. Treats, first, of several species of charities, such as the building of a caravansary, and digging of tanks and wells for the accommodation of travellers; secondly, of religious duties diurnal and periodical, of the various kinds of sacraments, and of ceremonies propitious or expiative, in which are included the holy incantations [muntram] wherewith temples are sanctified and images of deities deified and adorned; and lastly, of the nature of the godhead and his attributes, of souls [autmam], elements [bhootam], and other principles [tatwam], and of contemplation, &c.——*Siddhaunta cowmoody* (सिद्धान्तकौमुदी - siddhántakaumudí, San.). From (siddhánta, san. theorem + kaumudí, san. moonlight). Grammar, by Bhattojy deecshitan; being a practical arrangement of Paniny's [q.v.] sootrams [q.v.] with a commentary.——*Siddhauntam* (सिद्धान्त - siddhánta, San.). From (siddha, san. established + anta, san. end). Established truth. Theorem. In astronomy a treatise on that science. There is a numerous train of astronomical siddhauntams, of which four are reputed to be of divine origin, viz., Soorya, Bramha, Powlastya, Soma. By some authorities nine are named, viz., Bramha, Soorya, Soma, Brihaspaty, Garga, Naurada, Parausharा, Poolastya, Vasishta. The Soorya siddhauntam is the best known of all hindoo astronomical works. A comparatively modern one is Arya siddhauntam by Arya bhatta [q.v.]. This is preferred by Tamuls to Soorya siddhauntam. The Travancoreans again have a Siddhauntam of their own. Certain elementary differences can be seen as follows:—According to the Arya siddhauntam of Arya bhatta [q.v.] there are 1577917500 Bhoomy sauvana [q.v.] days called Yoog dinam [q.v.] in a Mahayoog [q.v.] or 4320000 years. Hence one year = 365d 15g 31v 15p indian time, 365d 6h 12m 30s european time. The same solar year according to the copies of the Arya siddhauntam preserved in Bengal, is $\frac{1577917800}{4320000}$ =

365d 15g 31v 17p 6s. This year is unknown in the Peninsula. According to the Soorya siddhauntam there are 1577917828, yoog dinams, hence the year is = 365d 15g 31v 31p 24s indian time, and 365d 6h 12m 36s 34f european time. According to the Travancore siddhaunties, there are 1577917320 yoog dinams, and the year is 365d 15g 31v 30p indian time, and 365d 6h 12m 36s european time [ahargaman, jyotisham, mausam].——*Siddhaunta shikhaumany* (सिद्धान्तशिखामणि - siddhántashikhámani, San.). From (siddhánta, san. established truth + shikhámani, san. crest-jewel). A treatise on philosophical Hindooism by Shiva pracausa deshican, a poet of Conjeeveram, seventeenth century.——*Siddhaunta shiromany* (सिद्धान्तशिरोमणि - siddhántashirómani, San.). From (siddhánta, san. established truth + shirómani, san. crest-jewel). Work on astronomy by Bhascara-charry [jyotisham].——*Siddhaunty* (சித்தாந்தி - shittándi, Tam.). From (siddha, san. accomplished + anta, san. end). An astronomer [jyotisham, nacshatram]; as Joshy is astrologer [peyar].——*Siddhaurtan* (सिद्धार्थ - siddhárt'ha, San.). From (siddha, san. accomplished + art'ha, san. object). One who has attained perfection; epithet of Booddha [q.v.].——*Siddhee* (سدهی - siddhí, Hind.); from use among siddhar or adepts. Same as Bhang [q.v.] drink.——*Siddheshwaram coil* (சித்தேசுவரன்கோவில் - shittésuvarangóvil, Tam.). From (siddhéshvara, san. shiva, the lord of the siddhas + kóvil, tam. temple). Mountain, Place of pilgrimage, much resorted to on new moon [amavausyay] days; Salem dist., Salem tal.; lat 11° 38′; long. 78° 04′; from Salem W. 8 miles. At the western end of the Cunjoomullay hills, contains pure mineral water springs.——*Siddhy* (सिद्धि - siddhi, San.; சித்தி - shitti, Tam.). An object to be attained. Supernatural power of which eight are enumerated:—animay, power of becoming an atom; mahimay, large; laghimay, light; garimay, heavy; praupty, attainment; praucaumyam, freedom of will not transferable; eeshitwam, lordliness; vashitwam, dominion. Title also means perfection, heavenly bliss, gift.——*Sidhout* (సిద్ధవట్టము - siddhavattamu, Tel.). See sep. title.——*Soorya siddhauntam* (सूर्यसिद्धान्त - súryasiddhánta, San.). A celebrated astronomical work said to have been revealed by the sun [sooryan] himself [jyotisham].——*Sowcar* (ساهوکار - sáhúkár, Hind.). From (sádhu, san. right + kár, pers. doer). A banker or money-lender. Nearly the same as Chetty [q.v.].

SAUF (صاف - sáf, *Hind.*). From (saffa, ar. to be even or clear). Fair copy in office business.

SAUL (शाल - shála, *San.*). From (shal, san. to praise); valuable timber tree. Botanically the Shorea genus, dipterocarpeæ [vricsham, 24]. Large, glabrous, mealy, or pubescent resinous trees, natives of tropical asia; leaves entire or wavy-edged; flowers yellow, sweet-smelling, and in axillary or terminal panicles; fruit one-seeded; wood generally close-grained; heart-wood brown, hard or very hard; hopea [caung] is an allied genus. The species of shorea best known to the natives are shown below.——*Common saul* (शाल - shála, San. and Mahr.; سال - sál, Hind. and Dec.; ಅಶ್ವಕರ್ಣ - ashvakarna, Can.; గుగ్గిలపుచెట్టు - guggilapuchettu, Tel.; ସଲ୍ୱ - salvá, Oor.; മുളപ്പൂമരുതു - mulappúmarutu, Mal.; දුම්මල - dummala, Singh.; குங்கிலியமரம் - kungiliyamaram, Tam.). San. as above. Hind. from sanscrit. Can. from (ashva, san. horse + karna, san. ear). Tel. from (guggilamu, tel. dammer + chettu, tel. tree). Mal. from (mula, mal. sprout + pú, mal. flower + marutu, mal. the tree, terminalia); perhaps in allusion to the seeds sprouting before falling from the tree. Singh. means resin of the tree. Tam. from (kungiliyam, tam. resinous gum + maram, tam. tree), dammer tree. San. also (ashvakarna), meaning horse's ear, from leaves; (sarjjaka), meaning pouring forth; (kaushikáhva), meaning named cowshicam; (kárshya), meaning lessening; (sasyasamvara), meaning covered with fruits. Hind. also (sákhar); (dohnah), meaning the resin; (damar), meaning the resin; (sálwa); (sákhu) [teak]; (sakoh). Dec. also (rál), meaning the resin. Can. also (áshina); (ásu); (guggulamara). Tel. also (véginachettu); (inumaddi), meaning iron + terminalia arjuna, bedd. [black murdah]; (nallamaddi), meaning black + terminalia arjuna, bedd. Oor. also (soringhi). Mal. also (marámaram), meaning tree of trees; (kunkilyamaram), meaning dammer tree. Singh also (hal), from sanscrit. Title otherwise Black dammer, Black muddy, Horse-ear [spogel], Indian dammer. Botanically Shorea [saul] robusta, gærtn., dipterocarpeæ [vricsham, 24]. Alias Vatica robusta. Tree, 100–150 feet; calyx five-sepalled, afterwards enlarging into long wings; petals five twisted in the bud, rather silky outside; leaves cordate-oblong, entire, on short petioles; calyx pubescent as well as the branches of the panicles; panicles terminal and axilary; ovary three-celled; cells two-seeded; seeds single; flowers yellow; fragrant. Tall, sparsely-branched, deciduous; one of the largest and most useful trees in india; seed ripens at commencement of rains. Whitish aromatic resin [raul] exudes; devoid of taste or smell, sparingly soluble in alcohol, entirely so in ether, and perfectly in turpentine [carpoora teilam] and the fixed oils [yennay]; occurs in small rough pieces, from a pale creamy color to a dark brown, nearly opaque, and very brittle; known as raul [q.v.] or dhoonah [q.v.]. Oil is expressed from the ripe seed. The saul seed falls actually sprouting from the tree; the plants form patches of forest, quite impenetrable. The resin unites with the fixed oils and forms medicinal plasters; superior kind is substitute for pine [cheer] resins of european pharmacopœias; applied to ulcers and chilblains, acting as a stimulant; thrown over fire gives out thick volumes of fragrant smoke, and is used for fumigating sick rooms; quoted in pharm. non-officinal. The wood is burnt for incense in temples; also the resin; aromatic oil [attar] procured from resin by dry distillation; resin used as substitute for dammer [q.v.] by boat-builders; for tanning [chamrah] purposes the bark is generally used along with terminalia [murdah], mimusops [csheericay] and phyllanthus [aumlacam], or with the bark of peepul [q.v.], babool [q.v.], and mango [q.v.]; ashes used as mordant [cauram]; plant gives fibre [naur]. Yields timber as much as 60 feet in length and with a girth of $4\frac{1}{2}$ feet; lasts a very long time under ground or under water, almost unequalled for sleepers, proof against white-ants [q.v.]; strong, tough, coarse-grained and fibrous, not easily worked, and when dressed has a hard horny surface, and fibres appear to be interlaced with each other; superior to teak [q.v.] in transverse strength and direct cohesive power, but subject to shrinkage; very heavy, so that it cannot be floated without more buoyant aids, and is, on that and some other accounts, inferior to teak; valuable for engineering purposes, largely used in gun carriages and for house-building and ship-building, but warps in plank.——*River saul* (नदीसर्ज - nadísarja, San.). From habitat. Same as White murdah.——*Taloora saul* (ಬಿಲೆಬೋವು - bilebóvu, Can.; ಕರ್ಮರ - karmara, Too.; జాలారి - dzálári, Tel.; കരിമരുതു - karimarutu, Mal.; தலூரா - talúra, Tam.). Title from tamul. Can. from (bili, can. white + bóvu, can. the tree). Too. from (kari, too. black + mara, too. tree). Tel. from (jála, tel. net + áre, tel. bauhinia racemosa, lam.) [yellow mountain ebony]. Mal. from (kari, mal. black + marutu, mal. the tree, terminalia) [black murdah]. Tam. corrupted from teloogoo. Can. also (bilebhógi), meaning white + the tree; (jálárimara); (jelaranda). Tel. also (himsra). Title otherwise Bastard saul, Jarallea, Lac tree [ceylon oak], Peach saul. Botanically Shorea [saul] talura, roxb., dipterocarpeæ [vricsham, 24]. Specific from tamul. Alias Saul jarallea; Shorea laccifera, robusta, roxburghii; Vatica chinensis, laccifera. Saul, from (shála, san. shorea robusta, gærtn.); Jarallea probably from teloogoo. Large tree; leaves coriaceous, oblong, obtuse or emarginate, and often emarginate at the base; panicles numerous from the axils of the fallen leaves; branches and pedicels glabrous; stamens fifteen; anther bristle very long; flowers yellow; flowering in march-april. Gives a lac [q.v.]. Wood grey, extremely hard, smooth, with small dark-colored irregularly-shaped heart-wood; much used for house-building.——*Tambaga saul* (کالا ڈامر کا پیڑ - káládámarképer, Hind.; کالا ڈامر کا جھاڑ - káládámarkájhár, Dec.; నల్లగుగ్గిలపుచెట్టు - nallagugilapuchettu, Tel.; തമ്പകം - tampakam, Mal.; தம்புகைமரம் - tambugaimaram, Tam.). Title from malayalam. Hind. from (kálá, hind. black + dámar, hind. dammer + per, hind. tree). Dec. from hindostany. Tel. from (nalla, tel. black + guggilamu, tel. dammer + -chettu, tel. tree). Mal. from (chempu, mal. redness + akam, mal. inside). Tam. from malayalam. Tel. also (nalladammarumánu), meaning black + dammer + tree; (thambá). Tam. also (tambam); (karuppudámarmaram), meaning black dammer tree; (kangu), meaning dark tree. Title otherwise Dammer tree, Tambam. Giving Black dammer, Dammer. Botanically Shorea [saul] tumbuggaia, roxb., dipterocarpeæ [vricsham, 24]. Specific name from malayalam. Alias Vatica tumbuggaia. Large tree; leaves long-petioled, ovate-cordate; panicles terminal; stamens about hundred with bearded anthers; sepals enlarging into wings; flowers yellow; flowering in march-april. A dammer [q.v.] exudes from trunk. Wood smooth, harder than that of common saul, but similar in structure; used for house-building, particularly for door-frames and posts, and for rafters.

SAULEY (సాలె - sále, *Tel.*). From (sálu, tel. cloth). Weavers of tel. origin [salem]. The corresponding terms are:—Tam. keikkala, Can. jeydar, Mal. chaulyan. They are divided into Shacoona sauley who are Sheivas, and Pudmasauley who are Veishnavas [jauty]. Numbers about 200,000.——*Chittisauley* (చిట్టిసాలె - chittisále, Tel.). From (chiru, tel. small + sále, tel. weaver). An inferior class of weavers.——*Puttsauley* (పట్టుసాలె - pattusále, Tel.). From (pattu, tel. silk). Silk [puttoo] weavers. See vol. II, 230.——*Salampore* (శాలంబరిగుడ్డ - shalambarigudda, Tel.). From (sále, tel. weaver + pura, san. town), weaver's town. A kind of cotton [q.v.] cloth formerly manufactured at Nellore; half the length of ordinary Poonjam [palampore, poonjam].——*Saulore* (సాలూరు - sálúru, Tel.). See sep. title.

SAULORE (సాలూరు - sálúru, *Tel.* sálúru *). From (sále, tel. weaver caste + úru, tel. village) [sauley].——**(1)** Division; Vizagapatam district; area 380 square miles; population Non-agency, 83,699; Agency, 7,002; language Teloogoo. Boundaries:—east, Bobbily and Parvatipore divisions; south, Gajapatinugger division; west, Pottinghy division; north, Parvatipore division. A plain intersected by numerous small ranges of hills and dotted with granite [caroom cull] bosses of great height; soil fertile, black clay [calimunn], black and red sand [manal]. Very large Brinjarry [q.v.] trade with jeypore and central provinces in salt [ooppoo], grain [dhaunyam], lace [calaubat], gallnuts [maachicoy], turmeric [country saffron], &c. Irrigation by tanks, rivers being on too low level. Camping ground at Ramabhadrapooram. Places of archæological interest :—Pauchipenta, Saulore. The leading places, &c., in the division are the following.——*Chemoodoo* (చెముడు - chemudu, Tel.). See sep. title.——*Langoolya* (లాంగూలియా - lánguliyá, Tel.). See sep. title.——*Macwa* (మకువ - makuva, Tel.). Means desire. Village; pop. 2,722; lat. 18° 40′; long. 83° 19′; from Saulore N.N.E. 12 miles; from Vizagapatam N. 65 miles. Ruined mud fort. Many weavers formerly lived here. Now a decaying village.——*Pauchipenta* (పాచిపెంట - páchipenta, Tel.). See sep. title.——*Ramabhadrapooram* (రామభద్రపురము - rámabhadrapuramu, Tel.). From (rámabhadrudu, tel. proper name + pura, san. city). Village; pop. 2,777; lat. 18° 29′; long. 83° 19′; from Saulore E.S.E. 5 miles; from Vizagapatam N. 54 miles. Ruined fort. Important halting place for carts going from Saulore and Parvatipore to Vizianagram, &c.——*Saulore* (సాలూరు - sálúru, Tel.). See below.——**(2)** Deputy tahsildarry; Vizagapatam district. Pay Rs. 100.——**(3)** Zemindarry; Vizagapatam dist., Saulore division; pop. 64,148. Came under the Poosapauties [q.v.], when Jeypore ceded all the old hill zemindarries to Seetaram raj. At period of first establishment of English, Sanyausy rauz of Saulore headed a rebellion against Vizianagram, in the course of which he lost one of his hoondahs, Macwa, but was allowed to retain country about Saulore. On his death in 1774, the whole zemindarry was confiscated by Poosapauties, who imprisoned his three sons, Bhogy rauz, Bootchy rauz and Ramchendra rauz in the fort at Devapully. In 1793 they were released and a small allowance settled on them. On death of Vijiaram rauz in 1794, Saulore was granted on cowle [q.v.] to Ramchendra rauz, eldest son of the last Zemindar. He died in 1801, and the permanent settlement was made with Sanyausy rauz, his son. The zemindars of Saulore are Ooriyas, but read and write Teloogoo. Pesbcush Rs. 35,954.——**(4)** Town, Head-quarters of Zemindar and Deputy tahsildar, Sub-registrar's office, a German mission chapel; Vizagapatam dist., Saulore division; pop. 12,917; lat. 18° 30′; long. 83° 15′; from Coraputt S.E. 36 miles; from Madras N.E. 420 miles; from Narsapatam N.E. 68 miles; from Parvatipore S.W. 23 miles; from Vizagapatam N. 55 miles; from Vizianagram N.N.W. 30 miles. Old mud fort. Granted by Vishwambhara deo of Jeypore to a chieftain of the Conda rauz caste, whom he honored with the title of Boliyaurosimha. Does great trade with Jeypore and Central provinces.

SAUMAUN (سامان - sámán, *Hind.*). From persian. Articles, furniture, baggage [saranjaum].

SAUNY (ثانی - sání, *Hind.*). From arabic, second. A companion. Sauny puttahdar is a co-puttahdar [sa].

SAURA (చార - tsára, *Tel.*). Stripe.——*Saurapotoo* (చారపోతు - tsárapótu, Tel.). From (above + pótu, tel. a male mate). Leptorhytaon jara, lycodontidæ [vazhalay], ophidii colubriformes, ophidia [sarpam], reptilia [sarpy, 15], of naturalists [jantoo]. Distinguish from Rat snake [q.v.], though that has the same native name.

SAURAH (سارا - sárá, *Hind.*). Means princess. Abraham's wife. Female alam, as Saurah bee, alam + alaumat [ism].

SAURASAM (सारस - sárasa, *San.*). From (saras, san. lake) [sar]. Gruidæ family, pressirostres, grallatores, aves [pacshy, 40], of naturalists [jantoo]. Cranes. Fly with outstretched necks; very loud, trumpet-like call. Highly gregarious; nidificate on the ground. There is a Tamul proverb:—படித்தவனுக்கும் படியாதவனுக்கும், கொக்குக்கும் அன்னத்துக்கும் வித்தியாசம்போல—"the difference between the learned "and the unlearned is as great as that between a crane and a "swan [hamsam]." Friar Jordanus, the Quilon Bishop of the fourteenth century, has the following:—"there is also another "big bird, not like a kite [chillam], which flies only at night, "and utters a voice in the night season like the voice of a man "wailing from the deep." The species best known to the natives are shown below.——*Common crane* (बक - baka, San.; कळ्ळ - kallam, Mahr.; کرکی - kurkí, Ar.; کلنگ - kulang, Pers., Hind. and Dec.; جنجنگ - jinjang, Malay; కొంగ - konga, Tel.; നാര - nára, Mal.; கொக்கு - kokku, Tam.). San. from (vak, san. to go crookedly). Pers. from (khulanj, pers. crooked). Mal. from (nara, mal. to grow white). Tam. from the cry. Ar. also (ghurník). Tel. also (kólangi); (gúdakonga), meaning mean + crane. Tam. also (nárai), meaning whiteness. Grus cinerea, gruidæ [saurasam], pressirostres, grallatores [pacshy, 40], of naturalists. Alias Ardea grus; Grus antigone. Forehead and cheeks nude, with black bristly hairs; crown nude, dull orange red; occiput, throat and forepart of neck, of deep blackish grey; between eyes, sides of head and upper part of neck white, as is greater part of back of the neck, color impure and with reddish tinge; all upper part of body and lower plumage dark ashy blue; quills and greater coverts dull black; secondaries and tertiaries grey, black tipped, latter narrowing to point with barbs of uppermost feathers disunited, all arching down and forming elegant tuft of floating plumes which it is able to erect at pleasure. Bill glaucous green at the base, blackish green in the middle, the tip dark horny; irides yellowish red, reddish brown in some; legs and feet dull black. Length 3 to 3½ feet; extent 6 feet; wing 21 inches; bill at front 4; weight about 12 lb. Young birds want naked patch on head, neck is dingy grey without white, and colors generally are more dull. Visits India in numerous flocks during the cold weather. Feeds chiefly on grain, committing great havoc in the wheat [geung] fields, also eats shoots of plants and flowers and occasionally insects [poochy] and reptiles [sarpy]. Feeds chiefly in the morning; leaves this country early, generally before end of March; eggs two, greenish color, with brownish spots; tolerably good eating.——*Cyrus crane* (सारस - sárasa, San.; سارهنس - sárhans, Hind.; سارس - sáras, Dec.). Title corruption from deccany. San. from (saras, san. lake). Hind. from sanscrit. Dec. from sanscrit. Title otherwise Sarus crane. Grus antigone, gruidæ [saurasam] pressirostres, grallatores [pacshy, 40], of naturalists. Alias Ardea antigone; Grus orientalis, torquata. Head and neck naked and covered with numerous crimson papillæ, clad with few scant black hairs, which accumulate into broad ring on neck and form a sort of mane down nape of neck; ear-coverts white; below this neck whitish grey, gradually passes into pale blue or french grey, which is color of whole plumage, quills and inner webs of the tail-feathers being dusky slaty. At breeding season, in April, they assume pure white collar, immediately below crimson papillose skin of neck, which also becomes brighter in color; and in old birds the tertiaries and some of the scapulars become white and are lengthened, hanging over gracefully, and exceeding the tail. Bill pale sea green, brownish at tip; irides orange red; legs and feet pale rosy red. Length about 52 inches; extent nearly 8 feet; wing 26 inches; tail 9¼; bill at front 6½; weight 17 or 18 lb. Found throughout the greater part of India; rare south of the Godavery; chiefly found in pairs, occasionally several together; feeds less exclusively perhaps on grain than the other cranes met with in India, and is very generally found not far from water; breeds on some island or spot nearly surrounded by water, laying two eggs only, very pale bluish green with reddish spots. Nest sometimes commenced below water, and raised above surface; young have head and neck dull ferruginous. Old birds when sitting, or with their young, very bold. Its fine trumpet-like call, uttered when alarmed or on the wing, can be heard a couple of miles. Young not bad eating, but old birds are worthless for the table.——*Demoiselle crane* (करकची - karakuchí, Mahr.; کرکرا - karkará, Hind.; ಕಾರ್ಕೊಂಚೆ - kárkonche, Can.; వడకొరక - vadakoraka, Tel.). Title from plumage, and tuft of long black feathers hanging from back of head. Can. from (káru, can. black + krauñcha, san. curlew). Hind. also (karronch), from (krauñcha, san. the bird). Can. also (konga). Anthropoides virgo, gruidæ [saurasam], pressirostres, grallatores [pacshy, 40], of naturalists. Alias Ardea virgo. Forehead, face, sides of head, neck and lengthened breasts, plumes, black; tuft of white decomposed feathers extending backwards and outwards from eye; general plumage fine purplish grey; quills black; greatly elongated tertiaries and scapular dusky slaty, drooping. Bill greenish at base, yellowish in middle, inclining to pink at tip; irides fine ruby red; legs black. Length about 30 inches; extent 5 feet, wing 19 inches; tail 6½ to 7; bill at front $2\frac{3}{10}$; weight about 6 lb. Young birds have no black, and want the white ear-tuft; found throughout greater part of India, more rare in extreme south; never seen in Malabar. Cold weather visitor generally, only coming in late in October; associates in numerous flocks, from fifty to five hundred; chiefly frequents vicinity of rivers; very destructive to grain fields; fly with great regularity, either in long continuous line, or in double wedge-shaped and then utter their fine clanging note frequently. Breeds on ground in Northern Asia, laying two olive grey eggs speckled with rufous. Male bird watches whilst female is incubating, and fights boldly if attacked. Dance among themselves, and will often seize hold of any small article toss it up in the air, and catch it as it descends; also occasionally eat mice [shoondely], snakes [paumb], &c., lifting them up and dashing them down on the ground till quite dead.

SAUTAUNY (சாத்தானி - sháttáni, *Tam.*). From (chaitanya, san. the vaishnava reformer). A class of Veishnavites. Musicians and mendicants. They are followers of Cheitanyan, a religious teacher of the fifteenth century, and of his disciple Sanautanan. They have views similar to those of the Beisnab reformers of Bengal. Do not wear the sacred thread [poonool] or tuft of hair [coodoomy]. Many of them in Southern india worship Permaul [q.v.], an incarnation of Vishnoo [q.v.], perambulate the street morning and evening, and accept alms from all but the lowest castes, often exacting the same by threats of burning themselves with a lamp. The temple servants are generally taken from the Sautauny class. They are skilled in weaving flowers into garlands. They are generally attached to Vishnoo temples; while the Pundaurams [q.v.] are attached to Sheiva temples. One of the Sautauny sects burn their dead; the others bury their dead in the sitting posture up to the head, then burst the head by throwing cocoanuts [q.v.] on it, and heap it over with earth [shavacaud, shoodcaud]. Their philosophic principle is Vishishtaudweitam. See vol. I (77), (86), (90); II, 231. There is a Teloogoo proverb:—సాతానిపంచాయతి—"a sautauny dispute;" they admit as members of their body all classes amongst the worshippers of vishnoo, who consequently dispute each others rank in assemblies; so a dispute which cannot be easily settled.——*Sautautha* (சாத்தாத - sháttátha, obl., Tam.). From (sháttu, tam. to wear); as not wearing sacred thread [poonool] or tuft of hair [coodoomy]. Same as Sautauny; but the words are not really connected.

SAUVARAM (సావరము - sávaramu, *Tel.*). From (chávar, hind. a measure of land). The home lands [havelly]. That portion of a zemindarry [q.v.] which proprietor retains in his own hands, Shery [q.v.] being lands which are let out to tenants.

SAWAUL (سوال - sawál, *Hind.*). From (saala, ar. to ask). A question.

SAWAUR (سوار - sawár, *Hind.*). From (asp, pers. horse + wár, pers. suffix of affinity). A horseman, trooper.——*Sawaury* (سواری - sawárí, Hind.). From persian. Riding. Any mode of conveyance, especially a palankeen [q.v.]. A mounted retinue. A sawaury horse is a riding horse.

SAYER (سایر - sáir, *Hind.*). From (sair, ar. current). Current or customary. Sources of revenue in addition to the land-tax, as customs, transit duties, licenses, fees, house-tax, market-tax, &c. Sayer chowky is a custom-house station. See vol. I, 112.

SCAMMONY (سقمونيا - sakmúniyá, *Ar.*, *Pers.* and *Hind.*; సకుమునియా - sakumuniyá, *Tel.*; சகமுனியா - shagamuniyá, *Tam.*). Title from syriac through arabic. Ar. also (mahmúdah), meaning excellent. Tel. also (mámúdá). Tam. also (mámúthá), from arabic. Greek σκαμμώνιον; erroneously derived from σκάμμα, a trench, as if from excavation made around the root. Title otherwise Gum scammony, Syrian bind-weed. Botanically Convolvulus [tauly] scammonia, linn., convolvulaceæ [vricsham, 93]. Perennial, deciduous, ligneous or herbaceous twiner; leaves sagittate, truncate behind; peduncles rounded, three-flowered, flowers whitish-purple, flowering in july and august; hedges of greece and the levant. Gum resin [googal], obtained by incision from root is glossy, of the color of raw silk [puttoo], and easily friable, with a peculiar heavy odour, and a bitterish, slightly acrid taste; this is scammony. Medicinally cathartic and anthelmintic; substituted for british jalap [q.v.] and rhubarb [indian rhubarb]; gives to pharm. the dried root, scammoniæ radix; also the gum-resin [googal], scammonium; officinal.

SCAND (स्कन्द - skand, *San.*). To leap.——*Scandan* (स्कन्द - skanda, San.). From (skand, san. to leap); as fond of exercise. Younger son of Shiva [soobramanyan]. The name Scandan is in little use except that the Scaundapooraunam [q.v.] thence takes its title. Caurtikeyan [q.v.] in Northern india and Soobramanyan [q.v.] in Southern india are more frequent. See also Cundasawmy.——*Scanda shashty* (స్కందషష్ఠి - skanda-shasht'hi, Tel.). Means the god scandan + sixth lunar day. Lunar [chaundramaunam] festival [pundigay, 3a], subject to intercalation [adhicam]. Begins on first day of waxing moon [shooclapacsham] in eighth lunar month Caurteecam [mausam] and lasts for seven days. Principal day is sixth, between 22nd October and 21st November, in commemoration of defeat of Shoorapudman, a giant whom Scandan vanquished after combat of six days. The seventh day, the image is carried in procession [maryauday, sambauran].

SCAR LEAF (வட்டிலை - vattilai, *Tam.*). From spots on leaf. Same as Face plant.

SCIMITAR POD (गरंबी - garambí, *Mahr.*; ಹಲ್ಲೆಕಾಯಿಬಳ್ಳಿ - hallekáyiballi, *Can.*; ಪಲ್ಲೆಬೂರು - pallebúru, *Too.*; టీకాతివ్వ - tíkátivva, *Tel.*; പെരുംകാക്കവള്ളി - perumkákkavalli, *Mal.*; පුස්වැල - pusvela, *Singh.*; இரிக்கி - irikki, *Tam.*). Title from appearance of legumes. Can. from (halle, can. vegetable + káyi, can. fruit + balli, can. creeper). Too. from (palle, too. large bean + búru, too. creeper). Tel. from (tíká, hind. the ornament + tivva, tel. creeper). Mal. from (peru, mal. large + kákkavalli, mal. crow-creeper). Singh. from (pus, singh. empty + vela, singh. creeper); hollow creeper. Tam. from (iri, tam. to destroy); medicinal. Tel. also (gilatíga); (tandramánu). Tam. also (tellu), meaning clearing, medicinal; (shillu). Title otherwise Creeping babool, Creeping mimosa, Faba marina, Lady nut tree, Match box bean, Shillo, West indian cocoon, West indian filbert tree. Botanically Entada scandens, benth., leguminosæ [vricsham, 48]. Alias Acacia scandens; Entada monostachya, pursætha, rheedii; Mimosa entada, scandens. A gigantic climbing shrub, remarkable for its legumes which are several feet long, 4–5 inches broad; and surrounded with a thick, very firm, polished entire rim, which is found to remain like a picture-frame when the less durable jointed body of the legume has disappeared; the joints are 10–30, one-seeded, ligneous, swelled in the centre, transversely furrowed, greenish ash-color when ripe; the seeds are more or less heart-shaped, flattened, about 2 inches in diameter, with a shining brown testa, which is 1/8th of an inch thick, and very tough and horny; it encloses two large, equal cotyledons which adhere to it; the radicle is patelliform, and lodged at the umbilicus of the seed; the substance of the cotyledons is white and insipid; when a thin section is cut and a drop of water placed upon it, the water immediately becomes milky, and the opacity of the section is much diminished. The seeds are emetic, and a paste prepared from them is applied medicinally to glandular swellings.

SCORPION (بچھو - biççhú, *Hind.*). Prefix.——*Scorpion fish* (سینگی - síngí, Hind.; بچھو مچھی - biççhúmaççhí, Dec.; ಚೇಳುಮೀನು - chélumínu, Can.; తేలుచేప - téluchépa, Tel.; ସିଂଘି - singhí, Oor.; കാരിമീൻ - kárimín, Mal.; தேளி - téli, Tam.). A short flat-headed eel having something like a scorpion's nippers, hence the name. Hind. from (síng, hind. horn); from its pectoral spine. Dec. from (biççhú, hind. scorpion + maççhí, hind. fish). Can. from (chélu, can. scorpion + mínn, can. fish). Tel. means scorpion fish. Oor. from hindostany. Mal. from (kári, mal. doer + mín, mal. fish). Tam. from (tél, tam. scorpion). Tel. also (márupu). Saccobranchus fossilis, siluridæ [kizhautty], physostomi, teleostei [matsyam, 35], of naturalists [jantoo]. Alias Saccobranchus singio; Silurus biserratus, fossilis, laticeps, microcephalus, singio. Singio from hindostany. Freshwater; colors leaden, sometimes with two longitudinal yellowish bands; the young occasionally reddish; wounds from the pectoral spine of this fish are dreaded as they are reputed very poisonous, occasioning tetanus; as soon as captured, the offensive spine is broken off by blows with a stake; fishermen dread it so much that they would prefer cutting the meshes of their nets and allowing it to escape than endeavour to remove it uninjured; as food the flesh is esteemed for its invigorating qualities, and tanks are frequently stocked with them during the rainy season; when food is plentiful they fatten well, if the reverse they become lanky, thus altering the comparative height of the body to that of its length; attaining a foot or more in length. No other common species here.——*Scorpion sting* (തേൾകട - télkata, Mal.; தேட்கொடுக்கி - tédgodukki, Tam.); from fruits like scorpion's sting. Same as Indian heliotrope.

SCREW (پیچ - pech, *Hind.*). Prefix.——*Screw bean* (مسقیط پیچدار - miskítipechdár, Hind.). From shape of pods. Same as Screw mesquit.——*Screw-pine* (केतकी - kétakí, San.; केवडा - kévadá, Mahr.; बोंडयि - bóndayi, Concany; كاذى - kází, Ar.; كدر - kadar, Pers.; کیوڑہ - keurah, Hind. and Dec.; پندن - pandan, Malay; ಕೇದಿಗೆ - kédige, Can.; ಕೇದಯಿ - kédayi, Too.; మొగలి - mogali, Tel.; കൈത - kaita, Mal.; වැටකෙයියා - vatakeyiyá, Singh.; தாழை - tázhai, Tam.). Title from screw-like arrangement of the long, spine-edged, sedge-like leaves on summit of the stems and pine-apple [ananas] like fruit. San. from (chit, san. to shine) [kait], from fragrant flowers. Mahr. from sanscrit. Can. from sanscrit. Too. from sanscrit. Tel. from (mogga, tel. bud), from flower not expanding like all other flowers [dyeing mulberry]. Mal. from sanscrit. Singh. from (vata, singh. hedge + keyiyá, singh. screw-pine, pandanus). Tam. from (tazhai, tam. to flourish with foliage). Conc. also (kédagi). Ar. also (kadar). Hind. also (ketgí), from sanscrit; (gaganphúl), meaning sky flower. Can. also (tále); (kyádige); (gédige); (mundige). Too. also (mundeyi). Tel. also (gádzangi); (gédangimogali); (goddzangi). Mal. also (tázha), meaning wide-spreading; (palliyambu), meaning royal arrow. Singh. also (múdukeyiyá), meaning sea + screw-pine, pandanus; (vataké). Tam. also (mundagam), meaning branchless plant; (musalí), meaning pestle like, from branchless stem. Title otherwise Caldera bush, Fragrant screw pine, Green spined screw spine, Keora oil plant, Ketaky, Mogaly, Moreton bay bread fruit, Nicobar breadfruit, Pandang oil plant, Tauzhay. Botanically Pandanus odoratissimus, linn. fil., pandanaceæ [vricsham, 150]. Pandanus from malay. Alias Arthrodactylis spinosa; Keura odorifera. Keura from hindostany. Large spreading shrub, 10 feet or more, bushy, ramous; roots issuing from lower parts of the stem or larger branches; leaves confluent, stem clasping, closely imbricated in three spiral rows round the extremities of the branches, tapering to a fine triangular point, smooth, shining, margin and back armed with sharp spines—those on the margin point towards the apex, those below in various ways; flowers male and female in terminal racemes on different plants; in female flowers no other corolla or calyx than the termination of the three rows of leaves forming three imbricated fascicles of white floral leaves, standing at equal distance round the base of the young fruit; fruit something in appearance like a pine-apple [ananas], orange-colored, composed of numerous drupes, detached when ripe, and covered with a deeper orange-colored skin, interior filled with rich-looking yellow pulp, intermixed with strong fibres; seed one, oblong, smooth; flowers small, pale yellow, very fragrant; flowers seldom visible, but the large red fruit, much like a pine-apple, is conspicuous. Extends over a large space by sending down aerial roots from branches; blossoms during rainy season with panicles of large, white, sheath-like leaves, enclosing spongy-looking bundles of closely packed minute flowers, with sandal [q.v.] perfume; thrives in low swampy ground; fringes the coast in many places, and is often planted in belts, but takes up much room, forms dense thickets, and harbours venomous reptiles [mogily cobra]; the lands in which chayroot [q.v.] is cultivated are often protected from drifts by means of this shrub, it is a very strong sand-binder [manal]. Flower offered to mauriyamman [q.v.], also to vishnoo [q.v.]; but is not acceptable to shiva [q.v.]. Floral leaves eaten either raw or boiled; lower pulpy part of drupes sometimes eaten; flowers with catechu [q.v.] and spices, form substance used in paun [q.v.]; pulp of fruit is used as famine food. From flowers is made keora oil [attar]; mats [boriyah], baskets [tokrah] and hats [topee] are made from the fusiform roots, as also a coarse brush for white-washing houses; farina of the male flowers is used as a perfume; natives bestrew their heads with it, as europeans do with perfumed powder; leaves composed of tough, longitudinal fibres, white and glossy, employed for covering huts, making matting, as well as for cordage; fibre [naur] very short in the staple, not being above an inch long; thick roots so soft and spongy as to be employed as corks [solah]. There is a Tamul proverb:—கடற் கரைத் தாழங்காய் இழ் தொங்கி என்ன மேல் தொங்கினென்ன—"what matters it whether the wild pine fruit on the seashore "hangs high or low?" being useless. There is another:—வேளைக்கு உதவாத பிள்ளை தாழங்காய்க்குச் சரி—"a "child who does not help in an emergency is like the fruit of "the screw-pine." Other common species are:—fascicularis, furcatus, lævis. For creeping screw-pine see Tirootauly. For foreign screw-pine see Ananas. For large screw-pine see Foreign aloe.——*Screw-tree* (आवर्त्तनी - ávartaní, San.; धामनी - dhámaní, Mahr.; توا بر توا - tawábartawá, Ar.; كشت بركشت - kishtbarkisht, Pers.; مروڑی - marorí, Hind. and Dec.; ಎಡಮುರಿಗಿಡ - edamurigida, Can.; వలంబిరి - valambiri, Tel.; ମୁରିମୁରି - murimuri, Oor.; വലമ്പിരി - valampiri, Mal.; ලීනියා - líniyá, Singh.; வலம்புரி - valamburi, Tam.). Title from twisted capsules. San. from (ávrit, san. to twist); from twisted capsules. Ar. from (tawá, ar. fold + bar, pers. over + tawá, ar. fold). Pers. from (kisht, pers. chain + bar, pers. over + kisht, pers. chain). Hind. from (marorí, hind. anything twisted), from use of its fruit in gripes, or from its screw-like capsules. Can. from (eda, can. left + muri, can. turn). Mal. from tamul. Tam. means turned to the right [roodrauck tree, valamboory]. San. also (mrigashringa), meaning deer's horn. Mahr. also (kévana); (varkáti). Pers. also (pechak), meaning little twists. Hind. also (maroríphallí), meaning gripes + pod; (jonkphallí), meaning leech + pod. Can. also (bhútakaralu), meaning goblin + entrail; (kádukalnárugida), meaning wild stone + hemp plant, cannabis sativa, linn.; (chachalu); (kywalla). Tel. also (shyámali), meaning black; (ádashyámali), meaning female + the tree; (kávanchi); (nuliti), meaning small; (gubbadára); (nulitada), meaning small + grewia tiliæfolia, vahl. [round-leaved tadda]. Mal. also (íshvaramúli), meaning divine root; (íshvaramulla), meaning divine jasminum sambac, ait. [isharmool]. Title otherwise Deer's horn, Devil's entrails, Eeshwaramooly, Isora, Twisted horn, Twisted stick, Valamboory. Botanically Helicteres isora, linn., sterculiaceæ [vricsham, 23]. Specific from (íshvaramúli, mal. the plant). Alias Helicteres jamaicensis roxburghii; Isora corylifolia. Shrub, 12 feet; leaves broad, slightly cordate roundish, obovate, suddenly and shortly acuminated, serrate, toothed, upper side scabrous, under tomentose, like english hazel; pedicles two to four together, forming an almost sessile, axillary corymb; petals reflexed; capsule cylindrical, spirally twisted, pubescent; flowers brick-colored. The fruit consists of five slender angular carpels, twisted like a corkscrew, and together forming a cone about $1\frac{1}{2}$ to 2 inches long; the carpels are pubescent, and of a greenish brown color; they contain a single row of dark brown angular seeds; the internal surface is of a light greenish hue and highly polished; taste mucilaginous; the root bark is of a dark-brown color, and is very thickly studded with small round warts so as to present almost the appearance of shagreen. A liniment from powder of the capsule, mixed with castor-oil [aumanac] applied in medicine to sore-ears; seed vessels used internally in bilious affections with other medicines, the screw of plant being taken to indicate applicability to colic. Fibre [naur] from bark is strong, white, and very useful for cordage, rough sacking, and canvas; curtain blinds of verandahs [q.v.] of native houses are made from this. Wood white, soft; branches used for fuel, fencing and thatching; used for producing fire by friction. No other common species here.

SEA BREEZE (دریا کی ہوا - daryákíhawá, *Hind.*; ಸಮುದ್ರದಘಾಳಿ - samudradaghálí, *Can.*; ಕಡಲ್‌ಘಾಳಿ - kadalghálí, *Too.*; సముద్రపుగాలి - samudrapugálí, *Tel.*; കടൽകാററു - katalkáttu, *Mal.*; கடற்காற்று - kadargáttu, *Tam.*). Title as blowing from the sea. Hind. from (daryá, hind. sea + hawá, hind. breeze). Can. from (samudra, san. sea + ghálí, can. breeze). Too. from (kadal, too. sea + ghálí, too. breeze). Tel. from (samudra, san. sea + gáli, tel. breeze). Tam. from (kadal, tam. sea + káttu, tam. wind). A local wind. Occurs along the east coast, and for a few miles inland. Sets in about noon and continues for sometime after sunset. At the distance of ten or twenty miles from the sea it arrives late in the afternoon, and is already heated by the tract of country over which it has passed. Called in old Anglo-indian, the Doctor. There is something of the same sort on the W. coast. See vol. II, 3 [land-wind, monsoon, vayoo].

SEB (सेव - séva, *San.*; شجر تفاح - shajarituffáh, *Ar.*; درخت سیب - darakhtiseb, *Pers.*; سیو کا پیڑ - seukáper, *Hind.*; سیب کا جہاڑ - sebkájhár, *Dec.*; ಸೇವುಗಿಡ - sévugida, *Can.*). Title from persian. San. from persian. Ar. from (shajar, ar. tree + tuffáh, ar. apple). Pers. from (darakht, ar. tree + seb, pers. apple). Hind. from (séva, san. apple + per, hind. tree). Dec. from hindostany. Hind. also (sahjnákábínj), referring to seeds. Greek μηλέα. Title otherwise Apple. Botanically Pyrus malus, linn., rosaceæ [vricsham, 49]. Alias Malus communis. Deciduous fruit tree, 20 feet high; leaves ovate, oblong, acuminate, serrated, smooth; umbel sessile; claws shorter than the calyx; styles smooth; flowers reddish white, flowering in april and may; fruit usually globose, always umblicate at the base, and not narrowed into the peduncle; flesh firm, brittle and acidulous, never stony, containing, besides sugar [q.v.] and malic acid, gum, pectine and albumine; malic acid is contained in considerable quantity; at bangalore bears well, but inferior to the english and american apple. For species communis or pear, see Amrood. Compare the following apples:—Ægle marmelos, golden apple and wood-apple; Anacardium occidentale, cashew apple; Ananas sativus, pine-apple; Anona palustris, alligator apple; Anona squamosa, custard-apple and sugar-apple; Chrysophyllum roxburghii, star-apple; Citrullus colocynthis, bitter apple; Citrus medica, var. limetta, adam's apple; Cydonia vulgaris, cretan apple and golden apple; Datura fastuosa, thorn apple; Eugenia jambos, east indian rose-apple; Eugenia malaccensis, malay apple and malay rose-apple; Feronia elephantum, elephant-apple; Lycopersicum esculentum, love-apple; Momordica dioica, balsam-apple; Punica granatum, carthagenian apple; Solanum melongena, jew's apple and mad-apple; Spondias dulcis, otaheite apple; Tabernæmontana coronaria, adam's apple; Tabernæmontana dichotoma, eve's apple. See gloss. paragraphs.

SEBESTEN (शेलु - shélu, *San.*; سپستان - sapistán, *Pers.*; బొటుకు - botuku, *Tel.*; വിരി - viri, *Mal.*; நறுவிலி - naruvili, *Tam.*). Title from persian [sag]. San. from (shél, san. to shake); from curing diseases. Pers. from (sag, pers. dog + pistán, pers. nipple). Tam. from (naruvu, tam. odour + ul, tam. having), from pleasant-tasted fruit. Title otherwise Lobesten. Botanically the Cordia genus, boragineæ [vricsham, 92]. Trees or shrubs; leaves alternate, stalked; flowers in dichotomous corymbs or clusters; drupe ovoid or ellipsoid, with one to four cells each with a seed. The species best known to the natives are shown below. Other s. indian species indigenous or naturalized are:—Cordia macleodii, h. f. and t.; found in godavery forests; heart-wood light-brown, mottled with darker veins, even-grained, vey hard, strong, tough and elastic; seasons well and works easily; used for furniture, picture-frames, and other ornamental work; fishing-rods; something like maple; much used in central india. Cordia monoica, roxb.; small tree; flowers white; drupe oval, as large as a black-currant [angoor], smooth yellow filled with mucilaginous pulp; yields a strong close-grained wood, but small and crooked. Cordia subcordata, lamk., tahiti tow tree; tree; flowers white, suffused with red; introduced from the moluccas. Cordia tectonifolia, wall.; small tree with handsome scarlet flowers in gardens in the plains, introduced from the west indies [golden sebesten].——*Cuba sebesten* (విరిగె - virige, Tel.). Tel. from (virugu, tel. to break), from its brittleness. Title otherwise Rough-leaved sebesten. Botanically Cordia [sebesten] sebestana, l., boragineæ [vricsham, 92]. Small tree, 15 feet, native of cuba; ovate, acute or elliptic, entire, rough coarse leaves; large cymes of bright scarlet flowers produced at ends of branches, followed by pure white fruits. Wood aromatic when burnt.——*Golden sebesten* (பொன்னறுவிலி - ponnaruvili, Tam.). Title from scarlet flowers. Tam. from (pon, tam. gold + naruvili, tam. cordia sp.). Botanically Cordia [sebesten] speciosa, willd., boragineæ [vricsham, 92]. Small tree with handsome scarlet flowers in gardens in the plains, introduced from the west indies. Compare species tectonifolia, above.——*Large sebesten* (शेलु - shélu, San.; مخیطة کبیر - makhítahikabír, Ar.; سپستان کلان - sapistánikalán, Pers.; بڑالسوڑا - barálasorá, Hind.; بڑی گوندنی کا جہاڑ - barígondníkájhár, Dec.; నక్కెరు - nakkéru, Tel.; വലിയവനിച്ചി - valiyavaniçci, Mal.; பெரியநறுவிலி - periyanaruvili, Tam.). Title from size of tree and berry. San. from (shél, san. to shake), from curing diseases. Ar. from (makhítah, ar. cordia myxa, linn. + kabír, ar. large). Pers. from (sag, pers. bitch + pistán, pers. breasts + kalán, pers. large). Hind. from (bará, hind. large + lasorá, hind. cordia myxa, linn.). Dec. from (barí, hind. large + gondní, hind. fruit of cordia myxa, linn. + jhár, hind. tree). Tel. from (nakka, tel. fox + éru, tel. to pick up) [false sandal, narrow-leaved sebesten]. Mal. from (valiya, mal. large + vaniççi, mal. diospyros embryopteris, pers.). Tam. from (periya, tam. big + naruvili, tam. cordia sp.). San. also (bahuváraka), meaning preventing much, medicinal; (gandhapushpa), meaning fragrant blossomed; (bhútadruma), meaning devils' tree; (bhútavriksha), meaning devil's tree; (shítap'hala), meaning having cold fruit; (shíta), meaning cold; (shléshmántaka), meaning phlegm destroying; (pichhila), meaning slippery, from clammy pulp; (uddála), meaning bursting out; (dvijakutsita), meaning despised by bramins or birds; (shátaka), meaning thinning, weakening diseases. Hind. also (barálaslasá); (barálasorá); (lasorá); (gondní). Tel. also (bankanakkera), meaning gum + the tree; (iriki), meaning narrow, from small wood; (peddanakkéru), meaning large + the tree; (úrunakkera), meaning village + the tree; (peddabotuku), meaning large + the tree cordia. Mal. also (periyamari), meaning large + indigofera tinctoria, linn.; (naruvari), meaning fragrant cordia. Tam. also (vidimaram), corruption from malayalam; (verasu). Title otherwise Broad leaved sebesten. Botanically Cordia [sebesten] obliqua, willd., borogineæ [vricsham, 92]. Alias Cordia latifolia. Tree, 12-25 feet; leaves roundish, cordate, entire, repand, three-nerved, smooth above, scabrous beneath; calyx villous, campanulate, with an unequally-toothed mouth; corolla short, campanulate; segments five; panicles terminal and lateral; flowers numerous; small, white; drupe pale-straw color, covered with whitish bloom; nut surrounded with soft clammy pulp. Has numerous spreading branches, and the young shoots are angular and smooth; small, round, reddish-colored, pleasant-tasted glutinous fruit, called sebesten plum. Fruit is medicinally expectorant and astringent; medical use same as cordia myxa, linn. [small sebesten]. The fruit is eaten. Matches made from the bark; plant gives fibre [naur]. Wood here very inferior, and of small size. There is a variety obliqua, willd., var. wallichii; tree tolerably common throughout western forests and in mysore; technically hardly distinct from the common cordia myxa, linn. [small sebesten], but the densely woolly leaves will distinguish it; timber is serviceable and in use with the natives.——*Narrow-leaved sebesten* (भोकर - bhókara, Mahr.; گوندنی کا جہاڑ - gondníkájhár, Dec.; చిన్నబొటుకు - chinnabotuku, Tel.; நறுவிலி - naruvili, Tam.). Dec. from (gondní, hind. cordia + jhár, hind. tree). Tel. from (chinna, tel. small + botuku, tel. cordia). Tam. from (naruvu, tam. odour + ul, tam. having). Tel. also (nakkéru), meaning fox + picking up [false sandal, large sebesten]. Botanically Cordia [sebesten] rothii, rœm. and sch., boragineæ [vricsham, 92]. Alias Cordia angustifolia, cuneata, reticulata. Tree, 12-15 feet; leaves nearly opposite, lanceolate, obtuse or emarginate, scabrous; calyx campanulate, obscurely four-toothed; corolla-tube longer than the calyx; limb four-partite, with revolute edges; panicles terminal, corymbose; stamens four; flowers small, white; drupe round, smooth, yellow; nut surrounded with mucilaginous pulp. Decoction [kwantam] of the bark astringent and used as gargle; in pharm. non-officinal. Pulp of fruit eaten. Liber or inner bark made into rope; gives a gum [gond]. Wood grey, compact, hard; elastic, making good poles for carriages, &c.——*Small sebesten* (शेलु - shélu, San.; भोंकर - bhómkara, Mahr.; शर्पेल - sharpala, Conc.; مخيط - makhítah, Ar.; سپستان - sapistán, Pers.; چھوٹالسوڑا - chhotálasorá, Hind.; چھوٹی گوندنی کا جہاڑ - chhotígondníkájhár, Dec.; ಮಣ್ಣಡಿಕೆ - mannadike, Can.; కిట్సవిరిగి - kítsavirigi, Tel.; ଗୋଣ୍ଡି - gondi, Oor.; ചെറുവിരി - cheruviri, Mal.; ලොලු - lólu, Singh.; சிறுநறுவிலி - shirunaruvili, Tam.). Title from tree and berry being smaller. San. from (shél, san. to shake), meaning subduer of diseases. Pers. from (sag, pers. bitch + pistán, pers. breasts); from fruit's resemblance. Hind. from (chhotá, hind. small + lasorá, hind. the fruit). Dec. from (chhotí, hind. small + gondní, hind. fruit of cordia + jhár, hind. tree). Can. from (mannu, can. earth + adike, can. areca catechu, linn.). Mal. from (cheru, mal. small + viri, mal. cordia). Tam. from (shiru, tam. small + naruvili, tam. cordia sp.). San. also (bhúkampadáruka), meaning earthquake + tree; (bahuváraka), meaning many + cover, from therapeutic value; (shléshmántaka), meaning phlegm destroyer; (bhúshélu), meaning earth + the plant; (kshudrashléshmántaka), meaning small + phlegm destroyer; (bhútadruma), meaning devil's tree; (súkshmap'hala), meaning having minute fruits; (laghupichhila), meaning small cordia; (laghushíta), meaning small + cold, cordia obliqua, willd. Ar. also (dabak). Pers. also (pistánisag), meaning teats of a bitch, from fruit. Hind. also (chhotálaslasá), meaning small cordia; (lasorá); (gondí). Can. also (challemara); (chotte). Tel. also (chinnanakkéru), meaning small + the tree, cordia obliqua, willd.; (chinnabotuku), meaning small + the tree, cordia; (naravanji). Mal. also (cheruvaniççi), meaning small + the tree, diospyros embryopteris, pers.; (kotta); (vidimaram), corruption of (virimaram) cordia tree. Singh. also (lóla). Tam. also (naruvili), meaning odour + having. Title otherwise Assyrian plum, Devil's tree, Dog teat, Earthquake tree, Phlegm killer, Sebesten plum, Sepistan plum, Smooth leaved cordia, Smooth leaved myxa. Botanically Cordia [sebesten] myxa, linn., boragineæ [vricsham, 92]. Alias Cordia africana, brownii, dichotoma, domestica, ixiocarpa, latifolia, officinalis, sebestena; Sebestena officinalis. Tree, 8-10 feet; leaves oval, ovate, or obovate, repand, smooth above, rather scabrous beneath; calyx tubular, widening towards the mouth, torn as it were in three to five divisons; divisons of corolla revolute; drupes globular, smooth, yellow; panicles terminal and lateral; nut four-celled, tetragonal, cordate at both ends, surrounded with transparent viscid pulp; flowers small, white. Common, much in cultivation about native villages; trunk generally crooked, bark grey and cracked, branches forming a dense shady head; fruit grows in clusters and consists of a drupe, the pulp of which is soft and clammy. Dried fruit yields on maceration plentiful mucilage, of emollient nature, useful in diseases of breast and urethra; fruit is gently aperient; bark is a mild tonic; the seeds are a good remedy in ringworm, being powdered and mixed with oil and so applied; substituted for british glycirrhiza [atimathooram]; gives to pharm. fruit and bark, non-officinal. When ripe, fruit eaten by the natives and also pickled; smell of the nuts when cut is heavy and disagreeable; kernel taste like filberts [findak]. Bark made into ropes, fibre [naur] used for caulking boats, ropes, and fuses; gives a fixed fat oil [yennay]. Wood one of the best for producing fire by friction, ploughs made out of it; generally set down by natives as only fit for firewood, it however furnished the timber from which the egyptian mummy cases were made.

SECUNDER (سکندر - sikandar, *Hind.*). Persian for Alexander the Great, called also (sikandarirúmí), meaning alexander the grecian; also (sikandaribinfilikús), meaning son of philip.——*Secunderabad* (سکندر آباد - sikandarábád, Hind.). From (above + ábád, hind. city). A cantonment in the Nizam's territories, the head-quarters of the Hyderabad subsidiary force, situated in lat. 17° 26′ N. and long. 78° 32′ E.; 397 miles from Madras. The city of Hyderabad lies six miles to the southward, separated from the Residency usually called the Chudderghaut by the river Moosy.——*Secunder shah* (سکندر شاہ - sikandarsháh, Hind.). From (above + royal title). Nizam of Hyderabad, 1803 to 1829, with Chundoo laul as minister. Received large accession of territory for service in Mahratta [q.v.] and Pindarry [q.v.] wars. See vol. I, 10; II, 252.

SEEGORE (ಸೀಗೂರು - sígúru, *Can.* sígúr *). From (siguri, can. a kind of fan + úru, can. village).—"*a*" Village deserted about twenty years ago, Hill; Neilgherry dist., Todanaud div.; lat. 11° 32′; long. 76° 45′; height 6,778 feet; from Ootacamund N. 9 miles. Chuttram [q.v.]. The Seegore forest lies to the east, and the Mysore road, comprising the tract of country between base of Neilgherries and Moyaur river. Its area is about 40 square miles. The timber trees are inferior, the tract being almost beyond influence of S.W. monsoon [q.v.]. Good sandal-wood [sandal]. The tract is unhealthy.—"*b*" River; Neilgherry dist., Todanaud division. About 2,900 feet above level of sea; formed by the Ootacamund stream, one branch from Marlemund and another from between Marlemund and Bilicull. Joins the Bhawanny at Barra, about 7 miles from Seegore to the right of Teppacadav.—"*c*" Pass; Neilgherry dist., Todanaud division; lat. 11° 31′; long. 76° 44′; from Ootacamund N. 8 miles. Runs down north side of hills from Mootnaud to near the village of Seegore. The head of the pass is 4¾ miles from Ootacamund, the road being fairly level. The descent is about 7 miles in length. About half way down is Cullhutty, with picturesque waterfall. From foot of ghaut [q.v.] to Teppacadav on Mysore frontier the distance is 10½ miles. The Moyaur is crossed by a wooden bridge constructed in 1841. Near this point the road into Wynaud branches off. The town of Mysore by this route is 69 miles from Ootacamund. The road for 25 miles passes through much dense jungle, in which large game abounds. The gradient of this ghaut never exceeds 1 foot in 10, the average being 1 in 12. It is bridged with timber structures throughout. It is partly metalled. It was constructed in 1838, and took the place of the old path by Bilicull further to the east. At one time it was the favorite approach to the Hills by the visitors from the northern parts of the Presidency and Madras. It is still much used for the carriage of teak [q.v.] and other timber to the hills. Near the foot is an important group of cromlechs [paundoo cull], and at the head is a fortification consisting of a wall joining two circles.—"*d*" Coffee [q.v.] estate, Seegore, Neilgherries. 8 miles from Ootacamund at the foot of the ghaut. 150 acres.

SEEMA (सीमा - símá, *San.*; ಶೀಮೆ - shíme, *Can.*; సీమ - síma, *Tel.*; சீமை - shímai, *Tam.*). Means boundary. Tract of country. Cona seema is the corner country. Byle seema is the outside country. Often a foreign country, especially Europe or England [europe, faranghee, firangy, paranghy, rata, vilanyaty].——*Shivaur* (शिवार - shivára, Mahr.; శివారు - shiváru, Tel.). From (shimva, mahr. border). Hamlet.

SEER (شیر ماھی - shermáhí, *Hind.*; చందామచేప - tsandámuchépa, *Tel.*; ମଞ୍ଜିରମୋ - manjiramo, *Oor.*; ചമ്പാൻ - champán, *Mal.*; மாப்பிலாச்சை - máppiláççai, *Tam.*). Title from portuguese serra, because of the serrated appearance of the rows of finlets behind the second dorsal and anal fins. Oor. corruption from tamul below. Mal. from (sanpan, chinese. three planks); fishing boat, hence fish. Tam. from (má, tam. black + piláççai, tam. ostracion genus). Tel. also (vandzu). Mal. also (arakkiya). Tam. also (ahkulah); (kónam); (vañjiram), meaning strong head; (vellará), meaning white snake; (vellirál), meaning white shrimp. Title otherwise Indian salmon, Vanjiram, Vellarah. The genus Cybium, scombridæ, acanthopterygii, teleostei, pisces [matsyam, 19], of naturalists [jantoo]. Cybium commersonii, alias Scomber commersonii, konam, maculosus; konam from tamul is the coromandel fish. Lateral line at first bends down, then passes direct to centre of caudal where it ends in soft raised keel between bases of either lobe; colors bluish above, silvery below; first dorsal black to end of seventh spine, behind which it is pure white, having narrow black upper edge; basal half of pectoral black; after death numerous vertical undulating lines and spots appear on sides; during life they are rather indistinct; sea, not estuaries; mouth full of teeth; most delicate eating of all marine fishes, under a foot in length they are dry, from $1\frac{1}{2}$ to $2\frac{1}{2}$ feet excellent, above this coarse. Oil might be used like cod or shark [soorah] liver oil. Cybium guttatum is the ceylon species.

SEER (سیر - ser, *Hind.*; ഷേർ - shér, *Mal.*; சேரு - shéru, *Tam.*). From persian.—"*a*" Measure of weight. 40 seers = 1 maund [niray, 2e]. There are two seers, cutcha and pucka, 40 of the former making a Madras maund, and 40 of the latter an Indian maund. The former is 8 pollums and the latter $26\frac{2}{3}$ pollums. The cutcha seer weighs $9\frac{2}{3}$ oz. avoir. and the pucka 2 lbs. avoir. The cutcha seer weighs 24 tolahs, while a pucka seer weighs 80 tolahs.—"*b*" Measure of capacity. 4 pows = 1 seer [slavay, 3e]. Approximate actual value, 1 seer = 70 cubic inches. By seer is generally meant the pucka seer, which is $\frac{3}{4}$ of the Madras puddy. In Cuddapah the seer is 118 cubic inches. In Bellary and Mysore $73\frac{1}{4}$ cubic inches, and in Tinnevelly $71\frac{3}{4}$ cubic inches. In Bellary there is another seer which is $94\frac{1}{2}$ cubic inches. The Adony seer is 92 cubic inches. In Vizagapatam the seer is equal to $78\frac{3}{4}$ cubic inches and is the same as tavva. See vol. I, 609; II, 506.

SEETAY (सीता - sítá, *San.*; సీత - síta, *Tel.*; சீதை - shíthai, *Tam.*). Means furrow; as born of the furrow of the field. Compare Auudaul, one of the Alwars [q.v.]. Wife of Rama [q.v.] and the daughter of Janacan [q.v.], king of Mitilay [ramayanam]. There is a Tamul proverb:—சீதை பிறக்கவும் இலங்கை அழியவும்—"the birth of Seetay was the ruin of "Lunka [q.v.]." Hindoo female proper name [peyar]. Familiarly Sheela. In composition also male proper names, as Seetayya, Seetappa. Plant first term. Ex., where transl. is of second term:—Anona squamosa (sítáp'hala), fruit; Cassytha filiformis (sitammapógunúlu), mother + line of thread; Ipomæa angustifolia (sítammavárisavaramu), mother + false hair, (sítasavaramu), false hair; Pergularia minor (sítámanóharamu), pleasing; Spondias mangifera (sítavrikshamu), tree. See gloss. paragraphs. ——*Seetammah* (సీతమ్మ - shítamma, Tel.; சீதம்மா - shíthammá, Tam.). From (above + ammá, tam. mother, titular affix). Hindoo female proper name [peyar].——*Seetampett* (సీతంపేట - shítampéta, Tel.). From (shítamma, tel. proper name + péta, tel. suburb). Ghaut [q.v.]; Vizagapatam dist., Palcondah tal. One of the principal roads from Vizagapatam into Ganjam. Practicable for wheeled traffic.——*Seetanuddy* (ಸೀತಾನದಿ - sítánadi, * Can.). From (above + nadí, san. river). River; South canara dist., Oodipy tal. Rises in the ghauts beyond Someshwaram to the north-east of Oodipy talook. Joins the Swarnanuddy at Maubeal, and the two rivers form a backwater. Navigable as far as Cokkarney, about 11 miles inland from the coast. Barcore on its bank.——*Seetappa gowniraur* (సీతప్పగవనివారు - sítappagavanivāru, Tel.). Name + title. First of the present Poonganore zemindars. Originally settled at Varigapully in Chittore talook and founded Soogatore and built a fort there.——*Seetaraman* (சீதாராமன் - shítháráman, Tam.). From (above + ráma, san. rama). Hindoo 2nd or pers. name [peyar].——*Seetaramasawmy* (சீதாராமசாமி - shíthárámasámi, Tam.). From (above + ráma, san. the hero + svámí, san. master). Hindoo 2nd or pers. name [peyar].——*Seetaram raj* (సీతారామరాజు - sitárámarázu, Tel.). Name + third name. The brother and diwaun [q.v.] of Vijiaram rauz. See vol. I, 54; II, 132.——*Seeta's candle* (سیتا کا پنجیری - sítákápanjerí, Hind.). Same as Country lavender.——*Seeta's heart joy* (సీతామనోహరము - sítámanóharamu, Tel.). Same as Creeper champak.——*Seeta's knot* (సీతసవరము - sítasavaramu, Tel.; തലനീളി - talanfli, Mal.). Title from filiform habit. Tel. from (sítá, san. rámá's wife + savaramu, tel. false hair); cf. cottaun, hedge cotton. Mal. from (tala, mal. head + nílu, mal. to grow long); from supposed property of accelerating growth of hair. Tel. also (sítammavárisavaramu), meaning seetay + mother + title of respect + false hair; (lanjasavaramu), meaning concubine + false hair; (kondasítasavaramu), meaning hill + the plant; (kondasítammasavaramu), meaning hill + the plant; (gontemagomaruchettu), meaning gontema, the village deity + beauty + plant; (alumukáda), meaning weed + stem. Mal. also (vérilláttáli), meaning rootless creeper. Botanically Ipomæa [calamby] angustifolia, jacq., convolvulaceæ [vricsham, 93]. Alias Convolvulus denticulatus, filicaulis, filiformis, hastatus, medium, prostratus, simplex; Ipomæa bidentata, denticulata, filicaulis, filiformis. Stem elongated, rarely twining, filiform, angular; leaves linear or linear-lanceolate, shortly petioled, hastate and denticulate at the base, quite smooth; peduncles longer than the leaf, one to two-flowered; pedicels clavate; sepals ovate-acuminate; corolla small, pale-yellow, with a crimson eye; flowering nearly all the year.——*Seeta's thread* (आकाशभव - ákáshabhava, San.; निर्मूली - nirmúlí, Mahr.; کشوث - kashús, Ar. and Pers.; آکاس بیل - ákásbel, Hind.; آکاس پون - ákáspawan, Dec.; సీతమ్మపోగునూలు - sitammapógunúlu, Tel.). Title from airy roots. San. from (ákásha, san. sky + bhú, san. to be). Mahr. means rootless. Ar. from greek κάσσυθα. Hind. from (ákás, hind. heaven + bel, hind. creeper). Dec. from (ákás, hind. heaven + pawan, hind. flying). Tel. from (sítá, san. the goddess + amma, tel. mother + pógu, tel. line + núlu, tel. thread). San. also (ákáshapávana), meaning sky purifier. Ar. also (aftímún). Hind. also (nilátár), meaning blue thread. Dec. also (amarwal), meaning sky creeper. Title otherwise Air plant [cottaun], Dodder, Sky creeper. Botanically Cuscuta reflexa, roxb., convolvulaceæ [vricsham, 93]. Alias Cuscuta verrucosa. Generic from arabic. Parasitic herb; stem funicular; flowers loosely racemose, each flower pedicelled; sepals acutish, ovate-oblong; corolla tubular, lobes minute, acute, externally reflexed; anthers sub-sessile at the throat of the corolla; scales inserted at the base, fimbriated; styles short; capsule baccate; flowers small, white. Seeds carminative, and an anodyne; a cold infusion is given as a depurative. The dried plant used as a dye [shauyam]. The natives have a proverb that he who finds the roots of this plant will become possessed with boundless wealth and the power of invisibility. Other common species are:—chinensis, hyalina.——*Seeta's yarn* (సీతమ్మపోగునూలు - sítammapógunúlu, Tel.). From thread-like habit of growth. Same as Cottaun.——*Seetaupaty* (சீதாப்பதி - shítháppathi, Tam.). From (above + pati, san. husband). Rama, husband of Seetay. Hindoo 2nd or pers. name [peyar].——*Seetavullabhan* (సీతావల్లభుడు - sítávallabhudu, Tel.). From (above + vallabha, san. husband). Rama, husband of Seetay. Hindoo 2nd or pers. name [peyar].——*Seetayyah* (సీతయ్య - sítayya, Tel.). From (above + ayya, tel. master), rama the lord of seetay. Hindoo 2nd or pers. name [peyar].

SEIF (سیف - saif, *Ar.*). From (sáfa, ar. to strike). Sword. In lacabs; as Seif ool moolk, sword of the kingdom [ism].

SEM (سیم کا گوند - semkágond, *Hind.*). From (semal, hind. red-cotton tree + gond, hind. gum). Otherwise Semla gum. Gum from species of bauhinia [mountain ebony], resembling gum arabic [q.v.].

SENNA (سناء - saná, *Ar.*, *Pers.*, *Hind.* and *Dec.*; నేలతంగేడు - nélatangédu, *Tel.*; സുന്നാ - sunná, *Mal.*; நிலாவாரை - nilávárai, *Tam.*). Title from mount sinai, through arabic. Tel. from (néla, tel. ground + tangédu, tel. cassia auriculata, linn.). Mal. from arabic. Tam. from (nilam, tam. ground + ávárai, tam. cassia auriculata, linn.). Botanically certain Cassia species [soovarnacam], leguminosæ [vricsham, 48]. Leaves, when carefully dried, have faint, rather sickly odour and a slightly bitter, sweetish, and nauseous taste; are characterized by peculiar extractive matter, which on being boiled passes into a resinous substance resisting action of water; are the sennæ alexandrinæ folia of chemists; as met with in the bazaars are often of very inferior quality, consisting of broken pieces of old leaves, pieces of stem, and other rubbish; also adulterated with a very similar-looking leaf of the solenostemma argel, hayne, asclepiadeæ [vricsham, 88], this leaf being thicker and stiffer than senna. Senna was first used by arabian physicians and through them introduced into europe. Infusion of dried leaves or leaflets is in medicine a safe and efficient purgative; usual form is in infusion in boiling hot water; natives quicken its operation, with addition of castor-oil [aumanac]; infusion of senna with epsom salts [bhaidy ooppoo] constitutes black draught; alexandrian and tinnevelly senna alone officinal in pharmacopœia of india. In commerce three kinds are distinguished:—first Alexandrian senna; secondly Bombay or mocha or east indian senna; thirdly Tinnevelly senna. See the various heads below. The first class or Alexandrian is the most used in europe, and the third or Tinnevelly is the most used in india; the second class, which is botanically a branch of the third, is out of use here in spite of its names.——*Aleppo senna* (भूतलपोत - bhútalapóta, San.; भुईतरवड - bhuítaravada, Mahr.; سناء حلبی - sanáihalabí, Ar. and Pers.; سنا - saná, Hind.; సనాముఖి - sunámukhi, Tel.; സുന്നാമക്കി - sunnámakki, Mal.; නිලාවරි - nilávari, Singh.; நிலாவாரை - nilávárai, Tam.). Title from original port of export to europe. San. from (bhú, san. earth + talapóta, san. cassia sophera). Mahr. from (bhuí, mahr. earth + taravada, mahr. cassia auriculata, linn.). Ar. from (saná, ar. senna + halab, ar. aleppo). Tel. means senna of mecca. Mal. means senna of mecca. Singh. from tamul. Tam. from (nilam, tam. ground + ávárai, tam. cassia auriculata, linn.). Hind. also (sunnámakkí), meaning mecca senna. Tel. also (nélatangédu), means ground + cassia auriculata, linn. Singh. also (sanakola). Title otherwise Ground tungaid, Italian senna, Obovate senna. Botanically Cassia [soovarnacam] obovata, collad., leguminosæ [vricsham, 48]. Alias Cassia burmanni, obtusa, senna; Senna obtusa. Semi-shrubby or herbaceous perennial; sometimes an annual; stem 2–3 feet high, erect, smooth, pale green, somewhat zigzag, with long spreading branches; leaves alternate, spreading; leaflets opposite, in three to six pairs, pale glaucous green, about 1 inch long, the upper one often rather large than the lower; flowers rather large, bright yellow; grows in dry sandy ground. The first kind of senna known, having been introduced by the moors [q.v.] into europe. This together with nubian constitutes Alexandrian senna.——*Alexandrian senna* (سناء اسکندری - sanáiiskandarí, Hind.). Title from original place of export to europe. Title otherwise Officinal senna. General term for product of Cassia acutifolia, delile [nubian senna], and Cassia obovata, collad. [aleppo senna]. Constitutes the bulk of the senna consumed in Europe. Angustifolia [tinnevelly senna] gives all sennas not included under Alexandrian.——*Bombay senna* (بمبئی کی سنا - bombaíkísaná, Hind.). Title from place of import. Product of the original variety of angustifolia [tinnevelly senna].——*Country senna* (ناٹ کی سنا - nátkísaná, Hind.). Same as Tinnevelly senna.——*East indian senna* (هندی سنا - hindísaná, Hind.). The original variety of angustifolia; but in spite of name, has been superseded by the Tinnevelly variety. ——*Foreign senna* (ولایتی سنا - viláitísaná, Hind.). Same as Nubian senna, acutifolia, part of Alexandrian.——*Indian senna* (هندی سنا - hindísaná, Hind.). Same as Tinnevelly senna, angustifolia.——*Italian senna* (سناء بلدی - sanáibaladí, Hind.). Hind. means city senna. Same as Aleppo senna, obovata, part of Alexandrian.——*Lotus senna* (भूपद्म - bhúpadma, San.). From resemblance of flowers. Same as Tinnevelly senna, angustifolia.——*Mocha senna* (سناء مکی - sanáimakkí, Hind.). From place of export. Product of the original variety of angustifolia [tinnevelly senna].——*Nubian senna* (سنا مکی - sanámakkí, Ar., Pers. and Hind.; سنا مکی - sunnámakkí, Dec.; ನೆಲಾವರಿಕೆ - nelávarike, Can.; సీమతంగేడు - símatangédu, Tel.; சூரத்துநிலாவிரை - shúrattunilávirai, Tam.). Title from habitat. Ar. from (saná, ar. senna, cassia + makkí, ar. of mecca). Can. from (nela, can. ground + ávarike, can. cassia auriculata, linn.). Tel. from (síma, tel. foreign + tangédu, tel. the plant, cassia auriculata, linn.). Tam. from (shúrattu, tam. surat, the city + nilávirai, tam. tinnevelly senna, cassia angustifolia, vahl.). Ar. also (saná), (sanáihijází), meaning hijauz senna. Tel. also (nélaponna), meaning ground + calophyllum inophyllum, linn., probably from leaf; (nélatangédu), meaning ground + cassia auriculata, linn.; (súrattutangédu), meaning surat, the city + cassia auriculata, linn. Tam. also (shímainilávirai), meaning foreign + senna, cassia angustifolia, vahl. Title otherwise Acute-leaved senna, African senna, Foreign senna, Ground tungaid, Kordofan senna, Sennaar senna, Surat senna. Botanically Cassia [soovarnacam] acutifolia, delile, leguminosæ [vricsham, 48]. Small shrub, about 2 feet high; stem much as in obovata [aleppo senna]; leaves alternate, spreading; leaflets opposite, in four or five pairs, $\frac{3}{4}$–$1\frac{1}{4}$ inch long, rather thick, pale green; flowers bright yellow, a little smaller than obovata; native of tropical africa, principally nubia and especially sennaar and kordofan, probably extends westwards, reported from timbuctoo; does not occur in arabia or india. Leaves are the principal component part of alexandrian senna.——*Surat senna* (صورت کی سنا - súratkísaná, Hind.). From place of import. Same as Nubian senna, acutifolia.——*Tinnevelly senna* (भूपद्म - bhúpadma, San.; सोनामुखी - sónámukhí, Mahr.; सोनामक्कि - sónámakki, Conc.; سناء هندی - sanáihind, Ar.; سناء هندی - sanáihindí, Pers.; هندی سنا - hindísaná, Hind.; ناٹ کی سنا - nátkísaná, Dec.; ನೆಲಾವರಿಕೆ - nelávarike, Can.; నేలతంగేడు - nélatangédu, Tel.; നിലവാക - nilaváka, Mal.; සනකොල - sanakola, Singh.; நிலாவிரை - nilávirai, Tam.). Title from habitat of chief present variety. San. from (bhú, san. earth + padma, san. lotus, nelumbium speciosum, willd.); perhaps from resemblance of flowers. Mahr. and Conc. means mocha senna. Ar. from (saná, ar. senna + hind, ar. indian). Pers. from arabic. Hind. from (hindí, ar. indian + saná, hind. senna). Dec. from (nát, hind. country + saná, hind. senna). Can. from (nela, can. ground + ávarike, can. cassia auriculata, linn.). Tel. from (néla, tel. ground + tangédu, tel. cassia auriculata, linn.). Mal. from (nila, mal. ground + váka, mal. albizzia lebbek, benth.). Tam. from (nilam, tam. ground + ávirai, tam. cassia auriculata, linn.). San. also (bhúmihárí), meaning earth + taking, small shrub; (st'halótpala), meaning ground lily. Ar. also (sanáihijází), meaning hijauz senna; (sanáijabalí), meaning mountain senna. Hind. also (sunnámakkí), meaning mocha senna; (hindísanákápát), meaning indian senna leaf. Can. also (nelávare), meaning earth + cassia auriculata, linn. Tel. also (nélaponna), meaning ground + calophyllum inophyllum, linn., probably from leaf. Tam. also (nilavágai), meaning ground + albizzia lebbek, benth., from resemblance of leaf; (náttunilávirai), meaning country + the plant. Title otherwise Arabian senna, Bombay senna, Country senna, East indian senna, Ground tungaid, Indian senna, Lotus senna, Mocha senna, Narrow-leaved senna, Officinal senna. Botanically Cassia [soovarnacam] angustifolia, vahl., leguminosæ [vricsham, 48]. Alias Cassia elongata, lanceolata; Senna angustifolia, officinalis. Annual small shrub; stem erect, smooth; leaves narrow, equally pinnated; leaflets four to eight pairs, lanceolate, nearly sessile, slightly mucronate, smooth bright-green above, rather downy beneath; petioles without glands; racemes axillary and terminal, erect, stalks longer than the leaves; petals bright yellow; legumes pendulous, oblong, membranous, about $1\frac{1}{2}$ inch long, straight, tapering abruptly to the base, rounded at the apex, deep brown, many-seeded; agreeing with cassia acutifolia, delile [nubian senna], in general characters of its stem and leaves; flowers a little smaller than cassia obovata, collad. [aleppo senna]. Of senna yielded by this plant there are two varieties:—"*a*" Arabian, mocha, bombay, or east indian senna; collected in south arabia and exported from mocha, aden, and other ports in red sea to bombay; regarded as inferior kind of senna; consists of leaflets of present plant, often brown and decayed from having been dried without care, mixed with a variable proportion of legumes, stalks, and flowers of same plant; leaflets readily known by length and narrowness.—"*b*" Tinnevelly senna proper; originally from arabian seeds; from cultivation in south india the plant grows more luxuriantly than in its wild state and forms the officinal tinnevelly senna; fine variety; free from legumes, stalks and adulteration; consists of large, thin, entire leaflets, from one to two or more inches long, and sometimes half an inch broad at widest part; yellowish green color on upper surface, and similar but somewhat duller tint on under surface; odour and taste closely resemble Alexandrian senna; commonly exported from tuticorin; the finest senna of commerce. The plant is cultivated in red or black loam; dry ground prepared in april by ploughing and manuring [yeroo]; seed sown next month broadcast and ploughed in; weeds cleared; much water not required; leaves plucked after three months and dried in the shade; produce brought to market two weeks after.

SESAMUM (سمسم - simsim, *Ar.*). From egyptian. Same as Gingelly.

SESBAN (जयन्ती - jayantí, *San.*; سيسبان - saisbán, *Ar.*). Title from arabic. San. from (jí, san. to conquer); medicinal. Pea-tree. Botanically the Sesbania genus, leguminosæ [vricsham, 48]. Soft-wooded tropical shrubs or herbs; leaves pinnate, long, very narrow, with numerous leaflets; flowers in axillary racemes, usually yellow; pods long, narrow, cylindrical or flattened, containing many seeds. The species best known to the natives are shown below. Title comprises also species from genera bauhinia and parkinsonia.——*Common sesban* (राज - rája, San.; शेवरी - shévarí, Mahr.; راسن - rásin, Hind.; رواسن - ravásin, Dec.; ಕರಿಜಿನಂಗಿ - karijínangi, Can.; సొమింత - sóminta, Tel.; ചെമ്പ - chempa, Mal.; செம்பை - shembai, Tam.). San. from (ráj, san. to shine). Mahr. from hindostany. Can. from (kari, can. black + jínangi, can. the plant, æschynomene aspera, linn.). Tam. from (shem, tam. red), from flowers [parangyvail]. San. also (jayanti), meaning conquering; (vaijayanta), meaning indra's banner; (nádéyí), meaning river-born. Hind. also (jet); (jaintí) from sanscrit. Dec. also (ravásing) from (shewú). Can. also (arasinajínangi), meaning saffron + pith plant. Tel. also (sómanti); (dzalugu). Mal. also (kitannu), meaning a ditch; (nellittáli), meaning phyllanthus + creeper. Tam. also (karuñjembai), meaning blackness + the plant. Title otherwise Bastard sensitive plant, Chempay, Danchy, Jayanty, Sesban, Sominta. Botanically Sesbania [sesban] ægyptiaca, pers., leguminosæ [vricsham, 48]. Alias Æschynomene indica, sesban; Coronilla sesban; Dolichos æschynomene, sesban. Small tree, unarmed; leaves abruptly pinnate, about three times longer than broad; leaflets ten to eighteen pairs, oblong-linear, obtuse, slightly mucronate; racemes axillary, lax, pendulous, about the length of the leaves, three to twelve-flowered; legumes linear, slender, much contracted between the seeds, twisting when ripe; calyx five-cleft; corolla papilionaceous; keel obtuse; petals distinct at the base; flowers yellow, flowering nearly all year; rapid growing; common near cultivation. Seeds applied in ointment to eruptions, also stimulant emmenagogues; leaves as a cataplasam to promote suppuration. Leaves and branches lopped for cattle [maud] fodder. Suitable for hedges [vaily]; fibre [naur] from bark; makes the best charcoal [adoopp kary] for gunpowder. Wood white, extremely soft; not durable; used to boil jaggery [q.v.]; furnishes poles as a substitute for bamboo [q.v.]. There are two varieties, one which has leaflets fifteen to eighteen pairs, flowers orange, and vexillum purple on the outside; and the other, leaflet ten to twelve pairs, vexillum yellow speckled, with black dots and lines.——*Foreign sesban* (சீமைச்செம்பை - shímaiççembai, Tam.). Same as Parangy vail.——*Prickly sesban* (जयन्ती - jayantí, San.; कानशेवरी - kánashévarí, Mahr.; ಮುಳ್ಳುಜೀನಂಗಿ - mullujínangi, Can.; ఎఱ్ఱజీలుగ - errajíluga, Tel.; കിടങ്ങു - kitannu, Mal.; முட்செம்பை - mudchembai, Tam.). Title from prickles. San. from (jí, san. to conquer). Mahr. means wild sesban. Can. from (mullu, can. thorn + jínangi, can. pith plant). Tel. from (erra, tel. red + jíluga, tel. pith plant, æschynomene aspera, linn.). Tam. from (mul, tam. thorn + shembai, tam. sesbania ægyptiaca, pers.). Tam. also (nírççembai), meaning water + sesbania ægyptiaca, pers. Title otherwise Red solah. Botanically Sesbania [sesban] aculeata, pers., leguminosæ [vricsham, 48]. Alias Æschynomene bispinosa, cannabina, sesban, spinulosa; Coronilla aculeata. Herbaceous, erect; stem and petioles sprinkled with small cartilaginous points; leaflets twenty to forty pair, linear, obtuse, mucronate; racemes peduncled, erect, lax, about half the length of the leaves; legumes erect, nearly terete, sharp-pointed; flowers rather large, on slender pedicels, yellow, purple-dotted; flowering in august and september. A hardy plant, grows from 6–10 feet high. Cultivated on account of fibres [naur] of the bark; they are from 6–7 feet long, but unless cut at a very early period they are coarser and more harsh than hemp [kinnab]; made into ropes and fishing nets [yalay]. There are varieties, cannabina and paludosa.——

West indian sesban (अगस्ति - agasti, San. and Mahr, ; اگتی - agtí, Hind. ; اگتی کا جھاڑ - agtíkájhár, Dec. ; ಅಗಸೆ - agase, Can. and Too. ; అవిసి - avisi, Tel. ; അകത്തി - akatti, Mal. ; කතුරුමුරුංගා - katurumurungá, Singh. ; அகத்தி - agatti, Tam.). Title from habitat. San. from (agastya, san. the sage so called). Hind. from sanscrit. Dec. from sanscrit. Tel. from sanscrit. Singh. from (katuru, singh. venom curer + murungá, singh. moringa pterygosperma, gærtn.). Tam. from sanscrit [alsee]. San. also (vaka), meaning growing crookedly, from flowers; (vranári), meaning enemy of sores; (st'húlapushpa), meaning large-flowered. Hind. also (basna), referring to red variety. Can. also (agache). Tel. also (agisi); (avise); (uma); (tella-avisi), meaning white + the tree; (erraavisi), meaning red + the tree. Tam. also (aççam), meaning timidity, constantly shaking. Title otherwise Agastya's plant, Agatty, Buko, Great-flowered agatty, Tree bean, West indian pea tree. Botanically Sesbania [sesban] grandiflora, pers., leguminosæ [vricsham, 48]. Alias Æschynomene coccinea, grandiflora; Agati grandiflora; Coronilla grandiflora; Dolichos arboreus. Agati from tamul. Tree, 30–35 feet; long bare stems; leaves abruptly pinnated, leaflets numerous; calyx campanulate, slightly two-lipped; corolla papilionaceous, vexillum oval, oblong, keel large, falcate, with petals free at the base and apex; racemes axillary, two to four-flowered; flowers large, pendulous, scarlet or white; legumes pendulous, very long, many-seeded, contracted between the seeds; short-lived, soft-wooded tree, cultivated near villages; flowers march to april. The bark is much fissured longitudinally, of a greyish-brown externally, the dry suber nearly equal to the living portion in thickness; in the fissures may be seen numerous small tears of a garnet-red when fresh, but soon becoming almost black by exposure to the air; the outer portion of the living bark is of a red color, and is loaded with the same kind of gum [gond] in a soft state. The bark is bitter and is used in medicine as a tonic; an infusion of the leaves is a useful cathartic; the natives put the juice of the leaves in the nostrils in bad fevers on the day of the paroxysm; the juice of the flowers is also squeezed into the eyes for expelling dimness of vision. Leaves and tender pods are eaten in curries [q.v.]; cattle [maud] are partial to them. Plant much employed on account of rapid growth for training the betel [q.v.] plant; inner bark gives a fibre [naur]; gum [gond] dark-colored, yielded scantily, resembling kino [q.v.]; used as avenue [shaulay] tree. Wood white, soft, not durable; grown as a substitute for bamboo [q.v.]; useless except for fuel. The red variety is coccinea.——*Wild sesban* (అడవిఅవిశె - adaviavishi, Tel.). Same as Purple mountain ebony and Small-flowered mountain ebony.

SEVEN PAGODAS (सप्तक्षेत्र - saptakshétra, *San.*; மாவலிப்புரம் - mávalippuram, *Tam.*). Title from the ruined pagodas there found. Sanscrit also (mahábalipura), meaning mahabaly's town. Indigenous name is Mullayore, meaning mulla's town; see below. Appears also as Mahbalipooram, Mauvellipore, Maumalaipooram, and Mullapoory cshetram. Village; Chingleput dist., Chingleput tal.; pop. 1,076; acres 2,245; lat. 12° 37′; long. 80° 14′; from Chingleput E.S.E. 15 miles; from Madras S. 33 miles; from Sydapett S. 28 miles; from the sea W. ½ mile. Midway between Sadras and Covelong and between the East coast canal [q.v.] and the sea. Reached by the Canal. Light on a rock; lat. 12° 36′ 52·36″; long. 80° 14′ 01·69″; red; fixed; 17 miles range; visible from all directions seaward; small grey turret; to warn vessels off the Tirporore reef. According to Bramins, in the Tretayoog [q.v.] it was the city of a great king, which was submerged by the sea, six temples being overwhelmed. Mahbaly [q.v.] the king by penance and austerity had obtained possession of the whole universe. Becoming elated by his greatness he omitted to perform the customary religious ceremonies to the gods [deva]. Vishnoo [q.v.] becoming incarnate [avatar] in the person of a dwarf [vaumanan], and in this form appearing before Mahbaly, asked as a boon as much of his possessions as he could pace in three steps [trivicraman]. This the king granted, upon which the dwarf grew larger, and continued to expand till he filled the whole universe, thus depriving the monarch of all his possessions except hell [pautaulam], which he was allowed to keep. This legend probably represents the victory of Hindoos of the Veishnava [q.v.] sect over some powerful indigenous ruler. Another Sanscrit legend connected with the place is as follows. There were two raucshasans [q.v.] named Chatoorangan and Balarangan, who lived in Chatoorangaputnam or Sadras [q.v.]. These cleared the forest from Mylapore to Cuddalore. Mahbaly chuckravurty is said to have been their descendant. According to Stalapooraunam [q.v.] one Mullaishan ruled in early times. He mocked a Bramin, and was metamorphosed into an alligator [mugger]. Mulla is a titular name of an aboriginal Teloogoo people. In the Kaliyoog [q.v.] Singama naidoo, zemindar [q.v.] of the Velgotwaur [velgoty] family, ruled here. In that time, during a famine, many artificers resorted hither and wrought on the mountain a variety of works during two or three years. Singama naidoo built a palace on the hill, of which a few fragments only now remain. The Jeinas [q.v.] had an ascendancy in this neighbourhood. Seventy-two headmen among them rode in palankeens [q.v.]. A mud-shower descended and destroyed their towns, and the sea overflowed them. From Mylapore to Cuddalore not one stone upon another now remains of their habitations. It is evident on the whole that this was an old settlement of the Pullavas [q.v.]. Then the Bramins settled in it and made a great town, moving later to Mylapore. The remains here are probably the earliest known examples of the Dravidian style of architecture [maunasauram, staupatyam] of Southern india. The sculptures were the work of artists from the Northern provinces. The granite [caroom cull] remains consist of the following:—the nine raths [q.v.] or isolated temples cut out of a single boulder; the thirteen caves excavated out of the rocks at Mauvellipore and two more at Saulvancooppam; the great bas-relief of Arjoonan's [q.v.] penance; several structural temples, the most important of which is the shore temple, which has long served as a landmark for shipping.—"*a*" Of the nine raths the most southern is called that of Dharma rajan [q.v.], the next that of Bheeman [q.v.], the third that of Arjoonan, and the fourth that of Drowpady [q.v.]. These four are situated in one line, extending about 160 feet north and south. The fifth is called after the twins Sahadevan and Nacoolan. The sixth, the Ganesh [q.v.] rath, is some little distance from the others and near it are the remaining three, in an incomplete condition. The most nearly finished of all the nine is the Ganesh rath. It measures 19 feet by 11 feet 3 inches, and its height is 28 feet. It is in three stories and the details are elegant. The most northerly of the large group of raths is that of Drowpady. It is square in plan measuring only 11 feet each way, and with a curvilinear roof rising to about 18 feet in height. The Bheema rath measures 48 feet in length by 25 in breadth, and is about 26 feet in height. The roof of this rath is cracked right through, owing to the insufficient strength of the pillars that support it. The Arjoonan and Dharma rajan raths are identical in general appearance, the only difference being that the first is much smaller than the other. Arjoonan's rath is a square, measuring 11 feet 6 inches each way, and its height is about 20 feet. Dharma rajan's rath measures 26 feet 9 inches by 28 feet 8 inches, and its height is rather more than 35 feet. In general appearance it is a building of four stories arranged in a pyramidal form. The rath named after Sahadevan and Nacoolan measures 18 feet by 11 feet, the height being 16 feet. The remaining three raths are in an extremely unfinished condition.—"*b*" The rock-caves are thirteen in number. One of the most striking peculiarities of these caves is the extreme tenuity of their pillars and generally of their architectural details, when compared with those of other groups of caves. This probably arises from the excavators having literally copied the forms they found employed in wooden structures. As these caves are scattered promiscuously on both sides of a low ridge of hills, it is difficult to classify them clearly. The following are the most important in the order in which they occur, beginning at the southern end of the ridge, nearly opposite the great group of raths. Dharma rajan's mantapam [q.v.] is a cave measuring 17 feet by 12½ with four pillars; Yamapoory of Mahishamardiny [q.v.] mantapam is a fine cave 33½ feet by 15 feet; on the south wall is a large bas-relief of Vishnoo [q.v.] as Narayanan [q.v.], lying on the huge serpent Anantan [q.v.], rolled up so as to form a couch, and bending her many heads, like an umbrella over the divinity; in the same hall is also an image of Shiva [q.v.] together with Parvaty [q.v.], and an infant between them and an elaborate group representing Cauly [q.v.] with many arms riding on a lion [simham] and surrounded by many attendants, as pursuing a giant with the head of an ox; at the other end of the hall is a finely sculptured tablet representing the combat between Mahishausooran [q.v.] and Doorga [q.v.]; near this is a small Shiva temple with bas-reliefs of Shiva [q.v.] and his son Soobramanyan [q.v.]. The temple dedicated to the boar [varauham] avatar [q.v.] of Vishnoo is still used for worship. Krishna's mantapam measures 48 feet by 23; here he is found in the form of Krishnan [q.v.], holding with one of his arms the mountain Govardhanam over a number of Gopies [q.v.], Gopaular [q.v.] and cows [go], to protect them from a great thunderstorm, caused by Indran [q.v.], because the shepherds and shepherdesses had, agreeably to the instruction of Krishnan, ceased to worship him. The mantapam [q.v.] of the Puncha pandavas [q.v.] is a large but unfinished cave. A Veishnava cave contains, amongst other subjects, a representation of Vishnoo's varauha avatar, viz., a large human figure with the head of a boar [varauham] and with Lutchmy [q.v.] as a natural woman on his lap; there is also here one of Shree lutchmy seated on a lotus [nelumbo] flower with elephants [q.v.] pouring water over her. Three miles north of the last of these thirteen caves are the two caves of Saulvancooppam. One is called the Atichundeshwaran mantapam. The other is a small cell cut out of a rock, with nine simham [q.v.] or yauly [q.v.] heads round the front of it.—"*c*" The great bas-relief of Arjoonan's penance is a most remarkable object. It represents him doing penance, standing on one leg and having his hands folded over his head, together with that of Shiva, who with many attendants appears to the ascetic [kirautarjooneeyam]. It is carved on two masses of granite [caroomcull] rock, measuring about 90 feet long by 30 feet average height. Between the two rocks was formerly the serpent statue of the Nauga rajah [q.v.], the head of which overshadowed by a seven-hooded serpent has fallen to the ground. The surface of the rock is covered with figures of gods, men, and animals, in basso-relievo, representing scenes taken from the Mahabhaurat [q.v.]. The name by which the whole is now called is taken from one of the most spirited groups of figures, supposed to represent Arjoonan praying to Krishnan, after a long fast.—"*d*" The Aulyam or Shore temple is a singular monument, and, if not the most early, is one of the best examples of structural primitive Dravidian architecture [maunasauram, staupatyam]. Standing on the edge of the sea it has suffered much from the action of the wind and salt-water. Part of the building lies ruined in the surf, and a solitary pillar is left erect in the midst of fallen blocks of stone. This temple was dedicated to both Shiva and Vishnoo. This and the usual stone pillar in front of such temples lying in the sea, as well as fragments of images, large quantities of stone and broken bricks lying about, some partially buried in the sea, plainly show that at one time buildings existed to the eastward, but have been overwhelmed by the sea. By tradition, the whole coast from Mylapore to Mauvellipore was overflowed by the sea, and many towns were destroyed. The monolith temples consist of chambers cut out of the solid rock, and with figures and inscriptions in ancient character; only one of them is now on the land. Rocks partly covered at high water are carved with the figures of tigers [pooly]. See vol. I (20).

SEWIYAUN (سیویان - sewiyán, *Hind.*). Vermicelli, which Mahomedans prepare between hands instead of a press.

SHAB (شب - shab, *Hind.*). Night [leil, rautry].——*Shabcharaugh* (माणिक्य - mánikya, San.; عقيق احمر - akíkiahmar, Ar.; شبچراغ - shabcharágh, Pers. and Hind.; మాణిక్యము - mánikyamu, Tel.; മാണിക്കം - mánikkam, Mal.; மாணிக்கம் - mánikkam, Tam.). San. from (manika, san. name of a town). Ar. from (akik, ar. gem + ahmar, ar. red). Pers. from (shab, pers. night + charágh, pers. lamp). Hind. from persian. Tel., Mal. and Tam. from sanscrit. Carbuncle. Precious stone of the ruby [laul] kind [ratnam]. The λιθία διαφανέα found according to the Periplus in Ceylon and exported in every variety from Mouziris [cranganore] and Nelkunda [cullada] were probably carbuncles.——*Shab e baraut* (شب برات - shabibarát, Hind.). From (above + barát, record); from belief that actions and fortunes of men for coming year are then registered. Compare hindoo Chittray powrnamy. Night of fourteenth Shabaun [maheena]. Called also Leilat ool moobaurak, or blessed night. Sufficiently described at vol. I (97).——*Shabgasht* (شب گشت - shabgasht, Hind.). From (above + gasht, pers. perambulation). Nocturnal perambulation. On the tenth khun [q.v.] of the Moharram [q.v.] all the alams [q.v.] and taboots [q.v.] are carried on men's shoulders, attended by fakeers [q.v.]; and a perambulation is made very slowly in great pomp and state. The lower orders do this in the evening, and the higher at midnight. The streets are illuminated and every kind of sport takes place.

SHABDAM (शब्द - shabda, *San.*; சத்தம் - shattam, *Tam.*). Sound; said in hindoo philosophy to be eternal and universal. Declinable word. Oral evidence or verbal authority; one of the four processes according to nyauyam [q.v.], by which the mind arrives at true and accurate knowledge; the other three being pratyacsham or perception by the senses, anoomaunam or inference, and oopamaunam or comparison [pramaunam].——*Shabdaurta calpataroo* (शब्दार्थकल्पतरु - shabdárt'hakalpataru, San.). From (above + art'ha, san. meaning + kalpataru, san. all-giving tree of paradise). A dictionary of Sanscrit with explanations in Teloogoo by Maumidy vencayya, author of Andhra deepacam. The words are arranged first under finals. Next according to syllables; words of two syllables apart, those of three syllables apart. Finally each of these sub-divisions is alphabetically arranged according to initials. Thus in looking for Sa-ma-yah, reader first turns to Y, then to the triliteral class under Y, and then to the initial S in that class [acaraudy, nigantoo].

SHAC (शक् - shak, *San.*). To be able, to know.——*Saca* (शक - shaka, San.). See sep. title.——*Shacoonam* (शकुन - shakuna, San.; சகுனம் - shagunam, Tam.). From (shak, san. to know). Omen. The following coming or being carried in front of a person starting on a journey, or as soon as he has left his house or place of business with some object in view, are propitious omens:—a married woman, a virgin, a dancing girl, two bramins, music, flower, fruit, fish, flag, umbrella, sugar-cane, boiled-rice, milk, flesh, fire, toddy, an elephant, a horse, cows, cloth, a king, pearl, consecrated rice, parched rice-corn, a dead body, a regiment or troop, an indian bangle seller, and two pitchers full of water. The following passing by or coming in front of a person as he is going out on business or otherwise, or happening suddenly, are unlucky omens:—a widow, a bramin, three comaties, two shoodras, a tiger, a snake, a bundle of firewood on one's head, a sickle, a pick-axe, a crowbar, a pot of oil, a new pot, a man in disguise, butter-milk, curdled milk, one sneezing stumbling and falling down, dust caused by a fierce blast of wind, one with dishevelled hair, unseasonable rain, thunderbolt, a person with a newly-shaven head and mourning. If a person asks another, while he is going out or starting on a journey or on business, not to go, to eat, or to wait saying 'I shall also go with you,' 'where are you going?' and so forth; also if one loses on the way what he had in his waist, and if the person still continues his journey; he will meet with some calamity and will not gain his desired object. Under such circumstances the native often retraces his steps to the place whence he started, waits for some time, and then resumes his journey. There are many omens regarding beasts, birds and other animals. A deer [mrigam], a musk-rat [q.v.] or a blind mouse [shoondely], a guana [oodoomoo], a skylark [vaunambaudy], a quail [batair], a kite [chillam], a falcon [pattry], a large owl [ooloocam], a mongoose [q.v.], a squirrel [anil], and a dog [nye], passing by the side of one's left hand, forbode something propitious; a crow [caurvam], a narayanan bird [blue heron], a jack-daw, a fox [lomree], a parrot [totah], a bloodsucker [q.v.], a paddy bird [q.v.], a peacock or pea-hen [mayil], a cow [pashoo], a buffalo [khoolgah], and a civet-cat [poonoogoo poonay], passing by the side of one's right hand, are good omens; but a snake [paumb], a cat [poonay], and a horse [ghorah] should not pass cross-wise. The natives consider the sitting of an owl [ooloocam] on their house-top, or its perching on the bough of a tree either in or close to their house, as inauspicious; one screeching of an owl forebodes certain death, two success in undertakings, three that a girl will be added to the family by marriage, four that there will be a disturbance in a short time, five that the person hearing it will have to travel, six the advent of guests, seven mental distress, eight sudden death, and nine a highly favorable result. The chirping of a lizard [chipkalee] is a great point. If a lizard chirps once when a native is meditating on any undertaking, it denotes thorough failure; if twice consecutively, it signifies success; if thrice, or five or seven times, it signifies, sedition; if six, nine, ten or eighteen times, it indicates gain of wealth; if eight or twelve times, it predicts death; if eleven or fourteen times, it foretells success; if thirteen times, it shows that the person who heard it will leave his country to go elsewhere. The Pandoos, in the Mahabhaurat [q.v.] heard a lizard chirp thirteen times consecutively and had to leave Hastinapooram. The chirping of a lizard fifteen times consecutively denotes that the person who heard it will be kept in confinement. Seetay [q.v.], the wife of Rama [q.v.], having heard a lizard chirp fifteen times was carried away by Ravanan [q.v.]. The chirping of a lizard sixteen times denotes success. Hanooman [q.v.] after having heard a lizard chirp sixteen times, crossed the sea and liberated Seetay. If a lizard chirps seventeen or nineteen times, it signifies success. Rama after having heard a lizard chirp seventeen times, built Rama's bridge [adam's bridge], and attacked Ravanan. On his having heard a lizard chirp nineteen times he succeeded in completely vanquishing Ravanan. If a lizard chirps twenty times, it foretells a certain success. Shiva [q.v.], having heard the same, attacked and overpowdered the asoorans of Tripooram [q.v.]. The fall of a lizard is another point. A lizard falling on one's head purports sedition and dispute; its falling on the face forebodes the visit of relatives; its falling on the upper lip implies wasting of wealth; its falling on the lower lip signifies gain of wealth; its falling on the right ear denotes longevity; its falling on the left ear indicates profit in trade; its falling on the eyes signifies entry into a newly-built house; its falling on the chin foretells punishment from the king; its falling on the mouth indicates fear; its falling on the neck forebodes the vanquishing of an enemy; its falling on the right arm signifies comfort and peace of mind; its falling on the left arm signifies enjoyment with the other sex; its falling on the right wrist forebodes grief and sorrow; its falling on the left wrist foreshows renown; its falling on the breast denotes gain of wealth; its falling on both the sides indicates considerable gain; its falling on the thighs forebodes the death or the killing of a father; its falling on the knees or the ankle signifies prosperity; its falling on the heels denotes travelling; its falling on the bosom foreshows that something serious will happen; its falling on the knot of hair on the head foreshows fear of an enemy. There is a Tamul proverb:—விறகு கட்டுக்காரனுக்கு நாரை வலம் ஆனால் ஒரு பணம் விற்கிறது ஒன்றேகாற்பணம் விற்கும்—"if a "crane [paddy bird] cross a firewood man from left to right "what he sells ordinarily for a fanam will fetch a fanam [q.v.] "and a quarter." The following is a Hindostany proverb:—کیا مکھی نے چھینک دیا—"did a fly sneeze?" If one gives over anything, for natives will not begin anything if one sneeze, but will wait a while. For omens of trees and flowers see Phool. For omens of twilight see Sundhyay. For omens of the seasons see Caur, Caurtey, Mausam and Mazhay.——*Shacoontalay* (शकुन्तला - shakuntalá, San.). From (shakunta, san. bird + lá, san. to take); as fostered by birds. From the story that she was protected by birds till found by Canwan who brought her up. Wife of Dooshyantan and mother of Bharatan [q.v.]. Drama by Calidass [q.v.].——*Shacran* (शक्र - shakra, San.). From (shak, san. to be powerful). Indran; also Shiva [q.v.].——*Shactibhactan* (शक्तिभक्त - shaktibhakta, San.). From (shakti, san. feminine energy personified + bhakta, san. adorer). Worshipper of the Shacty [q.v.].——*Shacty* (शक्ति - shakti, San.; சத்தி - shatti, Tam.). From (shak, san. to be able).—"*a*" Power, energy, of which three and five are enumerated. The three powers are:—Itchah shacty, the power of affection which is friendly to life; Nyanna shacty, the power of the knowledge of good and evil; Kriyah shacty, the power of creating worlds. The five powers are:—Chit shacty, knowledge; Parah shacty, vital operation; Itchah shacty, the combination of the five elements; Nyauna shacty, the power of perception; Kriyah shacty, skill or power to perform a thing [matam].—"*b*" So the power or energy of a deity, personified as a female and considered as his wife. Parvaty [q.v.] is the shacty of Shiva [q.v.], Lutchmy [q.v.] of Vishnoo [q.v.], Saraswaty [q.v.] of Bramha [q.v.]. The two former are universally recognized, while Saraswaty enjoys much more homage than her husband Bramha. The female forms of Roodran [q.v.], white and black, are termed in the Vishnoo pooraunam [q.v.], shacties. A vast variety of inferior female beings of malevolent character and formidable aspect receive the worship of the multitude. It is needless to say that the Shacty or feminine energy system has pervaded all atheistic forms. The Grecian mysteries were the secret rites of this system, and connected with human sacrifices. Names of the feminine energy, corresponding with shacties of the Hindoos, were Juno, Venus, Ceres, Hecate, Proserpine, Artemis. The worship in the great temple at Ephesus was of this character. Among the Latins the system had but a limited range. The rites however of the Bona dea and the worship of Vesta were of this description. Here among the Hindoos, the worship of the female principle has some reflection in the later Vedams [q.v.], in which the will or purpose to create the universe is represented as originating from the creator, and co-existent with him as his bride and part of himself. The Sauma vedam [q.v.], speaking of the divine cause of creation, says, "he felt "not delight, being alone; he wished another, and instantly "became such; he caused his own self to fall in twain, and thus "became husband and wife; he approached her, and thus were "human beings produced." This first manifestation of divine power is termed Itchah roopam, personified desire; and the creator is designated as Swetchah mayan, united with his own will. In the Saunkhyam [q.v.] philosophy, Pracrity [q.v.] or Moolapracrity is defined to be a female entity of eternal existence and independent origin, distinct from the supreme spirit [autmam, poorsham], productive though no production, and the plastic origin of all things, including even the gods; hence she has come to be regarded as the mother of gods and men. In the Vedauntam [q.v.] philosophy, in which all created things are held to be illusory, the Shacty or active will of the deity is designated as Mauyay [q.v.] or illusion. In all the Pooraunams [q.v.] this pracrity or mauyay bears a prominent part. In the Bramha veivartam pooraunam, one section, the Pracrity khandam, is devoted to the subject, and the legends relating to the principal modifications of the female principle are there narrated. The adoration took its most material form in consequence of the publication of the Tantrams [q.v.], a class of works in which the female energy is worshipped through what is there styled the maternal organ, regarded as a symbol of self-existent and productive nature. The adherents of the Tantram ritual are termed Shauctas or worshippers of the energy. They do not, at least in Southern india, form themselves into a separate class or sect, nor do they generally wear any characteristic mark. Their whole doctrinal theory may be defined thus briefly; the extinction of desire is the great aim of hindooism; the other sects seek it by the mortification of the passions, the shauctas by their gratification. There are two modern divisions of the Shauctas; first, the Dacshinacharries [q.v.], right-hand worshippers, or Bhactas, devoted ones, who worship the goddess Parvaty [q.v.] or Doorga [q.v.] openly, and without impure practices; secondly, the Vaumacharries [q.v.], left-hand worshippers, or Caulas, ancestral ones, who perform their rites in secret. The sacred books appealed to by the first are the Nigamam [q.v.]; by the second the Augamam [q.v.]. See vol. I (76), (79), (86), (108). For the male energy in nature see Paty.——*Shauctan* (शाक्त - shákta, San.). Worshipper of the Shacty.——*Shaukiny* (शाकिनी - shákiní, San.). From (shak, san. to have power). Female demons attendant on Cauly [q.v.].——*Shunk* (शंकु - shanku, San.). From (shak, san. to know). Distinguish from chunk [q.v.]. A gnomon. For astronomy this is a straight rod, pole or pillar of stone, as seen in front of every pagoda [q.v.], placed perpendicularly on a horizontal plane. The astronomers trace a meridional line [raikhay] by describing concentric circles from the point on which the centre of the pillar rests on the ground. Whatever be its height, the Shunk is divided into 12 ungoolams or digits, and each ungoolam [q.v.] is sub-divided into 60 vyangoolams [q.v.]. It thus serves as a scale for measuring the Chauyay [q.v.], the length of the meridional shadow; and a rod is accordingly made of the same dimensions and divisions for that purpose. In marking alternately the points where the top of the shadow cuts any of the concentric circles, native astronomers choose the time of 5, 6 and 7 dandams [caulam, 6], or Indian hours of the Moortam [q.v.] account 60 to a day, before and after noon [madhyaunam, ooroomam]. This being done the arcs [chaupam] are bisected, the meridian line [raikhay] is traced, and the four Dics [q.v.] or cardinal points, with the Ashtadics [q.v.] or the four intermediate divisions [tisay], are easily determined. By help of problems if the altitude [avanataumsham] of the pole [dhroovam] be given, the Ravy sauyanam [q.v.], or sun's longitude reckoned from the equinoctial point [craunty pautam, maishauyanam, vishoo] may be found from day to day, by means of the Madhyama chauyay [q.v.] or meridian shadow. The length of the shadow being known the sun's zenith distance [nataumsham] may be found. The meridian zenith distance [oordhwanataumsham], and the latitude [acsham] of the place being known, the sun's declination [craunty] may be found. The obliquity [paramaupamacramam] of the ecliptic [crauntymundalam] being always taken by native astronomers as 24°, and the sun's declination being given, the hypothenuse [carnam] or arc of the ecliptic between the sun [sooryan] and equinoctial points [craunty pautam, vishoo], called the Ravy sauyanam, is easily found [jyotisham, sauyanam].

SHACOOR (شکور - shakúr, *Hind.*). From (shakara, ar. to thank). Grateful. An epithet of God [allah]. Mahomedan alam; as Abd oosh shacoor, slave of god.

SHADAY (சடை - shadai, *Tam.*). Matted hair [jatay].——*Shadaimoody* (சடைமுடி - shadaimudi, Tam.). From (jatá, san. matted hair + mudi, tam. head). Shiva [q.v.].——*Shadaiyakkan* (சடையக்கன் - sadaiyakkan, Tam.). From (shadaiyan, tam. a man with a matted hair). The same as Dalavoy saitoopaty [q.v.].

SHAFEE (شفیع - shafí, *Ar.*). From (shafia, ar. to intercede). Intercessor. Title of Mahomet. Common alam, as Mahomed shafee, double alam. Feminine form, Shafia, as Shafia begum, alam + alaumat [ism].

SHAH (شاه - sháh, *Pers.*). A king. Title assumed by saints [walee] and peers [q.v.] who founded the system of making mooreeds [q.v.], as Shah madaur. Syed alaumat out of respect, especially of masheikh [q.v.] classes, as Shah hoossain, alaumat + alam. Also part of lacab, as Shahsawaur, a brave cavalier [ism]. Suffix in compound as Padshah, throne + master.——*Shah badee ood deen* (شاه بدیع الدین - sháhbadíuddín, Hind.). A celebrated walee [q.v.] commonly known as Zinda shah madaur or Madaur, the living prince, supposed to be still living [chiranjeevy]. Died on 17th of Jamaudy ool owval [maheena] which is day of his Oors [q.v.].——*Shah boolbool* (بلبل - bulbul, Ar.; هزارداستان - hazárdástán, Pers.; شاه بلبل - sháhbulbul, Hind. and Dec.; తోకపికిలిపిట్ట - tókapikilipitta, Tel.; இராப்பாடிக்குருவி - iráppádikkuruvi, Tam.). Pers. from (hazár, pers. thousand + dástán, pers. notes) [madras boolbool]. Hind. means royal boolbool. Tel. means tailed boolbool. Tam. from (irá, tam. night + pádu, tam. to sing + kuruvi, tam. small bird). Ar. also (andalíb). Dec. also (husainíbulbul), meaning beautiful bird; (sultáníbulbul), meaning royal bird. Tam. also (válgondalátti), meaning tail + crest; from long tail. The Paradise flycatcher. Tchitrea paradisi, myiagrinæ, muscicapidæ [macsha grauhy], dentirostres, insessores [pacshy, 20], of naturalists [jantoo]. Alias Muscipeta indica, paradisi. For Leucocerca albofrontata of this sub-family, see Mynautty.——*Shahbunder* (شاه بندر - sháhbandar, Hind.). From (above + bandar, ar. seaport). Harbourmaster, custom-house agent [bunder].——*Shah in shah* (شاهنشاه - sháhinsháh, Hind.). King of kings. Imperial title.——*Shahnaye* (شهنائی - sháhnáí, Pers.). From (above + náí, pers. tube). Means chief instrument. Mahomedan clarionet [naugaswaram], with leaf mouth-piece [sangeetam].——*Shahrokh* (شاه رخ - sháhrokh, Hind.). From (above + rokh, pers. face). Having a royal countenance. Mahomedan servant's name [ism].——*Shahtra* (شاهتره - sháhtra, Pers.). From (above + tara, pers. garden herb). Same as Pitpapra.——*Shahy* (شاهی - sháhí, Hind.). Royal. Shahy peisa are irregular shaped pieces of thick copper, weighing about 150 grains, still numerous in the Hyderabad country. For Mahomedan dynasties so called see sep. title.——*Shahzauda* (شاه زاده - sháhzádah, Hind.). From (above + zádah, pers. born). Prince [rajcoomar].

SHAHAD (मधु - madhu, *San.*; मध - madha, *Mahr.*; عسل - asal, *Ar.*; انگبین - angabín, *Pers.*; شهد - shahad, *Hind.*; مدو - madu, *Malay*; ಜೇನು - jénu, *Can.*; తేనె - téne, *Tel.*; തേൻ - tén, *Mal.*; මීපැණි - mípani, *Singh.*; தேன் - tén, *Tam.*). San. means sweetness. Singh. from (mí, singh. honey + pani, singh. juice). Tam. from (tém, tam. sweetness). Honey. Mel of chemists. Vegetable product, and occurs chiefly in the nectaries of various flowers. The bee collects it and brings it to the hive to store it up for the food of the community. Honey is here nearly always the produce of wild bees, brought from the jungles. Its quality depends on the nature of plants from which the bees extract it. It differs much in color and flavor in different tracts of country, also in flavor. That colored darkish green is unwholesome. In Cuddapah there is a kind of honey, which in place of being liquid in the comb, is hard and candied, and of the form of cells, and drops out like sugar plums. Its peculiar character is ascribed to the bees, which are small, feeding on flowers and sweetish bitter fruit of the Mimusops hexandra, roxb. [monkey-face paulay]. Honey gathered from Strobilanthes species and Mesua ferrea [naugachampak] is specially good. Honey from the flower of the prickly-pear [q.v.] is hot. Medicinally honey is emollient and slightly laxative; used in gargles; native use, detergent and nutritive. Pharm. preparations are clarified honey, mel depuratum; simple ointment, unguentum simplex; and ceromel. For the honey-bee see Tainee; for wax see Mom.

SHAHAR (شهر - shahar, *Hind.*). From persian. A large town [cusbah, pooram]. Shahargasht is going in procession round a town, a very favorite ceremony with natives on great occasions [oorvalam, pradacshinam].

SHAHAUB (شهاب - shaháb, *Ar.*). Meteor [nacshatram, 10]. Part of lacab; as Shahaub ood deen, meteor of the faith [ism].

SHAHAUDAT (شهادت - shahádat, *Hind.*). From (shahida, ar. to witness). Martyrdom.——*Shahaudat kah roz* (شهادت كا روز - shahádatkároz, Hind.). From (above + roz, pers. day). Day of martyrdom. The tenth day of Moharram [q.v.]. This is the day in which the alams [q.v.] are to be taken out to some place near water, representing the plain of Carbalah near the Euphrates, and to be there thrown into the water to represent loss of the military array in the river. Practically the people generally bring back and keep till next year.——*Shahidy* (شاهدى - sháhidí, Hind.). From (shahida, ar. to testify). Evidence, witness [pramaunam, sautchy].

SHAH BAUSH (شاه باش - shádbásh, *Hind.*). From (shád, pers. glad + bash, pers. to be); to be victorious. Bravo, well done!

SHAHY (شاهى - sháhí, *Hind.*). Royal [shah]. So title of dynasty [raj], specially the five offshoots of the Bahmany [q.v.]. ——*Adil shahy* (عادل شاهى - ádilsháhí, Hind.). After adil shah, the founder. Mussalman dynasty, first offshoot of Bahmany, at Beejapore from 1489 till 1672. See vol. I (148), foot-note (4); II, 251.——*Ahmed shahy* (احمد شاهى - ahmadsháhí, Hind.). After ahmed shah, the founder. Same as Imaud shahy. Branch of Bahmany dynasty in Berar. See vol. I (148), foot-note (3); II, 252.——*Bareed shahy* (بريد شاهى - barídsháhí, Hind.). After bareed shah, the founder. Branch of Bahmany dynasty, at Beedar. See vol. I (148); foot-note (7); II, 252.——*Cootb shahy* (قطب شاهى - kutbsháhí, Hind.). After cootb shah, the founder. Branch of Bahmany dynasty, at Golcondah. See vol. I (148), foot-note (6); II, 252.——*Imaud shahy* (عماد شاهى - imádsháhí, Hind.). After imaud shah or ahmed shah, the founder. Same as Ahmed shahy. Branch of Bahmany dynasty in Berar.——*Nizam shahy* (نظام شاهى - nizámsháhí, Hind.). After nizam shah, the founder. Branch of Bahmany dynasty at Ahmednugger. See vol. I (148), foot-note (5); II, 252.

SHALANGAY (சலங்கை - shalangai, *Tam.*). From tinkling sound. Bells worn by dancers on ankles [goongra, nagay].

SHALGHAM (شلجم - shaljam, *Ar.*; شلغم - shalgham, *Pers.*, *Hind.* and *Dec.*; సరసావాలు - sarasávālu, *Tel.*). Title from deccany. Tel. from (sarshapa, san. mustard + ávālu, tel. mustard brassica juncea, h. f. and t.). Greek γογγύλη ἥμερος and ῥάπυς. Title otherwise Turnip. Botanically Brassica [sarshapam] campestris [sarsoon], linn., sub.-sp. rapa, linn., cruciferæ [vricsham, 10]. Alias Brassica rapa. Root tuberous; lower leaves hispid, not glaucous, upper glabrous and glaucous; petals deciduous. Acclimatised. Medicinally cooling, and gently aperient. The root and tops eaten as vegetables [keeray]; bramins however dislike it from a suspicion of its relation to animal matter. Oil of no value. Several varieties even of this sub-species.

SHALOOCAH (شلوكا - shalúká, *Hind.*). From (shil, pers. little). Two pinafores, one worn on the breast, the other on the back, and fastened above and below the shoulders. For children.

SHAM (शम् - sham, *San.*). To appease; to sacrifice. Happiness.——*Sankhvel* (शङ्खपुष्पी - shankhapushpí, San.; शङ्खवेल - shankhavéla, Mahr.; കഞ്ചാങ്കോര - kañchánkóra, Mal.). Title from mahratta [chunk]. San. from (shankha, san. conch shell + pushpa, san. flower) [crow creeper]; from flower. Mahr. from (shankha, san. couch shell + véla, mahr. creeper). Mal. from (kañjá, tam. cannabis sativa, linn. + kórai, tam. cyperus) [fragrant toolsy]. San. also (kambupushpí), meaning conch shell + flower; (kambumáliní), meaning conch shell + garland; (dantótpala), meaning tooth + flower, from white color. Title otherwise Conch flower [crow creeper], Shell creeper. Botanically Canscora decussata, roem. et sch., gentianaceæ [vricsham, 90]. Generic name from malayalam. Alias Pladera decussata. Stem about a foot high, perfectly erect four-sided, angles very sharp or rather membrane-winged, smooth, ramous, branches always opposite, cross-armed, in other respects like the stem; leaves opposite, spreading, sessile, lanceolate, sharp-pointed, entire, smooth, three-nerved, size various; flowers terminal and axillary, peduncled, the terminal ones three-fold, the axillary single, white; peduncles four-sided; calyx large, four-toothed, four-sided, four-winged; corol funnel-shaped, border irregular, three-parted, the two upper segments equal and orbicular, the lower one two-parted, with a deep groove, in the groove is lodged the fourth or large stamen; filaments four, inserted into the mouth of the tube, the lowermost longer than the other three; style single; stigma two-cleft, segments recurved; capsule one-celled, many-seeded. The different species of canscora are bitterish annual plants which grow in moist situations during, or immediately after the rainy season; they have pink, yellow or white flowers. The present species is medicinally laxative, alterative, and nervine tonic.——*Shaman* (சமன் - shaman, Tam.). From (shamana, san. destroyer). Yaman [q.v.], regent of south [ashtadic], god of justice and of death.——*Shambaran* (शम्बर - shambara, San.). From (sham, san. happiness + vri, san. to screen). Demon of drought.——*Shambaraury* (शम्बरारि - shambarári, San.). From (shambara, san. the demon + ari, san. enemy). Manmatan [q.v.].——*Shambhoo* (சம்பு - shambu, Tam.). Shiva, the happiness maker. Applied to males and females. Hindoo 2nd or pers. name [peyar].——*Shamee* (शमी - shamí, San.; شمى - shamí, Hind.; జమ్మి - dzammi, Tel.; வன்னி - vanni, Tam.). San. from (sham, san. to sacrifice); used in sacrifice as fuel from its power of retaining heat. Hind. from sanscrit. Tel. from sanscrit [manna jhow]. Tam. from (vahni, san. fire). San. also (priyadarshaní), meaning good-looking. Tam. also (parambai); (shambu). Title otherwise Edible prosopis, Parambay, Vanny. Botanically Prosopis [shivah] spicigera, linn., leguminosæ [vricsham, 48]. Alias Adenanthera aculeata; Prosopis spicata. Somewhat arboreous, armed with scattered prickles, occasionally wanting; leaves rarely simply pinnated, usually bipinnate with one to two pair of pinnæ; leaflets seven to ten pair, oblong, linear, obtuse, glabrous; spikes axillary, several together, elongated, filiform; legumes cylindric, filled with mealy pulp; calyx five-toothed; petals five, distinct; flowers small, yellow. A large thorny bush, thriving in black-cotton soil [regar]; mysore, coromandel; foliage and wood closely resemble acacia sundra [sundra]; very slow growth; flowers in hot weather; pod is about an inch in circumference, and from six to twelve long. Pod medicinally astringent and stimulant. Pod contains a large quantity of a brown, mealy, sweetish substance, which is eaten; flavor of carob [q.v.] tree; eaten in different ways, green or dry, raw and alone; boiled with salt [ooppoo], onions [piyauz] and ghee [q.v.] and eaten with bread, or mixed with tyre [q.v.]; pod also sometimes used as fodder for camels [ottagam], cattle [maud], and goats [velland]. Bark used in tanning [chamrah]; a gum [gond] exudes resembling gum arabic [q.v.]. Timber is dark red in color, straight and close-grained, hard and durable, and superior to teak [q.v.] in strength, much used for building purposes and cart wheels, occasionally for furniture, and makes excellent fuel.——*Shankham* (शंख - shankha, San.). From (sham, san. to soothe) [chunk]. Conch [q.v.].——*Shaumbhavy* (शाम्भवी - shámbhaví, San.). Feminine of shambhoo. Parvaty [q.v.].——*Shauntam* (शान्त - shánta, San.). From (sham, san. to be calm). Peace.——*Shaunty* (शान्ति - shánti, San.; ಶಾಂತಿ - shánti, Too.; ശാന്തി - shánti, Mal.). From (sham, san. to be appeased). Means tranquillity. The office of priest [acharry, poojarry, poorohit] in a temple [coil, pagoda]. In astrology [jyotisham, nacshatram] a sign meaning that the deity must be appeased. Also a religious song chanted by lamp light and in procession. In Tooloo same as Belleric myrobalan.——*Shengoo* (कुण्डली - kundalí, San.; سگ پات - sagpát, Hind.; سگ كا پتا - sagkápattá, Dec.; తెల్లుప్పి - tellauppi, Tel.; சங்கு - shangu, Tam.). San. from (kundala, san. ring), rolling creeper. Hind. from (sag, hind. dog + pát, hind. leaf). Dec. from hindostany. Tel. from (tella, tel. white + uppi, tel. capparis sepiaria, linn.). Tam. from (shankha, san. conch shell), from white color of ripe fruit. San. also (trikantajáta), meaning born with three spines. Tam. also (mulluççangu), meaning thorn + the plant; (kanniram). Title otherwise Four spined monetia, Shangilay. Botanically Azima tetracantha, lam., salvadoraceæ [vricsham, 86]. Alias Fagonia montana; Monetia barlerioides, tetracantha. Stem scarcely any, but branches innumerable, opposite, spreading in all directions, forming a close impenetrable bush, something like furze; young branches four-sided; thorns axillary, four-fold, spreading, very sharp, from 1–2 inches long; leaves opposite, short-petioled, reflexed, oval, acute; male flowers axillary, numerous, female axillary, solitary, sessile, between the two thorns; berry globular, of the size of a pea [calanyam], when ripe white, succulent, edible; seeds two; the plant is in flower and fruit the greater part of the year. Leaves medicinally stimulant, and given to puerperal women immediately after confinement. They are administered in the following manner by the villagers:—the leaves with an equal quantity of neem [q.v.] leaves, and a little powdered brick [shengal], are finely ground and given twice a day for the first two days, no food being allowed; for the next six days the woman gets a little boiled rice [q.v.] and pepper water [mullagatawny] once a day, and is allowed to drink warm water after the meal; she is not allowed to sleep after her food during the day, and if thirsty must quench her thirst by eating betel [q.v.] leaves and areca nut [q.v.]; from the seventh day she gets her ordinary food; it is also the practice among the rural classes to give 2 to 4 ounces of neem [q.v.] oil soon after delivery, with roasted asafœtida [q.v.], and the woman is made to take daily for a month from the morning of the third or fourth day a bolus of a stimulating confection, called nadaycauyam in tamul, which is supposed to keep off cold from the system. The leaves are also administered with food as a remedy for rheumatism, and their juice to relieve cough. The root is considered to have the same properties as the leaves, and to be also diuretic; it is given in dropsy along with other drugs. The following formula is used by veidyans [q.v.]:—take of the root bark ℥x, tribulus terrestris, linn. [nerinjy] fruit, root of trianthema monogyna, linn. [shauranay] and cephalandra indica, naud. [indian caper] āʒi, belleric and chebulic myrobalans [q.v.] āʒss, iron [auhan] dross ℥x, goat's urine ℥viii, water four seers; make a decoction and keep it for several days in the oven; dose 2 to 3 ounces twice a day in as much water. A decoction of the root, leaves and bark with an equal quantity of Acorus calamus, linn. [vashamboo], ginger [q.v.], ajwaun seeds [ajwaun], and salt [ooppoo], is recommended as a remedy for chronic diarrhœa; and 1 to 1½ ounces of the juice obtained from the root bark, with three ounces of goat's [vellaud] milk [paul], twice a day as a diuretic in dropsy.——*Shumbha* (शम्भ - shambha, San.). From (sham, san. happiness + bhú, san. to become). Otherwise Vajram or vajrayoodham. Indran's thunderbolt [indran, vajram]. Said to have been made of the back-bone of a rishy. Distinguish from Shumbah, rice, and Shamba, saturday.——*Shumbhavaty* (ಶಂಭವತಿ - shambhavati, Can.). From (shambha, san. indra's thunderbolt + vat, san. suffix of possession). River; South canara dist., Mangalore tal. River on which Moolky is situated. Takes its rise at the foot of the Western ghauts [q.v.] and is navigable about 10 miles from Moolky in rainy weather. Is dammed for irrigation. ——*Shun* (शम् - sham, San.). Happiness [sham].——*Shuncara bhaushyam* (शङ्करभाष्य - shankarabháshya, San.). From (shankara, san. proper name + bháshya, san. commentary). A work by Shuncaracharry [shuncaran], a comment on the Vedantism of Vyausan [q.v.].——*Shuncaracharry* (शङ्कराचार्य - shankarácharya, San.). Same as Shuncaran.——*Shuncaran* (शङ्कर - shankara, San.; சங்கரன் - shangaran, Tam.). From (above + kara, san. doer). Epithet of Shiva, the happiness maker. Hindoo 2nd or pers. name [peyar].—"*a*" The name of the celebrated South indian teacher of Vedaunta sheivism, successor to the northern philosopher Comaurila bhatt; generally called Shuncaracharry. He was a native of Caulady a village on Periyaur about 20 miles S.E. of Cranganore in Travancore, a posthumous child of a Bramin mother. He led a wandering life, and engaged in successful controversy with various sects, whether of the Sheiva, Veishnava, or less orthodox persuasions. In the course of his wanderings he established a mutt [q.v.] at Shringairy, on the Western ghauts [q.v.], near the sources of the Toongabudra. Towards the close of his life he went to Cashmere. Shuncaran is said to have had four principal disciples, in the popular traditions called Pudmapaudan, Hastamalacan, Sooreshwaran or mandanan, and Trotacan. For the philosophy see Adweitam, for the sect see Smarta.—"*b*" The Chola puttayam states that Shuncaran came to Conjeeveram, and there placed an earthen lingam [q.v.]; most probably the humble origin of the since large temple of Yecaumbareshwaran [q.v.] and Caumautchy [q.v.], local names of Shiva and Parvaty. Among his works is the Caumautchy ashtacam or octave in praise of the wanton-eyed goddess; but whether he was more than a passing pilgrim at Conjeeveram is doubtful. He is next traced at Tripatty, fixing there a lingam [q.v.] of crystal [palingoo, spaticam]. The symbol here was designated Chundramowleeshwaran or deity with the moon on his head, and the Nacshtra maulay, or lunar mansion [nacshatram] garland, is said to have been written by him in honor of the deity. The Shuncara vijayam gives a list of the sects he opposed and conquered; being Booddhists, Jeinas, Chaurvaucans, Caupaulas and others. He wrote a work expressly intended to show that all the thousand names [sahasranaumam] of Vishnoo mean Shiva.—"*c*" Shuncaran wrote his own bhaushyam [q.v.] or commentary on the Vedams [q.v.], and on the sootrams [q.v.] of Vyausan [q.v.], and on the metaphysical part of the Bhagavat geeta [q.v.]. He insisted also that not merely are the Vedams alone an authoritative rule, but that the divinely revealed Smrities [q.v.] or codes of law should be regarded as Shabdam [q.v.] or authoritative testimony [pramaunam]. It is from following the Smrities that the disciples of Shuncaracharry are termed Smartas [q.v.] in distinction from the Shrowtas [q.v.], who admit the Vedams only as a rule.—"*d*" When dying, Shuncaracharry caused himself to be covered with dried cow-dung cakes [bratty] which by his orders were lighted and so reduced his body to ashes. This ceremony called Carishaugny is the most effective purifier of all remaining defects in life, stopping all transmigrations [samsauram]. See vol. I (76).—"*e*" Shuncara charitam, Shuncara katah, and Shunkara vijayam are well-known biographies of Shuncaracharry relating his controversies with heretical sects and his refutation of their doctrines [matam].——*Shuncaranarayanan* (சங்கரநாராயணன் - shangaranáráyanan, Tam.). Fram (shankara, san. shiva + náráyana, san. epithet of vishnu). Shiva and vishnoo combined in one [hariharan]. Hindoo 2nd or pers. name [peyar]. *Shuncaraneinarcoil* (சங்கரநாயிநாரக்கோயில் - shankaranáyinárkkóyil, Tam.). See sep title.——*Shungoonny* (ശങ്കുണ്ണി - shankunni, Mal.). From (shanku, mal. shankaran + unni, mal. infant). Shuncaran, the darling. Hindoo 2nd or pers. name [peyar].——*Shunkerry droog* (சங்ககிரித்துருக்கம் - shangagirittarukkam, Tam. saukaridrug *). From (shankha, san. conch + giri, san. mountain + durga, san. fort), white like conch shell [chunk]. Ancient name (kunnattúr), meaning hill + village.—"*a*" Deputy tahsildarry, Salem district. Pay Rs. 70.—"*b*" Village, Head-quarters of Deputy tahsildar, Railway station, Hill; Salem dist., Trichengode tal.; pop. 1,302; acres 6,727; lat. 11° 29′; long. 77° 54′; height 879 feet; from Madras S.W. 195 miles; from Namcull N.W. 25 miles; from Oossoor S. 87 miles; from Salem W.S.W. 24 miles; from Trichengode N.N.W. 5 miles; from Tripatore S.S.W. 85 miles; from Yercaud S.W. 32 miles. Some distance to the north-west of, and about 1½ miles away from the railway station. The droog, which rises to 2,345 feet above the sea, as viewed from the Railway is a great square white mass, whence its name. It is completely terraced with fortifications, attributed to Tippoo sultan, of which some must have been built by the English. Along the ascent creepers, trees, and prickly-pear [q.v.] grow in abundance; half way up to the left, on the side of a steep scarp is a musjid [q.v.]. The summit consists of a small plateau with a good supply of water stored in the rocks. Remarkably fine specimens of granite [caroom cull] veins pierce the gneiss on the exposed portion of the hill side; marble [shalavay cull] is found in the vicinity and several beds of lime stone [choonam cull] cross the railway close by. Ancient Shiva temple on the hill. Fort. Cave close to the musjid [q.v.]. Roman catholic chapel and unused cemetery. London mission school.

SHAMBA (شنبه - shambah, *Hind.*). From persian. Singly implies Saturday. The other days of a week [vauram] are designated by numerals prefixed, meaning so many days after Saturday. For Arabic names, also common, see Yowm.—"*a*" *Yekshamba* (یکشنبه - ekshambah, Pers.). From (ek, pers. one + above). Sunday [yowm ool ahad].—"*b*" *Doshamba* (دو شنبه - doshambah, Pers.). From (do, pers. two + above). Monday [yowm ool isnein].—"*c*" *Seh shamba* (سه شنبه - sehshambah, Pers.). From (seh, pers. three + above). Tuesday [yowm ool salausah].—"*d*" *Charshamba* (چهار شنبه - chahárshambah, Pers.). From (chahár, pers. four + above). Wednesday [yowm ool arbah].—"*e*" *Punjshamba* (پنج شنبه - panjshambah, Pers.). From (panj, pers. five + above). Thursday. Otherwise Joomeraut [yowm ool khamees].—"*f*" *Sesh shamba* (شش شنبه - seshshambah, Pers.). From (sesh, pers. six + above). Friday. Otherwise Jooma [yowm ool jooma].—"*g*" *Shamba* (شنبه - shambah, Pers.). Saturday [yowm ool sabt].

SHAN (شن - shan, *Pers.*). Suffix showing place; as Goolshan, flower + place.

SHANAGA (శనగ - shanaga, *Tel.*). From (chanaka, san. bengal gram). Same as Bengal gram.

SHANBOGUE (ಶಾನಭೋಗ - shánabhóga, *Can.*). From (shanáya, can. allowance of grain paid to the village accountant + bhóga, san. enjoyment). Village accountant [coolacurny], curnum [q.v.] of Carnatic [q.v.]. Corresponding terms are:—Tel. curnum, Mal. menon, Tam. kanakan. Hindoo third name [peyar].

SHANGARF (हिंगुल - hingula, *San.*; شنجرف - shanjarf, *Ar.*; شنگرف - shangarf, *Pers.*; هنگول - hingol, *Hind.*; شنگرف - shangraf, *Dec.*; گلوگا - galuga, *Malay*; ಇಂಗಲೀಕ - ingalíka, *Can.* and *Too.*; ఇంగిలీకము - ingilíkamu, *Tel.*; ചായില്യം - cháyilyam, *Mal.*; ජාතිලිංගම් - játilingam, *Singh.*; சாதிலிங்கம் - sháthilingam, *Tam.*). Title from persian. San. from (hingu, san. asafœtida + lá, san. to take), from resembling asafœtida [q.v.] in color. Hind. from sanscrit. Can. from sanscrit. Mal. from tamul. Tam. from (játi, san. caste + ilingam, tam. vermilion). Tam. also (ilingam), shining substance. Otherwise Impure bisulphate of mecury, Vermilion, Red sulphuret of mercury. Hydrargyri bisulphuretum of chemists. Mostly imported from China. A mineral substance, red, heavy, brilliant: found native in quicksilver [rasam] mines. Most common artificial, when thus made according to the Poorna sootram:—Twelve pagodas [q.v.] weight of sulphur [gandhac] is to be put into an earthen pot [chatty], and fused over a slow fire; when in a state of fusion, eighty pagodas weight of mercury [rasam] must be added to it, and the whole kept gently stirred until it is reduced to a black powder. Twelve pagodas weight more of sulphur and four pagodas weight of pewter [velly eeyam], cut into small pieces are to be added to the black powder, and the whole to be mixed with the same quantity of saltpetre [shorah]. All of these are to be put into a phial [cooppy], which must be sufficiently large to contain the medicines in the half of it. This vessel is then to be coated over with clay [calimunn] in the most complete manner. An oven is then to be made in the ground, over the mouth of which is to be put a broad hollow earthen pot, and in this pot is to be placed the cooppy [q.v.] containing the drugs; which is to be next covered over with sand [manal] up to its neck. The fire is then to be put into the oven and kept burning for twelve hours, after which the phial is to be taken off and kept till it is cool, when it may be broken, and in the neck will be found the shangarf in a lump. The mode of fumigating with shangarf is as follows:—Eight pagodas weight of bark of the root of the Calotropis gigantea [yercum], four pagodas weight of the charcoal [adoopp kary] of the wood of the same, four pagodas weight of shangarf, and one pagoda weight of common black pepper [q.v.], are all to be ground together, with the juice of the leaves of the Gossypium herbaceum [indian cotton] and, when well rubbed, to be formed into cakes and dried. The fumes of one of these cakes, while burning, to be inhaled daily, through a smoking pipe, either all at once or at two different periods in the twenty-four hours. Fumigation of this sort may be continued for five or six days, according to circumstances, and is efficacious in cancerous affections, in venereal ulcers of the throat and nose, and in a disease attended with a singular pricking pain in the skull. A pink, sometimes used as a dye [shauyam], but more frequently as a pigment vermillion, which may be prepared by reducing the one to a powder, or by chemical action. The article is used as a pigment [rangh].

SHANY (शनि - shani, *San.*). From (shanais, san. slowly), slow going planet. Otherwise Shaneischaran. The planet [graham] Saturn, ♄. Sidereal period of revolution [bhagauam] is 10,759d 5h 16m, or nearly 29½ terrestrial years. Inclination [natam] of orbit [cacsham] is 2° 28′ 29″. He is rêpresented in the arts as a black man, clothed in black garments, riding on a vulture [gidh], with four arms. The astrologers say :—if a person be born when the planet shany is in the same constellation [nacshatram] as the moon [chundran], he will be slandered, his riches dissipated, his son, wife, and friends destroyed; he will live at variance with others and endure many sufferings. Many stories are told of the adverse influence of this planet. There is a proverb :—அகப்பட்டவனுக்குஅஷ்டமத்துச்சனி ஓடிப்போனவனுக்கு ஒன்பதாம் இடத்து ராஜா—"he "who was caught was under the influence of saturn in the eighth. "sign [raushy], and he who escaped did so under the influence of "saturn in the ninth." Saturn situated in the eighth sign from that of one's birth is specially malignant; one is born in a sign if that sign is rising at hour of one's birth [lagnam, raushy]. ——*Saneechar* (سنيچر - saníchar, Hind.). From (shanaishchara, san. saturn, the slow-mover). Saturday [shany, vauram].—— *Shanivauram* (சனிவாரம் - shanivâram, Tam.). Saturday [vauram]. There is a Tamul proverb :—சனி நீராடு—"bathe "on saturdays;" in some parts of the country, men bathe on Saturday, while women bathe on Friday or Monday; to bathe frequently on Tuesday is regarded as fatal. There is another :— சனிப் பிணம் தனிப்போகாது—"a Saturday corpse goes "not alone;" to avert evil tamulians bury a fowl [moorghy] when a death happens on Saturday.

SHAR (شعر - shar, *Hind.*). Hair.——*Shar ool jin* (شعر الجن - sharuljinn, Ar.). Means fairy hair. Same as Indian maiden hair.

SHARA (شرح - sharah, *Hind.*). From (sharaha, ar. to lay open). Remarks.

SHARA (شرع - shara, *Hind.*). Literally an open road, i.e. of means to an eternal life. Religious law of God.——*Sharayee* (شرعی - sharaí, Hind.). From (shara, ar. law). Long drawers [pyjauma] reaching down to the ankles, worn by the strictly pious. The same as Izaur [q.v.].——*Shareeyat* (شريعت - sharíat, Hind.). From (shara, ar. road). The law of islam [q.v.], including both the teaching of the Koran [q.v.] and the traditions of the prophet; consisting of such ordinances as those of fasting [roza], prayer [namauz], pilgrimage [haj], giving the poor rate [zakaut], and other acts of piety [deen].

SHARAM (शर - shara, *San.*). From (shrí, san. to injure) [shooran, shringam].—"*a*" Injury, arrow. Reed.—"*b*" From sharp edges of leaves, botanically the Saccharum genus, graminaceæ [vricsham, 156]. Grown mostly in warm countries; inflorescence in loose panicles, often very ornamental, spikelets more or less lanceolate; glumes, two-valved, two-flowered, enveloped in long wool. The species best known to the natives are :—munja [moonj], officinarum [sugar-cane], procerum [wild sugar-cane], sara [moonshee grass], spontaneum [naunal]. Other s. indian species indigenous or naturalized are :—exaltatum, fuscum, propinquum.——*Sara* (शर - shara, San.). From (shrí, san. to split in pieces). Same as Moonshee grass.—— *Sharad* (शरद् - sharad, San.). From (shrí, san. to destroy); from destroying leaves of trees. Autumn [ritoo].——*Sharauvaty* (ಶರಾವತಿ - sharávati, Can.; sharavati, Mys. gov.). From (shara, san. arrow + vat, san. suffix of possession); from its rise in amboo teertam, the arrow fountain, generated by a stroke of rama's [q.v.] arrow. River; rises at Amboo teertam near Nonabaur in the Teertahully talook, Shimoga district, Mysore, precipitating itself down the celebrated falls of Gersoppah [q.v.]; discharges into the sea at Honore in N. canara.——*Sharbhalingam* (சரபலிங்கம் - sharabalingam, Tam.). From (sharabha, san. fabulous animal + linga, san. phallic emblem of shiva); lingam as worshipped by a sharbham [q.v.]. Hindoo 2nd or pers. name. Common among non-bramins [peyar].——*Sharbham* (शरभ - sharabha, San.). From (shrí, san. to hurt). A fabulous animal supposed to be a bird with eight legs, regarded as foe of the lion [simham]. Also deer [mrigam] with eight legs.——*Sharcaray* (शर्करा - sharkará, San.). From (shrí, san. to cut); a piece. Candied sugar [q.v.]. One of the seven oceans [samoodram] of mythology [bhoogolashastram].—— *Shareeram* (शरीर - sharíra, San.). From (shrí, san. to decay). Body [cshetram]. According to the Vedauntam [q.v.] philosophy, there are three shareerams or corporeal forms :—Caurana shareeram, corpus causans, Sooeshma shareeram, the fine material form, and Stoola shareeram, the gross body, made up of the limbs which are perceivable. The latter two are the corpora causata. The Stoola shareeram perishes at death, but Soocshma shareeram, the immediate organ of the soul, accompanies it through all its transmigrations [samsauram], and is capable of sensations of enjoyment and suffering. The corpus causans is the original type or embryo of the body as existing with the soul in its original state. Compare Puncha cosham.——*Sharvanamoottoo* (சரவணமுத்து - sharavanamuttu, Tam.). From (shara, san. reed + vana, san. forest + muttu, tam. pearl). Hindoo 2nd or pers. name. Common among non-bramins [peyar].——*Sharvanan* (சரவணன் - sharavanan, Tam.). From (shara, san. reed + vana, san. forest). Scandan who was born out of a reed lake. Hindoo 2nd or pers. name. Common among non-bramins [peyar].——*Shauradanuddy* (శారదానది - shâradánadi, Tel.). From (shárada, san. goddess sarasvatí + nadí, san. river). Otherwise Ankapully river. River; Vizagapatam dist., Veeravilly and Ankapully divisions, Sarwasiddhy tal. Rises in the Madgole hills, and flowing west past Ankapully and Cassimcote, reaches the sea at Wattauda. Much used for irrigation, being crossed by six large anicuts [q.v.]. Total length about 45 miles.——*Shauraday* (शारदा - sháradá, San.). From (sharad, san. autumn); autumn deity. Saraswaty [q.v.].

SHARAT (شرط - shart, *Hind.*). Condition, contract. Begheir sharat is unconditionally.

SHARB (شرب - sharb, *Hind.*). General term for any non-alcoholic beverage [abshola, sherbet]. The following is a key list of the principal of such beverages in general use in southern india arranged under the botanical names of the plants which give them :—Ægle marmelos, bael, fruit sherbet; Andropogon schœnanthus, lemon grass, grass tea; Camellia theifera, tea from leaf; Coffea arabica, coffee, decoction from seed, tea from leaf; Coriandrum sativum, coriander, tea from seed; Erythroxylon coca, coca, tea from leaf; Hemidesmus indicus, indian sarsaparilla, decoction from root-bark; Ocimum canum, hoary basil, tea from leaf; Tectona grandis, teak, tea from leaf; Woodfordia floribunda, godaury, tea from leaf.——*Sharaub* (सुरा - surá, San.; شراب - sharáb, Ar.; دارو - dárú, Hind.; ಸಾರಾಯಿ - sáráya, Can.; సారాయి - sárâyi, Tel.; ചാരായം - charâyam, Mal.; சாராயம் - shârâyam, Tam.). San. from (su, san. to distil). Ar. from (sharb, ar. to drink); whence sherbet. Drav. from (sára, san. essence). General term for volatile substances collected by distillation; the intoxicating principle of which is alcohol. The alcohol of commerce is the product of the alcoholic or vinous fermentation of sugar [q.v.]. Cane-sugar [sugar-cane] or sucrose, not directly fermentable, is first converted into grape [angoor] sugar, and this into ethyl alcohol and carbonic acid, with some other secondary products, as glycerine. When the alcohol amounts to about 25 per cent. of the fermenting solution of sugar, the process is spontaneously arrested, and distillation is necessary in order to obtain a dilution containing a higher percentage. The various products of such fermentation and distillation are called spirits [arrack]. They differ in strength, but still more in flavor; which depends either upon certain ethers developed during the manufacture or upon substances purposely added to them. Of such spirits there is a very great variety. The six principal in use in Southern india are arrack [q.v.], mohwah [q.v.], spirit brandy, gin, rum and whisky. Of these arrack and mohwah spirit are the only two indigenous. The following alcoholic articles are in the Indian pharm. :— "*a*" Alcohol; volatile liquid, obtained by distillation of rectified spirit with lime [choonam]; colorless and free from empyreumatic odour; entirely volatile by heat, is not rendered turbid when mixed with water, does not cause anhydrous sulphate of copper [mayil toottam] to assume blue color when left in contact with it; used in chemical analysis.—"*b*" Spiritus ætheris nitrosi; alcoholic solution of nitrous ether; transparent nearly colorless, with slight tinge of yellow, mobile, inflammable, peculiar penetrating apple like [seb] odour, sweetish cooling sharp taste.— "*c*" Spiritus rectificatus; alcohol, with sixteen per cent. of water; obtained by distillation of fermented saccharine fluids; colorless, transparent, mobile, inflammable, of peculiar pleasant odour, and strong spirituous burning taste; burns with blue flame without smoke.—"*d*" Spiritus tenuior; Proof spirit; composed of rectified spirit, five pints, and distilled water, three pints; powerful diffusible stimulant; in overdoses poisonous; proof spirit may be prepared from fermented juice or arrack [q.v.] obtained from palmyra [q.v.] or cocoanut [q.v.] palms.— "*e*" Spiritus vini gallici; spirit of French wine; brandy; obtained by distillation of French wine; pale, or of very slight brownish-yellow tint; peculiar vinous aromatic odour.——*Sherbet* (شربت - sharbat, Hind.). From (sharaba, ar. to drink). Lemonade [sharb]. Beverage made of the juice of limes [q.v.], pomegranates [anaur], pineapples [ananas], or other fruit [pazham] mixed with water and sugar [q.v.], rose water [goolaub] being added. It is either sweet or sweetish sour; when sour it is called Abshola [q.v.].

SHARF (شرف - sharf, *Ar.*). Upholder. Part of lacab; as Sharfood dowla, upholder of the empire. Feminine form is Sharfoo; as Sharfoo bee, female alam + alaumat [ism].—— *Sharaufat* (شرافت - sharáfat, Ar.). From (sharafa, ar. high). Nobility. Prefixed to an alam forms a lacab; as Sharaufat ally nobility of ally [ism].——*Shareef* (شريف - sharíf, Hind.). From (sharafa, ar. high). Noble, exalted, highness. Title of that descendant of the prophet who is the Governor of Mecca; now applied as a title of honor to any descendant of the prophet, and also affixed or prefixed to the children whose father is a Sheikh and mother a Syed. Feminine form is Shareefa; as Shareefa begum, alam + alaumat [ism].

SHARMAN (शर्मा - sharmá, *San.*). Means happy. A not common Bramin title. Connected originally with ceremonies.

SHASTRAM (शास्त्र - shástra, *San.*). From (shás, san. to instruct) [shaus]. Works of literature and science in general [ilm]. Shastry is a learned man [acharry, pundit].——**(1)** The following are the principal abstract terms for the arts and sciences, shown for convenience with the English first.——*Algebra* (बीजगणित - bíjaganita, San.).——*Archery* (धनुर्विद्या - dhanurvidyá, San.).——*Architecture* (स्थापत्य - st'hápatya, San.).——*Arithmetic* (अङ्कगणित - ankaganita, San.).——*Astrology* (ज्योतिश्शास्त्र - jyótishshástra, San.).——*Astronomy* (खगोलशास्त्र - khagólashástra, San.).——*Biography* (चरित्र - charitra, San.).——*Chemistry* (रसायनशास्त्र - rasáyanashástra, San.).——*Chronology* (कालगणित - kálaganita, San.).——*Dancing* (भरतशास्त्र - bharatashástra, San.).——*Fencing* (शस्त्रविद्या - shastravidyá, San.).——*Geography* (भूगोलशास्त्र - bhúgólashástra, San.).——*Geometry* (क्षेत्रगणित - kshétraganita, San.).——*Grammar* (व्याकरणशास्त्र - vyákaranashástra, San.).——*History* (चरित्र - charitra, San.).——*Hydraulics* (जङ्गमजलशास्त्र - jangamajalashástra, San.).——*Hydrostatics* (स्थावरजलशास्त्र - st'hávarajalashástra, San.).——*Law* (धर्मशास्त्र - dharmashástra, San.).——*Logic* (तर्कशास्त्र - tarkashástra, San.).——*Mechanics* (यन्त्रशिल्प - yantrashilpa, San.).——*Moral philosophy* (नीतिशास्त्र - nítishástra, San.).——*Music* (सङ्गीतशास्त्र - sangítashástra, San.).——*Natural science* (प्रकृतितत्त्वशास्त्र - prakrititattvashástra, San.).——*Optics* (चाक्षुषशास्त्र - chákshushashástra, San.).——*Painting* (चित्रलेखनविद्या - chitralékhanavidyá, San.).——*Perspective* (यथादर्शनचित्रलेखनविद्या - yat'hádarshanachitralékhanavidyá, San.).——*Philosophy* (तत्त्वशास्त्र - tattvashástra, San.).——*Physic* (वैद्यशास्त्र - vaidyashástra, San.).——*Physiology* (शारीरकशास्त्र - shárírakashástra, San.).——*Pneumatics* (वायुशास्त्र - váyushástra, San.).——*Poetry* (काव्य - kávya, San.).——*Rhetoric* (अलङ्कारशास्त्र - alankárashástra, San.).——*Sculpture* (तक्षणशिल्प - takshanashilpa, San.).——*Theology* (वेदान्तशास्त्र - védántashástra, San.).——*Trigonometry* (त्रिकोणगणित - trikónaganita, San.).——**(2)** *Cuppal shastram* (கப்பற்சாத்திரம் - kapparchâttiram, Tam.). From (kappal, tam. ship + above). A treatise on navigation. Contains directions concerning mode of building ships [dhony]. The suitable times for sailing are stated. The observation of the stars and lunar mansions [nacshatram] is enforced with reference to everything; even to the dropping of an anchor, which must be only as the stars ordain.——*Dharma shastram* (धर्मशास्त्र - dharmashástra, San.). From (dharma, san. duty, justice + above). Law.——*Shilpa shastram* (शिल्पशास्त्र - shilpashástra, San.). From (shilpa, san. mechanics + above). Treatises on shilpam [q.v.]. Directions for laying the foundations of houses [veed] and other buildings and raising the superstructure. Astrology [jyotisham] is brought in. These are numerous in Sanscrit. Remains of those entitled Caushyapam, Maunasauram, Pauncharautram, Sacalaudhicauram, Sanatcomauram, Sauraswatyam, Veikhaunasam, Vishwacarmeeyam are met with here. The Maunasauram [q.v.] is the most perfect.

SHAT (शड् - shat, *San.*). Six.——*Salsette* (سالست - sálsat, Hind.). Corruption of (shatshashti, san. sixty-six); from the number of villages it contained. An island immediately north of Bombay. Also the maritime provinces of Goa.——*Salsette hemp* (سالست کا نار - sálsatkánár, Hind.). Same as Sunn.——*Shadacsharam* (षडक्षर - shadakshara, San.). From (above + akshara, san. letter). Muntram [q.v.] consisting of six characters. Sacred to Soobramanyan [q.v.], as the Punchaucsharam [q.v.] is sacred to Shiva [q.v.].——*Shadanga* (ಷಡಂಗ - shadanga, Can.). From (above + anga, san. limb); epithet of the vedam. Title of Canarese bramins. Hindoo third name [peyar].——*Shadangam* (ഷഡംഗം - shadangam, Mal.). From (above + anga, san. part). The six cooling drugs:—Andropogon muricatus [cuscus], Cyperus rotundus [common sedge], Mollugo cerviana [hazaur danah], Pavonia odorata [peramootty], Santalum album [sandal], Zingiber officinale [ginger].——*Shadauranyam* (षडारण्य - shadáranya, San.). Six forests [arcot]; the wilderness of paradise, probably imagined in Cashmere.——*Shad darshanam* (षड्दर्शन - shaddarshana, San.). From (above + darshana, san. teaching). See Darshanam.——*Shadjam* (षड्ज - shadja, San.). From (above + já, san. to produce); produced by the six organs, tongue, teeth, palate, nose, throat and chest; or producing six other notes of scale. First of the seven primary notes in music [swaram].——*Shadrasam* (षड्रस - shadrasa, San.). Six flavors or tastes:—sweet, sour, salt, bitter, pungent and astringent.——*Shadritoo* (षड्तु - shadritu, San.). Six seasons; see Ritoo.——*Shadtily* (षड्तिली - shadtilí, San.). From (above + tila, san. sesamum indicum, dec.). One who performs six acts with gingelly [q.v.] seeds to obtain delivery from sin and poverty and secure a place in heaven [swargam]. These are Tilodvartanam, bathing in water containing the seed; Teilasnaunam, anointing body with pounded seeds; Tilahomam, burnt offering of seeds; Tilapradam, offering the seeds to the dead; Tilabhojanam, eating the seeds; Tilavaupanam, throwing out the seeds.——*Shadvargam* (षड्वर्ग - shadvarga, San.). From (above + varga, san. grouping). Six modes of division of the ecliptic [craunty mundalam] for horoscopic [jautacam, jenmaputtricay] purposes. These are:—Raushy [q.v.] or sign, in which the ecliptic is divided into twelve equal parts of 30° each; Horah [q.v.] in which each sign is divided into two equal parts of 15° each; Dricaunam [q.v.] in which a sign is divided into three equal parts of 10° each; Navaumsham in which a sign is divided into nine equal parts of 3° 20′ each; Dwaudashaumsham, in which a sign is divided into twelve equal parts of 2° 30′ each; and Trimshaumsham, in which a sign is divided into thirty equal parts of a degree each. See Dashavargam [vargam] where the modes are extended to ten, and further particulars are given.——*Shashty* (षष्ठि - shasht'hi, San.). From (shat, san. six). The sixth. Lunar [chaundramaunam] festival [pundigay, 3e]. The sixth tity [q.v.] of either the waxing [shooclapacsham] or waning [krishnapacsham] moon [chundran] in any month. The sixth or twenty-first day of the lunar month [scanda shashty, soobbaroya shahsty].——*Shatank* (சடங்கு - shadangu, Tam.). From (above + anga, san. limb), ceremonial done according to the mode prescribed in the six Vedaungams [q.v.]. Now in use only among non-bramins. Any ceremony.——*Shatsamayam* (षट्समय - shatsamaya, San.). Six systems of religion; see Samayam.——*Shatstalattaun* (சட்தலத்தான் - shaddalattán, Tam.). From (above + st'hala, san. place). Six-place people; epithet of Sheivas as they mark six places of the body where Shiva dwells. Moolaudhauram or pubic parts, Swaudhishtaunam or umbilical region, Manipooram or pit of the stomach, Anauhatam or root of the nose, Vishooddham or the hollow between the frontal sinuses, Aunyaukhyam or fontanel.——*Shodasham* (षोडश - shódasha, San.). From (above + dasha, san. ten); sixteen. Ceremony performed on the twelfth day after death, when sixteen bramins are fed. Also applied to a gift [daunam] of sixteen kinds made at a shrauddham [q.v.]; compare Dashadaunam.——*Shunmookham* (சண்முகம் - shanmugam, Tam.). From (above + mukha, san. face). Soobramanyan [q.v.], the six-faced god. Hindoo 2nd or pers. name. Common among non-bramins. Compare Armoogam [peyar].——*Shunmookhasoondram* (சண்முகசுந்தரம் - shunmugasundaram, Tam.). From (above + mukha, san. face + sundara, san. beautiful); beautiful soobramanyan. Hindoo 2nd or pers. name. Common among non-bramins [peyar].

SHATAM (शत - shata, *San.*). Hundred.——*Shakaukool* (शतमूली - shatamúlí, San.; शतावली - shatávalí, Mahr.; शीतेचवारि - shítéchavári, Conc.; شقاقل - shakákul, Ar., Pers., Hind. and Dec.; ಹಲುಮಕ್ಕಳತಾಯಿಬಳ್ಳಿ - halumakkalatáyiballi, Can.; ಉದುರಿಬೂರು - uduribúru, Too.; తల్లగడ్డ - tsallagadda, Tel.; ശതാവരി - shatávari, Mal.; හාතාවාරිය - hátávâriya, Singh.; தண்ணீர்முட்டான் - tannírmuttán, Tam.). Title from arabic. San. from (shata, san. hundred + múla, san. root); from shaggy root. Mahr. from (shata, san. hundred + ávalí, san. row). Arabic corrupted from sanscrit. Can. from (hala, can. many + makkalu, can. children + táyi, can. mother + balli, can. creeper). Too. from (uduru, too. hanging down + búru, too. creeper). Tel. from (tsalla, tel. buttermilk + gadda, tel. root). Mal. from (shata, san. hundred + ávri, san. to cover). Tam. from (tannír, tam. water + vidu, tam. to issue); holds cool water; also diuretic. San. also (áshádhí), meaning produced in the malayam mountain; (késhí), meaning hairy; (shatávarí); (varí), meaning covering. Hind. also (sadáborí); (satáwar), meaning asparagopsis ascendens, kunth. Can. also (majjigegadde), meaning buttermilk + lump; (áshádiyaballi), meaning malayam mountain + creeper. Tel. also (pillitíga), meaning cat + creeper, small; (erraváludutíga), meaning red + hanging + creeper; (pillipesara), by corruption; (pillipítsara), meaning cat + the plant. Mal. also (shatávali), meaning hundred rows. Singh. also (barí), meaning best plant. Tam. also (paniyinákku), meaning snake + tongue; (shathávéri), meaning hundred-rooted. Title otherwise Buttermilk root, Cat creeper, Racemose asparagus, Shatauvary, Water root, Wild carrot. Botanically Asparagopsis [shatamooly] floribunda, kth., liliaceæ [vricsham, 136]. Alias Asparagus racemosus. A straggling climbing shrub; branches striated; foliage like juniper [abhal]; leaves fascicled, linear, falcate; thorns solitary, reflexed; racemes many-flowered, axillary; flowers profuse small, white, fragrant. Bark is poisonous; leaves boiled and mixed with ghee [q.v.] applied externally to promote suppuration in boils and tumours; tuberous root demulcent, refrigerant, diuretic, aphrodisiac, alterative, anti-diarrhœatic, and anti-dysenteric; demulcent in veterinary medicine; prevents confluence of small-pox; in impotence is used as morabba [q.v.] or preserve.——*Shatacam*

(शतक - shataka, San.). Means a collection of hundred. A collection of epigrams, which have one uniform refrain. There are many such as Vemana shatacam, Soomaty shatacam, &c. There is a Tamul proverb :—வைராக்கிய சதகம் சதகங் களில் வி சேஷம் —" the most distinguished of shatacams is "that on self-control."——*Shatagooppy* (சதகுப்பி - shathaguppi, Tam.). From (above + pushpa, san. flower). Same as Sowa. ——*Shatamooly* (शतमूली - shatamúlí, San.). From (above + múla, san. root). Botanically the Asparagopsis genus, liliaceæ [vricsham, 136]. Herbs or undershrubs, branched. The species best known to the natives are :—ascendens [indian salep], floribunda [shakaukool], officinalis [naug down], sarmentosa [soofaid moosly].——*Shata roopay* (शतरूपा - shatarúpá, San.). From (above + rúpa, san. shape). The female portion of Bramha [q.v.], type of many forms, same as Mauyay.——*Shatranj* (شطرنج - shatranj, Hind.). From (sad, ar. hundred + rang, ar. stratagem). Chess [chatrangam, chowsar]. The pieces are :—Shah, king ; farzeen, queen ; feel, bishop ; asp or sawaur, knight ; rookh, castle ; piyauda, pawn.

SHATAN (शठ - shat'ha, *San.*). Deceiver, rogue.——*Shadagopan* (சடகோப்பன் - shadagóppan, Tam.). From (above + kópa, san. anger). Otherwise (shat'hári), meaning rogue + foe, enemy of the wicked. Vishnoo who is angry against rogues. Also specially a Veishnava devotee so called [nummalwar]. Hindoo 2nd or pers. name ; common among Veishnavas [peyar].

SHATROO (शत्रु - shatru, *San.*). From (shad, san. to perish). Enemy.——*Shatroognan* (शत्रुघ्न - shatrughna, San.). From (above + han, san. to kill). Brother of Rama [q.v.].

SHAUDY (شادی - shádí, *Hind.*). Means joy. Mahomedan marriage with all its ceremonies and festive rejoicings. It is contracted after the female attains her age and when the bridegroom is between twenty and twenty-five. The cost on the bride's side averages Rs. 2,000, and on that of the bridegroom Rs. 1,000. The following is a brief description of the ceremonies :—" *a* " Betrothal. In case the contracting parties are strangers, the information required by the bridegroom's party of a family in which it is proposed to marry, is conveyed by professional female go-betweens. After such preliminaries a relation of the bridegroom goes to the bride's house to get the consent of the bride's family. This obtained privately, a day is appointed for announcing it publicly. The friends and relations of the bridegroom then proceed to the bride's house with betel-nut [q.v.], sugar [q.v.], flowers [phool], and jewels [zewar] as presents to the bride, and return, after obtaining the consent of her guardian. The object of this is to bind the parties.—" *b* " Ceremonies before Nicka [q.v.]. The wedding commences on an appointed day and lasts five or six days. The two first days are devoted to minor ceremonials. On the third day the wedding dress, jewels for the bride provided by the bridegroom, with painted earthen pots containing sugar-candy [candy], almonds [baudam], dates [kharjooram], raisin [angoor], &c., are carried from the house of the bridegroom to that of the bride. The friends and relations who accompany the processions are entertained at the bride's house, and return after ceremonies. The bride's jewels, articles of toilet, furniture, &c., and the bridegroom's wedding dress are similarly carried to the bridegroom's house from that of the bride on the fourth day. About 4 o'clock in the morning of the fifth the bridegroom proceeds to the bride's house in procession and arrives there at dawn. His admission into the bride's house is opposed till some present is given to a relation of the bride's and then he is taken to the Diwaun khana.—" *c* " The nicka [q.v.] ceremony, the only ceremony enjoined according to law, is then solemnised at a propitious hour. The cauzy [q.v.] appoints two individuals as witnesses on the part of bridegroom and desires them to obtain orders of the bride's guardian regarding the nicka. They return accompanied by a vakeel [q.v.] appointed on the bride's side. The dowry [mahar] to be paid by the bridegroom is then settled. The consent of the bridegroom is then taken, and nicka is read. Supplications are then offered by the cauzy [q.v.]. Towards the evening, the bridegroom goes into the zenana [q.v.], and carries the bride to his own house in procession. Five successive Fridays are kept as honey-moon, and entertainments are given ; on the first four at the bride's and on the fifth at the bridegroom's [janauza, mootah, nicka].

SHAUFEE (شافعی - sháfaí, *Hind.*). From (shafa, ar. to intercede). Intercessor. Founder of one of the four principal Mahomedan sects [cowm], comprising chiefly the Nivayats [q.v.] and Lubbays [q.v.]. He reduced Muslim [q.v.] jurisprudence to order and made it a science [soonnee].

SHAUL (शाल् - shál, *San.*). To shine.——*Salustry* (سالوتری - sálútarí, Hind.). From (sálíhótra, san. name of bramin who wrote a treatise on veterinary art). Horse-doctor.——*Saul* (शाल - shála, San.). See sep. title.——*Saula* (శాల - shála, Tel.). From (shal, san. to shine) ; large hall or house. A house ; suffix in compounds, as Dhurramsaula, meaning charity + house.——*Saulo* (سالو - sálú, Hind.). Fine turkey-red calico.——*Semal* (سیمل - semal, Hind.). From (shálmalí, san. the tree, bombax malabaricum, dec.). Same as Red-cotton tree. White semal is same as Silk-cotton tree. For semal gum see Sem gum.——*Shaulam* (शाल - shála, San.). From (shál, san. to praise). The saul [q.v.] tree.——*Shaulancauyanan* (शालङ्कायन - shálankáyana, San.). From (shála, san. the saul tree + anka, san. mark + ayana, san. abode) ; one born in a place noted for saul trees. Nundy [q.v.], the sacred bull. Name of the dynasty [raj] of kings at Vengy [q.v.]. See vol. 1 (139) ; II, 80.——*Shaulay* (शाल - shála, San. ; شالا - shálá, Hind. ; శాల - shála, Tel. ; ശാല - shála, Mal. ; சாலை - shálai, Tam.). Place, hall, school. So avenue. The planting of large trees along the highways and of groves or topes [q.v.] for halting places has from the most ancient times been a popular custom. The bramins say that he who plants a tree lives long. The trees may be of almost any description. A great number are banyans [q.v.] ; but these by sending their roots in different directions down along the trunk and from the branches into the road spoil it for wheel carriages ; when the props are cut away, as is customary by the road side, the tree itself is liable to be uprooted. Tamarinds [q.v.] and mangoes [q.v.] supply the place of banyans [q.v.] near villages. In storms the Portia [q.v.] suffers most of all the avenue trees, and trees grown from cuttings are more extensively damaged than seedlings. The casuarinas [chowkmaram] with their acicular foliage yield to the gale and suffer the least. Trees with soft or brittle wood as Carica papaya, linn. [papaw] ; Melochia velutina, bedd. ; Millingtonia hortensis, lin. f. [indian cork] ; Moringa pterygosperma, gærtn. [moringa] ; Sesbania grandiflora, pers. [west-indian sesban], &c. ; are either entirely prostrated or have their branches strewed about. Plan pursued in making avenues is usually to have circular pits dug 6 feet deep and 6 feet in diameter, which are filled with fresh soil ; round these, mud walls are raised 3 feet high to protect the young plants from cattle. The plants must be watered and looked after for about five years. The following is a tolerably complete list of trees used for avenue-planting in southern india :—Adenanthera pavonia, false red sanders ; Albizzia lebbek, common sirissa ; Anthocephalus cadamba, cadamba ; Artocarpus integrifolia, common jack ; Bombax malabaricum, red-cotton tree ; Carica papaya, papaw ; Casuarina equisetifolia, whip tree ; Cedrela toona, toon ; Dalbergia sissoo, sissoo ; Eugenia jambolana, common jaumoon ; Ficus bengalensis, banyan ; Ficus religiosa, peepul ; Ficus retusa, chinese banyan ; Ficus tsiela, tsiela ; Guazuma tomentosa, roodrauck tree ; Mangifera indica, mango ; Melia azadirachta, margosa ; Mesua ferrea, nauga champak ; Millingtonia hortensis, indian cork ; Moringa pterygosperma, indian horse-radish ; Parkia biglandulosa, nitta ; Pithecolobium dulce, corcapilly ; Poinciana elata, indian poinciana ; Poinciana regia, flamboyant ; Polyalthia longifolia, asoca ; Pongamia glabra, indian beech ; Protium caudatum, hill kilooway ; Sesbania grandiflora, west-indian sesban ; Sterculia fœtida, bastard poon ; Tamarindus indica, tamarind ; Terminalia arjuna, arjoon tree ; Terminalia catappa, country almond ; Thespesia populnea, portia.——*Shaulicay* (शालिका - sháliká, San.). From (shála, san. shorea robusta, gærtn.) ; from leaves like saul. Title otherwise French honeysuckle, Tick trefoil, West indian honeysuckle. Botanically the Desmodium genus, leguminosæ [vricsham, 48]. Herbs, shrubs or small trees ; chiefly tropical ; pods much like the blade of a penknife in form, size and thickness ; flowers greenish white, pink or purple. The species best known to the natives is Indian medicago [q.v.]. Other species are :—biarticulatum, capitatum, cephalotes, diffusum, gangeticum, heterophyllum, latifolium, laxiflorum, parvifolium, polycarpum, pulchellum, reniforme, rottleri, rufescens, scalpe, triquetrum, umbellatum, wightii.——*Shauliyan* (சாலியன் - sháliyan, Tam.). From (shálika, san. weaver). Weavers, chiefly of coarse colored cloths for women's wear [chaulyan, jauty].——*Shaulmaly* (शाल्मली - shálmalí, San.). The silk-cotton tree. An island lying east of Lunka [q.v.]. Also one of the Sapta dweepams [q.v.] ; supposed to extend from the Euxine to the shores of the Baltic and Adriatic seas.——*Shauly* (சாலி - sháli, Tam.). Domestic hindoo 2nd or pers. name [peyar]. As suffix means possessing ; as booddhishauly, possessing wisdom.

SHAUM (شام - shám, *Hind.*). From persian. Evening [sundhyay].

SHAUMAY (अणु - anu, *San.* ; ساوان - sávan, *Hind.* ; سانوا - sánwá, *Dec.* ; ಸಾಮೆ - sáme, *Can.* ; చామలు - tsámalu, *Tel.* ; ସୁନିଅ - suniva, *Oor.* ; ചാമ - cháma, *Mal.* ; சாமை - shámai, *Tam.*). Title from tamul [shyaumam]. San. means small. Mal. from (shyámá, san. dark-brown millet) [shyaumay]. Hind. also (kutkí) [black cootkee, cootkee]. Tel. also (nallatsámalu), meaning black + the plant. Tam. also (tinai) [tinay]. Title otherwise Deccan grass, Little millet, Sanwah. Botanically Panicum [priyangoo] miliare, lam., graminaceæ [vricsham, 156]. Alias Milium effusum ; Panicum attenuatum. Leaves smooth, panicle oblong, bowing with the weight of the grain ; branches alternate ramous capillary ; angular, hispid ; flowers oval, paired upon a common pedicel, with unequal partial pedicels ; calyces, glumes smooth, striated lengthways with nerves ; corol accompanied with a neutral valve ; seed oval, striated, smooth, shining, brown. Annual grass, 2-3 feet high, producing many erect branching culms from a single seed ; found only cultivated. Grown on account of the grain as a field crop ; cultivated in red soil; dry ground prepared in south in chittray [mausam] or april, on coromandel in shrauvanam or august and bhaudrapadam or september, on w. coast as soon as monsoon [q.v.] sets in, or from the first maidom or april till fifteenth yedavam or may; the ground is ploughed three or four times and levelled; seed sown in south in auvany or august, on coromandel in shrauvanam or august and bhaudrapadam or september; on w. coast between the first maidom or april and fifteenth yedavam or may according as the monsoon [q.v.] sets in; sown broadcast; depends solely upon rainfall; full-grown crop much resembles grass with ears; when the seeds are full ripe, the leaves and the stems become yellow; the plants attain a height of about 2 feet; cut after three months; brought to threshing ground after cutting and trodden by cattle; average price, 30 imperial seers for 1 rupee. Seed is diet in the higher lands; cattle [maud] fond of straw.——(1) *Shaumay grass* (ಸಣ್ಣಪುರುಳೆಹುಲ್ಲು - sannapurulehullu, Can.; ചാമപ്പുൽ - chámappul, Mal.; பூப்புல் - púppul, Tam.). Title from resemblance. Can. from (sanna, can. small + puruli, can. parrot + hullu, can. grass), the large being poæoides. Mal. from (cháma, mal. panicum frumentaceum, roxb. + pul, mal. grass). Tam. from (pú, tam. flower + pul, tam. grass), from leaves having fringes of long delicate white hairs. Hind. also (puluka). Botanically Eragrostis [coosham] plumosa, retz., graminaceæ [vricsham, 156]. Alias Poa plumosa, decipiens. Culms filiform, branched, spreading at the base, erect above, 1–2 feet; leaves, linear long hairy at the throat of the sheath; rays of the ovate-oblong diffuse, panicle scattered, horizontal, hairy at the insertions; spikelets depending, pedicelled, four to six-flowered; inner valves ciliated; in tufts on pasture ground; cattle [maud] eat it. Wild shaumay grass, called in hindostany chinkah, is verticillata.——(2) *Large shaumay* (श्यामाक - shyámáka, San.; ساوان - sáwán, Hind.; سانوا - sánwá, Dec.; ಸಾಮೆ - sáme, Can.; ಸಾಮೆದರಿ - sámedari, Too.; చామలు - tsámalu, Tel.; ചാമ - cháma, Mal.; சாமை - shámai, Tam.). San. from (shyáma, san. dark-brown). Hind., &c., from sanscrit meaning panicum miliare, lam. San. also (kódrava), meaning growing with little water [khoda]. Hind. also (kodro), meaning paspalum scrobiculatum, linn. Can. also (háraka). Tel. also (bontatsámalu), meaning large + the plant; (barigelu); (peddaúdagaddi), meaning large + panicum flavidum, retz. Tam. also (nelluppil), meaning paddy grass; (varagu) [varagoo]. Title otherwise Deccan grass, Semolina. Botanically Panicum [priyangoo] frumentaceum, roxb., graminaceæ [vricsham, 156]. Alias Oplismenus frumentaceus. Culms erect, ramous, a little compressed, smooth, from 2–4 feet high; leaves large, margins hispid; panicle erect, oblong, rigid, composed of numerous, secund, condensed, incurved spikes; they entirely surround the common rachis, and sometimes tend to be verticelled; rachis, common five or six-sided, a little hairy; partial three-sided, waved; flowers almost always three from the same point, one sessile, the second short-pedicelled, and the third a little longer pedicelled; calyx, with all the glumes three-nerved; the two large daggered; corol with a third neutral valve; seed ovate, pointed, smooth. The quickest growing of all millets [q.v.]; invariably sown alone, reaped about the third month; yields a wholesome and nourishing grain, which is of special utility to the poorer classes in affording, by its early ripening a supply of cheap grain before the main autumn food crop is harvested; stalks are used as fodder for cattle [maud].——*Red shaumay* (ಕೋಣನತಲೆಹುಲ್ಲು - kónanatalehullu, Can.; కారుఓద - káruóda, Tel.; കവറപ്പുല്ല - kavarappullu, Mal.; சிவப்புச்சாமை - shivappuççámai, Tam.). Title from color of seed. Can. from (kóna, can. buffalo + tale, can. head + hullu, can. grass). Tel. from (káru, tel. forest + óda, tel. panicum brizoides, jacq.). Mal. from (kavara, san. braid of hair + pullu, mal. grass), from growing in tufts; cf. coratty pausy. Tam. from (shivappu, tam. red + shámai, tam. panicum frumentaceum, roxb.). Tam. also (mattangáyppul), meaning pleasure + fruit + grass. Botanically Panicum [priyangoo] egyptiacum, retz., graminaceæ [vricsham, 156]. Alias Dactyloctenium ægyptiacum; Eleusine ægyptiaca. Creeping at the base; spikes four to eight, corymbose, smooth; florets twin, unequally pedicelled; accessory valve of the glume minute or wanting, the rest unequal, nerved and ciliated on the margin. Scarce, growing in tufts; west coast; used as food in famine and somewhat like raggy [q.v.]; cattle [maud] are fond of it.——*Wild small shaumay* (ಕಾಡುಸಣ್ಣಸಾಮೆ - kádusannasáme, Can.). Can. from (kádu, can. wild + sanna, can. small + sáme, can. panicum miliare, lam.). Botanically Panicum [priyangoo] antipodum, sp., graminaceæ [vricsham, 156]. Alias Isachne australis.——*Wild white shaumay* (ಕಾಡುಬಿಳಿಸಾಮೆ - kádubilisáme, Can.). Title from color of leaves. Can. from (kádu, can. wild + bili, can. white + sáme, can. panicum miliare, lam.). Botanically Panicum [priyangoo] prostratum, lam., graminaceæ [vricsham, 156]. Alias Panicum setigerum. Culm creeping, branched, 1–2 feet, nodes pubescent; sheaths glabrous or ciliated; leaves lanceolate from a cordate base, ciliated at the base, 1–2 inches long; racemes four to fifteen, crowded, alternate, much longer than the interstices; spikelets twin and solitary, oval, acute, smooth; lower glume a quarter the length of the flowers; hermaphrodite floret cuspidate-mucronate, slightly wrinkled. Grows amongst bushes and under shade of trees; when exposed to weather the leaves are smooth shining green, and when under trees of a pale color; cattle [maud] are fond of it.

SHAUMBOO (சாம்பு - shámbu, *Tam.*). Means striking. Drum [paray].——*Shaumbaun* (சாம்பான் - shámbán, Tam.). Meaning drum-beater. Cf. Maula. A tribal title of the Tamul pariahs [q.v.]. Pettaun shaumbaun or blessed pariah was one of the sixty-three devotees of shiva [aroopatt moover]; also appellation of nundan [q.v.].

SHAUMIL (شامل - shámil, *Hind.*). From (shamala, ar. to include). Additions to Shist [q.v.], especially that made in Canara by the Bednore and Mysore governments. Shaumilaut are lands which have never been divided, but are held in common [samoodauyam].

SHAUNDOO (ചാന്തു - chántu, *Mal.*; சாந்து - shándu, *Tam.*). From (sháttu, tam. to smear). Mortar. Aray shaundoo, from (arai, tam. to grind) is ground mortar, or stucco. Caroom shaundoo, from (karum, tam. black) is clay used as plaster. Munn shaundoo is mud mortar. Ven shaundoo is white mortar [cauray].

SHAUNY (गोमय - gómaya, *San.*; گوبر - gobar, *Hind.*; ಸಗಣಿ - sagani, *Can.*; ಅಂಬಿ - ambi, *Too.*; పేడ - péda, *Tel.*; ചാണകം - chánakam, *Mal.*; ගොම - góma, *Singh.*; சாணி - sháni, *Tam.*). Title from tamul from (chhagana, san. dried cowdung). San. from (gó, san. cow + maya, san. belonging to). Cowdung. Held in high estimation by all natives. With it they besmear the mud floors and walls of houses, with a view to cleanliness and to its pleasant odour. They also make it into balls, which being burnt the ashes form a whitish powder [tirneer, vibhoory], and sheiveites rub this over their foreheads horizontally [tripoondram]. Where cowdung is plentiful it is used as manure [yeroo]. Also fuel [bratty]. Shauny paul, from (pál, tam. juice) is juice or essence extracted from cowdung used for sealing a heap of corn in the threshing floor [calam].

SHAUR (சாறு - sháru, *Tam.*). Juice, toddy.——*Shaunaun* (ചാണാൻ - chánán, Mal.; சாணான் - shánán, Tam.). From (sháru, tam. toddy). The corresponding terms are:—Can. billawa, Tel. yeediga, Mal. ilavan. A low caste very numerous in Tinnevelly, whose hereditary occupation is that of cultivating and climbing the palmyra [q.v.] palm, the juice of which they boil into a coarse sugar [jaggery]. They are also styled Naudaun [q.v.], and they append to their names the term Graumany [q.v.] as a tribal title. The Shaunaur have a tradition that they came from the north of Ceylon. The Haleypeik of the upper canarese country and the Billawar below the ghauts [q.v.] are nearly allied to them. The majority of the Shaunaur confine themselves to the labor appointed to their race, but a considerable number have become cultivators of the soil, as landowners or farmers, or are engaged in trade. In Madras a settlement of Tinnevelly shaunaur have adopted rice boiling as an occupation. They are everywhere a hard-working, industrious people, eating freely of fish and flesh, and drinking the toddy [q.v.] or palm wine; in the sandy seacoast wastes of the south of the peninsula, they have widely extended the cultivation of the palmyra [q.v.] tree; they claim a seigniorage over these tracts, and they are largely occupied in extracting the palm wine. In appearance they are a dark-skinned race, with low foreheads, sunken eyes, and prominent cheek-bones. The dravidian demonolatry, or devil-worship, is retained by the shaunaur more than by any other caste; see vol. I (80); of all indian tribes however they number most converts to christianity. On the east coast they are divided into three minor divisions, Tennan shaunaur, Panan shaunaur, and Eetchan shaunaur, the prefix in each case denoting the kind of trees from which they draw toddy; cocoanut [q.v.], palmyra [q.v.] and wild date [q.v.]. The division refers merely to occupation and indicates no social distinction. Around Madras the Shaunaur are divided into two classes, the higher and the lower; the latter are called Pully shaunaur. There is nothing very peculiar about the habit, custom, or dress of the Shaunaur to separate them from other Hindoo castes, apart from their occupation. The Shaunaun, when accoutred, has first in importance among his appointments, the Arivaul petty or knife-box, made from the sheath of the spathe and bound round tight with two binders of rattan [q.v.]. A strongly plaited rope is permanently fastened to one side of the Arivaul petty; the short arm of it has a much smaller loop; when fastened round the waist, the longer arm is passed inside the small loop of the short arm. Through the loop of the long arm, the toddy-drawer passes the end of his waist-cloth and ties it into a knot. Next in importance is the Yairpetty, into which the toddy-drawer empties the toddy collected in the pot or chatty [q.v.] up the tree. It is made of palmyra fibre closely plaited, and, when moistened, is water-tight. Two wooden collar shavings, about two inches broad, encircle the mouth of the Yairpetty, one inside and one outside; between them the plaited wicker-work is run up and made fast. To keep the Yairpetty in its bulged, bottle-like form, a piece of rattan about half-way down is woven in, and encircles the vessel like the hoop of a barrel. The Yairpetty hangs suspended at the waist. It takes nearly a year's practice to make a man master of the curious mode of climbing, after which the loftiest trees are ascended in a minute with surprising ease. After a hard morning's work, the left arm always aches more than the other limb, showing that there is more strain on it than anywhere else. When an accident befalls a toddy-drawer, it is usually occasioned by his left hand missing its hold on the tree and slipping aside, which brings him to the ground instantly, often with fracture or injury of that limb. When the spathe is a month or a month and-a-half old the toddy-drawer begins his labors by binding the sheath to prevent its expansion, after which he cuts about an inch off the end, and then gently hammers the flowers which are thereby exposed. Finally, he binds up the end with a broad strip of fibre and descends. This process he continues morning and evening and for fifteen days, a thin slice being cut away on each occasion. During this time also, by shaving away a portion of the under part of the sheath, he trains it to bend over. The exact term of days during which the spathe undergoes this initiatory preparation varies in different places, and depends upon surrounding circumstances; but the time when a spathe is ready to yield toddy will be easily known by the chattering of birds, the crowding of insects, the dropping of the juice, and other unmistakeable signs. When ready, the end of the spathe is fixed into a Coodoovay or small pot, and a small slip of leaf is pricked into the flowers to catch the oozing liquor, and to convey the drops, without wasting, clear into the vessel. When the spathe begins to yield toddy, the shaunaun ceases to hammer it. It will give toddy for about a month, during which time, every morning and evening, he mounts the tree, empties the toddy into his Yairpetty, binds the spathe an inch lower down, smears the end of it with his Paulay muttay, and shaves a little away, then pricks in the slip of leaf, and ties the Coodoovay on again. The man who ascends the tree is generally a paid servant, receiving about rupees seven a month. He will attend to thirty or forty trees. Forty trees yield about twelve madras measures of juice, seven in the morning and five in the evening. During the heat of the day the spathe does not yield so freely as in the night. Twelve measures for forty trees is at the rate of a little more than one-fourth of a measure to each tree. A first rate tree in a good soil, and carefully tended, will produce one measure during the night, and three-fourths or one-half of that quantity during the day; but, taking one tree with another, a quarter of a measure is a fair average. Some trees, under favorable circumstances, continue yielding at this rate throughout the year, others only for six months. It is not prudent however to draw all that is possible from them, as they thus soon become barren. Every morning and evening, when the shaunaun goes to draw the toddy, a servant or some one connected with the owner or contractor for the trees, accompanies him with a chatty [q.v.], into which is emptied the toddy from the Yairpetty. When all the trees have been visited, and the toddy measured into the chatty or Cull paunay, it is carried away to the bazaar rented by the contractor from Government at a fixed price. There are some 500,000 shaunaur in the presidency, mostly in Tinnevelly. See vol. I (35), (54), (68), (128); II, 131, 231.——*Shaunautty* (சாணாத்தி - shánátti, Tam.). Female of Shaunaur caste [jauty].

SHAURICAY (शारिका - shárika, *San.*). From (sri, san. to go) [sar]; from active habit. Merulidæ family dentirostres, insessores, aves [pacshy, 21], of naturalists [jantoo]. Thrushes. Divided into :—Myiotherinæ, ground thrushes, small, with short wings and tails, nidificate in bushes on the ground, or on rocks near water. Merulinæ, true-thrushes, and black-birds, sombre colors, many black; frequenting woods and gardens; flight is somewhat undulating, but strong and vigorous. Timalinæ, babblers; divided into finch-thrushes, jay-thrushes and shrike-babblers; quaker and wren-babblers; creeper-thrushes; laughing-thrushes; true-babblers and reed-thrushes. The species best known to the natives are shown below, but others are very numerous.——*Blue-rock thrush* (पांडु - pándu, Mahr.; شاما - shámá, Hind.; పొడకచ్చిపిట్ట - podakaççipitta, Tel.). Tel. from (poda, tel. spot + kaççe, tel. quarrel + pitta, tel. bird). Petrocossyphus cyaneus, merulinæ, merulidæ. Alias Petrocincla affinis, longirostris, maal, pandoo. Pandoo from mahratta. Male throughout dull indigo [q.v.] or antwerp blue, more or less marked dusky; familiar bird, perching on a house-top; agreeable song; the 'sparrow that sits alone on the house-top' of the bible.——*Dausary bird* (దాసరిపిట్ట - dásaripitta, Tel.). From (dásari, tel. veishnavite mendicant + pitta, tel. bird), from stripe on face resembling caste mark of the mendicant. Tel. also (námálapitta), meaning striped + bird. Title otherwise Southern scimitar bird. Pomatorhinus horsfieldii, timalinæ, merulidæ. Above deep olive-brown; white superciliary stripe; neck in front, breast and middle of abdomen white; flanks, vent and under tail-coverts olive-brown; bill yellow, dusky, above green; legs dusky green; shy and wary; usually in pairs, the male calling out hoot, hoot, hoot, while the females answer hooee.——*Dung bird* (کھیرا - khairá, Hind.; చింద - chinda, Tel.; கள்ளிக்குருவி - kallikkuruvi, Tam.). Title from picking up grain from dung. Tam. from (kalli, tam. euphorbia tirucalli, l. + kuruvi, tam. small bird); from resort. Tel. also (sida). Tam. also (panrikkuruvi), meaning pig + bird; (píkkuruvi), meaning dung-bird. Title otherwise White-hoaded babbler. Malacocircus griseus, timalinæ, merulidæ. Alias Malacocircus affinis. Head, lores and nape fulvescent or dirty whitish; found in every hedge, avenue, and garden; occasionally seen seeking insects or grain from heaps of dung; cry a whispering sort of chatter, no song; flight slow and laborious; breeding at all times from january to july, and even later; the female of black and white crested cuckoo [koel], coccystes melanoleucos, selects this bird to act as foster parent to her own egg.——*Golden-thrush* (نورنگا - naurangá, Hind. and Dec.; పొన్నంగి - ponnangi, Tel.). Hind. from (nau, hind. nine + rang, hind. color). Tel. from (ponnu, tel. gold + anga, san. body); from color of body. Title otherwise Yellow-breasted ground thrush. Pitta bengalensis, myiotherinæ, merulidæ. Alias Pitta brachyura, triostegus. Common; in the carnatic [q.v.] chiefly occurs in beginning of hot weather, when land-winds first begin to blow; progresses by hopping; in general silent.——*Grass bird* (గడ్డిపిట్ట - gaddipitta, Tel.). Title from resort. Tel. from (gaddi, tel. grass + pitta, tel. bird). Chætornis striatus, timalinæ, merulidæ. Alias Dasyornis locustelloides. Above olive or yellowish brown; beneath white, tinged earthy brown on breast, and with a few dark specks; in long grass and rice fields.——*Neilgherry black bird* (பீக்காக்கை - píkkákkai, Tam.). Tam. from (pí, tam. the cry + kákkai, tam. crow); in imitation of cry. Merula simillima, merulinæ, merulidæ. Male entirely black, conspicuously darker on head and back of neck; somewhat lighter beneath, tinged with dusky-brownish; female dusky olive-brown above; same, but lighter, beneath; bill, eyelids and gape, deep orange; legs dusky-yellow; claws yellow; irides dark brown; young bird resembles the female, but is spotted; very similar to the european bird, differs in being rather smaller in size, not quite so deep a black, and in having yellow instead of brown legs; neilgherry and pulney hills; feeds much on indian winter cherry [q.v.] agreeable song.——*Red-headed thrush* (تین رنگ کا کستوری - tínrangkákastúrí, Hind. and Dec.; ఎర్రపొన్నంగి - erraponnangi, Tel.). Hind. from (tín, hind. three + rang, hind. color + kastúrí, hind. thrush); red head, upper plumage leaden, lower plumage dusky white. Tel. from (erra, tel. red + ponnangi, tel. thrush); from color of head. Title otherwise White winged ground-thrush. Geocichla cyanotus, merulinæ, merulidæ. Peculiar to southern india, extending as far as goomsoor on the east coast, and to bombay on the west side; most abundant in forests of malabar and wynaud; is not rare in the jungles of the eastern ghauts; prefers bamboo-jungles, feeds on the ground, and generally perches low; food is chiefly insects [poochy], ants [choomtee], cockroaches [jhingoor] and beetles [zeerangy]; not unfrequently, also stony fruit. Agreeable song.

SHAUS (शास् - shás, *San.*). To protect, rule, enact, teach.——*Shastram* (शास्त्र - shástra, San.). See sep. title.——*Shausanam* (शासन - shásana, San.). From (shás, san. to enact). An inscription on stone or copper [aursham]. The following is specimen of an ordinary Tamul inscription on stone, being taken from the inner gopooram [q.v.] of the temple [coil, pagoda] of Soobramanyan [q.v.] at Tirparacooncram, four miles south of Madura :—சாலியவா கன சகார்த்தம் ஞளாயசஹூறு மேல் செல்லா நின்ற பரீதாபிஹூ பங்குனிமீ சஉ புதன் கிழமை யும் சுக்கிலபட்சத்தில் துதிகைரோவதி நட்சத்திர முஞ் சூலநாம யோகமும் பாலவாகரண (முங்) கூடிய சுபதினத்தில் அசாதகேபிலே நபாபுசாயபு அவர்கள் ராட்சியம் ஆளுகிறநாளையில் மாடல்கூடின மதுரைச் சிமை அமீ காதர்சாயபு அவர்கள் மாமுலத்துச்செய்கிற போதும் துரைபாண்டி பதிஞலுதலத்தில் திருப்பரங் குன்றம் தலத்தில் நடந்தவயனம் அசாது திரிசுரபுரம் நபாபுசாயபு அவர்கள் திவானிசுரூயஹ்ரிகோபாலராய ரவர்கள் ஞளையில் தலத்தில் ரிசுமிட்டு வெள்ளைக்காரர் பாளையம்வந்து இரங்கி சொக்கநாதர் கோவிலும் இடித் து பழனியாண்டவன் கோவிலையும் இடித்து ஊரையும் ஒப்புக்கொண்டு ஆஸ்தானமண்டபம் கைக்கொண்டு அட்சகோபுரவாசல் கதவையும்வெட்டி கலியாணமண் டபத்துக்கு வருகிறபக்குவத்தில் திருவிழாவும் நின்று தலமும் ஊரும் எடுபட்டுப்போரதா யிருக்கிறதென்று தலத்தாரில் சுந்தரபட்டர் தெய்வேந்திரபட்டர் குட்டி பட்டிபட்டர் சிதம்பரம்பிள்ளை விழுப்பாதராயர் ஆறு நிறுபாகக்காரர் உள்ளிட்டாரும் நாட்டாண்மை முத்து கருப்பபிள்ளை உள்ளிட்டாரும் காவல் ஆறு கரைப்பேர் உளளிட்டாரும்கூடி வயிராவி முத்துக்கருப்பன்மகன் குட்டியைக் கோபுரத்திலேரி விழச்சொல்லி அவன் விழுந்து பாளையம் வாங்கிப்போனபடியினலே அவனுக் கு ரத்தகாணிக்கை பட்டயம் எழுதிக் கொடுத்தோம் ரத்தகாணிக்கை நிலம் தெங்கால் புரவில் அம்மாபாகத் துக்குத்தெற்கு மதுரை பாதைக்கும் குளத்துக்கரைக்கும் கிளக்கு வீரப்பபிள்ளை தெப்பகுளத்துக்கு மேற்கு தெப் பக்குளம் வாய்க்காலுக்கு வடக்கு இன்னன்கெல்லைக் குள்ப்பட்ட திருத்தலநிலம் ஒருமாவும் கிர்ஷ்ணபுரம் குடியிருப்புக்குமேற்கு சுந்தரபட்டர் ஆண்டிச்செய்க்கி கிழக்கு சரவணப் பெருமாள்பட்டர் திருத்தலுக்கும் வாய்க்காலுக்கும் தெற்கு மதுரைப்பாதைக்கும் வடக்கு

இன்னுஞ் கெல்கைக்குள்ப்பட்ட ணாரடிநிலம் ஒருமாவும் ஆக ரெண்டுசெய்யும் உளவடை மேல்வாரம் கட்டுச் சுவந்திரம் சர்வசுத்தமானியம்பண்ணி கோவிலில் நித்தியப்படி அளைப்படி அரிசி சாதமும் கொடுத்து கிராமத்துவரி நலொட்டுவரி ஆயும் உள்பட சுத்தமானியமாய் கல்லுங்காவேரி புல்லும்பூமியும் சந்திராதித்தியருள்ளவரைக்கும் புத்திரபவுத்திர பாரம்பரியாய் ஆண்டுகொள்வாராகவும் இதுக்கு விகாதம் பண்ணினவன் கெங்கைக்கரையில் காராம்பசுவைக் கொன்றதோஷத்தில் போவாராகவும் குமரன் துணை—"On the fortunate day Wednesday, the fourth tity [q.v.] of the month of "Pungoony [mausam] or March in the year Paritaupy [brihaspaty chuckram, paridhauvy], which was current after the "1714th elapsed year of the Shalivahanasaca [q.v.], and on the "second day of the light fortnight [shooclapacsham] in which "the asterism [nacshatram] of Raivaty [q.v.], the yogam [q.v.], "named shoolam [q.v.], and the caranam [q.v.] baulavam were "in conjunction, while Asauta kepilay nawaub sahib avergal was "ruling over the kingdom, and while Ameer cawder sahib "avergal was ruling over the dominion of the Madura country "which has many palaces, the following event occurred in holy "place of Tirparacoondram, which is one of the fourteen holy "places of Toray paundy [q.v.], &c. In the time of the "diwaunship of Raja shree gopaula royer avergal, under Asad "nawaub sahib of Trichinopoly, a regiment of Europeans came "and destroyed the Chokkanautan [q.v.] temple, and even the "temple of Pulney aundy [q.v.], seized the town, took into their "hands the Astauna mantapam [q.v.], broke the gates of the "Atcha gopooram [q.v.], and were approaching the Calyauna "mantapam [q.v.]. Of the residents of that holy place, Soondra "bhattar, Devendra bhattar, Coottiputty bhattar, Chidambaram "pillay, Viloopauta royer, the six managers with their followers, "the chief Mootcarooppa pillay with his followers, the six "watchmen with their followers, all these seeing that the town "and its holiness would be destroyed and that the festivals "[ootsavam, pundigay] would be discontinued, asked one Cootty, "the son of Veirauvy mootcarooppan, to ascend the tower and "jump down; and as the regiment went away as soon as he fell, "they gave him this written document as a favor for the blood. "The lands given in favor of the blood shed are:—in the village "of Tengaulpooravoo, the land situated to the south of Ammapaukam, to the east of the way to Madura and the tank bank, "to the west of Veerappa pillay teppacoolam tank, and to the "north of the teppacoolam channel; thus: one mah [q.v.] of the "temple land within these four limits, and one mah of land in "the borders of this town, which land is situated to the west of "the inhabited portion of Krishnapooram, to the east of the "Aunditchey land belonging to Soondra bhattar, to the south of "the channel and the mended land of Sharvana permaul bhattar, "and to the north of the way to Madura, thus one mah [q.v.] of "land within these four limits. We, in total, give you two cheys "[q.v.] of land with the right of ploughing and collecting the "crops yourself without giving any portion of it to your superiors, "and we have also ordered that that quantity of cooked rice, "which half a measure of raw rice [q.v.] can give to be given to "you daily from the temple. The village shall pay your tax "with its tax. Thus in free gift may you, so long as last the "stone and Cauvery, the grass and earth, and the sun and moon, "enjoy these privileges, and transmit them to your sons and "grandsons. He who obstructs this charity shall go in the sin "of one who has killed a black cow on the banks of the Ganges. "May Coomaran [q.v.] help us!" For a shausanam of west coast see Jonaca.——*Shaustauv* (ശാസ്താവു - shástávu, Mal.). Means protector. A deity worshipped in Malabar born of Shiva [q.v.] and Vishnoo [q.v.]. Chief place of worship, Aryancauv [ayen].——*Shauttan* (சாத்தன் - sháttan, Tam.). From (shás, san. to protect); protector. Death demon [bhootam]. Form of shaustauy.——*Shauttore* (சாத்தூர் - sháttúr, Tam.). See sep. title.

SHAUTTORE (சாத்தூர் - sháttúr, *Tam.* sátúr*). From (sháttan, tam. aiyyanár, the village deity + úr, tam. village) [shaus].——**(1)** Talook, Tinnevelly district. Tahsildar's pay Rs. 150. Area 570 square miles. Population 184,329. Language Tamul. N.E. of district. Bounded north by Tirmungalam talook and Ramnaud zemindarry of Madura district, west by Shreevillipoottore talook, east and south-east by Ottapidauram talook, and south-west by Shuncaraneinarcoil talook. The northern portion, which is flat or slightly undulating, includes a large part of the wide valley of the Shauttore. This part of the country is bare for miles together, the only trees being the babool [q.v.] thorn and a few tope [q.v.] trees. To the south and west there is more variety and the country rises. The drainage flows partly south-east towards Ottapidauram and Tuticorin. Coilputty, a station of the South indian railway, stands on the water-shed [nadee] between. The northern and eastern villages are parts of the black cotton [regar] plain. To the south and west the country is broken up by ridges of gneiss or quartz [vencull] supporting large areas of red loam and sand. The red soil covers a considerably larger area than the black soil. Of the black soil about half is fair, one-tenth is good, and the rest poor, gravelly and salt. Of the red, half is fair and the rest sandy. Cotton [q.v.] is the staple produce of the northern and eastern parts; cumboo [bajrah], gram [q.v.], tobacco [pogauk], chillies [q.v.], and vegetables are also grown. The villages in the south and south-west are better provided with trees. The soil is mostly poor, the staple cultivation in dry lands being cumboo [bajrah] and gram [q.v.] under wells; raggy [q.v.], chillies [q.v.], vegetables [keeray], and rice [q.v.] under tanks. Much business done in cleaning and pressing cotton. Tobacco prepared for chewing and sent to Travancore. As in Ottapidauram, the water in the wells is brackish and apt to fail in the hot weather. Most of the villages have small tanks or Oornies [q.v.] for storage of water. There are five river-fed tanks and fifty-nine rain-fed tanks in the Government villages, the irrigated area being only 3,320 acres. There are 990 old wells and many new ones. The Shauttore river collects the water of many streams rising in Shreevillipoottore talook and in South madura. It is crossed by the high road and South indian railway by bridges 150 to 200 yards long close to Shauttore. It is full only in floods during the north-east monsoon [q.v.], at which time it occasionally carries a heavy flood, but is too sudden and occasional to be of much use for irrigation. Zemindarries:—Gollaputty, Munnarcottah, Nullamoottanputty, Ovayannickanputty, Panvanly, Sevvalputty, Shennelgoody, Vandy mittah, Yelayirampunnay. Places of archæological interest:—Colavarputty, Coondalacoott, Nemmainy, Panaiyadiputty, Shauttore, Tirtancaul, Veippalputty, Vembacottah, Viroothooputty, Woudipoolinaickanore, Yercangoody. Principal trig. station:—Coilputty. The leading places, &c., in the talook are the following.——*Coilputty* (கோவிற்பட்டி - kóvirbatti, Tam.). See sep. title.——*Gollaputty* (கொல்லபட்டி - kollappatti, Tam.). From (golla, can. cowherd + patti, tam. village). Zemindarry, Village; pop. 2,093; acres 10,722; lat. of village 9° 20′; long. 77° 59′; from Shauttore E.S.E. 2 miles; from Tinnevelly N. 45 miles. Weekly fair on Sundays. An anicut across the Veippaur. Peshcush Rs. 3,223.——*Mailpoothore* (மேலப்புதூர் - mélapputhúr, Tam.). From (mél, tam. west + puthu, tam. new + úr, tam. village). Village; pop. 885. Baptist mission station.——*Munnarcottah* (மன்னார்க்கோட்டை - mannárkkóttai, Tam. mannárkóta *). From (mannan, tam. king + kóttai, tam. fort). Zemindarry, Village; pop. 749; square miles 48; lat. of village 9° 27′; long. 78° 02′; from Shauttore N.N.E. 7 miles; from Tinnevelly N.N.E. 52 miles. Peshcush Rs. 5,093.——*Servalputty* (செவ்வல்பட்டி - shevvalbatti, Tam. sevalpati *). From (shevval, tam. red + patti, tam. Village). Zemindarry, Village; pop. 1,771; acres 20,354; lat. of village 9° 18′; long. 77° 46′; from Shauttore W.S.W. 13 miles; from Tinnevelly N. 40 miles. Peshcush Rs. 6,122.——*Shauttore* (சாத்தூர் - sháttúr, Tam.). See below.——*Shivacaushy* (சிவகாசி - shivagási, Tam. sivakási*). From (shiva, san. the god + káshi, san. benares). Town; pop. 12,184; acres 679; lat. 9° 27′; long. 77° 50′; from Shauttore N.W. 11 miles; from Tinnevelly N. 50 miles. Chiefly inhabited by Shaunaur [q.v.] who carry on active trade with Travancore, chiefly tobacco [pogauk] and cotton [q.v.]. Fine reservoir with pavilion in centre. Festival in May. Weekly fair on Tuesday.——*Vaudy mittah* (வாடிமிட்டா - vádimittá, Tam. vádimitta *). From (vádi, tam. enclosure + mitta, tel. estate). Zemindarry, Village; pop. 320; square miles 21; lat. of village 9° 28′; long. 77° 56′; from Shauttore N.N.W. 8 miles; from Tinnevelly N.N.E. 52 miles. Peshcush Rs. 5,440.——*Vembacottah* (வெம்பக்கோட்டை - vembakkóttai, Tam.). From (vembu, tam. to be scorched + kóttai, tam. fort). Village; pop. 987; acres 3,647; lat. 9° 20′; long. 77° 48′; from Shauttore W. 10 miles; from Tinnevelly N. 42 miles. Cattle [maud] and sheep [aud] thrive. Common cloths manufactured.——*Viroothooputty* (விருதுப்பட்டி - viruthuppatti, Tam.). See sep. title.——*Yelayirampunnay* (ஏழாயிரம்பண்ணை - ézháyirambannai, Tam.). From (ézhu, tam. seven + áyiram, tam. thousand + pannai, tam. farm establishment). Town, Zemindarry; pop. 4,298; acres 5,650; lat. 9° 16′; long. 77° 52′; from Shauttore S.W. 8 miles; from Tinnevelly N.N.E. 38 miles. Weekly fair on Wednesday. Peshcush Rs. 5,022.——**(2)** Village, Railway station, Head-quarters of Tahsildar; Tinnevelly dist., Shauttore tal.; pop. 2,887; acres 1,980; lat. 9° 21′; long. 77° 58′; height 208 feet; from Madras S.S.W. 295 miles; from Palamcottah N.N.E. 44 miles; from Shermadevy N.N.E. 51 miles; from Shreevillipoottore E.S.E. 23 miles; from Tinnevelly N. 45 miles; from Tuticorin N.N.W. 41 miles. On north bank of Veippaur. Former centre of zemindarry [q.v.] of great antiquity. On a mantapam [q.v.] 4½ miles east are sculptured figures. Five miles north-east is an old temple on a rock, built over a statue found at Coondalacoott. Near this is a temple of Chokkalinga sawmy. Near this is a high ground, the site of an ancient city, where sepulchral urns [mady moottaur tauzhy] and pottery, broken ornaments, &c., are found.

SHAUVAGAM (சாவகம் - shávagam, *Tam.*). Javanese.

SHAUVY (సావి - sávi, *Tel.*; சாவி - shávi, *Tam.*). From (shá, tam. to die). Crops withered for want of moisture [sookty]. Poollary shauvy is remission when grazing lands themselves are shauvy [poollary]. Neor shauvy is blight from floods [vellam].

SHAUYAM (राग - rága, *San.*; لون - laun, *Ar.*; رنگ - rang, *Pers.* and *Hind.*; ಛಾಯೆ - chháye, *Can.*; చాయ - tsáya, *Tel.*;

ചായം - chháyam, *Mal.*; சாயம் - sháyam, *Tam.*). San. from (rañj, san. to color); Drav. from (chháya, san. color). Dye. The methods of dyeing practised by the Tamulians are generally tedious and complicated, yet they have long possessed the art of giving beautiful and permanent colors to cotton [q.v.] goods. The country supplies all the raw materials for producing a variety of colors, and the workmen have long been acquainted with various mordants [cauram]. They are able to impart durable colors in reds, blacks and blues, and their various modifications; but the deep greens, yellows and other colors are more fugitive. From the diversity of subtsances used as dyes including metals, woods, flowers, roots, barks, leaves, fruits, lichens, insects, &c., there is considerable variation in the methods. This variety is increased by the different nature of the materials to be dyed, viz., animal substances, as wool [pushm], silk [puttoo] and leather [chamrah]; or vegetable materials, as cotton [q.v.], flax [alsee] and wood.——**(1)** The following are cotton yarn-dyeing processes under heads of principal colors.—"*a*" For red. Dissolve a small quantity of ashes, procured by burning the milk-hedge tree [round milk-hedge] in water, filter and add an equal quantity of sheep's droppings and gingelly [q.v.] oil to the solution. Soak the yarn in the mixture twice a day for twenty days, drying the yarn in the sun during the intervals. Wash the yarn white in pure water and dry. Steep it in a mixture of chayroot [q.v.] powder, and cassa [q.v.] leaf, coarsely powdered, for three successive days both morning and evening, drying the yarn during the day, steep the yarn again for five days, morning and evening, in a mixture of chayroot powder and drying it for five successive days and on the sixth night, boil the yarn in a closely covered vessel for twelve hours, and wash it in pure water on the following morning, when a fast red color will be found. If the yarns dyed by the above process be steeped for some time in a solution of indigo [q.v.], a deep purple color will be produced. If white yarn prepared as above detailed be soaked for five successive days, both morning and evening, in a solution of Shoorool puttay [pappily], and the yarn dried in the sun and boiled as prescribed for red, a shade of light purple color will be produced.—"*b*" For blue. If a mixture made of powdered choonam [q.v.] and extract of Cassia tora, linn. [chakondah], be put into an earthen vessel, partly buried in the earth and the yarn be steeped in it for eight days, different shades of black will arise. The mixture must be constantly stirred while dyeing. When a light preparation of the mixture is made and the yarn soaked in it three times a day, sky blue color arises.—"*c*" Black. If white yarn be soaked in a paste made of Cadookye powder, Terminalia chebula, retz. [chebulic myrobalan], and green vitriol [annabhaidy] and again steeped in a bath of tank mud, it will take various shades of black color, according to intensity of dye.—"*d*" Pink. If powdered Coosumbah flower, Carthamus tinctorius, linn. [bastard saffron], be well washed with water and mixed with Appalacauram [q.v.] then trodden with the feet, strained, and fixed by adding lime-juice [lime], bleached yarn soaked in this mixture gains a good rose color.—"*e*" For orange. Mix turmeric [country saffron] powder in water, soak the bleached yarn in this mixture and dry, soak the yarn again in the Coosumbah [bastard saffron] mixture mentioned under pink.—"*f*" For yellow. Mix a quantity of turmeric powder in water, soak the yarn for twenty-four hours, squeeze and let it dry, repeat the operation for four successive days, then soak the yarn again in a solution of turmeric [country saffron] powder with alum [padicauram], morning and evening, squeeze the yarn and let it dry.—"*g*" For straw color. Soak the yarn in a solution of turmeric powder and water four or five times, squeeze and steep the yarn again in a solution of lime-juice [lime] and fresh water for about an hour, squeeze it well, and dry.—"*h*" For green. Soak the bleached yarn in a solution of indigo [q.v.], dry and then steep it in a solution of turmeric [country saffron] powder and water for forty-eight hours, wash the yarn in a mixture of lime-juice [lime] and water and dry it in the shade.—"*i*" For orange, again. Tie a quantity of Arnatto seeds [monkey country saffron] in a piece of cloth, soak it in water for twelve hours, squeeze the coloring matter out in a basin of fresh water, add cocoanut [q.v.] water, lime-juice [lime] and alum [padicauram] powder, steep the yarn in the mixture for four hours and then boil it for an hour, squeeze and let it dry.——**(2)** The following are methods of dyeing silk [puttoo] yarn.—"*a*" To bleach it. Steep the silk in a solution of choonam [q.v.] and dhobys' earth [q.v.] for twenty-four hours, wash the yarn in fine water and then soak it in alum [padicauram] for an hour and again for two hours in a mixture of soap [sauboon] and indigo [q.v.] when the yarn will be bleached to a white color, wash and let it dry.—"*b*" For a red color. Tie a quantity of stick lac [q.v.] coarsely powdered in a strong cloth, and macerate it in warm water, bruising it occasionally with a wooden hammer, till it ceases to yield any coloring matter; add to the liquor a small quantity of tamarind [q.v.] pulp and alum [padicauram] powder, boil the silk in this mixture for two hours, and wash, when a deep red color will be produced.—"*c*" For a crimson color. Make a mixture of small dyeing mulberry [q.v.] seeds, add alum [padicauram] and boil the silk, which has been previously bleached and dyed deep red, for an hour, squeeze and dry.—"*d*" For an orange color. Make a mixture of Fuller's earth [dhoby's earth] and kamela [q.v.] powder, add a small quantity of alum [padicauram] and boil the silk, which has been previously bleached and dyed red, for two hours, when cold squeeze and dry.——**(3)** The following are the mineral ingredients used in dyeing by the tamulians; but it is difficult to say where each is a mordant [cauram], and where it is a dye-stuff:—Abruck; mica or talc [abruck, talc]; well known for its metallic lustre and its peculiar cleavage, splitting into thin plates; in a roughly powdered form used by dyers and washermen to sprinkle on cloth so as to give it a sparkling appearance. Anna bhaidy [q.v.]; sulphate of iron; a dye or rather a mordant used with organic products to give a black or dark brown dye; this salt, associated with organic matter, produces the following colors, black, blue-black, dark-green, dark-brown, brown and slate grey; used in dyeing, tanning [chamrah] and painting [rangh] and in the manufacture of ink [mashy, shye] and prussian blue. Cauvy [q.v.]; ochre; dyes a brownish red. Choonam [q.v.]; lime; used in calico-printing with gums [gond] as a resist paste; this is an auxiliary of dye different from a mordant. Gandhac ooppoo [q.v.]; sulphate of soda; this is an auxiliary of dye different from a mordant, used like soap [sauboon] to wash fabrics before dyeing them. Ghil arminy [q.v.]; armenian bole; dyes a nankeen color. Hartaul [q.v.]; orpiment or golden pigment; used in dyeing yellow. Iroomboo pody [q.v.]; iron filings; used with vinegar [candy] and the bark of terminalia [antyaparny, murdah] alata for dyeing black. Jautilingam [shangarf]; cinnabar; a good pink, sometimes used as a dye, but more frequently as a pigment vermilion prepared by reducing the ore to a powder or by chemical action. Mara ooppoo [jhar ka namak]; carbonate of potash; used in dyeing and bleaching. Mayil toottam [q.v.]; blue vitriol; employed in making ink [mashy, shye] and in the process of cotton [q.v.] and linen [alsee] printing; used as a mordant and an auxiliary and in leather [chamrah] dyeing along with lime [choonam] to produce a light blue. Navachauram [nowshaudar]; sal ammoniac; this, with salts of copper [taumram] and catechu [q.v.], yield a permanent bronze color. Ooppoo [q.v.]; common salt; used with other articles. Padicauram [q.v.]; alum; most common indian mordant; used especially with madder [munjeet] and turmeric [country saffron]. Pooraun cauvy [q.v.] cull; yellow ochre; occasionally used as a dye under the name of ramraj; also called zard or pillimitty. Pottle ooppoo [shorah]; saltpetre; in solution is used in wool-dyeing. Shivappoo cauvy [q.v.]; red ochre; extensively used by hindoo devotees in dyeing cloths of a dull orange color; largely used by dyers for other colors; earth is simply powdered and mixed with water into which cotton cloth is steeped. Sujjee khaur [q.v.]; carbonate of soda; used in extracting the crimson dye from safflower [bastard saffron]; also in bleaching. Tooroo [iroomboo tooroo]; rust of iron [auhan]; used in dyeing black. Vellay toottam [q.v.]; white vitriol, sulphate of zinc. Zangaur [q.v.]; verdigris; used in dyeing black orange shade, green, and with sal ammoniac [nowshaudar], blue.——**(4)** The only animal substance used by the tamulians as a dye is lac [q.v.]; used chiefly in coloring leathers [chamrah].——**(5)** The following are two key-lists in the briefest possible terms of the principal vegetable dye substances of s. india for which vernacular names are known; further information must be traced in the glossary paragraphs through the small-type cross references at end of this volume; see also vricsham, 7 for the method of expressing the products, &c., of plants in the dravidian languages.—"*a*" Acacia arabica, babool, bark; Acacia catechu, catechu, cutch; Acacia farnesiana, cassie-oil plant, bark; Acacia leucophlœa, white babool, leaf; Adenanthera pavonina, false red sanders, wood; Adhatoda vasica, malabar nut, leaf; Ægle marmelos, bael, rind; Ailanthus excelsa, coromandel ailanto, gum; Albizzia stipulata, stone sirissa, bark; Aloe vulgaris, barbadoes aloe, aloes; Alpinia galanga, greater galangal, root; Althæa officinalis, hollyhock, leaf; Anogeissus latifolia, vekkauly, gum; Anona reticulata, bullock's heart, fruit, leaf; Areca catechu, areca, nut; Artocarpus hirsuta, anjely, bark; Artocarpus integrifolia, bread fruit, wood; Artocarpus lakoocha, lakoocha, root; Basella cordifolia, heart-leaved malabar night-shade; Basella rubra, red malabar night-shade; Berberis aristata, berberry root, wood; Bixa orellana, monkey turmeric, seed; Bombax malabaricum, red-cotton tree, gum; Bruguiera gymnorhiza, tree mangrove, bark; Butea frondosa, bengal kino, flowers; Cæsalpinia sappan, sappan, wood; Calotropis gigantea, mudar, sap; Carthamus tinctorius, safflower, flower; Cassia auriculata, tungaid, bark; Cassia tora, chakondah, seed; Casuarina equisetifolia, whip tree, bark; Cedrela toona, toon, flower; Chickrassia tabularis, chickrassy, flower; Clitoria ternatea, crow creeper, flower; Coscinium fenestratum, false calumba, wood; Crozophora plicata, round pepper, fruit; Curcuma longa, turmeric, root; Cuscuta reflexa, seeta's thread, dried plant; Cynometra ramiflora, iripa, wood; Diospyros embryopteris, gaub, fruit, bark; Erythrina indica, common coral tree, flower; Eugenia jambolana, common jaumoon, bark; Excæcaria sebifera, china tallow, leaf; Ficus religiosa, peepul, leaf; Garcinia cambogia, malabar gambogo, gum; Garcinia mangostana, mongosteen, flower; Garcinia morella, ceylon gamboge, gum; Glycirrhiza glabra, liquorice, root; Hibiscus rosa-sinensis, china rose bendy, flower; Hibiscus syriacus, syrian bendy, flower; Indigofera argentea, var. cœrulea, wild indigo, leaf; Indigofera tinctoria, common indigo, leaf; Jatropha glandulifera, adul oil, leaf; Kandelia rheedii, cand e mangrove, bark ; Lagenaria vulgaris, bottle gourd, tendril ; Lagerstrœmia parviflora, loose strife, bark ; Lawsonia alba, henna plant, leaf ; Mallotus philippensis, kamela, fruit ; Mangifera indica, mango, bark, leaf ; Manihot utilissima, tapioca, leaf ; Melia azadirachta, margosa, leaf ; Melia azedarach, large neem, leaf ; Mesua ferrea, nauga champak, flower ; Michelia champaca, champak, flower ; Mimusops elengi, ilanjy, bark ; Morinda citrifolia, ach root, root-bark ; Morinda umbellata, small ach root, root-bark ; Moringa pterygosperma, indian horse-radish, wood ; Myrica sapida, box myrtle, bark ; Nipa fruticans, java thatch, fruit ; Nyctanthes arbortristis, coral jasmine, flower ; Ochrocarpus longifolius, soora poon, flower ; Oldenlandia umbellata, chayroot, root ; Phyllanthus emblica, emblic myrobalan, fruit ; Phyllanthus multiflorus, poolah, root ; Plecospermum spinosum, cority, wood ; Portulaca oleracea, indian purslane, leaf ; Pterocarpus marsupium, malabar kino, gum ; Pterocarpus santalinus, red sanders, wood ; Punica granatum, pomegranate, flower ; Rubia cordifolia, munjeet, root ; Semecarpus anacardium, marking nut, bark ; Soymida febrifuga, rohan tree, bark ; Symplocos racemosa, lodh, bark ; Tamarindus indica, tamarind, leaf ; Terminalia arjuna, arjoon, bark ; Terminalia belerica, belleric myrobalan, fruit ; Terminalia catappa, country almond, bark ; Terminalia chebula, chebulic myrobalan, fruit ; Terminalia paniculata, flowering murdah, fruit ; Terminalia tomentosa, var. typica, black murdah, bark ; Thespesia populnea, portia, fruit, sepals, calyx ; Toddalia aculeata, lopez root, root bark ; Trapa bispinosa, water caltrops, flower ; Trigonella fœnum-græcum, fenugreek, seed ; Ventilago madraspatana, pappily, root-bark ; Woodfordia floribunda, godaury, flower ; Wrightia tinctoria, paula indigo, leaf ; Wrightia tomentosa, ground paulay, sap ; Zizyphus xylopyrus, nutty bair, bark.—"*b*" Ach root, morinda ; Adul oil, jatropha ; Ailanto, ailanthus ; Almond, terminalia ; Anjely, artocarpus ; Arjoon, terminalia ; Babool, acacia ; Bael, ægle ; Bair, zizyphus ; Bendy, hibiscus ; Berberry, berberis ; Box myrtle, myrica ; Bread fruit, artocarpus ; Bullock's heart, anona ; Caltrops, trapa ; Calumba, coscinium ; Cassie oil, acacia ; Catechu, acacia ; Chakondah, cassia ; Champak, mesua, michelia ; Chayroot, oldenlandia ; Chickrassy, chickrassia ; China tallow, excæcaria ; Coral tree, erythrina ; Cority, plecospermum ; Crow creeper, clitoria ; Fenugreek, trigonella ; Galangal, alpinia ; Gamboge, garcinia ; Gaub, diospyros ; Godaury, woodfordia ; Gourd, lagenaria ; Henna, lawsonia ; Hollyhock, althæa ; Horse-radish, moringa ; Ilanjy, mimusops ; Indigo, indigofera, wrightia ; Iripa, cynometra ; Jasmine, nyctanthes ; Jaumoon, eugenia ; Java thatch, nipa ; Kamela, mallotus ; Kino, butea, pterocarpus ; Lakoocha, artocarpus ; Liquorice, glycirrhiza ; Lodh, symplocos ; Loose strife, lagerstrœmia ; Lopez root, toddalia ; Malabar nut, adhatoda ; Mango, mangifera ; Mangosteen, garcinia ; Mangrove, bruguiera, kandelia ; Margosa, melia ; Marking nut, semecarpus ; Mudar, calotropis ; Munjeet, rubia ; Murdah, terminalia ; Myrobalan, phyllanthus, terminalia ; Neem, melia ; Night-shade, basella ; Pappily, ventilago ; Paulay, wrightia ; Peepul, ficus ; Pepper, crozophora ; Pomegranate, punica ; Poolah, phyllanthus ; Poon, ochrocarpus ; Portia, thespesia ; Purslane, portulaca ; Red cotton, bombax ; Rohan, soymida ; Safflower, carthamus ; Sanders, adenanthera, pterocarpus ; Sappan, cæsalpinia ; Seeta's thread, cuscuta ; Sirissa, albizzia ; Tamarind, tamarindus ; Tapioca, manihot ; Toon, cedrela ; Tungaid, cassia ; Turmeric, bixa, curcuma ; Vekkauly, anogeissus ; Whip tree, casuarina.

SHAV (शव् - shav, *San.*). To alter; go.——*Savarinautan* (சவரிநாதன் - shavarináthan, Tam.). From (shabara, san. mountaineer + nát'ha, san. lord) ; shiva who assumed the form of a mountaineer. Commonly shortened into Showry. Hindoo 2nd or pers. name. Common among non-bramins [peyar].——*Severy* (శబరి - shabari, Tel.). Means a female mountaineer. Sanscrit name (shabarinadí), meaning shabary, an attendant of seetay + river. River ; Vizagapatam dist., Mulkangherry tal. Tributary of Godavery. Rises in Eastern ghauts [q.v.] in Jeypore and passes through a rocky channel, joins the Godavery at Coonavaram in lat. 17° 34′ N., and long. 81° 18′ E. It has two perpetual tributaries, Sillair and Socoolair. Navigable for about 25 miles from the junction.——*Shabalam* (शवल - shabala, San.). From (shav, san. to alter) ; mottled, pied. The Indian cerberus.——*Shabara* (शबर - shabara, San.). From (shav, san. to go), wandering tribe. Any mountaineer [sowrah].——*Shabara chintaumany* (शबरचिन्तामणि - shabarachintámani, San.). From (shabara, san. mountaineer + chintá, san. thought + mani, san. gem). Code of destructive magic. The following are literal extract translations :—"*a*" "Owm ! Hreem ! Hrom ! "hail, O goddess of Malayalam, who possessest us in a moment ! "come, come ! On a Sunday let the conjurer obtain the corpse "of a girl, and at night let him place it at the foot of a tree. "Let him place it on the altar. Then let him use the abovesaid "spells one hundred times on a Sunday, and it will be inspired "by a devil whom he must appease with flesh and wine to the "full. Offer him everything he demands, and he will grant all "you desire. This spell is all powerful. It came from Malaya- "lam."—"*b*" "Carnautacam process of causing death, infallible "if recited in a cemetery [shoodcaud]. Om ! Hoom ! Glowm ! "ghost, who delightest in human flesh and blood, and eatest the "honeyed cake ; destroyer of thousands ! devourer of number- "less living creatures, devour each a man ; devour him, drink his "blood ! eat, eat his flesh ! Ha ! How ! Hoom ! Phat ! This "supreme spell is to be recited in a cemetery ; the sacrificer "must be naked ; he must stand on a shroud, and facing the "south. In the wane of the moon [krishna pacsham] he must "commence it, and continue through the fortnight reciting the "spell in the order called the dark path. Then will the queen "of demons obey his call and come surrounded by her ghosts. "She will ask him what he requires, and he must say, the death "of my foe. She will graciously reply that she will bring it "about. She will immediately undertake it. Then let the "sorcerer frame the name of his enemy into a spell, and thus "bring about his death by reciting it one hundred times. Of "this there can be no doubt." For Chintaumany, the tamul classic see that head.——*Shawl* (شال - shál, Hind. ; ಶಾಲು - shálu, Can. ; శాలువ - sháluva, Tel. ; സാല്വ - sálva, Mal. ; சால்வை - shálvai, Tam.). From (savala, san. variegated). The Thibetan goats [vellaud] which bear the fine substance, of which shawls are made, are called Changra. Their colors are various ; a faint black, a bluish tinge, and often a shade something lighter than that of a fawn. The shawls are manufactured in Cashmere, whither the material is carried from Thibet [pushmeenah].——*Shawl fruit tree* (شال کے پنڈو کا جھاڑ - shálkepandúkájhár, Hind.). From soft spines of capsules. Same as Monkey country saffron.——*Showrimala* (ശൌരിമല - shaurimala, Mal.). From (shabarí, san. female devotee so called + mala, mal. mountain). Sanscrit name (shabaryáshrama), meaning shabary's hermitage. Peak ; Travancore state, Quilon division, Chenganore tal. Shrine dedicated to Shaustauv [q.v.], largely resorted to for religious vows. Country round consists of dense forest abounding in wild animals.——*Shwaunum* (श्वान - shvána, San.). From (shvi, san. to go). Dog. The genus Canis, canidæ [cookooram], digitigrada, carnivora, mammalia [sastanam, 12], of naturalists [jantoo]. The feral species known to the natives are aureus [jackal], dukhunensis [dhole], pallipes [konye]. For domestic dog see Nye.——*Sowrah* (సవర - savara, Tel.). From (shav, san. to go) ; wandering tribe [shabara]. Kolarian hill-tribe in Vizagapatam and Ganjam, especially latter. Language spoken by about 180,000. See vol. I (5), (30), (48), (57), (59), (69), (109) ; II, 78. Distinguish from Sowrah, the Bramin tribe.

SHEELAY (वस्त्र - vastra, *San.* ; لباس - libás, *Hind.* ; ಗುಡ್ಡೆ - gudde, *Can.* ; గుడ్డ - gudda, *Tel.* ; ശീല - shíla, *Mal.* ; சீலை - shilai, *Tam.*). Title from (chíra, san. strip of cloth). San. from (vas, san. to wear). Tel. from (gudi, tel. round) ; as worn round body. Clothes. For usage see vol. I (98). The greater proportion whether Hindoo or Mahomedan, are articles untouched by needle or scissors. These articles leave the loom [tarry] in a state ready to be worn, and have their analogues in European shawls [q.v.], plaids, and scarfs. The principal of these are the loonghees [q.v.], dhoties [q.v.] and turbans [puggry] worn by men, and the sauries [q.v.] worn by women. Nearly always of cotton [q.v.]. When dyed the colors are fast and admit of constant and rough washing. The portions which are concealed when the garment is on the wearer are rarely decorated. Mahomedans wear clothes made out of piece-goods by the aid of scissors and needles. Jackets, coats, and trousers for men ; and bodices, trousers, and skirts or petticoats, for women. There also occur loom-made brocades and hand-embroideries. For Hindoo clothes, see :—Caul shetty, Chintz, Chokkye, Dhoty, Doopty, Dungry, Gingham, Goodda, Lungooty, Moory, Pootcooly, Ravy, Shaurang, Sullah, Tarp. For Mahomedan clothes, see :—Bafta, Bandana, Boorca, Cabah, Camees, Casheeda, Chapkan, Charkhauny, Choga, Cholee, Chudder, Coortah, Coortee, Cufnee, Cummerbund, Daglah, Dastauna, Dhanak, Dhoopchown, Dohar, Doputta, Doriyah, Doshaula, Duster, Goolbadan, Goorgy, Izaur, Jauma, Jhauran, Jhoobba, Jodah, Joree, Khaudee, Khes, Kincob, Lahngah, Loonghee, Makmull, Mandeel, Meetaun, Meyjodoo, Mirzayee, Mushroo, Muslin, Neemah, Neinsook, Palampore, Phoolcaury, Pishwauz, Puggry, Pushmeenah, Putty, Pyjauma, Pyrahan, Rizye, Roomaul, Sadry, Salampore, Saulo, Saury, Shaloocah, Sharayee, Soojnee, Soosy, Tafetta, Tahband, Toombaun, Yek putta.

SHEER (شیر - shír, *Hind.*). From persian. Milk [csheeram, paul]. Sheerbiranj, from (biranj, pers. rice), is a mess of rice [q.v.] and milk [paul]. Sheerdeh, from (deh, pers. giver), is a wet nurse. Sheer i boordah, from (burídah, pers. separated), is coagulated milk. Sheer i maudiyaun, from (mádiyán, pers. mare), is mare's milk. Sheer khoormah, from (khurma, pers. date), is dates [kharjooram] and milk, used in breaking the last fast [roza] of the Ramzaun [q.v.]. Sheer khowr, from (khuár, pers. eater), is a suckling babe. Sheerkist is manna [q.v.]. Sheer maul, from (mál, pers. kneaded), is bread kneaded with milk. Sheer mayeh, from (máyah, pers. substance), is rennet [paneer mayeh].

SHEETAM (शीत - shíta *San.*). San. from (shí, san. to rest). Cold, cool. Phlegm. One of the three humours. For other two see Pittam and Vautam. From Sheetam are derived twenty human diseases. Such as the following :—paleness of the lips, swelling of the tongue in a manner that prevents speaking, a sensation of the limbs as if they were bruised, obstruction of the nose, paleness of the blood, itch, frequent sneezing, coughing, &c. [veidyan].——*Sheetal cheeny* (سیتل چینی - sítalchíní, Hind.).

From (sítal, hind. cool + chíní, hind. chinese pepper). Same as pimento in Bengal [china pepper], cubebs in Madras [cubeb pepper].——*Sheetalpaty* (शीतलपत्रिका - shítalapatriká, San.; سيتل پتی - sítalpatí, Hind.). Title from hindostany. San. from (shítala, san. cold + patrika, san. leaf); from stems, cool mats made. Hind. from sanscrit. San. also (bhadrá), meaning auspicious; (bhadrabalá), meaning auspicious + the shrub, sida cordifolia, linn.; (bhadródaní), meaning auspicious + the plant, sida cordifolia, linn.; (balá), meaning strong [balah]; (baláhvá), meaning called balah; (kalyáníní), meaning auspicious. Title otherwise Forked phrynium. Botanically Maranta dichotoma, wall., marantaceæ [vricsham, 143]. Alias Phrynium dichotomum. Stems straight, 3–6 feet, very smooth polished; branches numerous, dichotomous, spreading, jointed at every division; leaves alternate, petioled, ovate-cordate, smooth, entire, acute, with fine parallel veins; petioles sheathing; racemes terminal, usually solitary, jointed, a little flexuose; flowers in pairs on a common pedicel, from the alternate joints of the rachis; calyx three-leaved; border of corolla double, exterior of three equal, recurved segments, interior of five unequal ones far extending above the rest; flowers large, white. Split stems are tough, and from them are made mats [boriyah]; stems give also a fibre [naur]. Maranta arundinacea is west indian or true arrowroot; cultivated here; the article is white, odourless, and tasteless, in the form either of a light opaque white powder or of small pulverulent masses; inferior arrowroot may be distinguished from genuine, by its yellow tinge and by its not thickening in boiling water; for the production of arrowroot, the rhizomes are dug up, they are then ground and the pulp washed to remove the starch, this is drained and finally dried with a gentle heat. For native arrowroots see Tikhar or Malabar arrowroot.

SHEEVAL (சீவல் - shíval, *Tam.*). From (shívu, tam. to slice). Literally paring. Areca-nut [q.v.] parings, in use along with betel-leaf [betel-pepper] and choonam [q.v.].

SHEIKH (شيخ - shaikh, *Hind.*). From (shákha, ar. to grow old). A chief, a venerable old man, a superior of an order of dervishes [q.v.]. The designation of those Mussalmans [q.v.] who profess to be descended from the first [aboo bakr] or second [oomr] caliphs or from the prophet's uncle Abbaus [q.v.]. They class themselves according to their Arab origin as Ansaury, Faurooky, Koreshee, Moohaujir, and Siddeeky. The principal of these are:—Sheikh koresh, of which class are the prophet and all his companions and descendants; Sheikh siddeeky, descendants of aboo bakr; and Sheikh faurooky, descendants of oomr. Sheikh is the title generally applied to the principal teachers among the Soofee [q.v.]. In Arabia and Syria, the hereditary or elected chief of a tribe is also called Sheikh. In India this title is given to all who are not Syeds [q.v.], Moghuls [q.v.], or Patauns [q.v.], and to all descendants of Mahomedan converts; as Sheikh ally, alaumat + alam. The Sheikhs therefore are of the most varied origin, and are engaged in all avocations, military and civil. About 55,000 in Presidency; of which North arcot, Bellary, Cuddapah, and Kurnool have the most [mahomedan]. See vol. II, 233.

SHEITAUN (شيطان - shaitán, *Hind.*). From (shatan, ar. to rebel). Greek σατανᾶς. Egyptian Set, god of discord. Devil [pey]. Term of abuse. Plant first term. Ex.:—Abroma augusta, devil's cotton; Alstonia scholaris, devil's tree; Argemone mexicana, devil's fig; Datura stramonium, devil's trumpet; Ferula narthex, devil's dung; Ficus dæmonum, devil fig; Ficus oppositifolia, devil fig; Laminaria saccharina, devil's apron; Martynia diandra, devil's claw; Nigella hispanica, devil in a bush; Urtica crenulata, devil's nettle. See gloss. paragraphs.

SHEKHADAH (سیکڑا - saikará, *Hind.*). Percentage. Especially a grant of pasture in proportion to holdings or cultivation.

SHEKK (செக்கு - shekku, *Tam.*). From (chakra, san. wheel) [chuckram]. Oil-press [gaunam].——*Shekk moottay* (செக்கு முட்டை - shekkumuttai, Tam.). From (above + muttai, tam. egg). An egg-shell like spoon filled with oil; contribution levied by proprietors from each oil-press.

SHEL (செல் - shel, *Tam.*). To go.——*Selvadoray* (செல்வதுறை - shelvathurai, Tam.). From (shelvam, tam. prosperity + turai, tam. prince). Hindoo 2nd or pers. name. Common among non-bramins [peyar].——*Selvam* (செல்வம் - shelvam, Tam.). From (shel, tam. to go); increase, prosperity. Wealth [shellam].——*Selvanayagam* (செல்வநாயகம் - shelvanáyagam, Tam.). From (shelvam, tam. wealth + náyaka, san. master). Hindoo 2nd or pers. name. Common among non-bramins [peyar].——*Selvarauz* (సెల్వరాజు - selvarádzu, Tel.). From (shelvam, tam. wealth + rádzu, tel. king). Hindoo 2nd or pers. name [peyar].——*Shelavoo* (செலவு - shelavu, Tam.). Leave, permission to depart; expense [curts].——*Shellacootty* (செல்லக்குட்டி - shellakkutti, Tam.). From (shellam, tam. favorite + kutti, tam. child). Favorite child. Applied to males and females. Proper name [peyar].——*Shellum* (செல்லம் - shellam, Tam.). Fortune. Favorite. Name applied to males and females [payer, selvam].——*Shellammah* (செல்லம்மா - shellammá, Tam.). From (shellam, tam. favorite + ammá, tam. mother, titular affix). Favorite child.——*Shellaye* (செல்லாயி - shelláyi, Tam.). Proper name. Term of endearment to children among the higher classes. Female proper name among the lower classes [peyar].——*Shelly* (செல்லி - shelli, Tam.). Feminine form of shellan; non-bramin female proper name [peyar].——*Shelvy* (செல்வி - shelvi, Tam.). From (shelvam, tam. prosperity). Lutchmy [q.v.].

SHEM (لال - lál, *Hind.*; ಕೆಂಪು - kempu, *Can.*; ఎఱ్ఱ - erra, *Tel.*; செம் - shem, *Tam.*). Red, good [chem]. Plant first term, often joining two genera, in the former sense. Ex., where transl. is of second term:—Albizzia odoratissima (yerrachinta), tamarindus indica; Amarantus spinosus (erramulugóranta), barleria prionitis; Anacardium occidentale (kempugéru), semecarpus anacardium; Aristolochia indica (errakalabanda), aloe indica; Baliospermum montanum (erradundiga), jatropha glandulifera; Barringtonia acutangula (kempukanaginamara), nerium odorum; Breynia rhamnoides, var. genuina (errapurugudu), phyllanthus multiflorus; Capsicum annuum (kempumenasu), piper nigrum; Carthamus tinctorius (shendurukkam), crocus sativus; Cinnamomum iners (shembilá), artocarpus integrifolia; Crossandra undulæfolia (erravádámbramu), dædalacanthus nervosus; Daucus carota (kempumullangi), raphanus sativus; Erythroxylon monogynum (shembuliççai), hibiscus cannabinus; Indigofera enneaphylla (kenneggilu), tribulus terrestris; Ipomæa quamoclit (kempumallige), jasminum sambac; Nymphæa lotus (kendávare), nelumbium speciosum; Ochna squarrosa (erradzuvvi), ficus tsiela; Orygia decumbens (shivappuççaranai), trianthema monogyna; Pterocarpus santalinus (kempugandha), santalum album; Pupalia atropurpurea (errauttaréni), achyranthes aspera; Rhynchosia viscosa (errachikkudu), dolichos lablab; Sesbania aculeata (errajíluga), æschynomene aspera; Sterculia urens (errapuniki), gyrocarpus jacquini; Trichosanthes palmata (lálindráyan), citrullus colocynthis. See gloss. paragraphs.——*Sendoorkum* (செந்துருக்கம் - shendurukkam, Tam.). From (above + turukkam, tam. crocus sativus, linn.). Same as Bastard saffron.——*Seyaur* (செய்யாறு - sheyyáru, Tam.). From (sheyya, tam. red + áru, tam. river). Sanscrit name (kamandalanadí), meaning water jar + river. Rises in the Jawaudies and passes through Polore talook, after which it is sometimes called, and running by the town of Arnee, drains the jagheer and joins the Cheyaur, the tributary of Palaur outside the jagheer [q.v.].——*Shaumanty* (सेवान्तिका - sévantiká, San.; शेवती - shévatí, Mahr.; शेवन्ते - shévanté, Conc.; داودی - dáúdí, Ar.; درخت گل چینی - darakhtigulichíní, Pers.; گل چینی کا پیڑ - gulchíníkáper, Hind.; گل چینی کا جھاڑ - gulchíníkájhár, Dec.; ಶಾವಂತಿಗೆ - shávantige, Can.; ಶೇವಮತ್ತಿಗೆ - shómattigo, Too.; చేమంతి - chémanti, Tel.; ജെവന്തി - jevanti, Mal.; ලාවුලුගස් - lávulugas, Singh.; சாமந்தி - shámandi, Tam.). Title from tamul. San. from (sév, san to serve), useful. Mahr. from sanscrit. Pers. from (darakht, pers. tree + gul, pers. flower + chíní, pers. chinese). Hind. from (gul, pers. flower + chíní, pers. chinese + per, hind. tree). Dec. from (gul, pers. flower + chíní, pers. chinese + jhár, hind. tree). Tel. from (cheyyi, tel. hand + banti, tel. bouquet); from form of flower; by corruption from sanscrit. Mal. from tamul. Singh. from (lávulu, singh. chrysophyllum roxburghii, g. don. + gas, singh. plant). Tam. from (shem, tam. red + andi, tam. evening) [country baboona]; by corruption from sanscrit. San. also (sugandhiká), meaning good + scented; (shatapatratarani), meaning hundred-petalled rose; (atimuktá), meaning surpassing pearl, is white variety [madablota, nemmy]; (chandrikámalliká), meaning moonlight + jasmine; (sévatí), meaning useful, also applied to indian white rose [q.v.]. Pers. also (darakhtigulidáúdí), meaning david's flower tree. Hind. also (dáúdí), meaning david's tree. Tel. also (erracbémanti), meaning red + the plant; (pattsachémanti), meaning yellow + the plant; (chámanti). Tam. also (akkirágáram), from similarity of flowers to akalkarah [q.v.] plant; (shevvandi), meaning red + evening. Title otherwise Chinese flower, Christmas flower, Crown daisy, David's flower, Garden chrysanthemum, Indian chamomile, Sicilian chrysanthemum. Botanically Chrysanthemum coronarium, linn., compositæ [vricsham, 74]. Alias Chrysanthemum roxburghii; Pyrethrum indicum. Common in gardens. Flowers, when dried, form substitute for chamomile [baboona]; root, when chewed, communicates tingling sensation to tongue like pellitory [akalkarah]; plant administered in conjunction with black pepper [q.v.] in gonorrhœa. Indian shaumanty is chrysanthemum indicum, fruticose; flowers smallish, yellow; fragrant; flowers made into garlands and offered to vishnoo [q.v.] and shiva [q.v.]. White shaumanty is chrysanthemum carinatum, two or three varieties, showy annual, daisy like flowers as large as watch, white or yellow rays and dark-brown eye.——*Shekkilaun* (சேக்கிழான் - shékkizhán, Tam.). From (shé, tam. good + kizhán, tam. owner, title of headman in certain villages). Called also Aran mozhy tevan; born a Vellaula at Coonnatore in the Tonday [q.v.] country, Pooliyore cottam; poet and politician; king Anapauya cholan made him prime minister; wrote lives and action of the sixty-three Tirtondar, or special votaries of Shiva [aroopatt moover], an epic poem, Tirttondar pooraunam in seventy-two cantos; when the king heard of it he sent both author and work on an elephant [q.v.] in royal procession [ooryalam, shahargasht] through Chidambaram.——*Shembadavan* (செம்படவன் - shembadavan, Tam.). From (above + padavan, tam. boat man). Fisherman. In Canara and Malabar, Moocwa. In Teloogoo districts Boy, Besta, Chaupacoolam. In Tinnevelly, Patnava, Parava, and Valaiya. They fish along the seashore and in the marine lagoons [cauyal]. See vol. II, 231 [jauty].——*Shembiyan* (செம்பியன் - shembiyan, Tam.). From (shem, tam. good); good king. A name for Chola [q.v.] rulers.——*Shemmanatty* (செம்மணத்தி - shemmanatti, Tam.). From (shem, tam. red + manam, tam. fragrance); from red fragrant wood. Same as Deccany deodar.——*Shempunjy* (செம்பஞ்சி - shembañji, Tam.). Red-cotton wool [q.v.].——*Shen* (ചെം - shem, Mal.; செம் - shem, Tam.). Red, good, pure. Prefix in place names, as Shencottah, meaning red fort [chem].——*Shencottah* (ചെങ്കോട്ട - chenkótta, Mal.). From (chem, mal. red + kótta, mal. fort).—"*a*" Talook, Travancore state, Quilon division; population 30,477. Extreme length, N. to S., is 16 miles; its breadth, E. to W., is unequal running into Tinnevelly in a narrow strip of country 19 miles in length. Sub-divided into eight maniyams [q.v.] and consisting of seventy caras [q.v.] or villages. Bounded N., E. and S. by the British district of Tinnevelly, and W. by Putnapooram and Nedoovengaud talooks. The talook is a plateau. Soil is red and productive of good grain. Timber is brought from Travancore forest and sold in Tinnevelly side. Every paddy-field is watered by small artificial canals and reservoirs. The only portion of Travancore territory lying on the eastern side of the ghauts [q.v.]. Inhabited entirely by Tamul people.—"*b*" Town, Talook head-quarters; Travancore state, Quilon division; Shencottah tal.; pop. 9,294; lat. 8° 59′; long. 77° 18′; from Alleppey E.S.E. 70 miles; from Cottayam S.E. 64 miles; from Madras S.S.W. 350 miles; from Nagarcoil N.N.W. 55 miles; from Paravore S.E. 105 miles; from Quilon E. 45 miles; from Trivandrum N.N.E. 40 miles; from the sea E. 47 miles. On main road from Quilon to Tencaushy, east of Periyacoil pass. Separated from other inhabited parts of Travancore by a wide extent of forest. Extensive Bramin population. Centre of coffee [q.v.] trade. Mission station. ——*Shendan* (சேந்தன் - shéndan, Tam.). From (shéndu, tam. redness). Soobramanyan [sheyyaun, soobramanya]. Author of Divaucaram [q.v.]. Member of the Madura college [q.v.].——*Shengal* (इष्टका - ishtaká, San.; ईंट - íta, Mahr.; خشت - khisht, Pers.; اينٹ - ínt, Hind.; ایٹ - ít, Dec.; بتا - bata, Malay; ಇಟ್ಟಿಗೆ - ittíge, Can.; ಇಟ್ಟಿಗೆ - ittige, Too.; ఇటిక - itike, Tel. ഇഷ്ടിക - ishtaka, Mal.; செங்கல் - shengal, Tam.). Title from tamul. San. from (yaj, san. to sacrifice), from use of bricks to make altars in yanyams [q.v.] or sacrifices. Mahr., &c., from sanscrit. Tam. from (shem, tam. red + kal, tam. stone). Brick. To make this, reddish earth is mixed with water, thrown into a wooden mould placed on ground, and smoothed over, then taken out of the mould, dried and burnt in a kiln [shoclay]. Sun-dried unburnt bricks of a very large size were formerly employed by the natives in building; these were often 2½ feet in length by 15 inches in breadth and 7 or 8 inches in thickness; the basement and a great deal of the interior of mantapams [q.v.] of temples [coil] have been so built, the masonry being placed over this foundation; in some old forts the lower part of the walls is built of unburnt bricks and the upper part of hewn stones.——*Shengan maul* (செங்கண்மால் - shénganmál, Tam.). From (above + kan, tam. eye + mál, tam. greatness). The red-eyed Vishnoo.——*Shengan maul maidan* (செங்கண்மால் மைந்தன் - shenganmálmaindan, Tam.). From (above + kan, tam. eye + mál, tam. great + maindan, tam. son). Manmatan [q.v.] in the form of pradyoomnan or mighty one, son of krishnan [q.v.] and roocminy [q.v.].——*Shengode* (செங்கோடு - shengódu, Tam.). Means red mountain. Ancient town. Shencottah in Travancore.——*Shengol cadavool* (செங்கோற்கடவுள் - shengórkkadavul, Tam.). From (shem, tam. just + kól, tam. rod + kadavul, Tam. god). Yaman [q.v.], the god of death and of justice.——*Shenjadaiyeeshar* (செஞ்சடையீசர் - sheñjadaiyísar, Tam.). From (above + jatá, san. matted hair + ísha, san. lord). Shiva [q.v.].——*Shen tamul* (செந்தமிழ் - shendamizh, Tam.). Pure, correct tamul. The ancient or classical dialect of Tamul [q.v.] in which nearly all the higher literature has been written. Contains scarcely any Sanscrit [q.v.]. Once spoken in and about Madura. A grammar [lacshanam] of this dialect was compiled by Beschi [veera maumoony] in Latin, which is translated into English [bhaushay]. See vol. I (52).——*Sheppaun* (சேப்பான் - sheppán, Tam.). Means red man. Feminine sheppy. Pariah proper name [peyar].——*Shevvapett* (செவ்வாய்ப்பேட்டை - shevváyppéttai, Tam.). From (shevváy, tam. tuesday + péttai, tam. suburb); from the fair on tuesdays. Village; Salem dist., Salem tal.; lat. 11° 40′; long. 78° 11′; from Salem W. 1½ miles. Western part of the town of Salem.——*Shevvazhy* (செவ்வழி - shevvazhi, Tam.). From (shemmai, tam. beauty + vazhi, tam. place). Ground near the sea.——*Shevvye* (செவ்வாய் - shevváy, Tam.). From (above + váy, tam. mouth). Red one. The day of the planet [graham] Mars [coojan, mungalan]; Tuesday [vauram].——*Shey* (சே - shé, Tam.). Redness [chem, shem].——*Sheyyaul* (செய்யாள் - sheyyál, Tam.). From (sheyya, tam. red). Lutchmy [q.v.].——*Sheyyaun* (சேயான் - shéyán, Tam.). From (shem, tam. red). Soobramanyan [shendan, soobramanyan].

SHEMBAH (سیمبہ - sembhá, *Hind.*). From (shémba, mahr. mucus). Glanders. The horse [ghorah], and mule [katcher] are liable to this and it is communicable not only to them but the human subject. When the specific poison affects principally the air passages, the disease is termed glanders; when the skin, areolar tissue, and lymphatics are attacked, it is called farcy [bail]. The former is rapid and violent in its course, which invariably terminates in death. Its characteristic symptoms are the abundant discharge, sometimes bloody or purulent, from the nostrils; and the eruption of small painful lenticular tumors, chiefly on the nostrils; neck, and shoulders. In farcy the same eruption occurs; the limbs are swollen and the symptoms generally are less severe. Damp ill-ventilated stables, improper food, excessive fatigue, and other depressants of health predispose to the reception of the specific poison; the principal vehicle for which is the discharge from the nostrils. This forcibly ejected in fine spray may infect stables, food, litter, vessels, &c., and so communicate the disease to healthy animals. A beast suffering from glanders is generally at once killed and everything possible done to destroy the specific poison which it has generated as in the case of rinderpest [vishajooram].

SHENDHY (शिंदी - shindí, *Mahr.*). Means toddy. Same as Wild date.——*Sondy* (సొండి - sondi, Tel.). From (sendhí, hind. toddy). A caste of distillers and toddy-drawers in Ganjam. The following are sub-divisions:—Gowndla, Shegidy, Siolo, Sondy, Yauta. Number about 35,000 [jauty]. See vol. I, 74.

SHENIYAN (சேணியன் - shéniyan, *Tam.*). From (shén, tam. sky); from weaving colored cloths. Weaver caste. The corresponding terms are:—Tel. sauley, Can. jeyda, Mal. chaulyau. Numbers about 18,000.

SHER (ചേർ - cher, *Mal.*). Junction [chair].——*Sherogar* (சேர்வைக்காரன் - shérvaikkáran, Tam.). From (shérvai, tam. company of soldiers + kára, san. doer). Petty ruler. Retainer under a poligar [q.v.]. See vol. I, 57 [maroothoo].——*Sherp* (சேர்ப்பு - shérppu, Tam.). From (shéru, tam. to unite). Coast [caray].——*Sherpan* (சேர்ப்பன் - shérppan, Tam.). Ruler of a maritime tract [coomary sherpan, neydal].——*Shertala* (ചേർത്തല - chérttala, Mal.). From (chér, mal. junction + tala, mal. place). Otherwise Sharretala.—"*a*" Talook, Travancore state, Cottayam division. Population 113,704. Extreme length, N. to S., 25 miles. Extreme breadth, E. to W., 7 miles. Sub-divided into seven praverties [q.v.] and containing thirty-eight caras [q.v.] or villages. Bounded N. by Cochin state, E. by Vembanaud lake, S. by Ambalapoya talook, W. by the Indian ocean. Sandy and low. Soil fertile. Coir industry. Irrigation by means of canals.—"*b*" Town, Head-quarters of talook; Travancore state; Cottayam division, Shertala tal.; pop. 21,152; lat. 9° 41′; long. 76° 54′; from Alleppey N. 13 miles; from Cottayam W. 13 miles; from Madras S.W. 355 miles; from Nagarcoil N.W. 126 miles; from Paravore S.S.E. 33 miles; from Quilon N.N.W. 56 miles; from Trivandrum N.N.W. 91 miles; from the sea E. 3 miles. At Southern extremity of an inland branch of the backwater, by means of which communication is maintained with Alleppey, Cochin, and the interior. Population consists of Bramins [q.v.], Nayars [q.v.], Concanies [q.v.], Syrians [q.v.] and Shannaurs [q.v.]. About the centre on the west side is a large old Syro-Roman church. A colony of black Jews [jonaca] once settled here, but their synagogue is now in ruins. Annual festival in April, for eight days. Remarkable temple to Bhagavaty [q.v.].——*Shervaicauran* (சேர்வைக்காரன் - shérvaikkáran, Tam.). Means Captain. Title of Maravar [sherogar].——*Shervay* (சேர்வை - shérvai, Tam.). An army [dandam, dandoo].

SHER (சேறு - shéru, *Tam.*). Mud [cher].——*Shett caul* (சேற்றுக்கால் - shéttukkál, Tam.). From (above + kál, tam. field). Land trampled, ploughed, and puddled for sowing rice after irrigation. Wet ploughing system [coodapa] of cultivation [vellaumay] as opposed to dry ploughing system [pooldy caul, veligada].——*Shoranore* (ചെറുവണ്ണൂർ - cheruvannúr, Mal. shoranur*). From (cheruman, mal. slave + úr, mal. village). Village, Railway station; Cochin state, Talapully tal.; pop. 1,116; lat. 10° 46′; long. 76° 19′; height 98 feet; from Beypore S.E. 41 miles; from Ernacolum N. 53 miles; from Trichore N.N.E. 16 miles; from Madras S.W. 312 miles; from Vadacancherry N.N.E. 6 miles; from the sea E. 22 miles. The south-west line of the Madras railway touches Cochin state here. A line is projected hence to Cochin.

SHERAM (சேரம் - shéram, *Tam.*). Same as Cheram.——*Salem* (சேலம் - shélam, Tam.). See sep. title.——*Shermadevy* (சேரமாதேவி - shérmáthévi, Tam. shermádevi*). From (chéra, san. ruler of that country + mahádéví, san. the great queen); after a princess of madura, whom he married. Town, Head-quarters of Head assistant collector; Tinnevelly dist., Ambasamoodram tal.; pop. 9,333; acres 2,040; lat. 8° 41′; long. 77° 36′; from Ambasamoodram E. 8 miles; from Madras

S.S.W. 352 miles; from Palamcottah W. 12 miles; from Shreevillipoottore S. 56 miles; from Tinnevelly W. 9 miles; from Tuticorin S.W. 41 miles. On south bank of Tamrapurny. Includes Coilputty. Former head-quarters of talook of same name. Very fertile. Old Shiva temple. A cenotaph in memory of Paundyan [q.v.] rulers is worshipped by the Maravar [q.v.].——*Shevaroy hills** (சேர்வராயன்மலை - shérvaráyanmalai, Tam.). From (shéran, tam. chera race + iráyan, tam. king + malai, tam. mountain).—"*a*" Deputy tahsildarry, Salem district. Pay Rs. 150.—"*b*" Hill, Sanitarium; Salem dist., Salem tal.; pop. 1,136; area 147 square miles; lat. 11° 49′; long. 78° 16′; average elevation 4,500 feet. Highest point in the green hills 5,410 feet; from Madras S.W. 166 miles; from Namcull N. 41 miles; from Oossoor S.E. 68 miles; from Salem N.N.E. 11 miles; from Tripatore S. 52 miles; from Yercaud N. 3 miles. For description, see vol. II, 124.

SHERE (شیر - sher, *Pers.*). Lion. Prefixed to an alam forms a lacab; as Shere ally, the lion of god [hyder, ism].——*Shere mahomed khan* (شیر محمد خان - shermuhammadkhán, Hind.). From (above + alam + khitaub alaumat). The first fowjdar [q.v.] of Chicacole circar [q.v.], which included the modern Ganjam, sent by the Cootb shahy [q.v.] dynasty. Built the large mosque [musjid] at Chicacole. See vol. II, 77.——*Shergadah* (శేరుగడ - shérugadá, Tel. sérgadá *). From (sher, hind. mah. proper name + gadá, tel. fort). Ancient zemindarry, Village; Ganjam dist., Zemindarry tracts; pop. 11,562; square miles 30; lat. of village 19° 31′; long. 84° 39′; from Chetterpore W.N.W. 27 miles; from Russellcondah S. 29 miles. Small zemindarry, south-west of Dhauracote, and north-east of Chinna kimedy. Peshcush [q.v.] Rs. 5,555. Yearly revenue Rs. 18,314. Number of villages thirty-eight. Fertile. High road between Aska and Ichapore skirts the town. Rooshcoolya canal enters estate at 12th mile of its course.

SHERY (శేరి - shéri, *Tel.*). From (sherah, ar. rate). Land let out by proprietor or zemindar to ryots or tenants, while Sauvaram [q.v.] is land held by the proprietor [havelly]. Distinguish from the dravidian Cherry.

SHESHAN (शेष - shésha, *San.*; சேடன் - shédan, *Tam.*). From (shish, san. to remain). A serpent [naugam, sarpam]. Especially the thousand-headed serpent resting on which Vishnoo [q.v.] reclined on the primeval waters [anantan, audisheshan, pralayam]. Familiarly Sheshoo, Chaitchoo. Hindoo 2nd or pers. name. Feminine form is Sheshy [peyar].——*Shaisham* (शेष - shésha, San.). From (shish, san. to leave). Remainder [bauky]; in mathematics.——*Sheshachellam* (శేషాచలము - shéshá-chalamu, Tel.). From (shésha, san. the serpent god + achala, san. mountain). Range of hills; Cuddapah dist., Poollampett, Voilpaud and Royachoty tals.; lat. 14° 13′ to 14° 31′ N.; long. 78° 01′ to 79° 02′; from Cuddapah S.; from Poollampett W. This range strikes off from the Palcondahs 15 miles south of the Pennair in a westerly direction and skirts the east and north-east of Cuddapah district, effectually shutting in the sub-division. No isolated peaks; but when seen from a distance, the whole range presents the appearance of one long horizontal line skirting the horizon. In the centre of the country thus enclosed there are a number of isolated hills very rocky and entirely bare of vegetation. About Goorramcondah, these hills present an especially picturesque appearance, and the old palace of Goorramcondah forms a favorite halting-place. Near Madanapully, about 2,900 feet above the sea, the hills present the appearance of a continuous range, and are covered with vegetation, though with but few forest trees. Thirteen miles from Madanapully in a northerly direction, near Caunaulamadoogoo, is the highest peak in the sub-division known as Horsleycondah. These hills are separated from the Veligondas by the Bullipully pass. Seshachellam also indicates specially the Tripatty hill. Is also a Hindoo 2nd or pers. name [peyar].——*Sheshagiry* (சேசகிரி - shésagiri, Tam.). From (above + giri, san. mountain). The Tripatty hill. Hindoo 2nd or pers. name [peyar].——*Sheshammah* (శేషమ్మ - shéshamma, Tel.). From (above + amma, tel. mother, titular affix). Familiarly sheshy, chaitchy, chaitcham, chaitchoo. Hindoo female proper name [peyar].——*Shesha naugam* (शेषनाग - shéshanága, San.). From (above + nága, san. serpent). The Sheshan serpent [audisheshan].——*Sheshashayanan* (శేషశయనుడు - shéshashayanudu, Tel.). From (above + shayana, san. bed). Vishnoo [q.v.], lying on Sheshan [anantashayanan, sheshaudharan]. Hindoo 2nd or pers. name [peyar].——*Sheshaudharan* (சேசாதரன - shésátharan, Tam.). From (above + dhara, san. support). Vishnoo [q.v.], supported by sheshan [sheshashayanan]. Hindoo 2nd or pers. name [peyar].——*Sheshaudry* (சேசாத்திரி - shésáttiri, Tam.). From (above + adri, san. mountain). The Tripatty hill. Hindoo 2nd or pers. name [peyar].——*Sheshavarna tevan* (சேடவருணத்தேவன் - shédavarunattévan, Tam.). From (above + varna, san. color + tévan, tam. title). Otherwise Moottoo vijaya raghoonauta periya wodeya tevar. The first zemindar of Shivagunga. See vol. I, 56 [charitram].——*Sheshayyah* (శేషయ్య - shéshayya, Tel.). From (above + ayya, tel. master, titular affix), vishnoo, the lord of Sheshan [q.v.]. Familiarly Sheshoo. Hindoo 2nd or pers. name [peyar].——*Shist* (شست - shist, Hind.). From (shishta, san. remainder). Sum due. The assessment [teervay] on land. Distinguish from Kist. Shist bauky are outstanding balances.

SHEY (செய் - shey, *Tam.*). As verb, to make. As noun, cultivated or cultivable land, especially rice field [chey].——*Sheygaul* (செய்கால் - sheygál, Tam.). From (above + kál, tam. place). Land capable of cultivation.——*Sheygaul carambay* (செய்கால்கரம்பு - sheygálgarambu, Tam.). From (above + kál, tam. place + karambai, tam. sterile ground). Land lying waste, though capable of cultivation.——*Sheygay* (செய்கை - sheygai, Tam.). From (above + kai, tam. suffix of condition). Practical orthography.——*Sheyyool* (செய்யுள் - sheyyul, Tam.). From (above + ul, tam. suffix of action). Verse [pah].

SHI (शि - shi, *San.*). To attenuate, sharpen, weaken.——*Shimbicam* (शिम्बिक - shimbika, San.). San. from (shi, san. to sharpen, to attenuate), from weakening or expelling wind, bile, &c. Bean. Those most commonly cultivated for the european table are phaseolus vulgaris, linn. [lobyah], and phaseolus lunatus, linn. [country lobyah]; of these here are several varieties, named variously as kidney or french beans, haricot, duffin, vellore or butter beans, &c.; the natives have no particular names for them both being exotics. Another is the hussar or sword bean, Canavalia ensiformis, dec. [tambattam], of which also there are several varieties, differing in the color of their flowers and seeds; the white-seeded variety is considered the most wholesome, and is cultivated both by europeans and natives. The Goa bean, psophocarpus tetragonolobus, dc., is occasionally used. Cf. also Dolichos biflorus [madras horse-gram] and Vigna catiang [cow gram].——*Shimby* (शिम्बी - shimbí, San.). From (shi, san. to sharpen), from being a hot food-stuff. Botanically the Dolichos genus leguminosæ [vricsham, 48]. Herbaceous or shrubby plants, with twining stems and trifoliate leaves, and flowers in racemes; pods flat, neither winged, nor nerved; throughout tropical and temperate regions of asia, africa; originally natives of india. The species best known to the natives are:—biflorus [madras horse-gram], falcatus [wild horse-gram], lablab [country bean].——*Sissoo* (शिंशपा - shimshapá, San.; سیسم - sásam, Ar.; سیسو - sísú, Hind.; شیشم - shísham, Dec.; ಬಿರಿಡಿಮರ - biridimara, Can.; సిస్సు - sissu, Tel.; ସିସୋବ - sissova, Oor.; ഇരുവിൾ - iruvil, Mal.; நூக்கம் - núkkam, Tam.). Title from hindostany. San. from (shi, san. to attenuate); from medicinal wood as weakening diseases. Hind. and Dec. from arabic. Tel. from hindostany. Oor. from sanscrit. Mal. from (iru, mal. dark + ul, mal. inside) [dark vail]. Tam. from (nugai, tam. to slacken); from elastic wood; also from weakening diseases. Hind. also (talí); (sísam). Can. also (shishmabáge); (agurumara); (irugundimávu), meaning dark wood mango. Tel. also (yerrasissu), meaning red variety, from brown heart-wood. Tam. also (shisumaram), meaning sissoo tree; (piççai), from (pichhá, san. gum, the tree as yielding gum). Title otherwise Sheham, Sissum. Botanically Dalbergia [yooga pattricay] sissoo, roxb., leguminosæ [vricsham, 48]. Specific name from hindostany. Tree, 50 feet; leaves pinnate; leaflets three to five, alternate orbicular or obcordate, with a short sudden acumination, slightly waved on the margin, when young pubescent; panicles axillary, composed of several short secund spikes; flowers almost quite sessile; stamens nine, united into a sheath open on the upper side; style very short; legumes stalked, linear lanceolate, three-seeded; flowers small, yellowish white; flowers at beginning of hot season; flowers perfume the air in evening; introduced from bengal; grows rapidly; never wild. Raspings of the wood are alterative in medicine; gives an empyreumatic medicinal oil [yennay]. Young trees are browsed by cattle [maud] and goats [velland]; planted extensively as an avenue [shaulay] tree. Sap-wood small, white; heart-wood brown with darker longitudinal veins, close and even-grained, very hard; annual rings not distinctly marked, alternating dark and light-colored bands, which run into each other; wood seasons well, does not warp or slip; highly esteemed for all purposes where strength and elasticity are required; white-ants [q.v.] seldom attack it; it was the favorite wood for gun carriages as long as the supply of large timber lasted.——*Sissum* (شیشم - shísham, Dec.). From (sásam, arabic). Same as Sissoo.

SHIAH (شیعه - shiah, *Hind.*). From (shai, ar. follower). Means follower of ally, son-in-law of the prophet. Also called Teen yaury meaning the disclaimer of the three companions; Imaumiyah from belief that God does not leave mankind at any time without a man who acts as imaum; Asnah ashariyah or duodecimians from accepting the leadership of the twelve imaums [q.v.]. The second [soonnee] great division of Mahomedans, who believe Ally to have been the first legitimate successor of Mahomet. The soonnees call shiahs Rafzee [q.v.] or heretics; on the other hand the shiahs call the soonnees Khaurjee [q.v.] or schismatics. Shiahs are opposed to the Soonnees like the Protestants of europe to Roman catholics. They reject the traditions of the soonnees, having separated from them about 363 years after Mahomet's hijra [q.v.], A.D. 985, under one of the Abbausiya caliphs [q.v.], or descendants of Abbaus, Mahomet's uncle who ruled as Caliphs over Baghdad and Persia from A.D. 749 to 1258. They deny the caliphate of the first three successors of Mahomet, Aboo bakr, Omar, and Osman, the first two being Mahomet's fathers-in-law and the third his son-in-law, who ruled at Medina. They regard these three as usurpers of the successorship to the caliphate, which they declare belonged only to another son-in-law, the fourth caliph, Ally, husband of the prophet's daughter Fatimah and father of Hassan and Hoossain. Beginning with Ally, shiahs recognize a succession of twelve imaums, whereas the soonnees begin with Aboo bakr. As regards imaumat [q.v.] itself the Shiahs maintain that it was a legacy bequeathed to Ally and his descendants by Mahomet and that it consequently descends by express appointment in the apostolic line and that election does not apply. This the soonnees do not believe. The shiahs also hold that the imaum must be masoom or sinless. The twelfth Imaum, Mahdee [q.v.] is believed by one sect to be still alive and expected to reappear; these are known as the Mahdivy [q.v.]. Another sect believe that Mahdee has appeared and gone and are styled the Gheir mahdee. On the death of the sixth imaum the majority of the shiahs acknowledged his second son as imaum, but a minority following the eldest son's son Ismail seceded and formed the Ismail sect of shiahs. These again, on a dispute as to succession between two brothers, at the close of the eleventh century, divided into two branches; the Nazarene, represented in india by the Khojas [q.v.], and the Mustalian, represented in india by the Bohras [q.v.]. The doctrine of the shiahs, as it developed itself in Persia, was influenced in some measure by the ancient religion of Zoroaster which preceded it in that country. There the shiah tenets ultimately gave birth to a kind of spiritual philosophy called soofeeism [soofee]; so similar to the indian vedauntam [q.v.] that it is based upon two ideas, viz., nothing really exists but God, while all besides is illusion [mauyay], and union with God is the highest object of human effort. The shiahs keep with great solemnity the anniversary of the death in battle of Hoossain, son of Ally, on a particular day in the moharram [q.v.] or first month [maheena] of the mahomedan lunar year. Hassan is supposed to have been poisoned by a woman at the instigation of yazeed; but Hoossain was killed at Carbalah by Yazeed, son of the first Oommiya caliph, commonly called Mooauviya, who, supported by Mahomet's favorite wife Ayeesha, daughter of Aboo bakr, opposed the succession of Ally, assumed the government, and transferred the caliphate to Damascus. Hence the shiahs perform pilgrimages to Carbalah rather than to Mecca. The bigoted amongst the shiahs on the eighteenth Zihauj make three images of dough filled with honey to represent Aboo bakr, Omar, and Osman, and thrust knives into them. Shiahs admit the principle of religious compromise called Takiyah [q.v.] or pious fraud, whereby a Shiah may deny the peculiarities of his religion to save himself. There are minor differences between soonnees and shiahs in liturgical ceremonies and civil law. Shiahs often marry by the Mootah [q.v.] ceremony for a brief period, which the soonnees consider haraum [q.v.]. The Turks, Egyptians, and Indian mahomedans are mostly soonnees, while the Persians are shiahs. The shiah sect in india are considerable in Oudh and Hyderabad of Scind. There are two particular sub-sects amongst shiahs, viz., followers of principles and followers of traditions, the difference between the two being as to the weight to be attached to the exposition of Moojtahids [q.v.] the former repudiating their authority and the latter obeying them. Total number about 45,000 in presidency [mahomedan, soonnee].

SHICSHAY (शिक्षा - shikshá, *San.*). From (shiksh, san. to teach). The science which teaches proper pronunciation and especially the laws of euphony peculiar to the Vedams [q.v.]. The second Vedaungam [q.v.]. Since the chief virtue of the Vedic texts was in their oral repetition, these phonetic manuals were of great value to priests or devotees. The title is used in dravidian languages for Punishment.

SHIGRAM (शीघ्र - shíghra, *San.*). Means quick. In astronomy [jyotisham], parallax. A small hack palankeen-carriage, used mainly in Madras [jutkah].

SHIKA (சீயக்காய் - shíyakkáy, *Tam.*). Means cleaning pod, from use as soap in washing hair. Same as Soap-pod.

SHIKAR (شکار - shikár, *Hind.*). Hunting, so the thing hunted. A shikarry is a sportsman. Shikar khanah is a preserve.

SHIKAST (شکست - shikast, *Hind.*). From (shikastan, pers. to break). Broken; decayed; a running handwriting.

SHIKHAY (शिखा - shikhá, *San.*). Crest. Top-knot [conday, coodoomy].——*Shekharan* (சேகரன் - shégaran, Tam.). From (shikhara, san. head). Suffix in proper names, as Chundrashekharan. Hindoo 2nd or pers. name [peyar].——*Shikharam* (शिखर - shikhara, San.). From (shikha, san. head). Pinnacle, tower [calasham, coil].——*Shikhaumany* (சிகாமணி - shigámani, Tam.). From (above + mani, san. jewel). Crest-jewel. Hindoo 2nd or pers. name [peyar].

SHIL (शिल् - shil, *San.*). To practice.——*Shilpam* (शिल्प - shilpa, San.). Mechanical science, especially sculpture and architecture [maunasauram, shastram].——*Shilpy* (शिल्पी - shilpí, San.). A mechanic.

SHIL (சில் - shil, *Tam.*). Small.——*Shilamban* (சிலம்பன் - shilamban, Tam.). Hill-god. Soobramanyan [q.v.]. Also chief of hilly tracts [coorinjy, desham, poorooppan].——*Shilamboo* (சிலம்பு - shilambu, Tam.). From (shil, tam. small). Hill.

SHILANDY (कनकचंप - kanakachampa, *San.*; ಮುಡಮರ - múdamara, *Can.*; సున్నూరు - sunúru, *Tel.*; କୋନିୟର - koniara, *Oor.*; சிலந்தி - shilandi, *Tam.*). Title from tamul. San. from (kanaka, san. gold + champa, san. bauhinia variegata, linn.). Tam. means knobbed; from leaves. Can. also (narole). Tel. also (tammichettu); (erradzuvvi), meaning red + ficus tsiela, roxb.; (kakamochettu). Tam. also (sherundi); (shengódu), meaning red branched. Title otherwise Golden champak, Red jovy, Tummy tree, Yellow flowered ochna. Botanically Ochna squarrosa, linn., ochnaceæ [vricsham, 34]. Alias Ochna lucida, obtusata. Small tree; leaves from narrow-oblong to oblong-ovate, obtuse or acute, serrated; racemes springing from the apex of a short, lateral, almost leafless shoot; pedicels elongated; sepals oval; petals and ovaries seven to twelve; stigma capitate; anthers linear, elongated; flowers yellow fragrant; flowering in february and march. Wood reddish-brown, moderately hard, close-grained; warps and splits. Another species is wightiana.

SHILAY (शिला - shilá, *San.*; சிலை - shilai, *Tam.*). From (shi, san. to sharpen). Stone. The fixed idol [vigraham] of a temple [coil, pagoda] usually of black granite [caroom cull], not removed for processions [pradacshinam]; Moola vigraham [q.v.] or the principal idol as opposed to Ootsava vigraham or the festival idol carried about in processions. In tamul the latter is known as Yezhoondarool nauyagar or the move-about lord [maunasauram].——*Shilahaura* (शिलाहार - shiláhára, San.). Dynasty, probably Dravidian, that ruled in the Northern concan [q.v.] from about 810 to 1260 A.D.——*Shilah vamsham* (शिलावंश - shilávamsha, San.). Dynasty of the ancient rulers of Nundapore. See vol. I, 61.——*Shilajit* (शिलाजित् - shilájit, San.; سلاجیت - salájít, Hind.; ಶಿಲಾಜತ್ತು - shilájittu, Can.; శిలాజిత్తు - shilájittu, Tel.; சிலாசத்து - shilásattu, Tam.). San. from (shilá, san. stone + jí, san. to conquer); fossil exudation [blue-flowered chiretta, himalayan chiretta]. San. also (shilájatu), meaning stone lac; supposed to issue from stones of mountains in hot weather. Title otherwise Mineral caoutchouc, Mineral tallow, Mineral tar, Mineral wax. Bitumen; substance exuding from rocks in hot weather, produced in mountains where iron [auhan] abounds; a dark sticky unctuous substance, in appearance like the vegetable bdellium [q.v.], taste bitter, smell like stale cow's urine; medicinally alterative tonic, specially useful in urinary diseases, diabetes, gravel, anæmia, consumption, cough and skin diseases. Asphalt is solid bitumen; black or brownish black, insoluble in alcohol but soluble in naphtha [nift]; otherwise jew's pitch, mineral pitch. Petroleum is fluid bitumen, otherwise mineral naphtha, persian naphtha or rock naphtha [munn teilam]. Carpoor shilajit, from (karpúra, san. camphor + above) is a foliated granular gypsum of a reddish grey color; soft, translucent, and easily broken; an impure variety of alabaster; imported; when pounded, sprinkled over excoriations and ichorous ulcers. See vol. II, 39.——*Shilastaupanam* (शिला-स्थापन - shilást'hápana, San.). From (above + st'hápana, san. erecting). A ceremony. Setting a stone or stones at a funeral ceremony to personify a deceased ancestor [pitry], whose spirit is supposed to enter and remain in it while the ceremonies are performed. Done on the second day after death [shoodcaud]. See vol. II, 237.——*Shilaubhishaicam* (शिलाभिषेक - shilábhishéka, San.). From (above + abhishéka, san. ablution). Part of funeral ceremony [shoodcaud]. See vol. II, 237.——*Shilodvausanam* (शिलोद्वासन - shilódvásana, San.). From (above + udvásana, san. abandoning). Setting free of the stones [shilastaupanam]. Thrown into water on the tenth day, after which all the relatives bathe. See vol. II, 237.——*Silauras* (शिलारस - shilárasa, San.; میعه سائله - míahisáilah, Ar.; سلارس - siláras, Hind. and Dec.; رسمال - rasamála, Malay; நெரியாசிப்பால் - neriyásippál, Tam.). Title from hindostany. San. from (shilá, san. stone + rasa, san. juice). Ar. from (míah, ar. storax + sáilah, ar. liquid). Tam. from (niryása, san. resin + pál, tam. milk). General term for the gum-resin of either Altingia excelsa, noronha [java storax], Liquidambar orientale [indian storax], or Styrax officinale [true storax].——*Sillair* (సిల్లేరు - silléru, Tel.). From (shilá, san. stone + éru, tel. river); from its course through mountainous country. River; Vizagapatam dist., Jeypore zemindarry, Mulkangherry magisterial division. Rises in Jeypore hills. Flows east then north to Oomauda where it turns west and finally south-west and joins the Severy at Motoo, about 20 miles north-east of the junction of the latter with the Godavery. Total length, about 150 miles. The course is tortuous and through mountainous country. Forms the boundary between Rekapully talook and Mulkangherry talook of the district of Vizagapatam.

SHIMBEAM (شین بین - shínbaín, *Hind.*). A corruption from burmese (shín, to join side by side + byín, plank). A thick plank used in constructing the side of a ship. It is not sawn, but split from green trees.

SHINGLE TREE (ಹೌಲಿಗೆ - haulígo, *Can.*; மலைக்கோன் - malaikkón, *Tam.*). Title from use for roofing. Can. from (hauru, can. lightness), light timber. Tam. from (malai, tam. mountain + kóu, tam. king). Can. also (kalinji). Title otherwise King of the mountains, Pink cedar, Red cedar. Botanically Acrocarpus fraxinifolius, wight, leguminosæ [vricsham, 48]. Large tree, deciduous, often having large buttresses, bark light grey, young parts golden pubescent; leaves glabrous, bipinnate; pinnæ three pairs with a terminal one; leaflets equally pinnate, four to six, opposite pair ovate, acuminate; racemes many-flowered; flowers dull greenish-red; calyx and corolla minutely golden-pubescent outside. Timber flesh-colored, shrinks in seasoning; light and much resembles Cedrela toona, roxb. [toon], has a cedelaceous smell; much used by planters for roofing as shingles, building purposes, furniture, &c.

SHIR (சிறு - shiru, *Tam.*). Small [cher, chinna, chit, chota, coor]. Prefix in place names; as in Shirvayal, meaning small field.——*Seetaur* (சிற்றாறு - shittáru, Tam. sítár *). From (shiru, tam. small + áru, tam. river). River; Tanjore dist., Nunnilam and Negapatam tals. Branches from the Vettaur at Cangalancherry. A small river irrigating a portion of Nunnilam talook.——*Shiroocoody* (சிறுகுடி - shirugudi, Tam.). From (above + kudi, tam. village). Village of hilly tracts [coorchy].——*Shiroomullay* (சிறுமலை - shirumalai, Tam. sirumalai *). From (shiru, tam. small + malai, tam. hill). Mountain; Madura dist., Dindigul tal.; lat. 10° 07′ to 10° 18′; long. 77° 58′ to 78° 07′; height 4,522; from Dindigul S.S.W. 5 miles; from Madura N.N.W. 23 miles. A few miles east of the Pulneys. Extreme length about 20 miles. The undulating plateau at its top is cool and agreeable. Rather feverish. Noted for plantains [q.v.].——*Shitt* (சிற்று - shittu, Tam.). From (shiru, tam. small). Small. Prefix in place names; as Shittarasore, meaning the small royal village.——*Shree choornam* (శ్రీచూర్ణము - shríchúrnamu, Tel.). From (above + chihna, san. clarion). Form is a corruption. Trumpets blown with one mouth in pairs before a priest [acharry, mahant] or in the temple [coil, pagoda].——*Siroogooppa* (శిరుగుప్ప - shiruguppa, Tel. siruguppa *). From (shiru, tel. small + kuppa, tel. mound).—"*a*" Deputy tahsildarry, Bellary district. Pay Rs. 70.—"*b*" Village, Deputy tahsildar's station; Bellary dist., Bellary tal.; pop. 5,478; acres 7,417; lat. 15° 32′; long. 76° 56′; from Adony W. 28 miles; from Bellary N. 34 miles; from Hospett N.E. 42 miles; from Hurpanhully N.E. 82 miles; from Madras N.W. 288 miles; from Tadpatry W.N.W. 90 miles. On S. bank of Toongabudra. Site of anicut [q.v.] by which large channels [q.v.] are taken off Toongabudra. Weekly market.——*Sirwail* (చిరువెళ్ల - chiruvella, Tel.). See sep. title.

SHIRAH (شيره - shírah, *Hind.*). Means juice. Indian ink [mashy, shye] made with lamp-black [caujal]; the blackness of this never diminishes unless injured by wet.

SHIRRY (ಸಿಡಿ - sidi, *Can.*; సిడి - sidi, *Tel.*; செடில் - shedil, *Tam.*). From (sidi, tel. hook). A beam of wood traversing on upright post upon a pivot, to the ends of which persons are fastened to be whirled round at the hook-swinging festivals [shedil]. Churruck of Bengal. The volunteer for this is first brought to the river or tank, in which he is plunged, he then proceeds accompanied by the poojarry [q.v.] and bajantry [q.v.] to the temple, where he prostrates himself before the god, is perfumed with sandal [q.v.], is decorated with flowers, receives a benediction from the priest, goes three times round the temple with the same attendants, and afterwards performs a similar circuit round the Shirry itself. He is then suspended in the air by passing a hook through the sinews of his back. The hook is at the end of a chain which hangs from horizontal beam. The operation is said to be to a great extent painless [maryauday].——*Shedil* (செடில் - shedil, Tam.). From (sidi, tel. hook). Same as Shirry.

SHIVA (शिव - shiva, *San.*; சிவன் - shivan, *Tam.*). From (shvi, san. to thrive). ζεύς of Greeks; Jupiter of Romans; Osiris of Egyptians. Osiris and Isis correspond with Shiva and Parvaty.——**(1)** The history of Sheivism in relation to Southern india has been given in the foot-note on the history of Hindoo religion at vol. I (73) to (76). At the present day the followers of Shiva consider him to be the highest god and merely call him Eeshwaran or supreme being. Though Shiva is the term generally used in these pages, yet Eeshwaran [q.v.] is the name that would be heard among sheiveites. The office of Roodran [q.v.] or destruction is given to Shiva but this character is much attenuated by legend. In the creed of the people it is the village goddesses who represent the furies and destruction, and Shiva has never been assimilated in that character. The followers of Shiva form, in the southern part of the peninsula, the great majority, and are distinguished from the others by the mark of burnt cowdung [tirneer, vibhooty] on their foreheads. Their principal and often repeated form of prayer [muntram] is Namashivauya which is called Punchauesharam [q.v.], 5 characters, and means, salutation to Shiva. Among the Sheivas there are many different sects. Sixteen divisions are specially recognised:—abhaidam, addhwam, anaudy, anoo, antaram, audy, bhaidam, goonam, kriyah, maha, naulpaudam, nirgoonam, nyannam, oordhwam, shooddham and yogam. See also Samayam.——**(2)** Shiva is represented in the temple by the lingam [q.v.] alone. In the arts he is represented by manifold images. Most frequently this is by a human figure in a standing posture, with four arms and hands, two of which he lifts up, holding in one a deer [mrigam] and in the other a mazhoo [q.v.] or battle-axe, and two he keeps empty. He is of gigantic stature, his color is white or ashy; he has a perpendicular eye [trinetran] on his forehead, which when opened emits destructive fire; the crescent moon [chundran] is on his forehead, and the goddess gungay [q.v.] in his hair; he wears the hide of an elephant [q.v.] and the skin of a tiger [pooly]; he bears a necklace of human skulls [cuncaulan], and deadly serpents [vausooky] are entwined about his arms; in his hands he holds various emblems, the most redoubtable of which is a shoolam [q.v.] or trident, and next a strangulative cord [pausham], whence the epithet pashoopaty [q.v.], lord of life; there are certain peculiarly destructive times when he dances for joy [taundavam]. He has two human prototypes. The first appears in Shiva, as the husband of Saty [q.v.] who was, daughter of Dacshan [q.v.]. The second type occurs when Shiva reappears at the churning the milk-sea, swallows the poison [neelacuntan] of the serpent Vausooky [q.v.], and remains for a night in the apparent stupor of death but recovers [coormam, pradosham]. The fact of chundran [q.v.] or the moon being placed on the forehead of shiva, shows some connection; as of bramha [q.v.] with the earth, and of vishnoo [q.v.] with the sun; somavauram [q.v.] or monday is a special day with sheivas; the more so if any religious duty or observance fall thereon; the chief sheiva processions [ootsavam] take place in the night of the full moon [powrnimay]. Shiva is sometimes represented with five faces. His wife is Parvaty [q.v.]. His sons are Vigneshwaram [q.v.], Soobramanyan [q.v.] and Veerabhadran [q.v.]. His heaven is Keilausam [q.v.] in the Himalayas. He is also represented as sitting on a bull [nundy], together with his consort Parvaty. The bull on which he rides is called Rishabham [q.v.], and Nundikeshwaran [nundy], which may be seen in all pagodas that are built in honor of Shiva. In front of the larger ones, the bull is under a portico in a lying posture with his face towards the temple [coil, pagoda].——**(3)** Shiva's principal names are the following:—Ambica bhaugan or the ambicay or parvaty-sided; Anandan or the blissful; Ananta nautan or the infinite lord; Andivurnan or the twilight-colored; Annaumalay nautan or the lord of arnauchellam or the red hill lord [trinomalee]; Aulamar cadavool or the banyan [q.v.] god; Bhoota nautan or the lord of the demons; Bhoovaneshanautan or the lord of the world; Bramha or the supreme one; Cadavool or the supreme being; Cadookeiyan or he who wears a garland of the cassia fistula [common condray]; Calinga royan or calinga king; Capauly or the skull-wearer; Caulacaulan or the conqueror of caulan or yaman [q.v.], the king of death; Caulatty appan or the calastry father; Cauliyodaudy or the dancer with cauly; Cauyauronan or his name at negapatam; Chandra shekharan or the moon-crested; Chidambara moorty or the supernal sky form; Coondravilly or the hill archer, as having made mount meroo his bow; Cuncaulan or the bone-wearer; Cunnisoody or the garland-wearer; Devamany or the divine gem; Eeshaunan or the universal ruler; Gungavenyan or he whose hair is adorned with the river ganges; Haran or the supremely powerful; Ireiyone or king; Jyoty or the light; Keilaiyauly or the lord of keilausam; Mahashivan or the great shiva; Maheswaran or the great lord; Maraimoothal or the author of the vedams [q.v.]; Masilauthavar or the spotless; Maudevan or the great god; Maunidamendy or he who holds a deer in his hand; Maunyaula moorty or the great lord of the world; Mooccunnan or the three-eyed; Moonnone or the ancient one; Mungay bhaugan or the virgin-sided; Nakkan or the naked; Namban or the supremely desirable; Nundikeshwaran or the bull-lord; Nanjooraicuntan or he who had poison in his throat; Nateshan or the dancing lord; Nauribhaugan or the female-sided; Nautan or the lord; Neelacuntan or the blue-throated; Nirmalan or the spotless; Nityan or the eternal one; Oooma sahitan or he who is united with oomay [q.v.] or parvaty; Punchamookhan or the five-faced; Paraman or the highest; Paramashivan or the celestial shiva; Parameshwaran or the sublime lord; Parashoopauny or the battle-axe wearer; Pariyairy or the horse-rider; Parvaty cozhnan or the husband of parvaty; Pashoopaty or the lord of souls; Paundarungan or the white-colored dancer; Peyodaudy or the dancer with a demon; Pillaityaugar or the child-giver; Pinauca pauny or the trident bearer; Pingacan or he who wears matted hair; Piraisoody or the crescent-moon crested; Pongaravanindon or he who is adorned with a raging serpent; Poorauntacan or the city destroyer; Roodran or the furious or the disperser of tears; Sadaushivan or the eternal shiva; Shadaimoody or he who is crowned with entangled locks; Shambhoo or the happiness maker; Shaurndauray cauttavar or the protector of them who take refuge with him; Shenjadaiyeeshar or the red-locked lord; Shokkanautan or the handsome lord; Shoodalaiyaudy or the dancer on the place where dead bodies are burnt; Shoolapaunyan or the trident wearer; Shuncaran or the author of good; Swargauaickan or the lord of heaven; Tatparan or the self-existent; Taundava moorty or the dancing god; Varan or the giver of gifts; Vishwanautan or the lord of the world; Vriddhauchella moorty or the ancient hill god; Yecaumbaran or lord of the undivided garment; Yendolan or the eight-shouldered; Yogy or the ascetic, &c.—— **(4)** The images to be found in Shiva pagodas [q.v.] are the following.—"*a*" Aroopatt moover [q.v.], or the sixty-three persons who were taken visibly into bliss [mocsham] by Shiva, wherefore they are now adored with him in his pagodas [q.v.]. These are to be found only in very large pagodas.—"*b*" Ashtadio paulacans [q.v.], or the regents of the eight cardinal points, who enjoy some adoration.—"*c*" Ayyar, the lord, an image having the form of a man.—"*d*" Bheiravan [q.v.], who is represented by a human form quite naked, and said to be an incarnation of Shiva himself. Bheiravan is also often represented with the head of a dog, and the dog though otherwise regarded as unclean, is his vehicle [vauhan].—"*e*" Chidambareshwaran, or Shiva himself, represented as dancing, with his wife standing beside him.—"*f*" Chundra shekharan, or Shiva; the form in which he is carried about at festivals, riding with his wife on an ox.—"*g*" Chundra sooryan, or the sun and moon, represented in some pagodas by certain figures and images, and in others by two burning lamps. For, to a certain extent, the Tamulians worship also the sun and the moon, and make even offerings to them. On Sunday some fast in honor of the sun, which fast is called Nyayitkizhamay-vratam [q.v.], Sunday fast, or simply Nyayir [q.v.] sun. On Sunday fast especially women who wish to get male children, and to be preserved from widowhood. Fasting on Sunday is also recommended for sore-eyes; and the Sunday is the best day for taking purgatives. And so natives have also fasts at certain phases of the moon. But the other planets [graham] they adore only with a few observances.—"*h*" Dwaurapaulacas or door-keepers, and Coondodaran, the bearer of Shiva's umbrella. —"*i*" Lingam standing in the innermost part of the pagoda and adored daily three times with offerings, meant in honor of Shiva and Shacty.—"*j*" Maha lutchmy, Vishnoo's wife, a figure of stone, standing in a separate small temple and enjoying some adoration. The conjunction indicates a very early stage when there was no rivalry.—"*k*" Nundikeshwaran, the bull. He is one of the nearest to Shiva and receives therefore some adoration.—"*l*" Parvaty's image, called Ammay, or mother and adored in the same manner as Shiva.—"*m*" Soobramanyan with his two wives, Vulliyammay and Devayaunay.—"*n*" Soondramoorty, also one of those who, on account of their holy life, have a place near Shiva.—"*o*" Dandeshwara neinaur, a man who, by his holy life on earth, obtained a place near Shiva and is therefore adored with him.—"*p*" Vigneshwaran. Some of the images are made of stone, others of metal; those made of stone remain always in the same place, whereas those made of metal are carried about in the streets at festivals on wooden vehicles [vauhan], representing birds and animals [poonyaprauny]. The large pagodas [coil, pagoda] have large cars [rath], on which the images of the gods are carried about once every year. These cars have six wheels and the form of a tower, and on all sides there are carvings, representing the stories concerning Shiva. At festivals when they are dragged they are adorned with shells, &c.; and on each there are, besides the idol, Bramins, dancing-girls, and musicians. They differ as to size; some are very large, so large that for each one from 500 to 1,000 men are required to drag it. In connection with every large pagoda there are five cars; the first for Shiva, the second for Ammay or Parvaty, the third for Vigneshwaran, the fourth for Soobramanyan, and the fifth for Dandeshwaraneinaur; and at processions they follow each other in this order, Vigneshwaran, Soobramanyan, Shiva, Ammay, Dandeshwaran.—— **(5)** The festivals celebrated in honor of Shiva are very numerous, for at every one of the 1,008 places where he is believed to have appeared, an anniversary of the event is celebrated, at which the respective story is acted. But two annual festivals, named Tircalyaunam [pundigay, 6d] sacred wedding, and Maurgaly tirmanjanam [pundigay, 6d] or the anointing of idols in the month Maurgaly [mausam] or December-January, when it is done with more than usual solemnity, are celebrated all over the land. The latter is best known at Chidambaram, where it is celebrated in honor of Nateshan, the dancing lord; that is to say Shiva dancing in emulation with Bhadra cauly [q.v.]. In honor of Shiva there are also various fast days observed, viz. :—"*a*" every Monday, and particularly Mondays in the month Caurteecam or November-December; Monday is the moon's day, and the moon is associated with Shiva and worn by him as a head ornament;—"*b*" the thirteenth day from every new and full moon, called Pradosha vratam;—"*c*" the Varsha pirapp [pundigay, 6d], i.e., the New-year's day;—"*d*" a fast in the month Maushy or February-March, named Shivarautry [pundigay, 6a], i.e., shiva's night; when natives watch the whole night and observe a very strict fast, supposed to be exceedingly meritorious;—"*e*" a fast in the month Auvany or August-September, called Auvany moolam [pundigay, 5b];—"*f*" a fast for women in the month Arpisy or October-November, called Kedaura vratam [pundigay, 6b]. From the observance of these fasts great benefit is expected; but as a rule they are not strict fasts; one regular meal besides milk and sweetmeats being allowed; and most of them are not observed by all the followers of Shiva, but only by the Bramins and those who are specially orthodox.—— **(6)** The books written in honor of Shiva are very numerous. There is, in the first place, a set of sacred Sheiva works, named Augamams [q.v.], twenty-eight in number, containing copious directions for the various rites of worship and much other abstruse matter not deemed proper to be read by the vulgar. There are further many local Pooraunams [stala pooraunam], which contain the stories said to have happened at the 1,008 places sacred to Shiva; and there are moreover the great Pooraunams [q.v.], secondary sacred writings, which treat for the greater part of Shiva. Of the local and the great Pooraunams, and other Sheiva books, those best known are the following:—"*a*" Annaumalay nautan vannam, i.e., annaumalay nautan's ode.—"*b*" Arnagiry antandy, containing 100 hymns about Shiva, in which the end of every line forms the beginning of the following one.—"*c*" Caushy caundam, a part of the Scaunda-pooraunam in which are related the wonders performed by Shiva at Caushy, or Benares.—"*d*" Canyauronar oolah, relating his deeds as Cauyauronan at Negapatam.—"*e*" Chidambara maulay, a collection of hymns about his deeds at Chidambaram.—"*f*" Marcandeya pooraunam, in which is related the story of a Bramin's son, who was destined by Shiva to become only 16 years old, that is to say to remain always 16 years old without dying. But Yaman, the king of death, not knowing in what sense he should become only 16 years old, came to fetch him when he was of that age; upon which Shiva came forth out of a lingam, and killed him, restoring him however afterwards again to life, in consequence of the intercession of the gods.—"*g*" Mathooray pooraunam, which is also called Aroopatt naul vilei-yaudal pooraunam, because it contains an account of the sixty-four plays of Shiva as Swarganaickan at Madura.—"*h*" Nenjvidoo tooth, setting forth Shiva's praise.—"*i*" Ottara bodhacam, setting forth his praise and mighty deeds as Mylapore poorshan at St. Thomé or Mylapore.—"*j*" Paramarahasya maulay, containing 100 hymns in honor of Shiva, by Namashivauyam.—"*k*" Periya pooraunam, i.e., the large pooraunam, containing many stories about Shiva's sixty-three special devotees [aroopatt moover]. —"*l*" Sawmiperil vunnam, i.e., ode on the lord.—"*m*" Scaunda-pooraunam, which contains, among other stories, one about Shiva's marriage with Parvaty; and one about Shoorapudman, who, by severe penance, obtained great power from Shiva, but became afterwards tyrannical in consequence of which the gods had a great war with him, and in this he was finally slain.—"*n*" Shivarautry pooraunam, containing the story that gave occasion for the annual fast of this name.—"*o*" Tairoornda vauchacam, in which is related how Shiva revived a certain king's son at Warriore, over whose body a carriage had gone, because his own carriage had gone over a calf.—"*p*" Tirvarore oolah, relating his deeds as Tyaugaroyar in Tirvarore.—"*q*" Tirvencata pooraunam, containing diffuse stories about Shiva at Tirvengadam. The temple at Tirvengadam or Tripatty was taken possession of by Ramaunoojan [q.v.] for Vishnoo [q.v.] in the twelfth century.—"*r*" Vanthavore pooraunam which contains many stories about Shiva at Vauthavore, where he appeared as teacher of Tennavan bramharoyan, the writer of the Maunikya vauchacam, who spent an immense sum of money in building pagodas and tanks, and did many miracles by the help of Shiva.—"*s*" Vazhippatt, a poetical composition which is chanted when one dies, containing prayers to Shiva, that he may soothe the pains of death and receive the soul into bliss.—"*t*" Vriddhauchella pooraunam, containing the stories that are said to have happened at Vriddhauchellam.—"*u*" Yecaumbaranautar oolah, procession-hymns about the wonders which Shiva did as Yecaumbara nautan. All these books are written in poetry. For the followers of Shiva see Sheiva siddhauntam below.—— **(7)** The rivalry between Veishnavism and Sheivism is incessant. The Veishnavite acknowledges but one God; he speaks of Vishnoo as if there were no other God. So with the devotee of Shiva even in a greater degree; he transposes the name into the neuter Shivam, and expresses thus his belief that his deity is the one great essence, without sex or corporeal shape [autmam]. The Bhaugavatam thus denounces the worshippers of Shiva:—"Those who profess "the worship of Bhavan, and those who follow their doctrines, "are heretics and enemies of the sacred Shastrams." On the side of shiva, the Pudma pooraunam says:—"From even looking at "Vishnoo, the wrath of Shiva is kindled, and from his wrath, we "fall assuredly into a horrible hell; let not therefore the name of "Vishnoo ever be pronounced." There is however a Tamul proverb:—அரியும்சிவனும் ஒன்று அல்ல என்கிறவன் வாயில் மண்—"Vishnoo and Shiva are one; let sand be put "into the mouth of him who denies it [matam]." The strange conjunction of rival gods under the same roof, or at least within the same temple wall, is exemplified at the well-known pagoda [q.v.] at Trivettore close to the town of Madras, where Shiva is adored under the name Audipooreeshwaran, known as Tyaugaraja sawmy. One corner of his pagoda has been taken possession of by a Shacty [q.v.] or plebeian goddess called Tripoora soondary, but vulgarly Vuttapauray nauchiyaur. The god has a Shiva bramin as his priest and has his spouse Parvaty with him. But the Shacty or pariah goddess has for priest an Otchan [q.v.]. This goddess's feast lasts ten days, during which Shiva and his spouse receive no worship. All Hindoos, even those the most respectable classes in the town of Madras, flock to this pagoda. This god's name, Tyaugarajan, has become a common proper name. The universal sacrifice of Sarwa medham [yaugam] is offered to shiva. He is the only god to whom animal sacrifices are offered. The Vilvam [bael] tree is sacred to him, and chaplets of the leaves and flowers are worn by him. Two or more horizontal lines [vibhooty] made of ashes of cowdung [shauny] or sandal [q.v.] wood, either with or without a single dot or Pottoo [q.v.], on the forehead, typical of Shiva's third eye, are marks of a Sheiva. The Sheiva sect was confirmed by Shuncaracharry [shuncaran]. A Veera sheiva is a lingayet [q.v.].——**(8)** Shiva is also a common plant first term, in the sense of the plant being sacred to him or useful in destroying diseases or white in color or tri-partite in leaf or seeds like his phallus emblem. Ex., where transl. is of second term :—Datura fastuosa, var. alba (shivapriyá), dear; Indigofera aspalathoides (shivanárvémbu), (shivanimba), melia azadirachta; Methonica superba (shivaraktiballi), red + creeper, (shivashakti), power; Parkia biglandulosa (shivalingamara), emblem + tree; Rauwolfia serpentina (shivanábhiballi). poison + creeper; Sphæranthus amaranthoides (shivakkarandai), ocimum basilicum; Terminalia chebula (shivá) auspicious. See gloss. paragraphs.——**(9)** As regards trees sacred to Shiva, Ægle marmelos, corr. [bael] is, as above indicated, the principal. To him are also dedicated the Saraca indica, linn. [bengal ashocam], Cæsalpinia pulcherrima, swartz. [gold mohur tree], Jasminum sambac, ait. [arabian jasmine], Guettarda speciosa, linn. [indian zebra wood], Calophyllum inophyllum, linn. [common poon], Origanum marjorana, linn. [marwah], Ixora coccinea, linn. [jungle geranium], Nerium odorum, soland. [gannair], Chrysanthemum indicum, dec. [shaumanty]. For other sacred plants see Poonyoshadhy. ——**(10)** *Sheivam* (शैव - shaiva, San.). From (shiva, san. the god). Any one of the sixteen orthodox systems of the Sheiva religion, mentioned above.——*Sheiva siddhauntam* (शैवसिद्धान्त - shaivasiddhánta, San.). From (above + siddhánta, san. doctrine). The orthodox philosophy of the tamul Sheivas. Its standards are the twenty-eight Augamams [q.v.]. The Sheivas claim ten of the eighteen great Pooraunams [q.v.]; but only an abridgment of one of them, the Scaunda pooraunam, has yet been printed in Tamul.—"*a*" In the Sheiva philosophy, as in Ramaunoojan's veishnavite system, there are three eternal entities, Paty [q.v.], Pashoo [q.v.], Pausham [q.v.]; deity soul, matter. God and the soul are declared to be distinct. Matter cannot proceed from spirit; therefore the world was not developed from the deity. The great object set before men is to seek deliverance from the bondage of matter by Nyaunam [q.v.], divine knowledge. The soul will then be united to God, and freed from future births [mocsham, samsauram].—"*b*" The Sheivas suppose that there are four stages in religious life before union with God can be obtained. These are called Charitay, Kriyay, Yogam, and Nyaunam; resulting in Maha nyaunam. There are definite rules to guide the disciples through these successive steps. Their due observance will bring the soul to one of the heavens of the gods. Charitay results in the heaven called Saulokyam [q.v.], i.e., the state of being with god; Kriyay ends in Sauroopyam [q.v.], i.e., the state of being in the image of god; Yogam conducts to Saumeepyam [q.v.], i.e., nearness to god; Nyaunam leads to Sauyoojyam [q.v.], i.e., union with god. Charitay signifies history, and is nearly synonymous with pooraunam [q.v.]; hence this stage may be denominated the pooraunic or historic; the eighteen great pooraunams are the books of direction in this stage; it is the popular idolatry of india; the soul is under the influence of the external body, called stoola shareeram [q.v.], or body of sense [indriyam]. Kriyay [q.v.] means action; the lingam [q.v.] is supposed to be the symbol of god's mode of operating; it is the chief external object of worship in this stage; the soul is under the influence of its second body, called lingashareeram [q.v.]. Yogam [q.v.] signifies meditation; this is the ascetic stage; it is characterised by a peculiar course of dreamy meditations: the soul is chiefly under the influence of its third body, called autma shareeram [q.v.], soul-like body; it is in this state that the soul has dreams and visions in sleep, which readily indicates the dreamy mode of meditation, and the spiritual visions obtained in this stage; the aids of the yogam course are necessary to help the soul on into the light of wisdom; in this stage the soul is in darkness; and yet it has attained to some idea of the light desired, and struggles for it; hence the yogy's neglect of his body. Nyaunam [q.v.] means wisdom; the soul is now under the influence of the fourth body, having escaped from the entanglements of the three exterior bodies; this body is denominated paramautma shareeram, the heavenly soul-like body; the breath communicates with this fourth body; the great object is to get a vision of god; this is sought to be attained in the following way; the nyauny seats himself on a tiger-skin or some other sacred article; having closed all the orifices of the body except the right nostril, he throws, by the power of thought, the awful name of the deity, om [q.v.], or namashivauya, upon the breath a few inches before the nose; he then draws in a full breath and closes the nostril as long as possible; while this form of god is thus floating around in the region of the soul, the soul is engaged in intense meditation, looking for a vision of deity; when the breath can be no longer retained, it is exhaled by the opposite nostril, when that is again closed, and the soul is left to meditate on the deities enthroned in his body; after a long course the light breaks in, the vision is obtained; the deity is seen in the form of a circular light, with an intensely bright spot, or luminous ring, in the centre; the man has now passed into light, and sees things as they are; he hears a divine sound, sees the five mystic letters [punchaucsharam] and receives a consciousness of the essential union between his soul and god, that they are one in essence, now separated only as the air in an earthen vessel is from that without; break the vessel, and they are one; he has now become a nyauny, or wise man; he has escaped entirely from the influence of his senses, appetites, and passions, and even from the influence of his intellectual powers; let his body do what it will, yet his soul sins not; he still inhabits the body and controls it at pleasure, but his soul receives no influence in return.—"*c*" A man may die in this stage, or pass into the condition of maha nyaunam, or great wisdom; if he dies in this stage he will be born but once more, and then a nyauny in the higher stage; in maha nyaunam the visions of the soul are all bright, undefined, formless splendour; the man is now a god; he waits only for the look of deity to annihilate his body, when the souls will pass away pure, and again become one with the eternal essence.——*Shivabhacticauran* (சிவபத்திக்காரன் - shivabattikkáran, Tam.). From (above + bhakti, san faith + kára, san. doer). A Sheiva devotee.——*Shivacaumy* (शिवकामी - shivakámí, San.). From (above + káma, san. desire). Parvaty [q.v.].——*Shivachidambaram* (சிவச்சிதம்பரம் - shivaççithambaram, Tam.). Shiva at chidambaram. Hindoo 2nd or pers. name. Common among non-bramins [peyar].——*Shivacode* (శివకోడు - shivakódu, Tel.). From (above + kódu, tel. pool).—"*a*" Deputy tahsildarry, Godavary district. Pay Rs. 70.—"*b*" Village, Deputy tahsildar's station; Godavery dist., Narsapore tal.; acres 2,987; lat. 16° 28′; long. 81° 52′; from Cocanada S.W. 43 miles; from Coonavaram S.S.E. 83 miles; from Ellore E.S.E. 50 miles; from Madras N.N.E. 250 miles; from Narsapore E.N.E. 9 miles; from Rajahmundry S. 37 miles; from the sea N. 7 miles.——*Shivacomauran* (சிவக்குமாரன் - shivakkumáran, Tam.). From (above + kumára, san. child). Scandan [q.v.], child of Shiva [q.v.]. Hindoo 2nd or pers. name. Common among non-bramins [peyar]. ——*Shivadootun* (சிவதூதன் - shivathúthan, Tam.). From (above + dúta, san. servant). Shiva's messengers.——*Shivaganam* (शिवगण - shivagana, San.). From (above + gana, san. crowd) Deities attendant on Shiva [ganam].——*Shivagherry* (சிவகிரி - shivagiri, Tam. sivagiri *). From (above + giri, san. mountain). Zemindarry, Town; Tinnevelly dist., Shuncaraneinarcoil tal.; pop. of zemindarry 8,987; of village 7,888; acres of zemindarry 87,632; village 47,717; lat. of town 9° 21′; long. 77° 28′; from Shuncaraneinarcoil N.W. 14 miles; from Tinnevelly N.N.W. 46 miles. The zemindarry [q.v.] is to the north-west of the talook [q.v.]. Peshcush Rs. 54,580. Number of villages, twenty-six. ——*Shivagooroo* (சிவகுரு - shivaguru, Tam.). From (above + guru, san. preceptor). Scandan, preceptor of Shiva [gooroonautan]. Hindoo 2nd or pers. name. Common among non bramins [peyar]. Otherwise Shivagooroonautan.——*Shivagunge* (சிவகங்கை - shivagangai, Tam.). See sep. title.——*Shivagungay* (ಶಿವಗಂಗೆ - shivagange, Can.; shivagangabetta, Mys. Gov.). From (above + gangá, san. ganges); from sacred fountains on the hill. Sanscrit name (kakudgiri), meaning hump + hill; also (dakshinakáshí), meaning southern benares. Sacred hill in north-west of Nelamungala talook, Bangalore district, Mysore, 4,559 feet. On the east its outline resembles a bull, on the west Ganesh [q.v.], on the north a serpent, and on the south a lingam [q.v.].——*Shivah* (शिवा - shivá, San.). Means auspicious. Botanically the Prosopis genus, leguminosæ [vricsham, 48]. Allied to acacia [cantalam]. Erect trees or shrubs with scattered prickles; leaves twice pinnate, with small narrow leaflets; flowers small, green or yellowish; pod more or less thickened, straight or variously twisted, indehiscent. The species best known to the natives are:—dulcis [manilla tamarind], glandulosa [mesquit], pubescens [screw mesquit], spicigera [shamee].——*Shivajee* (ಶಿವಾಜಿ - shivájí, Can.). From (above + jí, hind. sir). Hindoo 2nd or pers. name. Common among Madhwas and Mahrattas [peyar]. Name of the founder of the Mahratta [q.v.] kingdom. Born 1627. Seized the hill fort of Tornea while 19, Murdered the Bejapore general. Plundered Surat and English and Dutch factories there. Assumed the title of Rajah, coined money, collected a fleet of ships, and sacked Barcelore. Defeated Aurungzeeb's general and declared independence. Invaded Carnatic [q.v.]; took Bellary, Kurnool, Jingee, Vellore. In the conduct of government he was assisted by eight ministers called Asht purdhans [pradhaun], of which Peshwah [q.v.] was the chief. Died 1680 [charitram]. See vol. I (117), (144), (149), (166); II, 253.——*Shiva locam* (शिवलोक - shivalóka, San.). From (above + lóka, san. world). Another name of Satyalocam. ——*Shivam* (சிவம் - shivam, Tam.). Supreme essence [bramh] without sex or corporeal shape.——*Shiva matam* (शिवमत - shivamata, San.). From (above + mata, san. creed). The creed of Sheivites.——*Shiva maulay* (शिवमाला - shivamálá, San.). From (above + málá, san. garland). Rosary of Saraswaty [q.v.]. ——*Shivanadiyaun* (சிவனடியான் - shivanadiyán, Tam.). Sixty-three special votaries of Shiva [aroopatt moover].——*Shivanandam* (சிவாநந்தம் - shivánandam, Tam.). From (above + ánanda, san. happiness); one who is happy in shiva. Hindoo 2nd or pers. name [peyar].——*Shivanautan* (சிவநாதன் - shivanáthan, Tam.). From (above + nát'ha, san. lord), shiva, the lord. Hindoo 2nd or pers. name [peyar].——*Shivapadam* (சிவப்பதம் - shivappatham, Tam.). From (above + pada, san. foot). Same as shiva locam. Hindoo 2nd or pers.

name [peyar].——*Shivappan* (சிவப்பன் - shivappan, Tam.). From (above + appan, tam. father). Shiva, the father. Hindoo 2nd or pers. name [peyar].——*Shivappa naick* (ಶಿವಪ್ಪ ನಾಯಕ - shivappanáyaka, Can.). Name + third name. Name of Dalavoy [q.v.] and afterwards greatest prince of Ikkairy [q.v.] family. Defeated the Jeina [q.v.] rajahs of Tooloovam and acquired Canara; captured the Portuguese settlements at Mangalore, Barcelore, and Honore.——*Shivaramakrishnan* (சிவராமக்கிருட்டிணன் - shivarámakkiruttinan, Tam.). From (above + ráma, san. the hero + krishna, san. the god). Common among smartas [q.v.] who consider shiva and vishnoo the same. Compound Hindoo 2nd or pers. name [peyar].——*Shivaraman* (சிவராமன் - shivaráman, Tam.). From (above + ráma, san. the god). Rama who worshipped shiva, as at rameshwaram. Compound Hindoo 2nd or pers. name [peyar].——*Shivarautry* (சிவராத்திரி - shivaráttiri, Tam.). From (above + rátri, san. night). The fourteenth lunar day [tity] in the dark half [krishnapacsham] of every month, sacred to Shiva. But Maha shivarautry [q.v.] is generally meant.——*Shivasamoodram* (ಶಿವಸಮುದ್ರ - shivanasamudra, Can.). From (above + samudra, san. ocean). Properly called Heggoorra. Ancient town, Island, Water-falls; Coimbatore dist., Collegaul tal.; lat. 12° 16′; long. 77° 13′; from Coimbatore N. 89 miles; from Collegaul N.N.E. 9 miles. On the south-east border of the Tirmacoodloonarsapore talook, Mysore district, Mysore. The Cauvery here branches into two streams, each of which makes a descent of about 200 feet in a succession of picturesque rapids and waterfalls. The principal island embraced within these torrents, called Shivasamoodram is about 3 miles long by ¾ of a mile broad. On the western branch of the river, which forms the boundary between Mysore and Coimbatore, are the Gaganachookky falls; these waters divide round another small island called Yetticooroo. The falls on the eastern branch of the river are called the Burra chookky and display a great volume of water. The founder of the temples of Someshwarasawmy and Rungasawmy and the city was Tiroo chola roya, King of Keralam [q.v.]. After the death of his grandson the place was deserted till Gunga roya, a petty chief of Mysore, restored it. Gunga roya committed suicide in the falls, after a reign of sixty years. In 1791, at the time of the advance of the British army upon Seringapatam, Tippoo sultan laid waste the surrounding country, and drove all the inhabitants and the cattle into this island. Subsequently the whole area became overgrown with jungle, and the old stone bridges connecting it with the main land were impassable. About 1824, their repair was undertaken by a confidential servant of the Residency of Mysore, named Ramasawmy moodelliar. He expended several thousand pounds on the work, and was rewarded by the British government with the title of Janopacaura caum curta, or public benefactor. He also received a jagheer [q.v.] from the British government, and seven villages from the Mysore state. The new bridges are built on pillars of hewn stone founded in the rocky bed of the stream, and connected by stone girders. Both the temples are elaborately sculptured and contain inscriptions. The stones of an old Jeina [q.v.] temple were used for building the bridge over the Cauvery. There is a large mosque [musjid]. A bungalow [q.v.] where European visitors are entertained by jagheerdar. During the winter months island is malarious [aroovy].——*Shiva's blood* (भवरक्त - bhavarakta, San.). From red dye of flowers. Same as Saffron.——*Shivashuncaran* (சிவசங்கரன் - shivasangaran, Tam.). From (above + shankara, san. shiva); meaning shiva the happiness-maker. Hindoo 2nd or pers. name [peyar].——*Shiva vaucyam* (शिववाक्य - shivavákya, San.). From (above + vákya, san. word). A Tamul poem on theism. The author belonged to the sect of the Siddhar [q.v.], and taught a pure theism, retaining the name of Shiva. According to the legend, Shiva vaucyan, so called after his book, became a Veishnava [q.v.] and even a christian at the time of the apostle Thomas [q.v.]; but not being satisfied, he returned to Sheivism. Sheiva pundaurams [q.v.] destroy all copies they can lay hold of. The Dharma sabhay in Madras printed an interpolated edition, in which the meaning of the original is changed into the contrary. Genuine copies are very rare. The following is a specimen passage:—பண்டுநான்பறித்தெறிந்த பன்மலர்களெத்தனை பாழிலேசெபித்துவிட்ட மந்திரங்களெத்தனை மிண்டனாய்த் திரிந்தபோதிறைத்த நீர்களெத்தனை மீளவுஞ்சிவாலயங்கள் சூழவந்ததெத்தனை அண்டர்கோனிருப்பிடமறிந்துணர்ந்தஞானிகள் கண்டகோயிற்றெய்வமென்று கையெடுப்பதில்லையே. நீனாயுள்ளி நீரில்விட்டு நீர்நினைந்தகாரிய மாரை யுன்னி நீரெல்லாமவத்திலேயிறைக்கிறீர் வேரையுன்னிவித்தையுன்னி வித்திலேமுளைத்தெழுந்த சீரையுன்னவல்லிராய் சிவபதங்கள்சேரலாம். அரியுமல்லவரனுமல்லவயனுமல்லவப்புறங் கருமைவெண்மைசெம்மையுங் கடந்துநின்றகாரணம் பெரியதல்லசிறியதல்லபெண்ணுமாணுமல்லவே துரியமுங் கடந்துநின்ற தூரதூரதூரமே. சாதியாவதேதடா சலந்திரண்டநீரல்லோ பூதமைந்துமொன்றல்லோ புலன்களைந்துமொன்றல்லோ காதுவாழிகாறைகம்பி சூடகம்பொன்னொன்றல்லோ சாதிபேதமோதுகின்ற தன்மையென்னதன்மையே. கறந்தபால்முலைபுகா கடைந்தவெண்ணெய்மோர்புகா வுடைந்தசங்கினோசையு முயிர்களுமுடல்புகா வடிந்தவோரடையினியுதிர்ந்தபூ மரம்புகா விறந்துபோனமானிட ரினிப்பிறப்பதில்லையே—"Formerly how many flowers have I "gathered and scattered? How many prayers have I repeated "in vain worship? While yet in the prime of my life, how much "water have I poured out? And moreover, how often have I "encompassed the holy places of Shiva? This I have left off, for "the wise who know the true God, the Lord of heavenly beings, "believe not the idol [shilay, vigraham] of the temples apparent "to the eyes to be God, nor lift up to it their hands [poojah]. "While taking up the water and throwing it again into the "water what is the object on which you think? On whatsoever "you think you have thrown all the water vainly. Think on the "root, think on the seed and on the benefit arising from that "seed; when you are thus able to think, you may approach the "feet of God [sundhyauvandanam]. It is not Hary [q.v.], it "is not Haran [q.v.], it is not Ayan [bramha]; far beyond the "black of Vishnoo [q.v.], the white of Shiva [q.v.] or the red "of Bramha [q.v.] soars the everlasting cause; it is not great, "it is not small, neither is it male nor female; beyond every "state of corporeal being it is farther, farther, and farther still "[autmam]. What, O wretch, is caste [jauty]? Is not water an "accumulation of fluid particles? Are not the five elements "[bhootam] and the five senses [indriyam] one? Are not the "several ornaments for the neck, the breast, and the feet "equally gold? What then is the peculiar quality supposed to "result from difference in caste? As milk once drawn cannot "again enter the udder, nor butter churned be recombined "with milk; as sound cannot be produced from a broken conch "[chunk], nor the life be restored to its body; as a decayed leaf "and a fallen flower cannot be reunited to the parent tree; so "a man once dead is subject to no future birth [samsauram]." ——*Shivayyan* (சிவய்யன - shivayyan, Tam.). From above + aiyyan, tam. master). Hindoo 2nd or pers. name [peyar].

SHIVAGUNGA (சிவகங்கை - shivagangai, *Tam.* sivaganga*). From (shiva, san. the god + gangá, san. ganges) [shiva]. Sanscrit name (dakshinakálípura), meaning south + cauly, the deity + town.——**(1)** Zemindarry, Madura district. Peshcush Rs. 2,57,430. For description see vol. 1, 56. Places of archæological interest:—Carshaucoolam, Cauleiyaur coil, Cholapooram, Coonnacoody, Coottaunda, Kizhangattore, Manalore, Maudapooram, Ooracoody, Oorvatticottay, Orciyore, Pashalay, Piraumullay, Shaittore, Shargany, Shivagunga, Tircoolacoody, Tircoottore, Tirpauchatty, Tirpoovanam, Tripatore, Vadooganautapooram, Vembangoody, Yamaneshwaram, Yilayangoody. Principal trig. station:—Shembaulavayal. The leading places, &c., in the talook are the following.——*Cauleiyaur coil* (காளையார்க்கோவில் - kálaiyárkkóvil, Tam.). From (kálaiyár, tam. shiva, the bull man + kóvil, tam. temple); temple of shiva as caulay eeshwaran or bull-lord. Sanscrit name (sómanát'hamangala), meaning moon + lord + prosperity. Village; lat. 9° 51′; long. 78° 41′; from Madura E.S.E. 36 miles; from Shivagunga E. 10 miles. Large ancient Shiva temple with inscriptions. Hamlet of Ooroovaudy.——*Cauraicoody* (காரைக்குடி - káraikkudi, Tam. káraikudi*). From (kárai, tam. thorny webera, canthium parviflorum, lamk. + kudi, tam. village). Village; pop. 5,541; lat. 9° 52′; long. 78° 50′; from Madura E.S.E. 44 miles; from Shivagunga E. 21 miles. Next in importance to Devacottah as the abode of Nautcottay chetties [q.v.].——*Coonnacoody* (குன்னக்குடி - kunnakkudi,* Tam.). From (kunram, tam. hill + kudi, tam. village). Village, Place of pilgrimage; pop. 2,021; lat. 10° 07′; long. 78° 45′; from Madura E. 42 miles; from Shivagunga N.E. 23 miles. Two miles from the border of Poodoocottah state. Old Shiva temple with inscriptions of the Paundy [q.v.] dynasty [raj].——*Manalore* (மணலூர் - manalur,* Tam.). From (manal, tam. sand + úr, tam. village). Sanscrit name (manipura), meaning gem + town. Village; pop. 1,017; lat. 9° 52′; long. 78° 16′; from Madura E.S.E. 8 miles; from Shivagunga W. 19 miles. The Bramins have transferred here the Manipooram of the Mahabhaurat [q.v.] the Paundyan [q.v.] capital.——*Mauna madura* (மானாமதுரை - mánámathurai, **Tam.** mánamadura*). From (mán, tam. greatness + á, tam. negative particle + mathurai, tam. town so called); little Madura. But supposed to be a corruption from (vánaramathurai), meaning monkey madura, from tradition that hanooman [q.v.] halted here with his monkey allies on his way to lunka [q.v.]. Village, Additional district moonsif's station; pop. 3,997; lat. 9° 41′; long. 78° 29′; from Madura S.E. 28 miles; from Shivagunga S. 11 miles. Pots [chatty] and bell-metal [cunts] manufactured.——*Piraumullay* (பிரமலை - pirámalai, Tam.). From (pirán, tam. lord, shiva + malai, tam. mountain). Village; pop. 2,175; lat. 10° 15′; long. 78° 29′; from Madura N.E. 30 miles; from Shivagunga N. 27 miles. Old Shiva temple richly sculptured with inscriptions of Paundy [q.v.] and Vijianugger [q.v.] dynasties [raj].——*Shembaulavayal* (செம்பாளைவயல் - shembálaivayal, Tam.). From (shembálai, tam. red paddy so called + vayal, tam. field). Trig. station; lat. 10° 02′ 31·69″; long. 78° 57′ 49·01″; height 109 feet; from Shivagunga E.N.E. 32 miles; from Tripatore E.S.E. 23 miles.——*Shivagunga*

(சிவகங்கை - shivagangai, Tam.). See below.——*Tircoottore* (திருக்கோட்டூர் - tirukkóttúr, Tam.). From (tiru, tam. holy + kódu, tam. hill-top + úr, tam. village). Village; pop. 2,045; lat. 10° 04′; long. 78° 36′; from Madura E.N.E. 31 miles; from Shivagunga N. 16 miles. Shiva temple with inscription dated A.D. 1679, regarding the Saitoopaties [q.v.] of Ramnaud.——*Tirpoovanam* (திருப்பூவனம் - tiruppúvanam, Tam. tirupuvanam *). From (tiru, tam. sacred + pú, tam. flower + vana, san. grove). Sanscrit name (pushpavana), meaning flower garden. Village; pop. 5,455; lat. 9° 50′; long. 78° 18′; from Madura S.E. 12 miles; from Shivagunga W. 16 miles. Ancient Shiva temple elaborately sculptured with numerous inscriptions and copper-plate grant [shausanam].——*Tripatore* (திருப்பத்தூர் - tiruppattúr, Tam.). See sep. title.——*Veigay* (வைகை - vaigai, Tam.). See sep. title.——*Yamaneshwaram* (இயமனேசுவரம் - iyamanésuvaram, Tam.). From (yamana, san. the god yama + íshvara, san. lord). Village; pop. 4,420; lat. 9° 32′; long. 78° 39′; from Madura S.E. 42 miles; from Shivagunga S.S.E. 21 miles. Ancient Cauly [q.v.] temple with inscription.——*Yilayangoody* (இளையாங்குடி - ilaiyángudi, Tam. ilayángudi *). From (ilaiyán, tam. younger brother + kudi, tam. village). Village; pop. 5,239; lat. 9° 37′; long. 78° 40′; from Madura S.E. 40 miles; from Shivagunga S.S.E. 18 miles. On the bund of the tank stands a Jeina [q.v.] stone figure. Old Shiva temple by Rajendra choleshwaran, with inscriptions of the Chola [q.v.] dynasty [raj].——**(2)** Deputy tahsildarry, Madura district. Pay Rs. 100.——**(3)** Town, Head-quarters of Deputy tahsildar and sub-registrar, District moonsif's station; Madura dist., Shivagunga zemindarry; pop. 8,809; lat. 9° 51′; long. 78° 32′; from Dindigul S.E. 50 miles; from Kodaykarnal E.S.E. 71 miles; from Madras S.S.W. 255 miles; from Madura E. 25 miles; from Rameshwaram W.N.W. 68 miles; from Ramnaud N.N.W. 40 miles. Residence of the zemindar. Ancient Shiva temple with inscriptions and copper-plate shausanam [q.v.].

SHIYALLY (சிய்யாழி - shiyyázhi, *Tam.* shiyáli *). From (shír, tam. beauty + kázhi, tam. town, so called). Tam. also (kázhi), meaning cauly, the deity; also (pugalúr), meaning asylum + town; also (pugali), meaning same; also (tiruppugali), meaning holy + asylum + place; also (shanbai), meaning champah, proper name + place. Sanscrit name (shríkálípura), meaning holy + cauly, the deity + town.——**(1)** Talook, Tanjore district. Tahsildar's pay Rs. 150. Area 171 square miles; pop. 119,804; language Tamul. N. coast of district. Boundaries; N. Coleroon, E. sea, W. Mayavaram talook and Coleroon, S. Mayavaram talook. Open level country. Soil sandy loam. Cloth-weaving, rattan [q.v.] works, and mat [boriyah] making; export of paddy [q.v.] and rice [q.v.]. Irrigation by Ayyavayyanaur, Caloomalaiyaur, Cauveriyaur, Moodavanaur, Poodoomunniyaur, Poravycaul, Rajah vycaul, Tirnagary vycaul. Places of archæological interest:—Atchaulpooram, Cauveryputnam, Condattore, Devicottah, Keelnangoor, Marvattore, Sayauvanam, Shiyally, Tirmeilaudy, Tirnagary, Tozhoothore, Trivengaud, Vailoor, Veitheeshwarancoil. Principal trig. stations:—Cauveryputnam beacon, Taundacoolam beacon, Tirnagary, Trimalvausal. The leading places, &c., in the talook are the following.——*Aneicaura chuttram* (ஆணிக்காரச்சத்திரம் - ánikkáraççattiram, Tam. ánaikárachattram *). From (ánaikkáran, tam. proper name + satra, san. choultry). Sanscrit name (gópálasamudram), meaning cowherd god + ocean; also (hanumantapura), meaning the monkey god + town. Village, Railway station; pop. 2,431; lat. 11° 20′; long. 79° 46′; from Shiyally N.N.W. 7 miles; from Tanjore N.E. 54 miles; from the sea W. 8 miles. Comprises the villages of Gopaulsamoodram and Hanoomantapooram. Bridge over the Coleroon. Noted for rattan [q.v.] works and mats [boriyah]. Small chuttram [q.v.] on northern bank of Coleroon. ——*Atchaulpooram* (ஆச்சாள்புரம் - áççálburam, Tam.). From (áççál, tam. párvatí, the mother of the world + pura, san. town). Sanscrit name (shivalókatyágapura), meaning shiva's world + abandoning + town. Village; pop. 1,941; acres 1,370; lat. 11° 20′; long. 79° 48′; from Shiyally N.N.W. 6 miles; from Tanjore N.E. 53 miles; from the sea W. 5 miles. Noticeable for its defence in 1749 against the Tanjore army. Old Shiva temple with inscriptions in Tamul [q.v.] and Grantam [q.v.]. During the war between the English and French, implements, ammunition, &c., were preserved in the temple.——*Cauveryputnam* (காவேரிப்பட்டணம் - kávérippattanam, Tam.). See sep. title.——*Codiyampolliem* (கொடியம்பாளையம் - kodiyambálaiyam, Tam.). From (kodiyan, tam. cruel man + pálaiyam, tam. camp). Village, Port; pop. 880; lat. 11° 23′ N.; long. 79° 51′; from Madras S.S.W. 120 miles; from Porto novo S.S.E. 9 miles; from Shiyally N.N.E. 11 miles; from Tanjore N.E. 61 miles. Near the mouth of the Coleroon; the northern most part of Tanjore district. Devicottah is close to it.——*Coleroon* (கொள்ளடம் - kolladam, Tam.). See sep. title.——*Devicottah* (தீவுக்கோட்டை - tívukóttai, Tam.). See. sep. title.——*Manigraumam* (மணிக்கிராமம் - manikkirámam, Tam.). From (mani, san. gem + gráma, san. village). Village; pop. 1,412; acres 989; lat. 11° 10′; long. 79° 52′; from Shiyally E.S.E. 8 miles; from Tanjore E.N.E. 52 miles; from the sea W. 3 miles. ——*Neydavausal* (நெய்தவாசல் - neydavásal, Tam.). From (neydal, tam. maritime tract + vásal, tam. entrance). Village; pop. 1,113; lat. 10° 10′; long. 79° 53′; from Shiyally E.S.E. 8 miles; from Tanjore E.N.E. 55 miles; from the sea W. 1¼ miles. Salt station.——*Shiyally* (சிய்யாழி - shiyyázhi, Tam.). See below.——*Taundacoolam beacon* (தாண்டக்குளம் - tándakkulam, Tam.). Trig. station; lat. 11° 19′ 9·13″; long. 79° 52′ 34·82″; from Shiyally N.E. 9 miles; from Pazhayapolliem E. 3 miles; from Poothooputnam E. 2 miles; from Vaittangoody N.N.E. 4 miles; from the sea W. ⅛ mile.——*Tirnagary* (திருநகரி - tirunagari, Tam.). From (tiru, tam. holy + nagarí, san. town). Sanscrit name (bilváranya), meaning bael [q.v.] tree, ægle marmelos, corr. + forest. Village; pop. 1,641; acres 2,150; lat. 11° 14′; long. 79° 51′; from Shiyally E. 4 miles; from Tanjore N.E. 53 miles; from the sea W. 3 miles. Old Vishnoo temple. Trig. station in lat. 11° 13′ 29·95″; long. 79° 50′ 30·26″; from Neppattore N.W. ¾ mile; from Shiyally E.S.E. 4 miles; from the sea W. 4 miles.——*Trimal vausal* (திருமுல்லைவாசல் - tirumullaivásal, Tam.). From (tiru, tam. sacred + mullai, tam. wood land + vásal, tam. entrance). Village, Port; pop. 3,643; lat. 11° 14′; long. 79° 53′; from Codiyampolliem S.S.E. 10 miles; from Madras S.S.W. 129 miles; from Shiyally E. 7 miles; from Tanjore N.E. 56 miles; from Tranquebar N. 14 miles. At the mouth of an estuary. Old Shiva temple. Trig. station in lat. 11° 14′ 16·45″; long. 79° 53′ 23·51″; from Shiyally E. 7 miles.——*Trivengaud* (திருவெண்காடு - tiruvengádu, Tam.). From (tiru, tam. sacred + ven, tam. white + kádu, tam. jungle). Sanscrit name (shvétáranya), meaning white forest. Village, Place of pilgrimage; pop. 2,639; acres 3,128; lat. 11° 11′; long. 79° 51′; from Shiyally S.E. 7 miles; from Tanjore E.N.E. 52 miles; from the sea W. 3 miles. Important place of Shiva worship. Festival in February.——*Vadaputty melaputty* (வடபாதிமேற்பாதி - vadabáthimérbáthi, Tam.). From (vada, tam. north + páthi, tam. half + mél, tam. west + páthi, tam. half). Sanscrit name (shríkálípura), meaning holy + cauly, the goddess + town. Village; pop. 4,989; lat. 11° 14′; long. 79° 44′; from Shiyally W. 4 miles; from Tanjore N.E. 48 miles; from the sea W. 11 miles.——*Veitheeshwarancoil* (வைத்தீசுவரன்கோவில் - vaittísuvarangóvil, Tam. vaithísvarankoil *). From (vaidya, san. a physician + íshvara, san. lord + kóvil, tam. temple). Sanscrit name (vaidyanát'hapura), meaning shiva, the lord of physicians + town. Village, Railway station, Place of pilgrimage; pop. 4,155; lat. 11° 12′; long. 79° 45′; height 22 feet; from Shiyally S.W. 4 miles; from Tanjore N.E. 47 miles; from the sea W. 10 miles. Old and large Shiva temple with inscriptions and two copper-plate grants.——**(2)** Town, Head-quarters of talook and District moonsif, Railway station; Tanjore dist., Shiyally tal.; pop. 6,715; acres 1,532; lat. 11° 14′; long. 79° 47′; height 21 feet; from Combaconam N.E. 32 miles; from Madras S.S.W. 131 miles; from Mayavaram N.E. 11 miles; from Munnargoody N.N.E. 43 miles; from Negapatam N.N.W. 32 miles; from Tanjore N.E. 51 miles; from the sea W. 7 miles. Large Shiva temple on a low hill with inscriptions. Mats [boriyah] made here by Lubbays [q.v.] similar to those of Palghaut but much cheaper. German lutheran mission station.

SHLAISHAY (श्लेष - shlésha, *San.*). From (shlish, san. to adhere); double meaning from context. Paronomasia.——*Shlaisha cauvyam* (శ్లేషకావ్యము - shléshakávyamu, Tel.). From (above + kávya, san. poem). A kind of poetry, each stanza of which conveys a double meaning.

SHLOCAM (श्लोक - shlóka, *San.*). From (shlók, san. to compose). A couplet. Also a Sanscrit epic metre, consisting of four verses of eight syllables each or two lines of sixteen syllables each.

SHOE FLOWER (සපත්තුමල - sappattumala, *Singh.*). From use of flowers in blacking shoes. Same as China rose bendy.

SHOL (சொல் - shol, *Tam.*). Word [mozhy]. A saying or proverb. Declaration, promise. The following are from Cooral:—*நிறைமொழி மாந்தர் பெருமை நிலத்து மறைமொழி காட்டி விடும்*—"the hidden words of the men whose "words are full of effect, will show their greatness to the world."—*சொல்லுக சொல்லிற் பயனுடைய சொல்லற்க சொல்லிற் பயனிலாச் சொல்*—"speak what is useful, and speak "not useless words."—*நாநல மென்னு நலனுடைமை யந்நலம் யாநலத் துள்ளதூஉ மன்று*—"the possession of that "goodness which is called the goodness of speech is even to "others better than any other goodness."—*திறனறிந்து சொல்லுக சொல்லை யறனும் பொருளு மதனினூஉங் கில்*—"understand the qualities of your hearers and then make your "speech; for superior to this there is neither virtue nor wealth."—*சொலல்வல்லன் சோர்விலன் அஞ்சா னவனை யிகல்வெல்லல் யார்க்கு மரிது*—"it is impossible for any one to conquer "him by intrigue who possesses power of speech, and is neither "faulty nor timid."—*பலசொல்லக் காமுறுவர் மன்றமாசற்ற சிலசொல்ல றேற்றா தவர்*—"they will desire to utter "many words, who do not know how to speak a few faultless "ones."—*உணர்வ துடையார்முற் சொல்லல் வளர்வதன் பாத்தியு ணீர்சொரிந் தற்று*—"lecturing to those who have "the ability to understand for themselves is like watering a bed "of plants that are growing of themselves."—உளரொனிறு மில்லாரோ டொப்பர் களனஞ்சிக் கற்ற செலச்சொல்லா தார்—"those who through fear of the assembly are unable "to set forth their learning in an interesting manner, though "alive, are yet like the dead."—நிலத்திற் கிடந்தமை கால் காட்டுங் காட்டுங் குலத்திற் பிறந்தார்வாய்ச் சொல்—"as the sprout indicates the nature of the soil, so the speech "of the noble indicates that of their birth."

SHOLAH (ಶೋಲೆ - shóle, *Can.*; சோலை - shólai, *Tam.*). A shruberry; as opposed to tope [q.v.] which is a plantation of tall trees. Not to be confounded with solah [q.v.], the soft root of Æschynomene aspera, linn. To plant a sholah is one of the thirty-two kinds of charity [santaunam, shaulay]. In Anglo-indian usage, a wooded ravine; especially on the Neilgherries or in the Wynaud.——**(1)** The sholahs on the Neilgherries are innumerable, and hold up the water supplying that tract. The best known of these to the English are the following, to which the native names are given and the distance from Ootacamund. ——*Aramby plantation* (ಅಗ್ಗಲುಶೋಲೆ - aggálushóle, Can.; குரங்குச்சோலை - kuranguççólai, Tam.). Can. from (aggala, can. great). Tam. from (kurangu, tam. monkey). 1¾ miles N.W. Same as Monkey sholah.——*Aundy plantation* (ಪಿಚಲುಶೋಲೆ - píchalushóle, Can.; ஆண்டிச்சோலை - ándiççólai, Tam.). Can. from (pichula, can. tamarind tree). Tam. from (ándi, tam. the caste). Four miles W. by S.——*Baikie wood* (ಬೈಕಿಶೋಲೆ - baikishóle, Can.; பெயிக்கிசோலை - peyikkisólai, Tam.). Three miles W. by S.——*Briar sholah* (ಆನೆಕುಂದುಗೋಡುಮಂದುಶೋಲೆ - ánekundugódumandushóle, Can.; செம்மண்ணுக்குளிச்சோலை - shemmannukkuliççólai, Tam). Can. from (áne, can. elephant + kundru, tam. rock + kódu, can. hill + mandu, can. todah village). Tam. from (shem, tam. red + man, tam. earth + kuzhi, tam. pit). Eight miles W. by N.——*Brooklands* (ಪಿಳ್ಳೇತಾಚಿಮಂದುಶೋಲೆ - pillétáchimandushóle, Can.; பிள்ளைத்தாச்சிமந்து - pillaittáççimandu, Tam.). Can. from tamul. Tam. from (pillaittáyççi, tam. woman with child). 3¾ miles N. by W.——*Cully plantation* (ಮಾವಿದಿಮಂದುಶೋಲೆ - mávidimandushóle, Can.; கள்ளிச்சோலை - kalliççólai, Tam.). Can. from (mávi, can. mango + mandu, can. todah village). Tam. from (kalli, tam. milk-hedge). Also Aganaud. 3½ miles W. by N. Same as Katerfelto sholah. ——*Druid sholah* (ಕವ್ವೆಗಾಡುಮಂದುಶೋಲೆ - kavvegádumandushóle, Can.; கவ்வெக்காடுமந்துசோலை - kavvekkádumandusólai, Tam.). Can. from (kave, can. two + kádu, can. forest + mandu, can. todah village). Tam. same. 3½ miles W. by S.——*Fair lawns* (ಕವ್ವೆಶೋಲೆತಿರಿಯೇರಿಶೋಲೆ - kavveshóletireyérishóle, Can.; கவ்வெசோலை - kavvesólai, Tam.). Can. from (kave, can. two + tiru, tam. holy + yér, can. buffalo). Tam. from (kave, can. two). S.W. 3¼ miles by cart road; but by bridle-path, W.S.W. 2½ miles.——*Governor's sholah* (ಕುಂದಗೋಡುಶೋಲೆ - kundagódushóle, Can.; கவர்னர்சோலை - kavarnarsólai, Tam.). Can. from (kundru, tam. rock + kódu, can. hillock). W. by S. 5 miles.——*Hanging sholah* (ನೇರಗೋಡುಮಂದುಶೋಲೆ - néragódumandushóle, Can.; நேர்க்கோடுமந்து - nérkkódumandu, Tam.) Can. and Tam. from (nér, tam. straight + kódu, can. hillock + mandu, can. todah village). Eight miles N.W.; 3 miles as crow flies.——*Jackal sholah* (ನರಿಶೋಲೆ - narishóle, Can.; நரிசோலை - narisólai, Tam.). Can. and Tam. from (nari, tam. jackal). Can. also (mallishóle), meaning jasmine. 2½ miles W. by S.——*Katerfelto sholah* (ಮಲೆವಿದಿಮಂದುಕೋಡುಶೋಲೆ - malevidimandukódushóle, Can.). Can. from (male, can. hill + vithai, tam. great + mandu, can. todah village + kódu, can. peak). 3½ miles W. by N. Same as Cully plantation.——*Monkey sholah* (ಕೊರಂಗುಶೋಲೆ - korangushóle, Can.; கொரங்குச்சோலை - koranguççólai, Tam.). Vernacular mean the same. 1¾ miles N.W. Same as Aramby plantation.——*Porcupine sholah* (ಮೇಲ್ ಕವ್ವೆಶೋಲೆ - mélkavveshóle, Can.; மேல்கவ்வெசோலை - mélgavvesólai, Tam.). Can. and Tam. from (mél, tam. above + kavai, tam. cross-road). Four miles W.S.W.——*Porlock sholah* (ಆನೆಕಾಲುಮಂದುಶೋಲೆ - ánekálumandushóle, Can.; ஆனைக்காலுமந்துசோலை - ánaikkálumandusólai, Tam.). Can. and Tam. from (áne, can. elephant + kálu, can. leg + mandu, can. todah village). 5¼ miles W. by S.——*Rally wood sholah* (ಅಗನಾಡುಮಂದುಶೋಲೆ - aganádumandushóle, Can.; அகநாடுமந்துசோலை - aganádumandusólai, Tam.). Can. and Tam. from (agam, tam. interior + nádu, tam. country + mandu, can. todah village). W. 5¼ miles.——*Rockwood spinney* (ಬೆಟ್ಟುಮಂದುಶೋಲೆ - bettumandushóle, Can.; பெட்டுமந்துசோலை - pettumandusólai, Tam.). Can. and Tam. from (betta, can. hill + mandu, can. todah village). E. 13 miles.——*Rocky cover* (ಕೊಂಬುತೂಕುಮಂದುಶೋಲೆ - kombutúkumandushóle, Can.; கொம்புதூக்கிமந்து - kombuthúkkimandu, Tam.). Can. and Tam. from (kombu, can. branch of tree + túgu, can. to hang up + mandu, can. todah village). E. 10 miles.——*Sheffield plantation* (ಉಳ್ಳನಾಡುಶೋಲೆ - ullanádushóle, Can.; காளப்பன் சோலை - kálapansólai, Tam.). Can. from (ul, tam. interior + nádu, tam. country). Tam. from (kálappa, can. proper name). W. by S. 3½ miles.——*Staircase sholah* (ಗದ್ದೆಗಾಡುಮಂದುಶೋಲೆ - gaddegádumandushóle, Can.; காடிமந்துசோலை - kádimandusólai, Tam.). Can. from (gadde, can. wet land + kádu, can. forest + mandu, can. todah village). Tam. from (kádu, tam. forest + mandu, can. todah village). W. 6 miles.——**(2)** *Sholah pigeon* (ചോലപ്രാവു - chólaprávu, Mal.). See Capotam.

SHONACAM (சோனகம் - shónagam, *Tam.*). From (yavana, san. ionian). The country of Yavanas [q.v.] or Greeks, but sometimes applied to Bactria and Arabia [jonaca]. One of the fifty-six countries [bhoogolashastram]. As one of the eighteen languages it refers to Hindostany [bhaushay]. See vol. 1 (1).

SHONAY (சோணை - shónai, *Tam.*). From (shóna, san. red). Trinomallee hill.

SHOOBH (शुभ् - shubh, *San.*). To shine.——*Shajnah* (سہجنا - shajná, Hind.). Corruption of (shóbhañjana, san. moringa). Same as Moringa.——*Shobhanam* (शोभन - shóbhana, San.). From (shubh, san. to shine). Auspicious.——*Shobhanaudry* (சோபனாத்திரி - shóbanáttiri, Tam.). From (shóbhana, san. auspicious + adri, san. mountain). Epithet of Veicoontam or Keilausam. Hindoo 2nd or pers. name [peyar].——*Shoobhaungy* (शुभाङ्गी - shubhángí, San.). From (shubha, san. handsome + anga, san. limb). Raty, wife of Manmatau [q.v.].

SHOOCH (शुच - shuch, *San.*). To be grieved or afflicted; to shine.——*Shocam* (शोक - shóka, San.). From (shuch, san. to afflict). Feverishness; one of the effects of Manmatan's arrows [cauma baunam].——*Shooclam* (शुक्ल - shukla, San.). From (shuch, san. to shine). Bright, white.——*Shoocla pacsham* (शुक्लपक्ष - shuklapaksha, San.). Means bright fortnight. The half of a lunar month from new to full [pacsham].——*Shooclaudy* (शुक्लादि - shukládi, San.). From (shukla, san. bright + ádi, san. beginning). Otherwise mookhyam [q.v.]. The S. indian mode of reckoning [maunam] a month by beginning with the day following the conjunction of the sun and moon [arcaindoosangamam]; so that the full moon [powrnimay] falls on the fifteenth day [tity] of the month, and the Amavausyay [q.v.] on the thirtieth [jyotisham, krishnaudy, mausam, tity].——*Shoocran* (शुक्र - shukra, San.). From (shuch, san. to shine). The planet [graham] Venus, ♀. Male, the gooroo [q.v.] of the giants [asooran]. Always seen near sun [sooryan]. Is called a Morning star when visible in east just before sunrise, and Evening star when visible in west just after sunset. Former case is where planet is moving from inferior to superior conjunction [sangamam]. Sidereal period of revolution [bhaganam] is 224d 16h 50m. Inclination [natam] of orbit [cacsham] to ecliptic [craunty mundalam] is 3⅓°. In Sanscrit the word means the regent and the planet also, but the tamuls retaining Shoocran as the gooroo [q.v.] call the planet Velly. Shoocra vauram and Velly kizhamay both mean Friday. The astrologers say:—if a person be born under the planet shoocran, he will have the faculty of knowing things past, present, and future; he will have many wives, and a kingly umbrella, the emblem of royalty [chattram], and other kings will worship him. The following are Varauha mihiran's astrological remarks on the movements of shoocran:—"If shoocran should disappear "or reappear in the several veeties [q.v.] beginning from the "northernmost one the condition of the world will respectively "be first very excellent, second excellent, third good, fourth fair, "fifth moderate, sixth tolerable, seventh poor, eighth very poor, "ninth miserable. Shoocran disappears when within 10 "degrees from the sun and reappears beyond that limit; if "shoocran should be visible before sunset there will be fear in "the land; if visible throughout the day, mankind will suffer "from hunger and from disease; if visible at midday in "conjunction with the moon [chundran], the king's army and "capital city will suffer. If shoocran should pass through the "constellation of kritticay [q.v.], the earth will be so much "inundated with water as to make its surface even; if shoocran "should pass through the constellation of rohiny [q.v.], earth "will assume the same appearance of death and devastation as "if she was going through the ceremony of caupaulicam for the "expiation of the sin of murder; if shoocran should enter the "constellation of mrigashiras [q.v.], juice and crops will suffer; "if he should enter the constellation of ardray [q.v.], the people "of cosalam [q.v.] and of calingam [q.v.] will suffer and there "will be abundance of rain [mazhay]; if shoocran should enter "the constellation of poonarvas [q.v.], the people of ashmacam "and of vidarbham will become lawless; if shoocran should "enter the constellation of pooshyam [q.v.], there will be good "rain, singing and dancing parties will suffer; if shoocran "should enter the constellation of aushlaisham [q.v.], there "will be much suffering from serpents [sarpam]; if shoocran "should pass through the constellation of magham [q.v.], "elephant [q.v.] keepers or ministers will suffer and there will "be abundance of rain; if shoocran should pass through the "constellation of poorvaphalgoony [poobbam], hillmen and the "people of poolindam will perish and there will be abundance "of rain; if he should pass through the constellation of oottara-

"phalgoony [oottaram], the people of cooroo, of jaungalam "and of paunchaulam will perish, and there will also be rain; "if he should pass through the constellation of hastam [q.v.], "the cowravas and painters will suffer, there will be no rain, "well-diggers [wodda] and birds [pacshy] will suffer; if he "should enter the constellation of chitta [q.v.], there will be "good rain; if he should enter the constellation of swaunty "[q.v.], there will be much rain, servants, merchants and "boatmen will become wicked and lawless; if he should enter "the constellation of vishaukham [q.v.], there will be good rain "and tradesmen will suffer; if he should enter the constellation "of anoosham [anooraudhay], rulers will be at strife; if he "should enter the constellation of jyeshtay [q.v.], the chief "rulers will suffer; if he should enter the constellation of "moolam [q.v.], physicians that deal in medicinal plants will "suffer; in each of these three last cases there will be drought "in the land; if shoocran should enter the constellation of "poorvashaudham [q.v.], the creatures of water will suffer; "if he should enter the constellation of oottarashaudham [q.v.], "diseases will increase; if he should enter the constellation of "shravanam [q.v.], diseases of the ear will afflict mankind; if "he should enter the constellation of dhanishtay [q.v.], heretics "will suffer; if shoocran should enter the constellation of shatabhishay [q.v.], drunkards and dealers in liquor will suffer; "if he should enter the constellation of poorvabhaudram [q.v.], "gamblers will suffer as well as the cowravas and the paunchaulas, "and there will be rain [mazhay] in the land; if shoocran "should enter the constellation of oottarabhaudram [q.v.], "fruits [pazham] and roots will be injured; if he should enter "the constellation of raivaty [q.v.], travellers will suffer; if he "should enter ashwiny [q.v.], horsekeepers will suffer; if he "should enter bharany [q.v.], hill men [kirautan] and the yavanas "[q.v.] will suffer." Shoocran is said in Hindoo mythology to have possessed the power of raising the dead. He is represented in the arts as a white man seated on a water-lily [indian water-lily].——*Shoodra* (शूद्र - shúdra, San.). From (shuch, san. to be afflicted). The fourth theoretical caste of the Hindoos. Shoodras are said in the Visnuoo pooraunam [q.v.] to have been produced from the feet of Bramha [q.v.]. Their duties are to wait on the three upper castes. They may also engage in trade and mechanical labor. In Southern india it is only Bramins [q.v.] who use the term. See vol. I (32), (37), (61), foot-note. They are here practically all Hindoos who are not bramins [jauty].——*Sooshindram* (शुचीन्द्र - shuchíndra, San.; ശുചീന്ദ്രം - shuchíndram, Mal.). From (shuchi, san. purified + indra, san. the god); indran who was cursed by Gowtaman [q.v.] for his intimacy with Gowtaman's wife was relieved of his curse at this place. Town, Place of pilgrimage; Travancore state, Pudmanaubhapooram division, Agasteeshwaram tal; pop. 6,535; lat. 8° 9′; long. 77° 31′ E.; from Alleppey S.E. 119 miles; from Cottayam S.S.E. 116 miles; from Madras S.S.W. 386 miles; from Nagarcoil S.E. 3 miles; from Paravore S.S.E. 160 miles; from Quilon S.E. 77 miles; from Trivandrum E.S.E. 41 miles; from the sea E. 12 miles. About 8 miles north-west of Cape comorin, and on the main road to Trivandrum. Large Bramin population. Large temple to Bramha [q.v.], Vishnoo [q.v.], and Maheshwaran [q.v.]; built in Carnatic [q.v.] style and profusely decorated with figures of Hindoo pantheon [maunasauram]. Many rocks in the temple with very ancient inscriptions. Inside the temple there is the image of a large bull [nundy] of white color built purely of chunk [q.v.] powder. Next to Pudmanaubhasawmy's temple at Trivandrum, that at Sooshindram is the most largely endowed pagoda [q.v.] in the state. From the top of pagoda [q.v.], the sea is visible.

SHOODDH (शुध् - shudh, *San.*). To cleanse.——*Shodhanam* (शोधन - shódhana, San.). From (shuddh, san. to clear). Literally purity. Reduction, in mathematics [ganitam].——*Shooddhadinam* (शुद्धदिन - shuddhadina, San.). From (shuddha, san. bright + dina, san. day). Birthday. Initial feria of the year [aharganam, samvatsaram].——*Shooddham* (शुद्ध - shuddha, San.). Bright. Same as Shooclam. Shoocla pacsham was originally called Poorva pacsham, former half, or Apooryamauna pacsham, waxing half. The bright lunar fortnight [pacsham]. At this time in the seventh lunar month of Aushwinam [mausam] between 15th September and 16th October, the Dusserah [q.v.] begins [aushwina shooddham].——*Sotha* (سوتها - sothá, Hind.). Among Thugs, the inveigler.

SHOODOO (சுடு - shudu, *Tam.*). To burn.——*Shoodalaiyaudy* (சுடலையாடி - shudalaiyádi, Tam.). From (above + talai, tam. place + ádu, tam. to play). Shiva [q.v.] the dancer on the burning ground [shoodcaud].——*Shoodalay* (சுடலை - shudalai, Tam.). From (above + talai, tam. place). A burning ground [shoodcaud].——*Shoodalay maudan* (சுடலைமாடன் - shudalaimádan, Tam.). From (above + talai, tam. place + mádan, tam. a devil). A goblin. See vol. I (81).——*Shoodcaud* (சுடுகாடு - shudugádu, Tam.). Burning ground. See Caud.——*Shoodcaud siddhan* (சுடுகாட்டுசித்தன் - shudugáttusittan, Tam.). From (shudugádu, tam. burning ground + siddha, san. accomplished); from practising their arts in the burning ground. A tribe of jugglers and fortune-tellers, who carry about human bones to work charms and incantations with. The descendants of a Maha poorsha named Mulla siddhayya, a Jangam [q.v.] of Parvaty mullicarjoonam on the Kistna, are still looked upon as their gooroos [q.v.].——*Shoolay* (சூளை - shúlai, Tam.). From (shudu, tam. to burn). Furnace, kiln [collvye].

SHOOJAH (شجاع - shujá, *Ar.*). From (shaja, ar. to be bold). Intrepid. Part of lacab; as Shoojah ood deen, intrepid in religion [ism].——*Shoojaut* (شجاعت - shujáat, Ar.). Valour. Prefixed to an alam forms a lacab; as Shoojaut ally, valour of ally [ism].

SHOOL (शूल - shúl, *San.*). To pierce.——*Shoolam* (शूल - shúla, San.). Trident. Also in astrology the supposed position of the trident at any given time, varying with the days of the week [vauram], hence called vaura shoolam; it is considered unlucky to set out on a journey in those days in the direction in which it lies and the reverse. For the direction of the trident in the days of the week see Tisay.——*Shoolapaunyan* (சூலப்பாணியன் - shúlappániyan, Tam.). From (shúla, san. trident + páni, san. hand). Shiva [q.v.].——*Shooly* (சூலி - shúli, Tam.); having trident. Bhadra cauly [q.v.].

SHOOLLY (சுள்ளி - shulli, *Tam.*). Ebony [q.v.] tree.——*Shoolliteev* (சுள்ளித்தீவு - shullittívu, Tam.). From (above + tívu, tam. island). Islets; Tinnevelly dist., Ottapidauram tal.; lat. 8° 56′ to 8° 57′; long. 78° 18′ to 78° 19′; from Ottapidauram E. 17 miles; from Tinnevelly E.N.E. 43 miles. A group of islets to the S.S.E. of the entrance of Veippaur river.

SHOOLY (சுழி - shuzhi, *Tam.*). Circle. A curl or circular mark indicating one's fortune. The natives say as follows. One will be brave and enterprising who has a shooly in the right ear turning to the right; but a shooly in the left ear sloping towards the left implies want of intellect and the state of being poor; he will be a man of fortune who has a shooly in the right side of the head; if a person has a shooly in the middle of the head, he will have ordinary wealth [samoodricam, shacoonam]. The circlets of hair on horses [ghorah] and cattle [maud] also are observed carefully.

SHOOMAUR (شمار - shumár, *Hind.*). From (shumurdan, pers. to calculate). More or less. Shoomaury is a census [khana shoomaury].

SHOONDAY (विदारी - vidárí, *San.*; कलांट - kallánta, *Conc.*; کالا میوہ - kálámewah, *Hind.*; ಕಲ್ಲತ್ತಿ - kallatti, *Can.*; రసగడిమాను - rasagadimánu, *Tel.*; ചുണ്ട - chunta, *Mal.*; சுண்டை - shundai, *Tam.*). Title from tamul. San. from (vidrí, san. to split open); from breaking swellings [cashmere tree, giant potato]. Hind. from (kálá, hind. black + mewá, hind. fruit). Can. from (kallu, can. stone + atti, can. ficus glomerata, miq.). Tel. from (rasa, tel. juice + gada, tel. stem + mánu, tel. tree). Mal. from tamul. Tam. from (shundu, tam. small) [shoondely]. San. also (pat'hi), meaning road plant. Can. also (sondegida). Mal. also (malañchunta), meaning wild solanum. Tam. also (malaiççundai), meaning mountain + the plant. Title otherwise Choondakye, Double colored solanum, Pubescent solanum. Botanically Solanum [cooly] verbascifolium, linn., solanaceæ [vricsham, 94]. Alias Solanum adulterinum, bicolor, erianthum, pubescens. Shrubby; leaves ovate-oblong, acuminate, entire, tomentose, surfaces discolored; axils leafless; corymbs subterminal, dichotomous, peduncled; calyx half five-cleft; flowers pale yellow or dirty white; flowering nearly all the year. Small tree with a thick shady head; every part covered with a powdery white tomentum. Fruit, small, round, yellow; used in curries [q.v.]. There is a Tamul proverb:—சுண்டைக்காய் அரைப்பணம் சுமைக்கூலி முக்கால் பணமா? சுண்டைக்காய் அளவு சாப்பிடுகிறது பாதியா வைக்கிறது பாதியா?—"of food about the size of a choondakye, "am I to eat half and leave half?"——*Elephant shoonday* (चान्द्री - chándrí, San.; गुल्ला - gullá, Conc.; ಬಿಳಿಗುಳ್ಳ - bilegulla, Can.; గుళ్ళబదనె - gullabadane, Too.; ములక - mulaka, Tel.; വെള്ളോട്ടുവഴുതിന - vellóttuvazhutina, Mal.; ஆனைச்சுண்டை - ánaiçcundai, Tam.). Title from size of fruit. San. from (chandra, san. moon), from fruits and flowers. Can. from (bili, can. white + gulla, can. solanum). Too. means solanum + brinjaul. Tel. from (mullu, tel. thorn + káya, tel. fruit), from thorns on fruit sheath. Mal. from (vella, mal. white + ótu, mal. rind + vazhutina, mal. brinjaul, solanum melongena, linn.). Tam. from (ánai, tam. elephant + shundai, tam. solanum verbascifolium, linn.). San. also (chandrika), meaning moonlight, from white flowers [haleem, snake root]; (chandra), meaning moon [snake root]; (garbhadá), meaning impregnating; (garbhabhí), meaning roaring; (priyamkarí), meaning doing good; (ráma), meaning delightful; (kshétradútí), meaning land spy; (shvétakantakári), meaning white + the plant, solanum xanthocarpum, schrad.; (lakshmaná), meaning marked; (mahaushadhí), meaning effective medicine [lussoon]; (nákulí), meaning pertaining to mongoose [galangal]; (nisnéhapushpá), meaning not oily + flower; (shvétakanta), meaning white thorn. Can. also (gulla). Mal. also (ánaççunta), meaning large + solanum. Title otherwise Hairy nightshade, Wild brinjaul. Botanically Solanum [cooly] ferox, linn., solanaceæ [vricsham, 94]. Alias Solanum hirsutum, lasiocarpum, mammosum, quadriloculare. Perennial, herbaceous, woody at the base; leaves paired, cordate, sinuately angled, woolly tomentose and prickly on both sides; peduncles intra-foliaceous and like the short pedicels calyx and berries, hairy; flowering in august and september. Used medicinally in fever and rheumatism. Gives a species of wild brinjaul eaten on malabar coast. For indicum see Indian nightshade.——*Hill shoonday* (కొండఉస్తె - kondauste, Tel.; மலைச்சுண்டை - malaiçcundai, Tam.). Tel. from (konda, tel. hill + uste, tel. solanum pubescens, willd.). Tam. from (malai, tam. mountain + shundai, tam. solanum verbascifolium, linn.). Botanically Solanum [cooly] torvum, swz., solanaceæ [vricsham, 94]. Shrub 8–12 feet high, or flowering as a herb; leaves 6 by 4 inches, lobes shallow rarely deep, softly hairy above, never prickly; petiole 1 inch, peduncles usually extra-axillary, short; racemes many-flowered, often dichotomous; pedicels often $\frac{1}{4}$–$\frac{1}{2}$ inch; calyx-lobes in flower $\frac{1}{8}$ inch, lanceolate, sparingly hairy; corolla 1–1$\frac{1}{4}$ inches diameter; lobes $\frac{1}{2}$ inch, triangular, pubescent without; ovary and style glabrous; berry yellow; calyx lobes patent, not half as long as the berry; seeds scarcely $\frac{1}{16}$ inch diameter, smooth. Used as vegetable.——*Prickly shoonday* (अलर्क - alarka, San.; वेलवांगी - vélavángí, Mahr.; ಕಾಕಮುಂಚಿ - kákamunchi, Can.; ముండ్లముస్తె - muudlamuste, Tel.; തുതവളം - tútavalam, Mal.; වැල්තිබ්බටු - valtibbatu, Singh.; தூதுவளை - túthuvalai, Tam.). Title from state of stem. San. from (al, san. to adorn + arka, san. calotropis gigantea, r. br.) [yercum]. Mahr. from (véla, mahr. creeper + vángí, mahr. solanum melongena, linn.). Can. corruption of (kákamáchi, san. solanum nigrum); from resemblance of fruit to the red variety. Tel. from (mullu, tel. thorn + uste, tel. solanum pubescens, willd.). Mal. from tamul. Singh. from (val, singh. creeper + tibbatu, singh. solanum indicum, linn.). Tam. from (túthu, tam. small stone + ul, tam. having), from stone-like berry within the lobe. San. also (achúdá), meaning not crested. Can. also (ambasonde), meaning arrow + solanum verbascifolium, linn.; (mullumusta). Tel. also (uste); (tel-lauste), meaning white + solanum pubescens, willd.; (uççinta). Tam. also (kúthalam), meaning prickly leaf; (túdulai), meaning stone + having; from stone-like berry within the lobe of fruit. Title otherwise Three-lobed nightshade. Botanically Solanum [cooly] trilobatum, linn., solanaceæ [vricsham, 94]. Alias Solanum acetosæfolium. Climbing shrub; stem armed with numerous very sharp recurved prickles; leaves remote, panduriformly three to five lobed, smooth on both sides; petioles and veins armed; peduncles prickly, leaf-opposed, solitary, few-flowered, terminal, and axillary; corolla deeply five-cleft, bluish purple; berries small, globose, red, drooping. Root, leaves are bitter, prescribed in consumptive cases in electuary, decoction, or powder; berries and flowers are given internally in decoction for coughs. Leaves [keeray] eaten, having been previously sprinkled with salt and water.——*Rameshwaram shoonday* (गण्डीर - gandíra, San.; రామేశ్వరఉస్తె - rámeshvarauste, Tel.; சுண்டை - shundai, Tam.). San. from (ganda, san. boil + ír, san. to go); useful in boils. Tam. from (shundu, tam. small). San. also (shvétamahatí), (shvétasimhí), (shvétavártákí), (shvétabrihatí), all meaning white + solanum melongena, linn.; (shvétap'halá), meaning white fruit. Tel. also (kásiuste), meaning benares + the plant; (uste). Title otherwise Oostey. Botanically Solanum [cooly] pubescens, willd., solanaceæ [vricsham, 94]. Shrubby, unarmed, clothed all over with short, somewhat viscid tomentose pubescence; leaves ovate, acute, entire or sub-repand; racemes corymbose, lateral; the lower anther larger; flowers blue, berries red. Stimulant in medicine.

SHOONDELY (बालमूषिक - bálamúshika, *San.*; تكس - tikus, *Malay*; ಸಣ್ಣಿಲಿ - sannili, *Can.*; చిట్టెలుక - chitteluka, *Tel.*; ചുണ്ടെലി - chundeli, *Mal.*; ගිරිකා - giriká, *Singh.*; சுண்டெலி - shundeli, *Tam.*). San. from (bála, san. small + múshika, san. rat). Can. from (sanna, can. small + ili, can. rat). Tel. from (chiru, tel. small + eluka, tel. rat). Singh. from (giriká, san. swallower). Tam. from (shundu, tam. smallness + eli, tam. rat) [shoonday]. Title otherwise Mouse. Mus [moosham] urbanus, muridæ, rodentia, mammalia [sastanam, 17], of naturalists [jantoo]. Under the head of ordinary mice, as distinguished from Field mice with short tails [varappoo shoondely]; Tree mice with long tails [mara shoondely], and Spiny mice whose fur is mixed with spines [moolloo shoondely], this is the chief representative. Called the Common indian mouse. It differs conspicuously from the Common english mouse in its smaller ears and much longer tail. It has also larger eyes, and smaller feet. The fur too is of very different texture. Above dusky reddish brown, below paler and more or less rufescent; feet paler. Another house-mouse is the Large-footed mouse, Mus crassipes of naturalists. The feet particularly large, and like the tail well furnished with coarse short setæ. Indian species not here found are:—bactrianus, darjeelingensis, erythronotus, homourus, pachycercus, sublimis, tytleri.——*Mara shoondely* (तरुबालमूषिक - tarubálamúshika, San.; شجر موش - shajarmúsh, Pers.; جهار کا چوها - jhárkáchúhá, Hind.; ಮರದಿಲಿ - maradaili, Can.; మానెలుక - máneluka, Tel.; മരച്ചുണ്ടെലി - maraççundeli, Mal.; மரச்சுண்டெலி - maraççundeli, Tam.). San. from (taru, san. tree + bálamúshika, san. small rat). Pers. from (shajar, pers. tree + músh, pers. mouse). Hind. from (jhár, hind. tree + chúhá, hind. rat). Can. from (mara, can. tree + ili, can. rat). Tel. from (mánu, tel. tree + eluka, tel. rat). Tam. from (maram, tam. tree + shundeli, tam. mouse). Title otherwise Tree mouse. Mus [moosham] oleraceus, muridæ, rodentia, mammalia [sastanam, 17], of naturalists [jantoo]. This belongs to a group of some small arboreal, long tailed mice, diminutives of the Tree rat [maravely]. Above light rufous or pale chestnut; lips, feet, and lower parts, pure white; tail almost nude, very long; muzzle slightly rounded; head of moderate length; ears ovate. Particularly prevalent in the south of India, where it frequents trees, and very commonly palm [taur] trees. It occasionally places its nest in the thatch of houses, on beams, &c. Akin is the Neilgherry tree mouse; Mus nilagiricus of naturalists; above deep but bright chestnut brown, beneath bright fawn yellow, with a distinct line of demarcation between the two colors; head rather elongated; ears long, oval; tail somewhat hairy. Indian species not here found are:—Mus badius or bay tree mouse, Mus gliroides or cherrapoonjee tree mouse, Mus peguensis or pegu tree mouse.——*Moolloo shoondely* (शल्यबालमूषिक - shalyabálamúshika, San.; خار موش - khármúsh, Pers.; ಕಲ್ಲಿಲಿ - kallili, Can.; గిజిలిగాడు - gijeligádu, Tel.; കല്ലെലി - kalleli, Mal.; முள்ளுச்சுண்டெலி - mulluççundeli, Tam.). San. from (shalya, san. thorn + bálamúshika, san. small rat). Pers. from (khár, pers. thorn + músh, hind. mouse). Can. from (kallu, can. stone + ili, can. rat). Mal. from (kal, mal. stone + eli, mal. rat). Tam. from (mullu, tam. spine + shundeli, tam. mouse). Tel. also (leggade); (kalleluka), meaning stone + rat. Title otherwise Spiny mouse.—"*a*" Leggada platythrix, muridæ, rodentia, mammalia [sastanam, 17], of naturalists [jantoo]. Generic from teloogoo. This is the chief representative of a class of field-mice which have fine fur mixed with numerous spines. Somewhat flattened. It is only found in S. India. Above light sandy brown or light brown mixed with fawn; beneath pure white, the white separated from the brown by a well-defined pale fawn line. The flattened spines are transparent on the back, beneath smaller, and form with the fur a thick close covering. The head is long, the muzzle pointed, the ears rather large oblong, rounded. Lives entirely in the red gravelly soil in a burrow of moderate depth, generally on the side of a bank. When the animal is inside the entrance is closed with small pebbles. Inside is a bed of small pebbles on which it sits. The Yanaudies [q.v.] state that one variety uses small sticks to sit on instead of stones, and give it a distinct appellation.—"*b*" Nearly affined is the Dusky spiny mouse, Leggada spinulosa of naturalists. Of a dark dusky color above, with fulvous tips to the softer fur; below, and all the feet dull whitish, upper rodential tusks orange, the lower white. Whiskers long and fine, the posterior and longer of these black for the basal half or more, the rest white.—"*c*" Also the Small spiny mouse, Leggada lepida of naturalists. Above pale sandy brown, pure white below, separated from the upper color by an exact line. The spines are small, fine, transparent, and of a dusky tinge tipt with fawn. The head very long, and muzzle pointed. Ear large ovate, naked. Tail naked. Limbs rather long, fine. This mouse is preyed on by the common Indian roller or Indian jay [q.v.], and is used as a bait to catch that bird with bird-lime.—"*d*" Indian species not here found are:—Hapalomys longicaudatus, Leggada jerdoni or himalayan spiny mouse, Mus chevrieri, Mus confucianus, Mus flavipectus or yellow-breasted rat, Mus griseipectus or grey-breasted rat, Mus onang-thomæ or kiangsi rat, Mus pygmæus or pigmy mouse.——*Varappoo shoondely* (केदारबालमूषिक - kédárabálamúshika, San.; موش دشتی - múshidashtí, Pers.; വരമ്പുച്ചുണ്ടെലി - varampuççundeli, Mal.; வரப்புச்சுண்டெலி - varappuççundeli, Tam.). San. from (kédára, san. field + bálamúshika, san. mouse). Pers. from (músh, pers. mouse + dasht, pers. forest). Tam. from (varappu, tam. field-ridge + shundeli, tam. mouse). Pers. also (múshisahrí), meaning desert mouse. Title otherwise Field mouse. Mus [moosham] cervicolor, muridæ, rodentia, mammalia [sastanam, 17], of naturalists [jantoo]. Ordinary field-mice have the tail shorter than head and body; fur not spinous. The above is the chief representative. Above dull fawn or yellowish gray; below sordid white; lining of ears and extremities pale; tail short; ears large, hairy. Another is the Earthy field mouse, Mus terricolor of naturalists. Above variable according to the soil, light fawn brown, more or less rufescent; under parts white, abruptly separately from the hue of the upper parts. Indian species not here found are:—Beaveni or beaven's mouse, Cunicularis or little rabbit mouse, Erythrotis or cherrapoonjee red-eared mouse, Fulvidiventris, Kakhyenensis or kakhyen mouse, Nitidulus or shiny little house mouse of Pegu, Peguensis or pegu field mouse, Viculorum or kakhyen house mouse.

SHOONDY (लज्जालु - lajjálu, *San.*; लाजरी - lájarí, *Mahr.*; لجالو - lajálu, *Hind.*; شرمندی - sharmindí, *Dec.*; ಮುದುಗುದಾವರೆ - mudugudávare, *Can.*; നാചികെഡൈ - náchikedai, *Too.*; అత్తపత్తి - attapatti, *Tel.*; തീണ്ടാർമണി - tíntármani, *Mal.*; මහනිදිකුඹ - mahanidikumba, *Singh.*; சுண்டி - shundi, *Tam.*). San. from (lajja, san. shyness). Mahr. and Hind. from sanscrit. Dec. from (sharm, pers. shame + possessive particle); from sensitiveness of leaf. Can. from (mudugu, can. to sink + dávare, can. the plant, lotus). Too. from (náchike, too. shame + dai, too. tree). Tel. from (atta, tel. mother-in-law + patti, tel. cotton).

Mal. from (tíndu, mal. to touch + mázhku, mal. to languish); fading at the touch. Singh. from (maha, singh. large + nidikumba, singh. the plant, mimosa pudica, linn.). Tam. means that which shrinks. San. also (añjalikáriká), meaning joining the hands in prayer, in allusion to the folding leaves when fading; (varáhakrántá), meaning attracting hogs; (sharabha), meaning injuring [sharbham]; (namaskári), meaning prostrating; (lajjávatí), meaning shy plant; (sámangá), meaning having contracted limbs [munject]; (khadirá), meaning having small leaves like acacia catechu, willd. [biswool, catechu, sundra]. Mahr. also (lájálú), meaning bashful. Hind. also (lajwantí), meaning shameful; (siyálkántá), meaning sensitive thorn. Can. also (náchike), meaning shame; (mutlamurike), meaning touch + shrinking; (muttidaremuniva), meaning if touched + be angry. Tel. also (nidrakanti), meaning sleep + eye [water shoondy]; (peddanidrakanti), meaning large + the plant; (munugutámara), meaning sinking + the plant, nelumbium speciosum, willd.; (muttavapulagamu), meaning great grandmother + pudding [common balah, lance-leaved balah, peramootty, shrubby balah]; (bódatsandra), meaning bald + acacia sundra, dec.; (undra); (ventra) Mal. also (tottáváti), meaning fading at the touch; (tíndármázhi), meaning languishing at the touch. Singh. also (nidikumba). Tam. also (tottáççurungi), meaning to touch + to shrink; (karuppuyindiriyakkodi), meaning black + sense + creeper; (tottálvádi), meaning fading when touched; (indiriyakkodi), meaning sensitive creeper; (indu). Title otherwise Sensitive plant. Botanically the Mimosa genus, leguminosæ [vricsham, 48]. Chiefly tropical; mostly herbs, undershrubs or climbers; scarcely any grow into trees; many are prickly; leaves are twice pinnate, usually with a large number of very small leaflets, but in a few species the leaflets are much larger and reduced to eight in the whole leaf; in many species the leaves are sensitive, that is to say closing downwards when touched and only recovering their position after a time greater or less according to climate, season, weather or vigour of individual; some of the species ripen seed, others may be increased by cuttings from points of young shoots. The species best known to the natives are:—hamata, pudica, rubicaulis. Pudica is a native of brazil long naturalized here; decoction of root is useful in gravellish complaints; leaves and root in piles and fistula; the tapering thin roots contain ten per cent. of tannin of such a nature as to form a good black-ink [mashy] with salts of iron [auhan].——*Water shoondy* (पाणीलाजरी - pánílájarí, Mahr.; నిద్రకంటి - nidrakanti, Tel.; நீர்ச்சுண்டி - nírçcundi, Tam.). Title from habitat. Mahr. from (pání, mahr. water + lájarí, mahr. shy plant, mimosa genus). Tel. from (nidra, tel. sleep + kannu, tel. eye). Tam. from (nír, tam. water + shundi, tam. mimosa genus); water mimosa. Tel. also (nírutalavapu), meaning water touching; (chinnanidrakanti), small + the plant. Tam. also (shundakkírai), meaning mimosa + vegetable. Title otherwise Floating desmanthus, Floating sensitive plant, Shoonda keeray. Botanically the Neptunia genus, leguminosæ [vricsham, 48]. Herbs without prickles floating in water; leaves bipinnate; flowers in globular heads; pods broad, flat, short, edible. The species best known to the natives are:—oleracea, triquetra.

SHOONYAM (शून्य - shúnya, *San.*). From (shvi, san. to swell), swollen, hollow. Empty. Also cypher in arithmetic.——*Shoonyaurgham* (शून्यार्घ - shúnyárgha, San.). From (above + argha, san. price). Scarcity; or a time unfavorable for agricultural [vellaumay] undertakings, predicted in the calendar [punchaungam, vriddhyaurgham].

SHOORAN (शूर - shúra, *San.*). From (shúr, san. to hurt) [sharam]. Hero; demon so called.——*Shooramungalam* (சூரமங்கலம் - shúramangalam, Tam.). From (shúran, tam. proper name + mangala, san. prosperity). Village; Salem dist., Salem tal.; pop. 1,716; acres 391; lat. 11° 40′; long. 78° 09′; height 923 feet; from Salem W.N.W. 4 miles. Suburb of Salem. Railway station.——*Shoorsamhaura moorty* (शूरसंहारमूर्ति - shúrasamhóramúrti, San.). From (above + samhára, san. killing + múrti, san. embodiment). Soobramanyan [q.v.], the destroyer of shoora pudmausooran [samhauran].——*Shoory* (சூரி - shúri, Tam.). Heroine; Mauriyamman [q.v.].——*Showrya lutchmy* (शौर्यलक्ष्मी - shauryalakshmí, San.). From (above + lakshmí, the goddess). The goddess of heroism [ashta lutchmy].——*Showryam* (शौर्य - shaurya, San.). From (shúra, san. hero). Valour.——*Sooran* (سورن - súran, Hind.). Hurting; from caustic root. Plant name common to:—Amorphophallus campanulatus; Colocasia esculenta; Tacca pinnatifida. See gloss. paragraphs.

SHOOROOL (சுருள் - shurul, *Tam.*). Curl.——*Shoorooliyaur* (சுருளியாறு - shuruliyáru, Tam. suruliyár*). From (shurulai, tam. curl + áru, tam. river). River; Madura dist., Periyacoolam tal. Rises partly in the high mountains near Varshanaud and partly in the Travancore hills. After a meandering course of about 30 miles down the valley it meets the Veigay, 6 miles north of Guntamanaickanore, just after receiving the Teniyaur.

SHOORPAM (शूर्प - shúrpa, *San*.). From (shúrp, san. to measure); a kind of wicker work receptacle which when agitated serves as a fan for winnowing corn. Winnowing basket. Also a winnowing fan.——*Shoorpanakhay* (शूर्पणखा - shúrpanakhá, San.). From (above + nakha, san. nail); having nails like winnowing fans. Sister of Ravanan [q.v.]. Now applied to any monstrous or hideous female.

SHORAH (شعرا - shorá, *Pers.*). Pl. of (sháir, pers. poet). Part of lacab; as Malik oosh shorah, king of poets, laureate.

SHORAH (यवक्षार - yavakshára, *San.*; घोरमीठ - shóramít'ha, *Mahr.*; ابكر - abkar, *Ar.*; شوره - shorá, *Pers., Hind.* and *Dec.*; سانداو - sándawa, *Malay*; ಪೆಟ್ಲುಪ್ಪು - petluppu, *Can.*; సురాకారము - surákáramu, *Tel.*; വെടിയുപ്പ് - vetiyuppu, *Mal.*; වෙඩිලුනු - vedilunu, *Singh.*; பொட்டிலுப்பு - pottiluppu, *Tam.*). Title from persian. San. from (yava, san. barley + kshára, san. alkali). Mahr. from hindostany. Pers. from (shor, pers. saline substance). Can. from (pottulu, can. to burst + uppu, can. salt). Tel. from (shorá, hind. nitre + kshára, san. alkali). Mal. from (veti, mal. explosion + uppu, mal. salt). Singh. means explosive salt. Tam. from (pottil, tam. pistol + uppu, tam. salt). San. also (suvarchilavana), meaning good + lustre + salt, from use in fireworks. Can. also (sóruppu), meaning nitre + salt. Tel. also (petluppu), meaning to explode + salt. Tam. also (vediyuppu), meaning to explode + salt; (púmikkúrmai), meaning earth + sharpness. Saltpetre. Also called Nitrate of potash. Potassæ nitras of chemists. A salt composed of nitric acid [shorey ka tezaub] and potash [jharka namak]. Procured impure in great quantities from the earth containing it [sooracaurapoo sowdoo]. Production greatest during period when hot winds blow. Obtained artificially, in some parts, from earth of old walls, scrapings of roads, cow-pens, and other places where cattle [maud] have urinated. Crude saltpetre is made in factories on high mounds of earth. A factory includes several steeping pits on a high level, a catchment pit below, a masonry conduit from the former falling into the latter at a sharp angle, one or more evaporating pans, and the necessary implements. The steeping pits are round pits, 1 or 2 feet deep. The catchment pit is a deep pit built of masonry. The evaporating pans are rectangular shallow pans paved ½ or 1 inch thick with choonam [q.v.]. Nitrous earth is collected and taken on carts to the factory. This is done only in the hot and rainless months. The earth stored at the factory is eventually thrown into the steeping pits and there stamped down. Each pit holds some half a cart load. Then water is poured over. Between the steeping pits and the conduit, palmyra [q.v.] web or other fibrous substance is placed, and sand or husk is plastered over it. The fluid in the pits must then percolate to enter the conduit. If steeping begins one morning the percolation is finished the next. The liquid is then baled out, and poured into the evaporating pans to the depth of two or three inches. Evaporation is complete in three days, and the pan is then incrusted with saltpetre, in some parts in masses [pauray], and in some parts in crystals [palingoo]. The incrusted nitre is scraped with an iron instrument, removed in pots and stored in heaps. It is then sold to merchants. Crude nitre sells at about 8 rupees per pootty [q.v.] weighing 20 maunds [q.v.]. Crude nitre is subsequently purified by dissolving it in boiling water, removing the scum after the liquid has been allowed to settle, straining the solution through calico [q.v.] and setting aside to crystallise. Pure specimens should be in white crystalline masses or fragments, colorless, and of a peculiar, cool, saline taste. Medicinally refrigerant, diuretic and diaphoretic when administered in solution freely diluted; irritant if given in the solid form or in concentrated solution; and poisonous in very large doses. Externally applied in solution it produces great cold and acts like ice. Employed by natives in the preparation of gunpowder from ancient times. Also for cooling water and wine in hot season. Also in conjunction with alum [padicauram] and salt [ooppoo], used by goldsmiths in the process of brightening gold ornaments. Used in dyeing [shauyam].

SHOZHAM (சோழம் - shózham, *Tam.*). Same as Cholam.——*Sholinghur** (சோளங்கிப்புரம் - shólangippuram, Tam.). From (chóla, san. chola king + linga, san. idol + pura, san. town). Tam. also (tirukkadigai), meaning holy + vedam; also (kadigai), meaning vedam. Sanscrit name (chólalingapura), means the same; also (ghatikáchala), meaning soapstone + mountain. Village, Mountain, Place of pilgrimage; North arcot dist., Wallajahpett tal.; pop. 6,416; acres 2,411; lat. 13° 07′; long. 79° 28′; from Chittore E.S.E. 24 miles; from Wallajahpett N.N.E. 14 miles. An extensive town. A Chola rajah here found a natural lingam [q.v.] and built a temple over it called Choleshwaram temple. It was here that Athonday [q.v.] was encouraged by a vision to resume his contest with the Coorumbar [q.v.], by whom he had been at first defeated. In the neighbourhood, in 1781, was fought the battle between Coote and Hyder in which the latter was defeated. Besides that of Choleshwaran there is another temple, to Bhactavatsalan, built by a Vijianugger king. A fine mantapam [q.v.], resembling those of Vellore and Virinjipooram, has been begun; the pillars lie half buried in the soil. Outside the town is temple of Narsimhasawmy upon summit of loftiest hill. A flight of stone steps, built by Royajee leads to the summit. Pilgrims visiting Tripatty and Conjeeveram generally visit this temple, remaining in Sholinghur three or four days. There are fourteen holy peaks in vicinity, but this is the holiest. At foot of Royajee's ascent is a charitable institution, founded by him and called Anna daunam. Only Bramins are fed; the worshippers in the temple, who stay sometimes for years, receive a daily dole. On Sundays in Caurtigay [mausam] or november, 200 Bramins resident in town are fed. Close to the choultry [q.v.] is a well dug at Royajee's expense as deep as the temple is high.. Many teertams [q.v.]. Chief is Bramha teertam, in which people bathe on Thursdays. Festival about May. —*Shozhagam* (சோழகம் - shózhagam, Tam.); means south. South wind. Chola country. Sect of Bramins. Cf. Choliya for Mahomedans.

SHRADDHAY (श्रद्धा - shraddhá, *San.*; சிரத்தை - shirattai, *Tam.*). From (shrat, san. faith). Faith, belief, piety [bhucty]; implicit belief in the words of a gooroo [q.v.] or priest, much inculcated in modern Vedauntam [q.v.] books.——*Sharadan* (சரதன் - sharathan, Tam.). From (sharatham, tam. faithfulness from shraddha, san. faith). Pariah proper name [peyar].——*Shattaimoony* (சட்டைமுனி - shattaimuni, Tam.). From (shattai, tam. esteem + muni, san. sage). Very ancient Sheiva ascetic, one of Agastyan's converts [agastyan]. Author of Nyaunanoor a work on theology, Calpa noor a medical work and Vauta nigantoo a treatise on alchemy [rasauyanam].——*Shrauddham* (श्राद्ध - shráddha, San.). Obsequies paid to the manes [pitry] of deceased ancestors. Hindoos are enjoined to offer a ball of rice or cake, pindam [q.v.], to the ghosts of their ancestors, as far back as the third generation. This ceremony is performed on the day of the new moon [amavausyay]. The first shrauddham is performed the day after the ten days of mourning are over. It is usual to repeat it once a month for the first year and after that once a year. The offering of water, tarpanam [q.v.], is in like manner to be performed daily to appease the dead. These ceremonies were known to the Greeks and Romans. Grihya sootram [q.v.] mentions four kinds of shrauddham:—Paurvana or monthly, to ancestors for three generations on the day of conjunction [arcaindoo sangamam] or new moon [amavausyay]; Caumya or voluntary, performed for object of desire; Aubhyoodayica, performed as thank-offerings on occasion of family rejoicing as at samscaurams [q.v.]; Yecoddishtam or special, having reference to one person recently deceased and not to ancestors generally. These are sometimes classified as:—Nitya or perpetual, daily offerings to ancestors in general; Naimittica or occasional; Caumya or voluntary; Vriddhy, performed on occasions of rejoicing; Sapindadauna, offerings to all individual and general ancestors; Paurvana, offerings to manes on new moon [amavausyay] and full moon [powrnimay]; Goshty, for the advantage of a number of learned persons; Shooddhy, for the purification of one from defilement; Carmaunga, forming part of initiatory ceremonies [samscauram]; Daivica, for gods; Yautray, held by a person going on a journey; Pooshty, to promote health and wealth. Auma shrauddham or raw shrauddham is performed by shoodras where instead of cooked meals raw articles are given. Shrauddha devan is yaman [q.v.], the lord of pitry locam [q.v.] or spirit-world.

SHRAM (श्रम् - shram, *San.*). To be wearied, mortify.——*Shamanan* (சமணன் - shamanan, Tam.). From (shramana, san. jaina devotee). Same as Shramanan [carnautaca rajakkal].——*Shramam* (श्रम - shrama, San.). Labor, austerity.——*Shramanan* (श्रमण - shramana, San.; சமணன் - shamanan, pers. sing.; சமணர் - shamanar, pers. pl., Tam.). From (shram, san. to mortify). The Jeina [q.v.] sect. Since the word Σαρμᾶνας the form used by Clemens of Alexandria, corresponds exactly with the Sanscrit, it is to be surmised that the forms Γαρμᾶνας and Γερμᾶνας, which are found in all the MSS. of Strabo, are incorrect, Γ having been wrongly written for Σ. See vol. I (63).——*Shravanabelgola* (ಶ್ರವಣಬೆಳಗೊಳ - shravanabelagola, Can.; shravanbelgolabetta, Mys. Gov.). From (shramana, san. jaina + belgola, can. white tank); from a splendid tank built by Jeinas. Village, Hill, Place of pilgrimage, Hassan district, Mysore, between two rocky hills in Chenroypatna talook, 8 miles southeast of the cusbah [q.v.]. Chief seat of the Jeina [q.v.] sect.

SHRAVANAM (श्रवण - shravana, *San.*). From (shru, san. to hear). Hearing; that which is heard; Vedam [q.v.]. Twenty-second hindoo lunar mansion [nacshatram].——*Shrauvacan* (श्रावक - shrávaka, San.). From (shru, san. to hear); disciple. Jeinas [q.v.] who engage in secular occupations, as opposed to Yaties [q.v.] or monks.——*Shrauvanam* (श्रावण - shrávana, San.). Belonging to shravanam, the twenty-second asterism. Fifth lunar month. Lunar [chaundramaunam] festival [pundigay, 3c], subject to intercalation [adhicam]. See Oopaucarmam.——*Shrauvana powrnimay* (శ్రావణపౌర్ణమి - shrávanapaurnamí, Tel.). Means fifth lunar month + full moon day. Same as Auvany avittam.——*Shrooty* (श्रुति - shruti, San.). From (shru, san. to hear). Revelation, as opposed to Smrity [q.v.] or tradition. The three divisions of the Vedams [q.v.], or Muntram [q.v.], Bramhanam [q.v.], and Oopanishad [q.v.], all come under the head of shrooty. It consists more generally of knowledge heard by Rishies [q.v.], and by them orally transmitted; or if committed to writing, then written down exactly as heard without any intervention of human authorship.——*Shrotriem* (श्रोत्रिय - shrótriya, San.). For learning and teaching shrooty. Lands, or a village, held at a favorable rate. Properly an assignment of land or revenue to a Bramin learned in the vedams [q.v.], but latterly applied generally to similar assignments to native servants of Government as a reward for past services [inam]. See vol. I, 112.——*Shrowtam* (श्रौत - shrauta, San.). Pertaining to Shrooty. Sacrificial rules.——*Soonauvany* (سناؤنی - sunáuní, Hind.). From (sunáná, hind. to cause to hear). Reading out of petitions [arzee], &c.

SHREE (श्री - shrí, *San.*). From (shrí, san. to mature). Sometimes wrongly written Stree [q.v.]; cf. shrotriem appearing as stotriem. Holiness, prosperity. Also personification of such in Lutchmy [q.v.], wife of Vishnoo [q.v.], born like the grecian Aphrodite from the sea [samoodram]. Every city has its own tutelar Shree or prosperity, which in former times was represented by an image with a temple of its own. The word is used also as an abstract prefix of reverence to the names of deities, holy places, sacred books, spiritual teachers, &c. Cf. Tir, which is probably only a dravidian corruption of Shree. See vol. I (74). Shree is also a common plant first term in the sense of holy, beautiful, or excellent. Ex., where transl. is of second term:—Ægle marmelos (shríp'hala), fruit; Corypha umbraculifera (shrítála), borassus flabelliformis; Ficus religiosa (shrívriksha), tree; Heliotropium indicum (shríhastiní), elephant; Pinus longifolia (shrívása), abode; Premna integrifolia (shríparna), leaf; Santalum album (shrígandha), fragrance. See gloss. paragraphs.——*Seringapatam* (سرنگ پٹن - sirangpatan, *Hind.*; ಶ್ರೀರಂಗಪಟ್ಟ - shrírangapatna, *Can.*; seringapatam, Mys. Gov.). From (shrí, san. holy + ranga, san. vishnu + pattana, san. city). Town in 12° 26′ N. lat., 76° 44′ E. long., at the western or upper end of an island in the Cauvery, about 3 miles in length from west to east and 1 in breadth. The head-quarters of the Seringapatam talook, Mysore district, Mysore; stands on the Bangalore-Mysore high road, 75 miles south-west from the former and 10 north-east from the latter.——*Shiroor* (ಶಿರೂರು - shirúru, Can.). From (shiri, can. lakshmí, the goddess + úru, can. village). Village, Sub-port; South canara dist., Coondapore tal.; pop. 3,258; lat. 13° 54′; long. 74° 38′; from Beidoor N.N.W. 3 miles; from Bhatcull S.E. 6 miles; from Bombay S.S.E. 360 miles; from Coondapore N.N.W. 20 miles; from Mangalore N.N.W. 72 miles; from Oodipy N.N.W. 40 miles; from the sea E. 1 mile. A small port on a creek which forms the north limit of the Presidency. The ruins of ancient Shiroor are extensive.——*Shiry* (శిరి - shiri, Tel.). Corruption of Shree. Suffix in place names, as Yellashiry, meaning wealthy village on the boundary.——*Shreecaucoolam* (శ్రీకాకుళము - shríkákulamu, Tel.). From (shrí, san. holy + kákóla, san. boar). Zemindarry, Village, Place of pilgrimage; Kistna dist., Sullapully zemindarry; pop. 2,822; lat. of village 16° 12′; long. 80° 53′; from Masulipatam W. 18 miles; from the sea W. 22 miles; from Sullapully N.W. 8 miles. On left bank of Kistna. Bramins here first settled in this district at the invitation of the three-eyed Pullava [q.v.] monarch. Festival held in Veishaukham [mausam] or May [chicacole].——*Shreecauntan* (శ్రీకాంతుడు - shríkántudu, Tel.). From (above + kánta, san. husband). Epithet of Vishnoo [q.v.], the husband of Lutchmy [q.v.]. Hindoo 2nd or pers. name [peyar].——*Shree cauryam* (ശ്രീകാര്യം - shríkáryam, Mal.). From (above + kárya, san. action). Office of a pagoda [q.v.] manager.——*Shree choornam* (ஸ்ரீச்சூரணம் - shiriççúranam, Tam.). From (above + chúrna, san. powder). Sacred powder of the veishnavas [naumam]. Cf. the corruption Shree choornam under Shir.——*Shreecoormam* (శ్రీకూర్మము - shríkúrmamu, Tel.). From (shrí, san. holy + kúrma, san. tortoise, incarnation of vishnu).—"*a*" Zemindarry; Ganjam dist., Chicacole tal.; pop. 18,283; acres 8,934.—"*b*" Village, Place of pilgrimage; Ganjam dist., Chicacole tal.; pop. 2,444; lat. 18° 16′; long. 84° 03′; from Chetterpore S.W. 97 miles; from Chicacole E.S.E. 7 miles; from the sea W. 3 miles. Belongs to Vizianagram zemindarry in Vizagapatam district. At extreme south of district on the coast. Temple to Coormam [q.v.] avatar [q.v.] of Vishnoo [q.v.]. Image in shape of tortoise. Temple formerly Sheiva, changed into Veishnava by Ramaunoojacharry [ramaunoojan]. Only place of pilgrimage for Teloogoos in Ganjam district.——*Shree cuntan* (श्रीकण्ठ - shríkant'ha, San.). From (above + kant'ha, san. throat). Epithet of the blue-throated shiva [q.v.]. Hindoo 2nd or pers. name [peyar].——*Shreedharan* (श्रीधर - shrídhara, San.). From (above + dhri, san. to hold); husband of lutchmy. Vishnoo.——*Shreeharicote* (శ్రీహరికోట - shríharikóta, Tel. sríharikót*). Sanscritized from (chíkirénî, tel. tree, albizzia amara, boivn. + kóta, tel. fort); from trees being abundant. Sanscrit name (shríharikóta), meaning holy + vishnoo + fort. Tract of country; Nellore dist., Goodoor tal.; pop. 11,149; lat. 13° 34′ to 14° 00′; long. 80° 12′ to 80° 18′; from Goodoor E. 23 miles; from Nellore S.S.E. 34 miles. Southernmost portion of Goodoor talook. A long low island or bank of alluvial and marine deposits rising only some few feet above the water level. Washed on the east by the sea and on the west by Poolicat lake. Stretches from Coromandel [q.v.] on the south to Doogarauzpatam on the north, where it is separated from the mainland by a narrow channel. Transferred from the Madras district in 1865. It is about 35 miles long and 6 miles broad in its widest part. Covered with dense jungle and forms one of the chief sources of supply of firewood for the Madras market.

The soil is almost pure sand. Climate unhealthy, with much elephantiasis owing to scanty and stagnant water-supply. Along the Poolicat lake a narrow strip of land is under rice [q.v.] cultivation. Round the huts scanty crops of raggy [q.v.] and chayroot [q.v.] are raised by sinking earthenware wells. The trees are pollarded, and to a great measure recover themselves in seven years. Chiefly interesting as being one of the homes of the Yanaudies [q.v.], a wild tribe, of whom there are several thousands in the district. No village of this name. Tradition states that an old city, which was founded here by Trishunkoo [q.v.] of the Solar race, has been submerged.——*Shree jayanty* (శ్రీజయంతి - shríjayanti, Tel.). Means holy + day of rejoicing. Veishnava name. Compare Gocoolaushtamy, the Smarta designation. Same as Krishna jayanty.——*Shreemat* (श्रीमत् - shrímat, San.). From (above + mat, san. possessing). Or Shreeman. Title not of southern usage. Also used as an expletive in opening of letters; in Mahratta and Canarese inscriptions, this is of uniform occurrence. In Tamul, inscriptions [jonaca, shausanam] are commenced with Swastishree [peyar].——*Shreemooshnam* (சிரீமுட்டணம் - shirímuttanam, Tam.). From (shrí, san. beauty + mush, san. to excel); surpassing in beauty. Sanscrit name (jhillikávana), meaning cricket, gryllus genus + forest. South arcot dist., Chidambaram tal.; pop. 2,810; acres 1,973; lat. 11° 23′ 54″; long. 79° 27′; from Chidambaram W. 20 miles; from Cuddalore S.W. 32 miles; from the sea W. 28 miles. South of the Vellaur. The Vishnoo [q.v.] temple is one of the eight great Veishnava shrines and considered next to Shreerungam for sanctity. The main part of the building was built by a Naick [q.v.] of Tanjore. The temple has some very fine carvings in black trap [padicutt cull]. Annual festivals are Maushimagham [pundigay, 5b] in Maushy [mausam] or February and Cheitrotsavam [pundigay, 2d] in Chittray [mausam] or April. During the former the idol [shilay, vigraham] is carried to Killay, where great numbers of people follow it and bathe in the sea. At convenient stages during the journey the idol stops for a few hours and its followers are fed by charitable people. The Cheitrotsavam is the ordinary ten days' annual festival which is held at all large pagodas [q.v.].——*Shreenivausan* (சிரீநிவாசன் - shirínivásan, Tam.). From (above + nivása, san. abode). Vishnoo [q.v.] who dwells with Lutchmy [q.v.]. Familiarly sheenan, sheenoo, sheemautchoo. Hindoo 2nd or pers. name [peyar].——*Shree padam* (श्रीपद - shrípada, San.). From (above + pada, san. foot). Sacred foot-steps on rocks, worshipped [dharmarajacull, kadam, paudam]. See vol. I (87).——*Shreepermatore* (சிரீப்பெரும்பூதூர் - shirípperumbúthúr, Tam. sríperumbudur *). From (shrí, san. holy + perum, tam. large + bhúta, san. devil + úr, tam. village). Familiarly Peroondore. Sanscrit name (bhútapurí), meaning demon + town. "*a*". Deputy tahsildarry, Chingleput district. Pay Rs. 70.—"*b*" Town, Place of pilgrimage, Deputy tahsildar's station; Chingleput dist., Conjeeveram tal.; pop. 5,956; acres 4,792; lat. 12° 58′; long. 80° 01′; from Chingleput N. 19 miles; from Conjeeveram E.N.E. 19 miles; from Madras W. 24 miles; from St. Thomas' mount W. 17 miles; from Sydapett W. 19 miles. On high western trunk road. Belonged to old talook of Manimungalam, and was for some years after 1860 cusbah [q.v.] of Conjeeveram talook. Birth place of Ramaunoojacharry [ramaunoojan]. Vishnoo [q.v.] temple. Shiva [q.v.] temple older.——*Shreeraman* (శ్రీరాముడు - shrírámudu, Tel.). From (above + ráma, san. the hero). Holy rama. Hindoo 2nd or pers. name [peyar].——*Shree rama navamy* (శ్రీరామనవమి - shrírámanavami, Tel.). From (above + ráma, san. the hero + navamí, san. the ninth lunar day). Lunar [chaundramaunam] festival [pundigay, 3a], subject to intercalation [adhicam]. The ninth day of the waxing moon [shooclapacsham] of the first lunar month Cheitram [mausam] between 23rd March and 21st April. Festival lasts nine days, celebrated in temples of Vishnoo [q.v.]. Each evening god goes in procession through streets on different vehicles [vauhan], and on return of procession he is exposed in a mantapam [q.v.], to receive offerings of people. It is not a Dravidian festival, and was introduced into the country by the Mahrattas. On this day Rama was born as a Cshatriya at Ayodhyay under star [nacshatram] Poonarvas [maryauday, poonarvas]. See vol. I (92).——*Shreerungam* (சிரீரங்கம் - shirírangam, Tam. srírangam *). From (shrí, san. holy + ranga, san. pleasure place). Sanscrit name (ádiranga), meaning first + pleasure-place [rungasawmy]. Veishnava name (namberumálsannithi), meaning our great god + presence; also (kóvil), meaning temple; also (tiruvarangam), meaning same as title. Town, Island, Place of pilgrimage; Trichinopoly dist., Trichinopoly tal.; pop. 21,632; acres 975; lat. 10° 52′; long. 78° 45′; from Ariyalore S.W. 32 miles; from Madras S.W. 185 miles; from Moosiry E.S.E. 18 miles; from Trichinopoly N.N.W. 4 miles. Between the Cauvery and Coleroon. The town is famous for its Vishnoo [q.v.] temple with which it is almost conterminous. The temple is certainly the largest in the south of India. The entire mass of building consists of seven enclosures, the outermost wall of which measures 3,072 feet by 2,521 feet. In the centre of whole is the shrine of Runganauta sawmy. This shrine is surrounded by a wall measuring 240 feet by 181 feet; the second enclosure is 426 feet by 295 feet; and the third 767 feet by 503 feet. Europeans are not allowed to enter these enclosures. The fourth, in which is the thousand-pillar mantapam [q.v.], to which the great idol [shilay, vigraham] is brought every year during the Veicoonta yecaudasby [pundigay, 3a], festival, measures 1,235 feet by 849 feet. The hall of thousand columns measures 450 feet by 130 feet. The number of columns is sixteen in front by 60 in depth, consequently they are not more than 10 feet apart. Over the gates of the fourth enclosure are three gopoorams [q.v.], of which the eastern is the finest in the whole temple. It is known as the vellay or white gopooram [q.v.] and is 146 feet 6 inches in height. There is an unfinished outer gopooram of immense size, which, if completed, would have risen to the height of 300 feet. There are altogether fifteen gopoorams. Of these there are four in each of the three outer walls and three in the one next in order. There is at present no gate or gopooram on the western side of this enclosure; but tradition states that the gate formerly existing was blocked up because a number of the inhabitants of the portion of the town had entered through it and plundered the pagoda [q.v.]. The gate, over which is the vellay gopooram, leads into a yard to the south of the thousand-pillar mantapam, in which the only good specimens of stone carving in the temple are to be found. During the annual festival, this yard is covered by a pandaul [q.v.] erected at a cost of about Rs. 3,000. Running round the fourth enclosure is a street in which are ordinary dwelling-houses and shops. The fifth wall measures 1,653 feet by 1,270 feet. Outside is a second street, and then a wall of 2,108 feet in length by 1,846 feet in breadth. This wall is surrounded by a third street, and then comes the seventh and last wall. This wall is built of fine cut-stone, and is 20 feet 8 inches in height and 6 feet broad at the top. Another object of interest is a gopooram with a painted ceiling depicting the boar incarnation of Vishnoo and other subjects. In another Mantapam the temple jewels are shown to visitors. Some of them are very fine specimens of goldsmith's work. Several of the oldest of these were presented to the temple by Vijaya runga chokkanauta naick of Madura. The accumulated wealth in gold, silver, and precious stones is valued at between 12 and 15 lakhs [q.v.] of rupees. In his retirement here, Ramaunoojan worked out the system of the Veishnavite religion. He died here about the middle of the eleventh century. About 1½ miles from the great Vishnoo temple is a Shiva pagoda [q.v.]; which, although much smaller, surpasses the larger building in beauty and architectural dignity. There are many inscriptions on the walls of this temple, one dated A.D. 1481-82. Annual festival in December attracts natives from all parts of India [jambookeshwaram]. There is a Tamul proverb :—சீரங்கத்துக் காகமானாலும் கோவிந்தம் பாடுமா?—" though hatched at Shreerungam, will a crow sing "the praises of Govindan?" the qualities of the evil will not change. From 1751 to 1755 the island and its pagodas were the frequent objects of the contests between the French and the British. In those contests several rocks, the Golden, Pine, French, and Sugar loaf were the points of battles.——*Shreerungan* (சிரீரங்கன் - shirírangan, Tam.). From (above + ranga, san. vishnu of the island or pleasure place), holy vishnoo. Hindoo 2nd or pers name. In the neuter form applied to a female; it is then familiarly contracted into sheerungoo or sheerangy [peyar].——*Shreerunga nautan* (श्रीरङ्गनाथ - shríranganát'ha, San.). From (shríranga, san. the place + nát'ha, san. lord). Vishnoo at Shreerungam.——*Shreerungaroyer* (శ్రీరంగరాయలు - shrírangaráyalu, Tel.). From (above + ranga, san. island + ráya, tel. king). Representative of the then waning Vijianugger line and Rajah of Chundragherry. Granted to the English in 1640 the settlement of Madrasputnam [madras]. On his defeat by Golcondah army, sought refuge with the Rajah of Bednore, who made him governor of Sakroyputna [charitram]. See vol. I (161), 532; II, 66, 91.——*Shreevatsam* (श्रीवत्स - shrívatsa, San.). From (above + vasta, san. favorite); the favorite of lutchmy [q.v.]. A mark or curl of hair on the breast of Vishnoo [q.v.]. It is white and is represented in pictures by a symbol resembling a cruciform flower. For omens from curl marks see Shooly.——*Shreeveicoontam* (சிரீவைக்குண்டம் - shirívaikkundam, Tam. srívaikuntham *). From (above + vaikunt'ha, san. the heaven of vishnu).—"*a*" Sub-magistracy, Tinnevelly district. Pay Rs. 100.—"*b*" Town, Talook head-quarters; Tinnevelly dist., Tencaray tal.; pop. 7,209; acres 1,701; lat. 8° 38′; long. 77° 58′; height 141 feet; from Madras S.S.W. 340 miles; from Palamcottah E.S.E. 14 miles; from Shermadevy E. 24 miles; from Shreevillipoottore S.S.E. 63 miles; from Tinnevelly E.S.E. 17 miles; from Tuticorin W.S.W. 21 miles; from the sea W. 16. On left bank of Tamrapurny. Veishnava holy place. Ten principal temples. Vishnoo [q.v.] temple and Keilausa nauta temple, are large and important. Underneath the Vishnoo temple, tradition says, is a hidden building. Jeina [q.v.] statue. A peculiar class of people resident here called the Cottay vellaular whose females never on any pretext leave the limits of the fort in which they live. Two car festivals in March and July. Festivals at the Vishnoo pagoda [q.v.] in January, February, and April. Roman catholic chapel. Gives its name to an anicut [q.v.].——*Shreeveishnava* (श्रीवैष्णव - shrívaishnava, San.). From (above + vaishnava, worshipper of vishnu). The followers of Ramaunoojan [q.v.]; otherwise called Ramaunoojeeyans, or Shree sampradayees [q.v.]. They form the bulk of Vishnoo worshippers in the east and south, as the Madhwacharries [madhwa] do on the central tableland and the west coast. The

Braminical heads of the sect are called Jiyyar or Jiyyangar [q.v.]. Their worship is addressed to Vishnoo [q.v.] and to Lutchmy [q.v.], and their respective incarnations [avatar], either singly or conjointly; and the sect consists of corresponding sub-divisions, as Narayanan, Lutchmy, Lutchminarrain, Rama, Seetay, Seetaraman, Krishnan, Roocminy, or other modifications of the name of Vishnoo and his consort. The muntram [q.v.] of the Ramaunoojan sect is the six syllable muntram [q.v.], Om ramauya nama, or Om salutation to Rama. To the Acharries [q.v.], or supreme teachers of this sect, the rest perform the Ashtaunga dandawat pranaumam [ashtaungam, pranaumam] or prostration of the body with the application to the ground of eight parts, the forehead, breast, hands, knee, and insteps of the feet. The principal authorities of this sect are the comments of the founder on the Sootrams of Vyausan [q.v.] and other Vedic works. They are written in Sunscrit, and are the Shree bhashyam, Geeta bhashyam, Vedaurta sangraham, Vedaunta pradeepam, and Vedaunta sauram. Besides these, the works of Vencatacharry are of great repute, as the Sootra bhashyam and Shatadooshiny and others. The Chunda mauroota veidicam and Trimshata dhyaunam are also works of authority, as is the Pauncharautram [q.v.] of Nauradan. Of the Pooraunams [q.v.] they acknowledge only six as authorities; the Vishnoo, Nauradeeyam, Gauroodam, Pudmam, Varauham and the Bhaugavatam. The other twelve are regarded as Taumasam [q.v.] or originating in the principles of darkness and passion. Besides these, the Ramaunoojeeyans have a variety of popular works in the dialects of the south, one of which the Gooroo pauramparay contains an account of the life of Ramaunoojan. For the founder see Ramaunoojan, for the philosophy see Vishishtaudweitam. See also vol. I (85), (89) [matam].——*Shree vencateshan* (श्रीवेङ्कटेश - shrívénkatésha, San.). From (above + vénkata, san. the mountain + ísha, san. lord). Vishnoo.——*Shreevillipoottore* (ஸ்ரீவில்லிப்புத்தூர் - shirívillipputtúr, Tam.). See sep. title.——*Shreevullabhan* (ஸ்ரீவல்லபன் - shirívallaban, Tam.). From (above + vallabha, san. husband). Lutchmy's husband. Hindoo 2nd or pers. name [peyar].——*Srisheilam* (శ్రీశైలం - shríshailam, Tel.). From (above + shaila, san. mountain). Colloquially Parvatam [q.v.] or the special hill among the local people. Village, Place of pilgrimage; Kurnool dist., Nundicotcore tal.; lat. 16° 05′; long. 78° 55′; height 1,439 feet; from Kurnool E.N.E. 56 miles; from Nundicotcore N.E. 42 miles. In Nullamullay forests close to gorge of Kistna. The great temple here is, in spite of inaccessibility, one of the most renowned in S. india and pilgrims visit it from Central india. The image was formerly a small oblong roundish white stone with dark rings fixed in a silver case. The Rohillas stole it, and the present stone was obtained from Benares. The temple is situated high above the rocky banks of the Kistna, and surrounded on all sides by temples [coil, pagoda], mantapams [q.v.], long flights of stone steps on hill-sides, and other monuments. The earliest actual record of the temple relates to a visit by the Chaloukya [q.v.] ruler Treilocyan, in A.D. 1058. It was richly endowed by Hindoo nobles and was in a prosperous condition till the arrival of the Mahomedans in seventeenth century, who resumed inams [q.v.] and levied a tax on pilgrims. Up to 1794, unknown to Europeans. The image is, owing to the darkness of the inner part of the temple, exhibited to the visitor by means of a mirror called Darpanam or cunnaudy [q.v.] for which a large fee is charged. It is the water lingam [q.v.]. The earth lingam is at Conjeeveram, and the air lingam at Chidambaram or Rameshwaram [punchalingam]. The poojarries [q.v.] are Jangams [q.v.]. The principal places connected with Srisheilam are the temples on both banks of the river, 5 miles north; a temple $1\frac{1}{2}$ miles south; the temple of Alakeshwara coobairan, 2 miles south-east; the temple at Shikharam, 4 miles south-east; the temple at Collamnullah, 4 miles south; the temple of Nakkamulla, 6 miles south by west; and the temple of Nungalooty, 15 miles south-west. Seven miles north, on the Nizam's side of the river, is the site of the deserted city and fort of Chundragoortyputnam, a place formerly of great importance, said to measure 10 square miles in circumference. At Shivarautry {pundigay, 6a] in February or March a great festival takes place, which is attended by pilgrims from all parts of the country, who muster about twenty to thirty thousand. A fee is collected by the renters, and another fee by the Chentsoos [q.v.]. This festival is followed by another in honor of Ambah devy, and the whole lasts nearly two months. The Srisheilam plateau has long been the grazing ground of the cattle [maud] of the coast districts of Nellore and Kistna in hot weather and in seasons of drought.——*Sylhet* (سلهٹ - silhat, Hind.). From (shrí, san. auspicious + hatta, san. market). A district in Assam, N.E. of Bengal.——*Sylhet varnish* (भल्लातक - bhallátaka, San.). Product of Marking-nut [q.v.] tree.

SHREEVILLIPOOTTORE (ஸ்ரீவில்லிப்புத்தூர் - shirívillipputtúr, *Tam.* srívilliputúr*). From (shrí, san. holy + villi, tam. bowman + puthu, tam. new + úr, tam. village) [shree]; named after a hunter, who discovered the shrine amidst the jungle. Tam. also (villipputtúr); also (náççiyárkkóvil), meaning maiden + temple, referring to aundaul [q.v.]. Sanscrit name (gódápurí), meaning the earth-born + town, referring to aundaul; also (shrídhanushpura), meaning holy + bow + town. ——**(1)** Talook, Tinnevelly district. Tahsildar's pay Rs. 200. Area 585 square miles. Population 190,517. Language Tamul. N.W. of district. Bounded north by Tirmungalam and Periyacoolam talooks of Madura district, west by the ghauts, south by Shuncaraneinarcoil talook, and east by Shauttore. The country to the west undulates considerably owing to the numerous streams which descend from the mountains. It contains many palmyras [q.v.] and a considerable number of mango [q.v.] and tamarind [q.v.] topes [q.v.]. The principal feature of this portion is a deep bay in the mountains 6 miles north of Shreevillipoottore, containing the village of Watrap. From this village a mountain pass [ghaut] leads over into the Cumbum valley of Madura district, whence there is a road viâ Peermaid into Travancore. Another pass leads from the Shauttore zemindarry in the south-west angle of the talook over mountains densely forested and over 4,000 feet in height into a wide plateau, many square miles of which are grass and through which flows the Periyaur on its way to the sea in Travancore. A few miles north of this path is the site of the dam by which it is proposed to turn the waters of the Periyaur over a low ridge in the range into the Cumbum valley of Madura district. The forests of the sources of this river are yearly searched for cardamoms [q.v.] by the Travancore government. Peermaid and the low country of Travancore may be reached by this road also. The eastern half of the talook has few trees. Occasionally poor topes of tamarind [q.v.] are met with and thickets of babool [q.v.] thorn are found in most tanks and river beds. The lofty tower of Shreevillipoottore pagoda [q.v.] is a landmark from almost every part of the talook. Rather more than half of the talook, including the villages lying to the west, belongs to the red clay loam and sand series. The easterly villages form a portion of the cotton plain, and half a black cotton soil [regar] or one of black soil mixed with gravel and salt earth [sowdoo]. The mountains above Shauttore as well as above Shreevillipoottore and Watrap, contain valuable timbers of several kinds. Cumboo [bajrah], gram [q.v.] and dholl [q.v.] are the products of the dry lands [poonjah], and rice [q.v.], plantains [q.v.], and cocoanuts [q.v.] of the wet [nunjah], in the western portion of the talook. Cotton [q.v.], cumboo [bajrah] and gram [q.v.] are grown on the dry lands in the eastern portion. The irrigated lands, which are few, grow rice, and with the aid of wells tobacco [pogauk] and chillies [q.v.]. Irrigation has been carefully attended to in early times in the western villages of this talook, and the streams which descend from the ghauts [q.v.] at Rajahpolliem, Shauttore, Shreevillipoottore, and Watrap have been utilised by anicuts [q.v.] and channels [q.v.] and tanks [q.v.] to store the water in. There are 38 anicuts [q.v.], 25 principal river channels [q.v.], and 253 tanks [q.v.], of which about one-half are partially supplied by river channels. Zemindarries:—Collancondaun, Shettore. Places of archæological interest:—Cholapooram, Collancondaun, Cottangoolam, Cummaulancoolam, Devastaunam, Keel rajacoola ramangraumam, Madavaurvilaugam, Mauranairy, Nadicoody, Poothoopolliem, Rajahpolliem, Sammandapooram, Shettore, Shreevillipoottore, Vengamullore, Yethircottay. Principal trig. stations:—Peymullay, Vauzhaicoolam. The leading places, &c., in the talook are the following.——*Atchandavilattaun* (அச்சந்தவிளத்தான் - açcandavilattán, Tam.). From (açcam, tam. fear + tavizhttán, tam. deliverer), place of refuge. Village; pop. 3,199; acres 4,697; lat. 9° 26′; long. 77° 42′; from Shreevillipoottore S.S.E. 6 miles; from Tinnevelly N. 48 miles. On left bank of Cayalgoody river. Temple.——*Cholapooram* (சோழபுரம் - shózhavaram, Tam.). From (chóla, san. the dynasty so called + pura, san. city). Village; pop. 2,887; acres 5,504; lat. 9° 23′; long. 77° 36′; from Shreevillipoottore S.S.W. 10 miles; from Tinnevelly N. 45 miles. On road to Shuncaraneinarcoil. Two old Shiva and Vishnoo temples, with inscriptions. Weekly fair on Thursdays.——*Collancondaun* (கொல்லங்கொண்டான் - kollangundán, Tam.). From (kollam, tam. high ground + kondán, tam. he who possesses). Village, Head-quarters of zemindar; pop. 2,335; acres 7,383; lat. 9° 25′; long. 77° 34′; from Shreevillipoottore S.W. 10 miles; from Tinnevelly N.N.W. 47 miles. Two large ancient Shiva and Vishnoo temples, with inscriptions. Peshcush Rs. 24.——*Devastaunam* (தேவத்தானம் - tévattánam, Tam.). From (déva, san. god + st'hána, san. place). Village; pop. 1,954; lat. 9° 24′; long. 77° 30′; from Shreevillipoottore S.W. 14 miles; from Tinnevelly N.N.W. 48 miles. Fine Shiva temple with inscriptions.——*Madavaurvilaugam* (மடவார்விளாகம் - madavárvilágam, Tam.). From (madavál, tam. woman + világam, tam. battle-field). Village; pop. 2,483; lat. 9° 30′; long. 77° 40′; from Shreevillipoottore S. ¼ mile; from Tinnevelly N. 53 miles. Suburb of Shreevillipoottore. Fine pagoda [q.v.] and tower dedicated to Shiva [q.v.]. Annual car festival [ratotsavam] in May. Inscriptions in temple.——*Peymullay* (பேய்மலை - péymalai, Tam.). From (péy, tam. devil + malai, tam. hill). Sanscrit name (dharmádri), meaning justice + mountain. Hill; lat. 9° 33′; long. 77° 34′; from Shreevillipoottore W.N.W. 8 miles; from Tinnevelly N. 57 miles. Trig. station in lat. 9° 33′ 12″; long. 77° 33′ 36″; height 5,575 feet; from Shreevillipoottore W.N.W. 8 miles; from Vauzhaicoolam N. 52 miles.——*Rajacoolaraman* (இராசகுலராமன் - irásakularáman, Tam.). From (rájakula, san. royal family + ráma, san. proper name); after a paundyan of that name. Village; pop. 3,408; acres 220; lat. 9° 24′; long. 77° 41′; from Shreevillipoottore S. 8 miles; from Tinnevelly N. 46 miles. On Tinnevelly road.——*Rajahpolliem* (இராசாப்பாளையம் - irásáppálaiyam, Tam.). From (rájá, san. king + pálaiyam, tam. fortified village). Town; pop. 13,301; acres 1,184; lat. 9° 27′; long. 77° 36′; from Shreevillipoottore S.W. 7 miles; from Tinnevelly N. 50 miles. On the Shreevillipoottore-Tinnevelly road. Inhabited chiefly by people who came from the old Vijianugger state. Old Shiva [q.v.] temple. Fine tamarind [q.v.] tope [q.v.] to the north. Large tank with ancient temple on its bank. Iron [auhan], agricultural and other implements made.——*Shettore* (சேத்தூர் - shéttúr, Tam. sétur *). Mean's saitocpaty's village. Zemindarry, Town; pop. 7,665; acres 22,492; lat. 9° 25′; long. 77° 31′; from Shreevillipoottore S.W. 12 miles; from Tinnevelly N.N.W. 48 miles. The estate is at S.W. corner of talook. Well irrigated from mountains. Zemindar [q.v.] is of Marava caste. Peshcush Rs. 12,536, rental, Rs. 36,240. Old Shiva [q.v.] temple in the village with inscriptions.——*Shreevillipoottore* (ஸ்ரீவில்லிப்புத்தூர் - shirívillipputtúr, Tam.). See below.——*Vauzhaicoolam* (வாழைக்குளம் - vázhaikkulam, Tam.). From (vázhai, tam. plantain + kulam, tam. tank). Trig. station in lat. 8° 48′ 17·94″; long. 77° 39′ 56·02″; from Paurapully S.W. 62 miles; from Shreevillipoottore S. 48 miles.——*Watrap* (வத்திராயிருப்பு - vattiráyiruppu, Tam.). See sep. title.——*Yethircottay* (எதிர்க்கோட்டை - ethirkkóttai, Tam.). From (ethir, tam. opposite + kóttai, tam. fort); pop. 1,830; acres 4,707; lat. 9° 23′; long. 77° 47′; from Shreevillipoottore S.E. 11 miles; from Tinnevelly N. 44 miles. Inscription on a rock.——**(2)** Town, Head-quarters of General deputy collector, Tahsildar, District moonsif; Tinnevelly dist., Shreevillipoottore tal.; pop. 21,448; acres 1,622; lat. 9° 31′; long. 77° 40′; height 651 feet; from Madras S.W. 302 miles; from Palamcottah N. 54 miles; from Shermadevy N. 56 miles; from Tinnevelly N. 53 miles; from Tuticorin N.W. 60 miles. On an open plain on road leading viâ Shencottah and Courtallam through Aryancauv pass. Aurautchiputty, with a population of 3,807, forms part of Shreevillipoottore. Old Vishnoo [q.v.] temple, handsomely sculptured, and an old Shiva [q.v.] temple. Both temples have fine gopoorams [q.v.] and a number of inscriptions. Small temple to Krishnasawmy, with inscriptions. The old palace of the Naicks [q.v.] has been converted into a cutcherry [q.v.]. Car procession [ratotsavam] in August. Another for bathing in January. Coarse cotton cloths woven. Vishnoo temple on a rock in the west. Much frequented on Saturdays [poorattaushy shany kizhamay] in September.

SHRINGAM (शृङ्ग - shringa, San.). From (shrí, san. to injure) [sharam, shooran]. Horn; peak.——*Shaurngam* (शार्ङ्ग - shárnga, San.). From (shringa, san. horn); as made of horn. The bow of Vishnoo [codandam].——*Shaurngapauny* (शार्ङ्गपाणि - shárngapáni, San.). From (shárnga, san. bow + páni, san. hand). Vishnoo, the Shaurngam-bearer. Hindoo2nd or pers. name [peyar].——*Shingy* (శింగి - shingi, Tel.). From (shringa, san. peak). Mountain.——*Shringairy* (ಶೃಂಗೇರಿ - shringéri, Can.; shringeri, Mys. Gov.). From (shringa, san. peak + giri, san. mountain). Sanscrit name (rishyashringagiri), meaning rishyashringan, the sage + mountain. Town, Place of pilgrimage, Cuddore district, Mysore, on the left bank of the Toonga, in 13° 25′ N. lat., 75° 18′ E. long., in the Coppa talook. 8 miles south-west of Hariharpore, the cusbah [q.v.]. Most important of mutts [q.v.] founded by Shuncaran [q.v.].——*Shringy* (शृङ्गी - shringí, San.). Horned. Plant second term. Ex., where transl. is of first term:—Gymnema sylvestre (méshashringí), sheep; Helicteres isora (mrigashringa), deer; Odina wodier (ajashringí), sheep; Pistacia integerrima (karkatashringí), crab; Rhus succedania (karkatashringí), crab; Terminalia chebula (karkatashringí), crab. See gloss. paragraphs.——*Sing* (سینگ - síng, Hind.; கொம்பு - kombu, Tam.). Hind. from (shringa, san. horn). Horn. Horns are obtained from the following:—Antelope bezoartica [jinka]; Axis maculatus or Spotted deer [cheetal]; Bos indicus, or Domestic cattle [maud]; Bubalus arni, or Buffalo [khoolgah]; Capra hircus, or Domestic goat [aud]; Cervulus muntjac, or Jungle sheep [q.v.]; Gavæus gaurus, or Bison [gowr]; Gazella bennettii, or Ravine deer [q.v.]; Hemitragus hylocrius, or Ibex [saddle back]; Rusa aristotelis, or Samber [q.v.]. The horns of deer [murigam], called antlers, are solid processes from the frontal bone and possess the properties of true bone; periodically shed by absorption of the bony base, after which a new pair grows with great rapidity. The horns of the ox, buffalo, &c., are hollow and are never shed; deposited in layers or bony cores composed principally of albumen. Horns of wild animals are more prominent than in domesticated races. They are generally larger in males. For Ivory see Dant.——*Singauram* (శింగారము - singáramu, Tel.). From (shringára, san. beauty). Beauty. Also as a name short for Singauravailoo.——*Singauravailoo* (శింగారవేలు - singáravélu, Tel.). From (shringára, san. beauty + vélu, tam. familiar form of vélan, tam. skanda, the lance-bearer). Hindoo 2nd or pers. name. Common among non-bramins [peyar].——*Singhaura* (शृङ्गाटक - shringátaka, San.; शिंगाडा - shingádá, Mahr.; سنگھاڑہ - singhárah, Hind.; سنگارا - singárá, Dec.; పందిగడ్డ - pandigadda, Tel.; കരിമ്പോള - karimpóla, Mal.; ඉකිලිය - ikiliya, Singh.; பன்றிமொந்தான்கிழங்கு - panrimóndángizhangu, Tam.). Title from deccany. San. from (shringa, san. horn + at, san. to go), from horned fruit. Mahr. from sanscrit. Hind. from (síng, hind. horn). Dec. from hindostany. Tel. from (pandi, tel. pig + gadda, tel. root). Mal. from (kari, mal. black + póla, mal. the water plant, geodorum dilatatum, r. br.). Tam. from (panri, tam. pig + mó, tam. to smell + kizhangu, tam. esculent root). San. also (kubjaka), meaning crooked; (jalakantaka), meaning water thorn. Hind. also (pániphal), meaning water fruit. Tel. also (parikegadda). Tam. also (panrimottai), meaning pig + lump. Title otherwise Paneephul, Pig root, Water caltrops, Water chestnut, Water thorn. Botanically Trapa bispinosa, roxb., onagraceæ [vricsham, 59]. Alias Trapa bicornis. Herbaceous, floating; upper leaves and petioles tomentose beneath, lower leaves opposite, others alternate, floating leaves rather quadrate, serrulately toothed; calyx villous, limb four-partite; petals four; crown of the ovary eight-furrowed, the margins curled; fruit two-horned; horns opposite, conical, very sharp, barbed backwards; petioles furnished with a large bladder in the middle; ovary two-celled, surrounded by a cap-shaped crown; flowers smallish, white; found on tanks. The nut grows under the water after the flowers decay, and is of a triangular shape, and covered with a tough brown integument, adhering strongly to the kernel, which is white and esculent. Nuts used in bilious affections and diarrhœa; also in form of poultices. Kernel of nut white, sweetish and farinaceous, eaten, raw and cooked. Flower gives a dye [shauyam]. No other common species here. For land caltrops see Nerinjy.——*Srungavarapoocote* (శృంగవరపుకోట - sbringavarapukóta, Tel.). See sep. title.

SHUBBEER (شبیر - shabbír, *Ar.*). Another name of Hassan, the grandson of the prophet. Alam taken by Shiahs, as Shubbeer hoossain, double alam [ism].

SHUBBER (شبر - shabbar, *Ar.*). Another name of Hoossain, the grandson of the prophet. Alam taken by Shiahs, as Shubber ally, double alam [ism].

SHUM (شم - sham, *Hind.*). Tail.——*Shumsheer* (شمشیر - shamshír, Pers.). From (above + sher, pers. lion). Scimitar. Prefixed to an alam makes a lacab; as Shumsheer ally, the sword of ally [ism].

SHUMS (شمس - shams, *Pers.*). Sun [sooryan]; known amongst the Mahomedans as the celestial cook, with its orbit in the fourth heaven [najm]. One born at the hour of the week assigned to its influence [zyecha] will be wealthy, passionate, generous, annually indisposed, and little famed for pious works. Part of lacab; as Shums ood deen, the sun of religion [ism].

SHUNCARANEINARCOIL (சங்கரநயினார்கோயில் - shangaranayinárkkóyil, *Tam.* sankaranainárkoil *). From (shankara, san. shiva, the pleasure-giver + nayinár, tam. lord + kóvil, tam. temple) [sham]. Sanscrit name (shankaranáráyanapura), meaning town of shiva and vishnoo in one [hariharan].——**(1)** Talook, Tinnevelly district. Tahsildar's pay Rs. 200. Area 718 square miles. About one-half is Government and the rest zemindarry and inam. Population 213,779. Language Tamul. N.W. of district. At the foot of the ghauts [q.v.]. Bounded south by Tencausby and Tinnevelly talooks; east by Ottapidauram talook; west by the Southern ghauts; and north by Shreevillipoottore talook. Soil is red and black. In general the talook is bare of trees. The red country is broken into valleys and ridges by numerous small torrents and streams descending from the mountains, and is well supplied with channels leading from these streams and with tanks supplied by the channels [q.v.]. Its principal wealth is its irrigated lands, as the dry cultivation is poor excepting under wells, where good crops of cholum [q.v.] and raggy [q.v.] are occasionally seen. The black cotton [regar] country is almost one-fourth of the talook in extent and is a portion of the great cotton plain which occupies the north and north-east portion of the district. The plains are broken only by a few scattered topes [q.v.] of poor tamarinds [q.v.] and of the babool [q.v.] found in almost all the tank-beds throughout the cotton plains [regar]. The greater portion of the cotton soil is poor. Trade is trifling. Raw cotton [q.v.] is the only export; and rice [q.v.] and articles of European manufacture, chiefly cloth, the principal imports. There are no manufactures of importance. In the higher lands, much of which are of fair quality, cholum [q.v.] cumboo [bajrah] and gram [q.v.] are sown in the north-east monsoon [q.v.] months, and large areas are generally left fallow. Rice [q.v.], plantain [q.v.] gardens and betel [q.v.] vines are the products grown under irrigation. The supply of water in the south-west monsoon [q.v.] is trifling and uncertain and confined to a few villages quite at the foot of the range. The main supply is from the north-east monsoon [q.v.], which breaks usually with considerable force on the range and fills all the streams, channels, and tanks generally two or three times, in which case a good crop is secured. Zemindarries:—Alagapoory, Auvoodaiyaupooram, Coolashekhara mungalam, Eechandah, Nadoovacoorchy, Notchicolam, Panayore, Poygaycoottaulapairy, Shivagherry, Soobramanyapooram, Tala vancottah, Tirvettaynullore, Trimalnaick poothoocoody, Vada mullaypooram, Vailayoodhapooram, Veeriroop, Vellaulacoolam. These except Talavancottah are portions of the ancient zemindarry of Chokkamputty sold up in 1867. Places of archæological interest:—Carivalamvandanullore, Daurcapooram, Shuncaraneinarcoil, Tenmullay, Veerashikhaumany. Principal trig. stations :—Caurishauttan, Periyore mullay. The leading places, &c., in the talook are the following.——*Alagapoory* (அழகாப்புரி - azhagáppuri, Tam.). From (azhagu, tam. beauty + purí, san. town). Zemindarry, Village ; pop. 1,347 ; square miles 1¼ ; lat. of village 9° 13′ ; long. 77° 40′ ; from Shuncaraneinarcoil E.N.E. 6 miles ; from Tinnevelly N. 33 miles. Peshcush Rs. 669.——*Auvoodaiyaupooram* (ஆவுடையாப்புரம் - ávudaiyáppuram, Tam.). From (ávudaiyár, tam. lingam and yóni, emblem of shiva + pura, san. town). Zemindarry, Village ; pop. of zemindarry 6,960 ; lat. of village 9° 20′ ; long. 77° 35′ ; from Shuncaraneinarcoil N. 11 miles ; from Tinnevelly N.N.W. 43 miles. Zemindarry consists of three villages. Peshcush Rs. 2,941.——*Carivalamvandanullore* (கரிவலம்வந்தநல்லூர் - karivalamvandanallúr, Tam.). From (kari, san. elephant + valamvá, tam. to circumambulate + nal, tam. good + úr, tam. village). Village ; pop. 3,975 ; acres 4,554 ; lat. 9° 16′ ; long. 77° 35′ ; from Shuncaraneinarcoil N. 7 miles ; from Tinnevelly N.N.W. 38 miles. On road to Shreevillipoottore. Temple to Paulvunnanauta sawmy, with inscriptions of Psundy [q.v.] dynasty in Grantam [q.v.] and Tamul [q.v.]. The lingam [q.v.] was once of crystal [palingoo cull], hence name of the deity, milk-colored lord. Three car festivals annually.——*Caurishauttan* (காரிசாத்தான் - kárisáttán, Tam.). From (kári, tam. blackness + sháttan, tam. the god aiyyanár). Village ; pop. 1,619 ; acres 3,779 ; lat. 9° 17′ ; long. 77° 36′ ; from Shuncaraneinarcoil N.N.E. 8 miles ; from Tinnevelly N. 39 miles. Trig station in lat. 9° 16′ 59·56″ ; long. 77° 37′ 29·94″ ; height 915 feet ; from Mahomed sahibpooram S. 7 miles ; from Shuncaraneinarcoil N.N.E. 8 miles.——*Coolashekhara mungalam* (குலசேகரமங்கலம் - kulaségaramangalam, Tam.). From (kulashékhara, san. proper name + mangala, san. prosperity). Village, Head-quarters of Mittahdar ; pop. 5,733 ; lat. 9° 05′ ; long. 77° 30′ ; from Shuncaraneinarcoil S.S.W. 8 miles ; from Tinnevelly N.N.W. 28 miles. Peshcush Rs. 2,029.——*Cooroovicolam* (குருவிக்குளம் - kuruvikkulam, Tam.). From (kuruvi, tam. smal bird + kulam, tam. tank). Village ; pop. 5,679 ; acres 10,203 ; lat. 9° 10′ ; long. 77° 43′ ; from Shuncaraneinarcoil E. 9 miles ; from Tinnevelly N. 31 miles. Shiva temple. Coarse cloths manufactured.——*Ecchandah* (ஈச்சந்தா - íççandá, Tam.). From (íñju, tam. the date tree, phœnix farinifera, roxb. + távu, tam. place). Zemindarry, Village ; pop. 1,859 ; lat. of village 9° 04′ ; long. 77° 34′ ; from Shuncaraneinarcoil S.S.W. 8 miles ; from Tinnevelly N.N.W. 26 miles.——Peshcush Rs. 557.——*Nadoovacoorchy* (நடுவக்குறிச்சி - naduvakkuriççi, Tam.). From (naduvu, tam. middle + kuriççi, tam. village). Zemindarry, Village ; pop. of zemindarry 1,125 ; square miles 16¼ ; lat. of village 9° 06′ ; long. 77° 33′ ; from Shuncaraneinarcoil S.S.W. 6 miles ; from Tinnevelly N.N.W. 29 miles. Zemindarry ; consists of ten villages. Peshcush Rs. 1,527.——*Panayore* (பனையூர் - panaiyúr, Tam.). From (panai, tam. palmyra tree, borassus flabelliformis, linn. + úr, tam. village). Zemindarry, Village ; pop 2,520 ; lat. of village 9° 16′ ; long. 77° 33′ ; from Shuncaraneinarcoil N.N.W. 7 miles ; from Tinnevelly N.N.W. 39 miles. Peshcush Rs. 1,399.——*Periyore* (பெரியூர் - periyúr, Tam.). From (periya, tam. great + úr, tam. village). Village ; pop. 1,585 ; acres 2,481 ; lat. 9° 15′ ; long. 77° 33′ ; from Shuncaraneinarcoil N.N.W. 6 miles ; from Tinnevelly N.N.W. 38 miles. Almost in ruins. Trig. station in lat. 9° 12′ 15·61″ ; long. 77° 32′ 13·57″ ; height 1,378 feet ; from Malaiyadiputty W. 18 miles ; from Shuncaraneinarcoil N.W. 4 miles.——*Pooliyangoody* (புளியங்குடி - puliyangudi, Tam.). From (puli, tam. tamarind tree, tamarindus indica, linn. + kudi, tam. village). Town ; pop. 7,233 ; acres 1,525 ; lat. 9° 10′ ; long. 77° 26′ ; from Shuncaraneinarcoil W. 10 miles ; from Tinnevelly N.N.W. 37 miles. On old Madura road. Two temples of Vishnoo [q.v.] and Soobramanyan [q.v.]. Two annual car festivals [ratotsavam]. Cloths, reed [coray] mats [boriyah], iron [auhan], and jaggery [q.v.] manufactured.——*Shivagherry* (சிவகிரி - shivagiri, Tam.). See sep. title.——*Shuncaraneinarcoil* (சங்கரநயினார்க்கோயில் - shangaranayinárkkóyil, Tam.). See below.——*Soobramanyapooram* (சுப்பிரமணியபுரம் - shuppiramaniyappuram, Tam.). From (subrahmanya, san. the pious god skanda + pura, san. town). Zemindarry, Village ; pop. 390 ; acres 309 ; lat. of village 9° 21′ ; long. 77° 31′ ; from Shuncaraneinarcoil N.N.W. 13 miles ; from Tinnevelly N.N.W. 44 miles. Irrigated by Palavore channel. Peshcush Rs. 880.——*Talavancottah* (தலைவன்கோட்டை - talaivangóttai, Tam.). From (talaivan, tam. chieftain + kóttai, tam. fort). Zemindarry, Village ; pop. 1,696 ; acres 5,710 ; lat. of village 9° 11′ ; long. 77° 30′ ; from Shuncaraneinarcoil W. 6 miles ; from Tinnevelly N.N.W. 36 miles. Peshcush Rs. 2,732.——*Tirvettaynullore* (திருவேட்டைநல்லூர் - tiruvéttainallúr, Tam.). From (tiru, tam. sacred + véttai, tam. hunt + nal, tam. good + úr, tam. town). Village, Head-quarters of Mittahdar ; pop. 4,751 ; lat. 9° 08′ ; long. 77° 27′ ; from Shuncaraneinarcoil W.S.W. 9 miles ; from Tinnevelly N.W. 34 miles. Peshcush Rs. 1,645.——*Trimalnaickpoothoocoody* (திருமலைநாயக்கன்புதுக்குடி - tirumalainàyakkanbuthukkudi, Tam.). From (tirumalainàyakkan, tam. proper name + puthu, tam. new + kudi, tam. village). Zemindarry, Village ; pop. 2,333 ; acres 394 ; lat. of village 9° 10′ ; long. 77° 26′ ; from Shuncaraneinarcoil W. 10 miles ; from Tinnevelly N.N.W. 37 miles. Peshcush Rs. 2,069.——*Vasoodevanullore* (வாசுதேவநல்லூர் - vásuthévanallúr, Tam. vásudévanallúr*). From (vásudéva, san. epithet of krishna + nal, tam. good + úr, tam. village). Town ; pop. 5,926 ; acres 3,523 ; lat. 9° 15′ ; long. 77° 27′ ; from Shuncaraneinarcoil W.N.W. 10 miles ; from Tinnevelly N.N.W. 40 miles. On Madura-Travancore road. Ancient temple. Festival in June. Weekly fair on Wednesday.——*Veerashikhaumany* (வீரசிகாமணி - vírasigámani, Tam.). After a person of that name. Village ; pop. 2,118 ; acres 3,211 ; lat. 9° 06′ ; long. 77° 31′ ; from Shuncaraneinarcoil S.W. 8 miles ; from Tinnevelly N.N.W. 30 miles. Rock cut caves and sculpture.——*Vellaulacoolam* (வெள்ளாளன்குளம் - vellálangulam, Tam.). From (vellálan, tam. man of that caste + kulam, tam. tank). Zemindarry, Village ; pop. 1,257 ; lat. of village 9° 03′ ; long. 77° 32′ ; from Shuncaraneinarcoil S.S.W. 10 miles ; from Tinnevelly N.W. 26 miles. On road to Tencaushy. Peshcush Rs. 429.——*Yilaiyarasanendal* (இளவரசனேந்தல் - ilavarasanéndal, Tam.). From (ila, tam. young + arasan, tam. king + éndal, tam. high ground). Town ; pop. 4,015 ; acres 4,245 ; lat. 9° 13′ ; long. 77° 50′ ; from Shuncaraneinarcoil E.N.E. 17 miles ; from Tinnevelly N.N.E. 34 miles. Group of agricultural hamlets. Granted in the time of Gentoo [q.v.] kings to certain Cummavaur [q.v.]. ——**(2)** Town, Head quarters of Tahsildar and Sub-registrar, Place of pilgrimage ; Tinnevelly dist., Shuncaraneinarcoil tal. ; pop. 8,566 ; acres 6,019 ; lat. 9° 10′ ; long. 77° 35′ ; height 602 feet ; from Madras S.W. 325 miles ; from Palamcottah N.N.W. 33 miles ; from Shermadevy N. 33 miles ; from Shreevillipoottore S.S.W. 24 miles ; from Tinnevelly N.N.W. 32 miles ; from Tuticorin W.N.W. 49 miles. On a plain 10 miles east of the road from Madura to Travancore. Ancient Shiva temple with good stone-carving and inscriptions, and known as the Shuncara lingam. Shiva is worshipped under the combined form of Vishnoo and Shiva [shuncaranarayanan] and Veishnavas worship as well as Sheivas. Fine tank with temple in the middle. Large bell in the gopooram [q.v.], the latter having numerous inscriptions. Car festivals [ratotsavam] in February and July. Weekly fair on Thursday.

SHWETAM (श्वेत - shvéta, *San.*). From (shvit, san. to be white). White.——*Shwetanuddy* (சுவேதநதி - shuvéthanathi, Tam.). From (above + nadí, san. river) ; on account of the limestone [choonam cull] it contains. River ; Salem dist., Ahtoor tal. Rises in the Collimullays and, fed by many torrents converging above Tammamputty, carries off the rainfall of the northern slopes of the Putchamullays. It runs in an easterly direction and then enters Perambalore tolook, Trichinopoly district.——*Shwetaumbaran* (श्वेताम्बर - shvétámbara, San.). From (above + ambara, san. apparel) ; white-robed ; epithet of Jeina [q.v.] mendicants as distinguished from digambaran or sky-clad mendicants. The Shwetaumbarans assert that females can attain nirvaunam [q.v.] or liberation. The Digambarans [q.v.] are more common in Southern india. See vol. I (95) [matam].——*Shyainacam* (श्येनक - shyénaka, San.). See sep. title.——*Shyainam* (श्येन - shyéna, San.). See sep. title.

SHYAINACAM (श्येनक - shyénaka, *San.*). Means small hawk [shwetam]. Buzzards. Buteoninæ, falconidæ [bheroondam], raptores, aves [pacshy, 2], of naturalists [jantoo]. Bill short, broad at base, much curved, cere occupying more than half its length ; wings long ; tarsi long, with broad transverse scales in front and behind ; toes rather short. The species best known to the natives are shown below. For hawks see Shyainam. ——*Dastmal* (دستمل - dastmal, Hind. ; పిల్లిగద్ద - pilligadda, Tel. ; பூனைப்பருந்து - púnaipparundu, Tel.). Title from hindostany. Tel. from (pilli, tel. cat + gadda, tel. kite). Tam. from (púnai, tam. cat + parundu, tam. kite) ; from noiseless flight. Hind. also (pattái), meaning striped ; (girgitmár), meaning bloodsucker + killer. Tel. also (tellachépagadda), meaning white + fish + kite ; (golpuli), of yerkalas. Title otherwise Pale harrier. Circus swainsonii, buteoninæ. Alias Circus albescens, dalmaticus, pallidus ; Falco herbœcola. Differs from the common harrier, chiefly in the paler plumage, the white throat and breast, and in the banded rump ; comes in at the beginning of the cold season, september to october, and disappears in march or april for the purpose of breeding ; frequents open, stony plains and cultivated ground ; flight usually slow, a few beats alternating with a sailing motion. The same native names are given to Montagne's harrier, Circus cineraceus, buteoninæ.——*Tisah* (تیسا - tísá, Hind. ; బుడమగద్ద - budamagadda, Tel.). Tel. from (budama, tel. plant, solanum verbascifolium, linn. + gadda, tel. kite) ; small kite. Title otherwise White eyed buzzard. Poliornis teesa, buteoninæ. Specific name from hindostany. Alias Astur hyder ; Buteo teesa. Brown above, paler and rufescent on the head, with a white eyebrow, beneath white ; flight like that of the kestril [narzee] ; flies low ; not unfrequently runs along the ground ; has a peculiar plaintive cry ; easily domesticated.

SHYAINAM (श्येन - shyéna, *San.*). Means white [shwetam]. Hawks. Accipitrinæ, falconidæ [bheroondam], raptores, aves [pacshy, 2], of naturalists [jantoo]. Bill short, much arched and deeply waved ; wings mostly long ; tail large ; tarsi long, large scales in front. The species best known to the natives are shown below. For buzzards see Shyaimacam.——*Baushah* (باشه - báshak, Ar.; باشه - báshah, Pers.; باشا - báshá, Hind.; ಬಣ್ಣದಡೇಗೆ - bannadadége, Can.; వర్ణపుడేగ - varnapudéga, Tel.; പറന്തു - parantu, Mal.). Ar. from (bashaka, ar. to seize). Pers. and Hind. from arabic. Can. from (banna, can. color + dége, can. hawk). Tel. from (varna, san. color + déga, tel. hawk). Mal. from (para. mal. to fly). Male bird is:—Hind. (báshin). Title otherwise European sparrow hawk. Accipiter nisus, accipitrinæ. Alias Accipiter dussumierii, fringillarius, nisosimilis, subtypicus. Young yellowish brown above, beneath ochrey white; adult blackish or brownish grey above, white on the eyebrow and nape; adult female differs from the male in being paler and browner above, and in the lower parts being whiter; cold weather visitant coming in regularly about beginning of october, leaving again about february or march; common; trained to falconry.——*Bauz* (باز - báz, Ar., Pers., Hind. and Dec.; డేగ - déga, Tel.; പെരുമ്പുള്ളു - perumpullu, Mal.). Ar. from (bazá, ar. to stretch out neck for prey). Tel. from (digu, tel. to descend), from swooping on its prey. Mal. from (peru, mal. great + pul, mal. bird). Male bird is:—(jurrah). Title otherwise Goshawk. Astur palumbarius, accipitrinæ. Alias Falco gallinarius. Young bird brown above, feathers edged with paler hue on head, often rusty with dark central spot; nape whitish; wings and tail light brown, latter with an ashy tinge banded with darker brown; beneath rusty white long dark-brown streaks throughout; streak over the eye and cheeks, also white with brown streaks; adult uniform light brown above with greyish tinge; beneath white, cross bands of rich hair or yellowish brown; tail has three conspicuous broad brown bands and a fourth indistinct one near the base; not common; trained to falconry.——*Besrah* (بیسرا - besrá, Hind.; ಉರುಚಿಟ್ಲು - urchitlu, Can.; వశిష్ఠపడేగ - vashisht'hapudéga, Tel.). Hind. from (be, pers. without + sar, pers. head). Can. from (úru, can. country + chitlu, can. hawk). Tel. from (vashisht'ha, san. the sage + déga, tel. hawk); superior hawk. Male bird is:—Hind. (dhotí). Title otherwise Sparrow hawk. Accipiter virgatus, accipitrinæ. Alias Accipiter affinis, besra, dussumierii, fringillarius. Young bird dark brown above, tinged with dusky on the cheeks and ears; beneath white; adult bird has above deep and glossy olive brown with blackish or slaty tint; with increasing age the brown of the upper parts become dark slaty, blackish on the head; in the female, after the first moult, the breast is marked with oval light yellow brown drops; adult male differs from female in being more grey on the upper parts; somewhat difficult to train. Another species of sparrow-hawk, Khan besrah or king hawk, is found in jungly country in south arcot and chingleput, bordering on tanjore and trichinopoly; known to the teloogoo shikarries [q.v.] as cansarpoo daiga or bronze-colored hawk.——*Gor besrah* (گور بیسرا - gorbesrá, Hind.; ಕೋಗಿಲೆಡೇಗೆ - kógiledége, Can.; కోకిలడేగ - kókiladéga, Tel.). Hind. from (gaurá, hind. male sparrow + besrá, hind. falcon). Can. from (kógile, can. cuckoo + dége, can. hawk), from resemblance to cuckoo [koel] in lower plumage. Hind. also (mánakbesrá); (koteswar), meaning mountain lord. Title otherwise Crested goshawk. Astur trivirgatus, accipitrinæ. Alias Astur cristatus, indicus, palumbarius. Young bird brown above, pale edgings to feathers, eyebrows white, white or rufous about the nape; below white, spotted on the breast, abdomen; flanks with dark brown spots, least numerous in the male; tail pale ashy brown, with dark broad bands; narrow dark line down centre of the chin and throat; adult, upper plumage glossy dark brown, in some with olivaceous tinge, in older birds with dark slaty hue; found in hilly regions; hunts in pairs.——*Shikrah* (شکره - shikrah, Pers.; شکرا - shikrá, Hind. and Dec.; ಜಾಲಿಡೇಗೆ - jálidége, Can.; జాలెడేగ - dzáledéga, Tel.; சின்ன வல்லூறு - shinnavallúru, Tam.). Pers. from (shikár, pers. game). Tel. from (dzálemu, tel. swift motion in a straight line + déga, tel. hawk). Tam. from (shinna, tam. small + vallúru, tam. falcon). Male bird is:—Hind. (chipak). Micronisus badius, accipitrinæ. Alias Accipiter dukhunensis, fringillaroides, scutarius; Astur bifasciatus; Falco brownii, dussumierii. Young bird dark reddish or dusky brown above, feathers edged with rufous, most broadly so in the male; tail light ashy brown with dark bands, beneath white; male has usually fewer spots than the female; adult bird pale ashy grey above, darkest on the head, dusky reddish nape, conspicuous when the head is bent forwards; tail with the two centre feathers and the two outer ones not barred; beneath white, plumage not assumed before fourth or fifth year; very common; general food lizards [chipkalee]; commonly trained to falconry.

SHYAUMAM (श्याम - shyáma, *San.*). From (shyai, san. to go). Dark-blue.——*Shaumay* (சாமை - shámai, Tam.). Little millet. See sep. title.——*Shyaumalatay* (श्यामलता - shyámalatá, San.; دودھی - dúdhí, Hind.; నల్లతీగ - nallatíga, Tel.; പാല്വള്ളി - pálvalli, Mal.). San. from (shyáma, san. dark-blue + latá, san. creeper). Tel. from (nalla, tel. black + tíga, tel. creeper). Mal. from (pál, mal. milk + valli, mal. creeper). San. also (shárivá), meaning of various colors [indian sarsaparilla]; (shyámá), meaning dark-blue [shaumay, tottila]. Tel. also (illukatte), meaning house + twig; (muntagajjanamu); (sahadévichettu), meaning with + sporting + plant; climbing plant [lance-leaved balah, wild jeerah]. Botanically Ichnocarpus frutescens, br., apocynaceæ [vricsham, 87]. Alias Apocynum frutescens; Echites frutescens. Extensive climber; leaves very variable, 2–3 by $\frac{3}{4}$–$1\frac{1}{2}$ inches, petiole $\frac{1}{4}$ inch, cymes 1–3 inches, axillary and in terminal panicles, rusty-pubescent, branches short, trichotomously divided or three-flowered, pedicels longer or shorter than the corolla, calyx-lobes ovate, obtuse or sub-acute, eglandular; corolla about $\frac{1}{4}$ inch in diameter, purplish, twice as long as the calyx, lobes twice as long as the tube, falcate, acuminate, mouth and margins sparingly bearded; disc-glands, five, erect, slender, capitate, much longer than the hairy ovary; style very short; follicles 3–6 by $\frac{1}{6}$ inch, very slender, cylindric, curved, acute; seeds $\frac{1}{2}$ inch, very slender, not peaked; coma scanty, white. The roots are somewhat similar in appearance to those of hemidesmus [indian sarsaparilla], but have not the same coumarin odour; the bark is of a dark brown color, and adheres closely to the wood, which is much harder, and differs in structure from that of hemidesmus in having a large central pith; the roots are seldom branched, but here and there a few fine fibres are given off; they are almost tasteless. For the properties and uses of this plant, see Hemidesmus [indian sarsaparilla].——*Shyaumay* (श्यामा - shyámá, San.). Means dark-blue, from color. A form of Doorga [q.v.] worshipped by shauctas [cauly, yaumaulamma]. For birds of this name see sep. title.

SHYAUMAY (श्यामा - shyámá, *San.*). From (shyáma, san. dark-blue) [shyaumam]. Robins. Saxicolinæ, sylviadæ [calacuntam], dentirostres, insessores, aves [pacshy, 23], of naturalists [jantoo]. The species best known to the natives are shown below.——*Dayar* (دیر - daiyar, Hind. and Dec.; చారలగాడు - tsáralagádu, Tel.; ഭൂമികുലുക്കി - bhúmikulukki, Mal.). Tel. from (tsára, tel. stripe + gádu, tel. personal suffix). Mal. from (bhúmi, mal. earth + kulukku, mal. to shake); from sound. Tel. also (peddanallanchi), meaning large + robin. Title otherwise Magpie Robin. Copsychus saularis, saxicolinæ. Alias Dahila docilis; Gryllivora intermedia. Caged for its song, as also for its pugnacious qualities.——*Malabar robin* (شاما - shámá, Hind. and Dec.; పొడనల్లంచి - podanallanchi, Tel.). Tel. from (poda, tel. variegated color + nallanchi, tel. robin). Tel. also (tókanallanchi), meaning tail + robin; from long tail. Kittacincla macroura, saxicolinæ. Alias Gryllivora longicauda. Almost always solitary; song, chiefly heard just before and after sunset, of great power, surpassed by no indian bird. In confinement imitates notes of other birds, and of various animals with ease and accuracy; caught in great number and caged for its song; usually fed on paste made of parched chenna [varagoo] mixed with the yolk of hard-boiled eggs, few maggots or insects are given occasionally; will also eat pieces of raw meat in lieu of insects [poochy].——*Washer-woman robin* (کلچری - kalchurí, Hind. and Dec.; నల్లంచి - nallanchi, Tel.; வண்ணாத்திக்குருவி - vannáttikkuruvi, Tam.). Title from habit of jerking up its tail like a washer-woman in washing. Hind. from (kálí, hind. black + churí, hind. sparrow). Tel. from (nalla, tel. black + latsanamu, tel. beauty). Tam. from (vannátti, tam. washer-woman + kuruvi, tam. small bird). Title otherwise Indian black robin. Thamnobia fulicata, saxicolinæ. Alias Thamnobia leucoptera. Mostly found about villages, pagodas [q.v.], old buildings, and mud walls, also common on rocky and stony hills, and in groves of palmyra [q.v.] or date palms [kharjooram]. Male has sweet but small song; occasionally caged.

SI (सि - si, *San.*). To bind.—*Saitoo* (सेतु - sétu, San.; திருவணை - tiruvanai, Tam.). San. means bund. Tam. means holy bund. The ridge of rocks between Ceylon and the southern extremity of the Coromandel coast [rameshwaram]; hence chief of Ramnaud or Maravar [q.v.] derived their title of Saitoopaty or lord of the bridge. Asaitookhandam or Imasaitooparyantam are common phrases to express india from Himalayas to Rameshwaram. See vol. I (2).——*Saitoopaty* (சேதுபதி - shéthuppathi, Tam.). From (sétu, san. bund + pati, san. lord). Title of the principal chief of Marava [q.v.] tribe, means guardian of the approaches at Adam's bridge to Rameshwaram. First said to have been conferred by Rama on the ancient Marava race, who became lords paramount of southern india till they were overborne by coorumbas [q.v.]. At first independent, then brought under subjugation by naicks [q.v.], regained independence on subversion of naick dynasty, and now zemindars [q.v.]. Had a coinage [naunyam] of their own; and their device was monkey [bandar] and garoodan [charitram, garoodan]. Vol. I (124), 56. Also Hindoo 2nd or pers. name [peyar].——*Senaupaty* (सेनापति - sénápati, San.). From (sená, san. army + pati, san. lord). A general; name of Soobramanyan [q.v.].——*Senay* (सेना - séná, San.). From (si, san. to bind). Army [dandam, dandoo, paday, shervay].——*Synigoonta* (సైనిగుంట - shyánigunta, Tel.). From (sainya, san. army + gunta, tel. tank). Village, Ghaut; North arcot dist., Goodiyattam and Pulmanair tals.; lat. 13° 05′; long. 78° 52′; from Chittore W.S.W. 21 miles; from Goodiyattam N.N.W. 9 miles. The pass [ghaut] leads from Goodiyattam talook to Pulmanair, where it unites with the road from Mogily.

SIALLY (سیالی - siyálí, *Hind.*; దారిగుమ్మడి - dárigummadi, *Tel.*). Tel. from (dári, tel. way + gummadi, tel. pumpkin). Hind. also (biláikand); (bidaríkand); (badarbillí); (sural). Title otherwise Daury goommady, Tuberous french honeysuckle. Botanically Pueraria tuberosa, dc., leguminosæ [vricsham, 48]. Alias Hedysarum tuberosum. Stems shrubby, the branches finely grey downy; stipules minute, deciduous, cordate-ovate; leaflets membranous, roundish, $\frac{1}{2}$–1 foot long, green, glabrescent above, densely clothed with whitish adpressed hair beneath; flowers in dense, virgate, leafless, often panicled racemes, reaching 6–9 inches long; pedicels very densely fascicled; calyx $\frac{1}{3}$–$\frac{1}{4}$ inch long, densely silky; corolla short, blue, not quite twice the calyx; limb of standard orbicular, distinctly spurred; pod 2–3 inches long, membranous, flat, three to six-seeded, clothed with long grey silky bristly hairs. The tubers vary in size and shape; pyriform or spindle-shaped, ranging in size from a small pear [amrood] to a large turnip [shalgham]; developed upon the roots of the plant, and are composed of the woody layers of the root spread out and separated by a large addition of soft cellular tissue; the external surface of the tuber is brown and scurfy from exfoliation of the tuberous coat; the cut surface is white and spongy, and shows several concentric rings of woody fibres, and numerous well-marked medullary rays; the taste is somewhat acrid, slightly bitter, and very mucilaginous; the color is not affected by ferric chloride or solution of iodine. Root has acrid properties, and is used medicinally as a cataplasm to reduce swellings of the joints.

SICCA (سکہ - sikkah, *Hind.*). From persian. Stamp, impression. Applied as an adjective to the silver currency of the moghuls, whose Sicca rupee [q.v.] was the general standard of value until superseded by the Company's rupee [q.v.]. The Sicca rupee as last coined weighed 192 grains, of which 176 were pure silver; its exchange value was about 2*s.* 2*d.* The Company's rupee, which introduced uniformity of coinage over British india in 1835, contained only 165 grains silver. Hence the Sicca bore to the Company's rupee the proportion of 16 : 15 nearly. See vol. I, 615. Sicca sunnud is a stamped grant [sunnud].

SIDDY (సిద్ది - siddi, *Can.*). Liquid measure. $1\frac{1}{2}$ coodtays = 1 siddy [alavay, 4c]. Approximate actual value, 1 siddy = $15\frac{3}{4}$ cubic inches. S. Canara. Compare Teloogoo chitty, Tamul olluck. See vol. I, 609; II, 508.

SIDHOUT (సిద్ధవట్టము - siddhavattamu, *Tel.* siddhavattam *). From (siddha, san. hermit + vata, san. banyan tree, ficus bengalensis, linn.) [saudh]. San. name (dakshinakáshí), meaning southern benares [tenoaushy].——**(1)** Talook, Cuddapah district. Tahsildar's pay Rs. 150. Area 606 square miles. Length from north to south from 19 to 27 miles, and breadth from east to west from 18 to 30 miles. Population 66,810. Language Teloogoo. E. of district. Bounded north by Badwail talook, east by Atmacore and Raupore talooks of Nellore district, south by Poollampett talook, south-west by Royachoty talook, and west by Cuddapah talook. The hills are the Lunkamalas, and the Mullayacondah and Palcondah ranges. The cultivable ground is found only in two valleys running parallel from the north. Madras railway traverses southern portion. Half the cultivated land is good, and a quarter middling. The best land is in Pennair valley, where water is obtainable by sinking wells. Except in valleys but little land is cultivated, owing to the vast masses of hills. Soil is divided into red, sandy, black, salt and stony. In addition to ordinary grains produced, the principal products are indigo [q.v.] and cotton [q.v.] and turmeric [country saffron]. Indigo goes to Madras and turmeric to Bombay. In the eastern portion the Cheyair forms a junction with the Pennair. The Saglair flows through the northern portion, previous to its junction with the Pennair. The Toommalair flows through the eastern portion down the Wobalam valley, and joins the Pennair below the junction of the Saglair. There are no river channels [q.v.], and the only benefit derived from the four rivers is the moisture of the sub-soil in the valleys. Camping grounds, Sidhout and Vontimittah. Places of archæological interest :—Goondlamoola, Gungaperore, Joty, Pennaperore, Punchalingaulacona, Sidhout, Vengopaulsawmy temple, Vontimittah, Wobalam, Wogore. The leading places, &c., in the talook are the following.——*Aurapoya canama* (ఆరేపాయకనమ - árepáyakanama, Tel.). From (áre, tel. bauhinia racemosa, lam. + páya, tel. portion + kanama, tel. pass). Ghaut; from Cuddapah E. 12 miles; from Sidhout N. 3 miles. In the Lunkamalas.——*Bagarapett* (బాకరాపేట - bákarápéta, Tel.). From (bhákara, tel. proper name + péta, tel. suburb). Village, Hamlet of Peddapully; pop. 2,724 including Peddapully; acres 6,022 including Peddapully; lat. 14° 25′; long. 79° 00′; from Cuddapah E. 10 miles; from Sidhout S. 4 miles.——*Bandicanama* (బండికనమ - bandikanama, Tel.). From (bandi, tel. cart + kanama, tel. pass). Ghaut [q.v.]. Between Sidhout and Cuddapah talooks.——*Capardeshlacona* (కపర్దేశ్వర్లకోన - kapardéshvarlakóna, Tel.). From (kaparda, san. the long locks of shiva + íshvara, san. lord + kóna, tel. ravine). Valley. In Lunkamalas. Shiva temple ruined and a waterfall.——*Cheyair* (చెయ్యేరు - cheyyéru, Tel.). See sep. title.——*Cooroogoontapully* (కురుగుంటపల్లి - kuruguntapalli, Tel.). From (kuru, tel. small + gunta, tel. tank + palli, tel. village). Village; pop. 3,498; acres 17,078; lat. 14° 24′; long. 79° 12′; from Cuddapah E.S.E. 23 miles; from Sidhout E.S.E. 13 miles.——*Cottore* (కొత్తూరు - kottúru, Tel.). From (kotta, tel. new + úru, tel. village). Village; pop. 1,732; acres 21,010; lat. 14° 28′; long. 79° 20′; from Cuddapah E.S.E. 31 miles; from Sidhout E.S.E. 21 miles.——*Joty* (జ్యోతి - jyóti, Tel.). Means light. Village; pop. 476; acres 11,276; lat. 14° 29′; long. 78° 58′; from Cuddapah E. 6 miles; from Sidhout W.N.W. 4 miles. On the Pennair. A subterranean passage said to run from a temple to the Nityapoojacona temple in the Lunkamalas. Temple now neglected, and half buried in sand. A mile west are two ruined pagodas [q.v.] of Narsimhasawmy.——*Lunkamala* (లంకమల - lankamala, Tel.). See sep. title.——*Nityapoojacona* (నిత్యపూజకోన - nityapújakóna, Tel.). From (nitya, san. daily + pújá, san. worship + kóna, tel. ravine). Valley. In the Lunkamalas. Remarkable for a huge overhanging rock able to afford shelter to 10,000 people, and a small pagoda [q.v.]. Festival in Caurtigay [mausam] or November and on Shivarautry [pundigay, 6a]. A water-fall in valley [aroovy].——*Pennair* (పెన్నేరు - pennéru, Tel.). See sep. title.——*Punchalingaulacona* (పంచలింగాలకోన - panchalingálakóna, Tel.). From (pañcha, san. five + linga, san. lingam + kóna, tel. ravine); from five lingams, discovered in a cave here. Sanscrit name (pañchalingáchala), meaning five + lingam + mountain. Valley. In the Mullayacondahs. Resorted to by pilgrims, especially on Mondays in Caurtigay [mausam] or november. In the roof of the cave are stalactites.——*Ramaupooram* (రామాపురము - rámápuramu, Tel.). From (ráma, san. the god + pura, san. town). Village; pop. 2,559; acres 14,389; lat. 14° 37′; long. 79° 12′; from Cuddapah E.N.E. 24 miles; from Sidhout N.E. 17 miles.——*Saglair* (సగిలేరు - sagiléru, Tel.). See sep. title.——*Sidhout* (సిద్ధవట్టము - siddhavattamu, Tel.). See below.——*Someshwaram* (సోమేశ్వరము - sóméshvaramu, Tel.). See Somashila.——*Soonkesala* (సుంకేసుల - sunkésula, Tel.). See sep. title.——*Toommalair* (తుమ్మలేరు - tummaléru, Tel.). See sep. title.——*Veligonda* (వెలిగొండ - veligonda, Tel.). See sep. title.——*Vengopaulsawmicondah* (వేణుగోపాలస్వామికొండ - vénugópálasvámikonda, Tel.). From (vénugópála, san. the cowherd krishna playing upon a flute + svámí, san. lord + konda, tel. hill). Hill; lat. 14° 34′; long. 79° 01′; from Cuddapah E.N.E. 12 miles; from Sidhout N. 7 miles. Vengopaulsawmy pagoda.——*Vontimittah* (ఒంటిమిట్ట - vontimitta, Tel.). See sep. title.——*Yellacondah* (యెల్లకొండ - yellakonda, Tel.). From (yella, tel. boundary + konda, tel. hill). Hill.——*Yellampett* (యెల్లంపేట - yellampéta, Tel.). From (yallamma, tel. proper name + péta, tel. suburb). Village; lat. 14° 24′; long. 79° 15′; from Cuddapah E.S.E. 27 miles; from Sidhout E.S.E. 17 miles. At confluence of Cheyair and Pennair. Inhabited by rich Cumma [q.v.] and Balije [q.v.] merchants. Temple and festival. Trade in indigo [q.v.] and thread [nool] dyed blue [shauyam].——**(2)** Town, Divisional and Talook head-quarters, Hills; Cuddapah dist., Sidhout tal.; pop. 3,446; acres 6,720; lat. 14° 28′; long. 79° 01′; from Cuddapah E. 10 miles; from Madanapully N.E. 70 miles; from Madras N.W. 131 miles. Of some importance and considerable sanctity. Owing to resemblance in its position on left bank of Pennair, and to relative position of some neighbouring villages and rivers, is called Dacshina caushy as above noted. Originally dependency of Chitwail rajah, and held by a member of the Matly family. Subsequently, under the Nizam's dynasty, residence of the Pataun nawaub, and joined to the province of Cuddapah. This dynasty was put an end to by Hyder ally and the fort was pulled down. After Colonel Munro's departure in 1807, Sidhout was for some time the residence of the Collector; but the head-quarters were subsequently moved to Cuddapah. The fort shows traces of Hindoo and Mahomedan architecture. It was originally founded by Ananda rauz, a relative of the reigning Chitwail rajah, in 1225 of Shalivahanan [q.v.]. Famed for the excellence of its melons [common melon], the cultivation of which is carried on during January, February and March in the dry sandy bed of the Pennair. There are seven different kinds of melons.——**(3)** Hills. These are a continuation of the great clayslate and sandstone [manal cull] range of the Nullamullays that commences in the Nizam's dominions, north of the Kistna, and appears to terminate to the S.E. at Nagary. The Pennair flows through them by a gap similar to that by which the Kistna finds its way through them farther north. Sidhout is situated in this pass on the left bank of the river, along which the road from Cuddapah lies, after crossing the rocky belt of the Nullamullay range. This valley is irrigated by the Pennair, and full of cultivation; shady topes [q.v.] and mahomedan makauns are interspersed throughout its extent. In the hills there is a variegated kind of sandstone, with both waving and acutely bent lines of alternate red and white, resembling on a large scale those in agate [akeek]. Many of the pillars in the fort gates are constructed of it, and have the appearance at a distance of a curiously veined wood. It is stated that during the Moghul government diamonds [vajram] were dug at a place in the hills, and also near the village of Darjepully. At the south-eastern base of the Nundicanama ghaut [q.v.] between Cuddapah and Sidhout, flints [teetatty cull] used by the Cuddapah nawaubs [q.v.] were formerly dug; they lie near the surface in flattish rugged masses imbedded in red soil and angular gravel [kankar]. The subjacent rock is sandstone.

SIFARSH (سفارش - sifárish, *Hind.*). From (sipurdan, pers. to recommend). Recommendation.

SIKH (शीख - shíkha, *Mahr.*). From (shishya, san. disciple); so called as following their gooroos [q.v.]. The name of a religious sect founded in Punjab at the end of fifteenth century by Naunak shah, a hindoo reformer.

SILENT VALLEY (വള്ളഘട്ടം - vállaghattam, *Mal.*). So named by Europeans who first used it as a shooting ground. Malabar dist., Valavanaud tal. Large tract of mountain forest and grass land jenm [q.v.], property of government, situated on western slopes of Coondahs, most inaccessible. Over 70 square miles. At northern extremity of valley lay the Wallaghaut coffee [q.v.] estates now abandoned. The old Sisparra ghaut [q.v.] crosses north end of valley.

SILK (سلک - silk, *Hind.*). Balance [bauky]. Silk bundy is adjustment of balances due to Government.

SILLAH (سلاح - siláh, *Hind.*). Arms [khitaub].——*Sillahdar* (سلاحدار - siláhdár, Hind.). One who wears arms; but particularly a soldier of irregular cavalry, who provides his own arms and horse.

SIMBOLEE (سمبولی - simbolí, *Hind.*). Oil of Murraya kœnigii, spr., Curry-leaf tree.

SIMHAM (सिंह - simha, *San.*; شیر - sher, *Hind.*). San. from (hims, san. to hurt). Lion. The lion was once prevalent in S. india; now confined to Cuttywar. Personal name Sing [q.v.] derived from this. Shere [q.v.] and Hyder [q.v.] also mean lion, Shere being applied both to the tiger [pooly] and the lion. There is a Tamul proverb:—மிருகங்களில் ஆனை பெரிது, அதினும் சிங்கம் வலிது—"among beasts an elephant [q.v.] "is the biggest and a lion the strongest." A lion was the signet of the Cadamba [q.v.] kings [raj]. For sign of the zodiac see Raushy. Simham is a suffix in proper names; as Narsimhan, Ramasimhan [peyar].——*Seilan* (سیلان - sailán, Hind.). Arabic form of malay or dravidian Ceylon.——*Serendib* (سراندیب - sarandíb, Hind.). Arabic corruption of the sanscrit Simhala [q.v.] dweepam or Ceylon in the earlier middle ages. Appears also as Selandib and Sarandeep.——*Shingan* (சிங்கன் - shingan, Tam.). From (simha, san. lion). Hindoo 2nd or pers. name. Feminine form is Shingy. Common among lower orders [peyar]. ——*Shingapermaul* (சிங்கப்பெருமாள் - shingapperumál, Tam.). From (above + perumál, tam. vishnu, the great god), vishnoo in his narsimhan [q.v.] or man-lion avatar [q.v.]. Hindoo 2nd or pers. name [peyar].——*Shingaroyacondah* (సింగరాయకొండ - shingaráyakonda, Tel.). From (singaráyadu, tel. proper name + konda, tel. hill). Sanscrit name (simháchala), meaning lion + hill. Shrotriem village; Nellore dist., Cundoocore tal.; pop. 933; acres 3,115; lat. 15° 14′; long. 80° 04′; from Cundoocore E. 9 miles; from Nellore N. 54 miles; from the sea W. 4 miles. Between the Munnair and Palair. Ancient Vishnoo temple to Narsimhasawmy. Through a cave temple on the hill said to be a passage to the adjacent pagoda [q.v.], but the entrance is blocked by a large stone image. Festival of Varauhasawmy held in April. Private choultry [q.v.]; traveller's bungalow [q.v.]. Two temples to Narsimhasawmy and Varauhasawmy. Worship is chiefly to the latter. The stones found in the neighbouring hill, partly red and partly white, are said to have been so made by Seetay [q.v.], to answer the purpose of Cooncoomam and Pasoopoo [country saffron].——*Simhalam* (सिंहल - simhala, San.). From (simha, san. lion). Sanscrit version of malay or dravidian Ceylon.——*Simhastam* (सिंहस्थ - simhast'ha, San.). From (above + st'ha, san. to stand). The time during which Jupiter [brihaspaty] is in sign [raushy] Leo; inauspicious, and in it marriages are prohibited.——*Simhauchellam* (సింహాచలము - simháchalamu, Tel.). From (above + achala, san. hill); resembling a lion couchant. Sanscrit name (simhádri), meaning same. Village, Hill, Place of pilgrimage; Vizagapatam dist., Vizagapatam division; pop. 2,254; lat. 17° 46′; long. 83° 18′; from Vizagapatam N.N.W. 6 miles; from the sea W. 7 miles. Remarkable temple. The shrine, picturesquely situated in a wooded glen containing springs and cascades, is to the varauha [q.v.] incarnation [avatar] of Vishnoo [q.v.]. Improved by the Gajapaty [q.v.] kings of Orissa 600 years ago. About 200 years ago endowed by the Poosapauties [q.v.]. Now in charge of Maharajah of Vizianagram, who has a house and rose [gool] garden with fountains. Maharajah has built a choultry [q.v.]. In the temple is the Cuppa stambham or Frog's pillar. It is hollow at the upper end, caused by a frog issuing therefrom. Revered by barren women, who embrace it and pour gifts before it. Half way up hill is gateway called Hanoomadwauram. Much carving defaced by Mahomedans. Alasauny peddanna records a visit to Simhanchellam made by Krishnaroya. Picnics to this spot by the English of Waltair [aroovy].——*Simhausanam* (सिंहासन - simhásana, San.). From (above + ásana, san. seat). Throne with figures of lions carved on supports. But there is also lotus [nelumbo] or pudma simhausanam, elephant [q.v.] or gaja simhausanam, conch shell [chunk] or shunkha simhausanam, goose [hamsam] or hamsa simhausanam, antelope [mrigam] or mriga simhausanam, horse [ghorah] or haya simhausanam, &c.——*Sing* (سنگ - singh, Hind.; సింగు - singu, Tel.). A lion; name borne by military castes. Title of the Rajpoots [q.v.] and Sikhs [q.v.]. Hindoo third name [peyar]. ——*Singapore* (سنگپور - singapúr, Hind.). Means lion + town. Island and town at the southern extremity of the Malayan peninsula [straits]. Compare:—Æschynomene aspera, singapore bat plant; Arenga saccharifera, singapore sago; Cedrela toona, singapore cedar.——*Singhala dweepam* (सिंहलद्वीप - simhaladvípa, San.). From (simhala, san. ceylon + dvípa, san. island). Ceylon [q.v.].

SINJID (عناب - unnáb, *Ar.*; سنجد - sinjid, *Pers.*). Title from persian. Ar. from (anuba, ar. sprightly), from appearance of fruit. Ar. also (arák). Pers. also (sinjidijílání), meaning the tree growing in jeelaun in persia. Greek παλίουρος. Title otherwise Common zizyphus, Jujube, Long plum, Round plum. Botanically Zizyphus [badary] vulgaris, lamk., rhamneæ [vricsham, 41]. Alias Zizyphus flexuosa. Shrub or small tree, with rigid spreading boughs and stiff branches, which are often unarmed, the whole plant quite glabrous; prickles usually geminate, the straight one often over 1 inch long, stout; flowers few, fascicled in the axils of the leaves; petals cucullate; disk thin, obscurely five-lobed; ovary two-celled, styles two, united to the middle; fruit globose or oblong, succulent, red or black, shining. Fruit has thin rind like that of an apple [seb], and bears a stone in the centre; between stone and rind is a crisp, refreshing substance like that of a juicy apple, but with no very marked flavor. The dried fruit which comes from china is from 1–1½ inch long and ¾ inch broad; skin red, much shrivelled; pulp adherent to the stone, spongy, sweet and yellow; stone $\frac{7}{10}$th inch long, very hard and rugose, apex sharp-pointed; shell very thick; seed oblong, flat, of a chestnut color, 4–10 inch long and $\frac{3}{10}$th inch broad. The fruit which comes from the persian gulf is somewhat smaller. This shrub is said to be the thorn from which Christ's crown of thorn was made. The bark of the tree is used medicinally to clean wounds and sores, the gum in certain affections of the eyes, and the leaves when chewed destroy the power of the tongue to appreciate the taste of disagreeable medicines. From pulp is made the confection sold by chemists under the name of jujubes. Two varieties; tree that bears the oval fruit has oval leaves, one that bears the round fruit has round leaves.

SIPAH (سپاه - sipáh, *Hind.*). From (asp, pers. horse). An army [dandam, dandoo, paday, shervay].——*Sepoy* (سپاهی - sipáhí, Hind.). From (sipáh, pers. an army). Through portuguese. A foot soldier, especially a native Indian, disciplined and dressed in the European style, as distinguished from a British soldier.——*Sibbundy* (سهبندی - sihbandí, Hind.). From (above + bandí, pers. recruitment). Militia for garrisons of forts, guard in towns and villages, and collection of revenue. So an establishment of clerks, peons, &c.

SIRAUJ (سراج - siráj, *Hind.*). From (saraja, ar. to adorn). Lamp [chiraugh]. Title of the prophet. Part of lacab; as Sirauj ood deen, lamp of the faith [ism].

SIRAUT (صراط - sirát, *Hind.*). From arabic. Road; a bridge extended over the midst of hell [dozak], which according to Mahomedan belief is sharper than a sword and thinner than a hair, and across which the Moslems [q.v.] pass into paradise [bheest].

SIRISSA (शिरीष - shirísha, *San.*; سرس - siris, *Hind.*; வாகை - vágai, *Tam*). Title from sanscrit through hindostany. San. from (shrí, san. to break); from brittle branches, also medicinal. Tam. from (vágu, tam. beauty). Botanically the Albizzia genus, leguminosæ [vricsham, 48]. Large trees spread through the tropics of the old world; leaves bipinnate; flowers in globose heads; pods large, thin, flat, strap-shaped, straight. The species best known to the natives are shown below.—— *Common sirissa* (शिरीष - shirísha, San.; मोठाशिरस - mót'háshirasa, Mahr.; سلطان الاشجار - sultánulashjár, Ar.; درخت ذکریا - darakhtizakariyáh, Pers.; سرس کا پیڑ - siriskáper, Hind.; سرش کا جہاڑ - sirishkájhár, Dec.; ಬಾಗೆ - bâge, Can. and Too.; దిరిసెన - dirisona, Tel.; ଟିନିୟା - tiniya, Oor.; വെൾവാക - velváka, Mal.; මාරා - mârá, Singh.; காட்டுவாகை - káttuvágai, Tam.). San. from (shrí, san. to break), from brittle branches or dispersing swellings, &c. Mahr. from (mót'há, mahr. large + shirasa, mahr. albizzia). Ar. from (sultán, ar. king + shajr, ar. tree). Pers. from (darakht, pers. tree + zakariyá, ar. zacharia). Hind. from sanscrit. Dec. from hindostany. Tel. from sanscrit. Mal. from (vel, mal. white + váka, mal. albizzia odoratissima, benth.); from small white flowers. Tam. from (kádu, tam. forest + vágai, tam. albizzia). San. also (munipriya), meaning dear to sages; (prit'hushringí), meaning large-branched; (mridupushpa), meaning soft flowered; (kapítaná), meaning monkey gladdening [wild mango]; (shukapushpa), meaning parrot flower; (shukapriya), meaning dear to parrots; (shukadruma), meaning parrot tree. Hind. also (sirijkájhár); from corruption. Can. also (kadache), meaning escape from danger; (kalbághi), meaning stone + the tree; (bénga), properly pterocarpus marsupium, roxb. [vengay]; (bághi). Tel. also (telladirisena), meaning white + the tree; (chinduva), meaning beautiful; (girisemu), by corruption from sanscrit. Oor. also (sirisha). Mal. also (nenméni), meaning rice-body. Tam. also (velvéngai), meaning white + tree, pterocarpus marsupium, roxb.; (vágai), meaning beautiful; (shirídam), from sanscrit; (adukkuvágai), meaning pile + the tree, dense spread of branches; (periyavágai), meaning large + the tree. Title otherwise Egyptian acacia, Forest vaugay, Large vaugay, Parrot tree, Sirios, Siris acacia, Sirissa neem, Sultan's tree, White-flowered sirissa. Botanically Albizzia [sirissa] lebbek, benth., leguminosæ [vricsham, 48]. Alias Acacia lebbek, serissa, sirissa, speciosa; Albizzia latifolia; Mimosa serissa, sirissa, speciosa. Serissa from sanscrit through hindostany. Tree, 30–40 feet, unarmed; with dense wide spreading head; young branches flexuose; leaves bipinnated; pinnæ one to four pair; leaflets four to nine pair, obtuse, oval, glabrous, unequal; peduncles axillary, each with a globular head of flowers on short pedicels, one to four together; calyx long, tubular; petals five, united to beyond the calyx; stamens very long, monadelphous; legumes flat and thin, remotely eight to ten-seeded; flowers small, white, fragrant especially at night; of rapid growth; puts leaves just before hot season, flowers soon after. Gives gum [gond] not soluble in water, but merely forming a jelly; resembles gum-arabic [q.v.]. Seeds form part of an anjanam [caujal] for ophthalmic diseases; oil [yennay] from seeds is useful in leprosy [cooshtam]; bark applied to injuries to the eye; gum in pharm. non-officinal. Leaves and twigs are good fodder. Good for avenues [shaulay], but branches are brittle and suffer in wind; bark used in tanning [chamrah]. Timber hard and durable, light reddish-brown color, darker veins, not liable to warp or crack; used for naves of wheels, pestles and mortars, picture frames, furniture, parts of boats, &c., and the heart-wood makes good charcoal [adooppkary].——*Dark sirissa* (कृष्णाशिरीष - kríshnashirísha, San.; ಸುಜ್ಜಲುಮರ - sujjalumara, Can.; చికిరేణి - chíkiréni, Tel.; உஞ்சமரம் - úñjamaram, Tam.). Title from color of wood. San. from (krishna, san. black + shirísha, san. albizzia lebbek, benth.). Can. from (ujjala, can. shining + mara, can. tree). Tel. from (chíki, tel. black + rénu, tel. zizyphus jujuba, lamk.). Tam. from (uriñju, tam. to absorb + maram, tam. tree); from absorbing oil from hair as a sponge. Can. also (belkambi), meaning growing + branch, with the side branches on. Tel. also (nallarégu), meaning black + zizyphus jujuba, lamk. Tam. also (arappumaram), meaning mohwah seed oil-cake tree, from leaves applied to similar use of washing oil from hair; (usilai), meaning sharpness [biswool]; (turiñjil), meaning to be close; (shurañji), meaning rancid oil + to extirpate, from clearing rancidity; (shíkkírán), meaning washing tree. Title otherwise Black bair, Black jujube, Black sirissa, Chickrainy, Oil-cake tree, Oonjal, Oosilay, Washing tree, Woonja. Botanically Albizzia [sirissa] amara, boiviu., leguminosæ [vricsham, 48]. Alias Acacia amara, wightii; Albizzia wightii; Mimosa amara, pulchella. Tree, 30 feet, unarmed; branches terete; young shoots, petioles, and peduncles, and under side of the leaflets clothed with yellowish tomentum; leaves bipinnate; pinnæ eight to ten pair, with a gland on the petiole and between the last pair; leaflets twenty to thirty pair; stipules lanceolate; peduncles solitary or aggregated, long and filiform in the axils of the upper leaves, and racemose from the abortion of the leaves; flowers small yellow in globular heads; corolla five-cleft; stamens long, numerous, monadelphous; legumes flat, thin, broadly linear, three to six-seeded. Grows most rapidly as coppice. Seeds medicinally astringent; oil [yennay] from seeds given for leprosy [cooshtam]; flowers externally applied to eruptions and swellings; leaves useful in ophthalmia; gives to pharm. woonja bark, non-officinal. Leaves are fodder for cattle [maud]. Natives use leaves for washing hair; gives a true gum [gond] of medium quality. Wood dark-brown, mottled, very handsome, strong, fibrous, stiff, close-grained, hard and durable, superior to saul [q.v.] and teak [q.v.] in transverse strength and direct cohesive power. ——*Fragrant sirissa* (शिरीष - shirísha, San.; रानशिरस - ránashirasa, Mahr.; سلطان الاشجار - sultáuulashjár, Ar.; درخت ذکریا - darakhtizakariyá, Pers.; سرس - siris, Hind.; سرش کاجهاڑ - sirishkájhár, Dec.; ಬಚಾರಿ - bachári, Can.; చిందుగ - chinduga, Tel.; ଟିନିୟା - tiniya, Oor.; വാക - váka, Mal.; සූරියමාරා - súriyamárá, Singh.; கருவாகை - karuvágai, Tam.). Title from scent of flowers. San. from (shrí, san. to break); from brittle branches or clearing ulcers and swellings. Mahr. from (rána, mahr. forest + shirísha, san. albizzia). Ar. from (sultán, ar. king + shajr, ar. tree). Pers. from (darakht, pers. tree + zakariyá, ar. zacharia). Hind. from sanscrit. Dec. from hindostany. Tel. from (chennu, tel. beauty) [stone sirissa]. Mal. means beauty. Tam. from (karumai, tam. blackness + vágai, tam. albizzia). Mahr. also (shirasa), by corruption from sanscrit. Can. also (pullibáge), meaning spot + the tree, albizzia lebbek, benth. Tel. also (telasu); (yerrachinta), meaning red + tamarindus indica, linn., from brown wood. Mal. also (karintakara), meaning black + cassia tora, linn. Tam. also (katturiñjil), meaning stone + albizzia amara, boiv. [stone sirissa]; (shilaiyúñjamaram), meaning stone + albizzia amara, boiv.; (vágai), meaning beautiful. Title otherwise Fragrant acacia, Red tamarind, Vaugay. Botanically Albizzia [sirissa] odoratissima, benth., leguminosæ [vricsham, 48]. Alias Acacia lomatocarpa, marginata, odoratissima; Albizzia micrantha; Mimosa marginata, odoratissima. Deciduous tree, 30–40 feet, unarmed; leaves bipinnated; pinnæ three to four pair; leaflets ten to forty pair, narrow, oval, oblique, glabrous, pale on the under side; panicles terminal and axillary, the ultimate divisions cymose, or somewhat umbellate; heads of flowers small, globose; stamens monadelphous; legume flat, thin, thick-margined, about ten-seeded; flowers pale yellow, very fragrant; flowers in hot season; grows rapidly; common. Gives dark brown gum [gond] in rounded tears, tasteless, and soluble in water; resembles babool [q.v.] gum. Juice of bark applied externally in leprosy [cooshtam] and ulcers. Lenves used for fodder. Wood is hard, coarse-gained, equal to teak [q.v.] in strength, of a dark reddish-brown or brown color, and takes a good polish; much used for building and cabinet purposes, naves and felloes of wheels, &c.——*Hill sirissa* (سفید سرس - sufedsiris, Hind.; ಚಿಕುಲ್ಮರ - chikulmara, Can.; తెల్లసాపర - tellasápara, Tel.; கொண்டவாகை - kondavágai, Tam.). Title from habitat. Tel. from (tella, tel. white + sápara, the tree so called). Tam. from (konda, tel. mountain + vágai, tam. albizzia). Tel. also (pedpaççeru), meaning large + tree, dalbergia paniculata, roxb.; (tellachinduga), meaning white + albizzia odoratissima, benth. Title otherwise Doon sirios tree. Botanically Albizzia [sirissa] procera, var. elata, baker, leguminosæ [vricsham, 48]. Alias Acacia elata; Mimosa elata. Large tree; pinnæ three to six pair; leaflets six to ten pair, sub-sessile, opposite, oblong, emarginate, smooth on both sides; petioles with a ridge on the upper side and one large oblong concave gland near the base, and generally one between the last one to three pair of leaflets; panicles axillary, generally compouud, composed of several pedicelled globular heads of white flowers; legume linear, pointed, smooth, leafy; six to eight-seeded; flowering in may and june; the timber is of good quality. Bark used in tanning [chamrah]. Timber straight, lengthy, and of large girth; when seasoned, it floats in water; wood red, hard and durable.——*Stone sirissa* (سرن - siran, Hind.; ಬಾಗೆ - báge, Can.; చిందుగ - chinduga, Tel.; කබල්මාරා - kabalmárá, Singh.; கற்றுரிஞ்சில் - katturiñjil, Tam.). Title from quality of wood. Tel. from (chennu, tel. beauty) [fragrant sirissa]. Tam. from (kal, tam. stone + turiñjil, tam. albizzia amara, boiv.) [fragrant sirissa]. Tel. also (kondacheragu). Singh. also (hulanmárá). Title otherwise Boomayza, Chindooga, Cubalmara, Stipulated acacia. Botanically Albizzia [sirissa] stipulata, boivin., leguminosæ [vricsham, 48]. Alias Acacia stipulata; Mimosa stipulacea, stipulata. Tree, 40–50 feet, unarmed; leaves bipinnated; young shoots irregularly angled; pinnæ six to twenty pair; petioles tomentose; leaflets numerous, semi-hastate, sides very unequal; peduncles aggregated; panicles terminal and in the upper axils; heads of flowers globose; corolla tubular, five-cleft; stamens very long, monadelphous at the base; legumes thin, flat, glabrous; seeds six to twelve; flowers white and rose-colored. One of the largest of the genus; common, particularly in s. canara; very rapid grower. Gives a gum [gond]. Branches lopped for fodder. Bark gives a dye [shauyam]. Timber strong, compact, stiff, coarse-grained and fibrous, light reddish-brown color, used for building purposes, naves of wheels, &c.

SIRWAIL (చిరువెల్ల - chiruvella, *Tel.* sirvel*). From (chiru, tel. small + velli, tel. stream) [shir].——(1) Talook, Kurnool district. Tahsildar's pay Rs. 150. Area 613 square miles. Population 65,168. Language Teloogoo and Hindostany. S. of district. Bounded N. by Nundiaul talok; E. by Nullamullays; W. by Coilcoontla talook; S. by Proddootore talook, Cuddapah district. Forms the lower portion of the Coondair valley. The E. portion of talook runs parallel to Nullamullays along foot of hills, and is irrigated by small rain-fed tanks [q.v.]. The whole talook is a flat open country. Water found at small depth. The W. half is black-cotton [regar] soil and is within influence of Cuddapah-Kurnool canal, which is here carried over a low ridge throwing water on either side. The E. half, adjoining sandstone [manal cull] hills of Nullamullays, is red ferruginous soil [serval munn]. It is cut up by stream valleys, filled with fine jungle. The principal tanks in the talook are in Alamore, Boyalcoontla, Chennore, Chinna cambalore, Condamauyapulley, Mittapulley, Moottiaul pand, Peddacambalore, Peroor, Roodravaram, Shreerungapooram, Sirwail, Yaudavauda, Yerragoody dinney. Camping grounds:—Chaugulmurry, Deebagoontla, Nullagoontla, Yerragoontla. Products are paddy [q.v.], areca [q.v.], great millet [cholum], italian millet [tinay], raggy [q.v.], horse-gram [q.v.], chillies [q.v.], indigo [q.v.] and cotton [q.v.]. The produce of villages near Nundiaul is carried to Nundiaul market while that of villages near Chaugulmurry is taken to Proddootore and Cuddapah. Indigo manufactories; and indigo is exported to Cuddapah and Madras. Piece-goods, European goods and Chinaware are imported from Cuddapah and Proddootore. Timber is exported to Coilcoontla talook and portion of Cuddapah district. In the villages at the foot of Nullamullays smelting of native iron [auhan]. A good variety of iron ore is obtained from the thin intercalated bands or seams among ferruginous quartz [vencull] of the Nullamullays. The ore worked here is generally a massive shaly iron sandstone

[manal cull]. Weekly markets at Mahadevapooram, Roodravaram and Sirwail. Places of archæological interest :—Ahobalam, Caloogotlapully, Chaugulmurry, Chinna bojanam, Chintacoonta, Digoova ahobalam, Lingamdinney, Mahadevapooram, Pasarapaud, Roodravaram, Zoolapulley. Principal trig. station :—Ahobalam. The leading places, &c., in the talook are the following.——*Ahobalam* (అహోబలం - ahóbalam, Tel.). See sep. title.——*Bauchepully* (బాచెపల్లి - báchepalli, Tel.). From (báchi, san. adze + palli, tel. village). Village; pop. 1,344; acres 3,783; lat. 15° 05′; long. 78° 40′; from Chaugulmurry N.N.E. 9 miles; from Kurnool S.S.E. 63 miles. Timber depôt. Formerly native iron [auhan] manufactory.——*Chaugulmurry* (చాగలమర్రి - chágalamarri, Tel.). See sep. title.——*Chintacoonta* (చింతకుంట - chintakunta, Tel.). From (chinta, tel. tamarind tree, tamarindus indica, linn. + kunta, tel. pond). Tel. also (peddachintakunta), meaning large village, so called. Village; pop. 1,480; acres 7,031; lat. 15° 09′; long. 78° 32′; from Chaugulmurry N.N.W. 15 miles; from Kurnool S.S.E. 54 miles. Temple of Paundarunga sawmy. Irrigated by Cuddapah-Kurnool canal and a tank. Canal bungalow [q.v.].——*Mahadevapooram* (మహాదేవపురం - mahádévapuram, Tel.). From (mahá, san. great + déva, san. god + pura, san. city). Village; pop. 1,200; acres 2,927; lat. 15° 23′; long. 78° 40′; from Chaugulmurry N. 29 miles; from Kurnool S.E. 48 miles. At entrance of W. Nundicanama pass [ghaut]. Weekly fair on Tuesday.——*Moottiaulpaud* (ముత్యాలపాడు - mutyálapádu, Tel.). From (mutyálu, tel. proper name + pádu, tel. village). Village; pop. 1,593; acres 6,422; lat. 15° 03′; long. 78° 39′; from Chaugulmurry N. 5 miles; from Kurnool S.S.E. 65 miles. Former residence of a poligar [q.v.]. Runga naidoo, Cauvalgar [q.v.] of Moottiaulpaud, served under the Vijianuggor rajahs with 700 peons [q.v.]. Family now extinct. Mission house.——*Nullamullay* (నల్లమల - nallamalá, Tel.). See sep. title.——*Oblapully* (ఓబలపల్లి - óbalapalli, Tel.). From (óbulu, tel. proper name + palli, tel. village). Village; pop. 1,209; acres 2,549; lat. 15° 09′; long. 78° 36′; from Chaugulmurry N.N.W. 12 miles; from Kurnool S.S.E. 57 miles. Country cloths.——*Roodravaram* (రుద్రవరం - rudravaram, Tel.). From (rudra, san. contraction for pratáparudra + pura, san. town). Sanscrit name (rudrapura), meaning shiva + town. Village; pop 2,600; acres 3,740; lat. 15° 15′; long. 78° 39′; from Chaugulmurry N. 19 miles; from Kurnool S.E. 54 miles. Iron-smelting. Ruined Shiva temple built by Prataupa roodran [prataupan] of Warangal, thirteenth century. Comaties [q.v.] largely reside. Weekly fair on Monday.——*Sirwail* (చిరువెల్ల - chiruvella, Tel.). See below.——*Vakkalair* (వక్కలేరు - vakkaléru, Tel.). From (vakka, tel. branch + éru, tel. river). River. Tributary of Coondair. Rises in Nullamullay about Pacherla, flows through jungles to Mahadevapooram whence it runs S. and receives Bhavanausy near Chaugulmurry and then falls into Coondair. Runs six months in a year.——*Vaumicondah* (వామికొండ - vámikonda, Tel.). From (vámi, tel. hay rick + konda, tel. hill). Hill; lat. 15° 01′; long. 78° 43′; from Chaugulmurry N.E. 7 miles; from Kurnool S.S.E. 69 miles. Near Chintalcheroo.——
(2) Village; Kurnool dist., Sitwail tal.; pop. 2,729; acres 11,608; lat. 15° 19′; long. 78° 35′; from Chaugulmurry N. 25 miles; from Cumbum W.S.W. 42 miles; from Kurnool S.E. 47 miles; from Madras N.W. 192 miles; from Nundiaul S.S.E. 12 miles; from Pyaupaly E. 53 miles. Former head-quarters of talook. Garden, the favorite resort of late Nawaub of Kurnool. Irrigated by a tank and Kurnool-Cuddapah canal. Weekly fair on Sunday.

SISPARRA (ചിച്ചിപ്പാറ - chiççippára, *Mal.*). From (chíçci, mal. smooth + pára, mal. a rock). Village, Peak, Ghaut; height 6,742 feet; Neilgherry dist., Coondah div.; lat. 11° 12′; long. 76° 29′; from Ootacamund S.W. 22 miles. The peak is the most interesting feature in the western region of the Neilgherries. It stands at the head of the pass [ghaut]. The pass at the south-west angle of the plateau was begun in 1832 and completed in 1838, the Pioneers being employed for the work. Once used as the tappaul [q.v.] line between Ootacamund and the West coast, but abandoned owing to the severity of the climate of the Coondahs. It starts at Sholacull in Nelambore at the base of the hills, and ascends through a wooded ravine for a distance of 11½ miles to the crest of the Coondahs at Sisparra. From this point to Ootacamund the distance is 31½ miles; from Sholacull to Woontore 10 miles, and from thence to Arriyacode, on the Beypore river, 14½ miles. The gradient in parts is very steep. The view from the head of the pass, with the tower-like Sisparra rock on the right, is perhaps the grandest on the hills. There was formerly a bungalow [q.v.] at the place, but it was burnt down some years ago and has not been rebuilt.——*Sisparra creeper* (कालदल - káladala, San.; കാക്കപ്പൂ - kákkappú, Mal.; වල්කොතලා - valkotalá, Singh.; காக்காய்ப்பூச்செடி - kákkáyppúççedi, Tam.). San. from (kála, san. dark + dala, san. petals), from dark flowers. Mal. from (kákka, mal. crow + pú, mal. flower). Tam. from (kákkáy, tam. crow + pú, tam. flower + shedi, tam. plant); from dark purple flowers. Title otherwise. Crow flower, Smooth torenia. Botanically Torenia asiatica, l., scrophularineæ [vricsham, 95]. Alias Torenia hians, vagans. Diffuse, glabrous or slightly hairy; leaves petioled, ovate or ovate-lanceolate, serrate-crenated; calyx elongated, acute at the base, ribs five, nearly equal or three narrow-winged; corolla more than twice as long as the calyx; appendage of the anterior filaments subulate; flowering in the rainy season. Herbaceous pot-plant; bears small, bell-formed, pale, purple flowers, with a large blotch of dark clear, purple on the lower lobe, sparkling like enamel. Juice of leaves a cure for gonorrhœa. There is a variety hirsuta. Other common species are :—cordifolia, parviflora.

SITAUR (ستار - sitár, *Hind.*). From (seh, pers. three + tár, pers. string). A guitar with movable frets; properly with three strings, sometimes has more [sangeetam].

SIVOY (سوائی - siváí, *Hind.*). Without, extra. Sivoy jumma is extra demand on lands brought to account after the regular Jummahbundy [q.v.] has closed; also stands for temporary or irregular items of revenue [teervay]. See vol. I, 112.

SIYAH (سیاه - siyáh, *Pers.*). Black.—"*a*" Plant first term often joining two genera. Ex., where transl. is of second term:—Carum nigrum (siyáhzírah), cuminum cyminum; Curculigo orchioides (siyáhmúslí), asparagopsis sarmentosa; Nigella sativa (siyáhdánah), seed, (siyáhbiranj), rice. See gloss. paragraphs.—"*b*" Plant second term. Ex., where transl. is of first term:—Carum carui (zírahisiyáh), cuminum cyminum; Justicia gendarussa (panjangushtisiyáh), vitex negundo; Solanum nigrum (angúrrúbáhisiyáh), vitis vinifera + fox. See gloss. paragraphs.—"*c*" Mammal first term. Ex., where transl. is of second term:—Felis caracal (siyáhgosh), ear; Macacus silenus (siyáhbandar), monkey of macacus genus. See gloss. paragraphs.——*Shye* (मसि - masi, San.; نقس - niks, Ar.; سیاهی - siyáhí, Pers. and Hind.; منگسی - mangsí, Malay; ಶಾಯಿ - sháyi, Can.; ಶಾಯಿ - sháyi, Too.; శిరా - shirá, Tel.; മഷി - mashi, Mal.; மை - mai, Tam.). San. from (matsya, san. fish); as originally obtained from cuttle-fish. Pers. from (siyáh, pers. black). Mal. from sanscrit. Ink. Composed of gall-nuts [manchicoy], copperas [mayil toottam], gum [gond], and logwood, according to purposes. Varieties are printing ink, writing ink, marking ink, indian ink, &c. [mashy, shirah].——*Siyahgosh* (سیاه گوش - siyáhgosh, Hind.). Means black-eared. Same as Caracal.

SMASHAUNAM (श्मशान - shmashána, *San.*). From (shman, san. body + shána, san. resting place). The place where bodies are burned [shoodcaud].

SMRITY (स्मृति - smriti, *San.*; மிருதி - miruthi, *Tam.*). From (smri, san. to recollect). Portion of sanscrit Vedic literature. Recollection, or that which is remembered and handed down by tradition, as distinguished from audition. This is founded on shrooty [q.v.] or direct revelation as its primary basis, and only possesses authority in so far as it is in harmony with such revealed truth. The essence of smrity however is considered to be that it was delivered memoriter by human authors and put into the form of human composition. In its widest acceptation, smrity may be said to include six principal subjects or departments, as follows.—"*a*" Six Vedaungams [q.v.] or limbs for supporting the Vedam [q.v.], or in other words helps to aid the student in reading, understanding, and applying it to sacrificial rites. They are:—Calpam [q.v.], ceremonial directory, comprising rules relating to the vedic ritual and the whole complicated process of sacrifices [yanyam], which rules are called shrowta sootram [q.v.], because they are vedic and relate directly to the application of the muntram [q.v.] and bramhanam [q.v.] portion of shrooty, being especially guides to the bramhanams; Shicshay [q.v.], the science of pronunciation; Chandas [q.v.], metre; Nirooctam [q.v.], exposition of difficult vedic words; Vyaucaranam [q.v.], grammar; Jyotisham [q.v.], astronomy, including arithmetic [ganitam] and mathematics, especially in connection with astrology.—"*b*" The Smarta sootram [q.v.], a comprehensive term for such rules as do not relate to Shrowtam or Vedic ceremonies, which were usually on a grand scale and public in their character; but rather to religious acts of a private and personal kind, falling naturally under two divisions, viz., family or domestic rites, Kriyay, performed at stated periods, and conventional usages and everyday practices, Samayauchauram; on which account these Smarta sootrams must be separated into two classes, Kriyah sootram and Samayauchaurica sootram.—"*c*" The Dharma shastrams [q.v.] or law books, and especially the Laws of Menoo [q.v.], and other inspired law-givers, supposed to have grown out of the Smarta sootrams. The Mitaucsharam [q.v.], a work on inheritance, by Vinyauneshwaran, on the institutes of Yaunyavalcyan [q.v.], is the chief of these in Southern india. There are also several digests, as the Dauyabhaugam or a treatise on inheritance by Jeemoota vauhanan, that by Jnggernath, &c.—"*d*" The Itihausams [q.v.] or legendary poems, under which head can be placed as portions of Smrity the two great epic poems called Ramayanam [q.v.] and Mahabhaurat [q.v.], and then for convenience, as following and depending on these, but not as properly smrity, the artificial poems, Cauvyam [q.v.], and erotic poems and the dramas, almost all of which in their subject-matter are closely connected with the two great epics.—"*e*" The eighteen Pooraunams [q.v.] or ancient legendary histories and traditions, with their train of eighteen inferior Pooraunams or Oopapooraunams [q.v.] and subsequent Tantrams [q.v.].—"*f*." The Neetishastrams [q.v.] or ethical and didactic writings of all kinds, including collections of fables and moral precepts. See vol. I (56).——*Smarta* (स्मार्त - smárta, San.). From (smriti, san. recollection). Traditional. A bramin following the traditional law based on Smrity. Usually applied to the followers of Shuncaracharry [shuncaran]. The great majority of sheiva bramins are smartas. They are divided into two classes according to their profession; Veidicas and Lowkicas or niyogies. The Veidicas are generally employed in performing the vedic ceremonies, and officiate as village and domestic priests [acharry, poorohit]. The Lowkicas are often village curnums [jauty]. See vol. I (76); II, 225.——*Smartacaul* (स्मार्तकाल - smártakála, San.). From (above + kála, san. time). The extreme time to which the memory of man may extend. ——*Smárta sootram* (स्मार्तसूत्र - smártasútra, San.). From (smárta, san. belonging to smriti + sútra, san. aphorism). A portion of smrity [q.v.]. A comprehensive term for such rules as do not relate to Shrowtam [q.v.] or Vedic ceremonies, but rather to religious acts of a private and personal kind falling naturally under two divisions, viz., Kriyay or family or domestic rites performed at stated periods, and Samayauchauram or conventional usages and every-day practices.

SMUGGLER'S PASS. (ഗൂഢച്ചുരം - gúdhachuram, *Mal.*). From (gúdha, san. secret + churam, mal. pass.). Mal. also (kottiyúrchuram), meaning the place so called + pass. Pass [ghaut]; Malabar district, Cottayam talook. From Dindimala to Manattana.

SNAKE (सर्प - sarpa, *San.*). Prefix.——*Snake gourd* (पटोल - patóla, San.). See sep. title.——*Snake root* (सर्पगन्धा - sarpagandhá, San.; چھوٹا چاند - chhotáchánd, Hind.; ಸೂತ್ರನಾಭಿ - sútranábhi, Can.; పాటలగంధి - pátalagandhi, Tel.; ചുവന്നാവില്പൊരി - chuvannávilpuri, Mal.; ඒකාවේරිය - ekávériya, Singh.; சேவன்னமில்பொரி - shóvannamilbori, Tam.). Title from cure against snake bites. San. from (sarpa, san. serpent + gandha, san. smell). Hind. from (chhotá, hind. small + chánd, hind. moon); from its white flowers. Can. from (sútra, san. thread + nábhi, san. poison). Tel. from (pátala, san. pale-red + gandha, san. smell). Mal. from (chuvanna, mal. red + avilpuri, mal. the plant, rauwolfia). Tam. from malayalam. San. also (chandriká), meaning moonlight [elephant shoonday, haleem]; (chandrashúra), meaning moon + the plant, amorphophallus campanulatus, blume; (vásupushpá), meaning having beautiful flower; (charmahantrí), meaning skin destroying; (nandaní), meaning delighting; (pashuméhanakáriká), meaning causing flow of urine in cows; (vásara); (káraví), meaning stimulant [black jeerah, oolinja]. Hind. also (chandra), meaning moon [elephant shoonday]. Can. also (chandrika), meaning moonlight; (shivanábhi), meaning shiva + poison; cf. bachnaug. Tel. also (pátalagaruda), meaning pale-red + braminy kite. Mal. also (vanduvázha), meaning beetle residing; (tálúnni), meaning stem + fixed; (amilpori). Title otherwise Indian serpent wood, Pautala gundhy, Red-flowered snake wood, Small moon plant, Snake wood plant, Three-leaved ophioxylon. Botanically Rauwolfia serpentina, benth., apocynaceæ [vricsham, 87]. Alias Ophioxylon serpentinum, trifoliatum. Twining; calyx five-cleft; corolla funnel-shaped, with long tube, thick in the middle, five-cleft, limb oblique; anthers almost sessile inserted in the middle of the tube; leaves three-four-five in a whorl, cuneate-oblong, acute, sometimes drooping; pedicels and calyxes red; drupe black, size of a pea [calauyam], twin or solitary by abortion; nut wrinkled, one-seeded; flowers white, with the tube pale rose-lilac. Common small shrub, two feet high; leaves narrow, lanceolate, smooth, shining green; corymbs of numerous small pure-white flowers on fine coral-red footstalks; fruit shining black; root crooked, tapering, from ½ an inch in diameter downwards; bark soft, corky, marked by longitudinal fissures, light brown; wood brittle, showing rings and medullary rays visible to the naked eye; taste very bitter; odour of the fresh root acrid; the suber upon transverse section presents when magnified the appearance of a piece of honeycomb, viz., alternate rows of long tubular cells and compressed cells; the inner portion of the bark consists of a delicate parenchyma, loaded with starch, and traversed by indistinct medullary rays; the wood is remarkably starchy. Bitter root prescribed medicinally for snake bites and scorpion stings; ordered in decoction, and powder applied externally to the injured part; used also as a febrifuge; also to promote delivery, like ergot of rye; root quoted in pharm., non-officinal. Other common species are:—beddomei, densiflora.——*Snake-stone* (सर्पमणि - sarpamani, San.; مارمہر - mármuhr, Hind.; ಹಾವುಕಲ್ಲು - hávukallu, Can.; పామురాయి - pámuráyi, Tel.; വിഷക്കല്ല് - vishakkal, Mal.; பாம்புக்கல் - pámbukkal, Tam.). Hind. from (már, pers. snake + muhrah, ar. shell). Tam. also (vidakkal), meaning poison + stone. A substance, the application of which to the part where a snake-bite has taken effect is supposed to draw out the poison. Various substances have this reputation. They are usually of a porous kind, and when they have been chemically examined have proved to be made of charred bone or some similar product.——*Snake-wood tree* (کچلا لتا - kuchlálatá, Hind.; నాగముసడి - nágamusadi, Tel.; മോതിരക്കാഞ്ഞിരം - mótirakkáññiram, Mal.). Title from cure in snake bites. Hind. from (kuchlá, hind. strychnos nux-vomica, linn. + latá, hind. creeper). Tel. from (nága, san. snake + musadi, tel. strychnos nux-vomica, linn.). Mal. from (mótiram, mal. ring + káññiram, mal. strychnos nux-vomica, linn.); from moustache-like tentacles. Tel. also (kausukandíra); (tigamushti), meaning creeper + strychnos nux-vomica, linn. Mal. also (cherukáttuvallikkáññiram), meaning small + wild + creeper + nux-vomica. Title otherwise Climbing koochlah, Climbing nux-vomica, Lignum colubrinum, Pao da cobra. Botanically Strychnos [mooshty] colubrina, linn., loganiaceæ [vricsham, 89]. Alias Strychnos bicirrhosa. Climbing shrub; calyx five parted; corolla tubular, with a five parted spreading limb; leaves opposite, from oval to oblong, bluntly acuminate, three-nerved; berries globose, pulpy, many-seeded; tendrils lateral, simple; corymbs terminal, composed of two to three pairs of villous branches; flowers small, greenish yellow; berry as large as an orange [q.v.]; rind yellowish. Stem of great size, often from 8 to 12 inches in diameter; bark ash-colored; few flowered; root is woody and covered with iron-colored bark; yields one sort at least of lignum colubrinum; wood and root contain strychnia; fruit also poisonous. The general structure of the bark resembles that of strychnos nux-vomica [poison nut], but it is of a rusty color, and the small lenticels upon it, instead of being pale, are of a bright rusty brown; the pieces of wood vary much in size, and are more knotty and crooked than those of strychnos nux-vomica [poison nut]; they are often as thick as a man's arm; the texture of the wood is closer, harder and of a deeper color; when touched with nitric acid [shorey ka tezaub] it turns of a reddish orange; under the microscope the zone of stone-cells in the bark is seen to be wider and more irregular than in strychnos nux-vomica, and the cells themselves are bright yellow, and larger. Wood given medicinally in substance for intermittent fevers; root has purgative qualities; wood and root remedy for bite of cobra [q.v.] brayed in rice-water; given in small doses internally and also applied externally; wood also anthelmintic.

SNAKE GOURD (पटोल - patóla, *San.*). Title from length of fruit in common kinds, sometimes tortuous. San. from (pat, san. to encircle). Botanically the Trichosanthes genus, cucurbitaceæ [vricsham, 62]. Scandent herbs; leaves three to nine-lobed; flowers white, large, beautifully fringed; fruit long or roundish, fleshy; seeds flat, irregular shaped, packed in pulp. The species best known to the natives are shown below.——*Bitter snake gourd* (महाकाल - mahákála, San.; कंवडळ - kamvadala, Mahr.; حنظل احمر - hanzaliahmar, Ar.; حنظل سرخ - hanzalisurkh, Pers.; لال اندراین - lálindráyan, Hind.; لال اندراون - lálindrávan, Dec.; ಅವಗುಡೆ - avagúde, Can.; అవ్వగూడ - avvagúda, Tel.; കാക്കത്തൊണ്ടി - kákkattonti, Mal.; තිත්තහොන්ඩල - tittahondala, Singh.; குறட்டை - kurattai, Tam.). Title from taste. San. from (mahá, san. great + kála, san. black, poison), from dark pulp of fruit supposed poisonous; see below. Ar. from (hanzal, ar. colocynth, citrullus colocynthis, schrad. + ahmar, ar. red), from extreme bitterness of fruit. Pers. from (hanzal, ar. colocynth + surkh, pers. red). Hind. from (lál, hind. red + indráyan, hind. colocynth). Dec. from hindostany. Tel. from (avva, tel. grandmother + gúda, tel. prolapsus uteri); from the fruit. Mal. from (kákka, mal. crow + tonti, mal. cephalandra indica, naud.). Singh. from (titta, singh. bitter + hondala, singh. the tree, modecca palmata, lam.). Tam. from (kurandu, tam. to be crumpled); from lobed leaves. Ar. also (anbaghol). Hind. also (makal), from sanscrit. Dec. also (godápandú), meaning kernel + fruit. Can. also (kákemandali), meaning crow + rebuke; (kágemáraballi), meaning crow + beat + creeper. Tel. also (ábuvva); (kákidonda), meaning crow + cephalandra indica, naud. Tam. also (shavari); (ángurattai), meaning male corattay. Title otherwise Bitter gourd, Corattay, Cowndal, Makal, Palmated gourd, Round snake gourd. Botanically Trichosanthes [snake gourd] palmata, roxb., cucurbitaceæ [vricsham, 62]. Alias Modecca bracteata; Trichosanthes anguina, laciniosa. Modecca from (mutukku, mal. the plant, modecca palmata, lam.). Climbing; leaves palmately lobed, toothed; tendrils three cleft; male flowers racemose; female ones solitary in the same axils as the male, or occasionally racemose; calyx five cleft; segments deeply toothed or serrated; corolla fringed, five petalled; flowers large, white. The fruit is round, oval, or pyriform, the size of a small apple [seb], crimson when fresh, of a dull orange [q.v.] color when dry, marked at one end by a deep cicatrix with sharp raised edges, at the other there is a prominence to which a portion of the stalk sometimes remains attached; in the dry fruit, which has a thin brittle very bitter shell, the segments of pulp with their seeds are loose, so that the contents of the gourd rattle; if a dry segment be soaked in water it soon softens, yielding a dark green pulp which smells like savine, and has an acrid and bitter taste; the seeds, ranging in number from sixty to hundred in each fruit, are flat, but very irregular in shape, generally somewhat triangular, and average $\frac{3}{10}$ths of an inch in length; they have a hard blackish shell, and sweet oily kernel; the vine is perennial, often as thick as a man's arm; it has a warty grey bark, marked by seven deep longitudinal fissures, which correspond to the medullary divisions between seven wedge-shaped woody and vascular bundles into which the stem is divided; the vine is not bitter; the flowers are slightly fetid. The fruit mixed with cocoanut [q.v.] oil is medicinally a specific in earache, but it is not eatable being considered poisonous; the root too is reckoned poisonous; it is used in diseases of cattle [pashoorogam], such as inflammation of the lungs, &c.; gives to pharm. rind of fruit, non-official, purgative.——*Common snake gourd* (चिचिण्ड - chichinda, San.; पडोल - padóla, Mahr.; पड्डूळ - paddúla, Conc.; چچینڈا - chichendá, Hind.; چچونڈا - chichondá, Dec.; ಪಡವಲಬಳ್ಳಿ - padavalaballi, Can.; ಪಟ್ಲಕಾಯಿ - patlakáyi, Too.; పొట్ల - potla, Tel.; പടോലം - patólam, Mal.; පොඩිවිලඟු - podivilangu, Singh.; புடல் - pudal, Tam.). Mahr. from (patóla, san. the plant). Hind. from sanscrit. Dravid. from (patóla, san. the plant). San. also (patóla), meaning encircling. Hind. also (parwar), meaning trichosanthes nervifolia, linn. Malay also (petálanlar); (petalriular). Can. also (patla); (adlaballi). Tel. also (polla); (lingupotla), meaning emblem of shiva + the plant. Title otherwise Chichonda, Club-gourd, Padole, Poodal, Snake cucumber, Snake-plant, Snake vegetable. Botanically Trichosanthes [snake gourd] anguina, linn., cucurbitaceæ [vricsham, 62]. Alias Cucumis anguinus. Plant trained to a frame or trellis; of exceedingly rapid growth; bears a large greenish-white, club-formed gourd, of the length of a man's arm and about four inches thick. Seeds are cooling medicine. Gourd eaten, sliced and dressed like french beans [lobyah]; used in curries [q.v.]; often cut into lengths filled with a preparation of minced meat.——*Palwal snake gourd* (पटोल - patóla, San.; पडोल - padóla, Mahr.; پرور - parwar, Hind.; پلول - palwal, Dec.; కొమ్ముపొట్ల - kommupotla, Tel.; പടോലം - patólam, Mal.; கொம்புப்புடல் - kombuppudal, Tam.). Title from deccany. San. from (pat, san. to encircle). Mahr., &c. from sanscrit. Tel from (kommu, tel. horn + potla, tel. trichosanthes anguina, linn.); from the fruit. Tam. from (kombu, tam. horn + pudal, tam. trichosanthes anguina, linn.), from short, sharp fruit. Hind. also (banpotal), meaning forest variety. Botanically Trichosanthes [snake gourd] dioica, roxb., cucurbitaceæ [vricsham, 92]. Stems twining, more or less woolly and scabrous; leaves 3 by 2 inches, harsh, sinuate-dentate, not lobed; petiole ¾ inch; tendrils 2-fid; male peduncles in pairs; calyx-tube 1¾ inches narrow; fruit 2-3½ inches, oblong, acute, orange red; seeds ⅜-½ inch, half ellipsoid, compressed, corrugate on margin; plant diœcious. Climbing annual; bears large, white flowers; gourd oblong, smooth, two to four inches long, green when unripe, yellow or orange when ripe. Used medicinally like cucumerina. Unripe fruit and tender tops, eaten in curries [q.v.]; also boiled whole, or in quarters.——*Short snake gourd* (پرور - parwar, Hind.; پلول - palwal, Dec.; కొమ్ముపొట్ల - kommupotla, Tel.; പടോലം - patólam, Mal.; கொம்புப்புடல் - kombuppudal, Tam.). Title from fruit short and thick like horn and also growing in pairs. Hind. and Dec. from (patóla, san. trichosanthes genus). Tel. from (kommu, tel. horn + potla, tel. trichosanthes anguina, linn.); from fruit short and thick like horn. Mal. from (pat, san. to encircle). Tam. from (kombu, tam. horn + pudal, tam. trichosanthes anguina, linn.). Title otherwise Horn poodul. Botanically Trichosanthes [snake gourd] nervifolia, linn., cucurbitaceæ [vricsham, 62]. Alias Trichosanthes dioica. Stem smoothish; leaves cordate-acuminate, minutely, and sharply bristle-toothed, smooth, marked beneath with prominent veins and nerves; tendrils two-cleft; male flowers long-pedicelled; peduncle sometimes branched; female flowers solitary; fruit ovate; malabar. Medicinally like dioica [palwal snake].——*Wild snake gourd* (पटोल - patóla, San.; रानपडोल - ránapadóla, Mahr.; काडपड्डूळ - kádapaddúla, Conc.; جنگلی چچینڈا - janglíchichendá, Hind.; جنگلی چچونڈا - janglíchichondá, Dec.; ಕಹಿಪಡವಲ - kahipadavala, Can.; ಕಾಟುಪಟ್ಲಕಾಯಿ - kátupatlakáyi, Too.; అడవిపొట్ల - adavipotla, Tel.; പടോലം - patólam, Mal.; තිත්තපටොල - tittapatóla, Singh.; பேய்ப்புடல் - péyppudal, Tam.). Title from habitat. San. from (pat, san. to encircle). Mahr. from (rána, mahr. wild + padavala, mahr. snakegourd). Hind. from (janglí, hind. wild + chichinda, san. snake gourd, trichosanthes anguina, linn.). Dec. from hindostany. Can. from (kahi, can. bitter + padavala, can. the plant, trichosanthes anguina, linn.). Too. from (kátu, too. wild + patlakáyi, too. the plant, trichosanthes anguina, linn.). Tel. from (adavi, tel. jungle + potla, tel. trichosanthes anguina, linn.). Singh. from (tikta, san. bitter + patóla, san. the plant). Tam. from (péy, tam. devil + pudal, tam. snake plant, trichosanthes anguina, linn.). San. also (tiktap'hala), meaning bitter fruit; (tiktaka), meaning bitter. Can. also (sannapadavala), meaning small + the plant, trichosanthes anguina, linn.; (kádáduballi), meaning jungle + sheep + creeper; (bettapadavala), meaning hill + the plant. Tel. also (chédupotla), meaning bitter + trichosanthes anguina, linn.; (chétipotla), meaning bitter + trichosanthes anguina, linn. Mal. also (kaippappatólam), meaning bitter + snake gourd; (péppatólam), meaning devil's gourd; (káttupatólam), meaning forest + snake gourd. Singh. also (dummella). Tam. also (káttuppéyppudal), meaning forest + the plant. Title otherwise Cucumber-like snake gourd, Devil's gourd, Doommella, Hair flower, Jagged hair blossom, Torn trichosanthes, Wild poodal. Botanically Trichosanthes [snake gourd] cucumerina, linn., cucurbitaceæ [vricsham, 62]. Alias Trichosanthes laciniosa. Annual, climbing; leaves broadly cordate, three to seven angled, toothed or serrated, pubescent or glabrous; tendrils three-cleft; male flowers disposed in something like umbels; female ones solitary on short peduncles, often from the same axils as the males; fruit ovate, pointed; petals five, ciliated; calyx five-cleft; flowers small, white; found everywhere. Fruit, oblong, one to four inches long; striated with white and green when unripe, and red when ripe. Tender shoots and dried capsules bitter and aperient; in decoction with sugar [q.v.] given to assist digestion; seeds antifebrile and anthelmintic; juice of the leaves expressed is emetic and that of root very purgative. Fruit contains red pulp which is very bitter and eaten unripe in curries [q.v.].

SNAUNAM (स्नान - snána, *San.*). From (sná, san. to bathe). Bathing, ablution, purification. Seven kinds of ceremonial Snaunam are enumerated. Ablution is stringently carried out by Hindoos, less so by Mahomedans. With Hindoos bathing is an indispensable prerequisite to first meal of day, and washing hands and feet before evening meal. For idol bathing see Abhishaicam.

SNOW (చనువు - tsannuvu, *Tel.*). Means authority, currency. Hence a snow-rupee.

SNOWDON (ದೇವಶೋಲೆಬೆಟ್ಟ - dévashólabetta, *Can.*). Vern. from (dévashóla, can. estate so called. + betta, can. hill). Can. also (dérbetta), meaning god + hill. Hill; Neilgherry dist., Todanaud div.; lat. 11° 26′; long. 76° 46′; height 8,299 feet; from Ootacamund N.E. 3 miles. Formerly known as Devasholahbett; also as Terbetta. Almost a perfect cone; the line of its northern slope, a fall of some 1,500 feet, being remarkably even, though steep [dodabetta].

SOAPNUT (फेनिल - p'hénila, *San.*; रिठा - rit'há, *Mahr.*; रिंठ्या - rintyá, *Conc.*; فندق هند - fundukihind, *Ar.*; بندق - bunduk, *Pers.*; ریٹھے کا پیڑ - rithekáper, *Hind.*; ریٹھے کا جھاڑ - ríthekájhár, *Dec.*; رارق - rarak, *Malay*; ಅಂಟವಾಳ - antavála, *Can.*; ನುರೆಕಾಯಿ - nurekáyi, *Too.*; కుంకుడు - kunkudu, *Tel.*; മുക്തമയ - muktamaya, *Oer.*; ഉറുവഞ്ചി - urvvañchi, *Mal.*; පෙනෙල - penela, *Singh.*; பூவந்தி - púvandi, *Tam.*). Title from saponaceous pulp round seed. San. from (p'héna, san. foam); from capsules. Mahr. from (rishta, san. the tree). Conc. from mahratta. Ar. from (funduk, ar. filbert, corylus avellana, linn. + hind. ar. india). Pers. from arabic. Hind. and Dec. from (rishta, san the tree). Can. from (antu, can. gum + vala, can. affix implying possession). Too. from (nure, too. foam + káyi, too. seed). Mal. corruption of (púviraññi); from (pú, mal. flower + iraññi, mal. mimusops elengi, linn.). Singh. from sanscrit. Tam. from (pú, tam. flower + andi, tam. evening); from color of nuts. San. also (arishta), meaning not injuring [black datura, neem]; (rishta), by corruption. Mahr. also (ringí). Pers. also (ratah), from sanscrit. Hind. also (rishta), from sanscrit; (arishta), from sanscrit. Can. also (kúgate); (thalemaradu); (púchikotte); (aradála); (antarale). Tel. also (kúkudu). Mal. also (punnakkotta), meaning seeds of poon tree, calophyllum inophyllum, linn.; (chavakkáymaram), meaning soap tree; (púviriññi), meaning flowering ilanjy. Tam. also (ponnán-gottaimaram), meaning gold + seed + tree; (manippungu), meaning bead + pongamia glabra, vent.; (paççaikkottaimaram), meaning sticky + seed + tree; (neykkottán), meaning ghee + seed, from unctuous nuts. Title otherwise Bead poongam, Downy-leaved soap-berry, Emarginated soap-berry, Monkey's blood, Notch-leaved soapnut, Reetah, Rintah, Soap-berry, Soap-tree. Botanically Sapindus trifoliatus, linn., sapindaceæ [vricsham, 43]. Alias Sapindus emarginatus, laurifolius. Pulp round the seed saponaceous, whence generic name. Tree, middling size; petiole pubescent; leaves abruptly pinnate; leaflets two to three pairs; oblong, retuse or emarginate, entire, upper side glabrous, under very downy; racemes in terminal panicles; calyx segments five, oblong; petals five, oval, outside densely hairy, margin very woolly, with a small woolly appendage on each side about the middle, inside nearly glabrous, or with a few scattered hairs about the middle; ovary densely hairy; fruit one to four, generally three-lobed, lobes very hairy on the inside at the insertion of the seeds; flowers small, white; flowering in october-november; common in dry jungles. The dry fruit or soap-nut as it is called is generally sold in the bazaar, single, spheroidal, about ¾ inch in diameter, wrinkled and reddish brown or brownish yellow in color, with a large, heart-shaped, whitish and woody scar at the base; the scar is divided into two slanting surfaces with a thin and prominent ridge, indicating the attachment of two other nuts originally; the pericarp is about a line and a half thick, with a soft, viscid, and translucent pulp; however long it may be exposed to the sun it does not get sufficiently dry to be pulverised; the inner membrane or shell enclosing the seed is thin, tough, translucent and leathery; the taste of the pulp is sweetish bitter, and the smell bears some resemblance to that of a very ripe and decomposing mango [q.v.], or the compound extract of colocynth [bitter water melon], butyric acid; the active principle of the soap-nut is saponin, which occurs to the extent of about 10 per cent. in the pulp; the seed of the fruit is roundish, black, smooth, and about the size of a large pea [calauyam]; and the kernel thereof is yellowish or pale-white, oily and sweetish in taste. The pericarp or pulp, and kernel of the fruit is in medicine internally, emetic, nauseant and expectorant; through the nose, a remedy in hemicrania, asthma, hysteria and epilepsy; externally, detergent, and a remedy for the stings and bites of poisonous insects [poochy], as scorpion [tail], centipede [kankhajoor], &c. The pulp or pericarp of soap-nut can only be administered conveniently in the form of draught, which is easily prepared by rubbing and bruising it in one or two ounces of water and passing the same through cloth; a thick solution of the drug for dropping into the nose is prepared in the same way with a very small quantity of water; the juice may be strained and kept in a bottle for use for a day or two, or squeezed into the nostrils then and there through the cloth; in preparing the paste or poultice of this medicine, vinegar [caudy] or lime-juice [lime] should be used instead of water. Doses; from one drachm and a half to two drachms as an emetic; from twenty to forty grains as a nauseant; and from ten to eighteen grains as an expectorant. Substituted; for ipecacuanha, sulphate of zinc [vellay toottam], squill and senega as an emetic, nauseant, and expectorant; for carbonate of ammonia, hypodermic injection of morphia, and liquor ammoniæ, as a remedy through the nose and as a local application. Capsule has a detergent quality when bruised, forming suds if agitated in hot water; used as a soap [sauboon] for washing the hair, silk, &c.; makes the hair lustrous, has however a corrosive action; stem gives a gum [gond]; the hard tough nuts take a fine polish and are employed for necklaces [maulay] and beads [munkah]. Wood used for posts, door frames, and the construction of carts; pale yellowish, close and elegantly grained, hard but not durable, and cracks if exposed. Other common species are:—attenuatus, erectus, mukorossi, obovatus; wood of these inferior.——*Rusty soap-nut* (ریٹھا - rítha, Hind.; ఇసుకరాశి - isukaráshi, Tel.; ମୁକ୍ତାମୟା - muktamoyá, Oor.; மணிப்புங்கம் - manippungam, Tam.). Title from color of wood. Hind. from (arishta, san. soap-nut tree, sapindus trifoliatus, linn.). Tel. from (isuka, tel. sand + ráshi, san. heap). Tam. from (mani, tam. bead + pungu, tam. pongamia glabra, vent.), from small similar berries. Tel. also (undurugu); (tavati); (tasati). Title otherwise Reetah. Botanically Erioglossum edule, bl., sapindaceæ [vricsham, 43]. Alias Erioglossum rubiginosum; Moulinsia rubiginosa; Sapindus fraxinifolius, rubiginosa. Tree; younger parts clothed with rusty pubescence; leaves abruptly pinnate; leaflets four to six pair, oblong-lanceolate, acuminated, entire, slightly hairy beneath; racemes in terminal panicles; calyx unequal; petals four, the fifth deficient, glabrous, with a distinct claw; limb cordate-oblong; scale attached to the petals by the margin, very woolly, with a woolly appendage at its back overtopping the scale; stamens on one side, woolly; ovary deeply three-lobed, hairy; style longish berries one to two, rarely three, nearly unconnected; flowers small, white; flowering in march. Timber straight, strong and durable, chocolate-colored towards the centre, useful for great variety of purposes. No other common species here.

SOAP-POD (सप्तला - saptalá, *San.*; शिककाई - shikakái, *Mahr.*; सिकायि - sikáyi, *Conc.*; سیکاکائی کا پڑ - síkákáikáper, *Hind.*; سیکے کائی کا جھاڑ - síkekáikájhár, *Dec.*; ಶೀಗೆ - shíge, *Can.*; ଶିଗେ - síge, *Too.*; సీకాయ - síkáya, *Tel.*; ചീനിക്കായ - chínikkáya, *Mal.*; சீயக்காய் - shíyakkáy, *Tam.*). Title from use of pods. San. from (sapta, san. seven + lá, san. to take); from thickest bushy habit. Mahr. and Hind. from tamul. Tel. assumed from (chikku, tel. rancidity of oil + káya, tel. pod); from removing rancid smell of oil in the head; but really see tamul. Mal. assumed from (chíni, mal. chinese foreign + káya, mal. fruit); but really see tamul. Tam. from (shí, tam. to cleanse + káy, tam. fruit); cf. clearing nut tree. San. also (charmakashá), meaning skin injurer, from thorns; (bhúrip'héna), meaning much + froth; (vimalá), meaning cleanser; (sátalá), meaning happy plant. Mahr. also (télashénga), meaning oil + pod, as used in oil bathing. Mal. also (ínna), by corruption. Title otherwise Charmaghas, Oil-pod tree, Shika, Shikauya, Soap acacia, Soap pod wattle, Tamarisk leaf-acacia, Washing-pod tree. Botanically Acacia [cantalam] concinna, dc., leguminosæ [vricsham, 48]. Alias Acacia abstergens, rugata, saponaria; Mimosa abstergens, concinna, intsia, rugata, saponaria, tamariscifolia. Intsia from (íncha, mal. acacia intsia, willd.). Climbing; branches irregularly angled, tomentose, armed with numerous recurved prickles; leaves bipinnated; pinnæ six to eight pair; leaflets numerous, linear, somewhat semi-hastate, mucronate; petioles with hooked prickles below; panicles terminal and axillary, with globular heads of flowers three to five together in the axils of a small bract or leaf, peduncled; stamens distinct; legumes large, succulent, contracted between the seeds; valves wrinkled on the surface when dry; flowers small, white; a hedge plant. The long flat pods or legumes, have taste resembling soap-nut, sapindus trifoliatus, linn. [soap nut]; more acid, less bitter, have singular pungency. Medicinally deobstruent, expectorant; commonly ordered in jaundice and other biliary derangements; small leaves have pleasant acidity, frequently put into pepper-water to keep bowels open or work off bile. Leaves are used in cookery as substitute for tamarinds [q.v.]. Pods are detergent, used for washing the hair to kill vermin; natives use them for marking the forehead [pottoo, tilacam].

SOCOOLAIR (సొకులేరు - sókuléru, *Tel.*). From (sóku, tel. to touch + éru, tel. river). River; Godavery dist., Rekapully talook. A tributary of the Severy. Rises in the eastern ghauts [q.v.], flows through the Rekapully talook and joins the Severy at Moocanore.

SODA GRASS (کلسنار - kalasnár, *Hind.*; సోడా - soda, *Tel.*). Botanically Panicum [priyangoo] paludosum, roxb., graminaceæ [vricsham, 156]. Culm branched, erect, swollen under the water, and there emitting roots from the joints; leaves linear, glaucescent, hispid, sheaths bearded at the mouth; panicle oval, diffuse, thin, composed of scattered, subalternate ramous branches, angles sharp, finely pointed; flowers oblong, twin, partial pedicels unequal; seed oblong, smooth, brown; usually growing in water.

SODY (چھوری - chhorí, *Hind.*). From (chhorná, hind. to relinquish). Relinquishment of puttah [q.v.] holdings, abatement of a charge.

SOLA (సోల - sóla, *Tel.*).—"*a*" Measure of capacity. 4 giddas = 1 sola; 2 solas = 1 tavva [alavay, 3b]. In Ganjam $13\frac{1}{2}$ cubic inches, in Vizagapatam $39\frac{1}{4}$ cubic inches, in Godavery $17\frac{1}{2}$ cubic inches, in Kistna 35 cubic inches.—"*b*" Bazaar weight. 15 tolahs = 1 sola; 4 solas = 1 adda [niray, 2b]. Approximate actual value 1 sola = 6 oz. $2\frac{2}{5}$ drs. avoir. Ganjam. See vol. I, 609; II, 510, 511, 512, 516, 519.

SOLAH (दमन - damana, *San.*; भेंड - bhénda, *Mahr.*; شولا - sholá, *Hind.*; بھینڈ - bhend, *Dec.*; ಟಣಕಲಿಗಿಡ - tanakaligida, *Can.*; జీలుగబెండు - jílugabendu, *Tel.*; നെല്ലിത്താളി - nellittáli. *Mal.*; මහදියසියඹලා - mahadiyasiyambalá, *Singh.*; நெட்டிச்செடி - nettiççedi, *Tam.*). Title from hindostany. San. from (dam, san. to pacify) [absinth]. Mahr. means pith. Tel. from (jílugu, tel. fine + bendu, tel. pith plant); from softness. Mal. from (nelli, mal. phyllanthus emblica, linn. + táli, mal. creeper). Singh. from (mahá, san. large + diya, singh. water + siyambalá, singh. tamarindus indica, linn.). Tam. from (netti, tam. pith + shedi, tam. plant). Hind. also (phúlshola), meaning light pith. Can. also (alaginagida), meaning shaking + tree. Tel. also (nírujíluga), meaning water + pith plant; (tigajíluga), meaning creeper + pith plant; (bendu), meaning pith plant. Mal. also (áttukatésham), meaning river + cork, millingtonia hortensis, linn. f. Tam. also (netti), meaning breaking with a crackle or pith; (kokkéri), meaning heron + to ascend; (áttunetti), meaning river + the plant; (takkaiççedi), meaning plug + tree, from use of pith as stoppers for bottles; (shadaiççedi), meaning bushy hair + plant; (shadai), meaning hairy; (kidai); (kidaiççi). Title otherwise Netty shrub, Pith plant, River cork, Rough-stemmed bastard sensitive plant, Singapore hat-plant, Sponge wood, Water tamarind. Botanically Æschynomene aspera, linn., leguminosæ [vricsham, 48]. Alias Æschynomene aquatica, indica, lagenaria; Hedysarum lagenarium. Perennial, floating, erect, sometimes branched; leaves unequally pinnated; leaflets numerous, linear, obtuse; racemes axillary, few-flowered; calyx five-cleft, two-lipped, bibracteolate; peduncles and pedicels rough with hairs; legumes four to seven-jointed, on long stalks, with prickly tubercles on the middle of each joint, margins striated, crenulated; flowers brownish orange; light, white-colored, corky-looking wood; grows on margins of tanks, &c. Plant used in decoction in dropsy. Leaflets used as greens [keeray]; famine food. Chief use is for its pith; largely used by fishermen for floats and cork-jackets; also cut into paper-like sheets and made into temporary decorations around idols during festivities; europeans use it for making cases for tumblers containing ice, being a bad conductor; similarly for making pith hats, which are extremely light and keep the head cool; also to pad the roofs of palankeens [q.v.]. There is a stanza from Nauladiyaur:—நீருட்பிறந்து நிறம்பசியதாயினும் ஈரங் கிடையகத்தில் லாகும் - ஒரும் நிறைப்பெருஞ்செல் வத்து நின்றக்கடைத்தும் அறைப்பெருங்கவன்றுருடை த்து—"the world has those whose hearts are hard as rock "though in the midst of abounding wealth; the solah plant "though born in water and green in color has no moisture "within."——*Black solah* (నల్లజీలుగ - nallajíluga, Tel.). Same as Lowly chakondah.——*Foreign solah* (సీమజీలుగ - símajíluga, Tel.). Same as Parangyvail.——*Hill solah* (కొండజీలుగ - kondajíluga, Tel.). Same as Bastard sago palm.——*Red solah* (ఎర్రజీలుగ - errajíluga, Tel.). Same as Prickly sesban.

SOLGA (సోలగ - sólaga, *Tel.*). Measure of capacity. 4 seers = 1 solga; 4 solgas = 1 maunam [alavay, 3c]. Approximate actual value, 1 solga = 280 cubic inches. Bellary. Compare Moonta of nellore, Cooncham of godavery and kistna, Cooncham or Toom of ganjam. See vol. I, 609; II, 508.

SONA (سونا - soná, *Hind.*). From (svapna, san. sleep). Sleep, rest.——*Sonapore* (సొన్నాపురము - sonnápuramu, Tel.). From (soná, hind. rest + pura, san. town). Village, Port, Sea-customs station; Ganjam dist., Berhampore tal.; pop. 1,424; acres 1,899; lat. 19° 07′; long. 84° 50′; from Barwah N.N.E. 22 miles; from Berhampore S. 14 miles; from Chetterpore S.W. 21 miles; from Gopalpore S.S.W. 20 miles; from Madras N.N.E. 506 miles. Two miles from Soorlah salt factory and connected with Berhampore by a branch road leading into the high road between Ichapore and Berhampore. Also connected by road with Sonapore in the Central provinces, distant about 105 miles. Now unimportant, although in 1768 the principal shipping place in Ichapore province. The anchorage is with the flagstaff bearing W.N.W. The Bauhoodah falls into the sea at Sonapore and forms sandy bars which offer great obstruction to shipping. The trade that formerly went to Sonapore is now gradually finding its way to Barwah. The soil around Sonapore was much injured by inundations from the sea in 1825, which have rendered it brackish and unfertile. Good edible oysters [auly] are found. Trig. station in lat. 19° 06′ 44·70″; long. 84° 49′ 28·70″; from Sonapore N. 1½ miles; from Berhampore S. 13 miles; from the sea W. ½ mile.——*Sooptee* (सुपती - supatí, Mahr.; కొండవెంపలి - kondavempali, Tel.). Title from mahratta. Mahr. from (svap, san. to sleep); from intoxicating fish. Tel. from (konda, tel. hill + vempali, tel. the plant, tephrosia purpurea, pers.). Mahr. also (supi), meaning drowsy tree. Title otherwise Cork leaved tephrosia. Botanically Mundulea suberosa, benth., leguminosæ [vricsham. 48]. Alias Cytisus sericeus; Robinia sennoides, suberosa; Tephrosia sericea, suberosa. Arborescent; young shoots tomentose; bark corky and cracked; leaves pinnated; leaflets six to eighteen pair, elliptic-oblong, obtuse, clothed on the under side with silky pubescence; calyx campanulate, shortly five-toothed; keel straightish; vexillum pubescent; legume long, straight, silky-pubescent, contracted between the seeds; racemes terminal; flowers in pairs, long-pedicelled; flowers in june and july. Densely silky on the branches; lilac or rosy flowers succeeded by a long silky pod, containing kidney-shaped seeds; very ornamental when in flower, as it is perfectly covered with blossoms; common about subalpine jungles; the leaves resemble senna [q.v.] leaves. Seeds used to poison fish [common emetic nut, indian berry, indian oak, marotty, round milk-hedge, tejbul, walsoora, zanzibar indigo]; inner bark of green color has same effect.

SONF (मधुरिका - madhuriká, *San.*; बडीशेप - badíshépa, *Mahr.*; راز يانج - ráziyánaj, *Ar.*; باديان - bádiyán, *Pers.*; سونف - sonf, *Hind.* and *Dec.*; పెద్దజీలకర్ర - peddajílakarra, *Tel.*; දෙවදුරු - dévaduru, *Singh.*; பெருஞ்சீரகம் - peruñjíragam, *Tam.*). Title from deccany. San. from (madhura, san. sweet) [sowa]. Mahr. from (barísonf, hind. the plant). Tel. from (pedda, tel. large + jílakarra, tel. cumin, cuminum cyminum, linn.). Singh. from (déva, singh. king + duru, singh. cumin); large cumin. Tam. from (perum, tam. great + jíraka, san. cumin). Pers. also (wálánibuzurg), meaning large fennel. Hind. also (pánmuhori), meaning betel-leaf fennel; (barísonf), meaning large fennel. Singh. also (rataenduru), meaning foreign cumin. Tam. also (shógikkírai), meaning sowa vegetable [sowa]; (narchíragam), meaning good cumin. Greek μάραθον. Title otherwise Arak baudyaun, Finicho, Indian fennel, Sweet fennel. Botanically Fœniculum vulgare, gærtn., umbelliferæ [vricsham, 67]. Alias Anethum fœniculum, panmorium; Fœniculum officinale, panmori, panmorium; Ozodia fœniculacea; panmori from hindostany. Perennial, glabrous, glaucous; stem striated; leaves many-cleft; lobes linear-setaceous; umbels twelve to twenty-rayed; involucel and involucre wanting; fruit oblong, laterally compressed, without a beak; flowers yellow; common in gardens, raised from seed. Aromatic seeds medicinally stimulant, aromatic, and carminative; root purgative; leaves diuretic; gives to pharm. aqua fœniculi, a vehicle for other drugs; leaves used by natives as seasoning, and by europeans in garnishing; fennel oil [yennay] from roots. The fennel seeds of commerce are:—German or saxon fennel, Indian fennel, Sweet or roman fennel, Wild or bitter fennel. Sonf is hindostany for Anise [q.v.] seed also.

SONT (शुण्ठी - shunt'hí, *San.*; سونٹ - sont, *Hind.*). San. from (shunt'h, san. to dry). Dry ginger [ginger].

SOO (सु - su, *San.*). Good. Plant first term. Ex., where transl. is of second term:—Allium cepa (sukandaka), root; Alpinia galanga (sugandhá), smell; Aristolochia indica (sunanda), enjoyment; Calophyllum inophyllum (surangí), color; Carissa carandas (sushéna), cluster; Cassia fistula (suvarnaka), color; Costus speciosus (subandhu), friend; Crinum amœnum (sudarshana), sight; Eclipta alba (suparna), leaf; Hemidesmus indicus (sugandhí), smell; Ipomæa turpethum (sushénaká), binding; Jasminum angustifolium (supújá), deserving; Mangifera sylvatica (suraktaka), red; Mesua ferrea (suvarna), color; Musa paradisiaca (sup'halá), fruit; Myrica sapida (sugandhi), smell; Ochrocarpus longifolius (surangí), color; Sida cordifolia (suvarna), color; Thespesia populnea (supárshvaka), side; Tribulus terrestris (sudamshtra), tooth; Vitex trifoliata (surasa), juice; Webera corymbosa (sup'hala), fruit; Zizyphus jujuba (sup'hala), fruit. See gloss. paragraphs.——*Shavveeram* (شويرم - shavíram, Hind.; شوير - shavír, Dec.; సౌవీరము - sauvíramu, Tel.; හොයන්දුන් - hoyandun, Singh.; சவ்வீரம் - shavvíram, Tam.). Vern. from (su, san. good + víra, san. strength) [soorma]. Corrosive sublimate. Otherwise Bisulphate of mercury, Perchloride of mercury [rasam]. Hydrargyri perchloridum of chemists. As sold in bazaars is less crystalline and more dull and opaque than the salt in use in hospitals, and occasionally contains a small quantity of sub-chloride or calomel [rascapoor]. The following process for making it is taken from the Poorna sootram:—First make Rasa paspam [q.v.] of the strength that will be formed by using the proportions of sixteen pagodas [q.v.] weight of sulphur [gandhac], eighty pagodas weight of quicksilver [rasam], and half a measure of common salt [ooppoo]. Then to eighty pagodas weight of this Rasa paspam add the same quantity of roasted salt. To these again are to be added the following substances; forty pagodas weight of roasted sulphate of copper [mayil toottam], twenty pagodas weight of alum [padicauram], twenty pagodas weight of nitre [shorah], twenty pagodas weight of the alkaline effloresced earth pooneer [q.v.], ten pagodas weight of sulphate of iron [annabhaidy], and five pagodas weight of sal ammoniac [nowshaudar]. All these to be well rubbed together till formed into an uniform powder, which is to be put into a phial sufficiently large to hold the whole in one-half of it; after which it is to be well coated round with clay, and set over an oven, where it is to be kept for thirty-six hours, taking care that the fire though slow is strong; the phial is then to be broken, and in the mouth of it will be found the Shavveeram in a lump. Veidyans [q.v.] use thus. Internally; in small and continued doses alterative, stimulating the urinary, cutaneous and salivary secretions; in large doses powerful irritant poison. Externally stimulant and mildly caustic; remedy in secondary syphilis, cutaneous eruptions, epilepsy, ophthalmia, cynanche and rheumatism; also in hydrocephalus, dropsical affections, glandular enlargements, hemeralopia and hepatic affections; locally used in gonorrhœa, gleet and leucorrhœa as an injection, in ophthalmia as collyrium, in skin diseases as a lotion or wash. Substituted for british perchloride of mercury. Used generally by natives in too strong doses, which are sometimes, when the preparation is pure and active, attended with dangerous effects; causes severe ulceration of the gums and cheeks resulting finally in permanent cartilaginous-like adhesions between the gums and cheeks. The mode of administering Shavveeram according to the Poorna sootram is as follows:—The weight of a grain of paddy [q.v.] of Shavveeram may be given, for three days together, morning and evening, mixed with a little of the juice of green ginger [q.v.], or about half a pagoda [q.v.] weight of common jaggery [q.v.]. This quantity, taken for the period mentioned, will affect the mouth, and is efficacious in thirteen kinds of convulsion, in disorders attended with much phlegm [sheetam], in venereal affections, in some kinds of asthma, and in scrofulous complaints.——*Shooppoo* (சப்பு - shuppu, Tam.). Familiar contraction of Soobramanyan [q.v.]. Proper name applied to males and females.——*Shooppoottye* (சப்புத்தாயி - shupputtáyi, Tam.). From (shuppu, tam. contraction of subrahmanya + táy, tam. mother). Female proper name [peyar].——*Soobba* (సుబ్బ - subba, Tel.; சப்பா - shuppá, Tam.). Snake. Proper name common to both sexes. Also suffix in proper names [peyar]. Similarly:—Soobbakka, from (akka, tel. sister); Soobbammah, from (amma, tel. mother), familiarly soobby; Soobbannan, from (annan, tam. elder brother), familiarly oobbannan; Soobbaramayyan, from (ráma, san. the hero + aiyyan, tam. master).——*Soobbaroya* (ಸುಬ್ಬರಾಯ - subbaráya, Can.). From (subba, can. snake + ráya, can. king). The sovereign serpent. See vol. I (83).——*Soobbaroya shashty* (సుబ్బరాయషష్ఠి - subbaráyashasht'hi, Tel.). Means serpent king + the sixth lunar day. Otherwise Kookkey shashty. Lunar [chaundramaunam] festival [pundigay, 3a]; subject to intercalation [adhicam], on sixth day of waxing moon [shooclapacsham] of ninth lunar month Margashiram [mausam] between 19th November and 20th December, when women give offerings to serpents [naugam]. Serpent worship consists in making Pradacshinams [q.v.] round the hole of the serpent and pouring milk [paul] into it [maryauday].——*Soobhadray* (सुभद्रा - subhadrá, San.). From (above + bhadra, san. auspicious). Sister of Krishnan [q.v.].——*Soobramanya* (ಸುಬ್ರಹ್ಮಣ್ಯ - subrahmanya, Can.). After the god. Part of Cookkey village, Place of pilgrimage; South canara dist., Ooppinangady tal.; pop. 440; lat. 12° 40′; long. 75° 39′; from Coondapore S.E. 90 miles; from Mangalore E. 55 miles; from Oodipy S.E. 74 miles; from Poottore S.E. 28 miles. Below the ghauts [q.v.]. One of principal seats of serpent [naugam] worship in india. In the temple are two images of a serpent and a six-faced deity, which stand side by side in the garbhaulyam [garbhagriham]. A large cattle [maud] fair during annual festival in November and December. Garnets [tamrah] are found in Comauradhaury river 3 miles from temple. For the hill see Pooshpaghorry.——*Soobramanyan* (सुब्रह्मण्य - subrahmanya, San.; சப்பிரமணியன் - shuppiramaniyan, Tam.). From (above + brahmanya, san. piety); the eminently pious. ἄρης of Greeks, Mars of Romans, Papremis of Egyptians. Familiarly Many, Shooppaly, Shooppauloo, Shooppauny. Younger son of

Shiva [q.v.], the elder being Vigneshwaran [q.v.]. Soobramanyan is called Caurtikeyan [q.v.] in the north, and Scandan [q.v.] in books; see also below for other names. He is the god of war.—"*a*" Soobramanyan is represented in the arts by an image with six heads and twelve arms. But because such an image is difficult to be made either of stone or of metal, he is usually found in the pagodas [q.v.] with one head and four arms only, of which he lifts two up, holding with them the celebrated vail [q.v.] or lance with which he slew Shooran [q.v.], while the remaining two of his four hands are empty. On his head he wears a crown, and his ears, neck, breast, arms, hands, as well as the lower part of his body, and his legs, are adorned like those of the other gods. His standing-place is a flower, to his right and left stand his two wives, near him a peacock [mayil], his vehicle [vauhan]. In the Shiva pagodas his image stands in a separate small temple and receives daily special offerings, together with the lingam [q.v.] and Shiva. In the places where he performed miracles he has pagodas of his own, and obtains three times the same offerings as Shiva.—"*b*" The Tamulians say that Soobramanyan is one with Shiva, so that whosoever worships him worships Shiva himself. He has therefore like Shiva many names. Among those which are peculiar to him, and which he has obtained because of his deeds and miracles, the principal are:—Armoogam or shunmookhan or the six-faced; Ausaun or priest or teacher; Cadamban or he to whom the flower-tree, barringtonia racemosa, blume [common indian oak], is sacred; Caurtikeyan or as nursed by the kritticay [q.v.] or pleiades; Chetty or the merchant, as which he appeared at madura; Comauran or the youth; Comaurasawmy or the son-god; Goohan or he who dwells in a mountain cavern; Gungamaindan or gungay's son; Haran magan or hara's son; Mayonmaroogan or mayon's son-in-law; Meilairy vailan or the lancer who rides the peacock; Mooroogeshan or the young lord; Mooroogan or mooroogappan or the younger son; Moottoocomauran or moottoocomaura sawmy or the pearl son; Pulneyvailan or the lancer of pulney; Scandan or cundasawmy; Senaupaty or the commander-in-chief; Sharvanan or as having originated in the lake sharvanam or reed forest; Shevaca permaul or the soldier-prince; Sheyaun and shendan or the ruddy one; Shilamban or the mountaineer; Shoora samhaura moorty or the destroyer of shooran; Varaippagaverindone or he who splits mountains by the thrusts of his lance; Veeravailan or the hero lancer; Vailayoodhan or the lancer; Vendan or the king; Vishaukhan or as born under the vishaukham [q.v.] lunar mansion [nacshatram]. Regarding Soobramanyan as Caurtikeyan, it is said that the gods, persecuted by giants, implored the help of Shiva, who then assumed six faces, and caused six sparks of fire to dart out of his six central eyes. The sparks were cast into a pond at Trittany, about 50 miles north-west of Madras, and became six infants, which were nursed by the six mothers, who form the constellation Kritticay [kritticay, nacshatram] or the Pleiades [caurtikeyan]. When Parvaty in turn took them in her arms, they assumed one united body, having six heads. This deity afterwards slew the giants.—"*c*" Soobramanyan being fond of fortresses, mountains, and hills, his principal pagodas [coil, pagoda] are built on mountains, and during his yearly festival bonfires are lit on them throughout the land.—"*d*" Among the books that treat of Soobramanyan the principal one is the Scaunda pooraunam [q.v.], in which there is, besides his war with Shooran, related at great length how he was sent by his father to frustrate the sacrifice of Dacshan [q.v.], who intended to place another god on the throne of Shiva, and how he was then at the instigation of Dacshan delayed on his way by damsels, who entertained him with song and music. The Devadausies [q.v.] are said to be betrothed and married to him. Among the books written in honor of Soobramanyan there are besides the Scaunda pooraunam to be mentioned:—Tirpoogazh, i.e., divine praise, in which more especially soobramanyan's deeds at calastry are extolled; its author is arnagiry nautan, who, being at first only a drum-player in one of soobramanyan's pagodas, became a devotee of the god; in consequence of which soobramanyan is said to have given him great gifts. Scandaunoo bhooty, i.e., superhuman knowledge of scandan, likewise a poem setting forth soobramanyan's glory and praise by the same author. Comauranpillay tirnaumam, a collection of songs in which he is extolled under the name of comauran. Comauraperil vunnam, a long poem in honor of soobramanyan. All these books are learned by heart and sung by children at school.—"*e*" Several places are considered to be in a special manner sacred to this god. Those which are of importance in this Presidency are the following:—Tricheeralavye or trichendore in Tinnevelly, Tirvauvinangoody the mountain town of pulney, Triveracam near pondicherry, Soobramanya in south canara, Trittany in carvetnugger, Tirporore in chingleput. See vol. I (79).—"*f*" Soobramanyan has two wives, Vulliyammay [vully] daughter of Indran [q.v.] and Devayaunay [q.v.] brought up by hunters. The image of the former is painted brown, and that of the latter yellow; but each is represented in a natural form with two arms and hands, holding in the left hand a lotus [nelumbo] flower, while the right arm hangs down. Each one wears also a crown on her head, and jewels in her nose, as well as the sign of the sacred ashes [vibhooty] on her forehead, and is on the whole adorned like the other goddesses. These two wives of Soobramanyan have no pagodas of their own, but stand in his pagodas, the one to his right hand and the other to his left. They partake of the offerings made to him, and the festivals celebrated in his honor are also meant for them. There are also many people who fast in their honor every Tuesday. They are mentioned in various books; and about Vulliyammay two special books have been written, the Vulliyammay venbah, a collection of 295 songs; and the Vulliyammanaur, a poem containing her history and a description of her glory.—"*g*" Soobramanyan is worshipped in the month Caurtigay [mausam] or november on which occasion numerous images are made, these after the ceremony of worship being cast into the river. Vows and offerings are made to him by Hindoo females to obtain children, especially sons. When the moon [chundran] enters the third star of the constellation [kritticay, nacshatram], a great feast is held and lamps are placed in every door-way [matam].—"*h*" Soobramanyan is common Hindoo 2nd or pers. name.——*Soodarshanan* (சுதர்சனன் - shutharisanan, Tam.). From (above + darshana, san. sight), beautiful. Epithet of the discus [chuckram] of krishnan [q.v.] or vishnoo [q.v.]. Also epithet of shiva [q.v.]. Hindoo 2nd or pers. name [peyar].——*Soogandham* (सुगन्ध - sugandha, San.). Fragrance. Plant first term often joining two genera. Ex., where transl. is of second term:—Alpinia galanga (sugandhavachá), acorue calamus. Kœmpferia galanga (sugandhavachá), acorus calamus; Nardostachys jatamansi (sugandhamuste), cyperus rotundus. See gloss. paragraphs.——*Soogandhy* (सुगन्धी - sugandhí, San.). Fragrant. Plant name common to Hemidesmus indicus and Myrica sapida. See gloss. paragraphs.——*Soogreevan* (सुग्रीव - sugríva, San.). From (above + grívá, san. neck). A monkey king, the king of Kishkindyay, [q.v.] the ally of Rama [q.v.]. Probably a Coorumba [q.v.] chief. See vol. I (115).——*Soomeroo* (सुमेरु - suméru, San.). A region over the north Pole [oottara dhroovam], where Indran [q.v.] presides over the Sooras [q.v.] or Devatays [deva]. South pole is Coomeroo, which see.——*Soomookhan* (சுமுகன் - shumugan, Tam.). From (above + mukha, san. feet), handsome faced; epithet of ganesh [q.v.], garoodan [q.v.] and shiva [q.v.]. Hindoo 2nd or pers. name [peyar].——*Soondary* (सुन्दरी - sundarí, San.). From (sundara, san. beauty). Parvaty [q.v.]. The Sowndarya lahary or sea of beauty is a panegyrical poem by Shuncaracharry [shuncaran] praising Parvaty [q.v.]. The shacty [q.v.] worshippers use the names Baulasoondary and Tripoora soondary, meaning Young parvaty and Parvaty at the time when the tripoorans [q.v.] or three cities were destroyed.——*Soondram* (सुन्दर - sundara, San.; சுந்தரம் - shundaram, Tam.). From (su, san. good + dara, san. body). Beauty. Name applied to males and females. Familiarly Shoondoo, Shoondye. Also suffix in proper names as Somasoondram, Meenautchisoondram [peyar].——*Soondran* (சுந்தரன் - shundaran, Tam.). One of the sixty-three devotees [aroopatt moover] of Shiva [q.v.] who was also one of the three authors of Devauram [q.v.], the Tamul vedam. Contemporary of Appar and Sambandhan. Champion for the Sheiva faith against the Jeinas [q.v.]. Real name Numbiyauroorau. Bramin of Audisheiva sect at Tirnauvalore. Died young at Caroor in the Chera [q.v.] country.——*Soondra paundy teran* (சுந்தரப்பாண்டியத்தேவன் - shundarappándiyattévan, Tam.). From (sundara, san. beautiful + pándiyan, tam. king, so called + tévan, tam. title). Marco polo's Sender bandi dewar. Originally a Sheiva [q.v.] then became a Jeina [q.v.], and was finally reconverted to Sheivism by the miracles performed by Nyauna sambandhan, a Sheiva teacher belonging to the Chola [q.v.] country, who was invited to Madura by Soondran's wife, herself a Chola princess. On this occasion he impaled eight thousand Jeinas. Before his reconversion to Sheivism he was a hunchback, and hence called Cobja or Coon, but on his reconversion he was straightened, and hence his name was changed to Soondran, the beautiful. He was the last sovereign of the old line of Paundya [q.v.] or Chola-Paundya kings. See vol. I (120); II, 96 [charitram].——*Soondraraman* (சுந்தரராமன் - shundararáman, Tam.). From (sundara, san. beautiful + ráma, san. the hero). Hindoo 2nd or pers. name [peyar].——*Soondraramayyan* (சுந்தரராமையன் - shundarayrámayyan, Tam.). From (sundara, san. beautiful + ráma, san. the hero + aiyyan, tam. master). Hindoo 2nd or pers. name [peyar].——*Soondrashivan* (సుందరశివుడు - sundarashivudu, Tel.). From (sundara, san. beautiful + shiva, san. shiva). Hindoo 2nd or pers. name [peyar].——*Soondravaradan* (சுந்தரவரதன் - shundaravarathan, Tam.). From (sundara, san. beautiful + varada, san. giver of gift); vishnoo, the beautiful. Hindoo 2nd or pers. name [peyar].——*Soondree* (सुन्दरी - sundarí, San. सुंद्री - sundrí, Mahr.; سندری - sundrí, Hind.; එතුන - etuna, Singh.). Title from hindostany. San. from (sundara, san. beautiful). Hind. from sanscrit. Title otherwise Looking glass plant, from silvery under-surface of leaves. Botanically Heritiera littoralis, dryand, sterculiaceæ [vricsham, 26]. Alias Balanopteris tothila. Tree; leaves oval, rounded at the base; panicles axillary; flowers small, red; sea coast. Wood strong, fibrous and flexible, tolerably close and straight-grained, not durable, light red, turning to reddish brown; not easily worked, used for poles and shafts of carriages, spokes of wheels; makes excellent firewood. Another species is Papilio, a very large tree.——*Soopaury* (سوپاری - súpárí, Hind.). Same as Betel-nut.——*Soorabhy* (सुरभी - surabhí, San.). Means sweet-smelling. The cow of plenty; also called Caumadhain [q.v.].——*Sooshaina*

(సుసేనుడు - sushénudu, Tel.). From (above + séná, san. army). Epithet of Vishnoo [q.v.], who has a good army. Hindoo 2nd or pers. name [peyar].——*Soovarnacam* (सुवर्णक - suvarnaka, San.). From (above + varna, san. color); from flowers. Botanically the Cassia genus, leguminosæ [vricsham, 48]. Erect shrubs or trees, rarely herbs; leaves simple, abruptly pinnate; flowers usually large and showy, in axillary racemes and terminal panicles; pod very variable, flat or cylindrical; of considerable importance from a medical point of view; the genus is much scattered in vernacular terminology. The species best known to the natives are:—absus [black horse-gram], acutifolia [nubian senna], alata [foreign agatty], angustifolia [tinnevelly senna], auriculata [tungaid], fistula [common condray], glauca [tree condray], marginata [red condray], obovata [aleppo senna], occidentalis [casoudy], pumila [lowly chakondah], siamea [yellow condray], sophera [stinking casoudy], tomentosa [hill tungaid], tora [chakondah]. Other s. indian species indigenous or naturalized are:—Berryana; tree; flowers yellow; flowering towards end of year. Kleinii; suffruticose; flowers small, yellow; travancore. Mimosoides; suffruticose; flowering in rainy season. Montana; large shrub. Timoroensis; large shrub common on neilgherries, &c. Wallichiana; suffruticose, branched; flowering in rainy season.——*Soovurma* (സുവർമ്മം - suvarmmam, Mal.). From (above + varmam, mal. mail). Hindoo 2nd or pers. name [peyar].——*Sowbhaugyam* (சௌபாக்கியம் - shaubákkiyam, Tam.). From (above + bhágya, san. good fortune). Hindoo 2nd or pers. name. Applied to males and females. Also taken by native christians [peyar].——*Surat* (صورت - súrat, Hind.). From (above + ráshtra, san. country). Pulipula of Ptolemy. An ancient town on the banks of the Tapty. See vol. I (139), (157).——*Swarna dweepam* (सुवर्णद्वीप - suvarnadvípa, San.). Means gold + island. Perhaps Ireland [britastaun].——*Swarnam* (स्वर्ण - svarna, San.). From (above + varna, san. color). Gold. Proper name common to both sexes among the lower orders. Feminine Swarny, which commonly appears as Shorany [peyar]. ——*Swarnamookhy* (స్వర్ణముఖి - svarnamukhi, Tel. swarnamukhi *). From (svarna, san. gold + mukha, san. face); named from its rise in the tripatty hills, styled the meroo or the golden mountain. River; North arcot and Nellore districts. Rises near Agastyauchala parvatam in the Chundragherry hills in North arcot district in lat. 13° 28′; long. 79° 09′; just beyond the south-east border of Chundragherry talook; near Paucala, where a gigantic figure of Hanooman [q.v.] is engraved upon a rock. Thence the water rises and flows into a tank, and from the surplus of this it continues. Flowing eastwards nearly parallel to the Northern pennair but veering more to the north-east through Calastry and Vencatagherry zemindarries, it is joined by the Raulla caulwa at Renigoonta. It then flows north-east through Polore division, north-east and east through Goodoor talook and after being joined by the Maumidy caulwa at Goodaly, passes through the villages of Vaucaud, Yargautipulley, Balireddipollem and Poochalapulley, and falls into the Bay of Bengal near Siddhavaram in Goodoor talook at lat. 14° 07′; long. 80° 11′ a little north of Poolicat lake. Has a course of 78 miles through North arcot and 21 miles through Nellore. There is no depth of water at the mouth. Fourteen miles up the river there is a dam, from which channels take off. The East coast canal crosses the river about five or six furlongs from the beach. The chief affluents are the Calyaunanuddy and the Bheemanuddy. The river is held in much reverence. One of the feet of Shiva [q.v.] is supposed to rest upon it, and consequently to celebrate the annual ceremonies [shrauddham] of a deceased parent near its banks is a very meritorious act. The bed is completely dry for the greater part of the year, but during the rainy season in October and November it has a large volume of water. Owing however to its rapid fall this river is seldom in flood for more than a few days at a time.——*Swarnanuddy* (ಸುವರ್ಣನದಿ - suvarnanadi, Can. swarnanadi *). From (svarna, san. gold + nadi, san. river). River; South canara dist., Oodipy tal. Rises in the hills beyond the south-eastern boundary of Oodipy talook; wide but shallow. Navigable as far as Bajey, about 12 miles inland.——*Swarnaudauyam* (स्वर्णादाय - svarnádáya, San.). From (svarna, san. gold + ádá. san. to take). Rent or revenue receivable in money, not in kind [cundauyam].——*Swasticam* (स्वस्तिक - svastika, San.). From (svasti, san. welfare). The front-mark 卐 distinguishing the Tantric sects. Identical with the greek Trigliph. Jeina [q.v.] mark of good luck. A mansion of a particular shape surrounded by a terrace or portico or verandah [q.v.] on north, west and south, with the door on the east.——*Swaustyam* (स्वास्थ्य - svást'hya, San.). From (above + as, san. to be). Lands held by Bramins in their villages or agrahaurams [q.v.] free of rent [inam].

SOO (सु - 'su, *San.*). To distil; generate.——*Sauvanam* (सावन - sávana, San.). From (sava, san. libation). Libatory. A sauvanam day is a natural or civil day from sunrise to sunrise, because libations made each morning or sunrise, besides noon and sunset [dinam, naul, roz, sooryan]. In order to determine its length in sidereal time for every day in the year, there must be established:—What the sun's declination [craunty] is when his longitude or ravy sauyanam [q.v.] is Is; IIs; and IIIs. The laguam [q.v.], or its right ascension when his longitude is in the said points of the ecliptic [craunty mundalam]. The agram [q.v.] or amplitude of the sun [sooryan] under the same circumstances. The charam [q.v.] or ascensional difference under the same circumstances. The oollagnam [q.v.] or oblique ascension of each sign [raushy] of longitude [sauyanam] counted from the equinoctial points [craunty pautam, vishoo], for the particular latitude [vicshaipam] which is to be computed for [jyotisham].——*Savam* (सव - sava, San.). From (su, san. to extract); extraction of somam [q.v.]. Juice, libation.——*Savitry* (सवितृ - savitri, San.). From (su, san. to generate). A name of Sooryan [q.v.]; also of Saraswaty [q.v.].——*Somachellam* (சோமாசலம் - shómáççalam, Tam.). From (sóma, san. moon + achala, san. mountain.). Applies to Chundragherry. Hindoo 2nd or pers. name [peyar].——*Somam* (सोम - sóma, San. and Mahr.; سوملتا - somlatá, Hind.; ಸೋಮಬಳ್ಳಿ - sómaballi, Can.; పుల్లతీగ - pullatíga, Tel.; സോമവല്ലി - sómavalli, Mal.; මුවකිරිය - muvakíriya, Singh.; கொடிக்கள்ளி - kodikkalli, Tam.). Title from sanscrit [hom]. San. from (su, san. to distil); from juice used in sacrifices. Hind. from (sómalatá, san. the plant), meaning moon creeper. Can. from (sóma, can. moon + balli, can. creeper). Tel. from (pulla, tel. sour + tíga, tel. creeper), from acid taste of creeper. Mal. from (sóma, san. moon + valli, mal. creeper). Singh. from (muva, singh. deer + kíriya, singh. milky plant). Tam. from (kodi, tam. creeper + kalli, tam. euphorbia tirucalli, linn.). San. also (sómalatá), meaning moon creeper; (padmakásht'ha), meaning lotus wood. Can also (hambukalli), meaning creeping + milky-hedge, euphorbia tirucalli, linn. Tel. also (tígajemudu), meaning creeper + euphorbia tirucalli, linn.; (kondapála), meaning hill + milky plant. Title otherwise Creeping milk hedge, Hom of zendavesta, Moon creeper, Poolla teegay, Sour creeper. Botanically Sarcostemma brevistigma, w. and a., asclepiadæ [vricsham, 88]. Alias Asclepias acida; Sarcostemma acidum, viminale. Twining; leafless; umbels terminal or terminating the short lateral branches; calyx and pedicels glabrous; outer stamineous corona ten-plicate, ten-crenate; leaflets of inner corona gibbous on the back, equal to the gynostegium; flowers small, white; flowering in june, august; indigenous to the punjaub and bolaun pass, candeish, the western ghauts and the coromandel coast. The plant yields a quantity of milky juice. Among the ancient aryans a fermented liquor was prepared by mixing its juice, strained through a sieve of goat's hair, with barley [jow] and ghee [q.v.]; this wine was drunk at all their religious ceremonies [yanyam], and was used as an intoxicant by the rishies [q.v.], who in the very early age of hindooism combined it at their meals with beef; for the worship of this beverage the arrangement of the vedam [q.v.] known as the sauma vedam was made; the juice of the plant was regarded as a kind of amritam [q.v.], conferring eternal life and vigour both on gods and men, and is represented as primeval and all-pervading, and finally identified with the supreme being himself; in later times soman was the moon, the ruler of planets [graham], plants, sacrifices [yanyam] and penances [mooskiraut, sharaub]. The raw juice is so mild that travellers suck the tender shoots to allay thirst. Bundles of this put into the trough of the well from which a sugar-cane [q.v.] field is watered, together with bag of common salt [ooppoo], will extirpate white-ants [q.v.] without injuring the sugar-cane. Other common species are:—brunonianum, intermedium.——*Soman* (सोम - sóma, San.; சோமன் - shóman, Tam.). From (su, san. to generate); see somam. The moon [choma, chundran]. Represented in the arts as a white man sitting on a water-lily [indian water-lily], or in a chariot drawn by an antelope [jinka] or by ten horses [ghorah] of the whiteness of jasmine [q.v.]. Hindoo 2nd or pers. name. Familiarly Somoo. Common among non-bramins [peyar].——*Somanautan* (சோமநாதன் - shómanáthan, Tam.). From (sóma, san. moon + nát'ha, san. lord). Shiva, the moon-lord; as wearing crescent moon on head, or as worshipped by the moon. Hindoo 2nd or pers. name [peyar].——*Somarauz* (సోమరాజు - sómarádzu, Tel.). From (sóma, san. moon + rájá, san. king). Hindoo 2nd or pers. name [peyar].——*Somashila* (సోమశిల - sómashila, Tel.). From (sóma, san. the god shiva + shilá, san. stone). Sanscrit name (sóméshvara), meaning shiva, the moon-lord. Village; Nellore dist., Atmacore tal.; pop. 484; acres 1,079; lat. 14° 30′; long. 79° 21′; from Atmacore W.S.W. 23 miles; from Nellore W. 45 miles. Shrotriem [q.v.] village. At foot of Veligondas where Pennair enters Nellore district. Celebrated temple to Someshwaran with festival in May lasting five days. Government spent one lac [q.v.] of rupees for construction of anicut [q.v.], but abandoned it as not profitable.——*Somasoondran* (சோமசுந்தரம் - shómasundaram, Tam.). From (sóma, san. moon + sundara, san. an epithet of shiva); shiva with the moon on his head. Hindoo 2nd or pers. name [peyar].——*Soma vauram* (सोमवार - sómavára, San.). From (sóma, san. moon + vára, san. day). Monday [vauram].——*Someshwaram* (సోమేశ్వరము - sóméshvaramu, Tel.). From (sóma, san. moon + íshvara, san. lord); from shiva, the moon lord. Same as Somashila.——*Someshwaran* (सोमेश्वर - soméshvara, San.). From (sóma, san. moon + ishvara, san. god). Shiva.——*Sompett* (సోంపేట - sómpéta, Tel. sómpet *). From (sóma, san. shiva, the moon-lord + péta, tel. suburb).— "*a*" Deputy tahsildarry, Ganjam district. Pay Rs. 70.—

"*b*" Town, Deputy tahsildar's station; Ganjam dist., Jalantra and Cheekaty zemindarries; pop. Cheekaty talook 1,760; Cheekaty 1,636; acres 422; lat. 18° 56′; long. 84° 38′; from Balligooda S.S.E. 95 miles; from Berhampore S.S.W. 29 miles; from Chetterpore S.W. 40 miles; from Chicacole N.E. 63 miles; from Madras N.N.E. 485 miles; from Russellcondah S. 70 miles; from the sea W. 5 miles. Off high road between Berhampore and Chicacole, but connected with it by a road distant 2 miles from public bungalow [q.v.] at Cunchily. The road to Sompett is continued to the neighbouring port of Barwah, from which Sompett is distant 6 miles. Old temple of Someshwaran. A large swamp near Sompett affords shooting. Contains Paulavalsa, Pudmye, Raty beacon, Yalmel, trig. stations.——*Somraj* (سومراج - somráj, Hind.). Shining white like the moon. Plant name common to:—Pæderia fœtida and Vernonia anthelmintica; see gloss. paragraphs.——*Somyaujee* (సోమయాజి - sómayáji, Tel.). From (sóma, san. the plant + yájí, san. sacrificer). Generally a title among bramins who perform a sacrifice [peyar,'yanyam]. So Hindoo 2nd or pers. name.——*Sooradah* (సురడా - suradá,* Tel.). From (surá, san. water + gada, oor. fort), from situation.—"*a*" Deputy tahsildarry; Ganjam district. Pay Rs. 100.—"*b*" Town, Deputy tahsildar's station; Ganjam dist., Goomsoor tal.; pop. 4,022; acres 685; lat. 19° 45′; long. 84° 29′; from Balligooda S.E. 46 miles; from Berhampore N.N.W. 38 miles; from Chetterpore W.N.W. 44 miles; from Chicacole N.N.E. 106 miles; from Madras N.N.E. 530 miles; from Russellcondah S.W. 17 miles. On Rooshcoolya. Formerly a zemindarry [q.v.]. The zemindar having died without issue in 1830, estate was purchased by Dhananjaya bhoonj, Zemindar of Goomsoor, in 1333 for Rs. 8,000 and merged in Goomsoor talook. Ruined fort.——*Soorah devy* (सुरादेवी - surádéví, San.). From (surá, san. wine + déví, san. goddess). The goddess of wine. Sometimes used to signify the year.——*Sooray* (सुरा - surá, San.). From (su, san. to extract juice). Wine [angoor].

SOOBAH (صوبه - súbah, *Hind*). From arabic. A province, especially of the Moghul empire; as the soobah of Deccan, Bengal, &c. Acbar's empire was divided into fifteen soobahs, twelve in Hindostan [q.v.] and three in the Deccan [q.v.]. Compare Zillah. Soobahdar is the governor of a province. Also native military officer corresponding to english Captain. The soobahdar-major used to be the native commissioned officer of the highest rank in an infantry or cavalry regiment, then came in order the soobahdar, the jemadar, the havildar, and the naick. For the corresponding officers of irregular cavalry, see under Rissaldar. Under the new organization each of the eight companies of an infantry regiment has one soobahdar, one jemadar [q.v.], five havildars [q.v.], and five naicks [q.v.].

SOOBHAUN (سبحان - subhán, *Hind.*). From (sabaha, ar. to praise). Praise. As an attribute of God, all perfect [allah]. Common alam, as Abd oos soobhaun, slave of god [ism].

SOOCSHMAM (सूक्ष्म - súkshma, *San.*). From (súch, san. to pierce); sharp. Subtle or atomic.——*Soocshma shareeram* (सूक्ष्मशरीर - súkshmasharíra, San.). From (above + sharíra, san. body). One of the three shareerams or corporeal forms according to the Vedauntam [q.v.] philosophy, the fine material form; the other two being the Caurana shareeram and the Stoola shareeram [q.v.]. Compare Cosham and Punchacosham.

SOOFAID (سفید - sufed, *Pers.*). White. Plant first term often joining two genera. Ex.:—Eriodendron anfractuosum (sufedsembal), white bombax malabaricum.——*Soofaid moosly* (سفید موسلی - sufedmúslí, Hind.). Means white asparagopsis. See sep. title.——*Soofaid soombal* (शङ्खविष - shankhavisha, San.; سم الفار - sammulfár, Ar.; مرگ موش - margmúsh, Pers.; سفید سنبل - sufedsumbul, Hind.; سنکیا سنبل - sankiyásumbul, Dec.; ورنگن پوتھی - waranganputih, Malay; ಪಾಷಾಣ - páshána, Can. and Too.; తెల్లపాషాణము - tellapáshánamu, Tel.; വെള്ളപ്പാഷാണം - vellappáshánam, Mal.; සුදුපාෂාණම් - sudupásánam, Singh.; வெள்ளைப்பாடாணம் - vellaippádánam, Tam.). Title from hindostany. San. from (shankha, san. conch + visha, san. poison); poison white like conch. Ar. from (samm, ar. poison + fár, ar. rat). Pers. from (marg, pers. death + músh, pers. rat). Hind. from (sufed, hind. white + sumbul, ar. arsenic). Dec. from (sankh, hind. conch + sumbul, pers. arsenic). Malay from (warangan, malay, arsenic + putih, malay, white). Tel. from (tella, tel. white + páshánamu, tel. arsenic). Mal. from (vella, mal. white + páshánam, mal. arsenic). Singh. from (sudu, singh. white + páshána, san. arsenic). Tam. from (vellai, tam. white + pádánam, tam. arsenic). San. also (shvétapáshána), meaning white stone. Ar. also (shuk); (turábulhálik), meaning fatal earth. Hind. also (sumbulkhár), meaning arsenic acid. Tel. also (shankhapáshánamu), meaning conch shell + arsenic. White arsenic. Otherwise Arsenious acid, White oxide of arsenic. Arsenicum album, Acidum arseniosum of chemists. An anhydrous acid, obtained by roasting arsenical ores and purified by sublimation; as found in bazaars is not pure, and is an import; some comes from china. Is an irritant poison. Veidyans [q.v.] employ thus; alterative tonic and antiperiodic in medicinal doses, and powerfully poisonous in larger quantities; useful in ague, ticdouloureux, hemicrania, chorea, epilepsy, hooping cough, asthma, and some chronic skin diseases, including leprosy [cooshtam]; also employed in chronic rheumatism, cancer, uterine congestion, menorrhagia, snake bites, and chronic catarrhal affections; substituted for british quinine [koinah]. Pharm. has acidum arseniosum, alterative, tonic, antiperiodic, in large doses powerfully poisonous; preparations, liquor arsenicalis or fowler's solution, liquor arsenici hydrochloricus. Used in the manufacture of glass [cunnaudy], dyeing [shauyam], &c. [paushaunam].

SOOFEE (صوفی - súfí, *Hind.*). From (súfah, ar. a tribe of arabs). Mystic philosophers amongst Mahomedans named after certain members of the Soofa arab tribe, who engaged themselves exclusively in the service of the Mecca temple. Here nearly equivalent to Masheikhs [q.v.]. Of all systems of philosophy, which after the death of the prophet influenced the conception of the several classes of the Moslem [q.v.] society, Soofeeism stands pre-eminent. It was founded on the teachings of the prophet himself, given to a select few of whom Ally and Aboo bakr were the chief in regard to the esoteric significance to be attached to the words of the koran [q.v.] and as based on the inner conviction of divine pervasion, with strict instructions to them not to divulge it. Cf. Maud. Soofeeism did not develop itself during the lifetime of the prophet; for performance of duty was then considered the most important observance. Till about the tenth century these mysteries passed from soul to soul, when they were divulged, and from their similarity to the new platonic ideas regarding the union of human intellect with universal reason attracted the attention of the numerous Shiite [shiah] gnostics then existing in Persia; and thence as a consequence of intercourse with India Soofeeism began to be diffused in other channels and departed from its original aim. Mysticism as practised by fakeers [q.v.] of the present day is an offshoot of the above. Alghazzauly commonly called algazel in europe, Jelalooddeen of masnavee, the lyric Hafiz, the moralist Saady and the romance-writer Nizamy, were all Soofees. The system is akin to the south indian Vedantism [vedauntam]. The following are the doctrinal views:—"*a*" God only exists; He in all things, and all things in him.—"*b*" All visible and invisible beings are an emanation from him, and are not really distinct from him.—"*c*" Religions are matters of indifference; they however serve as leading to realities. Some for this purpose are more advantageous than others, among which is Al islam, and of this Soofeeism is the true philosophy.—"*d*" There does not really exist any difference between good and evil, for all is reduced to unity and God is the real author of the acts of mankind.—"*e*" It is God who fixes the will of man; man therefore is not free in his actions.—"*f*" The soul existed before the body, and is confined within the latter as in a cage. Death therefore should be the object of the wishes of the Soofee, for it is then that he returns to the bosom of divinity.—"*g*" It is by this metempsychosis that souls which have not fulfilled their destination here below are purified and become worthy of reunion with God.—"*h*" Without the grace of God, or Fazl ool lah, no one can attain to spiritual union, but this can be obtained by fervently asking for it.—"*i*" The principal occupation of the devout, whilst in the body, is meditation on the Wadaunyat or unity of God, the remembrance of God's names, and the progressive advancement in the Tareekat or journey of life, so as to attain unification with God.—"*j*" The following are the stages of Tareekat. The first stage is humanity or nasoot, in which the disciple must live according to the law or shareeyat and observe all the rites, customs, and precepts of his religion. The second is the nature of angels or malacoot, for which there is the pathway of purity. The third is the possession of power or jabroot, for which there is knowledge or maurifut. The fourth is extinction or fanah, that is to say absorption into the deity, for which there is truth or hakeekat. Compare the four stages of tamul sheivism under Sheiva siddhauntam.—"*k*" There are three aids necessary to conduct the traveller on his path:—attraction or Injizaub; devotion or Ibaudat; elevation or Oorooj.

SOOGAULY (సుకాలి - sukáli, *Tel.*). Anotbher name of Lumbaudies [q.v.].——*Soocaury* (సుకారి - sukári, Tel.). Same as Soogauly.

SOOHAUG (سهاگ - suhág, *Hind.*). Short for Moosa soohaug, founder of a class of fakeers [q.v.].——*Soohaugiya* (سهاگیه - suhágiyah, Hind.). An order of fakeers. Followers of Moosa soohaug. They wear a cap and some female ornaments on the wrists, and are generally musicians and songsters, play upon tambore [q.v.], sitaur [q.v.], veenay [q.v.], &c.

SOOJEE (سوجی - súјí, *Hind.*) The fine flour made from the heart of wheat [geung], used to make bread [rotee] for English tables. It is prepared by grinding between two millstones which are not in close contact. Also a kind of porridge made with the above.

SOOJNEE (سوزنی - sozní, *Hind.*). From (sozan, pers. needle). A thick material of dark red cotton, with large diaper pattern in bleached cotton [q.v.], woven in the colored material. Used as a counterpane [palampore].

SOOKHAM (सुख - sukha, *San.*). From (sukh, san to please). Happiness, ease.——*Sooggy* (ಸುಗ್ಗಿ - suggi, Can.). From (sukhi, san. happy). Harvest [fusl] time.——*Sookhavausy* (सुखवासी - sukhavási, San.). From (above + vásí, san. one who lives). One who lives at his ease by rented lands.

SOOKKAUN (سکان - sukkán, *Hind.*). From (sakana, ar. to rest). A rudder.——*Secunny* (سکانی - sukkání, Hind.). From (sukkán, ar. helm). Steersman or quartermaster.

SOOKTY (سوکهتی - súkhtí, *Hind.*). Means parched. Withered crop [shauvy].

SOOLEY (ಸೂಳೆ - súle, *Can.*). From (shúlá, san. harlot). Dancing girl [dausy].——*Soolekerey* (ಸೂಳೆಕೆರೆ - súlekere, Can.; sulekere, Mys. Gov.). From (above + kere, can. tank). The largest tank in Mysore; in middle of the Chennagherry talook, Shimoga district. Margin 40 miles round.——*Soolcorpett* (సూళూరుపేట - súlúrupéta, Tel.).* From (above + úru, tel. village + péta, tel. suburb). Village, Head-quarters of Deputy tahsildar; Nellore dist., Polore division tal.; pop. 1,265; lat. 13° 42′; long. 80° 04′; from Madras N.N.W. 48 miles; from Naidoopett S.S.E. 17 miles; from Nellore S. 52 miles; from Ongole S. 125 miles; from Polore E. 1¾ mile; from Raupore S.E. 47¾ miles. Chief town of one of the two southern divisions of Vencatagherry zemindarry on the great northern road. Manufacture of handkerchiefs [roomaul]. On the left bank of the Caulingy river and on the great trunk road [polore].

SOOLIMAN (سلیمان - sulaimán, *Ar.*). Solomon. Mahomedan alam, as Sooliman khan, alam + alaumat [ism].——*Sooliman moorghy* (गरुड - garuda, San. and Mahr.; سلیمان مرغی - sulaimán murghí, Hind.; ಗರುಡ - garuda, Can.; മലമുഴക്കി - malamuzhakki, Mal.). San. from (garut, san. wing + dí, san. to fly) [braminy kite, garoodan]. Hind. means solomon's fowl. Can. like sanscrit. Mal. from (mala, mountain + muzhakku, mal. to cause to resound). Hind. also (hemráí), meaning gold + king; (banráí), meaning forest king; (gararpakh), meaning braminy kite bird. Bucerotidæ family, fissirostres, insessores, aves [pacshy, 11], of naturalists [jantoo]. Hornbills. Bill enormous, arched or curved; often with appendage or casque on upper mandible; usually live in pairs, most associating, at times, in small flocks; live almost entirely on fruit, which they swallow whole, tossing it up in the air after separating it from the tree, and catching it again. Nestle in holes of trees, laying three or four white eggs; and male bird plasters the female up in the hole with mud, only allowing her bill to protrude, by which he feeds. The voice is harsh.—"*a*" The Great hornbill or Rhinoceros hornbill is Homraius bicornis. Alias Buceros cavatus, homrai. A silent bird, making merely a deep but not very loud croak; flies with repeated flappings of its wings; noise of its wings can be heard more than a mile distant; at the root of tail above is a small sac, in which is a bundle or pencil of short bristles, forming a brush, from which exudes a yellow oily secretion, and with this the bird appears to dress the white wing-spot; is sacred to Vishnoo [q.v.]; does not reach its full size under two or three years.—"*b*" The Malabar pied hornbill is Hydrocissa coronata, alias Buceros pica, malabaricus, monoceros. Black; beneath pure white; very fond of the fruit of the koochlah or Strychnos nux-vomica [poison nut]; very noisy.—"*c*" The Common grey hornbill is Meniceros bicornis, alias Buceros ginginianus, cineraceus, griseus, oxyurus. Has a loud sharp cry; the flesh is used medicinally to alleviate the pangs of child birth.—"*d*" The jungle grey hornbill is Tockus gingalensis, alias Buceros pyrrhopygus; Malabar.

SOOMMAH (சும்மா - shummá, *Tam.*). Means without putting the burden on one's head. So quietly, in a leisurely way. As an exclamation, keep quiet [choop].

SOONGNAH (سونگنی کا نمک - súngnekánamak, *Hind.*; నవాసారుప్పు - navásárauppu, *Tel.*; நவச்சாரக்கிராணம் - navaççárakkiránam, *Tam.*). Hind. from (súngná, hind. smelling + namak, hind. salt). Tel. from (navásáramu, tel. sal ammoniac + uppu, tel. salt). Tam. from (navaççáram, tam. sal ammoniac + ghrána, san. smell). Volatile salt of sal ammoniac [nowshaudar]. Sal volatile of chemists. Smelling salts. Prepared by natives in the following manner:—sal ammoniac [nowshaudar], one pollum [q.v.]; chalk [sheemay choonam], two pollums; dry ingredients carefully, then mix and sublime with strong heat. Veidyans [q.v.] do not administer internally, but use as local stimulant to nose, in fainting fits, languors, and hysteria.

SOONKAM (సుంకము - sunkamu, *Tel.*). From (shulka, san. duty). Duty on goods [choongam].

SOONKOO (సుంకు - sunku, *Tel.*). Flower.——*Soonkesala* (సుంకేసల - sunkésala, Tel.). Means the tiger bean flower [soonkeshwaram]. As having many of these trees.—"*a*" Village; Kurnool dist., Ramalcottah tal.; pop. 416; acres 1,668; lat. 15° 52′; long. 77° 52′; from Kurnool W.N.W. 16 miles. Anicut constructed across Toongabudra, which supplies the Kurnool-Cuddapah canal. Partially breached in 1864.—"*b*" Gap in Eastern ghauts, through which Cheyair finds its way to Pennair [cheyair].——*Soonkeshwaram* (ಸುಂಕೇಸರ - sunkásari, Can.; సుంకేశ్వరము - sunkéshvaramu, Tel.; வாதநாராயணம் - váthanáráyanam, Tam.). Title from teloogoo. Can. from teloogoo. Tel. from (sunku, tel. blossom + íshvara, san. lord), from the great number of beautiful red flowers. Tam. from (váta, san. nervous disease + náráyana, san. the deity); useful in rheumatism, grows near water's edge. Can. also (nírangi); (sunkatti), by corruption. Tel. also (chitikéshvaramu); (sunkésala), by corruption. Title otherwise Indian poinciana, Tiger bean so called from general appearance. Botanically Poinciana [ratnagandhy] elata, linn., leguminosæ [vricsham, 48]. Alias Cæsalpinia elata; Poinciana indica. Arboreous, unarmed; leaflets linear, obtuse; flower-buds obovate-oblong, acute; calyx more or less pubescent or shortly villous, particularly on the inside; sepals coriaceous, equal, lanceolate, acute; æstivation valvular; petals fringed; ovary villous; legume flat-compressed, several-seeded. A large tree; bears in the hot season racemes of the large, gaudy, yellow flowers; abundant in a planted state in avenues [shaulay], topes [q.v.], gardens, native cemeteries [shavacaud], &c. Gum [gond] dark-colored and mucilaginous. Leaves good for rheumatism and flatulence; used by women after confinement. Leaves used for manuring indigo [q.v.]; tree used as a protection for the footings of rivers and channel banks; grows quickly, gives a good shade; gives a gum. Wood yellow, tolerably close and even-grained, easily worked and gives smooth surface, warps slightly, but never cracks.

SOONNAT (سنہ - sunnah, *Hind.*). From (sunan, ar. path). Traditions [hadees], especially those which record the sayings or doings of the prophet [mahomed] on questions religious, moral, ceremonial, and doctrinal. By Soonnees considered as supplement to Koran [q.v.]; rejected as apocryphal by Shiahs [q.v.].——*Soonnee* (سنی - sunní, Hind.). From (sunnat, ar. law). One of the two main religious divisions of Mahomedans [q.v.]. Their tenets are, deference to tradition [hadees], and affirmation of lawful succession of the first four Caliphs [q.v.], Aboo bakr, Omar, Osman, and Ally, in opposition to the Shiahs [q.v.], who denounce the three first as usurpers. Soonnees are sometimes termed Yaury, or votaries of the four friends [charyanree]. Most educated Indian mahomedans are Soonnees. The Soonnees maintain with respect to the alleged express appointment by Mahomed of Ally as his immediate successor, that if it had been so Aboo bakr would not have been unanimously recognized imaum and that Ally himself would not have hesitated to assert his right as he did later on when Mooauviyah disputed his succession, while on the contrary the nomination of Aboo bakr to lead the prayers during the prophet's illness and the readiness with which Ally then took the oath of allegiance point to a different conclusion. As to the general question of appointment or election of imaum the Soonnees hold that, as the office is for the benefit of the community, it is dependent on the choice of the people and need not be restricted to the family of Mahomed, the first three Caliphs not having been so restricted; nor must he necessarily be the most excellent just or virtuous of all, distinction in this respect being difficult. They believe that the last imaum [mahdee] is not yet born and will appear with the coming of Jesus at the Resurrection. They believe in saints [walee], ijmah [q.v.], keeyah [q.v.] and traditions which stand the test of certain rules of criticism as supplementary to Koran [q.v.]. Soonnees are sub-divided into four sects, named after four eminent orthodox Imaums or doctors of the law [moojtahid], who decided in conformity with Koranic ordinances and traditions handed down in regular succession questions regarding which Mahomet had given no explicit direction, and whom such sects implicitly obey in regard to the construction and interpretation of law [takleed]. These are as follows:—"*a*" Aboo haneefa, born A.H. 80. Called also Imaum i auzam or the highest Imaum. Founder of the first school. He admitted very few traditions as authoritative in his system, which claims to be a logical development from the Koran and permits the right of private judgment. His doctrines prevail all over India, Egypt, Central asia and Turkey, and are followed largely by syeds [q.v.], sheikhs [q.v.], pataans [q.v.] and moghuls [q.v.].—"*b*" Maulik, born A.H. 93, founded his system on the customs of Medina. He arranged and systematized the traditions current there, and formed a historical and traditional system of jurisprudence embracing the whole sphere of life. His tenets are not known to prevail in India.—"*c*" Shaufee, born A.H. 150. An eclectic system from the works of the two previous Imaums, and requiring a considerable number of traditions in proof of any single point. In offering prayer the followers put the hands on the breast or shoulder, the thumbs touching the lobes of the ear. His doctrines have some currency along the sea-coast; the Nivayats [q.v.] and Lubbays [q.v.] belong to this sect.—"*d*" Ibn e hambal, born A.H. 164, professed excessive veneration for the Koran as uncreated and eternal. There are none of this sect in India.

SOOR (शूकर - shúkara, *San.*; خنزیر - khinzír, *Ar.*; خوک - khok, *Pers.*; سور - súwar, *Hind.*; بابی - babi, *Malay*; ಹಂದಿ - handi, *Can.*; ಪಂಜಿ - panji, *Too.*; పంది - pandi, *Tel.*; പന്നി - panni, *Mal.*; ඌරා - úrá, *Singh.*; பன்றி - panri, *Tam.*). Title from hindostany. San. from (shú, san. grunt + kri, san. to make). Ar. from (khuzara, ar. contracted eyes). Hind. from sanscrit. Singh. from (varáha, san. boar). Tam. from (pari, tam. to dig). Dec. also (burájánwar), meaning bad animal. Title otherwise Pig. Sus indicus, suidæ, artiodactyla, ungulata, mammalia [sastanam, 22], of naturalists [jantoo]. The domesticated pig. Common breed met with here, not much prized, long legged, not easily fattened; better kind often brought from China, with shorter legs. Very inferior to the tame hog of Europe. It is however used extensively by the lowest castes for food. The melted fat of pigs is used by them as a substitute for ghee [q.v.]. The lard from the flank is used as in Europe for ointments and plasters. From the lard is expressed a clear oil.——*Jungly soor* (वराह - varáha, San.; डुकर - dukara, Mahr.; جنگلی سور - janglísúwar, Hind.; بابيوتن - babiutan, Malay; ಹಂದಿ - handi, Can.; ಕಾಡುಪಂಜಿ - kádupanji, Too.; పంది - pandi, Tel.; ବରିହା - bariha, Oor.; കാട്ടുപന്നി - kāttupanni, Mal.; වලුරා - valúrá, Singh.; காட்டுப்பன்றி - káttuppanri, Tam.). San. from (vrih, san. to root up). Mahr. from (súkara, san. hog). Hind. from (janglí, hind. wild + súwar, hind. hog). Malay from (babi, malay, hog + utan, malay, wild). Too. from (kádu, too. wild + panji, too. pig). Mal. from (kátu, mal. forest + panni, mal. hog). Singh. from (val, singh. wild + úrá, singh. hog). Tam. from (kádu, tam. forest + panri, tam. hog). Tam. also (kunrikkannau), meaning goomchy [q.v.] seed + eye; from the redness of its eyes; (eruzhi), meaning burning eyed. The feral type of Sus indicus, or the Indian wild boar. Head longer and more pointed than in the European or German boar; the plane of the forehead straight and not concave; ears small and pointed; tail more tufted; the malar beard well marked. The Indian is altogether a more active looking animal; the German having a stronger and heavier appearance. The same differences are perceptible in the domesticated individuals of the two countries. Length of a tolerably fine boar, 5 feet to root of tail which is one foot. Stands a little over 30 inches high at the shoulder. Color of the adult, brownish black, scantily covered with black hairs. Besides the black recumbent mane of the occiput and back, and the whiskers and the bristles above and below the eyes, there is a bundle of long black bristles on the throat, and the hairs of the throat and chest are reversed. The tail is scantily covered with short hairs, and the apex compressed, with long lateral bristles like those of the elephant [q.v.], arranged like the rings of an arrow. The young is more hairy, of a tawny or fulvous color and striped with dark brown. The hairs of the throat, chest, abdomen and elbows, in the two latter places very long, are black on the basal and white at the apical half. Found wherever there is sufficient shelter either of long grass, low jungle, or forest. Does much damage to crops. Has been detected feeding on the carcass of a dead elephant [q.v.]. Spearing the wild boar is a favorite sport. The speed of the wild hog for a short distance is surprising. In Madras a long spear is used lancewise. The bristles of the boar are removed while the animal is still alive and used by goldsmiths [tattann] and Poojarry [q.v.] bramins to clean their jewels [nagay] and idols [shilay, vigraham] with. Indian species not here found are:—Porcula salvania or pigmy hog of the saul forests, Sus andamanensis or andaman island pig, Sus moupinensis, Sus scrofa or european wild boar.——*Shookaram* (शूकर - shúkara, San.). San. means hog; hog-attracting. Title otherwise Club-moss. Botanically Selaginella imbricata, spreng., lycopodiaceæ [vricsham, 158].

SOORAH (சுறா - shurá, *Tam*). From (shuruthi, tam. swift). Sea-shark. The genus Carcharias, carchariidæ, selachoidei, plagiostomata, chondropterygii, pisces [matsyam, 46], of naturalists [jantoo]. The species of this genus best known to the natives are:—black, gray, red, white. Cf. also:—dun, fawn colored, great white, hammer-headed, malabar, two-spotted, yellow, zebra, which are of other genera. Sharks are found all along the coast of the presidency; in some years much more numerous than in others. This is due to the presence or absence of shoals of smaller fish, as sardines. Captured to a large extent both for the oil obtained from their livers and on account of the flesh of those of medium size, which is salted and sold to the poor; their fins likewise are exported to china, where due to the gelatine contained in them they are in request for making soups; the skins of some forms are employed as shagreen for scabbards of swords; in most localities they are captured by baits secured to a rough hook, which is attached to a chain; the most frequent accidents occurring are after the fish has been hooked and lifted into the fisherman's boat; corpses are almost immediately attacked by sharks; multitudes of the young are daily caught, and the numbers of the ferocious creatures are kept down in this way; as it is, they are sufficiently dangerous, carrying off those gathering shells for the manufacture of lime [choonam], or diving in the sea outside the rocks for shell-fish, or fishermen who may fall into the water; if a shark once seizes a man it never lets go, but in rare cases agile men may escape with the loss of one or both hands, or a leg. Flesh supposed by hindoo medical writers to have peculiar virtues in several diseases; particularly noticed by agastyan [q.v.], in his work ayiram, as a diet in rheumatic affections. The name Fresh-water shark [q.v.] has been given to several of the siluridæ [kizhautty], as indicative of their voracity.——*Black shark* (जटाजूट - jatájúta, Mahr.; కొఱముట్టెసొర - korramuttesorra, Tel.; மணிச்சுறா - maniççurá, Tam.). Title from dorsal deep black. Mahr. means hair tuft on head. Tel. from (korra, tel. dart + mutte, tel. snout + sorra, tel. shark, carcharias genus); from long snout. Tam. from (mani, tam. black + shurá, tam. shark, carcharias genus). Tel. also (sigasorra), meaning tuft of hair in the head + shark, carcharias genus. Title otherwise Jutjot. Carcharias [soorah] menisorrah, carchariidæ, selachoidei, plagiostomata, chondropterygii [matsyam, 46], of naturalists. Specific name from tamul. Alias Carcharias malabaricus, tjutjot; Prionodon menisorrah; tjutjot from mahratta. Very small groove at the angle of the mouth extending a short distance on to the upper jaw; gray above, white below; upper half of second dorsal deep black; calicut; twelve feet or more.——*Dun shark* (పాలసొర - pálasorra, Tel.). Tel. from (pála, tel. white + sorra, tel. shark, carcharias genus). Mustelus manazo, carchariidæ, selachoidei, plagiostomata, chondropterygii [matsyam, 46], of naturalists [jantoo]. Alias Mustelus vulgaris. Snout produced and pointed; well-developed labial fold at the angles of the mouth; reddish gray superiorly, becoming dull white beneath; posterior extremity of the caudal of a dark color; sea. No other common species here.——*Fawn-colored shark* (बालवाल - bálavála, Mahr.; బొక్కిసొర - bokkisorrah, Tel.; എട്ടി - étti, Mal.; குரங்கன்சுறா - kurangansurá, Tam.). Tel. from (bokki, tel. toothless + sorra, tel. shark, carcharias genus). Mal. from (étta, mal. elder); mischievous. Tam. from (kurangam. tam. deer + shurá, tam. shark, carcharias genus); from fawn color [zebra shark]. Mahr. also (dantáli), meaning prominent toothed. Tel. also (rágisorra), meaning copper + shark. Title otherwise Dentel shark, Dog fish. Chiloscyllium indicum, scylliidæ, plagiostomata, chondropterygii [matsyam, 47], of naturalists [jantoo]. Alias Chiloscyllum plagiosum, tuberculatum; Hemiscyllium malayanum; Scyllium freycineti, griseum, hasseltii, ornatum, phymatodes, plagiosum; Squale dentelé; Squalus caudatus, indicus, gronovianus, tuberculatus; Synchismus tuberculatus; dentelé from mahratta. Head rather depressed, flatter inferiorly than superiorly; lips surround the mouth, the lower labial fold being continuous; colors vary exceedingly; usually gray with dark, even black, cross-bands, which may or may not include white spots; sometimes the cross-bands break up into spots or bands, having dark edges; or the fish is simply of a reddish brown color; sea to the malay archipelago. No other common species here.——*Gray shark* (పాలసొర - pálasorra, Tel.). Tel. from (pála, tel. white + sorra, tel. shark, carcharias genus). Carcharias [soorah] macloti, carchariidæ, selachoidei, plagiostomata, chondropterygii [matsyam, 46], of naturalists. Alias Hypoprion macloti. Short groove at the angle of the mouth, not extending on to the upper jaw; nostrils nearer to the opening of the mouth than to the end of the snout; gray or brown, becoming dull white beneath; the fins gray, the caudal nearly black in its posterior half; outer half of first dorsal dark; pectoral and ventral with a light edge; sea.——*Great white shark* (سفید شورا - sufedshorá, Hind.; வெள்ளைச்சுறா - vellaiççurá, Tam.). Hind. from (sufed, hind. white + shorá, hind. shark, carcharias genus). Tam. from (vellai, tam. white + shurá, tam. shark, carcharias genus). Pristis zysron, pristidæ, batoidei, plagiostomata, chondropterygii [matsyam, 48], of naturalists [jantoo]. Alias Pristis dubius, pectinatus. Sandy-brown, becoming lighter beneath; sea; at least 20 feet. Pristis cuspidatus is the Saw-fish.——*Hammer-headed shark* (చప్పసొర - tsappasorrah, Tel.; കൊമ്പൻസ്രാവ് - kombanshrávu, Mal.; கொம்பன்சுறா - kombansurá, Tam.). Tel. from (tsappa, tel. flat + sorra, tel. shark, carcharias genus). Mal. from (kombu, mal. tusk + shrávu, mal. shark, carcharias genus). Tam. from (kombu, tam. tusk + shurá, tam. shark, carcharias genus); cf. macrones aor. Zygæna blochii, carchariidæ, selachoidei, plagiostomata, chondropterygii [matsyam, 46], of naturalists [jantoo]. Alias Sphyrna blochii; Zygæna laticeps. Nostril much nearer the mouth than the eye; deep gray or brownish-gray, becoming lighter beneath; the fins are usually of a slightly deeper color than the body; commonest form on the malabar coast where it attains very large size; sea. Zygæna malleus is the English hammer-headed shark.——*Malabar shark* (कालगगिल - kálagagli, Mahr.; వాలుగ - váluga, Tel.; മങ്കിവാള - mankívála, Mal.). Mahr. from (kála, san. black + gagli, mahr. callichrous bimaculatus); from fins. Tel. from (válu, tel. long). Mal. from (mannu, mal. to grow pale + vála, mal. wallago attu). Callichrous [butter fish] malabaricus, siluridæ [kizhautty], physostomi, teleostei [matsyam, 35], of naturalists [jantoo]. Alias Silurus malabaricus; Wallago malabaricus; Wallago from teloogoo. Lower jaw strongly prominent; deep grayish-brown shot with purple, fin membranes densely spotted with black; malabar coast up to 20 inches in length. For another callichrous see Two spotted shark.——*Red shark* (సెంసొర - semsorrah, Tel.; செஞ்சுறா - sheñjurá, Tam.). Tel. means red shark. Tam. from (shem, tam. red + shurá, tam. shark, carcharias genus). Tam. also (paruváyççurá), meaning great + mouth + shark, carcharias genus. Carcharias [soorah] acutus, carchariidæ, selachoidei, plagiostomata, chondropterygii [matsyam, 46], of naturalists. Alias Scoliodon acutus; Squalus russellii. Nostrils nearer to mouth than to the end of the snout; gray or bronze above, white below; fins gray, the posterior edge of pectoral, outer edges of ventral, anal and posterior half of caudal, white; upper edge of caudal dark, as is also its posterior lobe; sea; on malabar coast attain considerable size.——*Two-spotted shark* (गगिल - gagli, Mahr.; ಗೊಡ್ಲೆ - godle, Can.; దుకుడుము - dúkudúmu, Tel.; ପବ୍ତା - pobtá, Oor.; சொட்டைவாளை - shottaiválai, Tam.). Title from black spots. Tam. from (shottai, tam. depressed spot + válai, tam. wallago [attu]. Tel. also (váluga), meaning long fish. Tam. also (shélavālai). Title otherwise Butter fish. Callichrous [butter fish] bimaculatus, siluridæ [kizhautty], physostomi, teleostei [matsyam, 35], of naturalists [jantoo]. Alias Callichrous affinis, canio, ceylonensis, chechra, immaculatus, nebulosus; Ompok siluroides; Phalacronotus siluroides; Pseudosilurus bimaculatus; Schilbe pabo; Silurus bimaculatus, canio, chechra, duda, indicus, microcephalus, mysoricus; Wallago microcephalus; wallago from teloogoo. Fresh-water; eyes opposite angle of the mouth, lower jaw very prominent; colors silvery shot with purple, a black spot on the shoulder behind the gill-opening and above the middle of the pectoral fin; in some specimens this black spot is much better defined than in others; occasionally the caudal fin is tipped with black; dark tipped caudal fins are uncommon inland; at least a foot and-a-half in length; excellent food, considerably used by europeans. For another callichrous see Malabar shark.——*White shark* (పాలసొర - pálasorra, Tel.). Tel. from (pála, tel. white + sorra, tel. shark, carcharias genus), cf. mustelus manazo. Tel. also (nallasorra), meaning black + shark, carcharias genus. Carcharias [soorah] laticaudus, carchariidæ, selachoidei, plagiostomata, chondropterygii [matsyam, 46], of naturalists. Alias Carcharias palasorrah, macrorhynchus; Scoliodon laticaudus; Squalus pala-sorrah. Uniform gray superiorly, white beneath; pectoral of a deep gray, having a white outer edge, as have also the ventral and anal, posterior portion of caudal fin dark gray or nearly black; sea; at least two feet in length.——*Yellow shark* (కిట్టలసొర - kittalasorra, Tel.; வழுவன்சுறா - vazhuvansurá, Tam.). Tel. from (gitta, tel. claw of a scorpion or crab + sorra, tel. shark, carcharias genus). Tam. from (vazhu, tam. to slip + surá, tam. shark, carcharias genus), from slipperiness of body; cf. silundia. Galeocerdo rayneri, carchariidæ, selachoidei, plagiostomata, chondropterygii [matsyam, 46], of naturalists [jantoo]. Alias Galeocerdo tigrinus. Dark gray superiorly, dull white beneath; cheeks and lower surface of the snout yellowish; body, from a short distance behind the gill-openings, with numerous large black spots and vertical bars; fins gray, the first dorsal with irregular vertical bands; attains considerable size, not numerous; exceedingly fierce, very cunning and swells itself out so as to appear like a floating mass of animal substance, and having thus decoyed its prey it immediately attacks it; eats everything, even sea-snakes; sea; attaining upwards of 12 feet in length. No other common species here.——*Zebra shark* (शिन्वाल - shinvála, Mahr.; పులిమేకము - pulimekamu, Tel.; குரங்கன்சுறா - kuranganusurá, Tam.). Title from markings. Tel. from (puli, tel. tiger + mekamu, tel. beast), markings; cf. trygon uarnak. Tam. from (kurangam, tam. deer + shurá, tam. shark, carcharias genus); from fawn color [fawn-colored shark]. Title otherwise Tiger shark. Stegostoma tigrinum, scylliidæ, selachoidei, plagiostomata, chondropterygii [matsyam, 47], of naturalists [jantoo]. Alias Scyllium heptagonum; Squale tigre; Squalus cirrosus, fasciatus, longicaudus, tigrinus; Stegostoma carinatum, fasciatum. Head as broad as long; upper lip very thick, like a quadrangular pad, with a barbel on either side; distinct labial fold round the angle of the mouth, which is slightly nearer the eye than to the end of the snout; color, young, white or buff, in the form of markings, the fish appearing black, with narrow white lines or bands across the head and body, between which are white spots; these take on various forms in different examples; adults tawny, with more or less transverse bands of rounded spots, the color of the fish being brownish; favorite food of this fish is molluscs [chippy] and crustacea [kavachiny]; sea; 10–14 feet; common at madras. No other common species here.

SOORINJAUN (سورنجان - súrinján, Ar., Pers., Hind. and Dec.; షురింజాన్ - shurinján, Tel.; சுரிஞ்சான் - shuriñján, Tam.). Ar. also (lobatibarbarí), meaning barbary doll; (akanah). Title otherwise Barbary doll, Hermodactyl, Mercury's finger. Botanically Colchicum sp., liliaceæ [vricsham, 136]. Flowers, which spring from an under ground bulb, resemble crocus saffron [q.v.]. Of two kinds, sweet and bitter. Medicinally tonic.

SOORKH (سرخ - surkh, Pers.). Red. Plant second term often joining two genera. Ex., where transl. is of first term:—Capsicum annuum (pilpilisurkh), piper nigrum; Plumbago rosea (shítrakisurkh), plumbago zeylanica; Pterocarpus santalinus (sandalisurkh), santalum album; Tamarix articulata (gazisurkh), tamarix gallica; Trichosanthes palmata (hanzalisurkh), citrullus colocynthis. See gloss. paragraphs.——*Soorkee* (سرخی - surkhí, Hind.). Means redness. Pounded brick [shengal] used to mix with lime [choonam] so as to form a hydraulic mortar [cauray].

SOORMA (सौवीर - sauvíra, San.; الكحل - alkuhl, Ar.; كحل - kuhl, Pers.; سرمه - surmah, Hind.; انجن - anjan, Dec.; کنگنگ - kingang, Malay; ಅಂಜನ - añjana, Can. and Too.; అంజనరాయి - anjanaráyí, Tel.; അഞ്ഞനക്കല്ല് - aññanakkallu, Mal.; අඤ්ජන - añjana, Singh.; அஞ்சனக்கல் - añjanakkal, Tam.). Title from hindostany. San. from (suvíra, san. the name of a country along the indus); cf. shavveeram. Can. from (anjana, san. collyrium). Tel. from (anjana, san. collyrium + ráyi, tel. stone). Mal. from (añjana, san. collyrium + kal, mal. stone). Tam. from (añjana, san. collyrium + kal, tam. stone). Ar. also (ismad). Tel. also (nílánjanamu), meaning black + collyrium; (kátukaráyi), meaning lamp black + stone. Singh. also (hoyandun). Antimony. Properly Sulphuret of antimony. Antimonii sulphuretum, Antimonium sulphuratum of chemists. Metal [loham] of a lead gray color; met with compact and in rhombic prisms. A galena, or sulphuret of lead, is often sold for it in the bazaars; this is in a cubic form. For distribution, see vol. II, 33; greater part of native antimony met with is now brought from Siam; was exported from Egypt to Mouziris [cranganore] and Nelkunda [cullada] according to the Periplus. Medicines are prepared from soorma in four different ways:—"*a*" by trituration in metallic state, united with sulphur [gandhac]; hence prepared sulphur of antimony;—"*b*" by action of heat with phosphate of lime; hence antimonial powder;—"*c*" by action of alkalies; hence brown antimoniated sulphur;—"*d*" by action of acids; hence tartar emetic. The sulphate is used as an emetic by veidyans [q.v.]. In veterinary practice one part of antimony, and two each of nitre [shorah] and sulphur [gandhac] are used in cutaneous disease, four drachms of the powder daily in gram [q.v.]. Employed in composition of printing types; used by Mahomedans for dyeing [shauyam] and cooling the eyes and for painting the eye-brows and eye-lashes.

SOOSTY (سستی - sustí, Hind.). From persian. Laziness.

SOOSY (سوسی - súsí, Hind.). Striped calico [q.v.] woven with colored thread; also mixture of cotton [q.v.] and silk [puttoo]. Used extensively by Lubbays [q.v.] for trouserings and petticoats [sheelay].

SOOTRAM (सूत्र - sútra, San.; சூத்திரம் - shúttiram, Tam.). From (siv, san. to sew). Thread. So a rule or aphorism, as being shown in a string of rules. The whole ritual, grammatical, metrical, and philosophical literature of this country is written in such aphorisms, and their object is extreme brevity. In the grammatical Sootrams not a single letter is allowed which can by any contrivance be dispensed with, and moreover in these Sootrams letters and syllables are often used symbolically, like algebraic signs, to indicate ideas which would otherwise require a whole sentence or more to express them in full. The Sootrams are really mere memorial suggestions of the briefest possible kind, skilfully contrived for aiding the recollection of teachers. Historically speaking, all Sootrams are post-vedic. The most celebrated of all commentators on the Sootrams was Shuncaracharry [shuncaran]. See vol. I (74). According to the tamul Nunnool [q.v.] a sootram is a poetical composition containing much matter in as few words as possible, without injury to the force or minuteness of the sense, and appearing as clear as the reflection of a large object in a small mirror. The course or concatenation in which, according to the same, sootrams proceed from one another is of four kinds:—Fluviatic, or as a straight flowing river; Leonine, or as a lion [simham] which is supposed to see before and behind; Ranatic, or as the jumping of a frog [bhaicam], leaving intermediate space between one subject and another; and Aquiline, or as the darting of an eagle or kite [chillam] to seize upon its prey. Sootrams are generally written in tamul in the verse Ausryappah [q.v.] or Agaval, of which there are four kinds. Most Nunnool sootrams are written in the kind called Nilaimandila ausryappah. A few are in the verse called Nairisay venbah [q.v.].

SOOTRIYAUN (ستریان - sutriyán, Hind.). A dish consisting of wheat flour [soojee] made into paste, formed into small cakes and boiled in water with meat, &c.

SOPPA (చొప్ప - tsoppa, Tel.). The stalk of cholum [q.v.].

SOUDAN (سودان - saudán, Hind.). Means negro-land. The large tract of country from Atlantic ocean to Abyssinia south of Sahara; sometimes restricted to regions bordering Niger.——*Soudan seed* (حب السودان - habbussaudán, Ar.). Same as Black horse-gram.

SOUTH (दक्षिण - dakshina, San.; தென் - ten, Tam.). Prefix [ten].——*South arcot* (தென்னார்க்காடு - tennárgádu, Tam.). Otherwise Cuddalore or Munjacooppam zillah [q.v.]. Revenue district; situated on the Coromandel coast; between 11° 09′ and 12° 35′ N. lat., and between 78° 40′ and 80° 3′ E. long.; bounded N. by North arcot and Chingleput districts, E. by Bay of Bengal, S. by Tanjore and Trichinopoly districts, W. by Salem district; square miles 5,218; pop. 2,162,851; language Tamul. Contains rivers Coleroon, Guddilam, Jinjee, Paravanaur, Ponniaur, Vellaur. Ports Cuddalore, Mercaunum, Pondicherry and Porto novo; mountains Cullroyen range, Jawaudy hills, and Trinomallee hill. The whole area of the district is represented by the following sub-areas:—Chidambaram talook, Cuddalore talook, Cullacoorchy talook, Pondicherry territory, Tindivanam talook, Tricalore talook, Trinomallee talook, Villoopooram talook, Vriddhauchellam talook. For general administrative purposes, the district is distributed between the following revenue and magisterial officers, who have their head-quarters at the places shown. The extent of the range or jurisdiction is shown where necessary. The pay set opposite the subordinate officers gives the grade of the corresponding charge:—Collector, Cuddalore; Sub-collector, Tindivanam, in charge of Tindivanam, Trinomallee and Villoopooram talooks; Head assistant collector, Vriddhauchellam, in charge of Vriddhauchellam and Chidambaram talooks; General deputy collector, Tricalore, in charge of Tricalore and Cullacoorchy talooks. Tahsildars; Chidambaram, Rs. 250; Cuddalore, Rs. 225, this talook includes the mittahs [q.v.] of Alaginuttam, Chennappa naicken polliem and Nadooveraputt; Cullacoorchy, Rs. 175; Tindivanam, Rs. 225; Tricalore, Rs. 200; Trinomallee, Rs. 150, this talook includes the Zemindarry [q.v.] of Vettavalam; Villoopooram, Rs. 250, this talook includes the mittah of Mundacaputt; Vriddhauchellam, Rs. 200. Deputy tahsildars; Bhoovangherry, Rs. 70, range situated north of the Vellaur in Chidambaram talook; Chengam, Rs. 70, range situated in Trinomallee talook; Jinjee, Rs. 70, range situated in Tindivanam talook; Mercaunum, Rs. 70, range situated in Tindivanam talook; Munnargoody, Rs. 70, range situated in Chidambaram talook; Oolandoorpett, Rs. 70, range situated in Tricalore talook; Panrooty, Rs. 70, range situated in Cuddalore talook; Tittagoody, Rs. 70, range situated in Vriddhauchellam talook; Vaunore, Rs. 70, range situated in Villoopooram talook. Similarly judicial officers:—Judge, Cuddalore; District moonsifs, Chidambaram, Cuddalore, Tricalore, Villoopooram, Vriddhauchellam. Contains Registration subdistricts; Chengam, Chidambaram, Coorinjipaudy, Cuddalore, Cullacoorchy, Jinjee, Mercaunum, Munnargoody, Oolandoorpett, Panrooty, Tindivanam, Tricalore, Trinomallee, Vaunore, Villoopooram, Vriddhauchellam. Contains Forest ranges; Chidambaram, Cuddalore, Cullacoorchy, Jinjee, Tindivanam, Tricalore, Trinomallee, Villoopooram and Vriddhauchellam. Contains Municipalities Cuddalore and Chidambaram. Contains District board and Talook boards; Cuddalore embracing Cuddalore talook; Vriddhauchellam embracing Vriddhauchellam and Chidambaram talooks; Tricalore embracing Tricalore and Cullcoorchy talooks; Tindivanam embracing Villoopooram, Tindivanam and Trinomallee talooks. The following general references should be made to the preceding volumes:—general geography, I (1) to (29); general ethnology, I (29) to (109); general history, I (110) to (188); physical geography, II, 1; meteorology, II, 3; geology, II, 8; fauna, II, 21; flora, II, 26; mineralogy, II, 29. The following references in the preceding volumes will furnish details special to the district:—latitudes, and longitudes II, 47; particulars about towns, II, 48; coast survey, II, 160; light-houses, II, 168; comparative population, II, 172; location of revenue officers, II, 379; revenue settlement of the district, II, 406; registrars' and sub-registrars' station, II, 420; ports, II, 423; salt factories, II, 426; rain-gauge station, II, 428; police divisions, II, 431; maps published, II, 436; survey topographical lists, II, 443; hospitals and dispensaries, II, 447; missionary stations, II, 455; head-quarter stations of gazetted officers, II, 461; incidence of taxation, II, 463; weights and measures of the district, II, 507; zemindarries contained, II, 294; special public works, I, 404. A special gazetteer account of the whole district is given at II, 56. For the detailed topography of the district, reference should be made to the talook notices in the present volume, viz.:—Chidambaram, Cuddalore, Cullacoorchy, Pondicherry, Tindivanam, Tricalore, Trinomalee, Villoopooram, Vriddhauchellam.——*South canara* (ದಕ್ಷಿಣಕನ್ನಡ - dakshinakannada, Can.; തെക്കൻകർണ്ണാടകം - tekkankarnnátakam, Mal.). Colloquially Mangalore zillah [q.v.]. Revenue district; situated on the western coast; between 12° 06′ and 13° 58′ N. lat., and between 74° 37′ and 75° 44′ E. long.; bounded N. by North canara of Bombay, E. by Mysore and Coorg, S. by Malabar district, W. by Indian ocean; square miles 3,902; pop. 1,056,081; languages Tooloo, Canarese and Malayalam. Contains rivers Netrauvaty, Goorpore, Gungavully, Chundragherry; ports south to north, Hosdroog, Baicull, Cassergode, Coombla, Manjeshwar, Mangalore, Moolky, Padbidry, Yermaul, Ootchil, Caup, Oodiyauvar, Malpey, Barcore, Coondapore, Naickancuttey, Beidore, Shiroor; mountains Western ghauts; sanitaria none in district but two bungalows exist just beyond the boundary in Mysore on Coothireymookh. The whole area of the district is represented by the following sub-areas:—Cassergode talook, Coondapore talook, Mangalore talook, Oodipy talook, Ooppinangady talook. For general administrative purposes the district is distributed between the following revenue and magisterial officers, who have their head-quarters at the places shown. The pay set opposite the subordinate officers gives the grade of the corresponding charge. Collector, Mangalore. Assistant collector, Mangalore. Head assistant collector, Coondapore, in charge of Coondapore and Oodipy talooks. General deputy collector, Poottore, in charge of Cassergode and Ooppinangady talooks. Tahsildars; Cassergode, Rs. 200; Coondapore, Rs. 150; Mangalore, Rs. 225; Oodipy, Rs. 225; Ooppinangady, Rs. 175. Deputy tahsildars; Amindivy, called the Monigar, Rs. 70, range situated south-west of Mangalore talook in the sea; Beltangady, Rs. 70, range situated in northern part of Ooppinangady talook; Buntwaul, Rs. 70, range situated in south-eastern portion of Mangalore talook; Caurcal, Rs. 70, range situated in south-eastern portion of Oodipy talook; Mangalore, Rs. 100, jurisdiction extending over the town of Mangalore and adjacent villages; Neeleshwar, Rs. 70, range situated in southern part of Cassergode talook. Similarly judicial officers:—Judge, Mangalore. Subordinate judge, Mangalore. District moonsifs; Mangalore, with jurisdiction extending over a greater part of Mangalore talook and a portion of Cassergode; Cassergode with jurisdiction over the Cassergode talook with the exception of the portions assigned to Mangalore and Poottore moonsifs, respectively; Coondapore, with jurisdiction extending over the Coondapore talook and a small portion of Oodipy; Oodipy with jurisdiction extending over the Oodipy talook excepting the portions assigned to the Moonsifs of Coondapore and Caurcal; Caurcal with jurisdiction extending over portions of Oodipy and Mangalore talooks and also a small portion of Ooppinangady talook; Poottore with jurisdiction extending over the whole of Ooppinangady talook, excepting the small portion assigned to the Moonsif of Caurcal, and portions of Cassergode and Mangalore talooks. Contains Registration sub-districts, Beidore, Beltangady, Bramhahwar, Buntwaul, Cassergode, Caurcal, Coondapore, Hosdroog, Mangalore, Manjeshwar, Moodbidry, Moolky, Oodipy, Ooppinaugady, Vittal. Contains five Forest ranges, Cassergode, Mangalore, Ooppinangady, Oodipy and Coondapore. Contains Municipality, Mangalore. Contains District board, and five Talook boards. The following general references should be made to the preceding volumes:—general geography, I (1) to (29); general ethnology, I (29) to (109); general history, I (110) to (188); physical geography, II, 1; meteorology, II, 3; geology, II, 8; fauna, II, 21; flora, II, 26; mineralogy, II, 29. The following references in the preceding volumes will furnish details special to the district:—latitudes and longitudes, II, 47; particulars about towns, II, 48; coast survey, II, 146; light-houses, II, 168; comparative population, II, 172; location of revenue officers, II, 380; registrars' and sub-registrars' stations, II, 420; ports, II, 424; rain-gauge stations, II 428; police divisions, II, 431; maps published, II, 436; hospitals and dispensaries, II, 447; head-quarter stations of gazetted officers, II, 461; incidence of taxation, II, 463; weights and measures of the district, II, 508. A special gazetteer account of the whole district is given at II, 62. For the detailed topography of the district, reference should be made to the talook notices in the present volume, viz.:—Cassergode, Coondapore, Mangalore, Oodipy, Ooppinangady.——*South coast canal* (உப்புவாய்க்கால் - uppuváykkál, Tam.). Canal; Chingleput district, Sydapett and Chingleput talooks. Runs south from the Adyar to Mercaunam in S. arcot district. During the famine of 1876–78 this and Cochrane's canal [q.v.] were united in Madras [buckingham canal].

SOWA (शतपुष्पा - shatapushpá, *San.*; शोप - shópa, *Mahr.*; شبت - shibit, *Ar.*; شود - shod, *Pers.*; سوا - suvá, *Hind.*; سوئی - soí, *Dec.*; ಸಬ್ಬಸಿಗೆ - sabbasige, *Can.*; సోపు - sópu, *Tel.*; ശതകുപ്പ - shatakuppa, *Mal.*; ශතපුෂ්ප - shatapushpa, *Singh.*; சதகுப்பி - shathaguppi, *Tam.*). Title from hindostany. San. from (shata, san. hundred + pushpa, san. flower); from numerous flowers [anise]. Ar. from persian. Hind. from (shályéya, san. the plant). Dec. from hindostany. Tel. from hindostany. Mal. from sanscrit. Tam. from malayalam. San. also (mishréya), meaning introduced from misry [q.v.] or egypt; (madhurá), meaning sweet [sonf]; (chámarapushpiká), meaning fan + flower. Ar. also (sibit). Hind. also (soyah). Can. also (salup'hagida). Tel. also (sóyikúra); (peddasadápa), meaning large + the plant, ruta graveolens, linn., var. angustifolia; (sadápa). Singh. also (hinenduru). Tam. also (shóyikkírai), meaning sowa + vegetable [sonf]. Greek ἄνηθον. Title otherwise Anet, Bishop's weed, Common dill, Dill, Hog's fennel, Shatagooppy, Soy, Sulphurwort, Yampa of north american indians. Botanically Peucedanum graveolens, benth., umbelliferæ [vricsham, 67]. Alias Anethum graveolens, sowa; Peucedánum sowa. Annual, 2–4 feet, erect; glabrous; leaves decompound, alternate; leaflets filiform; petioles sheathing below; stem smooth, covered with whitish pubescence; petals roundish, entire; umbels terminal, without involucels; stamens about the length of the petals; fruit oblong, compressed, almost destitute of a membranaceous margin; seeds two; flowers yellow; flowering in february—april; flattened elliptical seed, with brown and slightly convex backs and pale membranous margin; aromatic, sweetish odour, unpleasant, moderately warm and pungent taste; frequently sold in bazaars for caraway [q.v.] seeds; the seeds yield a valuable oil [yennay], prepared by distillation. Bruised and boiled in water and mixed with roots, seeds are applied externally in rheumatism; leaves, applied warm and moistened with oil, hasten suppuration; gives to pharm. dried fruit, anethi fructus, properties similar to those of carum carui, linn. [caraway], but more grateful to the taste; preparations, oleum anethi, aqua anethi; officinal. Seeds are a chief ingredient in curry-powder [curry]; leaves also. No other common species here. For Anise see that head, for Indian dill or omum see Ajwaun, for Caraway see that head.

SOWDOO (చవుడు - tsavudu, *Tel.*; சவடு - shavadu, Tam.). From (tsavi, tel. taste). Tam. is borrowed term. Saline material in earth [munn]. The decomposition of rocks through the action of the atmospheric oxygen and carbonic acid [vayoo] gives origin ultimately to soluble sulphates, carbonates, and chlorides. These are carried away by the rivers. In the fresh water alluvial plains such salts have accumulated during the lapse of centuries, to an extent sufficient to give rise, by chemical changes in the soil, to the sowdoo efflorescence, the heat of the sun drawing the salts to the surface. The efflorescences consist of three groups:—"*a*" the neutral, which contain no carbonate of soda; these consist chiefly of sodium chloride and sulphate, and frequently magnesium sulphate ;—"b" the alkaline, which contain carbonate of soda, and alkaline chlorides and sulphates, but no lime or magnesium salts ;—"c" the nitrous efflorescences ; these generally contain no alkaline carbonate, but consist chiefly of nitrate of lime and alkaline chlorides, while others contain alkaline nitrate, chloride and sulphate ; they are developed where the soil has become loaded with organic nitrogenous matter. Sowdoo is thus a very variable compound. The ingredients and their relative proportions vary in different places, exactly as the well waters at different spots differ in saline contents. Soils containing a large percentage, from 30 to 50 per cent. of carbonate of soda, abound all over the country and are habitually collected by the people for use as dhobies' earth [q.v.], and in dyeing [shauyam], and for the manufacture of soap [sauboon] and of glass bangles [gauzoo] ; it is purified by a simple process of lixiviation. The following are the five principal. Distinguish from Sujjee khaur or barilla, and Jharkanamak or potash.——*Gauzoo sowdoo* (గాజుచవుడు - gádzutsavudu, Tel. ; வளையலமண் - valaiyalman, Tam.). Tel. from (gádzu, tel. glass bangle). Tam. from (valaiyal, tam. glass bangle + man, tam. earth). Bangle earth. A soda soil. Color fawn ; appearance sandy. Used almost exclusively in the manufacture of the several varieties of glass bangles [gauzoo] so largely worn by the native women of this country ; the color of the bangle being dependent on the composite, iron [auhan] for red bangles, copper [taumram] for green, indigo [q.v.] for blue, &c. The crude common salt [ooppoo] educed from bangle earth is supposed to possess medicinal properties ; also culinary.——*Ooppoo sowdoo* (ఉప్పుచవుడు - upputsavudu, Tel. ; உப்புமண் - uppuman, Tam.). Tel. from (uppu, tel. salt). Tam. from (uppu, tam. salt + man, tam. earth). Earth giving educed or lixiviated or washed common salt [ooppoo]. Spoils masonry if admitted in chopnam [q.v.] ; witness dilapidated appearance of houses near sea-coast where salt air acts on the mortar [cauray] ; its presence makes all soils sterile ; used for cattle affected by foot and mouth-disease [caulvye comaury], being rubbed on the tongue ; cattle [maud] are also driven into salt swamps to stand there ; wild animals have their salt licks ; also used as a foundation for stacking cowdung bratties [q.v.] to keep out white-ants [q.v.].——*Paulasowdoo* (పాలచవుడు - pálatsavudu, Tel.). Tel. from (pála, tel. white + above). A soil containing carbonate of soda. Similar in appearance to dhobies' earth [q.v.], with which it is closely allied. Used as manure [yeroo] with leaves of tungaid [q.v.], or with refuse pulp of the neem [q.v.] fruit, after the oil has been expressed ; in the Ceded districts [q.v.], where grass is scarce, worked up into a consistency and spread on the roofs of houses as a substitute for thatch [pooneer].——*Soonnapoo sowdoo* (సున్నపుచవుడు - sunnaputsavudu, Tel. ; உவர்மண் - uvarman, Tam.). Tel. from (sunnamu, tel. lime + above). Tam. from (uvar, tam. salt + man, tam. earth). Dhobies' earth [q.v.], Fuller's earth. A special kind of soda [munn cauram] soil. —*Sooracaurapoo sowdoo* (సూరేకారపుచవుడు - súrákáraputsavudu, Tel. ; வெடியுப்புமண் - vediyuppuman, Tam.). Tel. from (súrákáramu, tel. saltpetre + above). Tam. from (vediyuppu, tam. saltpetre + man, tam. earth). A soil containing saltpetre [shorah] or potash with its nitrate. This produces saltpetre [shorah] and country soap [sauboon]. Color mouse ; appearance sandy. Collected in the village streets, off mud walls, &c., where it is the result of frequent staling in the village. Used as a manure [yeroo]. On special occasions acts as a vermicide in tobacco [pogauk] cultivation.

SPATICAM (स्फटिक - sp'hatika, *San.* ; بلور - billaur, *Hind.* ; స్ఫటికము - sp'hatikamu, *Tel.* ; പളുങ്ക - palunku, *Mal.* ; பளிங்கு - palingu, *Tam.*). San. from (sp'hat, san. to burst), easily splitting [spootam]. Hind. means crystal. Mal. and Tam. means crystal. Tam also (velléttukkal), meaning white + leaf + stone. Crystal quartz. They are of various colors ; white, brown, yellow, lilac, &c., but the white are the most common. A yellow crystal resembles a real topaz [pookhrauj], and a lilac-colored crystal is occasionally passed off as an amethyst [martees]. Black crystals are not commonly found in Southern india, but are found in Ceylon. A milk-colored crystal is also found in Ceylon [pálingoocull, ratnam].——*Csheera spaticam* (क्षीरस्पटिक - kshírasp'hatika, San. ; دودهیاپتهر - dúdhyápatthar, Hind. ; గోపాలరాయి - gópálaráyi, Tel.). San. from (kshíra, san. milk). Hind. from (dúdhyá, hind. milk-like + patthar, hind. stone). Tel. from (gópála, tel. short for gópálapatnamu, town so called + ráyi, tel. stone). Opal. Greek ὀπάλλιος. An amorphous form of silica, having a resinous lustre. Precious opal has a peculiar play of colors. Generally met with in large masses in the Nizam's dominions. When first dug out of the earth it is soft, but it hardens and diminishes in bulk by exposure to the air ; some emitting various colored rays, with a particular effulgency, when placed between the eye and the light. It is of a milky white color, but of an inferior quality to what is called the Noble opal of Hungary. Most of the opals found in Southern india are hydrophanes, becoming opaque after some exposure to the atmosphere [ratnam].

SPEAR GRASS (ಕರಿವುನಗದಹುಲ್ಲು - karivunagadahullu, *Can.* ; ఎడ్డి - eddi, *Tel.* ; பன்றிப்புல் - panrippul, *Tam.*). Title from being long and stiff. Can. from (karuva, can. calf + nagu, can. to laugh + hullu, can. grass) ; from being greedily eaten by cattle. Tel. means rude. Tam. from (panri, tam. pig + pul, tam. grass). Tam. also (valamburippul), meaning gyration + grass ; as the aristæ are very sensitive to moisture, if one of its awns be moistened with saliva or water it immediately begins to turn round in the hand and continues to do so for some time. Title otherwise Hygrometric grass, Twist grass. Botanically Andropogon [beard grass] contortus, linn., graminaceæ [vricsham, 156]. Alias Heteropogon contortus ; Stipa spicata. Culm erect, branched, 1–2 feet between, round and two-edged ; sheaths and nodes smooth ; leaves flat, setaceous, acuminated, rough ; spike solitary, terminal, cylindric, drooping ; rachis smooth below, where it is occupied by male and neuter flowers, above covered with short brown hairs ; awns twisted together ; common ; grows in tufts on pasture ground. Cattle [maud] eat it when fresh ; makes good hay when the seeds fall off. Used as a fibre [naur].

SPOGEL (इसबगोल - isabagóla, *Mahr.* ; بزر قطونا - bazrikatúná, *Ar.* ; اسبغول - isbaghol, *Pers.* and *Hind.* ; اسبغول - isabghol, *Dec.* ; ಇಸಬಗೋಲು - isabagólu, *Can.* ; ಇಸಬಕೋಲ್ - isabakul, *Too.* ; ఇసపగాలచెట్టు - isapagálachettu, *Tel.* ; இசப்புக்கோல் - isappukkól, *Tam.*). Title from persian. Ar. from (bazr, ar. seed + katúná, ar. fleawort). Pers. from (asp, pers. horse + ghol, pers. ear) ; from shape of leaf. Dec. from persian. Tel. and Tam. from hindostany. Pers. also (shikamdarídah), meaning belly-cleaving. Can. also (visamugólu). Tam. also (isgól). Greek ψύλλιον, as seeds not unlike fleas. Latin psyllium. Title otherwise Fleawort, Horse ear [common saul], Ispaghul. Botanically Plantago ovata, forsk., plantagineæ [vricsham, 104]. Alias Plantago decumbens, ispaghula. Annual ; stem short, if any, branches ascending, 2–3 inches long ; leaves alternate, linear-lanceolate, three-nerved; somewhat woolly, channelled towards the base, stem-clasping, 6–8 inches long ; peduncles axillary, solitary, erect, slightly villous, the length of the leaves ; spikes solitary, terminal ; flowers numerous, imbricated, small, dull white ; bracts one-flowered, with green keel and membranaceous sides ; calyx four-leaved, with membranaceous margins ; corolla four-cleft, segments ovate, acute ; capsule ovate, two-celled ; seeds solitary ; flowering in november to january ; habitat persia ; cultivated during cold season for the seeds. The seeds are boat shaped, about ⅛ of an inch long and rather less than $\frac{1}{16}$ broad, translucent, with a pinkish tinge and a faint brown streak upon the convex side ; the concavity is covered with a thin white membrane ; soaked in water they become coated with an abundant adherent mucilage which is free from taste and odour ; the epidermis of the seeds is composed of polyhedral cells, the walls of which are thickened by secondary deposits, the source of the mucilage ; between it and the albumen is a thin brownish layer ; the albumen is formed of thick walled cells which contain granular matter ; procurable in most bazaars. Gives to pharm. the seeds, ispaghulæ semina ; demulcent, mildly astringent ; officinal. Another species is major.

SPONGE WOOD (بینڈ - bhend, *Hind.* ; ಬೆಂಡು - bendu, *Tel.*). Title from soft wood. Same as Solah.

SPOOTAM (स्फुट - sp'huta, *San.*). From (sp'hut, san. burst open) ; plain. In astronomy visible or apparent ; in contradistinction to both madhyamam [q.v.] or mean or calculated, and aspootam or invisible or real. Thus in celestial latitude and longitude, spootam are all the incidents as calculated from the shifting point given by the polar axis of the earth projected, while aspootam are the same as calculated from the more real pole of the heavens given by the pole of the ecliptic. It is because there are no trustworthy records of the latter class of observations that it is so difficult to identify the fixed stars mentioned in the hindoo shastrams [nacshatram, sauyanam, vicshaipam].——*Spaticam* (स्फटिक - sp'hatika, San.). See sep. title.

SQUILL (वनपलाण्डु - vanapalándu, *San.* ; रानकांदा - ránakándá, *Mahr.* ; कोळकंदो - kólakandó, *Conc.* ; اشقيل هندى - iskílihindí, *Ar.* ; پیاز دشتی هندی - piyázdashtíihindí, *Pers.* ; کاندا - kándá, *Hind.* ; جنگلی پیاز - janglípiyáz, *Dec.* ; ಕಾಡುಬೆಳ್ಳುಳ್ಳಿ - kádubellulli, *Can.* ; ಬೊಗ್ಗುಳ್ಳಿ - boggulli, *Too.* ; నక్కఉల్లి - nakkaulli, *Tel.* ; കാട്ടുള്ളി - káttulli, *Mal.* ; වල්ලූනු - vallúnu, *Singh.* ; நரிவெங்காயம் - narivengáyam, *Tam.*). Title from arabic. San. from (vana, san. forest + palándu, san. onion, allium cepa, linn.). Mahr. from (rána, mahr. wild + kándá, mahr. onion). Ar. from (iskíl, ar. squill + hindí, ar. indian). Pers. from (piyáz, pers. onion + dashtí, pers. forest + hindí, pers. indian). Hind. from (kanda, san. bulbous root). Dec. from (janglí, hind. wild + piyáz, hind. onion). Can. from (kádu, can. wild + bellulli, can. garlic, allium sativum, linn.). Tel. from (nakka, tel. fox + ulli, tel. onion). Mal. from (kátu, mal. forest + ulli, mal. onion). Singh. from (val, singh. wild + lúnu, singh. onion). Tam. from (nari, tam. jackal + vengáyam, tam. onion). Ar. also (ansalihindí), meaning indian officinal squill ; (baslulfárihindí), meaning indian rat-killing onion ; (baslulbarrihindí), meaning indian forest onion. Pers.

also (piyázimúshihindí), meaning indian rat-killing onion. Hind. also (janglipiyáz), meaning wild onion. Dec. also (kandrá), from sanscrit meaning bulbous root. Can. also (kádírulli), meaning wild + onion; (náyulli), meaning dog + garlic; (adaviírulli), meaning jungle + onion. Tel. also (adavitella-gadda), meaning jungle + garlic, allium sativum, linn. Mal. also (kántánna), meaning methonica superba, lam. + fruit. Tam. also (káttuvelvengáyam), meaning forest + white + onion. Title otherwise Indian squill, Jackal onion, Jungle onion, Rat onion, Sea onion. Botanically Urginia indica, kunth., liliaceæ [vricsham, 136]. Alias Scilla indica. Scilla from arabic. Bulb perennial, truncated, white, about the size of a large apple [seb]; leaves numerous, radical, ensiform, nearly flat, smooth, 6–18 inches in length; scape erect, round, smooth, and, including the raceme, about 2–3 feet in length; raceme erect, very long; flowers remote, long-pedicelled, drooping; when in blossom the plant is entirely destitute of leaves; grows in sandy plains on coast. The bulbs are white, the size of an orange [q.v.], inodorous, nearly tasteless, resemble in appearance and qualities the root of the true squill, urginia scilla, steinh., being nauseous and bitter; not so large nor so round as the latter, but have similar fleshy scales; sometimes dark in color, owing to not having been properly dried. Substituted medicinally for the officinal squills; possess little action when old and large; expectorant and diuretic; in pharm. non-officinal. Other common species are:—coquesta, coromandeliana.

SRUNGAVARAPOOCOTE (శృంగవరపుకోట - shringavarapukóta, *Tel.*). From (shringa, san. peak + pura, san. town + kóta, san. fort) [shringam].—(1) Division; Vizagapatam district; area, 438 square miles exclusive of agency tracts; population 129,323; language Teloogoo. E. central inland of district. Boundaries:—north, Pottinghy and Gajapatinugger talooks; east, Vizianagram and Bimlipatam division; south, Vizagapatam division; west, Veeravilly division. Flat, gradually rising towards the north-eastern ghauts which skirt the northern boundary. Smaller hills occur all over division at intervals. Chittivalsa river, also called Gostany passes through north-eastern portion. Soil very fertile. Parts are clayey and saltish. The chief industry is agriculture. Srungavarapoocote is reputed for its lacquered wares. At Lakkavarapoocote bell-metal [cunts] vessels are made. The usual industries of weaving and pottery [chatty] exist all over the division. Exports, paddy [q.v.], rice [q.v.], jaggery [q.v.], and skins [chamrah] and horns [sing] to Vizagapatam, myrobalans [q.v.] and niger seed [ramtil] to Bimlipatam. Imports raggy [q.v.], gingelly [q.v.], niger [ramtil], myrobalans [q.v.] and horns [sing] from the hills. Irrigation, seven channels branching from the Chittivalsa river and a hill stream called Chilkalagedda in the north and east. Tanks fed by rainfall elsewhere. The north-west portion is occupied by the agency villages and hills rising to 5,300 feet at Gaulicondah. Camping grounds; Anlmanda, Bheemasingy, and Cottavalsa daubaul. Places of archæological interest:—Bonangby, Caushipore, Condagoody, Cottaum, Dharmavaram, Goodivauda, Lakkavarapoocote, Reiga, Shreerampooram, Somapooram, Srungavarapoocote. Principal trig. stations:—Coomrye, Goomroo, Mariky, Vizagapatam N.E. base, Vizagapatam S.E. base. The leading places, &c., in the division are the following. ——*Anantagherry* (అనంతగిరి - anantagiri, Tel.). From (ananta, san. vishnu, the eternal + giri, san. mountain). Village; pop. including suburbs 1,823; height 3,111 feet. On crest of Gaulicondah hills, here the boundary between Vizianagram and Pauchipenta zemindarries. Coffee [q.v.] estate belonging to Maharajah of Vizianagram.——*Annam rauzpett* (అన్నంరాజుపేట - annamrádzupéta, Tel.). From (annamrádzu, tel. proper name + péta, tel. suburb). Village; pop. 2,543. Former residence of a branch of Vizianagram family, by whom Shree vengopaulsawmy was established here and a large pagoda [q.v.] built. The latter has an endowment of Rs. 3,630 derived from lands.——*Bonanghy* (బొనంగి - bónangi, Tel.). Village; pop. 2,613; lat. 18° 09′; long. 83° 16′; from Srungavarapoocote N.E. 6 miles; from Vizagapatam N. 30 miles. Copper plate grant dated A.D. 1586.——*Caushipore* (కాశీపురము - kásipuramu, Tel.). From (káshi, san. benares + pura, san. town). Zemindarry, Village; pop. 1,359 including hamlets; lat. of village 18° 13′; long. 83° 10′; from Srungavarapoocote N. 8 miles; from Vizagapatam N.N.W. 36 miles. Old fort and ancient stone statues. Fair every Wednesday. Peshcush Rs. 600. ——*Chittivalsa* (చిట్టివలస - chittivalasa, Tel.). See sep. title. ——*Coomrye* (కుమురాయి - kumuráyi, Tel.). From (kummu, tel. smouldering ashes + ráyi, tel. stone). Trig. station; lat. 18° 14′ 39·52″; long. 83° 06′ 39·80″; height 3,984 feet; from Condeba E. 1¾ miles; from Srungavarapoocote N.N.W. 10 miles.——*Cottaum* (కొట్టము - kottámu, Tel.). Means cattle shed. Village; pop. 2,197; lat. 18° 06′; long. 83° 15′; from Srungavarapoocote E.S.E. 6 miles; from Vizagapatam N. 27 miles; from Vizianagram W. 12 miles. Chief station in Bonanghy talook of Vizianagram zemindarry.——*Dharmavaram* (ధర్మవరము - dharmavaramu, Tel.). From (dharma, san. piety + pura, san. city). Town; pop. 3,274; lat. 18° 07′; long. 83° 14′; from Srungavarapoocote E. 3 miles; from Vizagapatam N.N.W. 29 miles. Old temple with copper images [shilay, vigraham]. Another built 300 years ago. Seat of Sanyausayyan, a disciple of Shiva. Bestowing issue is his particular power.——*Gaulicondah* (గాలికొండ - gálikonda, Tel.). See sep. title.——*Goodivauda* (గుడివాడ - gudiváda, Tel.). From (gudi, tel. temple + váda, tel. village). Village; pop. 2,094; lat. 18° 02′; long. 83° 09′; from Srungavarapoocote S.S.W. 6 miles; from Vizagapatam N.N.W. 24 miles. Also name of a talook of Vizianagram zemindarry. Illegible inscriptions at the temple of Bramhalingam.——*Goomroo* (గుమురు - gumuru, Tel.). Means a cluster. Trig. station; lat. 17° 56′ 08·68″; long. 83° 16′ 35·09″; height 1,452 feet; from Srungavarapoocote S.S.E. 13 miles.——*Jaumy* (జామి - jámi, Tel.). From (jammi, tel. a tree, prosopis spicigera, linn.). Village; pop. 5,066; lat. 18° 03′; long. 83° 18′; from Srungavarapoocote E.S.E. 9 miles; from Vizagapatam N. 24 miles. On the Gostany. Former head-quarters of a talook. Indigo factory.——*Lakka varapoocote* (లక్కవరపుకోట - lakkavarapukóta, Tel.). From (lakka, tel. lac + pura, san. town + kóta, san. fort). Village; pop. 2,132; lat. 18° 02′; long. 83° 13′; from Srungavarapoocote S.S.E. 6 miles; from Vizagapatam N.N.W. 24 miles. Chief station in Vapadah talook of Vizianagram zemindarry. Three ancient temples. In a courtyard of the Veerabhadran [q.v.] temple are some inscribed slabs [shausanam].——*Mariky* (మరికి - mariki, Tel.). Means soapstone basin. Trig. station; lat. 18° 03′ 01·82″; long. 83° 06′ 42·82″; height 2,110 feet; from Srungavarapoocote S.W. 6 miles.——*Poonyagherry* (పుణ్యగిరి - punyagiri, Tel.). See sep. title.——*Reiga* (రైగ - raiga, Tel.). From (régada, tel. black-cotton soil). Village; pop. 852; lat. 18° 00′; long. 83° 02′; from Srungavarapoocote S.W. 13 miles; from Vizagapatam N.W. 28 miles. Rock-cut cave dedicated to Grihaulingeshwaran.——*Royavalsa* (రాయవలస - ráyavalasa, Tel.). See sep. title.——*Vapadah* (వపాద - vapadá, Tel.). Village; pop. 1,530; lat. 18° 04′; long. 83° 15′; from Srungavarapoocote S.E. 5 miles; from Vizagapatam N.N.W. 25 miles. Also name of a talook of Vizianagram zemindarry.——*Vizagapatam north end base* (విశాఖపట్టణము - visbákhapattanamu, Tel.). Trig. station; lat. 18° 01′ 02·91″; long. 83° 16′ 10·54″.——*Vizagapatam south end base* (విశాఖపట్టణము - vishákhapattanamu, Tel.). Trig. station; lat. 17° 55′ 38·16″; long. 83° 14′ 09·41″.—(2) Deputy tahsildarry; Vizagapatam district. Pay Rs. 70.—(3) Town, Deputy tahsildar's station; Vizagapatam dist., Srungavarapoocote division; pop. 5,715; lat. 18° 06′; long. 83° 11′; from Coraputt S.E. 54 miles; from Madras N.E. 390 miles; from Narsapatam N.E. 46 miles; from Parvatipore S.S.W. 25 miles; from Vizagapatam N.N.W. 30 miles; from Vizianagram W. 18 miles. Ruined fort, belonged formerly to the giant king Simhabala. A mile west is a steep hill with a waterfall, near which is a ruined building of two storeys.

SS (शालिवाहनशक - shálivåhanashaka, *San.*). An abbreviation for Shalivahana [q.v.] saca [q.v.].

STA (स्था - st'há, *San.*). To stand.——*Stala cauval* (தலக்காவல் - talakkával, Tam.). From (st'hala, san. place + kával, tam. guard). System of guarding a tract of country against open marauders [desha cauval, inam].——*Stala curnum* (స్థలకరణము - st'halakaranamu, Tel.). From (st'hala, san. place + karanamu, tel. accountant). The accountant of a district [deshpandya].——*Stala jemadar* (స్థలజమాదారుడు - st'halajamádárudu, Tel.). From (st'hala, san. place + jamádárudu, tel. peon). Head peon [q.v.] of village.——*Stalam* (स्थल - st'hála, San.). From (st'ha, san. to stand firm). A place; terra firma. A holy place or place of pilgrimage [teertam]. ——*Stala pooraunam* (स्थलपुराण - st'halapurána, San.). From (st'hala, san. place + purána, san. history). Local pooraunam. See Pooraunam.——*Stalawar* (స్థళవారు - st'alaváru, Can.). A record showing the particulars of each field or parcel of land. ——*Stambham* (स्तम्भ - stambha, San.). From (stambh, san. to fix). Post. In architecture [staupatyam] same as Lant [lant, maunasauram].——*Stan* (ستان - sitán, Pers.). From (st'hána, san. place). Suffix denoting place; as Hindostan, hindoo + place.——*Staunam* (स्थान - st'hána, San.). From (st'há, san. to stand). Place, act of abiding; dignity. In Malabar called also Coorvaulcha [q.v.], and denotes the status and attendant property of the senior rajahs [q.v.] in the Malabar covilagams [q.v.] or palaces. The theory is that when a rajah attains to the rank of first, second, third, fourth, &c., in the family, he resigns his place in the common covilagam [q.v.] or palace, in which he was brought up, and lives apart on the special property set apart for his staunam or dignity. Practically while taking their staunam the rajahs retain an influence in the covilagam. Accumulations made by a stauny himself are at his absolute disposal, but if undisposed of in his lifetime pass to the covilagam or family in which he was born. The real Staunam property is inalienable except in cases of the gravest necessity and for the benefit of the staunam. As regards debts contracted by a stauny, his position is essentially different from that of a carnaven [q.v.] of a Malabar tarwaud [q.v.]. The carnaven is the accredited agent of the family, and a creditor dealing with him gives credit not to the individual but to the family in all matters apparently and ordinarily within the scope of a carnaven's authority. On the other hand, a creditor dealing with a stauny gives a personal credit only. The creation of a staunam, with property appurtenant thereto, indicates a stage when joint ownership was developing into individual ownership. Many Nayar [q.v.] families of respectability have adopted the customs of the rajahs and created staunams to be filled by the senior member of one house or of several houses connected with one another by community of pollution [poola sambandham]. In a wider sense, the word staunam has the same meaning as mirassy [q.v.] on the eastern coast, and is used to denote the position of some religious functionary, hereditary officer of state, &c., who by virtue of his office enjoys land rent-free. ——*Staunican* (स्थानिक - st'hánika, San.). From (st'hána, san. office). Principal Bramin attached to a pagoda [q.v.].——*Stauny* (സ്ഥാനി - st'háni, Mal.). A dignitary.——*Staupatyam* (स्थापत्य - st'hápatya, San.). From (st'ha, san. ground + pati, san. lord). Cf. Greek ἀρχιτέκτων. Architecture. The Staupatya vedam is one of the four Oopavedams [q.v.]. The indigenous styles are Dravidian, called also Carnatic, occupying all south, and the Chalookyan in north of presidency. The Booddhist style is an adaptation of these two. The Jeina style is in the interior mostly Dravidian, but shows on the west coast foreign elements introduced from N.E. India. The Muhomedan or Saracenic style is entirely foreign. Rishy [q.v.] agastyan [q.v.], who probably brought one of the first Bramin colonies into S. india, wrote a treatise on architecture, or one goes by his name. Other ancient Sanscrit treatises were composed collectively called Shilpa shastram, but few traces remain. One treatise called Maunasauram, and seven others less well known, are extant [maunasauram, shilpashastram]. The Tamuls have no such works, but they have many traditional principles [oor, veed].—"*a*" The Dravidian or Carnatic style comprises nine-tenths of the architectural objects in the whole of peninsular India, though it is actually confined for the most part to a small angle of it in the south. The style shows the ancient inhabitants of the south to have been one of the chief building races of the world. The Dravidians are constructive as the Aryans [q.v.] are literary. The typical Dravidian style consists of a square base ornamented with pilasters externally and containing the cell in which the image or emblem of the deity is placed. Above this rises a pyramid, the general outline of which is straightlined, but always divided into storeys; in small temples [coil, pagoda] generally three, but frequently, as in the great pagoda [q.v.] at Tanjore, into as many as fourteen storeys. Upwards the building terminates in a small dome of polygonal or circular shape. The second feature belonging to Dravidian temples consists in the great gateways, or gopoorams [q.v.], which are frequently more important in size than the vimaunams [q.v.] or pyramids themselves. They form the entrance through the large circumvallating wall [praucauram]. Their outline and general design is the same as that of the temples, except that in plan they are generally twice as wide as they are deep, and are always crowned by an oblong roof instead of a circular dome [goombaz]. In the Dravidian style again the temple almost invariably includes, beside the vimaunam [q.v.] or towered shrine and the gopoorum or gateway, the mantapam [q.v.] or porch leading to the shrine; the choultry [q.v.] or pillared hall; numerous other buildings; elegant stambhams [q.v.] or pillars bearing the images or flags [dhwajam] of the gods, or numberless lamps all connected with the temple worship and service [poojah]; tanks and gardens and avenues [shaulay] of palms [taur] and sacred trees [poonyoshadhy]; all within the temple enclosure. The Dravidian form of design has apparently arisen from a form of building in receding terraces which prevailed in earlier times, though existing only in wood. In such early forms it is to be concluded that the basement was probably a pillared hall like those of Booddhist [booddha] monasteries [vihauram] found in Burmah at the present day. Above this was apparently a smaller hall, with detached cells in the edge of the platform on which it stood; though whether these were chapels, or sleeping apartments, or cooking rooms, cannot now be determined. In the oldest buildings belonging to the style, the cells are still observable detached from the vimaunam [q.v.] and used as chapels. Later the cells are only semi-detached, and afterwards they become mere ornaments of the pyramid. Another feature by which this style is to be recognized is the double curve of the cornices. In all other Indian styles the cornice is straight-lined and sloping downwards to throw off the wet. In the Dravidian style they are universally formed with a double curvature. In connection with this style, it is necessary to point out that no Dravidian architect uses the arch as part of his art. According to a Tamul proverb, an arch never sleeps. An arch in fact contains in its principle an active force, always tending to thrust outwards. A pillar supporting a beam is on the contrary in stable equilibrium; and the Tamulians prefer it, though its use frequently limits their interiors to an undesirable extent. When they find it necessary to cover larger spaces than can be done by single stones, they bracket out one stone beyond another, as was done in ancient Etruria and Greece, till the stones approach near enough to be covered by one stone. The special exhibition of Dravidian architecture known as the south-east style arose under the Chola [q.v.] or Tanjore king in the eleventh century A.D., when nearly all the great temples to Shiva in Southern india were built, and it continued in use in the twelfth and thirteenth centuries, during which time the great temples to Vishnoo were erected. Up to the beginning of the sixteenth century these temples remained almost unchanged; but at that time all Southern india became subject to the kings of Vijianugger, and Krishnaroya, A.D. 1509–30, rebuilt or added to most of the great buildings of the south. The chief feature of the architecture of this later period is the construction of the enormous gopoorams [q.v.] which are so conspicuous at Conjeeveram, Chidambaram, and Shreerungam. All these were built by Krishnaroya; they do not form part of the original south-east style, but were intended as fortifications to protect the shrines from foreign invaders. The following may be taken as a descriptive catalogue of the chief present South indian specimens of Dravidian architecture.—"*i*" First the Dravidian rock-cut temples at Mauvellipore [seven pagodas].—"*ii*" Secondly, Dravidian temples of the ordinary description. Those at Chidambaram; Combaconam, Conjeeveram, Madura, Peroor, Rameshwaram, Shreerungam, Tanjore, Tinnevelly, Trivellore, and Vijianugger may be taken as typical. The temple at Chidambaram is one of the most venerated, and has also the reputation of being one of the most ancient temples in Southern india. This temple has been aggregated at different ages. At Combaconam there is a fine gopooram [q.v.]. The two towns, Great and Small Conjeeveram, possess groups of temples as picturesque and nearly as vast as any to be found elsewhere. The great temple at the first-named place possesses some remarkable gopoorams. At Madura the most important of Trimal naick's original buildings is the celebrated choultry [q.v.] which he built for the reception of the presiding deity of the place. The great temple at Madura is however a larger and far more important building than the choultry, and it also owes all its magnificence to Trimal naick. Although the temple at Peroor, near Coimbatore, can only rank among the second class as regards size, it possesses a portico of extreme interest to architectural history. Of Rameshwaram it may be said that in no other temple has the same amount of patient industry been exhibited. It was begun and finished on a previously settled plan, as regularly and as undeviatingly carried out as that at Tanjore, but on a principle diametrically opposed to it. It is double the dimensions of Tanjore and has ten times its elaboration. The chief ornament of this temple resides in its corridors. Shreerungam is certainly the largest, and, if its principle of design could be reversed, would be one of the finest temples in the south of India. Here the central enclosure is quite as insignificant as that at Trivellore, which see below. Tanjore has a very celebrated temple. In nine cases out of ten, Dravidian temples are a fortuitous aggregation of parts, arranged without plan, as accident dictated at the time of their erection. The principal exception to this rule is to be found at Tanjore. The great pagoda there was commenced on a well-defined plan, which was persevered in till its completion. One of the peculiarities of the Tanjore temple is that all the sculptures of the gopoorams belong to the religion of Vishnoo, while everything in the courtyard is dedicated to the worship of Shiva. Tinnevelly temple also has the advantage of having been built on one plan, and at one time without subsequent alteration or change. The great thousand-pillared portico in the temple is well known. Trivellore is about 30 miles west of Madras. The nucleus was a small village temple drawn to the same scale as the plan of Tanjore. It however at some subsequent period became enriched and a second or outer court was added. Additions were again made at some subsequent date. For Vijianugger see that title-heading and Humpy. The buildings mentioned in the above catalogue are in number rather more than one-third of the great Dravidian temples known to exist in the Presidency. Of the remainder, none have vimaunams [q.v.] like that of Tanjore, nor corridors [praucauram] like those of Rameshwaram; but several have gopoorams [q.v.] quite equal to or exceeding those mentioned above, and many have mantapams [q.v.] of great beauty and extent. Several, such as Auvidayaurcoil, Tauramungalam, Virinjipooram, and others, possess features unsurpassed by any in the south, especially the first-named, which may, perhaps, be considered as one of the most elegant of its class as well as one of the oldest.—"*iii*" Thirdly forts. Among the most remarkable of these are those of Dindigul, Jinjee, Oodayagherry, Palamcottah, Penoocondah, Seringapatam, Trichinopoly, and Vellore; with the droogs [q.v.] or hill forts in the Baramahaul, Mysore, Canara, &c. Many of these are very ancient. The works of Jinjee are specially interesting [aursham, chauvady, coil, dewal, droog, goody, gopooram, mantapam, pagoda, rath, stambham, vimaunam].—"*b*" Chalookyan architecture is easily distinguished from either the Dravidian or the North indian. In plan the temples are generally star-shaped and of sixteen sides. The typical characteristic is that four of these sides are flat and form the principal faces, and between each of these are three facets arranged angularly. The same principle pervades the design of the spire, which is always rectilinear in outline, and generally made up of miniature repetitions of itself heaped one over the other. The peculiarity however which is more characteristic of the style than the outline of its form, is the great richness and beauty of the details with which the buildings are elaborated. The most celebrated temples are those at Halabeed in Mysore. The Nizam's territory was the original central seat of the Chalookya power [chalookya].—"*c*" Booddhist architecture consists of caves, elaborated by artifice for purposes of religious occupation;

pillars or stambhams [q.v.]; carved rails enclosing spaces, an adaptation of the indigenous cromlechs [paundoocull] or circles of stones [azhauram]; topes [q.v.] or stoopams [q.v.], an adaptation of the indigenous tumulus and erected for commemorative purposes; monasteries or vihaurams [q.v.]; and temples or cheityams [q.v.]. The number of Booddhist remains existing anywhere in India is small, and particular interest attaches to them, as they are assumed to be the earliest specimens of developed Indian architectural art. No pillars or built specimens are now found standing, but the style has been reconstructed in theory from remains. The pillars bore inscriptions on the shafts and emblems or animals on the capitals. The carved rails were the principal vehicle for ornamentation. They enclosed sacred trees, shrines and pillars; and in later periods topes [q.v.]. The topes themselves were at first commemorative of a locality merely; in later periods they had for their central construction a dagoba [q.v.] or shrine containing a relic. This dagoba is an adaptation in masonry with domical surface of the earthen tumulus. The vihaurams [q.v.] or sangharaumams [q.v.] or monasteries were buildings containing cells for monks. It is supposed that they were sometimes built in storeys. The cheityams [q.v.] or assembly halls had an ogee roof, and in internal arrangement closely resembled Christian churches. In Southern india Booddhist remains are found near the Kistna river in the Godavery and Kistna districts. The remains in other parts stated to be Booddhist [booddha] are probably of a later date or Jeina [q.v.]. Rock-cut monasteries are found near the Kistna; for instance, at Goontoopully and Naugoolapully in the Ellore talook of the Godavery district. There are no pillars. There are several stoopams or topes in ruins in the abovenamed locality. Examples are the following:—in the Godavery district Saugipaud in the Bheemavaram talook; in the Kistna district Goodivauda in the talook of that name; Ghuntashaula in the Sullapully zemindarry; and Bhattiprole in the Repully talook. The most important stoopam [tope], however, is the well-known one at Amravatty, 20 miles north-west of Guntoor. No vihaurams [q.v.] or cheityams [q.v.] are yet known. From a technical point of view it is not correct to speak of the Booddhist as a separate architectural style. It is only a special exhibition of the indigenous styles of the country, the Dravidian and Chalookya [baur, cheityam, dagoba, goomta, laut, tope, vihauram].—"*d*" In Southern india there are two classes of temples erected by the Jeinas [q.v.], called Bettas [q.v.] and Basties [q.v.]. In the interior they are almost all of the Dravidian style. A special style however belonging to the Jeina religion is found all along the west coast below the ghauts [q.v.], from Goa to Cochin, and sporadically also in the central plateau of India. This is sometimes called the Canarese style. A celebrated temple of this class is that at Moodbidry in South canara. The architecture resembles the Nepaulese. The sloping stone roof which the pillars support is a novelty in Indian architecture very rarely met with. Another peculiarity is the Thibetan character of the wooden roof, which forms a second storey and protects the lower roof from the effects of the weather. This would be more appropriate in a country where snow falls than where protection has to be given against rain alone. The bells which hang from each angle of the roof are a characteristic form found everywhere in Thibet and the Himalaya. This intrusive style is not yet adequately explained [basty, betta].—"*e*" To the south of the Nerbudda there are three well-marked Saracenic styles. First, that of the Bahmany dynasty. Beginning at Goolburga, A.D. 1347, and afterwards at Beedar, A.D. 1426, they adorned their capitals with edifices of great magnificence and well-marked individuality, before they were absorbed, in A.D. 1525, in the great Moghul empire. Next to these was the still more celebrated Adil shahy dynasty [raj.] of Beejapore, A.D. 1489–1672. Their style differed most essentially from all those above enumerated, and was marked by a grandeur of conception and boldness in construction unequalled by any edifices erected in India. The third southern style is that of the Cootb shahy dynasty of Golcondah, A.D. 1512–1672. Their tombs are splendid and form one of the most striking groups in India, but show evident signs of a decadence that was invading art at the age when they were erected [goombaz, meenaur, takiya, &c.].——*Stauvaram* (स्थावर - st'háara, San.). From (st'há, san. to stand). Immovable. Opposite of Jangamam [jangam]. Stauvara sott in tamul is fixed or real property. Stauvara lingam is an immovable lingam [q.v.], or that fixed in the temples [coil, pagoda].——*Stiram* (स्थिर - st'hira, San.). Fixed. Epithet of the four fixed caranam, [q.v.].——*Stity* (स्थिति - st'hiti, San.). From (st'há, san. to stand). Anything to stand on; property [sott]. Suffix in compounds; as Bhoo stity, meaning earth + property.——*Stooladeham* (स्थूलदेह - st'húladéha, San.). From (st'húla, san. gross + déha, san. body). Visible material body [shareeram].——*Stoolam* (स्थूल - st'húla, San.). Gross, as distinguished from soocshmam [q.v.] or subtle.

STAR PAGODA (பூவராகன் - púvarágan, *Tam.*). Means flower + pagoda; from star impression on the reverse. Madras coin [naunyam, pagoda]. See vol. I, 616.

STICKING GRASS (لپٹا - laptá, *Hind.*; ಸಣ್ಣ ಅಂಟುಪುರುಳೆ ಹುಲ್ಲು - sannaantupurulehullu, *Can.*; చికిలింతగడ్డి - chikilintagaddi, *Tel.*; ஒட்டுப்புல் - ottuppul, *Tam.*). Title from sticking to clothes. Hind. from (lapatná, hind. to stick to). Can. from (sanna, can. small + antu, can. gum + purulu, can. parrot + hullu, can. grass). Tel. from (chikili, tel. beautiful + gaddi, tel. grass). Tam. from (ottu, tam. to stick + pul, tam. grass); from sticking to clothes. Tam. also (kuthiraivárchámai), meaning horse + tail + panicum miliare, lam. Title otherwise Horse tail millet, Rough panic grass. Botanically Panicum [priyangoo] verticillatum, linn., graminaceæ [vricsham, 156]. Alias Setaria verticillata. Culms below resting on the ground and rooting, above weak, leaning to one side, smooth; leaves sheathing, linear-lanceolate, a little downy, margins hispid, mouths of the sheaths hairy; spikes cylindric, compound sub-verticelled; bristles of the involucels reversely hispid; hermaphrodite florets rather smooth; common about rubbish heaps. Requires a good soil and shade; cattle eat it before the flower spikes are formed; seeds eaten by small birds.

STORAX (اصطرك - ustarak, *Ar.*). Greek στύραξ. Fragrant resin from several trees; see below.——*Indian storax* (सिह्लक - sihlaka, San.; ضرو - darrú, Ar.; سلارس - siláras, Hind. and Dec.; رسمال - rasamála, Malay; ಬೆಳೋರಿ - belóri, Can.; శిలారసముచెట్టు - shilárasamuchettu, Tel.; நெரியாசிப்பார்செடி - neriyásippárchedi, Tam.). Title from habitat. San. from (sil, san. to gather); from exudation gathered from tree. Ar. from syriac. Hind. from (shilárasa, san. the plant). Tel. from (shilárasa, san. liquid storax + chettu, tel. tree). Tam. from (niryása, san. resin + pál, tam. milk + shedi, tam. tree). San. also (shilárasa), meaning stone juice; compare silauras. Ar. also (maiahisáilah), meaning the liquid storax; (míahilubani), meaning milky storax. Tam. also (erigásuççedi), meaning burning + inspissated juice + plant; (neriyarisippárchedi), meaning brittle + rice-like drops + milk plant; from brittle dry transparent balsamic drops of plant, chewed by natives as a preservative to their teeth. Title otherwise Indian silauras, Lord wood. The balsam is Bookher oil, Copal balsam, Incense oil, Liquidambar, Liquid storax, Rose malloes, Solid storax, Sweet gum. Botanically Liquidambar orientale, miller, hamamelideæ [vricsham]. Deciduous, 60 feet high; leaves palmate, lobed; recesses at the base of the veins villous; flowers apetalous. Umbrageous tree resembling a plane; the resin or storax from bark is opaque and semi-fluid, styrax liquidus of chemists; the dried and compressed bark is made into fragrant cakes formerly known as cortex thymiamatis. Gives to pharm., the balsam purified by rectified spirit and straining, styrax præparatus; contains volatile oil [yennay], styrol, crystallizable principle, styracine, and cinnamic acid; stimulant, expectorant; officinal; much used also in native medicine; substituted for british balsam of peru and citrine ointment. No other species here.——*Java storax* (शिलारस - shilárasa, Mahr.; لبنى - lubna, Ar. and Pers.; سلارس کا پیڑ - siláraskáper, Hind.; سلارس کا جھاڑ - siláraskájhár, Dec.; శిలారసము - shilárasamu, Tel.; நெரியாசிப்பால் - neriyásippál, Tam.). Title from habitat. Mahr. from (shilá, san. stone + rasa, san. juice). Ar. from (laban, ar. juice). Hind. from (siláras, hind. storax + per, hind. tree) [true storax]. Dec. from hindostany. Tel. from (shilá, san. stone + rasa, san. juice). Tam. from (niryása, san. gum + pál, tam. milk). Mahr. also (shílakusuma), meaning stone + flower. Tel. also (shilávásamu), meaning stone + habitation. Title otherwise Java silauras. Botanically Altingia excelsa, noronha, hamamelideæ [vricsham]. Alias Liquidambar altingia. 60–100 feet high; leaves 3–4½ inches, glabrous on both surfaces, or with tufts of hairs in the axils of the nerves beneath. Gigantic tree; native of java; bark is bitter, hot, and aromatic, and when wounded affords a storax; see indian storax for properties.——*Liquid storax* (میعہ سائلہ - míahisáilah, Hind.). Same as Indian storax.——*True storax* (شجر اصطرك - shajariustarak, Ar.; درخت میعہ - darakhtimíah, Pers.; سلارس کا پیڑ - siláraskáper, Hind.; سلارس کا جھاڑ - siláraskájhár, Dec.). Title from product. Ar. from (shajar, ar. tree + ustarak, ar. storax). Pers. from (darakht, pers. tree + míah, ar. storax). Hind. from (siláras, hind. storax + per, hind. tree) [java storax]. Dec. from hindostany. Title otherwise Officinal storax, True silauras. Hebrew libneh. Poplar of the Bible. Botanically Styrax [dhoopam] officinale, linn., styraceæ [vricsham, 84]. Deciduous shrub, 1–2 feet high; leaves ovate, beneath villous; racemes simple, shorter than the leaf; flowers white, flowering in July. Plant of the levant, greece, palestine, syria; yields a solid resin somewhat resembling benzoin [q.v.]; agreeable odour, pleasant, subacidulous, aromatic, slightly pungent taste. This product occurs in three different forms; in grains, in soft masses, in brittle masses. Storax in grains, the rarest and purest of all, in transparent, yellowish-white or reddish-yellow grains, the size of a small bean, the consistence of wax [mom], and capable of consolidating into a thick mass; odour strong, penetrating, and very agreeable; taste aromatic and bitter. Storax in soft mass, or amygdaloid storax softer than the preceding species, easily fusible, with brown fracture, displaying almond-like yellowish tears; odour very sweet, like benzoin, taste sweet and perfumed. Massive hard storax; light brown, yellow, and reddish brown, friable, sometimes slightly tenacious, softens under the teeth; more odourless than that of the two preceding; this variety is very impure. The better kinds of storax burn with a white flame; they are soluble, except the impurities, in alcohol and ether. Medicinally stimulant and expectorant; now little used.

STOTRAM (स्तोत्र - stótra, *San.*). From (stu, san. to praise). Strings of names by which different gods are worshipped. Stotra pautacan is a bard attached to native courts.

STRAITS (اسٹریٹس - strets, *Hind.*). Otherwise Malacca straits. The channel that separates Malayan peninsula from Sumatra. The Straits settlements are British colonies to the north, with head-quarters at Singapore [q.v.]. See vol. I, 31.

STREE (स्त्री - strí, *San.*). Woman. A common dravidian error for Shree [q.v.], which has no connection; cf. stotriem for shrotriem. Polygamy is not frequently found s. in india; and usually when a man marries a second wife while his first is still alive, it is because the latter is barren or has an incurable disease. But the first wife remains even then mistress of the house, and the second is regarded as her younger sister who is to serve her. In the Cooral [q.v.] the women of South india are highly spoken of because of their many virtues.——*Stree dhánam* (స్త్రీధనము - strídhanamu, Tel.). From (above + dhana, san. property). Dowry. Property belonging to a woman, which follows a law of succession different from that which regulates other property. For Mahomedan dowry see Mahar.

STYLE PLANT (पाथरी - pát'harí, *Mahr.*; వాడతెడ్డాకు - vádateddáku, *Tel.*; எழுத்தாணிப்பூண்டு - ezhuttánippúndu, *Tam.*). Title from appearance of flowers. Mahr. from (páta, mahr. line + ari, mahr. row); flagelliform leaf. Tel. from (váda, tel. boat + teddu, tel. oar + áku, tel. leaf); flagelliform leaf. Tam. from (ezhuttáni, tam. style + púndu, tam. plant); from flower shooting up in the form of a style. Tam. also (kadargozhuppai), meaning sea + flourisher. Title otherwise Sarment lettuce. Botanically Launea pinnatifida, cass., compositæ [vricsham, 74]. Alias Lactuca sarmentosa; Microrhynchus sarmentosus; Prenanthes sarmentosa. Stems twiggy, filiform, procumbent, here and there bearing roots and leaves; leaves close together, sinuately pinnatifid; lobes, obtuse or subacute; peduncles one-headed, somewhat shorter than the leaf, bearing at the apex subimbricated scaly bracts, scariose at the margin; flowers yellow; in sandy places. Sand-binder [manal]; a widely diffused humble plant, with long flagelliform runners; juice mixed with karanj [q.v.] seed oil largely used as an external application in rheumatism; juice also used as a sodorific for children.

SUDDER (صدر - sadr, *Ar.*). From (sadara, ar. to lead). Chief. Part of lacab; as Sudder ood deen, chief of religion [ism].——*Sudder adawlut* (صدر عدالت - sadradálat, Hind.). From (above + adálat, ar. court). The supreme court, the name of the highest court established under the East india company in each Presidency, and consisting of two sides, known as the Sudder diwauny adawlut or Chief civil court and the Sudder nizaumat or Fowjdarry adawlut, the Chief criminal court. The Sudder adawluts have been replaced by High courts [adawlut].——*Sudder ameen* (صدر امین - sadramín, Hind.). From (above + amín, ar. arbitrator). Formerly a native civil judge. Some of a higher grade were distinguished as Principal sudder ameens.——*Sudder o mofussil* (صدر و مفصل - sadromufassal, Hind.). From (above + mufassal, ar. separate). Town and country.

SUGAR (शर्करा - sharkará *San.*; سکر - sukkar, *Ar.*; شکر - shakar, *Pers.*; شکر - shakkar, *Hind.*; ಸಕ್ಕರೆ - sakkare, *Can.*; చక్కెర - tsakkera, *Tel.*; പഞ്ചസാര - pañchasára, *Mal.*; சருக்கரை - sharkkarai, *Tam.*). Both title and vernaculars from sanscrit. San. means piece; granulated sugar. Saccharum of chemists. Chiefly product of Saccharum officinarum, l., gramínaceæ [sugar-cane]. Extracted however if necessary by process from several other plants; as from arenga [gomooty], bassia [mohwah], borassus [palmyra], calotropis [yercum], caryota [bastard sago palm], cocos [cocoanut], corypha [talipot], phœnix [kharjooram], and sorghum [cholum]. Sugar is either crystallized or amorphous. White, brown, and pink candy [q.v.], and white and brown sugar are examples of the first; and barley-sugar of the second. Muscovado or raw-sugar is a mixture of crystalline and amorphous sugar. For the different kinds of sugar see below under Sugar-cane. Crystallized sugar should be nearly white, dry, and entirely soluble in water; the last quality shows freedom from the ordinary adulterations, sand, and flour; the white powdery sugar obtainable in most bazaars generally contains a considerable proportion of insoluble material. Sugar includes on the average about .5 per cent. of water, the uncrystallizable part of the juice constituting either treacle or molasses which is about 23 per cent. Sugar when concentrated is highly antiseptic, it is frequently employed in the preservation of vegetable, animal, and medicinal substances; in cases of poisoning by copper [taumram], arsenic [paushanam], or corrosive sublimate [shavveeram], it acts as antidote, and white sugar finely pulverised is occasionally sprinkled upon ulcers with unhealthy granulations; pure cane sugar is medicinally demulcent, nutritive, and dietetic; root is also demulcent and diuretic; sugar and treacle largely used in native medicines; gives to pharm. saccharum purificatum; also treacle the uncrystallised residue of the refining of sugar, theriaca; also syrupus simplex. Unrefined sugar is offered at the shrines of gods, and presented by inferiors to superiors as mark of respect.——(1) *Sugar apple* (سفرجل شیرین - safarjalishírín, Hind.). Same as Common anona.——*Sugar bean* (شکر لوبیا - shakkarlobiyá, Hind.). Same as Country lobyah.——*Sugar-cane* (इक्षु - ikshu, San.; ऊस - úmsa, Mahr.; قصب السکر - kasabussukkar, Ar.; نی شکر - naishakar, Pers.; گنا - ganná, Hind. and Dec.; تبو - tabu, Malay; ಕಬ್ಬು - kabbu, Can.; கரும்பு - karimbu, Too.; చెరుకు - cheruku, Tel.; ଆଖୁ - áku, Oor.; കരിമ്പ് - karimbu, Mal.; උක් - uk, Singh.; கரும்பு - karumbu, Tam.). Title from product. San. from (ish, san. to desire). Mahr. from sanscrit. Ar. from (kasab, ar. reed + sukkar, ar. sugar). Pers. from (nai, pers. reed + shakar, pers. sugar). Mal. means dark color. Singh. from sanscrit. San. also (rasála), meaning ornamented by juice [hurrially, mango]; (mahárasa), meaning great juice; (shastra), meaning weapon, as of cauman; (pundraka), meaning auspicious, applies to the red variety. (kántáraka), meaning produced in forest, the red variety. Mahr. also (úsa). Hind. also (ûkh). Dec. also (gánda). Tel. also (árukanupulakranuga), meaning six + joint + sugar-cane; (kanupulacheruku), meaning joint + sugar-cane; (pottikanupulacheruku), meaning short + joint + sugar-cane; (lávucheruku), meaning thick + sugar-cane; (tellacheruku), meaning white + sugar-cane. Tam. also (ukkiragandi), meaning strong smell. Title otherwise Gannah, Juicy reed, Ookh, Sugar reed. Botanically Saccharum [sharam] officinarum, linn., gramínaceæ [vricsham, 156]. Culm 6–12 feet; panicles terminal, spreading, erect, oblong, 1–3 feet long, of a grey color from the large quantity of long soft hairs surrounding the flowers, ramifications alternate, very ramous, expanding; flowers hermaphrodite in pairs, one sessile the other pedicelled; calyx two-leaved, smooth; corolla one-valved, membranaceous, rose-colored. Strong cane-stemmed grass, one of the largest, culms marked in spaces by knots or large and swollen joints, large feathery plume of flowers; wild and cultivated; thrives from the equator to the 32° of latitude; the sucrose is contained in the loose cellular inodorous juicy pith with which the stalk is filled; this gives the best known of commercial sugars. Raw sugar, or goor [q.v.], is variable in purity; sugar-cane jaggery [q.v.] is the crude inspissated juice of the sugar-cane often substituted for treacle; refined sugar, or muscovado, is goor refined so as to afford a sugar of very white color, solid, hard, friable, brilliant in some parts, scarcely diaphanous, sonorous, phosphorescent by friction in the dark; loaf sugar is the product of the evaporation of the syrup of refined sugar; candy [q.v.] is crystallized sugar, the crystals are four-sided, with dihedral or sometimes trihedral summits; molasses is uncrystallizable sugar, liquid, thick, of deep color, strong smell, about 1½ per 100 of the whole produce of the cane; caramel is burnt sugar; rum is the alcoholic liquid obtained by the fermentation of molasses. The sugar-cane was originally a native of india, and has been known here from time immemorial; introduced into general use in europe by the saracens and through the crusades; stated not to have been known to the ancient greeks and latins, but lucan has the line, quique bibunt tenera dulces ab arundine succos; the periplus speaks of μέλι τὸ καλάμινον, τὸ λεγόμενον σάκχαρ; and strabo stated that reeds in india yielded honey [shahad] without bees [tainee]; the theory that σάγκαρον meant tabasheer [q.v.] is not sustainable. The cane grows well on a good loam [pasalay munn] or light clay [calimunu]; the season of planting is soon after the commencement of the rains [mazhay]; the chief requisites are frequent ploughing of the soil, much manuring [yeroo], and careful removal of weeds; and in those varieties requiring much moisture the land must occasionally be artificially watered; a too wet or too dry season is injurious to the sugar-cane; the crops suffer much from the depredations of wild animals, particularly elephants [q.v.], wild hogs [soor], jackals [q.v.], besides caterpillars [cumbly poochy] and worms [keerah]; white-ants [q.v.] are also destructive. Ground prepared for this cultivation in south in maushy [mausam] or february, on coromandel in cheitram or april, on w. coast in chingom or august and cunny or september; seed sown in south in veiyaushy or may, on coromandel in cheitram or april, on w. coast in chingom or august and cunny or september; no nursery; the top knot of the cane is cut and put in water for three days; afterwards it is covered with straw, when it sprouts within five days and is washed and planted; while under growth is weeded and watered; cane is of blue color when fit to be cut one year after; cut at bottom with a sharp knife. For extraction of juice by the mill see Aulay. The following is the ordinary process for separating the sugar from the cane juice; the juice is first boiled, adding choonam [q.v.] at the rate of three ounces for every twenty-four pucka seers [q.v.]; when the contents of the boiler feel waxy to the touch, they are poured off into chatties [q.v.] with a six inch mouth and having small holes at the bottom; the syrup in the molasses drains through these holes; in this state the mass is kept usually for six or eight months, or for at least six weeks at any rate; any remaining syrup in the mass is then drained off by placing it in bamboo [q.v.] baskets, and squeezing it in a cloth; the sugar is then dissolved in water, and boiled a second time, adding from time to time a little ghee [q.v.] and milk [paul] to clarify the sugar; after it has been sufficiently boiled, the sugar is put again into wide mouthed pots having holes at the bottom, and left to cool and crystalize; any remaining syrup in the sugar drains away through these holes; the outside of the pots is coated over with cowdung [shauny]; a creeping water plant, hydrilla verticillata, rich., is placed on the top of the sugar to make the sugar white and remove any syrupy or black substance; sometimes these plants are also placed at the bottom of the sugar; the plants are renewed every day for five or six days; the sugar is then thoroughly dried and kept for use. To make sugar-candy, the second of the above boilings is curtailed, and the syrup is poured into pots, in which are placed thin slips of bamboo [q.v.]; cloth is then tied over the mouths of these pots, and they are stood for forty days on paddy husk; the sugar crystallizes round these slips. This is the method generally adopted by natives for the manufacture of sugar in south india; in some places however sugar is manufactured according to the european method, and with the help of steam machines; the process for instance employed at aska is the so-called diffusion-process, and consists in chopping up the sugar-cane into small shavings by rapidly revolving knives, the juice being then extracted by a thorough saturation in water, and the saturated juice being boiled down into sugar after undergoing various process of cleaning and refining. Cattle [maud] and horses [ghorah] eat sugar-cane readily; it is fattening, and makes excellent fodder; stalks are chewed by natives. Several varieties cultivated here; some being grown entirely for the manufacture of sugar, others for eating raw; the latter are as a rule thicker, softer, and more juicy than the former. There is a Tamil proverb:—பெருங் குலத்தில் பிறந்தாலும் புத்தி அற்றவன் கரும்புப் பூப்போல—"though born in a high "family, a fool is like a sugar-cane flower"; sugar-cane should be cut before it flowers; the flower destroys value of the cane and a fool kills reputation of the family. And another:—களர் நிலத்தில் கரும்புவை—"plant sugar-cane in calar [q.v.] or "alkaline soil." And another:—ஆனிஆனை வாலொத்த கரும்பு—"in june sugar-cane is like an elephant's tail;" referring to its stem. The cooral says:—சொல்லப் பயன்படு வர் சான்றோர் கரும்புபோற் கொல்லப் பயன்படு கீழ்—"the great bestow their alms as soon as they are informed; "but the mean, like the sugar-cane, only when they are tortured "to death." Compare the following, where transl. is of second term:—Aloe littoralis (ikshuramalliká), meaning sweet juice + giving + jasmine; Hygrophila spinosa (ikshugandhá), smell; Ipomæa digitata (ikshugandhá), smell; Saccharum spontaneum (ikshugandhá), smell; Tribulus terrestris (ikshugandhá), smell; see gloss. paragraphs. Wild sugar-cane, or Devil sugar-cane as in the vernaculars, is botanically Saccharum [sharam] procerum, kœnig., graminaceæ [vricsham, 156]; very lofty grass; leaves are given in cow [pashoo] confinement; culms and leaves are food for elephants [q.v.]; yields but little sugar; makes roofs for houses, rafts for crossing rivers, railings for enclosures, and biers to carry dead bodies. Wild sugar-cane is also a name given to Naunal [q.v.].——*Sugar millet* (शर्कराजूर्ण - sharkarájúrna, San.). Same as Sweet cholum.——*Sugar-palm* (شکرتار - shakkartár, Hind.). Same as Gomooty.——(2) The following are the varieties of cane sugar in the bazaar.——*Boorah shakkaray* (بوراشکر - búráshakkar, Hind.; బూరాశక్కెర - búrátsakkera, Tel.; തരിപ്പഞ്ചസാര - tarippañchasára, Mal.; பூராச்சருக்கரை - púráççarukkarai, Tam.). Hind. from (búrá, hind. powder-like + shakkar, hind. sugar). Mal. from (tari, mal. grain + pañchasára, mal. sugar). Tam. also (naváttuççarukkarai), meaning candy + sugar, from its appearance like powdered sugar-candy. Finest native sugar in white crystals. From Ashtagram and Aska. ——*Cand shakkaray* (قند کی شکر - kandkíshakkar, Hind.; కండశక్కెర - kandatsakkera, Tel.; கன்சருக்கரை - kansarukkarai, Tam.). Hind. from (kand, ar. sugar-candy + shakkar, hind. sugar). Loaf sugar.——*Naut shakkaray* (देशशर्करा - déshasharkará, San.; مخطومی شکر - makhtúmíshakkar, Hind.; ಉರುಸಕ್ಕರೆ - úrasakkare, Can.; నాటుశక్కెర - nátutsakkera, Tel.; നാട്ടുപഞ്ചസാര - náttupañchasára, Mal.; நாட்டுச்சருக்கரை - náttuççarukkarai, Tam.). Hind. from (makhtúmí, hind. country + shakkar, hind. sugar). Hind. also (lálshakkar), meaning red sugar. Tel. also (bellaputsakkera), meaning jaggery + sugar. Tam. also (shivappuççarukkarai), meaning red + sugar; also (shélañjarukkarai), meaning salem town + sugar. Country sugar, whitey brown.——*Raub shakkaray* (راب شکر - rábshakkar, Hind.; రాప్శక్కెర - ráptsakkera, Tel.; இராப்சருக்கரை - irábsarukkarai, Tam.). Hind. from (ráb, hind. syrup + shakkar, hind. sugar). Unrefined moist sugar.——*Vellay shakkaray* (श्वेतशर्करा - shvétasharkará, San.; چینی شکر - chínishakkar, Hind.; ಬಿಳಿಸಕ್ಕರೆ - bilisakkare, Can.; తెల్లశక్కెర - tellatsakkera, Tel.; വെൺപഞ്ചസാര - venpañchasára, Mal.; வெள்ளைச் சருக்கரை - vellaiççarukkarai, Tam.). Hind. from (chíní, hind. chinese + shakkar, hind. sugar). Mal. also (chínippañchasára), meaning chinese sugar; also (vensharkkara), meaning white sugar. Tam. also (shíniççarukkarai), meaning china + sugar; also (shíni), same. White sugar.

SUJJEE (سجی - sajjí, *Hind.*). Impure carbonate of soda. Same as Sowdoo.——*Sujjee khaur* (सर्ज्जिक्षार - sarjjikshára, San.; सज्जीखार - sajjíkhára, Mahr.; سجی کھار - sajjíkhár, Hind.; సజ్జక్షారము - saddzákáramu, Tel.; ഉമരിക്ഷാരം - umariççáram, Mal.; சச்சிக்காரம் - shaççikkáram, Tam.). Title from hindostany. San. from (sarjji, san. natron + kshára, san. alkali). Hind. from (sajjí, hind. impure carbonate of soda + khár, hind. alkali). Tel. from sanscrit. Mal. from (umari, mal. salicornia brachiata, roxb. + cháram, mal. ashes). Tam. from sanscrit. Tel. also (lótásaççi), meaning vessel + natron. Barilla or impure carbonate of soda prepared by burning the following plants, all of which belong to Chenopodiaceæ:—Anthrocnemum indicum, moq.; Salicornia brachiata, roxb. [chook]; Salsola kali, willd.; Suæda indica, moq.; Suæda nudiflora, moq. [indian saltwort]. Distinguish from potash [jharka namak]. Distinguish from the carbonate of soda made from the minerals Oovarmunn cauram [q.v.] and Poongauram [q.v.]. Barill as medicine is primarily antacid, secondarily alterative. Used in dyeing [shauyam].——*Sujjee matty* (سجی مٹی - sajjímattí, Hind.). From (above + mattí, hind. earth). Any sowdoo [q.v.] soil.

SULLA (చల్ల - tsalla, *Tel.*). Cool. Also buttermilk.——*Salivendra* (చలివేంద్ర - tsalivéndra, Tel.). From (above + pandili, tel. shed). Water pandaul [inam] where water is given gratis to travellers.——*Sullapully* (చల్లపల్లి - tsallapalli, Tel.). From (tsalla, tel. buttermilk + palli, tel. village). Tel. also (dévarákóta), meaning god's fort. Zemindarry; Kistna dist., Bunder tal.; pop. 58,925; square miles 192. Otherwise called Devarcote. The ancestors of the family called Yerlagadda were cultivators of the Cumma caste who settled in the district three centuries ago. Yerlagadda goornova naidoo procured the zemindarry of Devarcote in A.D. 1576. In 1732 during the incursions of Asaf jah, the estate was taken under the Fowjdar's management for a time. After the French had established themselves at Masulipatam in 1751 they obtained from Salaubut jung a grant of the Acoolamannud and Goodoor pergunnahs [q.v.] as a jagheer [q.v.] and allowed Yerlagadda codandaraman a pension for maintenance. When the English in 1759 expelled the French from Masulipatam, Codandaraman again assumed the title of zemindar but was forced to fly to Condaveed. He died in 1791 and Government recognised as Zemindar the eldest son Vencatramana naidoo. In 1798 he was deposed and his adopted son Ankanna was proclaimed Zemindar. He built the temple at Shivagunga close to Masulipatam at an enormous cost, and erected a house in the Sullapully fort for Rs. 1,32,000 on the model of one at Benares. Estate since then twice under Court of Wards. The young Rajah in 1851 pulled down the temple his grandfather had built at Shivagunga and began to reconstruct it of Condapully granite [caroom cull]. Places of archæological interest:—Ayyanky, Cauza, Ghuntashaala, Nidmole, Pedda cullepully, Shreecaucoolam, Yanamlacoodroo.

SULLAH (سیلا - selá, *Hind.*). Gauze for turbans [mull, puggry, turban].

SULTAN (سلطان - sultán, *Ar.*; സുല്ത്താൻ - sultán, *Mal.*). From (saluta, ar. to predominate). Strength or might, used in the sense of ruler. This arabian title, first taken by Mahmood of ghuznee, fell quickly into disesteem even among the turks themselves, having been assumed by many of their petty rulers. Many of the native princes of the malay archipelago assumed it after their conversion to mahomedanism, in lieu of the sanscrit name of Rajah [q.v.] or the native ones of Ratoo and Pangheran. It was taken by the princes of Bantam, and the only considerable independent malay prince of Borneo now uses it. The word is taken as alam; as Sultan khan, alam + plaumat [ism]. The Sultauny was a system of coins [fanam, naunyam, pagoda] so called in Mysore under Tippoo sultan.——*Sultan's basil* (سلطان الرياحين - sultánurrayáhín, Ar.). Same as Fragrant toolsy.——*Sultan's battery* (ഗണപതിവട്ടം - gánapatiyattam, Mal.). Title from the fort of tippoo sultan. Vern. from (ganapati, san. the deity + vattam, mal. circle). Town; Malabar dist., Wynaud tal.; lat. 11° 40′; long. 76° 17′; from Calicut N.E. 43 miles; from Manantoddy S.E. 19 miles. In Ganapativuttam amshom. Tippoo sultan had a fort here. British regiment stationed in early part of present century.——*Sultan's canal* (സുല്ത്താൻതോട് - sultántótu, Mal.). From (sultán, ar. ruler + tótu, mal. channel). Canal; Malabar dist., Chiracal tal.; lat. 12° 01′ to 12° 02′ N.; long. 75° 15′ to 75° 17′ E. Artificial work, about two miles in length, executed in 1766 by Ally rajah [audy rajah], husband of the Beeby of Cannanore, when managing the Colattiry domains for Hyder ally. Connects Mount delly river with the backwater formed at the mouth of the Taliparamba and Belliapatam rivers, and thus gives uninterrupted water communication at all seasons. Formerly boats going to or from the north had to go out to sea at this point. ——*Sultan's tree* (سلطان الاشجار - sultánulashjár, Ar.). Title from height. Same as Common sirissa.——*Sultan well* (سلطان باوڑی - sultánbáuri, Hind.). From (above + báurí, hind. well). Well on river-bank, with channel [q.v.] to bring water close for percolation or entry.——*Sultauna* (سلطانہ - sultána, Ar.). Female form of sultan.——*Wild sultan seed* (حب السلاطين صحراٸی - habbusalátínisahráí, Ar.). Same as Wild jamalgota.

SUMACH (سماق - sumák, *Hind.*). From arabic meaning high; grown on elevated lands. Botanically the Rhus genus, anacardiaceæ [vricsham, 45]. Shrubs, bushes and trees; leaves usually compound; flowers small; fruits small, nearly dry or slightly juicy, containing a single bony one-seeded stone; wood grey, soft, often streaked, with a yellow or brown heart-wood. The species best known to the natives are shown below.—— *American sumach* (سماق امریکا - sumákiamrikali, Ar.). Same as Divy divy.——*Red lac sumach* (कर्कटशृङ्गी - karkatashringí, San.; काकडशिंगी - kákadashingí, Mahr.; کاکڑا سنگی - kákrásingí, Hind. and Dec.; కాకరశింగి - kākarashingi, Tel.; கர்க்கடகச்சிங்கி - karkkádagaççingi, Tam.). Title from varnish. San. from (karkata, san. crab + shringa, san. claw), from galls like scorpion's or crab's claw [kakrasinghy]. Mahr., &c., from sanscrit. San. also (shringí), meaning horn-like. Title otherwise Crab's claw, Japanese tallow sumach, Japanese varnish. Botanically Rhus [sumach] succedanea, linn., anacardiaceæ [vricsham, 45]. Alias Rhus acuminata. Tree about 30 feet high, everywhere glabrous, except the panicle in some varieties; leaves crowded at the ends of the branches, 6–18 inches; petiole terete, slender; leaflets 2–5 by $1\frac{1}{2}$–$2\frac{1}{2}$ inches, petiolulate, elliptic-oblong, or oblong, or ovate-lanceolate, tip very slender; base rounded or acute, straight or oblique; nerves numerous, slightly arched, slender; panicles axillary, half the length of the leaves, slender, lax, with a very few scattered hairs, or glabrous; flowers $\frac{1}{12}$ inch diameter, yellow green; pedicel slender; sepals broadly ovate, obtuse; petals much longer, oblong, or obtuse; disk five-lobed; drupes $\frac{1}{4}$ inch diameter, in drooping panicles, gibbous, compressed epicarp very thin, bursting irregularly; stone compressed, bony, surrounded with wax. The horn-like excrescences caused by insects on the branches are called kakrasinghy [q.v.]; they are large, hollow, thin-walled, generally cylindrical, tapering to either extremity. The excrescences are medicinally tonic, expectorant; quoted in pharm., non-officinal, like oak galls [mauchicoy]. A varnish is yielded; the seed gives on being pressed an oil, which soon congeals to the consistence of tallow, and from which in japan candles are prepared.——*Tanner's sumach* (سماق الدباغین - summákuddabbághín, Ar.; سماق - sumák, Pers.; مچھلی - machhlí, Hind.). Title from use. Ar. means tanner's sumach. Pers. from arabic. Hind. means fish or sinew. Ar. also (timtim). Ar. also (samákíl). Pers. also (sumákishakkí), meaning doubtful sumach; (máhi), meaning fish. Hind. also (tatrak); (tamátír). Greek ῥοῦς ἐρυθρή. Title otherwise Elm leaved sumach, European sumach, Fish sumach, Mutchly, Varnish tree. Botanically Rhus [sumach] coriaria, linn., anacardiaceæ [vricsham, 45]. The leaves are about a foot long, pinnate, with from five to seven pairs of leaflets and an odd one, like the leaves of the common elm; the petioles and midribs of the leaflets are covered with a reddish brown tomentum; the leaflets are hairy and very astringent. Fruit is imported in large quantities from persia; considered of good quality when odour is strong, color of a lively green, well ground, and free from stalks. The dry fruit is so small and flat that it looks like a seed; it is either circular or oblong; generally about a line and-a-half in diameter, and half a line in thickness; it is covered with a very thin and light pericarp, which is reddish-brown or rust-colored, odourless, slightly astringent in taste, and can be easily removed from the seeds by rubbing between the hands; the seeds are about one-half smaller in size, almost always oblong, very hard, slightly inclining to be kidney-shaped and possess no particular taste or smell. The pericarp of the seeds and the leaves are medicinally astringent. Compound powder;- take of the pericarp of the seeds of rhus coriaria, butea-gum [palaus] and the gum of odina wodier [wodier], in powder, each ten drachms; the fruit of carum roxburghianum [ajmood ajwann], in powder, five drachms; cinnamon bark [cinnamon], in powder, four drachms; and opium [aphainam], in powder, one drachm; mix well, pass the powder through a fine sieve, rub it lightly in a mortar and keep it in a closed bottle. Dose; from five to forty grains; forty grains contain one grain of opium. Substituted for pulv. ipecac. compositus, pulv. kino compositus, and pulv. cretæ aromat. cum opio. Leaves and fruit are boiled down, and a liquid extract obtained; this used as an astringent; leaves made into poultices applied to the abdomen in diarrhœa of children; leaves and fruit used as styptic, astringent, and tonic. Fruit is acid. Dried and pulverized leaves furnish a tan; and ounce contains about .75 grains of tannin; of all astringents it bears the greatest resemblance to galls [mauchicoy].

SUMPAUJEY (ಸಂಪಾಜೆ - sampáje, *Can.*). Part of Bylehully village, ghaut; South canara dist., Ooppinangady tal.; pop. 216; from Mangalore E. 54 miles; from Poottore S.E. 30 miles. The ghaut [q.v.] connects S. canara with Coorg. Wheeled traffic.

SUNDAVOLE (చందవోలు - tsandavólu, *Tel.*). From (tsandu, tel. proper name + prólu, tel. town). Tel. also (velnádu), meaning outside + country. Village; Kistna dist., Repully tal.; pop. 2,819; acres 4,626; lat. 16° 01′; long 80° 39′; from Masulipatam W.S.W. 35 miles; from Repully W. 15 miles; from the sea N. 9 miles. Of great antiquity. Mentioned in Hindoo ballads and poems. Mound outside the village contains Booddhist [booddha] remains. Temple built by Chola [q.v.] kings, with inscriptions, dated A.D. 1154, 1171 and 1176. Gold coins [naunyam] have been found.

SUNDOOR (సొండూరు - sondúru, *Tel.* sandúr). From (sandu, tel. gap + úru, tel. village) [sa]. Ghaut village near Bheemagundy pass.——(1) Territory, Bellary. An independent state and pays no peshcush. For description, &c., see vol. II, appendix XII. Places of archæological interest:—The temple of Comaurasawmy, Ramanmullay, Sundoor. Principal trig. station:—Ramanmullay. The leading places, &c., in the territory are the following.——*Bheemagundy* (భీమగండి - bhímagandi, Tel.). From (bhíma, san. fearful; one of the five pándavas + gandi, tel. pass). Ghaut; lat. 15° 06′; long. 76° 38′; from Bellary W. 21 miles; from Sundoor N.E. 3 miles. One of the three passes by which the Sundoor state is entered, through which runs the main road from Bellary to Ramandroog. Yettinhutty is at the entrance.——*Comaurasawmy's hill* (ಕುಮಾರಸ್ವಾಮಿಗುಡ್ಡ - kumárasvámigudda, Can.). From (kumára, san. skanda, the son-god + svámí, san. lord + gudda, can. hill). Hill, Place of pilgrimage; lat. 15° 01′; long. 76° 37′; height 2,965 feet; from Bellary W.S.W. 25 miles; from Sundoor S.S.E. 5 miles. South of Ramanmullay overlooking Sundoor valley; used as a sanitarium. Ancient temple of Comaurasawmy on the hill, much visited by pilgrims from all parts of India. The jatrah [pundiguy, 6d] is triennial. The temple of Parvaty is of stone to the summit and has a wagon-shaped roof like that of the Bheema rath [q.v.] at Mauvellipore.——*Oblagundy* (ఓబలగండి - ublagandi, Tel.). From (aóbilamu, tel. name of a hill + gandi, tel. pass). Pass; lat. 15° 03′; long. 76° 42′; from Bellary W.S.W. 18 miles; from Sundoor S.W. 4 miles. W. pass from Ramandroog plateau. A stream forms main feeder of Darojee lake.——*Ramandroog* (ರಾಮನದುರ್ಗ - rámanadurga, Can.). See sep. title.——*Ramanmullay* (ರಾಮನಮಲೆ - rámanamale, Can.). From (ráma, san. the god + male, can. hill). Sanscrit name (rámagiri). Trig. station; lat. 15° 07′ 34·57″; long. 76° 30′ 26·65″; height 3,256 feet; from Bellary W. 30 miles; from Sundoor W.N.W. 6 miles.——*Sundoor* (సొండూరు - sondúru, Tel.). See below.——*Yettinhutty* (ಯತ್ತಿನಹಟ್ಟಿ - yettinahatti, Can.). From (ettu, can. bullock + hatti, can. cattle-pen). Village; pop. 1,548; lat. 15° 08′; long. 76° 32′; from Bellary W. 21 miles; from Sundoor N.E. 5 miles.——(2) Village, Head-quarters of the Sundoor Rajah; Bellary dist., Sundoor territory; pop. 4,347; lat. 15° 00′; long. 76° 36′; height 1,815; from Adony S.W. 60 miles; from Bellary W. 25 miles; from Hospett S.E. 16 miles; from Hurpanhully E.N.E. 43 miles; from Madras W.N.W. 286 miles; from Tadpatry W. 96 miles. After capture of Gooty in 1779, Hyder ally took Sundoor, and built strong fort called Krishna nugger near entrance of valley by Bheemagundy pass.

SUNDRA (खदिर - khadira, *San.*; लालखैर - lálakhaira, *Mahr.*; لال کہیر - lálkhair, *Hind.*; ಕಗ್ಗಲಿಮರ - kaggalimara, *Can.*; చండ్ర - tsandra, *Tel.*; കരിങ്ങാലി - karinnáli, *Mal.*; கருங்காலி - karungáli, *Tam.*). Title from teloogoo. San. from (khad, san. to be firm); from hard durable wood [biswool, catechu, shoondy]. Mahr. from hindostany. Hind. from (lál, hind. red + khair, hind. acacia catechu, willd.). Can. from (kaggu, can. firm + mara, can. tree). Mal. from tamul. Tam. from (karumai, tam. blackness + kál, tam. foot). San. also (hóma-vriksha), meaning sacrifice + tree; (mridupatrika), meaning soft + leaf. Tel. also (nallatsandra), meaning black + the tree. Title otherwise Caroongauly. Botanically Acacia [cantalam] sundra, dec., leguminosæ [vricsham, 48]. Specific name from teloogoo. Alias Acacia chundra; Mimosa chundra. Tree, 20–30 feet; branches armed with recurved stipulary prickles, sometimes unarmed; leaves bipinnated; pinnæ fifteen to twenty pair; leaflets numerous, small, linear; spikes one to three together, axillary, peduncled, shorter than the leaves, many-flowered; corolla five-cleft; stamens distinct; flowers small, yellow; legumes thin, flat, lanceolate; seeds few; flowers July to August. Scarcely more than a variety of Acacia catechu, willd. [catechu], from which it differs in its fewer leaflets, total absence of pubescence, and the dark-brown color of its branchlets. Yields a gum similar to catechu gum [gond]. Wood tolerably close-grained and durable; dark red color, veined with a darker shade of streaks, very heavy, used for beams and posts, ploughs, mortars and pestles, and is good for piles and sleepers; not attacked by insects; apt to split with nails.——*Bald sundra* (బోడచండ్ర - bódatsándra, Tel.). Same as Shoondy.——*Foreign white sandra* (சீமைவெள்வேல் - shímaivelvél, Tam.). Same as Anasandra [q.v.].——*White sundra* (शमी - shamí, San.; धवलखैर - dhavalakhaira, Mahr.; ಮುಗಳಿ - mugali, Can.; తెల్లచండ్ర - tellatsandra, Tel.; கொவிள் - kovil, Tam.). Title from flowers. San. from (sham, san. to destroy); cf. prosopis spicigera, linn. [shamee]. Mahr. from (dhavala, san. white + khaira, mahr. acacia catechu, willd.). Tel. from (tella, tel. white + tsandra, tel. acacia sundra, dec.). Can. also (banni), properly prosopis spicigera, linn. Botanically Acacia [cantalam] suma, kurz., leguminosæ [vricsham, 48]. Alias Mimosa suma. Tree, armed with straight stipulary thorns; pinnæ ten to twenty pair, with a large concave gland above the base of the petiole, and two or three between the last two to three pairs of pinnæ; spikes one to six, axillary; legume linear, thin, six to eight-seeded; flowers white; a very common tree, remarkably conspicuous for its white bark; flowering in the rainy season. Has a very hard wood.

SUNN (शण - shana, *San.*; सण - sana, *Mahr.*; सोणबु - sónabu, *Conc.*; سن - san, *Pers.* and *Hind.*; جنب - janab, *Dec.*; ಸಣಬು - sanabu, *Can.*; జనుము - dzanumu, *Tel.*; ଚୋନିପୋତ୍ତ - chonipotta, *Oor.*; വാക്ക - vakka, *Mal*; හණ - hana, *Singh.*; சணல் - shanal, *Tam.*). Title from hindostany. San. from (shán, san. to give). Pers., &c., from sanscrit. Tel. from sanscrit [jute]. Mal. from (valka, san. bark of tree). Singh. from sanscrit. Tam. from sanscrit. San. also (karnashúla), meaning earache; (dhanabári), meaning carrying away wealth; (satinaka), meaning powerful. Hind. also (patsan), meaning corchorus olitorius fibre; (viláitia-krekánár), meaning foreign calotropis fibre. Can. also (henna). Mal. also (chanam); (káttutantalakkotti), meaning wild crotalaria retusa, linn.; (pulivaññi), meaning sour reed. Tam. also (shanappai); (mañji); (kuttiram); (vakkunár), meaning bark fibre. Title otherwise Bengal hemp plant, Bombay hemp, Brown hemp, Concany hemp, Earache plant, False hemp, Gunny, Indian hemp, Janab hemp, Jubbulpore hemp, Madras hemp, Rusty crotolaria, Salsette hemp, Shanal hemp, Striated stalked crotalaria, Sunn hemp, Taag hemp, Travancore flax, Wucknaur. Botanically Crotalaria [ghantaravam] juncea, linn., leguminosæ [vriesham, 48]. Alias Crotalaria benghalensis, fenestrata, porrecta, sericea, tenuifolia, viminea. Small plant, 4–8 feet, erect, branched, more or less clothed with shining silky pubescence or hairs; branches terete, striated; stipules and bracts setaceous; leaves from narrow linear to ovate-lanceolate, acute; calyx deeply five-cleft, densely covered with rusty tomentum, the three lower segments usually cohering at the apex; racemes elongated, terminating every branch; flowers distant; legumes sessile, oblong, broader upwards, about twice the length of the calyx, tomentose and many-seeded; flowers yellow; flowering nearly all year; flowers resemble spanish broom. Menoo [q.v.] says:—"the sacrificial thread [poonool] of a bramin must be of "cotton [q.v.], so as to be put on over his head in three strings; "that of a cshatriya, must be of sunn thread; that of a veisya, "must be of woollen thread." Cultivated in sandy soil, dry; ground prepared on coromandel in caurteecam [mausam] or november and margashiram or december, on w. coast in cunny or september; ploughed dry; seed sown on coromandel in caurteecam or november and margashiram or december, on w. coast in cunny or september; no nursery; scattered through zaddigam [q.v.] mixed with early zonna [cholum] seeds; plant if necessary propped by poles; full-grown crop as tall as zonna or a man's height; pulled up after three months; the fruit bearing part of the plant is cut off and thrown away; the remaining stem is dried in the sun for two days, after which it is dipped in water for three days and again dried in the sun for about three days; the bark is taken from the stem; average price 10 imperial seers for 1 rupee. The fibre is exported from madras under the name of Madras hemp, and from bombay under that of Brown hemp. Seeds used in medicine to purify the blood; narcotic; used in rheumatism. Fibres make strong hemp for cordage, canvas and paper; take tar [keel] easily; when properly prepared, they are much valued in the home markets; in this country they are used for fishing-nets, cordage, canvas, gunny bags, &c.; they are much stronger if left in salt water; with gunny [q.v.] bags, when old, natives make the greater part of their paper [caugaz].——*Shaunam* (शाण - shána, San.). From (shana, san. hemp). Sacred thread [poonool].

SUNNUD (سند - sanad, *Hind.*). From (sanada, ar. to lean against). A document conveying to an individual emoluments, titles, privileges and offices, or the government rights to revenue from land, &c., under the seal of the ruling authority. A sicca sunnud is a stamped grant.——*Sunnud i milkyat i istimrar* (سندملکیت استمرار - sanadimilkiyatiistimrár, Hind.). From (above + milkiyat, ar. proprietary right + istimrár, ar. perpetual). Document by which the British government recognised the ownership of zemindars [q.v.] at a fixed assessment, current chiefly in the Northern circars [q.v.]. See vol. I, 112.

SUNT (سنت کی لکڑی - santkílakrí, *Hind.*). Wood of the Babool [q.v.].

SURPRISE GRASS (چرچرا - chirchirá, *Hind.*; ಅಕ್ಕಬಹುಲ್ಲು - akkabahullu, *Can.*; பிசாசு - pisásu, *Tam.*). Title from crackling sound. Hind. means achyranthes aspera, linn. [indian burr]. Can. from (akkaba, can. surprising + hullu, can. grass). Tam. means devil. Can. also (biliakkabahullu), meaning white + surprising + grass; (ganduakkabahullu), meaning male + surprise grass. Tam. also (melampari). Botanically Panicum [priyangoo] javanicum, poir., graminaceæ [vricsham, 156]. Alias Milium sanguinale; Panicum sanguinale. Culms creeping near the base; the rest erect, smooth, one and-a-half foot high; leaves long, narrow, smooth; racemes sub-digitate, three to eight; spikelets alternate in two series, unequally pedicelled; glumes glabrous; sheaths hairy; western coast. When green yields fair fodder, but is unfit for hay-making as it has no undergrowth.

SUTTENAPULLY (సత్తెనపల్లి - śattenapalli,* *Tel.*). From (satyanna, tel. proper name + palli, tel. village) [sat].——(1) Talook, Kistna district. Tashildar's pay Rs. 175. Area 714 square miles. Population 138,617. Language Teloogoo. E. centre part of district. Bounded north by the Kistna, east by Guntoor talook, west by Pulnaud talook, and south by Narsarowpett talook. On the west the Kistna flows round a range of hills, a continuation of the Pulnaud limestone [choonam cull] formation with remarkable outliers near Achammapett and Beeravullipoya. The road from Guntoor to Pulnaud traverses the talook, passing by Medicondore and Suttenapully; there is a road from Amravatty to Guntoor; and the road from Guntoor to Narsarowpett passes through the south-eastern corner at Firangipooram. In wet weather the black soil [regar] and the water-courses are almost impassable. The most conspicuous object is the hill fortress of Bellamcondah, whose castle-like cliffs stand out prominently to the west of Crossoor. Within sight are the neighbouring fortresses of Condapully and Condaveed; so that the talook must have been a debatable ground in the sixteenth century, when Condapully was the frontier post of Golcondah and Condaveed the frontier post of Vijianugger, while Bellamcondah was taken and retaken, being held at one time by Mussalman at another by Hindoo. Great extent of black soil producing heavy crops of cotton [q.v.], and in this black soil the gneissic rock protrudes here and there, sometimes in picturesque profile, as in the eminence overlooking Crossoor. The most interesting spot is the town of Amravatty with the neighbouring village of Dharanicottah in the north-eastern corner. Industries and Commerce.—Agricultural industry, commerce in cloth and indigo [q.v.]. Irrigation by rain-fed tanks [q.v.]. Places of archæological interest:—Ameenbandah, Amravatty, Bellamcondah, Caumepully, Chintapully, Colalpoody, Crossoor, Dharanicottah, Firangipooram, Garikipaud, Goodipoody, Kaitvaram, Moongode, Mullayyapollem, Panidem, Pedda makkena, Poonoro, Rajpollem, Siripooram, Yeddanapoody, Yincomesla. Trig. stations:—Beeravullipoya, Canchelbode, Chikry, Dhoolipaulla, Lagadapaud, Mannem, Medarsaul, Poolichinta, Worvacull. The leading places, &c., in the talook are the following.——*Achammapett* (అచ్చమ్మపేట - aççammapéta, Tel.). From (aççamma, tel. proper name + péta, tel. suburb). Village; pop. 2,084; lat. 16° 37′; long. 80° 10′; from Crossoor N. 7 miles; from Masulipatam W.N.W. 70 miles. Scene of the murder in 1764 of Jugganna, father of Vasireddy vencataudry naidoo. His widow Achamma, sacrificed herself upon the funeral pile, and the village was called Achammapett. Formerly considerable trade in cloth, still commercial place.——*Amravatty* (అమరావతి - amarávati, Tel.). See sep. title.——*Beeravullipoya* (బీరవల్లిపాయ - bíravallipáya, Tel.). From (bíra, tel. plant, luffa acutangula, roxb. + valli, san. creeper + páya, tel. stream). Village; pop. 1,430; lat. 16° 26′; long. 80° 02′. Natural fortress of limestone [choonam cull] to which surrounding villagers retired in 1816 before the Pindarries. An irrigation tank. Trig. station in lat. 16° 27′ 17·92″; long. 80° 02′ 34·04″; height 1,294 feet; from Bellamcondah S. 3 miles; from Suttenapully W.N.W. 11 miles.——*Bellamcondah* (బెల్లంకొండ - bellamkonda, Tel.). See sep. title.——*Cauchelbode* (కాచెలబోడు - káchelabódu, Tel.). From (káchi, tel. solanum nigrum, linn. + bódu, tel. hillock). Trig. station; lat. 16° 30′ 42·59″; long. 80° 01′ 06·89″; from Suttenapully N.N.W. 14 miles.——*Chikry* (చిక్రి - chikri, Tel.). Trig. station; lat. 16° 35′ 40·48″; long. 80° 07′ 01·31″; height 801 feet.——*Chintapully* (చింతపల్లి - chintapalli, Tel.). From (chinta, tel. tamarind tree, tamarindus indica, linn. + palli, tel. village). Village; pop. 1,176; acres 2,697; lat. 16° 42′; long. 80° 11′; from Crossoor N. 10 miles; from Masulipatam W.N.W. 71 miles. On right bank of Kistna. Once capital of Vasireddy zemindars [q.v.]. In 1794 garrisoned by a battalion of sepoys [q.v.]. The zemindar then changed his residence to Amravatty. The fort was 250 yards by 160, and had six bastions with two entrances. It is now in ruins. Inscription south of the village dated A.D. 1239. The grandsons of Vencataudry naidoo's nephew and the great grandsons of Vencataudry naidoo lived here in receipt of pensions. Ferry.——*Collore* (కొల్లూరు - kollúru, Tel.). See sep. title.——*Crossoor* (క్రోసూరు - krósúru, Tel. krósur *). From (krósha, san. distance of call + úru, tel. village). Village, Talook head-quarters; pop. 2,088; acres 6,006; lat. 16° 33′; long. 80° 11′; from Bezwada W. 30 miles; from Guntoor N.W. 27 miles; from Madras N. 240 miles; from Masulipatam W.N.W. 67 miles; from Vinoocondah N.E. 42 miles. Many old temples. Large irrigation tank.——*Dharanicottah* (ధరణికోట - dharanikóta, Tel.). See sep. title.——*Dhoolipaulla* (ధూళిపాళ్ల - dhúlipálla, Tel.). From (dhúli, san. dust + pádu, tel. village). Trig. station; lat. 16° 25′ 59·52″; long. 80° 07′ 57·31″; height 249 feet; from Suttenapully N.W. 5 miles.——*Firangipooram* (ఫిరంగిపురము - p'hirangipuramu, Tel.). From (farangí, hind. europeans + pura, san. town). Village, Hill, Railway station; pop. 3,594; acres 3,303; lat. 16° 17′; long. 80° 18′; from Crossoor S.S.E. 91 miles; from Masulipatam W. 53 miles. Village is at north end of detached hill. Temple of Veerabhadran [q.v.] with three inscriptions, one of which dated A.D. 1409 records the construction of a tank by the wife of Veera narrain vaima vibhoo in the days of the Reddies. Since 1816 head-quarters of the Catholic missions from Pulnaud to Repully.——*Goodipoody* (గుడిపూడి - gudipúdi, Tel.). From (gudi, tel. temple + púdi, tel. village). Village; pop. 1,845; acres 4,393; lat. 16° 26′; long. 80° 16′; from Crossoor S.S.E. 10 miles; from Masulipatam W.N.W. 62 miles. Temple with five inscriptions, two dated A.D. 1160, others 1163, 1237, and 1243.——*Kistna* (కృష్ణ - krishna, Tel.). See sep. title.——*Lagadapaud* (లగడపాడు - lagadapádu, Tel.). From (lagudu, tel. hawk + pádu, tel. village). Trig. station; lat. 16° 29′ 19·91″; long. 80° 16′ 52·15″; height 225 feet; from Goojjerlapoody E. 2 miles; from Suttenapully N.E. 9 miles.——*Mannem* (మన్నెం - mannem, Tel.). Means hilly land. Trig. station; lat. 16° 22′ 23·62″; long. 79° 55′ 25·42″; height 1,210 feet; from Suttenapully W. 17 miles.——*Maudala* (మాదల - mádala, Tel.). Means a citron, citrus medica, linn. Village; pop. 2,826; acres 7,753; lat. 16° 22′; long. 80° 10′; from Crossoor S. 12 miles; from Masulipatam W.N.W. 68 miles. Old Shiva temple. An irrigation tank.——*Medarsaul* (మేదరసాల - médarasála, Tel.). From (médari, tel. basket weaver + sálu, tel. line). Trig. station; lat. 16° 42′ 02·81″; long. 80° 05′ 59·06″.——*Medicondore* (మేడికొండూరు - médikondúru, Tel.). From (médi, tel. fig tree, ficus glomerata, miq. + konda, tel. hill + úru, tel. village). Village; pop. 1,894; acres 5,056; lat. 16° 20′; long. 80° 20′; from Crossoor S.E. 17 miles; from Masulipatam W.N.W. 56 miles. On Guntoor-Pulnaud road.——*Moongode* (మునుగోడు - munugódu, Tel.). From (munu, tel. front + kódu, tel. rivulet). Village; pop. 1,311; acres 3,491; lat. 16° 34′; long. 80° 17′; from Crossoor E.N.E. 7 miles; from Masulipatam W.N.W. 62 miles. 8 miles west of Amravatty. Now decayed. Inscriptions of reign of Vishnoovardhanan [q.v.], and that of Gonka a Chola [q.v.], regent. Fine tamarind tope [q.v.] and numerous stone circles [azhauram] in the neighbourhood.——*Munney sultan pollem* (మన్నేసుల్తానుపాలెము - mannésultánupálemu, Tel.). From (mannemu, tel. highland + sultán, ar. prince + pálemu, tel. fortified village). Village; pop. 364; acres 941; lat. of village 16° 34′ 55″; long. 80° 00′ 54″; from Crossoor W.N.W. 12 miles; from Masulipatam W.N.W. 81 miles. Title bestowed by the Nizam upon the Chintapully zemindar for subduing certain poligars [q.v.]. An irrigation tank.——*Panidem* (పణిదెము - panidemu, Tel.). From (pannidamu, tel. wager). Village; pop. 1,890; acres 5,035; lat. 16° 28′ 00″; long. 80° 13′ 54″; from Crossoor S.S.E. 6 miles; from Masulipatam W.N.W. 65 miles. Three inscriptions recording private grants, two dated A.D. 1102 and 1282. Another east of the village records a grant by the wife of Kota kaita rajah in A.D. 1231. ——*Pautibunda* (పాటిబండ - pátibanda, Tel.). From (pádu, tel. a village + banda, tel. rock). Village; pop. 2,161; acres 3,107; lat. 16° 28′; long. 80° 20′; from Crossoor E.S.E. 12 miles; from Masulipatam W.N.W. 55 miles. The majority of the cultivators are Catholics [siripooram]. Fine Christian church. Festival on January 6th. Adjoining is a mass of black rock crowned by Hindoo temples.——*Peddacoorpaud* (పెద్దకూరపాడు - peddakúrapádu, Tel.). From (pedda, tel. large + kúra, tel. kitchen vegetable + pádu, tel. village). Village; pop. 2,801; acres 8,890; lat. 16° 28′; long. 80° 18′; from Crossoor E.S.E. 9 miles; from Masulipatam W.N.W. 61 miles. Largest village in talook.——*Poolichinta* (పులిచింత - pulichinta, Tel.). From (puli, tel. sour + chinta, tel. tamarind, tamarindus indica, linn.). Trig. station; lat. 16° 45′ 02·92″; long. 80° 06′ 15·04″; height 1,106 feet; from Poolichinta N.N.E. 2 miles; from Suttenapully N.N.W. 25 miles. ——*Siripooram* (సిరిపురము - siripuramu, Tel.). From (siri, tel. wealth + pura, san. town). Village; pop. 2,193; acres 4,065; lat. 16° 25′; long. 80° 20′; from Crossoor S.E. 14 miles; from Masulipatam W.N.W. 57 miles. Christians here from a remote period. Festival on January 1st. Ruined temple near tank with inscription of A.D. 1165, relating how the Chalookya [q.v.] kingdom passed into the hands of the Cholas. Inscription in Teloogoo records that Cendamaneed, son of Gopa patro, on horseback crossed over the rock from west to east. Indigo plantations.——*Suttenapully* (సత్తెనపల్లి - sattenapalli, Tel.). See below.——*Velpoor* (వేల్పూరు - vélpúru, Tel.). From (vélpu, tel. deity + úru, tel. village). Village; pop. 1,577; acres 5,106; lat. 16° 35′; long. 80° 10′; from Crossoor N. 8 miles; from Masulipatam W.N.W. 68 miles. Ancient pagodas [q.v.].——*Worra cull* (ఓరువకల్లు - óruvakallu, Tel.). Means touch stone. Trig. station; lat. 16° 35′ 33·17″; long. 80° 12′ 24·25″.——**(2)** Village; Kistna dist., Suttenapully tal.; pop. 2,788; acres 3,100; lat. 16° 24′; long. 80° 11′; from Crossoor S. 10 miles; from Masulipatam W.N.W. 66 miles. Residence of zemindar of the Manoor family. Has mud fort, a strong erection with bastions at the angles and a rampart to the eastern face, where was the entrance built by Pedda vencatakrishnamma, zemindar of Chilcaloorpaud during the time of Basaulat jung. Talook [q.v.] cutcherry [q.v.] buildings under construction. Irrigation tank. On the Guntoor-Pulnaud road. A centre of trade. The Manoor zemindars, until lately zemindars of Suttenapully and Chilcaloorpaud, are Bramins. They have an imperial grant dated 1707, the last year of Aurungzeeb's reign, appointing them zemindars and Sheristadars [q.v.] of Moortezahnugger circar [q.v.]. They make use of the title Majmoodar [q.v.] in addition to their family name.

SUTTIMUNGALAM (சத்தியமங்கலம் - shattiyamangalam, *Tam.* satyamangalam *). From (satya, san. truth epithet of vishnu + mangala, san. prosperity) [sat]. Sanscrit name (satyapuri), meaning vishnoo, the truthful + town.——**(1)** Talook, Coimbatore district. Tahsildar's pay Rs. 200. Area 1,185 square miles. About 40 miles from N. to S. and 60 from E. to W. Nearly 600 square miles is hill and forest, 389 acres surveyed. Population, 151,313. Languages, Tamul, Canarese, Teloogoo and Hindostany. The northernmost talook below ghauts. Bounded N. by Collegaul talook; N.W. by Chaumrajnugger talook of Mysore; S., S.E., and S.W. by Pulladam, Erode and Coimbatore talooks respectively; E. by Bhawauny; W. by Goondloopett talook of Mysore. On the N., N.E., N.W., and W. it is enclosed by mountain ranges; the Neilgherries lying to W., and the ghauts S. of the Mysore plateau to the N.W. and N. Through the ghauts [q.v.] are the Guzzelhutty, Hassanore and Talamullay passes, routes through which Hyder and Tippoo launched their armies into the plains during the Mysore wars. Climate bad. Does not benefit by Palghaut gap. Elephants [q.v.] abundant above ghauts [q.v.]. Bhawauny noted for fish. Forests important. Soils are chiefly red loam and red sand, black soils not occupying above 8 per cent. of the area. Dry crops are cholum [q.v.], cumboo [bajrah], shaumay [q.v.], tinay [q.v.], raggy [q.v.], varagoo [q.v.], castor [aumanac], pulses [dholl] and mustard [rayaun]. Garden crops are the same with the addition of wheat [geung] and exception of shaumy [q.v.], varagoo [q.v.], pulses [dholl] and mustard [rayaun]. Wet crops [q.v.] are devaroyen shumbab, shaday shumbah and caur paddy [q.v.]. The yield of paddy [q.v.] under the two great channels is very heavy. Trade chiefly exportation of grain and importation of cloths, salt, and miscellaneous goods. The sandal-wood of the forests above ghauts are extensive and famous. Large numbers of small cattle [maud] bred in Hassanore hills. Bhawauny flows through talook. Joined by three affluents, Moyaur which unites 10 miles west of Guzzelhutty, the Tattapallam and the Gandypollem. Bhawauny is in highest flood from June to August. Bridge across river at Suttimungalam. Project to dam the flood waters of the Bhawauny a short distance above Suttimungalam, and to form a lake capable of irrigating a very large area in centre of district. The chief cultivation is dependent on the old anicut [q.v.]. The two chief channels [q.v.] are the Tadapully channel and the Arcancottah both regulated by head sluices. Places of archæological interest:—Attiltoray, Caniyampolliem, Cawnitippancottay, Codoovairy, Danaickencottah, Gootyaulattore, Guzzelhutty, Negamam, Peroondalayore, Rungasawmy's peak, Shengalaray, Sirvalore, Suttimungalam, Talamalaicottay, Vellacoil. Principal trig. stations:—Cambatroyen, Comaulicaradoo, Oorgamullay, Tittamullay. The leading places, &c., in the talook are the following.——*Arcancottah* (அரக்கங்கோட்டை - arakkangóttai, Tam.). From (arakkan, tam. a giant + kóttai, tam. fort). Channel. Taken off Bhawauny on N. bank at Codivairy anicut opposite to Tadapully channel. Falls into Bhawauny at Permoogay. Length, 24 miles.——*Bhawauny* (பவானி - paváni, Tam.). See sep. title.——*Cambatroyen* (கம்பத்தராயன் - kambattaráyan, Tam.). From (kambattam, tam. agriculture + iráyan, tam. king). Trig. station; lat. 11° 35′ 27·35″; long. 77° 18′ 46·63″; height 5,571 feet; from Coottaulatore S.W. 8 miles; from Suttimungalam N.N.E. 6 miles.——*Comaulicaradoo* (கோமாளிக்கரடு - kómálikkaradu, Tam.). From (kómál, tam. mistress + karadu, tam. rugged ground). Trig. station; lat. 11° 25′ 44·83″; long. 77° 32′ 23·40″; height 757 feet; from Coogalore S. 4 miles; from Suttimungalam E.S.E. 18 miles.——*Congarapolliem* (கொங்கரப்பாளையம் - kongarappálaiyam, Tam.). From (kongan, tam. the kongu king + pálaiyam, tam. fortified village). Village; pop. 1,628; acres 2,691; lat. 11° 31′; long. 77° 24′; from Coimbatore N.N.E. 45 miles; from Suttimungalam E. 8 miles. Near Oorgamullay trig. station. Market on Sunday.——*Coogalore* (கூகலூர் - kúgalúr, Tam.). From (kúgai, tam. owl + úr, tam. village). Village; pop. 4,630; acres 6,588; lat. 11° 29′; long. 77° 32′; from Coimbatore N.E. 49 miles; from Suttimungalam E. 17 miles. Shiva [q.v.] and Vishnoo [q.v.] temple [coil] built by a Chera [q.v.] king.——*Coottaulatore* (குத்தாளத்தூர் - kuttálattúr, Tam.). From (kuttálam, tam. bauhinia racemosa, lam. + úr, tam. village). Village; pop. 4,260. Near Cambatroyen trig. station.——*Coshanam* (கோசணம் - kósanam, Tam.). Probably a corruption from sanscrit. Sanscrit name (kóshalápuri), meaning cosalam, ancient city of oude + town. Village; pop. 2,835; acres 5,122; lat. 11° 22′; long. 77° 24′; from Coimbatore N.E. 37 miles; from Suttimungalam S.E. 12 miles. Near Tittamullay trig. survey station.——*Danaicken cottah* (டணாயக்கன்கோட்டை - tanáyakkangóttai, Tam.). See sep. title.——*Dimmam* (ದಿಮ್ಮಂ - dimmam, Can.). See sep. title.——*Gopichettipolliem* (கோப்பிசெட்டிப்பாளையம் - kóppisettippálaiyam, Tam.). Means gopichetty's village. Village; pop. 2,104; acres 1,375; lat. 11° 27′; long. 77° 29′; height 859 feet; from Coimbatore N.E. 45 miles; from Suttimungalam E.S.E. 13 miles. Best wet land of talook.——*Guzzelhutty* (ಗೆಜ್ಜಲಹಟ್ಟಿ - gejalhatti, Can.). See sep. title.——*Hassanore* (ஆசனூர் - ásanúr, Tam.). See sep. title.——*Honnholey* (ಹೊನ್ನುಹೊಳೆ - honnuhole, Can.). See sep. title.——*Moyaur* (மொய்யாறு - moyyáru,

Tam.). See sep. title.——*Numbiyore* (நம்பியூர் - nambiyúr, Tam.). From (nambi, tam. one of that caste + úr, tam. village). Village; pop. 7,145; acres 11,952; lat. 11° 22′; long. 77° 22′; from Coimbatore N.E. 36 miles; from Suttimungalam S.S.E. 11 miles.——*Oorgamullay* (உருகமலை - urugamalai, Tam.). From (uraga, san. snake + malai, tam. mountain). Trig. station; lat. 11° 36′ 57·63″; long. 77° 23′ 26·18″; height 4,879 feet; from Congarapolliem N. 7 miles; from Suttimungalam N.E. 10 miles. ——*Peroondalayore* (பெருந்தலையூர் - perundalaiyúr, Tam.). From (perum, tam. large + talai, tam. head + úr, tam. village). Village; pop. 3,892; acres 4,832; lat. 11° 28′; long. 77° 37′; from Coimbatore N.E. 53 miles; from Suttimungalam E. 22 miles. End of rice-producing tract with tank known as Auantasaugaram filled by Tadapully channel. Old Shiva [q.v.] temple [coil].——*Poonjah pooliyamputty* (புஞ்சைப்புளியம்பட்டி - puñjaippuliyambatti, Tam.). From (puñjai, tam. dry land + puli, tam. tamarind tree, tamarindus indica, linn. + patti, tam. cattle-fold). Village; pop. 1,937; acres 2,869; lat. 11° 21′; long. 77° 13′; from Coimbatore N.N.E. 28 miles; from Suttimungalam S.S.W. 13 miles. Weekly market on Thursday.——*Sirvalore* (சிருவலூர் - shiruvalúr, Tam.). From (shiru, tam. small + val, tam. strength + úr, tam. village). Sanscrit name (vyághrapura), meaning tiger + town. Village; pop. 3,965; acres 6,035; lat. 11° 22′; long. 77° 30′; from Coimbatore N.E. 42 miles; from Suttimungalam E.S.E. 17 miles. On road from Peroondoray railway station to Suttimungalam. Old Vishnoo [q.v.] temple. Shiva [q.v.] temple [coil]. Weekly market on Tuesday.——*Suttimungalam* (சத்தியமங்கலம் - sattiyamangalam, Tam.). See below.——*Tadapully* (தடப்பள்ளி - tadappalli, Tam.). From (tadam, tam. hill slope + palli, tam. village). Village; pop. 1,756; acres 1,671; lat. 11° 28′; long. 77° 22′; from Coimbatore N.N.E. 41 miles; from Suttimungalam E.S.E. 6 miles. The channel of this name is taken off Bhawauny on S. bank at Codivairy anicut [q.v.]. It ends in Anantasaugaram tank in Peroondalayore. Length 48 miles.——*Taulavaudy* (தாளவாடி - tálavádi, Tam.). See sep. title.——*Tittamullay* (திட்டமலை - tittamalai, Tam.). From (tittai, tam. mound + malai, tam. mountain). Trig. station; lat. 11° 20′ 45·48″; long. 77° 23′ 54·27″; height 1,218 feet; from Coshanam S. 1½ miles; from Suttimungalam S.E. 13 miles.——**(2)** Village, Divisional and talook head-quarters; Coimbatore dist., Suttimungalam tal.; pop. 3,574; acres 2,039; lat. 11° 30′; long. 77° 17′; from Coimbatore N.N.E. 40 miles; from Erode W.N.W. 35 miles; from Madras W.S.W. 230 miles; from Ootacamund E. 36 miles; from Pollachy N.N.E. 61 miles. On the Bhawauny, here more than 100 yards broad. Guzzelhutty and Hassanore ghauts [q.v.] lead to uplands from here. Old mud fort, built by son in-law of Trimal naick of Madura, commanded the fords at the foot of the Guzzelhutty pass, and was of strategic importance in Mysore wars. Taken by the Mysore generals in 1657; captured by Colonel Wood in 1768; recaptured by Hyder in 1769. In 1790 Colonel Floyd occupied Suttimungalam, and between the fort and Danaicken cottah fought a severe battle with Tippoo. Two ancient Shiva [q.v.] and Vishnoo [q.v.], temples.

SWAM (स्व - sva, *San.*). Latin suus. One's own.——*Saeen* (سائیں - sáín, Hind.). From (svámí, san. lord). Title of a religious mendicant.——*Sauny* (సాని - sáni, Tel.). Corruption of Sawminy, meaning a woman of rank; affix to names of dancing girls [dausy], as Rungasauny, Camalasauny [peyar]. Distinguish from Sauny, companion.——*Sawmy* (स्वामी - svámí, San.). From (svam, san. own). Lord; master; title given to idols [shilay, vigraham], especially shiva [q.v.] or soobramanyan [q.v.]; often borne by individuals. Used as a term of address, especially to bramins. Also suffix in Tamul and Madhwa proper names [peyar]. Sawmibhogam, from (bhógam, san. enjoyment), is proprietor's right; share of produce paid to Mirassidar [q.v.] by tenant cultivator [mail vauram, mitchauram, ryot]. Sawmyam is right of property [cawny]; suffix in compounds as Ashtabhoga [q.v.] sawmyam.——*Shaumoo* (சாமு - shámu, Tam.). Familiar form of (svámí, san. lord. Hindoo 2nd or pers. name [peyar]. ——*Sott* (சொத்து - shottu, Tam.). From (sva, san. property). Property [porool, stity]. Chara or jangama sott is movable property, while Stira or stauvara sott is immovable property.——*Soymida* (पत्राङ्ग - patránga, San.; रक्तरोडा - raktaródá, Mahr.; روهن - rohan, Hind.; روهن كا جهاڑ - rohankájhár, Dec.; ಸ್ವಾಮಿಮರ - svámimara, Can.; సోమిద - sómida, Tel.; సోహన - sóhan, Oor.; செம்மரம் - shemmaram, Tam.). Title from teloogoo. San. from (patra, san. leaf + anga, san. body). Hind. from (róhana, san. the plant). Dec. like hindostany. Can. from (svámí, san. superior + mara, can. tree). Tel. corrupted from canarese. Tam. from (shem, tam. red + maram, tam. tree). San. also (róhana), meaning red. Hind. also (rohitaka), meaning red [rohitacam]. Tel. also (chévamánu), meaning red heartwood + tree [malay red wood]; (súmi). Tam. also (shurakkalli), meaning fever + euphorbia; (vandumaram), meaning beetle tree. Title otherwise Bastard cedar, Coromandel redwood, Febrifuge mahogany, Indian mahogany, Indian redwood, Red cedar, Rohan tree. Botanically Soymida febrifuga, adr., juss., meliaceæ [vricsham, 36]. Generic name from teloogoo. Alias Swietenia febrifuga, soymida. Tree, 60 feet; petals five, shortly unguiculate; calyx five-toothed; leaves abruptly pinnate; leaflets opposite, three to six pair, oval-oblong, obtuse; panicles terminal or axillary from the upper leaves; capsules five celled; seeds numerous, winged; flowers small, greenish white; flowering in march-april. Bark is of a dull red color, epidermis rough and gray, fracture fibrous and woody; breaks easily, pleasant, bitter taste, with slight degree of austerity. In bazaars nux-vomica bark or koochlah [poison nut] is sold for the soymida; this is thin, black internally, very brittle, is grey externally, and stained with bright rust-colored spots; the infusion of nux-vomica bark is nearly colorless. Gives to pharm. soymidæ cortex, bitter amorphous principle; astringent, tonic, and antiperiodic; preparation, decoctam soymidæ; officinal, like cinchona [koinah]. Decoction of bark dyes brown of various shades according as the cloth is prepared. Yields valuable dull red colored wood highly prized by natives for building purposes, durable and strong, well adapted for all indoor work, apt to split on exposure to the sun, grain tolerably close not even, and does not work smoothly. No other common species here.——*Swa bhauvam* (स्वभाव - svabháva, San.; சுபாவம் - shubávam, Tam.). From (above + bháva, san. state). Nature, characteristic, or property of perceptible things. ——*Swacarmam* (स्वकर्म - svakarma, San.). From (above + kri, san. to do). One's own business.——*Swadesham* (स्वदेश - svadésha, San.). From (above + désha, san. country). One's country.——*Swadesha madhya paridhy* (स्वदेशमध्यपरिधि - svadéshamadhyaparidhi, San.). From (above + désha, san. country + madhya, san. middle + paridhi, san. circumference). The circumference of the terrestrial equator [niracsham]. This element is used in the resolution of all gnomonic problems [shunk], and for fixing the longitude [deshauntaram] of places. ——*Swadesha paridhy* (स्वदेशपरिधि - svadéshaparidhi, San.). From (désha, san. country + paridhi, san. circumference). The circumference of a circle of longitude [deshauntaram] in any point on the globe [golam] of the earth removed from the equator [niracsham] or which has latitude [acsham]. The degrees [bhaugam] of these small circles of the sphere are taken to be in the direct ratio of the cosines of the latitudes [acsham]; and resolved into assignable quantities from the dimensions of the equatorial circle, held to contain 5,059 yojanams [jyotisham, yojanam].——*Swadhay* (स्वधा - svadhá, San.). From (above + dhá, san. to place). Self-contained Pracrity [q.v.] or nature.——*Swadhyauyam* (स्वाध्याय - svádhyáya, San.). From (above + adhyáya, san. reading). Repeating prayers [japam].——*Swajauty* (स्वजाति - svajáti, San.). From (above + játi, san. class). One's own people.——*Swaroopam* (स्वरूप - svarúpa, San.; சொரூபம் - shorúbam, Tam.). From (above + rúpa, san. form). Natural state or condition, an idol [vigraham] or image [moorty], person. In malabar a dynasty, answering to vamsham [q.v.] on the other coast. The Calicut zamorin [q.v.] rajah's family is called the Nediyiroopp [q.v.] swaroopam, that of the Cadatnaud rajah is the Porlattiry [q.v.] swaroopam, that of the Chiracal rajah is the Colattiry [q.v.] or Colaswaroopam, that of Cottayam or Cotiote is the Pooranautcara or Poorattara [pooranaud] swaroopam, that of the Cooroombranaud is the Cooroombarattiry or Coorumbiyattiry swaroopam. The Valavanaud rajah is the Arnottoor [arangott] swaroopam, the Cochin rajah is the Perimpadapp [q.v.] swaroopam, the Travancore rajah is the Tripah or Tripah swaroopam [q.v.]. In general usage it means only the Colattiry, Zamorin, Cochin and Travancore rajahs.——*Swosampaudanam* (സ്വസമ്പാദനം - svasampádanam, Mal.). From (above + sampádana, san. earning). Self-acquired property. The self-acquisitions of an individual member of a Malabar family are at his absolute disposal during his lifetime, and the last survivor of a joint family has the same power over the family property as if it were his self-acquisition. At the death of the acquirer, all acquisions which he has not disposed of form part of the family property.——*Swatantram* (स्वतन्त्र - svatantra, San.). From (above + tantra, san. dependence). Independent property. Perquisites due to village officers [merah].——*Swayam* (स्वय - svaya, San.). Self.——*Swayambh* (स्वयम्भू - svayambhú, San.; சுயம்பு - shuyambu, Tam.). From (svayam, san. self + bhú, san. to be). Shiva, the self-existent. Hindoo 2nd or pers. name [peyar].——*Swayambhoo lingam* (स्वयम्भूलिङ्ग - svayambhulinga, San.). From (svayam, san. self + bhú, san. to be + linga, san. phallus). Lingam [q.v.] made of a rock not placed but forming part of the ground.——*Swayam pracausham* (स्वयम्प्रकाश - svayamprakásha, San.). From (svayam, san. self + prakásha, san. light). Self-inherent light. The deity.——*Swayamvaram* (स्वयंवर - svayamvara, San.). From (svayam, san. self + vri, san. choose). The choice of a husband in a public assembly of suitors and others [calyaunam].

SWAR (स्वर् - svar, *San.*). From (sur, san. to shine). Heaven. ——*Soora* (सुर - sura, San.). Divine. Plant first term often joining two genera. Ex., where transl. is of second term:—Barringtonia speciosa (suraponna), calophyllum inophyllum; Calophyllum inophyllum (surahonnémara), mallotus philippensis; Cedrus deodara (suradru), tree; Grangea maderaspatana (suraparna), leaf; Leea hirta (surapádi), foot; Ochrocarpus longifolius (suraponna), calophyllum inophyllum. See gloss. paragraphs.——*Sooram* (सुर - sura, San.). From (sur, san. to shine, rule). Measure of sidereal or star time. 60 soorams = 1 param or indian second [caulam, 4, 5]. Approximate actual value, 1 sooram = $\frac{1}{160}$th of a second. Same as alipalam [caulam, 6].——*Sooran* (सुर - sura, San.). From (sur, san. to shine). A divinity. See Asooran.——*Soorinainy* (సూరినేని - súrinéni, Tel.). From (súri, tel. sun + náyadu, tel. caste title). Family name of zemindars [q.v.] of Meilaveram in Kistna district. Originally renters of Condapully killadar [q.v.].——*Sooryacaunty* (सूर्यमुखी - súryamukhí, San. ; सूर्यकान्ति - súryakánti, Mahr. ; آذریون - ázariyún, Ar. ; آفتاب پرست - áftábparast, Pers ; سورج مکھی - súrijmukkhí, Hind. ; سورج کاجھاڑ - súrijkájhár, Dec. ; ಸೂರ್ಯಕಾಂತಿ - súryakánti, Can. and Too. ; సూర్యకాంతి - súryakánti, Tel. ; സൂര്യകാന്തം - súryakántam, Mal. ; சூரியகாந்தி - shúriyagándi, Tam.). Title from tamul. San. from (súrya, san. sun + mukha, san. face), sun-facing. Mahr. from (súrya, san. sun + kánti, san. desire), sun-desiring [one-leaf nelumbo]. Ar. from (ázar, ar. fire + yún, pers. color). Pers. from (áftáb, pers. sun + parast, pers. worshipper). Hind. from (súrij, hind. sun + mukh, hind. face). Dec. from (súrij, hind. sun + jhár, hind. tree). Drav. from (súrya, san. sun + kánti, san. desire). San. also (ádityabhaktá), meaning sun worshipper [dog vailay]. Pers. also (vartáj). Can. also (hottutiruganagida), meaning sun + turning + plant. Tel. also (poddutirugudu), meaning sun + turning ; (ádityabhaktichettu), meaning sun + devotion + tree [dog vailay] ; (súryávartamu), meaning sun + turning. Title otherwise Golden flower of peru, Sun-flower. Botanically Helianthus annuus, linn., compositæ [vricsham, 74]. Alias Helianthus indicus. Leaves all cordate three-nerved ; peduncle thick ; heads cernuous. Shrub ; ornamental annual ; flower very large yellow. Gives a clear, fluid drying oil [yennay], like that of groundnut [q.v.], used in native medicine. The seeds form a good food for poultry ; the leaves and stalks furnish a strong fibre, and the refuse or marc from the seeds, after the oil has been extracted, yields a good cake [ponnauk] for cattle. The Jerusalem artichoke, a corruption of gira sole, italian for turn-sun, is Helianthus tuberosus, linn., native of brazil, cultivated as vegetable for roots, similar to small potatoes [q.v.] ; not to be confounded with the true garden artichoke, Cynara scolymus, linn.——*Soorya devan* (సూర్యదేవుడు - súryadévudu, Tel.). From (súrya, san. sun. + déva, san. lord). Rajah of Orissa in the twelfth century who, according to the chronicles of Orissa, founded, as a subordinate seat of Government, the present town of Amravatty. See vol. I (10).——*Sooryamoorty* (சூரியமூர்த்தி - shúriyamúrtti, Tam.). From (súrya, san. sun + múrti, san. form) ; sun deity. Hindoo 2nd or pers. name [peyar] ——*Sooryan* (सूर्य - súrya, San.). From (suvar, san. heaven + ya, san. goer). The sun ☉. One of the vedic gods ; he is there savitry, the producer ; to him is dedicated the gayatry [q.v.] ; his place is in the sky, while that of agny [q.v.] is on earth, and that of indran [q.v.] is in the atmosphere. ἀπόλλων of Greeks ; Apollo of Romans ; Horus of Egyptians. Sooryan is otherwise Vivaswat, Ravy, and Audityan. Of the worship of the elements there is no trace in the history, language, or usages of any portion of the Tamul people. On the other hand it is to be mentioned that Indran [q.v.] is worshipped on the first, and Sooryan the sun on the second day of Pongal [pundigay, 6d] the great Tamul festival commemorating the winter solstice [oottarauyanam] ; the observances being imported. The purely solar festivals are when the sun enters a new sign [raushy], especially the days of the equinoxes [crauntypautam, maishauyanam, vishoo] and solstices [dacshinauyanam, oottarauyanam], the day of a solar eclipse [grahanam], and the day of conjunction of sun and moon [amavausyay]. From Ravy comes Ravivauram for Sunday [vauram]. The Jyotish tatwam, a Hindoo work on astrology, says that if a person is born when Ravy is rising, he will possess an anxious mind, be subject to disease and other sufferings, be an exile, a prisoner, and suffer the loss of wife, children, and property [jyotisham, matam, nacshatram]. See vol. I (74). Sooryodayam is sunrise, sooryaustam or sooryaustamanam is sunset. The following abstract table shows the average times of sunrise [sooryodayam] and sunset [sooryaustamanam] throughout the year in latitude 13° [nacshatram] :—

Month and date.		Sunrise.	Sunset.
		A.M.	P.M.
January	1	6 24	5 43
,, ...	15	6 28	5 50
,, ...	31	6 28	5 59
February	14	6 25	6 4
March	1	6 18	6 8
,, ...	15	6 11	6 9
,, ...	16	6 10	6 9
,, ...	17	6 9	6 9
,, ...	31	5 59	6 10
April	15	5 48	6 11
May	1	5 40	6 14
,, ...	15	5 36	6 16
,, ...	31	5 34	6 21
June	15	5 36	6 26
July	1	5 39	6 28
,, ...	15	5 42	6 29
,, ...	31	5 47	6 25
August	15	5 49	6 20
September	1	5 50	6 10
September	15	5 50	5 59
,, ...	23	5 50	5 52
,, ...	24	5 51	5 51
,, ...	26	5 51	5 50
,, ...	30	5 51	5 48
October	15	5 52	5 40
November	1	5 55	5 32
,, ...	15	6 1	5 29
,, ...	30	6 8	5 30
December	15	6 16	5 35
,, ...	31	6 24	5 43

Varauha mihiran has the following regarding sun spots :—"The dark spots on the sun known as kaits [q.v.], the sons of "rahoo [q.v.], are taumasam, keelacam and the like, and are 33 "in number ; how they affect the earth depends upon their color, "position and shape ; when the spots appear on the solar disc "the waters will get disturbed ; the sky will be filled with dust ; "high winds capable of breaking down the tops of mountains "and of trees will carry pebbles and sand along their course ; "the trees will fail to yield in their appropriate seasons, birds "and animals will appear to be burning ; there will be an appear-"ance of false fire all round, and lightning [minnal] and earth-"quake [mahy campam] will afflict mankind ; the princes of "the countries in which the spots are visible will be afflicted "with miseries ; even rishies [q.v.], reduced to mere skeletons "by starvation, giving up their pious course of life, with fleshless "infants in their arms, deprived of their property by highway "men, with long sighs, closed eyes, emaciated bodies, and with "their sight dimmed with the tears of sorrow will proceed with "difficulty to other lands ; men reduced to mere bones and "ashamed to beg will be harassed both by their own princes and "by the princes of other lands ; some will begin to speak dispar-"agingly of the character and deeds of their own sovereign ; "even though there should be indications of good rain [mazhay], "the clouds will yield little rain ; the rivers will fail and "food crops [vellaumay] will be found only here and there." Sooryan is a common plant first term. Ex., where transl. is of second term :—Crozophora plicata (súryávartá), turning ; Gynandropsis pentaphylla (súryávartá), turning ; Helianthus annuus (súryakántam), dsire, (súryamukhí), face ; Hibiscus hirtus (súryamani), jewel ; Hibiscus mutabilis (súryakánti), desire ; Hygrophila spinosa (súryabhíra), fearing ; Ionidium suffruticosum (súryakánti), desire ; Ipomæa quamoclit (súryaratnamu), precious stone. See gloss. paragraphs.——*Sooryanarrain* (சூரியநாராயணன் - shúriyanáráyanan, Tam.). From (súrya, san. sun + náráyana, san. vishnu) ; sun who is vishnoo [q.v.] in another form. Hindoo 2nd or pers. name [peyar].——*Soorya vamsham* (सूर्यवंश - súryavamsha, San.). From (súrya, san. sun + vamsha, san. race). The race of the sun, the name of the Aryan dynasty of which Rama [q.v.], the hero of the Ramayanam [q.v.], was a member. They ruled in Oudh and Tirhoot, and are supposed to have preceded the Lunar race or Chundravamsham [q.v.]. See vol. I (114). The three rajpoot [q.v.] tribes of the solar race are :—"*a*" Grahilote or Gahlot, with twenty-four shaukhays or branches, of which the Sisodiya is the most distinguished. The Rana of Oodayapore or Mewaur is a Grahilote.—"*b*" Rahtore, said to be descended from Rama by Cooshan, his second son. It has twenty-four branches, and the rajah of Jodhpore belongs to this tribe.—"*c*" Kachwaha also sprung from Cooshan. The rajah of Jeypore is of this tribe. It has twelve gotrams [q.v.] or houses.——*Sowrah* (सौर - saura, San.). From (súrya, san. sun). Sect of the Dravida [q.v.] or Southern bramins ; followers of Sooryan, only occasionally found in this presidency. Distinguish from Sowrah the tribe [shabara].——*Swarga dwauram* (స్వర్గద్వారం - svargadváram, Tel.). Means heaven + gate. Same as Veicoonta yecaudashy.——*Swargam* (स्वर्ग - svarga, San.). Heaven, the residence of Indran [q.v.], the space between the sun [sooryan] and the polar star [dhroovam].—"*a*" When the soul has attained its full purity, it is then according to the doctrine of the Bramins, susceptible of five degrees of eternal joy and happiness :—Saulokyam, being in the same world as god, Saunnidhyam, the presence of god, Saumeepyam, approximation to god, Sauroopyam, participation in the divine essence, Sauyoojyam, union with god [mocsham, saulokyam].—"*b*" The damned on the other hand are exposed in Naracam [q.v.] or hell to dreadful torments. The Pretam, or souls of the damned, have to expect there :—Tapanam, pain ; Aveechy, internal anguish ; Samhauram, sufferings and punishment for their sins ; Caulasootram, an extraordinary length of time, which does not end till full atonement has been made for their sins ; Teevra vedanay, torments effected by fire ; Peeday, a malignity and exasperation of their minds. The inspection of the damned belongs to Yaman [q.v.], the god who restrains ; or Shrauddha devan, the god of obsequial offerings.—"*c*" The five principal places where good works are rewarded are :—Mocsham, the true abode of the blessed in the highest heaven, where parabramh [q.v.], the god of gods, has his residence. Bramha locam, the heaven of the god bramha [q.v.], to which those ascend who have particularly devoted themselves to the service of this god. Keilausam [q.v.], the heaven of shiva [q.v.]

or mahadevan [q.v.], to which his adherents attain. Veicoontam [q.v.], the heaven of vishnoo [q.v.], which is peculiarly destined for the worshippers of that deity. Indralocam, or swargam, the heaven of devendran [q.v.]; this is situated in the air; it is consequently the lowest of all, and is appointed for the reception of those who on earth devoted themselves to the service of any deity. The Mocsham is the only one of these heavens from which souls [autmam] have no need of again descending to the earth, for in it they are already cleansed, and have attained to the highest degree of perfection. From all the rest they are occasionally sent down; but they again ascend to them, according as their past conduct in life has been meritorious or deserving punishment. Souls [autmam] transmigrate also sometimes into animal bodies, and hence the prohibition to kill animals [samsauram].——*Swarganaicken* (स्वर्गनायक - svarganáyaka, San.). From (svarga, san. heaven + náyaka, san. leader). Shiva.——*Swar locam* (स्वर्लोक - svarlóka, San.). Same as Swargam.

SWARAM (स्वर - svara, *San.*). From (svri, san. to sound). A note in the musical scale.——*Soorbut* (சுரபத்து - shurabattu, Tam.). From (svara, san. music + vat, san. possessive suffix). Stringed instrument played with plectrum of ivory [dant] or wood [sangeetam].——*Swara graumam* (स्वरग्राम - svaragráma, San.). From (above + gráma, san. gamut). The musical gamut, comprising the seven notes shadjam, rishabham, gaundhauram, madhyamam, punchamam, dheivatam, and nishandam, which are all respectively denoted by their initial letters or syllables, viz., sa, ri, ga, ma, pa, dha and ni [raugam].

SWAUDOO (स्वादु - svádu, *San.*). From (svad, san. to relish). Sweet.——*Swaudoocantacam* (स्वादुकण्टक - svádukantaka, San.). From (svádu, san. sweet + kantaka, san. thorn); sweet thorn. Botanically Flacourtia genus, bixineæ [vricsham, 14]. Small trees or shrubs, met with in tropical asia, africa, and america; nearly all armed with thorns; fruits succulent. The species best known to the natives are:—cataphracta [indian plum], inermis [tomitomi], montana [attack], ramontchi [mauritius plum], ramontchi, var. sapida [ceylon plum], sepiaria [forest bair].

SWAUGA (سہاگا - sohágá, *Hind.*). Borax [vengauram]. Cutcha swauga is crude, Pucka swauga is prepared, borax.

SYAND (स्यन्द् - syand, *San.*). To trickle, flow, shed.——*Sendoor* (सिन्दूर - sindúra, San.; اسرنج - isrinj, Ar.; سرنج - surinj, Pers.; سندور - sindúr, Hind.; سیندور - sendúr, Dec.; سدلانگم - sadalánggam, Malay; ಸಿಂಧೂರ - sindhúra, Can. and Too.; సిందూరము - sindúramu, Tel.; സിന്ദൂരം - sindúram, Mal.; සින්දූර - sindúra, Singh.; செந்தூரம் - shendúram, Tam.). San. from (syand, san. to trickle). San. also (nágasambhava), meaning produced from lead. Tel. also (errasindúramu), meaning red + the powder. Tam. also (shivappuççendúram), meaning red + the powder. Abbreviation for Eeya sindooram, Red lead. Otherwise Minium, Red oxide of lead [eeyam]. Plumbi oxidum rubrum of chemists. A mineral drug; sometimes made into plasters. A red paint [rangh]. Abruck sendoor, from (abhraka, san. talc), is prepared talc consisting of a powder of brick-dust color and a saline earthy taste chemically silicate of magnesia with iron [auhan] in excess. Aya sendoor, from (ayas, san. iron), is red oxide of iron [auhan]. Eeya sendoor, from (íyam, tam. lead), is red oxide of lead; otherwise vanga sindooram, the present article. Gandhac sendoor, from (gandhaka, san. sulphur), is calcined brimstone [gandhac]. Rasa sendoor, from (rasa, san. mercury), is red precipitate of mercury [rasam]. Taumra sendoor, from (támra, san. copper), is a red chemical preparation of copper [taumram]. Tunga sendoor, from (tangam, tam. gold), is a red chemical preparation from gold [pon].——*Sind* (سندھ - sindh, Hind.). From (syand, san. to flow). The river Indus; also the country so called.——*Sindoocam* (सिन्दुक - sinduka, San.). From (syand, san. to shed); used medicinally. Title otherwise Chaste tree. Botanically the Vitex genus, verbenaceæ [vricsham, 102]. Trees or shrubs chiefly tropical; shoots hairy or tomentose; leaves opposite, digitately three to five foliolate; inflorescence terminal and axillary or wholly axillary; drupe globose or obovoid; wood hard, close-grained. The species best known to the natives are:—alata [peacock gingelly], altissima [wild peacock gingelly], leucoxylon [field notchy], negundo [notchy], pubescens [tall notchy], trifolia [water notchy]. Compare also in other genera:—Clerodendron inerme (nírnoççi), water notchy; Jatropha curcas (kárnoççi), black notchy; Justicia gendarussa (karunoççi), black notchy; Vernonia anthelmintica (nírnoççi), water notchy. See gloss. paragraphs.——*Sondahnamak* (सैन्धव - saindhava, San.; ملح الحجر - milhulhajar, Ar.; نمك سنگ - namakisang, Pers.; سيندا نمك - sendánamak, Hind.; سوندا نمك - sondánamak, Dec.; ఇందుప్పు - induppu, Tel.; ഇന്തുപ്പ് - intuppu, Mal.; இந்துப்பு - induppu, Tam.). Title from deccany. San. from (sindhu, san. the river indus). Ar. from (milk, ar. salt + hajar, ar. stone). Pers. from (namak, pers. salt + sang, pers. stone). Hind. from (sindhu, san. indus + namak, hind. salt). Dec. from hindostany. Drav. from (sindhu, san. indus + uppu, tel. salt). Hind. also (sendálon), meaning indus salt. Tel. also (saindhavalavanamu), meaning sindh + salt; (sindhudéshapuuppu), meaning sindh + salt; (chandruduppu), meaning moon + salt; (rátiuppu), meaning rock salt. Tam. also (shindudésavuppu), meaning sindh + salt; (shayíndavalavanam), meaning sindh + salt; (indunáttuppu), meaning sindh + salt; (shómanuppu), meaning moon + salt. Rock salt [ooppoo]. An impure chloride of sodium; occurs in large masses varying in weight from 2 or 3 to 8 or 10 lbs.; dull or brownish-white externally, white and crystalline internally, of a pure saline taste; procurable in all bazaars [q.v.]. Though a mere variety of common salt [ooppoo], possessed medicinally of far stronger purgative properties. Used in native medicine for men, cattle [maud], and horse [ghorah].

SYAUD (स्याद् - syád, *San.*). If there be.——*Syaudvaudy* (स्याद्वादी - syádvádí, San.). From (above + vad, san. to argue). The Jeinas [q.v.] as assertors of probabilities or of what may be; also called Saptavaudies [q.v.], assertors of seven propositions.

SYCE (سائیس - sáís, *Hind.*). From (saasa, ar. to tend). A horsekeeper or groom. Bengal term. In madras Horsekeeper is more common, and in bombay Ghorawallah.

SYDAPETT (سعيداباد - saídábád, *Hind.*; சைதாப்பேட்டை - shaithápp̄éttai, *Tam.* saidápet *). From (saíd, ar. mah. name + péttai, tam. suburb) [syed].——**(1)** Talook, Chingleput district. Tahsildar's pay Rs. 175. Area 841 square miles. Population 224,472. Language Tamul, Teloogoo. N. coast of district. Bounded E. by Bay of Bengal; N. by Ponnairy and Trivellore talooks; W. by Trivellore and Conjeeveram talooks; and S. by Chingleput talook. The general appearance is flat and uninteresting, but here and there the otherwise flat expanse is studded by ridged or conical hills of no great elevation, on many of which is either a pagoda [q.v.] or a bungalow [q.v.]. Well supplied with roads. The chief are the Great southern trunk road, the High western trunk road, and the Great northern trunk road. The Madras and South indian railways traverse the talook. The Buckingham canal [q.v.] runs along the whole length of the coast. Rainfall averages 42 inches. The soil is of various qualities, being as a rule better in proportion to distance from the sea. Sand [manal], red ferruginous loam [sevval munn], and alluvial [adaimunn, vandalmunn] soils represent the degrees of progressive fertility. Weaving is carried on in several villages, but only for the supply of local wants. In one or two villages red handkerchiefs [roomaul] and Mussalman cloths are manufactured for export, finding their way chiefly to Penang and Singapore. The only noticeable feature as to crops is the taking up of hitherto unremunerative sandy wastes at the seaside for casuarina [chowkmaram] plantation; this tree flourishes on such soils, and being a quick grower and commanding a ready sale as firewood [lukdy], its cultivation has since 1862–63 been a favorite form of investment. Rivers are the Adyar, Cooum and Corteliaur; the last does not contribute directly to the irrigation of the talook, being a mere drainage stream, but water is raised by baling to a small extent. The only two irrigation works of any importance are Red hills and Chembrambaukam tanks. Petty zemindarries:—Chembrambaukam, Chokkanullore, Corattore, Maumbalam, Motharambaid, Palanjore, Pullavaram, Shittoocaud, Shoranjery, Tircoilputt, Tirmanam, Tookkanamputt, Trimalrajapooram, Vanyalnullore. Places of archæological interest:—Coonnatore, Little mount, Maungaud, Mauthavaram, Poonamallee, Poottore, St. Thomas' Mount, St. Thomé, Tinnanore, Tirmoollavauyil, Tirvarcaud, Trivettore. Principal trig. stations:—Andaurcooppam, Eenjambaukam, Ennore beacon, Ennore D.P.W., Manaly, Maungaud, Manthavaram, Mauttore, Nanmungalam, Peroombauk, Red hills, St. Thomas' mount, Shadayan cooppam, Teeyambaukam, Vadapoorambaukam, Vilaungaudpaukam, Yelandacherry. The leading places, &c., in the talook are the following.——*Adyar* (அடையாறு - adaiyáru, Tam.). See sep. title.——*Ambattore* (அம்பத்தூர் - ambattúr, Tam. ambatúr *). From (ambu, tam. the lime tree, citrus medica, linn. + úr, tam. village). Village, Railway station; pop. 1,068; acres 1,924; lat. 13° 06′; long. 80° 14′; height 60 feet; from Sydapett N. 6 miles; from the sea W. 9 miles. Contains large tracts of stone quarry. Ambattore naud formed part of Pozhal cottam [q.v.] in the ancient Tondaimundalam [q.v.].——*Andaurcooppam* (ஆண்டார்க்குப்பம் - ándárkkuppam, Tam.). From (ándán, tam. lord + kuppam, tam. village). Trig. station; lat. 13° 11′ 26·60″; long. 80° 18′ 4·53″; from Shadayan cooppam N.N.W. 2 miles; from Sydapett N. 12 miles; from the sea W. 4 miles.——*Aroombaukam* (அரும்பாக்கம் - arumbákkam, Tam.). From (arumai, tam. scantiness + pákkam, tam. village). Village; pop. 513; acres 456; lat. 13° 05′; long. 80° 16′; from Sydapett N. 4 miles; from the sea W. 6 miles.——*Avady* (ஆவடி - ávadi, Tam. avadi *). From (á, tam. cattle + vadi, tam. corruption of kudi, tam. village). Village, Railway station; lat. 13° 07′; long. 80° 11′; height 80 feet; from Sydapett N.W. 9 miles; from the sea W. 12 miles. Represents the old Augoody naud. Hamlet of Parookwaukam village.——*Ayanaupooram* (அயனப்புரம் - ayanáppuram, Tam.). From (aiyyanár, tam. the village deity, so called + pura, san. city). Shrotriem, Village; pop. 5,235; acres 1,421; lat. 13° 06′; long. 80° 18′; from Sydapett N. 5 miles; from the sea W. 4

miles. Sanitarium.——*Chembrambaukam* (செம்பரம்பாக்கம் - shembarambákkam, Tam.). See sep. title.——*Chokkanullore* (சொக்கநல்லூர் - shokkanallúr, Tam.). From (shokkan, tam. shiva, the beautiful + nal, tam. good + úr, tam. village). Zemindarry, Village; pop. 184; acres 280; lat. of village 13° 05'; long. 80° 08'; from Sydapett N.W. 11 miles; from the sea W. 15 miles. Peshcush Rs. 359.——*Cochrane canal* (கொக்கரேன் வாய்க்கால் - kokkarénváykkál, Tam.). See sep. title.——*Codambaukam* (கோடம்பாக்கம் - kódambákkam, Tam.). See sep. title.——*Coonnatore* (குண்ணத்தூர் - kunnattúr, Tam.). From (kunram, tam. hill + úr, tam. village). Zemindarry, Peshcush Rs. 123. Village; pop. 1,419; acres 2,369; lat. 13° 00'; long. 80° 10'; from Sydapett S.W. 8 miles; from the sea W. 12 miles. ——*Coottambaukam* (குத்தம்பாக்கம் - kuttambákkam, Tam.). From (kuttam, tam. a pond + pákkam, tam. village). Village; pop. 2,217; acres 1,883; lat. 13° 03'; long. 80° 05'; from Sydapett W. 13 miles; from the sea W. 17 miles. Noted for its fertility. ——*Cooum* (கூவம் - kúvam, Tam.). See sep. title.——*Corattore* (கொரட்டூர் - korattúr, Tam.). From (kurattai, tam. a creeper, trichosanthes palmata, roxb. + úr, tam. village). Zemindarry, Village; pop. 526; acres 562; lat. of village 13° 05'; long. 80° 05'; from Sydapett W. 14 miles; from the sea W. 18 miles. Peshcush Rs. 323.——*Cuttivaukum* (கத்திவாக்கம் - kattivákkam, Tam.). See sep. title.——*East coast canal* (கிழக்கரைவாய்க்கால் - kízhkkaraiváykkál, Tam.). See sep. title. ——*Eenjambaukam* (ஈஞ்சம்பாக்கம் - íñjambákkam, Tam.). From (íñju, tam. date tree, phœnix farinifera, roxb. + pákkam, tam. village). Trig. station; lat. 12° 54' 51·18"; long. 80° 17' 38·41"; height 29 feet; from Cholanginullore N.E. 2 miles; from Sydapett S. 8 miles; from the sea W. 2 miles.——*Ennore* (எண்ணூர் - ennúr, Tam.). See sep. title.——*Guindy park* (கிண்டித்தோட்டம் - kindittóttam, Tam.). See sep. title. ——*Little mount* (சின்னமலை - shinnamalai, Tam.). See sep. title.——*Manaly* (மணலி - manali, Tam.). Means a bitter kitchen herb, gisekia pharnaceoides, l. Trig. station; lat. 13° 10' 29·80"; long. 80° 18' 40·62"; from Shekkaud N. 1 mile; from Sydapett N.E. 10 miles; from the sea W. 4 miles.——*Maumbalam* (மாம்பலம் - mámbalam, Tam.). From (má, tam. mango tree, mangifera indica, linn. + ambalam, tam. an open space). Zemindarry, Village; pop. 6,007; acres 501; lat. 13° 02'; long. 80° 17'; from Sydapett N. 1 mile; from the sea W. 4 miles. Peshcush Rs. 597. Gives its name to Marmelong [q.v.] bridge. ——*Maungaud* (மாங்காடு - mángádu, Tam.). From (má, tam. the mango tree, mangifera indica, linn. + kádu, tam. forest). Village; pop. 4,946; acres 1,397; lat. 13° 02'; long. 80° 11'; from Sydapett W. 7 miles; from the sea W. 12 miles. Old Shiva temple with Grantam [q.v.] inscriptions, Maungaud naud formed part of Pooliyore cottam [q.v.], in the ancient Tondaimundalam [q.v.]. Trig. station in lat. 13° 00' 24·72"; long. 80° 08' 25·49"; height 174 feet; from Moonangattalay W. 2 miles; from Sydapett W. 8 miles; from the sea W. 12 miles. ——*Mautharvaram* (மாதவரம் - máthavaram, Tam.). From (máthu, tam. woman + pura, san. town). Sanscrit name (mádhavapura), meaning vishnoo + town. Village; pop. 4,601; acres 4,301; lat. 13° 09'; long. 80° 17'; from Sydapett N. 9 miles; from the sea W. 5 miles. Near Red hills tank, ancient fortress of the Coorumbar [q.v.] before their conquest by the Cholas [q.v.]. Sanitarium. Trig. station in lat. 13° 9' 13·15"; long. 80° 16' 5·17"; from Shembyam N.W. 4 miles; from Sydapett N. 9 miles; from the sea W. 7 miles.——*Mauttore* (மாத்தூர் - máttúr, Tam.). From (máttu, tam. barter + úr, tam. village). Trig. station; lat. 13° 10' 38·73"; long. 80° 17' 37·29"; from Manjambaukam N.W. 1¼ mile; from Sydapett N. 11 miles; from the sea W. 6 miles.——*Motharambaid* (மொதரம்பேடு - motharambédu, Tam.). From (móthiram, tam. ring + pédu, tam. village). Zemindarry, Village; pop. 89; acres 109; lat. of village 13° 05'; long. 80° 06'; from Sydapett W. 12 miles; from the sea W. 17 miles. Peshcush Rs. 52.——*Nanmungalam* (நன்மங்கலம் - nanmangalam, Tam.). From (nal, tam. good + mangala, san. prosperity). Trig. station; lat. 12° 55' 33·99"; long. 80° 13' 05·07"; height 233 feet; from Medavauk W. 3 miles; from Sydapett S.S.W. 8 miles; from the sea W. 7 miles.—— *Nundambaukam* (நந்தம்பாக்கம் - nandambákkam, Tam.). From (nandan, tam. cowherd + pákkam, tam. village). Otherwise Mount nundambaukam. Village; pop. 332; acres 652; lat. 13° 01'; long. 80° 15'; from Sydapett W. 2 miles; from the sea W. 6 miles.——*Ooroor* (ஊரூர் - úrúr, Tam.). From (úru, tam. to ooze as water + úr, tam. village). Village; acres 719; lat. 13° 01'; long. 80° 20'; from Sydapett S.E. 4 miles; from the sea W. ½ mile.——*Peroombauk* (பெரும்பாக்கம் - perumbákkam, Tam.). From (perum, tam. big + pákkam, tam. village). Trig. station; lat. 12° 53' 01·81"; long. 80° 14' 12·27"; height 262 feet; from Arasankalany N. ¾ mile; from Sydapett S. 10 miles; from the sea W. 4 miles.—— *Poonamallee* (பூந்தமல்லி - púndamalli, Tam.). See sep. title. ——*Pozhal* (புழல் - puzhal, Tam.). See sep. title.——*Pullavaram* (பல்லாவரம் - pallávaram, Tam.). See sep. title.—— *Red hills tank* (புழலேரி - puzhaléri, Tam.). See sep. title.—— *Saint Thomas' mount* (பரங்கிமலை - parangimalai, Tam.). See sep. title.——*Shadayan cooppam* (சடயன்குப்பம் - shadayanguppam, Tam.). From (shadayan, tam. proper name + kuppam, tam. village). Trig. station; lat. 13° 11' 11·02"; long. 80° 20' 1·65"; from Cadapaukam S.E. 1½ miles; from Sydapett N.E. 12 miles; from the sea W. 3 miles.——*Shauttancaud* (சாத்தங்காடு - sháttangádu, Tam.). From (sháttan, tam. the god aiyyanár + kádu, tam. forest). Village; pop. 3,758; acres 2,048; lat. 13° 10'; long. 80° 21'; from Sydapett N. 10 miles; from the sea W. 2 miles.——*Shembyam* (செம்பியம் - shembiyam, Tam.). From (shembiyan, tam. title of the chola ruler). Village; pop. 3,651; acres 446; lat. 13° 07'; long. 80° 19'; from Sydapett N. 7 miles; from the sea W. 4 miles.——*Shittoocaud* (சித்துக்காடு - shittukkádu, Tam.). From (shiru, tam. small + kádu, tam. forest). Zemindarry, Village; pop. 895; acres 912; lat. of village 13° 07'; long. 80° 06'; from Sydapett W. 13 miles; from the sea W. 17 miles. Peshcush Rs. 1,023.——*Shorancherry* (சோராஞ்சேரி - shóránjéri, Tam.). From (shózhan, tam. the king + shéri, tam. village). Zemindarry, Village; pop. 1,428; acres 1,829; lat. of village 13° 06'; long. 80° 08'; from Sydapett N.W. 12 miles; from the sea W. 15 miles. Peshcush Rs. 2,461.——*Sirvalore* (திருவள்ளூர் - shiruvallúr, Tam.). From (shiruvalli, tam. a creeper, dioscorea aculeata, linn. + úr, tam. village). Village; pop. 2,969; acres 222; lat. 13° 07'; long. 80° 18'; from Sydapett N. 6 miles; from the sea W. 4 miles.—— *Sydapett* (சைதாப்பேட்டை - shaithápp**é**ttai, Tam.). See below.——*Sydapett government farm* (روشن باغ - roshanbágh, Hind.). See Roshanbaug.——*Teeyambaukam* (தீயம்பாக்கம் - tíyambákkam, Tam.). From (tíyan, tam. a hunter + pákkam, tam. village). Trig. station; lat. 13° 11' 14·90"; long. 80° 16' 33·25"; from Mauttore W. 3 miles; from Sydapett N. 12 miles; from the sea W. 7 miles.——*Tinnanore* (தின்னனூர் - tinnanúr, Tam.). From (tinnan, tam. strong man, a hunter + ur, tam. village). Sanscrit name (shrínivásapura), meaning town where shree or lutchmy abides. Title otherwise Tirnindravore, meaning lutchmy + halt + village. Jagheer village, Railway station; pop. 3,115; acres 3,657; lat. 13° 07'; long. 80° 05'; height 117 feet; from Madras W. 17 miles; from Sydapett W.N.W. 14 miles; from the sea W. 18 miles. Vishnoo [q.v.] temple [coil, pagoda] with inscriptions.——*Tirmanam* (திருமணம் - tirmanam, Tam.). From (tiru, tam. sacred + manam, tam. fragrance). Zemindarry, Village; pop. 890; acres 293; lat. of village 13° 06'; long. 80° 07'; from Sydapett W. 11 miles; from the sea W. 15 miles. Peshcush Rs. 728.——*Tirneer mullay* (திருநீர்மலை - tirunírmalai, Tam.). From (tiru, tam. sacred + nír, tam. water + malai, tam. hill). Village; pop. 1,156; acres 1,452; lat. 12° 58'; long. 80° 11'; from Sydapett W.S.W. 8 miles; from the sea W. 10 miles. Vishnoo [q.v.] temple [coil] on top of hill.——*Tirvaumyore* (திருவான்மியூர் - tiruvámeyúr, Tam.). From (tiru, tam. holy + válmíki, san. the sage + úr, tam. village). Sanscrit name (válmíkipura), meaning valmeeky + city. Shrotriem village, Place of pilgrimage; pop. 1,669; acres 1,260; lat. 12° 59'; long. 80° 20'; from Sydapett S.E. 5 miles; from the sea W. ½ mile. An important Bramin settlement, similar to Mylapore. Shiva [q.v.] temple [coil] with handsome square tank attached. Birth place of Valmeeky [q.v.].—— *Trivettore* (திருவொற்றியூர் - tiruvottiyúr, Tam.). See sep. title.——*Vadapoorambaukam* (வடப்புரம்பாக்கம் - vadappurambákkam, Tam.). From (vadappuram, tam. northern side + pákkam, tam. village). Trig. station; lat. 13° 10' 22·44"; long. 80° 16' 13·46"; from Mauthavaram N.W. 2 miles; from Sydapett N. 10 miles; from the sea W. 7 miles.——*Vauyalnullore* (வாயலா நல்லூர் - váyalánallur, Tam.). From (váyil, tam. gate + nal, tam. good + úr, tam. village). Zemindarry, Village; pop. 963; acres 984; lat. of village 13° 05'; long. 80° 08'; from Sydapett W. 11 miles; from the sea W. 15 miles. Peshcush Rs. 1,511. ——*Vilaungavdpaukam* (விளாங்காடுப்பாக்கம் - vilángáttuppákkam, Tam.). From (vilá, tam. the wood-apple tree, feronia elephantum, corr. + kádu, tam. forest + pákkam, tam. village). Trig. station; lat. 13° 11' 28·07"; long. 80° 15' 54·31"; from Mauthavaram N.W. 4 miles; from Sydapett N. 12 miles; from the sea W. 8 miles.——*Yelandacherry* (இலந்தச்சேரி - elandaççéri, Tam.). From (ilandai, tam. the jujube tree, zizyphus jujuba, lamk. + shéri, tam. village). Trig. station; lat. 13° 12' 45·54"; long. 80° 19' 43·67"; from Cadapaukam N. 1½ miles; from Sydapett N.E. 12 miles; from the sea W. 4 miles.—— *Yernavore* (ஏரணாவூர் - éranávúr, Tam.). From (ézhu, tam. seven + aran, tam. jungle + á, tam. cattle + úr, tam. village). Shrotriem village; pop. 528; acres 1,478; lat. 13° 12'; long. 80° 22'; from Sydapett N.E. 13 miles; from the sea W. ¾ mile. In 1742 held at a pepper-corn rent on shrotriem [q.v.] tenure under a grant from Nawaub saudat oollah khan, Soobahdar of Arcot, dated 4th November 1742. Confirmed by Moghul's firmaun [q.v.], 12th August 1765.——**(2)** Town, Head-quarters of the Collector, also of the Divisional officers, the District forest officer and the Talook offices and Division deputy collector, Railway station; Chingleput dist., Sydapett tal.; pop. 5,702; acres 287; lat. 13° 02'; long. 80° 17'; height 26 feet; from Chingleput N. 28 miles; from Conjeeveram N.E. 37 miles; from Madras S.W. 6 miles; from St. Thomas' mount N.E. 2 miles; from the sea W. 5 miles. On the Mount road. Since 1859 head-quarters of the Collector. His office and treasury are located in Homes' gardens.

SYED (سيد - saiyid, *Hind.*). From Arabic. Lord, prince, noble. Hence it has become an alaumat [q.v.] or tribal title; see vol. I (106). The title is taken by all descendants of Ally and Fatimah, and also by the children of the other wives of Ally. Ally had altogether nine wives, by whom he had fourteen sons and eighteen daughters. Ally and Fatimah's descendants through Hassan and Hoossain are styled Hassanee and Hoossainy; and Ally's offspring by the other wives, Alavee. Syeds are also styled Meer or prince. Syed women are Seidaunee; the syed race Saudaat. The offspring of a Syed and another mahomedan woman is Shareef [q.v.] or noble. Indian syeds are met with serving as soldiers or in civil avocations, and also following religious duties. Many are Mowlvies [q.v.] or Peers [q.v.], but the poor follow all callings. Amongst the women of the Syeds of Madras most can read the Arabic koran [q.v.] and the Hindostany books of belief and devotion, but they cannot write; about 400 or 500 of them are good needlewomen and embroiderers. Syeds usually give their daughters to men only of their own class, but they will take wives from the other classes of Mussalmans. There was a dynasty of Syeds at Delhi from 1414 to 1451 A.D. The small principality of Bunganapully in the Ceded districts [q.v.] is ruled by Syeds. About 23,000 in presidency, much the greater number being in Bellary and Coimbatore.——*Seedee* (سيدى - sídí, Hind.). From (saiyid, ar. lord). Descendant of natives of Africa on W. coast employed on ships. Formerly held high positions under the Mahomedan sovereigns of the Deccan [q.v.]. Cf. the Spanish Cid.——*Sydapett* (சைதாப்பேட்டை - shaithâppéttai, Tam.). See sep. title.——*Sydapore* (సైదాపురము - saidápuramu, Tel.). From (saíd, hind. fortunate + pura, san. town). Sanscrit name (siddhéshvarapura), meaning siddheshwaran, the deity + town. Village; Nellore dist., Raupore tal.; pop. 1,447; acres 7,287; lat. 14° 11′; long. 79° 47′; from Nellore S.W. 25 miles; from Raupore E. 14 miles. Formerly the seat of the zemindar [q.v.] of the Zoopully family and head-quarters of one of the Western pollems [q.v.]. Shaurngadharan, a prince whose limbs were mutilated, recovered the use of them at this place. Utensils of soft stones [sowcaura cull] manufactured and sent in large quantities to other districts. A temple on a hill called Siddeshwara condah, 3 miles away. Large tank. Vencatagherry river irrigates gardens. On road from Goodoor to Raupore.——*Syed abdool cauder jeelauny* (سيد عبدالقادرجيلانى - saiyidabdulkádirjílání, Hind.). From (saiyid, ar. tribal title + abd, ar. slave + kádir, ar. god + jílán, ar. birth-place) [abdool cawder]. The highest of the Mahomedan saints [walee] and divines and founder of the Cawdiriya order of fakeers [q.v.].——*Syed ahmed* (سيد احمد - saiyidahmad, Hind.). Mahomedan proper name; alaumat + alam [ism].

SYRIA (شام - shám, *Ar.*). Country to the north of Arabia, opposed to Yemen which lies to the south.——*Sooryauny* (سريانى - suryání, Hind.). Syrian christian [syrian].——*Syrian* (സുറിയാനി - suryáni, Mal.). Otherwise Syrian christian. This sect found in Malabar and Travancore are called by the other natives Sooryaunies, that is to say Syrians; or Nasraunies [q.v.], that is to say Nazarenes; by Europeans, they are styled Christians of St. Thomas [q.v.].—"*a*" Their own traditions attribute their origin to the Apostle Thomas [st. thomas], who visited India in the first century and preached the Gospel there, making numerous converts, these being joined some centuries afterwards by other Christians from Syria. They may be styled generally the Syrian christians of Malabar, having their analogues in the Syrian christians of Persia. Favorable treatment was accorded to these early Christians, whether colonists or indigenous, by the rulers of the Malabar coast. The privileges given to them are recorded in inscriptions on copper plates which are still in the possession of the Syrians, and preserved in their college at Cottayam. Fac-similes again of these taken by Buchanan Hamilton are in the public library of the Cambridge university, along with copies of similar grants to the chief of the ancient Jewish colony at Cochin [jonaca]. The Syrian plates are nearly ten inches in length and four in breadth, with large letters distinctly graven on both sides. The character is the ancient Vattezhoot [q.v.], common to both Tamul and Malayalam. These grants confer upon the Syrian headman possession of a village, with permission to use certain ornaments and musical instruments, and emblems of authority; to collect particular taxes and duties allotted to him; and to exercise jurisdiction over his own tribe. The dates of these documents are expressed in such ambiguous language that it is difficult to determine their exact period. The Syrians proved serviceable allies to the native rulers, and were therefore treated well and attained to considerable political influence. They were allowed to bear arms, and were regarded as equal in caste to the Nayars [q.v.]. In A.D. 547, the Christian church in Malabar was visited by Cosmas, an Egyptian merchant, who gives some account of their discipline and worship. It is also asserted, in ancient Anglo-Saxon chronicles, that in A.D. 883 King Alfred sent Sighelm, Bishop of Sherburn, to India, to visit these Christians and present gifts at the shrine of St. Thomas, near Madras. He is said to have successfully performed this noteworthy enterprise, and to have returned laden with gems [ratnam] and spices. After the arrival of the Portuguese on the western coast of India, early in the sixteenth century, the Roman catholic priests desired to effect the subjection of this sect to the Papal authority. At first, measures of conciliation were pursued. In 1545 Franciscan friars were sent by the Archbishop of Goa to open a seminary for Syrian youths, who were afterwards ordained as priests but the Syrians refused to admit these to their churches. Stronger measures were then resorted to. Plots were laid to seize Mar Joseph, the Syrian metraun [q.v.], whose influence against Rome was conspicuous. He was made prisoner and sent to Portugal in 1558; but promising to bring over his people to the Church of Rome, he was allowed by the Queen to return to India. On his arrival, he again taught the ancient doctrines. He was recaptured and sent to Rome, where he died. Another metraun, Mar Simeon, who had been sent to India by the Patriarch of Mosul, was taken to Cochin, sent to Rome, and tried as a heretic by the Inquisition. There is reason to believe that he ended his days in Portugal in captivity. In 1525 Alexis da Menezes, who was about to proceed to Goa as Archbishop, received a brief from Pope Clement VIII directing him to make strict inquiry into the faith and obedience of the Syrian bishop and his flock, and to prevent any bishops or priests from Syria from reaching Malabar. Early in 1599 Menezes, attended by Portuguese troops, reached Cochin, and summoned the Syrian Archdeacon George, the late metraun [q.v.] being now dead, to appear before him. The archdeacon at first refused allegiance to the authority of the Church of Rome, but was at last wearied by the perseverance and zeal of Menezes and the threats of the Portuguese power and was induced to sign an acknowledgment of the Pope's supremacy. Menezes visited in person many of the Syrian churches, but they for the most part refused to submit to his authority. The assembling of a council, or synod, was now resolved on. The synod met at Diamper, near Cochin, on 20th June 1599. It was attended by the Romish archbishop, the Syrian archdeacon and 153 Cattanars [q.v.], many Roman priests, and some chief persons among the Portuguese. Decrees were there passed confirming the doctrines of Rome, and repudiating those which had hitherto been held and proclaimed by the Syrian Church. The Roman sacraments and celibacy were established, the ancient records and historical documents of the Syrian Church were destroyed, and a Latin bishop was appointed; but it was found necessary to consent to the continued use of the Syriac language in public worship. Thus were the Syrian christians reduced to a nominal conformity to the Roman church, and brought in reality into subjection to the Portuguese power. This state of things continued for about fifty years. In 1653 many of the Syrians revolted from the Roman power, excluded the Roman priests from their churches, and appointed their archdeacon as metraun, until they could obtain a bishop from their patriarch. When the expected bishop, Mar Attala, at last reached the shores of India, he was taken prisoner and sent to Goa, where he was consigned to a dungeon in the Inquisition, and at last burnt as a heretic A.D. 1654. A few years afterwards the Dutch seized upon Cranganore; and thence forward the Portuguese power declining, the Syrians enjoyed freedom from external violence. Still many continued to adhere to the Church of Rome. In this way arose the two bodies that now exist; the Syrians proper, who retain to a large extent the doctrine and ritual of the ancient church, but to whom the Roman party have attached the title 'Poottancoor' [q.v.], or the new assemblage; and the Romo Syrians, who are under the authority of, and directly connected with, the Church of Rome, governed by the Bishop of Verapoly, and who call themselves 'Pazhayacoor' [q.v.], or the old assemblage.—"*b*" The Syrian hierarchical order and ritual system bear some resemblance to that of the Copts, or, native Egyptian christians. They are governed by a metraun, or metropolitan bishop, who is appointed by the Patriarch of Antioch. The cattanars [q.v.], or priests perform the services of the church, celebrate marriages, bury the dead, &c. They do not receive stated pay, but derive their support from the contributions of the people on festival days, and from marriage and burial fees, &c. The ordinary dress of the priesthood is a long white coat of cotton cloth, tied or buttoned in front, and loose white trousers. The hair is shaven in the form of a tonsure, and the beard is usually worn long.—"*c*" Previous to the Jesuit crusade against the Syrian church, the latter rejected many Papal doctrines such as the dogmas of Papal supremacy and the authority of traditions, the doctrines of transubstantiation and purgatory, &c. They had no images in their churches, nor were extreme unction or auricular confession practised by them. The sacraments they regarded as three, viz., Baptism, Orders, and the Lord's Supper. The clergy were allowed to marry; the bread was dipped in the wine, and the communion thus administered in both kinds. But after that attack the Syrians were led to receive many Roman doctrines which are still retained, though the authority of the church of Rome is repudiated. Transubstantiation, the worship of the Virgin Mary, the invocation of saints, and prayers for the dead are now allowed. The Syrian christians are sometimes called Nestorians; that is to say followers of the doctrine which maintains that Christ was two distinct persons as well as of two distinct natures. It appears that this was their doctrine in the sixth and seventh centuries; but in the eighth century a Jacobite, or Monophysite bishop came from Alexandria, and the Syrian christians thus became dependent on the Jacobite see of Antioch. The Jacobites, so called after Jacobus Baradæus, an opponent of Nestorianism in the sixth century, contend that in Christ there is but one nature, the human nature being absorbed in the divine, not, say they, like oil and water, but like water and wine, which become mingled and united. This doctrine was readily adopted by the Syrians of Malabar, who thus proceeded from one extreme to the other. The term Nestorian does not now properly apply to them.—"*d*" The Patriarch of Antioch, to whom the Syrians render obedience, is one of the four great Patriarchs of the Eastern christian church, viz., of Constantinople, Alexandria, Antioch, and Jerusalem; of whom the first is supreme. There are three prelates in Syria that claim the title and rank of patriarchs of Antioch; but the head of the Asiatic Jacobite, is he who resides generally in a monastery not far from the city of Mardin in Turkey, in N. lat. 37° 15′; E. long. 40° 40′; his spiritual dominion is extensive. He has an associate in the government, to whose care, under the general direction of the patriarch, are entrusted the more distant eastern churches, and who resides in a monastery at Mosul in Mesopotamia, near the ruins of Nineveh. All the patriarchs of this sect assume the name of Ignatius, and their associates that of Basil.—"*e*" The ancient liturgy in general use throughout the Syrian churches, called St. James's Order, has been translated more than once into English. The small Malayalam prayer books used by the Syrians contain prayers for several occasions, and short prayers to be offered in the course of the public service; but no translation of the prayers offered by the cattanar [q.v.] in the celebration of the mass. Though the Syrian christians speak and write Malayalam as their mother tongue, the style of their religious works in this language is very peculiar, being intermixed with Syriac words in a pure or modified form. Their technical and theological terms are all Syriac. A few of the principal terms are as follows:—Gospel, Evangelion; Epistle, Yeucarttah; Psalm, Masmoorah; Apostle, Shleeha; Prophet, Nibyah; Deacon, Meshamshana; Priest, Cattanar; Parish priest, Casheesha; Bishop, Mar; Sexton, Cappiaur; Doctor, Rambaun; Angel, Maulauk; Baptism, Mamodeesa; Mass, Coorbaun; Unction, Ooprisimah; Chancel, Madoobbah; Nave, Haycalah; Holy Ghost, Roohaúda coodisha; Jesus Christ, Yaisoo masheeha; Father, Bawa.—"*f*" The personal disputes and party contentions which have occurred in the more recent internal history of this church have excited attention. Rival priests have visited the distant Patriarch of Antioch with their representations, afterwards returning to Malabar to carry on their disputes in the church itself. At various periods several bishops also have simultaneously put forward antagonistic pretensions to primatial authority. In 1848 there were five bishops in Malabar, each describing the others as unauthorized intruders.—"*g*" The Syrian christians are comparatively fair in complexion. Many are engaged in trading and agricultural pursuits, and some are possessed of much wealth. Several of their number occupy good positions as English teachers, astronomers, lawyers, and clerks. Property among the Syrian christians devolves to legitimate children alike by first or second marriage, sons inheriting the bulk of the property in equal shares; daughters can claim only dowry, and are, therefore, not responsible for debts on the estate. The father cannot quite disinherit any of his children, but may, while alive, distribute his property to them by gift in any reasonable manner or proportion that he pleases. If there are no sons, all goes to the daughters, or brothers, or next heirs; if no near relatives, to the church. Persons without children may bequeath all their property to the church, but this is not allowed if they have children. A widow with a family may enjoy her late husband's property till her sons come of age; if she remarries, nothing is given her [jauty]. See vol. I (96); II (100).——*Syrian bead tree* (حب الشام - habbushshám, Hind.). Same as Large neem.——*Syrian bind weed* (لبلاب شامی - lablábishámí, Hind.). Same as Scammony.——*Syrian cassia* (قثائشامی - kissáishámí, Pers.). Same as Carob.——*Syrian hibiscus* (ليلك شامی - lailakishámí, Hind.). Same as Syrian bendy.——*Syrian rue* (سداب شامی - sadábishámí, Hind.). Same as Harmal.

T (ट - ṭa, टा - ṭá, त - ta, ता - tá, *San.*; ٹ - ṭe, ط - toe, ت - te, *Hind.*; ட - ṭa, தா - tá, *Tam.*). San. ता for Lutchmy [q.v.]. Hind. ث symbol for 400. Hind. ط numerically symbol for 9, and astronomically the sign [raushy] Capricorn [jaddy, macaram]. Denotes 400 in arithmetic.

TABOOT (تابوت - tábút, *Hind.*). Arabic meaning a chest. Otherwise Taziya. Applied to a bier or coffin. Especially a model of the mausoleum of Hoossain [q.v.], carried in the Moharram [q.v.] processions. It consists of a bamboo [q.v.] frame-work, the interstices being filled up with network of paper, often pasted on mica [abruck]. But every variety of materials is employed, even silver [velly], ivory [dant], ebony [q.v.], sandal-wood [sandal], cedar [deodar], &c. Within it are placed alams [q.v.] or flags to represent those of Hassan and Hoossain; lights are placed within it to illuminate it. At the close of the Moharram [q.v.] procession, the taboots should properly be thrown into waters, or if there is not sufficient water they should be buried. But see Shahaudat kah roz. See vol. I (96).

TACCA (تكا - ṭakka, *Malay*). Same as Otaheite salep.

TACORAH (تكورا - takorá, *Hind.*). From (tak, imitative sound). Small kettle drum [paray].

TACSH (तक्ष् - taksh, *San.*). To cut.——*Tacshacan* (तक्षक - takshaka, San.). An artificer. One of the eight serpents [naugam] of mythology.——*Tutchacole* (தச்சக்கோல் - taççakkól, Tam.). From (taççan, tam. carpenter + kól, tam. rod). Carpenter's rod. Linear measure. 44 ungoolams = 1 tutchacole [alavay, 1a]. Approximate actual value, 1 tutchacole = 33 inches. Used in Madura and Tinnevelly. Compare Guz, Ilauhee guz. See vol. I, 609; II, 505, 515, 519.——*Tutchamoolam* (தச்சமுழம் - taççamuzham, Tam.). Carpenter's cubit. Same as Tutchacole.——*Tutchan* (तक्षक - takshaka, San.; بڑھائی - barhaí, Hind.; ಬಡಗಿ - badagi, Can.; వడ్లవాడు - vadlavádu, Tel.; ആശാരി - áshári, Mal.; தச்சன் - taççan, Tam.). Carpenter. One of the village servants [balootah]. Repairs ploughs there, and makes wooden door-frames. The higher class can imitate the most elaborate details, either of art or manufacture. Wood-carving for architectural use is practised with more or less success in almost every village in S. india. Sandal-wood [sandal] carving is carried in Mysore and Travancore and on the Malabar coast generally. According to the Brihatsamhitay [q.v.] of Varauha mihiran [q.v.] the woods most esteemed for furniture are:—Cedrus deodara, loud. [deodar], Dalbergia latifolia, roxb. [malabar blackwood], or bombay blackwood, Diospyros embryopteris, pers., [gaub], Gmelina arborea, linn. [cashmere tree], Mesua ferrea, linn. [nauga champak], Michelia champaca, linn. [champak], Ougeinia dalbergioides, benth. [nemmy], Santalum album, linn. [sandal], Shorea robusta, gærtn. [common saul], Tectona grandis, linn. f. [teak], and Terminalia tomentosa, bedd., var. typica [black murdah]. Artocarpus integrifolia, willd. [common jack], and Cedrela toona, roxb. [toon], both now much used are not named in the list. The Shilpa shastram [q.v.] on mechanics and architecture and some of the pooraunams [q.v.] give detailed directions for felling the trees at particular seasons when their circulation is inactive, and for seasoning the wood afterwards, so as to prevent unequal contractions and cracks in drying. Sandal-wood is according to these authorities the most auspicious of woods for furniture, especially when mounted with gold and jewels. The woods practically most used for furniture are:—for common furniture, chittagongwood [chickrassy], teakwood [teak] toon [q.v.], jack [q.v.]; for carved and ornamental furniture, ebony [q.v.], blackwood [q.v.], satinwood [q.v.], kyabocawood [mochcoondam]. The following are two key-lists of the different kinds of woods [maram] used by the native carpenters of s. india for which vernacular names are known; further information must be traced in the glossary paragraphs through the small-type cross references at the end of this volume; see also vricsham, 7, for the method of expressing the products, &c., of plants in the dravidian languages:—"*a*" Acacia arabica, babool; Acacia ferruginea, anasandra; Acacia sundra, sundra; Adinia cordifolia, model wood; Albizzia lebbek, common sirissa; Anogeissus latifolia, vekkauly; Anthocephalus cadamba, cadamba; Areca catechu, areca; Artocarpus hirsuta, anjely; Artocarpus integrifolia, bread fruit; Bassia longifolia, common mohwah; Berrya ammonilla, trincomalee tree; Borassus flabelliformis, palmyra; Calophyllum inophyllum, common poon; Cedrela toona, toon; Chickrassia tabularis, chickrassy; Chloroxylon swietenia, satinwood; Cocos nucifera, cocoanut; Dalbergia latifolia, malabar blackwood; Diospyros ebenum, ceylon ebony; Diospyros melanoxylon, coromandel ebony; Diospyros montana, forest gaub; Eriodendron anfractuosum, silk cotton; Erioglossum edule, rusty soapnut; Erythrina indica, common coral tree; Erythroxylon monogynum, deccany deodar; Eugenia jambolana, var. caryophyllifolia, clove-leaved jaumoon; Melia azadirachta, margosa; Morinda umbellata, small ach root; Psidium guyava, var. pyriferum, white guava; Pterocarpus marsupium, malabar kino; Pterocarpus santalinus, red sanders; Santalum album, sandal; Schrebera swietenoides, weaver's beam; Shorea robusta, common saul; Soymida febrifuga, rohan tree; Tamarindus indica, tamarind; Tectona grandis, teak; Terminalia belerica, belleric myrobalan; Terminalia catappa, country almond; Terminalia tomentosa, var. typica, black murdah; Thespesia populnea, portia; Xylia dolabriformis, burmah ironwood; Zizyphus jujuba, bair.—"*b*" Ach root, morinda; Almond, terminalia; Anasandra, acacia; Anjely, artocarpus; Babool, acacia; Bair, zizyphus; Blackwood, dalbergia; Bread fruit, artocarpus; Cadamba, anthocephalus; Chickrassy, chickrassia; Cocoanut, cocos; Coral tree, erythrina; Deodar, erythroxylon; Ebony, diospyros; Gaub, diospyros; Guava, psidium; Ironwood, xylia; Jaumoon, eugenia; Kino, pterocarpus; Margosa, melia; Model wood, adina; Mohwah, bassia; Murdah, terminalia; Myrobalan, terminalia; Palmyra, borassus; Poon, calophyllum; Portia, thespesia; Rohan, soymida; Sandal, santalum; Sanders, pterocarpus; Satinwood, chloroxylon; Saul, shorea; Silk cotton, eriodendron; Sirissa, albizzia; Soapnut, erioglossum; Sundra, acacia; Tamarind, tamarindus; Teak, tectona; Toon, cedrela; Trincomalee tree, berrya; Vekkauly, anogeissus; Weaver's beam, schrebera.——*Tutcholy* (തച്ചോളി - taççóli, Mal.). From (taççan, mal. carpenter + óli, mal. term of respect). Name of a tarwaud [q.v.] in Cadatnaud in North malabar.——*Tutcholy pauti* (തച്ചോളിപ്പാട്ട് - taççólippáttu, Mal.). From (taççóli, mal. the family so called + páttu, mal. song).

Originally ballad relating the deeds of Tutcholy meppayil coonny othainan. Now a generic term. One Tutcholy pautt commemorates the Pychee rajah's rebellion; another, Tippoo sultan.

TADDA (धर्मण - dharmana, *San.*; धामण - dhámana, *Mahr.*; دهامن - dháman, *Hind.*; తడశలు - tadashalu, *Can.*; తడ - tada, *Tel.*; ଧାମଣ - dhamonó, *Oor.*; ചടച്ചി - chataççi, *Mal.*; දමනිය - damniya, *Singh.*; சடச்சி - shadaççi, *Tam.*). Title from tel. San. from (dhanvá, san. dry soil); from habitat. Mahr. and Hind. from san. Can. and Tel. corrupted [tadoo] from tamul. Mal. from (chata, mal. hairlock), from fibrous bark. Singh. from (damanawá, singh. to tame), devil tamer; from the priest binding the devil he wishes to compel to his service to this tree [falsah]. Tam. from (shadai, tam. matted hair); from fibrous bark [solah]. Can. also (batale). Tel. also (charachi), by corruption from tamul. Tam. also (úná). Title otherwise Lime tree leaved grewia, Matted hair plant, Tame devil. Botanically Grewia [dharmanam] tiliæfolia, vahl., tiliaceæ [vricsham, 27]. Alias Grewia arborea. Tree; leaves five-nerved, roundish-cordate, bluntly toothed, usually oblique at the base, under side sometimes pubescent; stipules auricled on one side at the base; peduncles numerous, three to five-flowered; sepal twice as long as the petals; stigma four-lobed; drupes two-lobed; each lobe with two hemispherical three-celled nuts; flowering during the hot season. Handsome tree; luxuriant foliage; very common; bark thick, white internally, covered externally by a thin grey suber which readily peels off, showing a slightly rough, green surface beneath. Fruit edible, having agreeable acid flavor; leaves make fodder; bark used as cordage. Timber highly prized for strength and elasticity; used for building purposes, bows, buggy shafts, walking sticks, and a variety of other uses; light and rather soft, flexible and fibrous, coarse-grained and durable, of a light pinkish color turning to light brown, easily worked.——*Bird tadda* (గువ్వదడ - guvvadada, Tel.). Title from small size. Tel. from (guvva, tel. bird + tada, tel. grewia tiliæfolia, vahl.). Tel. also (pótushálmali), meaning male + silk-cotton tree, bombax malabaricum, dec.; (peddatarraki); (gubbadara). Botanically Grewia [dharmanam] abutilifolia, juss., tiliaceæ [vricsham, 27]. Alias Grewia aspera. Tree; leaves irregularly and coarsely toothed, roundish-cordate, occasionally lobed; peduncles about half as long as the petiole, three to four-flowered; sepals oblong, longer, than the petals; drupes four-lobed, pubescent and hairy; nuts four, one to two-celled; flowers greenish-white; flowering throughout the year; common. Gives fibre [naur] and wood.——*Round-leaved tadda* (నులితడ - nulitada, Tel.; நெய்ச்சிட்டி - neyççitti, Tam.). Tel. means small tadda [screw tree]. Tam. from (ney, tam. ghee + shitti, tam. small measure). Tel. also (jánachettu); (jenachettu). Title otherwise Jauna. Botanically Grewia [dharmanam] orbiculata, rottl., tiliaceæ [vricsham, 27]. Alias Grewia rotundifolia. Shrub; leaves five to six-nerved, roundish-cordate, or ovate, hoary and softly velvety on both sides, crenulated; peduncles several together, three-flowered; sepals linear; petals slightly two-toothed; stylo longer than the stamens; stigma four-lobed, crenulated; drupes slightly two-lobed, with one to two usually two-celled nuts in each; flowers purple. Nearly allied to grewia tiliæfolia, vahl. [tadda]; wood of moderate strength.——*Small tadda* (సిరిజాన - sirijána, Tel.; କୁଲୋ - kuló, Oor.; அங்கோலம் - ángolam, Tam.). Tel. means small + jauna tree. Tel. also (kólupu); (jána); (jibilikachettu); (tadikachuvva). Title otherwise Small jauna. Botanically Grewia [dharmanam] excelsa, vahl., tiliaceæ [vricsham, 27]. Alias Grewia bicolor, lævigata, rothii, savifolia. Shrub; leaves ovate-oblong, sharply serrulated, under side hoary, tomentose; peduncles two to three, much longer than the petioles, sepals linear, twice the length of the petals; style filiform; stigma dilated; drupe globose, glabrous, with two one to two-celled nuts; flowering during the rainy season; fruit ripens a few months later; fruit small, agreeable to taste. Gives fibre; has a light, ash-colored wood, with a straight grain, hard and strong, much used.

TADOO (தடு - tádu, *Tam.*). To intervene. To resist.——*Tadauthakye* (தடாதகை - tadáthagai, Tam.). From (above + á, tam. negative particle + kai, tam. hand). Irresistible hand. An epithet given in the pooraunam [q.v.] of the Sheiva temple at Madura [tirvilaiyaudal] to Meenautchy [q.v.], who went out to meet and fought with Shiva her future husband.——*Tadda* (తడ - tada, Tel.). Means impediment. Village; Nellore dist., Polore division tal.; lat. 13° 35′; long. 80° 04′; from Nellore S. 60 miles; from Polore S. 8 miles; from Raupore S.E. 54 miles. Has a canal port on the backwater ½ mile from the village. Is on the trunk road from Nellore to Madras. Private chuttram [q.v.] and a Conair [q.v.] pond.——*Talay* (தலை - talai, Tam.). Field-partition [tank].——*Taity* (ٹٹی - tatti, Hind.; தட்டி - tatti, Tam.). From (tadu, tam. to hinder). Any screen. Especially a screen made of the roots of the fragrant cusous [q.v.] grass, with which door or window openings are filled up in the season of hot winds [land wind]; the screens being kept wet and the wind blowing through them.

TADPATRY (تارپتری - tárpatri, *Hind.*; తాడిపత్రి - tádiparti, *Tel.* tadpatri *). From (tádi, tel. palmyra tree, borassus flabelliformis, linn. + parti, tel. village) [taulam]. Original name is Taulapully.——**(1)** Talook, Anantapore. Tahsildar's pay Rs. 200. Area 641 square miles. Population 112,656. Languages Teloogoo and Canarese. N.E. of district. Boundaries:—north, Coilcoontla and Putticondah talooks of Kurnool district; east, Jummalmadoogoo in Cuddapah district, and Coilcoontla in Kurnool; south, Poolivendla in Cuddapah and Anantapore talook; west, Anantapore and Gooty. The country is flat, except on the eastern boundary, where a low range of hills separates it from the Cuddapah and Kurnool districts. Through the centre of the talook the river Pennair flows, and on either side of it are plains of black-cotton soil [regur]. There is hardly any red soil in the talook. Cotton [q.v.] is the principal crop, but a fine kind of cholum [q.v.] is also grown. Tadpatry and Yellanore are the chief markets, and grain and cloths are sent to Bellary and Cuddapah. A large quantity of the cotton grown in the talook is sent down to Madras. The only tanks [q.v.] of any size are the singular double tank at Royalcheroo and one at Bhogasamoodram. Many irrigation channels [q.v.] are taken off from the river. There are ninety-three villages in the talook, which is a small number for the area. Places of archæological interest:—Arcativaimla, Arvaid, Aulore, Cadanacull, Chaugal, Chillavauripully, Chinna polamoda, Coommanamala, Coommeta, Coormaujipett, Cullore, Dauditota, Dosavaid, Goddoomurry, Goottoor, Mullagoondla, Eittore, Pappore, Pautapully, Peddapappore, Pedda polamoda, Polamoda, Saulavaimla, Sadzaldinney, Shanagalgoodoor, Shingavaram, Tadpatry, Velamacore, Vennapoosalapully, Yaudiky, Yellanore. Principal Trig. station:—Nelgonda. The leading places, &c., in the talook are the following.——*Aulore* (ఆలూరు - álúru, Tel. álúr *). From (álu, tel. cattle + úru, tel. village). Village, Place of pilgrimage; pop. 957; acres 5,968; lat. 14° 55′; long. 78° 06′; from Anantapore E.N.E. 33 miles; from Tadpatry E. 3 miles. Cave with a spring in a mountain valley 2 miles.——*Bhogasamoodram* (భోగసముద్రము - bhógasamudramu, Tel.). From (bhóga, tel. proper name + samudra, san. ocean). Called after Bhogamma. Village; pop. 1,375; acres 5,229; lat. 15° 01′; long. 78° 03′; from Anantapore N.E. 35 miles; from Tadpatry N. 7 miles. Large tank.——*Chitravaty* (చిత్రావతి - chitrávati, Tel.). See sep. title.——*Chookkalore* (చుక్కలూరు - tsukkalúru, Tel.). From (tsukka, tel. small spot + úru, tel. village). Village; pop. 1,148; acres 2,889; lat. 14° 57′; long. 78° 02′; from Anantapore N.E. 30 miles; from Tadpatry N.N.W. 3 miles.——*Cona oopalpaud* (కోనవుప్పలపాడు - kónavuppalapádu, Tel.). From (kóna, tel. ravine + uppalamu, tel. salt marsh + pádu, tel. village). Village; pop. 720; acres 8,539; lat. 15° 06′; long. 77° 56′; from Anantapore N.E. 35 miles; from Tadpatry N.N.W. 15 miles.——*Dauditota* (దాడితోట - dáditóta, Tel.). From (dádi, tel. army + tóta, tel garden). Village; pop. 2,119; acres 10,309; lat. 14° 36′; long. 78° 00′; from Anantapore E.S.E. 24 miles; from Tadpatry S. 22 miles.——*Igdore* (ఇగుదూరు - igudúru, Tel.). Village; pop. 871; acres 3,339; lat. 14° 58′; long. 77° 59′; from Anantapore N.E. 30 miles; from Tadpatry N.W. 6 miles. Large channel.——*Mootchoocottah* (ముచ్చుకోట - muttsukóta, Tel.). From (muttsu, tel. thief + kóta, tel. fort). Village; pop. 1,608; acres 9,696; lat. 14° 51′; long. 77° 55′; from Anantapore E.N.E. 21 miles; from Tadpatry W.S.W. 10 miles. Yhipy [q.v.] jungles.——*Nagarore* (నగరూరు - nagarúru, Tel.). From (nagaru, tel. palace + úru, tel. village). Village; pop. 1,309; acres 5,147; lat. 15° 00′; long. 77° 52′; from Anantapore N.E. 26 miles; from Tadpatry W.N.W. 13 miles.——*Nelgonda* (నెలగొండ - nelagonda, Tel.). From (néla, tel. ground + konda, tel. hill). Trig. station; lat. 14° 51′ 09·57″; long. 77° 57′ 45·65″; from Anantapore N.E. 25 miles; from Tadpatry S.W. 7 miles.——*Nittore* (నిట్టూరు - nittúru, Tel.). From (nidu, tel. long + úru, tel. village). Village; pop. 1,535; acres 16,616; lat. 15° 03′; long. 77° 59′; from Anantapore N.E. 34 miles; from Tadpatry N.N.W. 10 miles.——*Nundiaulpaud* (నంద్యాలపాడు - nandyálapádu, Tel.). From (nandi, san. bull god + álaya, san. temple + pádu, tel. village). Village; pop. 989; acres 2,954; lat. 14° 55′; long. 78° 02′; from Anantapore N.E. 29 miles; from Tadpatry W. 1½ miles. Site of the Tadpatry railway station.——*Peddapappore* (పెద్దపప్పూరు - peddappúru, Tel.). From (pedda, tel. large + pappu, tel. dholl + úru, tel. village). Village; pop. 1,513; acres 2,025; lat. 14° 56′; long. 77° 55′; from Anantapore N.E. 24 miles; from Tadpatry W. 10 miles. Good silk cloth woven.——*Peddayeckalore* (పెద్దయెక్కలూరు - peddayekkalúru, Tel.). From (pedda, tel. great + ekkali, tel. mound + úru, tel. village). Village; pop. 1,978; acres 3,706; lat. 14° 56′; long. 77° 52′; from Anantapore N.E. 22 miles; from Tadpatry W. 12 miles. Weekly market.——*Pennair* (పెన్నేరు - pennéru, Tel.). See sep. title.——*Royalcheroo* (రాయలచెరువు - ráyalcheruvu, Tel.). See sep. title.——*Shanagalgoodoor* (శనగలగూడూరు - shanagalagúdúru, Tel.). From (shanagalu, tel. bengal gram, cicer arietinum, linn. + gúdúru, tel. place so called). Village; pop. 3,447; acres 12,018; lat. 14° 49′; long. 78° 05′; from Anantapore E.N.E. 30 miles; from Tadpatry S.S.E. 7 miles.——*Tadpatry* (తాడిపత్రి - tádiparti, Tel.). See below.——*Yaudiky* (యాడికి - yádiki, Tel.). See sep. title.——*Yellanore* (యెల్లనూరు - yellanúru, Tel.). From (ella, tel. boundary + úru, tel. village). Village; pop. 3,403; acres 9,860; lat. 14° 42′; long.

78° 07′; from Anantapore E. 31 miles; from Tadpatry S.S.E. 15 miles. On Chitrauvaty, and founded more than 600 years ago by Chikka wodeyar. Its old name was Vellalore. In seventeenth century became the residence of a Mahomedan chief, from whom it was taken by one of the Cuddapah poligars [q.v.].——*Zootoor* (ఝూటూరు - dzútúru, Tel.). From (dzúti, tel. rogue + úru, tel. village). Village; pop. 3,482; acres 6,691; lat. 14° 57′; long. 77° 57′; from Anantapore N.E. 27 miles; from Tadpatry W.N.W. 7 miles.——**(2)** Town, Talook head-quarters, Subordinate judge's court; Anantapore dist., Tadpatry tal.; pop. 10,283; acres 7,554; lat. 14° 55′; long. 78° 03′; height 783 feet; from Anantapore E.N.E. 30 miles; from Bellary E.S.E. 74 miles; from Gooty S.E. 28 miles; from Madras N.W. 200 miles; from Penoocondah N.E. 64 miles. On right bank of Pennair which flows close underneath its walls. The railway station is at Nundiaulpaud, 2½ miles off. Town was founded by Ramalingam naidoo, a subordinate of the Vijianugger kings, 400 years ago. After Talicote [q.v.] the country round Tadpatry was subdued by the Cootb shahy [q.v.] dynasty [raj], and a Mahomedan governor was appointed. Afterwards the town was captured by Moraury row, and still later by Hyder ally. A great trading centre, and on this account and also on account of its peculiar sanctity, one authority reckoning it next to Benares, it has always been a thriving town. Silk [puttoo] and cotton [q.v.] cloths are woven which are sent to Bangalore and towards Bombay. There is a small trade with Cuddapah in cotton [q.v.] and indigo [q.v.]. Ramalingam naidoo built the temple on the river bank dedicated to Rameshwaran. The other temple in the town called that of Chintaroya was built by his grandson, Timma naidoo, who founded several other villages in the neighbourhood. These two temples are elaborately decorated with sculptures representing the adventures of Krishnan [q.v.], Rama [q.v.], &c. Among the bas-reliefs [jalee] is a figure holding a Grecian bow. The temple on the river bank is the finest, but is not finished. The gopooram [q.v.] of the other temple [coil, pagoda] was struck by lightning some years ago and split in half.

TAEEFA (طايفه - táifah, *Hind.*). From (taafa, ar. to go round). A dancing girl [cunchany, dausy].

TAFAUWAT (تفاوت - tafáwat, *Hind.*). From (fauta, ar. far as under) [firkah]. Discrepancy.

TAFETTA (تافته - táftah, *Hind.*). From (táftan, pers. to twist). A fabric of twisted thread, made both in silk [puttoo] and cotton [q.v.]. Has a wavy lustre [sheelay].

TAFREEK (تفريق - tafrík, *Hind.*). From (fark, ar. separation) [firkah]. Distribution. Extra contribution imposed on villagers. For Maraumut tafreek see Maraumut.

TAFSEEL (تفصيل - tafsíl, *Hind.*). From (fasala, ar. to divide). Particulars [vivaram].

TAFSEER (تفسير - tafsír, *Hind.*). From (fisr, ar. to explain). A commentary, especially on the Koran [q.v.].

TAFWEEZ (تفويض - tafwíz, *Hind.*). From (fáza, ar. to delegate). Delegation of authority [takdeer]. The doctrine of absolute liberty with regard to the choice of right and wrong maintained by certain sects of Mahomedans.

TAGAR (தகர் - tagar, *Tam.*). To break.——*Tagarum* (कस्तीर - kastíra, San.; قلعى - kalaí, Ar.; ارزيز - arzíz, Pers.; كتهيل - katthíl, Hind.; رنگا - rangá, Dec.; تيما - timah, Malay; ತಗರ - tagara, Can.; ತಮರ - tamara, Too.; తగరము - tagaramu, Tel.; തകരം - takaram, Mal.; සුදුඊයම් - suduíyam, Singh.; தகரம் - tagaram, Tam.). Title from tamul. San. from (kásh, san. to shine). Hind. from sanscrit. Mal. from tamul. Singh. from (sudu, singh. white + íyam, tam. lead). Tam. from (tagar, tam. to break to pieces), easily cut. San. also (trapu), meaning bashful, on account of its melting easily; (ranga), meaning tin; (vanga). Ar. also (rasás). Malay also (timahpútih), meaning white tin; (timasari), meaning flower tin. Mal. also (vellíyam), meaning white lead. Tam. also (vellíyam), meaning white lead. Greek κασσίτερος from sanscrit. Tin. Stannum of chemists. Soft, white, brilliant, and inelastic metal [dhautoo, loham]. Its surface is but slowly impaired on exposure to the atmosphere. Is alloyed with copper [taumram], zinc [tootnaug], &c., forming compounds. Black tin is tin and iron [auhan] combined. A valuable pewter [cull eeyam] is antimony [soorma] seventeen parts and tin eighty-three parts. κασσίτερος was exported from Egypt to Monziris [cranganore] and Nelkunda [cullada] according to the Periplus, but now chiefly brought here from Indian archipelago. Pulvis stanni is known to hakeems [q.v.]; considered anthelmintic; it is purified for medicine by melting it over the fire and pouring the melted fluid into the milky juice of calotropis gigantea [yercum]. Various common uses; chief is in tinning different metals [loham], such as iron [auhan] and copper [taumram]. Tagara raikk is tinfoil; used for ornamenting images, fans, pictures, &c.——*Tagaray* (தகரை - tagarai, Tam.). Means to destroy, useful remedy. Same as Chakondah.

TAGARAM (तगर - tagara, *San.*). Botanically the Tabernæmontana genus, apocynaceæ [vricsham, 87]. Trees or shrubs natives of tropical regions; leaves opposite, entire, mostly smooth, and short-stalked; flowers white, fragrant; fruits consist of two ovoid or oblong or kidney-shaped, smooth or ribbed, dry or fleshy follicles; seeds buried in pulp. The species best known to the natives are shown below. Other s. indian species indigenous or naturalized are:—citrifolia, crispa.——*Adam's apple* (तगर - tagara, San. and Mahr.; تگر - tagar, Hind.; دودهموگرا - dúdhmográ, Dec.; ನಂದಿಬಟ್ಲು - nandibatlu, Can.; ಕೊಕ್ಕೆ - kokke, Too.; నందివర్ధనము - nandivardhanamu, Tel.; നന്തിയാർവട്ടം - nantiyárvattam, Mal.; තුවරලා - tuvaralá, Singh.; நந்தியாவட்டம் - nandiyávattam, Tam.). Title as the companion of eve's apple [q.v.]. Hind. from sanscrit. Dec. from (dúdh, hind. milk + mográ, hind. jasmine, jasminum sambac, ait.). Can. from (nandi, san. pleasing + batla, can. circle). Tel. from (nandi, san. happiness + vardhana, san. increasing). Mal. from tamul. Tam. from (nandyávarta, san. the plant). San. also (nandyávarta), meaning delight + turning; (vishnupriya), meaning vishnoo + favorite; (nandivriksha), meaning happiness + plant [toon]; (tárávata), meaning star-like. Hind. also (chándní), meaning moonlight. Can. also (nanjavatta), by corruption. Tel. also (grandhitagarapuchettu), probably sanscritized corruption of (gandhatagarapuchettu), meaning fragrant + the tree. Tam. also (adukkunandiyávattai), meaning layer + plant; from double petals; (perunandiyávattai), meaning large + the plant. Title otherwise Broad leaved rose bay, Burra tagar, Ceylon jasmine, Chandnee, Indian rose bay, Milky jasmine, Moonbeam, Tagar, Wax flower. Botanically Tabernæmontana [tagaram] coronaria, br., apocynaceæ [vricsham, 87]. Alias Nerium coronarium, divaricatum; Tabernæmontana divaricata. A shrub six to eight feet leaves opposite, unequal, elliptic-oblong, acute at the base, obtusely acuminated; peduncles from the forks twin, erect, dichotomous, four to six-flowered; flowers white, fragrant at night; flowering nearly all the year; found wild in western jungles, much cultivated in gardens and about temples. Flower religious. Juice of leaves dropped into eyes in ophthalmia. Wood white, moderately hard, close-grained. One garden variety has double flowers.——*Eve's apple* (ഉതളം - utalam, Mal.; දිවිකදුරු - divikaduru, Singh.; காட்டலரி - káttalari, Tam.). Title from resemblance to half-eaten small apple [seb], as well as from being native of ceylon, near which paradise supposed to be situated; the fruit, wholesome once, became a deadly poison after having been tasted by eve. Mal. compare odallam. Singh. from (divi, singh. heaven + kaduru, singh. the forbidden plant, general name for dog's bane). Tam. from (kádu, tam. forest + alari, tam. nerium odorum, soland.). Tam. also (pálai), meaning milky plant [dita, edible paulay, ground paulay, monkey-face paulay, nakchiknoo silk cotton, nauga champak, pauchonty, paula indigo, paulay silk cotton, tellicherry bark]. Title otherwise Forbidden fruit [pummelow], Mango like cerbera. Botanically Tabernæmontana [tagaram] dichotoma, roxb., apocynaceæ [vricsham, 87]. Alias Cerbera manghas; Manghas latescens; manghas from mango. Shrub; leaves oblong, acute at the base, obtuse at the apex, coriaceous; petiole dilated at the base, amplectant; cymes terminal, dichotomous, many-flowered, nearly equalling the leaf; peduncles naked, long; bracts ovate, small; calycine lobes ovate, obtuse; segments of the corolla somewhat longer than the tube; follicles recurved, acutish, orange-colored; flowers yellowish-white, slightly fragrant; flowering nearly all the year. Large spreading shrub; broadly lanceolate, rigid, yellow-green leaves, nine or ten inches long; fragrant flowers, similar to vinca alba; fruit like a mango [q.v.] both in color and shape, one side more concave than the other; seeds size of large chestnuts. Seeds of fruit powerfully narcotic; leaves and bark purgative; fruit externally applied as cataplasm in diseases of the skin. Oil [yennay] from seeds.

TAGARAUR (تكرار - takrár, *Hind.*). From (karra, ar. to repeat). Altercation [tantah].

TAGHEIR (تغير - taghír, *Hind.*). From (ghaira, ar. to change). Dismissal [bartarf, mokoop].

TAGLOOB (تغلب - tagallub, *Hind.*). From (ghaluba, ar. to over-power). Cheating.

TAH (ته - tah, *Hind.*). Below. Tahband is a petticoat.

TAHITI (تاهيتى - táhití, *Hind.*). Chief of the Society islands. Same as Otaheite.——*Tahiti arrowroot* (காராக்கருணை - kárákkarunai, Tam.). Same as Otaheite salep.

TAHREER (تحرير - tahrír, *Hind.*). Fr. (harra, ar. write). Fee.

TAHSIL (تحصيل - tahsíl, *Hind.*). From (hasala, ar. to collect). Collections. Tahsildar is the native collector of revenue and sub-magistrate in charge of a talook [q.v.]. Tahsildar nautacam is a tamul drama by Vishwanautan to ridicule the vices of a Tahsildar.

TAIL (वृश्चिक - vrishchika, *San.*; विंचू - vinchú, *Mahr.*; عقرب - akrab, *Ar.*; كژدم - kazdum, *Pers.*; بچھو - biçchú, *Hind.* and *Dec.*; كلا - kala, *Malay*; ಚೇಳು - chélu, *Can.*; ತೇಲ್ - tel, *Too.*; తేలు - télu, *Tel.*; തേൾ - tél, *Mal.*; ගෝනුස්සා - gónussá, *Singh.*; தேள் - tél, *Tam.*). Title from tamul. San. from (vrashch, san. to wound). Ar. from (akraba, ar. to twist). Hind. from sanscrit. Mal. from (chel, mal. sharp). Tam. also (nattuváykkáli), meaning lobster-mouthed-legged one. Scorpion.

Some are black colored, but the usual tints are various shades of brown. Plant first term meaning that fruits are like scorpion's tail or the plant is antidote to scorpion-bite or the touch is burning like scorpion sting. Ex., where transl. is of second term :—Heliotropium indicum (télumani), gem ; Martynia diandra (télukondi), sting ; Tragia involucrata (télumanichettu), gem + tree. See gloss. paragraphs.

TAINEE (मधुकर - madhukara, *San.* ; मधमाशी - madhamáshí, *Mahr.* ; نحل - nahl, *Ar.* ; زنبورعسل - zambúriasal, *Pers.* ; شہد کی مکھی - shahadkímakkhí, *Hind.* and *Dec.* ; لابہ - lábah, *Malay* ; ಜೇನುನೊಣ - jénunona, *Can.* ; తిగకెలెంజి - tigatakelenji, *Too.* ; తేనీగ - ténìga, *Tel.* ; തേനീച്ച - téníçça, *Mal.* ; මීපා - mípá, *Singh.* ; தேனீ - téní, *Tam.*). Title from tamul [tem]. San. from (madhu, san. honey + kri, san. to do). Mahr. from (madhu, san. honey + makshiká, san. fly). Pers. from (zambúr, pers. bee + asal, pers. honey). Hind. from (shahad, hind. honey + makkhí, hind. fly). Can. from (jénu, can. honey + nona, can. fly). Too. from (tiga, too. honey + kelenji, too. fly). Tel. from (téne, tel. honey + íga, tel. fly). Mal. from (tén, mal. honey + íçça, mal. fly). Singh. from (mí, singh. honey + pá, san. to drink). Tam. from (tén, tam. honey + í, tam. fly). Honey bee. Apis mellifica, aphidæ, hemiptera, hemimetabola, insecta [poochy], of naturalists [jantoo]. Not domesticated here. Some construct their nests in trees, others frequent rocks, and one kind often takes up its abode about the doors or windows of buildings. The natives have a belief that when a swarm of bees builds its nest on a building, it is a sign of some of the inmates being about to change their residence. Honey [shahad] and wax [mom] are chiefly collected by jungle tribes, and when robbing the nests they smear their bodies with a substance which prevents the bees from stinging them. The Yanaudies [q.v.] and Chentsoos [q.v.] of the East coast climb into apparently inaccessible places and over perpendicular cliffs in some places from 100 to 200 feet high. This they do by means of a plaited rope made of young bamboos [q.v.] tied together. The rope being fastened on the top of the cliff, 100 or 200 feet above, by means of a peg driven into the ground, or by a tree, the man swings suspended in the air, armed with a basket and stick. He first burns some brushwood or grass under the hive, which is then relinquished by the majority of the bees. This accomplished, he swings the rope until it brings him close to the hive, which he pokes with his stick, at the same time holding out his basket to catch the pieces broken off from the hive. When the basket is full he shakes the rope, and is drawn up by his companions. The bamboo ropes are never taken away, nor are they used a second time, a fresh one being made on each occasion and at each place. They are to be seen hanging for years until they decay and fall down of themselves. There is a Tamul proverb :—மலைத்தேன் முடவனுக்கு வருமா ?—"will mountain honey come to the lame "man ?" do not expect too much. The indigenous honey-making bees of Southern India have been referred to the following kinds.——*Flower bee* (पुष्पलिट् - pushpalit, San. ; ಕೊಂಬುಜೇನುಹುಳ - kombujénuhula, Can. ; జుంటితేనీగ - dzuntiténíga, Tel. ; ചെറുതേനീച്ച - cheruténíçça, Mal. ; சிறுதேனீ - shiruthéní, Tam.). San. from (pushpa, san. flower + lih, san. to lick). Can. from (kombu, can. branch + jénu, can. honey + hula, can. insect). Tel. from (dzunnu, tel. cheese + téníga, tel. honey bee). Tam. from (shiru, tam. small + tén, tam. honey + í, tam. fly). Apis floralis, aphidæ, hemiptera, hemimetabola, insecta [poochy], of naturalists. Chiefly confined to the plains, but appears in Wynaud. In habits resemble Apis indica [tree bee].——*Hill bee* (ಹೆಜ್ಜೇನುಹುಳ - heddajénuhula, Can. ; కొండతేనీగ - kondaténíga, Tel. ; മലന്തേനീച്ച - malanténíçça, Mal. ; மலைத்தேனீ - malaitténí, Tam.). Can. from (hedda, can. large + jénu, can. honey + hula, can. insect). Others mean hill bee. Apis dorsata, aphidæ, hemiptera, hemimetabola, insecta [poochy], of naturalists. Found amongst low hills and in forests. Invariably lodges on the branches of trees and in clefts of rocks and has favorite haunts. Although the honey [shahad] be taken year after year, a swarm always occupies the old locality. Comb often several feet in length and over an inch in thickness. Honey collected mostly in the hot season. The sting is painful and dangerous. Apis dorsata, var. testacea, smith, is a large variety, widely distributed, not recognised as distinct from the ordinary large rock bee by natives ; comb, honey, &c., identical with the ordinary Apis dorsata. Apis dorsata, var. zonata, fuer, is dun colored ; resembles the other varieties of dorsata.——*Mosquito bee* (ಸೊಳ್ಳೆಜೇನುಹುಳ - sollejénuhula, Can. ; ముసురుతేనీగ - musuruténíga, Tel. ; கொசுத்தேனீ - kosutténí, Tam.). Title from small size. Can. from (sollo, can. musquito + jénu, can. honey + hula, can. insect). Tel. from (musuru, tel. to swarm + téníga, tel. honey bee). Tam. from (kosu, tam. mosquito + tén, tam. honey + í, tam. fly). Tam. also (pondutténí), meaning crevice + bee ; (shiruthéní), meaning small bee. Apis nigrocincta, aphidæ, hemiptera, hemimetabola, insecta [poochy], of naturalists. Confined to the plains and low rocky hills. Builds its nest in crevices of rocks, hollows of trees and ruined buildings. The quantity of honey [shahad] is small and not good.——*Tree bee* (ತುಡುವಿಜೇನುಹುಳ - tuduvijénuhula, Can. ; పుల్లతేనీగ - pullaténíga, Tel. ; കൊമ്പുതേനീച്ച - komputténíçça, Mal. ; கொம்புத்தேனீ - kombutténí, Tam.). All mean branch + bee. Apis indica, aphidæ, hemiptera, hemimetabola, insecta [poochy], of naturalists. Is mostly confined to the plains and low hill ranges, but appears also on the Neilgherries. Attaches its combs to branches or establishes itself in hollows of the trunks of trees. Sting not severe.

TAIR (తేరు - téru, *Tel.* ; தேர் - tér, *Tam.*). An idol car [rath]. For mirage or peytair see under Pey.——*Tairottam* (தேரோட்டம் - teróttam, Tam.). Means car + running. Otherwise Ratotsavam. Any Car festival [pundigay, 6d].

TAJAMMOOL (تجمل - tajammul, *Ar.*). From (jamala, ar. to adorn). Adorned, dignified. Prefixed to an alam forms a lacab ; as Tajammool hoossain, dignity of hoossain [ism].

TAKBEER (تکبیر - takbír, *Hind.*). From (kibr, ar. great). [cabeer]. Repeating the Mahomedan creed [deen, imaun].

TAKDEER (تقدیر - takdír, *Hind.*). From (kadara, ar. to measure). Predestination ; the decree of good and evil [tafweez]. Compare the hindoo Carmam and Samsauram.

TAKEE (تقی - takí, *Ar.*). From (taká, ar. to fear) ; God-fearing, pious. Lacab of the ninth Imaum [q.v.]. Common alam ; as Takee hoossain, double alam [ism].——*Takeeya* (تقیہ - takíyah, Hind.). From (taká, ar. to fear). Caution. An outward conformity with an alien religious belief, a practice held to be permissible by the shiahs [q.v.].

TAKEED (تاکید - tákíd, *Hind.*). From (akada, ar. to tie fast). Injunction. Written order, generally from superior to inferior.

TAKHALLOOS (تخلص - takhallus, *Hind.*). From (khalasa, ar. freed). Descriptive names of poets which they assume in consequence of the unpoetical consonance of their own proper names, these not entering into the measure of a verse. Usually found in concluding distich of a poem. Rare in Arabic, oftener in Persian. Takhalloos refers either to the native place of the poet, or to his original trade, profession, special accomplishments, habits, &c. Sometimes taken as an honorary title conferred by patron. See vol. I (106), cl. (6) [ism].

TAKHT (تخت - takht, *Hind.*). From pers. Throne [pad].

TAKIYA (تکیہ - takiyah, *Hind.*). From persian. A pillow. The tomb [durgah] of a Mahomedan saint [walee].

TAKKAULY (தக்காளி - takkáli, *Tam.*). From (takka, tam. fit, proper + ál, tam. to possess) ; of good quality ; medicinal shrub. Botanically Physalis genus, solanaceæ [vricsham, 94]. Annual or perennial herbs ; leaves alternate or twin, entire or lobed ; flowers solitary, extra-axillary ; berry covered by a connivent inflated calyx, globose, two-celled, placentæ thick seeds many, reniform, compressed ; embryo fleshy. The species best known to the natives are :—minima [small indian winter cherry], peruviana [indian winter cherry].

TAKLEED (تقلید - taklíd, *Hind.*). From (kalada, ar. to invest with authority) [gheir mookallid]. The doctrine of following the exposition and interpretation of law [shareeyat] of certain doctors [moojtahid]. Held by soonnees [q.v.].

TAL (تل - tal, *Hind.*). Low [taul].——*Talaghaut* (تل گھاٹ - talghát, Hind.). From (above + ghát, hind. hill-pass). Lowlands [payeen ghaut].

TALA (തല - tala, *Mal.* ; தலை - talai, *Tam.*). Head, and hence prominent. Prefix in place names ; as Talacaud, meaning principal forest.——*Talamullay* (தலைமலை - talaimalai, Tam.). From (talai, tam. head + malai, tam. hill). Hill, Head assistant's division ; Trichinopoly dist., Moosiry tal. ; lat. 11° 05′ ; long. 78° 22′ ; from Moosiry N.W. 12 miles ; from Trichinopoly N.W. 30 miles. Detached and conspicuous from the railway. Sanitarium for Europeans. On summit a pagoda [hill-station, pagoda].——*Talapully* (തലപ്പള്ളി - talappalli, Mal.). From (tala, mal. chief + palli, mal. village). Talook, Cochin state ; pop. 113,114. Principal places :—Caccaud, Chemmandatta, Coonnancoolam, Kellarcaud, Matchaud, Moolloorkara, Pazhayanore, Porcalam, Shoranore, Tirvillamala, Venganellore, Yermayputty.——*Talavausal* (தலைவாசல் - talaivásal, Tam.). From (talai, tam. head + vásal, tam. entrance). The chief entrance to the Mysore territory. Village ; Salem dist., Ahtoor tal. ; pop. 1,065 ; acres 772 ; lat. 11° 35′ ; long. 78° 48′ ; from Ahtoor E. 10 miles ; from Salem E. 40 miles. On the Vasishtanuddy and on South arcot frontier. Travellers' bungalow [q.v.]. Indigo [q.v.] factory.——*Talay* (தலை - talai, Tam.). Head. Talay vary is a poll-tax.——*Taliyary* (తలారి - talári, Tel. ; தலையாரி - talaiyári, Tam.). From (talai, tam. head + personal suffix). A head village watchman whose duty it is to give information of offences, guide travellers, &c. [cauvalgar]. See vol. I (102), 154.——*Tellicherry* * (തലശ്ശേരി - talashshéri, Mal.). From (tala, mal. head + shéri, mal. village). Sanscrit name (shvétáranyapuri), meaning white + forest + town ; this name still survives in tirvangaud, a part of the town.—"*a*" Town, Port, Head-quarters of Judge, Sub-collector, Sub-judge, District moonsif, Tahsildar, and District registrar, Lighthouse ;

Malabar dist., Cottayam tal.; pop. 27,196; lat. 11° 45′; long. 75° 32′; height 70 feet; from Bombay S.S.E. 516 miles; from Calicut N.N.W. 39 miles; from Cannanore S.E. 12 miles; from Dharmapatam S.E. 2 miles; from Cottayam S.W. 6 miles; from Madras W.S.W. 336 miles; from Malapooram N.W. 61 miles; from Manantoddy W. 34 miles; from Palghaut N.W. 102 miles; from Ponnany N.N.W. 71 miles; from Talye N.N.W. 1½ miles. Site picturesque, open to sea on west, and on opposite side backed by wooded hills interspersed with valleys and watered by a fine river. Has been called the Montpellier of India. The native town lies to the south. The limits of the port are:—north, boundary pillar 1½ miles north of the custom house; south, boundary pillar 1½ miles south of the custom house; east, seashore between them to within 50 yards of high-water mark, spring tides; west, space enclosed by the two lines running due west from the boundary pillars to nine fathoms water. Light on the fort wall near the beach; lat. 11° 44′ 50″; long. 75° 28′ 30″; white; fixed; 8 miles range. Visible from all directions seaward. Small masonry tower. A harbour light. The best anchorage for large vessels is with the flagstaff N.E. by N. in six fathoms and about 2 miles off shore. Coasting craft come into the bay, lying south of a reef of rocks, which at a distance of about a 1,000 yards from shore runs parallel to the coast line. Vessels of six hundred or eight hundred tons in ballast have been known to pass the monsoon [q.v.] under shelter of this reef. Factory established under a chief and factors by the President of Surat, being the first pepper [q.v.] settlement on the Malabar coast [q.v.], 1683. Factory strengthened 1688. Formal grant obtained for the fort from the Chiracal rajah, 1708. On several occasions between 1708 and 1761 the company obtained from the Colattiry [q.v.] rajah and other local chiefs grants of land in and near Tellicherry, and some important privileges such as right to collect customs, administer justice, &c., within these grants. Limits of settlement extended on south side after a successful war with the Coorangote nayar, 1719. Settlement reduced from a chiefship to a residency, 1776. Besieged by Sirdar khan, Hyder's fowjdar [q.v.] with Chiracal rajah, 1780. H.M.S. Superb of seventy-four guns was lost at Tellicherry in November 1781. Successful sortie under Major Abingdon and the siege raised, 1782. The Chiefship re-established, 1784. Chiefship abolished and the settlement placed directly under the Supervisor of Malabar, 1794. The citadel, still in excellent preservation, stands on rising ground close to the sea and north of the town. The old residency is now occupied by the Sub-collector. Principal modern exports are coffee [q.v.], pepper [q.v.], ginger [q.v.], cardamoms [q.v.], and sandal [q.v.] wood; and imports are rice [q.v.] and salt [ooppoo]. Hindoo pagoda [q.v.] in Tirvangaud dedicated to Shree rama commonly called Brass pagoda, on account of roof. Travellers' bungalow [q.v.].—"*b*" River; Malabar dist., Cottayam tal.; lat. 11° 46′ N.; long. 75° 33′ E. Also called Codoly river, from fort of that name commanding the bay at its mouth. Navigable for boats for only 3½ miles. Small country craft enter its mouth and lie above bridge which spans it. Formerly important as affording protection to English factory at Tellicherry on N. and E. landward sides. It still forms boundary of French Aldée of Pandacull. Total length, about 14 miles. ——*Tellicherry bark* (कुटज - kutaja, San.; कुडा - kudá, Mahr.; لسان العصا فير المر - lisánulasáfírulmurr, Ar.; اندر جو تلخ - indarjauitalkh, Pers.; كڑوا اندر جو - karváindarjú, Hind. and Dec.; ಕೊರಸಿಗ - korisiga, Can.; కొడిశ - kodisha, Tel.; ପତ୍ରକର୍ବାନ - patrakarvan, Oor.; കടകപ്പാല - kutakappála, Mal.; කිරිවැල්ල - kirivallá, Singh.; கசப்புவெப்பாலை - kasappuveppálai, Tam.). Title from place of export. San. from (kutila, san. curled + jan. san. to be born); from curled roots; cf. echites. Mahr. from sanscrit. Ar. from (lisán, ar. tongue + asáfír, ar. sparrows + murr, ar. bitter), from resemblance of seed or bean. Pers. from (indrayava, san. the seed + talkh, pers. bitter), as opposed to sweet inderjow from wrightia tinctoria, r. br. [paula indigo]. Hind. from (karvá, hind. bitter + indrayava, san. seed of the plant). Can. and Tel. from sanscrit, by corruption. Oor. from (patra, san. leaf + karvá, hind. bitter); plate leaf + bitter inderjow; cf. (vistrákupála), below in teloogoo. Mal. from (kutaku, mal. the gháts near coorg + pála, mal. milky plant). Singh. from (kiri, singh. milk + vallá, singh. wrightia zeylanica, br.). Tam. from (kasappu, tam. bitter + vedbálai, tam. wrightia tinctoria, r. br.). San. also (kalingá), meaning useful; (chírí), meaning clothed. Mahr. also (dhavalakuda), meaning white conessi tree. Ar. also (tíwáj). Pers. also (zabánikunjashkitalkh), meaning tongue + sparrow + bitter. Hind. also (karaija), meaning sweet inderjow; (dúdhíkílakrí), milk-giving stick. Can. also (kodasiga), from sanscrit by corruption. Tel. also (manupála), meaning earth + milky plant; (kalingamu), from sanscrit [chaltah]; (kolamukki); (peddaankudu), meaning large + the tree; (pálakodisha), meaning milk + the tree; (chédukodisha), meaning bitter + the tree; (ankudu) [gambier, paula indigo]; (pála) [dita, edible paulay, eve's apple, ground paulay, monkey-face paulay, nakchiknee silk cotton, nauga champak, pauchonty, paula indigo, paulay silk cotton]; (kákakodisa), meaning crow + the tree; (indravrikshamu), meaning indra's tree; (vistrákupála), meaning plate leaf + the tree. Oor. also (karva), meaning bitter. Mal. also (kaippakkotakappála), meaning bitter + the plant; (venpála), meaning white + milk plant; (pálappatta), meaning milk plant + bark. Tam. also (veppálai), meaning white + milky plant; (kulappálai), meaning coorg + the plant. Title otherwise Bitter inderjow, Bitter oleander, Bitter sparrow tongue, Codaga plant, Conessi bark, Coorchy bark, Coorg milk plant, Corte de pala, Medicinal echites, Wild bitter. Botanically Holarrhena antidysenterica, wall., apocynaceæ [vricsham, 87]. Alias Chonemorpha antidysenterica; Echites antidysenterica; Holarrhena codaga, pubescens; Nerium antidum; Wrightia antidysenterica. Codaga from malayalam. Large jungle shrub; leaves bright green on each side, opposite, entire, elliptic, very obtuse at the base, acute or abruptly acuminated at the apex; calycine lobes lanceolate; corolla cup-shaped, tube dilated between the base and the middle, throat contracted; stamens inserted between the base and middle of the tube; cymes many-flowered, terminal; flowers puberulous, white; follicles a foot long; common. The young bark is grey and nearly smooth; on the older branches it is externally of a brown color, and scarred from the exfoliation of portions of the suber; internally it is of a cinnamon color, and the cambium layer when present smooth and nearly white; the root bark resembles that of the older stems, but is of a deeper and more rusty brown color. The leaves of paula indigo [q.v.] are so like those of tellicherry bark especially when young that they may be mistaken; a distinction is however the numerous pointed glands on the petiole at the base of the leaf of the present article. Seeds of tellicherry bark are of a cinnamon [q.v.] brown color, convex on one side, and concave and marked with a longitudinal pale line on the other, covered with a downy tuft, resembling the down of the thistle; easily broken, bitter to the taste, and of a heavy unpleasant odour; something like oats [vilauyaty jow]; these also often confounded with seeds of paula indigo. The astringent and bitter bark is a remedy in dysentery, hence specific name; substituted for british cinchona [koinah] bark and ipecacuanha; seeds are astringent and anthelmintic; a thick, scarlet-colored medicinal oil; bark and seeds both in pharm., non-officinal. Leaves used as fodder or litter; ashes used as mordants [cauram]; wood white, soft, even-grained, used for carving and turning. Another species is Mitis.

TALABONE (తలబోను - talabónu, *Tel.*; குழவிப்பாம்பு - kuzhavippámbu, *Tam.*). Tam. from (kuzhavi, tam. roller + pámbu, tam. snake). Title otherwise Bamboo fish. Murænesox talabon, murænidæ [vilaung], physostomi, teleostei [matsyam, 42], of naturalists [jantoo]. Specific name from teloogoo. Alias Conger telabon; Murænesox exodon and serradentata, lanceolata. Upper surface of back and head olive, becoming brown posteriorly; abdomen dull white, becoming silvery inferiorly. The throat, cheeks, and gill covers with golden reflections; vertical fins with dark margins. Sea; 10 feet or more. No other common species here.

TALAM (तल - tala, *San.*). For Stalam [q.v.]. Floor.——*Talautalam* (तलातल - talátala, San; தராதலம் - taráthalam, Tam.). From (above + atala, san. bottomless). The fourth of the seven regions of Pautaulam [bhoogolashastram]. Mauyay [q.v.] reigns over this having been raised to that dignity by Shiva [q.v.] after the destruction of the three cities [tripooran]. ——*Talee* (തളി - tali, Mal.). Means local. Apart from the Punniyore and Chovoor distinction, the Numboory [q.v.] bramins who entered the W. coast formed themselves into four principal and several other petty talees or associations under the Permauls [q.v.], retaining for this purpose in their own hands various executive and fiscal prerogatives. The four principal talees were located at Cranganore, which place all the Permauls with the members of those four talees made their chief abode. These members were called Taliyaudry. Some of the places where the petty talees were originally located still bear the affix; as Calicut talee, Chenganaud talee, Neeleshwara talee, &c. The power and influence of the Permauls however gradually increased, while those of the talees decayed. Distinguish from Talee, the woman's marriage necklace, which is quite another word [taur].——*Taliparamba* * (തളിപ്പറമ്പ - talipparampa, Mal.). From (tali, mal. temple + paramba, mal. high ground). So called after the chief temple of Colatnaud. Sanscrit name (lakshmípura), meaning lutchmy the goddess + town.—"*a*" Deputy tahsildarry, Malabar district. Pay Rs. 70.—"*b*" Town, Amshom, Deputy tahsildar's, Sub-registrar's and Cavvye moonsif's station, Place of pilgrimage; Malabar dist., Chiracal tal.; pop. 9,906; lat. 12° 03′; long. 75° 24′; from Calicut N.N.W. 60 miles; from Cannanore N. 13 miles; from Madras W. 342 miles; from Malapooram N.N.W. 82 miles; from Manantoddy W.N.W. 46 miles; from Palghaut N.W. 122 miles; from Ponnany N.N.W. 93 miles; from Tellicherry N.N.W. 22 miles; from the sea E. 12 miles. Three ancient and important temples, known as Caunyarangaud, Taliparamba and Trichambaram. Rock-cut sepulchres near Travellers' bungalow [q.v.]. Important festival at Trichambaram in March.—"*c*" River; Malabar dist., Chiracal tal.; lat. 12° 16′ N.; long. 75° 33′ E. Rises from lower slopes of W. ghauts. After passing Taliparamba, main branch is joined by one from the east, and the two together spread out into an extensive sheet of water. Bending slightly to the north and passing under a ruined fort of Colattiry the united streams then suddenly turn at Payyangaudy due south and run parallel to the sea till they meet the Belliapatam river, united to which they force for themselves a passage to the sea through the sand shoals thrown up by the littoral currents. A large tract of fertile garden land has been formed by the continuous action of the littoral currents damming up the mouth of this river. Length about 51 miles. The main branch is navigable at all seasons for boats as far as the lower slopes of the ghaut [q.v.] mountains.——*Taliyaudry* (തളിയാതിരി - taliyátiri, Mal.). Head of a talee.

TALAUB (تالاب - táláb, *Hind.*). From persian. A tank [q.v.] for irrigation [airy, cheroo, kerey].

TALC (طلق - talk, *Ar.*). Same as abruck [q.v.]. Not co-extensive with European term, which is a mineral also capable of foliation, but more greasy and less elastic than Abruck [q.v.] or foliated mica, appearing in commerce as tailor's chalk [balapam]; and generally appearing naturally in the massive form, when it is called steatite or soapstone [sowcaura cull].

TALEEL (تعليل - tatíl, *Hind.*). From (alla, ar. to assign a cause). Agnosticism; specially that of the ancient pagan arabs.

TALICOTE (తాళికోట - tálikóta, *Tel.*). Town, Bombay; lat. 16° 28′ 10″; long. 76° 21′ 10″. Scene of battle in 1565 in which the empire of Vijianugger was overthrown by a confederacy of the mahomedan kings of the Deccan [q.v.], Adil shahy of Beejapore, Cootb shahy of Beder, and Nizam shahy of Ahmednugger [ram rauz]. See vol. I (153).

TALOOK (تعلقه - talukah, *Hind.*; ತಾಲೂಕು - tálúku, *Can.*; తాలూకా - tálúká, *Tel.*; താലൂക്ക് - tálúkka, *Mal.*; தாலூக்கா - tálúkká, *Tam.*). From (alaka, ar. belong to). A dependency. In this Presidency as in Bombay it is the sub-division of a district [zillah], presided over by a Tahsildar [q.v.]. In Bengal it is applied to tracts of proprietary land, sometimes not distinguishable from zemindarries [q.v.], and sometimes subordinate to zemindars [q.v.]. A Talook sheristadar [q.v.] is here the second officer in a tahsildar's office. The following is a list of the talooks into which the zillahs [q.v.] or administrative districts of the Presidency are divided, showing the district to which each belongs. These are all directly administered by the Government through the Tahsildar. Outside so-called Government talooks are however other areas either not so directly administered, and specially administered, and therefore designated by a special name. Such are added to the list. The entire list shows the segments into which the entire Presidency area is geographically divided. Where there is no special designation, it will be understood that the area is an ordinary Tahsildar's talook:—Adony, bellary; Ahtoor, salem; Amalaupooram, godavery; Ambasamoodram, tinnevelly; Anantapore, anantapore; Ankapully division, vizagapatam; Arcot, north arcot; Arnee jagheer, north arcot; Atmacore, nellore; Aulore, bellary; Baupatla, kistna; Bellary, bellary; Berhampore, ganjam; Bezwada, kistna; Bhadrachellam, godavery; Bhawauny, coimbatore; Bheemavaram, godavery; Bimlipatam division, vizagapatam; Bissemcuttack division, vizagapatam; Bobbily division, vizagapatam; Budwail, cuddapah; Bunder, kistna; Bunganapully, native state, kurnool; Cadiry, cuddapah; Calastry zemindarry, north arcot; Calicut, malabar; Canigherry, nellore; Caricaul territory, tanjore; Caroor, coimbatore; Carvetnugger zemindarry, north arcot; Cassergode, south canara; Cauvaly, nellore; Cheepoorpully division, vizagapatam; Chicacole, ganjam; Chidambaram, south arcot; Chingleput, chingleput; Chiracal, malabar; Chittore, north arcot; Chundragherry, north arcot; Cocanada division, godavery; Cochin, malabar; Coilcoontla, kurnool; Coimbatore, coimbatore; Collegaul, coimbatore; Combaconam, tanjore; Conjeeveram, chingleput; Coodligy, bellary; Coolitalay, trichinopoly; Coondah division, neilgherries; Coondapore, south canara; Cooroombranaud, malabar; Coraputt division, vizagapatam; Coringa division, godavery; Cottayam, malabar; Cuddalore, south arcot; Cuddapah, cuddapah; Cullacoorchy, south arcot; Cumbum, kurnool; Cundoocore, nellore; Cungoondy zemindarry, north arcot; Darshy division, nellore; Dharaupooram, coimbatore; Dharmapoory, salem; Dharmavaram, anantapore; Dindigul, madura; Ellore, godavery; Erode, coimbatore; Gajapatinugger division, vizagapatam; Golcondah, vizagapatam; Goodivauda, kistna; Goodiyattam, north arcot; Goodoor, nellore; Goomsoor, ganjam; Goonapore division, vizagapatam; Guntoor, kistna; Gooty, anantapore; Hindoopore, anantapore; Hoovinhadgully, bellary; Hospett, bellary; Hurpanhully, bellary; Jeypore division, vizagapatam; Jummalmadoogoo, cuddapah; Krishnagherry, salem; Krittivenn zemindarry, kistna; Lingagherry zemindarry, kistna; Madaksira, anantapore; Madanapully, cuddapah; Madrantacam, chingleput; Madras town; Madura, madura; Maliah tracts, ganjam; Mangalore, south canara; Marcapore, kurnool; Mayavaram, tanjore; Meilavaram zemindarry, kistna; Mailore, madura; Merkoonaud division, neilgherries; Moongaula zemindarry, kistna; Moosiry, trichinopoly; Mulkangherry division, vizagapatam; Munnargoody, tanjore; Namcull, salem; Nangoonairy, tinnevelly; Narsapore, godavery; Narasarowpett, kistna; Negapatam, tanjore; Nellore, nellore; Noozveed zemindarry, kistna; Nowrungapore division, vizagapatam; Nundiaul, kurnool; Nundicotcore, kurnool; Nundigauma, kistna; Nunnilam, tanjore; Ongole, nellore; Odamalpett, coimbatore; Oodayagherry, nellore; Oodayarpolliem, trichinopoly; Oodipy, south canara; Ooppinangady, south canara; Oossoor, salem; Ootancaray, salem; Ottapidauram, tinnevelly; Padair division, vizagapatam; Palcondah, vizagapatam; Palghaut, malabar; Paranginaud division, neilgherries; Parvatipore division, vizagapatam; Peddapore, godavery; Penoocondah, anantapore; Perambalore, trichinopoly; Periyacoolam, madura; Pittapore division, godavery; Podily division, nellore; Pollachy, coimbatore; Polore, north arcot; Polore division, nellore; Pondicherry territory, south arcot; Ponnairy, chingleput; Ponnany, malabar; Poodoocottah territory, trichinopoly; Poolivendla, cuddapah; Poolampett, cuddapah; Poonganore zemindarry, north arcot; Pottinghy division, vizagapatam; Proddootore, cuddapah; Pulladam, coimbatore; Pulmanair, north arcot; Pulnaud, kistna; Pulney, madura; Putticondah, kurnool; Puttoocottah, tanjore; Rajahmundry, godavery; Ramalcottah, kurnool; Ramachendrapooram, godavery, Ramnaud zemindarry, madura; Raupore, nellore; Rekapully, godavery; Repully, kistna; Royachoty, cuddapah; Royadroog, bellary; Royagada division, vizagapatam; Rumpa division, godavery; Salem, salem; Sarwasiddhy, vizagapatam; Saulore division, vizagapatam; Shauttore, tinnevelly; Shivagunga zemindarry, madura; Shiyally, tanjore; Shreevillipoottore, tinnevelly; Shunkaraneinarcoil, tinnevelly; Sidhout, cuddapah; Sirwail, kurnool; Srungavarapoocote division, vizagapatam; Sullapully zemindarry, kistna; Sundoor territory, bellary; Suttenapully, kistna; Suttimungalam, coimbatore; Sydapett, chingleput; Tadpatry, anantapore; Tanjore, tanjore; Tanookoo, godavery; Tencaray, tinnevelly; Tencaushy, tinnevelly; Tindivanam, south arcot; Tinnevelly, tinnevelly; Tirmungalam, madura; Todanaud division, neilgherries; Toony division, godavery; Tricalore, south arcot; Trichengode, salem; Trichinopoly, trichinopoly; Trinomallee, south arcot; Tripatore, salem; Tritrapoondy, tanjore; Trivellore, chingleput; Valavanaud, malabar; Valloor zemindarry, kistna; Veeravilly division, vizagapatam; Vellore, north arcot; Vencatagherry division, nellore; Villoopooram, south arcot; Vinoocondah, kistna; Vissanapett division, kistna; Vizagapatam division, vizagapatam; Vizianagram division, vizagapatam; Voilpaud, cuddapah; Vriddhauchellam, south arcot; Wallajahpett, north arcot; Wandiwash, north arcot; Wynaud, malabar; Wynaud south-east division, neilgherries; Yernagoodem, godavery; Yernaud, malabar; Zemindarry tracts, ganjam. See vol. II, 378.——*Talookdar* (تعلق دار - taallukdár, Hind.). From (above + dár, pers. holder). Petty zemindar [q.v.]. None in this presidency.

TAM (तम् - tam, *San.*). Faint.——*Tamal* (तमाल - tamála, San.). From (tamas, san. dark). Same as Cassia cinnamon.——*Tamas* (तमस् - tamas, San.). From (tam, san. to suffocate). Ignorance. The earth's shadow [chauyay] in an eclipse [grahanam].——*Tambauk* (తంబాకు - tambáku, Tel.; തമ്പാക്ക - tampákku, Mal.; தம்பாக்கு - tambákku, Tam.). Title portuguese corruption of (támbaga, malay, from támraka, san. copper). Otherwise tombac from french. Pinchbeck, three parts zinc [tootnaug] to sixteen copper [taumram]; brass [pittalay] being one zinc two copper. Is ruddy like gold [pon].——*Tambool* (ताम्बूल - támbúla, San.; تنبول - tambúl, Hind.). From (tam, san. to faint away). Betel-leaf. Tambooly is a seller of betel [q.v.], tobacco [pogauk], &c.——*Tamogoonam* (तमोगुण - tamóguna, San.). The quality of darkness or malignity [goonam]. The Prabhoolinga leelay makes it inherent in Parvaty [q.v.] as a component part. Some ascribe it to Shiva [q.v.]. As to its influence on transmigration see Samsauram.——*Tamracherry* (താമരശ്ശേരി - támarashshéri, Mal.; támrachéri *). From (támara, mal. lotus, nelumbium speciosum, willd. + shéri, mal. village). Village, ghaut; Malabar dist., Calicut tal.; lat. 11° 25′; long. 75° 59′; from Calicut N.E. 16 miles; from Chevayore N.E. 12 miles; from the sea E. 15 miles. Ghaut [q.v.] on road from Calicut to Goodalore. In Kedavore amshom. Palace belonging to Cottayam rajah. Close to it is a tank 240 by 144 feet. The ghaut is one of Tippoo's military roads. Leads from Calicut through South wynaud to Mysore, and was the line selected by Colonel Wellesley for the operation against the Pychy rajah. Now much used for the export of coffee [q.v.].——*Tamrachoodan* (ताम्रचूड - támrachúda, San.). From (támra, san. copper + chúda, san. crest). Shiva.——*Tamrah* (ياقوت رمانی - yákútirummání, Pers.; تامرا - támrá, Hind.). Pers. from (yákút, ar. garnet + rummán, ar. pomegranate, punica granatum, linn.); from color. Hind. from (támbá, hind. copper), meaning inferior. Garnet, which is from the Latin granatum, 'grained.' A mineral, crystallizing in the isometric or cubical system, and composed of silicate of alumina and lime of iron; the alumina often replaced by sesquioxide of iron and the lime by magnesia of some other oxide. There are two distinct kinds, the precious and the common. The color of the first is of various shades of red, and hence the name of the mineral [dhautoo], from its supposed resemblance to the flower of the pomegranate [anaur], with sometimes a tinge of yellow or blue, or a smoky aspect. The color of the common garnet is of various shades of brown and green. Garnets are found in Ceylon, in Southern india, and in Burmah Black garnets are occasionally to be met with in Ceylon and in the ghauts [q.v.] near Cape comorin [ratnam].——*Tamrapurny* (താമ്രപർണ്ണി - támraparni, Mal.; தாம்பிரப்பருணி - támbirapparuni, Tam. támbraparni *). From (támra, san. copper red + parní, san. a tree, as having leaves); after the red sandalwood trees about its source. Otherwise Tamravanny, or copper-hued, from sand. Real tamul name is Porny simply, and the sanscrit terms are an invention.—"*a*" Tam. also (porundam), meaning mountain stream; also (áni), from auny [mausam] or june, the third solar month as it overflows in the month of June. Greek σωλήν, meaning chunk [q.v.]. In the Mahavanso Tamrapurny [tamravurnam] is said to have been the name of the first setttlement formed by Vijaya and his followers in Ceylon, from which the name came to be applied to the whole island, and hence Greek ταπροβάνη. The settlement of Tamrapurny was near Putlam on the western coast of Ceylon, nearly opposite the mouth of this river in Tinnevelly. Hence perhaps the confusion of names. River; Tinnevelly dist., Ambasamoodram, Tinnevelly, Tencaray tals. Rises in the Western ghauts in lat. 8° 36′ N., and long. 77° 19′ E. Leaving the ghauts [q.v.] in the celebrated Paupanausam fall, it runs in a south-easterly direction to Shermadevy, then north-east between Tinnevelly and Palamcottah, then again south and east falling into the Gulf of Manaar in lat. 8° 40′, long. 78° 10′ close to Poonnacauyal. It receives the Chittaur on the left side in lat. 8° 47′, long. 77° 51′. Other affluents are the Gatananuddy, Manimooctah, Putchayaur and Ramanuddy. Total length, 70 miles. This river like the Cauvery, but unlike most south indian streams, is fed by both monsoons [q.v.], and is seen in full flood twice a year. It flows through a narrow and densely populated but very rich alluvial valley, originally formed by itself through the process of denudation, and then filled up by itself in later periods through the process of sedimentary deposition. With its feeders, it irrigates 65,000 acres of land. There are eight anicuts [q.v.]. For description of these, see vol. I, 404. There is a bar at the mouth of the river preventing the entrance of shipping. 35 miles higher up it is crossed by a fine bridge, connecting Tinnevelly and Palamcottah. Two waterfalls on main stream, Paupanausam and Baunateertam, and one on a tributary Paumbanaroovy. Most chunks [q.v.] used in commerce are found in the sea adjacent to mouth of this river. Every portion of the stream is sacred, but bathing at the water-falls in the upper part of its course is specially meritorious. Another river of the same name, distinguished as the western Tamrapurny, has its source close to this and flows westward into Travancore; see next clause.—"*b*" Otherwise Coolitora, meaning deep ford. River; Travancore state, Pudmanaubhapooram division. Rises in the mountains north of Mahendragherry. Passing first through wild tract, it enters the plains at Tirvattaur, and after a south-westerly course of 23 miles receives the Coday. Reaches the sea at Tengyeputnam. Length 37 miles. Narrow and occasionally rocky bed. Seven miles of its course are navigable, but timber is floated a greater distance; boats only ascend as far as Coolitora. Nunjenaud owes much of its fertility to the waters intercepted by dams at Ponmana, which are conducted partly to the Palayaur; a second channel flows by Pudmanaubhapooram and runs an equally fertile course. Not directly used for cultivation.——*Tamravurnam* (ताम्रवर्ण - támravarna, San.). From (támra, san. copper + varna, san. color), from red color of earth. One of the nine divisions of Bhaurata varsham or Northern india; Ceylon, by transfer.——*Taprobane* (ताम्रपर्ण - támraparna, Tam.). San. from (támra, san. copper + parna, san. leaf). Greek ταπροβάνη [tamrapurny]. Ceylon. Word used by Milton.——*Taumaray* (தாமரை - támarai, Tam.). From (támarasa, san. red lotus). Lotus or water-lily; held sacred. Lutchmy [q.v.] is the lotus [nelumbo] born. It is the poetic flower of the Hindoos. For different varieties of taumaray see Nelumbo.——*Taumbam* (तांब - támba, Mahr.). From (támra, san. copper). The genus Lutjanus, percidæ [panayairy], acanthopterygii, teleostei, pisces [matsyam, 1], of naturalists [jantoo]. Sea-fish. Insipid as food, extensively salted. The species best known to the natives are :—argenti. maculatus [red rock cod], bengalensis, erythropterus, fulviflamma, jahngarah, johnii, lineolatus, marginatus [bride fish], rivulatus, sebæ. ——*Taumbil* (तंबिल - tambila, Mahr.). From (támba, mahr. red); from appearance. Same as False bummelo.——*Taumram* (ताम्र - támra, San.; तांब्र - támbra, Mahr.; نحاس - nohâss, Ar.; مس - mis, Pers.; تانبا - támbá, Hind. and Dec.; تامبگ - támbaga, Malay; ತಾಂಬ್ರ - támbra, Can.; ಚೆಂಬು - chembu, Too.; రాగి - rági, Tel.; ചെമ്പ - chempu, Mal.; තඹ - támba, Singh.; செம்பு - shembu, Tam.). Title from sanscrit. San. from (tám, san. to faint), as losing color when put in fire. Hind. from sanscrit. Can. from sanscrit. Tel. from (rága, san. redness). Mal. from tamul. Singh. from sanscrit. Tam. from (shem, tam. red + pon, tam. metal). San. also (támraka). Tel. also (támbramu). Copper. Cuprum of chemists. The only red-colored metal [loham]. Malleable and ductile, and has a disagreeable taste and smell when rubbed. In dry air becomes covered with a film of sub-oxide of copper, and in moist air with a green crust the carbonate. Found in Jeypore, Travancore, Nellore, &c.; but greater part exposed for sale comes from other countries. χαλκὸς which may have been either copper or brass was exported from Egypt to west coast according to the Periplus. Is either procured in metallic state, when it is crystallized in form of native copper; or sulphuretted, in combination with iron [auhan], or with iron and arsenic [panshaunam]. The sulphurets are the most abundant ores. Copper fused with tin [tagaram] forms bronze and bell-metal [cunts]; with zinc [tootnaug], or the oxide of zinc, called calamine [madal toottam], it forms brass [pittalay], which the natives know how to prepare in a simple way. Another alloy is pinchbeck [tambauk]. The natives also use an alloy of copper mixed with gold [pon], like the ancient Aes corinthium. The medicinal powder of copper or Taumra paspam [q.v.] is made by plunging copper coin made red hot into acid juice expressed from leaves of tamarind [q.v.] tree; this repeated several times, after which the coin is melted in crucible, with sulphur [gandhac] thrown into it at two different times; this mass is ground, moistening it with the juice of lemons [q.v.], which renders it white. There is another native preparation, which contains copper, egg shells, muriate of ammonia, corrosive sublimate [shavveeram], borax [vengauram], orpiment [hartaul], mercury [rasam] and lime [choonam]; this being administered in leprosy [cooshtam] and cutaneous affections. Clean copper vessels are with safety used for carrying or lifting drinking water, but copper cooking vessels are dangerous, as fatty and acidulous substances dissolve the metal which then gets oxidised and becomes poisonous. For sub-acetate of copper or verdigris, see Zangaur. For sulphate of copper or copperas or blue-stone, see Toottam. Taumram as meaning copper colored is a common plant first term. Ex., where transl. is of second term :—Bauhinia variegata (támrapushpi), flower; Nicotiana tabacum (támrakúta), head; Rubia cordifolia (támbravalli), creeper. See gloss. paragraphs.

TAM (தம் - tam, *Tam.*). Oblique form of (tám), they, themselves. Own.——*Tambaun* (തമ്പാൻ - tampân, Mal.). Short for Tumbiraun.——*Tammenapatam* (తమ్మెనపట్నం - tammenapatnamu, Tel.). From (tammudu, tel. brother + pattana, san. town). Built by a brother of krishna deva royel. Village; Nellore dist., Goodoor tal.; acres 9,097; lat. 14° 14′; long. 80° 09′; from Goodoor E.N.E. 18 miles; from Nellore S.S.E. 17 miles; from the sea W. 2 miles. Abounds in palmyra [q.v.] trees.——*Tanam* (తనము - tanamu, Tel.; தனம் - tanam, Tam.). From (tán, tam. one's self). Nature. Suffix in compounds as Puttitanam, meaning looseness of conduct + nature.——*Tumbidoray* (தம்பித்துரை - tambitturai, Tam.). From (tambi, tam. younger brother + turai, tam. prince). Hindoo 2nd or pers. name. Common among non-bramins [peyar].——*Tumbiraun* (തമ്പുരാൻ - tamburán, Mal.). From (tam, mal. one's own + purán, mal. lord). A prince, a lord, especially male in a royal family. Title of Cochin rajah. Means also in religion supreme god. Term of address among the inferior castes towards members of the superior castes [peyar]. Also headman of a convent. Periya tumbiraun is a form of Shiva, sometimes represented by an image of burnt clay or plaster, worshipped by washermen [dhoby] and others. For Coil tumboorauns see that head.——*Tumboo* (தம்பு - tumbu, Tam.). Familar form of tumby, brother. Hindoo 2nd or pers. name Title of address among Teloogoo shoodras in Tamul districts [peyar].——*Tumboosawmy* (தம்புசாமி - tambusámi, Tam.). Hindoo 2nd or pers. name. Common among non-bramins [peyar].——*Tumbratty* (തമ്പുരാട്ടി - tampurátti, Mal.). Female in a royal family.——*Tumbraukkal* (തമ്പ്രാക്കൾ - tambrákkal, Mal.; தம்பிராக்கள் - tambirákkal, Tam.). Plural of tumbiraun. Male of a royal family; title of high priest, as Alwancherry tumbraukkal. ——*Tumby* (തമ്പി - tampi, Mal.; தம்பி - tambi, Tam.). From (tan, mal. one self + pin, mal. after). A younger brother. A title assumed by the sons of the Rajahs of Travancore. Term of familiar address among non-bramins. Also suffix in proper names among non-bramins as Chinnatumby, Nullatumby [peyar].——*Tummanna* (తమ్మన్న - tammanna, Tel.). From (tammudu, tel. younger brother + anna, tel. elder brother, a title). Hindoo 2nd or pers. name [peyar].——*Tundacoor* (തന്തക്കൂറ - tantakkúru, Mal.). From (tanta, mal. father + kúr, mal. share). Inheritance by the father's side. ——*Tundavazhy* (തന്തവഴി - tantavazhi, Mal.). From (tanta, mal. father + vazhi, mal. line). Father's line.——*Tunday* (തന്ത - tanta, Mal.). From (tan, mal. one's own + táyi, mal. parent). Father.——*Tungatchy* (തങ്കച്ചി - tankaççi, Mal.). A younger sister. Daughter of rajah on the West coast. These who, like sons, have no titles of rank, are first married in childhood by a Tirmalpaud [q.v.]; when one attains to maturity, cloth is given by some one who takes her to wife. The nieces on the other hand, who, like nephews, have the titles of Highness and Ranee are married when young to Coil tumboorauns [coil tumbooraun, maryauday, peyar].

TAMANA (تمن کا تیل - támankátel, *Hind.*). Poon oil.

TAMARIND (तिन्त्रिणी - tintriní, *San.*; चिंच - chincha, *Mahr.* and *Conc.*; تمرهند - tamarihind, *Ar.*; تمرهندی - tamarihindí, *Pers.*; انبلی کا پیڑ - anblíkáper, *Hind.*; املی کا جھاڑ - amlíkájhár, *Dec.*; اسم - asam, *Malay*; ಹುಣಿಶೆ - hunishe, *Can.*; ಪುಂಕೆ - punke, *Too.*; చింత - chinta, *Tel.*; କୋୟାଁ - koyán, *Oor.*; പുളി - puli, *Mal.*; සියඹලා - siyambalá, *Singh.*; புளி - puli, *Tam.*). Title from arabic. San. from (tim, san. to become wet), from exciting saliva in the mouth. Mahr. from (chiñcha, san. tamarind tree). Ar. from (tamar, ar. date, phœnix dactylifera, linn. + hindí, ar. indian). Pers. from arabic. Hind. and Dec. from (ámliká, san.

the plant). Tel. like mahratta. San. also (ámlikâ), meaning sour plant [sour auray]; (chiñchá), meaning paining, as from sourness; (shukta), meaning sour; (tintidí), by corruption. Mahr. also (amlí), meaning sour. Ar. also (húmar), meaning red referring to the seed; (sabárá), meaning acid. Hind. also (tintirí), from sanscrit. Malay also (kamal); (neghka); (asamjawa); (asamkranj). Can. also (hulimara), meaning sour + tree; (neralamara), meaning shade + tree [common jaumoon]; (hulise); (unaramara); (unanamará); (karangi); (kamal); (asam). Oor. also (tentúli), from sanscrit. Mal. also (madhurappuli), meaning sweet tamarind; (válanpuli), meaning sword tamarind, from pod. Tam. also (indam); (mugini). Greek ὀξυφοινίκα. Title otherwise Amlee, Aumlicah, Chinch, Chinta, Pooliyamaram, Pooly. Botanically Tamarindus indica, linn., leguminosæ [vricsham; 48]. Alias Tamarindus occidentalis, officinalis. Tree, 80 feet; calyx limb bilabiate, reflexed; petals 3, alternate with the segments of the upper lip of the calyx; seven short stamens all sterile, the others longer, fertile; leaves abruptly pinnated; leaflets numerous; legumes linear, more or less curved, one-celled, many-seeded; seeds compressed, bluntly four-angled; flowers in racemes with straw-colored calyx, and yellow petals streaked with red, purple filaments and brown anthers. A common slow-growing, long-lived, and handsome tree; circumference to 25 feet; one of the largest trees in india, with an umbrageous head; common both wild and cultivated; the pod is thick, oblong, 4 to 6 inches long, curved, compressed between each seed, smooth, of greyish-rusty color, externally formed of a double envelope; seeds large, shining, angular, and flat, and covered with a dark pulp; the odour of the pulp is vinous, the taste acid, somewhat astringent, and saccharine; pod is connected with the seeds by tough strings or fibres; from seeds is expressed a clear, bright, fluid oil [yennay]. Commercially there are two kinds of tamarind products:—brown and red tamarinds, the west indian tamarinds, the pulp preserved in sugar [q.v.], this is the form chiefly sold in the shops in england; and black or east indian tamarinds, not preserved in sugar, this is the black pulp as prepared and sold here. There is a considerable export trade of tamarinds from madras; little attention however is paid to the preparation of the fruit in this country; it is simply deprived of its outer covering and then stored in mass; it therefore contains seeds, stringy fibres, and often pieces of the pod. Cultivated in red soil; pits are dug and seed inserted by hand; no nursery; the plants are watered when young; produce obtained after twelve years by persons climbing trees and shaking branches or beating with sticks; produce exposed to sun for four days and then beaten with sticks which separate the shells. Medicinally kernels of seeds reduced to fine powder and boiled form a tenacious paste, this smeared on skin promotes suppuration in indolent boils; seed sometimes given by veidyans [q.v.] in dysentery as a tonic; the pulp is laxative and stomachic, and quenches thirst, increases the action of the sweet purgatives cassia [q.v.] and manna [q.v.], and weakens that of resinous cathartics; pulp substituted for british tartaric and citric acids; a decoction of the acid leaves employed externally in cases requiring repellent fomentation, and for preparing collyria; the tamarind is generally antiscorbutic; gives to pharm. tamarindi pulpa; enters into the composition of confectio sennæ, officinal. Tamarinds are preserved in two ways; by throwing hot sugar from the boiler on the ripe pulp, or by putting alternate layers of tamarinds and powdered sugar into a stone jar; by this last means they preserve their color and taste better; they contain sugar, mucilage, citric acid, tartaric and malic acids; the young leaves are used in pepper-water; the green fruit is an ingredient in chutneys [q.v.]; pulp of ripe fruit is used in curries [q.v.]; also used for sherbet [q.v.]; in times of scarcity the poor eat tamarind fruit and stones; after being roasted, then soaked in water, the dark outer skin comes off, leaving the seeds below white, soft, and in taste not unlike a field bean; these are boiled or fried, and eaten. Black tamarinds are used for adulterating tobacco [pogauk]; a strong infusion mixed with sea salt is used by silversmiths in a mixture for cleaning silver [velly]; the pulverised seeds boiled into a paste with thin glue form one of the strongest wood cements [pattoo]; an infusion of leaf imparts a green color to silk [puttoo] previously dyed with indigo [q.v.]; alone it makes a yellow or reddish hue; used in coloring especially along with safflower [bastard saffron]; flowers also; natives have a prejudice against sleeping under the tree; the acid damp affects the cloth of tents [derah] pitched under it; many plants do not grow under its shade; very largely planted in avenues [shaulay] and topes [q.v.], also round villages for its fruit and shade. Heart-wood generally of small diameter, very hard, close-grained and sometimes finely veined of a dark-reddish hue; hard to be worked, much used for turnery purposes and for pestles, oil presses [gaunam], sugar crushers [aulay], carpenter's mallets and planes, and many other purposes; one of the best fuels for brick kilns [shoolay] as it burns whilst green; excellent for gunpowder charcoal [adoopp kary]; heart-wood is only procurable from very old trees; sap wood is of a dirty white not durable and if not seasoned in water gets worm-eaten; from the liability to become hollow in centre, it is difficult to get a tamarind plank of any width. The three following are varieties according to quality of pulp:—sweet-fruited, sour-fruited, rose-colored; the last makes the best preserve. There is a Tamul proverb:—ஆளை ஆள் அறியவேண்டும் மீனைப் புளியங்காய் அறியவேண்டும்—"man must be tested by man and fish by tamarind "fruit." There is another:—வெறும் புளி தின்றால் பற்கூசும்—"tamarinds if eaten alone will set the teeth on edge." And another:—புளியம்பழத்துக்குப் புளிப்புப்புகுதவிடவருகிறாயோ—"do you try to infuse sourness into tamarind "fruit." And another:—பொங்குங்காலம் புளி பூக்கும் மங்குங்காலம் மா காய்க்கும்—"in propitious seasons the tama-"rind flowers, in times of scarcity the mango fruits." The following is a Hindostany proverb:—گڑیون کی بیاہ میں چنچونکے جیل—"at a doll's marriage the gifts are tamarind seeds;" said of the very poor; tamarind seeds are very small. There is a Teloogoo proverb:—నంచికాలానికి చింతలు చెడుకాలానికి మామిళ్లు—"in a good season look for tamarinds, in a bad for mangoes "[q.v.]." No other species here.——**(1)** *Tamarind fish* (புளிமீன் - pulimín, Tam.). Fish soured with tamarind [q.v.] juice eaten as a relish. The fish are cut in transverse slices, and preserved in kegs.——*Tamarind stone* (రాతిచింత - ráticbinta, Tel.). Tel. from (ráyi, tel. stone + chinta, tel. tamarind tree, tamarindus indica, linn.). Otherwise called Wood stone. Found in great abundance at the village of Tirvacaray, 15 miles west by north from Pondicherry. Supposed to be a petrifaction of the tamarind tree. Retains the appearance of the ligneous texture and is susceptible of a fine polish.——**(2)** *Bitter tamarind* (ಕೈಪೇರಿಪುಳಿ - kaipéripuli, Too.). Same as Monkey lime.——*Bramin tamarind* (பாப்பாரப்புளி - páppárappuli, Tam.). Tam. corruption from (papparappuli), meaning goozerat tamarind. Same as Baobab.——*Carpenter's tamarind* (املی - amlí, Hind.; పిల్లగుముడు - pillagumudu, Tel.; ମୁନିଆରି - muniári, Oor.; ஆசாரிப்புளி - ásárippuli, Tam.). Title from use of wood. Tel. from (pilla, tel. small + gumudu, tel. gmelina asiatica, linn.). Tam. from (áchárya, san. teacher + puli, tam. tamarindus indica, linn.). Botanically Antidesma [amla shaucam] diandrum, tulasne, euphorbiaceæ [vricsham; 118]. Small tree with smooth, grey bark; shoots glabrous or rusty pubescent; leaves very variable, obtuse acute, or acuminate, the longest 5 by 1 inch, the largest 5 by 2 inches, the smallest 1 by $\frac{3}{3}$ inch, thin in texture, rarely slightly pubescent beneath, yellowish green when dry, base always acute, nerves faint; petiole $\frac{1}{10}$–$\frac{1}{8}$ inch, stipules slender; racemes always quite glabrous; bracts short, oblong, obtuse, glabrous, lowest often the longest; flowers minute, a few here and there sessile; disk lobed and quite glabrous; flower very small, greenish. Leaves are acid and eaten, resemble sorrel [auray] and are made into chutney [q.v.]; ripe berries eaten. Wood pinkish-grey, hard, close-grained.——*Crow tamarind* (काकचिंच - kákachiñcha, San.). Title from growing wild and leaf resembling tamarind. Same as Indian liquorice.——*Elephant tamarind* (ஆனைப்புளி - ánaippuli, Tam.). Title from size. Same as Baobab.——*False tamarind* (ಜಾರಿಗೆಹುಳಿ - járigehuli, Can.). Same as Ceylon gamboge.——*Foreign tamarind* (ولایتی املی - viláitiamlí, Hind.; సీమచింత - símachinta, Tel.). Same as Baobab, Malabar gamboge, and Corcapilly.——*Gorakh's tamarind* (گورك چنچا - gorakchinchá, Hind.). Tree under which gorakh taught. Same as Baobab.——*Hill tamarind* (மலைப்புளி - malaippuli, Tam.). Same as Yellow mangosteen.——*Khorassan tamarind* (خراسان کی املی - khurásánkíamlí, Hind.). Same as Portia.——*Malabar tamarind* (കുറുക്കമ്പുളി - kurukkampuli, Mal.). Mal. means short fruit tamarind. Same as Malabar gamboge.——*Pot tamarind* (കുടമ്പുളി - kutampuli, Mal.). From being preserved in pots. Same as Malabar gamboge.——*Red tamarind* (ఎర్రచింత - errachinta, Tel.). Title from reddish brown color of wood. Same as Fragrant sirissa.——*Ship tamarind* (వాడచింత - vádachinta, Tel.). Same as Malabar gamboge.——*Sour tamarind* (పుల్లచింత - pullachinta, Tel.). Same as Malabar mountain ebony and Sour auray.——*Square tamarind* (ചതുരപ്പുളി - chaturappuli, Mal.). From angular fruit. Same as Coromandel gooseberry.——*Water tamarind* (දියසියඹලා - diyasiyambalá, Singh.). Same as Solah.——*White tamarind* (ಬಿಳಿಹುಳಿ - bilihuli, Can.). Same as Small poolay.

TAMAUSH (تماشا - tamáshá, *Hind.*). From (mashí, ar. to walk together). Spectacle.

TAMBATTAM (कोशफल - kóshap'hala, *San.*; गवरी - gavarí, *Mahr.*; کھر سنبل - kharsambal, *Hind.* and *Dec.*; ಶಂಬೆಗಿಡ - shambegida, *Can.*; తమ్మ - tamma, *Tel.*; വാളമര - válamara, *Mal.*; தம்பட்டை - tambattai, *Tam.*). Title from tamul. San. from (kósha, san. sheath + p'hala, san. fruit). Hind. from (khara, san. sharp + shimbí, san. the plant), sword bean. Mal. from (vál, mal. sword + amara, mal. bean, dolichos lablab, linn.); from long flat pods. San. also (shimbí), meaning pod [shimby]. Hind. also (barásem), meaning the large dolichos lablab, linn.; (mukhamsem); (chhotísem), meaning small dolichos; (sufedkharsambal), meaning white sword bean; (lálkharsambal), meaning red sword bean. Can. also (tamatigida). Tel. also (chamma); (tellatamma), meaning white + plant; (yerratamma), meaning red + the plant. Mal. also (kanavázha). Tam. also (kózhiyavarai), meaning fowl + dolichos lablab, linn.; (shivapputtambattai), meaning red + the plant; (vellaittambattai), meaning white + the plant; (válavarai), meaning sword + dolichos, from sword-shaped pod. Title otherwise Fowl's bean, Hussar bean, Jamaica horse-bean, Jamaica overlook, Sabre-podded horse-eye bean, Sword bean. Botanically Canavalia ensiformis, dec., leguminosæ [vricsham, 48]. Canavalia, from (kanavázha, mal.). Alias Canavalia gladiata, incurva; Dolichos ensiformis, gladiatus; Malschia gladiata. Perennial shrub, twining; leaves pinnately trifoliate; leaflets cordate-ovate, rather acute; calyx unequally bilabiate, upper lip largest, lower lip acutely three-toothed; corolla papilionaceous; vexillum bicallous at the base; keel falcate at a right angle, petals distinct; racemes axillary, many-flowered; flowers in pairs, or threes, purplish; legumes five to ten times longer than broad. An extensive climber ascending to the summit of the loftiest trees; flowers in the rainy season; the pod is large, flat, sword-shaped, full nine inches long, and more than an inch and a quarter wide; seeds large, some bright red, others white; a common plant in hedges and thickets; when cultivated requires very strong stakes. Pod, though coarse-looking, when sliced and boiled exceedingly tender, little inferior to french beans [lobyah]; most wholesome, extensively used at the tables of europeans; plucked when half-ripe; compare the use of dolichos biflorus, linn. [madras horse gram], and vigna catiang, endl. [cow gram]. Varieties, with seeds and flowers of different colors; that with large white seeds and flowers is the most wholesome. Other common species are:—mollis, obtusifolia.

TAMBORE (تنبور - tambúr, *Hind.*). From (tonbá, hind. a small gourd). A sort of lute; no frets [sangeetam].

TAMOORY (താമൂതിരി - támútiri, *Mal.*). A corruption of (sámudri, san. sea king). Same as Zamorin.

TAN (तन् - tan, *San.*). Extend.——*Taag* (ताग - tága, Mahr.). From (tantuka, san. thread). Same as Sunn.——*Tanoo* (तनु - tanu, San.). From (tan, san. to extend). Slender.——*Tanoo madhyaumbaul* (தனுமத்தியாம்பாள் - tanumattiyámbál, *Tam.*). From (tanu, san. slender + madhya, san. waist + ambá, san. mother). Parvaty [q.v.].——*Tantram* (तन्त्र - tantra, San.). From (tan, san. to weave). Thread. Thence ritual. The name of a class of works founded on one of the oopanishads [q.v.]. Properly a Tantram, like a Pooraunam [q.v.], ought to treat of five subjects; viz., the creation, the destruction of the world, the worship of the gods, the attainment of all objects especially of six superhuman faculties [siddhy], the four modes of union [saulokyam] with the supreme spirit [bramh]. A great variety of other subjects however are introduced, and all extant tantrams deal as a first subject with the female energy of deity, personified in the person of his shacty [q.v.] or wife. There are a few tantrams which make Vishnoo's wife or Randhay [q.v.] the object of devotion, but the great majority of them are devoted to one of the manifold forms of Parvaty [q.v.] the shacty [q.v.] of Shiva [q.v.] and they are commonly written in the form of a dialogue between these two last named deities. There are five requisites for tantram worship, the five Macaurams or five m's:—Madyam, wine; Maumsam, flesh; Matsyam, fish; Moodrah, parched grain and mystic gesticulations; Meitoonam, intercourse between the sexes. Each shacty is said to have a twofold nature, white and black, gentle and ferocious; but the former are not known in S. india. The later tantrams are merely handbooks or manuals of magic and witchcraft, and collections of muntrams for producing and averting evils. The following are specimens of what they contain:—praise of the female energy; spells for bringing people into subjection; for making them enamoured; for unsettling their minds; for fattening; for destroying sight; for producing dumbness, deafness, and fevers; for bringing on miscarriage; for destroying crops.; for preventing various kinds of evil; methods of breathing in certain rites; language of birds, beasts, &c. The tantrams are exceedingly numerous. The principal are the Shyaumah rahasyam, Roodra yaumalam, Muntra mahodadhy, Shauradah tilacam, and Calicah tantram. The Coola choodaumany and Coolaurnavam are allied works. Tantric worship came from North-eastern india. The Shauctas [q.v.] or worshippers of the Shacties are divided into two classes, Dacshinacharries and Vaumacharries, the right-handed and the left-handed; see those heads. The followers of the tantrams profess to consider them as a fifth vedam [q.v.]. See vol. I (87). [matam].——*Tantra vaurticam* (तन्त्रवार्त्तिक - tantravárttika, San.). From (tantra, san. ritual + vártika, san. commentary). A celebrated Mimaumsam [q.v.] treatise by Comaurila bhatt, forming a commentary on the Jeiminy sootrams. It contains earliest known mention in Sanscrit of Dravidian languages.——*Tanty* (தந்தி - tandi, Tam.). From (tantu, san. string). Wire [taur].——*Tanty cullan* (தந்திக்கள்ளன் - tandikkallan, Tam.). From (tandi, tam. wire + kallan, tam. thief). Thug [q.v.].——*Tauga* (تاگا - tágá, Hind.). Hind. from (tantuka, san. thread). Cotton thread. Cutchatauga is rough thread or lamp cotton [q.v.].——*Tauntrica* (तान्त्रिक - tántrika, San.). Follower of the tantram doctrine.

TAN (தண் - tan, *Tam.*). Cool, water.——*Tandalam* (தண்டலம் - tandalam, Tam.). From (above + talam, tam. place). Grove [tope].——*Tannote* (തണ്ണോട്ടു - tannóttu, Mal.). Oblique form of Tannagam. From (tan, mal. water + akam, mal. inside). Hill; Malabar dist., Wynaud tal.; lat. 11° 32'; long. 76° 01'; from Calicut N.E. 24 miles; from Manantoddy S. 18 miles. Overhangs Tamracherry pass [ghaut] into Wynaud.——*Tunniketch* (தண்ணிக்காரிச்சி - tannikkáriççi, Tam.). From (tannír, tam. water + káratti, tam. woman-servant). Female water-carrier in the kitchen.——*Tunny* (தண்ணீர் - tannír, Tam.). Means cool + water. A general term for water. For different kinds of water see Neer.——*Tunny paumb* (जलव्याल - jalavyála, San.; پانی کا سانپ - páníkásámp, Hind.; నీరుహావు - níruhávu, Can.; నీళ్లపాము - níllapámu, Tel.; നീർക്കോലി - nírkkóli, Mal; தண்ணீர்ப்பாம்பு - tannírppámbu, Tam.). Title and Tam. from (tannír, tam. water + pámbu, tam. snake). San. from (jala, san. water + vyála, san. snake). Hind. from (pání, hind. water + sámp, hind. snake). Tel. from (níllu, tel. water + pámu, tel. snake). Mal. from (nír, mal. water + kól, mal. stick). Water-snake. Especially the Tropidonotus plumbicolor, colubridæ [paumb]. Fresh-water snakes are distinguished by the position of the nostrils, which are placed on the top of the snout and by a tapering tail.

TANAKK (زيتون - zaitún, *Hind.*; పొనుకు - ponuku, *Tel.*; தணக்கு - tanakku, *Tam.*). Title from tamul. Hind. means olive [zeitoon]. Tam. from (tana, tam. to go), from use of wood as floats or catamarans [golden silk cotton, odul]. Tel. also (kummaraponuku), meaning potter + the tree; (tanuku); (éruponuku), meaning river + the tree. Tam. also (shendanakku), meaning red + tanakk tree; (kadavu), meaning catamaran tree; (karamanikkáymaram), meaning dark + seed + fruit + tree; (kalámaram). Title otherwise Catamaran wood tree, Potter's tree, Red tanakk. Botanically Gyrocarpus jacquini, roxb., combretaceæ [vricsham, 55]. Alias Gyrocarpus acuminatus, americanus, asiaticus, rugosus, sphenopterus. Large tree; leaves crowded about the extremities of the branchlets, broad cordate, three-nerved often slightly lobed, above smooth, below downy, with two pits on the upper side of the base; petioles downy; panicles terminal, divisions two forked; hermaphrodite flowers solitary, sessile in the division of the panicle; calyx five-sepalled, segments unequal, interior pairs large, wedge-shaped, three-toothed, expanding into two long membranaceous wings; flowers small, yellow; capsule globular, wrinkled, one-celled, one-valved, size of a cherry [q.v.], ending in two long lanceolate membranaceous wings; flowering in december–january. Necklaces [maulay] and rosaries are made from the seeds; the seeds are used by the potters to polish their earthen vessels [chatty]. Wood is very light, soft, and white, much used at Condapully for making light cauvady [q.v.], boxes and toys [moochee wood], takes paint and varnish, also preferred before all other woods for making catamarans [q.v.].——*White tanakk* (پولکی - polkí, Malay; తెల్లపొనుకు - tellaponuku, Tel.; பூத்தாளி - púttáli, Tam.). Title from color of wood. Tel. from (tella, tel. white + ponuku, tel. gyrocarpus jacquini, rox.). Tam. from (pú, tam. flower + táli, tam. running plant, convolvulus). Tam. also (vendáli), meaning white + running plant, convolvulus. Botanically Givotia rottleriformis, griff., euphorbiaceæ [vricsham, 118]. Small tree, much branched; leaves orbicular-ovate, acuminate, coarsely repand-toothed, membranaceous, stellately tomentose, above afterwards glabrescent, indumentum at first whitish, then tawnyish or somewhat rusty; petioles with few glands above the middle; panicles exceeding the leaves, alternately bearing branches; bracts long linear; segments of the calyx obovate, glabrous within; petals obovate; hypogynous disc urceolar, lobed, pubescent; filaments hairy at the base, about twice as long as the anthers; ovary puberulous; styles stiff, spreading, two-cleft to the middle; fruit oblong-ellipsoid, minutely ashy-tomentose; seeds globose, ellipsoid, smooth, pale. Common in dry subalpine forests; seed yields an oil [yennay] valuable for fine machinery; has a light, soft wood, like mango [q.v.] wood, useful for toys, imitation fruit, boxes, &c., and catamarans [q.v.], it takes paint [rangh] very well. No other species here.

TANDAL (తండలు - tandalu, *Tel.*; தண்டல் - tandal, *Tam.*). Tam. from (tandu, tam. to collect). Money collection [inam, vasool].——*Tandalgar* (தண்டற்காரன் - tandargáran, Tam.). From (above + kri, san. to do.). Village revenue collector [moodipp cauran].

TANDOO (தண்டு - tandu, *Tam.*). From (danda, san. column). Army [dandam, dandoo, paday, shervay].——*Tandoomaury* (தண்டுமாரி - tandumári, Tam.). From (above + mári, tam. goddess of small-pox). Village goddess.——*Taundah* (ٹانڈا - tándá, Hind.). From (danda, san. column of troops) [dandam]. A large body of travellers or traders travelling together for mutual security. Movable encampment.

TANGAL (തങ്ങൾ - tannal, *Mal.*). From the malay. Moplah [q.v.] priests, supposed to be syeds [q.v.], and who exercise considerable influence. Under a Tangal are several Lubbays [q.v.], one in each mosque [musjid], who conduct the worship kill sheep [aud] for food with due ceremonial, and conduct marriages.

TANIKY (تنقيح - tankíh, *Hind.*). From (naķaha, ar. to extract the marrow). Examination.

TANJORE (تنجاور - tanjáwar, *Hind.*; தஞ்சாவூர் - tañjávúr, *Tam.*). From (tañjam, tam. asylum + úr, tam. village). Tam. also (tañjai), meaning shelter + place; also (tañjamánagaram), meaning shelter + great + city; also (tañjapuri), meaning shelter + town; also (tañjákkúr), meaning asylum + village. Sanscrit name (tungapura), meaning town of toongeshwaran, or shiva, lord of hills, whose lingam [q.v.] was set up under this name by coolottoonga cholan; also (brihadíshvara), meaning great lord, after the great lingam brought by caricaulan from nerbudda. ——(1) Revenue district; situated on the Coromandel coast; between 9° 49′ and 11° 25′ N. lat., and between 78° 45′ and 79° 54′ E. long.; bounded N. by Coleroon river; E. by Bay of Bengal; S. by Bay of Bengal and Madura district; W. by Madura and Trichinopoly districts; square miles 3,708; pop. 2,228,114; language Tamul. Contains rivers Cauvery, Coleroon; ports Adiramputnam, Ammaputnam, Caricaul, Cautmauvady, Codiyampolliem, Cottapatam, Gopaulputnam, Krishnaujiputnam, Moottoopett, Nagore, Negapatam, Point calimere, Topetoray, Tranquebar, Trimal vausal, Velangauny. The whole area of the district is represented by the following sub-areas:—Caricaul territory, Combaconam talook, Mayavaram talook, Munnargoody talook, Negapatam talook, Nunnilam talook, Puttcocottah talook, Shiyally talook, Tanjore talook and Tritrapoondy talook. For general administrative purposes the district is distributed between the following revenue and magisterial officers, who have their head-quarters at the places shown. The pay set opposite the subordinate officers gives the grade of the corresponding charge:—Collector, Tanjore; Sub-Collector, Combaconam, in charge of Combaconam, Mayavaram and Shiyally talooks; Head assistant collector, Negapatam, in charge of Negapatam and Nunnilam talooks; General deputy collector, Munnargoody, in charge of Munnargoody and Tritrapoondy talooks; General deputy collector, Tanjore, in charge of Tanjore talook; Assistant collector, Tanjore, in charge of Puttoocottah talook. Tahsildars; Combaconam, Rs. 250; Mayavaram, Rs. 225; Munnargoody, Rs. 200; Negapatam, Rs. 250; Nunnilam, Rs. 250; Puttoocottah, Rs. 175; Shiyally, Rs. 150; Tanjore, Rs. 250; Tritrapoondy, Rs. 225. Deputy tahsildars; Arantaungy, Rs. 70, range situated in the south of Puttoocottah talook; Combaconam, Rs. 100, range situated in the centre of the talook; Codavausal, Rs. 70, range situated in the western portion of the Nunnilam talook; Needamungalam, Rs. 70, range situated in the northern portion of the Munnargoody talook; Negapatam, Rs. 100, range situated in the north-eastern portion of the Negapatam talook; Tanjore, Rs. 100, range situated in the centre of the Tanjore talook; Tirvadamaroothore, Rs. 70, range situated in the east of the Combaconam talook; Tranquebar, Rs. 70, range situated in the south-eastern part of the Mayavaram talook; Tirvarore, Rs. 70, range situated on the western extremity of the Negapatam talook; Trivaudy, Rs. 70, range situated in the northern portion of the Tanjore talook; Vedaranyam, Rs. 70, range situated in the south-eastern part of the Tritrapoondy talook; Vullam, Rs. 70, range situated in the south and west of the Tanjore talook. Similarly judicial officers:—Judge, Tanjore. Sub-Judges, Combaconam, Negapatam and Tanjore. District Moonsifs, Combaconam, Mayavaram, Munnargoody, Negapatam, Puttoocottah, Shiyally, Tanjore, Tirvarore, Tritrapoondy, Trivaudy, Valangimaun. Contains Registration sub-districts, Arantaungy, Auditchapooram, Combaconam, Madyarjoon, Mayavaram, Milattore, Munnargoody, Negapatam, Nunnilam, Paupanausam, Peralam, Puttoocottah, Sawmymullay, Shiyally, Tanjore, Tircautpully, Tirpoondy, Tirvarore, Tranquebar, Tritrapoondy, Trivaudy, Valangimaun, Vedaranyam and Vullam. Contains Forest ranges, Northern and Southern. Contains Municipalities, Combaconam, Mayavaram, Munnargoody, Negapatam, Tanjore. Contains District board; and Talook boards, Tanjore embracing Tanjore talook, Combaconam embracing Combaconam, Mayavaram and Shiyally talooks, Negapatam embracing the talooks of Negapatam and Nunnilam, Munnargoody embracing Munnargoody and Tritrapoondy talooks, Puttoocottah embracing the talook of Puttoocottah. The following general references should be made to the preceding volumes:—general geography, I (1) to (29); general ethnology, I (29) to (109); general history, I (110) to (188); physical geography, II, 1; meteorology, II, 3; geology, II, 8; fauna, II, 21; flora, II, 26; mineralogy, II, 29. The following references in the preceding volumes will furnish details special to the district:—latitudes and longitudes, II, 47; particulars about towns, II, 48; coast survey, II, 159; lighthouses, II, 169; comparative population, II, 172; location of revenue officers, II, 390; registrars' and sub-registrar's stations, II, 421; ports, II, 423; salt factories, II, 426; rain-gauge stations, II, 428; police divisions, II, 431; maps published, II, 436; survey topographical lists, II, 443; hospitals and dispensaries, II, 447; missionary stations, II, 455; head-quarter stations of gazetted officers, II, 461; incidence of taxation, II, 463; weights and measures of the district, II, 518; zemindarries, II, 300; special public works, I, 399. A special gazetteer account of the whole district is given at II, 126. For the detailed topography of the district, reference should be made to the talook notices in the present volume, viz.:—Caricaul, Combaconam, Mayavaram, Munnargoody, Negapatam, Nunnilam, Puttoocottah, Shiyally, Tanjore, Tritrapoondy.

——(2) Talook, Tanjore district. Tahsildar's pay, Rs. 250. Area 689 square miles; population 410,447; language Tamul. W. of district. Boundaries:—North by Coleroon and Combaconam talook, east by Combaconam and Munnargoody talooks, south by Puttoocottah talook and Poodoocottah territory, west by Trichinopoly talook and Poodoocottah territory. Except the south and south-western portions which are elevated the talook is a level country sloping towards the east. The low lands are clayey, while parts of the elevated land are rocky and the rest sandy mixed with red loam. Industries:—Silk-weaving, fine arts, pith [solah] works, painting, sculpture, copper-work wrought in silver; silk and woollen carpets and ordinary cloth. Commerce:—Paddy [q.v.], dholl [q.v.], groundnut [q.v.] and other articles produced in the talook, opium [aphainam], European liquors and cloths of different sorts. Irrigated by the Cauvery, Coodamoorty, Vadavaur, Vennaur and Vettaur, and some minor tanks. The South indian railway enters the talook on the north and leaves it viâ Tanjore city on the west, with a branch from Tanjore city eastward to Negapatam. Zemindarries:—Conoor, Cullacottay, Gandharvacottah. Places of archæological interest:—Adanjiyore, Agaram, Candiyore, Carooppore, Caungayamputty, Cazhoomungalam, Coilady, Comapooram, Conairirajapooram, Cooriyaputty, Covilore, Covilputt, Cutchamungalam, Maroovore, Maungoody, Naimam, Nodiyore, Nulloocherry, Paroodiyapparcoil, Pashoopaticoil, Perambore, Poothoocoodiyadapaudy, Poransacoody, Rajagherry, Shoolamungalam, Siddharcoody, Tanjore, Tingalore, Tircautpully, Tirpandirty, Tirvaulampozhy, Tirvedacoody, Trichendoray, Trivaudy, Vaunarangoody, Vendayamputty, Vishnampett, Vullam. Principal trig. stations:—Arasaputt, Cakkaracottah, Particottah, Poovattore, Rauramoodracottah. The leading places, &c., in the talook are the following.——*Ammapett* அம்மாப்பேட்டை - ammáppéttai, Tam. ammápet*). From (ammá, tam. title of a woman + péttai, tam. village). Town, Railway station; pop. 3,804; lat. 10° 47′; long. 79° 22′; height 106 feet; from Tanjore E. 13 miles. Weaving centre. Fairs every Sunday.——*Arasaputt* (அரசப்பட்டு - arasappattu, Tam.). From (arasu, tam. peepul tree, ficus religiosa, linn. + pattu, tam. village). Trig. station; lat. 10° 43′ 31·18″; long. 79° 20′ 49·19″; height 103 feet.——*Ayyampett* (அய்யம்பேட்டை - ayyambéttai, Tam. ayyampet*). From (aiyyan, tam. the god ayyanár + péttai, tam. village). Town, Railway station; pop. 7,695; lat. 10° 53′; long. 79° 14′; height 114 feet; from Tanjore N.N.E. 8 miles. Includes suburb of the Shoolamungalam and Manojiappa chauvady. Seat of weaving [nesavoo]. Silk [puttoo] cloths and carpets [satranjee] of silk floss, and mats [boriyah] of rushes [coray] are largely made.——*Bhootalore* (பூதலூர் - púthalúr, Tam. búdalúr*). From (bhúta, san. demon + úr, tam. village). Sanscrit name (buddhipura), meaning intellect city. Village, Railway station; pop. 2,054; acres 2,055; lat. 10° 47′; long. 79° 01′; height 188 feet; from Tanjore W. 11 miles. Includes the suburb of Covilputt. Colonel Smith took possession of the pagoda [q.v.] in 1773, when marching from Trichinopoly against Tanjore.——*Cakkaracottah* (கக்கரக்கோட்டை - kakkarakkóttai, Tam.). From (kal, tam. stone + karai, tam. boundary + kóttai, tam. fort). Trig. station; lat. 10° 36′ 17·59″; long. 79° 15′ 08·80″; height 107 feet.——*Cauvery* (காவேரி - kávéri, Tam.). See sep. title.——*Coilady* (கோவிலடி - kóviladi, Tam.). From (kóvil, tam. temple + adi, tam. foot). The temple adjoins that of Shreerungam. Town; pop. 2,273; acres 2,372; lat. 10° 51′; long. 78° 56′; from Tanjore W.N.W. 17 miles. Two old Shiva and Vishnoo temples. Formerly a Deputy tahsildar and Sub-magistrate's station. The Grand anicut [q.v.] is five miles from Coilady.——*Coleroon* (கொள்ளிடம் - kolladam, Tam.). See sep. title.——*Cullacottay* (கல்லாக்கோட்டை - kallákkóttai, Tam.). From (kal, tam. stone + kóttai, tam. fort). Zemindarry, Village; pop. 1,750; lat. of village 10° 31′; long. 79° 09′; from Tanjore S. 19 miles. Peshcush Rs. 1,701. ——*Cunnandagoody* (கண்ணந்தக்குடி - kannandakkudi, Tam.). From (kan, tam. eye + andam, tam. beauty + kudi, tam. village). Village; pop. 1,428; lat. 10° 39′; long. 79° 19′; from Tanjore S.E. 14 miles. Mission station. Country seat of the Rajah's family. A bungalow [q.v.] for European travellers.——*Cutchamungalam* (கச்சமங்கலம் - kaççamangalam, Tam.). From (kaççam, tam. a fish + mangala, san. prosperity). Village; pop. 1,404; acres 608; lat. 10° 50′; long. 78° 56′; from Tanjore W.N.W. 17 miles. Includes suburbs of Tripyore and Mahadevapooram. Old Shiva temple. Site of an ancient anicut [q.v.]. The dam is across the Vennaur where the Pillay vyçaul channel branches from its north and the Ananta cauvery channel from its south bank.——*Gandharvacottah* (கந்தருவக்கோட்டை - kandaruvakkóttai, Tam.). See sep. title.——*Manamboochauvady* (மானோம்புச்சாவடி - mánómbuççávadi, Tam.). From (má, tam. great + nómbu, tam. festival + shávadi, tam. choultry). Village; lat. 10° 47′; long. 79° 11′; from Tanjore S.E. $1\frac{1}{2}$ miles. Included in Municipality of Tanjore. Mostly inhabited by silk-weavers [putnool]. European and Eurasian quarter of Tanjore town.——*Mauriyammancoil* (மாரியம்மன் கோவில் - máriyammangóvil, Tam.). From (máriyamman, tam. the village deity + kóvil, tam. temple). Village; pop. 2,299; lat. 10° 47′; long. 79° 14′; from Tanjore E. 4 miles. Old temple of Mauriyamman [q.v.].——

Milattore (மிலட்டூர் - milattúr, Tam.). From (mél, tam. west + áru, tam. river + úr, tam. village). Town and a Sub-registrar's station; pop. 6,804; acres 7,483; lat. 10° 52′; long. 79° 17′; from Tanjore N.E. 9 miles. On the Vellaur and in the most fertile part of the Cauvery delta [conamoogam]. Considerable Bramin [q.v.] population.——*Ortnaud* (ஒரத்தநாடு - orattanádu, Tam.). From (óram, tam. side + nádu, tam. country). Town, Post office; pop. 3,035; lat. 10° 38′; long. 79° 18′; from Tanjore S.E. 14 miles. Chuttram [q.v.] erected by Rajah sarbhojee in 1800 in honor of his concubine Moocta bye, whose name it bears. Fairs every Saturday.——*Particottah* (பரித்திக்கோட்டை - parittikkóttai, Tam.). From (parutti, tam. cotton, gossypium herbaceum, linn. + kóttai, tam. fort). Trig. station; lat. 10° 41′ 40·36″; long. 79° 26′ 56·59″; height 67 feet; from Munnargoody W. 4 miles; from Tanjore E. 19 miles.——*Ponvausal* (பொன்வாசல் - ponvásal, Tam.). From (pon, tam. gold + vásal, tam. gate). Village; pop. 1,472; acres 1,189; lat. 10° 54′; long. 79° 08′; from Tanjore N.W. 9 miles.——*Poovattore* (பூவத்தூர் - púvattúr, Tam.). From (pú, tam. flower + attu, tam. small + úr, tam. village). Trig. station; lat. 10° 34′ 30·31″; long. 79° 20′ 40·98″; height 82 feet.——*Rauramoodracottah* (இராராமுத்திரைக்கோட்டை - irárámuttiraikkóttai, Tam.). From (iráyar, tam. king + mudrá, san. seal + kóttai, tam. fort). Trig. station; lat. 10° 45′ 59·75″; long. 79° 15′ 10·41″; height 137 feet; from Mauriyamman coil S.E. 2 miles; from Tanjore E. 6 miles.——*Shaulyamungalam* (சாலியமங்கலம் - sháliyamangalam, Tam. sáliyamangalam). From (sháliyan, tam. one of the weaver caste + mangala, san. prosperity). Village, Railway station; pop. 1,336; acres 1,391; lat. 10° 47′; long. 79° 19′; height 121 feet; from Tanjore E. 10 miles. Ordinary weaving.——*Shingiputty* (சிங்கிப்பட்டி - shingippatti, Tam.). From (shingi, tam. female of the kurava tribe + patti, tam. village). Village; pop. 1,670; acres 4,245; lat. 10° 43′; long. 79° 00′; from Tanjore W.S.W. 13 miles. Former head-quarters of Deputy tahsildar and Sub-magistrate. Centre of tract inhabited by Cullar [q.v.]. Traveller's bungalow [q.v.].——*Tircautpully* (திருக்காட்டுப்பள்ளி - tirukkáttuppalli, Tam.). From (tiru, tam. sacred + kádu, tam. forest + palli, tam. village). Sanscrit name (agníshvara), meaning fire-lord, Shiva. Village, Sub-registrar's office; pop. 2,382; acres 681; lat. 10° 51′; long. 79° 00′; from Tanjore W.N.W. 13 miles. The Coodamoorty branches at this place from the Cauvery. Colonel Smith took possession of the fort in 1773, when marching from Trichinopoly against Tanjore. Old Shiva temple built by a Chola king and containing inscriptions. Fort in ruins. Fairs every Thursday.——*Tittey* (திட்டை - titte, Tam.). Means elevated ground. Village, Railway station; pop. 971; acres 878; lat. 10° 50′; long. 79° 14′; height 128 feet; from Tanjore N.E. 4 miles.——*Trivaudy* (திருவாடி - tiruváthi, Tam.). See sep. title.——*Tutchancoorchy* (தச்சங்குறிச்சி - taççanguriççi, Tam.). From (taççan, tam. a carpenter + kuriççi, tam. village). Village, Hill; pop. 1,006; acres 2,449; lat. 10° 40′; long. 79° 02′; from Tanjore S.W. 13 miles. Out of the hill granite [caroom cull] stones are dug.——*Vellaur* (வெள்ளாறு - velláru, Tam.). See sep. title.——*Velhiarpooram* (வேதியர்ப்புரம் - véthiyarppuram, Tam.). From (véthiyan, tam. missionary + pura, san. city). Village; pop. 985; lat. 10° 43′; long. 79° 16′; from Tanjore S.E. 8 miles. Sub-station of Wesleyan methodist society. S.P.G. mission school formerly here was abolished some years ago.——*Vullam* (வல்லம் - vallam, Tam.). See sep. title.——*Yelangaud* (இளங்காடு - elangádu, Tam.). From (ilamai, tam. tenderness + kádu, tam. forest). Village; pop. 2,375; lat. 10° 50′; long. 78° 58′; from Tanjore W.N.W. 15 miles. Centre of Cullar [q.v.].——**(3)** Deputy tahsildarry, Tanjore district. Pay Rs. 100.——**(4)** Town, Head-quarters of Judge, Division, Talook, Deputy tahsildar, District moonsif, Sub-judge, Local fund engineer, Executive engineer, District surgeon, Superintendent of Police, Railway station; Tanjore dist., Tanjore tal.; pop. 54,390; lat. 10° 48′; long. 79° 11′; height 193 feet; from Combaconam S.W. 20 miles; from Madras S. 174 miles; from Mayavaram S.W. 41 miles; from Munnargoody W.N.W. 22 miles; from Negapatam W. 47 miles. The European and East indian quarters are in the suburb of Manamboo chauvady [q.v.], south-east of the fort. The native town outside the fort extends also northward about two miles to the Jamboo cauvery channel north of the Vennaur. Its greatest length south and north is about 4, and its greatest breadth east and west about 3 miles. Railway junction for Negapatam. Six miles west is Vullam, the residence of the Collector. For history see vol. II, 126. In 1860 the head-quarters of the Collector, then at Tranquebar, were removed to Tanjore; and in 1863 the District court, till then at Combaconam, was also removed to this station. Tanjore is the principal seat of the S.P.G. in the district. The memory of Schwartz is preserved by a marble monument, executed by Flaxman, which stands in the church in the small fort opposite to the Shivagunga tank. The fort, in which is situated the palace of the late Rajah, now in the occupation of his family, is the most thickly-populated part of the town, and is the residence of the principal inhabitants. It is surrounded by thick masonry walls and a deep moat, and covers an area of 530 acres; the walls are however being gradually removed. This fort also contains a fine library of 8,000 Sanscrit manuscripts. The great temple is one of the oldest in the south and has been preserved with little alteration [stanpatyam]. The temple consists of two courts, one a square of about 250 feet originally devoted to minor shrines; but when the temple was fortified by the French in 1777 it was converted into an arsenal and has not been reconsecrated. The temple itself stands on a courtyard 500 feet long by about 250 in breadth. The walls of the temple are covered with inscriptions [shausanam]. Nearly all belong to the reign of Veera cholan. On entering through the two gateways at the east end of the enclosure, there is a small temple, where sacrifices are offered. A figure of the great bull Nundy [q.v.], in solid granite [caroom-cull] over 12 feet high, is directly in front of, and covered by, a mantapam [q.v.]. Further west is the great vimaunam [q.v.] containing the lingam [q.v.], with tower, 200 feet high. The base of the building is covered with inscriptions in old Tamul of the eleventh century, and one of them records the conquest by Veera cholan of Bengal and Northern india. The perpendicular part of its base measures 82 feet square. The pyramid rises in thirteen storeys to a height of 190 feet. The sculptures on the gopoorams [q.v.] relate to Vishnoo [q.v.], while everything in the courtyard is dedicated to Shiva [q.v.]. The shikharam [q.v.] of the great gopooram [q.v.] is composed of a single block of granite 25½ feet square, which was placed in position by means of an inclined plane commencing from the village of Shaurapullam, 4 miles north-east of the town. To the north-west of the enclosure is the temple of Soobramanyan [q.v.]. East of that is a Chundikaishan temple, and further east a small temple to Doorga [q.v.]. At the east fort gate is a tower called the clock-tower, with a curious device for marking the time. During the days of native government Tanjore was a principal seat of manufacturing industry as well as of fine arts. The latter have to a great extent disappeared, but manufactures, chiefly silk-weaving, continue to be carried on to a considerable extent. The Putnoolcaurar [putnool], an early colony from Goozerat, form a principal section of the population of the outside town. They turn out dyed silk [puttoo] yarn of fair quality and make fine carpets [satranjee] of silk floss. Tanjore is also noted for native jewellery [nagay, zewar], pith [solah] toys, lace-work [sarigay], embroidery and flower garlands. The principal workmen at Tanjore are brick-masons. The following are the travelling distances by road from Tanjore to different places:—

To	Via	Miles	Furlongs
Adiramputnam	Gandharvacottah and Puttoocottah ...	48	5
Bangalore	Trichinopoly, Salem and Oossoor ...	242	1
Bellary	Trichinopoly, Salem and Bangalore ...	429	4
Calicut	Trichinopoly, Palghaut and Malapooram.	281	4
Cannanore	Trichinopoly, Palghaut and Calicut ...	340	5
Chidambaram ...	Combaconam	71	2
Chingleput	Combaconam, Panrooty and Vicravaundy.	161	3
Chingleput	Combaconam, Cuddalore and Pondicherry.	175	7
Coimbatore	Trichinopoly, Caroor and Caungyam ...	160	1
Combaconam ...	Paupanausam	23	4
Dindigul	Trichinopoly	98	1½
Madras	Combaconam, Vicravaundy and Chingleput.	196	2
Madras	Combaconam, Cuddalore, Pondicherry and Chingleput.	210	6
Madura	Poodoocottah and Tripatore	102	0
Negapatam	Tirvarore	56	0
Point Calimere ...	Munnargoody and Tritrapoondy ...	68	1
Poodoocottah ...	Gandharvacottah	36	2
Puttoocottah ...	Cullacottay	41	0
Rameshwaram ...	Puttoocottah, Tondy and Ramnaud ...	166	4
Ramnaud	Puttoocottah and Tondy	129	4
Salem	Trichinopoly and Namcull	124	1
Trichinopoly ...	Vullam	37	2
Vellore	Combaconam, Panrooty and Villoopooram.	167	1

TANK (ಕೆರೆ - kere, *Can.*; చెరువు - cheruvu, *Tel.*; ചിറ - chira, *Mal.*; ஏரி - éri, *Tam.*). Portuguese Tanque, Latin Stagnum. Anglo-indian for artificial lake, being a natural depression converging at a point and banked up so as to retain the water. Sometimes in part at any rate excavated. The country abounds with these. The larger are supplied by channels [q.v.] brought from rivers [aur]. The smaller are filled by local rains [mazhay], and do not retain water for more than three or four months. When great drought prevails, small pits are dug in the beds of the tanks. Cultivation of tank-beds silts them up rapidly.

TANNAH (تھانہ - thána, *Hind.*). From (st'hána, san. a place). A station, especially a police station [chowky]. Tannahdar is a station-house officer.

TANOOKOO (తనుకు - tanuku, *Tel.*). Means burning. The eastern portion of the talook is identified with old Lunka seema and the western with old Pentapaud seema.——**(1)** Talook, Godavery district. Tahsildar's pay Rs. 200. Area 372 square miles. Composed of 180 villages, 88 being Government, 65 zemindarry [q.v.], and 27 shrotriem [q.v.] agraharams [q.v.]. Population 204,048. Language Teloogoo. In the south of the district. Bounded:—north by Ellore and Yornagoodem tolooks, south by Narsapore and Bheemavaram talooks, east by the Vasishta branch of the Godavery and Amalaupooram talook, and west by Colair lake and Ellore talook. Generally flat, but productive and healthy. Soil is of eight different sorts:—alluvial, permanently improved, regar [q.v.] pure, regar loamy, regar sandy, red clay, red loamy, and red sandy [munn]. Products are chiefly paddy [q.v.], gram [q.v.], gingelly [q.v.] and lamp-oil [q.v.] seeds, hemp [kinnab], coriander [cassibor], fenugreek [maitee], mustard [rayaun], zonna [cholum], cumboo [bajrah], raggy [q.v.], tobacco [pogauk], chillies [q.v.], onions [piyauz], garlic [lussoon], turmeric [country saffron] and cotton [q.v.]. No special industry, the chief trâde being in paddy, grain and cotton. There is also toddy drawing and manufacture of arrack [q.v.] and jaggery [q.v.] from toddy [q.v.]. There is a perfect supply of anicut [q.v.] irrigation [panchal]. The chief canals are the Caucarparroo canal, the Vencayya canal, part of the Ellore canal, Gostanuddy canal and the Attily canal. These are available both for irrigation and navigation. From these several branch channels [q.v.] have been cut for the supply of water. Zemindarry:—Nidadvole. Places of archæological interest:—Attily, Cantair, Caucarparroo, Caunore, Chebrole, Condwapaud, Cundavilly, Doovva, Iragavaram, Mandapauca, Maumoodore, Maurcandapaud, Mooccaumala, Moonipulley, Mullepoody, Mulleshwaram, Nidadvole, Paikair, Pandlaparroo, Paulangy, Pendyaul, Penoogonda, Penoomuntra, Pentapaud, Pipparroo, Rameshwaram, Relangy, Taitaly, Tanookoo, Vaimavaram, Velpoor, Vijayeshwaram, Vipparroo, Yilindraparroo, Zoottiga. The leading places, &c., in the talook are the following.——*Attily* (అత్తిలి - attili, Tel.). From (atti, tel. fig tree, ficus glomerata, miq.). Sanscrit corruption (átréyapurí), meaning atreyan, the sage + town. Town; pop. 7,365; acres 5,338; lat. 16° 41′; long. 81° 39′; from Cocanada W.S.W. 45 miles; from Tanookoo S.W. 7 miles. Two old temples. Once had a fort. The Attily canal 15¾ miles long is navigable to this village. Weekly market on Thursdays and Fridays.——*Caucarparroo* (కాకరపఱ్ఱు - kákarapafru, Tel.). From (kákara, tel. momordica charantia, linn. + parra, tel. swamp). Village, Canal; pop. 1,912; acres 1,487; lat. 16° 46′; long. 81° 47′; from Cocanada W.S.W. 34 miles; from Tanookoo E.N.E. 4 miles. Two old temples founded by Rajah narendran, a Chola king. Old temple of Seetay. The canal is a branch of the western main delta canal. Much resorted to for bathing in the Godavery. Mango [q.v.] and plaintain [q.v.] gardens abound.——*Chettipett* (శెట్టిపేట - shettipéta, Tel.). From (shetti, tel. merchant caste + péta, tel. suburb). Zemindarry village; pop. 1,987; acres 2,082; lat. 16° 52′; long. 81° 43′; from Cocanada W. 37 miles; from Tanookoo N. 8 miles. Weir in connection with the Western delta main canal, which separates here into the Caucarparroo and Ellore canals. Head-quarters of Executive engineer, western division.——*Cundavilly* (ఖండవిల్లి - khandavilli, Tel.). From (khandamu, tel. sugar-candy + palli, tel. village). Village; pop. 4,171; acres 3,386; lat. 16° 43′; long. 81° 48′; from Cocanada W.S.W. 35 miles; from Tanookoo S.E. 5 miles. Old temple. On Vasishta godavery. Has an extensive lunka [q.v.]. Plaintain [q.v.] and mango [q.v.] gardens abound.——*Doovva* (దువ్వ - duvva, Tel.). Means dust. Village; pop. 4,029; acres 4,446; lat. 16° 47′; long. 81° 39′; from Cocanada W.S.W. 42 miles; from Tanookoo W.N.W. 5 miles. Temples of great antiquity. A river named Veyyair runs by the side.——*Godavery* (గోదావరి - gódávari, Tel.). See sep. title.——*Gostanuddy* (గోస్తనది - góstanadi, Tel.). See sep. title.——*Mooccaumala* (ముక్కామల - mukkámala, Tel.). From (mukku, tel. nose + mala, tel. hill). Government village; pop. 2,096; acres 2,024; lat. 16° 45′; long. 81° 48′; from Cocanada W.S.W. 34 miles; from Tanookoo E. 5 miles. Old temples.——*Nidadvole* (నిడుదవోలు - nidudavólu, Tel.). See sep. title.——*Penoogonda* (పెనుగొండ - penugonda, Tel.). From (penu, tel. great + konda, tel. hill). Town; pop. 4,179; acres 2,749; lat. 16° 39′; long. 81° 47′; from Cocanada S.W. 38 miles; from Tanookoo S.S.E. 8 miles. North of Narsapore canal on the road to Rajahmundry. This road called Forbes' road joins the river bank at Caucarparroo. Former residence of a zemindar [q.v.]. Four temples. Large temple of Comaties [q.v.] largely resorted to by the caste [jauty].——*Pentapaud* (పెంటపాడు - pentapádu, Tel.). See sep. title.——*Rameshwaram* (రామేశ్వరం - rámeshvaram, Tel.). From (ráma, san. the god + íshvara, san. lord); after shiva, rama's lord. Village, Place of pilgrimage; pop. 997; acres 977; lat. 16° 39′; long. 81° 41′; from Cocanada W.S.W. 44 miles; from Tanookoo S.S.W. 7 miles. On the Gostanuddy. Temple of Rameshwara sawmy. Ancient temples. Largely attended festival at Shivarautry [pundigay, 6a].——*Relangy* (రేలంగి - rélangi, Tel.). From (rellu, tel. reed, saccharum spontaneum, linn. + angu, tel. beauty). Zemindarry village; pop. 5,467; acres 3,927; lat. of village 16° 42′; long. 81° 41′; from Cocanada W.S.W. 42 miles; from Tanookoo S.W. 5 miles. On the Gostanuddy. Ancient temple.——*Tanookoo* (తణుకు - tanuku, Tel.). See below.——*Teeparroo* (తీపఱ్ఱు - típarru, Tel.). From (tippa, tel. elevation + arru, tel. neck). Zemindarry village; pop. 1,333 acres 1,027; lat. 16° 47′; long. 81° 47′; from Cocanada W.S.W. 34 miles; from Tanookoo N.E. 4 miles. On the Godavery.——*Velpoor* (వేల్పూరు - vélpúru, Tel.). From (vélpu, tel. angel + úru, tel. village). Town; pop. 6,649; acres 2,057; lat. 16° 43′; long. 81° 42′; from Cocanada W.S.W. 40 miles; from Tanookoo S.S.W. 3 miles. On the Gostanuddy. Temple with two inscriptions.——*Vijayeshwaram* (విజయేశ్వరము - vijayéshvaramu, Tel.). From (vijaya, san. victory + íshvara, san. lord). Zemindarry; pop. 1,286; acres 663; lat. 16° 55′; long. 81° 46′; from Cocanada W. 33 miles; from Tanookoo N.N.E. 12 miles. Two old temples held sacred. The Vijayeshwaram division of the Godavery anicut [q.v.], constructed in 1849, extended from Maddore island to Chigooroo island, adjoining the right bank of the river. The whole breadth of the river at this spot is 7,000 yards, or 4 miles.——*Zoottiga* (జుత్తిగ - dzuttiga, Tel.). From (dzutta, tel. a span). Zemindarry village; pop. 1,195; acres 1,880; lat. 16° 39′; long. 81° 42′; from Cocanada W.S.W. 43 miles; from Tanookoo S. 7 miles. Ancient temples. Inscriptions. Situated on the Gostanuddy.——(2) Village, Talook head-quarters. It contains the District moonsif's court and the Sub-registrar's office; Godavery dist., Tanookoo tal.; pop. 3,801; acres 3,988; lat. 16° 45′; long. 81° 44′; from Cocanada W.S.W. 38 miles; from Coonavaram S.S.E. 62 miles; from Ellore E. 38 miles; from Madras N.N.E. 264 miles; from Narsapore N. 21 miles; from Rajahmundry S.S.W. 18 miles. Temples of Keshava sawmy and of Siddheshwarasawmy.

TANTAH (ٹنٹا - tantá, *Hind.*). Disturbance [tagaraur].

TAP (तप् - tap, *San.*). To heat.——*Tapas* (तपस् - tapas, San.; تپس - tapas, Hind.; தவசு - tavasu, Tam.). Penance. Its merit is proportioned to its length and severity. Its power controls alike gods and men. There are three modes of merit [mocsham]:—carmam [q.v.], bhacty [q.v.], nyaunam [q.v.], or works, faith, wisdom. Carmam includes sacrifices [yanyam], pilgrimage [yautray], bathing [snaunam] and penance. Compare the following from Cooral [q.v.], which inclines however always to internal rather than to external self-mortification:—உற்ற நோய் நோன்ற லுயிர்க்குறுகண் செய்யாமை யற்றே தவத்திற் குரு—"the nature of religious discipline consists "in the endurance by the ascetic of the sufferings which it brings "on himself, and in abstaining from giving pain to others."—வேண்டிய வேண்டியாங் கெய்தலாற் செய்தவ மீண்டு முயலப் படும்—"religious discipline is practised in this world, "because it secures the attainment of whatever one may wish to "enjoy in the world to come."—தவஞ்செய்வார் தங்கருமஞ் செய்வார்மற் றல்லா ரவஞ்செய்வா ராசையுட் பட்டு—"those discharge their duty who perform austerities, all others "accomplish their own destruction through the entanglement "of desire."—சுடச்சுடரும் பொன்போ லொளிவிடுந் துன்பஞ் சுடச்சுட நோற்கிற் பவர்க்கு—"just as gold is "purified when heated in the fire, so will those shine who have "endured the burning of pain in frequent austerities."—தன்னுயிர் தானறப் பெற்றானை யேனைய மன்னுயி ரெல்லாந் தொழும்—"all other creatures will worship him who has "attained the control of his own soul."—தவமறைந் தல்லவை செய்தல் புதன்மறைந்து வேட்டுவன் புட்சிமிழ்த் தற்று—"he who hides himself under the mask of an ascetic "and commits sins, is like a sportsman who conceals himself in "the thicket to catch birds."—புறங்குன்றி கண்டனைய ரேனு மகங்குன்றி மூக்கிற் கரியா ருடைத்து—"the world contains "persons whose outside appears as the red berry of the abrus "[indian liquorice], but whose inside is as black as the nose of "that berry."—மழித்தலு நீட்டலும் வேண்டா வுலகம் பழித்த தொழித்து விடின்—"there is no need of a shaven "crown nor of tangled hair, if a man abstain from those deeds "which the wise have condemned."—கொல்லா நலத்தது நோன்மை பிறர்தீமை சொல்லா நலத்தது சால்பு—"penance consists in the goodness that kills not, and perfection "in the goodness that tells not others' faults."—சால்பிற்குக் கட்டளை யாதெனிற் றோல்வி துலையல்லார் கண்ணுங் கொளல்—"the touch-stone of perfection is to receive a defeat "even at the hands of one's inferior."——*Tapolocam* (तपोलोक - tapólóka, San.). From (tapas, san. penance + lóka, san. world). One of the seven upper worlds [locam]. The sphere of penance, inhabited by Veibbraujans or deified sages shining with high penitential merit and lustre and who are unconsumable by fire.——*Taptapauny* (తప్తపాని - taptapáni, Tel.). From (tapta, san. hot + pániya, san. water). Village; Zemindarry tracts, Chinna kimedy zemindarry; lat. 19° 28′; long. 84° 26′; from Chetterpore W.N.W. 40 miles; from Russellcondah S.S.W. 33 miles. Hot water spring half way up Eastern ghaut [q.v.] above Poodamary. The temperature is 110°, and strong sulphurous vapour. Occasional pilgrimages. Source of the Godahaddoh which eventually falls into the Rooshcoolya.——*Taupasan* (तापस - tápasa, San.). Sage. Cf.:—Cordia sp. (tapasimara), sage's tree; Terminalia catappa (tápasataruvu), sage's tree. See gloss. paragraphs.——*Tupsee* (تپسی - tapsí, Hind.). From long hairs about the mouth looking like a penitent. The Robaul [q.v.]. Otherwise the Pilgrim fish, from going up ganges to benares; also Mango fish, from abounding in the ganges about mango season.

TAPKAH (ٹپکا - tapká, *Hind.*). From (tapakná, hind. to drop). Dripping of water. The best wells in hill forts.

TAPPAH (ٹپہ - tappah, *Hind.*). Means a leap. A ballad, or a mode in music.

TAPPATTAY (ڈھپٹی - dhaptí, *Hind.*; తప్పెట - tappeta, *Tel.*; தப்பட்டை - tappattai, *Tam.*). From (tappu, tam. to clap). A large drum [paray].

TAPPAUL (ٹپال - tappál, *Hind.*). From (táppá, mahr. place where letters are stamped + álaya, san. house). A halting place [majil]. Post stage. Thence, the letters delivered [anchey].

TAR (تر - tar, *Hind.*). Moist.——*Tarai* (ترائی - tarái, Hind.). Marshy ground.——*Tooranj been* (ترنجبین - turanjbín, Ar.). From (above + angabín, pers. honey). Arabian manna.

TARAF (طرف - taraf, *Hind.*). From arabic. A side, quarter. Division of a talook [firkah, talook, tookady]. Compare Zillah. A tarafdar means often generally a superintendent.

TARAM (طرح - tarah, *Hind.*; తరము - taramu, *Tel.*; தரம் - taram, *Tam.*). From (tara, san. suffix of comparison). Sort, kind or class. Especially applied to the classification of soils [munn]. As the latter have been assessed with regard to their classification the word is sometimes loosely and improperly used for the assessment [teervay] itself. Taram cummy is a reduction from taram assessment. Taramdar is a person who superintends the classing of lands, classifier. Taram jausty is an extra tax. Tara teervay is the assessment assigned to a particular class of land. See vol. I, 112.

TARCAM (तर्क - tarka, *San.*). From (tark, san. to infer). Logic [mantik]. A regular argument or complete syllogism, nyauyam [q.v.], consists of five members, avayavam, or component parts. First, the Proposition, pratinyay; second, the Reason, haitoo or apadesham; third, the Instance, oodauharanam or nidarshanam; fourth, the Application, oopanayam; fifth, the Conclusion, nigamanam. Example:—This hill is fiery; for it smokes; what smokes, is fiery, as a culinary hearth; accordingly the hill is smoking; therefore it is fiery.

TARDOOD (تردد - taraddud, *Hind.*). From (radda, ar. to go to and fro). Exertion, cultivation [vellaumay].

TARIFF (تعریف - taríf, *Hind.*). From (arafa, ar. to know). Determination, table of rates of duties.

TARISS (தரிசு - tarisu, *Tam.*). From (tari, tam. to stop); place where cultivation is suspended. Waste land [bunjar, haul, paul].——*Terriote* (തരിയോത്ത് - tariyóttu, Mal.). Oblique form of Tariyagam. From (tari, mal. uncultivated + akam, mal. inside). Village; Malabar dist., Wynaud tal.; lat. 11° 39′; long. 76° 03′; from Calicut N.E. 32 miles; from Manantoddy S. 10 miles. Has a Chuttram [q v.].

TARJOOMA (ترجمہ - tarjumah, *Hind.*). From (tarjamah, ar. to interpret). Translation [mozhipeyarpp]. Tarjoomaun is a translator [doobaush], whence Dragoman [q.v.].

TARLAH (తర్లా - tarlá, *Tel.* tarlá*). Ancient zemindarry, Village; Ganjam dist.; pop. 27,035; pop. of village 1,010; area 55 square miles; lat. of village 18° 48′; long. 84° 27′; from Chetterpore S.W. 54 miles; from Chicacole N.E. 47 miles; from the sea W. 9 miles. South of Mundasa. Bounded south by Tekkaly, and west by Parlakimedy. The family originally came from Nagpore and entered the service of the kings of Orissa. The first zemindar's father was killed in battle at Conjeeveram, and Poorshottama gajapaty deo made over the estate to his son, Sadausena soor in A.D. 1436. Number of villages about sixty. Tolerably level and well supplied with water. Peshcush [q.v.] Rs. 4,000. Contains Moorkhy trig. station.

TAROW (ٹھراؤ - tharáo, *Hind.*; ఠరావు - t'harávu, *Tel.*). From (t'haraném, mahr. to become fixed). Settlement. The fixed assessment [teervay] of a village based on average collections for the preceding sixteen or seventeen years. Otherwise Sarausary [q.v.] system. Especially the assessment in Canara settled by the English in A.D. 1819. See vol. I, 112.

TARP (ತರ್ಪ - tarpa, *Can.*). Waist cloth of Todahs [q.v.].

TARPANAM (तर्पण - tarpana, *San.*). From (trip, san. to be satisfied). Satisfaction. Propitiatory libations of water to manes of a deceased [pitry], with Til [q.v.] seeds and Coosham [q.v.] grass. Otherwise Neer cadan or water duty; also Oodaca kriyay or water ceremony; also Pitry yanyam or sacrifice to ancestors. Done every Amavausyay [q.v.] and at other times [pundigay, 6d].

TARRY (वेम - véma, *San.*; تانت - tánt, *Hind.*; మగ్గము - maggamu, *Tel.*; തറി - tari, *Mal.*; தறி - tari, *Tam.*). Title from tamul. San. from (vé, san. to weave). Hind. from (tantu, san. thread). Loom [nesavoo].

TARWAR (तरवड - taravada, *Mahr.*; ترور - tarwar, *Hind.*). Same as Tungaid.

TARWAUD (തറവാട - taraváṭu, *Mal.*). From (tara, mal. village + pátu, mal. place) [teroo]. Originally one of the heads in the Shoodra village or tara [q.v.] of Malabar. Hence the place of abode of such householder. Hence the joint family as opposed to the village community. In former times each petty rajah under the great Swaroopam [q.v.] rajahs ruled his own portion of territory, designated a Naud [q.v.] or country, and was styled Naudvauly [q.v.] or Boynore [vauzhnore]. Subordinate to the Naudvaulies came other still smaller rulers, who as Deshavaulies administered each his own Deshom [q.v.], which might be styled a parish. Subordinate to the Deshom came the Tara. Sub-divisions of the Tara were the family Tarwauds. Sub-divisions of the Tarwauds were the Tauveries [q.v.]. A Tarwaud corresponds with what the Romans called a gens; with this distinction that whereas in Rome all members of the gens traced their descent from a common ancestor, in Malabar the members of a tarwaud trace their descent from a common ancestress. The large tarwauds set apart property for the common use. So long as that common property exists, an indefinite number of private families may be comprised in the tarwaud. Every member of a tarwaud has an equal share in the common stock; the infant as much as the aged. No member can claim his share, but the tarwaud as a body can make such division as it pleases of the common stock. When partition takes place, the tarwaud becomes disintegrated into as many tarwauds as the members may have settled to form among themselves. This process of disintegration goes on continually, except among the highest classes, who pride themselves in maintaining a large common stock. But even among the highest classes there are as above said in the tarwauds sub-divisions, locally known as Tauveries or branches [tauvery]. A member, with perhaps some assistance from the common stock but more usually with the assistance obtained from his father who under the Maroomakkatoyem [q.v.] system stands in no recognized legal relation to his children, leaves the tarwaud house and lives apart, taking with him one or more female relatives usually a sister or sisters and thus founding a separate tauvery. When a tauvery branch of a Rajah's family is thus founded, it is styled a Covilagam [q.v.]. That word inflected becomes Covilagatt and in speaking the word is pronounced as if it were Coilote; hence the word Culote as written in the old records. Within the tarwaud the entire property is managed by its senior member [carnaven] for the benefit of the family [anandraven]. In inheritance of status in the tarwaud, all tarwauds follow the Maroomakkatoyem [q.v.] rule or descensus a matrice. In theory the property is held to vest in the females only, the males having right of management and claim to support. Practically the males are co-sharers with the females. All members of the family, even the remotest, are entitled to maintenance. The rights of the junior members of a Malabar family are the right of the males to succeed to the headship by seniority, and the right of the males and females to be supported in the family house. A separate maintenance is not allotted to a junior member who voluntarily and without lawful excuse separates himself or herself from the family [maryauday]. See vol. II, 104.——(1) The following are the principal Tarwauds in North malabar, with the talook indicated.——*Aralatt numbiyaur* (അറളത്ത് നമ്പ്യാർ - aralattunampyár, Mal.), Cottayam.——*Arattil cundote numbiyaur* (അറത്തിൽ കണ്ടോത്ത് നമ്പ്യാർ - arattilkantóttunampyár, Mal.), Cottayam.——*Arayat numbiyaur* (അരയത്ത് നമ്പ്യാർ - arayattunampyár, Mal.), Chiracal.——*Arayedatt numbiyaur* (അരേടത്തു നമ്പ്യാർ - arétattunampyár, Mal.), Chiracal.——*Arikkara nayar* (അരിക്കരനായർ - arikkaranáyar, Mal.), Cooroombranaud.——*Ayicote mauvilye numbiyaur* (അഴിക്കോട്ട് മാവിലായിനമ്പ്യാർ - azhikkóttumáviláyinampyár, Mal.), Chiracal.——*Ayilat numbiyaur* (ആയില്യത്ത് നമ്പ്യാർ - áyilyattunampyár, Mal.), Chiracal.——*Capiyatt numbiyaur* (കപിയത്ത് നമ്പ്യാർ - kapiyattunampyár, Mal.), Chiracal.——*Caunyirote kidauv* (കാഞ്ഞിരോട്ട് കിടാവ് - kaññiróttukitávu, Mal.), Cooroombranaud.——*Chaulal veetil numbiyaur* (ചാലലവീട്ടിൽനമ്പ്യാർ - chálalavíttilnampyár, Mal.), Chiracal.——*Chaulayil cundote numbiyaur* (ചാലയിൽ കണ്ടോത്ത് നമ്പ്യാർ - chálayilkantóttunampyár, Mal.), Chiracal.——*Chauttote numbiyaur* (ചാത്തോത്ത് നമ്പ്യാർ - cháttóttunampyár, Mal.), Chiracal.——*Cheriyaut numbiyaur* (ചെറിയത്ത് നമ്പ്യാർ - cheriyattunampyár, Mal.), Cooroombranaud.——*Coonnat veetil numbiyaur* (കുന്നത്തുവീട്ടിൽ നമ്പ്യാർ - kunnattuvíttilnampyár, Mal.), Chiracal.——*Coonnatt edattil numbiyaur* (കുന്നത്തെടത്തിൽനമ്പ്യാർ - kunnattetattilnampyár, Mal.), Cottayam.——*Cooroocaut coorpoo* (കുറുക്കാട്ടുകുറുപ്പ് - kurukkáttukuruppu, Mal.), Cooroombranaud.——*Cootauly tayatveetil numbiyaur* (കൂടാളിതായത്ത് വീട്ടിൽനമ്പ്യാർ - kútálitázhattuvíttilnampyár, Mal.). Cottayam.——*Coottipoorat poolairy coorpoo* (കുറ്റിപ്പുറത്തുപൂലേരിക്കുറുപ്പ് - kuttippurattupúlérikkuruppu, Mal.), Cooroombranaud.——*Coottyanttore maunikatt numbiyaur* (കുറ്റിയാറ്റൂർമാണിക്കത്ത് നമ്പ്യാർ - kuttiyáttúrmáṇikkattunampyár, Mal.), Chiracal.——*Coottyauttorekelote numbiyaur* (കുറ്റിയാറ്റൂർ കേളോത്തു നമ്പ്യാർ - kuttiyáttúrkélóttunampyár, Mal.), Chiracal.——*Cottaurat numbiyaur* (കൊട്ടാരത്ത് നമ്പ്യാർ - kottárattunampyár, Mal.), Cottayam.——*Coykil yedattil numbi-*

yaur (കൊഴക്കിൽ എടത്തിൽനമ്പ്യാർ - kozhukiletattilnampyár, Mal.), Cottayam.——*Culyaut numbiyaur* (കല്യാട്ട് നമ്പ്യാർ - kalyáttunampyár, Mal.), Chiracal.——*Cundote nayar* (കുണ്ടോട്ടു നായർ - kantóttunáyar, Mal.), Cooroombranaud.——*Keipattore yedam nayar* (കൈപ്പട്ടൂരെടംനായർ - kaipattúretamnáyar, Mal.), Cooroombranaud.——*Keipautt kidauv* (കൈപ്പാട്ടുകിടാവ് - tkaippáttukitávu, Mal.), Cooroombranaud.——*Keithairy chandrote numbiyaur* (കൈതേരിചന്ത്രോത്ത് നമ്പ്യാർ - kaitérichantróttunampyár, Mal.), Cottayam.——*Keithairy kelote numbiyaur* (കൈതേരികേളോത്ത് നമ്പ്യാർ - kaitérikélóttunampyár, Mal.), Cottayam.——*Keithairy yedattil numbiyaur* (കൈതേരിഎടത്തിൽനമ്പ്യാർ - kaitérietattilnampyár, Mal.), Cottayam.——*Mangoottil nayar* (മങ്കൂറ്റിൽനായർ - mankúttilnáyar, Mal.), Cooroombranaud.——*Manmily kidauv* (മറിമില്ലികിടാവ് - manmilikkitávu, Mal.), Cooroombranaud.——*Moorehilote croopoo* (മൂച്ചിലോട്ടുകുറുപ്പ് - múrççilóttukuruppu, Mal.), Cooroombranaud.——*Naurangapooral nayar* (നാരങ്ങാപ്പുറത്തുനായർ - nárannáppuratunáyar, Mal.), Cottayam.——*Nettore chauttote numbiyaur* (നെട്ടൂർചാത്തോത്ത് നമ്പ്യാർ - nettúrchátt́ottunampyár, Mal.), Chiracal.——*Ningilairy numbiyaur* (നിങ്കിലേരി നമ്പ്യാർ - ninkilérinampyár, Mal.), Cottayam.——*Nullacundy corote numbiyaur* (നല്ലകണ്ടികോരോത്ത് നമ്പ്യാർ - nallakantíkoróttunampyár, Mal.), Chiracal.——*Padinyautt edattil nayar* (പടിഞ്ഞാറെടത്തിൽ നായർ - pattiññáttetattilnáyar, Mal.), Cooroombranaud.——*Panoly numbiyaur* (പനോളിനമ്പ്യാർ - panólinampyár, Mal.), Cottayam.——*Parycurattedavan numbiyaur* (പരിയാരത്തെടവൻനമ്പ്യാർ - pariyárattetavannampyár, Mal.), Chiracal.——*Pooliairy ola* (പുളിയേരി ഓല - puliyérióla, Mal.), Cooroombranaud.——*Poolyote nayar* (പുളിയോത്ത് നായർ - paliyóttunáyar, Mal.), Cooroombranaud.——*Poonooredattil kidauv* (പൂനൂരെടത്തിൽകിടാവ് - púnúretattilkitávu, Mal.), Cooroombranaud.——*Poothoocherry kidauv* (പുതുശ്ശേരി കിടാവ് - putushshérikitávu, Mal.), Cooroombranaud.——*Punyote numbiyaur* (പന്നിയോട്ട് നമ്പ്യാർ - panniyóttunampyár, Mal.), Cottayam.——*Puttanore yedattil numbiyaur* (പട്ടാനൂർഎടത്തിൽ നമ്പ്യാർ - pattánúretattilnampyár, Mal.), Cottayam.——*Tekkedatt nayar* (തെക്കേടത്ത് നായർ - tekkétattunáyar, Mal.), Cooroombranaud.——*Tirwott poolairy croorpoo* (തിരുവത്ത് പൂലേരി കുറുപ്പ് - tiruvattupúlérikuruppu, Mal.), Cooroombranaud.——*Tutchinayinola* (തച്ചിനായിനോല - taççináyinóla, Mal.), Cooroombranaud.——*Vannatancundy numbiyaur* (വണ്ണത്താങ്കണ്ടി നമ്പ്യാർ - vannattánkantinampyár, Mal.), Cooroombranaud.——*Vauricara nayanaur* (വാരിക്കര നായനാർ - várikkaranáyanár, Mal.), Chiracal.——*Vauyote kidauv* (വായോത്ത് കിടാവ് - váyóttukitávu, Mal.), Cooroombranaud.——*Velloora chautote numbiyaur* (വെള്ളുവച്ചാത്തോത്ത് നമ്പ്യാർ - velluvachátt́ottunampyár, Mal.), Cottayam.——*Velloovapoothiya veetil numbiyaur* (വെള്ളുവ പുതിയ വീട്ടിൽ നമ്പ്യാർ - velluvaputiyavíttilnampyár, Mal.), Chiracal.——*Vengayil nayanaur* (വേങ്ങയിൽനായനാർ - vénnayilnáyanár, Mal.), Chiracal.——*Venmineery kidauv* (വെൺമിനിരികിടാവ് - venminírikitávu, Mal.), Cooroombranaud.——*Yelamana nayar* (എളമനനായർ - elamananáyar, Mal.), Cooroombranaud.——(2) The following are similarly the principal tarwauds in South malabar.——*Autrapaut curtauv* (ആത്രപ്പാട്ട് കർത്താവ് - átrappáttukarttávu, Mal.), Valavanaud.——*Cadoocauvil nedoongaudy* (കടുക്കാവിൽ നെടുങ്ങാടി - katukkávilnetunnáti, Mal.), Valavanaud.——*Calavore nayar* (കളവൂർ നായർ - kalavúrnáyar, Mal.), Yernaud.——*Calpully plauppara* (കല്പള്ളിപ്പലാപ്പറ - kalpallipuláppara, Mal.), Yernaud.——*Cuppadat* (കപ്പടത്ത് - kappatattu, Mal.), Palghaut.——*Caumbrat* (കാമ്പ്രത്ത് - kámprattu, Mal.), Palghaut.——*Caunyirampaudat* (കാഞ്ഞിരമ്പാടത്ത് - kánñirampátattu, Mal.), Valavanaud.——*Caurampully* (കാരമ്പള്ളി - kárampalli, Mal.), Calicut.——*Chauttalingat* (ചാത്തലിങ്ങത്ത് - chättalinnattu, Mal.), Palghaut.——*Chembat munnaudiyaur* (ചെമ്പത്ത് മന്നാടിയാർ - champattumannátiyár, Mal.), Chittoor.——*Chemmalacherry aloovingal* (ചെമ്മലശ്ശേരി അലുവിങ്ങൽ - chammalashshérialuvinnal, Mal.), Calicut.——*Cheroocara nayar* (ചെറുകരനായർ - cherukaranáyar, Mal.), Palghaut.——*Cheroovalat* (ചെറുവലത്ത് - cheruvalattu, Mal.), Calicut.——*Codanat* (കോതനാത്ത് - kótanattu, Mal.), Palghaut.——*Colakampaudat munnaudiyaur* (കൊളക്കമ്പാടത്ത് മന്നാടിയാർ - kolakkumpátattumannátiyár, Mal.), Palghaut.——*Colapully nayar* (കൊളപ്പള്ളി നായർ - kolappallináyar, Mal.), Palghaut.——*Congalat munnaudiyaur* (കോങ്കലത്ത് മന്നാടിയാർ - kónkalattumannátiyár, Mal.), Palghaut.——*Congode* (കോണോട്ട് - kónnóttu, Mal.), Palghaut.——*Coolamcolly* (കുളംകൊള്ളി - kulamkolli, Mal.), Calicut.——*Coolatore warriar* (കുളത്തൂർവാരിയർ - kulattúrváriyar, Mal.), Valavanaud.——*Coottampully numbiyaur* (കുത്തമ്പള്ളിനമ്പ്യാർ - kuttámpallinampyár, Mal.), Ponnany.——*Cootticaut vallody* (കുറ്റിക്കാട്ട് വള്ളോടി - kuttikkáttuvallóti, Mal.), Valavanaud.——*Coottichira nayar* (കുറ്റിച്ചിറനായർ - kuttiççiranáyar, Mal.), Ponnany.——*Coottiprat* (കുറ്റിപ്പുറത്ത് - kuttippurattu, Mal.), Yernaud.——*Coyicot agattaith* (കോഴിക്കോട്ടകത്തേത്ത് - kozhikkóttakattétu, Mal.), Ponnany.——*Keiprat* (കൈപ്രത്ത് - kaiprattu, Mal.), Calicut.——*Kenaut* (കേനാത്ത് - kénáttu, Mal.), Palghaut.——*Manattanaut* (മനത്താനാത്ത് - manattánattu, Mal.), Calicut.——*Mannattore* (മണ്ണത്തൂർ - mannattúr, Mal.), Calicut.——*Mañyalauvil nayar* (മഞ്ഞളാവിൽനായർ - maññalávilnáyar, Mal.), Ponnany.——*Moondagaparambat* (മുണ്ടകപ്പറമ്പത്ത് - muntakapparampattu, Mal.), Calicut.——*Moondukal munnil yedam* (മുണ്ടക്കൽ മണ്ണിൽഎടം - muntakkalmannileťam, Mal.), Calicut.——*Mooriyat warriar* (മൂരിയത്ത് വാരിയർ - múriyattuváriyar, Mal.), Valavanaud.——*Moothirakal panikkar* (മുതിരക്കൽ പണിക്കർ - mutirakkalpanikkar, Mal.), Ponnany.——*Moottacoottil naraut* (മുത്തക്കുറ്റിൽ നാരാത്തു - múttakúttilnárattu, Mal.), Calicut.——*Nellye warriar* (നെല്ലായിവാരിയർ - nelláyiváriyar, Mal.), Valavanaud.——*Neydilat* (നേയ്തിലത്ത് - néytilattu, Mal.), Palghaut.——*Odangote munnaudiyaur* (ഒതുണ്ണോട്ട് മന്നാടിയാർ - otunnóttumannátiyár, Mal.), Palghaut.——*Oolnaud panikkar* (ഉള്ളനാട്ട് പണിക്കർ - ullanáttupanikkar, Mal.), Ponnany.——*Padinyaurpaud numbiyaur* (പടിഞ്ഞാറപ്പാട്ട് നമ്പ്യാർ - patiññárappáttunampyár, Mal.), Ponnany.——*Panamanna keiraut* (പനമണ്ണകൈരാട്ട് - panamannakairáttu, Mal.), Valavanaud.——*Paravattu munnaudiyaur* (പരവത്ത് മന്നാടിയാർ - paravattumannátiyár, Mal.), Palghaut.——*Paulacoonnat colye* (പാലക്കുന്നത്തുകൊളായി - pálakkunnattukoláyi, Mal.), Calicut.——*Paulacoonnatnungolatt* (പാലക്കുന്നത്തുനങ്ങോലത്തു - pálakkunnattunannólattu, Mal.), Calicut.——*Paulakal* (പാലക്കൽ - pálakkal, Mal.), Calicut.——*Paulaprat numbiyaur* (പാലപ്പുറത്ത് നമ്പ്യാർ - pálappurattunampyár, Mal.), Valavanaud.——*Paulmoly chauliyaudat* (പാലമൊളിചാലിയാടത്ത് - pálamolicháliyátattu, Mal.), Calicut.——*Payyanaut coonnat pannikkar* (പയ്യനാട്ട് കുന്നത്ത് പണിക്കർ - payyanáttukunnattupanikkar, Mal.), Yernaud.——*Pooliyancoolat munnaudiyaur* (പുളിയങ്കുളത്ത് മന്നാടിയാർ - puliyankálattumannátiyár, Mal.).——*Poonnoly corote* (പൂന്നോളി കോറോത്ത് - púnnólikoróttu, Mal.), Yernaud.——*Sootrakal yillat* (സൂത്രായ്ക്കൽ ഇല്ലത്ത് - sútráykkalillattu, Mal.), Yernaud.——*Talakauppil nayar* (തലക്കാപ്പിൽനായർ - talakkáppilnáyar, Mal.), Ponnany.——*Tekkinyyedatt nayar* (തെക്കിനിയേടത്ത് നായർ - tekkiniyétattunáyar, Mal.), Ponnany.——*Tillamannauttil* (തില്ലമന്നാട്ടിൽ - tillamannáttil, Mal.), Palghaut.——*Tutchaumat nedoongaudy* (തച്ചാമത്ത് നെടുങ്ങാടി - taççámattunetunnáti, Mal.), Valavanaud.——*Vadacherry munnaudiyaur* (വടശ്ശേരിമന്നാടിയാർ - vatashshérimannátiyár, Mal.), Palghaut.——*Vaulayore yeraudy* (വാഴയൂർ ഏറാടി - vázhayúréráti, Mal.), Yernaud.——*Yelayaut* (എളയാട്ട് - elayáttu, Mal.), Palghaut.

TASDIK (تصدیق - tasdik, *Hind.*). From (sidk, ar. truth). Attestation.

TASHEEA (تصحیح - tashíh, *Ar.*). From (sahha, ar. to verify). Muster.——*Tasheea nauma* (تصحیح نامہ - tashíhanámah, Hind.). From (above + námah, pers. deed). Deed conferring the privilege of maintaining cavalry [sawaur] under Mahomedan rulers.

TASSAH (ٹھپا - thassá, *Hind.*). From (thánsná, hind. to stuff). A mould, seal, stamp [moodray, sicca].

TAT (तत् - tat, *San.*). That.——*Tadbhavam* (तद्भव - tadbhava, San.). From (above + bhava, san. birth). Means sprung from that. A Dravidian word derived from Sanscrit, but much altered; as in English from ratio, reason. If a word is only altered in the termination, this is denominated Tatsamam [q.v.] or equivalent; as in the English from ratio, ration. Some Sanscrit words, like some Latin or Greek words in English, are used without any alteration [bhaushay].——*Tadeikyam* (तदैक्य - tadaikya, San.). From (above + aikya, san. union). Unity, or the union of identification [sauyoojyam], as Samyogam is that of contiguity [matam].——*Tanmavtram* (तन्मात्र - tanmátra, San.). From (above + mátra, san. measure), only so much; merely that. That in which its own peculiar property resides without change or variety. Subtile element of matter, of which there are five, viz:—Shabdam, sound; Sparsham, torch;

Roopam, form ; Rasam, taste ; Gandham, smell. These are the archetypes or rudimentary principles from which the five gross elements, otherwise Maha bhootam or Puncha bhootam [q.v.], are evolved ; correspond nearly to the πρῶτα στοιχεῖα of Plato. For more details see Saunkhyam and Tatwam.——*Tatparam* (तत्पर - tatpara, San.). From (above + para, san. beyond). A speck. Measure of solar time. 100 trooties or atoms = 1 tatparam or speck ; 30 tatparams = 1 nimisham or twinkling [caulam]. Approximate actual value, 1 tatparam = $\frac{2}{675}$ of an english second.——*Tatparan* (तत्पर - tatpara, San.). From (above + para, san. best). Shiva [q.v.], the self-existent.——*Tatsamam* (तत्सम - tatsama, San.). From (above + sama, san. equal). Means equal to that. Pure sanscrit words [tadbhavam]. The Atarvana vyaucaranam or grammar has as follows :—" The " adherents of Andhra vishnoo who then resided on the banks " of the Godavery spoke Tatsamam words. In the course of " time these words, not being properly articulated by the " unlearned, by the change or obliteration of letters, or by " being contracted, a fourth, or a half, became Tadbhavams " [q.v.]. Those words consisting of nouns, verbals, and verbs, " created by the God Bramha [q.v.], before the time of " Hary [q.v.], the lord of Andhram, are called Atchams or pure."——*Tatwabodhacar* (तत्त्वबोधक - tattvabódhaka, San. ; தத்துவபோதகன் - tattuvabóthagan, Tam.). From (tatva, san. truth + bhódhaka, san. teacher). Robert de Nobili. Roman catholic missionaries accompanied the Portuguese expeditions to India, and one of these a jesuit Robert de Nobili or Nobilibus nephew of Cardinal Bellarmine, proceeded to Madura in 1606. He was a distinguished Sanscrit and Tamul scholar. The following is a list of his writings :—Anitya nitya vyatyausam, Aumma nirnayani, Cadavool nirnayam, Dooshana dhicauram, Jesoonauthar charitram, Muntramaulay, Muntra vyaukhyaunam, Neetitchol, Nitya jeeva sallaupam, Nyauna deepicay, Nyaunopadesha caundam, Parama sootchmaubhiprauyam, Poonar jenmaucshaipam, Prapuncha virodha vyatyausam, Satyaveda lutchanam, Shacoona nirvauranam, Tapashatam, Tatwa cunnaudy. He founded a mission at Madura A.D. 1624 during the reign of Trimal naick [q.v.]. He was supported by the College of Rome de propaganda fide, founded in 1622 by Pope Gregory XV [veeramaumoony].——*Tatwam* (तत्त्व - tattva, San.). From (above + twa, san. suffix of quality). Primordial and eternally existing essence. The saunkhyas reckon twenty-five tatwams or metaphysical entities. For the catalogue see Saunkhyam. The sheivas postulate ninety-six tatwams or constituent principles in nature or operations whether of deity or of creatures, including elements, bodily and mental organs, faculties, matter, &c. According to the Chatoor acarauthy [q.v.] they are the five bhootams [q.v.] or elements, the five poolans or objects of senses [vishayam], the five organs of action or carmendriyam [q.v.], the five organs of perception or nyaunendriyam [q.v.], the four intellectual faculties or antah caranam [q.v.]; these twenty-four being called autmatatwam or powers of the soul [autmam]; the ten naudies or nerves, the five states of soul or avastays [q.v.], the three principles of moral evil, the three cosmic qualities or goonams [q.v.], the three mundalams or regions of sun, moon and fire, the three humours of body [pittam, sheetam, vautam], the eight vicaurams or predominant passions, the six audhaurams or stations of soul [shatstalattaun], the seven dhautoos or constituent elements of body, the ten vayoos [q.v.] or vital airs, the five coshams [q.v.] of soul, the nine doors or vents of body.——*Tatwa nyaunam* (तत्त्वज्ञान - tatvañána, San.). From (tatva, san. truth + ñána, san. knowledge). Philosophy.——*Tatwa vivechiny* (तत्त्वविवेचिनी - tattvavivéchiní, San.). From (tatva, san. truth + vivich, san. to discriminate). **Vernacular newspaper.**

TATAUCAM (तटाक - tatáka, *San.*). From (tat, san. to rise). Pond deep enough for the lotus [nelumbo] and other aquatic flowers [indian water-lily].

TATT (ٹٹو - tattú, *Hind.*). A pony [ghorah]. There is a Tamul proverb :—எண்ணப்பட்ட குதிரை எல்லாம் மண்ணைப் போட்டுக்கொள்ள, தட்டுவாணிக்குதிரை வந்து கொள்ளுக்கு அழுகிறதாம்—" whilst horses of the first class lick the ground the miserable tatt is neighing for gram [q.v.]."

TATT (தட்டு - tattu, *Tam.*). To beat.——*Tatta* (తట్ట - tatta, Tel.). Flat.——*Tattammavauroo* (తట్టమ్మవారు - tattammaváru, Tel.). From (tatta, tel. flat + ammaváru, tel. small-pox) ; flat eruptions. Measles.——*Tattaun* (தட்டான் - tattán, Tam.). From (tattu, tam. to beat). Goldsmith. The corresponding terms are :—Tel. cumsala, Can. acasauly, Mal. tattaur [jauty].——*Tuttapaumb* (دریاکاساںپ - daryákásámp, Hind. ; ಸಮುದ್ರಹಾವು - samudrahávu, Can. ; తట్టపాము - tattapámu, Tel. ; കടല്പാമ്പ - katalpámbu, Mal. ; கடற்பாம்பு - kadarbámbu, Tam.). Hind. from (daryá, hind. sea + sámp, hind. snake). Can. from (samudra, can. sea + hávu, can. snake). Tel. from (tatta, tel. flat + pámu, tel. snake). Mal. and Tam. from (katal, tam. sea + pámbu, tam. snake). The terms may be considered representative of the family Hydrophidæ, ophidii, colubriformes venenosi, ophidia [sarpam], reptilia [sarpy, 28], of naturalists [jantoo]. The Tuttapaumbs or Hydrophidæ pass their whole life in the water ; soon die when brought on shore. Most striking feature in the organization is their elevated and compressed tail. The hind part of the body, and sometimes forwards to beyond the middle of its length, is also compressed, and the belly forms a more or less sharp ridge. Their tail answers all the purposes of the same organ in a fish, and their motions in the water are almost as rapid as they are uncertain and awkward when removed out of their proper element. Their nostrils are placed quite at the top of the snout, as in crocodiles [mugger] and in fresh-water snakes [tunny paumb], so that they are enabled to breathe whilst the entire body and the greater part of the head are immersed in the water. They have very capacious lungs, by retaining a portion of the air in these extensive lungs, they are enabled to float on the surface of the water without the slightest effort. The scales of the sea-snakes are different from those of other snakes ; they overlap one another in only a few species. The eye is small, with round pupil, which is so much contracted by the light when the snake is taken out of the water that the animal becomes blinded and is unable to hit any object it wants to strike. The tongue is short. Food consists entirely of small fish. All these animals are killed by the poison of the snake before they are swallowed ; belong to the most poisonous species of the whole order. They are extremely shy and swim away on the least alarm ; cannot endure captivity ; viviparous. The young are more brightly colored than the adult. They have formidable enemies in the sea-eagles [machrangah], in sharks [soorah], and in other large raptorial fishes. The greatest size some species attain is about 12 feet. They are all venomous, and inhabit the salt-water estuaries and tidal streams. The fishermen know their dangerous properties and carefully avoid them. The Platurus is a transitional stage between the sea and land snakes. The following are the chief South indian known genera :—Enhydrina [vaulakidy]; Hydrophis [chittal]; Pelamis [nullavaulagily] ; Platurus [sea bungaur].

TATTOO (தத்து - tattu, *Tam.*). Leap.——*Tatta* (തത്ത - tatta, Mal.). From (tattu, tam. to hop). Parrot.——*Tattamungalam* (തത്തമംഗലം - tattamannalam, Mal.). From (tatta, mal. parrot + mangala, san. prosperity). Village ; Cochin state, Chittoor tal. ; pop. 8,741 ; lat. 10° 41′ ; long. 76° 45′ ; from Chittoor S.W. 3 miles ; from Trichore E.N.E. 34 miles ; from Ernacolum N.E. 56 miles ; from the sea E. 51 miles. The Ponnany river goes by the name of Tattamungalam near this place.——*Tattoo kily* (جراد - jarád, Ar. ; ملخ - malakh, Pers. ; ٹڈا - tiddá, Hind. and Dec. ; ಮಿಡತೆ - midite, Can. ; మొంటె - monte, Tel. ; మిడత - midata, Tel. ; വെട്ടുകിളി - vettukili, Mal. ; தத்துக்கிளி - tattukkili, Tam.). Title from tamul. Ar. from (jarada, ar. to destroy herbage). Tel. from (midiyu, tel. to hop). Mal. from (vettu, mal. to cut + kili, mal. bird). Tam. from (tattu, tam. to leap + kili, tam. grasshopper). Tam. also (vettukkili), meaning cut + grasshopper, from destroying herbage [tiddah]. Grasshopper. Belongs to family gryllidæ, orthoptera, hemimetabola, insecta [poochy], of naturalists [jantoo].

TAUB (تاب - táb, *Hind.*). From (tábídan, pers. to shine). Light. Mahtaub is the firework called Bengal light.——*Taubdaun* (تابدان - tábdán, Hind.). From (above + dán, pers. holder). Sky-light.

TAUHIR (طاهر - táhir, *Ar.*). From (tahara, ar. to be pure). The unsullied. Name of one of the sons of Mahomet. Also lacab of the prophet. Common alam, as Tauhir ally, double alam ; Tauhir khan, alam + alaumat [ism].

TAUJ (تاج - táj, *Hind.*). From persian. A cap, generally conical [topee]. Crown. Part of lacab ; as Tauj ood deen, crown of faith ; Tauj oon nissa begum, diadem of ladies [ism].

TAUK (தாக்கு - tákku, *Tam.*). From (tagai, tam. to restrain), place marked by limits. Place ; plot of ground ; rice field [talay].

TAUKK (தாக்கு - tákku, *Tam.*). To outweigh.——*Taukkunung* (தாக்கணங்கு - takkanangu, Tam.). From (above + anangu, tam. beauty). Lutchmy [q.v.] ; the goddess whose beauty excels all others.

TAUL (தால் - tál, *Tam.*). Dandling.——*Taulautt* (தாலாட்டு - tálattu, Tam.). From (above + áttu, tam. to rock). Cradle song. Sung to the gods, when at annual festivals [pundigay] they are swung in cradles [oonjal tirnaul]. Mothers also repeat them to their children.

TAUL (தாழ் - tázh, *Tam.*). Low [tal].——*Taulvauram* (தாழ்வாரம் - tázhváram, Tam.). From (above + váram, tam. side). Verandah [q.v.] with sloping roof.

TAULIB (طالب - tálib, *Ar.*). From (talaba, ar. to demand). A petitioner. Lover. Prefixed to an alam forms a lacab ; as Taulib ally, lover of ally [ism].

TAULY (ಗೌರೀಬಳ್ಳಿ - gauríballi, *Can.* ; தாளி - táli, *Tam.*). Title otherwise Bindweed. Botanically the Convolvulus genus, convolvulaceæ [vricsham, 93]. Herbs or undershrubs, erect prostrate or twining, sometimes spinous ; leaves entire toothed or lobed, capsule globose, usually four-seeded ; seeds glabrous, usually smooth. The species best known are :—arvensis [deer's foot], scammonia [scammony]. Other s. indian species indigenous or naturalized are :—flavus, parviflorus, pluricaulis, rottlerianus.

TAUMANY (தாமணி - támani, *Tam.*). From (damaní, san. subduing). A long line with smaller one attached for fastening cattle. Common word in spite of its origin. Applied also to 'sheet' in boat tackle.

TAUN (تهان - thán, *Hind.*). A piece of cloth or lace, &c. Commercial term for piece-goods.

TAUNDAVAM (ताण्डव - tándava, *San.*). From (tad, san. to beat); from violent treading of ground. Dance ——*Taundava moorty* (ताण्डवमूर्ति - tándavamúrti, San.). From (above + múrti, san. embodiment). Shiva [q.v.] in his dancing attitude.

TAUNDRY (தான்றி - tánri, *Tam.*). Belleric myrobalan.——*Taundry kye* (தானறிக்காய் - tánrikkáy, Tam.). The fruit of the same.

TAUNG (தாங்கு - tángu, *Tam.*). To support.——*Taungal* (தாங்கல் - tángal, Tam.). From (tángu, tam. to support). Pond.——*Taungy* (தாங்கி - tángi, Tam.). One that supports. Plant second term indicating place of growth. Ex., where transl. is of first term :—Andrographis echioides (kóburandángi), tower; Sida carpinifolia (malaithángi), hill. See gloss. paragraphs.

TAUR (कपालनालिका - kapálanáliká, *San.*; పంటి - panti, *Tel.*; താർ - tár, *Mal.*; தார் - tár, *Tam.*). Title from tamul. San. from (kápála, san. cup + náliká, san. hollow reed); from form. Tel. means a pot; from the resemblance in form. Large spindle-like bamboo [q.v.] frames, round which thread is wound prior to skeining [ausmaun, nesavoo].

TAUR (تار - tár, *Hind.*). From (tal, san. to fix) [taulam]. Palmyra [q.v.] palm.——*Tadpatry* (తాడిపర్తి - tádiparti, Tel.). See sep. title.——*Talee* (தாலி - táli, Tam.). From (tála, san. palmyra), from the original practice of wearing for this purpose palmyra [q.v.] leaf dipped in saffron [country saffron] water. Title is usually spelt like this, but distinguish from Talee a numboory association which is quite another word [talam]. A piece of gold, forming either the centre or the sole ornament of a necklace, which is tied on the neck of the bride by the bridegroom at the time of marriage [calyaunam]; practice common to all the people of S. india [mungala sootram]. The talee is worn till the woman becomes a widow and is then removed by the husband's relations. Many talees are made of two small pieces which separate. Some are cup-shaped. Some are flat and oval. Some have the figures of Vigneshwaran [q.v.], Lutchmy [q.v.], lingam [q.v.], sun [sooryan] and moon [chundran], &c., engraved on them. The talee is fastened round the neck by a string dyed yellow with saffron [country saffron, lutchah, maryauday].——*Talipot* (श्रीताल - shrítála, San.; बजरबट्टू - bajarabattú, Mahr.; तलतमाड्डो - talatamáddó, Conc.; بجربتو - bajarbattú, Hind. and Dec.; ಶ್ರೀತಾಳೆ - shrítále, Can.; ପନୋଳି - panóli, Too.; శ్రీతాళము - shrítálamu, Tel.; കുടപ്പന - kutappana, Mal.; තල - tala, Singh.; தாளிப்பனை - tálippanai, Tam.). Title from (tála, san. palm + patra, san. leaf); properly applies to leaf, so to tree. San. from (shrí, san. holy + tála, san. palm); from leaves being employed to write on with iron style. Hind. from mahratta. Can. from sanscrit. Mal. from (kuta, mal. umbrella + pana, mal. palm), from leaves used in making native umbrellas. Tam. from (tála, san. palm + panai, tam. palmyra tree, borassus flabelliformis, linn.). San. also (alpáyushí), meaning short-lived; (karáliká), meaning large; (tálí), meaning small palm [palmyra] Can. also (baini). Tel. also (dridhatálamu), meaning strong + palm. Mal. also (tálippana); (sítálam), meaning holy palm. Tam. also (kudaippanai), meaning umbrella + palmyra tree, borassus flabelliformis, linn.; (kúndarbanai), meaning woman's hair + palmyra tree, borassus flabelliformis, linn. [bastard sago-palm]; (shrítthálam), meaning holy + palm; (talappamaram), meaning palm + tree; (talappam), meaning palm tree. Title otherwise Ceylon fan palm, Codapanay, Fan palm, Great fan palm, Holy palm, Java fan palm, Umbrella palm. Botanically Corypha umbraculifera, linn., palmaceæ [vricsham, 149]. Trunk 60–70 feet; leaves sublunate, palmate-pinnatifid, plaited; segments forty to fifty pair; petioles armed; inflorescence pyramidal, equalling the trunk of the tree; calyx three-toothed; petals three; ovary three-celled, one-seeded. Each of its enormous fan-like leaves, when laid upon the ground, will form a semi-circle of 16 feet in diameter, and cover an area of 200 superficial feet; the tree flowers but once and dies; stem smooth; flowers green-yellowish, very fragrant; berries spherical, smooth, green, succulent, oily; met with in ceylon and malabar. A kind of sago [q.v.] from the pith of the trunk. Small bowls and other ornaments made from the nuts, and when polished and colored red, are passed off for coral [moongah]; leaves made into fans, mats [boriyah], and umbrellas, and used for thatching; leaves used for native books [grantam], like palmyra [q.v.] leaves, and are written on with an iron style; seeds used as beads by the tauthar [q.v.] or dausaries [q.v.]. Wood soft, with a hard rind composed of black vascular bundles [taur]. No other species here. ——*Tallapoody* (తాళ్లపూడి - tállapúdi, Tel.). From (tádu, tel. palmyra, borassus flabelliformis, linn. + púdi, tel. village). Village, Tahsildar's head-quarters; Godavery dist., Yernagoodem tal.; pop. 1,123; lat. 17° 07′; long. 81° 43′; from Cocanada W.N.W. 28 miles; from Coonavaram S.E. 41 miles; from Ellore N.E. 46 miles; from Madras N.N.E. 288 miles; from Narsapore N. 47 miles; from Rajahmundry N.N.W. 10 miles. Tahsildar's head-quarters were formerly at Yernagoodem.——*Talura palm* (ताली - tálí, San.; تارجهار - tárjhár, **Hind.**). Title from bengalee. Distinguish from Taloora saul [saul]. Title otherwise Tara palm. Botanically Corypha taliera, roxb., palmaceæ [vricsham, 149]. Stem 30 feet; fronds orbicular, palmately pinnatifid, segments forty to fifty pairs; spadix ovate-pyramidal, erect, very large, 20 feet; flowers white, fragrant; berries ovate-globose, olive or yellowish green. Flowering in march and april. Uses same as talipot [q.v.].——*Taulam* (ताल - tála, San.). San. from (tal, san. to fix). Originally the palmyra, so generally the Palm class of trees. Belonging to the division of Endogens or Monocotyledons, which comprises also the grasses, sedges [coray], lilies, orchids, and screw-pines [q.v.] and which also stands intermediate between the highest and lowest orders of the vegetable kingdom [vricsham]. In external structure as well as in their internal organization, palms approach the grasses. Cf. the bamboo [q.v.], as a representative of the grasses, by the side of a rattan [q.v.] as a representative of the palms. In habit, the two orders have much in common; their leaves are formed upon exactly the same plan, the only difference being that those of the palms are generally divided. Even the silicious secretions [tabasheer], characteristic of grasses, are observable in rattans. As to flowers, those of the grasses are those of the palms with the floral envelopes removed and only the bracts remaining. Compare tamul Pool [pill] applied to palmyra [q.v.] which is otherwise known as poolpaty grass lord, and pool tauly grass taulam. Compare the sanscrit Trinarajam, grass king, applied to palmyra [q.v.], cocoanut [q.v.], bamboo [q.v.] and sugar-cane [q.v.]. Compare the sanscrit Trinadroomam or Trinavricsham, grass tree, applied to various species of palms, as palmyra [q.v.], cocoanut [q.v.], areca [q.v.], date [kharjooram], talipot [q.v.], and screw-pine [q.v.]. Palms are perennial and woody plants; they are never annual and herbaceous. Most of them attain the size and assume the aspect of trees. The foliage generally forms a crown at the end of the trunk. The leaves, supported on petioles, or leaf stalks, sheathing at the base, are alternate, coriaceous, and often of gigantic size. Palms, after having arrived at the proper age, flower either every year until they die, or only once during the whole course of their existence. The spathe, or sheath enclosing the flowers, consist of one or many valves, is occasionally of a woody texture and presents the phenomenon of bursting suddenly open with an audible report. The fruits being drupaceous, are nut-like, or berried often covered with a fibrous rind, are almost of every color, and occasionally very numerous. Compared with the size of the plants, they are generally small; some are in this respect like peas [calauyam]. The cocoanut is one of the largest. In the tropics the palms can satisfy every want, and almost every luxury. Sugar [q.v.] is obtained from the Palmyra [q.v.], Cocoanut [q.v.], Date [kharjooram], and Gomooty [q.v.]; starch [nishastah] from the Palmyra [q.v.], Sago [q.v.] palm, and Gomooty [q.v.]; oil [yennay] from the Cocoanut; fibre [coir] from the Cocoanut and Gomooty; and toddy [q.v.] from the Palmyra, Date, Cocoanut, and Gomooty; and nearly all of these species have an eatable fruit and cabbage. But great as are the gifts of the order, the cocoanut alone concentrates them all in itself. For the principal palms of S. india see Areca, Cocoanut, Date [kharjooram], Gomooty, Palmyra, Rattan, Sago [q.v.] palm, Talipot.——*Taulavaudy* (தாளவாடி - tálavádi,* Tam.). From (tála, san. palmyra tree, borassus flabelliformis, linn. + vádi, tam. garden). Sanscrit name (tálaváti), meaning same.—"*a*" Deputy tahsildarry, Coimbatore district. Pay Rs. 70. Head-quarters, Gopichettipolliem.—"*b*" Village, Deputy tahsildar's station; Coimbatore dist., Suttimungalam tal.; pop. 860; lat. 11° 45′; long. 77° 10′; from Coimbatore N. 53 miles; from Erode N.W. 57 miles; from Madras W.S.W. 234 miles; from Ootacamund N.E. 36 miles; from Pollachy N. 78 miles; from Suttimungalam N.N.W. 18 miles.——*Taula vilausam* (தாளவிலாசம் - tálavilásam, Tam.). From (above + vilása, san. play). A singhalese poem on the palmyra [q.v.] palm. *Taulisam* (तालीश - tálísha, San.). Title otherwise Dye pine, Himalayan deal tree, Himalayan silver fir, King pine, Webb's pine. Botanically Abies webbiana, lindl., coniferæ [vricsham]; the leaves and twigs are medicinal; for british liquor ammoniæ acetatis, squill [q.v.] and benzoic acid [sambrauny poo].——*Taulispatry* (تالیسپتری - tálíspatrí, Hind.). The leaf of the Taulisam. The term is however used for that of Cinnamomum iners [country cinnamon], from resemblance.——*Taurbund* (تاربن - tárban, Hind.). From (tár, hind. palmyra + ban, hind. tope). Palmyra tope.——*Tautaparty* (తాటిపర్తి - tátaparti, Tel.). From (tádi, tel. palmyra, borassus flabelliformis, linn. + parti, tel. village). Village, Ghaut; Vizagapatam dist., Veeravilly division, Madgole zemindarry; lat. 18° 02′; long. 82° 45′; from Chodavaram N. W. 20 miles; from Vizagapatam N.W. 45 miles. Better known as Minamullore. This village is at the head of the pass and Tautaparty at the foot. Leads across Eastern ghauts [q.v.] from Vizagapatam to hill Madgole. ——*Toddy* (تاڑی - tárí, Hind.). See sep. title.

TAUR (تار - tár, *Hind.*). Wire [tanty].——*Taurcush* (تارکش - tárkash, Hind.). From (above + kash, pers. drawer), means wiredrawer. A workman who does the coarse drawing of tinsel wire.

TAURAH (तारा - tárá, *San.*). From (stri, san. to scatter rays of light). Star. Taurah bye was wife of Rajaram, the third Mahratta king of Sattapura.——*Taurah matsyam* (तारामत्स्य - tárámatsya, San.). Star-fish [kavachiny].——*Tauray* (தாரை - tárai, Tam.). From (tára, san. high shrill note). Long reed instrument [sangeetam].

TAURAM (താരം - táram, *Mal.*). A copper coin [naunyam], value 1½ pies. Current at the time of arrival of Portuguese in Calicut.

TAUREEK (تاریخ - táríkh, *Hind.*). From (arakha, ar. to date). Date [taidy]. History [ilm].

TAUT (తాత్ - tát, *Tel.*). Army [dandam, dandoo, paday, shervay].——*Taut rajah* (తాత్రాజా - tátrájá, Tel.). The Rajah of the army; as opposed to Paut rajah, the Rajah of the turban [q.v.] or crown. Chief of the Tooamool zemindarry, a feudatory of Jeypore.

TAUTHAN (தாதன் - táthan, *Tam.*). From (dása, san. servant). Same as Dausary.

TAVVA (తవ్వ - tavva, *Tel.*). Measure of capacity. 2 solas = 1 tavva; 2 tavvas = 1 maunica [alavay, 3b]. In Ganjam 26¼ cubic inches; in Vizagapatam 78¾ cubic inches; in Godavery, 35 cubic inches; in Kistna, 70 cubic inches, the same as pucka seer; in Nellore, 61¼ cubic inches. See vol. I, 609; II, 510, 511, 512, 513, 520.

TAWYID (تائید - táíd, *Hind.*). From (áda, ar. to corroborate). Help. Part of lacab; as Tawyid ood deen, the help of religion [ism].

TAY (تی - te, *Malay*; තේ - té, *Singh.*). Chinese through Malay. Old Anglo-indian prounnciation of Tea [q.v.].

TAYAUR (تیار - taíyár, *Hind.*). Ready.

TAZIYA (تعزیہ - taziyah, *Hind.*). From (azá, ar. to mourn). Same as Taboot. Taziya khana is same as Ashoorkhana [q.v.].

TEA (चहा - chahá, *Mahr.*; شاه - sái, *Ar.*; چاى - chái, *Pers.*; چاه - chá, *Hind.*; تي - te, *Malay*; ಚಾಗಿಡ - chágida, *Can.*; ಚಾ - chá, *Too.*; తేయాకుచెట్టు - téyákuchettu, *Tel.*; ചായ - cháya, *Mal.*; තේ - té, *Singh.*; தேயிலை - téyilai, *Tam.*). Title from malay; cf. tay. Mahr. from persian. Ar., &c., from chinese. Tel. from (té, tel. tea + áku, tel. leaf + chettu, tel. plant). Mal. from chinese through hindostany. Tam. from (té, tam. tea + ilai, tam. leaf). Ar. also (shái). Tel. also (nallatéyáku), meaning black tea + leaf. Tam. also (paççaittéyilai), meaning green + tea; (karupputtéyilai), meaning black + tea. Title otherwise Char, China tea, Tay. Botanically Camellia theifera, griff., ternstromiaceæ [vricsham, 23]. Alias Camellia viridis; Thea assamica, cantoniensis, chinensis, viridis; Theabohea stricta. Shrubby; leaves lanceolate, flat, serrated, three times longer than broad; sepals five to six; petals six to nine; flowers axillary, solitary, erect, white; fruit nodding, dehiscent; capsule tricoccous. Evergreen with thin, grey bark, alternate, very short-stalked leaves, saw-edged and of a deep shining green; flowers resemble those of a bramble, one inch in diameter, produced in great abundance if not pruned. The alkaloid of tea, called theine, is identical with that of coffee [q.v.] or caffeine; the theine is variable in quantity in different teas, south indian samples containing more than those from china and japan; the percentage ranges from one to more than six. Plant was introduced from china to assam in 1830; thence extended to cachar, sylhet, &c.; introduced in s. india in 1837; the peculiarities of madras teas, as contrasted with china teas, are their much greater strength and stronger aroma. In cultivating, small plantations are preferable to large; a rich loamy soil is best; the object is to insure deep soil, free from rocks and stones; a tolerably moist climate, such as may be found at elevations of from 2,500 to 5,000 feet above the level of the sea, is most suitable, and in localities free from all influence of hot winds in summer; the estimated number of seedlings for one acre is about 1,000; for cultivation the ground is cleared as much as possible, marked out in lines, and holes dug at proper distances; plants may be kept in the nursery till they are six months old; after transplanting and when plants are eighteen months old, they are cut down to a short height, and from that time the young shoots are plucked as they appear and manufactured into tea; the bushes require pruning and topping; ground must be kept clean; the young leaves are used and the tree is not allowed to seed as a rule; the flush is ready at intervals varying from seven to fourteen days; produce is manufactured and ready for market in about six weeks. For Neilgherry tea-planting see vol. I, 292. Tea leaves are divided into two classes, green and black, both the products of the same plant but differently prepared for use; the former contains a larger proportion both of theine and of tannin than the latter, their composition in other respects being nearly identical; the green tea leaf is prepared when the plant is in its less mature state, while it contains a quantity of viscid and to a certain degree narcotic juice. Green teas which are or have been commonly met with in s. india are; gunpowder, very strong, being the leaf rolled quite round; hyson, a small leaf, closely curled and bluish green; bloom tea, light green and has loose leaf; singlo, similar; green tea is comparatively little used, owing to its high price, its powerful action on the nervous system when genuine, and its great liability to pernicious adulteration. There are three principal varieties of black tea; in the third or fourth year of the plant's age or later the young shoot is plucked as soon as three leaves have appeared on it; the uppermost leaf scarcely expanded when dried gives pekoe, the second about thirty-six hours old gives souchong, the third of forty-eight to sixty hours' growth gives congoo; a fourth leaf is sometimes plucked and yields bohea, but the proportion of theine diminishes from the topmost leaf downwards and is insignificant in this last variety which is rarely brought to market; all these varieties of leaf are plucked and dried together and separated subsequently by sieves of different-sized meshes, pekoe and souchong passing through the first sieve, leaving congoo behind, and being separated from each other by a further sieving; thus the different kinds of black tea may be distinguished by the different sizes of the leaves expanded by infusion. Leaves slowly dried retain more green color than those that are dried rapidly; the green tea is carefully dried by exposure to the open air in the shade, the black by means of artificial heat in shallow pans over a charcoal fire. The above named classificatory terms are all Chinese. The adulterations of tea leaves are of two kinds, the substitution of leaves of other plants, and the introduction of exhausted tea leaves re-rolled and dried; if green tea be adulterated, put a piece of gall [mauchicoy] into the liquor, which will turn it to a deep-bluish color, this it will not do unless there be either vitriol or copperas [mayil toottam] in it as galls do not tincture the proper tea; counterfeit black tea produces a deeper color by infusion than the real tea, a little copperas put into it will turn it to a light blue, which otherwise ought to be of a deep blue inclining to black; it is with the small, white, pleasant-scented flowers of the osmanthus fragrans, lour., that the chinese give a peculiar flavor to their best teas. The uses of tea need not be here mentioned, but it is to be observed that its narcotic effects on man increase towards the equator. The oil from seeds resembles that of olive [zeitoon], burns with a clear, bright light, and is free from unpleasant odour; not edible but can be utilised in the manufacture of a superior kind of soap [sauboon]. Wood grey, soft. There are at present date three varieties of plant, viz., china, assam, and a hybrid between those two; the china is hardiest, but the hybrid most prolific of leaf and therefore most cultivated. For other leaves used as tea see Sharb.——**(1)** *Tea grass* (ಚಾಹುಲ್ಲು - cháhullu, Can.). Title from use of fresh leaves. Same as Roussa grass.——**(2)** *Ceylon tea* (چاسیلان - cháisailán, Hind.). Same as Nerija.——*Indian tea* (چاهندی - cháihindí, Hind.). Same as Fragrant toolsy.——*Shiranjy tea* (చిరంజి - chiranji, Tel.). Same as Godaury.——*Wild tea* (بانرا - bánrá, Hind.; ಹುಲುನಿ - huluni, Can.; නෙයදස්ස - neyadassa, Singh.). Title from leaf like tea-leaf. Hind. also (gonta); (deurá). Botanically Eurya japonica, thun., ternstrœmiaceæ [vricsham, 23]. In leaf and general appearance much resembles tea plant; wood brown, soft, close, grained, sometimes used for fuel.

TEAK (शाक - shâka, *San.*; सागवान - sâgavâna, *Mahr.*; टिक्यारूकु - tikyárúku, *Conc.*; ساج - sáj, *Ar.*; سال - sál, *Pers.*; ساکھو - sákhú, *Hind.*; ساگوان - ságwán, *Dec.*; جتی - jati, *Malay*; ತೇಗು - tégu, *Can.*; ತೆಕ್ಕಿ - tekki, *Too.*; టేకు - téku, *Tel.*; ଶିଂଗରୁ - singaru, *Oor.*; തേക്ക - tékka, *Mal.* and *Singh.*; தேக்கு - tékku, *Tam.*). Title from malayalam. San. from (shak, san. to be powerful). Mahr. from hindostany. Ar., &c., from sanscrit [common saul]. San. also (nauvriksha), meaning ship + tree. Can. also (jádi), meaning superior; (ságwan). Tel. also (peddatéku), meaning large + the tree. Mal. also (játi), meaning superior. Title otherwise Indian oak, Saag, Shaucam, Ship tree. Botanically Tectona grandis, linn., verbenaceæ [vricsham, 102]. Alias Tectona theca; Theca ternifolia. Theca from malayalam. Large tree, with an ash-colored and scaly bark; young shoots four-sided, channelled; leaves opposite, oval, scabrous above, whitish and downy beneath; panicles terminal, large, cross-armed, divisions dichotomous, with a sessile fertile flower in each cleft, the whole covered with a colored farina; peduncles quadrangular, sides deeply channelled; flowers numerous, small, white; calyx and corolla five to six-cleft; stamens often six; ovary round, hairy, four-celled; cells one-seeded; nut very hard. Grows straight, and with lofty cross-armed panicles of showy white flowers; flowering in rains; the principal forests are in malabar, canara, travancore; the vertical range of the tree is from the sea-level up to 3,000 feet, but it always avoids exposed situations; in twenty-five years the teak attains the size of two feet in diameter and is considered serviceable timber, but it requires eighty years to arrive at maturity; yields a kind of resin [raul] resembling that of canarium strictum, roxb. [black dammer]; the seeds are of the size and shape of sesamum [gingelly] seeds; they are very oily, but the difficulty of extracting them from the nuts makes the oil expensive; it is a bland, fatty oil [yennay], free from any peculiar odour. The teak takes up from the soil a quantity of silica, hence sandstone [manal cull] and granite [caroom cull] soils are the favorite places for it; to this large secretion of silica must be attributed the strength and durability of the timber; very easily raised from seed; end of august is the proper time to commence cutting down the tree, when the cambium will have been expended; in malabar carried down streams to coast. Plaster of the powdered wood is used medicinally in bilious headaches and for the dispersion of inflammatory swellings; taken internally in doses of 90 to 200 grains, it is beneficial in dyspepsia with burning pain in the stomach arising from an overflow of bile, also as a vermifuge; the charred wood quenched in poppy [aphainam] juice and reduced to a smooth paste is applied to swellings of the eyelids, and to strengthen the sight; the bark is astringent, and the oil of the nuts, which is thick and has an agreeable odour, is used for making the hair grow and removing itchiness of the skin; flowers are diuretic; seeds have similar property; the tar extracted from the wood is used as an application to the sores of draught cattle to prevent maggots breeding. Young teak is not injured by elephants [q.v.]; the tree affords no fodder for animals. Foliage supplies a red dye [shauyam]; oil is applied to woodwork of all sorts, either alone as a natural varnish [rangh] or in combination with certain resins [raul]. Sap-wood white and small; heart-wood when cut green has pleasant and strong aromatic fragrance and a dark golden yellow color, which on seasoning soon darkens into brown mottled with darker streaks, hard, exceedingly durable, and strong; wood does not split, crack, warp, shrink, or alter its shape when once seasoned; does not suffer in contact with iron [auhan], and is rarely if ever attacked by white-ants [q.v.]; durability is due to the aromatic oil contained in the wood; it works easily and takes a good polish; it has some resemblance to oak [belote]; great quantities are used on the western coast for ship-building, for which it is superior to any other kinds of wood, even oak; after the best straight timber has been taken, the crooked pieces called shin-logs are used for many other useful purposes; malabar teak is ranked higher for ship building than tenasserim or pegu teak, on account of its greater durability and power of resisting dry rot; the teak which grows on the sides and tops of mountains is far superior to that which grows in the black heavy soil of the low grounds, though it takes a longer time to attain the same dimensions.——*Bastard teak* (جھوٹا ساگوان - jhútáságwán, Hind.). Same as Common coral tree.——*Cooml teak* (గుమ్మడుతేకు - gumudutéku, Tel.). Same as Cashmere tree.——*Dog teak* (நாய்த்தேக்கு - náyttékku, Tam.). Same as Small chaltah.——*Firebrand teak* (चाम्हारी - chámhárí, Mahr.; ನಾರಲೆ - nárale, Can.; నగరుచెట్టు - nagaruchettu, Tel.; බූසෙරු - búséru, Singh.; கொள்ளிக்கட்டைத்தேக்கு - kollikkattaittékku, Tam.). Title from color of wood. Tam. from (kollikkattai, tam. firebrand + tékku, tam. teak, tectona grandis, linn. f.). Can. also (íjimara). Tel. also (navuru). Tam. also (podaganárimaram). Botanically Premna [jayah] tomentosa, willd., verbenaceæ [vricsham, 192]. Alias Cornutia corymbosa; Premna flavescens. Small tree; branchlets, young leaves, and cymes everywhere tomentose; leaves petioled, ovate or ovate-oblong, long-acuminate, entire, venoso-rugous, stellato-pubescent on both sides, sparingly above, copiously beneath; panicles large, terminal, many-flowered, compact; flowers small, white. Leaves medicinally diuretic and are given internally and applied externally in dropsy; natives using them soaked in goat's [vellaud] urine or in onion [piyauz] juice; sometimes chebulic myrobalans [q.v.] are added if the bowels are costive. Wood light-brown, the color of teak but lighter, moderately hard, smooth, close and even-grained, seasons and polishes well.——*Saffron teak* (ಅರಸಿನತೇಗ - arasinatéga, Can.). Title from color of wood. Same as Yellow cadamba.——*Small teak* (சிறுதேக்கு - shirutékku, Tam.). Same as Knotted bhraungy.——*Strong teak* (வத்தேக்கு - vattékku, Tam.). Same as Sappan.——*Venteak* (बोंडग - bóndaga, Mahr.; ಬೆಂಡೇಕು - bendéku, Can.; ನಂದಿ - nandi, Coorg; చెన్నంగి - chennangi, Tel.; വെന്തേക്ക - ventékku, Mal.; வெண்தேக்கு - vendékku, Tam.). Title from malayalam. Can. from (bili, can. white + tégu, can. teak). Tel. from (chennu, tel. beauty + arga, san. body). Mal. from (ven, mal. white + tékku, mal. teak). Tam. from (ven, tam. white + tékku, tam. tectona grandis, linn. f.); from light-colored wood. Can. also (bellanuttemara); (bilinandi); (bilindu). Tam. also (kaççaikkattai), meaning tender + wood; (velvilá), meaning white + feronia elephantum, corr. Title otherwise Ben teak, White teak, White wood apple. Botanically Lagerstrœmia [cadaly] lanceolata, wall., lythraceæ [vricsham, 58]. Alias Lagerstrœmia microcarpa. Large tree; western forests; leaves from elliptic to ovate, often attenuated or acute at the base, obtusely pointed at the apex, glabrous above, pale beneath, often vary finely downy; panicles axillary and terminal, glabrous or hoary, with minute pubescence; flowers very numerous, white; calyx white outside, with hoary pubescence; six outer stamens longer than the others; capsule scarcely an inch long. Wood light-colored, straight fibred, and elastic; much used for building, flooring, rafters, &c.; if left exposed soon attacked by white-ants [q.v.].——*White teak* (வெண்டேக்கு - vendékku, Tam.). Same as Venteak.

TEAPOY (سہ پائی - sihpáe, *Hind.*). From (sih, pers. three + páe, pers. foot). A small three-legged table [charpoy].

TEE (തീ - ti, *Mal.*). Fire.——*Teeneer* (தீநீர் - tínír, Tam.). Distilled water [neer].——*Teeyauttoonny* (തീയാട്ടുണ്ണി - tíyyáttunni, Mal.). From (above + átu, mal. to dance + unni, mal. boy). Otherwise Teeyaudy. Firedancer; degraded from Bramins [q.v.] because they jump through fire in honor of Bhadra cauly [q.v.].

TEECAY (टीका - tíká, *San.*). From (tík, san. to explain). Commentary.

TEEK (ٹھیک - thík, *Hind.*). Proper, exact.

TEEN (தீன் - tín, *Tam.*). From (tin, tam. to eat). Food.——*Teeny* (ತಿನಿ - tíni, Can.; తిని - tíni, Tel.; തീന് - tín, Mal.; தீனி - tíni, Tam.). From (tin, tam. to eat). The general name for any meal or for food. The English have adopted it for dinner. Compare Teymez. The night meal [khanah] is universal in Southern india. The following is a Hindostany proverb:—خدا بھوکا اٹھاتا ہے پر بھوکا سلا تا نہیں "God wakes the hungry, "but does not send the hungry to sleep." A complete account of the dietary of the natives of s. india was given at vol. I (101), foot-note.——*Tinay* (திணை - tinai, Tam.). See sep. title.

TEER (தீர் - tír, *Tam.*). To decide.——*Teerp* (తీర్పు - tírpu, Tel.; തീര്പ്പ് - tírppu, Mal.; தீர்ப்பு - tírppu, Tam.). A decision [feisal, insauf].——*Teervay* (తీర్వ - tírva, Tel.; தீர்வை - tírvai, Tam.). From (tír, tam. to decide). What is fixed; tax, especially on land.——*Teervay cummy* (தீர்வைகம்மி - tírvaigammi, Tam.). Remissions granted on irrigable lands cultivated with a dry crop [dry grain], but which otherwise would have been left waste [tariss].——*Teervay jausty* (తీరువజాస్తి - tíruvajásti, Tel.). From (tírvai, tel. tax + jásti, tel. excess). Charge for water from a Government source taken to dry or to garden lands. The charge varies according to the class of tank [q.v.] or channel [q.v.] from which the water is taken [fusljausty]. See vol. I, 112.

TEERTAM (तीर्थ - tírt'ha, *San.*). From (trí, san. to cross). Ford; place of sacred waters; special spot along the courses of sacred streams or in the vicinity of sacred springs; sacred object; worthy person; epithet of Shiva [q.v.], Arghan [arhat]; title to saints and pious persons; also suffix in proper names as Ananta teertan, Rama teertan [peyar].——*Teertacaran* (तीर्थकर - tírt'hakara, San.). From (above + kri, san. to make). The saint who has made the passage of the world; epithet of a Jinan [q.v.], who is with jeinas [q.v.] what a Booddha [q.v.] is with booddhists. Also called Jagat prabhoo, lord of the world; Sarwanyan, omniscient; Adheeshwaran, supreme lord; and Devautidevan, god of gods. In the Trishashty poorannam, a jeina work, sixty-three good dispositions are specified, and he who attains to the whole of them is Teertacaran. Of these deified human beings, the jeinas reckon twenty-four, and each teertacaran is considered to be at the head of a long period of time [avasarpiny, ootsarpiny], like the hindoo Menoo [q.v.], and worshipped as such. An ancient list is as follows:—Nirvauny, Sagaran, Nalanautan, Vimala prabhoo, Shreedharan, Soodantan, Amala prabhoo, Oodaran, Angiran, Soomaty, Sindhoo, Coosoomanjany, Shiva gungay, Ootsauhan, Ganeshwaran, Parameshwaran, Vimaleshwaran, Rasodharan, Crooshtan, Gana moorty, Siddhamaty, Shreebhadran, Atricatan, Shaunty. A mediæval list, and that now most generally recognized, is as follows, adding the sign or symbol of each:—Rishabhan, bull; Ajitan, elephant; Sambhavan, horse; Abhinandanan, an ape; Soomaty, curlew; Padmaprabhan, a lotus; Soopaurthivan, the swasticam 卐; Chundraprabhan, the moon; Pooshpadantam, macaram; Sheetalan, shree vatsam; Shreyaumshan, a rhinoceros; Vasoopoojan, a buffalo; Vimalan, a boar; Anantan, a falcon; Dharman, vajram, a thunderbolt; Shaunty, an antelope; Coontoo, a goad; Aran, nandavartam, a compound swasticam; Mahy, a jar; Moonisoovratan, a tortoise; Namy, neelotpalam, blue water-lily; Nemy, a shell; Parshwanautan, a serpent; Maha veeran, or Vardhamaunan, a lion. The mediæval twenty-four have colors ascribed to them; the perfection of color in hindoo books is the hiranyam or gold color; this is ascribed to nine of them; the others are red, fair, blue and black. Furthermore, as the spirit of the prophecy is possessed by teertacarans, these have foretold by name a future series of twenty-four as follows:—Mahapudman, Saradevan, Soopaurshwan, Swayam prabhan, Sadautmabhooty, Deva pootan, Coolapootran, Oodancan, Crooshtan, Jaya keerty, Moonisoovratan, Aran, Nepanampan, Nishcashauyan, Vimalacan, Nirmasah, Chitragooptan, Samaudhigooptan, Swayambhoo, Anoovantacan, Jayan, Vimalan, Devapaulan, Anantaveeryan. Colossal statues of the Teertacarans are placed in the courtyards of the jeina temples [basty]. The best-known is at Shravanabelgola near Chenroyputna in Mysore; its height is 70 feet, 3 inches. There is another at Caurcal on the west coast. See vol. I. (95) [matam]. For jeinism or religion of the jeins see Jeina.——*Teerta yautray* (തീർത്ഥയാത്ര - tírt'hayátra, Mal.). From (above + yátrá, san. journey). A pilgrimage [haj, yautray].

TEETAR (تیتر - títar, *Hind.*). From imitative sound [tittiram]. Perdicinæ, tetraonidæ [tittiram], rasores, aves [pacshy, 33], of naturalists [jantoo]. Partridges. The species best known to the natives are shown below.——*Black partridge* (कालातितर - kálátítara, Mahr.; دراج اسود - durrájiaswad, Ar.; تیتر سیاه - títarisiyáh, Pers.; کالا تیتر - kálátítar, Hind. and Dec.; ಚಕೋರ - chakóra, Can.; కక్కెరకోడి - kakkerakódi, Tel.; କାଉଡ଼ୁଚୋଡ଼ି - kaudzuchódi, Oor.). Mahr. from (kálá, mahr. black + títara, mahr. partridge). Ar. from (durráj, ar. partridge + aswad, ar. black). Pers. from (títar, hiud. partridge + siyáh, pers. black). Hind. from (kálá, hind. black + títar, hind. partridge). Tel. from (kakkera, tel. crane + kódi, tel. fowl). Oor. means partridge fowl. Title otherwise Painted partridge. Francolinus pictus, perdicinæ [teetar], tetraonidæ [tittiram], rasores [pacshy, 33], of naturalists. Forehead, lores, face, broad supercilium, and ear-coverts ferruginous-chestnut; top of head dark brown with pale edgings; neck all round pale ferruginous; upper part of back and scapulars deep brown, feathers edged laterally creamy white, this gradually passing into markings of wings, which are chestnut with black bands; lower back, rump and upper tail-coverts marked with undulating lines of black and white; tail deep brown, feathers finely cross-barred at base; beneath throat is white, with longitudinal dark lines; whole of rest of lower surface variegated black and white, each feather white, with two dark cross-bands, shaft and tip black; these dark bands gradually narrow towards vent; under tail-coverts chestnut, feathers of flanks and sides of rump tinged with pale ferruginous; bill blackish; irides dark brown; legs yellow-red; length 12 inches. Female differs in having a somewhat ferruginous tinge beneath, and in the throat being more or less rufous; not known on malabar coast; affects open plains with scattered bushes. Chiefly occurs in pairs. Cock-bird has guttural call or broken crow, chee-kee-kerray—chee-kee-kerray, heard a long way off, answered on all sides. ——*Girzah partridge* (گیرزا - gírzá, Hind.; گیرزا - gerzá, Dec.; గెరిజపిట్ట - gerijapitta, Tel.). Title otherwise Jungle bush quail. Perdicula cambayensis, perdicinæ [teetar], tetraonidæ [tittiram], rasores [pacshy, 33], of naturalists. Alias Coturnix pentah; Perdicula rubicola. Male above rich dark reddish brown, mottled dull rufous; long yellowish or rufous white supercilium, narrowly edged black, indistinct pale line from gape; between this and supercilium rufous brown; shafts of feathers of back of neck and back white; many feathers of back with black markings; scapulars and wing-coverts richly marked on inner webs with pale creamy white and black; primaries red-brown, with fulvous or tawny spots; tail with black bars; beneath chin rich chestnut, rest of under surface white, tinged rufescent on lower abdomen, flanks, vent and lower tail-coverts, with numerous cross bars of black, small on throat and sides of neck, increasing on breast and abdomen, and disappearing towards the vent; bill dusky with reddish tinge; irides light brown; legs yellow-red; length 6½ inches. Female has lower plumage rufous, with whitish shafts in some and black markings of upper plumage less distinct; throat generally darker rufous than rest of lower plumage. Found in wooded districts; rare in low carnatic [q.v.]; found in coveys, all rise at once with a loud whirring noise, uttering cries of alarm, and after a short flight drop down again into the jungle.——*Indian partridge* (तित्तिरि - tittiri, San.; دراج - durráj, Ar.; تیتر - títar, Pers., Hind. and Dec.; ತಿತ್ತಿರಿ - tittiri, Can.; కౌజు - kaudzu, Tel.; ആൾകാട്ടി - álkátti, Mal.; கவுதாரி - kavuthári, Tam.). Ar. from (daraja, ar. to go on foot step by step). Pers. from sanscrit. Tel. from (kapinjala, san. partridge). Mal. from (ál, mal. man + kátti, mal. pointer). Male bird is:—(haikután, ar.). Hind. also (gorátítar), meaning white partridge. Ortygornis ponticerianus, perdicinæ [teetar], tertraonidæ [tittiram], rasores [pacshy, 33], of naturalists. Alias Perdix orientalis. Head above olive brown, rufous on forehead, over eyes, and on nape; lores and face also rufous, with black specks; ear-coverts silky hair-brown; upper plumage, including wing-coverts, upper tail-coverts and central tail-feathers speckled brown, each feather being rich red brown with three bars of creamy yellow, and paler and somewhat olive brown at tip; primaries pale brown; outer tail-feathers rich chestnut brown, with dusky brown terminal band, pale tipped; beneath chin and throat whitish with small dark brown spots, forming triangular mark; rest of lower plumage ochreous white or creamy, most pronounced on breast; with numerous minute cross-bars of brown, somewhat broader on breast and sides of neck, where it mingles with upper plumage; lower tail-coverts ferruginous; bill dusky plumbeous; irides hazel brown; legs dull red; length about 12½—13 inches; male strongly spurred, generally one spur on each leg, occasionally two, second at base of first; females not spurred. Frequents alike bush-jungle, and cultivated lands; associates in coveys, difficult to flush, rises with a whirr; call a loud shrill cry, compared to the word 'pateela-pateela-pateela,' quickly repeated, preceded by a single note uttered two or three times, each time with higher intonation; in flight not unlike English partridge; kept by Mussalmans in cages, sometimes for fighting, as it is highly pugnacious; partridges with double spurs are esteemed the most for fighting; also used as a decoy for wild birds. Common during the season that the small, dry grains [q.v.] are ripe; inferior as food to the same bird in Europe, being dry, and rather insipid. Of partridges, veidyans [q.v.] say, the flesh of the cock bird occasions bile, while that of the hen strengthens the body. Mahomedans hold eggs of partridge in high estimation.——*Lowah partridge* (قطا - katá, Ar.; سنگخواره - sangkhwárah, Pers.; لوا - lawá, Hind. and Dec.; ಲಾವ - láva, Can.; లావుక - lávuka, Tel.; செங்காடை - shongádai, Tam.). Title from deccany. Ar. from its call. Pers. from (sang, pers. stone + khwárah, pers. eater); said to swallow stones. Dec. means iron. Tel. from deccany. Tam. from (shem, tam. red + kádai, tam. quail). Can. also (lavuga). Title otherwise Rock bush quail. Perdicula asiatica, perdicinæ [teetar], tetraonidæ [tittiram], rasores [pacshy, 33], of naturalists. Alias Coturnix argoondah. Male, upper plumage brownish rufous, feathers minutely freckled and lineolated with black and tawny; feathers of head and neck tipped black, and som; of scapulars and wing-coverts with irregular black blotches; primaries dark brown with tawny bars on outer webs; tail with lateral feathers also barred; narrow white line passses over eye from base of bill, bordered by dusky, and another short line below this from gape; rest of the face, chin and throat bright rufous; whole lower parts, including sides of neck, white with numerous cross bars of black, tinged with rufous on flanks, lower belly and thigh-coverts; bill dark slaty; irides brown; orbits pale; legs red; length 6½ inches. Female differs in having upper surface more uniform rufous brown, and the whole of lower parts pale rufous albescent on vent. Frequents rocky hills with low scrub jungle; flesh perfectly white, used for fighting among mussalmans [q.v.].——*Small lowah partridge* (ککنی لوا - koknílawá, Hind. and Dec.; ನವಿಲುರೆಕ್ಕೆಬೆಬ್ಬಕ್ಕಿ - navilurekkebebbakki, Can.). Hind. from (kokní, small + lawá, hind. bush quail). Can. from (navilu, can. peacock + rekke, can wing + heççu, can. superior + hakki, can. bird). Title otherwise Painted bush-quail. Perdicula erythrorhyncha, perdicinæ [teetar], tetraonidæ [tittiram], rasores [pacshy, 33], of naturalists. Male forehead, lores, and crown of head black; white frontal band continued as supercilium over each eye; upper plumage rich olive brown, with black lunules; scapulars, wing-coverts and secondaries with large patches of black, shaft pale yellow, and faint cross lines of same; primaries brown, outer webs barred dark rufous; tail brown with black spots, barred with narrow pale yellow lines; beneath chin pure white, bordered black; rest of lower parts rufous, passing into olive brown on sides of neck, spots of black on breast, increasing in size on sides of neck and breast; feathers of flanks with large spots of deep black tipped with white; bill and legs fine red; irides yellow brown; length 6½ inches. Female differs in having chin, supercilium, forehead and face rufous, in place of white; head brown instead of black. Found on high lands; rise with less whirr than other bush quails, plumage generally being softer and not so firm.

TEEV (തീവ് - tívu, *Mal.*; தீவு - tívu, *Tam.*). From (dvípa, san. island). Island [divy, dweepam]. The chief islands of the Presidency are the Laccadive and Maldive islands, consisting of low coral reefs [atoll], south-west of presidency and Ceylon. In the Bay of Bengal there are Rameshwaram and Manaar between the presidency and Ceylon.——*Teeyan* (തീയ്യൻ - tíyyan, Mal.). Means islander. Tribal-title. Numerically the strongest section of the Malabar population. They form the mass of the field laborers, but their chief avocation is to collect and make coarse sugar [jaggery] from the juice of the palm [taur]. They follow polyandric customs. Both men and women are generally handsome, with strong muscular frames; able to undergo much fatigue, and talkatively inclined. The women sometimes carry a small piece of muslin [q.v.] over the shoulder, and draw it across the breast when a European approaches, but the custom of the caste is to leave the bosom bare. The Teeyar follow the rule of descent a matrice [maroomakkatoyem]. They are supposed to have come from Ceylon. Cf. Dweepar. See vol. I (16), (110), and II, 99 [jauty].——*Teeyatty* (തീയത്തി - tíyatti, Mal.). Teeya woman.

TEILA (ತೈಲ - taila, *Can.*). From (taiyal, tam. beauty). Makes compound personal names; as Teilapa, cadamba ruler of Banavausy and Haungal, A.D. 1099—1124.——*Teily* (தைலி - taili, Tam.). Name of the goddess at Veitheeshwarancoil near Tanjore. Hindoo female proper name [payar].

TEILAM (तैल - taila, *San.*; तेल - téla, *Mahr.*; دهن - duhn, *Ar.*; روغن - raughan, *Pers.*; تیل - tel, *Hind.*; ತೈಲ - taila, *Can.*; ତୈଳ - taila, *Oor.*; తైలము - tailamu, *Tel.*; തൈലം - tailam *Mal.*; தைலம் - tailam, *Tam.*). Title from sanscrit [til]. San. from (tilá, san. sesamum seed). Mahr. from sanscrit. Ar. from (duhna, ar. to anoint). Hind. from sanscrit. Drav. from sanscrit.

Oleo-resin. A sub-division of resins [raul]. Oleo-resins are resins [raul] combined with volatile oil [yennay]; on distillation the oil passes over, leaving a resin behind [gond, raul]. The Tamulians include also balsams [q.v.] under Teilam. The following are two key-lists in the briefest possible terms of the oleo-resins, and balsams of s. india for which vernacular names are known:—further information must be traced in the glossary paragraphs through the small type cross-references at end of this volume; see also vricsham, 7, for the method of expressing the products, &c., of plants in the dravidian languages.—"*a*" Altingia excelsa, java storax, balsam from bark; Balsamodendron roxburghii, indian bdelluim, gum-resin; Buchanania latifolia, chironjee, varnish; Cedrus deodara, deodar, wood oil; Chloroxylon swietenia, satin wood, wood oil; Dalbergia sissoo, sissoo, wood oil; Dipterocarpus turbinatus, gurjan, oil from wood; Erythroxylon monogynum, deccany deodar, wood oil; Holigarna longifolia, holigarna, oil from fruit; Liquidambar orientale, indian storax, resin from bark; Melaleuca leucadendron, cajeput, oil from leaf; Odina wodier, wodier, varnish; Semecarpus anacardium, marking nut, black varnish from nut shell; Tectona grandis, teak, wood oil.—"*b*" Bdellium, balsamodendron; Cajeput, melaleuca; Chironjee, buchanania; Deodar, cedrus, erythroxylon; Gurjan, dipterocarpus; Marking nut, semecarpus; Satinwood, chloroxylon; Sissoo, dalbergia; Storax, altingia, liquidambar; Teak, tectona; Wodier, odina. ——*Carpoora teilam* (सरलरस - saralarasa, San.; دهن الكافور - duhnulkáfúr, Ar.; عرق كافور - arkikáfúr, Pers.; كافور كا تيلم - káfúrkátailam, Hind.; ಕರ್ಪೂರತೈಲ - karpúratsila, Can. and Too.; కర్పూరతైలము - karpúratailamu, Tel.; കർപ്പൂരതൈലം - karppúratailam, Mal.; கற்பூரத்தைலம் - karppúrattailam, Tam.). Title from tamul. San. from (sarala, san. pinus longifolia, roxb. + rasa, san. juice). Ar. from (duhn, ar. oil + káfúr, ar. camphor). Pers. from (ark, ar. extract + káfúr, ar. camphor). Hind., &c., mean camphor + oil. Hind. also (gandabaríjekátel), meaning oil of pinus longifolia, roxb. Turpentine [ganda firoza] oil. Also called Spirits of turpentine. Oleum terebinthinæ of chemists. The essential oil drawn from turpentine by distillation. Used by moochees [q.v.] in preparing paints and varnishes [rangh].——*Munn teilam* (भूमितैल - bhúmitaila, San.; قفراليهود - kafralyahúd, Ar. and Pers.; مٹی کا تیل - mittíkátel, Hind. and Dec.; ಮಣ್ಣುಯೆಣ್ಣೆ - mannuyenne, Can.; ಮಣ್ಣೆಣ್ಣೆ - mannenne, Too.; మంటితైలము - mantitailamu, Tel.; മണ്ണെണ്ണ - mannenna, Mal.; மண்ணெண்ணெய் - mandailam, Tam.). Title from tamul. San. from (bhúmi, san. earth + taila, san. oil). Ar. from (kafr, ar. pitch + yahúd, ar. jew). Hind. from (mittí, hind. earth + tel. hind. oil). Drav. means earth + oil. San. also (prit'hivitaila), meaning earth oil. Mahr. also (mattíkatél), meaning earth + oil. Tel. also (bhúmitailamu), meaning earth + oil; (mantinúne), meaning earth + oil. Mal. also (mantáilam), meaning earth oil. Tam. also (shiláthailam), meaning rock + oil; (mannenney), meaning earth oil. Petroleum or fluid bitumen [shilajit]. Otherwise Rock oil. Naphtha [q.v.] and Kerosene oil are finer varieties. Rock oils are liquids formed by the slow decomposition of organic remains, animal or vegetable, or both combined. Munn teilam occurs, semi-liquid somewhat of the consistence of treacle tenacious, semi-transparent of a deep sherry-red or nearly opaque, tar-like brown with a peculiar though not unpleasant aromatic odour and pungent acrid taste; exudes spontaneously from the rocks in volcanic regions, and collects on the surface of certain lakes; can be obtained in nearly every bazaar [q.v.] in the country. The tamul doctors order it as an external application in rheumatic complaints, as also in cases of epilepsy, hysteria, and palsy, in all which affections it is rubbed on the part with the hand in the form of a liniment. Useful in all skin diseases, especially when of a parasitic origin. When mixed with earth or ashes, it serves for fuel. Useful in destroying bugs [moott poochy] in old wood, and in removing white-ants [q.v.]

TEIYIB (طيب - taiyib, *Ar.*). Good, name of a son of Mahomet. Common alam, as Teiyib ally, double alam [ism].

TEJAS (तेजस् - téjas, *San.*; தேயசு - téyasu, *Tam.*). From (tij, san. to sharpen). Light [jyoty] or fire [agny].——*Tejbul* (तुम्बुरु - tumburu, San.; فاغرة - fághirah, Ar.; كبابكشادهدهن - kabábikushádehdahan, Pers.; تجبل - tijbal, Hind.; ಜಿಮ್ಮೆ - jimme, Can.). Title from hindostany. San. means coriander, coriandrum sativum, linn.; from flavor and size of fruit. Ar. means mouthed. Pers. from (kabáb. pers. cubebs, piper cubeba, linn. f. + kushádah, pers. open + dahan, pers. mouth). Hind. from (téja, san. pungency + p'hala, san. fruit); from aromatic fruit. Title otherwise Indian toothache tree. Botanically Zanthoxylum [toomroo] alatum, roxb., rutaceæ [vricsham, 32]. Alias Zanthoxylum hostile. Small shrub, armed with straight thorns; leaves pinnate, opposite; leaflets oblong, acuminated at both ends, entire; petioles unarmed; panicles terminal or sub-axillary; flowers small greenish; flowering in the hot season. Seeds and bark aromatic, tonic; aromatic fruit used as a condiment [vadagam]; twigs serve as tooth-brushes; capsules and seeds used for intoxicating fish [common emetic nut, indian berry, indian oak, marotty, round milk-hedge, sooptee, walsoora, zanzibar indigo].——*Tejpat* (तेजपत्त्र - téjapattra, San.; تيج پات - tejpát, Hind.). From (téja, san. pungency + pattra, san. leaf). Leaf of cinnamomum tamala, nees. [cassia cinnamon]. The folium indicum of the english Pharmacopœia. Same as Malabathrum.——*Tendoo* (تيندو - tendú, Hind.). From (tindu, san. from tij, san. to sharpen), from acid exudation of tree. Same as Coromandel ebony.

TEKKALY (టెక్కలి - tekkali, *Tel.* tekkali*). Means robbery.—"*a*" Deputy tahsildarry; Ganjam district. Pay Rs. 100.—"*b*" Proprietary estate; Ganjam dist.; pop. 112,015; square miles 172; lat. 18° 36'; long. 84° 17'; from Bulligooda S.S.E. 109 miles; from Berhampore S.W. 60 miles; from Chetterpore S.W. 71 miles; from Chicacole N.E. 30 miles; from Madras N.E. 470 miles; from Russellcondah S.S.W. 93 miles; from the sea W. 9 miles.

TEL (తెలి - teli, *Tel.*). Brightness [teiu].——*Telaga* (తెలగ - telaga, obl., Tel.). A teloogoo-speaking man.——*Telaganya* (తెలగాణ్య - telagányh, obl., Tel.). From (telugu, tel. language so called + ánemu, tel. country). A class of Smarta [q.v.] bramins [bramin, jauty].——*Telingan* (தெலுங்கன் - telungan, Tam.). A teloogoo man.——*Telingana* (تلنگانه - telingánah, Hind.). From (telingá, hind. telugu people + affix showing relationship). Mahomedan name for Teloogoo country. The eastern part of Telingana was from the beginning of the ninth to nearly the end of the eleventh century in the hands of an obscure race of princes known by the name of Yaudava [q.v.]. The grants of the rajahs of this dynasty date from A.D. 808 to A.D. 1080. The capital was at Narrainpooram and the two chief places were Chundragherry and Tripatty. According to tradition there were eighteen rulers of this line, but little or nothing is known about them. In the western part of the country the Chalookya [q.v.] family were the reigning princes. The parent stock established itself at Calyaun on the borders of Carnautam [q.v.] and Maharashtram [q.v.]. This dynasty was contemporary with the earlier Ballaula [q.v.] sovereigns, and they appear to have reigned from the end of the tenth to the end of the twelfth century. Religious disputes dismembered the kingdom, and the last king Bijjala [q.v.] was deposed by his minister, who was soon after assassinated by some fanatics of the Lingayet [q.v.] sect. Another branch of the Chalookya [q.v.] family ruled over Calingam [q.v.], which is the north-eastern portion of Telingana extending along the sea-coast from Dravira to Orissa. This dynasty lasted throughout the whole of the twelfth and thirteenth centuries, when it was overthrown by one of the Ganapaty [q.v.] kings of Andhram [q.v.]. Andhram was the name of the inland part of Telingana, and the capital of this state was at Warangal, about 80 miles north-east of Hyderabad. Tradition gives the names of Vicramadityan [q.v.] and Shalivahanan [q.v.] as some of the earliest monarchs; after them came the Chola [q.v.] rajahs, who were succeeded about A.D. 515 by a race called Yavana [q.v.]. There were nine rajahs of this house and they reigned until the middle of the tenth century. About this time notice first appears of the family of the Ganapaty rajahs, but they did not become famous till the end of the next century. The rajah at this time was Cancateeya [q.v.], from whom the whole dynasty is sometimes named. He is first mentioned as an officer of state of a feudatory of the Chalookya [q.v.] kings. This dynasty was at its greatest power about the end of the thirteenth century, when, according to local tradition, the whole of the country south of the Godavery was subject to it. Friar jordanus, the quilon bishop of the fourteenth century, has the following:—"there be "also other kings, as the king of telenc, who is very potent and "great; the kingdom of telenc abounds in corn [dhaunyam], "rice [q.v.], sugar [q.v.], wax [mom], honey [shahad] and "honey comb, pulse [dholl], eggs, goats [vellaud], buffaloes "[khoolgah], bee-hives, milk [paul], butter, and in oils [yennay] "of diverse kinds, and in many excellent fruits [pazham], more "than any other part of the Indies [india];" Telenc was Andhram [charitram, raj]. See vol. I (10), (147).——*Teloogoo* (తెలుగు - telugu, Tel.). Andhram [q.v.] of Sanscrit writers. Vadoogoo [q.v.] of the tamuls. Formerly called by Portuguese and English Gentoo [q.v.]. Trilingam [q.v.] is a modern Sanscrit pedantic name. Teloogoo originated in Canarese. The ancient Teloogoo rulers are spoken of as Carnautaca [q.v.] doraloo. The use of Sanscrit is the chief feature of its vocabulary. The pronunciation of Sanscrit among the Teloogoos corresponds with the purest pronunciation used at Benares. Teloogoos have always emigrated to other parts of Southern india, but there are no signs of a converse immigration. Teloogoo is the softest of all the Eastern languages, with the exception of the Malay, which has been called the Italian of Asia, but Teloogoo is a very poor language in everything except outward appearances; it is philologically the weakest of the Dravidian languages [bhaushay]. There is a native proverb:—"The Mahratta is sand; the Hindee is dust; the Canarese "is musk; the Teloogoo is honey; the Ooriya is strength." See vol. I (41), (43), (47), (48); II, 185-192, 193.——*Teloogoo new year* (యుగాది - yugádi, Tel.). Vernacular means commencement of yoog [q.v.]. Otherwise Samvatsaraudy. Lunar [chaundra maunam] festival [pundigay, 6d], subject to intercalation [adhicam]. The first day [tity] of the waxing moon [shooclapacsham] in the first lunar month Cheitram [mausam] between 14th March and 12th April. The natives celebrate its return as a holiday. After having anointed themselves and bathed they offer the flower of the margosa [neem] tree with tamarind [q.v.] juice and sugar [q.v.] to their household deities and afterwards partake of the same themselves. Alms are then distributed among the poor, and during the day the people divert themselves in the hope of being happy through the year, as they believe their happiness during the year depends on the manner in which they begin it [maryauday, new year, samvátsaram, tamul new year, yoogaudy]. See vol. I (92).

TELINI FLY (चन्द्रक - chandraka, *San.*; ذراريح هندى - zaráríhihindí, *Ar.*; ذبان هندى - dabánihindí, *Pers.*; تيلنى مكهى - telnímakkhí, *Hind.*; எரிவண்டு - erivandu, *Tam.*). Title from hindostany. San. means eye in peacock's tail; from variegated gold color. Ar. from (zaráríh, ar. cantharis or spanish fly + hindí, ar. indian). Pers. from (dabán, pers. cantharis + hindí, ar. indian). Hind. from (telní, hind. specific name + makkhí, hind. fly). Tam. from (eri, tam. to burn + vandu, tam. beetle). Hind. also (badbokízírangí), meaning bad smelling cantharis. Also called Blistering beetle. Mylabris cichorii, meloidæ, coleoptera, holometabola, insecta [poochy], of naturalists [jantoo]. Feeds on flowers of cucurbitaceous plants, especially on Hibiscus esculentus [common bendy]. Insect about an inch in length and the third of an inch broad; the elytra or wing-cases of an obscure yellow, with three large somewhat zigzag transverse black bands; the first band is interrupted and sometimes reduced to three or four spots. Have medicinally irritant and vesicant properties, the active principle being the same with that of the officinal cantharides, viz., cantharidine. Is a substitute for Spanish fly, cantharis vesicatoria. The following other species also are substitutes for cantharides:—Mylabris indica, Mylabris melanura, Mylabris humeralis, Mylabris proxima, Mylabris orientalis, Lytta assamensis, and Epicauta nepalensis.

TELKACHA (تلخيه - talkhaiya, *Hind.*). Means bitter plant. Same as Indian caper.

TEM (தேம் - tém, *Tam.*). Sweetness [madhoo, tel].——*Tain* (தேன் - tén, Tam.). From (tém, tam. sweetness). Honey [shahad]. Plant first term. Ex., where transl. is of second term:—Ficus carica (ténatti), ficus glomerata; Guazuma tomentosa (ténbaççai), greenness, (téngáymaram), fruit + tree; Holopetala integrifolia (ténbúççimaram), meaning honey bee + tree. See gloss. paragraphs.——*Tainee* (தேனீ - téní, Tam.). See sep. title.——*Tainimullay* (தேனேமலை - ténémalai, Tam.). From (tén, tam. honey + malai, tam. mountain). Range of hills; North arcot dist., Calastry zemindarry; East of Naugalaupooram and running westerly towards Madanambaid and then northerly towards Vaunellore.——*Tainiyaur* (தேனியாறு - téniyáru, Tam.). From (téní, tam. honey bee + áru, tam. river). River; Madura dist., Periyacoolam tal. Tributary of the Shoorooliyaur. Rises in the Travancore hills and drains the Bodinaickanore valley, which lies between the Travancore and Pulney ranges. Joins the Shoorooliyaur at Allingaram after irrigating one Government village and two villages of the Bodinaickanore zemindarry by means of anicuts [q.v.].——*Tamizhmoony* (தமிழ்முனி - tamizhmuni, Tam.). From (tamizh, tam. the language + muni, tam. sage). Agastyan [q.v.].——*Tamizh mullay* (தமிழ்மலை - tamizhmalai, Tam.). Means tamul mountain. Mount Pothiyam [pothigay], the reputed residence of the sage Agastyan [q.v.] father of the tamul language.——*Tamul* (தமிழ் - tamizh, Tam.). Means sweetness. The Tamul language. An old name by which the people have always themselves called it. Cf. the meaning of Teloogoo and Tooloo. See also Dravida. In the Indian segment of the Roman maps called the Peutinger tables, there is a considerable country covered by two names, Andre indi and Damirice, plainly the Teloogoo and Tamul countries. In another place in the same map a district is called Scytia Dymirice, and it appears to have been this word which, by a mistake of Λ for Δ, Ptolemy wrote Λυμιρίκη. The anonymous geographer of Ravenna repeatedly mentions Dimirica as one of the three divisions of India [q.v.], and the one farthest to the east; giving Madura as one of the cities. Cf. ἀριάκη, the Mahratta or Aryan-speaking country [bhaushay]. For tamul grammar see Lacshanam; for tamul poets see Pauvalan. See vol. I (43), (47), (48), (52), (53); II, 185-192, 205, 209.——*Tamul new year* (வருடப்பிறப்பு - varudappirappu, Tam.). Means year + birth. Title otherwise Varsha pirapp, Varsha sancramanam, Varsha sancramam, Samvatsaraudy [pundigay, 6d]. This falls on April 12, the first day of the first solar [madhyamasowra maunam] month Chittray [mausam]. It is observed in the same way as the Teloogoo new year; but no anointment takes place, the day being dedicated on the part of the Bramins [q.v.] to the spirits of departed ancestors [tarpanam]. On the other hand a good work performed on this day is considered to be worth a hundred done at any other time [maryauday, new year, samvatsaraudy, tologoo new year, yoogaudy]. See vol. I (92).——*Tamul vedam* (தமிழ்வேதம் - tamizhvétham, Tam.). Same as Devaram, and Tirvyemozhy. Also Cooral [q.v.] of tirvulloovar [q.v.], so called in eulogy. ——*Tembauvany* (தேம்பாவணி - tέmbávani, Tam.). From (above + pá, tam. verse + ani, tam. ornament). A Tamul poetical work by Beschi [veera maumoony]. The following are specimens of this remarkable work.—"*a*" While the holy family are crossing the desert on their return from Egypt, the Saviour is represented as enumerating in prophecy the several devotees, who in succeeding times are there to devote themselves to austerities. Ejesia mariyal celebrated in the extract is St. Mary the Egyptian, the first female recluse on record in the Christian church. She was discovered by St. Zosimus in the desert beyond Jordan, where she had passed forty-seven years:—அவாவென மதத்தின்சீற்றத் தறிவெனப்பாகன் வீழ்த்த வுவாவென வுடலைக் கைக்கொண் டுக்கநற் றோட்டி மாற்றி யிவாவன தவக்க வட்டை யிட்டுறு விரதத்தூணின் மவாவனமுனிவன் சேர்த்தி வானமும் வியப்பச்செய்வான். வீட்டருநாட்டிற்கேற்ற விழுப்பொருளாகநாடி யீட்டருஞ் சிலைக்குப்பை யேறறிநல் லுயிரோடூக்கைப் பூட்டரு மேராய்ப் பூட்டிப் புரைநசைச் சேற்றுட் செல்லா வாட்டருந் தவதசின்பண்டி மதித்தகன் கதியிற்சேர்ப்பான். தேனிமிர்முல்லையாசத் திருந்தறத்தொகுதிநட்டு நானிமிர்தவத்திற் காத்த நொறிப் பொறிவேலிகோலி மேனிமிரொழுக்கநீரை விட்டருண் மணலைப்பாய்த்தி வானிமிருலகிறைறும் வனத்திறுங் கசோரன்பூப்பான். ஆசறிய தவச்செந்தீயி லைம்பொறி யிரும்பிட்டுத் தேயறறியதெருளின் ஞான விரதமிட்டாய பைம்பொன் றேற்றியமறையச்சாசச் சீலநன்பணிகள் சேர்த்திப் போற்றியதேவமார்பிற் புரோதரனணிப்பூணுவான். தீயவுநலவுமுள்ளிற் றேறியபெண்ணிற்றேறலாயவுமரிதே முன்னாரழிந்த நாண்வேலிதாவி யேவுங் காமத்தழ்ந்த வெசிசியமரியாள் பின்னர் தூயவுமரிதிவோர்ந்து துறந்திவணெடுநா ணிற்பாள். கண்ணமயின் மற்றியாருங் கண்டதன்பிழைகாண்பாரா ருண்மையினுற்றபாவ நுதலியுட் டானே கண்ட வுண்மையிலுணர்ந்தவுக்கமுளதிறகாகவெட்டிப் பெண்மையின் போர்வைநாணம் பிரிவிலள் போர்த்து நோற்பாள். காமமே பறவைத் தேர்மேற் கசடெனும் பாலைசேர்ந்தாள் வீமமே பறவைத் தேர்மேல் விளைதவக்குறிஞ்சி ஞான வாமமே பறவைத் தேர்மேல் வளரறமுல்லை சேர்ந்தென் னாமமே பறவைத் தேர்மே லயாபவானாட்டைச்சேர்வாள்—"When by the outrageous fury of the "passions the driver has fallen from his seat, Mahauvana moony "having seized and mounted the elephant, which is the body, "governing him by the strong hook of resolution, will bind "him to the pillar of constancy by the rope of penance, and fill "all heaven with admiration. Desirous of obtaining the wealth "peculiar to the kingdom of heaven, Madittagan having heaped "on the car of unceasing penitence a load of holiness and yoked "to it as oxen his body and soul, avoiding the quagmire "of sinful desire he will arrive at salvation. Having planted "the honey-dropping jasmine-vine of perfect virtue; having "surrounded it with a hedge of subdued senses, to protect it by "penance supported by religion; having let in the water of "strict discipline and spread around it the sand of grace, "Asoren will flourish as a garden whose fragrance reacheth to "heaven. Blowing the red furnace of penance and placing "therein the iron of the five senses, adding the mercury of "bright wisdom, Poorodaran poured the pure gold thus obtained "into the mould of religion, and, having enchased it with precious "jewels of virtue, he became an ornament for the breast of the "God he adored. Though women may inwardly resolve on good "or bad, it is difficult for them to persist in their resolution; "thus, though the egyptian Mary overleaping the fence of "modesty had at first plunged into the sea of carnal desire, yet "at last having determined to perform austerities with the "purest devotion, she will retire from the world and long "remain here. The eye perceives not the color by which it is "darkened, and who are they who see their own faults apparent "to all others? but she remembering of herself her minutest "sins and borne on the wings of mental resolution, produced by "reflecting on the truth she perceived, gave herself up to "devotion covered only by the mantle of female modesty. On "the flying chariot of desire she arrived at the desert of sin; "on the flying chariot of fear she repaired to the mountains "of patience; on the flying chariot of resplendent wisdom she "entered the grove of growing virtue; and on the flying "chariot of my name she shall enter the kingdom of heaven."—"*b*" The following is the description of the country of Judæa:—புள்ளுலாம்விசும்பிடை தொறும்பொரும்படை பொருவ வெள்ளுலாமழை வெண்கொடியுருக்கொடு விளங்கித் தெள்ளுலாந்திரை திளைப்பவுண்டெழுந்துயர் பரந்து வள்ளுலாங்கரு மதகரியினமெனத்தோன்ற. போர்புறங்கொடு பொருந்தலுரத்திறெய்த்தொளிர் வேற் சீர்புறங்கொடு திசைதொறுமிருளறமின்னி வார் புறங்கொடு வளர்முரசொலியெனவதிர்ந்து நீர்புறங் கொடு நீன்முகில் முழங்கின மாதோ. படையெனச் செருப் பகைதரப்படர்ந்தனவல்லாற் கடையெனச் செறி கருணையோடுற்றியவள்ளற் கொடையெனச் செழுங் குன்றொடு வயின்றொறுங்குளிர மிடையெனச் சொரி வியன்முகில்வளைவிலபொழிய— "As in an army "arrayed for battle, over all the sky, where the birds rove, white "clouds appear resembling white banners; but, having filled

"themselves with the clear waves of the ocean, they spread "abroad and seem like a mighty herd of black and furious "elephants [q.v.]. Like bright spears glancing from the breasts "of enemies in the field of battle, they dart their lightnings "dissipating darkness in every quarter and, trembling as it were "by the reverberating sound of leather-bound cymbals, the black "and watery clouds thunder aloud. Though at first taking the "appearance of an army prepared for horrid battle, at length, "as the liberal-minded bestow their gifts, diffusing coldness "over the mountains and the whole expanse of the earth, the "extended clouds pour down abundant rain [mazhay]."—"c" The following is in praise of the Saviour:—மருட்டுருவலியுரு
வே மருளுறு சினவுருவே அருட்டரு தயையுருவே யள
வறு திருவுருவே தெருட்டரு கலையுருவே செயிரறுமனு
வுருவே பொருட்டருமணியுருவே பொழிமணவடிதொழு
தேன். உரையிலகலை நிலையே யுயரறமடை யுரையே
கரையிலபடர்கடலே கதியுயிர்பெறுகரையே வரையில
சுகநிலையே வளர்தவ மடைவரையே புரையிலமனு
மகனே புதுமலரடிதொழுதேன். மருமலிமலர்நிழலே
மறைமலியுயர்பயனே திருமலிகரமுகிலே சிவமலிதனி
முதலே இருமலிபுகழ்குளரோ யிணையொடு தொழுமடியே
குருமலியுறநிறையே கொழுமலரடி தொழுதேன்—"O "thou who hast the power to cause dread, but art not disturbed "by thine anger! O thou by whose mercy grace is vouchsafed "and unnumbered blessings are confirmed! O thou who art the "knowledge which giveth understanding, who in the human "form destroyedst sin! Who art a precious jewel set in gold! "I worship thy feet diffusing fragrance! O thou who possesseth "knowledge not conveyed by words, and art the word by which "the highest virtue is conferred! O thou who art a broad ocean "without a shore, and the shore attained by beautified spirits! "O thou who art eternal happiness without limit, and the limit "to be attained only by unceasing devotion! O thou the Son of "Man without an equal, I worship the newly blown flower of "thy feet! O thou whose protecting grace resembles the shade "of fragrant flowers, who art the exalted sense of the Scripture, "whose hand, bounteous as the clouds, dispenses felicity, who "art alone the cause of salvation, whose feet those dwelling in "the two worlds adore and adorn with flowers, who art both the "teacher and the path of virtue, I worship the blooming flower "of thy feet [bhaushay]." See vol. I (57).

TEN (തെൻ - ten, *Mal.*; தென் - ten, *Tam.*). South [dacshinam, tisay].——*Tekk* (തെക്ക - tekku, Mal.). From (ten, tam. south); dative turned to nominative. South [dacshinam, terkk, tisay].——*Temmala* (തെന്മല - temmala, Mal.). From (above + mala, mal. mountain). Hill; Malabar dist., Palghaut tal. On south edge of Palghaut gap. Continuation of the Madura hills, and the Pollachy and Anamullay ranges. It includes the Agamala, Poottoondimala, Vellauttimala, &c., and descends towards the coast into the Palcode and Putticaud hills. Above this southern range lies a high land range of ghauts [q.v.], and forest country running southward which terminates in Cape comorin.——*Tencaray* (தென்கரை - tengarai, Tam.). See sep. title.——*Tencaushy* (தென்காசி - tengási, Tam.). See sep. title.——*Tendisaykone* (தென்றிசைக்கோன் - tenrisaikkón, Tam.). From (above + dik, san. direction + kón, tam. king). Yaman [q.v.], the god of death and the regent of the south [ashtadicpaulacan].——*Tengalay* (தென்கலை - tengalai, Tam.). Means southern branch. Southern or original sect of the Ramaunoojeeyans [q.v.]; followers of the ritual and interpretation of Manavaula maumoony [q.v.] of Conjeeveram; as opposed to Vadagalays [q.v.] or northern sect of the same. The difference between the two is explained in detail in the foot-note on Hindoo sects at vol. I (89). See Manavaula maumoony, Vadagalay, and Vedaunta charry. The founder of the Tengalay sect was Manavaula maumoony, who lived about 300 years ago. He was the son of Krishnamacharry and a native of Alwar tirnagary in the Tinnevelly district. He was also called Ramya jamautry moony. The three principal seats of the priests of the Tengalay sect are in Vaunamamullay [nangoonairy], called in sanscrit Totaudry, in the tinnevelly district; Shreerungam [q.v.] in the trichinopoly district; and Tripatty [q.v.] in the north arcot district [jauty].——*Tenga yair* (തെന്നയേറു - ténnayéru, Mal.). From (ténna, mal. cocoanut + éru, mal. throw). Cocoanut [q.v.] feast of Malabar. Luni-solar [chaundramaunam] festival [pundigay, 6d]. Held in new moon [amavausyay] of fifth solar month of Chingom [mausam], i.e., between 15th August and 14th September. At this time the S.W. monsoon [q.v.] is supposed to have terminated, cocoanuts [q.v.] and other fruits are therefore taken to the sea and launched into it. After this ceremony, the coast is considered open for country crafts from Bombay southwards.——*Tengye* (టెంకాయ - tenkáya, Tel.; തെന്ന - ténna, Mal.; தேங்காய் - téngáy, Tam.). From (above + káy, tam. ripening fruit); as introduced from Ceylon. Cocoanut [q.v.].——*Tenkizhakk* (தென்கிழக்கு - tengizhakku, Tam.). South-east [ashtadic, tisay].——*Tenmerkk* (தென்மேற்கு - tenmérgu, Tam.). South-west [ashtadic, tisay].——*Ten mozhy* (தென்மொழி - tenmozhi, Tam.). Southern speech. Tamul, as opposed to Vadamozhy or Sanscrit the northern speech.——*Ten mullay* (தென்மலை - tenmalai, Tam.). Southern mountain. Pothiguy [q.v.], the supposed residence of Agastyan [q.v.]. Vadamullay or northern mountain being Meroo [q.v.] or Tripatty [q.v.].——*Tennal* (தென்னல் - tennal, Tam.). South wind [long shore wind].——*Tennaunday mullay* (தென்னண்டைமலை - tennándaimalai, Tam.). From (above + ándai, tam. ruler + malai, tam. mountain); the hill seat of government in the south. Hill; Salem dist., Salem and Ootancaray tals.; lat. 11° 52′; long. 78° 31′; from Salem N.E. 25 miles. Continuation of the Shevaroy hills. On the north-east of the Munjavaudy pass it is known as the Arnoottimullay and farther north again in Ootancaray talook as the Chittairimullay, and may be said to extend as far as Teertamullay itself, towards which it is known as Caurapandy mullay, Maukkal, Tarsalmullay and Vellay mullay. The range is divided by two breaks into three parts of very different sizes. The southern part, the Tennaunday mullay proper, which is by far the largest, is divided from the northern part by a very steep valley The lofty ridge thus cut off is known as the Caurapandy mullay, and is itself fairly separated from the Teertamullay by a deep saddle-shaped depression. The Tennaunday mullay proper is deeply cut into by four great ravines, one on the north side at Taltooky, a second on the east in which the village of Dandamputty is situated, and the third and fourth on the south side. From these two, which unite just before their opening into the Salem-Ahtoor valley, emerges the Vellaur river. On the portion known as the Chittairimullay, the gooroo [q.v.] lives who has spiritual charge of all the salem Malayaulies.——*Tenpaundy* (தென்பாண்டி - tenbándi, Tam.). From (above + pándi, tam. pándiya country). One of the twelve districts in the Tamul country in which bad Tamul or Codoon tamul is spoken. Same as Naunjinaud.——*Tenpoolattaur* (தென்புலத்தார் - tenbulattár, Tam.). From (above + pulam, tam. place). The inhabitants of the southern region, to whom ceremonies for the dead are performed. Yaman [q.v.] is their king; hence his name is Tendisaykone [q.v.], the king of the southern region. The expression may indicate the equatorial origin of the Dravidians. The tamul Cooral [q.v.] has the following:—தென்புலத்தார் தெய்வம்விருந்தொக்கலு னென்றுங் கைம்புலத்தாறோம்பறலை—"the chief duty of "the householder [gribastan] is to preserve the five-fold rule "towards the spirits of the south, the gods, his guests, his "relations, and himself [mahayanyam, yanyam]."——*Tenraltairone* (தென்றற்றேரோன் - tenrattérón, Tam.). From (tenral, tam. south wind + tér, tam. car). One who has the south-wind [tennal] as his car [ruth, tair]. Manmatan [q.v.].——*Terkk* (தெற்கு - tergu, Tam.). The south [tisay].

TENALLY (తెనాలి - tenáli, *Tel.*). From (ténu, can. lofty + áli, can. ridge).—"*a*" Deputy tahsildarry, Kistna district. Pay Rs. 70.—"*b*" Village, Deputy tahsildar's station; Kistna dist., Repully tal.; pop. 6,074; acres 7,080; lat. 16° 15′; long. 80° 41′; from Bezwada S. 19 miles; from Guntoor E.S.E. 14 miles; from Madras N. 218 miles; from Masulipatam W. 32 miles; from Repully N.W. 20 miles; from Vinoocondah E. 62 miles; from the sea N. 24 miles. On the Nizampatam canal. Temples with inscriptions. In the enclosure of the Ramalingeshwarasawmy temple is a colossal image, Boodhist [booddha] or Jeina [q.v.]. Birth-place of Ramalingam, teloogoo poet [cavy] of the court of Krishna deva royel.

TENCARAY (தென்கரை - tengarai, *Tam.* tenkarai *). From (ten, tam. south + karai, tam. shore) [ten].——**(1)** Talook, Tinnevelly district. Tahsildar's pay Rs. 250. Area 542 square miles. Number of villages 153. Population 287,603. Language Tamul. S. coast of district. Bounded N. by Ottapidauram talook, E. by sea, S. by sea and Nangoonairy talook, W. by Nangoonairy and Tinnevelly talooks. The talook may be taken as an epitome of the whole district, as the district is of the presidency. Palmyra [q.v.] forest spreads over all the extreme southern villages, and the Tamrapurny valley has magnificent alluvial belts of rich and well-watered lands on either side. The northern and north-eastern villages above the river are bare, except for a few babool [q.v.] thickets. To the south the country, while bare for miles, is on the whole so covered with the palmyra [q.v.] palm as to deserve being included in the palmyra forest. The coast villages also abound with the babool [q.v.] or acacia [cantalam, vail]. The river valley here as elsewhere abounds in its higher lands with topes [q.v.] of mangoes [q.v.], ilooppay [mohwah], cocoanut [q.v.] and other trees. Black-cotton soil [regar] is found to the north, red sand and red clay to the south and west, tairy [q.v.] or blown sand on the sandstone [munal cull] and clay stone ridges parallel to the coast, and white sand on the sea-coast. There are also rocky ridges both of quartz [vencull] and of gneiss and quarries of the finest stone to be found in the district, the clay stones of the tairy formation. Cotton [q.v.], cholum [q.v.] and bengal gram [q.v.] are the products of the cotton soil, rice [q.v.] only of the river belt; palmyras [q.v.], dry rice [q.v.] and horse-gram [q.v.] of the sandy uplands to the south; and plaintains [q.v.], chillies [q.v.], cocoanuts [q.v.] and vegetables of the ooze or spring [oorny] irrigated lands which skirt the tairy ridge. On the sea-coast, a large population, chiefly Paravar and

Roman catholics, is engaged in fishing. At Cauyalputnam is an extensive salt-pan [ooppalam] tract, whence salt [ooppoo] is conveyed by cart to the inland villages of the talock, as well as to Tinnevelly and thence to other places. Large numbers of Shaunaur [q.v.] in the southern and eastern villages are engaged in the manufacture of palmyra [q.v.] jaggery [q.v.]. Four main channels [q.v.], two on either bank of the river from the Maroothoor and Shreeveicoontam anicuts [q.v.], irrigate the rice lands of the talook, supplying 56 river-fed tanks [q.v.] besides a large area of channel-fed lands. There are also 221 rain-fed tanks. River-irrigated lands extend to 34,549 acres and watered from rain-fed tanks to 10,135 acres. The Maroothoor anicut [q.v.] is an ancient work; Shreeveicoontam recent. The talook has two recognized sea-ports, viz., Cauyalputnam and Coolashekharaputnam. Places of archæological interest:—Akkashaulay, Alwar tirnagary, Auditchanullore, Auttore, Caroongoolam, Caunam, Cauyal, Congaroyacoorchy, Coolashekharaputnam, Coorangany, Cooroombore, Cuttaurimungalam, Keel vullanaud, Korkay, Manapaud, Mauramungalam, Maurtaundapacherry, Moorpanaud, Naul mauvady, Percongoolam, Peroor, Pooliyangoody, Poothoocoody, Pullacoorchy, Pulliputt, Rettay tripatty, Shairacoolam, Shendamungalam, Sholaycoodiyiroopp, Shreeveicoontam, Tencaray, Tentirpairy, Tolappanpunnay, Tricalore, Trichendore, Vadakk caurcherry, Vagoottauncooppam, Veiravam, Vulnaud hill. Principal Trig. stations:—Pillaivalay, Trichendore mantapam, Vulnaud, Yittamoly. The leading places, &c., in the talook are the following.——*Alwar tirnagary* (ஆழ்வார்த்திருநகரி - ázhvárttirunagari, Tam. álvártirunagari *). From (ázhván, tam. vaishnava devotee + tiru, tam. holy + nagarí, san. city); called after nummaulwar who was born there [alwar]. Tam. also (kurugúr). meaning vishnoo, the dwarf + town; also (kurungai), meaning vishnoo, the dwarf + place; also (tirungari), meaning holy + city. Also erroneously Alwar tinnevelly. Town, Place of pilgrimage; pop. 5,077; lat. 8° 36′; long. 77° 59′; from Shreeveicoontam S.E. 4 miles; from Tinnevelly E.S E. 21 miles; from the sea W. 11 miles. Important town, on right bank of Chindintooray. Large and ancient Vishnoo temple with inscriptions. Annual festivals in February and May.——*Auditchanullore* (ஆதிச்சநல்லூர் - áthiççanallúr, Tam.). From (áditya, san. sun + nal, tam. good + úr, tam. village). Sanscrit name (ádityapura), meaning sun town. Village, Hill; pop. 721; from Shreeveicoontam S. 20 miles; from Tinnevelly S.E. 32 miles; from the sea N. 2 miles. Ancient sepulchral urns found here, containing bones and pottery [mady moottaur tauzhy].——*Aulandalay* (ஆலந்தலை - álandalai, Tam.). From (álam, tam. the banyan tree, ficus bengalensis, linn. + talai, tam. field). Village; lat. 8° 28′; long. 78° 10′; from Shreeveicoontam E.S.E. 18 miles; from Tinnevelly E.S.E. 34 miles. Harbour. A hamlet of Trichendore.——*Auttore* (ஆத்தூர் - áttúr, Tam.). From (áru, tam. river + úr, tam. village). Town; pop. 2,901; acres 2,057; lat. 8° 37′; long. 78° 07′; from Shreeveicoontam E. 11 miles; from Tinnevelly E.S.E. 28 miles; from the sea W. 4 miles. Near mouth of Tamrapurny. Temple with inscriptions. Festivals in February and July.——*Cadautchapooram* (கடாட்சப்புரம் - kadádchappuram, Tam.). From (katáksha, san. favor shown by the glance + pura, san. town). Village; pop. 2,696; acres 2,764; lat. 8° 26′; long. 78° 0′; from Shreeveicoontam S.S.E. 15 miles; from Tinnevelly S.E. 29 miles; from the sea W. 6 miles. Mission station.——*Caraychoott* (கரைச்சுத்து - karaiççuttu, Tam.). From (karai, tam. shore + shuttu, tam. circuit). Town; pop. 5,937; acres 4,443; lat. 8° 25′; long. 78° 05′; from Shreeveicoontam S.S.E. 17 miles; from Tinnevelly S.E. 31 miles; from the sea W. 3 miles. Considerable trade in jaggery [q.v.] and rice [q.v.].——*Cauyal* (காயல் - káyal, Tam.). See sep. title. ——*Cauyalputnam* (காயற்பட்டணம் - káyarbattanam, Tam.). See sep. title.——*Christianagaram* (கிறிஸ்துவநகரம் - kiristtuvanagaram, Tam.). Christ's town. Village; lat. 8° 26′; long. 78° 04′; from Shreeveicoontam S.S.E. 16 miles; from Tinnevelly S.E. 31 miles; from the sea W. 3 miles. Mission station. A hamlet of Caraychoott.——*Coolashekharaputnam* (குலசேகரப்பட்டணம் - kulaségarappattanam, Tam.). See sep. title.——*Korkay* (கொற்கை - korgai, Tam.). See sep. title.——*Manapaud* (மணப்பாடு - manappádu, Tam.). See sep. title.——*Mauramungalam* (மாறமங்கலம் - máramangalam, Tam.). See sep. title.——*Meynaunapooram* (மெய்ஞானப்புரம் - meyñánappuram, Tam.). See sep. title.——*Moodalore* (முதலூர் - muthalúr, Tam.). From (muthal, tam. first + úr, tam. village). Village; pop. 2,852; acres 2,833; lat. 8° 25′; long. 78° 00′; from Shreeveicoontam S.S.W. 15 miles; from Tinnevelly S.E. 28 miles; from the sea W. 8 miles. Built by Shaunaur [q.v.] converts in 1799. They were converted in 1797 by one of their own caste, who became a Christian at Taujore and was sent as a catechist. ——*Nazareth* (நாசரத்து - násarattu, Tam.). See sep. title. ——*Nulloor* (நல்லூர் - nallúr, Tam.). From (nal, tam. good + úr, tam. village). Village; pop. 1,978; acres 1,776; lat. 8° 35′; long. 78° 06′; from Shreeveicoontam E.S.E. 11 miles; from Tinnevelly E.S.E. 28 miles; from the sea W. 6 miles.——*Palaya cauyal* (பழையகாயல் - pazhaiyagáyal, Tam.). See sep. title.——*Pannambauray* (பன்னம்பாறை - pannambárai, Tam.). From (panai, tam. palmyra tree, borassus flabelliformis, linn. + párai, tam. rock). Village; pop. 1,532; acres 5,687; lat. 8° 28′; long. 77° 59′; from Shreeveicoontam S. 11 miles; from Tinnevelly S.E. 25 miles; from the sea W. 12 miles. Quarry for cut-stone. ——*Pillaivalay* (பிள்ளைவிளை - pillaivalai, Tam.). From (pillai, tam. a member of the caste + vilai, tam. high dry ground). Trig-station; lat. 8° 42′ 23·24″; long. 78° 11′ 19·04″; height 21 feet; from Palaya cauyal N.E. 4 miles; from Tencaray E.N.E. 15 miles; from the sea W. ⅛ mile.——*Poonnacauyal* (புன்னக்காயல் - punnakkáyal, Tam.). See sep. title.——*Sawyerpooram* (சாயெர்ப்புரம் - sáyerppuram, Tam. sawyerpuram *). Called after a missionary. Village; pop. 4,047; acres 1,054; lat. 8° 41′; long. 78° 05′; from Shreeveicoontam E.N.E. 9 miles; from Tinnevelly E. 24 miles; from the sea W. 7 miles. Mission station founded by Dr. Pope.——*Shataunconlam* (சாத்தான்குளம் - sháttángulam, Tam. sátánkulam *). From (sháttan, tam. aiyyanár, the god + kulam, tam. tank). Town; pop. 5,430; acres 5,315; lat. 8° 26′; long. 77° 57′; from Shreeveicoontam S. 14 miles; from Tinnevelly S.E. 25 miles; from the sea W. 12 miles. Many money lenders.——*Shirtondanullore* (சிறுத்தொண்டநல்லூர் - shiruttondanallúr, Tam.). From (shiruttondan, tam. a shaiva devotee + nal, tam. good + úr, tam. village). Town; pop. 5,914; acres 1,013; lat. 8° 38′ N.; long. 78° 04′ E.; from Shreeveicoontam E. 8 miles; from Tinnevelly E.S.E. 24 miles; from the sea W. 7 miles. ——*Shreeveicoontam* (சிரீவைக்குண்டம் - shirívaikkundam, Tam.). See sep. title.——*Tamrapurny* (தாம்பிரப்பருணி - támbirapparuni, Tam.). See sep. title.——*Tencaray* (தென்கரை - tengarai, Tam.). See below.——*Tricalore* (திருக்களூர் - tirukkalúr, Tam.). From (tiru, tam. holy + kazhu, tam. eagle + úr, tam. village). Village; pop. 1,984; acres 1,107; lat. 8° 35′; long. 78° 00′; from Shreeveicoontam S.E. 5 miles; from Tinnevelly E.S.E. 20 miles; from the sea W. 12 miles. Vishnoo and Shiva temples.——*Trichendore* (திருச்செந்தூர் - tiruççendúr, Tam.). See sep. title.——*Veerapaundiyanputnam* (வீரப்பாண்டியன்பட்டணம் - vírappándiyanbattanam, Tam.). From (vírapándya, san. the pándiya king víran + pattana, san. town). Village, Port; pop. 1,968; acres 2,274; lat. 8° 31′; long. 78° 10′; from Cauyalputnam S.S.W. 3 miles; from Madras S.S.W. 343 miles; from Shreeveicoontam E.S.E. 17 miles; from Tinnevelly E.S.E. 33 miles; from Trichendore N. 2 miles. On Gulf of Manaar. The Trichendore reef affords sheltered anchorage to coasters off this town, which is second only to Tuticorin.——*Vulnaud* (வல்லநாடு - vallanádu, Tam.). From (val, tam. strong + nádu, tam. country). Village, Hill; pop. 2,365; acres 1,437; lat. 8° 43′; long. 77° 53′; from Shreeveicoontam N.N.W. 6 miles; from Tinnevelly E. 11 miles; from the sea W. 21 miles. Of considerable antiquity. Old urn-burying places [mady moottaur tauzhy] in the hill. Annual car festival. Trig. station in lat. 8° 42′ 48·13″; long. 77° 55′ 37·16″; height 1,023 feet; from Tencaray N.N.W. 8 miles; from Vulnaud E. 3 miles; from the sea W. 19 miles.——*Wodangoody* (ஓடன்குடி - odangudi, Tam.). From (ódam, tam. ferry boat + kudi, tam. village). Village, Port; lat. 8° 26′; long. 78° 05′; from Coolashekharaputnam N.W. 2 miles; from Madras S.S.W. 350 miles; from Nangoonairy E. 26 miles; from Tinnevelly S.S.E. 31 miles; from Vijayaputty N.E. 25 miles. On Gulf of Manaar, about 41 miles N.E. of Cape comorin.——*Yittamoly* (இட்டமொழி - ittamozhi, Tam.). From (ittu, tam. small + mózhai, tam. underground stream). Trig. station; lat. 8° 22′ 27·41″; long. 77° 55′ 24·24″; height 219 feet; from Arasore W.N.W. 3 miles; from Tencaray S. 18 miles; from the sea W. 13 miles.——**(2)** Town; Tinnevelly dist.; pop. 5,956; acres 1,876; lat. 8° 36′; long. 77° 59′; from Madras S.S.W. 344 miles; from Palamcottah E.S.E. 16 miles; from Shermadevy E. 26 miles; from Shreevillipoottore S.S.E. 65 miles; from Tinnevelly E.S.E. 19 miles; from Tuticorin S.W. 20 miles; from the sea W. 14 miles. On right bank of Tamrapurny.

TENCAUSHY (தென்காசி - tengási, *Tam.* tenkási *). From (ten, tam. south + káshi, san. benares) [ten]. Sanscrit name (dakshinakáshi), meaning the same.——**(1)** Talook, Tinnevelly district. Tahsildar's pay Rs. 175. Area 374 square miles. Population 154,940. Language Tamul. W. of district. Bounded south by Ambasamoodram talook; east by Shuncaraneinarcoil and Tinnevelly talooks; west by the Western ghauts; and north by Shuncaraneinarcoil talook. This tract was ruled by several independent kings in the time of the Paundy [q.v.] dynasty [raj]. Many of the richest villages in the bay formed by the mountains around Courtallam belong to the Travancore government [shencottah], which in ancient times, and when Tinnevelly was constantly plunged in war, temporarily possessed a considerable area here, as well as in the extreme south of the district. The country is undulating with a succession of hills and valleys. Red clays and loams prevail to the west, sandy and poor soil to the east and south. At the northern boundary a few villages belong to the black cotton series, being outlying patches of the great black cotton plain [regar] of north-eastern Tinnevelly. Agriculture is the chief pursuit of the people; weaving is also prevalent but is declining. Jaggery [q.v.] is manufactured to a small extent. Trade in rice [q.v.] and cloth is carried on with Travancore and coffee [q.v.]; and spices, the products of the western ghauts [q.v.], are also exported from this talook. The Chittaur, with its various branches, drains an extent of mountains not much less than the basin of the Tamrapurny, and though a much smaller river, irrigates a large area in many villages spread over a wide bay enclosed by a bend in the direction of the range, as well as along its course eastward to the limits of the talook and beyond till it joins the Tamrapurny a few miles north-east of Tinnevelly town. The villages near the foot of the mountains obtain two crops [vellaumay], one from each monsoon [q.v.]; those further out only one in the north-east monsoon. The river and its affluents are crossed by numerous anicuts [q.v.] feeding irrigation channels [q.v.] and many tanks [q.v.]. Zemindarries:—Aunacoolam, Chokkamputty, Coolayanairy, Coonnacoody, Cumbanairy poothoocoody, Manadicherry, Neinaur agaram, Oormeniyalagyaun, Ootoomullay, Shivanaudanore, Shooranday, Sillarayporavoo, Veirauvicoolam, Vullam. Places of archæological interest:—Courtallam, Panboolly, Shivalaurcoolam, Shooranday, Tencaushy, Yilanjy. The leading places, &c., in the talook are the following.——*Aulangoolam* (ஆலங்குளம் - álangulam, Tam.). From (álam, tam. banyan tree, ficus bengalensis, linn. + kulam, tam. tank). Village; pop. 2,591; acres 3,022; lat. 8° 52′; long. 77° 33′; from cusbah E.S.E 15 miles. Travellers' bungalow [q.v.], and chuttram [q.v.].——*Cadayanullore* (கடையநல்லூர் - kadaiyanallúr, Tam.). From (kadaiyan, tam. a man of the laboring class + nal, tam. good + úr, tam. village). Town; pop. 8,200; acres 5,650; lat. 9° 05′; long. 77° 23′; from Tencaushy N.N.E. 8 miles; from Tinnevelly N.W. 34 miles. Trading town east of a ridge of low hills of same name at junction of Travancore and Atchancoil passes [ghaut]. Cloths largely manufactured by Lubbays [q.v.] for exportation to Travancore. Chuttram [q.v.]. On main road from Courtallam to Madura.——*Chittaur* (சிற்றாறு - shittáru, Tam.). See sep. title.——*Chokkamputty* (சொக்கம்பட்டி - shokkambatti, Tam.). From (shokkan, tam. shiva, the beautiful + patti, tam. village). Village; pop. 6,215; acres 30,363; lat. 9° 08′; long. 77° 24′; from Tencaushy N.N.E. 12 miles; from Tinnevelly N.W. 36 miles. Seat of an ancient zemindarry [q.v.] recently dismembered and now held in eighteen mittahs [q.v.]. Old zemindar's palace in ruins.——*Coolashekharaputty* (குலசேகரப்பட்டி - kulaségarappatti, Tam.). From (kulashékhara, san. the family head, proper name + patti, tam. village). Coolashekharan's hamlet. Village; acres 5,618; lat. 8° 57′; long. 77° 25′; from Tencaushy E.S.E. 5 miles; from Tinnevelly N.W. 26 miles. Chuttram [q.v.]. On main road from Courtallam to Tinnevelly. Inhabited principally by Shaunaur [q.v.] who carry on extensive manufacture of palmyra [q.v.] jaggery [q.v.] and sugar-candy [sugar].——*Coolayanairy* (குலையனேரி - kulaiyanéri, Tam.). From (kolaiñan, tam. a hunter who lives by killing + éri, tam. tank). A mittah village; pop. 1,849; lat. 9° 01′; long. 77° 28′; from cusbah E.N.E. 9 miles. One of eighteen mittahs into which old Chokkamputty zemindarry has been split up. Peshcush Rs. 674.——*Courtallam* (குற்றாலம் - kuttálam, Tam.). See sep. title.——*Cumbanairy poothoocoody* (கம்பனேரிப்புதுக்குடி - kambanérripputhukkudi, Tam.). From (kamban, tam. proper name + éri, tam. tank + puthu, tam. new + kudi, tam. village). Zemindarry village; pop. 3,506; square miles $1\frac{1}{16}$; lat. of village 9° 04′; long. 77° 24′; from Tencaushy N.N.E. 9 miles; from Tinnevelly N.W. 32 miles. One of the eighteen mittahs [q.v.] into which old Chokkamputty zemindarry [q.v.] has been split up. Peshcush Rs. 20,063.——*Krishnaupooram* (கிருஷ்ணாபுரம் - kiruttinappuram, Tam.). From (krishna, san. god vishnu + pura, san. town). Village; pop. 3,683; acres 4,344; lat. 9° 06′; long. 77° 23′; from Tencaushy N.N.E. 10 miles. Inhabited by bramins and has a tank Hanoomanta teertam.——*Melpavoor* (மேலப்பாவூர் - mélappavúr, Tam.). From (mél, tam. west + pávu, tam. yarn + úr, tam. village). Town; pop. 2,156; acres 2,174; lat. 8° 57′; long. 77° 25′; from Tencaushy E. 5 miles; from Tinnevelly N.W. 26 miles. On the right bank of a canal from the Chittaur. Large irrigation tank.——*Oormeniyalagyaun* (ஊர்மேனியழகியான் - úrméniyazhagiyán, Tam.). From (úr, tam. village + méni, tam. color + azhagu, tam. beauty); a beautiful village. Zemindarry village; pop. 2,345; lat. of village 9° 02′; long. 77° 24′; from Tencaushy N.E. 6 miles; from Tinnevelly N.W. 30 miles. One of eighteen mittahs [q.v.] into which old Chokkamputty zemindarry [q.v.] has been split up. Peshcush Rs. 2,122.——*Ootoomullay* (ஊற்றுமலை - úttumalai,* Tam.). From (úttu, tam. spring + malai, tam. hill). Zemindarry village; pop. 2,630; acres 74,049; lat. of village 8° 59′; long. 77° 34′; from Tencaushy E.N.E. 15 miles; from Tinnevelly N.N.W. 21 miles. One of the most important zemindarries in district, consisting of fifty-two villages and 79,850 acres, and paying a peshcush [q.v.] of Rs. 26,962. Contains a considerable area of well-watered land under Chittaur river. Zemindar [q.v.] belongs to Maravar [q.v.] caste, and is a descendant of one of the ancient Tinnevelly poligars [q.v.]. The seat of zemindarry [q.v.] has since been transferred to Veerakeralampoothore a zameen [q.v.] village on the banks of the Chittaur, 7 miles south-west of Ootoomullay.——*Shivanaudanore* (சிவநாடானூர் - shivanádánúr, Tam.). From (shivanádán, tam. proper name + úr, tam. village). Zemindarry village; pop. 1,532; lat. of village 8° 54′; long. 77° 24′; from Tencaushy S.E. 5 miles; from Tinnevelly W.N.W. 25 miles. One of eighteen mittahs into which old Chokkamputty zemindarry has been split up. Peshcush Rs. 474.——*Shooranday* (சுரண்டை - shurandai, Tam.). From (shuram, tam. barren tract + andai, tam. vicinity). Village; pop. Ayan shooranday 4,189; Zameen shooranday 3,290; acres 6,028; lat. 8° 58′; long. 77° 28′; from Tencaushy E.N.E. 8 miles; from Tinnevelly N.W. 25 miles. Shiva temple with inscriptions. Weekly fair on Monday. Mission bungalow [q.v.]. Peshcush Rs. 668.——*Tencaushy* (தெங்காசி - tengási, Tam.). See below.——*Veerakeralampoothore* (வீரக்கேரளம்புதூர் - vírakkéralambuthúr, Tam.). From (vírakkéralan, tam. proper name + puthu, tam. new + úr, tam. village); after Veerakeralan one of the princes of Travancore. Zemindarry, Village; pop. 5,198; lat. of village 8° 56′; long. 77° 29′; from Tencaushy E. 10 miles; from Tinnevelly N.W. 22 miles. See Ootoomullay above.——**(2)** Town, Talook head-quarters; Tinnevelly dist., Tencaushy tal.; pop. 12,861; acres 3,813; lat. 8° 58′; long. 77° 21′; from Madras S.W. 344 miles; from Palamcottah W.N.W. 34 miles; from Shermadevy N.W. 26 miles; from Shreevillipoottore S.S.W. 44 miles; from Tinnevelly N.W. 31 miles; from Tuticorin W. 59 miles. On Tinnevelly-Quilon road and in left bank of Seetanuddy. Formerly fortified, but fortifications destroyed during poligar [q.v.] war in 1790. Old Shiva temple with inscriptions. A number of rude stone monuments are to be seen. Five dolmens [coday cull] in the temple of Vishwanauta sawmy. Sepulchral urns [mady moottaur tauzhy] abound. Of the five large temples in present use, three are to Shiva [q.v.] and two to Vishnoo [q.v.]. Of these, Caushy vishwanauta sawmy is finest and best sculptured. Two car festivals [ratotsavam]. Old Roman catholic church built in 1786, at which a festival is celebrated in September. Is a busy centre of trade. One-third of the population are Lubbays [q.v.], principally employed in manufacture of cloths exported to Travancore. Two bridges across Chittaur. There is a Tamul proverb:—தெங்காசி ஆசாரம் திருநெல்வேலி உபசாரம்—"the manners of Tencaushy, and the ceremoniousness of Tinnevelly;" both are hollow. The following are the travelling distances by road from Tencaushy to different places:—

To	Viá	Miles and Furlongs.	
Palamcottah ...	Aulangoolam	34	4
Palamcottah ...	Cadayam	38	3
Panagoody ...	......	54	0
Quilon	Cottacaray	63	6
Trivandrum ...	Cottacaray	94	3

TENKY (पाकत - pákata, *Mahr.*; తెంకి - tenki, *Tel.*; திருக்கை - tirukkai, *Tam.*). Tam. from (tirugu, tam. to twist); twisted or rugged one. Title otherwise Ray, Skate, Thornback. The genus Trygon, trygonidæ, batoidei, plagiostomata, chondropterygii, pisces [matsyam, 50], of naturalists [jantoo]. Sting rays. Body smooth or with tubercles; color very variable. The species best known to the natives are the Shark tenky and the Tiger tenky to which they add several other genera; see below.——*Banded tenky* (ముకాలతెంకి - múkalatenki, Tel.; சப்பைத்திருக்கை - shappaittirukkai, Tam.). Tel. from (múka, tel. crowd + tenki, tel. ray, trygon genus), from going in shoals. Tam. from (shappai, tam. flat + tirukkai, tam. thornback, trygon genus). Tel. also (rájntenki), meaning shining ray fish. Tam also (tappukkúli), meaning small drum + stunted ore. flat. short one. Myliobatis nienhofii, myliobatidæ, batoidei, plagiostomata, chondropterygii [matsyam, 51], of naturalists. Alias Raja and Mookarah tenkee; Raja fasciata, nieuhofii. Raja tenkee from teloogoo; mookarah tenkee from teloogoo. Fleshy prolongation of snout short; body smooth; olive superiorly, tinged externally with reddish hue and a dark outer margin to the disk; young have about seven blue bands across the disk and two more between or close to the eyes; as the fish increases in size, first the bands on the head disappear and finally those on the body; sea. Myliobatis aquila is Eagle ray or Whip ray.——*Black-tail tenky* (राज - rája, San.; ఈలతెంకి - ílitenki, Tel.; തിരണ്ടി - tiranti, Mal.; கருவாற்றிருக்கை - karuváttirukkai, Tam.). San. from (ráj, san. to shine); from variegated back. Tel. from (íla, tel. shyness + tenki, tel. ray, trygon genus). Mal. from (tira, mal. wave + andu, mal. to approach). Tam. from (karumai, tam. blackness + vál, tam. tail + tirukkai, tam. thorn, back, trygon genus). Ætobatis narinari, myliobatidæ, batoidei, plagiostomata, chondropterygii [matsyam, 51], of naturalists. Specific name perhaps from bengalee. Alias Ætobatis flagellum, indica, laticeps, latirostris; Goniobatis flagellum, macroptera; Myliobatis eeltenkee, narinari; Raja flagellum, guttata, narinari, quinqueaculeata; Stoasodon narinari. Eeltenkee from teloogoo; raja from sanscrit. Comparative proportions vary greatly with age; grayish-olive sometimes greenish-olive or leaden-gray above, usually covered from beyond the occiput with numerous dirty-white or bluish spots edged with black; abdominal surface white; tail black; iris golden-green, teeth greenish-yellow; in the immature the back is of a deep leaden color, and the spots hardly apparent; seas and estuaries upwards of 6 feet in width;

eaten raw and salted; livers employed to produce oil and fins exported to china with those of other rays, skates and sharks [soorah]; no other common species here.——*Bristly tenky* (राज - rája, San.; முள்ளந்திருக்கை - mullandirukkai, Tam.). Title from spines. San. from (ráj, san. to shine). Tam. from (mul, tam. thorn + tirukkai, tam. thornback, trygon genus). Title otherwise Sting ray. Urogymnus asperrimus, trygonidæ, batoidei, plagiostomata, chondropterygii [matsyam, 50], of naturalists. Alias Anacanthus asperrimus; Raja asperrima; Rhachinotus africanus; Urogymnus africanus. Raja from sanscrit. Snout scarcely projecting; body densely covered with small heart-shaped scales, between which are numerous thorns which are generally erect, and are continued posteriorly to the first fifth of the tail, where they cease; on the pectoral fins are numerous small conical spines, irrespective of those over the body amongst the tubercles; greenish above, white beneath; sea; no other common species here.——*Flat tenky* (மட்டத்திருக்கை - mattattirukkai, Tam). Tam. from (mattam, tam. flat + tirukkai, tam. thornback, trygon genus). Tam. also (kuruvittirukkai), meaning small bird + thornback. Rhinoptera adspersa, myliobatidæ, batoidei, plagiostomata, chondropterygii [matsyam, 51], of naturalists. Notch on snout shallow; greenish brown superiorly, becoming lighter at the edges of the disk; sea; no other common species here.——*Large tenky* (తెంకికుంచె - tenkikunche, Tel.; பெருந்திருக்கை - perundirukkai, Tam.). Tam. from (perum, tam. big + tirukkai, tam. thornback, trygon genus). Tel. also (rájatenkikunche); (rájatenki), maning bright ray fish. Tam. also (tappukkuttittirukkai), meaning small tabour + short + thornback, trygon genus. Pteroplatea micrura, trygonidæ, batoidei, plagiostomata, chondropterygii [matsyam, 50], of naturalists. Alias Dasyatis microura; Pastinaca annulata, kunsul; Pteroplatea annulata; Raja tenkee kunsul, micrura, pæcilura; Trygon pæcilurus. Raja tenkee from teloogoo Skin smooth; reddish-brown; tail annulated with white and brown; superiorly in the centre of each light ring there is generally a brown spot; young are covered all over with small brown spots; sea; no other common species here.——*Shark tenky* (गोवालपाकत - góválapákata, Mahr.; ترکامچّهی - tirkámaççhí, Hind.; వాలుగతెంకి - válugatenki, Tel.; ஆடுவாலாண்டிருக்கை - áduválándirukkai, Tam.). Hind. from tamul, meaning tenky fish. Tel. from (váluga, tel. wallago attu + tenki, tel. ray, trygon genus). Tam. from (ádu, tam. to shake + vál, tam. tail + tirukkai, tam. thorn back, trygon genus). Trygon sephen, trygonidæ, batoidei, plagiostomata, chondropterygii [matsyam, 50], of naturalists. Alias Hypolophus sephen; Raja sancur, sephen; Trygon forskalii. Length of tail three to four times that of the body; snout more obtuse in adults; upper surface of head and body and base of tail covered by thick, concave, or flat-headed, several-sided tubercles; upper surface of immature is reddish-brown; in adult lead-colored, becoming black in two-thirds of the tail; sea; grows to a large size; most common during south-west monsoon, when it approaches shore; from the skin of its back some of the shagreen of commerce used to be prepared; wounds inflicted by the spine of its tail are dangerous.——*Tiger tenky* (పులితెంకి - pulitenki, Tel.; ଶଂକୁଶ - sankush, Oor.; சோணகத்திருக்கை - shónagattirukkai, Tam.). Title from brown markings. Tel. from (puli, tel. tiger + tenki, tel. ray, trygon genus); cf. stegostoma tigrinum. Tam. from (jónaka, mal. mahomedan + tirukkai, tam. thornback, trygon genus); cf. trichiurus haumela. Title otherwise English ray. Trygon uarnak, trygonidæ, batoidei, plagiostomata, chondropterygii [matsyam, 50], of naturalists. Alias Pastinachus uarnak; Raja uarnak; Trygon ellioti, gerrardi, macrurus, pareh, pastinacoides, russellii, uarnacoides, undulatus, variegatas. Tail three to four times as long as body; colors vary according to age; up to when breadth of disk is about 9 inches the body is of a yellowish brown darkest along the back, and the abdomen white; a short distance beyond the commencement of the tail it is irregularly annulated with alternate narrow light brown, and broad or narrow dark brown rings; as age increases, black spots appear on body, and when it has attained 3 feet across its disk it is light brown or greenish-olive, covered with lighter and in some almost white spots, or reticulated with white lines, whilst the anterior extremity of the tail also shows the remains of the rings; the adult is uniformly brownish or greenish-olive; iris golden; occasionally there are light spots on the posterior portion of the disk; in the cold season, these fish are perceived springing out of water; they devour large quantities of small fish; seas and estuaries; immature captured in backwaters; wounds from their caudal spines are much dreaded; attain 5 feet or more across disk. Trygon vastinaca is Sting ray or Fire flaire.

TEPPAM (తెప్ప - teppa, *Tel.*; தெப்பம் - teppam, *Tam.*). From (télu, tel. to float). Floating raft, catamaran [catamaran, inam].——*Teppacoolam* (தெப்பக்குளம் - teppakkulam, Tam.). From (above + kulam, tam. tank). A square stone tank [q.v.] for religious uses, especially for the floating festival [conair].

TEROO (தெரு - teru, *Tam.*). From (tiri, tam. to walk). Street.——*Tara* (തറ - tara, Mal.). Similar to (teru, tam.). A village or quarter. The tara was formerly the Nayar [q.v.] territorial unit of organization for civil purposes. The taras were governed by representatives of the Nayar caste, styled carnavens [q.v.] or elders. When combined in deliberation, the taras formed a coot [q.v.] or assembly of the naud [q.v.]. Is the west coast equivalent of the village east of the ghauts [q.v.]. See vol. II, 104.——*Tarwaud* (തറവാട് - taravátu, Mal.). See sep. title.——*Toorla* (తుర్ల - turla, Tel.). From (turru, tel. village). Locative plural. Suffix in place names; as Ventoorla, meaning village of the ears of corn.——*Toorty* (తుర్తి - turti, Tel.). Oblique form of (turru, tel. village); cf. toorla. Village.

TETTAH (தேற்று - téttá, *Tam.*). From (tír, tam. to clean). Same as Clearing nut.

TEVAN (தேவன் - tévan, *Tam.*). The tamul form of the sanscrit Deva or god. There is a tradition that they are supposed to be descended from Indran [q.v.]. Plural is Tevar. The tribal designation of the Marava race in Ramnaud, Madura, Shivagunga, and Tinnevelly [marava].——*Tegnapatam* (தேவனாம்பட்டணம் - tévanámbattanam, Tam.). Native name of the site of Fort St. David.

TEY (தே - té, *Tam.*). Grace.——*Teppermaul* (தேப்பெருமாள் - tépperumál, Tam.). From (above + perumál, tam. vishnu, the great god). Vishnoo, the gracious god. Hindoo 2nd or pers name. Common among non-bramin veishnavites [peyar].

TEYMEZ (تیمیز - temez, *Hind.*). Breakfast [khanah, teeny].

TEZAUB (अम्ल - amla, *San.*; تیزاب - tezáb, *Pers.* and *Hind.*; اسام - asám, *Malay*; ಹುಳಿ - huli, *Can.*; ପୁଲିପୁ - pulipu, *Too.*; పులుసు - pulusu, *Tel.*; പുളിപ്പ് - pulippu, *Mal.*; புளிப்பு - pulippu, *Tam.*). Title from persian. San. means sour. Pers. from (tez, pers. corrosive + áb, pers. water). Mal. from tamul. Tam. from (puli, tam. sourness). Acid, mineral or vegetable [drauvacam]. Taste is sour; in the stronger kinds acrid and corrosive; combines with water in every proportion, with a condensation of volume and evolution of heat; volatilised or decomposed at a moderate heat; changes the purple colors of vegetables to a bright red; unites in definite proportions with the alkalies [cauram], earths [munn], and metallic oxides [paspam], and forms salts [ooppoo]. The following are principal tezaubs [poolipp]. For Benzoic acid, see Sambrauny poo; for Arsenious acid, Soofaid soombal; for Citric acid, Yelimitchay poolipp.——*Gandhac tezaub* (गन्धकद्रावक - gandhakadrávaka, San.; ماءالکبریت - máulkibrít, Ar.; تیزاب گوگرد - tezábigogird, Pers.; گندک کا تیزاب - gandakkátezáb, Hind. and Dec.; ಗಂಧಕದ್ರಾವಕ - gandhakadrávaka, Can.; గంధకద్రావకము - gandhakadrávakamu, Tel.; ഗന്ധകദ്രാവകം - gandhakadrávakam, Mal.; ගන්ධකරස - gandhakarasa, Singh.; கந்தகத்திராவகம் - kandagattirávagam, Tam.). Title from hindostany. San. from (gandhaka, san. sulphur + drávaka, san. essence). Ar. from (má, ar. water + kibrít, ar. sulphur). Pers. from (tezáb, pers. acid + gogird, pers. sulphur). Hind. from (gandak, hind. sulphur + tezáb, pers. acid). Tel. from sanscrit. Singh. from (gandhaka, san. sulphur + rasa, san. essence). Pers. also (arkigogird), meaning sulphur essence. Hind. also (gandhakkáitr), meaning essence of sulphur. Sulphuric acid. Otherwise Vitriolic acid, Oil of vitriol, Spirits of vitriol. Acidum sulphuricum of chemists. Colorless oily fluid, acrid, corrosive, and intensely sour. Procured by burning a mixture of about eight parts of sulphur [gandhac] and one of nitre [shorah] in a furnace so placed that the resulting fumes may pass into close chamber containing water; the water gradually becomes a dilute sulphuric acid, and the acid itself is procured by evaporation; its manufacture here is very ancient. Is a corrosive poison. Astringent properties render it a valuable medicine in weakness, and relaxation of the digestive organs.——*Namak tezaub* (लवणद्रावक - lavanadrávaka, San.; ماءالملح - máulmilh, Ar.; تیزاب نمك - tezábinimak, Pers.; نمك کا تیزاب - namakkátezáb, Hind. and Dec.; లవణద్రావకము - lavanadrávakamu, Tel.; ഉപ്പുദ്രാവകം - uppudrávakam, Mal.; ලුණුරස - lunurasa, Singh.; உப்புத்திராவகம் - upputtirávagam, Tam.). Ar. from (má, ar. water + milh, ar. salt). Pers. from (tezáb, pers. acid + nimak, pers. salt). Hind. from (namak, pers. salt + tezáb, pers. acid). Tel. from (lavana, san. salt + drávaka, san. essence). Singh. means salt + essence. Mal. and Tam. from (uppu, tam. salt + drávaka, san. liquid). Pers. also (arkinimak), meaning salt essence. Muriatic acid. Otherwise Marine acid, Spirit of salt, Hydrochloric acid, Chlorohydric acid. Acidum hydrochloricum of chemists. Pungent colorless incombustible gas with intensely acid properties; in solution, much used as a solvent. When pure it is colorless. Veidyans [q.v.] prepare it in the following manner:—take of common salt [ooppoo] 8 pollums [q.v.], of alum [padicauram] 6 pollums, of bengal gram vinegar [caudy] 8 pollums; let the common salt and alum be first well dried and pounded together, then add the other ingredient, and distill till the whole of the muriatic acid is disengaged and condensed in the receiver. Used diluted in medicine as antalkaline and tonic; acts locally as a caustic. Used specially as a solvent of metals [loham].——*Shoreyka tezaub* (यवक्षारद्रावक - yavaksháradrávaka, San.; ماءالابقر - máulabkar, Ar.; تیزاب شوره - tezábishorá, Pers.; شوری

کا تیزاب - shorekátezáb, Hind. and Dec.; ಸೋರುಪ್ಪುದ್ರಾವಕ - sóruppudrávaka, Can.; పెట్లుప్పుద్రావకము - petluppudrávakamu, Tel.; വെടിയുപ്പുദ്രാവകം - vetiyuppudrávakam, Mal.; වෙඩිලුණුරස - vedilunurasa, Singh.; பொட்டிலுப்புத்திராவகம் - pottilupputtirávagam, Tam.). Title from hindostany. San. from (yavakshára, san. saltpetre + drávaka, san. essence). Ar. from (má, ar. water + abkar, ar. nitre). Pers. from (tezáb, pers. acid + shorá, pers. nitre). Hind. from (shorá, hind. saltpetre + tezáb, pers. acid). Can. from (sóruppu, can. saltpetre + drávaka, can. acid). Tel. from (petluppu, can. saltpetre + drávaka, san. essence). Mal. from (vetiyuppu, mal. saltpetre + drávaka, san. essence). Singh. from (vedilunu, singh. saltpetre + rasa, san. essence). Tam. from (pottiluppu, tam. saltpetre + drávaka, san. liquid). Pers. also (arakishorá), meaning saltpetre essence. Nitric acid. Otherwise Aqua fortis. Acidum nitricum of chemists. Dense, colorless fluid; emits white, disagreeable fumes; taste is extremely sour and acrid, and the skin is idelibly tinged a yellow color by it. Veidyans [q.v.] prepare it as follows:—take of saltpetre [shorah] 20 pollums, of alum [padicauram] 16 pollums, of bengal gram vinegar [candy] 18 pollums; mix and distill with an increasing heat till the whole of the acid is condensed in the receiver; the operation is conducted in common earthen vessels; the product is a mixture of nitrous and nitric acids. A corrosive poison; when diluted, it forms a lotion for indolent ulcers. Employed in chemical processes in dyeing [shauyam] and in medicine Impure nitric acid is Tezaub i noocrah.——*Sirkeyka tezaub* (سرکے کا تیزاب - sirkekátezáb, Hind.). Hind. from (sirkah, pers. vinegar + above). Acetic acid. Otherwise Methyloxalic acid, Methylformic acid, Pyroligneous acid, Wood acid, Wood vinegar. Acidum aceticum of chemists. Obtained by the fermentation of saccharine matter and the distillation of wood. ——*Tezaub i faurook* (تیزاب فاروق - tezábifárúk, Hind.). From (above + fárúk, ar. distinguishing). Nitro muriatic acid. Otherwise Aqua regia, Nitro hydrochloric acid. A mixture of nitric and hydrochloric acid, which will dissolve gold [pon] and platinum [goorootwam].——*Tezaub i noocrah* (تیزاب نقرہ - tezábinukrah, Hind.). From (above + nukrah, pers. silver). Impure nitric acid [shoreyka tezaub].

THAKOOR (ٹھاکر - thákur, *Hind.*). Chief. Also barber. There is a Hindostany proverb:—نائی کی برات میں سبھی ٹھاکر— "in a barber's marriage procession all are thakoors."

THUG (स्थग - st'haga, *San.*; ٹھگ - thug, *Hind.*; ತಂತಿಕಳ್ಳ - tantikalla, *Can.*; ఉర్లవాడు - urlavádu, *Tel.*; உரித்துலுக்கன் - urittulukkan, *Tam.*). Title from sanscrit. San. means a cheat. Can. from (tanti, can. wire + kalla, can. thief), from stretching wire across the road, over which travellers trip and fall, though this is not their usual method. Tel. from (uri, tel. noose + vádu, tel. personal suffix), from using noose. Tam. from (uri, tam. noose + tulakkan, tam. mahomedan). Hind. also (phánsigar), meaning noose doer or strangler. A robber and assassin of a peculiar class, who sallying forth in a gang of smaller or larger numbers, and in the character of wayfarers either on business or pilgrimage, fall in with other travellers on the road, and having gained their confidence take a favorable opportunity of strangling them by throwing a turban [q.v.] or handkerchief [roomaul] from behind round their necks. This is the name best known in the north. Thugs have slang terms and phrases; and Ramoosy [q.v.], or slang phraseology of thugs, is the same all over india, being extremely ancient. The thugs state that in immolating the victims they obey the deity of their worship, namely the goddess Bhawauny [q.v.]; notwithstanding the adherence to hindoo rites of worship observable among them, a very considerable number are mussalmans [q.v.]. The symbol of worship is a pickaxe of iron, known by the name of Nishaun [q.v.]; with every gang there is carried a Nishaun, which is their standard. Previous to commencing an expedition, the Nishaun is taken into the open fields, in the expectation of an omen [shacoonam]; if an owl [ooloocam], jay [indian jay], jackal [q.v.], or ass [gadhah], calls out, or moves to the right-hand side, the omen is looked upon as favorable; but if to the left, it is considered unfavorable and the project is abandoned. Thugs disdain every species of stealing that has not been preceded by the perpetration of murder; they adopt no other method of killing but strangulation; the implement is a handkerchief [roomaul] or any other convenient strip of cloth; after a murder they invariably bury the body immediately. The crime is hereditary in families; they recruit their numbers from all classes. In every gang of thugs there are one or more Jemadars [q.v.] who hold that rank in consequence of their wealth and influence; the jemadars assigns to every thug the particular duty he is to undertake. Next to the jemadar, the most important person is the Bhuttote, or strangler; his handkerchief is a piece of fine strong cotton [q.v.] cloth, about a yard long; at one end a knot is made, and the cloth is kept ready for use in front of the waist band; the handkerchief is called Roomaul [q.v.]; the bhuttote follows the person, and on the pre-concerted signal being given, the handkerchief is seized, with the knot in the left hand, and right hand being some inches further up; in which manner it is thrown over the head of the person to be strangled from behind; the two hands are crossed as the victim falls. To aid the bhuttote, another thug is appointed under the denomination of Sumsoeah; to seize the person by the wrists if he be on foot, and by one of his legs if he be on horseback, and so to pull him down. A convenient spot to murder is denominated a Bhill. Of mussalman thugs, some are to be found of every sect, Sheikh [q.v.], Syed [q.v.], Moghul [q.v.] and Pataun [q.v.]; among the hindoos, the castes chiefly to be met with are Bramins [q.v.], Rajpoots [q.v.] and Holeyar [q.v.]. All, as above said, worship Bhawauny [bhawauny, jauty].

TICCA (ٹھیکا - thiká, *Hind.*). Fare, fixed price on contract. Ticcagharry is a hired carriage.

TICKOR (ٹکور - tíkor, *Hind.*). Distinguish from Tikhar under Teak. Botanically Garcinia [ractaumram] pedunculata, roxb., guttiferæ [vricsham, 22]. Tree, 60 feet; leaves opposite, short-petioled, oblong or obovate-oblong, entire, smooth on both sides, with large parallel veins; flowers terminal, peduncled; male ones numerous, forming small trichotomous panicles on separate trees; females solitary; calyx of two opposite pairs of nearly equal sepals; petals four, alternate with the segments of the calyx, and nearly of the same length; berry large, round, smooth, yellow when ripe; seeds ten, reniform, arillate Fruit very large; rich yellow when ripe; exceedingly acid; used in curries [q.v.] and for acidulating water.

TIDAL (திடல் - tidal, *Tam.*). Rising ground; a flat shoal in a river.

TIDDAH (शलभ - shalabha, *San.*; टोळ - tóla, *Mahr.*; جراد - jarád, *Ar.*; ملخ - malakh, *Pers.*; ٹڈا - tiddá, *Hind.* and *Dec.*; ಮಿಡತೆ - midite, *Can.*; మొంటె - monte, *Too.*; మిడత - midata, *Tel.*; വെട്ടുകിളി - vettukili, *Mal.*; வெட்டுக்கிளி - vettukkili, *Tam.*). Title from hindostany. San. from (shal, san. to shake). Ar. from (jarada, ar. to strip off herbage). Tel. from (midiyu, tel. to hop). Mal. from (vettu, mal. to cut + kili, mal. bird). Tam. from (vettu, tam. to cut + kili, tam. grasshopper) [tattoo kily]. Tam. also (mazhaikkili), meaning grain grasshopper, locust appearing before rains; (tavittukkili), meaning bran-brown locust, the small locust. Terms synonymous with family Locustidæ, orthoptera, hemimetabola, insecta [poochy], of naturalists [jantoo]. Locusts. Upwards of twenty species are known. They appear in large flights, committing great damage during progress. The small locust is edible.

TIGALA (ತಿಗಳ - tigala, *Can.*). From (tikka, can. stammering). The canarese for Tamulian.

TIGER (व्याघ्र - vyághra, *San.*). Prefix [pooly].——*Tiger's claw* (विंचू - vinchú, Mahr.; بچھو - bicçhú, Hind.; తేలుకొండి - télukondi, Tel.; தேள்கொடுக்கு - télgodukki, Tam.). Title from color and spots of flowers. Mahr. from (vrishchika, san. scorpion). Hind. means scorpion, from curved hooks of fruit resembling scorpion's tail. Tel. from (télu, tel. scorpion + kondi, tel. sting). Tam. from (tél, tam. scorpion + kodukku, tam. sting). Hind. also (bálhjorí). Tel. also (garudamukku), meaning braminy kite + beak. Title otherwise Devil's claw, Garoodan's beak, Scorpion sting. Botanically Martynia diandra, glox., pedalineæ [vricsham, 100]. Bush 3–4 feet with large coarse leaves, of rampant growth; flowers two inches, white, pale, rose-colored, stained with orange below on the inside, and stained on the limb above with five central dark purple spots; rather disagreeable odour; the seed pods are size of an almond [baudam], black, with two long horns proceeding from one end. ——*Tiger's foot* (మేకమడుగు - mekamadugu, Tel.; പുലിച്ചുവട് - puliççuvatu, Mal.; දිවිඅඩිය - diviadiya, Singh.; சிவதை - shivathai, Tam.). Title from resemblance of leaf. Tel. from (mekamu, tel. beast + adugu, tel. foot). Mal. from (puli, mal. tiger + chuvatu, mal. foot mark). Singh. from (divi, singh. tiger + adiya, singh. foot). Tam. from (shiva, tam. to redden). Singh. also (divipasuru), meaning tiger's foot; (divipahuru), meaning tiger's claws. Tam. also (púnaikkírai), meaning cat greens, from silky hairy leaves. Title otherwise Cat's greens, Tiger's claw. Botanically Ipomæa [calamby] pestigridis, linn., convolvulaceæ [vricsham, 93]. Alias Convolvulus pestigridis. Stems round, hairy; leaves palmately five to seven-lobed; lobes ovate-acute, silky and hairy; peduncles many-flowered, as long as the leaf; heads of flowers surrounded by six to eight ovate-linear hairy bracts; corolla white, hairy; common in hedges, flowering nearly all the year. Sand-binder [manal]. ——*Tiger's milk* (अगरु - agaru, San.; گیوا - gewá, Pers.; کیوگهرو - kayugahru, Malay; తెల్లచెట్టు - tellachettu, Tel.; ଗୁଣ - gnua, Oor.; കമ്മട്ടി - kammatti, Mal.; තෙලකිරිය - telakíriya, Singh.; அகில் - agil, Tam.). Title from quality of juice and smoke. San. from (a, san. privative suffix + guru, san. heavy), light [eagle-wood]. Malay from (kayu, malay, wood + gahru, malay, from sanscrit). Tel. from (tella, tel. white + chettu, tel. tree). Mal. from (karma, san. work + kri, san. to perform); used for procuring abortion. Tel. also (tillachettu), from tamul; (chilla). Tam. also (tillai), meaning seashore tree. Title otherwise Blinding tree, Cametty eagle-wood, Gava, Gheria, Spurgewort. Botanically Excæcaria [agaroo] agallocha, müller, var. camettia, euphorbiaceæ [vricsham, 118]. Alias Arbor excœcans; Commia cochin-chinensis; Excæcaria camettia. Excæcaria, producing blindness. Agallocha, from false supposition that it yielded eagle-wood [q.v.]. Camettia from malayalam. Small tree or shrub; leaves ovate or elliptic; obtuse at the base, entire or crenate-serrulate; male spikes amentiform, dense-flowered, cylindric; female racemes shorter than the male spikes, and in separate branches, both axillary, solitary, or rarely twin; bracts destitute of distinct glands; male calyx sessile, covered by the bract, female sepals ovate, with one gland on both sides of the base inside; anthers long-exserted after flowering; capsule sulcately three-lobed; flowers greenish; sea-coast tree; common in salt backwaters [cauyal]. Juice which exudes from green bark is poisonous and blinding; even smoke has same effect; juice applied to inveterate ulcers; leaves also in decoction; a caoutchouc [pauchonty] may be prepared from juice. Wood only used for fuel and charcoal [adooppkary]; very soft; spongy.

TIKRY (पुनर्नवा - punarnavá, *San.*; घेटोळी - ghétólí, *Mahr.*; ٹکڑی - tikrí, *Hind.*; ٹھکری کا جھاڑ - thikríkájhár, *Dec.*; ಬಳೆವಡಕಿಗಿಡ - baḷevadakigida, *Can.*; అటికమామిడి - atikamámidi, *Tel.*; തവിഴാമ - tavizháma, *Mal.*; மூக்கறட்டை - múkkarattai, *Tam.*). Title from hindostany. San. from (punar, san. again + nava, san. new); growing when cut [shauranay]. Can. from (bale, can. surrounding + vadaku, can. fracture + gida, can. plant). Tel. from (atika, tel. pot + mámidi, tel. mangifera indica, linn.); used as potherb. Mal. from (tavizhu, mal. to creep along); spreading. Tam. from (múkku, tam. nose + arattu, tam. to wail). San. also (sinádiká), meaning having white leaf-stalks; (shót'haghní), meaning swelling destroyer; (punarbhava), meaning again born; applied specially to the red variety. Hind. also (gadhaparná); (sánt). Can. also (sanádikágida), meaning nervous plant; (bekkinaajjeballi), meaning cat + arabian jasmine, jasminum sambac, ait. + creeper. Tel. also (ádaatukumámidi), meaning female + the plant. Mal. also (tazhutáma); (tamizháma), by corruption. Tam. also (kadiyirattam), meaning intensity + blood; (periyamúkkarattai), meaning large + the plant; (sháttaranai); (shatticçáranai), meaning vomiting + trianthema monogyna, linn.; from root as an emetic. Title otherwise Cat's jasmine, Female pot mango, Pot mango, Spreading hogweed, Vomit shauranay. Botanically Bœrhaavia repens, linn., var. diffusa, nyctagineæ [vricsham, 105]. Alias Bœrhaavia diandra, diffusa, polimorpha. Low creeping plant with many diffused stalks, about two feet long; flowers pale rose-colored, much scattered on long branching peduncles from the axils and at the end of the branches; seeds brown, oblong, striated, very rough; leaves ovate, rather roundish, bright green above, whitish below; sometimes curled at the edges; white, or rose-colored flowers; flowering all year. Root given medicinally in powder as laxative and in infusion as vermifuge; taste slightly bitter and nauseous; a good expectorant, and prescribed in asthma; taken largely, acts as an emetic; poultice of leaves useful in abscesses; in pharm. nonofficinal. Small round leaves at joint of stalks are eaten. The variety procumbens is American or Upright hogweed, small red flowers. Other common species are:—repanda, verticillata.

TIL (तिल - tila, *San.*; تل - til, *Hind.*). From (til, san. to anoint). Gingelly seed [teilam]. Cf. Ramtii.——*Teilam* (तैल - taila, San.). See sep. title.——*Tel* (تیل - tel, Hind.). From (tila, san. sesa num indicum, linn.). Oil [yennay]. Telee is an oil man.——*Tilacam* (तिलक - tilaka, San.). Mark, compared to a seed of sesamum. A mark on the forehead and between the eyebrows, either as an ornament or a sectarial distinction [naumam, pottoo], generally the latter [matam]. Hence any ornament. Means also spotted or freckled. In composition expresses greatness or distinction. Plant name common to:—Cinnamomum iners, Clerodendron phlomoides, Vitex alata; see gloss. paragraphs.

TILLAY (தில்லை - tillai, *Tam.*). From (tirai, tam. sea), the tree affecting seashore situations. The plant Excæcaria agallocha [tiger's milk]. So Chidambaram, from the tree being there found.——*Tillainayagam* (தில்லைநாயகம் - tillainâyagam, Tam.). From (above + náyaka, san. lord). Epithet of Shiva, as worshipped at Chidambaram. Hindoo 2nd or pers. name. Common among non-bramins [peyar]. Appears short as Tillay.

TIMINGILAM (वाजातिमि - vájatimi, *San.*; مگرمچھی - magarmaççhí, *Hind.*; ತಿಮಿಂಗಿಲ - timingila, *Can.*; తిమింగిలము - timingilamu, *Tel.*; തിമിംഗിലം - timingilam, *Mal.*; சிறைத் திமிங்கிலம் - shiraittimingilam, *Tam.*). San. from (vája, san. wing + timi, san. whale). Hind. from (magar, hind. alligator + maççhí, hind. fish). Tel. from (timi, san. whale + gila, san. devourer). Tam. from (shirai, tam. fin + timingilam, tam. whale devourer). Title otherwise Finback, Finner, Pikewhale, Rorqual. Balænoptera indica, balænidæ, cetacea, mammalia [sastanam, 31], of naturalists [jantoo]. Mysticete or Whalebone whales are distinguished from sperm whales which belong to the family Physeteridæ by having baleen or whalebone in their mouths instead of teeth. They comprise genus Balæna or right-whales, and genus Balænoptera or fin-whales. The Right-whales have no fin on the back. They are not found in the intertropical seas. Fin-whales are distinguished by their longer and narrower bodies, rather smaller heads being one-fourth instead of one-third the length of the body, smaller mouths, shorter baleen, plaited throats, and smaller flippers; they have a dorsal fin behind the middle of the back, and the root of the tail is compressed laterally. They are more muscular and active animals than the Right-whales, and have a less amount of blubber and much shorter whalebone, consequently are not so much sought after by whalers, as the risk in attacking them is not compensated for by the commercial results. Many of them grow to enormous size, far exceeding any of the Right-whales. The whalebone hanging from roof of mouth on each side of tongue forms a sieve through which the animal strains his food from the vast gulps of water he takes in whilst feeding. The lower jaw has neither teeth nor baleen, but is furnished with fleshy lips. The Maldives and Seychelles are the head-quarters of such whalers as seek these whales. Nearchus, in B.C. 327, mentions having met with these whales in the Persian gulf. In 1858 one of 90 feet was standard at Quilon. American ships call at Cochin for stores during their cruises after these animals. But they are little hunted, being active and dangerous, and yielding indifferent whalebone, which is generally obtained from the Right whale. Whalebone is an albuminous tissue resembling horn [sing] and hair and forming the transition between those two substances. For the sperm-whale see Hoot.

TIMIRY (திமிரி - timiri, *Tam.*). From (timir, tam. dullness). Village; North arcot dist., arcot tal.; pop. 4,459; acres 2,874; lat. 12° 50′; long. 79° 21′; height 722 feet; from Arcot S.S.W. 6 miles; from Chittore S.S.E. 30 miles. On Arnee road. Small fort built by Timmakkaul, sister of Bommy reddy, who constructed the Vellore fort. After Mahomedans obtained possession of place, it was given, with a jagheer [q.v.] worth a lakh [q.v.] of rupees [q.v.], by the emperor Mahomed shah to a son of one of his ministers. Afterwards resumed by Nawaub Mahomed ally. Captured by Clive in 1751, and held by British till 1758, when it surrendered to D'Estainge. Major Munro recovered the town in 1760. Peroontimiry naud meant the great Timiry country, part of Palcoondra cottam in the ancient Tondaimundalam [q.v.].

TIMMA (తిమ్మడు - timmadu, *Tel.*). Monkey god. Feminine Timmy. Familiarly Timmoo. Hindoo 2nd or pers. name [peyar]. Similarly Timmappa, Timmayya. Timmy reddy was the ruler of Vellore locally believed to have built the fort of Arcot.

TINAY (कंगु - kangu, *San.*; वरी - vari, *Mahr.*; वरयि - varayi, *Conc.*; دخن - dukhn, *Ar.*; ارزن - arzan, *Pers.*; کنگنی - kangní, *Hind.*; کنگونی - kanguní, *Dec.*; ನವಣೆ - navane, *Can.*; ನವಣೆ - navane, *Too.*; కొఱ్ఱ - korra, *Tel.*; କଙ୍ଗୁ - kangu, *Oor.*; തിന - tina, *Mal.*; තනහල් - tanahal, *Singh.*; தினை - tinai, *Tam.*). Title from tamul [teen]. San. from (kank, san. to go); useful seed [bajrah]. Arabic; cf. seed toolsy. Hind. and Dec. from sanscrit. Tam. from (tin, tam. to eat). San. also (priyangu), meaning valued plant; (shyámá), meaning dark brown [shaumay, white datura]. Pers. also (ghal); (ulam). Hind. also (chenna), meaning cicer arietinum, linn. [bengal gram]; (rálá), meaning a variety of millet; (rál), panicum miliaceum, linn.; (kangu); (bírtiya); (kálákangní), meaning black variety. Can. also (kango); (árike); (tene); (sámeakki); (nernakki). Tam. also (korali), meaning inferior [mecca cholum, white tinay]; (shendinai), meaning red millet; (açcittinai), meaning acheen millet, a small variety from acheen; (anilváttinai), meaning squirrel-tail millet, a kind of white variety with ears supposed to resemble the tail of the squirrel [anil]. Greek κέγχρος; late greek ἔλυμον. Latin milium. Title otherwise Bengal grass, Cangny, Caucam, Chinese corn, Corra, Fine panic grass, Italian millet. Botanically Panicum [priyangoo] italicum, linn., gramineacæ [vricsham, 156]. Alias Echinolæna erythrosperma; Panicum erythrospermum, glomeratum; Pennisetum italicum; Setaria italica, melinis. Cereal; culms erect, 3–5 feet, round, smooth; roots issuing from the lower joints; margins of leaves hispid; mouths of sheaths bearded; spikes nodding; spikelets scattered; pedicels two to four-flowered, with smooth intermediate bristles; seeds small, roundish, straw-colored, pericarp brittle, with a round and partially pellucid grain. Cultivated in red loam; dry ground prepared in south in auvany [mausam] or august, on coromandel in aushweejam or october and caurteecam or november two months later; the land is ploughed four or five times, sheep-folded and cowdung applied; seed sown in south in arpisy or october, on coromandel in caurteecam or november and margashiram or december; sown broadcast while under growth two hoeings are used and there must be rain after each hoeing; cut after three or four months by hand or sickles, the sheaves are dried and brought to the threshing floor [calam]; then they are beaten with sticks and seeds are winnowed from the chaff; produce brought to market at once; average price, 16 imperial seers for 1 rupee. Boiled with milk, makes light diet for invalids. Good for pastry; nutritious, rather heating, sometimes parched; the quantity of straw, about 10 feet long and an inch in circumference, makes a fair compensation for the meanness of the ear. Two varieties; one straw yellow and the other reddish yellow. There is a Tamul proverb:—மலை அக்

தினை சுவாமிக்குத் தினை அத்தனை புஷ்பம்—"a flower, as "small as a millet-seed, is dedicated to an idol as large as a "mountain;" the grain is small.——*Black tinay* (ಕರಿಕೊರಲೆ - karikorale, Can.; కారుసొద - kárusoda, Tel.; கருந்தினை - karundinai, Tam.). Title from color of seed. Can. from (kari, can. black + korale, can. panicum glaucum, linn.). Tel. from (káru, tel. wild + soda, tel. panicum paludosum, roxb.). Tam. from (karumai, tam. blackness + tinai, tam. the millet). Botanically Panicum [priyangoo] indicum, linn., graminaceæ [vricsham, 156]. Culm prostrate, thin, branched; sheaths glabrous; leaves linear, glabrous or scattered above with a few hairs; thyrses very narrow, rays simple, very short, shorter than the spikelets; spikelets ovate, acute, glabrous; lower glume a half shorter than the florets, three-upper ones seven to eleven-nerved. Useless for feeding purposes; will not make hay, as it has but little undergrowth.——*Forest tinay* (ಕಾಡುನವಣೆ - kádunavane, Can.). Same as Wild coraly.——*Jackal tinay* (నక్కకొర్ర - nakkakorra, Tel.). Title from inferiority of plant. Tel. from (nakka, tel. fox + korra, tel. panicum italicum, linn.). Tel. also (nakirigaddi). Botanically Panicum [priyangoo] helvolum, l., graminaceæ [vricsham, 156]. Alias Panicum glaucum. Culm branched, 6 feet, sterile branches shorter; leaves towards the base, above beset with spreading white hairs; spike simple, about 7 inches, florets without order; involucels one-flowered, bristles fascicled, greyish-yellow; hermaphrodite flower striated longthways; on cultivated land.——*Trembling tinay* (చెంగలిగడ్డి - chengaligaddi, Tel.; தினை - tinai, Tam.). Tel. from (tsangu, tel. to tremble as by wind + gaddi, tel. grass), from slender stalk. Tam. from (tin, tam. to eat). Botanically Panicum [priyangoo] ciliare, retz., graminaceæ [vricsham, 156]. Spikes four to five, digitate, undivided; leaves lanceolate, waved, rather hairy; sheaths smooth; florets imbricated; outer valve of the glume very minute, nerveless; inner one half the length of the flower.——*White tinay* (ಬಿಳಿಕೊರಲೆ - bilikorale, Can.; నకిరిగడ్డి - nakirigaddi, Tel.; கொரலி - korali, Tam.). Title from color of seed. Can. from (bili, can. white + korale, can. panic seed, panicum italicum, linn.). Tam. from (kuru, tam. short); small grain. Can. also (korali), meaning small grain; (korre), meaning panic seed. Tel. also (nakkakorra), meaning fox + panicum italicum, linn.; (verritsámalu), meaning mad + panicum frumentaceum, roxb. Tam. also (vellaittinai), meaning white tinay. Title otherwise Coraly [mecca cholum, tinay]. Botanically Panicum [priyangoo] glaucum, linn., graminaceæ [vricsham, 156]. Alias Setaria glauca. Culm erect, branched; leaves internally slightly scabrous, subglaucescent, scabrous at the margin; spike cylindric; involucre with many bristles much longer than the one to four-nous spikelets; glumes glabrous; hermaphrodite floret transversely waved; male two-paleaceous. Staple food with hill tribes on the neilgherries.

TINCAL (تنکال - tinkál, *Hind.*). Tibetan word. Crude borax [swauga, vengauram].

TINDAL (تنڈیل - tandel, *Hind.*; തണ്ടൽ - tandal, *Mal.*). From (tandu, mal. oar + vali, mal. to pull). The head of a body of men, especially of a gang of laborers or the crew of a ship. Thence captain of a native vessel [nacodah, nahah, serang].

TINDIVANAM * (திண்டிவனம் - tindivanam, *Tam.*). From (tintidí, san. tamarind tree, tamarindus indica, linn. + vana, san. jungle). Sanscrit name (tintidívana), meaning same.——**(1)** Talook, South arcot district. Tahsildar's pay Rs. 225. The South indian railway runs through the talook from north to south for about 17 miles, with three railway stations. Population 316,018; language Tamul. N. coast of district. Boundaries:—N. Polore and Wandiwash talooks, N. Arcot district, and Madrantacam talook in Chingleput; E. Bay of Bengal; S. French territory, and Villoopooram talook; W. Polore in N. Arcot and Trinomallee talooks. The talook is a plain rising gradually westwards from the coast and broken near Jinjee by a cluster of small hills over an area of about 40 square miles. Soils principally regar [q.v.] and sundry and sedimentary origin. Manufacture of jaggery [q.v.] and cloths, and trade in indigo [q.v.] and groundnut [q.v.]. The latter is chiefly sent to Pondicherry for export. Irrigation by tanks [q.v.] with some anicuts [q.v.] across Varauhanuddy and Condamore rivers. Camping grounds:—Saram, Vilangampaudy, near Chundoor and Jinjee. Places of archæological interest:—Auttipaukam, Avalore, Chaivore, Chittanore, Conimere, Devanore, Dhautaupooram, Eyil, Gengapooram, Jinjee, Kedangal, Melacherry, Moonnore, Olacore, Permacoil, Permandore, Pervalore, Shauttambaudy, Shembaid, Shingavaram, Shirvalore, Tayanore, Teevanore, Tindivanam, Tondore, Veeranamore. Principal trig. stations:—Jinjee rock, Permacoil. The leading places, &c., in the talook are the following.——*Ariancooppam* (அரியன்குப்பம் - ariyanguppam, Tam.). See sep. title.——*Aulapaukam* (ஆலப்பாக்கம் - álappákkam, Tam.). From (ál, tam. banyan tree, ficus bengalensis, linn. + pákkam, tam. village). Pop. 972; acres 570; lat. 12° 10′; long. 79° 58′; from Cuddalare N.N.E. 32 miles; from Tindivanam E.S.E. 19 miles; from the sea W. 1¼ miles.——*Chuckly droog* (சக்கிலித்துருக்கம் - shakkilitturukkam, Tam.). From (shakkili, tam. one of that caste + durga, san. fort). Sanscrit name (mátangadurga), meaning chundaulan + fort. Hill. A fortified hill most difficult of ascent one mile from Jinjee.——*Chundoor* (சந்தூர் - shandúr, Tam.). From (shandu, tam. a place where four roads meet + úr, tam. village). Pop. 1,488; acres 1,591; lat. 12° 07′; long. 79° 38′; from Cuddalore N.N.W. 30 miles; from Tindivanam S.S.W. 9 miles; from the sea W. 22 miles.——*Chundrayya doorgam* (చంద్రయ్యదుర్గము - chandrayyadurgamu, Tel.). From (chandrayya, tel. proper name + durga, san. fort). Hill. One of the three peaks of Jinjee.——*Conimere* (கூனிமேடு - kúnimédu, Tam.). See sep. title.——*Jinjee* (செஞ்சி - shenji, Tam.). See sep. title.——*Kilyanore* (கிளியனூர் - kiliyanúr, Tam.). From (kiliyál, tam. proper name + úr, tam. village); called after kilyaul, the daughter of a ruler who founded the village. Pop. 2,026; acres 3,877; lat. 12° 06′; long. 79° 48′; from Cuddalore N. 26 miles; from Tindivanam S.E. 11 miles; from the sea W. 10 miles. An ancient ruler had five daughters; Kilyaul, Nullaul, Oolagaul, Peraul and Teilaul. He founded five villages after their names. The others, viz., Nullavore, Oolagaupooram, Peravore, and Teilaupooram also lie within a radius of 4 miles.——*Krishnagherry* (கிருட்டிணகிரி - kiruttinagiri, Tam.). From (krishna, san. black + giri, san. mountain); called after a person of that name. Hill; lat. 12° 16′; long. 79° 27′; from Cuddalore N.W. 43 miles; from Tindivanam W. 16 miles; from the sea W. 39 miles. One of the three hills of Jinjee.——*Malayanore* (மலையனூர் - malaiyanúr, Tam.). From (malaiyan, tam. hill-chief, epithet of the chéra rulers + úr, tam. village). Village, Place of pilgrimage; pop. 2,144; acres 1,610; lat. 12° 20′; long. 79° 22′; from Cuddalore N.W. 51 miles; from Tindivanam W.N.W. 23 miles; from the sea W. 24 miles. Large annual bullock [maud] fair held during Ancaulamman [q.v.] festival about March every year.——*Meilam* (மயிலம் - mailam,* Tam.). From (mayil, tam. peacock). Sanscrit name (mayúrapura), meaning peacock + town. Village, Place of pilgrimage; pop. 1,505; acres 1,374; lat. 12° 07′; long. 79° 40′; height 162 feet; from Cuddalore N.N.W. 28 miles; from Tindivanam S. 8 miles; from the sea W. 19 miles. Annual festival in July. Cattle [maud] fair. Pilgrims resort at Caurtigay [pundigay, 5c] to worship Soobramanya sawmy whose temple is on top of Meilam hill.——*Mercanum* (மரக்காணம் - marakkánam, Tam.). See sep. title.——*Olacore* (ஒலக்கூர் - olakkúr, Tam.). From (ulakkai, tam. waste + úr, tam. village). Railway station; pop. 2,377; acres 4,124; lat. 12° 19′; long. 79° 46′; height 129 feet; from Cuddalore N. 39 miles; from Tindivanam N.E. 6 miles; from the sea W. 20 miles. West of village at foot of hill are stones with inscriptions.——*Paumbayaur* (பாம்பையாறு - pámbaiyáru, Tam.). From (pámbu, tam. snake + áru, tam. river). River. Tributary of the Varaubanuddy.——*Permacoil* (பெருமுக்கல் - perumukkal, Tam.). See sep. title.——*Rajagherry* (இராசகிரி - irásagiri, Tam.). From (rájá, san. king + giri, san. mountain). Hill. One of three hills of Jinjee.——*Saram* (சாரம் - sháram, Tam.). Means fertility; lat. 12° 17′; long. 79° 45′; from Cuddalore N. 38 miles; from Tindivanam N.E. 4 miles; from the sea W. 20 miles. Camping ground.——*Shingavaram* (சிங்கவரம் - shingavaram, Tam.). From (simha, san. lion + varam, san. town). Sanscrit name (simhapura), means same. Hill, Place of pilgrimage; pop. 469; acres 1,044; lat. 12° 17′; long. 79° 27′; from Cuddalore N.W. 45 miles; from Tindivanam W.N.W. 17 miles; from the sea W. 40 miles. Old Vishnoo temple, partly rock-cut. North is another temple in ruins with many inscriptions.——*Tindivanam* (திண்டிவனம் - tindivanam, Tam.). See below.——*Tirnautar coondroo* (திருநாதர்க்குன்று - tirunátharkkunru, Tam.). From (tiru, tam. sacred + nát'ha, san. lord + kunru, tam. hill). Hill. Contains Jeina [q.v.] sculptures.——*Tondayaur* (தொண்டியாறு - tondiyáru, Tam.). See sep. title.——*Tondore* (தொண்டூர் - tondúr, Tam.). From (tondu, tam. divine service + úr, tam. village). Pop. 871; acres 1,134; lat. 21° 21′; long. 79° 31′; from Cuddalore N.N.W. 48 miles; from Tindivanam N.W. 15 miles; from the sea W. 40 miles. Three rock-cut caves and sculptures. Jeina [q.v.] statue.——*Varauhanuddy* (வராகநதி - varáganathi, Tam.). See sep. title.——**(2)** Town, Railway station, Head-quarters of Sub-collector and talook; South arcot dist., Tindivanam tal.; pop. 9,191; acres 840; lat. 12° 14′; long. 79° 42′; height 145 feet; from Chidambaram N. 56 miles; from Cuddalore N.N.W. 36 miles; from Madras S.S.W. 71 miles; from Tricalore N.E. 36 miles; from Vriddhauchellam N.N.E. 54 miles; from the sea W. 22 miles. Consists of a congeries of hamlets, viz., Avarapaukam, Cauverypauk, Gidangal, Jafferabad, Moorongapaukam and Tindivanam proper. Gidangal was formerly fortified. There was a Soobahdar [q.v.] at Tindivanam in the service of the Mahrattas when Ramrauz ruled at Jinjee. The pagoda [q.v.] is sacred to Tintrineevana eesbwarasawmy. Considerable trade in tanning skins [chamrah], and in groundnut [q.v.] sent to Pondicherry for export.

TINGAL (ತಿಂಗಳು - tingalu, *Can.*; திங்கள் - tingal, *Tam.*). From (tigazh, tam. to shine). The moon [chundran]. A month [maheena, mausam] in general. Monday [vauram]. 4 kizhamays or weeks = 1 tingal, 12 tingals = 1 aundoo or year [caulam, 1].

TINNEVELLY (திருநெல்வேலி - tirnnelvéli, *Tam.*). From (tiru, tam. sacred + nel, tam. paddy + véli, tam. village) [tir]. Sanscrit name (malakúta), meaning sin + peak; also (dárukávana), meaning wooden figure + forest; from the lingam [q.v.] in the wood worshipped by rishies [rishy] here.——**(1)** Revenue district; situated on the extreme southern and eastern part of the Presidency; between 8° 08′ and 9° 44′ N. lat. and between 77° 15′ and 78° 25′ E. long.; bounded N. by Madura district, E. by Madura district and Gulf of Manaar, S. by Gulf of Manaar, W. by Southern ghauts; square miles 5,389; pop. 1,916,095; language Tamul. Contains rivers Chittaur, Tamrapurny, Veippaur; ports Cauyalputnam, Tuticorin, Veippaur; mountains Southern ghauts; sanitaria Courtallam, Trichendore. The whole area of the district is represented by the following sub-areas:—Ambasamoodram talook, Nangoonairy talook, Ottapidauram talook, Shauttore talook, Shreevillipoottore talook, Shuncaraneinarcoil talook, Tencaray talook, Tencaushy talook, Tinnevelly talook. For general administrative purposes the district is distributed between the following revenue and magisterial officers, who have their head-quarters at the places shown. The pay set opposite the subordinate officers gives the grade of the corresponding charge:—Collector, Palamcottah; Sub-collector, Tuticorin, in charge of Tencaray and Ottapidauram talooks; Head assistant collector, Shermadevy, in charge of Ambasamoodram, Nangoonairy and Tencaushy talooks; General deputy collector, Shreevillipoottore, in charge of Shreevillipoottore, Shuncaraneinarcoil and Shauttore talooks; Assistant collector, Tinnevelly, in charge of Tinnevelly talook. Tahsildars; Ambasamoodram, Rs. 225; Nangoonairy, Rs. 200; Ottapidauram, Rs. 150; Shauttore, Rs. 150; Shreevillipoottore, Rs. 200; Shuncaraneinarcoil, Rs. 200; Tencaray, Rs. 250; Tencaushy, Rs. 175; Tinnevelly, Rs. 225. Deputy tahsildars; Coolashekharaputnam, Rs. 100, range situated in the south of Tencaray talook; Palamcottah, Rs. 70, range situated in the south of Tinnevelly talook; Raudhaupooram, Rs. 70, range situated in the south of Nangoonairy talook; Tuticorin, Rs. 100, range situated in the east of Ottapidauram talook; Vilauticoolam, Rs. 70, range situated in the north of Ottapidauram talook; Viroothooputty, Rs. 70, range situated in the north of Shauttore talook; Watrap, Rs 70, range situated in the north of Shreevillipoottore talook. Sub-magistrate, Shreeveicoontam, Rs. 100, jurisdiction extending over the whole of Tencaray talook excepting Coolashekharaputnam range. Similarly judicial officers:—Judge, Palamcottah; Subordinate judge, Palamcottah. District moonsifs, Tuticorin with jurisdiction extending to the Ottapidauram talook, Shreevillipoottore with jurisdiction extending to the Shreevillipoottore and Shauttore talooks, Ambasamoodram with jurisdiction extending to Ambasamoodram, Tencaushy and Nangoonairy talooks excluding Raudhaupooram division, Tinnevelly with jurisdiction extending to the Tinnevelly and Shuncaraneinarcoil talooks, Shreeveicoontam with jurisdiction extending to Tencaray talook and Raudhaupooram division of Nangoonairy talook. Similarly Public works officers:—Executive engineer, Palamcottah, in charge of the division, which consists of Tencaray sub-division comprising Tencaray and Ottapidauram talooks; Shermadevy sub-division comprising Ambasamoodram, Tencaushy and Shuncaraneinarcoil talooks; head-quarter sub-division comprising Tinnevelly, Nangoonairy, Shreevillipoottore and Shauttore talooks. Contains Registration sub-districts:—Alwar tirnagary, Ambasamoodram, Cadayam, Cayataur, Coilputty, Moorpanaud, Nangoonairy, Ottapidauram, Palamcottah, Pettah, Raudhaupooram, Skatauncoolam, Shauttore, Shermadevy, Shivacaushy, Shivagherry, Shooranday, Shreevillipoottore, Shuncaraneinarcoil, Tencaray, Tencaushy, Trichendore, Tuticorin, Vilauticoolam, Viroothooputty, Watrap. Contains Forest ranges northern, southern and central. Contains Municipalities Palamcottah, Tinnevelly, Tuticorin. Contains District board and Talook boards, Tuticorin T. B. embracing Tencaray and Ottapidauram talooks, Shermadevy T. B. embracing Tencaushy, Ambasamoodram and Nangoonairy talooks, Shreevillipoottore T. B. embracing Sreevillipoottore, Shuncaraneinarcoil and Shauttore talooks, Tinnevelly T. B. embracing Tinnevelly talook. The following general references should be made to the preceding volumes:—general geography, I (1) to (29); general ethnology, I (29) to (109); general history, I (110) to (188); physical geography, II, 1; meteorology, II, 3; geology, II, 8; fauna, II, 21; flora, II, 26; mineralogy, II, 29. The following references in the preceding volumes will furnish details special to the district:—latitudes and longitudes, II, 47; particulars about towns, II, 48; coast survey, II, 158; lighthouses, II, 169; comparative population, II, 172; location of revenue officers, II, 391; revenue settlement of the district, II, 417; registrars' and sub-registrars' stations, II, 422; ports, II, 423; salt factories, II, 426; rain-gauge stations, II, 428; police divisions, II, 431; maps published, II, 436; survey topographical lists, II, 443; hospitals and dispensaries, II, 447; missionary stations, II, 455; head-quarter stations of gazetted officers, II, 461; incidence of taxation, II, 463; weight and measures of the district, II, 518; zemindarries, II, 300; special public works, I, 401. A special gazetteer account of the whole district is given at II, 130. For the detailed topography of the district, reference should be made to the talook notices, in the present volume, viz.:—Ambasamoodram, Nangoonairy, Ottapidauram, Shauttore, Shreevillipoottore, Shuncaraneinarcoil, Tencaray, Tencaushy, Tinnevelly.——**(2)** Talook, Tinnevelly district. Tahsildar's pay Rs. 225. Area 327 square miles. Contains 143 villages, of which 10 are Government, 40 inam. Population 184,728. Language Tamul. Centre of district. Bounded N. by Shuncaraneinarcoil and Ottapidauram talooks, E. by Ottapidauram and Tencaray talooks, S. by Nangoonairy talook, W. by Ambasamoodram and Tencaushy talooks. Consists, as respects soil and general features, of two distinct portions, viz., the valleys of the Tamrapurny and Chittaur and the high and dry lands which lie between these rivers and on either side of them. The dry lands, south of the Tamrapurny and Chittaur, are of the red and sandy series, and cultivated but once in the rainy season, yielding poor crops of gram [q.v.] or shaumay [q.v.]. These lands are largely left fallow. There are a considerable number of palmyra [q.v.] topes [q.v.] scattered about in this portion, which may be considered the northern limit of the Palmyra forest. Some villages of the north-eastern portion belong to the black cotton [regar] series, being at southern edge of these extensive plains. Most of the garden cultivation under wells belongs to this group; cotton [q.v.], cholum [q.v.] and gram [q.v.] are the staple crops of this soil, besides tobacco [poguak], chillies [q.v.], and vegetable [keeray] under wells. On either side of the Tamrapurny is a broad belt, a quarter to half a mile wide, of irrigated land, which yearly bears two unfailing crops of rice [q.v.]; plantains [q.v.], betel [q.v.] gardens, cocoanuts [q.v.] also abound, and in the higher portions of the river alluvial fine topes [q.v.] of mangoes [q.v.], iluppay [mohwah] and other trees. Trade is comparatively small; the chief item is rice, which in favorable seasons is exported in large quantity to the dry talooks of Tinnevelly. A considerable import business in Europe cotton [q.v.] and other articles is also carried on. Cloths of a superior description are woven in Melapolliem. Metal utensils are made in Tinnevelly. Water is derived from the Tamrapurny by means of three channels [q.v.], viz., the Codagam, Polliem, Tinnevelly, leading from anicuts [q.v.] on the river. These are supplemented by ninety tanks [q.v.], which they supply in their course. The Chittaur supplies eight channels in the talook, and these again twenty-six to tanks scattered about over the north-eastern portion wherever there was found by the ancient rulers of the province a suitable site for such a reservoir. The Putchayaur feeds twenty-nine tanks but only in the pishaunam [q.v.] or October monsoon [q.v.] season, and joins the Tamrapurny near the western boundary of the talook. There are also seventy-five rain-fed tanks filled in the October rains [mazhay] and cultivated but once. Camping grounds:—Palamcottah, Ponnacoody, Seetaparpanullore, and Shadhikhan chuttram. Places of archæological interest:—Coonnattore, Gungaycondaun, Krishnaupooram, Maunapaday veed, Maunore, Oograncottay, Palamcottah, Pullicottah, Shoottamully, Tinnevelly, Trimalpooram. Principal Trig. stations:—Coonnattorepottay, Coottaitutty, Palamcottah base, east end, Palamcottah base, west end, Taulaiyoottpottay. The leading places, &c., in the talook are the following.——*Chindintooray* (சிந்துப்பூந்துறை - shinduppúndurai, Tam.). From (shindu, tam. river + pú, tam. flower + turai, tam. ford). Village; pop. 2,254; acres 364; lat. 8° 44′; long. 77° 45′; from Tinnevelly E. 2 miles. On left bank of Tamrapurny. Celebrated pagoda [q.v.]. In bed of river is the Shiva teertam mantapam [q.v.] where floating festival takes place in January. Gives its name to a mutt [q.v.].——*Chittaur* (சிற்றாறு - shittáru, Tam.). See sep. title.——*Coonnattorepottay* (குன்னத்தூர்ப்பொத்தை - kunnattúrp-pottai, Tam.). From (kunnattúr, tam. place so called + pottai, tam. hillock). Trig. station; lat. 8° 41′ 45·89″; long. 77° 42′ 54·16″; height 470 feet; from Coonnattore S. ⅛ mile; from Tinnevelly S.S.W. 2 miles.——*Coottaitutty* (குட்டைத்தட்டி - kuttaittatti, Tam.). From (kuttai, tam. pond + tatti, tam. defence). Trig. station; lat. 8° 51′ 24·59″; long. 77° 38′ 20·35″; height 595 feet; from Tinnevelly N.W. 12 miles; from Yettaungoolam W. 1½ miles.——*Gunyaycondaun* (கங்கைக்கொண்டான் - kangaikkondán, Tam. gangaikondán *). From (gangá, san. ganges river + kondán, tam. he who obtained); from gungaycondaun, the real name of soondra paundyan, the chola king. Sanscrit name (gangádharapura), meaning shiva, the ganges bearer + town. Village, Railway station; pop. 2,971; acres 11,195; lat. 8° 51′; long. 77° 49′; height 139 feet; from Tinnevelly N.N.E. 11 miles. Large ancient Shiva temple on banks of river, richly sculptured with inscriptions.——*Manaar* (மன்னார் - mannár, Tam.). See sep. title.——*Manapaday veed* (மணப்படைவீடு - manappadaivídu, Tam.). From (manam, tam. marriage + padai, tam. multitude + vídu, tam. house). Sanscrit name (kalyánapura), meaning marriage city. Village; pop. 678; acres 329; lat. 8° 46′; long. 77° 48′; from Tinnevelly E.N.E. 6 miles. Of considerable antiquity on right bank of Tamrapurny. The ancient Calyaunapooram. Temple with inscriptions.——*Maroothoor* (மருதூர் - maruthúr, Tam.). From (marutham, tam. terminalia tomentosa, bedd., var. typica + úr, tam. village). Village; pop. 769; acres 715; lat. 8° 45′; long. 77° 51′; from Tinnevelly E.N.E. 9 miles. Very ancient village on right bank of Tamrapurny, across which is an anicut.——*Melapolliem* (மேலப்பாளையம் - mélappálaiyam, Tam. melapálaiyam *). From (mél, tam. western + pálaiyam, tam. fortified village). Town; pop. 7,661; acres 1,334; lat. 8° 42′; long. 77° 45′ 13″; from Tinnevelly S.E. 2¼ miles. Site of a

Vijianugger ruler's encampment. Superior cloths woven.——*Narsinganullore* (நரசிங்கநல்லூர் - narasinganallúr, Tam.). From (narasimha, san. man-lion, incarnation of vishnu + nal, tam. good + úr. tam. village). Village; pop. 2,349; acres 1,479; lat. 8° 45′; long. 77° 39′; from Tinnevelly W. 6 miles. On left bank of Aryanaickanpooram canal. On north is high rising ground. Chiefly inhabited by herdsmen and artizans and a few Paravar [q.v.] roman catholics.——*Oograncottay* (உக்கிரங்கோட்டை - ukkirangóttai, Tam.). From (ugra, san fierce + kóttai, tam. fort); called after oogra paundyan. Village; pop. 1,877; acres 2,365; lat. 8° 54′; long. 77° 38′; from Tinnevelly N.N.W. 14 miles. Lies on N. bank of Chittaur and is most N.W. village of talook. Shiva temple. Inscription of Paundy [q.v.] dynasty [raj] on a rock called Anaimottaypanray.——*Palamcottah* (பாளையங்கோட்டை - pálaiyangóttai, Tam.). See sep. title.——*Pettah* (பேட்டை - péttai, Tam.). Suburb. Town, Post office; pop. 9,642; acres 1,199; lat. 8° 43′; long. 77° 42′; from Tinnevelly W. 3 miles. Large trading Mahomedan population.——*Seeriliperry* (சிவிலிப்பேரி - shivilippéri, Tam.). From (shivili, tam. proper name + éri, tam. tank); after seevily, an ancient ruler of the place. Village; pop. 3,229; acres 6,389; lat. 8° 47′; long. 77° 51′; from Tinnevelly E.N.E. 9 miles. At junction of the Tamrapurny and Chittaur. Temple to Krishnasawmy. Cattle [maud] fair in April. Weekly fairs on Monday. Paravar [q.v.] roman catholics have a chapel.——*Shoottamully* (சுத்தமல்லி - shuttamalli, Tam.). From (shuddha, san. pure + malli, san. jasmine, jasminum sambac, ait.). Village; pop. 3,062; acres 2,945; lat. 8° 42′; long. 77° 41′; from Tinnevelly S.W. 5 miles. On canal of same name. Divided by canal and bridge into two parts. Important anicut across Tamrapurny. Shiva temple with inscriptions. Car festivals in April and October.——*Tamrapurny* (தாம்பிரப்பருணி - támbirapparuni, Tam.). See sep. title.——*Taulaiyoottpottay* (தாழையூற்றுப்பொத்தை - tázhaiyúttuppottai, Tam). From (tázhai, tam. screw-pine, pandanus odoratissimus, linn. + útru, tam. spring + pottai, tam. hillock). Trig. station; lat. 8° 48′ 55·17″; long. 77° 45′ 54·91″; height 489 feet; from Taulaiyoott E. 1½ miles; from Tinnevelly N.N.E. 7 miles.——*Tinnevelly* (திருநெல்வேலி - tirunelvéli, Tam.). See below.——**(3)** Town, Headquarters of Tahsildar and District moonsif, Railway station; Tinnevelly dist., Tinnevelly tal.; pop. 24,768; acres 1,093; lat. 8° 44′; long. 77° 44′; height 213 feet; from Madras S.S.W. 344 miles; from Palamcottah W. 4 miles; from Shermadevy E. 9 miles; from Shreevillipoottore S. 54 miles; from Tuticorin W. 36 miles by rail. 1½ miles from the left bank of the Tamrapurny. Largest town in district but administrative headquarters of district are at Palamcottah on other side of the river. When the district was subject to the Naicks [q.v.] of Madura, their governor lived in state at Tinnevelly. About 1560, Vishwanautan, the founder of the Naick [q.v.] dynasty [raj] of Madura, rebuilt the town, and erected many temples, &c. Terminus of a branch of the South indian railway. Active centre of Protestant mission in South india. It has lately been created a diocese and bishop appointed. Car procession in July. Weekly fair on Thursday. Large Shiva temple beautifully sculptured and containing many inscriptions. Is on a typical pattern [maunasauram, staupatyam]. Divided into equal portions, of which one is to Shiva [q.v.], the other to Paravaty [q.v.]. The great thousand-pillared portico in the temple consists of a mass of pillars, 10 deep and extending to 100 in length, without any break or any open space or arrangement. There is a fine Mahomedan tomb raised in memory of a chief who died here. A substantial bridge of 11 arches of 60 feet span crosses the river, connecting Tinnevelly and Palamcottah.

TIPPA (తిప్ప - tippa, *Tel.*; திப்பை - tippai, *Tam.*). Mound [dibba].

TIPPOO (ٹیپو - típú, *Hind.*). Name of a saint, whose tomb is at Arcot, the patron saint of Hyder ally, who named his son Tippoo [tippoo sultan] after him. Mahomedan alam; as Tippoo bee, alam + alaumat [ism].——*Tippoo sultan* (ٹیپو سلطان - típúsultán, Hind.). From (above + sovereign title). Son of Hyder ally, ruler of Mysore, whose capital was Seringapatam. Succeeded to the throne of Mysore, January 2, 1783. The Nizam and Mahrattas united to overthrow his power, 1786. Attacked Travancore and was defeated, December 29, 1789. He successfully renewed the attempt, 1790. Treaty of peace, March 18, 1792. Fresh misunderstandings, November 8, 1798. War declared, February 1799. Action at Malvully in which the Sultan's troops were defeated, March 6, 1799. Seringapatam taken; death of Tippoo, May 4, 1799 [charitram]. See vol. I (183)—(185), 20.

TIR (ತಿರು - tiru, *Can.*; തിരു - tiru, *Mal.*; திரு - tiru, *Tam.*). The Dravidian dialectal change from Shree [q.v.]. An adjective signifying venerable, divine, or sacred; prefixed to many names. A prefix to holy places; as Tripatore, Tripatty. Also to religious books and to names of writers on religion. Also name of Lutchmy.——*Teriry* (ತೆರಿರಿ - teriri, Can.). Short for tiriyairy [q.v.]. Temple of the Todah [q.v.] tribe.——*Tinnevelly* (திருநெல்வேலி · tirunelvéli, Tam.). See sep. title.——*Tircalicoondram* (திருக்கழுக்குன்றம் - tirukkazhukkunram, Tam. tirukalikundram*). From (tiru, tam. sacred + kazhu, tam. kite + kunram, tam. hill). Tam. also (kazhukkunram), meaning kite + hill. Sanscrit name (pakshitírt'ha), meaning bird + sacred place; also (gridhráchala), meaning vulture + mountain; also (védagiri), meaning sacred writing + mountain [narsimhacondah]; also (védáchalam), meaning the same. Village, Hill, Place of pilgrimage; Chingleput dist., Chingleput tal.; pop. 3,566; acres 2,722; lat. 12° 36′; long. 80° 07′; height 500 feet; from Chingleput S.E. 8 miles; from Sydapett S. 30 miles; from the sea W. 9 miles. Half way between Chingleput and coast on road to Sadras. Hill is termination of a ridge. Was endowed by Cholan [q.v.] and Paundyan [q.v.] rulers, its soil and water furnishing a cure of leprosy [cooshtam]. Still place of pilgrimage. Former head-quarters of a Tahsildar [q.v.]. On hill stands part of a temple to Shiva, main building and offices being in town at foot. The idol is Vedagiry eeshwaran, the hill is Vedachellam. The temple was once Jeina [q.v.] and is mentioned by Taranautan in his Thibetan history of Indian booddhism [booddha], under the name of Pacshiteertam or Bird convent. Every day two birds of the kite [gridhram] species come to the hill and are fed by a pundauram [q.v.]. They are believed to be Rishies [q.v.], condemned to bathe every morning in Ganges at Benares, to take food at Tircalicoondram, and to sleep at Rameshwaram. Indran [q.v.] is said to anoint the god by sending down a thunderbolt [vajram] once in twelve years which falls exactly on the top of the conical tower in which the god is placed making a circuit around the god thrice without injuring the building or any person in it. There is a tank called Shankha teertam or chunk [q.v.] shell pond. It is said that once in twelve years a chunk shell comes out of this pond. Two or three days before, a roaring noise comes from the waters which assume a frothy appearance. The people watch carefully and take out the shell with ceremony. Trig. station in lat. 12° 36′ 30·95″; long. 80° 6′ 5·23″; from Chingleput S.E. 8 miles; from the sea W. 9 miles [mahadeva mullay].——*Tircalyaunam* (திருக்கலியாணம் - tirukkaliyánam, Tam.). Sacred wedding. Marriage of a god [pundigay, 6d]. Especially festival for Shiva's marriage with Parvaty. The festival lasts usually nine or ten days, during which the daily offering are made on a larger scale; and Shiva [q.v.], Parvaty [q.v.], Vigneshwaran [q.v.], Soobramanyan [q.v.], &c., are carried about morning and evening in the streets.——*Tircanchy* (திருக்காஞ்சி - tirukkánji, Tam.). From (tiru, tam. holy + káñji, tam. the town). Sanscrit name (káñchi). Another name of Canjy or Cutchy [q.v.].——*Tircaumayyan* (திருக்காமய்யன் - tirukkámayyan, Tam.). From (above + káma, san. love short for kámákshi, or párvatí + aiyyan, tam. master, titular affix). Hindoo 2nd or pers. name [peyar].——*Tircaurtigay* (திருக்கார்த்திகை - tirukkárttigai, Tam.). Means holy + third lunar asterism. Same as Caurtigay.——*Tirchoornam* (திருச்சூரணம் - tiruccúranam, Tam.). From (above + chúrna, san. powder). Holy paste to mark the forehead with [naumam, shree choornam].——*Tiriyairy* (ತಿರಿಯೇರಿ ಮಂದು - tiriyérimandu, Can.). From (above + ér, can. buffalo + mandu, can. todah village). Sacred mund [q.v.] of the Todahs [q.v.]. There are about nineteen Tiriyairies on the hills.——*Tirmagal* (திருமகள் - tirumagal, Tam.). From (above + magal, tam. daughter). The divine daughter; Lutchmy [q.v.].——*Tirmagalmaindan* (திருமகள்மைந்தன் - tirumagalmaindan, Tam.). From (above + magal, tam. daughter + maindan, tam. son). Manmatan [q.v.] in his birth as Pradyoomnan, or the radiant deity, son of krishnan [q.v.] and roocminy [q.v.].——*Tirmagan* (திருமகன் - tirumagan, Tam.). From (above + magan, tam. son). Krishnan [q.v.] or Vishnoo [q.v.].——*Tirmalasawmy* (திருமலைசாமி - tirumalaisámi, Tam.). From (above + malai, tam. mountain + svámí, san. lord). Epithet of Shiva, the lord of Keilausam, the holy mountain. Also of Vishnoo as lord of Tripatty. Hindoo 2nd or pers. name [peyar].——*Tirmaley* (తిరుమల - tirumala, Tel.; திருமலை - tirumalai, Tam.). From (tiru, tam. holy + malai, tam. hill). Tam. also (tiruvéngadam), means holy vencatam; also (véngadam), meaning white mountain; also (vadavéngadam), meaning north vencata as distinguished from Tenvengadam or the Alagar hills near Madura; also (vadamalai), meaning north + mountain. Sanscrit name (shésháchala), meaning sheshan, the serpent + mountain; also (vénkatáchala), means vishnoo, the sin destroyer + hill; also (vénkatádri); also (venkatagiri) [vengadam]; also (añjanáchala), meaning anjanay, the mother of hanooman + mountain; also (anjanágiri). Village, Hill, Place of pilgrimage; North arcot dist., Chundragherry tal.; pop. 1,517; acres 31,166; lat. 13° 41′; long. 79° 24′; from Chittore N.N.E. 37 miles; from Chundragherry N.N.E. 7 miles. Otherwise called Upper tripatty. On top of range and near its S.W. angle, 6 miles from Lower tripatty. Is in shape of a parallelogram and is ill-built. Most buildings are choultries [q.v.]; some modern, built by rajahs of Mysore and Cochin and zemindars of Calastry and Vencatagherry; but most are long stone corridors [praucauram] skirting streets and rudely carved. Opposite to the temple are shops. Around the town a belt of gardens contain mango [q.v.], jack [q.v.], tamarind [q.v.], orange [q.v.], sandal [q.v.], champak [q.v.], &c., for use of temple. The range has several peaks, each sacred. Near Sheshachellam peak stands the temple, and the whole range is called after this peak. Several teertams [q.v.];

principal is Toomboor cona. Different ascents to hills, most frequented being from Lower tripatty and from Chundragherry. The temple is simple, but richest shrine in S. india. The jewels, &c., are worth about 50 lakhs [q.v.], and it has the same in cash [q.v.]. Originally dedicated to Shiva [q.v.], now a temple of Vishnoo [q.v.]. Ramaunoojacharry [ramaunoojan] effected this change. The principal temple was formerly larger than now; main street of modern town being outer praucauram [q.v.], of which ruined gopoorams [q.v.] remain at four corners. Adjoining the temple are the principal bathing pool called the Sawmy-pooshcarny, the thousand-pillared mantapam [q.v.], &c. The whole is very much decayed. The idol [shilay, vigraham], which has no consort, is a figure of Shiva converted into Vishnoo by addition of chunk [q.v.] and chuckram [q.v.] in gold [pon]. No European has yet entered the temple gate. The divinity has 1,008 names. The chief are Shreenivasa sawmy, Vencatachellapaty, Vencateshwarasawmy and Sheshachellapaty. Hindoos from bengal call him Baulajee [q.v.]. In front of the adytum and anteroom is a mantapam [q.v.] supported on stone pillars, in the middle of which is a brass vessel in which hangs a bag open at the bottom and suspended from the roof. Into this money and jewels are thrown. On either side of it hangs a gong [q.v.]; that on the left side when struck utters the name Govindan [q.v.], and its companion on the right Narayanan [q.v.]. On the way up there are three portals, at the first of which Christians and Mahomedans must stop. Temple records state that the principal part of the temple was built by Tondiman chuckravurty athonday, son of Coolotoonga cholan, in the year 499 of the Kaliyoog [q.v.] or B.C. 3100, when it was prophesied that worship would continue for only 5,000 years. By this only five years remain. A village called Tondaimundalam still exists not far from the town. A monastery belonging to the mahant [q.v.] is on rising ground, where beiraugies [q.v.] are fed. Under Mahomedans, revenues of temple were all paid to ruling power of the country. There are three authorities on the establishment of the temple, the two jiyyangars [q.v.] and the mahant [q.v.]. Of these the great and the small jiyyangar [q.v.] are the most holy, and regarded almost as divinities. They are the religious heads. The mahant is the secular head. He is always a northern bramin, surrounded by beiraugies, one of whom he nominates during his life time to be his successor. The importance of this office has greatly increased since 1843, when Government surrendered management. The principal festival, Bramhotsavam [pundigay, 6a], in which the marriage of the sawmy with Pudmauvaty is celebrated, is in September. It lasts ten days. The most popular procession is that of Garooda ootsavam [pundigay, 6a] on fifth day; on the ninth day when the car [q.v.] goes round the town the people disperse. Other periodical feasts are Shivarautry [pundigay, 6a], Mooccoty ootsavam [pundigay, 3e], and Rata saptamy [pundigay, 3e]. The number of pilgrims on ordinary days amounts to 200 or 300; during the annual festival, 50,000. The pilgrims perform their vows on Upper tripatty hill, then visit the idol below and return to their homes. The principal part of the vow in the up-hill temple consists in shaving completely the heads of men and women indiscriminately. A very large part walk up the hill, but the rich go in small portable cots [dhooly]. Sickness and the desire of male offspring are the chief causes which induce persons to make a vow to the Tripatty idol; when the object is attained the vow must be fulfilled at some time, but not necessarily at once. Hindoos visit it as pilgrims from great distances, usually in bands and of all ages under a leader, the members of the party calling out Govindan [q.v.]. Offerings are made of every degree of value; gems, jewels, gold and silver cloths, always the hair of the head, from the lame a silver leg, from the blind a gold or silver eye, &c. Its immense revenues are derived from offerings, and there are villages and lands held by the officers of the temple. The gifts of pilgrims are recorded as a repayment of the nuptial expenses of the idol. The great Sheiva vedantist Shuncaracharry [shuncaran] resided here for some time. There is a Tamul stanza:—இரணியராட்டா னிரணியனீரைந் தலையன்கஞ்சன் முரணியகோட்டி னகத்திற்சரத்தன் மூன்றுளிற்றஞ்சத், தரணியிற்குத்தி யிடந்தெய்த்தைத் தவன் சர்ப்பவெமபன், அரணியகேழ லரிராகவன்கண் ணனுகிவந்தே—"the god of tripatty is he who, assuming the "forms of a hog [varauha avatar], of a lion [narsimha avatar], "of rama [q.v.], and of krishnan [q.v.], pierced, lacerated, shot "and kicked, by means of his tusk, claws, arrow and feet; "so that these four personages, hiranyaucshan, hiranyan, the "ten-headed ravanan [q.v.], and cumsan, were killed."——*Tirmalpaud* (തിരുമുൽപ്പാട് - tirumulppátu, Mal.). From (above + mun, mal. front + pátu, mal. chief, a title). Rank of a Bramin [q.v.] or Cshatriya [q.v.]. A member of a royal family. ——*Tirmanass* (തിരുമനസ്സ് - tirumanassu, Mal.). From (above + manas, san. will). Holy will, an honorific form of addressing a king [peyar].——*Tirmanjan* (திருமஞ்சன் - tirumañjau, Tam.). From (above + majjana, san. ablution). Hindoo 2nd or pers. name [peyar].——*Tirmanjanam* (திருமஞ்சனம் - tirumañjanam, Tam.). From (above + majjana, san. bathing). Bathing the idols [shilay, vigraham]. For this it is the practice to bring water from sacred tanks, wells or rivers [teertam]. The water is usually brought on the head of a Bramin [q.v.] accompanied by music in large temples.——*Tirmany moottaur* (திருமணிமுத்தாறு - tirumanimuttáru, Tam.). From (tiru, tam. sacred + mani, tam. beauty + muktá, san. pearl + áru, tam. river). Tam. also (tirumaniyáru); also (manimuttáru). Sanscrit name (manimuktánadí), meaning crystal + pearl + river. River; Salem dist., Salem, Trichengode and Namcull tals. Rises in the Shevaroy hills, and flowing through the western portion of the talook, passes by Paramatty and Salem supplying on its way the Idoomban coolam tank, and joins the Cauvery near Yeddayaur.——*Tirmaul* (திருமால் - tirumál, Tam.). From (above + mál, tam. greatness). Vishnoo [q.v.]. ——*Tirmoodisheragar* (திருமுடிச்சேவகர் - tirumudiççévagar, Tam.). From (above + mudi, tam. crown + sévaka, san. servant). The warrior with the sacred crown. Ayenaur [ayen] as tutelary god of a village [grauma devatay].——*Tirmoomboo* (തിരുമുമ്പ - tirumumpu, Mal.). From (above + mumpu, mal. presence). Title among bramins of Chiracal who have adopted the Maroomakkatoyem [q.v.] law of inheritance [dauyam]. Hindoo third name [peyar].——*Tirmozhy* (திருமொழி - tirumozhi, Tam.). Sacred word or speech [tirvye, tirvye mozhy]. ——*Tirmullay* (திருமலை - tirumalai, Tam.). From (above + malai, tam. mountain). Epithet of Keilausam [q.v.] and of Tripatty [q.v.]. Hindoo 2nd or pers. name [peyar].——*Tirmungalam* (திருமங்கலம் - tirumangalam, Tam.). See sep. title.——*Tirmunn* (திருமண் - tiruman, Tam.). From (above man, tam. earth). Clay with which Veishnavas draw lines on their foreheads [naumam].——*Tirnarayanan* (திருநாராயணன் - tirunáráyanan, Tam.). From (above + náráyana, san. vishnu, the mover on waters). Hindoo 2nd or pers. name [peyar].——*Tirnaul* (திருநாள் - tirunál, Tam.). Means sacred day [pundigay, 6d]. Any festival day. Veishnavite term and corresponds to the Ootsavam [q.v.] of Sheiveites. Also called Tirvizhah. Tirnauleipovaun is a festival-goer, specially applied to nundan [q.v.], the pariah [q.v.] devotee of shiva [q.v.], who obtained mocsham [q.v.] at chidambaram on the occasion of his visiting it on the tirvauthiray festival [ardrah darshanam]; he is one of the sixty-three devotees of shiva [aroopatt moover].—— *Tirnaumam* (திருநாமம் - tirunámam, Tam.). See Naumam. ——*Tirnavoya* (തിരുനാവായ - tirunáváya, Mal.). From (tiru, mal. holy + náva, san. ship). Sanscrit name (shrínavayógipura), meaning holy + nine + saint + town; also (shrínávápura), meaning holy + ship + town. Village, Place of pilgrimage; Malabar dist., Ponnany tal.; pop. 8,925. Close to railway at 382nd mile from Madras, about half way between Coottipooram and Tiroor stations. Here is a bund [q.v.] across some fields, where formerly the Maha magham [q.v.] festival used to take place at the enthronement of the kings every twelve years. The last occurred 180 years ago. Near the road from Codacull to Coottipooram, and about 20 yards from the spot where the king used to stand during the ceremonies, is a rockcut cave. Old temple in the village dedicated to Rama [q.v], the most famous in the district.——*Tirneer* (திருநீறு - tiruníru, Tam.). From (above + níru, tam. burnt ashes). Burnt ashes [neeroo] of cowdung [shauny] used by Sheivites to smear the body with [vibhooty].——*Tiroor* (തിരൂര് - tirúr, * Mal.). From (tiru, mal. good fortune + úr, mal village). Village, Railway station, Travellers' bungalow, Market on Sundays; Malabar dist., Ponnany tal.; pop. 5,734; lat 10° 56'; long. 75° 59'; height 17 feet; from Calicut S.S.E. 24 miles; from Ponnany N. 10 miles; from the sea E. 4 miles. Present terminus of the Canal viâ Ponnany to Cochin.——*Tiroorangaudy* (തിരൂരങ്ങാടി - tirúrannáti, Mal. tirurangadi *). From (tiru, mal. prosperous + úr, mal. village + annáti, mal. bazaar). Bazaar in the prosperous Chernaud.—"*a*" Deputy tahsildarry, Malabar district. Pay Rs. 70.—"*b*" Town, Deputy tahsildar's station; Malabar dist., Yernaud tal.; lat. 11° 03'; long. 75° 58'; from Calicut S.S.E. 18 miles; from Cannanore S.S.E. 67 miles; from Madras W.S.W. 326 miles; from Malapooram W. 9 miles; from Manantoddy S. 51 miles; from Munjery W.S.W. 14 miles; from Palghaut W.N.W. 52 miles; from Ponnany N. 17 miles; from Tellicherry S.S.E. 52 miles; from the sea E. 5 miles. Remains of a fort where a victory was gained by General Hartley over Tippoo's troops in 1790.——*Tirpanimautt* (திருப்பணிமாற்று - tiruppanimáttu, Tam.). From (above + pani, tam. work + máttu, tam. to change). Repairs in temples.——*Tirpauvauday* (திருப்பாவாடை - tiruppávádai, Tam.). From (above + pávai, tam. woman + ádai, tam. dress). A long cloth on which offerings of rice [q.v.] are presented to idols [shilay, vigraham].—— *Tirporore* (திருப்போரூர் - tiruppórúr, Tam. tiruporúr *). From (tiru, tam. sacred + pór, tam. war + úr, tam. village); from caurtikeyan, the god of war; tam. also (pórúr), meaning war + village; also (póri), meaning war place. Village, Place of pilgrimage; Chingleput dist., Chingleput tal.; pop. 2,186; acres 1,538; lat. 12° 44'; long. 80° 14'; from Chingleput E. 14 miles; from Madras S. 25; from Saidapett S. 21 miles; from the sea W. 3 miles. On East coast canal. Former cusbah [q.v.] or a talook, subsequently station of a deputy tahsildar [q.v.]. Shiva pagoda [q.v.]. Crowds flock to its monthly festivals called Kritticay [caurtey, pundigay].——*Tirshooly* (திருச்சுழி - tiruççuzhi, Tam. tirushuli *). From (tiru, tam. holy + shuzhi, tam. circle). Tam. also (shuzhigai), meaning toddy. Sanscrit name (trishúlapura), meaning trident town; also (pannagakshétra), meaning serpent + sacred place; also (káléshvarakshétra), meaning shiva + lord + sacred place.—"*a*" Deputy tahsildarry, Madura district. Pay Rs. 100.—"*b*" Village, Head-quarters of Deputy tahsildar and sub-registrar; Madura dist., Ramnaud zemindarry; pop. 3,769; lat. 9° 32′; long. 78° 15′; from Dindigul S.S.E. 60 miles; from Kodaykarnal S.E. 66 miles; from Madras S.S.W. 280 miles; from Madura S.S.E. 27 miles; from Rameshwaram W.N.W. 78 miles; from Ramnaud W.N.W. 44 miles; from the sea S.E. 32 miles. On the south bank of the Goondaur. Head-quarters of a talook. Of great antiquity and much resorted to by pilgrims. Large sculptured Shiva temple built by Paraucráma paundyan. Several fine bathing reservoirs. Two miles east on a small hill is an old Shiva temple. Three annual festivals in April, July and August. Weekly market on Wednesday.——*Tirvadamaroothore* (திருவிடைமருதூர் - tiruvidaimaruthúr, Tam. tiruvadamarudúr *). From (tiru, tam. sacred + idai, tam. middle + marutham, tam. terminalia tomentosa, bedd. + úr, tam. town). Place in the middle of which is an arjoon tree. Sanscrit name (madhyárjuna), meaning middle + arjoon tree, terminalia tomentosa, bedd. [murdah].—"*a*" Deputy tahsildarry, Tanjore district. Pay Rs. 70.—"*b*" Village, Deputy tahsildar's station, Railway station; Tanjore dist., Combaconam tal.; pop. 2,580; lat. 11° 00′; long. 79° 30′; height 73 feet; from Combaconam E.N.E. 6 miles; from Madras S.S.W. 153 miles; from Mayavaram S.W. 15 miles; from Munnargoody N. 23 miles; from Negapatam W.N.W. 31 miles; from Tanjore E.N.E. 25 miles. Residence of some of the Tanjore family. Old and well sculptured Shiva temple with fine gopooram [q.v.], containing inscriptions.——*Tirvadaunay* (திருவாடானை - tiruvádánai, Tam.). From (tiru, tam. holy + ádu, tam. sheep + ánai, tam. elephant); from the temple idol with head of a goat and body of elephant [q.v.].—"*a*" Deputy tahsildarry, Madura district. Pay Rs. 70.—"*b*" Village, Head-quarters of Deputy tahsildar and Sub-registrar; Madura dist., Ramnaud zemindarry; pop. 1,110; lat. 9° 47′; long. 78° 58′; from Dindigul E.S.E. 76 miles; from Kodaykarnal E.S.E. 100 miles; from Madras S.S.W. 243 miles; from Madura E.S.E. 56 miles; from Rameshwaram N. 42 miles; from Ramnaud N. 29 miles; from the sea W. 10 miles. On the road from Shivagunga to Tondy. Old sculptured Shiva temple surrounded by a wall with two copper-plate shausanams [q.v.], dated A.D. 1679, recording grants by Hiranya garbha saitoopaty. Annual festival in April. Weekly market on Monday.——*Tirvallam* (തിരുവല്ലം - tiruvallam, Mal.). From (tiru, mal. holy + vallabha, san. lord). Village, Place of pilgrimage; Travancore state, Trivandrum division, Neittincara tal.; lat. 8° 21′; long. 77° 07′; from Neittincara S. 4 miles; from Trivandrum S.E. 12 miles; from the sea E. 3 miles. Situated at the junction of the Caramana and Kiliyaur and about four miles to the south of Trivandrum. Pagoda [q.v.] to Bramha [q.v.]. Considered by Malayaulies as sacred as Gayay in N. india.——*Tirvancode* (തിരുവാങ്കോട് - tiruvánkótu, Mal.). From (tiru, mal. goddess of prosperity + vázhu, mal. reside + kótu, mal. fort). Sanscrit name (shrivarddhanapurí), meaning lutchmy + prosperity + town. Town; Travancore state, Pudmanaubhapooram division, Yerraneel tal.; pop. 7,402; lat. 8° 14′; long. 77° 21′; from Yerraneel N. 3 miles; from Trivandrum S.E. 28 miles; from the sea N. 8 miles. Once the capital of Travancore. Two miles to the south of Pudmanaubhapooram. Gives its name to the whole state. Former residence of the court, now almost deserted. Trivandrum, the modern capital, was in former days merely the summer residence of the rajah. Ruins of an old fortress. It is now largely inhabited by Mahomedans, most of whom deal in bell-metal [cunts] vessels. Has a mosque [musjid] where the Chandanacoodam [sandal] ceremony is annually performed. Has a very old Shiva temple.——*Tirvanjicoolam* (തിരുവഞ്ചിക്കുളം - tiruvañchikkulam, Mal.). From (tiru, mal. prosperous + vañchi, mal. the country so called + kóvilakam, mal. palace). Mal. also (tiruvañcházhimukham), meaning holy + vanchy, the country so called + sea + face; the prosperous sea-port of the vanchy country. Sanscrit name (jayarátéshvara), meaning victory + giving + shiva, the lord. Village; Cochin state, Moocoondapooram tal.; lat. 10° 13′; long. 76° 15′; from Irinyaulacode S. 10 miles; from Ernacolum N.N.W. 16 miles; from the sea E. 4 miles. Ancient capital of Keralam [q.v.]. The temple to Shiva, by Cherma permaul.——*Tirvarore* (திருவாரூர் - tiruvárúr, Tam.). From (tiru, tam. holy + ár, tam. the tree, cassia fistula, linn. + úr, tam. village); holy place with condray [q.v.] trees. Tam. also (árúr), meaning condray tree, cassia fistula, linn. + village; it also means village of bauhinia racemosa, lam. whose flowers are sacred to shiva as well; also (kamalai), meaning lotus + place. Sanscrit name (kamalálaya), meaning lotus [nelumbo], temple. Otherwise Trivelore.—"*a*" Deputy tahsildarry, Tanjore district. Pay Rs. 70.—"*b*" Town, Railway station, Moonsif's station; Tanjore dist., Negapatam tal.; pop. 9,415; acres 1,011; lat. 10° 47′; long. 79° 41′; height 39 feet; from Negapatam W. 15 miles; from Tanjore E. 33 miles; from the sea W. 14 miles. Sacred to Shiva. Noted for temple and car festival. Former cusbah [q.v.] of a talook [q.v.] now merged in Negapatam talook. Wesleyan mission station. There is a Tamul proverb:—அரிசிப்பொதியுடன் திருவாரூர்—"tirvarore with a bag of rice." Spoken of a double benefit. And another:—காசியிலிறக்க முத்தி கமலையிற்பிறக்கமுத்தி—"death at Caushy, birth at Camalay obtains salvation." Referred to by certain astronomical tables. According to Hindoo geography it lies 3° 32′ 58″ E. of Lunka [q.v.] in longitude [deshauntaram] and in 10° 44′ N. latitude [acsham].——*Tirvauchacam* (திருவாசகம் - tiruvásagam, Tam.). From (above + váchaka, san. word). Collection of hymns to Shiva [q.v.] by Maunicavauchacan [q.v.]. Still current. There is a Tamul proverb:—திருவாசகத்திற்கு உருகாதார் ஒரு வாசகத்திற்கும் உருகார்—"those who are unaffected by Tirvauchacam will "not be moved by any other composition [devauram]." Cf. the Naulauyira prabandham to Vishnoo [q.v.]. See vol. I (56).——*Tirvausal* (திருவாசல் - tiruvásal, Tam.). From (above + vásal, tam. gateway). The gateway [gopooram] of temple [coil, pagoda.]——*Tirvausy* (திருவாசி - tiruvási, Tam.). From (above + vási, tam. contraction of vásigai, tam. garland). The arch or bow over the head of an idol [shilay, vigraham].——*Tirvauthiray* (திருவாதிரை - tiruváthirai, Tam.). From (tiru, tam. auspicious + árdrá, san. sixth lunar mansion). Same as Ardrah darshanam.——*Tirveeraroyan* (തിരുവീരരായൻ - tiruvírarâyan, Mal.). From (above + vira, mal. a hero + ráyan, mal. a king). Hindoo 2nd or pers. name [peyar].——*Tirvengadam* (திருவேங்கடம் - tiruvéngadam, Tam.). From (above + vénkata, san. the mountain). Tripatty, the holy mountain [tirmaley]. Hindoo 2nd or pers. name [peyar].——*Tirvengadamoodgiyal* (திருவேங்கடமுடையாள் - tiruvéngadamudaiyál, Tam.). The possessor of Tripatty, Lutchmy [q.v.].——*Tirvengadasawmy* (திருவேங்கடசாமி - tiruvéngadasámi, Tam.). From (above + venkata, san. mountain + svámí, san. master). Lord of holy tripatty. Hindoo 2nd or pers. name [peyar]. Similarly Tirvengadiah.——*Tirvilaiyaudal* (திருவிளையாடல் - tiruvilaiyádal, Tam.). From (above + vilaiyádal, tam. sport). Sacred sports [leelay] of the deity, applied to the 64 sports of Shiva as Soondreshwaran at Madura. Otherwise Madura pooraunam [q.v.]. By Paranjoty tumbiraun [q.v.], a Pundauram [q.v.] or Sheiva priest, in reign of Hary veera paundyan, in the Shalivahanan [q.v.] year 973 or A.D. 1051. Paraphrase in tamul of sanscrit legend Halausya mahautmyam [q.v.], a section of the Scaundapooraunam [q v.]. See vol. I (123).——*Tirvilakkammay* (திருவிளக்கம்மை - tiruvilakkammai, Tam.). The goddess of the sacred lamps; Lutchmy [q.v.].——*Tirvore* (తిరువూరు - tiruvúru, Tel.). From (tiru, tam. holy + úru, tel. village). Zemindarry, Village, Deputy tahsildar's station; Kistna dist., Vissanapett division; pop. 2,796; lat. of village 17° 07′; long. 80° 39′; from Bezwada N. 41 miles; from Guntoor N. 57 miles; from Madras N. 275 miles; from Masulipatam N.N.W. 71 miles; from Vinoocondah N.E. 94 miles. The zemindars of this place claim descent from the Vellanky family [calagara]. Peshcush Rs. 4,396.——*Tirvulloovan* (திருவள்ளுவன் - tiruvalluvan, Tam.). The holy pariah. Literary name of author of Cooral [q.v.]. Real name unknown. His parents were Bhagavan and Adiyaul, a Bramin and a Pariah. Brought up by a Vulloovan [q.v.], or priest of the Pariah [q.v.] caste, at Mylapore. Tirvulloovar lived during the lifetime of Oogra vazhoothy paundyan, whose reign was the last in which the Madura college existed. He worked at the loom [tarry], wrote his Cooral, and took it to the Madura college [q.v.]. He has many titles, as Deva poolavan divine poet, Moothal pauvalar first of poets, Pernavalar great poet, etc. [pauvalan]. When he died his body was according to his own desire exposed outside the town to be eaten by crows [caurvam]. See vol. I (55).——*Tirvye* (திருவாய் - tiruváy, Tam.). From (above + váy, tam. word). Word of a deity [tirmozhy, tirvye mozhy].——*Tirvyemozhy* (திருவாய்மொழி - tiruváymozhi, Tam.). From (above + váy, tam. mouth + mozhi, tam. word). Otherwise Prabandham. Four thousand stanzas by veishnava alwars [q.v.]. Called, by veishnavas the Tamul vedam. In four books. The first part sacred words, relates the story of Krishnan's child-hood, and contains hymns in praise of temples. The second part, called the great sacred words, is chiefly about Veishnava temples. The third part is termed words of the sacred mouth; the divinity of Vishnoo, how to meditate on him, a message sent to the deity by a bird, duty of men to the deity, are some of the subjects. The fourth part contains prayers to Vishnoo, meditations, &c. Compare the Sheiva tirvauchacam [q.v.]. See vol. I (56). There is a Tamul proverb:—படிக்கிறது திருவாய்மொழி, இடிக்கிறது பெருமாள் கோவில்—"to read Tirvyemozhy and to break down the "temple of Vishnoo;" hypocrisy.——*Travancore* (തിരുവിതാംകൂർ - tiruvitánkúr, Mal.). See sep. title.——*Tricalore* (திருக்கோயிலூர் - tirukkóyilúr, Tam.). See sep. title.——*Trichendore* (திருச்செந்தூர் - tiruççendúr, Tam. tiruchendúr *). From (above + shéndan, tam. skanda + úr, tam. village). Tam. also (alaiváy), meaning wave + mouth; also (tiruççíralaiváy), meaning holy + beauty + wave + mouth; also (shendi), corruption of (jayanti, san.), meaning doorga, the victorious; also (shendil), meaning same. Sanscrit name (jayantípura), meaning doorga + town. Town, Port, Place of pilgrimage; Tinnevelly dist., Tencaray tal.; pop. 9,689; acres 9,482; lat. 8° 30′; long. 78° 10′; from Coolashekharaputnam N.E.

8 miles; from Madras S.S.W. 344 miles; from Shreeveicoontam E.S.E. 18 miles; from Tinnevelly E.S.E. 34 miles; from Veerapandiyanputnam S. 1½ miles. On Gulf of Manaar. Large and important temple built out into the sea, much frequented and containing excellent sculpture. On the shore, a few miles south is a group of sixteen pillars, each bearing an inscription. One of the six places sacred to Soobramanyan [q.v.]. Annual festival in March, when a cattle [maud] fair also takes place. Trig. station at Trichendore mantapam in lat. 8° 29′ 46·36″; long. 78° 10′ 17·22″; height 50 feet; from Tencaray E.S.E. 16 miles; from Trichendore E. ½ mile; from the sea W. ½ mile.——*Trichengode* (திருச்செங்கோடு - tiruççhengódu, Tam.). See sep. title.——*Trichinopoly* (திருச்சிராப்பள்ளி - tiruççináppalli, Tam.). See sep. title.——*Trichore* (തൃശ്ശിവപ്പേരൂർ - trishshivappérúr, Mal.). From (above + shiva, san. the god + peru, mal. great + úr, mal. village). Sanscrit name (parashuráamapurí), meaning parshooraman, the hero + town; also (shríshivaméru), meaning holy + shiva, the god + the mountain, so called.—"*a*" Talook, Cochin state; pop. 104,695. Principal places:—Andicaud, Arimbore, Arnautkara, Cotticaud, Moondore, Olloor, Oorgam, Peringotekara, Permanam, Putticaud, Trichore, Veeyore, Yedacoony, Yenamacull.—"*b*" Town, Head-quarters of Peshcar, Divisional officer, Zillah judge, Tahsildar and Moonsif, Telegraph office; Cochin state, Trichore tal.; pop. 11,638; lat. 10° 32′; long. 76° 15′; height 29 feet; from Bangalore S.W. 190 miles; from Bombay S.S.E. 588 miles; from Chetwye E. 12 miles; from Chittoor W.S.W. 37 miles; from Chowghaut E.S.E. 13 miles; from Cochin city N. 38 miles; from Ernacolum N. 38 miles; from Madras W.S.W. 325 miles; from Tripoontora N.N.W. 41 miles; from the sea E. 13 miles. Very old town on the Malabar coast said to have been founded by Parshooraman sixth incarnation [avatar] of Vishnoo. Chief centre of Braminism. The site is advantageous, being close to the eastern coast of the backwater by which it communicates with Chowghaut, Calicut, and the city of Cochin; by land the only route is that proceeding north-east to Palghaut, being a defile through jungles infested with wild elephants and other wild animals, and very unhealthy from November to March. The town is considered healthy. The Cochin rajah has a fine country residence situated within a ruined mud fort. The fortifications erected in 1774 have been destroyed. A detachment of Native infantry under the British government is stationed here. Active trade with Palghaut and Cochin. One Malayalam weekly paper and one monthly magazine published here.—"*c*" Lake; Cochin state; Trichore tal.; lat. 10° 25′ to 10° 35′ N.; long. 76° 09′ to 76° 15′ E.; from Ernacolum N. 30 miles. Otherwise called Yenamacull mouth. Of great value, and deserves notice, if only for the singular struggle of human industry against the forces of nature, which the cultivation of its bed demands. From the subsidence of the floods of one year to the commencement of the following rains the time is barely sufficient for the garnering of a crop. At the close of the rains the water in the lake, which is protected from tidal influences by a masonry dam at Yenamacull, is drained off by ceaseless labor day and night with Persian wheels [chuckram] aided not unfrequently by patent pumps driven by portable steam-engines. Every foot of reclaimed ground is protected by fences of wattle and mud and is planted up with rice seedlings [nautt]. Spaces are left between the fields, and into these channels the water drawn from the fields is poured; so that boats have to be employed for visiting the different fields, the dry beds of which lie some three or four feet below the level of the water in the canals. The bulwarks of the fields are frequently breached and the unmatured crop drowned [colpoonjah]. A small portion only of this lake lies in British territory. The major portion belongs to the Cochin state. The original dam was formed during the eighteenth century by united efforts of the Zamorin and Cochin rajahs. It is now annually repaired at the joint cost of the British and Cochin governments.——*Trimal* (திருமலை - tirumalai, Tam.). From (above + malai, tam. mountain). Epithet of Tripatty.——*Trimal deva* (తిరుమలదేవ - tirumaladéva, Tel.). From (tirumalai, tam. the holy mountain + déva, san. god). Name of two rajahs of Vijianugger of the Rama rajah dynasty [charitram].——*Trimal naick* (திருமலைநாயக்கன் - tirumalaináyakkan, Tam.). Name + third name. Naick [q.v.] ruler of Paundya [q.v.]. A.D. 1623—1659. See vol. I (121), (154); vol. II, 96, 250. Fifteen rulers of the Naick race are enumerated as having borne sway over Madura and Tinnevelly between 1559 and 1736. By far the most distinguished was this prince, whose magnificent tastes are attested by the buildings he erected at Madura, especially his palace, a Saracenic structure which is the grandest building of its kind in Southern india [maunasauram, stanpatyam]. What is now a palace was originally little more than the hall of audience. He erected another palace of much smaller dimensions, but in the same style of architecture at Shreevillipoottore in Tinnevelly, where, it is said, he liked to reside occasionally. The remains of this palace are now utilized as the Tahsildar's cutcherry [q.v.]. The greater part of Trimal naick's reign however was disfigured by exhausting and impolitic wars [charitram].——*Trimal saitoopaty* (திருமலைசேதுபதி - tirumalaisethuppathi, Tam.). Name + title. Otherwise Raghoonaut tevar. Ruler of Ramnaud from 1645 to 1670. Drove back a Mysore invasion. Introduced the Navarautry [pundigay, 6d] festival at Ramnaud. See vol. I (124).——*Trimal shree runga* (తిరుమలశ్రీరంగ - tirumalashríranga, Tel.). From (tirumala, tel. holy hill, tripatty + shrí, san. holy + ranga, san. island, also vishnu), vishnoo, the god of shreerungam at tripatty. Rajah of Vijianugger of the Rama rajah dynasty. A.D. 1564—1585. See vol. II, 251.——*Trinomallee* (திருவண்ணாமலை - tiruvannámalai, Tam.). See sep. title.——*Tripah* (തൃപ്പ - tripa, Mal.). From (tri, mal. fortunate + pá, san. to protect). Title of Travancore rajah.——*Tripah swaroopam* (തൃപ്പാസ്വരൂപം - trippásvarúpam, Mal.). From (tripa, san. auspicious ruler + svarúpa, san. dynasty). The dynasty of Travancore or Venaud.——*Tripassore* (திருப்பாசூர் - tiruppásúr, Tam.). From (above + pásu, tam. green + úr, tam. village). Sanscrit name (vamsháranya), meaning bamboo + forest.—"*a*" Zemindarry; Chingleput dist., Trivellore tal.; pop. 2,656; square miles 3; lat. 13° 09′; long. 79° 56′. Peshcush Rs. 2,554.—"*b*" Village; Chingleput dist., Trivellore tal.; pop. 2,656; acres 1,685; lat. 13° 09′; long. 79° 56′; from Sydapett N.W. 25 miles; from Trivellore W. 2 miles. Formerly a cantonment and station for cadets in Company's service, more recently same for pensioned European soldiers. The old fort served as a protection to adjacent country from ravages of neighbouring poligars. Captured by Sir Eyre Coote in 1781. Old Shiva temple with Chola inscriptions. The level of the plain is 183 feet above the sea.——*Tripatore* (திருப்பத்தூர் - tiruppattúr, Tam.). See sep. title.——*Tripatty* (తిరుపతి - tirupati, Tel.; திருப்பதி - tiruppathi, Tam. tirupati*). From (above + pathi, tam. village). Sanscrit name (govindarájapattana), means town of the king govindan or vishnoo.—"*a*" Deputy tahsildarry, North arcot district. Pay Rs. 70.—"*b*" Town, Head-quarters of Deputy tahsildar and District moonsif; North arcot dist., Chundragherry tal.; pop. 14,242; acres 7,182; lat. 13° 38′; long. 79° 28′; height 635 feet; from Arnee N. 67 miles; from Chittore N.E. 36 miles; from Chundragherry E.N.E. 8 miles; from Madras W.N.W. 70 miles; from Ranipett N. 49 miles; from Vellore N.N.E. 53 miles. On the road from Madras to Cuddapah, at foot of Eastern ghauts [q.v.], in valley between Tripatty hills and those of Carvetnugger. Swarnamookhy passes a mile south. Lower tripatty in contradistinction to that on the hill. Is an extremely old town with ruined temples. There are 15 temples, many insignificant. The chief are of Govindarajasawmy and Ramasawmy. The former sawmy is brother of Vencateshwaran, and in his honor Tripatty is sometimes called Govindrajputnam. In September the town is full, owing to Bramhotsavam [pundigay, 6a] feast at Upper tripatty. In April or May is the Gungah yautray [pundigay, 6a] feast, 10 days. A waterfall, Capila teertam, descends from hill north of town, up to corridors of stone supported upon carved pillars. It is the duty of every pilgrim to bathe in Capila teertam before ascending the hills, and if he can swim to go and sit upon a figure of Hanooman [q.v.] over which the water falls [aroovy]. Bazaars brisk. There is a Tamul proverb:—திருப்பதிக்குப் போனாலும் துடைப்பம் ஒரு காசு—"though taken to Tripatty, a broom "will fetch only a cash." For Upper tripatty, the place of pilgrimage, see Tirmaley.——*Tripoontora* (തൃപ്പൂണിത്തുറ - trippúnittara, Mal.). From (above + púnuka, mal. to embrace + tara, mal. village). Sanscrit name (shrípúrnapura), means fortune + full + town. Latin Tropinæ. Village; Cochin state, Canyanore tal.; lat. 9° 57′; long. 76° 23′; from Chittoor S.S.W. 60 miles; from Cochin E.S.E. 7 miles; from Ernacolum E.S.E. 5 miles; from Madras S.W. 340 miles; from Trichore S.S.E. 41 miles; from the sea E. 7 miles. Enclosed village. Residence of the Royal family of Cochin.——*Tritrapoondy* (திருத்துறைப்பூண்டி - tirutturaippúndi, Tam.). See sep. title.——*Trittany* (திருத்தணி - tiruttani, Tam. tirutani*). From (above + tanigai, tam. ancient name for the place). Sanscrit name (kshanikáchala), means leisure + mountain. Ancient Tamul name (tanigai), place of relief.—"*a*" Sub-magistrate's division, Carvetnugger zemindarry, North arcot district. Pay Rs. 100.—"*b*" Village, Hill, Railway station, Place of pilgrimage, Headquarters of Zemindar's revenue talook and of Sub-magistrate's division; North arcot dist., Carvetnugger zemindarry; pop. 3,504; lat. 13° 11′; long. 79° 40′; height 283 feet; from Arnee N.N.E. 42 miles; from Carvetnugger S.S.E. 20 miles; from Chittore E. 34 miles; from Madras W. 47 miles; from Ranipett N.E. 25 miles; from Tripatty S.S.E. 35 miles; from Vellore E.N.E. 36 miles. In south of zemindarry. The town includes four villages, Amoortapooram, Mattamgraumam, Nullanigoonta, and Trittany proper. Mattamgraumam the most holy. Name from mutts [q.v.], choultries [q.v.], and mantapams [q.v.]. The temple stands upon a low range of hills. To Soobramanya sawmy, with wives Devasenay or devayaunay [q.v.] and Vulliyammay [q.v.]. The ascent is by two flights of stone steps on the east and west. Almost all the houses are of local stone. There are nine Teertams [q.v.]:—Agastyan, Bramha, Comaura, Indra, Naurada, Rama, Sapta rishy, Shesha, and Vishnoo. In the temple itself is Keilausa teertam. There are also nine separate lingams [q.v.]. On S. of hill are the seven pools, around which are built the temples of the seven celebrated virgins and Veerabhadra sawmy. Trade in grain and cloths during the Nacshatram [q.v.], feasts once in every lunar month. Particularly in Audy or july, Caurtigay or november, and Maushy [mausam] or february. Bramhotsavams [pundigay,

6a] for ten days in Maushy or february and Chittray [mausam] or april.—"*c*" River; North arcot dist., Carvetnugger zemindarry. Takes its source in Sholinghur hills, runs east and joins Cooshastaly near Arcot-cooppam. Flows between August and December. Crossed by the railway bridge N. of Trittany railway station.——*Trivandrum* (തിരുവനന്തപുരം - tiruvanantapuram, Mal.). From (above + ananta san. serpent, the eternal one + pura, san. city). Sanscrit name (anantashayana), meaning vishnoo, whose bed is the serpent god and to whom pagoda is dedicated as tutelary deity of maharajahs of travancore.—"*a*" Revenue division, Travancore state; pop. 352,679. The smallest of the four divisions, divided into 4 talooks.—"*b*" Talook, Travancore state, Trivandrum division; pop. 102,986. Subdivided into ten praverties [q.v.] or adhicaurams, and containing eighty-eight caras [q.v.] or villages. Bounded N. by Nedoovengaud talook, E. by Neittincara talook, S. by the Indian ocean and W. by Cherankeel talook. Presents a variety of aspects; consisting of hills, valleys, mountains, riversides, seashore, &c.—"*c*" Town, Headquarters of Resident, Divisional and Judges' head-quarters, Place of pilgrimage, Cantonment. It is the capital of the Travancore state, the residence of H.H. The Maharajah, Head-quarters of the Travancore government. Seat of the Huzoor [q.v.] cutcherry [q.v.] and other public offices, of the High court and of the chief educational institutions of Government including a college educating up to the highest standard. Travancore state, Trivandrum division, Trivandrum tal.; pop. 41,173 including the fort, fort alone 3,521; lat. 8° 28′; long. 76° 59′; from Alleppey S.S.E. 80 miles; from Bombay S.S.E. 760 miles; from Cannanore S.E. 255 miles; from Cottayam S.S.E. 80 miles; from Madras S.W. 386 miles; from Nagarcoil W.N.W. 38 miles; from Paravore S.S.E. 123 miles; from Quilon S.E. 37 miles; from the sea E. 2 miles; from Veily E.S.E. 5 miles. The Caramana and Kiliyaur intersect the town; and several other minor streams find their way to the sea in the vicinity. As the outfall is imperfect, lower parts of town are unhealthy. Several public buildings, country houses of the Maharajah and princes, houses of European and wealthy natives, &c., are built on isolated laterite [q.v.] hills rising from 50 to 200 feet above sea-level and commanding beautiful scenery. The fort and a great part of the native town are on the low level. The fort, which is of no military value, is surrounded by a high wall. There are extensive Bramin streets both in the fort and in suburbs adjoining the same. The Kiliyaur feeds a large tank within the fort which is largely used by the public. Within the fort are the palaces of the Maharajah and of the princes and princesses of the ruling family, and the great temple of Pudmanaubhan. These buildings are picturesque, and display the local characteristics of high-pitched gables projecting ridges, deep eaves, overhanging balconies, verandahs [q.v.] with massive wooden pillars and elaborate wood-carving, testifying alike to the profusion of timber in the State and the skill of its artisans. The temple is crowned with a lofty tower over its entrance, from the summit of which there is fine view of the surrounding country. The temple is of great antiquity, and is held in the highest regard. The temple enjoys a land revenue of Rs. 75,000, and is almost independent of the State. The frequent religious ceremonies required of Travancore princes, which can only be performed with efficacy at the shrine of Pudmanaubhan, will probably long necessitate the residence of the Maharajah in the immediate neighbourhood of the temple. The cantonment with Nayar brigade is north of town. The town is opened on all sides by well-formed roads covering a space of ground over 6 miles in length. An observatory was built by the Maharajah in 1836. The first astronomer was appointed in 1837. In 1854 a branch observatory was established on Agastya mullay, but in 1865 this establishment was broken up. The main observatory is now under native management. The most interesting modern building is the Napier museum, which has been erected in the public gardens, on plans embracing the prominent features of Malayalam architecture. Among the well built public buildings may be mentioned the public offices, the college and the preparatory school, the residency at Tekkaud and the General hospital. There is no regular port; the surf on the coast is high, and the few vessels which touch have to lie out a long way from the shore. A succession of canals running along the coast to the north connects the local backwaters, and puts the town in direct communication with the great backwater system of northern Travancore and Cochin and with the Madras railway. There was formerly a break at Warkully, about 20 miles north of Trivandrum, where high laterite headlands abut on the sea. Heavy works consisting of two tunnels have been completed at a cost of 18 lakhs and have surmounted this.——*Trivaudy* (திருவாதி - tiruváthi, Tam. tiruvádi *). From (above + ádi, san. shiva). The first god. Tam. also (tiruvaiyár), meaning holy + five + river. Sanscrit name (pañchanada), meaning five rivers. They are the Coleroon, the Cauvery proper, the Coodamoorty, the Vellaur and the Vennaur all running parallel within the breadth of six miles.—"*a*" Deputy tahsildarry, Tanjore district. Pay Rs. 70.—"*b*" Town, Head-quarters of Deputy tahsildar and Registrar, and Moonsif's court; Tanjore dist., Tanjore tal.; pop. 7,907; acres 1,227; lat. 10° 53′; long. 79° 09′; from Combaconam W.S.W. 19 miles; from Madras S.S.W. 169 miles; from Mayavaram W.S.W. 39 miles; from Munnargoody W.N.W. 27 miles; from Negapatam W.N.W. 50 miles; from Tanjore N.N.W. 7 miles. On the right bank of the Cauvery in the midst of the most richly cultivated and productive rice-fields in the delta [conamoogam] of that river. In this neighbourhood, the river margins and isolated spots of dry and elevated ground produce immense quantities of vegetables and green-crops; while village sites are covered with thick clumps of high trees, such as cocoanut [q.v.], mango [q.v.], tamarind [q.v.] and ilooppay [mohwah], and with bamboo [q.v.] bushes, which grow to a great height. Paddy [q.v.] land in this neighbourhood sells at about Rs. 500 an acre, but in some cases it cannot be had at even double this price. Shivajee halted here in his first descent on Tanjore. Before 1860 this was head-quarters of the Trivaudy talook. One of the principal centres of Braminical religion with a large temple, which is held more than ordinarily sacred, and is considered to impart special merit to ablutions in the Cauvery at this particular spot. It is the general resort of aged and pious Bramins, who terminate their existence here. Old Shiva temple with Chola inscription. On sacred and festival days, in April and January, streams of visitors may be seen flowing into the town from Tanjore.——*Trivellore* (திருவள்ளூர் - tiruvallúr, Tam.). See sep. title.——*Trivettore* (திருவொற்றியூர் - tiruvottiyúr, Tam.). From (above + áthi, tam. shiva, the first one + úr, tam. village). Sanscrit name (ádipura), meaning shiva, the first one + town. Town, Place of pilgrimage; Chingleput dist., Sydapett tal.; pop. 7,429; acres 1,726; lat. 13° 10′; long. 80° 22′; from Sydapett N.N.E. 11 miles; from the sea W. ¾ mile. Visited by Fryer in 1673 and mentioned in his Travels. He calls it Triblitore. Cuttiwaukum, Shauttancaud and Trivettore were granted on 25th September 1708 by a Purwauna [q.v.] from Davood khan, Nawaub [q.v.] and Fowjdar [q.v.] of the Carnatic [q.v.] portion of the Golcondah soobah [q.v.]. Resumed by Nawaub saad ool lah khan, 1713. Firmaun [q.v.] from the emperor Feroksere, cancelling this resumption and confirming the grant, 5th January 1716. Confirmed again by the general firmaun of the Moghul, 12th August 1765. Old Shiva temple with inscriptions. Grand annual festival during February.——*Trivettore* (திருவத்தூர் - tiruvattúr, Tam. tiruvetipuram *). From (above + ottumai, tam. joint + úr, tam. village). Tam. also (ottiyúr), meaning clubbed village; also (otti), meaning dependent village. Sanscrit name (védapurí), means city of the sacred writing. Otherwise Wottiyore and Wotty. Village, Place of pilgrimage; North arcot dist., Arcot tal.; pop. 1,866; includes five villages which form the town; acres 728; lat. 12° 39′; long. 79° 35′; from Arcot S.E. 23 miles; from Chittore S.E. 50 miles. Close to N. bank of Cheyaur. Once of importance as head-quarters of the old Trivettore talook and of a District moonsif. Originally a stronghold of Jeinas [q.v.]. When they denied truth of Shiva [q.v.] religion, it was agreed that the rival Vedams [q.v.] should be subjected to ordeal by being dropped into Cheyaur. The Jeina vedams floated down the river as far as Anaputtoor, while the Bramin vedams moved against the stream for 2 miles to Cheyyautvendraun. Some Jeinas were therefore hanged, some cut to pieces, some crushed in oil mills. These executions are represented by sculptures on walls of temple. A sculpture, 8 feet high cut out of a single stone and placed under a small mantapam [q.v.] in the temple, represents a palmyra [q.v.] tree bearing male blossoms on one side and female blossoms on the other. Held to be work of Shiva as a representation of himself and Parvaty [q.v.], in one body as Ardha naureeshwaran [ardhanaury].——*Trivetty* ((திருவதி - tiruvathi, Tam. tiruvadi *). From (above + pathi, tam. place). Place of pilgrimage; South arcot dist., Cuddalore tal.; pop. 5,068; acres 2,841; lat. 11° 46′; long. 79° 37′; height 166 feet; from Cuddalore W.N.W. 14 miles; from the sea W. 15 miles. On the Guddilam. Former head-quarters of a Deputy tahsildar. In June 1750, during the absence of Nauzir jung and Mahomed ally at Arcot, Dupleix possessed himself of the place. Mahomed ally with the assistance of a body of English troops marched to retake it in the July following. The commander refused to surrender, but the Nawaub declined the assault, and the English returned to Fort st. david. Mahomed ally's army was routed by Dupleix in the neighbourhood and the latter at once marched on and took Jinjee. In 1752, after the death of Chundah sahib, the garrison surrendered to the English, who with Mahomed ally's forces encamped here; from this the English made excursions into the country to secure the districts for the Nawaub [q.v.]. In September 1752, Major Lawrence marched hence to attack Wandiwash which was ransomed. On the 3rd January 1753, the united forces of the French and Mahrattas, the latter under Moraury row, entrenched themselves on the banks of the Pennair in sight of Trivetty. They attacked Lawrence on the 9th May, but were repulsed. On the 1st of April the English force under Lawrence defeated the Mahrattas and the French. Lawrence and most of his troops were now summoned to Trichinopoly, as were most of the French force. The remainder attacked Trivetty in April 1753 and, after having been driven back twice, succeeded in taking the Pettah [q.v.], owing to mutiny in the garrison. After the capture of Vardoor in April 1769, Trivetty surrendered without resistance to a small English force.

TIRAUNA (कर्णिकार - karnikára, *San.*; ರಾಯಬೋರೆ - ráyabóre, *Can.*; కొండపాపట - kondapápata, *Tel.*; କଚୁରିଆଚାଲ - kachúriyachál, *Oor.*; കുപ്പിപ്പു - kuppippú, *Mal.*; തരണ - tarana,

Singh.; திருநப்பழம் - tirunáppazham, *Tam.*). Title from singhalese. San. means resembling an ear-ring [hemp bendy, kaniyaur]. Can. from (ráya, can. king, hence large + bóre, can. the jujube tree, zizyphus jujuba, lamk.). Tel. from (konda, tel. hill + pápata, tel. pavetta indica, linn.). Mal. from (kuppi, mal. bottle + pú, mal. flower). San. also (vyádhiripu), meaning enemy to disease; (drumótpala), meaning tree + water-lily, nymphæa lotus, linn.; (pragrahá), meaning stretching forth; (kritamála), meaning made into garland; (parivyádha), meaning struck on all sides; (rájataru), meaning king's tree [common condray]; (sup'halá), meaning having good fruit [plantain]; (pádapótpala); meaning tree + water-lily. Can. also (páputigida), properly pavetta. Tel. also (bommapápata), meaning doll + pavetta indica, linn.; (kommi). Mal. also (puliyáyini), meaning sour, artocarpus hirsuta, lamk. Tam. also (kurá); (kódilam); (velvedchi), meaning white + ixora coccinea, linn. Title otherwise Bottle flower tree, Commy, Tree water-lily. Botanically Webera corymbosa, willd., rubiaceæ [vricsham, 71]. Alias Canthium coryinbosum; Cupia corymbosa; Gardenia pavetta; Ixora alba; Pavetta wightiana; Polyozus maderaspatanus; Rondeletia asiatica; Stylocoryne webera; Tarenna zeylanica. Webera asiatica, cerifera, zeylanica. Pavetta from (pávattai, tam. pavetta indica, linn.); Tarenna from singhalese. Shrub, glabrous; leaves polished leathery, lanceolate oblong; shining; corymbs trichotomous, terminal; calyx five-cleft; tube of corolla short, twice the length of the calyx tube, widened and bearded at the mouth, segments of limb recurved, villous at the base along the middle, about twice as long as the tube; berry two-celled; cells four to eight seeded; flowers small white, afterwards, cream-colored, fragrant; young shoots are frequently covered with resinous exudation [raul]; the fruit is a small black berry, edible. Hard wood, but very small; used in ceylon for fishing boats. There are other species:—lucens, monosperma.

TIRMUNGALAM (திருமங்கலம் - tirumangalam,* *Tam.*). From (tiru, tam. holy + mangala, san. prosperity) [shree, tir]. —(1) Talook, Madura district. Tahsildar's pay Rs. 200. Area 745 square miles. Population 264,621. Language tamul; a coarse sort of Teloogoo is spoken by Reddies. S. inland part of district. Bounded on the north by Dindigul and Madura talooks, on the east by Madura talook, Shivagunga and Ramnaud zemindarries, on the south by Ramnaud zemindarry, Shauttore and Shreevillipoottore talooks of Tinnevelly district, on the west by Periyacoolam talook. The talook is one vast plain with rugged rocks and verdure here and there. The western boundary consists of a chain of hills which are a continuation of the Western ghauts [q.v.]. Soil generally fertile, but suited better for dry than for wet crops [q.v.]. The soils are black cotton soil [regar], red soil, and gravelly soil. No Industry of note, except dyeing [shauyam], for which Tirmungalam town is remarkable. Tanks [q.v.] mostly fed by rain [mazhay] and a few by the jungle streams called Goondaur and Gowndanuddy. Camping grounds:—Callottputty, Culligoody and Tirmungalam. Places of archæological interest:—Calloottputty, Cattacaroop-panputty, Cooppalnuttam, Devancoorchy, Mailattimaunikam, Poottore, Shilarputty, Sindooputty, Tidiyan, Vicramungalam. Principal trig. stations:—Gopaulsawmy pagoda, Shathooragherry. The leading places, &c., in the talook are the following.——*Carmattore* (கருமாத்தூர் - karumáttúr, Tam.). From (karu, tam. black + máthu, tam. woman + úr, tam. village); from the amman. Village; pop. 3,452; acres 4,025; lat. 9° 56′; long. 77° 58′; from Madura W. 12 miles; from Tirmungalam N.N.W. 8 miles.——*Culligoody* (கள்ளிக்குடி - kallikkudi, Tam. kalligudi*). From (kalli, tam. milk-hedge, euphorbia tirucalli, linn. + kudi, tam. village). Village, Railway station; pop. 3,327; acres 4,808; lat. 9° 56′; long. 78° 00′; height 362 feet; from Madura S.S.W. 19 miles; from Tirmungalam S.S.W. 9 miles.——*Doddappa naickanore* (தொட்டப்பநாயக்கனூர் - tottappanáyakkanúr, Tam.). From (doddappanáyakudu, tel. proper name + úr, tam. village). Zemindarry, Village; pop. 5,627; lat. 9° 56′; long. 77° 53′; from Madura W.N.W. 26 miles; from Tirmungalam N.W. 13 miles. Peshcush of zemindarry Rs. 2,179.——*Goondaur* (குண்டாறு - kundáru, Tam.). See sep. title.——*Gopaulsawmy pagoda* (கோபாலசாமிக்கோவில் - kóbálasámikkóvil, Tam.). From (kóbálasámi, tam. deity + kóvil, tam. pagoda). Sanscrit name (garudaparvata), meaning braminy kite + mountain. Trig. station; lat. 9° 39′ 18·70″; long. 77° 50′ 27·02″; height 671 feet; from Mothagam S.S.W. 1¾ miles; from Paurapufty E. 1½ miles; from Tirmungalam S.W. 17 miles.——*Jotila naickanore* (சோதிலநாயக்கனூர் - shóthilanáyakkanúr, Tam.). From (shóthilinganáyakkan, tam. proper name + úr, tam. village). Zemindarry, Village; pop. 1,486; square miles 5¼; lat. of village 9° 55′; long. 77° 49′; from Madura W. 24 miles; from Tirmungalam W.N.W. 15 miles. Peshcush Rs. 1,070.——*Keelcottah* (கீழக்கோட்டை - kílakkóttai, Tam.). From (kízh, tam. east + kóttai, tam. fort). Zemindarry, Village; pop. 667; square miles 3; lat. of village 9° 47′; long. 78° 03′; from Madura S.W. 11 miles; from Tirmungalam S.S.E. 3 miles. Peshcush Rs. 480.——*Melacottah* (மேலக்கோட்டை - mélakkóttai, Tam.). From (mél, tam. west + kóttai, tam. fort). Zemindarry, Village; square miles 1¾; lat. of village 9° 47′; long. 78° 02′; from Madura S.W. 11 miles; from Tirmungalam S. 3 miles. Peshcush Rs. 910.——*Nadoocottah* (நடுக்கோட்டை - nadukkóttai, Tam.). From (nadu, tam. central + kóttai, tam. fort). Zemindarry, Village; pop. 787; square miles 1⅓; lat. of village 9° 48′; long. 78° 02′; from Madura S.W. 12 miles; from Tirmungalam S.S.E. 2 miles. Peshcush Rs. 773.——*Oosilamputty* (உசிலம்பட்டி - usilambatti, Tam.). See sep. title.——*Oottapa naickanore* (உத்தப்பநாயக்கனூர் - uttappanáyakkanúr, Tam.). From (uttappanáyakkan, tam. proper name + úr, tam. village). Zemindarry, Village; pop. 3,223; acres 10,391; lat. of village 10° 02′; long. 77° 50′; from Madura W.N.W. 24 miles; from Tirmungalam N.W. 20 miles. Zemindarry pays peshcush [q.v.] of Rs. 2,583.——*Peraiyoor* (பேரையூர் - péraiyúr, Tam. peraiyúr *). From (pér, tam. large + ai, tam. place + úr, tam. village). Zemindarry, Village; pop. 3,480; lat. of village 9° 44′; long. 77° 50′; from Madura S.W. 26 miles; from Tirmungalam W.S.W. 14 miles. Zemindarry [q.v.] pays peshcush [q.v.] of Rs. 11,857. ——*Pooliyangoolam* (புளியங்குளம் - puliyangulam, Tam.). From (puli, tam. tamarind tree, tamarindus indica, linn. + kulam, tam. tank). Zemindarry, Village; pop. 2,811; square miles 5; lat. of village 9° 40′; long. 77° 57′; from Madura S.W. 23 miles; from Tirmungalam S.S.W. 13 miles. Peshcush Rs. 1,931.——*Poottore* (புத்தூர் - puttúr, Tam.). From (puthu, tam. new + úr, tam. village). Village; pop. 7,625; lat. 2° 57′; long. 77° 51′; from Madura W. 21 miles; from Tirmungalam N.W. 14 miles. Old shiva temple with inscriptions.——*Shandaiyoor* (சந்தையூர் - shandaiyúr, Tam.). From (shandai, tam. market + úr, tam. village). Zemindarry, Village; pop. 1,311; lat. of village 9° 42′; long. 77° 48′; from Madura S.W. 30 miles; from Tirmungalam W.S.W. 17 miles. Peshcush of zemindarry Rs. 3,697.——*Shathooragherry* (சதுரகிரி - shathuragiri, Tam.). From (chatura, san. square + giri, san. mountain). Sanscrit name (chaturáchala), meaning same. Trig. station; lat. 9° 44′ 20·30″; long. 77° 43′ 07·26″; height 4,172 feet; from Shauptore W.S.W. 5 miles; from Tirmungalam W.S.W. 22 miles.——*Shauptore* (சாப்டூர் - sháppattúr, Tam. sáptúr *). From (shá, tam. death + pattu, tam. village + úr, tam. village). Zemindarry, Village; pop. 2,540; lat. of village 9° 46′; long. 77° 47′; from Madura W.S.W. 27 miles; from Tirmungalam W.S.W. 16 miles. Zemindarry pays peshcush [q.v.] of Rs. 8,833. ——*Sindooputty* (சிந்துப்பட்டி - shinduppatti, Tam.). From (shindu, tam. river + patti, tam. village). Village; pop. 1,370; acres 1,821; lat. 9° 53′; long. 77° 55′; from Madura W. 16 miles; from Tirmungalam W.N.W. 9 miles. Temples with Paundy [q.v.] inscriptions.——*Tirmungalam* (திருமங்கலம் - tirumangalam, Tam.). See below.——*Vicramungalam* (விக்கிரமங்கலம் - vikkiramangalam, Tam.). From (vikrama, san. proper name + mangala, san. prosperity). Village; pop. 2,284; acres 3,092; lat. 10° 01′; long. 77° 58′; from Madura N. 14 miles; from Tirmungalam W.N.W. 12 miles. Inscriptions of Paundy dynasty at the Shiva temple.——*Yeloomullay* (எழுமலை - ezhumalai, Tam.). From (ezhumai, tam. height + malai, tam. mountain). Zemindarry, Village; pop. 4,820; lat. of village 9° 52′; long. 77° 44′; from Madura W. 28 miles; from Tirmungalam W. 19 miles. Peshcush of zemindarry Rs. 3,612.—(2) Town; Railway station, Talook head-quarters, Sub-registrar's office, Madura dist., Tirmungalam tal.; pop. 6,451; acres 77; lat. 9° 49′; long. 78° 02′; height 416 feet; from Dindigul S. 37 miles; from Kodaykarnal S.E. 44 miles; from Madras S.S.W. 270 miles; from Madura S.W. 11 miles; from Rameshwaram W.N.W. 98 miles; from Ramnaud N.W. 66 miles. Vellaula [q.v.] colony established in 1566 by Ariya naick moodelly, deputy of Vijianugger.

TIROO (திரு - tiru, *Tam.*). To turn.——*Tirootauly* (पर्णक - parnaka, San.; ऐरण - airana, Mahr.; ತಗ್ಗಿಬಳ್ಳಿ - taggiballi, Can.; తెక్కలి - tekkali, Tel.; തിരുതാളി - tirutáli, Mal.; தழுதாழை - tazhutházhai, Tam.). Title from malayalam. San. from (parna, san. leaf). Can. from (taggu, can. low + balli, can. creeper). Mal. from (tiru, mal. to turn + táli, mal. creeper), twisting creeper. Tam. from (tazhuvu, tam. to entwine + tázhai, tam. screw-pine, pandanus odoratissimus, linn.). San. also (vátaghní), meaning wind + destroyer. Tel. also (talúki); (tukadi); (tilaka), meaning ornamental as the forehead mark [country cinnamon, peacock gingelly]; (nelli) [buffalo moonnay, curry moonnay]. Tam. also (váthamadakki), meaning wind + suppresser; useful in flatulency. Title otherwise Creeping screwpine, Wind killer. Botanically Clerodendron [bhaurgam] phlomoides, linn. f., verbenaceæ [vricsham, 102]. Alias Volkameria multiflora. Shrub or small tree, branchlets terete, and like the petioles and peduncles, whitish tomentose; leaves membranaceous, opposite, petioled, ovate, or ovate-rhomboid, acuminate, somewhat obtuse, entire at both ends, irregularly and bluntly serrated in the middle; glabrous above, puberulous beneath; panicles terminal, large, fastigiate, leafy below; cymes trichotomous, lax; bracteoles oblong; clayx glabrous, campanulate-ventricose, half five-cleft, segments sub-ovate, acute; tube of the corolla subglandulose, thrice the length of the calyx; flowers white; flowering nearly all the year; very sweet-scented particularly at night. Juice of leaves somewhat bitter, and medicinally alterative; prescribed in syphilitic complaints and rheumatism. There is a variety with red flowers.——*Tirye* (திராய் - tiráy, Tam.). See sep. title.

TIRTIRA (ترترا - tharthará, *Hind.*; నూనెబుడ్డిగాడు - núnebuddigádu, *Tel.*). Hind. means shaking; from motion of its tail. Tel. from (núne, tel. oil + buddi, tel. bottle + gádu, tel. personal suffix); from glossy black of back and wings. Ruticilla rufiventris, ruticillinæ, sylviadæ [calácuntam], dentirostres, insessores [pacshy, 23], of naturalists [jantoo]. Alias Phænicura atrata; Ruticilla indica, nipalensis. Frequents groves, gardens, old buildings and houses; feeds on the ground, on various insects.

TIRYAUK (تریاک - tiryák, *Hind.*). From (rík, ar. spittle of serpents). Theriaca andromachi, or Venice treacle. A medicine in the form of an electuary supposed to be an antidote to the poison of venomous animals. Invented or introduced into europe by Andromachus of Crete. It was a mixture of seventy ingredients, some inert, others antagonistic to one another. The title revived by some native practitioners [hakeem, veidyan].

TIRYE (ग्रीष्मसुन्दर - gríshmasundara, *San.*; చాతరాశి - chátaráshi, *Tel.*; ചെറുചോനകപ്പുല്ലു - cheruchónakappullu, *Mal.*; திராய் - tiráy, *Tam.*). Title from tamul [tiroo]. San. from (gríshma, san. summer + sundara, san. beauty). Mal. from (cheru, mal. small + chónakappullu, mal. the grass, medicago esculenta). Tam. from (tiri, tam. to ramble); from straggling habit [pitpapra]. San. also (gríshmajá), meaning born in summer. Tel. also (pilakasáre). Tam. also (perundiráy), meaning large + the plant; (oduvadakki), meaning boil subduer [cooppamainy]. Title otherwise Bed straw plant, Carpetweed, Indian chickweed. Botanically Mollugo [parpatam] spergula, linn., ficoideæ [vricsham, 66]. Alias Mollugo parviflora, verticellata; Pharnaceum mollugo, parviflorum. Small herbaceous plant; stem very straggling and branched; leaves more or less succulent, oblong or obovate, mucronate, alternated towards their base; pedicels one-flowered, several together, forming a simple sessile umbel; stamens three to five or ten; petals narrow, cleft to the middle, or none; seeds rough with numerous tubercles; flowers small, white; flowering nearly all year. Bitter leaves medicinally stomachic, aperient and antiseptic; leaf used as famine food.——*Small tirye* (చిరుచాతరాశి - chirichátaráshi, Tel.). Tel. from (chiru, tel. small + chátaráshi, tel. mollugo spergula, linn.). Title otherwise Australian tooth flower, the petals having on either side a small tooth-like process. Botanically Dentella repens, forst., rubiaceæ [vricsham, 71]. Alias Hedyotis repens; Oldenlandia repens. Herbaceous, annual, tufty, creeping; stems filiform, branched; leaves oblong, attenuated at the base; glabrous or with the petioles ciliated at the base; corolla funnel-shaped; tube longer than the calyx-limb, slightly hairy on the inside near the base; limb five-cleft, spreading; segments ovate, acute, with an acute tooth on each side above the middle; stigmas two, long narrow-linear, slightly spreading; flowers white, small, axillary, solitary, alternate, very shortly-pedicelled; common in moist places, shady banks of rivers and water-courses throughout the country.——*Wild tirye* (पर्पटक - parpataka, San.; ಪರ್ಪಟಕ - parpátaka, Can.; వెర్రిచాతరాశి - verrichátaráshi, Tel.; ପିତଗୋହଂ - pitagoham, Oor.; குத்துத்திராய் - kuttuttiráy, Tam.). Tel. from (verri, tel. wild + chátaráshi, tel. mollugo spergula, linn.). Tam. from (kuttu, tam. upright + tiráy, tam. the plant); low-erect plant. San. also (kshétraparpati), meaning field + mollugo. Title otherwise Wild indian chickweed. Botanically Mollugo [parpatam] stricta, linn., ficoideæ [vricsham, 66]. Alias Mollugo linkii, paniculata, pentaphylla, radiata, triphylla; Pharnaceum pentaphyllum, strictum, triphyllum. Annual, glabrous, stems diffuse at the base, afterwards erect, angled; leaves linear-lanceolate, pointed; panicles elongated, many-flowered; stamens three; petals wanting; seeds minutely tubercled; flowers small, white.

TISAY (திசை - tisai, *Tam.*). From (dish, san. to point out). Point of the compass. Quarter, region [dic]. Ascertaining direction is a matter of importance in many details of native daily life. Special directions are prescribed in hindoo shastrams for bathing, worshipping household gods, eating and sleeping; for instance one should not sleep with the head to the north as that is the position for a corpse. Shoolam is the supposed position of the trident of shiva [q.v.] at any given time according to the days of the week, hence called vaura shoolam, during which it is considered unlucky to set out on a journey in the direction in which it lies and the reverse. Compare Trishoolam. Direction again is an important factor in settling the import of omens [shacoonam]. On occasions of festivals [pundigay], especially festivals of village deities [grauma devatay], before beginning the festival proper care is taken first to guard the place on all sides by fortifying the eight cardinal points with incantations [muntram] and by invoking the protection of their regents; this is done by turning to each point repeating the incantation indranya nama or salutation to indran [q.v.], beginning with the east and making prostrations to him as the regent and offering him oblation [baly], and then turning to the next point; this ceremony is called in sanscrit dicbandhanam and in tamul tisay cutt, both meaning binding the cardinal points. For the method of fixing directions in hindoo astronomy, see Shunk. For detailed information about the eight cardinal points and their regents as protectors of the earth see Ashtadic and Ashtadic paulacan. For the mythological elephants of the cardinal points, considered as supporters of the earth, see Ashtadic gajam. For the importance of directions in connection with the site and construction of houses see Veed. For the direction of the signs of the zodiac see Raushy. For the native method of ascertaining bearings at sea see Dhony. For direction among mahomedans compare Rijaul ool gheib and Janauza. The following are the different vernacular names for the points of the compass; with their presiding deities, &c., in the hindoo system according to hindoo shastrams:—

No.	English.	Sanscrit.	Arabic.	Persian.	Hindostany.	Canarese.	Tooloo.	Teloogoo.	Malayalam.	Tamul.	Presiding deities [ashtadic paulacan].	Animals of the quarters [ashtadic].	Elephants of the quarters [ashtadic gajam] in pairs.	Direction of shoolam [shoolam, trishoolam] on week days.
1	North ...	Oottaram ...	Shoomaul ...	Shoomaul ...	Oottar ...	Badagoo ...	Badakye ...	Oottaram ...	Vadakk ...	Vadakk ...	Coobairan ...	Elephant [q.v.] ...	Saurvabhoomam, Anjanay.	Shevvye, boodhan.
2	North-east.	Eeshaunyam.	Shoomaul oosh sharkee.	Shoomaul mashrik.	Eesaun ...	Eeshaunyam.	Moodye badakye.	Eeshaunyam.	Vadakkizhakk.	Vadakizhakk.	Eeshaunan.	Hare [mosal] ...	Soopradeepam, Anjanauvaty.	Boodhan.
3	East ...	Poorvam ...	Mashrik ...	Mashrik ...	Poorab ...	Moodloo ...	Moodye ...	Toorp ...	Kizhakk ...	Kizhakk ...	Indran ...	Kite [braminy kite] ...	Eirauvatam, Apramay.	Tingal, shany.
4	South-east...	Agneyam ...	Joonoob oosh sharkee.	Joonoob mashrik.	Dakkhan poorab.	Temmoodloo.	Moodye tenkye.	Agneyam ...	Tekkizhakk.	Tenkizhakk.	Agny ...	Cat [poomy] ...	Poondareecam, Capilay.	Vyauzham, shany.
5	South ...	Dacshinam.	Joonoob. ...	Joonoob ...	Dakkhan ...	Tenka ...	Tenkye ...	Dhcshinam.	Tekk...	Terkk ...	Yaman ...	Lion [simham] ...	Vaumanam, Pingalay.	Vyauzham.
6	South-west.	Neirritam...	Joonoob ool-gharbee.	Joonoob maghrib.	Dakkhan pacham.	Tempadoovaloo.	Tenkye puddye.	Neirritam ...	Tekk-padinyaur.	Tennerkk ...	Nirrity ...	Dog [nye] ...	Coomoodam, Anoopamay.	Tingal, velly.
7	West ...	Pashchimam.	Maghrib ...	Maghrib ...	Pacham ...	Padoovaloo.	Puddye ...	Padumara ...	Padinyaur ...	Merkk ...	Varoonan ...	Snake [paumb]. ...	Anjanam, Taumracurny.	Nyayir, velly.
8	North-west.	Vauyavyam.	Shoomaul ool-gharbee.	Shoomaul maghrib.	Oottar pacham or bauyeb.	Vauyavyam.	Badakye puddye.	Vauyavyam.	Vadakk-padinyaur.	Vadamerkk.	Vayoo ...	Rat [ely] ...	Pooshpadantam, Soodanty.	Nyayir, shevvye.

The following are the same with their etymologies.——*Agneyam* (आग्नेय - ágnéya, San.; ಆಗ್ನೇಯ - ágnéya, Can.; ఆగ్నేయము - ágné-yamu, Tel.). From (agni, san. fire); from the presiding deity. South-east.——*Badagoo* (ಬಡಗು - badagu, Can.). From (vadakku, tam. north). North. *Badakye* (ಬಡಕಾಯಿ - badakayi, Too.). From (vadakku, tam. north). North.——*Badakye puddye* (ಬಡಕಾಯಿಪಡ್ಡಾಯಿ - badakayipaddáyi, Too.). North-west.——*Bauyeb* (بايب - báeb, Hind.). From (váyavya, san. the quarter) [vauya-vyam]. North-west.——*Dacshinam* (दक्षिण - dakshina, San.; దక్షిణము - dakshinamu, Tel.). Means right. Applied by the Aryans to the country on their right hand. South.——*Dakkhan* (دکهن - dakkhan, Hind.). From sanscrit. South [dacshinam]. Cf. Deccan.——*Dakkhan pacham* (دکهن پچهم - dakkhanpaççham, Hind.). From (dakshinapashchima, san. south-west). South-west.——*Dakkhan poorab* (دکهن پورب - dakkhanpúrab, Hind.). From (dakshinapúrva, san. south-east). South-east.——*Eesaun* (ایسان - ísán, Hind.). From (íshána, san. shiva, the presiding deity). North-east [eeshaunyam].——*Eeshaunyam* (ईशान्य - íshánya, San.; ಈಶಾನ್ಯ - íshánya, Can.; ఈశాన్యము - íshányamu, Tel.). From (íshána, san. shiva); from the presiding deity. North-east. Cf. Eesaun.——*Joonoob* (جنوب - junúb, Ar. and Pers.). From (janab, ar. side). South.——*Joonoob maghrib* (جنوب مغرب - junúbmaghrib, Pers.). South-west.——*Joonoob mashrik* (جنوب مشرق - junúbmashrik, Pers.). South-east.——*Joonoob ool gharbee* (جنوبی الغربی - junúbiulgharbí, Ar.). South-west.——*Joonoob oosh sharkee* (جنوبی الشرقی - junúbiyushsharkí, Ar.). South-east.——*Kizhakk* (കിഴക്ക - kizhakku, Mal.; கிழக்கு - kizhakku, Tam.). From (kízh, tam. downward). East.——*Maghrib* (مغرب - maghrib, Ar. and Pers.). From (gharaba, ar. to set), direction of sun-setting. West.——*Mashrik* (مشرق - mashrik, Ar. and Pers.). From (sharaka, ar, to rise); direction of sunrising. East.——*Merkk* (மேற்கு - mérgu, Tam.). From (mél, tam. above). West.——*Moodloo* (ಮೂಡ್ಲು - múdlu, Can.). From (múdu, can. to rise). East.——*Moodye* (ಮೂಡಾಯಿ - múdayi, Too.). From (múdu, can. to rise). East.——*Moodye badakye* (ಮೂಡಾಯಿಬಡಕಾಯಿ - mudayibadakayi, Too.). North-east.——*Moodye tenkye* (ಮೂಡಾಯಿತೆನ್ಕಾಯಿ - mudayitenkáyi, Too.). South-east.——*Neirritam* (नैऋत - nairrita, San.; నైరృతము - nairritamu, Tel.). From (nirriti, san. the presiding deity). South-west.——*Oottar* (اتر - uttar, Hind.). From sanscrit. North [oottaram].——*Oottaram* (उत्तर - uttara, San.; ఉత్తరము - uttaramu, Tel.). From (ut, san. up + tara, san. comparative suffix). North. Cf. Oottar.——*Oottar pacham* (اتر پچهم - uttarpachchham, Hind.). From (uttarapashchima, san. north-west). Also called Bauyeb. North-west.——*Pacham* (پچهم - paççham, Hind.). From (pashchima, san. west). West [pashchimam].——*Padinyaur* (പടിഞ്ഞാറ - patiññáru, Mal.). From (patiyu, mal. to sink + ñáyar, mal. sun). West.——*Padoovaloo* (ಪಡುವಲು - paduvalu, Can.). From (padu, can. to lie down). West.——*Pashchimam* (पश्चिम - pashchima, San.). Means behind. West. Cf. Pacham.——*Poorab* (پورب - púrab, Hind.). From (púrva, san. east). East [poorvam].——*Poorvam* (पूर्व - púrva, San.). Means front; so called by the conquering Aryans [q.v.] who came from the west. East. Cf. Poorab.——*Puddye* (ಪಡ್ಡಾಯಿ - paddáyi, Too.). From (padu, can. to lie down). West.——*Shoomaul* (شمال - shimál, Ar. and Pers.). From (shamala, ar. left hand); i.e., of mecca. North.——*Shoomaul maghrib* (شمال مغرب - shimálmaghrib, Pers.). North-west.——*Shoomaul mashrik* (شمال مشرق - shimálmashrik, Pers.). North-east.——*Shoomaul ool gharbee* (شمالی الغربی - shimáliyulgharbí, Ar.). North-west.——*Shoomaul oosh sharkee* (شمالی الشرقی - shimáliyushsharkí, Ar.). North-east.——*Tekk* (തെക്ക - tekku, Mal.). South.——*Tek kizhakk* (തെക്ക കിഴക്ക - tekkukizhakku, Mal.). South-east.——*Tekk padinyaur* (തെക്ക പടിഞ്ഞാറ - tekkupatiññáru, Mal.). South-west.——*Temmoodloo* (ತೆಂಮೂಡಲು - temmúdalu, Can.). South-east.——*Tempadoovaloo* (ತೆಂಪಡುವಲು - tempaduvalu, Can.). South-west.——*Tenka* (ತೆಂಕ - tenka, Can.). South.——*Ten kizhakk* (தென்கிழக்கு - tengizhakku, Tam.). South-east.——*Tenkye* (ತೆನ್ಕಾಯಿ - tenkáyi, Too.). From tamul. South.——*Tenkye puddye* (ತೆನ್ಕಾಯಿಪಡ್ಡಾಯಿ - tenkáyipaddáyi, Too.). South-west.——*Ten merkk* (தென்மேற்கு - tenmérgu, Tam.). South-west.——*Terkk* (தெற்கு - tergu, Tam.). South.——*Vada kizhakk* (வடகிழக்கு - vadagizhakku, Tam.). North-east.——*Vadakk* (വടക്ക - vatakku, Mal.; வடக்கு - vadakku, Tam.). North [vada].——*Vadak kizhakk* (വടക്ക കിഴക്ക - vatakkukizhakku, Mal.). North-east.——*Vadakk padinyaur* (വടക്ക പടിഞ്ഞാറ - vatakkupatiññáru, Mal.). North-west.——*Vada merkk* (வடமேற்கு - vadamérgu, Tam.). North-west.——*Vauyavyam* (वायव्य - váyavya, San.; ವಾಯವ್ಯ - váyavya, Can.; వాయవ్యము - váyavyam, Tel.). From (váyu, san. air deity); from the presiding deity. North-west. Cf. Bauyeb.

TISSO (تیسو کا پهول - tesúkáphúl, *Hind.*). Palaus flower.

TITT (திட்டு - tittu, *Tam.*). Hillock.——*Tittagoody* (திட்டக்குடி - tittakkudi, Tam. titagudi *). From (tittai, tam. elevation + kudi, tam. village). Sanscrit name (vasisht'hak-shétra), meaning vasishtan, the sage + sacred place.—"*a*" Deputy tahsildarry, Vriddhauchellam talook, South arcot district. Pay Rs. 70.—"*b*" Deputy tahsildar's head-quarters; pop. 2,245; acres 318; lat. 11° 24′; long. 79° 10′; from Chidambaram W. 38 miles; from Cuddalore S.W. 48 miles; from Madras S.W. 140 miles; from Tindivanam S.S.W. 67 miles; from Tricalore S.S.W. 38 miles; from Vriddhauchellam S.W. 16 miles. Important Shiva temple.

TITTIRAM (तित्तिर - tittira, *San.*). From sound. Tetraonidæ family, rasores, aves [pacshy, 33], of naturalists [jantoo]. Partridges and quails. Form is heavy, stout, and massive; neck short; bill stout and short; often no difference between sexes; game plumage; affect open grass lands, moors, fields, and low scattered jungle; associate in bevies, and in flocks in winter; flesh of all is good and high flavored. Sub-family Tetraoninæ, or grouse, not here represented. The following are the sub-families which occur:—"*a*" Perdicinæ. Tarsus not feathered; orbits plumed or wanting nude eyebrow of grouse; tarsus often spurred. Moderate or small size, frequenting fields, pastures, reeds, moors, and rocky hill sides, very rarely preferring forests or jungles. Beak is generally short and tolerably compressed, margin entire, and nostrils protected by a hard scale. Lay numerous eggs, and feed on grain, berries, insects [poochy], and small molluscs [chippy]. Several distinct types of form. Partridges occurring may be divided into Francolins, Chakors, Grey-partridges, Wood-partridges, and Bush-quails [teetar].—"*b*" Coturnicinæ, Quails. Wings pointed, rather long; bill moderate; tarsi not spurred; small size. Sexes differ somewhat in coloration [batair].——*Teetar* (تیتر - títar, Hind.). See sep. title.

TITY (तिथि - tit'hi, *San.*). From (at, san. to move). A lunar [chaundramaunam] day.—"*a*" A mean tity is the time during which the moon moves through 12° of her synodical orbit [cacsham] supposed to be divided into 360°; its duration is therefore 59g 3v 38p hindoo time [caulam, 4], or 23h 37′ 27⅛″ european time. Of these there are very nearly 371 in a solar year. Teloogoo astronomers allow something more for the length of the mean tity which according to them is of 59g 3v 40p 23s. Sixty-four mean tities are very nearly equal to sixty-three solar days, and this difference of one day is the occasion of the expunged tities, which in the calendars are called Avamauham or Sprik, and which recur once in about sixty-four days. When no tity begins or ends in a solar day, the preceding tity is repeated in the calendar [punchaungam], and the same numeral answers to two solar days [dinam]; it is then called Adhy or Adhicam [q.v.]. When two tities end in the same solar day, the intermediate tity is expunged and called Cshayam [q.v.]. The synodical month is divided into two parts [pacsham], consisting of fifteen tities each; the first fourteen tities of each part are named after the numerals from one to fourteen; the last tity of each part, that is, the 15th and 30th of the month, are called respectively Powrnimay [q.v.] and Amavausyay [q.v.], or Amavausyay and Powrnimay, according as the Shooclaudy [q.v.] or Krishnaudy [q.v.] method is followed. See also Mookhyam and Gownam. The following is the list of Tities:—Pratamay or Paudyamy, Dwiteeyay or Vidiya, Triteeyay or Tadiya, Chatoorty or Chowty, Punchamy, Shashty, Saptamy, Ashtamy, Navamy, Dashamy, Yecaudashy, Dwaudashy, Trayodashy, Chatoordashy, Poonnama or powrnimay for shooddham, and Amavausyay for bahoolam [jyotisham]. The following is the scale:—2 caranams or half lunar days = 1 tity; 15 tities = 1 pacsham or lunar fortnight [caulam, 4]. Compare Nairam [caulam, 1].—"*b*" All religious and funeral rites are regulated by tities; so much so that in common usage a tity means an anniversary day [shraud-dham]. The astrological lords of the fifteen lunar days are respectively:—first Bramha [q.v.], second Vidhautry, third Hary [q.v.], fourth Yaman [q.v.], fifth Moon [chundran], sixth Soobramanyan [q.v.], seventh Indran [q.v.], eighth Vasoo [q.v.], ninth Sarpam, tenth Dharman [q.v.], eleventh Shiva [q.v.], twelfth Savitry [q.v.], thirteenth Manmatan [q.v.], fourteenth Cauly [q.v.] and fifteenth Vishwedevah [q.v.]. The new-moon day [amavausyay] is sacred to the Pitries [q.v.]. A person should commence works suited to the devas presiding over particular lunar days. The first, sixth and eleventh lunar days are known as Nundam [nundy]; the second, seventh, and twelfth lunar days are known as Bhadram; the third, eighth and thirteenth lunar days are known as Vijayam [jayay]; the fourth, ninth, and fourteenth lunar days are known as Rictam; and the fifth, tenth and fifteenth lunar days are known as Poornam. Works directed to be done in particular Nacshatrams should be done on lunar days sacred to the lords of those Nacshatrams [q.v.].—"*c*" The same remarks apply to Caranams [q.v.] and Moohoortams [q.v.].—"*d*" Caranam is half a lunar day, and is according to circumstances either Adhroovam movable, or Dhroovam fixed; see Caranam. The astrological lords of the seven movable caranams, Bavam, Baulavam, Cowlavam, Teitilam, Garam, Vanikk, and Vishty or bhadram, are respectively Indran [q.v.], Bramha [q.v.], Mitran, Aryaman, Bhoo [q.v.], Shree [q.v.] and Yaman [q.v.]. These seven when eight times repeated occupy the space from the second-half of the first day in the moon's increase [shooclapacsham] to the first-half of the fourteenth day in its wane [krishnapacsham]. The astrological lords of the four fixed caranams, Shacoony, Chatooshpadam, Naugavam, Kimstoognam, are Cauly, Vrisham, Sarpam and Vayoo. These begin from the second-half of the fourteenth day of the waning moon [krishnapacsham]. In a Bava caranam according to shastrams should be done deeds of an auspicious, a movable or a fixed character, as well as deeds for the promotion of a person's health and comfort. In a Baulava caranam should be done acts of charity and acts of help to bramins. In a Cowlava caranam should be done joyful deeds and those for the acquisition of friends. In a Teitila caranam should be done deeds liked by the public at large, and houses should be built. In a Gara caranam lands should be tilled, seeds sown, houses built, and the like. In a Vanikk caranam, works of a fixed nature should be done, as well as dealings with merchants. In a Vishty or bhadra caranam, auspicious deeds should not be done but acts aimed at the ruin of enemies; those connected with poison will be done. In a Shacoony caranam a person should do acts for the increase of his health and comfort, should take medicine, and should learn and repeat the moola muntrams [q.v.] or magical formulæ. In a Chatooshpada caranam a person should do deeds connected with cows, bramins, the pitries, and the king. In a Nauga caranam a person will do works of a fixed nature, cruel deeds, acts of stealth and wicked deeds. In a Kimstoogna caranam, a person should do any work for the increase of his health and comfort, as well as auspicious deeds.—"ε" A Moohoortam [q.v.] is 48 minutes. The 12 hours of day and 12 hours of night are each divided into 15 Moohoortams. The 15 day-Moohoortams are sacred respectively to:—1st Roodran [q.v.], 2nd Sarpam, 3rd Mitran, 4th Pitries [q.v.], 5th Vasoo [q.v.], 6th Vara, 7th Vishwodevah [q.v.], 8th Vidhy, 9th Bramha [q.v.], 10th Indran [q.v.], 11th Indraugny, 12th Deityan [q.v.], 13th Varoonan [q.v.], 14th Aryaman and 15th Bhagan. The 15 night-Moohoortams are sacred respectively to:—1st Eeshwaran [q.v.], 2nd Ajapaudan, 3rd Ahirboodnay, 4th Pooshan [q.v.], 5th Nausatyan, 6th Yaman [q.v.], 7th Vanhy, 8th Dhantry, 9th Shashy, 10th Anditvan [q.v.], 11th Gooroo [q.v.], 12th Atchootan, 13th Arcan [q.v.], 14th Twashtry and 15th Vayoo [q.v.]. Of the 15 night-Moohoortams, the 1st, 2nd, 6th, and 7th, should be rejected for all auspicious purposes. ——*Taidy* (తేది - tédi, Tel.). From (tit'hi, san. lunar day). A date [taureek], according to solar account.

TOCUSSA (توکسا - tukassá, *Hind.*). African for raggy.

TODAH (ತೊಡವ - todava, *Can.*). From (toru, tam. a herd). A hill tribe found on the Neilgherries, who have passed there at some excessively ancient date from the low hills N.E. of Neilgherries.—"*a*" Their language is a dialect of old Canarese. It has more sounds than any other Dravidian dialect, and some of these are peculiar to it, seeming to have been modified by the position and habits of the tribe; they chiefly converse for instance in the open air calling to each other from one hill top to another. The language was once highly inflectional, but has lost most of its inflections, the people as the result of isolation not having replaced them by significant particles or auxiliaries to the same extent as the other South indian tribes, and the language having thus dwindled down to a mere skeleton. A few tamul forms were introduced by the poligars [q.v.]. Of teloogoo influence there is no trace. Nor is there a resemblance in Todah to malayalam in any of the points where that dialect differs from its sisters. The pectoral pronunciation of the Todahs in speaking their language is the reason why so many Europeans, who heard them speak, formerly believed that it had no relationship at all with any of the S. indian languages. The whole life of a Todah being concentrated in his buffaloes [khoolgah] it is difficult to discover among them words for abstract terms. Most of their verbs have only one tense, and they help themselves by adverbs of time to express the future and past tenses. They have no pure "a" as it occurs in other Indian languages but their "a" is pronounced as "a" in tall. They use no written character, and have never apparently done so; they are wholly illiterate [bhaushay]. There is a slight difference in the dialects even of the different tribes of the Todahs.—"*b*" The Todahs are considered by the other hill tribes to be the lords of the soil, and are accordingly paid a tribute in kind by them in acknowledgment of this right; they themselves say that they came from the jungle tract of inferior hills situated between the canarese and tamul districts, in the direction of the hassanore pass in the eastern ghauts [q.v.], north-east of the neilgherries; though this was their origin, they with their buffaloes [khoolgah] approached the hills from the western side.—"*c*" Notwithstanding the long residence of the todahs in a cold, cloudy mountain region, the color of their skin is considerably darker than that of the more modern hill race, the badagas, a race of people who immigrated from the canarese country more recently, and is many shades darker than that of the majority of the natives of the malabar coast; the darkness of the complexion of the todahs tends to prove that they came originally from the eastern or sunburnt side of the range of ghauts [q.v.]. The mode of wearing the hair also points the same way; the luxuriant crop of hair, which is their pride, differs but little from the rough, shaggy and unkempt hair of many of the pariah [q.v.] and wandering castes of the carnatic [q.v.] and deccan [q.v.], except that it is oiled and combed. The hazel or brown eye of the Todah is also met with in the wild castes of the eastern plains. The todahs surpass all the other tribes in physique and dignity of bearing, but they are not so tall as the badagas; still they may be spoken of as tall, the height of the men averaging 5 feet 3·30 inches, that of the women 5 feet 0·25 inches; their features may best be described as european, with roman noses and bright hazel eyes, good teeth and an abundance of rather coarse but glossy black hair, which is worn in a crop by the men and in long thick ringlets by the women; the expression of their countenances is open, fearless, and agreeable, and their smile invariably pleasant although rather vacant; their faces have sometimes a general resemblance to the jewish type, but nothing whatever in their customs or traditions connects them with the jews [jónaca]; the ideas once held on this point are quite fanciful; as regards strength of body they will not bear comparison with the teloogoo caupoos [q.v.] and palankeen [q.v.] bearers [boy]. The dress of the todahs is simple in the extreme, but not ungraceful; it consists of a coarse species of cloth woven at coimbatore, and white when new, having one or two bars of color, generally red, woven into it at each end; by the men it is worn wound round the body, so as to form a kilt or petticoat, leaving the legs nearly bare; then it is brought under the right arm and the end is thrown over the left shoulder; in general effect it is not unlike a roman toga; the men also wear the lungooty [q.v.] or waist cloth called by them coov or kone; they never on any occasion wear a turban [q.v.]. The female dress consists of the same kind of cloth, but it is merely thrown over the shoulders and held together in front, and is not worn so gracefully as by the men; women also wear heavy brass armlets generally two on one arm, called toovagy, weight about 5 lb.; they have necklaces of twisted hair or black thread with silver clasps, and here and there a bead or a bunch of cowry [q.v.] shells, and sometimes a silver chain; they wear silver bracelets of rather a pretty pattern, and silver rings on their fingers and thumbs, also iron bracelets of peculiar design, one like a snake; sometimes a silver chain is worn round the waist, to which is attached a small silver box opening with a screw, and used for carrying small coins; their hair-dressing is the most elaborate feature of their toilette, and the curling of their ringlets on long sticks occupies a considerable time every evening. From the entire want of records among these people it is impossible to ascertain with exactness what is in general their length of life, but it is supposed that a few of the todahs have attained the age of ninety, or even a hundred years, and in one or two instances a new set of teeth, it is said, has appeared after that period.—"*d*" The religion of the Todahs is wholly rudimental. Such words as god, sin, ghost are almost pure sanscrit, whilst the words which relate to ideas, which they have borrowed from the badagas [q.v.], are canarese [q.v.]. They have a distinct idea of a life after death to be spent in a country, sometimes called 'the other district;' as their buffaloes [khoolgah] are their chief food in this world, they kill a sufficient number at each funeral [kerd] to supply the dead with milk in the next; the spirits of men and buffaloes are supposed to leap together into the other world from macoorty peak; the todah has an awe of anything unusual or beyond his comprehension, and soon exalts such things into objects of reverence. The actual worship of the todahs is confined to one material object, the sacred buffalo-bell, which is hung round the neck of the best buffalo of the sacred herd, and is looked upon by them as the representative of hiredeva [q.v.] or the chief deity; besides this deity they have quite a pantheon of presiding gods, one in fact for each mund [q.v.], and a hunting god called baidagan [q.v.] whose temple is at numbalagode in wynaud; the latter is the son of dirkish, the son of yen, the first todah, and is now, they say, attended by bramins [q.v.]; but to these gods they do not pray; some old men make salaam [q.v.] to the rising sun [sooryan] and at some seasons to the moon [chundran] and fast at eclipses [grahanam], and occasionally they prostrate themselves at the door of the paultchy [q.v.], but no one except the poojarry [q.v.] attempts anything beyond this; 'may all be well,' or 'may the buffaloes be well' is the only form of prayer; in fact the names of their gods, like some of their funeral ceremonies, seem more like remains of an extinct religion than parts of a living creed; it is also a curious fact that the todah does not pray by deputy; his priest, so far from offering up prayers for the people, regards himself as a god who does not need to pray. In spite of this apparent apathy, one division of the todahs, the Peikies, is devoted to the priesthood. There are five kinds of priests. The highest are the paulauls [q.v.] a mixture of herdsmen and priests; they live in isolated holy munds [q.v.] or groves called tiriyairy [q.v.]; no female may approach the mund [q.v.], and no man may converse with the paulaul except from a distance, much less touch him; his own father must bow down before him; he is attended by a herdsman called the canvalaul or watchman, who is also an ascetic, but by no means so holy as the paulaul, being merely his servant; he may converse with the paulaul, but may not touch him; both paulaul and canvalaul are generally married men, and only lead a celibate life during their term of office; the preparation which a paulaul must undergo is by no means light; the aspirant is expected to retire to the jungles and there to live for eight days without any clothing to protect him from the severity of the weather and with hardly any food; after thirty days of this exposure in the wilds, he is allowed to enter upon his duties, and from henceforth he inhabits a small hut in the lonely tiriyairy mund; the office of paulaul is seldom, if ever, held for life; there are instances of its being held for fourteen years, but the ordinary period is from two to three years; the dress of a paulaul [q.v.] consists of a scanty black cloth; these are woven by the badagas [q.v.] of jackanairy. Priests of the second order are called varzhaul; they go through the same ceremonies as the paulaul, but hold office for a shorter period and are employed as milkmen; they wear only the lungooty [q.v.]. The next two orders seem to be identical with the varzhaul but their designation depends upon the munds to which they belong; they are called respectively kokvauly and coorpooly. The last, paulcapauls, i.e., milk watchers, are a lower order; they are not obliged to lead a celibate life and may wear the pootcooly [q.v.]. The paulaul appropriates all the milk of the sacred herd; it is considered too holy to be sold as milk, but what remains when the paulaul and cauvalaul have had their shares is made into ghee [q.v.], and in that state sold to the laity and the badagas. There are two kinds of temples. One, called boa [q.v.] or boath, is a conical-roofed building surrounded by a wall; there are four boas in the hills:—manboa at moottinaud mund about four miles from ootacamund on the left of the seegore road; kinej, at the tiriyairy mund, near sholore; tarzcauv, at the tiriyairy mund on the coondahs; metterzbva, near brikaputsy; there was formerly a fifth called katedva near macoorty, but it is now in ruins; the boa temples do not seem properly to belong to the todahs, but to some earlier race; they are not attended by priests of the highest, but of the second grade. The second kind of temple is called a paultchy; it resembles an ordinary house, but is larger; there are two varieties, one is merely a dairy house, such as every mund possesses, the other is something more, and its importance appears to depend upon the relics it contains; these are called coorpoos and the paultchy in which they are kept is looked upon as a shrine; munds where they are found are called yetad, or great munds, in contradistinction to boory, or common munds.—"*e*" The todahs are essentially a pastoral people, and in a measure nomadic, that is to say the inhabitants of each mund or village possess one or two other munds, and move from one to the other as they may find it convenient or necessary to do so, either to secure pasture for their herds or shelter from the monsoons which are more felt in some localities than in others; they never make any attempt to cultivate their lands; the goodoo [q.v.], which they levy in kind from the badagas [q.v.] and kotahs [q.v.], supplies them with grain, and beyond this they depend entirely upon their large herds of buffaloes [khoolgah] for support; besides their simple household duties, the women do a coarse kind of embroidery in blue and white thread obtained from the low country; they use neilgherry nettle-thread for sewing their cloths and english needles. The polyandry of the todahs, being that of several brothers or near kinsmen having one wife is a less gross institution than that existing among other polyandrists in south india; polyandry is now on the decline, and those men who can afford it have each their own wife; female infanticide, undoubtedly existed as a practice among them, but has now ceased; they claim the children on the principle of seniority, thus, the first child is given to the eldest brother, the second to the next and so on; inheritence ordinarily goes in the male line, not in the female as amongst the polyandrist of the west coast; it is remarkable, however, that in regard to the sacred buffaloes [khoolgah], the descent is through the females. Their mode of saluting one another is peculiar to themselves; a woman when she meets a man, lifts his feet, first one and then the other, to her head as she crouches before him; in the case of an old woman, the ceremony reversed, and she places her foot on the head of the man. Badagas are called mauv, or fathers-in-law, by the todahs in token of respect; a badaga greets a todah by laying his hand on the head of the latter. The todahs burn their dead, and bury weapons and personal ornaments with the remains [shavacaud]; their cemetery and place of funeral sacrifice is a green spot, partially enclosed by a stone wall, rendered gloomy by a thick wood on one side and lofty hills on the other; it is their practice to sacrifice buffaloes on the demise of a todah, and a strongly-walled area is set apart for the reception of these animals, whose bones and horns are strewed on the ground; the funeral procession enters the green and moves towards the centre; the deceased is dressed in a new garment and mantle, and arrayed in all the ornaments which he had worn during life; he is carried on a bier formed of branches and herbs, and followed by a number of mourners, male and female, who chant the lament, whilst others carry wood for the funeral pile and provisions for the evening meal; a herd of buffaloes is driven into the walled area, and the men, armed with clubs, enter with exciting shouts, and perform a wild dance amongst the buffaloes; these soon became excited to the highest pitch, and, at a signal, a bell is attached to the neck of each infuriated animal; two young men throw themselves on the animal's neck; seize it by its horns, and others run to their assistance, and eight or ten men then hang on the neck of one animal, whilst others increase its rage by blows of their clubs, and goad it on with yells and gestures; three or four animals are thus attacked at one time, and the bell attached to the neck of each; but meanwhile the general assemblage which line the walls are weeping, exulting, or sending forth shrieks of horror whenever a man is wounded, a buffalo overpowered, or a relative in imminent danger; on the next day, the victims are finally sacrificed; the men strike the animals behind the horns with a wood-cutter's axe, and a single blow always produces death; after the sacrifice, several wild dances follow, during which the men feign to cut and lacerate themselves; on the third day, the deceased is burned on the funeral pile. There are no marriage ceremonies among them; the eldest brother of a family applies for a young girl to her mother, and, on consent being obtained, two buffaloes are given by the father of the girl as a provision for her; the bridegroom also gives her a few buffaloes according to his circumstances; afterwards the bridegroom, followed by all his brothers, conducts her home. Todahs all live in small communities, not exceeding a dozen persons, and their habitations are usually 6 feet high, and 6 feet wide, being curious oblong huts, formed of bamboos [q.v.], bent into long, narrow gothic arches, covered neatly with thick thatch, and closed at both ends with wicker work of bamboo, and plastered over with mud; in one end there is a small opening, close to the ground, not quite 2 feet high, and 15 inches wide, through which the inhabitants creep; three or four huts form the hamlet or mund as it is called, usually placed in a highly picturesque and luxuriant spot, affording shelter to themselves, and food for their cattle; in each mund there is a separate hut of a better structure and materials, and larger size than the others, devoted to their religious rites. The poorer class serve those who are in good circumstances, and live upon their earnings, added to what they receive from the badagas as tribute; they never serve any but their own caste.—"*f*" The numbers of the Todahs is considerably under 1,000. They are divided into two classes, Devaulayaul and Tarserzhaul. The first consists of the Peiky clan, corresponding in some slight respect to the Bramins; the second consists of the four remaining clans, called respectively Pekhans, Coottans, Kennans and Todies. None of the clans intermarry.—"*g*" See vol. I (14) (36), (69); II, 108, 233.——*Todamund* (ತೋದಮಂದು - tódamandu, Can.). The village of todahs.——*Todanaud* (ತೋದನಾಡು - tódanádu, Can.). Division, Neilgherries; area 216,903 acres; pop. 14,489, exclusive of Ootacamund municipality. Occupies the whole of the plateau north-west of the other three nauds, the tableland at the foot of the northern slopes. The Ouchterlony valley may now be regarded as appertaining to this naud [q.v.]. Consists of the minor divisions of Boodnattam, Seegore, Sembanattam and Todanaud. Divided by the hill tribes into two divisions known as Mailnaud and Keelnaud. The town of Ootacamund lies within Mailnaud, though the southern portion of the settlement, including the Lawrence asylum appertains to Merkoonaud. Boundaries:—N. Moyaur river, S. Paranginaud, Merkoonaud and Coondahs, E. Paranginaud and Coimbatore district, W. Malabar district, Ouchterlony valley and S.E. Wynaud.

TODAY (தொடை - todai, *Tam.*). Thigh.——*Tadappanay* (തുടപ്പന - tutappana, Mal.). Means thigh + palm; as high as thigh. Same as Indian sago palm.

TODDALY (काञ्चन - káñchana, *San.*; जंगलीकाळीमिरची - jangalíkálímirachí, *Mahr.*; गाळायि - gáláyi, *Conc.*; جنگلی کالی مرچ کا پیڑ - janglíkálímirchkáper, *Hind.*; جنگلی کالی مرچی کا جھاڑ - janglíkálímirchíkájhár, *Dec.*; ಕಾಡುಮೆಣಸು - kádumenasu, *Can.*; ಕಾಡುಕಾರೆ - kádukáre, *Too.*; కొండకసింద - kondakasinda, *Tel.*; తుండుపర - tundupara, *Oor.*; തുടലി - tutali, *Mal.*; කුඩුමිරිස් - kudumiris, *Singh.*; மிளகரணை - milagaranai, *Tam.*). Title from malayalam. San. means golden; from orange color of fruit [champak, purple mountain ebony, white mountain ebony]. Mahr. from hindostany. Hind. from (janglí, hind. wild + kálí, hind. black + mirch, hind. pepper, piper nigrum, linn. + per, hind. tree); from pungency of berries. Dec. from hindostany. Can. from (kádu, can. wild + menasu, can. black pepper, piper nigrum, linn.). Too. from (kádu, too. wild + káre, too. thorny webera, canthium parviflorum, lamk.). Tel. from (konda, tel. hill + kasinda, tel. cassia occidentalis, linn.). Mal. from (tutar, mal. chain) [small bair]. Singh. from (kudu, singh. small + miris, singh. pepper). Tam. from (milagu, tam. pepper, piper nigrum, linn. + arani, tam. jungle). San. also (dahana), meaning burning; from pungent berries. Hind. also (kánj), from sanscrit; (dahan), from sanscrit meaning burning, referring to pungent berries. Dec. also (lopazkájhár). Can. also (káduhákukáre), meaning wild + thorny webera. Tel. also (mirapakándra), meaning pepper + plant so called; (varagóki); (varrakashimi). Mal. also (kára), meaning black [cauray]; (kákkattutali), meaning crow + plant; (mulakutánni), meaning pepper + terminalia belerica, roxb. Title otherwise Lopez root, Milagarandy, Prickly scopolia, Prickly toddalia. Botanically Toddalia aculeata, pers., rutaceæ [vricsham, 32]. Generic name from malayalam. Alias Paullinia asiatica; Scopolia aculeata; Toddalia asiatica, floribunda, nitida, rubricaulis. Six feet; stem and branches prickly; leaflets sessile, from oblong to broad-lanceolate, crenulate, glabrous; midrib beneath, and petioles prickly or occasionally unarmed; racemes simple or compound; fruit five-furrowed, with three to five perfect cells; petals five, spreading; leaves alternate, digitately trifoliate; flowers small, white, fragrant. Ramous prickly shrub; common on coromandel; stem irregular, bark corky, branches exceedingly numerous, climbing; prickles innumerable.

The flowers are white, scented, in racemes, and are succeeded by three to five-celled orange-colored berries as large as a pea [calauyam], and having a hot peppery taste when unripe; the dry berries are dark brown or nearly black, and have a pungent, aromatic, and very agreeable flavor like citron [q.v.]. The bark is about $\frac{1}{16}$th of an inch thick, and consists of a soft, yellow, corky external layer, wrinkled longitudinally, a thin bright yellow layer, and a firm brown middle cortical layer and liber. The root is woody and in cylindrical flexuose pieces, from ½-2 inches in diameter. The root-bark occurs in hollow pieces, varying in length from 2-5 inches, and in thickness from ¾ to 1½ lines; it is more or less flexuous, often partially quilled, and covered with a yellowish corky epidermis; it possesses no particular odour, but is bitter in taste; in the fresh state it is aromatic and pungent and has an odour of citron [q.v.]. The root-bark is medicinally antiperiodic, antipyretic, diaphoretic, carminative and tonic. Decoction; take of the root-bark, in coarse powder, six ounces; water, two pints and-a-half; boil on a slow fire till the liquid is reduced to one pint and strain when cool. Tincture; take of the root-bark, in coarse powder, six ounces; proof spirit, one pint; macerate for seven days in a closed vessel with occasional agitation; filter and add more spirit to make one pint. Watery extract; take of the root-bark in coarse powder one portion; water, six portions; boil till the liquid is reduced to one-third; strain the latter through cloth while hot and evaporate it on a sand-bath to the consistence of an extract. Simple powder; the root-bark pulverized in the ordinary way after scraping off the corky epidermis, and passed through a fine sieve or cloth. Doses; of decoction, from two to six fluid ounces; of tincture, from two to four fluid drachms; of watery extract, from forty to eighty grains; of simple powder, from one to two drachms. Substituted; for quinine [koinah] and other alkaloids of cinchona [koinah]. as an antiperiodic; for warburg's tincture, antipyrin, antifebrin, phenacetin and pulv. jacobi vera, as a diaphoretic and antipyretic; and for gentian [chiretta] and calumba [q.v.], as a tonic. One of the most valuable drugs in this country; medical properties very analogous to berberry [q.v.]; all the parts are febrifugal; under the name of lopez-root, once enjoyed celebrity in europe as a remedy for diarrhœa; gives to pharm. toddaliæ radix, aromatic tonic, and stimulant, antiperiodic; like cusparia bark, official. The fresh leaves are eaten raw in stomach complaints. The ripe berries are as pungent as pepper [q.v.] and make excellent pickles [chutney]. Fresh leaves eaten raw. The root-bark contains a yellow coloring matter [shauyam]. The wood is hard, yellow, and without taste or smell; its pores are arranged in a concentric manner, and the medullary rays are numerous and narrow. Another species is bilocularis.

TODDY (मधु - madhu, *San.*; سیندی - sendí, *Hind.*; ಹೆಂಡ - henda, *Can.*; కల్లు - kallu, *Tel.*; കള്ള് - kallu, *Mal.*; கள்ளு - kallu, *Tam.*). Title from inflected form of teloogoo for palmyra [taulam]. San. means sweet. A saccharine juice obtained by the excision of the spadix or young flowering branch of the palmyra [q.v.], cocoanut [q.v.], and other palms [taur]; when the juice exudes and drops into earthern pots [chatty], which are attached to the stem to receive it [shaunaur]. Taken fresh from the tree, early in the morning before the sun is up, it forms a pleasant drink [neerah]. When exposed to the air it undergoes various fermentation and becomes the common intoxicating drink of the lower classes. The following are the views of the Cooral about drunkenness:—உட்கப் படாஅர் ஒளியிழப்பர் எஞ்ஞான்றுங் கட்காதல் கொண்டொழுகு வார்—"those who always thirst after drink will neither inspire fear "in others nor retain the light of their fame."—உண்ணற்க கள்ளை யுணிலுண்க சான்றோரான் எண்ணப் படவேண்டா தார்—"let no liquor be drunk; if it is desired, let it be "drunk by those who care not for the esteem of the puncti-"lious."—ஈன்றாள் முகத்தேயும் இன்னாதா லென்மற்றுச் சான்றோர் முகத்துக் களி—"intoxication is painful even in "the presence of one's mother; what will it not then be in that "of the wise?"—நாணென்னு நல்லாள் புறங்கொடுக்குங் கள்ளென்னும் பேணாப் பெருங்குற்றத் தார்க்கு—"the "fair maid of modesty will turn her back on those who are "guilty of the great and abominable crime of drunkenness."—துஞ்சினார் செத்தாரின் வேறல்லர் எஞ்ஞான்று நஞ்சுண்பார் கள்ளுண் பவர்—"they that sleep resemble the dead; "likewise they that drink are no other than poison-eaters."—உள்ளொற்றி யுள்ளூர் நகப்படுவர் எஞ்ஞான்றுங் கள்ளொற்றிக் கண்சாய் பவர்—"those who always intoxicate "themselves by a private indulgence in drink, will have their "secrets detected and laughed at by their fellow-townsmen:"—களித்தானைக் காரணங் காட்டுதல் கீழ்நீர்க் குளித்தானைத் தீத்துரீஇ யற்று—"reasoning with a drunkard is like "going under water with a torch in search of a drowned man." Other uses near towns are for making arrack [q.v.], sugar [q.v.], and vinegar [caudy]. The name is the origin of the Scottish term for punch. The different toddies, particularly that of the cocoanut, are used by bakers as a leaven for raising bread. Veidyans [q.v.] prescribe it in consumptive cases [mooskiraut, sharaub]. There are toddies also from juice of bark of the fig [atty] and other trees, mostly used in medicine. —(1) *Toddy bird* (بیہیا - baiyá, Hind.). Title from its attachment to toddy tree or palmyra [q.v.] where it hangs its curious pensile nests. Same as Weaver bird.——*Toddy cat* (ताडीमार्जार - tádímárjára, San.; उद - úda, Mahr.; جہاڑکتا - jhárkákuttá, Hind.; میو سنگ - musang, Malay; ಕರಿಬೆಕ್ಕು - karibekku, Can.; మానుపిల్లి - mánupilli, Tel.; മരപ്പട്ടി - marappatti, Mal.; උගුඩුවා - ngudnvá, Singh.; வெருகு - verugu, Tam.). Title from supposed fondness for toddy. San. from (tádi, san. palm + márjara, san. cat). Mahr. from (udra, san. otter). Hind. from (jhár, hind. tree + kuttá, hind. dog). Can. from (kari, can. black + bekku, can. cat). Tel. from (mánu, tel. tree + pilli, tel. cat). Mal. from (maram, mal. tree + patti, mal. bitch). Tam. strictly means a tom cat or male cat. Malay also (pandung), meaning night-robber. Title otherwise Common tree cat, Fitchet, Pole cat, Screw tail; called in Ceylon the Palm cat. Paradoxurus niger, viverrinæ, viverridæ, digitigrada, carnivora, mammalia [sastanam, 11], of naturalists [jantoo]. Alias Paradoxurus hermaphroditus, hirsutus, musanga, typus; Platyschista pallasii; Viverra nigra. General color brownish black, with some dingy yellowish stripes on each side, more or less distinct, and sometimes not noticeable; a white spot, above and below each eye, and the forehead with a whitish band in some; a black line from the top of the head down the centre of the nose is generally observable, variations are owing to the state of abrasion of the fur, which is yellowish at the base and blackish at the tip. individuals occur with the tail spirally twisted, so that the extremity has the lower surface uppermost; and, it was an individual similar to this on which the genus was founded. There is a Tamul proverb:—வாழுநர் வீட்டில் மரநாய் கட்டினாற்போல—"as a toddy-"cat was tied up in a house occupied by a prosperous family;" it being considered an inauspicious animal. It infests houses, especially where there is a ceiling of cloth. Lurks by day among the fronds of the cocoanut [q.v.] palms, rolled up as a ball. It will live for months in confinement on vegetable food, but preferring flesh. It is said to consume toddy [q.v.]. Indian species not here found are:—Paradoxurus hermaphroditus or terai musang, Paradoxurus grayii or hill musang, Paradoxurus aureus or golden musang.——*Toddy palm* (सुरमाड - suramáda, Mahr.). Title from product. Same as Bastard sago palm.——**(2)** The following are the different toddies, the principal being the Cocoanut [q.v.] and Palmyra [q.v.].——*Cocoanut toddy* (नारिकेलमधु - nárikélamadhu, San.; ناریلی - nárelí, Hind.; ತೆಂಗಿನಹೆಂಡ - tenginahenda, Can.; టెంకాయకల్లు - tenkáyakallu, Tel.; തെങ്ങിൻകള്ള് - tenninkallu, Mal.; தென்னங்கள்ளு - tennangallu, Tam.). Product of Cocos nucifera, linn. [cocoanut], palmaceæ. The best of the palm-toddies.——*Date toddy* (खर्जूरमधु - kharjúramadhu, San.; سیندی - sendí, Hind.; ಈಚಲಹೆಂಡ - íchalahenda, Can.; ఈతకల్లు - ítakallu, Tel.; ഈന്തിൻകള്ള് - íntinkallu, Mal.; ஈச்சங்கள்ளு - íççangallu, Tam.). Product of Phœnix sylvestris, roxb. [wild date], palmaceæ. Coarse, but better than palmyra [q.v.]. Much used in Mysore.——*Fig toddy* (उडुम्बरमधु - udumbaramadhu, San.; گلرکا نیرا - gullarkánírá, Hind.; ಅತ್ತಿಹೆಂಡ - attíhenda, Can.; అత్తికల్లు - áttikallu, Tel.; അത്തിക്കള്ള് - attikkallu, Mal.; அத்திக்கள்ளு - attikkallu, Tam.). Product of Ficus glomerata, miq. [cluster fig], moraceæ. Used by veidyans [q.v.] as a powerful tonic.——*Margosa toddy* (निम्बमधु - nimbamadhu, San.; نیم کا نیرا - nímkánírá, Hind.; ಬೇವುಹೆಂಡ - bévuhendá, Can.; వేపకల్లు - vépakallú, Tel.; വേപ്പുങ്കള്ള് - véppankallu, Mal.; வேப்பங்கள்ளு - véppangallu, Tam.). Product of Melia azadirachta, linn. [neem], meliaceæ. Veidyans [q.v.] prescribe as stomachic.——*Palmyra toddy* (तालमधु - tálamadhu, San.; تاڑی - tárí, Hind.; ತಾಳೆಹೆಂಡ - tálehenda, Can.; తాటికల్లు - tátikallu, Tel.; പനങ്കള്ള് - panankallu, Mal.; பனங்கள்ளு - panangallu, Tam.). Product of Borassus flabelliformis, linn. [palmyra], palmaceæ. The worst of the palm-toddies. Good only for distilling arrack [q.v.].——*Peepul toddy* (पिप्पलमधु - pippalumadhu, San.; گلرکا نیرا - gullarkánírá, Hind.; ಅರಸೆಹೆಂಡ - araséhenda, Can.; రావికల్లు - rávikallu, Tel.; അരയാലിൻകള്ള് - arayálinkallu, Mal.; அரசங்கள்ளு - arasangallu, Tam.). Product of Ficus religiosa, linn. [peepul], moreceæ. Use medicinal.——*Prickly-pear toddy* (विदरमधु - vidaramadhu, San.; چپل سیندھ کی تاڑی - chappalsendhkítárí, Hind.; ಮುಳ್ಳುಗಳ್ಳಿಹೆಂಡ - mulligallihenda, Can.; నాగజెముడుకల్లు - nágájemudukallu, Tel.; നാഗതാളിക്കള്ള് - nágatálikkallu, Mal.; சப்பாத்துக்கள்ளு - shappáttukkallu, Tam.). Product of Opuntia dillenii, haw. [prickly-pear], cacteæ. A purgative.——*Sago-palm toddy* (ماڑی کی سیندی - márikísendí, Hind.; ಬೈನೀಹೆಂಡ - bainihenda, Can.; చిరుగుకల్లు - chirugukallu, Tel.; ഇരുമ്പനങ്കള്ള് - írumpanankallu, Mal.; கூந்தற்பனங்கள்ளு - kúndarbanangallu, Tam.). Product of Caryota urens, linn. [bastard sago palm], palmaceæ. Inferior and chiefly used on Malabar coast.

TODE (തോട് - tótu, *Mal.*). From (tóndu, mal. to dig). Artificial canal. Suffix in place names as Andattode.——*Toty* (ತೋಟಿಗ - tótígu, Can.; தோட்டி - tótti, Tam.). From (tóndu, tam. to dig). Digger [wodda]; village servant of low caste, who waits upon the villagers generally, is set to watch the crops, and assists in measuring them, &c.; menial domestic servant [inam]. See vol. I, 154, 158.

TOGAR (తొగరు - togaru, *Tel.*). Red color.——*Togar mogaly* (తొగరుమొగలి - togarumogali, Tel.). Meaning red color + pandanus odoratissimus, linn. Same as Dyeing mulberry.

TOGH (طوغ - togh, *Turk.*). Standard.——*Toghdar* (حباری - bubára, Ar.; هوبره - húbarah, Pers.; توغدار - toghdár, Hind. and Dec.; బట్టమేక - battaméka, Tel.; நீலநாரை - nílanárai, Tam.). Title from deccany. Ar. from (hubara, ar. ash-color). Pers. from arabic. Hind. from turkish, meaning standard-bearer; from feathers in front.. Tel. from (batta, tel. stripe + méka, tel. goat). Tam. from (níla, san. blue + nárai, tam. stork). Male bird is:—Ar. (kharab). Hind. also (sohau); (gaganbher), meaning sky lamb; (gurain). Tel. also (burrachirata), meaning gourd shell + leopard. Title otherwise Indian bustard. Eupodotis edwardsii, otididæ, pressirostres, grallatores [pacshy, 35], of naturalists [jantoo]. Alias Otis nigriceps. Male, top of head with crest black; face, nape, and whole neck white, feathers somewhat lengthened and hackled in front; back and upper plumage, including shoulder of wings and the inner wing-coverts, pale olive brown, or buff, beautifully mottled and variegated with minute lines of black; outer wing-coverts black, white tipped; greater coverts slaty-grey, also tipped with white, as is winglet; primaries dark slaty, more dusky on outer edges, white-tipped; tail as back with dark subterminal band not always, distinct on central feathers; blackish brown band across breast; lower parts, with thigh-coverts, white; flanks dark olive brown; vent and lower tail-coverts same but lighter; bill dusky above, yellowish beneath; irides pale yellow with brownish specks; legs and feet dingy pale yellow; length 4½–5 feet. Female one-third less at least, white of neck less pure, generally, rufous about face and eyes; pectoral band incomplete, abdomen less pure white, flanks paler brown more spotted; length 3½ feet. Fully grown adult male stands above 4 feet. Gular sac able to hold about three quarts of water. Not known on malabar coast; frequents open plains; when raised, generally takes long flight, sometimes three or four miles.——*Toghlak* (تغلق - toghlak, Hind.). From turkish, meaning standard bearer. The third of the Ghory dynasties [charitram]; see vol. I (143).

TOHFA (تحفه - tohfah, *Hind.*). From (tahafa, ar. to present). Tribute from inferior to superior [bhet, caunicay, nuzzer, wolfa].

TOKKY (తొక్కి - tokki, *Tel.*). Human sacrifice festival formerly held among the Sowrahs. See vol. I (72). This festival was annually held, and forty or fifty villages united in its celebration, choosing one village by turn for the site of operation. It was held in honor of Jaugrata devatay, the local numen. The most important part of the preparation was made four or five months before the time fixed on for the festival, by selecting some friendless man or woman of the age of twenty-five or twenty-six years, who was put into confinement, being highly fed and allowed the free use of intoxicating beverages. At the time of sacrifice, this victim was taken out in public procession for eight or nine successive days, proceeding round the village wherein the sacrifice was to be held. The precise act was held at four o'clock in the morning, or an hour or two before sunrise. The victim was then killed by a weapon termed gandagoddaly, and the blood was used as an offering to the idol [shilay, vigraham]. The person was always kept in a state of intoxication, and was usually insensible at the time of sacrifice. The Sowrahs considered that by this sacrifice they increased the fertility of their lands and rendered their villages more valuable [sowrah]. Compare Poorshamedham or human sacrifice under Yanyam.

TOKRAH (पिटक - pitaka, *San.*; توکرا - tokrá, *Hind.*; ಪುಟಿಕೆ - putike, *Can.*; గంప - gampa, *Tel.*; കൊട്ട - kotta, *Mal.*; கூடை - kúdai, *Tam.*). Title from hindostany. San. from (pit, san. to collect). Can. from sanscrit. Tam. from (kúdu, tam. to collect). Basket. Generally manufactured by the Coravars [q.v.] and Yerkalas [q.v.]. But bamboo [q.v.] baskets are made by Maidaries [q.v.]. The following is a key-list of the articles generally used for basket-work in this Presidency:—Bambusa arundinacea, common bamboo, split stem; Bambusa stricta, male bamboo, split stem; Borassus flabelliformis, palmyra, leaf; Calamus rotang, country rattan, stem; Caryota urens, bastard sago palm, leaf stalk; Cocos nucifera, cocoanut, leaf; Maba buxifolia, neilgherry satin-wood, split stalk; Phœnix sylvestris, wild date, fibrous leaflets, fibre from petioles; Saccharum sara, moonshee grass, split stalk; Salix babylonica, weeping willow, branches and twigs; Salix tetrasperma, indian willow, twigs; Tephrosia purpurea, zanzibar indigo, split stalk; Vitex negundo, notchy, split stalk.

TOL (تول - tol, *Hind.*). Bengalee word for a Sanscrit college.

TOL (தொல் - tol, *Tam.*). Old.——*Tolgauppyam* (தொல்காப்பியம் - tolgáppiyam, Tam.). From (above + kávya, san. poem). Tamul grammar [lacshanam] by Tolgauppyan of Madura, pupil of Agastyan [q.v.], whose large grammar, consisting of 80,000 rules, he abridged, reducing the number to 8,000. The Tolgauppyam complete should consist of three parts; on letters, words and prosody, or rather versification as an art. Of these the last part cannot be found complete. Tolgauppyam has had three commentaries written upon it by Nutchinarkiny, Yilampooran, and Shenauvareiyan [nunnool]. See vol. I (49).——*Tonnool* (தொன்னூல் - tonnúl, Tam.). From (above + núl, tam. science). Ancient science or book. Tamul grammar [lacshanam] by Beschi [veeramaumoony]; based on Nunnool, but the arrangement different.

TOLE (തോൽ - tól, *Mal.*). Hide [chamrah].——*Tolcollan* (തോൽകൊല്ലൻ - tólkollan, Mal.). From (above + kollan, mal. artificer). Tanner [jauty].

TOMATO (تماتی - tamátí, *Malay*). Same as Europe brinjaul.

TOMAUN (تومان - tomán, *Hind.*). Persian gold coin, answering to the english sovereign.

TOMI-TOMI (تومی تومی - tomitomi, *Malay*; ವುಬ್ಬೊಲು - vubbolu, *Can.*; ලොවිලොවි - lovilovi, *Singh.*; சொத்தைக் களா - shottaikkalá, *Tam.*). Title from malay. Tam. from (shottai, tam. decayed + kalá, tam. the plant, carissa genus). Tam. also (shottai). Title otherwise Lovi-lovi. Botanically Flacourtia [swaudoocantacam] inermis, roxb., bixineæ [vricsham, 14]. Young branches puberulous; leaves 4–8 by 2–3½ inches, base acute or rounded, shining, thin, coriaceous, midrib below pubescent; petiole ⅓–½ inch; disk covered with orange fleshy glands; ovary five-celled, cells two-ovuled; stigmas four to eight, two-lobed; fruit size of a cherry [q.v.], red, acid, pyrenes eight to ten. Tree from moluccas; flowers small greenish, flowers in hot weather, ripens fruit in september; berry very smooth; used in cookery, but inferior to flacourtia cataphracta, roxb. [indian plum].

TOM-TOM (తప్పెట - tappeta, *Tel.*; தம்பட்டம் - tambattam, *Tam.*). Small drum. There are several kinds, generally made of jack-wood [jack], and covered with deer-skin [mrigam], from which the hair has been removed. The skin is laid on in a wet state, and dried in the sun. There is a Tamul proverb:—உரல் போய் மத்தளத்தோடே முறையிட்டதுபோல—"as the "mortar went to the tom-tom with its complaints;" the mortar is beaten at one end only, whereas the tom-tom is beaten at both ends. Compare Paray.

TONDAY (தொண்டை - tondai, *Tam.*). From (áthondai, tam. a creeper, capparis horrida). The Tonday country. Also called Valanaud [q.v.], meaning fertile country. Ancient Chola province between E. ghauts and Palaur, corresponding with modern districts of N. & S. Arcot. See vol. I (13), (141). The following is the Dravidian legendary history. After the deluge [pralayam] the country was a vast forest inhabited by wild beasts.. A wild race of men arose, who destroying the wild beasts dwelt in certain districts. There were then no forts, only huts, no kings, no religion, no civilisation, no books; men were naked savages; no marriage institutions. Many years after the Coorumbar [q.v.] arose in the Carnauta [q.v.] country; they had a certain kind of religion, they were murderers, they derived the name of Coorumbar from their cruelty. Some of them spread into Dravida desham as far as the Tondaimundalam country. They are now found near Ootramallore, but more civilised. They ruled the country some time, but falling into strife among themselves they at length agreed to select a chief who should unite them altogether. They chose a man who had some knowledge of books, who was chief of the Dravida [q.v.] country, and was called Coorumba prabhoo and Pozhal rajah. He built a fort in Pozhalore. He divided the Coorumba [q.v.] land into twenty-four parts and constructed a fort in each district. While they were ruling, there was a commerce carried on by ships. As the merchants of Cauveripoomputnam sought trading intercourse with them, the Coorumbar built the following forts for trade:—Aulambaray, Cuddalore, Mercaunum, Meyyore, Pattipoolam, Shaulacooppam, Shaulapaukam; whence, by means of merchants from Cauveripoomputnam and the Coorumbar a commercial intercourse by vessels was carried on. They flourished in consequence, and while without any religion a Jeina ascetic came and turned them to the Jeina [q.v.] credence. The basty [q.v.] which the Pozhal [q.v.] king built after the name of that ascetic is still remaining, together with other basty and some Jeina images in different places; but some are dilapidated and some destroyed by the hatred of the Bramins [q.v.]. They were similar to the Jeinas of the present day. They were shepherds, weavers, lime-sellers, traders. While living thus, various kings of civilised countries made inroads upon them, as the Chola [q.v.] and Paundyan [q.v.] kings and others; and being a wild people who cared not for their lives, they successfully resisted their invaders and had some of the invading chiefs imprisoned in fetters, in front of the Pozhal fort. Besides, they constrained all young people to enter the Jeina religion; in consequence of which vexation a cry arose in the neighbouring countries. At length Athonday of Tanjore formed the design of subduing them; and, he invading them, a fierce battle was fought in front of the Pozhal fort, in which the Coorumba king's troops fought and fell with great bravery, and two-thirds of Athonday's army were cut up. He retreated to a distance overwhelmed with grief and the place where he halted is still called Cholan paid. While thinking of returning to Tanjore, Shiva that night appeared to him in a dream and promised him victory over the Coorumbar, guaranteed by a sign. The sign occurred and the Coorumba troops were the same day routed with great slaughter; the king was taken, the Pozhal fort was thrown down, and its bell-metal [cunts] gate was fixed in front of the shrine at Tanjore. A temple was built where the sign occurred, and a remarkable pillar of the fort was fixed there; the place is called Trimal vaasal. A sort of commemorative ceremony is practised there. After more fighting the other forts were taken and the Coorumbar destroyed. Athonday placed the Vellaular [q.v.] as his deputed authorities, having called them into the country to supply the deficiency of inhabitants from the Tooloova [q.v.] desham. They are called Tooloova vellaular to the present day. Some were brought from the Chola [q.v.] desham, still called Chola vellaular. He called from the north certain Bramins by birth, whom he fixed as accountants. The Condeicutty vellaular were appointed by him. He acquired the name of Chuckravurty from rescuing the people from their troubles. The name of Coorumba bhoomy was discontinued, the country was called Tondaimundalam and common consent ascribes to Athonday the regulation of the country. The following list shows the twenty-four cottams [q.v.] and seventy-nine nauds [q.v.]:—Aumore cottam; coomily naud, padoovore naud. Cadigay cottam; naugavaid naud, paraunjy naud, peroongaunjy naud. Calattore cottam; cooroombranaud, nadoonaud, pauttore naud, vullipoora naud. Cauliyore cottam; cauliyore naud, pauvore naud, tirpoolivana naud, vitpaid naud, yerikeel naud. Chundricay cottam; aroongobla naud, aulatore naud, polore naud, valacoolam naud. Coondraputra cottam; maugaula naud, mungala naud, nindray naud. Eecautt cottam; caucalore naud, cutchy naud. Eethore cottam; aramorangah naud. Manavorecottam; cunnore naud, illatore naud, pausaulay naud, permoor naud, poorisay naud. Ootcaud cottam; coondra naud, neevalore naud, pauleiyore naud, tammanore naud. Padoovore cottam; arcaud naud, shengoondram naud. Palcoondra cottam; meyyore naud, parasore naud, peroontimiry naud, singamportavala naud, tutchore naud. Peiyore cottam; cunny naud, shenore naud, vengaly naud, vitputty naud. Pooliyore cottam; amarore naud, coondratore naud, cottore naud, maungaud naud, peroor naud. Pozhal cottam; ambattore naud, augoody naud, auttore naud, nayar naud, yezhoomore naud. Shembore cottam; moogoondore naud, puttana naud, pireiyore naud. Shengautt cottam; athigattore naud, pennalore naud. Sircaray cottam; oynda naud. Daumal cottam; cariveed naud, vadacaray vullam naud. Veloor cottam; mauttore naud, nenmely naud, ozhcaray naud. Vengada cottam; coodacaray naud, pottapy naud, tondiman naud. Vengoondra cottam; arasore naud, maroothaud naud, nulloor naud, pernagar naud, tellaur naud. Yeyil cottam; conairy naud, maugaralnaud, tandaga naud. Yilangautt cottam; maragoona naud, ponnore naud, tennatore naud [charitram].——*Tondaimundalam* (தொண்டைமண்டலம் - tondaimandalam, Tam.). The realm of Tonday.——*Tondayaur* (தொண்டியாறு - tondiyáru, Tam.). From (above + áru, tam. river). River; South arcot dist., Tindivanam and Villoopooram tals.; Tributary of the Varauhanuddy.——*Tondeeran* (தொண்டீரன் - tondíran, Tam.). The chief of the Tonday country.——*Tondiman* (தொண்டமான் - tondamán, Tam.). From (above + mán, tam. suffix of possession). Title of the chiefs of Poodoocottah in Trichinopoly district. See vol. I, 40.

TONDRAL (தோன்றல் - tónral, *Tam.*). From (tónru, tam. to appear), conspicuous one. Title of the ruler in a forest tract [desham, moollay].

TONDY (തൊണ്ടി - tondi, *Mal.*). Thick rind.——*Tondy teragam* (തൊണ്ടിതേരകം - tonditterakam, Mal.). Mal. from (above + térakam, mal. ficus asperrima, roxb.). Mal. also (tonti), meaning thick-skinned. Title otherwise Downy callicarpa, Folhas da raspa macho, Groot rijf blad, Woolly callicarpa. Botanically Callicarpa lanata, linn., verbenaceæ [vricsham, 102]. Alias Callicarpa americana, cana, tomentosa. From 20–40 feet in height, the young branches are cinnamoneous [cinnamon], shaggy and woolly, the leaves 4–8 inches long, ovate lanceolate, stellately tomentose beneath; if the tomentum is removed, numerous oil glands are visible; both leaves and bark are faintly aromatic and bitterish, and afford much mucilage when boiled. Has in medicine mucilaginous emollient and diuretic properties; is also sub-aromatic and bitter; leaves boiled in milk [paul] are used as a wash for aphthæ of the mouth; bark and root boiled in water yield a decoction which is used to lessen febrile heat and remove hepatic obstruction and herpetic eruptions; leaves, roots, and bark are used by the natives of ceylon in skin diseases.

TONDY (தொண்டி - tondi,* *Tam.*). Means toddy. Village, Port; Madura dist., Tirvaudaunay tal.; pop. 3,823; lat. 9° 45′; long. 79° C4′; from Damodaraputnam S.W. 5 miles; from Madras S.S.W. 246 miles; from Madura E.S.E. 62 miles; from Numboodalay N.E. 1½ miles; from Ramnaud N.N.E. 28 miles. On Palk's bay connected by road with the interior. Inhabitants are principally Mussalmans [q.v.], but there are also a few Caraiyaur [q.v.]; the former are engaged in manufacturing long-cloths, and the latter are fishermen. Inland commodities, consisting of grain, tamarinds [q.v.], cloths, &c., are exported, as also chunks [q.v.], in great abundance. Trade with Colombo. Government treasure is generally shipped for Madras by steamer from here.

TONGA (ٹانگا - tángá, *Hind.*). A two-wheeled, four-seated low carriage of strong construction for use on rough ground; drawn by a pair of ponies abreast.

TONGUE (நாக்கு - nákku, *Tam.*). Prefix. For bull's tongue see Gowzabaun. For naukkmeen see Indian sole.——*Tongue grass* (நாக்கறுத்தான்புல் - nákkaruttánbul, Tam.). From sharp blades. Same as Darbhay.

TONJON (تام جہام - támjhám, *Hind.*). Hind. from (thám, hind. support + jháng, san. thigh). A sedan or portable chair, open in front and on each side, carried by single pole [dandam], on men's shoulders [dhooly].

TOOCAJEE (ತುಕೋಜೀ - tukóji, *Can.*). From (tukái, mahr. párvati + jí, hind. master). Mahratta name [peyar].

TOOGLOOT (ತುಗ್ಲುಟಿ - tugluti, *Can.*). Hill quagmire.

TOOK (தூக்கு - túkku, *Tam.*). Means weight. Bazaar weight. 1¼ vissos = 1 took; 2 tooks = 1 yeday [niray, 2a]. Approximate actual value, 1 took = 3 lbs. 13 oz. 11⅔ drs. avoir. Tamul districts. See vol. I, 609; II, 507, 509.

TOOKADY (ٹکری - tukrí, *Hind.*). From (tukrá, hind. a piece). A division or district [firkah, taraf, zillah]. Tookry, corruption of tookridar, is a village-watcher.

TOOLAM (तुला - tulá; *San.*; துலம் - tolam, *Tam.*). From (tul, san. to weigh). Balance.——*Tolah* (तुला - tulá, San.; تولہ - tolah, Hind.). From (tul, san. to weigh). A weight formerly regarded as equivalent to the weight of the sicca [q.v.] rupee or 179·666 troy grains. Now fixed at 180 troy grains, the weight of the current rupee [q.v.]. British rupees 38·9 weigh 1 lb. avoir. 350 tolahs = 9 lb. Weight of a florin is 174·54 grains. According to Mahomedan calculations tolah = 12 maushams. According to Sanscrit calculations tolah = 8 maushams. See vol. I, 609; II, 505.——*Tool* (طول - tul, Hind.; తుల - tula, Tel.). From (tul, san. to weigh). The measurement of a heap of grain by means of a cord over the top.——*Toolabhauram* (तुलाभार - tulábhára, San.). From (tulá, san. balance + bhára, san. weight). A ceremony performed once in the life-time of each maharajah [q.v.] retained at Travancore. The Maharajah is seated on one scale of an ornamental balance, with his sword and shield; and in the other scale his weight is heaped in gold coins [naunyam] having the name of the god inscribed thereon, which are afterwards distributed to the Bramins [q.v.] in various proportions according to their dignity and claims. One ruler performed this ceremony a second time in silver at the end of his reign.——*Toolaum* (തുലാം - tulám, Mal.; துலாம் - tulám, Tam.). Bazaar weight. 100 pollums = 1 toolaum; 20 toolaums = 1 bhauram [niray, 2d]. Approximate actual value, 1 toolaum = 25 pounds avoir. Variable. The Tamul toolaums are much smaller. Same as Shiroopuddy in Tinnevelly. Compare Maund. See vol. I, 609; II, 509, 515, 518, 519.——*Toolsy* (तुलसी - tulasí, San.). See sep. title.——*Toolyabhauga* (తుల్యభాగ - tulyabhága, Tel.). From (tulya, san. equal + bhága, san. division). A mouth of the Godavery; near Chollangy.

TOOLOO (ತುಳು - tulu, *Can.*). Means mild. Language once prevalent throughout Canara, but now spoken mostly in the neighbourhood of Mangalore. Holds a position midway between Canarese and Malayalam, but more resembles former [bhaushay]. See vol. I (51).——*Tooloo rajyam* (തുളുരാജ്യം - tulurájyam, Mal.). From (above + rájya, san. kingdom). Northern keralam [q.v.] from Gocurnam to Cassergode river. See vol. I (127).——*Tooloovam* (ತುಳುವ - tulu, Can.; തുളുവം - tuluvam, Mal.; துளுவம் - tuluvam, Tam.). From (tulu, can. the language). Canara from Chundragherry river in south to Bhadragherry river in north. One of the fifty-six countries [bhoogola shastram].——*Tooloovan* (ತುಳುವನು - tuluvanu, Can.; துளுவன் - tuluvan, Tam.). Inhabitants of the Tooloo country. Tooloova bramins [q.v.] belong neither to Gowda [q.v.] nor Dravida [q.v.]. They do not intermarry with the other Bramins on the Malabar coast. They resemble the Numboories [q.v.]. They are divided between the sects of Shuncaracharry [shuncaran] and Madhwacharry [madhwa].

TOOLSY (तुलसी - tulasí, *San.*). From (tul, san. weigh); grave, holy [toolam]. Title otherwise Basil. Botanically the Ocimum genus, labiatæ [vricsham, 103]. Strongly scented herbs, undershrubs or shrubs. The species best known to the natives are shown below. Includes also one species of melissa and two of sphæranthus. Toolsy as a name is applied to males and females among Madhwas [peyar].——(1) *Toolasingam* (துளசிங்கம் - tulásingam, Tam.). From (above + simha, san. lion, short for narsimha, the man-lion god); meaning vishnoo as crowned or adorned with toolsy garland. Hindoo 2nd or pers. name [peyar].——*Toolsajee* (تلساجی - tulsájí, Hind.). Holy basil + mahratta honorific title. Son of Prataup sing, rajah of Tanjore, 1765–1787. Tanjore captured and the rajah taken prisoner by Oomdat ool oomrah, who was aided by the English. Subsequently reinstated. Nagore settlement, consisting of 277 villages, was ceded and Tanjore became a protected state. See vol. I, 50; II, 126.——*Toolsimany tauvadam* (துளசி மணித்தாவடம் - tulasimanittávadam, Tam.). From (above + mani, san. bead + tázh, tam. pendent + vadam, tam. string). A rosary [maulay] of toolsy.——*Toolsy bye* (ತುಳಸಿಬಾಯಿ - tulasibáyi, Can.). From (above + báyi, can. title). A ranee of Indore, well known in history.——*Toolsy toongaury* (తులసితుంగారి - tulasitungári, Tel.). From (above + tunga, san. high + giri, san. mountain). Range of hills; Vizagapatam district, Jeypore zemindarry, Mulkangherry magisterial division; separate Ramgherry and Mulkangherry zemindarries. Stretch into the state of Bustar. Average elevation 3,000 feet. Highest peak, Toolsy, 3,928 feet.——(2) *Common toolsy* (तुलसी - tulasí, San.; तुळशी - tulashí, Mahr.; कालितुलसि - kálitulasi, Conc.; بادروج - bádrúj, *Ar.*; تلسی - tulsí, Hind. and Dec.; سالسی - sálasi, Malay; ತುಳಶಿ - tulashi, Can.; ಕಪ್ಪುತುಳಚಿ - kapputulachi, Too.; తులసి - tulasi, Tel.; തുളസി - tulasi, Mal.; මදුරුතලා - madurutalá, Singh.; துளசி - tulasi, Tam.). Title from hindostany. San. from (tul, san. to weigh), meaning of great weight or importance. Mahr. from sanscrit. Conc. from (kála, san. black + tulasí, san. the plant). Ar. means ocimum basilicum, linn. Hind. from sanscrit. Malay from sanscrit. Too. from (kappu, too. black + tulasí, san. basil). Tel. from sanscrit. Mal. from sanscrit. Singh. from. (maduru, singh. the mount méru + talá, singh. basil). Tam. from sanscrit. San. also (bháratí), meaning indian; (bhútaka), meaning demon plant, useful in incantations; (divyá), meaning divine; (krishnamúla), meaning dark-rooted; (ájaka), meaning pertaining to goat; (parnása), meaning leaf + dropping, from shedding old leaves; (arjaka), meaning procuring, from utility; (surasá), meaning good juice [notchy]; (krishnatulasí), meaning black basil. Hind. also (kálátulsí), meaning black toolsy; (krishnatulsí), meaning black toolsy; (varindá), by corruption (barandá), from (brindá, san. holy basil). Dec. also (tulsíkámankah), meaning toolsy bead; (tulsíkíjar), meaning toolsy root. Can. also (karitulashi), meaning black + basil; (kálatulashi), meaning black + basil; (kural). Tel. also (gaggera); (nallagaggera), meaning black + the plant; (nallatulasi), meaning black + toolsy plant; (brinda). Mal. also (nallatrittávu), meaning good basil; (shivatulasi), meaning shiva's basil. Tam. also (alangai), meaning shining, from use as garlands to deities; (pirundam), from (brindá, san. holy basil); (karundulasi), meaning black + holy basil. Title otherwise Holy basil, Monk's basil, Purple stalked basil, Sacred basil. Botanically Ocimum [toolsy] sanctum, linn., labiatæ [vricsham, 103]. Alias Basilicum agreste; Lumnitzera tenuiflora; Ocimum frutescens, hirsutum, inodorum, monachorum, scutellarioides, tenuiflorum, tomentosum, villosum, zeylanicum; Plectranthus monachorum. Small plant, 1–2 feet; stems and petioles pilose, dull red purple; profusely branched; branches also clothed with dark purple hairs; leaves same color, 1½ inches long, 1 inch broad, petiolate, oval, obtuse, toothed, pubescent; floral leaves sessile, shorter than the pedicels; racemes slender, simple or branched at the base; calyx shorter than the pedicels, smoothish, upper tooth obovate, concave; corolla hardly exceeding the calyx; flowers small, fragrant, pale purple; generally cultivated in pots, in gardens and near pagodas [q.v.]. Sacred to vishnoo [q.v.]; said to have been produced from hair of a nymph beloved by him as krishnan [q.v.]; the veishnava rosaries [maulay] are composed of 108 beads made of the wood; oaths are made on leaves steeped in water; these are held in the hand, and after the oath are swallowed; venerated by hindoos like the vervein was amongst the romans; may be often seen occupying a prominent position in front of hindoo houses; when thus kept it has to be watered and worshipped daily. Medicinally much like fragrant toolsy; dried plant aromatic stimulant, expectorant and diaphoretic; used mixed with lime-juice [lime], in cutaneous affections and ringworm; in pharm non-officinal. There is a Canarese proverb:—ಮಾಡೋದು ದುರಾಚಾರ, ಮನೆಯ ಮುಂದೆ ವೃಂದಾವನ—"acts wickedly, but rears a toolsy in front of his house."——*Fever toolsy* (சுரக்கரந்தை - shurakkarandai, Tam.). Title from cure against fever. Tam. from (jvara, san. fever + karandai, tam. sweet basil, ocimum basilicum, linn.). Tam. also (shivakkarandai), meaning shiva + sweet basil. Title otherwise Ceylon toolsy. Botanically Sphæranthus [moondy] amaranthoides, burm., compositæ [vricsham, 74]. Alias Oligolepis amaranthoides; Sphæranthus zeylanicus. Annual, glabrous; leaves lanceolate entire, serrated, glabrous, shortly decurrent; capitula ovate-globose, subsessile; peduncles very short, wingless; bracts very much acuminated, involucre usually one scale to each flower, that of the hermaphrodite much larger and forming a common involucre to the capitulum, those of the females linear-obtuse, mucronate or truncated, folded round the flower and adhering to the pedicel. Found in rice fields; used in fever and cutaneous diseases.——*Fragrant toolsy* (वर्वर - varvara, San.; सबजा - sabajá, Mahr.; कामकस्तूरि - kámakastúri, Conc.; شاهسفرم - sháhasfaram, Ar.; ریحان - raihán, Pers.; سبزه - sabzah, Hind. and Dec.; سالسی - sálasi, Malay; ಬಿಳಿಕಮ್ಮಗಗ್ಗರಿ - bilikammagaggari, Can.; ನಾಯಿತುಳಚಿ - náyitulachi, Too.; వేపుడుపత్స - vépudupattsa, Tel.; ଧଳତୁଳସି - dhálatulasi, Oor.; വെള്ളത്തുളസി - vellattulasi, Mal.; සුවඳතලා - suvandatalá, Singh.; திருநீற்றுப்பச்சை - tiruníttuppaççai, Tam.). Title from qualities of all parts of plant. San. from (vri, san. to cover) [babool, knotted bhraungy, vailay]. Mahr. from hindostany. Conc. from (káma, san. desire + kastúri, san. musk). Ar. from (sháh, pers. king + asparam, pers. basil, ocimum). Pers. from (ráih, ar. fragrance). Hind. from (sabz, pers. green). Malay from (tulasí, san. basil). Can. from (bili, can. white + kammagaggari, can. the plant, ocimum sanctum, linn). Too. from (náyi, too. dog + tulachi, too. the holy basil, ocimum sanctum, linn.). Tel. from (vétsu, tel. to fry + pattsa, tel. green). Oor. means white basil. Mal. from (vella, mal. white + tulasí, san. holy basil). Singh. from (suvanda, singh. fragrant + talá, singh. basil). Tam. from (tiru, tam. holy + níru, tam. ashes + paççai, tam. plant); from its fragrant evergreen leaves used in perfuming sacred ashes [tirneer, vibhooty]. San. also (vishvatulasí), meaning world + holy basil; (ájaka), meaning relating to goat; (gambhíra), meaning secret, from supposed virtues; (gandhap'hanijjhaka), meaning fragrant basil; (mañjariká), meaning having a cluster of flowers; (arjaka), meaning procuring, useful. Mahr. also (tukumaráí), meaning the seed of the plant; (pándharítulasí), meaning white basil. Ar. also (sultánurrayáhín), meaning king of ocimum species; (raihánimutlak), meaning absolute sweet basil; (asábiulfatiyát), meaning fingers of a girl; (badrúj); (bakalatul'zabb), meaning porpoise potherb. Pers. also (názbú); (dabánsháb); (angushtikhúnizakn), meaning finger + blood + chin. Hind. also (janglítulsí), meaning wild holy basil; (bábarí), by corr. from sanscrit; (bábrítulsí); (mane), (kálátulsí), meaning black toolsy. Dec. also (ujlítulsí), meaning white basil. Malay also (sulasi). Can. also (kámakastúri), meaning desire + musk; (nírutulasi), meaning water + basil; (náyitulasi), meaning dog + basil; (rámatulasi), meaning the hero + basil. Too. also (kámakastúri), meaning desire + musk. Tel. also (bhútulasi), meaning ground + toolsy plant; (tellatulasi), meaning white + toolsy plant; (vibúdipatri), meaning sacred ashes + leaf; (nírutulasi), meaning water + toolsy plant; (kukkatulasi), meaning dog toolsy; (rudrajada), meaning shiva + matted hair. Mal. also (tiruníttuppaçça), meaning holy + ashes + green; (paççapushpam), meaning greenish flower; (nákkanni), meaning dog-eyed; (rámatulasi), meaning rama's basil; (kátturématulasi), meaning wild rama's basil; (tulasittrittávu), meaning holy basil. Tam. also (kañjángórai) [persian toolsy, white toolsy], cf. sankhvel; (tiruníttuppattiri), meaning holy + ashes + leaf; (karandai); (uruttirasadai), meaning shiva + matted hair; (náyttulasi), meaning dog + holy basil; (mañjilikkán), meaning rice-field plant; (shunaikkarandai), meaning sharp + the plant. Greek ὤκιμον. Title otherwise Ciliated basil, Holy ashes leaf, Indian tea, Roodra's hair, Royal basil, Sabzah, Sweet basil, Wild mint. Botanically Ocimum [toolsy] basilicum, linn., labiatæ [vricsham, 103]. Alias Basilicum indicum, Ocimum album, americanum, anisatum, caryophyllatum, ciliatum, hispidum, hispidulum, integerrimum, lanceolatum, laxum, minimum, pilosum. Herbaceous, erect, glabrous; leaves petiolate, ovate or oblong, narrowed at the base, slightly toothed; petioles ciliated; racemes simple; calyxes longer than the pedicels; upper teeth ovate, concave, shortly acuminated; whorls about six, rarely ten-flowered; flowers small, white; flowering nearly all year; whole plant aromatic fragrant. Juice of leaves used for ringworm, and bruised leaves for scorpion stings; juice of leaves is squeezed into ear in earache; seeds and flowers stimulant, diuretic and demulcent; seed are a favorite medicine with hindoo women for relieving the afterpains of parturition; seeds steeped in water swell and form a jelly; leaves and seeds in pharm. non-officinal. Plant often used for seasoning in cookery; infusion of leaves dried in shade used as a tea [q.v.]; an aromatic ethereal oil is obtained from the root. There are several varieties. Compare the following compounds, where translation is of first term:—Brachycome assamica (shirugotta'kkarandai), small + seed; Grangea maderaspatana (shinnappúkkottaikkarandai), small + flower + seed; Laggera aurita (nárungarandai), smell; Melissa officinalis (pársigañjángórai), persian; Salvia plebia (káttukkañjángórai), wild; Sphæranthus amaranthoides (shivakkarandai), shiva, (shurakkarandai), fever; Sphæranthus indicus (kódálakkarandai), meaning axe-like, from use against disease, (kottaikkarandai), seed, (vittunukkarandai), vishnoo. See glossary paragraphs.——*Mecca toolsy* (مکہ سبزہ - makkahsabzah, Dec.). Same as Persian toolsy.——*Persian toolsy* (مفرح القلب - mufarrihulkalb, Ar.; بادرنگبویه - bádrangbóyah, Pers.; رام تلسی - rámtulsí, Hind.; مکہ سبزہ - makkahsabzah, Dec.; பார்சிகஞ்சாங்கோரை - pársigañjángórai, Tam.). Title from habitat. Ar. from (mufarrih, ar. stimulant + kalb, ar. heart). Pers. from (bádrang, pers. ocimum canum, sims. + búyah, pers. fragrant). Hind. from (rám, hind. rama + tulsí, hind. holy basil, ocimum sanctum, linn.) [rama toolsy]. Dec. from (makkah, hind. mecca + sabzah, hind. sweet basil, ocimum basilicum, linn.). Tam. from (pársi, tam. persia + kañjángórai, tam. white-basil, ocimum canum, sim.). Ar. also (bakalatulfaristún); (bakalatulutrujiyat), meaning citrus medica, linn. + potherb; (habakituranján), meaning citrus + mint, mentha pulegium, linn. Hind. also (billílotan), meaning valerian spikenard, nardostachys jatamansi, dec. Tam. also (kañjángórai), meaning white basil, ocimum basilicum, linn. [fragrant toolsy, white toolsy]; cf. sankhvel. Greek μελισσόφυλλον, μελιτταῖνα. Title otherwise Arabian balm, Balm mint, Citrago, Mecca toolsy. Botanically Melissa officinalis, linn., labiatæ [vricsham, 103]. Perennial deciduous creeper ligneous or herbaceous, 1 foot high; leaves ovate-acute, serrated; whorls halved, subsessile; bracts oblong, stalked; flowers white, flowering in june and october; originally brought from arabia; flower white or pale yellow; employed as a tea [q.v.] and diluent in fevers; expectorant, febrifuge, stomachic.——*Rama toolsy* (रामतुलसी - rámatulasí, San.; रामतुळशी - rámatulashí, Mahr.; فرنجمشك - faranjmishk, Ar.; پلنگمشك - palangmishk, Pers.; رام تلسی - rámtulsí, Hind. and Dec.; ರಾಮತುಳಸಿ - rámatulasi, Can.; రామతులసి - rámatulasi, Tel.; കാട്ടുതൃത്താവ് - káttutrittávu, Mal.; எலுமிச்சந்துளசி - elumiççandulasi, Tam.). Title from sanscrit. San. from (ráma, san. white + tulasí, san. holy basil, ocimum sanctum, linn.), from ash-colored stems. Mahr. from sanscrit. Ar. from (faranj, ar. frank + mishk, ar. musk). Pers. from arabic. Hind. from (rám, hind. rama + tulsí, hind. holy basil) [persian toolsy]. Can. and Tel. from sanscrit. Mal. from (kátu, mal. forest + trittávu, mal. holy basil). Tam. from (elumiççai, tam. lemon tree, citrus medica, linn., var. acida, brandis + tulasí, san. holy basil); from fragrance. San. also (arjaka), meaning procuring. Tel. also (nimmatulasi), meaning lime + toolsy plant. Mal. also (rámatulasi). Tam. also (perundulasi), meaning big + holy basil. Title otherwise Frank musk, Garden clove, Large basil, Lemon basil, Shrubby basil. Botanically Ocimum [toolsy] gratissimum, linn., labiatæ [vricsham, 103]. Alias Ocimum frutescens, petiolare, zeylanicum. Stem rather glabrous; leaves petioled, ovate-acute, crenated or coarsely toothed, narrowed at the base, glabrous or pubescent along the veins; floral leaves like bracts, lanceolate-acuminate, hastate at the base; racemes simple or slightly branched, pubescent; calyx pedicelled; lateral teeth minute, upper united into a bimucronate lip; corolla scarcely longer than the calyx; stamens exserted; flowers white or pale-yellow; common in gardens, flowering all the year. Leaves have a remarkably grateful lemon [q.v.] odour and taste, and are a cooling remedy in gonorrhœa; a decoction of seeds is demulcent; gives to pharm. seeds, non-officinal. Leaves made into chutney [q.v.].——*Rough toolsy* (अर्जक - arjaka, San.; తెల్లగగ్గెర - tellagaggera, Tel.; குழிமிட்டான் - kuzhimittán, Tam.). Title from villose leaf. San. from (arj, san. to procure); from being useful and medicinal. Tel. from (tella, tel. white + gaggera, tel. holy basil, ocimum sanctum, linn.). Tam. from (kuzhisi, tam. pot + vidu, tam. to set), as growing in pot. Title otherwise Rough basil. Botanically Ocimum [toolsy] sanctum, linn., var. hirsuta, labiatæ [vricsham, 103]. Alias Ocimum villosum. Aromatic small herb, clothed with white or pale green hairs; leaves ovate, oblong, crenate, serrate, obtuse, from 1 to 2 inches long.——*Seed toolsy* (मुण्डितिका - munditiká, San.; मुंडी - mundí, Mahr.; कळंचो - kalanchó, Conc.; كمادريوس - kamázariyús, Ar.; كمادريوس - kamádariyús, Pers.; منڈی - mundí, Hind.; مونڈی - múndí, Dec.; ಕರಂಡೆ - karande, Can. and Too.; బోడతరము - bódataramu, Tel.; അടക്കമണിയൻ - atakkamaniyan, Mal.; මුඩමහන - mudamahana, Singh.; கொட்டைக்கரந்தை - kottaikkarandai, Tam.). Title from officinal part. San. from (mund, san. to shave). Mahr. from sanscrit. Ar. from greek. Pers. from arabic. Hind. and Dec. from sanscrit. Can. from (karandai, tam. fragrant toolsy). Mal. from (atakka, mal. areca nut + mani, mal. grain); from sub-globular flowers. Singh. from (muda, singh. bald + mahana, singh. ascetic); perhaps from the globular flowers. Tam. from (kottai, tam. seed + karandai, tam. sweet basil, ocimum basilicum, linn.). Ar. also (dukhn) [tinay]. Pers. also (zakhmihayát), meaning life wound. Hind. also (mundíbutí), meaning the globe-thistle herb. Can. also (múdugattina); (bódukodalc). Tel. also (bódasaramu). Mal. also (mínánkanni), meaning fish eye. Singh. also (atmudamahana). Tam. also (vittunukkarandai), meaning vishnoo + sweet basil, ocimum basilicum, linn.; (tiriloki), meaning indran, a valuable plant; (kódálakkarandai), meaning axe-like basil, from being a curative. Title otherwise Bald ascetic, Fish eye, Indian globe-thistle, Vishnoo caranday. Botanically Sphæranthus [moondy] indicus, linn., compositæ [vricsham, 74]. Alias Sphæranthus africanus, hirtus, mollis. Annual, winged; leaves sessile, decurrent, long-obovate, bristly-serrated, downy and glutinous; heads of flowers solitary, leaf-opposed or terminal; peduncles winged; flowers rose-colored or purple; common in rice-fields, flowering nearly all the year; the whole plant is remarkably fragrant. Small oblong seeds brown, with delicate whitish bristles are anthelmintic, prescribed in powder; powder of root stomachic; bark ground small and mixed with whey a remedy for piles. There is a Tamul proverb :—விடாச்சுரத்துக்கு விஷ்ணுகரந்தை—"vishnoo caranday is a specific "remedy for continued fever."——*Upland toolsy* (మెట్టతులసి - mettatulasi, Tel.). Same as Wild toolsy.——*White toolsy* (विश्वतुलसी - vishvatulasí, San.; بادروج ابيض - bádrújiabyaz, Ar.; ريحان كوهى - raihánikohí, Pers.; سفيد تلسى - sufedtulsí, Hind.; ككا تلسى - kukkátulsí, Dec.; ನಾಯಿತುಳಸಿ - náyitulasi, Can.; కుక్కతులసి - kukkatulasi, Tel.; നാക്കണ്ണി - nákkanni, Mal.; හිංතලා - híntalá, Singh.; கஞ்சாங்கோரை - kañjángórai, Tam.). Title from leaf. San. from (vishva, san. world + tulasí, san. holy basil, ocimum sanctum, linn.). Ar. from (bádrúj, ar. wild basil + abyaz, ar. white). Pers. from (raihán, pers. sweet basil, ocimum basilicum, linn. + koh, pers. mountain). Hind. from (sufed, hind. white + tulasi, san. basil). Dec. from teloogoo. Can. from (náyi, can. dog + tulasí, san. holy basil). Tel. from (kukka, tel. dog + tulasí, san. holy basil). Mal. from (náya, mal. dog + kan, mal. eye). Tam. from (kañjá, tam. plant, cannabis sativa, linn. + kórai, tam. the plant, cyperus rotundus, linn.) [fragrant toolsy, persian toolsy]; cf. sankhvel. San. also (arjaka), meaning procuring. Pers. also (turrahi khurásání), meaning khorassan basil. Hind. also (janglítulsí), meaning wild basil; (bábú); (kálátulsí), meaning black toolsy. Tel. also (krishnatulasi), meaning black + toolsy plant. Tam. also (náyttulasi), meaning dog + holy basil; (tulasi). Title otherwise Hoary basil, White basil. Botanically Ocimum [toolsy] canum, sims., labiatæ [vricsham, 103]. Alias Ocimum album, americanum, stamineum. Stem herbaceous, erect, pubescent; leaves petioled, ovate, removed at both ends, denticulate or entire, rather hoary beneath; petioles ciliated; verticils of the fruit bearing raceme, numerous, approximated; calyx small, a little ciliated; flowers white; common everywhere, flowering at all seasons. Shrub about a foot high, chiefly grown in native gardens; leaves have pleasant aromatic taste and smell. Gives tea [q.v.] like fragrant toolsy [q.v.].——*Wild toolsy* (جنگلی تلسی - janglítulsí, Hind. and Dec.; ಕರಿಕಮ್ಮಗಗ್ಗರಿ - karikammagaggari, Can.; మెట్టతులసి - mettatulasi, Tel.; കാട്ടുതുളസി - káttutulasi, Mal.; காட்டுத்துளசி - káttuttulasi, Tam.). Title from hindostany. Hind. from (janglí, hind. wild + tulsí, hind. holy basil). Can. from (kari, can. black + kammagaggari, can. holy basil). Tel. from (metta, tel. high land + tulasí, san. holy basil). Mal. from (kátu, mal. forest + tulasí, san. holy basil). Tam. from (kádu, tam. forest + tulasí, san. holy basil, ocimum sanctum, linn.). Can. also (kastúrikammagaggari), meaning musk + basil; (kádutulasi), meaning wild + ocimum. Tel. also (lakshmitulasi), meaning lutchmy the goddess + ocimum. Title otherwise Upland toolsy, Wild basil. Botanically Ocimum [toolsy] adscendens, willd., labiatæ [vricsham, 103]. Alias Ocimum cristatum, indicum; Plectranthus indicus. Stem prostrate; branches pubescent; leaves petioled, ovate-oblong, obtuse, slightly toothed, narrowed at the base, pubescent; floral leaves like bracts, deciduous; racemes simple; calyx in fruit drooping, the tube striated; wings of the upper tooth reaching to the middle of the calyx; lateral teeth truncated, lower very shortly setaceous, acuminated; corolla twice the length of the calyx; stamens much exserted; flowers pale rose; common, flowering in the rains; scentless.

TOOM (తూము - túmu, *Tel.*; தூமு - túmu, *Tam.*).—"*a*" Measure of capacity. The indian Bushel. 4 coonchams = 1 toom; 20 tooms = 1 pootty or candy [alavay, 3 b]. Very variable. In Bellary 2 cubic feet 1,234 cubic inches; in Cuddapah 1 cubic foot 582 cubic inches; in Ganjam 227½ cubic inches; in Godavery 1,120 cubic inches; in Kistna 1 cubic foot 1,632 cubic inches; in Nellore 2 cubic feet 464 cubic inches. Teloogoo people in the south translate mercaul into toom. Same as Cooncham in Ganjam. See vol. I, 609; II, 508, 510, 511, 512, 513, 516, 519.—"*b*" Bazaar weight. 4 addas = 1 toom; 4 tooms = 1 navitey [niray, 2b]. Approximate actual value, 1 toom = 6 lbs. 4 oz. avoir. Ganjam. Same as Dhadiyam or Yettoo. Compare Yeday.

TOOMBAY (தும்பை - tumbai, *Tam.*). Botanically Leucas genus, labiatæ [vricsham, 103]. Herbs or shrubs; natives of tropical asia and africa; flowers white, rarely purple. The species best known to the natives are shown below. Includes also one species of each of the genera:—alhagi, andrographis, anisomeles, dysophylla, impatiens, trichodesma.——*Benares toombay* (காசித்தும்பை - kásittumbai, Tam.). Same as Gool mindie.——*Black toombay* (കരിന്തുമ്പ - karintumba, Mal.). Title from flowers. Same as Malabar catmint.——*Donkey toombay* (چھوٹا خرفا - chhotákhurfá, Dec.; గువ్వగుత్తి - guvvagutti, Tel.; கழுதைத்தும்பை - kazhuthaittumbai, Tam.). Title from growing in waste places. Dec. from (chhotá, hind. small + khurfá, hind. purslane, portulaca oleracea, linn.). Tel. from (guvva, tel. bird + gutti, tel. cluster). Tam. from (kazhuthai, tam. ass + tumbai, tam. plant, leucas). Title otherwise Indian borage, Small purslane. Botanically Trichodesma indicum, br., boragineæ [vricsham, 92]. Alias Borago indica. Diffuse or erect; stem shortly villous; leaves usually opposite, narrow-lanceolate, half-stem-clasping, sessile; pedicels opposite-flowered or lateral one-flowered; calyx villous, acutely auricled at the base, lobes increased by a subulate point; limb of the corolla spreading, reflexed; flowers pale blue; grown in waste places. Is repute in snake-bites; diuretic; blood purifier; cold infusion of leaves is depurative; in pharm. non-officinal. Ceylon borage is zeylanicum; leaves used as emollient poultice; in pharm. non-officinal.——*Dung toombay* (പിത്തുമ്പ - píttumba, Mal.). Same as Coromandel chiretta.——*Flower toombay* (द्रोणपुष्पी - drónapushpí, San.; تمبا - tumbá, Hind.; ಒಲ್ಲೆತುಂಬೆ - olletumbe, Can.; పూలతుమ్మి - púlatummi, Tel.; காசித்தும்பை - kásittumbai,

Tam.). San. from (dróna, san. cup + pushpa, san. flower). Hind. from tamul. Can. from (olle, can. good + tumbe, can. leucas). Tel. from (puvvu, tel. flower + tummi, tel. leucas indica, r. br.); to distinguish from fruit bearing kind. Tam. from (káshí, san. shining, also benares + tumbai, tam. the plant); from shining flowers. Tam. also (péyttumbai), meaning devil + the plant. Botanically Leucas [toombay] linifolia, spreng., labiatæ [vricsham, 103]. Alias Leonurus indicus, lavandulæfolia; Phlomis linifolia, zeylanica. Herbaceous, erect, slightly pubescent or tomentose; leaves oblong-linear, entire or remotely serrated; verticels dense, sub-equal, many-flowered; bracts linear, hoary; calyx elongated above, mouth very oblique, lower teeth very short, upper longest; flowers white; the fresh juice is employed in headache and colds.——*Hill toombay* (மலைத்தும்பை - malaittumbai, Tam.). Tam. from (malai, tam. mountain + tumbai, tam. the plant, leucas, sp.). Tam. also (kavizhttumbai), meaning stooping + the plant. Botanically Leucas [toombay] procumbens, desf., labiatæ [vricsham, 103]. Alias Nepeta indica; Phlomis biflora. Herbaceous; diffuse; leaves ovate-lanceolate, sub-serrate, glabrous; verticils two to six-flowered; bracts minute; calyx tubular, throat equal, teeth lanceolate-subulate, erect; flowers white; flowering nearly all the year.——*Large toombay* (तुंबी - tumbí, Mahr.; పెద్దతుమ్మి - peddatummi, Tel.). Tel. from (pedda, tel. large + tummi, tel. leucas indica, r. br.). Botanically Leucas [toombay] cephalotes, spreng., labiatæ [vricsham, 103]. Alias Leucas capitata; Phlomis cephalotes. Herbaceous; hairy and pubescent; leaves ovate, or oblong, subserrate, green; verticils subsolitary, large, globose, densely many-flowered; bracts ovate-lanceolate, acute, imbricated; calyx striated and subvillous at the apex; mouth oblique, teeth subulate, short; uppermost leaves coming out of the top of the verticel; flowering nearly all the year. Flowers sacred to shiva [q.v.] leaves eaten [keeray]; gives an oil.——*Rough toombay* (तुंबी - tumbí, Mahr.; تمبی کا پتا - tumbikápattá, Hind.; ತುಂಬೆ - tumbe, Can.; தும்பை - tumbai, Tam.). Title otherwise Bitter leucas. Botanically Leucas [toombay] aspera, spreng., labiatæ [vricsham, 103]. Alias Phlomis aspera, esculenta, plukenetii, wightiana. Herbaceous; hairy and pubescent; leaves oblong or linear, subcrenate, green; verticils dense, equal; bracts oblong-linear or subulate, hairy; calyx smooth at the base, striated at the apex, subincurved, mouth oblique, teeth short; flowers white; flowering nearly all the year. The dried plant, an application for itch and other skin diseases; reputed antidote for snake bites; quoted in pharm. non-official; leaves used as greens [keeray].——*Ship toombay* (കപ്പത്തുമ്പ - kappattumba, Mal.). Same as Arabian manna.——*Small toombay* (சன்னத்தும்பை - shannattumbai, Tam.). Tam. from (shannam, tam. smallness + tumbai, tam. leucas indica, r. br.). Botanically Leucas [toombay] rosmarinifolia, benth., labiatæ [vricsham, 103]. Suffruticose; branches villous with adpressed hairs; leaves sessile, linear, quite entire, scabrously hairy above, white-tomentose or hoary beneath, hispid at the rib; bracts lanceolate-linear; throat of the villous calyx truncated, villous; teeth very short, somewhat spreading; flowering nearly all the year.——*Wild toombay* (కారుతుమ్మి - kárutummi, Tel.). Tel. from (káru, tel. forest + tummi, tel. the plant, leucas indica, r. br.). Botanically Dysophylla cruciata, benth., labiatæ [vricsham, 103]. Alias Dysophylla tetraphylla; Mentha quadrifolia. Hirsute with soft spreading hairs; stems long, procumbent, somewhat simple; leaves in fours, rarely in fives or sixes, lanceolate or sublinear, obtuse, quite entire, revolute at the margin; floral ones lanceolate, nearly equalling the flowers; teeth of the villous calyx rather obtuse, sub-erect.

TOOMBY (தும்பி - tumbi, *Tam.*). Means beetle; from colored markings. The genus Pterois, scorpænidæ, acanthopterygii, teleostei, pisces [matsyam, 7], of naturalists [jantoo]. The species best known to the natives are shown below.——*Black toomby* (රතුගිනිමහා - ratuginimaha, Singh.; கருந்தும்பி - karundumbi, Tam.). Title from dark markings. Singh. means from (ratu, singh. red + ginimaha, singh. pterois volitans). Tam. from (karumai, tam. blackness + tumbi, tam. pterois genus). Pterois [toomby] miles, scorpænidæ, acanthopterygii, teleostei [matsyam, 7], of naturalists. Alias Macrochyrus miles; Pterois geniserra, muricata; Scorpæna miles. Interorbital space convex but not deeply so; scales present in interorbital space and on nape; colors red, with many dark vertical bands much wider than ground-color, in first two-thirds of body ground-color appears like narrow light bands; in last third of body the dark bands are wider apart with from one to three intermediate narrow ones; head banded, bands mostly radiating from eye, two of an S. shape over chest; white spot surrounded by black in axilla; dorsal spines with from five to six dark rings; soft dorsal, caudal, and anal covered with small black spots; pectoral with large black blotches on lighter ground; ventral nearly black, with white and light brown spots; sea; 14 inches in length.——*Flying toomby* (कोंबडा - kómbadá, Mahr.; కోడిపుంజు - kódipundzu, Tel.; പറവ - parava, Mal.; ගිනිමහා - ginimaha, Singh.). Tel. from (kódi, tel. fowl + pundzu, tel. cock). Mal. means flying. Singh. from (gini, singh. fire + maha, singh. fish); from pinky brown color and from dread of its wound. Title otherwise Red fire fish. Pterois [toomby] volitans, scorpænidæ, acanthopterygii, teleostei [matsyam, 7], of naturalists. Alias Gasterosteus volitans; Pseudomonopterus volitans; Scorpæna mahe, volitans. Interorbital space deeply concave, it and nape scaleless, or with very rudimentary scales; traversed by two low ridges; reddish, with vertical brown bands having narrower and lighter intermediate ones; three or four broad ones radiate from eye; one passes over nape, and seven or eight more are present on body, the third and fourth usually coalescing under middle of pectoral fin; black mark in axilla, having pure white spot in centre; dorsal spines annulated with black; soft dorsal, caudal, and anal spotted; pectoral greyish with light-colored spots; ventral slate-colored with white spots; sea.

TOOMMA (తుమ్మ - tumma, *Tel.*). A general name for certain Acacias [babool, cantalam, vail].——*Toomaracote* (తుమ్మరకోట - tummarakóta, Tel.). From (above + ráyi, tel. stone + kóta, tel. fort).—"*a*" Deputy tahsildarry, Kistna district. Pay Rs. 70.—"*b*" Village, Deputy tahsildar's station, Kistna dist., Pulnaud tal.; pop. 2,048; acres 4,725; lat. 16° 33′; long. 79° 30′; from Dauchepully W. 19 miles; from Guntoor W.N.W. 68 miles; from Madras N.N.W. 243 miles; from Masulipatam W.N.W. 113 miles; from Vinoocondah N.N.W. 38 miles. Fort was surprised in 1793 by a rabble of about one thousand peons [q.v.], who came across from the Nizam's side of the river. They killed the garrison of Company's sepoys [q.v.] and tortured the towns people to make them disclose hidden treasure, but were put to flight by a detachment sent from Vinoocondah. Fine mosque [musjid] and durgah [q.v.].——*Toommalair* (తుమ్మలేరు - tummaléru, Tel.). From (above + éru, tel. river). River; Cuddapah district, Sidhout talook. Rises in Budwail talook. Flows through the north-eastern portion of Sidhout talook and joins the Pennair below the junction of the Saglair near Bookkayapully.——*Toommalapenta* (తుమ్మలపెంట - tummalapenta,* Tel.). From (above + penta, tel. heap). Village, Port; Nellore dist., Cauvaly tal.; pop. 3,271; acres 13,045; lat. 14° 54′; long. 80° 07′; from Cauvaly E. 5 miles; from Chennayapollem S. 6 miles; from Madras N. 125 miles; from Nellore N. 32 miles; from Zoovvaldinney N. 6 miles. Open roadstead. Formerly a salt factory. Vishnoo temple of Keshava permaul in ruins. Large tank [q.v.], six miles long, with bund [q.v.] on both sides. Numerous palmyra [q.v.] trees. Good sport in neighbourhood.

TOOMROO (तुम्बुरु - tumburu, *San.*; تومرو - tumrú, *Hind.*). From (kustumbaru, san. coriander seed); from size and aroma of seeds. Toothache tree. Botanically the Zanthoxylum genus, rutaceæ [vricsham, 32]. Shrubs or trees, often armed with stout prickles; leaves alternate, three-foliolate or unequally pinnate; leaflets opposite or alternate, entire or crenate, often oblique, dotted; flowers small, in axillary or terminal stalked broad or narrow cymes, white pink or greenish; fruit of 1 to 5 globose coriaceous or fleshy one-seeded carpels; seeds blue or black-shining. The species best known to the natives are:—alatum [tejbul], rhetsa [q.v.]. Other s. indian species indigenous or naturalized are:—ovalifolium, tetraspermum.

TOON (तुन्न - tunna, *San.*; تون - tún, *Hind.* and *Dec.*; ತುಂಡು - tundu, *Can.*; ನೊಗೆ - nogé, *Coorg*; నంది - nandi, *Tel.*; ମହାଲିମ୍ବୋ - mahalimbo, *Oor.*; അരണ - arana, *Mal.*; துனுமரம் - túnumaram, *Tam.*). Title from sanscrit through hindostany. San. from (tud, san. to give pain); as eaten by elephants. Hind. from sanscrit. Can. from (tundu, can. short). Tel. from (nandivriksha, san. the tree) [turbith]. Oor. means large neem. Mal. from (arani, san. the tree, producing fire by attrition, premna integrifolia, linn.). Tam. from sanscrit. San. also (nandivriksha), meaning happy tree [adam's apple]; (kubéraka), meaning bad + body; (apíta), meaning not yellow; (kántalaka), meaning eaten by elephants; (patuka); (kachha), meaning destroyed; (kánta), meaning shining; (nandaka), meaning happy one. Hind. also (mahánim), meaning large melia azadirachta, linn. [large neem]. Can. also (kempugandagheri); (suolamura). Coorg also (belandi). Tam. also (shandanavémbu), meaning sandal, santalum album, linn. + neem tree, melia azadirachta, linn. Title otherwise Bastard cedar, Chittagong wood [chickrassy], Happy tree, Indian cedar, Indian mahogany, Moulmein cedar, Sandal neem, Singapore cedar, White cedar. Botanically Cedrela toona, roxb., meliaceæ [vricsham, 36]. Alias Cedrela hexandra, serrata. Specific name from sanscrit. Tree 50 to 60 feet; trunk quite erect; bark smooth and grey; branches numerous, forming a large shady head; leaves abruptly pinnate; leaflets six to twelve pairs, ovate-lanceolate, acuminated, slightly undulated on the margins, quite entire or slightly and distinctly toothed, glabrous; calyx small, five cleft; petals five, ciliated; panicles drooping, terminal; capsule oblong, five celled; dehiscent. Flowers very numerous, small, white and possessing a fragrance like fresh honey [shahad]; prevalent in south canara. Bark powerfully astringent in medicine; though not bitter is a fair substitute for peruvian bark [koinah], particularly when united with powdered bonduc [q.v.] nut. The bark contains a resinous matter, a brown astringent true gum [gond], and a gummy brown extractive matter resembling ulmine. Seeds used to feed cattle. Good avenue [shaulay] tree; flower yields a red and a yellow dye [shauyam] used for dyeing cotton [q.v.]. The timber is like a poor mahogany; brick-red, soft, shining, even but open-grained, fragrant, seasons readily, does not split nor warp; annual rings distinctly marked by a belt of large and numerous pores; durable not eaten by white-ants [q.v.]; valued and universally used for furniture of all kinds, door panels and carving; often sold in madras under the general name of chittagong wood [q.v.]; it is the most valuable of the woods known by that commercial name. No other common species here.

TOOND (తుండు - tundu, *Tel.*; துண்டு - tundu, *Tam.*). From (tundi, tam. to cut). A piece of anything.——*Toondam* (துண்டம் - tundam, Tam.). From (tunu, tam. to cut). Section; a small channel.——*Toondchit* (துண்டுச்சீட்டு - tunduççíttu, Tam.). From (above + shíttu, tam. note). A small note [chit].——*Toond irsaul* (துண்டிர்சால் - tundirsál, Tam.). From (above + irsál, hind. remittance). A remittance made frequently.——*Toondooravuram* (துண்டுவாரம் - tunduváram, Tam.). From (above + vára, san. quantity). The share of the landlord from lands cultivated by temporary cultivators [mailvauram].——*Toony* (తుని - tuni, Tel.). See sep. title.

TOONGA (తుంగ - tunga, *Tel.*). Same as Common sedge.——*Round toonga* (గుండతుంగ - gundatunga, Tel.). Same as Club grass.

TOONGABUDRA (تمبدرا - tumbadrá, *Hind.*; తుంగభద్ర - tungabhadra,* *Tel.*). From (tungá, san. river so named meaning high or excellent + bhadrá, san. river so named, meaning auspicious). River; Bellary and Kurnool districts. Formed by the junction of the Toonga and Bhadra. Both rise near the south-west frontier of Mysore, on the eastern slopes of the high range of hills bordering South canara. Their junction takes place in lat. 14° north, and long. 75° 42′ east, in Mysore, in front of the Bramin village of Coodaly in Shimoga district. The united stream, flowing north and north-east, forms the northern boundary of Bellary district and of Madras presidency. Shortly after receiving the Hagary in Bellary district, it becomes the boundary between Kurnool district and the Doab. It then runs due east to Kurnool where it unites with the Hindry, and winding northward, and thereby becoming particularly holy, joins the Kistna at Coodaly sangam, 16 miles N.N.E. of Kurnool, in lat. 15° 58′; long. 78° 18′. Total length, 400 miles. Chief tributaries on the left bank are the Coomadvaty and the Wurdah, both rising in the north of Mysore and traversing the southern portion of Dharwar district; and on the right bank, the Hagary in Bellary and the Hindry in Kurnool. Though running low during the hot weather, in the south-west monsoon or from June to October the river is over half a mile in breadth, with a depth of from 15 to 25 feet. Timber is then floated down it from the western forests. The stream is rapid, but is fordable from the end of December to the end of May, when it becomes clear and is then 300 yards in breadth and little more than knee deep. When not fordable, it is crossed by means of basket boats. The boats are generally from 6 to 11 feet in diameter. The bed consists of sand and pebbles, and opposite Kurnool it is very rocky. The average fall of the river is one foot and-a-half per mile. Its water is to a considerable extent used for irrigation. The Vijianugger kings built seven gigantic dams across the river to the east and west of Anagoondy. From these dams irrigation canals are led along both sides of the river. In 1860 an anicut was thrown across the river by the Irrigation canal company at Soonkesala. The river abounds in crocodiles [mugger], and it is reputed to have the sweetest water in India. There is a Teloogoo proverb:—గంగా స్నానం తుంగా పానం—"bathe in the ganges and drink in the "toonga." The chief towns on the banks of the river are:—Hurrihur in Mysore; Humpasaugar, Hospett, Humpy, Ramporam, and Cumply, in Bellary district; and Kurnool. At Hurrihur it is crossed by a fine bridge of stone and bricks, constructed in 1868, and by the Railway bridge recently constructed. The Madras railway crosses it at Rampore in Bellary by a bridge built on 52 piers. The Southern mahratta railway crosses it by a bridge at Hosoor in Hospett talook.

TOONY (తుని - tuni, *Tel.*). From (tuniya, tel. piece) [toond]. ——**(1)** Division, Godavery. Area 320 square miles. Population 81,601. Language Teloogoo. E. coast of district. Bounded:—north by Golcondah talook, Vizagapatam district; east by Sarwasiddhy talook, Vizagapatam district; south by Bay of Bengal and Pittapore division; west by Peddapore talook. The northern side contains forests and hills. The chief of the hills are Naugal hill, Totapully hill and Penoocondah hill. Soil red loamy but of indifferent quality mixed with gravel in some places. Agriculture the chief occupation of the people. Preparation of jaggery and manufacture of jewellery [nagay, zewar] give employment to many. All sorts of grains, jaggery [q.v.], tamarind [q.v.], honey [shahad], skins [chamrah], &c., are brought for sale to Toony market. These are exported to Vizagapatam district, Rajahmundry and Cocanada by bandies [q.v.]. Irrigated by spring channels [q.v.], jungle streams, and tanks [q.v.]. Camping grounds:—Annavaram and Toony. Zemindarry:—Cottaum. Places of archæological interest:—Bendapoody, Narendraputnam, Naumagherry. Principal trig. station:—Cuppacondah, Goondaulamma, Lutchmeepooram, Naugaula. The leading places, &c., in the division are the following.——*Annavaram aurempoody* (అన్నవరంఅరెంపూడి - annavaramárempúdi, Tel.). From two villages clubbed. Mokhausa village. Camping ground, Proprietor's choultry, Travellers' bungalow; pop. 2,854; lat. 17° 17′; long. 82° 27′; from Cocanada N.N.E. 26 miles; from Toony W.S.W. 10 miles. Pampauty river irrigates.——*Cottaum* (కొట్టము - kottámu, Tel.). Means a shed. Zemindarry village; pop. 1,534; lat. 17° 27′; long. 82° 30′; from Cocanada N.N.E. 38 miles; from Toony N.W. 9 miles. Peshcush Rs. 26,422.——*Cuppacondah* (కప్పకొండ - kappakonda, Tel.). From (kappa, tel. frog + konda, tel. hill). Trig. station; lat. 17° 20′ 09·18″; long. 82° 31′ 03·46″; height 1,102 feet; from Cottore S.W. 1¾ miles.——*Goondaulamma* (గుండాలమ్మ - gundálamma, Tel.). From (gundamu, tel. deep gorge + amma, tel. mother). Trig. station; lat. 17° 31′ 30·04″; long. 82° 21′ 51·74″; height 2,671 feet; from Lododdy N.E. 2 miles.——*Lutchmeepooram* (లక్ష్మీపురము - lakshmípuramu, Tel.). From (lakshmí, san. the goddess + pura, san. town). Trig. station; lat. 17° 00′ 13·56″; long. 81° 37′ 09·27″; height 332 feet; from Hamsavaram W.S.W. 63 miles.——*Naugaula* (నాగాల - nágála, Tel.). From (nága, san. snake). Trig. station; lat. 17° 21′ 31·03″; long. 82° 13′ 13·87″; height 1,657 feet; from Simsore N. 1¾ miles.——*Toony* (తుని - tuni, Tel.). See below. ——*Totapully* (తోటపల్లె - tótapalle, Tel.). From (tóta, tel. garden + palle, tel. village). Zemindarry village; pop. 112; lat. of village 17° 18′; long. 82° 20′; from Cocanada N. 25 miles; from Toony W.S.W. 17 miles. The estates of Totapully and Jaddangy were formerly held under the Zemindar of Peddapore, on whose behalf they were bound to provide an armed force to repel incursions from the hills.——**(2)** Deputy tahsildarry, Godavery district. Pay Rs. 100.——**(3)** Village; Godavery dist., Toony division; pop. 7,773 including Toonypetts, Veeravaram and Toony proper; lat. 17° 21′; long. 82° 35′; from Cocanada N.E. 34 miles; from Coonavaram E.S.E. 84 miles; from Ellore E.N.E. 104 miles; from Madras N.N.E. 325 miles; from Narsapore N.E. 82 miles; from Rajahmundry E.N.E. 56 miles. Principal market for transport of goods to Vizagapatam.

TOONY (തൂണി - túni, *Mal.*). From (dróna, san. a measure). —"*a*" A hollow piece of bamboo [q.v.] used as measure of grain. 6 nauzhies = 1 toony [alavay, 3d]. Approximate actual value, 1 toony = 170½ cubic inches. It is a measure of seed sufficient to sow 100 yards of rice field and contains 86,400 seed grains. Same as Cootty.—"*b*" Measure of capacity. 2 pathakks = 1 toony; 3 toonies = 1 calam [alavay, 3a]. Varies with the mercaul.

TOOR (تور - tuvvar, *Dec.*). From (tuvarí, san.). Same as Dholl [common dholl].——*Tora* (തോര - tóra, Mal.). From (tuvara, san. dholl plant). A linear measure indicating the space occupied by such a seed. 8 yenmanies = 1 tora; 8 toras = 1 viral [alavay, 1d]. Approximate actual value, 1 tora = ·09375 inch. Same as San. yavam, Hind. jow, Can. yavey, Tam. nel.

TOORANJ (துரிஞ்சி - turiñji, *Tam.*). From persian. Same as Citron.

TOORAY (துறை - turai, *Tam.*). A kind of Tamul verse. It consists of four lines, each of five feet, and always takes ஏ at its close. The grammar [lacshanam] Caurigay, treating of poetry, is in this metre.

TOORINJIL (துரிஞ்சில் - turiñjil, *Tam.*). From (turu, tam. to be thick); from dense foliage. Same as Dark sirissa.——*Toorinjalaur* (துரிஞ்சலாறு - turiñjaláru. Tam.). From (above + áru, tam. river). River; South arcot dist., Trinomallee and Tricalore taks. Jungle stream. Rises in a hill in Trinomallee talook and joins the Ponniaur at Manampoondy in Tricalore talook. Has water even in hot weather, as there are good springs. Shiva temple on western band at Velancoolam.

TOORSY (துருசி - turusi, *Tam.*). From (turu, tam. rust). Sulphate of copper [toottum].

TOORTOORY (ترتری - turturí, *Hind.*; తుతార - tutára, *Tel.*). Imitative. A kind of trumpet [sangeetum].

TOORTY (துருத்தி - turutti, *Tam.*). From (driti, san. a leather bag). Bagpipe. This comprises the entire skin [chamrah] of a sheep [aud] or goat [vellaud], freed of hair, and having all the openings closed, excepting two pipes of reed, one of which is inserted in the neck, and the other at one of the extremities; one is to blow with, and the other through which the air issues, produces a low, moaning sound [magady, jeenboorra].

TOORVOO (துரவு - turavu, *Tam.*). From (tura, tam. to dig). An unwalled well [doroovoo].

TOOTH-BRUSH TREE (पीलु - pílu, *San.* and *Mahr.*; اراكجبلي - arákijabalí, *Ar.*; درخت مسواك - darakhtimiswák, *Pers.*; چهوٹا پیلو - chhotápílú, *Hind.* and *Dec.*; ಗೋನಿಮರ - gónimara, *Can.*; వరగోగు - varagógu, *Tel.*; களர்வா - kalarvá, *Tam.*). Title from use. San. from (píl, san. to check), medicinal; cf. coomby. Ar. from (arák, ar. the tooth-brush tree + jabal, ar. hill). Pers. from (darakht, pers. tree + miswák, pers.

tooth brush). Hind. from (chhotá, hind. small + pílú, san. the tree + jhár, hind. tree). Can. from (góni, can. sack + mara, can. tree). Tel. from (vara, san. superior + gógu, tel. the hemp plant, hibiscus cannabinus, linn.). Tam. from (kalar, tam. brackish soil), from habitat. San. also (gauli), meaning white, from wood. Hind. also (pílú), from sanscrit. Tel. also (chinnavaragógu), meaning small + the plant; (pinnavaragógu), meaning small + the plant; (gónechettu), meaning gunny bag + plant. Tam. also (shirugalarvá), meaning small + the tree; (ubá); (ugá), meaning to please, from the leaf; (kárgolmaram), meaning sea-side tree. Title otherwise Kikuel oil plant [curry leaf tree], Mahomedan tooth brush tree, Mustard tree, Sack tree, Small calarvah. Giving Oogah fruit. Mustard seed of scripture. Botanically Salvadora persica, linn., salvadoraceæ [vricsham, 86]. Alias Cissus arborea; Embelia burmanni, grossularia; Pella ribesioides; Rivina paniculata; Salvadora indica, wightiana. Small thick-stemmed, soft-wooded tree; trunk generally crooked from eight to ten feet high to the branches, and one foot in diameter; bark deeply cracked; branches numerous, spreading, pendulous at their extremities; leaves opposite, petioled, oval or oblong, entire, very smooth, shining on both surfaces, veinless; panicles terminal, and from the exterior axils; flowers small, numerous, greenish yellow; berry minute, smooth, red, juicy, one-seeded; calyx four-toothed, corolla one-petalled. Flowering and fruiting nearly all year; common in low lands particularly in salt soil. The root-bark when fresh is of a light brown color and nearly smooth, studded with scabrous corky warts, either single or arranged in transversely extended patches; the substance and inner surface of the bark is white and soft; fracture short; odour like cress; taste warm and pungent. Fruits are medicinally deobstruent, carminative and diuretic; leaves used in poultice to relieve pain of tumours, piles, &c.; wood used as a tooth brush to strengthen the gums; the bark used in decoction in low fever, tonic and stimulant; bruised bark of the root vesicant; in snake-bites, seeds administered internally, purgative; gives to pharm. leaves, bark, and fruit, non-officinal. Berries have aromatic smell and taste, not unlike garden cress [haleem]; shoots and leaves are pungent, eaten as salad and given as fodder to camels. Gives an oil [yennay]. Wood white and soft. The small branches and roots of other plants especially those with colorless sap are used as tooth brushes by Hindoos. The following are in general use:—Acacia catechu [catechu]; Achyranthes aspera [indian burr]; Ægle marmelos [bael]; Albizzia lebbek [sirissa]; Anthocephalus cadamba [cadamba]; Butea frondosa [palaus]; Calotropis gigantea [yercum]; Feronia elephantum [wood-apple]; Mangifera indica [mango]; Wrightia tinctoria [paula indigo]; Zizyphus jujuba [bair].——*Large tooth-brush tree* (पीलू - pílu, Mahr.; اراك برى - arákibarrí, Ar.; درخت مسواك - darakhtimiswák, Pers.; بڑا پیلو - barápílú, Hind.; پیلو کا جھاڑ - pílúkájhár, Dec.; పెద్దవరగోగు - peddavaragógu, Tel.; பெருகளர்வா - perugalarvá, Tam.). Ar. from (arák, ar. tooth-brush tree, salvadora persica, linn. + barr, ar. forest). Pers. from (darakht, pers. tree + miswák, pers. tooth brush). Hind. from (bará, hind. large + pílu, san. tooth-brush tree, salvadora persica, linn.). Dec. from (pílu, san. tooth-brush tree, salvadora persica, linn. + jhár, hind. tree). Tel. from (pedda, tel. large + varagógu, tel. the plant, salvadora persica, linn.). Tam. from (perumai, tam. greatness + kalarvá, tam. the plant, salvadora persica, linn.). San. also (rasana), meaning tongue, applies to the leaves. Tam. also (kárgolmaram), meaning sea-side tree. Title otherwise Calarvah, Miswauk. Botanically Salvadora oleoides, dcne., salvadoraceæ [vricsham, 16]. Alias Salvadora indica. Tree; leaves broad, ovate oval, obtuse, glabrous; panicles terminal and axillary, diffuse; flowers longish-pedicelled; bracts somewhat persistent; berry about twice the length of the calyx, red, embraced by the withering corolla; flowers white; common everywhere, in low damp ground. Oil [yennay] expressed from seeds is a bright green fat of the consistence of butter; in bazaar much adulterated. Oil is medicinally stimulant; root-bark is vesicant; both in pharm. non-officinal. Fruit dried for future use, and has then appearance and flavor of currants; leaves serve as fodder for camels [ottagam]. Galls used as mordant [cauram]. Wood light-red, moderately hard, with small, irregular, purple heart-wood.

TOOTROO (توترو - totrú, *Hind.*). Imitative. Turtle doves. Turturinæ, columbidæ [capotam], gemitores, aves [pacshy, 29], of naturalists [jantoo]. The species best known to the natives are shown below.——*Common dove* (होला - hólá, Mahr.; فاختہ - fákhtah, Ar., Pers., Hind. and Dec.; చిట్టిబెల్లగువ్వ - chittibellaguvva, Tel.; தவிட்டுப்புறா - tavittuppurá, Tam.). Ar. from (fakhtu, ar. light of the new moon), from its color. Tel. from (chiru, tel. small + bellaguvva, tel. dove). Tam. from (tavidu, tam. bran + purá, tam. pigeon); from pale color. Ar. also (urfiyah). Pers. also (kúkú), from its call. Hind. also (tutrúfákhtah). Tel. also (tavatiguvva), meaning bran + dove; from color. Turtur cambayensis. Alias Turtur maculicollis, senegalensis. Above brown; head and upper part of neck pinkish vinaceous; wing-coverts, except towards scapulars, pure light grey; winglet, primaries, and their coverts, dusky; secondaries tinged grey; tail with middle feathers brown; others black at base, white for nearly their terminal half; beneath neck and breast pinkish vinaceous, paling below, passing to white on belly and lower tail-coverts; sides of neck with patch on each side, nearly meeting, black at base, rufous tipped, black hardly apparent except when neck is stretched; bill blackish; irides dark brown, with whitish inner circle; legs lake red; length 10½ inches; tail graduated to upwards of an inch, and feathers slightly narrowed towards their tips; abundant in low bushy jungles; its coo is a dissyllabic sound, repeated four or five times successively.——*Ring dove* (قمری - kumrí, Ar., Pers., Hind. and Dec.; పెద్దబెల్లగువ్వ - peddabellaguvva, Tel.; മണിപ്രാവു - maniprávu, Mal.; மணிப்புறா - manippurá, Tam.). Title from black collar. Ar. from (akmar, ar. dusky white). Tel. from (pedda, tel. large + bellaguvva, tel. dove). Mal. from tamul. Tam. from (mani, tam. blackness + purá, tam. pigeon); from black collar. Male bird is:—Ar. (sákihurr), from cry of young one. Pers. also (kúkú), from cry. Hind. also (dhorfákhtah), meaning squint-eyed dove. Beng. also (halhak); (kahalaki); (pankghughu). Turtur risoria. Head delicate pale vinous-grey, whitish on forehead; nape vinaceous; narrow black collar on nape set off with whitish above, slightly so below; upper plumage uniform light grey-brown; edge of wing pure ashy; primaries dusky, slight whitish margins bordering their tips; middle tail feathers uniform with back above; lateral feathers marked black about middle, passing to greyish on basal half, and to white on terminal, these successively more pronounced externally; beneath very pale vinaceous, whitish on throat, passing to light greyish towards vent, lower tail-coverts pure ashy; wings underneath greyish-white; bill black; irides crimson; orbital skin whitish; feet dark pink-red; length 13 inches; common in neighbourhood of cultivation; the coo may be expressed by kookookoo, kookookoo.——*Spotted dove* (چیتل فاختہ - chítalfákhtah, Hind.; పొడబెల్లగువ్వ - podabellaguvva, Tel.; പുള്ളിപ്രാവു - pulliprávu, Mal.; புலிப்புறா - pulippurá, Tam.). Hind. from (chítal, hind. spotted deer + fákhtah, hind. dove). Tel. from (poda, tel. spot + bellaguvva, tel. dove). Mal. from (pulli, mal. spotted + práva, mal. pigeon). Tam. from (puli, tam. tiger + purá, tam. pigeon). Hind. also (kangskiri); (chitta), meaning spotted deer; (chitrúfákhtah), meaning leopard dove. Mal. also (pulipráva), meaning tiger pigeon. Beng. also (chavalghughu); (teliaghughu). Turtur suratensis. Alias Turtur ceylonensis, tigrina. Head pale vinaceous, greyish on forehead; upper parts generally dusky, each feather with two pale rufous isabelline terminal spots, enlarging and spreading up each side of feather upon wing-coverts, blackish contracting to central streak, having broad pale vinaceous lateral borders; edge of wing, with some nearest coverts, light grey; tail with central feather brown; outermost ones black at base, white for terminal half, others intermediate in coloring; lower parts pale vinaceous, more or less albescent on throat, passing to white on vent and lower tail-coverts; bill dull leaden-black; irides dark hazel, surrounded by reddish sclerotic; legs dark purplish red; length about 12 inches; nearly as familiar as common dove, entering gardens, feeding on roads, near houses; the coo is something like oot-raow-oo—oot-raow-oo.

TOOTTAM (तुत्थ - tutt'ha, *San.*; துத்தம் - tuttam, *Tam.*). From (tud, san. to pain). Vitriol, or glass-like oil.——*Madal toottam* (دستہ - dastah, Hind.; மடற்றுத்தம் - madattoottam, Tam.). Title and Tam. from (madal, tam. leaf + above), from scaly appearance in ore. Cadmia of Pliny. Calamine, so called from having reedy appearance when melted. Otherwise Carbonate of zinc, Zinc spar. Carbonas zinci impurus of chemists. Used as astringent lotion to ulcers, &c.——*Mayil toottam* (तुत्थाञ्जन - tutt'háñjana, San.; زاج اخضر - zájiakhzar, Ar.; زاك سبز - zákisabz, Pers.; نیلا تھو تھا - nílát'hút'há, Hind.; مہورتتہ - mhortuttah, Dec.; ترسی - tursí, Malay; ಮೈಲುತುತ್ತ - mailtutta, Can.; మయిలుతుత్తము - mayilututtamu, Tel.; തുരിശു - turishu, Mal.; පල්මානික්කං - palmánikkam, Singh.; மயிற்றுத்தம் - mayittuttam, Tam.). Title from tamul. San. from (tutt'ha, san. vitriol + añjana, san ointment). Ar. from (záj, ar. copperas + akhzar, ar. blue). Pers. from (zák, pers. copperas + sabz, pers. green). Hind. from (nílá, hind. blue + thútha, hind. vitriol). Dec. from (mhor, hind. peacock + tuttah, hind. vitriol). Can. and Tel. from tamul. Mal. from (turuvu, mal. rust). Tam. from (mayil, tam. peacock + tutt'ha, san. blue vitriol), from color. Ar. also (kalkand). Mal. also (mayiltuttam). Tam. also (turisu), meaning rust. Copperas. Otherwise Sulphate of copper, Blue stone, Blue vitriol, Cyprian vitriol, Roman vitriol. Cupri sulphas, Cuprum vitriolatum, Vitroleum. Appears in crystalline masses of an elegant sapphire blue color, hard, compact, and semi-transparent; when perfectly crystallised, of a flattish rhomboidal, decahedral figure; taste nauseous. Procurable in most bazaars; should be without any light-green or whitish powder adherent on the surface; not known to occur in nature, but is largely made in s. india from copper [taumram] ore by pulverising the ore, which is then thrown into earthen vessels filled with water, and after filtration the crystals form. In large doses is an irritant poison; chronic poisoning may occur from the use of copper vessels in preparing food; in medicinal doses sulphate of copper is astringent, and in sufficient quantity emetic; externally it is escharotic, and is also used in solution as a lotion or collyrium. In veterinary practice, as tonic in drachm doses daily;

as caustic either in powder or in solution. Applied in solution to floors and matting to check or prevent the attacks of white-ants [q.v.]; used in leather-dyeing [shauyam] along with lime [choonam] to produce a light blue. Green copperas is sulphate of iron [annabhaidy]. White copperas is sulphate of zinc [vellay toottam]. For the sub-acetate of copper see Zangaur.——*Tootnaug* (नाग - nága, San. ; तुत्तिनाग - tuttinága, Mahr. ; جست - jast, Hind. ; جس - jas, Dec. ; تامبگا پوتیه - támbagaputih, Malay ; ಸತ್ತು - sattu, Can. ; తుత్తినాగము - tuttinágamu, Tel. ; നാഗം - nágam, Mal. ; துத்துநாகம் - tuttunágam, Tam.). Title from tamul. San. from (naga, san. mountain). Mahr. from (tutt'ha, san. blue vitriol + nága, san. lead). Malay from (támbaga, malay, copper + putih, malay, white). Tel. from (tutt'ha, san. blue vitriol + nága, san. lead). Mal. from sanscrit. Tam. from (tutt'ha, san. blue vitriol + nága, san. lead), from bluish grey color. San. also (yashada), meaning bright. Zinc. Zincum of chemists. Bluish-white metal which slowly tarnishes in the air, forming a film of oxide which prevents further oxidation; malleable, and when rubbed with the fingers emits a peculiar smell. Zinc, oxidized in the ore, is called calamine [madal toottam]; its constituent parts are varying proportions of oxide of zinc and carbonic acid [kary poolipp]. Zinc has been discovered in southern districts combined with sulphur [gandhac] and iron [auhan], forming what is called blende; the greater part however is brought from cochin-china, or china, where both the calamine and blende are common; it is from the last, or the sulphuret, that this metal is usually obtained for commerce, and it is then called spelter; the metal may be procured pure by dissolving this zinc of commerce in diluted sulphuric acid [tezaub], and immersing a plate of zinc for some hours in the solution, which is then filtered and decomposed by carbonate of potassa, and the precipitate ignited with charcoal [adoopp kary] in an iron pot. Pharm. has various and well known articles. Used in the arts chiefly in the fabrication of brass [pittalay] and other gold-colored mixtures, and in making bronze, by fusing together tin [tagaram], copper [taumram], and zinc; it is now applied to many of the purposes for which copper was formerly used; oxide of zinc is a substitute for white lead, as a pigment not liable to change and not subject to those deleterious consequences so frequently attendant on preparations of lead [eeyam]; gold [pon], silver [velly], platina [goorootwam], and nickel, are rendered brittle by it, but with bismuth and lead it enters into no combination in fusing; of all known bodies, except manganese [q.v.], zinc unites the most readily with oxygen, hence it acts very rapidly on acids [tezaub]. For white vitriol or sulphate of zinc see Vellaytoottam.——*Tootnaug paspam* (नागभस्म - nága-bhasma, San. ; دستا - dastá, Hind. ; جس - jas, Dec. ; ಸತ್ತುಭಸ್ಮ - sattubhasma, Can. ; తుత్తినాగభస్మము - tuttinágabhasmamu, Tel. ; നാഗഭസ്മം - nágabhasmam, Mal. ; துத்துநாகப்பற்பம் - tuttunágapparbam, Tam.). Title and Tam. from (tuttunágam, tam. zinc + bhasma, san. ashes). Latin, lana philosophica. Flowers of zinc. Native preparation is as follows:—Zinc is fused in an earthern pot, green leaves of the Euphorbia nereifolia [leafy milk-hedge] being thrown into the melted mass, which is constantly stirred with an iron spoon; it inflames in the usual manner, leaving ashes, which are kept in the fire till they acquire a fine white color; only finest parts of these are preserved for medical use, and are separated from the rest by sifting through a piece of fine muslin [q.v.]. Tootnaug paspam is employed by veidyans [q.v.] in gonorrhœa, &c.——*Vellay toottam* (سفید توتا - sufedtútah, Hind. ; سفید تتہ - sufedtuttah, Dec. ; ಬಿಳಿತುತ್ತಾ - bilítuttá, Can. ; పాలతుత్తము - pálatuttamu, Tel. ; പാൽതുത്തം - páltutt'ham, Mal. ; வெள்ளைத்துத்தம் - vellaittuttam, Tam.). Title and Tam. from (vellai, tam. white + tutt'ha, san. blue vitriol), from color. Hind. from (sufed, hind. white + tútah, hind. vitriol). Dec. from hindostany. Mal. from (pál, mal. milk + tut'ha, san. vitriol). Tam. also (páttuttam), meaning milk white vitriol. Sulphate of zinc. Otherwise White vitriol. Zinci sulphas of chemists. A salt formed by the union of sulphuric acid [tezaub] with the oxide of zinc. In large doses an irritant poison; in moderate doses emetic; in small doses a nervine tonic and antispasmodic. In veterinary practice, combined with sugar of lead, as lotion to sprains, &c., a drachm of the latter to a scruple of the former in a bucket of water. Hindoos and Mahomedans only know it through their connection with Europeans. Used in dyeing [shauyam].

TOOTTY (चक्रभेंड - chakrabhénda, *Mahr.* ; مشطالغول - mashtulghaul, *Ar.* ; درخت شانه - darakhtishánah, *Pers.* ; کنگوئی کا جہاڑ - kangoikájhár, *Hind.* ; ڈبے کا جہاڑ - dabbekájhár, *Dec.* ; ಹೇರುತ್ತಿಗಿಡ - hétuttigida, *Can.* ; ఉర్కి - urki, *Too.* ; తుత్తిరి - tuttiri, *Tel.* ; തുത്തി - tutti, *Mal.* ; අනෝදා - anódá, *Singh.* ; துத்தி - tutti, *Tam.*). Title from tamul. Mahr. from (chakra, san. wheel + bhéndá, mahr. the okro plant, hibiscus esculentus, linn.); from circular fruit and leaves like okro leaf. Ar. from (masht, ar. comb + ghaul, ar. demon); from shape of leaves. Pers. from (darakht, pers. tree + shánah, pers. comb). Hind. from (kangoí, hind. comb + jhár, hind. tree). Dec. from (dabbá, hind. oil bag + jhár, hind. tree). Can. from (héru, can. great + tuttigida, can. the tree) [shrubby balah]. Tel. and Mal. from tamul. Tam. from (tu, tam. to eat). Ar. also (daishár). Can. also (shrímudrigida), meaning beauty + seal + plant, from circular fruit; (kisangigida), meaning red + branch + plant; (gidutingi); (hetakisa); (tuttigida). Tel. also (tutti), means to eat; (tuttiribenda), meaning plant + hibiscus esculentus, linn.; (núgubenda), meaning down + the plant; (adavibenda), meaning forest + the plant; (bottabenda), meaning hamper + the plant. Mal. also (úram), meaning creeping; (vellúram), meaning white + creeper; (káttúram), meaning forest + creeper. Tam. also (perundutti), meaning big + the plant; (paniyárattutti), meaning cake + the plant. Title otherwise Cake mallow, Comb tree, Country liquorice [indian liquorice], Country mallow, Demon's comb, Indian mallow, Indian marsh mallow, Round bendy. Giving Balbij seeds. Botanically Abutilon indicum, g. don., malvaceæ [vricsham, 25]. Shrub, 2–3 feet; leaves cordate, somewhat lobed, soft, shortly tomentose, unequally toothed; calyx five-cleft, without an involucel; pedicels erect, axillary, longer than the petioles, jointed near the flowers; corolla spreading; capsules truncated; carpels eleven-twenty, acute, not awned, hairy; flowers longish, orange-colored; flowering nearly all year. The seeds are small, being about a line in length and half a line in breadth and thickness; ash-colored when fresh, brown if old; somewhat kidney-shaped; odourless; taste mucilaginous. The bark occurs in long, thin, tough, fibrous strips, which are very strong; externally it is striated and covered by a cinnamon-colored epidermis, internally it is white and striated; the taste is feebly astringent and bitter. The leaves, seeds and bark are medicinal; leaves emollient, seeds demulcent and slightly diuretic; decoction of leaves for external use, by boiling fresh leaves with water, one handful to one pint; simple powder of seeds prepared as usual; doses of powder, from one to two drachms, three or four times in the twenty-four hours; substituted for marsh-mallow, copaiba, uva ursi and buchu. Boiled milk, whisked with the fibrous twigs, coagulates. Stem yields a fibre [naur], clean and strong, fit for rope. There is a variety, distinguished by blue or purple color of its stem, branches, petioles, &c., and found growing in hedges, called black tootty. Crispum, g. don., is a species called creeping tootty; has a yellow, middle-sized flower. Graveolens, w. &. a., is a strong smelling species, flowers large, orange with a dark centre. Muticum, g. don., alias tomentosum, has flowers large, light orange. Polyandrum, schlecht, is called Peepul-leaved tootty; flowers largish, yellow. The last two have long silky fibre, resembling hemp [kinnab], fit for ropes.——*Double thread tootty* (இரட்டைக்குத்தி - irattagattutti, Tam.). Same as Musk bendy.——*Foreign tootty* (गुलखैरा - gulakhairá, Mahr. ; خطمی - khitmí, Ar. ; خیرو - khairo, Pers. ; خطمی کا پیڑ - khitmíkáper, Hind. ; خطمی کا جہاڑ - khitmíkájhár, Dec. ; சீமைத்துத்தி - shímaittutti, Tam.). Title from being introduced from western asia or europe. Mahr. from (gul, mahr. red + khairo, pers. marsh mallow). Hind. from (khitmí, ar. marsh mallow + per, hind. tree) [small foreign tootty]. Dec. from hindostany. Tam. from (shímai, tam. foreign + tutti, tam. abutilon indicum, g. don.). Hind. also (gulikhairokájhár), meaning marsh mallow flower tree. Greek ἀλθαία. Title otherwise Goolkheir, Guimauve, Holly hock, Marsh mallow. Botanically Althæa officinalis, linn., malvaceæ [vricsham, 25]. Stem erect, 2–3 feet; leaves ovoid, angular, base scarcely cordate, unequally toothed; stipules linear-subulate; flowers 1–2 inches diameter, rosy; bractioles half the length of the sepals. By nature a perennial, in this country an annual; the calyx is thick, and covered with simple hairs, very closely set, and arranged in star-like tufts; the flower has five petals, which in the dry articles are bluish green at the base, the blades being purple; both calyx and flowers are mucilaginous; the carpels are large and pubescent. The different parts of the plant used here are generally imported from persia. Seeds medicinally demulcent, diuretic, febrifuge; flowers cooling and diuretic; roots, radix altheæ, astringent and demulcent, boiled with sugar form a decoction used in coughs, &c.; leaves used as a poultice or fomentation, mixed with oil, applied to burns or sores caused by snake-bites. Leaves yield blue coloring matter [shauyam] not inferior to indigo [q.v.]; stem gives fibre [naur]. The species rosea is the English holly hock; with three or four varieties named according to color of flower as red, white, purple, &c. The althæa of portuguese at goa is the root of Grewia scabrophylla, roxb. The roots of shoe-flower [q.v.] are dried and sold in shops as substitute for Foreign tootty.——*Lowly tootty* (నేలతుత్తి - nélatutti, Tel.). Same as Dwarf balah.——*Small foreign tootty* (خبازی - khubází, Ar. ; خطمی کوچک - khitmíkochak, Pers. ; ಸಣ್ಣಬಿಂದಿಗೆ - sannabindige, Can.). Ar. from (khubz, ar. bread), from flat round fruit. Pers. means small, althæa officinalis, linn. Can. from (sanna, can. small + bindige, can. metallic water vessel). Ar. also (khatmí), meaning althæa officinalis, linn. [foreign tootty]; from similarity of properties; (anjíl). Pers. also (nánikulágh), meaning crow's bread. Greek μαλάχη χεραῖα. Title otherwise Common mallow, Marsh mallow, Maul, Maws, Round dock. Botanically Malva [khoobauzy] sylvestris, linn., malvaceæ [vricsham, 25]. Annual, 1–3 feet high; leaves cordate rounded, lobed; petiole 4–5 inches; peduncles about 1 inch; bractioles ovate, entire, shorter than the bell-shaped calyx; corolla $1\frac{1}{2}$ inches diameter; petals notched, claw bearded; carpels reticulated, downy or glabrous. Carpel and seed are medicinal.——*Wild tootty* (காட்டுத்துத்தி - káttuttutti, Tam.). Same as Wild jute.

TOOTY COORA (कलम्बी - kalambí, *San.*; తూటికూర - túti-kúra, *Tel.*; വള്ളൽ - vallal, *Mal.*; කංකුන් - kankun, *Singh.*; வள்ளை - vallai, *Tam.*). Title from teloogoo. San. from (ka, san. water + lamb, san. to hang); aquatic. Tel. from (tútu, tel. hole + kúra, tel. pot-herb); from the eye in flower. Mal. means encompassing. Tam. from (val, tam. beauty). Mal. also (mundavalli), meaning branchless creeper [moon-flower]. Title otherwise Aquatic convolvulus, Creeping bindweed. Botanically Ipomœa [calamby] aquatica, forsk., convolvulaceæ [vriesham, 93]. Alias Convolvulus adansonii, repens, reptans; Ipomæa repens, reptans. Stems creeping and rooting, fistulous, smooth; leaves sagittate, lanceolate; petioles glabrous; peduncles one to five flowered, nearly as long as the petioles; sepals ovate, glabrous; corolla tubulose, campanulate, rose color; flowering nearly all the year. A creeping annual, found about the borders of tanks and moist places. Tender tops and leaves are much eaten [keeray].

TOPASS (തോപ്പാശി - tópáshi, *Mal.*). Corruption of the hindostany doobash [q.v.]. A native Christian sprung from a Portuguese father and Indian mother; in the early history of the Company extensively enlisted as soldiers; now used on ships.

TOP BOAT (गुप्तिनौका - guptinauká, *San.*; چھتکا پروا - chhatkáparvá, *Hind.*; కప్పుపడవ - kappupadava, *Tel.*; കേവുവള്ളം - kévuvallam, *Mal.*; கூட்டுப்படகு - kúttuppadagu, *Tam.*). Tel. from (kappu, tel. cover + padava, tel. boat). Boats provided with movable tops and floorings for passengers; these can be removed when it is wished to use the boats for cargo only; the tops are carried on stanchions, and can be made fairly weather-tight by tarpaulins. Vary in size from three to seven tons, and carry about sixteen native passengers.

TOPE (स्तूप - stúpa, *San.*). San. from (stúp, san. to pile up). Title is an Anglo-Indian corruption through the Pali, on the analogy of the tamul Tope [q.v.] which means a grove. Booddhist ring temple. These form one of the three groups of Booddhist [booddha] buildings erected in India since the time of Asoca; the other two groups being Cheityams [q.v.] which in form and purpose are almost identical with the early churches of the Christians, and Vihaurams [q.v.] or monasteries. They are the derivative successors of the funeral tumulus, which, from the earliest age to which antiquarian knowledge extends, the Turanian races are found to have raised over the graves of their dead. There are two peculiarities which distinguish the Booddhist tope from ordinary tumuli [aursham]. The first is that being of brick [shengal] or stone [cull], they could readily be made of a rounded or domical form, while the earthen tumulus was generally straight-lined. The second peculiarity is that, instead of being the last resting place of a body, they had now become depositories of relics only. In addition to its primary and general use as a relic shrine, the Booddhist tope was also not uncommonly used as a memorial tower to mark a sacred spot. Of the 84,000 topes which Asoca is traditionally said to have erected, it is gathered from the Chinese travellers that one-half at least were erected to mark spots where Booddha [q.v.] or some Bodhisatwan [q.v.] had performed a miracle, or done an act worthy of note. Booddhist topes occur in the valley of the Kistna [amravatty, staupatyam].

TOPE (توپ - top, *Hind.*). From the turkish. A cannon. Tope khauna is an arsenal.——*Toopauky* (توپک - túpak, Hind.). Turkish word. A small cannon. A musket.

TOPE (తోపు - tópu, *Tel.*; தோப்பு - tóppu, *Tam.*). From (togu, tam. to collect). A grove of many kinds of trees; usually however of mango [q.v.] or tamarind [q.v.] trees; largely planted in charity as one of the seven santaunams [q.v.] or meritorious acts [inam, tandalam, tote].——*Topetoray* (தோப்புத்துறை - tópputturai, Tam.). From (above + turai, tam. seaport). Town, Port, Customs house, Sea; Tanjore dist., Tritrapoondy tal.; pop. 2,921; lat. 10° 24′; long. 79° 54′; from Madras S. 186 miles; from Tanjore S.E. 54 miles; from Tritrapoondy S.E. 17 miles; from Vedaranyam N. 2 miles; from Velangauny S. 19 miles; from the sea W. 1 mile. At the mouth of the Adappaur. The trade with Ceylon considerable. Inhabited largely by Lubbays [q.v.].——*Toppoor* (தொப்பூர் - toppúr, Tam.). From (above + úr, tam. village); from margosa [neem] grove. Tam. also (véppádi), meaning margosa tree, melia azadirachta, linn. + village. Zemindarry, Village, Pass; Salem dist., Dharmapoory tal.; pop. 851; lat. of village 11° 56′; long. 78° 06′; height 1017 feet, from Dharmapoory S.S.W. 16 miles; from Salem N.N.W. 20 miles. On the north of the river of the same name, which is bridged a little to the west of the old fort. The pass [ghaut] is southernentrance to Dharmapoory talook. Scene of Tippoo's flight from a British force on the 18th November 1790. The pass is approachable on this quarter by two routes, the one from Salem viâ Omalore and the other from the Ahtoor ghaut and Shevaroy hill railway station viâ Caudyamputty, both converging near Deevatiputty. From Toppoor the ghaut [q.v.] road winds north in numerous zigzags. From Deevatiputty towards Toppoor the rise is gentle, but after leaving Toppoor, between the 195th and 190th mile stones, near the latter of which is Munro's goonta [q.v.], the ascent is considerable, the ghaut attaining its greatest elevation between the 190th and 191st mile stones. Between the 189th and 188th mile stones the country is more open, and a vast plateau some 30 to 20 miles in extent opens out.

TOPEE (ٹوپی - topí, *Hind.*). From (topná, hind. to cover). Skull-cap, made up from various materials, worn temporarily as a substitute for the turban [puggry]. A common form is a cap of dyed cotton cloth, which sits close to the head and descends with two flaps over the ears. The Moplahs wear a stiff cap made of twisted silk [puttoo] thread, or of pasteboard; around which a roomaul [q.v.] is sometimes wound. There is no special or made-up head-dress among women; the embroidered skull-cap however is occasionally used. Term generally used for european hats and caps. Topee wallah now denotes a european; originally all, persians and moghuls, who wore turbans.——*Topicull* (தொப்பிக்கல் - toppikkal, Tam.). From (above + kal, tam. stone). Hat stone; another name of Coday cull [paundoocull].

TOPRAH (توبره - tobrah, *Hind.*). Horse's nose bag for food.

TORANAM (तोरण - tórana, *San.*). From (tur, san. to go forward). Passage. An arched gateway [gopooram].

TORAY (ತೊರೆ - tore, *Can.*; തുറ - tura, *Mal.*; துறை - turai, *Tam.*). From (turu, tam. to crowd); place of resort. A river ford. More commonly the haven of a sea, or port. Suffix in place names, as Audootoray, Tonitoray, Topetoray. The principal sea-ports are, on the east coast, Ganjam, Mansoorcottah or Gopalpore, Calingapatam, Bimlipatam, Vizagapatam, Cocanada and Coringa, Masulipatam, Madras, Cuddalore, Porto novo, Tranquebar, Negapatam and Nagore, Paumben, Tuticorin; and on the west coast, Alleppey, Cochin, Ponnany, Beypore, Calicut, Quilandy, Badagara, Tellicherry, Cannanore and Mangalore. See the foot-note at page 253 of volume I with regard to changes in the coast. For a complete list of the ports and sub-ports of this Presidency arranged from east to west, see vol. II, appendix LXIV. Toray also means a place of descent into a tank or stream [ghaut].——*Toorayore* (துறையூர் - turaiyúr, Tam.). From (above + úr, tam. town). Sanscrit name (tírt'hapurí), meaning ford + city.—"*a*" Deputy tahsildarry, Trichinopoly district: Pay Rs. 100.—"*b*" Zemindarry; Trichinopoly dist., Moosiry tal.; pop. 7,467. Formerly extended 80 miles from east to west, and 40 miles from south to north being in effect a large country. The polliem [q.v.] was overrun by the Mysoreans and the French. In 1755 the new chief was deposed and one of his cousins put in his place. From Toorayore the French marched against the poligars of Ariyalore and Oodayarpolliem. Captain Calliaud, then commanding in Trichinopoly, advanced against them, and they were left unmolested. In 1756 the Toorayore poligar [q.v.] again failing to pay his tribute was deposed by the French, his immediate predecessor taking his place. The poligar expelled by the French in 1757 was befriended by the poligars of Ariyalore and Oodayarpolliem, and in 1758, with the assistance of the English, the reigning chief of Toorayore was expelled and escaped to Mysore. The latter continued to plunder the country between Toorayore and Ootatoor. In November 1758, three of the five companies garrisoning Toorayore were recalled to Trichinopoly. The deposed poligar took advantage of this opportunity, and captured the town. He then made terms with the Nawaub, who confirmed him in the Government. In 1773, the son of the poligar quarrelled with his father and sought the aid of the Nawaub [q.v.]. On agreeing to raise the peshcush [q.v.] of the polliem from 1,50,000 to 1,75,000 rupees, the young chief was in 1786 appointed poligar, and his father removed to Madras. The latter on offering to increase the peshcush to 2,00,000 rupees if the estate was placed under his authority was restored to the polliem in 1787. In 1789 the son, by the offer of 1,00,000 rupees as a present to the Nawaub and on engaging to pay the same peshcush [q.v.] as his father had agreed to, was again reinstated. The young chief being unable to fulfil his engagements was removed in 1793, and his father placed in the management of the polliem for the third time, having previously engaged to pay a peshcush of 2,75,000 rupees. The polliem in its impoverished state was unable to pay this increased tribute and in 1795 the old chief and his son became reconciled and took refuge in Tanjore, where the father soon afterwards died. His son in 1796 taking advantage of the disturbances in Oodayarpolliem and the distracted state of the country collected a considerable number of men, and laid waste all parts of the polliems. He agreed however to retire to Tanjore, on promise of a monthly allowance of Rs. 1,000 from the Nawaub and permission to levy annually an assessment on the inhabitants of Toorayore, which was to bear a proportion of 25 per cent. to the revenue of the State. This arrangement continued till the assignment of the Carnatic [q.v.] to the Company. Present peshcush Rs. 700.—"*c*" Town, Deputy tahsildar's station, Head assistant collector's division; Trichinopoly dist., Moosiry tal.; pop. 7,467; lat. 11° 09′; long. 78° 40′; from Ariyalore W. 32 miles; from Madras S.W. 172 miles; from Moosiry N.N.E. 8 miles; from Shreerungam N.N.W. 21 miles; from Trichinopoly N. 25 miles. Largest village in talook. Residence of Toorayore zemindar. The head-quarters of the old Toorayore talook was Cannanore, a village 6 miles from Toorayore on the road to Moosiry. Large tank with curious half-ruined three-storeyed building in centre, formerly occasional residence of the Zemindar [q.v.]. Small hill with elaborately sculptured Vishnoo temple.

TORCH TREE (مشعل کا جہاڑ - mashalkájhár, *Hind.*). From use of boughs. Same as Large jungle geranium.

TORYE (తురాయి - turáyi, *Tel.*). Means an ornament for the head. Same as Gold mohur tree.

TOTAH (शुक - shuka, *San.*; ببغا - babaghá, *Ar.*; طوطی - túti, *Pers.*; توتا - totá, *Hind.* and *Dec.*; نوری - nuri, *Malay*; ಗಿಣಿ - gini, *Can.*; చిలుక - chiluka, *Tel.*; തത്ത - tatta, *Mal.*; ගිරවා - giravá, *Singh.*; கிளி - kili, *Tam.*). Title from deccany. Pers. from (tút, pers. mulberry); from its appearing in that season. Hind. and Dec. from persian. Tel. from sanscrit. Mal. from (tattu, mal. to leap). Tam. from (killu, tam. to take up as with the beak). Tam. also (kilippillai), meaning parrot + affix to the names of small birds. Parrots. Palæorninæ, psittacidæ [keeram], scansores, insessores [pacshy, 12], of naturalists [jantoo]. There is a Tamul proverb :—சொன்னதைச் சொல்லும் கிளிப் பிள்ளை—"the parrot will utter what it is taught." The species best known to the natives are shown below.——*Lahbar totah* (कीर - kíra, San.; राघू - rághú, Mahr.; لہبر توتا - lahbartotá, Hind.; చిలుక - chiluka, Tel.; തത്ത - tatta, Mal.; கிளி - kili, Tam.). Title from hindostany. San. from (kír, san. to lisp). Mahr. from (rága, san. color). Hind. from (lahbar, hind. parrakeet so called + totá, hind. parrot). Tel. from (shuka, san. parrot). Mal. from (tattu, mal. to trip). Tam. from (killu, tam. to take up as with the beak). Tel. also (rámachiluka), meaning beautiful + parrot. Title otherwise Rama's parrot, Rose-ringed parrakeet. Palæornis torquatus, palæorninæ [totah], psittacidæ [keeram] scansores, insessores [pacshy, 12], of naturalists. Colors as in Roy totah, without the red shoulder spot; black band in front extends under the chin; bill cherry-red [cherry]; irides pale yellow; feet cinereous, length 16½ inches; female wants the rose collar, but has a bright emeraldine narrow green collar in its place; extremely common; habitually found about towns and villages; destructive to grain and fruit gardens; has a harsh cry; owls [ooloocam] attack these birds by night. ——*Madangowr totah* (مدنگور توتا - madangúrtotá, Hind.; مدنہ توتا - madanatotá, Dec.; கருங்கிளி - karungili, Tam.). Title from hindostany. Hind. from (madana, san. delighting + gaura, san. yellowish white + totá, hind. parrot). Dec. from (madana, san. pleasing + totá, hind. parrot). Tam. from (karumai, tam. blackness + kili, tam. parrot). Title otherwise Black parrot, Blue-winged parrakeet. Palæornis columboides, palæorniæ [totah], psittacidæ [keeram], scansores, insessores [pacshy, 12], of naturalists. Alias Palæornis melanorhynchus. Head, hind neck, plumage beneath generally pale dove-grey, purest on head and cheeks; verdigris-green patch on forehead, lores and below eye; black collar round neck, meeting at chin; in front of this a verdigris-green [zangaur] collar, which widens on upper part of neck; lower part of back, rump and upper tail-coverts blue-green; wing-coverts and scapulars dark blue-green; feathers edged pale; quills darkish blue, faintly edged with green externally, and dusky on the inner webs; tail-coverts, with centre feathers, blue, tipped with yellowish-white; next pair blue on outer web, greenish near base, tipped yellow; all others green externally, yellow internally; beneath all tail-feathers yellow; lower abdomen, vent, and under tail-coverts, pale verdigris-green; female wants the collar, or has only a faint indication of it; the bill is black; bill cherry-red above, dusky beneath; legs greenish plumbeous; length 15 inches; frequents only loftiest trees; associates in small flocks; cry mellow, subdued.——*Roy totah* (رائی توتا - ráítotá, Hind. and Dec.; పెద్దచిలుక - peddachiluka, Tel.; பெரியகிளி - periyagili, Tam.). Hind. from (ráí, hind. prince + totá, hind. parrot); from large size and color. Tel. from (pedda, tel. large + chiluka, tel. parrot). Tam. from (periya, tam. big + kili, tam. parrot). Tel. also (kerieuri), from ghond. Title otherwise Alexandrine parakeet. Palæornis alexandri, palæorninæ [totah], psittacidæ [keeram], scansores, insessores [pacshy, 12], of naturalists. Alias Palæornis nipalensis. Adult male, green, brilliant, emeraldine on head and face, duller on the back, paler beneath, dingy on the breast, yellowish on chin and lower tail-coverts; quills bluish, tail with two centre feathers bright green at base, pale bluish-green for remaining two thirds, tipped yellowish; outer feathers light green on outer webs, yellowish-green internally; black stripe crossing round behind the ears, demi-collar of peach-rose on nape and sides of neck; dark red spot on shoulders of wings, some feathers of wing narrowly edged with dusky; narrow line from nostrils to eye tinged with black; bill deep red, yellowish beneath; feet plumbeous; irides pale yellow; length 21 inches, female wants the collar of the male, generally less brightly colored; beak very large and strong; taken to europe by alexander; feeds on fruits and grain.——*Tooria totah* (توریاتوتا - turiátotá, Hind. and Dec.; రామచిలుక - rámachiluka, Tel.; சிவப்புத்தலைக்கிளி - shivapputtalaikkili, Tam.). Title from hindostany. Tel. from (ráma, san. beautiful + chiluka, tel. parrot). Tam. from (shivappu, tam. redness + talai, tam. head + kili, tam. parrot). Hind. also (faryádí), meaning plaintive or complainer; (kákátuá). Title otherwise Rama's parrot, Rose-headed parrakeet. Palæornis rosa, palæorninæ [totah], psittacidæ [keeram], scansores, insessores [pacshy, 12], of naturalists. Alias Palæornis bengalensis, cyanocephalus, flavicollaris. Adult male, head and face pale roseate, tinged with plum [auloo chah] bloom posteriorly and inferiorly; black spot from base of lower mandible, uniting into narrow complete collar, meeting its opposite one at chin, which is thus broadly black; behind the collar, hind neck verdigris-green [zangaur]; upper portion of back yellow-green; lower back, rump, upper tail-coverts, pale blue-green; wings green, with small red spot on lesser coverts; shoulders bluish-green; webs of most quills dusky; tail, with two centre feathers, cobalt blue, tipped white; next pair blue also tipped white; others pale green on outer webs, yellowish internally; plumage beneath bright siskin, or yellow-green; some less brightly colored, more of uniform green with less yellow; old males have cap much brighter deeper colored than juniors; female head plum-blue, wants the black collar; yellow demi-collar in front and on the sides; breast is much tinged with oil yellow; young birds green throughout; centre tail-feathers always blue, usually faint indication of pale collar of the female; length 14–15 inches; flight very swift.——*Totakahauny* (طوطا کہانی - totákahání, Hind.). Tales of a parrot. Book of thirty-eight didactic tales related by a parrot one each evening to its mistress, thereby dissuading her from turning her affections towards a stranger during the absence of her husband on a journey.

TOTE (తోట - tóta, *Tel.*; தோட்டம் - tóttam, *Tam.*). Tam. from (tódu, tam. collection). A garden, an orchard [baugh, tope].——*Totacaul* (தோட்டக்கால் - tóttakkál, Tam.). From (above + kál, tam. place). Land on which garden products, as chillies [q.v.], tobacco [pogauk], turmeric [country saffron], &c., are raised [baughayet, vellaumay].

TOTTILA (प्रियंगु - priyangu, *San.*; ತೊಟ್ಟಿಲಕಾಯಿ - tottilakáyi, *Can.*). San. from (priya, san. beloved + anga, san. body [priyangoo]. Can. from (tottu, can. peduncle of leaf or fruit + illa, can. having not + káyi, can. fruit). San. also (shyámá), meaning black [shaumay, shyaumalatay, white datura]; (kántatva), meaning shining; (nandiní), meaning gladdening; (p'haliní), meaning fruit-bearing; (latá), meaning creeper. Title otherwise Priyangoo. Botanically Aglaia roxburghiana, miq., meliaceæ [vricsham, 36]. Alias Milnea roxburghiana. A large tree with pinnate leaves and yellow flowers; fruit ½–⅔ inch in diameter, sub-globose, very minutely pilose, one to two celled and seeded, buffcolored when fresh, brown and wrinkled when dry; it consists of a thin shell inclosing one or two brown seeds, covered by a pink fleshy aril; the seeds are flat, of somewhat irregular outline, with one side slightly convex; they are nearly half an inch in diameter and remarkably acid and astringent; when dry they have an aromatic odour. The fruit is used in native medicine, cooling and astringent, and useful in inflammatory, bilious, and febrile complaints; also beneficial in leprosy [cooshtam]; seeds are the part to which its medicinal reputation is due.

TOTTIYAN (தொட்டியன் - tottiyan, *Tam.*). From (tottiyam, tam. witchcraft); from the practice of magic. People originally from the north, settled in Coimbatore [jauty]. Some 60,000 in number. See vol. II, 228.

TOURMALINE (तोरमल्ली - tóramallí, *Mahr.*; ترملی - turmali, *Hind.*; తోరమల్లె - tóramalle, *Tel.*; තෝරමල්ලි - tóramalli, *Singh.*; துவரைமல்லி - tuvaraimalli, *Tam.*). All from singhalese. Mineral presenting brown, blue, green and red colors; the blue called indicolite, the red bubellite; green and red esteemed in jewelry when clear and large; crystals when heated exhibit electric polarity; ceylon jewellers apply it to zircon or ceylon or madura diamonds.

TOWHEED (توحید - tauhíd, *Hind.*). From (wahada, ar. to declare to be one). Unity of god.

TOWVAY (தௌவை - tauvai, *Tam.*). Elder sister. Goddess of misfortune [moodevy]. There is a Tamul proverb :— தௌவையின் மனத்துக்கு ஒவ்வுதல் இல்லை—"nothing "gives satisfaction to towvay."

TRAIL GRASS (ಮಂಚಡಕಾಲುಹುಲ್ಲು - manchadakáluhullu, *Can.*; కొండజెరి - kondajeri, *Tel.*; കൊണ്ടപ്പുല്ല് - kondappullu, *Mal.*; மயிர்கொண்டைப்புல் - mayirgondaippul, *Tam.*). Title from spreading habit. Can. from (mancha, can. cot + kálu, can. leg + hullu, can. grass). Tel. from (konda, tel. hill + jerri, tel. centipede). Mal. from (konda, mal. tuft of hair + pullu, mal. grass). Tam. from (mayil, tam. peacock + kondai, tam. crest + pul, tam. grass), from flowering head. Can. also (hennuganjalugarikehullu), meaning female + cluster + a kind of bent grass. Tel. also (adavigódhumalu), meaning wild wheat, triticum vulgare, vill. Tam. also (kudaippul), meaning umbrella + grass. Title otherwise Bearded chloris, Centipede grass, Peacock crest grass, Trailing grass, Umbrella grass, Wild wheat. Botanically Chloris barbata, swartz., graminaceæ [vricsham, 156]. Alias Andropogon barbatus; chloris caribæa. Culm one foot, compressed, branched; leaves acute, a little hairy above; spikes digitate, four to twelve, spikelets sessile; imbricated, hermaphrodite; corolla ciliated, awned, neuter of two-awned valves; very common; grows in large tufts; resembles hurrially [q.v.]. Cattle eat it till in flower; may be converted into hay [ghaus]. Other species are:—digitata, montana, roxburghiana, tetrameris, wightiana.

TRANQUEBAR* (தரங்கம்பாடி - tarangambádi, *Tam.*): From (taranga, san. wave + pádi, tam. village). Place against which the waves dash.—"*a*" Deputy tahsildarry, Tanjore district. Pay Rs. 70.—"*b*" Village, Deputy tahsildar's station; Tanjore dist., Mayavaram tal.; pop. 4,947; lat. 11° 02′; long. 79° 54′; from Caricaul N. 8 miles; from Combaconam E.N.E. 32 miles; from Madras S.S.W. 143 miles; from Mayavaram E.S.E. 14½ miles; from Munnargoody N.E. 36 miles; from Negapatam N. 18 miles; from Tanjore E.N.E. 50 miles; from Trimal vausal S. 14 miles. Surrounded by walls and protected by the Dansborg, which being white, as well as most of the houses, the place is conspicuous when viewed from the sea. There is a slight curvature in the shore here, concave towards the sea. In 1616 the first Danish vessel that visited India sent by the Danish east india company, established in 1612, was wrecked off Tranquebar. The captain obtained for the Company Tranquebar with land around, 5 miles long and 3 miles broad, at an annual rent of Rs. 4,000 paid to the Rajah of Tanjore. A fort was built. In 1624, Tranquebar became the property of the king of Denmark, to whom the Company owed money. For supplying arms to the Nawaub of Arcot, Hyder ally in 1780 exacted a fine of Rs. 1,40,000 from the Danes. Tranquebar was taken by the English with all other Danish settlements in India in 1807, but restored in 1814. Bought by the English in 1845, for Rs. 12,50,000. From 1845 to 1860 Tranquebar was the head-quarters of the Collector, now transferred to Tanjore; and from 1860 to 1874 it contained the District and Sessions court, afterwards removed to Negapatam. In 1878 the North tanjore district court, which had been in abeyance for two years, was re-established at Tranquebar. Since again discontinued. Tranquebar is also interesting as the first settlement of Protestant missionaries in India. See vol. I, 622. In 1847 the mission passed from the Danes to the Leipzic evangelical lutheran mission, who have a printing press. The fort is on the shore, separated from the cultivated land by a broad sandy tract. It is a square, of which the shore forms one side, and on which the sea is gradually encroaching, having already swept away the first church built by Ziegenbalg. All the European houses are within the fort, and the absence of compounds gives the place an appearance unusual in an Indian station. The bulk of the native population live outside the fort. The walls are well preserved, and the former citadel, the Dansborg, is now used as a jail. The fort also contains two Protestant churches, and a small Roman catholic church, under the jurisdiction of the Archbishop of Goa. The principal Catholic church is outside the fort; and belong to the Vicariates apostolic of Pondicherry. In the fort is an old Shiva [q.v.] temple with an inscription. The temple authorities possess a copper-plate grant. Another temple dedicated to Vishnoo [q.v.] contains a copper-plate grant [shausanam], dated A.D. 1609. A number of carved Dutch tombstones are to be seen in the cemetery, some very handsomely sculptured. In Danish times Tranquebar was a busy port, and contained a number of Danish families. Under English rule the revenue increased rapidly; and as the port affords better anchorage than Negapatam, it soon drew away the trade of the latter place. The completion of the South indian railway line from Negapatam to Tanjore in 1861 and to Trichinopoly in 1862 restored the tráde to Negapatam, and Tranquebar is now almost ruined. Tranquebar tower forms a trig. station; lat. 11° 01′ 23·06″; long. 79° 53′ 53·57″; from Mayavaram E.S.E. 14 miles.

TRAVANCORE (തിരുവിതാംകൂർ - tiruvitánkúr, *Mal.*). From (tiru, mal. goddess of prosperity + vázhu, mal. to reside + kúr, mal. part) [shree, tir]. Sanscrit name (shrívardhanapurí), meaning lutchmy + prosperity + town. Tam. name (tiruvázhumgódu), meaning the place where the goddess of prosperity resides. —(1) Native state; situated on the south-west extremity of the presidency; between 8° 4′ and 10° 22′ N. lat., and between 76° 13′ and 77° 38′ E. long.; bounded N. by Cochin state and Coimbatore district, E. by Madura and Tinnevelly districts, S. and W. by the Indian ocean; pop. 2,401,158; language Malayalam. Rivers:—Atchancoil, Coolitora, Cullada, Pambah, Periyaur. Ports:—Alleppey, Anjengo, Caracoolam, Cauttore, Colachel, Manacodam, Manacoody, Paliport, Paravore, Poondora, Poovaur, Poracaud, Quilon, Rajakkal mungalam, Tengyeputnam, Vilinjam. Mountains:—Anamullays, Cardamom hills, Travancore hills. The whole area of the state is represented by the following talooks:—Agasteeshwaram, Ambalapoya, Aulangaud, Caroonaugapully, Caurtigapully, Chenganore, Cherankeel, Chungacherry, Coonnat naud, Coonnatore, Cottaura cara, Cottayam, Cullcoolam, Mauvelicara, Meenachel, Mocatpoya, Nedoovengaud, Noittincora, Paravore, Putnapooram, Quilon, Shencottah, Shertala, Tiroovalla, Todoopoya, Tovaula, Trivandrum, Velavancode, Wycome, Yaittmanore, Yerraneel. For administrative purposes, the state is also divided into the following divisions:—Southern or Pudmanaubhapooram division, Trivandrum division, Quilon division, and Northern or Cottayam division. The following general references should be made to the preceeding volumes:—general geograpy, I (1) to (29); general ethnology, I (29) to (109); general history, I (110) to (188); physical geography, II, 1; meteorology, II, 3; geology II, 8; fauna, II, 21; flora, II, 26; mineralogy, II, 29. The following references in the preceding volumes will furnish details special to the district:—particulars about towns, II, 48; coast survey, II, 149; light-houses, II, 168; ports, II, 423. A special gazetteer account of the whole district is given at II, 133 and 287. Places of archæological interest:—Agasteeshwaram, Alagya paundyapooram, Anantapooram, Anjengo, Aramana, Atchancoil, Aurdeshaputt, Bramhapooram, Cadiapatam, Capiyara, Chenganore, Colachel, Coolatore, Cottaur, Cottayam, Cullada, Cullcoolam, Madaulam, Mail pidaugay, Maudavoreparra, Mauvelicara, Nadoovoo pidaugay, Nattaulam, Neendacara, Parakye, Periyacoil, Ponmana, Poorayore, Sooshindram, Tairoor, Taulacoody, Tirnundicara, Tiroovalla, Tirvancode, Tirvattaur, Tovaula, Tricaroor, Tungacherry, Vadacherry, Valavancode, Yerraneel. The leading places, &c., in the state are the following.——*Agasteeshwaram* (അഗസ്തീശ്വരം - agastíshvaram, Mal.). See sep. title.——*Alagya paundyapooram* (അഴകിയപാണ്ഡ്യപുരം - azhakiyapándyapuram, Mal.). From (azhakiya, mal. beautiful + pándya, san. the kingdom so called + pura, san. city); the beautiful city of the paundyan chief. Village; Pudmanaubhapooram division, Tovaula tal.; lat. 8° 18′; long. 77° 29′; from Tovaula N.N.W. 7 miles; from Trivandrum E.S.E. 35 miles; from the sea N. 15 miles. Extensive Agrahaurams [q.v.]. The Naunjy coravar, who had for some time sovereignty of Nannjinand [q.v.] were succeeded by Moodelliars [q.v.] with head-quarters here. ——*Alleppey* (ആലപ്പുഴ - álappuzha, Mal.). See sep. title.——*Alwye* (ആലുവായ - áluváya, Mal.). See sep. title.——*Ambalapoya* (അമ്പലപ്പുഴ - ambalappuzha, Mal.). See sep. title.——*Anamoody* (ആനമുടി - ánamuti, Mal.). See sep. title.——*Anjanaud* (അഞ്ചനാട് - añchanátu, Mal.). See sep. title.——*Anjengo* (അഞ്ചുതെങ്ങ് - añchutennu, Mal.). See sep. title.——*Aramboly* (ആരുവാമൊഴി - áruvámozhi, Mal.). See sep. title.——*Aripaud* (അരിപ്പാട് - arippátu, Mal.). From (ari, mal. vishnu, the god + páti, mal. village); from the temple of shreekrishnan. Village, Tahsildar's station; Quilon division, Caurtigapully tal.; pop. 6,104; lat. 9° 17′ N.; long. 76° 30′ E.; from Alleppey S.S.E. 16 miles; from Cottayam S.S.W. 21 miles; from Madras S.W. 365 miles; from Nagarcoil N.W. 100 miles; from Paravore S.S.E. 60 miles; from Quilon N.N.W. 28 miles; from Trivandrum N.N.W. 63 miles; from the sea E. 4 miles. In a fertile and populous tract. Sacred shrine of Soobramanyan [q.v.], supported by the State. Annual festival in April lasts ten days.——*Aryancauv* (ആരിയങ്കാവ് - áriyankávu, Mal.). See sep. title.——*Ashamboo* (അശമ്പു - ashambu, Mal.). See sep. title.——*Ashtamoody* (അഷ്ടമുടി - ashtamuti, Mal.). See sep. title.——*Atchancoil* (അച്ചൻകോവിൽ - aççankóvil, Mal.). See sep. title.——*Áttingal* (ആറ്റുങ്ങൽ - áttunnal, Mal.). See sep. title.——*Aulangaud* (ആലങ്ങാട് - álannátu, Mal.). See sep. title.——*Bhootapaundy* (ഭൂതപ്പാണ്ടി - bhútappánti, Mal.). From (bhúta, san. demon + pándya, san. pándyan king). Village; Tahsildar's and Registrar's station; pudmanaubhapooram division, Tovaula tal.; lat. 8° 16′; long. 77° 29′; from Alleppey S.E. 111 miles; from Cottayam S.S.E. 109 miles; from Madras S.S.W. 380 miles; from Nagarcoil N. 6 miles; from Paravore S.S.E. 152 miles; from Quilon S.E. 71 miles; from Trivandrum E.S.E. 36 miles; from the sea N. 12 miles. At the foot of the ghauts [q.v.] and about 8 miles north-west of Aramboly pass. Ancient town, once in the possession of the Paundyan [q.v.] rajahs. Old pagoda [q.v.] on the bank of a small stream branching off from the Palayaur. Remarkable for its monkeys [bandar]. Extensive agrahaurams [q.v.].——*Cadambanaud* (കടമ്പനാട് - kadambanátu, Mal.). From (kadamba, san. a tree, anthocephalus cadamba, miq. + nátu, mal. country). Village; Quilon division, Coonnatore tal.; lat. 9° 06′; long. 76° 44′; from Coonnatore N. 2 miles; from Trivandrum N.N.W. 45 miles; from the sea E. 13 miles. Ancient Syrian [q.v.] church.——*Cadapooram* (കടപ്പുറം - katappuram, Mal.). From (katal, mal. sea + puram, mal. side). Village; Quilon division, Tiroovalla tal.; pop. 11,916; lat. 9° 20′; long. 76° 35′; from Cochin S.E. 46 miles; from Quilon N. 31 miles; from Tiroovalla S.S.W. 3 miles; from Trivandrum N.N.W. 64 miles; from the sea E. 11 miles.——*Catiapatam* (കടിയപട്ടണം - katiyapattanam, Mal.). See sep. title.——*Candiyore* (കണ്ടിയൂർ - kantiyúr, Mal.). From (kanti, mal. high ground + úr, mal. village). Village; Quilon division, Mauvelicara tal.; lat. 9° 15′; long. 76° 35′; from Mauvelicara W. 1 mile; from Trivandrum N.N.W. 59 miles; from the sea 8 miles. Ancient village near Mauvelicara. Once the field of a battle in which Travancore obtained a decisive victory over the Cauyancollam rajah, this leading to the annexation of the latter principality to the state. Large ancient pagoda [q.v.] and palace.——*Capiyore* (കപിയൂർ - kapiyúr, Mal.). From (kapi, san. monkey + úr, mal. village);

so called from the pagoda dedicated to hanooman, the monkey chief. Village; Quilon division, Tiroovalla tal.; pop. 15,300; lat. 9° 24′; long. 76° 39′; from Tiroovalla E.N.E. 4 miles; from Trivandrum N.N.W. 66 miles; from the sea E. 17 miles. On the Manimala. Inhabited by Nayars. Large pagoda [q.v.] to Hanooman [q.v.] and reservoir. There is a regular street of Nayar [q.v.] houses.——*Caracoolám* (കരക്കുളം - karakkulam, Mal.). From (kara, mal. village + kulam, mal. tank). Village, Port; Trivandrum division, Nedoovengaud tal.; pop. 4,425; lat. 8° 34′; long. 77° 01′; from Anjengo E.S.E. 16 miles; from Bombay S.S.E. 750 miles; from Trivandrum N.N.E. 7 miles; from Veily E.N.E. 8 miles; from Nedoovengaud S.S.W. 3 miles. ——*Caramana* (കരമന - karamana, Mal.). See sep. title.——*Cardamom hills* (ഏലമല - élamala, Mal.). See sep. title.——*Caroonaugapully* (കരുനാഗപ്പള്ളി - karunágappalli, Mal.). From (karu, mal. black + nága, san. serpent + palli, mal. village). Talook, Quilon division; lat. 8° 56′ to 9° 11′; long. 76° 31′ to 76° 40′; pop. 101,039. The talook is sub-divided into 8 praverties [q.v.] and consists of 104 caras [q.v.] or villages. It is bounded N. by Caurtigapully talook, E. by Mauvelicara and Coonnatore talooks, S by Quilon talook, W. by the Indian ocean. Its greatest length, N. to S., is 15 and its greatest breadth, E. to S., is 8 miles. Its area 89 square miles. Thickly populated. Soil alluvial. Good screw-pine [q.v.] mats [bóriyah] are made. The talook is well watered and irrigated by small canals. The village of same name is in lat. 9° 05′; long. 76° 35′; from Cochin S.E. 63 miles; from Padanayarcoolangara N. 1 mile; from Trivandrum N.N.W. 48 miles; from the sea E. 3 miles; on the coast at the northern extremity of an extensive inlet communicating with the sea. There are hills of the same name. ——*Caumapooram* (കാമപുരം - kámapuram, Mal.). From (káma, san. indian god of love + pura, san. city). Town; Quilon division, Ambalapoya tal.; lat. 9° 18′; long. 76° 28′; from Ambalapoya S.E. 7 miles; from Quilon N.N.W. 31 miles; from Trivandrum N.N.W. 65 miles; from the sea E. 3 miles. A pagoda [q.v.]. Travellers' bungalow [q.v.].——*Caunyirapully* (കാഞ്ഞിരപ്പള്ളി - káññirappalli, Mal.). From (káññiram, mal. strychnos nux-vomica, linn. + palli, mal. village). Village; Cottayam division, Chungacherry tal.; pop. 19,520; lat. 9° 34′; long. 76° 50′; from Chungacherry E.N.E. 19 miles; from Trivandrum N. 75 miles; from the sea E. 32 miles. Trading town at foot of a ghaut [q.v.], and on the main road from Cottayam to Madura. Christians and Lubbays [q.v.]. Fra. Paolino di S. Bartolomeo mentions it specially. Romo-syrian church [syrian]. ——*Caurtigapully* (കാർത്തികപ്പള്ളി - kárttikappalli, Mal.). From (krittiká, san. the asterism of that name + palli, mal. village); called after the king born under caurtigay [q.v.]. Talook; Quilon division; pop. 81,969. Sub-divided into 10 praverties and comprises 93 caras or villages. It is bounded N. by Ambalapoya talook, E. by Chenganore and Mauvelicara talooks, S. by Caroonaugapully talook and W. by the Indian ocean. Its greatest length, N. to S., is 15 miles and its greatest breadth, E. to W., is 7 miles. Its area is 70 square miles. Soil alluvial. Well watered by canals and rivulets. The village of same name is in lat. 9° 16′; long. 76° 30′; from Aripaud S. 1¾ miles; from Trivandrum N.N.W. 63 miles; from the sea E. 3 miles. Syrian [q.v.] church and town encompassed by a mound.——*Cauttore* (കാട്ടൂർ - káttúr, Mal.). From (kátu, mal. forest + úr, mal. village). Village, Port; Cottayam division, Shertala tal.; lat. 9° 34′; long. 76° 22′; from Alleppey N. 5 miles; from Bombay S.S.E. 675 miles; from Cottayam W.S.W. 13 miles; from Trivandrum N.N.W. 84 miles; from Shertala S. 8 miles. ——*Cauyancollam* (കായങ്കുളം - káyankulam, Mal.). See sep. title.——*Chenganore* (ചെങ്ങന്നൂർ - chennannúr, Mal.). See sep. title.——*Cherankeel* (ചിറയിൻകീഴ് - chirayinkízh, Mal.). See sep. title.——*Chungamnaud* (ചങ്ങനാട് - channamanátu, Mal.). From (sangama, san. joining + nádu, mal. country). Village; Cottayam division, Aulangaud tal.; pop. 8,023; lat. 10° 10′; long. 76° 23′; from Aulangaud N.N.E. 4 miles; from Trivandrum N.N.W. 120 miles; from the sea E. 12 miles. Extensive Nayar village, with celebrated ancient temple in ruins.——*Codamungalam* (കൊടമംഗലം - kotamangalam, Mal.). From (kodai, tam. gift + mangala, san. prosperity). Town; Cottayam division, Mooatpoya tal.; pop. 7,876; lat. 10° 4′; long. 76° 40′; from Mooatpoya N.N.E. 6 miles; from Coimbatore S.S.W. 68 miles; from Trivandrum N. 109 miles; from the sea E. 27 miles. On the Mooatpoya river. Formerly of importance on account of trade with Tinnevelly and Dindigul. Chief seat of Mahomedans. ——*Codayaur* (കോതയാർ - kótayár, Mal.). See sep. title.——*Codwully* (കൊടുവള്ളി - kotuvalli, Mal.). From (kotu, mal. steep + palli, mal. village). Village; Cottayam division, Paravore tal.; pop. 7,542; lat. 10° 07′; long. 76° 18′; from Paravore S.S.E. 3 miles; from Trivandrum N.N.W. 120 miles; from the sea E. 4 miles. Handsome pagoda [q.v.] with annual festival.——*Colachel* (കൊല്ലച്ചൽ - kollaççal, Mal.). See sep. title.——*Comorin* (കന്യാകുമാരി - kanyákumári, Mal.). See sep. title.——*Connemow* (കുന്നുമാവ് - kunnumávu, Mal.). See sep. title.——*Cooleliy* (കുലെല്ലി - kulelli, Mal.). From (kulayalli, mal. palm-blossoms). Village; lat. 9° 12′; long. 76° 56′; from Trivandrum N. 49 miles; from Tinnevelly W.N.W. 63 miles; from the sea E. 29 miles.——*Coolitora* (കുഴിത്തുറ - kuzhittura, Mal.). See sep. title. ——*Coondaly* (കുണ്ടലി - kuntali, Mal.). From (kundu, mal. deep + azhi, mal. river-mouth). Town; lat. 10° 9′; long. 77° 12′; from Trivandrum N. 114 miles; from Coimbatore S.E. 60 miles. ——*Coondara* (കുണ്ടറ - kuntara, Mal.). Means dungeon. Town; Quilon division, Cottaura cara tal.; lat. 8° 58′; long. 76° 44′; from Cottaura cara W.S.W. 6 miles; from Trivandrum N.N.W. 37 miles; from the sea E. 10 miles. A small but somewhat regular town, situated amidst some fine open heights.——*Coonnatnaud* (കുന്നത്തുനാട് - kunnattunátu, Mal.). From (kunnu, mal. hill + nátu, mal. country). Talook; Cottayam division; pop. 109,625. The greatest length, N. to S., is 20 miles. Greatest breadth, E. to W., is 18 miles. Sub-divided into 11 praverties and consists of 166 caras or villages. Bounded N. by Aulangaud talook, E. by Mooatpoya talook, S. and W. by the Cochin territory. Irrigated by the Alwye river.——*Coonnatore* (കുന്നത്തൂർ - kunnattúr, Mal.). From (kunnu, mal. hill + úr, mal. village). Talook, Quilon division; pop. 62,700. Greatest length, N. to S., 14 miles. Greatest breadth, E. to W., 25 miles. Sub-divided into 9 praverties and contains 123 caras or villages. Bounded N. by Mauvelicara and Chenganore talooks, E. by the hills, S. by Pudmanaubhapooram, Cottaura cara and Quilon talooks, and W. by Caroonaugapully talook. Irrigated by Cullada river. The Village and tahsildar's station is in lat. 9° 4′ N.; long. 76° 44′ E.; from Alleppey S.E. 37 miles; from Cottayam S.S.E. 37 miles; from Madras S.W. 365 miles; from Nagarcoil N.W. 78 miles; from Paravore S.S.E. 79 miles; from Quilon N.N.E. 13 miles; from Trivandrum N.N.W. 44 miles; from the sea E. 12 miles. A large but irregular town. There is another village of same name in Pudmanaubhapooram division, Velavancode tal.; lat. 8° 18′; long. 77° 14′; from Coolitora S.S.W. 2 miles; from Trivandrum S.E. 21 miles; from the sea N. 6. miles.——*Coonny alam* (കുഞ്ഞിയലം - kuññiyalam, Mal.). From (kuññi, mal. small + alam, mal. salt marsh). Portion of cardamom [q.v.] hills.——*Cottacoolangara* (കോട്ടക്കുളങ്ങര - kóttakkulannara, Mal.). From (kótta, mal. fort + kulam, mal. tank + kara, mal. shore). Village; Cottayam division, Aulangaud tal.; lat. 10° 13′; long. 76° 25′; from Aulangaud N.E. 8 miles; from Trivandrum N.N.W. 123 miles; from the sea E. 15 miles. Large Nayar village.——*Cottaur* (കോട്ടാർ - kóttár, Mal.). See sep. title.——*Cottaura cara* (കൊട്ടാരക്കര - kottárakkara, Mal.). From (kottáram, mal. palace + kara, mal. village). Talook; Quilon division; pop. 55,924. The greatest length, N. to S., is 21 miles and greatest breadth, E. to W., is 10 miles. Sub-divided into 8 praverties and consists of 137 caras or villages. Bounded N. and E. by Putnapooram talook, S. by Nedoovengaud and Cherankeel talook and W. by Quilon talook. Soil is laterite [q.v.]. The town and Head-quarters of talook is in lat. 9° 00′; long. 76° 49′; from Alleppey S.E. 44 miles; from Cottayam S.S.E. 44 miles; from Madras S.W. 365 miles; from Nagarcoil N.W. 71 miles; from Paravore S.S.E. 86 miles; from Quilon E.N.E. 14 miles; from Trivandrum N.N.W. 38 miles; from the sea E. 16 miles. Straggling town, surrounded by picturesque scenery. Pagoda [q.v.], palace and the most southern Syrian [q.v.] church.——*Cottayam* (കോട്ടയം - kóttayam, Mal.). See sep. title.——*Covalam* (കോവളം - kóvalam, Mal.). Means headland. Mal. also (rattara), meaning double village [rattera]. Village, Port; Trivandrum division, Trivandrum talook. The small bay affords tolerable landing in fine season.——*Cuddamuttam* (കടമറ്റം - katamattam, Mal.). From (katá, mal. last + mattu, mal. limit). Village; Cottayam division, Mooatpoya tal.; lat. 9° 59′; long. 76° 33′; from Mooatpoya W. 5 miles; from Trivandrum N.N.W. 105 miles; from the sea E. 18 miles. Christians have a large church and a village.——*Cullada* (കല്ലട - kallata, Mal.). See sep. title.——*Cullcoolam* (കൽക്കുളം - kalkkulam, Mal.). From (kal, mal. stone + kulam, mal. tank). Talook; Pudmanaubhapooram division; pop. 60,908. Its greatest length, N. to S., is 24 miles; and its greatest breadth, E. to W., is 10 miles. Sub-divided into 8 praverties [q.v.] and containing 108 caras [q.v.] or villages. Bounded N. by the Tinnevelly district, E. by Tovaula talook, S. by Yerraneel talook, and W. by Velavancode talook. Slopes to the south and west. Had a sanitarium known as Moottcooly vayal, where there is a Circar [q.v.] bungalow [q.v.]. Contains Pudmanaubhapooram. Small fresh-water lake called Cauyalcara, 6 miles from Pudmanabhapooram. Weaving on a small scale, agriculture chief industry. River-fed and rain-fed tanks [q.v.]. ——*Diamper* (ഉദയംപേരൂർ - udayampérúr, Mal.). See sep. title. ——*Irore* (ഇരൂർ - irúr, Mal.). From (iru, mal. two + úr, mal. village). Village; Quilon division, Tiroovalla tal.; pop. 20,615; lat. 9° 21′; long. 76° 46′; from Tiroovalla E. 11 miles; from Trivandrum N.N.W. 60 miles; from the sea E. 24 miles. Mart frequented by Tinnevelly merchants.——*Itticara* (ഇത്തിക്കര - ittikkara, Mal.). See sep. title.——*Ivica* (അഴിമുഖം - azhimukham, Mal.). See sep. title.——*Jyemánnam* (ജൈമനം - jaimanam, Mal.). From (jaya, san. victory + mannam, mal. judgment seat). Title otherwise Eimanam, by corruption. Village;

Cottayam division, Yaittmanore tal.; pop. 9,702; lat. 9° 37′; long. 76° 32′; from Yaittmanore W.S.W. 6 miles; from Trivandrum N.N.W. 83 miles; from the sea E. 13 miles. Dense Nayar population scattered in extensive plantations. Pagoda picturesquely caps the summit of a low insulated top.——*Kericaud* (കേറിക്കാട് - kérikkátu, Mal.). From (kéram, mal. cocoanut, cocos nucifera, linn. + kátu, mal. forest). Quilon division, Caurtigapully tal.; lat. 9° 11′; long. 76° 32′; from Aripaud S. 7 miles; from Trivandrum N.N.W. 58 miles; from the sea E. 3 miles. A small Nayar village on the east coast of the Cauyancollam lake.——*Kilimanore* (കിളിമാനൂർ - kilimánúr, Mal.). From (kili, mal. parrot + mán, mal. deer + úr, mal. village). Village; Trivandrum division, Cherankeel tal.; pop. 6,595; lat. 8° 46′; long. 76° 55′; from Attingal N.N.E. 6 miles; from Trivandrum N.N.W. 20 miles; from the sea E. 12 miles. On road from Trivandrum to Shencottah, viâ Nedoovengaud. Residence and jenm [q.v.] property of Coil tumbooraum [q.v.], who are allied to the Travancore royal family by marriage.——*Kiliyaur* (കിളിയാർ - kiliyár, Mal.). From (kili, mal. parrot + áru, mal. river). River; Trivandrum division, Nedoovengaud and Trivandrum talooks. Small river rising in the Nedoovengaud forests and after a devious but generally a southerly course joining the Caramana at Trivallam near Trivandrum. Length, 15 miles. Irrigates a small tract of rice [q.v.] land.——*Kistnapooram* (കൃഷ്ണപുരം - krishnápuram, Mal.). From (krishna, san. the god + pura, san. town). Village, District moonsif's station; Quilon division, Caroonaugapully tal.; pop. 13,608; lat. 9° 9′; long. 76° 34′; from Quilon N. 18 miles; from Cauyancollam S.E. 2 miles; from Padanayarcoolangara N. 6 miles; from Trivandrum N.N.W. 54 miles; from the sea E. 4 miles. Former military station of the Cauyancollam rajahs. Here the Cauyancollam army was defeated by Travancore. Contains a palace and a large square fort in good repair to the west. Temple of Krishnasawmy. Annual festival lasting thirty days. Its once active sea-borne trade has now disappeared. Canal leads to Cauyancollam.——*Kyepully* (കൈപ്പള്ളി - kaippalli, Mal.). From (kai, mal. branch + palli, mal. village). Village; Cottayam division, Yaittmanore tal.; pop. 9,611; lat. 9° 40′; long. 76° 33′; from Yaittmanore W. 4 miles; from Trivandrum N.N.W. 85 miles; from the sea E. 14 miles. Small church and an interesting scenery.——*Laulam* (പള്ളിപ്പെട്ട - pallippétta, Mal.). From (palli, mal. church + pétta, mal. bazaar). Called also Paula, Pully or Paulah. Town, Tahsildar's station; Cottayam division, Meenachel tal.; pop. 8,168; lat. 9° 43′; long. 76° 44′; from Alleppey N.E. 28 miles; from Cottayam N.E. 14 miles; from Madras S.W. 335 miles; from Nagarcoil N.N.W. 115 miles; from Parayore S.E. 43 miles; from Quilon N. 55 miles; from Trivandrum N.N.W. 85 miles; from the sea E. 26 miles; from Cochin S.E. 35 miles. On a fine navigable stream. Capital of Meenachel district. Inhabited almost entirely by Romo-syrian christians of the earlier persuasion. Many are engaged in the areca-nut [q.v.], pepper [q.v.] trade, which form the chief articles of traffic. The town is accessible by the Cottayam river. ——*Mahendragherry* (മഹേന്ദ്രഗിരി - mahéndragiri, Mal.). See sep. title.——*Manacoody* (മണക്കുടി - manakkuti, Mal.). See sep. title.——*Manarchaul* (മനാർച്ചാല - manárççála, Mal.). See sep. title.——*Manimala* (മണിമല - manimala, Mal.). From (mani, san. gem + mala, mal. hill). River; Quilon and Cottayam divisions, Tiroovalla and Chungacherry talooks. Small river which rises in the Coodamoorty hills and joins the Pambah at Tiroovalla. Useful for sugar-cane [q.v.] cultivation. Navigable for about 35 miles. Culloorpaura and Tiroovalla are on its banks. After receiving several small streams it unites with the Pambah about 15 miles above the mouth of that river. It afterwards separates from that river and flows into the Vembanaud lake by several mouths.——*Margary alam* (മക്കരി അളം - markariyalam, Mal.). Portion of Cardamom hills.——*Mauvelicara* (മാവേലിക്കര - mávélikkara, Mal.). See sep. title.——*Meenachel* (മീനച്ചിൽ - mínaççil, Mal.). See sep. title.——*Meilaudy* (മൈലാടി - mailáti, Mal.). From (mayil, mal. peacock + átu, mal. to play). Village; Pudmanaubhapooram division, Tovaula tal.; lat. 8° 09′; long. 77° 33′; from Bhootapaundy S.S.E. 9 miles; from Trivandrum E.S.E. 43 miles; from the sea N. 6 miles. Considerable village near the base of the southern hills. Contains the first Protestant missionary church built in Travancore, viz., in 1810.——*Mooatpoya* (മൂവാറ്റുപുഴ - múvattupuzha, Mal.). See sep. title. ——*Moondipolliem* (മുണ്ടിപ്പാളയം - muntippálayam, Mal.). From (mundiyan, mal. dwarf, forest deity + pálayam, mal. camp). Town; lat. 9° 11′; long. 76° 54′; from Trivandrum N. 49 miles; from the sea E. 27 miles.——*Moottam* (മുട്ടം - muttam, Mal.). See sep. title.——*Mundacaud* (മണ്ടക്കാട് - mantakkátu, Mal.). From (manta, mal. skull + kátu, mal. jungle). Village; Pudmanaubhapooram division, Yerraneel tal.; lat. 8° 14′; long. 77° 18′; from Yerraneel W.N.W. 4 miles; from Trivandrum S.E. 27 miles; from the sea N. 4 miles. Situated on the coast a little inland, a few miles to the north-east of Colachel. Shrine with annual festival.——*Munjaudicara* (മഞ്ചാടിക്കര - mañchátikkara, Mal.). From (mañcháti, mal. adenanthera pavonina, linn. + kara, mal. village). Town; Cottayam division, Chungacherry tal.; pop. 12,024; lat. 9° 27′ N.; long. 76° 34′ E.; from Chungacherry N.W. 1 mile; from Trivandrum N.N.W. 72 miles; from the sea E. 13 miles. Trading town between Madura and Cottayam.——*Munnanjainy* (മന്നഞ്ചേനി - mannañchéni, Mal.). From (mannan, mal. king + chéni, corruption of chéri, mal. village). Village; Cottayam division, Shertala tal.; lat. 9° 55′; long. 76° 18′; from Shertala N.N.W. 17 miles; from Trivandrum N.N.W. 108 miles; from the sea E. ½ mile. Pagoda [q.v.] and a street of bazaar [q.v.]. Once a mart. Large vessels may approach it.——*Munnpully* (മന്നപ്പള്ളി - mannappalli, Mal.). See sep. title.——*Munyaly* (മഞ്ഞളി - maññali, Mal.). From (mañña, mal. yellow). Village; Cottayam division, Aulangaud tal.; lat. 10° 09′; long. 76° 18′; from Aulangaud N.W. 3 miles; from Trivandrum N.N.W. 122 miles; from the sea E. 6 miles. Large market.——*Munyappara* (മഞ്ഞപ്പാറ - maññappara, Mal.). From (mañña, mal. yellow + para, mal. large field). Village; Cottayam division, Aulangaud tal.; pop. 7,993; lat. 10° 13′; long. 76° 30′; from Aulangaud E.N.E. 12 miles; from Trivandrum N.N.W. 122 miles; from the sea E. 20 miles. Small Christian village with church. Capital of one of the divisions of Aulangaud. The neighbouring country has been partly deserted.——*Nagarcoil* (നാഗർകോവിൽ - nágarkóvil, Mal.). See sep. title.——*Nairanam* (നേരണം - néranam, Mal.). Village; Quilon division, Tiroovalla tal.; lat. 9° 21′; long. 76° 30′; from Tiroovalla W.S.W. 7 miles; from Trivandrum N.N.W. 68 miles; from the sea E. 7 miles. One of the most ancient Syrian [q.v.] churches.——*Navoycoolam* (നാവായിക്കുളം - náváyikulam, Mal.). From (nál, mal. four + váya, mal. mouth + kulam, mal. tank). Town; Trivandrum division, Cherankeel tal.; pop. 6,028; lat. 8° 47′; long. 76° 49′; from Attingal N.N.W. 6 miles; from Trivandrum N.N.W. 23 miles; from Tinnevelly W. 61 miles; from the sea E. 7 miles.——*Nedoovengaud* (നെടുവങ്ങാട് - netuvannátu, Mal.). From (netu, mal. long + van, mal. large + kátu, mal. forest). Often called Yellavaloornaud, a state, the race of whose chief is now extinct. Talook; pop. 52,211; Sub-divided into 8 praverties [q.v.] and consisting of 68 caras [q.v.] or villages. Greatest length, N. to S., 25 miles; greatest breadth, E. to W., 29 miles. Bounded N. by Cottaura cara and Putnapooram talooks, E. by Tinnevelly district, S. by Neittincara talook and W. by Trivandrum and Cherankeel talooks. There is a waterfall at Aroovy cara and a sanitarium at the Ponmoody hills. Bamboo mat [boriyah] making. There are no tanks, but some rivers. The Village and Tahsildar's station is in lat. 8° 37′; long. 77° 03′; from Alleppey S.E. 74 miles; from Cottayam S.S.E. 74 miles; from Madras S.W. 375 miles; from Nagarcoil N.W. 41 miles; from Paravore S.S.E. 117 miles; from Quilon S.E. 33 miles; from Trivandrum N.N.E. 10 miles; from the sea E. 13 miles. Pagoda [q.v.].——*Neittincara* (നെയ്യാറ്റിങ്കര - neyyáttinkara, Mal.). From (ney, mal. ghee + áru, mal. river + kara, mal. village). Talook; Trivandrum division; area 213 square miles; villages or caras, 151; pop. 110,410; Sub-divided into 10 praverties and containing 151 caras or villages. Greatest length, N. to S. 25 miles. Greatest breadth, E. to W., 16 miles. Bounded N. by Tinnevelly district, E. by Velavancode talook, S. by the Indian ocean, and W. by Trivandrum and Nedoovengaud talooks. Weaving coarse cloth. There are some tanks and a river, viz., Neyyaur. The town and Tahsildar's station; pop. 23,107; is in lat. 8° 24′; long. 77° 08′; from Alleppey S.E. 89 miles; from Cottayam S.S.E. 89 miles; from Madras S.W. 385 miles; from Nagarcoil W. 28 miles; from Paravore S.S.E. 131 miles; from Quilon S.E. 47 miles; from Trivandrum E.S.E. 11 miles; from the sea E. 8 miles. Large Nayar [q.v.] town with pagoda [q.v.] and Cottauram [q.v.].——*Neyttode* (നെയ്തോട് - neytótu, Mal.). From (ney, mal. ghee + tótu, mal. canal). Village; Cottayam division, Aulangaud tal.; lat. 10° 10′; long. 76° 27′; from Aulangaud E.N.E. 8 miles; from Trivandrum N.N.W. 119 miles; from the sea E. 16 miles. Celebrated pagoda.——*Neyyaur* (നെയ്യാർ - neyyár, Mal.). From (ney, mal. ghee + áru, mal. river). Sanscrit name (ghritamálá), meaning ghee + garland. River; Trivandrum division, Nedoovengaud and Neittincara talooks. Rises near Agastyacootam peak, passes through Neittincara and Nedoovengaud, and flows south-west into the sea near Poovaur having previously dilated into a small lagoon. Length, 35 miles. Not much used for cultivation. The river is rapid and navigable for boats for only 8 miles from its mouth, boats not proceeding beyond Neittincara, though timber rafts may be floated down from the hills. A succession of small water-falls occurs in the early part of its course, and it descends into the plains in a cataract of considerable size [aroovy].——*Ochira* (ഓച്ചിറ - óççara, Mal.). See sep. title.——*Oodayagherry* (ഉദയഗിരി - udayagiri, Mal.). See sep. title.——*Ooloor* (ഉള്ളൂർ - ullúr, Mal.). From (ul, mal. interior + úr, mal. village). Village; Trivandrum division, Trivandrum tal.; pop. 6,614; lat. 8° 32′; long. 76° 58′; from Cape comorin N.W. 52 miles; from Trivandrum N. 4 miles; from the sea E. 5 miles. Temple to Soobramanya sawmy [soobramanyan]. Annual festival. The Maharajah visits the pagoda [q.v.] on Tircaurtigay [pundigay,

5c] in December.——*Padanayarcoolangara* (പടനായർകുളങ്ങര - patanáyarkulannara, Mal.). From (patanáyar, mal. náyar sepoy + kulannara, mal. tank side); a place for nayar sepoys. Village, Head-quarters of Tahsildar and Registrar; Quilon division, Caroonaugapully tal.; lat. 9° 04′; long. 76° 35′; from Alleppey S.S.E. 32 miles; from Cottayam S. 36 miles; from Madras S.W. 370 miles; from Nagarcoil N.W. 84 miles; from Paravore S.S.E. 77 miles; from Quilon N.N.W. 12 miles; from Trivandrum N.W. 48 miles; from the sea E. 3 miles. About 3 miles east of the main line of water communication from Quilon to Cochin. Former possession of the Cauyancollam rajahs and used by them as a military station.——*Palayaur* (പഴയാർ - pazhayár, Mal.). See sep. title.——*Paliport* (പള്ളിപ്പുറം - pallippuram, Mal.). See sep. title.——*Pambah* (പമ്പാനദി - pampánadi, Mal.). See sep. title.——*Paravore* (പറവൂർ - paravúr, Mal.). See sep. title.——*Paulore* (പാലൂർ - pálúr, Mal.). From (pál, mal. milk + úr, mal. village). Village; Pudmanaubhapooram division, Yerraneel tal.; lat. 8° 15′; long. 77° 16′; from Yerraneel W.N.W. 7 miles; from Trivandrum S.E. 24 miles; from the sea N. 5 miles.——*Peeravanam* (പിറവനം - píravanam, Mal.). From (pír, hind. saint + vana, san. forest). Title otherwise Piravam. Village; Cottayam division, Mooatpoya tal.; lat. 9° 53′; long. 76° 23′; from Mooatpoya S.W. 10 miles; from Trivandrum N.N.W. 100 miles; from the sea E. 15 miles. On the margin of a fine river. Church and pagoda.——*Peermaid* (പീരുമേട് - pírumétu, Mal.). See sep. title.——*Perambavore* (പെരുമ്പാവൂർ - perumpávúr, Mal.). From (perum, mal. large + pál, mal. milk + úr, mal. village). Title otherwise Perambalore. Town, Tahsildar's station; Cottayam division, Coonnatnaud tal.; lat. 10° 07′; long. 76° 31′; from Alleppey N.N.E. 43 miles; from Cottayam N. 36 miles; from Madras S.W. 325 miles; from Nagarcoil N.N.W. 145 miles; from Paravore E.S.E. 17 miles; from Quilon N. 83 miles; from Trivandrum N.N.W. 116 miles; from the sea E. 18 miles. Capital of a district.——*Periyaur* (പെരിയാർ - periyár, Mal.). See sep. title.——*Poonalore* (പുനലൂർ - punalúr, Mal.). From (punal, mal. river + úr, mal. village). Village; Quilon division, Putnapooram tal.; lat. 9° 01′; long. 76° 58′; from Putnapooram S.E. 7 miles; from Trivandrum N. 37 miles; from the sea E. 27 miles. On Cullada or Poonalore river, on the main road from Quilon to Shencottah. The river is crossed by a suspension bridge. Seat of a paper-mill.——*Poondora* (പൂന്തുറ - púntura, Mal.). From (pú, mal. flower + tura, mal. harbour). Village, Port; Trivandrum division, Trivandrum tal.; lat. 8° 25′; long. 77° 00′; from Bombay S.S.E. 760 miles; from Trivandrum S. 5 miles. Port of Trivandrum.——*Poonyautt* (പുണ്യാറ് - punyátt, Mal.). From (punya, san. virtue + áru, mal. river). Title otherwise Poonnautt. Village; Cottayam division, Meenachel tal.; lat. 9° 40′; long. 76° 50′; from Laulam S.E. 8 miles; from Quilon N.E. 54 miles; from Trivandrum N. 81 miles; from Tinnevelly N.W. 87 miles; from the sea E. 33 miles. Residence of the chief of that name. A few Nayar [q.v.] habitations.——*Pooracadav* (പുറക്കടവ് - purakkatavu, Mal.). From (pura, mal. outside + katavu, mal. landing place). Village; Cottayam division, Paravore tal.; pop. 7,698; lat. 10° 12′; long. 76° 22′; from Paravore N.E. 8 miles; from Trivandrum N.N.W. 123 miles; from the sea E. 12 miles. Residence of the nominal rajah of Paravore. Being a numboory [q.v.] his presence attracts great number of Bramins [q.v.].——*Pooraly* (പുരളി - purali, Mal.). See sep. title.——*Poovaur* (പൂവാർ - púvár, Mal.). From (pú, mal. flower + áru, mal. river). Village, Port; Trivandrum division, Neittincara tal.; lat. 8° 19′; long. 77° 07′; from Neittincara S.S.W. 6 miles; from Bombay S.S.E. 768 miles; from Paravore S.S.E. 136 miles; from Quilon S.E. 50 miles; from Trivandrum S.E. 14 miles. Small crafts are built. A salt [ooppoo] bankshaul [q.v.].——*Porvolly* (പോരുവഴി - póruvazhi, Mal.). From (póru, mal. war + vazhi, mal. way). Village; Quilon division, Coonnatore tal.; pop. 7,957; lat. 9° 05′; long. 76° 42′; from Coonnatore W.N.W. 2 miles; from Trivandrum N.N.W. 45 miles; from the sea E. 10 miles. Important mart and large town.——*Pudmanaubhapooram* (പത്മനാഭപുരം - patmanábhapuram, Mal.). See sep. title.——*Pullipooram* (പള്ളിപ്പുറം - pallippuram, Mal.). From (palli, mal. church + puram, mal. backside). Village; Trivandrum division, Trivandrum tal.; pop. 7,695; lat. 8° 36′; long. 76° 54′; from Trivandrum N.W. 10 miles; from the sea E. 3 miles. Betel [q.v.] cultivation.——*Pundalam* (പന്തളം - pantalam, Mal.). From (pan, mal. beautiful + talam, mal. plateau). Village; Quilon division, Mauvelicara and Chenganore tals.; pop. 29,666; lat. 9° 14′; long. 76° 43′; from Chenganore E. 9 miles; from Mauvelicára E. 9 miles; from Trivandrum N.N.W. 55 miles; from the sea E. 18 miles. Originally called Iroor swaroopam. Now residence of the Rajah of that name, a nominal chief. Several pagodas [q.v.].——*Putnapooram* (പത്തനാപുരം - pattanápuram, Mal.). From (pattanáva, corruption of padmanábha, san. vishnu, the lotus navelled + pura, san. city). Sanscrit name (padmanábhapura), meaning the same. Talook, Quilon division; pop. 37,094, its area about 400 square miles. Greatest length, N. to S., 24 miles and the greatest breadth, E. to W., 16 miles. Sub-divided into 7 praverties and containing 80 caras or villages. Bounded N. by Coonnatore and Chenganore talooks, E. by Shencottah talook, S. by Nedooven-gaud talook and W. by Cottaura cara talook. Tea [q.v.] and cocoa [q.v.] are cultivated on the hills. The village and Tahsildar's station is in lat. 9° 5′; long. 76° 54′; from Alleppey S.E. 45 miles; from Cottayam S.E. 42 miles; from Madras S.W. 357 miles; from Nagarcoil N.N.W. 72 miles; from Paravore S.S.E. 84 miles; from Quilon N.E. 22 miles; from Trivandrum N. 41 miles; from Tinnevelly W.N.W. 62 miles; from the sea E. 25 miles. Mart frequented by Tinnevelly merchants.——*Quilon* (കൊല്ലം - kollam, Mal.). See sep. title.——*Ramamungalam* (രാമമംഗലം - rámámannalam, Mal.). From (ráma, san. the god + mangala, san. prosperity). Village; Cottayam division, Mooatpoya tal.; pop. 9,953; lat. 9° 56′; long. 76° 32′; from Mooatpoya W.S.W. 7 miles; from Trivandrum N.N.W. 102 miles; from the sea E. 15 miles; A conspicuous pagoda [q.v.] on the bank of the river.——*Rauny* (റാന്നി - ráni, Mal.). From (rájñí, san. queen). Village; Quilon division, Chenganore tal.; pop. 6,624; lat. 9° 22′; long. 76° 49′; from Chenganore E.N.E. 15 miles; from Trivandrum N. 62 miles; from the sea E. 27 miles. On a rock overhanging the Pambah. Belongs to the Syrians [q.v.].——*Red cliffs* (വർക്കലക്കുന്നു - varkkalakkunnu, Mal.). See sep. title.——*Shaunaurgoody* (ശാന്നാർകുടി - shánár-kuti, Mal.). From (shánán, mal. toddy drawer + kuti, mal. habitation). Village, Port; Pudmanaubhapooram division, Agasteeshwaram tal.; lat. 8° 6′; long. 77° 36′; from Bombay S.S.E. 794 miles; from Cadiapatam E. 17 miles; from Mannacoody N.E. 5 miles; from Trivandrum E.S.E. 48 miles; from Sooshindram S.E. 7 miles. In the bay N.E. of Cape comorin.——*Shencottah* (ചെങ്കോട്ട - chenkótta, Mal.). See sep. title.——*Sheranellore* (ശേരാനെല്ലൂർ - shéránellúr, Mal.). From (chéra, mal. the kingdom + nel, mal. paddy + úr, mal. village). Village; Cottayam division, Connatnaud tal.; pop. 10,720; lat. 10° 11′; long. 76° 31′; from Perambavore N. 4 miles; from Trivandrum N.N.W. 118 miles; from the sea E. 21 miles. Nayar village on the Periyaur. Pagoda.——*Shertála* (ചേർത്തല - chérttala, Mal.). See sep. title.——*Showrimala* (ശൗരിമല - shaurimala, Mal.). See sep. title.——*Sooshindram* (ശുചീന്ദ്രം - shuchíndram, Mal.). See sep. title.——*Tamrapurny* (താമ്രപർണ്ണി - támraparnni, Mal.). See sep. title.——*Taulacoody* (താഴക്കുടി - tázhakkuti, Mal.). From (tázha, mal. screwpine, pandanus odoratissimus, linn. f. + kuti, mal. hut). Village; Pudmanaubhapooram division, Tovaula tal.; pop. 5,830; lat. 8° 14′; long. 77° 30′; from Bhootapaundy S. 3 miles; from Trivandrum E.S.E. 37 miles; from the sea N. 10 miles. Tank. Noted for its earthenware. Near it there once were extensive stables known as Maudhavaulayam belonging to Travancore kings.——*Tengyé-putnam* (തേങ്ങാപ്പട്ടണം - tenkaipattanam, Mal.). From (ténkáy, tam. cocoanut, cocos nucifera, linn. + pattana, san. city). Mal. also (tánkapattanam), meaning gold + village by corruption. Village, Port; Pudmanaubhapooram division, Velavancode tal.; lat. 8° 14′; long. 77° 13′; from Coolitora S.S.W. 6 miles; from Bombay S.S.E. 778 miles; from Colachel N.N.W. 7 miles; from Trivandrum S.E. 23 miles; from Vilinjam S.E. 16 miles. At the mouth of the river Tamrapurny, behind Enciam island and between Trivandrum and Cape comorin.——*Tircodatanam* (തൃക്കോടിത്താനം - trikkótattanam, Mal.). From (tri, mal. holy + kóti, mal. west + tánam, mal. place). Sanscrit name (shrí-kótist'hána), meaning prosperity + corner + place. Seat of prosperity. Village; Cottayam division, Chungacherry tal.; lat. 9° 26′; long. 76° 36′; from Chungacherry E.S.E. 3 miles; from Trivandrum N.N.W. 70 miles; from the sea E. 15 miles. Large Nayar [q.v.] population. Temple.——*Tirnundicara* (തിരുനന്ദിക്കര - tirunandikkara, Mal.). From (tiru, mal. holy + nandi, san. shiva's bull + kara, mal. village). Village; Pudmanaubhapooram division, Cullcoolam tal.; lat. 8° 24′; long. 77° 20′; from Trivandrum E.S.E. 24 miles; from the sea E. 22 miles. Celebrated pagoda [q.v.] to Shiva [q.v.]. Rock of peculiar geological formation.——*Tiroovalla* (തിരുവല്ല - tiruvallá, Mal.). From (tiru, mal. holy + villu, mal. bow). After rama, the bowman. Sanscrit name (vallabhagráma), meaning vallabha, the lord + village; vishnoo, the lord of lutchmy; Quilon division; pop. 103,007. Dimensions:—extreme length, N. to S., 9 miles; extreme breadth, E. to W., 25 miles. Sub-divided into 8 praverties [q.v.] and consisting of 150 caras [q.v.] or villages. Bounded N. by Chungacherry talook, E. by the hills, S. by Chenganore talook, and W. by Ambalapoya talook. Several small canals from the Manimala and Pambah rivers. The town and head-quarters of talook are in lat. 9° 22′; long. 76° 36′; from Aleppey E.S.E. 17 miles; from Cottayam S. 15 miles; from Madras S.W. 360 miles; from Nagarcoil N.W. 98 miles; from Paravore S.S.E. 57 miles; from Quilon N. 32 miles; from Trivandrum N.N.W. 65 miles; from the sea E. 14 miles. On the Manimala. Previous to 1796 of commercial note, but has declined since capture of Cochin by British. Large antique pagoda [q.v.], only exceeded by Trivandrum. Syrian [q.v.] christian church.——*Tirpárapp* (തൃപ്പരപ്പ് - tripparappu, Mal.).

From (tri, mal. holy + parappu, mal. expansion). Village; Pudmanaubhapooram division, Cullcoolam tal.; lat. 8° 23′; long. 77° 18′; from Trivandrum E.S.E. 21 miles; from the sea N. 15 miles. A small village near Tirvattaur. Being at foot of hills, is used for training elephants [q.v.]. Pagoda to Shiva near a cataract on Codayaur.——*Tirvallam* (തിരുവല്ലം - tiruvallam, Mal.). See sep. title.——*Tirvancode* (തിരുവാങ്കോട് - tiruvánkótu, Mal.). See sep. title.——*Tirvattaur* (തിരുവട്ടാർ - tiruvattár, Mal.). From (tiru, mal. holy + vattam, mal. circle + áru, mal. river). The river Tamrapurny here winds round the pagoda. Village, Place of pilgrimage; Pudmanaubhapooram division, Cullcoolam tal.; pop. 10,073; lat. 8° 20′; long. 77° 19′; from Pudmanaubhapooram N.W. 7 miles; from Trivandrum E.S.E. 23 miles; from the sea N. 11 miles. Ancient village. On the Tamrapurny. Ancient Vishnoo pagoda.——*Todoopoya* (തൊടുപുഴ - totupuzha, Mal.). From (totu, mal. to bite + puzha, mal. river). Talook; Cottayam division; pop. 24,321. Extreme length, N. to S., 40 miles. Extreme breadth, E. to W. 30 miles. Sub-divided into 5 praverties and containing 88 caras or villages. Bounded N. by Mooatpoya talook and the Cochin state, E. and S. by the hills and Chunganacherry talook, W. by Meenachel and Mooatpoya talooks. Irrigated by Todoopoya river. The village is at foot of ghauts [q.v.] almost entirely inhabited by Mahomedans engaged in trade. Much mountain produce is collected here.——*Tooravore* (തുറവൂർ - turavúr, Mal.). From (tura, mal. frequented place + úr, mal. village). Village; Cottayam division, Shertala tal.; pop. 18,187; lat. 9° 46′; long. 76° 22′; from Shertala N.N.W. 6 miles; from Aleppey N. 18 miles; from Trivandrum N.N.W. 97 miles; from the sea E. 2 miles. Within a few miles of the coast, on a long narrow strip of sandy tract inhabited by Concanies who have settled here for trade. Concany [q.v.] pagoda [q.v.].——*Toraule* (തോവാഴ - tóvázha, Mal.). Talook; Pudmanaubhapooram division; pop. 30,260; extreme length, N. to S., 19 miles; extreme breadth, E. to W., 12 miles. Sub-divided into 6 pidaugas [q.v.] and containing 158 caras [q.v.] or villages. Bounded on the N. and E. by the Tinnevelly district, S. by Agasteeshwaram talook, W. by Cullcoolam talook; physical aspect. The northern portion is covered with dense forests. Fertile. Coffee [q.v.] and tea [q.v.] are produced in the hills. Palayaur, Poottanaur, and Anantanaur rivers. Anicuts across the Palayaur. The village is in lat. 8° 14′; long. 77° 33′; from Bhootapaundy S.E. 5 miles; from Trivandrum E.S.E. 41 miles; from the sea N. 11 miles. Pagoda [q.v.] and Ootpera [q.v.]. Has an extensive Conjee [q.v.] house for feeding the poor.——*Travancore hills* (തിരുവിതാംകൂർമല - tiruvitánkúrmala, Mal.). See sep. title.——*Tricoonnapoya* (തൃക്കുന്നപ്പുഴ - trikkunnappuzha, Mal.). From (tri, mal. holy + kunnu, mal. hillock + puzha, mal. river). Village; Quilon division, Caurtigapully tal.; pop. 5,771; lat. 9° 15′; long. 76° 27′; from Aripaud S.W. 4 miles; from Trivandrum N.W. 64 miles; from the sea E. ½ mile. Belongs to the Yidapully rajah. On the bank of the canal connected with Cauyancollam lake. Pagoda under water. Palace.——*Trippappore* (തൃപ്പാപ്പൂർ - trippáppúr, Mal.). From (trippáppa, mal. holy father, the dynasty of travancore rajahs + úr, mal. village). Village, Place of pilgrimage; Trivandrum division, Trivandrum tal. Small ancient village from which royal family name of Tripaudatt swaroopam [q.v.] is derived.——*Trivandrum* (തിരുവനന്തപുരം - tiruvananta-puram, Mal.). See sep. title.——*Tungacherry* (തങ്കശ്ശേരി - tankashshéri, Mal.). See sep. title.——*Tunnymook* (തണ്ണീർമുക്ക് - tannírmukk, Mal.). From (tannír mal. water + mukku, mal corner). Village; Cottayam division, Shertala tal.; pop. 12,048; lat. 9° 41′; long. 76° 26′; from Shertala E.S.E. 3 miles; from Trivandrum N.N.W. 90 miles; from the sea E. 7 miles. On a low cape opposite Codayvaichore promontory. Pagoda [q.v.] and Chowky [q.v.].——*Vanjipoya* (വഞ്ഞിപ്പുഴ - vaññip-puzha, Mal.). From (vaññi, mal. a species of wild thorny creeper + puzha, mal. river); from the weeds that abound in the paramba. Zemindarry village, Yidavaga, or dependency attached to the Travancore state; Quilon division, Chenganore talook. In by-gone days female members of the Travancore royal family once took refuge in this place.——*Vaulrampooram* (ബാലരാമപുരം - bálarámapuram, Mal.). From (bálaráma, san. hindoo proper name, name of a former maharajah of travancore + pura, san. city). Town; Trivandrum division, Neittincara tal.; lat. 8° 25′; long. 77° 5′; from Neittincara W.N.W. 4 miles; from Trivandrum E.S.E. 7 miles; from the sea E. 6 miles. Modern and flourishing town, founded by Oommany tumby.——*Vaumanapooram* (വാമനപുരം - vámanapuram, Mal.). See sep. title.——*Vauriyore* (വാരിയൂർ - váriyúr, Mal.). From (vári, san. water + úr, mal. village). Village; Pudmanaubhapooram division, Agasteeshwaram tal.; lat. 8° 08′; long. 77° 36′; from Sooshindram E. 6 miles; from Trivandrum E.S.E. 46 miles; from the sea W. 1¼ miles. On the coast north-east of Cape comorin. Salt manufactured on a small scale.——*Veily* (വെലി - vaili, Mal.). Village, Port; Trivandrum division, Trivandrum tal.; lat. 8° 31′; long. 76° 55′; from Bombay S.S.E. 760 miles; from Caracoolam W.S.W. 8 miles; from Trivandrum W.N.W. 5 miles. Near mouth of a small backwater of same name.——*Veippore* (വൈപ്പൂർ - vaippúr, Mal.). From (veppu, mal. deposit + úr, mal. village). Village; Quilon division, Tiroovalla tal.; lat. 9° 27′; long. 76° 44′; from Tiroovalla E.N.E. 11 miles; from Trivandrum N.N.W. 69 miles; from the sea E. 25 miles. On the Manimala; church.——*Velavancode* (വേലവങ്കോട് - velavankótu, Mal.). From (vélavan, mal. spear-man + kótu, mal. fort). Talook; Pudmanaubhapooram division; pop. 69,688. Extreme length, N. to S., 24 miles; extreme breadth, E. to W., 7 miles. Sub-divided into 8 praverties and containing 114 caras or villages. Bounded N. by Tinnevelly district, E. by Cullcoolam and Yerraneel talooks, S. by the Indian ocean and W. by Neittincara talooks. The Tamrapurny which flows through the talook is of little use to cultivation. The village is in lat. 8° 18′; long. 77° 14′; from Coolitora W.S.W. 1 mile; from Trivandrum S.E. 20 miles; from the sea E. 7 miles.——*Vellangore* (വെള്ളങ്കൂർ - vellankúr, Mal.). From (vellam, mal. water + kúr, mal. share). Village; lat. 10° 3′; long. 76° 28′; from Trivandrum N.N.W. 111 miles; from Cochin E.N.E. 14 miles; from the sea E. 14 miles.——*Vembanaud* (വെമ്പനാട് - vempanátu, Mal.). See sep. title.——*Verapoly* (വരാഹപ്പുഴ - varáhappuzha, Mal.). See sep. title.——*Vijiapooram* (വിജയപുരം - vijayapuram, Mal.). From (vijaya, san. victory + pura, san. city). Village; Cottayam division, Cottayam, tal.; pop. 15,619; lat. 9° 36′; long. 76° 38′; from Cottayam E. 5 milas; from Trivandrum N.N.W. 80 miles; from the sea E. 18 miles. Large Nayar [q.v.] village with conspicuous págoda [q.v.].——*Vilinjam* (വിഴിഞ്ഞം - vizhiññam, Mal.). Village; Trivandrum division, Neittincara tal.; lat. 8° 23′; long. 77° 02′; from Neittincara W. 7 miles; from Trivandrum S.S.E. 7 miles. Small fishing village on the coast. Vessels take in cargoes of fish. Former seat of a Dutch factory.——*Waddiyaur* (വടിയാർ - vatiyár, Mal.). From (vati, mal. to empty + áru, mal. river). River in which so many rivers empty their contents. Village; Cottayam division, Wycome tal.; pop. 8,645. Large market town. Formerly of great note.——*Warkully* (വർക്കല - varkkala, Mal.). See sep. title.——*Wuttacottah* (വട്ടക്കോട്ട - vattakkótta, Mal.). From (vatta, mal. round + kótta, mal. fort). Village; Pudmanaubhapooram division, Agasteeshwaram tal.; lat. 8° 07′; long. 77° 36′; from Sooshindram E. 7 miles; from Trivandrum E.S.E. 48 miles; on the seashore. Fort near Cape comorin built into the sea, now deserted.——*Wycome* (വൈക്കം - vaikkam, Mal.). See sep. title.——*Yaittmanore* (ഏറ്റുമാനൂർ - éttumánúr, Mal.). From (éttumán, mal. bullman, epithet of shiva + úr, mal. village). Talook; Cottayam division; pop. 79,058. Extreme length, N. to S., 12 miles, extreme breadth, E. to W., 25 miles; sub-divided into 6 praverties [q.v.] and containing 76 caras [q.v.] or villages. Bounded N. by Wycome talook and the Cochin State, E. by Mooatpoya and Meenachel talooks, S. by Cottayam talook and W. by the Vembanaud lake. Irrigated by the Meenachel river. The village, Tahsildar's station, Place of pilgrimage is in lat. 9° 40′; long. 76° 36′; from Alleppey N.E. 20 miles; from Cottayam N.N.E. 7 miles; from Nagarcoil N.N.W. 116 miles; from Paravore S.S.E. 40 miles; from Quilon N. 53 miles; from Trivandrum N.N.W. 84 miles; from the sea E. 18 miles. Chiefly occupied by Puttar [q.v.] bramins engaged in traffic. Celebrated Shiva temple. Annual festival. As place of pilgrimage next in importance to Wycome.——*Yeddowa* (ഇടവഴി - itavazhi, Mal.). From (ita, mal. middle + vazhi, mal. way). Village, Port; Trivandrum division, Cherankeel tal.; lat. 8° 46′; long. 76° 45′; from Attingal W. 9 miles; from Trivandrum N.W. 25 miles. A small village two miles from Warkully. Boxes and other materials of cane [rattan] manufactured.——*Yerraneel* (ഇരണിയൽ - iraniyal, Mal.). See sep. title.——*Yidapully* (ഇടപ്പള്ളി - itappalli, Mal.). See sep. title.——**(2)** *Travancore hills* (തിരുവിതാംകൂർമല - tiruvitámkúrmala, Mal.). Hills; Travancore state. The portion of Western ghauts [q.v.] or Sahya parvatam, which is situated along eastern frontier of Travancore, running by side of the following talooks:—Tovaula, Cullcoolam, Velavancode, Neittincara, Nedoovengaud, Cottaura cara, Putnapooram, Shencottah, Chenganore and Todoopoya. This range forms also the extreme southern portion of Eastern ghauts. The course of the Travancore hills is very irregular, forming a concourse of distinct ridges rather than a single chain. The outline in the north is bold, but tolerably uniform, a few cliffs and conical summits alone breaking its regularity. Towards south it is broken into every variety of form. Westwards and southwards from these high ridges the country presents a succession of clusters of hills of various heights, more or less distinct from each other, and of low but intricate chains and spurs. The highest hills are usually naked in their summits, and a large portion of their slopes is also free from forests. The ravines and bases of the mountain are covered with dense forests of lofty trees, which abound with wild animals. From these hills to the sea-coast and borders of the lake, especially in the more southern districts, these highlands gradually slope downwards to an undulating tableland, which falls gently to the level of the plains. Amongst the labyrinth of mountains there are some rough elevated tablelands, but the transition from hill to dale is, in most cases, too rapid to allow of any large extent of waving upland. The form of the separate hills is generally in the northern parts rather round with considerable but gradual declivities, than precipitous; but towards the south, bleak and craggy tops of very irregular shape are frequent. The valleys dilate in width as the elevation of the hills diminishes. The more important ridges in the mountainous parts are steep and precipitous in their declivity, narrow in their summits and furrowed by chasms or ravines whose contracted breadth scarcely allows space for the winding rivulets which drain them. The hills lying between Periyaur and Dindigul enclose within their recesses some small open elevated plains copiously watered and affording pasturage for cattle of the neighbouring country and enjoying a good climate for a part of the year. Average altitude of summits of these ghauts [q.v.] is about 4,000 feet. Amongst the more important of the summits are the following:—Agastyacootam, Anamullay, Anwartamala, Chunganaud, Codiyattore mala, Cullanaud peak, Mahendragherry, Maroothamala, Nedoombauray, Paupanausam peak, Poermaid, Periyamullay.——*Travancore lines* (നോട്ടുകോട്ട - notunkótta, Mal.). Means long fort. A mud wall, with stone bastions and forts at intervals, extending from Paliport to the Ghauts a distance of 40 miles, constructed in 1766 by Travancore government as a means of protection from the encroachments of Mysorians. Here in 1789 Tippoo was repulsed in an attempt to force an entrance through the wall. Ruins visible here and there. Also another from Arambolly to sea on Tinnevelly frontier.

TRAVELLER'S PALM (நீர்வாழை - nírvágai, *Tam.*). Title from usefulness. Tam. from (nír, tam. water + vázhai, tam. plantain, musa paradisiaca, linn.), from leaves like plantain and holding water at their bases. Title otherwise Madagascar palm. Botanically Ravenalia. madagascariensis, som., musaceæ [vricsham, 142]. Thick succulent stem, long, broad leaves like those of the plantain [q.v.], only less fragile, and rising not round the stalk but in two lines on opposite sides; tree presents appearance of a large open fan; many thirty feet from the ground to lowest leaves; containing fresh water in thick firm ends of the stalks of the leaves. No other species here.

TREE SNAKE (गोनास - gónása *San.*; جهاڑ کا سانپ - jhárkásámp, *Hind.*; చెట్టురుకుపాము - chetturukupámu, *Tel.*; കൊമ്പേരിമൂർഖൻ - kompérimúrkhan, *Mal.*; கொம்பேறிமூக்கன் - kombérimúkkan, *Tam.*). Title from haunt. San. from (gó, san. cow + nására, san. nose); ox-nosed. Hind. from (jhár, hind. tree + sámp. hind. snake). Tel. from (chettu, tel. tree + uruku, tel. to leap + pámu, tel. snake). Mal. from tamul. Tam. from (kombu, tam. branch + éru, tam. to climb + múkku, tam. nose). Tel. also (parugudupámu), meaning running + snake. The terms may be considered co-extensive with the family Dendrophidæ ophidii colubriformes, ophidia [sarpam], reptilia [sarpy, 20], of naturalists [jantoo]. However many other snakes mount trees. The Dendrophidæ have the body and tail much compressed or very slender and elongate; head generally elongate, narrow, flat, depressed, distinct from the slender neck; snout rather long, obtuse or rounded in front; cleft of the mouth wide; nostril lateral; eye of moderate size or large with round pupil; shields of the head normal; scales generally narrow and much imbricate; ventral shields generally with two keels, rising on the sides; subcaudals two-rowed; no large fang either in front or in the middle of the upper jaw. Diurnal species, living in trees, feeding chiefly on tree-lizards. There is a Tamul proverb:—சுடுகாட்டுப் புகையைப் பார்க்கும் கொம்பேறி மூக்கன்—"the tree snake looks anxiously for the smoke of "the funeral pyre;" referring to certainty of death. The two South indian genera are Clerysopelea and Dendrophis [combairy mookkan].

TRI (त्रि - tri, *San.*). Three. Prefix in place names; as Tricootam, meaning three peaks.——*Tadiya* (తదియ - tadiya, Tel.). Corruption of (tritíyá, san. third). Third tity [q.v.] of either waxing or waning moon [pacsham] of any mouth [acsha tadiya]. Same as Triteeyay.——*Teora* (تیورا - teurá, Beng.). From (triputi, san. lathyrus sativus, linn.). Same as Casauree.——*Teory* (تیوری - teori, Beng.). From (trivrit, san. turbith). Same as Turbith.——*Teyrah* (تیرا - terá, Hind.). Thirteen.——*Teyrah teyzee* (تیرا تیزی - terátezí, Hind.). From (terá, hind. thirteen + tezí, hind. bitter day). Observances on the first thirteen days of Safar [maheena] especially by lower classes. See vol. I (96).——*Trayam* (त्रय - traya, San.). Three.——*Trayodashy* (త్రయోదశి - trayódashi, Tel.). From (traya, san. three + dash, san. ten). Lunar [chaundramaunam] festival [pundigay, 3e]. The thirteenth tity [q.v.] of the waxing [shooclapacsham] or the waning [krishnapacsham] moon of any month. Thirteenth or twenty-eighth lunar day.——*Treiraushy* (त्रैराशि - trairáshi, San.). From (above + ráshi, san. quantity). The common rule of three.——*Treivarnica* (त्रैवर्णिक - traivarnika, San.). From (above + varna, san. caste). A generic name for the three superior castes. Also sometimes for Comaties [q.v.], as people of the third caste [jauty].——*Tretay* (त्रेता - trétá, San.). From (tri, san. three). The second age of the four ages or yoogs [q.v.] of the world represented by the series 4, 3, 2 and 1.——*Tribhoovanamulla* (ತ್ರಿಭುವನಮಲ್ಲ - tribhuvanamalla, Can.). From (above + bhuvana, san. world + malla, san. wrestler). Cadamba [q.v.] royal title.——*Tricalasham* (त्रिकलश - trikalasha, San.). From (above + kalasha, san. peak). Island [britastaun].——*Tricalingam* (त्रिकलिङ्ग - trikalinga, San.). From (above + kalinga, san. the country so called). The three Calingams [trilingam].——*Tricarashoory* (திரிகரசூரி - tirigarasúri, Tam.). From (above + kara, san. hand + shúrí, san. heroine). One of the seven matrons [mautah] in the temple of Ayenaur [ayen].——*Trijyay* (त्रिज्या - trijyá, San.). From (jyá, san. sine). Literally sine of three; meaning of three signs [raushy] or 90 degrees [bhaugam]. Radius.——*Trijye* (త్రిజ్యే - trijáyi, Tel.). Mahratta word. One-third of the assessment [trishwaicam].——*Trikonam* (त्रिकोण - trikóna, San.). From (above + kóna, sam angle). Triangle. Sama trikonam is equilateral; Vishama trikonam is scalene; Dwisáma trikonam is isosceles. Coty is the upright side of a right-angled triangle [mookkonam]. The equilateral triangle in Hindoo mythology, when the apex points downwards, is symbolical of Vishnoo [q.v.], considered as the principle of humidity, to descend being the property of water. When with the apex upwards, it is a symbol of Shiva [q.v.] as fire.——*Trilingam* (त्रिलिङ्ग - trilinga, San.). Country of the three lingams [q.v.]. Sanscrit corruption for Tricalingam, or the three Calingams [q.v.]. By Appacavy regarded as the derivation of Teloogoo, which is fanciful; there is no reason why the teloogoos should not have a name for their own language, as have each of the other dravidian nations [calingam, lingam, teloogoo]. Trilingam occurs in the Amara cosham, Bramhottara khandam, chapter xvi, applied not to language but to the Tripoondram [q.v.], or triple line drawn by sheiveites across the forehead. See vol. I (3), (132).——*Trilocam* (त्रिलोक - trilóka, San.). Three worlds [locam]; earth, sky, and heaven.——*Trilochanan* (त्रिलोचन - trilóchana, San.). From (above + lóchana, san. eye). Three-eyed Shiva. Name of a Pahlava [q.v.] king. See vol. I (129).——*Trimoorty* (त्रिमूर्ति - trimúrti, San; திருமூர்த்தி - tirumúrtti, Tam.). From (above + múrti, san. form). Moommoorty [q.v.] among the Tamulians. Hindoo trinity of gods. It was foreshadowed in the Vedic association of the three gods, Agny [q.v.], Vayoo [q.v.] and Sooryan [q.v.]; fire, wind and sun. Philosophers endeavoured to unite the conflicting claims of Shiva [q.v.] and Vishnoo [q.v.], and first conceived of Hariharan [q.v.], who combined the two. Then the original Bramha [q.v.] was added, making a triad. The acceptance of the triad as an article of creed was of late growth and special to Southern india. Philosophically the Trimoorty implies the unity of the three principles of creation, preservation, destruction. When represented, the Trimoorty is one body with three heads; in the middle that of Bramha, at its right that of Vishnoo, at its left that of Shiva. The symbol of the Trimoorty is the mystical syllable Om [q.v.]. The Bhaugavata pooraunam [q.v.] specially maintains the essential oneness of the three deities. The Vayoo pooraunam says that the three names signify the sautwicam, raujasam, and taumasa goonams [q.v.] or qualities. By other authorities Bramha is the earth, Vishnoo the sun, and Shiva the moon. By others again Bramha is time, Vishnoo is water, and Shiva is fire. Some poets make Bramha the sky by day, Vishnoo dark blue the sky at night, and Shiva pale or ashy the sky by moonlight. The legend of the Veishnava pooraunams is that from the navel of Narayanan [q.v.] or the original first cause sleeping on the sea, a lotus [nelumbo] stalk proceeded, in the flower of which Bramha was born, who made Vishnoo and Shiva to preserve and destroy. The Hebrews held the existence of three sephiroth or lights in the one deity; these were represented by three yods on the letter shin or by three yods in a circle. See vol. I (74), (78) [matam]. Trimoorty also serves as a Hindoo 2nd or pers. name [peyar].——*Trincomalee* (திருக்கோணமலை - tirukkónamalai, Tam.). From (above + kóna, san. corner + malai, san. mountain). A port with a fine harbour on the E. coast of Ceylon [q.v.]. Distinguish from Trinomallee.——*Trincomalee tree* (సరళదేవదారు - saraladévadáru, Tel.; හල්මිලිල - halmilila, Singh; திருக்கோணமலைமரம் - tirukkónamalaimaram, Tam.). Title after the town in ceylon. Tel. from (sarala, san. straight + dévadáru, san. tree, erythroxylon monogynum, roxb.). Tam. from (tirukkónamalai, tam. trincomalee + maram, tam. tree). Singh. also (somendilla). Tam. also (shayandalai), by corruption from singhalese. Title otherwise Ceylon ash, Trincomalee red wood. Botanically Berrya ammonilla, roxb., tiliaceæ [vricsham, 27]. Specific from singhalese. Large tree; leaves 4–8 by 2½–3 inches; petiole 1½ and upwards; stipules ensiform; pedicels 1 inch, pubescent; calyx ⅓ inch; downy; petals linear-oblong, twice the length of the calyx filaments half the length of the petals; ovary-ovate; style short, stigma three-cleft; capsule six-winged, rounded, wings netted, villose; seeds one to four in each cell; flower small, white, with gold-colored anthers; common, cultivated. Heart-wood dark red, very hard, close-grained, but apt to split; it has even when old a smooth, rather damp feel; very durable; used for carts, agricultural implements and spear-handles, and for masulah [q.v.] boats; inferior to saul [q.v.] for spokes and to babool [q.v.] for some other purposes, but is comparatively light and easily worked; largely imported into madras from ceylon;

answers all the purposes of ash in england.——*Trinetra cadamba* (ತ್ರಿನೇತ್ರಕದಂಬ - trinétrakadamba, Can.). From (above + nétra, san. eye + kadamba, san. member of the dynasty so called). Also called Jayanta trilochana. Founder of the Cadamba [q.v.] family of Bavanausy.——*Tripalam* (त्रिफल - trip'halá, San.). See sep. title.——*Tripatagay* (त्रिपथगा - tripat'hagá, San.). From (above + pa'tha, san. way + gam, san. to go). The mythological Ganges as flowing through the three worlds [trilocum]. Sometimes identified in astronomy with the Milky way [kahkashaun].——*Tripitacam* (त्रिपिटक - tripitaka, San.). From (above + pitaka, san. basket). The Booddhist sacred canon, written in the ancient language called Pali [q.v.]. Its name denotes its distribution under three divisions. The first basket contains all that has reference to morality or Vinayam; the second contains the Sootrams, i.e., the discourses of Booddha [q.v.]; the third includes all works treating of dogmatic philosophy or metaphysics. The second and third baskets are sometimes comprehended under the general name of dharmam or law, and it has become usual to apply to the third basket the name of Abhidharmam, or bye-law. See vol. I (95).——*Tripoondram* (त्रिपुण्ड्र - tripundra, San.). From (above + pundra, san. line). A name given by Sheivas to the triple horizontal, or in a few cases curvilinear, lines of ashes marked on the forehead, shoulders, and breast of votaries. Compare Keet naumam. Smartas [q.v.] add a black spot [pottoo, tilacam] on the centre of the middle line to designate the feminine energy [shacty]. The marks should properly be made with the ashes taken from the fire of an Agny hotra bramin. But they may be the ashes of burnt cowdung from an oblation offered to the idol. See Gopichandanam, Pottoo, Ungooly toranam, Vibhooty. See vol. I (86) [matam].——*Tripocran* (त्रिपुर - tripura, San.). From (above + pura, san. town). A giant in the form of three towns whom Shiva destroyed. Relates to some historic incident. Tripoora soondary, from (above + sundara, san. beautiful) is parvaty, term of very frequent usage by the shactibhactans. Tripoora soondran is Shiva.——*Tripooty* (त्रिपुटी - triputí, San.). From (above + puti, san. fold). The three qualities, viz., knowledge, that which is to be known, and the knower or the soul——*Trishashty* (त्रिषष्टि - trishashti, San.). From (above + shashti, san. sixty). A man who has attained the sixty-three special dispositions among the Jeinas [q.v.], becoming after death a Teertacaran [q.v.]——*Trishoolam* (त्रिशूल - trishúla, San.). From (above + shúla, san. pike). A trident, the weapon of Shiva [shoolam]. Compare the Chuckram [q.v.] of Vishnoo [q.v.], the Vajram [q.v.] of Indran [q.v.]. The trishoolam is considered to be in continual motion over the face of the universe to guard and preserve its creatures. To oppose its course is to incur immediate death. Its motion is regular, but varies according to the days in the week [vauram]. Thus on Monday and Saturday, Shiva holds his trident from the east. No one should, on these days, travel in that direction. It is unlucky to proceed towards the west on Sundays and Fridays, to the northward on Tuesdays and Wednesdays, and to the southward on Thursdays [shoolam, tisay, vauram].——*Trishwaicam* (त्रिष्वेक - trishvéka, San.). From (trishu, san. in three + éka, san. one). Revenue grant in which one-third part of the produce is given for rent [trijye]. See vol. I, 112.——*Triteeyay* (తృతీయ - tritíya, Tel.; திரிதியை - tirithiyai, Tam.). Lunar [chaundramaunaur] festival [pundigay, 3e]. The third tity [q.v.] of the waxing [shooclapacsham] or the waning [krishnapacsham] moon of any month. The third and the eighteenth days of the lunar month [acshaya tadiya].——*Tritwam* (त्रित्व - tritva, San.; திரித்துவம் - tirittuvam, Tam.). From (above + tva, san. suffix of quality). Trinity, threeness [moommay]. See Trimoorty.——*Trivicraman* (त्रिविक्रम - trivikrama, San.). From (above + vikráma, san. step). Vishnoo, who measured the three worlds by three steps [vaumanan]. There are several interpretations of the three steps; some say that they mean morning, noon and evening, as Vishnoo was originally a solar deity.——*Trivicrama roya* (ತ್ರಿವಿಕ್ರಮರಾಯ - trivikramaráya Can.). From (above + vikrama, san. step + rájú, san. king). Chera King in Malabar.——*Triyacshan* (त्र्यक्ष - tryaksha, San.). From (above + aksha, san. eye). Shiva, the three-eyed god.——*Triyambacan* (त्र्यम्बक - tryambaka, San.). From (above + ambaka, san. eye). Shiva, the three-eyed god. Hindoo 2nd or pers. name [peyar].——*Turbith* (त्रिवृत् - trivrit, San.; तेड - téda, Mahr.; तिगडे - tigadé, Conc.; تربد - turbud, Ar.; نسوت - nisút, Hind.; تکرا - tikrá, Dec.; ತಿಗಡೆ - tigade, Can.; తెగడ - tegada, Tel.; ത്രികോല്പക്കൊന്ന - trikólpakkonna, Mal.; [illegible] - trastaválu, Singh.; சிவதை - shivathai, Tam.). Title from arabic. San. from (tri, san. three + vrit, san. to exist), from three-fold property antiphlegmatic, antibilious and cathartic. Ar. from sanscrit. Tel. means cutting; from the purgative property. Mal. from (tri, san. three + kól, mal. stick + pakunna, mal. the plant). Tam. from (shiva, tam. to become red); perhaps from brownish root. San. also (triputá), meaning three + fold, from three folds covering young shoots; (trivritá), meaning covered by three folds; (nandí), meaning gladdening [toon]; (laghuróchaní), meaning slightly stomachic; (kumbhadhátrí), meaning pot preserver; (sarvánubhúti), meaning perception of all tastes, from the sweet, acrid root; (aruná), meaning red [munjeet, galangal]; (paripákiní), meaning digestive; (réchaní), meaning purgative [chebulic myrobalan]; (masúravidalá), meaning split like ervum. lens, linn.; (saralá), meaning purgative; (sushénaká), meaning binding tight; cf. caroudah. Mahr. also (dúdhakalamí), meaning milk + ipomea hederacea, jack; (dudhání), meaning milky. Ar. also (habbulzangí), meaning black seed. Hind. also (teurí), by corruption; (dúdkulmí), from mahratta; (nákpattar); (pithorí). Can. also (áltigudu); (dévadanti), meaning deity + croton tiglium; (bilenágadanti), meaning white + elephant + croton tiglium. Tel. also (tellategada), meaning white + the plant; (talantutíga), meaning head + anointing + creeper; (errategada), meaning red + the plant. Mal. also (chíváka). Singh. also (trivrit). Tam. also (kunagandi); (paganrai), meaning creeper. Title otherwise Indian jalap, Indian rhubarb, Square-stalked bind weed, Teory, Turpeth root. Botanically Ipomœa [calamby] turpethum, r. br., convolvulaceæ [vricsham, 93]. Specific name from arabic. Alias Convolvulus gandichaudii, riedlei, turpethum. Perennial, twining; stem angular, winged, glabrous or a little downy; leaves alternate, cordate, ovate, acuminatad, sometimes entire or angularly sinuated or crenated; peduncles axillary, one to four flowered, bracteate at the apex; outer sepals the largest, ovate roundish; corolla twice as long as the calyx, white; capsule four-sided, four-celled; seeds round, black, one in each cell; flowers white, with a tinge of cream color. Root long, fleshy, thickness of finger, brownish; in dried state sweetish yet nauseous taste; a resinous substance exudes from root when wounded, altogether soluble in spirits of wine, has a taste at first sweetish, afterwards slightly acid. The turbith of commerce consists of the root and stem of the plant cut in short lengths, usually from ½–2 inches in diameter; the central woody portion is often removed by splitting the bark on one side; the exterior surface has a twisted rope-like or columnar appearance, and is of a dull grey color; a transverse section shows a porous surface of a dirty white color, and loaded with pale yellowish white resin; through this substance pass numerous bundles composed of large vessels and woody fibre; the drug is free from smell, but has a nauseous taste, which is only perceptible after it has been sometime in the mouth. Bark medicinally purgative, rubbed up with milk free from nauseous taste or smell; substituted for british jalap [q.v.] and rhubarb [indian rhubarb]; in pharm. non-officinal. Cattle do not eat it. Gives a dye [shauyam]. Two varieties, white and black; black poisonous.

TRICALORE (திருக்கோயிலூர் - tirukkóyilúr, *Tam.* tirukoilúr *). From (tiru, tam. holy + kóyil, tam. temple + úr, tam. village); from the vishnoo temple [shree, tir]. Sanscrit name (krishnapura), means vishnoo + town; also (krishnáranya), meaning vishnoo + forest.——**(1)** Talook, South arcot district. Tahsildar's pay Rs. 200; area 584 square miles; pop. 257,132. Language Tamul. Centre of district. Boundaries:—north, Trinomallee and Villooporam talooks; east, Villoopooram and Cuddalore talooks; south, Vriddhanchellam talook; west, Cullacoorchy talook. Talook is a plain intercepted by two rivers Ponniaur and Guddilam which run parallel to each other. Soil sandy and clayey. Agriculture; cloth and indigo [q.v.] manufacture, trade in cloth and sundry articles. Irrigation by wells, tanks, Ponniaur, Guddilam, Toorinjalaur anicuts [q.v.] and river channels [q.v.]. Camping grounds Arasore, Asanore, and Oolandoorpett. Places of archæological interest:—Arcandalore, Aumore, Collore, Devanore, Graumam, Jambaday, Meyyore, Oolandaundarcoil, Pervidayaur, Shendamungalam, Siddhilingam, Tayanore, Tirnaumanullore, Tirpalpandal, Tirvennanullore, Tricalore, Yedeiyore, Yelavanausore. Principal trig. stations:—Kiliyore rock, Oolandoorpett, Shendamungalam. The leading places, &c., in the talook are the following.——*Coovaugam* (கூவ்வாக்கம் - kúvvákkam, Tam.). From (kúvu, tam. to crow as a cock + pákkam, tam. village); from sacrifice of fowls. Village; pop. 1,291; acres 1,980; lat. 11° 49′; long. 79° 24′; from Cuddalore W. 29 miles; from Tricalore S.E. 14 miles. Annual festival in honor of Coottaundaur, a village god, at which thousands of sheep [aud] and fowls [moorghy], are sacrificed. Also noted for bullock [maud] fair, largely attended.——*Guddilam* (கடிலம் - kadilam, Tam.). See sep. title.——*Kiliyóre rock* (கிளியூர் - kiliyúr, Tam.). From (kili, tam. parrot + úr, tam. village). Trig. station; lat. 11° 47′ 54·13″; long. 79° 17′ 17·00″; height 328 feet; from Kiliyore S. 1 mile; from Tricalore S.S.E. 12 miles.——*Malattaur* (மலட்டாறு - malattáru, Tam.). See sep. title.——*Manaloorpett* (மணலூர்ப்பேட்டை - manalúrppéttai, Tam.). From (manal, tam. sand + úr, tam. village + péttai, tam. village). Village pop. 2,922; acres 1,833; lat. 12° 00′; long. 79° 08′; from Cuddalore W.N.W. 50 miles; from Tricalore W.N.W. 8 miles. On the north bank of the Ponniaur [q.v.]. Two Hindoo temples and two mosques [musjid]. From twenty to thirty thousand pilgrims attend the annual Ponniaur ootsavam festival, when the image [shilay, vigraham] of Shiva [q.v.] is brought from Trinomallee. Superior native cloths are manufactured and silk-dyeing [shauyam] is carried on.——*Oolandoorpett* (உளுந்தூர்ப்பேட்டை - ulundúrppéttai, Tam.). See sep. title.——*Ponniaur* (பெண்ணையாறு - pennaiyáru, Tam.). See sep. title.——*Shendamungalam* (சேந்தமங்கலம் - shéndamangalam, Tam.). From (shéndan, tam. the god skanda + mangala, san. prosperity). Trig. station lat. 11° 43′ 43·65″; long. 79° 24′ 48·21″; height 265 feet; from Shendamungalam S. 1 mile; from Tricalore S.S.E. 20 miles. ——*Tirnarooncoondram* (திருநறுங்குன்றம் - tirunarungunram, Tam.). From (tiru, tam. holy + naru, tam. fragrant + kunram, tam. hill). Pop. 243; acres 1,446; lat. 11° 49′; long. 79° 20′; from Cuddalore W.N.W. 32 miles; from Tricalore S.S.E. 12 miles. Jeina [q.v.] temple on a hillock by the side of a large reservoir, visited by pilgrims from all parts of India.——*Tirnaumanullore* (திருநாமநல்லூர் - tirunámanallúr, Tam.). From (tiru, tam. holy + námam, tam. name + nal, tam. good + úr, tam. village). Pop. 1,902; acres 2,495; lat. 11° 52′; long. 79° 27; from Cuddalore W.N.W. 29 miles; from Tricalore S.E. 13 miles. Inscriptions of Chola [q.v.] dynasty [raj].——*Tirvennanullore* (திருவெண்ணநல்லூர் - tiruvennanallúr, *Tam.). From (tiru, tam. holy + vennai, tam. butter + nal, tam. good + úr, tam. village). Place of pilgrimage; pop. 3,469; acres 1,607; lat. 11° 52′; long. 79° 24′; from Cuddalore W.N.W. 29 miles; from Tricalore S.E. 13 miles. Shiva and Vishnoo temples. Sugar [q.v.] factory.——*Toorinjalaur* (துறிஞ்சலாறு - turinjalâru, Tam.). See sep. title.——*Tricalore* (திருக்கோயிலூர் - tirukkóyilúr, Tam.). See below.——*Yelavanausore* (எலவானசூர் - elavánásúr,* Tam.). From sanscrit. Sanscrit name (lavanásurapura), meaning lavanan, an asooran + town. Pop. 2,450; acres 2,685; lat. 11° 43′; long. 79° 14′; height 358 feet; from Cuddalore W. 39 miles; from Tricalore S. 17 miles. Former head-quarters of Tahsildar. Large Shiva temple, and smaller one dedicated to Hanooman [q.v.]. In the Shiva temple, the nundies [q.v.] do not face towards Shiva as they ordinarily do but are placed with their tails towards him. It is said that the reason of this is that Shiva ordered the bulls to be ready for war with an asooran [q.v.]. Fort said to have existed here——(2) Town Head-quarters of talook and Deputy collector, South arcot dist., Tricalore tal.; pop. 5,732; acres 2,606; lat. 11° 58′; long. 79° 15′; height 456 feet; from Chidambaram N.W. 50 miles; from Cuddalore W.N.W. 41 miles; from Madras S.W. 107 miles; from Tindivanam S.W. 36 miles; from Vriddhauchellam N.N.W. 32 miles. On the south bank of the Ponniaur. Large and elaborately sculptured Vishnoo temple of Trivicraman with inscriptions. Old Mahomedan mosque [musjid]. Shiva temple with gopooram [q.v.] of eight storeys. It is said that a portion of the temple was a century ago used for storing Government salt [ooppoo]. Weekly fair on Wednesday. In the bed of the river is a large boulder on which stands a temple. In the suburb of Keelore is an old Shiva temple, and near Keelore on a small hill on the opposite side of the river is a deserted temple.

TRICHENGODE (திருச்செங்கோடு - tiruççengódu, *Tam.* tiruchengód *). From (tiru, tam. holy + shem, tam. red + kódu, tam. peak) [shree, tir]. Sanscrit name (nágáchalapura), meaning snake + mountain + town.——(1) Talook, Salem district. Tahsildar's pay Rs. 225. Area 637 square miles. Averages about 25 miles in length and breadth, extremes being 35 miles from east to west and 33 miles from north to south. Population 248,679. Language Tamul. S.W. of district. Between N. lat. 11° 15′ and 11° 45′ and E. long. 77° 44′ to 78° 15′. Bounded north and north-east by Salem talook; south and south-east by Namcull talook; and west by the Cauvery, which separates it from Coimbatore district. The talook is exceptional in its configuration as compared with the rest of the district, being one bleak glaring plain with only a few hills, of which Shunkerrydroog only is of importance, and no hill ranges. The centre is high ground sloping towards the Cauvery; on the north and east are two valleys in which run the Sharabhunganuddy and Tirmany meottaur. Poolamputty hill is in the north-west corner. Soil red. Weaving goes on in all large villages, more especially at Trichengode. Raggy [q.v.] is the staple of consumption. Trichengode enjoys a great reputation for its milch cows [pashoo], which though small fetch from 35 to 50 rupees or even more. Exports are paddy [q.v.], horse-gram [q.v.], gingelly [q.v.] seed, cumboo [bajrah], ghee [q.v.], palmyra [q.v.] jaggery [q.v.] and lamp oil [q.v.]. Imports are salt [ooppoo], jaggery [q.v.], wheat [geung], betel-nut [q.v.], raggy [q.v.], tobacco [pogauk], saffron [country saffron], plantains [q.v.] and coriander [cassibor] seed. The only rivers are the Sharabhunganuddy and the Tirmany moottaur. There are ferries at Calavadangam, Cauveryputty agrahauram, Cokkaroyanpettah, Conairyputty agrahauram, Jalacantapooram, Kailamputty, Molasy, Mungalam, Nedooncoolam, Pillagowndenputty, Poolamputty-cauvery, Pulipolliem agrahauram, Puttalore, Samayasagily agrahauram, Shiloovamputty and Yerayamungalam. The following are the principal irrigation works in the talook:—Auvaniperore-veppamputty anicut, Chinnappanputty anicut, Connaiyaur anicut, Mullasamoodramkeelmookhan large tank, Mungalam tank, Navany tank, Parootiipully amritasaugaram tank, Yedapaudy anicut, Yeloor tank. Camping grounds:—Chinnappanputty, Comaurapolliem, McDonald's choultry, Pullipolliem, Shunkerry droog. Zemindarries:—Animor mittah, Carmanore mittah, Cautpolliem, Chinnamanaly, Cokkaley, Cokkaroyanpettah, Comauramungalam, Comaurapolliem, Conganapooram, Cottay varoothamputty, Culyauny, Gowndenpolliem, Iroogalore, Manapauray, Minnampully, Molipully, Moonjanore, Morangam, Oonjiny, Palamode, Periyamanaly, Poottore, Shittalandore, Shuncagherry, Toccavaudy. Places of archæological interest:—Aundipolliem, Auvaniperore, Cadayampett, Carveppamputty, Comauramungalam mittah, Comaurapolliem, Devanancoorchy, Molipully, Palayapolliem, Poolamputty, Rajahpolliem, Shittalandore, Shunkerrydroog, Trichengode, Varagooranputty, Vellirivully, Woddaputty, Yedagansaulay, Yedapaudy. Principal trig. station:—Moroor. The leading places, &c., in the talook are the following.——*Animore mittah* (அனிமூர்மிட்டா - animúrmitta, Tam. animúrnutta *). From (ani, tel. battle + úr, tel. village + mitthá, hind. estate). Zemindarry, Village; pop. 751; square miles 14; lat. of village 11° 20′; long. 77° 55′; from Salem S.W. 31 miles; from Trichengode S.S.W. 4 miles. Peshcush Rs. 6,401.——*Cánacagherry* (கனகிரி - kanagagiri, Tam.). From (kanaka, san. gold + giri, san. mountain). Village; pop. 602; acres 773; lat. 11° 34′; long. 78° 03′; from Salem W. 13 miles; from Trichengode N. 15 miles.——*Carmanore mittah* (கருமனூர்மிட்டா - karumanúrmittá, Tam. karumanurmitta *). From (karumán, tam. blacksmith + úr, tam. village + mitthá, hind. estate). Zemindarry, Village; pop. 1,456; square miles $9\frac{7}{16}$; lat. of village 11° 27′; long. 78° 03′; from Salem S.W. 19 miles; from Trichengode N.E. 9 miles. Peshcush Rs. 5,558.——*Gaulipputty* (காளிப்பட்டி - kálippatti, Tam.). From (káli, san. the goddess + patti, tam. cattle-fold). Village; pop. 2,253; lat. 11° 31′; long. 78° 05′; from Salem S.W. 13 miles; from Trichengode N.E. 14 miles. About 5,000 persons attended the Cundaswamy car festival held about 21st January. At this festival pilgrims carry cauvadies [q.v.] in fulfilment of vows.——*Cautpolliem* (காட்டுப்பாளையம் - káttuppálaiyam, Tam.). From (kádu, tam. forest + pálaiyam, tam. fortified village). Zemindarry, Village; pop. 200; lat. of village 11° 27′; long. 78° 05′; from Salem S.S.W. 17 miles; from Trichengode E.N.E. 11 miles. Peshcush Rs. 657.——*Cauvery* (காவேரி - kávéri, Tam.). See sep. title.——*Chinnamanaly* (சின்னமணலி - shinnamanali, Tam.). From (shinna, tam. small + manali, tam. plant, gisekia pharnaceoides, linn.). Zemindarry, Village; pop. 1,255; lat. of village 11° 35′; long. 77° 53′; from Salem W.S.W. 23 miles; from Trichengode N.N.W. 15 miles. Peshcush Rs. 1,538.——*Cokkaley* (கொக்கலே - kókkalé, Tam.). From (kokku, can. crane + halli, can. village). Zemindarry, Village; pop. 1,659; square miles 5; lat. of village 11° 22′; long. 78° 06′; from Salem S.S.W. 21 miles; from Trichengode E. 11 miles. Peshcush Rs. 2,425.——*Cokkaroyanpettah* (கொக்கராயன்பேட்டை - kokkaráyanbéttai, Tam. kokaráyanpet *). Means cokkaroyen's village. Sanscrit name (brahmapuri), meaning bramha's town. Zemindarry, Village; pop. 2,001; square miles $23\frac{1}{4}$; lat. of village 11° 19′; long. 77° 50′; from Salem S.W. 35 miles; from Trichengode W.S.W. 9 miles. Peshcush Rs. 8,661.——*Comauramungalam* (குமாரமங்கலம் - kumáramangalam, Tam. komáramangalam *). From (kumára, san. skanda + mangala, san. prosperity). Zemindarry, Village; pop. 2,911; square miles $9\frac{1}{4}$; lat. of village 11° 24′; long. 77° 58′; from Salem S.W. 25 miles; from Trichengode N.E. 2 miles. Peshcush Rs. 5,901. ——*Comaurapolliem* (குமாரப்பாளையம் - kumárappálaiyam, Tam.). From (kumára, san. skanda, the god + pálaiyam, tam. fortified village). Zemindarry, Village; pop. of village 1,863; acres 3,539; lat. 11° 26′; long. 77° 44′; from Salem W. S.W. 36 miles; from Trichengode W.N.W. 15 miles. Inhabited chiefly by Canarese weavers. Copper-plate grant [shaasanam]. Peshcush Rs. 3,648.——*Conganapooram* (கொங்கணபுரம் - konganappuram, Tam. konganapuram *). From (kónkana, san. people, so called + pura, san. town). Zemindarry, Village; pop. 1,453; square miles $12\frac{5}{8}$; lat. of village 11° 34′; long. 77° 57′; from Salem W.S.W. 19 miles; from Trichengode N. 14 miles. Peshcush Rs. 8,429.——*Culyauny* (கல்லியாணி - kalliyáni, Tam.). From (kalyání, san. an epithet of párvati). Zemindarry, Village; pop. 1,474; square miles $4\frac{1}{2}$; lat. of village 11° 24′; long. 78° 11′; from Salem S. 18 miles; from Trichengode E. 17 miles. Peshcush Rs. 1,848.——*Gowndenpolliem* (கவுண்டன்பாளையம் - kavundanbálaiyam, Tam.). Means gownden village. Zemindarry, Village; pop. 2,657; square miles $6\frac{3}{8}$; lat. of village 11° 22′; long. 77° 59′; from Salem S.W. 26 miles; from Trichengode E.S.E. 3 miles. Peshcush Rs. 3,088.——*Iroogalore* (இருகாலூர் - irugálúr, Tam.). From (iru, tam. two + kál, tam. channel + úr, tam. village). Tam. also (iruvádchippattanam), meaning irvautchy flower, jasminum sambac, ait. + town. Zemindarry, Village; pop. 2,257; square miles 7; lat. of village 11° 31′; long. 78° 00′; from Salem S.W. 18 miles; from Trichengode N.N.E. 10 miles. Peshcush Rs. 2,801.——*Marapauray* (மரப்பாறை - marappárai, Tam.). From (maram, tam. tree + párai, tam. rock). Zemindarry, Village; pop. 2,546; square miles 5; lat. of village 11° 25′; long. 78° 06′; from Salem S.S.W. 19 miles; from Trichengode E.N.E. 11 miles. Peshcush Rs. 2,708.——*McDonald's choultry* (மகுடன்சாவடி - magudansávadi, Tam.). See sep. title.——*Minnampully* (மின்னம்பள்ளி - minnámballi, Tam.). From (min, tam. lightning + palli, tam. village). Zemindarry, Village; pop. 2,058; square miles 4; lat. of village 11° 26′; long. 78° 08′; from Salem S.S.W. 17 miles; from Trichengode E.N.E. 14 miles. Peshcush Rs. 3,368.——*Molipully* (மோளிப்பள்ளி - mólippalli, Tam.). From (móle, can. a bank + palli, tam. village). Zemindarry, Village; pop. 1,362; square miles 8; lat. of village 11° 19′; long. 78° 01′; from Salem S.S.W. 27 miles; from Trichengode

S.E. 6 miles. Vishnoo temple with inscriptions. Peshcush Rs. 5,022.——*Moonjanore* (ಮುಂಜನೂರು - munjanúru, Can.; முஞ்சனூர் - muñjanúr, Tam.). From (munjana, can. ploughshare + úru, can. village). Zemindarry, Village; pop. 1,555; square miles 3; lat. of village 11° 27′; long. 78° 09′; from Salem S.S.W. 16 miles; from Trichengode E.N.E. 15 miles. Peshcush Rs. 1,530.——*Morangam* (மொறங்கம் - morangam, Tam.). Zemindarry, Village; pop. 896; square miles 2; lat. of village 11° 26′; long. 78° 07′; from Salem S.S.W. 17 miles; from Trichengode E.N.E. 13 miles. Peshcush Rs. 1,750.——*Moroor* (மோரூர் - mórúr, Tam.). From (mór, tam. buttermilk + úr, tam. village). Village; pop. 4,039; acres 5,163; lat. 11° 25′; long. 77° 55′; from Salem S.W. 26 miles; from Trichengode N.N.W. 3 miles. Trig. station in lat. 11° 24′ 14·23″; long. 77° 55′ 54·88″; height 1,643 feet; from Rajahpolliem E. 1½ miles; from Trichengode N. 2 miles.——*Navany* (நவனி - navani, Tam.). From (navane, can. panicum italicum, linn.). Village; pop. 4,063; acres 5,056; lat. 11° 22′; long. 78° 11′; from Salem S. 20 miles; from Trichengode E. 16 miles.——*Nedooncoolam* (நெடுங்குளம் - nedungulam, Tam.). From (nedu, tam. long + kulam, tam. tank). Village; pop. 361; acres 1,473; lat. 11° 36′; long. 77° 47′; from Salem W. 29 miles; from Trichengode N.W. 19 miles.——*Oonjiny* (உஞ்ஜினி - uñjini, Tam.). From (uñju, can. worn out + ane, can. bund). Zemindarry, Village; pop. 1,996; square miles 4; lat. of village 11° 21′; long. 78° 00′; from Salem S.S.W. 26 miles; from Trichengode E.S.E. 5 miles. Peshcush Rs. 2,639.——*Palamode* (பாலமேடு - pálamédu, Tam.). From (pálam, tam. bridge + médu, tam. high ground). Zemindarry, Village; pop. 1,563; square miles 2½; lat. of village 11° 27′; long. 78° 06′; from Salem S.S.W. 17 miles; from Trichengode E.N.E. 12 miles. Peshcush Rs. 2,782.——*Periyamanaly* (பெரியமணலி - periya-manali, Tam.). From (periya, tam. great + manali, tam. gisekia pharnaceoides, linn.). Zemindarry, Village; pop. 640; lat. of village 11° 22′; long. 78° 07′; from Salem S.S.W. 21 miles; from Trichengode E. 12 miles. Peshcush Rs. 1,353.——*Poolamputty* (பூலாம்பட்டி - púlámbatti, Tam.). From (púlá, tam. plant, phyllanthus multiflorus, willd. + patti, tam. cattle-fold). Village, Hill; pop. 1,967; acres 4,483; lat. 11° 40′; long. 77° 49′; from Salem W. 27 miles; from Trichengode N. N.W. 20 miles. Old Shiva temple with inscriptions. The hill is covered with scrub jungle.——*Poottore* (புத்தூர் - puttúr, Tam. putúr*). From (puttu, tam. ant-hill + úr, tam. village). Sanscrit name (valmíka-pura), meaning ant-hill + town. Zemindarry, Village; pop. 1,190; square miles 23; lat. of village 11° 18′; long. 78° 08′; from Salem S.S.W. 26 miles; from Trichengode E.S.E. 14 miles. Peshcush Rs. 12,189.——*Pulliрolliem* (பள்ளிப்பாளையம் - pallippálaiyam, Tam.). From (palli, tam. member of the palli caste + pálaiyam, tam. fortified village). Sanscrit name (dvára-kápuri), meaning dwarca + town. Village, Railway station; pop. 3,176; acres 5,147; lat. 11° 22′; long. 77° 47′; from Salem S.W. 35 miles; from Trichengode W. 11 miles. On the Cauvery. Tall menhir [paundoocull]. In a field is a closed cromlech [paundoocull] and five cairns [paundoo-coozhy], the latter surrounded with stone circles [azhauram].——*Shittalandore* (சித்தளந்தூர் - shittalandúr, Tam.). From (shiru, tam. small + alandai, tam. tank + úr, tam. village). Zemindarry, Village; pop. 2,966; square miles 6¾; lat. of village 11° 19′; long. 77° 58′; from Salem S.W. 29 miles; from Trichengode S.S.E. 5 miles. Peshcush Rs. 3,675.——*Shuncagherry* (சங்ககிரி - shangagiri, Tam.). From (shankha, san. conch + giri, san. mountain), white like conch shell. Zemindarry, Village; pop. 2,491; square miles 10½; lat. of village 11° 28′; long. 77° 55′; from Salem W.S.W. 24 miles; from Trichengode N.N.W. 7 miles. Peshcush Rs. 3,104.——*Shunkerrydroog* (சங்ககிரித்துருக்கம் - shangagiritturukkam, Tam.). See sep. title.——*Tirmany moottaur* (திருமணிமுத்தாறு - tirumanimuttáru, Tam.). See sep. title.——*Toccavaudy* (தொக்கவாடி - tokkavádi, Tam.). From (tokku, tam. small + vádi, tam. an enclosure). Zemindarry, Village; pop. 1,362; square miles 7; lat. of village 11° 22′; long. 77° 53′; from Salem S.W. 30 miles; from Trichengode W.S.W. 4 miles. Peshcush Rs. 2,968.——*Trichengode* (திருச்செங்கோடு - tiruççengódu, Tam.). See below.——*Yedagansaulay* (எடங்கண்சாலை - edan-gansálai, Tam.). From (idam, tam. left side + kan, tam. affix of place + shálai, tam. road). Village; pop. 4,772; acres 5,651; lat 11° 38′; long. 78° 02′; from Salem W.S.W. 12 miles; from Trichengode N.N.E. 18 miles. Old Shiva temple with inscription.——*Yedápaudy* (எடப்பாடி - edappádi, Tam.). From (idaiyan, tam. shepherd + pádi, tam. village). Sanscrit name (gópálapura), meaning cow-herd city. Village; pop. 4,803; acres 2,389; lat. 11° 35′; long. 77° 53′; from Salem W.S.W. 23 miles; from Trichengode N.N.W. 15 miles. Inhabited chiefly by weavers. Old Shiva temple. Brass vessels are largely manufactured.——*Yeloor* (ஏழூர் - élúr, Tam.). From (ézhu, tam. seven + úr, tam. village). Village; pop. 3,647; acres 4,404; lat. 11° 21′; long. 78° 09′; from Salem S.S.W. 22 miles; from Trichengode E. 14 miles.——**(2)** Town, Head-quarters of Tahsildar, Hill; Salem dist., Trichengode tal.; pop. 7,511; acres 2,854; lat. 11° 23′; long. 77° 57′; height 1,901 feet; from Madras S.W. 197 miles; from Namcull N.W. 21 miles; from Oossoor S. 94 miles; from Salem S.W. 27 miles; from Tripatore S.S.W. 89 miles; from Yercaud S.W. 36 miles. At the foot of a rock some 1,200 feet above the plan. The town lies to the north of the hill. The droog is a bare square-looking mass with some red stains on its sides, like the streaks on the wall of the pagoda [q.v.]. It is from this that the name is derived; compare etymology at head. The town is healthy as a rule, but the water-supply is inferior. Shiva pagoda of great repute with inscription dated A.D. 1600, much frequented by pilgrims; especially at new moon days and during the car feast. Trade is in weaving, grain, and making sandalwood [sandal] balls.

TRICHINOPOLY (திருச்சிறுப்பள்ளி - tiruççináppalli, Tam.). From (tiru, tam. holy + shiná, tam. plant, cissampelos pareira, linn. + palli, tam. village) [shree, tir]. Sanscrit name (trishirahpura), meaning trishiran, the giant + town. Tel. name (chirutapalli), meaning hunting leopard + village. Tam. name (shivandippuram), meaning the flower plant, chrysanthemum indicum, linn. + town, from the garden near the rock; also (shivandiyúr). Mahomedan name (natharnagar), meaning nutter, name of saint + city. Greek ὀρθοῦρα; see Warriore.——**(1)** Revenue district; situated inland; between 10° 07′ and 11° 31′ N. lat., and between 78° 11′ and 79° 33′ E. long.; bounded N. by Salem and South arcot districts, E. by Tanjore district, S. by Poodoocottah state and Madura district, W. by Coimbatore district; square miles 4,733; pop. 1,372,717; language Tamul. Contains rivers Amravatty, Cauvery, Coleroon, Vellaur; mountains Putchamullay; sanitarium Tálamullay. The whole area of the district is represented by the following sub-areas:—Coolitalay talook, Moosiry talook, Oodayarpolliem talook, Perambalore talook, Poodoocottah territory, and Trichinopoly talook. For general administrative purposes the district is distributed between the following revenue and magisterial officers, who have their head-quarters at the places shown. The pay set opposite the subordinate officers gives the grade of the corresponding charge:—Collector, Trichinopoly; Assistant collector, Trichinopoly or Head-quarter Deputy collector, in charge of Trichinopoly talook; Head Assistant Collector, Moosiry, in charge of Moosiry and Coolitalay talooks; General deputy collector, Ariyalore, in charge of Perambalore and Oodayarpolliem talooks. Tahsildars; Coolitalay, Rs. 150; Moosiry, Rs. 225; Oodayarpolliem, Rs. 200; Perambalore, Rs. 175; Trichinopoly, Rs. 250. Deputy tahsildars; Keelpaloovore, Rs. 70, range situated in the south-west of Oodayarpolliem talook; Laulgoody, Rs. 100, range situated in the north-east of Trichinopoly talook; Manapauray, Rs. 70, range situated in the south of Coolitalay talook; Toorayore, Rs. 100, range situated in the north of Moosiry talook; Sub-magistrate, Trichinopoly, Rs. 100, jurisdiction extending over 52 villages. Similarly judicial officers:—Judge, Trichinopoly. District moonsifs; Ariyalore with jurisdiction extending over Perambalore and Oodayarpolliem, talooks; Coolitalay with jurisdiction extending over Coolitalay and Moosiry talooks; Trichinopoly Principal and Additional District moonsifs, with jurisdiction extending over the Trichinopoly talook. Similarly Public works officers:—District engineer, Trichinopoly; Sub-divisional officer, Assistant engineer, Moosiry. Contains Registration sub-districts Ariyalore, Coolitalay, Jayancondacholapooram, Laulgoody, Manapauray, Moosiry, Perambalore, Shreerungam, Toorayore, Trichinopoly, Warriore. Contains Forest ranges Coolitalay, Moosiry, Oodayarpolliem, Perambalore, Trichinopoly. Contains Municipalities Shreerungam, Trichinopoly. Contains District board and Talook boards:—Trichinopoly Talook board embracing Trichinopoly talook, Moosiry Talook board embracing Moosiry and Coolitalay talooks, Ariyalore Talook board embracing Perambalore and Oodayarpolliem talooks. The following general references should be made to the preceding volumes:—general geography, I (1) to (29); general ethnology, I (29) to (109); general history, I (110) to (188); physical geography, II, 1; meteorology, II, 3; geology, II, 8; fauna, II, 21; flora, II, 26; mineralogy, II, 29. The following references in the preceding volumes will furnish details special to the district:—latitudes and longitudes, II, 47; particulars about towns, II, 48; comparative population, II, 172; location of revenue officers, II, 391; revenue settlement of the district, II, 418; registrars' and sub-registrars' stations, II, 422; rainguage stations, II, 428; police divisions, II, 431; maps published, II, 436; survey topographical lists, II, 443; hospitals and dispensaries, II, 447; missionary stations, II, 455; head-quarter stations of gazetted officers, II, 461; incidence of taxation, II, 463; weights and measures of the district, II, 519; zemindarries, II, 301. A special gazetteer account of the whole district is given at II, 136. For the detailed topography of the district, reference should be made to the talook notices in the present volume, viz.:—Coolitalay, Moosiry, Oodayarpolliem, Perambalore, Poodoocottah, Trichinopoly.——**(2)** Talook, Trichinopoly district. Tahsildar's pay Rs. 250. Area 542 square miles. Pop. 360,829. Language Tamul. Greatest length from E. to W. about 36 miles; greatest breadth from N. to S. about 30 miles. S. of district. Divided into two almost equal portions by Cauvery, which crosses its entire length from W. to E. Bounded on N. by Moosiry and Perambalore talooks, on E, by Oodayarpolliem talook, Tanjore talook, on S. by Poodoocottah territory and on W. by Coolitalay talook. Prior to 1861 the portion of the talook lying north of the river was termed Laulgoody, and that to the south Conaud talook. Of the 437 villages 49 are inam [q.v.]. There are no zemindarry [q.v.] villages. To the south are 15 villages, known as the Iloppore division, separated from the rest of the district by Poodoocottah territory. On the whole very flat, and no hills of importance. South indian railway runs across talook from W. to E. and across the S.W. extremity. The soil of greater portion of fields irrigated by the Cauvery and its channels has been enriched by alluvial deposit. In the Ilooppore division the soil is hard and gravelly, interspersed with tracts of land impregnated with saltpetre [shorah]. There is however considerable cultivation under tanks [q.v.] in this portion. Paddy [q.v.] is principal grain. The most important dry grains [q.v.] are cholum [q.v.], varagoo [q.v.] and cumboo [bajrah]; oil-seeds [yennay], raggy [q.v.], gram [q.v.], dholl [common dholl] are also grown, and sugar-cane [q.v.], indigo [q.v.] and cotton [q.v.] are cultivated, especially north of the Coleroon. A large amount of rice is exported every year principally to Madura. Principal sources of irrigation are the Cauvery and its channels [q.v.], of which the following are the most important :—Ayyan vycaul, Nauttvycaul, Pervala vycaul, Poothoo vyttalay, Wyacondaun, and Yelanda vyttalay. The principal tanks are Coottapaur, Kileyore, and Vaulavondauncottay. Camping grounds :—Alloor, Naugamungalam, Pettah vyttalay, Samayaupooram, Shilayautty, Poovacoody. Places of archæological interest :—Anacaray, Jambookeshwaran, Javantinautapooram, Keel ambil, Laulgoody, Malavanore, Maungoody, Pitchaundarcoil, Poottore, Samayaupooram, Shreerungam, Tirmullaynullore, Tirpalatoray, Tirvausy, Trichinopoly, Trivellary, Warriore, Wyacondaun, Yelmanore, Yeroombeshwaram. The leading places, &c., in the talook are the following.——*Ambil* (அம்பில் - ambil, Tam.). From (ambu, tam. pleasure + il, tam. house). Sanscrit name (prémapurí), meaning love + town. Village; pop. 938; acres 429; lat. 10° 52′; long. 78° 57′; from Trichinopoly E.N.E. 13 miles. On Coleroon. Birth place of Shendan [q.v.].——*Amravatty* (அமராவதி - ámarávathi, Tam.). See sep. title.——*Aulambaudy* (ஆலம்பாடி - álambádi, Tam.). From (álam, tam. the banyan tree, ficus bengalensis, linn. + pádi, tam. village). Village; pop. 869; acres 1,079; lat. 10° 54′; long. 79° 03′; from Trichinopoly E.N.E. 21 miles. On the left bank of Coleroon. Occupied by a small British garrison in 1768 which was dispossessed by Hyder ally.——*Cauvery* (காவேரி - kávéri, Tam.). See sep. title.——*Coleroon* (கொள்ளிடம் - kolladam, Tam.). See sep. title.——*Cottapaur* (குட்டப்பார் - kuttappár, Tam.). From (kuttam, tam. littleness + pár, tam. rock). Village; pop. 1,959; acres 2,465; lat. 10° 48′; long. 78° 51′; from Trichinopoly E. 6 miles. Tank.——*Iloppore* (இலுப்பூர் - iluppúr, * Tam.). From (iluppai, tam. mohwah tree, bassia longifolia, linn. + úr, tam. village). Town; pop. 3,593; acres 2,386; lat. 10° 31′; long. 78° 41′; from Trichinopoly S. 21 miles.——*Iroongalore* (இருங்களூர் - irungalúr, * Tam.). From (irungu, tam. plant, sorghum vulgare, pers. + kal, tam. stone + úr, tam. village). Village; pop. 1,280; acres 1,687; lat. 10° 57′; long. 78° 50′; from Trichinopoly N.N.E. 10 miles.——*Jambookeshwaram* (जम्बुकेश्वर - jambukéshvara, San.). See sep. title.——*Laulgoody* (இலாலுக்குடி - ilálukkudi, Tam.). See sep. title.——*Motooputty* (மேட்டுப்பட்டி - méttuppatti, Tam.). From (médu, tam, high ground + patti, tam. village). Village; pop. 618; acres 760; lat. 10° 54′; long. 78° 55′; from Trichinopoly E.N.E. 12 miles. Mission station.——*Munnatcha nellore* (மண்ணச்சநெல்லூர் - mannaççanellúr, Tam.). From (man, tam. great + aççan, tam. master + nel, tam. paddy + úr, tam. village). Village; pop. 3,310; acres 388; lat. 10° 55′; long. 78° 45′; from Trichinopoly N. 7 miles. Taken from the French in 1752; recaptured by them in 1759.——*Poollambaudy* (புள்ளம்பாடி - pullambádi, Tam.). From (pullam, tam. a sickle + pádi, tam. village). Town; pop. 3,726; acres 2,587; lat. 10° 57′; long. 78° 58′; from Trichinopoly E.N.E. 16 miles. Mission centre.——*Shreerungam* (ஸ்ரீரங்கம் - shrirangam, Tam.). See sep. title.——*Tirveroombore* (திருவரம்பூர் - tiruvarambúr, Tam. tiruverumbúr*). From (tiru, tam. holy + erumbu, tam. ant + úr, tam. town). Sanscrit name (pipílikéshvarapura), meaning ant + lord + town. Village, Railway station; pop. 1,042; acres 520; lat. 10° 48′; long. 78° 50′; height 230 feet; from Trichinopoly E.S.E. 5 miles. Important, formerly as commanding road from Trichinopoly to Tanjore. Strongly built Shiva temple on a low rock. Rock-cut cave under temple.——*Trichinopoly* (திருச்சிராப்பள்ளி - tiruççináppalli, Tam.). See below.——*Trivellary* (திருவெள்ளறை - tiruvallarai, Tam.). From (tiru, tam. beautiful + vellarai, tam. white rock). Sanscrit name (shvétádri), meaning white mountain. Village, Place of pilgrimage; pop. 400; acres 827; lat. 10° 58′; long. 78° 43′; from Trichinopoly N.N.W. 10 miles. Fine pagoda [q.v.] with curious rock-cut caves probably Booddhist [booddha].——*Warriore* (உறையூர் - oraiyúr, Tam.). See sep. title.——*Wyacondaun* (உய்யக்கொண்டான் - uyyakkondán, Tam.). From (uy, tam. to prosper + kondán, tam. he who obtained). Means a place of thriving colonists. The principal irrigating channel of the district. It takes off from the Cauvery 18 miles west of Trichinopoly, and irrigates about 25,500 acres. In December 1809 this channel burst in several places, and was with greatest difficulty repaired. In May 1828 a similar accident occurred and sixteen villages had to be left uncultivated.——*Wyacondaun tirmullay* (உய்யக்கொண்டான்திருமலை - uyyakkondándirumalai, Tam.). From (uy, tam. to prosper + kondán, tam. he who obtained + tiru, tam. holy + malai, tam. mountain). Village; pop. 785; acres 324; lat. 10° 49′; long. 78° 43′; from Trichinopoly W. 3 miles. Small village with strongly fortified Shiva temple on the walls of which the marks of cannon shot are still visible. It was repeatedly taken and retaken by the English and French, being an outpost of considerable strength. *Yelmanore* (எழுமனூர் - ezhumanúr, Tam.). From (ellamman, tam. a deity + úr, tam. village). Village, Railway station; pop. 296; acres 312; lat. 10° 53′; long. 78° 38′; height 254 feet; from Trichinopoly W.N.W. 10 miles. On S. bank of Cauvery, where Coleroon branches. Resorted to for bathing by a large number of people in Arpisy [mausam] or October.——**(3)** Sub-magistracy, Trichinopoly district. Pay Rs. 100.——**(4)** Town, Cantonment, Head-quarters of Collector, Judge, Railway station; Trichinopoly dist., Trichinopoly tal.; pop. 90,609; acres 3,052; lat. 10° 49′; long. 78° 46′; height 274; from Ariyalore S.W. 34 miles; from Madras S.S.W. 191 miles; from Moosiry E.S.E. 20 miles; from Shreerungam S. 4 miles. On the Cauvery about half a mile from its right bank. The Mahomedans call it Nutternagar, from a saint Nutter whose tomb still exists. Its position on banks of Cauvery and proximity to holy island of Shreerungam render it a place of great attraction to natives from all parts of India. For history see district notice in vol. II, 136. The principal monuments are the following :—the rock, and its temples; the teppacoolam, at the foot of the rock to the west; a fortified pagoda at Wyacondaun tirmullay; Chundah sahib's tomb; the Daur ool imaura, palace of the Nawaubs [q.v.] of the Carnatic [q.v.] and mosque [musjid]; the tank where Bishop Heber was drowned; the great temple of Shreerungam; the temple of Jambookeshwaran. Previous to the demolition of the ramparts in 1845 the rock formed the citadel of a large fort, one mile long by half a mile wide. Now only the fortifications of the rock remain. The rock is of syenite, 600 feet above the alluvial plain from which it rises, and is a very striking object viewed from a distance. The ascent to the rock is partly by a covered stone staircase and partly by steps cut in the rock itself. Upon it is a Shiva temple and at the top a small temple dedicated to Pillaiyaur or Ganapaty [vigneshwaran]. In August a festival at this temple attracts a crowd of pilgrims. The teppacoolam [q.v.] has steps down to the edge of the water. In the centre is a mantapam [q.v.] or pillared porch. The houses round the tank were once occupied by Europeans, and one is pointed out as having been Clive's residence. The different gateways or gopoorams [q.v.] are covered with inscriptions, but at present nothing is known of the history and date of the buildings. The districts of Madura and Trichinopoly were constantly devastated by the incursion of the Mahomedans, and it is probably due to this that the pagoda was fortified and made a stronghold. The peculiar design renders the place specially interesting, apart from its more modern associations. The remains of Chundah sahib, murdered in 1752 by Manikjee commander of the Tanjore force in alliance with the English, are interred at the shrine of Nutter owlia. The tomb of this latter saint has the appearance of having been converted out of the materials of Hindoo buildings, and may have been erected about the time of the invasion of Malik caufoor, who came from Delhi in A.D. 1310. Chundah sahib built the dome of the edifice. The railings round the two tombs in the building are of pierced metal-work of very singular design. The group of palaces and gardens, known as the Daur ool imaura, was built about A.D. 1660 by Chokka naick, when he removed his capital from Madura to Trichinopoly. The architecture is Saracenic [maunasauram, staupatyam]. Trichinopoly is the largest city south of Madras and of considerable commercial importance being situated at the trijunction of the Madras, Madura and Erode branches of the South indian railway. The town is famed for the skill of its inhabitants in the manufacture of hardware, cutlery, and jewellery [nagay, zewar]; their harness and saddlery are also excellent in workmanship and materials. Large quantities of cheroots [q.v.] are manufactured from tobacco [pogauk] of superior quality, grown in the neighbouring districts. It is the residence of a Roman catholic bishop. There are several Roman catholic churches, two of which are large and important. The S.P.G., Wesleyans, Lutherans, and Jesuits, have missions here and two first grade colleges, S.P.G. and Saint Joseph's. The cantonment is about 3 miles south-west of the fort, on an extensive open plain studded with masses of granite [caroom cull]. It is extensive, covering an area of from 6 to 8 miles in circuit. The following are the travelling distances by road from Trichinopoly to different places :—

To	Viâ	Miles and Furlongs.	
Adiramputnam ...	Puttoocottah	64	7
Avanashy ...	Caroor and Caungyam	104	0
Bangalore ...	Namcull, Salem and Oossoor	204	7
Bellary	Namcull, Salem, Bangalore and Hiriyore.	392	2
Calicut	Caroor, Palghaut and Malapooram ...	246	6
Calicut	Caroor, Coimbatore, Palghaut and Malapooram.	244	2
Cannanore ...	Coimbatore, Palghaut and Calicut ...	303	3
Caroor	......	49	4
Caungyam ...	Caroor	87	1
Chidambaram ...	Anicut and Combaconam	100	2
Chingleput ...	Volcondapooram, Oolandoorpett and Tindivanam.	165	4
Cochin	Caroor, Coimbatore and Palghaut ...	245	6
Cochin	Caroor, Dharaupooram and Palghaut ...	248	2
Coimbatore ...	Caroor, Caungyam and Pulladam ...	128	7
Combaconam ...	Capistalam	52	4
Cuddalore ...	Volcondapooram and Vriddhauchellam.	111	3½
Cuddalore ...	Combaconam and Chidambaram ...	125	6
Cuddalore ...	Poollambaudy, Shauttatope and Panrooty.	121	1
Dindigul	Manapauray	60	7½
Erode	Caroor	89	5
French rocks ...	Caroor, Hassanore and Seringapatam ...	226	0
Hassanore ...	Caroor, Erode and Suttimangalam ...	147	3
Madras	Volcondapooram, Oolandoorpett, Tindivanam and Chingleput.	200	3
Madras	Govindrajpett, Panrooty, Tindivanam and Chingleput.	218	3
Madras	Combaconam, Cuddalore, Pondicherry and Chingleput.	239	6
Madura	Toovarancoorchy and Mailore	81	0
Madura	Dindigul	101	1
Mangalore ...	Palghaut, Calicut and Cannanore ...	389	4
Mangalore ...	Caroor, Hassanore, Mysore and Mercara.	370	1
Mercara	Caroor, Hassanore, and Mysore ...	284	3
Mettapolliem ...	Caroor and Avanashy	137	7
Munnargoody ...	Vullam	59	2
Mysore	Caroor and Hassanore	210	0
Namcull	Tottiyam	55	3
Negapatam ...	Tanjore and Tirvarore	93	2
Ootacamund ...	Caroor, Avanashy and Mettapolliem ...	170	1¾
Palamcottah ...	Madura	176	6
Palamcottah ...	Dindigul and Madura	196	7
Palghaut	Caroor and Coimbatore	159	6
Palghaut	Caroor and Dharaupooram	162	2
Point calimere ...	Munnargoody	105	3
Pondicherry ...	Combaconam and Cuddalore	137	5
Pondicherry ...	Volcondapooram, Oolandoorpett and Cuddalore.	123	2½
Pulladam ...	Caroor and Caungyam	106	7
Pullavaram ...	Volcondapooram, Tindivanam and Chingleput.	188	3
Quilon	Madura, Palamcottah and Trivandrum	308	2
Quilon	Madura, Shreevillipoottore and Aryancauv ghaut.	234	5
Quilon	Dindigul, Goodalore ghaut and Peermaid.	275	5½
Rameshwaram ...	Madura and Ramnaud	186	4
Ramnaud ...	Madura	159	4
Ranipett	Volcondapooram, Tindivanam and Wandiwash.	179	7
Salem	Namcull	87	7
Seringapatam ...	Caroor, Hassanore and Mysore	219	4
Shiyally	Combaconam	87	5
Shreevillipoottore	Madura and Cullpauty	127	8
Suttimangalam ...	Caroor and Erode	126	7
Tanjore	Vullam	37	2
Tranquebar ...	Combaconam and Perambore	88	7
Trivandrum ...	Madura, Shreevillipoottore, Aryancauv ghaut and Cotacaray.	265	2
Vellore	Volcondapooram, Villoopooram, Jinjee and Arnee.	177	6
Volcondapooram	Paudalore	40	2½

TRINAM (तृण - trina, *San.*). From (trin, san. to injure), as eaten by animals. Grass [ghaus, ghiyah].——*Trinarajan* (तृणराज - trinaraja, San.). Means king of grasses. Same as Palmyra.

TRINOMALLEE (திருவண்ணாமலை - tiruvannámalai, * *Tam.*). From (tiru, tam. sacred + aruna, san. red + malai, tam. mountain) [shree, tir]. Tam. also (annámalai), meaning same as sanscrit; also (arunai), meaning same. Sanscrit name (arunáchala), meaning red + mountain; also (arunagiri), meaning same; from red flowers of the butea frondosa [palaus] trees once found on the hill. Distinguish from Trincomalee.——(1) Talook, South arcot district. Tahsildar's pay Rs. 150. Includes the mittah of Vettavalam. Area 1,010 square miles. Population 205,403. Language Tamul. N.W. of district. Boundaries:—N. Tripatore talook, Salem district, Polore talook, North Arcot; E. Tindivanam and Villoopooram talooks; S. Tricalore and Cullacoorchy talooks; W. Ootancaray talook, Salem district. Regar [q.v.] and sandy soil [manal]. Cheyaur irrigates a portion of the Chengam division by three anicuts [q.v.] across at Chengam, Cottacoolam, and Yerayore. Places of archæological interest:—Auvore, Bhootamungalam, Caunjy, Chengam, Cullote, Gungavaram hills, Keel sangam, Malamanjanore, Malayanore, Manicull, Mekkanore, Moodiyanore, Peroongalattore, Shekkady, Shiviyampett, Tandausampett, Taunapaudy, Trinomallee, Varagore, Vayalore, Vettavalam. The leading places, &c., in the talook are the following.——*Auvore* (ஆவூர் - ávúr, Tam.). From (á, tam. cow + úr, tam. village). Acres 1,555; lat. 12° 08′; long. 79° 16′; from Cuddalore N.W. 46 miles; from Trinomallee S.E. 11 miles. Inscriptions.——*Chengam* (செங்கம் - shengam, Tam.). See sep. title.——*Jawaudy* (சவாதி - shaváthi, Tam.). See sep. title.——*Ponniaur* (பெண்ணையாறு - pennaiyáru, Tam.). See sep. title.——*Toorinjalaur* (துரிஞ்சலாறு - turiñjaláru, Tam.). See sep. title.——*Trinomalee* (திருவண்ணாமலை - tiruvanná-malai, Tam.). See below.——*Vettavalam* (வேட்டவலம் - véttavalâm, Tam.). See sep. title.——(2) Town, Head-quarters of talook, Hill. South arcot dist., Trinomallee tal.; pop. 12,155; acres 4,222; lat. 12° 15′; long. 79° 07′; height 2,669; from Chidambaram N.W. 70 miles; from Cuddalore W.N.W. 57 miles; from Madras S.W. 100 miles; from Tindivanam W. 38 miles; from Tricalore N.N.W. 19 miles; from Vriddhauchellam N.N.W. 50 miles. The first town on the road from the Baramahaul [q.v.] through the Chengam pass, and roads diverge north, south and to the coast. It is thus the entrepôt of trade between South arcot and the country above the ghauts [q.v.], and its fortified hill was always an important military point. The town is well built. The hill consists of three fortified peaks. The isolated Trinomallee peak is covered with jungle and accessible only on foot. From the top of the hill a natural column rises perpendicularly, which Sheiva bramins hold to be a lingam [q.v.]. It is the subject of a legend in the Scandapoorannam. Between 1753 and 1791 it was besieged on ten separate occasions and was six times taken, thrice by assault; besieged unsuccessfully by Moortezah ally khan in 1753, occupied by the French in 1757, recaptured by Krishna row in August 1758, retaken by the French in September, taken by the British in 1760. From 1760 it was a British post, on which Colonel Smith fell back in 1767, as he retired through the Chengam pass before Hyder ally and the Nizam. Here he held out till reinforced, when he signally defeated the allies. The last time it was taken was in January 1791 by Tippoo. Trinomallee is one of the five main Shiva centres [punch lingam]. The Caurtigay [pundigay, 5c] feast in November and December lasts ten days. From the nature of the soil and rock the hill appears red before sun-rise. An annual ceremony takes place in the plain below the hill by setting fire on the hill to a large torch. After some rites a light is kindled towards dark in the evening, when immediately the top of the torch on the hill becomes ignited. This is taken as a miracle. The staple articles of commerce at the festival are cattle [maud], woollen cloths [cumbly], and brass [pittalay] utensils. There is a tamul proverb:—விஷ்ணுவைப் பெரிது என்பார் ஸ்ரீரங்கத்தில், சிவனைப் பெரிது என்பார் அருணாசலத்தில்—"the inhabitants of shree-"rungam say that vishnoo is great, those of arnauchellam say "that shiva is great." The following are the travelling distances by road from Trinomallee to different places:—

To	Viâ	Miles and Furlongs.	
Cuddalore ...	Mangaloorpett	64	5
Mercaunum ...	Jinjee and Tindivanam	46	4
Pondicherry ...	Jinjee and Tindivanam	67	1
Pondicherry ...	Jinjee, Devanore, Meilam	64	2
Vellore	Polore	51	5

TRIPALAM (त्रिफला - trip'halá, *San.*; ترپهلا - tirphala, *Hind.*; ತ್ರಿಫಲ - trip'hali, *Can.*; త్రిఫలము - trip'halamu, *Tel.*; ത്രിഫല - trip'hala, *Mal.*; திரிபலம் - tiribalam, *Tam.*). From (tri, san. three + p'hala, san. fruit); three myrobalans [tri]. The fruit of two species of indian Terminalia [belleric myrobalan, chebulic myrobalan], and one Phyllanthus [emblic myrobalan]. In each case a winged drupe of a dingy yellow color, and containing a hard stone. The myrobalans [q.v.] have been a common dyeing material in this country from time immemorial; with alum [fatakree, padicauram], they yield a good durable yellow [shauyam] and with salts of iron [annabhaidy], a black color little inferior to that produced by oak galls [mauchicoy]; they also make good ink [mashy, shye]; kernels of the nuts are eaten by the natives; in large quantities they produce intoxication; used in almost all diseases. Term Tripalam applied also:—to three spices, nutmeg [jauty], areca nut [q.v.], and cloves [lavangam]; and to three sweet fruits, grape [angoor], pomegranate [anaur], and date [kharjooram].——*Belleric myrobalan* (विभीतक - vibhítaka, San.; बेहडा - béhadá, Mahr.; गोटिंग - gótinga, Conc.; شجر بليلج - shajaribalílaj, Ar.; درخت بليلہ - darakhtibalílah, Pers.; بہیڑلے کا پیڑ - bharlekáper, Hind.; بلدے کا جہاڑ - baldekájhár, Dec.; ملکہ - malaka, Malay; ತಾರೆ - táre, Can.; ಶಾಂತಿಮರ - shántimara, Too.; తాడి - tádi, Tel.; ତର - tara, Oor.; താന്നി - tánni, Mal.; බුළු - bulu, Singh.; தான்றி - tánri, Tam.). Title from arabic. San. from (vi, san. preposition of intensity + bhí, san. to fear), from supposed haunt of devils. Mahr. from sanscrit. Ar. from (shajar, ar. tree + balílaj, ar. belleric myrobalan). Pers. from arabic. Hind. and Dec. from sanscrit. Mal. from tamul. San. also (aksha), from seeds used as dice; (tusha), meaning pleased with little water; (karshap'hala), meaning furrow-fruited; (bhútávása), meaning devil's abode; (kalidruma), meaning caly's tree, the haunt of goblins; cf. bonduc. Hind. also (bhairekáper), meaning myrobalan tree; (balrekájhár), meaning myrobalan tree, cf. belleric above. Malay also (kadondong). Can. also (tari); (shánti); (yebela); (bhirda). Too. also (dandi). Tel. also (tándi); (táni); (tándra). Tam.

also (káttiluppai), meaning forest + bassia longifolia, linn. [wild mohwah]; (akkandam); (ambalatti), meaning growing in open space. Title otherwise Baldah, Bedda, Bhirda, Devil's abode, Shaunty, Taniky, Taundry, Taurey. Botanically Terminalia [antya parny] belerica, roxb., combretaceæ [vricsham, 55]. Alias Myrobalanus belerica; Terminalia punctata. Tree, 100 feet; leaves about the extremities of the branchlets, long-petioled, obovate, quite entire, glabrous; spikes axillary, solitary, almost as long as the leaves; bisexual flowers sessile; male shortly pedicellate; drupe obovate, obscurely five-angled, fleshy, covered with greyish silky down; flowers fetid, small, greyish green. Has straight trunk and spreading head; narrow lance-like leaves, growing in tufts at the tops of the branches; flowering in march-april; common forest tree. The belleric myrobalan is the dried ripe drupe or fruit; it is about the size of an olive [zeitoon], of yellowish grey color, obovate shape, and marked with five longitudinal furrows; downy; size when dry of a gallnut [mauchicoy], and dirty-brown color; very astringent. Insipid gum [gond], resembling gum arabic [q.v.], issues from trunk when wounded; soluble in water, but inflammable, and will burn like a candle. Powder of the dried fruit is medicinally astringent in small doses and cathartic in large ones; in pharm. non-officinal; astringency nearly equal to that of emblic myrobalan; mixed with honey [shahad], the kernel of the nut is used in ophthalmia. Fruit eaten when fresh by goats [vellaud], sheep [aud], cattle [maud], deer [mrigam] and monkeys [bandar]; kernels eaten by natives, and slightly intoxicating. Oil [yennay] expressed from seed used for strengthening hair; fruit used in the arts as the basis of several colors [shauyam]; by itself forms a dingy yellow dye; employed in making ink [mashy]; also used in tanning [chamrah]; gum of no use. Wood white and rather soft, but durable; answers for packing-cases, sometimes hollowed out for canoes. There are three varieties of the belerica:—typica, leaves without glands at the apex of the petiole; belerica proper, leaves with two glands at the apex of the petiole and laurinioides.——*Chebulic myrobalan* (हरीतकी - harítakí, San.; हिरडा - hiradá, Mahr.; شجر هليلج - shajarihalílaj, Ar.; درخت هليله - darakhtihalílah, Pers.; هرڑے کا پیڑ - harrekáper, Hind.; هلدے کا جھاڑ - haldekájhár, Dec.; ಅಳಲೆಮರ - alalemara, Can.; ಅಣಿಲೆಮರ - anilemara, Too.; కరక - karaka, Tel.; କରେଢ଼ - karedha, Oor.; കടുക്കായ - katukkáya, Mal.; අරළු - aralu, Singh.; கடு - kadu, Tam.). Title from arabic meaning cabool myrobalan. San. from (hri, san. to remove); from clearing bowels. Mahr. from sanscrit. Ar. from (shajar, ar. tree + halílaj, ar. chebulic myrobalan). Pers. from (darakht, pers. tree + halílah, pers. chebulic myrobalan). Hind. from (harrá, hind. chebulic myrobalan + per, hind. tree). Dec. from (haldá, hind. chebulic myrobalan + jhár, hind. tree). Can. from (alale, can. gallnut + mara, can. tree). Too. from (anile, too. gallnut + mara, too. tree). Tel. means black color, probably from the black color given by the fruits [wild papaw]. Mal. from tamul. Tam. meaning sharpness. San. also (pat'hyá), meaning agreeing with; (káyast'há), meaning supporting the body; (pancharasá), meaning five tastes; (abhayá), meaning relieving from fear; (avyat'há), meaning relieving from pain; (pútaná), meaning cleansing; (amritá), meaning nectar [emblic myrobalan, goolancha, wild bachnaug]; (pránadá), meaning life-giver; (sudhá), meaning nectar; (bhishakpriyá), meaning physician's favorite [goolancha]; (haimavatí), meaning produced on the himalayas [vashanboo]; (réchakí), meaning purgative [turbith]; (shréyasí), meaning leading to happiness [elephant long pepper]; (shivá), meaning auspicious [purple datura]; (harí), meaning yellow; (hémavatí), meaning golden colored; (chétakí), meaning reminding; (vijayá), meaning conquering; (jayá), meaning victorious [jayah]; (pramat'há), meaning destroying; (amóghá), meaning efficacious; (jívaníyá), supporting life; (nandiní), meaning happy; (róhiní), meaning red. Ar. also (shajarihalílajiasfar), meaning yellow myrobalan tree; (halílajikábulí), meaning cabool chebulic; (halílajíaswad), meaning black chebulic myrobalan. Pers. also (darakhtihalílahizard), meaning yellow myrobalan tree; (halílahikalán), meaning small myrobalan; (halílahisiyáh), meaning black myrobalan. Hind. also (pileharkáper), meaning yellow myrobalan tree; (harkáper), meaning chebulic myrobalan tree. Dec. also (halrekájhár), meaning chebulic myrobalan tree; (harlekájhár), meaning chebulic myrobalan tree; (pílehalekájhár), meaning yellow myrobalan tree. Can. also (aralekáyemara), meaning gallnut + tree; (anilekáyi); (kárekáyi); (herdekáyi); (atala); (pillamaradu); (allimara). Tel. also (karakamaddi), meaning gallnuts + terminalia arjuna, bedd.; (velamakaraka), meaning white + the tree; (pillamaddi), meaning small + terminalia arjuna, bedd.; (shringitíga), meaning top + creeper; (kappatíga), meaning frog + creeper [creeper mooshty]. Title otherwise Black myrobalan, Caraga, Common myrobalan, Country gall nut, Doum palm of egypt, Galled myrobalan, Haritakee, Indian myrobalan, Ink-nut tree, Negroo's olive, Oval-leaved terminalia, Yellow myrobalan. Botanically Terminalia [antya parny] chebula, retz., combretaceæ [vricsham, 55]; specific from hind. meaning from cabool. Alias Melanoxylon cadikamarum; Myrobalanus chebula; Terminalia myrobalanus citrina, reticulata. Cadikamaram from mal. Tree, 40-50 feet; trunk rarely straight, short; bark, ash-colored; branches numerous and spreading; leaves nearly opposite, shortly petioled, ovate oblong, obtuse or cordate at the base, quite entire, when young clothed with glossy silky hairs, particularly above, adult ones glabrous, sometimes glaucous, upper surface inconspicuously dotted, under closely reticulated with purplish veins; glands one on each side at the apex of the petiole; spikes terminal, often panicled; drupes oval, glabrous; nut irregularly and obscurely five-furrowed; flowers numerous small, whitish, fetid; found throughout forests, sometimes planted; from cabool, where it is very abundant. Fruit is Chebulic myrobalan. These are arranged into six classes, the fruit dried when just formed and the size of cumin-seed [jeerah], the fruit dried when the size of a barley-corn [jow], the fruit dried when the size of a raisin and black larger than last and greenish, the fruit near maturity and yellow, the fruit at full maturity. Chebulic myrobalans are of an ovoid shape, about an inch in length, sometimes tapering towards the lower extremity, round or obscurely five or six-sided, more or less furrowed longitudinally, smooth, of a yellowish-brown color, and astringent taste. They contain about 45 per cent. tannin, also gallic acid, mucilage and a brownish yellow coloring matter; the black articles contain an oleo-resin of a green color soluble in alcohol, ether, petroleum, spirit and oil of turpentine; named myrobalanin, is colored red by nitric acid [shorey ka tezaub]. Fictitious myrobalans of very large size are manufactured by glueing slices of the pulp upon a natural fruit. From seeds is expressed a clear, transparent, almost colorless fluid oil [yennay]; galls also are found on the leaves, the tender leaves being punctured by an insect and its eggs deposited therein, which by extravasation of the sap, become enlarged into hollow glands of various shapes and sizes; these more astringent than the fruit. When Indran [q.v.] was drinking amritam [q.v.] in heaven a drop of the fluid fell on the earth and produced the plant. Fruit, gall nuts, and flowers are all used medicinally; fruit is cathartic in large doses and astringent in smaller ones; substituted for british rhubarb, jalap, gallic and tannic acids; gall nuts used like oak [belote] galls; well rubbed with an equal proportion of catechu [q.v.] are used in aphthous complaints; flowers powdered are astringent, expectorant, febrifuge; all in pharm. officinal; medicinally in fine same as terminalia belerica, roxb. [belleric myrabolam] but more generally used. Leaves eaten by cattle; kernels also eaten and taste like filberts [findak], in large quantities produce intoxication. The galls with iron salts give a black dye [shauyam]; with turmeric [country saffron] and indigo [q.v.], a green; and with catechu, a brown; used in preparation of ink [mashy] along with iron [auhan]; with alum [padicaram], gives a yellow dye; used by chucklers in tanning and preparing leather [chamrah]; fruit more astringent than that of terminalia belerica, roxb., much more used by natives in arts and manufactures; plant gives a gum [gond]. Wood very hard, brownish-grey, with a greenish or yellowish tinge, fairly smooth and close-grained, seasons well, and takes a good polish. There is a Tamul proverb:—கடுக்காய்க்கு அகணி நஞ்சு சுக்கிற்குப்புறணி நஞ்சு—"the kernel of the gall-nut "and the skin of dried ginger are poisonous." The two are rejected before using in medicine.——*Citrine myrobalan* (هرڑا - harrá, Hind.). Same as Harra.——*Emblic myrobalan* (आमलकी - ámalakí, San.; अवळा - avalá, Mahr.; आवळो - ávaló, Conc.; املج - amlaj, Ar., آمله - ámlah, Pers.; آنوله - áunlah, Hind., Dec.; ನೆಲ್ಲಿ - nelli, Can. and Too.; ఉసిరిక - usirike, Tel.; ଔଁଳା - ohalu, Oor.; നെല്ലി - nelli, Mal. and Singh.; நெல்லி - nelli, Tam.). Title from sanscrit. San. from (ámla, san. sour). Ar. from persian. Pers. and Hind. from sanscrit; cf. tamarind. Mahr., &c., from sanscrit. Drav. from (nel, mal. rice), from small leaves. San. also (amritá), meaning nectar [chebulic myrobalan, goolancha, wild bachnaug]; (dhátrí), meaning nourishing; (ámrap'halá), meaning sour fruit; (ádip'halá), meaning first fruit; (tishyap'halá), meaning pooshyam [caurtey] fruiting; (vayast'há), meaning keeping or preserving health. Hind. also (aungra); (aruli). Oor. also (gondhona) [buffalo moonnay]. Tam. also (káttunelli), meaning forest + the plant; (tóppi); (tóppunelli), meaning garden + the plant. Greek μυροβάλανος ἐμπλέτζ, μυροβάλανος ἐμβλικὰ. Title otherwise Awla, Garden gooseberry, Nelly, Shrubby phyllanthus. Botanically Phyllanthus [aumlacam] emblica, linn., euphorbiaceæ [vricsham, 118]. Alias Cicca emblica; Emblica officinalis; Myrobalanus emblica. Tree; crooked, thick as a man's body; leaves alternate, bifarious, pinnate, flower-bearing; leaflets numerous, alternate, linear-obtuse, entire; petioles striated, round; calyx six-parted; flowers in the male very numerous in the axils of the lower leaflets and round the common petiole below the leaflets; in the female few, solitary, sessile, mixed with some males in the most exterior floriferous axils; stigmas, three; drupe globular, fleshy, smooth, six-striated; nut obovate-triangular, three-celled; seeds two in each cell; flowers small, greenish yellow. Cultivated in native gardens; flowers like common peel. Fresh emblic myrobalans are globular, fleshy, smooth, six-striated, of a yellowish-green color, and sometimes as large as a walnut [acroot]; they contain an obovate obtusely triangular, three-celled nut, each cell of which contains two triangular seeds; the taste of the pulp is acid, astringent, and somewhat acrid; the dried fruit is the size of a cob nut, sub-hexagonal, wrinkled, of a grey-black color if it has been collected when immature, but yellowish brown if mature; the latter upon pressure breaks up into six parts, each of which consists of a section of the pulp and nut, and contains one triangular brown seed. Fruit in fresh state has purgative properties, but when dry astringent, contains a large proportion of gallic acid; the exudation from the incisions on the fruit is used as an external application in inflammation of the eye; fruit substituted for british gentian [chiretta] and calumba [q.v.]; flowers are refrigerant and aperient; the seeds in infusion are cooling remedy; infusion of leaves applied to sore eyes; bark of root mixed with honey [shahad] applied to aphthas; bark used in diarrhœa; gives to pharm. dried fruit, like oak galls [mauchicoy], extract from wood, like catechu [q.v.]. Fruit made into pickle [chutney]. Bitloban [q.v.] is prepared by melting together impure muriate of soda and emblic myrobalans.; fruit used as an adjunct to hair-dyes; black dye [shauyam] obtained from the fruit, along with myrobalans and sulphate of iron [annabhaidy]; chips of the wood clear muddy water; cf. clearing nut; branches sometimes placed in wells to impart a pleasant flavor to the water; the bark is used for tanning purposes [chamrah]; gives a gum [gond]. Has a wood very hard and durable, stands water well, is used for gun stocks, color reddish. There is a Tamul proverb:—உள்ளங்கையில் நெல்லிக்கனிபோல—"like the "nelly berry in the palm of the hand;" said of something unmistakably evident, from transparent skin and pulp of fruit. ——*Indian myrobalan* (هليلج هندى - halílajihindí, Hind.). Same as Chebulic myrobalan.——*Wild almond myrobalan* (جنگلى بادام - janglíbádám, Hind.). Same as Catapang.——*Yellow myrobalan* (پيلا هرّا - piláharrá, Hind.). Same as Harra.

TRIPATORE (திருப்பத்தூர் - tiruppattúr, *Tam.* tirupatur*). From (tiru, tam. holy + pathi, tam. place + úr, tam. village) [shree, tir].——(1) Talook, Salem district, Tahsildar's pay Rs. 200. Area 539 square miles. Population 188,826. Language Tamul. N.E. of district between N. lat. 12° 16′ and 12° 47′ and between E. long. 78° 27′ to 79° 04′. Extreme length from north to south about 31 and from east to west about 40 miles. Bounded north by Goodiyattam and Vellore talooks, North arcot, east by Polore talook of North arcot and Trinomallee talook in South arcot, south by Ootancaray talook, and west by a portion of the latter talook and by Krishnagherry. The talook may be compared to an isosceles triangle with the apex to the north-east and the base running from north-west to south-east. The greater part is plain country, blending to the south and south-west with Ootancaray and Krishnagherry. West and east the Baramahaul hills and the Jawaudy respectively separate the talook from Krishnagherry and South arcot. To the north centre the Yelagherry hills enter the talook like a wedge. The soil is composed of regar [q.v.], chiefly loamy, and red soil. The formation is gneissic of the quartzo-felspathic variety. Chief industries are trade in grains, oil-seed [yennay] and skins [chamrah], tanning [chamrah], and dealings in barks for dyeing [shauyam] and tanning [chamrah]. Chief products are cumboo [bajrah] and raggy [q.v.], the staple grains used as food, wheat [geung], cholum [q.v.], varagoo [q.v.], shaumay [q.v.], gingelly [q.v.], dholl [common dholl], oolandoo [black gram], horse-gram [q.v.], and beans [country bean]; these are grown on dry lands and hills. In wet lands and gardens, rice [q.v.], tobacco [pogauk], chillies [q.v.], cocoanut [q.v.], areca-nut [q.v.], ground-nut [q.v.], plantains [q.v.], and sugarcane [q.v.] are raised. Coffee [q.v.] is produced in small quantities on the Jawaudy. Paddy [q.v.] is exported to Calicut, rice to Avanashy and Bangalore, and wheat to Madras. The Yelagherry or Vaniyambaudy wheat is noted for fineness. Areca-nut [areca] and yarn are imported from Shirmoogay and Berar. Pepper [q.v.] comes from Palghaut and salt [ooppoo] from Madras. Ghee [q.v.], lamp-oil [q.v.], dholl [q.v.] and jaggery [q.v.] are also exported in different directions, and tamarind [q.v.] fruit goes to Pondicherry and Madras. Auvauramputtay [tungaid], hides [chamrah] and ghee [q.v.] are imported from the adjoining talook of Ootancaray. The chief rivers are the Palaur, which flows through the north-western corner, and the Paumbaur, which flows through the centre and south with their tributaries. There are ferries at Vaniyambaudy at different points on the Palaur and its branches. The principal tanks are Tripatore periyairy tank, which succumbed to the cyclone of may 1874; Agrahauram tank; Irnamputt yegilairy which burst in the cyclone of may 1872; the Vaniyambaudy naugalairy; the Koratty periyairy; and the Coonitchy periyairy. Camping grounds:—Alangauyam, Mottore, Nunnery, Poohoopett, Tripatore, Vaniyambaudy. The camping ground at Muttrapully is indifferent. Zemindarries:—Alanjicolam, Amboor pettah, Anayairy, Bommeycooppam, Candily, Casinaickamputty, Cathirimungalam, Caucangaray, Chiccanacooppam, Chinnacandily, Chinna veppamputt, Cunnaulaputty, Devastaunam, Lakkinaickamputty, Madanancherry, Moocanore, Nuttam, Pauchal, Periyagaram, Poottaharam, Pulliputty, Rauchamungalam, Shammaudicooppam, Shelathampully, Tauthavully, Tiriyaulam, Yelagherry-mittah, Yilayanagaram. Places of archæological interest:—Madagadappa droog, Vaniyambaudy, Yelagherry hill. The leading places, &c., in the talook are the following.——*Agrahauram* (அக்கிரகாரம் - akkiragáram, Tam.). From (agra, san. first + hára, san. gift). Village; pop. 1,896; acres 1,776; lat. 12° 33′; long. 78° 33′; from Salem N.N.E. 66 miles; from Tripatore N.W. 6 miles.——*Alangauyam* (ஆலங்காயம் - álangáyam, Tam.). From (álam, tam. the banyan tree, ficus bengalensis, linn. + kayam, tam. tank). Village; pop. 3,200; acres 1,285; lat. 12° 37′; long. 78° 48′; from Salem N.N.E. 77 miles; from Tripatore N.E. 15 miles. Near the Jawaudy hills; weekly fair on Thursdays.——*Alanjicolam* (அலஞ்சிக்குளம் - alañjikkolam, Tam.). From (azhinjil, tam. sage-leaved alangium, alangium lamarckii, thw. + kulam, tam. tank). Zemindarry, Village; pop. 560; square miles 5. Peshcush Rs. 781.——*Amboor pettah* (ஆம்பூர்ப்பேட்டை - ambúrpéttai, Tam. amburpet*). From (ambúr, tam. a place so called + péttai, tam. suburb). Zemindarry Village; pop. 279; square miles 19; lat. of village 12° 41′; long. 78° 40′; from Salem N.N.E. 77 miles; from Tripatore N.N.E. 14 miles. The village now forms part of the town of Vaniyambaudy. Peshcush Rs. 3,977.——*Anayairy* (ஆனையேரி - anaiyéri, Tam.). From (anai, tam. dam + éri, tam. tank). Zemindarry, Village; pop. 778; square mile 1; lat. of village 12° 28′; long. 78° 37′; from Salem N.N.E. 62 miles; from Tripatore S.S.E. 2 miles. Peshcush Rs. 891.——*Aundyappanore* (ஆண்டியப்பனூர் - ándiyappanúr, Tam.). Means aundy appan's village. Village; pop. 2,041; acres 1,100; lat. 12° 32′; long. 78° 45′; from Salem N.N.E. 70 miles; from Tripatore N.E. 9 miles.——*Authiyore* (ஆதியூர் - áthiyúr, Tam.). From (ádi, san. first + úr, tam. village); as being before tripatore. Sanscrit name (ádipura), meaning first town. Village; pop. 1,682; acres 1,381; lat. 12° 28′; long. 78° 36′; from Salem N.N.E. 52 miles; from Tripatore S.S.W. 1¾ miles.——*Bommeycooppam* (பொம்மைக்குப்பம் - pommaikkuppam, Tam. bommayakuppam*). From (bomma, tel. proper name + kuppam, tam. village). Zemindarry, Village; pop. 1,193; square miles 14; lat. of village 12° 28′; long. 78° 40′; from Salem N.N.E. 64 miles; from Tripatore E.S.E. 4 miles. Peshcush Rs. 5,461.——*Candily* (கந்திலி - kandili, Tam.). From (kandu, can. black + halli, can. village); from the granite quarries in the neighbourhood. Zemindarry, Village; pop. 1,103; square miles 6; lat. of village 12° 29′; long. 78° 30′; from Salem N.N.E. 60 miles; from Tripatore W. 8 miles. Granite [caroom cull] quarries in neighbourhood. Peshcush Rs. 1,448.——*Casinaickamputty* (காசிநாயகம்பட்டி - kasináyagambatti, Tam.). Means caushy naicken's village. Zemindarry, Village; pop. 553; square miles 4; lat. of village 12° 29′; long. 78° 35′; from Salem N.N.E. 62 miles; from Tripatore W.S.W. 3 miles; Peshcush Rs. 1,099.——*Cathirimungalam* (கதிரிமங்கலம் - kathirimangalam, Tam.). From (kathiram, tam. the ebony tree, acacia sundra, dec. + mangala, san. prosperity). Zemindarry, Village; pop. 790. Peshcush Rs. 658.——*Caucangaray* (காகங்கரை - kágangarai, Tam.). From (kágam, tam. crow + karai, tam. bank). Mittah village; pop. 1,123; acres 3,146; lat. 12° 26′; long. 78° 31′; height 1,242 feet; from Salem N.N.E. 57 miles; from Tripatore S.W. 8 miles. Railway station. Weekly market on Fridays. Peshcush Rs. 833.——*Chinnacandily* (சின்னக்கந்திலி - shinnakkandili, Tam.). From (shinna, tam. little + kandili, tam. town so called). Zemindarry, Village; pop. 409; square miles 3; lat. of village 12° 29′; long. 78° 29′; from Salem N.N.E. 60 miles; from Tripatore W. 9 miles. Peshcush Rs. 457.——*Chinna veppamputt* (சின்னவேப்பம்பட்டு - shinnavéppambattu, Tam.). From (shinna, tam. small + vémbu, tam. margosa, melia azadirachta, linn. + pattu, tam. village). Zemindarry, Village; pop. 692; square miles 5¾; lat. of village 12° 38′; long. 78° 39′; from Salem N.N.E. 74 miles; from Tripatore N.N.E. 11 miles. Peshcush Rs. 1,689.——*Janapaur* (சணப்பார் - shanappár, Tam.). From (dzanumu, tel. hemp, crotalaria juncea, linn. + áru, tam. river). River. Branch of Palaur, from which it branches off above Vaniyambaudy; it rejoins it at the town.——*Jawaudy* (சவ்வாதி - shavváthi, Tam.). See sep. title.——*Jollarpett* (சொலார்ப்பேட்டை - sholárppéttai, Tam.). See sep. title.——*Ketaundaputty* (கேதாண்டப்பட்டு - kéthándappattu, Tam.). From (kéthándan, tam. proper name + patti, tam. village). Inam village, Railway station; pop. 832; lat. 12° 39′; long. 78° 37′; height 1,232; feet; from Salem N.N.E. 72 miles; from Tripatore N. 11 miles.——*Koratty* (கொரட்டி - koratti, Tam.). From (kurattai, tam. a gourd, trichosanthes palmata, roxb.). Village; pop. 1,065; acres 1,669; lat. 12° 25′; long. 78° 36′; from Salem N.N.E. 59 miles; from Tripatore S. 5 miles. Copper [tammram], shaushanam [q.v.] preserves the genealogy [vamsham] of certain Tooloova [q.v.] kings and records that Tripatore was a sub-division of the district of Meyyal in the kingdom of Moolwye. It also gives grounds for the inference that Andainaud was the ancient name of the Jawaudies. Car festival in March. Weekly market on Wednesdays.——*Madanancherry* (மதனாஞ்சேரி - mathanáñjéri, Tam.). From (madana, san. proper name + shéri, tam. village). Zemindarry, Village; pop. 653; lat. of village 12° 43′; long. 78° 39′; from Salem N.N.E. 78 miles; from Tripatore N. 16 miles. Peshcush Rs. 390.——*Maudapully* (மாடப்பள்ளி - mádappalli, Tam.). From (mádam, tam. house + palli, tam. village). Village; pop. 2,441; acres 851; lat. 12° 29′; long. 78° 39′; from Salem N.N.E. 64 miles; from Tripatore E. 2 miles. Large tank.——*Moocanore* (மூக்கனூர் - múkkanúr, Tam.).* From (múkkan, tam. proper name + úr, tam. village). Zemindarry, Village; pop. 1,062; square miles 2½;

lat. of village 12° 32′; long. 78° 34′; from Salem N.N.E. 65 miles; from Tripatore N.W. 4 miles. Peshcush Rs. 876.——*Mottore* (மோட்டூர் - móttúr, Tam.). From (módu, tam. high ground + úr, tam. village). Village; pop. 725; acres 694; lat. 12° 34′; long. 78° 45′; from Salem N.N.E. 72 miles; from Tripatore E.N.E. 11 miles. Weekly market on Wednesdays.——*Muttrapully* (மட்டரப்பள்ளி - mattarappalli, Tam.). From (mattam, tam. flatness + tarai, tam. ground + palli, tam. village). Village; pop. 1,266; acres 1,009; lat. 12° 25′; long. 78° 39′; from Salem N.N.E. 61 miles; from Tripatore S.S.E. 6 miles. Weekly market on Tuesdays; on left bank of the Paumbaur.——*Nauttarampully* (நாட்டரம்பள்ளி - náttaramballi, Tam.). From (nádu, tam. country + arai, tam. rock + palli, tam. village). Village; pop. 1,661; acres 1,167; lat. 12° 35′; long. 78° 33′; from Salem N.N.E. 68 miles; from Tripatore N.N.W. 5 miles. Weekly market on Tuesdays.——*Nuttam* (நத்தம் - nattam, Tam.). Means village. Mittah village; pop. 1,128; acres 5,294; lat. 12° 25′; long. 78° 31′; from Salem N.N.E. 56 miles; from Tripatore S.W. 9 miles. Large temple, yearly car festival in April. Peshcush Rs. 2,597.——*Palaur* (பாலாறு - pálárn, Tam.). See sep. title.——*Paraundapully* (பாராண்டப்பள்ளி - parándappalli, Tam.). From (párai, tam. rock + andai, tam. vicinity + palli, tam. village). Village; pop. 784; acres 598; lat. 12° 30′; long. 78° 32′; from Salem N.N.E. 62 miles; from Tripatore W. 5 miles. Temple and weekly market on Sundays.——*Patchore* (பச்சூர் - paççúr, Tam.). From (paççai, tam. green + úr, tam. village). Tam. also (athanigavunippalli), meaning proper name + village. Village; pop. 1,042. Railway station.——*Paumbaur* (பாம்பார் - pámbár, Tam.). See sep. title.——*Peramputt* (பேராம்பட்டு - pérámbattu, Tam.). From (pér, tam. large + pattu, tam. village). Village; pop. 1,720; acres 1,475; lat. 12° 23′; long. 78° 38′; from Salem N.N.E. 57 miles; from Tripatore S. 8 miles. Festival in October.——*Periyagaram* (பெரியகரம் - periyagaram, Tam.). From (periya, tam. large + agaram, tam. village). Zemindarry, Village; pop. 1,029; square miles $4\frac{3}{16}$; lat. of village 12° 29′; long. 78° 34′; from Salem N.N.E. 62 miles; from Tripatore W. 3 miles. Peshcush Rs. 1,755.——*Poothoopett* (புதுப்பேட்டை - puthuppéttai, Tam.). From (puthu, tam. new + péttai, tam. suburb). Tam. also (amanángóvil), meaning jeina + temple. Village; lat. 12° 32′; long. 78° 35′; from Salem N.N.E. 64 miles; from Tripatore N.W. 5 miles. Weekly market on Sundays.——*Poottaharam* (புத்தகரம் - puttagaram, Tam.). From (puthu, tam. new + agaram, tam. village). Zemindarry, Village; pop. 895; square miles $2\frac{3}{16}$; lat. of village 12° 30′; long. 78° 33′; from Salem N.N.E. 63 miles; from Tripatore W.N.W. 4 miles. Peshcush Rs. 927.——*Pulliputty* (பள்ளிப்பட்டி - pallippatti, Tam.). From (palli, tam. member of the caste + patti, tam. cattle-fold). Zemindarry, Village; pop. 549; square miles $3\frac{4}{16}$; lat. of village 12° 42′; long. 78° 39′; from Salem N.N.E. 78 miles; from Tripatore N.N.E. 15 miles. Peshcush Rs. 545.——*Rauchamungalam* (రాచమంగలం - rátsamangalam, Tel.). From (rádzu, tel. king + mangala, san. prosperity). Zemindarry, Village; pop. 658; square miles $1\frac{3}{4}$; lat. of village 12° 27′; long. 78° 37′; from Salem N.N.E. 61 miles; from Tripatore S. 3 miles. Peshcush Rs. 1,037.——*Shammandicooppam* (சம்மந்திக்குப்பம் - shammandikkuppam, Tam.). From (shammandi, tam. relation + kuppam, tam. hamlet). Zemindarry, Village; pop. 278; square miles 2; lat. of village 12° 43′; long. 78° 41′; from Salem N.N.E. 80 miles; from Tripatore N.N.E. 17 miles. Peshcush Rs. 1,409.——*Shelathampully* (சலதம்பள்ளி - shalathamballi, Tam.). From (jalada, san. clond + palli, tam. village). Zemindarry, Village; pop. 664; square miles $9\frac{7}{16}$; lat. of village 12° 29′; long. 78° 39′; from Salem N.N.E. 64 miles; from Tripatore E.S.E. 3 miles. Peshcush Rs. 3,324.——*Shevattore* (செவாத்தூர் - sheváttúr, Tam.). From (shem, tam. red + áru, tam. river + úr, tam. village). Village; pop. 822; acres 1,999; lat. 12° 26′; long. 78° 33′; from Salem N.N.E. 58 miles; from Tripatore S.W. 6 miles.——*Tiriyaulam* (திரியாலம் - tiriyálam, Tam.). From (tri, san. three + álam, tam. banyan tree, ficus bengalensis, linn.). Zemindarry, Village; pop. 408; square miles 15; lat. of village 12° 34′; long. 78° 35′; from Salem N.N.E. 67 miles; from Tripatore N.N.W. 5 miles. Peshcush Rs. 4,504.——*Tripatore* (திருப்பத்தூர் - tiruppattúr, Tam.). See below.——*Vaniyambaudy* (வாணியம்பாடி - vániyambádi, Tam.). See sep. title.——*Vellacoottay* (வெள்ளக்குட்டை - vellakkuttai, Tam.). From (vellai, tam. white + kuttai, tam. small tank). Inam village; pop. 2,470; acres 3,394; lat. 12° 39′; long. 78° 44′; from Salem N.N.E. 77 miles; from Tripatore N.E. 14 miles.——*Yelagherry* (ஏலகிரி - élagiri, Tam.). See sep. title.——*Yelagherrymittah* (ஏலகிரிமிட்டா - élagirimitta, Tam. yelagirimitta *). From (élu, tel. to reign + giri, san. mountain + mittá, tel. estate). Zemindarry, Village; pop. 928; square miles $19\frac{4}{8}$; lat. of village 12° 33′; long. 78° 38′; from Salem N.N.E. 67 miles; from Tripatore N.N.E. 4 miles. On west of Yelagherry hills. Peshcush Rs. 5,891.——*Yilayanagaram* (இளையாநகரம் - ilaiyánagaram, Tam.). From (ilaiyál, tam. lakshmí, the younger + nágara, san. town). Zemindarry, Village; pop. 186; square miles $2\frac{3}{16}$; lat. of village 12° 43′; long. 78° 40′; from Salem N.N.E. 79 miles; from Tripatore N.N.E. 16 miles. Peshcush Rs. 333.——**(2)** Town, Head-quarters of Head assistant collector, Assistant superintendent of Police, District moonsif, and talook, Railway station; Salem dist., Tripatore tal.; pop. 16,499; acres 2,305; lat. 12° 30′; long. 78° 36′; height 1,275 feet; from Madras W.S.W. 121 miles; from Namcull N.N.E. 91 miles; from Oossoor E.S.E. 53 miles; from Salem N.N.E. 63 miles; from Yercaud N.N.E. 55 miles. On south-west line of Madras railway. The native town, east of trunk road, is rich and well-built. Europeans live on west side nearer railway station. The centre of a net-work of roads leading to Alangauyam, Dharmapoory, Krishnagherry, Madras, Ootancaray, Salem, Shingaurapett, and Vaniyambaudy. The town is healthy and the water-supply good. Tope [q.v.] in which most of the public offices are situated. Taken by British and recaptured by Hyder ally in 1767. French mission apostolic represented by a missionary, who resides at Coyilore, two miles away. Trade chiefly in grains [dhaunyam], cloths, lamp-oil [q.v.] and hides [chamrah], for curing which latter there are two or three large tanneries in the hands of Chetties [q.v.] and Lubbays [q.v.]. Tripatore tank [q.v.] is one of the largest in the district receiving the drainage of 75 square miles.——**(3)** Deputy tahsildarry, Madura district. Pay Rs. 100.——**(4)** Village, Deputy tahsildar's station, Sub-registrar's station; Madura dist., Shivagunga zemindarry; pop. 5,446; lat. 10° 07′; long. 78° 39′; from Dindigul E.S.E. 46 miles; from Kodaykarnal E. 76 miles; from Madras S.S.W. 232 miles; from Madura E.N.E. 36 miles; from Rameshwaram N.W. 75 miles; from Ramnaud N.N.W. 54 miles; from Shivagunga N.N.E. 20 miles. Ancient Shiva temple with two inscriptions, first dated in the third year of Tribhoovana chuckravurty paraucrama paundya tevar, the second in the tenth year of Tribhoovana chuckravurty shreevullabha tevar.

TRITRAPOONDY (திருத்துறைபூண்டி - tirutturaippúndi, *Tam.* tiruturaipúndi *). From (tiru, tam. sacred + taru, sar. tree + púndi, tam. place) [shree, tir]. Place of the holy tree. Sanscrit name (bilvavana), meaning the bael tree, ægle marmelos, corr. + forest.——**(1)** Talook, Tanjore district. Tahsildar's pay Rs. 225. Area 485 square miles. South coast of the district. Population 180,308. Language mostly Tamul. Boundaries; N. Negapatam talook. E. Negapatam talook and sea. S. sea. W. Puttoocottah and Munnargoody talooks. Flat level sloping towards the east and south. Soil loamy. Weaving, tobacco [pogauk] trade and salt [ooppoo] manufacture, exportation of rice [q.v.] and paddy [q.v.] to Ceylon. Irrigation by the Coraiyaur, Paumanaiyaur, and their branches Adappaur and Harichendranuddy. Places of archæological interest:—Carpacanautarcoolam, Cautchanam, Jaumboovanoday, Nautchicoolam, Punnayteroo, Shittambore, Tandalcherry, Tircollicaud, Tritrapoondy, Vadacaud, Yidoombauvanam. Principal trig. stations:—Vaunavan mahadevy beacon, Point calimere beacon. The leading places, &c., in the talook are the following.——*Adappaur* (அடப்பாறு - adappáru, Tam.). From (adaippu, tam. obstruction + áru, tam. river). Sanscrit name (kadambanadí), meaning the cadamba tree, anthocephalus cadamba, miq. + river; also (agastyanadí), meaning agastyan + river. River. Branch of the Moollaiyaur.——*Agastyapully* (அகஸ்தியான்பள்ளி - agattiyánballi, Tam.). From (agastya, san. the sage + palli, tam. village). Sanscrit name (agastyáshrama), meaning agastyan, the sage + hermitage. Village; pop. 3,316; acres 2,310; lat. 10° 22′; long. 79° 54′; from Tanjore E.S.E. 56 miles; from Tritrapoondy S.E. 18 miles; from Vedaranyam S. ½ mile; from the sea W. 1 mile. Temple of Agasteeshwaran.——*Calimere point* (கள்ளிமேடு - kallimédu, Tam.). See sep. title.——*Codicaray* (கோடிக்கரை - kódikkarai, Tam.). From (kódi, tam. corner + karai, tam. shore). Sanscrit name (ádisétu), meaning first bund. Village, Sanitarium, Place of pilgrimage; pop. 2,077; acres 1,744; lat. 10° 17′; long. 79° 52′; from Tanjore S.E. 57 miles; from Tritrapoondy S.S.E. 21 miles; from the sea N. ¾ mile. Beacon column. Tobacco [pogauk] largely cultivated.——*Coraiyaur* (கோரையாறு - kóraiyáru, Tam.). See sep. title.——*Jaumboovanoday* (சாம்புவானோடை - shámbuvánódai, Tam.). From (jámbaván, san. the bear god in hindu myth. + ódai, tam. water course). Village; pop. 2,366; acres 3,022; lat. 10° 25′; long. 79° 34′; from Moottoopett N. 3 miles; from Tanjore S.E. 37 miles; from Tritrapoondy S.W. 11 miles; from the sea N. 7 miles. Old musjid [q.v.] with inscriptions. Extensive cocoanut [q.v.] topes [q.v.].——*Moottoopett* (முத்துப்பேட்டை - muttuppéttai, Tam.). See sep. title.——*Palk's bay* (பாக்குக்குடாக்கடல் - pákkukkudákkadal, Tam.). See sep. title——*Talanayar* (தலைஞாயிறு - talaiñáyiru, Tam.). From (talai, tam. first + ñáyiru, tam. sun). Village; pop. 1,752; acres 799; lat. 10° 34′; long. 79° 49′; from Tanjore S.E. 44 miles; from Tritrapoondy E. 9 miles; from the sea W. 6 miles. Large Bramin village. Surrounded with lakes known as Cottagams, which abound with teal [common teal, varatam] and wild duck [q.v.] in the cold weather. Old Vishnoo temple.——*Tillavilaugam* (தில்லைவிளாகம் - tillaivilágam, Tam.). From (tillai, tam. tiger's milk tree, excæcaria agallocha, mueller, var. camettia + vilar, tam. fertility + agam, tam. place). Village; pop. 2,715; acres 3,606; lat. 10° 25′; long. 79° 36′; from Tanjore S.E. 38 miles; from Tritrapoondy S.W. 11 miles; from the sea N. 7 miles. About twenty-five years ago large-sized idols [shilay, vigraham] of Rama [q.v.], Lutchmanan [q.v.], and Seetay [q.v.] were found under ground. A small temple has since been constructed for them.——*Topetoray* (தோப்புத் துறை - tópputturai, Tam.). See sep. title.——*Tritrapoondy* (திருத்துறைபூண்டி - tirutturaippúndi, Tam.). See below. ——*Vada cuttalay* (வடக்கட்டளை - vadakkattalai, Tam.). From (vada, tam. north + kattalai, tam. portion). Town; pop. 3,059; from Tanjore S.E. 54 miles; from Tritrapoondy S.E. 17 miles; from the sea W. 3 miles.——*Vaunaran mahadevy beacon* (வானவன்மகாதேவி - vánavanmagáthévi, Tam.). From (vánavan, tam. celestial + mahá, san. great + déví, san. goddess). Trig. station; lat. 10° 31′ 56·71″; long. 79° 53′ 58·66″; from Tritrapoondy E. 15 miles; from Covilputt S.E. 1½ miles. On the seashore.——*Vedaranyam* (வேதாரணியம் - vétháraniyam, Tam.). See sep. title.——*Vidoombauranam* (இடும்பாவனம் - idumbávanam, Tam.). From (idumban, tam. name of a giant + vana, san. forest). Sanscrit name (hidimbavana), meaning same. Village; pop. 2,479; acres 9,396; lat. 10° 25′; long. 79° 39′; from Tanjore S.E. 39 miles; from Tritrapoondy S.S.W. 8 miles; from the sea N. 8 miles. Old Shiva temple with inscriptions in the gopooram [q.v.].——**(2)** Head-quarters of Tahsildar, District moonsif and D.P.W. Sub-division; Tanjore dist., Tritrapoondy tal.; pop. 2,666; acres 1,359; lat. 10° 32′; long. 79° 41′; from Combaconam S.E. 33 miles; from Madras S. 180 miles; from Mayavaram S. 38 miles; from Munnargoody S.E. 15 miles; from Negapatam S.W. 20 miles; from Tanjore E.S.E. 38 miles; from the sea. W. 14 miles. On the Moollaiyaur, which irrigates a great portion of the talook. Old Shiva temple with inscriptions. Well attended weekly market.

TRIVELLORE (تلوالور - tilválúr, *Hind.*; திருவள்ளூர் - tiruvallúr,* *Tam.*). From (tiru, tam. holy + val, tam. beauty + úr, tam. village) [shree, tir]. Tam. also (evvulúr), meaning which + house + village. Sanscrit name (víksháranya), meaning sight + forest; also (kingrahapurí), meaning which + house + city; also (kingrahanagara), meaning same. Otherwise Yevvoolore.——**(1)** Talook, Chingleput district. Tahsildar's pay Rs. 175. Area 508 square miles. Population 170,939. Language Tamul, Teloogoo. N.W. of district. Bounded east by Sydapett and Ponnairy talooks; east and north by Calastry and Vencatagherry zemindarries; west by Vencatagherry, Calastry and Carvetnugger zemindarries; and south by Conjeeveram talook. The talook generally is flat and uninteresting, but it is altogether the best wooded in the district. At the northern end the Naugalaupooram and Suttivaid hills relieve the monotonous plain. The rainfall, which averages about 61 inches, is the highest in the district. The soil is generally either sandy, or red ferruginous loam. The soils soak up so much moisture that in spite of the heavy rainfall, the talook is no better off in the quality of its dry crops [dry grain] than neighbouring tracts with stiff black soil and less than half the rainfall [mazhay]. The principal crops are paddy [q.v.], raggy [q.v.], indigo [q.v.], varagoo [q.v.] and cumboo [bajrah]. Weaving is carried on in many villages, but only for the supply of local demand. English cloth is dyed for male and female garments. Red handkerchiefs [roomaul] and Mussalman cloths are manufactured in Suttivaid division. These are sent to Bangalore, whence they find their way to Madras, Penang and Singapore. Rivers are the Corteliaur, which flows eastward through the centre of the talook; the Aranyaunddy, which runs across its northern borders; the Cooum, which supplies irrigation to several villages near the line of railway; and in the Suttivaid division of the talook a jungle stream called the Yellappa naidoo pettah stream which irrigates Amboor, Colattore, Pandore, and a few other villages in that part. Petty zemindarries:—Autpaukam, Caucalore, Colundalore, Coonnatore, Eivailyaharam, Keivandore, Mailaharam, Mauthancooppam, Nungumbaukum, Paunambaukam, Shembaid, Shenjey, Siroovanore, Tirvore, Tripassore, Vengal, Yekatore. Places of archæological interest:—Allicore, Cambaukam droog, Caradipoottore, Cottacooppam, Madavilaugam, Manjacarnay, Maulandore, Naugalaupooram, Nambaukam, Ootcottay, Paunambaukam, Periyapolliem, Pondavaukam, Poothoor, Rajanagaram, Raman coil, Ramgherry, Shenjey, Shirvaid, Shittambaukam, Suttivaid, Tirvore, Tomore, Tripassore, Trivellore. Principal trig. stations:—Cambaukum droog, Shembaid. The leading places, &c., in the talook are the following.——*Cadambatore* (கடம்பத்தூர் - kadambattúr, Tam. kadambatúr *). From (kadambu, tam. a tree, barringtonia acutangula, gærtn. + úr, tam. village). Village, Railway station; pop. 1,119; acres 528; lat. 13° 06′; long. 79° 56′; height 170 feet; from Sydapett N.W. 25 miles; from Trivellore S.W. 4 miles.——*Calattore* (களத்தூர் - kalattúr, Tam.). From (kalam, tam. threshing floor + úr, tam. village). Tam. also (kalandai), meaning threshing floor + place; also (tirukkalandai), meaning holy + threshing floor + place. Village; pop. 990; acres 2,241; lat. 13° 39′; long. 80° 01′; from Sydapett N.W. 46 miles; from Trivellore N. 35 miles.——*Cambaukum* (காம்பாக்கம் - kámbákkam, Tam.). See sep. title.——*Caucalore* (காகளூர் - kágalúr, Tam.). From (kákóli, tam. the ashoca tree, saraca indica, linn. + úr, tam. village). Zemindarry, Village; pop. 945; square miles 2½; lat. of village 13° 09′; long. 79° 59′; from Sydapett N.W. 21 miles; from Trivellore E. 1½ miles. Peshcush Rs. 986. Caucalore naud formed part of Eecautt cottam in the ancient Tondaimundalam [tonday].——*Corteliaur* (கொர்த்தலையாறு - korttalaiyáru, Tam.). See sep. title.——*Eecaud* (ஈக்காடு - íkkádu, Tam.). From (í, tam. bee + kádu, tam. forest). Village; pop. 1,820; acres 2,467; lat. 13° 10′; long. 79° 59′; from Sydapett N.W. 22 miles; from Trivellore N.E. 1½ miles.——*Naugalaupooram* (நாகலாப்புரம் - nágaláppuram, Tam.). See sep. title.——*Nungumbaukum* (நுங்கம்பாக்கம் - nungambákkam, Tam.). From (nungama, tel. proper name + pákkam, tam. village). Zemindarry, Village; pop. 961; square miles 2; lat. of village 13° 04′; long. 79° 58′; from Sydapett W. 22 miles; from Trivellore S. 5 miles. Peshcush Rs. 540.——*Pattrapermatore* (பட்டரப்பெருமதூர் - pattarapperumathúr, Tam.). From (patti, tam. cattle-fold + éri, tam. tank + perum, tam. great + pathi, tam. place + úr, tam. village). Village; pop. 2,321; acres 3,313; lat. 13° 09′; long. 79° 53′; from Sydapett N.W. 28 miles; from Trivellore W. 6 miles.——*Paunambaukam* (பானம்பாக்கம் - pánambákkam, Tam.). From (pánam, tam. toddy + pákkam, tam. village). Zemindarry, Village; pop. 366; square mile 1; lat. of village 13° 06′; long. 79° 54′; from Sydapett W. 26 miles; from Trivellore S.W. 5¾ miles. Peshcush Rs. 275. Ancient Shiva temple built by a Chola king.——*Periyapolliem* (பெரியபாளையம் - periyappálaiyam, Tam.). From (periya, tam. great + pálaiyam, tam. fortified village). Village; pop. 1,539; acres 785; lat. 13° 19′; long. 80° 7′; from Madras N.W. 22 miles; from Sydapett N.W. 23 miles; from Trivellore N.E. 15 miles. Old Doorga [q.v.] temple to Bhawauny [q.v.]. Annual festival in Audy [mausam] or july when pilgrims perform vows by going round temple clothed in garments of margosa [neem] leaves and sacrificing sheep [aud] and fowls [moorghy].——*Ramancherry* (இராமஞ்சேரி - irámañjéri, Tam.). From (ráma, san. proper name + shéri, tam. village). Village; pop. 3,264; acres 3,813; lat. 13° 12′; long. 79° 51′; from Sydapett N.W. 31 miles; from Trivellore N.W. 8 miles.——*Shembaid* (செம்பேடு - shembédu, Tam.). From (shem, tam. red + pédu, tam. village). Zemindarry, Village; pop. 975; square miles 4; lat. of village 13° 15′; long. 80° 03′; from Sydapett N.W. 21 miles; from Trivellore N.E. 9 miles. Peshcush Rs. 877. Trig. station in lat. 13° 15′ 22·70″; long. 80° 01′ 11·17″; height 244 feet; from Vada madura W. 5 miles; from Trivellore N.N.E. 9 miles.——*Shenjey* (செஞ்சி - sheñji, Tam.). From (shem, tam. red + shey, tam. field). Zemindarry, Village; pop. 812; square miles 1⅝; lat. of village 13° 05′; long. 79° 53′; from Sydapett W. 27 miles; from Trivellore S.W. 7 miles. Peshcush Rs. 1,027. Old Shiva temple built by a Chola king with inscriptions.——*Suttivaid* (சத்தியவேடு - shattiyavédu, Tam.). See sep. title.——*Tirvore* (திருவூர் - tiruvúr, Tam. tiruvúr *). From (tiru, tam. holy + úr, tam. village). Zemindarry, Village; pop. 6,673; square miles 19; lat. of village 13° 07′; long. 80° 01′; from Sydapett N.W. 18 miles; from Trivellore E. 5 miles. Peshcush Rs. 7,784. Three inscriptions of Vijianugger and Mysore dynasties in front of a ruined Shiva temple.——*Trippassore* (திருப்பாசூர் - tiruppásúr, Tam.). See sep. title.——*Trivellore* (திருவள்ளூர் - tiruvallúr, Tam.). See below.——*Vada madura* (வடமதுரை - vadamathurai, Tam.). Means north madura. Village; pop. 2,509; acres 4,772; lat. 13° 17′; long. 80° 06′; from Sydapett N.W. 23 miles; from Trivellore N.E. 13 miles. Tank of ten months' capacity, the largest in the talook.——*Velliyore tambrapaukam* (வெள்ளியூர்த்தாம்பிரப்பாக்கம் - velliyúrttámbirappákkam, Tam.). From (velliyúr, tam. village so called + támbirappákkam, tam. village so called). Village; pop. 1,507; acres 2,694; lat. 13° 13′; long. 80° 04′; from Sydapett N.W. 19 miles; from Trivellore N.E. 9 miles. Site of an anicut [q.v.] on the Corteliaur, from which a channel [q.v.] is taken off to supply Red hills tank [q.v.].——*Vengal* (வெங்கல் - vengal, Tam.). From (ven, tam. white + kal, tam. stone). Zemindarry, Village; pop. 2,075; square miles 5¼; lat. of village 13° 15′; long. 80° 04′; from Sydapett N.W. 21 miles; from Trivellore N.E. 10 miles. Peshcush Rs. 1,693.——*Yekatore* (ஏகாட்டூர் - égáttúr, Tam.). From (ézh, tam. seven + kádu, tam. forest + úr, tam. village). Zemindarry, Village; pop. 1,649; square miles 3; lat. of village 13° 07′; long. 79° 57′; from Sydapett N.W. 23 miles; from Trivellore S.W. 3 miles. Peshcush Rs. 2,837.——**(2)** Town, Place of pilgrimage, Railway station, Talook head-quarters, District moonsif's station, Telegraph office, Sub-registrar's office; Chingleput dist., Trivellore tal.; pop. 5,023; acres 264; lat. 13° 09′; long. 79° 58′; height 151 feet; from Chingleput N. 31 miles; from Conjeeveram N.E. 25 miles; from Madras W. 26 miles; from St. Thomas' mount N.W. 22 miles; from Sydapett N.W. 23 miles. Town is about two miles north of railway station. The large Vishnoo temple at each new moon [amavausyay] attracts crowds of natives from Madras, who perform ablutions [snaunam] in the tank. There are two specially great fixed festivals, Bramhotsavam [pundigay, 6a] on the new-moon day in Tye [mausam], or january and floating festival on that in Auny [mausam] or june. The nucleus from which the present building sprung was a small village pagoda [q.v.] containing a double shrine, under the name of Veera raghava sawmy, dedicated to Vishnoo and his wife. This stands in a cloistered court, measuring 192 feet by 156 feet, with one tower or gopooram [q.v.] in the front wall. Another court was afterwards added, measuring 470 feet square, with two towers in the walls. Some time afterwards a third and last court was added, measuring 940 feet by 701 feet, ornamented with five towers and containing several new shrines. It was designed to erect a mantapam [q.v.] or hall of thousand pillars in this outer court. The builders set up 688 of these, about half of which were covered in, when want of funds stopped further progress. This is the head-quarters of the Ahobala mutt [q.v.], the head of which is styled Jiyyar [q.v.], the high priest of Vadagalays [q.v.]. There is also a Shiva temple called Teerteshwara sawmy's pagoda [q.v.] older than the Vishnoo temple.

TROOTY (त्रुटि - truti, *San.*). From (trut, san. to fall asunder). An atom. Measure of solar time. 100 trooties = 1 tatparam or speck [caulam]. Approximate actual value, 1 trooty = $\frac{1}{33750}$th of an English second. Compare Paramaunoo.

TSIANA (ചട്ട - channa, *Mal.*). Title corruption from malayalam, which is short for (channakkúva, mal.). Arabian costum.

TSIELA (पिंपर - pimpara, *Mahr.*; ಬಿಳಿಬಸರಿ - bilibasari, *Can.*; జువ్వి - dzuvvi, *Tel.*; ചേലമരം - chélamaram, *Mal.*; ඉතෙටු - ehetu, *Singh.*; இச்சி - içci, *Tam.*). Title from malayalam. Mahr. means peepul tree, ficus religiosa, linn. Can. from (bili, can. white + basari, can. ficus infectoria, roxb.). Mal. from (chéla, mal. cloth + maram, mal. tree); bark made into a kind of cloth; cf. sack tree. Tel. also (peddadzuvvi), meaning large + the tree. Tam. also (kuruvál), meaning short + banyan tree, ficus bengalensis, linn.; (shittál), meaning small banyan tree. Title otherwise Itchy, Jovy, Short banyan. Botanically Ficus [atty] tsiela, roxb., moraceæ [vricsham, 121]. Specific name from malayalam. Alias Ficus amplissima. Large spreading tree without aerial roots; leaves 2 to 4½ inches; nerves indistinct, from eight to ten pairs; petiole 1¼ to 2 inches; stipules ovate acuminate, ½ to 1 inch; male flowers few, sessile; sepals three ovate, acuminate, longer than the single stamen; anther broadly ovate, filament longer thick; gall flower sessile or pedicelled; female mostly sessile; sepals of both three, ovate shorter than the achene; fertile and gall achenes ovate-reniform, fertile broadest; style in both long, stigma cylindric. Fruit receptacles axillary, paired, sessile, round, turbinate, smooth, the size of a cherry [q.v.]; common in subalpine tracts; the juice of the root and fruit is remedy in sore eyes; much planted as an avenue tree [shaulay]; bark gives fibre [naur].——*Hill tsiela* (కొండజువ్వి - kondadzuvvi, Tel.). Tel. from (konda, tel. hill + dzuvvi, tel. ficus tsiela, roxb.). Botanically Ficus [atty] tuberculata, roxb., moraceæ [vricsham, 121]. Small tree; leaves short-petioled, oblong, entire, acute, rough; fruit-receptacles paired, peduncled, roundish, size of a large pea [calauyam], tubercled.——*Red tsiela* (ఎఱ్ఱజువ్వి - erradzuvvi, Tel.). Same as Shilandy.——*Small tsiela* (పుత్రజువ్వి - putradzuvvi, Tel.). Tel. from (putra, san. son, diminutive term + dzuvvi, tel. ficus tsiela, roxb.), meaning small species; cf. putranjeeva. Title otherwise Willow fig tree. Botanically Ficus [atty] benjamina, linn., urticaceæ [vricsham, 119]. Alias Ficus pendula, striata; Urostigma benjamineum. Branchlets slender, flexuose, weak, hanging; petioles round, rather short; leaves ovate or elliptic-ovate, acuminate, coriaceous, like parchment, surrounded by a smooth margin, veins capillary, horizontal, united into an arched nerve; fruit axillary, sessile, like peas [calauyam]; bracts, three, ovate-obtuse deciduous; fruit smooth, shining, greenish yellow, with a dash of purple.——*White tsiela* (తెల్లజువ్వి - telladzuvvi, Tel.). Same as Rough coorvitchy.

TSJINKIN (چینی حنا - chíníhiná, *Pers.*). China mindie.

TUCCAUVY (تقاوی - takávi, *Hind.*). From (kavi, ar. strong). A reinforcement. Advance of money to ryots [q.v.] to enable them to buy seed and stock for cultivation [vellaumay]. See vol. I, 112.

TULLY (తళి - tali, *Can.*). Means good breed, applied to a cow. Village; Salem dist., Oossoor tal.; pop. 1,868; acres 850; lat. 12° 35′; long. 77° 42′; from Oossoor S.W. 15 miles; from Salem N.N.W. 72 miles. The locality is feverish, the town being situated in a hollow close to the tank bed. Large agricultural centre. Trade in grain in large quantities, oil-seed [yennay], betel-nut [q.v.], and garden produce [vellaumay].

TUNGACHERRY (തങ്കശ്ശേരി - tankashshéri, *Mal.* tangachéri*). From (chankan, mal. a fisherman + chéri, mal. village). Title otherwise Chungacherry, especially the third and fourth items.—"*a*" Sub-magistracy; Malabar dist., Cochin tal. Pay Rs. 70.—"*b*" Village; Malabar dist., Cochin tal.; pop. 1,715; lat. 8° 54′ N.; long. 76° 37′ E.; from Cochin S. 75 miles; from Ernaculum S.S.E. 76 miles; from Madras S.W. 380 miles; from Trichore S.S.E. 112 miles; from Tripoontora S. 72 miles; from Trivandrum N.N.W. 38 miles; from the sea E. ½ mile. Originally a fort built in a head-land of laterite [q.v.] jutting into the sea. Portions of the old wall are still visible as also ruins of an old Portuguese tower and belfry. Bounded north and north-east by Travancore territory, west, south and south-east by the sea, adjoins Quilon on the west. Tungacherry reef extends 1½ miles to the south-west and 3 miles to the west of Tungacherry point, and 6 miles along the coast to the northward. The bank should not be approached by vessels under 13 fathoms of water by day or 17 fathoms at night. Town level, crowded with houses, very thickly planted with cocoanut [q.v.], bread-fruit [jack], and other trees. Lies on the margin of the sea and bears the appearance of decay. The population betrays the mixture of a foreign race. Portuguese possession from 1552 to 1665, then captured by the Dutch. Came under the English government on the capture of Cochin in 1795, and like that town is attached to the Malabar collectorate. The tract has been leased to the Travancore government for an annual rent of Rs. 2,447. In civil judicial matters the people are subject to the District moonsif's court at Anjengo, which is again subordinate to the District court of South malabar. For criminal matters there is a resident Subordinate magistrate under the immediate orders of the Deputy magistrate of Cochin. There are two sections of Roman catholics here, one owing allegiance to the Goa mission and the other to the Propaganda mission of Verapoly. Church of the latter is very old. Two cemeteries built by Dutch. Coir-yarn [coir] manufactured.—"*c*" Talook; Travancore state, Cottayam division; pop. 74,154. Its greatest length, N. to S. is 12 miles and its greatest breadth, E. to W., is 25 miles. It is sub-divided into 7 praverties [q.v.] and contains 64 caras [q.v.] or villages; boundaries. The talook is bounded N. by Cottayam and Meenachel talooks, E. by the hills, S. by Tiroovalla talook and W. by Ambalapoya talook and the Vembanaud lake; physical aspect is in some parts hilly and in others low with paddy [q.v.] fields; soil is exceedingly productive. Good brass [pittalay] vessels are made at Chungacherry. Trade with Alleppey, Cochin and other places in pepper [q.v.], turmeric [country saffron] and cloth. The talook has the largest number of pepper [q.v.] vines and the most extensive sugar-cane [q.v.] cultivation in the whole state.—"*d*" Town, Tahsildar's station; Travancore state, Cottayam division, Chungacherry tal.; pop. 12,961; lat. 9° 27′; long. 76° 35′; from Alleppey E.S.E. 14 miles; from Cottayam S. 10 miles; from Madras S.W. 355 miles; from Nagercoil N.W. 103 miles; from Paravore S.S.E. 52 miles; from Quilon N. 37 miles; from Trivandrum N.N.W. 70 miles; from the sea E. 13 miles. Built on rising ground on the eastern border of the Cootnaud delta. Innumerable canals lead to it. Communication with Dindigul valley across the hills and by water with Quilon, Alleppey, &c. Former capital of Chungacherry rajahs. Also the seat of a family of Coil tumboorauns [q.v] who are allied to the royal family by marriage. Inhabited mostly by Syrian christians, who form an industrious class. There are several Syrian [q.v.] churches. Noted for a large fair, where all varieties of productions of the country are brought for sale, mostly vegetables. Good bronze vessels are made here, also brass [pittalay] boxes.

TUNGAID (तिमिरहरी - timiraharí, *San.*; तरवड - taravada, *Mahr.*; تروڑ - tarwar, *Hind.* and *Dec.*; ಒಳ್ಳೆತಂಗಡಿ - olletangedi, *Can.*; తంగేడు - tangédu, *Tel.*; ആവിരം - áviram, *Mal.*; රනවරා - ranavará, *Singh.*; ஆவாரை ávárai, *Tam.*). Title from teloogoo. San. from (timira, san. morbid affection of eye + hri, san. to destroy). Can. from (olle, can. good + tangedi, can. cassia auriculata, linn.). Mal. from tamul. Can. also (tangedi); (ávarike); (chákusivagida); (taravadagida). Mal. also (ponnáviram), meaning golden + the plant. Tam. also (ávirai). Title otherwise Auvauray, Eared cassia, Tanner's cassia, Tarwar, Tungedy [dark vail]. Botanically Cassia [soovarnacam] auriculata, linn., leguminosæ [vricsham, 48]. Alias Senna auriculata. Shrub; young branches, petioles, and peduncles pubescent; leaflets eight to twelve pairs, with a gland between each pair, oval, obtuse or retuse, mucronate, upper side glabrous, under slightly pubescent; racemes axillary, nearly as long as the leaves, many-flowered, approximated towards the ends of the branches; pedicels compressed; sepals slightly hairy; legumes compressed, straight; flowers three to five together, bright yellow. Very common, with dense foliage, easily distinguished by the ear-like appendage between each pair of leaflets; abundant large yellow flowers; much found in plains and sterile tracts. The bark as generally met with is about as thick as cinnamon [q.v.], nearly smooth, externally reddish-brown, internally olive-green; it occurs in small strips or quills; taste sweetish, and moderately astringent; sections examined under the microscope show a deposit of crystals arranged like rows of beads in the course of the vessels, otherwise, there is nothing remarkable. The seeds are smooth, flat, of an oval, oblong, or obscurely triangular form, obtusely pointed at one end; their color is brown, or dull olive-green; they are tasteless and inodorous. Bark employed medicinally in place of oak-bark [belote] for gargles, enemas, &c.; seeds are a local application in ophthalmia or country sore eyes; resin [raul] medicinal; flowers astringent. Added to jaggery [q.v.] water when arrack [q.v.] is being formed. Bark and small unpeeled branches much used for tanning [chamrah] and dyeing [shauyam]; it dyes leather a buff color on the whole the best indigenous astringent for tanning purpose; when the government tannery existed at Hoonsoor, it was used almost exclusively there for tanning purposes; the root is employed in tempering iron [auhan] with steel [wootz]; tooth-brushes are made from the branches; flowers yield yellow coloring matter, but not used economically. There is a Tamul proverb:—ஆவாரை இலையும் ஆபத்துக்

குதவும்—"even the leaves of the auvauray may be useful in "misfortune;" they are eaten in famine.——*Foreign tungaid* (हॊडिरतनगंधि - hódiratnagandhi, Conc.; گل مہر - gulmuhr, Hind.; گل مہر - gulmohr, Dec.; ದೊಡ್ಡರತ್ನಗಂಧಿ - doddaratnagandhi, Can.; సీమతంగేడు - símatangédu, Tel.; അലസിപ്പൂവു - alasippúvu, Mal.; மயிர்கொன்றை - mayirgonrai, Tam.). Title from being introduced from madagascar. Hind. from (gul, pers. flower + muhr, hind. peacock) [gold mohur tree]. Dec. from hindostany. Can. from (dodda, can. large + ratna, can. gem + gandhi, can. scent). Tel. from (síma, tel. foreign + tangédu, tel. cassia auriculata, linn.). Mal. from (alasuka, mal. to miscarry + púvu, mal. flower); perhaps from the loose petals. Tam. from (mayil, tam. peacock + konrai, tam. cassia fistula, linn.). Title otherwise Flamboyant, Mascarene, Peacock's pride, Royal gold mohur, Royal peacock-flower, Royal poinciana. Botanically Poinciana [ratnagandhy] regia, bojer., leguminosæ [vricsham, 48]. Alias Cæsalpinia regia. A large tree, with showy-colored flowers; introduced from madagascar, still confined to gardens and avenues [shaulay]; does not attain a great size. Gives a gum [gond]. Wood white, soft, light, and loose-grained. The same title is also applied to Yellow condray. For other red gaudy flowered trees see:—Anaur, Bastard saffron, China rose bendy, Common coral tree, Gendah, Indian pink, Indian shot, Indian water-lily, Jaffer goondy, Jungle geranium, Lotus bendy, Moorgha, Nelumbo, Palaus, Purple mountain ebony, Rangoon creeper, Red cotton tree, Soonkeshwaram, Wild bachnaug.——*Gold tungaid* (పమిడితంగేడు - pamiditangédu, Tel.). Title from flower. Same as Gold mohur tree.——*Ground tungaid* (నేలతంగేడు - nélatangédu, Tel.). Same as Tinnevelly senna.——*Hill tungaid* (ಸೊಗಡತಗಚೆ - sogadatagache, Can.; மலையாவாரை - malaiyávárai, Tam.). Title from habitat. Can. from (sogadu, can. fetid smell + tagache, can. cassia tora, linn.). Tam. from (malai, tam. mountain + ávárai, tam. cassia auriculata, linn.).—"*a*" Botanically Cassia [soovarnacam] tomentosa, linn., leguminosæ [vricsham, 48]. Alias Cassia multiglandulosa. Large shrub; branches tomentose; leaflets six to eight pair, usually with a gland between each pair, linear-oblong, mucronate, a little unequal at the base, pubescent above, tomentose beneath; racemes in the upper axils as long as the leaves, forming a leafy corymbiform panicle; legumes long, linear, compressed, mucronate, tomentose; seed somewhat kidneyshaped, horizontal; neilgherries.—"*b*" The same title is also applied to Yellow condray.—"*c*" Botanically Sophora glauca, lesch., leguminosæ [vricsham, 48]. Alias Edwardsia madraspatana; Sophora madraspatana. Shrub; leaves irregularly pinnated; leaflets nineteen to twenty-three, elliptical, mucronate, upper side glaucous and velvety, under villous; racemes terminal, crowded; flowers middle-sized, white tinged with rose; neilgherries, flowering nearly all the year. Other species are:—heptaphylla, interrupta, tomentosa.—"*d*" Same as Dark vail.

TUNKAH (تنخواہ - tankhwáh, *Hind.*). From (tan, pers. body + khwáh, pers. demanding). Draft for payment of allowance, &c., made upon an inhabitant; salary [talab].

TUNKAM (टङ्क - tanka, *San.*; تنک - tankah, *Hind.*). From (tank, san. to bind). Instrument. So a stamped coin or weight. —"*a*" Chief silver coin of the Delhi sovereign, substantially the same as the rupee of the later days. 4 dubs = 1 silver fanam; 4 silver fanams = 1 silver tunkam. There was also a gold tunkam coin and a copper.—"*b*" Epithet applied to the finest gold or that of 10½ touch.—"*c*" Goldsmith's weight. 16 dubs = 1 tunkum; 1¼ tunkams = 1 cutcha seer [niray, 3b]. Approximate actual value, 1 tunkam = 7 oz. 4 dwts. Here a tunkam is the weight of the value in copper, of a gold tunkam. See vol. I, 609; II, 512.——**(1)** *Tungam* (തങ്കം - tankam, Mal.; தங்கம் - tangam, Tam.). Gold [pon]. In composition denotes excellence or goodness. Hindoo female proper name. Familiarly Tungy. Compare Canacam, Bungaur, Ponnoo [peyar].——*Tungarauz* (தங்கராசு - tangarásu, Tam.). From (tangam, tam. gold + rájá, san. king). Hindoo 2nd or pers. name [peyar]. ——*Tungasawmy* (தங்கசாமி - tangasámi, Tam.). From (tangam, tam. gold + svámí, san. lord, titular affix). Golden or dear lord. Hindoo 2nd or pers. name. Common among non-bramins [peyar].——*Tungaveilov* (தங்கவேலு - tangavélu, Tam.). From (tangam, tam. gold + vél, tam. spear), soobramanyan with the ornamental spear. Hindoo 2nd or pers. name. Common among non-bramins [peyar].——*Tunka cash* (టంకకాసు - tankakásu, Tel.). A gold ducat.——*Tunkasaula* (టంకశాల - tankasála, Tel.). From (above + shálá, san. hall). Place where coins are minted.——**(2)** *Pudma tunkam* (पद्मटङ्क - padmatanka, San.). Means lotus coin, from lotus [nelumbo] figure in the centre. Ancient gold coin weighing from 55 to 70 grains [naunyam].——*Rama tunkam* (రామటంకము - rámatankamu, Tel.). From (ráma, san. the hero + tanka, san. the coin). Large cup-shaped gold metal with elaborate representations of Rama [q.v.] and Seetay [q.v.] sitting in state, surrounded by numerous attendants, among whom Hanooman [q.v.] is conspicuous. Prized by Veishnava bramins as objects of household worship and now often manufactured. They occur in different sizes; the largest should weigh 4 tolahs [q.v.] or 720 grains, being a double Rama tunkam, and is very rare; the next, 360 grains; the third, 180 grains.

TURBAN (دلبند - dulband, *Hind.*). From (dul, pers. a girdle + band, pers. a band). The head-dress of the Mahomedan [q.v.], since borrowed by Hindoos [duster, puggry].

TURK (ترک - turk, *Hind.*; துருக்கன் - turukkan, *Tam.*). Meaning native of turkey, european or asiatic. For purposes of distinction the former is called (rúmí) the roman, and the latter turk. Hence a soldier or warrior. South indian name for Mahomedans.——*Toolacan* (ತುರುಕ - turuka, Can.; తురక - turaka, Tel.; துலுக்கன் - tulukkan, Tam.). Corruption of Turk. Mahomedan. Plant first term meaning introduced by mahomedans or simply foreign, often joining two genera. Ex., where transl. is of second term:—Anacardium occidentale (turakagérumara), semecarpus anacardium; Jatropha curcas (turukaharalagida), ricinus communis; Olax scandens (turakavépa), melia azadirachta. See gloss. paragraphs.——*Turkey aloes* (صبر رومی - sibrirúmí, Hind.). Same as Bombay aloe.——*Turkey cumin* (کمون رومی - kamúnirúmí, Ar.). Same as Caraway.——*Turkey gram* (துலுக்கப்பயறு - tulukkappayaru, Tam.). Same as Moorman's gram.——*Turkey red* (لال گارا - lálgárá, Hind.; తోపు - tópu, Tel.; വിലാത്തിച്ചുവപ്പു - viláttiççuvappu, Mal.; தோம்பு - tómbu, Tam.). Title from source of the dyed article. Hind. from (lál, hind. red + gárá, hind. long cloth). Mal. from (viláití, hind. foreign + chuvappu, mal. red). Tam. means red color. First known as Adrianople red. Cotton [q.v.] cloth dyed with pure madder [munjeet] dye; popular, on account of the fast color [shauyam].——*Turkey wheat* (حنطۂ رومی - hintahirúmí, Ar.). Same as Mecca cholum.

TURMERIC (هلدی - haldí, *Hind.*). Same as Country saffron. ——*Tree turmeric* (మానిపసుపు - mánipasupu, Tel.). Same as Berberry.——*Turmeric wood* (هلداؤ - haldáu, Hind.). Title from color of wood. Same as Yellow cadamba.

TUSMA (تسمہ - tasmah, *Hind.*). Leathern strap, tied round the loins, to which the lungooty [q.v.] is fastened before and behind. Worn only by fakeers [q.v.]. Compare Dawauly [q.v.] of string.

TUSSER (تسر - tassar, *Hind.*). From (tasara, san. shuttle). An inferior silk [puttoo], the product of Antheræa mylitta, drury, found especially in the Carnatic [q.v.] uplands. These caterpillars are about four inches long, green, with reddish spots and a reddish yellow band running lengthways. They feed on several plants, including the teak [q.v.], the bair [q.v.], the saul [q.v.], and semal trees [red-cotton tree], and the castor-oil plant [aumanac], and produce ten-fold as much as an ordinary silkworm. They hang their gray-white cocoons on the branches by thick hard cords of silky matter, so that they look like fruit. The cocoons are killed by placing in boiling water, then taken to the market, and reeled like the ordinary silk cocoon. The raw silk is either employed alone or mixed with cotton [q.v.]. The Tusser silk fabrics are of an uniform greyish drab color, and have a glossy appearance due to the fact that the fibre is flat and not round as is that of ordinary silk. Tissues are exported largely. This silk moth cannot be domesticated.

TUTICORIN * (தூத்துக்குடி - túttukkudi, *Tam.*). From (túttu, tam. to scatter + kudi, tam. habitation). The final n was added for some such euphonic reason as turned Cotchy into Cochin and Coomary into Comorin. Sanscrit name (mandiranagara), meaning sea city.—"*a*" Deputy tahsildarry, Tinnevelly district. Pay Rs. 100.—"*b*" Town, Port, Railway terminus, Head-quarters of Sub-collector, Deputy tahsildar and District moonsif, Assistant superintendent of Police, Lighthouse; Tinnevelly dist., Ottapidauram tal.; pop. 25,107; acres 1,855; lat. 8° 48′; long. 78° 12′; height 6 feet; from Cauyal N. 17 miles; from Madras S.S.W. 324 miles; from Ottapidauram S.E. 12 miles; from Palamcottah E.N.E. 30 miles; from Shermadevy E.N.E. 41 miles; from Shreevillipoottore S.E. 60 miles; from Tinnevelly E. 33 miles; from Veippaur S.S.W. 17 miles. On the north-west shore of the Gulf of Manaar near Paumben passage and between the mouths of the Tamrapurny and Veippaur. The general appearance is unattractive. Chief port of the district. There is a fine harbour for boats, since extended, and a short public jetty as well as several private ones. The anchorage for ships, about two and-a-half miles out is sheltered on the west, north, and south by the mainland of Tinnevelly, and on the east by a group of islets, extending about 8 miles from north to south. In the north-east monsoon it is especially well-protected. Light, north extreme of Hare island or Paundyan teev, 2½ miles east of Tuticorin; lat. 8° 47′ 10″; long. 78° 11′ 20″; white; fixed; 14 miles range; visible from all directions seaward; sandstone column, colored brown, lantern white; guide to the anchorage. The Dutch obelisk light is in lat. 8° 47′ 17″ N. and long. 78° 11′ 17″ E. Tuticorin was first a Portuguese settlement about 1540; taken by the Dutch 1658; taken from the Dutch by the English 1782; restored to the Dutch 1785 in consequence of the treaty of 2nd September 1783; again taken by the English in 1795; captured and held for a short time by the Poligar of Punchaulamcoorchy during the last Poligar war in 1801; ceded to the Dutch in 1818; and again ceded back to the English in 1825. In 1700 the Jesuits spoke of Tuticorin as having 50,000 inhabitants but the place has decreased in importance since then. It is still the centre of pearl [moty] and conch [chunk] shell fishery. The trade is chiefly in cotton [q.v.], and there are several steam cotton-presses and spinning mills. Coffee [q.v.] from the ghaut [q.v.] estates, salt [ooppoo], chillies [q.v.], and palmyra [q.v.] jaggery [q.v.] are other exports. Imports are chiefly English piece-goods and yarn, paddy [q.v.], rice [q.v.], metals [loham], and betel-nuts [q.v.]. Much rice, as well as cattle [maud], horses [ghorah], sheep [aud] and poultry are sent to Ceylon. There are several European merchants. Trade has much increased since the opening in 1875 of the South indian railway, of which Tuticorin is a terminus. Water-supply is derived from the Tamrapurny, being brought from a reservoir 4 miles distant in open channels and masonry conduits and stored in dipping wells and tanks. The local wells are all salt. Of the inhabitants about 30 per cent. are Parava [q.v.] roman catholics, fishermen by profession. Tuticorin is the chief town and residence of their headman. There are several Catholic churches and a convent of European nuns. Old cemetery with elaborately-carved Dutch tomb-stones, having coats of arms on them.

TVAK (त्वक् - tvak, *San.*). Means bark. Same as Cinnamon. ——*Tabasheer* (तवक्षीर - tavakshíra, San.; طباشیر - tabáshír, Ar. and Pers.; بنس لوچن - banslochan, Hind.; طباشیر - tabáshír, Dec.; వెదురుప్పు - veduruppu, Tel.; වංශරෝචනා - vamsharóchaná, Singh.; மூங்கிலுப்பு - múngiluppu, Tam.). Title from arabic. San. from (tvak, san. rind + kshíra, san. milk). Ar. from sanscrit. Hind. from (báns, hind. bamboo + lochan, hind. eye); as obtained from bamboo joint. Dec. from sanscrit. Tel. from (veduru, tel. bamboo + uppu, tel. salt). Singh. from (vamsha, san. bamboo + róchana, san. digestive). Tam. from (múngil, tam. bamboo + uppu, tam. salt). San. also (vamshalóchana), meaning bamboo + eye; (vamsharóchaná), meaning bamboo + manna, the appetizer; (róchana), meaning the appetizer. Singh. also (unamakulu), meaning bamboo + pipeclay. Otherwise Bamboo manna, Bamboo salt, Banslochan. A white secreted silicious matter, found in the joints of the female bamboo [q.v.]. It has some medicinal repute here among hakeems and veidyans, being deemed tonic and astringent. At a red heat it fuses into a transparent glass [cunnaudy]. Will be found fully described under Common bamboo.——*Tikhar* (تیکھر - tíkhar, Hind.). From (tavakhíra, mahr. from tvakshíra, san. bamboo milk). Distinguish from Tickor. Native arrowroot, from the roots of several species of curcuma [haridrah].

TWIST GRASS (வலம்புரிப்புல் - valamburippul, *Tam.*). From twisting motion. Same as Spear grass.

TYAUGAM (त्याग - tyága, *San.*). From (tyaj, san. to give up). Gift [daunam, varam]. Renouncing world.——*Tyaugadroog* (தியாகத்துருக்கம் - tiyágatturukkam, Tam. tyágadrug *). From (tiyágan, tam. shiva, the giver + durga, san. fort). Town, Hill; South arcot dist., Cullacoorchy tal.; pop. 2,986; acres 2,181; lat. 11° 45′; long. 79° 07′; height 740 feet; from Cuddalore W. 46 miles; from Cullacoorchy E. 8 miles. At intersection of roads from Arcot to Trichinopoly and from Salem to Cuddalore. Once strongly fortified. Like the fortress of Trinomallee, Tyaugadroog formed one of the bulwarks against invasion from above the ghauts [q.v.]. In October 1757, after the capture of Trinomallee by the French, the latter attacked Tyaugadroog but were repulsed. They subsequently captured it in 1759. Given to Hyder ally in 1760, but restored in September of the same year. The British recaptured it in 1761. An attack by Tippoo in 1790 was repulsed. Village is an important trade centre. ——*Tyaugaroyan* (தியாகராயன் - tiyágaráyan, Tam.). From (above + rájá, san. king); lord of all gifts or of ascetics. Epithet of Shiva at Tirvettore. Hindoo 2nd or pers. name [peyar]; often written unrecognizably Theagaroyan. Similarly Tyaugeshan. Familiarly Tyaugoo.——*Tyaujyam* (त्याज्य - tyájya, San.). From (tyaj, san. to abandon). That portion of a Nacshatram [q.v.] which is deemed unlucky is called Varjyam [q.v.], and the period of its duration is the Tyaujyam of the Varjyam. It is called Divy [q.v.] when it occurs at day time; and Ravy [q.v.] when at night. The instant of its commencement is registered in every Punchaungam [q.v.], its mean duration is about 4 ghadiyas [q.v.] or 1′ 36″ European time, so that the beginning being known the end may be supposed, with sufficient accuracy for practical purposes, without actual computation. Its true duration is more or less, according as the moon's continuance in the same Nacshatram happens to be more or less than 60 ghadiyas [q.v.]. Pending the tyaujyam all voluntary business should be suspended [jyotisham].

TYE (தை - tai, *Tam.*). From (tishya, san. eighth lunar mansion); from the full moon [powrnimay] being in or near that nacshatram [q.v.]. Tenth solar month [mausam].——*Tye amavausyay* (தையமாவாசியை - taiyamávásiyai, Tam.). Means the tenth tamul solar month + new moon day. Luni-solar [chaundramaunam] festival [pundigay, 5a]. The new moon [amavausyay] falling in tenth solar month Tye [mausam], i.e., between 12th January and 11th February, observed by Tamulians. Favourable days for Shrauddham [q.v.] to deceased ancestors [pitry], and presents to Bramins, are any new moon from July to December [dacshinauyanam], but Tye amavausyay is the chief [maryanday].——*Tye poosham* (தைப்பூசம் - taippúsam, Tam.). Means the tenth tamul solar month + name of the eighth nacshatram. Luni-solar [chaundramaunam] festival [pundigay, 5b]. Day of full moon [powrnimay], when the moon is in the constellation Pooshyam [q.v.], in the tenth solar month Tye [mausam], i.e., between 12th January and 11th February. Festival specially at Pulney. Sacred to Soobramanyan [q.v.]. The day is considered auspicious for purposes of education, next after the Dusserah [q.v.]. The harvest feast is observed on the same day in Vishnoo temples [maryanday].

TYE (தாயி - táyi, *Tam.*). Means mother. Hindoo female proper name. Also suffix in female proper names as Shooppootye, Vanattye [peyar].——*Tauvery* (തായ്വഴി - távazhi, Mal.). From (above + vazhi, mal. line). Branch. Relationship by the mother's side. A branch of a Malabar tarwaud [q.v.] which has separated more or less from the parent stock.——*Tayaman naley* (தாயுமானநலே - táyumánanalé, Tam.). From (táyumánavan, tam. shiva, who became mother to an orphan + nale, tam. proper name). Naley, the Sheivite. First founder of the Chola [q.v.] kingdom settled at Trichinopoly, then surrounded by a vast wilderness. He had a son called Vencholan, from connecting the Cauvery river with the Vennaur, and thereby fertilizing an enlarged extent of country.

TYNAUT (تعینات - taínát, *Hind.*). From (aín, ar. to particularize). Attendance. So a peon [q.v.], body-guard, &c.

TYPHOON (طوفان - túfán, *Hind.*; తుపాను - tupánu, *Tel.*; புசல் - pusal, *Tam.*). Arabic. Otherwise cyclone. Revolving storm especially at sea [monsoon].

U (उ - u, ऊ - ú, *San.*; உ - u, ஊ - ú, *Tam.*). San. stands for Shiva [q.v.]. Tam. short is symbol for the numeral 2 [yen].

ULL (அள்ளு - allu, *Tam.*). A handful of grain given to village servants [balootah] and others as remuneration for their services [oolyam].

ULSOOR (ಅಲಸೂರು - alsúru, *Can.*). From (halasu, can. jack tree, artocarpus integrifolia, willd. + úru, can. village). Otherwise written Halsore. An artificial lake in Bangalore. Supplies cantonment with water which is pumped to the top of a rock and thence distributed by pipes.

UMBRELLA (குடை - kudai, *Tam.*). Plant prefix. From similar appearance, or from leaves used in making umbrellas [coday].——*Umbrella grass* (குடைப்புல் - kudaippul, Tam.). From tufted growth. Same as Trail grass.——*Umbrella palm* (குடைப்பனை - kudaippanai, Tam.). From use of leaf. Same as Talipot.——*Umbrella thorn* (குடைவேல் - kudaivél, Tam.). From habit of growth. Same as Coday vail.——*Umbrella tree* (چھتری کا جھاڑ - chhatríkájhár, Hind.). From use of leaves. Same as Screw-pine.

UNGOOLAM (अंगुल - angula, *San.*). From (ang, san. to mark). Finger.—"*a*" Finger-breadth. Linear carpenter's measure. The commonest scale is:—8 yavams or barley corns = 1 ungoolam; 12 ungoolams = 1 jaun or span [alavay, 1]; approximate actual value, 1 ungoolam = ·82 english inch; same as viralcaday. There are many ways of measuring an ungoolam. With the original meaning:—by measuring the circumference of the second joint of the thumb, half of which is an ungoolam; by measuring from tip of nail to first joint of thumb, half of which is an ungoolam; by taking actual width of tip of thumb, which is an ungoolam. By grains of principal cereal [dhaunyam] of the locality, such as paddy [q.v.]:—by placing 3 such grains in a line; by placing 8 such grains breadthwise side by side. By seeds of principal pulse of the locality, such as common dholl [q.v.]:—eight of these in a line = 1 ungoolam. See vol. I, 609; II, 505.—"*b*" As 12 ungoolams = 1 span [jaun], ungoolam comes to mean 12th of anything. In this sense it is sub-divided into 60 vyangoolams [alavay, 1]. See Shunk.—"*c*" Ungooly toranam, from (above + torana, san. ornamental archway), is three semi-circular lines drawn across the forehead, made with sandal [q.v.] or ashes of burnt cowdung [vibhooty], denoting a worshipper of Shiva [shiva, tripoondram]. Compare Keetnaumam of veishnavites [naumam].

UNJANUCKLE (அஞ்சனக்கல் - añjanakkal, *Tam.*). Means collyrium or black stone. Anglo-indian for Soorma.

URS (ಅರಸು - arasu, *Can.*). Means king. Caste-title of the relatives of the Maharajah of Mysore.

V (व - va, वा - vá, *San.*; و - wáu, *Hind.*; வ - va, வா - vá, *Tam.*). San. short Varoonan [q.v.]. Hind. symbol for 6; Friday the sixth day of the week [vauram]; sign [raushy] Libra [meezaun, toolaum]. Tam. short a sign for ¼ [caul]. The Northern Hindoo pronounces a B, where the southern prefers a V. The two letters simultaneously occur only in border districts. No B is found in the names of places situated in the Chingleput, South arcot, Tanjore, Trichinopoly, Madura, Tinnevelly, and Malabar districts; while in South canara, Ganjam and Mysore a V is seldom used.

VA (வா - vá, *Tam.*). To come.——*Varavoo* (வரவு - varavu, Tam.). Coming. Income, receipt [vasool].——*Varmaunam* (வருமானம் - varumánam, Tam.). From (above + má, san. to measure). Source of income.——*Varwa* (వరవ - varava, Tel.). Channel [caulvye, vaug, vyecaul].——*Vauram* (వారము - váramu, Tel.; வாரம் - váram, Tam.). Share [coroo]. Share of agricultural produce in kind [merah]. Rent of land. Coodivauram, from (kudi, tam. subject + above), the share of the cultivator. Mailvauram, from (mél, tam. above + above), the upper or government or government assignee's share. Oodeivauram, from (udai, tam. owning + above), the whole produce. See vol. I, 112. Distinguish from sanscrit Vauram, day or week.

VADA (വട - vata, *Mal.*; வட - vada, *Tam.*). Means the fading quarter. From the comparatively infertile character of the region in and about the north of the tamul country; tripatty being supposed to be the northern limit of the tamul country, thence called vadamullay [q.v.]. See vol. I (50). North [ashtadic, bada].——*Vadagalay* (வடகலை - vadagalai, Tam.). From (above + kalá, san. portion); northern branch. Those of the northern school among the Shreeveishnavas, followers of Vedauntacharry; as opposed to Tengalays, followers of Manavaula maumoony. The difference between the two sects has been fully explained in the foot-note on Hindoo sects at Vol. I (89). See Tengalay, Manavaula maumoony, Shreeveishnava and Vedauntacharry.——*Vadakk* (வடக்கு - vadakku, Tam.). A dative converted to nominative. The north quarter [ashtadic, tisay].——*Vadamala* (വടമല - vatamala, Mal.). From (above + mala, mal. mountain). Range of hills; Malabar dist., Palghaut and Valavanaud talś. At northern edge of Palghaut gap. Stretch from the Culladicode hill on the west to within seven miles of Coimbatore town. About 30 miles long. Highest point, Valiya carmala; now known as Cunnaudy comban because a survey party took observations there. The highest peak at eastern end is Paraputty, and that at western end is Oodayagherry. Between Cunnaudy comban, which is in the middle, and Paraputty there is a spar connecting the range with Condoomala, a precipitous hill which rises straight up from the cultivation, 6,700 feet. The ridge is steep and the summit is without tableland. Links connect it with the Coondahs.——*Vadamalaivaunan* (வடமலைவாணன் - vadamalaivánan, Tam.). From (above + malai, tam mountain + vázhnan, tam. inhabitant). Name of Vishnoo, as lord of Tripatty.——*Vada mozhy* (வடமொழி - vadamozhi, Tam.). Northern speech or sanscrit, as opposed to Tenmozhy or tamul.——*Vadamullay* (வடமலை - vadamalai, Tam.). From (above + malai, tam. mountain). Tripatty, the northern mountain, the northern limit of the tamul country. See vol. I (50). Also Mount meroo [q.v.]. Hindoo 2nd or pers. name. Common among non-bramins. Even pariahs [peyar]. Tenmullay on other hand or southern mountain is Pothiyam [pothigay].——*Vadatchol* (வடசொல் - vadasol, Tam.). Northern or Sanscrit words. These are Tatsamam [q.v.] and Tadbhavam [q.v.].——*Vadoogan* (வடுகன் - vadugan, Tam.). Tamul name for a Teloogoo-speaking man. Distinguish from Vadoogan or Bheiravan. The Teloogoos invaded the Tamul country from Vijianugger [humpy] during later middle ages, but especially in sixteenth century [jauty].——*Vadoogoo* (வடுகு - vadugu, Tam.). Teloogoo country and language.

VADAGAM (वटक - vataka, *San.*; ಸಂಡಿಗೆ - sandige, *Can.*; వడియాలు - vadiyálu, *Tel.*; കൊണ്ടാട്ടം - kondáitam, *Mal.*; வடகம் - vadagam, *Tam.*). San. from (vat, san. to divide). Tel. and Tam. from sanscrit. Mal. from (kondátuka, mal. to enjoy). A condiment; consists of pulse [dholl], onions [piyauz], mustard [rayaun], curry-leaf [q.v.], garlic [lussoon], &c., pounded together and made into balls; when required for use, a portion is fried in ghee [q.v.] and used for seasoning curry [q.v.].

VADOOGAN (வடுகன் - vadugan, *Tam.*). From (vatu, san. boy). Bheiravan [q.v.], form of Shiva [q.v.]. Distinguish from Vadoogan, a northerner [vada].——*Vadoogantye* (வடுகந்தாய் - vaduganday, Tam.). From (above + táy, tam. mother). Mauriyamman [q.v.].——*Vadoogy* (வடுகி - vadugi, Tam.). Mauriyamman [q.v.]. Otherwise Caud caul [q.v.].

VADY (வடி - vadi, *Tam.*). To sharpen.——*Vadivailoo* (வடிவேலு - vadivélu, Tam.). From (above + vél, tam. spear). Epithet of Scandan [q.v.], who holds a sharp lance. Hindoo 2nd or pers. name. Common among non-bramins [peyar].——*Vadivauttah* (வடிவாத்தா - vadiváttá, Tam.). From (vadivu, tam. beauty + áttál, tam. mother). Village goddess Mauriyamman [q.v.]; compare Comala vully.——*Vadivoo* (வடிவு - vadivu, Tam.). Beauty.

VAGEIRAH (وغيره - vaghairah, *Hind.*). From (wa, ar. and + ghairuhu, ar. the others). Etcetera.

VAHEED (وحيد - vahíd, *Ar.*). From (ahad, ar. one). Alone. Part of lacab; as Vaheed oon nissa, unique lady [ism].

VAIL (வேல் - vél, *Tam.*). From (vel, tam. to conquer) [vel]. Spear. So Acacia [cantalam] species, from sharp thorns. There is a Tamul proverb:—வேம்புக்குப் பல் அழகு, வேலுக்குப் பல்இறுக்கும்—"when cleaned with a margosa "[neem] stick the teeth look beautiful, when cleaned with a "vail stick they are made firm." There is another:—வேல் வைத்துப் பயிர் ஆக்குவோர் இல்லை—"no one cultivates "the vail tree" [toomma].——**(1)** *Vailan* (வேலன் - vélan, Tam.). Means Soobramanyan [q.v.], the lance-bearer. Pariah proper name [peyar].——*Vailauyoodhan* (வேலாயுதன் - véláyuthan, Tam.). From (above + áyudha, san. weapon). Soobramanyan.——*Vailoo* (வேலு - vélu, Tam.; വേലു - vélu, Mal.). Familiar form of vailauyoodhan and other names of which it forms a part. Hindoo 2nd name. Also suffix in proper names among non-bramins; as Colandayvailoo, Ratnavailoo, Vadivailoo [peyar].——**(2)** *Black vail* (கருவேல் - karuvél, Tam.). Same as Babool.——*Caroovail* (கருவேல் - karuvél, Tam.). Means black acacia. Same as Babool.——*Coday vail* (हिवर - hivara, Mahr.; குடைவேல் - kudaivél, Tam.). Title from tamul. Mahr. from (himva, mahr. cold, damp); it is undesirable to sit under shade of this tree [velvail]. Tam. from (kudai, tam. umbrella + vél, tam. acacia sp.); from large thorns. Title otherwise Elephant thorn, Jungle nail, Tomentose acacia, Umbrella thorn. Botanically Acacia [cantalam] tomentosa, willd., leguminosæ [vricsham, 48]. Alias Mimosa kleinii, tomentosa. Tree armed with large stipulary spines; young shoots petioles and peduncles covered with yellowish down; pinnæ ten to twelve pair, with an oblong gland below the lowest, and an umbilicate one between each of the one to two last pair; leaflets numerous, linear, obtuse, pubescent beneath; peduncles axillary, one to four together, with four small bracts about the middle; heads of flowers globose, stamens distinct; stigma dilated; legume flat, thin, linear-falcate, six to eight-seeded; flowers white, rather offensive smell; flowering nearly all the year; found sparingly. Has a tough and strong wood; used for fuel.——*Creeper vail* (கொடிவேலம் - kodivélam, Tam.). Same as Divy-divy.——*Dark vail* (कनकाकुली - kanakákulí, San.; जांब - jámba, Mahr.; جامبا - jambá, Hind.; ಹೊನ್ನಾವರಿಕೆ - honnávariko, Can.; ಶಿವ್ವೊ - shivvo, Coorg; కొండతంగేడు - kondatangédu, Tel.; ଭୋଜ - bója, Oor.; ഇരുവിൾ - iruvil, Mal.; இருவேல் - iruvél, Tam.). Title from color of wood. San. from (kanaka, san. gold + ákula, san. filled). Mahr. compare [common jaumoon, malacca jaumoon, rose apple]. Can. from (honnu, can. gold + ávarike, can. the plant, cassia auriculata, linn.). Tel. from (konda, tel. hill + tangédu, tel. cassia auriculata, linn.). Mal. from (iru, mal. dark + ul, mal. inside) [sissoo]. Tam. from (irul, tam. dark + vél, tam. acacia). Can. also (bettadávarike), meaning hill + the plant, cassia auriculata, linn.; (jambe); (tirvamara). Tel. also (bója); (tangédu) [tungaid]. Title otherwise Burmah iron wood, Hill tungaid, Iron wood [cassa, chowkmaram, deccany deodar, foreign ilanjy, nauga champak, yellow condray], Irool. Botanically Xylia dolabriformis, benth., leguminosæ [vricsham, 48]. Alias Acacia xylocarpa; Inga xylocarpa; Mimosa coorganensis, xylocarpa. Tree, 60 feet, unarmed; leaves conjugately pinnated; leaflets two to four pairs, with an odd one on the outside below the pairs, ovate-oblong, acute; peduncles in pairs, axillary, long; flowers globose-capitate; legumes ovate-oblong, hatchet-shaped, woody, many-seeded; flowers small white, flowering in hot season. Oil from seeds; red resin [raul]. Wood very dark red fading to dark-brown, heavy, hard, close-grained, and not easily worked; when planed up the surface has an unctuous feel and not very agreeable smell. No other common species here.——*Dung vail* (பீவேல் - pívél, Tam.). From fetid gum. Same as Piyvail.——*Foreign white vail* (சீமைவெள்வேல் - shímaivelvél, Tam.). Same as Anasandra.——*Green vail* (பச்சைவேல் - paççaivél, Tam.). From green trunk. Same as Parangy vail.——*Ooday vail* (బుడతుమ్మ - buddatumma, Tel.; உடை - udai, Tam.). Title from tamul. Tel. from (budda, tel. rupture + tumma, tel. acacia arabica, willd.). Tam. from (udu, tam. arrow); from large thorns. Tel. also (sále). Title otherwise Arrow thorn tree. Botanically Acacia [cantalam] planifrons, w. & a., leguminosæ [vricsham, 48]. Alias Acacia roxburghii; Mimosa eburnea, horrida. Tree; branches crowded at the summit, spreading and umbrella-like; thorns stipulary, short, conical and curved, and very long, terete or angled and channelled on the sides; pinnæ five to six pair; leaflets ten to twelve pair, very small, linear, obtuse, glabrous; petioles, compressed, flat on the lower side, ciliated, without glands; peduncles axillary, aggregated, shorter than the leaves, with bracts at the base; heads of flowers globose; legumes tumid, spirally curved; very common in southern districts. Wood hard and strong; heart-wood red, sap-wood white; used for agricultural implements and fuel.

There is a Tamul proverb:—உடைமுள்ளுக்கு எதிரே உதைக்கலாமா—"can you kick against the thorns of the arrrow "thorn?"——*Parangy vail* (సీమజిలుగ - símajíluga, Tel.; பரங்கிவேல் - parangivél, Tam.). Tel. from (síma, tel. european + jíluga, tel. pith plant, æschynomene aspera, linn.). Tam. from (parangi, tam. foreign + vél, tam. acacia sp.), as introduced from west indies. Hind. also (chendúphul), meaning tassel + flower. Tam. also (shéli); (shembai), meaning red [common sesban]; (nallavél), meaning good + acacia; (shímaiççembai), meaning foreign + sesbania ægyptiaca, pers.; (paççaivél), meaning green + acacia. Title otherwise Barbadoes flower fence, Foreign solah, Green babool, Jerusalem thorn, West-indian prickly broom. Botanically Parkinsonia aculeata, l., leguminosæ [vricsham, 48]. A tree-like shrub, from 15–20 feet high, clear, vivid, polished green trunk and stems with pinnate foliage of minute leaflets; nearly always in blossom with racemes of small, yellow flowers; hedge [vaily] plant; yields white fibre [naur]; wood used for fuel. No other common species here.——*Piyvail* (विट्खदिर - vitkhadira, San.; गुबाभूळ - gúbábhúla, Mahr.; कुस्रिझाड - kusrijháda, Conc.; گوہ ببول - gúhbabúl, Hind.; گو کیکر - gúkíkar, Dec.; ಕಸ್ತೂರಿಜಾಲಿ - kastúrijáli, Can.; కంపుతుమ్మ - kamputumma, Tel.; പീവേലം - pívélam, Mal.; பீவேல் - pível, Tam.). Title from tamul. San. from (vish, san. malodour + khadira, san. acacia catechu, willd.); from strong scented flowers. Mahr. from (gú, mahr. excrement + bábhúla, mahr. acacia). Hind. from (gúh, hind. excrement + babúl, hind. acacia). Dec. from (gú, hind. excrement + kíkar, hind. acacia). Can. from (kastúri, san. musk + jáli, can. acacia sp.); from sweet-scented flowers. Tel. from (kampu, tel. bad odour + tumma, tel. acacia). Mal. from tamul. Tam. from (pí, tam. dung + vél, tam. acacia). San. also (ariméda), meaning insufferable + exudation; from fœtid gum. Mahr. also (gúkinkara), meaning fœtid acacia. Hind. also (viláitíkíkar), meaning foreign acacia; (viláitíbabúl), meaning foreign acacia, being an american naturalised species; (gandbabúl), meaning stinking acacia. Can. also (sannajáli), meaning small + acacia sp.; (karijáli), meaning black + acacia sp. Tel. also (nágatumma), meaning serpent + acacia; (piyyitumma), meaning dung + the tree; (kastúritumma), meaning musk + the tree; (murikitumma), meaning dirt + the tree. Tam. also (píkkaruvél), meaning dung + black + the tree; (vęthavalli). Greek λεύκη ἄκανθος. Title otherwise Cassie-oil plant, Custoory babool, Fetid mimosa, Small acacia, Sponge tree, Stinking acacia, West-indian black-thorn. Botanically Acacia [cantalam] farnesiana, willd., leguminosæ [vricsham, 48]. Alias Acacia indica; Farnesia odora; Mimosa farnesiana, indica, scorpioides; Vachellia farnesiana. Shrub or small jungle tree, armed with stipulary thorns; calyx five-toothed; corolla tubular; stamens distinct; leaves bipinnated; pinnæ four to eight pair; leaflets linear, ten to twenty pair, nearly glabrous; petioles and peduncles more or less pubescent; legumes cylindrical, fitted with pulp and two rows of seeds; flowers globular, size of bullet, two to three together, each on an axillary peduncle, small, yellow, smell resembling wall flowers; flowers in december and january. Gives to pharm. piyvail bark, mentioned but non-officinal; also gum [gond]. Makes a good fence [vaily] if properly pruned; strong-scented, yellow flower-heads yield the otto [attar] known as cassie; the bark gives an inky dye [shauyam]. Wood white, close-grained, used for naves, ship knees, tent-pegs, ploughs, &c.——*Vellay moolvail* (देवबाभळ - dévabábhala, Mahr.; بہیس - bhais, Dec.; ಹೊಟ್ಟೆಜಾಲಿ - hottéjáli, Can.; పక్కెతుమ్మ - pakketumma, Tel.; வெள்ளைமுள்வேல் - vellaimulvél, Tam.). Title from tamul. Mahr. from (déva, san. god + bábhala, mahr. acacia arabica, willd.); from white thorns. Dec. means buffalo. Can. from (hotte, can. belly + jáli, can. acacia sp.). Tel. from (pakke, tel. tamarix gallica, linn. + tumma, tel. acacia). Tam. from (vellai, tam. white + mul, tam. thorn + vél, tam. acacia sp.); from white thorns. Title otherwise Buffalo-thorn, Silver-thorned acacia, Tamarisk acacia. Botanically Acacia [cantalam] latronum, willd., leguminosæ [vricsham, 48]. Alias Mimosa cornigera, latronum. Somewhat arboreous; thorns numerous, stipulary, very large, united at the base; pinnæ three to five pair, with a gland on the petiole; leaflets six to fifteen pair, very small, narrow-linear, obtuse, without glands; spikes axillary usually in pairs, longer than the leaves, many-flowered; stamens distinct; legume flat, thickish, oval-falcate, three to four-seeded; flowers white, becoming yellowish, fragrant; flowering in the rainy season; from some unknown cause the tree at a certain stage ceases to elongate; the branches then increase horizontally to a considerable extent, forming a flat umbrella-like top. Covers large arid tracts; gives fibre [naur]; used for fuel.——*Velvail* (सोमवल्क - sómavalka, San.; हिवर - hivara, Mahr.; سفید کیکر - sufedkíkar, Hind.; اجلی کیکر - ujlíkíkar, Dec.; ಬಿಳೇಜಾಲಿ - biléjáli, Can.; తెల్లతుమ్మ - tellatumma, Tel.; ଗୋୟର - goyira, Oor.; വെൾവേലം - velvélam, Mal.; අඳර - andara, Singh.; வெள்வேல் - velvél, Tam.). Title from tamul. San. from (sóma, san. moon + valka, san. bark); from whitish bark. Mahr. from (híma, san. snow); from whiteness [coday vail]. Hind. from (sufed, hind. white + kíkar, hind. acacia arabica, willd.). Dec. from (ujlí, hind. white + kíkar, hind. acacia arabica, willd.). Can. from (bili, can. white + jáli, can. acacia sp.). Tel. from (tella, tel. white + tumma, tel. acacia). Mal. from tamul. Tam. from (vel, tam. white + vél, tam. acacia sp.); from color of bark. San. also (shvétavarvara), meaning white acacia arabica, willd. Hind. also (sharábkíkíkar), meaning spirits' acacia, bark used to flavor native spirits; (pattekíkíkar), meaning arrack acacia; (sufedbabúl), meaning white acacia. Mal. also (venkarinnáli), meaning white + acacia catechu, willd. Singh. also (katuandara), meaning thorny acacia; (mahaandara), meaning large acacia. Title otherwise Arrack acacia, Kateerah gum tree [golden silk cotton], Panicled acacia, White babool, White-bark acacia, White toomma. Botanically Acacia [cantalam] leucophlæa, willd., leguminosæ [vricsham, 48]. Alias Acacia alba; Mimosa alba, horrida, leucophlæa. The specific name from whitish color of bark. Tree, armed with stipulary thorns; leaves bipinnated; pinnæ seven to twelve pair, leaflets numerous, oblong-linear, slightly pubescent; panicles terminal or from the upper axils; branches and peduncles shortly tomentose; corolla five-cleft; stamens distinct; legumes narrow, long, curved, shortly tomentose when young; heads of flowers globose; flowers small, pale yellow; flowers june to september. Gum [gond] resembles gum bussorah [q.v.]. Gives to pharm. velvail bark, mentioned but non-officinal; astringent like that of acacia arabica willd. [babool]; used in native medicine. Young pods and seeds and even the whitish bark are eaten in times of scarcity; bark used to flavor native spirits [sharaub], and to increase quantity of alcohol from the sugar [arrack]. A fibre [naur] from the bark by maceration after four or five days' beating; it is used for large fishing-nets [valay] and coarse kind of cordage, being tough and strong; leaves give a black color as dye [shauyam]. Timber hard and strong, much like babool, but closer-grained and of a deeper color; used for the same purposes; makes excellent fuel for locomotive purposes.——*White vail* (வெள்வேல் - velvél, Tam.). Same as Velvail.

VAILAY (सूर्य्यावर्त्त - súryávarta, *San.*; तिळवणी - tilavaní, *Mahr.*; शिर्काल - shirkála, *Conc.*; ہرہر - hurhur, *Hind.*; ہلہل - hulhul, *Dec.*; ನಾರಂಬೇಳೆ - nárambéle, *Can.*; వామింట - váminta, *Tel.*; വേള - véla, *Mal.*; වේලා - vélá, *Singh.*; வேளை - vélai, *Tam.*). Title from tamul [vem]. San. from (súrya, san. sun + ávarta, san. turning); cf. soorycaunty. Can. from (náru, can. to smell + béle, can. the plant). Tel. from (vámu, tel. omum, carum copticum, benth. + antu, tel. to stick), viscous plant with peculiar odour. Mal. and Tam. from (vé, tam. to burn); from vesicant leaves. San. also (arkapushpiká), meaning sun + flower; (varvara), meaning covering, medicinal [babool, fragrant toolsy, knotted bhraungy]. Can. also (shirikála), from concany; (tilónigida), from mahratta. Tel. also (ajagandhi), meaning goat + smelling; cf. ajwaun. Mal. also (taivéla), meaning young + the shrub; (káttukatuku), meaning wild mustard, brassica juncea, h. f. t.; (nallavéla), meaning good + the shrub; (kárvvéla), meaning black variety. Tam. also (náykkadugu), meaning dog + mustard; (taivélai), meaning the month + the plant; (nallavélai), meaning good + the plant. Title otherwise Black vailay, Dog mustard, Five-leaved cleome. Botanically Gynandropsis pentaphylla, dc., capparideæ [vricsham, 11]. Alias Cleome pentaphylla; Gymnogonia pentaphylla; Gynandropsis affinis; Podogyne pentaphylla; Sinapistrum pentaphylla. Annual, 1 foot; calyx sepals four, spreading; petals four, open, not covering the stamens; stem more or less covered with glandular pubescence or hairs; middle leaves five-foliolate, lower and floral leaves trifoliolate; leaflets obovate, puberulous, entire, or slightly serrulate; flowers white or flesh-colored, with pink stamens and brown anthers; siliqua stalked. Common weed in gardens and fields, flowering nearly all the year; the whole plant is viscid and covered thickly with glandular hairs; it has a strong peculiar odour like the black currant leaf or asafœtida [q.v.]; the seeds are black, of the same shape and size as those of cleome viscosa [dog vailay], but rougher; they have a very faint flavor of mustard [rayaun]. The plant when crushed in the fresh state develops an acrid volatile oil [yennay] having the properties of garlic [lussoon] or mustard [rayaun] oil; the dried plant exhausted by alcohol yields a deep green tincture, this on evaporation leaving a brown soft resin [raul] which has no irritant action when applied to the skin. The seeds, leaves and roots are medicinal, the seeds anthelmintic and rubefacient, the leaves remedy for diseases of the ear, the root febrifuge. The seeds are prescribed internally in powder with sugar [q.v.], and externally in poultice or paste by bruising them with vinegar [caudy], lime-juice [lime] or hot water. For the use of the ear, the juice of the leaves is pressed out by bruising them without water. The root is employed in decoction, prepared thus:—take of the root, cut into small pieces and bruised, three ounces; water, one pint and a half; boil on a slow fire till the liquid is reduced to one pint, and strain when cool. Doses; of the powder, from thirty grains to one drachm, morning and evening for two days, followed on third morning by castor [aumanac] oil; of the decoction, from one to three fluid ounces, four or five times a day. Substituted; the seeds for the mustard [rayaun] imported from europe, and for santonin [absinth]; the leaves for glycerine; the root for pulv. antimonialis. Leaves eaten in curries [q.v.] and used as famine food; pungent taste. Seeds yield oil [yennay]. A variety with rose-colored flowers, in flower gardens. Another species called

Triphylla.——*Dog vailay* (आदित्यभक्ता - ádityabhaktá, San. ; वेडमोहरी - védamóhari, Mahr. ; शिरिकाल - shirikála, Conc. ; هرهر - hurhur, Hind. ; هلهل - hulhul, Dec. ; ಕಾಡುಸಾಸಿವೆ - kádusásive, Can. ; ಸಂತೆಮಿ - santemi, Too. ; నేలావామింట - nélavámınta, Tel. ; കാട്ടുകടുക - káttukatuku, Mal. ; වලබ - valaba, Singh. ; நாய்வேளை - náyvélai, Tam.). Title from tamul. San. from (áditya, san. sun + bhaj, san. to serve) [sooryacaunty]. Mahr. from (véda, mahr. mad + móharí, mahr. mustard). Can. from (kádu, can. jungle + sásive, can. mustard). Tel. from (néla, tel. ground + váminta, tel. gynandropsis pentaphylla, dec.) ; from the small compressed, netted surfaced, hottish tasted seeds. Mal. from (kátu, mal forest + katuku, mal. mustard, brassia juncea, h. f. and t). Singh. from (val, singh. wild + aba, singh. mustard). Tam. from (náy, tam. dog + vélai, tam. plant, gynandropsis pentaphylla, dec.) ; from pungent leaves. San. also (shvánavarvara), meaning dog + gynandropsis pentaphylla, dc. ; (shunakavarvara), meaning dog + gynandropsis pentaphylla, dc. ; (arkakántá), meaning sun loving. Mahr. also (kánap'hutí), meaning ear + breaking open, from its use in curing deafness ; (pivalátilavaní), meaning yellow + the plant, gynandropsis pentaphylla, d.c. Hind. also (chhoríajwán), meaning false ajwaun ; (janglíhurhur), meaning wild cleome. Dec. also (janglíhulhul), meaning wild cleome. Can. also (náyibele), meaning dog + the plant, gynandropsis pentaphylla, d.c. ; (huççusásive), meaning mad + mustard plant. Tel. also (kukkávâlu), meaning dog + mustard, brassica juncea, h. f. and t. ; (peddaváminta), meaning large + gynandropsis pentaphylla, dec. ; (kukkaváminta), meaning dog + gynandropsis pentaphylla, dec. Mal. also (áryavéla), meaning noble + gynandropsis ; (náyvéla), meaning dog + gynandropsis ; (náykatuku), meaning dog + mustard. Tam. also (náykkadugu), meaning dog + mustard, inferior mustard, from feeble taste of seed ; (káttukkadugu), meaning forest + mustard ; (peruvélai), meaning big + gynandropsis pentaphylla, dec. Herbe puante or Brede puante of french settlements in east ; Bredo mamma of portuguese. Title otherwise Deaf mustard, Dog mustard, Viscid celadine, Wild mustard. Botanically Cleome viscosa, linn., capparideæ [vricsham, 11]. Alias Cleome dodecandra, epilobioides, icosandra, viscosa ; Polanisia icosandra, viscosa. Small plant, 2–3 feet ; stem covered with viscid glandular hairs ; leaves three to five foliolate ; leaflets obovate-cuneate or oblong, pubescent, scarcely longer than the petiole ; siliqua terete, striated, rough with glandular hairs, sessile, acuminated ; flowers small yellow ; flowering nearly all year. One of the commonest weeds in fields, particularly those of indigo [q.v.] ; flowers curious for the great distance the pistil with the seed-vessel at the end projects out from among the stamens ; flowers are clumped several together in a tuft-like head on the summit of the plant ; the whole plant pubescent and extremely viscid ; many of the hairs are surmounted by a round gland, from which a reddish viscid secretion exudes ; the plant has a powerful odour like black currants ; the capsules are from 2–3½ inches long, striated, pubescent, tapering towards the point, which is surmounted by the style ; the seeds are dark brown or nearly black, reniform, and granular, about the size of black mustard [rayaun] seed ; the leaves have a pungent flavor, and the seed a feeble taste of mustard. Seeds are medicinally anthelmintic, rubefacient and vesicant ; leaves rubefacient, vesicant and remedy for diseases of ear. Seeds used internally in powder with sugar [q.v.], and externally in poultice by bruising with vinegar [caudy], lime-juice [lime] or hot water. Leaves applied to skin in poultice or paste by bruising them with vinegar, lime-juice or hot water ; juice for use of ear is pressed out by bruising and rubbing them without water. Dose of powder, from thirty grains to a drachm, twice a day for two days, followed on third morning by purgative. Substituted ; the seeds for santonin [absinth] and mustard [rayaun] flour from europe ; leaves for last-named and for glycerine. Seeds are, as a drug, same as gynandropsis pentaphylla [vailay], but leaves much superior. Fresh plant eaten as greens, and has a warm taste like mustard ; seeds used in curries [q.v.] like mustard [rayaun]. Seeds, when subjected to very powerful pressure, yield an oil [yennay] which is of a light, olive green color ; ashes used as mordant [cauram]. As this plant and Vailay [q.v.] are often confounded, the following distinctions can be noticed :—Cleome viscosa ; siliqua flat, striated, pubescent, and sessile or short-stalked ; flowers yellow ; stem and branches quite covered with viscid, glandular hairs ; smell very fœtid and strong. Gynandropsis pentaphylla ; siliqua round, glabrous ; stalk generally long and sometimes as long as the siliqua itself ; flowers almost always white ; stem and branches slightly covered with glandular hairs ; smell fœtid, but generally very indistinct ; seeds more rough. Other species of cleome are :—aspera, burmanni, tenella. Purple dog vailay, or blue as called in vernacular, is cleome chelidonii, linn. ; erect growing pot plant, large rose colored flowers ; moist soil by borders of rice-fields ; flowering in rainy season ; seed used like viscosa. Tye vailay so called from the month, otherwise cat's cleome, is cleome felina. Small vailay, otherwise simple-leaved cleome, is cleome monophylla, linn. ; flowers small, pale rose-colored ; common weed in waste places.——*Gram vailay* (கொள்ளுக்காய்வேளை - kollukkáyvélai, Tam.). From resemblance to horse-gram. Same as Zanzibar indigo.

VAIMA (వేమ - véma, *Tel.*). From (vé, san. to sew). A loom [tarry].——*Vaimareddy* (వేమారెడ్డి - vémareddi, Tel.). From (above + reddi, tel. caste title). Title of rulers of Condaveed. One attained to some distinction after the fall of Warangal [raj]. See vol. I (150).

VAITASAM (वेतस - vétasa, *San.*). From (vé, san. to plait) ; useful in plaiting. Botanically the Calamus genus, palmaceæ [vricsham, 149]. Canes. Climbing palms [taur] ; sometimes occur as stunted erect bushes, constituting impenetrable clumps ; at other times by their prickly tendrils clasping trees of the forest they ascend as climbers, attaining a length of even 600 feet ; stems, leaves and tendrils are covered with spines and prickles ; fruit hangs in large clusters, inner succulent layer of which is edible ; stem when freshly cut contains much liquid ; roots and young shoots edible ; outer layer of canes very strong and to this is due their strength ; many species, from girth of goose-quill to that of a stout walking-stick. The species best known to the natives are :—draco [sumatra dragon's blood], fasciculatus [walking-stick rattan], rotang [country rattan]. Other s. indian species indigenous or naturalized are :— erectus, extensus, gracilis, latifolius, pseudo-rotang.

VAJ (वज् - vaj, *San.*). To be strong.——*Vajracaroor* (వజ్రకరూరు - vajrakarúru, Tel.). From (vajra, san. diamond + karúru, tel. village so named). Village ; Anantapore dist., Gooty tal. ; pop. 2,473 ; acres 11,265 ; lat. 15° 02′ ; long. 77° 26′ ; from Anantapore N.N.W. 28 miles ; from Gooty W.S.W. 18 miles. Diamond [vajram] mines worked in former days by Tippoo. Europeans recently carried on operations.——*Vajram* (वज्र - vajra, San. ; الماس - almás, Ar. ; هيرا - hírá, Hind. ; ವಜ್ರ - vajra, Can. ; రవ - rava, Tel. ; വൈരക്കല്ല് - vairakkallu, Mal. ; வயிரம் - vayiram, Tam.). San. from (vaj, san. to be hard). Ar. from (lamasa, ar. sparkle). Hind. from (hírá, san. indra's thunderbolt). Tel. means a particle. Diamond. Crystallised mineral, the most valuable gem [ratnam]. Occurs in single or unattached crystals, sometimes with plain, but more frequently with rounded surfaces. Colors commonly white or grey, sometimes red, brown, yellow, green, blue and black ; the two last rare. Chiefly found disseminated in gravel [kankar] or embedded in sandstone [manal cull]. Generally brought from Golcondah, Bundelcund, Borneo, and Sumbulpore in Orissa. These are reckoned superior in transparency and purity to those of Brazil. The Maturese diamond of Ceylon, or yellow tourmaline [q.v.], is a topaz [pookhrauj] of a greenish-yellow color. ἀδάμας or dimonds were exported from Mouziris [cranganore] and Nelkunda [cullada] according to the Periplus. The Tamulians value diamonds in jewellery [nagay] for their decorative effect, but they also prize them as a talisman ; this is specially so when the natural crystal is so perfect and clear that it requires only to have its natural facets polished ; this is what jewellers call a point diamond. The rose diamond is a hemisphere covered with facets ; and the brilliant, cut above with thirty-two facets, and below with twenty-four. Diamonds are classed by natives as follows :—Bramin, white pure water ; Cshatriya, rose or reddish ; Veisya, smoky ; Shoodra, dark and impure. Diamond powder is much used in native medicine. It is purified by being enclosed within a lemon [q.v.] and boiled in the juice of Sesbania grandiflora [sesban]. The powder acts as a powerful alterative tonic. It is also and more familiarly known as a powerful mechanical poison. There is a Tamul proverb :—வைரத்தை வைரம் கொண்டே அறுக்கவேண்டும்—"a diamond must be cut with a diamond." Diamonds are weighed by the carat [q.v.] as in England ; and rough or unwrought diamonds are generally valued according to the square of their carat weight. Wrought diamonds are supposed to have lost half their original weight and therefore they are valued according to the square of double their actual weight. See vol. II, 29.—"*a*" Vajram means also the thunderbolt, the weapon of indran [q.v.] ; otherwise Vajrauyoodham. Sometimes described as quoit-shaped like the Chuckram [q.v.] of vishnoo [q.v.], and sometimes as consisting of two transverse bolts. Vajrapauny, from (páni, san. hand), is indran [q.v.] himself. Varauha mihiran [q.v.] says that when two winds come in collision, that which being struck falls on the earth is known as a thunderbolt.—"*b*" Vajram means also glue. This is of three kinds ; skin or leather glue, bone glue, and fish glue also termed isinglass [meen vajram]. Dubbers for holding oils and other fluids are made of gelatine prepared by boiling cuttings of skins [chamrah] shaped on earthen moulds.—"*c*" Meen vajram, meaning fish glue, is Isinglass. Commercial term for the swimming or air-bag of the sturgeon, Accipenser huso, and of some other fishes. According to the form in which it is prepared it is termed leaf, staple, ribbon, or book isinglass. Soluble in water, insoluble in alcohol. Ichthyocolla of chemists. The following are Isinglass-yielding fish here :—Accipenser huso, Corvina miles, Lates calcarifer [cock up], Lobotes erate, Osteogeniosus militaris [cat keliroo], Otolithus biauritus, maculatus, ruber, versicolor, Polynemus indicus [screw-pine robaul], Pristipoma hasta [caukkan], Sciæna maculata [striped cuttalay].—"*d*" Vajram in the sense of adamantine is plant first term. Ex., where transl. is of second term :—Cannabis sativa (vajradru), tree ; Euphorbia antiquorum (vajrakantaka), thorn ;

Euphorbia tirucalli (vajradruma), tree; Euphorbia tortilis (vajratunda), stem; Vitis quadrangularis (vajrakanda), root, (vajravallí), creeper. See gloss. paragraphs.

VAJAH (وضع - vaza, *Hind.*). From (vaza, ar. to place down or remove). Deduction [minhah].

VAJEE (وجيه - vajíh, *Ar.*). Support. Part of lacab; as Vajee ood deen, support of religion [ism].

VAKEEL (وكيل - vakíl, *Hind.*). From (vakala, ar. to entrust). Delegate, agent. An authorized attorney. A pleader in a court of justice.——*Vakaulat* (وكالت - vakálat, Hind.). Agency. Vakaulat nauma is a power-of-attorney [adhicaurapatram, adhicaurapatricay].

VAL (வல் - val, *Tam.*). Strength. Beauty.——*Valam* (வலம் - valam, Tam.). From right arm being stronger of the two. Cf. dacshinam, dexter. Right.——*Valam* (வளம் - valam, Tam.). Fertility.——*Valamboory* (வலம்புரி - valamburi, Tam.). Turned to the right, from screw-like pods or markings on fruits. Plant name common to:—Eriolæna candollei; Guazuma tomentosa; Holicteres isora. See gloss. paragraphs. For the valamboory chunk see under Chunk.——*Valanaud* (வளநாடு - valanádu, Tam.). From (valam, tam. fertility + nádu, tam. country). Ancient name of Tondaimundalam [q.v.].——*Valanaudan* (வளநாடன் - valanádan, Tam.). Owner of fertile tract. Title of Chola rulers. See vol. I (141).——*Valangay* (வலங்கை - valangai, Tam.). From (valam, tam. right + kai, tam. hand). Right-hand [yidangay]. Righthand faction. See vol. I (67), (69); II, 229 [jauty].——*Valavan* (வலவன் - valavan, Tam.). Means strong one. Vishnoo.——*Valavan* (வளவன் - valavan, Tam.). Owner of a fertile tract. The same as Valanaudan.——*Valavanaud* (വള്ളുവനാട് - valluvanátu, Mal.). See sep. title.——*Valay* (வலை - valai, Tam.). See sep. title.——*Valiya* (വലിയ - valiya, Mal.). From (val, tam. powerful). Large. Plant first term, often joining two genera. Ex., where transl. is of second term:—Cordia obliqua (valiyavaniççi), diospyros embryopteris; Pupalia atropurpurea (valiyakotuvéli), plumbago zeylanica; Vitis latifolia (valiyaparpátakam), mollugo cerviana. See gloss. paragraphs.——*Vallanang* (வல்லணங்கு - vallanangu, Tam.). From (above + anangu, tam. woman). The malevolent goddess Bhadra cauly [q.v.].——*Vallinam* (வல்லினம் - vallinam, Tam.). Hard letter. One of the three tamul classes of letters [mey]. க், ச், ட், த், ப், ற். None of these can end a word. See vol. I (52); II, 205, 209.——*Vilaugam* (விளாகம் - világam, Tam.). From (vilar, tam. fertility + agam, tam. home). Suffix in place names. Also means battle-field.——*Vullam* (வல்லம் - vallam,* Tam.). From (val, tam. hillock + agam, tam. place). Sanscrit name (indrakílaparvata), meaning indran, the god + shiva + mountain; after a shrine of shiva erected by indran. Tam. also (valliyammainagaram), meaning vully ammay, the mother of caulacunta cholan, the founder + town.—"*a*" Deputy tahsildarry, Tanjore district. Pay Rs. 70.—"*b*" Town, Head-quarters of Collector, Registrar, Deputy tahsildar and Sub-magistrate; Tanjore dist., Tanjore tal.; pop. 8,097; acres 2,030; lat. 10° 43′; long. 79° 06′; from Combaconam S.W. 27 miles; from Madras S.S.W. 180 miles; from Mayavaram S.W. 48 miles; from Munnargoody W. 27 miles; from Negapatam W.S.W. 53 miles; from Tanjore S.W. 7 miles. On an elevated level. Considerable trade in dholl [common dholl] and ground nut [q.v.]. Strong fort built presumably by the Naick [q.v.] rajahs in the sixteenth or seventeenth century. Taken by the English for the Nawaub [q.v.] of the Carnautaca [q.v.] payeen ghaut [q.v.] in 1771, and remained in their occupation until its restoration to rajah Toolsajee together with the whole Tanjore country in 1776. Very few traces of the fort, except the moat, now remain. The population consists chiefly of Nuttamaudies [nuttamaur] and Lubbays [q.v.]; the former engaged in agriculture and the latter in trade. Old Shiva temple with a number of inscriptions. The temple tank is of great depth. Mission station. Quartz crystals [palingoo cull] found here are made into spectacles.——*Vulloovan* (வள்ளுவன் - valluvan, Tam.). From (vallu, tam. to be able). Pariah priest common to the Pariahs [q.v.] and Pullar [q.v.]. The Vulloovan is consulted when horoscopes [jenma puttricay] are to be cast. He wears the braminical thread or poonool [q.v.]. The Vulloova kone of Valavanaud formerly presided at the great assembly of Keralam [q.v.], when a new Permaul [q.v.] was chosen every twelfth year [mahamagham] to rule over the whole of Malayalam [jauty]. See vol. I (68).——*Vully* (வள்ளி - valli, Tam.). From (val, tam. beauty). Consort of Soobramanyan [q.v.]. The principal goddess in Triplicane, who as amman [q.v.] presides over the cshetram [q.v.] and to whom the temple compound belongs, is Vedavully; the god Partasauraty or vishnoo is only lodging there as her guest. In Trivellore the amman is called Canacavully; in chidambaram Pankajavully; in shreemooshnam Ambojavully. In combaconam there are two, Comalavully and Vijayavully. In munnargoody is a Champakavully. In tirmaul iroom sholay as well as in negapatam there is a Soondravully, &c. [matam]. Vully is female proper name among the lower orders; also suffix in female proper names, as Comalavully, Vijayavully [peyar].——*Vundan* (வண்டன் - vandan, Tam.). From (val, tam. strength). An impudent man. Vundapey, impudence devil, is one of the Tamulian devils [pey].

VAL (வள் - val, *Tam.*). To surround.——*Valaiyal* (வளையல் - valaiyal, Tam.). Glass bangle [gauzoo]. For valaiyal ooppoo see under Ooppoo and Poongauram.——*Valloor* (వల్లూరు - vallúru, Tel. vallur *). From (valle, tel. cloth + úru, tel. village).—"*a*" Zemindarry, Kistna dist., Bezwada tal.; pop. 5,047; square miles 56. The zemindarry [q.v.] dates its rise from Bommadevara nauganna naidoo, employed in the Transport department of the British army in 1798-99. He amassed a considerable fortune and in 1803 purchased the Havelly [q.v.] estates of Valloor and Goodoor. In February 1807 he was granted the monopoly of the Transport service inland from Masulipatam, and this he and his descendants enjoyed for more than half a century. It was the timely aid afforded by one of his successors that enabled Sir George Whitlock to proceed through Central india, when movements were paralysed for lack of transport. Peshcush [q.v.] Rs. 20,493.—"*b*" Village; Kistna dist., Valloor zemindarry; pop. 4,070; lat. 16° 21′; long. 80° 49′; from Bezwada S.E. 16 miles; from Guntoor E. 22 miles; from Madras N. 226 miles; from Masulipatam W.N.W. 24 miles; from Vinoocondah E.N.E. 72 miles. On the Kistna. Zemindar's palace.——*Vattam* (വട്ടം - vattam, Mal.; வட்டம் - vattam, Tam.). Mal. from (vatu, mal. round). Circle. Small district comprising three or four villages under one headman [amshom]. Cf. Taraf. Plant first term meaning round. Ex., where transl. is of second term:—Acalypha spiciflorus (vattattáli), creeper; Macaranga indica (vattattámarai), nelumbium speciosum. See gloss. paragraphs.——*Vatta royasam* (வட்டராயசம் - vattaráyasam, Tam.). From (vattam, tam. circle + ráyasamu, tel. secretaryship). Clerk under Revenue inspector.——*Vattatauly* (വട്ടത്താളി - vattattáli, Mal.). Mal. from (vatta, mal. round + táli, mal. convolvulus). Botanically Acalypha [maumsicay] spiciflorus, linn., euphorbiaceæ [vricsham, 118]. Alias Acalypha hispida; Caturus spiciflorus. Shrub; leaves long-petioled, cordate, serrate; flowers axillary, spiked, pendulous, longer than the leaves; calyx three-cleft; styles three; capsule tricoccous. The leaves, beaten up with green tobacco-leaf [pogauk] and infusion of rice [q.v.], administered to ulcers; the flowers a specific in diarrhœa, either in decoction or conserve.——*Vattezhoot* (വട്ടെഴുത്ത - vattezhuttu, Mal.). Means round letter, as opposed to Kolezhoot or pointed character. The truncated form of Kolezhoot [q.v.]. The original Tamul alphabet once used in all the peninsula south of Tanjore and also in South malabar and Travancore. Its origin has not hitherto been well traced. The Vattezhoot alphabet remained in use in Malabar up to the end of the seventeenth century among the hindoos, and since then in the original form of the Kolezhoot [q.v.] or stick-writing it is the character in which the hindoo sovereigns have their grants [shausanam] drawn up. See vol. I (44), (49), (116), (120), (125), (127) [bhaushay].——*Vattil* (வட்டில் - vattil, Tam.). From (vatti, tam. to be round). A clepsydra [ghuntay, ghurry]. For Nauzhigay vattil see sep. title.——*Vattoovally* (शेंडवेल - shéndavéla, Mahr.; घार्पूल् - ghárp'húl, Cono.; ಘಾರಬುವ್ವ - ghárabuvvu, Can.; വട്ടുവള്ളി - vattuvalli, Mal.). Mal. from (vattu, mal. round + valli, mal. creeper); from leaves. Mahr. also (máravéla), meaning exuberant creeper. Title otherwise Torique with portuguese, Pensbout with dutch. Botanically Cosmostigma racemosum, wight., asclepiadeæ [vricsham, 88]. Leaves large, rather coriaceous, smooth, ovate-cordate acuminate, but sometimes rounded with an obtuse tip, readily distinguished by a group of small, brown, dusty, prominent glands at the junction of the petiole with the leaf; roots from ½ to 1 inch in diameter, externally light brown and scabrous; fracture starchy and friable, a transverse section shows them to be composed of a central woody column and a very thick greyish-white cortex; in the circumference, and sparingly scattered through the root, light yellow brown hard cells are seen; the root has no taste, and a faint ipecacuanha-like [indian ipecacuanha] odour, which is more marked in the seeds; the latter are contained in a large, smooth, green follicle; large woody climber running over high trees. Has a medicinal reputation on west coast where its leaves cure ulcerous sores and root bark is administered internally in indigestion; root bark in five grain doses three times a day found an efficient cholagogue. The flowers [phool] are sweet and are eaten by the natives.——*Vilaiyaudal* (விளையாடல் - vilaiyádal, Tam.). From (vilaiyádu, tam. to sport) Sport of gods; in other words a miracle [leelay]. For the miracles of Shiva at Madura see Tirvilaiyaudal.——*Vilaiyaudoo* (விளையாடு - vilaiyádu, Tam.). To move in a circle. To sport.

VALAVANAUD (വള്ളുവനാട് - valluvanátu, *Mal.* walawanád *). From (valluvan, mal. member of the caste so called + nátu, mal. country) [val]. Talook; Malabar district. Tahsildar's pay Rs. 200. Area 963 square miles. Language Malayalam; in Attapaudy valley, Tamul. E. inland of district. Bounded north by Yernaud talook and portion of Neilgherry district; east by Coimbatore talook; south by Palghaut talook, Cochin state and Ponnany talook; and west by Ponnany and Yernaud talooks. Soil is chiefly red loam, except where black alluvial clay [calimunn] is found in the valleys. Extends along the foot of the

Western ghauts [q.v.], many spurs of which run into it. A part of Aracoorchy amshom lies east of the ghaut and is known as Attapaudy valley, which contains the head waters of Bhawauny river. The area of this valley is about 200 square miles. The whole talook may be said to be one series of hills and dales, the latter being cultivable with paddy [q.v.], while the borders of the former are covered with gardens, containing jack [q.v.], areca [q.v.], and various other trees, in the midst of which stand the houses of the people. Madras railway passes through the talook. Staple produce is rice [q.v.], though areca [q.v.], jack [q.v.], and plantain [q.v.] are also grown largely and cocoanuts [q.v.] on a small scale. Principal rivers are Ponnauy, which forms southern boundary of the talook; Malapooram or Anakkayam river, which forms northern boundary; and Munnarcaud or Tootha, tributary of Ponnany. All these are perennial and largely used for floating timber in rafts from hills to the coast during the rainy season and are also passable for small boats except in the hot season. Places of archæological interest:—Alliparamba, Angaudipooram, Aracoorchy, Arakkparamba, Aunamangaud, Cadambalipooram, Carim poya, Cauracaud, Cauryavuttam, Chalavara, Chettanullore, Choonangaud, Colapully, Colattore, Comauramboottore, Coolcullore, Coonnattara, Cothaccorchy, Cottapaudam, Cottore, Culladicode, Melattore, Moolanyore, Moondacotecoorchy, Moondamookha, Moothootala, Moottedatt maudamba, Mungada, Nadoovuttam, Nemminy, Paunga, Perindalman, Peroor, Plaundole, Ponmana, Poolacherry, Pullipooram, Shree krishnapooram, Tekkamungalam, Tencara, Tirvalancoonn, Tutchamparra, Tutchanautcara, Vadakoombram, Valambore, Vallappoya, Vellinauly, Vettattore, Yelamboolacherry, Yeledatt maudamba. Principal trig. stations:—Anangamala, Prancode. The leading places, &c., in the talook are the following.——*Anangamala* (അനങ്ങമല - anannamala, Mal.). From (ananga, san. indian cupid + mala, mal. hill); picturesque hill. Hill; lat. 10° 49′ N.; long. 76° 26′ E.; from Calicut S.E. 50 miles; from Perindalman S.E. 14 miles. A long precipitous isolated rocky hill, a conspicuous landmark. There are one or two small coffee [q.v.] gardens on its slopes. Trig. station in lat. 10° 49′ 10·90″; long. 76° 25′ 49·66″; height 1,298 feet; from Perindalman S.E. 14 miles; from Cothacoorchy E. 3 miles.——*Angaudipooram* (അങ്ങാടിപ്പുറം - annátippuram, Mal. angádipuram *). From (annáti, mal. bazaar + puram, mal. beyond). Village; pop. 7,680; acres 625; lat. 10° 59′; long. 76° 16′; from Calicut S.E. 36 miles; from Perindalman N.W. 1½ miles. Important market town connected by a good road with Calicut. The fort, maintained till 1800, is now a ruin. Dolmens [coday cull]. Scene of one of the most desperate of the Moplah [q.v.] outrages in 1849. Temple called Tirmandhauncoonn on the top of a hill. Of great sanctity. In Moplah outrage of 1849, insurgents occupied this temple.——*Anginda* (അങ്കിന്ദ - ankinta, Mal.). Peak; lat. 11° 11′; long. 76° 30′ E.; height 7,828 feet; from Calicut E. 46 miles; from Perindalman N.E. 21 miles. On the southern edge of the Neilgherry plateau.——*Attapaudy* (അട്ടപ്പാടി - attappáti, Mal.). See sep. title.——*Carimpoya* (കരിമ്പുഴ - karimpuzha, Mal.). From (kari, mal. black + puzha, mal. river). Village; pop. 5,478; lat. 10° 55′; long. 76° 28′; from Calicut E.S.E. 49 miles; from Perindalman E.S.E. 13 miles. The seat of the Yeralpaud or second rajah of Zamorin [q.v.] family. Hindoo author, Toonchatezhoottatchan [q.v.], lived here. Chetties [q.v.] manufacture thin cloths, patterns peculiar to natives of Malabar and similar though inferior in quality to those manufactured in Tinnevelly; cloth known by name of Carimpoya pauv.——*Cherpalcherry* (ചെര്പ്പുള്ളശ്ശേരി - cherppullashshéri, Mal.). See sep. title.——*Colattore* (കുളത്തൂര് - kulattúr, Mal.). From (kulam, mal. tank + úr, mal. village). Village; pop. 4,421; lat. 10° 56′; long. 76° 10′; from Perindalman W.S.W. 8 miles; from Calicut S.E. 32 miles. Scene of Moplah [q.v.] outbreaks against the Colattore warrior, the first of which occurred in 1851 and the second in 1873.——*Culladicode* (കല്ലടിക്കോട് - kallatikkótu, Mal.). From (kallu, mal. stone + ati, mal. base + kótu, mal. peak). Peak; lat. 10° 53′; long. 76° 37′; from Calicut E.S.E. 58 miles; from Perindalman E.S.E. 24 miles. Considered the stormiest peak in Malabar. There is a Malayalam proverb:—കല്ലടിക്കോടൻകറുത്താൽകരുകപ്പുഴനിറഞ്ഞു—"if Culladicode grows "angry the Carooga river will be swollen."——*Lukkidy* (ലക്കിടി - lakkiti, Mal. lakkidi *). Means wood. The site of one of the stockades of Hyder. Village in Peroor amshom, Railway station; pop. 5,478; lat. 10° 45′; long. 76° 28′; height 142 feet; from Calicut S.E. 56 miles; from Perindalman S.E. 19 miles. On the opposite side of the river in the Cochin state lies one of the most famous Hindoo temples [devasom] in Malabar called Tirvillamala cshetram dedicated to Shree rama [q.v.].——*Melattore* (മേലാറ്റൂര് - méláttúr, Mal.). From (mél, mal. high + áru, mal. river + úr, mal. village). Village; pop. 7,691; lat. 11° 04′; long. 76° 20′; from Calicut E.S.E. 36 miles; from Perindalman N.N.E. 7 miles. Scene of Moplah [q.v.] outrages.——*Munnarcaud* (മണ്ണാര്ക്കാട് - mannárakkátu, Mal. mannárghat *). From (mannár, mal. king + kátu, mal. forest). Town; pop. 12,378; lat. 11° 00′; long. 76° 30′; from Calicut E.S.E. 50 miles; from Perindalman E. 15 miles by road 18. Centre of commerce in olden times.——*Pattaumby* (പട്ടാമ്പി - pattámbi,* Mal.). Village in Neytirimungalam amshom, Railway station; pop. 4,147; lat. 10° 48′; long. 76° 14′; height 87 feet; from Calicut S.S.E. 41 miles; from Perindalman S.S.W. 12 miles. Weekly market on Tuesdays.——*Pauraul* (പാറാല് - párál, Mal.). From (pára, mal. rock + ál, mal. banyan, ficus bengalensis, linn.). Village; pop. 2,924; lat. 10° 55′; long. 76° 21′; from Calicut S.E. 41 miles; from Perindalman S.E. 5 miles. In the Moplah [q.v.] outrage of Colattore in 1873 the insurgents came from this place. They started on the expedition after attacking and severely wounding the Velichapaud or oracle attached to the Hindoo temple.——*Perindalman* (പെരിന്തല്മണ്ണ - porintalmannu, Mal.). See sep. title.——*Pleundole* (പ്ലാന്തോട് - plántól, Mal.). From (pula, mal. jack tree, artocarpus integrifolia, willd. + mávu, mal. mango tree, mangifera indica, linn. + tótu, mal. water-course). Village, Ferry; pop. 3,695; lat. 10° 54′; long. 76° 15′; from Calicut S.E. 37 miles; from Perindalman S.S.W. 5 miles. Residence of ancient hereditary physician family called Plaundole moossad [q.v.].——*Ponnany* (പൊന്നാനി - ponnáni, Mal.). See sep. title. ——*Prancode* (പ്രാണക്കോട് - pránakkótu, Mal.). From (prána, san. life + kótu, mal. end); from the solitude. Hill; lat. 10° 59′ N.; long. 76° 20′ E.; height 1,792 feet; from Calicut S.E. 38 miles; from Perindalman E.N.E. 4 miles. The summit of a small densely-wooded range of hills. Trig. station in lat. 10° 58′ 46·65″; long. 76° 20′ 01·31″; height 1,792 feet; from Perindalman E.N.E. 4 miles; from Angaudipooram E. 4 miles. ——*Pundalore* (പന്തലൂര് - pantalúr, Mal.). See sep. title.——*Shoranore* (ചെറുവണ്ണൂര് - cheruvannúr, Mal.). See sep. title.——*Silent valley* (വള്ളഘട്ടം - vállaghattam, Mal.). See sep. title.——*Siroovauny* (ശിറുവാണി - shiruváni, Mal.). From (shiru, mal. small + bhaváni, san. the river). River in the Attapaudy valley. Rises on the northern slopes of the mountains north of Palghaut and flows northwards till it joins the Bhawauny.——*Toothacull* (തൂതക്കല് - tútakkal, Mal.). From (túta, mal. milk-pot + kal, mal. suffix of place). River. Rises near Munnarcaud and flows S.W. till it joins the Ponnany river, a few miles E. of Coottipooram railway station, where is spanned by a large railway bridge.——*Vadamalay* (വടമല - vatamala, Mal.). See sep. title. ——*Vaunyamcoolam* (വാണിയംകുളം - vániyankulam, Mal.). From (vániyan, mal. trader + kulam, mal. tank). Village; pop. 6,227; lat. 10° 47′; long. 76° 22′; from Calicut S.E. 50 miles; from Perindalman S.S.E. 15 miles. Travellers' bungalow [q.v.]. Basel mission station and school. Weekly market for cattle [maud]. ——*Wottapollem* (ഒറ്റപ്പാലം - ottappálam, Mal. ottapálam *). From (otta, mal. single + pálam, mal. bridge); from the single log of wood which once formed the bridge. Village in Choonangaud amshom, Railway station, Moonsif's station; pop. 8,583; lat. 10° 47′; long. 76° 25′; height 116 feet; from Calicut S.E. 51 miles; from Perindalman S.E. 17 miles. Weekly market on Saturday.

VALAY (जाल - jála, *San.*; جال - jálá, *Hind.*; ಬಲೆ - bale, *Can.*; వల - vala, *Tel.*; വല - vala, *Mal.*; வலை - valai, *Tam.*). San. from (jala, san. water). Drav. from (val, to pull) [val]. Net. The following are the principal kinds of net made use of by Madras fishermen.——*Caray valay* (కంధలము - kandhalamu, Tel.; അരിപ്പുവല - arippuvala, Mal.; கரைவலை - karaivalai, Tam.). Tel. from (kande, tel. roll of thread). Mal. from (ari, mal. to sift + vala, mal. net). Tam. from (karai, tam. shore + valai, tam. net). Dragnet. Consists of a cotton [q.v.] bag with fine meshes in the centre, and wide meshes of knotted coir [q.v.] rope at either end to lead the fish into the central bag. The upper ropes are supported by wooden floats, and the under ones kept down by stone sinkers, so as to make a kind of wall of rope. A great quantity of cordage is used for this net, which almost fills a small boat, being sometimes half a mile in length. One end is left on shore in the hands of a few helpers, and the other end carried to sea by boat, and then payed out in a semi-circle; after an hour or two it is dragged into shore by ten or twenty men and boys. The two ends of the net are equally pulled, boys shouting and beating the water in the middle to drive the fish into the bag as it nears the shore. Large quantities of fish are taken in these nets.——*Cattoo valay* (ఈడ్పుము - ídpumu, Tel.; ചവിട്ടുവല - chavittuvala, Mal.; கட்டுவலை - kattuvalai, Tam.). Tel. from (ídtsu, tel. to pull). Mal. from (chavittu, mal. to tread + vala, mal. a net). Tam. from (kattu, tam. to bind + valai, tam. net). A fishing net. Open at both ends but the narrow end is tied when in use. It is set in streams with the mouth distended by a hoop or by pegs.——*Cayitt valay* (കയറുവല - kayattuvala, Mal.; கயிற்று வலை - kayittuvalai, Tam.). Means rope + net. For catching large fish in deep water or rapid streams.——*Dobbood valay* (దొబ్బుడువల - dobbuduvala, Tel.). From (dobbu, tel. to push + vala, tel. net). A triangular hand net pushed forward in still water.——*Kyevalay* (సన్నపువల - sannapuvala, Tel.; ചെറുവല - cheruvala, Mal.; கைவலை - kaivalai, Tam.). Tel. from (sannapu, tel. thin + vala, tel. net). Mal. from (cheru, mal. small + vala, mal. net). Tam. from (kai, tam. hand + valai, tam. net). Small casting net.——*Oodoovalay* (కట్లవల - katlavala, Tel.; உடுவலை - uduvalai, Tam.). Tel. (from kattu, tel. band +

vala, tel. net). Tam. from (udu, tam. to encircle + valai, tam. net). This is about 40 yards in length; it is tied across a stream in shallow parts.——*Poosalavalay* (పూసలవల - púsalavala, Tel.). Tel. from (púsa, tel. bead + vala, tel. net). A dragnet with a large mesh.——*Tevvalay* (దయ్యపువల - dayyapuvala, Tel.; പെരുവല - peruvala, Mal.; தெவ்வலை - tevvalai, Tam.). Tel. from (dayyamu, tel. devil + vala, tel. net). Mal. from (peru, mal. large + vala, mal. net). Tam. from (tev, tam. opposing power + valai, tam. net). This is used in deep and shallow water and spreads to a distance of about 80 yards. It requires about twenty men to use it, who drag it along the water, gradually forming a semi-circle, when the fish thus imprisoned are captured by means of the Cayitt valay.——*Veechvalay* (తాటము - tátamu, Tel.; വീശുവല - víççuvala, Mal.; வீச்சுவலை - víççuvalai, Tam.). Tel. from (tádu, tel. rope). Mal. from (víshu, mal. to cast + vala, mal. net). Tam. from (vísu, tam. to throw + valai, tam. net). The common cast-net of Southern india. It is circular, varying between nine and twelve yards in diameter, with its edges weighted with iron beads. It is made of stiff cotton [q.v.] thread. The fisherman who has to use the net gathers it in his hand and casts it on the surface of a pond or tank. The weight of the iron beads makes the edges of the net sink at once to the bottom, while the central network remains afloat. The fisherman then begins to take in the net, inch by inch, by slowly pulling up a cord attached to the centre of the net, and when the whole net is landed, the folds are well shaken and any fish which are found are taken out.

VALLABHAN (वल्लभ - vallabha, *San.*). Means master. Teloogoo bramin of the Veishnava [q.v.] sect, who lived in the sixteenth century, and established the worship of Baulagopaulan, the infant Krishnau [q.v.], associated with his mistress Raudhay [q.v.]. Amongst other articles of creed, he taught that privation forms no part of sanctity, and that it is the duty of the teacher and of his disciples to worship the deity, not in solitude and mortification, but in the pleasures of society and the enjoyment of the world. The Vallabhacharry sect is scarce here. The forehead marks are two red perpendicular lines joined by semicircle at root of nose, with red spot [pottoo, tilacam] between [naumam]. See vol. I (85).——*Vallabham* (वल्लभ - vallabha, San.). Beloved or liked by. Plant second term. Ex., where transl. is of first term:—Mangifera indica (kámavallabha), cupid; Pentapetes phœnicea (arkavallabha), sun; Zizyphus jujuba (rájavallabha), king. See gloss. paragraphs.——*Vallabha rajah* (വല്ലഭരാജാ - vallabharájá, Mal.). Means powerful king, but really sanscritized form of (valluva rájá), king of Valavanaud. The Vellattiry rajah, see vol. II, 101. Distinguish from Vallabhy.——*Vallabhy* (वल्लभी - vallabhí, San.). From (vallabha, san. chief). Dynasty. The name of an era [q.v.] which began in Samvat [q.v.] 375 or 319 A.D. S. indian form of Ballabhy [q.v.].

VALMEEKY (वाल्मीकि - válmíki, *San.*). From (valmíka, san. ant hill). Author of sanscrit Ramayanam [poottacondah].

VALSA (వలస - valasa, *Tel.*; வலசை - valasai, *Tam.*). From (vellu, tel. to go). Emigration of people in a body from village through fear of calamity. So colony established.

VAN (वन् - van, *San.*). To sound, seek.——*Vamsha choodaumany* (वंशचूडामणि - vamshachúdámani, San.). From (vamsha, san. family + chúdá, san. top-knot + mani, san. gem). Otherwise Vamsha shekharan. Paundyan [q.v.] king in whose time the Madura college [q.v.] was established. See vol. I (120).——*Vamshadhavra* (వంశధార - vamshadhára, Tel.). From (vamsha, san. bamboo, bambusa arundinacea, willd. + dhárá, san. stream). River; Vizagapatam dist., Jeypore zemindarry, Goonapore magisterial division. Rises in the Bissemcuttack hills and flows south-south-east into Ganjam district, which it enters at Battily in the Kimedy country. Hence it follows a south-easterly course, until it falls into the Bay of Bengal at Calingapatam. Total length about 170 miles, for nearly half of which it is navigable by country boats during the rains, but with difficulty only. Near its mouth the river is three-quarters of a mile broad. Unbridged.——*Vamsham* (वंश - vamsha, San.).—"*a*" Bamboo. Ancient linear measure. 10 hastams or cubits = 1 vamsham [alavay, 1f]. Approximate actual value, 1 vamsham = 15 feet.—"*b*," A line of pedigree, from its resemblance to the succession of joints in a bamboo [q.v.]. Cf. genealogical tree in english. Genealogy is one of the five topics [punchalutchanam] which every pooraunam [q.v.] is supposed to treat of. The other four are sargam, pratisargam, manwantaram and vamshannoocharitam. The Aryans [q.v.] before they were divided into the castes [jauty] established by the Code of Menoo [q.v.] are spoken of as belonging to either the solar race Soorya vamsham, or the lunar race Chundra vamsham. The solar race, which is stated to have reigned subsequently in Oudh, was the more celebrated, and the Rama [q.v.] of the Ramayanam [q.v.] is its great hero.——*Vamshyam* (वंश्य - vamshya, San.). From (vamsha, san. spine). Vertebrata. Animals [jantoo] having a back-bone or vertebral column. The back-bone consists of a number of bony pieces called vertebræ, which, together with the bones of the head or cranium, form a strong longitudinal hollow axis for the reception and support of the brain and spinal cord. The other bones of the vertebrate skeleton consist of the ribs and sternum forming the hæmal arch, and those which afford support to, and those which enter into the composition of the limbs. The skeleton of all vertebrate animals is internal, and besides serving as a bony case for the protection of the organs of digestion, circulation, and respiration and the nervous system, it also forms a frame-work for the muscles by which the various movements of the limbs, &c., are effected. The limbs are never more than four in number, and they are always turned away from the side of the body on which the nervous system is located. The vertebrate sub-kingdom [oopaganam] includes in ascending scale the classes [vargam] of Fishes [matsyam], Batrachians [bhaicam], Reptiles [sarpy], Birds [pacshy], and Mammals [sastanam]. For invertebrate see Nirvamshyam.——*Vana bhojanam* (वनभोजन - vanabhójana, San.). Taking food in the forest, or by substitution in a tope [tope, tote] or garden. Luni solar [chaundramaunam] festival [pundigay, 6d] held on the full moon [powrnimay] in the 8th solar month Caurtigay [mausam], i.e., between 15th November and 13th December. Feast held in topes [q.v.] and gardens, in the month of November, with the object of increasing their produce. Also called Caurtigay powrnimay [q.v.].——*Vana cookkootam* (वनकुक्कुट - vanakukkuta, San.). From (vana, san. wood + kukkuta, san. cock). Scolopacidæ family, longirostres, grallatores, aves [pacshy, 41], of naturalists [jantoo]. Bill typically long, slender, in many, somewhat soft towards tip, in others hard throughout; wings lengthened, as are tertials; tail short; tarsus moderately long; toes slightly united by very short web. Plumage brown, of various shades above, white, more or less tinged brown or ashy beneath. Snipes [oollaun] and sand-pipers [oollangy] form a continued series, graduating into each other, with various modifications of the bill, as to length, strength, hardness, and form. Divided as follows.—"*a*" Scolopacinæ, snipes. Bill long, straight, rather soft, swollen at tip, which is gently bent over the lower mandible; tail varying in the number of feathers. Have the richest plumage of the family, dorsals and scapular feathers being often streaked with black and yellow. Bills are highly sensitive and soft at tip, and in drying shrivel up so as to appear punctured. Feed on worms and soft larvæ, chiefly nocturnal in habits, and have large eyes set far backwards, giving them peculiar physiognomy; mostly affect concealment, and some of them even frequent woods [oollaun]:—"*b*" Limosinæ, godwits. Bill much lengthened, soft at tip, straight or slightly turned upwards; mostly of large size; plumage plain; distinct web between the outer toes. Approach snipes [oollaun] in form of bill and softness of tip, differ much in coloration, wanting their rich plumage. Frequent open ground, not affecting concealment; are diurnal.—"*c*" Numeninæ, curlews. Bill very long, curved downwards; differ from Godwits in their curved beaks, the summer plumage not varying from the winter garb.—"*d*" Tringinæ, stints, &c. Bill short or moderate, soft, and somewhat flexible, occasionally dilated or curved; wings long; tail short; legs moderately short; toes usually divided to base, or with very rudimentary web. Differ from Godwits by shorter bill and legs; and from Sand-pipers by shorter and softer bills, combined with greater delicacy of tact, which is equal to that of Godwits, but less than that of the Snipes. Tendency to associate in flocks; feed in marshes, paddy-fields, edges of tanks, rivers, &c., affect concealment or cover more perhaps than the sand-pipers [oollangy]. Live on soft insects [poochy], worms [keerah], larvæ, small crustacea [kavachiny] and molluscs [chippy]. Most have marked change of plumage in summer, becoming darker above and rufous beneath; and in one species the male, which is larger than the female, is ornamented with a fine ruff.—"*e*" Totaninæ, sandpipers. Bill moderately long, slender, with tip hard and pointed, slightly ascending in some; tarsi slender, rather long; feet elongate; outer toe joined by web to the middle one. Change of plumage in summer slight in some, in others to black or dusky beneath and not to rufous. Sand-pipers run along the muddy and pebbly banks of rivers or lakes and seas, and pick up various small crustacea [kavachiny] and molluscs [chippy] generally from the surface of the ground, not inserting their bills deeply like snipes [oollaun] and stints. Several are solitary habits, a few gregarious; are all winter visitants to India, breeding in Northern and Central europe and Asia, laying four eggs, green or greenishwhite with numerous spots [oollangy].——*Vanajam* (वनज - vanaja, San.). The water-born. A lotus [nelumbo].——*Vanam* (वन - vana, San.; వనం - vanam, Tel.; വനം - vanam, Mal.; வனம் - vanam, Tam.). From (van, san. to sound). Wilderness; uncultivated ground surrounding a town. Also means water.——*Vanaspaty* (वनस्पति - vanaspati, San.). From (vana, san. forest + pati, san. lord); applied to large tree generally. In botany a Cryptogam [vricsham].——*Vanatye* (வனத்தாயி - vanattáyi, Tam.). From (vana, san. forest + táy, tam, mother); woodland deity. Female proper name among the lower orders [peyar].——*Vanchikshmah* (വഞ്ചിക്ഷ്മാ - vañchikshmá, Mal.). From (vanchi, mal. boat + kshmá, san. land). The country of Travancore.——*Vanchy* (വഞ്ചി - vañchi, Mal.). Raft of bamboo [q.v.]. Boat [munjy].——*Vanitay* (वनिता - vanitá, San.). From (van, san. to seek); sought after, desired. Woman.——*Vaniteshwary* (वनितेश्वरी - vanitéshvarí, San.). From (vanitá, san, woman +

ishvarí, san. goddess). Daughter of a Chola [q.v.] king and wife of Coon paundyan [soondra paundy tevar]; converted her husband from the Jeina [q.v.] to Sheivite faith [charitram, sambandhan]. See vol. I (120).——*Vaunaprastan* (वानप्रस्त - vánaprast'ha, San.). From (vana, san. forest + prast'ha, san. marching towards). A Bramin [q.v.] of the third order [aushramam] who has passed through the stages of student [bramhacharry] and householder [grihastan] and has left his house and family for the woods.——*Vaunaram* (वानर - vánara, San.). From (vana, san. forest + nara, san. man); man-like animal in the forest. Monkey [bandar].——*Vaunardhwajam* (वानरध्वज - vánaradhvaja, San.). Monkey flag. Arjoonan's [q.v.] flag; also that of the Cadambas [q.v.]. See vol. I (115).——*Vaunaspatyam* (वानस्पत्य - vánaspatya, San.). Belonging to (vanaspati, san. forest lord). In botany a phanerogam [vricsham].——*Vaunausy* (வாணசி - vánási, Tam.). From (vanavási, san. forest residence). An ancient large town at the western limits of Paundy. Near Omalore in salem talook, salem district.

VAND (वन्द् - vand, *San.*). To salute.——*Vanda* (वन्दा - vandá, San.). Means saluting, a parasite. Generic botanical name [rasnah].——*Vandanam* (वन्दन - vandana, San.). Obeisance, salutation [namas, salaam]; usually by touching the feet.

VANJA (వంజ - vanja, *Tel.*). From (vandhya, san. barren). Barren spot [bunjar].

VANKA (వంక - vanka, *Tel.*). From (vangu, tel. to bend); from zigzag course. A small stream.

VANTAN (वन्त - vanta, *San.*). Pl. of vat, meaning possession. Suffix in compounds; as Booddhivantan, meaning wisdom + possessor.

VANTHAM (வனிதம் - vanitham, *Tam.*). From (vanai, tam. to adorn); beauty, elegance. Place suffix, as in Yelauyirampunnay vantham.

VAR (वर - var, *San.*). To screen, cover, surround, envelop; to restrain; to prevent; to choose; to love, desire.——*Varadacharry* (वरदाचार्य - varadácharya, San.). From (vara, san. desire + dá, san. to give + áchárya, san. teacher, titular affix) [pauvalan]. A title. Bramin poet and dramatist. Disciple of Vedauntacharry [q.v.], head of the Vadagalays [q.v.] at Conjeeveram. In old age wrote Vasanta tilacam [q.v.], known popularly by the name of Ammaul baunam. The subject is a general description of Conjeeveram at the May festival. Varadacharry lived towards the close of the sixteenth century, and died aged 54 at Conjeeveram.——*Varadan* (வரதன் - varathan, Tam.). From (vara, san. desire + dá, san. to give). Epithet of Shiva. Also of Vishnoo at Conjeeveram. Hindoo 2nd or pers. name; in compounds, as Soondravaradan, Vencatavaradan [peyar].——*Varadappa naick* (ವರದಪ್ಪನಾಯಕ - varadappanáyaka, Can.). From (varada, san. vishnu + appa, can. title). Ruler of Madura and tributary of Vijianugger. A.D. 1544–1545. See vol. II, 250.——*Vara lutchmy vratam* (వరలక్ష్మీవ్రతం - varalakshmivratam, Tel.). Means boon + lutchmy, the goddess + vow. Lunar [chaundra maunam] festival [pundigay, 6b], subject to intercalation [adhicam]. Kept on Friday which precedes full moon of fifth lunar month Shrauvanam [mausam] between 1st and 30th August. Women worship Lutchmy [q.v.] in their houses and pray not to become widows. Those who have once kept it contract an obligation to celebrate it perpetually both themselves and their descendants. The women tie a thread of yellow cotton [q.v.] round the right wrist [ananta chatoordashy, kedaury gowry vratam, maryauday].——*Varam* (वर - vara, San.). From (vri, san. to choose). Gift [daunam, tyangam]. Best.——*Varan* (वर - vara, San.). From (vri, san. to desire). The best. Shiva.——*Varatam* (वरट - varata, San.). See sep. title.——*Varatoongan* (வாதுங்கன் - varathungan, Tam.). From (vara, san. best + tunga, san. high). Name of a Paundyan [q.v.] king; see vol. I (124).——*Varna coty* (वर्णकोटि - varnakóti, San.; బరణకోటి - barnakóti, Tel.). From (varuna, san. water + kóti, san. end); limit of water. The third assumed city of Sanscrit astronomers. Supposed to lie under the equator at 90° from Lunka [q.v.].——*Varoonam* (वरुण - varuna, San.). See sep. title.——*Varoonan* (वरुण - varuna, San.). From (vri, san. to encompass). Greek οὐρανός. One of the oldest Vedic deities. The god of the waters, clouds and rain [mazhay]. Regent of west [ashtadicpaulacan]. See vol. I (78).——*Varroo* (వర్రు - varru, Tel.). From (vári, san. water). Stream.——*Varsham* (वर्ष - varsha, San.). From (vri, san. to surround). Any large division of a continent. Distinguish from Varsham [q.v.], rain or year.——*Vauram* (वार - vára, San.). Week. See sep. title.——*Vauroonam* (वारुण - váruna, San.). From (varuna, san. the god of waters). The west. One of the nine divisions of Bhaurata varsham [navakhandam] or Northern india [jamboo dweepam].——*Verandah* (برآمده - barámadah, Hind.); the second syllable of title formerly pronounced much broader; from (vara, san. surrounding). An open pillared platform round a house.——*Vratam* (व्रत - vrata, San.). From (vri, san. to choose); self-chosen, act of austerity. Otherwise nomboo [q.v.] in Tamul. Vow [pundigay, 6d]. Mostly confined to females, during which a fast is observed. Undertaken with a view to accomplish various objects in life, as wealth, learning, offspring, long life, virtue, &c. Some of the principal Vratams observed are as follows:—Vinauyaca vratam, otherwise vinauyaca poojay, Vara lutchmy vratam, Ananta vratam, Kedaura gowry vratam, Rishy punchamy vratam, &c. [q.v.]. The release from Vratam is called Oodyaupanam; it is closed by a strict religious ceremony performed to secure its benefits which would otherwise be lost. The benefits are attainable either in this life or the future [maryauday].——*Vrautyan* (व्रात्य - vrátya, San.). From (vráta, san. multitude), as having been cast away and compelled to be of the multitude, for failing to perform the essential ceremonies. A Bramin [q.v.] who has lost caste [jauty] through non-observance of the vedams [q.v.]. See Vol. I (73).——*Varman* (വർമ്മൻ - varmman, Mal.). Means armour. Cognomen of rajahs among Paundies [q.v.], Cholas [q.v.], and Cheras [q.v.].

VARAGOO (वरक - varaka, *San.*; ارزن - arzan, *Pers.*; چینا - chíná, *Hind.*; رالا - rálah, *Dec.*; ಬರಗು - baragu, *Can.*; ಸಾಮೆ - sáme, *Too.*; వరగ - varaga, *Tel.*; കുറൻപുല്ല - kúranpullu, *Mal.*; வரகு - varagu, *Tam.*). Title from tamul. San. from (vara, san. desirable). Mal. from (kúran, mal. sharp + pullu, mal. grass). Tam. means dry crop. San. also (shyámaka), meaning black [shaumay]; (chína), meaning china grain, as foreign; (anu), meaning small. Hind. also (kodro), meaning paspalum scrobiculatum, linn. [khoda]; (chínághás), meaning panicum grass; (wárí), from sanscrit; (sáwán), meaning panicum miliare, lam.; (shámakh), from sanscrit. Can. also (navane) [tinay]; (sháme) [shaumay]. Tel. also (barigelu). Tam. also (panivaragu), meaning dew + the plant; (kádaikkanni), meaning quail + eye; (shámai) [shaumay]; (kadavuni), by corruption. Title otherwise Chenna, Common millet, Indian millet, Indian oats, Little millet, Pany varagoo, Quail eye, True millet, Wild kidney bean. Botanically Panicum [priyangoo] miliaceum, linn., graminaceæ [vricsham, 156]. Alias Panicum asperrimum, milium. Cereal; erect, annual, about 2 feet high, with rather broad, hairy leaves and a much divided nodding panicle; seeds oval, slightly compressed, brilliant, about a line in length, bark or envelope blackish, brown or fair, parenchyme, white, of sweet taste; native of arabia; slow growing; needs but little rain. Cultivated as dry crop; grows best on an elevated, dry, light, rich soil, and is generally sown after the rains [mazhay]; ground prepared in south in auny [mausam] or june, on coromandel in ashaudham or july and shrauvanam or august; twice or thrice ploughed; seed sown in south in audy or july, on coromandel in ashaudham or july and shrauvanam or august; sown broadcast and ploughed in, or by a seed drill [gorroo] and the soil gone over with a harrow [goontaca]; while under growth no special treatment is necessary; full grown crop is ½ yard high; cut after six or eight months by sickles; carried to the threshing floor [calam] and trodden by bullocks [maud], and buffaloes [khoolgah]; grain is separated from the chaff by winnowing pans; produce brought to market three months after cutting; average price, 36 imperial seers for 1 rupee. Lands that have been under zonna [cholum], sadza [bajrah], indigo [q.v.], or corra [tinay], are generally prepared for varagoo; it commands the greater portion of the ryot's labor and resources, for almost all the manure [yeroo] goes to this crop, and the land is invariably well prepared; crop seldom met with in poorer soils. The grain is digestible and nutritious; inferior to panicum italicum, linn. [tinay], and fetches lower price; boiled and eaten with milk [paul] and sugar [q.v.]; it contains about nine per cent. of nitrogenous matter and fifty-nine of starch; alimentary, but the pericarp is with much difficulty separated from the grain; here deprived of the husk and used whole as rice, or ground into meal and flour and made into bread; in england it is used for feeding small birds; makes tolerable cattle fodder [ghaus] for village cattle [maud]. There is a Tamul proverb:—மக்கள் களவும் வரகுபதரும் சரி—"the dishonest tricks of children "and the husks of varagoo are alike;" both are obstinate.——*Wild varagoo* (ಕಾಡುಬರಗುಹುಲ್ಲು - kádubaraguhullu, Can.; கொறணி - korani, Tam.). Can. from (kádu, can. wild + baragu, can. panicum miliaceum, linn. + hullu, can. grass). Botanically Panicum [priyangoo] remotum, retz., graminaceæ [vricsham, 156]. Alias Panicum petiveri. Culm branched, creeping at the base, ascending, apex slender; leaves linear-acuminate, and with the sheaths glabrous; raceme decompound, lax, partial ones alternate, thin, secund scabrous; spikelets twin, distant, oval, puberulous; podicels longish, naked; glumes unequal, obtuse; lower one twice shorter; neuter floret two-valved; hermaphrodite one oblong, muticous, transversely lightly waved and wrinkled, striated lengthways, equalling the upper glume. Moderately good fodder, but unsuited for hay [ghaus].

VARAM (వరము - varamu, *Tel.*; வரம் - varam, *Tam.*). From (pura, san. town). Suffix in place names, as Dharmavaram, charity + town. Distinguish from Varam [var], best.

VARATAM (वरट - varata, *San.*). From (vara, san. best + at, san. to go); from gait [var]. Anatidæ family, lamellirostres, natatores, aves [pacshy, 50], of naturalists [jantoo]. Bill broader at base than high, shallow, depressed, of nearly equal width throughout, wider at tip; nostrils sub-basal or nearly median; tarsus moderately short, set far back on body. Differ from family anseridæ [hamsam] by possessing a longer, shallower bill and shorter tarsus, and having the lamellæ of the bill more highly developed. Sexes usually differ much in color; males of many assume female plumage for a short period immediately after breeding season, resuming their proper coloring at autumn moult; feed partly on vegetable matter and partly on minute worms, larvæ, &c. Divided as follows.—"*a*" Anatinæ, true ducks and teal; hind toe not bordered by a membrane; head of moderate size; neck long and more or less slender; bill usually of even width throughout, or wider at tip, not raised at base; legs set a little more forward than in the next group, and they can walk tolerably well; wings of most are long, and they fly rapidly.—"*b*" Fuligulinæ, pochards, sea ducks or diving ducks; hind toe short, bordered by more or less wide web; wings shorter than in last sub-family; feet large, web reaching to very end of toes, and wide; tail generally short, rounded, somewhat wedged; have larger head and shorter neck than true ducks; walk badly in consequence of very backward position of legs, but swim well and dive freely; only one moult; many are exclusively marine ducks, others partially; few are mostly fresh water, and to this last section belong all the indian species. The species of the two sub-families best known to the natives are shown below. ——*Common teal* (مرغابی - murghábí, Pers.; پانی کی بدق - pánikíbadak, Hind. and Dec.; చిలువ - chiluva, Tel.; ଶିଳେଚୋଡ଼ା - silechodai, Oor.; கிளுவை - kiluvai, Tam.). Pers. from (murgh, pers. fowl + áb, pers. water). Hind. from (pání, hind. water + badak, hind. duck). Tam. from (kila, tam. to rise). Tam. also (shiravi), meaning winged. Querquedula crecca, anatinæ, anatidæ [varatam], lamellirostres, natatores [pacshy, 50], of naturalists. Male, crown of head, cheeks, front and sides of neck ferruginous brown; on sides of head, inclosing eye, large patch of deep glossy green, passing off backwards to nape in form of broad band; back and scapulars with transverse undulating lines of black and white, some longer scapulars creamy-yellow, with portion of their outer webs velvet black; tail hair-brown, feathers edged white; wing-coverts brown, tinged grey; speculum, formed by tips of secondary coverts, deep green in middle, velvet black at sides, bordered above by broad yellowish white bar; chin black; lower part of neck in front, and breast reddish or creamy-white, with round black spots; abdomen white; lower tail-coverts blackish-brown, bordered at sides with yellowish-white; bill blackish; irides hazel-brown; legs greyish brown; length 14½ inches; female has head, neck and all upper parts dusky-brown, feathers broadly edged pale reddish brown; throat, cheeks and band behind eyes yellowish-white, spotted black; speculum as in male, and under parts yellowish-white. One of the most abundant as well as earliest visitors, frequents both tanks and rivers, often in immense flocks, flight amazingly rapid, strictly night-feeding, large numbers netted or caught. Sometimes caught alive by man wading with head above water concealed in large earthen chatty [q.v.].——*Domestic duck* (वरट - varata, San.; بط - bat, Ar., اردك - urdak, Pers.; بدك - badak, Hind. and Dec.; బాతు - bátu, Tel.; വാത്ത് - váttu, Mal.; சீமைவாத்து - shímaiváttu, Tam.). Tam. from (shímai, tam. european + váttu, tam. goose). Anas domestica, anatinæ, anatidæ [varatam], lamellirostres, natatores, aves [pacshy, 50], of naturalists [jantoo]. Plumage very variable, greatly differing from the wild duck [q.v.], but the males retain the curled feathers of the tail found in the wild ones. In form the domestic duck is more dull and less elegant than the wild, domestication having deprived it of the lofty gait, long tapering neck, and sprightly eyes.——*Golden eye duck* (నల్లచిలువ - nallachiluva, Tel.). Tel. from (nalla, tel. black + chiluva, tel. wild duck). Title otherwise Tufted duck. Fuligula cristata, fuligulinæ, anatidæ [varatam], lamellirostres, natatores [pacshy, 50], of naturalists. Alias Anas fuligula. Head and neck, including the long pendent, silky crest, glossy black with green and purple reflections; back wings, and rump black; rest of the lower parts pure white; the vent black; speculum formed by the secondaries, white, with a narrow greenish-black edge; tertials glossy green. Bill dark bluish grey, the tip black; irides golden yellow, leg leaden, the webs dusky. The female has the colors somewhat duller and more brown; the crest not so long; speculum smaller, and the lower parts spotted with brown. The young want the crest, and have the base of the bill and region of the eyes varied with white. Very common; late in leaving; frequents open tanks keeping away from edges; generally found in small or moderately sized parties.——*Wild duck* (جنگلی بدق - janglíbadak, Hind. and Dec.; నీళ్లబాతు - níllabátu, Tel.; நீர்வாத்து - nírváttu, Tam.). Hind. from (janglí, hind. wild + badak, hind. duck). Tel. from (níllu, tel. water + bátu, tel. duck). Tam. from (nír, tam. water + váttu, tam. goose). Title otherwise Mallard. Anas boschas, anatinæ, anatidæ [varatam], lamellirostres, natatores, aves [pacshy, 50], of naturalists [jantoo]. Male, bill yellowish green; head and neck of a deep shining green; a white collar round the neck; part of the breast and shoulders of a deep vinous chestnut; breast and belly gray, marked with speckled lines of a dusky hue; scapulars white, elegantly barred with brown; spot on the wing rich purple; tail feathers twenty-four; four middle deep black, strongly curled upwards; irides red or hazel-brown; legs orange-yellow, length 24 inches; 2½ pounds in weight; female differs greatly from the male; very good eating.

VARAUHAM (वराह - varáha, *San.*). From (vrih, san. to root up). A boar [soor]. Hindoo 2nd or pers. name [peyar].——*Varahah* (వరహా - varahá, Tel.). Means boar. Pagoda [q.v.]; teloogoo form. 2 maudas = 1 varahah [naunyam, 2b]. Approximate actual value, 1 varahah = 4 rupees. Not current. Same as kurruck varahah or pagoda. Compare San. dharanam, Hind. hoon, Tam. varauhan. See vol. I, 609.——*Varauha avatar* (वराहावतार - varáhávatára, San.). From (above + avatára, san. incarnation). The third or boar incarnation of Vishnoo [avatar]. The Vishnoo pooraunam [q.v.] thus succinctly describes it:—"At the close of the Pudma calpam [q.v.] the supreme "Narayanan [q.v.], the incomprehensible, the sovereign of all "creatures, lying within the form of Bramha [q.v.], awoke from "his sleep of night, and beheld the universe void. Then he the "lord, concluding that within the waters lay the earth, and being "desirous to raise it up, created another form for that purpose; "and as in preceding Calpams [q.v.] he had assumed the shape "of a fish [matsyam] or a tortoise [coormam], so in this he took "the form of a boar, and plunged into the ocean; while the "goddess earth, beholding him thus descending to the sub-"terraneous regions, bowed in devout adoration and glorified "the god. Then being praised by the earth, he emitted a low "murmuring sound, like the chanting of the Saumavedam [q.v.]; "and the mighty boar [jungly soor], whose eyes were like "the lotus [nelumbo], and whose body, vast as the Neelam "mountain, was of the dark color of the lotus leaves, uplifted "upon his ample tusks the earth from the lowest regions." Another Veishnava legend tells the story as follows. The three persons of the trinity [trimoorty] at one time disputed as to who had the pre-eminence. Bramha [q.v.], who, from the summit of the lotus where he was seated, saw nothing in the universe, believed himself the first of creatures. He descended into the stem of the lotus, and finding at last Narayanan or Vishnoo asleep, he asked him who he was. "I am the first-"born," replied Vishnoo. Bramha disputed this title and even attacked him. But during the struggle, Mahadevan or Shiva threw himself between them, saying, "It is I who am the "first-born. Nevertheless I will recognise as my superior him "who is able to see the summit of my head or the sole of my "feet." Vishnoo, as hidden or infernal moon, transforming himself into a wild boar, pierced through the ground and penetrated to the infernal regions, where he saw the feet of Mahadevan. On his return Mahadevan saluted Vishnoo as the first born of the gods. Some say that as the cause of this avatar an asooran [q.v.] named Hiranyaucshan stole the vedams [q.v.], rolled up the earth as a mat, and hid himself with the vedams in the sea. Vishnoo took the form of a boar, slew the asooran, recovered the vedams, and reinstated the world. This has the appearance of relating to some large national struggle [matam].——*Varauha mihiran* (वराहमिहिर - varáhamihira, San.). From (above + mihira, san. sprinkler). Means male boar. An astronomer, one of the nine gems of the court of Vicramadityan [navaratnam]. Born at Oojjein A.D. 530 and died in 587. Author of Brihat samhitay [q.v.] and Brihad jautacam [q.v.]. On the moon, he says:—"One-half of the moon [chundran], "whose orbit [cacsham] lies between the sun [sooryan] and the "earth [bhoomy], is always bright by the sun's rays; the other "half is dark, by its own shadow [chauyay]; like the two sides "of a pot standing in the sunshine." On eclipses, he says:—"The true explanation of the phenomena is this: in an eclipse "[grahanam] of the moon he enters into the earth's shadow "[chauyay]; in a solar eclipse the same things happen to the "sun. Hence the commencement of a lunar eclipse does not "take place from the west side, nor that of a solar eclipse from "the east." For more details about eclipses according to him see Rahoo. He said that solar spots indicate famine in the land.——*Varauhan* (வராகன் - varágan, Tam.). Means boar, having impression of vishnoo in that incarnation. Hoon [q.v.] of mahomedans. Pagoda [q.v.] coin of english. The most celebrated coin symbol of Southern india. Originally the badge of the Chalookya [q.v.] families of Calyaun and Rajahmundry, it passed from them to the later Cholans, was subsequently adopted by the Royer [q.v.] dynasty [raj] of Vijianugger, and is still found on the seals of some of the petty local chiefs in the Carnatic [q.v.]. In teloogoo the abbreviated form of expressing this coin in writing is by the letter ×, from the first letter of gadyaunakam as ×o, meaning one pagoda. The Canarese mode is ಗು the first syllable of ಗುಳಿಗೆ gulige, ancient name of small spherical coins. In Tamul, வ the first syllable of the present word. The following is the scale of the varauhan:—22½ fanams = 1 varauhan [naunyam, 2a]. Approximate actual value, 1 varauhan = 3½ rupees. Not current; mostly used in book transactions by the grain merchants at madras. Same as Hind. hoon; Pagoda; Star pagoda. Compare kurruck varahah for pagoda used in circars [q.v.] and ceded districts [q.v.].——*Varauhaniday* (வராகனிடை - varáganidai, Tam.). From (varagán, tam. pagoda + edai, tam. weight). Weight of a pagoda [q.v.]. Tamul goldsmith's weight. 9 panatookkams = 1 varauhaniday; 10 varauhaniday = 1 pollum [niray, [3a. Approximate actual value, 1 varauhaniday = 54 grains. Very commonly used. Compare Hind. miscal, Tam. cutlay pagoda.

——*Varauhanuddy* (వరాహనది - varáhanadi, Tel.; வராகநதி - varáganathi, Tam. varáhanadi *). From (above + nadí, san. river). Tel. also (pandéru), meaning hog + river.—"*a*" River; Vizagapatam dist., Golcondah, Sarwasiddhy tals. Also called Pundaur. Rises in the Eastern ghauts [q.v.] 20 miles north-west of Narsapatam, takes a south-easterly course for about 45 miles and falls into the sea with the Shaurada nuddy at Wattauda. Extensively used for irrigation. There are eight anicuts [q.v.]; three belonging to Government, four to proprietors, and the Gubbauda anicut 18 miles from head of the river and within 1½ miles of Narsapatam.—"*b*" River; South arcot dist., Tindivanam and Villoopooram tals. Also known as Shuncaraubharany and Jinjee. Issues from the Malayanore tank, and past Jinjee receives the Tondayaur and Paumbayaur, and flows into the sea by two mouths near Ariancooppam and Chinna viraumputnam.—"*c*" River; Madura dist., Periyacoolam tal. Tributary of the Veigay. Rises in the Upper pulneys on marshy land called Berijam near Fort Hamilton, irrigates the village of Tencaray and Taumaray coolam by an anicut taken off at the foot of the hills; and after being joined by Cullaur and Pambaur waters the village of Mailmungalam and three others, emptying itself into the Veigay at Goollapooram.——*Verapoly* (വരാപ്പുഴ - varáppuzha, Mal.). From (above + puzha, mal. river). Village, Island; Travancore state; Cottayam division, Paravore tal.; pop. 8,613; lat. 10° 4′; long. 76° 19′ E.; from Paravore S.S.E. 7 miles; from Cochin N.E. 8 miles; from Trivandrum N.N.W. 116 miles; from the sea E. 5 miles. Important place near the northern frontier. Formerly belonged to Cochin. Seat of one of the earliest Roman Catholic missions in India. Gives its name to the Vicariate Apostolic of Verapoly established in 1659. The Archbishop resides here. Extensive buildings along the river consist of schools, convents, &c. Head-quarters of the Carmelite mission. Church of St. Joseph, commenced about 1673, is a miniature representation of St. Peter's at Rome.

VARAUNGY (ورانگی - varángi, *Mahl.*). Female assembly. A division of a village in Minicoy for the purposes of administration. Boys till they are old enough to join the male assemblies are admitted to this [attiry].

VARAWA (వరవ - varava, *Tel.*; കതിരാൻ - katirán, *Mal.*). Mal. from (katir, mal. beauty). The genus Teuthis, teuthididæ, acanthopterygii, teleostei, pisces [matsyam, 8], of naturalists [jantoo]. The species best known to the natives are java and verniculata.

VARAY (வரை - varai, *Tam.*). Hill. Varayaud is ibex [saddle back]; the specific name is spelt Warrayato.

VARGAM (वर्ग - varga, *San.*). From (vrij, san. to exclude). In natural history a class. For category, see Padaurtam; for elementary substance, see Dravyam; for matter, see Bhootam; for organic and inorganic, see Indriyam and Anindriyam; for organic kingdom, see Ganam [jantoo, vricsham]; for organic class, see present head; for organic order, see Santaunam; for organic family, see Coolam; for organic genus, see Jauty; for organic species, see Bhaidam. Oopa prefixed to either of the above means a sub-head. For inorganic minerals, see Dhautoo. Vargam also means the square of a number.——*Dashavargam* (दशवर्ग - dashavarga, San.). The ten ways of astrologically dividing the ecliptic [craunty mundalam].—"*a*" The following are the ten. Raushy [q.v.] is a sign; for the lords of raushies see diagram under raushy, k. Horah; each sign is divided into two equal parts of 15° each; the two horahs of the odd signs are respectively the solar and lunar horahs or have sooryan [q.v.] and chundran [q.v.] respectively for their lords, while the two of the even signs are respectively the lunar and solar horahs or have chundran and sooryan respectively for their lords; according to gargan and others the lords of the two horahs are respectively the lords of the sign and of the eleventh sign. Dricaunam; each sign is divided into three equal parts of 10° each; the lords of the dricaunams of a sign are respectively the lords of that sign, of the fifth sign and of the ninth sign; according to gargan and others the lords of the dricaunams are respectively the lords of the sign, of the twelfth sign and of the eleventh sign from it. Navaumshams; each sign [raushy] being divided here into nine equal parts and there being twelve signs, there are in all 12 × 9 or 108 such divisions in the ecliptic [craunty mundalam]; the ecliptic contains 27 × 4 or 108 stellar quarters or nacshatrapaudams [nacshatram]; it follows therefore that a navaumsham is equal to a nacshatrapaudam, that is one-fourth of a lunar mansion; the 108 navaumshams beginning from the first point of aries [maisham] bear the same names as the twelve signs of the zodiac counted over and over again; the first navaumsham of maisham [q.v.] is maisham itself, that of vrishabham [q.v.] is macaram [q.v.], that of mitoonam [q.v.] is toolaum [q.v.], and that of carcatacam [q.v.] is carcatacam itself; the same order holds for the 4 signs from simham [q.v.] to vrishchicam [q.v.] and for the 4 from dhanoos [q.v.] to meenam [q.v.]; in other words the four sets of trikonam or triangular signs begin with the same navaumshams; that is the trikonam signs of maisham, simham, dhanoos begin with the navaumsham of maisham; vrishabham, canyay, macaram begin with the navaumsham of macaram; mitoonam, toolaum, coombham begin with the navaumsham of toolaum; and carcatacam, vrishchicam, meenam begin with the navaumsham of carcatacam. The last navaumshams of catacam or carcatacam, vrishchicam and meenam are known as ricsha sandhies [ricsham]; the lords of the navaumshams are the same as the lords of the raushies, see the square diagram under raushy. Dwaudashaumshams; the twelve parts into which each sign is divided bear the same names as those of the signs of the zodiac; the name of the first dwaudashaumsham of a particular sign is the name of the sign itself; so that the twelve dwaudashaumhams of maisham are maisham, vrishabham, mitoonam, &c., ending with meenam; those of vrishabham are vrishabham, mitoonam, carcatacam, &c., ending with maisham; those of mitoonam are mitoonam, carcatacam, simham, &c., ending with vrishabham and so on. Trimshaumsham is division of a sign of the zodiac into thirty equal parts, each part being a degree [bhaugam]; their lords are as below; five, five, eight, seven and five degrees of these thirty divisions are respectively those of mars, saturn, jupiter, mercury and venus in the odd signs; in the even signs their order is reversed; the odd signs are maisham, mitoonam, simham, toolaum, dhanoos, and coombham, the even signs are vrishabham, carcatacam, canyay, vrishchicam, macaram and meenam; in the odd signs the first five degrees are the trimshaumsham of mars [coojan, mungalan]; the next five are those of saturn [shany]; the next eight are those of jupiter [brihaspaty]; the next seven are those of mercury [boodhan]; and the last five are those of venus [shoocran]; in the even signs the first five are those of venus; the next seven are those of mercury; the next eight are those of jupiter [brihaspaty]; the next five are those of saturn [shany]; and the last five are those of mars. Saptamaumsham is division of a sign of the zodiac into seven equal parts; the lords of the 7 parts of the odd signs are respectively the lords of the 7 signs of the zodiac commencing from the odd sign; and the lords of the 7 parts of the even signs are respectively the lords of the 7 signs of the zodiac beginning from the 7th sign from the even sign. Dashaumsham is division of a sign of the zodiac into ten equal parts; the lords of the 10 parts of the odd signs are respectively the lords of the 10 signs of the zodiac commencing from the odd sign, and the lords of the 10 parts of the even signs are respectively the lords of the 10 signs commencing from the 10th sign from the even sign. Shodashaumsham is division of a sign of the ecliptic into 16 equal parts; the lords of the 16 parts of the odd signs are the lords of the 12 signs commencing from the odd sign together with bramha, vishnoo, roodran, and sooryan; the lords of the 16 parts of the even signs are the lords of the 12 signs commencing from the even signs together with sooryan, roodran, vishnoo and bramha. Shashtyaumsham is division of a sign of the ecliptic into 60 equal parts; the 60 parts of the odd signs are those of 1, ghoram; 2, raucshasam; 3, devam; 4, coobairam; 5 racshognam; 6, kinnaram; 7, bhrashtam; 8, coclagnam; 9, garalam; 10, agny; 11, mayam; 12, pretapooreesham; 13, apaumpaty; 14, devaganesham; 15, calay; 16, ahy; 17, amritaumsham; 18, chundram; 19, mridoo; 20, comalam; 21, pudmam; 22, latchmy; 23, vaugeesham; 24, digambaram; 25, devam; 26, aurdram; 27, calinausham; 28, cshiteeshwaram; 29, camalaucauram; 30, mundautmajam; 31, mrityoo; 32, caulam; 33, dauvaugny; 34, ghoram; 35, aumayam; 36, cantacam; 37, shooddham; 38, amritam; 39, poornachundram; 40, vishapradigdham; 41, calinausham; 42, mookhyam; 43, vamshacshayam; 44, ootpatacam; 45, calahroopam; 46, sowmyam; 47, mridoo; 48, soosheetalam; 49, damshtraucaraulam; 50, indoomookham; 51, praveenam; 52, caulaugny; 53, dandauyoodham; 54, nirmalam; 55, shoobham; 56, ashoobham; 57, atisheetalam; 58, shooddham; 59, payodhibhramanam; 60, indooraikhay; and the 60 parts of the even signs are the above in the inverse order, that is to say, beginning from indooraikhay and ending in ghoram.—"*b*" A planet which at any time occupies what is considered his particular house [raushy], or his horah, or his dricaunam, or his navaumsham, or his dwaudashaumsham, &c., according to the above scheme, is said to be in his vargam. A planet occupies two vargams when he is in his house or raushy and in his horah, i.e., when he is lord of the sign as well as of the horah division of the sign. So three vargams, when planet is in his raushy, his horah and his dricaunam, i. e., when he is lord of the sign, of the horah division of that sign and of the dricaunam division of the same sign. And so on similarly. A planet occupying two vargams is said to be in paurijautaumsham; if he occupies three vargams, he is said to be in oottamaumsham; if four vargams, in gopooraumsham; if five vargams, in simhausanaumsham; if six, in parvataumsham; if seven or eight, in devalocaumsham; if nine, in eirauvataumsham; and if ten, in veishaishicaumsham.—"*c*" The vargottamá or best places are:—the first navaumshams of the four movable signs maisham, carcatacam, toolaum, and macaram; the 5th navaumshams of the four fixed signs, vrishabham, simham, vrishchicam, and coombham; the 9th navaumshams of the four movable and fixed signs, mitoonam, canyay, dhanoos, and meenam [raushy].——*Varjyam* (वर्ज्य - varjya, San.). From (vrij, san. to abandon). A certain unlucky portion of a nacshatram [q.v.]. See Tyaujyam.

VARNAM (वर्ण - varna, *San.*). From (varn, san. to color).—"*a*" Color. The Hindoos enumerate five colors, viz., white, black, red, golden and green. The twelve zodiacal signs [raushy] are as to color respectively:—Maisham red, Vrishabham white,

Mitoonam of the color of the parrot [totah], Carcatacam of the color of pautaly or trumpet flower [panthiry], Simham black white, Canyay variegated in color, Toolaum black, Vrishchicam of gold color, Dhanoos of the color of the husk of paddy [q.v.], Macaram white red, Coombham of the color of mongoose [q.v.], and Meenam of the color of fish. Similarly Sooryan [q.v.] is of a red and dark-brown color, Chundran [q.v.] is white, Coojan [q.v.] is both red and white, Boodhan [q.v.] is green like the color of the bent grass [hurrially], Brihaspaty [q.v.] is yellow like molten gold, Shoocran [q.v.] is neither very white nor very black, and Shany is black [q.v.]; these planetary colors are useful in ascertaining the color of stolen articles and in determining the color of the flowers to be used in the worship of the planets [graham].—"*b*" Caste. The word used in the older Sanscrit writings as applied to the four principal divisions. The Chatoorvarnam, or four castes, as found established in the code of Menoo [q.v.] are:—Bramin [q.v.], the sacerdotal and learned class, the members of which may be, but are not necessarily, priests [acharry, purohit]; Cshatriya [q.v.], the regal and warrior caste; Veisya [q.v.], trading and agricultural caste; Shoodra [q.v.], servile caste, whose duty is to serve the other three. The first three castes are called dwijan [q.v.], that is to say, twice-born or regenerate, from their being entitled to investiture [oopanayanam] with the sacred thread [poonool] which effects a second birth. The Bramins maintain that their caste alone remains, that the other three have been lost or degraded, and it is generally believed that there are no pure Cshatriyas or Veisyas now existing. The numerous castes which have sprung up from the intercourse of people of different castes or from other causes are called Varnasancaram, [q.v.] or mixed castes [anooloma, pratiloma]. See vol. I (65) [jauty]. There is a stanza from Shivavaucyam [q.v.]:—சா॥ இயாவதேத டா சலந்திரண்டநீரல்லோ, பூதமைந்துமொன்றல்லோ புலன்களைந்துமொன்றல்லோ, காதுவாழிகாறைகம்பி சூடகம்பொன்னொன்றல்லோ, சாதிபேதமோதுகின்ற தன்மையென்னதன்மையே.—"what, o wretch, is caste? is not water an accumulation of fluid particles? are not five elements [bhootam] and the five senses [indriyam] one? are not the several ornaments of the neck, the breast, and the feet equally gold? what then is the peculiar quality declared by difference in caste?"——*Vanney* (వన్నె - vanne, Tel.). From (varna, san. color). Touch of precious metals [loham, mautt]. Compare Carat.——*Varnamaulay* (अक्षरन्यास - aksharanyása, San.; వర్ణమాల - varnamála, Tel.; അക്ഷരമാല - aksharamála, Mal.; நெடுங்கணக்கு - nedunganakku, Tam.). Title and Tel. means letter + series. San. from (akshara, san. letter + nyása san. placing). Mal. from (akshara, san. letters + málá, san. garland). Tam. means long + account. Alphabet. See vol. I (52); II, 205, 209 [bhaushay, yezhoot]. The following table shows the alphabets of, or connected with, southern india, set opposite the roman alphabet. The order of the letters is that of the Sanscrit [q.v.]:—

Classification of the letters.	Roman.	Asoca [q.v.] inscriptions.	Sanscrit [q.v.] or Devanagry [q.v.].	Kolezhoot [q.v.].	Tamul [q.v.].	Malayalam [q.v.].	Canarese [q.v.].	Teloogoo [q.v.].
Vowels.	a	𑀅	अ	[illegible]	அ	അ	ಅ	అ
	á	𑀆	आ	[illegible]	ஆ	ആ	ಆ	ఆ
	i	𑀇	इ	[illegible]	இ	ഇ	ಇ	ఇ
	í	—	ई	[illegible]	ஈ	ഈ	ಈ	ఈ
	u	𑀉	उ	[illegible]	உ	ഉ	ಉ	ఉ
	ú	𑀊	ऊ	[illegible]	ஊ	ഊ	ಊ	ఊ
	ri	—	ऋ	—	—	ഋ	ಋ	ఋ
	rí	—	ॠ	—	—	ൠ	ೠ	ౠ
	lri	—	ऌ	—	—	ഌ	—	ఌ
	lrí	—	ॡ	—	—	ൡ	—	ౡ
	e	𑀏	—	[illegible]	எ	എ	ಎ	ఎ
	é	—	ए	[illegible]	ஏ	ഏ	ಏ	ఏ
	ai	𑀐	ऐ	[illegible]	ஐ	ഐ	ಐ	ఐ
	o	𑀑	—	[illegible]	ஒ	ഒ	ಒ	ఒ
	ó	—	ओ	[illegible]	ஓ	ഓ	ಓ	ఓ
	au	—	औ	[illegible]	ஔ	ഔ	ಔ	ఔ
	am	—	अं	[illegible]	—	അം	ಅಂ	అం
	ah	—	अः	—	—	അഃ	ಅಃ	అః
Gutturals.	k	𑀓	क	[illegible]	க	ക	ಕ	క
	kh	𑀔	ख	—	—	ഖ	ಖ	ఖ
	g	𑀕	ग	—	—	ഗ	ಗ	గ
	gh	𑀖	घ	—	—	ഘ	ಘ	ఘ
	n	—	ङ	[illegible]	ங	ങ	ಙ	ఙ
Palatals.	ch	𑀘	च	[illegible]	ச	ച	ಚ	చ
	chh	𑀙	छ	—	—	ഛ	ಛ	ఛ
	j	𑀚	ज	—	—	ജ	ಜ	జ
	jh	𑀛	झ	—	—	ഝ	ಝ	ఝ
	ñ	𑀜	ञ	[illegible]	ஞ	ഞ	ಞ	ఞ
Linguals.	ṭ	𑀝	ट	[illegible]	ட	ട	ಟ	ట
	ṭh	𑀞	ठ	—	—	ഠ	ಠ	ఠ
	ḍ	𑀟	ड	—	—	ഡ	ಡ	డ
	ḍh	𑀠	ढ	—	—	ഢ	ಢ	ఢ
	ṇ	𑀡	ण	[illegible]	ண	ണ	ಣ	ణ
Dentals.	t	𑀢	त	[illegible]	த	ത	ತ	త
	th	𑀣	थ	—	—	ഥ	ಥ	థ
	d	𑀤	द	—	—	ദ	ದ	ద
	dh	𑀥	ध	—	—	ധ	ಧ	ధ
	n	𑀦	न	[illegible]	ந	ന	ನ	న
Labials.	p	𑀧	प	[illegible]	ப	പ	ಪ	ప
	ph	𑀨	फ	—	—	ഫ	ಫ	ఫ
	b	𑀩	ब	—	—	ബ	ಬ	బ
	bh	𑀪	भ	—	—	ഭ	ಭ	భ
	m	𑀫	म	[illegible]	ம	മ	ಮ	మ
Semi-vowels.	y	𑀬	य	[illegible]	ய	യ	ಯ	య
	r	𑀭	र	[illegible]	ர	ര	ರ	ర
	l	𑀮	ल	[illegible]	ல	ല	ಲ	ల
	ḷ	—	—	—	—	ള	ಳ	ళ
	v	𑀯	व	[illegible]	வ	വ	ವ	వ
	h	𑀳	ह	—	—	ഹ	ಹ	హ
Miscellaneous.	s	𑀲	स	—	—	സ	ಸ	స
	sh	—	श	—	—	ശ	ಶ	శ
	sh	—	ष	—	—	ഷ	ಷ	ష
	ksh	—	क्ष	—	—	ക്ഷ	ಕ್ಷ	క్ష
	ḻ	—	—	[illegible]	ள	—	—	—
	ṟ	—	—	[illegible]	ற	റ	—	ఱ
	zh	—	—	[illegible]	ழ	ഴ	—	—
	ṉ	—	—	[illegible]	ன	—	—	—

The Cooral says:—அகர முதல எழுத்தெல்லாம் ஆதி பகவன் முதற்றே உலகு—"as all letters have the letter A "for their first, so the world has the eternal God for its first." And again:—எண்ணென்ப வேனை யெழுத்தென்ப விவ்விரண்டுங் கண்ணென்ப வாழுமுயிர்க்கு—"letters and "numbers are the two eyes of man."——*Varnasancaram* (वर्णसङ्कर - varnasankara, San.). From (above + sam, san. together + kri, san. to do). A mixed caste, as from a Bramin father and Shoodra mother, or reverse [anooloma, jauty, pratiloma].——*Vunnam* (வண்ணம் - vannam, Tam.). From (varna, san. color). A kind of Tamul verse, consisting of eight equal stanzas.

VAROONAM (वरुण - varuna, *San.*). Title means water; water plant [var]. Title otherwise Osier, Sallow, Willow. Botanically the Salix genus, salicaceæ [vricsham, 126]. Trees or shrubs, natives of north temperate regions; leaves undivided, notched at the edges or even, stalked and varying in shape from linear to round; wood white, soft, smooth, light; bark bitter; reproduced by cuttings; growth rapid. The species best known to the natives are shown below. The common english osier is Viminalis.——*Aromatic willow* (خلاف - khiláf, Ar.; بيد مشك - bedmushk, Pers., Hind. and Dec.). Title from flowers. Ar. means contrary; from its growing in a locality other than its origin, having been carried thither by torrents. Pers. from (bed, pers. cane, calamus rotang, linn. + mushk, pers. musk). Pers. also (khiláfibalkhí), meaning balkh hedge willow. Title otherwise British sallow, Goat willow, Great sallow, Hedge willow, Musk cane. Botanically Salix [varoonam] caprea, linn., salicaceæ [vricsham, 126]. Tree 25-30 feet, flowering before leafing; trunk attaining 3–4 feet girth, often a shrub; leaves 2–4 inches, dark green above, margins often recurved, base cuneate rounded or cordate; male catkins very stout, sweet-scented; female 2-3 inches; capsule ½ inch. Flowers yield, on distillation, an aromatic attar [q.v.] which has stimulant properties; in pharm. non-officinal.——*Indian willow* (वरुण - varuna, San.; वाळुंज - válumja, Mahr.; پانی جما - pánijamá, Hind.; جمتی کی بیل - jamtíkíbel, Dec.; ನಿರವಂಜಿ - niravanji, Can.; ఏటిపాల - étipála, Tel.; ആറ്റുപാല - áttupála, Mal.; ஆற்றுப்பாலை - áttuppálai, Tam.). San. means water, hence plant growing near it. Hind. from (páni, hind. water + jamá, hind. close). Dec. from (jamtí, hind. the willow creeper, salix + bel, hind. creeper) [jamtee]. Can. from (níru, can. water + anju, can. to be alarmed). Tel. from (éru, tel. river + pála, tel. milky plant). Mal. from (áru, mal. river + pála, mal. milk-plant). Tam. from (áru, tam. river + pálai, tam. milky plant). Hind. also (bed), meaning cane [rattan]; (bent), meaning cane. Dec. also (jamtíkápattá), meaning salix leaf. Tel. also (étipisinika), meaning river + clerodendron inerme, gærtn. Title otherwise Four-seeded willow, River paulay. Botanically Salix [varoonam] tetrasperma, roxb., salicaceæ [vricsham, 126]. Alias Salix ichnostachya. Small tree; leaves alternate, lanceolate; entire; stipules leafy; catkins lateral, peduncled, male long, lax, and few-flowered, female cylindric, rather dense, elongated; peduncle three to six leaved; scales oblong, spathulate, puberulous; capsule long-pedicelled, ovoid, glabrous; always found near water. Bark febrifuge; in pharm. non-officinal. Leaves lopped and given to cattle as fodder. Twigs made into baskets [tokrah]. Timber used for fire-wood; also for gunpowder charcoal [adooppkary].——*Majnoon's willow* (بيد مجنون - bedimajnún, Pers., Hind. and Dec.; ஆற்றுப்பாலை - áttuppálai, Tam.). Title from long, slender, drooping branches. Pers. from (bed, pers. calamus rotang, linn. + majnún, pers. a celebrated lover). Tam. from (áru, tam. river + pálai, tam. milky plant). Hind. also (pánijamá), meaning close to water; (siyálimajnún), meaning majnoon's plant. Hebrew oreb. Title otherwise Weeping willow. Botanically Salix [varoonam] babylonica, linn., salicaceæ [vricsham, 126]. Tree attaining 50 feet; trunk 12 feet in girth, flowering and leafing together; males much commoner than females; leaves 3–6 inches, midrib prominent; male catkins ½–1 inch; bracts lanceolate; female as long, bracts as in male; capsule $\frac{1}{12}$ inch, pale-green. Branches and twigs largely used for baskets, wattles, weirs, &c. Wood soft, smooth and white; small twigs used for rope bridges.

VARSHAM (वर्ष - varsha, *San.*). From (vrish, san. rain). Rain [mazhay]; the rainy season [ritoo]. Also a year, for which the following is the scale:—2 ayanams or half-years = 1 varsham or year of men, 360 varshams = 1 devavarsham or year of god [caulam, 2]; same as San. samvatsaram [caulam, 4], Hind. saul, Tam. aundoo [caulam, 1]. Bramha varsham means bramha's year or 12 bramha's months [caulam, 2]. Deva varsham means year of the gods; the following is the scale:—360 varshams or year of men = 1 devavarsham or year of the gods; 12,000 devavarshams = 1 maha yoog [q.v.] or great age [caulam, 2]. Distinguish from Varsham, division of a continent.——*Vrisham* (वृष - vrisha, San.). From (vrish, san. to generate). Bull of Shiva [q.v.] or Nundy [q.v.]. Same as Rishabham [q.v.] and Vrishabam [q.v.].

VARTAM (वर्त - varta, *San.*). From (vrit, san. to exist). Existence.——*Vartacam* (ವರ್ತಕ - vartaka, Can.). From (vártá, san. business). Trade.——*Vartamaunam* (वर्तमान - vartamána, San.). News [acbaur].——*Vartanay* (वर्तन - vartana, San.). Fees.

VARY (வரி - vari, *Tam.*). Line.——*Varapp* (வரப்பு - varappu, Tam.). From (vari, tam. to draw line). Limit, a ridge in corn field [talay].——*Varshaleiyaur* (வரிசலையாறு - varisalaiyáru, Tam.). From (varisai, tam. row + alai, tam. wave + áru, tam. river). River; Madura dist.; Ramnaud zemindarry. Narrow and rapid stream. Rises in the high lands near Praumullay in Shivagunga zemindarry, and, being fed by numerous jungle streams, supplies the large lake at Tripatore, and after an easterly course crosses the high road from Poodoocottah to Shivagunga. Thence continuing easterly about a mile, flows south and crosses the road from Cunnagoody to Tripatore, where it unites with a channel [q.v.] flowing from the northern Calingula of Tripatore lake. It continues its course to Marootham pilleiyaurcoil, and flowing east-south-east four miles, receives the Tirmany moottaur channel from the west about 1 mile south of Nadoocottah. It then flows east, widens in its way, and passes by Cullar yelavancottah, where it enters Ramnaud zemindarry. It then flows north-easterly towards Devacottah, where it separates into two branches, which, uniting about a mile to the east, run north of the fort of Hanoomantagoody and south of the village. It again separates into two branches. The northern runs easterly three miles, and then separates into two streams, taking an east by south course for 10 miles, and falls into the Paumbenaur, below Andavattore; the lower branch is known as the Paushiyaur, from the village Paushiputnam, situated on the coast near the junction of this channel with the sea. The southern branch pursues a south-easterly course about 17 miles from Hanoomantagoody; passing by Cumboocottah and Audavattore it supplies several tanks, and crossing the high road to Ramnaud discharges itself into the sea.——*Varshanaud mullay* (வரிசைநாட்டுமலை - varisaináttumalai, Tam.). From (varisai, tam. row + nádu, tam. country + malai, tam. hill). Sanscrit name (varshagiri), meaning border mountain. Village, Range of hills; Madura dist., Periyacoolam tal.; pop. 1,199; lat. 9° 44′; long. 77° 33′; from Madura W.S.W. 42 miles; from Periyacoolam S. 27 miles. The range runs north-east from the spurs of the Travancore hills for about 40 miles and then turns suddenly to the south-east. Also called Andiputty range. Belongs to the zemindarry of Guntamanaickanore. Feverish and not suited for habitation.——*Viriyan* (விரியன் - viriyan, Tam.). See sep. title.

VARY (وری - varí, *Hind.*; வரி - vari, *Tam.*). Tax. Talay vary is poll-tax; Veet vary is house tax. For Poollary or tax on pasture-land see sep. title. See also Vauram.

VAS (वस् - vas, *San.*). To shine; to dwell.——*Vasantam* (वसन्त - vasanta, San.). From (vas, san. to shine). Spring [ritoo]. Vasantan is spring personified or Manmatan [q.v.].——*Vasanta tilacam* (वसन्ततिलक - vasantatilaka, San.). From (vasanta, san. spring + tilaka, san. mark). A poem describing Conjeeveram during the May festival by Varadacharry [q.v.]. Popularly known as Ammaul baunam.——*Vasishta godavery* (वसिष्ठगोदावरी - vasisht'hagódávarí, San.). Called after the sage vasishtan [q.v.]. River; Godavery dist., Amalapooram and Narsapore tals. Branch of the Godavery, falls into the sea near Antarvedhy. Islands in this river fertilised every year by the freshes.——*Vasishtan* (वसिष्ठ - vasish'tha, San.). From (vasu, san. wealth + isht'ha, san. superlative termination); master of all desire. The sage. One of the seven great rishies [q.v.] who escaped the deluge [nacshatram, pralayam]. The Nyauna vausishtam in Tamul is a storehouse of Vedantic learning [alvandar].——*Vasishtanuddy* (வசிட்டநதி - vasittánathi, Tam.). From (vasisht'ha, san. the sage, so called + nadí, san. river); vasishta moony, being supposed to have performed a yaugam [q.v.] in ancient times near Bailore. Tam. also (vellár), meaning white river; also (pérár), meaning great river. River; Salem and S. arcot districts. Also called Northern vellaur and Peraur.——*Vasoo* (वसु - vasu, San.). Living, thriving, prosperity, wealth.——*Vast* (वस्तु - vastu, San.). From (vas, san. to dwell). Soul, reality; as in Parauparavast. That upon which one lives, and hence property.——*Vatsaram* (वत्सर - vatsara, San.). A Jovian year composed of about twelve terrestrial years [brihaspaty]. Also period of five years [yoog].——*Vausam* (वास - vása, San.). From (vas, san. to live); living. Suffix in compounds; as Cala vausam, meaning threshing-floor + living, threshing fees.——*Vausana vully* (वासनवल्ली - vásanavallí, San.). From (vásana, san. fragrance + vallí, san. creeper). Botanically the Cocculus genus, menispermaceæ [vricsham, 5]. Climbing or sarmentose shrubs; flowers panicled; fruit a drupe with a bony shell containing a curved seed. The species best known to the natives are:—palmatus [calumba], villosus [jamtee]. Other s. indian species indigenous or naturalized are:—Laurifolius on anamullays; Leæba, substitute for indian berry; Macrocarpus, malabar.——*Vausoodevan* (வாசுதேவன் - vásuthévan, Tam.). From (vasu, san. wealth + déva, san. god). A patronymic from Vasoodevan, father of Krishnan; epithet of Krishnan [q.v.]. Hindoo 2nd or pers. name [peyar].——*Vausooky* (वासुकि - vásuki, San.). From (vasuka, san. kóshyapa). One of the eight serpents [naugam] of mythology. Was used as a cord round mount

Mandaram [q.v.], when by it the devans [q.v.] and asoorans [q.v.] churned the milk sea [samoodram] in the Coormam [q.v.] avatar [q.v.]. The snake vomited poison into the vessel containing the amritam [q.v.], and Shiva drinking it [shivarautry] his neck became blue and so continues [neelacuntan].——*Vausy* (वासी - vásí, San.). From (vas, san. to dwell). Inhabitant. Suffix in compounds; as Sookhavausy meaning happiness + inhabitant, permanent tenant.

VASIREDDY (వాసిరెడ్డి - vásireddi, *Tel.*). From (vási, tel. famous + reddi, tel. caste title). Family of the Cumma [q.v.] caste, in the kistna district, where they occupied a prominent position for a long time. The ancestor of the family, Vasireddy veerappa naidoo, obtained from the king of golcondah a sunnud [q.v.] appointing him deshmookh [q.v.] of the pergunnah [q.v.] of Nundigauma. The famous Vencataudry was of this family. The estate was resumed by the Government, and the family pensioned.

VASOOL (وصول - vasúl, *Hind.*). From (vasala, ar. to realize). Collection [varavoo]. Vasool bauky is uncollected balance. Dowle vasool bauky is demand, collection and balance. See vol. I, 112.——*Vasoolat* (وصولات - vasúlát, Hind.). The total collected under every description. Mesne profits.

VAU (वा - vá, *San.*). To blow.——*Vaumacharry* (वामाचारी - vámáchárí, San.). From (váma, san. good + áchar, san. to observe) [vaumam]. A follower of the left-hand ritual of the tantrams [q.v.]. Compare Dacshinacharry. See vol. I (87).——*Vaumam* (वाम - váma, San.). From (vá, san. to blow, to excite); happy, favorable. Literally beauty. Also reverse or left. One of the six religious systems [oochamayam] of Sheivas, which regards the female principle [shacty] in nature as the primeval form of deity and teaches its worship [sheiva siddhauntam].——*Vauma maurgam* (वाममार्ग - vámamárga, San.). From (váma, san. good + márga, san. way). Left hand ritual.——*Vaumana avatar* (वामनावतार - vámanávatára, San.). From (vámana, san. dwarf + avatára, san. incarnation). The dwarf or fifth incarnation [avatar] of Vishnoo [q.v.]. In this Vishnoo assumed the form of a dwarf, and coming to Mahbaly [q.v.], a chuckravurty [q.v.] or universal sovereign, asked as much land in gift as his foot could cover in three steps. The grant being made, the dwarf assumed the Trivicraman [q.v.] form; one foot being on the ground, another on Mahbaly's neck, and the third in the heavens [padiyalandone]. As Mahbaly was a virtuous sovereign, he was not destroyed, but was made a king in the infernal regions [pautaulam]. The Tamulians celebrate annually a festival in November, at which they burn a palmyra [q.v.] tree before the pagodas [q.v.] and act the story of Mahbaly [mattam]. See vol. I (79).——*Vaumanam* (वामन - vámana, San.). The beautiful. A variety of shalagram [q.v.]. Also one of the eight elephants of mythology [ashtadicgajam].——*Vaumanan* (वामन - vámana, San.). Means reverse or crooked. A dwarf. Vishnoo [q.v.] in his dwarf incarnation [avatar]. Hindoo 2nd or pers. name. Common among the Madhwas [peyar].——*Vaumanapoorам* (വാമനപുരം - vámanapuram, Mal.). From (vámana, san. vishnu; the dwarf + pura, san. town).—"*a*" Town; Travancore state, Trivandrum division, Nedoovengaud tal.; pop. 8,240.—"*b*" River; Travancore state, Trivandrum division, Nedoovengaud and Cherankeel talooks. Also known as the Attingal. Rises at the foot of the Parambacode hills and after running west 23 miles through a hilly tract between high banks and over a sandy and occasionally rocky bed it reaches the town that gives its name and from thence flows into the Anjengo lake, which is formed chiefly by its waters. Length, 35 miles. Navigable for 13 miles above its mouth up to the town that gives it its name. Timber [maram], bamboo [q.v.], &c., find an easy passage during the monsoons [q.v.].——*Vaumeshwaran* (वामेश्वर - váméshvara, San.). From (váma, san. good + íshvara, san. lord). Shiva [q.v.].——*Vautam* (वात - váta, San.). San. from (vá, san. to blow). Vital air or wind; specially one of the three affections or humors of body [shareeram] recognised in hindoo shastrams, the other two being Pittam or bile and Sheetam or phlegm. For the vital airs or principles constituting animal life in man see Vayoo. From vautam are derived eighty human diseases. Such as the following:—swelling of the sides of the neck, scurviness of the skin that looks like ashes strewed upon it, swelling of the foot and legs, griping of the bowels, swelling of the knees, protuberance of the veins and sinews, swelling in the abdomen, half-sided headache or megrim, sensation of stinging in the feet together with a contraction of the same parts, a pain of the abdomen with the sensation of its being covered with wounds, spasmodic contraction of the throat, preventing respiration, constant shaking of the head, violent headache, inflexibility of the fingers, &c. [veidyan].——*Vayoo* (वायु - váyu, San.). From (vá, san. to blow). Air. Gas. The invisible fluid surrounding the earth [bhoomy]. Distinguish from Aucausham, the fifth element of the hindoos. Vedic god of wind. Often identified with Indran [q.v.]. His other names are Pavanan the purifier, Gandhavauhan bearer of perfumes, and Satatagam ever moving. One of the five elements [bhootam] among hindoos. One of the guardians of the cardinal points [ashtadic, ashtadicpaulacan, tisay]. For the vital airs or principles so called in hindoo philosophy constituting animal life see Puncha praunam. See vol. I (74), (78). Jalavayoo is hydrogen; Ooppoovayoo is nitrogen; Praunavayoo is oxygen; Cary poolipp vayoo is carbonic acid gas.

VAUDA (వాడ - váda, *Tel.*). Means that which goes fast. Ship. Plant first term as meaning imported. Ex.:—Garcinia cambogia (vádachinta), foreign tamarind.

VAUDA (వాడ - váda, *Tel.*). Fragrance. Plant first term. Ex., where transl. is of second term:—Dædalacanthus nervosus (vádámbramu), cloth or covering; Plumeria acutifolia (vádagannéru), nerium odorum; Walsura ternata (vádavalasa), guizotia abyssinica. See gloss. paragraphs.——*Vaudaumbram* (వాడాంబ్రము - vádámbramu, Tel.; நீலமுள்ளி - nílamulli, Tam.). Tel. from (váda, tel. fragrance + ambara, san. sky); fragrant sky blue flowers. Tam. from (níla, san. blue + mulli, tam. any thorny plant). Tel. also (nílámbramu), meaning blue sky. Title otherwise Fragrant sky blue, Thorny sky blue. Botanically Dædalacanthus nervosus, t. anders, acanthaceæ [vricsham, 101]. Alias Eranthemum nervosum, pulchellum; Justicia pulchellum. A bush, with large, blackish green leaves, and profusion of deep azure blue flowers on large pencilled ears. There are other species, montanus and purpurascens.

VAUDAM (वाद - váda, *San.*). From (vad, san. to speak). Utterance.——*Vaudy* (वादी - vádí, San.). San. from (vad, san. to speak). Plaintiff, complainant [firyaudy]; praty vaudy being defendant.——*Vaudyam* (वाद्य - vádya, San.). From (vad, san. to speak). Musical instrument. Instrumental music itself. One of the three parts into which books on Indian music [sangeetam] are generally divided, the other two being Gaunam [q.v.] and Nrityam [q.v.].

VAUDOO (వాడు - vádu, *Tel.*). Suffix of agency; as goorrapvaudoo, meaning horse + doer, horsekeeper, groom.——*Vaur* (వారు - váru, Tel.). Plural of (vádu, tel. he); people. Suffix in compounds, as:—Cummavaur, meaning cumma caste people; Maumidy vaur, the maumidy family.

VAUDY (वाट - váta, *San.*; വാടി - váti, *Mal.*; வாடி - vádi, *Tam.*). From (vat, san. to surround). Enclosure or garden. A village.

VAUG (వాగు - vágu, *Tel.*). From (véga, san. flood). Water course [caulvye, varwa, vyecaul].——*Vaucaud* (వాకాడు - vákádu, Tel.). From (váka, tel. stream + kádu, tel. jungle). Sanscrit name (varadapurí), means vishnoo, the gift-giver + town. Village; Nellore dist., Goodoor tal.; pop. 2,119; acres 3,608; lat. 14° 00'; long. 80° 06'; from Goodoor S.E. 17½ miles; from Nellore S.S.E. 32 miles; from the sea W. 6½ miles. On Doogarauzpatam road between Kota and Doogarauzpatam. Lutheran mission station.

VAUGAY (வாகை - vágai, *Tam.*). From (vágu, tam. beauty). Same as Sirissa.

VAUHAN (वाहन - váhana, *San.*). From (vah, san. to carry). Vehicle; especially of the different gods. Antelope [jinka], vehicle of Vayoo [q.v.] and Chundran [q.v.] the moon; buffalo [khoolgah], vehicle of Yaman [q.v.]; bull or nundy [q.v.], vehicle of Shiva [q.v.] and Parvaty [q.v.]; dog [nye], vehicle of Shiva as Bheiravan [q.v.]; elephant [q.v.] or eirauvatam [q.v.], vehicle of Indran [q.v.], and sometimes all the guardians [ashtadicpaulacan] of the eight points [ashtadic, tisay] of the compass are represented on elephants; garoodan [q.v.], the king of the birds, the vehicle of Vishnoo [q.v.], and represented as the special enemy of the naugams [q.v.]; horse [ghorah], vehicle of Shiva as Bheiravan [q.v.], also of Coobairan [q.v.]; lion [simham], vehicle of Parvaty; macaram [q.v.], the mythical sea-monster or whale [timingilam], vehicle of Varoonan [q.v.] and sometimes of Manmatan [q.v.], and when the latter rides on a parrot [totah], he bears the macaram as his standard [dhwajam]; parrot, vehicle of Manmatan; ram [maisham], vehicle of Aguy [q.v.]; serpent, sheshanaugam, called also Anantan [q.v.], the infinite, the king of the naugams [q.v.] or serpents and lord of the infernal regions called pautaulam [q.v.], a vehicle of vishnoo; swan or goose or Hamsam [q.v.], vehicle of Saraswaty [q.v.] and Bramha [q.v.] Saraswaty being sometimes represented on a white peacock [mayil] and sometimes on a paddy-bird [q.v.]; tiger [pooly], vehicle of Parvaty; vulture [gridhram], or crow [caurvam], vehicle of Shany [matam]. See Poonyaprauny.

VAUK (वाक् - vák, *San.*). From (vach, san. to speak). Speech [shol]. Vaukkaul is tamul form for Saraswaty [q.v.]; compare Naumagal. Vaukmoolam, from (múla, san. root) is a deposition [kyfiyat].——*Vajtoorky* (وج ترکی - vajjiturkí, Dec.). Meaning Turkish sweetflag. Same as Atees.——*Vashamboo* (वचा - vachá, San.; वेखंड - vékhanda, Mahr.; وج - vajj, Ar.; اگرترکی - agariturkí, Pers.; وچ - vach, Hind.; بچ - bach, Dec.; ಬಜೆಗಿಡ - bajegida, Can.; వస - vasa, Tel.; വയമ്പ - vayampu, Mal.; වදකහ - vadakasá, Singh.; வசம்பு - vasambu, Tam.). Title from tamul. San. from (vach, san. to speak); as clearing the throat. Mahr.

and Ar. from sanscrit. Pers. from (agar, pers. aloe wood, aquilaria agallocha, linn. + turkí, pers. turkish). Hind., Dec., Can. and Tel. from sanscrit. Singh. from (vada, san. speech + kasá, singh. turmeric, curcuma longa, roxb.); throat clearing turmeric. Tam. from sanscrit. San. also (vijayá), meaning the victorious [kinnab]; (gólómí), meaning earth's hair, from root fibres; (jatilá), meaning hairy plant; (kharasára), meaning pungent juice; (ugragandhá), meaning strong-scented [piyauz]; (haimavatí), meaning pertaining to himalayas [chebulic myrobalan]. Hind. also (gandkílakrí), meaning scent wood. Can. also (nárubérugida), meaning fibre + root + plant. Tel. also (erravasa), meaning red + the plant; (vadaja), meaning speech + to give. Tam. also (shadakkóthan), meaning bushy haired, from the root fibres; (shadinam), meaning having entangled hair. Greek ἄκορον. The κάλαμος ἀρωματικὸς of Dioscorides and κάλαμος of Theophrastus, and Sweet cane of Bible, formerly identified with sweet flag, are now identified with Roussa grass, Andropogon martini, roxb. Title otherwise Myrtle flag, Myrtle grass, Myrtle sedge, Sweet-flag. Botanically Acorus calamus, linn., araceæ [vricsham, 152]. Alias Acorus aromaticus, odoratus. Perennial, semi-aquatic; rhizome thick, with long roots; leaves erect, 2–3 feet, sword-shaped; stalk leaf-like, but thicker below the spadix; spadix a foot above the root, spreading, 2–3 inches long, covered with a mass of numerous thick-set pale-green flowers, fragrant when bruised; petals six; capsules three-celled; whole plant has strong, sweet, aromatic smell; native of ceylon and malabar. The root stock occurs in pieces of various lengths, about the thickness of the thumb, rather flattened, spongy, provided with numerous sheath-like ringed appendages; odour peculiar and aromatic; taste bitterish, warm and somewhat acrid. In medicine the root-stock is carminative, stomachic, stimulant, diaphoretic, tonic and febrifuge; an insectifuge and insecticide, especially with fleas [telloopoochy]; on the malabar coast a bath made of an infusion of the root is a remedy for leprosy [cooshtam]; used for british peppermint [poodeenah], cinchona [koinah] bark, james' powder and sulphurous acid; quoted in pharm. non-officinal. In veterinary practice, ground well with water into a fine paste and rubbed in for killing lice or fleas. The leaves are never eaten by cattle [maud]. The leaves contain an essential oil [yennay], used by perfumers, mixed with farina of rhizomes, in the manufacture of hair-powders; they are also used for tanning leather [chamrah]; also commonly deposited amongst books and clothing to prevent the ravages of insects [poochy]; root-stock gives a dye [shauyam]. Vashamboo is often confounded with orris root. No other species here.——*Vaukyam* (वाक्य - vákyá, San.). From (vach, san. to speak). Sentence. Mode of computation [maunam] in astronomy [jyotisham]. The elements from which the Vaukyam rules and tables are constructed are extracted from the Arya siddhauntam [q.v.]. Vaukyam process computations are directly for the apparent [spootam], without previously obtaining the mean places [madhyamagraham] of the stars [nacshatram]; and refer to the time of sun rising [sooryan], instead of mean midnight, as is directed in the Soorya siddhauntam [q.v.].

VAUL (வால் - vál, *Tam.*). From (vali, tam. to bend). Tail.——*Vaul taragoo* (வாற்றகு - váttaragu, Tam.). From (above + taragu, tam. tax). Tax on cattle [maud].——*Vauly* (वालि - váli, San.; ವಾಲಿ - váli, Can.). From (vála, san. tail), tailed one. Otherwise Bauly. A chief at Kishkindyay [q.v.], the elder and crowned brother of the monkey king Soogreevan [q.v.]. The brothers disputed, and Rama [q.v.] taking part with the younger slew Vauly and installed Soogreevan, who became his ally. Sometimes confounded with sanscrit Baly [q.v.], the Deityan [q.v.] king, to suppress whom Vishnoo [q.v.] became manifest in his dwarf [vaumanan] avatar [q.v.].——*Vauly coody* (வாலிகுடி - váligudi, Tam.). From (váli, tam. the monkey + kudi, tam. house). Another name of Paundicoozhy [q.v.].——*Volcondapooram* (வாலிகண்டபுரம் - váligandappuram, Tam.). From (váli, san. the monkey chief + kanda, tam. visited + pura, san. city); rama [q.v.] is said to have met vauly, the monkey chief. Village; Trichinopoly dist., Perambalore tal.; acres 2,670; lat. 11° 19′; long. 78° 59′; from Perambalore N.N.E. 7 miles; from Trichinopoly N.N.E. 38 miles. Till 1861 headquarters of a talook comprising northern portion of Perambalore talook [q.v.]. Formerly seat of a nawaub [q.v.]. Remains of mosques [musjid] and temples. One of the most important forts on the road from Madras to Trichinopoly. The Conairiyaur is adjacent. Place of cattle-breeding [maud].

VAUL (வாள் - vál, *Tam.*). From (val, tam. sharpness). Sword. Varauha mihiran says that a sword 50 inches long is a good one and one 25 inches long is a bad one; also that marks along the back of the sword of the shape of the bilva [bael] tree, a platter, an umbrella, a shiva lingam [q.v.], pendants, a lotus [nelumbo], a banner, and a weapon of war, are indicative of prosperity.——*Vaulakidy* (دریا کا سانپ - daryáksámp, Hind.; వాలకిడి - válakidi, Tel.; வாளைக்கடியன் - válaikkadiyan, Tam.). Tam. from (válai, tam. fish, wallago attu + kadi, tam. to bite). Title otherwise Vaulakadyen. Genus Enhydrina hydrophidæ [tuttapaumb], ophidii colubriformes venenosi, ophidia [sarpam], reptilia [sarpy, 28] of naturalists [jantoo]. Sea-snakes. Poisonous; differs from Hydrophis, for which see Chittal, in the deep cleft in the lower jaw, where the mandibles do not unite and the fold of integument connecting them forms a deep notch. The only species here known is Enhydrina bengalensis. Alias Enhydrina valakadyen; Hydrophis bengalensis, schistosa, subfasciata; Hydrus valakadyen. The following is the description of the appearance of the species. Head rather short, of moderate width; neck and body moderately elongate. Rostral shield very small, lobuliform, its projecting point fitting into a corresponding cavity of the lower jaw; the fourth upper labial shield below the eye; mental shield very narrow and long, situated in a groove; anterior lower labials much elongate; throat covered with scales, without shields. One post-ocular, sometimes divided into two. Neck surrounded by forty-eight series of scales. Scales scarcely imbricate hexagonal, each provided with a short keel; ventral shields not, or but little, different from the scales of the adjoining series; they are 824–314 in number. Terminal scale of the tail rather large. The young has broad black rhombic bands across the back, which become fainter with age and finally disappear entirely. The fang of Enhydrina is short, but well marked; the groove is open part of its length, but not throughout. The body somewhat compressed, the belly carinate; the tail flat and compressed, almost like a fish's fin; the nostrils vertical; the eyes small. The poison is very virulent. It measures from 36–48 inches.——*Vaulappan* (வாளப்பன் - válappan, Tam.). From (above + appan, tam. father). Mountain deity worshipped by the Coonnoova [q.v.], a tribe on Pulney hills.——*Vaulay* (வாளை - válai, Tam.). See sep. title.——*Vaulgeicondole* (வாள்கைக்கொண்டோள் - válgaikkondól, Tam.). From (above + kai, tam. hand + kol, tam. to hold). Parvaty [q.v.], who holds a sword in her hand.

VAULAY (शिवडा - shivadá, *Mahr.*; వాలుగ - váluga, *Tel.*; ବୁଆଳି - buálí, *Oor.*; വാള - vála, *Mal.*; வாளைமீன் - válaimín, *Tam.*). Title from tamul [vaul]. Tel. from (válu, tel. long). Mal. from (vál, mal. sword). Tam. from (vál, tam. sword + mín, tam. fish). Title otherwise Fresh-water shark. Wallago attu, siluridæ [kizhautty], physostomi, teleostei, [matsyam, 35], of naturalists [jantoo]. Generic name from teloogoo. Specific name ooriyah. Alias Callichrus macrostomus; Schilbe boalis; asotus, athu, attu, boalis, mülleri, wallago; Wallagoo asotus, Silurus mülleri, russelii. Snout rather produced; air-vessel moderate size, somewhat heart-shaped, situated in front portion of abdomen, and attached to the anterior vertebræ; colors uniform, fins sometime covered with fine dots; throughout india; attains at least six feet in length, and is good eating, but is a voracious and not very cleanly feeder. Well known to south indian sportsmen. No other common species here.——*Barber vaulay* (भालत - bhálat, Mahr.; ولکتتا - valaktattá, Hind.; ପୁଲି - pulli, Oor.; அம்பட்டன்வாளை - ambattanválai, Tam.). Title from being like barber's knife. Oor. means a slice. Tam. from (ambattan, tam. barber + válai, tam. wallago attu). Mahr. also (chambári). Tam. also (shottaiválai), meaning depression + wallago attu. Title otherwise Barber's knife. Notopterus kapirat, notopteridæ, physostomi, teleostei [matsyam, 41], of naturalists [jantoo]. Alias Clupea sinura; Gymnotus notopterus; Mystus badjee, kapirat; Notopterus bontianus, pallasii. Scales those on the cheeks much larger than those on body; silvery, darkest on the back; some gloss of yellow about the head; numerous fine grayish spots everywhere; upper surface of dorsal whitish; eyes golden; fresh and brackish waters of india; grow to 2 feet or more in length. No other common species here.——*Moorman's vaulay* (సవార - savára, Tel.; ପୁଟିୟା - puttiyá, Oor.; പാമ്പാട - pámpáta, Mal.; சோனகவாளை - shónagaválai, Tam.). Title implies inferiority; cf. trygon uarnak. Tel. means beauty. Mal. from (pámbu, mal. snake + áta, mal. garment). Tam. from (jónaka, mal. mahomedan + válai, tam. wallago attu). Title otherwise Hairtail, Sabre fish, Silvery hairtail. Trichiurus haumela, trichiuridæ, acanthopterygii, teleostei [matsyam, 14], of naturalists [jantoo]. Alias Clupea haumela; Enchelyopus haumela; Trichiurus lepturus, malabaricus. Lower jaw considerably longer; lateral-line gradually descends until above commencement of anal fin, where it is in the lower third of the body; colors grayish along back, silvery on sides and beneath; dark mark along edge of preorbital; fins pale yellow, upper half dorsal dark, due to numerous fine black dots; sea and estuaries; 3 feet in length; extremely voracious, devouring its own species, as well as other kinds of fish and crustacea [kavachiny]. No other common species here.——*Thorny vaulay* (వాలుగ - váluga, Tel.; କୁଣ୍ଡ - kunda, Oor.; முள்ளுவாளை - mulluválai, Tam.). Title from spines. Tel. from (válu, tel. long). Tam. from (mul, tam. thorn + válai, tam. wallago attu). Tam. also (kíruválai), meaning to cut + wallago attu, from its biting at every thing near it. Chirocentrus dorab, chirocentridæ, physostomi, teleostei [matsyam], of naturalists [jantoo]. Alias Chirocentrus nudus; Clupea dentex, dorab; Esox chirocentrus. Upper lip terminating anteriorly in a short mesial flap; lower jaw the longer; air-vessel small, elongated and cellular; bluish-green along the back; silvery on the sides and abdomen; through the sea; attains at least 12 feet in length; when captured it bites at everything near it. No other common species here.

VAUN (வான் - ván, *Tam.*). Sky [vin]. Rain [maunam, mazhay].——*Vaunapaumb* (వానపాము - vánapámu, Tel.). Tel.

from (above + pámu, tel. snake). The chameleon snake. Tropidonotus stolatus, linn., colubridæ [paumb], ophidii colubriformes, ophidia [sarpam], reptilia [sarpy, 17] of naturalists [jantoo].——*Vauna shastram* (வானசாத்திரம் - vánasáttiram, Tam.). From (above + shástra, san. science), science of the sky or firmament; astronomy; see Jyotisham. For astrology the following glossary titles can be consulted. For horoscope, Jautacam and Jenmaputtricay. For influence at birth of lunar asterisms and other constellations, Nacshatram. For influence of lagnams [q.v.] or raushies on births, Raushy and Vargam. For the astrology of the seasons, Caurtey, Mausam, Mazhay and Yoog. For house building, Veed. For influence of planets, Graham, Raushy, Vargam, Vauram and Yoog. For omens of flowers and trees, Phool. For omens of birds and animals, Shacoonam. For omens of the twilight skies, Sundhyay. For astrology of marks of body, Saumoodricam and Shooly. For planets, see the information under each separate title of the seven planets. For miscellaneous astrological information see Punchaungam, Shoolam, Tity, Trishoolam, Varnam, Vaul, Vil, Yogam.——*Vaunore* (வானூர் - vánúr, Tam.). From (vánavan, tam. a jeina + úr, tam. town).—"*a*". Deputy tahsildarry, Villoopooram talook, South arcot district. Pay Rs 70.—"*b*" Head-quarters of Deputy tahsildar; pop. 2,535; acres 3,231; lat. 12° 01′; long. 79° 47′; from Chidambaram N. 42 miles; from Cuddalore N.N.W. 21 miles; from Madras S.S.W. 80 miles; from Tindivanam S.S.E. 15 miles; from Tricalore E.N.E. 35 miles; from Villoopooram E.N.E. 16 miles; from Vriddhauchellam N.E. 44 miles; from the sea W. 8 miles. Captured in 1760 by the British under Sir Eyre Coote. Abode of Vaunavas or Jeinas [q.v.]. Now the people call themselves Moodelliar [q.v.].——*Vaunpayir* (வான்பயிர் - vánbayir, Tam.). From (above + payir, tam. crop). Articles of cultivation excepting grain, as fruit trees and vegetables [vellaumay].——*Vin* (விண் - vin, *Tam.*). Sky [vaun], cloud [maigham].——*Vindoe* (விண்டு - vindu, Tam.). Vishnoo [q.v.] the sky colored.——*Vinmoozhoothauly* (விண்முழுதாளி - vinmuzhuthâli, Tam.). From (above + muzhuthu, tam. all + ál, tam. to rule). Indran [q.v.], the ruler of the whole sky.——*Vinoocondah* (వినుకొండ - vinukonda, Tel.). See sep. title.

VAUNDY (பாண்டி - pándi, *Tam.*). A paundyan [q.v.] place. Suffix in place names; as Vicravaundy [paundy].

VAUNIYAN (வாணியன் - vániyan, *Tam.*). From (vanik, san. merchant). The corresponding terms are:—Tel. gaundla, Can. gauniga, Mal. checkaula. Tamul oil-monger caste. To be distinguished from Vunniyar [q.v.]. About 320,000 in Presidency; extending north to Godavery and west to Malabar. Ilay vauniya, meaning leaf traders, are a caste of traders in betel [q.v.] leaf and vegetables, &c., numbering some 25,000 [janty]. See vol. I (67); II, 227.——*Vaniyambaudy* (வாணியம்பாடி - vániyambádi,* Tam.). From (above + pádi, tam. village). Sanscrit name (vánípura), meaning saraswaty + town.—"*a*" Deputy tahsildarry, Salem district. Pay Rs. 70.—"*b*" Town, Deputy tahsildar's head-quarters. Railway station; Salem dist., Tripatore tal.; pop. 15,838; acres 905; lat. 12° 41′; long. 78° 40′; height 1,156 feet; from Madras W.S.W. 115 miles; from Namcull N.N.E. 105 miles; from Oossoor E. 53 miles; from Salem N.N.E. 77 miles; from Tripatore N. 13 miles; from Yercaud N.N.E. 68 miles. On the Palaur, in the two islands formed by the bifurcation of the river. The town is almost entirely Mussalman and is a great centre of trade, the Lubbays [q.v.] and Mussalmans [q.v.] having branch establishments in Bombay, Poona, Madras, Sholapore and elsewhere. Captured by Hyder ally in 1767, but he retired before an English force the same year. Trade is chiefly in grain, cloths, hides [chamrah], and oil [yennay]. For the curing of the hides there are some fifteen large tanneries [chamrah]. The town is healthy and the water-supply good. There is a weekly market at which cattle [maud] are sold. Ponniyamman [amman] festival in August.

VAUNTY (వాంతి - vánti, *Tel.*). From (vam, san. vomit). Vomiting.——*Vaunty bhaidy* (विषूचिका - vishúchiká, San.; قی جلاب - kaíjuláb, Hind.; ವಾಂತಿಭ್ರಾಂತಿ - vántibhránti, Can.; వాంతిభ్రాంతి - vántibhránti, Tel.; നടപ്പുദീനം - natappudínam, Mal.; வாந்திபேதி - vándibéthi, Tam.). Title and Tamul means vomiting + purging. San. from (vi, san. intensive prefix + súchika, san. hinting); hinting at instant death. Hind. from (kaí, ar. vomiting + juláb, ar. purging). Can. from (vánti, san. vomiting + bhránti, san. delirium). Tel. from (vánti, san. vomiting + bhránti, san. delirium). Mal. from (natappu, mal. walking + dínam, mal. disease); epidemic disease. Mal. also (talattatti), meaning head + striking. Tam. also (vidabéthi), meaning poison + purging. Cholera. Generally make its appearance when rains [mazhay] have failed and consequently crops [dry grain, vellaumay, wet crop] deficient, and supplies bad and high priced. Poor people then in a half-starved condition, and in the state to imbibe the poison [veidyan].

VAUPS (واپس - vâpas, *Hind.*). From pers. Back again.]

VAURAM (वार - vára, *San.*). From (vri, san. to cover) [var]. Distinguish from dravidian Vauram [va]. Time.—"*a*." A day used in composition, as Somavauram, Monday [kizhamay]. Hence a week. 7 dinams or days = 1 vauram, or week; 2 vaurams = 1 paesham or fortnight [caulam]. Same as Hind. haftah [caulam]. For rationale of week nomenclature see vol. I, 610.—"*b*" The shastrams recognize planetary years; the rule in these is that the planet [graham] in whose week day the new moon [amavausyay] falls in the lunar month of Cheitram [mausam] or april is the regent of the year which then commences. Varauha mihiran has the following about the astrology of the planetary years:—"If sooryan [q.v.] should be the lord of the "year, month or day, there will be crops only here and there, "the forests will be full of wild, carnivorous animals seeking "for prey; springs will yield but little water; rivers will fail; "and diseases and medicine will not gain much in strength; the "heat of the sun will be felt intolerable even in the dewy season; "clouds though resembling mountains in size will not yield "much rain; the sky will be full of heavenly bodies of lost "lustre; ascetics and cows will be afflicted with miseries; "princes will range over the land in military order with proud "elephants, horses, foot-soldiers and other strength, armed with "bows, swords, cudgels and engaged in attacking countries as "they march. If chundran [q.v.] should be the lord of the year, "the sky will be filled with clouds moving like mountains and of "the color of the black cobra [q.v.], collyrium [caujal], or the "bee [tainee], and filling the whole earth with water and the "sky with the roar of thunder; the tanks will appear beautiful "by the presence in them of the lotus [nelumbo] and the white "lily [indian water lily], the groves will be full of flower trees "rendered attractive by the humming of black bees [zeerangy]; "cows [pashoo] will yield abundance of milk [paul], and will "thrive; wives will please their husbands by acts of love for "ever; there will be an abundant growth of wheat [geung], "rice [paddy], barley [jow] and other grains [dhaunyam] and "also of excellent sugar-cane [q.v.]; the towns and mines will "flourish; the surface of the earth will be marked by the "construction of raised brick-works over the sites of sacrificial "rites [yanyam, yaugam], the sky will be filled with the sound "of vedic hymns [vedum] chanted by persons engaged in such "rites; and the earth will be under the protection of good "rulers. If mungalan [q.v.] should be the lord of the year there "will be fear from destructive fires gaining in strength by the "winds that blow over them and consuming villages, towns and "forests; mankind will suffer from the attacks of robbers, and "there will be heard everywhere cries of distress and there will "also be loss of property and cattle; though gigantic clouds "may float together in the sky, they will yield little rain; crops, "even though they might be grown in wet places, will become "dry, and if they happen to grow and ripen at all, they will be "cut and carried away by robbers; rulers will little attend to "the protection of their subjects; bilious complaints will afflict "mankind; there will also be deaths from snake bites and crops "will suffer blight or be otherwise injured. If boodhan [q.v.] "should be the lord of the year, the arts of jugglery and sorcery "will thrive; rogues will prosper; towns and villages will "flourish; musicians, writers, mathematicians and persons "skilled in the use of arms will abound in the land and rulers "will exchange rare and valuable gifts; mankind will be truth"ful; vedic studies [vedam] will flourish; criminal courts will "administer justice according to the code of menoo [q.v.]; there "will be found students of the higher metaphysics, yoga vidyay "[yogam] and bramha nyaunam [q.v.], in many places seeking "their way to salvation [mocsham], and there will also be found "students of logic [nyauyam] and the like sciences [shastram]; "buffoons, messengers, poets, children, hermaphrodites, makers "of perfumes, and persons living on banks, over waters and in "mountains will prosper; medicinal plants will thrive. If "brihaspaty [q.v.] should be the lord of the year, the sound "of vedic hymns [vedam] chanted aloud by bramins [q.v.] in "sacrificial rites [yanyam; yaugam], will fill the sky, cause "distress to the enemies of the rites, and bring joy to the minds "of the devas [q.v.] that partake of the offerings [homam]; "abundance of excellent crops will mark the earth, large numbers "of elephants [q.v.], horses [ghorah], cows [pashoo] and foot"soldiers will thrive; there will be an increase of wealth; "mankind will be happy under the protection of just rulers and "the earth will assume an appearance as bright as the starry "heavens; the sky will be full of various huge clouds yielding "abundance of rain [mazhay]; crops will thrive and there will "be prosperity in the land. If shoocran [q.v.] should be the lord "of the year, rice-crops [paddy] and sugar-canes [q.v.] will "flourish, low grounds will be filled with rain water, tanks will "appear beautiful on account of the lotus [nelumbo] growing in "them; and the earth will assume an appearance as attractive "as a woman bedecked with jewels; rulers will achieve success "in war; the sky will be filled with the sound of the joy of "triumph from the soldiers of the army; all good men will be "happy and wicked men will dwindle and perish; towns and "villages will thrive and the earth will be under the protection "of just rulers; the spring season [ritoo, vasantam] will be "marked by husbands frequently imbibing delightful honey "[shahad], wine [sharaub], in the company of their wives; "pleasant music from the flute and the lyre will delight the ear "and mankind will partake of their meals in company with

" visitors, friends and kinsmen, and the god of love [manmatan] " will revel in triumph. If shany [q.v.] should be the lord of the " year, the land will suffer from wicked men, bands of robbers " and large wars ; cows will perish ; wealth will disappear ; there " will be heard the cries of people mourning for the death of " their kinsmen in civil strife ; severe epidemics will break out " and afflict people ; clouds will be dispersed by winds ; trees " will suffer from disease ; the sky will be filled with dust " concealing from view the discs of the sun and moon ; tanks will " become dry and rivers will fail ; crops found growing here and " there will perish for want of water ; and in other places they " will thrive only when fed by the slight rain sent down by " indran [q.v.]."—" c " As to sex :—Mercury and Saturn are hermaphrodite planets ; Mercury being female hermaphrodite and Saturn being male hermaphrodite ; the Moon and Venus are female planets ; and the rest are male planets. . As to elements :—the Sun and Mars are fire ; Mercury is earth ; Jupiter is ether ; the Moon and Venus are water ; and Saturn is air. As to caste :—Venus and Jupiter are bramins ; Mars and the Sun are cshatriyas ; the Moon is a veisya ; Mercury is a shoodra ; and Saturn is a chundaulan. As to temper :—the Moon, the Sun and Jupiter are of satwagoonam [q.v.] or good temper ; Mercury and Venus are of rajogoonam [q.v.] or passionate temper ; Mars and Saturn are of tamogoonam [q.v.] or dark temper.—" d " The following are the different vernacular names for days of week, with hours of Rahoocaulam [q.v.] and Goolicacaulam [q.v.] in each. See vol. I, 610, 613 :—

	English.	Sanscrit.	Arabic.	Persian.	Hindostany.	Canarese.	Coorg.
1	Sunday	Bhaunoo vauram ...	Yowm ool ahad ...	Yekshamba ...	Itwar	Auditya vauram ...	Narauchey.
2	Monday	Soma vauram ...	Yowm ool isnein ...	Doshamba ...	Peer	Soma vauram	Tingalauchey.
3	Tuesday	Mungala vauram ...	Yowm ool salausah...	Sehshamba ...	Mungal ...	Mungala vauram ...	Chovvauchey.
4	Wednesday ..	Boodha vauram ...	Yowm ool arbah ...	Chahaurshamba ...	Charshamba ...	Boodha vauram ...	Podanauchey.
5	Thursday ...	Brihaspaty vauram ...	Yowm ool khamees...	Punjshamba ...	Joomeraut ...	Brihaspaty vauram ...	Bailauchey.
6	Friday	Shoocra vauram ...	Yowm ool jooma ...	Jooma	Jooma	Shoocra vauram ...	Bollyauchey.
7	Saturday	Shany vauram ...	Yowm ool sabat ...	Shamba	Haftah	Shany vauram	Chanyauchey.

	Tooloo.	Teloogoo.	Malayalam.	Tamul.	Lords.	Rahoo caulam.	Goolica caulam.
1	Eitvaura ...	Audy vauram ...	Nyayir	Nyayir	Sun	From 4½ P.M. to 6 P.M. ...	From 3 P.M. to 4½ P.M.
2	Somaura ...	Soma vauram ...	Tingal	Tingal	Moon ...	From 7½ A.M. to 9 A.M. ...	From 1½ P.M. to 3 P.M.
3	Angaura ...	Mungala vauram ...	Chovva	Shevvye ...	Mars ...	From 3 P.M. to 4½ P.M. ...	From 12 NOON to 1½ P.M.
4	Boodhaura ...	Boodha vauram ...	Boodhan	Boodhan ...	Mercury ...	From 12 NOON to 1½ P.M. ...	From 10½ A.M. to 12 NOON.
5	Gooroovaura ...	Besta vauram ...	Vyauzhan ...	Vyauzhan ...	Jupiter ...	From 1½ P.M. to 3 P.M. ...	From 9 A.M. to 10½ A.M.
6	Shoocraura ...	Shoocra vauram ...	Velly	Velly	Venus ...	From 10½ A.M. to 12 NOON. ...	From 7½ A.M. to 9 A.M.
7	Shany vaura ...	Shany vauram ...	Shany	Shany	Saturn ...	From 9 A.M. to 10½ A.M. ...	From 6 A.M. to 7½ A.M.

" *e* " The following are the same with their etymologies.——*Angaura* (ಅಂಗಾರ - angára, Too.). From (angáraka, san. mars). Tuesday.——*Auditya vauram* (ಆದಿತ್ಯವಾರ - ádityavára, Can.). From (áditya, san. sun). Sunday.——*Audy vauram* (ఆదివారము - ádiváramu, Tel.). Sunday.——*Bailauchey* (ಬೇಳಾಚೆ - béláche, Coorg). From (vyázham, mal. jupiter + ázhcha, mal. day). Thursday.——*Besta vauram* (బెస్తవారము - bestaváramu, Tel.). From (brihaspati, san. jupiter). Thursday.——*Bhaunoo vauram* (भानुवार - bhánuvára, San. ; ಭಾನುವಾರ - bhánuvára, Can.). From (bhánu, san. sun). Sunday.——*Bolly auchey* (ಬೊಳ್ಳಿಆಚೆ - bolliáche, Coorg). From (velli, mal. venus + ázhcha, mal. day). Friday.——*Boodhan* (ബുധൻ - budhan, Mal. ; புதன் - puthan, Tam.). Means mercury. Wednesday.——*Boodhaura* (ಬುಧಾರ - budhára, Too.). From (budha, san. mercury + vára, san. week day). Wednesday.——*Boodha vauram* (बुधवार - budhavára, San. ; ಬುಧವಾರ - budhavára, Can. ; బుధవారము - budhaváramu, Tel.). From (budha, san. mercury). Wednesday.——*Brihaspaty vauram* (बृहस्पतिवार - brihaspativára, San. ; ಬೃಹಸ್ಪತಿವಾರ - brihaspativára, Can. ; బృహస్పతివారము - brihaspativáramu, Tel.). From (brihaspati, san. jupiter). Thursday.——*Chahaurshamba* (چهارشنبه - chahárshambah, Pers.). From (chahár, pers. four + shambah, pers. saturday). Wednesday.——*Chanyauchey* (ಚನಿಆಚೆ - chaniáche, Coorg). From (shani, mal. saturn + ázhcha, mal. day). Saturday.——*Charshamba* (چارشنبه - chárshambah, Hind.). From (chár, pers. four + shambah, pers. saturday). Wednesday.——*Chovva* (ചൊവ്വ - chovva, Mal.). Means redness, hence Mars. Tuesday.——*Chovvauchey* (ಚೊವ್ವಆಚೆ - chovuáche, Coorg). From (chovva, mal. mars + ázhcha, mal. day). Tuesday.——*Doshamba* (دو شنبه - doshambah, Pers.). From (do, pers. two + shambah, pers. saturday). Monday.——*Eitvaura* (ಐತ್ವಾರ - aitvára, Too.). From (áditya, san. sun + vára, san. week day). Sunday.——*Gooroo vauram* (ಗುರುವಾರ - guruvára, Too. ; గురువారము - guruváramu, Tel.). From (guru, san. jupiter). Thursday.——*Hafta* (هفته - haftah, Hind.). From (haft, pers. seven). Saturday.——*Itwar* (اتوار - itwár, Hind.). From (áditya, san. sun + vára, san. day). Sunday.——*Jooma* (جمعه - juma, Ar.). From (jama, ar. to collect). Friday.——*Joomeraut* (جمعرات - jumarát, Hind.). From (juma, ar. friday + rát, hind. night). Friday eve. Thursday.——*Mungal* (منگل - mangal, Hind.). Tuesday.——*Mungala vauram* (मङ्गलवार - mangalavára, San. ; ಮಂಗಳವಾರ - mangalavára, Can. ; మంగళవారము - mangalaváramu, Tel.). From (mangala, san. mars). Tuesday.——*Narauchey* ನಾರಾಚೆ - náráche, Coorg). From (náyar, mal. sun + ázhcha, mal. day). Sunday.——*Nyayir* (ഞായർ - ñáyar, Mal. ; ஞாயிறு - ñáyiru, Tam.). Sunday.——*Peer* (پیر - pír, Hind.). Monday.——*Podanauchey* (ಪೊದನಾಚೆ - podanáche, Coorg). From (budha, san. mercury + ázhcha, mal. day). Wednesday.——*Punj shamba* (پنج شنبه - panjshambah, Pers.). From (panj, pers. five + shambah, pers. saturday). Thursday.——*Seh shamba* (سه شنبه - sehshambah, Pers.). From (seh, pers. three + shambah, pers. saturday). Tuesday.——*Shamba* (شنبه - shambah, Pers.). Saturday.——*Shany* (ശനി - shani, Mal. ; சனி - shani, Tam.). Meaning saturn. Saturday.——*Shany vauram* (शनिवार - shanivára, San. ; ಶನಿವಾರ - shanivára, Can. ; ಶನಿವಾರ - shanivára, Too. ; శనివారము - shaniváramu, Tel.). From (shani, san. saturn), Saturday.——*Shevvye* (செவ்வாய் - shevváy, Tam.). Meaning mars. Tuesday.——*Shoocraura* (ಶುಕ್ರಾರ - shukrára, Too.). From (shukra, san. venus + vára, san. week day). Friday.——*Shoocra vauram* (शुक्रवार - shukravára, San. ; ಶುಕ್ರವಾರ - shukravára, Can. ; శుక్రవారము - shukraváramu, Tel.). From (shukra, san. venus). Friday.——*Somaura* (ಸೋಮಾರ - sómára, Too.). From (sóma, san. moon + vára, san. week day). Monday.——*Soma vauram* (सोमवार - sómavára, San. ; ಸೋಮವಾರ - sómavára, Can. ; సోమవారము - sómaváramu, Tel.). From (sóma, san. moon). Monday.——*Tingal* (തിങ്കൾ - tinkal, Mal. ; திங்கள் - tingal, Tam.). Means moon. Monday.——*Tingalauchey* (ತಿಂಗಳಾಚೆ - tingaláche, Coorg). From (tinkal, mal. moon + ázhcha, mal. day). Monday.——*Velly* (വെള്ളി - velli, Mal. ; வெள்ளி - velli, Tam.). Meaning venus. Friday.——*Vyauzhan* (വ്യാഴം - vyázham, Mal. ; வியாழன் - viyázhan, Tam.). Meaning jupiter. Thursday.——*Yek shamba* (یکشنبه - ekshambah, Pers.). From (ek, pers. one + shambah, pers. saturday). Sunday.——*Yowm ool ahad* (يوم الاحد - yaumulahad, Ar.). From (yaum, ar. day + ahad, ar. one). Sunday.——*Yowm ool arbah* (يوم الاربعاء - yaumularbaá, Ar.). From (yaum, ar. day + arbaá, ar. four). Wednesday.——*Yowm ool isnein* (يوم الاثنين - yaumulisnain, Ar.), From (yaum, ar. day + isnain, ar. two). Monday.——*Yowm ool jooma* (يوم الجمعه - yaumuljuma, Ar.). From (yaum, ar. day + juma, ar. meeting) ; from its being prayer day ; Friday.——*Yowm ool khamees* (يوم الخميس - yaumulkhamis, Ar.). From (yaum, ar. day + khamís, ar. fifth). Thursday.——*Yowm ool sabat* (يوم السبت - yaumussabt, Ar.). From (yaum, ar. day + sabt, ar. rest). Sabbath day. Saturday.——*Yowm ool salausah* (يوم الثلاثا - yaumussalásá, Ar.). From (yaum, ar. day + salásá, ar. three). Tuesday.

VAURS (وارث - váris, *Hind.*). From (virs, ar. inheritance). Heirship. Under Mahomedan law, a testator, if he leaves any relations, can only dispose of one-third of his net property by will ; and therefore unless his debts, funeral expenses, &c., exhaust the estate, there is necessarily in almost all cases an intestacy as to a considerable portion. The general principles of Mahomedan inheritance are as follows. There is no distinction between real and personal property. There is no right of primogeniture, so that for instance if a man leave three sons, the eldest will take no more than each of the other two. There is no right by representation. Thus, if a man leaves as his only relations one son and a grandson through another son, the surviving son will take all, and the grandson will have no claim as the representative of his deceased parent. There is no distinction between ancestral property and property which the deceased has himself acquired. Persons who may succeed to property by virtue of relationship or marriage to the deceased are divided into three classes, viz. :—sharers, residuaries, and distant kindred. The first two classes are frequently mentioned under the common name of heirs. Sharers are those who are entitled to a prescribed fractional part; e.g., a wife under certain circumstances takes $\frac{1}{4}$; a father $\frac{1}{6}$; a daughter $\frac{1}{2}$, &c. Residuaries are those who take no prescribed fractional part, but divide the residue among them after the sharers are satisfied, and the whole if there are no sharers. Distant kindred are all relations who are neither sharers nor residuaries. When there are no sharers or residuaries the distant kindred take the whole among them according to certain rules. The above is the Soonnee law, Soonnees [q.v.] being the great majority in this presidency. For hindoo inheritance see Dauyam.

VAUVILY (వావిలి - vávili, *Tel.*). Same as Water notchy.

VAUZH (வாழ் - vázh, *Tam.*). To flourish.——*Valdavore* (வழுதாவூர் - vazhuthávúr, Tam.). From (vazhuthi, tam. epithet of the pándiyan kings + úr, tam. village). South arcot dist., Villoopooram tal.; pop. 2,218; acres 1,373; lat. 11° 59′; long. 79° 45′; from Cuddalore N.N.W. 18 miles; from Villoopooram E.N.E. 14 miles; from the sea W. 9 miles; from Pondicherry W.N.W. 9 miles. Fortified by the French, and formed one of the supports of their capital, Pondicherry. One of the main redoubts of the Pondicherry fortifications still bears the name of Valdavore. On the 18th December 1758 the united forces of Krishna row and Mahomed yoosoof, after threatening Pondicherry, cut the bund [q.v.] of the great tank of Valdavore and this being in the height of the monsoon [q.v.] a large extent of cultivation was destroyed. Valdavore was captured in 1760 by the British, but restored to the French in 1763. An old ruined fort the residence of a minister of a ruler of Jinjee, contains several subterranean cells. On the west stand three sculptured stone figures larger than life, representing Rama [q.v.], Lutchmanan [q.v.], and Seetay [q.v.].——*Vauzhnore* (വാഴുന്നോർ - vázhunnór, Mal.). From (vázhu, mal. to rule + ór, mal. pers. affix); ruler. A naudvauly or governor of a naud [q.v.] under old malabar rulers; now a title of members of some families [tarwaud]; otherwise Boynore, by corruption.——*Vauzhvoo* (வாழ்வு - vázhvu, Tam.). From (vázhu, tam. to flourish). Prosperity. Suffix in place names [mungalam].——*Vazhoothy* (வழுதி - vazhuthi, Tam.). From (vazhuttu, tam. to praise). Epithet of the Paundy [q.v.] kings.

VAVVAUL (अजिनपत्र - ajinapatra, *San.*; बटुरी - baturí, *Mahr.*; خفاش - khaffásh, *Ar.*; شپره - shapparah, *Pers.*; گدل - gadal, *Hind.*; لوا - lava, *Malay*; ಕಣ್ಣುಕಪ್ಪಟೆ - kannukappate, *Can.*; ಬಾವೊಲಿ - bávoli, *Too.*; గబ్బిలము - gabbilamu, *Tel.*; ବାଦରା - bádará, *Oor.*; കടവാതിൽ - katavátil, *Mal.*; வவ்வால் - vavvál, *Tam.*). San. from (ajina, san. skin + patra, san. wing). Ar. from (khafisha, ar. small eye). Pers. from (shab, pers. night + parah, pers. flying). Can. from (kannu, can. eye + kappate, can. wrapper). Tel. from (gabbu, tel. stench + bila, san. hole). Oor. from (vátuli, san. flying fox). Mal. from (katal, mal. sea + vátil, mal. bat). Tam. from (vavvu, tam. to seize), to steal; as appearing in dusk. The ordinary bat, and may be considered co-extensive with the family Vespertilionidæ, cheiroptera, mammalia [sastanam, 6], of naturalists [jantoo]. These have simple nostrils as in the frugivorous bats with no complications of foliated cutaneous appendages; the muzzle is conical, moderately long, and clad with fur; the ears wide apart. There is a Tamul proverb :—வெளவாலுக்கு இரவில் கண் தெரியும்—"bats can see in the dark." Another :—வெளவால் தலை நரித் தலைபோல்—"the head of a bat resembles that of "a jackal [q.v.]." Another: வெளவால் போலத் தொங்குகிறான்—"he hangs like a bat." Another:—வெளவால்அடைகிற வீட்டில் குடி இருப்பது எப்படி—"how can one dwell in "a house frequented by bats." Bats are generally referred to by Tamulians as unclean animals, or as illustrative of unsightly things; though with the Chinese they are regarded as creatures of good omen [shacoonam].—"*a*" The first of the family is the Coromandel bat, Scotophilus coromandelicus. Alias Vespertilio imbricatus, coromandelicus; Vesperugo abramus. Ears rather large, broad :tragus lunate, or slightly curved forwards, and obtuse and rounded at the tip; a minute præmolar above, situated laterally internally, not visible from without; two lower præmolars; two pair of upper incisors about equal in size; fur short; above, dingy fulvous brown, beneath grayish fulvous; in some dark brown both above and below. This minute bat usually conceals itself in the roofs of dwelling houses, in holes in the thatch, under tiles, &c. Akin to the English Pipistrelle.—"*b*" Next is the Large yellow bat, Nycticejus heathii. Ears shorter than the head, straight, oblong, with rounded tip, sub-emarginate posteriorly, lobed; tragus linear, slightly curved, fur short, soft, shining; above, bright olivaceous with a tinge of ferruginous or golden brown; beneath pale and slightly greenish yellow. Roosts both in houses and trees.—"*c*" Next is the Common yellow bat, Nycticejus temminckii. Ears short, rounded; tragus moderate curved inwards; above, castaneous-olive, or rufous, or rufo-fulvous; beneath flavescent, or fulvous. A very common species, appearing early in the evening. It collects by hundreds in hollow trees, and feeds chiefly on whiteants [q.v.].—"*d*" Next is the Hoary bat, Nycticejus canus. Light dusky above, with the tips of the hairs pale grayish or fulvous; lighter beneath; sometimes variegated with bright ferruginous. Very common.—"*e*" Last is the Painted bat, Kerivoula picta. Fur fine, woolly; above yellowish red, or golden rufous; beneath less brilliant and more yellow; wing membranes inky black with rich orange stripes along the fingers, extending in indentations into the membrane. When disturbed in the day-time, looks like a butterfly [pautarny] called in Northern india the orange bat. It conceals itself in the folded leaf of the plantain [q.v.], and its Ceylonese name is Kehelvoulha, meaning plantain bat, whence the scientific term. The colors of this bat are adapted to its hiding place.—"*f*" Indian allied species not here found are :—Barbastellus communis, Harpiocephalus auratus, cyclotis, griseus, harpia, leucogaster, suillus or pigbat, Kerivoula hardwickii, pallida, papillosa, Miniopterus schreibersii, Myotis murinus, parvipes, theobaldi, Noctulinia noctula, Nycticejus atratus or sombre bat, castaneus or chestnut bat, luteus or bengal yellow bat, nivicolus or alpine bat, ornatus or harlequin bat, Nyctophilus geoffroyi, Plecotus auritus or homochrous, Scotophilus emarginatus, fuliginosus or smoky bat, heathii, leisleri or hairy-armed bat, lobatus or lobe-eared bat, ornatus, pachyomus, pallidus, serotinus or silky bat, temminckii, Vespertilio emarginatus, formosus, longipes, montivagus, muricola, murinoides, mystacinus, nepalensis, Vesperugo affinis, annectans, atratus, dormeri, leucotis, maurus, noctula, pachyotis, pachypus, tickelli.—"*g*" For the Noctule bats, see Chamgadal; for the Vampires see Kaffaush.

VAYIDAH (وعده - vadah, *Hind.*). From (vada, ar. to promise). Stated period for the payment of a sum of money, or other purpose [kist].

VAZHALAY (വഴല - vazhala, *Mal.*; வழலை - vazhalai, *Tam.*). From (vazhalu, tam. to put off), that which peels off skin; snake. ——**(1)** The term may be considered co-extensive with the family Lycodontidæ ophidii colubriformes, ophidia [sarpam], reptilia [sarpy, 23] of naturalists [jantoo]. The Vazhalays are nocturnal snakes, yet feed exclusively on skinks, which they must catch during the day. They are groundsnakes. The following are the chief species in Southern india :—"*a*" Leptorhytaon jara, called by the teloogoos a saurapotoo or striped mate, like the rat-snake [q.v.]. Alias Coluber bipunctatus, jara; Leptorhytaon jarapotoo; Lycodon jara. Brown above, each scale with two white dots; generally a white collar; lower parts uniform white. —"*b*" Lycodon anamallensis. Greyish brown, with small, white, brown-edged cross bars on back of the trunk; sides indistinctly reticulated with whitish; no collar; each labial with a brown spot; lower parts uniform white.—"*c*" Lycodon aulicus. Alias Coluber aulicus; Lycodon hebe. The common brown snake. Var. *a*. Uniform brown above, without collar. Var. *β*. Uniform brown above, with a white collar. Var. *γ*. Brown or greyish brown, with traces of a white network, with a white collar. Var. *δ*. Ferruginous or chestnut-brown, with white, brown-edged cross bars on the back; this is the most common. One of the most common snakes of Southern india; scarce on the coasts of the south-eastern parts. Formidable enemies of skinks, which form almost its sole food; of fierce habits and defends itself vigorously. About 3 feet long and the thickness of a man's finger. Sometimes mistaken for the Krait, which see.—"*d*" Lycodon striatus called by the Teloogoos Gauzoo tutta, or glass-snake. Alias Coluber malignus, striatus. Snout much depressed; black or brown, with or without whitish collar; body and tail with white cross bands, sometimes bifid on the sides, sometimes reduced to a vertebral series of white spots.—"*e*" Ophites albofuscus. Alias Sphecodes albofuscus. Light reddish, with numerous brown cross bands; a reddish white collar.——**(2)** The Tamulians distinguish the following.——*Black vazhalay* (கருவழலை - karuvazhalai, Tam.). Called the king of serpents. ——*Blood vazhalay* (இரத்தவழலை - irattavazhalai, Tam.). The bite of which causes vomiting of blood.——*Cundam caroovazhalay* (கண்டங்கருவழலை - kandangaruvazhalai, Tam.). Tam. from (kandam, tam. division + karu, tam. black). A name for Bungarus caeruleus or Krait [q.v.], whose black body is divided into divisions by thin white arches.——*Red vazhalay* (செவ்வழலை - shevvazhalai, Tam.). The red kind.

VEDAM (वेद - véda, *San.*; بيد - bed, *Hind.*). From (vid, san. to know) [vid]. Knowledge. Hence any sacred writings. Especially those of the ancient Aryan [q.v.] hindoos. Only a small portion of the Aryan vedams is now generally read among Bramins. They are in obsolete Sanscrit. The few Bramins who live by the Vedams commit twenty or thirty chapters to memory, which are recited at certain ceremonies in weddings [calyaunam], funerals [shoodcaud], and yanyams [q.v.]. Those recluses who study divinity read various commentaries called

Bhaushyam [q.v.]. The Smartas read the Shuncara bhaushyam. The Veishnavas read the Ramaunooja bhashyam, and the Madhwas read the Madhwa bhaushyam. Bramins say of the vedams that they were knowledge which issued like breath from the self-existent being bramh [q.v.], perceived by rishies [q.v.], by them orally transmitted, and eventually reduced into writing by vyausan [q.v.]. The old original sanscrit Vedam consisted of the following four parts:—Muntram [q.v.] or prayer and praise embodied in samhitays [q.v.] or compilations, texts and metrical hymns. Bramhanam [q.v.] or ritualistic precept and illustration written in prose. Oopanishad [q.v.], or nyaunam [q.v.], mystical or secret doctrine, appended to the aforesaid bramhanam in prose and occasional verse. Aranyacam belonging to the forest; intended for bramins in retreat and closely connected with the oopanishads. The Muntram or primary portion was comprised in five principal samhitays or collections of muntrams, called respectively rig, teittireeyam, vaujasaneyin, saumam, atarvam; of these the rigveda samhitay, containing one thousand and seventeen hymns, is the oldest and most important, while the atarva veda samhitay is generally held to be the most recent and is perhaps the most interesting; moreover these are the only two vedic hymn books worthy of being called separate original collections; the last hymn of the third book of the samhitay of the rig vedam consists of six invocations by the rishy vishwamitran [q.v.], one of which is the celebrated gayatry [q.v.], or verse of eight syllables, known as the holiest verse of the vedams and the mother of the vedams, which it is the duty of every bramin to repeat at all his devotions [sundhyauvandanam]. The two samhitays of the yajoorvedam, viz., teittireeyam and vaujasaneyin or black and white and the sauma vedam, borrow largely from the rig, and are manuals the necessity for which grew out of the ritual gradually elaborated by the hindoo aryans [q.v.]. Only seventy-eight verses in the sauma vedam are untraceable to the present recension of the rig; the greatest number of its verses are taken from the ninth mundalam [q.v.] of the rig, which is in praise of the somam [q.v.] plant, the sauma vedam being a collection of liturgical forms for the somam ceremonies of the oodgautry [q.v.] priests, as the yajoos is for the sacrifices performed by the adhwaryoo priests. For Bramhanam see that head. For Oopanishad see that head. Aranyacams are certain chapters of the bramhanams [q.v.] so awe-inspiring and obscure that they were required to be read in the solitude of forests; properly each bramhanam had its aranyacams; but the mystical doctrines they contained were so mixed up with extraneous subjects that the oopanishads [q.v.] appear to have been added with the object of investigating more definitely such obstruse problems as the origin of the universe, the nature of the deity, of the soul, and the reciprocal connection of spirit and matter. The Samhitays, Bramhanams, Oopanishads, and Aranyacams of the vedams are designated as Shrooty [q.v.], or heard; and all other hindoo sacred scriptures are simply Smrity [q.v.] or recollected, distinguished from the heard or directly revealed word. The three great schools of hindoo philosophy [darshanam] and their three supplementary schools, the Nyauyam [q.v.] and Veishaishicam [q.v.], the Saunkhyam [q.v.] and Yogam [q.v.], and the Poorva mimaumsam [q.v.] and Oottara mimaumsam [q.v.] or vedauntam [q.v.], all implicitly accept the divine authority of the vedams, but explain them differently. Vedic literature at present day extant consists of, first, Samhitays and Bramhanams and commentaries &c. on them, belonging to the Rig vedam, Krishna or black yajoor vedam, Shooclam or white yajoor vedam, Sauma vedam, and Atarva vedam; secondly Sootrams and Prayogams for special rites; thirdly Oopanishads; fourthly Vedaungams. For more modern works see Sanscrit. Agny [q.v.] or god of fire, Indran [q.v.] or lord of the firmament, the Maroots [q.v.] or personified winds, Varoonam [q.v.] or the god of the sea, Mitran [q.v.] or the sun, and the two Ashwins [ashwiny] or sons of the sun, are the chief deities addressed in the old vedams. The worship of the ancient aryans [q.v.] consisted, as the samhitays [q.v.] show, of oblations and libations of clarified butter [ghee] and of the expressed juice of the somam [q.v.] plant. It is by no means clear whether the authors of the vedams possessed any clear ideas of the divine unity; whether they entertained any belief in a creator and ruler of the universe, certainly does not appear from any passage hitherto met with. There is a division which separates bramins into four distinct classes, each appertaining to one of the four aryan vedams; in their ceremonies that is to say they follow the rituals or instructions of one or other of the four vedams; five of the principal gotrams [q.v.] observe the sauma vedam, five others the rig vedam, five others the yajoor vedam, and five the atarva vedam; the rest of the bramins of all gotrams [q.v.] follow the yajoor vedam; but in the ordinary intercourse of life little attention is paid to this distinction [matam]. The vedam in a more general sense than the above is sometimes classed into fourteen divisions:—the four original vedams; the six angams [q.v.] of grammar, astronomy, &c.; the pooraunams [q.v.] as the eleventh class; and the mimaumsam [q.v.] or theology, nyauyam [q.v.] or logic, and dharmam [q.v.] or law, as the remaining three. The Itihausams [q.v.] and Pooraunams [q.v.], are sometimes considered as a fifth Vedam. The aryan Vedams have never been translated into tamul, except a few hymns as specimens, which have appeared in periodicals. The Tirvauchacam [q.v.] and Tirvyemozhy [q.v.] are called the Tamul vedams of the Sheivas and Veishnavas respectively. The Dravida prabandham [q.v.] is held in superior veneration by the Veishnavas. But these are original productions. The two following verses are inserted as being remarkable passages in the Nyauna vausishtam [q.v.]:—சடுமனவன்பேய் கனலிற் கொடிதாகு மலைகளிலுங்கடத்தற் கொண்ணு, நெடுவயிரத்தினும் வலிது கடல்பருகி மேருவினை வேரோடேர்த்திச், சடுங்கனலை விழுங்கிலு நிறுத்தரிது புலன்முழுதுந் தோன்றுமூலங் கெடுமுலகிதுண்டெனிலுண் டிலதாகில்லை, இதனைக்கெடுத்தல் வேண்டும்.—"This powerful "devil of a deceitful heart is fiercer than fire, more impassable "than the mountains, and harder than adamant, sooner might "the ocean be emptied, mount meroo [q.v.] be rooted up, and "the burning flames be swallowed down, than the mind be "restrained; it is the agent that operates through the senses; "at its bidding this destructive world stands and vanishes; "therefore it is the mind that must be first subdued."—கருத்தெனு மான்மருண்டோடி விடயமெனுங் குழியில் விழக் காயமென்னு, மருத்தலத்தி லெவ்வனமாங்கடுங்கான லெழுந்துமிக வளாந்திற்கும், பெருத்தவுயரிளமை நலமெவ்வளவு அவ்வளவும் பெருகாநிற்கு, மருத்திகளு மெவ்வளமவ்வளவும் விளைத்தெழுந்த மிகவநர்த்தஞ் செய்யும்.—"As the deer [mrigam] like the bewildered mind "runs over the plain, and falls into the pit of the senses, so in "this body, compared to a barren soil, youthful lusts, like bright "mirage rising, will continue to produce numberless evils; the "forbidden pleasure of youth will increase in proportion as "they are cherished; and cherished desires will, in proportion "to youthful lusts, grow rapidly and cause destruction." There is a Tamul proverb:—நாதமும் கீதமும் ஒத்திருப்பது போல, வேதமும் போதமும் ஒத்திருக்க வேண்டும்—"as a melody and a song are in harmony, so must instruction be "in harmony with the vedam." And another:—வேதத்தை அறியாத கிழவன் வீண்—"the old man that knows not "the vedams is worthless." Among Native christians vedam is applied to Christianity. The bible is called Vedam or veda poostacam; and Vedacauran is a christian, especially a roman catholic. See vol. I (73), (87).——**(1)** *Vedachellam* (வேதாசலம் - véthásalam, Tam.). From (above + achala, san. mountain). The hill at Tircalicoondram, place of pilgrimage. Hindoo 2nd or pers. name [peyar].——*Vedagiry eeshwaran* (वेदागिरीश्वर - védagiríshvara, San.). Shiva at Tircalicoondram.——*Vedamaunicam* (வேதமாணிக்கம் - véthamánikkam, Tam.). From (above + mánikya, san. ruby). The gem of the vedam, Proper name. Common among non-bramins [peyar].——*Vedanayagam* (வேதநாயகம் - véthanáyagam, Tam.). From (above + náyaka, san. lord). Bramha [q.v.], the deity of the vedam. Hindoo 2nd or pers. name. Common among non-bramins. Also a native christian name. Similarly Vedacunn, Vedamoottoo [peyar].——*Vedaranyam* (வேதாரணியம் - vétháraniyam, Tam.). From (above + aranya, san. forest). Tam. also (tirumaraikkádu), meaning holy + vedam + forest; also (maraisai), meaning vedam + lodge.—"*a*" Deputy tahsildarry, Tanjore district. Pay Rs. 70.—"*b*" Town, Port, Deputy tahsildar's station, Salt manufactory, Sub-registrar's office; Tanjore dist., Tritrapoondy tal.; pop. 13,438; acres 223; lat. 10° 23′; long. 79° 54′; from Calimere point N.W. 6 miles; from Combaconam S.E. 50 miles; from Madras S. 188 miles; from Mayavaram S.E. 51 miles; from Munnargoody S.E. 33 miles; from Negapatam S. 27 miles; from Tanjore E. 55 miles; from Topetoray S. 2 miles; from Tritrapoondy S.E. 18 miles. Near Point calimere. Well endowed Shiva temple containing inscriptions. Tobacco [pogauk] is cultivated. There is a Tamul proverb:—வேதாரணியத்தில் பாம்பு கடிக்கிறதும் இல்லை, வேதாரணியத்தில் பாம்புகுறைகிறதும் இல்லை—"at Vedaranyam snakes "[sarpam] do not bite, nor do they cease to abound;" indicating its sanctity.——*Veda samauj* (वेदसमाज - védasamája, San.). From (above + samája, san. gathering). S. indian form of the Bramha samauj.——*Vedaugny* (वेदाग्नि - védágni, San.). From (above + agni, san. fire). The three kinds of sacred fire [agny], viz.:—Gaurhaptyam, the house-holder's perpetual fire; Ahavaneeyam, the prepared fire for daily oblations [homam]; and Dacshinam, sacred fire placed towards the south.——*Vedaungam* (वेदाङ्ग - vedánga, San.). From (above + anga, san. limb). Member of the vedams. Six Sanscrit books explanatory of the Vedams:—Shicshay or pronunciation, by Paniny; Chandas or metre, by Pingalan; Vyaucaranam or grammar, by Paniny; Nirooctam, a glossarial comment; Jyotisham or astronomy; Calpam or vedic ceremonial. These are written in the Sootram [q.v.] style. The four Vedams, the six Angams, with Mimaumsam theology, Nyauyam logic, Dharmam the institutes of law, and the Pooraunams, constitute the fourteen principal branches of knowledge. See Smrity.——*Vedauntacharry* (வேதாந்தாசாரி - véthándásári, Tam.). From (above + anta, san. end + áchárí, san. title). The head of the Vadagalay [q.v.] or innovating party among the Shree veishnavas [q.v.], otherwise Ramaunoojeeyans [ramaunoojan]; in which capacity he opposed Manavaula maumoony [q.v.] at Conjeeveram. He laid claim to a divine commission to reform the customs of southern Bramins and to introduce northern rules and traditions. See Tengalay.

The Vadagalays wear the simple naumam [q.v.] on the forehead; the Tengalays draw the centre line down on the bridge of the nose. When Vedauntacharry had carried his reforms as far as practicable, he retired to a hermitage near Conjeeveram, with his wife and his disciple Varadan. Vedantacharry wrote many theological and hymnological tracts; the Vedaunta bhaushyam, or comment on the system of Vyausan [q.v.] and on the Bhagavat geeta [q.v.], is a large and important work. He also wrote a popular drama entitled Sancalpa sooryodayam or sunrise of accuracy, in which virtues and vices are brought on the stage with appropriate language, dress, and action, the tendency being to inculcate the Veishnava system. Its Sheiva rival was the Prabodhachandrodayam by Appayya deeeshitar. He died at Conjeeveram. See vol. I (85), (89).——*Vedauntam* (वेदान्त - védanta, San.). From (above + anta, san. end). A system of pantheistic philosophy or psychology inferred from scattered texts of the vedams, and thence named their end or substance. One of the six darshanams [q.v.] or systems of philosophy, so called from its being founded on the Oopanishads [q.v.], which are the end of the vedam. It is otherwise called the Oottara mimaumsam [q.v.], and is attributed to Baudarauyanan, otherwise called Vyausan [q.v.], which is a general term for philosophic compilers. Its position in the history of S. indian religion has been shown in the foot-note on the History of Religion at vol. I (74). It is the only surviving main philosophy, being the basis alike of Adweitam [q.v.], Dweitam [q.v.], and Vishishtaudweitam [q.v.]. The Vedauntam offers many parallels to the idealism of Plato, as opposed to the Nyauyam [q.v.] which much resembles Aristotle. The object of the whole system is stated in one compound word, viz., Bramha jinyausay or Bramh inquisitiveness, or the desire of knowing Bramh [q.v.] the only really existing being [parauparavast]. The knower of Bramh attains the supreme good and supreme object of man [poorshaurtam]; τὸ ἀγαθόν, τὸ ἄριστον. In the second aphorism of the system Bramh is defined to mean that from which the production of this universe results. Shuncaran [q.v.] adds a fuller definition:—Bramh is that all-knowing, all-powerful cause from which arises the production, continuance, and dissolution of the universe, which universe is modified by name and form, contains many agents and patients, is the repository of actions and effects, and the form of its arrangement cannot be conceived even by the mind. The aphorisms of the system which follow, as far as the 28th, proceed to define and describe the character of god as the supreme soul [paramautman] of the universe. That the supreme being is omniscient follows from the fact that he is the source of the Vedam. As from that being every soul [autmam] is evolved, so to that same being does every soul return. How can souls be merged into pracrity [q.v.], for then the intelligent would be absorbed in the unintelligent? He, the supreme being, consists of joy [anandam]. This is clear from the Vedam, which describes him as the cause of joy, for as those who enrich others must be themselves rich, so there must be abundant joy with him who causes others to rejoice. Again he, the one god, is the light. He is within the sun and within the eye. He is the ethereal element [peroovely]. He is the life and the breath of life. He is the life with which Indran [q.v.] identified himself when he said to Pratardanam, 'I am the life, consisting of perfect knowledge; worship me as the life immortal.' From other portions of the aphorisms it appears that the τὸ ἕν, or one universal essence called Bramh, is to the external world what yarn is to cloth, what milk to curds, what earth to a jar, and gold to a bracelet. He is both creator and creation, actor and act. He is also existence, knowledge, and joy [satchidaunandam], but is at the same time without parts, unbound by qualities, without action, without emotion, having no consciousness such as is denoted by 'I' and 'Thou,' apprehending no person or thing, nor apprehended by any, having neither beginning nor end, immutable, the only real entity [parauparavast]. Such a creed as this does not necessarily imply what the later Vedantists teach, that the world is all Mauyay [q.v.], a mere illusion. That theory, now so popular, receives little countenance in the Oopanishads [q.v.], being rather imported from Booddhism [booddha]. A true Vedantist, though he affirms that Bramh alone is real, allows a Vyauvahauricam or practical existence to souls [autmam], the world [jagat], and Eeshwaran [q.v.], as distinguished from Pauramaurticam, real and Prautibhausicam, apparent or illusory existence. But how can it be maintained that an impure world is the manifestation of a pure spiritual essence? To avoid this difficulty, the supreme spirit [parabramh] is represented as ignoring himself by self-imposed ignorance [anyaunam], in order to draw out from himself the separate individuated souls [jeevautman] and various appearances, which, although really parts of his own essence, constitute the apparent phenomena of the universe. Hence the external world [jagat], the living souls [jeevam] of individual men and even the personal god [eeshwaran, paramautman] are all described as created by a power which the Vedantist calls Avidyay, the ἄγνοια of Plato, or false knowledge. Of this power there are two distinct forms of operation, viz., first that of envelopment or Auvaranam, which, enveloping the soul, causes it to imagine that it is liable to mundane vicissitudes, that it is an agent or a patient, that it rejoices or grieves, &c., as if a person under a delusion were to mistake a rope for a snake; secondly that of projection or Vicshaipam which, affecting the soul in its state of pure intelligence, raises upon it the appearance of a world, producing first the five subtle elements [tanmautram] and drawing out from them seventeen subtle bodies, also called Linga shareeram [q.v.], comprising the five organs [indriyam] of sense, the five organs of action, the five vital airs [praunam] with booddhy [q.v.] and manas [q.v.], and the five gross elements [bhootam] in the same order as in the Saunkhyam [q.v.], hence the soul mistakes itself for a mere mortal, as it mistook the rope for a snake. When the personal soul is set free from this self-imposed ignorance by a proper understanding of the truth [avastay], through the Vedauntam philosophy, all illusion vanishes and the identity of the Jeevautman [q.v.] and of the whole phenomenal universe with the Paramautman [q.v.], or one only really existing spirit, is re-established. With regard to the envelopments, the individuated soul, when separated off from the supreme soul, is regarded as enclosed in a succession of cases or coshams [q.v.] which as it were fold one over the other, like the coats of an onion [piyauz]. The first or innermost sheath is called the Vinyaunamaya cosham or sheath composed of mere intellection, associated with the organs of perception [nyaunendriyam]; this gives the personal soul its first conception of individuality. The second case is called the Manomayam or sheath composed of mind, associated with the organs of action [carmendriyam]; this gives the individual soul its powers of thought and judgment. The third envelope is called the Praunamayam or breathing sheath, i.e., the sheath composed of breath and the other vital airs associated with the organs of action. The fourth case is called the Annamayam or covering supported by food, i.e., the corporeal form or gross body [stoola shareeram]; the three preceding sheaths, when combined together, constituting the subtle body [soocshma shareeram]. A fifth case, called Anandamayam or that composed of supreme bliss, is also named, although not admitted by all; it must be regarded as the innermost of all, and ought, therefore, when five are enumerated, to be placed before the Vinyaunamayam. In many points the Vedauntam agrees with the Saunkhyam [q.v.], a philosophy strange to southern india. The order of creation in both is nearly the same, though the Originant in one case is Pracrity, in the other Avidyay, or false knowledge [anyaunam]. See vol. I (74) [matam]. Compare Virgil, Æneid VI, 724, &. Principio caelum ac terras, camposque liquentes lucentemque globum lunae, titaniaque astra, spiritus intus alit, totamque infusa per artus mens agitat molem et magno secorpore miscet.——*Vedaunta rasauyanam* (वेदान्तरसायन - védánta-rasáyana, San.). From (védánta, san. the philosophy so called + rasa, san. essence + ayana, san. place). A Teloogoo poem in four books written by a Roman catholic christian named Anandan, son of Mungalagiry timmayya, about A.D. 1700. In the first book the author endeavours to confute Bramins and other idolators on their own ground. The second book brings the history as far as the birth of Christ; having commenced with the fall. The third gives a brief selection from the Gospels describing the baptism, the descent of the Holy spirit, whom the author using latin words denominates Sancta spirita, the temptation, some miracles particularly the raising of Lazarus, the Last supper, and the departure to the Mount of Olives. The betrayal of Christ to the Jews concludes this book. The fourth book describes the crucifixion and subsequent events. The author now teaches the doctrine of purgatory, for which he uses the hindoo phrase Pitry locam [q.v.]. Then are described the Saviour's resurrection and appearance to the Maries, and the journey to Emmaus. Then follow brief accounts of the ascension, and the descent of the Holy spirit. Then the beatification of the Virgin, Peter being left on earth as head of the Church. On the wrath of God and the intercession of the Redeemer. The Last judgment. Conclusion, containing a summary of the points in the creed, with poetical version of the ten commandments. The author calls the mount of olives Nandana vanam. He names Peter Royappan, from Rye a king, but also with meaning of stone as in original. He calls James Yaugappan, and John Arlappan [tembauvany].——*Vedauntin* (वेदान्ती - védántí, San.). A follower of the Vedauntam philosophy.——*Veidica* (वैदिक - vaidika, San.). Class of Smarta [q.v.] bramins who follow no worldly occupation, and are supported by charity. The converse of Lowkica, or Bramins engaged in the business of the world. Many of the Veidica class now engage however in tuition.——

(2) *Atarva vedam* (अथर्ववेद - at'harvavéda, San.). From at'har, san. fire). The fourth and most recent of the four vedams. The vedam of the Shactibhactans [q.v.], or worshippers of the female energy [shacty], who make the universe to be developed by an inherent power in matter and use feminine terms and symbols. It has been termed the Black vedam. Does not exist in S. india, and by this term either the Koran or the Bible is always intended by a Tamulian.——*Ayoor vedam* (आयुर्वेद - áyurvéda, San.). From (áyus, san. life). Ancient inspired medical work. By some described as portion of the fourth or Atarva vedam. It was communicated by Bramha [q.v.] to Dacshan [q.v.] the Prajaupaty [q.v.], and by him to the two Ashwins [ashwiny] or sons of Sooryan [q.v.]. They became medical attendants of the gods [deva]. Cf. two sons of Esculapius and their descent from Apollo. Ayoor vedam consisted of 100 sections of 1,000 stanzas each; it was divided into eight main parts:—Shalyam, art of extracting extraneous substances forced into the human frame; Shaulakyam, of external organic affections, such as diseases of the eyes, ears, &c.; Canya chikitsay, of application of healing art to body in general; Bhoota vidyay, of restoration of faculties from a deranged state, by demoniacal possession; Cowmaura bhrityam, care of infancy, treatment of puerperal disorders in mothers and nurses; Agadam, of administering antidotes; Rasauyanam, chemistry or alchemy; Vaujeecaranam, increase of human race [veidyan].——*Krishna yajoor vedam* (कृष्णयजुर्वेद - krishnayajurvéda, San.). From (krishna, san. dark + yajurvéda, san. the veda so called); because in this, the separation of the samhitay [q.v.] or collection of mantrams and Bramhanam portion is greatly obscured. This is the oldest collection of the yajoor vedam as taught by Veishampauyanan.——*Oopavedam* (उपवेद - upavéda, San.). Means inferior vedam. Title given to works of supposed inspired origin :—as Ayoor vedam, the science of life or medicine; Dhanoor vedam, the science of the bow, or military science; Gaundharva vedam, the science of music, from the heavenly musicians. See vol. I (62), (73).——*Rig vedam* (ऋग्वेद - rigvéda, San.). From (rich, san. to chant). The oldest and most important of the four vedams; called the first. The hymns are amongst the oldest writings known to mankind. They are generally short, and are addressed to the great powers of nature; that is to say to Indran [q.v.] the god of the firmament, to fire [agny], to the sun [sooryan], and to the moon [chundran]. As regards the latter, they are more especially devoted to the praise of the Somam [q.v.], or moon plant, the juice of which plays a prominent part in many of the vedic hymns. This juice was fermented and formed into an intoxicating beverage, which was held in high esteem. The total number of hymns in the Rig vedam is about 1,020. Their composition was the work of many men and of long periods of time. The language of the hymns, besides being archaic, is very involved and elliptical, abounding with epithets of which it is difficult now to see the force, and with obscure metaphors and comparisons. The chief desires expressed are for riches, victory, and various temporal blessings. Moral sentiments rarely occur; the hymns addressed to Varoonan [q.v.] contain the most. The following hymn, addressed to Agny [q.v.], the god of fire, and the Maroots [q.v.] or the stormgods, may be taken as a specimen :—"Thou art called forth to this "fair sacrifice for a draught of milk; with the Maroots come "hither O agny! No god indeed, no mortal, is beyond the might "of thee, the mighty one; with the Maroots, &c., &c. They who "know of the great sky, the Vishwedevah without guile; with "the Maroots, &c. The wild ones who sing their song, unconquerable by force; with the Maroots, &c. They who are brilliant, "of awful shape, powerful, and devourers of foes; with the "Maroots, &c. They who in heaven are enthroned as gods, in "the light of the firmament; with the Maroots, &c. They who "toss the clouds across the surging sea; with the Maroots come "hither, &c. They who shoot with their darts across the sea with "might; with the Maroots, &c. I pour out to thee for the early "draught the sweet juice of Somam [q.v.]; with the Maroots, "&c." The Rig is divided into eight parts called ashtacams or caundams, each of which is sub-divided into as many lectures or adhyayanams. Another mode of division also runs through the volume, distinguishing ten books or mundalams [q.v.], which are sub-divided into more than a hundred chapters or anoovaucam and comprise a thousand hymns, or invocations or sooctam. A further sub-division of more than two thousand sections or vargam [q.v.] is common; it is suited to both methods. The whole contains above 10,000 verses, or rather stanzas of various measures. Some passages are in the form of dialogue, and in such cases the interlocutors are alternately considered as rishy [q.v.] or "he by whom the muntram is spoken," and devatay [q.v.] or "he who is therein mentioned." The number of Samhitays of the Rig vedam is reckoned in the Pooraunams [q.v.] as sixteen.——*Sauma vedam* (सामवेद - sámavéda, San.). From (sham, san. to pacify), from tranquillizing utterance while chanting. The third of the four vedams and in Bhagavat geeta [q.v.] is called best of all. Is little more than a recast of the Rig vedam. While the Rig is in regular metre to be recited aloud; and the Yajoos consists chiefly of prose to be inaudibly muttered; the Saumam contains a certain rhythm, or mode, sung to music, and the name is also generally employed to designate a hymn. Compare Varautha avatar.——*Shoocla yajoor vedam* (शुक्लयजुर्वेद - shuklayajurvéda, San.). From (shukla, san. white + yajurvéda, san. the véda so called); because the separation between the samhitay [q.v.] or collection of muntrams [q.v.] and the bramhanams [q.v.] is clearly distinguished. This is the later collection of the Yajoor vedam as taught by Yaunyavalcyans who received it from the sun [sooryan] who assumed the form of a horse while constructing it. Hence the followers of this vedam are called Vaujin.——*Teittireeya vedam* (तैत्तिरीयवेद - taittiríyavéda, San.). Otherwise Teittareeya samhitay of the black Yajoor vedam, as handed down by Tittiry of the school of Veishampauyanan.——*Vaujasaneyin vedam* (वाजसनेयिवेद - vájasanéyivéda, San.). From (vájasanéyin, san. a patronymic of yáñavalkya). Otherwise Vaujasaneyin samhitay as being originally given out by sun in the form of vaujee or horse or Shoocla yajoor vedam.——*Yajoor vedam* (यजुर्वेद - yajurvéda, San.). From (yajus, san. sacrifice + above). The second of the four vedams; comprehends the science of religious rites and ceremonies, such as fasts, festivals, purifications and sacrifices. Formed out of the Rig. Appears in two forms, as black [krishna yajoor vedam] and white [shoocla yajoor vedam].

VEDDAH (வேடன் - védan, *Tam.*). From (védu, tam. hunting). Also appears as Baida, Beyda and Veydan. The name of a very wild aboriginal tribe in Travancore and Malabar and found also in Ceylon. They inhabit the hills and forests, and live by hunting. Formerly sold and bought as slaves. Their usages, worship, and superstitions greatly resemble those of the Poolayar [q.v.]. These and allied tribes were doubtless the earliest inhabitants of the peninsula, giving way before the Coorumbar [q.v.]. In Hindoo writings the term is synonymous with everything low under a human form. The language of the Veddahs in Ceylon is a dialect of Singhalese, that is to say Dravidian, and free from Sanscrit or Pali, but the vocabulary is very limited. They occupy there a district about 90 miles long and 45 miles broad in the south-eastern side of the island; said to be a remnant of the Yakkho, the Sanscrit name for the aborigines of Ceylon, who, after the conquest of the island by Vijaya and his followers, were driven into the wilds. The Bisadæ, or Besadæ, which in mediæval Greek are called Vesadæ, are alluded to in the tract of Palladius de moribus brachmanorum, written about A.D. 400, and the same name is applied by Ptolemy to a similar race inhabiting northern India. The Veddahs have no knowledge of God, nor of a future state, and have no temples, idols, altars, prayer or charms, but have a devil worship. They do not bury their dead but cover them with leaves in the jungle. See vol. I (35).——*Veddasundoor* (வேடசந்தூர் - védasandúr, Tam.). From (above + sandhi, san. meeting + úr, tam. village).—"*a*" Deputy tahsildarry, Madura district. Pay Rs. 70.—"*b*" Village, Head-quarters of Deputy tahsildar and Sub-registrar; Madura district, Dindigul talook; pop. 6,863; acres 8,563; lat. 10° 32′; long. 78° 00′; from Dindigul N. 12 miles; from Kodaykarnal N.E. 37 miles; from Madras S.S.W. 234 miles; from Madura N.W. 44 miles; from Rameshwaram N.W. 126 miles; from Ramnand N.W. 100 miles. In 1796 detatched from Ammayanaickanore polliem. Good tobacco [pogauk] grown.——*Veddaulay* (வேடாலை - védálai, Tam.). From (above + ál, tam. banyan tree, ficus bengalensis, linn.). Village, Port; Madura dist., Ramnaud zemindarry tal.; lat. 9° 16′; long. 79° 09′; from Madras S.S.W. 274 miles; from Madura E.S.E. 80 miles; from Marcauyaputnam W. 1¼ miles; from Mantapam W.S.W. 3 miles; from Ramnaud E.S.E. 19 miles. South of Tonitoray promontory. Formerly a port of some note for native craft. Famous in Portuguese history for victory gained there by Martin Alfonso de sousa, Capitão Mór do Mar, over the Zamorin [q.v.]. Inhabited chiefly by Mussalmans [q.v.] and Shaunaur [q.v.], the former carrying on a good trade. Chayroot [q.v.] dye [shauyam] is manufactured.——*Vettavalam* (வேட்டவலம் - véttavalam, Tam.). From (véttai, tam. hunting + valam, tam. strength). Zemindarry; South arcot dist., Trinomallee tal.; pop. 4,275; lat. 12° 07′; long. 79° 17′; height 1,741 feet; from Cuddalore N.W. 44 miles; from Trinomallee S.E. 14 miles. The only zemindarry [q.v.] in South arcot. Granted to the original holder, more than two centuries ago for his services in clearing it of robbers.——*Veydan* (വേടൻ - védan, Mal.; வேடன் - védan, Tam.). A hunter [veddah].

VEENAY (वीणा - víná, *San.*; بين - bín, *Hind.*; ವೀಣೆ - víne, *Can.*; వీణ - vína, *Tel.*; வீணை - vínai, *Tam.*). San. from (vi, san. to move), as played by fingers. Hind. and Drav. from sanscrit. The Indian lute. Instrument of the guitar kind. A gourd is attached to the end where the pegs are fixed for tightening the strings; the other end consists of a hollow wood-work serving for sounding board, over which the strings pass. There are four strings, two of steel and two of brass passing over the frets and finger-board; on these the notes are produced. Three other thin strings of steel are attached to the side for the purpose of being struck by the little finger to keep time. The compass of the instrument, beginning from the lowest note produced on the farthest brass string, to the highest one on the smaller steel wire, is 3½ octaves. The extent on any one string is 2 octaves, At 12 frets for an octave there are 24 fixed frets of steel or bell-metal. The veenay of northern india, called Roodra veenay, has a gourd at each end. Veenays are made chiefly of blackwood [q.v.] or jackwood [jack], which woods give the best tone. They are generally much carved and ornamented, the long neck of the instrument ending in a carved dragon. The gourd is rested upon a cushion in playing. There is no fixed pitch for tuning the strings [sangootam]. They have much sweetness but little power; astonishing manual skill is often displayed upon them; the player sometimes sings to his or her own accompaniment on the veenay.——*Mookha veenay* (ముఖవీణ - mukhavína, Tel.), Means face lute. Clarionet [naugaswaram].

VEERAM (वीर - víra, *San.*). From (vír, san. to be powerful). Heroism.——*Veerabhadran* (वीरभद्र - vírabhadra, San.), From (above + bhadra, san. auspicious), the good warrior. Son of Shiva, the destroyer of Dacshan's sacrifice [dacshan]. Veerabhadran was a son of Shiva, created from the mouth, or according to some the hair, of his father, for the purpose of destroying the above sacrifice. Shiva [q.v.] had married one of the daughters of Dacshan, called Saty [q.v.] or Parvaty [q.v.] in her next birth. Dacshan commenced a horse-sacrifice [ashwa medham]. Being incensed with Shiva on account of his habits, Dacshan had intended contrary to custom to offer the sacrifice to Vishnoo [q.v.] and so Shiva was not among the invited. Saty went to the sacrifice uninvited, and having received a cold welcome threw herself into the sacrificial fire and perished. Shiva exasperated created Veerabhadran to avenge himself, who destroyed the sacrifice striking off Dacshan's head. The gods interceded with Shiva on behalf of Dacshan who was reanimated; but as his head could not be found it was replaced by that of a ram. The story is intended to intimate the struggle between Sheivites and Veishnavites, in which at first the latter but finally the former acquired the ascendancy. It is also a favourite subject of Hindoo sculpture. See vol. I, (71), (78).——*Veeracull* (ವೀರಕಲ್ಲು - vírakallu, Can.). From (above + kallu, can. stone). A sculptured stone erected in honor of a person killed in battle, similar to european Menhir [aursham].——*Veera maumoony* (வீரமாமுனி - víramámuni, Tam.). From (above + má, tam. great + muni, san. sage). Also called Ismauthy sanyausy [q.v.], the chaste devotee. Tamul name of Beschi, a native of Italy and a Jesuit. Having been appointed to East india mission, he arrived in 1700 at Goa. He proceeded to Auvore in Trichinopoly, where he studied Tamul, Sanscrit, Teloogoo, Hindostany and Persian. Held subordinate political offices in the earlier part of his life, and eventually after 1736 became Diwaun [q.v.], under Chundah sahib, Nawaub [q.v.] of Trichinopoly. He abandoned use of animal food and employed Bramins [q.v.] to prepare his meals. He adopted habit of religious devotee, and on his visitations to his flock assumed all the pageantry of a gooroo [q.v.]. He wore purple flowing garments, a white turban [q.v.], and yellow slippers. In his hand he carried a silver-mounted cane. In his ears and fingers he wore rings set with precious stones. He travelled on a white horse [ghorah] or in a palankeen [q.v.]. One servant held a purple silk umbrella over him, while another fanned him with peacock [mayil] feathers. He was seated on a tiger [pooly] skin; and a retinue followed. When he was the diwaun [q.v.] of Chundah sahib, he was styled Ismauthy sanyausy [q.v.], and obtained for his maintenance four villages yielding an annual revenue of 1,200 rupees. He founded a church at Conangooppam ariyanore. In honor of the Virgin mary he composed the very remarkable sacred poem Tembauvany [q.v.]. He also founded a church at Tircauvalore, near Ariyalore, and on the Madonna there composed three poems; Tircauvalore calambagam, Annay azhoongal antaudy and Adeicala maulay. Wrote also Kittairy ammaul ammaunay, a poem; Vediyar oloocam, in prose, Veda vilakkam, in prose, &c. Also a dictionary, Tamul and French, another Tamul and Portuguese, a third Tamul and Latin, Chatoor acarauthy [q.v.] or the four dictionaries, a Tamul work relating to the higher dialect His grammar of the coloquial dialect was written in Latin, dated Mission of Madura, 29th January 1728, and printed at Tranquebar in 1739. To this he soon afterwards added his grammar of the high dialect [shen tamul], written in 1730, a standard work. Modern works have not superseded these. He also wrote for natives a grammar called Tonnool [q.v.] in opposition to Nunnool [q.v.]. Beschi was diwaun until the year 1740, when Trichinopoly being besieged by the Mahratta army under Moraury row, and Chundah sahib being taken prisoner, he escaped, and fled to Cauyalputnam, then belonging to Dutch. He there remained till his death in 1742. His name is still remembered in Cauyalputnam.——*Veeran* (வீரன் - víran, Tam.). Hero. Feminine Veery. Non-bramin proper name. Also by irony term of insignificance and contempt. Compare Cauttaun [peyar].——*Veerappan* (வீரப்பன் - vírappan, Tam.). From (above + appan, tam. father). Hindoo 2nd or pers. name. Common among non-bramins. Also term of contempt [peyar].——*Veerappanaick* (வீரப்பநாயக்கன் - vírappanáyakkan, Tam.). From (above + appan, tam. father + náyaka, san. leader). Veerappan, the leader. Name of a king of Madura. See vol. I (121).——*Veeraraghavan* (வீரராகவன் - víarágavan, Tam.). From (above + rághava, san. ráma of the raghu race). Hindoo 2nd or pers. name [peyar].——*Veera rajendrapett* (ವೀರರಾಜೇಂದ್ರಪೇಟೆ - vírarájéndrapéte, Can.; വീരരാജേന്ദ്രപ്പേട്ട - vírachandrappétta, Mal.; virarajendrapet, coorg gov.). Otherwise Veerajpett by corruption. Town in north lat. 12° 12', east long. 75° 51', on the main road, 16 miles south of Mercara, head-quarters of Yedenaulknaud talook. Founded in 1792 by Rajah dodda veera rajendra, the hero of Coorg independence, on the spot where he had met General Abercromby in the previous year. In 1805 a colony of native immigrants from the Concan [q.v.] settled here under a Roman catholic priest from Mangalore. Large weekly market.——*Veerasawmy* (வீரசாமி - vírasámi, Tam.). From (above + svámi, san. lord). Epithet of Soobramanyan [q.v.], the veteran lord. Hindoo 2nd or pers. name [peyar].——*Veerashaishay* (वीरशेषा - vírashésha, San.). From (above + shésha, san. remainder). Fees given by the bridegroom to the temple at marriages.——*Veerasheiva* (वीरशैव - virashaiva, San.). From (above + shaiva, san. relating to shiva). The same as Lingayets; which see. The epithet Veera from their ferocity in their warfare against the Jeinas [q.v.] and Booddhists [booddha], and to this day they are intolerant enemies of the Bramins [q.v.]. The Veerasheivas are chiefly found in the Canarese country [jauty]. See vol. I (84).——*Veeraunam* (வீராணம் - víránam, Tam.). From (vírannan, tam. proper name + nattam, tam. village). Tank; South arcot dist., Chidambaram tal.; lat. between 11° 17' and 11° 25'; long. between 79° 33' and 79° 36'; from Chidambaram W. 10 miles; from Cuddalore S.S.W. 26 miles; from the sea W. 17 miles. The largest irrigation tank in the district, irrigating upwards of 34,000 acres. Improved during Mahomedan rule. Lies in the limits of 10 villages:—Agarapoottoore, Carnaucaranullore, Collamullay, Laulpett, Mailpauthy, Nuttamullay, Podanjore, Rayanullore, Shooddhamully, Tirchinapooram, Vaunamadevy.——*Veeravailan* (வீரவேலன் - víravélan Tam.). From (above + vél, tam. lance); hero with the lance. Soobramanyan [q.v.].——*Veeravausaram* (వీరవాసరం - víravásaram,* Tel.). From (above + vása, san. dwelling + pura, san. town); so called after veerabhadran [q.v.] an incarnation of shiva worshipped in a large temple. Town; Godavery dist., Bheemavaram tal.; pop. 5,664; acres 7,037; lat. 16° 32'; long. 81° 40'; from Bheemavaram E. 6½ miles; from Cocanada S.W. 49 miles; from Coonavaram S.S.E. 74 miles; from Ellore E.S.E. 35 miles; from Madras N.N.E. 250 miles; from Narsapore N.W. 8 miles; from Rajahmundry S.S.W. 34 miles. Talook head-quarters transferred to Bheemavaram. English factory established in 1634, withdrawn in 1662, re-established in 1677, and abandoned in 1702. Ceded with Circars [q.v.], 1768. Very old temple and fort built by a former zemindar [q.v.]. Near the temple of Vishweshwara sawmy stands a Dhwaja stambham [q.v.], close to which is a stone Nundy [q.v.] with an inscription.——*Veeravilly* (వీరవల్లి - víravilli, Tel.). See sep. title.——*Veeroye* (வீரராயன் - víaráyan, Tam.). Title of the zamorin. Gives name to an old coinage [naunyam], especially a fanam [fánam, poodameny].——*Veery* (வீரி - víri, Tam.). Heroine; Bhadra cauly [q.v.]. Non-bramin female proper name; also Veerye [peyar].——*Veeryam* (वीर्य - virya, San.). Fortitude; one of the six pauramitays or transcendent perfections of conduct which take to the shores of Nirvaunam [q.v.]. The other five are daunam or charity, sheelam or goodness, shaunty or patience, dhyaunam or meditation, pranyay or knowledge [booddha].

VEERAVILLY (వీరవల్లి - víravilli, *Tel.*). From (víra, san. hero + palli, tel. village) [veeram]. Division, Vizagapatam district; area 555 square miles; population 197,866; language Teloogoo. Central inland talook of district. Boundaries:—east, Ankapully and Srungavarapoocote talooks; south, Ankapully and Golcondah talook; west Golcondah and Padair talooks; north, Srungavarapoocote talook. Plains interspersed with small hill ranges. Soil fertile and black in color. Agriculture is chief industry. Common food grains, jaggery [q.v.] and hill products, such as gallnuts [mauchicoy], piplee [long pepper], wax [mom], honey [shahad]. Irrigation by rivers and tanks. Shaurada takes its rise in this talook. Places of archæological interest:—Arjoonagherry, Chodavaram, Madgole, Mooddore, Peddapolliem, Sanganore, Tautaparty, Zoottauda. Principal trig. stations:—Coralbiding, Cuppacondah, Jeeracondah. The leading places, &c., in the division are the following.——*Chidicauda* (చిడికాడ - chídikáda, Tel.). From (chídi, tel. tree, semecarpus anacardium, linn. + kada, tel. place). Porprietary estate, Village; pop. 2,377; lat. of village 17° 55'; long. 82° 56'; from Chodavaram N.N.W. 7 miles; from Vizagapatam N.W. 29 miles. Peshcush Rs. 1,750.——*Chodavaram* (చోడవరము - chódavaramu, Tel.). See sep. title.——*Coralbiding* (కొఱ్ఱబిడింగి - kóralbidingi, Tel.). From (korra, tel. grain, panicum italicum, linn. + budige, tel. pot). Trig. station; lat. 18° 08' 02·05"; long. 82° 24' 24·25"; from Chodavaram N.W. 42 miles.——*Cuppacondah* (కప్పకొండ - kappakonda, Tel.). From (kappa, tel. frog + konda, tel. hill). Trig. station; lat. 17° 56' 52·82"; long. 82° 39' 37·47"; height 5,214 feet; from Chodavaram W.N. W. 21 miles.——*Gavaravaram* (గవరవరము - gavaravaramu, Tel.). From (gavara, tel. member of the caste + pura, san. town). Village; pop. 2,199; lat. 17° 53'; long. 82° 49'; from Chodavaram W.N.W. 10 miles; from Vizagapatam W.N.W. 36 miles; from Vizianagram W.S.W. 44 miles. Chief station of Aulmanda talook of Vizianagram zemindarry in the Narsapatam division.——*Jeeracondah* (జీరకొండ - jírakonda, Tel.). From (jíraga, tel. owl + konda, tel. hill). Trig. station; lat. 18° 01' 37·96"; long. 82° 51' 36·64"; height 4,182 feet; from Chodavaram N.N.W. 16 miles; from Madgole N. 8 miles.——*Juggannautapooram* (జగన్నాథపురము - jagannát'hapuramu, Tel.). From (jagannát'hudu, tel. proper name + pura, san. town). Proprietary estate, Village; pop. 4,914; lat. of village 17° 52'; long. 83° 02'; from Chodavaram N.E. 4 miles; from Vizagapatam W.N.W. 22 miles. Peshcush Rs. 3,104.——*Madgole* (మాడుగుల - mádugula, Tel.). See sep. title.——*Shaurada nuddy* (శారదానది - sháradánadi, Tel.). See sep. title.——*Tautaparty* (తాటపర్తి - tátaparti, Tel.). See sep. title.

VEETY (वीथि - vít'hi, *San.*). From (ví, san. to extend). Street [teroo]. Section of path of the sun [sooryan] and planets [graham] amongst the lunar asterisms [nacshatram]. The ecliptic [craunty mundalam] is divided into nine divisions known as Veeties or paths. Each division consists of three constellations [nacshatram] beginning from the lunar mansion Ashwiny [q.v.]. These divisions are technically known as, first Naugam or serpent, second Gajam or elephant, third Eirauvatam the divine elephant or serpent, fourth Vrishabham [arshabhoo] or bull, fifth Go or cow, sixth Jauradgavam or old ox, seventh Mrigam or deer, eighth Ajam or ram, ninth Dahanam or fire.

The veeties belong to the fixed ecliptic [craunty mundalam]. Of the nine Veeties the first three are known as the northern, the next three as the central, and the last three as the southern; these three sets are called Avastaunams [q.v.]. Again in the case of each three the first is known as the northern, the second as the central, and the last as the southern According to some the topical designation of a Veety follows that of the Yoga taurah [yogam] or chief star of the particular constellation; so that if the star should be on the north of the ecliptic, the veety is known as the northern one, if on the ecliptic, it is known as the central one, and if on the south of the ecliptic, it is known as the southern one [nacshatram]. ——(1) The following are the Avastaunams alphabetically.——*Eirauvatam* (ऐरावत - airávata, San.). Indran's elephant. 1st avastaunam.——*Jauradgavam* (जारद्गव - járadgava, San.). Old ox. 3rd avastaunam.——*Veishwaunary* (वैश्वानरी - vaishvánarí, San.). Fire. 2nd avastaunam.——(2) The following are the Veeties alphabetically.——*Ajam* (अज - aja, San.). Goat. 2nd veety of 3rd avastaunam Jauradgavam.——*Arshaboo* (अंर्षभू - arshabhú, San.). From (rishi, san. sage + bhú, san. to be). 1st veety of 2nd avastaunam Veishwaunary.——*Dahanam* (दहन - dahana, San.). Burning. 3rd veety of 3rd avastaunam Jauradgavam.——*Eirauvatam* (ऐरावत - airávata, San.). Indran's elephant. 3rd veety of 1st avastaunam, Eirauvatam.——*Gajam* (गज - gaja, San.). Elephant. 2nd veety of 1st avastaunam Eirauvatam.——*Go* (गो - gó, San.). Cow. 2nd veety of 2nd avastaunam Veishwaunary.——*Jauradgavam* (जारद्गव - járadgava, San.). Old cow. 3rd veety of 2nd avastaunam Veishwaunary.——*Mrigam* (मृग - mriga, San.). Deer. 1st veety of 3rd avastaunam Jauradgavam.——*Naugam* (नाग - nága, San.). Elephant. 1st veety of 1st avastaunam Eirauvatam.

VEIDYAN (वैद्य - vaidya, *San.*). From (vid, san. to know) [vid]. Hindoo physician [hakeem, ospitry].——(1) S. india is abundantly supplied with country medicines; that is to say simple, energetic, and appropriate remedies, adapted for treatment of tropical diseases. The use of these is long anterior to Arab practice. Practitioners are of all castes and of all religious sects. Veidya einnoor, by Agastyan [q.v.], medical shastram [q.v.] in Tamul verse is in the hands of every veidyan. Other Tamul books are Dhanwantary cauvyam, Bhogar shastram, and Teraiyar vaugadam; all of them printed. The works of Characan [q.v.] and Sooshrootan are in Sanscrit. These are known to the races speaking Malayalam, Canarese, Mahratta and Goozeratty; but they have never been translated into Tamul, nor in their entirety in Teloogoo. The Ashtaunga hridayam, literally heart of eight sections, is a compilation by Vaukbhatan or Baubatan, from works of Characan and Sooshrootan, and is in repute amongst Malayalam veidyans. These style themselves Ashtaunga hridaya veidyans, while Tamuls of that coast are Chintaumany veidyans, following Agastyan. The plan followed by Tamulian medical writers is always uniform. They preface the work with a topographical memoir descriptive of the climate and soil of some locality [desham], and follow this up with materia medica, noticing the seasons for gathering vegetable drugs, the modes of preparing them and their doses. They describe the pulse, give rules for diagnosis and prognosis with careful instructions as to diet and regimen. These books are generally in eight sections, which have a parallel in the Greek and Latin medical works. According to them the harmonious action of the five elements [bhootam] and their qualities constitutes health. The body is said to contain three humors; air [vautam], bile [pittam], phlegm [sheetam], which are the pillars of the system; if deranged the same are the cause of disease and death. There are eighty diseases caused by derangements of the air; forty by those of bile; twenty by those of phlegm; and sixteen by combination. A shastram says:—"As the moon "sheds moisture, and abstracts the sun's rays, which dry up and "bestow energy upon the earth, and the air moves from place to "place, so phlegm [sheetam] bestows moisture, bile [pittam] "withdraws it by its heat and air [vautam] wafts it about in the "microcosm or animal body [shareeram]; bramha [q.v.], the "creator of the world, is full of the rajogoonam [q.v.] and "resembles air [vautam]; while bile [pittam] resembles vishnoo "[q.v.] and, is like him full of satwagoonam [q.v.]; in like "manner phlegm [sheetam] resembles shiva [q.v.] with his "inactive qualities [tamogoonam], and is the destroyer of the "body [trinity]." To reduce these humours when super-abundant and increase them when wanting, are the principles upon which the system of cure is based. To accomplish such objects a strict regimen is enforced, and certain articles of food and particular medicines are prescribed to increase or diminish these elements. The diagnosis of veidyans defines and distinguishes symptoms with great accuracy. Diagnosis they arrange under the seven following heads:—temperature of the body; appearance of the eyes; mode of speaking; color of the face and body; state of the urine; state of the stools; state of the tongue. Some of their notions of prognosis are excellent. As an example, favorable symptoms:—when the natural tones of the patient's voice remain unaltered; when he wakes from sleep without agitation; and when eating rather cools than heats his frame. They have less knowledge of anatomy. From one of the principal authorities comes the statement that the navel is the origin of all the vessels and is the principal seat of life. The instrumental part of surgery is of eight kinds:—Chedanam, excision; Laikhanam, drawing lines, applicable to scarification and inoculation; Vyadhanam, puncturing; Yaishanam, probing; Ahauryam, extraction of solid bodies; Visrauvanam, extraction of fluids; Sevanam, sewing; Bhaidanam, division. The mechanical means are termed Yantrams [q.v.], including a great variety of instruments; such as tongs or sandamsham, needles or soochy, teeth instruments or danta shankoo, saws or cara patram, tubular instruments or naudy, lancets or mandalaugram, knives or ardha dhauram, bistovries or cotaudicam. Of bandages there are fourteen kinds; of rods and sounds, and instruments for eradicating nasal polypi or nacram a great variety. Actual cautery with heated metals is very commonly employed by veidyans, who also use a cautery prepared with hot seeds, combustible substances, or inflamed boiling fluids of a gelatinous or mucous consistence. No operations in surgery of any nicety are now ventured on, but dislocated joints are replaced and fractured limbs set by a class of men who also apply leeches [attay], &c. The veidyans being Shoodras are not permitted to peruse the sacred vedams [ayoorvedam]. Particular gods superintend different parts or functions of the body, and to them prayers are offered up before operations are performed or medicines exhibited. The following are the chief:—Agny or fire, the tongue; Bramha or creator, the soul; Chundran or moon, understanding; Dhroovam or stars, the eyebrows; Indran or firmament, strength; Samoodram or ocean, the navel; Sooryan or sun, sight; Varoonan or water, understanding; Vayoo or air, life; Vishnoo or preserver, courage. The Tamul medical works are written in Ilakkanam [lacshanam]; liberal license being permitted, as in the Greek, in transposing, altering and occasionally altogether taking away certain letters, in order to harmonize and vary the rhythm. The following specimens are from Agastya veidya einnoor:—"Signs of a "bilious and irritable habit; a person of what is called a "bilious habit, generally becomes grey very early in life; he "is easily made to perspire; his eyes are often inflamed, while "his body is pale; he is impatient, perverse, opiniative, and "consequential; and for the most part very amorous; the "conversation of such an individual is unguarded; he is addicted "to falsehood, fond of abstruse studies, yet is he more partial "still to the praises that are bestowed on himself. Causes of "fever [jwaram]; an exposure to the heat of the sun, at an early "hour of the morning, while fasting; eating voraciously any "food of a very hot nature, when the body has been previously "weakened by extreme hunger or fatigue; drinking stagnated "water, into which withered leaves have fallen; taking a full "meal without appetite, unseasonable weather; sudden vicissi-"tudes of temperature; wooded, ill-ventilated valleys; neglected "adoration of krishnan [q.v.]; air one has not been accustomed "to, whether that of the plains or mountains; the malign influ-"ence of an evil spirit or devatay [q.v.]; checked perspiration; "fear; grief; sleepless nights; long-continued constipation; in "a word, whatever exposes our mortal frame to deviations from "its natural and accustomed movements, or clogs nature so much "that it requires great agitation and consequent heat to bring "the body back to sound health. What constitutes a good "physician; the sages of antiquity or mahá rishies [q.v.] have "thus handed down to us the qualities which constitute a good "physician; he must be a person of strict veracity, and of the "greatest sobriety and decorum, holding intercourse with no "woman except his own wife; he ought to be thoroughly skilled "in all the commentaries on the ayoor vedam [q.v.], and be "otherwise a man of sense and benevolence; his heart must be "charitable; his temper calm and his constant study how to do "good; such an individual is properly called a good physician, "and such a physician ought still daily to improve his mind by "an attentive perusal of scientific books or vaugadam; when a "patient expresses himself peevishly or hastily, a veidyan so "endowed will not thereby be provoked to impatience; he "remains mild yet courageous, and cherishes a cheerful hope of "being able to save the sufferer's life; he is frank, communi-"cative, impartial and liberal, yet ever rigid in exacting an "adherence to whatever regimen or rules he may think it neces-"sary to enjoin; should death come upon us, under the care of "this earthly saint, it can only be considered as inevitable fate, "and not the consequence of presumptuous ignorance." The tamul Cooral has the following:—மிகினுங் குறையினு நோய் செய்யு நூலோர் வளிமுதலா வெண்ணியமூன்று—"if food and work are either excessive or deficient, the three "things enumerated by writers, flatulence [vautam], biliousness "[pittam] and phlegm [sheetam], will cause one disease."—மருந்தென வேண்டாவாம் யாக்கைக் கருந்திய தற்றது போற்றி யுணின்—"no medicine is necessary for him who eats "after assuring himself that what he has already eaten has been "digested."—அற்றா லளவறிந் துண்க வஃதுடம்பு பெற்றா னெடிதுய்க்குமாறு—"if one's food has been digested let one "eat with moderation; for that is the way to prolong the life of "an embodied soul."—மாறுபா டில்லாத வுண்டி மறுத் துண்ணி னூறுபா டில்லை யுயிர்க்கு—"there will be no "disaster to one's life, if one eats with moderation food that is "not disagreeable."—இழிவறிந் துண்பான்க ணின்பம்போ னிற்குங்கழிபே ரிரையான்க ணோய்—"as pleasure dwells "with him who eats moderately, so disease dwells with the "glutton who eats voraciously."—தீயள வன்றித் தெரியான் பெரிதுண்ணி னோயள வின்றிப் படும்—"he will be afflicted "with numberless diseases, who eats immoderately, ignorant of "the rules of health."—நோய்நாடி நோய்முத னாடி யது தணிக்கும் வாய்நாடி வாய்ப்பச் செயல்—"let the physi- "cian enquire into the nature of the disease, its cause and its "method of cure and treat it faithfully according to medical "rule."—உற்றா னளவும் பிணியளவுங் காலமுங் கற்றான் கருதிச் செயல்—"the learned physician should ascertain the "condition of his patient, the nature of his disease, and the season "of the year and then proceed with his treatment."—உற்றவன் றீர்ப்பான்மருந்துழைச் செல்வானென் றப்பானாற் கூற்றே மருந்து—"medical science consists of four parts, viz., "patient, physician, medicine and compounder; and each of "these again contains four sub-divisions."——**(2)** The following are two key-lists in the briefest possible terms of the principal vegetable drugs employed by veidyans for which vernacular names are known; further information must be traced in the glossary paragraphs through the small-type cross references at end of this volume; see also vricsham, 7, for the method of expressing the products, &c., of plants in the dravidian languages.—"*a*" Abies webbiana, himalayan silver fir, leaf, twig; Abrus precatorius, indian liquorice, root, seed; Abutilon indicum, country mallow, leaf; Acacia arabica, babool, gum, bark; Acacia catechu, catechu, cutch; Acalypha fruticosa, chinny, infusion of leaf; Acalypha indica, cooppamainy, leaf; Achyranthes aspera, indian burr, whole plant; Aconitum ferox, indian aconite, root; Aconitum heterophyllum, atees, root; Acorus calamus, sweet-flag, root; Adansonia digitata, baobab, pulp, bark; Adhatoda vasica, malabar nut, leaf, flower; Ægle marmelos, bael, pulp, root-bark, leaf; Ærua lanata, woolly ærua, decoction of root; Agave americana, american aloe, root; Ailanthus excelsa, coromandel ailanto, bark; Ailanthus malabarica, malabar ailanto, gum resin, bark; Alangium lamarckii, ancola, root-bark; Alhagi maurorum, arabian manna, manna; Allium cepa, onion, bulb; Allium sativum, garlic, bulb; Aloe littoralis, coromandel aloe, juice of pulp; Aloe socotrina, bombay aloe, aloes; Aloe vulgaris, barbadoes aloe, inspissated juice of leaf, pulp of leaf; Alpinia galanga, greater galangal, root; Alpinia officinarum, lesser galangal, root; Amarantus campestris, field spinach, decoction of root; Amarantus spinosus, thorny spinach, leaf, root; Ammannia baccifera, blistering ammannia, whole plant; Anacardium occidentale, cashew, oil from nut; Anacyclus pyrethrum, pellitory, root; Anamirta cocculus, indian berry, fruit; Andrographis paniculata, french chiretta, root and stem; Andropogon muricatus, cuscus, root; Andropogon schœnanthus, lemon grass, oil, leaf; Anisochilus carnosus, country lavender, leaf; Anisomeles malabarica, malabar catmint, leaf; Anthemis nobilis, chamomile, dried flower heads; Aquilaria agallocha, eagle wood, wood; Arachis hypogæa, groundnut, oil; Areca catechu, areca, catechu; Argemone mexicana, mexican poppy, oil; Argyreia speciosa, broad-leaved bind-weed, leaf; Aristolochia bracteata, indian worm killer, whole plant; Aristolochia indica, isharmool, root; Artemisia vulgaris, indian absinth, dried plant; Asparagopsis ascendens, indian salep, dried tuberous root; Asparagopsis floribunda, shakaukool, tuberous root; Asparagopsis sarmentosa, climbing asparagus, fresh tuberous root; Astragalus verus, tragacanth, gum; Averrhoa carambola, coromandel gooseberry, leaf, root, fruit; Balsamodendron mukul, mookul bdellium, bdellium; Balsamodendron myrrha, myrrh, gum, seed; Balsamodendron opobalsamum, balm of gilead, gum-resin; Balsamodendron roxburghii, indian bdellium, gum-resin; Bambusa arundinacea, common bamboo, tabasheer; Barleria prionitis, common nail-dye, juice of leaf; Barringtonia racemosa, common indian oak, bud, root, fruit; Bassia longifolia, common mohwah, bark and flower; Bauhinia tomentosa, wild mountain ebony, seed, leaf, root-bark; Berberis aristata, berberry, root-bark, watery extract; Bixa orellana, monkey turmeric, pulp, seed; Bœrhaavia repens, var. diffusa, spreading hog weed, root; Bombax malabaricum, red cotton-tree, gum-resin; Borassus flabelliformis, palmyra, toddy; Boswellia serrata, yellow dammer, gum-resin; Boswellia serrata, var. glabra, yellow dammer, gum-resin; Brassica alba, white mustard, seed; Brassica nigra, black mustard, seed; Breynia rhamnoides, var. genuina, poolah shrub, leaf, root-bark; Buchanania latifolia, chironjee, kernel; Butea frondosa, bengal kino, seed, flower, gum, juice of seed; Cacalia kleinia, hart's ear, bark, flower; Cæsalpinia bonducella, bonduc, seed; Cæsalpinia sappan, sappan, wood; Calamus draco, sumatra dragon's blood, resin; Calophyllum inophyllum, common poon, oil; Calotropis gigantia, mudar, root bark, milky juice; Canarium commune, elemi, resin; Canarium strictum, black dammer, dammer; Cannabis sativa, indian hemp, dried flowering tops; Canthium parviflorum, thorny webera, bark, young shoot; Capsicum annuum, common chilly, dried ripe fruit; Cardiospermum halicacabum, balloon vine, leaf, root; Carica papaya, papaw, milky juice, seed; Carthamus tinctorius, safflower, oil, seed, flower; Carum carui, caraway, fruit; Carum copticum, ajwaun, fruit; Carum roxburghianum, ajmood ajwaun, fruit; Cassia absus, black horse gram, seed; Cassia alata, ring-worm shrub, leaf; Cassia angustifolia, tinnevelly senna, leaf; Cassia auriculata, tungaid, bark, seed; Cassia fistula, indian laburnum, pulp; Cassia obovata, aleppo senna, leaf; Cassia tora, chakondah, leaf; seed; Celastrus paniculata, malkangany, oil; Cephalandra indica, indian caper, root; Chrysanthemum coronarium, indian chamomile, flower; Cicer arietinum, bengal gram, vinegar; Cichorium intybus, indian endive, seed; Cinnamomum camphora, camphor cinnamon, camphor; Cinnamomum tamala, cassia cinnamon, cassia lignea, buds; Cinnamomum zeylanicum, ceylon cinnamon, bark, leaf; Citrullus colocynthis, colocynth, dried pulp; Citrus aurantium, var. aurantium proper, sweet orange, rind, fruit; Citrus medica, var. acida, sour lime, fruit; Citrus medica, var. medica proper, citron, fruit; Cleome viscosa, wild mustard, seed, leaf, juice; Clerodendron inerme, sangcooppy, juice of root and leaf; Clerodendron phlomoides, tirootauly, juice of leaf; Clerodendron serratum, knotted bhraungy, root, leaf; Clitoria ternatea, crow creeper, seed, root; Cochlospermum gossypium, golden silk cotton, gum; Cocos nucifera, cocoanut, oil; Coffea arabica, coffee, seed; Colchicum autumnale, wild colchicum, corm, seed; Convolvulus scammonia, scammony, resin; Coptis teeta, mishmee bitter, root; Corallocarpus epigæa, snake caper, root; Cordia myxa, small sebesten, fruit; Cordia obliqua, large sebesten, fruit; Coriandrum sativum, coriander, seed; Coscinium fenestratum, false calumba, wood; Costus speciosus, arabian costus, rhizome; Cratæva religiosa, garlic pear, leaf; Crinum asiaticum, poison lily, leaf; Crocus sativus, saffron, stigmas; Crotalaria juncea, sunn, seed; Crotalaria verrucosa, forest giligitcha, juice of leaf; Croton tiglium, purging croton, oil, seed; Cucumis melo, common melon, seed; Cucumis melo, var. utilissimus, country melon, seed; Cucumis sativus, common cucumber, seed; Cucumis trigonus, country cucumber, root; Cucurbita maxima, great pumpkin, seed; Cuminum cyminum, cummin, seed; Curculigo orchioides, weevil root, root; Curcuma angustifolia, malabar arrowroot, starch; Curcuma aromatica, round zedoary, rhizome; Curcuma longa, turmeric, rhizome; Curcuma zedoaria, long zedoary, root; Cydonia vulgaris, quince, seed; Cynodon dactylon, hurrially, root, leaf; Cyperus rotundus, common sedge, root; Dæmia extensa, hedge cotton, whole plant; Datura fastuosa, purple datura, leaf, seed; Datura fastuosa, var. alba, white datura, leaf; Daucus carota, carrot, seed; Dichrostachys cinerea, ashy babool, root; Diospyros embryopteris, gaub, fruit; Dipterocarpus turbinatus, gurjan, wood oil; Dorema ammoniacum, gum ammoniac; Dracontium polyphyllum, wild telinga potato, root; Dregea volubilis, nakchiknee silk cotton, leaf, root, tender stalk; Eclipta alba, bhangrah, whole plant, seed; Ehretia buxifolia, rough coorvitchy, root; Elettaria cardamomum, cardamom, capsule; Embelia ribes, byebarang, berry; Enicostema littorale, small chiretta, whole plant; Epicarpurus orientalis, stunted jack, bark, milky juice; Eriodendron anfractuosum, silk cotton, gum, bark, root; Erythroxylon monogynum, deccany deodar, young leaf, tender shoot; Eugenia caryophyllata, clove tree, flower buds; Eugenia jambolana, common jamoon, fruit, bark; Eugenia jambolana, var. caryophyllifolia, clove-leaved jamoon, fruit; Euphorbia nereifolia, leafy milk-hedge, milky juice; Euphorbia tirucalli, round milk-hedge, root; Euphorbia tortilis, twisting milk-hedge, milky juice; Evolvulus alsinoides, chickweed, whole plant; Feronia elephantum, wood-apple, gum; Ferula narthex, asafœtida, gum; Ficus bengalensis, banyan, milky juice, bark; Ficus carica, european fig tree, fruit; Ficus racemosa, country fig, bark, seed; Ficus religiosa, peepul, bark, seed; Flacourtia cataphracta, indian plum, leaf, young shoot, bark; Garcinia morella, ceylon gamboge, gum; Gardenia gummifera, decamallee, resin; Gardenia lucida, decamallee, resinous exudation; Glycirrhiza glabra, liquorice, root; Glycosmis pentaphylla, conjy, wood; Gmelina asiatica, small cashmere tree, leaf; Gnaphalium indicum, indian cudweed, root; Gossypium arboreum, tree cotton, cotton, root; Gossypium barbadense, american cotton, cotton, root; Gossypium herbaceum, indian cotton, cotton, root; Grangea maderaspatana, madras absinth, leaf; Gymnema sylvestre, small indian ipecacuanha, leaf; Gynandropsis pentaphylla, dog mustard, leaf; Helicteres isora, screw tree, capsule, seedvessel; Helleborus niger, black hellebore, root; Helmia bulbifera, malacca yam, root; Hemidesmus indicus, indian sarsaparilla, root; Herpestis monniera, water hyssop, leaf, root, stalk; Hibiscus esculentus, common bendy, fresh immature capsules; Hibiscus rosa-sinensis, china rose bendy, flower, leaf; Holarrhena antidysenterica, tellicherry bark, bark, seed, root; Hordeum vulgare, barley; Hydnocarpus venenata, fish poison tree, oil, kernel; Hydrocotyle asiatica, indian pennywort, leaf, root; Hygrophila spinosa neermoolly, root, leaf; Hyoscyamus niger, henbane, seeds; Illicium anisatum, star anise, fruit; Indigofera argentea, wild indigo; Indigofera aspalathoides, shiva's neem, leaf, flower, tender shoot; Indigofera enneaphylla, red nerinjy, whole plant; Ionidium suffruticosum, one-leaf lotus, leaf, tender stalk, root; Ipomæa hederacea, kaladanah, seed; Ipomæa quamoclit, indian pink, root; Ipomæa turpethum, indian jalap, root; Jasminum angustifolium, wild jasmine, root; Jasminum sambac, arabian jasmine, flowers; Jatropha curcas, physic-nut, oil; Juniperus communis, juniper, berry; Justicia tranquebariensis, tranquebar gendarussa, juice of leaf; Lageuaria vulgaris, bottle gourd, seed; Lawsonia alba, henna plant, leaf, seed, root; Lepidium sativum, cress, seed; Leucas indica, wild tombay, whole plant; Linum usitatissimum, flax, seed, oil; Lippia nodiflora, creeping vervain, leaf, tender stalk; Liquidambar orientale, indian storax, storax; Lodoicea seychellarum, double cocoanut, kernel; Luffa acutangula, common luffa, seed; Mallotus philippensis, kamela, powder from pod; Mangifera indica, mango, seed, bark; Melaleuca leucadendron, cajeput, oil; Melia azadirachta, margosa, bark, gum, seed, toddy; Melia azedarach, large neem, root-bark;

Melissa officinalis, persian toolsy, flower; Mentha arvensis, common mint, leaf; Michelia champaca, champak, bark; Mimusops elengi, ilanjy, bark; Mimusops hexandra, monkey face paulay, fruit, wood; Mirabilis jalapa, false jalap, root, leaf; Mollugo cerviana, hazaur danah; Mollugo spergula, indian chickweed, leaf; Momordica dioica, bristly balsam apple, root; Morinda umbellata, small ach root; Moringa pterygosperma, indian horse-radish, root, bark, gum; Mucuna pruriens, common cowitch, root, leaf, pod; Murraya kœnigii, curry-leaf tree, leaf; Musa paradisiaca, plantain, leaf; Myrica sapida, box myrtle, bark; Myristica fragrans, common nutmeg, nut; Myristica malabarica, malabar nutmeg, kernel; Nardostachys jatamansi, indian spikenard, root; Nelumbium speciosum, sacred lotus, filament, seed, leaf, juice of leaf and flower stalk, petals, root; Nicotiana tabacum, tobacco, leaf; Nigella sativa, small fennel, seed; Nymphæa lotus, red indian water-lily, flower, root and seed; Nymphæa odorata, purple indian water-lily; Ocimum basilicum, sweet basil, seed, flower, juice of leaf; Ocimum sanctum, sacred basil, leaf; Ocimum sanctum, var. hirsuta, rough basil, leaf; Oldenlandia umbellata, chayroot, leaf; Orchis mascula, salep, root; Ormocarpum sennoides, wild moringa, root, root-bark; Oryza sativa, paddy, rice; Osbeckia aspera, forest bengal gram; Oxalis corniculata, sorrel, leaf, tender stalk, flower; Papaver somniferum, opium poppy, opium, poppy-head, seed; Pavetta indica, pavetta, root; Pavonia odorata, peramootty, root; Pavonia zeylanica, shittamootty, root; Pedalium murex, elephant nerinjy, fresh plant; Peganum harmala, syrian rue, seed; Peucedanum graveolens, dill, leaf, seed, root; Phœnix farinifera, small date, gum; Phyllanthus emblica, emblic myrobalan, fruit, seed; Phyllanthus maderaspatensis, madras phyllanthus; Phyllanthus multiflorus, poolah, root; Phyllanthus niruri, var. genuinus, neeroory, root, leaf, young shoot; Picrorhiza kurrooa, bitter root, root; Pimenta officinalis, pimento, bark, berry; Pimpinella anisum, anise, seed; Piper betel, betel pepper, juice of leaf; Piper cubeba, cubeb pepper, dried berry; Piper longum, long pepper, dried berry; Piper nigrum, black pepper, dried berry; Pistacia lentiscus, mastic, resin; Pithecolobium dulce, corcapilly, seed, fruit; Plantago ovata, spogel, seed; Plumbago zeylanica, ceylon lead-wort, root; Polygala senega, senegal nangay, dried root; Polygonum barbatum, alligator's nose, leaf, seed; Pongamia glabra, indian beech, oil, leaf, root; Portulaca quadrifida, small indian purslane, juice; Premna integrifolia, moonnay, whole plant, root, leaf; Prosopis spicigera, shamee, pod; Prunus amygdalus, almond, nut; Psoralea corylifolia, bawchee, seed; Pterocarpus marsupium, malabar kino, gum; Pterocarpus santalinus, red sanders, wood; Punica grantum, pomegranate, root bark, rind, seed; Quercus infectoria, dyer's oak, gall; Randia dumetorum, common emetic nut, nut; Raphanus sativus, country radish, seed, root; Rheum emodi, indian rhubarb, root; Rheum moorcroftianum, indian rhubarb, root; Ricinus communis, castor oil, oil, root; Rosa centifolia, cabbage rose, flower; Rubia cordifolia, munjeet, root; Saccharum officinarum, sugar-cane, sugar, treacle; Sansevieria roxburghiana, bowstring hemp, root, juice of tender shoots; Santalum album, sandal, wood; Sapindus trifoliatus, soap nut, capsule, root; Securinega leucopyrus, white honey shrub, root; Semecarpus anacardium, marking nut, juice; Sesamum indicum, gingelly, oil; Sida carpinifolia, lance-leaved balah, root, leaf; Smilax china, common china root, root; Solanum indicum, indian night-shade, root; Solanum melongena, brinjaul, leaf, seed; Solanum nigrum, indian hounds' berry, leaf, root, seed; Solanum pubescens, rameshwaram shoonday, root; Solanum trilobatum, prickly shoonday, root, leaf, berry, flower; Solanum xanthocarpum, prickly brinjaul, dried plant, root, seed; Soymida febrifuga, rohan tree, bark; Sphæranthus amaranthoides, fever toolsy, whole plant, root, bark; Sphæranthus indicus, seed toolsy, whole plant, root, bark; Stereospermum chelonoides, pauthiry, root, flower; Strychnos nux-vomica, poison nut, leaf, bark, seed; Strychnos potatorum, clearing-nut, nut; Styrax benzoin, gum benjamin, benzoin; Swertia chirata, himalayan chiretta, dried stalk with root; Tamarindus indica, tamarind, pulp; Tephrosia purpurea, zanzibar indigo, root; Terminalia belerica, belleric myrobalan, fruit; Terminalia catappa, country almond, fruit; Terminalia chebula, chebulic myrobalan, fruit, flower; Terminalia tomentosa, var. typica, black murdah, juice of leaf; Thespesia populnea, portia, fruit; Thevetia nereifolia, exile tree, bark; Tinospora cordifolia, goolancha, dried tender shoots, leaf, fresh juice, root, stem; Toddalia aculeata, lopez root, root-bark; Tragia cannabina, small caunjory, root; Tragia involucrata, caunjory, root, juice, fruit; Trianthema monogyna, shauranay, root; Tribulus terrestris, land caltrops, fruit, leaf, root; Trichosanthes cucumerina, wild snake gourd, tender shoots, dried capsule, seed, juice of leaf and of root; Trichosanthes palmata, bitter snake gourd, root, fruit; Trigonella fœnumgræcum, fenugreek, seed; Triticum vulgare, wheat; Tylophora asthmatica, indian ipecacuanha, leaf, root; Uncaria gambier, gambier, catechu; Urginia indica, squill, bulb; Vateria indica, piney, dammer; Ventilago madraspatana, pappily, bark; Vernonia anthelmintica, wild cummin, seed; Vitex negundo, notchy leaf, dried fruit; Vitex trifolia, water notchy, leaf; Vitis carnosa, acid naralay, root; Vitis quadrangularis, piranday, leaf and young shoots; Vitis vinifera, grape vine, raisins; Wedelia calendulacea, yellow bhangrah, leaf; Withania somnifera, asgand, fruit, root and leaf; Wrightia tinctoria, paula indigo, bark and seeds; Zingiber officinale, ginger, rhizhome; Zizyphus glabrata, carookvauly; Zizyphus jujuba, bair, kino, root, bark, leaf, seed and fruit.—"*b*" Absinth, artemisia, grangea; Ach root, morinda; Aconite, aconitum; Ailanto, ailanthus; Ajwaun, carum; Alligator's nose, polygonum; Almond, prunus, terminalia; Aloe, agave; Ammoniac, dorema; Ancola, alangium; Anise, illicium, pimpinella; Arrowroot, curcuma; Asafœtida, ferula; Asgand, withania; Asparagus, asparagopsis; Atees, aconitum; Babool, acacia, dichrostachys; Bael, ægle; Bair, zizyphus, Balah, sida; Balm, balsamodendron; Balsam apple, momordica; Bamboo, bambusa; Banyan, ficus; Baobab, adansonia; Barley, hordeum; Basil, ocimum; Bawchee, psoralea; Bdellium, balsamodendron; Beech, pongamia; Bendy, hibiscus; Benjamin, styrax; Berberry, berberis; Bhangrah, eclipta, wedelia; Bhraungy, clerodendron; Bindweed, argyreia; Bitter root, picrorhiza; Bonduc, cæsalpinia; Box myrtle, myrica; Brinjaul, solanum; Burr, achyranthes; Byebarang, embelia; Cajeput, melaleuca; Caltrops, tribulus; Calumba, coscinium; Caper, cephalandra, corallocarpus; Caraway, carum; Cardamom, elettaria; Carookvauly, zizyphus; Carrot, daucus; Cashew, anacardium; Cashmere tree, gmelina; Castor, ricinus; Catechu, acacia; Catmint, anisomeles; Caunjory, tragia; Chakondah, cassia; Chamomile, anthemis, chrysanthemum; Champak, michelia; Chayroot, oldenlandia; Chickweed, evolvulus, mollugo; Chilly, capsicum; China root, smilax; Chinny, acalypha; Chiretta, andrographis, enicostema, swertia; Chironjee, buchanania; Cinnamon, cinnamomum; Citron, citrus; Clearing nut, strychnos; Clove, eugenia; Cocoanut, cocos, lodoicea; Coffee, coffea; Colocynth, citrullus; Conjy, glycosmis; Cooppamainy, acalypha; Coorvitchy, ehretia; Corcapilly, pithecolobium; Coriander, coriandrum; Cotton, bombax, cochlospermum, dæmia, eriodendron, gossypium; Cowitch, mucuna; Cress, lepidium; Crow creeper, clitoria; Cucumber, cucumis; Cudweed, gnaphalium; Cummin, cuminum, vernonia; Curry-leaf, murraya; Cuscus, andropogon; Dammer, boswellia, canarium; Date, phœnix; Decamallee, gardenia; Deodar, erythroxylon; Dill, peucedanum; Dragon's blood, calamus; Eagle wood, aquilaria; Ebony, bauhinia; Elemi, canarium; Emetic nut, randia; Endive, cichorium; Exile tree, thevetia; Fennel, nigella; Fenugreek, trigonella; Fig, ficus; Fir, abies; Fish poison, hydnocarpus; Flax, linum; Galangal, alpinia; Gambier, uncaria; Gamboge, garcinia; Garlic, allium; Garlic pear, cratæva; Gaub, diospyros; Gendarussa, justica; Giligitcha, crotalaria; Gingelly, sesamum; Ginger, zingiber; Goolancha, tinospora; Gooseberry, averrhoa; Gourd, lagenaria, trichosanthes; Gram, cassia, cicer, osbeckia; Ground nut, arachis; Gurjan, dipterocarpus; Hart's ear, cacalia; Hazaur danah, mollugo; Hellebore, helleborus; Hemp, cannabis, sanseviera; Henbane, hyoscyamus; Henna, lawsonia; Hog weed, boerhaavia; Horse radish, moringa; Hounds' berry, solanum; Hurrially, cynodon; Hyssop, herpestes; Ilanjy, mimusops; Indian berry, anamirta; Indigo, indigofera, tephrosia, wrightia; Ipecacuanha, gymnema, tylophora; Isharmool, aristolochia; Jack, epicarpurus; Jalap, ipomæa, mirabilis; Jasmine, jasminum; Jaumoon, eugenia; Juniper, juniperus; Kaladanah, ipomæa; Kamela, mallotus; Kino, butea, pterocarpus; Laburnum, cassia; Lavender, anisochilus; Leadwort, plumbago; Lemon grass, andropogon; Lily, crinum; Liquorice, abrus, glycirrhiza; Lopez root, toddalia; Lotus, ionidium, nelumbium; Malabar nut, adhatoda; Malkangany, celastrus; Mallow, abutilon; Mango, mangifera; Manna, alhagi; Margosa, melia; Marking nut, semecarpus; Mastic, pistacia; Melon, cucumis; Mexican poppy, argemone; Milk-hedge, euphorbia; Mint, mentha; Mishmee, coptis; Mohwah, bassia; Moonnay, premna; Moringa, ormocarpum; Mudar, calotropis; Munjeet, rubia; Murdah, terminalia; Mustard, brassica, cleome, gynandropsis; Myrobalan, phyllanthus, terminalia; Myrrh, balsamodendron; Nail dye, barleria; Nangay, polygala; Naralay, vitis; Neem, indigofera, melia; Neermoolly, hygrophila; Neeroory, phyllanthus; Nerinjy, indigofera, pedalium; Night shade, solanum; Notchy, vitex; Nutmeg, myristica; Oak, barringtonia, quercus; Onion, allium; Orange, citrus; Paddy, oryza; Palmyra, borassus; Papaw, carica; Pappily, ventilago; Paulay, mimusops; Pauthiry, stereospermum; Peepul, ficus; Pellitory, anacyclus; Pennywort, hydrocotyle; Pepper, piper; Peramootty, pavonia; Physic nut, jatropha; Pimento, pimenta; Piney, vateria; Pink, ipomæa; Piranday, vitis; Plantain, musa; Plum, flacourtia; Poison nut, strychnos; Pomegranate, punica; Poolah, breynia, phyllanthus; Poon, calophyllum; Poppy, papaver; Portia, thespesia; Potato, dracontium; Pumpkin, cucurbita; Purslane, portulaca; Quince, cydonia; Radish, raphanus; Rhubarb, rheum; Ring-worm shrub, cassia; Rohan, soymida; Rose, rosa; Rue, peganum; Safflower, carthamus; Saffron, crocus; Salep, asparagopsis, orchis; Sandal, santalum; Sanders, pterocarpus; Sangcooppy, clerodendron; Sappan, cæsalpinia; Sarsaparilla, hemidesmus; Scammony, convolvulus; Screw tree, helicteres; Sebesten, cordia; Sedge, cyperus; Senna, cassia; Shakaukool, asparagopsis; Shamee, prosopis; Shauranay, trianthema; Shittamootty, pavonia; Shoonday, solanum; Soap nut, sapindus; Sorrel, oxalis; Spikenard, nardostachys; Spinach, amarantus; Spogel, plantago; Squill, urginia; Storax, liquidamber; Sugar-cane, saccharum; Sunn, crotalaria; Sweet flag, acorus; Tamarind, tamarindus; Tellicherry bark, holarrhena; Tirootauly, clerodendron; Tobacco, nicotiana; Toolsy, melissa, sphæranthus; Toombay, leucas; Tragacanth, astragalus; Tungaid, cassia; Turmeric, bixa, curcuma; Vervain, lippia; Vine, cardiospermum, vitis; Water-lily, nymphæa; Webera, canthium; Weevil root, curculigo;

Wheat, triticum; White honey, securinega; Wood-apple, feronia; Wormkiller, aristolochia; Yam, helmia; Zedoary, curcuma.——(3) The following is a key-list of the principal animal drugs employed by veidyans:—Amber-grisea [amber]; Bombyx, silk-worm [puttoopoochy]; Calculus cisticus bovis, cow bezoar [gorochanay]; Calculus cisticus camelinus [gorochanay]; Castoreum, musk [custoory]; Cera, wax [mom]; Coccus cacti, linn., cochineal insect [kirmiz]; Coccus lacca, lac [q.v.]; Lac, cow's milk [paul]; Mel, honey [shahad]; Moschus, musk [custoory]; Mylabris cichorii, fabr., telini [q.v.]; Peacock's feathers [mayil]; Ragoom ayeo, lizard [chipkalee]; Silk-worm's nests [puttoo poochy]; Turtle's shell [aumay].——(4) The following is a key-list of the principal mineral drugs employed by veidyans:—Acidum arseniosum [paushaunam]; Alumen [padicauram]; Ammonii chloridum [nowshaudar]; Antimonium sulphuratum [soorma]; Argentum [velly]; Arsenicum auri pigmentum [wurkee hartaul]; Arsenicum flavum [hartaul]; Arsenicum oxidum album [soofaid soombal]; Arsenicum rubrum [manoshilay]; Aurum [pon]; Bezoar [q.v.]; Bolus armenia rubra [ghilarminy]; Creta præparata [sheemay choonam]; Cupri sulphas [mayil toottam]; Fel vitri [valaiyal ooppoo]; Ferri oxidum magneticum [cauntam]; Ferri peroxidum hydratum [iroomboo tooroo]; Ferri sulphas [anna bhaidy]; Gypsum [carpoor shilajit]; Hydrargyri bisulphuretum [shangarf]; Hydrargyri oxidum rubrum [rasasindooram]; Hydrargyri perchloridum [shavveeram]; Hydrargyri subchloridum [rascapoor]; Plumbi carbonas [vellyeeyam]; Plumbi oxidum rubrum [sendoor]; Plumbi oxidum [moordarsing]; Potassæ nitras [shorah]; Potassæ tartras acida [draucsha ooppoo]; Sodæ biboras [vengauram]; Sodæ carbonas [sujjeekhaur]; Sodii chloridum [ooppoo]; Limestone [sookkaunoull]; Sulphur [gandhac]; Tabasheer [q.v.]; Zinci sulphas [vellaytoottam]; Zincum [tootnaug].——(5) The following is a list of the principal diseases according to the veidyans, with some particulars of their medical diagnosis where that differs essentially from the european.——*Agny vranam* (अग्निव्रण - agnivrana, San.; انگارکا داغ - angárkádágh, Hind.; ಸುಟ್ಟಘಾಯ - suttagháya, Can.; నిప్పుగాయము - nippugáyamu, Tel.; തീപ്പുണ്ണ് - típpunnu, Mal.; நெருப்புப்பட்டபுண் - neruppuppattabun, Tam.). San. from (agni, san. fire + vrana, san. wound). Hind. from (angár, hind. fire + dágh, pers. wound). Can. from (sutta, can. burnt + gháya, can. wound). Tel. from (nippu, tel. fire + gáyamu, tel. wound). Mal. from (tí, mal. fire + pun, mal. wound). Tam. from (neruppu, tam. fire + padu, tam. to touch + pun, tam. ulcer). Burn. There are four degrees:—Plooshtam, in which there is severe pain, and change of color on the part. Door dagdham, when accompanied with blisters, with much redness and pain. Sama dagdham, when it is black and does not produce much pain. Aty dagdham, when the part is separated with the destruction of the vessels, &c., with fever, thirst, faintness, and the wound heals slowly.——*Ajeernam* (अजीर्ण - ajírna, San.; بدهضمی - badhazmí, Hind.; ಅಜೀರ್ಣ - ajírna, Can.; అజీర్ణము - ajírnamu, Tel.; അജീർണ്ണം - ajírnnam, Mal.; அசீரணம் - asíranam, Tam.). Title from sanscrit. San. from (a, san. negative prefix + jrí, san. to digest). Hind. from (bad, pers. bad + hazmí, pers. digestion). Drav. from sanscrit. Indigestion. When this occurs, there is a disinclination to exertion, with giddiness; the body is heavy, the color of the skin bad, and there is no passage of air; such a person does not like his food, his understanding is impaired, and his bowels are either constipated or there are copious dejections. The unfavorable symptoms are fainting, delirium, vomiting, copious discharge of saliva from mouth, with languor and giddiness. Varieties:—Auma ajeernam, in which the body feels heavy with a flow of saliva and phlegm from the nose; the eyelids swell, and there are eructations of the substances eaten, some time before. Vishtabdha ajeernam, in which the air is deranged, producing severe pain in the stomach with flatulency. The stomach swells, there are no dejections, no air escapes, and the person remains stupid, with his understanding impaired, and pain over the body. Vidagdha ajeernam, in which the bile is deranged, the person has sour eructations, complains of thirst, is giddy and often doses, has pain in the abdomen, and free perspiration over the body which feels hot.——*Alasacam* (अलसक - alasaka, San.; استسقاء طبلی - istiskáiktablí, Hind.; ಹೊಟ್ಟೆಉಬ್ಬುವಿಕೆ - hotteubbuvike, Can.; కడుపుబ్బసము - kadupubbasamu, Tel.; വയറുവീർപ്പ് - vayaruvírppu, Mal.; வயிற்றுப்புசம் - vayittuppusam, Tam.). Title from sanscrit. San. from (alasa, san. inactive). Hind. from (istiská, ar. dropsy + tabal, ar. drum); from the appearance of the patient's belly. Can. from (hotte, can. belly + ubbuvike, can. swelling). Tel. from (kadupu, tel. belly + ubbu, tel. to swell). Mal. from (vayar, mal. belly + vírppu, mal. swelling). Tam. from (vayiru, tam. belly + uppusam, tam. swelling). Tympanitis. The abdomen becomes enlarged and tight, with a rumbling noise and the air passes upwards, followed by a constipation of fæces and air; with great thirst, eructations, and pain in the stomach.——*Antruvriddhy* (अन्त्रवृद्धि - antravriddhi, San.; رودےکی بیماری - rodekíbímárí, Hind.; బుడ్డ - budda, Tel.; അന്ത്രവൃദ്ധി - ántravriddhi, Mal.; வளிப்பிடுக்கு - valippidukku, Tam.). Title from sanscrit. San. from (antra, san. intestines + vriddh, san. to increase). Hind. from (rodá, hind. gut + bímárí, hind. disease). Tel. means a bubble. Mal. from sanscrit. Tam. from (vali, tam. air + pidukku, tam. testicle). Rupture.——*Apasmauram* (अपस्मार - apasmára, San.; صرع - sara, Ar.; مرگی - mirgí, Hind.; ಅಪಸ್ಮಾರರೋಗ - apasmáraróga, Can.; కాకిసోమాల - kákisómála, Tel.; സന്നിവലി - sannivali, Mal.; காக்காய்வலி - kákkáyvali, Tam.). Title from sanscrit. San. from (apa, san. negative prefix + smiri, san. to remember). Ar. from (sara, ar. to throw down). Tel. from (káki, tel. crow + somma, tel. faintness). Mal. from (sanni, mal. convulsions + vali, mal. pull). Tam. from (kákkáy, tam. crow + vali, tam. convulsion); probably from the peculiar affection of vision during fit. Epilepsy. Sudden loss of sense, loss of sight, and the person falls down with convulsions. There are four kinds:—Vautaja apasmauram; the symptoms are followed by shivering, grinding of the teeth, foaming at the mouth, and hurried respiration, and to the patient every object appears obscured, red, and confused. Peitica apasmauram; the symptoms are accompanied with a yellowness of the body and countenance; to the patient everything appears of a yellowish color, the sputa is of the same color and the eyes appear red; the patient has great thirst and everything feels hot as if enveloped in flames. Capha apasmauram; the symptoms are whiteness of the countenance and body, the saliva and foam are of the same color, the body is cold, and the patient shivers; the person sees everything white, and as it appears to approach near him, he faints; these fits cease very slowly. Sannipauta apasmauram; all the symptoms of the other varieties are present; this is incurable if not recent, as the person becomes weak and emaciated, and the fits are frequent, and accompanied with severe convulsive movements of the body; the eye brows contract frequently with the eye lids, and the eyes move rapidly.——*Apdtaunacam* (अपतानक - apatánaka, San.; تشنج - tashannuj, Hind.; ಸನ್ನಿರೋಗ - sanniróga, Can.; మాంద్యజన్ని - mándyadzanni, Tel.; സന്നിവ്യാധി - sannivyádhi, Mal.; மாந்தசன்னி - mándasanni, Tam.). Title from sanscrit. San. from (apa, san. prefix of negation + tan, san. to extend). Hind. from (shanija, ar. to contract). Can. from (sanni, can. convulsions + róga, can. disease). Tel. from (mándyamu, tel. sluggishness + dzanni, tel. convulsions). Mal. from (sanni, mal. convulsions + vyádhi, san. disease). Tam. from (mándya, san. slowness + shanni, tam. shortened form of sannipáta, san. derangement of three humours). Convulsions. When air is much deranged and passes into the different vessels, it produces contractions of the body.——*Arshum* (अर्श - arsha, San.; بواسير - bawásír, Hind.; مولم - múlam, Dec.; ಮೂಲರೋಗ - múlaróga, Can.; మూలం - múlam, Tel.; മൂലരോഗം - múlarógam, Mal.; மூலம் - múlam, Tam.). Title from sanscrit. San. from (ri, san. to destroy). Hind. from (básúr, ar. tumour). Tel. means root. Can. and Mal. from (múlam, san. root + róga, san. disease). Tam. from (múla, san. root), from growth of tumours about the verge of anus. Piles. There are six varieties of this disease according as it is produced from deranged air [vautam], bile [pittam], phlegm [sheetam], the three humours deranged at the same time, diseased blood and the last form is congenital or hereditary.——*Ashmary* (अश्मरी - ashmarí, San.; سنگ مثانہ - sangimasánah, Hind.; ಅಶ್ಮರಿರೋಗ - ashmariróga, Can.; రాతిమేహము - rátiméhamu, Tel.; കല്ലടപ്പ് - kallatappu, Mal.; கல்லடைப்பு - kalladaippu, Tam.). Title from sanscrit. San. from (ashma, san. stone + rá, san. to give). Hind. from (sang, hind. stone + masánah, ar. bladder). Tel. from (ráyi, tel. stone + méhamu, tel. venereal affection). Mal. and Tam. from (kal, tam. stone + adai, tam. to be choked). Gravel.——*Astysrauvam* (अस्थिस्राव - ast'hisráva, San.; جريان مذی - jiryánimazí, Hind.; ಬಿಳುಪು ಹೋಗುವಮೇಹ - bilupuhóguvaméha, Can.; అస్థిరోగము - astirógamu, Tel.; അസ്ഥിസ്രാവം - ast'hisrávam, Mal.; எலும்புருக்கி - elumburukki, Tam.). Title from sanscrit. San. from (ast'hi, san. bone + srav, san. to flow). Hind. from (jiryán, ar. flowing + mazí, ar. whitish). Can. from (bilupu, can. whites + hógu, can. to discharge + méha, san. urinary). Tel. from (ast'hi, san. bone + róga, san. disease). Tam. from (elumbu, tam. bone + urukku, tam. to melt). Whites.——*Atisauram* (अतिसार - atisára, San.; پیچش - pechish, Hind.; ಉಷ್ಣಹೊರ್ಕಡೆ - ushnahorkade, Can.; నెత్తురుబంక - netturubanka, Tel.; അർശസ് - arshas, Mal.; சீதக்கடுப்பு - shíthakkaduppu, Tam.). Title from sanscrit. San. from (ati, san. intensive prefix + sri, san. to flow). Hind. from (pechídan, pers. to twist). Can. from (ushna, san. heat + horkade, can. ease nature). Tel. from (netturu, tel. blood + banka, tel. slime). Mal. from (arsha, san. piles); by mistake to dysentery. Tam. from (shítham, tam. mucus + kadu, tam. to ache). Dysentery. There are six varieties of the disease:—Vauta atisauram; there is much pain; the dejections are of a dark yellow colour, frothy, dry and frequent, and in small quantities mixed with the indigested substances, which have been eaten, pain is felt in the anus on the expulsion of air and the urine is scanty. Pitta atisauram; the dejections which have a bad smell, are hot and of a red yellowish colour like the water in which flesh has been steeped; there is also thirst, dozing, heat of body, free perspirations and tenesmus at the time of the evacuation, inflammation of the rectum with violent fever. Shlaishma atisauram; the patient dozes, the dejections are white, thick and constipated, mixed with phlegm [sheetam]; there is no appetite. Tridosha atisauram; the symptoms of this are a mixture of the above three. Shokabhaya atisauram ; the person has the internal fire of pakvaushayam or chyle receptacle or small intestines deranged by the watery vapours which are formed by grief, and passing into the pakvaushayam mix with the fire, and derange the bright blood of the part ; this blood is mixed with the dejections, often becomes putrid, and is expelled with them ; in other cases it is deranged by itself ; sometimes it has a bad smell, in other cases it has not ; if the dejections are frequent, the cure will be very difficult. Auma atisauram ; this is produced by mucus which deranges the aumashayam or chyme receptacle or stomach and is discharged frequently of various colors.——*Bhagandaram* (भगन्दर - bhagandara, San. ; ناسور - násúr, Hind. ; ಆಸನಪವಿತ್ರ - ásanapavitra, Can. ; ఆసనపవిత్రము - ásanapavitramu, Tel. ; ആസനപവിത്രവ്രണം - ásanapavitravranam, Mal. ; பவுத்திரம் - pavuttiram, Tam.). Title from sanscrit. San. from (bhaga, san. sexual organ + dar, san. to rend). Hind. from (nasara, ar. tearing flesh with a beak). Can. and Tel. from (ásana, san. anus + pavitra, san. rubbing). Mal. from (ásana, san. anus + pavitra, san. rubbing + vrana, san. wound). Tam. from (pavitra, san. rubbing). Fistula.——*Calah shotam* (कलाशोथ - kaláshót'ha, San. ; استسقازقی - istiskázikkí, Hind. ; విషపాండు - vishapándu, Tel. ; நீர்க்கோவை - nírkkóvai, Tam.). Title from sanscrit. San. from (kalá, san. cellular tissue + shót'ha, san. swelling, dropsy). Hind. from (istiská, ar. dropsy + zik, ar. water bag) ; from the appearance of the patient's belly. Tel. from (visha, san. poison + pándu, san. whiteness). Tam. from (nír, tam. water + kó, tam. to string). Anasarca.——*Candoo* (कण्डु - kandu, San. ; خارشت - khárisht, Pers. ; کھجلی - khujlí, Hind. ; ಖಜ್ಜಿ - khajji, Can. ; గజ్జి - gajji, Tel. ; ചൊറി - chori, Mal. ; சிரங்கு - shirangu, Tam.). Title from sanscrit. San. from (kand, san. to scratch). Pers. from (kharídan, pers. to itch). Hind. like canarese. Can. and Tel. from (kachhu, san. itch). Mal. means to scratch. Tam. from (shira, tam. to destroy). Itch [cooshtam].——*Carnashoolam* (कर्णशूल - karnashúla, San. ; درد گوش - dardigosh, Pers. ; کانکادرد - kánkádard, Hind. ; ಕಿವಿನೋವು - kivinóvu, Can. ; చెవిపోటు - chevipótu, Tel. ; ചെവികുത്ത - chevikutta, Mal. ; காதுநோவு - káthunóvu, Tam.). Title from sanscrit. San. from (karna, san. ear + shúla, san. pain). Pers. from (dard, pers. pain + gosh, pers. ear). Hind. from (kán, hind. ear + dard, pers. pain). Can. from (kivi, can. ear + nóvu, can. ache). Tel. from (chevi, san. ear + podutsu, tel. to pierce). Mal. from (chevi, san. ear + kuttu, mal. to pierce). Tam. from (káthu, tam. ear + nó, tam. to pain). Ear-ache. There are several varieties. Carnashoolam proper ; the vital air [vautam] in ear being deranged and confined in its passage by the other humours produces severe pain in the organ and is very difficult to cure. Carna samsrauvam ; this is produced by blows on the ear, by bathing in water during which water enters the ears, or by a boil in the part which suppurates. Carna gootacam ; this is produced by the wax in the ear becoming hard. Pratinanham ; the wax in the ear melts and passes out of the nose or mouth accompanied with much pain in the head. Crimy carnacam ; this is produced when worms form in the ear by flies depositing their eggs in it. Carna vidradhy ; there is great pain, burning and tightness in the ear with a discharge of yellow pus or blood. Carnapaucam ; by the derangements of bile [pittam], abscesses are formed in the ear. Praticarnacam ; this is produced by the deranged phlegm [sheetam] being discharged from the ear with a disagreeable smell.——*Carpang* (विसर्पिका - visarpiká, San. ; کرپان - karpán, Hind. ; కరపాణి - karapáni, Tel. ; കരപ്പാൻ - karappán, Mal. ; கரப்பான் - karappán, Tam.). Title from tamul. San. from (vi, san. intesive prefix + srip, san. to creep). Tel. and Mal. from tamul. Tam. from (karai, tam. to emaciate). See sep. title.——*Caumalay* (कामला - kámalá, San. ; یرقان - yarkán, Hind. ; ಕಾಮಾಲೆ - kámále, Can. ; కామాలి - kámáli, Tel. ; കാമാല - kámála, Mal. ; காமாலை - kámálai, Tam.). Title from sanscrit. San. from (káma, san. beauty + lu, san. to destroy). Drav. from sanscrit. Jaundice. This is produced by eating after an attack of anaemia such things as produce much bile [pittam] ; the increased bile enters the blood and flesh and produces especially yellowness of the eyes, the skin, the nails, and the face, accompanied with drowsiness, loss of strength, thirst and indigestion.——*Causam* (कास - kása, San. ; کھانسی - khánsí, Hind. ; ಕೆಮ್ಮು - kemmu, Can. ; దగ్గు - daggu, Tel. ; ചുമ - chuma, Mal. ; இருமல் - irumal, Tam.). Title from sanscrit. San. from (kás, san. to cough). Hind. from sanscrit. Tel. from the sound. Tam. from (irumu, tam. to cough). Cough. This is produced by smoke or dust entering the mouth and nostrils, by fighting, by great fatigue, by dry food, by articles of food entering the air passages or by resisting the calls of nature ; these causes derange the vital air [vautam] in the chest and trachea, by which the air which passes through the air passages to the mouth produces a peculiar noise ; the disease may likewise be produced by the ruptures of the respiratory organs, and by the deranged humours ; all these varieties of cough pass to consumption, if neglected. There are five sorts of Causam :—Vautica causam ; the symptoms are the change of voice, the dry and frequent cough with pain in the temples, head, stomach and chest ; the face becomes sallow, and the person becomes weak. Pittacausam ; in this the mouth is dry and bitter and the breath is hot with fever ; the person complains of thirst and severe pain over the body ; the expectoration is sour and of a yellowish color, and the skin becomes yellow and hot. Capha causam ; in this the mouth is full of mucus with headache, loss of appetite, languor, frequent cough with thick mucus expectoration ; the person cannot labor, has frequent fits of coughing, the body is heavy and weak, he has no appetite. Cshatacausam ; this is caused by excessive venery, fatigue, carrying heavy weights, going great distances when unaccustomed, and violent exercise upon horseback or elephants ; by these the air passages are injured or ulcerated when the patient is first attacked with dry cough followed by spitting of blood, pain in the throat and chest, which is increased by pressure ; the joints and other parts of body are painful, as if pins were penetrating it, fever, difficulty of breathing, thirst, hoarseness. Cshayacausam ; see under Cshayam.——*Chardicausam* (छर्दिकास - chhardikása, San. ; ککوان کی کھانسی - kakwánkíkhánsí, Hind. ; ನಾಯಿಕೆಮ್ಮು - náyikemmu, Can. ; కక్కువాయిదగ్గు - kakkuváyidaggu, Tel. ; എക്കച്ചുമ - ekkachuma, Mal. ; கக்குவான் - kakkuván, Tam.). Title from sanscrit. San. from (chhard, san. to vomit + kása, san. cough). Hind. from (kakku, tel. to vomit + váyi, tel. mouth + khánsí, hind. cough). Can. from (náyi, can. dog + kemmu, can. cough). Tel. from (kakku, tel. to vomit + vayi, tel. mouth + daggu, tel. cough). Mal. from (ekku, mal. to come up + chuma, mal. cough). Tam. from (kakku, tam. to vomit). Hooping cough.——*Cooshtam* (कुष्ठ - kusht'ha, San. ; جذام - juzám, Hind. ; ಕುಷ್ಠರೋಗ - kusht'haróga, Can. ; పెద్దరోగము - peddarógamu, Tel. ; കുഷ്ഠം - kushtam, Mal. ; குட்டம் - kuttam, Tam.). Hind. from (jazama, ar. to cut off). Tel. from (pedda, tel. great + róga, san. illness). Leprosy. This is the ἐλεφαντίασις of the Greeks. See sep. title.——*Cshavatoo* (क्षवथु - kshavat'hu, San. ; گلے کا درد - galekádard, Hind. ; ಗಂಟಲುಹುಣ್ಣು - gantluhunnu, Can. ; గొంతునొప్పి - gontunoppi, Tel. ; തൊണ്ടപുണ്ണ - tondapunna, Mal. ; தொண்டைநோவு - tondainóvu, Tam.). Title from sanscrit. San. from (kshu, san. to sneeze). Hind. from (galá, hind. throat + dard, pers. pain). Can from (gantlu, can. throat + hunnu, can. ulcer). Tel. from (gontu, tel. throat + noppi, tel. pain). Mal. from (tonda, mal. throat + pun, mal. sore). Tam. from (tondai, tam. throat + nóvu, tam. pain). Sore throat.——*Cshayam* (क्षय - kshaya, San. ; دق - dik, Hind. ; ಕ್ಷಯ - kshaya, Can. ; క్షయము - kshayamu, Tel. ; ക്ഷയം - kshayam, Mal. ; சயம் - shayam, Tam.). Title from sanscrit. Sanscrit from (kshi, san. to destroy). Hind. from (dikk, ar. to become thin). Drav. from sanscrit. Consumption. Also called Raja yacshmay meaning the king of disease, Shosham meaning drying up, and Cshatam meaning rupture or ulcer of the respiratory organs. Characterized by coughing accompanied with bloody expectoration. This is produced by grief ; by the evacuations being retained ; by great loss of the humours of the body ; by performing unusual and unnatural actions as ineffectually endeavouring to raise heavy weights ; by violent exercises ; by eating bad food at unusual times in unusual quantities ; by fasting ; by boils and sores in the chest. The disease commences by the person being emaciated and debilitated ; difficult breathing and pain over the body comes on, with cough, and a discharge of mucus, from the mouth and nose ; the palate is dry, vomiting and loss of appetite takes place from the internal heat being diminished ; there is also derangement of the mind, jaundice, cough with expectoration, and the loss of taste and smell ; the patient sleeps continually, and the eyes become of a pearl white color ; the person is fond of animal food. The following symptoms also indicate the presence of this disease :—the patient's voice changes, he sees in his dream crows [caurvam], parrots [totah], porcupines [kharpoosht], peacocks [mayil], vultures [gidh], monkeys [bandar], and lizards [chipkalee] ; and he supposes he is mounted upon these animals ; he sees also dry beds of rivers, dry trees, as if destroyed by storms and by fire ; the characteristic symptoms are pain in the shoulders, and sides of the chest ; a burning feverish sensation in the palms of the hands and soles of the feet is felt, which extends over the body.——*Cshoodrakrimy* (क्षुद्रकृमि - kshudrakrimi, San. ; کرم - kirm, Hind. ; చిరిపురుగులు - chiripurugulu, Tel. ; சிறுபூச்சி - shirubúççi, Tam.). Title from sanscrit. San. from (kshudra, san. small + krimi, san. worm). Hind. from (krimi, san. worm). Tel. from (chiri, tel. small + purugu, tel. worm). Tam. from (shiru, tam. mall + púççi, tam. worm). Worms, Ascarides.——*Cshoodramasooricay* (क्षुद्रमसूरिका - kshudramasúriká, San. ; گوبری - gobrí, Hind. ; ಚಿಕ್ಕಮ್ಮನರೋಗ - chikkammanaróga, Can. ; చిన్నమ్మవారు - chinnammaváru, Tel. ; അഞ്ചാംപനി - añchámpani, Mal. ; சின்னம்மை - shinnammai, Tam.). Title from sanscrit. San. from (kshudra, san. insignificant + masúriká, san. small-pox). Can. from (chikka, can. small + amma, can. goddess of small-pox + róga, can. disease). Tel. from (chinna, tel. small + ammavári, tel. small-pox). Mal. from (añchu, mal. five + pani, mal. fever). Tam. from (shinna, tam. small + ammai, tam. mother). Measles.——*Dadroo* (दद्रु - dadru, San. ; داد - dád, Hind. ; ಪಡದಾಮರೆ - padadámare, Can. ; పాడదామర - podadámara, Tel. ; പുഴുക്കടി - puzhukkati, Mal. ; படர்தாமரை - padardámarai, Tam.). Title from sanscrit. San. from (dri, san. to tear). Hind. from sanscrit.

Can. like tamul. Tel. from (poda, tel. spot + támara, tel. lotus plant). Mal. from (puzhu, mal. worm + kaṭi, mal. to bite). Tam. from (padar, tam. to spread + támarasa, san. red-coloured lotus). Ring-worm [cooshtam].——*Danta shoolam* (दन्तशूल - dantashúla, San.; درد دندان - dardidandán, دانتکادرد - dántkádard, Hind.; ಹಲ್ಲುನೋವು - hallunóvu, Can.; పంటినొప్పి - pantinoppi, Tel.; പല്ലുകുത്തു - pallakuttu, Mal.; பல்லுநோவு - pallunóvu, Tam.). Title from sanscrit. San. from (danta, san. tooth + shúla, san. pain). Pers. from (dard, pers pain + dandán, pers. tooth). Hind. from (dánt, hind. tooth + dard, hind. pain). Can. from (hallu, can. tooth + nóvu, can. pain). Tel. from (pallu, tel. tooth + noppi, tel. pain). Mal. from (pal, mal. tooth + kuttu, mal. to pierce). Tam. from (pal, tam. tooth + nóvu, tam. pain). Toothache. The varieties are :—Daulanam; in this the tooth becomes very painful. Crimy dantacam; this is caused by a small black decayed part of the tooth which is painful and discharges matter with swelling, and much pain. Bhanjanacam; the mouth is turned to one side and the teeth broken, as in spasm. Danta harsham; in this the person cannot bear cold, or hot applications; cool air and sour articles produce much pain. Danta sharcaray; the teeth are dirty, dried up and deformed, like the scale of fishes. Capaulicah; the tartar increases and the teeth become loose, and eventually drop out. Shyauvadantam; the teeth become of a dark color, as if burnt in the fire. Hanoomocsham; in this dislocation of the lower jaw is caused.——*Doerghakrimy* (दीर्घकृमि - dírghakrimi, San.; لمبی کینڈوی - lambegendwo, Hind.; నిడివిపురుగు - nidivipurugu, Tel.; நீளப்பூச்சி - nílappúççi, Tam.). Title from sanscrit. San. from (dírgha, san. long + krimi, san. worm). Tel. from (nidivi, tel. long + purugu, tel. worm). Tam. from (nílam, tam. length + púççi, tam. worm). Tape worms.——*Dooshtavranam* (दुष्टव्रण - dushtavrana, San.; خراب پھوڑا - kharábphorá, Hind.; ಕೆಟ್ಟಹುಣ್ಣು - kettahunnu, Can.; గుంటపుండు - guntapundu, Tel.; കുന്തം - kuntam, Mal.; அழிபுண் - azhibun, Tam.). Title from sanscrit. San. from (dushta, san. corrupted bad + vrana, san. wound). Hind. from (kharáb, hind. bad + phorá, hind. ulcer). Can. from (ketta, can. bad + hunnu, can. ulcer). Tel. from (gunta, tel. pit + pundu, tel. ulcer). Tam. from (azhi, tam. to decay + pun, tam. ulcer.) Foul ulcer.——*Doshajwaram* (दोषज्वर - dóshajvara, San.; تپ زہری - tapizahrí, Hind.; ವಿಷಮಶೀತಜ್ವರ - vishamashítajvara, Can.; కృష్ణదోషము - krishnadóshamu, Tel.; കാച്ചപ്പനി - káççappani, Mal.; அதிசுரம் - attisuram, Tam.). Title from sanscrit. San. from (dósha, san. disorder of the humours + jvara, san. fever). Hind. from (tap, hind. fever + zahrí, pers. poisonous); Can. from (vishama, san. latent + shíta, san. cold + jvara, san. fever). Tel. from (krishna, san. black + dósha, san. disorder of the humours). Mal. from (káyu, mal. to be hot + pani, mal. fever). Tam. from (ast'hi, san. bone + jvara, san. fever). Typhus fever.——*Ganda maulay* (गण्डमाला - gandamálá, San.; گنڈمالا - gandmálá, Hind.; ಗಂಡಮಾಲೆ - gandamále, Can.; కంఠమాల - kant'hamála, Tel.; കണ്ഠമാല - kant'hamála, Mal.; கண்டமாலை - kandamálai, Tam.). Title and Tam. from sanscrit. San. from (ganda, san. cheek + mála, san. garland). Hind. from sanscrit. Tel. from (kant'ha, san. neck + málá, san. garland). Scrofula. In this disease many small tumours like plums appear in the axilla, neck, back, and groins; these are produced by diseased fat and phlegm [sheetam], they suppurate slowly, and continue to appear and suppurate for a long period, when it is called apachy; when not attended by any bad constitutional disease it is curable, but when accompanied with coryza, with pain in the sides, cough, fever, and vomiting, it is incurable.——*Gomasooricay* (गोमसूरिका - gómasúriká, San.; گائی کی سیتلا - gáíkísítlá, Hind. ಗೋವಸೂರಿ - góvasúri, Can.; ఆవమ్మవారు - ávammavάru, Tel.; ഗോവസൂരി - góvasúri, Mal.; கோவைசூரி - kóvaisúri, Tam.). Title from sanscrit. San. from (gó, san. cow + masúriká, san. small-pox). Hind. from (gái, hind. cow + sítlá, hind. pox). Tel. from (ávu, tel. cow + ammavάru, tel. small-pox). Cow pox.——*Grahany* (ग्रहणी - grahaní, San.; اسہال - ishál, Hind.; ಅತಿಸಾರ - atisára, Can.; అతిసారము - atisáramu, Tel.; ഗ്രഹണി - grahani, Mal.; கிராணிக்கழிச்சல் - kiránikkazhiççal, Tam.). Title from sanscrit. San. from (grahaní, san. an imaginary organ between the stomach and intestine). Hind. from (sahala, ar. to loosen). Can. and Tel. from (ati, san. intensive prefix + sára, san. essence). Tam. from (grahaní, san. disease so called + kazhi, tam. to pass stools). Diarrhœa. Before this disease commences the patient complains of lassitude and weakness of the body, accompanied with noise in the intestines, sour and bitter eructations, and a bad taste in the mouth; when a singing of the ears, œdema in the hands and feet, with pain in the joints, vomiting, fever, thirst, loss of appetite, and a heaviness and burning sensation of the body occurs, in old cases, the prognosis should be guarded.——*Hanoostambham* (हनुस्तम्भ - hanustambha, San.; دانتکیلی - dántkílí, Hind.; ಶೆಳವುಸನ್ನಿ - shelavusanni, Can.; జన్ని - dzanni, Tel.; സന്നിപാതം - sannipátam, Mal.; சன்னி - shanni, Tam.). Title from sanscrit. San. from (hanu, san. jaw + stambha, san. fixedness). Hind. from (dánt, hind. tooth + kílí, hind. key). Can. from (shelavu, can. pulling + sanni, can. convulsion). Tel., Mal. and Tam. from (sannipáta, san. disorder of the three humours). Lockjaw. This is caused when the air is deranged by a person speaking very loud, or by eating large mouthfuls of meat, or hard things, or laughing much or gaping or sleeping uncomfortably or bearing heavy weights. This affects the lower jaw or half the face and neck, which it draws laterally, and the head shakes; the person cannot speak, there is a deformity of the eye, nose, mouth and neck, with pain in these parts, as also in the chin and teeth, and the senses [indriyam] are in an unhealthy state; the dangerous symptoms of this disease are when the person is weak, the pain severe, and he cannot move his eyelids, nor speak distinctly, when the mouth is turned to one side, and with the shaking of the part of the body, as the head, has continued for three or more years.——*Hikkay* (हिक्का - hikká, San.; ہچکی - hichkí, Hind.; ಬಿಕ್ಕಲು - bikkalu, Can.; వెక్కిల్లు - vekkillu, Tel.; എക്കിൾ - ekkil, Mal.; விக்கல் - vikkal, Tam.). Title from sanscrit. San. from (hikk, san. to make an indistinct sound). Tel. from the sound. Mal. from (ekku, mal. to come up). Tam. from (vikku, tam. to hickup). Hickup. This disease is produced by nearly the same causes as Shwausam [q.v.] and Caussam [q.v.]. The precursory symptoms are a heaviness of the throat and chest, and astringent taste in the mouth, and a rumbling noise in the belly. There are five kinds of Hikkay :—Annajay; this form is produced by taking too much food and drink. Yamalay; in this form the passage of the air proceeds, after a considerable time, with eructations of air, and the head and neck shake at the moment. Cshoodray; this takes place slowly, is not strong, and proceeds from the scrobiculous cordis. Gambheeram; in this form the hiccup commences from the navel, is strong, and very noisy, and is always accompanied with other severe or fatal symptoms. Mahaty; there is frequent hiccup, which produces pain in the vital parts, and shakes the whole body. The unfavorable symptoms are when hiccup is accompanied with fixed eyes, as if drawn up by some one; when there is great weakness, and the patient's arms and legs are thrown out, with frequent sneezing; when combined with other diseases, as delirium, fainting and great thirst, it will be fatal.——*Hritdauham* (हृद्दाह - hriddáha, San.; معدے کا جلن - medekájalan, Hind.; ಎದೆಉರಿಯು - yedeuriyu, Can.; రొమ్మమంట - rommumanta, Tel.; നെഞ്ഞുകലിക്ക - neññukalikka, Mal.; குலையெரிவு - kulaiyerivu, Tam.). Title from sanscrit. San. from (hrid, san. heart + dah, san. to burn). Hind. from (medah, hind. stomach + jalan, hind. burning). Can. from (yede, can. breast + uriyu, can. burn). Tel. from (rommu, tel. heart + mandu, tel. to burn). Mal. from (neññu, mal. heart + kali, mal. to mix). Tam. from (kulai, tam. viscera + eri, tam. to burn). Heart-burn.——*Laulaushayashotam* (लालाशयशोथ - láláshayashót'ha, San.; گلے آنا - galeáná, Hind.; ಬಂಗಾರಬಾವು - bangárabávu, Can.; జలుబుగడ్డ - dzalubugadda, Tel.; മുണ്ടിനീർ - muntinír, Mal.; குளிர்மைக்கட்டி - kulirmaikkatti, Tam.). Title from sanscrit. San. from (lála, san. saliva + áshaya, san. receptacle + shót'ha, san. swelling). Hind. from (galá, hind. neck glands + áná, hind. to come). Can. from (bangára, can. gold + bávu, can. swelling); from gold being the cure. Tel. from (dzalubu, tel. catarrh + gadda, tel. boil). Mal. from (mundi, mal. swelling of the glands of the neck + nír, mal. water). Tam. from (kulir, tam. coldness + katti, tam. boil). Mumps.——*Madhoo maiham* (मधुमेह - madhuméha, San.; ذیابیطس - ziyábitas, Hind.; ಬಹುಮೂತ್ರ - bahumútra, Can.; బహుమూత్రము - bahumútramu, Tel.; പ്രമേഹം - praméham, Mal.; நீரழிவு - nírazhivu, Tam.). Title from sanscrit. San. from (madhu, san. sweet + méha, san. urine). Hind. from Greek. Can. and Tel. from (bahu, tel. much + mútra, san. urine). Mal. from (pra, san. intensive prefix + méha, san. urine). Tam. from (nír, tam. water + azhivu, tam. decay). Diabetes. This disease is ushered in by the appearance of morbid secretions about the teeth, ears, nose and eyes; the hands and feet are very hot and burning, and the surface of the skin is shining as if oil had been applied to it; this is accompanied with thirst and a sweet taste in the mouth; the urine is sweet.——*Mahodaram* (महोदर - mahódara, San.; استسقاء بطنی - istiskáibataní, Hind.; ಮಹೋದರ - mahódara, Can.; మహోదరము - mahódaramu, Tel.; മഹോദരം - mahódaram, Mal.; மகோதரம் - magótharam, Tam.). Title from sanscrit. San. from (maha, san. great + udara, san. belly). Hind from (istiská, ar. dropsy + batan, ar. belly). Drav. from sanscrit. Ascites. In this disease the abdomen becomes large, the umbilicus prominent, and appears shining as if anointed and full of water, and like it moves about, and gives a sound like a leather bag. There is weakness, loss of appetite, languor, constipation, burning and great thirst.——*Maiha vyaudhy* (मेहव्याधि - méhavyádhi, San.; خراب مرض - kharábmarz, Hind.; ಮೇಹವ್ಯಾಧಿ - méhavyádhi, Tel.; മൂത്രരോഗം - mútrarógam, Mal.; மேகவியாதி - mégaviyáthi, Tam.). Title from sanscrit. San. from (maiha, san. urine + vyádhi, san. disease). Hind. from (kharáb, hind. bad + marz, ar. disease). Tel. and Tam. from sanscrit. Mal. means urine + disease. Venereal disease.——*Masoory* (मसूरी - masúrí, San.; سیتلا - sítlá, Hind.; ಶಿದುಬುರೋಗ - shiduburóga, Can.; పెద్దమ్మవారు - peddammavάru, Tel.; വസൂരി - vasúri, Mal.;

பெரியம்மை - periyammai, Tam.). Title from sanscrit. San. from (masura, san. lentil, vicia hirsuta, koch.). Hind. from (shítalá, san. small-pox). Can. from (shidubu, can. the pustule of small-pox + róga, can. disease). Tel. from (pedda, tel. large + ammaváru, tel. small-pox). Mal. from sanscrit. Tam. from (periya, tam. big + ammai, tam. mother). Small-pox.——*Mookha paucam* (मुखपाक - mukhapáka, San.; تپ‌خالہ - tapkhálá, Hind.; ವಾತಗ್ರಂಥಿ - vátagranthi, Can.; అక్షరం - aksharam, Tel.; അക്കരം - akkaram, Mal.; அச்சரம் - aççaram, Tam.). Title from sanscrit. San. from (mukha, san. face + páka, san. inflammation). Hind. from (tap, hind. fever + khálah, pers. effects). Can. from (váta, san. wind + grant'hi, san. knot). Tel. means letters of the alphabet; from the resemblance. Mal. and Tam. from (akshara, san. indestructible). Thrush.——*Moorchay* (मूर्छा - múrchhá, San.; سکتہ - saktah, Hind.; ಸನ್ನಿರೋಗ - sanniróga, Can.; సన్నిపాతము - sannipátamu, Tel.; സന്നിപാതം - sannipátam, Mal.; அசதிசன்னி - asathisanni, Tam). Title from sanscrit. San. from (murchh, san. to faint). Hind. from (sakata, ar. to become still). Can. from (sanni, can. convulsion + róga, can. disease). Tel. from (sannipat, san. to fall down). Mal. from (sannipáta, san. disorder of the three humours). Tam. from (asathi, tam. suddenness + sannipáta, san. disease of the three humours). Apoplexy. This is produced by deranged air [vautam], bile [pittam] and phlegm [sheetam], which pass to the place where life is situated, and overpower all the functions of both mind and body, and the person suddenly falls down and remains as if dead or like a piece of wood; if not immediately and properly treated, such a person will die.——*Mootra kritchram* (मूत्रकृच्छ्र - mútrakrichhra, San.; پیشاب‌ٹپکنا - píshábtapakná, Hind.; ಮೂತ್ರಕೃಚ್ಛ್ರ - mútrakrichhra, Can.; మూత్రకృచ్ఛ్రం - mútrakriççham, Tel.; மூத்திரக்கிருச்சரம் - múttirakkiruççam, Tam.). Title from sanscrit. San. from (mútra, san. urine + krichhra, san. difficulty). Hind. from (píshab, pers. urine + tapakná, hind. to drip). Drav. from sanscrit. Urine difficulty.——*Mootrasrauvam* (मूत्रस्राव - mútrasráva, San.; سلسل‌بول - silsilibol, Hind.; ಬಹುಮೂತ್ರ - bahumútra, Can.; తెల్లనీరుడుమేహము - tellanírudumèhamu, Tel.; നീരൊഴിവു - nírozhivu, Mal.; நீரொழுக்கு - nírozhukku, Tam.). Title from sanscrit. San. from (mútra, san. urine + srav, san. to flow). Hind. from (silsil, ar. frequent running down + bol, pers. urine). Can. from (bahu, san. much + mútra, san. urine). Tel. from (tella, tel. white + níru, tel. water + méha, san. urine). Mal. from (nír, mal. water + ozhivu, san. flow). Tam. from (nír, tam. water + ozhugu, tam. to flow). Urine incontinence.——*Mootraughautam* (मूत्राघात - mútrágháta, San.; پیشاب‌بند - píshábband, Hind.; ಮೂತ್ರಬಂಧನ - mútrabandhana, Can.; నీరుకట్టు - nírukattu, Tel.; മൂത്രബന്ധം - mútrabandham, Mal.; நீர்க்கட்டு - nírkkattu, Tam.). Title from sanscrit. San. from (mútra, san. urine + ághâta, san. stoppage). Hind. from (píshab, pers. urine + band, pers. stoppage). Can. from (mútra, san. urine + bandhana, san. stoppage). Tel. from (níru, tel. water + kattu, tel. to bind). Tam. from (nír, tam. water + kattu, tam. to bind). Urine stoppage.——*Mootravriddhy* (मूत्रवृद्धि - mútravriddhi, San.; فتق - fatak, Hind.; ಬುದ್ದೆರೋಗ - budderóga, Can.; నీరుశూల - nírushúla, Tel.; ജലശൂലരോഗം - jalashúlarógam, Mal.; நீர்ச்சூலை - nírççúlai, Tam.). Title from sanscrit. San. from (mútra, san. urine + vriddhi, san. increase). Hind. from (fataka, ar. to split). Can. from (budde, can. rupture + róga, disease). Tel. from (níru, tel. water + shúla, san. acute pain). Mal. from (jala, san. water + shúla, san. acute pain + róga, san. disease). Tam. from (nír, tam. water + shúla, san. acute pain). Hydrocele [antravriddhy].——*Naudy vranam* (नाडीव्रण - nádívrana, San.; نارو - nárú, Hind.; నారకురుపు - nárakurupu, Tel.; நரம்புச்சிலந்தி - narambuççilandi, Tam.). Title from sanscrit. San. from (nádí, san. nerve + vrana, san. wound). Hind. from (nára, tel. fibre). Tel. from (nára, tel. fibre + kurupu, tel. ulcer). Tam. from (narambu, tam. tendon + shilandi, tam. boil). Guinea worm. This most frequently appears in the feet and legs. At the end of six weeks the presence of the animal is revealed by tumours; then wounds appear, caused by the dissemination of the eggs.——*Naugakrimy* (नागकृमि - nágakrimi, San.; گینڈوے - gendwe, Hind.; ఎముడికపాము - emidikapámu, Tel.; நாக்கப்பூச்சி - nákkappúççi, Tam.). Title from sanscrit. San. from (nága, san. snake + krimi, san. worm). Tel. from (imudu, tel. to settle + pámu, tel. snake). Tam. from (nángu, tam. to shrink + púççi, tam. worm). Tel. also (élikapámu), meaning rag snake, narrow and strip-like. Round worms.——*Netrashoolam* (नेत्रशूल - nétrashúla, San.; آنکھیں‌آنا - ánkhenáná, Hind.; ಕಣ್ಣುಶೂಲೆ - kannushúle, Can.; కన్నునొప్పి - kannunoppi, Tel.; കണ്ണോവു - kannóvu, Mal.; கண்ணோவு - kannóvu, Tam.). Title from sanscrit. San. from (nétra, san. eye + shúla, san. acute pain). Hind. from (ánkhen, hind. eyes + áná, hind. to come). Can. from (kannu, can. eye + shúla, san. pain). Tel. from (kannu, tel. eye + noppi, tel. pain). Mal. and Tam. from (kan, tam. eye + nóvu, tam. pain). Ophthalmia.——*Oonmaudam* (उन्माद - unmáda, San.; دیوانگی - díwánagí, Hind.; ಹುಚ್ಚುಹಿಡಿತ - huççuhidita, Can.; పిచ్చి - piççi, Tel.; ഭ്രാന്തു - bhrántu, Mal.; பயித்தியம் - payittiyam, Tam.). Title from sanscrit. San. from (unmad, san. to be mad). Can. from (huççu, can. madness + hidita, can. hold). Tel. from (pitta, san. bile). Mal. from (bhram, san. to be perplexed). Tam. from (pitta, san. bile). Madness.——*Oopadamsham* (उपदंश - upadamsha, San.; ٹاکی - táki, Hind.; ಉಷ್ಣವ್ರಣ - ushnavrana, Can.; పొక్కు - pokku, Tel.; ഉഷ്ണപ്പുണ്ണു - ushnappunnu, Mal.; கிரந்திப்புண் - kirandippun, Tam.). Title from sanscrit. San. from (upadamsh, san. to eat). Can. from (ushna, san. heat + vrana, san. wound). Tel. from (pokku, tel. to blister). Mal. from (ushna, mal. heat + punnu, mal. wound). Tam. from (grant'hi, san. swelling and hardening of the vessels as in varicocele + pun, tam. ulcer). Chancre.——*Pacshaughautam* (पक्षाघात - pakshágháta, San.; فالج - fálij, Hind.; ನಡುಗುರೋಗ - nadugurόga, Can.; పక్షవాయువు - pakshaváyuva, Tel.; പക്ഷവാതം - pakshavátam, Mal.; பக்கவாதம் - pakkavátham, Tam.). Title from sanscrit. San. from (paksha, san. side + ághâta, san. stroke) Hind. from (falaja, ar. to divide). Can. from (nadugu, can. shake + róga, san. disease). Tel. from (paksha, san. side + váyu, san. wind). Mal. and Tam. from (paksha, san. side + váta, san. air). Palsy. There are two varieties of this disease, one affecting one side of the body and another affecting one half of the body taken transversely; when air affects the vessels and nerves of one side, it produces this disease; the person loses the power of that part, which is without feeling and with looseness of the joints; when there is great weakness of the essential parts of the body, as after hemorrhagia in parturition or injuries, the disease is incurable.——*Patalum* (पटल - patala, San.; موتیابند - motiyábind, Hind.; ಪರೆ - pare, Can.; పొరలు - poralu, Tel.; പടലം - patalam, Mal.; படலம் - padalam, Tam.). San. from (patala, san. cover). Hind. from (motiyá, hind. pearl shaped + bind, hind. drop). Can. from (pare, can. web on the eye). Tel. means film. Mal. and Tam. from sanscrit. Cataract. Also called Linganaushan. In this disease the whole crystalline lens is affected, and if not very deep, the person can see the moon, star and lightning; when air is much increased the patient sees every object red, and when bile is affected, he can see the sun, the rainbow and lightning; in other cases everything appears black, variegated, and like the feather of a peacock [mayil]; when affected by phlegm, every object appears as if covered with oil and white; when the three humours are deranged, everything appears spotted as of a mixture of different colors; when blood is deranged every object appears red and dark.——*Pitta masooricay* (पित्तमसूरिका - pittamasúriká, San.; کانجیان - kánjiniyán, Hind.; ಶೀತಳಶಿಡುಬು - shítalashidubu, Can.; తట్టమ్మవారు - tattammavárú, Tel.; നീർക്കോൾവൻ - nírkkolván, Mal.; கொத்தமல்லியம்மை - kottamálliyammai, Tam.). Title from sanscrit. San. from (pitta, san. heat + masúriká, san. small-pox). Tel. from (tatta, tel. flat + ammaváru, tel. small-pox). Mal. from (nír, mal. water + kol, mal. to contain). Tam. from (kottamalli, tam. coriander seed + ammai, tam. mother). Chicken-pox [masoory].——*Rajah vispotam* (राजविस्फोट - rája-visp'hóta, San.; راجپھوڑا - rájphorá, Hind.; ರಾಜಹುಣ್ಣು - rájahunnu, Can.; రాచపుండు - rátsapundu, Tel.; രാജകുരു - rájakuru, Mal.; பக்கப்பிளவை - pakkappilavai, Tam.). Title from sanscrit. San. from (rája, san. king + visp'hóta, san. boil). Hind. from (rája, san. king + phorá, hind. boil). Can. from (rája, san. king + hunnu, can. boil). Tel. from (rája, san. king + pundu, tel. boil). Mal. from (rája, san. king + kuru, mal. boil). Tam. from (pakkam, tam. side + pilavai, tam. cancre). Called also Rajah boil. Carbuncle.——*Romaunticam* (रोमान्तिक - rómántika, San.; മണല്വാരി - manalvári, Mal.). San. from (róma, san. hair + anta, san. end). Mal. from (manal, mal. sand + mári, mal. small-pox). Measles. Produced by vitiated phlegm [sheetam] and bile [pittam]; the symptoms are fever followed by an eruption of small red papillæ, like the roots of hairs; these appear over the body, accompanied with loss of appetite and cough.——*Sannipauta jwaram* (सन्निपातज्वर - sannipátajvara, San.). Title and San. from (sannipáta, san. falling down + jvara, san. fever). Typhus fever. This a dangerous form of fever; at one time the patient is hot, at other times cold, with pains in the bones, and joints, the eyes are watery and hollow, he is always dozing, but cannot sleep at night, has no memory, is often delirious, sometimes he is laughing and crying, is always coughing, has quick breathing, the tongue is black like charcoal, and irregular like that of a cow, with pain; blood, phlegm [sheetam] air [vautam] and bile [pittam] flow from the mouth; the urine is secreted in small quantities with costiveness and no perspiration, great thirst, noises in the throat, so that there is a difficulty in comprehending what the sick person says, with round elevations, and central depressions of a blue and red color, over the surface of the body; after the first stage, should the fever continue severe, it will generally be fatal, and at the last stage of the fever the lower part of the ear swells; this is supposed to be a fatal sign; those who live till the twenty-second day generally recover.——*Sarpadamsham* (सर्पदंश - sarpadamsha, San.; سانپ‌کاٹنا - sánpkátná, Hind.; ಹಾವುಕಡಿತ - hávukadita, Can.; పాముకాటు - pámukátu, Tel.; വിഷംതീണ്ടൽ - vishamtíndal, Mal.; பாம்புக்கடி - pámbukkadi, Tam.). Title from sanscrit. San. from (sarpa, san. serpent + dash, san. to bite). Hind. from (sánp, hind. snake + kátná, hind.

to bite). Can. from (hávu, can. snake + kadita, can. biting). Tel. from (pámu, tel. snake + karatsu, tel. to bite). Mal. from (visha, san. poison + tíndu, mal. to touch). Tam. from (pámbu, tam. snake + kadi, tam. to bite). Snake bite. The poison of serpents is very acid and hot, and for preventing its effects everything cooling should be employed. The serpents are divided into five classes:—Darveecaram or hooded snakes [cobra]; the bite of this leaves a black color in the wound, with the symptoms of various air diseases; the skin, eyes, nails, teeth, urine and fæces, and the part which is bitten, becomes black, with roughness of the body and heaviness of the head, pain in the joints, weakness in the loins, back and neck, gaping, shivering, alteration of voice, languor, hiccough, thirst, foaming and sluggishness of the circulation; and the secretions and all the external passages are closed. Mandaly [viriyan], or serpents with figures of round arches on their bodies; the bites of this class of serpents produce in the part a yellow color; it swells, is painful and soft, accompanied with the following symptoms, thirst, stupidity, fainting, fever, blood is discharged from the mouth and anus, and gangrene occurs in the bitten part; these serpents are shining, and are marked with different circles over the body. Raujilam; serpents with longitudinal lines; these produce swelling, a glistening gray-color of the part, and the blood is thick, accompanied with the various symptoms of diseased phlegm [sheetam]; they are distinguished by the longitudinal lines along their bodies. Nirvisham [paumb]; these are serpents without poison. Vyantarajam; serpents which combine the peculiarities of several of the others. The following cases will be rarely cured; when no blood follows on cutting the part, and when the person is senseless so that no weals are produced by the strokes of a whip, or horripilation after throwing cold water on the body; the following symptoms are likewise unfavorable, when the tongue is black, the hair falls off, the nose and mouth become changed in their shape, the voice is altered, and the bitten part becomes black and red, or tetanus [hanoostambham] supervenes, when thick mucus proceeds from the mouth, or when the blood is discharged from the mouth and anus, and there are the wounds of four teeth. Treatment; when the extremities are bitten immediately apply a tight bandage above the bitten part, so as to prevent the poison entering into the system; when this cannot be done so, the bitten part is to be cut out; in all cases cutting out the part, sucking the wound with a horn, or burning the part is highly proper; when the mouth is used for sucking place a piece of bladder over it first and then suck; then antidotes must be used to prevent the effects of the poison; when the poison has reached the head, the person should be bled, and in the succeeding stages emetics and strong errhines should be used.——*Shilocpadam* (शिलीपद - shilípada, San.; هتی کا پاؤں - hattíkápáún, Hind.; ಆನೆಕಾಲು - ánékálu, Can.; ఏనుగకాలు - énugakálu, Tel.; പെരിങ്കാൽ - perinkál, Mal.; ஆனைக்கால் - ánaikkál, Tam.). Title from sanscrit. San. from (shila, san. stone + pada, san. leg). Hind. from (hattí, hind. elephant + páún, hind. leg). Can. from (áne, can. elephant + kálu, can. leg). Tel. from (énuga, tel. elephant + kálu, tel. leg). Mal. from (perum, mal. large + kál, mal. leg). Tam. from (ánai, tam. elephant + kál, tam. leg). Cochin leg. This disease is most frequent in those countries where there is much stagnant water and in cold damp situations; the patient's groin first swells, and becomes very painful with fever; the swelling then slowly descends to the foot and the part affected becomes hard and rough; this is incurable, after it has remained upwards of a year, or is very large, and when the skin is much affected, as indicated by continual discharge, the itchy or painful nature of the swelling, and its discoloration. See Cochin leg.——*Shirapaumay* (शिर:पामा - shirahpámá, San.; گنج - ganj, Hind.; ತಲೆಹುಣ್ಣು - talehunnu, Can.; మాడ - máda, Tel.; കഷണ്ടി - kashandi, Mal.; பொடுகு - podugu, Tam.). Title from sanscrit. San. from (shiras, san. head + pámá, san. itch). Can. from (tale, can. head + hunnu, can. scald). Tam. from (podi, tam. to powder), from scaly parings. Scald head.——*Shirashoolam* (शिरःशूल - shirashshúla, San.; سرکادرد - sarkádard, Hind.; ತಲೆನೋವು - talenóvu, Can.; తలనొప్పి - talanoppi, Tel.; തലവേദന - talavédana, Mal.; தலைநோவு - talainóvu, Tam.). Title from sanscrit. San. from (shiras, san. head + shúla, san. pain). Hind. from (sar, hind. head + dard, hind. pain). Can. like tamul. Tel. from (tala, tel. head + noppi, tel. pain). Mal. from (tala, mal. head + védana, san. pain). Tam. from (talai, tam. head + nóvu, tam. pain). Tam. also (talaivali). Head-ache. There are eleven varieties:—Vautaja shirorogam; in this the head is suddenly affected with pain, which is severe at night; but it is diminished by hot applications, and bandages. Pittaja shirorogam; in this variety the head is hot as if burning charcoal was placed over it, and there is an appearance of smoke proceeding from the mouth; the pain is diminished when the head is kept cool and during the night. Caphaja shirorogam; in this variety the head is heavy and dull, and it cannot be turned about; the head feels cool, and the eyelids and mouth are swollen. Saunnipauticam; in this variety the symptoms of the foregoing varieties are combined. Ractaja shirorogam; in this variety the symptoms are the same as those of pittaja shirorogam, but the pain is so severe that the head cannot be touched, or bent forward. Cshayaja shirorogam; this variety is produced by a diminution of brain or fat, phlegm, or blood in the head; this produces great uneasiness and pain; this pain is increased by hot applications, by smoke, by errhines, and by blood-letting. Krimija shirorogam; worms sometimes produce severe pain in the head, of a kind as if an animal was eating, or tearing the head; a watery red or bloody discharge flows from the nose, and the patient's life is to be considered as in danger. Sooryauvartam; in this variety when the sun rises the eyes and brow feel pain, and it continues and increases, while the sun is above the horizon; it diminishes in the evening and towards night. Anantavantam; the symptoms are great pain, particularly in the eyebrows, temples, and cheeks; it also produces shaking of the head, pain in the lower jaw, and diseases of eyes. Ardhauvabhedacam; the attack occurs sometimes every fortnight, in other cases every tenth day, or in other cases every day; the half of the neck, brow, temples, ears, eyes, are very painful; when severe, as it often is, like that of poison, or as if burnt, and the sight and hearing become imperfect; this disease is very obstinate, and most distressing. Shankhacam; severe pain is produced in the temples and head, which becomes hot; this form is dangerous like poison; when the person cannot swallow, he will die in three days; but if he lives beyond this time, medicines may then be given for the cure.——*Shiromalam* (शिरोमल - shirómala, San.; بفا - bafá, Hind.; ಚುಂಡು - chundu, Can.; చుండు - tsundu, Tel.; താരണം - táranam, Mal.; சுண்டு - shundu, Tam.). Title from sanscrit. San. from (shiras, san. head + mala, san. dirt). Tel. from (tsundú, tel. to be shrivelled). Mal. from (tárana, san. crossing). Tam. from (shundu, tam. sediment). Dandriff.——*Shoocramaiham* (शुक्रमेह - shukraméha, San.; سوزاک - sozák, Hind.; ಮೇಹಹುಣ್ಣು - méhahunnu, Can.; సెగరోగము - shagarógamu, Tel.; മൂത്രദോഷം - mútradósham, Mal.; வெள்ளை - vellai, Tam.). Title from sanscrit. San. from (shukla, san. white + méha, san. urine). Hind. from (soz, pers. burning). Can. from (méha, san. venereal + hunnu, can. ulcer). Tel. from (sega, tel. heat + róga, san. disease). Mal. from (mútra, san. urine + dósha, san. disorder). Tam. means white. Gonorrhœa.——*Shwausam* (श्वास - shvása, San.; ضيق النفس - zíkunnafs, Ar.; دمه - dammah, Hind.; ಉಬ್ಬಸ - ubbasa, Can.; ఉబ్బసము - ubbasamu, Tel.; നെഞ്ഞടെപ്പടിനം - neññateppadínam, Mal.; சுவாசகாசம் - shuvásagásam, Tam.). Title from sanscrit. San. from (shvas, san. to breathe). Ar. from (zík, ar. difficulty + nafs, ar. breath). Hind. from (dam, hind. breath). Tel. from (ubbu, tel. to swell). Mal. from (neññu, mal. chest + ateppu, mal. closing). Tam. from (shvása, san. breathing + kása, san. cough). Can. also (névasa). Asthma. There are five varieties of asthma. Mahashwausam; the air is confined in the air passages by the phlegm [sheetam]; the patient respires with difficulty and with noise; he becomes low spirited, his eyes are always moving about; his mouth open, with constipation of urine and fæces; he speaks with difficulty. Oordhwashwausam; the patient respires with difficulty and effort; the air passages being closed by phlegm [sheetam], and the air trying to escape gives much pain; his eyes are directed upwards, he cannot see; sometimes he faints, his mouth remains dry with restlessness and severe pain over the body; the respiration becomes more and more difficult, and he dies. Chinna shwausam; this form occurs in fits at irregular intervals; in these cases he is sometimes still, and cannot breathe; the vital parts are much affected and very painful; he is constipated in his bowels, with much perspiration and drowsiness; he complains of much pain in the bladder, which is very hot, his eyes are always rolling about and red; great debility, low spirits, mouth dry, bad color of the skin, delirium; such persons quickly die. Tamaca shwausam; in this variety the air passes in, but is not discharged easily; the vessels of the neck and air passages are affected, with a collection of mucus in their passages; catarrh is produced, as indicated by yellow spotam in the mouth and snoring, with great uneasiness and difficulty in breathing; when he coughs he often faints, but on mucus being discharged he feels easier; at times he cannot sleep, does not speak, and when he does he complains of much pain in the sides and chest; he is easiest in the sitting position and likes hot things; his eyes are turned upwards, he perspires much in the forehead, his mouth is dry, and the body swings about, as if he was riding upon an elephant; this disease is increased in cloudy, rainy and cold weather; when this form is combined with fever and dozing it forms pratamacam. Cshoodra shwausam; this is produced by dry food and exercise; in this form there is less difficulty in breathing and there is no pain nor uneasiness; it does not prevent deglutition, nor the action of the senses, and only produces difficulty in breathing on running, &c.——*Shwetacooshtam* (श्वेतकुष्ठ - shvétakusht'ha, San.; برص - baras, Ar.; کوڑ - kor, Hind.; ಶ್ವೇತಕುಷ್ಠ - shvétakusht'ha, Can.; తెల్లకుష్టు - tellakushtu, Tel.; പാണ്ഡുരോഗം - pándurógam, Mal.; வெள்ளைக்குட்டம் - vellaikkuttam, Tam.). Title from sanscrit. San. from (shvéta, san. white + kusht'ha, san. leprosy). Tel. from (tella, tel. white + kusht'ha, san. the disease). Mal. from (pándu, san. white + rógam, san. disease). Tam. means white leprosy. Leprosy, white. This is the λεύκη of the Greeks [cooshtam]. For albinos see Venpaundy.——*Swaragnam* (स्वरघ्न - svaraghna, San.; سوکھی کھانسی - súkhíkhánsí, Hind.; ಗಂಟಲುಮುಲ್ಲುರೋಗ - gantlumulluróga, Can.; కింకవాయువ - kinkaváyuva, Tel; മുൾവ്യാധി - mulvyadhi, Mal.; இளை - ilai, Tam.). Title from sanscrit. San. from (svara, san. sound + han, san. to destroy). Hind. from (súkhí, hind. dry + khánsí, hind. cough). Can. from (gantlu, can. throat + mullu, can. thorn + róga, san. disease). Tel. from (kinka, tel. choking sound + váyu, san. wind). Mal. from (mul, mal. thorn + vyádhi, san. disease). Croup. This is produced when phlegm [sheetam] stops the passage of air, and causes dryness of the throat, hoarseness, difficulty in breathing and great uneasiness.——*Taptodacavranam* (तप्तोदकव्रण - taptódakavrana, San.; گرم پانی کاداغ - garmpánikádágh, Hind.; ಬಿಸಿನೀರುಬಿದ್ದು ಆದಗುಳ್ಳೆ - bisinírubidduádagulle, Can.; వెన్నీల్లుపడ్డపుండు - vónnillupaddapundu, Tel.; പൊള്ളൽ - pollal, Mal.; சுடுபுண் - shudubun, Tam.). Title from sanscrit. San. from (tapta, san. hot + udaka, san. water + vrana, san. wound). Hind. from (garm, hind. hot + páni, hind. water + dágh, hind. wound). Can. from (bisiníru, can. hot water + biddu, can. fallen + áda, can. caused + gulle, can. blister). Tel. from (védi, tel. hot + níllu, tel. water + padu, tel. to fall + pundu, tel. ulcer). Mal. from (pollu, mal. to swell). Tam. from (shudu, tam. to burn + pun, tam ulcer). Scald [agny vranam].——*Taupa jwaram* (तापज्वर - tápajvara, San.; گرم تپ - garmtap, Hind.; ದೋಷಜ್ವರ - dóshajvara, Can.; తాపజ్వరము - tápajvaramu, Tel.; ത്രിദോഷപ്പനി - tridóshappani, Mal.; தாபசுரம் - tábasuram, Tam.). Title from sanscrit. San. from (tápa, san. hot + jvara, san. fever). Can. from (dósha, san. malignant + jvara, san. fever). Mal. from (tridósha, san. derangement of the three humours + pani, mal. fever). Tel. and Tam. from sanscrit. Fever, ardent or remittent.——*Valmeekam* (वल्मीक - valmíka, San.; سرطان - sartán, Hind.; ಹುತ್ತ - hútu, Can.; కొరుకు - koruku, Tel.; അർബുദം - arbudam, Mal.; புற்று - puttu, Tam.). Title from sanscrit. San. means ant-hill. Hind. means cancer, from the resemblance of tumours like legs of the animal. Tel. from (koruku, tel. to bite off). Mal. from (arb, san. to injure). Tam. means ant-hill. Cancer. Tumours in the soles of the feet or palms of the hand, or in a joint or in the neck, axilla, and other parts; they increase by degrees, like the hills of white ants [q.v.] and are surrounded with painful and itchy ulcers, and accompanied with a discharge.——*Vauta rogam* (वातरोग - vátaróga, San.; وجع مفاصل - vajimafásil, Hind.; ವಾತರೋಗ - vátaróga, Can.; కీల్లవాయువు - kíllaváyuva, Tel.; വാതം - vátam, Mal.; சீதவாதக்கடுப்பு - shíthaváthakkaduppu, Tam.). Title from sanscrit. San. from (váta, san. wind + róga, san. disease). Hind. from (vaja, ar. pain + mafásil, ar. joints). Can. from (váta, san. wind + róga, san. disease). Tel. from (kilu, tel. joint + váyu, san. wind). Mal. from (vá, san. to blow). Tam. from (shíta, san. cold + váta, tam. air + kaduppu, tam. pain). Rheumatism. The general symptoms are pain over the body, loss of appetite, thirst, languor, heaviness, fever, burning sensation in the wrist, ankle, neck, hip, knee and loins and in all the joints, with swelling, and redness, itching and rigidity of the part.——*Vibandham* (विबन्ध - vibandha, San.; قبض - kabz, Hind.; ಮಲಬದ್ಧ - malabaddha, Can.; మలబద్ధము - malabaddhamu, Tel.; മലബന്ധം - malabandham, Mal.; மலச்சிக்கு - malaççikku, Tam.). Title from sanscrit. San. from (vi, san. intensive prefix + bandh, san. to tie). Hind. from (kabaza, ar. to grasp). Can. and Tel. from (mala, san. excrement + bandh, san. to bind). Mal. from (mala, san. excrement + bandh, san. to bind). Tam. from (mala, san. excrement + shikku, tam. obstacle). Costiveness. This is somewhat different from alasacam [q.v.], as there is no swelling nor tightness of the abdomen; nor is the indigested food either rejected by vomiting or by stool; but is retained in the abdomen causing much pain there, and likewise producing various diseases in different parts of the body; this is always difficult to cure.——*Vidradhy* (विद्रधि - vidradhi, San.; بڑادنبل - barádumbal, Hind.; ಒಳವ್ರಣ - olavrana, Can.; విద్రధి - vidradhi, Tel.; മഹാവ്രണം - mahávranam, Mal.; விப்புருதி - vippuruthi, Tam.). Title from Sanscrit. San. from (vi, san. intensive prefix + drí, san. to tear). Hind. from (bará, hind. large + dumbal, hind. boil). Can. from (ola, can. inner + vrana, san. ulcer). Mal. from (mahá, san. great + vrana, san. wound). Tam. from sanscrit. Abscess.——*Visarpam* (विसर्प - visarpa, San.; شرجا - sharjá, Hind.; ದದ್ದುರೋಗ - dadduróga, Can.; అక్కి - akki, Tel.; കഴലപ്പനി - kazhalappani, Mal.; அக்கி - akki, Tam.). Title from sanscrit. San. from (vi, san. intensive prefix + srip, san. to creep). Hind. means lion. Can. from (daddu, can. eruption + róga, san. disease). Tel. and Tam. from (agni, san. fire). Mal. from (kazhala, mal. swelling + pani, mal. fever). Erisipelas. The symptoms are slight swelling of the whole body, which passes from one part to another, fever, the swelling is red with vesications; when the inflammation is deep, the flesh and vessels are destroyed: and it discharges a matter like a mixture of water and clay; such cases are incurable.——*Vishama jwaram* (विषमज्वर - vishamajvara, San.; ٹھنڈتپ - thandtap, Hind.; ವರಿಸೆಜ್ವರ - varisejvara, Can.; చలిజ్వరము - tsalijvaramu, Tel.; ഒന്നരാടൻപനി - onnarátanpani, Mal.; குளிர்காய்ச்சல் - kulirgáyççal, Tam.). Title from sanscrit. San. from (vishama, san. intermittent + jvara, san. fever). Hind. from (thand, hind. cold + tap, hind. fever). Can. from (varise, can. turn + jvara, san. fever). Tel. from (tsali, tel. cold + jvara, san. fever). Mal. from (onnarátan, mal. on alternate days + pani, mal. fever). Tam. from (kulir, tam. cold + káyççal, tam. fever). Fever, intermittent. The general symptoms are as follows; when the paroxysm occurs at uncertain periods, the patient feels first cold, then hot, and afterwards perspires; there are five varieties. Santata jwaram, this affects the chyle and blood, and continues for seven, ten, or twelve days; followed by an interval and again occurs, and remains for several days. Satata jwaram; this has two paroxysms daily, one at night, and another during the day. Anyedyooshcam; in this variety the paroxysm of fever recurs at the same hour daily. Triteeyacam; in this variety the fever returns at an interval of one day. Chautoortacam; in this variety, the paroxysms of the fever occur every fourth day.——*Vishoochicay* (विषूचिका - vishúchiká, San.; هيضه وبائی - haizahiwabái, Hind.; ವಾಂತಿಭೇದಿ - vántibhédi, Can.; వాంతిభ్రాంతి - vántibhránti, Tel.; നീർത്തിരിപ്പ് - nírttirippu, Mal.; குருவாந்திபேதி - kurúravándibéthi, Tam.). Title from sanscrit. San. from (vi, san. intensive prefix + súch, san. to indicate). Hind. from (haizah, ar. looseness of bowels + wabá, ar. cholera). Can. from (vánti, san. vomiting + bhédi, san. purging). Tel. from (vánti, tel. vomiting + bhránti, san. fear). Mal. from (nír, mal. water + tiri, mal. to turn). Tam. from (krúra, san. fierce + vánti, san. vomiting + bhédi, san. loosening the bowels). Cholera morbus. There is pain as from indigestion [ajeernam], in the abdomen followed by frequent stools and vomitting, great thirst and pain in the abdomen, fainting, giddiness yawning and cramps in the legs; the color of the body is altered accompanied with shivering, pain in the chest and head-ache; the unfavorable symptoms are the lips, teeth and nails become blackish, the person insensible, with frequent vomiting; the eyes become sunken, voice feeble, and the joints loose, with great debility; the most fatal symptoms are want of sleep, restlessness, shivering, no secretion of urine and insensibility [vaunty bhaidy].——*Vispotam* (विस्फोट - visp'hóta, San.; دنبل - dumbal, Hind.; ನೆತ್ತರಗಡ್ಡೆ - nettaragadde, Can.; కురుపు - kurupu, Tel.; കുരു - kuru, Mal.; சிலந்தி - shilandi, Tam.). San. from (vi, san. intensive prefix + sp'hut, san. to burst open). Can. from (nettaru, can. blood + gadde, can. lump). Mal. means shooting. Boil.——*Vranam* (व्रण - vrana, San.; پھوڑا - phorá, Hind.; ಹುಣ್ಣು - hunnu, Can.; పుండు - pundu, Tel.; പുണ്ണ് - punnu, Mal.; புண் - pun, Tam.). San. from (vran, san. to wound). Ulcer, simple. Ulcers are either produced from exterior or internal causes; the deranged humours and blood produce them. The varieties are:—Vautica vranam; this is characterized by its black or red appearance, it is superficial, and discharges a cold, mucilaginous and scanty discharge; the pain is also peculiar, being of a crackling stiff kind; this pain is severe and does not affect the flesh. Peitica vranam; this is of a yellowish blue color, and is surrounded by a red color and yellow eruptions, spreads quickly, and discharges a hot and red matter with a burning pain. Caphaja vranam; there is much itchiness, and the ulcer is deep seated; the vessels and nerves of the part are affected, and it is hard and white without much pain, and the discharge is white, cold, mucilaginous and thick. Ractaja vranam; the ulcer becomes red and is surrounded with black vessels; the smell is like that of a horse stable; with much pain, great heat, and it discharges blood and is accompanied with symptoms of bile [pittam].——*Vridhnam* (वृध्न - vridhna, San.; بد - bad, Hind.; ತೊಡೆವಾಳೆ - todevále, Can.; వోడిసెగడ్డ - vódisegadda, Tel.; അരക്ലേശം - araklésham, Mal.; அரையாப்பு - araiyáppu, Tam.). Title from sanscrit. San. from (vridh, san. to increase). Tel. from (odi, tel. loins + gadda, tel. boil). Mal. from (ara, mal. waist + klésha, san. pain). Tam. from (arai, tam. waist + áppu, tam. wedge). Bubo.——*Vrishchicadamsham* (वृश्चिकदंश - vrishchikadamsha, San.; بچھوکاٹنا - biççhúkátná, Hind.; ಚೇಳುಕುಟುಕು - chélukutuku, Can.; తేలుకొట్టు - télukottu, Tel.; തേൾകൊത്ത് - télkotta, Mal.; தேள்கடி - télgadi, Tam.). Title from sanscrit. San. from (vrishchica, san. scorpion + dash, san. to bite). Hind. from (biççhú, hind. scorpion + kátná, hind. to bite). Can. from (chélu, can. scorpion + kututsu, can. to sting). Tel. from (télu, tel. scorpion + kuttu, tel. to sting). Mal. from (tél, mal. scorpion + kottu, mal. to sting). Tam. from (tél, tam. scorpion + kadi, tam. to bite). Scorpion sting. There are three varieties of these bites, according as they are mild, strong and very strong; scorpions generated in dung hills are not so poisonous as those generated in bricks and dry places; those generated in the putrid carcases of serpents and other venomous animals have the most violent poisons; the symptoms of the bites of these resemble those produced by the bites of serpents [sarpadamsham]; the weak kinds produce pain, swelling, followed by shivering and fever, with perspiration and stiffness of the body; the second class produce swelling of the tongue so as to prevent swallowing, fainting and much pain.——*Yakrit rogam* (यकृद्रोग - yakridróga, San.; کلیجے کا درد - kálíjekádard, Hind.; ಪಾರ್ಶ್ವಶೂಲಿ - párshvashúli, Can.; పక్కశూల - pakkashúla, Tel.; പക്കശൂലി - pakkashúli, Mal.; பக்கசூலை - pakkasúlai, Tam.). Title from sanscrit. San. from (yakrit, san. liver + róga, san. disease). Hind. from (kalíjah, hind. liver + dard, hind. pain). Can. from (párshva, san. side + shúla, san. pain). Tel. from (pakka, tel. side + shúla, san. pain). Mal.

from (pakka, mal. side + shúla, san. pain). Tam. from (pakkam, tam. side + shúla, san. pain). Liver disease. This occurs when the liver is swelled; in this form the air [vautam], bile [pittam] and phlegm [sheetam] are deranged and the disease is severe; this is to be treated by opening the vein at the bend of the right arm, after ghee [q.v.] has been given and perspiration has been promoted.——(6) The following are the forms of prescription among veidyans.——*Abhyangam* (अभ्यङ्ग - abhyanga, San.; ضماد - zimád, Ar.; ليپ - lep, Hind.; ಅಡಿವಾಳ - adivála, Can.; తైలము - tailamu, Tel.; കുഴമ്പ് - kuzhampu, Mal.; துவாலை - tuválai, Tam.). Title from sanscrit. San. from (abhi, san. over + anga, san. body). Ar. from (zamada, ar. to bind a wound). Hind. from (lip, san. to anoint). Tel. from (tila, san. gingelly seed). Mal. from (kuzha, mal. to mix). Tam. from (tuval, tam. to adhere as oil). Liniment for the whole body.——*Choornam* (चूर्ण - chúrna, San.; سفوف - safúf, Ar.; بكني - bukní, Hind.; ಚೂರ್ಣ - chúrna, Can.; చూర్ణము - chúrnamu, Tel.; ചൂര്‍ണ്ണം - chúrnan, Mal.; சூரணம் - shúranam, Tam.). Title from sanscrit. San. from (chúrn, san. to grind). Ar. from (saffa, ar. to eat). Drav. from sanscrit. Powder; this is more properly speaking a compound powder of several well-dried plants; prepared by pounding dry substances in a mortar with a pestle, and passing the powder through the cloth; generally sugar [q.v.] is mixed with powders for use.——*Ghooticay* (घुटिका - ghutiká, San.; حب - habb, Ar.; گولی - golí, Hind.; ಗುಳಿಗೆ - gulige, Can.; మాత్ర - mátra, Tel.; ഗുളിക - gulika, Mal.; குளிகை - kuligai, Tam.). Title from sanscrit. San. from (ghut, san. to preserve). Ar. means grain or seed. Mal. and Tam. from sanscrit. Pill; this is usually prepared by reducing a decoction [kwautam] of vegetable substances to a thick consistence and then adding some powders for making a pill-mass; sometimes pill-masses are made of powdered medicines with the addition of treacle [jaggery] or honey [shahad].——*Kwautam* (क्वाथ - kvát'ha, San.; جوشانده - joshándah, Pers.; کاڑا - kárá, Hind.; ಕಷಾಯ - kasháya, Can.; కషాయము kasháyamu, Tel.; കഷായം - kasháyam, Mal.; கசாயம் - kasáyam, Tam.). Title from sanscrit. San. from (kvat'h, san. to boil). Pers. from (josh, pers. boiling + nidah, pers. present participial suffix). Hind. from (karshana, san. drawing). Mal. and Tam. from (kash, san. to rub). Decoction. This is as a general rule prepared by boiling one part of vegetable substances with sixteen parts of water, till the latter is reduced to one-fourth; the medicines should first be pounded small, then boiled over a slow fire, and the decoction strained through cloth; when decoctions are prepared with dry substances, eight parts of water are recommended to be used; decoctions are administered with the addition of salt [ooppoo], honey [shahad], sugar [q.v.], treacle [jaggery], alkalies [cauram], clarified butter [ghee], oil [yennay], or some medicinal powders.——*Laihyam* (लेह्य - léhya, San.; حلوا - halwá, Hind.; ಲೇಹ್ಯ - léhya, Can.; లేహము - léhamu, Tel.; ലേഹം - léham, Mal.; இலேகியம் - ilégiyam, Tam.). Title from sanscrit. San. from (lih, san. to lick). Hind. from (halau, ar. sweet). Drav. from sanscrit. Electuary. Laihyam is composed of drugs in powder or decoction [kwautam], and some oil [yennay] or ghee [q.v.], honey [shahad], sugar [q.v.], or old jaggery [q.v.]; the sugar or the jaggery is made into a pure syrup of a thick consistence, with the addition of the decoction; when the syrup is hot, and when the decoction is not mixed with it, the powdered things, ghee, and honey are mixed, and the resulting thick mass is taken out of the vessel and preserved for use.——*Pauntam* (फाण्ट - p'hánta, San.; خیسانده - khísándah, Hind.; ಊಟೆ - úte, Can.; ఊట - úta, Tel.; ശീതകഷായം - shíta-kasháyam, Mal.; கசாயம் - kasáyam, Tam.). Title from sanscrit. San. from (p'han, san. to run). Hind. from (khísánidan, pers. to steep). Tel. from (úru, tel. to soak). Mal. from (shíta, san. cold + kasháya, san. decoction). Tam. from (kash, san. to rub). Infusion. This is prepared by steeping one part of powdered herbs in eight parts of hot water, for twelve hours during the night. Sheetacashayam or cold infusion is prepared by steeping one part of a drug in six of water for the night and straining the fluid in the morning. Pauneeyam is a weak sort of decoction prepared by boiling one part of medicinal substances in thirty-two of water till the latter is reduced to one-half; this preparation is usually taken adlibitum for appeasing thirst or some such object. Pramatyay is a sort of decoction in which the medicines are first reduced to a pulp and then boiled in eight parts of water, till the latter is reduced to one-fourth; this is administered with the addition of honey [shahad]. Csheerapaucam or decoction in milk; the proportions in this preparation, are one part of medicine, eight of milk [paul], and thirty-two of water; the materials are boiled together, till the water is evaporated and the milk alone remains; the decoction is then strained.——*Pralaipam* (प्रलेप - pralépa, San.; مرهم - marham, Hind.; ಮುಲಾಮು - mulámu, Can.; మలాము - malámu, Tel.; മുറിമരുന്ന് - murimarunnu, Mal.; பூச்சு - púççu, Tam.). Title from sanscrit. San. from (pra, san. intensive prefix + lip, san. to smear). Tel. from (mulammá, hind. gilding). Mal. from (muri, mal. wound + marunnu, mal. medicine). Tam. from (púsu, tam. to daub). Plaster.——*Snehanam* (स्नेहन - snehana, San.; ضماد - zimád, Hind.; ತೈಲ - taila, Can.; తైలము - tailamu, Tel.; തൈലം - tailam, Mal.; தைலம் - tailam, Tam.). Title from sanscrit. San. from (snih, san. to be adhesive). Hind. from (zimada, ar. to bind a wound). Drav. from (tila, san. plant, sesamum indicum, linn). Liniment; this is usually prepared by mixing with oil four times the quantity of milk, whey, cow's urine, &c.; then boil, and when the watery part is evaporated, certain fragrant medicines are added, and it is then strained through cloth.——(7) The following key-lists show the Sanscrit terms for medicinal powers with all the plants yielding them which are known as such to European science in this country; further information must be traced in the glossary paragraphs through the small-type cross references at end of this volume; see also vricsham, 7, for the method of expressing the products, &c., of plants in the dravidian languages.——*Aucshepagnam* (आक्षेपघ्न - ákshépaghna, San.; دافع تشنج - dáfaitashannuj, Hind.; இசிவுநோப்பி - isivu-noppi, Tam.). San. from (ákshépa, san. convulsion + han, san. to destroy). Hind. from (dáfa, ar. antidote + tashannuj, ar. convulsion). Tam. from (isivu, tam. convulsion + noppu, tam. to hinder). Antispasmodics, from:—Adhatoda vasica, nees. [adhatoday], Andropogon schœnanthus, rox. [lemon grass], Artemisia vulgaris, linn. [indian absinth], Cannabis sativa, linn. [kinnab], Carum copticum, benth. [ajwaun], Datura fastuosa, linn. [purple datura]; Draconitum polyphyllum, linn. [wild telinga potato], Euphorbia nereifolia, linn. [leafy milk-hedge], Ferula narthex, bois. [asafœtida], Gardenia gummifera, linn. [decamallee], Gynandropsis pentaphylla, dec. [vailay], Lobelia nicotianæfolia, heyne [wild pogauk], Nardostachys jatamansi, dec. [jatamansy], Nicotiana tabacum, linn. [pogauk], Papaver somniferum, linn. [opium poppy].——*Chedanam* (छेदन - chhédana, San.; مفتحات بلغم - mufattihátibalgham, Hind.; கோழையறுப்பான் - kózhaiyaruppán, Tam.). San. from (chhid, san. to cut). Hind. from (mufattihát, ar. opener + balgham, ar. phlegm). Tam. from (kózhai, tam. phlegm + aru, tam. to cut). Expectorants, from:—Acalypha indica, linn. [cooppamainy], Adhatoda vasica, nees. [adhatoday], Altingia excelsa, noronha [java storax], Anisochilus carnosus, wall. country lavender], Balsamodendron mukul, hooker [mookul bdellium], Bœrhaavia repens, linn., var. diffusa [tikry], Crinum asiaticum, linn. [poison bamboo], Dæmia extensa, r. br. [hedge cotton], Dorema aureum, stocks [ooshak], Ocimum basilicum, linn. [fragrant toolsy], Ocimum sanctum, linn. [common toolsy], Polygala telephioides, willd. [large nangay], Solanum xanthocarpum, schr. and wendl. [prickly brinjaul], Tylophora asthmatica, w. et a. [indian ipecacuanha], Urginia indica, kunth [squill].——*Cooshtagnam* (कुष्ठघ्न - kusht'haghna, San.; مصفی خون - musaffíkhún, Hind.; கரப்பாங்கொல்லி - karappángolli, Tam.). San. from (kusht'ha, san. leprosy + han, san. to destroy). Hind. from (musaffí, ar. purifier + khún, pers. blood). Tam. from (karappán, tam. disease so called + kol, tam. to kill). Antiscorbutics, from:—Citrus aurantium, linn., var. bergamia, brandis [bergamot orange], Musa paradisiaca, linn. [plantain], Phyllanthus emblica, linn. [emblic myrobalan.——*Deepanam* (दीपन - dípana, San.; مفرحات - mufarrihát, Hind.; காரம் - káram, Tam.). San. from (díp, san. to burn). Hind. from (faraha, ar. to make happy). General stimulant, from:—Anacardium occidentale, linn. [cashew], Andropogon schœnanthus, roxb. [lemon grass], Bassia latifolia, roxb. [wild mohwah], Bassia longifolia, linn. [common mohwah], Borassus flabelliformis, linn. [palmyra], Cannabis sativa, linn. [kinnab], Caryota urens, linn. [bastard sago palm], Celastrus paniculatus, willd. [malkangany], Cocos nucifera, linn. [cocoanut], Nardostachys jatamansi, dc. [jatamansy], Peganum harmala, linn. [barmal], Rubia cordifolia, linn. [munjeet], Salix caprea, linn. [aromatic willow], Salvadora persica, linn. [tooth-brush tree], Vitex negundo, linn. [notchy], Vitex trifolia, linn. [water notchy].——*Jwaragnam* (ज्वरघ्न - jvaraghna, San.; دافع تپ - dáfaitap, Hind.; காய்ச்சலடக்கி - káyççaladakki, Tam.). San. from (jvara, san. fever + han, san. to destroy). Hind. from (dáfa, ar. curer + tap, hind. fever). Tam. from (káyççal, tam. fever + adakku, tam. to suppress). Febrifuges, from:—Aconitum heterophyllum, wall. [atees], Acorus calamus, linn. [vashamboo], Adansonia digitata, linn. [baobab], Alstonia scholaris, r. br. [dita], Aristolochia bracteata, retz. [indian worm-killer], Aristolochia indica, linn. [isharmool], Berberis asiatica, roxb. [berberry], Cæsalpinia bonducella, flem. [bonduc], Cæsalpinia coriaria, willd. [divy divy], Cedrela toona, roxb. [toon], Clerodendron infortunatum, gærtn. [saraswaty's leaf], Ficus oppositifolia, gasp. [devil fig], Helleborus niger, linn. [black cootkee], Holarrhena antidysenterica, r. br. [tellicherry bark], Justicia gendarussa, linn. [common gendarussa], Melia azadirachta, linn. [neem], Michelia champaca, linn. [champak], Papaver somniferum, linn. [opium poppy], Piper nigrum, linn. [black pepper], Plumbago zeylanica, linn. [chitramoolam], Salix tetrasperma, roxb. [indian willow], Soymida febrifuga, juss. [soymida], Strychnos colubrina, linn. [snake wood tree], Strychnos nux-vomica, linn. [poison nut], Thevetia nereifolia, juss. [yellow gannair], Toddalia aculeata, pers. [toddaly].——*Keetagnam* (कीटघ्न - kítaghna, San.; قاطعات كرم - kátiátikirm, Hind.; பூச்சிகொல்லி - púççigolli, Tam.). San. from (kíta, san. insect + han, san. to destroy). Hind. from (kátiát, ar. dispeller + kirm, pers. worm). Tam. from (púççi, tam. insect + kollu, tam. to kill).

Insecticides, from :—Acorus calamus, linn. [vashamboo], Anamirta cocculus, w. et. a. [indian berry], Melia azadirachta, linn. [neem], Saussurea lappa, clarke [costum], Vernonia anthelmintica, willd [wild jeerah].——*Krimignam.*(कृमिघ्न - krimighna, San. ; قاطعات ديدان - kátiátidídán, Hind. ; புழுகொல்லி - puzhugolli, Tam.). San. from (krimi, san. insect + han, san. to destroy). Hind. from (kátiát, ar. dispeller + dídán, ar. tape worm). Tam. from (puzhu, tam. worm + kollu, tam. to kill). Anthelmintics from :—Alstonia scholaris, r. br. [dita], Areca catechu, linn. [areca], Aristolochia bracteata, retz. [indian worm-killer], Butea frondosa, roxb. [palaus], Carica papaya, linn. [papaw], Clerodendron infortunatum, gærtn. [saraswaty's leaf], Cucurbita pepo, dec. [common pumpkin], Garcinia morella, desr. [Ceylon gamboge], Gisekia pharnaceoides, linn. [manaly], Holarrhena antidysenterica, wall. [tellicherry bark], Mallotus philippensis, mull. [kamela], Mangifera indica, linn. [mango], Melia azadirachta, linn. [neem], Melia azedarach, linn. [large neem], Mucuna pruriens, dc. [common cowitch], Peganum harmala, linn. [harmal], Punica granatum, linn. [anaur], Quisqualis indica, linn. [rangoon creeper], Rauwolfia serpentina, benth. [snake root], Vernonia anthelmintica, willd. [wild jeerah].——*Laulah srawvy* (लालास्रावी - lálásráví, San. ; مويد رياق - muaiyyidiriyák, Hind. ; உமிழ்நீர்ப்பெருக்கி - uminírpperukki, Tam.). San. from (lála, san. saliva + srav, san. to flow out). Hind. from (muayyid, ar. strengthener + riyák, ar. saliva). Tam. from (uminir, tam. saliva + perukku, tam. to cause to increase). Silagogues, from :—Chrysanthemum coronarium, linn. [shaumanty], Moringa pterygosperma, gærtn. [moringa], Plumbago rosea, linn. [chitramoolam], Plumbago zeylanica, linn. [chitramoolam], Solanum xanthocarpum, schrad. and wendl. [prickly brinjaul].——*Mootralam* (मूत्रल - mútrala, San. ; مدرات - mudirrát, Hind. ; சிறுநீர்ப்பெருக்கி - shirunírpperukki, Tam.). San. from (mútra, san. urine). Hind. from (darra, ar. to flow copiously). Tam. from (shirunír, tam. urine + perukku, tam. to cause to increase). Diuretics, from :—Achyranthes aspera, linn. [indian burr], Cissampelos pareira, linn. [indian pareira], Crinum asiaticum, linn. [poison bamboo], Dipterocarpus turbinatus, gærtn. [gurjan], Hemidesmus indicus, r. br. [indian sarsaparilla], Herpestis monniera, h. b. et k. [water zoofah], Hibiscus esculentus, linn. [common bendy], Hygrophila spinosa, t. and. [neermoolly], Luffa acutangula, roxb., var. amara, roxb. [bitter luffa], Moringa pterygosperma, gærtn. [moringa], Pedalium murex, linn. [elephant nerinjy], Phyllanthus niruri, muller [neeroory], Santalum album, linn. [sandal], Solanum nigrum, linn. [indian hounds' berry], Solanum xanthocarpum, schr. & wendl. [prickly brinjaul], Tribulus terrestris, linn. [nerinjy], Urginia indica, kunth. [squill], Withania somnifera, dun. [asgand].——*Netra roga deepanam* (नेत्ररोगदीपन - nétraróga-dípana, San. ; مفرحات امراض چشم - mufarrihátiamrázichashm, Hind. ; கண்ணோய்க்காரம் - kannóykkáram, Tam.). San. from (nétra, san. eye + róga, san. disease + dípana, san. stimulant). Hind. from (mufarrihát, ar. stimulants + amráz, ar. diseases + chashm, pers. eye). Tam. from (kan, tam. eye + nóy, tam. disease + káram, tam. hot thing). Stimulant applications in affections of the eye, from :—Argemone mexicana, linn. [bramhadand], Berberis aristata, dec. [berberry], Cassia absus, linn. [black horse-gram], Cassia auriculata, linn. [tungaid].——*Nirvaupanam* (निर्वापन - nirvápana, San. ; مبردات - mubarridát, Hind. ; குளிர்ச்சி - kulirççi, Tam.). San. from (nirvap, san. to sprinkle). Hind. from (baruda, ar. to become cold). Tam. from (kulir, tam. coldness). Refrigerants, from :—Adansonia digitata, linn. [baobab], Aloe indica, royle [common indian aloe], Aloe litoralis, kœn. [coromandel aloe], Borassus flabelliformis, linn. [palmyra], Cicer arietinum, linn. [bengal gram], Citrus aurantium, linn., var. bergamia, brandis [bergamot orange], Cocos nucifera, linn. [cocoanut], Hibiscus rosasinensis, linn. [china rose bendy], Santalum album, linn. [sandal], Tamarindus indica, linn. [tamarind].——*Niryausam* (निर्यास - niryása, San. ; صمغ - samagh, Ar. ; گوند - gond, Hind. ; பிசின் - pisin, Tam.). San. from (nir, san. out + yas, san. to strive). Gums, from :—Acacia arabica, willd. [babool], Acacia farnesiana, willd. [piyvail], Albizzia lebbek, benth. [common sirissa], Anacardium occidentale, linn. [cashew], Cochlospermum gossypium, dc. [golden silk cotton], Feronia elephantum, corr. [wood-apple], Odina wodier, roxb. [wodier]. For complete list of gums see Gond; see also Gum.——*Prasava saudhanam* (प्रसवसाधन - prasavasádhana, San. ; مخرج جنين - mukhrijijanín, Hind. ; பிரசவசாதனம் - pirasavasáthanam, Tam.). San. from (prasava, san. generating + sádhana, san. effecting). Hind. from (mukhrij, ar. expeller + janín, ar. foetus). Tam. from sanscrit. Parturifacients, from :—Cannabis sativa, linn. [kinnab], Aristolochia bracteata, retz. [indianworm-killer], Piper longum, linn. [long pepper], Rauwolfia serpentina, benth. [snake root].——*Praty copanam* (प्रतिकोपन - pratikópana, San. ادويه امالہ - adviahiimálah, Hind. ; எதிரழற்சி - ethirazharchi, Tam.). San. from (prati, san. counter + kup, san. to provoke). Tam. from (ethir, tam. opposite + azhal, tam. to burn). Counter-irritants, from :—Anacardium occidentale, linn. [cashew], Andropogon schœnanthus, roxb. [lemon grass], Anisomeles malabarica, r. br. [malabar catmint], Argyreia speciosa, sweet [seashore paulay], Baliospermum montanum, mull. [wild jamalgota], Brassica juncea, h. f. and t. [rayaun] Capsicum minimum, roxb. [bird's eye chilly], Croton oblongifolius, roxb. [devil's goad], Croton tiglium, linn. [jamalgota], Euphorbia antiquorum, linn. [square milk-hedge], Euphorbia tirucalli, linn. [round milk hedge], Gynandropsis pentaphylla, dc. [vailay], Jatropha curcas, linn. [wild aumanac], Jatropha glandulifera, roxb. [adul oil], Moringa pterygosperma, gærtn. [moringa], Myrica sapida, wall. [maroo-tham], Myristica fragrans, houtt. [common nutmeg], Myristica malabarica, lam. [malabar nutmeg], Piper betel, linn. [betel pepper], Piper chaba, hunter [chaab pepper], Piper longum, linn. [long pepper], Piper nigrum, linn. [black pepper], Plumbago rosea, linn. [chitramoolam], Plumbago zeylanica, linn. [chitramoolam], Salvadora persica, linn. [tooth-brush tree], Semecarpus anacardium, linn. [marking nut], Vateria indica, linn. [piney].——*Rasauyanam* (रसायन - rasáyana, San. ; مغيرات - mughaiyyirát, Hind. ; இரசாயனம் - irasáyanam, Tam.). San. from (rasa, san. essence + ayana, san. abode). Hind. from (ghaira, ar. to alter). Tam. from sanscrit. Alteratives, from :—Agave americana, linn. [american aloe], Calotropis gigantea, r. br. [yercum], Calotropis procera, r. br. [yercum], Clerodendron serratum, spreng. [knotted bhraungy], Corallocarpus epigæa, hook. [braminy kite caper], Echium sp. [gowzabaun], Eclipta alba, hassak. [bhangrah], ehretia buxifolia, roxb. [rough coorvitchy], Euphorbia antiquorum, linn. [square milk-hedge], Gynocardia odorata, r. br. [chaulmoogra], Hemidesmus indicus, r. br. [indian sarsaparilla], Hydnocarpus venenata, gærtn. [marotty], Hydrocotyle asiatica, linn. [indian pennywort], Ichnocarpus frutescens, r. br. [shyaumalatay], Smilax china, linn. [common china root], Smilax glabra, roxb. [large china root], Smilax lancæfolia, roxb. [indian china root], Smilax ovalifolia, roxb. [oval-leaved china root].——*Ritoo janacam* (ऋतुजनक - ritujanaka, San. ; مدرات حيض - mudirrátihaiz, Hind. ; இருதுப்பெருக்கி - iruthupperukki, Tam.). San. from (ritu, san. menstrual evacuation + janaka, san. generating). Hind. from (mudirrát, ar. promoter + haiz, ar. menstrual discharge). Tam. from (ritu, san. menstrual evacuation + perukku, tam. to increase). Emmenagogues, from :—Aloe indica, ryole [common indian aloe], Aloe litoralis, kœnig. [coromandel aloe], Andropogon muricatus, retz. [cuscus], Aristolochia bracteata, retz. [indian worm-killer], Aristolochia indica, linn. [isharmoól], Carica papaya, linn. [papaw], Peganum harmala, linn. [harmal], Plumbago rosea, linn. [chitramoolam], Ruta graveolens, linn. [sadauf], Sesamum indicum, dec. [gingelly].——*Shamacam* (शामक - shamaka, San. ; مزلقات - mazlikát, Hind. ; தணிப்பு - tanippu, Tam.). San. from (sham, san. to grow calm). Hind. from (zalaka, ar. to slip). Tam. from (tani, tam. to mitigate). Demulcents, from :—Abrus precatorius, linn. [indian liquorice], Amarantus spinosus, linn. [thorny spinach], Asparagopsis ascendens, kunth. [indian salep], Canarium commune, linn. [elemi], Clitoria ternatea, linn. [crow-creeper], Cordia myxa, linn. [small sebesten], Cordia obliqua, willd. [large sebesten], Curculigo orchioides, gærtn. [black moosly]; Cydonia vulgaris, pers. [bedauna], Gmelina asiatica, linn. [cashmere tree], Gracilaria lichenoides, grev. [cadal pausy], Heliotropium indicum, linn. [indian heliotrope], Hibiscus esculentus, linn. [common bendy], Ocimum basilicum, linn. [fragrant toolsy], Ocimum gratissimum, linn. [rama toolsy], Oryza sativa, linn. [paddy], Pedalium murex, linn. [elephant nerinjy], Plantago ovata, forsk. [spogel], Sesamum indicum, dec. [gingelly], Terminalia catappa, linn. [catapang], Trichodesma zeylanicum, r. br. [donkey toombay].——*Shamanam* (शमन - shamana, San. ; مسكنات - musakkinát, Hind. ; கொதிப்பாற்றி - kothippátti, Tam.). San. from (sham, san. to grow calm). Hind. from (sakana, ar. to allay). Tam. from (kothippu, tam. heat + áttu, tam. to mitigate). Sedatives, from :—Aconitum ferox, wall. [bachnaug], cannabis sativa, linn. [kinnab], Datura fastuosa, linn., var. alba [white datura], Hyoscyamus niger, linn. [persian ajwaun], Nicotiana tabacum, linn. [tobacco], Papaver somniferum, linn. [opium poppy], Santalum album, linn. [sandal], Saussurea lappa, clarke [costum], withania somnifera, dun. [asgand].——*Shonita staupanam* (शोणितस्थापन - shónitast'hápana, San. ; مقبضات خون - mukabbizátikhún, Hind. ; இரத்தமடக்கி - irrattamadakki, Tam.). San. from (shónita, san. blood + st'hápana, san. fixing). Hind. from (mukabbizát, ar. binder + khún, pers. blood). Tam. from (rakta, san. blood + adakku, tam. to restrain). Styptics, from :—Borassus flabelliformis, linn. [palmyra], Cocos nucifera, linn. [cocoanut], Colocasia antiquorum, schott. [kachwee].——*Spotaca pralepanam* (स्फोटकप्रलेपन - sp'hótakapralépana, San. ; منفطات - munaffitát, Hind. ; دواء آبلہ آور - davááblilahawur, Hind. ; கொப்புளிக்குமருந்து - koppulikkumarundu, Tam.). San. from (sp'hótaka, san. boil + pralépa, san. plaster). Ar from (nafata, ar. blister). Hind. from (davá, ar. medicine + ábilah, ar. boil + áwur, pers. raiser). Tam. from (koppuli, tam. to rise in blisters + marundu, tam. medicine). Vesicants, from ;—Brassica juncea, h. f. & t. [rayaun], Plumbago rosea, linn. [chitramoolam], Plumbago zeylanica, linn., [chitramoolam], Salvadora persica, linn. [tooth-brush tree].——*Stambhanam* (स्तम्भन - stambhana, San. ; قابضات - kábizát, Hind. ; துவர் - tuvar, Tam.). San. from (stambh, san. to fix firmly). Hind. from (kabaza, ar. to grasp firmly). Tam. from (tuvara, san. astringent). Astringents, from :—Acacia arabica, willd. [babool], Acacia catechu, willd. [catechu], Ægle marmelos. corr. [bael], Areca catechu, linn. [areca], Bombax malabaricum, dec. [red cotton tree], Butea frondosa, roxb.

[palaus], Cæsalpinia coriaria, willd. [divy-divy], Cæsalpinia sappan, linn. [sappan], Cassia auriculata, linn. [tungaid], Casuarina equisetifolia, forst. [chowk maram], Cordia rotlii, rœm and sch. [narrow-leaved sebesten], Diospyros embryopteris, pers. [gaub], Eucalyptus resinifera, smith [australian gum tree], Eugenia jambolana, lam. [common jaumoon], Feronia elephantum, corr. [wood-apple], Garcinia mangostana, linn. [mangosteen], Holarrhena antidysenterica, wall. [tellicherry bark], Lawsonia alba, lam. [mindie], Mangifera indica, linn. [mango], Odina wodier, roxb. [wodier], Phyllanthus emblica, linn. [emblic myrobalan], Psidium guyava, linn., var. pomiferum, linn. [guava], Psidium guyava, linn. var. pyriferum, linn. [guava], Pterocarpus marsupium, roxb. [vengay], Punica granatum, linn. [anaur], Rhus succedania, linn. [red lac sumach], Tamarindus indica, linn. [tamarind], Tamarix articulata, vahl. [red jhow] Tamarix gallica, linn. [manna jhow], Terminalia chebula, retz. [chebulic myrobalan], Terminalia tomentosa, bedd. var. typica [black murdah].——*Stanya janạnam* (स्तन्यजनन - stanyajanana, San.; مدرات لبن - mudirrátilaban, Hind.; பாற்பெருக்கி - párberukki, Tam.). San. from (stanya, san. milk + janana, san. generating). Hind. from (mudirrát, ar. promoter + laban, ar. milk). Tam. from (pál, tam. milk + perukku, tam. to increase). Lactagogues, from:—Jatropha curcas, linn. [wild aumanac], Ricinus communis, linn. [aumanac].——*Stanya shoshanam* (स्तन्यशोषण - stanyashóshana, San.; قاطعات لبن - kátiátilaban, Hind.; பாற் சுருக்கி - párchurukki, Tam.). San. from (stanya, san. milk + shush, san. to dry). Tam. from (pál, tam. milk + shurukku, tam. to lessen). Lactifuges, from:—Jasminum sambac, aiton. [arabian jasmine], Piper betel, linn. [betel pepper].——*Svedanam* (स्वेदन - svédana, San.; معرقات - muarrikát, Hind.; வேர்வைவாங்கி - vérvaivángi, Tam.). San. from (swid, san to sweat). Hind. from (arak, ar. perspiration). Tam. from (vérvai, tam. sweat + vángu, tam. to admit). Sudorifics, from:—Acorus calamus, linn. [vashamboo], Andropogon muricatus, retz. [cuscus], Andropogon schœnanthus, roxb. [lemon grass], Anisochilus carnosus, wall. [country borage], Anisomeles malabarica, r. br. [malabar catmint], Anisomeles ovata, r. br. [malabar catmint], Berberis asiatica, roxb. [berberry], Calotropis gigantea, r. br. [yercum], Calotropis procera, r. br. [yercum], Celastrus paniculatus, willd. [malkangany], Crinum asiaticum, linn. [poison bamboo], Cyperus pertenuis, roxb. [straight sedge], Cyperus rotundus, linn. [common sedge], Eupatorium ayapana, vent. [ayappanay], Hemidesmus indicus, r. br. [indian sarsaparilla], Justicia gendarussa, linn. [common gendarussa], Moringa pterygosperma, gærtn. [moringa], Ocimum sanctum, linn. [common toolsy], Papaver somniferum, linn. [opium poppy], Plumbago zeylanica, linn. [chitramoolam], Scindapsus officinalis, schott [elephant long pepper], Tylophora asthmatica, w. et. a. [indian ipécacuanha], Zingiber officinale, roscoe [ginger].——*Taurah vivàuranam* (ताराविवारण - tárá-vivárana, San.; كشائندة ثقبة چشم - kusháindahisukbahichashm, Hind.; விரிகண்மணி - viriganmani, Tam.). San. from (tárá, san. pupil of the eye + vivri, san. to make clear). Hind. from (kusháindah, pers. opener + sukbah, ar. hole + chashm, pers. eye). Tam. from (viri, tam. to expand + kanmani, tam. apple of the eye). Mydriatics, from:—Datura fastuosa, linn. var. alba. [white datura].——*Teilam* (तैल - taila, San.; تيل - tel, Hind.; எண்ணெய் - enney, Tam.). San. from (tila, san. sesamum). Tam. from (el, tam. plant sesamum indicum, linn. + ney, tam. ghee). Oils, from:—Aleurites triloba, forst. [lumbang nut], Anacardium occidentale, linn. [cashew], Arachis hypogæa, linn. [ground nut], Bassia butyracea, roxb. [butter mohwah], Bassia latifolia, roxb. [wild mohwah], Bassia longifolia, linn. [common mohwah], Calophyllum inophyllum, linn. [common poon], Canarium commune, linn. [elemi], Cocos nucifera, linn. [cocoanut], Garcinia indica, chois. [mate mangosteen], Moringa pterygosperma, gærtn. [moringa], Sesamum indicum, dec. [gingelly], Terminalia catappa, linn. [catapang]. For oils generally see Yonnay.——*Tikta soogandhy balyam* (तिक्तसुगन्धिबल्य - tiktasugandhibalya, San.; مقويات خوشبو و تلخ - mukavviyátikhushbowatalkh, Hind.; கைப்புமணவியவலியுருத்தி - kaippumanaviyavaliyurutti, Tam.). San. from (tikta, san. bitter + sugandha, san. aromatic + balya, san. tonic). Hind. from (mukavviyát, ar. tonics + khushbo, pers. aromatic + talkh, pers. bitter). Tam. from (kaippu, tam. bitterness + manam, tam. smell + vali, tam. strength + uruttu, tam. to produce). Tonics, Bitter and Aromatic, from:—Aconitum heterophyllum, wall. [atees], Acorus calamus, linn. [vashamboo], Ailanthus excelsa, roxb. [coromandel ailanto], Andrographis paniculata [french chiretta], Antiaris saccidora, dalz. [sack tree], Aristolochia indica, linn. [isharmool], Artemisia vulgaris, linn. [indian absinth], Berberis asiatica, dc. [berberry], Cæsalpinia bonducella, flem. [bonduc], Chrysanthemum coronarium, linn. [shaumanty], Cissampelos pareira, linn. [indian pareira], Clerodendron infortunatum, gærtn. [saraswaty's leaf], Cocculus villosus, dec. [jamtee], Coptis teeta, wall. [mamiraun], Cordia myxa, linn. [small sebesten], Cordia obliqua, willd. [large sebesten], Coscinium fenestratum, coleber [false calumba], Cratœva religiosa, forst. [nirval], Cyperus pertenuis, roxb. [straight sedge], Cyperus rotundus, linn. [common sedge], Enicostema littorale, blume [small chiretta], Erythræa roxburghii, g. don. [roxburgh's chiretta], Eupatorium ayapana, vent. [ayappanay], Exacum bicolor, roxb. [purple chiretta], Ficus oppositifolia, gasp. [devil fig], Luffa acutangula, roxb. var. amara [bitter luffa], Mesua ferrea, linn. [nauga champak], Michelia champaca, linn. [champak], Ophiorrhiza mungos, linn. [mongoose snake root], Picrorhiza kurrooa, benth. [cootkee], Rauwolfia serpentina, benth. [snake root], Sida carpinifolia, linn. [lance-leaved balah], Strychnos nux-vomica, linn. [poison nut], Swertia affinis, clarke [blue flowered chiretta], Swertia chirata, ham. [himalayan chiretta], Swertia decussata, nimmo. [mahableshwar chiretta], Thalictrum foliolosum, dc. [momiree], Tinospora cordifolia, miers. [goolancha], Tinospora crispa, miers. [goolancha], Toddalia aculeata, pers. [toddaly], Trichosanthes nervifolia, linn. [short snake-gourd] Trichosanthes palmata, roxb. [bitter snake-gourd].——*Tilaparneeya deepanam* (तिलपर्णीयदीपन - tilaparníyadípana, San.; مفرحات تربنتينيه - mufarrihátitirbintíniyah, Hind.; கர்ப்பூரதைலக்காரம் - karppúrathailakkáram, Tam.). San. from (tilaparna, san. turpentine + dípana, san. stimulant). Hind. from (mufarrihát, ar. stimulants + tirbintíniyah, ar. terebinthinate). Tam. from (karpúra, san. camphor + taila, san. oil + káram, tam. hot thing). Terebinthinate Stimulants, from:—Ailanthus malabarica, dc. [malabar ailanto], Balsamodendron mukul, hook. [mookul bdellium], Calophyllum inophyllum, linn. [common poon], Canarium commune, linn. [elemi], Canarium strictum, roxb. [black dammer], Cedrus deodara, loud. [deodar], Dipterocarpus turbinatus, gærtn. [gurjan], Dorema aureum, stocks. [ooshak], Pinus longifolia, roxb. [cheer], Shorea robusta, roxb. [common saul], Vateria indica, linn. [piney].——*Toovara balyam* (तुवरबल्य - tuvarabalya, San.; مقويات قابض - mukavviyátikábiz, Hind.; துவர்வலியுருத்தி - tuvarvaliyurutti, Tam.). Title from sanscrit. San. from (tuvara, san. astringent + balya, san. tonic). Hind. from (mukavviyát, ar. tonics + kábiz, ar. astringent). Tam. from (tuvara, san. astringent + vali, tam. strength + uruttu, tam. to produce). Tonics, Astringent, from:—Alstonia scholaris, r. br. [dita], Carapa moluccensis, lam. [crab oil plant], Cedrela toona, roxb. [toon], Diospyros melanoxylon, roxb. [coromandel ebony], Flacourtia cataphracta, roxb. [indian plum], Holarrhena antidysenterica, wall. [tellicherry bark], Hymenodictyon excelsum, wall. [wild anaur], Melia azadirachta, linn. [neem], Mimusops elengi, linn. [ilanjy], Rhus succedanea, linn. [red lac sumach], Soymida febrifuga, juss. [soymida], Terminalia chebula, retz. [chebulic myrobalan].——*Trak roga deepànam* (त्वग्रोगदीपन - tvagrógadípana, San.; محركات امراض لحمى - muharrikátiamrázilahmí, Hind.; தோல்நோய்க்காரம் - tólnóykkáram, Tam.). San. from (tvak, san. skin + róga, san. disease + dípana, san. stimulant). Hind. from (muharrikát, ar. stimulants + amráz, ar. diseases + lahmí, ar. relating to skin). Tam. from (tól, tam. skin + nóy, tam. disease + káram, tam. hot thing). Stimulant applications in Skin diseases, from:—Argemone mexicana, linn. [bramhadand], Cassia alata, linn. [foreign agatty], Cassia occidentalis, linn. [casondy], Cassia sophera, linn. [stinking casondy], Cassia tora, linn. [chakondah], Cedrus deodara, loud. [deodar], Ficus bengalensis, gasp. [banyan], Heliotropium indicum, linn. [indian heliotrope], Pongamia glabra, vent. [karanj], Rhinacanthus communis, nees [snake jasmine], Santalum album, linn. [saǹdal], Thespesia populnea, corr. [portia].——*Vamunum* (वमन - vamana, San.; مقيات - makíyát, Hind.; வாந்திமருந்து - vándimarundu, Tam.). San. from (vam, san. to vomit). Hind. from (kai, ar. vomiting). Tam. from (vánti, san. vomiting + marundu, tam. medicine). Emetics, from:—Acalypha indica, linn. [cooppamainy], Bassia latifolia, roxb. [wild mohwah], Bassia longifolia, linn. [common mohwah], Brassica juncea, h. f. and t. [rayaun]; Calotropis gigantea, r. br. [yercum], Calotropis procera, r. br. [yercum], Crinum asiaticum, linn. [poison bamboo], Ficus oppositifolia, gasp. [devil fig], Randia dumetòrum, lamk. [common emetic nut], Tylophora asthmatica, w. et a. [indian ipecacuanha], Urginia indica, kunth. [squill], Withania coagulans, dun. [asgand].——*Vautagnam* (वातघ्न - vátaghna, San.; مفششيات - mufashshiyát, Hind.; வாதமடக்கி - váthamadakki, Tam.). San. from (váta, san. wind + han, san. to destroy). Hind. from arabic meaning wind expelling. Tam. from (váta, san. air + adakku, tam. to suppress). Carminatives, from:—Acorus calamus, linn. [vashamboo], Alpinia nutans, roscœ. [galangal], Amomum aromaticum, roxb. [wild cardamom], Andropogon schœnanthus, roxb. [lemon grass], Anisomeles malabarica, r. br. [malabar catmint], Anisomeles ovata, r. br. [malabar catmint], Artemisia vulgaris, linn. [indian absinth], Carum copticum, benth. [ajwaun], Carum roxburghianum, benth. [ajmood ajwaun], Chrysanthemum coronarium, linn. [shaumanty], Cinnamomum iners, reinw. [country cinnamon], Cinnamomum tamala, nees. [cassia cinnamon], Cinnamomum zeylanicum, breyn. [ceylon cinnamon], Coleus aromaticus, benth. [country borage], Cratæva religiosa, forst. [nirvala], Cuminum cyminum, linn. [jeerah], Curcuma amada, roxb. [mango ginger], Curcuma aromatica, salisb. [round zedoary], Curcuma zedoaria, roscoe [long zedoary], Cyperus pertenuis, roxb. [straight sedge], Cyperus rotundus, linn. [common sedge], Elettaria cardamomum, maton [cardamom], Eugenia caryophyllata, willd. [lavangam], Eupatorium ayapana, vent. [ayappanay], Feronia elephantum, corr. [wood-apple], Fœniculum vulgare, gærtn. [sonf], Hedychium spicatum, smith [europe zedoary], Kœmpferia galanga, linn. [indian galangal], Kœmpferia rotunda, willd. [false zedoary], Murraya kœnigii, spr. [curry-leaf], Myristica fragrans, houtt. [common nutmeg],

Nigella sativa, linn. [black jeerah], Peucedanum graveolens, bth. [sowa], Piper betel, linn. [betel pepper], Piper chaba, hunter [chaab pepper], Piper longum, linn. [long pepper], Piper nigrum, linn. [black pepper], Solanum xanthocarpum, sch. & wendl. [prickly brinjaul], Vernonia anthelmintica, willd. [wild jeerah], Withania coagulans, dun. [country asgand], Withania somnifera, dun. [asgand], Zanthoxylum alatum, roxb. [tejbul], Zingiber cassumunar, roxb. [cassumunar], Zingiber officinale, roscoe [ginger], Zingiber zerumbet, smith [false ginger]. ——*Viraichanam* (विरेचन - viréchana, San.; مسهلات - mushilát, Hind.; பேதிமருந்து - péthimarundu, Tam.). San. from (vi, san. intensive prefix + rich, san. to purge). Hind. from (sahala, ar. to loosen). Tam. from (bhédi, san. to pass stool + marundu, tam. medicine). Purgatives, from :—Acalypha indica, linn. [cooppamainy], Aleurites triloba, forst. [lumbang nut], Alhagi maurorum, desv. [arabian manna], Aloe indica, royle [common indian aloe], Aloe litoralis, kœnig. [coromandel aloe], Argemone mexicana, linn. [bramhadand], Baliospermum montanum, mull. [wild jamalgota], Cassia alata, linn. [foreign agatty], Cassia fistula, linn. [common condray], Cassia obovata, collad. [tinnevelly senna], Clitoria ternatea, linn. [crow-creeper], Croton oblongifolius, roxb. [devil's goad], Croton tiglium, linn. [jamalgota], Cucumis sativus, linn. [common cucumber], Cucumis trigonus, roxb. [country cucumber], Garcinia morella, desrous [ceylon gamboge], Helleborus niger, linn. [black cootkee], Ipomæa hederacea, jacq. [kaladanah], Ipomæa sepiaria, kœn. [laldanah], Ipomæa turpethum, r. br. [turbith], Jatropha curcas, linn. [wild aumanac], Mirabilis jalapa, linn. [false jalap], Rheum emodi, wall. [indian rhubarb], Ricinus communis, linn. [aumanac], Salvadora persica, linn. [tooth-brush tree], Sesbania grandiflora, pers. [west indian sesban], Tamarindus indica, linn. [tamarind], Terminalia chebula, retz. [chebulic myrobalan], Trichosanthes nervifolia, linn. [short snake gourd].——*Vishagnam* (विषघ्न - vishaghna, San.; تریاق - tiryák, Hind.; விடமுறி - vidamuri, Tam.). San. from (visha, san. poison + han, san. to destroy). Tam. from (visha, san. poison + muri, tam. to break). Antidotes to bites of snakes and other animals, from :—Achyranthes aspera, linn. [indian burr], Aristolochia indica, linn. [isharmool], Dæmia extensa, r. br. [hedge cotton], Eupatorium ayapana, vent. [ayappanay], Euphorbia nereifolia, linn. [leafy milkhedge], Gymnema sylvestre, r. br. [indian ipecacuanha], Leucas aspera, spreng [rough toombay], Ophiorrhiza mungos, linn. [mongoose snake root], Rauwolfia serpentina, bth. [snake root], Salvadora persica, linn. [tooth-brush tree], Strychnos colubrina, linn. [snake wood tree], Trichodesma indicum, r. br. [donkey toombay].——*Vrana vidradhi deepanam* (व्रणविद्रधिदीपन - vranavidradhidípana, San.; محرکات قروح - muharrikátikurúh, Hind.; புண்ணழற்றி - punnazhatti, Tam.). San. from (vrana, san. wound + vidradhi, san. abscesses + dípana, san. stimulant). Hind. from (muharrikát, ar. stimulant + kurúh, ar. ulcers). Tam. from (pun, tam. ulcer + azhattu, tam. to irritate). Stimulant to ulcers, abscesses, &c., from :—Argemone mexicana, linn. [bramhadand], Borassus flabelliformis, linn. [palmyra], Eupatorium ayapana, vent. [ayappanay], Gardenia gummifera, linn. [décamallee], Hydrocotyle asiatica, linn. [indian pennywort], Melia azadirachta, linn. [neem], Mirabilis jalapa, linn. [false jalap], Myristica malabarica, lam. [malabar nutmeg], Vitex negundo, linn. [notchy], Vitex trifolia, linn. [water notchy].——*Vrimhanam* (बृंहण - vrimhana, San.; ادویہ تغذیہ - adviyahitaghziyah, Hind.; புட்டிகரம் - puttigaram, Tam.). San. from (vrih, san. to grow). Hind. from (adviyah, ar. medicines + taghziyah, ar. nutritive). Tam. from (pushti, san. plumpness + kri, san. to do). Nutritives, from :—Cocos nucifera, linn. [cocoanut], Gracilaria lichenoides, greville [cadal pausy].

VEIGAY (வைகை - vaigai,* *Tam.*). From (vai, tam. swiftness + kai, tam. course). Sanscrit name (végavatí), meaning rapid river. River; Madura district, Periyacoolam, Dindigul, Madura talooks, and Ramnaud zemindarry. Principal river of the district draining the north of the Tamrapurny basin into Madura. Consists of two main arms, the Veigay proper and the Shoorooliyaur. The Veigay proper rises in the spur of the Western ghauts [q.v.] in the south-western corner of Madura district. It traverses the mountains for about 30 miles, precipitating itself at the foot of Guntamanaickanore hill. Then flows north-easterly for about 20 miles, receives the Tainy which drains the Bodinaickanore valley, and unites with the Shoorooliyaur about 6 miles north of Guntamanaickanore and south of Allinagaram. The Shoorooliyaur [q.v.] rises in the western mountains at the southern corner of the Dindigul valley. It runs parallel to the Veigay, with a greater body of water, until that river has commenced its inclination to the north-east when the two streams unite. After the junction the river turns abruptly to the east for about 25 miles to Jayampolliem, and after receiving the Varauhanuddy and the Munjal enters Madura talook 8¾ miles north-west of Sholavandaun. From this point it takes a south-easterly course, flowing along a shallow sandy bed from 200 to 400 yards wide, in an almost direct line right across the district for 100 miles, and passing Sholavandaun, Tovarimaun, Madura, Tirpoovanam where it becomes very broad, and Mauna madura. Then turning south a few miles it proceeds east and enters Ramnaud zemindarry on the west. Here for about 8 miles it forms a part of the general boundary between Ramnaud and Shivagunga zemindarries in a course nearly due east. It comes with a full stream between Paramacoody and Yamaneshwaram, and flows south-east 3 miles. It then turns east for 4 miles, and south for 3½ when it is considerably diminished in width in consequence of numerous cuts from it for the purpose of irrigation. Now confined in a narrow bed it continues eastward in a winding course for 8 miles, and then spreads into the large Periyacoolam lake. A small channel on the north continues easterly. Retaining its name it proceeds eastward for 6 miles, losing itself in a salt-marsh, nearly 5 miles in length and about a mile and a half in breadth. At the east end of the marsh the river again reappears and proceeds in a south-easterly direction about 5 miles; thence it takes a serpentine course and falls into Palk's strait north-west of Tonitoray headland below Attangaray in lat. 9° 23′, long. 79° 2′. Total length about 140 miles. Principal towns on its banks are Madura and Ramnaud. The bed is nearly dry during the greater portion of the year even at Madura, 100 miles from its mouth, and dry all the year round at Ramnaud. The freshes last usually only three or four days. Scanty supplies of water are procured by digging small holes and channels in the bed, which retains at all times a certain amount of moisture. Near the point where it enters Madura district is the Pairanay anicut [q.v.], where a considerable portion of its waters is diverted into a channel [q.v.] taken off from its left bank. Two and three-quarter miles lower down the Chittanay anicut empties into a channel on its right bank, the greater part of its greatly diminished stream. The river is bridged by the South indian railway near Madura. There is a Tamul proverb :—வைகை ஆற்றுத் தண்ணீர் வேகம் அதிகம்—"the current in the "veigay is great." And another :—வைகை ஆற்று வெள்ளத்தில் பாலம் நிலைக்கிறது இல்லை—"when the veigay is in "flood, its bridges do not stand" [aroovy].

VEIPPAUR (வைப்பாறு - vaippáru, *Tam.* vaippár). From (vaippu, tam. greatness + áru, tam. river).—"*a*" Village, Port; Tinnevelly dist., Ottapidauram tal.; pop. 1,998; acres 8,752; lat. 9° 1′; long. 78° 17′; from Madras S.S.W. 312; from Ottapidauram E.N.E. 17 miles; from Tinnevelly E.N.E. 43 miles; from Tuticorin N.N.E. 16 miles; from Vembaur W.S.W. 9 miles. On Gulf of Manaar. At the mouth of the river of the same name, a little to north of Tuticorin. Ancient village. Early Dutch factory. Salt factory formerly here was abandoned owing to difficulties of communication. Old Shiva temple. Annual car festival.—"*b*" River, Tinnevelly district, Ottapidauram talook. Rises near the western frontier on the eastern declivity of the Eastern ghauts [q.v.] in about lat. 9° 42′, long. 77° 43′. Flowing easterly, and in some places south-easterly, for about 80 miles, during part of which it runs parallel to the north borders of Tinnevelly; it falls into the Gulf of Manaar in lat. 9° 01′, long. 78° 19′, near the town of the same name.

VEIRAVAM (வைரவம் - vairavam, *Tam.*). From (bhairava, san. a form of shiva). One of the six orthodox religious systems [cootchamayam] of the Sheivas in which Bheiravan is made supreme [sheiva siddhauntam].

VEISYA (वैश्य - vaishya, *San.*). From (vish, san to settle down on). Cf. Lat. vicus and Greek οἶκος, and English 'wick' at end of towns. The third primitive caste of the Aryans whose means of subsistence, according to Menoo [q.v.], were agriculture, trade, and the keeping of cattle [jauty]. In other words they were :—Bhoo veisyar, cultivators; Dhana veisya or vauniya or merchant caste; Go veisya or shepherd class.

VEL (വെൾ - vel, *Mal.*; வெள் - vel, *Tam.*). White, pure, free.—"*a*" Plant first term. Often joining two genera. Ex., where transl. is of second term :—Acacia intsia (vellindaugodi), mimosa rubicaulis; Acacia latronum (vellaimulvél), thorn + acacia; Anogeissus latifolia (vellainágamaram), eugenia jambolana; Azima tetracantha (tellauppi), capparis sepiaria; Calycopteris floribunda (tellavadala), combretum decandrum; Celosia argentea (veluttaatakkamániyan), sphæranthus indicus; Celtis wightii (tellakákamushti), sponia wightii; Cucumis melo, var. utilissimus (vellagummadi), cucurbita maxima; Ehretia buxifolia (telladzuvvi), ficus tsiela; Enicostema littorale (vellarugu), cynodon dactylon; Eriodendron anfractuosum (bilibúragadamara), bombax malabaricum; Ficus asperrima (tellabarranki), epicarpurus orientalis; Gardenia lucida (tellamanga), randia dumetorum; Givotia rottleriformis (tellaponiku), gyrocarpus jacquini; Gomphrena globosa (tellapeddagóranta), large + lawsonia alba; Lagerstrœmia lanceolata (vendékku), tectona grandis; Mesua ferrea (veluttachampakam), michelia champaca; Nymphæa lotus (bilidávare), nelumbium speciosum; Oldenlandia heynii (tellanélavému), andrographis paniculata; Oroxylum indicum (veluttapátiri), stereospermum chelonoides; Pancratium zeylanicum (tellagáta), diospyros sylvatica; Plumeria acutifolia (veluttarali), nerium odorum; Securinega leucopyrus (tellapurugudu), phyllanthus multiflorus; Symphorema involucratum (tellapippali), piper longum; Trianthema pentandra (biliganajali), plant, cæsalpinia mimosoides; Vitis lanceolaria (tellagumudu), gmelina asiatica; Webera corymbosa (velvedchi), ixora coccinea; See gloss. paragraphs.—"*b*" Fish first term. Ex., where transl. is of second term :—Ailia coila (vellakorada), ophiocephalus punctatus; Barbus ticto (vennattai), snail; Chela (vellaikkendai), carp, barbus genus; Cirrhina cirrhosa (vengondai), carp, barbus genus; Cybium guttatum (vellirá), shrimp;

Labeo fimbriatus (vengendai), carp, barbus genus; Lutjanus fulviflamma (vellaiççempalli), lutjanus johnii; Macrones cavasius (vellaikkeliru), macrones genus; Pristis zysron (vellaiççurá), carcharias genus; Sciæna albida (vellaikkattalai), pristipoma dussumieri; Trachynotus baillonii (vellótu), shell. See gloss. paragraphs.—"*c*" Mammal first term. Ex., where transl. is of second term:—Felis chaus (vellabokku), cat, felis genus; Gazella bennettii (velimán), deer, cervidæ; Gerbillus indicus (yelleli), rat, mus genus; Macacus sinicus (vellamanti), monkey, macacus genus; Portax pictus (venperumán), big + deer, cervídæ. See gloss. paragraphs.——*Vaily* (बाड़ - bár, Hind; కంచె - kanche, Tel.; വേലി - véli, Mal.; வேலி - vêli Tam.).—"*a*" Hedge; village.—"*b*" Superficial measure. 20 mahs = 1 vaily [alavay, 2a]. Approximte actual value, 1 vaily = 6·6157 acres. Tanjore. Compare cootchel. See vol. I, 609; II, 518.—"*c*" Plant first term from growing on hedges or serving for hedges. Ex., where transl. is of second term:—Dæmia extensa (vélipparutti), gossypium herbaceum; Justica betonica (vélimúngil), bambusa arundinacea.; Manihot utilissima (vélikkizhannu), root; Sida humilis (vélippási), moss. See gloss. paragraphs.—"*d*" The following are two key-lists of the plants principally used for field enclosures in s. india; further information must be traced in the glossary paragraphs through the small-type cross references at end of this volume; see also vricsham, 7, for the method of expressing the products, &c., of plants in the dravidian languages.—Acacia arabica, babool; Acacia concinna, soap-pod; Acacia farnesiana, cassie oil plant; Agave americana, american aloe; Balsamodendron berry, kiloovay; Bambusa arundinacea, common bamboo; Bambusa nana, dwarf bamboo; Bambusa spinosa, thorny bamboo; Cæsalpinia bonducella, bonduc; Cæsalpinia pulcherrima, gold mohur tree; Cæsalpinia sappan, sappan; Cæsalpinia sepiaria, mysore thorn; Capparis aphylla, common caper; Dendrocalamus tulda, bengal bamboo; Epicarpurus orientalis, stunted jack; Euphorbia antiquorum, square milk-hedge; Euphorbia tirucalli, round milk-hedge; Gmelina asiatica, small cashmere tree; Jatropha curcas, physic nut; Opuntia dillenii, prickly-pear; Pandanus odoratissimus, screw-pine; Parkinsonia aculeata, jerusalem thorn; Pithecolobium dulce, corcapilly; Scutia indica, small bair; Toddalia aculeata, lopez root. Aloe, agave; Babool, acacia; Bair, scutia; Bamboo, bambusa, dendrocalamus; Bonduc, cæsalpinia; Caper, capparis; Cashmere tree, gmelina; Cassie oil, acacia; Corcapilly, pithecolobium; Gold mohur, cæsalpinia; Jack, epicarpurus; Jerusalem thorn, parkinsonia; Kiloovay, balsamodendron; Lopez root, toddalia; Milk-hedge, euphorbia; Physic nut, jatropha; Prickly-pear, opuntia; Sappan, cæsalpinia; Screw-pine, pandanus; Soap-pod, acacia; Thorn, cæsalpinia.——*Vayal* (വയൽ - vayal, Mal.; வயல் - vayal, Tam.). From (veli, tam. open place). Field. Plant first term. Ex., where transl. is of second term:—Heliotropium ovalifolium (vayargodukki), sting; Hygrophila spinosa (vayalchulli), thorny plant; Phaseolus trilobus (vayappayaru), pulse. See gloss. paragraphs.——*Vekkauly* (धव - dhava, San.; धावडा - dhávadá, Mahr.; धौरा - dhaurá, Hind.; ದಿಂಡಿಗಮರ - dindigamara, Can.; చిరిమాను - chirimánu, Tel.; ଧୋବୁ - dhóbu, Oor.; දවු - davu, Singh.; வெக்காலி - vekkáli, Tam.). Title from tamul. San. from (dhav, san. to flow), washed, cleared, bright; from wood. Mahr. from sanscrit. Hind. from sanscrit [satin wood]. Can. from (dindu, can. thick + mara, can. tree). Tel. from (chiru, tel. small + mánu, tel. tree). Tam. from (vel, tam. white + kál, tam. post); from grey wood. San. also (bakavriksha), meaning crane tree, from resemblance of fruit to head of a crane. Hind. also (dhává), meaning woodfordia floribunda, salisb. Can. also (dinduga); (dindlumara); (bejalu); (dindal). Tel. also (yellamaddi), meaning boundary + tree, terminalia arjuna, bedd. Oor. also (dhaura). Tam. also (namai), meaning chariot-wheel, from use of wood; (vellainágamaram), meaning white + eugenia jambolana, lamk. Title otherwise Chirimaun. Botanically Anogeissus [dhavam] latifolia, wall., combretaceæ [vricsham, 55]. Alias Conocarpus latifolia. Valuable timber tree, common, attains large size; leaves alternate or nearly opposite, quite entire; limbs of calyx five cleft; petals none; leaves without glands, elliptical or obovate, obtuse, emarginate, glabrous; peduncles branched, bearing several heads of flowers sometimes thickly aggregated; fruit coriaceous, somewhat scaly, globular; seed solitary; flowers small, greenish pale. Exudes a gum [q.v.] which occurs in clear straw-colored elongated tears adhering into masses, sometimes honey-colored or brown from impurities. Leaves used by tanners [chamrah]; gum used with certain dye [shauyam] stuffs in cloth printing. Wood grey, hard, shining, smooth, with a small purplish-brown, irregularly shaped, extremely hard heartwood; sapwood in young trees and branches yellow; annual rings marked by darker lines; highly valued on account of its great strength and toughness; used for axe handles, poles for carrying loads, axles, in the construction of furniture, agricultural implements, and in ship-building; gives good fuel [lukdy] and an excellent charcoal [kary]. In the variety Villosa the leaves are rusty villose on both surfaces, and in the variety Parvifolia they are very small and silky pubescent.——*Velama* (వెలమ - velama, Tel.). From (veli, tel. outside). A principal tribe of Teloogoo cultivators; popularly supposed to have descended from ancient hill chieftains. Numbers about 350,000, chiefly up east coast. Teloogoo zemindars [q.v.] are mostly of this caste [janty]. Some divisions are:—Audivelama, from (ádi, san. first); Coppoola velama, from (koppu, tel. the tuft into which a hindoo woman arranges her hair); Pudmavelama, from (padmá, san. lotus goddess lakshmí). See vol. I (67); II, 228.——*Velapaly soonkam* (వెలపలిసుంకము - velapalisuukamu, Tel.). From (velapala, tel. outside + sunkamu, tel. duty). Export duty.——*Velgode* (వెలుగోడు - velugódu, Tel.). From (velugu, tel. hedge + vídu, tel. town); border town. Village; Kurnool dist., Nundicotcore tal.; pop. 2,783; acres 24,581; lat. 15° 43′; long. 78° 37′; from Kurnool E. 36 miles; from Nundicotcore S.E. 22 miles. On the borders of Nullamullay forests. In middle of 16th century a strong fort built here by fugitive zemindar [q.v.] from Golcondah, the ancestor of the present Rajahs of Vencatagherry. One of its bastions was known as that of the seven sisters. The story is that, in order to give permanence to the fort, seven daughters-in-law of the founder sacrificed themselves with their children; one of them, who had no child of her own, carrying a Pariah boy Atchanna whom she found in the street. In memory of the latter fact the zemindar's family is still known by the name of Atchanna, and respect is shown to the Pariahs [q.v.] on the occasion of marriages in the zemindar's family. One of the principal marts for forest timber [maram].——*Velgoty* (వెలుగోటి - velugóti, Tel.). From (velugódu, tel. village so called). A family name of the rajah of Vencatagherry [velgode, velgoty canama].——*Velgoty canama* (వెలుగోటికనమ - velugótikanama, Tel.). From (velugu, tel. hedge + vídu, tel. town + kanama, tel. ravine). Pass; Kurnool dist., Nundicotcore tal.; lat. 15° 42′; long. 78° 46′; from Kurnool E.S.E. 47 miles; from Nundicotcore E.S.E. 34 miles. Pass [ghaut] over nullamullays north of Nundicanama, and between Velgode in the Coondair and Bolloopully in the Cumbum valley; about 2,250 feet at the highest point. Sometimes used as the shortest route between Cumbum and the country to the west of the hills, but it is not fit for cart traffic. Two watering places about half-way across. The best part of the Nullamullay forest is about this canama; largely frequented by timber merchants, who have depôts for sale of wood at Velgode.——*Veligada* (వెలిగడ - veligada, Tel.). From (veli, tel. outside + kada, tel. place). Dry land [poonjah]. Dry ploughing [pooldycaul]. Same as Gaddavary. For wet land see Mauganny and Nunjah; for wet ploughing see Coodapa and Shettcaul——*Veligarum* (வெளிகரம் - veligaram, Tam.). From (veli, tam. open plain + agaram, tam. agricultural village). Sanscrit name (shukrapuri), means town of venus. Village, Place of pilgrimage, Mountain, River; North arcot dist., Carvetnugger zemindarry, Trittany division; pop. 1,136; lat. 13° 20′; long. 79° 28′; from Carvetnugger S.S.W. 7 miles; from Chittore E.N.E. 23 miles; from Trittany N.W. 16 miles. Shiva temple on hill. Pilgrims come on Mondays in Caurtigay [mausam] or November, and Shivarautry [pundigay, 6a]. On S. bank of Cooshastaly, 2 miles west of Pulliputt.——*Veligonda* (వెలికొండ - veligonda, Tel.). From (veli, tel. exterior + konda, tel. hill). Range of hills. The eastern edge of the Eastern ghauts [q.v.] and forms the boundary between Cuddapah and Nellore districts. Starts from Nagary nose in N. arcot and runs due north parallel to the Nullamullays till it ends about 10 miles to the east of Marcapore, about the same latitude as the Yerramalas in the west. The hills cross out again at the Goondlacumma in the form of a low-lying range known locally as Yerracondas, and terminate in an attenuated corner in the north-east on the confines of Kistna district. Composed chiefly of sandstone [manal cull], and covered with stunted trees and brush-wood, but with little valuable timber. Mark an ancient sea boundary. Towards the east the sides are abrupt and bare, towards the west they slope into valleys and join other hills. Average elevation about 3,000 feet.——*Velivaude* (వెలివాడ - velivåda, Tel.). From (veli, tel. outside + váda, tel. street). Outer part of village tenanted by Pariahs [parcherry, pariah].——*Vellaiyan* (வெள்ளையன் - vellaiyan, Tam.). Means white man. Proper name [peyar].——*Vellaiyauneiyoorty* (வெள்ளையானையூர்த்தி - vellaiyánaiyúrtti, Tam.). From (vellai, tam. white + yánai, tam. elephant + yúrtti, tam. rider). The rider of the white elephant, Ayenaur [ayen]. Also Indran [q.v.] as riding on Eirauvatam [q.v.], the white elephant [q.v.].——*Vellalore* (வெள்ளலூர் - vellalúr, Tam.). From (vellam, tam. flood + úr, tam. village). Village; Coimbatore dist., Coimbatore tal.; pop. 5,831; acres 3,992; lat. 10° 59′; long. 77° 04′; from Coimbatore S.E. 5 miles. In May 1842 were found in an earthen pot 522 Roman denarii, chiefly of reigns of Augustus and Tiberius, with a few of Caligula and Claudius. The earthen vessel was like the common terra cotta lotah [q.v.] of the present time, but was broken to pieces. Many paundicoozhies [q.v.] containing well-made earthen vessels found here. Market place.——*Vellam* (வெள்ளம் - vellam, Tam.). Flood, irrigation.——*Vellattiry* (വെള്ളാട്ടിരി - vellåttiri, Mal.). From (vellanátu, mal. ancient principality + tiri, mal. holy, title). The title of the South malabar rajah. Otherwise Vulloovaconattiry or Valavanaud [q.v.] or Arangott [q.v.] rajah [colattiry]. See vol. II, 101.——*Vellaula* (வெள்ளாளன் - vellálan, Tam.). From (vellam, tam. water + ál, tam. to rule). Otherwise (vélála), meaning benefit ruler. Agricultural caste. The corresponding terms are:—Tel. Reddy; Can. Bunt of canara and Okkaliga of mysore; Mal. Nayar. Vellaular hold the first place among the

Tamul agriculturists, as the Reddies [q.v.] do among the Teloogoos. During the period of the Paundyan [q.v.] kings no other classes were permitted to hold landed property. However there is this Tamul proverb :—*கள்ளன் மறவன் கலந்த அகமுடையான் மெள்ள மெள்ள வந்து வெள்ளாழன்.*—"the cullan, "maravan, and agambadiyaun, rising slowly became by degrees "the vellaulan." The Vellaular believe that they came from the north. They call themselves Veisya [q.v.], of the Bhoovamsham or agricultural section. They take the honorific appellation of Moodelly [q.v.] or Moodelliar [q.v.]. They do not use animal food or intoxicating liquors; polygamy is unknown, the widows do not re-marry, and they burn their dead [shoodcaud]. They are mostly of the Sheiva sect, but the chief objects of their worship are village gods [grauma devatay], and they keep the Pongal [q.v.] and Deepauvaly [q.v.] festivals. The Caurcautt vellaular of the Madura hills, or vellaular who watch the seasons, have institutions resembling Maroomakkatoyem [q.v.]. There is a Tamul proverb :—*வெள்ளாளன் கிரந்தமும் பார்ப்பான் தமிழும் விழல் விழலே*—"the sanscrit of a vellaula, and the tamul of a bramin are equally "faulty." There is another :—*வெள்ளாளர் செய்யாத வேளாண்மை வேளாண்மை அல்ல*—"agriculture not performed by vellaular is no agriculture;" numbers about 2 millions. The following stanza is from Manavaula narayana shatacam :—*அந்தணர்கள் கருமமுஞ் ஜெகராஜ புஜபலமு மவனி வர்த்தகலாபமும், அனைவர்க்குமேன்மையுந் தருமமுந் தானமு மன்பின் மங்கையரின்பமும், புந்திதெளிநியம முஞ் சாத்திரமுமாகம புராணமொடு சகலகலையும், பொய்யாதவுண்மையுங் கீர்த்திப்பிரதாபமும் புகழ்கின்ற தேவர்நிலையும், விந்தைபுரிமானமுங் குலமரபுநீதியும் விதரணமுதற் சகலமும், வேளாளர்குவளைபுனை காராளர்தங்களுட மேழியின் பெருமையன்றோ, மந்தர மெனம் புயசவுந்தர முகுந்தனே மணவாள நாராயணன், மனதிலுறையலர்மேலு மங்கைமணவாளனே வரதவேங்கடராயனே.*—"The vellaular, by the effect of "their ploughing maintain the prayers of the bramins, the "strength of kings, the profits of merchants, the welfare of all; "charity, donations, the enjoyments of domestic life and "connubial happiness, homage to the gods, the shastrams [q.v.], "the vedams [q.v.], the pooraunams [q.v.], and all other books, "truth, reputation, renown, the very being of the gods, things "of good report or integrity, the good order of castes, and "manual skill, all these things come to pass by the merit of the "vellaulan's plough [yair]." See vol. I (36), (67); II, 227, 234.

——*Vellaumay* (வெள்ளாண்மை - vellámai, Tam.). From (vellam, tam. water + ânmai, tam. possession). Husbandry.—"*a*" The principal crop is rice [q.v.], which when growing and before it is husked is called paddy [q.v.]. Rice is also termed a wet grain from the great quantity of moisture necessary for bringing it to maturity [wet crop]. The grains other than rice, and the pulses, are called dry crops from their requiring less water [dry grain, dholl]. The particular seasons of the year founded to be the most proper for sowing different crops depend upon the climate of the locality, and whether it is within the influence of the south-west or of the north-east monsoon [caur, caurtey, mausam, monsoon]. For seasons of rice cultivation see Paddy. As to dry grains [q.v.] :—On the east coast, the greater number are sown about the beginning of what are called the first rains; that is to say towards the end of june, or in july, and are reaped in september; others are put into the ground in october, and being in high situations, suffer little from the heavy rains of november, and are usually got in december; a third kind, such as panipayar [q.v.], &c., are not sown till after the rains [mazhay], these being nourished by the dews [pany] that fall heavy in february and being reaped in the beginning of march. On hill-ranges the general system of cultivation is as follows; a few acres of jungle are burnt and cleared, the ground scratched up, and a few seeds scattered; the first season a fair crop is obtained, the second year the crop is inferior, and in the third season it is scarcely worth gathering; the field is then deserted and another patch cleared in the same manner, the relinquished land not being returned to till ten or twelve years have elapsed [coomry, ponacaud].—"*b*" The following are the principal crops grown by cultivators in the presidency grouped under different heads;—Cereals :—barley [jow], cholum [q.v.], coraly [white tinay], cumboo [bajrah], khoda [q.v.] millet, large shaumay [q.v.], maize [mecca cholum], millet [q.v.], paddy [q.v.], raggy [q.v.], tinay [q.v.], varagoo [q.v.], wheat [geung]. Condiments :—areca [q.v.] palm, betel leaf [betel pepper], black mustard [cauly rayaun], cardamom [q.v.], chilly [q.v.], coriander [cassibor], cumin [jeerah], fenugreek [maitee], garlic [lussoon], ginger [q.v.], indian mustard [rayaun], onion [piyauz], pepper [q.v.], tamarind [q.v.], turmeric [country saffron], white mustard [soofaid rayaun]. Drugs and narcotics :—anise [q.v.], bengal hemp [sunn], bishop's weed [ajwaun], cinchona [koinah], coffee [q.v.], indian hemp [kinnab], opium [aphainam], senna [q.v.], tea [q.v.], tobacco [pogauk]. Dyes :—chayroot [q.v.], indigo [q.v.], morinda [indian mulberry], munjeet [q.v.], safflower [bastard saffron]. Fibres :—american aloe [q.v.], cotton [q.v.], flax [alsee], hemp bendy [q.v.], jute [q.v.], sunn [q.v.]. Garden produce :—areca [q.v.], brinjaul [q.v.], cashew [q.v.], chinese lablab [guar], cocoanut [q.v.], common bendy [q.v.], cucumber [oorvauroo], elephant yam [q.v.], grape [angoor], guava [q.v.], indian kale [kachvee], jack [q.v.], lime [q.v.], malabar arrowroot [q.v.], mango [q.v.], melon [oorvauroo], plantain [q.v.], pomegranate [anaur], potato [q.v.], pumpkin [carcauroo], sweet potato [q.v.], sweet water melon [q.v.], tapioca [malda dye], telinga potato [q.v.]. Oils :—castor-oil [aumanac], gingelly [q.v.], groundnut [q.v.], linseed [alsee], mohwah [q.v.], mustard [rayaun], ramtil [q.v.], rape [rarasarsoon], safflower [bastard saffron]. Pulses :—bean [country bean], bengal gram [q.v.], black gram [q.v.], cow gram [q.v.], dholl [q.v.], field gram [q.v.], green gram [q.v.], horse-gram [q.v.], moorman's gram [q.v.], pea [calauyam]. Starches :—arrowroot [malabar arrowroot], elephant-foot yam [elephant yam], potato [q.v.], sweet potato [q.v.]. Sugars :—date [kharjooram], palmyra [q.v.], sugar-cane [q.v.].—"*c*" The following are two alphabetical key-lists to the crops; further information must be traced in the glossary paragraphs through the small-type cross-references at end of this volume; see also vricsham, 7, for the method of expressing the products, &c., of the plants in the dravidian languages :—Allium cepa, onion; Allium sativum, garlic; Amorphophallus campanulatus, telinga potato; Anacardium occidentale, cashew; Arachis hypogæa, groundnut; Areca catechu, areca; Artocarpus integrifolia, bread fruit; Bassia latifolia, wild mohwah; Bassia longifolia, common mohwah; Borassus flabelliformis, palmyra; Brassica alba, white mustard; Brassica campestris, subsp. napus, rape; Brassica juncea, indian mustard; Brassica nigra, black mustard; Cajanus indicus, common dholl; Camellia theifera, tea; Cannabis sativa, indian hemp; Capsicum frutescens, shrubby chilly; Carthamus tinctorius, safflower; Carum copticum, ajwaun; Cassia angustifolia, tinnevelly senna; Cassia obovata, aleppo senna; Cicer arietinum, bengal gram; Cinchona officinalis, crown bark; Cinchona succirubra, red bark; Citrullus vulgaris, sweet water melon; Citrus medica, var. acida, sour lime; Citrus medica, var. limetta, sweet lime; Cocos nucifera, cocoanut; Coffea arabica, coffee; Colocasia antiquorum, indian kale; Corchorus capsularis, jute; Corchorus olitorius, wild jute; Coriandrum sativum, coriander; Crotalaria juncea, sunn; Cucumis melo, common melon; Cucumis sativus, common cucumber; Cucurbita maxima, great pumpkin; Cuminum cyminum, cummin; Curcuma angustifolia, malabar arrowroot; Curcuma longa, turmeric; Cyamopsis psoralioides, chinese lablab; Dolichos biflorus, madras horse-gram; Dolichos lablab, country bean; Elettaria cardamomum, cardamom; Eleusine coracana, raggy; Gossypium herbaceum, indian cotton; Guizotia abyssinica, ramtil; Hibiscus cannabinus, hemp bendy; Hibiscus esculentus, common bendy; Hordeum vulgare, barley; Indigofera tinctoria, common indigo; Ipomæa batatas, sweet potato; Linum usitatissimum, flax; Mangifera indica, mango; Manihot utilissima, tapioca; Morinda citrifolia, ach root; Morinda umbellata, small achroot; Musa paradisiaca, plantain; Nicotiana tabacum, tobacco; Oldenlandia umbellata, chayroot; Oryza sativa, paddy; Panicum frumentaceum, large shaumay; Panicum glaucum, coraly; Panicum italicum, italian millet; Panicum miliaceum, little millet; Panicum miliare, shaumay; Papaver somniferum, opium poppy; Paspalum scrobiculatum, khoda millet; Pennisetum spicatum, spiked millet; Phaseolus aconitifolius, moorman's gram; Phaseolus mungo, green gram; Phaseolus mungo, var. radiatus, black gram; Phaseolus trilobus, field gram; Phœnix dactylifera, arabian date; Phœnix sylvestris, wild date; Pimpinella anisum, anise; Piper betel, betel pepper; Piper nigrum, black pepper; Pisum sativum, garden pea; Psidium guyava, var. pomiferum, red guava; Psidium guyava, var. pyriferum, white guava; Punica granatum, pomegranate; Ricinus communis, castor-oil; Rubia cordifolia, munjeet; Saccharum officinarum, sugar-cane; Sesamum indicum, gingelly; Solanum melongena, brinjaul; Solanum tuberosum, potato; Sorghum vulgare, cholum; Tamarindus indica, tamarind; Trigonella fœnum-græcum, fenugreek; Triticum vulgare, wheat; Typhonium orixense, elephant yam; Vigna catiang, cow gram; Vitis vinifera, grape vine; Zea mays, maize; Zingiber officinale, ginger.—Ach root, morinda; Ajwaun, carum; Anise, pimpinella; Arrowroot, curcuma; Bark, cinchona; Barley, hordeum; Bean, dolichos; Bendy, hibiscus; Bread fruit, artocarpus; Brinjaul, solanum; Cardamom, elettaria; Cashew, anacardium; Castor, ricinus; Chayroot, oldenlandia; Chilly, capsicum; Cholum, sorghum; Cocoanut, cocos; Coffee, coffea; Coraly, panicum; Coriander, coriandrum; Cotton, gossypium; Cucumber, cucumis; Cummin, cuminum; Date, phœnix; Dholl, cajanus; Fenugreek, trigonella; Flax, linum; Garlic, allium; Gingelly, sesamum; Gram, cicer, dolichos, phaseolus, vigna; Groundnut, arachis; Guava, psidium; Hemp, cannabis; Indigo, indigofera; Jute, corchorus; Kale, colocasia; Lablab, cyamopsis; Lime, citrus; Maize, zea; Mango, mangifera; Melon, citrullus, cucumis; Millet, panicum, paspalum, pennisetum; Mohwah, bassia; Munjeet, rubia; Mustard, brassica; Onion, allium; Paddy, oryza; Palmyra, borassus; Pea, pisum; Pepper, piper; Plantain, musa; Pomegranate, punica; Poppy, papaver; Potato, amorphophallus, ipomæa, solanum; Pumpkin, cucurbita; Raggy, eleusine; Ramtil, guizotia; Rape, brassica; Safflower, carthamus; Senna, cassia; Shaumay, panicum; Sugar-cane, saccharum; Sunn, crotalaria; Tamarind, tamarindus; Tapioca, manihot; Tea, camellia; Tobacco, nicotiana; Turmeric, curcuma; Vine, vitis; Wheat, triticum; Yam, typhonium.—"*d*" The following are tabular lists showing the seasons of principal crops on the three coasts [q.v.] :—

General head of crop.	Name of crop.	Number of months to mature.	Ploughing season.	Sowing season.	Reaping season.
1	2	3	4	5	6
	Seasons of different crops on South coast.				
Wet or nunjah [q.v.] crops.	Auna comban, paddy	6	Poorataushy, September ...	Arpisy, October	Maushy and Pungoony, February and March.
	Cauday caloottan, paddy ...	6	Poorataushy, September ...	Arpisy, October	Pungoony, March.
	Caur, paddy	3	Chittray, April	Veiyaushy, May	Audy, July.
	Cooroovay, paddy...	3	Chittray, April	Veiyaushy, May	Audy, July.
	Mosanam, paddy	3	Poorataushy, September ...	Arpisy, October	Maurgaly, December.
	Neela shumbah, paddy	6	Auvany, August	Auvany, August	Maurgaly and Tye, December and January.
	Pishaunam, paddy	6	Audy, July	Auvany, August	Tye, January.
	Shumbah, paddy	5	Audy, July	Auvany, August	Maurgaly, December.
	Tirvarangam, paddy	7	Audy, July	Audy, July	Maurgaly, December.
	Vary shumbah, paddy	5	Pungoony and Chittray, March and April.	Chittray, April	Auvany, August.
	Vauday shumbah, paddy ...	5	Auvany, August	Auvany, August	Maurgaly, December.
Dry or poonjah [q.v.] crops.	Bengal gram [q.v.], cicer arietinum, linn.	4	Caurtigay, November ...	Maurgaly, December	Pungoony, March.
	Black gram [q.v.] phaseolus, mungo, var. radiatus, linn.	3	Poorataushy, September ...	Arpisy, October	Tye, January.
	Castor oil, ricinus communis, linn. [aumanac].	6	Chittray, April	Auvany, August	Maushy, February.
	Chilly, capsicum annuum, linn. [common chilly].	5	Audy and Auvany, July and August.	Auvany and Poorataushy, August and September.	Tye, Maushy and Pungoony, January, Febraary and March.
	Cholum [q.v.], sorghum vulgare, pers.	4	Chittray and Veiyaushy, April and May.	Veiyaushy and Auny, May and June.	Poorataushy and Arpisy, September and October.
	Coriander, coriandrum sativum, linn. [cassibor].	3	Poorataushy, September ...	Caurtigay, November	Maushy, February.
	Cotton [indian cotton], gossypium herbaceum, linn.	4 to 6	Poorataushy, September ...	Arpisy, October	Maushy and Pungoony, February and March.
	Country bean [q.v.], dolichos lablab, linn.	3	Auny and Audy, June and July.	Audy and Auvany, July and August.	Maushy and Pungoony, February and March.
	Cow gram [q.v.], vigna catiang, endl.	6	Auny and Audy, June and July.	Audy and Auvany, July and August.	Maurgaly and Tye, December and January.
	Dholl, cajanus indicus, spreng. [common dholl].	6	Auny and Audy, June and July.	Audy and Auvany, July and August.	Maurgaly and Tye, December and January.
	Fenugreek, trigonella fœnum-græcum, linn. [maitee].	4	Arpisy and Caurtigay, October and November.	Caurtigay and Maurgaly, November and December.	Maushy and Pungoony, February and March.
	Gingelly [q.v.], sesamum indicum, dec., first crop.	4	Caurtigay, November ...	Maurgaly, December	Pungoony, March.
	Do. second crop	4	Pungoony, March	Chittray, April	Audy, July.
	Green gram [q.v.], phaseolus mungo, linn.	6	Chittray, April	Veiyaushy, May	Arpisy, October.
	Ground nut [q.v.], arachis hypogæa, linn.	6	Auny and Audy, June and July.	Audy and Auvany, July and August.	Maushy and Pungoony, February and March.
	Horse-gram, dolichos biflorus, linn. [madras horse-gram].	3	Poorataushy and Arpisy, September and October.	Arpisy and Caurtigay, October and November.	Tye and Maushy, January and February.
	Indian mustard, brassica juncea, h. f. and t. [rayaun].	4	Pungoony, March	Chittray, April	Audy, July.
	Indigo, indigofera tinctoria, linn. [common indigo].	3	Poorataushy and Arpisy, September and October.	Arpisy and Caurtigay, October and November.	Chittray and Veiyaushy, April and May.
	Italian millet, panicum italicum, linn. [tinay].	3	Auvany, August	Arpisy, October	Tye, January.
	Khoda [q.v.] millet, paspalum scrobiculatum, linn.	6	Audy, July	Audy and Auvany, July and August.	Tye, January.
	Raggy [q.v.], eleusine coracana, gærtn.	4	Veiyaushy, May	Auny, June	Arpisy, October.
	Shaumay [q.v.], panicum miliare, lam.	3	Audy, July	Auvany, August	Caurtigay, November.
	Spiked millet, pennisetum spicatum, delile. [bajrah].	3	Auvany, August	Poorataushy and Arpisy, September and October.	Maurgaly and Tye, December and January.
	Sugar-cane [q.v.], saccharum officinarum, linn.	12	Chittray, April	Veiyaushy, May	Chittray, April.
	Sunn [q.v.], crotalaria juncea, linn.	5	Auny, Audy and Auvany, June, July and August.	Audy, Auvany and Poorataushy, July, August and September.	Caurtigay, Maurgaly and Tye, November, December and January.
	Tobacco, nicotiana tabacum, linn. [pogauk], first crop.	5	Audy, July	Auvany and Poorataushy, August and September.	Maurgaly and Tye, December and January.
	Do. second crop	5	Auvany and Poorataushy, August and September.	Arpisy and Caurtigay, October and November.	Maushy and Pungoony, February and March.
	Turmeric, curcuma longa, roxb. [country saffron].	9	Veiyaushy and Auny, May and June.	Auny and Audy, June and July.	Tye and Maushy, January and February.

General head of crop.	Name of crop.	Number of months to mature.	Ploughing season.	Sowing season.	Reaping season.
1	2	3	4	5	6
	Seasons of different crops on Golcondah coast.				
Wet poonausa [q.v.] or moodroo [q.v.].	Calinga shumbah, paddy ...	4	Ashaudham and Shrauvanam, July and August	Shrauvanam and Bhaudrapadam, August and September.	Margashiram, December.
	Eeshwaracora, paddy	5	Ashaudham to Bhaudrapadam, July to September.	Bhaudrapadam to Caurteecam, September to November.	Maugham and Phaulgoonam, February and March.
	Mosanam, paddy	5	Shrauvanam and Bhaudrapadam, August and September.	Shrauvanam and Bhaudrapadam, August and September.	Pooshyam and Maugham, January and February.
	Pedda sannavary, paddy ...	6	Ashaudham and Shrauvanam, July and August.	Ashaudham to Bhaudrapadam, July to September.	Maugham, February.
	Pishaunam, paddy	6	Jyeshtam and Ashaudham, June and July.	Jyeshtam to Shrauvanam, June to August.	Margashiram and Pooshyam, December and January.
	Sugar-cane [q.v.], saccharum officinarum, linn.	11	Cheitram, April	Cheitram, April	Phaulgoonam, March.
	Tirvarungavary, paddy	6	Shrauvanam and Bhaudrapadam, August and September.	Shrauvanam and Bhaudrapadam, August and September.	Maugham, February.
	Vauda sannavary, paddy ...	5	Ashaudham and Shrauvanam, July and August.	Shrauvanam and Bhaudrapadam, August and September.	Maugham, February.
Wet peiroo [q.v.].	Pedda kesary, paddy	4	Caurteecam and Margashiram, November and December.	Caurteecam and Margashiram, November and December.	Maugham and Phaulgoonam, February and March.
	Potty kesary, paddy	3	Pooshyam and Maugham, January and February.	Pooshyam and Maugham, January and February.	Phaulgoonam and Cheitram, March and April.
	Potty nullavary, paddy	3	Pooshyam and Maugham, January and February.	Pooshyam and Maugham, January and February.	Phaulgoonam and Cheitram, March and April.
Dry poonausa [q.v.] or moodroo [q.v.].	Castor oil, ricinus communis, linn. [aumanac].	5	Ashaudham and Shrauvanam, July and August.	Shrauvanam and Bhaudrapadam, August and September.	Maugham and Phaulgoonam, February and March.
	Cholum [q.v.], sorghum vulgare, pers.	5	Jyeshtam and Ashaudham, June and July.	Shrauvanam, August	Margashiram, December.
	Cotton, gossypium herbaceum [indian cotton].	...	Ashaudham, July	Shrauvanam, August	Maugham to Cheitram, February to April.
	Dholl, cajanus indicus, spreng. [common dholl].	3	Jyeshtam and Ashaudham, June and July.	Shrauvanam, August	Phaulgoonam, March.
	Gingelly [q.v.], sesamum indicum, dec.	3	Jyeshtam, June	Ashaudbam, July	Bhaudrapadam, September.
	Green gram [q.v.], phaseolus mungo, linn.	5	Jyeshtam and Ashaudham, June and July.	Shrauvanam, August	Pooshyam, January.
	Indigo, indigofera tinctoria, linn. [common indigo].	3	Ashaudham, July	Shrauvanam, August	Aushweejam and Pooshyam, October and January.
	Italian millet, panicum italicum, linn. [tinay].	4	Ashaudham, July	Shrauvanam, August	Caurteecam, November.
	Khoda [q.v.] millet, paspalum scrobiculatum, linn.	5	Ashaudham, July	Shrauvanam, August	Pooshyam, January.
	Shaumay [q.v.], panicum miliare, lam.	3	Ashaudham, July	Shrauvanam, August	Aushweejam, October.
	Spiked millet, pennisetum spicatum. delile [bajrah].	3	Jyeshtam, June	Ashaudham, July	Bhaudrapadam, September.
	Veliraggy, eleusine coracana, gærtn. [raggy].	4	Ashaudham and Shrauvanam, July and August.	Shrauvanam and Bhaudrapadam, August and September.	Margashiram, December.
	Velivary, oryza sativa, linn. [paddy].	4	Ashaudham and Shrauvanam, July and August.	Shrauvanam and Bhaudrapadam, August and September.	Margashiram, December.
	Wheat, triticum vulgare, pers. [geung].	3	Ashaudham and Shrauvanam, July and August.	Caurteecam, November ...	Maugham, February.
Dry peiroo [q.v.].	Bengal gram [q.v.], cicer arietinum, linn.	4	Caurteecam and Margashiram, November and December.	Margashiram, December ...	Phaulgoonam, March.
	Black gram [q.v.], phaseolus mungo, var. radiatus, linn.	3	Aushweejam, October ...	Caurteecam and Margashiram, November and December.	Maugham and Phaulgoonam, February and March.
	Castor oil, ricinus communis, linn. [aumanac].	4	Margashiram, December.	Pooshyam, January	Cheitram and Veishaukham, April and May.
	Cholum [q.v.], sorghum vulgare, pers.	5	Ashaudham to Bhaudrapadam, July to September.	Aushweejam and Caurteecam, October and November.	Phaulgoonam, March.
	Coriander, coriandrum sativum, linn. [cassibor].	3	Bhaudrapadam and Aushweejam, September and October.	Caurteecam, November ...	Maugham, February.
	Cow gram [q.v.], vigna catiang, endl.	3	Aushweejam, October ...	Caurteecam and Margashiram, November and December.	Maugham and Phaulgoonam, February and March.
	Flax, linum usitatissimum, linn. [alsee].	3	Bhaudrapadam and Aushweejam, September and October.	Caurteecam, November ...	Maugham, February.
	Horse-gram, dolichos biflorus, linn. [madras horse-gram].	4	Aushweejam, October ...	Caurteecam and Margashiram, November and December.	Maugham and Phaulgoonam, February and March.
	Indian mustard, brassica juncea, h. f. and t. [rayaun].	4	Bhaudrapadam and Aushweejam, September and October.	Caurteecam, November ...	Maugham, February.
	Little millet, panicum miliaceum, linn. [varagoo].	3	Ashaudham to Bhaudrapadam, July to September.	Aushweejam and Caurteecam, October and November.	Pooshyam, January.
	Sunn [q.v.], crotalaria juncea, linn.	4	Aushweejam, October ...	Caurteecam, November ...	Phaulgoonam, March.
Garden crops.	Chayroot [q.v.], oldenlandia umbellata linn.	6	Caurteecam, November ...	Margashiram, December ...	Veishaukham, May.
	Chilly, capsicum annuum, linn. [common chilly].	...	Bhaudrapadam and Aushweejam, September and October.	Aushweejam and Caurteecam, October and November.	Pooshyam to Phaulgoonam, January to March.

General head of crop.	Name of crop.	Number of months to mature.	Ploughing season.	Sowing season.	Reaping season.
1	2	3	4	5	6
			Seasons of different crops on Golcondah coast—continued.		
Garden crops—*cont.*	Onion, allium cepa, linn. [piyauz].	3	Aushweejam, October.	Caurteecam, November ...	Pooshyam, January.
	Paulapoo zonna, sorghum vulgare, pers., red sort [cholum].	3	Cheitram, April	Cheitram, April	Jyeshtam, June.
	Raggy [q.v.], eleusine coracana, gærtn.	4	Aushweejam and Caurteecam, October and November.	Caurteecam and Margashiram, November and December.	Phaulgoonam, March.
	Tobacco, nicotiana tabacum, linn. [pogauk].	5	Aushweejam and Caurteecam, October and November.	Caurteecam and Margashiram, November and December.	Cheitram, April.
			Seasons of different crops on West coast.		
Nunjah [q.v.], wet crops.	Anna shumbah, paddy ...	5	Meenam and Maidom, March and April.	Maidom, April	Chingom, August.
	Arcory, paddy	5	Carcatacam, July ...	Carcatacam, July	Vrishchicam, November.
	Aryan, paddy	4	Carcatacam, July ...	Carcatacam, July	Toolaum, October.
	Aunacomban, paddy	5	Cunny, September ...	Cunny, September	Macaram, January.
	Bengal shumbah, paddy ...	5	Meenam and Maidom, March and April	Maidom, April	Chingom, August.
	Calama, paddy	5	Maidom, April	Maidom, April	Cunny, September.
	Carippauly, paddy	4	Maidom, April	Maidom, April	Carcatacam, July.
	Cheera, paddy	6	Maidom, April	Maidom, April	Cunny, September.
	Chembaun, paddy	4	Macaram, January	Macaram, January	Maidom, April.
	Chennel, paddy	4	Macaram, January	Macaram, January	Maidom, April.
	Chornauly, paddy...	4	Mitoonam, June	Mitoonam, June	Chingom, August.
	Congan cheera, paddy	4	Toolaum, October	Toolaum, October	Macaram, January.
	Modan, paddy	4	Maidom, April	Maidom, April	Carcatacam, July.
	Moondagampaula, paddy ...	5	Chingom, August	Chingom, August	Dhanoo, December.
	Pulliyaul, paddy	6	Maidom, April	Maidom, April	Cunny, September.
Poonjah [q.v.], garden crops, annual.	Balsam apple, momordica charantia, linn. [carolah].	2½	Vrishchicam, November ...	Vrishchicam, November ...	Macaram, January.
	Bengal gram [q.v.], cicer arietinum, linn.	5	Chingom, August	Chingom, August...	Dhanoo and Macaram, December and January.
	Black gram [q.v.], phaseolus mungo, linn., var. radiatus linn.	4	Yedavam, May	Yedavam, May	Chingom and Cunny, August and September.
	Common bendy [q.v.], hibiscus esculentus, linn.	2	Toolaum and Vrishchicam, October and November.	Toolaum and Vrishchicam, October and November.	Dhanoo and Macaram, December and January.
	Cotton, gossypium herbaceum, linn. [indian cotton].	5	Mitoonam to Cunny, June to September.	Toolaum, October	Coombham, February.
	Cow gram [q.v.], vigna catiang, endl.	5	Yedavam, May	Yedavam, May	Cunny, September.
	Cucumber, cucumis sativus, linn. [common cucumber].	2	Cunny and Macaram, September and January.	Cunny and Macaram, September and January.	Vrishchicam and Meenam, November and March.
	Elephant yam [q.v.], typhonium orixense, schott.	10	Dhanoo and Coombham, December and February.	Coombham, February	Vrishchicam, November.
	Gingelly [q.v.], sesamum indicum, dec.	4	Carcatacam, July	Chingom, August...	Dhanoo, December.
	Ginger [q.v.], zingiber officinale, rosc.	8	Vrishchicam, November ...	Yedavam, May	Dhanoo, December.
	Great pumpkin, cucurbita maxima, linn. [carcauroo].	5	Toolaum and Vrishchicam, October and November.	Toolaum and Vrishchicam, October, and November.	Coombham, February.
	Green gram [q.v.], phaseolus mungo, linn.	4	Yedavam, May	Yedavam and Mitoonam, May and June.	Chingom and Cunny, August and September.
	Indian kale, colocasia antiquorum, schott. [kachvee].	6	Maidom and Coombham, April and February.	Maidom and Coombham, April and February.	Vrishchicam and Carcatacam, November and July.
	Snake gourd, trichosanthes anguina, linn. [common snake gourd].	2	Vrishchicam, November ...	Vrishchicam, November ...	Macaram, January.
	Sugar-cane [q.v.], saccharam officinarum, linn.	10	Chingom, August	Chingom and Cunny, August and September.	Yedavam, May.
	Turmeric, curcuma longa, roxb. [country saffron].	10	Vrishchicam, November ...	Vrishchicam, November ...	Toolaum, October.
	Wax gourd [q.v.], benincasa cerifera, savi.	2	Meenam and Vrishchicam, March and November.	Meenam and Vrishchicam, March and November.	Yedavam and Macaram, May and January.
	Wing-stalked yam, dioscorea alata, linn. [large yam].	10	Coombham, February ...	Coombham, February	Vrishchicam, November.
Poonjah, garden crops, perennial.	Areca [q.v.], areca catechu, linn.	7 years.	Coombham, February ...	Coombham and Meenam, February and March.	......
	Cocoanut [q.v.], cocos nucifera, linn.	8 do.	Coombham, February ...	Coombham and Meenam, February and March.	......
	Jack, artocarpus integrifolia, linn. [common jack].	8 do.	Maidom, April	Yedavam, May	......
	Pepper, piper nigrum, linn. [black pepper].	4 do.	Maidom and Yedavam, April and May.	Mitoonam, June	......

—"*e*" The tamul Cooral has the following :—சுழன்றுமேர்ப் பின்னது உலக மதனு லுழந்தும் உழவேதலை—"agriculture, "though laborious, is the most excellent form of labour; for, "people, though they go about in search of various employ- "ments, have at last to resort to the farmer."—உழுவா ருலகத்தார்க் காணி யஃதாற்ரு தெழுவாரை யெல்லாம் பொறுத்து—"agriculturists are the linch-pin of the world, "for they support all other workers who cannot till the soil."—உழுதுண்டு வாழ்வாரே வாழ்வார்மற் றெல்லாந் தொழுதுண்டு பின் செல் பவர்—"they alone live who live by agri- "culture; all others lead a cringing, dependent life."—பலகுடை நீழலுந் தங்குடைக்கீழ்க் காண்ப ரலகுடை நீழலவர்—"patriotic farmers desire to bring all other states under "the control of their own king."—இரவா ரிரப்பார்க்கொன் றீவர் கரவாது கைசெய்தூண் மாலை யவர்—"those whose "nature is to live by manual labour will never beg but give "something to those who beg."—உழவினார் கைம்மடங்கி னில்லை விழைவதூஉம் விட்டேமென் பார்க்கு நிலை—"if the farmers' hands are slackened, even the ascetic state will "fail."—தொடிப்புழுதி கஃசா வுணக்கிற் பிடித்தெருவும் வேண்டாது சாலப் படும்—"if the land is dried so as to "reduce one pollum [q.v.] of earth to a quarter, it will grow "plentifully even without a handful of manure [yeroo]."—ஏரினு நன்றா லெருவிடுதல் கட்டபி னீரினு நன்றதன் காப்பு—"manuring is better than ploughing; after weeding, watching is "better than watering."—செல்லான் கிழவ னிருப்பி னிலம் புலந் தில்லாளி னூடி விடும்—"if the owner does not per- "sonally attend to his cultivation, his land will behave like an "angry wife and yield him no pleasure."—இலமென் றசைஇ யிருப்பாரைக் காணி னிலமென்னு நல்லா ணகும்—"the "maiden, earth, will laugh at the sight of those who plead "poverty and lead an idle life."—இன்மையி னின்னாத தியாதெனி னின்மையி னின்மையே யின்னா தது—"there is "nothing that afflicts one like poverty."—தாளாண்மை யென்னுந் தகைமைக்கட் டங்கிற்றே வேளாண்மை யென்னுஞ் செருக்கு—"the lustre of munificence will dwell "only with the dignity of laboriousness or efforts." There is a Tamul proverb :—தொழுதூண் சுவையி லுழுதூணினிது—"to cultivate and eat is more palatable than to serve and "eat;" And another :—சீமைத்தேடி வேளாமைத்தேடு—"if you "seek wealth see to agriculture." And another :—உழுதவன் கணக்குப்பார்த்தால் உழவுகோற்கூட மிச்சமில்லை—"if "a cultivator examines his accounts, even the ox-goad is not left." And another :—ஓதுவாரெல்லா முழுவான் தலைக்கடையில்—"all learned men may be found at the entrance of the plough- "man's house." And another :—மேலாமினுக்கியைக்கொண்டவன்கெட்டான் மேட்டிலே பயிரிட்டவன் கெட்டான்—"he who marries a woman of great beauty will be ruined, "he who sows on high ground, will be impoverished."——*Vellaur* (வெள்ளாறு - vellâru, Tam. vellâr*). From (vel, tam. white + âru, tam. river).—"*a*" River; Salem and South arcot districts. The Northern vellaur; otherwise Vasishta nuddy. Formed by the streams of the Tennaunday mullay and Cullroyen hills in Salem district. Flows through the Ahtoor pass into the plain of South arcot, and across the latter district into the sea at Porto novo. It forms the boundary between South arcot and Trichinopoly for a considerable distance. Above Vriddhau-chellam, it receives the Manimooctah nuddy. Total length about 135 miles. The river is bridged where it crosses the trunk roads, and also by the South indian railway near Porto novo. The trunk road bridge near Porto novo was destroyed by floods and has not been rebuilt. Thirteen anicuts cross the Vellaur in Salem district, and two in South arcot. This river was formerly the boundary between the old Bhoovangherry and Chidambaram talooks of South arcot district.—"*b*" River, Trichinopoly and Tanjore districts. The Southern vellaur. This, formerly adopted as the common boundary of the Paundyans [q.v.] and Cholans [q.v.], rises in the hills near Maroongapoory in the Trichinopoly district, takes a south-easterly course through the Native state of Poodoocottah, and falls into the sea in Palk strait, south of Point calimere. It was an old custom prevalent amongst the Nautcottay chetties [q.v.] that their women should never be allowed to cross this Vellaur, it being considered an act of bad omen [shacoonam] for women to cross boundaries. Comes down for six or seven days only in year during two monsoons [q.v.].——*Vellay* (வெள்ளை - vellai, Tam.). White. Pariah proper name. Compare Belloo, Biliya [peyar].——*Vellola* (വെള്ളോല - vellóla, Mal.). From (above + óla, mal. leaf). Blank leaf. Unregistered document [dastavaiz].——*Velly* (வெள்ளி - velli, Tam.). See sep. title.——*Velnaud* (వెల్నాడు - velnâdu, Tel.). From (voli, tel. outside + nâdu, tel. country). Ancient name of the Sundavole country, Repully talook, Kistna district.——*Velnauty* (వెల్నాటి - velnâti, obl., Tel.). From (velnâdu, tel. country so called). A class of Smarta [q.v.] bramins [q.v.] originally from Velnaud in Kistna. Numbers about 30,000.——*Vely* (వెలి - veli, Tel.; வெளி - veli, Tam.). Outside.——*Ven* (வெண் - ven, Tam.). Same as Vel. White. Pure.——*Venaud* (വേണാട് - vénâtu, Mal.). From (ven, mal. white + nâtu, mal. country). Seventeenth district [naud] of Keralam [q.v.], one of the twelve districts of low Tamul.* Part of Mooshicam. Now Travancore.——*Venbah* (வெண்பா - venbâ, Tam.). From (ven, tam. pure + pâ, tam. verse). A particular kind of Tamul verse; the best verse as distinguished from other varieties. One kind, used in the Cooral [q.v.], resembles the distich, since it consists of two lines; of these, the first must contain four feet and the second three. But the following kind of venbah from Nauladi-yaur is most in use:—வெய்ய-குரற்றோன் றி-வெஞ்சினவே-றுட்கொளினும் பெய்யு - மழைமுகிலைப் - பேணுவரால் - வையத்திருள் பொழியும்-குற்றம - பலவெனினும்-யார்க்கு ம்பொருள்பொழிவா-மேற்றே-புகழ்—"As the clouds "which send forth a fearful sound and big with angry thunder- "bolt are yet cherished for the rain they pour down, so in the "world he who liberally distributes his wealth is praised, though "his many crimes spread darkness around him." Most of the ethical works are in the last metre [bhaushay].——*Venca* (వెంక - venka, Tel.). Short for vencata, the sacred mountain. Name applied to males and females. Familiary Vencoo, Venky [peyar].——*Vencajee* (ونكاجى - venkâjî, Hind.). From (venka, short for vénkata, san. the tripatty hill + jî, hind. mahratta honorific title). Half brother of Shivajee and founder of the Mahratta [q.v.] dynasty [raj] of Tanjore. Also known as Yeckojee. See vol. I, 50.——*Vencammah* (వెంకమ్మ - venkamma, Tel.). From (venka, tel. tripatty hill + amma, tel. mother, titular affix). Hindoo female proper name [peyar].——*Vencannah* (వెంకన్న - venkanna, Tel.). From (venka, tel. tripatty hill + anna, tel. brother, titular affix). Hindoo 2nd or pers. name [peyar].——*Vencappah* (వెంకప్ప - venkappa, Tel.). From (venka, tel. tripatty hill + appa, tel. father, titular affix). Hindoo 2nd or pers. name [peyar].——*Vencasawmy* (வெங்காசாமி - vengásâmi, Tam.). From (venka, tel. tripatty hill + svâmí, san. lord); lord of venca or vencatam, the tripatty hill. Hindoo 2nd or pers. name [peyar].——*Vencatachellam* (வெங்கடாசலம் - vengadâsalam, Tam.). From (vénkata, san. tripatty hill + achala, san. mountain); vencatam, the mountain. Tripatty [tirmaley]. Hindoo 2nd or pers. name [peyar].——*Vencatachellam choultry* (వెంకటాచలసత్రం - venkatâchalasatram, Tel.). From (venkatâchalam, tel. proper name + satramu, tel. choultry). Village, Railway station; Nellore dist., Goodoor tal.; pop. 2,079; lat. 14° 20′; long. 79° 58′; from Goodoor N.N.E. 14 miles; from Nellore S.S.W. 9 miles; from the sea W. 15 miles. On trunk road.——*Vencatachella-moorty* (வெங்கடாசலமூர்த்தி - vengadâsalamúrtti, Tam.). From (vénkata, san. tripatty hill + achala, san. hill + múrti, san. embodiment). Vishnoo, the deity on the vencatam mountain.——*Vencatachellapermaul* (வெங்கடாசலப்பெருமாள் - venga-dâsalapperumâl, Tam.). From (vénkata, san. tripatty hill + achala, san. hill + perumâl, tam. vishnu, the great god). Vishnoo at Tripatty.——*Vencatacunniah* (వెంకటకన్నయ్య - venkatakan-nayya, Tel.). From (vénkata, san. tripatty hill + kanna, tel. shortened from kanniyamma, tel. the deity + ayya, tel. master, titular affix). Hindoo 2nd or pers. name [peyar].——*Vencata-gherry* (వెంకటగిరి - venkatagiri, Tel.). From (vénkata, san. tripatty hill + giri, tel. hill); means vencatam mountain. Hindoo 2nd or pers. name [peyar]. For zemindarry, see sep title.——*Vencatagherrycottah* (వెంకటగిరికోట - venkatagirikóta, Tel.). From (venkatagiri, tel. proper name + kóta, tel. fort).—"*a*" Deputy tahsildarry, North arcot district. Pay Rs. 70.—"*b*" Village, Head-quarters of Deputy tahsildar; North arcot dist., Pulmanair tal.; pop. 683; acres 1,857; lat. 13° 00′; long. 78° 32′; from Arnee W.N.W. 58 miles; from Chittore W.S.W. 43 miles; from Madras W. 121 miles; from Pulmanair S.W. 22 miles; from Ranipett W. 57 miles; from Tripatty W.S.W. 76 miles; from Vellore W. 44 miles. Formerly a large place, but known for fever. In 1865 Deputy tahsildar moved to Krishna-pooram, but afterwards returned. Site of town lately moved to higher ground at west. Ruins of a fort between old and new town, built by Vencatagherry naidoo, a poligar [q.v.]. An ancestor Nullama naidoo four centuries ago settled at Wogoo 5 miles to east, and built a fort called Bheiravoony droog after Bheiravadeva. Shorty afterwards he moved nearer to Vencata-gherrycottah and built a new village Byrapully and another fort. His descendant founded Vencatagherrycottah, where the family ruled until they were dispossessed. Soil of the neighbourhood is rich, much sugarcane [q.v.] cultivated. Weekly fair. Sugar [q.v.], tamarind [q.v.] and gram [q.v.] are exported. Travellers' bungalow [q.v.].——*Vencatajagam* (వెంకటజగము - venkatajagamu, Tel.). From (vénkata, san. tripatty hill + jagamu, tel. short for jagannât'ha, san. lord of the world), vishnoo the lord of the world on tripatty hill. Hindoo 2nd or pers. name [peyar].——*Vencatakrishnan* (வெங்கடகிருட்டிணன் - vengadagiruttinan, Tam.). From (vénkata, san. tripatty hill + krishna, san. the hero); means vishnoo as krishnan. Hindoo 2nd or pers. name [peyar].——*Vencatam* (वेङ्कट - vénkata, San.; வேங்கடம் - véngadam, Tam.). Sanscritized from (vengadam, from ven, tam. white + kadam, tam. hill-slope), because of the grey sandstones [manal cull] about tripatty hills. The hill at Tripatty.——*Vencatammah* (వెంకటమ్మ - venkatamma, Tel.). From (vénkata, san. tripatty hill + amma, tel. mother, titular affix). Hindoo female proper name [peyar].——*Vencatanarsanna* (వెంకటనరసన్న - vonkatanarasanna, Tel.). From (vénkata, san. tripatty hill + narasu, tel. familiar contraction of narasimha, san. man-lion god + anna, tel. brother, titular affix); vishnoo in narsimhan [q.v.] avatar [q.v.]. Hindoo 2nd or pers. name [peyar].——*Vencatanarsingan* (வெங்கடநரசிங்கன் - vengadanarasingan, Tam.). From (vénkata, san. tripatty hill + narasimhan, san vishnu, the man lion god); vishnoo as narsimhan. Hindoo 2nd or pers. name [peyar].——*Vencatapaty* (వెంకటపతి - venkatapati, Tel.). From (vénkata, san. tripatty hill + pati, san. lord); vishnoo the lord of vencatam or tripatty. Hindoo 2nd or pers. name [peyar].——*Vencatappa* (వెంకటప్ప - venkatappa Tel.). From (vénkata, san. tripatty hill + appa, tel. father, titular affix). Hindoo 2nd or pers. name [peyar].——*Vencatasheshan* (வெங்கடேசன் - vengadasésan, Tam.). From (vénkata, san. tripatty hill + shésha, san. the serpent); sheshan, the vishnoo's serpent. Hindoo 2nd or pers. name peyar.——*Vencatasoobboo* (வெங்கடசுப்பு - vengadasuppu, Tam.). From (vénkata, san. tripatty hill + subba, can. serpent); sheshan, the vishnoo's serpent. Hindoo 2nd or pers. name [peyar].——*Vencateshan* (வெங்கடேசன் - vengadésan, Tam.). From (vénkata, san. tripatty hill + ísha, san. lord); vishnoo, lord of vencatam or tripatty. Hindoo 2nd or pers. name [peyar].——*Vencateshwaran* (வெங்கடேசுவரன் - vengadésuvaran, Tam.). From (venkata, san. tripatty hill + íshvara, san. lord); vishnoo, lord of vencatam or tripatty. Hindoo 2nd or pers. name [peyar].——*Vencateshwara permaul* (வெங்கடேசுவரப்பெருமாள் - vengadésuvarapperumál, Tam.). From (vénkata, san. tripatty hill + íshvara, san. lord + perumál, tam. vishnu, the great god). Vishnoo.——*Vencatprasaud* (వెంకటప్రసాదు - venkataprasádu, Tel.). From (vénkata, san. tripatty hill + prasáda, san. gift); the favoured of vishnoo. Hindoo 2nd or pers. name [peyar].——*Vencatraman* (வெங்கடராமன் - vengadaráman, Tam.). From (vénkata, san. tripatty hill + ráma, san. the hero); vishnoo as rama. Familiarly Vencatt, Vengoo. Hindoo 2nd or pers. name [peyar].——*Vencatramaunoojam* (வெங்கடராமானுசம் - vengadarámánusam, Tam.). From (vénkata, san. tripatty hill + rámánuja, san. name of the hindoo reformer); Ramaunoojan, the vishnoo devotee. Hindoo 2nd or pers. name [peyar].——*Vencatratnam* (வெங்கடரத்தினம் - vengadarattinam, Tam.). From (vénkata, san. tripatty hill + ratna, san. gem); the precious mountain of tripatty. Hindoo 2nd or pers. name [peyar].——*Vencatrungan* (வெங்கடரங்கன் - vengadarangan, Tam.). From (vénkata, san. tripatty hill + ranga, san. vishnu); vishnoo on vencatam or tripatty. Hindoo 2nd or pers. name [peyar].——*Vencatt* (வெங்கட்டு - vengattu, Tam.). Colloquial for vencatam or tripatty hill. Familiar contraction of Vencatraman. Hindoo 2nd or pers. name [peyar].——*Vencayya* (వెంకయ్య - venkayya, Tel.). From (venka, tel. tripatty hill + ayya, tel. master, titular affix). Hindoo 2nd or pers. name [peyar].——*Vencoba* (ವೆಂಕೋಬ - venkóba, Can.). From (venka, can. tripatty hill + bá, mahr. familiar form of bápa, mahr. father, affix of endearment and respect). Hindoo 2nd or pers. name [peyar].——*Vengadam* (வேங்கடம் - véngadam, Tam.). From (ven, tam. white + kadam, tam. hill slope), from grey sandstones [manal cull] about the hill. One of the names of the sacred hill of Tripatty [tirmaley]. Vengada cottam was a division of the ancient Tondaimundalam [q.v.].——*Vengalanimilay* (வெண்கலநிமிளை - vengalanimilai, Tam.). Title from Tam. from (vengalam, tam. bell-metal + nimilai, tam. pyrite). Tam. also (ambarai). Bismuth. Medicinally tonic.——*Vengoo* (வெங்கு - vengu, Tam.). Familiar form of Vencatam, the sacred mountain. Corrupted into Mangaun masculine and Mangy feminine. Hindoo 2nd or pers name [peyar]. Common to both sexes. Otherwise Vongy.——*Venpaundoo* (श्वेतपाण्डु - shvétapándu, San.; گورے لوگ - gorelog, Dec.; తెల్లపాండు - tellapándu, Tel.; வெண்பாண்டு - venbándu, Tam.). Title and Tam. from (ven, tam. white + pándu, san. jaundice). San. from (shvéta, san. white + pándu, san. skin disease). Tel. from (tella, tel. white + pándu, san. skin-disease). Albinos. These are to be met with occasionally; the color of the skin is not partially white; the whole outward surface is so, which gives the person somewhat the look of a dead European who had not been much exposed to the sun; the hair is like flax [alsee], the iris is of the palest grey tint, and the pupil itself, in place of being dark, has a sub-rubied appearance and is commonly of very narrow circumference, owing, it is to be supposed, to the extreme sensibility of the retina which is so remarkable in these people that the function of vision is but imperfectly performed in open day, or until they have been brought into some shady corner; their constitutions are usually delicate, the smell of their perspiration is very fetid; they are in their nature timid and irritable, and are seldom known to live to an advanced age; the females are said rarely to bear children, but when they do their offspring is of the natural color of the coast to which they belong [veidyan].——*Veppaulay* (வெட்பாலை - vedbálai, Tam.) From (vel, tam. white + pálai, tam. milky plant). Botanically the Wrightia genus, apocynaceæ [vricsham, 87]. Shrubs or small trees, with often slender cord-like branches; leaves opposite; flowers red, white or yellow, in terminal cymes; fruit consists of two long distinct or cohering follicles, containing numerous seeds furnished with a tuft of silky hairs at the lower ends. The species best known to the natives are:—tinctoria [paula indigo], tomentosa [ground paulay].——*Vunnaun* (வண்ணான் - vannán, Tam.). From (venmai, tam. white). Tamul washermen. The corresponding terms are:—Hind. dhoby; Tel. saucala; Can. agasa; Mal. veloottaidan. Numbers about 300,000. See vol. I (68); vol. II, 232, 236 [jauty].——*Wynaud* (വയനാട് - vayanátu, Mal.). See sep. title.

VEL (வெல் - vel, *Tam.*). To conquer.——*Vail* (வேல் - vél, Tam.). See sep. title.——*Vellore* (வேலூர் - vélúr, Tam.). See sep. title.——*Vetticodiyone* (வெற்றிக்கொடியோன் - vettikkodiyón, Tam.). From (vetti, tam. victory + kodi, tam. flag). Name of a vernacular newspaper.——*Vettivergay* (வெற்றிவேற்கை - vettivérgai, Tam.). From (vetti, tam. victory + vél, tam. lance + kai, tam. hand); from opening words. A moral treatise in tamul, by Ativeera rama pandiyan [q.v.].——*Vetty* (வெற்றி - vetti, Tam.). From (vel, tam. to conquer). Victory. Vetty maulay is a chaplet of victory, warrior's wreath. The dravidians have different garlands for different grades of heroism; and eight such are known among them:—vetchy or jungle geranium [q.v.] for seizing enemies' cattle [maud], the first act of aggression in war; caranday or fragrant toolsy [q.v.] for recovering one's own cattle seized by an enemy; vanjy or goolancha [q.v.] for going against an enemy; caunjy or indian elm [q.v.] for taking up a post against an advancing enemy; notchy [q.v.] for defending one's fort; oolinay or small poolay [q.v.] for taking an enemy's fort; toombay [q.v.] for fighting an enemy in battle and vaugay or sirissa [q.v.] for gaining a victory in battle.

VELANGA (मुचुकुन्द - muchukunda, *San.*; مچکند - machkand, *Hind.*; లోలుగ - lóluga, *Tel.*; ଗିରିଙ୍ଗ - giringa, *Oor.*; වෙලංග - velanga, *Singh.*). Title from singh. San. from (much, san. to abandon + kunda, san. jasminum pubescens, willd.). Hind. from sanscrit. Oor. also (bélo). Tam. also (ottinmaram). Title otherwise Various-leaved pterospermum. Botanically Pterospermum [moch coondam] suberifolium, lamk., sterculiaceæ [vricsham, 26]. Alias Pentapetes suberifolia; Pterospermum canescens. Tree; leaves cuneate-oblong, obliquely cordate at the base, coarsely toothed, densely pubescent beneath; peduncles axillary, three-flowered; involucel leaves three, linear, entire, very caducous; capsule obovoid, acutish, covered on the outside with a dense, scurfy pubescence; flowers large, white, fragrant; southern districts, flowering from march to may. Flower made into a paste with caunjika or rice vinegar [caudy] forms an application for hemicrania; wood light red, moderately hard, tough; used for building carts and other purposes.

VELLORE * (வேலூர் - vélúr, *Tam.*). From (vél, tam. bábul tree, acacia arabica, willd. + úr, tam. village) [vel]. Sanscrit name (vélapurí), meaning grove + town. Tel. name (ráyavéluru), means king's vellore.——**(1)** Talook. North arcot district. Tahsildar's pay Rs. 175. Area 455 square miles. Population 192,937. Language Tamul. Length east to west 35 miles, breadth 12. S. centre of district. Bounded west and north by Goodiyattam, from which separated by Palaur; east by Arcot; south by Arnee jagheer, Polore talook, and Tripatore talook of Salem district. The northern portion, along right bank of Palaur, is flat and open; but most of rest is covered with hill ranges proceeding from Jawaudies, which occupy eastern and southern parts. Chief elevations are Chuckly droog, Keilausagherry and Periyamullay. Most extensive valley is Agaram. Forests cover ⅕th of area. Teak [q.v.] and blackwood [q.v.], vengay [q.v.], atchah [q.v.], nullamaddy [black murdah], tella maddy [white murdah] and namay [nemmy]. Climate of hills and valleys is feverish. Soils are in the valleys rich loam and red and black clays [calimunn] mixed with sand [manal] and gravel [kankar]; in the level country proportion of sand greater and fertility less, while in some parts soda [sowdoo] and salt [ooppoo] occur and make ground barren. Trade is great, chiefly in grains [dhaunyam] and jaggery [q.v.]. Most at cusbah [q.v.] whence produce exported to Madras and Calicut. Forest produce exported, particularly bamboos [q.v.]. Malayaulies inhabiting Jawaudies gather bark [q.v.], lac [q.v.], honey [shahad] and wax [mom]. Besides iron [auhan], lime [choonam], and building stone [cull], saltpetre [shorah] is found and was until lately manufactured. Iron worked slightly in Pankkam and Pukkampolliem. Industries are cloth and coray [q.v.] mat [boriyah] weaving; making of brass [pittalay] vessels; and manufacture of paper, indigo [q.v.] and gunny [q.v.]. Common cloths are produced, notably in Amboor, Pullicondah and Vellore. Coray mats chiefly at Agaramcherry and Pullicondah by Lubbays. Manufacture of brass utensils and plates confined to Vellore where Cummaular are employed in it. Paper industry is dying out. Gunny [q.v.] is made in Pullicondah by Janapar, and indigo [q.v.] produced in Vellore town. Rivers are Agaram and Palaur. Tanks are few. The principal are Chedpairy, Chedvaulay and Torapaudy. Places of archæological interest:—Amboor, Cholapooram, Keilausagherry, Pullicondah, Velapaudy, Vellore, Virinjipooram. Principal trig. station:—Keilausagherry. The leading places, &c., in the talook are the following.——*Abdoollahpooram* (அப்துல்லாப்புரம் -

abdullâppuram, Tam.). From (abdulláh, hind. proper name + pura, san. town). Village; pop. 496; acres 520; lat. 12° 55′; long. 79° 08′; from Chittore S. 21 miles; from Vellore W. 4 miles. Ruins of palace built by Abdoollah khan, last of the family of Beejapore sultans, who reigned in Vellore and who removed his court here.——*Agaram* (அகரம் - agaram, Tam.). Means agricultural village. Village, River; pop. 2,421; acres 4,685; lat. 12° 49′; long. 78° 56′; from Chittore S.S.W. 31 miles; from Vellore W.S.W. 18 miles. Rises in Jawaudies and flows N. into Palaur.——*Amboor* (ஆம்பூர் - ámúr, Tam.). See sep. title.——*Aryandampoondy* (அருகந்தம்பூண்டி - arugandambúndi, Tam.). From (arigandam, tam. an iron frame worn on the neck for performing a vow + púndi, tam. village). Village; pop. 1,670; acres 937; lat. 12° 56′; long. 79° 11′; from Chittore S. 20 miles; from Vellore N. ½ mile. Tombs of Tippoo's family.——*Canyambaudy* (கணியம்பாடி - kaniyambádi, Tam.). From (kaniyan, tam. member of that caste + pádi, tam. village). Village; pop. 2,467; acres 2,515; lat. 12° 49′; long. 79° 11′; from Chittore S. 28 miles; from Vellore S. 8 miles. Choultry [q.v.].——*Cholapooram* (சோழவரம் - shózhavaram, Tam.). From Caricaulan the Chola king. Village; pop. 1,133; acres 3,965; lat. 12° 49′; long. 79° 08′; from Chittore S. 28 miles; from Vellore S.S.W. 8 miles. Vishnoo temple built by Chola [q.v.] king, Caricaulan.——*Chuckly droog* (சக்கிலித்துருக்கம் - shakkilitturukkam, Tam.). From (shakkili, tam. shoe-maker + durga, san. fort). Hill. Chief peak of Jawaudy hills. Hill fort.——*Keilausagherry* (கைலாசகிரி - kailásagiri, Tam.). From (kailása, san. paradise of shiva + giri, san. hill). Hill; lat. 12° 50′; long. 79° 07′; from Chittore S. 26 miles; from Vellore S.W. 8 miles. Hill fort improved by Mahrattas. Small bungalow [q.v.] in the fort. Trig. station in lat. 12° 50′ 19·07″; long. 79° 06′ 48·51″; height 2,743 feet; from Oossoor S. 1¾ miles; from Vellore S.W. 7 miles.——*Keilausaputnam* (కైలాసపట్నము - kailásapatnamu, Tel.). From (kailása, san. paradise of shiva + pattana, san. town). Village. At the base of Keilausagherry. Ancient town, royal residence with Chola kings, now effaced.——*Oossoor* (ஊசூர் - úsúr, Tam.). Hind. name (husainábad), meaning town of hoossain. Village; acres 1,249; lat. 12° 52′; long. 79° 06′; from Chittore S. 25 miles; from Vellore S.W. 7 miles. Noted for grapes [angoor] and pomegranates [anaur].——*Ootchicamullay* (உச்சிகைமலை - uççigamalai, Tam.). See sep. title.——*Palaur* (பாலாறு - páláru, Tam.). See sep. title.——*Pullicondah* (பள்ளிக்கொண்டை - pallikkondai, Tam.). See sep. title.——*Torapaudy* (தொரப்பாடி - torappádi, Tam.). From (turai, tam. ford + pádi, tam. village). Village; pop. 1,371; acres 1,262; lat. 12° 54′; long. 79° 10′; from Chittore S. 22 miles; from Vellore S.S.W. 2 miles. Tank. Central jail.——*Velupaudy* (வேலப்பாடி - vélappádi, Tam.). From (vél, tam. babul tree, acacia arabica, willd. + pádi, san. village). Sanscrit name (bálápurí), meaning parvaty + town. Village; pop. 3,623; acres 960; lat. 12° 54′; long. 79° 11′; from Chittore S. 22 miles; from Vellore S. 1⅓ miles. Suburb of Vellore. Ruined temple on hill called Bhawauny or Baulacondah, residence of Chola chief at the time Bommy reddy built the fort.——*Vellore* (வேலூர் - vélúr, Tam.). See below.——*Virinjipooram* (விரிஞ்சிபுரம் - viriñjippuram, Tam.). See sep. title.——**(2)** Deputy tahsildarry. North arcot district. Pay Rs. 70.——**(3)** Town, Headquarters of Sub-collector, Tahsildar and Deputy tahsildar, District moonsif; North arcot dist., Vellore tal.; pop. 44,925; acres 714; lat. 12° 55′; long. 79° 11′; height 700 feet; from Arnee N.N.W. 20 miles; from Chittore S. 21 miles; from Madras W. 78 miles; from Ranipett W. 13 miles; from Tripatty S.S W. 53 miles. Often called Rye ellore or royal ellore to distinguish from Ellore in Godavery known as Ooppellore or salt ellore. Original settlement Velapaudy. Includes ten villages. A mile south of Palaur. Heat great, owing to radiation from rocky hills. Station very healthy. Ancient fortress. In sixteenth century the Royer [q.v.] retired here before the allied Sultans of Beejapore and Golcondah. In 1646 Mahomedan. In 1677 captured by Shivajee. Davood khan in 1708 ousted the Mahrattas after four and a half months' siege. In 1710 given by Dost ally to his son-in-law, whose son Moortezah ally murdered Sufder ally here in 1741. For more than 20 years stronghold of Moortezah ally who rebelled against Nawaub of Arcot and English allies. About 1765 occupied by an English garrison. In 1768 threatened by Hyder ally. In 1780 Hyder invested the place, which held out for two years till siege raised by advance of army from Madras and Hyder's death. In 1791 basis of Lord Cornwallis' march on Bangalore. After fall of Seringapatam in 1799, Tippoo's twelve sons and eight daughters, were detained here. On morning of 10th July 1806 native troops rose against European part of garrison, consisting of two companies of 69th regiment. Attack totally unexpected; Colonel Gillespie, with a party of 19th dragoons, restored order, but Europeans massacred were 113. Among them Colonel Fancourt and thirteen other officers. 350 mutineers fell in the attack, and 500 were made prisoners. Two sons of Tippoo were implicated and the family was removed to Bengal. The fort is a perfect specimen of military architecture nearly an exact square. The old entrance was by a winding roadway with massive gates, and protected by a draw-bridge. The ditch is supplied with water by a subterranean drain connecting with bathing tank of Sooryagoonta. Has alligators [mugger]. Five mahauls [q.v.], known as Candy, Goomsoor, Pachah begum, Palcondah and Tippoo, are occupied by Candian pensioners, descendants of Tippoo's relatives, the ex-Palcondah zemindar [q.v.], and others. Temple near north-east corner of the fort. The best sculpture is in the Calyaunamantapam. Three fortified peaks overlooking the town are Gajarowghur, Mortizghur and Sajjarowghur. Sajjarowghur and Gajarowghur were built by Mahrattas, and Mortizghur by the last killadar [q.v.] of Vellore. The following are the travelling distances by road from Vellore to different places :—

To	Viâ	Miles and Furlongs.	
Amboor	Pullicondah	30	5
Arnee	Canyambaudy	23	4
Bangalore ...	Amboor, Krishnagherry and Oossoor ...	129	5
Bangalore ...	Goodiyattam, Naicknairy ghaut and Colaur.	118	0
Bangalore ...	Goodiyattam, Pulmanair and Colaur ...	126	5
Bellary	Goodiyattam, Pulmanair and Anantapore.	244	7½
Bellary	Chittore, Pulmanair and Anantapore ...	250	4½
Bellary	Goodiyattam, Naicknairy ghaut and Anantapore.	279	0
Bellary	Pulmanair, Colaur and Anantapore ...	284	0
Bellary	Chittore, Royachoty, Tadpatry and Gooty.	259	0
Berhampore ...	Nellore, Bezvada and Chicacole ...	685	4
Cadiry	Pulmanair and Madanapully	124	4
Calastry	Ranipett and Poottore	84	7
Calastry	Chittore and Tripatty	89	6
Cannanore ...	Krishnagherry, Bangalore, Seringapatam and the Periyambaudy ghaut.	328	4
Chingleput ...	Ranipett and Wallajahbad	64	1
Chittore	Narharipett	22	0
Chundragherry ...	Chittore	55	7
Coimbatore ...	Tripatore, Munjavaudy ghaut, Salem and Erode.	223	6
Coimbatore ...	Tripatore, Toppoor ghaut, Omalore and Bhawauny.	227	7
Coimbatore ...	Munjavaudy ghaut, Salem and Bhawauny.	225	5
Colaur	Pulmanair	84	7
Colaur	Goodiyattam and Naicknairy ghaut ...	76	6
Conjeeveram ...	Ranipett	43	5
Cuddalore ...	Ranipett, Wandiwash and Pondicherry.	112	3
Cuddalore ...	Arnee, Jinjee and Villoopooram ...	107	2
Cuddalore ...	Trinomallee, Manaloorpett and Panrooty.	115	6
Cuddapah ...	Chittore and Royachoty	123	3
Cuttack	Nellore, Bezvada, Chicacole and Berhampore.	802	1
French rocks ...	Krishnagherry, Bangalore and Maddore	206	6
Goodiyattam ...	Pullicondah	20	1
Gooty	Pulmanair, Cadiry and Anantapore ...	212	5½
Gooty	Chittore, Royachoty and Tadpatry ...	213	6
Jinjee	Arnee	55	1
Kamptee ...	Cuddapah, Kurnool, Secunderabad and Nirmal.	700	0½
Kircambaudy ...	Chundragherry and Tripatty ...	73	5
Kurnool	Chittore and Cuddapah	246	3
Kurnool	Pulmanair, Cadiry, Anantapore and Gooty.	272	4½
Madras	Ranipett and Poonamallee	84	3
Madanapully ...	Pulmanair	75	0½
Mangalore ...	Bangalore and Munjarabad	349	5
Mercara	Bangalore and Seringapatam ...	286	3
Nellore	Ranipett, Poottore and Calastry ...	142	6
Nellore	Chittore and Calastry	147	5
Palamcottah ...	Arnee, Villoopooram, Trichinopoly and Madura.	258	6
Pondicherry ...	Arnee and Tindivanam	93	1
Pondicherry ...	Arnee, Devanore and Meilam ...	97	5
Poonamallee ...	Ranipett	71	7
Poonganore ...	Pulmanair	61	0½
Pulmanair ...	Goodiyattam	42	3
Pulmanair ...	Narharipett	45	4
Quilon	Trichinopoly and Madura	412	3
Ranipett	......	13	6
Royachoty ...	Chittore	91	0
Sadras	Ranipett and Chingleput	84	5
Salem	Tripatore and Munjavaudy ghaut ...	125	1
Salem	Tripatore and Toppoor ghaut ...	136	3
Secunderabad. ...	Royachoty, Cuddapah and Kurnool ...	382	2
Secunderabad ...	Pulmanair, Anantapore, Gooty and Kurnool.	408	3½
Tindivanam ...	Arnee and Wandiwash	67	3
Trichinopoly ...	Arnee, Jinjee, Villoopooram and Volcondapooram.	177	6
Trinomallee ...	Polore	51	5
Tripatore ...	Vaniyambaudy	55	1
Tripatty	Chittore and Chundragherry	66	6
Vaniyambaudy ...	Pullicondah	41	1
Wallajahbad ...	Ranipett	50	1

VELLY (रजत - rajata, *San.*; रुपें - rupém, *Mahr.*; فضه - fizzah, *Ar.*; نقره - nukrah, *Pers.*; روپا - rúpá, *Hind.* and *Dec.*; پيرك - perak, *Malay*; ಬೆಳ್ಳಿ - belli, *Can.*; ಬೊಳ್ಳಿ - bolli, *Too.*; వెండి - vendi, *Tel.*; വെള്ളി - velli, *Mal.*; රිදී - ridí, *Singh.*; வெள்ளி - velli, *Tam.*). Title from tamul [vel.]. San. means white. Mahr. and Hind. from sanscrit. Mal. from tamul. Tam. from (vel, tam. white). San. also (rúpya), meaning wrought silver; (tára), meaning radiant. Pers. also (sím). Malay also (sálaka). Silver. Argentum of chemists.—"*a*" White lustrous metal, which does not oxidise in air or water, but becomes darkened by contact with sulphuretted hydrogen. Rarely got altogether pure, but generally contains small portions of other metals [loham]. In malleability and ductility it exceeds all metals, except gold [pon]. For local distribution, see vol. II, 35. Only preparation used in medicine is the nitrate of silver [caudicauram]. Silver-wire [calaubat] is made as fine as a hair; a silken thread is then covered with it for embroidering muslins [q.v.].—" *b* " A velly is also name of a coin. 10 peisas = 1 velly; 5 vellies = 1 rupee [naunyam, 2d]. Approximate actual value, 1 velly = 3 annas 4 pies. Malabar. Compare Hind. powlab, Can. caul, Tel. doogoolam.——**(1)** *Velly caur* (வெள்ளிக்காறு - vellikkáru, Tam.). From (above + káru, tam. bar). Silver in bars.——*Velly eeyam* (வெள்ளீயம் - vellíyam, Tam.). From (above + íyam, tam. lead). Tin [tagaram].——*Velly moolaum* (வெள்ளி முலாம் - vellimulám, Tam.). From (above + mullamma, ar. plating). Silver gilt [moolaum].——*Velly raikk* (ورق الفضة - varakulfizzah, Ar.; ورق نقره - varakinukrah, Pers.; روپیری ورق - rúperívarak, Hind.; روپیری تگٹ - rúperítagat, Dec.; ಬೆಳ್ಳಿರೇಕು - bellíréku, Can.; వెండిరేకు - vendiréku, Tel.; വെള്ളിത്തകിട് - vellittakitu, Mal.; வெள்ளிரேக்கு - vellirékku, Tam.). Hind. from (rúpá, hind. silver + tagat, hind. leaf). Mal. from (velli, mal. silver + takitu, mal. metalic leaf). Pers. also (varakisím). Silver leaf. Employed by moochees [q.v.] in ornamenting pictures, images, fans. Veidyans [q.v.] and hakeems [q.v.] use as tonic, stomachic and aphrodisiac. Substituted for British oxide of silver.——*Velly sarigay* (روپیری کناری - rúperíkinárí, Hind.; వెండిజరి - vendidzari, Tel.; வெள்ளிச்சரிகை - velliçarigai, Tam.). Hind. from (rúpá, hind. silver + kinárí, hind. lace). Tel. from (vendi, tel. silver + zar, hind. lace). Silver lace [sarigay].——**(2)** *Caur velly* (கார்வெள்ளி - kárvelli, Tam.). Otherwise Carookkan velly. Meaning black silver. Impure silver.——*Chokka velly* (చొక్కపువెండి - tsokkapuvendi, Tel.; சொக்கவெள்ளி - shokkavelli, Tam.). Title and Tam. from (shokkam, tam. pure + velli, tam. silver). Tel. from (tsokkamu, tel. pure + vendi, tel. silver). Pure silver.——*Cull velly* (கல்வெள்ளி - kalvelli, Tam.). From (kal, tam. stone + above). Hard inferior silver mixed with much alloy. Also mixture of tin [tagaram] and iron [auhan].——*Moottoo velly* (नागभस्म - nágabhasma, San.; सीसभस्म - sísabhasma, Mahr.; اسفیداج - isfedáj, Ar.; سفید آب - sufedáb, Pers.; سفیده - safedah, Hind. and Dec.; تماه پوتح - timahputih, Malay; ಶೀಸಭಸ್ಮ - shísabhasma, Can.; వంగభస్మ - vangabhasma, Too.; సీసభస్మము - sísabhasmamu, Tel.; നാഗഭസ്മം - nágabhasmam, Mal.; முத்து வெள்ளை - muttuvellai, Tam.). Title from tamul. San. from (nága, san. lead + bhasma, san. ashes). Mahr. from (sísa, san. lead + bhasma, san. ashes). Ar. from persian. Pers. from (sufed, pers. white + áb, pers. water). Hind. from (safed, pers. white). Malay from (timah, malay, tin + putih, malay, white). Can. from (sísa, san. lead + bhasma, san. ashes). Too. from (vanga too. white oxide of lead + bhasma, san. ashes). Tel. from (sísa, san. lead + bhasma, san. ashes). Mal. from sanscrit. Tam. means pearl white. Tam. also (vellíyapparbam), meaning white-lead ashes; (vellai), meaning whiteness. White lead. Otherwise Ceruse, White oxide of lead. Plumbi carbonas of chemists [veidyan]. Usually made by suspending thin plates of lead [eeyam] over heated vinegar [caudy], the vapour of which corrodes the metal and converts it into a heavy white powder. A mineral drug; sometimes employed in the shape of plaster and forms an astringent and desiccant for ulcers and sores. Mixed with oil it forms paint [rangh].

VEM (வெம் - vem, *Tam.*). Hot.——*Vaigisa* (వేగిస - végisa, Tel.). From (vé, tam. to burn), tropical plant. Same as Common vengay.——*Vailay* (வேலை - vélai, Tam.). See sep. title.——*Vaimboo* (வேம்பு - vémbu, *Tam.*). Margosa [neem] tree. Hindoo proper name, male and female [peyar]; called after the margosa tree, the representative of bitterness; death should regard in consequence the child as too bitter and too worthless to carry it off [peyar].——*Vaimdonda* (వేమదొండ - vémadonda, Tel.). Means margosa caper. Same as Camel thistle.——*Vaimla* (వేముల - vémula, Tel.). From (vému, tel. margosa tree). Locative pl. Suffix in place names.——*Vainil* (வேனில் - vénil, Tam.). From (vem, tam. hot). Hot season, divided into Yila vainil or mild hot season and Moothir vainil or severe hot season [caurtey, ritoo].——*Vembayyan* (வேம்பையன் - vémbaiyyan, Tam.). Familiarly Vemban. Proper name [peyar].——*Vemana* (వేమన - vémana, Tel.). From (vému, tel. margosa tree + ana, tel. a personal suffix). Modern author of a large collection of popular aphorisms on moral subjects, lived at the beginning of the 18th century. By birth a caupoo [q.v.], native of south western parts of Telingana [q.v.]. The following are specimens:—జనన మరణములను సంధ్యలు తానులేదు సంధ్యలు తానులేదు జననిశూద్రు తల్లియాదరాలు వానెట్లు బాపడు—" the daily " prayers and the braminical cord [poonool] are wanting both at " birth and at the time of death; his mother never enjoyed " either of these; and if his mother be a shoodra, how can he " be a bramin?"—మొదట తన మతము వదలక తుదనెవ్వరి మతమునైన దూషింపకయుండ వదలుకయు కోర్కెల్లకు మురమున జరియించు వాడె, సుఖ్యుడగుకు—" he who in the first place swerves not from his " own religion; who in the second place reviles the creed of no " other man; and who cautiously refrains from forming any evil " desire; he shall live in happiness; he is the first of men." It cannot be said that the style is at all profound.——*Vembanaud* (വെമ്പനാട് - vempanátu, Mal.). From (vempu, mal. hot + nátu, mal. country). Sanscrit name (bimbalídésha). Backwater; Travancore state, Quilon and Cottayam divisions, Ambalapoya, Shertala, Wycome, Yaittmanore, Cottayam and Chungacherry tals. The largest backwater in Travancore. Extreme length is 32 miles; extreme breadth 9 miles; average breadth 2 miles. Lies east of Alleppey. The waters of the Pambah, Mooatpoya, and Meenachel rivers are emptied into it. On the east bank are the talooks of Chungacherry, Cottayam and Wycome and on the west Shertala.——*Vendun* (வேந்தன் - véndan, Tam.). From (vé, tam. to burn); powerful. Means king. Soobramanyan [q.v.].——*Veppaudy* (வேப்பாடி - véppádi, Tam.). From (vémbu, tam. margosa tree, melia azadirachta, linn. + pádi, tam. village). Another name of Toppoor river.

VENCATAGHERRY (వెంకటగిరి - venkatagiri,* *Tel.*). From (vénkata, san. vishnu, of the white hill + giri, san. mountain) [vel].——**(1)** Zemindarry, Nellore district. The whole Zemindarry consists of two divisions in the south of the district, Vencatagherry and Polore, and two divisions in the north, Darshy and Podily; also a number of villages scattered about in different government talooks. Total villages 730, besides 617 hamlets. The southern division comprises five talooks, viz., Manoobole, Mullam, Polore, Sagootore, Vencatagherry. The northern division consists of five talooks, viz., Cotcherlacote, Darshy, Maurella, Pelloor, Podily. Swarna, in Kistna district, belongs to the zemindar. With Calastry, Bomrauz or Carvetnugger, and Sydapore, the Zemindarry was in 1800 made into the British district of Western pollems [q.v.]. In 1808 Vencatagherry, Sydapore, and the Pamoor talook of Cakastry were transferred to Nellore district. The house of Vencatagherry was founded by Chevy reddy 28 generations ago. Chevy reddy's greatgrandson, Yerra yantsama naidoo, a great warrior, drove the Paundya rajahs of Madura from Conjeeveram. His successors distinguished themselves in all parts of Telingana [q.v.] as far north as Rajahmundry and as far south as Madras. In 1751, the zemindar assisted the English against Hyder ally, who destroyed the town in retaliation. The family has always been distinguished for its loyalty to the British. A sunuud e milkyat istimrar [q.v.] was forwarded to the zemindar with a letter from Lord Clive, dated 24th August 1802. The zemindar is the chief of the Velama [q.v.] caste. The present zemindar is the 28th of the line. The peshcush [q.v.] at present is Rs. 373,875. In 1689 Bungauroo yautsama naidoo was rewarded with the title of Rajah bahadur by the Court of Hyderabad. See vol. I, 56.——**(2)** Zemindarry deputy tahsildar's division, Nellore district. Pay Rs. 120. Area 426 square miles. Bounded on the north by Raupore talook and north-east by Goodoor talook, south by North arcot district and Polore division of the zemindarry, east by Polore division separated by Swarnamookhy, and west by the Veligonda range which separates it from the Cuddapah district. The division extends in a south-westerly direction by the side of Veligouda hills. It is traversed by the Vencatagherry river which rises in the Veligonda hills and flows westward as far as Baulayapulley in the division and thence turning eastward enters the Goodoor talook. The passes [ghaut] through the Veligondas lead over into the Cuddapah district. The principal pass is Gungalaity canama. The Vencatagherry droog is nearly highest point in the Veligondas, excepting Penchalcondah. The soil is generally regady [regar] and fertile. The southern and western portions are hilly with red earth soil and generally poor. The chief productions are dry grains [q.v.]. Indigo [q.v.] is cultivated; tobacco [pogauk] also. Cloths are woven at Manoolaulpett, Vencatagherry, and some few other villages. Bangle earth [gauzoo sowdoo] is plentiful, and many villagers live by making bangles [gauzoo] which are sent to Madras, &c. There is some sport in the division. It is irrigated by the Maumidy caulwa, Swarnamookhy, and the Vencatagherry river. The Vencatagherry river is used by digging spring channels [q.v.] and by constructing dams for irrigation. The waters of this river flow into the Goodoor madoogoo, and irrigates a large area in the Goodoor talook. The country to the north and east presents a plain surface, intersected by numerous jungle streams which feed the several tanks. Principal trig. stations:—Cayyoor, Goorramcondah. The leading places, &c., in the division are the following.——*Cayyoor* (కయ్యూరు - kayyúru, Tel.). From (kayya, tel. field + úru, tel. village). Village; lat. 14° 02′; long. 79° 42′; from Nellore S.W. 37 miles; from Raupore S.S.E. 15 miles; from Vencatagherry N.N.E. 7 miles. Large tank. Trig. station in lat. 14° 00′ 41·89″; long. 79° 42′ 00·86″; height 301 feet; from Vencatagherry N.E. 6 miles; from Vengopaulpooram S.E. 2 miles.——*Goorramcondah* (గుర్రంకొండ - gurramkonda, Tel.). From (gurramu, tel. horse + konda, tel. hill). Village; pop. 289; lat 14° 01′; long. 79° 52′; from Nellore S.W. 32 miles; from Raupore S.E. 23 miles; from Vencatagherry E. 16 miles. In the midst of thick jungle. Trig. station in lat. 14° 00′ 45·21″; long. 79° 52′ 37·04″; height 337 feet; from Goorramcondah E. 1 mile; from Vencatagherry E.N.E. 17 miles.——*Manoolaulpett* (మనులాలపేట - manulálapéta, Tel.). From (manulálá, tel. proper name + péta, tel. suburb). Pop. 626; lat. 13° 56′; long. 79° 28′; from Nellore S.W. 44 miles; from Raupore S. 19 miles; from Vencatagherry S.S.E. 2 miles. Large weaving place.——*Veligonda* (వెలిగొండ - veligonda, Tel.). See sep. title.——*Vencatagherry* (వెంకటగిరి - venkatagiri, Tel.). See below.——**(3)** Village, Head-quarters of Deputy tahsildar and Special sub-registrar; Nellore dist., Vencatagherry division; pop. 9,623; lat. 13° 58′; long. 79° 37′; height 286 feet; from Madras N.W. 78 miles; from Naidoopett W. 21 miles; from Nellore S.W. 43 miles; from Ongole S.S.W. 109 miles; from Raupore S.S.E. 17 miles. The chief town of one of the two southern divisions of the Vencatagherry zemindarry. Place of residence of the rajah, who owns the estate. Traveller's bungalow [q.v.]. It is surrounded by the Vencatagherry river which flows by it in two branches. Two temples, Vishnoo and Shiva. In June of every year a great car festival [ratotsavam] takes place for ten days. Railway station is 1½ miles from the town at Periyavaram.——**(4)** A hill fort; lat. 13° 58′; long. 79° 31′; height 3,080 feet; from Nellore S.W. 48 miles; from Raupore S.S.W. 16 miles; from Vencatagherry W. 8 miles. Fort on a hill 6 miles west of Vencatagherry. Formerly residence of the zemindar [q.v.]. Some buildings yet remain. Stone steps lead up. Now abandoned.——**(5)** River; see above. Called also (kaivalyanadi), meaning beatitude + river.

VENGAY (வேங்கை - véngai, *Tam.*). From (vé, tam. to burn) [vem]; tropical plant. Botanically the Pterocarpus genus, leguminosæ [vricsham, 48]. Trees, mostly tropical; leaves alternate pinnate; flowers showy yellow; pods flat, round or oval, thick in the middle and containing one to three seeds; yield gum kino [q.v.]. The species best known to the natives are:—indicus [padouk], marsupium [common vengay], santalinus [red sanders].——*Common vengay* (पीतसार - pítasára, San.; बिंबला - bimbalá, Mahr.; بجسر - bijesar, Hind. and Dec.; ಒಳ್ಳೆ ಹೊನ್ನೆ - ollehonne, Can.; ರಕ್ತಹೊನೆ - raktahone, Coorg; వేగిస - végisa, Tel.; വേങ്ങ - vénna, Mal.; ගම්මලු - gammalu, Singh.; வேங்கை - véngai, Tam.). San. from (píta, san. yellow + sára, san. essence); generally applied to sandalwood. Hind. from sanscrit. Dec. from sanscrit. Can. from (olle, can. good + honne, can. the tree). Tel. from (vé, tam. to burn), tropical plant. Mal. from tamul. Tam. from (vé, tam. to burn); tropical plant. Hind. also (pítasála), meaning yellow saul, shorea robusta, gærtn. Can. also (bénga), from tamul; (honne), meaning golden, from yellow stain when damp; (raktahonne), red variety; (dhindaga); (bibla). Tel. also (végi); (ógisa) [fig mango]; (égi); (peddégi), meaning large + the tree; (gándámrigamunetturuchettu), meaning rhinoceros + blood + tree; (símagándámrigamunetturuchettu), meaning foreign + the tree. Mal. also (karintakara), meaning black + cassia tora, linn.; (malantakara), meaning wild tora. Tam. also (kándámirugamirattam), meaning rhinoceros + blood [sumatra dragon's blood]; (kuriñji); (vandunnámalarmaram), meaning beetle + uneaten + flower + tree, flower tree untouched by beetles [champak]; cf. foreign agatty. Title otherwise Amboyna kino, Coorinjy, Indian dragon's blood, Indian kino, Malabar kino, Vaigisa. Botanically Pterocarpus [vengay] marsupium roxb., leguminosæ [vricsham, 58]. Alias Pterocarpus bilobus. Tree, 40–80 feet; leaves unequally pinnated; leaflets five to seven, alternate, elliptical, usually deeply emarginate, glabrous; panicles terminal; calyx five-cleft; corolla papilionaceous; petals long-clawed, waved or curled on the margins; stamens combined into a sheath, split down to the base on one side, and half-way down the other; legume long-stalked, surrounded by a membranaceous wing, 1 or rarely 2-seeded; flowers pale yellow, flowering in rainy season. Found in forest; cultivated in gardens; abundant throughout presidency; next to teak [q.v.] and blackwood [q.v.] the most valuable timber tree; size and manner of growth differ very much under different circumstances. Reddish gum resin [googal] exudes from wounds in the bark, known as malabar kino [q.v.]; consists of dark, blackish-red, angular fragments rarely larger than a pea [calauyam], easily splitting into still smaller pieces, which are seen to be perfectly transparent, of a bright garnet [tamrah] hue, and amorphous under the microscope; in cold water they sink, but partially dissolve by agitation, forming a solution of very astringent taste, and a pale flocky residue; the latter is taken up when the liquid is made to boil, and deposited on cooling in a more voluminous form; malabar kino dissolves almost entirely in spirits of wine ·838, affording a dark reddish solution, acid to litmus paper, which by long keeping sometimes assumes a gelatinous condition; it is readily soluble in solution of caustic alkali, and to a large extent in a saturated solution of sugar [q.v.]. This kino has been known in the european markets for upwards of a century, but was first imported from western africa and not from this country; prepared here at an early date for the european market in early part of present century on a plantation of the east india company called anjarcundy a few miles from tellicherry. For extraction a perpendicular incision with lateral ones leading into it is made in the trunk, at the foot of which is placed a vessel to receive the outflowing juice; this juice soon thickens, and when sufficiently dried by exposure to the sun and air is packed into wooden boxes for exportation. Physiological actions and therapeutic uses of malabar kino are similar to those of catechu [q.v.], but being milder in its operation it is better adapted for children and delicate females; substituted for british dragon's blood, botany bay kino, log-wood and rhatany; in pharm. officinal. Leaves, a favorite food of cattle [maud] and goats [velland]. The heart-wood makes a yellow dye [sbauyam]. Timber dark colored and strong, much prized for building purposes, in some parts fetches as high a price as teak [q.v.]; is durable, tolerably close-grained, brittle, not easily worked; when steeped gives a blue tinge to water; best timber for exposed venetians and weather boards; gives out a yellow stain when damp; attacked by the teredo navalis when used for the bottoms of ships; apt to warp if sawn green; the stem is valued for house-posts beyond any other, being impervious to white-ants [q.v.]; smaller portions are carved into images. See Butea species [palaus] for Bengal kino.——*Hill vengay* (மலைவேங்கை - malaivéngai, Tam.). Same as Thorny vengay.——*Lesser vengay* (జిత్తేగి - jittégi, Tel.). Same as Malabar black wood.——*Thorny vengay* (असन - asana, San.; असण - asana, Mahr.; کسی - kassi, Hind.; سن - sun, Dec.; ಅಸನಮರ - asanamara, Can.; కొరమద్ది - koramaddi, Tel.; କୋଷି - kosi, Oor.; മുള്ളുവേങ്ങ - mulluvénna, Mal.; කටකාල - katakála, Singh.; முள்வேங்கை - mulvéngai, Tam.). Title from thorns on large branches. San. from (as, san. to throw), from spreading branches. Can. from sanscrit. Tel. from (kóra, tel. sharp + maddi, tel. terminalia). Mal. from (mullu, mal. thorn + vénna, mal. the tree, pterocarpus marsupium, roxb.). Singh. from (katu, singh. thorny + kála, singh. butea frondosa, roxb.). Tam. from (mul, tam. thorn + véngai, tam. the tree). San. also (ashana), meaning same; (ásana), meaning same. Hind. also (khaja); (gauli); (asan). Can. also (gojé); (gunjanamara). Tel. also (koramánu), meaning sharp + tree; (duriyamaddi); (ánnemu); (karáratti); (vadisha); (gundebigulu), meaning heart + tightness; (patangamu); (shiriánnem), meaning small + the tree; (donkibúra). Oor. also (gaurkassi), red variety. Tam. also (malaivéngai), meaning mountain + the tree; (kamuji). Title otherwise Coramaddy, Cora murdah, Hill vengay. Botanically Bridelia retusa, muller, var. genuina, euphorbiaceæ [vricsham, 118]. Alias Bridelia crenulata, spinosa; Clutytia retusa, spinosa. Large deciduous tree, 30–40 feet; bark scabrous; branches numerous, spreading; thorns large, few, chiefly on the large branches; leaves oblong, alternate, pointed, entire, with conspicuous parallel veins running from centre to circumference; spikes axillary or terminal; flowers aggregate, small, greenish yellow, males and females together. When wounded, the bark exudes a blood-red juice, which stains the hands and is very astringent; the dry bark is externally of a light-brown color, and has small fungous protuberances of dead suber; internally it is smooth and fibrous, of a cinnamon [q.v.] color; taste purely astringent; if soaked in water it gives out much mucilage; the fibrous portion of the bark is very tough and strong. Bark is medicinally a strong astringent; leaves a vermifuge. Leaves eaten by cattle [maud]. Bark used in tanning [chamrah]. Wood a dirty red or copper color, very stiff, strong, close-grained and durable, not easily worked; stands the action of water. There are other varieties of retusa:—roxburghiana and squamosa. Another species of bridelia is Montana; moderate-sized, deciduous tree; flowers greenish; mountains on east of presidency; leaves lopped for cattle fodder; wood similar to retusa; hard, red and very durable. Another species is Stipularis; large shrub; flower small, yellowish green; wood greyish-brown, moderately hard.——*White vengay* (வெள்வேங்கை - velvéngai, Tam.). Same as Common sirissa.

VENGY (వెంగి - vengi, *Tel.*). The ancient name of southern Telingana [q.v.] between Godavery and Kistna rivers, the capital of which was situated about 5 miles north and a little west of Ellore on the road to Nagpore viâ Bhadrachellam, and exhibits now extensive remains of walls and fortifications with the ruins of the Chitraratsawmy goody still bearing the same name. The religion of the dynasty was Booddhist [booddha] as far as known. Two small modern villages occupy a trifling portion of the ancient site, which are still called Pedda vengy and Chinna vengy [charitram]. Compare Andhram and Calingam. See vol. I (13), (132).——*Vaigy* (వేగి - végi, Tel.). More modern form of Vengy, generally used for the town.

VENN (వెన్ను - vennu, *Tel.*). Back. Suffix in place names; as Tandivenn, meaning the rear place with palmyras.

VENOO (वेणु - vénu, *San.*). From (vé, san. to weave, sew); from original use. Bamboo [q.v.]; reed.——*Vengopaul* (वेणुगोपाल - vénugópála, San.). From (above + gópála, san. cowherd krishna). One of Krishnan's [q.v.] manifestations in which he is represented as playing upon a flute [pillan grovy] like a shepherd boy.

VEPPOO (വെപ്പ് - veppu, *Mal.*). From (vai, tam. to lay). A deposit. In Palghaut same as Otty. See vol. II, 104.——*Vypeen* (വൈപ്പി - vaippi, Mal.). From (veppu, mal. deposit). Mal. also (putiyaveppu), meaning place formed by new deposit. Town, Island; Cochin state, Cochin tal.; lat. 9° 58′; long. 76° 17′; from Bangalore S.W. 225 miles; from Cannanore S.E. 145 miles; from Cochin city N. 1 mile; from Chittoor S.W. 60 miles; from Ernacolum W.S.W. 1¾ miles; from Madras S.W. 346 miles; from Trichore S. 38 miles; from Tripoontora W. 7 miles. In 1341 the sea threw up the island on the north side of Cochin. The waters breaking through the banks of the Cochin river swept away the adjacent village and formed a large river and backwater and so spacious a harbour that large ships lie safely at anchor in the river on the north-east side of the town of Cochin. Vypeen is 13 miles long and 1 broad. It is bounded south and west by the Arabian sea, and on all other sides by the backwater. The natives date their era [saca] from the period of its origin. Zamorin [q.v.] defeated here in 1503, and throughout the Travancore wars with Mysore this was a disputed point. The southern portion belongs to the British. In the north is the fort of Ayicottah. Roman catholic church built in 1666. Colonized by Eurasian roman catholics.

VERPAN (வெற்பன - verban, *Tam.*). From (verbu, tam. hill). Chief of hilly tract [desham, porooppan, shilamban]. For Collyverpan or ruler of colly see sep. title.

VERRY (వెఱ్ఱి - verri, *Tel.*; வெறி - veri, *Tam.*). From (virai, tam. to shake). Mad, wild. Fermented toddy. Plant first term, indicating wild growth or inferiority, often joining two genera. Ex., where transl. is of second term:—Citrullus ciliatus (verriputtsa), cucumis trigonus; Guizotia abyssinica (verrinúgu), sesamum indicum; Oldenlandia heynei (verrinéla-vému), andrographis paniculata. See gloss. paragraphs.

VETAULAM (वेताल - vétála, *San.*). From (ava, san. away + ita, san. gone + álaya, san. house). A goblin who haunts cemeteries and animates dead bodies.——*Vetaula puncha vimshaty* (वेतालपञ्चविंशति - vétálapañchavimshati, San.). From (above + pañcha, san. five + vimshati, san. twenty). Twenty-five tales of a demon. By Jambhala bhattan. Original of the hindee Beitaul pacheesy [q.v.]. The stories are told by a Vetaulam to king Vicramadityan [q.v.], who tries to carry off a dead body occupied by the Vetaulam.——*Vetauly* (வேதாளி - véthâli, Tam.). A demoness.

VETTOO (വെട്ട - vettu, *Mal.*; வெட்டு - vettu, *Tam.*). Digging; to cut.——*Vettivair* (வெட்டிவேர் - vettivér, Tam.). From (above + vér, tam. root). Cuscus root.——*Vetty* (వెట్టి - vetti, Tel; வெட்டி - vetti, Tam.).—"*a*" Worthless, as deserving to be cut down.—"*b*" Hence also drudgery.—"*c*" Village scavenger. Village peon [q.v.]. Messenger. Acts as guide to public officers and travellers. Always pariah. Vettiyaun is the same. Commonly called Yetty [balootah].—"*d*" A cut road [rustah].

VI (वि - vi, *San.*). Intensive prefix; prefix of division, separation, negation, or privation; sign of sexagesimal division. ——*Veejam* (वीज - víja, San.). From (vi, san. intensive prefix + jan, san. to generate). Source, primary cause or principle. The mystical syllable which forms the essential part of the muntram [q.v.] of any deity. Veeja ganitam is algebra; see Ganitam. ——*Veesabuddy* (వీసబడి - vísabadi, Tel.). From (vísamu, tel. one-sixteenth + badi, tel. suffix of condition). A coparcenary village, of which the lands are allotted by sixteenths and fractions of sixteenths among the hereditary proprietors.——*Veesam* (ವೀಸ - vísa, Can.; వీసము - vísamu, Tel.; வீசம் - vísam, Tam.). From (vítham, tam. from vi, san. suffix of division + hita, san. placed); division, apportionment. The sixteenth of anything; a share.—"*a*" Linear measure used in measuring land. 5 mooras = 1 veesam; 16 veesams = 1 puggam [alavay, 1b]. Approximate actual value, 1 veesam = 8¼ feet.—"*b*" Superficial measure. In vizagapatam 16 parrahs = 1 veesam; 16 veesams = 1 catty [alavay, 2b]; approximate actual value, 1 veesam = 1·2173 acres. In Nellore, veesam is $\frac{1}{16}$ of a gorroo which is 3·161 acres. In Cuddapah veesam is $\frac{1}{16}$ of a coonta, 40 of which make an acre; and a veesam = $7\frac{9}{16}$ square yards. Compare Cawny, Vithaicottay.—"*c*" Liquid measure. 1¼ pucka seers = 1 veesam, 16 veesams = 1 audam [alavay, 4a]. Approximate actual value, 1 veesam = 82¼ cubic inches. About 1¼ pucka seer. See vol. I, 609; II, 519.——*Veetham* (வீதம் - vítham, Tam.). From (vihita, san. fixed). Rate.——*Veicoonta gaty* (वैकुण्ठगति - vaikunt'hagati, San.). From (vaikunt'ha, san. paradise + gati, san. going). Obtaining Veicoontam. Euphemistic for death. Compare Shiva locam.——*Veicoontam* (वैकुण्ठ - vaikunt'ha, San.; வைகுண்டம் - vaigundam, Tam.). From (vi, san. negative prefix + kunt'ha, san. indolence); ever fresh. The heaven of Vishnoo. There is a Tamul proverb:—அகப்பிலே விழுந்தமுதலைக்குஅதுவேவைகுண்டம்—"the moat into "which the alligator [mugger] has plunged is to itself veicoon-"tam." Compare Keilausam. Title used ironically for a dungeon. Also a Hindoo 2nd or pers. name [peyar], as short for next item. See vol. I (74).——*Veicoonta nautan* (वैकुण्ठनाथ - vaikunt'hanát'ha, San.). From (vaikunt'ha, san. paradise + nát'ha, san. lord). Vishnoo, the lord of Veicoontam.——*Veicoonta yecaudashy* (వైకుంఠైకాదశి - vaikunt'haikádashi, Tel.). Heaven of vishnoo + eleventh lunar day. Also called Swarga dwaura yecaudashy; also Swargavausal yecaudashy; also Mooccoty yecaudashy. Lunar [chaundra mausam] festival [pundigay, 3a], subject to intercalation [adhicam]. On eleventh day of waxing moon [shooclapacsham] of ninth lunar month Margashiram [mausam] between 26th November and 25th December and is a special festival of the Veishnavas. Fasting day for Bramins and Shoodras. Particularly sacred at Shreerungam [maryauday].——*Veidhrity* (वैधृति - vaidhriti, San.). From (vi, san. suffix of separation + dhrita, san. held); stopping place.—"*a*" The index [yogam] star of Raivaty [q.v.], the 27th lunar asterism, either η or ζ Piscium [nacshatram], meenam [q.v.]. Veidhrity is the hindoo First point of Aries [maisham] in the fixed sidereal zodiac [raushy chuckram]; see Madhyama sowra maunam and Nacshatram. Longitudes from this star are known as Nirayana spootam or Dhroovacam [q.v.] or fixed longitudes; the longitudes from the true vernal equinox [craunty pautam, maishanyanam, vishoo] being known as Sauyana [q.v.] spootam or longitudes liable to precession [craunty pauta gaty] error. The space between this star and the true vernal equinoctial point is known as Ayanaumsham [q.v.].—"*b*" Veidhrity is the term also for a particular position of the sun [sooryan] and moon [chundran] when they are on the same side of either solstice and of equal declination [craunty] but of opposite direction. This is considered a malignant aspect in astrology [jyotisham, vaunashastram].——*Veidooryam* (वैदूर्य - vaidúrya, San.; వైడూర్యము - vaidúryamu, Tel.). From (vidúra, san. very distant). An ancient country. —"*a*" Northern parts of Western ghauts [q.v.].—"*b*" Lapis lazuli. This silicious fossil, which the Greeks and Romans called cyaneus, is of a saxon-blue color, inclining to purple. It is only translucent at the edges and is variegated with bright yellow veins and speckles owing to pyrites [teecull]. Its powder furnishes the paint known in Europe by the name of ultramarine. One of the nine gems or Navaratnam [ratnam]. ——*Veinateyam* (వైనతేయము - vainatéyamu, Tel). Means garoodan. Godavery district, Amalaupooram talook. A mouth of the Godavery. Separates the Amalaupooram and Narsapore talooks. An irrigation canal from Lolla is taken to the Nagara khandam across Vasishta by means of an aqueduct about half a mile long near Gunnavaram.——*Veiraugyam* (वैराग्य - vairágya, San.). From (vi, san. privative prefix + rága, san. passion). Suppression of worldly passions, whether of affection or aversion [beiraugy].——*Veishaishicam* (वैशेषिक - vaishéshika, San.). From (vishish, san. to distinguish). A division of the Nyauyam school of philosophy. Attributed to an author Canaudan [q.v.], extending the Nyauyam [q.v.] to physical inquiries. The most interesting of all the systems, both from its practical character and from the parallels it offers to european philosophical ideas. It begins by arranging its inquiries under seven Padaurtams [q.v.], which, as they are more properly categories, i.e., an enumeration of certain general properties or attributes that may be predicated or affirmed of existing things, are now the generally received categories of neiyauyican. They are as follows:—Substance or dravyam; Quality or property or goonam; Act or action, carmam; Generality or community of properties, saumaunyam; Particularity or individuality, vishaisham; Co-inherence or perpetual intimate relation, samavauyam; Non-existence or negation of existence, abhauvam. Compare the ten aristotelian categories:—οὐσία, substance; ποσόν, how much? quantity; ποιόν, of what kind? quality; πρός τι, in relation to what? relation; ποιεῖν, action; πάσχειν, passiveness or passivity; ποῦ, where? position in space; πότε, when? position in time; κεῖσθαι, local situation; ἔχειν, possession. The seven veishaishicam categories are all subdivided.—"*a*" There are nine Dravyams [q.v.]:—earth, water, light, air, ether, time, space, soul the internal organ, and mind.—"*b*" There are seventeen Goonams [q.v.] or qualities:—color, savour, odour, tangibility, numbers, extensions, individuality, conjunction, disjunction, priority, posteriority, intellections, pleasure, pain, desire, aversion, and volition.—"*c*" The third category, Carmam [q.v.], act or action, is thus divided:—elevation literally throwing upwards, depression or throwing downwards, contraction, dilatation, and going or motion in general.—"*d*" The fourth category, Saumaunyam, generality, is said to be twofold, viz., higher or param and lower or aparam; the first being simple existence, applicable to genus; the second being substantiality, applicable to species.—"*e*" The fifth category, Vishaisham, particularity, belongs to the nine eternal substances of the first category, viz., mind, soul, time, place, and the five atoms [bhootam] of earth, water, light, air, and ether, all of which have an eternal ultimate difference, distinguishing each from the other.—"*f*" The sixth category, Samavauyam, co-inherence or intimate relation, is of only one kind. This relation is that which exists between a substance and its qualities, between atoms and what is formed out of them, or between any object and the general idea connected with it. Cf. tanmautram subtle atoms, and punchabhootam gross atoms therefrom, of Saunkhyam. In connection with this sixth category may be mentioned the Nyauyam [q.v.] theory of causation. A cause is declared to be that which invariably precedes an effect which otherwise could not be, and three kinds of causes are enumerated, viz.:—Co-inherence cause, or that resulting from intimate and constant relation; substantial cause, as threads are the substantial cause of cloth; this corresponds to the material cause of aristotle; Non-substantial cause, as the putting together of the threads is of cloth; this corresponds to the formal cause; Instrumental cause as the weaver's tools, the loom, or the skill of the weaver himself, &c., are of cloth; this corresponds to the efficient cause. Aristotle's four causes are:—Material cause, i.e., the matter ὕλη, from which anything is made, as marble of a statue, silver of a goblet; Formal cause, i.e., the specific form or pattern according to which anything is made, as a drawing or plan is the formal cause of the building of a house; Efficient cause, i.e., the origin of the principle of motion, ὅθεν ἡ ἀρχὴ τῆς κινήσεως, as the energy of a workman is the prime-mover in producing any work; Final cause, i.e., the purpose for which anything is made, the motive for its production or the end served by its existence.—"*g*" As to the seventh category in veishaishicam, Abhauvam or non-existence, four kinds are specified, viz. :—Antecedent, or the non-existence of anything before it began to exist, as a jar not yet made; Cessation of existence, as of a jar when it is smashed to pieces; Mutual non-existence as of a jar in cloth; Absolute non-existence, as of fire in a lake. See vol. I (74) [matam].——*Veitarany* (वैतरणि - vaitarani, San.). From (vi, san. intensive prefix + tar, san. to cross). The Indian styx.

——*Veivaswatan* (वैवस्वत - vaivasvata, San.). From (vivasvat, san. the brilliant one). The seventh Menoo [q.v.]. His son Icshwauk was head of the ancient aryan [q.v.] Solar race [sooryavamsham]. He much resembles the biblical Noah. The number of years elapsed since his appearance is by native shastrams stated to be 18,618,733.——*Vibhactam* (विभक्त - vibhakta, San.). From (above + bhaj, san. to divide). Divided; either the property or the sharer. Partitioned among separated heirs [avibhactam].——*Vibhaugam* (विभाग - vibhága, San.). From (above + bhaj, san. to divide). According to law, either the simple apportionment of the property of a deceased person amongst his heirs who may nevertheless hold the whole in common, or sometimes the several distribution of the shares amongst the sharers and their mutual separation. For undivided family see Avibhactam. For hindoo law of inheritance see Dauyam. For partition generally see Bhaugam. For mahomedan law of inheritance see Vaurs.——*Vibheeshanan* (विभीषण - vibhíshana, San.). From (above + bhíshana, san. terrifying). A younger brother of Ravanan [q.v.]. After the death of Ravanan [q.v.] he was raised by Rama [q.v.] to the throne of Lunka [q.v.]. He is one of the ever-living saints [chiranjeevy].

——*Vibhoo* (विभु - vibhu, San.). From (above + bhú, san. to exist). Powerful.——*Vibhooty* (विभूति - vibhúti, San.; விபூதி - vibúthi, Tam.). From (above + bhúti, san. wealth). The ashes of burnt cowdung [shauny]; made with ceremonies and muntrams [q.v.]. With these ashes the forehead, breast and shoulders are smeared in the case of Shoodras [q.v.] of the Sheiva class. Aundies [q.v.] or Sheiva ascetics have their face and all visible portions of their body smeared over with the ashes. Sheiva bramins draw three lines with them on their forehead mostly horizontal [tripoondram], but sometimes curvilineal [uugooly toranam]. On the central line Smartas [q.v.] place a dark circular spot [pottoo, tilacam]. Three lines or tripoondram [q.v.] are marked on the shoulders and breasts of all Sheiva or Smarta bramins. Most local Sheiva pooraunams [q.v.] have a section entitled Vibhooty mahatwam or mahimay, narrating the wonders done by its use [naumam, neer, tirneer].

——*Vicalay* (विकला - vikalá, San.). From (above + kalá, san. time). Indian minute. 6 praunacalays = 1 vicalay; 60 vicalays = 1 dandam or indian hour [caulam, 6]. Approximate actual value, 1 vicalay or indian minute = 24 english seconds. Same as San. vighaticay [caulam, 5], Hind. pal, Tam. vinaudy [caulam, 1].——*Vicauram* (विकार - vikára, San.). From (vikri, san. to change). Change from a natural state, applied to a product or production in cosmogony [saunkhyam]. Cf. Vicrity.

——*Vicramadityan* (विक्रमादित्य - vikramáditya, San.). From (vikrama, san. power + áditya, san. sun). Title assumed by numerous princes. But especially a ruler of Oojjein who gave his name to an era [saca] and who flourished some century and a half before Shalivahanan [q.v.]. Era begins 56 B.C. He has many names; as Vicrama sainan, powerful armied; Vicramasimhan, powerful lion; Vicramarcan as below; Vicraman. It is said that Oojjein was destroyed by earthquake [mahy campam] in his time. For his nine poets see Navaratnam.——*Vicramam* (विक्रम - vikrama, San.). From (above + kram, san. to step). Prowess. Vicraman is vishnoo [q.v.] in his vaumana [q.v.] avatar [q.v.]; cf. trivicraman. Vicraman is also short for vicramadityan. Has given names to many south indian rulers, especially of chola [q.v.] and paundyan [q.v.] dynasties [raj].——*Vicramarca charitram* (विक्रमार्कचरित - vikramárkacharita, San.). From (vikrama, san. prowess + arka, san. sun + charita, san. story). Or Dwautrimshat saulabhanjicay or the thirty-two games with the wooden puppet. Favorite collection of tales [kattay]. The original in sanscrit consists of 32 stories in prose. The author not known. They are supposed to be narrated by puppets placed on the throne of Vicraman, to king Bhoja when he attempted ascending it. Written by Gopooraux in eight books [hamsa vimshaty].——*Vicramarcan* (विक्रमार्क - vikramárka, San.). From (vicrama, san. prowess + arka, san. sun). Same as Vicramadityan.——*Vicramorvashy* (विक्रमोर्वशी - vikramórvashí, San.). From (vikrama, san. valour + úrvashí, san. the divine courtezan, so called), valour-won oorvashy. A drama by Calidass [q.v.]. In five acts, telling how Poorooravan by his valour rescued Oorvashy from a demon who carried her off, and afterwards married her.——*Vicravaundy* (விக்கிறவாண்டி - vikkiravándi, Tam. vikravándi *). Called after Vicrama paundyan. Railway station; South arcot dist., Villoopooram tal.; pop. 2,734; acres 3,152; lat. 12° 02′; long. 79° 35′; height 126 feet; from Cuddalore N.W. 27 miles; from Villoopooram N.N.E. 8 miles; from the sea W. 22 miles.——*Vicrayam* (विक्रय - vikraya, San.). From (above + krí, san to sell). Sale. Vicraya chit is a bill of sale, otherwise Vicraya shausanam.——*Vicrity* (विकृति - vikriti, San.). From (above + kri, san. to do). Change [vicauram]. In the Saunkhyam [q.v.] philosophy, a generated effect, not producing any other effect, and so distinguished from Pracrity [q.v.]. Also one of the 60 years of the Jovian cycle [brihaspaty chuckram, yoog].——*Vicshaipam* (विक्षेप - vikshépa, San.). From (above + kship, san. to throw).—"*a*" Projection; one of the two modes in which avidyay [anyaunam] or ignorance operates on the soul [autmam], the other being auvarnam [vedauntam]. This is that power of ignorance, which, affecting the soul in its state of pure intelligence [chit], raises upon it the appearance of a world [mauyay], producing first the five subtle elements [tanmautram] and drawing out from them seventeen subtle bodies and the five gross elements [bhootam, tatwam]. Compare Avastay.—"*b*" Celestial latitude, with double meaning according as theoretical or practical. In theoretical hindoo astronomy vicshaipam is exactly the same as in the european system, that is to say reckoned by taking great circles proceeding from the pole of the ecliptic [craunty mundalam], otherwise circles of celestial latitude, as circles of measurement [rishy raikhay]. In practical hindoo astronomy however the circles of measurement are great circles from the pole of the equator [naudy mundalam], otherwise declination or meridian circles [raikhay], which fall upon the ecliptic thus at an angle and not perpendicularly [golayantram]; vicshaipam then is an arc of the meridian passing through an object intercepted between the object and its intersection with the ecliptic, and is somewhat longer than the perpendicular to the ecliptic. In the former case the latitude or vicshaipam is called aspootam or invisible, in the latter case it is called spootam or visible. For terrestrial latitude see Acsham. For longitudes see Deshauntaram, Dhroovacam and Sauyanam; also Veidhrity and Vishoo.——*Videha moocty* (विदेहमुक्ति - vidéhamukti, San.). From (above + déha, san. body + mukti, san. deliverance). Complete deliverance [mocsham].——*Vidhy* (विधि - vidhi, San.). From (vidhá, san. to enjoin). Rule. Fate. Name of Bramha [q.v.]. Bramha is supposed to write the fate of each human being on the forehead. The crooked lines on the frontal bone of the skull are this writing. Talay yezhoot or writing on the head is commonly used for fate.——*Vighadiya* (विघटिका - vighatiká, San.; ವಿಘಳಿಗೆ - vighalige, Can.; విఘడియ - vighadiya, Tel.). From (vi, san. prefix of separation + ghat, san. to join). Division. Indian minute. Measure of sidereal or star time. 60 params or indian seconds = 1 vighadiya; 60 vighadiyas = 1 ghadiya or indian hour [caulam, 5]. Approximate actual value, 1 vighadiya = 24 english seconds. Same as San. vicalay [caulam, 6]; Hind. pal [caulam]; Tam. vinaudy [caulam, 1].

——*Vignam* (विघ्न - vighna, San.). From (above + han, san. to kill). Obstacle.——*Vigneshwaran* (विघ्नेश्वर - vighnéshvara, San.). From (vighna, san. obstacle + íshvara, san. lord). Implying a power to forbid success or fame; the idea of malevolence to be averted is connected with all deity in s. india; compare the village goddesses [amman]. Called in the north Ganesh [q.v.], by the english the Belly-god, and by the ordinary people of the country Pillaiyaur [q.v.] or the noble child. The elder son of Shiva [q.v.] and Parvaty [q.v.]. One of the most popular of the deities of southern india. He is a male Minerva, a Lar, and the Janus of the public ways; his image stands in every house, and is painted on every school boy's slate; he is supposed to preside in the above sense over good fortune and success, particularly in mercantile and farming operations. Vigneshwaran was originally born of beautiful shape; in a matrimonial dispute shiva [q.v.] reproached parvaty [q.v.] with infidelity, whereupon vigneshwaran interfered to protect her; on which the father seizing the sword of an attendant cut off his son's head at a blow; in consequence of this act parvaty was inconsolable; and all the deities reproached shiva so severely that he decided to replace the head by that of the first animal which should approach, which was an elephant [q.v.]; the elephant's head is probably the emblem of sagacity. Vigneshwaran is thus represented by a figure, half man and half elephant, but also in a sitting posture, and with a great belly; he wears a crown, while his ears are adorned with two flowers and two jewels, and his forehead with sacred ashes [vibhooty]; of his four arms he lifts two up, holding in the left hand a pausham [q.v.] or rope, and in the right a cootaury or elephant goad [ancooshapaushamaindy], and in the right one of his other two hands he holds a piece of his own elephant's tooth, which he himself broke when enraged, and in the left a pancake; round his neck he wears jewels of pearls and precious stones, and also on his arms and feet, and a garland hangs from his shoulders; not infrequently only half of his image, made of stone, is carved out, that is to say the elephant's head with trunk and ears, and the large belly; in some pagodas [coil, pagoda] he is found in a standing posture. Vigneshwaran has in all the pagodas of shiva a small temple, in which his image, made of stone or cast metal, is worshipped with offerings; but he has also pagodas of his own; indeed there is hardly a place inhabited by sheivas where there is not a pagoda in honor of vigneshwaran; these pagodas are small, usually consisting of one building only, and not surrounded by a wall, but standing free at roads and streets where everybody passes by; as he is thought to be shiva's most beloved son, he receives the same divine honor as shiva, and has also similar names; in shiva's pagodas, as well as in his own, offerings are made to him daily twice, thrice, or four times, which offerings do not differ from those made to shiva and parvaty; his image stands in almost every house, and is adored by men and women, usually only with devout addresses, but sometimes also with offerings and all the prescribed ceremonies, more especially when they are about to begin something important, inasmuch as they believe that their affairs do not prosper unless they are begun in his name; for instance, when they wish to make a special offering to shiva, they first ask his son to make it prosper; there is hardly a tamul book to be found, on the first page of which there are not some words in honor and praise of vigneshwaran. Vigneshwaran is not married. He has various names, the most common of which are the following:—Ambica tanayan or ambicay's son; Ancoosha paushamaindy or the wearer of an elephant goad and a cord; Auc vauhanan or he whose vehicle is a large rat; Aunay mookhavan or the elephant faced; Coonjaramoodaiyone or the elephant owner; Coonjaran or the elephant or the excellent; Coottaudoom pillaiyaur or the dancing son; Eeshamaundan or eeshan's or eeshwaran's son; Eingaran or the five-handed, the elephant's trunk being his fifth hand; Gaja mookhan or the elephant-faced; Ganapaty or lord of hosts; Gunga sootan or gungay's son; Modaca priyan or he who is fond of rice flour cakes; Mooccunnan or the three-eyed; Moonnone or the elder son; Perarоolaulan or the most gracious; Pillaiyaur or the son; Poyyauthameyyoodaiyore or the possesser of pure truth; Toombikeiyan or he who has an elephant's trunk; Vinauyaca moorty or lord; Vinayacan or lord. Among the annual fasts [oopavausam] observed in honor of Vigneshwaran, there are two principal. The first is the Pillaiyaur chatoorty [pundigay, 3a], when the tamulians fast for the purpose of getting understanding, and carry his image about in the streets, and worship him also in their houses. The second is Pillaiyaur nomb or pillaiyaur's fast observed more especially for the purpose of obtaining his blessing on the household; on this day the householders make pancakes, which after having first been offered to the god in the pagodas and houses, are eaten by themselves when the time for fasting is over. Vigneshwaran is adored and his image carried about in the streets at all the festivals of shiva [q.v.] and parvaty [q.v.]. Among the books written specially in his honor, the principal is the Vezhamockhatt or Pillaiyaur sindh. A legend is told to the effect that, when vyausan [q.v.] dictated the bhauratam [q.v.], this god wrote it down with such rapidity that vyausan was embarrassed, and bethought himself of giving out here and there passages of extraordinary difficulty, still called knots; when the amanuensis laid down his stylus, and pondered over the meaning, vyausan found time to go on with the thread of the subject. See vol. I (77), (79) [matam].——*Vigraham* (विग्रह - vigraha, San.). From (vigrah, san. to spread out). Idol [shilay].——*Vihauram* (विहार - vihára, San.). From (vihri, san. to walk about). Means a promenade. A Booddhist [booddha] convent. Like the Cheityams, these resemble very closely the corresponding institutions among Christians. In the earlier ages they accompanied, but were detached from, the Cheityams [q.v.]. In later times they were furnished with chapels and altars of their own in which the service could be performed, independently of the Cheityam halls, which may or may not be found in their proximity. Not to be confounded with Vimaunam [baur, cheityam, dagoba, goomta, laut, staupatyam, tope].——*Vijaya* (विजय - vijaya, San.). From (vi, san. prefix of excellence + jí, san. to conquer). Victorious. Favorite prefix in place names. Name of the founder of the Booddhist [booddha] civilisation in Ceylon. See vol. I (117).——*Vijaya dashamy* (విజయదశమి - vijayadashami, Tel.). Victory + tenth lunar day. Doorga [q.v.] is said to have conquered Mahishausooran on this day. The tenth day of Dusserah [q.v.].——*Vijayam* (विजय - vijaya, San.). From (above + jí, san. to conquer). Conquest. Proper name applied to both sexes [peyar].——*Vijayaraghavan* (விசயராகவன் - visayarágavan, Tam.). Means victorious rama. Hindoo 2nd or pers. name [peyar.]——*Vijaya runga chokkanauta naick* (விசயரங்கசொக்கநாத நாயக்கன் - visayarangasokkanáthanáyakkan, Tam.). Means vijayarungan, vishnoo, the victorious + chokkanautan, shiva, the holy lord, the special designation under which shiva is worshipped in madura. Last of the Naick [q.v.] dynasty [raj] of Madura A.D. 1704–1731. See vol. I (120); II, 250.——*Vijayarungan* (விசயரங்கன் - visayarangan, Tam.). Means victorious vishnoo. Hindoo 2nd or pers. name [peyar].——*Vijayay* (विजया - vijayá, San.). Epithet of Doorga [q.v.]. Parvaty [q.v.].——*Vijianugger* (విజయనగరము - vijayanagaramu, Tel.). From (vijaya, san. victory + nagara, san. city). Distinguish from the modern Vizianagram of Vizagapatam district. The ancient city which was the capital of the last and most important Hindoo kingdom existing in the peninsula of India during the late middle ages and ruled by the Roya [q.v.] dynasty [raj]. The corruption Vidyanagar or city of learning was applied after the place in the thirteenth century had become the seat of a great revival of hindooism under the famous Shayana maudhavan [q.v.], who amongst other works wrote commentaries on the vedams [q.v.]. Both the city and the kingdom were commonly called by the early portuguese Narsinga [q.v.] from Narsimhan about 1490—1508 who was rajah at the time of their first arrival. The place is now known as Humpy and is entirely in ruins [humpy]. The history of the dynasty will be found at vol. I (151) [charitram]. See also vol. II, 251.

——*Vilausam* (विलास - vilása, San.). From (above + las, san. to shine). Pastime. As applied to deities it means the same as the tamul Vileiyaudal [q.v.]. Also means superscription of letters, otherwise Mail vilausam. In trade it means a trademark.——*Viliptam* (विलिप्त - vilipta, San.). From (above + liptá, san. minute). Measure of time equal to one-sixtieth of a liptam or minute; one second.——*Vimaunam* (विमान - vimána, San.). From (above + má, san. to traverse). A chariot [rath, vauhan] of the gods, carrying them self-moving through the skies and serving also as a throne [simhausanam]. Later, the main body of a temple [coil, pagoda].——*Vinaickasoondram* (விநாயகசுந்தரம் - vináyagasundaram, Tam.). From (above + náyaka, san. leader + sundara, san. beauty). Vigneshwaran the beautiful. Hindoo 2nd or pers. name [peyar].——*Vinaickenteroo* (விநாயக்கன்தெரு - vináyakkanderu, Tam.). From (vináyaka, san. belly god, the leader of shiva's attendants + teru, tam. street). Island; Tanjore dist., Combaconam tal.; pop. 856; acres 998; lat. 11° 09′; long. 79° 30′; from Combaconam N.N.E. 14 miles; from Tanjore N.E. 33 miles. Formed by two branches of the Coleroon. Formerly belonged to Trichinopoly district. The site of the Lower coleroon anicut [q.v.].——*Vinaudy* (विनाडि - vinádi, San.; விநாடி - vinádi, Tam.). From (vi, san. division + nádí, san. time). Measure of solar time. 60 palams or indian seconds = 1 vinaudy; 60 vinaudies = 1 naudy or indian hour [caulam]. Approximate actual value, 1 vinaudy = 24 english seconds. Commonly used. Same as San. vighaticay [caulam, 5], vicalay [caulam, 6], Hind. pal [caulam].——*Vinauyaca chatoorty* (వినాయకచతుర్థి - vinayakachaturt'hi, Tel.). Means songod vigneshwaran, the remover of obstacles + fourth lunar day. Same as Pillaiyaur chatoorty.——*Vinauyaca moorty* (विनायकमूर्ति - vináyakamúrti, San.). From (above + náyaka, san. leader + múrti, san. deity). Vigneshwaran, the deity.——*Vinauyacan* (विनायक - vináyaka, San.). From (above + ní, san. to lead). Leader of Shiva's attendants [ganam]. Vigneshwaran [q.v.].——*Vinayam* (विनय - vinaya, San.). From (vi, san. away + ní, san. to lead): Modesty. Vinayadityan, from (áditya, san. sun) is a hoysala ballaula royal name. See vol. I (140). Vinayauditya yooddhamalla, from (yuddha, san. fight + malla, san. wrestler) is a western chalookya royal name.——*Vinnapam* (ಬಿನ್ನಹ - binnaha, Can.; விண்ணப்பம் - vinnappam, Tam.). From (viñápaná, san. representation). Petition [arzee, manoo].——*Vipalam* (विपल - vipala, San.). From (vi, san. prefix denoting division + pala, san. second). A moment or instant; a simple breathing. Indian second. Measure of solar time. 60 alipalams = 1 vipalam; 60 vipalams = 1 palam or indian minute [caulam, 6]. Approximate actual value, 1 vipalam = ·4 english seconds. Same as San. caushta calay [caulam, 6], param [caulam, 4, 5].——*Viprayogam* (विप्रयोग - viprayóga, San.). From (vi, san. negative prefix + prayóga, san. combination); separation or disunion. One of the effects of Manmatan's arrows [cauma baunam].——*Viraumam* (விராமம் - virámam, Tam.). From (vi, san. intensive prefix + ram, san. stop); ceasing; a stop denoting mute consonants. A small oblique stroke placed under a consonant to denote that it is quiescent, i.e., that it has no vowel inherent or otherwise pronounced after it. It occurs only as a stop at the end of a sentence ending in a consonant.——*Viraut* (विराट् - virát, San.). From (above + ráj, san. to shine). Same as Para bramh [q.v.], the primary cause, or an immediate progeny from Bramh [q.v.]. The universal form. The material universe. Compare Poorsham, Pracrity, Veishwaunary, Vishwam.——*Virinjipooram* (விரிஞ்சிபுரம் - viriñjippuram, Tam. virinjipuram *). From (viriñchi, san. the disposer, epithet of the trinity + pura, san. town). Village. Place of pilgrimage; North arcot dist., Vellore tal.; pop. 3,615; acres 720; lat. 12° 55′; long. 79° 03′; height 788 feet; from Chittore S.S.W. 21 miles; from Vellore W. 8 miles. Most sacred spot in talook. Mysore military outpost during siege of Vellore. Marks of cannon on temple walls. Carvings inside defaced, probably by Mahomedan soldiery. To Maurga sahauya eeshwaran. Centre shrine constructed by a Chola rajah. Mahamantapam and interior wall by a king Ballicomba royel, next wall with western gopooram [q.v.] and the hundred-pillared hall by Veeracumba royel. Carvings by Bommy reddy of Vellore and his sons. After Bommy reddy eastern gopooram was built by Atchoota royel, son of Krishna deva of Vijianugger [humpy]. Many improvements were effected by subsequent rulers. One of the four guardian Shacties [q.v.] posted by Bramha [q.v.] north, south, east and west of Conjeeveram, was worshipped here. Subsequently consecrated to Shiva [q.v.]. Devicapooram and Narrainavaram are other towns in which Shacties are worshipped. Five annual feasts celebrated, chief being Cada nyayir ootsavam held in Caurtigay [mausam] or november. Cloth by Keikkilar [q.v.]. Choultries [q.v.], numerous. Until lately saltpetre [shorah] manufactured.——*Viroopam* (विरूप - virúpa, San.). From (vi, san. suffix of privation + rúpa, san. shape). Ugly.——*Viroopaucshan* (विरूपाक्ष - virúpaksha, San.). From (virúpa, san. unnatural + aksha, san. eye) Fierce-eye. Shiva.——*Visargam* (विसर्ग - visarga, San.): From (visrij, san. to send forth). A symbol mark by two perpendicular dots; usually at the end of a word; it represents a hard and distinctly audible aspiration and is really a kind of sibilant, often taking the place of final s and r when these letters pass into aspirations; it must be preceded by a vowel, but cannot be followed by one; it is called visargam either from its liability to be rejected or from its being pronounced with a full emission of breath ——*Vishaisham* (विशेष - vishésha, San.). From (above + shish, san. to remain). Characteristic difference; particularity; one of the seven categories [padaurtam] of the Neiyauyicans [veishaishicam].——*Vishamam* (विषम - vishama, San.). From (above + sama, san. even). Means odd. A planet [graham] is said to be in Vishamam when it is in 90° from the apsides. The sun is in Vishamam, when he is in the equinoctial points [ayanam, craunty pautam].——*Vishaukhan* (விசாகன் - viságan, Tam.). From (above + shákha, san. branch); branching out. The sixteenth lunar asterism [nacshatram] as figured by a gateway or arch. Soobramanyan [q.v.], as born under that asterism.——*Vishayam* (विषय - vishaya, San.). From (vishi, san. to connect). An affair; an object of sense. For category, see Padaurtam; for elementary substance, see Dravyam; for matter, see Bhootam; for organic and inorganic, see Indriyam and Anindriyam; for organic kingdom, see Ganam [jantoo vricsham]; for organic class, see Vargam; for organic order, see Santaunam; for organic family, see Coolam; for organic genus, see Jauty; for organic species, see Bhaidam. Oopa prefixed to either of the above means a sub-head. For inorganic minerals, see Dhautoo. ——*Vishishta* (വിശിഷ്ട - vishishta, Mal.). From (above + shish, san. to distinguish). Noted for rank, learning or sanctity. Class of Bramins. They have other titles according to function and dignity, as Adootiry, Chomautiry, Akkitiry and Bhattatiry, officers of burnt sacrifice, ascetics, and so forth.——*Vishishtam* (विशिष्ट - vishishta, San.). Distinguished.——*Vishishtaudwéitam* (विशिष्टाद्वैत - vishishtádvaita, San.). Means adweitam modified. The doctrine that the soul [autmam], though identical in essence, is still practically different from the supreme being [paramautman] for all human purposes. Principally inculcated by the veishnavite Ramaunoojan, whose followers are called Ramaunoojeeyans or Shree veishnavas. The bramins of southern india are divided into three great sects according to philosophical tenets; those who believe there is but one soul, in short that everything is God, Adweitam; those who believe there are two souls, God and man, Dweitam; and those who take a medium course, and believe there is but one soul, which in man and created things is somewhat different from the divine soul, Vishishtaudweitam. Ramaunoojacharry [q.v.] accepted with the others the vedauntam [q.v.] system of Vyausan [q.v.]; but opposed the extreme construction put on it, and on the last part of the Bhagavat geeta [q.v.] by Shuncaracharry [shuncaran]. Shuncaracharry had maintained the perfect unity of the Paramautman [q.v.] and Jeevautman [q.v.], or the divine spirit and the human soul. He rejected sacrifice [yanyam, yaugam] and made nyaunam [q.v.] or γνῶσις the highest attainment; and the highest degree of it in his view was to be able to say Aham shiva, I am God. Ramaunoojan opposed these as extreme views, and held that the human soul is almost, but not quite, one with the deity. His chief argument was that the soul is finite, the deity infinite; and a finite being cannot become infinite. He also maintained the need of ritual homage and sacrifices; and was himself an ascetic, surnamed Yatirajan or king of ascetics. Ramaunoojan and Madhwacharry were apostles of the Vishnoo creed, while Shuncaracharry was an apostle of the Shiva creed. See Ramaunoojacharry for the author, Shree veishnava for the sect. See vol. I (74), (89) [matam].——*Viss* (வீசை - vísai, Tam.). From (vítham, tam. from vi, san. suffix of division + hita, san. placed); division, distribution, share. Apportioned weight. Measure of weight.—"*a*" The old scale ran:—10 pagoda weights = 1 pollum, 40 pollums = 1 viss, 8 viss = 1 maund of 25 lbs., 20 maunds = 1 candy.—"*b*" Using the mahomedan seer [q.v.] the scale is:—5 cutcha seers = 1 viss; 8 viss = 1 Madras maund [niray, 2e]. Approximate actual value, 1 viss = 3 lbs. 2 oz. avoir. Used everywhere except in Malabar and Tinnevelly. Same as Hind. punchair. See vol. I, 609; II, 506–518.——*Vitalam* (वितल - vitala, San.). From (vi, san. privation suffix + tala, san. surface). One of the seven lower worlds; see Bhoogola shastram.——*Vitasty* (वितस्ति - vitasti, San.). From (above + tams, san. to move); measured by the extended thumb and little finger; long span as distinguished from short span or pradesham [q.v.]. Span. Linear measure. 12 ungoolams = 1 vitasty; 2 vitasties = 1 hastam [alavay, 1f]. Approximate actual value, 1 vitasty = 9 inches. Same as San. gocarnam, Hind. bilisht, Can. guenoo, Tel. jena, Tam. jaun. Compare San. pradesham, Tam. adee, wottay.——*Vityausam* (व्यत्यास - vyatyása, San.). From (vyatyas, san. to invert). Difference. In Hindoo books three kinds of differences are mentioned:—Soobhaidam, the difference in a thing itself; Soojautybhaidam, the difference between one kind and another; Vijautybhaidam, difference of nature.——*Vivaica chintaumuny* (विवेकचिन्तामणि - vivékachintámani, San.). From (vivéka, san. discrimination + chintá, san. thought + mani, san. gem). Or jewel of knowledge. Contains an account of hindoo sects. Canarese prose work on Tatwa nyaunam by Nisacoonayogy, leaning to sheiva system of the better kind.——*Vivaicam* (विवेक - vivéka, San.). From (above + vich, san. separate). Discrimination, distinguishing reality from illusion [mauyay].——*Vivaram* (विवर - vivara, San.). From (vivri, san. to spread out). Particulars [tafseel].——*Vivartanam* (विवर्तन - vivartana, San.). From (vivrit, san. to turn round). Circumgyration, a rolling or going round a temple &c. as a penance [pradacshinam].——*Vivaswat* (विवस्वत् - vivasvat, San.). From (above + vas, san. to shine forth). The sun [sooryan]. For veivaswatan see sep. title.——*Vizagapatam* (విశాఖపట్టణము - vishákhapattanamu, Tel.). See sep. title.——*Vizianagram* (విజయనగరము - vijayanagaramu, Tel.). See sep. title.——*Vyactam* (व्यक्त - vyakta, San.). From (vi, san. intensive prefix + añch, san. to mark). Visible substance. For avyactam or unevolved primary matter, see Saunkhyam. ——*Vyangoolam* (व्यंगुल - vyangula, San.). From (vi, san. prefix of division + angula, san. finger); sub-division of a finger-breadth [ungoolam]. Linear measure. 60 vyangoolams = 1 ungoolam [alavay, 1f]. Approximate actual value, 1 vyangoolam = ·136 of an inch. Measure used in the computation of eclipses [grahanam] and in gnomonic [shunk] problems. ——*Vyaucaranam* (व्याकरण - vyákarana, San.). From (vi, san. prefix of separation + á, san. intensive prefix + kri, san. to do); undoing. Means analysis, applied first to linguistic analysis and then generally to grammar [lacshanam]. The grammar of Paniny [q.v.], which is the great standard of correct sanscrit, is usually taken to represent this vedaungam [q.v.]. ——*Vyaumam* (व्याम - vyáma, San.). From (vyáyam, san. to stretch out). Fathom; distance between the tips of the finger of either hand extended sideways. Linear measure. 3½ hastams = 1 vyaumam [alavay, 1f]. Approximate actual value, 1 vyaumam = 6 feet. Same as San. dandam, Hind. baum, Can. bauroo, Tel. niloovoo, Mal. and Tam. maur or bauham. ——*Vyaupauram* (व्यापार - vyápára, San.). From (vyápri, san. to be engaged in). Trade.——*Vyaupaury* (व्यापारी - vyápárí, San.). Another name for Madhwas [q.v.]. Distinguish from Golcondah vyaupauries who are Veishnavas by religion.——*Vyausam* (व्यास - vyása, San.). From (vyas, san. to throw across); extension, breadth. The diameter of a circle [chuckram, mundalam].——*Vyausan* (व्यास - vyása, San.). From (vyas, san. to arrange); means arranger or compiler. Title of compilers of the vedams [q.v.]. Vishnoo pooraunam [q.v.] gives a list of twenty eight Vyausans, the last of whom was the Vyausan called krishnadweipauyanan. He was a compiler of the vedams, as well as of the Mahabhaurat [q.v.]. Many of the individuals called by this name appear as the authors of different hymns of the vedams. It is very possible that the greater portion of them had a real existence, being the framers or teachers of hindoo religion, before a complete ritual was compiled.——*Vyausa poonnama* (వ్యాసపున్నమ - vyásapunnama, Tel.). Means the sage so called, founder of vedauntam + full moon day. Otherwise Vyausa poojah. Lunar [chaundra maunam] festival [pundigay, 3a], subject to intercalation [adhicam]. Festival on full moon [powrnimay] day of second lunar month Veishaukham [mausam] between 29th April and 28th May, when Bramin priests, engaged in reading Pooraunams [q.v.] during that month for the public benefit, are led in procession and worshipped. Kept in commemoration of Vyausan [q.v.], reputed author of the 18 principal and 18 inferior Pooraunams, and also of all the Muntrams [q.v.] or forms of prayer in existence. Also held in Ashaudham [mausam] or july [maryauday].——*Vyausasamoodram* (వ్యాససముద్రము - vyásasamudramu, Tel.). From (vyása, san. the sage + samudra, san. ocean). Tank; Cuddapah dist., Madanapully tal.; from Cuddapah S.W. 70 miles; from Madanapully W.N.W. 28 miles. Near Cundoocore. Tank fed by the Paupughny which flows through it. Finest tank in district, and formed by bunding two hills. It was built under the Vijianugger dynasty by a gooroo, Vyausan, to whom a shausanam [q.v.] was given, granting him the land as an inam [q.v.]. A scheme is in existence for conducting the surplus water to Pedda tippasamoodram and from thence to Runga samoodram.——*Vyavahauram* (व्यवहार - vyavahára, San.). From (vyavahri, san. to act). Practice, procedure. Practices of law and kingly government; these embrace the procedure of legal tribunals and all the rules of judicature and civil and criminal law [dharmam]. For precepts concerning dravidian mode of government see under Raj and Rajah.——*Vyavahaura maula* (വ്യവഹാരമാല - vyavahāramála, Mal.). From (vyavahára, san. law + málá, san. garland). Treatise on Malabar law, especially land-law. It contains the law of division of produce between the cultivator [coodiyaun] and proprietor [jenmy], without allusion to any assessment which did not at that time exist.——*Vyavasauyam* (व्यवसाय - vyavasáya, San.). From (vyavas, san. to labour). Cultivation [vellaumay].——*Vyavastay* (व्यवस्था - vyavast'há, San.). From (vyavast'há, san. to be settled). Legal opinion given by pundits [q.v.].

VICAUR (وقار - wikár, *Ar.*). From (vakara, ar. to be modest). Honor. Prefixed to an alam forms a lacab; as Vicaur ally, honor of ally. Mostly taken by Shiahs [ism].

VID (विद - vid, *San.*). To know.——*Vedam* (वेद - véda, San.). See sep. title.——*Veidyalingam* (வைத்திலிங்கம் - vaittilingam, Tam.). From (vaidya, san. physician + linga, san. phallic emblem of shiva); shiva as a physician [veidyanautan]. Hindoo second or pers. name. Common among non-bramins [peyar].——*Veidyam*

(वैद्य - vaidya, San.). From (vidyá, san. learning). Belonging to vedam [ayoor vedam]. Medicine.——*Veidyan* (वैद्य - vaidya, San.); one who is well versed in vedam [ayoorvedam]. Physician [hakeem]. See sep. title.——*Veidyanautan* (வைத்தி நாதன் - vaittináthan Tam.). From (vaidya, san. physician + nát'ha, san. lord). Epithet of Shiva, lord of physicians. Compare Veidyalingam. Hindoo 2nd or pers. name [peyar]. Familiarly contracted into Veitty or Veittoo or Veittah.——*Veidya shastram* (वैद्यशास्त्र - vaidyashástra, San.). From (vaidya, san. medicine + shástra, san. science). The art of healing. May be classified as follows:—"*a*" original samhitays to which a divine origin is ascribed;—"*b*" digests and compilations ascribed to human authors;—"*c*" vaujeecaranam, medico-magical;—"*d*" rasanyanam, almost exactly the same as the mediæval alchemy;—"*e*" tántric system;—"*f*" dictionaries of materia medica; for instance abhidhauna ratnamaulay is a well-known dictionary of materia medica, arranged according to the six rasams [q.v.];—"*g*" cookery and diet;—"*h*" veterinary medicine, of horses [ghorah] and of elephants [q.v.].——*Vidya lutchmy* (विद्यालक्ष्मी - vidyálakshmí, San.). From (vidyá, san. learning + lakshmí, san. the goddess). The goddess of knowledge. One of the eight kinds of wealth or lutchmy [ashta lutchmy].——*Vidyaudharan* (विद्याधर - vidyádhara, San.). From (vidyá, san. learning + dhri, san. to hold); holder of occult knowledge. Scholars in the world of gods. Good and evil spirits attending the deity.——*Vidyay* (विद्या - vidyá, San.). From (vid, san. to know). Knowledge. The tamul Cooral [q.v.] has the following:—அஃகி யகன்ற வறிவென்னும் யார்மாட்டும் வெஃகி வெறிய செயின்—"what is the advantage of extensive and accurate knowledge if a man through covetousness "act senselessly towards all."—கற்றதனா லாய பயனென்கொல் வாலறிவ னற்றாள் தொழாஅ ரெனின்—"what profit "have those derived from learning, who worship not the good "feet of him who is possessed of pure knowledge?"—பரியினு மாகாவாம் பாலல்ல வுய்த்துச் சொரியினும் போகா தம—"whatever is not conferred by fate cannot be preserved "although it be guarded with most painful care; and that, which "fate has made a man's own, cannot be lost, although he should "even take it and throw it away."—வகுத்தான் வகுத்த வகையல்லாற் கோடி தொகுத்தார்க்குந் துய்த்த லரிது—"even those who gather together millions will only enjoy them, "as it has been determined by the disposer of all things."—ஊழிற் பெருவலி யாவுள மற்றொன்று சூழினுந் தான்முந்துறும்—"what is stronger than fate? If we think of "an expedient to avert it, it will itself be with us before "the thought."—நுண்ணிய நூல்பல கற்பினு மற்றுந்தன் னுண்மை யறிவே மிகும்—"although a man may study the "most polished treatises, the knowledge which fate has decreed "to him will still prevail."—ஒருமைக்கட் டான்கற்ற கல்வி யொருவற் கெழுமையு மேமாப் புடைத்து—"the learning, "which a man has acquired in one birth, will yield him pleasure "during seven births."—அரங்கின்றி வட்டாடி யற்றே நிரம்பிய நூலின்றிக் கோட்டி கொளல்—"to speak in an "assembly of the learned without fullness of knowledge, is like "playing at chess on a board without squares."—கல்லா தவரு நனி நல்லர் கற்றார்முற் சொல்லா திருக்கப் பெறின்—"the unlearned also are very excellent men, if they know how to "keep silence before the learned."—உளரென்னு மாத்திரைய ரல்லாற் பயவாக் களரனையர் கல்லா தவர்—"the "unlearned are like worthless barren land: all that can be said "of them is, that they exist."—மேற்பிறந்தா ராயினுங் கல்லாதார் கீழ்ப்பிறந்துங் கற்றா ரனைத்திலர் பாடு—"the "unlearned, though born in a high caste, are not equal in dignity "to the learned, though they may have been born in a low "caste." Vidyashaulay is a school [madrissa, pullicootam].

VIDIYA (విదియ - vidiya, *Tel.*). From (dvitíya, san. second). Second day [tity] of the lunar fortnight [pacsham] in the month [mausam].

VIDOO (விடு - vidu, *Tam.*). To leave, release, abandon, remain.——*Valencoorny* (खरशिंग - kharashinga, Mahr.; ಘನಸಿಂಗ - ghanasinga, Can.; വിടങ്കുരണ - vitankurana, Mal.; வெடங்குறுணி - vedanguruni, Tam.). Title corruption from malayalam. Mahr. from (khara, mahr. sharp + shringa, san. horn), from long, cylindrical, incurved like horn, tubercled pod. Can. from (ghana, san. heavy + shringa, san. horn); from appearance of woody capsule. Mal. from (vitan, mal. inferior + kurana, mal log). Tam. from malayalam. Tam. also (alambalmaram), meaning sharp toothed tree; (shavadimaram), meaning collor bone tree, from shape of capsule. Title otherwise Walking-stick bignonia. Botanically Stereospermum [pautalam] xylocarpum, wight., bignoniaceæ [vricsham, 99]. Alias Bignonia xylocarpa; Spathodea xylocarpa; Tecoma xylocarpa. Arboreous, glabrous; leaves bi-tri-pinnate; petiole sharply angular, leaflets petioled, ovate or oblong-acuminated, membranaceous, reticulately veined; panicle corymbose; branches dichotomous; calyx unequally five-toothed; corolla campanulate, shortly tubular; lobes rounded; capsule round-linear, incurved, woody, tubercled; flowers white, fragrant; flowering in august. Leaves are deciduous in cold weather, rapid grower, ornamental; native of malabar. Natives extract from the wood a thick fluid of the color and consistence of stockholm tar, which they use as a remedy for scaly eruptions on the skin. Tender fruit edible. Sapwood large, grey; heartwood very hard, brown; wood tough and elastic, close-grained; used for cabinet-work; the wood is hard, but easily split; when sawn across it presents a yellow resinous surface; sections examined with the microscope show that the yellow color is due to a solid resinous deposit in the pitted vascular system.——*Veed* (వీడు - vídu, Tel.; വീട് - vítu, Mal.; வீடு - vídu, Tam.). From (vidu, tam. to remain).—"*a*" House. A native house consists generally of three detached huts; one serving as a sleeping room for the family, another for a working room and kitchen, and a third for a store room for goods and chattels. Built of mud and thatched; but in parts the roofs are of terraced earth laid on beams, with wattle and daub between. The ordinary description of hut is circular in shape, from about 12 to 20 feet in diameter; the walls are of mud, or wattle and daub, the roof pointed in the centre and thatched. There is but one door, and no other means of ventilation. Though a low-caste man may acquire wealth, his neighbours will not allow him to build a house with beams to support a roof, or to use tiles [wode] instead of thatch. The bramins' and comaties' houses are generally the best in every village. Except during the rains [mazhay] the cattle [maud] are always kept in the open air, but at that season they are admitted within doors, and among the poorer classes form a part of the family. Among the richer there are cattle sheds in the house enclosures. Among the wealthier the apartments of the females are always distinct, and the mahomedan practice of women being shut up is followed [gosha, purdah]. Among the middle and lower classes however the women mix freely in society, attend the market, assist in cultivation [vellaumay], bring water and firewood to the house, cook the food, attend to the cattle, and perform all the ordinary in-door and out-door avocations of life. Some of the houses of the well-to-do are ornamented with carved wood-work and ornamental devices on the walls. In some may be seen framed and glazed pictures, chiefly representations of the hindoo divinities. Both woollen and cotton carpets [cumbly, jamkhana] are also beginning to be more freely used, though mats [boriyah] are most common. The articles of furniture are generally confined to a few wooden cots, the bottoms of which are made of laced rope or tape, a few stools and boxes, sometimes a large jar or two for grain, a few brass [pittalay], bell metal [cunts], tin [tagaram] and earthen pots [chatty], and dishes for culinary purposes. Food is generally eaten on leaf plates, as caste requires that any earthen vessel which has been used for eating be broken and never used a second time for the same purpose. The Mahomedans are the only class who use crockery. The following are current shastram rules relating to the building of a house. Having selected a site, the frontage must be divided into nine equal parts, five being assigned to the right, and three to the left, the fourth division being reserved for the doorway. The enumeration begins on the left, and thus the fourth section is in the mansion of Mercury [boodham]. The occupant of such a house may become as wealthy as Coobairan [q.v.]. A person born under Gemini [mitoonam], Cancer [carcatacam] or Leo [simham] must build his house on a line stretching east and west, the entrance being placed easterly [dic, tisay]. A person born under Virgo [canyay], Libra [toolaum] or Scorpio [vrishchicam] must build on a line running north and south, the doorway being southerly. One born under Sagitarius [dhanoos], Capricorn [macaram] or Aquarius [coombham] must build west and east, placing the entrance westerly. If born under Pisces [meenam], Aries [maisham] or the Twins [mitoonam], he must build south and north, the door being placed northerly. A family occupying a house built contrary to these rules will be ruined [maryanday, maunasauram, stanpatyam]. There is a Tamul proverb:—வடக்குப்பார்த்தமச்சுவீட்டைப் பார்க்கிலும் தெற்குப்பார்த்த தெருத்திண்ணை நலது—"a pyall [q.v.] facing south is "preferable to a terraced house with a northern aspect."—"*b*" Also means happiness. Among tamulians there are enumerated four kinds or sources of happiness, termed respectively Aram, Porool, Inbam, Veed; or benevolent virtue, property, sensual pleasure, eternal bliss.——*Vidigole* (విడిగోలు - vidigólu, Tel.). The time of letting out cattle [maud], early morning.

VIL (வில் - vil, *Tam.*). Bow. Each of the ancient Dravidian dynasties [raj] had its particular symbol or standard [dhwajam]; that of the Cholans [q.v.] being a tiger [pooly], of the Paundyans [q.v.] a fish [meenam], and of the Cherans [q.v.] a bow, to which the Congoo [q.v.] dynasty added that of an elephant [q.v.] still retaining the bow. Vil also indicates the rainbow; of which Varauha mihiran says;—"The many-colored rays of the sun "[sooryan] falling upon the clouds and being broken by the "winds take the shape of the rainbow in the sky; in the opinion "of certain writers the rainbow is formed of the expired breath "of certain serpents of the divine order; if two rainbows "similar to each other should appear perfect, unbroken, bent "towards the earth, bright, glossy, thick and variegated in "color, there will be abundant rain [mazhay, vaunashastram]."——*Villavan* (வில்லவன் - villavan, Tam.). From (vil, tam. a bow); bowman. Another name for Cherans [q.v.].——*Villi-*

poottooran (வில்லிப்புத்தூரன் - villipputtúran, Tam.). From (villipputtúr, tam. place so called). Otherwise Saurwa bhowma iyengar. Veishnava bramin born at Shaniyore in the Coimbatore country. Wrote the Tamul mahabhaurat [q.v.] which includes first ten Parvams and consists of 3,373 stanzas. Nullapillay added 14,728 stanzas.——*Villoopooram* (விழுப்புரம் - villuppuram, Tam.). See sep. title.——*Villy* (வில்லி - villi, Tam.). From (vil, tam. bow). Manmatan [manmatan, oorvilly].

VIL (விள் - vil, *Tam.*). To break, burst.——*Vilaum gum* (விளாம்பிசின் - vilámbisin, Tam.). From Wood-apple tree [q.v.].——*Vilauticoolam* (விளாத்திக்குளம் - vilátukkulam, Tam. vilátikulam *). From (vilátti, tam. the wood-apple tree, feronia elephantum, corr. + kulam, tam. tank).—"*a*" Deputy tahsildarry, Tinnevelly district. Tahsildar's pay Rs. 70. —"*b*" Village, Deputy tahsildar's station; Tinnevelly dist., Ottapidauram tal.; pop. 1,964; acres 5,379; lat. 9° 08′; long. 78° 13′; from Madras S.S.W. 305 miles; from Ottapidauram N.E. 18 miles; from Palamcottah N.E. 41 miles; from Shermadevy N.E. 51 miles; from Shreevillipoottore E.S.E. 45 miles; from Tinnevelly N.E. 43 miles; from Tuticorin N. 23 miles; from the sea N.W. 11 miles. On the road from Tuticorin to Madras, near the right bank of the Veippaur. Old Shiva temple. Festivals in April and July. Weekly fair on Wednesday.——*Vilay* (விளை - vilai, Tam.). From (vil, tam. to break); place of culture. High dry ground [tidal].

VILAUDAT (ولادت - viládat, *Hind.*). Birth.——*Vilaudat e shareef* (ولادت شریف - viládatisharíf, Hind.). From (above + sharíf, ar. noble). Also called Mowlood [q.v.]. Birth of the prophet. A feast [eed] on 12th of Rabee ool owval [mahoena].

VILAUNG (جری - jirrí, *Ar.*; مار ماهی - mármáhí, *Pers.*; کچیا مچھلی - kachiyámachhlí, *Hind.*; تمبومچھی - tambúmaççhí, *Dec.*; పాముచేప - pámuchépa, *Tel.*; അരഗൻ - aragan, *Mal.*; விலாங்கு - vilángu, *Tam.*). Ar. from (jirra, ar. to stretch). Pers. from (már, pers. snake + máhí, pers. fish). Hind. from (kachiyá, hind. sickle + machhií, hind. fish). Tel. from (pámu, tel. snake + chépa, tel. fish). Tam. from (vilangal, tam. puddle). Tel. also (maluguchépa), meaning eel + fish. Tam. also (malangu), meaning easily confused fish. Eels. The family Muraenidæ [matsyam, 42] of naturalists [jantoo].

VILAUYET (ولایت - viláyat, *Hind.*). From (valá, ar. to be near). Native country. Come to be used for foreign country, England or Europe. Also Persia or Turkey.——*Vilauty pauny* (ولایتی پانی - viláitípání, Hind.). From (above + pání, hind. water). European water, soda-water.——*Vilauyaty* (ولایتی - viláiti, Hind.). English, European [europe, faranghee, firangy, foreign, seema]. The opposite word is Deshye.

VILLOOPOORAM (بیلپور - belpúr, *Hind.*; விழுப்புரம் - villuppuram, *Tam.* villupuram *). From (vil, tam. bow + pura, sán. town)[vil]. Bowman village; otherwise Belpore by corruption.——**(1)** Talook, South arcot district. Tahsildar's pay Rs. 250. Area 508 square miles. Population 301,746. Language Tamul. N. Centre coast. Boundaries:—N. Tindivanam talook; S. Cuddalore and Tricalore talooks; E. Bay of Bengal and French territory; W. Trinomallee, Cullacoorchy and Tricalore talooks. Talook generally flat. Soil black cotton [regar] and red. Manufacture of cloths. Irrigation by Paumbay river, Vicravaundy river, Varauhanuddy river, Alangaul channel, Ponniaur. Camping grounds at Punchamandevy, Vicravaundy and Villoopooram. Includes the mittah [q.v.] of Mundacaputt. Places of archæological interest:—Anangore, Anniyore, Coliyanore, Cundamungalam, Mundacaputt, Panaimullay, Panayapooram, Pareiyapooram, Paroor, Periya tutchore, Perambaukam, Poornasingapolliem, Tirvacaray, Trivamauttore, Valavanore, Valdavore, Veedoor, Villoopooram, Yermayavaram, Yeroombay. Principal trig. stations:—Cullaputt, Mulliputt rock. The leading places, &c., in the talook are the following.——*Anniyore* (அன்னியூர் - anniyúr, Tam.). From (annai, tam. mother + úr, tam. village). Pop. 1,723; acres 1,926; lat. 12° 04′; long. 79° 26′; from Cuddalore N.W. 34 miles; from Villoopooram N.W. 11 miles; from the sea W. 32 miles. Two old temples with inscriptions of Vijianugger [humpy] dynasty [raj] dated 1520 and 1560. Built by a ruler of Vellore.——*Cullaputt* (கள்ளப்பட்டு - kallappattu, Tam.). From (kallan, tam. thief + pattu, tam. village). Trig. station; lat. 11° 57′ 15·07″; long. 79° 36′ 20·71″; height 174 feet; from Coliyanore N.N.E. 1¾ miles; from Villoopooram E. 5 miles; from the sea W. 19 miles.——*Mulliputt rock* (மல்லிப்பட்டு - mallippattu, Tam.). From (malli, tam. jasmine + pattu, tam. village). Trig. station; lat. 11° 58′ 03·00″; long. 79° 25′ 01·60″; height 289 feet; from Maumbalaputt N. ¾ mile; from Villoopooram W.N.W. 8 miles; from the sea W. 32 miles.——*Mundacaputt* (மண்டகப்பட்டு - mandagappattu, Tam.). From (mandagam, tam. a public resting place + pattu, tam. village). Mittah; pop. 2,597; acres 1,453; lat. 11° 53′; long. 79° 43′; from Cuddalore N.W. 13 miles; from Villoopooram E.S.E. 12 miles; from the sea W. 10 miles. Peshcush Rs. 2,434.——*Panaimullay* (பனைமலை - panaimalai, Tam.). From (panai, tam. palmyra tree, borassus flabelliformis, linn. + malai, tam. mountain). Sanscrit name (tálagiri), means same. Village, Mountain; pop. 1,319; acres 2,468; lat. 12° 06′; long. 79° 25′; from Cuddalore N.W. 37 miles; from Villoopooram N.W. 13 miles; from the sea W. 35 miles. On the mountain is a well-built Shiva temple to Taulagherry eeshwaran.——*Panayapooram* (பனையப்புரம் - panaiyappuram, Tam.). From (panai, tam. palmyra tree, borassus flabelliformis, linn. + pura, san. town). Pop. 1,177; acres 1,237; lat. 12° 00′; long. 79° 35′; from Cuddalore N.W. 25 miles; from Villoopooram N.E. 5 miles; from the sea W. 20 miles. Sculptured Shiva temple with a tasdik [q.v.] allowance.——*Ponniaur* (பெண்ணையாறு - pennaiyáru, Tam.). See sep. title.——*Tirvacaray* (திருவக்கரை - tiruvakkarai, Tam.). From (tiru, tam. holy + agam, tam. place + karai, tam. bank). Sanscrit name (vakrakshetra), meaning vacran, the asooran + sacred place. Village; pop. 845; acres 1,716; lat. 12° 02′; long. 79° 42′; height 151 feet; from Cuddalore N.N.W. 23 miles; from Villoopooram N.E 12 miles; from the sea W. 14 miles. The place where Vacrausooran was killed by Vishnoo and Chundramowleeshwaran. On north bank of Ariancooppam river. Formerly a place of great importance. The principal streets can still be traced. Old Shiva temple with inscriptions. The tower over gateway consists of eight storeys. Large stone tank covering several acres of ground. The pagoda [coil, pagoda] was much injured by Hyder ally's army, on its retreat from Porto novo in 1781. Tirvacaray is remarkable for petrifications found on a rising ground of sandstone [manal cull] in the vicinity. Petrified trees are manufactured into beads [munkah], necklaces [maulay], bracelets, and other ornaments [nagay, zewar].——*Tondayaur* (தொண்டியாறு - tondiyáru, Tam.). See sep. title.——*Trivamauttore* (திருவாமாத்தூர் - tiruvámáttúr, Tam.). From (tiru, tam. holy + á, tam. cow + máthu, tam. mother + úr, tam. village). Sanscrit name (gómátripura), means cow + mother + town. Place of pilgrimage; pop. 1,230; acres 1,498; lat. 11° 58′; long. 79° 31′; from Cuddalore N.W. 26 miles. Old Shiva temple with inscriptions.——*Valavanore* (வளவனூர் - valavanúr, Tam.). From (valavan, tam. epithet of chola ruler, as king of a fertile country + úr, tam. village). Railway station; pop. 3,527; acres 2,376; lat. 11° 55′; long. 79° 38′; from Cuddalore N.W. 18 miles; from Villoopooram E.S.E. 6 miles; from the sea W. 17 miles. Largest revenue of any village in district. The size of the tank was diminished on account of Railway works. Two old temples with inscriptions.——*Valdavore* (வழுதாவூர் - vazhuthávúr, Tam.). See sep. title.——*Varauhanuddy* (வராகநதி - varáganathi, Tam.). See sep. title.——*Vaunore* (வானூர் - vánúr, Tam.). See sep. title.——*Veedoor* (வீடூர் - vídúr, Tam.). From (vídu, tam. emancipation + úr, tam. village). Sanscrit name (muktikshétra), meaning emancipation + sacred place. Pop. 2,414; acres 3,412; lat. 12° 04′; long. 79° 38′; from Cuddalore N.N.W. 26 miles; from Villoopooram N.E. 11 miles; from the sea W. 19 miles. Jeina [q.v.] temple in present use.——*Vicravaundy* (விக்கிரவாண்டி - vikkiravándi, Tam.). See sep. title.——*Villoopooram* (விழுப்புரம் - villuppuram, Tam.). See below.——**(2)** Town, Head-quarters of talook, Railway station. Pop. 7,950; acres 1,724; lat. 11° 57′; long. 79° 32′; height 143 feet; from Chidambaram N.N.W. 39 miles; from Cuddalore N.W. 24 miles; from Madras S.S.W. 93 miles; from Tindivanam S.S.W. 21 miles; from Tricalore E. 19 miles; from Vriddhauchellam N.N.E. 31 miles; from the sea W. 22 miles. On the Trichinopoly road. Junction of South indian railway for Pondicherry. On the 24th of July 1752 captured from the French. In the same year Dupleix retook the fort. On the 3rd April 1760, English regained possession. Two old temples with inscriptions and the ruins of a Jeina [q.v.] temple [basty]. Two mutilated Jeina images close to travellers' bungalow [q.v.].

VILLY (ಪಲ್ಲಿ - villi, *Tel.*). A corruption of (palli, tel. village). Suffix in place names [hully, milly, pully]; as Veeravilly, hero's town.

VILOOTHOO (راچھ - ráchh, *Hind.*; விழுது - vizhuthu, *Tam.*). From (vizhu, tam. to fall). Heddle [nesavoo].

VINAY (வினை - vinai, *Tam.*). Action. In philosophy the accumulation of moral actions, entailed as a consequence of deeds in former births [jenmam, pirapp]; the latent cause of transmigration [samsauram]; same as Carmam. In common usage it means evil, pain, or misfortune. The tamul Cooral [q.v.] has the following:—தீயவை தீய பயத்தலாற் றீயவை தீயினு மஞ்சப் படும்—"because evil produces evil, therefore should evil "be feared more than fire."—இலனென்று தீயவை செய்யற்க செய்யி னிலனாகு மற்றும் பெயர்த்து—"commit not evil, "saying, I am poor, if you do, you will become poorer still."—தீயவை செய்தார் கெடுத னிழறன்னை வீயா தடியுறைந் தற்று—"destruction will dwell at the heels of those who com-"mit evil even as their shadow that leaves them not."—வினை வலியுந் தன்வலியு மாற்றான் வலியுந் துணைவலியுந் தூக்கிச் செயல்—"let a man weigh well the strength of the deed "he purposes to do, his own strength, the strength of his "enemy, and the strength of the allies of both, and then let him "act."—துணைநல மாக்கந் தரூஉம் வினைநலம் வேண் டிய வெல்லாந் தரும்—"the efficacy of support will yield "only wealth; but the efficacy of action will yield all that is "desired."—ஊறொரா லுற்றபி னொல்காமை யிவ்விரண்டி னாறென்ப ராய்ந்தவர் கோள்—"not to perform a ruinous "act, and not to be discouraged by the ruinous termination of "an act, are the two maxims which, the wise say, form the princi- "ples of those who have investigated the subject."—கடைக் கொட்கச் செய்தக்க தாண்மை யிடைக்கொட்கி னெற்றா விழுமந் தரும்—"so to perform an act as to publish it only "at its termination is manliness; for to announce it beforehand "will cause irremediable sorrow."—சொல்லுதல் யார்க்கு மெளிய வரியவாஞ் சொல்லிய வண்ணஞ் செயல்—"to "say how an act is to be performed is indeed easy for any one; "but far more difficult it is to do according to what has been "said."—கலங்காது கண்ட வினைக்கட் டுளங்காது தூக்கங் கடிந்து செயல்—"an act that has been firmly resolved on "must be as firmly carried out without delay."—எனைத்திட்ப மெய்தியக் கண்ணும் வினைத்திட்பம் வேண்டாரை வேண்டா துலகு—"the great will not esteem those who "esteem not firmness of action, whatever other abilities the "latter may possess."—சூழ்ச்சி முடிவு துணிவெய்த லத்துணிவு தாழ்ச்சியுட் டங்குதல் தீது—"consultation ends in "forming a resolution to act; but delay in the execution of that "resolve is an evil."—தூங்குக தூங்கிச் செயற்பால தூங்கற்க தூங்காது செய்யும் வினை—"sleep over such actions as "may be slept over; but never over such as may not be slept "over."—பொருள்கருவி காலம் வினையிடனொ டைந்து மிருடீர வெண்ணிச் செயல்—"do an act after a due con- "sideration of the following five, viz., money, means, time, "execution and place."

VINDHYAM (विन्ध्य - vindhya, *San.*). From (vind, san. to divide). The chain of mountains which divides Upper from Southern india. The course of the Nerbudda indicates the direction of the principal range, but the mountainous tract spreads much more widely. It meets the Ganges in several places towards the north, and the Godavery is held to be its southern limit.

VINOOCONDAH (వినుకొండ - vinukonda, * *Tel.*). From (vinu, tel. sky + konda, tel. hill) [vin].——**(1)** Taloŏk, Kistna district. Tahsildar's pay Rs. 150. Area 643 square miles; population 82,445; language Teloogoo. S.W. of district. Bounded north by Pulnaud talook, east by Narsarowpett talook, south by Darshy division in Nellore district, west by Marcapore talook of Kurnool district. The road south from the Pulnaud and west from Narsarowpett meet at Vinoocondah, whence a road proceeds to Cumbum and Kurnool. Bellary-Kistna railway from Goontacull to Kistna passes through. Remains of vast antiquity are met with on every hand. Along the course of the Goondlacumma stone implements have been found similar to those found at Abbeville in the north of France. Dolmens [coday cull] abound and almost each village has inscriptions. The Goondlacumma flows through the southern portion. There are indications of the presence of copper [taumram] and iron [auhan] among the hills. Soil rocky; regar [q.v.] series predominate. Agricultural produce. Camping grounds:—Chintalcheroo, Velpoor, Vinoocondah. Places of archæological interest:—Agnigoondaula, Boggaram, Bollapalley, Canamarlapoody, Caurmanchy, Chintalcheroo, Cotsarla, Cottalore, Dondapaud, Eepoor, Gandiganamala, Garikipaud, Gocanacondah, Goommanampaud, Gootlapully, Inoomella, Madamunchipaud, Mookkellapaud, Moolacalore, Noozulla, Oommadivaram, Pedda cancherla, Pitchicalapollem, Potlore, Remidicherla, Royavaram, Saricondapollem, Shaunampoody, Shivapooram, Talaurlapully, Timmaupooram, Timmayyapollem, Tripooraupooram, Vaddemgoonta, Vanicoonta, Vellatore, Velpoor, Vinoocondah, Yainoogapollem. Trig. stations:—Cankiraula, Soodicondah, Yerracondah. The leading places, &c., in the talook are the following.——*Cankiraula* (కంకిరాల - kankirála, Tel.). From (kanika, tel. a kind of marble + ráyi, tel. stone). Trig. station; lat. 16° 22′ 00·00″; long. 79° 38′ 00·00″; ——*Caurmanchy* (కారుమంచి - kárumanchi, Tel.). From (káru, tel. season + manchi, tel. goodness). Village; pop. 2,342; acres 7,281; lat. 16° 04′; long. 79° 56′; from Masulipatam W. 80 miles; from Vinoocondah E. 10 miles. Shiva temple with inscription. ——*Cotsarla* (కొచ్చర్ల - koççarla, Tel.). From (kóta, san. fort + cherla, tel. village). Village; pop. 2,419; acres 4,993; lat. 16° 09′; long. 79° 48′; from Masulipatam W. 88 miles; from Vinoocondah N.N.E. 7 miles. Old fort built by relative of Chintapully zemindar.——*Dondapaud* (దొండపాడు - dondapádu, Tel.). From (donda, tel. cephalandra indica, naud. + pádu, tel. village). Village; pop. 1,168; acres 3,610; lat. 16° 03′; long. 79° 42′; from Masulipatam W. 95 miles; from Vinoocondah W. 5 miles. North is an embankment formerly connecting two hills and forming a tank which irrigated the country as far as Vinoocondah. Dolmens [coday cull].——*Goondlacumma* (గుండ్లకమ్మ - gundlakamma, Tel.). See sep. title.——*Inoomella* (ఇనుమెళ్ల - inumella, Tel.). From (inumu, tel. iron + ella, tel. boundary). Village; pop. 2,254; acres 5,016; lat. 16° 17′; long. 79° 52′; from Masulipatam W. 83 miles; from Vinoocondah N.N.E. 17 miles. Five deserted temples of great antiquity. Inscriptions connected with Chola and Warangal dynasties.——*Shaunampoody* (శానంపూడి - shánampúdi, Tel.). From (shánamma, tel. proper name + púdi, tel. village). Village; pop. 2,036; acres 6,846; lat. 16° 05′; long. 79° 53′; from Masulipatam W. 83 miles; from Vinoocondah E.N.E. 6 miles. Shrine of Hanooman [q.v.]. Inscription on a rock.——*Soodicondah* (సూదికొండ - súdikonda, Tel.). From (súdi, tel. needle + konda, tel. hill). Trig. station; lat. 16° 14′ 26·92″; long. 79° 44′ 27·04″; height 1,835 feet.——*Vaddemgoonta* (వడ్డెంగుంట - vaddemgunta, Tel.). From (odde, tel. a caste + gunta, tel. pond). Village; pop. 1,931; acres 3,911; lat. 16° 08′; long. 79° 45′; from Masulipatam W. 92 miles; from Vinoocondah N.N.W. 6 miles. Inscription on a rock near a temple, latter built by Cholans [q.v.].——*Velpoor* (వేల్పూరు - vélpúru, Tel.). From (vélpu, tel. deity + úru, tel. village). Village; pop. 2,483; acres 5,476; lat. 16° 10′; long. 79° 54′; from Masulipatam W. 81 miles; from Vinoocondah N.E. 11 miles. Two old temples, Shiva and Vishnoo.——*Vinoocondah* (వినుకొండ - vinukonda, Tel.). See below.——*Yerracondah* (ఎర్రకొండ - errakonda, Tel.). From (erra, tel. red + konda, tel. hill). Trig. station; lat. 16° 05′ 51·34″; long. 79° 44′ 47·86″; height 1,147 feet; from Vinoocondah N.W. 4 miles.——**(2)** Town, Hill, General deputy collector's and talook head-quarters, Place of pilgrimage, Railway station on Bellary-Kistna line; Kistna dist., Vinoocondah tal.; pop. 6,911; acres 9,073; lat. 16° 03′; long. 79° 47′, from Bezwada W.S.W. 66 miles; from Guntoor W.S.W. 50 miles; from Madras N. 205 miles; from Masulipatam W. 92 miles. Hill-fort, on a rock composed of quartz [vencull] and mica [abruck], built by Saugy gannama naidoo, governor under Veera pratapa poorshottama gajapaty, A.D. 1462-1496, to whom is also attributed a temple and a finely sculptured mantapam [q.v.]. The hill is an extinct volcano. The fort was captured by Krishnadeva roya of Vijianugger [humpy] during his victorious march along the Eastern coast. It was for some time in the possession of the Condaveed reddies [q.v.]. Captured by Hyder ool moolk, Golcondah general, in 1578, and for some time in the possession of Goonda row, zemindar of Narsarowpett. After the English took Masulipatam the fort was regarded as a place of considerable strength, and in the many petty quarrels, among local zemindars towards the close of last century, it afforded a secure place of refuge. The Company established a garrison here about 1790, as it was a large depôt for stores being advanced on the road to Hyderabad and within easy reach of the seaport of Motoopully. In 1808 the stores were removed to Masulipatam and the fortifications demolished. In 1816 the Pindarries [q.v.] ravaged the country and the townspeople took shelter on the hill. The oldest fort, on the west side of the hill, was built or repaired by Vishwambhara deo gajapaty and repaired again by Poliya vaima reddy of Condaveed. Lower down is the fort of Pochineed gunnamaneed, one of the Reddy [q.v.] chiefs; five ruined palaces. The third fort, at foot of hill, was built by Saugy gannama naidoo. Another fort, built 250 years ago, surrounds the town. Raghoonautasawmy temple. Temple of Narsimhan with inscriptions. Codanda ramasawmy temple. Temple of Ramalingam on the hill of immemorial antiquity. Large mosque [musjid]. Dolmens [coday cull] in the vicinity. Shocks of earthquake [mahy campam]. On the hill are two tanks, water all the year round.

VIPRAN (विप्र - vipra, *San.*). From (vip, san. to utter). Means chanter of hymns. Bramin [q.v.].——*Vipranarrain* (விப்பிரநாராயணன் - vippiranáráyanan, Tam.). From (above + náráyana, san. vishnu, the mover on waters); as bramin [q.v.] by birth and worshipper of vishnoo [q.v.]. The same as Tondaradipody alwar [q.v.].——*Vipravinody* (విప్రవినోది - vipravinódi, Tel.). From (above + vinódi, san. diverting). A small class of Bramins [q.v.] who have lost their caste and exhibit legerdemain to other bramins [jauty].

VIRAL (വിരൽ - viral, *Mal.*). From (viri, tam. to extend), Finger. Linear measure. 8 toras or dholl seeds = 1 viral; 12 virals = 1 chaun [alavay, 1d]. Approximate actual value, 1 viral = ¾ inch. Same as San. ungoolam, Tam. viralcaday.——*Viral, caday* (விரற்கடை - virargadai, Tam.). From (above + kadai, tam. end). A finger tip's breadth. Linear measure. 8 nels = 1 viralcaday; 12 viralcadays = 1 jaun [alavay, 1a]. Approximate actual value, 1 viralcaday = ·82 inch. Same as San. ungoolam, Mal. viral. See vol. I, 609; II, 505.

VIRAL (விறல் - viral, *Tam.*). From (vira, tam. to increase, to conquer). Strength.——*Viraly* (விறலி - virali, Tam.). A girl of sixteen years.——*Viroothoo* (விருது - viruthu, Tam.). From (viruda, san. praise). Badge of distinction. Banner [dhwajam, jenda].——*Viroothooputty* (விருதுபட்டி - viruthupatti, Tam. virudupati*). From (viruthu, tam. a banner + patti, tam. village).—"*a*" Deputy tahsildarry, Tinnevelly district. Pay Rs. 70.—"*b*" Town, Railway station, Deputy Tahsildar's head-quarters; Tinnevelly dist., Shauttore tal.; pop. 6,614; acres 1,587; lat. 9° 45′; long. 78° 00′; height 336 feet; from Madras S.S.W. 286 miles; from Palamcottah N.N.E. 60 miles; from Shauttore N. 16 miles; from Shermadevy N.N.E. 66 miles; from Shreevillipoottore E.N.E. 23 miles; from Tinnevelly N.N.E. 61 miles; from Tuticorin N.N.W. 55 miles. Large Shiva temple with several inscriptions. Weekly fair on Monday. Considerable trade in cotton [q.v.], tobacco [pogauk] and grains.

VIRIYAN (मातुलाहि - mátuláhi, *San.*; زهری سانپ - zahrí-sámp, *Dec.*; ಬಳೆಗಡಿಕೆನಹಾವು - balegadikinahávu, *Can.*; పెంజెర - penjera, *Tel.*; മണ്ഡലി - mandali, *Mal.*; விரியன் - viriyan, *Tam.*). Title from tamul [vary]. San. from (mátula, san. pomegranate, punica granatum. linn. + ahi, mal. serpent); from its spotted character. Dec. from (zahr, pers. poison + sámp, hind. snake). Can. from (bale, can. circle + gaduku, can. stout + hávu, can. snake). Tel. from (penu, tel. large + jerri, tel. centipede). Mal. from (mandala, san. circle), from its circles or coils. Tam. from (vari, tam. streak). Tel. also (katteda), meaning striped. Form the family Viperidæ, ophidii viperiformes, ophidia [sarpam], reptilia [sarpy, 30] of naturalists [jantoo]. The Viriyans or Viperidæ have the body robust; tail rather short, not prehensile; head broad or thick, generally scaly above, or incompletely shielded; no pit in the loreal region, eye of moderate size, with vertical pupil; viviparous; terrestrial snakes. The following are the only two species in Southern india :—Daboia elegans [chain viper]; Echis carinata [carpet snake]. Among Viriyans the Dravidians themselves distinguish the following.——*Ass viper* (గాడిదెకట్టెడ - gádidekatteda, Tel.; கழுதைவிரியன் - kazhuthaiviriyan, Tam.). So called on account of the slow manner in which it moves; it grows to a large size and is of a black color. Its bite is not deadly.——*Blood viper* (నెత్తురుకట్టెడ - netturukatteda, Tel.; രക്തമണ്ഡലി - raktamandali, Mal.; இரத்தவிரியன் - irattaviriyan, Tam.). The bite of this viper causes vomiting of blood.——*Burning viper* (మంటకట్టెడ - mantakatteda, Tel.; எரிவிரியன் - eriviriyan, Tam.). Called on account of the burning pain that follows its bite.——*Chain viper* (గొలుసుకట్టెడ - golusukatteda, Tel.; சங்கிலிவிரியன் - shangiliviriyan, Tam.). See sep. title.——*Coiled viper* (సురటకట్టెడ - suratakatteda, Tel.; சுருட்டைவிரியன் - shuruttaiviriyan, Tam.). See Carpet snake.——*Deaf viper* (చెముడుకట్టెడ - chemudukatteda, Tel.; செவிட்டுவிரியன் - shevittuviriyan, Tam.).——*Fire-brand viper* (కొరివికట్టెడ - korivikatteda, Tel.; கொள்ளிவிரியன் - kolliviriyan, Tam.).——*Grass adder* (కసువుకట్టెడ - kasuvukatteda, Tel.; புல்விரியன் - pulviriyan, Tam.).——*Joint viper* (కట్టెడ - katteda, Tel.; கட்டுவிரியன் - kattuviriyan, Tam.). It is striped black and white with the appearance of joints.——*Large glass viper* (பெருங்கண்ணாடிவிரியன் - perungannádiviriyan, Tam.).——*Large viper* (పెద్దకట్టెడ - peddakatteda, Tel.; பெருவிரியன் - peruviriyan, Tam.).——*Long viper* (పొడుగుకట్టెడ - podugukatteda, Tel.; நெடும்விரியன் - nedumviriyan, Tam.).——*Oil viper* (నూనెకట్టెడ - núnekátteda, Tel.; எண்ணெய்விரியன் - enneyviriyan, Tam.).——*Palmyra viper* (తాటికట్టెడ - tátikatteda, Tel.; பனைவிரியன் - panaiviriyan, Tam.).——*Pus viper* (சீக்கூட்டுவிரியன் - shíkkúttuviriyan, Tam.). Its bite causes pus to form in a boil.——*Red viper* (ఎఱ్ఱకట్టెడ - errakatteda, Tel.; செவ்விரியன் - shevviriyan, Tam.).——*Rope viper* (తాటికట్టెడ - tátikatteda, Tel.; கயிற்றுவிரியன் - kayittuviriyan, Tam.).——*Rough viper* (கரட்டுவிரியன் - karattuviriyan, Tam.). Blood viper of a reddish color.——*Scissors viper* (కత్తెరకట్టెడ - katterakatteda, Tel.; கத்திரிவிரியன் - kattiriviriyan, Tam.).——*Short viper* (పొట్టికట్టెడ - pottikatteda, Tel.; குறும்விரியன் - kurumviriyan, Tam.).——*Small viper* (చిన్నకట్టెడ - chinnakatteda, Tel.; சிறுவிரியன் - shiruviriyan, Tam.).——*Twisted viper* (మెలికకట్టెడ - melikakatteda, Tel.; முறுக்குவிரியன் - murukkuviriyan, Tam.).——*Two-headed viper* (రెండుతలలకట్టెడ - rendutalalakatteda, Tel.; இருதலைவிரியன் - iruthalaiviriyan, Tam.). The earth snake, Eryx johnii of naturalists. A very harmless reptile. See Irtalay maniyan which is the same thing.

VISH (विष् - vish, *San.*). To spread, pervade.——*Veinavam* (வைணவம் - vainavam, Tam.). From (vishnu, san. deity). Belonging to Vishnoo [q.v.]; also the Veishnava faith as opposed to Sheivam [q.v.] and Booddham [booddha].——*Veishnava* (वैष्णव - vaishnava, San.). The Beishnab of bengal. Follower of Vishnoo, or relating to Vishnoo.——*Veishwaunaran* (वैश्वानर - vaishvánara, San.). From (vishva, san. all + nara, san. man); common to all men. The active principle dwelling on the collected sum of solid matter, or he who is conscious of self-existence [viraut].——*Veishwaunary* (वैश्वानरी - vaishvánarí, San.). From (vishva, san. all + nara, san. man). The central avastaunam [q.v.] of the sun [sooryan] and moon [chundran, nacshatram].——*Vishajooram* (विषज्वर - vishajvara, San.; கோவாரி - kóvári, Tam.). From (visha, san. poison + jvara, san. fever). Tam. means cow epidemic. Tam. also (alari), meaning spreading disease; (kóvári), meaning cow + epidemic. Rinderpest of cattle [pashoorogam]. Appears to be capable of origination de novo, and once generated is communicable with great facility. Its earliest symptom is a spasmodic twitching of the muscles of the chest and neck, and sometimes of the hind-quarters, which resembles but is different from the accompanying or following rigor. The temperature rises to 105° F., subsequently falling as low as 88°. The pulse is little disturbed at first but afterwards becomes quick and weak. The respiration is accelerated, and labored when the respiratory muscles are involved in the spasm. The disease may last from one to sixteen days, its usual duration being from three to nine. By the natives palmyra [q.v.] toddy [q.v.] is given as a cure; also the tender leaves of Cassia auriculata [tungaid], the succulent portion of the aloe [q.v.] leaf, cummin seed [jeerah], onions [piyanz], and the tender bark of Balsamodendron berryii [kiloovay] well ground and mixed with vinegar [caudy]. Compare Shembah.——*Visham* (विष - visha, San.). From (vish, san. to pervade), Poison.——*Vishnoo* (विष्णु - vishnu, San.; بشن - bishn, Hind.; விட்டுணு - vittunu, Tam.). From (vish, san. to pervade). According to Matsya pooraunam [q.v.] the name alludes to his entering into the mundane egg [bramhaundam]; according to the Pudma pooraunam [q.v.] to his entering into or combining with pracrity [q.v.], as poorsham [q.v.] or spirit. In the Mahabhaurat [q.v.] the word is derived from the root (ví), signifying motion, radiance. Ζεὺς of greeks; Jupiter of Romans; Osiris of egyptians.—"*a*" The second of the hindoo triad [trimoorty]; the preserver. During the period of temporary annihilation [pralayam] he is supposed to sleep on the waters floating on the serpent Sheshan [q.v.]. Bramha [q.v.] is said to have sprung from a lotus [nelumbo], which originally grew from the navel of Vishnoo, and the Ganges [gungay] springs from his foot; the different Avatars [q.v.] are considered as emanations of this deity, and in Krishnan [q.v.] he is supposed to have been really and wholly incarnate. Lutchmy [q.v.] is his wife; and he is usually represented as a mild and benevolent deity. In the vedic period Vishnoo was a god of subordinate importance, generally connected with Indran [q.v.], and seldom celebrated by himself. He did not rise much higher in the bramhanam [q.v.] period, at least among the bramins [q.v.] and cshatriyas [q.v.]. Presently however he was elevated to be the supreme god. The pooranic legend is, that from the navel of Narayanan [q.v.], or the first cause beneath the water, a lotus flower rose to the surface, and bore Bramha [q.v.] the creator; who disposed or set all things in order from Mauyay [q.v.] or matter, and handed over the preservation to Vishnoo, and destruction to Roodran [q.v.], both eminent like himself from Narayanan. The idea of a shacty [q.v.] for Vishnoo did not belong to the original system. That was superadded at a much later date by pooraunams [q.v.], and possibly after observing the effect produced by the Sheiveite dogma of a female energy. In the Matsya avatar [q.v.], the eight persons that escaped the deluge, Satyavratan [q.v.] and the seven rishies [q.v.], were all males; and it was only in the next or Coorma avatar [q.v.] that Lutchmy [q.v.] was produced from the ocean [samoodram]. Most of the pooraunams [q.v.] belong to the Vishnoo faith. The Mahabhaurat [q.v.], Ramayanam [q.v.] and Harivamsham, were written by votaries of Vishnoo.—"*b*" Of the Vishnoo worship the doctrine of the avatars [q.v.] or incarnations, literally descents, is the most characteristic feature. Vishnoo, when danger threatened either the devas [q.v.] or their worshippers, assumed certain terrestrial forms to assist them. The doctrine of the avatars afforded an opportunity of identifying Vishnoo with favourite heroes of tradition. Such were Rama [q.v.] or Ramchendran [q.v.], who extended his conquests to Ceylon; and Parshooraman [q.v.] the axe-rama, a native hero of the deccan [q.v.] whom the bramins canonized as the destroyer of all the cshatriyas. In the Krishna [q.v.] avatar the worship of Vishnoo reached its climax. Krishna was probably an aboriginal hero of some of the northern tribes. In the Bhagavatgeeta [q.v.] he appears as the preacher of the ethical pantheistic doctrine [vedauntam], and proclaims himself as the supreme being. In the Geeta govindam prominence is given to the legends of his miraculous birth, his intercourse with the shepherds, and his life with the shepherdesses [gopy], the remembrance of which was celebrated by special religious festivals [ooryady]; but this was a later production. When booddhism had ceased to be dangerous to the bramins, Booddha [q.v.] himself was included among the avatars [q.v.] of Vishnoo. At the end of this age or kaliyoog [q.v.] Vishnoo is to appear as Calky [q.v.], to root out all wickedness.—"*c*" In south indian history Veishnavism shows itself in three stages. The first is the simple and primitive system; the second is with the addition of herolatry, in the persons of Ramchendran, and Krishnan; the third, with the further addition of the Puncharautram [q.v.]. The Veishnava system is much more modern in the peninsula than the Sheiva system. Traditionally, the Shreepermatore temple is said to be the first Veishnava temple in the south. The twelve Alwars [q.v.] were the twelve apostles of the creed, and they with great zeal led the way in the first establishment of the system. By their followers they are almost deified. They composed the works known as Tirmozhy or sacred word; being matter from the Vedams [q.v.], rendered into tamul in an obscure idiom [tirvyemozhy]. Some of the oldest monuments of the Veishnava faith in s. india may be found in the ruins of Mauvellipore or the Seven pagodas. Though symbols of Shiva [q.v.] and sculptured representations of Parvaty [q.v.] are found in the multitude of figures represented there in the various reliefs, yet the chief subjects are selected from the legends attached to the Veishnava faith; the dwarf [vaumanan] incarnation of Vishnoo may be particularized [matam].—"*d*" The idols and pictorial representations of Vishnoo exhibit him by a human figure with four arms and hands. In two of his hands he holds nothing, having them ready to give blessings, and of the other two, which he raises, he holds in the right the Chuckram [q.v.] or discus, and in the left the Chunk [q.v.] or conch-shell. The color of his body is usually dark-blue. On his head he wears a crown, and on his forehead a red sign of custoory [q.v.] or spot [pottoo, tilacam] of musk or the sign tirnaumam [q.v.]. His hair, ears, neck, breast, body, hands, and feet are adorned with pearls [moty], precious stones [ratnam], gold [pon], and silver [velly]. His robe is embroidered with gold. From his shoulders a garland hangs and he stands on a lotus [nelumbo] flower. In the pagodas [coil, pagoda] two great lamps are left burning near the idol [shilay, vigraham]. The image which is carried about in the streets at festivals is of cast metal; but the one in the innermost part of the pagoda, to which daily offerings are made, is of stone. In honor of Vishnoo many pagodas of various sizes have been erected. In larger ones of these the following images are to be found:—Vishnoo's image of stone in the innermost part, which is daily as often worshipped as the lingam [q.v.] in eeshwaran's pagodas; Vishnoo's figure of metal, which is after the offering adorned with various jewels and ornaments especially when it is to be carried about in the streets at festivals; Maha lutchmy [q.v.], his consort, who stands in a small apartment of her own, and is daily worshipped together with her husband; her image is made both of stone and of metal; Dwaurapaulacans [q.v.], two door-keepers of ill-favored appearance standing at the entrance to the innermost apartment; Shellar, vishnoo's herald, who has a small place of his own, obtains a share in the worship, and takes always the lead at processions at festivals; Vatchicauran, a saint who has a small temple of his own; Pannirand alwar [q.v.], or the twelve devotees. The bird Garoodan [q.v.], Vishnoo's vehicle [vauhan], is found in all pagodas sacred to Vishnoo; and in the large pagodas at particularly sacred places many more images, chiefly forms of Vishnoo, representing him in his different incarnations and appearances, are found and adored together with those mentioned above. Vishnoo's ten avatars or incarnations are to be seen under Avatar. At the places where Vishnoo appeared and performed miracles, great pagodas have been erected. The most celebrated are those of Conjeevaram, Tripatty and Shreerungam. These are by pre-eminence respectively called Permaul coil, Tirmaley, Coil.—"*e*" Owing to his various incarnations and appearances, Vishnoo has many names, of which the following may be mentioned:—Atchyootan or the imperishable one, Alagya manavaula permaul or the beautiful bridegroom, Ananta shayanan or he who sleeps on the serpent anantan, Audinarrain or the supreme narayanan [q.v.], Audy varauhan or the supreme boar, Aulileimail pullicondone or he who took his abode on a banyan [q.v.] leaf, Bramhanaipettadhautry or bramha's father, Canavan or husband, Cariyavan or the black one, Condal vunnan or the cloud-colored, Codandaraman or rama as having the great bow codandam, Cunnan, Damodaran or he who was bound with a rope, Devaky meindan or devaky's mighty son, Gopaulan, Govindan, Hary, Jalaja lochanan or the lotus-eyed, Kelvan or lover or husband, Keshavan or he who has fine hair, Ketanan or the standard-bearer, Krishnan or the black one, Lutchmipaty or lutchmy's lord, Maudhavan, Maha vishnoo, Mooraury or the foe of mooran, Moocoondan or the bestower of salvation. Mauyone or the illusive, Narayanan, or the mover on the water, Narsimha moorty or man-lion form, Nediyone or the tall one, Nemiyone or the wearer of the discus weapon, Nundagopan or gopaulan or govindan or cowherd, Oolagoonda pemmaun or the great one in whose mouth the world appeared, Oondipoottone or he whose navel flowered, Padiyalandone or he who traversed the universe with three steps, Pudmanaubhan or the lotus-naveled, Pandavark dootan or the messenger of the pandavas, Partasauraty or arjoonan's charioteer, Peetaumbaran or the wearer of a silk or gold-colored garment, Permaul or the great person, Punchauyoodhan or he who has five weapons, Raghavan or rama as grandson of raghoo, Rama or the beautiful one, Ramasawmy or the god rama, Ramchendran or the moon-like rama, Shaurngapauny or the bowman, Shreedharan or the bearer of lutchmy, Shreerunganaickan or the lord of shreerungam, Soorimookha shankhamendy or the chunk-bearer, Tirmagan or the holy son, Tirmaul or vishnoo as lord of illusion, Vadamalaivaunan or the dweller on the mount of tripatty, Valavan or the mighty one, Vanamauly or the wearer of a garland of the basil [toolsy] plant, Varadaraja permaul or the benign king, Vausoodevan or krishnan, the son of vasoodevan, Vaumanan or dwarf, Veicoontanautan or the lord of veicoontam, Vencateshwara permaul or vencatachellamoorty or lord of tripatty, Vindoo or wind or cloud.—"*f*" About Vishnoo a great number of books have been written, which are regarded as authoritative in matters of religion; and every large pagoda [coil, pagoda] has a local pooraunam, [q.v.], in which the story believed to have happened at the places is described. Among the books that treat of Vishnoo in tamul, the following may be mentioned:—Baula caunda ramayanam or a part of the ramayanam, treating of rama's youth; Bharata ammaunay or a book of the same contents with bhauratam but written in less difficult poetical language; Canjan ammaunay or a book containing the story of cumsan, krishnan's maternal uncle, who intended to kill krishnan when a child; Coodanthay antaudy, a prayer-book in praise of vishnoo at combaconum, otherwise tircoodanthay; Covil calambagam or a collection of 100 songs in honor of vishnoo, sung everywhere in the pagodas; Gajendra mocsham or a book about the elephant gajendran, which was attacked by a crocodile [mugger] while bathing, but was saved by vishnoo and transferred to bliss; Garooda punchaucsharam or a book of muntrams [q.v.], in which the bird garoodan [q.v.] the vehicle [vauhan] of vishnoo and destroyer of snakes, is invoked for enchanting snakes and counteracting their poison; Hanooman ammaunay, a part of the ramayanam [q.v.], treating of the ape hanooman [q.v.] who assisted rama [q.v.] in his war with ravanan [q.v.]; Indrajit patalam or a description of rama's war with indrajit, ravanan's son and the conqueror of indran; Krishnan tooth or a description of krishnan as ambassador of the pandoos [q.v.] to dooryodhanan [q.v.]; Mahabhaurat [q.v.], containing a description of the war of the five pandoos, assisted by krishnan [q.v.], with dooryodhanan and his brethren; Narrain shatacam containing prayers to vishnoo as narayanan; Naugapausha patalam about a noose similar to a snake, said to kill the enemy by itself; Permaul ammaunay, a collection of different stories concerning vishnoo; Pillay tamul or a collection of 1,000 songs about vishnoo's birth and childish plays; Ramajayam or a description of vishnoo's deeds in his incarnations; Ramayanam about rama, by the poet cumban; Sambanda pillay tirnaumam or 100 songs by tirmangay alwar [q.v.]; Shreerungaraja ammaunay containing diffuse stories about vishnoo; Tirpoogazh poem setting forth the praises of vishnoo; Varkaicovay a collection of songs; Vazhippatt prayers to vishnoo, and is read when a veishnava is about to die; Vencata maulay 100 songs about vishnoo's glory in general; Vishnoomel vunnam an ode on vishnoo; Yecaudashy pooraunam, the legend of the origin of the fast yecaudashy [q.v.].—"*g*" To Vishnoo two wives are ascribed, viz., Lutchmy and Bhoomidevy. In the opinion of the Veishnavas, Lutchmy is what Parvaty is with the Sheivas, namely the feminine power or energy of the supreme being, emanating from the masculine energy as a distinct being. And as Shacty [q.v.] or Parvaty [q.v.] is said to have multiplied into many shacties, so Lutchmy [q.v.] is said to have become Ashta lutchmy [q.v.] or eight Lutchmies. Maha lutchmy, Vishnoo's wife, is the chief one, in whom the other seven are both contained and worshipped. As the goddess of beauty and prosperity, Lutchmy is much reverenced even by the Sheivas, who have placed her image in Eeshwarans' pagodas; which honor they by no means confer on Vishnoo. Lutchmy is also said to have risen from the sea of milk [samoodram], when it was churned by the gods with the view of obtaining the beverage of immortality, named amritam [q.v.]. To Vishnoo are ascribed three sons, viz., Manmatan, Cooshan, and Lavan.—"*h*" The manner in which vishnoo is worshipped by the Veishnavas is very much like that in which Shiva is worshipped by the Sheivas; that is to say thrice every day offerings are made to the image in the pagodas, and privileged persons worship him also in their houses. The latter are called Tirnaumam teertam pannoogiravar, and must observe a particular diet, and not defile themselves with anything. Moreover, corresponding to the Sheiva order of Aundies [q.v.], there are the Veishnava orders of the Dausary [q.v.] and Beiraugies [q.v.]. The festivals that are celebrated in honor of Vishnoo are as numerous as his appearances and miracles. Two of his festivals are celebrated all over the land, viz., the Jayanty [q.v.] and Permaul tirnaul [q.v.]. The first falling in August is Krishnan's birth-day, at which the circumstances connected with his birth are acted in the pagodas. The duration of the festival depends on the revenues of the pagoda; in rich pagodas it lasts several days, in poor ones only one day. The other festival, Permaul tirnaul, lasts nine or ten days; it is however not like the Jayanty celebrated everywhere at the same time, but whenever it is most convenient to the people of a place. It is also called Tircalyaunam [q.v.], because Vishnoo's marriage with Lutchmy is acted on it, while Vishnoo and Lutchmy are carried about in the streets on great cars. The famous pagodas sacred to Vishnoo have each five cars [rath], of which the first is used for Vishnoo as rama [q.v.], the second for Lutchmy as seetay [q.v.], the third for Lutchmanan [q.v.], the fourth for Bharatan, and the fifth for Shatroognan. The three last named, or Rama's brothers, are regarded as partial incarnations of Vishnoo. Among the fasts observed in honor of Vishnoo there are three principal. First, Yecaudashy [q.v.] vratam, a fast on the eleventh day after every new [amavausyay] and full moon [powrnimay]; this is believed to be very meritorious; its observance however is optional. Secondly, Veicoontayecaudashy [q.v.], a fast observed once a year in december, when the people fast the whole day and adore Vishnoo, taking in the evening either pancakes, or merely water consecrated by the leaves of toolsy [q.v.], and spend the night in watching and meditating; this fast is also called Swargavausal yecaudashy, that is to say, the door to heaven; and Bheema yecaudashy [bheeshma yecaudashy], because it was instituted by Bheeman, one of the five Pandavas [q.v.]; Bheeman could not bear hunger, but in order to fast at least once in the year, he observed this fast. Thirdly, Pooratanshy shanikizhamay, a fast observed on the four saturdays of the month [mausam] of pooratanshy [pooratanshy shany kizhamay] or september-october. Among those who observe this fast many make a pilgrimage to the pagoda at Tripatty, where in the month of september a great festival is celebrated.—"*i*" The Veishnavas in the Tamul country wear on their foreheads the figure called Tirnaumam or holy name [naumam]. Besides this they paint on their arms two other signs, viz., the Chunk [q.v.] shell and Chuckram [q.v.] discus, weapons of Vishnoo. Their principal form of prayer, called Ashtaucsharam [q.v.] or eight characters, is thus Omnamonaraynnaya, or Om salutation to narayanan [q.v.].—"j" In Southern india, compared with the Sheivas, Veishnavas are only as about one to four. Their two principal divisions are Madhwacharries and Shreeveishnavas; the latter again being sub-divided into the Tengalays and Vadagalays. See all those heads. See vol. I (76), (85) [matam].——*Vishnoo bhactan* (विष्णुभक्त - vishnubhakta, San.). From (vishnu, san. the deity + bhaj, san. to adore). Worshipper of Vishnoo.——*Vishnoochittan* (ವಿಷ್ಣುಚಿತ್ತ - vishnuchitta, Can.). From (vishnu, san. the deity + chitta, san. mind), devoted to vishnoo. Also called Vijayandityan. Cadamba [q.v.] king of Goa. A.D. 1147—1175.——*Vishnoo craunty* (विष्णुक्रान्ता - vishnukrántá, San. and Mahr.; विष्णुक्रान्ति - vishnukránti, Conc.; ವಿಷ್ಣುಕ್ರಾಂತಿ - vishnukránti, Can.; విష్ణుక్రాంతము - vishnukrántamu, Tel.; വിഷ്ണുക്രാന്തി - vishnukránti, Mal. and Singh.; விஷ்ணுக்கிராந்தி - vittunukkirándi, Tam.). San. from (vishnu, san. the deity + kránta, san. surpassing); from blue flowers. San. also (añjanapushpa), meaning black flower; (satinálika), meaning small powerful plant, from supposed medicinal virtue; (aparájitá), meaning not conquered [crow-creeper]; (vishnugandhi), meaning vishnoo + fragrance; (vaishnava), meaning relating to vishnoo. Hind. also (sankpushpi), meaning conch shell flower [crowcreeper]. Can. also (niligida), meaning dark blue + plant. Tel. also (nallavishnukrántamu), meaning black + the plant. Singh. also (nilapushpi), meaning blue-flowered plant. Tam. also (vittunukkándi), meaning vishnoo colour or dark blue. Title otherwise Chickweed, Monkeywort, Vishnoo blue, Vishnoo plant. Botanically Evolvulus alsinoides, linn., convolvulaceæ [vricsham, 93]. Alias Evolvulus angustifolius, hirsutus, hirtus; Nama convolvuloides, evolvuloides. Procumbent; stem, scarcely any; branches numerous, covered when young with long, soft, white hairs; leaves alternate, bifarious, sub-sessile, oblong, entire, hairy on both sides; peduncles axillary, solitary, longer than the leaves, pointed near the middle, one to three flowered, erect while in blossom, afterwards drooping; calyx of five segments, lanceolate; corolla companulate; flowers small, blue with a white tube, like forget me not; in dry ground plant almost covers the soil. In vedic period was believed to promote conception; veidyans [q.v.] still consider it to possess virtues in bowel-complaints, and prescribe it in infusion; substituted for british cinchona [koinah] bark and logwood. Plant eaten as greens [keeray] during famine. No other common species here. The title Vishnoocraunty is also applied to the Crow-creeper [q.v.].——*Vishnoo deepam* (విష్ణుదీపం - vishnudípam, Tel.). Means vishnoo + light. Luni-solar [chaundramaunam] festival [pundigay, 6a]. Celebrated on the day after Caurtigay [q.v.], considered to be the day on which Balychuckravurty obtained immortality, he being one of the seven Chiranjeevies [q.v.]. The attendant festival lasts ten or eleven days, and at some places still longer [maryauday].——*Vishnoogopa varman* (ವಿಷ್ಣುಗೋಪವರ್ಮಾ - vishnugópavarmá, Can.), From (vishnu, san. the deity + gópa, san. protector + varman, san. coat, title), one who has vishnoo as his protecting deity. Name of Chera [q.v.] king in Malabar.——*Vishnoo matam* (विष्णुमत - vishnumata, San.). From (vishnoo, san. the deity + mata, san. creed). The creed of the Veishnavites.——*Vishnoo priyam* (विष्णुप्रिय - vishnupriya, San.). Means dear to vishnoo; the flowers offered to him. Same as Adam's apple.——*Vishnoo's navel* (திருமாலுந்தி - tirumálundi, Tam.). Same as Nelumbo.——*Vishnoo's tree* (நாராயணம் - náráyanam, Tam.). Same as Peepul.——*Vishnoovardhanan* (ವಿಷ್ಣುವರ್ಧನ - vishnuvardhana, Can.). From (vishnu, san. the deity + vardhana, san. increase). He who has propagated the vishnoo faith. Also called Bitty deva. Name of a Hoysala ballaula [q.v.] king. A.D. 1117—1137. See vol. I (130), (142).——*Vishwacarmeeyam* (विश्वकर्मीय - vishvakarmíya, San.). A treatise on architecture [staupatyam].——*Vishwacurman* (विश्वकर्मा - vishvakarmá, San.; விசுவகருமன் - visuvagaruman, Tam.). From (vishwa, san. all + kri, san. to do). Son of Bramha [q.v.]. ἥφαιστος of grecks; Vulcan of romans; Thoth of egyptians. He was also named Cowshican; from his attempting to create a man with three eyes in his head, from a cocoanut [q.v.] and other materials. The architect of the universe, and the fabricator of arms for the gods. He presides over the arts and trades.——*Vishwa goonah darsham* (विश्वगुणादर्श - vishvagunádarsha, San.). From (vishwa, san. all + guna, san. property + ádarsha, san. mirror). Mirror of the virtues of the work. By Vencatacharry, a native of Conjeeveram, lived about 1600. This work is almost the only modern S. indian production that shows originality. It is an imaginary voyage over India by two gandharvans [q.v.], one of whom praises, while the other decries, all he sees.——*Vishwam* (विश्व - vishva, San.; விசுவம் - visuvam, Tam.). From (vish, san. to pervade). All world. The universe, the τὸ πᾶν of the Greeks. Vishwaroopam is in philosophy universal substance, that which exists in all forms. Compare Viraat. Vishwam is a name assumed by the goldsmith caste [tattaun]; the first man from whom they claim their descent being Vishwa curman, the architect of the world, the hindoo vulcan. Proper name. Familiar contraction of names which it begins [peyar].——*Vishwa mitran* (विश्वामित्र - vishvámitra, San.). Means friend of all. One of the Rishies [q.v.], and the Gooroo [q.v.] of Ramachendran [q.v.]. He was seduced by Rambhay [q.v.] while engaged in austerities, at the instigation of Indran [q.v.].——*Vishwanautan* (विश्वनाथ - vishvanát'ha, San.). From (vishva, san. all + nát'ha, san. lord). Shiva [vishweshwaran]. Tamul dramatic author of this century; wrote Tahsildar nautacam [q.v.], and Dambacharry vilausam [q.v.].——*Vishwanauta naick* (விசுவநாதநாயக்கன் - visuvanáthanáyakkan, Tam.). Name + 3rd name. Founder of the Naick [q.v.] dynasty [raj], of Madura. See vol. I (121); II, 250.——*Vishwedevah* (विश्वेदेवाः - vishvédéváh, San.). From (vishva, san. all + déva, san. god). All the gods [deva] collectively. The personified gods; as love, perseverance, truth, riches and time.——*Vishweshwaran* (विश्वेश्वर - vishvéshvara, San.). From (vishva, san. all + íshvara, san. lord). Shiva [vishwanautan].——*Vissanapett* (విస్సన్నపేట - vissannapéta, Tel.). See sep. title.

VISHOO (విషు - vishu, *Tel.*; വിഷു - vishu, *Mal.*). Corruption of (dvishu, san. loc. pl. of dvi, san. two); means in two equal parts. The equinoctial point [ayanam, craunty pautam] or the first point either of Aries [maisham] or Libra [toolaum] into which the sun [sooryan] enters at the vernal or autumnal equinox respectively [maishauyanam, toolauyanam]. Solar [madhyama sowra maunam] festival [pundigay, 2b] at what passes for the vernal equinox [maishauyanam], and actually at the astronomical new year's day [new year, nowroz] calculated on the siderial principle. Otherwise Maha vishoo. Distinguish from Vishoo poonyacaulam or toolauyanam below. It stands now at 12th april against 21st march the real vernal equinox [maunam, mausam]. The Malayauly is very superstitious about his conduct on this day, and the first thing that comes under his observation on the morning of the day is believed to be significant of the luck that will attend him throughout the year, then commencing. Hence the collection beforehand in houses of costly and auspicious objcets, and hence the annual presents to superiors.——*Vishoo poonya caulam* (విషుపుణ్యకాలం - vishupunyakálam, Tel.; വിഷുവൽപുണ്യകാലം - vishuvatpunyakálam, Mal.). Means the equinoctial point + auspicious time; the autumnal equinox. Commonly Toola snaunam or ablution in the month of toolaum. The first day of seventh solar month Arpisy [mausam] or 16th Octobar. Solar festival [pundigay, 2b] when the sun [sooryan] is supposed to enter the sign [raushy] Toolaum ♎ [q.v.]. Much the same observances as for Vishoo [jyotisham, maryauday].——*Vishoovam* (विषुव - vishuva, San.). The equinoctial points; called also Ayanam, Dhroovam and Craunty pautam. Vishoovamundalam is equinoctial colure [maishauyanamundalam]. For solstitial colure see Yaumyottara vrittam.

VISSANAPETT (విస్సన్నపేట - vissannapéta, *Tel.*). From (vissanna, tel. proper name + péta, tel. suburb) [vish]. After one vissam rauz —(1) Division, Kistna. Area 324 square miles. Population 61,118. Language Teloogoo. N. of district. Boundaries east Noozveed division, south Bezwada talook and Nizam's dominions, west Nizam's dominions and Nundigauma talook, north Nizam's dominions. Physical aspect elevated and jungly. Soil partly sandy [manal] and partly red ferruginous [sevval munn]. Agriculture and timber trade. Irrigation by rain-fed tanks [q.v.]. Trig. stations:—Daulgutt, Jamalavoy droog. The leading places, &c., in the division are the following.——*Calagara* (కలగర - kalagara, Tel.). Means a plant, eclipta alba, hassk. Zemindarry, Village; pop. 664; lat. of village 17° 01′; long. 80° 49′; from Masulipatam N.N.W. 60 miles; from Tirvore S.E. 13 miles. The ex-zemindars belong to the Vellanky family, who still retain some territory in the north of the district and have some claims over villages within the Nizam's dominions. They trace their pedigree back to Rajah vellanky mulla row, who had authority in the three pergunnahs [q.v.] of Canacagherry, Jamalavoy, Medoorghaut under the Mussulman kings of Golcondah. In 1834, when arrears had accumulated upon the estate, it was subdivided and sold.——*Daulgutt* (దాల్గట్టు - dálgattu, Tel.). From (dálu, tel. brightness + gattu, tel. hill). Trig. station; lat. 16° 53′ 38·75″; long. 80° 50′ 41·95″; height 1,413 feet; from Condavarava W. 3 miles; from Vissannapett S. 4 miles.——*Gumpalagoodem* (గంపలగూడెము - gampalagúdemu, Tel.). From (gampa, tel. basket + gúdemu, tel. village). Zemindarry, Village; pop. 1,982; lat. of village 17° 00′; long. 80° 36′; from Masulipatam N.W. 68 miles; from Tirvore S.W. 10 miles. Zemindars belong to Vellanky family. Peshcush Rs. 2,586 [calagara]. Two temples.——*Inagadapa* (ఇనగడప - inagadapa, Tel.). From (inumu, tel. iron + kadapa, tel. threshold). Zemindarry, Village; pop. 943; lat. of village 16° 59′; long. 80° 33′; from Masulipatam N.W. 66 miles; from Tirvore S.S.W. 11 miles. Zemindars belong to Vellanky family [calagara]. Old temple. Peshcush Rs. 1,236.——*Jamalavoy droog* (జమలావాయిదుర్గము - dzamalaváyidurgamu, Tel.). See sep. title.——*Ootcore* (ఊటుకూరు - útukúru, Tel.). From (úta, tel. spring + úru, tel. village). Zemindarry, Village; pop. 1,239; lat. of village 17° 01′; long. 80° 28′; from Masulipatam N.W. 72 miles; from Tirvore S.W. 13 miles. Head-quarters of the zemindar of the same village. An old small fort. Peshcush Rs. 2,156.——*Pootrails*

(పుట్రేల - putréla, Tel.). From (putta, tel. ant-hill + régu, tel. tree, zizyphus jujuba, lamk.). Zemindarry, Village; pop. 1,504; lat. of village 7° 02'; long. 80° 45'; from Masulipatam N.N.W. 63 miles; from Tirvore S.E. 9 miles. Peshcush Rs. 510.——*Sanoobanda* (తనుబంద - tanubanda, Tel.). See sep. title.——*Tirvore* (తిరువూరు - tiruvúru, Tel.). See sep. title.——*Vissanapett* (విస్సన్నపేట - vissannapéta, Tel.). See below.——**(2)** Deputy tahsildarry, Kistna district. Pay Rs. 100.——**(3)** Zemindarry, village; Kistna dist., Vissanapett division; pop. 2,018; lat. of village 16° 57'; long. 80° 50'; from Musulipatam N.N.W 56 miles; from Tirvore S.S.E. 17 miles. Peshcush Rs. 4,886. Six irrigation tanks [q.v.]. Formerly head-quarters of the zemindar [q.v.].

VITHAY (விதை - vithai, *Tam.*). Seed [veejam, viray].——*Viraippaud* (விரைப்பாடு - viraippádu, Tam.). From (above + padu, tam. to fall); seed-fall or seed sowing; amount of seed required to sow a plot or field. Measure of ground by amount of seed required to sow it. Compare Vithaicottay.——*Viray* (விரை - virai, Tam.). Common form of vithay; see initial letter R. Seed [veejam, vithay]; one of the Dravidian terms for plant products added to the word-root [vricsham]. —*Vithaicottay* (விதைக்கோட்டை - vithaikkóttai, Tam.). From (above + kóttai, tam. quantity of grain made up in straw in the form of a wisp or dutch cheese). Superficial measure [viraippaud]. 21 mercauls = 1 vithaicottay [alavay, 2a]. Approximate actual value, 1 vithaicottay = 1·6208 acres. Used in Tinnevelly. Same as Dhaunya cottay. Compare teloogoo Veesam, tamul Cawny.

VITTALA (विठ्ठल - vitt'hala, *San.*). Vishnoo, especially at Punderpoor in Bombay presidency. Hindoo 2nd or pers. name. Common among Madhwas and Mahrattas [peyar].

VIZAGAPATAM * (اسحاقپٹن - ishákpatan, *Hind.*; విశాఖపట్టణము - vishákhapattanamu, *Tel.*). From (vishákha, san epithet of skanda + pattana, san. city) [vi]; from soobramanyan [vishaukhan] temple which once existed but now washed away by sea. Ancient name (tírt'hapurállu), meaning holy waters + rock.——**(1)** Revenue district; on Coromandel coast; between 17° 14' and 20° 06' N. lat., and between 81° 25' and 84° 06' E. long.; bounded N. by Ganjam district and Central provinces, E. by Ganjam district and the sea, S. by the sea and Godavery district, W. by Central provinces; square miles 17,223; pop. non-agency 1,943,211; agency 859,781; language Teloogoo and Ooriya. Contains rivers Chittivalsa, Gostany, Indrauvaty, Matchair, Naugauvaly, Shaurada nuddy, Sillair, Varauhanuddy, Vamshadhaura; ports Bimlipatam, Conauda, Pentacote, Poodimadaca, Vizagapatam; mountains Eastern ghauts and Neemgherries; sanitarium Keilausam. The whole area of the district is represented by the following sub-areas, where talook [q.v.]. means an ordinary ryotwarry [q.v.] area administered by a Tahsildar [q.v.], and division means a Zemindarry [q.v.] tract administered by a superior Deputy tahsildar:—Ankapully division, Bimlipatam division, Bissemcuttack division, Bobbily division, Cheepoorpully division, Coraputt division, Gajapatinugger division, Golcondah talook, Goonapore division, Jeypore division, Mulkangherry division, Nowrungapore division, Padair division, Palcondah talook, Parvatipore division, Pottinghy division, Royagada division, Sarwasiddhy talook, Saulore division, Srungavarapoocote division, Veeravilly division, Vizagapatam division, Vizianagram division. For general administrative purposes the district is distributed between the following revenue and magisterial officers, who have their head-quarters at the places shown. The pay set opposite the subordinate officers gives the grade of the corresponding charge:—Collector, Vizagapatam. Principal assistant collector, Narsapatam, in charge of Golcondah and Sarwasiddhy talooks and Veeravilly, Ankapully and Padair magisterial divisions. Senior assistant collector, Parvatipore, in charge of Parvatipore, Bobbily, Saulore, Goonapore, Royagada, and Bissemcuttack magisterial divisions. General duty deputy collector, Vizianagram, in charge of Palcondah talook and Vizianagram, Gajapatinugger, Cheepoorpully and Bimlipatam magisterial divisions. Huzoor general duty deputy collector, Vizagapatam, in charge of Vizagapatam and Srungavarapoocote magisterial divisions. Special assistant agent, Coraputt, in charge of Coraputt, Jeypore, Nowrungapore, Mulkangherry and Pottinghy magisterial divisions. Tahsildars; Golcondah, Rs. 150; Sarwasiddhy, Rs. 150. Deputy tahsildars; Ankapully, Rs. 100, Bimlipatam, Rs. 70, Bissemcuttack, Rs. 120, Bobbily, Rs. 100, Cheepoorpully, Rs. 70, Coraputt, Rs. 200, Gajapatinugger, Rs. 70, Goonapore, Rs. 200, Jeypore, Rs. 150, Mulkangherry, Rs. 150, Nowrungapore, Rs. 150, Padair, Rs. 120, Palcondah, Rs. 100, Parvatipore, Rs. 100, Pottinghy, Rs. 120, Royagada, Rs. 150, Saulore, Rs. 100, Srungavarapoocote, Rs. 70, Veeravilly, Rs. 70, Vizagapatam, Rs. 100, Vizianagram, Rs. 100. Similarly judicial officers:—Ordinary tracts. Judge, Vizagapatam; District moonsifs, Vizagapatam with jurisdiction extending over Vizagapatam, Bimlipatam and Ankapully; Yellamanchily with jurisdiction extending over Sarwasiddhy and Golcondah; Chodavaram with jurisdiction extending over Veeravilly and Srungavarapoocote; Vizianagaram with jurisdiction extending over Vizianagaram and Gajapatinugger; Rajam with jurisdiction extending over Palcondah and Cheepoorpully; Parvatipore with jurisdiction extending over Parvatipore, Saulore and Bobbily. Agency tracts:—Judge, Agent to the Governor. District moonsifs; Golcondah with jurisdiction extending over Golcondah talook agency portion; Narrainpatam with jurisdiction extending over Parvatipore division agency portion; Royagada with jurisdiction extending over Royagada and Bissemcuttack divisions; Goonapore with jurisdiction extending over Goonapore division; Coraputt with jurisdiction extending over Coraputt division; Jeypore with jurisdiction extending over Jeypore division; Mulkangherry with jurisdiction extending over Mulkangherry division; Nowrungapore with jurisdiction extending over Nowrungapore division; Pottinghy with jurisdiction extending over Pottinghy division; Srungavarapoocote with jurisdiction extending over Srungavarapoocote division agency portion. Similarly Public works officers:—Executive engineer, Waltair; Sub-Divisional officers, Coraputt, Vizianagram, Vizagapatam. Contains Registration sub-districts, Ankapully, Bimlipatam, Bobbily, Cheepoorpully, Gajapatinugger, Narsapatam, Palcondah, Parvatipore, Saulore, Srungavarapoocote, Chodavaram, Vizagapatam, Vizianagram and Yellamanchily. Contains Forest ranges Sarwasiddhy, Palcondah and Golcondah. Contains Municipalities, Ankapully, Bimlipatam, Vizagapatam, Vizianagram. Contains District board; and Talook boards; Vizagapatam embracing Vizagapatam division and the ordinary tracts of Srungavarapoocote division; Narsapatam embracing Golcondah talook excluding Agency tract, Sarwasiddhy talook and Ankapully and Veeravilly divisions; Vizianagram embracing Vizianagram, Bimlipatam, Gajapatinugger, Cheepoorpully and Palcondah exclusive of Agency tract divisions; and Parvatipore embracing Bobbily, Saulore and Parvatipore exclusive of Agency tract divisions. Ancient and hill zemindarries:—Andra, Belgaum, Bobbily, Causipore, Chemoodoo, Cooroopaum, Jeypore, Madgole, Merangy, Pauchipenta, Sangamvalasa, Saripully bheemavaram, Saulore, Vizianagram. Proprietary estates:—Allipooram, Ankapully, Appicondah, Bayyavaram, Bharanicam, Cassimcote, Cheepoorpully, Chidicauda, Condala agrahauram, Cooppily, Cooraunda condayyavalsa, Corprole, Eedoolpauca bonangy, Goodicherla, Juggampett ten villages, Jugganuautapooram, Kintalay, Maddilapollem, Maumidivauda, Melpauca, Moouagapauk, Muntena, Naccapilly, Oongarauda, Ooratla, Pandoor mullavaram, Pedda goommoolore, Poolleta, Rauvauda, Shermahomedpooram, Shreepooram, Shreerampooram, Siddeshwaram, Sowdvauda, Tungaid and Gotivauda, Waltair. The following general references should be made to the preceding volumes:—general geography, I (1) to (29); general ethnology, I (29) to (109); general history, I (110) to (138); physical geography, II, 1; meteorology, II, 3; geology, II, 8; fauna, II, 21; flora, II, 26; mineralogy, II, 29. The following references in the preceding volumes will furnish details special to the district:—latitudes and longitudes, II, 47; particulars about towns, II, 48; coast survey, II, 166; light-houses, II, 169; comparative population, II, 172; location of revenue officers, II, 391; registrars' and sub-registrars' stations, II, 422; ports, II, 423; salt factories, II, 426; rain-guage stations, II, 428; police divisions, II, 431; maps published, II, 436; hospitals and dispensaries, II, 447; head-quarter stations of gazetted officers, II, 461; incidence of taxation, II, 463; weights and measures of the district, II, 519; zemindarries contained, I, 54, and II, 301; agencies contained, I, 68. A special gazetteer account of the whole district is given at II, 139. For the detailed topography of the district, reference should be made to the talook notices in the present volume, viz.:—Ankapully, Bimlipatam, Bissemcuttack, Bobbily, Cheepoorpully, Coraputt, Golcondah, Goonapore, Gajapatinugger, Jeypore, Mulkangherry, Nowrungapore, Padair, Palcondah, Parvatipore, Pottinghy, Royagada, Saulore, Sarwasiddhy Srungavarapoocote, Veeravilly, Vizagapatam, Vizianagram.——**(2)** Division; Vizagapatam district; area 173 square miles; population 97,301; language Teloogoo. Central coast of district. Boundaries north Bimlipatam and Srungavarapoocote divisions; east and south Bay of Bengal; west Ankapully division. Studded with hills, valleys and swamps. Soil; northern portion rocky and gravelly, western sandy, impregnated with salt [ooppoo]. Vizagapatam is noted for its ivory [dant] and horn [sing] manufactures and for the manufacture of jewellery worn by natives. Poonjam [q.v.] cloths are made at Vizagapatam and superfine native cloths are woven at Allipore from imported yarn. The port of Vizagapatam has a large and increasing trade. The principal articles of export are jaggery [q.v.], seeds, drugs, skins [chamrah], and hides [chamrah], horns [sing], turmeric [country saffron] and poonjam cloth. Imports piece goods, paddy [q.v.] and rice [q.v.], metals [loham], oilmanstores, spices, teak [q.v.]. Irrigation, mainly rainfed tanks. The following are places of archæological interest within the division:—Appicondah, Maudhavadhaura, Narava, Pinagaudy, Shree simhauchellam, Vizagapatam. Principal trig. stations:—Cootcondah beacon, Peddacondah, Rishicondah beacon, Yarauda. The leading places, &c., in the division are the following.——*Allipooram* (అల్లిపురము - allipuramu, Tel.). See sep. title. ——*Appicondah* (అప్పికొండ - appikonda, Tel.). From (ap, san. water + konda, tel. hill). Proprietary estate, Village, Place of pilgrimage; pop. 735; lat. of village 17° 34'; long. 83° 13'; from Vizagapatam S.W. 11 miles; from the sea W. ½ mile. Peshcush Rs. 601. Formerly part of Cheepoorpully estate. Shrine to Shiva as Someshwaran; large yautray [q.v.] every Shivarautry [pundigay, 6a]. The performance of Aujya vaicshanam ceremony at this pagoda [q.v.] is lucky. Numerous pagodas [coil, pagoda] formerly but covered over with sand-drifts.——*Cooraúda condayyavalsa* (కూరాడకొండయ్యవలస - kúrádakondayyavalasa, Tel.). From (kúráda, tel. village so called + kondayyavalasa, tel. village so called). Means two village clubbed. Proprietary estate, Village; pop. 749; lat. of village 17° 39′; long. 83° 12′; from Vizagapatam W. 10 miles; from the sea W. 7 miles. Peshcush Rs. 681. ——*Cootcondah beacon* (కుత్తుకొండ - kutukonda, Tel.). From (kuttu, tel. neck + konda, tel. hill). Trig. station; lat. 17° 34′ 02·00″, long. 83° 12′ 51·49″; from Appicondah S. ¾ mile; from Vizagapatam S.W. 12 miles; from the sea W. ⅓ mile.——*Dolphin's nose* (డాల్ఫిన్నగ్రము - dálp'hinnagramu, Tel.). See sep. title.——*Keilausam* (కైలాసము - kailásamu, Tel.). See sep. title.——*Maddilapollem* (మద్దిలపాలెము - maddilapálemu, Tel.). From (maddela, tel. drum + pálemu, tel. fortified village). Zemindarry village; pop. 883; Peshcush Rs. 883.——*Padagaudy* (పడగాడి - padagádi, Tel.). From (padaga, tel. banner + váda, tel. village). Village; pop. 2,295; lat. 17° 46′; long. 83° 21′; from Vizagapatam N.N.E. 5 miles; from the sea W. 3 miles.——*Peddacondah* (పెద్దకొండ - peddakonda, Tel.). From (pedda, tel. great + konda, tel. hill). Trig. station; lat. 17° 51′ 02·42″; long. 83° 22′ 37·11″; from Maricavalsa N.W. 2 miles; from Vizagapatam N. 11 miles; from the sea W. 6 miles.——*Rishicondah* (ఋషికొండ - rishikonda, Tel.). See sep. title.——*Simhauchellam* (సింహాచలము - simháchalamu, Tel.). See sep. title.——*Vizagapatam* (విశాఖపట్టణము - vishákhapattanamu, Tel.). See below.——*Waltair* (వాల్తేరు - vâltéru, Tel.). See sep. title.——*Yarauda* (యారాడ - yárâda, Tel.). From (éru, tel. river + váda, tel. village). Trig. station; lat. 17° 40′ 07·90″; long. 83° 17′ 45·77″; height 1,174 feet; from Vizagapatam S.W. 4 miles; from the sea W. 2 miles.——**(3)** Zemindarry; Vizagapatam dist., Vizagapatam division; pop. 34,487.——**(4)** Deputy tahsildarry, Vizagapatam dist. Pay Rupees 100.——**(5)** Town, Municipality, Port, Head-quarters of Collector, Revenue divisional officer, Deputy inspector-general of police and Salt deputy and Assistant commissioners, Superintendent of Police, Talook magistrate, District and Moonsif's courts, Observatory, Telegraph office; Vizagapatam dist., Vizagapatam division; pop. 34,487; lat. 17° 42′; long. 83° 20′; from Bimlipatam S.W. 17 miles; from Calcutta S.W. 470; from Coraputt S.S.E. 84 miles; from Madras N.E. 372; from Masulipatam N.E. 174; from Narsapatam E. 45 miles; from Parvatipore S.S.W. 74 miles; from Poodimadaca N.E. 23 miles; from Vizianagram S.S.W. 29 miles. On the Orissa coast [q.v.] in a small bay, the south extremity of which is bounded by the Dolphin's nose and the northern extremity by Waltair. To the west lies a large swamp, which is being reclaimed by Roman catholic missionaries. The town is separated from the Dolphin's nose by a small river, which forms a bar where it enters the sea, but is passable for vessels of 300 tons during spring tides. The best anchorage in the roads is with the castle on Dolphin's nose, S.W. ½ W. to S.S.W.; Sugarloaf hill from N.E. ½ N. to N.N.E.; Doorga hill from W. by N. to W.N.W.; Fort flag staff from N.W. to W.N.W.; with the mouth of the river open 6½ to 8 fathoms. A ferry plies between the north and south sides of the river. A pontoon bridge was constructed over the river on the road to Ankapully in 1887, and is known as Turner bridge. Within the site of the old fort are public buildings. The pettah [q.v.] immediately adjoins fort on its north and west sides; but shut in by sandhills to north, and the swamp already mentioned. The climate is unfavorable to Europeans. According to tradition founded by an Andhra king, Coolotoonga cholan, about the middle of the twelfth century. With the rest of the Calinga country, it fell to the Mussalman invador, and formed part of the Chicacole circar [q.v.] when Europeans first appeared on the scene. About the middle of the seventeenth century, the East india company established its factory. Factory seized and English officers murdered by Moghul's orders on 13th September 1689, owing to rupture between Aurungzeeb and Company. Cowle [q.v.] for factory renewed by Zoolfacar khan the Moghul [q.v.] general in the Deccan [q.v.], 28th December 1690. Factory allowed to be fortified by the same authority, April 1692. Entered in the dead stock account taken on the union of the two East india companies in 1702. Attack by Fakr ool lah khan, a local Nawaub [q.v.], repulsed 8th November 1710. Firmaun [q.v.] from the Emperor Ferokshere confirming the possession of the settlement, 1716. In 1726 garrison raised to thirty soldiers. Neither Jaffer ally nor his Mahratta mercenaries, who sacked Bimlipatam and harried the whole countryside, touched Vizagapatam; and save for a few months in 1757, when Bussy occupied the town, the company had undisturbed possession. The Rajah of Vizianagram took it from the French, and restored it to the English on 12th September 1758. Grant confirmed by the Moghul's firmaun [q.v.], dated 12th August 1765. Finally ceded by the Nizam together with the rest of the Northern circars [q.v.], 23rd February 1768. As a sea-port, is gradually increasing in business. Imports chiefly of piece-goods and metals from England. Principal exports are grain [dhaunyam] and sugar [q.v.]. The special industries of the town, elk horn and ivory knick-knacks, and silver filigreework, are well known. Residence of a Roman catholic vicar apostolic. The town owes much to the Maharajah of Vizianagram and the Goday [q.v.] family of Vizagapatam. At Dolphin's nose are remains of an old castle and battery, to the east of which is a large shallow cave. On a hill overlooking the harbour are the temple of Venkateshwaran, the Durgah [q.v.], two Mussalman tombs, and a Catholic church. A celebrated Mahomedan saint lies buried in the Durgah [q.v.]. Every vessel passing the bar inwards or outwards salutes him by hoisting and lowering its flag three times; he being considered allpotent over the elements in the Bay of Bengal. Silver dhonies [q.v.] are presented at his shrine by Hindoo shipowners after a successful voyage. The following are the travelling distances by road from Vizagapatam to different places:—

To	Viâ	Miles and Furlongs.	
Aska	Chicacole and Berhampore	187	1½
Aska	Chicacole and Digoopoody	188	2½
Bangalore ...	Bezwada, Nellore, Chittore and Colaur.	617	7½
Bellary	Bezwada, Guntoor, Cumbum and Gooty.	525	2
Berhampore ...	Chicacole and Ichapore	163	1½
Bezwada	Rajahmundry and Ellore	215	2
Bobbily	Vizianagram	74	5½
Chetterpore ...	Chicacole and Berhampore	177	4½
Chicacole	Chittivalsa	64	1
Chingleput ...	Bezwada, Guntoor, Nellore and Madras.	522	5½
Cocanada	Cassimcote, Toony and Samulcottah ...	107	1
Condacambair ...	Narsapatam	110	4
Coraputt ...	Vizianagram and Pauchipenta ghaut ...	124	3
Cotepaud ...	Vizianagram, Pauchipenta ghaut and Coraputt	162	2
Cuddapah ...	Bezwada, Guntoor and Cumbum ...	446	5½
Cuttack	Chicacole, Berhampore and Khoordhah.	270	6½
Ganjam	Chicacole and Berhampore	182	1½
Golcondah ...	Cassimcote and Narsapatam	62	0
Guntoor	Rajahmundry and Bezwada	245	2½
Jagdalpore ...	Vizianagram, Pauchipenta ghaut, Cotepaud and Coraputt.	183	6
Jeypore	Vizianagram, Pauchipenta ghaut and Coraputt.	188	3
Jeypore	Bowdara, Arakoo and Daudee	130	4
Jeypore	Narsapatam, Madgole and Padair ...	175	4
Jeypore	Narsapatam, Ballapollem and Padair ...	181	4
Joonaghur ...	Vizianagram, Palcondah, Cottore and Mookoly.	235	5
Joonaghur ...	Chicacole and Mookoly	238	2
Kamptee ...	Vizianagram, Cotepaud, Jagdalpore and Weiragarh.	492	7½
Kimedy ..	Chicacole	104	6
Kimedy ...	Vizianagram and Palcondah	114	7
Madras ...	Rajahmundry, Bezwada and Nellore ...	489	6½
Masulipatam ...	Rajahmundry and Ellore	222	7½
Motoo ...	Narsapatam and Mulkangherry	177	4
Mulkangherry ...	Narsapatam and Golcondah	143	0
Mulkangherry ...	Narsapatam and Condacambair	125	4
Narsapatam ...	Cassimcote	51	4
Nellore ...	Rajahmundry, Ellore and Ongole ...	382	0½
Palcondah ...	Vizianagram	83	5
Parvatipore ...	Vizianagram and Bobbily	89	3½
Rajahmundry ...	Cassimcote and Toony	123	0
Russellcondah ...	Chicacole and Berhampore	211	1½
Ryepore ...	Chicacole, Berhampore, Khoordhah and Sonapore.	548	2½
Samulcottah ...	Cassimcote and Toony	99	1
Secunderabad ...	Rajahmundry, Bezwada and Sooryapett.	384	0½
Sironchah ...	Vizianagram, Cotepaud and Jagdalpore.	360	0
Sumbulpore ...	Chicacole, Berhampore, Khoordhah and Sonapore.	432	0½
Vaddigoodem ...	Narsapatam, Mulkangherry and Anantapully.	207	4
Vizianagram ...	Chittivalsa	36	4
Weiragarh ...	Vizianagram, Cotepaud and Jagdalpore.	385	7½

VIZIANAGRAM (ایجانگر - íjánagar, *Hind.*; విజయనగరము - vijayanagaramu, *Tel.* vizianagram *) [vi]. From founder vijayaram rauz, the fifth ancestor of the present maharajah. Also as the foundations were laid on a Jayavauram or Tuesday, on the tenth day or Vijaya dashamy [q.v.] of Dusserah [q.v.] feast, in the year Vijaya of the Hindoo Jovian cycle, 1713. A.D. [brihaspaty chuckram].——**(1)** Division; Vizagapatam district; population 166,658; language Teloogoo; E. inland talook of district. Boundaries:—east and south Bimlipatam division; west Srungavarapocote division; north-west, north and north-east Gajapatinugger and Cheepoorpully divisions. The surface is generally mixture of red ferruginous series and black cotton soil [regar]. The black soil has a substratum of nodular kankar [q.v.] besides the lufaceous kind scattered on the soil. Agriculture is principal industry, and gunnies [q.v.] are manufactured. Vizianagram is a centre of trade. The imports are grain from the Ganjam and Godavery districts and the Palcondah talook, hill produce such as oil seeds [yennay], hides [chamrah], horns [sing], wheat [geung], pepper [q.v.], root, &c., from the Parvatipore side and iron [auhan], cotton [q.v.] goods and English yarn from Madras, Calcutta and England. The exports are hides [chamrah], salt [ooppoo], oil seed [yennay], gingelly [q.v.] and indigo [q.v.]. Coomilay and Nelivada tanks [q.v.] deserve special notice. Places of archæological interest:—Bhogaupooram, Biyyaulpett, Coomilay, Gandraid, Mullicherla, Nellimarla, Rama teertam, Rellivalsa, Saurica, Shreepooram. Principal trig. stations:—Bora, Candivalsa. The leading places, &c., in the division are the following.——*Bodicondah* (బోడికొండ - bódikonda, Tel.). From (bódi, tel. bare + konda, tel. hill). Hill; from Vizagapatam north about 44 miles viâ Vizianagram. Old temple on hill to Shiva as Mullicarjoona sawmy.——*Bora* (బోర - bóra, Tel.). Means the jujube tree, zizyphus jujuba, lam. Trig. station; lat. 18° 09′ 48·00″; long. 83° 20′ 11·39″; height 468 feet;

from Vizianagram W.N.W. 8 miles.——*Candivalsa* (కండివలస - kandivalasa, Tel.). From (kandi, tel. pigeon pea, cajanus indicus, spr. + valasa, tel. colony). Trig. station; lat. 18° 08′ 11·92″; long. 83° 37′ 21·23″; height 1,766 feet; from Rama teertam E. 6 miles; from Vizianagram E. 11 miles.——*Canimetta condah* (కనిమెట్టకొండ - kanimettakonda, Tel.). From (kanu, tel. seeing + metta, tel. mound + konda, tel. hill). Hill.——*Coomilay* (కుమిల - kumila, Tel.). From (kummi, tel. grain basket + ila, tel. ground). Village; pop. 4,478; lat. 18° 06′; long. 83° 34′; from Vizagapatam N.N.E. 32 miles; from Vizianagram E. 7 miles. Former seat of a Maharajah of Vizianagram.——*Garikivalsa* (గరికివలస - garikivalasa, Tel.). From (garika, tel. bent grass, cynodon dactylon, pers. + valasa, tel. colony). Agrahauram; pop. 1,301; lat. 18° 07′; long. 83° 24′; from Vizagapatam N. 29 miles; from Vizianagram W. 4 miles. Granted as an agrahauram [q.v.] by a late Maharajah, as he was addicted to a chutney [q.v.] made of the Bent grass [hurrially] found here.——*Gostany* (గోస్తని - góstani, Tel.). See sep. title.——*Mullicherla* (మలిచర్ల - malicherla, Tel.). From (mala tel. hill + cherla, tel. village). Village; pop. 551. On road to Chintalavalsa. Shiva temple very old. Two inscriptions of Ananta vurma deva of Orissa dynasty [raj], dated A.D. 1139.——*Rama teertam* (రామతీర్థము - rámatírt'hamu, Tel.). From (ráma, san. the hero + tírt'ha, san. place of sacred waters). Village; pop. 981; lat. 18° 10′; long. 83° 32′; from Vizagapatam N.N.E. 34 miles; from Vizianagram N.E. 6 miles. Once a large and important temple.——*Rellivalsa* (రెల్లివలస - rellivalasa, Tel.). From (rellu, tel. a reed, saccharum spontaneum, linn. + valasa, tel. colony). Village; pop. 3,270; lat. 17° 53′; long. 83° 16′; from Vizagapatam N. 14 miles; from Vizianagram S.W. 20 miles. Inscription dated A.D. 1151. ——*Saurica* (సారిక - sárika, Tel.). Means a species of jay. Village; pop. 1,382; lat. 18° 05′; long. 83° 24′; from Vizagapatam N. 26 miles; from Vizianagram S.W. 4 miles. Inscription of Orissa dynasty [raj], dated, A.D. 1153.——*Vizianagram* (విజయనగరము - vijayanagaramu, Tel.). See below.——**(2)** Deputy tahsildarry; Vizagapatam district. Pay rupees 100.——**(3)** Zemindarry; Vizagapatam dist., Vizianagram division; pop. 147,210; square miles 294. For description vide vol. I, 54, footnote. Distinguish from the historic Vijianugger of the later middle ages. The zemindarry is divided into the following fourteen talooks [q.v.] or tannahs [q.v.], which are sub-divided into mittahs [q.v.]:—Vizianagram; Goodivauda, to the south of Vizianagram, chief station Revidy agraharam; Bonanghy to the west, chief station Cottiyam; Coomaram, north of Vizianagram, chief station Cheepoorpully, bounded by Bobbily and Saulore zemindarries; Gajapatinugger, the northernmost, adjoining on the west and north are Andra, Saulore and Bobbily zemindarries; Padagaudy to the south-west; Lakka varapoocote to the south-west; Almoondah, south-west of Lakka varapoocote, chief station Gavarasam; Chodavaram to the south-west, chief station Anandapooram; Paravada to the south, chief station Govindapooram; to the east, chief station Conauda; Cotapollem to the north-east, chief station Ranastalam, Shreecoormam, north of Chicacole; and Kotipully in the Godavery district.——**(4)** Town, Capital of Vizianagram zemindarry, Head-quarters of General duties Deputy collector, and Deputy tahsildar, Cantonment, Municipality; Vizagapatam dist., Vizianagram division; pop. 32,179; lat. 18° 07′; long. 83° 27′; from Coraputt S.E. 64 miles; from Madras N.E. 400 miles; from Narsapatam N.E. 60 miles; from Parvatipore S. 45 miles; from Vizagapatam N.N.E. 29 miles. The climate salubrious, but very warm for the district. One mile from cantonment, is the fort built by Bussy and lying midway is a large tank. The fort is entirely occupied by the palace and buildings of the Maharajah. A regiment of native infantry is stationed here. The station contains about twenty officers' houses. There is a small church. The following are the travelling distances by road from Vizianagram to different places:—

To		Viâ	Miles and Furlongs.	
Bangalore	...	Bezwada, Nellore, Chittore and Colaur.	641	2½
Bellary	...	Bezwada, Guntoor, Cumbum and Gooty.	548	5
Berhampore	...	Chicacole and Ichapore	158	1½
Berhampore	...	Palcondah and Chicacole	171	1½
Bezwada	...	Rajahmundry and Ellore	238	5
Bobbily	...	Maradaum	37	7½
Chetterpore	...	Chittivalsa and Chicacole	172	4½
Chicacole	...	Chittivalsa	59	1
Chicacole	...	Palcondah	72	1
Chingleput	...	Bezwada, Nellore and Madras	546	0½
Cocanada	...	Soobaraum, Toony and Samulcottah ...	130	4
Coraputt	...	Pauchipenta ghaut	87	7
Cotepaud	...	Pauchipenta ghaut and Coraputt ...	125	6½
Cuddapah	...	Bezwada, Guntoor and Cumbum ...	470	1½
Cuttack	...	Chicacole, Berhampore and Khoordhah.	274	6½
Ganjam	...	Chicacole and Berhampore	177	1½
Jagdalpore	...	Pauchipenta ghaut, Coraputt and Cotepaud.	147	2½
Jeypore	...	Pauchipenta ghaut and Coraputt ...	101	7
Jeypore	...	Bowdara and Daudee	113	3
Kamptee	...	Coraputt, Jagdalpore and Weiragarh ...	456	7
Kimedy	...	Palcondah	78	3
Madras	...	Rajahmundry, Bezwada and Nellore ...	513	1½
Masulipatam	...	Rajahmundry and Ellore	246	2½
Nellore	...	Rajahmundry, Bezwada and Ongole ...	405	3½
Palcondah	...	......	46	7
Parvatipore	...	Bobbily	52	7½
Rajahmundry	...	Soobaraum and Toony	144	3
Russellcondah	...	Chicacole, Berhampore and Aska ...	206	1½
Ryepore	...	Chicacole, Berhampore, Khoordhah and Sonapore.	543	2½
Samulcottah	...	Soobaraum and Toony	122	4
Secunderabad	...	Rajahmundry, Bezwada and Sooryapett.	407	3½
Secunderabad	...	Colapaud, Jagdalpore and Sironchah ...	489	5½
Sironchah	...	Pauchipenta ghaut, Cotepaud and Jagdalpore.	323	4
Sumbulpore	...	Chicacole, Berhampore, Khoordhah and Sonapore.	427	0½
Vizagapatam	...	Chittivalsa	36	4
Weiragarh	...	Pauchipenta ghaut, Cotepaud and Jagdalpore.	349	3½

VIZIER (وزیر - vazír, *Ar.*). From (vazza, ar. to support). Minister. Usually the principal minister [muntry, peshwah, pradhaun, pragada] under a Mahomedan prince. Prefixed to an alam forms a lacab; as Vizier ally, minister of ally [ism]. ——*Vizaurat* (وزارت - vizárat, Hind.). The office of prime minister [muntry].

VOILPAUD (వాయల్పాడు - váyalpádu, *Tel.* váyalpád *). From (vávali, tel. five-leaved chaste tree, vitex negundo, linn. + pádu, tel. village). Sanscrit name (válmíkyáshrama), meaning vaulmeeky, the sage + hermitage.——**(1)** Talook, Cuddapah district. Tahsildar's pay Rs. 175. Area 831 square miles. 45 miles from east to west, and 18 miles from north to south. Population 127,043. Language Teloogoo. S.E. of district. Bounded by Royachoty talook on the north, Madanapully and Cadiry talooks on the west, Chundragherry talook, Pooganore zemindarry of North arcot on the south, and Poollampett talook on the east. The eastern portion is similar to that of Royachoty, and forms part of the same tableland with a few detached hills until shut in on the east by the hills which divide the talook from the main division. Towards the west and the south-west the talook is broken up by rocky hills. The sugar-cane [q.v.] is noted. Trade in jaggery [q.v.]. The Bauhoodah nuddy and Punchanuddy run through the talook. The principal tanks are Agrahauram, Chinnagottigull, Murripaud, Saukiraivpully and Targonda. There are 174 Government, 18 private, and 195 dasbandam [q.v.] channels [q.v.]. The two largest of the latter are the Madicoorty peddacaulwa and Voilpaud peddacaulwa. There are twelve anicuts [q.v.] of inconsiderable size. The number of wells is very large. Places of archæological interest:—Culcada, Devalapully, Gandlore, Goorramcondah, Medicoorty, Ramaupooram, Targonda, Voilpaud. Principal trig. stations:—Goondaulacondah, Suttevauripolliem, Toomcondah. The leading places, &c., in the talook are the following.——*Agrahauram* (అగ్రహారము - agraháramu, Tel.). Means first gift. Bramin village. Village; pop. 1,063; acres 2,116; lat. 13° 37′; long. 79° 00′; from Cuddapah S. 60 miles; from Voilpaud E. 23 miles. Tank.——*Bauhoodah nuddy* (బాహుదానది - báhudanadi, Tel.). See sep. title. ——*Cheyair* (చెయ్యేరు - cheyyéru, Tel.). See sep. title.——*Chinnagottigull* (చిన్నగొట్టిగల్లు - chinnagottigallu, Tel.). From (chinna, tel. small + gotti, tel. an edible root, spathium chinense, lour. + kallu, tel. stone). Village; pop. 1,733; acres 4,468; lat. 13° 39′; long. 79° 08′; from Cuddapah S.S.E. 60 miles; from Voilpaud E. 31 miles. Tank.——*Chitticherla* (చిట్టిచర్ల - chitticharla, Tel.). From (chiru, tel. small + cheruvu, tel. tank). Village; pop. 2,354; acres 9,399; lat. 13° 40′; long. 79° 13′; from Cuddapah S.S.E. 61 miles; from Voilpaud E. 36 miles. Seat of an important poligar's family. The only remaining polliem [q.v.] in the Ceded districts [q.v.].——*Culcada* (కలకడ - kalakada, Tel.). From (kallu, tel. stone + kada, tel. place). Village, Place of pilgrimage; pop. 2,705; acres 10,089; lat. 13° 50′; long. 78° 50′; from Cuddapah S. 45 miles; from Voilpaud N.E. 17 miles. On the Chittore-Cuddapah road, on a tributary of the Bauhoodah. Pagoda [q.v.] with lingam [q.v.] brought from Sidhout when that fort was taken by the Mussalmans. The festival commences about the beginning of March. Here a branch of the Cheyair, which in the rainy weather is swollen to some size, suddenly falls into the ground and, after a subterranean passage of several hundred feet issues from a cavern 200 feet lower than the spot where it made its descent. It then continues its course between high precipitous rocks through a narrow passage only four or five yards in breadth. This spot is held especially sacred. By the side of the waterfall is a pool called Dayyaulmadoogoo or devil's fountain. Those possessed of devils are dipped.——*Doddipully* (దొడ్డిపల్లె - doddipalle, Tel.). From (doddi, tel. backyard + palle, tel. village). Village; pop. 1,856; acres 6,456; lat. 13° 38′; long. 78° 57′; from Cuddapah S. 59 miles; from Voilpaud E. 18 miles. Seat of an old poligar's family.——*Goondaulacondah* (గుండాలకొండ - gundálakonda, Tel.). From (gundamu, tel. gorge + konda, tel. hill). Trig. station; lat. 13° 45′ 23·05″; long. 78° 54′ 46·44″; from Soracauyalpett N.W. 2 miles; from Cuddapah S. 50 miles; from Voilpaud E.N.E. 18 miles.——*Goorramcondah* (గుర్రంకొండ - gurramkonda, Tel.). See sep. title.——*Goottapolliem* (గుట్టపాళెం - guttapálem, Tel.). From (gutta, tel. hill + pálemu, tel. fortified village). Village; pop. 1,626; acres 5,773; lat. 13° 35′; long. 78° 49′; from Cuddapah S. 61 miles; from Voilpaud E.S.E. 10 miles. Once the seat of a poligar [q.v.].——*Mahaul* (మహాలు - mahálu, Tel.). See sep. title.——*Marella* (మారెళ్ళ - márella, Tel.). From (márédu, tel. bael tree, ægle marmelos, corr.). Village; pop. 2,060; acres 10,277; lat. 13° 50′; long. 78° 59′; from Cuddapah S. 46 miles; from Voilpaud E.N.E. 25 miles. Former seat of a poligar [q.v.].——*Murripaud* (మఱ్ఱిపాడు - marripádu, Tel.). From (marri, tel. banyan tree, ficus bengalensis, linn. + pádu, tel. village). Village; pop. 1,437; acres 4,201; lat. 13° 42′; long. 78° 43′; from Cuddapah S. 55 miles; from Voilpaud N.N.E. 6 miles. Tank.——*Peelair* (పీలేరు - píléru, Tel.). See sep. title. ——*Punchanuddy* (పంచనది - panchanadi, Tel.). See sep. title. ——*Rompicherla* (రొంపిచెర్ల - rompicherla, Tel.). From (rompi, tel. bog + cheruvu, tel. tank). Village; pop. 2,221; acres 4,272, lat. 13° 40′; long. 79° 05′; from Cuddapah S.S.E. 58 miles; from Voilpaud E. 28 miles. Once the seat of a poligar [q.v.].——*Saukiraivpully* (చాకిరేవుపల్లి - tsákirévupalli, Tel.). From (tsáki, tel. washerman + révu, tel. ford + palli, tel. village). Village; pop. 716; acres 2,290; lat. 13° 43′; long. 78° 48′; from Cuddapah S. 54 miles; from Voilpaud E.N.E. 10 miles. Tank.——*Sheshachellum* (శేషాచలము - shésháchalamu, Tel.). See sep. title.——*Suttavauripolliem* (చత్తెవారిపాళెము - tsattevári pálemu, Tel.). From (tsattevárn, tel. a family + pálemu, tel. fortified village). Village; pop. 1,362; acres 3,963; lat. 13° 40′; long. 79° 10′; from Cuddapah S.S.E. 59 miles; from Voilpaud E. 33 miles. Once the seat of a poligar. Trig. station; height 2,497; lat. 13° 40′ 55·90″; long. 79° 10′ 15·08″.——*Talacona* (తలకోన - talakóna, Tel.). From (tala, tel. head + kóna, tel. ravine). Place of pilgrimage. Ravine in the Sheshachellam hills, in which is a waterfall said to wash away sins. Festival on Shivarautry [pundigay, 6a] and two succeeding days [aroovy]. ——*Talpoola* (తలుపుల - talupula, Tel.). From (talupu, tel. gate). Village; pop. 2,307; acres 11,514; lat. 13° 45′; long. 79° 03′; from Cuddapah S.S.E. 52 miles; from Voilpaud E.N.E. 26 miles. Once the seat of a poligar.——*Targonda* (తరిగొండ - tarigonda, Tel.). From (tari, tel. wet land + konda, tel. hill). Village, Place of pilgrimage; pop. 2,012; acres 4,614; lat. 13° 42′; long. 78° 41′; from Cuddapah S.S.W. 54 miles; from Voilpaud N. 4 miles. Narsimhasawmy temple. Formerly the cattle-stand of the Chitticherla poligar.——*Toomcondah* (తూముకొండ - túmukonda, Tel.). From (túmu, tel. sluice + konda, tel. hill). Trig. station; lat. 13° 40′ 20·05″; long. 78° 37′ 10·44″; height 3,601 feet; from Targonda W.S.W. 6 miles; from Voilpaud N.W. 4 miles.——*Voilpaud* (వాయల్పాడు - váyalpádu, Tel.). See below. ——*Yellootla* (యల్లుట్ల - yallutla, Tel.). From (ella, tel. boundary + úta, tel. spring). Village; pop. 1,462; acres 6,894; lat. 13° 50′; long. 78° 39′; from Cuddapah S.S.W. 47 miles; from Voilpaud N. 14 miles. Once the seat of a poligar.——*Yerravauripollem* (ఎఱ్ఱవారిపాళెం - erravári pálem, Tel.). From (erravárn, tel. a family + pálemu, tel. fortified village). Village; pop. 1,967; acres 4,823; lat. 13° 43′; long. 79° 11′; from Cuddapah S.S.E. 57 miles; from Voilpaud E. 34 miles. Once the seat of a poligar.——*Zillelmanda* (జిల్లెళ్ళమంద - jillellamanda, Tel.). From (jillédu, tel. swallow-wort, calotropis gigantea, r. br. + manda, tel. cattle herd). Village; pop. 1,154; acres 12,081; lat. 13° 53′; long. 79° 03′; from Cuddapah S.S.E. 43 miles; from Voilpaud N.E. 31 miles. Once the seat of a poligar.——**(2)** Town, Talook head-quarters; Cuddapah dist., Voilpaud tal.; pop. 4,016; acres 9,879; lat. 13° 38′; long. 78° 40′; from Cuddapah S.S.W. 60 miles; from Madanapully N E. 10 miles; from Madras W.N.W. 118 miles; from Sidhout S.S.W. 62 miles. Pagoda [q.v.] with endowment of Rs. 835 a year. Festival in March lasting ten days. Near the Bauhoodah nuddy. Till lately seat of a District moonsif's court close to Bauhoodah nuddy. Surrounded by gardens, and a place of considerable trade. Near it on the N.W. is a hill called Ancaulamma condah crowned by a tall square rock, which is a very conspicuous land mark for 10 miles round.

VOLE (వోలు - vólu, *Tel.*). Corruption of (prólu, tel. town). Town. Suffix in place names [pole, prole, wail].

VONTIMITTAH (వొంటిమిట్ట - vontimitta,* *Tel.*). From (onti, tel. single + mitta, tel. mound) [or]. Sanscrit name (ékashilánagara), meaning single + rock + city [warangal]. Village, Railway station; Cuddapah dist., Sidhont tal.; pop. 4,484; acres 13,175; lat. 14° 24′; long. 79° 04′; height 423 feet; from Cuddapah S.E. 15 miles; from Sidhout S.E. 7 miles. Large pagoda [q.v.] dedicated to Codanda ramasawmy, built or restored by a Vijianugger rajah in 14th century. Car festival [ratotsavam] in April. Ancient mantapam [q.v.] close to a tank west of the village. North of this are two caves in the hill. Finely sculptured old temple of Gopaulsawmy. Under a tree east of the village are a number of naugaculls [q.v.], &c. Produces indigo [q.v.] and turmeric [country saffron].

VOWTAUN (வவுத்தான் - vavuttán, *Tam.*), From (vayiru, tam. belly + án, tam. personal termination). Big-bellied man. Pariah proper name [peyar].

VRICSHAM (वृक्ष - vriksha, *San.*). From (vrih, san. to grow [vrih]). The most general term for a plant.——**(1)** A general sketch of the flora prevailing in the Presidency has been given in vol. II, appendix V. The present remarks compare the European and Dravidian systems of botanical terminology. Plants are arranged according to the natural system of Jussieu, De Candolle, and later writers in the first place in two main divisions called sub-kingdoms. The first sub-kingdom or Phanerogamia [vaunaspatyam] includes all plants commonly known as flowering plants, in which the sexual arrangement is apparent, with cypress [saro], pine [cheer] and casuarina [chowkmaram] trees, and grasses that have only minute flowers, or in which the flowers have not bright colors. The second sub-kingdom or Cryptogamia [vaunaspaty] includes those in which the sexual arrangement is not so clearly apparent, viz., ferns [parny], mosses [pausy], mushrooms [caulaun], sea-weeds [cadalpausy], and other allied plants. The Phanerogamia sub-kingdom is again divided into two classes; Angiosperms and Gymnosperms. Angiosperms are divided into two sub-classes; Dicotyledons and Monocotyledons. Dicotyledons are also called Exogens, because the new wood is always formed outside the old wood. Monocotyledons are also called Endogens for the opposite reason. Dicotyledons are so called from the presence in the seed of two seed leaves; as in the pea [calauyam], and the castor-oil [aumanac] seed. These plants have the veins of the leaves forming an irregular network, so that if a leaf is torn the edge is irregular. The flowers have the various whorls of organs generally in fours or fives. The wood is formed in concentric annual bundles around a central pith, and increases in size by additions formed between the wood and bark, and the bark is separable. Monocotyledons are so called from the presence of one leaf only in the seed. The leaves of this class have the veins running parellel, as may be seen in a plaintain [q.v.] leaf, sugar-cane [q.v.], or any other grass. The parts of the flowers are in threes, and the wood is formed in wire-like bundles, which soon discontinue to grow in thickness. These bundles are easily distinguished in the stem of the cocoanut [q.v.], in the sugar-cane [q.v.], and the bamboo [q.v.]. As these divisions are natural groups in which the individual members resemble each other in many points yet differ in some respects, no single character or mark can be given by which they can be absolutely distinguished. The sub-classes are even again subdivided on account of structural considerations. Thus under Dicotyledons there are Thalamifloræ, in which the petals are distinct, and the stamens are inserted on the receptacle; Calycifloræ, in which the petals are free or more or less united, and the stamens are perigynous or epigynous and inserted on the calyx; Gamopetalæ or Corollifloræ, in which the petals are united and the stamens situated upon the corolla, and Incompletæ where the perianth is single or none. Monocotyledons are sometimes grouped, according to the nature of their inflorescence, into Spadicifloræ, Petaloideæ, and Graminiferæ. Cryptogams have also certain groups. Thus:—"*a*" Vascular cryptogams; class Dichotomæ, with sub-classes Ligulatæ, and Lycopodicæ; class Filicineæ, with sub-classes Rhizocarpeæ, Filices and Stipulatæ; class Equisetineæ:—"*b*" Muscineæ; class Musci; class Hepaticæ:—"*c*" Thallophytes; class Carposporæ; class Oosporeæ; class Zygosporeæ; class Protophyta. The next division after this is into Natural Orders, which is the most practically recognised. The Natural Orders are represented almost universally by Latin feminine substantives in the plural number. After the Natural Order in botanical classification comes the Genus represented by Latin substantive. Below Genus comes Species, represented by a Latin adjective, or occasionally by a Latin substantive in the genitive case. The genus in the singular and the species following and grammatically agreeing with it form a term which should if there was a universal accord among botanists be sufficient to indicate any particular species. It is usual however to add the name of the author who is responsible for the classification of the plant; as sometimes, according to different usage, one Latin name may stand for more than one plant. Another term indicating a variety of the species is sometimes added to the species. The above is the European system of botanical classification. The Dravidians have no method of classification answering to natural order, genus and species. They divide all plants however into five great structural divisions; according as they are shrub, creeper, tree, grass, or herbaceous plant. A verbal root gives the abstract name of the plant, and to that root they suffix the term expressing one of the above five divisions. The terms for these five divisions in the different Dravidian languages can be seen under the heads of shrub, creeper, tree, grass, and herbaceous plant, in section 7 below. Examples are:—(róséshedi), a rosebush; (vellarikkodi), a cucumber; (púvarasamaram), a portia tree; (arugam pillu), dog's grass; (shanalpúnd), crotalaria. Again the Dravidians are careful, when they do not intend to indicate the whole plant, but only a part of it or one of its products, to express this by the word used. Similar to the five words indicating plant-divisions and like them to be suffixed to the abstract root, there are a large class of words indicating the parts or products of plants. Some of them can be seen in section 7 below under the heads:—bark, branch, bud, bunch, fibre, flour, flower, foliage, fruit, greens, gum, leaf, milk, nut, oil, root, seed, shoot, spathe, tuber, twig, unripe fruit. But there are many others, and in fact the number is indefinite, owing to the genius of these languages for composition. An example is the following:—in Tamul (má) is the verbal root of mango, and (mámaram) is the mango tree. But four terms can be substituted for (maram), giving the names of four different products. That is to say:—(mámpú), mango flower; (mámpiñju), mango fruit just forming; (mánkáy), unripe mango fruit; (mámpazham), ripe mango fruit. Again varieties of plants are very carefully expressed by the Dravidians through prefixes; see in section 7 below the heads, black, country, dry, foreign, garden, green, hill, large, red, small, sour, sweet, wild. There are many others of these also. An example is the following:—in Tamul (ámanakku) is the castor-oil, and (kátrámanakku) is the wild castor-oil or croton. By bearing in mind the three principles here named, of structural or plant division suffix, of part or product suffix, and of descriptive prefix, the apparent complexity of Dravidian botanical nomenclature will be extensively reduced. In this work vernacular identifications of the vegetable kingdom are shown under the word-root only, leaving the reader who consults the work to add suffixes and prefixes after consulting the sub-heads of the present paragraph; in no other way could the subject have been set out within any reasonable limits. It may be noted that the term in Tamul for a barren tree is (avakósi), for a fruitful tree (palitham), for a male tree (agamkázh), for a female tree (purakázh), for a tree which has fruit without flowers (kóni); and all the Dravidian languages have the same distinction. The Dravidians attach much value to botany, and there is a Tamul proverb:—மூலிகை அறிந்தால் மூன்று உலகமும் ஆளலாம்—"he who is acquainted with botany may govern the "three worlds [trilocam]."——**(2)** The following is a key-synopsis of the principal flora of the Presidency indigenous, naturalized, or introduced, classified down to species, and connecting the european and native terminology. Small capitals indicate Classes; small capitals in inverted commas indicate Sub-classes; italic indicates Orders; the Genera and Species are in ordinary type.—DICOTYLEDONS "THALAMIFLORÆ."—1 *Ranunculaceæ.*—Clematis smilacifolia, wall.; triloba, heyne; gouriana, roxb.; hedysarifolia, dec.; wightiana, wall. Naravelia zeylanica, dec. Anemone rivularis, ham. Thalictrum dalzellii, hook.; javanicum, bl. [momiree]; foliolosum, dc. [momiree]. Ranunculus reniformis, wall.; diffusus, dec.; wallichianus, w. and a. Helleborus niger, linn. [black cootkee]. Coptis teeta, wall. [mamiraun]. Nigella sativa, linn. [black jeerah]. Delphinium ajacis, linn. [nahfirmaun]; staphisagria, linn. [nahfirmaun]. Aconitum [bish] ferox, wall. [bachnaug]; napellus, linn. [wolf strangler]; heterophyllum, wall. [atees].—2 *Dilleniaceæ.*—Tetracera lævis, vahl. Acrotrema arnottianum, wight. Dillenia indica, linn. [chaltah]; bracteata, wight; pentagyna, roxb. [small chaltah]—3 *Magnoliaceæ.*—Illicium anisatum, linn. [star anise]. Michelia champaca, linn. [champak]; nilagirica, zenk. [neilgherry champak]. Kadsura wightiana, arn.—4 *Anonaceæ.*—Uvaria narum, wall.; zeylanica, linn. Artabotrys odoratissimus, r. br. [madmaunty]; zeylanicus, h. f. and t. Cananga odorata, h. f. and t. [ilang ilang]. Unona pannosa, dalz.; discolor, vahl.; lawii, h. f. and t.; viridiflora, bedd. Polyalthia longifolia, benth [ashocam]; coffeoides, benth. [doodooga]; fragrans, benth. [doodooga]; cerasoides, benth. [doodooga]; korinti, benth. [doodooga]; suberosa, benth. [doodooga]; rufescens, h. f. and t. [doodooga]; persicæfolia, benth. [doodooga]. Popowia beddomeana, h. f. and t. Phæanthus malabaricus, bedd. Goniothalamus thwaitesii, h. f. and t.; wynaadensis, bedd.; cardiopetalus, h. f. and t.; wightii, h. f. and t. Mitrephora heyneana, thw.; grandiflora, bedd. Anona [q.v.] squamosa, linn. [common anona]; reticulata, linn. [netted anona]; muricata, linn. [prickly anona]; cherimolia, mill. [anona]; palustris, wight [anona]. Milinsa indica, lesch. [black doodooga]; wightiana, h. f. and t. [black doodooga]; velutina, h. f. and t. [black doodooga]; nilagirica, bedd. [black doodooga]. Saccopetalum tomentosum, h. f. and t. Alphonsea lutea, h. f. and t.; zeylanica, h. f. and t.; madraspatana, bedd. Orophea uniflora, h. f. and t.; zeylanica, h. f. and t.; thomsoni, bedd.; erythrocarpa, bedd. Bocagea dalzellii, h. f. and t.—5 *Menispermaceæ.*—Tinospora tomentosa, miers [goolancha]; malabarica, miers [goolancha]; crispa, miers [goolancha]; cordifolia miers [goolancha]. Anamirta cocculus, w. and a. [indian berry]. Coscinium fenestratum, colebr. [false calumba]. Tiliacora racemosa, colebr. [creeper mooshty]. Cocculus [vausanavully] macrocarpus, w. and a. [vausanavully]; laurifolius, dc. [vausanavully]; villosus, dec. [jamtee]; leæba, dec. [vausanavully]; palmatus, dec. [calumba]. Stephania hernandifolia, walp.; rotunda, lour. Cissampelos pareira, linn. [indian pareira]. Cyclea burmanni, miers; peltata, h. f. and t. Pachygone ovata, miers.—6 *Berberideæ.* Berberis nepalensis, spr. [berberry]; aristata, dec. [berberry]; lycium, royle [berberry]; asiatica, rox. [berberry]; concinna, h. f. [berberry].—7 *Nymphæaceæ.*—Nymphæa [indian water-lily] alba, linn.; lotus, linn. [red indian water-lily]; lotus, linn., var. pubescens, h. f. and t. [white indian water-lily]; stellata, willd. [blue indian water-lily]; odorata, willd. [purple indian water-lily]. Euryale ferox, salisb. [makhanah]. Nelumbium speciosum, willd. [nelumbo].—8 *Papaveraceæ.*—Papaver [aphainam] rhœas, linn. [corn poppy]; somniferum, linn. [opium poppy]. Argemone mexicana, linn. [brambadand].—9 *Fumariaceæ.*—Fumaria parviflora, lamk. [pitpapra].—10 *Cruciferæ.*—Nasturtium officinale, br. [haleem]; palustre, dc. [haleem]; indicum, dec. Cardamine africana, linn.; subumbellata, hook.; hirsuta, linn. Brassica [sarshapam] nigra, koch. [cauly rayaun]; campestris, linn. [sarsoon]; campestris, linn., sub sp. campestris [cauly sarsoon]; campestris, linn., sub. sp. napus [rara sarsoon]; campestris, linn., sub. sp. napus, linn., var. toria [toriya sarsoon]; campestris, linn., sub. sp. rapa [shaigham]; juncea, h. f. and t. [rayaun]; alba, h. f. and t. [soofaid rayaun]; oleracea, linn. [kobee]; oleracea, linn., var. capitata [kobee]; oleracea, linn., var. sabauda [kobee]; oleracea, linn., var. sabaudagemifera [kobee]; oleracea, linn., var. sabellica [kobee]; oleracea, linn., var. botrytis [kobee]; oleracea, linn., var. botrytis cymosa [kobee]; oleracea, linn., var. caulorapa [kobee]. Capsella bursa-pastoris, mœnch. Lepidium sativum, linn. [haleem]. Raphanus sativus, linn. [country radish].—11 *Capparideæ.*—Cleome monophylla, linn. [dog vailay]; simplicifolia, h. f. and t.; tenella, linn. [dog vailay]; aspera, koen. [dog vailay]; burmanni, w. and a. [dog vailay]; felina, linn. [dog vailay]; viscosa, linn. [dog vailay]; chelidonii, linn. [dog vailay]. Gynandropsis pentaphylla, dec. [vailay.]; triphylla, dc. [vailay]. Cratæva religiosa, forst. [nirvala]; religiosa, forst., var. nurvala, ham. [nirvala]; religiosa, forst., var. roxburghii [nirvala]; tapia, l. [nirvala]. Cadaba trifoliata, w. and a.; indica, lamk. Capparis [caper] spinosa, linn. [europe caper]; grandiflora, wall. [caper]; zeylanica, linn. [ceylon caper]; heyneana, wall. [caper]; divaricata, lamk. [caper]; aphylla, roth. [common caper]; diversifolia, w. and a. [caper]; moonii, wight [caper]; roxburghii, dec. [caper]; grandis, linn. [raghota caper]; pedunculosa, wall. [caper]; longispina, h. f. and t.; parviflora, h. f. and t.; sepiaria, linn. [caper]; floribunda, wight [caper]; horrida, linn. [thorny caper]; acuminata, willd.; tenera, dalz.; erythrocarpus, gmel. [caper].—12 *Resedaceæ.*—Oligomeris glaucescens, camb.—13 *Violaceæ.*—Viola patrinii, dec.; distans, wall.; serpens, wall.; odorata, linn. [banafshah]; tricolor, linn. [banafshah]. Ionidium suffruticosum, ging. [one-leaf nelumbo]. Alsodeia zeylanica, thw.—14 *Bixineæ.*—Cochlospermum gossypium, dec. [golden silk cotton]. Bixa orellana, linn. [monkey country saffron]. Scolopia crenata, clos. Flacourtia [swandoo cantacam] inermis, roxb. [tomi-tomi]; montana, grah. [attack]; cataphracta, roxb. [indian plum]; ramontchi, l'herit. [mauritius plum]; ramontchi, l'herit., var. sapida [ceylon plum]; sepiaria, roxb. [forest bair]. Xylosma latifolium, h. f. and t. Gynocardia odorata, r. br. [chaulmoogra]. Hydnocarpus venenata, gærtn. [marotty]; wightiana, bl. [marotty]; alpina, wight [marotty].—15 *Pittosporeæ.*—Pittosporum tetraspermum, w. and a.; nilghirense, w. and a.; floribundum, w. and a.; dasycaulon, miq.—16 *Polygaleæ.*—Polygala [nangay] arillata, ham. [nangay]; javana, dec. [nangay]; crotalarioides, ham. [nangay]; leptalea, dec.; persicariæfolia, dec.; erioptera, dec. [nangay]; elongata, klein. [nangay]; chinensis, linn. [common nangay]; rosmarinifolia, w. and a. [nangay]; sibirica, linn.; telephioides, willd. [large nangay]; senega, linn. [senegal nangay]. Salomonia oblongifolia, dec. Xanthophyllum flavescens, roxb.—17 *Caryophylleæ.*—Saponaria vaccaria, linn. Cerastium indicum, w. and a.; vulgatum, linn. Stellaria paniculata, edgew; media, linn.; uliginosa, linn. Arenaria neilgerrensis, w. and a. Spergula arvensis, linn. Drymaria cordata, willd. Polycarpon lœflingiæ, benth. Polycarpæa corymbosa, lamk.; diffusa, w. and a.; spicata, w. and a.—18 *Portulaceæ.*—Portulaca oleracea, l. [indian purslane]; wightiana, wall. [indian purslane]; quadrifida, l. [small indian purslane]; tuberosa, roxb. [indian purslane]; suffruticosa, wight. Talinum cuneifolium, willd.—19 *Tamariscineæ.*—Tamarix [jhow] gallica, l. [manna jhow]; dioica, roxb. [cypress jhow]; articulata, vahl. [red jhow]; ericoides, rottl. [garden jhow].—20 *Elatineæ.*—Elatine americana, arn.; ambigua, wight. Bergia ammannioides, roxb.; verticillata, willd.—21 *Hypericineæ.*—Hypericum mysorense, heyne; hookerianum, w. and a.; humifusum, l.; nepaulense, choisy.; japonicum, thunb.—22 *Guttiferæ.*—Garcinia [ractaumram] mangostana, linn. [mangosteen]; indica, chois. [mate mangosteen]; cambogia, desrouss. [malabar gamboge]; cowa, roxb. [ractaumram]; pedunculata, roxb. [tickor]; morella, desrouss. [ceylon gamboge]; morella, desrouss., var. pedicellata [siam gamboge]; wightii, t. anders. [ractaumram]; travancorica, bedd. [ractaumram]; eugeniæfolia, wall. [ractaumram]; xanthochymus, hk. f. [yellow mangosteen]; ovalifolius, hk. f. Ochrocarpus longifolius, bth. [soora poon]. Calophyllum [poon] inophyllum, l. [common poon]; tomentosum, wight [malabar poon]; bracteatum, thw. [bracteate poon]; wightianum, wall. [small poon]; walkeri, wight; angustifolium, rox. [narrow-leaved poon]. Mesua ferrea, l. [nauga champak]. Pœciloneuron indicum, bedd.; pauciflorum, bedd.—23 *Ternstrœmiaceæ.*—Ternstrœmia japonica, thunb. Eurya japonica, thunb. [wild tea]. Gordonia obtusa, wall. Camellia theifera, griff. [tea].—24 *Dipterocarpeæ.*—Dipterocarpus turbinatus, gært. [gurjan]. Ancistrocladus heyneanus, wall. Vatica roxburghiana, bl. Shorea [saul] talura, roxb. [taloora saul]; robusta, gærtn. [common saul]; tumbuggaia, roxb. [tambaga saul]. Hopea [caung] odorata, rox. [caung]; parviflora, bedd. [water caung]; longifolia, dyer; wightiana, wall. [common caung]; glabra, w. and a. [caung]; racophlœa, dyer; malabarica, bedd. [caung]; dichotoma [caung]. Vateria indica, l. [piney].—25 *Malvaceæ.*—Althæa officinalis, linn. [foreign tootty]; rosea, linn. [foreign tootty]. Malva [khoobauzy] verticillata, l.; silvestris, linn. [small foreign tootty]; rotundifolia, linn. [wild bengal gram]. Malvastrum tricuspidatum, a. gray; spicatum, a. gray. Anoda hastata, l. Sida [balah] humilis, willd. [dwarf balah]; mysorensis, w. and a. [mysore balah]; schimperiana, hochst.; spinosa

l. [prickly balah]; carpinifolia, l. [lance-leaved balah]; rhombifolia, l. [common balah]; cordifolia, l. [shrubby balah]. Wissadula rostrata, planch.; leschenaultiana, master. Abutilon polyandrum, schlecht. [tootty]; asiaticum, g. don.; indicum, g. don. [tootty]; graveolens, w. and a. [tootty]; muticum, g. don. [tootty]; crispum, g. don. [tootty]; ramosum, guill. and per.; neilgherrense, munro. Malachra capitata, l. Urena lobata, l. [jungle cotton]; lobata, linn., var. scabriuscula, dec. [jungle cotton]; sinuata, l. [jungle cotton]; repanda, roxb. [jungle cotton]. Pavonia [mootty] glechomifolia, a. rich.; zeylanica, cav. [shittamootty]; odorata, willd. [peramootty]. Decaschistia trilobata, wight; crotonifolia, w. and a. Hibiscus [bendy] trionum, l. [bendy]; surattensis, l. [thorny hemp bendy]; furcatus, roxb. [hill bemp bendy]; hirtus, l. [jasmine bendy]; micranthus, l. [bendy]; solandra, l'her. [bendy]; canescens, heyne [bendy]; macrophyllus, rox. [bendy]; collinus, roxb. [hill bendy]; lunariifolius, willd. [bendy]; panduræformis, burm.; vitifolius, l. [vine-leafed bendy] cannabinus, l. [hemp bendy]; gibsoni, stocks; sabdariffa, l. [red hemp bendy]; ficulneus, l. [spreading bendy]; tetraphyllus, roxb.; angulosus, mast. [bendy]; abelmoschus, l. [musk bendy]; rugosus, mast. [bendy]; esculentus, l. [common bendy]; tiliaceus, l. [corkwood bendy]; rosasinensis, linn. [china rose bendy]; mutabilis, linn. [lotus bendy]; syriacus, linn. [syrian bendy]. Thespesia lampas, dalz. [portia]; populnea, corr. [portia]. Gossypium [carpausy] herbaceum, l. [indian cotton]; barbadense, l. [american cotton]; barbadense, linn., var. acuminatum, roxb. [peruvian cotton]; arboreum, l. [tree cotton]. Kydia calycina, roxb. Adansonia digitata, l. [baobab]. Bombax malabaricum, dc. [red cotton tree]. Eriodendron anfractuosum, dc. [silk cotton]. Cullenia excelsa, wight. Durio zibethinus, dec. [durian].—26 *Sterculiaceæ.*—Sterculia [cauvalam] fœtida, l. [bastard poon]; urens, roxb. [false kateerah]; villosa, rox. [odul]; guttata, roxb. [piymaram]; nobilis, r. br.; balanghas, l. [balanghas]; colorata, roxb. [wild papaw]; alata, roxb. [cauvalam]; populifolia, roxb. [cauvalam]. Heritiera littoralis, dryand. [soondree]; papilio, bedd. [soondree]. Kleinhovia hospita, l. Helicteres isora, l. [screw-tree]. Pterospermum [mochcoondam] suberifolium, lam. [velanga]; diversifolium, bl.; rubiginosum, heyne; acerifolium, willd. [kaniyaur]; semisagittatum, ham.; reticulatum, w. and a.; glabrescens, w. and a.; obtusifolium, wight. Eriolæna stocksii, h. f. and t.; hookeriana, w. and a.; candollei, wall.; quinquelocularis, wight. Pentapetes phœnicea, l. [mankena]. Melhania incana, heyne; cannabina, wight.; hamiltoniana, wall. Melochia corchorifolia, l.; velutina, bedd. Waltheria indica, l. Abroma augusta, l. Guazuma tomentosa, kunth. [roodrauck tree]. Buettneria herbacea, roxb. Leptonychia moacurroides, bedd.—27 *Tiliaceæ.*—Berrya ammonilla, roxb. [trincomalee tree]. Grewia [dharmanam] columnaris, sm. [dharmanam]; emarginata, w. and a. [dharmanam]; orientalis, l. [female bair]; umbellata, roxb.; heterotricha, mast.; populifolia, vahl. [dharmanam]; excelsa, vahl. [small tadda]; salvifolia, heyne [jaurah]; orbiculata, rottl. [round-leaved tadda]; tiliæfolia, vahl. [tadda]; asiatica, l. [falsah]; carpinifolia, juss.; pilosa, lam. [dog bran plant]; villosa, willd. [dharmanam]; multiflora, juss.; lævigata, vahl. [dharmanam]; ritchiei, mast.; bracteata, roth.; abutilifolia, juss. [bird tadda]; diplocarpa, thw. [dharmanam]; hirsuta, vahl. [bran plant]; polygama, roxb. [dharmanam]; microcos, l. [abrony]. Erinocarpus nimmoanus, grah. Triumfetta pilosa, roth. [chikty]; glabra, w. and a.; rhomboidea, jacq. [chikty]; rotundifolia, lam. [chikty]; annua, linn. [chikty]; neglecta, w. and a. [chikty]. Corchorus capsularis, l. [jute]; olitorius, l. [wild jute]; trilocularis, l.; urticæfolius, w. and a.; fascicularis, lam.; antichorus, rœusch.; acutangulus, lam. Elæocarpus [roodrauck] ganitrus, roxb. [roodrauk]; serratus, l. [roodrauck]; robustus, roxb.; cuneatus, wight [roodrauck]; lanceæfolius, roxb. [roodrauck]; oblongus, gærtn. [roodrauck]; amœnus, thw.; tuberculatus, roxb. [roodrauck]; aristatus, roxb.; rugosus, roxb.; monocera, cav.; ferrugineus, wight [roodrauck]; munroii, mast. [roodrauck].—28 *Lineæ.*—Linum usitatissimum, l. [alsee]; mysorense, heyne. Reinwardtia trigyna, planch.; tetragyna, planch. Hugonia mystax, l. [creeping falsah]. Erythroxylon monogynum, roxb. [deccany deodar]; lanceolatum, wight.—29 *Malpighiaceæ.*—Hiptage madablota, gærtn. [madablota]; parvifolia, w. and a. [madablota]. Aspidopterys roxburghiana, a. juss.; canarensis, dalz.; cordata, a. juss.—30 *Zygophylleæ.*—Tribulus cistoides, l.; terrestris, l. [nerinjy].—31 *Geraniaceæ.*—Monsonia senegalensis, guill. and per. Geranium nepalense, sweet. Oxalis corniculata, l. [sour auray]. Biophytum sensitivum, dc.; apodiscias, turcz.; reinwardtii, walp.; polyphyllum, munro. Averrhoa [lavaly] carambola, l. [coromandel gooseberry] bilimbi, l [blimbing]. Impatiens [goolmindie] beddomei, hk. f.; modesta, wight [gool mindie]; stocksii, h. f. and t. [gool mindie]; crenata, bedd. [gool mindie]; orchioides, bedd.; acaulis, arn. [gool mindie]; scapiflora, heyne [gool mindie]; rivalis, wight [gool mindie]; denisonii, bedd.; chinensis, l. [gool mindie]; gardneriana, wight [gool mindie]; setosa, h. f. and t. [gool mindie]; kleinii, w. and a. [gool mindie]; diversifolia, wall. [gool mindie]; ligulata, bedd. [gool mindie]; tenella, heyne [gool mindie]; inconspicua, benth. [gool mindie]; oppositifolia, l. [gool mindie]; lawii, h.f. and t.; tomentosa, heyne [gool mindie]; concinna, h.f.; latifolia, l. [gool mindie]; leschenaultii, wall. [gool mindie]; lucida, heyne; verticillata, wight [gool mindie]; goughii, wight [gool mindie]; viscosa, bedd. [gool mindie]; parvifolia, bedd. [gool mindie]; balsamina, l. [gool mindie]; scabriuscula, heyne [gool mindie]; repens, moon. [gool mindie]; pendula, heyne [gool mindie]; mysorensis, roth. [gool mindie]; munronii, wight [gool mindie]; dasysperma, wight [gool mindie]; flaccida, arn.; pulcherrima, dalz.; henslowiana, arn.; fruticosa, dc. [gool mindie]; jerdoniæ, wight [gool mindie]; parasitica, bedd.; auriculata, wight [gool mindie]; viridiflora, wight [gool mindie]; umbellata, heyne [gool mindie]; viscida, wight [gool mindie]; cordata, wight; grandis, heyne [gool mindie]; campanulata, wight [gool mindie]; travancorica, bedd.; uncinata, wight [gool mindie]; elegans, bedd. [gool mindie]; maculata, wight [gool mindie]; phœnicea, bedd.; tangachee, bedd.; leptura, hk.; wightiana, bedd. [gool mindie]; racemosa, dc. [gool mindie]; ballardi, bedd. Hydrocera triflora, w. and a.—32 *Rutaceæ.*—Ruta graveolens, l. [sadauf]. Bœnninghausenia albiflora, reich. Peganum harmala, l. [harmal]. Evodia roxburghiana, benth.; fraxinifolia, h.f. Melicope indica, wight. Zanthoxylum [toomroo] ovalifolium, wight [toomroo]; alatum, roxb. [tejbul]; tetraspermum, w. and a. [toomroo]; rhetsa, dc. [rhetsa]. Toddalia aculeata, pers. [toddaly]; bilocularis, w. and a. [toddaly]. Acronychia laurifolia, bl. Glycosmis pentaphylla, correa [conjy]. Murraya [caroo vaimboo] exotica l. [foreign conjy]; kœnigii, spr. [curry-leaf tree]. Clausena indica, oliv.; willdenovii, w. and a. Triphasia trifoliata, dc. [musk lime]. Limonia acidissima, l. [wild lime]; alata, w. and a. [wild lime]; bilocularis, rox. [wild lime]. Luvunga eleutherandra, dalz. Paramignya monophylla, wight. Atalantia monophylla, correa [monkey lime]; racemosa, w. and a. [monkey lime]; ceylanica, oliv.; missionis, oliv. [monkey lime]. Citrus [jambeeram] medica, l. [lime]; medica, linn., var. medica proper, brandis [citron]; medica, linn., var. limonum, brandis [lemon]; medica, linn., var. acida, brandis [sour lime]; medica, linn., var. limetta, brandis [sweet lime]; aurantium, linn. [orange]; aurantium, linn., var. aurantium proper, brandis [sweet orange]; aurantium, linn., var. bigaradia, brandis [bitter orange]; aurantium, linn., var. bergamia, brandis [bergamot orange]; decumana, l. [pummelow]; japonica, thunb. [cumquot]. Feronia elephantum, correa [wood-apple]; Ægle marmelos, correa [bael].—33 *Simarubeæ.*—Ailanthus [ailanto] glandulosa, desf. [japanese ailanto]; excelsa, roxb. [coromandel ailanto]; malabarica, dc. [malabar ailanto]. Samadera indica, gærtn. [samadarah]. Balanites roxburghii, planch [firework plant].—34 *Ochnaceæ.*—Ochna squarrosa, l. [shilandy]; wightiana, wall. [shilandy]; pumila, ham. Gomphia angustifolia, vahl.—35 *Burseraceæ.*—Boswellia [olibanum] serrata, roxb. [indian olibanum]; serrata, roxb., var. glabra [yellow dammer]; carterii, bird. [true olibanum]. Garuga pinnata, roxb. [garooga]. Balsamodendron [balsam] mukul, hk. [mookul bdellium]; roxburghii, arn. [indian bdellium]; berryi, arn. [kiloovay]; myrrha, nees. [bole]; kataf, kunth. [african bdellium]; opobalsamum, kunth. [balm of gilead]. Protium caudatum, w. and a. [hill kiloovay]; pubescens, w. and a. [hill kiloovay]. Canarium [cannary] commune, linn. [elemi]; strictum, roxb. [black dammer]. Filicium decipiens, thw. [pehimbia].—36. *Meliaceæ.*—Turræa virens, l.; villosa, benn. Naregamia alata, w. and a. [shrub orange]. Munronia wallichii, wight. Melia azadirachta, l. [neem]; azedarach, l. [large neem]; dubia, cav. [hill neem]. Cipadessa fruticosa, bl. Dysoxylum binectariferum, hk.; malabaricum, bedd.; beddomei, hiern. Sandoricum indicum, cav. [malay red wood]. Aglaia odorata, lour.; roxburghiana, miq. [tottila]; minutiflora, bedd. Lansium anamalayanum, bedd. [lanseh]; domesticum, jack. Amoora rohituka, w. and a. [rohitacam]; canarana, bth. and hk. f.; cucullata, roxb. [rohitacam]; spectabilis, miq. [rohitacam]; lawii, bth. and hk. f. [rohitacam]. Walsura [walsoora] ternata, roxb. [walsoora]; piscidia, roxb. [walsoora]. Heynea trijuga, roxb. Beddomea indica, hook.; simplicifolia, bedd. Carapa moluccensis, lam. [crab-oil plant]. Soymida febrifuga, adr. juss. [soymida]. Chickrassia tabularis, adr. juss. [chickrassy]. Cedrela toona, roxb. [toon]. Chloroxylon swietenia, dc. [satin wood].—37 *Chailletiaceæ.*—Chailletia gelonioides, hk. f.—38 *Olacineæ.*—Ximenia americana, willd. [false sandal]. Olax scandens, roxb.; wightiana, wall. Erythropalum populifolium, mast. Strombosia ceylanica, gardn. Anacolosa densiflora, bedd. Cansjera rheedii, gmel. Opilia amentacea, roxb. Gomphandra axillaris, wall.; polymorpha, wight. Apodytes benthamiana, wight; beddomei, mast. Mappia tomentosa, miers; fœtida, miers; ovata, miers; oblonga, miers. Miquelia dentata, bedd. Sarcostigma kleinii, w. and a. [pooyana].—39 *Ilicineæ.*—Ilex malabarica, bedd.; walkeri, wight and gardn.; denticulata, wall.; gardneriana, wight; wightiana, wall.—40 *Celastrineæ.*—Euonymus indicus, heyne; crenulatus, wall.; walkeri, wight; dichotomus, heyne; serratifolius, bedd.; paniculatus, wight; angulatus, wight. Glyptopetalum zeylanicum, thw.; grandiflorum, bedd. Microtropis latifolia, wight; ramiflora, wight; densiflora, wight; microcarpa, wight; ovalifolia, wight. Lophopetalum wightianum, arn. Kokoona zeylanica, thw. Pleurostylia wightii, w. and a. Celastrus paniculata, willd. [malkangany]. Gymnosporia [chintoo] ovata, wall. [chintoo]; rothiana, w. and a. [chintoo]; heyneana, w. and a.; wallichiana, spreng. [chintoo]; emarginata, roth. [small chintoo]; montana, roxb. [large chintoo]. Kurrimia paniculata, wall.; bipartita, laws. Elæodendron glaucum, pers. [nerija]. Hippocratea obtusifolia, roxb.; arnottiana, wight; grahami, wight; indica, willd. Salacia prinoides, dc.; brunoniana, w. and a.; reticulata, wight; macrosperma, wight; oblonga, wall.; fruticosa, heyne.—41 *Rhamneæ.*—Ventilago madraspatana, gærtn. [pappily]; calyculata, tul.; bombaiensis, dalz. Zizyphus [badary] jujuba, lamk. [bair]; glabrata, heyne [carook vauly]; nummularia, w. and a. [forest bair]; wynadensis, bedd. [badary]; vulgaris, lamk. [sinjid]; œnoplia, mill. [jackal bair]; xylopyrus, willd. [nutty bair]; napeca, willd.; incurva, roxb.; horrida, roth. [badary]; rugosa, lamk. [badary]. Rhamnus dahuricus, pall. [red rohitacam]; dahuricus, pall., var. hirsutus [red rohitacam]; wightii, w. and a. [red rohitacam]; catharticus, linn. [red rohitacam]. Scutia indica, brongn. [small bair]. Sageretia hamosa, brongn.; oppositifolia, brongn. Colubrina asiatica, brongn.; travancorica, bedd. Noltia africana, reich. Gouania microcarpa, dc.—42 *Ampelideæ.*—Vitis [draucshay] quadrangularis, wall. [piranday]; repens, w. and a. [draucshay]; discolor, dalz. [draucshay]; heyneana, wall.; pallida, w. and a. [draucshay]; glauca, w. and a.; gigantea, bedd.; repanda, w. and a. [draucshay]; adnata, wall. [draucshay]; linnæi, wall. [small acid naralay]; tomentosa, heyne [draucshay]; erioclada, w. and a. [draucshay]; lanata, roxb. [large naralay]; latifolia, roxb. [jungle angoor]; vinifera, linn. [angoor]; indica, l. [country angoor]; rheedei, w. and a. [draucshay]; setosa, wall. [bristly piranday]; carnosa, wall. [acid naralay]; canarensis, dalz.; roxburghii, w. and a. [draucshay]; himalayana, brand. [draucshay]; araneosus, dalz.; elongata, wall. [draucshay]; auriculata, roxb. [vegetable nerinjy]; tenuifolia, w. and a.; lanceolaria, roxb. [large acid naralay]; sulcata, laws.; pedata, vahl. [naralay]. Leea macrophylla, roxb.; cinerea, laws.; coriacea, laws.; crispa, willd.; aspera, wall.; sambucina, willd. [ratanhia]; integrifolia, roxb.; robusta, roxb.—43 *Sapindaceæ.*—Cardiospermum halicacabum, l. [oolinja]; canescens, wall. Hemigyrosa deficiens, bedd.; canescens, thw. [fig mango]. Erioglossum edule, bl. [rusty soapnut]. Allophylus cobbe, bl. Schleichera trijuga, willd. [ceylon oak]. Sapindus trifoliatus, l. [soapnut]; erectus, hiern. [soap nut]; mukorossi, geartn. [soap nut]; attenuatus, wall. [soap nut]; obovatus, w. & a. [soap nut]. Nephelium lappaceum, linn. [rambutan]; litchy, camb. [litchy]; longana, camb. [longan]; stipulaceum, bedd. Harpullia cupanoides, roxb. Dodonæa viscosa, l. [golla's plate]. Meliauthus major, l. Turpinia pomifera, dc.—44 *Sabiaceæ.*—Sabia malabarica, bedd. Meliosma wightii, planch.; simplicifolia, roxb.; arnottiana, wight.—45 *Anacardiaceæ.*—Rhus [sumach] mysorensis, heyne; succedania, linn. [red lac sumach]; coriaria, linn. [tanner's sumach]. Pistacia [pistah] integerrima, stewart [kakra singhy]; lentiscus, linn. [mastic]; terebinthus, linn. [turpentine pistah]; vera, linn. [edible pistah]. Mangifera indica, l. [mango]; sylvatica, roxb. [mango]; zeylanica, hook. Anacardium occidentale, l. [cashew]. Gluta travancorica, bedd. Buchanania latifolia, roxb. [chironjee]; angustifolia, roxb. [chironjee]; lanceolata, wight. [chironjee]. Solenocarpus indica, w. and a. Odina wodier, roxb. [wodier]. Semecarpus anacardium, l. [marking-nut]; travancorica, bedd.; auriculata, bedd. Holigarna arnottiana, hk. f.; ferruginea, march.; longifolia, rox. [holigarna]; grahamii, hk. f. [holigarna]; beddomei, hk. f. Nothopegia colebrookiana, bl.; travancorica, bedd.; aureo-fulva, bedd. Spondias [amrautam] dulcis, willd. [otaheite apple]; mangifera, willd. [wild mango]; acuminata, roxb.—46 *Moringeæ.*—Moringa pterygosperma, gærtn. [moringa]; concanensis, nimmo. [moringa]; aptera, gærtn. [moringa].—"CALYCIFLORÆ."—47 *Connaraceæ.*—Rourea santaloides, w. and a. Connarus monocarpus, l.; wightii, hk. f.; ritchiei, hk. f.—48 *Leguminosæ.*—Rothia trifoliata, pers. [jackal green gram]. Heylandia latebrosa, dc. Crotalaria [ghantaravam] biflora, l. [ghantaravam]; globosa, w. and a. [ghantaravam]; filipes, bth.; trichophora, bth.; stocksii, bth.; vestita, baker; prostrata, roxb. [ghantaravam]; humifusa, grah.; evolvuloides, wight [ghantaravam]; hirsuta, willd. [black giligitcha]; bifaria, l. [ghantaravam]; rubiginosa, willd. [ghantaravam]; pusilla, heyne [ghantaravam]; hirta, willd. [ghantaravam]; mysorensis, roth. [ghantaravam]; triquetra, dalz.; albida, heyne [hill giligitcha]; nana, burm. [ghantaravam]; linifolia, l. [black hill giligitcha]; tecta, roth.; calycina, schrank.; sessiliflora, linn. [ghantaravam]; chinensis, l.; speciosa, heyne [ghantaravam]; dubia, grah.; priestleyoides, bth.; lutescens, dalz.; peduncularis, grah.; retusa, l. [short giligitcha]; sericea, retz. [silky giligitcha]; leschenaultii, dc. [gantaravam]; formosa, grah. [ghantaravam]; barbata, grah. [ghantaravam]; longipes, w. and a.; salicifolia, heyne [ghantaravam]; lunata, bedd.; verrucosa, l. [forest giligitcha]; semperflorens, vent. [ghantaravam]; heyneana, grah. [ghantaravam]; leptostachya, bth.; juncea, l. [sunn]; obtecta, grah. [ghantaravam]; madurensis, wight [ghantaravam]; subperfoliata, wight [ghantaravam]; fulva, roxb. [ghantaravam]; pulcherrima, roxb. [ghantaravam]; lunulata, heyne [ghantaravam]; ramosissima roxb. [ghantaravam]; paniculata, willd. [ghantaravam]; medicaginea, lamk. [ghantaravam]; willdenoviana, dc. [ghantaravam]; trifoliastrum, willd. [nauga giligitcha]; notonii, w. and a. [ghantaravam]; rigida, heyne [ghantaravam]; orixensis, rottl. [stunted giligitcha]; lævigata, lamk.; clavata, w. and a. [ghantaravam]; striata, dc.; laburnifolia, l. [large giligitcha]; quinquefolia, l. [water giligitcha]; grahamiana, w. and a. [ghantaravam]; digitata, hk. [ghantaravam]. Trifolium repens, l. Parochetus communis, hamilt. Trigonella fœnum-græcum, l. [maitee]; corniculata, linn. [maitee]. Melilotus parviflora, desf. Cyamopsis psoralioides, dc. [guar]. Indigofera [neely] echinata, willd. [black nerinjy]; linifolia, retz. [neely]; cordifolia, heyne [neely]; triquetra, dalz.; glandulosa, willd. [neely]; enneaphylla, l. [red nerinjy]; uniflora, hamilt. [neely]; aspalathoides, vahl. [shiva's neem]; pentaphylla, l. [dog green gram]; tenuifolia, rottl. [neely]; viscosa, lamk. [dog neem]; pedicellata, w. and a. [neely]; trifoliata, l. [neely]; vestita, baker; trita, l. [neely]; subulata, vahl. [neely]; marginulata, grah. [neely]; paucifolia, delile. [neely]; parviflora, heyne [neely]; endecaphylla, jacq.; hirsuta, l. [large zanzibar indigo]; argentea, linn. [arabian indigo]; argentea, linn., var. cærulea [wild indigo]; tinctoria, l. [common indigo]; wightii, grah. [neely]; galegoides, dc.; atropurpurea, hamilt. [neely]; pulchella, roxb. [neely]; mysorensis, rottl. [neely]; anil, linn. [west indian indigo]. Psoralea corylifolia, l. [bawchee]. Millettia rubiginosa, w. and a.; splendens, w. and a.; racemosa, bth. Mundulea suberosa, bth. [sooptee]. Tephrosia tenuis, wall. [zanzibar indigo]; calophylla, bedd.; tinctoria, pers. [zanzibar indigo]; tinctoria, pers., var. incana [zanzibar indigo]; spinosa, pers. [zanzibar indigo]; senticosa, pers. [zanzibar indigo]; purpurea, pers. [zanzibar indigo]; purpurea, pers., var. maxima [zanzibar indigo]; purpurea, pers., var. pumila [zanzibar indigo]; hookeriana, w. and a. [zanzibar indigo]; villosa, pers; fusca, w. and a. [zanzibar indigo]. Sesbania [sesban] ægyptiaca, pers. [common sesban]; aculeata, pers. [prickly sesban]; aculeata, pers., var. paludosa [prickly sesban]; aculeata, pers., var. cannabina [prickly sesban]; procumbens, w. and a.; grandiflora, pers. [west indian sesban]; grandiflora, pers., var. coccinea [west indian sesban]. Astragalus verus, oliver [kateerah]. Geissapsis cristata, w. and a.; tenella, bth. Alhagi maurorum, desv. [arabian manna]. Zornia diphylla, pers. Stylosanthes mucronata, willd. Smithia sensitiva, ait.; geminiflora, roth.; purpurea, hk.; setulosa, dalz.; bigemina, dalz.; gracilis, bth.; capitata, dalz.; pycnantha, bth.; dichotoma, dalz.; blanda, wall. Æschynomene indica, l.; aspera, l. [solah]. Ormocarpum sennoides, dc. [wild moringa]. Leptodesmia congesta, bth. Eleiotis sororia, dc. Pycnospora hedysaroides, r. br. Pseudarthria viscida, w. and a. [three leaf poon]. Lourea vespertilionis, desv. Uraria picta, desv. [orila]; crinita, desv.; lagopoides, dc. [orila]; hamosa, wall. Alysicarpus monilifer, dc.; hamosus, edg.; vaginalis, dc.; bupleurifolius, dc.; longifolius, w. and a.; rugosus, dc.; tetragonolobus, edg.; pubescens, law.; belgaumensis, wight. Ougeinia dalbergioides, bth. [nemmy]. Desmodium [shaulicay] umbellatum, dc. [shaulicay]; cephalotes, wall. [shaulicay]; pulchellum, bth. [shaulicay]; biarticulatum, bth. [shaulicay]; triquetrum, dc. [shaulicay]; ormocarpoides, dc.; laxiflorum, dc. [shaulicay]; gardneri, bth.; dolabriforme, bth.; scalpe, dc. [shaulicay]; gangeticum, dc. [shaulicay]; latifolium, dc. [shaulicay]; wightii, grah. [shaulicay]; diffusum, dc. [shaulicay]; retroflexum, dc. [shaulicay]; capitatum, dc. [shaulicay]; rufescens, dec. [shaulicay]; polycarpum, dc. [shaulicay]; rotundifolium, baker; parviflorum, baker; triflorum, dc. [indian medicago]; reniforme, dc. [shaulicay]; heterophyllum, dc. [shaulicay]; rottleri, baker [shaulicay]; parvifolium, dc. [shaulicay]; gyrans, dc.; gyroides, dc. Arachis hypogæa, linn. [ground nut]. Abrus precatorius, l. [indian liquorice]; fruticulosus, wall. Cicer arietinum, linn. [bengal gram]. Vicia hirsuta, koch.; sativa, l.; faba, linn. [cabool country bean]. Ervum lens, linn. [masoor]. Lathyrus sativus, linn. [casauree]; odoratus, linn. [casauree]. Pisum sativum, linn. [calauyam]; arvense, linn. [calauyam]. Shuteria vestita, w. and a. Dumasia villosa, dc. Glycine [mausha parny] javanica, l. [maushaparny]; pentaphylla, dalz; soja, sieb. [maushaparny]; tomentosa, pursh. [horse gram shrub]. Teramnus labialis, spr. Mucuna [cowitch] monosperma, dc. [negro bean cowitch]; atropurpurea, dc. [buffalo cowitch]; gigantea, dc. [elephant cowitch]; hirsuta, w. and a.; pruriens, dc. [common cowitch]; capitata, w. and a. Erythrina [coral tree] indica, lam. [common coral tree]; stricta, roxb. [thorny coral tree]; ovalifolia, roxb. [devil coral tree]; suberosa, roxb. [white coral tree]. Galactia tenuiflora, w. and a. Spatholobus roxburghii, bth. Butea frondosa, roxb. [palaus]; superba, roxb. [palaus]. Canavalia ensiformis, dc. [tambattam]; mollis, wall. [tambattam]; obtusifolia, dc. [tambattam]. Pueraria tuberosa, dc. [sially]. Phaseolus [moodgam] lunatus, l. [country lobyah]; vulgaris, l., [lobyah]; adenanthus, meyer [wild green gram]; grahamianus, w. and a.; semi-erectus, l. [needle chakondah]; trilobus, ait. [field gram]; aconitifolius, jacq. [moorman's gram]; pauciflorus, dalz.; mungo, l. [green gram]; mungo, l. var. radiatus, l. [black gram]; trinervius, heyne [tufted green gram]; calcaratus, roxb. Vigna catiang, endl. [cow gram]; vexillata, bth. [cow gram]; wightii, bth.; pilosa, baker [cow gram]. Pachyrhizus angulatus, rich. [wayaka]. Clitoria ternatea, l. [crow creeper]; biflora, dalz. Dolichos [shimby] lablab, l. [country bean]; bracteatus, baker; biflorus, l. [madras horse gram]; ciliatus, klein.; falcatus, klein. [wild horse gram]. Psophocarpus tetragonolobus, dc. [goa bean]; palustris, desv. Atylosia candollei, w. and a. [jungle dholl]; lineata, w. and a.; albicans, bth.; rugosa, w. and a.; scarabæoides, bth. [jungle horse gram]. Cajanus indicus, spr. [common dholl]; indicus, spr., var. bicolor [common dholl]; indicus, spr., var. flavus [common dholl]. Dunbaria ferruginea, w. and a.; heynei, w. and a.; conspersa, bth. Cylista scariosa, ait. Rhynchosia [black dholl] rufescens, dc. [black dholl]; heynei w. and a. [black dholl]; nummularia, dc. [black dholl]; aurea, dc. [black dholl]; filipes, bth.; suaveolens, dc. [black dholl]; cana, dc. [black dholl]; beddomei, baker; cyanosperma, bth. [black dholl]; minima, dc. [black dholl]; velutina, w. and a. [black dholl]; viscosa, dc. [black dholl]; sericea, spanoghe.; acutissima, thw.; densiflora, dc. [black dholl]. Flemingia strobilifera, r. br.; lineata, roxb.; stricta, roxb.; grahamiana, w. and a.; congesta, roxb.; wallichii, w. and a.; involucrata, bth.; vestita, bth.; tuberosa, dalz. Dalbergia [yooga pattricay] sissoo, roxb. [sissoo]; latifolia, roxb. [malabar blackwood]; rubiginosa, roxb.; congesta, grah.; stocksii, bth.; sympathetica, nimmo; tamarindifolia, roxb.; lanceolaria, l. [caunooga]; volubilis, roxb.; paniculata, roxb. [yellow mountain ebony]; monosperma, dalz.; spinosa, roxb. Pterocarpus [vengay] indicus, willd. [padouk]; santalinus, l. [red sanders]; marsupium, roxb. [common vengay]. Pongamia glabra, vent. [karanj]. Derris scandens, bth.; robusta, bth. [creeper caunooga]; uliginosa, bth. [creeper caunooga]; oblonga, bth.; brevipes, baker; eualata, bedd.; heyneana, bth. [creeper caunooga]; platyptera, baker; canarensis, baker [creeper caunooga]; ovalifolia, bth. [creeper caunooga]; wightii, baker. Sophora tomentosa, l. [hill tungaid]; glauca, lesch. [hill tungaid]; heptaphylla, linn. [hill tungaid]; wightii, baker; interrupta, bedd. [hill tungaid]. Calpurnia aurea, baker. Ormosia travancorica, bedd. Cæsalpinia [coobairaucshy] bonducella, flem. [bonduc]; bonduc, roxb. [bonduc]; nuga, ait.; sappan, l. [sappan]; pulcherrima, swartz. [gold mohur tree]; sepiaria, roxb. [mysore thorn]; mimosoides, lam.; digyna, rottl.; coriaria, willd. [divy divy]. Mezoneurum cucullatum, w. and a. Pterolobium indicum, a. rich. Poinciana [ratnagandhy] elata, l. [soonkeshwaram]; regia, bojer. [foreign tungaid]. Parkinsonia aculeata, l. [parangy vail]. Wagatea spicata, dalz. [wagaty]. Cassia [soovarnacam] fistula, l. [common condray]; marginata, roxb. [red condray]; occidentalis, l. [casondy]; sophera, l. [stinking casondy]; tora, l. [chakondah]; tomentosa, l. [hill tungaid]; auriculata, l. [tungaid]; obovata, colld. [aleppo senna]; angustifolia, vahl. [tinnevelly senna]; alata, l. [foreign agatty]; siamea, lam. [yellow condray]; montana, heyne [soovarnacam]; timorensis, dec. [soovarnacam]; glauca, lam. [tree condray]; absus, l. [black horse gram]; pumila, lam. [lowly chakondah]; kleinii, w. and a. [soovarnacam]; mimosoides, l. [soovarnacam]; wallichiana, dec. [soovarnacam]; berryana, voigt [soovarnacam]; acutifolia, delile. [nubian senna]. Cynometra ramiflora, l. [iripa]; travancorica, bedd.; cauliflora, l. [iripa]. Hardwickia binata, roxb. [yaipy]; pinnata, roxb. [yaipy]. Saraca indica, linn. [bengal ashocam]. Tamarindus indica, l. [tamarind]. Humboldtia lauriflora, vahl.; unijuga, bedd.; brunonis, wall.; vahliana, wight. Bauhinia [mountain ebony] tomentosa, l. [wild mountain ebony]; acuminata, l. [white mountain ebony]; racemosa, lam. [small flowered mountain ebony]; malabarica, roxb. [malabar mountain ebony]; lawii, benth.; diphylla, hamilt. [mountain ebony]; retusa, ham. [nirpa mountain ebony]; vahlii, w. and a. [large mountain ebony]; macrostachya, wall. [mountain ebony]; ferruginea, roxb.; phœnicea, heyne; purpurea, l. [purple mountain ebony]; variegata, l. [variegated mountain ebony]; anguina, roxb. [snake-like mountain ebony]; cannabina [mountain ebony]; richardiana, wall. [mountain ebony]. Neptunia [water shoondy] oleracea, lour. [water shoondy]; triquetra, bth. [water shoondy]. Xylia dolabriformis, bth. [dark vail]. Entada scandens, bth. [scimitar pod]. Adenanthera pavonina, l. [false red sanders]. Prosopis [shivah] spicigera, l. [shamee]; dulcis, kunth. [manilla tamariud]; pubescens, benth. [screw mesquit]; glandulosa, tor. [mesquit]. Dicrostachys cinerea, w. and a. [ashy babool]. Parkia biglandulosa, w. et. a. [nitta]; roxburghii, g. don. [nitta]. Desmanthus virgatus, willd. [neer choondy]. Leucæna glauca, bth. [large chakondah]. Mimosa [shoondy] pudica, l. [shoondy]; rubricaulis, lam. [shoondy]; hamata, willd. [shoondy]; sepiaria, bth. Acrocarpus fraxinifolius, wight. [shingle tree]. Acacia [cantalam] farnesiana, willd. [piyvail]; planifrons, w. and a. [ooday vail]; Acacia arabica, willd. [babool]; eburnea, willd.; tomentosa, willd. [ooday vail]; leucophlæa, willd. [velvail]; suma, kurz. [white sundra]; catechu, willd [catechu]; sundra, dc. [sundra]; ferruginea, dc. [anasandra]; latronum, willd. [vellay moolvail]; concinna, dc. [soap-pod]; intsia, willd. [corindah]; pennata, willd. [biswool]; wightii, baker; melanoxylon, r. br. [australian black-wood]. Albizzia [sirissa] lebbek, bth. [common sirissa]; odoratissima, bth. [fragrant sirissa]; procera, bth.; procera, benth., var. elata, baker [hill sirissa]; stipulata, boivin. [stone sirissa]; amara, boivin. [dark sirissa]. Pithecolobium [auragvadham] dulce, bth. [corcapilly]; gemminatum, bth; umbellatum, bth. [auragvadham]; bigeminum, bth. [wild condray]; subcoriaceum, thw. [auragvadham]; saman, benth. [zamang]. Inga cynometroides, bedd.—49 *Rosaceæ.*—Parinarium indicum, bedd.; travancoricum, bedd. Prunus [auloo] amygdalus, baill. [baudam]; persica, hook. and f. [shaftauloo]; armeniaca, linn. [mishmish]; cerasus, linn. [cherry]; communis, huds. var. institia [albaca]; domestica, linn. [auloochah]. Pygeum wightianum, bl.; gardneri, hk. f. Rubus [gowry's fruit] moluccanus, l. [gowry's fruit]; ellipticus, sm. [gowry's fruit]; ellipticus, sm., var. hirta [gowry's fruit]; lasiocarpus, sm. [gowry's fruit]; racemosus, roxb.; rosæfolius, smith [gowry's fruit]. Fragaria indica, andr.; nilgerrensis, schld. Potentilla leschenaultiana, ser.; kleiniana, w. and a.; supina, l. Alchemilla indica, gard. Rosa [gool] damascena, mill. [damask rose]; centifolia, linn. [cabbage rose]; gallica, linn. [french rose]; indica, linn. [indian rose]; alba, linn. [indian white rose]; moschata, mill. [musk rose]; leschenaultiana, w. and a. Cydonia vulgaris, pers. [bedauna]. Eriobotrya japonica, lindl. [loquat]. Pyrus malus, linn. [seb]; communis, linn. [amrood]. Photinia lindleyana, w. and a.; notoniana, w. and a. Cotoneaster buxifolia, wall.—50 *Saxifrageæ.*—Vahlia viscosa, roxb.; oldenlandioides, roxb. Parnassia wightiana, wall.; mysorensis, heyne.—51 *Crassulaceæ.*—Tillæa pentandra, royle. Bryophyllum calycinum, salisb. Kalanchoe glandulosa, hochst.; floribunda, w. and a. [zakhm hayant]; grandiflora, w. and a. [zakhm hayant]; brasiliensis, camb.; laciniata, dc. [zakhm hayant].—52 *Droseraceæ.*—Drosera burmanni, vahl.; indica, l.; peltata, sm.—53 *Halorageæ.*—Serpicula indica, thw. Myriophyllum indicum, willd.; intermedium, dc. Callitriche stagnalis, scop.—54 *Rhizophoreæ.*—Rhizophora mucronata, lam. [white candel mangrove]; conjugata, l. [white candel mangrove]. Ceriops candolleana, arn. Kandelia rheedii, w. and a. [candel mangrove]. Bruguiera gymnorhiza, lamk. [tree mangrove]; eriopetala, w. and a. [tree mangrove]; caryophylloides, bl. [tree mangrove]; malabarica, arn.; parviflora, w. and a. [tree mangrove]. Carallia integerrima, dc. [caurally mangrove]; lanceæfolia, rox. [caurally mangrove]. Weihea ceylanica, baill. Blepharistemma corymbosum, wall.—55 *Combretaceæ.*—Terminalia [antya parny] catappa, l. [catapang]; belerica, roxb. [belleric myrobalan]; chebula, retz. [chebulic myrobalan]; citrina, rox. [harra]; arjuna, bedd. [white murdah]; tomentosa, bedd.; tomentosa, bedd., var. typica [black murdah]; tomentosa, bedd., var. coriacea [leathery murdah]; paniculata, roth. [flowering murdah]; alata, don. [antya parny]. Calycopteris floribunda, lamk. [white wodala]. Anogeissus [dhavam] latifolia, wall. [vekkauly]; acuminata, wall. [pauchimaun]. Lumnitzera racemosa, willd. [madagascar mangrove]. Combretum decandrum, roxb. [wodala]; acuminatum, roxb.; ovalifolium, roxb. [wodala]; extensum, roxb. Quisqualis indica, l. [rangoon creeper]; malabarica, bedd. Illigera obtusa, meissn. Gyrocarpus jacquini, roxb. [tanakk]. Juglans regia, linn. [acroot].—56 *Myrtaceæ.*—Melaleuca leucadendron, l. [cajeput]. Eucalyptus [australian gum tree] globulus, labill. [blue gum]; resinifera, smith. [red gum]. Psidium guyava, l. [guava]; guyava, l., var. pyriferum [guava]; guyava, l., var. pomiferum [guava]. Myrtus communis, linn. [foreign mindie]. Rhodomyrtus tomentosa, wight. [hill guava]. Eugenia [jamboo] malaccensis, linn. [malacca jaumoon]; munronii, wight [water jaumoon]; aquea, burm. [red jaumoon]; jambos, linn. [rose apple]; javanica, lamk. [java jaumoon]; beddomei, duthie; hemispherica, wight [jamboo]; læta, ham. [jamboo]; cylindrica, wight [jamboo]; arnottiana, wight [small jaumoon]; wightiana, wight [jamboo]; zeylanica, wight [ceylon jaumoon]; montana, wight [jamboo]; lissophylla, thw.; gardneri, thw. [jamboo]; caryophyllæa, wight [jamboo]; revoluta, wight; neesiana, wight [jamboo]; calophyllifolia, wight [jamboo]; rubicunda, wight [jamboo]; malabarica, bedd. [malabar jaumoon]; alternifolia wight [moy]; operculata, rox. [cherry jaumoon]; stocksii, duthie; jambolana, lam. [common jaumoon]; jambolana, lamk., var. caryophyllifolia [clove-leaved jaumoon]; heyneana, wall. [jamboo]; jossinia, duthie [jamboo]; floccosa, bedd. [jamboo]; codyensis, munro; macrosepala, duthie; calcadensis, bedd. [jamboo]; bracteata, roxb. [coromandel jaumoon]; rottleriana, w. and a. [jamboo]; argentea, bedd. [jamboo]; mooniana, wight [jamboo]; uniflora, linn. [jamboo]; microphylla, bedd. [jamboo]; singampattiana, bedd.; caryophyllata, willd [lavangam]; wynaadensis, bedd. [jamboo]. Pimenta acris, wight. [china pepper]. Barringtonia [indian oak] speciosa, forst. [andaman indian oak]; racemosa, bl. [common indian oak]; acutangula, gærtn. [small indian oak]. Careya herbacea, roxb. [coomby]; arborea, roxb. [coomby]; sphærica, roxb. [coomby].—57 *Melastomaceæ.*—Osbeckia truncata, don. [forest bengal gram]; cupularis, don. [forest bengal gram]; zeylanica, willd. [forest bengal gram]; hispidissima, wight [forest bengal gram]; gracilis, bedd.; aspera, bl. [forest bengal gram]; glauca, benth.; wightiana, benth. [forest bengal gram]; leschenaultiana, dc. [forest bengal gram]; reticulata, bedd.; octandra, dc. [forest bengal gram]; wynaadensis, c. b. clarke; kotigueda, naud. [forest bengal gram]. Melastoma malabathricum, l. Kendrickia walkeri, hk. f. Sonerila brunonis, w. and a.; pedunculosa, thw.; amabilis, triana.; travancorica, bedd.; speciosa, zenk.; grandiflora, wall.; elegans, wight.; versicolor, wight.; wallichii, benn.; rotundifolia, bedd.; bensoni, hk. f. Medinilla beddomei, c. b. clarke; malabarica, bedd. Memecylon wightii, thw.; amabile, bedd. [cassa]; gracile, bedd. [cassa]; procerum, thw. [cassa]; terminale, dalz. [cassa]; amplexicaule, roxb. [cassa]; deccanense, c. b. clarke; heyneanum, bth. [cassa]; angustifolium, wight [cassa]; edule, roxb. [cassa].—58 *Lythraceæ.*—Ammannia peploides, spr. [agnivendram]; rotundifolia, ham. [agnivendram]; tenuis, c. b. clarke [agnivendram]; floribunda, clarke [agnivendram]; rotala, f. mull. [agnivendram]; pentandra, roxb. [agnivendram]; baccifera, l. [agnivendram]; salicifolia, monti. [agnivendram]; cordata, w. and a. [agnivendram]; lanceolata, heyne [agnivendram]; multiflora, roxb. [agnivendram]; octandra, l. [agnivendram]. Woodfordia floribunda, salisb. [godaury]. Pemphis acidula, forst. Lawsonia alba, lamk. [mindie]. Lagerstrœmia [cadaly] indica, l. [china mindie]; parviflora, roxb. [chennangy]; lanceolata, wall. [venteak]; rottleri, c. b. clarke; flos-reginæ, retz. [adambo]. Sonneratia apetala, ham.; acida, l. [blatty]. Punica granatum, l. [anaur].—59 *Onagraceæ.*—Jussiæa repens, l. [lowly lavangam]; suffruticosa, l. [lowly lavangam]. Ludwigia parviflora, roxb.; prostrata, roxb. Circæa alpina, l. Trapa bispinosa, roxb. [singhaura].—60 *Samydaceæ.*—Casearia glomerata, rox. [anavinga]; graveolens, dalz. [anavinga]; esculenta, roxb. [mormassy]; coriacea, thw. [anavinga];

rubescens, dalz. [anavinga]; tomentosa, roxb. [anavinga]; wynadensis, bedd. [anavinga]. Homalium zeylanicum, bth.; travancoricum, bedd.—61 *Passifloreæ.*—Passiflora leschenaultii, dc. [jimiky]. Modecca wightiana, wall.; palmata, lam. Carica papaya, linn. [papaw].—62 *Cucurbitaceæ.*—Trichosanthes [snake gourd] palmata, roxb. [bitter snake, gourd]; dioica, roxb. [palwal snake gourd]; nervifolia, l. [short snake gourd]; cucumerina, l. [wild snake gourd]; anguina, l. [common snake gourd]; lobata, roxb. Gymnopetalum wightii, arn. Lagenaria vulgaris, seringe. [fakeer's bottle]. Luffa [luffa] ægyptiaca, mill. [oil-giving luffa]; acutangula, rox. [common luffa]; acutangular, rox., var. amara, rox. [bitter luffa]; echinata, rox. [snake luffa]; kleinii, w. and a. Benincasa cerifera, savi. [wax gourd]. Momordica charantia, l. [carolah]; dioica, roxb. [prickly carolah]; cochinchinensis, spr. [carolah]; cymbalaria, fenzl [carolah]. Cucumis [oorvauroo] trigonus, roxb. [country cucumber]; melo, l. [common melon]; melo, linn., var. momordica [mottled melon]; melo, linn., var. utilissimus [country melon]; sativus, l. [common cucumber]. Citrullus [indra vally] colocynthis, schrad. [bitter water melon]; vulgaris, schrad. [sweet water melon]. Cephalandra indica, naud. [indian caper]. Cucurbita [carcauroo] maxima, duchesne [great pumpkin]; moschata, duchesne [true musk melon]; pepo, dc. [common pumpkin]; ovifera, linn. [vegetable marrow]. Bryonia laciniosa, l. [neyoonny]. Mukia scabrella, arn. [mosmoosky]; leiosperma, thw. Zehneria baueriana, endl.; hookeriana, arn.; umbellata, thw. [rama's caper]. Rhynchocarpa fœtida, schrad. Corallocarpus epigæa, hk. f. [braminy-kite caper]. Ctenolepis garcini, naud. Zanonia indica, l. [penarvully].—63 *Begoniaceæ.*—Begonia cordifolia, thw.; fallax, dc.; integrifolia, dalz.; crenata, dryand.; canarana, miq.; subpeltata, wight; concanensis, a. dc.; trichocarpa, dalz.; albo-coccinea, hk.; floccifera, bedd.; malabarica, lamk.; malabarica, lamk., var. dipetala; malabarica, lamk., var. hydrophila; malabarica, lamk., var. malabarica.—64 *Datiscaceæ.*—Tetrameles nudiflora, r. br.—65 *Cacteæ.*—Opuntia dillenii, haw. [prickly pear].—66 *Ficoideæ.*—Sesuvium protulacastrum, l. Trianthema monogyna, l. [shauranay]; crystallina, vahl. [shauranay]; pentandra, linn. [shauranay]; decandra, l. [shauranay]. Orygia decumbens, forsk [red shauranay]. Mollugo [parpatam] hirta, thunb.; spergula, l. [tirye]; stricta, l. [wild tirye]; cerviana, seringe [hazaur danah]; disticha, seringe; nudicaulis, lamk. Gisekia pharnaceoides, l. [manaly].—67 *Umbelliferæ.*—Hydrocotyle javanica, thunb. [indian pennywort]; conferta, wight [indian pennywort]; rotundifolia, roxb. [indian pennywort]; asiatica, l. [indian pennywort]. Sanicula europæa, l. Bupleurum plantaginifolium, wight; mucronatum, w. and a.; distichophyllum, w. and a. Apium graveolens, linn. [karafs]; petroselinum, willd. [karafs]. Petroselinum sativum, wight [makdoonas]. Carum [ajmood] carui, l. [caraway]; stictocarpum, c. b. clarke; roxburghianum, bth. [ajmood ajwaun]; copticum, bth. [ajwaun]. Pimpinella heyneana, wall. [anise]; leschenaultii, dc. [anise]; candolleana, w. and a. [anise]; monoica, dalz.; lateriflora, dalz.; anisum, linn. [anise]. Seseli indicum, w. and a. Fœniculum vulgare, gærtn. [sonf]. Polyzygus tuberosus, dalz. Ferula [baulhicam] narthex, boiss. [asafœtida]; galbaniflua, boiss. [galbanum]; persica, wight. [sagapenum]. Dorema ammoniacum, don. [ooshak]; aureum, stocks [ooshak]. Peucedanum graveolens, bth. [sowa]; anamallayense, c. b. clarke. Heracleum hookerianum, w. and a.; rigens, wall.; sprengelianum, w. and a.; pedatum, wight. Coriandrum sativum, l. [cassibor]. Cuminum cyminum, l. [jeerah]. Daucus carota, linn. [gaujar].—68 *Araliaceæ.*—Aralia malabarica, bedd. Pentapanax leschenaultii, seem. Polyscias acuminata, seem. Heptapleurum rostratum, bedd.; racemosum, bedd.; venulosum, seem.; stellatum, gærtn.; wallichianum, c. b. clarke. Brassaia capitata, c. b. clarke.—69 *Cornaceæ.*—Alangium lamarkii, thw. [alanjy]. Mastixia arborea, c.b. clarke; pentandra, bl.—"COROLLIFLORÆ."—70 *Caprifoliaceæ.*—Viburnum punctatum, ham.; coriaceum, bl.; hebanthum, w. and a.; erubescens, wall. Lonicera leschenaultii, wall.; ligustrina, wall.—71 *Rubiaceæ.*—Anthocephalus cadamba, miq. [cadamba]. Adina cordifolia, hk. f. [yellow cadamba]. Stephegyne parvifolia, korth. [water cadamba]; tubulosa, hk. f. Nauclea purpurea, roxb.; missionis, wall. Uncaria gambier, roxb. [gambier]. Hymenodictyon excelsum, wall. [wild anaur]; obovatum, wall [wild anaur]. Cinchona [koinah] officinalis, linn. [koinah]; officinalis, l., var. uritusinga [koinah]; officinalis, l., var. condaminea [koinah]; officinalis l., var. crispa [koinah]; calisaya, wedd. [koinah]; lancifolia, mutis. [koinah]; micrantha, r. et. p. [koinah]; nitida, r. and p. [koinah]; peruviana, how. [koinah]; succirubra, pav. [koinah]. Wendlandia exserta, dc.; notoniana, wall.; lawii, hk. f.; angustifolia, wight. Dentella repens, forst. [small tirye]. Argostemma courtallense, arn.; verticillatum, wall. Neurocalyx wightii, arn. Fergusonia zeylanica, hk. f. Hedyotis fruticosa, l.; purpurescens, bedd.; stylosa, br.; articularis, br.; pruinosa, w. and a.; swertioides, hk. f.; beddomei, hk. f.; buxifolia, bedd.; albonervia, bedd.; travancorica, bedd.; hirsutissima, bedd.; verticillaris, w. and a.; viscida, bedd.; auricularia, l.; cærulea, w. and a.; nitida, w. and a. Oldenlandia [field parpatam] corymbosa, l. [wild chayroot]; diffusa, roxb.; heynii, br. [field parpatam]; crystallina, roxb. [field parpatam]; umbellata, l. [chayroot]; wightii, hk. f.; trinervia, retz. [field parpatam]; brachiata, wight; dichotoma, kœn. [counterfeit chayroot]; stocksii, hk. f.; aspera, dc. [field parpatam]; gracilis, dc.; stricta, l.; sbuteri, hk. f. [field parpatam]; paniculata, l. [field parpatam]; biflora, l. [field parpatam]; nudicaulis, roth. [field parpatam]. Anotis leschenaultiana, w and a.; decipiens, hk. f.; lancifolia, dalz.; rheedii, w. and a.; montholoni, hk. f.; quadrilocularis, thw.; carnosa, dalz.; fœtida, dalz.; ritchiei, hk., f.; wightiana, wall.; monosperma, w. and a. Ophiorrhiza mungos, l. [mongoose snake root]; harrisiana, heyne [mongoose snake root]; brunonis, w. and a. [mongoose snake root]; grandiflora, wight [mongoose snake root]; roxburghiana, wight [mongoose snake root]; eriantha, wight [mongoose snake root]; hirsutula, wight; pectinata, arn. Mussænda tomentosa, wight [moossanda]; frondosa, l. [moossanda]; corymbosa, rox. [moossanda]. Acranthera grandiflora, bedd.; anamallica, bedd. Adenosacme lawii, hk. f. Webera corymbosa, will. [tirauna]; monosperma, w. and a. [tirauna]; lucens, hk. f. [tirauna]; canarica, hk. f.; nilagirica, hk. f. Byrsophyllum tetrandrum, hk. f. Randia [emetic nut] uliginosa, dc. [grey emetic nut]; dumetorum, lamk. [common emetic nut]; malabarica, lamk. [bedaly emetic nut]; densiflora, benth.; gardneri, thw. [emetic nut]; rugulosa, thw.; candolleana, w. and a. [emetic nut]; speciosa, bedd. [emetic nut]. Gardenia [gandharajah] lucida, roxb. [decamallee]; gummifera, l.; latifolia, ait. [hill emetic nut]; coronaria, ham. [gandharajah]; turgida, roxb. [nunjoondam]; campanulata, rox. [gandharajah]; florida, linn. [cape jasmine]. Diplospora apiocarpa, dalz.; sphærocarpa, dalz. Scyphiphora hydrophyllacea, gærtn. Guettarda speciosa, l. [indian zebra wood]. Knoxia corymbosa, willd; mollis, w. and a.; heyneana, dc.; wightiana, wall. Octotropis travancorica, bedd. Canthium didymum, roxb. [black cauray]; umbellatum, wight; neilgherrense, wight [cauray]; ficiforme, hk. f.; travancoricum, bedd.; rheedii, dc.; angustifolium, roxb. [cauray]; parviflorum, lamk. [cauray]. Vangueria spinosa, roxb. Ixora [q.v.] acuminata, roxb. [ixora]; lanceolaria, colebr. [ixora]; notoniana, wall. [ixora]; johnsoni, hk. f.; polyantha, wight [ixora]; elongata, heyne; brachiata, roxb. [ixora]; parviflora, vahl. [large jungle geranium]; coccinea, l. [jungle geranium]; stricta, rox. [pink jungle geranium]; undulata, rox. [white jungle geranium]; barbata, rox. [ixora]; nigricans, br. [ixora]. Pavetta indica, l. [pavetta]; indica, l., var. tomentosa [pavetta]; hispidula, w. and a.; angustifolia, w. and a.; breviflora, dc.; brunonis, wall.; wightii, hk. f. Coffea wightiana, w. and a. [coffee]; travancorensis, w. and a. [coffee]; arabica, linn. [coffee]. Morinda citrifolia, l. [dyeing mulberry]; citrifolia, linn., var. citrifolia proper [dyeing mulberry]; citrifolia, linn., var. bracteata [dyeing mulberry]; citrifolia, linn., var. elliptica [dyeing mulberry]; tinctoria, roxb. [dyeing mulberry]; tinctoria, rox., var. tinctoria proper [dyeing mulberry]; tinctoria, rox., var. tomentosa [dyeing mulberry]; umbellata, l. [small dyeing mulberry]. Psychotria thwaitesii, hk. f.; congesta, w. and a.; macrocarpa, hk. f.; subintegra, w. and a.; truncata, wall.; dalzellii, hk. f.; elongata, wight; sarmentosa, bl.; madraspatana, hk. f.; divergens, kurz.; sulcata, wall.; bisulcata, w. and a.; connata, wall.; anamallayana, bedd.; johnsoni, hk. f.; nudiflora, w. and a. Chasalia curviflora, thw. Geophila reniformis, don. Lasianthus jackianus, w.; oblongifolius, bedd.; blumeanus, wight; ciliatus, wight; strigillosus, hk. f.; acuminatus, wight; parvifolius, wight; obovatus, bedd.; truncatus, bedd.; venulosus, wight; capitulatus, wight; dichotomus, wight. Saprosma indicum, dalz.; fragrans, bedd.; ceylanicum, bedd.; corymbosum, bedd. Pæderia fœtida, linn. [gandhaulee]. Hamiltonia suaveolens, roxb. Hydrophylax maritima, linn., f. Spermacoce stricta, l.; ocymoides, burm.; hispida, l. [madanaghanta]. Rubia cordifolia, l. [munjeet]. Galium rotundifolium, l.; mollugo, l. —72 *Valerianeæ.*—Nardostachys jatamansi, dec. [jatamansy]. Valeriana hardwickii, wall.; hookeriana, w. and a.; leschenaultii, dc.; beddomei, c. b. clarke.—73 *Dipsaceæ.*—Dipsacus leschenaultii, coult.—74 *Compositæ.*—Centratherum reticulatum, bth.; molle, bth.; courtallense, bth.; ritchiei, hk. f.; phyllolænum, bth.; tenue, clarke; hookeri, clarke. Lamprachænium microcephalum, bth. Adenoon indicum, dalz. Vernonia malabarica, hk. f.; beddomei, hk. f.; bracteata, wall. [wild jeerah]; peninsularis, clarke; cinerea, less. [wild jeerah]; divergens, bth. [wild jeerah]; chinensis, less. [wild jeerah]; candolleana, w. and a. [wild jeerah]; anthelmintica, willd. [wild jeerah]; elæagnifolia, dc. [wild jeerah]; salviæfolia, wight [wild jeerah]; indica, clarke [wild jeerah]; pectiniformis, dc. [wild jeerah]; arborea, ham. [wild jeerah]; volkameriæfolia, dc. [wild jeerah]; travancorica, hk. f. [wild jeerah]. Elephantopus scaber, l. [elephant's foot]. Adenostemma viscosum, forst. Ageratum conyzoides, l. Eupatorium ayapana, vent. [ayappanay]. Dichrocephala latifolia, dc.; chrysanthemifolia, dc. Cyathocline lyrata, cass. Grangea maderaspatana, poir. [madras absinth]. Myriactis wightii, dc. Erigeron linifolius, willd.; asteroides, roxb.; alpinus, l. Microglossa zeylanica, bth. Conyza viscidula, wall. stricta, willd.; adenocarpa, dalz. Blumea amplectens, dc.; bifoliata, dc.; wightiana, dc.; neilgherrensis, hk. f.; barbata, dc; glomerata, dc.; lacera, dc.; hieracifolia, dc.; laciniata, dc.; virens, dc.; membranacea, dc.; jacquimontii, hk. f.; oxyodonta, dc.; eriantha, dc.; malcolmii, hk. f.; belangeriana, dc.; malabarica, hk. f.; flexuosa, clarke; spectabilis, dc. Laggera alata, schultz.; pterodonta, bth. [wild country radish]; aurita, schultz. [wild country radish]. Pluchea tomentosa, dc. Nanothamnus sericeus, thoms. Epaltes divaricata, cass.; pygmæa, dc. Sphæranthus [moondy] amaranthoides, burm. [fever toolsy]; indicus, linn. [seed toolsy]. Blepharispermum petiolare, dc.; subsessile, dc. Anaphalis beddomei, hk. f.; oblonga, dc.; notoniana, dc.; leptophylla, dc.; aristata, dc; wightiana, dc.; marcescens, clarke; brevifolia, dc.; neelgerriana, dc.

Gnaphalium luteo-album, l. [buffalo carolah]; hypoleucum, dc. [buffalo carolah]; indicum, l. [buffalo carolah]; pulvinatum, delile [buffalo carolah]. Helichrysum buddleioides, dc.; wightii, clarke. Cæsulia axillaris, roxb. Vicoa auriculata, cass.; cernua, dalz.; vestita, bth. Pulicaria wightiana, clarke.; angustifolia, dc. Carpesium cernuum, l. Lagascea mollis, cav. Chrysogonum heterophyllum, bth.; arnottianum, bth. Xanthium strumarium, l. [burdock datura]. Siegesbeckia orientalis, l. [pig plant]. Eclipta alba, hassk. [bhangrah]. Sclerocarpus africanus, jacq. Blainvillea latifolia, dc. Wedelia calendulacea, less. [yellow bhangrah]; urticæfolia, dc. [yellow bhangrah]; biflora, dc. [yellow bhangrah]. Spilanthes acmella, l. Helianthus annuus, linn. [sooryacaunty]. Guizotia abyssynica, cass. [ramtil]. Synedrella nodiflora, gærtn. Glossocardia linearifolia, cass. Bidens pilosa, l.; decomposita, clarke. Glossogyne pinnatifida, dc. Gulinsoga parviflora, cav. Tridax procumbens, l. Achillea millefolium, l. Anthemis nobilis, linn. [baboona]. Chrysanthemum coronarium, linn. [shaumanty]; indicum, linn. [shaumanty]; carinatum, schous. [shaumanty]. Matricaria chamomilla, linn. [country baboona]. Cotula anthemoides, l.; hemisphærica, wall. Anacyclus pyrethrum, nees [akalkarah]. Centipeda orbicularis, lour. [nakchiknee]. Sphæromorphæa russeliana, dc. Artemisia parviflora, roxb.; vulgaris, l. [indian absinth]. Gynura nitida, dc.; lycopersicifolia, dc.; angulosa, dc.; pseudo-china, dc. Emilia sonchifolia, dc. [hare's ear]. Notonia grandiflora, dc.; balsamica, dalz.; walkeri, clarke. Senecio zeylanicus, dc.; nilgheryanus, dc.; lavandulæfolius, dc.; sexatilis, wall.; polycephalus, clarke; lessingianus, clarke; ludens, clarke.; hohenackeri, hk. f.; tenuifolius, burm.; hewrensis, hk.; edgeworthii, hk. f.; dalzellii, clarke; lawii, clarke; gibsoni, hk. f.; belgaumensis, clarke; araneosus, dc.; corymbosus, wall.; scandens, don.; candicans, dc. Echinops echinatus, dc. [camel thistle]. Cnicus wallichii, dc. Silybum marianum, gærtn. Saussurea candicans, clarke [costum]; lappa, clarke [costum]. Goniocaulon glabrum, cass. Tricholepis radicans, dc.; amplexicaulis, clarke; glaberrima, dc.; angustifolia, dc. Volutarella divaricata, bth. Centaurea melitensis, l. Carthamus tinctorius, l. [bastard saffron]. Dicoma tomentosa, cass. Cichorium intybus, linn. [indian endive]; endivia, l. [indian endive]. Picris hieracioides, l. Crepis japonica, bth.; acaulis, hk. f. Hypochæris glabra, l.; japonica, bth. Taraxacum officinale, wigg. Lactuca heyneana, dc.; scariola, linn., var. sativa [kahoo]; hastata, dc. Sonchus asper, vill.; oleraceus, l.; arvensis, l. Launæa nudicaulis, less.; pinnatifida, cass. [style plant]. Tagetis erecta, linn. [gendah].—75 *Goodenovieæ.*—Scævola kœnigii, vahl.; lobelia, l.—76 *Campanulaceæ.*—Lobelia trigona, roxb.; trialata, ham.; zeylanica, l.; nicotianæfolia, heyne. [wild pogauk]; excelsa, leschen. Cephalostigma schimperi, hochst.; flexuosum, h. f. and t. Wahlenbergia gracilis, dc. Sphenoclea zeylanica, gærtn. [water long pepper]. Campanula colorata, wall.; alphonsii, wall.; fulgens, wall.—77 *Vacciniaceæ.*—Vaccinium [hill carondah] nilgherrense, wight [hill carondah]; leschenaultii, wight [hill carondah].—78 *Ericaceæ.*—Gaultheria fragrantissima, wall. Rhododendron arboreum, sm. [neilgherry rhododendron].—79 *Plumbagineæ.*—Plumbago [chitramoolam] zeylanica, l. [chitramoolam]; rosea, l. [chitramoolam]; capensis, thunb. [chitramoolam]. Vogelia indica, gibs.—80 *Primulaceæ.*—Lysimachia leschenaultii, duby.; deltoides, wight. Anagallis arvensis, l. Centunculus tenellus, duby.—81 *Myrsineæ.*—Mæsa indica, wall.; dubia, wall. Myrsine capitellata, wall. Embelia ribes, burm. [byebarang]; adnata, bedd.; robusta, roxb.; viridiflora, schff.; gardneriana, wight. Ardisia courtallensis, wight; amplexicaulis, bedd.; pauciflora, heyne.; rhomboidea, wight; humilis, vahl. Antistrophe serratifolia, hk. f.—82 *Sapotaceæ.*—Sideroxylon tomentosum, roxb. [foreign ilanjy]. Isonandra villosa, wight; candolliana, wight; perrottetiana, wight; stocksii, clarke; lanceolata, wight. Dichopsis elliptica, bth. [panchonty]. Bassia [mohwah] latifolia, roxb. [wild mohwah]; longifolia, l. [common mohwah]; malabarica, bedd. [mohwah]; microphylla, hook [mohwah]; butyraceæ, roxb. [butter mohwah]. Mimusops [csheericay] elengi, l. [ilanjy]; roxburghiana, wight [jointed paulay]; hexandra, roxb. [monkey-face paulay]; kauki, linn. [edible paulay]. Achras sapota, linn. [foreign mohwah].—83 *Ebenaceæ.*—Maba nigrescens, dalz. [neilgherry satin wood]; buxifolia, pers. [neilgherry satin wood]; micrantha, hiern [neilgherry satin wood]. Diospyros [indian ebony] pruriens, dalz. [indian ebony]; montana, roxb. [forest gaub]; kaki, linn. [chinese gaub]; embryopteris, pers. [gaub]; foliolosa, wall. [indian ebony]; ovalifolia, wight [indian ebony]; ebenum, kœn. [ceylon ebony]; assimilis, bedd. [indian ebony]; sylvatica, roxb. [indian ebony]; microphylla, bedd. [indian ebony]; chloroxylon, roxb. [indian ebony]; oocarpa, thw. [indian ebony]; tupru, hamlt.; tomentosa, roxb. [sweet gaub]; melanoxylon, roxb. [coromandel ebony]; insignis, thw. [indian ebony]; hirsuta, linn. [calaminder wood]; candolleana, wight [indian ebony]; nilagirica, bedd. [indian ebony]; affinis, thw.; paniculata, dalz. [indian ebony].—84 *Styraceæ.*—Symplocos spicata, roxb. [lodh]; oligandra, bedd. [lodh]; ferruginea, rox. [lodh]; nervosa, a. dc. [lodh]; racemosa, rox. [lodh]; macrophylla, wall. [lodh]; monantha, wight [lodh]; anamallayana, bedd. [lodh]; microphylla, wight [lodh]; macrocarpa, wight; gardneriana, wight [lodh]; hohenackeri, clarke; beddomei, clarke; foliosa, wight [lodh]; rosea, bedd. [lodh]; acuminata, bedd. [lodh]; pulchra, wight [lodh]; obtusa, wall. [lodh]; pendula, wall. [lodh]; sessilis, clarke [lodh]. Styrax [dhoopam] benzoin, dryand [benzoin]; officinale, linn. [true storax].—85 *Oleaceæ.*—Jasminum [jasmine] sambac, ait. [arabian jasmine]; pubescens, willd. [musk jasmine]; rottlerianum, wall.; malabaricum, wight [jasmine]; arborescens, roxb. [tree jasmine]; roxburghianum, wall.; cordifolium, wall. [jasmine]; sessiliflorum, vahl.; angustifolium, vahl. [wild jasmine]; ritchiei, clarke; wightii, clarke; rigidum, zenk. [jasmine]; latifolium, roxb. [large jasmine]; trichotomum, heyne [jasmine]; auriculatum, vahl. [needle jasmine]; brevilobum, dc. [jasmine]; flexile, vahl. [jasmine]; calophyllum, wall. [jasmine]; humile, l. [golden jasmine]; grandiflorum, linn. [common jasmine]. Nyctanthes arbortristis, l. [coral jasmine]. Schrebera swietenioides, roxb. [weaver's beam]. Fraxinus ornus, linn. [sicilian manna]. Linociera malabarica, wall.; wightii, clarke; leprocarpa, thw.; intermedia, wight. Olea [jita] glandulifera, wall. [jita]; dioica, roxb. [indian olive]; polygama, wight [jita]; europæa, linn. [zeitoon]. Ligustrum walkeri, dcne.; roxburghii, clarke; neilgherrense, wight; perrottetii, dc.; decaisnei, clarke. Myxopyrum smilacifolium, bl.—86 *Salvadoraceæ.*—Salvadora persica, l. [tooth brush tree]; oleoides, dcne [large tooth-brush tree]. Azima tetracantha, lam. [shengoo]. Fagonia arabica, linn. [ooshtarkhaur].—87 *Apocynaceæ.*—Chilocarpus atroviridis, bl. Carissa carandas, l. [carondah]; spinarum, dc. [carondah]; paucinervia, dc. [carondah]; macrophylla, wall. [carondah]; suavissima, bedd. Rauwolfia serpentina, benth. [snake root]; densiflora, bth. [snake root]; decurva, hk. f.; micrantha, hk. f.; beddomei, hk. f. [snake root]. Hunteria corymbosa, roxb. Cerbera odollam, gærtn. [odallam]. Thevetia nereifolia, juss. [yellow gannair]. Kopsia fruticosa, a. dec. [cluster gannair]. Vinca pusilla, murr. Plumeria acutifolia, poir. [pagoda tree]. Ellertonia rheedii, wight. Alstonia [saptaparnam] scholaris, br. [dita]; venenatus, br. [wild gannair]. Holarrhena antidysenterica, wall. [tellicherry bark]. mitis, br. [tellicherry bark]; Tabernæmontana [tagaram] dichotoma, roxb. [eve's apple]; heyneana, wall.; coronaria, br. [adam's apple]; crispa, rox. [tagaram]; citrifolia, willd. [tagaram]. Parsonsia spiralis, wall. Vallaris heynei, spr. Wrightia [veppaulay] tinctoria, br. [paula indigo]; tomentosa, roem. and sch. [ground paulay], Nerium adorium, soland [gannair]. Strophanthus wightianus. wall. Beaumontia jerdoniana, wight. Chonemorpha macrophylla, don. Aganosma caryophyllata, don.; cymosa, don. Anodendron paniculatum, dc. Ichnocarpus frutescens, br. [shyaumalatay].—88 *Asclepiadeæ.*—Hemidesmus indicus, br. [indian sarsaparilla]; pubescens, w. and a. [indian sarsaparilla]. Cryptolepis buchanani, r. and s.; grandiflora, wight. Cryptostegia grandiflora, br. [paulay silk cotton]. Brachylepis nervosa, w. and a. Utleria salicifolia, bedd. Streptocaulon kleinii, w. and a. Decalepis hamiltonii, w. and a. Secamone emetica, br. Toxocarpus, roxburghii, w. and a.; kleinii, w. and a. Oxystelma esculentum, br. [needle paulay]. Calotropis gigantea, br. [yercum]; gigantea, r. br., var. alba [yercum]; procera, br. [yercum]. Asclepias curassavica, l. Pentatropis microphylla, w. and a. Dæmia extensa, br. [hedge cotton]. Holostemma rheedei, wall. Cynanchum alatum, w. and a; pauciflorum, br.; callialata, ham. Sarcostemma brevistigma, w. and a. [somam]; brunonianum, w. and a. [somam]; intermedium, dcne. [somam]. Gymnema sylvestre, br. [small indian ipecacuanha]; hirsutum, w. and a. [small indian ipecacuanha]; lactiferum, br. [small indian ipecacuanha]; tingens, w. and a. [small indian ipecacuanha]; montanum, hk. f.; elegans, w. and a. [small indian ipecacuanha]; heyneana [small indian ipecacuanha]. Marsdenia tinctoria, br.; brunoniana, w. and a. Pergularia pallida, wight; minor, andr. [creeper champak]. Tylophora fasciculata, ham. [indian ipecacuanha]; macrantha, hk. f.; iphisia, dcne. [indian ipecacuanha]; capparidifolia, w. and a.; pauciflora, w. and a. [indian ipecacuanha]; zeylanica, dcne.; tenuis, bl. [indian ipecacuanha]; mollissima, wight [indian ipecacuanha]; rotundifolia, ham.; dalzellii, hk. f.; asthmatica, w. and a. [indian ipecacuanha]. Cosmostigma racemosum, wight. [vattoovally]. Dregea volubilis, bth. [nakchiknee silk cotton]. Heterostemma tanjorense, w. and a. Olianthus disciflorus, hk. f.; beddomei, hk. f. Hoya pauciflora, wight; wightii, hk. f.; ovalifolia, w. and a.; pendula, wight. Leptadenia reticulata, w. and a. Brachystelma maculatum, hk. f.; volubile, hk. f.; beddomei, hk. f. Ceropegia pusilla, wight; spiralis, wight; fimbrifera, bedd.; lawii, hk. f.; bulbosa, roxb. [mandey]; juncea, roxb.; elegans, wall.; mysorensis, wight; tuberosa, roxb.; candelabrum, l.; elliottii, hk. f.; acuminata, roxb.; intermedia, wight; thwaitesii, hk.; hirsuta, w. and a.; ciliata, wight; decaisneana, wight; brevicollis, hk. f.; ensifolia, bedd.; albiflora, hk. f.; beddomei, hk. f. Frerea indica, dalz. Caralluma [caurallam] edulis, benth.; adscendens, br. [caurallam]; attenuata, wight [caurallam]; fimbriata, wall. [caurallam]. Boucerosia umbellata, w. and a.; crenulata, w. and a.; diffusa, wight; hitchinia, dcne.; pauciflora, wight.—89 *Loganiaceæ.*—Mitrasacme alsinoides, br.; polymorpha, br. Buddleia asiatica, lour. Fagræa obovata, wall. Strychnos [mooshty] colubrina, l. [snakewood tree]; dalzellii, clarke; rheedei, clarke; beddomei, clarke; axillaris, colebr. [mooshty]; cinnamomifolia, thw. [mooshty]; nux-vomica, l. [poison nut]; potatorum, l. [clearing nut]; ignatii, berg. [papeeta]. Gardneria ovata, wall.—90. *Gentianaceæ.*—Exacum tetragonum, rox. [purple chiretta]; perrottetii, griseb. [purple chiretta]; bicolor, roxb. [purple chiretta]; atropurpureum, bedd.; courtallense, arn. [purple chiretta]; wightianum, arn. [purple chiretta]; pedunculatum,

l. [purple chiretta]; pumilum, griseb ; sessile, l.; lawii, clarke; petiolare, griseb ; insignis [purple chiretta]; cochin-chinensis [purple chiretta]. Hoppea dichotoma, willd.; fastigiata, clarke. Enicostema littorale, bl. [small chiretta]. Erythræa roxburghii, don. [roxburgh's chiretta]. Canscora diffusa, br.; decurrens, dalz.; pauciflora, dalz.; sessiliflora, r. and sch.; decussata, r. and sch. [sankhvel]; perfoliata, lamk.; wallichii, clarke. Gentiana quadrifaria, bl. Pleurogyne minor, bth. Swertia [chiretta] chirata, ham. [himalayan chiretta]; angustifolia, ham. [himalayan chiretta]; pulchella, ham. [himalayan chiretta]; affinis, clarke [blue-flowered chiretta]; corymbosa, wight; trichotoma, wall.; decussata, nimmo [mahableshwar chiretta]; beddomei, clarke. Halenia perrottetii, griseb. Limnanthemum cristatum, griseb. [floating nelumbo]; indicum, thw. [floating nelumbo]; aurantiacum, dalz.; parvifolium, griseb. 91 *Hydrophyllaceæ.*—Hydrolea zeylanica, vahl. [river blatty].—92 *Boragineæ.*—Cordia [sebesten] myxa, l. [small sebesten]; obliqua, willd. [large sebesten]; obliqua, willd. var. wallichii [large sebesten]; monoica, roxb. [sebesten]; rothii, r. and sch. [narrow leaved sebesten]; perrottetii, wight; macleodii, hk. f. and t. [sebesten]; fulvosa, wight; octandra, dc.; subcordata, lamk. [sebesten]; tectonifolia, wall. [sebesten]; speciosa, willd. [golden sebesten]; sebestana, linn. [cuba sebesten]. Ehretia [coorvitchy] acuminata, br. [prickly coorvitchy]; lævis, roxb. [smooth coorvitchy]; ovalifolia, wight; wightiana, wall.; buxifolia, roxb. [rough coorvitchy]. Coldenia procumbens, l. Rhabdia lycioides, mart. Tournefortia heyneana, wall.; reticosa, wight; wightii, clarke. Heliotropium zeylanicum, lamk. [indian heliotrope]; supinum, l. [indian heliotrope]; supinum, l., var. malabarica; ovalifolium, forsk. [indian heliotrope]; rottleri, lehm.; paniculatum, br. [indian heliotrope]; strigosum, willd.; bracteatum, dc.; marifolium, retz.; scabrum, retz. [indian heliotrope]; indicum, l. [indian heliotrope]; Trichodesma indicum, br. [donkey toombay] amplexicaule, roth.; zeylanicum, br. [donkey toombay]. Cynoglossum furcatum, wall.; denticulatum, dc. Paracaryum cælestinum, bth.; malabaricum, clarke. Onosma bracteatum, wall. [gowzabaun].—93 *Convolvulaceæ.*—Erycibe paniculata, roxb. Rivea ornata, chois.; hypocrateriformis, chois. Argyreia [ajauntry] tiliæfolia, wight; speciosa, sweet [sea shore paulay]; involucrata, clarke; bracteata, chois.; pomacea, chois.; sericea, dalz.; leschenaultii, chois.; nellygherya, chois.; malabarica, chois. [malabar creeper]; hirsuta, arn.; pilosa, arn.; lawii, clarke; choisyana, wight; cymosa, sweet; cuneata, ker.; fulgens, chois. Lettsomia aggregata, roxb.; mysorensis, clarke; elliptica, wight; setosa, roxb. Ipomæa [calamby] bona-nox, l. [moonflower]; muricata, jacq. [false kaladanah]; grandiflora, lamk.; coccinea, l. [caushy ratnam]; quamoclit, l. [indian pink]; hederacea, jacq. [kaladanah]; purpurea, lamk. [calamby]; laciniata, clarke; dissecta, willd. [calamby]; uniflora, r. and s. [calamby]; calycina, bth.; barlerioides, bth.; digitata, l. [giant potato]; pentaphylla, jacq. [hill giant potato]; batatas, lam. [potato]; pileata, roxb.; wightii, chois. [calamby]; bracteata, wight [calamby]; pestigridis, l. [tiger's foot]; eriocarpa, br. [calamby]; stocksii, clarke; angustifolia, jacq. [seeta's knot]; tridentata, roth. [calamby]; chryseides, ker. [calamby]; reniformis, chois. [rat's ear]; rumicifolia, chois. [calamby]; obscura, ker. [calamby]; sepiaria, koen. [laldanah]; beladamboe, r. and s. [white adambo]; aquatica, forsk. [tooty coora]; staphylina, r. and s. [calamby]; campanulata, l. [calamby]; cymosa, r. and s.; turpethum, br. [turbith]; biloba, forsk. [red adambo]; vitifolia, sweet [calamby]; kentrocaulos, clarke; rhyncorhiza, dalz.; palmata, forsk. [calamby]; dasysperma, jacq. [calamby]. Exogonium purga, benth. [jalap]. Quamoclit pennata, ch. [quamoclit]. Hewittia bicolor, wight. Convolvulus [tauly] pluricaulis, chois [tauly]; rottlerianus, chois. [tauly]; arvensis, l. [deer's foot]; flavus, willd. [tauly]; parviflorus, vahl. [tauly]; tricolor [tauly]; scammonia, linn. [scammony]. Evolvulus alsinoides, l. [vishnoo craunty]. Porana paniculata, roxb.; racemosa, roxb. [drowpady's hair]; malabarica, clarke. Breweria cordata, bl.; evolvuloides, chois. Neuropeltis racemosa, wall. Cressa cretica, l. Cuscuta reflexa, roxb. [seeta's thread]; hyalina, roth. [seeta's thread]; chinensis, lamk. [seeta's thread].—94 *Solanaceæ.*—Solanum [cooly] nigrum, l. [indian hounds' berry]; dulcamara, linn. [cooly]; vagum, heyne; verbascifolium, l. [shoonday]; pubescens, willd. [rameshwaram shoonday]; bigeminatum, nees. [cooly]; læve, dunal.; denticulatum, bl. [cooly]; biflorum, lour. [cooly]; giganteum, jacq. [cooly]; ferox, l. [elephant shoonday]; wightii, nees. [cooly]; torvum, swartz. [hill shoonday]; indicum, l. [indian nightshade]; melongena, l. [brinjaul]; coagulans, forsk.; xanthocarpum, schrad. [prickly brinjaul]; trilobatum, l. [prickly shoonday]; gracilipes, dcne. [cooly]; tuberosum, linn. [potato]; spinosissimum, lodd. [cooly]. Lycopersicum esculentum, miller [europe brinjaul]. Physalis [takkauly] minima, l. [small indian wintercherry]; peruviana, l. [indian wintercherry]. Capsicum [chilly] frutescens, l. [shrubby chilly]; minimum, roxb. [bird's eye chilly]; grossum, willd. [caffree chilly]; annuum, linn. [common chilly]. Withania somnifera, dunal [asgand]; coagulans, dunal [asgand]. Nicandra physaloides, gærtn. Atropa belladonna, linn. [dog angoor]. Mandragora officinarum, wight. [mardoomgiyah]. Datura [q.v.] stramonium, l. [europe datura]; fastuosa, l. [purple datura]; fastuosa, linn. var. alba [white datura]; metel, l. [downy datura]. Hyoscyamus niger, linn. [persian ajwaun]. Nicotiana tabacum, l. [pogauk].—95 *Scrophularineæ.*—Celsia coromandeliana, vahl. Linaria ramosissima, wall. Antirrhinum orontium, l. Sutera glandulosa, roth. Mazus surculosa, don. Lindenbergia polyantha, royle.; urticæfolia, lehm. Adenosma malabaricum, hk. f.; capitatum, bth. Stemodia viscosa, roxb.; serrata, bth. Limnophila roxburghii, don.; conferta, bth.; diffusa, benth.; gratissima, bl.; hirsuta, bth.; hypericifolia, bth.; polystachya, bth.; sessiliflora, bl.; heterophylla, bth.; racemosa, benth.; gratioloides, br. Herpestis monniera, h. b. and k. [water zoofah]; hamiltoniana, benth.; floribunda, br. [water zoofah]. Dopatrium nudicaule, ham.; junceum, ham.; lobelioides, benth. Artanema sesamoides, benth. Torenia cordifolia, roxb. [sisparra creeper]; asiatica, l. [sisparra creeper]; vagans, roxb.; hirtella, hk.; bicolor, dalz.; parviflora, ham. [sisparra creeper]. Vandellia crustacea, benth.; hirsuta, benth.; scabra, benth.; erecta, benth.; pedunculata, bth. Ilysanthes hyssopioides, benth.; parviflora, benth.; minima, benth.; rotundifolia, benth. Bonnaya brachiata, link.; reptans, spr.; veronicæfolia, spr.; oppositifolia, spr.; tenuifolia, spr. Microcarpæa muscosa, br. Peplidium humifusum, del. Glossostigma pathulatum, arn. Scoparia dulcis, l. Picrorhiza kurrooa, benth. [cootkee]. Veronica anagallis, l. Buchnera hispida, ham. Striga orobanchoides, bth.; densiflora, benth.; lutea, lour.; euphrasioides, bth.; masuria, bth.; sulphurea, dalz. Rhamphicarpa longiflora, bth. Centranthera hispida, br.; procumbens, bth.; humifusa, wall. Sopubia delphinifolia, don.; trifida, ham. Micrargeria wightii, bth. Pedicularis perrottetii, bth.; zeylanica, bth.—96 *Orobanchaceæ.*—Æginetia indica, roxb.; pedunculata, wall. Christisonia tubulosa, bth.; subacaulis, gardn.; bicolor, gardn.; neilgherrica, gardn. Orobanche cernua, loeff.; nicotianæ, wight.; indica, ham.—97. *Lentibularieæ.*—Utricularia stellaris, l.; flexuosa, vahl.; exoleta, br.; albo-cœrulea, dalz.; arcuata, wight; affinis, wight; cœrulea, l.; reticulata, sm.; scandens, benj.; hirta, klein.; bifida, l.; wallichiana, wight.; racemosa, wall.; orbiculata, wall.—98 *Gesneraceæ.*—Æschynanthus perrottetii, dc. Didymocarpus rottleriana, wall.; tomentosa, wight; lyrata, wight; ovalifolia, wight; missionis, wall.; repens, bedd. Chirita hamosa, br. Klugia notoniana, dc. Jerdonia indica, wight. Epithema carnosum, bth. Isanthera permollis, nees.—99 *Bignoniaceæ.*—Millingtonia hortensis, linn. [indian cork]. Oroxylum indicum, vent. [pajanely]. Dolichandrone [water ailanto] rheedii, seem. [long leaved wody]; crispa, seem. [flowering pauthiry]; falcata, seem. [wody]; lawii, seem.; arcuata, clarke. [night paulay]. Heterophragma roxburghii, dc. Stereospermum [pautalam] chelonoides, dc. [pauthiry]; suaveolens, dc.; xylocarpum, wight. [valencoorny]. Pajanelia rheedii, dc. [pajanely].—100 *Pedalineæ.*—Pedalium murex, l. [elephant nerinjy]. Martynia diandra, glox. [tiger claw]. Sesamum indicum, dc. [gingelly]; laciniatum, klein.; prostratum, retz. [wild gingelly].—101 *Acanthaceæ.*—Thunbergia fragrans, roxb. [indra's creeper]; tomentosa, wall. [indra's creeper]; alata, bojer. [indra's creeper]; hawtayneana, wall. [indra's creeper]; grandiflora, rox. [indra's creeper]; coccinea, wall. [indra's creeper]; mysorensis, t. anders. [indra's creeper]; wightiana, t. anders [indra's creeper]. Elytraria crenata, vahl. Nelsonia campestris, br. Ebermaiera glauca, nees.; zeylanica, nees. Cardanthera uliginosa, ham.; balsamica, bth.; verticillata, bth.; pinnatifida, bth. Hygrophila polysperma, t. anders.; serpyllum, t. anders. [neer moolly]; stocksii, t anders.; salicifolia, nees. [neer moolly]; quadrivalvis, nees.; phlomoides, nees. [neer moolly]; incana, nees; spinosa, t. anders. [neer moolly]. Nomaphila stricta, nees. Calophanes nagchana, nees.; littoralis, t. anders.; vagans, wight; dalzellii, t. anders. Ruellia prostrata, lamk.; repens, l.; patula, jacq. Petalidium barlerioides, nees. Phaylopsis parviflora, willd. Dædalacanthus nervosus, t. anders [vaudaumbram]; roseus, t. anders; purpurascens, t. anders. [vaudaumbram]; montanus, t. anders. [vaudaumbram]. Hemigraphis dura, t. anders.; venosa, clarke; latebrosa, nees. Stenosiphonium diandrum, wight; confertum, nees.; setosum, t. anders.; russellianum, nees.; parviflorum, t. anders. Strobilanthes foliosus, t. anders.; kunthianus, t. anders.; gossypinus, t. anders.; canaricus, bedd.; cuspidatus, t. anders.; consanguineus, clarke; jeyporensis, bedd.; barbatus, nees.; heteromallus, t. anders.; wightianus, nees.; pulneyensis, clarke; neilgherrensis, bedd.; perrottetianus, nees.; zenkerianus, t. anders.; warreensis, dalz.; ciliatus, nees.; adenophorus, bedd.; decurrens, nees.; walkeri, nees.; caudatus, t. anders.; tristis, t. anders.; lupulinus, nees.; heyneanus, nees.; ixiocephalus, bth.; micranthus, wight; papillosus, t. anders.; andersonii, bedd.; luridus, wight; bolamputtensis, bedd.; asper, wight; sessilis, nees.; dupeni, bedd.; perfoliatus, t. anders.; newii, bedd.; sexennis, nees.; homotropus, nees.; violaceus, bedd.; gracilis, bedd.; rubicundus, t. anders.; amabilis, clarke. Calacanthus dalzelliana, t. anders. Blepharis asperrima, nees.; boerhaaviæfolia, pers.; molluginifolia, pers. Acanthus ilicifolius, l. Barleria [nail dye] prionitis, l. [common nail dye]; cuspidata, heyne [nail dye]; buxifolia, l. [nail dye]; mysorensis, roth. [nail dye]; noctiflora, l. [nail dye]; longiflora, l. [nail dye]; tomentosa, roth. [nail dye]; involucrata, nees. [nail dye]; pilosa, wall. [nail dye]; lawii, t. anders.; sepalosa, clarke.; montana, nees. [nail dye]; gibsoni, dalz. [nail dye]; grandiflora, dalz.; cristata, l. [large nail dye]; courtallica, nees. [nail dye]; strigosa, willd. [blue nail dye]; nitida, nees.; bispinosa, vahl. [nail dye]. Neuracanthus trinervius, wight; sphærostachyus, dalz.; neesianus, clarke. Crossandra undulæfolia, salisb. Asystasia coromandeliana, nees.; chelonoides, nees.; violacea, dalz.; crispata, bth.; travancorica, bedd. Eranthemum malabaricum, clarke. Andrographis [bhoonimbam] paniculata, nees. [french chiretta];

subspathulata, clarke; elongata, t. anders.; ovata, bth.; alata, nees.; stenophylla, clarke; wightiana, arn. [bhoonimbam]; macrobotrys, nees. [bhoonimbam]; viscosula, nees. [bhoonimbam]; neesiana, wight [bhoonimbam]; stellulata, clarke; lineata, nees. [bhoonimbam]; lobelioides, wight [bhoonimbam]; echioides, nees. [coromandel chiretta]; glandulosa, nees.; rothii, clarke; serpyllifolia, wight [bhoonimbam]; beddomei, clarke; affinis, nees. [bhoonimbam]. Haplanthus verticillaris, nees.; tentaculatus, nees. Gymnostachyum febrifugum, bth.; polyanthum, wight; glabrum, t. anders.; canescens, t. anders.; latifolium, t. anders.; tomentosum, t. anders. Diotacanthus grandis, benth.; albiflorus, benth. Lepidagathis [corandy] cristata, willd. [lowly corandy]. mitis, dalz.; trinervis, nees.; spinosa, wight; pungens, nees. [milk corandy]; prostrata, dalz.; diffusa, clarke; cuspidata, nees.; scariosa, nees. [corandy]; hyalina, nees.; fasciculata, nees. Monothecium aristatum, t. anders. Justicia [gendarussa] montana, wall. [gendarussa]; betonica, l. [gendarussa]; nilgherrensis, wall. [gendarussa]; trinervia, vahl.; glauca, rottl. [gendarussa]; tranquebariensis, l. [tranquebar gendarussa]; salsoloides, t. anders.; gendarussa, l. [common gendarussa]; wynaadensis, wall. [gendarussa]; glabra, koen. [gendarussa]; micrantha, wall.; quinqueangularis, koen. [gendarussa]; diffusa, willd. [gendarussa]; simplex, don. [gendarussa]; procumbens, l. [coromandel gendarussa]; bivalvis, rox. [gendarussa]. Adhatoda, vasica, nees. [adhatoday]; beddomei, clarke. Rhinacanthus communis, nees. [snake jasmine]. Dianthera leptostachya, benth. Ecbolium linneanum, kurz. [neelaumbram]; linneanum, kurz., var. rotundifolia [neelaumbram]; linneanum, kurz., var. dentata [neelaumbram]. Graptophyllum hortense, nees. [face plant]. Rungia sisparensis, t. anders.; wightiana, nees.; læta, clarke; latior, nees.; crenata, t. anders.; linifolia, nees.; apiculata, bedd.; repens, nees.; elegans, dalz.; parviflora, nees. Dicliptera papribracteata, nees.; beddomei, clarke; zeylanica, nees.; cuneata, nees.; leonotis, dalz. Peristrophe bicalyculata, nees. [chebeera]; undulata, nees. [chebeera]; lanceolaria, nees. [chebeera]; montana, nees. [chebeera]; tinctoria, nees.—102 *Verbenaceæ*.—Lantana indica, roxb. [wild cholum]; crenulata, otto.; trifolia, l. Lippia nodiflora, rich. [wild long pepper]. Bouchea hyderabadensis, walp. Stachytarpheta indica, vahl. Priva leptostachya, juss. Callicarpa lanata, l. [tondy teragam]. Tectona grandis, l. [teak]. Premna [jayah] cordifolia, roxb. [conjee moonnay]; corymbosa, rottl.; coriacea, clarke; villosa, clarke; purpurascens, thw.; integrifolia, linn. [moonnay]; tomentosa, willd. [firebrand teak]; integerrima, wight; latifolia, roxb. [buffalo moonnay]; wightiana, schauer; thyrsoidea, wight.; esculenta, roxb. [curry moonnay]; herbacea, roxb. [lowly jaumoon]. Gmelina arborea, l. [cashmere tree]; asiatica, l. [small cashmere tree]. Vitex [sindoocam] trifolia, l. [water notchy]; negundo, l. [notchy]; altissima, l. [wild peacock gingelly]; alata, heyne [peacock gingelly]; pubescens, vahl. [tall notchy]; leucoxylon, l. [field notchy]. Clerodendron [bhaurgam] inerme, gærtn. [sangcooppy]; phlomoides, l. [tirootauly]; serratum, spreng. [knotted bhraungy]; infortunatum, gærtn. [saraswaty's leaf]; siphonanthus, br. [bhraungy]. Symphorema involucratum, roxb.; polyandrum, wight. Sphenodesma paniculata, clarke. Avicennia officinalis, l. [ooppata mangrove].—103 *Labiatæ*.—Ocimum [toolsy] canum, sims. [white toolsy]; basilicum, l. [fragrant toolsy]; gratissimum, l. [rama toolsy]; adscendens, willd. [wild toolsy]; sanctum, l. [common toolsy]; sanctum, linn., var. hirsuta [rough toolsy]. Geniosporum elongatum, benth.; prostratum, benth. Acrocephalus capitatus, benth. Moschosma polystachyum, benth. Orthosiphon diffusus, benth; pallidus, royle; tomentosus, benth.; rubicundus, benth.; comosus, wight.; stamineus, benth. Plectranthus pulneyensis, hk. f.; walkeri, arn.; rivularis, wight; stocksii, hk. f.; wightii, benth.; nilghiricus, benth.; nepetæfolius, benth.; menthoides, benth.; incanus, link.; subincisus, benth.; coleoides, benth.; urticifolius, hk. f.; fruticosus, wight. Coleus spicatus, benth.; barbatus, benth.; aromaticus, benth. [country borage]; parviflorus, benth. [country borage]; malabaricus, benth. [country borage]. Anisochilus carnosus, wall. [country lavender; scaber, benth. [country lavender]; eriocephalus, benth. [country lavender]; wightii, hk. f.; paniculatus, benth.; dysophylloides, benth. [country lavender]; plantagineus, hk. f.; suffruticosus, wight [country lavender]; sericeus, benth. [country lavender]; robustus, hk f.; verticillatus, hk. f. Hyptis suaveolens, poit. Lavandula burmanni, benth. Pogostemon paniculatus, benth. [patchouli]; gardneri, hk. f.; plectranthoides, desf. [patchouli]; purpurascens, dalz.; parviflorus, benth. [patchouli]; patchouli, pell. [patchouli]; hirsutus, benth. [patchouli]; paludosus, benth. [patchouli]; wightii, benth. [patchouli]; mollis, benth. [patchouli]; rotundatus, benth. [patchouli]; vestitus, benth. [patchouli]; atropurpureus, benth. [patchouli]; speciosus, benth. [patchouli]; travancoricus, bedd. Dysophylla myosuroides, benth.; rugosa, hk. f.; auricularia, bl.; quadrifolia, benth.; cruciata, benth. [wild toombay]; stellata, benth.; gracilis, dalz.; griffithii, hk. f. Colebrookia oppositifolia, gr. Elsholtzia cristata, willd. Mentha [poodeenah] arvensis, linn. [poodeenah]; piperita, linn. [poodeenah]; viridis, linn. [poodeenah]; pulegium, linn. [poodeenah]; sativa, linn. [poodeenah]. Origanum [marwah] vulgare, linn. [marwah]; marjorana, linn. [marwah]; onites, wight [marwah]. Thymus serpyllum, linn. [ipar]; vulgaris, linn. [ipar]. Hyssopus officinalis, linn. [zoofah]. Micromeria capitellata, benth.; biflora, benth. Calamintha umbrosa, benth. Melissa officinalis, linn. [persian toolsy]. Meriandra bengalensis, linn. Salvia [indian sage] plebeia, br. [indian sage]; indica, linn. [indian sage]; gerardiana, benth. [indian sage]; officinalis, linn. [indian sage]. Scutellaria discolor, coleb.; violacea, heyne.; rivularis, wall. Brunella vulgaris, l. Anisomeles heyneana, benth.; ovata, br. [malabar catmint]; malabarica, br. [malabar catmint]. Leucas [toombay] urticæfolia, br.; nepetæfolia, benth.; lanata, benth.; chinensis, br.; montana, spr.; procumbens, desf. [hill toombay]; biflora, br.; marrubioides, desf.; angularis, benth.; pubescens, benth.; suffruticosa, benth.; rosmarinifolia, benth. [small toombay]; helianthemifolia, desf.; lanceæfolia, desf.; eriostoma, hk. f.; lamiifolia, desf.; vestita, benth.; hirta, spr.; ciliata, benth.; stricta, benth.; nutans, spr.; martinicensis, br.; cephalotes, spr. [large toombay]; zeylanica, br.; diffusa, benth.; wightiana, benth.; aspera, spr. [rough toombay]; linifolia, spr. [flower toombay]. Leonotis nepetæfolia, br. Gomphostemma eriocarpum, benth. Teucrium tomentosum, heyne.; wightii, hk. f.—104 *Plantagineæ*.—Plantago major, l. [spogel]; ovata, forsk. [spogel].—"INCOMPLETÆ."—105. *Nyctagineæ*.—Mirabilis jalapa, linn. [false jalap]. Boerhaavia repens, l.; repens, linn., var. diffusa [tikry]; crispa, heyne.; repanda, willd. [tikry]; verticillata, poir. [tikry]. Pisonia aculeata, l. [conky]; alba, spanoghe [conky].—106 *Amarantaceæ*.—Celosia argentea, l. [moorgha]; cristata, l. [moorgha]; pulchella, moq. [moorgha]; polygonoides, retz. [moorgha]. Banalia thyrsiflora, moq.; Allmania nodiflora, br.; albida, br. Digera arvensis, forsk. Amarantus [maurisham] spinosus, l. [thorny spinach]; paniculatus, l. [brown spinach]; caudatus, l. [rose spinach]; gangeticus, l. [garden spinach]; atropurpureus, roxb. [red spinach]; mangostanus, l.; caturus, heyne.; viridis, l. [stunted spinach]; blitum, l.; blitum, linn., var. oleraceus, linn. [common spinach]; polygamus, l.; tenuifolius, willd. [wild spinach]; campestris, willd. [field spinach]. Cyathula prostrata, bl. [small indian burr]. Pupalia atropurpurea, moq. [audayotty]; orbiculata, wight. [audayotty]; lappacea, moq. Psilotrichum nudum, moq.; calceolatum, moq. Nothosærua brachiata, wight. Ærua [poolay] javanica, juss. [large poolay]; scandens, wall. [poolay]; lanata, juss. [small poolay]; wightii, hk. f.; monsonia, mart. [poolay]. Achyranthes aquatica, br. [indian burr]; aspera, l. [indian burr]; rubrofusca, wight. [indian burr]; bidentata, bl. [indian burr]. Alternanthera sessilis, br. Gomphrena globosa, l. [jaffer goondy]; hispida, l. [jaffer goondy].—107 *Phytolaccaceæ*.—Suriana maritima, linn.—108 *Salsolaceæ*.—Chenopodium ambrosioides, linn. Beta vulgaris, linn. [paulak]. Spinacea oleracea, linn. [indian spinach]. Atriplex heterantha, r. w. Obione kœnigii, moq. Salicornia brachiata, roxb. [chook]; herbacea, linn. [chook]; arabica, wight. [chook]. Arthrocnemum indicum, moq. Suæda monoica, forsk.; indica, moq. [indian salt-wort]; nudiflora, moq. [seaside indian salt-wort]. Chenopodina indica, r. w. Caroxylon indicum, r. w. Kochia indica, r. w.—109 *Basellaceæ*.—Basella [malabar nightshade] rubra, linn. [red malabar nightshade]; rubra, linn., var. alba [white malabar nightshade]; cordifolia, lam. [heart-leaved malabar nightshade]; lucida, linn.—110 *Polygonaceæ*.—Polygonum [water gannair] barbatum, willd. [alligator's nose]; glabrum, willd. [water gannair]; minus, huds. [water gannair]; donii, meissn. [water gannair]; pedunculare, wall. [water gannair]; horridum, ham. [water gannair]; nepalense, meissn. [water gannair]; wallichii, meissn. [water gannair]; chinense, linn. [water gannair]; miquelianum, meissn. [water gannair]; roxburghii, meissn. [wobilinta]; flaccidum, roxb. [water pepper]; lanigerum, r. br. [water gannair]; tomentosum, willd. [river jasmine]; bisbiræ, hamilt. [water gannair]; rivulare, roth. [water gannair]; aviculare, linn. [hoonrauj]. Rheum moorcroftianum, royle [indian rhubarb]; emodi, wall. [indian rhubarb]; webbianum, royle [indian rhubarb]. Rumex nepalensis, spreng. [country sorrel]; dentatus, campd. [country sorrel]; vesicarius, linn. [country sorrel].—111 *Lauraceæ*.—Cinnamomum [cinnamon] wightii, meissn.; zeylanicum, breyn. [ceylon cinnamon]; tamala, nees [cassia cinnamon]; iners, reinw. [country cinnamon]; iners, var. trinerve, reinw.; sulphuratum, nees [cinnamon]; perottetii, meissn. [cinnamon]; camphora, nees [camphor cinnamon]; cecidodaphne, meissn. [cinnamon]; parthenoxylon, meissn. [martaban cinnamon]. Laurus nobilis, linn. [zafnee]. Persea gratissima, gært. [alligator pear]; nanmuh, gært. [nanmuh]. Alseodaphne semecarpifolia, nees. Phœbe wightii, meissn. Machilus macrantha, nees.; glaucescens, r. w. Haasia wightii, nees. Beilschmiedia roxburghiana, nees.; fagifolia, nees. Apollonias arnottii, nees. Cryptocarya wightiana, thwaites.; stocksii, meissn.; neilgherrensis, meissn. Tetranthera tomentosa, roxb. [meida lukdy]; tomentosa, roxb., var. glabrescens [meida lukdy]; ligustrina, nees. [meida lukdy]; ligustrina, nees., var. celastroides [meida lukdy]; panamonja, hamilt. [meida lukdy]; laurifolia, jacq. [meida lukdy]; laurifolia, jack., var. roxburghii [meida lukdy]; laurifolia, jack., var. platyphylla [meida lukdy]; laurifolia, jack., var. citrifolia [meida lukdy]; micrantha, meissn.; glauca, wall. [meida lukdy]; læta, wall. [meida lukdy]; venulosa, meissn. [meida lukdy]; wightii, nees. [meida lukdy]; monopetala, roxb. [meida lukdy]; oleoides, meissn. [meida lukdy]; cordifolia, meissn. [meida lukdy]; glabrata, wall. [meida lukdy]. Cylicodaphne wightiana, nees.; sebifera, blume.; oblonga, meissn. Actinodaphne hookeri, meissn.; lanata, meissn. Litsæa zeylanica, nees.; foliosa, nees.; scrobiculata, meissn. Cassytha filiformis, linn. [cottaun].—112 *Myristicaceæ*.—Myristica [jauty] fragrans, houtt. [common nutmeg]; laurifolia, hook. f. [jungle nutmeg]; malabarica, lam. [malabar nutmeg]; magnifica, bedd. [travancore nutmeg]; horsfieldii, blume [wild nutmeg]; farquhariana, wall. [jauty]; attenuata, wall. [jauty].—113 *Proteaceæ.*—Helicia nilagirica, bedd.—114 *Thymelæaceæ.*—Lasiosiphon eriocephalus, decaisne.; sisparensis, meissn.; speciosus, decaisne.; metzianus, miq. Aquilaria agallocha, rox. [eagle wood].—115 *Elæagnaceæ.*—Elæagnus kologa, schlecht.; conferta, roxb.— 116 *Santalaceæ.*—Pyrularia wallichiana, alph. dec. Osyris wightiana, wall. Thesium wightianum, wall. Santalum album, linn. [sandal].—117 *Aristolochiaceæ.*—Bragantia wallichii, r. br. Aristolochia [eeshwaram] bacteata, retz. [indian worm-killer]; indica, linn. [isharmool]; acuminata, lam.—118 *Euphorbiaceæ.*—Euphorbia [milk hedge] halophila, miq. [milk hedge]; pycnostegia, boiss. [milk hedge]; zornioides, boiss. [milk hedge]; elegans, spreng. [milk hedge]; fimbriata, boiss. [milk hedge]; pilulifera, linn.; bracteolaris, boiss. [milk hedge]; indica lam. [ammaun putcharisy]; notoptera, boiss. [milk hedge]; serpens, kunth. [milk hedge]; corrigioloides, boiss. [milk hedge]; sanguinea, hochst et steud. [milk hedge]; thymifolia, burm.; rosea, retz.; erythroclada, boiss. [milk hedge]; tirucalli, linn. [round milk hedge]; nereifolia, linn. [leafy milk hedge]; nivulia, ham.; antiquorum, linn. [square milk hedge]; tortilis, rottl. [twisting milk hedge]; trigona, haw. [milk hedge]; cattimandoo, w. elliott. [cuttimandoo]; acaulis, roxb. [milk hedge]; peltata, roxb.; dracunculoides, lam. [milk hedge]; oreophila, miq. [milk hedge]; pulcherrima, willd [milk hedge]. Actephila thomsoni, muller.; excelsa, muller. Sauropus albicans, muller.; quadrangularis, muller.; ceratogynum, baill. Antidesma [amla shaucam] ghæsembilla, muller. [gasambilla]; menasu, muller.; comptum, tulasne.; bunius, muller. [nolatauly]; diandrum, tulasne. [carpenter's tamarind]. Phyllanthus [aumlacam] littoralis, muller. [aumlacam]; zeylanicus, muller. [aumlacam]; nitidus, muller. [aumlacam]; lanceolarius, muller. [aumlacam]; tomentosus, muller. [aumlacam]; obliquus, muller. [aumlacam]; canaranus, muller. [aumlacam]; hohenhackeri, muller. [aumlacam]; fagifolius, muller. [aumlacam]; asperus, muller. [aumlacam]; diversifolius, muller.; neilgherrensis, muller. [aumlacam]; arboreus, muller. [aumlacam]; malabaricus, muller. [aumlacam]; perrotetianus, muller. [aumlacam]; velutinus, muller.; heyneanus, muller. [aumlacam]; wightianus, muller. [aumlacam]; longipes, muller. [aumlacam]; peltandra, muller. [aumlacam]; reticulatus, muller. [netted nelly]; emblica, linn. [emblic myrobalan]; polyphyllus, willd. [forest nelly]; juniperinoides, muller. [aumlacam]; pendulus, roxb. [white nelly]; maderaspatensis, muller. [lowly nelly]; rheedii, r. w. [aumlacam]; urinaria, linn. [neeroory]; miquelianus, muller. [aumlacam]; simplex, muller. [aumlacam]; macræi, muller. [aumlacam]; leschenaultii, muller. [aumlacam]; rotundifolius, muller. [aumlacam]; niruri, muller.; niruri, mull., var. genuinus [neeroory]; distichus, muller. [brazil cherry]; indicus, muller. [aumlacam]; fimbriatus, muller. [aumlacam]; baillonianus, muller. [aumlacam]; macrocalyx, muller. [aumlacam]; multiflorus, willd. [poolah]; cyanospermus, mueller [aumlacam]; stellatus, retz. [aumlacam]. Melanthesopsis patens, muller. [large neeroory]; patens, mull., var. oblongifolia [large neeroory]; patens, mull., var. turbinata [large neeroory]; patens, mull., var. vulgaris [large neeroory]; patens, mull., var. genuina [large neeroory]. Breynia rhamnoides, muller.; rhamoides, mull., var. genuina [poolah coral tree]. Putranjiva roxburghii, wall. [pootranjeeva]. Securinega obovata, muller. [white poolah]; leucopyrus, muller. [white poolah]. Baccaurea sapida, muller.; courtallensis, muller. Aporosa lindleyana, muller.; sphærocarpa, muller. Bischoffia javanica, muller.; javanica, mull., var. genuina [java cedar]. Cyclostemon indicus, muller. Hemicyclia sepiaria, w. and a.; venusta, thwaites. Bridelia retusa, muller.; retusa, mull., var. genuina [thorny vengay]; retusa, mull., var. squamosa [thorny vengay]; retusa, mull., var. roxburghiana [thorny vengay]; stipularis, blume. [thorny vengay]; montana, willd. [thorny vengay]; hamiltoniana, muller. Cleistanthus patulus, muller.; malabaricus, muller.; stipularis, muller. Lebidieropsis orbicularis, muller.; orbicularis, mull., var. collina [garrar]. Aleurites triloba, forst. [lumbang nut]. Croton [ghanta beejam] oblongifolius, roxb. [devil's goad]; reticulatus, muller. [ghanta beejam]; aromaticus, linn. [croton lac tree]; caudatus, muller. [ghanta beejam]; tiglium, linn. [jamalgota]; malabaricus, bedd. [ghanta beejam]; cascarilla [ghanta beejam]; scabiosus, bedd. [ghanta beejam]. Agrostistachys indica, dalz. Sarcoclinium longifolium, r. wight. Crozophora plicata, muller. [round pepper]. Symphyllia mallotiformis, muller. Claoxylon indicum, muller.; mercurialis, thwaites. Acalypha [maumsicay] paniculata, miq. [maumsicay]; fruticosa, forsk. [chinny]; capitata, willd. [maumsicay]; alnifolia, willd. [maumsicay]; indica, linn. [cooppamainy]; brachystachya, hornemann. [maumsicay]; malabarica, muller. [maumsicay]; fallax, muller. [maumsicay]; ciliata, muller. [maumsicay]; spiciflorus, linn. [vattatauly]. Tragia miqueliana, muller.; involucrata, muller. [caunjory]; cannabina, linn. [small caunjory]. Trewia nudiflora, linn. [caunchy]. Mallotus barbatus, muller. [kamela]; albus, muller. [kamela]; muricatus, muller. [kamela]; stenanthus, muller. [kamela]; aureo-punctatus, muller. [kamela]; lawii, muller. [kamela]; distans, muller. [kamela]; atrovirens, muller. [kamela]; philippensis, muller. [kamela]; repandus, muller. [kamela]; rhamnifolius, muell. [kamela]. Cleidion javanicum, blume. Macaranga digyna, muller. [round-leaved nelumbo]; indica, r. wight [round-leaved nelumbo]; flexuosa, r. wight [round-leaved nelumbo]; tomentosa, r. wight [round-leaved nelumbo]; peltata, muller. [round-leaved nelumbo]. Homonoya retusa, muller.; retusa, muller., var. genuina; retusa, muller., var. cuneata; riparia, lour. [wild gaunair]. Ricinus communis, linn. [aumanac]. Jatropha [nicoombham] glandulifera, rox. [rat aumanac]; multifida, linn. [small wild aumanac]; wightiana, muller.; curcas, linn. [wild aumanac]. Manihot utilissima, pohl. [malda dye]. Trigonostemon lawianus, muller. Givotia rottleriformis, griff. [white tanakk]. Codiæum umbellatum, muller. Baliospermum montanum, muller. [wild jamalgota]; calycinum, muller. Gelonium multiflorum, adr. juss.; lanceolatum, willd.; angustifolium muller. Sebastiania chamælea, muller. [creeping aumanac]. Excæcaria [agaroo] baccata, muller. [agaroo]; insignis, muller. [agaroo]; cochinchinensis, lour. [agaroo]; indica, muller. [agaroo]; oppositifolia, jack. [agaroo]; agallocha, muller. [tiger's milk]; sebifera, muell. [china tallow]. Dalechampia indica, r. w.; scandens, muller. Pedilanthus tithymaloides, poir. [adjutant's hedge].—119 *Urticaceæ.*—Fleurya interrupta, r. w. Girardina heterophylla, dalz. [neilgherry nettle]. Splitgerbera macrostachya, r. w. Elatostemma surculosum, r. w.; cuspidatum, r. w.; lineolatum, r. w.; ovatum, r. w.; oppositifolium, dalz. Debregeasia longifolia, wedd. [capsy]. Laportea terminalis, r. w. Pilea trinervia, r. w.; radicans, r. w. Chamabainia cuspidata, r. w. Forskolia urticoides, r. w. Urtica nivea, linn. [china grass]. Pouzolzia indica, r. w.; stocksii, r. w.; acuta, r. w.; ovalifolia, r. w.; mysorensis, r. w.; tomentosa, r. w.; heterocarpa, r. w.; bennettiana, r. w.; longifolia, r. w.; wightii, bennett.; concinna, r. w.; aspera, r. w.; dalzellii, r. w.; scabra, r. w.; caudata, bennett; wallichiana, r. w.; neilgherrensis, r. w.; trialata, r. w.; cymosa, r. w.; rotundifolia, r. w.; elliptica, r. w.; bicuspidata, r. w.; rostrata, r. w.; auriculata, r. w.; rheedii, r. w.; scabrida, r. w.; minor, r. w.; tuberosa, r. w.; vesicaria, r. w.; pilosa, r. w.; tetraptera, r. w.; johnsoniana, r. w.; pyramidata, r. w. Cannabis sativa, linn. [kinnab]. Plecospermum spinosum, trecul. [cority].—120 *Ulmaceæ.*—Holopetala integrifolia, planch. [indian elm]. Celtis roxburghii, planch. [white indian nettle]; wightii, planch. [white indian nettle]; serotina, planch. [white indian nettle]. Sponia wightii, planch. [indian nettle]; velutina, planch. [indian nettle].—121 *Moraceæ.*—Morus indica, linn. [indian mulberry]. Covellia guttata, r. w.; macrocarpa, r. w. Epicarpurus orientalis, blume. [stunted jack]; spinosa, r. w. Dorstenia indica, r. w. Stilpnophyllum elasticum, endl. [indian caoutchouc]. Ficus [atty] oppositifolia, willd. [devil fig]; glomerata, miq. [cluster fig]; dœmonum, vahl.; bengalensis, linn. [banyan]; religiosa, linn. [peepul]; infectoria, rox. [stone banyan]; pseudotjiela, miq.; benjamina, linn. [small tsiela]; nitida, miq.; cordifolium, dalz.; volubile, dalz.; acutiloba, miq. [atty]; asperrima, roxb. [bramha's banyan]; heterophylla, linn. [red fig]; repens, roxb. [creeper fig]; scandens, rox. [stone fig]; laccifera, roxb. [nooga]; rumphii, bl. [atty]; excelsa, vahl. [tall fig]; vagans, roxb. [hill peepul]; cunia, buch. [large bramha's banyan]; tomentosa, roxb. [hill banyan]; tuberculata, roxb. [hill tsiela]; comosa, roxb.; angustifolia, roxb. [atty]; racemosa, linn. [atty]; carica, linn. [anjeer]; guttata [atty]; citrifoli, lam. [wild banyan]; tsiela, rox. [tsiela]; macrocarpa, wight. [atty]; wightiana, wall. [atty]; arnottiana, miq. [wild peepul]; retusa, linn. [chinese banyan].—122 *Artocarpaceæ*—Antiaris saccidora, dalz. [sack tree]; Artocarpus [jack] hirsuta, lam. [wild jack]; lakoocha, roxb. [monkey jack]; integrifolia, willd. [common jack]; incisa, linn. [foreign jack].—123 *Podostemaceæ.*—Dicræa longifolia, r. wight; dichotoma, tul.; wightii, tul.; rigida, tul.; stylosa, r. wight. Hydrobryum griseum, tul. Mniopsis johnsonii, r. wight. Dalzellia ramosissima, r. wight; pulchella, tul.; longipes, tul.—124 *Chloranthaceæ.*—Chloranthus indicus, r. w. Sarcandra chloranthoides, gardner.—125 *Piperaceæ.*—Peperomia dindigulensis, miq.; heyneana, miq.; portulacoides, dietr. miq.; reflexa, dietr. miq.; courtallensis, miq.; wightiana, miq. Pothomorphe subpeltata, miq. Cubeba wallichii, miq. Chavica sphœrostachya, miq. Muldera wightiana, miq.; galeata, miq.; trichostachya, miq. Piper [pepper] sylvestre, lam. [pepper]; attenuatum, hamilt. [pepper]; trioicum, roxb. [pepper]; nigrum, linn. [black pepper]; nepalense, miq.; wightii, miq. [pepper]; arborescens, miq. [pepper]; argyrophyllum, miq. [pepper]; chaba, blume. [chaab pepper]; betel, linn. [betel pepper]; cubeba, linn. f. [cubeb pepper]; longum, linn. [long pepper].—126 *Saliaceæ.*—Salix [varoonam] tetrasperma, roxb. [indian willow]; caprea, linn. [aromatic willow]; babylonica, linn. [majnoon's willow].—127 *Casuarinaceæ.*—Casuarina equisetifolia, forst. [chowkmaram].—128 *Gnetaceæ.*—Gnetum scandens, roxb.—129 *Cycadaceæ.*—Cycas circinalis, linn. [indian sago palm].—130 *Roxburghiaceæ.*—Roxburghia gloriosoides, jones.—131 *Smilaceæ.*—Smilax [china root] ovalifolia, roxb. [oval-leaved china root]; macrophylla, roxb. [china root]; zeylanica, linn. [china root]; macula, royle [china root]; lanceæfolia, rox. [indian china root]; glabra, roxb. [large china root]; hohenhackeri, kunth. [china root]; officinalis, humb. [sarsaparilla china root]; china, linn. [common china root].—132 *Dioscoreaceæ.*—Dioscorea [auloo] sativa, linn. [common yam]; alata, linn. [large yam]; oppositifolia, linn. [betel yam]; tomentosa, hohenhacker. [thorny yam]; triphylla, linn.; pentaphylla, willd. [prickly yam]; aculeata, linn. [goa yam]; pulchella, roxb. [short yam]; crispata, roxb. [roodrauck yam]; purpurea, rox. [pondicherry yam]; globosa, rox. [humped yam]. Helmia bulbifera, kunth.

[malacca yam]; dæmona, kunth. [malacca yam]; hirsuta, kunth. [malacca yam]; tomentosa, kunth. [malacca yam].—133 *Alismaceæ.*— Sagittaria sagittifolia, linn. [pit nelumbo]; cordifolia, roxb. [pit nelumbo]; obtusifolia, linn. [pit nelumbo].—134 *Fluviales.*— Najas indica, chamisso. Potamogeton crispum, linn.; indicum, roxb. Spathium chinense, lour.; echinatum, roxb.—135 *Pontederaceæ.*—Monochoria hastæfolia, presl. [blue nelumbo]; vaginalis, presl. [blue nelumbo].—136 *Liliaceæ.*— Methonica superba, lam. [wild bachnaug]. Lilium wallichianum, roem. and schult. Sanseviera roxburghiana, schult. [marool]; lanuginosa, willd. [marool]. Aloe [aloe] indica, royle [common indian aloe]; socotrina, lamb. [bombay aloe]; litoralis, koen. [coromandel aloe]; vulgaris, lam. [barbadoes aloe]. Barnardia indica, r. w. Allium cepa, linn. [piyauz]; sativum, linn. [lussoon]. Urginia indica, kunth. [squill]; coromandeliana, r. w. [squill]; congesta, r. w. [squill]. Ledebouria hyacinthina, roth.; maculata, dalz. Asphodelus pauciflorus, r. w.; clavatus, roxb. Phalangium tuberosum, kunth.; attenuatum, r. w.; oligospermum, r. w.; parviflorum, r. w. Chlorophytum parviflorum, dalz.; glaucum, dalz. Dianella ensifolia, aiton. Asparagopsis [shatamooly] sarmentosa, kunth. [soofaid moosly]; rubricaulis, kunth.; floribunda, kunth. [shakaukool]; ascendens, kunth. [indian salep]; officinalis, linn. [naugdown]. Ophiopogon indicum, r. w. Peliosanthes courtallensis, r. w.; neilgherrensis, r. w. Colchicum autumnale, linn. [soorinjaun]. Yucca aloifolia, linn. [adam's needle].—137 *Melanthaceæ.*—Disporum leschenaultianum, don.; mysorense, r. w. Iphigenia indica, kunth.—138 *Juncaceæ.*— Juncus monticola, steudel.—139 *Commelynaceæ.*—Commelyna communis, linn. [calf's grass]; benghalensis, linn. [calf's grass]; salicifolia, roxb.; diffusa, burm.; polyspatha, r. w. [calf's grass]; obliqua, don. [calf's grass]. Aneilema nudiflorum, r. br.; compressum, dalz.; ochraceum, dalz.; pauciflorum, dalz.; elatum, dalz.; canaliculatum, dalz.; demorphum, dalz.; semiteres, dalz.; tuberosum, ham.; latifolium, r. w.; ensifolia, r. w.; terminalis, r. w.; nana, kunth.; pauciflora, r. w.; vaginata, r. br. Dithyrocarpus paniculatus, kunth.; petiolatus, r. w.; undulatus, r. w. Cyanotis hispida, dalz.; vivipara, dalz.; fasciculata, roem. and schult.; tuberosa, roem. and schult.; cristata, roem. and schult; axillaris, roem. and schult; pilosa, roem. and schult.; longifolia, r. w.; lanceolata, r. w.; rosea, r. w.; sarmentosa, r. w.; decumbens, r. w.; vaginata, r. w.; papilionacea, roem. and schult.; burmanniana, r. w. Aclisia indica, r. w. Dichæspermum lanceolatum, r. w.; repens, r. w. Dictyospermum montanum, r. w.; ovalifolium, r. w.; protensum, r. w. Heterocarpus hirsutus, r. w.; glaber, r. w. Flagellaria indica, linn. [wild rattan].—140 *Xyridaceæ.*—Xyris anceps, lam. [cotchilitty]; lappacea, heyne. [cotchilitty]; pauciflora, willd. [cotchilitty]; walkeri, r. w. [cotchilitty]; indica, linn. [cotchilitty]; nilagiriensis, steudel. [cotchilitty]; oryzetorum, miq. [cotchilitty].—141 *Orchidaceæ.*—Microstylis versicolor, lindl.; rheedii, lindl.; luteola, r. w. Cottonia macrostachys, r. w. Liparis olivacea, lindl.; atropurpurea, lindl.; walkeriæ, graham.; longipes, lindl.; biloba, r. w.; elliptica, r. w.; odorata, lindl. Eria polystachya, ach. rich.; pubescens, r. w.; pauciflora, r. w.; reticosa, r. w.; dalzelli, lindl. Pholidota imbricata, lindl. Josephia lanceolata, r. w.; latifolia, r. w. Cælogyne breviscapa, lindl.; odoratissima, lindl.; glandulosa, lindl.; nervosa, a. rich.; corrugata, r. w. Corymbis disticha, lindl. Bolbophyllum neilgherrense, r. w.; fuscopurpureum, r. w.; tremulum, r. w. Luisia tenuifolia, blume.; trichorhiza, blume.; brachystachys, blume. Vanda roxburghii, r. br. [rasnah]; spathulata, spreng.; pulchella, r. w. Oberonia brunoniana, r. w.; platycaulon, r. w.; lindleyana, r. w.; denticulata, r. w.; verticillata, r. w.; wightiana, lindl.; arnottiana, r. w. Chiloschista usneoides, lindl. Aporum anceps, lindl. Aggeianthus marchantioides, r. w. Lichenora jerdoniana, r. w. Dendrobium heyneanum, lindl.; barbatulum, lindl.; humile, r. w.; jerdonianum, r. w.; album, r. w.; ramosissimum, r. w.; graminifolium, r. w.; lawianum, lindl. Acampe wightiana, lindl.; congesta, lindl.; papillosa, lindl.; excavata, lindl. Euphrobosces pigmæa, griffith. Ania latifolia, lindl. Cirrhopetalum fimbriatum, hook.; albidum, r. w.; neilgherriense, r. w. Arundina bambusifolia, lindl. Geodorum purpureum, r. br.; dilatatum, r. br. Cymbidium aloifolium, swartz.; erectum, r. w.; pendulum, swartz.; aphyllum, swartz. Cyrtopera cullenii, r. w.; fusca, r. w. Eulophia [salep] virens, r. brown; carinata, lindl.; campestris, wall. [salep]; ramentacea, lindl.; macrostachya, lindl.; herbacea, lindl. [salep]. Calanthe masuca, lindl.; perotettii, a. rich.; veratrifolia, r. br. Sarcanthus peninsularis, dalz.; filiformis, r. w.; roseus, r. w. Podochilus malabaricus, r. w. Aerides wightianum, lindl.; crispum, lindl.; lindleyanum, r. w.; maculosum, lindl.; cylindricum, lindl.; tesselatum, r. w. Apetalon minutum, r. w. Platanthera lutea, r. w.; susannæ, lindl.; brachyphylla, lindl.; iantha, r. w.; affinis, r. w. Peristylus plantagineus, lindl.; goodyeroides, lindl.; spiralis, a. rich.; richardianus, r. w.; exilis, r. w. Cæloglossum secundum, lindl. Ate virens, lindl. Satyrium nepalense, don.; perottetianum, a. rich.; albiflorum, rich.; wightianum, lindl. Podanthera pallida, r. w. Diplocentrum longifolium, r. w.; congestum, r. w. Micropera maculata, dalz. Polystachya luteola, hooker.; purpurea, r. w. Saccolabium wightianum, lindl.; guttatum, lindl.; præmorsum, lindl.; ringens, lindl.; viridiflorum, lindl.; paniculatum, r. w. Tæniophyllum jerdonianum, r. w. Habenaria lindleyana, r. w.; heyneana, lindl.; rariflora, a. rich.; longicalcarata, a. rich.; crinifera, lindl.; montana, a. rich.; viridiflora, r. br.; cephalotes, lindl.; plantaginea, lindl.; platyphylla, spreng.; commelinifolia, wall.; foliosa, a. rich; elliptica, r. w.; ovalifolia, r. w.; fimbriata, r. w.; richardiana, r. w.; decipiens, r. w.; candida, dalz.; diphylla, dalz. Disperis neilgherrensis, r. w.; tripetaloidea, lindl. Pogonia carinata, lindl.; biflora, r. w. Vanilla aphylla, blume. Cnemidia angulosa, lindl. Spiranthes australis, lindl. Zeuxine brevifolia, r. w.; robusta, r. w.; emarginata, lindl. Monochilus longilabre, lindl. Cheirostylis flabellata, r. w. Goodyera procera, hooker.; ovalifolia, r. w. Anæctochilus setaceus, blume.—142 *Musaceæ.*—Musa ornata, roxb.; superba, roxb. [wild plantain]; paradisiaca, linn. [plantain]; textilis, nees. [demon plantain]. Ravenalia madagascariensis, sonn. [traveller's palm].—143 *Marantaceæ.*—Phrynium capitatum, willd. Maranta dichotoma, wall. [sheetalpaty]; virgata, wall.; arundinacea, linn. [sheetalpaty]. Canna indica, linn. [indian shot]; edulis, ker. [indian shot].—144 *Zingiberaceæ.*—Globba marantinoides, r. w.; ophioglossa, r. w. Costus speciosus, smith [arabian costum]. Zingiber [aurdracam] squarrosum, roxb. [aurdracam]; zerumbet, smith [false ginger]; cassumunar, rox. [cassumunar]; nimmonii, dalz. [aurdracam]; roseum, roscoe [aurdracam]; capitatum, rox. [jungle ginger]; officinale, roscoe [ginger]. Hedychium scaposum, nimmo.; flavescens, roscoe; coronarium, willd.; venustum, r. w.; cernuum, r. w.; spicatum, smith [europe zedoary]. Curcuma [haridrah] aromatica, salisb. [round zedoary]; neilgherrensis, r. w. [haridrah]; angustifolia, rox. [malabar arrowroot]; amada, roxb. [mango ginger]; zedoaria, roscoe [long zedoary]; pseudomontana, j. grah. [haridrah]; rubescens, roxb. [haridrah]; leucorrhiza, rox. [red malabar arrowroot]; montana, roxb.; reclinata, rox. [haridrah]; longa, rox. [country saffron]. Alpinia [galangal] rheedii, r. w. [galangal]; nutans, roscoe [galangal]; calcarata, roscoe; allughas, roscoe [galangal]; galanga, willd. [galangal]; officinarum, hance. [galangal]; khulinjan [galangal]. Kœmpferia [bhoochampak] rotunda, willd. [false zedoary]; galanga, linn. [indian galangal]; angustifolia, rox. [bhoochampak]. Elettaria cannæcarpa, r. w.; cardamomum, maton. [cardamom]. Amomum subulatum, roxb. [wild cardamom]; aromaticum, roxb. [wild cardamom]; maximum, roxb. [wild cardamom]; melegueta, roscoe [wild cardamom].—145 *Amaryllidaceæ.*—Crinum roxburghii, dalz. [poison bamboo]; asiaticum, linn. [poison bamboo]; ornatum, herb. [poison bamboo]; revolutum, herb. [poison bamboo]; pratense, herb. [poison bamboo]. Pancratium parvum, dalz.; verecundum, soland.; malabathricum, herb. Agave americana, linn. [american aloe]; vivipara, linn. [bastard aloe]. Fourcroya gigantea, vent. [foreign aloe].—146 *Hypoxidaceæ.*—Hypoxis leptostachya, r. w.; trichocarpa, r. w. Curculigo malabarica, r. w. [cauly moosly]; brevifolia, ait. [cauly moosly]; orchioides, gærtn. [cauly moosly]; recurvata, dryand [cauly moosly].—147 *Taccaceæ.*—Tacca pinnatifida, forst. [otaheite salep].—148 *Hydrocharidaceæ.*—Hydrilla verticillata, rich. Vallisneria alternifolia, roxb.; spiralis, linn. Blyxa octandra, rich. Ottelia alismoides, pers.—149 *Palmaceæ.*—Areca catechu, linn. [areca]. Seaforthia dicksonii, mart. Caryota urens, linn. [bastard sago palm]. Calamus [vaitasan] latifolius, roxb. [vaitasam]; rotang, linn. [country rattan]; pseudo-rotang, mart. [vaitasam]; fasciculatus, roxb. [walking stick rattan]; extensus, roxb. [vaitasam]; gracilis, roxb. [vaitasam]; erectus, roxb. [vaitasam]; draco, willd. [sumatra dragon's blood]. Borassus flabelliformis, linn. [palmyra]. Bentinckia condapanna, berry. Corypha taliera, roxb. [talura palm]; umbraculifera, linn. [talipot]. Licualia acutifida, mart. [penang lawyer]. Phœnix [kharjooram] sylvestris, roxb. [wild date]; farinifera, roxb. [small date]; acaulis, roxb. [stemless date]; dactylifera, linn. [arabian date]. Arenga saccharifera, labill. [gomooty]. Metroxylon sagu, rottl. [borneo sago palm]. Cocos nucifera, linn. [cocoanut]. Lodoicea seychellarum, labill. [sea cocoanut].—150 *Pandanaceæ.*—Pandanus odoratissimus, linn. [screw-pine]; fascicularis, lam. [screw-pine]; furcatus, roxb. [screw-pine]; lævis, rumph. [screw-pine]. Nipa fruticans, thunb. [attap].—151 *Pistiaceæ.*—Pistia stratiotes, linn. [rootless nelumbo]; ægyptiaca, schleid. [rootless nelumbo]; crispita, blume. [rootless nelumbo].—152 *Araceæ.*—Cryptocoryne spiralis, fischer; roxburghii, dalz. Arisæma curvatum, kunth.; leschenaultii, blume.; tortuosum, schott. Typhonium divaricatum, decaisne. [elephant yam]; cuspidatum, decaisne. [elephant yam]; bulbiferum, dalz. [elephant yam]; orixense, schott. [elephant yam]. Amorphophallus campanulatus, blume. [telinga potato]; sylvaticus, kunth. [telinga potato]; dubius, blume. [telinga potato]; bulbiferum, dalz; giganteus, blume. [telinga potato]; lyratus, kunth. [telinga potato]. Remusatia vivipara, schott. Colocasia [kachvee] antiquorum, schott. [kachvee]; nymphæifolia, kunth. [kachvee]; montana, kunth. [kachvee]; indica, roxb. [kachvee]. Dracontium polyphyllum, linn. [wild telinga potato]. Scindapsus pertusus, schott. [elephant long pepper]; officinalis, schott. [elephant long pepper]. Pothos scandens, linn. [elephant creeper]. Lasia loureirii, schott. Lagenandra toxicaria, dalz. Acorus calamus, linn. [vashamboo].—153 *Typhaceæ.*—Typha angustifolia, linn. [lesser elephant grass]; elephantina, roxb. [elephant grass].—154 *Eriocaulaceæ.*—Eriocaulon setaceum, linn.; consanguineum, kunth.; melaleucum, mart.; sexangulare, linn.; quinquangulare, linn.; wallichianum, mart.; dalzelli, dalz.; nilagirense, steudel.; robustum, steudel.; lanceolatum, miq.; bracteosum, steudel.—155 *Cyperaceæ.*—Cyperus [coray] punctatus, roxb.; pumilus, linn. [coray]; vulgaris, seib. [coray]; polystachyus, rottb. [coray]; puncticulatus, vahl. [flood sedge]; tortuosus, koen. [coray]; mucronatus, rottb. [coray]; pygmœus, rottb. [thorny sedge]; alopecuroides, rottb. [striped sedge]; castaneus, willd. [coray]; squarrosus, linn. [coray]; aristatus, rottb. [coray]; compressus, linn. [wet-land sedge]; haspan, linn. [coray]; difformis, linn. [coray]; iria, linn. [tail sedge]; niveus, retz. [coray]; arenarius, retz. [coray]; cephalotes, vahl. [coray]; tuberosus, rottb. [coray]; procerulus, n. ab e. [coray]; articulatus, linn. [coray]; semi-nudus, roxb. [coray]; corymbosus, rottb. [indian matting sedge]; dehiscens, n. ab e. [coray]; pangorei, rottb. [creeping grass sedge]; tenuiflorus, rottb. [coray]; rotundus, linn. [common sedge]; venustus, r. br. [fisherman's sedge]; exaltatus, retz.; verticillatus, roxb. [coray]; procerus, vahl. [water sedge]; retzii, n. ab e. [coray]; pennatus, lam. [coray]; dilutus, vahl.; distans, linn. [coray]; kyllingioides, vahl.; pusillus, vahl. [coray]; umbellatus, burm. [large sedge]; wightii, n. ab e. [coray]; pertenuis, roxb. [straight sedge]; roxburghii, n. ab e. [demon sedge]; nilagiricus, hochst. [coray]; atroferrugineus, steudel. [coray]; tenuispica, steudel. [coray]; petræus, hochst. [coray]; oryzeticola, steudel. [coray]; racemosus, retz. [coray]. Mariscus umbellatus, vahl.; paniceus, link.; kyllingioides, steudel. Courtoisia cyperoides, n. ab e. Kyllingia monocephala, linn.; brevifolia, rottb.; melanosperma, n. ab e.; triceps, rottb. Remirea pedunculata, r. br. Eleocharis chætaria, roem.; capitata, brown; atropurpurea, kunth.; plantaginea, brown; tumida, schult.; fistulosa, schult.; media, schult.; spiralis, brown. Scirpus [club grass] juncoides, roxb. [club grass]; mucronatus, linn. [club grass]; subulatus, vahl. [club grass]; kysoor, roxb. [club grass]; grossus, linn. [club grass]; maritimus, linn. [club grass]. Fuirena glomerata, lam.; uncinata, wall.; pentagona, w. and a. Isolepis curvula, kunth.; articulata, n. ab e.; prælongatus, n. ab e.; squarrosa, roem. and schult.; dipsacea, roem. and schult.; barbata, brown; gracillis, n. ab e. Fimbristylis [nalam] polytrichoides, vahl. [nalam]; schœnoides, vahl. [nalam]; bispicata, n. ab e. [nalam]; argentea, vahl. [nalam]; albicans, n. ab e. [nalam]; dichotoma, vahl. [nalam]; æstivalis, vahl. [nalam]; complanata, link. [nalam]; scaberrima, n. ab c. [nalam]; quinquangularis, kunth. [nalam]; miliacea, vahl. [nalam]; communis, kunth. [nalam]; ferruginea, vahl.; latifolia, kunth. [nalam]; chætorhiza, kunth. [nalam]; torta, kunth. [nalam]; wightiana, n. ab c.; uliginosa, hochst. [nalam]; capillacea, hochst. [nalam]; glabra, hochst. [nalam]; monticola, hochst. [nalam]; tenera, schult. [nalam]; gigantea [nalam]. Abilgaardia monostachya, vahl.; tristachya, vahl. Lipocarpha argentea, brown; sphacilata, kunth. Hemicarpha isolepis, n. ab e. Hypolytrum latifolium, rich. Rhyncospora articulata, schult. Scleria lithosperma, willd.; tessellata, willd.; orizoides, presl.; sumatrensis, retz.; androgyna, n. ab e.; parvula, steudel. Carex nubigena, don.; longicruris, nees. ab esenb.; longipes, don.; phacota, spreng.; myosurus, n. ab e.; ramosa, schkuhr.; meiogyna, n. ab e.; indica, linn.; filicina, n. ab e.; lindleyana, n. ab e.; wightiana, n. ab e.; rhaphidocarpa, n. ab e.; baccans, n. ab e.; ligulata, n. ab e.; mercarensis, hochst.; leucantha, boott.; macrophylla, hochst.; nilagerica, hochst.; platycarpa, hochst.; gemella, hochst.—156 *Graminaceæ.*—Oryza mutica, roxb. [nivvary]; sativa, linn. [paddy]; Potamochloa aristata, griffith. Coix lacryma, linn. [coratty pausy]; barbata, roxb. [coratty pausy]; gigantea, koen. [coratty pausy]. Paspalum scrobiculatum, linn. [khoda]; metzii, steud.; distichum, burm. [khoda]; nematodes, schult. Panicum [priyangoo] corymbosum, roxb. [priyangoo]; dilatatum, steudel. [priyangoo]; wallichianum, w. and a. [priyangoo]; conjugatum, roxb. [priyangoo]; cimicinum, retz. [priyangoo]; burmanni, retz. [wild hurrially]; peninsulanum, steud. [priyangoo]; acuminatissimum, steud. [priyangoo]; elatius, linn. [priyangoo]; colonum, linn. [matted purple grass]; dubium, steud. [priyangoo]; crus galli, linn. [wild darbhay]; stagninum, retz. [large purple grass]; lanceolatum, retz. [priyangoo]; asperum, wight. [priyangoo]; glaucum, linn. [white tinay]; helvolum, linn. [jackal tinay]; tomentosum, roxb. [priyangoo]; canaliculatum, nees. [priyangoo]; helopus, trin. [quilled purple grass]; grossarium, linn. [cumboo grass]; canaræ, steudel. [priyangoo]; flavidum, retz. [purple grass]; fluitans, retz. [paddy-field grass]; javanicum, poir. [surprise grass]; leptochloa, nees. [priyangoo]; prostratum, lam. [wild white shaumay]; nilagiricum, steud. [priyangoo]; oxyphyllum, hochst. [priyangoo]; interruptum, willd. [priyangoo]; curvatum, linn. [priyangoo]; remotum, retz. [wild varagoo]; paludosum, roxb. [soda grass]; multibrachiatum, hochst. [priyangoo]; mangaloricum, steudel. [priyangoo]; courtallense, nees. [priyangoo]; indicum, linn. [black tinay]; trigonum, retz. [priyangoo]; megalanthum, steud. [priyangoo]; nodibarbatum, hochst. [priyangoo]; metzii, hochst. [priyangoo]; brachyclume, hochst. [priyangoo]; kunthianum, w. and a. [priyangoo]; æquatum, nees. [priyangoo]; roxburghii, spreng. [priyangoo]; serrulatum, roxb. [priyangoo]; uliginosum, roxb.; tenue, roxb. [priyangoo]; montanum, roxb. [priyangoo]; ciliare, retz. [trembling tinay]; egyptiacum, retz. [red shaumay]; nepalense, spreng. [priyangoo]; verticillatum, linn. [sticky grass]; frumentaceum, roxb. [large shaumay]; antipodum, spr. [wild small shaumay]; italicum, linn. [tinay]; erucæforme, sib. [small raggy]; miliare, lam. [shaumay]; jumentorum, swz. [guinea grass]; repens, linn. [ginger grass]; miliaceum, linn. [varagoo]. Pennisetum alopecuros, nees. [bajrah]; hohenhackeri, hoschst. [bajrah]; holcoides, schult. [bajrah]; spicatum, delile. [bajrah]. Cenchrus biflorus, roxb. Trachyozus muricata, pers. Lappago aliena, spreng. Spinifex squarrosus, linn. [ravanan's whiskers]. Lopholepis ornithocephala, hook. Arundinella ciliata, roxb.; nervosa, roxb.; hirsuta, nees.; fuscata, nees.; mesophylla, nees.; setifera, steudel.; purpurea, hochst.; pilosa, hochst. Thyssanolœna agrostis, arn. and nees. Aristida depressa, retz.; hystrix, linn.; setacea, retz. [broom grass]. Vilfa coromandaliana, beauv.; diandra, trin.; orientalis, nees.; genuculata, nees.; mangalorica, hochst. Triachryum nilagiricum, steudel. Perotis latifolia, ait. Phragmites roxburghii, kunth. [large naunal]. Amphidonax heynii, nees.; benghalensis, nees.; bifaria, nees.; tenella, wight and arn. Michrochloa setacea, r. br. Chloris barbata, swartz. [trail grass]; tenella, roxb.; montana, roxb. [trail grass]; roxburghiana, schult. [trail grass]; tetrameris, trin. [trail grass]; wightiana, nees. [trail grass]; digitata, steudel. [trail grass]. Leptochloa calycina, kunth.; coromandelina, steudel.; verticillata, kunth. Eleusine indica, gærtn. [wild raggy]; coracana, gærtn. [raggy]. Dactyloctenium ægyptiacum, beauv. Cynodon dactylon, pers. [hurrially]; gracilis, nees. [hurrially]; virgatus, nees. [hurrially]. Melanocenchris rothiana, nees. Aira maderaspatana, nees.; filiformis, koen. Pommereulla cornucopiæ, linn. fil. [ant grass]. Eragrostis [coosham] nutans, retz. [coosham]; ciliata, nees. [wild coraly]; cynosuroides, retz. [darbhay]; viscosa, trin. [coosham]; bifaria, vahl. [squirrel ginger]; cretacea, nees. and arn. [coosham]; punctata, linn. [coosham]; mangalorica, hochst. [coosham]; tenella, linn. [coosham]; plumosa, retz. [shaumay grass]; stenophylla, hochst. [coosham]; procera, roxb. [coosham]; koenigii, kunth. [coosham]; nigra, nees. [coosham]; atropurpurea, hochst. [coosham]; parviglumis, hochst. [coosham]; verticillata, beauv. [shaumay grass]. Uniola indica, spreng. Dactylis lagopodioides, linn. Elythrophorus articulatus, beauv. Triticum vulgare, villars [geung]. Hordeum vulgare, linn. [jow]; vulgare, linn., var. distichum [jow]; vulgare, linn., var. hexandrum [jow]. Avena sativa, linn. [vilauyaty jow]. Tripogon bromoides, roth.; filiformis, nees.; griffithii, wight and arn.; unidentatus, nees. Festuca indica, retz. [cleft grass]. Bambusa [bamboo] vulgaris, schrad. [striped bamboo]; arundinacea, willd. [common bamboo]; spinosa, roxb. [thorny bamboo]; stricta, roxb. [male bamboo]; arundo, klein. [mahableshwar bamboo]; nana, roxb. [dwarf bamboo]. Melocanna rheedii, rupr. [berry bamboo]. Dendrocalamus tulda, nees. [bengal bamboo]. Arundinaria hispida, steudel. Oropetium thomæum, trin. Hemarthria coromandeliana, steudel. Ophiurus perforatus, trin. Rottboellia exaltata, linn.; lævis, retz. Manisuris granularis, swartz.; myurus, linn. Andropogon [beard grass] pertusus, willd. [beard grass]; serratus, retz. [beard grass]; striatus, klein.; contortus, linn. [spear grass]; hohenhackeri, hochst; oliganthus, hochst.; monandrus, roxb.; tridentatus, roxb.; simillimus, steudel. [beard grass]; arnottianus, nees.; aristatum, roxb.; rugosus, gærtn.; courtallensis, steud.; bladhii, retz. [beard grass]; bifoveolatus, steud.; lanceolatus, roxb.; scandens, roxb. [beard grass]; incurvatus, retz.; strictus, roxb.; confertiflorus, steud.; polyneuros, steud.; schœnanthus, roxb. [lemon grass]; iwarancusa, roxb. [ibharancoosha]; martini, roxb. [roussa grass]; punctatus, roxb.; pumilus, roxb.; controversus, steud. [beard grass]; parviflorus, roxb.; montanus, roxb. [beard grass]; glaber, roxb. [beard grass]; fascicularis, roxb. [beard grass]; muricatus, retz. [cuscus]; aciculatus, retz. [keshinee]; verticillatus, roxb.; increscens, steud.; peninsulæ, steud.; nodulibarbis, hochst.; breviaristatus, steud.; imberbis, retz. [beard grass]; pilosus, wight [nutt]; nardus, linn. [indian grass]. Sorghum vulgare, pers. [cholum]; saccharatum, pers. [sweet cholum]. Zea mays, linn. [mecca cholum]. Anthistiria cymbaria, roxb.; ciliata, linn.; wightii, nees.; linneana, steud.; arundinacea, roxb. Apluda aristata, linn. Imperata kœnigii, nees. [lalong grass]. Amblyachyrum mangalorense, hochst. Leersia hexandra, swz. [wild dholl]. Saccharum [sharam] spontaneum, linn. [naunal]; sara, roxb. [moonshee grass]; fuscum, roxb. [sharam]; procerum, roxb. [wild sugar-cane]; officinarum, linn. [sugar-cane]; exaltatum, roxb. [sharam]; munja, rox. [moonj]; propinquum, steud. [sharam]. —ACOTYLEDONS OR CRYPTOGAMIC OR FLOWERLESS.—157 *Filices.*—Various species [parny].—158 *Lycopodiaceæ.*—Classification of species here not yet effected [shookaram].—159 *Equisetaceæ.*—Classification of species here not yet effected [ashwa vauly].—160 *Musci.*—Classification of species here not yet effected [pausy].—161 *Fungi.*—Classification of species here not yet effected [caulaun].—162 *Lichenes.*—Classification of species here not yet effected [cull pausy].—163 *Algæ.*—Classification of species here not yet effected [cadal pausy].——**(3)** The following are the orders here concerned, arranged alphabetically, with the sanscrit equivalents, references to the key-synopsis, and a brief description of each.——*Acanthaceæ* (कण्टकीयसन्तान - kantakíyasantána, San.). San. from (kantaka, san. spine). 101. Herbs or shrubs, with large leafy bracts, in the axils of which the flowers are partly concealed; calyx composed of deeply imbricated sepals forming a broken whorl; placenta expands into hard processes which are hooked [adhatoday, bhoonimbam, chebeera, corandy, coromandel chiretta, face plant, french chiretta, gendarussa, indra's creeper, nail-dye, neelaumbram, neermoolly, snake-jasmine, vandaumbram].——*Algæ* (समुद्रशाकेयसन्तान - samudrasháképyasantána, San.). San. from (samudra, san. sea + sháka, san. herb). 163. Sea weeds, leafless, flowerless plants, usually, growing in water; many are nutritious [cadal pausy].——*Amarantaceæ* (अमरपुष्पीयसन्तान - amarapushpíyasantána, San.). San. from (a, san. prefix of negation + mri, san. to die

+ pushpa, san. flower), herbs which do not soon fade. 106. Amaranths. Herbs and shrubs, weeds, or occasionally showy annual plants, with inconspicuous apetalous flowers, in almost all cases of a scarious texture, most commonly of a white color, now and then pink, orange, and crimson [audayotty, indian burr, jaffer goondy, maurisham, moorgha, poolay].——*Amaryllidaceæ* (कुमारीयसन्तान - kumáríyasantána, San.). San. means maiden, alluding to cool fleshy leaves. 145. Amaryllids, Narcissuses. Bulbous, sometimes fibrous-rooted, plants; have fleshy leaves, which are either flat or slightly concave, and arise in a tuft from the root, or from the top of a short stem; flowers resemble lily family; many display poisonous properties; some are emetic and purgative and some yield useful fibres [american aloe, bastard aloe, foreign aloe, poison bamboo].——*Ampelideæ* (द्राक्षेयसन्तान - drákshéyasantána, San.). San. from (dráksbá, san. vine). 42. Vineworts. Otherwise vitaceæ. Shrubby plants climbing by tendrils; inhabitants of woods [angoor, draucshay, naralay, piranday, ratanhia, vegetable nerinjy].——*Anacardiaceæ* (अनुहृदीयसन्तान - anuhridíyasantána, San.). San. from (anu, san. like + hrid, san. heart), so called from the form of the nuts. 45. Anacards. Trees or shrubs having a resinous, milky, often caustic juice, dotless leaves, small inconspicuous flowers, with an ovary containing a single ovule suspended at the end of an erect cord. The juice often becomes black in drying. The fruit however in some cases is eatable [amrautam, cashew, chiroujee, holigarna, kakrasinghy, mango, marking nut, mastic, otaheite apple, pistah, sumach, wodier].——*Anonaceæ* (गण्डगात्रेयसन्तान - gandagátréyasantána, San.). Title from (anóna, singh. custard apple). San. from (gandagátra, san. custard apple). 4. Custard apples. Trees or shrubs, tropical in habits; many abound in a powerfully aromatic secretion, which renders the flowers fragrant; the leaves of others give forth a perfume; the dried fruit of many is highly aromatic; of others the fruit is succulent and abounds in juice [anona, ashocam, doodooga, ilangilang, madmaunty].——*Apocynaceæ* (अपशुनेयसन्तान - apashunéya-santána, San.). San. from (apa, san. from + shuna, san. dog). 87. Dogbanes. Trees or shrubs, usually milky, allied to the asclepiadeæ; natives of the tropics; flowers ornamental; many are poisonous, some are drastic purgatives; the bark sometimes tonic and febrifugal; acrid principle combined with milky juice; tannic and gallic acid occasionally present [carondah, dita, gannair, ground paulay, odallam, pagoda tree, paula indigo, saptaparnam, shyaumalatay, snake root, tagaram, tellicherry bark, veppaulay].——*Araceæ* (वाराहीयसन्तान - váráhíyasantána, San.). San. from (varáha, san. an esculent yam). 152. Arums. Herbs or shrubby plants, sometimes climbing, often with corms; fruit succulent; acridity prevails and many are irritant poisons; the corms sometimes supply starch, which is separated from the acrid matter by washing [elephant creeper, elephant long pepper, elephant yam, kachvee, telinga potato, vashamboo, wild telinga potato].——*Araliaceæ* (तरुरुहेयसन्तान - taruruhéya-santána, San.). Title from American araba, ivy. San. from (taru, san. tree + ruh, san. to grow). 68. Ivyworts. Trees or shrubs, rarely herbs; several are conspicuous for their broad large foliage; fruit consisting always of more carpels than two, and having no double epigynous discs; they have aromatic qualities, usually slight, but occasionally intense.——*Aristolochiaceæ* (श्रेष्ठप्रसवेयसन्तान - shrésht'hapraasavéyasantána, San.). San. from (shrésht'ha, san. best + prasava, san. delivery). 117. Birthworts. Herbs or climbing shrubby plants with axillary apetalous flowers. Resemble endogens in flowers, but exogens in stems and leaves. Have pungent, aromatic, and tonic properties [eeshwaram, indian worm-killer, isharmool].——*Artocarpaceæ* (अपूपफलेयसन्तान - apúpap'haléyasantána, San.). San. from (apúpa, san. bread + p'hala, san. fruit). 122. Bread-fruits. Trees or shrubs, with a milky juice, dense flower heads, and edible fruits. Many yield caoutchouc [jack, sack tree].——*Asclepiadeæ* (अश्विनीयसन्तान - ashvníyasantána, San.). San. from (ashviní, san. physicians of heaven), much valued medicinally. 88. Milkweeds. Allied to apocynaceæ; lactescent, often twining, shrubs or herbs; have acrid, stimulating, purgative, diaphoretic, and emetic properties; most yield milky juice [caurallam, creeper champak, hedge cotton, indian ipecacuanha, indian sarsaparilla, mandey, nakchiknee silk cotton, needle paulay, paulay silk cotton, somam, vattoovally, yercum].——*Basellaceæ* (उपोदिकेयसन्तान - upódikéyasantána, San.). Title from basella, the malabar name. San. from (upódiká, san. basella genus). 109. Malabar nightshades. Mostly herbaceous climbers, with more or less succulent leaves, and small inconspicuous flowers; the perianth is usually thick and fleshy, and the style is three-cleft. Calyx double, stamens perigynous, outer calyx consists of two bracts which are adnate to the perianth [malabar nightshade].——*Berberidæ* (बर्बरीयसन्तान - barbaríyasantána, San.). Title from Arab. berberis, wild. San. from. (barbara, san. wild). 6. Berberids. Small trees or shrubs, with dry or succulent fruits, the latter of which contain large quantities of malic acid; bark and wood bitter; occur in hilly regions [berberry].——*Bignoniaceæ* (पाटलीयसन्तान - pátalíyasantána, San.). San. from (pátala, san. trumpet flower tree). 99. Trumpet flowers. Trees or twining or climbing shrubby plants whose trumpet-shaped flowers are great beauty; distinguished by large flat seed-pods; large white or yellow, often malodorous, flowers prevail [indian cork, night paulay, pajanely, pautalam, pauthiry, valencoorny, water ailanto, wody].——*Bixineæ* (कुंकुमफलीयसन्तान - kunkumap'halíyasantána, San.). San. from (kunkumap'halá, san. saffron-fruited, arnotto, bixa orellana). Title otherwise flacourtiaceæ. 14. Arnottoes. Shrubs or small trees; some are bitter and astringent; others yield edible fruits [attack, ceylon plum, chaulmoogra, forest bair, golden silk cotton, indian plum, marotty, mauritius plum, monkey country saffron, swaudoocantacam, tomi-tomi].——*Boragineæ* (हृद्यङ्गमेयसन्तान - hridyangaméya-santána, San.). San. from (hridaya, san. heart + gam, san. to go); beloved. 92. Borageworts. Herbs or shrubs, with round stems, alternate, rough leaves; remarkable for mucilaginous properties; some yield dyes [shauyam], others are used as pot-herbs [coorvitchy, donkey toombay, gowzabaun, indian heliotrope, keeray, sebesten].——*Burseraceæ* (वोलेयसन्तान - vóléyasantána, San.). San. from (vóla, san. myrrh). 35. Myrrhs. Yielding several kinds of aromatic resinous substances called Balsam [balm of gilead, balsam, bdellium, black dammer, bole, caunary, elemi, garooga, kiloovay, olibanum, pehimbia, yellow dammer].——*Cacteæ* (नागफणीयसन्तान - nágap'haníyasantána, San.). San. from (nágap'hana, san. serpent's hood, opuntia dillenii, haw.). 65. Melon-thistles. Succulent, often spiny herbs; many are ornamental; the fruit of many is sub-acid; in some instances, insipid; the stems of some are eaten by cattle [prickly-pear].——*Campanulaceæ* (घण्टिकेयसन्तान - ghantikéyasantána, San.). San. from (ghanta, san. bell). 76. Bellworts. Herbaceous plants, valued for beauty of flowers [water long pepper, wild pogauk].——*Capparideæ* (करीरेयसन्तान - karíréyasantána, San.). San. from (karíra, san. capparis). 11. Capparids. Herbs, shrubs, or thorny trees. In their properties resemble crucifers. They have pungent, stimulant, and antiscorbutic qualities [caper, nirvala, vailay].——*Caryophylleæ* (कणिकफुल्लेयसन्तान - kanika-p'hulléyasantána, San.). San. from (kanika, san. grain + p'hulla, san. bloom). 17. Silenads or Cloveworts. Herbaceous plants often growing in tufts with grass-like leaves; opposite leaves and terminal flowers; inhabit mountains, hedges, rocks, and waste places.——*Casuarinaceæ* (कशकृशीयसन्तान - kashakrishíyasantána, San.). San. from (kasha, san. whip + krisha, san. slender); from long slender branches. 127. Beef-woods. Leafless trees, tropical or sub-tropical, having the aspect of equisetums [chowk maram]; they abound in australia; their wood is hard and heavy, and on account of its color is called beef-wood [chowkmaram].——*Celastrineæ* (हैमलेयसन्तान - haimaléyasantána, San.). San. from (haimala, san. winter), the fruit remaining on the tree all the winter. 40. Spindle trees. Shrubs or trees; more or less acrid and some of the plants yield oil [chintoo, malkangany, nerija].——*Combretaceæ* (हरीतकीयसन्तान - harítakíyasantána, San.). San. from (harítakí, san. terminalia chebula, retz.); the best known here of the order. 55. Myrobalans. Trees or shrubs; astringency, the prevalent principle [antyaparny, belleric myrobalan, catapang, chebulic myrobalan, dhavam, harra, madagascar mangrove, murdah, pauchimaun, rangoon creeper, tanakk, vekkauly, wodala].——*Commelynaceæ* (वत्सप्रियसन्तान - vatsapriyasantána, San.). San. from (vatsapriya, san. dear to calf, commelyna communis, linn.). 139. Spiderworts. Herbs, with flat leaves. Underground stems of many yield starch and are used for food [calf's grass, wild rattan].——*Compositæ* (संयुक्तपुष्पीयसन्तान - samyuktapushpíyasntána, San.). San. from (samyukta, san. united + pushpa, san. flower). 74. Otherwise Asteraceæ. Herbs or shrubs, sometimes assume arborescent forms; flowers generally yellow; bitterness prevails to a greater or less degree; this is accompanied with tonic, stimulant, aromatic and narcotic qualities [akalkarah, ayappanay, baboona, bastard saffron, bhangrah, buffalo carolah, burdock datura, camel thistle, costum, country radish, elephant's foot, fever toolsy, gendah, hare's ear, indian absinth, indian endive, kahoo, madras absinth, moondy, nakchiknee, pig plant, ramtil, seed toolsy, shaumanty, style plant, wild jeerah].——*Convolvulaceæ* (संवर्तितेयसन्तान - samvartitéyasantána, San.). San. from (sam, san. together + vrit, san. to roll). 93. Bindweeds. Herbs or shrubs, usually twining and lactescent. Very abundant; they twine round other shrubs or creep among the weeds of the seashore; brilliant wheel-shaped flowers, of pure white, blue, rose, purple and intermediate shades; characterized by purgative properties and contain some important medicinal plants [ajauntry, calamby, caushy ratnam, deer's foot, drowpady's hair, giant potato, indian pink, jalap, kaladanah, laldanah, malabar creeper, moon flower, quamoclit, rat's ear, red adambo, seashore paulay, scammony, seeta's knot, seeta's thread, sweet potato, tauly, tiger's foot, tooty coora, turbith, vishnoocraunty, white adambo].——*Cornaceæ* (शृङ्गेयसन्तान - shringéyasantána, San. from (shringa, san. horn), the wood being thought to be as hard as a horn. 69. Dogwoods. Trees or herbs usually with opposite leaves having no stipules; flowers in cymose clusters or in heads surrounded by an involucre; calyx adherent, its limb four-toothed, petals four valvate in bud; stamens alternate with petals; styles united into one; ovary two-celled; ovules solitary, pendulous; fruit a two-celled drupe; these plants are used as tonics and in ague [alanjy].——*Crassulaceæ* (स्थूलकेयसन्तान - st'húlakéyasantána, San.). San. from (st'húla, san. thick + ka, san. diminutive suffix), in allusion to the fleshy leaves and stems. 51. House-leeks. Succulent herbs or shrubs, found in the driest situations; acridity prevails; some are refrigerant, others astringent [zakhm hayaut].——*Cruciferæ* (क्रुशभरेयसन्तान - krúshabharéyasantána, San.). San. from (cross + bhri, san. to bear). Name from the cruciform disposition of the four petals. 10. Cabbages; Herbaceous plants; antiscorbutic and pungent and occasionally acrid; none are poisonous; the order contains many of the culinary vegetables in constant use; have much nitrogen and sulphur in their composition [country radish, halcom, kobee, rayaun, sarshapam, sarsoon, shalgham].——*Cucurbitaceæ* (कर्कटिकेयसन्तान - karkatikéyasantána, San.). San. from (karkatika, san. cucumis melo, linn., var. utilissimus, roxb.). 62. Gourds. Succulent, climbing plants; herbaceous, annual, very rarely perennial; the root of the annual is thin that of the perennial fleshy; possess a certain degree of acridity; in many cases however as in the melon [oorvauroo], the cucumber [oorvauroo], the vegetable marrow [q.v.], gourd [carcauroo], pumpkin [carcauroo] and squash [carcauroo], the fruit is edible when cultivated; the seeds are usually harmless [braminy kite, caper, carcauroo, carolah, fakeer's bottle, indian caper, indravally, luffa, mosmoosky, neyoonny, oorvauroo, penarvally, rama's caper, snake gourd, wax-gourd].——*Cycadaceæ* (अलकपत्रीयसन्तान - alakapatríyasantána, San.). San. from (alaka, san. curl + patra, san. leaf). 129. Cycads. Small palm-like trees or shrubs with unbranched stems. Have a mucilaginous juice, in which there is often much starch used for food [indian sago palm]. ——*Cyperaceæ* (खपुरेयसन्तान - khapuréyasantána, San.). San. from (khapura, san. cyperus pertenuis, roxb.). 155. Sedges. Grass-like or rush-like cæspitose plants; triangular stem without knots; found especially in marshes, ditches, and about running streams [club grass, coray, nalam].——*Dilleniaceæ* (भव्यकेयसन्तान - bhavyakéyasantána, San.). San. from (bhavya, san. dillenia indica, linn.). 2. Handsome flowering trees and shrubs; some of the former affording excellent timber; but the shrubs are usually climbing or prostrate; a few herbaceous plants also occur; flowers often yellow; are generally astringent; the fruit of most are acid and used in curries [chaltah, curry]. ——*Dioscoreaceæ* (आलुकेयसन्तान - álukéyasantána, San.). San. from (álu, san. dioscorea genus). 132. Yams [auloo]. Shrubs; climbing and sarmentaceous; roots large, tuberous; acridity prevails, but is often associated with starch [auloo, malacca yam]. ——*Dipterocarpeæ* (द्विपत्रगर्भेयसन्तान - dvipatragarbhéyasantána, San.). San. from (dvi, san. twice + patra, san. wing + garbha, san. fruit). 24. Dipterads. Almost exclusively Indian. Large, fine flowering trees, abounding in resinous juice; leaves alternate, marked with strong parallel veins [caung, gurjan, piney, saul]. ——*Ebenaceæ* (तिन्दुकेयसन्तन - tindukéyasantána, San.). San. from (tinduka, san. diospyros embryopteris, pers.). 83. Trees or shrubs, not lactescent; fruit, a round or oval berry; give hard and valuable timber; the bark of some is astringent, the fruit is in many catablo; the heart-wood of several species of diospyros [indian ebony] constitute different kinds of ebony [calaminder wood, gaub, indian ebony, neilgherry satin-wood]. ——*Equisetaceæ* (अश्ववालीयसन्तान - ashvavâlíyasantána, San.). Title from resemblance to horse tails. San. from (ashva, san. horse + vála, san. tail). 159. Horse tails. Plants having great resemblance to ferns; they are often perennial, new shoots being thrown up from creeping rhizomes; the spores germinate like ferns [parny]; shoots are jointed, the articulation having a toothed membranous sheath; fruit a terminal cone; good sand-binders [ashwa vauly, manal].——*Ericaceæ* (जाङ्गलेयसन्तान - jángaléyasantána, San.). San. from (jángala, san. heath). 78. Heathworts. Shrubs or under shrubs with evergreen, rigid, entire, whorled or opposite exstipulate leaves; calyx inferior, four to five-cleft; corolla four to five-cleft; stamens eight to ten or twice these numbers, hypogynous; anthers two-celled, with appendages, opening by pores; ovary surrounded by a disk or scales; fruits capsular, rarely berried; seeds numerous, albuminous. Divided into two sections; one in which fruits open loculicidally, rarely septicidally; buds naked; the other in which the fruits capsular, septicidal; buds scaly, resembling cones [neilgherry rhododendron].——*Euphorbiaceæ* (वज्रीयसन्तान - vajríyasantána, San.). San. from (vajra, san. euphorbia genus). 118. Spurgeworts. Trees, shrubs, or herbs; are generally acrid and poisonous, abounding in milky juice; starchy matter is procured from many as well as oils [yennay] and gutta [q.v.]; a few are garden plants, from the colored leaves surrounding the flowers [agaroo, amlashaucam, ammaun putcharisy, aumanac, aumlacam, brazil cherry, carpenter's tamarind, caunchy, caunjory, china tallow, chinny, cooppamainy, croton-lac tree, cuttimandoo, devil's goad, emblic myrobalan, garrar, gasambilla, ghantabeejam, jamalgota, java cedar, kamela, lumbang nut, malda dye, maumsicay, milk-hedge, neeroory, nelly, nicoombham, nolataulу, poolah, poolah coral tree, pootránjeeva, round-leaved nelumbo, round pepper, thorny vengay, tiger's milk, vattataulу, wild gannair, white tanakk].——*Ficoideæ* (उदुम्बरेयसन्तान - udumbaréyasantána, San.). San. from (udumbara, san. ficus glomerata, miq.). 66. Fig-marigolds. Succulent shrubs or herbs; some are esculent, while a few are diuretic; rich in alkaline carbonates; explained by their usually frequenting the seashore [hazaur danah, manaly, parpatam, shauranay, tirye]. ——*Filices* (पर्णीयसन्तान - parníyasantána, San.). San. from (parna, san. leaf). 157. Ferns. Two classes, evergreen and deciduous; the evergreen are most valued in cultivation; tree ferns grow on the Neilgherries [parny].——*Fluviales* (स्रोतोवहेयसन्तान - srótóvahéyasantána, San.). San. from (srótas, san. river + vah, san. to carry). 134. Naiads. Plants living in fresh or salt water, and having cellular leaves with parallel veins, and inconspicuous flowers, which are unisexual or hermaphrodite; fruit dry, one-celled, usually indehiscent.——*Fumariaceæ* (धूम्रेयसन्तान - dhúmréyasantána, San.). San. from (dhúmra, san. smoke); from the smell of some of the species. 9. Fumeworts. Have watery juice, and contain a bitter principle [pitpapra]. ——*Fungi* (शिलीन्ध्रेयसन्तान - shilíndhréyasantána, San.). San. from (shilíndhra, san. mushroom). 161. Mushrooms. Several nutritions, many poisonous [caulaun].——*Gentianaceæ* (कैरातेयसन्तान - kairátéyasantána, San.). San. from (kairáta, san. chiretta). 90. Gentianworts. Herbs, rarely shrubs; fruit, a capsule or berry; bitterness prevails; occasionally emetic and narcotic [chiretta, floating nelumbo, sankhvel].——*Geraniaceæ* (जलरञ्जेयसन्तान - jalarañjéyasantána, San.). San. from (jalarañja, san. crane); from the long beak-like prolongation of the axis. 31. Crane's bills. Herbs or shrubs; valued in gardens for flowers; have astringent and aromatic qualities [blimbing, coromandel gooseberry, goolmindie, lavaly, sour auray].——*Gnetaceæ* (काण्डदेवदारसन्तान - kándadévadárasantána, San.). San. from (kánda, san. joint + dévadára, san. pinus genus). 128. Joint firs. Small trees or creeping shrubs, with jointed stems and branches, with opposite reticulated, and sometimes scaly leaves; flowers monœcious or diœcious arranged in catkins or heads; the seeds of some of them are eaten.——*Graminaceæ* (घासेयसन्तान - ghéséyasantána, San.). San. from (ghása, san. grass). 156. Grasses. Lance-shaped herbs, generally with hollow stems; the roots are fibrous, and not to be confounded with the creeping stems sometimes wrongly called roots; generally erect, all destitute of true thorns; the most numerous and useful of plants; the seeds of the grasses contain flour; chaff is the pericarp; the seeds of all, those of the darnel alone excepted, are capable by cultivation of becoming alimentary; they constitute a twentieth of all known plants; they are usually social plants, forming herbage, sometimes becoming arborescent, 50 or 90 feet high; the cultivated grains, have been so long under cultivation that the native state of most is unknown; properties nutritive in a marked degree; some yield fragrant oils [attar], others produce sugar [ant grass, bajrah, bamboo, beard grass, broom grass, cholum, cleft grass, coosham, coraly, coratty pausy, cumboo, cuscus, dharbhay, geung, ginger grass, guinea grass, hurrially, ibharancoosha, indian grass, jow, keshinee, khoda, lalong grass, lemon grass, moonj, moonshee grass, naunal, nivvary, nutt, paddy, priyangoo, purple grass, raggy, ravanan's whiskers, roussa grass, sharam, shaumay, soda grass, spear grass, squirrel ginger, sticky grass, sugar-cane, surprise grass, tinay, trail grass, varagoo].——*Guttiferæ* (विन्दुपत्रीयसन्तान - vindupatríyasantána, San.). San. from (vindu, san. drop + patra, san. leaf). 22. Gamboges. Trees or shrubs with resinous juice, opposite leathery leaves, and often incomplete flowers. Fruit dry or succulent, one or many-celled. The plants are generally acrid, and yield a yellow gum-resin [googal]. Ornamental foliage [gamboge, mangosteen, nauga champak, poon, ractaumram, tickor].——*Hydrocharidaceæ* (उद्रहर्षीयसन्तान - udraharshíyasantána, San.). San. from (udra, san. water + harsh, san. to rejoice). 148. Frog-bits. Aquatic plants; with flowers in spathe, often incomplete; perianth of six leaves, the three inner petaloid; fruit dry or fleshy, and opening; seeds albuminous. ——*Hydrophyllaceæ* (उद्रफुल्लेयसन्तान - udrap'hulléyasantána, San.). San. from (udra, san. water + p'hulla, san. bloom). 91. Water-leaf. Herbs or small trees with alternate lobed hispid leaves; fruit a two-valved one-celled, or spuriously two-celled capsule; some are cultivated on account of their showy flowers [river blatty].——*Hypoxidaceæ* (अपाग्रेयसन्तान - apágréyasantána, San.). San. from (apa, san. beneath + agra, san. point); referring to the base of the capsule. 146. Herbs with a tuberous or fibrous perennial root, radical linear dry leaves, and tromerous flowers on scapes; fruit dry or berried; roots of some bitter and aromatic, and the tuber of a few are eaten [cauly moosly].——*Labiatæ* (तुलसीयसन्तान - tulasíyasantána, San.). San. from (tulasí, san. ocimum sanctum, linn.). 103. Mints [poodeenah]. Herbs or undershrubs; have no deleterious qualities; are generally aromatic and fragrant; odour depends on an essential oil [attar] containing camphor [q.v.]; some are tonics; many are used as carminatives and antispasmodics, and cultivated in gardens for culinary purposes [country borage, country lavender, indian sage, ipar, malabar catmint, marwah, patchouli, poodeenah, toolsy, toombay, zoofah].——*Lauraceæ* (तमालेयसन्तान - tamáléyasantána, San.). San. from (tamála, san. cinnamomum tamala, nees.). 111. Laurels. Trees; fruit, a berry or drupe; inhabiting cool places; in all cases more or less aromatic and fragrant; some are valuable for timber, others bear fruit that partake of the quality of the nutmeg [jautikye], a certain number are febrifuges, some yield a fixed as well as volatile oil [yennay] and an abundance of camphor [alligator pear, cinnamon, cottaun, meida lukdy, nanmuh, zafnee].——*Leguminosæ* (शमीयसन्तान - shamíyasantána, San.). San. from (shamí, san. legume); pulse. 48. Beans. Leguminous tribe. Herbs, shrubs, or trees. Distinguished by the fruit being a pod, the flowers as a rule bearing a resemblance to a pea-blossom in shape. The order is among the most extensive known, also one of the most important to man. However upon the whole it is poisonous, and those species which are used for food by man or animals are exceptions to the general rule, deleterious juices of the order not being in such instances sufficiently concentrated to prove injurious, and being in fact replaced to a considerable extent by either sugar [q.v.] or starch. All the varieties have pinnate leaves, small and papilionaceous flowers, appearing in axillary clusters of a purple hue; the calyx is cleft; segments, acute; standard, roundish and notched at the upper extremity; keel furnished with a sub-acute spur on both sides; stamens, arranged in two distinct bundles, nine and one; legume, continuous, one or more seeded; seeds, truncated, separated by spurious cellular partitions. Leguminosæ have been divided into three sub-orders; Papilionaceæ, Cæsalpinieæ, and Mimosæ [agatty, anasandra, arabian manna, auragvadham, australian blackwood, babool, bawchee, bengal ashocam, biswool, black nerinjy, bonduc, cabool country bean, calauyam, cantalam, casauree, casondy, catechu, caunooga, chakondah, condray, coobairaucshy, coral tree, corcapillay, corindah, country bean, cowitch, crow-creeper, dholl, divy divy, dog neem, ghantaravam, giligitcha, goa bean, gold mohur tree, gram, ground nut, guar, indian liquorice, indian medicago, indigo, iripa, karanj, kateerah, lobyah, maitee, malabar blackwood, manilla tamarind, masoor, maushaparny, mesquit, moodgam, mountain ebony, mysore thorn, neely, neer choondy, nemmy, nitta, orila, padouk, palaus, ratnagandhy, red nerinjy, red sanders, sappan, scimitar pod, senna, sesban, shamee, shaulicay, shingle tree, shivah, shiva's neem, shoondy, sially, sirissa, sissoo, soap-pod, solah, soonkeshwaram, sooptee, soovarnacam, sundra, sunn, tamarind, tambattam, three leaf poon, tungaid, vail, vengay, wagaty, wayaka, wild moringa, yaipy, yooga patricay, zamang].——*Lichenes* (शिलावल्केयसन्तान - shilávalkéyasantána, San.). San. from (shilávalka, san. lichens). 162. Lichens [cullpausy]. Perennials, spreading in the form of a crust over rocks, trees, or the surface of the earth; some yield to ammoniacal solutions a variety of brilliant colors [cull pausy, shauyam].——*Liliaceæ* (व्याघ्रनखीयसन्तान - vyághranakhíyasantána, San.). San. from (vyághra, san. tiger + nakha, san. claw). 136. Lilyworts. Herbs, shrubs, or trees; ornamental foliage; some are used as emetic and purgatives, others are stimulant and diaphoretic; some yield resinous [raul] and astringent matter, others supply valuable materials for manufactures [adam's needle, aloe, indian salep, lussoon, marool, naugdown, piyauz, shakaukool, shatamooly, soofaid moosly, soorinjaun, squill, wild bachnaug].——*Lineæ* (अतसीयसन्तान - atasíyasantána, San.). San. from (atasí, san. linum usitatissimum, linn.). 28. Flaxworts [alsee]. Showing a connection with malvaceæ in mucilaginous properties, and the strong fibre of the inner bark; seeds of all species are mucilaginous and oily [alsee, creeping falsah, deccany deodar]. ——*Loganiaceæ* (मुष्टीयसन्तान - mushtíyasantána, San.). San. from (mushti, san. strychnos nux-vomica, linn.). 89. Strychnias. Shrubs, herbs, or trees; are highly poisonous; in very minute doses act as tonics [clearing nut, mooshty, papeeta, poison nut, snake-wood tree].——*Lycopodiaceæ* (शूकरेयसन्तान - shúkaréyasantána, San.). San. from (shúkara, san. lycopodium). Lycopodium is called vegetable sulphur. 158. Clubmosses. Consist of minute yellow particles [shookaram].——*Lythraceæ* (लोहितेयसन्तान - lóhitéyasantána, San.). San. from (lóhita, san. red). 58. Loose-strifes. Herbs, rarely shrubs; astringency is met with in many plants; some furnish dyes [adambo, agnivendram, anaur, blatty, cadaly, chennangy, godaury, mindie, venteak]. ——*Magnoliaceæ* (चंपकेयसन्तान - champakéyasantána, San.). San. from (champaka, san. michelia champaca, linn.). 3. Frutescent or arborescent plants, with alternate, generally entire leaves, terminal or axillary flowers; contain an essential oil [attar] often united with a bitter substance; many cultivated for beauty of flowers [champak, star anise].——*Malpighiaceæ* (माधवीयसन्तान - mádhavíyasantána, San.). San. from (mádhaví, san. hiptage madablota, gærtn.). 29. Barbadoes cherries. Trees or shrubs, often climbing; generally astringent; many are handsome trees or climber with showy flowers [madablota]. ——*Malvaceæ* (मृद्वेयसन्तान - mridvéyasantána, San.). San. from (mridu, san. soft); alluding to the mucilaginous properties of the plants. 25. Mallowworts. Herbs, shrubs, or trees; found in great abundance; have flowers resembling the common hollyhock in shape, the five-colored portions of the flower being united at their base to a tube; most are herbs or shrubs with stalked leaves, the seeds are usually kidney-shaped; the uniform character is that of abounding in mucilage, and an entire absence of deleterious properties [balah, baobab, bendy, carpausy, cotton, durian, khoobauzy, mootty, portia, tootty, wild bengal gram].——*Marantaceæ* (शीतलपत्रीयसन्तान - shítalapatríyasantána, San.). San. from (shítalapatri, san. cold leaf, maranta dichotoma, wall.). 143. Arrowroots. Herbaceous plants closely allied to zingiberaceæ; amylaceous qualities prevail [indian shot, seetalpaty].——*Melanthaceæ* (मलिनप्रसूनेयसन्तान - malinaprasúnéyasantána, San.). San. from (malina, san. dirty + prasúna, san. fruit). 137. Colchicums. Herbs with bulbs, corms, or fasciculated roots, and white green or purple flowers; fruit a three-celled capsule; they are acrid, purgative, emetic, and sometimes narcotic in their qualities.——*Melastomaceæ* (मलिनास्येयसन्तान - malinásyéyasantána, San.). San. from (malina, san. dirty + ásya, san. mouth); in allusion to the berry staining the mouth when eaten. 57. Melastomads. Trees, herbs, or shrubs, with opposite ribbed leaves and showy flowers; fruit many-celled, either capsular or succulent; there are no unwholesome plants in the order, and the succulent fruit of several are edible [cassa, forest bengal gram].——*Meliaceæ* (मालकेयसन्तान - málakéyasantána, San.). San. from (málaka, san. melia azadirachta). 36. Bead trees. Are bitter, astringent, and tonic; some act as powerful purgatives and emetics [chickrassy, crab-oil plant, lanesh, malay red wood, neem, rohitacam, satinwood, shrub orange, soymida, toon, tottila, walsoora].——*Menispermaceæ* (मासकबीजेयसन्तान - másakabíjéyasantána, San.). San. from (mása, san. moon + bíja, san. seed). Trailing shrubs. 5. Moonseeds. Important to physicians, containing several valuable remedies, and more than one formidable poison; inhabit only warm climates; the stalk is sarmentaceous, the leaves alternate, petiolar, simple or compound, the flowers axillary; pervading principle is a bitter substance, associated with mucilage or starch, and a yellow coloring matter of great intensity; common in the woods and climb among the trees to a great height [calumba, creeper mooshty, goolancha, indian berry, indian pareira, jamtee, vausana vully].——*Moraceæ* (वटेयसन्तान - vatéyasantána, San.). San. from (vata, san. ficus bengalensis, linn.). 121. Mulberries. Trees or shrubs with a milky juice; leaves commonly rough and lobed; flowers small, unisexual, collected in heads, spikes or catkins. Fruit is a succulent sorosis or syconus. Plants abound in milky juice yielding caoutchouc [indian caoutchouc]. Fruit often bland, nutritious, while their bark yields fibres [anjeer, atty, banyan, indian cautchouc, indian mulberry, nooga, peepul, stunted jack, tsiela].——*Moringeæ* (मुरुङ्गीयसन्तान - murungíyasantána, San.). San. from (murungí, san. moringa pterygosperma, gærtn.). 46. Horse-radishes. Long legumes; allied to leguminosæ; trees with pinnate or tripinnate leaves; properties usually stimulant and pungent; almond contains oil [moringa, yennay].——*Musaceæ* (कदलीयसन्तान - kadalíyasantána, San.). San. from (kadali, san. musa paradisiaca, linn.). 142. Bananas. The plants have shoots proceeding from subterranean root-stalks, which form spurious stems composed of the sheathing leaf-stalks; fruit either a three-celled capsule or succulent and indehiscent; natives of warm and tropical regions, and supply a large quantity of nutritious fruit, while their leaves afford valuable fibres [naur, plantain, traveller's palm].——*Musci* (शैवलेयसन्तान - shaivaléyasantána, San.). San. from (shaivala, san. moss). 160. Mosses [pausy]. Leaves more or less pointed and lanceolate, imbricated or distichous; fruit ovate, opening horizontally by the opening of a terminal lid; mosses are either annual or perennial; in the latter case new branches are thrown out; require a great deal of moisture when in active growth; in agriculture or in the garden, noxious weeds; not of any great utility [pausy].——*Myristicaceæ* (जातीयसन्तान - játíyasantána, San.). San. from (játí, san. myristica fragrans, houtt.). 112. Nutmegs. Natives exclusively of the tropics; trees bearing appearance of laurels; from bark exudes a viscous juice; the fruit is the important part; are acrid and aromatic [jauty].——*Myrsineæ* (विडङ्गसन्तान - vidangasantána, San.). San. from (vidanga, san. embelia ribes, burm). 81. Ardisiads. Trees or shrubs. Fruit fleshy. Many are handsome, evergreen shrubs [byebarang].——*Myrtaceæ* (जाम्बवीयसन्तान - jámbavíyasantána, San.). San. from (jambu, san. eugenia jambolana, lamk.). 56. Myrtle-blooms. Trees or shrubs, prevailing principle is volatile oil [yennay] in calices, fruits, bark, and leaves; tannic acid also abounds [australian gum tree, blue gum, cajeput, china pepper, coomby, foreign mindie, guava, indian oak, jamboo, jaumoon, lavangam, moy, red gum, rose-apple].——*Nyctagineæ* (नक्तगेयसन्तान - naktagéyasantána, San). San. from (nakta, san. night + gam, san. to go). 105. Marvel of Perus. Herbs or shrubs; roots are purgative [conky, false jalap, tikry].——*Nymphæaceæ* (अम्बुजेयसन्तान - ambujéyasantána, San.). San. from (ambuja, san. waterborn, nymphæa lotus, linn.). 7. Water-lilies. Aquatic herbs with large showy flowers; chiefly inhabit quiet waters; attached to the earth by fibres, with elliptical or circular leaves floating on, or in the lotus [nelumbo] sometimes standing out of, the water; possesses bitter, astringent, and narcotic properties; the plants contain much starch in their rhizomes which are used for food in the same way as potatoes [indian water-lily, makhanah, nelumbo, potato].——*Ochnaceæ* (कनकचम्पेयसन्तान - kanakachampéyasantána, San.). San. from (kanakachampa, san. ochna squarrosa, linn.). 34. Ochnads. A small group of under-shrubs or trees allied to rutaceæ; bitter, tonic properties [shilandy]. ——*Olacineæ* (वासकेयसन्तान - vásakéyasantána, San.). Title from (vásaka, san. perfuming). 38. Olacads. Tropical or sub-tropical trees or shrubs, with simple alternate exstipulate leaves; fruit fleshy, one-celled, one-seeded [false sandal, poovana].——*Oleaceæ* (जितवृक्षेयसन्तान - jitavrikshéyasantána, San.). San. from (jitavriksha, san. olea). 85. Olivewort. Trees or shrubs; sweet smelling flowers; some have emollient and laxative properties; others are bitter, tonic, and febrifugal; some supply oil [yennay], others manna [indian olive, jasmine, jita, sicilian manna, weaver's beam, zeitoon].——*Onagraceæ* (वनरासभेयसन्तान - vanarásabhéyasantána, San.). San. from (vana, san. wild + rásabha, san. ass); from leaves resembling ass's ears. 59. Evening primroses. Herbs or shrubs; properties mucilaginous and astringent; some yield edible roots and fruits [lowly lavangam, singhaura].——*Orchidaceæ* (मुष्केयसन्तान - mushkéyasantána, San.). San. from (mushka, san. testicles); from similar root. 141. Orchids. Terrestrial or epiphytic herbs, or shrubs, with showy flowers. Groups of petals frequently resembling insects or birds. Cling to the trunks and limbs of trees, and to stones and bare rocks, where they vegetate among ferns and other shade loving plants. Fragrant, aromatic, tonic, and mucilaginous properties. The roots of some of the terrestrial species contain bassorin and constitute the nutritious substance called salep [q.v.]. Blue coloring matter like indigo [q.v.] is met with in the leaves and flowers of some [rasnah, salep].——*Orobanchaceæ* (इक्षुघ्नीयसन्तान - ikshughníyasantána, San.). San. from (ikshu, san. sugar-cane + han, san. kill); as supposed to kill plants on which they grow. 96. Broom-rapes. Herbaceous parasitical plants, having scales in place of leaves; fruit capsular, enclosed within withered corolla, two valved; seeds indefinite, minute. Attach themselves to roots, hence called root-parasites. General properties are astringency and bitterness, some used as tonics.——*Palmaceæ* (तालेयसन्तान - táléyasantána, San.). San. from (tála, san. borassus flabelliformis, linn.). 149. Palms. Arborescent plants [taur]; fruit, a nut or drupe or berry; chiefly tropical plants, requiring a mean temperature of 78° 2 to 81° 5 f.; some however extend to temperate regions; some have slender reed-like stems, others attain a considerable diameter; some have a low caudex, or a subterranean stem, while others have an erect trunk nearly 200 feet high; flowers arranged on a terminal or lateral branched stalk, enclosed at first in a large sheathing bract; the flowers are comparatively small; the known species amount to some six hundered of which a sixth part have fanshaped leaves; yield numerous important products, and are applied to a great many uses; supply starch [nishastah], sugar [q.v.], oil [yennay], wax [mom], and edible fruits [pazham]; their buds are eaten like vegetables; their leaves [cadjan] form coverings for habitations, and materials for manuscripts, the reticulum makes coarse cloth, and the saccharine juice is sometimes fermented, so as to form the spirit arrack [q.v.], or the palm-wine toddy [q.v.]; no true poison exists, but the fruits of caryota urens [kittal] are acrid [areca, bastard sago palm, borneo sago palm, cocoanut, gomooty, kharjooram, palmyra, rattan, sumatra dragon's blood, taur, vaitasam].——*Pandanaceæ* (केतकीयसन्तान - kétakíyasantána, San.). San. from (kétakí, san. pandanus odoratissimus, linn.). 150. Screwpines [q.v.]. Trees or bushes; stem low, and differs but little from that of palms; fruit either one-scaled fibrous nuts or many-seeded berries; the seeds are eatable, and the spermoderm contains numerous crystals; the flowers of some are fragrant [screwpine].——*Papaveraceæ* (अफेनीयसन्तान - ap'hénívasantána, San.). San. from (ap'héna, san. opium). 8. Poppyworts. Plants with fibrous roots; leaves alternate, simple, penni-nerved, toothed, or with pennate lobes; the flowers are white, red, or yellow, never blue; they contain a juice, of white, yellow, or blood-like color, medicinal; narcotic properties prevail; the seeds are universally oily [aphainan, bramhadand, yennay].——*Passifloreæ* (पीडापुष्पेयसन्तान - pídápushpéyasantána, San.). San. from (pída, san. suffering + pushpa, san. flower). 61. Passion-worts. Herbs or shrubs; astringent and narcotic qualities prevail; many however produce edible fruits [jimiky, papaw].——*Pedalineæ* (गजदंष्ट्रीयसन्तान - gajadamshtríyasantána, San.). San. from (gajadamshtra, san. elephant's tooth, pedalium murex, linn.). 100. Oil seeds. Glandular herbs, with exstipulate leaves and large bracteated flowers; allied to bignoniaceæ, have generally a heavy odour; seeds yield oil [yennay] as well as starchy matter [elephant nerinjy, gingelly, tiger claw].——*Piperaceæ* (पिप्पलीयसन्तान - pippalíyasantána, San.). San. from (pippalí san. piper longum, linn.). 125. Pepper worts. Shrubs or herbs, with joined stems; the stems of pepper have a peculiar arrangement of the woody matter in wedges and not in concentric zones; pungent and aromatic, owing to the presence of an acrid resin [raul], an oil [yennay], and a crystalline matter, piperin; seeds all of burning taste; some possess narcotic qualities, others are astringent [pepper].——*Pittosporeæ* (अरालबीजेयसन्तान - arálabíjéyasantána, San.). San. from (arála, san. resin + bíja, san. seed); the seeds being covered with resinous pulp. 15. Pittosporads. Trees or shrubs, with simple alternate exstipulate leaves, and symmetrical occasionally polygamous flowers; many of them are resinous, and in some instances the berries are eaten.——*Plantagineæ* (पादतलेयसन्तान - pádataléyasantána, San.). San. from (páda, san. foot + tala, san. surface). Sole of foot from a resemblance in the leaves. 104. Ribworts. Herbs; have bitter and astringent qualities; seeds of some are demulcent [spogel].——*Plumbagineæ* (चित्रमूलीयसन्तान - chitramúlíyasantána, San.). San. from (chitra-múla, san. plumbago). 79. Leadworts. Herbs or undershrubs; found in salt marshes and on the sea-coasts; have tonic, astringent, and acrid properties; some cause blistering [chitramoolam].——*Polygaleæ* (बहुक्षीरीयसन्तान - bahukshíríyasantána, San.). San. from (bahu, san. much + kshíra, san. milk); the plants yielding nourishment to cattle. 16. Milkworts. Trees, shrubs, or herbs, with scattered leaves; some medicinal [nangay].——*Polygonaceæ* (बहुजानुकेयसन्तान - bahujánukéyasantána, San.). San. from (bahu, san. much + jánu, san. knee); alluding to the jointed stems. 110. Buck-wheats. Herbs, rarely shrubs; fruit a triangular nut; acid, astringent and purgative qualities [alligator's nose, country sorrel, indian rhubarb, river jasmine, water gannair, water pepper, wobilinta].——*Pontederiaceæ* (नीलकुवलयसन्तान - nílakuvalayasantána, San.). San. from (nílakuvalaya, san. blue lily, monochoria vaginalis, presl.). 135. Aquatic plants. Stout herbs with creeping rhizomes, longstalked leaves and a one-leaved stem, terminated by a raceme of purplish-blue flowers [blue nelumbo].——*Portulaceæ* (क्षीरभृतीयसन्तान - kshírabhritíyasantána, San.). San. from (kshíra, san. milk + bhri, san. to bear); the species being milky plants; 18; purslanes; succulent herbs or shrubs; found in dry places; esculent and antiscorbutic qualities prevail; some have showy flowers which are ephemeral [indian purslane].——*Ranunculaceæ* (लिप्ताङ्गेयसन्तान - liptángéyasantána, San.). San. from (lipta, san. poisoned + anga, san. body) 1. Crowfoots. Herbaceous, shrubby, or rarely climbing plants, with fascicular, fibrous, or tuberous roots, and alternate, sometimes opposite, rarely amplexicaul leaves; chiefly found in hilly districts; the majority contain an acrid principle, volatile at the temperature of boiling water, and capable of producing inflammation if brought in contact with the skin; taste acrid; if swallowed, many occasion purging and death; others are bitter tonics; very showy flowers [atees, bachnaug, bish, black cootkee, black jeerah, jadwaur, mamiraun, momiree, nahfirmaun, wolf-strangler].——*Resedaceæ* (प्रसादीयसन्तान - prasádíyasantána, San.). San. from (prasad, san. to soothe). 12. Weldworts. Soft herbaceous plants, rarely shrubs.——*Rhamneæ* (राङ्कलेयसन्तान - ránkaléyasantána, San.). San. from (ránkala, san. thorn). 41. Buck thorns. Shrubs or trees; generally acrid and purgative; some are bitter, tonic, and astringent; others yield dyes [badary, bair, carook vauly, pappily, red rohitacam, sinjid].——*Rhizophoreæ* (मूलवाहीयसन्तान - múlaváhíyasantána, San.). San. from (múla, san. root + vah, san. to bear); in allusion to the strange manner of growth. 54. Mangroves [q.v.]. Tropical maritime trees; leaves opposite, entire, flowers axillary either solitary or in cymes or clusters; seeds are without albumen, and almost always germinate before falling off [mangrove].——*Rosaceæ* (सेवतीयसन्तान - sévatíyasantána, San.). San. from (sévatí, san. rose). 49. Roseworts. Trees, shrubs, or herbs; astringent properties exhibited by the bark and roots of most; prussic acid occurs in the sub-orders amygdaleæ and pomeæ; many of the plants supply edible fruits; flowers highly fragrant from essential oil [albaca, amrood, auloo, baudam, bedauna, cherry, gool, gowry's fruit, loquat, mishmish, seb].——*Rubiaceæ* (रक्तकेयसन्तान - raktakéyasantána, San.). San. from (raktaka, san. red). 71. Madders. Trees, shrubs, or herbs; furnishes many important products; have tonic, stimulant, febrifugal, emetic, and purgative properties; some species have intoxicating and even poisonous qualities; many of the plants of the order have flowers remarkable for their beauty and odour [cadamba, cape jasmine, cauray, chayroot, coffee, decamallee, dyeing mulberry, emetic nut, field parpatam, gambier, gandharajah, gandhaulee, indian zebra wood, ixora, koinah, madanaghanta, mongoose snake root, moossanda, munjeet, nunjoondam, pavetta, small dyeing mulberry, small tirye, tirauna, wild anaur].——*Rutaceæ* (ब्राह्मीयसन्तान - bráhmíyasantána, San.). San. from (brahmí, san. holy plant, ruta graveolens, linn.). 32. Rueworts. Herbs, shrubs, and trees; characterized by peculiar penetrating odour; employed medicinally as antispasmodics, tonics, and febrifuges [bael, caroo vaimboo, conjy, curry leaf, harmal, lime, orange, pummelow, rhetsa, sadauf, tejbul, toddaly, toomroo, wood-apple].——*Salicaceæ* (वरुणीयसन्तान - varuníyasantáná, San.). San. from (varuní, san. salix). 126. Willowworts. Trees or shrubs with alternate leaves; flowers diœcious; ovaries of females one-celled; the seeds in two-valved capsules have always a tuft of long white silky hairs [varoonam].——*Salsolaceæ* (क्षारवृक्षेयसन्तान - ksháravrikshéyasantána, San.). San. from (kshára, san. salt + vriksha, san. tree). 108. Saltworts. These are always confined to the sea coast, or to salt marshes or to other places where the soil is impregnated with salt [oovar munn]; they are herbaceous somewhat shrubby smooth or downy plants, with stems jointed or twining; leaves usually alternate, but occasionally opposite, stalkless, more or less cylindrical, membranaceous or fleshy; flowers very minute; many of them yield barilla [chook, indian salt wort, indian spinach, paulak, sujjee khaur].——*Salvadoraceæ* (गौलीयसंन्तान - gaulíyasantána, San.). San. from (gaulí, san. tooth brush tree). 86. Small trees or shrubs. Acrid and stimulant and some have properties like mustard [ooshtarkhaur, shengoo, tooth brush tree].——*Samydaceæ* (हस्तिदमनीसन्तान - hastidamanísantána, San.). San. from (hasti, san. elephant + dam, san. to tame), elephant tamer. 60. Tropical trees or shrubs, with alternate leaves generally marked with pellucid dots, and hermaphrodite flowers, usually small in axillary clusters [anavinga, mormassy].——*Santalaceæ* (चन्दनीयसन्तान - chandaníyasantána, San.). San. from (chandana, san. santalum album, linn.). 116. Sandalworts. Trees, shrubs or herbs; some are astringent, others yield edible fruit [sandal].——*Sapindaceæ* (हिन्दुफेनिलेयसन्तान - hindup'hénilévasantána, San.). San. from (hindu, san. hindu + p'hénila, san. foam). 43.

Soapworts. Trees, shrubs, or climbers with tendrils, rarely herbs; handsome garden plants; many have saponaceous qualities; some are astringent; others yield edible fruits and seeds, and not a few are poisonous [ceylon oak, fig mango, golla's plate, litchy, longan, oolinja, rambutan, soap-nut].——*Sapotaceæ* (सपाटेयसन्तान - sapátéyasantána, San.). San. from sapota, west indian name for several fruits. 82. Starapples. Trees or shrubs, often with milky juice; flowers scented; the fruit of many is edible; the bark is bitter and febrifugal; some furnish fatty matter [csheericay, edible paulay, ilanjy, jointed paulay, mohwah, monkey face paulay, pauchonty].——*Scrophularineæ* (गण्डमालीयसन्तान - gandamálíyasantána, San.). San. from (gandamála, san. scrofula). 95. Figworts. Herbs or undershrubs; more or less suspicious in their properties; some are acrid, others sedative; there are many showy garden plants [cootkee, sisparra creeper, water zoofah].——*Simarubeæ* (महातिक्तसन्तान - mahátiktasantána, San.). San. means great bitter. 33. Quassiads. Trees or shrubs; bitterness prevails, used as tonics [ailanto, firework plant, samadarah].——*Smilaceæ* (शारिवेयसन्तान - shárivéyasantána, San.). From (shárivá, san. sarsaparilla). 131. Sarsaparillas. Climbing thorny plants similar to liliaceæ, but differing from it in the netted veined leaves and in small berry-like fruit [china root].——*Solanaceæ* (बृहतीयसन्तान - brihatíyasantána, San.). San. from (brihatí, san. solanum). 94. Nightshades, Potatoes. Herbs or shrubs; some alimentary, some poisonous; some yield edible tubers and fruit, others are tonic, pungent, and stimulant [asgand, brinjaul, chilly, cooly, datura, dog angoor, indian hounds' berry, indian night shade, indian wintercherry, mardoom giyah, persian ajwaun, pogauk, potato, shoonday, takkauly].——*Sterculiaceæ* (विड्गन्धीवृक्षसन्तान - vidgandhívrikshasantána, San.). San. from (vid, san. excrement + gandha, san. smell), from bad smell of the typical species. 26. Silk cottons. Shrubs, or large trees with simple or compound leaves; resemble the malvaceæ in their properties [balanghas, bastard poon, cauvalam, false kateerah, kaniyaur, mankena, mochcoondam, odul, piymaram, roodrauck tree, screw tree, soondree, velanga, wild papaw].——*Styraceæ* (शिलाजेयसन्तान - shilájéyasantána, San.). San. from (shilájit, san. storax). 84. Storax-worts. Trees or shrubs chiefly tropical; leaves alternate, undivided, without stipules; flowers solitary, clustered or paniculated, often white and usually axillary; fruit drupaceous [benzoin, dhoopam, lodh, true storax].——*Taccaceæ* (सूरणसन्तान - súranasantána, San.). From malay tacca. San. means hurting, arum. 147. Taccads. Perennial herbs, sometimes large, with a tuberous root; leaves are all radical, entire or divided; flowers are greenish or brown; the tubers contain a great deal of starch, and are used as an article of diet [otaheite salep].——*Tamariscineæ* (झावुकेयसन्तान - jhávukéyasantána, San.). San. from (jhávu, san. tamarix genus). 19. Tamarisks. Shrubs or herbs, usually growing by the sea-side; have an astringent and slightly bitter and tonic bark [jhow].——*Ternstrœmiaceæ* (चहासन्तान - chahásantána, San.). San. from (chahá, san. camellia theifera, griff.). 23. Teas. Tropical plants with alternate leaves and hermaphrodite flowers; many of them are of great beauty [tea].——*Tiliaceæ* (रुद्राक्षेयसन्तान - rudrákshéyasantána, San.). San. from (rudráksha, san. elæocarpus). 27. Lindenblooms. Allied to malvaceæ, but distinguished by free stamens; trees or shrubs, very seldom herbaceous plants with handsome, usually white or pink, small flowers; possess mucilaginous qualities; many yield timber [tutchan], fibre [naur], and edible fruits [abrony, bran plant, chikty, dharmanam, falsah, female bair, jaurah, jute, pazham, roodrauck, tadda, trincomalee tree].——*Typhaceæ* (कच्छेयसन्तान - kachhéyasantána, San.). San. from (kachha, san. marsh). 153. Bulrushes. Aquatic, smooth, plants with creeping roots; rhizome yields starch and the pollen also eaten [elephant grass].——*Ulmaceæ* (छायदेयसन्तान - chháyadéyasantána, San.). San. from (chháya, san. shade + dá, san. to give). 120. Elmworts. Trees or shrubs with rough alternate leaves, furnished with stipules; and small green or brown hermaphrodite flowers in loose clusters or cymes; they are often very valuable timber trees [indian elm, indian nettle].——*Umbelliferæ* (छत्रवाहीयसन्तान - chhatraváhíyasantána, San.). San. from (chhatra, san. umbrella + vah, san. to bear). 67. Carrots. Otherwise apiaceæ; herbs, with solid or hollow stems; rare, except at considerable elevations; some are harmless and esculent; others are antispasmodic, owing to the presence of a gum resin [googal] containing a fetid sulphur [gandhac] oil; others again are carminative from containing a volatile oil [yennay]; of the s. indian species none have been found poisonous [ajmood, ajwaun, anise, asafœtida, baulhicam, caraway, cassibor, galbanum, gaujar, indian pennywort, jeerah, karafs, makdoonas, ooshak, sagapenum, sonf, sowa].——*Urticaceæ* (उष्णकेयसन्तान - ushnakéyasantána, San.). San. from (ushna, san. hot), from stinging sensation on contact. 119. Nettleworts. Trees, shrubs or herbs, with watery juice, stipulate leaves, often covered with stinging hairs; have small inconspicuous green flowers, which never form catkins; some have caustic juice connected with stinging hairs, others yield valuable fibres [naur]; occasionally narcotic qualities are present [capsy, china grass, kinnab, neilgherry nettle].——*Vacciniaceæ* (गोवृक्षेयसन्तान - góvrikshéyasantána, San.). San. from (gó, san. cow + vriksha, san. tree). 77. Cranberries. Stalks and flowers rich in tannic acid [bill carondah].——*Verbenaceæ* (अर्णेयसन्तान - arnéyasantána, San.). San. from (arna, san. tectona grandis, linn.). 102. Vervains. Herbs, shrubs or trees; valuable timber trees and ornamental shrubs; properties like labiates, but not medicinal or economical; some possess bitter, tonic and aromatic qualities [bhaurgam, bhraungy, cashmere tree, jayah, lowly jaumoon, moonnay, notchy, ooppata mangrove, peacock gingelly, sangooppy, saraswaty's leaf, sindoocam, teak, tirootauly, tondy teragam, wild cholum, wild long pepper, wild peacock gingelly].——*Violaceæ* (पुरुषरत्नीयसन्तान - purusharatníyasantána, San.). San. from (purusharatna, san. ionidium suffruticosum, ging.). 13. Violetworts. Herbs or shrubby plants; many possess peculiar fragrance; several contain emetic principle emetine and violine; usually blue flowers [banafshah, one-leaved nelumbo].——*Zingiberaceæ* (शृङ्गवेरकेयसन्तान - shringavérakéyasantána, San.). San. from (shringavéra, san. ginger). Otherwise Scitamineæ. 144. Gingerworts. Herbs; have aromatic, stimulating properties; flowers often gaudy, bracts sometimes finely colored; thrive in moist situations; no poisonous species [arabian costum, aurdracam, bhoochampak, cardamom, cassumunar, country saffron, galangal, ginger, haridrah, malabar arrow-root, zedoary].——*Zygophylleæ* (युगफुल्लीयसन्तान - yugap'hullíyasantána, San.). San. from (yuga, san. double + p'hulla, san. bloom); the leaves being in pairs. 30. Bean capers. Herbs, shrubs, or trees; diaphoretic and anthelmintic qualities; wood of the arborescent plants is hard and durable [nerinjy].——**(4)** The following are the genera here concerned, arranged alphabetically, with sanscrit equivalents and references to the list of orders just given and to the key-synopsis. Title heads in this glossary cover each genus clearly distinguished among the natives by a common generic or grouping term; vide the cross-references in square brackets immediately following the etymologies.——*Abrus* (गुञ्जाजाति - guñjájáti, San.). San. from (guj, san. to sound); from sound of dry pods. Leguminosæ, 48 [indian liquorice].——*Abutilon* (श्रीमुद्रिजाति - shrímudrijáti, San.). San. from (shrí, san. beauty + mudrá, san. seal), from circular fruit. Malvaceæ, 25 [tootty].——*Acacia* (कण्टलजाति - kantalajáti, San.). San. from (kanta, san. thorn); from prickly branches [cantalam]. Leguminosæ, 48 [anasandra, australian blackwood, babool, biswool, cantalam, catechu, corindah, soap pod, sundra, vail].——*Acalypha* (मांसिकाजाति - mámsikájáti, San.). San. from (mámsa, san. worm); worm-killer [maumsicay]. Euphorbiaceæ, 118 [chinny, cooppamainy, maumsicay, vattatauly].——*Achras* (द्वीपमधूकजाति - dvípamadhúkajáti, San.). San. from (dvípa, san. island + madhúka, san. bassia). Sapotaceæ, 82 [foreign mohwah].——*Achyranthes* (अपामार्गजाति - apámárgajáti, San.). San. from (apa, san. away + márga, san. way); as being shunned from its troublesome prickles. Amarantaceæ, 106 [indian burr].——*Aconitum* (विषजाति - vishajáti, San.). San. from (vish, san. to pervade) [bish]. Ranunculaceæ, 1 [atees, bachnaug, bish, jadwaur, wolf strangler].——*Acorus* (वचाजाति - vachájáti, San.). San. from (vach, san. to speak), from property of clearing throat. Araceæ, 152 [vashamboo].——*Acrocarpus* (वनराजजाति - vanarájajáti, San). San. means mountain king. Leguminosæ, 48 [shingle tree].——*Actiniopteris* (मयूरशिखाजाति - mayúrashikhájáti, San.). San. from (mayúra, san. peacock + shikhá, san. crest). Filices, 157.——*Adansonia* (गोरक्षकाम्रजाति - górakshakámrajáti, San.). San. means gorakh's tamarind. Malvaceæ, 25 [baobab].——*Adenanthera* (ताम्रकजाति - támrakajáti, San.). San. from (támra, san. copper); from bright red berries. Leguminosæ, 48 [false red sanders].——*Adhatoda* (वासकजाति - vásakajáti, San.). Title corruption from tamul. San. from (vása, san. perfume). Acanthaceæ, 101 [adhatoday].——*Adiantum* (मयूरकजाति - mayúrakajáti, San.). San. from (mayúra, san. peacock); from beauty [indian maiden hair]. Filices, 157 [indian maiden hair].——*Adina* (धाराकदम्बजाति - dhárákadambajáti, San.). San. from (dhri, san. to hold + kadamba, san. anthocephalus cadamba, miq.). Rubiaceæ, 71 [yellow cadamba].——*Ægle* (बिल्वजाति - bilvajáti, San.). San. from (bil, san. to break); destroys diseases. Rutaceæ, 32 [bael].——*Ærua* (कर्पूरमधुराजाति - karpúramadhurájáti, San.). Title from arabic. San. from (karpúra, san. camphor + madhura, san. sweet); from silvery looking leaves, sweet-scented flowers of some species [poolay]. Amarantaceæ, 106 [poolay].——*Æschynomene* (दमनजाति - damanajáti, San.). San. from (dam, san. to pacify). Leguminosæ, 48 [solah].——*Agaricus* (सर्पच्छत्रजाति - sarpachhatrajáti, San.). San. from (sarpa, san. serpent + chhatra, san. umbrella). Fungi, 161 [caulaun].——*Agave* (बृहत्कुमारीजाति - brihatkumáríjáti, San.). San. means large + aloe, from similar leaves. Amaryllidaceæ, 145 [american aloe, bastard aloe].——*Aglaia* (अग्लानजाति - aglánajáti, San.). San. means not languid, bright one. Meliaceæ, 36 [tottila].——*Ailanthus* (महानिम्बजाति - mahánimbajáti, San.). San. from (mahá, san. large + nimba, san. melia azadirachta, linn.) [ailanto]. Simarubeæ, 33 [ailanto].——*Alangium* (अङ्कोलजाति - ankólajáti, San.). Title corruption from tamul [alanjy]. San. from (ank, san. to mark); marked with spines. Cornaceæ, 69 [alanjy].——*Albizzia* (शिरीषजाति - shiríshajáti, San.). San. from (shrí, san. to break); from brittle branches [sirissa]. Leguminosæ, 48 [sirissa].——*Aleurites* (अक्षोटजाति - akshótajáti, San.). San. from (aksh, san. to pervade); from spreading roots. Euphorbiaceæ, 118 [lumbang nut].——*Alhagi* (दुरालभाजाति - durálabhájáti, San.). Title from (alháj, hind. the pilgrim). San. from (dur, san. prefix meaning difficulty + álabh, san. to touch); prickly bush. Leguminosæ, 48 [arabian manna].——*Allium* (गृञ्जनजाति - griñjanajáti, San.). San. from (grij, san. to roar). Liliaceæ, 136 [lussoon, piyauz].——*Aloe* (कुमारीजाति - kumáríjáti, San.). San. means maiden, plant with cool leaves [aloe]; Liliaceæ, 136 [aloe].——*Alpinia* (गन्धमूलजाति - gandhamúlajáti, San.). San. from (gandha, san. fragrance + múla, san. root); from aromatic rhizomes [galangal]. Zingiberaceæ, 144 [galangal].——*Alstonia* (सप्तपर्णजाति - saptaparnajáti, San.). San. means seven-leaved [saptaparnam]. Apocynaceæ, 87 [dita, saptaparnam, wild gannair].——*Althæa* (मृदुकजाति - mridukajáti, San.). San. from (mridu, san. soft); from medicinal property. Malvaceæ, 25 [foreign tootty].——*Amaranthus* (मारिषजाति - márishajáti, San.). San. from (mrísh, san. to endure) [maurisham]. Amarantaceæ, 106 [maurisham].——*Ammannia* (शिलाभेदजाति - shilábhédajáti, San.). San. means gravel + curing. Lythraceæ, 58 [agnivendram].——*Amomum* (स्थूलैलाजाति - st'húlailájáti, San.). Title from (hamámá, ar. to heat); all plants under this genus are more or less pungent or aromatic. San. from (st'húla, san. large + élá, san. eletteria cardamomum, maton.). Zingiberaceæ, 144 [wild cardamom].——*Amoora* (रोहितकजाति - róhitakajáti, San.). San. means red. Meliaceæ, 36 [rohitacam].——*Amorphophallus* (सूरणजाति - súranajáti, San.). San. from (súr, san. to hurt); from caustic root. Araceæ, 152 [telinga potata].——*Anacardium* (शोफहरजाति - shóp'haharajáti, San.). San. means morbid swelling + destroyer. Anacardiaceæ, 45 [cashew].——*Anacyclus* (अकराकरभाजाति - akarákarabhájáti, San.). San. from (akará, san. branchless + karabhá, san. pellitory). Compositæ, 74 [akalkarah].——*Anamirta* (काकमारीजाति - kákamáríjáti, San.). San. means crow-killer. Menispermaceæ, 5 [indian berry].——*Andrographis* (भूनिम्बजाति - bhúnimbajáti, San.). San. from (bhú, san. ground + nimba, san. melia azadirachta, linn.) [bhoonimbam]. Acanthaceæ, 101 [bhoonimbam, coromandel chiretta, french chiretta].——*Andropogon* (वेणीजाति - véníjáti, San.). San. means tuft of hair, from roots [beard grass]. Graminaceæ, 156 [beard grass, cuscus, ibharancoosha, keshinee, lemon grass, nutt, roussa grass, spear grass].——*Anisochilus* (कर्पूरवल्लीजाति - karpúravallíjáti, San.). San. from (karpúra, san. camphor + vallí, san. creeper). Labiatæ, 103 [country lavender].——*Anisomeles* (ओष्ठफलजाति - ósht'hap'halajáti, San.). San. means lip + fruit. Labiatæ, 103 [malabar catmint].——*Anogeissus* (धवजाति - dhavajáti, San.). San. from (dhav, san. to run); from exudation [dhavam]. Combretaceæ, 55 [dhavam, pauchimaun, vekkauly].——*Anona* (गण्डगात्रजाति - gandagátrajáti, San.). Title from malay. San. means pimple + fruit [anona]. Anonaceæ, 4 [anona].——*Anthemis* (बहुपुष्पाजाति - bahupushpájáti, San.). San. means many flowered. Compositæ, 74 [baboona].——*Anthocephalus* (कदम्बजाति - kadambajáti, San.). San. from (kad, san. to kill); from curing virtue. Rubiaceæ, 71 [cadamba].——*Antiaris* (वल्कलवृक्षजाति - valkalavrikshajáti, San.). San. means bark + tree. Artocarpaceæ, 122 [sack tree].——*Antidesma* (अम्लशाकजाति - amlashákajáti, San.). San. from (amla, san. sour + sháka, san. plant); sour plant [amlashaucam]. Antidesmads. Euphorbiaceæ, 118 [amlashaucam, carpenter's tamarind, gasambilla, nolatauly].——*Apium* (अजमोदजाति - ajamódajáti, San.). San. from (aja, san. goat + móda, san. smell). Umbelliferæ, 67 [karafs].—*Aquilaria* (अगरुजाति - agarujáti, San.). San. means not heavy, from wood. Thymelæaceæ, 114 [eagle wood].——*Arachis* (भूचणकजाति - bhúchanakajáti, San.). San from (bhú, san. ground + chanaka, san. bengal gram). Leguminosæ, 48 [ground nut].——*Areca* (पूगजाति - púgajáti, San.). Title from malayalam [areca]. San. from (pú, san. to clear); clears mouth. Palmaceæ, 149 [areca].——*Arenga* (अश्वरोमतालजाति - ashvarómatálajáti, San.). Title from malay. San. from (ashvaróma, san. horsehair + tála, san. palm), from black horsehair like fibres surrounding petioles of leaves. Palmaceæ, 149 [gomooty].——*Argemone* (ब्रह्मदण्डजाति - brahmadandajáti, San.). San. from (brahma, san. bramin + danda, san. staff). Papaveraceæ, 8 [bramhadand].——*Argyreia* (वृद्धदारकजाति - vriddhadárakajáti, San.). San. means old + tree [ajauntry]. Convolvulaceæ, 93 [ajauntry, malabar creeper, sea shore paulay].——*Aristida* (मार्जनीजाति - márjaníjáti, San.). San. means broom stick. Graminaceæ, 156 [broom grass].——*Aristolochia* (ईश्वरजाति - íshvarajáti, San.). San. from (ísh, san. to rule) [eeshwaram]. Aristolochiaceæ, 117 [eeshwaram, indian worm-killer, isharmool].——*Artabotrys* (हरचंपकजाति - harachampakajáti, San.). San. from (hri, san. to captivate + champaka, san. michelia champaca, linn.). Anonaceæ, 4 [madmaunty].——*Artemisia* (दमनजाति - damanajáti, San.). San. means conquering. Compositæ, 74 [indian absinth].——*Artocarpus* (पनसजाति - panasajáti, San.). San. from (pan, san. to praise); useful plant [jack]. Artocarpaceæ, 122 [jack].——*Asparagopsis* (शतमूलीजाति - shatamúlíjáti, San.). San. from (shata, san. hundred + múla, san. root) [shatamooly]. Liliaceæ, 136 [indian salep, shakankool, shatamooly, soofaid moosly].——*Astragalus* (क्षीरद्विपत्रजाति - kshíradvipatrajáti, San.). San. from (kshíra, san. milk + dvipatra, san. vetch). Leguminosæ, 48 [kateerah].——*Atalantia* (वनजंबीरजाति - vanajambírajáti, San.). San. means wild lime. Rutaceæ, 32 [monkey lime].——*Atropa* (अनिवर्तनजाति - anivartanajáti, San.). San. means not turning away. Solanaceæ, 94 [dog angoor].——*Atylosia* (वनाढकीजाति - vanádhakíjáti, San.). San. means wild dholl. Leguminosæ, 48 [jungle dholl, jungle horse-gram].——*Avena* (यवकजाति - yavakajáti, San.). San. from (yava, san. barley). Graminaceæ, 156 [vilauyoty jow].——*Averrhoa* (लवलीजाति - lavalíjáti, San.). San. from (lu, san. to cut) from sour taste of fruit [lavaly]. Geraniaceæ, 31 [blimbing, coromandel gooseberry, lavaly].——*Avicennia* (श्वेतसमुद्रबहुपदीजाति - shévatasamudrabahupadíjáti, San.). Verbenaceæ, 102 [ooppata mangrove].——*Azima* (कुण्डलिनीजाति - kundaliníjáti, San.). San. means bracelet. Salvadoraceæ, 86 [shengoo].——*Balanites* (इंगुदीजाति - ingudíjáti, San.). San. from (ing, san. to move). Simarubeæ, 33 [fire-work plant].——*Baliospermum* (दन्तीजाति - dantíjáti, San.). San. means tooth. Euphorbiaceæ, 118 [wild jamalgota].——*Balsamodendron* (मुरजाति - murajáti, San.). San. from (mura, san. myrrh) [balsam]. Burseraceæ, 35 [balm of gilead, balsam, bdellium, bole, kiloovay].——*Bambusa* (वंशजाति - vamshajáti, San.). Title from malay. San. from (van, san. to sound); from cracking sound of cluster [bamboo]. Graminaceæ, 156 [bamboo].——*Barleria* (झिण्टीजाति - jhintíjáti, San.) [nail dye]. Acanthaceæ, 101 [nail dye].——*Barringtonia* (समुद्रफलजाति - samudrap'halajáti, San.). San. from (samudra, san. sea + p'hala, san. fruit) [indian oak]. Myrtaceæ, 56 [indian oak].——*Basella* (हरित्पर्णजाति - haritparnajáti, San.). Title from canarese; see sep. title. San. means green leaf [malabar night shade]. Basellaceæ, 109 [malabar night shade].——*Bassia* (मधूकजाति - madhúkajáti, San.). San. from (madhu, san. sweet) [mohwah]. Sapotaceæ, 82 [mohwah].——*Bauhinia* (काञ्चनजाति - káñchanajáti, San.). San from (káñch, san. to shine); beautiful trees [mountain ebony]. Leguminosæ, 48 [mountain ebony].——*Benincasa* (कूष्माण्डजाति - kúshmándajáti, San.). San. means cooling + seed. Cucurbitaceæ, 62 [wax-gourd].——*Berberis* (दार्वीजाति - dárvíjáti, San.). San. means wooden. Berberidæ, 6 [berberry].——*Berrya* (सरलदेवदारीजाति - saraladévadáríjáti, San.). San. from (sarala, san. straight + devádáru, san. erythroxylon monogynum, roxb.). Tiliaceæ, 27 [trincomalee tree].——*Beta* (पालङ्कीजाति - pálankíjáti, San.). San. from (pála, san. nourish + ank, san. to mark); requiring great care and attention for growth. Salsolaceæ, 108 [paulak].——*Bignonia* (पाटलजाति - pátalajáti, San.). Bignoniaceæ, 99 [stunted neem].——*Bischoffia* (कृष्णमुष्टिजाति - krishnamushtijáti, San.). San. from (krishna, san. black + mushti, san. strychnos nux-vomica, linn.). Euphorbiaceæ, 118 [java cedar].——*Bixa* (कुंकुमफलजाति - kunkumap'halajáti, San.). San. from (kunkuma, san. saffron + p'hala, san. fruit). Bixineæ, 14 [monkey country saffron].——*Bœrhaavia* (पुनर्नवाजाति - punarnavájáti, San.). San. from (punar, san. again + navá, san. new); growing when cut. Nyctagineæ, 105 [tikry].——*Bombax* (शाल्मलीजाति - shálmalíjáti, San.). San. from (shál, san. to shine). Malvaceæ, 25 [red cotton tree].——*Borassus* (तालजाति - tálajáti, San.). San. from (tal, san. to fix). Palmaceæ, 149 [palmyra].——*Boswellia* (कुन्दुरुकीजाति - kundurukíjáti, San.). San. from (kunduru, san. olibanum) [olibanum]. Burseraceæ, 35 [olibanum, yellow dammer].——*Brassica* (सर्षपजाति - sarshapajáti, San.). San. from (sri, san. to go); from round seeds [sarshapam]. Cruciferæ, 10 [kobee, rayaun, sarshapam, sarsoon, shalgham].——*Breynia* (अरुणीजाति - aruníjáti, San.). San. means red. Euphorbiaceæ, 118 [poolah coral tree].——*Bridelia* (असणजाति - asanajáti, San.). San. from mahratta. Euphorbiaceæ, 118 [thorny vengay].——*Bruguiera* (कण्डलजाति - kandalajáti, San.). San. from tamul [candel]. Rhizophoreæ, 54 [tree mangrove].——*Bryonia* (घृतपायीजाति - ghritapáyíjáti, San.). San. means ghee + eater. Cucurbitaceæ, 62 [neyonny].——*Bryophyllum* (व्रणहारीजाति - vranaháríjáti, San.). San. means wound + curer. Crassulaceæ, 51.——*Buchanania* (प्रियालजाति - priyálajáti, San.). San. from (priya, san. dear). Anacardiaceæ, 45 [chironjee].——*Butea* (पलाशजाति - paláshajáti, San.). San. from (pal, san. to go). Leguminosæ, 48 [palaus].——*Cœsalpinia* (कुबेराक्षीजाति - kubérákshíjáti, San.). San. from (kubéra, san. the god + akshi, san. eye); from flowers [coobairaucshy]. Leguminosæ, 48 [bonduc, coobairaucshy, divy-divy, gold-mohur tree, mysore thorn, sappan].——*Cajanus* (आढकीजाति - ádhakíjáti, San.). San. from (ádhaka, san split pulse). Leguminosæ, 48 [common dholl].——*Calamus* (वेतसजाति - vétasajáti, San.). San. from (vé, san. to plait); from use of split stems [vaitasam]. Palmaceæ, 149 [rattan, sumatra dragon's blood, vaitasam].——*Callicarpa* (कल्यकार्पजाति - kalyakárpajáti, San.). Means beautiful + fruit, in allusion to the pretty berries. Verbenaceæ, 102 [tondy teragam].——*Calophyllum* (पुन्नागजाति - punnágajáti, San.). San. from (pums, san. male + nága, san. mesua ferea, linn.) [poon]. Guttiferæ, 22 [poon].——*Calotropis* (अर्कजाति - arkajáti, San.). San. means sun. Asclepiadeæ, 88 [yercum].——*Calycopteris* (उक्षिणीजाति - ukshiníjáti, San.). San. means sprinkling, from plant growing under shade. Combretaceæ, 55 [white wodala].——*Camellia* (चहाजाति - chahájáti, San.). Ternstrœmiaceæ, 23 [tea].——*Cananga* (कनंगजाति - kanangajáti, San.). Title from malay. San. from malay. Anonaceæ, 4 [ilangilang].——*Canarium* (कृष्णधूपवृक्षजाति - krishnadhúpavrikshajáti, San.). Title from malay. San. means black dammer tree [caunary]. Burseraceæ, 35 [black dammer, elemi, caunary].——*Canavalia* (कोशफलजाति - kóshap'halajáti, San.). Title from malayalam. San. from (kósha, san. sheath + p'hala, san. pod). Leguminosæ, 48 [tambattam].——*Canna* (सर्वजयाजाति - sarvajayájáti, San.). San. means all conquering. Marantaceæ, 143 [indian shot].——*Cannabis* (भङ्गाजाति - bhangájáti, San.). Title from arabic. San. from (bhañj, san. to break). Urticaceæ, 119 [kinnab].——*Canscora* (शङ्खवल्लीजाति - shankhavallíjáti, San.). Title from malayalam. San, means conch creeper. Gentianaceæ, 90 [sankhvel].——*Canthium* (नागबलाजाति - nágabalájáti, San.). San. means elephant + strength. Rubiaceæ, 71 [cauray].——*Capparis* (करीरजाति - karírajáti, San.). San. from (krí, san. to hurt); from prickles [caper]. Capparideæ, 11 [caper].——*Capsicum* (मरिचजाति - marichajáti, San.). San. from (mri, san. to kill); from pungent berries [chilly]. Solanaceæ, 94 [chilly].——*Carallia* (वनाञ्जनजाति - vanáñjanajáti, San.). Title from teloogoo. San. from (vana, san. forest + añjana, san. memecylon edule, roxb.). Rhizophoreæ, 54 [caurally mangrove].——*Caralluma* (वनार्द्रकजाति - vanárdrakajáti, San.). Title from teloogoo [caurallam]. San. from (vana, san. forest + árdraka, san. ginger). Asclepiadeæ, 88 [caurallam].——*Carapa* (परुषजाति - parushajáti, San.). San. means knotted. Meliaceæ, 36 [crab oil plant].——*Cardiospermum* (ज्योतिष्मतीजाति - jyótishmatíjáti, San.). Meaning shining. Sapindaceæ, 43 [oolinja].——*Careya* (कुंभीजाति - kumbhíjáti, San.). San. from (kumbha, san. pot); alluding to hollow on top of fruit. Myrtaceæ, 56 [coomby].——*Carica* (पप्पायजाति - pappáyajáti, San.). San. from west indian term. Passifloreæ, 61 [papaw].——*Carissa* (करमर्दजाति - karamardajáti, San.). San. from (kara, san. hand + mard, san. to crush). Apocynaceæ, 87 [carondah].——*Carthamus* (कुसुंभजाति - kusumbhajáti, San.). Title from arabic. San. from (kus, san. to embrace); from dye. Compositæ, 74 [bastard saffron].——*Carum* (सुषवीजाति - sushavíjáti, San.). San. from (su, san. well + su, san. to beget) [ajmood]. Umbelliferæ, 67 [ajmood, ajwaun, caraway].——*Caryota* (सुरातालजाति - surátálajáti, San.). San. from (surá, san. toddy + tála, san. palm); from large quantity of toddy. Palmaceæ, 149 [bastard sago palm].——*Casearia* (हस्तिदमनीजाति - hastidamaníjáti, San.). San. means elephant + taming. Samydaceæ, 60 [anavinga, mormassy].——*Cassia* (सुवर्णकजाति - suvarnakajáti, San.). San. from (su, san. good + varna, san. color); from flowers [soovarnacam]. Leguminosæ, 48 [black horse-gram, casondy, chakondah, condray, foreign agatty, senna, soovarnacam, tungaid].——*Cassytha* (आकाशवल्लीजाति - ákáshavallíjáti, San.). Means air + creeper. Lauraceæ, 111 [cottaun].——*Casuarina* (कशकृशीजाति - kashakrishíjáti, San.). San. from (kasha, san. whip + krisha, san. slender); from long, slender branches. Casuarinaceæ, 127 [chowk maram].——*Cedrela* (तुन्नजाति - tunnajáti, San.). San. from (tud, san. to give pain). Meliaceæ, 36 [toon].——*Celastrus* (वह्निरुचिजाति - vanhiruchijáti, San.). San. from (vahni, san. fire + ruchi, san. taste); from acrid and stimulating properties. Celastrineæ, 40 [malkangany].——*Celosia* (मयूरशिखाजातिं - mayúrashikhájáti, San.). San. means peacock + crest. Amaranthaceæ, 106 [moorgha].——*Celtis* (पद्मकवृक्षजाति - padmakavrikshajáti, San.). San. means lotus tree. Ulmaceæ, 120 [white indian nettle].——*Centipeda* (चिक्कणीजाति - chikkaníjáti, San.). San. means sneezing. Compositæ, 74 [nakchiknee].——*Cephalandra* (विंबिकाजाति - bimbikájáti, San.). San. from (bimba, san. ball). Cucurbitaceæ, 62 [indian caper].——*Ceratonia* (वक्रशृङ्गीजाति - vakrashringíjáti, San.). San. from (vakra, san. curved + shringa, san. horn); from pods like curved horns. Leguminosæ, 48 [carob].——*Cerbera* (विषवृक्षजाति - vishavrikshajáti, San.). San. means poisonous tree. Apocynaceæ, 87 [odallam].——*Chickrassia* (पर्वतनिम्बजाति - parvatanimbajáti, San.). Title from hindostany. San. from (parvata, san. hill + nimba, san. neem, melia azadirachta, linn.). Meliaceæ, 36 [chickrassy].——*Chloris* (हरित्तृणजाति - harittrinajáti, San.). San. means green grass. Graminaceæ, 156 [trail grass].——*Chloroxylon* (हरिद्रुजाति - hariddrujáti, San.). San. means yellow wood. Meliaceæ, 36 [satin wood].——*Chrysanthemum* (सेवन्तिकाजाति - sévantikájáti, San.). From (sév, san. to seek); from beautiful flowers. Compositæ, 74 [shaumunty].——*Cicer* (चणकजाति - chanakajáti, San.). San. from (chan, san. to give). Leguminosæ, 48 [bengal gram].——*Cichorium* (कासनीजाति - kásaníjáti, San.). San. from (kásní, hind. the plant). Compositæ, 74 [indian endive].——*Cinchona* (ज्वरहरिजाति - jvaraharijáti, San.). San. means febrifuge [koinah]. Rubiaceæ, 71 [koinah].——*Cinnamomum* (त्वक्जाति - tvakjáti, San.). San. means bark [cinnamon]. Lauraceæ, 111 [cinnamon].——*Cissampelos* (पाठाजाति - pát'hájáti, San.). San. from (pat'h, san. to declare). Menispermaceæ, 5 [indian pareira].——*Citrullus* (इन्द्रवल्लीजाति - indravallíjáti, San.). San. means indra's creeper [indravally]. Cucurbitaceæ, 62 [indravally].——*Citrus* (जंबीरजाति - jambírajáti, San.). San. from (jam, san. to eat) [jambeeram]. Rutaceæ, 32 [cumquot, jambeeram, lime, orange, pummelow].——*Cleome* (आदित्यभक्ताजाति - ádityabhaktájáti, San.). San. means sun + serving. Capparideæ, 11 [dog vailay].——*Clerodendron* (भार्गजाति - bhárgajáti, San.). San. means fiery [bhaurgam]. Verbenaceæ, 102 [bhaurgam, bhraungy, sangooppy, saraswaty's leaf, tirootauly].——*Clitoria* (शंखपुष्पीजाति - shankhapushpíjáti, San.). San. means conch-flower. Leguminosæ, 48 [crow-creeper].——*Cocculus* (वासनवल्लीजाति - vásanavallíjáti, San.), San. means fragrant creeper [vausana vully]. Menispermaceæ, 5 [calumba, jamtee, vausanavully].——*Cochlospermum* (आवृत्तबीजजाति - ávrittabíjajáti, San.). San. means twisted seed. Bixineæ, 14 [golden silk cotton].——*Cocos* (नारिकेलजाति - nárikélajáti, San.). San. from (nála, san. tube + kam, san. water + ír, san. to throw). Palmaceæ, 149 [cocoanut].——*Coffea* (कावजाति - kávajáti, San.). Title and San. from arabic. Rubiaceæ, 71 [coffee].——*Coix* (गवेधुजातिं - gavédhujáti, San.). San. means water + growing. Graminaceæ, 156 [coratty pausy].——*Colchicum* (विषमण्डलजाति - vishamandalajáti, San.). San. means poison + bulb. Liliaceæ, 136 [soorinjaun].——*Coleus* (पाषाणभेदीजाति - páshánabhédíjáti, San.). San. means stone breaking. Labiatæ, 103 [country borage].——*Colocasia* (कच्वीजाति - kachvíjáti, San.). San. means itching root [kachvee]. Araceæ, 152 [kachvee].——*Combretum* (वडलजाति - vadalajáti, San.). From (vadala, tel. combretum decandrum, roxb.). Combretaceæ, 55 [wodala].——*Commelyna* (वत्सप्रियजाति - vatsapriyajáti, San.). San. means calf + dear. Commelynaceæ, 139 [calf's grass].——*Convolvulus* (विदारीजाति - vidáríjáti, San.). From (vi, san. prefix of division + dri, san. to break); breaking out and spreading [tauly]. Bindweed. Convolvulaceæ, 93 [deer's foot, scammony, tauly].——*Coptis* (तिक्ताजाति - tiktájáti, San.). San. means bitter. Ranunculaceæ, 1 [mamiraun].——*Corallocarpus* (आकाशकन्दाजाति - ákáshakandájáti, San.). San. means air + root. Cucurbitaceæ, 62 [braminy kite creeper].——*Corchorus* (कालशाकजाति - kálashákajáti, San.). San. means black herb. Tiliaceæ, 27 [jute].——*Cordia* (शेलुजाति - shélujáti, San.). San. from (shi, san. to excite) [sebesten]. Boragineæ, 92 [sebesten].——*Coriandrum* (कुस्तुंबरींजाति - kustumbaríjáti, San.), Umbelliferæ, 67 [cassibor].——*Corypha* (श्रीतालजाति - shrítálajáti, San.). San. means holy palm. Palmaceæ, 149 [talipot, talura palm].——*Coscinium* (पीतद्रुजाति - pítadrujáti, San.). San. means yellow wood. Menispermaceæ, 5 [false calumba].——*Cosmostigma* (चक्रलताजाति - chakralatájáti, San.). San. means round creeper, from leaves. Asclepiadeæ, 88 [vattoovally].——*Costus* (कुष्टजाति - kusht'hajáti, San.). Title from sanscrit. San. means bad + spot. Zingiberaceæ, 144 [arabian costum].——*Cratæva* (वरुणजाति - varunajáti, San.). San. from (vri, san. to cover). Capparideæ, 11 [nirvala].——*Crinum* (विषमण्डलजाति - vishamandalajáti, San.). San. means poison bulb. Amaryllidaceæ, 145 [poison bamboo].——*Crotalaria* (घण्टारवजाति - ghantáravajáti, San.). San. means bell + sound [ghantauravam]. Leguminosæ, 48 [ghantauravam, giligitcha, sunn].——*Croton* (घण्टाबीजजाति - ghantábíjajáti, San.). San. means bell + seed [ghantabeejam]. Euphorbiaceæ, 118 [croton lac tree, devil's goad, ghantabeejam, jamalgota].——*Crozophora* (सूर्यावर्त्ताजाति - súryávartájáti, San.). San. means turning towards sun. Euphorbiaceæ, 118 [round pepper].——*Cryptostegia* (क्षीरीजाति - kshíríjáti, San.). San. means milky plant. Asclepiadeæ, 88 [paulay silk cotton].——*Cucumis* (उर्वारुजाति - urvárujáti, San.). San. from (uru, san. much + ár, san. to cause to flow); diuretic [oorvauroo] Cucurbitaceæ, 62 [oorvauroo].——*Cucurbita* (कर्कारुजाति - karkárujáti, San.). San. means white [carcauroo]. Cucurbitaceæ, 62 [carcauroo].——*Cuminum* (जीरकजाति - jírakajáti, San.). San. means digestive. Umbelliferæ, 67 [jeerah].——*Curculigo* (तालमूलीजाति - tálamúlíjáti, San.). San. means palm + root. Hypoxidaceæ, 146 [cauly moosly].——*Curcuma* (हरिद्राजाति - haridrájáti, San.). Title from arabic. San means yellow plant [haridrah]. Zingiberaceæ, 144 [country saffron, haridrah, malabar arrow-root, mango ginger, zedoary].——*Cuscuta* (आकाशभवजाति - ákáshabhavajáti, San.). San. means produced in sky. Convolvulaceæ, 93 [seeta's thread].——*Cyamopsis* (गोवारीजाति - góváríjáti, San.). San. from (guar, hind. guar bean). Leguminosæ, 48 [guar].——*Cyathula* (भूम्यपांगजाति - bhúmyapángajáti, San.). San. from (bhúmi, san. ground + apánga, san. indian burr); from prostrate stem. Amaranthaceæ, 106 [small indian burr].——*Cycas* (कामवृक्षजाति - kámavrikshajáti, San.). San. means desire + tree. Cycadaceæ, 129 [indian sago palm].——*Cydonia* (देशान्तरदाडिमजाति - déshántaradádimajáti, San.). San. means foreign pomegranate. Rosaceæ, 49 [beduana].——*Cynodon* (दूर्वाजाति - dúrvájáti, San.). San. from (durv, san. to injure). Graminaceæ, 156 [hurrially].——*Cynometra* (श्वयोनिजाति - shvayónijáti, San.). San. means dog's womb, in allusion to shape and consistence of legumes. Leguminosæ, 48 [iripa].——*Cyperus* (मुस्ताजाति - mustájáti, San.). San. from (mus, san. destroy) [coray]. Cyperaceæ, 155 [coray].——*Dœdalacanthus* (नीलाम्बरजानि - nílámbarajáti, San.). San. from (níla, san. blue + ambara, san. sky). Acanthaceæ, 101 [vandaumbram].——*Dœmia* (युग्मफलाजाति - yugmap'halájáti, San.). San. from (yugma, san. double + p'hala, san. fruit). Asclepiadeæ, 88 [hedge cotton].——*Dalbergia* (युगपत्रिकाजाति - yugapatrikájáti, San.). San. from (yuga, san. pair + patriká, san. leaflet) [yoogapattricay]. Leguminosæ, 48 [caunooga, malabar black-wood, sissoo, yellow mountain ebony, yoogapattricay].——*Datura* (धत्तूरजाति - dhattúrajáti, San.). Title from sanscrit. San. from (dhús, san. to embellish + túri, san. thorn apple) [datura]. Solanaceæ, 94 [datura].——*Daucus* (गर्जरजाति - garjarajáti, San.). San. means roaring. Umbelliferæ, 67 [gaujar].——*Debregeasia* (उष्णकेयजाति - ushnakéyajáti, San.). San. from (ush, san. to burn). Urticaceæ, 119 [capsy].——*Delphinum* (शङ्कीयजाति - shankíyajáti, San.). San. means dolphin, from supposed resemblance to that animal in the nectary. Ranunculaceæ, 1 [nahfirmaun].——*Dendrocalamus* (प्रियवंशजाति - priyavamshajáti, San.). San. means lover + bamboo. Graminaceæ, 156 [bengal bamboo].——*Dentella* (दन्तीयजाति - dantíyajáti, San.). San. means tooth, each side of segments of corolla is furnished with a small tooth. Rubiaceæ, 71 [small tirye].——*Derris* (करजवल्लीजाति - karajavallíjáti, San.). San. means pongamia glabra + creeper. Leguminosæ, 48 [creeper canooga].——*Desmanthus* (गुच्छपुष्पीयजाति - guchhapushpíyajáti, San.). San. means cluster + flower. Leguminosæ, 48 [neer shoondy].——*Desmodium* (शालिकाजाति - shálikájáti, San.). San. from (shála, san. shorea rubusta, gærtn.); from resemblance of leaves [shaulicay]. Leguminosæ, 48 [indian medicago, shaulicay].——*Dichopsis* (क्षीरस्रवजाति - kshírasravajáti, San.). San. means milk shedding. Sapotaceæ, 82 [panchonty].——*Dichrostachys* (वीरवृक्षजाति - víravrikshajáti, San.). San. means strong + tree. Leguminosæ, 48 [ashy babool].——*Dillenia* (भव्यजाति - bhavyajáti, San.). San. from (bhú, san. to be handsome). Dilleniaceæ, 2 [chaltah].——*Dioscorea* (आलूजाति - álújáti, San.). San. from (ri, san. to move); round [auloo]. Dioscoreaceæ, 132 [auloo].——*Diospyros* (तिन्दुकजाति - tindukajáti, San.). San. from (tij, san. to sharpen); from acid exudation [indian ebony]. Ebenaceæ, 83 [calaminder wood, gaub, indian ebony].——*Dipterocarpus* (करालजाति - karálajáti, San.). San. means opening wide. Dipterocarpeæ, 24 [gurjan].——*Dodonœa* (दीप्यदारुकजाति - dípyadárukajáti, San.). San. means ignitible wood. Sapindaceæ, 43 [golla's plate].——*Dolichandrone* (जलमाहानिम्बजाति - jalamahánimbajáti, San.). San. means water ailanto [water ailanto]. Bignoniaceæ, 99 [flowering pauthiry, night paulay, water ailanto, wody].——*Dolichos* (शिंबीजाति - shimbíjáti, San.). San. from (shí, san. to sharpen) [shimby]. Leguminosæ, 48 [country bean, madras horse gram, shimby, wild horse gram].——*Dorema* (जतुकसदृशीजाति - jatukasadrishíjáti, San.). San. means asafœtida + resembling, from gum. Umbelliferæ, 67 [ooshak].——*Dracontium* (काननकन्दजाति - kánanakandajáti, San.). San. means wild esculent root. Araceæ, 152 [wild telinga potato].——*Dregea* (मधुमालतिजाति - madhumálatijáti, San.). San. means sweet maulaty. Asclepiadeæ, 88 [nakchiknee silk cotton].——*Durio* (गन्धमार्जारफलीजाति - gandhamárjárap'halíjáti, San.). Title from malay. San. from (gandhamárjára, san. civet cat + p'hala, san. fruit); from smell of fruit. Malvaceæ, 25 [durian].——*Dysophylla* (दुर्गन्धपत्रजाति - durgandhapatrajáti, San.). San. means fetid leaves. Labiatæ, 103 [wild toombay].——*Ecbolium* (नीलांबरीजाति - nílámbaríjáti, San.). San. means sky-blue. Acanthaceæ, 101 [neelaumbram].——*Echinops* (उष्ट्रकण्टकजाति - ushtrakantakajáti, San.). San. means camel thorn. Compositæ, 74 [camel thistle].——*Eclipta* (केशराजजाति - késharájajáti, San.). San. from (késha, san. lock of hair + ráj, san. to shine); from giving hair a glossy appearance. Compositæ, 74 [bhangrah].——*Ehretia* (दन्तरङ्ग - dantaranga, San.). From (danta, san. tooth, ivory + ranga, san. color), from greyish white wood of the order [coorvitchy]. Boragineæ, 92 [coorvitchy].——*Elæocarpus* (रुद्राक्षजाति - rudrákshajáti, San.). San. from (rudra, san. shiva + aksha, san. eye). Tiliaceæ, 27 [roodrauck].——*Elæodendron* (जितफलीयजाति - jitap'halíyajáti, San.). San. means olive-fruited. Celastrineæ, 40 [nerija].——*Elephantopus* (गोजिह्वाजाति - gójihvájáti, San.). San. means cow's tongue. Compositæ, 74 [elephant's foot].——*Elettaria* (एलाजाति - élájáti, San.). Title from malayalam. San. from (il, san. to send); from correcting foul breath. Zingiberaceæ, 144 [cardamom].——*Eleusine* (रागीजाति - rágíjáti, San.). San. means red. Graminaceæ, 156 [raggy].——*Embelia* (विडङ्गजाति - vidangajáti, San.). San. from (vid, san. to break). Myrsineæ, 81 [byebarang].——*Emilia* (शशकर्णीजाति - shashakarníjáti, San). San. means hare's ear. Compositæ, 74 [hare's ear].——*Enicostema* (कैरातकजाति - kairátakajáti, San.). San. means small chiretta. Gentianaceæ, 90 [small chiretta].——*Entada* (खड्गपुटीजाति - khadgaputíjáti, San.). San. means scimitar pod. Leguminosæ, 48 [scimitar pod].——*Epicarpurus* (शाखोटजाति - shákhótajáti, San.). San. from (shákha, san. branch + óta, san. suffix meaning spreading). Moraceæ, 121 [stunted jack].——*Eragrostis* (कुशजाति - kushajáti, San.). Means strewn on ground [coosham]. Graminaceæ, 156 [coosham, darbhay, shaumay grass, squirrel ginger, wild coraly].——*Eriobotrya* (लोमस्तबकजाति - lómastabakajáti, San.). San. means woolly cluster of flower, alluding to woolly racemes. Rosaceæ, 49 [loquat].——*Eriodendron* (श्वेतशाल्मलीजाति - shvétashálmalíjáti, San.). San. from (shvéta, san. white + shálmali, san. bombax malabaricum, dec.). Malvaceæ, 25 [silk cotton].——*Ervum* (मसूरजाति - masúrajáti, San.). San. means ripening. Leguminosæ, 48 [masoor].——*Erythræa* (रक्तपुष्पाजाति - raktapushpájáti, San.). San. means red + flower. Gentianaceæ, 90 [roxburgh's chiretta].——*Erythrina* (मन्दारजाति - mandárajáti, San.). San. from (mand, san. to be beautiful) [coral tree]. Leguminosæ, 48 [coral tree].——*Erythroxylon* (रक्तदारुजाति - raktadárujáti, San.). San. means red + wood. Lineæ, 28 [deccany deodar].——*Eucalyptus* (कर्पूरवृक्षजाति - karpúravrikshajáti, San.). San. means camphor tree. Myrtaceæ, 56 [australian gum tree].——*Eugenia* (जम्बुजाति - jambujáti, San.). San. from (jam, san. to eat) [jamboo]. Myrtaceæ, 56 [jamboo, jaumoon, lavangam, moy, rose-apple].——*Eulophia* (सुशेखरजाति - sushékharajáti, San.). San. means handsome crest, alluding to labellum bearing elevated lines or ridges. See salep. Orchidaceæ, 141 [salep].——*Eupatorium* (विषहाजाति - vishahájáti, San.). San. means poison destroying, in allusion to the plant being first used by eupator king of pontus as antidote to poison. Compositæ, 74 [ayappanay].——*Euphorbia* (वज्रीजाति - vajríjáti, San.). San. from (vajra, san. adamant); from hard spines [milkhedge]. Euphorbiaceæ, 118 [ammaun putcharisy, cuttimandoo, milk-hedge].——*Eurya* (वनचहाजाति - vanachahájáti, San.). San. from (vana, san. forest + chahá, san. tea). Ternstrœmiaceæ, 23 [wild tea].——*Evolvulus* (विष्णुक्रान्ताजाति - vishnukrántájáti, San.). San. from (vishnu, san. the deity + kránta, san. surpassing); from blue flowers. Convolvulus, 93 [vishnoocraunty].——*Exacum* (विषारिजाति - vishárijáti, San.). San. means poison + enemy, from being supposed to possess the virtue of expelling poison. Gentianaceæ, 90 [purple chiretta].——*Excœcaria* (तिमिरकारिजाति - timirakárijáti, San.). San. means blinding, alluding to dangerous acrid juice [agaroo]. Euphorbiaceæ, 118 [agaroo, china tallow, tiger's milk].——*Exogonium* (रेचनीजाति - réchaníjáti, San.). San. means purgative. Convolvulaceæ, 93 [jalap].——*Fagonia* (दुस्पर्शाजाति - dusparshájáti, San.). San. from (dur, san. prefix of negation + sprish, san. to touch); from prickly nature. Salvadoraceæ, 86 [ooshtarkhaur].——*Feronia* (कपित्थजाति - kapitt'hajáti, San.). San. from (kapi, san. monkey + st'há, san. to stand). Rutaceæ, 32 [wood-apple].——*Ferula* (बाह्लिकजाति - bálhikajáti, San.). San. means produced in balk [baulhicam]. Umbelliferæ, 67, asafœtida [baulhicam, galbanum, sagapenum].——*Festuca* (यवसजाति - yavasajáti, San.). San. from (yavasa, san. meadow grass). Graminaceæ, 156 [cleft grass].——*Ficus* (न्यग्रोधजाति - nyagródhajáti, San.). San. from (nyak, san. downwards + ruh, san. to grow); from descending roots [atty]. Moraceæ, 121 [anjeer, atty, banyan, nooga, peepal, tsiela].——*Filicium* (पर्णवृक्षजाति - parnavrikshajáti, San.). San. means fern + tree, alluding to fern-like leaves. Burseraceæ, 35 [pehimbia].——*Fimbristylis* (नलजाति - nalajáti, San.). San. from (nal, san. to shine) [nalam]. Cyperaceæ, 155 [nalam].——*Flacourtia* (स्वादुकण्टकजाति - svádukantakajáti, San.). San. from (svádu, san. sweet + kantaka, san. thorn) [swaudoocantacam]. Bixineæ, 14 [attack, ceylon plum, forest bair, indian plum, mauritius plum, swaudoocantacam, tomi-tomi].——*Flugellaria* (कशीयजाति - kashíyajáti, San.). San. means whip-like, alluding to long flexible branches. Commelynaceæ, 139 [wild rattan].——*Fœniculum* (मधुरिकाजाति - madhurikájáti, San.). San. from (madhura, san. sweet). Umbelliferæ, 67 [sonf].——*Fourcroya* (बृहत्कुमारीजाति - brihatkumáríjáti, San.). San. means large aloe. Amaryllidaceæ, 145 [foreign aloe].——*Fraxinus* (वारणीयजाति - váraníyajáti, San.). San. means used for hedges, alluding to the use. Oleaceæ, 85 [sicilian manna]. *Fumaria* (धूमगंधीयजाति - dhúmagandhíyajáti, San.). San. means smoke + smelling, alluding to the peculiar odor of plant.

Fumariaceæ, 9 [pitpapra].——*Garcinia* (रक्ताम्रजाति - raktámrajáti, San.). San. from (rakta, san. red + ámra, san. mangifera indica, linn.) [ractaumram]. Guttiferæ, 22 [gamboge, mangosteen, ractaumram, tickor].——*Gardenia* (गन्धराजजाति - gandharájajáti, San.). San. from (gandha, san. fragrance + rája, san. king); from fragrant flowers [gandharajah]. Rubiaceæ, 71 [cape jasmine, decamallee, gandharajah, hill emetic nut, nunjoondam].——*Garuga* (कुनिम्बजाति - kunimbajáti, San.). San. means low or inferior neem. Burseraceæ, 35 [garooga].——*Girardina* (वृश्चिकतरुजाति - vrishchikatarujáti, San.). San. means scorpion tree, from prickly leaves painful to touch. Urticaceæ, 119 [neilgherry nettle].——*Gisekia* (वालुकाशाकजाति - válukáshákajáti, San.). San. means sand greens. Ficoideæ, 66 [manaly].——*Givotia* (श्वेततरणवृक्षजाति - shvétataranavrikshajáti, San.). San. means white raft wood tree. Euphorbiaceæ, 118 [white tanakk].——*Glycine* (माषपर्णीजाति - máshaparníjáti, San.). San. from (másha, san. phaseolus bean + parna, san. leaf) [maushaparny]. Leguminosæ, 48 [horse-gram shrub, maushaparny].——*Glycirrhiza* (यष्टीमधुकजाति - yashtímadhukajáti, San.). San. from (yashti, san. stick + madhu, san. sweet). Leguminosæ. 48 [atimathooram].——*Glycosmosis* (अश्वशाखोटजाति - ashvashákhótajáti, San.). San. from (ashva, san. horse + shákhóta, san. epicarpurus). Rutaceæ, 32 [conjy].——*Gmelina* (काश्मरीजाति - káshmaríjáti, San.). San. means produced in cashmere. Verbenaceæ, 102 [cashmere tree].——*Gnaphalium* (मृदुलोमाजाति - mridulómájáti, San.). San. means downy, alluding to soft down covering the plant. Compositæ, 74 [buffalo carolah].——*Gomphrena* (अम्लानजाति - amlánajáti, San.). San. means not fading. Amarantaceæ, 106 [jaffer goondy].——*Gossypium* (कार्पासीजाति - kárpásíjáti, San.). San. means cotton [carpausy]. Malvaceæ, 25 [carpausy, cotton].——*Gracilaria* (समुद्रशाकजाति - samudrashákajáti, San.). San. means sea greens. Algæ, 163 [agar agar].——*Grangea* (माचिपत्रीजाति - máchipatríjáti, San.). San. from (máchí, san. artemisia + patra, san. leaf). Compositæ, 74 [madras absinth].——*Graptophyllum* (लेख्यपत्रीयजाति - lékhyapatríyajáti, San.). San. means written leaf, alluding to appearance of leaves. Acanthaceæ, 101 [falce plant].——*Grewia* (धर्मणजाति - dharmanajáti, San.). San. from (dhanvá, san. dry soil); from habitat [dharmanam]. Tiliaceæ, 27 [abrony, brau plant, dharmanam, falsah, female bair, janrah, tadda].——*Guazuma* (रुद्राक्षीयजाति - rudrákshíyajáti, San.). San. from (rudráksha, san. the roodrauck tree + íya, san. belonging to). Sterculiaceæ, 26 [roodrauck tree].——*Guettarda* (हिमपुष्पजाति - himapushpajáti, San.). San. from (hima, san. dew + pushpa, san. flower). Rubiaceæ, 71 [indian zebra wood].——*Guizotia* (कालतिलजाति - kálatilajáti, San.). San. from (kála, san. black flower + tila, san. sesamum). Compositæ, 74 [ramtil].——*Gymnema* (मेषशृंगीजाति - méshashringíjáti, San.). San. from (mésha, san. sheep + shringa, san. horn); from fruit. Asclepiadeæ, 88 [small indian ipecacuanha].——*Gymnosporia* (नग्नबीजजाति - nagnabíjajáti, San.). San. means naked seed [chintoo]. Celastrineæ, 40 [chintoo].——*Gynandropsis* (सूर्य्यावर्त्तजाति - súryávartajáti, San.). San. from (súrya, san. sun + ávrit, san. to turn). Capparideæ, 11 [vailay].——*Gynocardia* (तण्डुलकणमुद्गरजाति - tandulakanamudgarajáti, San.). San. from (tandulakana, san. rice grain + mudgara, san. jasmine); from seeds of species. Bixineæ, 14 [chaulmoogra].——*Gyrocarpus* (तरणवृक्षजाति - taranavrikshajáti, San.). San. means raft wood tree. Combretaceæ, 55 [tanakk].——*Hardwickia* (अञ्जनजाति - añjanajáti, San.). San. from (añj, san. to shine). Leguminosæ, 48 [yaipy].——*Hedychium* (कर्पूरकचूरजाति - karpúrakachhurajáti, San.). Means camphor zedoary. Zingiberaceæ, 144 [europe zedoary].——*Helianthus* (सूर्यमुखीजाति - súryámukhíjáti, San.). San. from (súrya, san. sun + mukha, san. face). Compositæ, 74 [sooryacaunty].——*Helicteres* (आवर्त्तनीजाति - ávartaníjáti, San.). San. from (ávrit, san. to twist); from twisted carpels. Sterculiaceæ, 26 [screw-tree].——*Heliotropium* (हस्तिशुण्डाजाति - hastishundájáti, San.). San. from (hasti, san. elephant + shundá, san. trunk); from fruit. Boragineæ, 92 [indian heliotrope].——*Helleborus* (कटुरोहिणीजाति - katuróhiníjáti, San.). San. from (katu, san. pungent + ruh, san. to grow). Ranunculaceæ, 1 [black cootkee].——*Helmia* (वनकन्दजाति - vanakandajáti, San.). Means wild yam. Dioscoreaceæ, 132 [malacca yam].——*Hemidesmus* (अनन्ताजाति - anantájáti, San.). San. means endless. Asclepiadeæ, 88 [indian sarsaparilla].——*Hemigyrosa* (उडुम्बराम्रजाति - udumbarámrajáti, San.). San. means fig mango. Sapindaceæ, 43 [fig mango].——*Heritiera* (सुन्दरीजाति - sundaríjáti, San.). San. means beautiful. Sterculiaceæ, 26 [soondree].——*Herpestis* (ब्राह्मीजाति - brahmíjáti, San.). San. from (vrih, san. to grow). Scrophularineæ, 95 [water zoofah].——*Hibiscus* (भिण्डाजाति - bhindájáti, San.) [bendy]. Malvaceæ, 25 [bendy].——*Hiptage* (माधवीलताजाति - mádhavílatájáti, San.). San. means spring flower creeper. Malpighiaceæ, 29 [madablota].——*Holarrhena* (कुटजजाति - kutajajáti, San.). San. from (kutila, san. curled + jan, san. to be born). Apocynaceæ, 87 [tellicherry bark].——*Holigarna* (वनभल्लातकजाति - vanabhallátakajáti, San.). Title from canarese. San. means wild markingnut tree. Anacardiaceæ, 45 [holigarna].——*Holopetala* (समपत्रीयजाति - samapatríyajáti, San.). San. means even-leaved. Ulmaceæ, 120 [indian elm].——*Homonoya* (वनकरवीरजाति - vanakaravírajáti, San.). San. means wild oleander. Euphorbiaceæ, 118 [wild gannair].——*Hopea* (वनद्रुमजाति - vanadrumajáti, San.). San. means forest tree [caung]. Dipterocarpeæ, 24 [caung].——*Hordeum* (यवजाति - yavajáti, San.). San. from (yu, san. to attach). Gramineæ, 156 [jow].——*Hugonia* (लतापरुषजाति - latáparushajáti, San.). San. means creeper falsah. Lineæ, 28 [creeping falsah].——*Hydnocarpus* (कन्दफलजाति - kandap'halajáti, San.). San. means tuber + fruit. Bixineæ, 14 [marotty].——*Hydrocotyle* (मण्डूकपर्णीजाति - mandúkaparníjáti, San.). San. from (mandúka, san. frog + parna, san. leaf). Umbelliferæ, 67 [indian pennywort].——*Hydrolea* (लाङ्गलीजाति - lángalíjáti, San.). San. from (lángala, san. plough). Hydrophyllaceæ, 91 [river blatty].——*Hygrophila* (कोकिलाक्षजाति - kókilákshajáti, San.). San. from (kókila, san. cuckoo + aksha, san. eye); flowers. Acanthaceæ, 101 [neer moolly].——*Hyoscyamus* (पारसीकयमानीजाति - párasíkayamáníjáti, San.). San. means persian ajwan. Solanaceæ, 94 [persian ajwaun].——*Hyssopus* (हिस्सपजाति - hissapajáti, San.). Labiateæ, 103 [zoofah].——*Ichnocarpus* (श्यामलताजाति - shyámalatájáti, San.). San. means black creeper. Apocynaceæ. 87 [shyaumalaty].——*Illicium* (हारिणीजाति - háriníjáti, San.). San. means attracting, on account of agreeable smell and taste. Magnoliaceæ, 3 [star anise].——*Impatiens* (दुष्पत्रीजाति - dushpatríjáti, San.). San. from (dus, san. bad + patra, san, leaf) [goolmindie]. Geraniaceæ, 31 [goolmindie].——*Imperata* (बर्हिर्जाति - barhirjáti, San.). San. from (vrih, san. to pluck up). Gramineæ, 156 [lalong grass].——*Indigofera* (नीलीजाति - nílíjáti, San.). San. from (níla, san. blue) [neely]. Leguminosæ, 48 [black nerinjy, doggreen gram, dog neem, indigo, neely, red nerinjy, shiva's neem].——*Ionidium* (चारटीजाति - cháratíjáti, San.). San. from (char, san. to spread). Violaceæ, 13 [one-leaf nelumbo].——*Ipomæa* (कलम्बीजाति - kalambíjáti, San.). San. from (ka, san. water + lamb, san. to hang); aquatic bindweed [calamby]. Convolvulaceæ, 93 [calamby, caushy ratnam, giant potato, hill giant potato, indian pink, kaladanah, laldanah, moon flower, rat's ear, red adambo, seeta's knot, sweet potato, tiger's foot, tooty coora, turbith, white adambo].——*Ixora* (बन्धूकजाति - bandhúkajáti, San.). Title from malayalam. San. from (bandh, san. to bind); from campact corymbs [ixora]. Rubiaceæ, 71 [ixora].——*Jasminum* (मल्लिजाति - mallijáti, San.). Title from arabic. San. from (mall, san. to hold); from fragrant flower [jasmine]. Oleaceæ, 85 [jasmine].——*Jatropha* (निकुम्भजाति - nikumbhajáti, San.). San. from (ni, san. prefix of certainty + kumbha, san. pot); from oil-bearing seeds [nicoombham]. Euphorbiaceæ, 118 [nicoombham, rat aumanac, small wild aumanac, wild aumanac].——*Juglans* (आक्षोटजाति - ákshótajáti, San.). San. from (aksh, san. to pervade); from spreading roots. Combretaceæ, 55 [acroot].——*Jussiæa* (भूलवङ्गजाति - bhúlavangajáti, San.). San. from (bhú, san. earth + lavanga, san. eugenia caryophyllata, willd.). Onagraceæ, 59 [lowly lavangam].——*Justicia* (गन्धरसजाति - gandharasajáti, San.). San. from (gandha, san. fragrance + rasa, san. juice); from leaves [gendarussa]. Acanthaceæ, 101 [gendarussa]——*Kalanchoe* (हेमसागरजाति - hémaságarajáti, San.). San. from (héma, san. gold + ságara, san. sea). Crassulaceæ, 51 [zakhm hayant].——*Kandelia* (कन्दाजाति - kandájáti, San.). Title from malayalam. Means bulbous root. Rhizophoreæ, 54 [candel mangrove].——*Kæmpferia* (भूचम्पकजाति - bhúchampakajáti, San.). San. from (bhú, san. earth + champaka, san. michelia champaca, linn.) [bhoochampak]. Zingiberaceæ, 144 [bhoochampak, false zedoary, indian galangal].——*Kopsia* (गुल्मीकरवीरजाति - gulmíkaravírajáti, San.). San. means cluster gannair. Apocynaceæ, 87 [cluster gannair].——*Lactuca* (क्षीरीजाति - kshíríjáti, San.). San. means milky, on account of the milky juice exuding when the plant is broken. Compositæ 74 [kahoo].——*Lagenaria* (अलाबुजाति - alábujáti, San.). From (a, san. negative prefix + lamb, san. to sink); serves as buoys. Cucurbitaceæ, 62 [fakeer's bottle].——*Lagerstræmia* (सितशाकजाजि - sitashákajáti, San.). San. means white teak [cadaly]. Lythraceæ, 58 [adambo, cadaly, chennangy, china mindie, venteak].——*Laggera* (वनमूलकजाति - vanamúlakajáti, San.). San. means wild radish. Compositæ, 74 [wild country radish].——*Lansium* (मर्कटद्राक्षजाति - markatadrákshajáti, San.). Title from malay. San. from (markata, san. monkey + dráksha, san. grape); fruit the size of grape and eaten by monkeys. Meliaceæ, 36 [lanseh].——*Lantana* (क्षुद्रपुष्पीजाति - kshudrapushpíjáti, San.). San. means small-flowered. Verbenaceæ, 102 [wild cholum].——*Lathyrus* (त्रिपुटीजाति - triputíjáti, San.). San. from (tri, san. three + puta, san. pod); from triangular wedge-shaped pod. Leguminosæ, 48 [casauree].——*Launea* (लेखनीपुष्पजाति - lékhanípushpajáti, San.). San. means style flower plant. Compositæ, 74 [style plant].——*Laurus* (श्यामवृक्षजाति - shyámavrikshajáti, San.). San. from (shyáma, san. dark + vriksha, san. tree). Lauraceæ, 111 [zafnee].——*Lawsonia* (मेन्धिकाजाति - méndhikájáti, San.). Lythraceæ, 58 [mindie].——*Lebidieropsis* (नन्दिवृक्षजाति - nandivrikshajáti, San.). San. from (nandi, san. happiness + vriksha, san. tree). Euphorbiaceæ, 118 [garrar].——*Leea* (कुकुरजिह्वाजाति - kukurajihvájáti, San.). From (kukura, san. dog + jihvá, san. tongue). Ampelidæ, 42 [ratanhia].——*Leersia* (जांगलाढकीजाति - jángaládhakíjáti, San.). San means wild dholl. Graminaceæ, 156 [wild dholl].——*Lepidagathis* (कुरुण्टकसदृशीजाति - kuruntakasadrishíjáti, San.). San. from (kuruntaka, san. nail dye + sadrisha, san. resembling); nail dye like [corandy]. Acanthaceæ, 101 [corandy].——*Lepidium* (चन्द्रसूरजाति - chandrasúrajáti, San.). San. from (chandra, san. moon + shúra, san. the plant). Cruciferæ, 10 [haleem].——*Leucæna* (वृहत्चक्रमर्दकजाति - brihatchakramardakajáti, San.). San. means large chakondah. Leguminosæ, 48 [large chakondah].——*Leucas* (रुद्रपुष्पीजाति - rudrapushpíjáti, San.). San. from (rudra, san. the deity + pushpa, san. flower) [toombay]. Labiatæ, 103 [toombay].——*Limnanthemum* (शीतलीजाति - shítalíjáti, San.). Means cooling. Gentianaceæ, 90 [floating nelumbo].——*Limonia* (वननिंबूजाति - vananimbújáti, San.). San. means wild lime. Rutaceæ, 32 [wild lime].——*Linum* (अतसीजाति - atasíjáti, San.). Lineæ, 28 [alsee].——*Lippia* (वशीरजाति - vashírajáti, San.). San. from (vash, san. to long for). Verbenaceæ, 102 [wild long pepper].——*Lobelia* (देवनलजाति - dévanalajáti, San.). San. from (déva, san. divine + nala, san. reed). Campanulaceæ, 76 [wild pogauk].——*Lodoicea* (अब्धिनारिकेलजाति - abdhinárikélajáti, San.). San. means sea-cocoanut. Palmaceæ, 149 [sea cocoanut].——*Loranthus* (वृक्षादनीजाति - vrikshádaníjáti, San.) San. from (vriksha, san. tree + ad, san. to eat). Loranthaceæ [gooloom].——*Luffa* (कोशातकीजाति - kóshátakíjáti, San.). Title from arabic. San. from (kósha, san. pod + at, san. to go constantly) [luffa]. Cucurbitaceæ, 62 [luffa].——*Lumnitzera* (समुद्रबहुपादीजाति - samudrabahupádíjáti, San.). San. means sea + many footed mangrove. Combretaceæ, 55 [madagascar mangrove].——*Lycopersicum* (वृकफलीयजाति - vrikap'halíyajáti, San.). San. means wolf + fruit, alluding to its aphrodisiac quality. Solanaceæ, 94 [europe brinjaul].——*Maba* (पीततिन्दुकजाति - pítatindukajáti, San.). San. means yellow ebony. Ebenaceæ, 83 [neilgherry satin wood].——*Macaranga* (मकरांगजाति - makarángajáti, San.). Euphorbiaceæ, 118 [round-leaved nelumbo].——*Mallotus* (कम्पिल्लकजाति - kampillakajáti, San.). Title from nepaulese. San. from (kamp, san. to shake). Euphorbiaceæ, 118 [kamela].——*Malva* (वनचणकजाति - vanachanakajáti, San.). San. means wild bengal gram [khoobauzy]. Malvaceæ, 25 [foreign tootty, khoobauzy, wild bengal gram].——*Mandragora* (नरमूलजाति - naramúlajáti, San.). San. means man + root. Solanaceæ, 94 [mardoomgiyah].——*Mangifera* (आम्रजाति - ámrajáti, San.). San. from (am, san. to affect with sickness). Anacardiaceæ, 45 [mango].——*Manihot* (दारुकन्दजाति - dárukandajáti, San.). San. means wood + root. Euphorbiaceæ, 118 [malda dye].——*Maranta* (शीतलपत्रिकाजाति - shítalapatrikájáti, San.). San. from (shítala, san. cold + patra, san. leaf). Marantaceæ, 143 [sheetalpaty].——*Martynia* (व्याघ्रनखीजाति - vyághranakhíjáti, San.). San. means tiger's claw. Pedalineæ, 100 [tiger claw].——*Matricaria* (देशीगवाक्षसेमन्तीजाति - déshígavákshasémantíjáti, San.). San. means country + cow-eye rose, chamomile. Compositæ, 74 [country baboona].——*Melaleuca* (सितशाखीजाति - sitashákhíjáti, San.). San. means white branched. Myrtaceæ, 56 [cajeput].——*Melanthesopsis* (कृष्णपुष्पीयजाति - krishnapushpíyajáti, San.). San. means black flower. Euphorbiaceæ, 118 [large neeroory].——*Melia* (निम्बजाति - nimbajáti, San.). San. from (ni, san. to lead). Meliaceæ, 36 [neem].——*Melissa* (भ्रमरतुलसीजाति - bhramaratulasíjáti, San.). San. means bee basil, from resort of bees. Labiateæ, 103 [persian toolsy].——*Melocanna* (विषवंशजाति - vishavamshajáti, San.). San. means poison bamboo. Graminaceæ, 156 [berry bamboo].——*Memecylon* (कलायजाति - kaláyajáti, San.). San. means causing wind. Melastomaceæ, 57 [cassa].——*Mentha* (पुदिनाजाति - pudinájáti, San.). San. from (pudínah, hind. the plant). Labiatæ, 103 [poodeenah].——*Mesua* (नागकेसरजाति - nágakésarajáti, San.). San. from (nága, san. serpent + késara, san. filament). Guttiferæ, 22 [naugachampak].——*Methonica* (अग्निशिखाजाति - agnishikhájáti, San.). Title from malayalam. San. from (agni, san. fire + shikhá, san. flame); from crimson flowers. Liliaceæ, 136 [wild bachnaug].——*Metroxylon* (मातृदारुजाति - mátridárujáti, San.). San. means mother tree. Palmaceæ, 149 [borneo sago palm].——*Michelia* (चम्पकजाति - champakajáti, San.). San. from (champá, san. island in cambodia). Magnoliaceæ, 3 [champak].——*Miliusa* (शृगालवृक्षजाति - shrigálavrikshajáti, San.). San. means jackal tree. Anonaceæ, 4 [black doodooga].——*Millingtonia* (दारुमल्लिकाजाति - dárumallikájáti, San.). San. from (dáru, san. wood + mallika, san. jasminum). Bignoniaceæ, 99 [indian cork].——*Mimosa* (लज्जालुजाति - lajjálujáti, San.). San. from (lajjá, san. bashfulness); alluding to sensitiveness [shoondy]. Leguminosæ, 48 [shoondy].——*Mimusops* (क्षीरिकाजाति - kshírikájáti, San.). San. from (kshíra, san. milk) [csheericay]. Sapotaceæ, 82 [csheericay, edible paulay, ilanjy, jointed paulay, monkey face paulay].——*Mirabilis* (सन्ध्यारागजाति - sandhyárágajáti, San.). San. from (sandhyá san. evening + rága, san. color). Nyctagineæ, 105 [false jalap].——*Mollugo* (पर्पटजाति - parpatajáti, San.). San. from sound of seed bursting [parpatam]. Ficoideæ, 66 [hazaur danah, parpatam, tirye].——*Momordica* (कारवेल्लाजाति - kárávéllájáti, San.). San. means grown with effort. Cucurbitaceæ, 62 [carolah].——*Monochoria* (नीलकुवलयजाति - nílakuvalayajáti, San.). San. from (níla, san. blue + kuvalaya, san. water-lily). Pontederaceæ, 135 [blue nelumbo].——*Morinda* (आछुकजाति - áchhukajáti, San.). Rubiaceæ, 71 [dyeing mulberry].——*Moringa* (मुरङ्गीजाति - murangíjáti, San.). Title from dravidian. Moringeæ, 46 [moringa].——*Morus* (तूलजाति - túlajáti, San.). Moraceæ, 121 [indian mulberry].——*Mucuna* (कन्दुराजाति - kandurájáti, San.). San. means pungent [cowitch]. Leguminosæ, 48 [cowitch].——*Mukia* (अहिलेखनजाति - ahilékhanajáti, San.). San. from (ahi, san. snake + lékhana, san. mark); from stripes on fruit. Cucurbitaceæ, 62 [mosmoosky].——*Mundulea* (सुप्तिवृक्षजाति - suptivrikshajáti, San.). San. means drowsy tree, from effect on fishes. Leguminosæ, 48 [sooptee].——*Murraya* (कृष्णनिम्बजाति - krishnanimbajáti, San.). San. from (krishna, san. black + nimba, san. melia azadirachta, linn.) [caroovaimboo]. Rutaceæ, 32 [caroovaimboo, curry-leaf, foreign conjy].——*Musa* (कदलीजाति - kadalíjáti, San.). San. from (ka, san. water + dala, san. leaf); from watery sheath. Musaceæ, 142 [plantain].——*Mussænda* (श्वेतपत्रीजाति - shvétapatríjáti, San.). Title from singhalese San. from (shvéta, san. white + patra, san. leaf). Rubiaceæ, 71 [moossanda].——*Myristica* (जातीफलजाति - játíp'halajáti, San.). San. from (jan, san. to be born + p'hala, san. fruit) [jauty]. Myristicaceæ, 112 [jauty].——*Myrtus* (सुगन्धाजाति - sugandhájáti, San.). San. means perfume. Myrtaceæ, 56 [foreign mindie].——*Nardostachys* (जटामांसीजाति - jatámámsíjáti, San.) San. from (jatá, san, matted hair + mámsa, san. flesh). Valerianeæ, 72 [jatamansy].——*Naregamia* (त्रिपत्रीजाति - tripatríjáti, San.). Title from malayalam. San. from (tri, san. three + patra, san. leaf). Meliaceæ, 36 [shrub orange].——*Nasturtium* (नासावर्त्तीजाति - násávarttíjáti, San.). San. means nose-twisting, from acrid taste of plant, affecting muscles of nose. Cruciferæ, 10 [haleem].——*Nelumbium* (पद्मजाति - padmajáti, San.). Title from singhalese. San. from (pat, san, to go + ma, san. water). Nymphæaceæ, 7 [nelumbo].——*Nephelium* (लांगनजाति - lánganajáti, San.). San. means longan plant. Sapindaceæ, 43 [litchy, longan, rambutan].——*Neptunia* (तोयलज्जालुजाति - tóyalajjálújáti, San.). San. means water + mimosa [water shoondy]. Leguminosæ, 48 [water shoondy].——*Nerium* (करवीरजाति - karavírajáti, San.). San. means sword. Apocynaceæ, 87 [gannair].——*Nicotiuna* (ताम्रकूटजाति - támrakútajáti, San.). San. means copper + head. Solanaceæ, 94 [pogauk].——*Nigella* (कृष्णजीरकजाति - krishnajírakajáti, San.). San. from (krishna, san. black + jíraka, san. cuminum cyminum). Ranunculaceæ, 1 [black jeerah].——*Nipa* (नीपाजाति - nípájáti, San.). From the moluccas name of plant. Pandanaceæ, 150 [attap].——*Nyctanthes* (शेफालीजाति - shép'hálíjáti, San.). San, from (shép'ha, san. sleeping + ali, san. beetle); from fragrant flowers attracting beetle. Oleaceæ, 85 [coral jasmine].——*Nymphæa* (उत्पलजाति - utpalajáti, San.). San. from (ut, san. up + pal, san. to burst) [indian water-lily]. Nymphæaceæ, 7 [indian water lily].——*Ochna* (कनकचंपकजाति - kanakachampakajáti, San.). San. from (kanaka, san. gold + champaka, san. michelia champaca, linn.). Ochnaceæ, 34 [shilandy].——*Ochrocarpus* (सुरङ्गीजाति - surangíjáti, San.). San. from (su, san. good + ranga, san. color). Guttiferæ, 22 [soora poon].——*Ocimum* (तुलसीजाति - tulasíjáti, San.). San. from (tulasí, san. ocymum sanctum, linn.) [toolsy]. Labiatæ, 103 [toolsy].——*Odina* (जिङ्गिनीजाति - jinginíjáti, San.). Title from tamul. San. from (ji, san. to conquer). Anacardiaceæ, 45 [wodier].——*Oldenlandia* (क्षेत्रपर्पटीजाति - kshétraparpatíjáti, San.). San. from (kshétra, san. field + parpatí, san. mollugo) [field parpatam]. Rubiaceæ, 71 [chayroot, field parpatam].——*Olea* (जितवृक्षजाति - jitavrikshajáti, San.). San. from (zaitun, ar. olive) [jita]. Oleaceæ, 85 [indian olive, jita, zeitoon].——*Onosma* (गोजिह्वाजाति - gójihvájáti, San.). San. from (gó, san. bull + jihvá, san. tongue). Boragineæ, 92 [gowzabaun].——*Ophiorrhiza* (सर्पाक्षिजाति - sarpákshijáti, San.). San. from (sarpa, san. serpent + akshi, san. eye). Rubiaceæ, 71 [mongoose snake root].——*Opuntia* (नागफणीजाति - nágap'haníjáti, San.). San. means serpent's hood. Cacteæ, 65 [prickly pear].——*Orchis* (शृगालाण्डजाति - shrigálándajáti, San.). San. means fox's testicles. Orchidaceæ, 141 [salep].——*Origanum* (मरुवकजाति - maruvakajáti, San.). San. from (maru, san. desert), from habitat [marwah]. Labiatæ, 103 [marwah].——*Ormocarpum* (कानन - शेखरजाति - kánanashékharajáti, San.). Means wild moringa. Leguminosæ, 48 [wild moringa].——*Oroxylum* (पर्वतदारुजाति - parvatadárujáti, San.). San. means mountain wood, from habitat. Bignoniaceæ, 99 [pajanely].——*Orygia* (रक्तसारणाजाति-raktasáranájáti, San.). San. fram (rakta, san. red + sárané, san. trianthema). Ficoideæ, 66 [red shauranay].——*Oryza* (नीवारजाति - nívárajáti, San.). Title from tamul. San. from (nivri, san. to ward off). Gramiuaceæ, 156 [nivvary, paddy]. ——*Osbeckia* (अरण्यचणकजाति - aranyachanakajáti, San.). San. means wild bengal gram. Melastomaceæ, 57 [forest bengal gram].——*Ougeinia* (नेमिजाति - némijáti, San.). San. means wheel, from use of wood in wheel-making. Leguminosæ, 48 [nemmy].——*Oxalis* (चांगेरीजाति - chángéríjáti, San.). San. means causing teeth to loose their soundness. Geraniaceæ, 31 [sour auray].——*Oxystelma* (दुग्धिकाजाति - dugdhikájáti, San.). San. means milky. Asclepiadeæ, 88 [needle paulay]. ——*Pachyrhizus* (शंखालुजाति - shankhálujáti, San.). San. means conch + esculent root. Leguminosæ, 48 [wayaka]. ——*Pæderia* (प्रसारणीजाति - prasáraníjáti, San.). San. means stretching forth. Rubiaceæ, 71 [gandhaulee].——*Pajanelia* (अरलुजाति - aralujáti, San.). Title a corruption of malayalam, meaning soft anjely. San. from (aralu, san. the plant). Bignoniaceæ, 99 [pajanely].——*Pandanus* (केतकीजाति - kétakíjáti, San.). Title from malay. Pandanaceæ, 150 [screw-pine].—— *Panicum* (प्रियंगुजाति - priyangujáti, San.). San. from (priya, san. pleasing) [priyangoo]. Graminaceæ, 156 [cumboo grass, ginger grass, guinea grass, paddy-field grass, priyangoo, purple grass, shaumay, small raggy, soda grass, sticky grass, surprise grass, tinay, varagoo, wild dharbhay, wild hurrially].——*Papaver* (अहिफेनजाति - ahip'hénajáti, San.). San. means serpent + foam [aphainam]. Papaveraceæ, 8 [aphainam].——*Parkia* (शिवलिङ्गवृक्षजाति - shivalingavrikshajáti, San.). San. means shiva + phallic emblem + tree. Leguminosæ, 48 [nitta].——*Parkinsonia* (हरित्खदिरजाति - haritkhadirajáti, San.). Means green babool. Leguminosæ, 48 [parangy vail].——*Parmelia* (शैलेयजाति - shailéyajáti, San.). San. from (shilá, san. stone). Lichenes, 162 [cull pausy].——*Paspalum* (कोद्रवजाति - kódravajáti, San.). San. from (ku, san. prefix of deficiency + udra, san. water). Graminaceæ, 156 [khoda].——*Passiflora* (पीडापुष्पजाति - pídápushpajáti, San.). San. means passion + flower. Passifloreæ, 61 [jimiky]. ——*Pavetta* (काकछेदीजाति - kákachhédíjáti, San.). Title from tamul. San. means crow killer. Rubiaceæ, 71 [pavetta].—— *Pavonia* (बालजाति - bálajáti, San.). San. from (val, san. to cover) [motty]. Malvaceæ, 25 [mootty].——*Pedalium* (गजदंष्ट्रीजाति - gajadamshtríjáti, San.). San. means elephant's tooth. Pedalineæ, 100 [elephant nerinjy].——*Pedilanthus* (पादुकापुष्पीयजाति - pádukápushpíyajáti, San.). San. means slipper + flower, alluding to their shape. Euphorbiaceæ, 118 [adjutant's hedge].—— *Peganum* (विदेशमेन्धिकाजाति - vidéshaméndhikájáti, San.). San. means foreign mindio. Rutaceæ, 32 [barmal].——*Pennisetum* (कङ्गुजाति - kangujáti, San.). San. from (ka, san. water + gam, san. to come out). Graminaceæ, 156 [bajrah].——*Pentapetes* (बन्धुजीवकजाति - bandhujívakajáti, San.). San. means living in group. Sterculiaceæ, 26 [mankena].——*Pergularia* (लताचंपकजाति - latáchampakajáti, San.). San. means creeper champak. Asclepiadeæ, 88 [creeper champak].——*Peristrophe* (परिवर्तनीजाति - parivartaníjáti, San.). San. means turning in all directions, alluding to twisted anthers. Acanthaceæ, 101 [chebeera]. ——*Peucedanum* (मिश्रेयजाति - mishréyajáti, San.). San. from (mishra, san. egypt). Umbelliferæ, 67 [sowa].——*Phaseolus* (मुद्गजाति - mudgajáti, San.). San. from (mud, san. to be glad). Leguminosæ, 48 [gram, lobyah, moodgam, needle chakondah]. ——*Phœnix* (खर्जूरजाति - kharjúrajáti, San.). San. from (kharj, san. to cleanse) [kharjooram]. Palmaceæ, 149 [kharjooram]. ——*Phragmites* (पोटगलजाति - pótagalajáti, San.). San. means clasped to the mouth and made to move. Graminaceæ, 156 [large naunal].——*Phyllanthus* (आमलकजाति - ámalakajáti, San.). San. from (amla, san. sour) [aumlacam]. Euphorbiaceæ, 118 [aumlacam, brazil cherry, emblic myrobalan, neeroory, nelly, poolah].——*Physalis* (टंकारीजाति - tankáríjáti, San.). San. from (tam, san. imitative sound + kárí, san. doer) [takkauly]. Solanaceæ, 94 [indian winter cherry, takkauly].——*Picrorhiza* (कटुकाजाति - katukájáti, San.). San. means pungent. Scrophularineæ, 95 [cootkee].——*Pimenta* (चीनमरीचजाति - chínamaríchajáti, San.). San. means chinese pepper. Myrtaceæ, 56 [china pepper].——*Pimpinella* (शतपुष्पाजाति - shatapushpájáti, San.). San. means hundred-flower. Umbelliferæ, 67 [anise].——*Piper* (पिप्पलीजाति - pippalíjáti, San.). Title from sanscrit. San. from (prí, san. to nourish) [pepper]. Piperaceæ, 125 [pepper]. ——*Pisonia* (गणिकाजाति - ganikájáti, San.). San. means harlot plant. Nyctagineæ, 105 [conky].——*Pistacia* (कर्कटशृङ्गीजाति - karkatashringíjáti, San.). Title from arabic. San. means crab + horn [pistah]. Anacardiaceæ, 45 [kakra singhy, mastic, pistah].——*Pistia* (कुंभिकाजाति - kumbhikájáti, San.). San. from (kumbha, san. water pot). Pistiaceæ, 151 [rootless nelumbo]. ——*Pisum* (कलायजाति - kaláyajáti, San.). San. from (kam, san. wind + lá, san. to take). Leguminosæ, 48 [calauyam].—— *Pithecolobium* (आरग्वधजाति - áragvadhajáti, San.). San. from (araja, san. skin disease + vadh, san. to kill) [auragvadham]. Leguminosæ, 48 [auragvadham, corcapilly, wild condray, zamang]. ——*Plantago* (अश्वकर्णजाति - ashvakarnajáti, San.). San. means horse + ear, from leaf. Plantagineæ, 104 [spogel].——*Plecospermum* (कण्टकीवृक्षजाति - kantakívrikshajáti, San.). San. means thorny tree. Urticaceæ, 119 [cority].——*Plumbago* (चित्रजाति - chitrajáti, San.). San. means variegated [chitramoolam]. Plumbagineæ, 79 [chitramoolam].——*Plumeria* (सितचंपकजाति - sitachampakajáti, San.). San. means white champak. Apocynaceæ, 87 [pagoda tree].——*Pogostemon* (हरितपत्त्रीजाति - haritapattríjáti, San.). San. means green leaf tree. Labiatæ, 103 [patchouli].——*Poinciana* (रत्नगन्धिजाति - ratnagandhijáti, San.). San. means gem + fragrance [ratnagandhy]. Leguminosæ, 48 [foreign tungaid, ratnagandhy, soonkeshwaram].—— *Polyalthia* (अशोकजाति - ashókajáti, San.). San. from (a, san. negative prefix + shóka, san. sorrow). Anonaceæ, 4 [ashocam]. ——*Polygala* (अतिक्षीरीजाति - atikshíríjáti, San.). San. means very milky [nangay]. Polygaleæ, 16 [nangay].——*Polygonum* (नक्राङ्गजाति - nakrángajáti, San.). San. means alligator's limb [water gannair]. Polygonaceæ, 110 [alligator's nose, hoonraunj, river jasmine, water gannair, wobilinta].——*Polypodium* (बहुपादीजाति - bahupádíjáti, San.). San. means many foot. Filices, 157 [parny].——*Pommereulla* (ऊषतृण - úshatrina, San.). San. from (úsha, san. saline soil + trina, san. grass), from habitat. Graminaceæ, 156 [ant grass].——*Pongamia* (नाक्तमालाजाति - náktamálájáti, San.). San. from (nakta, san. night + al, san. to shine). Leguminosæ, 48 [karanj].——*Porana* (अश्वबालजाति - ashvabálajáti, San.). San. means horse tail. Convolvulaceæ, 93 [drowpady's hair].——*Portulaca* (लोणीजाति - lóníjáti, San.). San. from (lú, san. to cut); from acidity. Portulaceæ, 18 [indian purslane].——*Pothos* (पूगवल्लीजाति - púgavallíjáti, San.). Title from singbalese. San. means areca creeper, from fruit like areca. Araceæ, 152 [elephant creeper].——*Premna* (जयाजाति - jayájáti, San.). San. from (jí, san. to conquer) [jayah]. Verbenaceæ, 102 [fire brand teak, lowly jaumoon, moonnay].—— *Prosopis* (शिवाजाति - shivájáti, San.). San. means auspicious [shivah]. Leguminosæ, 48 [manilla tamarind, mesquit, shamee, shivah].——*Protium* (शैलाम्रजाति - shailámrajáti, San.). San. means hill mango, from fragrance. Burseraceæ, 35 [hill kiloovay].——*Prunus* (बादामजाति - bádámajáti, San.) [auloo]. Rosaceæ, 49 [albaca, auloo, baudam, cherry, mishmish].—— *Pseudarthria* (छद्मग्रन्थीयजाति - chhadmagrandhíyajáti, San.). San. means false + knot, alluding to jointed pedicels which easily break off. Leguminosæ, 48 [three-leaf poon].——*Psidium* (बहुबीजफलजाति - bahubíjap'halajáti, San.). San. means many seeded fruit. Myrtaceæ, 56 [guava].——*Psophocarpus* (नादिनीजाति - nádiníjáti, San.). San. means sounding, from rattling noise of pods. Leguminosæ, 48 [goa bean].——*Psoralea* (वाकुचीजाति - vákuchíjáti, San.). San. from (váta, san. wind + kuch, san. to contract). Leguminosæ, 48 [bawchee].——*Pterocarpus* (महाकुटजजाति - mahákutajajáti, San.). San. from (mahá, san. large + kutaja, san. holarrhena antidysenterica, wall.) [vengay]. Leguminosæ, 48 [padouk, red sanders, vengay].——*Pteroselinum* (विदेशाजमोदजाति - vidéshájamódajáti, San.). San. means foreign ajwaun. Umbelliferæ, 67 [makdoonas].——*Pterospermum* (मुचुकुन्दजाति - muchukundajáti, San.). San. from (much, san. to abandon + kunda, san. jasmine) [mochcoondam]. Sterculiaceæ, 26 [kaniyaur, mochcoondam, velanga].——*Punica* (दाडिमीजाति - dádimíjáti, San.). San. from (dal, san. to burst open). Lythraceæ, 58 [anaur].——*Pupalia* (खरपुष्पीजाति - kharapushpíjáti, San.). San. means sharp flowered, from bristly plant and flower. Amarantaceæ, 106 [audayotty].——*Putranjiva* (पुत्त्रञ्जीवजाति - putrañjívajáti, San.). Title from sanscrit. San. from (putra, san. son + jíva, san. life); necklace of fruit efficacious in children in keeping health. Euphorbiaceæ, 118 [pootranjeeva]. ——*Pyrus* (अमृतफलजाति - amritap'halajáti, San.). San. means elixir + fruit. Rosaceæ, 49 [amrood, seb].——*Quamoclit* (कामलताजाति - kámalatájáti, San.). San. means beautiful creeper. Convolvulaceæ, 93 [quamoclit].——*Quisqualis* (कौन्दीलताजाति - kaundílatájáti, San.). San. means jasmine creeper. Combretaceæ, 55 [rangoon creeper].——*Randia* (शल्यजाति - shalyajáti, San.). San. from (shal, san. to cover) [emetic nut]. Rubiaceæ, 71 [emetic nut].——*Raphanus* (मूलकजाति - múlakajáti, San.). San. from (múla, san. root). Cruciferæ, 10 [country radish].——*Rauwolfia* (सर्पगन्धाजाति - sarpagandhájáti, San.). San. from (sarpa, san. serpent + gandha, san. smell). Apocynaceæ, 87 [snake root].——*Ravenalia* (रावनालजाति - rávanálajáti, San.). From the madagascar. Name of plant. Musaceæ, 142 [traveller's palm].——*Rhamnus* (रक्तरोहित-

जाति - raktaróhitajáti, San.). San. means red amoora rohituka. Rhamneæ, 41 [red rohitacam].——*Rheum* (रेवसजाति - révasajáti, San.). Polygonaceæ, 110 [indian rhubarb].——*Rhinacanthus* (नागमल्लिकाजाति - nágamallikájáti, San.). San. from (nága, san. serpent + malliká, san. jasmine). Acanthaceæ, 101 [snake jasmine].——*Rhizophora* (सितकन्दाजाति - sitakandájáti, San.). San. means white + bulbous root. Rhizophoreæ, 54 [white candel mangrove].——*Rhododendron* (पाटलद्रुजाति - pátaladrujáti, San.). San. from (pátala, san. red + dru, san. tree); alluding to terminal bunches of flowers. Ericaceæ, 78 [neilgherry rhododendron].——*Rhodomyrtus* (रक्तिकाजाति - raktikájáti, San.). San. means red, alluding to color of flowers. Myrtaceæ, 56 [hill guava]——*Rhus* (कर्कटशृङ्गीजाति - karkatashringíjáti, San.). San. from (karkata, san. crab + shringa, san. horn); from galls like crab's claws [sumach]. Anacardiaceæ, 45 [sumach].——*Rhynchosia* (कालतुवरीजाति - kálatuvaríjáti, San.). San. means black dholl. Leguminosæ, 48 [black dholl].——*Ricinus* (एरण्डजाति - érandajáti, San.). San. from (ir, san. to go). Euphorbiaceæ, 118 [aumanac].——*Rosa* (तरुणीजाति - taruníjáti, San.). San. means tender [gool]. Rosaceæ, 49 [gool].——*Rothia* (शृगालमुद्गजाति - shrigálamudgajáti, San.). San. means jackal green gram. Leguminosæ, 48 [jackal green gram].——*Rubia* (मञ्जिष्ठाजाति - mañjisht'hájáti, San.). San. from (mañju, san. beautiful + isht'ha, san. superlative affix). Rubiaceæ, 71 [munjeet].——*Rubus* (गौरफलजाति - gaurip'halajáti, San.). San. from (gaura, san. red + p'hala, san. fruit) [gowry's fruit]. Rosaceæ, 49 [gowry's fruit].——*Rumex* (चुक्रिकाजाति - chukrikájáti, San.). San. means sour. Polygonaceæ, 110 [country sorrel].——*Ruta* (ब्राह्मीजाति - bráhmíjáti, San.). San. from (vrish, san. to grow). Rutaceæ, 32 [sadauf].——*Saccharum* (शरजाति - sharajáti, San.). San. from (shrí, san. to hurt); from sharp leaves [sharam]. Graminaceæ, 156 [moonj, moonshee grass, naunal, sharam, sugar-cane].——*Sagittaria* (बाणपत्रीयजाति - bánapatríyajáti, San.). San. means arrow-leaved. Alismaceæ 133 [pit nelumbo].——*Salicornia* (लवणीजाति - lavaníjáti, San.). San. from (lavana, san. salt); from habitat. Salsolaceæ, 108 [chook].——*Salix* (वरुणजाति - varunajáti, San.). San. means water [varoonam]. Salicaceæ, 126 [varoonam].——*Salvadora* (पीलुजाति - pílujáti, San.). San. from (píl, san. to check). Salvadoraceæ, 86 [tooth brush tree].——*Salvia* (कर्पूरपत्रजाति - karpúrapatrajáti, San.). San. means camphor leaf [indian sage]. Labiatæ, 103 [indian sage].——*Samadera* (नीपविशेषजाति - nípavishéshajáti, San.). San. means variety of cadamba [q.v.] tree. Title from singhalese. Simarubeæ, 33 [samadarah].——*Sandoricum* (रक्तचन्दनजाति - raktachandanajáti, San.). Title from malay. San. from (rakta, san. red + chandana, san. sandal wood); from red wood. Meliaceæ, 36 [malay red wood].——*Sanseviera* (मूर्वाजाति - múrvájáti, San.). San. from (múrv, san. to bind). Liliaceæ, 136 [marool].——*Santalum* (चन्दनजाति - chandanajáti, San.). Title from malay. San. from (chand, san. to gladden). Santalaceæ, 116 [sandal].——*Sapindus* (फेनिलजाति - p'hénilajáti, San.). San. from (p'héna, san. froth). Sapindaceæ, 43 [soap nut].——*Saraca* (रक्ताशोकजाति - raktáshókajáti, San.). San. from (rakta, san. red + a, san. negative prefix + shóka, san. sorrow). Leguminosæ, 48 [bengal ashocam].——*Sarcostemma* (सोमलताजाति - sómalatájáti, San.). San. means moon plant. Asclepiadeæ, 88 [somam].——*Sarcostigma* (वासकेयजाति - vásakéyajáti, San.). San. from (vásaka, san. perfuming). Olacineæ, 38 [poovana].——*Saussurea* (कुष्ठजाति - kusht'hajáti, San.). San. from (ku, san. bad + st'ha, san. spot). Compositæ, 74 [costum].——*Schleichera* (सिंहलसिंदूरवृक्षजाति - simhalasindúravrikshajáti, San.). San. means ceylon oak tree. Sapindaceæ, 43 [ceylon oak].——*Schrebera* (मुष्ककजाति - mushkakajáti, San.). San. from (mushka, san. testicle); from ashes used in cautery. Oleaceæ, 85 [weaver's beam].——*Scindapsus* (गजपिप्पलीजाति - gajapippalíjáti, San.). San. from (gaja, san. elephant + pippalí, san. long pepper). Araceæ, 152 [elephant long pepper].——*Scirpus* (कस्तेरुजाति - kastérujáti, San.). San. means resting in water [club grass]. Cyperaceæ, 155 [club grass].——*Scutia* (बदरवल्लीजाति - badaravallíjáti, San.). San. from (badara, san. zizyphus jujuba, lamk. + valli, san. creeper). Rhamneæ, 41 [small bair].——*Sebastiania* (लतामण्डजाति - latámandajáti, San.). San. means creeper aumanac. Euphorbiaceæ, 118 [creeping aumanac].——*Securinega* (श्वेतकांबोजीजाति - shvétakámbójíjáti, San.). San. from (shvéta, san. white + kámbójí, san. abrus precatorius, linn.). Euphorbiaceæ, 118 [white poolah].——*Semecarpus* (भल्लातकजाति - bhallátakajáti, San.). San. from (bhall, san. to hurt); from vesicant property. Anacardiaceæ, 45 [marking nut].——*Sesamum* (तिलजाति - tilajáti, San.). Title from arabic. San. from (til, san. to anoint). Pedalineæ, 100 [gingelly].——*Sesbania* (जयन्तीजाति - jayantíjáti, San.). Title from arabic. San. from (jí, san. to conquer) [sesban]. Leguminosæ, 48 [sesban].——*Shorea* (शालजाति - shálajáti, San.). San. from (shal, san. to praise) [saul]. Dipterocarpeæ, 24 [saul].——*Sida* (बलाजाति - balájáti, San.). San. from (bala, san. strength) [balah]. Malvaceæ, 25 [balah].——*Sideroxylon* (कालदारुजाति - káladárujáti, San.). Means iron wood. Sapotaceæ, 82 [foreign ilanjy].——*Siegesbeckia* (वाराहीजाति - váráhíjáti, San.). San. means pig, in allution to strong smell. Compositæ, 74 [pig plant].——*Smilax* (चीनयष्टीजाति - chínayashtíjáti, San.). San. means china stick [china root]. Smilaceæ, 131 [china root].——*Solanum* (कुलीजाति - kulíjáti, San.). San. from (kula, san. crowd); from cluster of fruits [cooly]. Solanaceæ, 94 [brinjaul, cooly, indian hounds' berry, indian night shade, shoonday].——*Sophora* (गिरितिमिरहरीजाति - giritimiraharíjáti, San.). San. from (giri, san. mountain + timiraharí, san. tungaid). Leguminosæ, 48 [hill tungaid].——*Sorghum* (देवधान्यजाति - dévadhányajáti, San.). San. from (déva, san. god + dhánya, san. grain). Graminaceæ, 156 [cholum].——*Soymida* (पत्राङ्गजाति - patrángajáti, San.). Title from teloogoo. San. from (patra, san. leaf + anga, san. body). Meliaceæ, 36 [soymida].——*Sphæranthus* (मुण्डीजाति - mundíjáti, San.). San. from (mund, san. to shave); from globose flowers [moondy]. Compositæ, 74 [fever toolsy, moondy, seed toolsy].——*Sphenoclea* (तोयपिप्पलीजाति - tóyapippalíjáti, San.). San. means water + long pepper. Campanulaceæ, 76 [water long pepper].——*Spinacia* (क्षारमारिषजाति - ksháramárishajáti, San.). San. means salt spinach. Salsolaceæ, 108 [indian spinach].——*Spinifex* (कण्टकपत्रिजाति - kantakapatríjáti, San.). San. means spine + leaf. Graminaceæ, 156 [ravanan's whiskers].——*Spondias* (आम्रातकजाति - ámrátakajáti, San.). San. from (ámra, san. mango + at, san. to go); resembling mango [amrautam]. Anacardiaceæ, 45 [amrautam, otaheite apple, wild mango].——*Sponia* (जीवन्तीजाति - jívantíjáti, San.). San. from (jív, san. to live). Ulmaceæ, 120 [indian nettle].——*Stephegyne* (तोयकदंबजाति - tóyakadambajáti, San.). San. means water cadamba. Rubiaceæ, 71 [water cadamba].——*Sterculia* (विड्गन्धवृक्षजाति - vidgandhavrikshajáti, San.). San. means excrement + smell + tree [cauvalam]. Sterculiaceæ, 26 [balanghas, bastard poon, cauvalam, false kateerah, odul, piymaram, wild papaw].——*Stereospermum* (पाटलीजाति - pátalíjáti, San.). San. from (pátala, san. red) [pautalam]. Bignoniaceæ, 99 [pautalam, pauthiry, valencoorny].——*Stilpnophyllum* (ज्वलत्पत्रजाति - jvalatpatrajáti, San.). San. means shining leaf. Moraceæ, 121 [indian cautchouc].——*Strychnos* (मुष्टिजाति - mushtijáti, San.). San. from (mush, san. to kill) [mooshty]. Loganiaceæ, 89 [clearing nut, mooshty, papeeta, poison nut, snakewood tree].——*Styrax* (धूपजाति - dhúpajáti, San.). San. means incense [dhoopam]. Styraceæ, 84 [benzoin, dhoopam, storax].——*Suæda* (क्षारवृक्षजाति - ksháravrikshajáti, San.). San. from (kshára, san. salt + vriksha, san. plant). Salsolaceæ, 108 [indian salt wort].——*Swertia* (कैरातजाति - kairátajáti, San.). San. from (kiráta, san. mountaineer) [chiretta]. Gentianaceæ, 90 [chiretta].——*Symplocos* (लोध्रजाति - lódhrajáti, San.). San. from (rudh, san. to stop). Styraceæ, 84 [lodh].——*Tabernæmontana* (तगरजाति - tagarajáti, San.) [tagaram]. Apocynaceæ, 87 [tagaram].——*Tacca* (सूरणजाति - súranajáti, San.). Title from malay. San. from (súr, san. to hurt). Taccaceæ, 147 [otaheite salep].——*Tagetes* (गन्धकपुष्पजाति - gandhakapushpajáti, San.). San. from (gandhaka, san. sulphur + pushpa, san. flower). Compositæ, 74 [gendah].——*Tamarindus* (तिन्त्रिणीजाति - tintriníjáti, San.). Title from arabic. San. from (tim, san. to wet). Leguminosæ, 48 [tamarind].——*Tamarix* (झावुजाति - jhávujáti, San.). San. from (jham, san. to eat) [jhow]. Tamariscineæ, 19 [jhow].——*Tectona* (शाकजाति - shákajáti, San.). Title from malayalam. San. from (shak, san. to be able). Verbenaceæ, 102 [teak].——*Tephrosia* (शरपुंखाजाति - sharapunkhájáti, San.). San. from (shara, san. arrow + punkha, san. pinion). Leguminosæ, 48 [zanzibar indigo].——*Terminalia* (अन्त्यपर्णीजाति - antyaparníjáti, San.). San. from (anta, san. end + parna, san. leaf) [antyaparny]. Combretaceæ, 55 [antyaparny, belleric myrobalan, catapang, chebulic myrobalan, harra, murdah].——*Tetranthera* (गजपिप्पलीजाति - gajapippalíjáti, San.). San. means elephant long pepper. Lauraceæ, 111 [moida lukdy].——*Thalictrum* (पशुमारणजाति - pashumáranajáti, San.). San. from (pasbu, san. cow + márana, san. death). Ranunculaceæ, 1 [momiree].——*Thespesia* (पारिषजाति - párishajáti, San.). Malvaceæ, 25 [portia].——*Thevetia* (सुवर्णकरवीरजाति - suvarnakaravírajáti, San.). San. from (suvarna, san. gold + karavíra, san. nerium odorum, sol.); from yellow flowers. Apocynaceæ, 87 [yellow gannair].——*Thunbergia* (इन्द्रवल्लीजाति - indravallíjáti, San.). San. means indra's creeper. Acanthaceæ, 101 [indra's creeper].——*Thymus* (तुलसीभेदजाति - tulasíbhedajáti, San.). San. means basil variety. Labiatæ, 103 [ipar].——*Tiliacora* (लतामुष्टिजाति - latámushtijáti, San.). Title from bengalee. San. from (latá, san. creeper + mushti, san. strychnos nux vomica, linn.). Menispermaceæ, 5 [creeper mooshty].——*Tinospora* (गुडूचीजाति - gudúchíjáti, San.). San. from (gud, san. to protect). Menispermaceæ, 5 [goolancha].——*Toddalia* (दहनजाति - dahanajáti, San.). Title from malayalam. San. means burning. Rutaceæ, 32 [toddaly].——*Torenia* (कालदलजाति - káladalajáti, San.). San. means dark + petals. Scrophularineæ, 95 [sisparra creeper].——*Tragia* (वृश्चिकालीजाति - vrishchikálíjáti, San.). San. means scorpion's friend. Euphorbiaceæ, 118 [caunjory].——*Trapa* (शृङ्गाटकजाति - shringátakajáti, San.). San. from (shringa, san. horn + at, san. to go). Onagraceæ, 59 [singhaura].——*Trewia* (पिण्डारजाति - pindárajáti, San.). San. from (pinda, san. morsel + ri, san. to go). Euphorbiaceæ, 118 [caunchy].——*Trianthema* (सारणाजाति - sáranájáti, San.). San. means purgative. Ficoideæ, 66 [shauranay].——*Tribulus* (गोक्षुरकजाति - gókshurakajáti, San). San. means cow's hoof. Zygophylleæ, 30 [nerinjy].——*Trichodesma* (लोमग्रन्थिजाति - lómagrant'hijáti, San.). San. means hair + knot, alluding to anthers being bound to each other by hairs. Boragineæ, 92 [donkey toombay].——*Trichosanthes* (पटोलजाति - patólajáti, San.). San. from (pat, san. to encircle) [snake gourd]. Cucurbitaceæ, 62 [snake gourd].——*Trigonella* (मेथिकाजाति - mét'hikájáti, San.). Leguminosæ 48 [maitee].——*Triphasia* (चीननारङ्गजाति - chínanárangajáti, San.). San. means chinese orange. Rutaceæ, 32 [musk lime].——*Triticum* (गोधूमजाति - gódhúmajáti, San.). San. from (gudh, san. to turn, as in mill). Gramineæ, 156 [geung].——*Triumfetta* (विदेशकीशपर्णीजाति - vidéshakíshaparníjáti, San.). San. means foreign burrweed. Tiliaceæ, 27 [chikty].——*Tylophora* (मूलिनीजाति - múliníjáti, San.). San. from (múla, san. root). Asclepiadeæ, 88 [indian ipecacuanha].——*Typha* (एरकजाति - érakajáti, San.). Typhaceæ, 153 [elephant grass].——*Typhonium* (कन्दजाति - kandajáti, San.). San. means bulbous root. Araceæ, 152 [elephant yam].——*Uncaria* (पाण्डुनिर्यासवृक्षजाति - pánduniryásavrikshajáti, San.). San. means pale cutch tree. Rubiaceæ, 71 [gambier].——*Urena* (वनकार्पासीजाति - vanakárpásíjáti, San.). San. means jungle cotton. Malvaceæ, 25 [jungle cotton].——*Urginia* (वनपलाण्डुजाति - vanapalándujáti, San.). San. from (vana, san. forest + palándu, san. allium cepa, linn.). Liliaceæ, 136 [squill].——*Urtica* (तपनजाति - tapanajáti, San.). San. means burning, from stinging property. Urticaceæ, 119 [china grass].——*Vaccinium* (गोवृक्षजाति - góvrikshajáti, San.). San. means cow + tree [hill carondah]. Vaccinaceæ, 77 [hill carondah].——*Vanda* (वन्दाजाति - vandájáti, San.). Title from sanscrit. San. from (vand, san. to praise). Orchidaceæ, 141 [rasnah].——*Vateria* (धूपदाजाति - dhúpadájáti, San.). San. means incense-giving. Dipterocarpeæ, 24 [piney].——*Ventilago* (रक्तवल्लीजाति - raktavallíjáti, San.). San. from (rakta, san. red + valli, san. creeper). Rhamneæ, 41 [pappily].——*Vernonia* (अग्निबीजजाति - agnibíjajáti, San.). San. from (agni, san. fire + bíja, san. seed). Compositæ, 74 [wild jeerah].——*Vicia* (विदेशशिम्बीजाति - vidéshashimbíjáti, San.). San. means foreign bean. Leguminosæ, 48 [cabool country bean].——*Vigna* (निष्पावजाति - nishpávajáti, San.). San. from (nir, san. prefix of intensity + páva, san. winnowing). Leguminosæ, 48 [cow gram].——*Viola* (नीलपुष्पीभेदजाति - nílapushpíbhédajáti, San.). San. means dark-blue flowered variety. Violaceæ, 13 [banafshah].——*Viscum* (वृक्षरुहीजाति - vriksharuhíjáti, San.). San. means tree grower. Loranthaceæ [pilloory].——*Vitex* (सिन्दुकजाति - sindukajáti, San.). San. from (syand, san. to shed) [sindoocam]. Verbenaceæ, 102 [notchy, peacock gingelly, sindoocam].——*Vitis* (द्राक्षाजाति - drákshájáti, San.). San. from (dru, san. to run); from juice [draucshay]. Ampelideæ, 42 [angoor, draucshay, naralay, piranday, vegetable nerinjy].——*Wagatea* (वाघंटीजाति - vághantíjáti, San.). Title and San. from mahratta. Leguminosæ, 48 [wagaty].——*Walsura* (मत्स्यघातीवृक्षजाति - matsyaghátívrikshajáti, San.). San. means fish killing tree. Title corruption from teloogoo [walsoora]. Meliaceæ, 36 [walsoora].——*Webera* (कर्णिकारजाति - karnikárajáti, San.). San. means resembling ear-ring. Rubiaceæ, 71 [tiraunа].——*Wedelia* (भृंगराजजाति - bhringarájajáti, San.). San. from (bhringa, san. beetle + rájá, san. king). Compositæ, 74 [yellow bhangrah].——*Withania* (अश्वगन्धाजाति - ashvagandhájáti, San.). San. from (ashva, san. horse + gandha, san. smell). Solanaceæ, 94 [asgand].——*Woodfordia* (धातकीजाति - dhátakíjáti, San.). San. from (dhátu, san. mineral). Lythraceæ, 58 [godaury].——*Wrightia* (हयमारकजाति - hayamárakajáti, San.). San. means horsekiller [veppaulay]. Apocynaceæ, 87 [ground paulay, paula indigo, veppaulay].——*Xanthium* (अरिष्टजाति - arishtajáti, San.). San. means perfect. Compositæ, 74 [burdock datura].——*Ximenia* (कुचन्दनजाति - kuchandanajáti, San.). San. means bad sandal tree. Olacineæ, 38 [false sandal].——*Xylia* (कनकाकुलीजाति - kanakákulíjáti, San.). San. from (kanaka, san. gold + ákula, san. filled). Leguminosæ, 48 [dark vail].——*Xyris* दद्रुमारीजाति - dadrumáríjáti, San.). San. means ringworm killer. Xyridaceæ, 140 [cotchilitty].——*Yucca* (सूचीपत्रीजाति - súchípatríjáti, san.). San. means needle leaved. Liliaceæ, 136 [adam's needle].——*Zanonia* (दीर्घपत्राजाति - dírghapatrájáti, San.). San. means long leaved. Cucurbitaceæ, 62 [penarvully].——*Zanthoxylum* (तुंबुरुजाति - tumburujáti, San.). San. from (kustumbaru, san. coriander seed); from similar seeds [toomroo]. Rutaceæ, 32 [rhetsa, tejbul, toomroo].——*Zea* (यवनालजाति - yavanálajáti, San.). San. means ionian reed. Gramineæ, 156 [mecca cholum].——*Zehneria* (कृष्णबिम्बिकाजाति - krishnabimbikájáti, San.). San. means dark caper. Cucurbitaceæ, 62 [rama's caper].——*Zingiber* (आर्द्रकजाति - árdrakajáti, San.). Title from sanscrit. San. from (árdra, san. moist) [aurdracam]. Zingiberaceæ, 144 [aurdracam, cassumunar, ginger].——*Zizyphus* (बदरीजाति - badaríjáti, San.). Title from arabic. San. from (bad, san. to be firm) [badary]. Rhamneæ, 41 [badary, bair, carook vauly, sinjid].——**(5)** Title heads in this glossary cover each species clearly distinguished by the natives; vide the cross references in square brackets in the key-synopsis, or the same at the end of each item in the above lists of orders and genera, or the small-type cross-references at end of this volume.——**(6)** The abbreviations of names of botanical authors used in this article and throughout the volume are the same as those given in standard works on that subject, and need not be here explained.——**(7)** The following items show the suffixes and prefixes, especially Dravidian, by adding which to the verbal root expressing the abstract name of the plant, the structural division to which the plant belongs, the part of the plant, the product from the plant, or the variety of the plant, may be indicated; as stated in the remarks under the first section above.——

Aerial-root (پارمبی - párambí, Hind.; ಊಡೆ - úde, Can.; ఊడ - úda, Tel.; വിഴുതു - vizhutu, Mal.; விழுது - vizhuthu, Tam.). Adventitious roots given off by climbing or erect stems; as in pepper [black pepper], banyan [q.v.] and screw-pine [q.v.]. Plant-part suffix.——*Bark* (वल्कल - valkala, San.; چھال - chhál, Hind.; ಪಟ್ಟೆ - patte, Can.; పట్ట - patta, Tel.; തൊലി - toli, Mal.; பட்டை - pattai, Tam.). Outer integuments of plant beyond the wood and formed of tissue parallel with it. Only true bark is that of exogens. Plant-plant suffix [bark, puttay].——*Berry* (वीजफल - víjap'hala, San.; دانہ - dánah, Hind.; ಕಾಯಿ - káyi, Can.; కాయ - káya, Tel.; കായ - káya, Mal.; சிறுகாய் - shirugáy, Tam.). Succulent seed vessel, filled with pulp in which seeds are immersed; as in solanum [cooly]. Plant-part suffix.——*Bitter* (तिक्त - tikta, San.; کڑوا - karvá, Hind.; ಖಯ್ಯಿ - khayyi, Can.; చేదు - chédu, Tel.; കൈപ്പു - kaippu, Mal.; கசப்பு - kasappu, Tam.). Descriptive prefix.——*Black* (कृष्ण - krishna, San.; کالا - kálá, Hind.; ಕಪ್ಪು kappu, Can.; నల్ల - nalla, Tel.; കറുപ്പു - karuppu, Mal.; கருப்பு - karuppu, Tam.). Descriptive prefix [calam, car, caroo, caulam, krishna, nulla].——*Blossom* (पुष्प - pushpa, San.; پھول - phúl, Hind.; ಹೂವು - húvu, Can.; పువ్వు - puvvu, Tel.; പൂവു - púvu, Mal.; பூ - pú, Tam.). Plant-part suffix [phool, poo, pooshpam].——*Blue* (नील - níla, San.; نیلا - nílá, Hind.; ನೀಲ - níla, Can.; నీలి - níli, Tel.; നീലം - nílam, Mal.; நீலம் - nílam, Tam.). Terms often stand for purple. Descriptive prefix [neel, oodah].——*Bud* (कलिका - kaliká, San.; کلی - kallí, Hind.; ಮೊಗ್ಗೆ - mogge, Can.; మొగ్గ - mogga, Tel.; മൊട്ടു - mottu, Mal.; அரும்பு - arumbu, Tam.). Elementary folded leaves or flowers. Plant-part suffix.——*Bulb* (कन्द - kanda, San.; گڈّہ - gaddah, Hind.; ಗಡ್ಡೆ - gadde, Can.; గడ్డ - gadda, Tel.; കിഴങ്ങു - kizhannu, Mal.; கிழங்கு - kizhangu, Tam.). Underground buds, resembling roots, and consisting of scales placed one over the other. Plant-part suffix [doompa, gadda].——*Bunch of fruit* (स्तबक - stabaka, San.; خوشہ - khoshah, Hind.; ಗೊನೆ - gone, Can.; గొల - gola, Tel.; കുല - kula, Mal.; குலை - kulai, Tam.). Same terms for bunches of flowers. Plant-part suffix.——*Bunch of plantains* (چیپ - chíp, Hind.; చీపు - chípu, Tel.; ചീർപ്പു - chírppu, Mal.; சீப்பு - shíppu, Tam.). Plant-part suffix.——*Bush* (गुल्म - gulma, San.; جھاڑی - jhárí, Hind.; ಹೊದರು - hodaru, Can.; పొద - poda, Tel.; പടർപ്പു - patarppu, Mal.; புதர் - puthar, Tam.). A shrub with branches rising from near the root. Suffix showing structural division.——*Capsule* (वीजकोशी - víjakóshí, San.; بونڈا - bondá, Hind.; ಕಾಯಿ - káyi, Can.; కాయ - káya, Tel.; കായ - káya, Mal.; காய் - káy, Tam.). Dry dehiscent seed-vessel or fruit; as cotton [indian cotton], camellia [tea]. Plant-part suffix.——*Cluster* (गुच्छ - guchha, San.; خوشہ - khoshah, Hind.; ಗೊಂಚಲು - gonchalu, Can.; గుత్తి - gutti, Tel.; കുല - kula, Mal.; கொத்து -kottu, Tam.). Plant-part suffix [cott].——*Country* (देश - désha, San.; ناٹ - nát, Hind.; ನಾಡು - nádu, Can.; నాటు - nátu, Tel.; നാട് - nátu, Mal.; நாடு - nádu, Tam.). Indigenous. Descriptive prefix [country, indian, naud].——*Creeper* (लता - latá, San.; بیل - bel, Hind.; ಬಳ್ಳಿ - balli, Can.; తీగె - tíge, Tel.; വള്ളി - valli, Mal.; கொடி - kodi, Tam.). A plant which grows, as a vine [angoor], clinging to ground or other means for support; stems emit roots at their nodes. Suffix showing structural division [cody, vally].——*Drupe* (अष्ठिफल - asht'hip'hala, San.; گٹھلی دار پھل - guthlídárphal, Hind.; ವಾಟೇಹಣ್ಣು - vátéhannu, Can.; ముట్టెపండు - muttepandu, Tel.; അണ്ടിക്കായ - antikkáya, Mal.; கொட்டைக்காய் - kottaikkáy, Tam.). Succulent fleshy fruit, with a hard.

shelled seed; as mango [q.v.] and almond [baudam]. Plant-part suffix.——*Dry* (शुष्क - shushka, San.; سوکھا - súkhá, Hind.; ಒಣ - ona, Can.; ఎండు - endu, Tel.; ഉണങ്ങിയ - unanniya, Mal.; காய்ந்த - káynda, Tam.). Descriptive prefix.——*Dry twig* (समित् - samit, San.; سوکھی ڈالی - súkhídálí, Hind.; ಚಿದುಗು - chidugu, Can.; చిదుగు - chidugu, Tel.; ചുള്ളി - chulli, Mal.; சுள்ளி - shulli, Tam.). Plant-part suffix [samit].——*Fibre* (तन्तु - tantu, San.; نار - nár, Hind.; ನಾರು - náru, Can.; నార - nára, Tel.; നാർ - nár, Mal.; நார் - nár, Tam.). Plant-product suffix [naur].——*Flour* (पिष्ट - pishta, San.; آٹا - átá, Hind.; ಹಿಟ್ಟು - hittu, Can.; పిండి - pindi, Tel.; പൊടി - poti, Mal.; மாவு - mávu, Tam.). Plant-product suffix.——*Flower* (पुष्प - pushpa, San.; پھول - phúl, Hind.; ಹೂವು - húvu, Can.; పువ్వు - puvvu, Tel.; പൂവു - púvu, Mal.; பூ - pú, Tam.). Assemblage of organs in a plant, of which stamens or pistils or both form part. Plant-part suffix [phool, poo, pooshpam].——*Flower-sheath* (पुष्पपुट - pushpaputa, San.; ಹೊಂಬಾಳೆ - hombále, Can.; പാള - pála, Mal.; பாளை - pálai, Tam.). Spathe. Encloses stamen and pistil when young and expanding exposes them to view when fully formed. Plant-part suffix.——*Foliage* (पर्ण - parna, San.; پتے - patte, Hind.; ಎಲೆ - ele, Can.; ఆకు - áku, Tel.; തഴ - tazha, Mal.; தழை - tazhai, Tam.). Plant-part suffix.——*Foreign* (विदेशीय - vidéshíya, San.; ولایتی - viláití, Hind.; ಶೀಮೆ - shíme, Can.; సీమ - síma, Tel.; വിലാത്തി - vilátti, Mal.; சீமை - shímai, Tam.). Descriptive prefix [europe, furanghee, firangy, parangy, seema, vilauyaty].——*Fruit* (फल - p'hala, San.; پھل - phal, Hind.; ಹಣ್ಣು - hannu, Can.; పండు - pandu, Tel.; പഴം - pazham, Mal.; பழம் - pazham, Tam.). Any seed-vessel. Plant-part suffix [palam, pazham].——*Garden* (आराम - áráma, San.; باغ - bágh, Hind.; ತೋಟ - tóta, Can.; తోట - tóta, Tel.; തോട്ടം - tóttam, Mal.; தோட்டம் - tóttam, Tam.). Descriptive prefix [baugh, maulee, tote, tope].——*Grass* (तृण - trina, San.; گھاس - ghás, Hind.; ಹುಲ್ಲು - hullu, Can.; కసువు - kasuvu, Tel.; പുല്ല് - pullu, Mal.; புல்லு - pullu, Tam.). An endogenous plant having simple leaves, a stem generally jointed and tubular, a husky calyx called glume, and the seed single. Suffix showing structural division [ghaus, pill].——*Green* (हरित - harita, San.; کچا - kaççá, Mal.; ಹಸರು - hasaru, Can.; పచ్చ - pattsa, Tel.; പച്ച - paçça, Mal.; பச்சை - paççai, Tam.). That is to say fresh. Descriptive prefix [haritam, putchay].——*Greens* (शाक - sháka, San.; ساگ - ság, Hind.; ಸೊಪ್ಪು - soppu, Can.; కూర - kúra, Tel.; ചീര - chíra, Mal.; கீரை - kírai, Tam.). Any leafy esculents; as cabbages [kobee]. Plant-product suffix [keeray].——*Gum* (निर्यास - niryása, San.; گوند - gond, Hind.; ಗೋಂದು - góndu, Can.; బంక - banka, Tel.; പശ - pasha, Mal.; பிசின் - pisin, Tam.). Plant-product suffix [gond, gum].——*Heart-wood* (کھیر - khair, Hind.; ಶೇಗು - shégu, Can.; చేవ - chéva, Tel.; കാതൽ - kátal, Mal.; சேகு - shégu, Tam.). Central part of the timber of exogens hardened or altered by age. Plant-part suffix.——*Herbaceous plant* (ओषधि - óshadhi, San.; بوٹی - búti, Hind.; ಮೂಲಿಕೆ - múlike, Can.; మూలిక - múlika, Tel.; ചെടി - chéti, Mal.; பூண்டு - púndu, Tam.). Plant with soft succulent stems or stalks which die to the root every year; of herbaceous plants, some are annual stem and root, some are biennial existing two years, others perennial existing for many years by their roots retaining vitality. Suffix showing structural division [poond].——*Hill* (पर्वत - parvata, San.; پہاڑی - pahári, Hind.; ಬೆಟ್ಟ - betta, Can.; కొండ - konda, Tel.; മല - mala, Mal.; மலை - malai, Tam.). That is to say growing on hills. Descriptive prefix [condah, hill, mala, pahaur, parvatam].——*Kernel* (बीजगर्भ - bíjagarbha, San.; چارولی - chárúlí, Hind.; ಪಪ್ಪು - pappu, Can.; పప్పు - pappu, Tel.; പരിപ്പ് - parippu, Mal.; பருப்பு - paruppu, Tam.). Plant-part suffix.——*Large* (महा - mahá, San.; بڑا - bará, Hind.; ದೊಡ್ಡ - dodda, Can.; పెద్ద - pedda, Tel.; വലിയ - valiya, Mal.; பெரிய - periya, Tam.). Descriptive prefix [maha, pedda, per].——*Leaf* (पत्र - patra, San.; پتا - pattá, Hind.; ಎಲೆ - ele, Can.; ఆకు - áku, Tel.; ഇല - ila, Mal.; இலை - ilai, Tam.). Plant-part suffix [patram].——*Leaf-bud* (पत्रपुट - patraputa, San.; چگر - chugur, Hind.; ಚಿಗುರು - chiguru, Can.; చిగురు - chiguru, Tel.; തളിർ - talir, Mal.; துளிர் - tulir, Tam.). Bud producing leaves. Plant-part suffix.——*Milk* (क्षीर - kshíra, San.; دودھ - dúdh, Hind.; ಹಾಲು - hálu, Can.; పాలు - pálu, Tel.; പാൽ - pál, Mal.; பால் - pál, Tam.). Milky juice. Plant-product suffix.——*Nut* (अष्टि - asht'hi, San.; گٹھلی - guthlí, Hind.; ವಾಟೆ - váto, Can.; గింజ - gindza, Tel.; കുരു - kuru, Mal.; கொட்டை - kottai, Tam.). Otherwise Achene, Glans. Hard indehiscent fruit containing only one seed. Plant-part suffix [cottay].——*Oil* (तैल - taila, San.; تیل - tel, Hind.; ಎಣ್ಣೆ - enne, Can.; నూనె - núne, Tel.; എണ്ണ - enna, Mal.; எண்ணெய் - enney, Tam.). Plant-product suffix [teilam, yennay].——*Pistil* (स्त्रैणकेसर - strainakésara, San.; ಹೂದಿಂಡು - húdindu, Can.; దిమ్మె - dimme, Tel.; அல்லித்தாள் - allittál, Tam.). The female part of a flower; consisting of ovary, style, stigma and ovules. Plant-part suffix.——*Pith* (گودا - gúdá, Hind.; ತಿರುಳು - tiralu, Can.; దవ్వ - davva, Tel.; ചോറ് - chóru, Mal.; சோறு - shóru, Tam.). The central column of cellular matter over which the wood is formed in exogens. Plant-part suffix.——*Plant* (उद्भिज्ज - udbhijja, San.; نبات - nabát, Hind.; ಗಿಡ - gida, Can.; చెట్టు - chettu, Tel.; ചെടി - cheti, Mal.; செடி - shedi, Tam.). Includes every thing which has vegetable life. General suffix.——*Pod* (शमी - shamí, San.; پھلی - phallí, Hind.; ಕಾಯಿ - káyi, Can.; కాయ - káya, Tel.; കായ - káya, Mal.; காய் - káy, Tam.). Seed-case of leguminous and cruciferous plants. Plant-part suffix [coy].——*Pollen* (पुष्परजस् - pushparajas, San.; زیرہ - zírah, Hind.; ಹೂವಿನಪುಡಿ - huvinapudi, Can.; పుప్పొడి - puppodi, Tel.; പൂപ്പൊടി - púppoti, Mal.; பூந்தூள் - púndúl, Tam.). The powdery or other matter usually contained in the cells of an anther by action of which on the stigma the fertilization of the ovules is accomplished. Plant-part suffix.——*Pulp* (مغز - maghz, Hind.; ಗೊಜ್ಜು - gojju, Can.; గుజ్జు - guddzu, Tel.; കഴമ്പ് - kazhampu, Mal.; சதை - shathai, Tam.). Juicy tissue found in the interior of plants. Plant-part suffix.——*Red* (रक्त - rakta, San.; لال - lál, Hind.; ಕೆಂಪು - kempu, Can.; ఎర్ర - erra, Tel.; ചൊവന്ന - chovanna, Mal.; சிவப்பு - shivappu, Tam.). Descriptive prefix [chem, laul, ractam, shem].——*Rhizome* (शिफा - ship'há, San.; بیکھ - bíkh, Hind.; ಗಡ್ಡೆ - gaddo, Can.; గడ్డ - gadda, Tel.; മൂലം - múlam, Mal.; அடிவேர் - adivér, Tam.). Prostrate or subterranean stem, emitting leaves at the growing point, and rootlets along the under surface. Plant-part suffix.——*Rind* (छल्ली - chhallí, San.; پوست - post, Hind.; ಸಿಪ್ಪೆ - shippe, Can.; తోలు - tólu, Tel.; തൊലി - toti, Mal.; தோல் - tól, Tam.). The external coat of a nut. Plant-part suffix.——*Root* (मूल - múla, San.; جڑ - jar, Hind.; ಬೇರು - béru, Can.; వేరు - véru, Tel.; വേർ - vér, Mal.; வேர் - vér, Tam.). Subterranean or descending axis of a plant. Plant-part suffix [moolam].——*Sapling* (वृक्षक - vrikshaka, San.; شاخ - shákh, Hind.; ಸೊಸಿ - sosi, Can.; అంటు - antu, Tel.; തൈ - tai, Mal.; போத்து - póttu, Tam.). Suffix showing structural division.——*Seed* (बीज - bíja, San.; بینج - bínj, Hind.; ಬೀಜ - bíja, Can.; విత్తు - vittu, Tel.; വിത്ത് - vittu, Mal.; விரை - virai, Tam.). Independent reproductive body containing an embryo or new plant when cast off by the parent. Plant-part suffix [viray].——*Shoot* (किसल - kisala, San.; کونپل - konpal, Hind.; ಚಿಗುರು - chiguru, Can.; చిగురు - chiguru, Tel.; തെളിർ - telir, Mal.; கொழுந்து - kozhundu, Tam.). Plant-part suffix.——*Shrub* (क्षुप - kshupa, San.; چھوٹا جھاڑ - chhotájhár, Hind.; ಗಿಡ - gida, Can.; చెట్టు - chettu, Tel.; ചെടി - cheti, Mal.; சிறுசெடி - shirusedi, Tam.). Differs from herbaceous plant, in consequence of ligneous character. Is less than a tree, having several permanent woody stems dividing from the bottom. Is not unlike a tree as to length of duration, but seldom rises higher than twelve feet. Divided into two classes, deciduous and evergreen. Deciduous are such as lose their foliage entirely at certain seasons, evergreen retaining the foliage until the new appears when it gradually falls off. Suffix showing structural division.——*Side-root* (بازو کی جڑ - bázúkíjar, Hind.; ಬದಿಬೇರು - badibéru, Can.; పక్కవేరు - pakkavéru, Tel.; பக்கவேர் - pakkavér, Tam.). Plant-part suffix.——*Small* (क्षुद्र - kshudra, San.; چھوٹا - chhotá, Hind.; ಚಿಕ್ಕ - chikka, Can.; చిన్న - chinna, Tel.; ചെറിയ - cheriya, Mal.; சிறு - shiru, Tam.). Descriptive prefix.——*Sour* (आम्ल - amla, San.; کھٹا - khattá, Hind.; ಹುಳಿ - huli, Can.; పులుసు - pulusu, Tel.; പുളി - puli, Mal.; புளிப்பு - pulippu, Tam.). Descriptive prefix [pooly].——*Spathe* (पुष्पपुट - pushpaputa, San.; پھول کا پالا - phúlkápálá, Hind.; ಹೊಂಬಾಳೆ - hombále, Can.; പാള - pála, Mal.; பாளை - pálai, Tam.). Flower-sheath. Plant-part suffix.——*Spirit* (सुरा - surá, San.; شراب - sharáb, Hind.; ಸಾರಾಯಿ - sáráyi, Can.; సారాయి - sáráyi, Tel.; ചാരായം - cháráyam, Mal.; சாராயம் - sháráyam, Tam.). See Sharaub. Plant-product suffix.——*Sprout* (अंकुर - ankura, San.; موڑکا - morká, Hind.; ಮೊಳೆ - mole, Can.; మొలక - molaku, Tel.; മുള - mula, Mal.; முளை - mulai, Tam.). A shoot from the seed or from the stump or root of a plant. Plant part suffix.——*Stamen* (पौरुषकेसर - paurushakésara, San.; پھول کی ڈنڈی - phúlkídandí, Hind.; ದಿಂಡು - dindu, Can.; దిమ్మె - dimme, Tel.; അല്ലി - alli, Mal.; அல்லி - alli, Tam.). The organ of the flower to which the pollen belongs. Plant-part suffix.——*Stem* (काण्ड - kánda, San.; پیڑ - per, Hind.; ಕಾಮು - kámu, Can.; కాడ - káda, Tel.;

തണ്ട - tandu, Mal.; தண்டு - tandu, Tam.). The part of a plant which bears or has borne leaves or their rudiments; the ascending axis of growth. Plant-part suffix.——*Stone-fruit* (आष्ट्रिफल - asht'hip'hala, San.; گٹھلی دارپھل - guthlídárphal, Hind.; ವಾಟೆಹಣ್ಣು - vátéhannu, Can.; ముట్టెపండు - muttepandu, Tel.; അണ്ടിക്കായ - antikkáya, Mal.; கொட்டைக்காய் - kottaikkáy, Tam.). Fruit with a hard body in it, which is produced by the ossification of the endocarp or lining of fruit. Plant-part suffix.——*Sweet* (मधुर - madhura, San.; میٹھا - míthá, Hind.; ಶೀಯಾಡ - shíyáda, Can.; తియ్యని - tiyyani, Tel.; മധുരം - madhuram, Mal.; தித்திப்பு - tittippu, Tam.). Descriptive prefix.——*Tap-root* (اصل جڑ - asljar, Hind.; ನಡುಬೇರು - nadubéru, Can.; కుంకటివేరు - kunkativéru, Tel.; ആണിവേർ - ánivér, Mal.; ஆணிவேர் - ánivér, Tam.). Simple conical root with branches growing from it. Plant-part suffix.——*Thorn* (कण्टक - kantaka, San.; کانٹا - kántá, Hind.; ಮುಳ್ಳು - mullu, Can.; ముల్లు - mullu, Tel.; മുൾ - mul, Mal.; முள்ளு - mullu, Tam.). Strongly pointed extremity of branch abortive petiole or abortive peduncle. Plant-part suffix [mooll].——*Tree* (वृक्ष - vriksha, San.; جھاڑ - jhár, Hind.; ಮರ - mara, Can.; మాను - mánu, Tel.; മരം - maram, Mal.; மரம் - maram, Tam.). Plant which is woody, branched and perennial; like a shrub, but of larger size, generally exceeding ten feet in height; and of a single stock instead of a cluster. Suffix showing structural division [maram].——*Tuber* (कन्द - kanda, San.; گڈّہ - gaddah, Hind.; ಗಡ್ಡೆ - gadda, Can.; గడ్డ - gadda, Tel.; കിഴങ്ങ് - kizhannu, Mal.; கிழங்கு - kizhangu, Tam.). Roundish underground succulent stem covered with buds from which new plants or tubers grow. Plant-part suffix.——*Twig* (उपशाख - upashák'ha, San.; پھانٹا - pháutá, Hind.; ಚಿಡುಗು - chidugu, Can.; చిడుగు - chidugu, Tel.; ചുള്ളി - chulli, Mal.; கழி - kazhi, Tam.). Plant-part suffix.——*Unripe fruit* (शलाटु - shalátu, San.; ناپختہ - nápukhtah, Hind.; ಕಾಯಿ - káyi, Can.; కాయ - káya, Tel.; പച്ചക്കായ - paççakkáya, Mal.; காய் - káy, Tam.). Plant-part suffix [coy].——*White* (श्वेत - shvéta, San.; سفید - sufed, Hind.; ಬಿಳಿ - bili, Can.; తెల్ల - tella, Tel.; വെള്ള - vella, Mal.; வெள்ளை - vellai, Tam.). Descriptive prefix [shwetam, vel].——*Wild* (अरण्य - aranya, San.; جنگلی - janglí, Hind.; ಕಾಡು - kádu, Can.; అడవి - adavi, Tel.; കാട്ട് - káttu, Mal.; காட்டு - káttu, káttu, Tam.). Not cultivated. Descriptive prefix [caud, jungle].——*Yellow* (पीत - pita, San.; پیلا - pílá, Hind.; ಹಳದಿ - haladi, Can.; పసుపు - pasupu, Tel.; മഞ്ഞ - maññа. Mal.; மஞ்சள் - mañjal, Tam.). Descriptive prefix [munjal].——*Young fruit* (پندا - pindá, Hind.; ಕಸುಗಾಯಿ - kasugáyi, Can.; పిందె - pinde, Tel.; ഇളങ്കായ - ilankáya, Mal.; பிஞ்சு - piñju, Tam.). Plant-part suffix.——

(8) The following items show the vernacular equivalents of leading terms connected with the principal divisions of botany.——*Acrogen* (अग्रेरुह - agréruha, San.). Sub-division of the cryptogamic plants [vanaspaty], or acotyledons; comprising equisetaceæ, ferns [parny], mosses [pacsy], &c.——*Annual* (वार्षिक - várshika, San.). Plants that flower, perfect their seeds and perish in the same season.——*Biennial* (द्विवार्षिक - dvivárshika, San.). Plants which require two years to develop their growth and then decay.——*Class* (वर्ग - varga, San.). Above order.——*Endogen* (अन्तरुह - antarruha, San.). Growing by addition of new wood to centre of the stem. Monocotyledonous flowering plants, such as grasses [ghaus, pill], palms [taulam], lilies [indian water lily], &c., with simple veined leaves, seeds with one cotyledon, and the wood if any not in concentric layers.——*Exogen* (बाह्यरुह - báhyaruha, San.). Growing by addition of outer parts of the stem. The same as dicotyledonous.——*Family* (कुल - kula, San.). Above genus.——*Flora* (वृक्ष - vriksha, San.). In latin, the goddess of flowers. The whole collection of plants inhabiting a given geographical area.——*Genus* (जाति - játi, San.). Above species.——*Habitat* (स्थान - st'hána, San.). The situation in which a plant grows in a wild state.——*Kingdom* (गण - gana, San.). Above class.——*Order* (सन्तान - santána, San.). Above family.——*Perennial* (दृढमूल - dridhamúla, San.). Plants growing for many seasons and flowering annually; their roots remain alive for a series of years. Perennials have herbaceous stems which continue yearly to flower and decay. A plant considered annual in a northern climate is in many cases biennial or even perennial in this; on the other hand perennials of the tropics often become annuals in a northern climate.——*Species* (भेद - bhéda, San.). Above variety.——*Sub-class* (उपवर्ग - upavarga, San.). Between class and order.——*Sub-family* (उपकुल - upakula, San.). Between family and genus.——*Sub-genus* (उपजाति - upajáti, San.). Between genus and species.——*Sub-kingdom* (उपगण - upagana, San.). Between kingdom and class.——*Sub-order* (उपसन्तान - upasantána, San.). Between order and family.——*Sub-species* (उपभेद - upabhéda, San.). Same as variety.——*Variety* (प्रभेद - prabhéda, San.). Same as sub-species.

VRIDDHAUCHELLAM (விருத்தாச்சலம் - viruttáççalam, *Tam.* vriddháchalam*). From (vriddha, san. ancient + achala, san. mountain) [vrih]. Tam. also (pazhamalai), meaning old hill; also (muthugunram), meaning same. Sanscrit name (vriddhakáshi), means ancient + benares city; also (vriddhagiri), meaning old hill or the first hill on earth.——**(1)** Talook, South arcot district. Tahsildar's pay Rs. 200; area 596 square miles; pop. 222,793. Language Tamul. S. of district. Boundaries:—N. Tricaloro and Cullacoorchy talooks, S. Oodayarpolliem and Perambalore talooks in Trichinopoly district, E. Cuddalore and Chidambaram talooks, W. Cullacoorchy talook and Ahtoor talook of Salem district and Perambalore in Trichinopoly district. Physical aspect generally flat. Black cotton [regar] and red soil. Manufacture of cumblies [q.v.] and coarse cloth. Irrigation from five anicuts [q.v.] and many tanks [q.v.]. Camping grounds are Cazhoothore and Tozhoothore. Places of archæological interest:—Coogeiyore, Gopaulpooram, Mangalore, Nulloor, Pennaudam, Tirvadatoray, Tittagoody, Tozhoothore, Vriddhauchellam. Principal trig. stations:—Caunauthacundaun, Covilancooppam, Sheppalanuttam. The principal places, &c., in the talook are the following.——*Caunauthacundaun* (கானுதகண்டான் - kánáthagandán, Tam.). Means he who has seen the unseen. Trig. station; lat. 11° 33′ 12·92″; long. 79° 23′ 49·70″; height 240 feet; from Gopoorapooram S.E. 1¼ miles; from Vriddhauchellam N.E. 3 miles.——*Cosappullam* (கொசப்பள்ளம் - kosappallam, Tam.). From (kusavan, tam. a potter + pallam, tam. valley). Pop. 481; acres 561; lat. 11° 25′; long. 79° 19′; from Cuddalore S.W 40 miles; from Vriddhauchellam S.S.W. 8 miles. The great Pelandoray [q.v.] anicut is in the vicinity.——*Covilancooppam* (கோவிலாங்குப்பம் - kóvilánguppam, Tam.). From (kóvilán, tam. priest + kuppam, tam. village). Trig. station; lat. 11° 37′ 17·09″; long. 79° 26′ 30·80″; height 323 feet; from Manacollay S.E. 1½ miles; from Vriddhauchellam N.E. 10 miles.——*Gomookhanuddy* (கோமுகநதி - kómuganathi, Tam.). See sep. title.——*Gopoorapooram* (கோபுராப்புரம் - kóburáppuram, Tam.). From (gópura, san. tower + pura, san. town). Pop. 927; acres 478; lat. 11° 34′; long. 79° 23′; from Cuddalore W.S.W. 30 miles; from Vriddhauchellam N.N.E. 4 miles. Shiva [q.v.] temple [coil] with inscriptions.——*Mangalore* (மங்களூர் - mangalúr, Tam.). From (mangala, san. prosperity + úr, tam. village). Pop. 2,391; acres 5,143; lat. 11° 31′; long. 79° 03′; from Cuddalore W.S.W. 53 miles; from Vriddhauchellam W. 21 miles. Large Shiva [q.v.] temple [q.v.].——*Manimooctah* (மணிமுத்தா - manimuttá, Tam.). See sep. title.——*Mehmatore* (மேமாத்தூர் - mémáttúr, Tam.). From (mél, tam. west + máttúr, tam. village, so called). Pop. 400; acres 1,705; lat. 11° 34′; long. 79° 16′; from Cuddalore W.S.W. 38 miles; from Vriddhauchellam N.W. 7 miles. Site of an anicut [q.v.] across the Manimooctah nuddy.——*Mungalampett* (மங்கலம்பேட்டை - mangalambéttai, Tam.). From (mangala, san. prosperity + péttai, tam. village). Pop. 1,705; area in acres 777; lat. 11° 38′; long. 79° 19′; from Cuddalore W.S.W. 33 miles; from Vriddhauchellam N. 8 miles. Buffalo [khoolgah] sacrifices are made to the village goddess [grauma devatay].——*Nulloor* (நல்லூர் - nallúr, Tam.). From (nal, tam. good + úr, tam. town). Pop. 845; acres 1,099; lat. 11° 34′; long. 79° 14′; from Cuddalore W.S.W. 40 miles; from Vriddhauchellam W.N.W. 10 miles. At the confluence of the Manimooctah and Mayooram. Old Shiva temple.——*Paroor* (பரூர் - parúr, Tam.). From (paru, tam. great + úr, tam. village). Pop. 5,971; acres 5,572; lat. 11° 34′; long. 79° 18′; from Cuddalore S.W. 36 miles; from Vriddhauchellam N.W. 6 miles. Interesting on account of the fossil beds of the Upper green sand and Gault formation found in the neighbourhood, generally known as the Trichinopoly deposit.——*Pelandoray* (பெலாந்துறை - pelándurai, Tam.). See sep. title.——*Pennaudam* (பெண்ணாடம் - pennádam, Tam.). From (pennai, tam. palmyra, borassus flabelliformis, linn. + kadam tam. garden). Sanscrit name (pushpáranyapura), meaning flower + garden + town. Pop. 3,599; acres 1,631; lat. 11° 25′; long. 79° 17′; from Cuddalore S.W. 42 miles; from Vriddhauchellam S.S.W. 9 miles. Old Shiva [q.v.] temple [coil] with inscriptions.——*Potramungalam* (போத்திரமங்கலம் - póttiramangalam, Tam.). From (pótti, tam. rivalry + tiru, tam. holy + mangala, san. prosperity); village erected in rivalry. Sanscrit name (pótrímangala), meaning boar + prosperity. Pop. 1,139; acres 1,519; lat. 11° 24′; long. 79° 12′; from Cuddalore S.W. 46 miles; from Vriddhauchellam S.W. 13 miles. The Bramins of this village call themselves Iyengars [q.v.], but are not recognised by the other Iyengars of Southern india.——*Rajendraputnam* (இராசேந்திரப்பட்டணம் - irásendirappattanam, Tam.). From (rájá, san. king + indra, san. lord + pattana, san. city); called after a person of that name. Pop. 315; acres 901; lat 11° 26′; long. 79° 24′; from Cuddalore S.W. 34 miles; from Vriddhauchellam S.S.E. 6 miles. At the extreme south of the district. Formerly belonged to Trichinopoly district, and was head-quarters of a sub-Magistrate. Transferred to South arcot with nine other villages in 1882. Shiva temple.——*Sheppalanuttam* (சேப்பளாநத்தம் - shéppalánattam, Tam.). From (shé tam. high + pulam, tam. high arable land + nattam,

tam., village). Trig. station; lat. 11° 32′ 35·57″; long. 79° 33′ 44·97″; height 129 feet; from Managathy E.N.E. 1 mile; from Vriddhauchellam E. 13 miles.——*Shirpaukam* (சிருப்பாக்கம் - shiruppákkam, Tam.). From (shiru, tam. small + pákkam, tam. village). Pop. 3,009; acres 4,378; lat. 11° 33′; long. 79° 02′; from Cuddalore W.S.W. 54 miles; from Vriddhauchellam W.N.W. 23 miles. On the route from Trichinopoly to Arcot.——*Teppoodayore* (தெப்புடையூர் - téppudayúr, Tam.). From (té, tam. deity + pudai, tam. snake-hole + úr, tam. village). Tam. also (pudayúr), meaning same. Pop. 362; acres 2,184; lat. 11° 30′; long. 79° 15′; from Cuddalore W.S.W. 41 miles; from Vriddhauchellam W. 8 miles. Large Shiva temple.——*Tittagoody* (திட்டக்குடி - tittakkudi, Tam.). See sep. title.——*Vasishtapooram* (வசிட்டப்புரம் - vasittappuram, Tam.). From (vasisht'ha, san. rishi so called + pura, san. city). Pop. 4,188; acres 1,083; lat. 11° 24′; long. 79° 10′; from Cuddalore W.S.W. 48 miles; from Vriddhauchellam S.W. 15 miles. Vishnoo [q.v.] temple worshipped by rishy [q.v.] Vasishtan [q.v.].——*Velancoolam* (வேளாங்குளம் - vélángulam, Tam.). From (vélán, tam. a potter + kulam, tam. tank). Pop. 3,892; acres 2,591; lat. 11° 36′; long. 79° 30′; from Cuddalore W.S.W. 22 miles; from Vriddhauchellam N.E. 11 miles. Large village inhabited by merchants and money lenders.——*Vellaur* (வெள்ளாறு - velláru, Tam.). See sep. title.——*Vriddhauchellam* (விருத்தாசலம் - viruttáççalam, Tam.). See below.——**(2)** Town, Head-quarters of talook and Head assistant collector; South arcot dist., Vriddhauchellam tal.; pop. 7,893, acres 1,914; lat. 11° 31′; long. 79° 22′; height 205 feet; from Chidambaram W.N.W. 26 miles; from Cuddalore W.S.W. 33 miles; from Madras S.S.W. 126 miles; from Tindivanam S.S.W. 54 miles; from Tricalore S.S.E. 32 miles. On the Manimooctah. First head-quarters of the Zillah court of the district. Being on road from Cuddalore to Trichinopoly, it was of importance as a strategical point in wars of Carnatic [q.v.]. In 1751 taken from Chunda sahib by the English; in same year invested by troops of neighbouring poligar [q.v.] who was driven off by an English force proceeding to Trichinopoly; 1753 the garrison consisting of only 50 sepoys [q.v.] surrendered to Hassan ally who had been sent by Dupleix; in 1760 Major Monson recaptured the fort. Vriddhauchellam is a sacred town, and many legends are connected with it. Large fortified temple [coil]. An annual fair is held called Maushimagham [pundigay, 5b] on the last day of which Pariah [q.v.] widows whose husbands died during preceding year formally remove their talees [q.v.]. There is a Tamul proverb:—விருத்தாசலம் போனால் திரட்பாவம் போகும்—"pilgrimage to vriddhauchellam will expiate accumulated sins." There are sandstone [manal cull] quarries.

VRIH (वृह् - vrih, San.). To grow——*Vricsham* (वृक्ष - vriksha, San.). See sep. title.——*Vriddham* (वृद्ध - vriddha, San.). From (vridh, san. to grow).——*Vriddhauchellam* (वृद्धाचल - vriddháchala, San.). From (vriddha, san. ancient + achala, san. hill). See sep. title.——*Vriddhauchella moorty* (वृद्धाचलमूर्ति - vriddháchalamúrti, San.). From (vriddháchala, san. the place so called + múrti, san. embodiment, deity). Shiva at Vriddhauchellam.——*Vriddhy* (वृद्धि - vriddhi, San.). From (vridh, san. to increase). Increase, especially of money interest [palisha]. Chuckravriddhy, from (chakra, san. wheel), is compound interest. Shikhay vriddhy, from (shikhá, san. a lock of hair, as growing continually), is interest at a usurious rate. Vriddhy is also a grammatical term for the increase of vowels [ooyir, varnamaulay] under certain conditions.——*Vriddhyaurgham* (वृद्ध्यार्घ - vriddhyárgha, San.). From (vriddha, san. old + argha, san. price). In calendar [punchaungam] the time favourable for agricultural operations [vellaumay]. For unfavourable time see Shoonyaurgham.——*Vrihat* (वृहत् - vrihat, San.). From (vrih, san. to grow). Great [brihat].

VROOTTAM (விருத்தம் - viruttam, *Tam.*). From (vritta, san. round). Expanded; applied to verse. This is the metre in which all the great poetical narrations are composed. It is divided into several kinds, all of which contain four lines. Specimens in Chintaumany [q.v.] and Cumba ramayanam [q.v.].

VUCKANAY (வக்கணை - vakkanai, *Tam.*). Means hard and round. Same as Forest gaub.

VULLY (വള്ളി - valli, *Mal.*; வல்லி - valli, *Tam.*). Shepherd village [pully].

VULLY (वल्ली - vallí, *San.*). From (val, san. to surround). Creeper. Plant first term., Ex., where transl. is of second term:—Ipomæa batatas (vallikkizhannu), esculent root; Scutia indica (vallívadarí), zizyphus jujuba; See gloss. paragraphs.

VUNNIYA (வன்னியன் - vanniyan, *Tam.*). Another name for the Pullies [jauty].

VURTY (వర్తి - varti, *Tel.*). A row. Suffix in place names.

VYE (வாய் - váy, *Tam.*). Way; mouth. Vye kanak is mental arithmetic. Vye paud is a formula. For Collvye or kiln see that head and Shoolay.——*Vausal* (வாசல் - vásal, Tam.). From (váy, tam. mouth). Entrance [baugaloo]. Suffix in places names. Trittoo vausal, from (tirudu, tam. to steal + above) is a sally port [namcull].——*Voya* (వాయ - váya, Tel.). From (váy, tam. mouth). Defile; suffix in place names.——*Vycaul* (வாய்க்கால் - váykkál, Tam.). From (váy, tam. way + kál, tam. channel). Water-course, channel, canal [casham, channel, oday]. The canals of this Presidency are not on such a large scale as those of some other parts of India. They are constructed chiefly in connection with the systems of irrigation in the Godavery, the Kistna, and the Cauvery deltas [conamoogam]. In each of these localities however there is a perfect net-work of irrigating canals, the larger channels serving also as lines of navigation. Along the eastern coast a salt-water canal runs [buckingham canal]. On the western coast the shallow parts of the Cochin backwater have been deepened, and an excellent channel of communication exists for nearly 200 miles, along which the rich products of Travancore and Malabar are transported to the sea [cauyal].——*Vyetalmala* (വയിത്തൽമല - vayitalmala, Mal.). From (vazhittala, mal. road side + mala, mal. mountain). Hill; Malabar dist., Chiracal tal.; lat. 12° 10′ N., long. 75° 34′ E.; height 4,500 feet. A long, level grassy mountain, standing almost at right angles to ghauts [q.v.] and ending precipitously on its western face. During April, May and October, thunder-storms of terrific violence rage on western summit. Supposed to be haunted by a demon.——*Vythery* (വൈത്തിരി - vaittiri, Mal. vayitri *). From (vazhi, mal. way + tiri, mal. turn).—"*a*" Deputy tahsildarry, Malabar district. Pay Rs. 125.—"*b*" Town, Deputy tahsildar's and Moonsif's station, Sub-registrar's office, telegraph office, Head-quarters of the Wynaud planters' association; Malabar dist., Wynaud tal.; pop. 3,280; acres 29,326; lat. 11° 33′; long. 76° 05′; from Calicut N.E. 26 miles; from Cannanore S.E. 48 miles; from Madras W.S.W. 304 miles; from Malapooram N. 33 miles; from Manantoddy S. 18 miles; from Palghaut N.W. 66 miles; from Ponnany N.N.E. 51 miles; from Tellicherry E.S.E. 39 miles. Chief town of South wynaud coffee [q.v.] country, near head of Tamracherry ghaut [q.v.], down which coffee is conveyed to coast. Temple known as Coonnattambalam now in ruins, Roman catholic chapel, and a chuttram [q.v.]. About a mile south-west lies Pookkode lake, natural sheet of water among hills. On the bank European planters have built a club, and there is a large store adjoining it.

W (و - váu, *Hind.*). Twenty-sixth letter of the Arabic and thirtieth of the Persian alphabet. In arithmetic 6. In ephemerides [punchaungam] stands for Friday [vauram] and sign [raushy] Libra [meezaun, toolaum].

WAGATY (वाघंटी - vághantí, *Mahr.*; ஒக்காதிக்கொடி - okkáthikkodi, *Tam.*). Means tiger-like, from curved thorns. Botanically Wagatea spicata, dalz., leguminosæ [vricsham, 48]. Climbing shrub; branches and petioles armed with recurved prickles; leaves bipinnate; pinnæ five-six pairs; leaflets five-six pairs, oblong, obtuse, coriaceous, shining above; spikes terminal; legumes linear, coriaceous, much swollen at the seeds and constricted between them; flowers scarlet and orange-colored; flowering in the hot season. No other species here.

WAHAUB (وهاب - wahháb, *Hind.*). From (wahaba, ar. to excel in liberality). Bestower. An attribute of God [allah]. Mahomedan alam; as Abdool wahaub, slave of the bestower [ism].——*Wahauby* (وهابی - wahhábí, Hind.). From (wahháb, ar. founder of the sect). A sect of Mahomedan revivalists founded by one Syed ahmed, son of Abdool wahaub, about the beginning of the century. They affirm the right of private judgment in the interpretation of the Koran [q.v.] and traditions [hadees, gheir mookallid]. They reject the belief of the Soonnees [q.v.] that Mahomet has already obtained the permission of God to intercede for his people. They hold it unlawful to illuminate the shrines [durgah] of departed saints [waleo], nor do they even perform any act of reverence at the prophet's tomb, nor observe the ceremonies celebrated on the anniversary of the prophet's birth [baurah wafaut]. They regard themselves as reformers, seeking to bring back Islam [q.v.] to its original purity. Syed ahmed tried to raise a standard of revolt against the English and proclaim jehaud [q.v.]. See vol. I (95).——*Wahib* (واهب - wáhib, Hind.). From (wahaba, ar. to excel in liberality). A donor.

WAH WAH (واه واه - váhváh, *Hind.*). Bravo [shah baush].

WAIL (వేలు - vélu, *Tel.*; வேலி - véli, *Tam.*). Town. Suffix in place names [prole, vole].

WAKF (وقف - wakf, *Hind.*). From (wakafa, ar. to stand). Charitable funds bequeathing and dedicating property to pious uses [devadauyam, dharmadauyam]. The plural is Owkauf.——*Wakeef* (وقيف - wakíf, Hind.). One who dedicates property to pious uses.

WALAYAUR (വാളയാർ - válayár, *Mal.* wálayár *). Means a running stream. Village, Railway station; Malabar dist., Palghaut tal.; pop. 7,213; lat. 10° 50′; long. 76° 53′; height 691 feet; from Calicut E.S.E. 77 miles; from Palghaut E.N.E. 14 miles. Forest on the line of rail. Worked for fuel and teak [q.v.] poles. Rest house built. Endowed choultry [q.v.].

WALEE (ولی - walí, *Hind.*). Often appears as Wally. Master, guardian. Attribute of God [allah]. Common alam; as Walee ahmed, double alam [ism]. So a saint. Walee ahad is heir-apparent [peer].

WALKING FISH (குறவை - kuravai, *Tam.*). Title from creeping on land. Tam from (kuru, tam. short). Family Ophiocephalidæ, acanthopterygii, teleostei, pisces [matsyam, 29] of naturalists [jantoo]. Otherwise Snake-headed fishes [doke, murrel].

WALLAH (والا - wálá, *Hind.*). Suffix denoting agency; as Ghorawallah, horse + keeper.——*Wallajah* (والاجاه - wáláján, Hind.). From (wálá, pers. superior + jáh, pers. dignity). Nawaub of Carnatic. Known in history as Mahomed ally [q.v.].——*Wallajahbad* (والاجاهباد - wáláján bád, Hind.; வாலாசாபாத் - válásábád, Tam. wálajábád*). From (wáláján, pers. the ruler + ábád, pers. city). Tam. also (tondaisívaram), meaning tonday the ruler + holy + town. Also known as Dandoo seevaram or army town, by corruption. Town, Railway station; Chingleput dist., Conjeeveram tal.; pop. 4,534; acres 1,590; lat. 12° 48′; long. 79° 53′; height 197 feet; from Chingleput N.W. 12 miles; from Conjeeveram E.S.E. 9 miles; from Madras S.W. 38 miles; from Sydapett S.W. 31 miles. On left bank of Palaur between Conjeeveram and Chingleput. Received its name from nawaub [q.v.] Wallajah in 1776. Became British cantonment about 1786. There were stationed here for many years a European regiment, a regiment of native cavalry, and two or three regiments of native infantry. On the plain which stretches north towards Tennairy a race course was laid out. The town was found unhealthy and was abandoned, but continued up to 1860 to be the head-quarters of a native veteran battalion. From its position, an emporium for trade of surrounding country. Lubbay [q.v.] merchants monopolise most of this. Weaving is carried on, and formerly Wallajahbad chintz [q.v.] was noted. Oil, grain, and other agricultural produce are now staple articles. Free church of Scotland has two schools inclusive of an industrial school in which carpentry is mainly taught, and bungalow [q.v.] which is allowed to be used by travellers.——*Wallajahpett* (வாலாசாப்பேட்டை - válásáppéttai, Tam.). See sep. title.——*Waul* (وال - wál, Hind.). Same as Wallah. Suffix denoting agent; as Cotwaul, meaning one in charge of a fort.

WALLAJAHPETT (والاجاهپیٹھ - wáláhpeth, *Hind.*; வாலாசாப்பேட்டை - válásáppéttai, *Tam.* wálajápet*). From (wáláján, pers. the ruler + péttai, tam. suburb) [wallah]. Otherwise Wallajahnugger. Also corrupted by hindoos into Baulujipett.——**(1)** Talook, North arcot district. Tahsildar's pay Rs. 250. Area 484 square miles. Population 239,349. Language Tamul. E. of district. Bounded north by Carvetnugger zemindarry, east by Conjeeveram talook of Chingleput district, south and west by Arcot and Goodiyattam talooks respectively. Palaur forms southern frontier line, Poyney on west, and Corteliaur eastern border. Present talook was two, Cauverypauk and Sholinghur, in 1861 with few villages of old Tirvallam talook formed into present division. It includes Argilavaudy mittah [q.v.]. For most part surface is flat and soil sandy, but in north hills occur, outliers of range in west of Carvetnugger. Elevation 500 feet, Sholinghur highest. All destitute of trees or shrubs. Firewood imported from Carvetnugger or Chittore. Climate dry and healthy. Soil poor, being black and red clay mixed with sand and gravel. Granite [caroom cull] is extensively quarried at Baunauvaram and Mahendravaudy where dressed and exported to Madras. Lime [choonam] in several places. Earth salt [ooppoo] once manufactured at Keelveethy; iron [auhan] at Codacull. Weaving [nesavoo] of cloths and carpets [jamkhana] and dyeing [shauyam] of cloth. Coarse cotton cloths produced chiefly in Sholinghur, Minnal and Panapaukam, and exported to Madras. In Wallajahpett better kinds from cotton [q.v.] and silk [puttoo]. Many dyers. Thin jamkhanas [q.v.] and thick woollen rugs, not unlike those of Mysore, are made. Painting on cloth to small extent. Two principal rivers Palaur and Poyney. Anicut [q.v.] across former in 1857, and across latter in 1861. Other stream is Corteliaur, which rises at surplus of Cauverypauk tank [q.v.] and flowing to north-east for 25 miles turns to north and for 10 miles forms eastern boundary. Five miles beyond border it is joined by Nagary river. Largest tank is Cauverypauk. Others are Mahendravaudy, Naugavaid, Peroongaunjy and Sholinghur. Places of archæological interest:—Arconum, Auyal, Baulaucoolam, Caricull, Cauray, Cauverypauk, Codacull, Goodmullore, Keelpoolam, Keelveethy, Mahendravaudy, Minnal, Nungamungalam, Panapaukam, Paranjy, Peroongaunjy, Poolivalam, Pooliyamungalam, Poyavore, Poyney, Pulloor, Sholinghur, Shooray, Tirmaulpore, Tirpaulcadal, Trimalpooram, Tuccoolam, Vellore, Vunnivaid. Principal Trig. stations:—Anandalay, Carimcote. The leading places, &c., in the talook are the following.——*Anandalay* (அனந்தலை - anandalai, Tam.). From (ayan, tam. chief + talai, tam. head); bramha's head. Sanscrit name (praudhadévarájapura), means city of the proud kings of the gods. Village; pop. 928; acres 2,980; lat. 12° 56′; long. 79° 25′; from Chittore S.E. 27 miles; from Wallajahpett E. 1¼ miles. Trig. station in lat. 12° 55′ 53·52″; long. 79° 26′ 14·60″; height 926 feet; from Wallajahpett E. 2 miles.——*Arconum* (ஆர்க்கோணம் - árkkónam, Tam.). See sep. title.——*Baunauvaram* (பாணவரம் - pánávaram, Tam.). From (bána, san. giant of that name + pura, san. town). Village, Railway station called sholinghur though 8 miles from that place; pop 1,124; acres 1,978; lat. 13° 01′; long. 79° 32′; height 417 feet; from Chittore E.S.E. 31 miles; from Wallajahpett N.E. 11 miles.——*Carimcote* (کریم کوٹ - karímkot, Hind.; కరిముకోట - karímukóta, Tel.). From (karím, hind. proper name + kóta, tel. fort). Trig. station; lat. 13° 02′ 36·94″; long. 79° 47′ 18·33″ height 338 feet; from Arconum S.E. 6 miles; from Wallajahpett E.N.E. 27 miles.——*Cauverypauk* (காவேரிப்பாக்கம் - kávérippákkam, Tam.). See sep. title.——*Hussanallipett* (حسن علی پیٹھ - hasanalípeth, Hind.; அசனல்லிப்பேட்டை - asanallippéttai, Tam.). From (hasanalí, hind. proper name + péttai, tam. suburb). Village; pop. 1,370; lat. 12° 56′; long. 79° 23′; from Chittore S.E. 26 miles; from Wallajahpett W. 2 miles. Absorbed into Ranipett.——*Mahendravaudy* (மகேந்திரவாடி - magéndiravádi, Tam.). From (mahá, san. great + indra, san. the god + vádi, tam. garden). Village; pop. 827; acres 1,323; lat. 12° 59′; long. 79° 35′; from Chittore E.S.E. 34 miles; from Wallajahpett E.N.E. 12 miles. Fine tank and traces of fort walls, and within enclosure a small temple excavated out of a large boulder. One of the fortified places of the Coorumbar [q.v.]. Tank originally larger than Cauverypauk.——*Minnal* (முன்னல் - munnal, Tam.). See sep. title.——*Naugavaid* (నాగవీడు - nágavídu, Tel.; நாகவேடு - nágavédu, Tam.). From (nága, san. serpent + vídu, tel. town). Sanscrit name (nágapurí), meaning snake + town. Village; lat. 13° 02′; long. 79° 40′; from Chittore E.S.E. 38 miles; from Wallajahpett E.N.E. 20 miles. Naugavaid naud was part of Cadigay cottam in Tondaimundalam [q.v.]. Important tank.——*Palaur* (பாலாறு - pálárn, Tam.). See sep. title.——*Panapaukam* (பனப்பாக்கம் - panappákkam, Tam.). From (panai, tam. palmyra tree, borassus flabelliformis, linn. + pákkam, tam. village). Sanscrit name (tálapurí), means palmyra town. It is said that the village once abounded in palmyras [q.v.]. Village; pop. 4,429; acres 852; lat. 12° 55′; long. 79° 36′; from Chittore E.S.E. 38 miles; from Wallajahpett E. 14 miles. Nine miles south by east of Sholinghur railway station. Old temple of Mayooranauta sawmy, built by Cholan. Inscriptions on the Praucauram [q.v.] wall, on the wall of the Moola staunam [q.v.], and on the shrine of Soobramanyan [q.v.].——*Paravattore* (பறவத்தூர் - paravattúr, Tam.). From (paravatti, tam. párvatí, proper name + úr, tam. village). Village; acres 1,180; lat. 13° 08′; long. 79° 33′; from Chittore E.S.E. 29 miles; from Wallajahpett N.E. 17 miles. This village was once ruled by a rajah, who had three daughters. Akkatchiyammaul, Jaunaky ammaul, and Parvaty ammaul. This after the eldest.——*Peroongaunjy* (பெருங்காஞ்சி - perungáñji, Tam.). From (peru, tam. great + káñji, tam. the city of that name); the great conjeeveram. Village, Mountain, Place of pilgrimage; pop. 2,662; lat. 13° 03′; long. 79° 27′; from Chittore E.S.E. 24 miles. From Wallajahpett N.N.E. 9 miles. Peroongaunjy naud was part of Cadigay cottam in Tondaimundalam [q.v.]. Village formerly Jeina [q.v.] stronghold. Old Shiva temple repaired by Mahrattas. Large tank.——*Poyney* (పోయిని - póyini, Tel.). See sep. title.——*Pulloor* (பள்ளூர் - pallúr,* Tam.). From (palli, tam. member of the caste + úr, tam. village). Village, Railway station; pop. 1,572; acres 2,742; lat. 12° 58′; long. 79° 43′; height 287 feet; from Chittore E.S.E. 43 miles; from Wallajahpett E. 21 miles. Ruined temples.——*Ranipett* (இராணிப்பேட்டை - iránippéttai, Tam.). See sep. title.——*Sholinghur* (சோளங்கிப்புரம் - shólangippuram, Tam.). See sep. title.——*Trittany* (திருத்தணி - tiruttani, Tam.). See sep. title.——*Tuccoolam* (தக்கூலம் - takkúlam, Tam.). From (tagai, tam. beauty + kulam, tam. tank). Village, Place of pilgrimage; pop. 3,930; acres 3,998; lat. 13° 01′; long. 79° 47′; from Chittore E.S.E. 46 miles; from Wallajahpett E.N.E. 25 miles. Six miles north of Pulloor railway station. East is an old Shiva temple, built by dependent of Chola kings. At the temple of Gungahdhareshwaran is a water-trough, which carries the water of a spring entirely round the Garbhaulayam [coil, maunasauram, pagoda] and out through the mouth of a stone bull [nundy] into a pond. Near this village lies the scene of the disastrous engagement between Bailey and Hyder ally in 1780 [poollalore].——*Wallajahpett* (வாலாசாப்பேட்டை - válásáppéttai, Tam.). See below.——

(2) Town, Municipality, Tahsildar's station; North arcot dist., Wallajahpett tal.; pop. 10,485; acres 319; lat. 12° 56′; long. 79° 25′; from Arnee N.N.E. 18 miles; from Chittore S.E. 27 miles; from Madras W. 64 miles; from Ranipett E. 2 miles; from Tripatty S. 49 miles; from Vellore E. 16 miles. Three miles north of Palaur. Cut into two portions by trunk road from Madras. Royajee, the prime minister of Mahomed ally, founded it towards close of last century, when he for the convenience of merchants built eighteen pettahs [q.v.] containing shops surrounding a small temple in the centre. Within short time Wallajahpett became one of busiest marts in S. india. Chief trade was in grains and cotton [q.v.], with Madras, Mysore, and Ceded districts [q.v.]. At the present day comparatively little trade. Weaving in silk [puttoo] and cotton [q.v.], dyeing [shauyam], carpet-making [jamkhana] and the manufacture of oils [yennay]. The grain trade has travelled to Vellore, and the railway carries cotton directly to Madras from Cuddapah and Bellary. On the eastern side of the town a Peoples' park.

WALSOORA (వాలరసి - válarasi, *Tel.*; வாலசுரா - válasúrá, *Tam.*). Title otherwise Fish poison tree [indian berry]. Botanically the Walsura genus, meliaceæ [vricsham, 36]. Trees; leaves one to five foliolate; leaflets opposite, quite entire, pale beneath; flowers small in axillary and terminal panicles; fruit pulpy, with short hairs, one rarely two-seeded. The species best known to the natives are:—Walsura piscidia, roxb., small tree; flowers yellowish-white color; bark thrown into ponds intoxicates fish, which are consequently easily taken [common emetic nut, indian berry, indian oak, marotty, round milkhedge, sooptee, tejbul, zanzibar indigo]; the fish not deemed unwholesome; timber large heavy and strong, white-colored. Walsura ternata, r., small tree; godavery forests.

WALTAIR* (వాల్తేరు - váltéru, *Tel.*). From (válu, tel. sloping + éru, tel. river). Village; Vizagapatam dist., Vizagapatam division; pop. 1,601; lat. 17° 44′; long. 83° 23′; from Vizagapatam N.E. 4 miles; from the sea W. ¼ mile. All the European officers stationed at Vizagapatam reside near Waltair, for the most part on high land over-looking the sea, some of the houses being about 200 feet above sea-level. The climate is exceptionally cool, land winds in the hot weather being unknown and the thermometer rarely rising above 88°. There is a large club and church. The views along the coast are very fine. Lawson's bay, north of Waltair, is flanked to the north by two picturesque conical hills.

WANDEROO (වඳුරා - vandurá, *Singh.*). From (vánara, san. monkey) [van]. Ceylon black monkey, Semnopithecus ursinus [siyah bandar].

WANDIWASH (வந்தவாசி - vandavási, *Tam.*). From (vanda, tel. hundred + vásí, san. inhabitant). Sanscrit name (dhavalagiri), meaning white hill.——**(1)** Talook, North arcot district. Tahsildar's pay Rs. 200. Area 466 square miles. Population 177,723. Language Tamul. S.E. of district. Bounded north by Arcot; east by Madrantacam talook of Chingleput district; south by Tindivanam talook of South arcot district; and west by Arnee and Polore. A level plain with very few rocky hills, two principal being Dhavalagherry close to cusbah [q.v.] and Nedoongoonam 17 miles to the west. Hardly any jungle. Soil poor. Has much sand and gravel mixed with red and black clays and is in parts impregnated with soda [sowdoo]. Industries are weaving of cotton [q.v.] cloths and coray [q.v.] mats [boriyah]. There are 1,000 looms [tarry] for cloth. Lubbays [q.v.] have looms for mats. The rush [coray] is cultivated upon irrigated land. The rush is split, dried, and dyed in red, yellow, black, and other colors, and is worked into patterns. Principal river Cheyaur, which enters talook [q.v.] on west and cutting off small corner forms boundary between it and Arcot. An anicut [q.v.] in 1856, which supplies 104 tanks [q.v.]. Also Sookhauuddy or Wandiwash river, which rises west of cusbah [q.v.] and flowing eastwards unites with Palaur in Chingleput district. Tanks are Ancavore, Marathaud, Poorisay, Sheeshamungalam and Vaulcaday. Places of archæological interest:—Aharacora cottah, Auvaniyaupooram, Dessore, Marathaud, Matam, Nedoongoonam, Ponnore, Sheeshamungalam, Sheeyamungalam, Tellaur, Terracole, Trimalpaudy, Vazhoor, Vengoonam, Vullam, Wandiwash. Principal Trig. station:—Ponnore. The leading places, &c., in the talook are the following.——*Ammayaputt* (அம்மயப்பட்டு - ammayappattu, Tam.). From (ammai, tam. village goddess + pattu, tam. village). Village; pop. 372. Weaving centre.——*Anaputtoor* (அனப்பத்தூர் - anappattúr, Tam.). From (ani, tam. beauty + pattu, tam. little village + úr, tam. village). Sanscrit name (aníkapatipura), means army + master + town; the village of great warrior. Village; pop. 1,334; acres 1,922; lat. 12° 38′; long. 79° 38′; from Ancavore E. 3 miles; from Chittore S.E. 52 miles; from Wandiwash N. 9 miles. Rama [q.v.] is said to have encamped here with his allies on way from Ceylon. ——*Ancavore* (அனக்காவூர் - anakkávúr, Tam.). From (ani, tam. beauty + ká, tam. grove + úr, tam. village). Sanscrit name (aníkapura), means army + town. Village; pop. 2,498; acres 3,801; lat. 12° 38′; long. 79° 35′; from Chittore S.E. 50 miles; from Wandiwash N.N.W. 10 miles. On southern bank of Cheyaur. Idol [shilay, vigraham] is Hanoomanteshwaran. ——*Auvaniyaupooram* (ஆவணியாப்புரம் - ávaniyáppuram, Tam.). From (ávaníyam, tam. market street + pura, san. town). Village, Hill; pop. 780; acres 1,364; lat. 12° 35′; long. 79° 26′; from Chittore S.S.E. 48 miles; from Wandiwash W.N.W. 16 miles. Small ancient temple on top of hill. Near is Cheyaur anicut.——*Cheyaur* (செய்யாறு - sheyyáru, Tam.). See sep. title.——*Cheyyautvondraun* (செய்யாற்றுவென்றான் - sheyyáttuvenrán, Tam.). From (sheyyáru, tam. the river, so called + venrán, tam. conqueror). Village; pop. 780; acres 1,419; lat. 12° 40′; long. 79° 33′; from Chittore S.E. 47 miles; from Wandiwash N.N.W. 12 miles. The Vedams [q.v.] of the Bramins [q.v.] here gained a victory over the Grantam [q.v.] of the Jeinas [q.v.], by floating against the current of the Cheyaur, in which the two were launched together.——*Dessore* (தேசூர் - tésúr, Tam.). From (tésu, tam. beauty + úr, tam. village). Village; pop. 3,250; acres 1,636; lat. 12° 26′; long. 79° 32′; from Chittore S.S.E. 60 miles; from Wandiwash W.S.W. 10 miles. Formerly chief residence of a jagheerdar [q.v.], whose fort is in ruins. The jagheer [q.v.] was resumed again by company in 1826. Cloth offered for sale. Tanneries [chamrah]. ——*Dhavalagherry* (धवलगिरि - dhavalagiri, San.). From (dhavala, san. white + giri, san. mountain). Otherwise Wandiwash hill. Mountain. North of Wandiwash fort. Composed of gray granite [caroom cull]. Two peaks, upon higher of which is built shrine to Dhavalagiry nautan. At foot is smaller temple built, in memory of Ratna bye, mother of a rajah of Canouj, who died here on way to Rameshwaram [vengoonam].——*Marathaud* (மறதாடு - marathádu, Tam.). Village; pop. 2,879; acres 4,625; lat. 12° 30′; long. 79° 43′; from Chittore S.E. 64 miles; from Wandiwash E.S.E. 4 miles. Tank.——*Ponnore* (பொன்னூர் - ponnúr, Tam.). From (pon, tam. gold + úr, tam. village). Village; pop. 1,905; acres 3,641; lat. 12° 28′; long. 79° 35′; from Chittore S.E. 60 miles; from Wandiwash S.W. 5 miles. Ponnore naud was part of Yilangautt cottam in Tondaimundalam [q.v.]. Large Shiva temple with inscriptions. Trig. station in lat. 12° 29′ 50·59″; long. 79° 33′ 59·99″; height 587 feet.——*Poorisay* (புரிசை - purisai, Tam.). Means fort wall. Sanscrit name (puríshvara), means town of the lord shiva. Village; pop. 1,370; acres 2,448; lat. 12° 35′; long. 79° 38′; from Chittore S.E. 55 miles; from Wandiwash N.N.W. 5 miles. Poorisay naud was part of Manavore cottam in Tondaimundalam [q.v.]. Tank. Here Rama [q.v.] directed Soogreevan [q.v.] to found a town to Shiva [q.v.].——*Sheeshamungalam* (சீசமங்கலம் - shísamangalam, Tam.). From (sísa, san. lead + mangala, san. prosperity). Sanscrit name (shrípurushamangala), means lutchmy, the deity + vishnoo, the god + village. Village; pop. 3,065; acres 4,244; lat. 12° 38′; long. 79° 23′; from Chittore S.S.E. 44 miles; from Wandiwash W.N.W. 20 miles. Bronze and stone images found.——*Sheeyamungalam* (சியமங்கலம் - shiyyamangalam, Tam.). From (shíyam, tam. lion + mangala, san. prosperity). Village; pop. 678; acres 1,614; lat. 12° 26′; long. 79° 31′; from Chittore S.S.E. 60 miles; from Wandiwash W.S.W. 11 miles. Once formed part of Dessore jagheer [q.v.]. Built by Chemboo rajah. Single rock-cut temple.——*Tellaur* (தெள்ளார் - tellár, Tam.). From (tel, tam. clear, + áru, tam. river). Village; pop. 2,193; acres 2,349; lat. 12° 24′; long. 79° 36′; from Chittore S.S.E. 65 miles; from Wandiwash S.S.W. 8 miles. Tellaur naud was part of Vengoondra cottam in Tondaimundalam [q.v.]. Now village on road to Tindivanam. Ruins of fort built by Nundan, rajah of Padavaid. Jeinas [q.v.] have a place of worship.——*Vengoonam* (வெங்குணம் - vengunam, Tam.). From (ven, tam. white + kunram, tam. hill). Sanscrit name (dhavalagiri), meaning same. Village, Hill; pop. 925; acres 1,780; lat. 12° 31′; long. 79° 39′; from Chittore S.E. 59 miles; from Wandiwash N. 1½ miles. Shiva temple on top of hill with Nagry [q.v.] inscriptions. Jeina [q.v.] temple [basty] in village. As also Shiva temple.——*Vullam* (வல்லம் - vallam, Tam.). From (val, tam. hillock + agam, tam. place). Sanscrit name (valmíka), means ant's nest. Shiva is said to have manifested himself here in this form. Village; pop. 1,465; acres 1,850; lat. 12° 31′; long. 79° 32′; from Chittore S.S.E. 55 miles; from Wandiwash W. 8 miles. Ancient temple by a Chola king. Inscription of Vijianugger dynasty. ——*Wandiwash* (வந்தவாசி - vandavási, Tam.). See below.——**(2)** Village, Tahsildar's station, Mountain; North arcot dist., Wandiwash tal.; pop. 5,185; acres 1,245; lat. 12° 30′; long. 79° 39′; height 1,021 feet; from Arnee E.S.E. 25 miles; from Chittore S.E. 60 miles; from Madras S.W. 2 miles; from Ranipett S.S.E. 35 miles; from Tripatty S. 79 miles; from Vellore S.E. 43 miles. A short distance north of Sookhanuddy. The scene of several important operations in Carnatic [q.v.] wars. The fort belonged to a member of the family of the Nawaub [q.v.] of Arcot. In 1752 it was attacked by Major Lawrence. In 1757 Colonel Aldercom destroyed the town, but failed to capture the fort. The French garrison twice in that year repulsed the English. A more energetic attack under Monson in 1759 was also unsuccessful. Immediately after this the French soldiers mutinied, and although they were speedily pacified the fort surrendered to Coote before the end of the year. In 1760 the French appeared before the fort and in the pitched battle which ensued the French were utterly routed and Bussy was taken prisoner. This victory was in itself and in its consequences the most important ever won over the French in India. In 1780 Lieutenant Flint by a bold stratagem saved the fort from falling into the hands of Hyder ally, and with very inadequate means held it for nearly three years against every device of the enemy. Twice he was relieved by Sir Eyre Coote, and twice at least he repelled most vigorous assaults. Fort probably built by Mahrattas. In ordinary Hindoo style, being rectangular, with circumference of a mile. A plantation of indigo [q.v.] within the walls. Traces of its many sieges remain. The jagheer [q.v.] was first given by the emperor Mahomed shah to Mahomed takee khan at the request of his father-in-law nawaub Dost ally. He was deposed by Wallajah because he and Chundah sahib had married sisters, and he had admitted French officers into the fort. After some years, Wallajah conferred it upon his daughter Daryah begum, who held it for some years. At the cession the Nawaub [q.v.] was in possession of the revenues, which therefore passed to the Company. Temple of Jhallacaunteshwara sawmy in which Runganauta sawmy is also worshipped, the idol [shilay, vigraham] being placed in the Calyauna mantapam [q.v.]. Wandiwash hill is better known as Dhavalagherry. Trade in grain. Mats [boriyah] and leather [chamrah] manufactured.

WAR (وار - wár, *Pers.*). Suffix denoting possession ; as Coolwar, whole + having.—— *Warry* (واری - wárí, Hind.). Suffix in compounds ; as ryotwarry, meaning that which pertains to ryots.

WARANGAL (ఒరుంగల్లు - orungallu, *Tel.*). From (oru, tam. single + kal, tam. stone) [or]. Sanscrit name (varnakula), meaning caste + collection ; (ékashilánagarí), meaning one + stone + city ; from the single stone wall round the town [vontimittah]. Ancient capital of the Andhram [q.v.] country [charitram]. The Hyderabad territory.

WARKULLY (വർക്കല - varkkala, *Mal.*). From (vara, mal. straight + kallu, mal. stone) [vary]. Sanscrit name (valkala), meaning bark of a tree, usually worn by sages ; by throwing his valkalam at this spot the sage nauradan [q.v.] indicated it as the fit place for the sapta rishies [q.v.] to reside and do penance. Also (janárdana), meaning vishnoo the man-afflicter or the destroying deity ; one of the names of vishnoo to whom the temple is dedicated. Greek πυῤῥὸν ὄρος. Village, Place of pilgrimage ; Travancore state, Trivandrum division ; Cherankeel tal. ; pop. 18,452 ; lat. 8° 44′ ; long. 76° 45′ ; from Attingal W.N.W. 8 miles ; from Trivandrum N.W. 24 miles ; from the sea E ½ mile. A bar of red laterite [q.v.], a short distance south of Quilon. It forms abrupt cliffs on the sea, without beach, and cliffs are still known to seamen as the Red cliffs [q.v.]. This is the only natural object which resembles a sea cliff from Mount delly to Cape comorin. The height of the actual cliff is only about 80 or 100 feet ; the hill immediately behind 283. Ancient village reputed for a Hindoo pagoda [q.v.] of great antiquity, dedicated to the worship of Janardanan or Vishnoo [q.v.], and situated on the summit of the headland of Warkully. To the temple is attached a remarkable tank. Hindoos from all parts of India resort to it as a place of pilgrimage, and it is as religiously important as Gayay in the north. In the vicinity, two water tunnels constructed by the Travancore government at a cost of 18 lakhs [q.v.] of rupees [q.v.] have removed the only barrier that existed to the line of water communication from Trivandrum to the north. There is a good camping ground at Warkully.

WARRIA (വാരിയ - váriya, obl. ; വാരിയൻ - váriyan, pers. sing. ; വാരിയർ - váriyar, pers. pl., *Mal.*). From (váru, mal. to clean). Temple servants in Malabar [jauty]. Hindoo third name [peyar].

WARRIORE (உறையூர் - oraiyúr, *Tam.*). From (urai, tam. abode + úr, tam. city). Sanscrit name (nichulapurí), meaning the tree, barringtonia acutangula, gærtn. + town. Ancient name (kózhi), meaning cock ; with a story of a cock attacking an elephant [q.v.] at this place [calicut] ; also (pugazh), town of praise. Greek ὀρθοῦρα βασίλειον σωρνάγης. Latin Orthura regia sornagos. Village, Assistant collector's division ; Trichinopoly dist., Trichinopoly tal. ; pop. included in the Trichinopoly municipality ; acres 335 ; lat. 10° 50′ ; long. 78° 44′ ; from Trichinopoly N.W. 2 miles. Suburb of Trichinopoly, and oldest part of city. A capital of Chola [q.v.] dynasty [raj.]. Site of the old artillery cantonment. Principally noted for the manufacture of cigars [cheroot] and jewelry [nagay, zewar].

WASYAT (وصیت - vasíyat, *Hind.*). From (wasí, ar. to couple together). A will, generally nuncupative.

WATRAP (வத்திராயிருப்பு - vattiráyiruppu, *Tam.* vartiráyiruppu*). From (varttaráyan, tam. proper name + iruppu, tam. dwelling).—"*a*" Deputy tahsildarry, Tinnevelly district. Pay Rs. 70.—"*b*" Town, Deputy tahsildar's station ; Tinnevelly dist., Shreevillipoottore tal. ; pop. 7,425 ; acres 6,440 ; lat. 9° 38′ ; long. 77° 41′ ; from Madras S.W. 289 miles ; from Palamcottah N. 9 miles ; from Shermadevy N. 65 miles ; from Shreevillipoottore N. 9 miles ; from Tinnevelly N. 62 miles ; from Tuticorin N.N.W. 67 miles. In a fertile valley on the Malabar boundary. Iron-smelting formerly conducted. The manufacture of coarse cloths, earthen pots [chatty], and coarse mats [boriyah] still carried on. Irrigation is good.

WATTAUDA (వత్తాడ - vattáda, *Tel.*). From (vattu, tel. draining + váda, tel. village). Village, Port ; Vizagapatam dist., Sarwasiddhy tal. ; pop. 1,020 ; lat. 17° 26′ ; long. 82° 55′ ; from Madras N.E. 342 miles ; from Pentacote N.E. 20 miles ; from Poodimadaca S.W. 10 miles ; from Vizagapatam S.W. 32 miles ; from Yellamanchily S. 8 miles ; fom the sea W. ½ mile. Small port between Pentacote and Poodimadaca. The Shaurada and Varauhanuddy empty themselves into the Bay of Bengal here. Considered by navigators boundary between Golcondah and Orissa coasts [q.v.].

WATTLE (சீமைவேலம்பட்டை - shímaivélambattai, *Tam.*). Tam. from (shímai, tam. european + vél, tam. tree, acacia arabica, willd. + pattai, tam. bark). Anglo-indian name for bark of various species of australian acacia, used for tanning [chamrah] ; chiefly Acacia decurrens, willd., Acacia melanoxylon, r. br. [australian black wood], and Acacia dealbata, link. All on Neilgherries.

WAUHID (واحد - wáhid, *Hind.*). From (ahad, ar. one). One. Attribute of God [allah]. Common alam ; as Wauhid ally, double alam ; Wauhid beg, alam + moghul alaumat [ism].

WAUJIB (واجب - wájib, *Hind.*). From (wajaba, ar. right). Proper, responsible. Prayers [namauz] &c. enjoined in the Koran [q.v.] and Hadees [q.v.], the non-observance of which constitutes sin [farz].

WAUJID (واجد - wájid, *Hind.*). From (vajada, ar. to discover). The finder. Attribute of God [allah]. Common alam ; as Waujid ally, double alam [ism].

WAUKAM (வாக்கம் - vákkam, *Tam.*). Corruption of Paukam [q.v.] ; as in Pursewaukum, butea frondosa village.

WAUKIF (واقف - wákif, *Ar.*). Acquaintance. Prefixed to an alam forms a lacab ; as Waukif ally, friend of ally, a Shiah [q.v.] name [ism].

WAUN (وان - wán, *Hind.*). From (vat, san. suffix of possession). Possessive suffix ; as Bandiwaun, meaning prison + keeper.—— *Wund* (وند - wand, Pers.). (From vanta, san. pl. of vat, san. suffix of possession). Suffix denoting relationship or resemblance ; as Khodawund, god + like.

WAUSIF (واصف - wásif, *Ar.*). From (wasafa, ar. to describe). Praiser. Prefixed to an alam forms a lacab ; as Wausif ally, praiser of ally [ism].

WAX GOURD (कूष्माण्ड - kúshmánda, *San.* ; कोहळ - kóhala, *Mahr.* ; कुवाले - kuvále, *Conc.* ; مجدبه - majdabah, *Ar.* and *Pers.* ; کوندھا - kondhá, *Hind.* ; پیٹھا - pethá, *Dec.* ; ಬೂದಿಕುಂಬಳ - búdikumbala, *Can.* ; ಕರುಕುಂಬಡ - karukumbada, *Too.* ; బూడిదెగుమ్మడి - búdidegummadi, *Tel.* ; കുമ്പളം - kumbalam, *Mal.* ; கலியாணப்பூசணி - kaliyánappúsani, *Tam.*). Title from nature of bloom. San. from (ku, san. prefix of diminution + úshma, san. heat + anda, san. seed) ; from cooling seeds [common pumpkin]. Mahr. from sanscrit. Ar. from (jadaba, ar. dry land). Hind. from sanscrit. Can. from (búdi, can. ashes + kumbala, can. great pumpkin). Tel. from (búdide, tel. ashes + gummadi, tel. cucurbita maxima, duch.). Mal. from sanscrit. Tam. from (kalyána, san. auspicious + púsani, tam. great pumpkin) ; as used in marriage. Hind also (kamrhá), (golkaddú), meaning round pumpkin ; (bhuttuá) ; (kadíma), (jalkamrhá), meaning water pumpkin, from watery juice ; (páníkamrhá), meaning water pumpkin. Can. also (bilékumbala), meaning white pumpkin. Tel. also (pendligummadi), meaning marriage + cucurbita maxima, duch. ; from use in marriage. Tam. also (shámbarbúsani), meaning ashes pumpkin ; (perumbúsani), meaning large pumpkin ; (kumbalam). Title otherwise Ashes pumpkin, Marriage pumpkin, White gourd, White gourd melon, White melon, White pumpkin. Botanically Benincasa cerifera, savi., cucurbitaceæ [vricsham, 62]. Alias Cucurbita alba, cerifera, hispida, pepo. Leaves 4–6 inches diameter ; petiole 3–4 inches ; male peduncle 3-4 inches, female peduncle 1–2 inches ; calyx-teeth when young often narrow, scarcely serrate ; fruit 1–1½ feet, cylindric, without ribs, hairy ultimately covered with a waxy bloom ; seeds ½ by ⅓ inch. Climbing frequently on roofs of huts ; flower large, yellow ; large, egg-shaped gourd, covered with pale greenish-white waxen bloom. Fruit medicinally alterative and styptic ; valuable antimercurial ; fresh juice from fruit given internally, while a slice of the fruit at the same time applied to the temples, is cure for internal hæmorrhage ; either with sugar [q.v.] or as an adjunct to other medicines in insanity, epilepsy, and nervous diseases. Fruit used as preserve ; also as vegetable ; young unripe fruit eaten in curries [q.v.] ; yields a wax from surface of fruit ; considered a type of fertility and presented at native marriage feasts ; oil from seeds, pale-colored. No other common species here. For cucumis genus see Oorvauroo ; for cucurbita genus see Carcauroo.

WAYAKA (शङ्खालु - shankhálu, *San.* ; ویکا - wayaka, *Hind.*). Title from fijian. San. from (shankha, san. conch + álu, san. esculent root) ; from color of root. Hind. also (shakarálú), meaning sugar root. Title otherwise Bulbous bean, Conch yam, Sugar root, Yaka. Botanically Pachyrhizus angulatus, rich., leguminosæ [vricsham, 48]. Alias Dolichos bulbosus. Stems wide turning, suffruticose, clothed with short deciduous pubescence ; leaflets large, membranous, glabrous, as broad as long, deeply or shallowly lobed in the upper half, the base deltoid ; racemes lax, ½–1 foot, lower nodes often prolonged into short branches ; bracteoles setaceous ; calyx ¼ inch as long as the pedicel ; corolla reddish 1 inch or more long ; pod 6–9 inches long, eight to twelve seeded, straight, glabrescent. Cultivated for large, tuberous root, or underground stem, 6 to 8 feet in length, thick as a man's thigh, and resembles a turnip [shalgham], in taste and consistence ; eaten both raw and boiled ; in cooked state dirty white color and insipid flavor.

WAZAURAT (وزارت - wazárat, *Hind.*). From (wizr, ar. to sustain). The office of prime minister [vizier].

WEAVER-BIRD (تنوط - tannaut, *Ar.* ; بئیا - baiyá, *Hind.* and *Dec.* ; పసుపుపిట్ట - pasupupitta, *Tel.* ; ഓലമാടി - ólamáti, *Mal.* ; மஞ்சள்குருவி - mañjalguruvi, *Tam.*). Title from building pensile nests by interweaving twigs and fibres [indian tailor-bird]. Hind. is contraction of (bayaderi a dancing girl); from the bird being trained to pluck the ticca mark off the foreheads of dancing girls. Tel. from (pasupu, tel. yellow + pitta, tel. bird); from color. Mal. from (óla, mal. leaf + mátu, mal. to build), from building nests on palmyras. Tam. from (mañjal, tam. turmeric + kuruvi, tam. small bird). Hind. also (chindorá). Tam. also (túkkananguruvi), meaning pendant + bird; (shindam), meaning dwarf. Title otherwise Baya, Baya sparrow, Toddy bird. Ploceus baya, ploceinæ, fringillidæ [boosa priyam], conirostres, insessores [pacshy, 27], of naturalists [jantoo]. Specific name from hindostany. Alias Ploceus artigula, phillippinus. Frequently taken young, tamed, and taught to pick up rings, or such like articles, dropped down a well; or to snatch the ticca mark off the forehead of a person pointed out. It is also taught occasionally to carry a note to a particular place, on a given signal. Exhibitors carry them about.

WEAVER'S BEAM (मुष्कक - mushkaka, *San.*; ಮಗ್ಗಾರ್ತಿಮರ - maggártimara, *Can.*; ಕಲ್ಗಂಟೆ - kalgante, *Coorg*; మొగ్గకోడి - múkodi, *Tel.*; ଜାଣ୍ଟିୟା - jantiya, *Oor.*; மொகலிங்கம் - mogalingam, *Tam.*). Title from use. San. from (mushka, san. testicle); from ashes used in cautery. Can. from (magga, can. weaver's loom + árti, san. pain + mara, can. tree). Tam. from (magga, can. loom + vilangu, tam. to shine). San. also (ghantá-pátali), meaning bell + red, from bell-shaped blossoms; (ghantá), meaning bell-shaped; (pátalí), meaning red [common bendy, edible paulay, jungle geranium, pauthiry]; (gólídha), meaning eaten by cows. Can. also (makárti). Tel. also (mogalingachettu) [one leaf nelumbo]; (makkam); (tondamukkidi), meaning chameleon + snout. Tam. also (mávilingai), meaning mango tree, mangifera indica, linn. + feronia elephantum, corr. [ashy babool, nirvala]. Title otherwise Mogalingam. Botanically Schrebera swietenioides, roxb., oleaceæ [vricsham, 85]. Large tree; leaves nearly opposite, imparipinnate, about a foot long, leaflets three to four pairs, opposite, obliquely-ovate or cordate, entire, pointed, smooth on both sides, the lower ones largest; calyx tubular, bilabiate corolla salver-shaped, with cylindrical tube, and three times larger than the calyx; segments five to seven, curved, truncated; capsule large, pear-shaped [amrood], scabrous, very hard, two-celled, opening from the apex; seeds four in each cell, compressed, and with a long membranaceous wing; panicles terminal, trichotomous; flowers small, white and brown variegated, very fragrant at night. Wood brownish-grey, hard, close-grained, polishes well; durable, does not warp or split; no heart-wood but irregular masses of purple or claret colored wood in the centre, and scattered throughout the tree; used by weavers for making their beams and for many other purposes. No other common species here.

WELLINGTON* (ಜಗತಾಳ - jagatálá, *Can.*). Called after the Duke of Wellington. Formerly Jackatalla [q.v.]. Town, Convalescent depôt for British soldiers, Military cantonment; Neilgherry dist., Paranginaud division; pop. 3,096; lat. 11° 22′; long. 76° 50′; height 6,160 feet; from Coonoor N. 1¾ miles; from Jackatalla S.E. 1⅜ miles; from Ootacamund E.S.E. 7 miles. For description see vol. II, 142 [hill-station].

WEST (مغرب - maghrib, *Hind*; పడమర - padamara, *Tel.*). Prefix.——*Western polliems* (పడమటిపాళెములు - padamatipálemulu, Tel.). Anglo-indian term for Calastry, Carvetnugger or bomrauz, Sydapore, and Vencatagherry zemindarries; which see under their separate heads. Sydapore has disappeared.——*West indian* (جزیرہ مغربی - jazírahimaghrabí, Hind.). Hind. means western island. From group of islands between N. and S. America. Prefixed to plant names here, indicates their native habitat. Ex.:—Acacia farnesiana, west indian black thorn; Anona reticulata, west indian custard-apple tree; Asclepias curassavica, west indian blood flower, west indian ipecacuanha; Canavalia obtusifolia, west indian sea-side bean; Entada scandens, west indian cocoon, west indian filbert tree; Erythrina indica, west indian coral tree; Gossypium barbadense, west indian cotton; Hibiscus esculentus, west indian ochro; Hibiscus sabdariffa, west indian red sorrel plant; Hura crepitans, west indian sand box tree; Indigofera anil, west indian indigo; Jussæa suffruticosa, west indian loose strife; Leucæna glauca, west indian lead tree; Maranta arundinacea, west indian arrowroot; Mimusops elengi, west indian medlar; Morus atropurpurea, west indian red mulberry tree; Parkinsonia aculeata, west indian prickly broom; Pimenta officinalis, west indian bayberry tree; Pisonia aculeata, west indian cock's spur; Pistia stratiotes, west indian water lettuce; Sesbania grandiflora, west indian pea tree; Sesuvium portulacastrum, west indian samphire purslane, west indian sea-side purslane; Solanum torvum, west indian turkey berry; Triumfetta annua, west indian burweed; Ximenia americana, west indian sea-side plum. See gloss. paragraphs.

WET CROP (تری کا اناج - taríkáanáj, *Hind.*; ಮಾಗಾಣಿಪೈರು - mágánipairu, *Can.*; మాగాణిపంట - mágánipanta, *Tel.*; നഞ്ചധാന്യം - nañchadhányam, *Mal.* நஞ்சைப்பயிர் - nañjaippayir, *Tam.*). Hind. from (tarí, pers. wet + anáj, pers. grain). Tel. from (mágáni, tel. wet land + panta, tel. cultivation). Mal. from (nañcha, mal. irrigated ground + dhánya, san. grain). Tam. from (nañjey, tam. wet land + payir, tam. crop). Rice crop [paddy, rice]. For dry crop see Dry grain. For cultivation of crops generally see Vellanmay.

WHIP (چابک - chábuk, *Pers.*). Prefix.——*Whip fish* (वाल - vála, Mahr.; గుర్రపుచబుకు - gurraputsabuku, Tel.; கடற்குதிரை - kadarguthirai, Tam.). Title from long, slender form. Tel. from (gurramu, tel. horse + tsabuku, tel. whip). Tam. from (kadal, tam. sea + kuthirai, tam. horse). Tam. also (karbámbu), meaning stone + snake. Title otherwise Pipe-fish. Syngnathus serratus, syngnathidæ, lophobranchii, teleostei [matsyam, 43], of naturalists [jantoo]. Alias Syngnathus subbookoo, typle; Trachyrhamphus cultirostris, serratus. Subbookoo from teloogoo, meaning whip. Eyes large, situated in the middle of the length of the head; body scarcely deeper than broad; shields without spines; light brown with light spots along the side, and the body banded in rings, tail fin black with a white lower edge; a dark mark at base of anterior dorsal rays; and a dark line along the middle of the fin; sea; very common. No other species here.——*Whip snake* (دھامن - dhámin, Hind.; ಹಸರುಹಾವು - hasaruhávu, Can.; పసరికపాము - pasarikapámu, Tel.; പച്ചപ്പാമ്പ - paççappámbu, Mal.; பச்சைப்பாம்பு - paççaippámbu, Tam.). Title from the slender body. Hind. from (dháv, san. to run quickly). Can. from (hasaru, can. green + hávu, can. snake). Tel. from (pasarika, tel. green + pámu, tel. snake). Mal. and Tam. from (paççai, tam. green + pámbu, tam. snake). Tam. also (kanguttippámbu), meaning eye + piercing + snake [pit viper]. The terms may be considered as co-extensive with the family Dryiophidæ, ophidii colubriformes, ophidia [sarpam], reptilia [sarpy, 21], of naturalists [jantoo]. The whip-snakes are distinguished by their excessively slender body, compared to the cord of a whip, by their prevalent green color with two white stripes on the belly. Movements are awkward on the flat ground, but graceful and rapid in their natural haunts among the branches of trees. The following are the South indian species:—"*a*" Passerita mycterizans. Alias Coluber mycterizans; Dryinus nasutus; Dryiophis nasuta. Bright grass-green, bronze shade on back; on the anterior part of trunk skin between scales is white or black, these colors forming alternate cross bands when the animal expands that portion of the body; yellow stripe runs along each side of the pale-green abdomen; sometimes brownish olive instead of green; length of more than six feet. Feeds on birds and lizards. Often found on trees, and so called a Tree-snake; but see that head. Said to attack passengers, aiming particularly at the eyes, but it is perfectly harmless.—"*b*" Tragops dispar. Males bright green; females bronzecolored; skin between the scales black; a yellowish line with a greenish inner edge runs along each side of the abdomen.—"*c*" Tragops fronticinctus. Alias Dryiophis fronticinctus. Form grass-green above, paler below, with a yellow band along each side of the belly.——*Whip tree* (சவுக்கு - shavukku, Tam.). From long slender branches. Same as Chowk maram.

WHITE (श्वेत - shvéta, *San.*). Common prefix. For white arsenic see Soofaid soombal. For white lead see Moottoo velly. For white pepper see Pepper. For white vitriol see Vellay toottam.——*White-ant* (पुत्तिका - puttiká, San.; ارضہ - arzah, Ar.; خورہ - khurah, Pers.; دیمک - dímak, Hind.; دیوک - díwak, Dec.; اناي اناي - anaianaí, Malay; ಗೆದಲು - chedalu, Can.; ଉରଳେ - orale, Too.; చెదలు - chedalu, Tel.; ചെതൽ - chetal, Mal.; கறையான் - karaiyán, Tam.). Title from color. San. from (puttala, san. doll), from its form. Ar. from (arz, ar. earth). Hind. from old persian. Tel. from (shit'hila, san. decayed). Mal. from (chel, mal. sharp). Tam. from (karai, tam. to tarnish). Tam. also (shellu). Termes bellicosus, termitidæ, neuroptera, hemimetabola, insecta [poochy], of naturalists [jantoo]. The portuguese Formigas brancas. A species of termite and not an ant [choomtee]. Being blind it is exposed to attack of other animals, on which account it ordinarily remains underground; if it must come above ground, as to feed on a tree, &c., it first throws up sufficient earth to act as a screen. This is the meaning of the familiar white-ant earth. The large mounds of earth 7 or 8 feet high which are found all over the country are caused in this way. To destroy the cells of white-ants and dig out their queen is the best way of getting rid of them. Other remedies are:—Equal parts of lime [choonam], tar [keel], and soap [sauboon] boiled together and smeared over places where they appear; the earth-oils [munnteilam] of burmah; the wood-oils [q.v.] from the various species of dipterocarpi. Mixture of 3 of gambier [q.v.] and 12 of dammer oil; from ½ lb. to 4 lb. of hartaul [q.v.], the yellow sulphuret of arsenic mixed with the concrete of masonry; a mixture of pounded arsenic [paushaunam] and aloes [q.v.], scraped soap, and dhoby's earth [q.v.] boiled in a large pot half full of water and when cold filled up with cold water; sulphate of copper or of arsenic mixed with lime next to timber. Small quantity of arsenic and flour moistened with molasses [jaggery], made into a dough and placed near their tumuli. There are Tamul proverbs:—அந்தி ஈசல் பூத்தால், அடைமழை அதிகரிக்கும்—"if white-ants take wing in the evening, rain will increase." —காலைச் செல் பூத்தால் அடுத்த மழை அடங்கும்—"should winged white-ants appear in morning, approaching rain will cease."—புற்றிலே ஈசல் புறப்பட்டாலும், மண்

ணிலெகறையான் கூடிஞனும் மழை வரவே வரும்—"when winged white-ants issue out of a hole and white-ants "swarm, it will certainly rain [mausam, mazhay]."—ஈசல் இறகு எல்லாவற்றிலும் மிருது—"the wing of a white-ant "is the softest of all things."—பாம்புக்குத்தச்சன்கறையான்—"the white ant is the carpenter of the snake;" these ant-hills are always the habitations of snakes [sarpam].——*White honey* (श्वेतकाम्बोजी - shvétakámbóji, San.; سفید مدھ کا پیڑ - sufedmadhkáper, Hind.; سفید مدھ کا جھاڑ - sufedmadhkájhár, Dec.; తెల్లపురుగుడు - tellapurugudu, Tel.; வெள்ளைப்பூலாஞ்சி - vellaippúláñji, Tam.). San. from (shvéta, san. white + kámbójí, san. abrus precatorius, linn.); from white round fruit. Tel. and Tam. mean white + poolah [q.v.]. Tam. also (varadbúlá), meaning dry ground poolah. Sweet juice taken from whitish fruit of Securinega leucopyrus, müller, euphorbiaceæ [vricsham, 118]. Cf. Black honey.

WHONNAY (ಹೊನ್ನೆ - honne, *Can.*). From (honnu, can. gold); from red brown wood. Same as Red sanders.

WIJAYO (विजय - vijaya, *San.*). A form of Vijaya, ancient Aryan colonist of Ceylon [vi]. See vol. I (2) [mahavanso].

WIND (باد - bád, *Hind.*). Prefix.——*Wind-berry* (بادبرنگ - báubarang, Hind.; వాయువిడంగము - váyuvilangamu, Tel.). Same as Byebarang.——*Wind stroke* (पक्षाघात - pakshágháta, San.; کمری - kamarí, Hind.; ಪಕ್ಷವಾತರೋಗ - pakshavátaróga, Can.; పార్శ్వవాయువు - párshvaváyuvu, Tel.; പക്ഷവാതം - pakshavátam, Mal.; திமிர்வாயு - timirváyu, Tam.). San. from (paksha, san. side + ágháta, san. blow). Hind. from (kamar, hind. the loins). Can. from (paksha, san. side + váta, san. wind + róga, san. disease). Tel. from (párshva, san. side + váyu, san. wind). Mal. from (paksha, san. side + váta, san. wind). Tam. from (timir, tam. stiffness + váyu, san. wind). Medically Paraplegia. Paralysis of the hind extremeties of horses [ghorah]; lumbar or transverse paralysis; of obscure origin and rarely curable [ashwarogam].

WIRAUSAT (وراثت - wirásat, *Hind.*). From (irs, ar. to inherit) [mirass, vaurs]. Heirship. Wirausat nauma is heir certificate.

WIRE GRASS (குஞ்சப்புல் - kuñjappul, *Tam.*). From erect smooth stems. Same as Wild raggy.

WOBILINTA (వొబిలింత - vobilinta, *Tel.*). Botanically Polygonum [water gannair] roxburghii, meissn., polygonaceæ [vricsham, 110]. Alias Polygonum elegans. Herb; many-stemmed, prostrate; branches very thinly striated; ochreæ hyaline, ciliated and torn, one-nerved near the margin; leaves longer than internode, spreading, linear, acute or linear-oblong, apiculated, slightly scabrous at the edge; axils three to five flowered; pedicels articulated below the middle, short; calyx keeled and trigonal, attenuated at the base; achenium shining, faces ovate-rhomb, obsolutely dotted at the apex and margin; common everywhere.

WODALA (ఒడల - odala, *Tel.*; ஓடைமரம் - ódaimaram, *Tam.*). Tam. from (ódai, tam. rivulet + maram, tam. tree). Tel. also (bandikóta); (gódepeyyara); (rampamárédu); (yádala); (bandikattutíga), meaning wheel + tyre + creeper. Botanically Combretum decandrum, roxb., combretaceæ [vricsham, 55]. Alias combretum roxburghii; Poivrea roxburghii. Shrub; unarmed, scandent; young parts villous; leaves opposite, oval-oblong, acuminated; spikes panicled; bracts lanceolate; calyx turbinately campanulate; petals ovate, mucronate; stamens short; fruit five-winged; flowers small, pale-greenish; mountains of coromandel, flowering in the cold season. Another species is ovalifolium.——*White wodala* (उकशी - ukashí, Mahr.; తెల్లవడల - tellavadala, Tel.). Title from color of wood. Mahr. from (uksh, san. to sprinkle); from plants loving shade and moisture as naregamia alata, w. and a., flourishing beneath it. Tel. from (tella, tel. white + vadala, tel. combretum decandrum, roxb.). Tel. also (gaddapútike), meaning root + plant, grewia; (bandimurugudu); (karravadala), meaning stain + combretum decandrum, roxb. Botanically Calycopteris floribunda, lam., combretaceæ [vricsham, 55]. Alias Getonia floribunda, nutans. Dense climbing shrub; leaves opposite, shortly petioled, elliptic or ovate, acuminate, entire; on the upper surface are thinly scattered long hairs which are most abundant at the edges; the under surface is rusty tomentose, the tomentum being collected in little tufts giving rise to a dotted appearance in the fully matured leaf; taste very astringent and somewhat bitter; the fruit is about ¼ inch in length, ovoid, five-ribbed, villous, one-seeded, and is surmounted by the enlarged calyx; cotyledons convolute; leaves yield 6·86 per cent. of tannin; flowers greenish-white; common in ghauts [q.v.]. Leaves are bitter and astringent, and are chewed by the natives and the juice swallowed as a remedy for colic; the root ground to a paste with that of croton oblongifolium, roxb. [devil's goad] is applied to bites of the snake echis carinata [carpet snake]; in jaundice fruit, and various spices, of each one part, are made into a compound powder; the fruit, with the root of grewia pilosa, lam. [dog bran plant], is rubbed into a paste with honey [shahad] and applied to ulcers. Wood yellowish-white, moderately hard, with numerous broad medullary patches of soft, pith-like texture. No other common species here.

WODDA (ಒಡ್ಡನು - oddanu, *Can.*; ఒడ్డె - odde, *Tel.*; ஒட்டன் - ottan, *Tam.*). From (ódbra, san. name of a country) [wottiyam]. Tank-diggers and quarry laborers. They furnish the greater part of the body of agricultural laborers, corresponding to the english navvy. As a rule they are strong and athletic, but often addicted to drinking. Some, distinguished as Cull wodda, are stone masons. In Madras they rear pigs [soor] and clean tanks and wells of mud. They are migratory and dwell in small huts of reed or fine grass, and move to any place where they can find employment. Numbers about 400,000; distributed everywhere See vol. II, 230 [jauty].——*Wottiyam* (ஒட்டியம் - ottiyam, Tam.). From (ódhra, san. ancient name of orissa). Orissa, whence the tank-diggers [wodda] come [bhoogolashastram].

WODE (ഓട് - ótu, *Mal.*; ஓடு - ódu, *Tam.*). Tile. In making these, clayey earth is mixed with black ashes and water. This prepared earth is thrown upon a mould and sliced off with a wooden bow. The earth which is left in the mould is taken out and dried upon trough-shaped receptacles. After drying well it is burnt, and the result is a pantile. Tiles are used for roofing houses and for the coping of walls. For bricks and brick-making see Shengal.

WODEYA (ಒಡೆಯ - odeya, *Can.*; உடையான் - udaiyán, *Tam.*). From (udai, tam. possession). Means lord. Has no connection with Oodaya or Wodda or Wodier. Hindoo third name. Tam. singular wodeyaun, title among potters [coosava] and sometimes of jeinas [q.v.] but generally takes the plural form [peyar]. Sub-division of the neilgherry Badagas [q.v.]. Also title borne by some hindoo tribes. Also title of Mysore and Coorg rulers [jauty].——*Codayarpolliem* (உடையார்ப்பாளையம் - udayárppálaiyam, Tam.). See sep. title.——*Wodayaroy acottah* (ಉದಯರಾಯಕೋಟೆ - udayaráyakóte, Can.). From (udayaráya, can. proper name + kóte, can. fort); after wodeya rajah of mysore. Hill, Paranginaud division; Neilgherry district. One of the three principal old forts of the Neilgherries. The other two are Hoolicull droog and Mailcottah. No ruins remain. Utilized by Hyder ally. A mile beyond the fort are noted dolmens [coday cull].——*Wodeiyaun saitoopaty* (உடையான்சேதுப்பதி - udaiyánséthuppathi, Tam.). Name + title. First Saitoopaty of Ramnaud; created by Moottookrishnappa naick of Madura. Fortified Ramnaud and Pogalore. See vol. I (124).

WODIER (जिङ्गिनी - jinginí, *San.*; शिंटी - shimtí, *Mahr.*; کشملہ - kashmalá, *Hind.*; بے شرم کا جھاڑ - besharamkájhár, *Dec.*; ಉದಿಮರ - udimara, *Can.*; గుంపెన - gumpena, *Tel.*; ଇନ୍ଦ୍ରାମାଇ - indrámai, *Oor.*; ഒതി - oti, *Mal.*; හික් - hig, *Singh.*; ஒதியம் - othiyam, *Tam.*). Title from tamul. San. from (ji, san. to conquer); useful in disease. Hind from sanscrit. Dec. from (be, pers. without + sharam, pers. shame + jhár, hind. tree); from the tree becoming naked in hot weather; for another shameless plant see conky. Can. from tamul. Mal. from tamul. Tam. from (uthi, tam. to swell), meaning increasing in size without strength. San. also (ajashringí), meaning goat + horn, fruit resembles goat's horn; (jívala), meaning animating; (nétraushadhi), meaning eye + medicine, juice being applied to sore eyes. Hind. also (jíngam). Can. also (sintimara); (poonil); (shimtee); (shimti); (púvil); (gojal). Tel. also (dampara); (oddimánu). Mal. also (uti); (kaliççam); (ennakkara), meaning oily sap. Singh. also (hok). Tam. also (appiriyatharu), meaning not + liked + tree; (ánaikkárai), meaning elephant + canthium parviflorum, lam., from food of elephants. Title otherwise Aunacauray, Elephant webera, Ging, Goompany, Jingam. Botanically Odina wodier, roxb., anacardiaceæ [vricsham, 45]. Generic from tamul. Alias Haberlia grandis; Rhus odina. Large deciduous tree; leaves alternate about the ends of the branches, unequally pinnated; leaflets three to four pair opposite, almost sessile, oblong-obvate, acuminated, glabrous, entire, paler below; calyx shortly four-lobed, segments rounded; petals five, oblong, spreading; drupe uniform, very hard, one-celled; seeds solitary, of the same shape as the nut; racemes terminal, fascicled; flowers small, greenish yellowish, externally purplish; commonly cultivated; dark-red gum [gond] exudes from bark. The gum occurs in bazaars partly in tears of a yellowish tinge, and partly in colorless angular fragments, which are full of fissures like gum arabic; it has disagreeable taste and is not astringent, about one-half of it is completely soluble in water, the remaining portion forms a slimy mucilage, but is not gelatinous; the soluble portion, which is feebly acid, is precipitated by alcohol, and in a less degree by oxalate of ammonium, not at all by perchloride of iron or borax [vencauram]. The bark of the younger plants is ash-colored and smooth externally, and very fibrous and of a flesh color internally; that of the older trees is very rough, scaly, generally about ⅝ of an inch in thickness, brown externally, and reddish-brown internally; the taste of the inner bark is slightly astringent, due to tannic acid. Gum beaten up with cocoanut milk and applied medicinally to sprains and bruises; pulverised bark, boiled in or mixed with oil, applied to ulcers and wounds; leaves boiled in oil externally applied to bruises; bark forms gargle; bark and gum are in pharm. non-officinal, as demulcent and tonic respectively. Decoction; take of the inner bark, in coarse powder, five ounces; water, three pints; boil on a slow fire till the liquid is reduced to one point, cool and strain. Dose, from one and-a-half to three fluid ounces, three or four times in the 24 hours. Substituted; the bark for tinctura myrrhæ, liquor plumbi sub-acetatis dilutus, alum, gentian and calumba; the gum for gum-acacia. Tree is pollarded for fodder, especially for elephants [q.v.]; used as avenue [shaulay] tree, but is bare of leaves for several early months in the hot season; gum used in cloth printing; bark yields coarse cordage and a good bast fibre and also is used in tanning [chamrah]. Outer wood is white and worthless; there is a Tamul proverb:—ஒதி பெருத்துத் தூணுகுமோ—"though the wodier grow large, "will it become a pillar?"; heart-wood of good seedling trees, deep reddish mahogany, useful for many purposes, excellent for cabinet purposes. No other common species here.

WODY (ഓടി - óti, *Mal.*). From (ótu, mal. to run) [ode]. Swift-going vessel. A large sea-boat.

WODY (వోడి - vódi, *Tel.*; നീർപ്പൊന്നല്യം - nírpponnalyam, *Mal.*; பெசலத்தி - pesalatti, *Tam.*). Mal. from (nír, mal. water + ponnalyam, mal. ailantus malabarica, dec.). Tam. from (pasalai, tam. paleness + atti, tam. fig tree, ficus); from whitish wood. Tel. also (uddi). Title otherwise Falcate trumpet flower. Botanically Dolichandrone [water ailanto] falcata, seem., bignoniaceæ [vricsham, 99]. Alias Bignonia falcata, spathacea; Spathodea falcata, longiflora, rheedii. Small tree; leaves unequally pinnate, two to three pair, oval, rounded, entire, slightly hairy; racemes terminal, few-flowered; calyx cylindrical, oblique; flowers white, about 1 inch long, fragrant; capsule linear, 1 foot oblong, various twisted. Fibre obtained; wood whitish; hard, close and even-grained, seasons well, shining and glossy; no heart-wood; annual rings indistinct; used for building and agricultural purposes.——*Long-leaved wody* (వోడి - vódi, Tel.; നീർപ്പൊന്നല്യം - nírpponnalyam, Mal.; දියදැඹ - diyadámga, Singh.; ஆட்டுக்கொம்பொதியமரம் - áttukkombothiyamaram, Tam.). Mal. from (nír, mal. water + ponnalyam, mal. ailantus malabarica, dec.). Tam. from (ádu, tam. sheep + kombu, tam. horn + othiyamaram, tam. odina wodier, roxb.); latter has fruits like goats' horn. Tel. also (udi). Tam. also (kanbillaimaram). Title otherwise Long-leaved trumpet flower. Botanically Dolichandrone [water ailanto] rheedii, seem., bignoniceæ [vricsham, 99]. Alias Bignonia longiflora; Spathodea longiflora, rheedii. Arboreous, glabrous; leaves unequally pinnate, three-paired; leaflets oval-lenceolate, acuminate, petiolulate, entire; racemes terminal, short, about three-flowered; corolla with a long slender tube, capsule siliquiform, subcylindrical, erect or more or less curved; corolla white, 5 to 6 inches, capsule about 8 inches long; septum thickened in the middle, hence the capsule is somewhat four-celled; wing of the seed thickish, opaque, truncated. Very showy when in blossom; a common species, especially in malabar. Nets [valay] made from fibres [naur] of branches and roots; a red decoction prepared from root preserves the nets. Timber light-colored, strong and serviceable, used for agricultural and building purposes.

WOLFA (علوفى - alúfa, *Hind.*; உலுப்பை - uluppai, *Tam.*). From (alaf, ar. subsistence). Present of fruits, grain, &c., made to a house where there is a wedding, to a high official on tour, or to superiors generally on festival or special occasions. Also supplies of vegetables, fruits, &c., to a dependent or guest [bhet, caunicay, nuzzer].

WOLF-STRANGLER (خانق الذئب - khánikuzzaib, *Ar.*). Ar. from (khánik, ar. strangler + zaib, ar. wolf). Ar. also (kátiluzzaib), meaning wolf killer; (khánikunnamr), meaning panther-strangler. These two animals particularized from quickness of action on them. Herba aconita of chemists. Greek ἀκόνιτον, Title otherwise Bear's foot, Common aconite, European aconite, Friar's cap, Helmet flower, Luckie's mutch, Monk's cowl, Monk's hood, Nepaul aconite, Soldier's cap, Turk's cap, Wolf's bane. Botanically Aconitum [bish] napellus, linn., ranunculaceæ [vricsham, 1]. The european aconite plant. Perennial, deciduous, herbaceous plant, 4 feet high; leaves divided down to petiole, with linear acute furrowed lobes; racemes cylindric, long; ovaries three, smooth; flowers blue, flowering in may and july; root resembles ferox. Gives to pharm. the dried root, aconiti radix, and the fresh leaves, aconiti folia, both officinal; preparation of the leaves and flowering tops is extract of aconite, extractum aconiti; active principle, an alkaloid, aconitia; powerfully sedative, anydone, and antiphlogistic, in large doses a virulent poison. For non-poisonous aconites see Atees and Jadwaur; for indian aconite see Bachnaug.

WONAM (ഓണം - ónam, Mal.). From (shravana, san. the twenty-second lunar asterism). In Tamul Tirwonam. Luni-solar [chaundramaunam] festival [pundigay, 5c], occurring in the 5th solar month chingom [mausam], i.e., between 15th August and 14th September, when the full moon [powrnimay] is in the constellation shravanam [q.v.]. It lasts for 10 days and is the greatest national feast of Malabar. This is the day on which Vishnoo as Parshooramau [q.v.] is supposed to still descend annually to earth. On this day the acknowledgment of fealty to the Permaul [q.v.] emperor was formerly renewed. Chermaun, the last of the Permaul rulers, set sail for Mecca on the Tirwonam day in 824-25 after fealty acknowledged [collam, maryauday]. At the present day the Ñayar women go from street to street singing songs, and the men take part in athletic sports.

WOOD (لكڑی - lakrí, *Hind.*). Common prefix.——*Wood-apple* (விளா - vilá, Tam.). See sep. title.——*Wood cock* (سيمتيتر - símtítar, Hind.). From frequenting wooded regions. Same as Indian wood cock.——*Wood-oil* لكڑی كا تيل - lakríkátel, Hind.; ಮರಎಣ್ಣೆ - maraenne, Can.; మానినూనె - máninúne, Tel.; மரவெண்ணெய் - maravenney, Tam.). Title from being obtained by incision in the heart-wood. Hind. from (lakrí, hind. wood + tel, hind. oil). Can. from (mara, can. tree + enne, can. oil). Tel. from (mánu, tel. wood + núne, tel. oil). Tam. from (maram, tam. wood + enney, tam. oil). Resinous or balsamic volatile oil. Defined under Yennay [q.v.]. The chief so-called articles are from:—Dalbergia sissoo, roxb., giving sissoo wood-oil [sissoo]; Dipterocarpus turbinatus, gærtn., giving gurjan balsam [gurjan]. Dryobalanops aromatica, gærtn., giving camphor wood-oil [malayan camphor]; Erythroxylon monogynum, roxb., giving shemmanatty wood-oil [deccany deodar]; Tectona grandis, linn. f., giving teakwood oil [teak]. Wood-oil is chiefly used as a natural varnish [rangh] either alone or with colored pigments; also as a substitute for tar [keel, zift] in paving seams of shippings and for preserving timber from white-ants [q.v.].——*Woodpecker* (لكڑ پھوڑ - lakarphor, Hind.). From habit. Same as Marangotty.——*Wood sorrel* (انبوتی - ambutí, Hind.). Same as Sour auray.——*Wood turmeric* (دارهلد - dárhald, Hind.). From yellow dye of wood. Same as Berberry.——*Wood warbler* (مرغ چمن - murghichaman, Hind.). Title from resort. Hind. means garden bird. See Calacuntam.

WOOD-APPLE (कपित्थ - kapitt'ha, *San.*; कवंठ - kavant'ha, *Mahr.*; बेल - béla, *Conc.*; كبيت - kabít, *Ar.* and *Pers.*; كت بيل - katbel, *Hind.*; كويت كا جهاڑ - kavítkájhár, *Dec.*; ಬೇಲದಮರ - béladamara, *Can.*; ಬೇಲ - béla, *Too.*; వెలగ - velaga, *Tel.*; କୋୟଟ - koyata, *Oor.*; വിളാവു - vilávu, *Mal.*; දිවුල් - divul, *Singh.*; விளா - vilá, *Tam.*). Title from fruit, the size of an apple, with a hard, woody rind [wood]. San. from (kapi, san. monkey + st'ha', san. to stand); monkeys affect the tree for fruits. Mahr. from sanscrit. Conc. means bael tree, ægle marmelos. Ar. from sanscrit. Hind. from (kát, hind. wood + bel, hind. ægle marmelos, corr.). Dec. from (kavíta, mahr. wood-apple + hár, hind. tree). Mal. from (vil, mal. to burst). Tam. from (vilavu, tam. to burst); fruit splits on falling down. San. also (gópakarnu), meaning cowherd's ear; (p'halasugandhi), meaning having fragrant fruit; (sangráhi), meaning gathering together, astringent; (bhúkapitt'ha), meaning ground + the tree; properly applies to a smaller variety; (dadhip'hala), meaning curd fruit, the fruit having the sour taste of curd [great pumpkin]. Hind. also (bhuinkatbel), meaning ground, ægle marmelos, linn. Dec. also (bhuínkavítkájhár), meaning ground wood-apple tree. Can. also (dantashat'ha), meaning tooth + rogue, from sour fruit [gaub, sour auray]; (gráhamara), meaning constipation + tree. Tel. also (nélavelaga), meaning ground + wood-apple; (pulivelaga), meaning sour + wood-apple; (parupuvelaga), meaning spreading wood-apple. Tam. also (vellil), from yellowish white wood; (kuttivilá), meaning small + the tree, strictly limonia acidissima, linn. [wild lime]; (nilavilá), meaning ground + the tree; (karuvilá), meaning black + feronia; applies to ægle marmelos, corr. whose fruit is darker. Title otherwise Curd fruit, Elephant apple, Monkey fruit, Elephant apple, because the fruit is like an elephant's skin. Balong of the portuguese. Botanically Feronia elephantum, corr., rutaceæ [vricsham, 32]. Alias Cratæva balanghas, vullanga. Vullanga, from tamul, meaning wood-apple. Handsome erect growing tree, 50–60 feet, armed with spines; leaves pinnated, smelling of aniseed; leaflets five to seven, obovate, almost sessile; petioles winged, pointed; racemes lax, axillary or terminal; calyx five-toothed; petals five; style scarcely any; flowers small, pale pink with crimson anthers smelling of aniseed; much cultivated, common in dry forests. Fruit as occurring is somelike the bael [q.v.], round, of a pale green color, and about the size of a cricket ball; when the hard shell-like rind is cracked, the interior is found full of a brown, soft, mealy kind of substance, rather acrid, having a strong smell of rancid butter, and not palatable, containing flat woolly seeds; fruit is extremely acid before maturity; is sometimes used to adulterate bael [q.v.] fruit. The pulp of the fruit contains citric acid and mucilage. The leaves yield to distillation a small quantity of essential oil similar to that obtained from bael leaves. Vilaum gum, a true transparent gum [gond], exudes from wounds in bark; this occurs in small roundish, oblong or tapering tears, or in broken pieces, varying in size from a pea [calauyam] to a soap-nut [q.v.]; generally colorless and transparent, sometimes opaque with numerous minute cracks on the surface; odourless, bland and mucilaginous in taste; much whiter and more transparent than acacia arabica [babool]. The root bark is thick, white and starchy; it has the odour of the leaves and contains essential oil [attar]. Young leaves medicinally stomachic and carminative, especially for children; ripe fruit useful in affections of the throat; sherbet [q.v.] made from fruit has alexipharmic properties; pulp applied externally is a remedy for the bites of venomous insects, if not obtainable the powdered rind may be used; astringent pulp of unripe fruit used in dysentery and diarrhœa; gum used as an adjunct to other medicines and especially for the purpose of suspending heavy powders, substituted for british gum arabic; in pharm. non-officinal; oil from leaves is a good substitute for oil of anise [q.v.]. Syrup; take of the pulp of the ripe fruit, ten ounces; mix well in thirty ounces of water and strain through cloth; add twenty ounces of refined sugar to the strained liquid, and apply heat till the sugar is dissolved and the liquid assumes the consistence of a thick syrup. Infusion; take of the fresh leaves, three ounces; boiling water, one pint; infuse in a closed vessel for two hours and strain. Doses; of mucilage, from two to four fluid ounces; of syrup, from four fluid drachms to one fluid ounce; of the infusion, from two to four fluid ounces. Substituted; the gum for the gum arabic and tragacanth [kateerah] imported from europe; the syrup for effervescing draughts, diluted phosphoric and sulphuric acids; the leaves for dill [sowa] and anise [q.v.]. Pulp of fruit makes an edible jelly [morabba], like black-currant; this has a peculiar flavor, agreeable but more astringent; also eaten raw with sugar [q.v.]. Gum used by dyers [shauyam] and painters, particularly miniatrre and chintz-painters; employed in making ink [mashy] and varnish [raugh], and by bricklayers in preparing certain cements and plaster [cauray]; it forms a stronger mucilage than gum arabic; forms a part of the gum ghautty [q.v.] and east india gum arabic of commerce. Wood yellowish-white, hard; annual rings distinctly marked by a white line; heavy and durable; is used for various purposes. There is a small variety of this tree, the properties of which are nearly the same. There is a Tamul proverb:—அருகாகப்பழுத்தாலும் விளாமரத்தில் வௌவால் சேராது—"although the fruit of the "wood-apple tree close by ripens, bats will not approach it." There is another:—விட்டுகடா ஆசை விளாம்பழத்து ஓட்டோடே—"the pleasure of wood apple ceases with the "shell."——*Dark wood-apple* (नीलकपित्थ - nílakapitt'ha, San.). Same as Mango.——*Dog wood-apple* (ನಾಯಿಬೇಲದಮರ - náyibéla-damara, Can.). From inferior but similar fruit. Same as Monkey lime.——*Large wood-apple* (महाकपित्थ - mahákapitt'ha, San.; மாவிலங்கை - mávilangai, Tam.). Same as Ashy babool, Bael, Nirvala, and Weaver's beam.——*Lowly wood-apple* (కుంది వెలగ - kundivelaga, Tel.). Same as Mysore balah.——*Robust wood-apple* (తోరెలగ - tórelaga, Tel.). Same as Wild lime.——*Water wood-apple* (നീർവിളാ - nírvilá, Mal.). Same as Nirvala.——*White wood-apple* (வெள்விளா - velvilá, Tam.). From light-colored wood. Same as Venteak.

WOONDY (उंदी - undí, *Mahr.*). Same as Soora poon.

WOONJA (உஞ்சப்பட்டை - úñjappattai, *Tam.*). From (uriñju, tam. to absorb + pattai, tam. bark); from absorbing oil from hair as sponge. Bark of Albizzia amara, boivin [dark sirissa].

WOOTZ (अयस् - ayás, *San.*; فولاد - fúlad, *Pers.*; فولاد - folád, *Hind.*; پولاد - polád, *Dec.*; کالولی - káluli, *Malay*; ಉಕ್ಕು - ukku, *Can.*; அலவு - alavu, *Too.*; ఉక్కు - ukku, *Tel.*; ഉരുക്കു - urukku, *Mal.*; உருக்கு - urukku, *Tam.*). Title from (uçça, san. high); superior, as forming metal for edge-tools. San. (i, san. to go). Tel. means strength. Mal. from tamul. Tam. from (urugu, tam. to melt); prepared iron. Malay also (málela); (waja). Tam. also (ehgu), meaning sharpness. Indian steel. Made especially in Salem. Steel is iron [auhan] combined with a small quantity of carbon [kary]. Brittle, resists the file, cuts glass, affords sparks when struck on flint, and retains the magnetic virtue for any length of time. It loses this hardness by being ignited, and cools very slowly. The σίδηρος ἰνδικὸς καὶ στόμωμα of the Periplus. Damascus sword blades were made from the wootz of S. india. The Arabian poets celebrate swords made of indian steel. Indian iron is mentioned in the Pandects as an article of commerce. Salmasius says that among the surviving Greek treatises was one περὶ βαφῆς ἰνδικοῦ σιδήρου. The art of converting iron into steel has been immemorially known to the more civilised nations of the Malay archipelago, and they have native names for it. Prepared here from small pieces of malleable iron made from magnetic ore, which are packed in crucibles with pieces of Cassia auriculata [tungaid] wood, and covered with leaves and clay [calimunu].

WOTTAM (ஒட்டம் - ottam, *Tam.*). From (ottu, tam. to stick on). A conical pile of earth left by tank diggers [wodda] as a measure of the depth to which they have dug.——*Wottay* (ஒட்டை - ottai, Tam.). Otherwise Wottay chann. A short span or span between the tips of the thumb and forefinger extended [pradesham]. Jaun [q.v.] is a long span, viz., between the tips of the thumb and little finger extended [vitasty].

WUCK (വക്ക - vakka, *Mal.*). From (valka, san. bark). Same as Sunn.——*Wucknaur* (வக்குநார் - vakkunár, Tam.). Fibre of Sunn.

WUNKA (వంక - vanka, *Tel.*). From (vankara, tel. crooked). Channel [vaug]; suffix in place names, as Booggawunka, meaning spring + channel.

WUNTOO (వంతు - vantu, *Tel.*). Literally a turn. A share, part or portion.——*Wuntoodar* (వంతుదారుడు - vantudárudu, Tel.). From (above + dár, hind. holder). The holder of a share. A petty superintendent, because he gets more than the one wuntoo or share which an ordinary labourer receives, and is therefore wuntoodar by pre-eminence.

WURD (ورد - vard, *Ar.*). Rose.——*Wurd i abyaz* (ورد ابیض - vardiabyaz, Hind.). From (above + abyaz, ar. white). Indian white rose [gool].——*Wurd i ahmar* (ورد احمر - vardiahmar, Hind.). From (above + ahmar, ar. red). Cabbage rose [gool].——*Wurd i ahmar i boostauny* (ورد احمر بستانی - vardiahmari-bustání, Hind.). From (bustán, ar. garden). Damask rose [gool].——*Wurd i jabalee* (ورد جبلی - vardijabali, Hind.). From (jabal ar. hill). French rose [gool].——*Wurd i seeny* (ورد صینی - vardisíní, Hind.). From (sín, ar. china). Indian rose [gool].

WURG (ವರ್ಗ - varga, *Can.*). From (vrij, san. to remove) [vargam]. Means division. A holding, an estate. Wurgdar is a landlord.

WURREE (واری - wárí, *Hind.*). From (varaka, san. desirable). Same as Varagoo.

WYCOME (വൈക്കം - vaikkam, *Mal.*). From (vai, mal. deposit). Alluvial soil. Sanscrit name (vyághrálaya), meaning vyaugran, the sage so called + temple [chidambaram].—"*a*" Talook; Travancore state, Cottayam division. Population 76,414. Extreme length, N. to S., 15 miles; extreme breadth, E. to W., 10 miles. Sub-divided into 7 praverties [q.v.] and containing 67 caras [q.v.] or villages. Bounded N. and E. by the Cochin territory, S. by Yaittmanore talook, and W. by the Vembanaud lake. Irrigation by means of canals.—"*b*" Town, Tahsildar's and Moonsif's station, Place of pilgrimage; Travancore state, Cottayam division; Wycome tal.; pop. 14,838; lat. 9° 45'; long. 76° 27'; from Alleppey N.N.E. 18 miles; from Cochin S.S.E. 18 miles; from Cottayam N.N.W. 13 miles; from Madras S.W. 350 miles; from Quilon N.N.W. 60 miles; from Nagarcoil N.N.W. 127 miles; from Paravore S.S.E. 30 miles; from Trivandrum N.N.W. 94 miles; from the sea E. 7 miles. On the eastern bank of Vembanaud lake. Formerly the residence of Vyaugra maha rishy [chidambaram]. Great Shiva pagoda [q.v.]. Thousands resort for vows on Ashtamy [pundigay, 5c] festival in November.

WYNAUD (വയനാട്ട് - vayanátu, *Mal.* wynaad*). From (vayal, mal. open field + nátu, mal. country) [vayal]. Sanscrit name (mayakshétra), meaning disrict of mayan, architect of the deityans [q.v.]—(1) Wynaud proper. Talook, Malabar district. Tahsildar's pay Rs. 200. Area 821 square miles. Balaghaut talook of district. Bounded north by Cottayam and Coorg, east by Mysore, south by Neilgherry district and Yernaud, and west by Calicut and Cooroombranaud and Cottayam. Originally consisted of three divisions, known as North wynaud, South wynaud and South-east wynaud. This latter portion, area 240 square miles, consisting of the amshoms of Numbalagode, Moonnanaud and Cherangode, was transferred to the Neilgherry district on 31st March 1877 [wynaud, south east]. The Ouchterlony valley, area 40 square miles, also formed part of S.E. Wynaud, but on the 1st September 1873 it was transferred to the Neilgherry district. A general account of the whole Wynaud country has already been given at vol. II, 143. The following are the principal mountains:—Balasore, Bramhagherry, Chambramala, Culpettamala, Dindimala, Morampora, Shashimala, Talamala, Terriotemala, Vauvoomala or Camel hump, Vellaramala, Yedacullmala, Yelambilairymala. Passes [ghaut] uniting the low country with the talook are:—Smugglers' pass from Dindimala to Manattana; Periya pass descending on Cannavam [cangote] in Cottayam talook, wheeled traffic; Yelatchooram pass or Cardamom mountain pass, leading to Coottiyaudy in Cooroombranaud talook; Coottiyaudy pass also descending on Coottiyaudy; Terriote pass likewise leading to Coottiyaudy; Tamracherry pass into Calicut talook, wheeled traffic; Cholaudy pass leading into the Nelambore valley; Carcoor pass into the Yernaud talook, wheeled traffic. Rivers:—Aulatore póya, Canayaucherry poya, Cholaudy river, Coonnat poya, Cubbany, Manantoddy poya, Panamaram poya, Poothoocherry poya, Sholaiyaur. Places of archæological interest:—Ganapativuttam, Moopnaud, Poothaudy, Tirnelly. Principal trig. station:—Naricaud. The leading places, &c., in the Malabar talook are the following.——*Balasore* (ബാലേശ്വരം - baléshvaram, Mal.). From (bala, san. strong + íshvara, san. lord). Sanscrit name also (bánásura), meaning baunam, the asooran; called after him. Peak; lat. 11° 42' N.; long. 75° 57' E.; height 6,762 feet; from Calicut N.N.E. 31 miles; from Manantoddy S.W. 9 miles. Isolated cone-shaped peak. Except on the lower portions, which have been cleared by Moplahs for coffee [q.v.] cultivation, it is densely wooded.——*Benny* (ബെന്നി - benni, Mal.). Forest; lies partly in S.E. Wynaud and partly in Malabar-wynaud. The latter portion is known as Trans-benny, whilst the former is called Benny.——*Bramhagherry* (ബ്രഹ്മഗിരി - brahmagiri, Mal.). See sep. title.——*Camel hump* (വാവുൾമല - vávúlmala, Mal.). See sep. title.——*Corote* (കോറോത്ത് - kórótt, Mal.). See sep. title.——*Cubbany* (കബ്ബനി - kabbani, Mal.). See sep. title.——*Culpetta* (കല്പെട്ട - kalpétta, Mal.). From (kal, mal. stone + pétta, mal. suburb). Town ; lat. 11° 38′ ; long. 76° 08′ ; from Calicut N.E. 33 miles. By road 45 miles ; from Manantoddy S.S.E. 12 miles. Large weekly market. Mostly inhabited by Tamul settlers. On high road from the Tamracherry pass [ghaut]. Bungalow [q.v.] and chuttram [q.v.].——*Lukkidy* (ലക്കിടി - lakkiti, Mal.). Means wood ; lat. 11° 31′ ; long. 76° 04′ ; from Calicut N.E. 24 miles ; from Manantoddy S. 19 miles. Head of the Tamracherry ghaut [q.v.] pass. Bungalow [q.v.], chuttram [q.v.] and ruins of the old Mysorean stockade from which it derives its name.——*Manantoddy* (മാനന്തവാടി - mánantaváti, Mal.). See sep. title.——*Naricaud* (നരിക്കാടു - narikkátu, Mal.). From (nari, mal. tiger + kátu, mal. forest). Village ; lat. 11° 33′ ; long. 76° 02′ ; from Calicut N.E. 24 miles ; from Manantoddy S.S.W. 16 miles. Trig. station in lat. 11° 32′ 26·88″ ; long. 76° 01′ 21·07″ ; height 5,095 feet ; from Manantoddy S.S.W. 16 miles.——*Padry* (പാതിരി - pátiri, Mal.). Means a christian priest. Forest ; lat. 11° 39′ ; long. 76° 15′ ; from Calicut N.E. 40 miles ; from Manantoddy S.E. 17 miles.——*Panamarticottah* (പനമരത്തിക്കോട്ട - panamarattikótta, Mal.). From (panamaram, mal. palm tree, borassus flabelliformis, linn. + kótta, mal. fort). Village ; lat. 11° 44′ ; long. 76° 07′ ; from Calicut N.E. 38 miles ; Manantoddy S.E. 6 miles. Formerly a military post.——*Perambaudy* (പെരമ്പാടി - perampáti, Mal.). See sep. title.——*Periya* (പേരിയ - périyá, Mal.). From (periya, mal. great). Pass ; lat. 11° 51′ N. ; long. 75° 51′ E ; from Calicut N.N.E. 40 miles ; from Manantoddy W.N.W. 13 miles. Leads from Tellicherry and Cannanore through North wynaud to Mysore.——*Poracaud* (പൊറക്കാട് - porakkátu, Mal.). From (pura, mal. outer + kátu, mal. jungle). Town ; lat. 11° 41′ ; long. 76° 12′ ; from Calicut N.E. 39 miles ; from Manantoddy S.E. 13 miles. Temple of repute.——*Ramapore* (രാമപുരം - rámapuram, Mal.). From (ráma, san. the god + pura, san. town).—" *a* " Village ; lat. 11° 46′ ; long. 76° 29′ ; from Calicut N.E. 55 miles ; from Manantoddy E. 28 miles.—" *b* " River ; Tributary of the Cubbany, into which it eventually flows after draining a large portion of South-east wynaud.——*Sisparra* (ചിച്ചിപ്പാറ - chiççippára, Mal.). See sep. title.——*Sultan's battery* (ഗണപതിവട്ടം - ganapativattam, Mal.). See sep. title.——*Tannote mala* (തണോട്ടമല - tanóttmala, Mal.). From (tan, mal. water + ótu, mal. to run + mala, mal. hill). Hill ; lat. 11° 32′ N. ; long. 76° 01′ E. ; from Calicut N.E. 24 miles ; from Manantoddy S. 18 miles. Overhanging the Tamracherry pass into Wynaud.——*Terriote* (തരിയോട്ടു - tariyóttu, Mal.). See sep. title.——*Tirnelly* (തിരുനെല്ലി - tirunelli, Mal.). From (tiru, mal. holy + nelli, mal. the tree, phyllanthus emblica, linn.). Sanscrit name (sahyámalakí), meaning sahyadry + the tree, phyllanthus emblica, linn. ; also (ámalakakshétra), meaning emblic myrobalan + sacred place ; also (siddhakshétra), meaning sage + sacred place. Village, Place of pilgrimage ; lat. 11° 55′ ; long. 76° 02′ ; from Calicut N.N.E. 47 miles ; from Manantoddy N. 8 miles. Temple in the Ellorenaud amshom [q.v.]. Lies in a valley of the mountains to the south of the Bramhagherry peak. Is known by three different names, Aumlaca temple, Siddha temple and Tirnelly temple. In connection with the temple are seven holy water fountains:—Goonnica teertam, Paupnaushy, Punchateertam, Rinamochiny teertam, Sahasravindoo, Shatavindoo, Varauham.——*Vythery* (വൈത്തിരി - vaittiri, Mal.). See sep. title.——*Yelambilairy* (എളമ്പിലേരി - elampiléri, Mal.). From (ela, mal. tender + pul, mal. grass + éri, mal. tank). Peak ; lat. 11° 31′ N. ; long. 76° 07′ E. ; height 6,806 feet ; from Calicut N.E. 28 miles ; from Manantoddy S.S.E. 21 miles. Precipitous needle-shaped hill in the heart of the best coffee-producing district in Wynaud. 5 miles S.E. of Vythery.——**(2)** South-east Wynaud. Division, Neilgherries ; area 240 square miles. Comprises the minor divisions of Cherangode, Moonnanaud, Numbalagode. Boundaries :—North by Malabar, Wynaud, Ganapativuttam amshom and Mysore. East by Todanaud. South by Yernaud talook, Malabar district. West by Yernaud talook and Moopnaud amshom. Contains small rounded hills separated by swamps or valleys. Many of the hills are covered with forest. Fever is prevalent from March to June. Soil good. Several coffee [q.v.] and cinchona [koinah] estates have been opened by European planters. The native ryots [q.v.] generally cultivate paddy [q.v.] in the swamps called nilams. There are several gold mining companies now working. There is considerable traffic between Mysore and Goodalore along the Goodalore-teppacaudoo road. All articles of food are obtained from Mysore. Weekly markets are at Goodalore, Devaulah, Pundalore and Cherambaudy. The division was as above said, transferred in 1877 from Malabar district to the Neilgherries and placed under the Head assistant collector. Contains a Moonsif's court.

X (क्ष - ksha, *San.*). San. the fourth or man-lion [narsimhan] incarnation [avatar] of Vishnoo [q.v.].

Y (य - ya, या - yá, *San.* ; ى - ye, *Hind.* ; ய - ya, யா - yá, *Tam.*). San. long Lutchmy [q.v.]. San. short Yaman [q.v.]. Hind. numerically symbol for 10 ; in almanacs [punchaungam] stands for jupiter [brihaspaty, najm] and sign [raushy] aquarius [coombham, dalo]. Tam. short the numeral 10.

YACOOB (يعقوب - yakúb, *Ar.*). Jacob. Mahomedan alam ; Yacoob ally, double alam [ism].

YACSHAN (यक्ष - yaksha, *San.*). From (yaksh, san. to worship). Demi-gods, attendants on Coobairan [q.v.]. Yacshy is the feminine.——*Yekky* (யெக்கி - yekki, Tam.). Corruption from (yakshí, san. demoness). Female devil [pey].

YADOO (यदु - yadu, *San.*). A king, progenitor of Yaudavas.——*Yaudava* (यादव - yádava, San.). The descendants of Yadoo. Otherwise Jauts. The principal branches were formerly settled in the west of Malwah, Rajpootana, and Goozerat. The Yaudavas of Dwaura samoodram or Halabeed [q.v.] in Mysore were commonly called Hoysala [q.v.] ballaulas [q.v.]. Another line of Yaudava kings arose in the northern part of the old Chalookya [q.v.] kingdom at the end of the twelfth century. They overcame the Calachooryas [q.v.] and became masters of all the western Deccan [q.v.], having their capital at Devagiry, the ancient Tagara, and now known as Dowlatabad in Hyderabad territory. The two dynasties contested till overthrown by Mahomedans in fourteenth century [charitram, jadow, raj]. See vol. I (139) ; II, 251. Yaudava is a caste-title taken by about 100,000 of the shepherd tribes, chiefly in the two Arcots and Chingleput ; but probably this is a mere corruption from their own dravidian title of Yiday [q.v.].

YAHYAH (يحيى - yahyá, *Ar.*). Jehu. Mahomedan alam ; as Yahyah hoossain, double alam [ism].

YAILAM (యేలము - yálam, *Tel.* ; ஏலம் - élam, *Tam.*). From arabic, meaning notification. Auction [haraaj].

YAIPY (अंजन - añjana, *Mahr.* ; انجن کا پیڑ - anjankáper, *Hind.* ; ಕಾರಚಿಗಿಡ - kárachigida, *Can.* ; ఏపె - épe, *Tel.* ; ஆச்சா - áççá, *Tam.*). Title from teloogoo. Mahr. from (añj, san. to shine) [cassa, champak]. Hind. from (añjana, mahr. the tree + per, hind. tree). Can. from (káru, can. black + áchigida, can. the plant). Tam. from (ár, tam. density, also lustre) ; from colored heavy wood. Can. also (karachu) ; (kamara) ; (kaula) ; (asanagurgi). Tel. also (náraépe), meaning fibre + the tree. Tam. also (káttudugu), meaning wild + the tree, acacia pennata, willd. Title otherwise Atchah, False frankincense tree. Botanically Hardwickia binata, roxb., leguminosæ [vriesham, 48]. Tree, bark deeply cracked, branches spreading ; leaves alternate, petioled, leaflets one pair, opposite, sessile, with a bristle between them, between semi-cordate and reniform, obtuse, entire, very smooth on both sides, three to six-veined at the base, when young tinged with red, stipules small, cordate, caducous ; panicles terminal and from the exterior axils ; flowers pedicelled, scattered, small, bracts minute, caducous ; calyx somewhat hoary outside, often dotted, yellowish within, filaments usually ten, rarely six to eight, anthers with or without an acute point between the lobes ; style filiform, stigma large, peltate ; legume lanceolate, 2–3 inches in length, two-valved, striated lengthwise, opening at the apex ; seed solitary in the apex of the legume ; found in forests to 3,500 feet elevation ; is easily raised from seed. From notches made in the heart of the trunk an oleo-resin [teilam] is obtained, balsamic in its properties and resembling copaiba balsam [q.v.], for which it is an efficient substitute ; called madeiyan sambrauny [q.v.], or false frankincense ; leaves given as fodder to cattle [maud] ; bark yields strong fibre [naur]. Sap-wood small, white ; heart-wood extremely hard, dark red, often with a purplish tinge, cross, and very close-grained ; about the hardest and heaviest wood in india ; extremely durable, liable to split, but does not warp ; used for bridge and house posts, ornamental work. Hardwickia pinnata, roxb., has similar properties.

YAIR (ಏರು - éru, *Can.* ; ഏർ - ér, *Mal.* ; ஏர் - ér, *Tam.*). A plough [calappay]. Also as much land as will occupy a plough [gorroo]. Yairaul attavanay, from (ál, tam. person + attavanai, tam. register), is a list of ploughs and laborers in the village. Yair caunicay is plough tax. Yair cocripp is daily account of ploughs at work. Yairezhoopatt, from (above + ezhubathu, tam. seventy), is a poem of 70 stanzas in praise of the plough, by Cumban [q.v.], written at the instance of a wealthy farmer.——*Yair poott* (ஏர்ப்பூட்டு - érppúttu, Tam.). From (above + púttu, tam. to yoke). Ploughing for the first time in the season on an auspicious day, begun with appropriate ceremonies. Otherwise Yaircutt, meaning same ; also Ponnair or golden plough.

YAISOO (യേശു - yéshu, *Mal.*). Jesus.——*Yaisoo masheeha* (യേശുമശിഹാ - yéshumashíha, Mal.). Jesus the Messiah, among the Malabar syrian [q.v.] christians.

YAITTAM (ایتم - etam, *Hind.*; ಯಾತ - yáta, *Can.*; ఏతము - étamu, *Tel.*; ഏത്തം - éttam, *Mal.*; ஏற்றம் - éttam, *Tam.*). From (éru, tam. to rise). A picottah [q.v.].——*Yaitampota* (ఏతముపోత - étamupóta, Tel.). From (above + póyu, tel. to pour). Irrigation by picottah [cheypota, yiraippoo].——*Yaitcole* (ഏത്തക്കോൽ - éttakkól, Mal.; ஏற்றக்கோல் - éttakkól, Tam.). From (above + kól, mal. rod). The bamboo [q.v.] thereof.——*Yaittachaul* (ஏற்றச்சால் - éttaççál, Tam.). From (above + shál, tam. bucket). The bucket thereof [mbote].——*Yiraippoo* (இறைப்பு - iraippu, Tam.). From (irai, tam. raise water). Irrigation [pauchal] by lift [yaitampota].

YAJ (यज् - yaj, *San.*). To sacrifice.——*Yajanam* (यजन - yajana, San.). Performing holy sacrifice.——*Yajoos* (यजुस् - yajus, San.; யசுரு - yasuru, Tam.). From (yaj, san. to sacrifice). The second of the four Vedams [q.v.].——*Yanyam* (यज्ञ - yaña, San.; யக்கியம் - yakkiyam, Tam.). Tam. also (eççam), by corruption. Prayers employed at periodic solemn rites, hence the periodic rites themselves [yaugam]. For daily rites of Bramins see Mahayanyam. The following ancient yanyams are mentioned in Shoocla yajoor vedam [q.v.]:—Darshapoornamausow, ceremonies performed at the new [amavausyay] and full moon [powrnimay] of every lunar [chaundramaunam] month [mausam]; Pitry medham, obsequies in commemoration of a deceased ancestor; Agnishtomam or praise of agny [q.v.], including jyotishtomam, drinking of the juice of somam [q.v.]; Vaujapeyam, drinking of an acetous mixture of meal and water; Rajasooyam or king making, the consecration of a king [rajah]; Sowtraumany in honor of sootrauman or indran [q.v.]; a substitute for soma sacrifice, spirituous liquors and milk [paul] used instead of somam [q.v.] juice; Ashwamedham or horse [ghorah] sacrifice; according to vedam [q.v.] in this sacrifice 609 animals of various prescribed kinds domestic and wild including bird [pacshy], fish [matsyam], reptiles [sarpy] are made fast, the tame ones to 21 posts and the wild ones in the intervals between the posts; after some prayers are finished these are set at liberty uninjured; later on a ceremony performed by cshatriyas [q.v.] ambitious of universal empire and consisting in the immolation of a horse; Poorshamedham or human sacrifice; according to vedam 185 men of various specified tribes, characters and professions are tied to 11 posts; after the recitation of certain hymns [muntram], they are all set at liberty uninjured; later on it consisted in the immolation of one man, traces of which lingered till recent times in the doorga poojay [q.v.] and meriah [q.v.] of the hill tribes; Sarwa medham or sacrifice of all, prayers and oblations for universal success. Five yanyams are enjoined by Menoo [q.v.] on every householder [grihastan] of the twice-born [dwijan] castes to be performed every day:—Bramhayanyam or the devotional act of teaching or repeating the vedams [q.v.] or other sacred texts; Devayanyam or worshipping the superior gods by oblations to fire or through fire the other gods [deva]; Pitry yanyam or worshipping the manes of ancestors or obsequial offerings; Manooshya yanyam or devotion due to men or the honoring of guest by acts of hospitality; Bhoota yanyam or the devotion due to beings in general, which is performed by throwing up into the air, generally at the door of the house, a baly [q.v.] or ball of rice, the remains of the morning and evening meal with mantrams [q.v.] or prayer addressed to gods, demi-gods, men, animals and even to spirits of trees, waters, &c. Yanyam in the abstract is conceived to be a kind of machinery, in which every piece must tally with the other; or a sort of large chain in which no link is allowed to be wanting; or a staircase by which one may ascend to heaven; or as a personage endowed with all the characteristics of the human body; it exists from eternity and proceeded from the supreme being, prajaupaty [q.v.] or bramh [q.v.] neuter, along with the trai-vidyay, i.e., the three-fold science; the creation of the world is even regarded as the fruit of a sacrifice performed by the supreme being; the yanyam exists as an invisible thing at all times; it is supposed to extend, when unrolled from the ahavaneeyam or sacrificial fire into which all oblations are thrown, to heaven, forming thus a bridge or ladder, by means of which the sacrifice can communicate with the world of gods and spirits, and even ascend when alone to their abodes.——*Yanyeshwaran* (எக்கியேசுவரன் - ekkiyésuvaran, Tam.). From (yaña, san. sacrifice + íshvara, san. lord); lord of sacrifice. Epithet of vishnoo. Hindoo 2nd or pers. name [peyar]. Familiarly Yanyan.——*Yanyopaveetam* (यज्ञोपवीत - yañópavíta, San.). From (yaña, san. sacrifice + upavíta, san. thread), as first worn after a homam before fire. The sacred thread [jandiram, janivaura, poonool].——*Yaugam* (याग - yága, San.). Occasional and special sacrifice [yanyam]. Consists in parting with a thing that it may belong to a deity whom it is intended to propitiate. It is of four sorts:—Ishty, a simple oblation; Pashoomantam, immolation of a victim; Somam, presentation of moon plant [somam] juice; Homam [q.v.], burnt offering. Shyaina yaugam or hawk sacrifice is performed for inflicting an injury on a foe; Chittray for acquisition of a cow; Oodbhid for possessing the same; Vishwajit or all-conquering for benefit in another world; and so many others.——*Yaugappah* (యాగప్ప - yágappa, Tel.). From (yága, san. sacrifice + appa, tel. father, titular affix). Hindoo 2nd or pers. name [peyar].——*Yaujee* (ಯಾಜಿ - yájí, Can.). Means sacrificer. Hindoo third name; also suffix in proper names as Somayaujee [peyar].——*Yaunyavalcyan* (याज्ञवल्क्य - yáñavalkya, San.). A patronymic from Yanyavalcan. Surnamed Vaujasaneyan. Wrote White yajoor vedam [q.v.], Shatapata bramhanam [q.v.] and Brihad auranyacam. Also author of the most important law book [smrity] next to that of Menoo [q.v.], this emanating from the White yajoor vedam [q.v.] as the code of the Maunavas did from the Black yajoor vedam [q.v.]. Yaunyavalcyan's work is more concise than that of Menoo [q.v.], being comprised in three books instead of twelve. The first book, consisting of 376 couplets, is chiefly on social and caste duties or auchauram [q.v.]; the second, consisting of 307 verses which have been transferred almost word for word to the Agny pooraunam [q.v.], is mainly on administrative judicature and civil and criminal law or vyavahauram [q.v.]; third, consisting of 335 verses, is principally on devotion, purification, expiation, penance or prauyaschittam [q.v.], &c. See vol. I (56).——*Yejmaun* (यजमान - yajamána, San.). Corruption of (yajamána, san. sacrificer). Properly means the householder at whose expense and on whose behalf a religious ceremony is performed [carnaven, inam]. Householder [grihastan], manager, master. The head of a family under aliya santauna [q.v.] law. Also Hindoo third name [peyar].

YAKA (یکا - yaka, *Hind.*). From fijian. Same as Wayaka.

YALLAH (یلاکاتیل - yalákátel, *Hind.*). From (piyal, hind.) which is from (priyála, san.), the first syllable being dropped out. Cf. Malabathrum, from (tamálapatram). Oil of Wild mohwah.

YAM (यम् - yam, *San.*). To restrain [dam]. Also to sustain.——*Yamadootan* (यमदूत - yamadúta, San.). From (yama, san. death + dúta, san. messenger). Yama's messengers [dootan].——*Yamalocam* (यमलोक - yamalóka, San.). From (yama, san. death + lóka, san. world). The world of death [locam].——*Yamam* (यम - yama, San.; இயமம் - iyamam, Tam.). From (yam, san. to restrain). Restraint of the appetites; a stage of yogam [q.v.].——*Yaman* (यम - yama, San.). The restrainer. The god of death. πλούτων of greeks; Pluto of romans; Serapis of egyptians. Yaman has for his watch-dogs the two Sarameyams, born of Saramay [q.v.], Indran's dog. See vol. I (78). Also called Dharma rajan [q.v.]. There is a Tamul proverb:—நமன் அறியாத உயிரும் நாரை அறியாத குளமும் உண்டோ?—"is there a soul that Yaman knows not, is there a "tank unknown to the crane?" And another:—எண்ணம் எல்லாம் பொய் எமன் ஓலை மெய்—"all our thoughts are "vain, the olay [q.v.] of Yaman is real" [ashtadicpaulacan, chitragooptan].——*Yamatarpanam* (యమతర్పణం - yamatarpanam, Tel.). Means yaman, the god of the dead + propitiation. Same as Deepauvaly.——*Yamoonay* (यमुना - yamuná, San.). The daughter of Yaman, the restrainer. Jumna river.——*Yamy* (यमी - yamí, San.). The twin sister of Yaman.——*Yantram* (यन्त्र - yantra, San.). From (yam, san. to sustain). Any machine. A mystical diagram [chuckram]. Yantra muntram is conjuring.——*Yatirajan* (யதிராசன் - yathirásan, Tam.). From (yati, san. ascetic + rájá, san. king). Hindoo 2nd or pers. name [peyar]. Title of Ramaunoojacharry [ramaunoojan], the antagonist of Shuncaracharry [shuncaran]. Also called Yembramaunar.——*Yatiraudz* (ఎతిరాజు - etirádzu, Tam.). From (yati, san. ascetic + rádzu, tel. king). Epithet of an alwar [q.v.]. Hindoo 2nd or pers. name among Veishnavites [peyar].——*Yatiyappan* (யதியப்பன் - yathiyappan, Tam.). From (yati, san. ascetic + appan, tam. father). Hindoo 2nd or pers. name [peyar].——*Yaty* (यति - yati, San.). From (yam, san. to restrain). A Sanyausy [q.v.] or ascetic of the strictest order [yogy]. The body of the Yaty is never burned, but buried, usually in a sitting posture; the head previously broken by a cocoanut [q.v.], and the body then covered with salt [ooppoo] and quicklime [choonam, shavacaud].——*Yaumam* (याम - yáma, San.). Measure of time [jyotisham, varauha mihiran]. $7\frac{1}{2}$ ghaticams = 1 yaumam; 8 yaumams = 1 dinam [caulam]. Approximate actual value, 1 yaumam = 3 hours. Same as San. praharam, Tel. jaumam, Tam. yaumam.——*Yaumyottaravrittam* (याम्योत्तरवृत्त - yámyóttaravritta, San.). From (yámya, san. south + uttara, san. north + vritta, san. circle), as marking the range of declination of sun, north and south. The solstitial colure. The equinoctial colure is vishoomundalam [q.v.] or maishauyanamundalam [q.v.].

YANAM (యానాము - yánámu, *Tel.*). Means sea beach.

French colony, Town, Port; Godavery dist., Cocanada division; pop. 4,971; lat. 16° 44′; long. 82° 15′; from Bendamoorlunka N.E. 26 miles; from Cocanada S. 15 miles; from Madras N.N.E. 278 miles; from Neelapully W. 1 mile. At the bifurcation of the Godavery and Coringa, about 9 miles above the embouchure of the former. Bounded by these rivers on the east and south and surrounded by British territory. Extends along the banks of the two rivers for two leagues and-a-half, and its breadth varies from 390 metres to 3 kilometres. The mouth of the Godavery is obstructed by sand banks which prevent the entrance of ships. The Coringa has a deep bed which at spring tides admits vessels of 200 tons. Founded shortly before 1750, in which year it was seized by order of Nizam nauzir jung. Its fortunes followed the vicissitudes of French history in Southern india. With other French possessions in India it was secured to the French by the treaty of 1814-15. Till 1857 the territory was farmed out to an agent called the farmer-general. In that year this system was superseded by the Government dealing directly with the ryots [q.v.]. The Chief, appointed by the President of the Republic, governs under the control of the Governor-General of the French possessions in India. He has under his orders a priest, a head of police and other administrative affairs, a collector of taxes who also acts as treasurer and receiver of unclaimed property, a medical man, and a registrar. The Chief fills the functions of president of the criminal court, of commerce, and of the magistracy and police. There is also a European civilian in charge of the registration of births, deaths, and marriages. In November 1839, a hurricane, accompanied by an inundation of the sea, destroyed all the official records. There are three schools :—a girls' school, superintended by four nuns of St. Joseph of Lyons, paid by the State ; a school for high-caste girls, under the same superintendence ; and a free school for boys. There is a jail and a dispensary. The soil is fertile. Abundance of rice [paddy] is cultivated. See vol. I (175), 3.——*Yanaudy* (యానాది - yánádi, Tel.). From (yánádamu, tel. seashore). An aboriginal tribe of northern coast districts, especially Nellore. They reside on the hills dividing Cuddapah from Nellore and North arcot ; but also still inhabit the jungles along the seashore of the Nellore district. They speak a dialect of Teloogoo. An account received from an old man of that tribe is, that of old one named Raghavan brought with him sixty families from Pauknaud district and located himself with them at Shreeharicote, and clearing the country formed Raghavapooram ; the people by degrees spread through a few adjoining districts. Yanaudics are small in stature with poor attenuated frames, and indicate evidently a very aboriginal survival. They live upon roots and what grain they can get in exchange for honey [shahad] and medicinal herbs ; they are useful servants in the forest department, where their knowledge of the forests is turned to good account, and they are often found as village night-watchers. The shreeharicote estate lapsed to the british government in 1835 ; till then, the yanaudies of that island were in a state of complete barbarism, did not know the use of money, were rarely seen, and lived on fruits, roots, and other jungle produce ; in order to civilise them, government employed them to gather jungle produce, and gave them in exchange rice [q.v.] and clothing. Numbers of the tribe about 85,000. See vol. I (36), 195 ; II, 75, 113.

YASHAB (सूर्यकान्त - súryakánta, *San.* ; يشب - yashab, *Hind.* ; ಜೀವರತ್ನ - jívaratna, *Can.* ; సూర్యకాంతి - súryakánti, *Tel.* ; സൂര്യകാന്തം - súryakántam, *Mal.* ; சூரியக்காந்தம் - shúriyakkándam, *Tam.*). Title from hindostany. San. from (súrya, san. sun + kánta, san. beloved). Can. from (jíva, san. life + ratna, san. gem) ; from bright red color. Jasper. Impure opaque-colored quartz [vencull], often of a bright red color, or striped red and black or white [ratnam].

YASHM (يشم - yashm, *Hind.* ; పచ్చరాయి - pattsaráyi, *Tel.* ; பச்சைக்கல் - paççaikkal, *Tam.*). Title from persian. Tel. from (pattsa, tel. green + ráyi, tel. stone). Tam. from (paççai, tam. green + kal, tam stone). Jade. Mineral, color greenish-white, passing into grayish-green and dark grass-green ; semi-transparent and cloudy ; fracture splintery and splinters white. Difficult to cut. Chinese fashion into cups, bracelets, &c. Imported.

YAUD (یاد - yád, *Hind.*). Memory.——*Yadust* (یاد داشت - yáddásht, Hind.). From (above + dásht, pers. keeper). A written memorandum [olay].——*Yaudgaur* (یادگار - yádgár, Hind.). From (above + gár, pers. keeping). Memorial. Prefixed to an alam forms a lacab ; as Yaudgaur ally, remembrance of ally [ism].

YAUDIKY (యాడికి - yádiki, *Tel.*).—"*a*" Deputy tahsildarry, Anantapore district, Tadpatry talook. Pay Rs. 70.—"*b*" Town, Deputy tahsildar's station ; pop. 4,699 ; acres 14,835 ; lat. 15° 03′ ; long. 77° 55′ ; from Anantapore N.E. 31 miles ; from Bellary E. 64 miles ; from Gooty E.S.E. 17 miles ; from Madras N.W. 210 miles ; from Penoocondah N.N.E. 70 miles ; from Tadpatry N.W. 13 miles. Built by Timmappa naidoo, founder of Tadpatry. Second town in importance in talook. 3 miles from Royalcheroo railway station. Celebrated temples.

YAULY (शरभ - sharabha, *San.* ; యాళి - yáli, *Tel.* ; യാഴി - yázhi, *Mal.* ; யாளி - yáli, *Tam.*). Title and Drav. from (vyála, san. hunting leopard). San. from (shri, san. to hurt) [sharbham]. Mythological animal [sharbbam] like a lion [simham] with an elephant's [q.v.] proboscis and tusks [dant].——*Yauliyoorty* (யாளியூர்த்தி - yáliyúrtti, Tam.). From (above + úr, tam. to ride). Name of Bhadra cauly [q.v.] or rider on a lion.

YAUMALAY (யாமளை - yámalai, *Tam.*). From (shyámalá, san. dark green) [shyaumay]. Bhadra cauly [q.v.].——*Yaumaulamma* (యామాలమ్మ - yámálamma, Tel.). Village deity.

YAUP (யாப்பு - yáppu, *Tam.*). From (yá, tam. to bind), binding words together [nool]. Poetry [pah] ; one of the five divisions of the Tamul grammar or lacshanam [q.v.].

YAUTRAY (यात्रा - yátrá, *San.*). From (yá, san. to go). Pilgrimage [jatrah].

YAUVAT (यावत् - yávat, *San.*). How much.——*Yauvattauvat* (यावत्तावत् - yávattávat, San.). From (above + távat, san. so much). The unknown quantity [caulak] in mathematics, as European 'x.' Known quantity is Roopam [q.v.].

YAUWAR (یاور - yáwar, *Pers.*). From (yárí, pers. intimacy + war, pers. suffix of possession). Aid, friend. Prefixed to an alam forms a lacab ; as Yauwar ally, friend of ally [ism].

YAUZH (யாழ் - yázh, *Tam.*). Ancient stringed musical instrument of the lute kind not now in use.——*Macara yauzh* (மகரயாழ் - magarayázh, Tam.). With the figure of the macaram [q.v.] fish.——*Pairyauzh* (பேர்யாழ் - périyázh, Tam.). Means great yauzh.——*Shacotayauzh* (சகோடயாழ் - shagódayázh, Tam.). In the shape of a wedge.——*Shengoty yauzh* (செங்கோட்டியாழ் - shengóttiyázh, Tam.). Of a beautiful red [sangeetam].

YECAM (एक - éka, *San.* ; ஏகம் - égam, *Tam.*). One [or, yek]. Unity, sign of Mahat [q.v.] ; a shastram says of it :—ஏகரூபி, சீவீசரசெகத்தாகத்தோன்றிணுஞ் சச்சிதானந்த இலட்சணமுடையவர்—"one undistinguished thing "possessing the attributes of existence, intelligence and joy "[satchidaunandam] though manifested diversely in jeevam "[q.v.] or life, eeshwaran [q.v.] or ruler and jagat [q.v.] or "matter [mauyay, pashoo, paty, pausham]."——*Yeca bhogam* (एकभोग - ékabhóga, San.). From (above + bhóga, san. enjoyment). The holding of a whole village by one man, as opposed to Pala bhogam or [q.v.] holding of land by each member of the village [graumam]. Also applied to single crop lands [yek fusly].——*Yecadamshtran* (एकदंष्ट्र - ékadamshtra, San.). From (above + damshtra, san. tusk). Single tusked. Name of Vigneshwaran [q.v.] as having one tusk, the fellow tusk being broken off in a fight with Caurtikeyan [q.v.], or according to another legend by Parshooraman [q.v.].——*Yecaucsharam* (एकाक्षर - ékákshara, San.). From (above + akshara, san. character). The sacred monosyllable Om [q.v.].——*Yecaudasha roodran* (एकादशरुद्र - ékádasharudra, San.). From (above + dasha, san. ten + rudra, san. deity). Eleven Roodrans [q.v.].——*Yecaudashy* (एकादशी - ékádashí, San. ; ఏకాదశి - ékádashi, Tel. ; ஏகாதசி - égáthasi, Tam.). From (above + dasha, san. ten). Lunar [chaundra maunam] festival [pundigay, 3e]. The eleventh lunar day [tity] in the bright and dark halves [pacsham] in the moon's orbit [cacsham]. It is observed by Bramins, especially Madhwa veishnavas [q.v.], as a strict fast. Local pooraunams [q.v.] are profuse on the benefits resulting from its observance. Appears to rest on hygienic grounds. There is a Tamul proverb :—ஏகாதசிக்கு மா இடித்தாற் போல—"like pounding flour for yecaudashy ;" said of something not required and irrelevant. The following Yecaudashies are specially observed:—Bheeshmam [bheeshma yecaudashy] in the bright fortnight [shooclapacsham] of tye [mausam] or january, Nirjalam or waterless in the bright fortnight of veiyaushy or may, Oottaunam [oottaunaicaudashy] or bodhanam in the bright fortnight of arpisy or october, Parivartanay or rolling in the bright fortnight of auvany or august, Shayanam or toly in the bright fortnight of auny or june, Veicoontam [veicoonta yecaudashy] in the bright fortnight of maurgaly [mausam] or december. Title also applies to a ceremony performed on the eleventh day after the death of a relative [shrauddham] ; during the previous ten days the relatives are supposed to be mourning, and in a state of ashowcham or impurity, so that no one can communicate with them ; when yecaudashy is performed the period of uncleanness ceases [maryauday].——*Yecaumbaran* (एकाम्बर - ékámbara, San.). From (above + ambara, san. cloth). Lord of the undivided garment ; meaning the visible heaven. Local tradition, derives it from (éka, san. single + ámra, san. mango tree), from an old mango tree in temple said to be the tree under which the lingam [q.v.] originally was. A name of Shiva at great Conjeeveram ; the shacty [q.v.] being Caumautchy. Yecaumbaram and Chidambaram had reference to the Booddhas [q.v.] or Jeinas [q.v.], formerly in the two localities.——*Yecaumbareshwaran* (ஏகாம்பரேசுவரன் - égámbarésuvaran, Tam.). From (above + ambara, san. cloth + íshvara, san. lord). Epithet of Shiva. Hindoo 2nd or pers. name [peyar].——*Yecauntalingam* (ஏகாந்தலிங்கம் - egándalingam, Tam.). From (ekánta, san. solitary + linga, san. emblem of shiva). Hindoo 2nd or pers. name [peyar].——*Yegammaul* (ஏகம்மாள் - égammál, Tam.). From (above + ammál, tam. mother). Village goddess.——*Yegauttaul* (ஏகாத்தாள் - égáttál, Tam.). From (above + áttál, tam. mother). The only mother ; a mother ; a form of Cauly [q.v.], and the tutelary goddess [grauma devatay] of the Black town of Madras.——*Yek* (ایک - ek, Hind.). One.——*Yek fusly* (ایک فصلی - ekfaslí, Hind.). From (above + faslí, ar. harvest year).

Producing only one crop [fusl] in the year [yeca bhogam].——*Yekka* (ایکا - ekká, Hind.). A small light two-wheeled carriage made chiefly of bamboo [q.v.]; it is drawn by a single horse [ghorah] or pony, the shafts meeting on the animal's back; it has no seat in the European sense, and is used only by natives. Compare Rekla.——*Yekputta* (ایک پٹا - ekpattá, Hind.). From (above + pattá, hind. breadth). Single width of scarf or loonghee [q.v.]. Those who can afford it prefer the more ample doputta [q.v.].——*Yeksaula* (ایک ساله - eksálah, Hind.). From (above + sál, pers. year). Annual [sanwar].——*Yekshamba* (ایکشنبه - ekshambah, Hind.). From (above + shambah, pers. saturday). Sunday [shamba, vauram].

YECAULY (ஏகாலி - égáli, *Tam.*). From (vé, tam. to boil + kári, tam. doer); one who steams. Corresponding terms are:—Tel. saucala, Can. agasa, Mal. veloottaidau. Tamul washerman [dhoby, jauty, vunnaun].

YECKOJEE (ایکوجی - ekkojí, *Hind.*). Colloquial corruption of Vencajee [q.v.].

YEDAY (எடை - edai, *Tam.*). From (edu, tam. to weigh). Weight in general. So a specific bazaar weight; 2 tooks = 1 yeday [niray, 2a]; approximate actual value, 1 yeday = 7 lbs. 11 oz. 7 drs. avoir.; compare Tel. dhadiyam, toom, yettoo.——*Yettoo* (ఎత్తు - yettu, Tel.). Bazaar weight; 2 visses = 1 yettoo; 4 yettoos = 1 maund [niray, 2b]; approximate actual value, 1 yettoo = 6¼ lbs. avoir.; same as San. dhurrah, Tel. dhadiyam, toom; compare Yeday; see vol. I, 609; II, 519.

YEEDIGA (ఈడిగ - ídiga, *Tel.*). From (ídtsu, tel. to draw). Teloogoo palm cultivator. The corresponding terms are:—Tam. shaunaun, Can. billava, Mal. ilavan. While the Tamulians in climbing tie their knives behind them, the Teloogoos tie them downwards on the right thigh. Tamulian drawers extract the juice from palmyras [q.v.] and cocoanuts [q.v.] and but rarely from the date [kharjooram], the Teloogoos from palmyras and dates but never from cocoanuts [jauty].

YEL (ఏలు - élu, *Tel.*). To rule.——*Yelagherry* (ஏலகிரி - élagiri, Tam. yelagiri *). From (above + giri, san. mountain); overruling or high. Hills; Salem dist., Tripatore tal.; acres 19,657; lat. 12° 31′ to 12° 38′ N.; long. 78° 38′ to 78° 45′ E.; from Salem N.N.E. 71 miles; from Tripatore N.N.E. 4 miles. On the N.E. border of the district separating it from the S.W. portion of South arcot. Somewhat triangular in shape, the base being south of a line from Vaniyambaudy through Vellacoottay to Alangauyam, and the apex of the triangle being towards Tripatore. The summit consists mainly of a ridge varying from 3,000 to 4,441 feet above the sea, and pierced on the south-east, a little north of the apex, by a remarkable cleft in the solid rock, which narrows up to a point near Attanauvore, where a tributary to the Paumbaur rises. The plateau looks as if it had been artificially flattened; and for a long distance towards the south flat terraces succeed each other on the very summit of the hill, which appear to have been originally cultivated. Brushwood is springing up over them. Following this plateau southwards, in an angle formed by the ridge which faces Tripatore, is a valley which is the richest part of the hill, but neglected. These hills contain six villages. On the Devamullay is a remarkable monolith [laut]. Under it are stone images of deities. Stone implements, chisels, axe-heads, hammers, and wedges have been found in the hills. The natives of the neighbourhood possess many of these, and they worship them, saying that they fell from the sky.——*Yelair* (ఏలేరు - éléru, Tel.). From (above + éru, tel. river). River; Godavery dist., Peddapore tal. and Cocanada division. Takes its rise in Doommacondah hill near Mattam bheemavaram in Goortaid mootah [q.v.]. During its course it is joined at Noonnamaumidy in the Rumpa country by the Caunair coming from Kotah side and the Maudair near Timmapooram in the Jaddangy tracts. After a course of about 60 miles, it crosses great northern trunk road at Yerravaram, a little below which it begins to form into branches. One of the branches which supplies water to many villages in Pittapore division joins sea at Ramannapollem near Ooppauda in Pittapore division. Another branch after supplying many villages in Peddapore talook for irrigation, goes via Peddapore to Samulcottah, where it divides into three branches, the Bheemanuddy, the Narayadoo, and the Merakayair, also called the main stream. It is bridged at Yerravaram, 15 vents of 36 spans each. A bridge across the Maudair is now in course of construction.——*Yeleshwaram* (ఏలేశ్వరము - éléshvaramu, Tel.). From (above + íshvara, san. lord); ruling eeshwaran, from a local deity. Tel. also (prattipádu), meaning cotton + village.—"*a*" Deputy tahsildarry, Godavery district. Pay Rs. 70.—"*b*" Village, Deputy tahsildar's station; Godavery dist., Peddapore tal.; pop. 4,945; acres 3,823; lat. 17° 17′; long. 82° 08′; from Cocanada N.N.W. 25 miles; from Coonavaram E.S.E. 58 miles; from Ellore N.E. 76 miles; from Madras N.N.E. 306 miles; from Narsapore N.N.E. 64 miles; from Peddapore N. 15 miles; from Rajahmundry N.E. 29 miles.

YELAILAM (ఏలలు - élalu, *Tel.*; ஏலேலம் - élélam, *Tam.*). From (vali, tam. to exert). The sound uttered by boatmen and others on the Coromandel [q.v.] coast when pulling together.——*Yelaila singan* (ஏலேலசிங்கன் - élélasingan, Tam.). From (above + simha, san. lion); lion of the surf. A wealthy fisherman and merchant, the disciple of Tirvulloovan [q.v.]. There is a Tamul proverb:—ஏலேல சிங்கன்பொருள் ஏழு கடலிற் போனாலும் திரும்பும்—"the property of yelailasingan, "though it pass over seven seas [samoodram], will return."

YELAM (एला - élá, *San.*). From (il, san. to send down); removing nausea. Cardamom.——*Yelattary* (ഏലത്തരി - élattari, Mal.). Means cardamom + seed. Hence Elettaria, generic term.

YELIMITCHAY (எலுமிச்சை - elumiççai, *Tam.*). From (límun, ar. lime). Lime [q.v.].——*Yelimitchay poolipp* (ನಿಂಬೆಹುಳಿ - nimbehuli, Can.; నిమ్మపులుసు - nimmapulusu, Tel.; எலுமிச்சம் புளிப்பு - elumiççambulippu, Tam.). Can. from (nimbi, can. lime + huli, can. acid). Tel. from (nimma, tel. lemon + pulusu, tel. acid). Citric acid. Obtained from lime-juice; met with in crystals [palingoo, spaticam]; employed by calico [q.v.] printers. For acids generally see Poolipp and Tezaub.

YELL (எள் - el, *Tam.*). The root means slender, slight. Sesamum [gingelly] seed, one of the nava dhaunyams or nine kinds of grain [dhaunyam]. Linear measure. 8 yells = 1 nell or paddy seed [alavay, 1a]. Approximate actual value, 1 yell = $\frac{1}{64}$th of a native inch or $\frac{3}{256}$th inch. Same as Mal. yenmany.——*Yenmany* (എണ്മണി - eumani, Mal.). From (above + mani, mal. grain). Sesamum seed. Linear measure. 8 yenmanies = 1 tora [alavay, 1d]. Approximate actual value, 1 yenmany = $\frac{3}{256}$ of an inch. Same as Tam. yell. See vol. I, 609.

YELLAY (ఎల్ల - ella, *Tel.*; எல்லை - ellai, *Tam.*). A boundary [inam]. Yellay cull is a boundary stone.——*Yelattore* (ഏലത്തൂർ - elattúr, Mal.). From (above + úr, mal. village).—"*a*" Village, Port; Malabar dist., Calicut tal.; pop. 3,817; lat. 11° 21′; long. 75° 46′; from Bombay S.S.E. 550 miles; from Calicut N.N.W. 7 miles; from Caupautt S.S.E. 3 miles; from Poothiyangaudy N.N.W. 3 miles. Small port at mouth of river of same name. Two ruined temples [coil, pagoda]. Connected with the Cullye river and backwaters [cauyal] and with the Beypore river beyond by the Conolly canal.—"*b*" River; Malabar dist., Calicut tal. Rises in the mountains west of the Tamracherry pass, near Poonoordeshom in lat. 11° 30′ N., and long. 75° 54′ E., and, after a devious course of about 32 miles through Malabar district, flows into the extensive backwater [cauyal] which communicates with the sea near Yelattore town, in lat. 11° 21′ N., long. 75° 46′ E. A shallow stream unsuited for boat traffic.——*Yellamanchily* (ఎల్లమంచిలి - yellamanchili, Tel.). From (above + manchi, tel. good). Sanscrit name (ilámañjari), meaning earth + garland. Town, Head-quarters of Tahsildar; Vizagapatam dist., Sarwasiddhy tal.; pop. 6,296; acres 2,796; lat. 17° 33′; long. 82° 54′; from Coraputt S.S.E. 86 miles; from Madras N.E. 340 miles; from Narsapatam E.S.E. 19 miles; from Parvatipore S.S.W. 91 miles; from Vizagapatam W.S.W. 30 miles; from Vizianagram S.W. 52 miles; from the sea N. 9 miles. Former seat of shepherd kings, who built pagodas [q.v.] of which ruins are visible, with a building called Nookpaupa maida. One pagoda on a rock has a figure of Veerabhadra [q.v.] sawmy a form of Shiva [q.v.]. Cave temple to Gopaulsawmy, with inscription 400 years old. On top of a hill is a ruined temple and an inscription [shausanam]. A jar containing copper coins [naunyam] of the old shepherd [yaudava] dynasty [raj] was found in the hill fort in 1863; on one side they bore the effigy of a bullock.——*Yellamma* (ఎల్లమ్మ - ellamma, Tel.). From (above + amma, tel. goddess). One of the best known of the village goddesses [graumadevatay]. If one is bitten by a poisonous serpent he calls on Yellamma; fishermen the same when in danger. She is represented in the arts in a sitting posture, with a red skin, a fiery face, and four arms and hands. On her head she wears a crown, round which there are serpents; on her forehead she has three streaks [tripoondram] of sacred ashes [tirneer, vibhooty], and on the whole she is adorned like the other goddesses. In her four hands she holds respectively a drum, called Damaroo [q.v.]; a trident, called Shoolam [q.v.]; a bundle of ropes, called Pausham [q.v.]; and the skull of Bramha's fifth head, which was cut off by Shiva [q.v.]. Of this skull [capaulam] it is said that it attracts all the bloodshed on earth, and nevertheless is never full; and inasmuch as the Graumadevatays [q.v.] receive animal sacrifices, they usually hold it in their hands. An image [shilay, vigraham] of the above description, cast of metal [loham], is found in her pagodas [q.v.]; but her principal image, to which offerings are made, is of stone, representing only her head, in the earth. The temples of Yellamma are numerous, but usually very small. The images found in them, besides that of herself, are the following:—Bhadra cauly; Jamadagny maharishy, her husband, who ordered her to be killed; Mullagashetty a hero who assists her in battle; Mautangy, the pariah woman on whose head yellamma's head was put; Parshooraman, her son, incarnation of vishnoo; Potrauz or bull-king, her herald; Ooyirtoondilcaurs, her servants who, having themselves died a violent death, catch those who die a violent death, and bring them into Yellamma's court; Vigneshwaran with his elephant's head. Besides these, there are sometimes also images of serpents [naugam] in her pagodas, to which the people make salutation. See vol. I (77) [matam].

——*Yellan* (எல்லன் - ellan, Tam.). Hindoo 2nd or pers. name [peyar].——*Yellannan* (எல்லண்ணன் - ellannan, Tam.). From (above + annan, tam. elder brother, titular affix). Hindoo 2nd or pers. name [peyar].——*Yellappan* (எல்லப்பன் - ellappan, Tam.). From (above + appan, tam. father, titular affix). Pariah proper name [peyar].——*Yellay mullay* (എല്ലമല - ellamala, Mal.). From (above + malai, tam. mountain).—"*a*" Hill; Neilgherry dist., Wynaud S.E. division; lat. 11° 26′; long. 76° 29′; from Goodalore S.W. 5 miles; from Ootacamund W.N.W. 17 miles. The north side of the Neilgherries towards Mysore rises about 3,500 feet above that tableland, with which it is connected by a neck about 15 miles in width. The isolation of the Neilgherries would be complete, but for this singular, sharp, and precipitous ridge of granite [caroom cull] peaks, which projects from the base of Yellay mullay on the western crest of the range and taking a west by north course towards the coast unites itself with the Western ghauts [q.v.].—"*b*" Coffee [q.v.] estate, Ouchterlony valley; Neilgherries. Acres 199.——*Yellayyan* (எல்லய்யன் - ellayyan, Tam.). From (above + ayyan, tam. master, titular affix). Hindoo 2nd or pers. name [peyar].

YELLOW (மஞ்சள் - mañjal, *Tam.*). Prefix.——*Yellow buttons* (جعفر گندی - jafarígundí, Hind.). Same as Jaffer goondy.——*Yellow-flower tree* (மஞ்சள்பூச்செடி - manjalbúççedi, Tam.). Same as Coral jasmine.——*Yellow root* (عروق الصفر - arúkussifr, Ar.). Same as Country saffron.——*Yellow wood* (دهورا - dhaurá, Hind.). Same as Satin wood.

YELY (எலி - eli, *Tam.*). Means dark one. Rat [ely].——*Yelicair* (ఎలికేరు - elikéru, Tel.). From (elika, tel. rat + éru, tel. river). River; Nellore dist., Cundoocore tal. Rises in Ammavauripollem shrotriem [q.v.] tank [q.v.]. Chief feeder to the Chaugolloo tank. Crossed by a bridge near Veereypulley. Disembogues two miles north of Ramapatam and three miles south of Teeya vaugoo channel [q.v.].

YEM (എൻ - en, *Mal.*; எம் - em, *Tam.*). My, our.——*Yembramanaur* (எம்பெருமானார் - emberumánár, Tam.). From (above + perumán, tam. king + ár, tam. plural suffix). Our lord. Hindoo 2nd or pers. name among Veishnavites [peyar]. Another name of Ramaunoojan [q.v.].——*Yembraun* (എമ്പ്രാൻ - embrán, pers. sing.; എമ്പ്രാന്മാർ - embránmár, pers. pl., Mal.). From (above + purán, mal. lord). Otherwise Yembrauntry. A class of sacrificing Bramins [q.v.] in South canara and in Travancore. Chiefly Tooloo [q.v.]. Officiate at Shoodra [q.v.] ceremonies. Largely employed in Travancore and Cochin as poojarries [q.v.] of temples [coil]. See vol. II, 100 [jauty].——*Yembrauntry* (എമ്പ്രാന്തിരി - embrántiri, Mal.). From (above + purán, mal. lord + tiri, mal. goddess of fortune). Title given to the Tooloo bramins in Malabar corresponding to Potty in Travancore. Hindoo third name [peyar].——*Yencarttah* (എൻകർത്താ - enkarttá, Mal.). My lord. Title.

YEN (எண் - en, *Tam.*). Number. Science of numbers or calculation. Arithmetic; mathematical astronomy [ganitam]. Seven [saptam] is regarded as the most lucky number, after which five [puncham] and other odd numbers have precedence. There is a Tamul proverb :—எண்ணும் எழுத்தும் கண்ணெனத் தகும்—"numbers and letters may be regarded as eyes." And another :—எண்ணெழுத்திகழேல்—"think not lightly "of numbers and letters [yezhoot]."——*Yennam* (എണ്ണം - ennam, Mal.). Counting. Charge for reaping, usually 10 per cent.; or if paid in kind, one sheaf out of ten.——*Yensoovady* (எண்சுவடி - ensuvadi, Tam.). From (above + shuvadu, tam. mark). The multiplication table.

YENAMACULL (ഏനാമാക്കൽ - énámákkal, *Mal.*). From (ínam, corruption of hína, san. low + váya, mal. mouth + kal, mal. case ending showing place), meaning low place at the mouth of the lake.—"*a*" Village; Malabar dist., Ponnany tal.; Syrian christians. In Venkitanga amshom [q.v.], about 8 miles south-east of Coottingal and four from Chittatkara. Important ancient Syro-roman catholic church [syrian]. Chief articles of trade are cocoanut [q.v.] and cocoanut oil.—"*b*" Fresh-water lake, Malabar dist., Ponnany tal., and large anicut 8 miles from the mouth of Chetwye river. The anicut [q.v.] keeps out the salt water and renders a wide expanse of land cultivable. The area protected mostly belongs to native Cochin. For description of lake see Trichore.

YENDA (ఎండ - enda, *Tel.*). Hot.——*Yendacaur* (ఎండకారు - endakáru, Tel.). Hot season [caur, coday, ritoo, vainil].

YENNAY (तैल - taila, *San.*; دهن - duhn, *Ar.*; روغن - raughan, *Pers.*; تیل - tel, *Hind.*; ಎಣ್ಣೆ - enne, *Can.*; నూనె - núne, *Tel.*; എണ്ണ - enna, *Mal.*; எண்ணெய் - enney, *Tam.*). San. from (tila, san. sesamum seed). Hind. from sanscrit. Tel. from (núvu, tel. sesamum seed + neyi, tel. ghee). Tam. from (el, tam. plant, sesamum indicum, linn. + ney, tam. ghee). The sanscrit and dravidian etymologies show the prevalence of gingelly [q.v.] oil. The terms however include all oils. In classification oils are first divided into three large classes according to the kingdom of nature whence they are derived; that is to say Animal [jantoo], Vegetable [vricsham], and Mineral [dhautoo].——**(1)** The following is a key-list of the principal animal oils of s. india:—Aumay yennay, turtle [cadalaumay] oil. Aut cozhooppoo, mutton [aud] suet. Boochy pitta nooney, boochy bird [kilkilah] oil. Carady ney, bear's [ricsham] grease. Cautt paumb yennay, wild serpent [paumb] oil. Ghee [q.v.]. Jella chaipa nooney, jella [q.v.] fish oil. Maun cozhooppoo, deer's [mrigam] lard. Mayil yennay, peacock's [mayil] fat. Meen yennay, fish-oil [malabar oil]. Mezhoogoo yennay, wax [mom] oil. Pashoo mautt caul yennay, neat's [pashoo] foot oil. Pooly ney, tiger's [pooly] fat. Pundry ney, hog's [soor] lard. Soorah ney, shark-liver [soorah] oil. Tavalay cozhooppoo, frog's [bhaicam] fat. Vaulooga chaipa nooney, vaulooga [vaulay] fish oil.——**(2)** The vegetable oils are obtained from seeds such as castor [aumanac], croton [jamalgota], gingelly [q.v.], ground-nut [q.v.], linseed [alsee], &c.; from fruit, as the olive [zeitoon]; from rind and leaves, as the orange [q.v.], lemon [q.v.], &c.; from flowers, as the neroli [bitter orange]; and from roots and wood, as sandal [q.v.], &c. The modes of extraction of vegetable oils vary with different circumstances; see below. Vegetable oils are generally sub-divided into three sub-classes:—fixed oils, fat or drying; volatile oils or essences or attars [q.v.]; wood oils [q.v.] or oleo-balsams.—"*a*" The first sub-class are fixed oils, or oils which communicate a permanently greasy stain to paper or cloth. These are best obtained by submitting the seeds or fruit to the strong pressure of a screw-press [gaunam]; this is called cold-drawing. The bruised mass may however instead, be submitted to heat, which facilitates the exudation; this is called hot-drawing. In the former case the oil must be afterwards clarified as it contains albuminous and mucilaginous matter; these are eliminated by gently boiling the expressed oil with a small quantity of water, taking care not to raise the heat beyond the boiling point of water, nor to continue the boiling after the water has been dissipated; this process coagulates the albumen and mucilage, which become precipitated in lumps carrying with them all other impurities; if the process of pressing and clarifying have been conducted with care, the oil is clear and colorless. The hot process which begins with boiling [aumanac, e] gives a greater yield, but the oil then soon becomes rancid and is never colorless. The ordinary vegetable fixed oils, more especially gingelly and cocoanut, are largely used by the natives in their daily diet; although they are for the most part uniform in their chemical composition, there is a considerable difference in their nutritive value, probably owing to physical conditions of form or aggregation, whereby some are more easily taken up into the system than others. "*i*" The first group of the above sub-class or the Fat oils form the ordinary bulk of the oils used. They are represented by such oils as Belgaum walnut [lumbang-nut], Bennut [moringa], Cashew-nut [cashew], Castor [aumanac], Catappa [catapang], Chironjee [q.v.], Cocoanut [q.v.], Colocynth [bitter water melon], Coorook [brambadand], Cotton [q.v.], Country cress [haleem], Croton [jamalgota], Cucumber [oorvauroo], Gamboge butter [mate mangosteen], Gingelly [q.v.], Gogoo [hemp bendy], Ground-nut [q.v.], Hemp seed [kinnab], Illoppay [mohwah], Karanj [q.v.], Margosa [neem], Marking-nut [q.v.], Malkangany [q.v.], Melon [oorvauroo], Modooga [palaus], Moorgana [mate mangosteen], Mustard [rayaun], Nauga champak [q.v.], Neeradimoott [marotty], Nux vomica [poison nut], Paugal [carolah], Physic-nut [wild aumanac], Piney [q.v.] tallow, Pinnay cottay [common poon], Poovennay [poovana], Pumpkin [carcauroo], Ramtil [q.v.], Rape [sarsoon], Safflower [bastard saffron], Soapnut [q.v.], Vernonia [wild jeerah], Viscid cleome [dog vailay], &c. Fat oil is contained in that part of the seed of plants which gives birth to the cotyledons; it is thus termed because it cannot be distilled without decomposition, and it is not until a temperature of between 500° and 600° is reached that it begins to boil and undergo decomposition, giving off acroleine and other compounds. "*ii*" The second group of the above sub-class or the Drying oils is represented by such oils as Hemp [kinnab] seed, Linseed [alsee], Poppy [opium poppy], &c. These dry quickly on exposure to the atmosphere and retain their transparency on solidifying. They form the basis of many paints and varnishes [rangh]; also of printing ink. Before they can be used in the arts they must be thoroughly deprived of all mucilaginous matters and brought into a state which will increase their affinity to combine with oxygen when exposed to the air in a thin stratum; this is effected by further boiling and adding from time to time the basic acetate of lead; that chemical re-agent combines with the mucilage and forms with it a new compound, which is thrown down; the boiling is continued briskly, and the heat allowed to reach to such a degree as will scorch a feather when dipped into the boiling oil; when the heat has arrived to this degree, it is allowed gradually to subside, and after it has cooled down the oil is drawn off clear, and allowed to repose in large cisterns until no further deposit takes place; it then becomes clear and transparent, and is fit for use. The older the oil the better its drying qualities.—"*b*" The second sub-class are Volatile oils, or oils which do not communicate a permanent stain to paper or cloth, the greasy stain being dissipated by heat; they are otherwise known as ethereal or essential oils [attar]; they can be distilled without decomposition and possess in a concentrated form the odour characteristic of the plants or vegetable substances whence obtained; they are for the most part insoluble or only with difficulty and sparingly soluble in water, but dissolve freely in ether, alcohol, fatty oils, and mineral oils. They are generally distilled, though a few are pressed, such as lemon [q.v.], orange [q.v.], and citron [q.v.]. The distillation is carried on in large copper stills; the fruit, seeds, leaves, flowers, or the whole plant, is put into the body of the still, and as much water is poured on as to cover the article to be operated upon; on the application of heat, the water impregnated with oil distils over and is collected in a receiver; the oil either floats on the top, or if heavier than water, as clove [lavangam] oil, it sinks to the bottom; in distilling oils heavier and less volatile than water, the heat must be above the boiling point of water, and to obtain this increased temperature common salt [ooppooo] is added to the water to increase its capacity for taking in heat, otherwise the oil will not distil over. These oils are principally used in perfumery [attar], and medicine; some are used in the arts as solvents of resins [raul]. Of vegetable substances producing volatile oils there is an immense variety, but with the exception of the oils of cassia [q.v.], cinnamon [q.v.], and roossa [grass oil], and the rose [gool] attar [q.v.], few are of any commercial importance, nor are they prepared in any quantity for consumption in this country. Scented oils erroneously termed volatile obtained by the repeated distillation of fragrant herbs, &c., into a receiver containing a portion of any fixed oil, to which the aroma is imparted, are prepared to some extent but chiefly for native use; sandal-wood oil [sandal] and the large variety of common attars [q.v.], which form the principal part of native perfumery are included in this class.—"*c*" The third sub-class are wood oils or oleo-balsams [teilam], or oils having the qualities of a fixed oil and a liquid resin [raul]. These form the connecting link between the oils and resins of the natural kingdom. They are a sort of empyreumatic liquid resin, consisting of a volatile oil holding in solution a resin, and are generally classed under the head of Balsams [q.v.]. They are obtained from various trees of the order dipterocarpeæ, some of which also yield the dammers [q.v.] of commerce. The mode of extraction is similar to that adopted for obtaining the solid resin and is nearly the same as that for tar [keel] in europe; about the end of the dry season, that is to say in march or april, several deep incisions are made with an axe into the trunk of the tree, and a large-sized piece scooped out; into this hole fire is placed and kept burning until the oil begins to run, when it is received into a bamboo [q.v.] and allowed to run slowly drop by drop; the oil, when freshly obtained from the tree and allowed to rest, separates into two layers, the upper consisting of a clear chestnut-colored liquid balsam [q.v.], and the lower being a flocculent deposit of the more solid resin [raul] of a light ash color. These wood-oils are much used as natural varnishes [rangh] for indoor work, especially in conjunction with dammer [q.v.], but are very brittle and require constant renewal; also employed by moochees [q.v.] in the preparation of pigments [rangh]. Many substances called wood oil by veidyans [q.v.] are little else than varieties of tar [keel] obtained by the destructive distillation of chips of various woods. Wood oil of a superior kind is brought from burmah.——**(3)** The following are two key-lists in the briefest possible terms of the principal vegetable oils of all kinds in s. india; further information must be traced in the glossary paragraphs through the small type cross-references at end of this volume; see also vricsham, **7**, for the method of expressing the products, &c., of the plants in the dravidian languages.—"*a*" Abrus precatorius, indian liquorice, seed, fixed fat; Acorus calamus, sweet flag, root, volatile; Adenanthera pavonina, false red sanders, seed, fixed fat; Albizzia lebbek, common sirissa, seed, fixed fat; Aleurites triloba, lumbang nut, kernel, fixed fat; Allium cepa, onion, seed, volatile; Allium sativum, garlic, bulb, volatile; Amomum subulatum, wild cardamom, seed, volatile; Amoora rohituka, rohitacam, seed, fixed fat; Anacardium occidentale, cashew, nut, fixed fat; Anamirta cocculus, indian berry, berry, fixed fat; Andropogon muricatus, cuscus, root, volatile; Andropogon nardus, citronella, fresh plant, volatile; Andropogon schœnanthus, lemon grass, grass, volatile; Anisochilus carnosus, country lavender, whole plant, volatile; Anisomeles malabarica, malabar catmint, whole plant, volatile; Aquilaria agallocha, eagle wood, chips of wood, volatile; Arachis hypogæa, ground-nut, seed, fixed fat; Argemone mexicana, mexican poppy, seed, fixed fat; Argyreia speciosa, broad-leaved bind-weed, whole plant, volatile; Artemisia vulgaris, indian absinth, whole plant, volatile; Atalantia monophylla, monkey lime, berry, volatile; Balanites roxburghii, fire-work plant, seed, fixed fat; Baliospermum montanum, wild croton, seed, fixed fat; Bassia latifolia, wild mohwah, seed, fixed fat; Bassia longifolia, common mohwah, seed, fixed fat; Bauhinia acuminata, white mountain ebony, seed, fixed fat; Bauhinia tomentosa, wild mountain ebony, seed, fixed fat; Bauhinia variegata, variegated mountain ebony, seed, fixed fat; Benincasa cerifera, wax gourd, seed, fixed fat; Bombax malabaricum, red-cotton tree, seed, fixed fat; Brassica campestris, subsp. campestris, colza, seed, fixed fat; Brassica juncea, indian mustard, seed, fixed fat; Brassica nigra, black mustard, seed, fixed fat; Buchanania latifolia, chironjee, seed, fixed fat; Butea frondosa, bengal kino, seed, fixed fat; Cæsalpinia bonducella, bonduc, seed, fixed fat; Calophyllum inophyllum, common poon, nut, fixed fat; Calophyllum tomentosum, malabar poon, seed, fixed fat; Calophyllum wightianum, small poon, seed, fixed fat; Camellia theifera, tea, seed, fixed fat; Cananga odorata, ilang-ilang, flower, volatile; Canarium commune, elemi, kernel, fixed fat; Cannabis sativa, indian hemp, seed, fixed drying; Carapa moluccensis, crab oil plant, seed, fixed fat; Carthamus tinctorius, safflower, flower and seed, fixed fat; Carum carui, caraway, seed, volatile; Carum copticum, ajwaun, seed, volatile; Celastrus paniculatus, malkangany, seed, fixed fat; Cerbera odollam, odallam, seed, fixed fat; Cinnamomum tamala, cassia cinnamon, leaf and bark, volatile; Cinnamomum zeylanicum, ceylon cinnamon, bark, volatile; Citrullus colocynthis, colocynth, seed, fixed fat; Citrullus vulgaris, sweet water melon, seed, fixed fat; Citrus aurantium, orange, rind, volatile; Citrus medica, var. limonum, lemon, rind, volatile; Citrus medica, var. medica proper, citron, rind, volatile; Cleome viscosa, wild mustard, seed, fixed fat; Cochlospermum gossypium, golden silk cotton, seed; Cocos nucifera, cocoanut, kernel, fixed fat; Cordia myxa, small sebesten, nut, fixed fat; Coriandrum sativum, coriander, seed, volatile; Croton oblongifolius, devil's goad, seed, fixed fat; Croton tiglium, purging croton, seed, fixed fat; Cucumis melo, common melon, seed, fixed fat; Cucumis sativus, common cucumber, seed, fixed fat; Cucumis trigonus, country cucumber, seed, fixed fat; Cucurbita maxima, great pumpkin, seed, fixed drying; Cucurbita moschata, true musk melon, seed, fixed drying; Cucurbita pepo, common pumpkin, seed, fixed drying; Cuminum cyminum, cummin, seed, volatile; Cynometra cauliflora, seed, fixed fat; Cynometra ramiflora, iripa, seed, fixed fat; Cyperus rotundus, common sedge, rhizome, volatile; Dalbergia lanceolaria, caunooga, seed, fixed fat; Dalbergia latifolia, malabar black wood, seed, fixed fat; Dalbergia sissoo, sissoo, wood, wood oil; Datura stramonium, europe datura, seed, fixed fat; Daucus carota, carrot, seed, fixed fat; Dichopsis elliptica, indian gutta-percha, seed, fixed fat; Diospyros embryopteris, gaub, seed, fixed fat; Dipterocarpus tubinatus, gurjan, wood, wood oil; Dolichos biflorus, madras horse gram, seed, fixed fat; Dryobalanops aromatica, malayan camphor, wood, wood oil; Elettaria cardamomum, cardamom, seed, volatile; Eriodendron anfractuosum, silk-cotton, seed, fixed fat; Erythroxylon monogynum, deccany deodar, wood, wood oil; Eucalyptus globulus, blue gum, leaf, volatile; Eugenia caryophyllata, clove tree, flower bud, volatile; Excæcaria sebifera, china tallow, kernel, fixed fat; Feronia elephantum, wood apple, leaf, volatile; Ferula narthex, asafœtida, root, volatile; Flacourtia cataphracta, indian plum, seed, fixed fat; Fœniculum vulgare, indian fennel, root, volatile; Garcinia indica, mate mangosteen, seed, fixed fat; Garcinia morella, ceylon gamboge, seed, fixed fat; Givotia rottleriformis, white tanakk, seed, fixed fat; Gossypium arboreum, tree cotton, seed, fixed fat; Gossypium barbadense, american cotton, seed, fixed fat; Gossypium herbaceum, indian cotton, seed, fixed fat; Guizotia abyssynica, ramtil, seed, fixed fat; Gymnosporia montana, large chintoo, seed, fixed fat; Helianthus annuus, sunflower, seed, fixed drying; Hibiscus cannabinus, hemp bendy, seed, fixed fat; Hibiscus ficulneus, spreading bendy, seed, fixed fat; Hibiscus sabdariffa, red hemp bendy, seed, fixed fat; Holarrhena antidysenterica, tellicherry bark, seed, fixed fat; Holopetala integrifolia, indian elm, seed, fixed fat; Hydnocarpus venenata, fish poison tree, kernel, fixed fat; Illicium anisatum, star anise, seed, volatile; Indigofera aspalathoides, shiva's neem, root, volatile; Indigofera tinctoria, common indigo, seed, fixed fat; Jasminum sambac, arabian jasmine, flower, volatile; Jatropha curcas, physic nut, nut, fixed fat; Jatropha glandulifera, adul oil, nut, fixed fat; Jatropha multifida, small physic nut, nut, fixed fat; Lactuca scariola, var. sativa, lettuce, seed, fixed fat; Lagenaria vulgaris, bottle gourd, seed, fixed fat; Lawsonia alba, henna plant, flower, volatile; Lepidium sativum, cress, seed, fixed fat; Leucas cephalotes, large toombay, seed, fixed fat; Linum usitatissimum, flax, seed, fixed drying; Luffa acutangula, common luffa, seed, fixed fat; Luffa ægyptiaca, oil-giving luffa, seed, fixed fat; Mallotus philippensis, kamela, seed, fixed fat; Mangifera indica, mango, seed, fixed fat; Matricaria chamomilla, german chamomile, whole plant, volatile; Melaleuca leucadendron, var. minor, cajeput, leaf, volatile; Melia azadirachta, margosa, seed, fixed fat; Melia azedarach, large neem, seed, fixed fat; Mentha piperita, peppermint, leaf, volatile; Mentha viridis, spearmint, leaf, volatile; Mesua ferrea, nauga champak, fixed fat from nut, oleo-resin from bark and root, and essential from flower; Michelia champaca, champak, oil from bark, and volatile from flower; Mimusops elengi, ilanjy, fixed from seed, and volatile from flower; Mimusops hexandra, monkey-face paulay, seed, fixed fat; Mimusops kauki, edible paulay, seed, fixed fat; Momordica charantia, balsam apple, seed, fixed fat; Moringa pterygosperma, indian horse radish, seed, fixed fat; Murraya kœnigii, curry-leaf tree, fixed fat from seed, essential from leaf; Myristica fragrans, common nutmeg, nut, volatile; Myristica malabarica, malabar nutmeg, nut, volatile; Nerium odorum, oleander, flower, volatile; Nicotiana tabacum, tobacco, seed, fixed drying; Nigella sativa, small fennel, seed, volatile; Nyctanthes arbortristis, coral jasmine, flower, volatile; Pandanus odoratissimus, screw-pine, flower, volatile; Papaver somniferum, opium poppy, seed, fixed drying; Persea gratissima, alligator pear, fruit, fixed fat; Peucedanum graveolens, dill, seed, volatile; Pimpinella anisum, anise, seed, volatile; Piper cubeba, cubeb pepper, berry, volatile; Piper nigrum, black pepper, berry, volatile ; Pithecolobium dulce, corcapilly, seed, fixed fat ; Pongamia glabra, indian beech, seed, fixed fat ; Prunus amygdalus, almond, nut, fixed fat ; Prunus persica, peach, kernel, fixed fat ; Psoralea corylifolia, bawchee, seed, fixed fat ; Pterocarpus marsupium, malabar kino, seed, fixed fat ; Putranjiva roxburghii, wild olive, seed, fixed fat ; Raphanus sativus, country radish, seed, fixed fat ; Ricinus communis, castor oil, seed, fixed fat ; Salvadora oleoides, large tooth-brush tree, seed, fixed fat ; Salvadora persica, tooth-brush tree, seed, fixed fat ; Samadera indica, neipa bark, kernel, fixed fat ; Santalum album, sandal, fixed fat from seed, and volatile from wood and root ; Sapindus trifoliatus, soapnut nut, nut, fixed fat ; Sarcostigma kleinii, poovana, fixed fat ; Schleichera trijuga, ceylon oak, seed, fixed fat ; Semecarpus anacardium, marking nut tree, nut, fixed fat ; Sesamum indicum, gingelly, seed, fixed fat ; Shorea robusta, common saul, seed, fixed fat ; Spinacia oleracea, indian spinach, seed, fixed fat ; Sterculia fœtida, bastard poon, seed, fixed fat ; Strychnos nux-vomica, poison nut, nut, fixed fat ; Styrax benzoin, benjamin, gum, volatile ; Tabernæmontana dichotoma, eve's apple, seed, fixed fat ; Tamarindus indica, tamarind, seed, fixed fat ; Tectona grandis, teak, wood, wood oil ; Terminalia belerica, belleric myrobalan, seed, fixed fat ; Terminalia catappa, country almond, kernel, fixed fat ; Terminalia chebula, chebulic myrobalan, seed, fixed fat ; Thespesia populnea, portia ; Thevetia nereifolia, exile tree, nut, fixed fat ; Trigonella fœnum-græcum, fenugreek, seed, fixed fat ; Vateria indica, piney tree, seed, fixed fat ; Vernonia anthelmintica, wild cumin, seed, fixed fat ; Vitex trifolia, water notchy, root, volatile ; Wrightia tomentosa, ground paulay, seed, fixed fat ; Xanthium strumarium, burdock datura, seed, fixed fat ; Xylia dolabriformis, burmah ironwood, seed, fixed fat.—"*b*" Absinth, artemisia ; Adul oil, jatropha ; Ajwaun, carum ; Alligator pear, persea ; Almond, prunus, terminalia ; Anise, illicium, pimpinella ; Asafœtida, ferula ; Balsam apple, momordica ; Bawchee, psoralea ; Beech, pongamia ; Bendy, hibiscus ; Benjamin, styrax ; Bindweed, argyreia ; Blackwood, dalbergia ; Blue gum, eucalyptus ; Bonduc, cæsalpinia ; Cajeput, melaleuca ; Camphor, dryobalanops ; Caraway, carum ; Cardamom, amomum, elettaria ; Carrot, daucus ; Cashew, anacardium ; Castor, ricinus ; Catmint, anisomeles ; Caunooga, dalbergia ; Chamomile, matricaria ; Champak, mesua, michelia ; China tallow, excæcaria ; Chintoo, gymnosporia ; Chironjee, buchanania ; Cinnamon, cinnamomum ; Citron, citrus ; Citronella, andropogon ; Clove, eugenia ; Cocoanut, cocos ; Colocynth, citrullus ; Colza, brassica ; Corcapilly, pithecolobium ; Coriander, coriandrum ; Cotton, bombax, cochlospermum, eriodendron, gossypium ; Crab oil, carapa ; Cress, lepidium ; Croton, baliospermum ; Cubeb, piper ; Cucumber, cucumis ; Cummin, cuminum ; Curry-leaf, murraya ; Cuscus, andropogon ; Datura, xanthium ; Deodar, erythroxylon ; Devil's goad, croton ; Dill, peucedanum ; Eagle wood, aquilaria ; Ebony, bauhinia ; Elemi, canarium ; Elm, holoptela ; Eve's apple, tabernæmontana ; Exile tree, thevetia ; Fennel, fœniculum, nigella ; Fenugreek, trigonella ; Firework plant, balanites ; Fish poison, hydnocarpus ; Flax, linum ; Gamboge, garcinia ; Garlic, allium ; Gaub, diospyros ; Gingelly, sesamum ; Gourd, benincasa, lagenaria ; Gram, dolichos ; Ground-nut, arachis ; Gurjan, dipterocarpus ; Guttapercha, dichopsis ; Hemp, cannabis ; Henna, lawsonia ; Horse radish, moringa ; Ilang, cananga ; Ilanjy, mimusops ; Indian berry, anamirta ; Indigo, indigofera ; Iripa, cynometra ; Iron wood, xylia ; Jasmine, jasminum, nyctanthes ; Kamela, mallotus ; Kino, butea, pterocarpus ; Lavender, anisochilus ; Lemon, citrus ; Lemon grass, andropogon ; Lettuce, lactuca ; Lime, atalantia ; Liquorice, abrus ; Lumbang, aleurites ; Malkangany, celastrus ; Mango, mangifera ; Mangosteen, garcinia ; Margosa, melia ; Marking nut, semecarpus ; Melon, citrullus, cucumis, cucurbita ; Mohwah, bassia ; Mustard, brassica, cleome ; Myrobalan, terminalia ; Neem, indigofera, melia ; Neipa bark, samadera ; Notchy, vitex ; Nutmeg, myristica ; Oak, schleichera ; Odallam, cerbera ; Oleander, nerium ; Olive, putranjiva ; Onion, allium ; Orange, citrus ; Paulay, mimusops, wrightia ; Peach, prunus ; Pepper, piper ; Peppermint, mentha ; Physic nut, jatropha ; Piney, vateria ; Plum, flacourtia ; Poison nut, strychnos ; Poon, calophyllum, sterculia ; Poovana, sarcostigma ; Poppy, argemone, papaver ; Portia, thespesia ; Pumpkin, cucurbita ; Radish, raphanus ; Ramtil, guizotia ; Rohitacam, amoora ; Safflower, carthamus ; Sandal, santalum ; Sanders, adenanthera ; Saul, shorea ; Screw-pine, pandanus ; Sebesten, cordia ; Sedge, cyperus ; Sirissa, albizzia ; Sissoo, dalbergia ; Soapnut, sapindus ; Spearmint, mentha ; Sun flower, helianthus ; Sweet flag, acorus ; Tamarind, tamarindus ; Tanakk, givotia ; Tea, camellia ; Teak, tectona ; Tellicherry bark, holarrhena ; Tobacco, nicotiana ; Toombay, leucas ; Tooth-brush tree, salvadora ; Wild cumin, vernonia ; Wood apple, feronia.——**(4)** The mineral oils found in the presidency are :—Earth oil from palghaut and coimbatore, Mud oil from mangalore, and Petroleum from burmah [munn teilam].

YENOO (ఏను - énu, *Tel.*). Five [ei].——*Yebalam* (ఏబలము - ébalamu, Tel.). From (above + palamu, tel. the measure) ; but it is equal to 10 of the modern pollums. Bazaar weight. 10 pollums = 1 yebalam ; 4 yebalams = 1 viss [niray, 2b]. Approximate actual value, 1 yebalam = 12½ oz. avoir. = 30 tolahs. See vol. I, 609.——*Yegauny* (ఏగాని - égáni, Tel.). From (above + káni, tel. one sixty-fourth). A copper coin. 2 roowas = 1 yegauny ; 2 yegaunies = 1 doody [naanyam, 2b]. Approximate actual value, 1 yegauny = 2 pies. Same as Dooggauny.

YENOOR (ಯೇಣೂರು - yénúru, *Can.*). From (énu, can. edge + úru, can. town). Title otherwise Venoor. Village ; South canara dist., Mangalore tal. ; pop. 421 ; lat. 13° 01′ ; long. 75° 11′ ; from Madras W. 350 ; from Mangalore E.N.E. 24 miles ; from Moodbidry E. 10 miles ; from the sea E. 24 miles. Monolithic Jeina [q.v.] statue [gomataroya] 35 feet high, one of the three as yet known ; see Caurcal. There is also a Jeina temple. Near the latter is a fine pillar [stambbam] made of one stone and richly sculptured. The doorway of the temple is finely decorated. Near the principal temple is another small Jeina shrine with pillars. At its base are some Naugaculls [q.v.] and a Veeracull [q.v.]. There are in all eight Jeina and one Braminical temple. A car festival [ratotsavam] in principal temple at beginning of March. Washing [abbishaicam] the statue is performed once every 60 years [brihaspaty]. Last performed in March 1887.

YEOMIAH (يوميه - yaumíyah, *Hind.*). From (yaum, ar. day) [yowm]. A money allowance or pension [inam] calculated originally at so much per diem.

YER (ഏർ - ér, *Mal.*). Bullock [yair]. *Yeddadoogoo canama* (ఎడ్డడుగుకనమ - eddadugukanama, Tel.). From (eddu, tel. bull + adugu, tel. foot print + kanama, tel. pass). Ghaut ; Cuddapah dist., Budwail tal. ; lat. 14° 52′ ; long. 78° 53′ ; from Budwail W.N.W. 17 miles ; from Cuddapah N. 27 miles. In the Nullamullays, connecting Proddootore and Budwail talooks.——*Yeddoo* (ఎద్దు - eddu, Tel.) Bull [maud].——*Yeralpaud* (ഏറാൽപ്പാട് - érálppátu, Mal.). Same as Yeraudipaud.——*Yeraudipaud* (ഏറാടിപ്പാട് - érátippátu, Mal.). From (above + ád, mal. country + pátu, mal. chief title). The title of the heir apparent of Zamorin's [q.v.] family. See vol. I, 52.——*Yernaud* (ഏറനാട് - éranátu, mal.). See sep. title.

YERCAUD (ஏர்க்காடு - érkkádu, *Tam.*). From (éri, tam. lake + kádu, tam. wood) ; lake-wood from the sacred grove near the lake. Village ; Salem dist., Salem tal. ; pop. 1,365 ; lat. 11° 47′ ; long. 78° 16′ ; height 4,828 feet ; from Salem N. 9 miles. For description, see vol. II, 145 [hill-station].

YERCUM (अर्क - arka, *San.* ; रुई - rui, *Mahr.* ; रूवि - rúvi, *Conc.* ; عشر - ushshar, *Ar.* ; خرك - kharak, *Pers.* ; مدار - madár, *Hind.* ; آگ کا جہار - ágkájhár, *Dec.* ; ಎಕ್ಕೆ - ekke, *Can.* ; ಎಕ್ಕಮಾಲೆ - ekkamále, *Too.* ; జిల్లేడు - jillédu, *Tel.* ; എരിക്ക - erikku, *Mal.* ; වරා - vará, *Singh.* ; எருக்கு - erukku, *Tam.*). Title from sanscrit through tamul. San. means sun from cuneiform shape of leaf. Mahr. from sanscrit. Ar. from (ush, san. to burn) ; from the dried twigs of plant being tied to the tail of wild bulls, and set fire to by ancient arabs in times of drought to induce rain. Hind. from (mandára, san. the purple flowered variety). Dec. and dravidian from sanscrit. San. also (pratápasa), meaning very hot, the white var. ; (shvétárka), meaning white + calotropis gigantea, r. br ; (vasuka), meaning abiding ; (ásp'hóta), meaning opening from all sides [arabian jasmine, wild jasmine] ; (ganarúpa), meaning multitude + shape ; (vikírna), meaning scattered ; (mandára), meaning minor disease + expeller [coral tree] ; (arkaparna), meaning sun + leaved ; (áditya), meaning sun ; (alarka), meaning adorning arcan, the white var. [prickly shoonday] ; (rudra), meaning shiva ; (súryapatra), meaning sun leaf. Ar. also (ushmor). Pers. also (darakhtizahrnák), meaning poisonous tree. Hind. also (akond) ; (akan) ; (safedák), meaning white calotropis ; (ák) [dyeing mulberry]. Dec. also (ákrá), by corr. from sanscrit. Tel. also (mandáramu) [white mountain ebony] ; (nallajillédu), meaning black + plant so called ; (tellajillédu), meaning white + plant so called ; (rátsajillédu), meaning king + the plant. Mal. also (vellerikku), meaning white + calotropis gigantea, r. br. Singh. also (múduvará), meaning ocean + the plant. Tam. also (vellerukku), meaning white + the plant. Title otherwise Bow-string hemp [marool] Curled-flowered swallow-wort, French cotton, French jasmine, Gigantic nettlewort, Gigantic swallow-wort, Lightning leaf, Madaur, Madaur silk cotton, Mudar, Sun plant, Vegetable mercury, Yercok. Botanically Calotropis gigantea, r. br., asclepiadeæ [vriesham, 88]. Alias Asclepias gigantea. Shrub, 6-10 feet ; leaves stemclasping, decussate, oblong-ovate, wedge-shaped, bearded on the upper side at the base, smooth on the upper surface, clothed with woolly down on the under side ; segments of corolla reflexed, with revolute edges ; stamineous corona five-leaved, shorter than the gynostegium ; leaflets keel-formed, circinately recurved at the base, incurved and subtridentate at the apex ; umbels sometimes compound, surrounded by involucral scales ; follicles ventricose, smooth ; seeds comose ; flowers rose-color and purple mixed ; flowering all year. Stem and branches covered with a fibrous, corky, soft bark ; stem abounds in acrid milky juice ; leaves opposite, 6 inches in length ; fruit full of fine silky hairs ; common in south, especially in sandy and barren soils. The root barks occur in bazaar in short quilled pieces ⅛ to ⅕ of an inch thick ; the outer surface is yellowish-grey, soft and corky, fissured longitudinally, and can be easily separated from the middle cortical layer, which is white, friable, and traversed by narrow brown liber rays ; the taste is mucilaginous, bitter and acrid, and the odour peculiar. From an alcoholic solution of powdered root, the spirit being then distilled off, is obtained a resinous decoction mudarine, which possesses the property of coagulating by heat and becoming again fluid by exposure to cold; mudarine is very bitter, soluble in alcohol and cold water, but insoluble in sulphuric ether or olive-oil [zeitoon]; dried bark of root is of greyish yellow color; an acrid milky juice flows from every part of the shrub when wounded. The roots are collected in april and may, and after washing are dried in open air without exposure to the sun, until the inherent milky juice becomes so far dried that it ceases to flow on incision made; the root bark is then carefully removed, dried, reduced to powder, and preserved in well-corked bottles. To procure the fibre, the straightest branches are cut and exposed to the weather for at least twenty-four hours; on the second and third day they are slightly beaten, the skin is then peeled and the stringy substance between the bark and the wood taken out; they are then dried in the sun; this slow process is necessarily expensive, but if the bark is steeped in water, it becomes discolored, and cutting will destroy it; the fibre is strong and possesses many of the properties of europe flax [alsee]; it can be spun into the finest thread for sewing or weaving cloth. The rind below outer crust of root pulverised and made into an ointment is medicinally efficacious in the treatment of old ulcers; powdered root-bark is internally alterative-tonic, diaphoretic and emetic, substituted for british ipecacuanha; the inspissated juice is used externally in almost all cutaneous affections, especially ring-worm and leprosy, this is more powerful than the root-bark; the juice mixed with common salt [ooppoo] is given in toothache; the juice of the young buds is given in ear-ache; the leaves warmed and moistened with oil are applied as a dry fomentation in abdominal pains, and form a good rubefacient; flowers are digestive, stomachic, tonic, useful in asthma, catarrh, and loss of appetite; dry leaves burnt for fumigating obstinate sores; these remedies have been used in hindoo medicine from time immemorial; gives to pharm. root-bark dried, calotropis cortex, alterative tonic, diaphoretic, and in large doses emetic, officinal. The plant is a poison for goats and sheep [aud]. Hairs from seeds used for stuffing pillows; milky sap on evaporation forms a caoutchouc [pauchonty]; the liquor called bar is prepared from this plant by the tribes of the western ghauts [q.v.]; root is used in manufacture of gunpowder charcoal [adoopp kary]; the silky floss which surrounds the seeds has been woven into shawls [q.v.] and handkerchiefs [roomaul] and even paper, besides a soft kind of thread [nool]; the fine strong fibre is a good substitute for flax [alsee], fit for cambric cloth, and twine, used for making fishing-lines by native fishermen; the milky juice imparts yellow color to the skin, and used by chucklers [q.v.] with lac [q.v.] in dyeing [shauyam] leather [chamrah] red; the powdered flowers adulterate safflower [bastard saffron]; fresh root is used as a toothbrush, considered by patauns [q.v.] to cure toothache; ashes used as mordant [cauram]. A variety alba, with white, cream-colored flowers; another species procera [black yercum], in northern districts. There is a Tamul proverb:—வெள்ளெருக்கும் வெள்ளாட்டுப்பாலுக்கும் கள்ளக்கருமேகம் காணாமற்போம்—"the treacherous disease which blackens "the skin will be thoroughly cured by white yercum and goats' "milk [paul.]".——*Ant-hill yercum* (పుట్టజిల్లేడు - puttajillédu, Tel.). Means ant-hill + yercum. Same as Ground paulay.——*Black yercum* (నల్లజిల్లేడు - nallajillédu, Tel.). Calotropis procera with pale-purplish flowers. See above.

YERKALA (ఎరుకల - erukala, *Tel.*). From (eruka, tel. fortune-telling). Call themselves Goory [q.v.], meaning fortune-tellers from marks on body. Called by mahomedans Corchewar. A branch of the Corava [q.v.] people. Nomad caste found wandering over the plains of southern india; numerous in the shreeharicote jungles. They are usually of a dark-brown color; the men are spare and light made, but hardy, with low forehead, small eyes, short nose; they wear only a strip of cloth [lungooty], and they tie their hair in a knot [conday] above their brow. The women are famous as fortune-tellers; they bring game and jungle produce for sale to madras; they live in grass, mat [boriyah], or reed huts, and make and sell mats and baskets [tokrah]; they are found on the outskirts of most towns; they also make wooden combs, work as laborers, and a few who have settled engage in cultivation; they rear pigs [soor], poultry, donkeys [gadhah], and dogs [nye], and eat the flesh of most animals; they admit polygamy, but do not re-marry their widows; numbers about 130,000 [jauty]. See vol. I (36), 195; II, 75, 113.

YERNAGOODEM (యెర్నగూడెము - yernagúdemu, *Tel.* yernagúdem *). From (errana, tel. proper name + gúdemu, tel. village) [yerra].——**(1)** Talook, Godavery district. Tahsildar's pay Rs. 150. Area 1,141 square miles. Consists of 99 Government villages, 98 Zemindarry and Proprietary villages, 17 Agrahaurams. Population 136,209. Language Teloogoo. W. of district. Bounded:—north by the Nizam's territory, south by Tanookoo talook, east by the Godavery, west by Ellore talook. Surface is rocky and jungly in most parts, but level towards the south and near the Godavery. Upper portions are very unhealthy and feverish in the rainy and cold seasons. Soil is of eight different kinds; alluvial, permanently improved, regar [q.v.] pure, regar loamy, regar sandy, red clay [calimunn], red loamy, and red sandy [munn]. Principal products are paddy [q.v.], gram [q.v.], gingelly [q.v.] and lamp oil [q.v.] seeds, cumboo [bajrah], zonna [cholum], raggy [q.v.], cotton [q.v.], timber, chillies [q.v.] and bamboos [q.v.]. Trade is chiefly in dry grains [q.v.], cotton [q.v.], oil seeds [yennay] and timber [maram], and jungle products. A few villages in the south are watered by the Ellore canal, and other parts of the talook are irrigated by means of tanks [q.v.] and mountain streams. Camping grounds:—Covoor, Nullacherla, Paugidy, Yernagoodem, on the trunk road. Zemindarries—Annadevarpaud, Anoomoolunka, Bayyanagoodem, Bheemole, Billoomilly, Calavalpully, Chidipy, Condagoodem, Cooroocore, Dhoonmutoonigoodem, Gangole, Gavaravaram, Gootaula, Gowriputnam, Guddigoodem, Gunnygull, Jangamreddygoodem, Lakkavaram, Malacapully, Nullamillipaud, Nundigoodem, Ooncaramilly, Pattesam, Payidimetta, Peddeham, Polavaram, Prakkilunka, Telikicherla, Tirgoodoometta, Tyanjampoody, Yaudavole, Yernagoodem. Places of archæological interest:—Anantapulley, Aurgole, Auroolla, Auvapaud, Comauradevam, Condrooprole, Covoor, Ganapavaram, Gootaula, Gopalpore, Guzzram, Lakkavaram, Pattesam, Polavaram, Prattipaud, Singarauzpollem, Taudepullegoodem, Taudimulla, Telikicherla, Yaudavole. Principal trig. stations:—Addacondah, Auvapaud, Hooracondah, Parimpoody, Paupicondah. The leading places, &c., in the talook are the following.——*Addacondah* (అడ్డకొండ - addakonda, Tel.). From (adda, tel. cross + konda, tel. hill). Trig. station; lat. 17° 13′ 50·75″; long. 81° 31′ 36·14″; height 1,375 feet; from Saugipaud N.W. 4 miles.——*Annadevarpaud* (అన్నదేవరపాడు - aunadévarapádu, Tel.). From (annadévara, tel. proper name + pádu, tel. village). Zemindarry, Village; pop. 2,147; lat. 17° 7′; long. 81° 40′; from Cocanada W.N.W. 41 miles; from Tallapoody W. 3 miles. Peshcush Rs. 3,728.——*Anoomoolunka* (అనుముల్లంక - anumullanka, Tel.). From (anumu, tel. a bean, dolichos lablab, linn. + lanka, tel. island). Zemindarry village; pop. 1,258; lat. of village 17° 02′; long. 81° 26′; from Cocanada W.N.W. 55 miles; from Tallapoody W.S.W. 20 miles. Peshcush Rs. 611.——*Auvapaud* (ఆవుపాడు - ávupádu, Tel.). From (ávu, tel. cow + pádu, tel. village). Trig. station; lat. 16° 53′ 05·99″; long. 81° 26′ 02·42″; height 196 feet; from Auvapaud S.W. 2 miles.——*Bayyanagoodem* (బయ్యనగూడెము - bayyanagúdemu, Tel.). From (bayyana, tel. proper name + gúdemu, tel. village). Zemindarry village; pop. 1,447; lat. of village 17° 07′; long. 81° 24′; from Cocanada W.N.W. 58 miles; from Tallapoody W. 20 miles. Peshcush Rs. 985.——*Bheemole* (భీమోలు - bhímólu, Tel.). From (bhíma, san. one of the five pándavás + prólu, tel. town). Zemindarry village; pop. 1,443; lat. of village 17° 09′; long. 81° 37′; from Cocanada W.N.W. 46 miles; from Tallapoody W.N.W. 7 miles. Peshcush Rs. 1,210.——*Billoomilly* (బిల్లుమిల్లి - billumilli, Tel.). From (billu, tel. satinwood, chloroxylon swietenia, dec. + palli, tel. village). Zemindarry village; pop. 1,580; lat. of village 17° 11′; long. 81° 26′; from Cocanada W.N.W. 57 miles; from Tallapoody W.N.W. 19 miles. Peshcush Rs. 1,619.——*Calavalpully* (కలవలపల్లి - kalavalapalli, Tel.). From (kaluva, tel. water lily, nymphæa lotus, linn. + palli, tel. village). Zemindarry village; pop. 2,124; lat of village 16° 57′; long. 81° 41′; from Cocanada W. 39 miles; from Tallapoody S. 11 miles. Peshcush Rs. 1,346.——*Chidipy* (చిడిపి - chidipi, Tel.). Means small. Zemindarry village; pop. 685; lat. of village 17° 05′; long. 81° 43′; from Cocanada W.N.W. 37 miles; from Tallapoody S. 2 miles. Peshcush Rs. 1,665.——*Covoor* (కొవ్వూరు - kóvúru, Tel.). From (gó, san. cow + úru, tel. village). Village; pop. 2,351; acres 4,521; lat. 17° 01′; long. 81° 46′; from Cocanada W.N.W. 33 miles; from Tallapoody S.S.E. 8 miles. On right bank of the Godavery, opposite to Rajahmundry. Ancient temple of Madana gopalsawmy said to have been established by Booddha [q.v.]. Temple of Choleshwara sawmy erected by a Chola king, as also temple of Aunjaneyan [hanooman]. Communication by ferry steamer with Rajahmundry.——*Doodcore* (దుడ్డుకూరు - duddukúru, Tel.). From (duddu, tel. rude + úru, tel. village). Village; pop. 1,262; acres 2,087; lat. 17° 02′; long. 81° 38′; from Cocanada W.N.W. 42 miles; from Tallapoody S.W. 8 miles.——*Ganapavaram* (గణపవరము - ganapavaramu, Tel.). From (ganapati, tel. belly god + pura, san. town). Village; pop. 690; acres 4,492; lat. 17° 12′; long. 81° 18′; from Cocanada W.N.W. 65 miles; from Tallapoody W.N.W. 28 miles.——*Gangole* (గంగోలు - gangólu, Tel.). From (ganga, tel. ganges + prólu, tel. town). Zemindarry village; pop. 829; lat. of village 17° 11′; long. 81° 37′; from Cocanada W.N.W. 46 miles; from Tallapoody N.W. 8 miles. Peshcush Rs. 1,264.——*Gavaravaram* (గవరవరము - gavaravaramu, Tel.). From (gavara, tel. a caste + pura, san. town). Zemindarry village; pop. 855; lat. of village 17° 07′; long. 81° 27′; from Cocanada W.N.W. 56 miles; from Tallapoody W. 16 miles. Peshcush Rs. 145.——*Godavery* (గోదావరి - gódávari, Tel.). See sep. title.——*Gootaula* (గూటాల - gútála,* Tel.). From (gútamu, tel. peg). Zemindarry village; pop. 3,633; lat. of village 17° 11′; long. 81° 41′; from Cocanada N.W. 42 miles; from Tallapoody N. 5 miles. Peshcush Rs. 6,741. Old fort dates from time of Reddies [q.v.].——*Gowriputnam* (గౌరిపట్నము - gauripatnamu, Tel.). From (gaurí, san. the goddess + pattana, san. town). Zemindarry village; pop. 899; lat. of village 17° 02′; long. 81° 40′; from Cocanada W.N.W. 40

miles; from Tallapoody S.W. 7 miles. Peshcush Rs. 1,853.——*Hooracondah* (హూరకొండ - hurakonda, Tel.). Trig. station; lat. 17° 18′ 12·72″; long. 82° 32′ 46·62″; from Lutchmeepooram E.N.E. 15 miles.——*Jangamreddygoodem* (జంగమరెడ్డిగూడెము - dzangamareddigúdemu, Tel.). From (dzangamareddi, tel. proper name + gúdemu, tel. village). Zemindarry village; pop. 1,187; lat. of village 17° 07′; long. 81° 20′; from Cocanada W.N.W. 62 miles; from Tallapoody W.N.W. 25 miles. Peshcush Rs. 499. ——*Lakkavaram* (లక్కవరము - lakkavaramu, Tel.). From (lakki, tel. proper name + pura, san. town). Zemindarry village; pop. 2,094; lat. of village 17° 03′; long. 81° 20′; from Cocanada W.N.W. 61 miles; from Tallapoody W.S.W. 25 miles. Peshcush Rs. 2,643. Deserted temple, dates from time of the Reddy chiefs, 1328 to 1427 A.D.——*Maudavaram* (మాధవరము - mádhavaramu, Tel.). From (mádhava, san. epithet of vishnu + pura, san. town). Town; pop. 2,712; acres 4,164; lat. 16° 53′; long. 81° 38′; from Cocanada W. 42 miles; from Tallapoody S.S.W. 16 miles.——*Naugavaram* (నాగవరము - nágavaramu, Tel.). From (nága, san. serpent + pura, san. town). Zemindarry village; pop. 5,339; lat. of village 17° 13′; long. 81° 21′; from Cocanada W.N.W. 63 miles; from Tallapoody W.N.W. 25 miles. The estate consists of 40 hill villages inhabited chiefly by Coyis [gond]. The village has a ruined fort.——*Nullacherla* (నల్లచర్ల - nallacharla, Tel.). From (nalla, tel. black + charla, tel. village). Village; pop. 2,435; acres 10,499; lat. 16° 56′; long. 81° 27′; from Cocanada W. 54 miles; from Tallapoody S.W. 22 miles.——*Nundigoodem* (నందిగూడెము - nandigúdemu, Tel.). From (nandí, san. shiva's bull + gúdemu, tel. village). Zemindarry village; pop. 804. Peshcush Rs. 364.——*Parimpoody* (పరింపూడి - parimpúdi, Tel.). From (pari, tel. army + púdi, tel. village). Trig. station; lat. 17° 12′ 41·04″; long. 81° 14′ 37·77″; height 689 feet; from Parimpoody S. 1 mile; from Narrainpooram S.W. 1½ miles.——*Pattesam* * (పట్టెసం - pattesam, Tel.). From (patte, tel. plank). Sanscrit name (vírabhadrakshétra), meaning veerabhadran, the god + sacred place. Zemindarry village. Place of pilgrimage; pop. 1,547; lat. of village 17° 13′; long. 81° 41′; from Cocanada W.N.W 42 miles; from Tallapoody N. 7 miles. Peshcush Rs. 5,244. The Godavery passes round the island of Pauta pattesam at this place. Pilgrims come here for the Maha shivarautry [pundigay, 6a] festival in February. Temples of great age.——*Paupicondah* (పాపికొండ - pápikonda, Tel.). From (pápí, san. sinner + konda, tel. hill). Trig. station; lat. 17° 15′ 31·90″; long. 81° 26′ 25·05″; height 1,832 feet; from Yernagoodem N. 20 miles.——*Polavaram* (పోలవరము - pólavaramu, Tel.). See sep. title.——*Potavaram* (పోతవరం - pótavaram, Tel.). From (pótu, tel. bull + pura, san. town). Village; pop. 2,334; acres 3,316; lat. 17° 01′; long. 81° 27′; from Cocanada W. 54 miles; from Tallapoody W.S.W. 19 miles. Former headquarters of Polavaram division Deputy tahsildar.——*Prakkilunka* (ప్రక్కిలంక - prakkilanka, Tel.). From (prakki, tel. reed + lanka, tel. island). Zemindarry village; pop. 1,123; square miles 1⅓; lat of village 17° 08′; long. 81° 42′; from Cocanada W.N.W. 39 miles; from Tallapoody N.W. 1 mile. Peshcush Rs. 1,770.——*Rauvimetta* (రావిమెట్ట - rávimetta, Tel.). From (rávi, tel. peepul tree, ficus religiosa, linn. + metta, tel. mound). Zemindarry village; pop. 902; square miles 4; lat. of village 16° 54′; long. 81° 41′; from Cocanada W. 38 miles; from Tallapoody S.S.W. 15 miles. Peshcush Rs. 1,630.——*Tallapoody* (తాళ్లపూడి - tállapúdi, Tel.). See sep. title.——*Telikicherla* (తెలికిచర్ల - telikicherla, Tel.). From (telika, tel. gingelly plant, sesamum indicum, dec. + charla, tel. village). Zemindarry village; pop. 1,110; lat. of village 16° 56′; long. 81° 31′; from Cocanada W. 50 miles; from Tallapoody S.W. 19 miles. Peshcush Rs. 943. Temple with inscriptions.——*Tirgoodoometta* (తిరుగుడుమెట్ట - tirugudumetta, Tel.). From (tirugu, tel. to turn + metta, tel. mound). Zemindarry village; pop. 978; lat. of village 17° 05′; long. 81° 41′; from Cocanada W.N.W. 40 miles; from Tallapoody S.W. 4 miles. Peshcush Rs. 1,856.——*Tyaujampoody* (త్యాజంపూడి - tyájampúdi, Tel.). From (tyága, san. gift + púdi, tel. village). Zemindarry village; pop. 1,198; lat. of village 16° 58′; long. 81° 34′; from Cocanada W. 46 miles; from Tallapoody S.W. 15 miles. Peshcush Rs. 2,791. ——*Yaudavole* (యాదవోలు - yádavólu, Tel.). From (yádava, tel. a race, so called; applied to shepherds + prólu, tel. town). Zemindarry village; pop. 3,892; lat. of village 17° 04′; long. 81° 31′; from Cocanada W.N.W. 50 miles; from Tallapoody W.S.W. 14 miles. Peshcush Rs. 2,161. Stone pillar [laut] with inscriptions [shausanam].——*Yernagoodem* (యెర్నగూడెము - yernagúdemu, Tel.). See below.——**(2)** Zemindarry village; Godavery dist., Yernagoodem tal.; pop. 2,162; lat. 16° 59′; long. 81° 33′; from Cocanada W. 47 miles; from Tallapoody S.W. 14 miles. Peshcush Rs. 1,725. On the road from Bezwada to Rajahmundry. Headquarters of the Tahsildar [q.v.] removed to Tallapoody owing to the unhealthiness of the place.

YERNAUD (ഏറനാട് - éranátu, *Mal.* ernad*). From (éru, mal. bullock + nátu, mal. country) [yer]. Sanscrit name (gópálapura), meaning cowherd + town; also (ábhíra), meaning cowherd place. The hebrew Ophir is probably a corruption of the latter. Talook, Malabar district. Tahsildar's pay Rs. 200. Area 811 square miles. S. centre coast of district. Bounded north by Calicut and Wynaud, east by Neilgherry district, south by Valavanaud and Ponnany, west by the sea. Comprises the two old talooks of Yernaud and Chernaud, amalgamated in 1860. 140 square miles under cultivation, remainder waste lands and hilly tracts. The eastern portion comprehends the Nelambore valley formed by the ghauts and the Coondah mountains. The most remarkable hills are the Vauvool range, Chekkmala or Checoonn hill, Pundalore hill whose ridge separates the Yernaud from Valavanaud taleok, Oorotemala hill, which formed the boundary of the old Chernaud talook. Soil of the western portion and on the heights is red laterite [q.v.], intermixed with gravel; in valleys of cultivation, a rich brown free from gravel [kankar]; so also in cultivated tracts in interior. Dense cocoanut [q.v.] belt usually not more than 4 miles wide extending along coast runs up for 12 or 15 miles into very nearly the heart of the talook about Malapooram. Pine-apple [ananas] nowhere flourishes better. Productions generally are rice [q.v.], several species of dry grain [q.v.] and pulses [dholl]; pepper [q.v.] is produced but not in abundance. Ginger [q.v.] is largely cultivated, areca [q.v.] palm is cultivated extensively about central parts, and grows luxuriantly on banks of all rivers, scarce to the east of Nelambore. Timber, bamboos [q.v.], honey [shahad], and bees' wax [mom] are obtained from forests. Iron [auhan] ore is found in different parts, chiefly in Chembracherry and Paundicaud amshoms [q.v.], but very little actually worked. Gold [pon] ore is found in beds of rivers and streams running down from ghauts [q.v.] into Nelambore valley. One principal branch of Beypore river is called Ponpoya or gold river. The manufactures are of little moment and consist of some cloth of an inferior quality. The cloths formerly famous as Shaliyat derived their name from Chaulyam. Oils from cocoanut and castor [aumanac], coir [q.v.] on the sea coast, jaggery [q.v.] and arrack [q.v.] from toddy [q.v.] are manufactured almost everywhere. Rivers are the Beypore and Cadaloondy. Places of archæological interest:—Alinyilam, Cadaloondy, Carippore, Cauracoonn, Caurand, Charye, Cheroocauv, Codevauvore, Cunnamungalam, Indyanore, Irimbooly, Irvetty, Munjery, Munnore, Nelambore, Niroomgythacottah, Nullore, Ooragam mailmoory, Palanjannore, Pommala, Pooliyacode, Tricalangode, Tricolam, Vandoor, Vencara, Vullicoonn. Principal trig. stations:— Checoonn, Oorotemala. The leading places, &c., in the talook are the following.——*Arriyacode* (അരിയക്കോട് - ariyakkótu, Mal.). From (ari, mal. small + kótu, mal. fort). Town; lat. 11° 14′; long. 76° 05′; from Beypore E.N.E. 17 miles; from Calicut E. 18 miles; from Munjery N.N.W. 10 miles; from the sea E. 19 miles. On the south bank of the Beypore river. The highest point to which the river is navigable in dry season. Has a colony of Mahomedan traders. Timber depôt established in 1797. Public bungalow [q.v.].——*Beypore* (ബേപ്പൂർ - béppúr, Mal.). See sep. title.——*Bhawauny* (ഭവാനി - bhaváni, Mal.). See sep. title.——*Cadaloondy* (കടലുണ്ടി - katalunti, Mal.). See sep. title.——*Carcoor* (കാർക്കൂർ - kárkkúr, Mal.). From (kár, mal. black + úr, mal. village). Ghaut [q.v.]; lat. 11° 28′; long. 76° 27′; from Calicut E.N.E. 44 miles; from Munjery N.E. 30 miles; from the sea E. 47 miles. Leads from Yernaud talook into Neilgherry district.——*Chaulyam* (ചാലിയം - cháliyam, Mal.). See sep. title. ——*Checoonn* (ചെക്കുന്ന് - chekkunnu, Mal.). From (cheru, mal. small + kunnu, mal. hill). Trig. station; lat. 11° 15′ 27·71″; long. 76° 08′ 22·58″; height 1,975 feet; from Munjery N. 10 miles; from the sea E. 22 miles. On the outskirts of Camel hump [q.v.] range.——*Condotty* (കുണ്ടുവട്ടി - kuntuvatti, Mal. kondótti *). From (konda, mal. tuft of hair + vettu, mal. to cut). Town, Place of Mahomedan pilgrimage; lat. 11° 09′; long. 76° 00′; from Calicut S.E. 14 miles; from Munjery W. 11 miles; from the sea E. 11 miles. Important Moplah [q.v.] town on road between Calicut and Malapooram. Residence of Condotty tangal [q.v.], Mahomedan high priest of the section of Moplahs [q.v.] known as Condotty kyecaur. The Tangals [q.v.] hold a personal inam [q.v.] of Rs. 2,734 per year and may keep seven pieces of cannon. Two mosques [musjid] largely attended. Public bungalow [q.v.].——*Cottacull* (കോട്ടക്കൽ - kóttakkal, Mal.). From (kótta, mal. fort + kal, mal. suffix of place). Village; lat. 10° 59′; long. 76° 04′; from Calicut S.E. 24 miles; from Munjery S.W. 11 miles; from the sea E. 10 miles. Fourteen miles from Munjery, seat of the Kizhakk covilagam [q.v.] rajahs, the second of the three branches of the Zamorin's [q.v.] family. Old fort, called Vencatacottah, small bungalow built by Rajah, weekly fair held. Areca-nut [areca], arrowroot [coova] flour and ginger [q.v.] form principal articles of trade. Military camping ground at Claury is two miles from this place. ——*Furruckabad* (فرخ آباد - farrukhábád, Hind.). See sep. title. ——*Macoorty* (ಮುಕುರ್ತಿಬೆಟ್ಟ - múkurtibetta, Can.). See sep. title. ——*Malapooram* (മലപ്പുറം - malappuram, Mal.). See sep. title. ——*Mambram* (മമ്പ്രം - mampram, Mal.). From (man, mal. loose, earth + puram, mal. side). Village, Place of Mahomedan pilgrimage; lat. 11° 15′; long. 76° 01′; from Calicut E. 14 miles; from Munjery N.W. 14 miles; from the sea E. 14 miles. Tomb of a Moplah tangal [q.v.]. Opposite to Tiroorangaudy, on the north bank of the river.——*Maumbaud* (മാമ്പാട് - mámbátu, Mal.). From (mávu, mal. mangifera indica, linn. + pátu, mal. village). Town; pop. 5,174; lat. 11° 15′; long. 76° 13′; from

Calicut E. 27 miles; from Munjery N. 10 miles; from the sea E. 28 miles. Place of timber trade. On Beypore river, four miles north of Nelambore.——*Munjery* (മഞ്ചേരി - mañchéri, Mal.). See sep. title.——*Neilgherry peak* (നീലഗിരിശിഖരം - nílagirishikharam, Mal.). See sep. title.——*Nelambore* (നിലമ്പൂർ - nilampúr, Mal.). See sep. title.——*Oorotemala* (ഊരോത്ത്മല - úróttmala, Mal.). From (úrakam, mal. the amshom so called + mala, mal. mountain). Hill; lat. 11° 5′; long. 76° 03′; from Calicut S.E. 19 miles; from Munjery W.S.W. 8 miles; from the sea E. 12 miles. Overlooking Malapooram. On the summit a small temple. Trig. station in lat. 11° 05′ 15·73″; long. 76° 03′ 05·60″; height 1,573 feet; from Munjery W.S.W. 8 miles; from Cunnamungalam W. 28 miles; from the sea E. 12 miles.——*Parpanangaudy* (പരപ്പനങ്ങാടി - parappanannáti, Mal.). See sep. title.——*Paundicaud* (പാന്തിക്കാട് - pántikkátu, Mal.). From (pánti, mal. bamboo, bambusa arundinacea, willd. + kátu, mal. forest). Village; pop. 6,999; lat. 11° 06′; long. 76° 17′; from Calicut E.S.E. 33 miles; from Munjery E. 8 miles; from the sea E. 27 miles. Public bungalow [q.v.], weekly market; iron [auhan] ore obtained.——*Payyanaud* (പയ്യനാട് - payyanátu, Mal.). From (payya, mal. flat + nátu, mal. country). Village; pop. 4,319; lat. 11° 06′; long. 76° 12′; from Calicut S.E. 27 miles; from Munjery E. 2 miles; from the sea E. 22 miles.——*Ponpoya* (പൊൻപുഴ - ponpuzha, Mal.). See sep. title.——*Tiroorangaudy* (തിരൂരങ്ങാടി - tirúrannáti, Mal.). See sep. title.——*Tricolam* (തൃക്കോലം - trikkolam, Mal.). From (tri, mal. holy + kulam, mal. tank). Village; pop. 10,540; lat. 11° 2′; long. 75° 57′; from Calicut S.S.E. 17 miles; from Munjery W.S.W. 15 miles; from the sea E. 4 miles. Shiva temple. Old fort occupied by Tippoo. Umbrella stones [coday cull] and ancient rock-cut tombs.——*Tricullore* (തൃക്കല്ലൂർ - trikkallúr, Mal.). From (tri, mal. holy + kal, mal. stone + úr, mal. village). Village; lat. 11° 15′; long. 76° 03′; from Calicut E. 16 miles; from Munjery N.W. 13 miles; from the sea E. 17 miles. Shiva temple on elevated ground; in this 12 Moplahs [q.v.] made a stand against the police and the military from the 27th to 29th December 1884; temple was captured and the fanatics killed after breaking open the loopholed barricaded doors with dynamite. The temple owns large property [devasom].——*Vandoor* (വണ്ടൂർ - vantúr, Mal. wandúr *). From (vantu, mal. beetle + úr, mal. village). Village, Sub-registrar's station; pop. 7,532; acres 8,249; lat. 11° 12′; long. 76° 17′; from Calicut E.S.E. 31 miles; from Munjery N.E. 10 miles; from the sea E. 30 miles. Public bungalow [q.v.] once used travelling by Sisparra route [ghaut] to the Neilgherries. Road not now maintained beyond Caly cauv, 8 miles E. of Vandoor. Mosque [musjid] and Shiva temple. Six dolmens [coday cull] and rude stone monuments.——*Yedacara* (എടക്കര - etakkara, Mal.). From (eta, mal. shepherd caste + kara, mal. village). Village; lat. 11° 21′; long. 76° 21′; from Calicut E.N.E. 36 miles; from Munjery N.E. 20 miles; from the sea E. 38 miles. On the river, 8 miles east of Nelambore. On an extensive plain of black rich soil, once thickly populated. Public bungalow.——*Yedawanna* (എടവണ്ണ - etavanna, Mal.). From (etam, mal. palace + vannam, mal. beauty). Town; lat. 11° 12′; long. 76° 11′; from Calicut E.S.E. 25 miles; from Munjery N. 7 miles; from the sea E. 24 miles. On the left bank of the Beypore, at the head of its navigable course. Considerable timber trade. Public bungalow [q.v.].

YEROO (ఎరువు - eruvu, *Tel.*; எரு - eru, *Tam.*). Manure. This divides into vegetable, animal and mineral.—"*a*" Vegetable manure comprises substances such as boughs and leaves of bushes and trees, indigo [q.v.] refuse, wood ashes, weeds, &c. These are simply thrown upon the land and dug or ploughed into the land in a fresh state. The plants containing milky sap [paulay] are preferred. Oil-cakes [ponnauk] especially of karanj [q.v.] are also used. Green leaves are used in case of paddy [q.v.] fields. The stubble of previous crop ploughed into the land serves to enrich it as it decays. The following is a list of the principal plants used as manure:—Adhatoda vasica [adhatoday]; Calotropis gigantea [yercum]; Cassia auriculata [tungaid]; Cedrella toona [toon]; Crotalaria juncea [sunn]; Datura fastuosa [purple datura]; Datura fastuosa, var. alba [white datura]; Dodonia viscosa [golla's plate]; Dolichos lablab [country bean]; Euphorbia tirucalli [round milk-hedge]; Holarrhena antidysenterica [tellicherry bark]; Indigofera tinctoria [common indigo]; Jatropha curcas [wild aumanac]; Mangifera indica [mango]; Melia azadirachta [neem]; Mirabilis jalapa [false jalap]; Ocimum sanctum [common toolsy]; Pongamia glabra [karanj]; Spondias mangifera [wild mango]; Tephrosia purpurea [zanzibar indigo].—"*b*" Animal manure consists mainly in the excreta of cattle [maud]. Sheep [aud] are folded on the lands to be cultivated. Red soils are manured by cattle-folding. Cow dung [shauny] is however not extensively used as manure as it is used for fuel [bratty]. In garden cultivation sheep's blood, garbage and stale fish are applied to betel [q.v.] and grape [angoor] vines.—"*c*" Mineral manures, such as lime [choonam], gypsum, nitrates, common salt [ooppoo], saline earth [sowdoo], &c., are only rarely used by the native cultivator. The fluviatile deposits found in the beds of channels and tanks [adaimunn] are however largely made use of. Common salt [ooppoo] is sometimes used for cocoanut [q.v.] trees.—"*d*" As a rule, garden lands are more frequently manured than others, and dry lands receive more frequent attention than wet. The amount of manure supplied varies according to locality and means of cultivator. The following is a fair average of the quantity of manure per acre:—Garden lands 3 to 6 tons; wet lands $1\frac{1}{2}$ to 3 tons; dry lands 0 to 1 ton. Garden lands are manured every year. Among wet lands those under veligada [q.v.] requiring more frequent application than those under coodapa [q.v.]; these last are manured every third, fourth or fifth year. The practice of diluting manure with large quantities of water is known to the ryots [q.v.] and various modes of making, altering and correcting soils are well understood. Regar [q.v.] land requires no manure.—"*e*" The following are Tamul proverbs:—பாயும் சலமுழுவதும் கட்டு பழய எரு வெடுத்துக்கொட்டு—"old muck and abundance of water."—காடுவெட்டி நஞ்சைபண்ணு, மாடுகட்டி வைக்கோல் போடு—"turn dry land into wet, pen your cattle in the field, "feed them with straw."—ஏரிலும் நன்றாலெருவிடுதல்.—"manure is better even than the plough."—ஆட்டெரு அந்தபோகம் மாட்டெரு மறுபோகம்—"sheep dung for "the immediate crop, cattle dung for the succeeding crop." There is a Teloogoo proverb:—ఎరువులేనిచేను, లేగలేనిపశువు నిష్ప్రయోజనము.—"a field without manure is as unproductive as a cow "[pashoo] without her calf."—"*f*" The following recipés for mixed manures are from the Brihat shaurngadharam:—"Mix with earth a variety of fragrant flowers; use the mixture "as manure to a tree of scentless flowers; pour at the roots the "juice of dhavam [godaury] and khadiram [cantalam]; smear "over the tree sandal [q.v.] paste, and expose the tree to the "smoke of ghee [q.v.]; its scentless flowers will become fragrant. "Use as manure to the roots of the cotton [q.v.] the leaves of "barley [jow], sesamum [gingelly] and of turmeric [country "saffron], and pour at the roots water prepared with a mixture "of these leaves; the plant will yield cotton throughout the year, "bright and red as fire. Mix with water the juice of the sugar-"cane [q.v.] and the root of the vidaury [giant potato]; heat the "mixture and rub it over the roots of any flowering tree [phool], "and pour at the roots the juice of the sugar-cane; the trees will "yield flowers at unusual seasons. Make cakes of a mixture of "madhooyashty [atimathooram], sugar [q.v.], coshtam [arabian "costum] and madhoopooshpam [mohwah], and cover with the "cakes the roots of fruit trees [pazham] and throw earth over "the parts; the fruits will grow without stones. Kill a goat "[velland] and immediately tie its shoulder skin over the "branches of fruit trees; the fruits will long remain unripe. "Pound in a stone mortar the bone of the monkey [bandar] "mixed with the juice of the elephant [q.v.] in rut; rub the "preparation over the roots of fruit trees; the fruits will remain "unripe for a year. Tie over the branches of fruit trees the "skin of an animal and grass; rub over the branches a mixture "of vidangam [byebarang], honey [shahad] and milk [paul]; "pour at the roots a mixture of milk [paul] and water; the "ripe fruits will adhere to the tree for a very long time. Mix "with milk [paul] the serum or marrow of flesh of the fish "[matsyam] and the hog [soor] as well as the flesh of the two "creatures; soak any seed in the mixture; dry it and expose "it to the smoke of ghee [q.v.]; the seed when sown will grow in "an unusual and wonderful manner. If the seed of the pome-"granate [anaur] be soaked in the blood of the cock [moorghy] "twenty-one times and dried each time, it will, the moment it "is put into the ground, grow and bear fruits in a wonderful "manner. Force into the root of the coomoodam [red indian "water-lily] a variety of colors, soak the root in urine, rub over "it ghee [q.v.] and honey [shahad], and then sow it in the soil, "it will grow and bear flowers of the several colors originally "put into the root. Mix together the buffalo's [khoolgah] dung "and urine, rub the mixture over the seed of the fruit of the "coomoodam [red indian water-lily] for seven days drying the "seed each time; if the seed be then sown into the ground, "it will grow as a karaveeram [gannair] plant. Soak the seed "of the pumpkin [wax gourd] or of the brinjaul [q.v.], or of the "serpent cucumber [snake gourd] and the like in the serum or "marrow of flesh of the fish or hog and dry the seed; if the "seed be then sown in good soil and watered it will bear fruits "of very large size and without stones. Soak the seed of the "castor-oil plant [aumanac] in the blood and serum of flesh of "the hog [soor] and dry it; soak it again in the oil of the ancolam "[alanjy] and dry it; if the seed be now sown in the soil, it "will grow and bear the fruits of caunavully [carolah]. Use as "manure to the root of the plantain [q.v.] the excrement of the "ass [gadhah] and the horse [ghorah]; burn dry twigs over the "root; the plantain will then yield fruits as large as the trunk of "the elephant [q.v.], and the fruits will appear as if to tear out "the tree. If the root of the plantain be drenched with the "blood or serum of flesh of the hog [soor] or with the decoction "of the fruit of the ancolam [alanjy], it will bear pomegranate "[anaur] fruits. If the rambhay or plantain [q.v.] be watered "with a liquid mixture consisting of the flesh, serum and blood "of man and the powdered tooth of the elephant [q.v.] and "water, the tree will yield mango [q.v.] fruits. Mix together "the shining decoction of the fruits of ancolam [alanjy], human "flesh, the milk [paul] of the goat [velland] and oil cakes "[ponnauk]; use the mixture as manure to the seed of the "mango [q.v.] put into the soil; the seed will grow out as "a spreading creeper like the vine [angoor] and will bear fruit "at all times. Form a mixture of krimiripoo [byebarang], of "barley [jow], of madhooyashty [atimathooram] and of jaggery "[q.v.], rub it over any tree yielding bitter fruit, after slightly "grazing the bark with a knife, pour at the root a mixture of "milk and water; the tree will thenceforth yield sweet fruits. "Soak any seed many times in human flesh and in the oil of the "ancolam [alanjy], drying the seed each time; take a quantity "of earth in the land, bury the seed in it and pour water over it; "the seed will grow that instant. Dig a pit, burn in it the bones "and the dung [shauny] of the cow [pashoo] and the hog [soor]; "remove the ashes; fill the pit with earth; plant in it the root "of the moolacam [country radish], the root will grow to the "size of the pit."

YERRA (ఎర్ర - erra, *Tel.*). Red.——*Yernagoodem* (ఎర్నగూడెము - yernagúdemu, Tel.). See sep. title.——*Yerracondah* (ఎర్రకొండ - errakondah, Tel.). From (above + konda, tel. hill). Hill, range; Nellore dist., Raupore, Atmacore, Oodayagherry talooks. Runs through the talooks of Raupore, Atmacore and Oodayagherry. Trig. station lat. 14° 42′ 42·34″; long. 79° 17′ 54·24″; height 1,825 feet; from Nundipaud S.W. 9 miles; from Oodayagherry S.S.W. 12 miles.——*Yerramala* (ఎర్రమల - erramala, Tel.). From (above + mala, tel. hill). Range of hills; Kurnool and Cuddapah dists., lat. 14° 31′ to 14° 58′; long. 78° 10′ to 78° 31′; height 1,478 feet. Commences at Yaumavaram in Jummalmadoogoo talook of Cuddapah district, and runs northward, ending about 8 miles from Kurnool near the Dornaul road. Length from 60 to 70 miles. Greatest width 20 miles. Eastern extensions are the Paunem, Baitamcheroo and Ooppalapaud hills. Generally flat-topped with scarped sides and all the hills inhabited. The flat tops are generally bare, but the slopes and plains are clothed with shrubs and stunted trees, but no valuable timber. Tammirauzpully ghaut [q.v.] in the north and Rampore ghaut in south are the two passes. The Nundiaul road passes over the former, and the new line between Gooty road and Nundicanama passes over the latter. In 1847 these hills afforded shelter to Narsimhareddy. The diamond [vajram] mines of Moonimadoogoo attracted attention of Moraury row and others. Other diamond mines in the range are Bunganapully and Ramalcottah. See vol. II, 86.——*Yerra pragada* (ఎర్రాప్రగడ - errápragada, Tel.). From (above + pragada, tel. prime minister, a title like ayya, assumed by niyógis of former days). Otherwise Prabandha parameshwaran. Lived 800 years ago in Goodoor, Cundoocore talook, Nellore district and translated from Sanscrit into Teloogoo latter half of Aranya parvam of Bhauratam [nannayyabhatt, ticcana].

YERRANEEL (ഇറണിയൽ - iraniyal, *Mal.*). From (irana, san. salt-soil).—"*a*" Talook; Travancore state, Pudmanaubhapooram division. Area 142 square miles. Population 112,116. Extreme length, N. to S., 8 miles; extreme breadth, E. to W., 18 miles. Sub-divided into 8 praverties [q.v.] and containing 158 caras [q.v.] or villages. Bounded N. by Cullcoolam talook, E. by Agasteeshwaram talook, S. by the Indian ocean and W. by Vilvancode talook. Agriculture and manufacture of jaggery [q.v.]. Weaving [nesavoo]. Considerable trade. Vulliyaur is the only channel [q.v.] for cultivation. There are some rainfed tanks [q.v.], chief being Cadiapatam.—"*b*" Town, Tahsildar's station; Travancore state, Pudmanaubhapooram division, Yerraneel tal.; pop. 18,420; lat. 8° 12′; long. 77° 21′; from Alleppey S.S.E. 109 miles; from Cottayam S.S.E. 108 miles; from Madras S.S.W. 390 miles; from Nagarcoil W.N.W. 8 miles; from Paravore S.S.E. 150 miles; from Quilon S.E. 67 miles; from Trivandrum S.E. 31 miles; from the sea N. 6 miles. About three miles west of the main road from Nagarcoil to Trivandrum. Chiefly inhabited by weavers and chetties [q.v.]. Residence of Travancore royal family before they removed to Pudmanaubhapooram. Old palace. History states that one of the Travancore kings suddenly disappeared when sleeping in the Yerraneel palace. Considerable inland trade. Noted for manufacture of cotton [q.v.] cloths. Large cattle market in the vicinity.

YETT (எட்டு - ettu, *Tam.*). Eight [ashtam].——*Yendolan* (எண்டோளன் - endólan, Tam.). From (above + tól, tam. shoulder). Shiva [q.v.].——*Yendoly* (எண்டோளி - endóli, Tam.). Bhadra cauly [q.v.]——*Yettappan* (எட்டப்பன் - ettappan, Tam.). From (above + appan, tam. father); possessing eight attributes or forms. Epithet of shiva [q.v.] who is identified with the five elements [puncha bhootam] and mind, ego and matter or according to the opening stanza of shacoontalay [q.v.] by Calidass [q.v.], the five elements and the sun, moon and sacrificing priest. Hence ashtamoorty or eight-formed for shiva.——*Yettiyaupooram* (எட்டையாபுரம் - ettaiyáppuram, Tam. etaiyápuram *). From (ettappanáyakkan, tam. the traditional founder of the family + pura, san. town). Zemindarry village; Tinnevelly dist., Ottapidauram tal.; pop. 6,321; area of zemindarry 241,089 acres; lat. of village 9° 09′; long. 78° 03′; from Ottapidauram N. 16 miles; from Tinnevelly N.E. 36 miles; from the sea N.W. 20 miles. The ancestors of the zemindar [q.v.], who belongs to the Cumbalattaur caste, came from Chundragherry in North arcot and settled first in Madura under the Paundyan [q.v.] kings, subsequently in the neighbourhood of their present principal residence, where they held a considerable estate and gradually increased its area. Towards the close of the last century Catabomu naick, then zemindar of Punchaulamcoorchy, rebelled against the British government on two occasions. The Yettiyaupooram zemindar for assistance in suppressing these rebellions was rewarded in 1803 with the estates of the Punchaulamcoorchy zemindar. He subsequently obtained the forfeited estates of other rebels by purchase, and has since further added to his property by purchase. The estates were managed for the present zemindar for several years by the Court of Wards till he came of age in 1878. In the Shiva temple close to the zemindar's palace is a copper plate inscription [shausanam] containing a proclamation issued by the zemindar on 20th October 1799, urging his subjects to submit to British authority. Present peshcush Rs. 88,349.

YEVAL (ஏவல் - éval, *Tam.*). From (évu, tam. to command). Command.——*Yevalcaura pey* (ஏவற்காரப்பேய் - évargárappéy, Tam.). From (above + kára, san. doer + péy, tam. devil). Name of a deity; a demon who serves Cauly [q.v.] as messenger.

YEZH (ஏழு - ézhu, *Tam.*). Seven [haft, saptam].——*Yenaud* (ஏநாடு - énádu, Tam.). From (above + nádu, tam. country). Country, south-west of Tonday [q.v.]; Trichinopoly and Tanjore. The Yenautt cheyaur was the Ponniaur [cheyair, cheyaur].——*Yezhoomore naud* (எழுமூர் நாடு - ezhumúrnádu, Tam.). From (above + úr, tam. village + nádu, tam. country); country about Egmore which originally consisted of seven villages. Part of Pozhal cottam in the ancient Tondaimundalam [q.v.]. Within the present Madras district.

YEZHOOT (எழுத்து - ezhuttu, *Tam.*). From (ezhuthu, tam. to write). A letter. So orthography or one of the five divisions of the tamul Lacshanam [q.v.]. In the sanscrit phonetic system, names of letters are formed:—by adding cauram or varnam to the sound; by the unchanged sound itself, e.g. a; by adding a or some other vowel to a consonant, by a special name e.g. raipham (r); names of classes of letters are also formed by the first of the class followed by vargam. In tamul, letters are divided:—into vowels, consonants, and vowel consonants; into initial, medial, and final; into short, long, demonstrative, and interrogative; into hard, soft, and medial; into relative, dependent, and substituted letters. The tamul alphabet consists of 12 vowels [ooyir] and 18 consonants [mey]; in all 30 letters. Letters peculiar to the tamul language are ற, ழ and ன; and letters borrowed from the sanscrit are ஜ j, ஸ s, ஷ sh, ஹ h, and க்ஷ ksha. The tamul Cooral [q.v.] has the following:—எண்ணென்ப வேனை யெழுத்தென்ப விவ்விரண்டுங் கண்ணென்ப வாழு முயிர்க்கு—"letters "and numbers are the two eyes of man." There is a Tamul proverb:—நப்போலவளை—"bend yourself like the letter "ந;" be humble [bhaushay].—And another:—எட்கிடை நெற்கிடை விட்டெழுத—"to write leaving space of a "sesamum seed [gingelly] between the letters and of a paddy "[q.v.] grain between the lines;" the correct order to be observed in writing [varnamaulay]. See vol. I (42), (44); II, 186–192, 205–210.——*Yezhoottiyal* (எழுத்தியல் - ezhuttiyal, Tam.). From (above + iyal, tam. nature). Orthography [iyal].

YIDAM (ഇടം - itam, *Mal.*; இடம் - idam, *Tam.*). From (idu, tam. to put). Place; house [mana]; formerly the distinctive name for the house of a Naudvauly [q.v.] of consequence. Also means left.——*Yedangaly* (ഇടങ്ങഴി - itannazhi, Mal.). From (itannu, mal. narrow + názhi, mal. the measure). Otherwise Yidangazhy.—"*a*" Measure of capacity. Also called Macleod seer. 4 nauzhies = 1 yedangaly; 10 yedangalies = 1 parrah [alavay, 3d]. Approximate actual value, 1 yedangaly = 113$\frac{3}{4}$ cubic inches. Used in the west coast. Yedangaly introduced by Mr. Macleod is used throughout North malabar and in some talooks of South malabar. A smaller Yedangaly or naudan contains 62 cubic inches or a third of a gallon; 24$\frac{1}{5}$ small yedangalies = 1 bushel, which is 2,218 cubic inches. The smaller measures are used in Yernaud and Wynaud. The Pauttom yedangaly is larger than the ordinary measure by 10 or 20 per cent. and issued by Jenmies [q.v.] to receive pauttom [q.v.]. Compare Puddy.—"*b*" A superficial measure denoting that extent of land in which a standard Yedangaly of seed may be sown. 4 nauzhies = 1 yedangaly; 10 yedangalies = 1 parrah [alavay, 2d]. Approximate actual value, 1 yedangaly = $\frac{1}{30}$ of an acre. North malabar. It is a varying measure and ranges from 55 to 72 per acre. See vol. I, 609; II, 516.——*Yeddatralpaud* (ഏടത്രാൽപ്പാട് - etatrálppátu, Mal.). From (edattúr, mal. the place + pátu, mal. chief, title). Title of the fourth prince of the Zamorin's family.——*Yidacoodiyaun* (ഇടക്കുടിയാൻ - itakkutiyán, Mal.). From (above + kutiyán, mal. tenant). An under-tenant.——*Yidaiyinam* (இடையினம் - idaiyinam, Tam.). Middle letter. One of the three Tamul classes. ய், ர், ல், வ், ழ், ள். Of these ய் and வ் only are initial; all are final [yezhoot]. See vol. I (52); II, 205, 209.——*Yidangay* (இடங்கை - idangai, Tam.). Means left hand. Especially the left-hand faction among s. indian caste and tribes. The division into right-hand and left-hand occurred simultaneously with the religious agitation which introduced into Southern india the now-prevailing Braminical supremacy. The imminent decay of the Jeina [q.v.] power opened a prospect. This movement was always confined to Southern india, its centre being at Conjeeveram, where there are to this day special halls for both parties, called Valangay mantapams [q.v.] and Yidangay mantapams. The influence of Jeinas was always strongest in towns; Bramins appealed to the agricultural classes [vellaulan]. In various localities the same castes embraced different sides, yet on the whole the principal parties on both sides are always the same. There is a saying that the Pariahs [q.v.] are not left-hand people, but belong to the Tamulians; the meaning is that, as the Tamulians or Vellaular [q.v.], the masters of the Pariahs, and the principal Shoodras [q.v.], are right-hand men, so are their dependants the Pariahs.—"*a*" On the right-hand are enumerated:—1, Vellaular [q.v.] and cavarays with the following insignia; white umbrella [chattram], white flag, curved fan, chowry [q.v.], aroogoo teevatty, plough, plough-flag, monkey-flag, cuckoo-flag, parrot-flag, bell [many], conch [chunk], wheel stick, big drum, green, blue lotus [indian water-lily] garland [maulay], autty [mountain ebony] flag, davanday, trumpet; 2, Vadooga vellaular, northern or teloogoo vellaular, with swan flag; 3, Reddies [q.v.] with plough flag; 4, Cummavaur [cumma] agricultural laborers, with bull flag; 5, Coontalavargal with chakor [teetar] flag; 6, Nuttamaur [q.v.] with auly [q.v.] flag; 7, Malayamaun [q.v.] with baritaulam or shree taulam [talipot] flag; 8, Comaties [q.v.], merchants, with cotton flag, macaratoranam drum, venmayir or chowry [q.v.], idimoorass; 9, Yidayar [q.v.], shepherds, with wheel; 10, Vadooga yidayar, teloogoo shepherds, with conch; 11, Cannadiyar, canarese shepherds, with tent, five-colored flag; 12, Pudma sauleys [q.v.], weavers, with tiger vehicle, male tiger flag; 13, Puttsauleys [q.v.], silk-weavers, with two-headed bird flag; 14, Vadooga sheniyar [q.v.], northern weavers, with jasmine flag, naugapausham, five-colored flag; 15, Jendravar [q.v.], teloogoo weavers, with crocodile; 16, Cannadiyasheniyar, canarese weavers, with wild jasmine [q.v.] garland, big eagle flag, vishiry tanday; 17, Putnoolcaurar [putnool], silk-thread weavers, with silk flag; 18, Shedar, weavers, with tortoise flag and colinjy [sweet orange] flag; 19, Shekk vauniyar [q.v.], oil-press mongers, with shaday chedy [solah], yell [gingelly] raushy, sesamum leaf garland, garooda [braminy kite] flag, drum; 20, Ilay vauniyar, leaf oil-mongers, with covay [indian caper] garland, drum, cuckoo flag; 21, Wonteddoo vauniyar, one bullock oil-mongers, with five-colored parrot flag; 22, Shanappar, hemp-dressers, with chowry [q.v.] flag; 23, Moochees [q.v.], painters, &c., with macaram [q.v.] flag; 24, Canchiyar, braziers, with bodhy [peepul] flag; 25, Vaitteicaur, basket-makers, with shikkiroo [moringa] flag, wooden-legged horse, sword flag; 26, Nary shokkiyar, fox-beggars, with dog [nye] flag; 27, Tamul coosavar [q.v.], potters, vadooga coosavar, teloogoo potters, coosa kanakar [q.v.]; 28, Mailacaur, fluters, with drum flag; 29, Nuttoovar, dancing masters, with cymbal flag; 30, Dausies [q.v.], dancing girls, with manmatan [q.v.] flag; 31, shaunaur [q.v.] and eezhar, toddy-drawers, with coorinjy [common vengay] flag, knife and ladder; 32, Coravar [q.v.], mountaineers, foresters, snake catchers, basket-makers, salt-sellers, with donkey flag; 33, Shookkaur chetty lumbaudy [q.v.], salt-sellers, with picturesque flag; 34, Vaitteicaurar, hunters, with sling flag; 35, Patnavar [q.v.] with tortoise flag; 36, Caraiyaur [q.v.], sea-coastmen, with fish flag; 37, Woddar [q.v.] road-makers and tank-diggers, from Orissa with spade flag; 38, Ooppaurar [q.v.], common tank-diggers, with pig flag; 39, Boyies [q.v.], bearers, with palankeen flag; 40, Paniseyvar [q.v.], menial servants with tauray [q.v.], trumpet flag; 41, Tamul vunnaur [q.v.] and vadooga vunnaur [saucala], tamul and teloogoo washermen, with curved knife, lotus garland and white elephant; 42, Tamul nauvithar [ambattan], tamul barbers, with toombay [q.v.] garland, animal with human face; 43, Vadooga nauvithar [mungala], teloogoo barbers, with nangaswaram [q.v.], musical instrument; 44, Dombars [q.v.], rope-dancers, with keday flag; 45, Mauriyamman poojarries [q.v.], mauriyamman priests, with small drum flag; 46, Poojarries [q.v], with hollow brass ring flag; 47, Iroolar [q.v.], wild foresters, with iron bar flag; 48, Arippoocaura cavaray, cavaray weavers, with lotus [q.v.] flag; 49, Vadooga pundauram [q.v], northern mendicants, with battleaxe flag; 50, Vanjooraur with pearl flag; 51, Coodcoodooppacaur, soothsaying beggars, with shacty [q.v.] flag; 52, Yanaudies [q.v.], forestmen, with hare flag; 53, Calauscaur [calassy], lascars, with cart flag; 54, Vely caroomaur [q.v.], excommunicated blacksmiths, with bellows and hammer flag; 55, Vely culltutchar [q.v.], excommunicated carpenters, with chisel flag; 56, Cuppal tutchar, ship carpenters, with adze flag; 57, Cuppal vadoogar, teloogoo sailors, with ship flag; 58, Pantar, bards with sword flag.—"*b*" The people and ensigns of the punchama or fifth or pariah class of the Valangay are:—1, Pavaniyar or palanigal, processionists, with damauram [damaroo], drum flag; 2, Vulloovar [q.v.], mavoottar and vettiyauns [q.v.], mahout [q.v.], pariahs [q.v.] and panda pariahs with white umbrella, white chowry, white flag, conch, vajra stick, trumpet or tamookkoo, drum or tappattay [q.v.], bankah [q.v.] or trumpet, tootaura [toortoory] or short trumpet, big tootaura, pariah music, five pots and white macaram or alligator festoons.—"*c*" On the left-hand are enumerated:—1, Berichetties [q.v.], bery merchants, with kite flag; 2, Nagara vauniyar [q.v.], town oil-mongers, with tondoo garland and garland of nine gems [ratnam]; 3, Keikkilar [q.v.], weavers, with tirvauray patram, adakkam, lance, male vulture, lion flag, bear flag, deer flag, peacock flag, cuckoo flag, drum; 4, Cummaular [q.v.], artisans, this class is composed of the tattaur [q.v.] or goldsmiths, cunnaur [q.v.] or braziers, shilpies [q.v.] or masons, collar [q.v.] or black smiths and tutchar [q.v.] or carpenters; with hammer, chisel, adze, compass, parrot flag, eagle flag, or white kite flag; 5, Pullies [q.v.] with big axe, crane feather, vengay [q.v.] garland [maulay], red lotus [indian water-lily] garland, crow flag, cloud-colored flag, fire flag, cock flag, vulture flag, fox flag, date flag, stone flag, green flag, hair-queue flag, drum and bow, coontauly, black flag.—"*d*" The people and ensigns of the fifth class of the Yidangay are:—1, Pullar [q.v.] with nelly [q.v.] garland and crab flag; 2, Chucklers [q.v.], leather-workers, with saffron screen, black garland, warrior sword, cocoa leaf, drum, curved stick [jauty].—"*e*" See vol. I (69).——*Yidangazhy* (ഇടങ്ങഴി - itannazhi, Mal.). Same as Yedangaly.——*Yidapully* (ഇടപ്പള്ളി - itappalli, Mal.). From (itam, mal. mansion + palli, mal. village). Town; Trav. state, Cottayam division, Coonnatnaud tal.; pop. 17,276; lat. 10° 01′; long. 76° 21′; from Perambavore W.S.W. 13 miles; from Trivandrum N.N.W. 112 miles; from the sea E. 6 miles. Capital of a small principality formed of several detached portions divided into two parts, viz., Yidapully tekkoombhaugam, population 13,093, and Yidapully vadakkoombhaugam, population 5,183. Near the northern frontiers of Travancore and about midway between Alwye and Tripoontora. Residence of the chief of the Yidavaga of that name, who is a Numboory [q.v.] bramin [q.v.] of rank. He is regarded as the family priest of the princes of Travancore. Palace of large and rustic structure, and a bazaar [q.v.] kept by Christians. Largely inhabited by Nayars [q.v.]. The soil is sandy [manal] and cocoanut [q.v.] trees grow in abundance.——*Yiday* (இடையன் - idaiyan, Tam.). Means middle class. The cowherd race in the southern districts. The corresponding terms are:—Tel. golla; Can. golla; Mal. yeraudy. They have as their tribal title Konan meaning king, also Sherveicauran meaning captain. The race are very numerous, but take a lower place in social life than the agricultural Vellaular [q.v.], who generally assume the title of Moodelly [q.v.]. Numbers about 600,000 [yaudava].——*Yidayan* (இடையன் - idaiyan, Tam.). A shepherd, cowherd [golla, inam].——*Yidayangoody* (இடையங்குடி - idaiyangudi, * Tam.). From (idaiyan, tam. a shepherd + kudi, tam. village). Village; Tinnevelly dist., Nangoonairy tal.; lat. 8° 19′; long. 77° 56′; from Nangoonairy S.E. 20 miles; from Tinnevelly S.S.E. 32 miles. The most important Protestant village in the district founded by Bishop Caldwell. Palmyra [q.v.] is largely cultivated.——*Yidaytchol* (இடைச்சொல் - idaiççol, Tam.). Particles or middle words, denoting adverbs, post-positions, and conjunctions. These are of eight kinds in the Nunnool [q.v.]. Cf. Ooritchol [shol].

YIDY (मेघनाद - méghanáda, *San.*; رعد - raad, *Ar.*; گرج - garaj, *Dec.*; النتر - alintar, *Malay*; ಗುಡುಗು - gudugu, *Can.*; తెడిలు - tedilu, *Too.*; ఉరుము - urumu, *Tel.*; ഇടി - iti, *Mal.*; இடி - idi, *Tam.*). San. from (mégha, san. cloud + náda, san. sound). Tam. from (idu, tam. to throw). Thunderbolt [vajram]. The Maigha sandaisha grantam says that when smoke, lightning, water, and wind combine together, and rise towards the regions in which reigns the prachunda wind, or wind that blows at a height above the surface of the earth, a friction is produced between these substances, which occasions the discharge of bolts with the accompanying thunder [caurtey, minnal].

YILAM (இளம் - ilam, *Tam.*). Tender [elliah].——*Yilaiyapermaul* (இளையப்பெருமாள் - ilaiyapperumál, Tam.). From (above + perumál, tam. vishnu, the great god). Hindoo 2nd or pers. name [peyar].——*Yilaiyaul* (இளையாள் - ilaiyál, Tam.). Means younger sister. Lutchmy [q.v.] the younger sister of Moodevy [q.v.]. She is also called Shreedevy [q.v.].——*Yilaiyaun* (இளையான் - ilaiyán, Tam.). Means a young man. Proper name [peyar].——*Yilaneer* (இளநீர் - ilanír, Tam.). Means tender water. Water of a tender cocoanut [q.v.].——*Yilangautt tariss* (இளங்காட்டுத்தரிசு - ilangáttuttarisu, Tam.). From (above + kádu, tam. forest + tarisu, tam. fallow land). Land left waste [bunjar, tariss] for ten years.

YIROOPP (இருப்பு - irrupu, *Tam.*). From (iru, tam. to sit). Abode; suffix in place names [coodiyiroopp].

YOO (यु - yu, *San.*). To mix, join, attach.——*Yamauny* (यमानी - yamáni, San.). Means pertaining to yavanas. Ajwaun.——*Yavam* (यव - yava, San.). From (yu, san. to attach); from grain attached to husk. Means barley corn [jow]—"*a*" Goldsmith's weight. 6 sarshapams or mustard seeds = 1 yavam; 3 yavams = 1 goonjam [niray, 3f]. Approx. actual value, 1 yavam = $\frac{3}{8}$th of a grain. According to some equal to $\frac{1}{2}$ of a goonjam = 12 mustard seeds. Compare Hind. jow.—"*b*" Linear measure. 8 yavams = 1 ungoolam [alavay, 1]. Approximate, actual value, 1 yavam = ·09375 inch. According to some $\frac{1}{8}$th of an ungoolam. Same as Hind. jow, Can. yavey, Mal. tora, Tam. nel. See vol. I, 609.——*Yavana* (यवन - yavana, San.). Formerly

Ionian or Asiatic greeks. Now any Mahomedan [jonaca, mussalman].——*Yonaca* (യോനക - yónaka, Mal.). Jew [jonaca].——*Yony* (योनि - yóni, San.). From (yu, san. to mingle). The place or element of birth, the womb. Alone, or in combination with the lingam [q.v.], it is an object of worship by the followers of the Shacty [q.v.].——*Yoonaun* (یونان - yúnán, Hind.). Ionia or ancient Greece; so called till subdued by the romans, after which the term Room [q.v.] was applied to the whole of the eastern roman empire at large. Cf. Yavana.——*Yoonauny* (یونانی - yúnání, Ar.). From (yúnán, ar. greece). Greek school of medicine, as opposed to misry [q.v.] or egyptian. A foreigner; the lowest class of Mahomedans [q.v.].

YOODH (युध् - yudh, *San.*). To fight.——*Yoodhishtiran* (युधिष्ठिर - yudhisht'hira, San.). From (above + st'hira, san. steady). The eldest son of Pandoo [q.v.]. Cf. Dharmarajan.

YOOG (युग - yuga, *San.*). From (yuj, san. to join) [yooj].—"*a*" Conjunction [sangam, sangamam, yogam] of planets [graham]. Sometimes their opposition. More generally a long period of years, at the expiration of which certain phenomena recur. See vol. I, 609.—"*b*" The Bramins divide the infinity of time [caulam] into four great ages, which they consider to be in constant revolution; these they denominate yoogs or conjunctions, implying cosmic cycles so delimitated. The first of these four ages is named Kritayoog referring to some conjunction which took place at the Kritam or creation [srishty]. It consists of 1,728,000 years. The second is denominated Tretayoog, the conjunction of the Tretay or three sacrificial fires, so called because the great sacrifice in which these fires are used was introduced during this period, which contains 1,296,000 years. The third is named Dwaupar yoog, a compound of two + 1 the next, that which followed the two first, viz., the third; this comprises 864,000 years. The fourth or present age is known by the name of Kaliyoog properly signifying vicious or sinful; to this age bramins assign a period of 432,000 years, of which 4,994 are already elapsed. If the years in the fourth age be doubled, the number of those in the third is given; if multiplied by three, the length of the second is found; and if multiplied by four, the product is the length of the first age.—"*c*" The Kritam, Tretay, Dwauparam, and Kaliyoog, correspond with the golden, silver, brazen, and iron ages of Greek and Latin writers.—"*d*" The predominant duties of the four yoogs are austere fervour in the Kritam age, knowledge in the Tretay, sacrifice in the Dwauparam, and liberality alone in the Kaliyoog.—"*e*" Some say that Kritam, Tretay, Dwauparam, and Kaly, are named from the marks on dice, the Kritam being the best throw of four points, and the Kaly the worst of one point.—"*f*" During each of the three first ages, mankind lost a part equal to one-fourth of truth [satyam] and moral rectitude [dharmam], until the last or wicked age in which man becomes wholly depraved and sinful. The third age or dwaupar is the renovated world described by Moses, in which is a chaos, or the wreck of a former world, and upon the surface of this moves the spirit of God. The Swayambh [q.v.] was the man-woman of the Hindoos, who was separated into a male and female, like Adam and Eve, and became the first progenitor of mankind. By both accounts, the life of man extended to one thousand years; and the days of the gods were as a thousand years of mortals [caulam, 2]. According to Menoo [q.v.], Noah lived in the third or in the beginning of the fourth yoog, when the age of man was fixed at one hundred years.——**(1)** The following are the yoogs in chronological order.—"*a*" *Kritayoog* (कृतयुग - kritayuga, San.). From (krita, san. good + above). Otherwise Satyayoog, or age of truth or virtue. The oldest or fourth yoog reckoning backwards consisting of four thousand eight hundred divine years, thus:—Kritayoog, proper, 4,000, Sundhyay, 400, Sundhyaumsham, 400, Total, 4,800. Otherwise 1,728,000 solar sidereal years. The golden age of the Hindoos, when virtue wholly prevailed, and the cow stood on its four legs.—"*b*" *Tretayoog* (त्रेतायुग - trétáyuga, San.). From (trétá, san. triad + above). The second oldest, or third yoog reckoning backwards, consisting of 36 thousand divine years; 1,296,000 solar sidereal years. The silver age of the Hindoos. Men were then tall and lived long; while vice was as one and virtue as three; the cow stood on three legs.—"*c*" *Dwaupar yoog* (द्वापरयुग - dváparayuga, San.). From (dvá, san. two + para, san, following + above). The second yoog, reckoning backwards. This age lasted 2,400 divine years; 864,000 mortal years. The Brazen age of the hindoos. In this equity and iniquity existed in equal portions. At end of Dwaupar yoog, the number of years elapsed since creation is 1955,880,000 as noted in punchaungams [q.v.].—"*d*" *Kaliyoog* (कलियुग - kaliyuga, San.). From (kali, san. evil + above). The latest age in every maha-yoog [q.v.]. It consists of 1,200 years of the gods. 432,000 mortal years. The date of the commencement of the present Kaliyoog is fixed at 3,102 B.C. 18th February, when Vishnoo [q.v.] returned to heaven after his incarnation [avatar] as Krishnan [q.v.]. It is the Iron age of the hindoos. During the currency of the present Kaliyoog all things will decline, and the deterioration of mankind will be general; the vedams [q.v.] will be disregarded; the minds of men will be wholly occupied in acquiring wealth; wealth will be spent solely on selfish gratifications; women will follow their inclinations and be fond of pleasure; men of all degrees will consider themselves equal to bramins [q.v.]; cows [pashoo] will be held in esteem only as they supply milk [paul]. These are a few of the evils, selected from the long catalogue of them contained in the Vishnoo pooraunam [q.v.], which are to prevail in the Kaly age. A few redeeming properties of the age are however mentioned; the efficacy of devotion [bhacty] to vishnoo [q.v.] is more strikingly manifested; the least moral merit obtains in this age greatest reward, and is by all classes most easily displayed. At present the number of years elapsed since creation is as noted in calendars [punchaungam] 1955, 884, 994.——**(2)**—"*a*" The following ancient dates in general chronology should be compared with reference to the Kaliyoog:—B.C. 5688 was according to the chronology of josephus the epoch assigned to the creation in accordance with the numbers of the ancient jewish bible. B.C. 5509 is the commencement of the era of constantinople, adopted by the œcumenical council held at constantinople in a.d. 381, as the date of the creation, in accordance with the chronology of julius africanus, and since maintained by the greek and armenian churches. B.C. 5439 is the commencement of the era of alexandria, adopted as the date of the creation in accordance with the interpretation of scripture adopted by the church council held at alexandria in the year a.d. 362. B.C. 5390 is the date of the creation according to the interpretation of scripture, followed in the septuagint version. B.C. 5369 is the period to which the indians carried back their history in the time of alexander the great, according to megasthenes, as cited by clement of alexandria. B.C. 4245 is the date of creation according to the chronological indications of the samaritan pentateuch. B.C. 4004 is the date of creation according to the reading of the received hebrew text of the old testament, which has been followed in the authorized english version. B.C. 3761 is the date of creation according to the orthodox jewish chronology of the bible; it is of all biblical chronological computations the most restricted, differing from that of josephus by 1,927 years, from that of the oriental churches by 1,748 years, from that of the alexandrain era by 1,678 years, from that of the septuagint by 1,629 years, from that of the samaritan text by 484 years, and from that of the english authorized version by 243 years.—"*b*" The following is from Sanchiouiatho:—"We must also condemn the Babylonians, "and those who in the region of Caucasus pretend to have "observed the heavens and courses of the stars; we must "condemn them of folly, or of vanity, or of impudence, who "assert that they have preserved upon monuments observations "extending back during an interval of 470,000 years."—"*c*" The following is from Eusebius:—"Among the Egyptians "there is a certain tablet called the Old chronicle, containing "thirty dynasties in 113 descents, during the long period of "36,525 years; the first series of princes was that of the Auritæ, "the second was that of the Mestræans, the third of Egyptians. "It runs thus. The reign of the gods according to the old "chronicle. To hephæstus is assigned no time as he is apparent "both by night and day; helius the son of hephæstus reigned "three myriads of years; then cronus and the other twelve "divinities reigned 3984; next in order are the demigods, in "number eight, who reigned 217 years; in all, thirty dynasties "and 36,525 years. Which number of years, resolved and "divided into its constituent parts, that is to say 25 times 1,461 "years, shows that it relates to the fabled periodical revolution "[bhaganam] of the zodiac [raushy chuckram] among the "Egyptians and Greeks; or its revolution from a particular "point to the same again, which point is the first minute of "the first degree of that equinoctial sign [raushy] called the "Ram [maisham], as it is explained in the Genesis of Hermes "and in the Cyrannian books."—"*d*" The following is from Pomponius Mela:—"The Egyptians, according to their own "accounts, are the most ancient of men, and they reckon in "their series of annals 330 kings who reigned above 13,000 "years; and they preserve, in written records the memory of "the event that since the commencement of the Egyptian race "the stars have completed four revolutions and the sun has "twice set where he now rises."—"*e*" The following is from the Pascal Chronicle:—The following is from Censorinus:—"The year which Aristotle calls the greatest, rather than the "great, is that in which the sun, moon and all the planets "complete their courses, and return to the same sign from which "they originally started together. The winter of this year is "the cataclysm, which we call the deluge; but its summer is "the ecpyrosis, that is to say the conflagration of the world. For "at these alternate seasons the world is burned and deluged. "Aristarchus supposes this periodical revolution to consist of "2,484 years; Aretes of Dyrrhachium of 5,552; Herodotus and "Linus of 10,800; Orpheus of 120,000; Cassandrus of 136,000. "Others suppose it to be infinite in duration, and that the "celestial bodies never again coincide in their original posi-"tions."—"*f*" Seneca has the following:—"Berossus, who thus "interprets the Babylonian tradition, says that these events "take place according to the course of the stars; and affirms it "so positively as to assign the time for the conflagration and the "deluge. He maintains that all terrestrial things will be "consumed, when the planets [graham], which now are travers-"ing their different courses, shall all coincide in the sign [raushy] "of Cancer [carcatacam], and be so placed that a straight line "could pass through all their orbs [golam]. But the inundation “will take place when the same conjunction of the planets [graham] shall occur in Capricorn [macaram]. The first in the summer, the last in the winter of the year [caulam].”—“*g*” Compare Madhyama sowra maunam.——**(3)** For modern chronological purposes the Kaliyoog begins with the sun's entrance [sancramanam] into the hindoo lunar mansion Ashwiny [q.v.], which happens now owing to the march of precession on the 12th of april [madhyama sowra maunam].——**(4)** A yoog of jupitor [brihaspaty] is a period of five terrestrial years [samvatsaram], or one-twelfth part of the whole cycle of sixty terrestrial years, or $\frac{1}{12}$ths of a jupiter revolution; this being an unnatural inversion of the ordinary periods shown under Brihaspaty. Under this mode of reckoning, the twelve yoogs are known as belonging respectively to the Devas, Vishnoo, Brihaspaty, Indran, Agny, Twashtry, Ahirboodnyay, Pitries, Vasoodevan, Soman, Indraugny, Ashwiny devah, Bhagan. The five years of each yoog are known as:—Samvatsaram, Parivatsaram, Idavatsaram, Anoovatsaram, Idvatsaram. These are sacred respectively to:—Agny [q.v.] fire, Arcan [sooryan] the sun, Chundran [q.v.] the moon, Prajaupaty [q.v.] the creator, Roodran [q.v.] the destroyer. The following are Varauha mihiran's remarks as to the seasonal, &c., prospects of the sixty years thus divided:—“Generally in every yoog, there will be good rain in the first year and at the beginning of the second year; excessive rain in the third year; moderate rain at the end of the rainy season of the fourth year; and slight rain in the fifth year. In the first four yoogs there will be prosperity in the land; in the next or middle four there will not be much of it; and in the last four mankind will suffer miseries. When brihaspaty reappears at the beginning of the constellation of dhanishtay [q.v.] in the month of mangham [mausam] or february march, the first year of the cycle of sixty years of brihaspaty known as prabhavam commences; in it all creatures will be happy; in the same year there will be drought in certain places and suffering from storm and fire; the crops will be injured; phlegmatic maladies [sheetam] will afflict mankind; nevertheless mankind will be happy; the next year is known as vibhavam; the third as shooclam, the fourth as pramodam [pramodootam] and the fifth as prajaupaty [prajotputty]; in each of these years mankind will be happier than in the next preceding year; in the same four years there will be good growth of the shauly [paddy] crop, of sugar-cane [q.v.], of barley [jow] and other crops in the land; mankind will be freed from all fears and they will live at peace, in happiness and without the vices of the kaliyoog [q.v.]. The five years of the second yoog are known as angiram [angeerasam], shreemookham, bhavam, yoovam and dhautoo; of these during the first three years mankind will enjoy happiness but during the last two they will not enjoy much of it; in the first three of the above five years there will be abundance of rain and mankind will be freed from fears and anxieties, in the last two years the rainfall will be moderate but disease and wars will afflict mankind. The five years of the third yoog sacred to indran [q.v.] are known as eshwaram, bahoodhaunyam [vegoodhaunyam], pramaudy, vicramam and vrisham [vishoo]; in the first two years mankind will enjoy the happiness of kritayoog [q.v.]; in the year pramaudy they will feel miserable, but in the years vicramam and vrisham [vishoo] they will again be happy. The first year of the fourth yoog is known as chittrabaun, in it mankind will be happy; the second is known as soobhaun; in it mankind will be neither happy nor miserable, there will however be disease in the land but no deaths in consequence; the next year is known as tauranam, in it there will be abundance of rain the next is known as paurtivam, in it crops [vellaumay] will thrive well and mankind will be happy; the fifth year is known as vyayam, in it amorous sensations will prevail over the land. The first year of the next yoog sacred to twashtry is known as sarwajit; the next year is known as sarwadhaury; the next three years are virodhy, vicrit and kharam; in the second of these, mankind will be happy and they will be afflicted with fears in the other years. The five years of the next yoog are nandanam, vijayam, jayam, manmatam, doonmookhy; during the first three years there will be happiness in the land; in manmatam mankind will feel neither happy nor miserable, and in the year doonmookhy they will feel miserable. The years of the seventh yoog are hevilamby, vilamby, vicaury, shaurwary and plavam; in the first of these years crops will generally be injured and there will be storm and rain; in the second year crops will not grow in abundance and the rainfall will not be much; in the third year mankind will be afflicted with fears and there will be much rain; in the fourth year there will be famine; in plavam, the fifth year, there will be prosperity in the land and also much rain [mazhay]. The first year of the next yoog sacred to vishwedevah is shobhacrit; the next year is known as shoobhacrit; the third is crodhy; and the remaining years are known as vishwauvasoo and paraubhavam; during the first two years mankind will be happy; during the third they will feel exceedingly miserable; and during the last two years they will be neither happy nor miserable; but in the year paraubhavam there will be fear from fire and suffering from weapons and from disease, the bramins and cows will also suffer. The first year of the ninth yoog is plavangam, the next year is known as keelakam, the third is known as sowmyam and the last two years are known as sadhauranam and rodhacrit [virodhikrit]; during the years keelakam and sowmyam mankind will be happy; in the year plavangam mankind will suffer much; in sadhauranam there will be slight rain and crops will suffer; in the fifth year there will be a variety of rainfall and crops will thrive. The first year of the next yoog sacred to indraugny is known as paridhauvy; the remaining years are pramaudy, anandam, raucshasam and analam [nalam]; in the year paridhauvy the madhyadesham will suffer, the ruling princes will perish, there will be slight rain and fear from fire; in the year pramaudy mankind will be disposed to be inactive, villagers will be at strife, red flowers and red seed will be destroyed; in the next year mankind will be happy; in the years raucshasam and analam [nalam] there will be deaths and decay in the land; in raucshasam again the summer crops will thrive, and in analam [nalam] there will be fear from fire and much suffering in the land. The five years of the eleventh yoog are pingalam, caulayoocty, siddhaurty, rowdry, doormaty; in the first year there will be much rain and fear from thieves and mankind will suffer from consumption of the lungs and asthmatic complaints; in the year caulayoocty mankind will suffer from various evils; but in siddhaurty they will be happy in more ways than one; in the year rowdry mankind will suffer much and there will be loss and rain in the land; in doormaty there will be moderate rain [mazhay]. In the twelfth yoog sacred to the god bhagan the first year is known as dooudoobhy, the crops will thrive well; the next year is known as oodgaury [roodrotcaury], in it the ruling sovereigns will perish and there will not be good rain; the third year is known as raucshasam [ractaucshy], in it there will be fear from the attack of tusked animals, and mankind will suffer from disease; the fourth year is known as crodhanam, in it there will be anger in the land and countries will be ruined in consequence of internal strife; the last year of the last yoog is cshayam [acshayam], there will then be much rain in the land the bramins [q.v.] will be afflicted with fear, and farmers will prosper, the veisyas [q.v.] and shoodras [q.v.] will be happy as also persons that deprive others of their property. Thus have been described briefly the effects of the sixty years of Brihaspaty's cycle [brihaspaty chuckram].”——**(5)** *Yoogaudy* (యుగాది - yugádi, Tel.). Means an age of the world + beginning. Generally used among those who follow the lunisolar [chaundramaunam] calendar [punchaungam], for beginning of the new year [q.v.] as anniversary of the epoch [samvatsaraudy, teloogoo new year].——*Yoog dinam* (युगदिन - yugadina, San.). The anniversary of the day on which the current Mahayoog [q.v.], and any one of the four lesser yoogs began; which anniversary is always noticed in the calendar [punchaungam].

YOOJ (युज् - yuj, *San.*). To join [jog].——*Yogam* (योग - yóga, San.; யோகம் - yógam, Tam.). From (yuj, san. to join).—“*a*” The third of the four stages of progress towards union with god. The eight kinds of yogam are:—Ausanam, position; Dhauranay, fixing the mind on a member of the body; Dhyaunam, silent meditation; Niyamam, religious observances; Pratyauhauram, restraining the sense; Praunayaumam, breathing in a particular way; Samaudhy, silent contemplative worship; Yamam, restraint of the appetites.—“*b*” Also the name of one of the ancient Darshanams [q.v.] or philosophies. The Yogam philosophy was propounded by Patanjaly [q.v.], of whom nothing is known, except that he was probably not the same person as the author of the Mahabhaushyam. The aim of the Yogam is to teach the means by which the human soul [autmam] may attain complete union [mocsham] with the supreme soul [paramautman]. This fusion or union of individual with universal spirit may be effected even in the body by the practice of Veiraugyam [q.v.], or complete suppression of the passions. This Veiraugyam is only to be obtained by Eeshwara pranidhaunam or the contemplation of the supreme being, who is defined to be a particular Poorsham [q.v.] or spirit unaffected by works [carmam], afflictions, &c., and having the appellation Pranavam [q.v.] or Om [q.v.]. The repetition of this monosyllable is attended with marvellous results, and the muttering of it with reflection on its meaning is conducive to a knowledge of the supreme and to a prevention of all the obstacles to Yogam. This mysticism pervades every sect of the Hindoos and is analogous to the Soofee [q.v.] reveries among Mussalmans [q.v.], and to the european system of Swedenborg [matam].—“*c*” Proper name common to both sexes, used in composition with distinctive suffixes, masculine and feminine [peyar].—“*d*” Conjunction [sangam, sangamam]. In astronomy, a period of variable length during which the joint motion [chanram, gaty] in longitude [dhroovacam, sauyanam] of the sun [sooryan] and moon [chundran] amounts to one nacshatram [q.v.] or 13° 20′. The duration of a mean yogam is $56^g\ 29^v\ 21^p$ [caulam, 5], answering to $23^h\ 47'\ 44''\ 24'''$ european time; but the apparent yogam varies in proportion with the sun and moon's respective apparent motions, which depend on the place of their apogees and afford a vast variety of combinations. Hence a yogam star is theoretically the junction or limiting star of a lunar mansion [nacshatram]. There are twenty-eight yogam stars including Abhijit [q.v.] in the lunar zodiac [raushy chuckram]. Harshanam [q.v.], Spica virginis, was the yogam which most attracted the attention of the more recent hindoo astronomers; probably on account of its convenient magnitude and declination [craunty], which latter at the beginning of the ninth century was 9° 38′ 13″ S. To this star they referred the beginning of the seventh month of the solar sidereal year, from which they concluded the beginning of the first month. It was by observations of the same star that Hipparchus first discovered in the second century before Christ the motion of the fixed stars from west to east, and in this respect it is possible that hindoo astronomy borrowed from the greek. As regards yogam stars being junction stars, this is in reality only very approximate; see Nacshatram and Madhyama sowramaunam. The following are the yogam stars in order of right ascension [lagnam], with the best conjectures that can be made as to the stars on the european system which they represent. They will be found alphabetically arranged under Nacshatram [q.v.]:—

Serial No.	Yogam.	Assumed corresponding star on European system.
1	Vishcambham	α Arietis, hamel.
2	Preety	35 Arietis.
3	Ayooshmat	η Tauri, alcyone.
4	Sowbhaugyam	α Tauri, aldebaran.
5	Shobhanam	λ Orionis.
6	Atigandam	α Orionis, betelgeux.
7	Soocarmam	β Geminorum, pollux.
8	Dhrity	δ Cancri.
9	Shoolam	α Cancri.
10	Gandam	α Leonis, regulus or cor leonis.
11	Vriddhy	δ Leonis.
12	Dhroovam	β Leonis.
13	Vyaughautam	δ Corvi.
14	Harshanam	α Virginis, spica.
15	Vajram	α Bootis, arcturus.
16	Siddhy	α Libræ, zubenesch.
17	Vyateepautam	δ Scorpii.
18	Vareeyas	α Scorpii, antares.
19	Parigham	λ or ν Scorpii.
20	Shivam	δ Sagittarii.
21	Siddham	τ Sagittarii.
21*a*	Abhijit	α Lyræ, vega.
22	Saudhyam	α Aquilæ, altair.
23	Shoobham	α Delphini.
24	Shooclam or Shoobhram ...	λ Aquarii.
25	Bramham	α Pegasii, markab.
26	Mahendram or Eindram ...	α Andromedæ, alpheratz.
27	Veidhrity	η or ζ Piscium.

—"*e*" Yogams also mean in an applied sense the concurrences of certain sauvanam or natural days [dinam, 2] of the week [vauram] of 7 days, with certain of the 27 lunar asterisms [nacshatram] occupied on those days by the moon; these giving without abhijit 189 permutations, as the lunar month exceeds 4 weeks and is always shifting in relation to the 4-week period. These permutations are ranked astrologically under 6 heads, which are held to give the astrological quality of the actual resulting day. Thus:—Amrita siddham, immortal and accomplished or perfect, the best; Amritam, immortal; Siddham, accomplished or perfect; Ootpautam, portentous; Mrityoo or maranam, death; Prabalaunishtam, excessively bad, the worst. The influence of these yogams do not operate during rahoo caulam [vauram], sancramanam [q.v.], tyaujyams [q.v.], and certain other periods. They are always entered against each day in the native calendar [punchaungam]. The following is the complete table of these yogams, it being called the Amritaudy yogam table. The assignment of qualities is according to the conflicting or mutually modifying or cumulative qualities of the presiding deity of the mansion [nacshatram] and the planetary lord of the week-day [vauram]:—

Nacshatram.	Sunday.	Monday.	Tuesday.	Wednesday.	Thursday.	Friday.	Saturday.
Ashwiny	S.	S.	A.S.	M.	A.	A.	S.
Bharany	P.	S.	S.	S.	S.	S.	S.
Kritticay	S.	M.	S.	A.	M.	S.	A.
Rohiny	S.	A.	A.	S.	O.	M.	A.S.
Mrigashiras	S.	A.S.	S.	S.	M.	S.	S.
Ardray	S.	S.	M.	S.	M.	S.	S.
Poonarvas	S.	A.	S.	S.	A.	S.	S.
Pooshyam	S.	S.	S.	S.	A.S.	O.	S.
Aushlaisham	S.	S.	S.	S.	S.	M.	M.
Magham	M.	M.	S.	S.	A.	M.	A.
Poobbam	S.	S.	S.	A.	S.	S.	S.
Ottaram	A.	S.	A.	A.	M.	S.	O.
Hastam	A.S.	S.	S.	M.	S.	A.	M.
Chitta	S.	P.	S.	S	S.	S.	M.
Swauty	S.	A.	S.	S.	A.	S.	A.
Vishaukham	O.	M.	M.	S.	S.	S.	S.
Anooraudhay	M.	S.	S.	A.S.	S.	S.	S.
Jyeshtay	M.	S.	O.	S.	P.	M.	S.
Moolam	A.	S.	A.	M.	S.	A.	S.
Poorvashaudham	S.	O.	S.	A.	S.	P.	S.
Oottarashaudham	A.	M.	P.	A.	S.	S.	S.
Shravanam	A.	A.	S.	S.	S.	M.	S.
Dhanishtay	M.	S.	S.	P.	S.	S.	S.
Shatabhishay	S.	S.	M.	S.	M.	S.	A.
Poorvabhaudram	S.	S.	M.	A.	S.	S.	M.
Oottarabhaudram	A.	S.	A.	S.	S.	S.	S.
Raivaty	A.	S.	S.	O.	S.	A.S.	P.

A. = Amritam; A.S. = Amrita siddham; M. = Mrityoo; O. = Ootpautam; P. = Prabalaunishtam and S. = Siddham.

——*Yoga nidray* (योगनिद्रा - yóganidrá, San.). From (yóga, san. union + nidrá, san. sleep). The sleep of devotion or abstraction, the active principle of illusion personified; also termed Mauyay [q.v.] and Maha mauyay, and also Anyaunam [q.v.] or ignorance. ——*Yogappan* (యోగప్ప - yógappa, Tel.). From (yogí, san. ascetic + appa, tel. father, titular affix). Hindoo 2nd or pers. name [peyar].——*Yogendran* (యోగీంద్రుడు - yógíndrudu, Tel.). From (yógi, san. a saint + indra, san. chief); chief among yogies. Hindoo 2nd or pers. name [peyar].——*Yogeshan* (யோகேசன் - yógésan, Tam.). From (yógí, san. sage + ísha, san. lord); lord among yogies. Hindoo 2nd or pers. name [peyar].——*Yogeshwaran* (யோகீசுவரன் - yógísnvaran, Tam.). From (yógi, san. a saint + íshvara, san. lord); lord among yogies. Hindoo 2nd or pers. name [peyar].——*Yogivullabhan* (யோகிவல்லபன் - yógívallaban, Tam.). From (yógí, san. sage + vallabha, san. friend); friend of yogies. Hindoo 2nd or pers. name [peyar]. ——*Yogy* (योगी - yógí, San.). A follower of the yogam [q.v.] system of philosophy. A sheiva ascetic [yaty]. The tamulian idea however is rather that of spiritual union with deity than that of asceticism. Compare the following from Cooral:—மலர் மிசையேகினான் மாணடி சேர்ந்தார் நிலமிசை நீடுவாழ் வார்—"they who are united to the glorious feet of him who "occupies swiftly the flower of the mind, shall flourish in the "highest of worlds."—வேண்டுதல்வேண்டாமை யிலானடி சேர்ந்தார்க் கியாண்டு மிடும்பை யில—"to those who "meditate the feet of him who is void of desire or aversion, evil "shall never come."—இருள்சேர் ருவினையுஞ் சேரா விறை வன் பொருள்சேர் புகழ்புரிந்தார் மாட்டு—"the two-fold "deeds that spring from darkness shall not adhere to those who "delight in the true praise of god."—பொறிவாயி லைந்தவித் தான் பொய்தீ ரொழுக்க நெறிநின்றார் நீடுவாழ் வார்— "those shall long prosper who abide in the faultless way of "him who has destroyed the five desires of the senses."—தனக் குவமை யில்லாதான் றாள்சேர்ந்தார்க் கல்லான் மனக் கவலை மாற்ற லரிது—"anxiety of mind cannot be removed, "except from those who are united to the feet of him who is "incomparable."—அறவாழி யந்தணன் றாள்சேர்ந்தார்க் கல்லாற் பிறவாழி நீந்த லரிது—"none can swim the sea "of vice, but those who are united to the feet of that gracious "being who is a sea of virtue."—கோளில் பொறியிற் குண மிலவே யெண்குணத்தான் றாளை வணங்காத் தலை— "the head that worships not the feet of him who is posses- "sed of eight attributes, is as useless as a sense without the "power of sensation."——*Yojanam* (योजन - yójana, San.; யோசனை - yósanai, Tam.). From (yuj, san. to join).—"*a*" A stage in travelling, league. Linear measure. 4 croshams = 1 yojanam [alavay, 1f]. Approximate actual value, 1 yojanam = 9 miles. Varies however with the crosham from 4 to 18 miles. Compare Hind. gow, Can. gauvada, Tel. aumada, Tam. cautham. See vol. I, 609.—"*b*" An astronomical measure, deduced from the ratio of the diameter of the earth [bhoomy] to the circumference [paridhy] of its equatorial circle [niracsham]. The Hindoo mathematicians divide the diameter of the earth into 1,600 parts, whence they have this expression $\sqrt{10 \times 1600^2} = 5059{\cdot}04$ yojanams for the value of the equatorial circle. An angle of one minute [calay] of a degree [bhaugam] is supposed to be subtended by 15 yojanams, at the mean distance of the moon [chundran]; so that dividing the earth's semi-diameter or 800 yojanams by 15, there is given 53′ 20″ for the moon's mean horizontal parallax [sheeghram]. It follows from this result that 53′ 20″ of the moon's orbit [cacsham] will measure 15 yojanams, and that her whole orbit or 360° will measure 324,000 yojanams. Hence 5,059 or the circumference of a great circle [mundalam, raikhay] of the terrestrial globe [bhoogolam] in yojanams, is to 800 yojanams its semi-diameter, as 324,000 or the circumference of the moon's orbit [cacsham] in yojanams is to 51,235 yojanams her mean distance from the earth. From which it follows that this distance according to the estimates of Hindoo astronomers is about 64 semi-diameters of the earth. As the moon is supposed to complete 57,753,336,000 sidereal revolutions [bhaganam] in a Calpam [q.v.], this number drawn into 324,000, gives 18,712,080,864,000,000 yojanams for her absolute motion during that time. It is a principle in Hindoo astronomy that the absolute motion of each planet [graham] in a day, or any other given time, is equal to the absolute motion of the moon in the same time. Hence if the absolute motion of the moon during a Calpam [q.v.] be divided by the number of mean revolutions [bhaganam] completed by any planet, during that period, it will give the Cacsham [q.v.], or circumference of the planet's orbit in yojanams. To convert degrees of latitude [acsham] and longitude [deshauntaram] into yojanams, Hindoos use the following proportion:—as 360° to the proposed number of degrees; so 5,059 yojanams or the circumference of the equatorial circle, to the number of yojanams sought. The shastrams sub-divide the yojanam into a great number of parts, in the following manner:—yojanam ÷ 4 croshams ÷ 1,000 dhanoos, or dandams ÷ 4 hastams, or cubits ÷ 2 vitasties, or spans ÷ 2 padams, or foot breadths ÷ 6 angoolams, or finger breadths ÷ 4 yavams. Some make the crosham = 2,000 dandams or half a yojanam, which agrees better with that in which the distances are usually computed [jyotisham].——*Yoocty* (युक्ति - yukti, San.; உத்தி - utti, Tam.). From (yuj, san. to join). Rule of criticism. There are according to the Nunnool [q.v.] thirty-two yoocties, which an author employs in reference to literary subjects:—"*a*" stating the author's aim beforehand;—"*b*" proper arrangement of parts of the antecedents and consequents;—"*c*" giving the substance or summary;—"*d*" specification or sub-division;—"*e*" adducing eminent examples and applying them to practice;—"*f*" reference to authorities;—"*g*" citations from ancient authors; —"*h*" mere mention of the principles of others;—"*i*" explication, or supplying terms to bring out the author's meaning; —"*j*" using related or compound words;—"*k*" using terms by which one thing is employed and another implied;—"*l*" subsequent explanation of what was previously introduced or left unsettled; —"*m*" applying one rule to another when subjects are similar;—"*n*" attaching one rule to another when the subjects depend on one another;—"*o*" rejection of obsolete usage;— "*p*" adoption of modern usage;—"*q*" frequent recurrence to a previously established hypothesis;—"*r*" transposition of words and subjects according to circumstances;—"*s*" using a particular expression to render a subject intelligible;—"*t*" making apparent a particular by a general subject;—"*u*" a hint put forth with a view to subsequent explanation;—"*v*" referring to a subject already explained;—"*w*" siding with one or other of two contrary authorities;—"*x*" producing examples for rules or opinions laid down;—"*y*" making adduced examples apparent;—"*z*" resolution of dubious passages;—"*aa*" inferring an omitted subject by its dependence upon what has been already stated;—"*bb*" adoption of, or acquiescence in, the opinions or conclusions of others;—"*cc*" continuation of the use of technical terms and phrases peculiar to an author;— "*dd*" an evident and easy transition from words to thoughts; —"*ee*" statement of all kindred subjects in one view for the sake of conciseness;—"*ff*" use of such terms, descriptions or definitions in a written work as may require the exercise of thought, and reference to other parts in order to comprehend them. True criticism consists in:—"*a*" showing the connection or consistency of the subject of a work with generally received opinions as well as with those of approved authors;—"*b*" in a nicety of judgment by the exercise of which fit places are awarded to appropriate topics.——*Yooga pattricay* (युगपत्त्रिका - yugapattriká, San.). From (yuga, san. pair + pattrika, san. leaflet); from leaflets in pairs. Blackwoods, otherwise East indian rosewoods. Botanically the Dalbergia genus, leguminosæ [vricsham, 48]. Hard-wooded, wing-leaved trees, native of east indies; pods thin, flat, not winged; timber employed for railway sleepers and valuable furniture. The species best known to the natives are:—lanceolaria [caunooga], latifolia [malabar blackwood] paniculata [yellow mountain ebony], sissoo [q.v.].

YOONOOS (يونس - yúnus, *Ar.*). Jonas. Mahomedan alam; as Yoonoos ally, double alam [ism].

YOOSOOF (يوسف - yúsuf, *Ar.*). Beautiful. Joseph. Adonis of the east. Common alam among Mahomedans; as Yoosoof beg, alam + alaumat [ism].

YOOVAM (युव - yuva, *San.*). Young.——*Yoova rajah* (युवराजा - yuvarájá, San.). From (above + rájá, san. king). The young rajah, eldest son of a rajah who succeeds to the raj [q.v.] by primogeniture [elliah rajah].

YOWM (يوم - yaum, *Ar.*). Day [shamba, vauram].—"*a*" *Yowm ool ahad* (يوم‌الاحد - yaumulahad, Ar.). From (ahad, ar. one). Sunday.—"*b*" *Yowm ool isnein* (يوم‌الاثنين - yaumulisnain, Ar.). From (isnain, ar. two). Monday.—"*c*" *Yowm ool salausah* (يوم‌الثلاث - yaumussalásá, Ar.). From (salásá, ar. three). Tuesday.—"*d*" *Yowm ool arbah* (يوم‌الاربعاء - yaumularbaá, Ar.). From (arbaá, ar. four). Wednesday.— "*e*" *Yowm ool khamees* (يوم‌الخميس - yaumulkhamís, Ar.). From (khamís, ar. fifth). Thursday.—"*f*" *Yowm ool joomah* (يوم‌الجمعه - yaumuljuma, Ar.). From (juma, ar. meeting). Friday.—"*g*" *Yowm ool sabat* (يوم‌السبت - yaumussabt, Hind.). From (sabt, ar. rest). Sabbath day or Saturday.

Z (ذ zál, ز ze, ض - zád, ظ - zoe, *Hind.*). Hind. ز - denotes 700 in arithmetic; contraction for the last Mahomedan mouth [maheena]. Hind. ز stands for the numeral seven [haft, saptam]; and for Saturday in almanacs [punchaungam] and the sign [raushy] Scorpion [akrab, vrishchicam]. Hind. ض symbol for 800. Hind. ظ symbol for 900.

ZABARJAD (गारुड - gáruda, *San.*; حجر ازرق - hajariazrak, *Ar.*; ياقوت كبود - yákútikabúd, *Pers.*; زبرجد - zabarjad, *Hind.*; ವೈಡೂರ್ಯ - vaidúrya, *Can.*; గరుడపచ్చ - garudapattsa, *Tel.*; വൈഡൂര്യം - vaidúryam, *Mal.*; படிகப்பச்சை - padigappaççai, *Tam.*). Title from hindostany. San. from (garuda, san. braminy kite); so called as antidote to snake-bite, garoodan being enemy of snakes. Ar. from (hajar, ar. stone + azrak, ar. blue). Pers. from (yákút, pers. garnet + kabúd, pers. blue). Can. from (vidúra, san. the mountain). Tel. from (garuda, san. braminy kite + pattsa, tel. emerald). Tam. from (sp'hatika, san. crystal + paççai, tam. green). Tam. also (shamuttiravannakkal), meaning sea + colour + stone. Otherwise Aqua marina. Beryl. Greek βήρυλλος. The πυννάτα ἐν ῇ βήρυλλος of Ptolemy was Seringapatam. A mineral composed of silicate of alumina and glucina, crystallizing in the hexagonal system, and usually occurring in hexagonal pyramids. Bluish-green stones brought from Ceylon and Pegu. They are so analogous in their properties and composition to emeralds or zamarrood [q.v.] that they have been called varieties, but chrome has not been discovered in the beryl, and to this is ascribed the rich green color of the emerald [ratnam]. See vol. II, 40.

ZABAUN (زبان - zabán, *Hind.*). From persian. Tongue, language.——*Zabaun bandee* (زبان بندى - zabánbandí, Hind.). From (above + bandí, pers. binding). Deposition of a witness [kyfiyat, vaukmoolam].——*Zabaunee* (زبانى - zabánú, Hind.). Means by mouth. Viva voce statement.

ZABH (ذبح - zabh, *Hind.*). From (zabaha, ar. to cut lengthwise). A sacrifice, slaughter agreeably to the Mahomedan law [halaul].

ZABL (ذبل - zabl, *Ar.*; پشت سنگپشت - pushtisangpusht, *Pers.*; كچكره - kachkarah, *Hind.* and *Dec.*; తాబేటిచిప్ప - tâbétichippa, *Tel.*; ആമയോട് - ámayótu, *Mal.*; ஆமையோடு - ámaiyódu, *Tam.*). Pers. from (pusht, pers. back + sangpusht, pers. tortoise). Hind. from (kachhapa, san. tortoise + karaka, san. cocoanut shell). Tel. from (tábélu, tel. tortoise + chippa, tell. shell). Mal. from tamul. Tam. from (ámai, tam. tortoise + ódu, tam. shell.). Tortoise shell. Procured from the species of sea tortoise called Caret, Testudo imbricata, linn. [cadal aumay].

ZABOOR (زبور - zabúr, *Hind.*). From hebrew. Psalms of David [davood].

ZABR (زبر - zabar, *Hind.*). Superior.——*Zabrdast* (زبردستى - zabardastí, Hind.). From (above + dast, pers. hand.). Force.

ZACRIYAH (زكريا - zakariyá, *Ar.*). Zakariah. Mahomedan alam, mostly taken by the Saits; as Zacriyah sait [ism].

ZADDY (జడ్డి - dzaddi, *Tel.*). Pole.——*Zaddigam* (జడ్డిగము - dzaddigamu, Tel.). From (dzaddi, tel. a pole). Bamboo [q.v.] drill for sowing [calappay, gorroo].

ZAFNEE (غار - ghár, *Ar.*; باهشتان - báhishtán, *Pers.*; ذافنى - záfní, *Hind.*). Title and Hind. from greek δάφνη. Title otherwise Bay, Poet's laurel, Portugal bay, Roman laurel, Sweet bay, Warrior's laurel. Not the Green bay tree of the bible. Botanically Laurus nobilis, linn., lauraceæ [vricsham, 111]. Berries are oval or sub-globular drupes about ½ to ¾ an inch long; when dry, they are greenish-black or blackish brown, slightly wrinkled, and fragile, the integuments, including the reddish-brown endocarp, being thin and brittle; the loose oval seed is easily separated into the two plano-convex brownish cotyledons, which have an aromatic, oily, and bitter taste. Leaves decrepitating when burned; berries deep blue while fresh, brown when dry; have sweet fragrant odour; bachelor, in the degrees, was derived from placing a crown of this in berry on the heads of successful students. For warrior's wreaths among dravidians see Vettimaulay.

ZAFR (ظفر - zafr, *Ar*). From (zafara, ar. to accomplish). Victory. Prefixed to an alam forms a lacab; as Zafr ally victory of ally [ism].

ZAHEER (ظهير - zahír, *Ar.*). From (zahara, ar. to be strong). Support. Part of lacab; as Zaheer ood deen, support of religion [ism].——*Zaheer ood dowla bahaudur*, G.C.S.I. (ظهيرالدولہ بہادر - zahíruddaulahbahádur, Hind.). Descriptive + khitaub alaumats. Second Prince of Arcot. A.D. 1874–1879. See vol. I, 45; II, 252.

ZAHR (زهر - zahr, *Hind.*). Poison.——*Zahrinaurel* (زهرى ناريل - zahrínárol, Hind.). Means poison + cocoanut. Same as Sea-cocoanut.

ZAHRA (زهره - zahra, *Ar.*). Means white, fair-complexioned. Daughter of Mahomet; familiarly fatimah [q.v.]; wife of Ally [q.v.] from whom descended the syeds [q.v.]. Common female alam, as Zahra bee, alam + alaumat [ism].

ZAKAUT (زكوٰة - zakát, *Hind.*). From (zakú, ar. to purify). Alms [kheirauty]. One of the five foundations of practical religion of Islam [q.v.], and consists in the bestowal in alms of a portion of property as a sanctification of the remainder under certain conditions. It is not incumbent on those who have debts, nor is it due upon the necessaries of life, and varies with reference to the different kinds of property in possession.

ZAKHM (زخم - zakhm, *Hind*). Wound.——*Zakhm hayaut* (हेमसागर - hémaságara, San.; घैमारि - ghaimári, Mahr.; زخم حيات كا پتا - zakhmhayátkáptté, Dec.; ತೊನ್ನ ಹದಕಿನಗಿಡ - tonnahadakinagida, Can.; മുറികൂടി - murikúti, Mal.; மலைக்கள்ளி -

malaikkalli, Tam.). Title from deccany. San. from (héma, san. gold + ságara, san. sea). Dec. from (zakhm, pers. wound + hayát, ar. life + pattá, hind. leaf). Can. from (tonnu, can. leprosy + haduku, can. stench + gida, can. plant). Mal. from (muri, mal. wound + kútu, mal. join); cf. indian worm-killer. Tam. from (malai, tam. mountain + kalli, tam. euphorbia tirucalli, linn.). San. also (ast'hibhaksha), meaning bone + eating; (parnabíja), meaning leaf-seed; from the leaves, when placed on moist place, taking root. Hind. also (hemságar) from sanscrit. Can. also (haradhachchaka). Mal. also (ilamarunnu), meaning leaf + medicine. Title otherwise Hill cully, Kidney-wort, Leaf seed, Leper's plant, Navelwort, Wound leaf. Botanically Kalanchoe laciniata, dec., crassulaceæ [vricsham, 51]. Alias Cotyledon laciniata. Leaves decompound and pinnatifid; the segments oblong, acute, coarsely toothed, upper ones nearly entire; sepals lanceolate, acuminated, spreading; cymes panicled; flowers yellow; flowering in the rainy season. Leaves valued as an application to wounds and sores; allay irritation and promote cicatrization. Other species are:—floribunda, grandiflora.

ZAMANG (زمنگ - zamang, *Hind.*). From Javanese. Title otherwise Genisaro tree, Rain tree, Saman tree, Uango tree, Venezula zamang tree. Botanically Pithecolobium [auragvadham] saman, benth., leguminosæ [vricsham, 48]. Alias Niga saman. Introduced from jamaica, extensively cultivated as an ornamental tree; sapwood white, heart-wood brown, soft, perishable.

ZAMARROOD (मरकत - marakata, *San.*; زمرد - zamarrud, *Ar.*, *Pers.*, *Hind.*; ಪಚ್ಚೆ - paççe, *Can.*; పచ్చ - pattsa, *Tel.*; മരതകം - maratakam, *Mal.*; பச்சைக்கல் - paççaikkal, *Tam.*). San. from (mara, san. death + tak, san. to deride); as a poison-killer. Can. and Tel. mean green. Tam. from (paççai, tam. green + kal, tam. stone). Tam. also (paççai), alone. Emerald. A sort of green sapphire [neelam] and altogether different from the occidental emerald. The oriental gem is harder than the American, though inferior in the richness and purity of its green color [ratnam].

ZAMEEN (زمين - zamín, *Hind.*). From (zam, pers. cold + suffix of relation). Earth, land [zemindar].——*Zameen cundah* (زمينى كندا - zamíníkandá, Hind.). Meaning ground + root. Same as Malacca yam.——*Zemindar* (زميندار - zamíndár, Hind.; జమీందారుడు - dzamíndárudu, Tel.; சமீந்தார் - shamíndár, Tam.). From (above + dár, pers. holder). Landholder. An officer, who under the Moghul [q.v.] Government was charged with the financial superintendence of the lands of a district; since made hereditary and independent [mittah, mootah]. See vol. I, 112.——*Zemindarry* (زمينداری - zamíndárí, Hind.). The office or jurisdiction of a zemindar [inam].

ZAMORIN (سامری - sámarí, *Hind.*; സാമൂതിരി - sámútiri, *Mal.*). From (sámudri, san. relating to sea), through portuguese. One of the Saumantans [q.v.]. A titular chief of Calicut, descendant of a royal family who once ruled over territories now comprising the greater part of the collectorate of Malabar. The Zamorin in 1513 sent a deputation to Portugal, and his native ambassador turned Christian and was knighted under the name of John of the cross, by John III; on returning to india, he was banished from the Zamorin's court. By a treaty of 18th August 1792, the Zamorin agreed to act on the civil rules which the East india company might introduce. Further changes were made by treaties of June 1793, September 1794, and 15th November 1806, the last of which gave a consolidated allowance to the Zamorin. Zamorin nediyiroopp moottarauty tirmalpaud is the fifth prince of the zamorin's family; Yidattore naud numbiyauttiry tirmalpaud is the fourth prince; Yernaud moonancoor numbiyauttiry tirmalpaud is the third prince; Yernaud yelancoor numbiyauttiry tirmalpaud is the second prince and heir apparent. See vol. I (16), (18), (129), 35, 51; and II, 103 [charitram].

ZAMZEM (زمزم - zamzam, *Hind.*). Means copious. Otherwise Hagar's well. Sacred well at Mecca; water greatly esteemed by Mahomedans and brought to this country. Compare Gungay.

ZANG (زنگ - zang, *Hind.*). Rust.——*Zangaur* (पित्तलता - pittalatá, San.; زنجار - zanjár, Ar., Pers., and Hind.; زنگال - zangál, Dec.; سانم - sánam, Malay; జంగాలపచ్చ - jangálapaççe, Can.; జంగాలప్పత్స - dzangálappattsa, Tel.; ചെങ്കലപ്പച്ച - chenkalappaçça, Mal.; வங்காளப்பச்சை - vangálappaççai, Tam.). Title from hindostany. San. from (pittalá, san. brass). Ar. from persian. Pers. from (zang, pers. rust). Tel. from (zangár, hind. verdigris + pattsa, tel. green). Mal. from (chenkalam, mal. red vessel, copper + paçça, mal. green). Tam. from (vangálam, tam. bengal + paççai, tam. green). Hind. also (pitrái), meaning copper like. Malay also (taitámbaga), meaning rust of copper. Tel. also (chilumu), meaning shedding. Mal. also (paççanílam), meaning green blue; (sénákám). Tam. also (shengalappaççai), meaning red + vessel + green; (kalimbu), meaning glutinous excretion. Verdigris. Sub-acetate of copper. Sub-acetas cupri of chemists. Rust of copper [taumram], of a beautiful bluish-green color, formed from the corrosion of copper by the acid [poolipp, tezaub] of fermented vegetables. Never used internally by veidyans [q.v.]; but as detergent and stimulating applications for ill-conditioned ulcers. Used in dyeing [shauyam] cotton [q.v.] black, orange and green; likewise in preparation of colors [rangh], chiefly greens, and with the assistance of sal ammoniac [nowshaudar] an excellent blue.

ZANJEER (زنجير - zanjír, *Hind.*). Chain. [jareeb]. Zanjeer zaumin is chain security, where all stand security for each other.

ZANZIBAR (زنگبار - zangbár, *Hind.*). From (zangí, Pers. blacks + bár, pers. region). Term once applied to the east coast of Africa; now restricted to the island where the sultan of Zanzibar lives. Plant first term; ex.:—Aloe socotrina, zanzibar aloe; Tephrosia purpurea, zanzibar indigo; see gloss. paragraphs.——*Zanj* (زنج - zanj, *Ar.*). Zingis of Ptolemy. An inhabitant of Zanzibar, or a negro in general.

ZAR (زر - zar, *Pers.*). Gold.——*Sarigay* (சரிகை - sharigai, Tam.). From (zar, pers. gold). Lace. Ornamental net-work, made of threads of silk [puttoo], flax [alsee], cotton [q.v.], or of gold [pon] or silver [velly] interwoven. A novelty hitherto confined to the Christian settlement, at Nagarcoil and a few other places. Pon sarigay is gold lace.——*Zarafshauny caugas* (زرافشانى كاغذ - zarafshánikághaz, Hind.). From (above + afshání, pers. sprinkled + kághaz, pers. paper). Gold-sprinkled paper, which natives use when addressing people of rank. Eedoos [q.v.] are generally written upon these.——*Zardozy* (زر دوزى - zardozí, Hind.). From (above + dozí, pers. sewing). Embroidery in gold thread [sarigay]. The cloth is stretched out in a horizontal bamboo [q.v.] frame of rude construction, raised about a couple of feet from the ground, and the figures intended to be worked or embroidered are drawn upon it by designers. The body of the design is copied from colored drawings. On woollen cloths [pushm] the outlines are traced with chalk [sheemay choonam], and on muslin [q.v.] with pencil. The embroiderers, seated upon the floor around the frame, ply the needle, which they do not draw towards but push from them. In place of scissors they commonly use a piece of glass or Chinaware to cut the threads. Gold [pon], silver [velly], tinsel [caukkay pon], and beetle [zeerangy] wings are used in embroidery [caurchoby].——*Zar i gool* (زرگل - zarigul, Hind.). From (above + gul, pers. rose). The yellow anthers of a rose [gool].——*Zar i kalb* (زرقلب - zarikalb, Hind.). From (above + kalb, pers. counterfeit). Base coin.——*Zar i nakd* (زر نقد - zarinakd, Hind.). From (above + nakd, pers. cash). Ready money.

ZARB (ضرب - zarb, *Hind.*). From (zaraba, ar. to strike). A blow. Zarb-i-arcot, means struck or coined at Arcot.

ZARISHK (زرشك - zirishk, *Hind.*). Rasoot [berberry].

ZAROOR (ضرور - zarúr, *Hind.*). From pers. Haste [jeldy].

ZARRAH (ذرة - zarrah, *Hind.*). Mustard seed [rayaun]. Goldsmith's weight. 6 zarrahs = 1 jow or barley corn [nitay, 3e]. A very small weight equal to $\frac{1}{16}$ of a goonj [goomchy] seed. Compare Sarshapam.

ZAUDA (زادة - zádah, *Hind.*). From (záídan, pers. to beget). Son. Haraumzauda, of illegitimate birth; rascal. Shahzauda, a king's son [rajcomaur].

ZAUHID (زاهد - záhid, *Ar.*). From (zuhda, ar. to abstain from). Pious. Prefixed to an alam forms a lacab; as Zauhid hoossain, pious hoossain. Feminine form is Zauhida [ism].

ZAUMIN (ضامن - zámin, *Hind.*). From (zamana, ar. to be responsible). Security [jaumeen]. Prefixed to an alam makes a lacab; as Zaumin ally, security of ally [ism].——*Zamaunat* (ضمانت - zamánat, Hind.). From (zamana, ar. to be responsible). Bail, security [jaumeen]. Zamaunat nauma is a deed of surety. Prefixed to an alam forms a lacab; as Zamaunat hoossain, security of hoossain [ism].

ZAUR (زار - zár, *Pers.*). Suffix denoting place or multitude; as Goolzaur, flower + place.

ZAVAUJIR (زواجر - zavájir, *Hind.*). Admonition. Short work on traditions, by Mowlvy sheikh adam, taught to children and females. Translation of Arabic work of Ibn e hajar e hateemy. The following is specimen:—حقتعالى تين شخص پر لعنت كرتا هے راشى — مرتشى — رايش راشى دينے والا — مرتشى لينے والا — رايش دونوں كے درميان ضمانت معرفت قبول كرنے والا

"The curse of God is upon three persons; him who takes bribes, "him who gives them, and him who consents to act as mediator "and to stand security [jaumeen, zaumin]."

ZEDOARY (زدوار - zadwár, *Ar.*). A general name for the roots of several species of Curcuma [haridrah], Hedychium, and Kœmpferia [bhoochampak].——*Camphor zedoary* (كپور كچرى - kapúrkachrí, Hind.). Same as Europe zedoary.——*Europe zedoary* (कापूरकचरी - kápúrakacharí, Mahr.; كپور كچرى - kapúrkachrí, Hind.; ولايتى كچور - viláitíkachúr, Dec.; సీమకిచ్చిలిగడ్డ - símakiççiligadda, Tel.; சீமைக்கிச்சிலிக்கிழங்கு - shímaikkiççilikkizhangu, Tam.). Mahr. from hindostany. Hind. from (kapúr, hind. camphor + kachúr, hind. curcuma zedoaria, roscoe), from its color and fragrance. Dec. from (viláití, hind. foreign

+ kachúr, hind. curcuma zedoaria, roscoe). Tel. from (síma, tel. foreign + kiççiligadda, tel. kœmpferia galanga, linn.). Tam. from (shímai, tam. foreign + kiççilikkizhangu, tam. kœmpferia galanga, linn.). Hind. also (sitrattí), meaning lesser galangal, alpinia officinarum, hance; (káfúrkachrí), meaning camphor zedoary. Tel. also (kiççiligadda), meaning orange citrus aurantium, linn. + root. Tam also (kiççilikkizhangu), meaning citrus aurantium, linn. + thick root; from aromatic root. Title otherwise Camphor zedoary, Capoor cutchrah, Orange root, Spiked garland flower. Botanically Hedychium spicatum, smith, zingiberaceæ [vricsham, 144]. Evergreen herbaceous, 3 feet high; spathes truncate, one-flowered; outer segments of corolla linear; lip roundish, two lobed, longer than the style; flowers yellow, flowering in june. Fragrant grass; its smell, taste, internal color, are like those of long zedoary; like long zedoary, root is generally found in the bazaar in circular slices, 1 or 1½ lines in thickness, and about 2 anna or ¼ rupee piece in circumference, very white with a reddish-brown edge, and fragrant. Resembles also the Lesser galangal [q.v.]; but is different in being very white internally, amylaceous in structure, fragrant, and slightly warm or aromatic in taste, but not peppery or pungent. Used medicinally for same purposes as long zedoary, but preferable to it; quoted, non-officinal, in pharm. Other common species indigenous are:—cernuum, coronarium, flavescens, scaposum, venustum.——*False zedoary* (भुमिचम्पक - bhúmichampaka, San.; भुईचांपा - bhuíchámpá, Mahr.; भुंयिचांपे - bhuyimchámpé, Conc.; ನೆಲಸಂಪಿಗೆ - nelasampige, Can.; కొండకలవ - kondakalava, Tel.; മലങ്കൂവ - malankúva, Mal.; යවකෙන්ද - yavakenda, Singh.; நேர்ப்பிசின் - nérppisin, Tam.). Title from this being supposed to be source of the zedoaries until roxburgh traced them to curcuma aromatica, salisb., and curcuma zedoaria, roscoe. San. from (bhúmi, san. ground + champaka, san. michelia champaca, linn.); from fragrant flowers. Mahr. from sanscrit. Can. from (nela, can. earth + sampige, can. the plant). Tel. from (konda, tel. hill + kalava, tel. water lily, nymphæa lotus, linn.). Mal. from (mala, mal. hill + kúva, mal. curcuma angustifolia, linn.). San. also (káshmarya), meaning produced in cashmere; cf. cashmere tree and costum; (bhúchampaka), meaning ground champak. Can. also (utpalbú); (kallakúve); (kumudagedde). Tel. also (gumudu) [giant potato, cashmere tree]. Mal. also (cheñchinírkizhannu), meaning red + water in which rice is cleaned + root, from color of the flower. Singh. also (kabasan). Title otherwise Ground champak, Kœmpferian zedoary. Botanically Kœmpferia [boochampak] rotunda, willd., zingiberaceæ [vricsham, 144]. Alias Kœmpferia longa. Deciduous tuberous rooted plant; leaves large oblong, colored; spikes radical, appearing before the leaves, which are oblong, waved, and usually stained underneath; upper segments of the inner series of the corolla lanceolate, acute, lower ones divided into two broad obcordate lobes; flowers near, fragrant, sessile, purplish white; scapes embraced by a few common sheaths, very short, greenish purple; calyx above, one-leafed, as long as the tube of the corolla, somewhat gibbous; apex generally two-toothed, and of a dotted purplish colour. Leaves die down towards end of november, and do not appear again till after the flower has finished flowering in april; the flowers with two petals white and two deep lilac of moderate size, are borne not more than two or three inches from the ground in a crowded manner, opening day by day in succession in the morning and fading by the evening and diffusing much fragrance; root bulbous, about thickness of a finger, ash-colored outside and white within; smells like ginger [q.v.] and tastes hot to the tongue. The whole plant, reduced to a powder, used as an ointment; useful in healing wounds, and taken internally removes coagulated blood or purulent matters; root is useful in anasarcous swellings and has a hot, ginger-like [ginger] taste; in pharm. non-officinal.——*Long zedoary* (शटी - shatí, San.; कचोरा - kachórá, Mahr.; زرنباد - zurumbád, Ar.; ژرنباد - zhurumbád, Pers.; کچورا - kachúrá, Hind.; کچور - kachúr, Dec.; کونتپدی - kunitpadi, Malay; ಕಚೋರ - kachóra, Can.; కచ్చూరము - kaççúramu, Tel.; കച്ചൂരം - kaççóram, Mal.; හරන්කහ - harankaha, Singh.; கர்ப்பூரக்கிச்சிலிக்கிழங்கு - karppúrakkiççilikkizhangu, Tam.). Title from shape of root. San. from (shat, san. to divide). Mahr. from (kachhúra, san. the plant). Ar. from persian. Hind. from (kachhúra, san. zedoary plant). Dec. from (kachhúra, san. zedoary plant). Can. from (kachhúra, san. zedoary plant). Tel. from sanscrit. Mal. from (kachhúra, san. the plant). Singh. from (aran, singh. forest + kaha, singh. turmeric, curcuma longa, roxb.). Tam. from (karpúra, san. camphor + kiççilikkizhangu, tam. orange root, heydichium spicatum). San. also (chóra), meaning thief; (dushpatra), meaning small-leaved [gool mindie]; (kachhúra), meaning itches burning; (nirvishá), meaning antidote to poison; (apavishá), meaning free from poison; (vishahá), meaning poison destroyer; (vanárishtá), meaning wild margosa, melia azadirachta, linn.; (vanaharidrá), meaning wild turmeric; (shólí), meaning wild turmeric; (shadgrant'hiká), meaning six-knotted; (gandhamúlí), meaning having fragrant root; (karbura), meaning variegated. Ar. also (arúkulkáfúr), meaning root of camphor from its smell. Pers. also (kazhúr). Hind. also (kakhura); (ámbihaldí), meaning curcuma aromatica, salisb.; (kapúrhaldí), meaning camphor + turmeric; (karpúrkacharí), meaning camphor zedoary. Dec. also (janglíhaldí), meaning wild turmeric. Malay also (tomon). Can. also (nirbisi); (kachu); (sappanga) [sappan]. Tel. also (kiççiligadda), meaning orange + root; from smell; (kachóramu); (tellakastúripasupu), meaning white + curcumam aromatica, salis.; (adavikachóramu), meaning wild zedoary. Mal. also (kaççólam) and (kaççúram), by corruption; (atavikkaççólam), meaning wild zedoary; (káttiñchikkúva), meaning wild + ginger, zingiber officinale, ros. + curcuma sp. Singh. also (hingurupiyali). Tam. also (púlángízhangu), meaning probably red root [malda dye]; (kiççilikkizhanguççedi). Title otherwise Broad-leaved zedoary, Camphor root, Camphor turmeric, Custoory munjal, Fragrant root, Musk turmeric, Orange root, Wild turmeric, Zerumbet. Botanically Curcuma [haridrah] zedoaria, roscoe, zingiberaceæ [vricsham, 144]. Alias Amomum latifolium, zerumbet; Curcuma officinalis, speciosa, zerumbet. Zerumbet from arabic. Height 3–4 feet; bulbs and palmate tubers pale straw-colored throughout; leaves broad lanceolate, with a dark-purple sheath down the middle; scape 5–6 inches long, distinct from the leafy stems; spike 4–5 inches long; flowers deep yellow and bright crimson tuft; native of the east indies. Root externally wrinkled and of an ash color, but internally of brownish red; odour fragrant like camphor [q.v.], taste biting; root generally exposed for sale cut into small round pieces about the third of an inch thick, inch and-a-half or two inches in circumference; best comes from ceylon. Rhizomes possess aromatic, stimulant and carminative properties; employed in native medicinal practice as a stomachic, and also applied to bruises and sprains; in pharm. non-officinal; used in veterinary practice. The dry root, powdered and mixed with the powdered wood of cæsalpinia sappan, l. [sappan], makes the red powder, called abeer [goolaul] which is used during holy [q.v.] festival; from its fragrant smell much used in conjunction with custoory munjal the root of the curcuma aromatica, salisb. [round zedoary], in bathings and purifications of hindoos.——*Round zedoary* (वनहरिद्रा - vanaharidrá, San.; आंबेहलदी - ámbéhaladí, Mahr.; आंबहलदि - ámbahaladi, Conc.; آنبےھلدی - ámbehaldí, Hind.; جنگلی ھلدی - janglíhaldí, Dec.; ಕಸ್ತೂರಿಅರಸಿನ - kastúriarasina, Can.; ಆನೆಮಂಜಲ್ - ánemanjal, Too.; కస్తూరిపసుపు - kastúripasupu, Tel.; കാട്ടുമഞ്ഞൾ - káttumaññal, Mal.; වල්කහ - valkaha, Singh.; கத்தூரிமஞ்சள் - kattúrimañjal, Tam.). Title from shape of root. San. from (vana, san. forest + haridrá, san. turmeric, curcuma longa, roxb.). Mahr. & Conc. from hindostany. Hind. from (ámbe, hind. spontaneous + haldí, hind. turmeric, curcuma longa, roxb.). Dec. from (janglí, hind. wild + haldí, hind. curcuma longa, roxb.). Can. from (kastúrí, san. musk + arasina, can. turmeric, curcuma longa, roxb.). Too. from (áne, too. elephant + manjal, too. turmeric). Tel. from (kastúrí, san. musk + pasupu, tel. turmeric, curcuma longa, roxb.). Mal. from (kátu, mal. forest + maññal, mal. turmeric). Singh. from (val, singh. wild + kaha, singh. curcuma longa, roxb.). Tam. from (kastúrí, san. musk + mañjal, tam. turmeric, curcuma longa, roxb.). San. also (nirvishá), meaning antidote to poison; (apavishá), meaning free from poison; (vishahá), meaning poison + destroyer; (jángalaharidrá), meaning forest turmeric. Mahr. also (ránahaladí), meaning wild turmeric. Ar. also (jadwár), meaning aconitum heterophyllum, wall. [jadwaur]. Hind. also (banhaldí), meaning forest turmeric; (nirbisi), meaning antidote to poison; (banharida), meaning forest turmeric. Can. also (kádarisina), meaning wild turmeric; (ambehaladigida), meaning scented turmeric. Tel. also (tellakastúripasupu), meaning white + the plant; (adavipasupu), meaning forest + turmeric. Mal. also (kastúrimaññal), meaning musk turmeric; (ánakkúva), meaning elephant + curcuma sp., is costus speciosus, smith. Singh. also (dadakaha), meaning wilderness + turmeric. Title otherwise Cochin turmeric, Musk turmeric, Red zedoary, Turmeric colored zedoary, Wild turmeric, Yellow zedoary. Botanically Curcuma [haridrah] aromatica, sal., zingiberaceæ [vricsham, 144]. Alias Amomum zedoaria; Curcuma zedoaria. Bulb small, and, with the long palmate tubers, inwardly yellow; leaves 2–4 feet in length, broad lanceolate, sessile on their sheaths, sericeous underneath; the whole plant of a uniform green; spikes 6–12 inches long; flowers aromatic, largish, pale rose-colored, with a yellow tinge along the middle of the lip; a wild turmeric having smell somewhat resembling musk [custoory]; grows in moist forests. Root color externally, dirty yellow; wrinkled, and, internally of a brownish red, possessing an agreeable fragrant smell, and a warm, bitterish, and aromatic taste. Root possesses tonic properties and is less heating than ginger [q.v.]; in pharm. but non-officinal. Root used as a perfume; it is mixed with the powder of sandalwood [sandal], with which hindoo women of rank rub their skins.

ZEELAN (سیلان - sailán, *Hind*). A corruption of the Sanscrit simhala or Ceylon [seilan, simham].

ZEERANGY (भ्रमर - bhramara, *San.*; زیرنگی - zírangí, *Dec.*; ತುಂಬಿ - tumbi, *Can.*; ಕುರ್ದಯಿ - kurdayi, *Too.*; తుమ్మెద - tummeda, *Tel.*; വണ്ട് - vantu, *Mal.*; வண்டு - vandu, *Tam.*). Title from deccany. San. from (bhram, san. to wander). Dec. from (zí, ar. possessor + rang, pers. color). Mal. from (val, mal. to whirl). Tam. from (val, tam. beauty). Terms for any insect of the beetle class of the order coleoptera, holometabola, insecta [poochy], of naturalists [jantoo]. There is a Tamul proverb:—வண்டு தூரத்திலே பூவின் வாசனையை அறியும்; அதுபோல, கற்றோர் தூரத்திலேயே ஒருவன் நடத்தையை அறிந்துகொள்வார்கள்—"As beetles smell at a "distance the fragrance of flowers, so the learned understand "one's character when he is at distance." The following are different kinds of beetle.——*Dung beetle* (وند - vand, Hind.; పేడపురుగు - pédapurugu, Tel.; பீவண்டு - pívandu, Tam.). Tel. from (péda, tel. cowdung + purugu, tel. insect). Tam. from (pí, tam. dung + vandu, tam. beetle). Geotrupes stercorarius, geotrupidæ, coleoptera, holometabola, insecta [poochy], of naturalists. The dung-feeding Lamellicorn beetles. They roll up pieces of excrementitious matter into the form of balls, in which they enclose their eggs, and the balls serve for the food of their young. Sometimes they bury the dung in the earth.——*Red beetle* (لالزیرنگی - lálzírangí, Hind.; ఎఱ్ఱజీరంగి - errajírangi, Tel.; செவ்வண்டு - shevvandu, Tam.). So called from the red mark on the upper part of its breast. Destructive to cocoanuts [q.v.].——*Stag beetle* (بهونرا - bhaunrá, Hind.). Different species of Lucanus, of the family lucanidæ, coleoptera, holometabola, insecta [poochy], of naturalists. These are especially destructive to living trees.——*Telini beetle* (تیلنی - telní, Hind.). See Telini fly.

ZEIN (زین - zaín, *Ar.*). From (zaina, ar. to adorn). Pride or glory. Prefixed to an alam forms a lacab; as Zein ool aubi deen, pride of the servants of god [ism].——*Zeenat* (زینت - zínat, Hind.). From (zaina, ar. to adorn). Beauteous. Ornament. Part of lacab, chiefly female; as Zeenat oon nissa, ornament of ladies [ism].——*Zeinab* (زینب - zainab, Ar.). From (zain, ar, to adorn). Name of the daughter of Mahomet; and of his granddaughter, sister of Hoossain. Common female alam; as Zeinab bee, alam + alaumat [ism].

ZEITOON (زیتون - zaitún, *Ar.* and *Pers.*; زیتون کا پیڑ - zaitúnkáper, *Hind.*; زیتون کا جہاڑ - zaitúnkájhár, *Dec.*; జైతూను - jaitún, *Tel.*; சைதூன் - shaithún, *Tam.*). From hebrew. Greek ἐλαία. Title otherwise Europeau olive, Olive. Giving Florence oil, Olive oil, Salad oil, Sweet oil. Botanically Olea [jita] Europæa, linn., oleaceæ [vricsham, 85]. Evergreen tree, 15 feet high; leaves lanceolate, pointed, entire, hoary beneath; branches angular not spiny; flowers white, flowering in June and August. Though called europæa, native of western asia; thrives introduced, but is unproductive; an evergreen tree, attaining extreme old age; oil obtained by pressing pulp of fruit; the tree which gave its name to the mount of olives. Gives to pharm. the oil expressed from the fruit, olivæ oleum, mild, emollient, antidote in cases of poisoning; officinal. Oil [yennay] used as food. Compare:—Canarium commune, chinese olive; Elæagnus conferta, wild olive; Olea dioica, indian olive, indian wild olive; Putranjiva roxburghii, wild olive; Terminalia chebula, negro's olive; see gloss. paragraphs.

ZENANA (زنانه - zanánah, *Hind.*). From (zan, pers. a woman). Apartments appropriated to women. A seraglio. The women in it [harem].

ZEND (زند - zand, *Hind.*). Meaning explanation. Old persian language. Zend avesta, meaning explanation of the law, was the book of the high priest or ruler Zoroaster [q.v.]. This inculcates worship of two gods, Light and Darkness, Ormuzd and Ahraman; Light creating good and Darkness creating evil. Disbelief is expressed in the eternity of the world, and in the unity of the creator.——*Zindeek* (زندیق - zindík, Hind.). From (zand, ar. book of zoroaster). Follower of Zoroaster.

ZERUMBET (زرنباد - zurumbád, *Ar.*). Long zedoary.

ZEWAR (زیور - zewar, *Hind.*). Ornament. Amongst Mahomedans the use of ornaments confined to females, males being prohibited from wearing any except the signet ring [nagay]. See vol. I (98).

ZI (ذی - zí, *Ar.*). Possessive prefix; as Zihaj, lord + pilgrimage. Cf. Zoo.

ZIFT (زفت - zift, *Ar.*). Pitch. Product of Cedrus deodara, loud. [deodar], and Pinus longifolia, rox. [cheer]. Residuum of tar [keel] inspissated by heat or boiled down to dryness. Black dammer [dammer] is here used for pitch.

ZIKR (ذکر - zikr, *Ar.*). From (zikara, ar. to remember). Recitation, oral or mental, of sacred tests, &c., concerning glorification of God [allah] practised by the various religious orders [fakeer, peer, soofee].——*Zaukir* (ذاکر - zákir, Hind.). From (zikr, ar. praise). The praiser of God. Prefixed to an alam forms a lacab; as Zaukir ally, praiser of ally [ism].

ZILLAH (ضلع - zilla, *Hind.*). From arabic meaning a rib; side, portion, division. The different terms for territorial revenue divisions and sub-divisions under native administrations were:—Desham, Prauntam, Soobah, Zillah, Pergunnah, Talook, Mahaul, Pettah, Sammat, Taraf, Cusbah, Mowza and Mazrah. Desham and Prauntam were the most general terms, expressing country or region; among the mahrattas it meant their own country proper, the middle country between the sahyadry, the balaghaut carnatic, and the godavery river; all outside this tract they called deshauntaram or foreign country. Soobah was a province. Zillah, pergunnah and talook differed but little originally, meaning shire or county; zillah was a larger division covering many talooks. Mahaul and Pettah were sub-divisions of a talook; canton or circuit. Sammat and Taraf were a collection of villages as the charge of revenue inspector. Cusbah was the principal or large town in a division; it properly meant the town proper or old town in contradistinction to the later additions and extensions. Mowza was a village; Mazrah a hamlet, an agricultural division of the village. As to present Zillahs, or districts, or collectorates:—Ganjam, Vizagapatam, Godavery and Kistna are collectively called the Northern circars [q.v.]; the following eight, viz., Nellore, Madras, North and South arcot, Trichinopoly, Tanjore, Madura and Tinnevelly make up the Carnatic [q.v.]; Cuddapah, Kurnool and Bellary are the Ceded districts [q.v.]. Zillahdar is a subordinate revenue officer under a Tahsildar [q.v.]. See vol. I, 62.

ZIMMEE (ذمی - zimmí, *Hind.*). From (zimma, ar. protection). A non-muslim, subject of a muslim [q.v.] government, who for the payment of capitation tax [jizia] becomes entitled to security of life and property with freedom and toleration.

ZINDA (زنده - zindah, *Pers.*). Living. Celebrated Persian hero. Used as alam; as Zinda sahib, alam + suffix [ism].

ZINGIBER (زنجبیل - zanjabíl, *Ar.*). Title from arabic which is from (shringabéra, san. the rhizome of ginger). The scientific genus [ginger]. Also a fountain in Paradise [bheest, paradise].

ZIYAH (ضیاء - ziyá, *Ar.*). Light. Prefixed to an alam forms a lacab; as Ziyah ool hukk, the light of God [ism].

ZIYAURAT (زیارت - ziyárat, *Hind.*). From (zára, ar. to visit). Also called phool, meaning flowers; from flowers being strewn that day over the grave. Ceremony of visiting the grave [gor] third day after burial when koran [q.v.] is read, alms are given, and flowers placed on the grave of the deceased [janauza].

ZIZYPHUS (زیزفون - zaizufún, *Ar.*). Generic. Same as Bair.

ZONNAVAUDA (జొన్నవాడ - dzonnaváda, *Tel.*). From (dzannamu, tel. sacrifice + váda, tel. village). Village; Nellore dist., Nellore tal.; pop. 575; acres 1,292; lat. 14° 29'; long. 79° 56'; from Nellore W.N.W. 6¼ miles; from the sea W. 19 miles. On the north bank of the Pennair. Shiva temple, favorite place of pilgrimage. This, Narsimhacondah, and Runganaick's temple at Nellore form a sacred triad. The Pennair flowing between this and Narsimhacondah is considered specially sacred there.

ZOO (ذو - zú, *Hind.*). Master.——*Zaut* (ذات - zát, Hind.). Feminine. Essence of God [allah]. In Mahomedan law means body connected with soul in opposition to material body.——*Zoolcada* (ذوالقعده - zulkadah, Hind.). Eleventh Mahomedan month [maheena].——*Zoolfacar* (ذوالفقار - zulfakár, Hind.). From (above + fakár, ar. cleaver). A double-edged sword, with small hollows in the edge, suitable for hacking suits of mail. Applied in particular to the sharp two-edged sword of an unbeliever which passed on to Mahomet on the death of the former in the battle at Badr with Mahomet; the latter subsequently transferring it to Ally. Prefixed to an alam forms a lacab; as Zoolfacar ally, the sword of ally, mostly taken by Shiahs [ism, shiah].——*Zoolfacar khan* (ذوالفقارخان - zulfakár-khán, Hind.). Alam + honorific title. A general of Aurungzeeb. Came to the Deccan [q.v.] 1690. Became the first Nawaub [q.v.] of the Carnatic [q.v.]. Granted to the Company rent free the villages of Egmore, Pursewaukum, &c., in 1692—See vol. I (169); II, 253 [charitram].——*Zoolhijja* (ذوالحجه - zulhijjah, Hind.). Last or twelfth Mahomedan month [maheena].——*Zool kernein* (ذوالقرنین - zulkarnain, Hind.). From (above + karnain, ar. two horns); master of two horns, East and West. Alexander the Great [secunder].

ZOOBDAT (زبده - zubdat, *Ar.*). From (zabada, ar. to churn). Cream; so select. Part of lacab; as Zoobdat ool moolk, the select of the state [ism].——*Zobeidah* (زبیده - zubaidah, Ar.). Wife of Haroun ar raschid, the original reciter of the Arabian nights. She is buried at Baghdad.

ZOOFAH (زوفاء یابس - zúfáiyábis, *Ar.* and *Pers.*; زوفاء - zúfá, *Hind.* and *Dec.*). Ar. from (zúfá, ar. hyssop + yábis, ar. dry). Hind. from arabic. Pers. also (ushnahidáúdi), meaning David's cuscuta. Greek ὕσσωπος. Hebrew Esof. Title otherwise Hyssop. Botanically Hyssopus officinalis, linn., labiatæ [vricsham, 103]. Deciduous undershrub, 2 feet high; leaves lanceolate; flowers racemose, whorled, one sided; middle lobe of corolla two-lobed entire; teeth of calyx erect; flowers blue, flowering in June and September. Brought to India from Syria; leaves stimulant, stomachic, emmenagogue and carminative; useful in hysteria and colic; also used as a poultice to bruises, especially of the eyes; sap of the leaves made into a syrup with sugar [q.v.] and honey [shahad], used as a vermifuge for roundworms.——*Water zoofah* (ब्राह्मी - brahmí, San.; बाम - báma, Mahr.; ब्राह्मी - brahmí, Conc.; سفید چمنی - sufedchamní, Hind. and Dec.; ನೀರುಬ್ರಹ್ಮಿ - nírubrahmi, Can.; సాంబ్రాణిచెట్టు - sámbránichettu, Tel.; ଉରିଷ୍ଣପର୍ଣ୍ଣୀ - urishnaparni, Oor.; பிரமி - brahmi,

Mal.; സുണാവില -sunuvila, Singh.; நீர்ப்பிரமி - nírppirami, Tam.). Title from habitat. San. from (vrih, san. to grow) [indian pennywort]. Mahr. and Conc. from sanscrit. Hind. from (sufed, hind. white + chamní, hind. garden flower). Can. from (níru, can. water + brahmí, san. the plant). Tel. from (sámbráni, tel. incense + chettu, tel. tree). Mal. from sanscrit. Tam. from (nír, tam. water + brahmí, san. the plant). San. also (jalabrahmí), meaning water + the plant; (tivra), meaning sharp. Hind. also (adhabirní); (jalním), meaning water margosa, melia azadirachta, linn. Mal. also (nírbrahmi), meaning water + the plant. Tam. also (piramiyappúndu), meaning the plant + herb; (pirami), meaning diabetes plant. Title otherwise Bauma, Bramy, Diabetes plant, Hedge hyssop, Indian bramy, Thyme-leaved gratiola, Water hyssop, Water neem. Botanically Herpestis monniera, h. b. et k., scrophularineæ [vricsham, 95]. Alias Bramia indica; Capraria connieria; Gratiola monnieria, portulacacea; Herpestis brownei, cuneifolia, procumbens, spathulata; Limosella calycina; Monniera brownei; Septas repens. Annual, creeping; leaves opposite, sessile, obovate, wedge-shaped or oblong, smooth, entire, fleshy, dotted with minute spots; peduncles axillary, alternate, solitary, shorter than the leaves, one-flowered; flowers smallish, pale blue; calyx five-cleft, exterior three segments larger than the others; corolla campanulate, five-parted, divisions equal; capsule ovate, two-celled, two-valved; seeds numerous; margins of tanks; flowering nearly all year. Root, stalks, and leaves are medicinally diuretic and aperient; expressed juice mixed with petroleum [munn teilam] is rubbed on parts affected with rheumatism; in pharm. non-officinal. Another species is floribunda.

ZOOHOOR (ظهور - zuhúr, *Ar.*). From (zahara, ar. to be conspicuous). Manifestation. Prefixed to an alam forms a lacab; as Zoohoor ahmed, manifestation of Ahmed [ism].

ZOOLM (ظلم - zulm, *Hind.*). From (zalama, ar. to act wrongfully). Force, oppression.——*Zoolmaut* (ظلمات - zulmát, Hind.). The region of darkness at one extremity of the world in which the fountain of immortality is said to exist.

ZOONNAUR (زنار - zunnár, *Ar.*). Greek ζωνάριον. Cord worn round the waist by the Eastern christians, Jews, and Magians. In india the Braminical thread [jandiram, janivaura, jaunwah, poonool].

ZOORRAIR (జుర్రేరు - dzurréru, *Tel.*). From (dzurru, tel. to dry up + éru, tel. river). River; Kurnool district, Coilcoontla and Bunganapully native state. Drains Coilcoontla talook and Bunganapully state. Rises in the Bunganapully territory and cutting through the town of Bunganapully, joins Coondair near Bheemoonipaud. The banks are studded with orchards and mango [q.v.] plantations.

ZOOVVY (జువ్వి - dzuvvi, *Tel.*). Same as Tsiela.——*Zoopully* (జూపల్లి - dzúpalli, Tel.). From (above + palli, tel. village). Zemindarry [q.v.] family. About 1544 A.D. Zoopully vencataroyaningaur obtained killadarship [q.v.] of Oodayagherry droog with certain russooms [q.v.] and inams [q.v.]. Seventy years later his great-grandson Narsaroyaningaur was made by the Nawaub [q.v.] rissaldar [q.v.] of 500 troops and granted the peshcush [q.v.] of 60 villages in Oodayagherry talook. Lutchmaroyaningaur, son of the latter, was beheaded by the Fowjdar [q.v.] of Nellore district who seized the Oodayagherry zemindarry [q.v.]. On the cession of the Carnatic [q.v.] to the British a pension of 100 pagodas [q.v.] a month was given to the family, to be diminished by one-third on each succeeding lapse. ——*Zoovvaldinney* (జువ్వలదిన్నె - dzuvvaladinne, Tel.). From (above + dinne, tel. mound). Village, Port; Nellore dist., Cauvaly tal.; pop. 2,114; acres 7,829; lat. 14° 49′; long. 80° 07′; from Cauvaly S.E. 9 miles; from Iskapully N.N.W. 6 miles; from Madras N. 117 miles; from Nellore N.N.E. 26 miles; from Toommalapenta S. 6 miles. Two temples, of Codandaramasawmy, and of Shiva. Climate healthy. Water good. Good mango [q.v.] and other topes [q.v.]. At the mouth of a salt water creek, crossed by the coast road. Chief export grain. Trig. station in lat. 14° 48′ 30·34″; long. 80° 6′ 13·22″; from Cauvaly S.S.E. 9 miles; from Moongamore E. 3 miles; from the sea W. 2 miles.

ZOR (زور - zor, *Hind.*). Strength.——*Zorawar* (زورآور - zoráwar, Pers.). From (above + war, pers. denoting agent). Vigorous. Prefixed to an alam forms a lacab; as Zorawar ally, vigorous ally [ism].

ZOROASTER (زر تشت - zartasht, *Hind.*). Means high priest. The founder of the Magian religion, some 3,000 years B.C. This was the national religion of Persia until supplanted by Mahomedans. The sacred book is Zend avesta [zend]. The Parsees [q.v.] are Magians.

ZUFT (ضبط - zabt, *Hind.*). From (zabata, ar. to keep) [zaubitah]. Attachment, distraint. Zufty is sequestrated.——*Zaubitah* (ضابطه - záhitah, Hind.). From (zabata, ar. to keep). A list [daub]. Rule, established practice or usage [maumool].

ZYE (زائی - záí, *Hind.*). Means born. Cf. Ibn. Afghan tribal termination.

ZYECHA (زايچه - záichah, *Hind.*). From (zái, pers. brought forth + chah, pers. diminutive sign); from original use in ascertaining the fortunes of a new-born child. Horoscope.— "*a*" Mahomedans distribute the hours of day and night of the seven days of the week [vauram] among the seven principal planets, which include sun and moon, as in the annexed table. The orbits of the planets are supposed to be in the following order, sun, venus, mercury, moon, saturn, jupiter, mars; and the progressive hours of the week beginning with 6 a.m., on sunday are assigned to them in that order in rotation. As the sunday day regents happen to coincide with the wednesday night regents, the table is clubbed; but to see the rotations continuously alternating day and night the columns have to be read in the order 1, 5, 2, 6, 3, 7, 4, 1, 5, 2, 6, 3, 7, 4. It may be added that in point of nomenclature mahomedans call sunday night, the night of monday, and so on; reckoning from sunset to sunset. However this does not affect the table, and the english designations are there given. When a person is born at a certain hour, it is considered that the person is born under the planet thus assigned to the hour, and his fortunes are then predicted according to the following canons:—Shums or sun, the person will be generous, irascible, respected in word, very wealthy, addicted to drinking, little inclined to do pious acts, long-lived and auspicious to parents. Zohra or venus, will be fond of music, of dress and scents, amorous, accomplished, of good voice, a good singer, a delight to men and women, will enrich himself at expense of others, and maintain his parents and relations. Ootaurid or mercury, will be wise, learned, of good memory, skilled in painting, affectionate, social, friendly, obliging and will exalt whom he likes and avoid whom he dislikes. Cumr or moon, will be a liar, drunkard, gambler, afraid of water, subject to cold and debility, a great traveller and exposed to danger to life in travelling, propitious to parents and friends. Zoohal or saturn, will be of dark complexion, thin, bilious, hasty, perverse, cruel, forgetful and a good warrior. Mooshtary or jupiter, will be good-looking, a judge, a king versed in arts and politics, will have many foes, but will overcome them, skilled in handicraft, drawing, writing, charitable, firm in mind, high-spirited and persevering. Mirreek or mars, will be a rapid talker, irascible, cruel, desirous of knowledge, ambitious, and covetous of neighbour's money:—

Sunday day, Wednesday night.	Monday day, Thursday night.	Tuesday day, Friday night.	Wednesday day, Saturday night.	Thursday day, Sunday night.	Friday day, Monday night.	Saturday day, Tuesday night.
1	2	3	4	5	6	7
6–7 (*a*)	6–7 (*d*)	6–7 (*g*)	6–7 (*c*)	6–7 (*f*)	6–7 (*b*)	6–7 (*e*)
7–8 (*b*)	7–8 (*e*)	7–8 (*a*)	7–8 (*d*)	7–8 (*g*)	7–8 (*c*)	7–8 (*f*)
8–9 (*c*)	8–9 (*f*)	8–9 (*b*)	8–9 (*e*)	8–9 (*a*)	8–9 (*d*)	8–9 (*g*)
9–10 (*d*)	9–10 (*g*)	9–10 (*c*)	9–10 (*f*)	9–10 (*b*)	9–10 (*e*)	9–10 (*a*)
10–11 (*e*)	10–11 (*a*)	10–11 (*d*)	10–11 (*g*)	10–11 (*c*)	10–11 (*f*)	10–11 (*b*)
11–12 (*f*)	11–12 (*b*)	11–12 (*e*)	11–12 (*a*)	11–12 (*d*)	11–12 (*g*)	11–12 (*c*)
12– 1 (*g*)	12– 1 (*c*)	12– 1 (*f*)	12– 1 (*b*)	12– 1 (*e*)	12– 1 (*a*)	12– 1 (*d*)
1–2 (*a*)	1–2 (*d*)	1–2 (*g*)	1–2 (*c*)	1–2 (*f*)	1–2 (*b*)	1–2 (*e*)
2–3 (*b*)	2–3 (*e*)	2–3 (*a*)	2–3 (*d*)	2–3 (*g*)	2–3 (*c*)	2–3 (*f*)
3–4 (*c*)	3–4 (*f*)	3–4 (*b*)	3–4 (*e*)	3–4 (*a*)	3–4 (*d*)	3–4 (*g*)
4–5 (*d*)	4–5 (*g*)	4–5 (*c*)	4–5 (*f*)	4–5 (*b*)	4–5 (*e*)	4–5 (*a*)
	5–6 (*a*)	5–6 (*d*)	5–6 (*g*)	5–6 (*c*)	5–6 (*f*)	5–6 (*b*)

a = Shums, sun; *b* = Zohra, venus; *c* = Ootaurid, mercury; *d* = Cumr, moon; *e* = Zoohal, saturn; *f* = Mooshtary, jupiter; *g* = Mirreek, mars.

—"*b*" The above table is also used in choosing a name for a new-born child; the initial or final letter of the planet under which it is born being taken for initial letter of the name intended to be given; thus if born under cumr or moon, the name may be either Cootb ood deen, pivot of religion, or Rookn ood deen, pillar of religion.—"*c*" When a marriage is arranged, the following table is consulted by masheikhs to see whether the parties will make a happy match. A person can be born under a zodiacal sign; that is to say the sign which is in the ascendant otherwise orient at the hour of his birth is his sign through life [raushy, 1j]. And each sign has in arabic astrology for quality a predominating element, thus:—I, V, IX are signs of fire; II, VI, X of earth; III, VII, XI of air; IV, VIII, XII of water. Compare the terrestrial applications of hindoo signs at Raushy (1) j. These signs and their elements are shown in columns 1 and 2 of the table. Again each sign has its planetary regent, these being identical with those in the hindoo system; see Raushy (1) k. While each planetary regent has a sex in that capacity, thus:—mars is hermaphrodite, or male for I, female for VIII; venus is hermaphrodite, or female for II, male for VII; mercury is hermaphrodite, or male for III, female for VI; moon is always female, having but one sign, IV; sun is always male, having but one sign, V; jupiter is hermaphrodite, or male for IX, female for XII; saturn is hermaphrodite, or female for X, male for XI. These differ from the sexes in the hindoo system; see Vauram, c. These planetary regents and their sexes are shown in columns 3 and 4 of the table. Certain letters of the arabic alphabet are again arbitrarily held to correspond with certain signs. Then by a combination of these different considerations with the initials of the names of the contracting parties the masheikhs tell their fortunes as a married couple:—

Sign of zodiac.	Its predominating element.	Planetary regent of the sign.	Its gender as such.	Alphabetical letters assumed to correspond with the sign.	Ditto transliterated in english.
1	2	3	4	5	6
I. Hamel, aries	Fire	Mirreek, mars	Male	ا, ل, ع, ى	a, l, y.
II. Sowr, taurus	Earth	Zohra, venus	Female ...	ب, و	b, v, w.
III. Jowzah, gemini	Air	Ootaurid, mercury	Male	ق, ك	k.
IV. Sartaun, cancer ...	Water	Cumr, moon	Female ...	ح ه	h.
V. Asad, leo	Fire	Shums, sun	Male	م	m.
VI. Soomboola, virgo ...	Earth	Ootaurid, mercury	Female ...	غ	gh.
VII. Meezaun, libra	Air	Zohra, venus	Male	ر ت ط	r, t.
VIII. Akrab, scorpio	Water ...	Mirreek, mars	Female ...	ص ز ن ظ ذ	z, n, s.
IX. Kows, sagittarius ...	Fire	Mooshtary, jupiter	Male	ف	f.
X. Jaddy, capricornus ...	Earth	Zoohal, saturn	Female ...	خج	kh, j.
XI. Dalo, aquarius	Air	Zoohal, saturn	Male	ش س ث ص	s, sh.
XII. Hoot, pisces	Water ...	Mooshtary, jupiter	Female ...	د	d.

—"*d*" The following table is used in sickness for ascertaining the probability of survival. In this case for ascertaining the zodiacal sign which rules the case the patient's alam [q.v.] and that of his mother are ascertained, and the numerical value of the consonants therein is calculated according to a certain formula. That is to say the consonants in this verse, 'abjad hawwaz, hutti, kalaman, safas karashat, sakhazzazigh,' which is supposed to enumerate the names of some celebrated kings of midian, are held to have the following numerical values:—
ا, a = 1; ب, b = 2; ج, j = 3; د, d = 4; ه, h = 5; و, v, w = 6; ز, z = 7; ح, h = 8; ط, t = 9; ى, y = 10; ك, k = 20; ل, l = 30; م, m = 40; ن, n = 50; س, s = 60; ع, a = 70; ف, f = 80; ص, s = 90; ق, k = 100; ر, r = 200; ش, sh = 300; ت, t = 400; ث, s = 500; خ, kh = 600; ذ, z = 700; ض, z = 800; ظ, z = 900; غ, gh = 1,000. Then the values of all the consonants of the two names are added together, and divided by 12 being the number of signs; if 1 remains the patient is under sign I or hamel, if 2 remains he is under sign II or sowr, and so on. But according to the sign thus ruling there are certain critical years of age for the patient, and these are shown in the table:—

Sex.	I Hamel.	II Sowr.	III Jowzah.	IV Sartaun.	V Asad.	VI Soomboola.	VII Meezaun.	VIII Akrab.	IX Kows.	X Jaddy.	XI Dalo.	XII Hoot.
	1	2	3	4	5	6	7	8	9	10	11	12
Male.	7	12	4	7	8	2	18	30	2	7	30	7
	13	30	12	9	16	...	...	39	...	15	...	...
	20	...	20	30	20	...	...	...	...	...	...	...
	...	...	30	...	40	...	...	...	...	...	...	...
	...	...	40	...	50	...	...	...	...	...	...	...
	...	...	50	...	...	...	...	...	...	...	...	...
Female.	1	5	2	4	5	16	17	4	2	3	1	2
	9	30	4	19	...	20	...	12	...	...	...	56
	20	...	10	30	...	40	...	3	...	...	...	30
	50	...	15	40	...	...	...	...	...	...	...	40

—"*e*" There are other tables for finding lucky and unlucky days of the month. A familiar fixed rule for this is to count the days of month on the 5 fingers of the hand beginning with little finger and then beginning again, thus 1—5, 6—10, &c.; the days which fall on middle finger are lucky. Monday, Wednesday, Thursday and Friday are lucky days of the week; the other three not so. For making journeys see Rijaul ool gheib.

ZYLE (ذيل - zail, *Hind.*). From (zála, ar. to have a tail), as the skirt of a garment reaching the ground. Otherwise zeyl by corruption. Appendix; supplement to a letter or book; margin of a book with annotations; any supplementary detail of particulars. Specification of rates in which rent is to be paid by a ryot [q.v.], whether in money or kind, annexed to the puttah [q.v.] granted by a zemindar [q.v.].

INDEX.

[*Words other than the first in the index not preceded by a hyphen indicate capital titles in the text. Words in the index preceded by a hyphen indicate italic sub-titles in the text under the word last preceding the hyphen. Numerical figures in the index not preceded by a hyphen indicate clarendon numbers in the text. Numerical figures in the index preceded by a hyphen indicate ordinary numbers in the text under the clarendon number given by the figure preceding. Single letters in the index indicate the sub-heads of matter in the text denoted by italic single letters within inverted commas.*

When either the commencement or the termination of a compound word falls quite naturally within the alphabetical arrangement of the main text, the reader is left to trace the word for himself; but in all other cases assistance is given through the index.]

B

C

D

G

H

J

K

L

M

O

P

Q

284

W

X

Y

Z

Numerals.